The Almanac of American Politics
★ 2004 ★

THE **Senators,** THE **Representatives**

AND THE **Governors:**

THEIR **Records** AND **Election Results,**

THEIR **States** AND **Districts**

Michael Barone
Richard E. Cohen

National
Journal
—GROUP—

Washington, D.C.

NATIONAL JOURNAL GROUP

Chairman: David G. Bradley
President and Publisher: John Fox Sullivan
Chief Operating Officer: William Wolf

Printed in the United States of America by United Book Press. Database design by Directional Data, Inc.; composition by Impressions Book and Journal Services Inc. Distributed to the trade by the University of Chicago Press.

Photographs by Richard A. Bloom, John Eisele, Liz Lynch and Bruce Reedy. For information regarding photographs, contact: National Journal, 1501 M Street, N.W., Washington, D.C. 20005. 202-739-8400. All rights reserved.

The Almanac of American politics. — 1972 –

v. : ill. ; 24 cm.

Biennial
Published by Gambit 1972– ; by National Journal 1988–

ISSN: 0362-076X
ISBN 0-89234-105-X (2004)
ISBN 0-89234-106-8 (pbk. : 2004)

1. United States. Congress—Biography.   2. United States. Congress—Committees.   3. Election districts—United States—Handbooks, manuals, etc.   I. Barone, Michael.   II. Ujifusa, Grant.   III. Matthews, Douglas.

JK1012 .A44
328.73/005

70-160417

THE ALMANAC OF AMERICAN POLITICS 2004

Author
Michael Barone

Co-Author
Richard E. Cohen

Editor
Charles Mahtesian

Founding Editor
Grant Ujifusa

Principal Contributing Writer
Louis Jacobson

Research Director
Molly Chapman Norton

Research Associates
Susan Davis, Zachary Patton

Researcher
Gregg Sangillo

Editorial Interns
Courtney Crimmins, Josh Kraushaar, Abby Samolis,
Brooke Schechtman, Lauren Wall

Presidential Election Results
Polidata

State Maps
Polidata

Congressional Election Results
Election Data Services Inc.

CONTENTS

6 **Contents**

8   **Contents**

12   **Contents**

GUIDE TO USAGE

The following guide provides a brief description of each section and a list of sources from which information was derived, both of which serve as a road map to understanding the meaning behind the figures. Some of the data will be updated regularly on the Almanac website. For information on how to subscribe to this free service, please see the insert card toward the middle of the book. Data in each category below is generated for *The Almanac of American Politics* by Polidata from data compiled by the United States Census Bureau, unless otherwise noted. Figures released by the Census may vary slightly from those used by the Almanac due to different methods of data aggregation or tabulation.

The People

Population.   All population figures, excluding voter registration, are from the Census Bureau, www.census.gov. Official April 1, 2000 Census figures are used for each state.

Area Size.   Area size is in square miles, including water.

State Native.   Refers to persons born in their state of residence as a % of all persons.

Non-Citizen.   Refers to persons foreign born and not a citizen as a % of all persons.

Language.   Refers to the % of households speaking that language. The abbreviation *Other Eur.* refers to Other Indo-European languages.

Race and Ethnic Origin.   For the 2000 Census, the Census Bureau asked people what their race or ethnic origin was. Race, as defined by the Census, reflects the individual respondent's perception of his or her racial identity and does not reflect any biological or anthropological definition. The basic racial categories are: American Indian or Alaska Native (designated in the box as *Native Am.*); Asian; Native Hawaiian or other Pacific Islander (*Hawaiian*); Black or African American; White; Two or more races (*Two + races*); Other non-Hispanic persons (*Other*). The race statistics used in the Almanac are drawn from respondents reporting only one race category, but the book includes a total for those who responded to more than one race category. Hispanic origin is defined as an ethnicity, and includes those who classified themselves in one of three specific Hispanic categories on the census form (Cuban, Mexican, Puerto Rican) or as of other Spanish/Hispanic origin. Persons of Latino or Hispanic origin may be of any race for Census purposes, but the Almanac includes only non-Hispanic Blacks in the Black population category and only non-Hispanic Whites in the White population category, so that the percentages add to 100%. The figures in the box are as a % of all persons in a state or congressional district.

Ancestry.   Ancestry refers to ethnic origin or descent; categories are drawn from Census-designated possible groups. The question was intended by the Census to provide data for groups that were not included in the Hispanic origin and race questions; thus it does not reflect diversity within Hispanic and Asian subgroups. The % figure is calculated by using the average number of responses to estimate the % of the population that shares this ancestry characteristic. NOTE: The *USA* designation refers to "American" as a unique ethnicity, if it was provided alone as a response without any other ethnicity. *Subsaharan* refers to the Census category of Subsaharan African. *West Indian* excludes Hispanic groups.

Military Veterans.   Refers to persons who were in the Armed Forces previously as a % of voting age persons. *Gulf War* % includes all veterans with service after 1990, but does not include those who also served in Vietnam.

Urban/Rural Population.   Refers to the % of total population that lives in areas defined as urban or rural by the Census Bureau.

Education.   *H.S. Grad* refers to persons with a high school diploma or higher, as a % of persons 25 years and older. *College Grad* refers to persons with a bachelor's degree or higher, as a % of persons 25 years and older.

Industry.   Refers to industry of occupation. The figure is of persons employed by that particular industry as a % of employed persons 16 years or older. Abbreviations: *Agri* (agriculture, forestry, fishing and mining); *Con* (construction); *Fin* (finance, insurance and real estate); *Info* (information); *Mfg* (manufacturing, durable and non-durable); *Prof* (professional and related services, including health and education); *Public* (public administration); *Trade* (trade, wholesale and retail); *Other* (primarily entertainment, recreation, hotel and food services).

Occupation.   Refers to type of job within industry. The figure is the % of employed persons 16 years and older in these occupations. *White collar* refers to management, professional, sales and administrative occupations. *Blue collar* refers to construction, production and transportation occupations. *Gray collar* refers to the balance of employed persons not classified as white or blue collar, such as farming, fishing and forestry or health care, protective service, food prep and personal care occupations.

Work Sector.   Refers to a classification of worker by economic sector. The figure is the % of employed persons 16 years and older. Abbreviations: *Private* (private for profit/not for profit wage/salary employers); *Govt* (federal, state and local government); *Self* (self-employed); *Family* (unpaid family workers).

Unemployment.   Unemployed civilians as a % of persons 16 years and older and as a % of the labor force.

Household Income/Poverty Status.   *Household Income* refers to household income in 1999, as a % of all households. *Poverty status* refers to % of persons below the poverty line.

Home Value.   Refers to self-estimated market value of owner-occupied units as % of owner-occupied housing units for which value was specified.

State Information.   Each legislature is referred to according to the proper name of its legislative body, followed by a breakdown by party membership.

Legislative Term Limits.   Refers to whether a state has term limits for state legislators.

Registered Voters.   Refers to the number of registered voters by party, as close as possible to the November 2002 election. The individual states' election bureaus or political parties provide these figures. Some states have no voter registration. *D* refers to Democrat; *R* refers to Republican; *I* refers to independent, unaffiliated and minor parties.

Cook Partisan Voting Index.   Refers to the Partisan Voting Index (PVI) as used by Charlie Cook, Washington's foremost political handicapper. The PVI is designed to provide a quick overall assessment of generic partisan strength. For this volume, the PVI includes only the 2000 presidential election as the partisan indicator. The PVI value is calculated by a comparison of the district percentage for the party nominee, compared to the national value for the party nominee. Based upon the two-party vote, the national values for 2000 are Bush 49.7% and Al Gore 50.3%. The positive value indicates a district with a partisan base above the national value for that party's 2000 presidential nominee. Thus a district with an R + 15 is a district that voted 15 percentage points higher for George W. Bush than the national value of 49.7%. Similarly, a district with a D + 15 is a district that voted 15 percentage points higher for Al Gore than the national value of 50.3%. An X + 00 indicates an evenly balanced district.

Biography.   This section lists when each governor, senator and representative was elected or appointed, date and place of birth, home, college education and degrees obtained (if any), religion, marital status and, if applicable, spouse's name. The number of terms listed reflects full, elected terms. Also listed is a brief outline of the politician's past elected offices, professional career and military service and his or her office addresses and telephone numbers. Committee and subcommittee assignments, as of June 3, 2003, are provided as well. (Note: On many committees, the chairman and ranking minority member are ex officio members of each subcommittee on which they do not hold a regular assignment.)

Ratings

Group Ratings.   The congressional rating statistics of 11 interest groups provide an idea of a legislator's general ideology and the degree to which the legislator represents different groups' interests. Not just a record of liberal/conservative voting behavior, these ratings come from a range of groups concerned with everything from single issues (environmental concerns) to the political interests of a particular sector (e.g., business). The order of the groups is such that the more "liberal" groups are on the left and the more "conservative" are on the right. Five groups, ACLU, ITIC, NTLC, CON and CHC provide one rating for the two-year congressional session. Following is a general description of each organization.

ADA   Americans for Democratic Action
   Liberal: Since its founding in 1947, ADA members have pushed for legislation designed to reduce inequality, curtail rising defense spending, prevent encroachments on civil liberties and promote international human rights. The ADA uses a broad spectrum of issues for its vote analysis.

ACLU   American Civil Liberties Union
   Pro-individual liberties: ACLU seeks to protect individuals from legal, executive and congressional infringement on basic rights guaranteed by the Bill of Rights. The ACLU ratings are published for every Congress; the 2002 ratings include the years 2001 and 2002.

AFS   American Federation of State, County and Municipal Employees (AFSCME)
   Liberal labor: As the nation's largest public employee and health care workers union, representing more than 1.3 million members, AFSCME is committed to achieving dignity and improving working conditions through collective bargaining. The AFSCME voting records are based on a representative sample of roll call votes from the First and Second Sessions of the 107th Congress.

LCV   League of Conservation Voters
   Environmental: Formed in 1970, LCV is the national, non-partisan arm of the environmental movement. LCV works to elect pro-environmental candidates to Congress. LCV ratings are based on key votes concerning energy, environment and natural resource issues.

CON   Concord Coalition
   Pro-balanced budget: The Concord Coalition is a nonpartisan, grassroots organization dedicated to eliminating the federal budget deficit and reforming entitlement programs. The Coalition, with members and active chapters in all 50 states, is determined to educate the American public about the dangers of the federal deficit.

ITIC   Information Technology Industry Council
   High technology industry: ITIC represents the leading U.S. providers of information technology products and services. ITIC's mission is to help shape policies that advance electronic commerce, open new markets, rely on market-based solutions, and foster innovation.

NTU   National Taxpayers Union
   Pro-taxpayer rights: NTU is the nation's largest and oldest taxpayers' rights group, representing 300,000 members in all 50 states. NTU analyzes every roll call vote taken during both sessions of Congress that significantly affects federal taxes, spending, debt, or regulatory impact.

COC   Chamber of Commerce of the United States
   Pro-business: Founded in 1912 as a voice for organized business, COC represents local, regional and state chambers of commerce in addition to trade and professional organizations.

ACU   American Conservative Union
   Conservative: Since 1971, ACU ratings have provided a means of gauging the conservatism of members of Congress. Foreign policy, social and budget issues are their primary concerns.

NTLC   National Tax-Limitation Committee
   Pro-tax limitation: NTLC was organized in 1975 to seek constitutional and other limits on taxes, spending and deficits. These ratings are based on budget issue votes and bills that would have a major impact on long-term government taxing and spending programs.

CHC   Christian Coalition
   Conservative: Pro-family citizen organization and national lobby founded in 1989 working for family-friendly public policy on a local, state and national level with over 1.5 million members.

National Journal Ratings.   *National Journal*'s rating system establishes an objective method of analyzing congressional voting. A panel of *National Journal* editors and staff initially compiled a list of congressional roll call votes and classified them as either economic, social or foreign policy-related. The interrelationship of these votes was shown by a statistical procedure called "principal components analysis," which revealed which "yea" votes and which "nay" votes fit a liberal or a conservative pattern. The votes in each of the three subject areas were computer-weighted to reflect the degree they fit the common pattern. All members of Congress who participated in at least half of the votes in each area received ratings; those who missed more that half the votes were not scored (shown as *). Absences and abstentions were not counted.

Members of Congress were then ranked according to relative liberalism and conservatism. Finally, they were assigned percentiles showing their rank relative to others in their chamber. Percentile scores range from a minimum of 0 to a maximum of 99. Because some members voted liberal or conservative on every roll call, however, there are ties at the liberal and conservative ends of each scale. For that reason, the maximum percentiles often turn out to be less than 99.

Election Results

Listed for each member of the House are results of the 2002 general, runoff and primary elections, as well as the 2000 general elections (results of any special elections are also listed). Gubernatorial and senatorial results are presented in a like manner. Votes and percentages are included, indicating the margin of victory (due to the process of rounding up and rounding down, some totals may equal more or less than 100%). Candidates receiving less than 4% of the total vote are grouped together and listed as "Other." Election returns were collected from the individual states. Where a state abbreviation and district number appear in parenthesis next to an election year, this indicates that the member ran in a differently numbered congressional district that year.

Prior Winning Percentage.   This feature provides winning percentage of the vote in past elections; in Senate profiles, the word "House" indicates the election that year was for the U.S. House. If no percentage is provided for an election year, it indicates that the member lost or did not run for reelection that year; generally this will occur where there has been a gap in service. An odd election year (e.g. 1989) indicates a special election; two elections in the same year indicate a special and a general election.

Presidential Vote.   The 1996 and 2000 presidential vote is included for each state. Results of the presidential primaries were provided by the states; caucus results are not provided. Due to redistricting, 1996 presidential vote results are unavailable for all 435 congressional districts. The 2000 presidential vote, however, is included here for each congressional district. It has been recompiled to reflect the presidential vote within the new district lines in effect for the 2002 election. Presidential vote by congressional district is estimated by Polidata, from political databases used in the 2001–2002 redistricting cycle in a number of states. Political stakeholders frequently use previous election results to assess the partisan base of proposed districts. However, unlike census datasets, which are developed by one entity, delivered in a standard format and available for each census block, these political databases are produced by different entities in each state, each of which may use different standards. In most cases these data were distributed to the census blocks based upon a population factor. In this manner, whenever a census block was assigned to a district, a certain number of estimated votes were carried with the block. It is from aggregations of the votes for the census blocks that the estimates for the districts were made. While estimates of votes are included, the percentage values generally provide the more reliable information. The votes for minor party candidates are included where available but are not consistent across all 50 states. The total of the congressional district votes may not add up to the total state vote, because some votes (overseas, military and some absentee and early votes) are not assigned to a congressional district.

Campaign Finance

All data are derived from candidates' campaign finance reports and party reports available from the Federal Election Commission (FEC). The dollar figure, in parentheses to the right of the election results, represents the candidates' net disbursements (expenditures) for the period beginning January 1, 2001, and ending December 31, 2002. *These figures may not include candidate loans that have been repaid, nor does it include any corrections or amendments filed with the FEC after May 2003.*

Abbreviations

ABC	Americans for Better Childcare Act	I	Independent
ACLU	American Civil Liberties Union	IC	Independent Conservative
ACP	A Connecticut Party	Ind	Independence Party
ACU	American Conservative Union	IAP	Independent American Party (NV)
ADA	Americans for Democratic Action,	IR	Independent-Republican Party (MN)
	Americans with Disabilities Act	ISTEA	Intermodal Surface Transportation
AFDC	Aid to Families with Dependent		Efficiency Act
	Children	IVP	Independent Voters Party
AFS	American Federation of State,	L	Liberal Party
	County & Municipal Employees	LCV	League of Conservation Voters
	(AFSCME)	LHOB	Longworth House Office Building
AI	Alaska Independent Party	Lib	Libertarian Party
AID	Agency for International	LU	Liberty Union
	Development	MFN	Most Favored Nation
ANWR	Arctic National Wildlife Refuge	NAFTA	North American Free Trade
AS	American Samoa		Agreement
BGH	Bovine Growth Hormone	NARAL	National Abortion Rights Action
C	Conservative Party (NY)		League
CAFE	Corporate Average Fuel Economy	NEA	National Endowment for the Arts
CFA	Consumer Federation of America	NFIB	National Federation of
CFC	Conscience for Congress		Independent Business
CCP	Change Congress Party	NL	Natural Law Party
CHC	Christian Coalition	NPA	No Political Affiliation Party (FL)
CHOB	Cannon House Office Building	NRCC	National Republican Congressional
CIA	Central Intelligence Agency		Committee
CNP	Constitution Party	NRSC	National Republican Senatorial
CPF	Constitution Party of Florida		Committee
COC	Chamber of Commerce of the	NTLC	National Tax-Limitation Committee
	United States	NTU	National Taxpayers Union
COLA	Cost of Living Adjustment	NTX	No New Taxes Party (MN)
CON	Concord Coalition	PDP	Popular Democratic Party (PR)
DCCC	Democratic Congressional	PNTR	Permanent Normal Trade Relations
	Campaign Committee	POP	Populist Party
DFL	Democratic-Farmer-Labor Party	PR	Puerto Rico
	(MN)	PRG	Progressive Party
DLC	Democratic Leadership Council	Ref	Reform Party
DNC	Democratic National Committee	RHOB	Rayburn House Office Building
DSCC	Democratic Senatorial Campaign	RLDS	Reorganized Church of the Latter
	Committee		Day Saints
DSOB	Dirksen Senate Office Building	RMM	Ranking Minority Member
EMILY	EMILY's List (Early Money is Like	RNC	Republican National Committee
	Yeast)	RP	Republican Moderate Party (AK)
ERISA	Employee Retirement Income	RSOB	Russell Senate Office Building
	Security Act	RTL	Right-to-Life Party
FEC	Federal Election Commission	S	Capitol Building Room, Senate side
FERC	Federal Energy Regulatory	SCH	School Choice Party
	Commission	SDI	Strategic Defense Initiative
GATT	General Agreement on Tariffs &	SOC	Socialist Party
	Trade	UAW	United Auto Workers
Green	Green Party	UCIT	United Citizens Party (SC)
H	Capitol Building Room–House side	VNS	Voter News Service
HMO	Stop HMO Abuses Party	WIC	Women and Infant Children
HSOB	Hart Senate Office Building	WF	Working Families

KEY VOTES OF THE 107TH CONGRESS

Key Votes.   The Key Votes section attempts to illustrate a legislator's stance on important votes where he or she must vote *for* or *against* a national issue. The process grossly over-simplifies the legislative system where months of debate, amendment, pressure, persuasion, and compromise go into a final floor vote. However, the voting record remains the best indication of a member's general ideologies and position on specific issues. Following is a list of key votes used. A member who was absent, voted present, or who was not in office at the time of a particular vote receives an "*". Roll-call data were drawn from Congressional Observer Publications at *www.proaxis.com/cop*, a private legislative tracking company.

House Votes, 107th Congress:
1. **Approve Bush Tax Cuts** (HR 1836) Approve conference report for $1.35 trillion in tax cuts. May 26, 2001. (240-154) (D: 28-153; R: 211-0; I: 1-1)
2. **Limit Patients' Bill of Rights** (HR 2563) Limit non-economic damages for liability awards in the patients' rights proposal. Aug. 2, 2001. (218-213) (D: 3-206; R: 214-6; I: 1-1)
3. **Campaign Finance Reform** (HR 2356) Reform campaign finance laws to eliminate most uses of soft money, raise contribution limits, and impose limitations on pre-election advertising targeted at candidates. Feb. 14, 2002. (240-189) (D:198-12; R: 41-176; I: 1-1)
4. **Ban ANWR Development** (HR 4) Maintain existing protection of the Arctic National Wildlife Refuge by striking language in the bill that repeals the prohibition against energy development in ANWR. Aug. 1, 2001. (206-223) (D: 171-36; R: 34-186; I: 1-1)
5. **Faith-Based Charities** (HR 7) Permit federal incentives for social services provided by religious organizations. July 19, 2001. (233-198) (D:15-193; R: 217-4; I: 1-1)
6. **Bar Gays in the Boy Scouts** (HR 2944) Bar funds for the District of Columbia to enforce anti-discrimination ruling against the Boy Scouts for expelling two gay Scouts. Sept. 25, 2001. (262-152) (D: 54-143; R: 207-8; I: 1-1)
7. **Ban Partial-Birth Abortion** (HR 4965) Ban what foes describe as "partial-birth" abortion, with criminal penalties for those who perform the procedure. July 24, 2002. (274-151) (D: 65-141; R: 208-9; I: 1-1)
8. **Arm Commercial Pilots** (HR 4635) Permit commercial airplane pilots to carry firearms and use force during a flight. July 10, 2002. (310-113) (D: 102-102; R: 206-11; I: 2-0)
9. **Trade Promotion Authority** (HR 3005) Extend "trade promotion authority" for the president to negotiate international trade agreements. Dec. 6, 2001. (215-214) (D: 21-189; R: 194-93; I: 0-2)
10. **Bar Funds for Intl. Court** (HR 4546) Bar funds for the International Criminal Court. May 10, 2002. (264-152) (D: 59-143; R: 204-8; I: 1-1)
11. **Authorize Force in Iraq** (HJRes 114) Authorize the use of U.S. military force against Iraq. Oct. 10, 2002. (296-133) (D: 81-126; R: 215-6; I: 0-1)
12. **Deny Home. Sec. Dept. Union** (HR 5005) Permit the president to deny employees of the Homeland Security Department from joining a union if their membership might jeopardize national security. July 26, 2002. (229-201) (D: 11-198; R: 217-2; I: 1-1)

Senate Votes, 107th Congress:
1. **Approve Bush Tax Cuts** (HR 1836) Cut taxes by $1.35 trillion over 10 years. May 23, 2001. (62-38) (D: 12-38; R: 50-0)
2. **Expand Patients' Rights** (S 1052) Expands patients' rights in dealing with insurers and health maintenance organizations. June 29, 2001. (59-36) (D: 50-0; R: 9-35; I: 0-1)
3. **Campaign Finance Reform** (HR 2356) Reform campaign finance laws to eliminate most uses of "soft money," raise contribution limits, and impose limitations on pre-

election advertising targeted at candidates. March 20, 2002. (60-40) (D: 48-2; R: 11-38; I: 1-0)

4. **Permit ANWR Development** (S 517) Cloture motion to end debate on proposal to allow oil and gas development in the Arctic National Wildlife Refuge. April 18, 2002. (46-54) (D: 5-45; R: 41-8; I: 0-1)

5. **Confirm Ashcroft as AG** Confirm John Ashcroft as Attorney General. Feb. 1, 2001. (58-42) (D: 8-42; R: 50-0)

6. **Bar Gays in the Boy Scouts** (S 1) Permit education funds to be withheld from schools that prohibit the Boy Scouts from using their facilities. June 14, 2001. (51-49) (D: 8-42; R: 43-6; I: 0-1)

7. **$ for Hate Crime Prosecution** (S 625) Cloture motion to end debate on a proposal to prosecute hate crimes. June 11, 2002. (54-43; failed to receive required 60 votes) (D: 49-1; R: 4-42; I; 1-0)

8. **Overseas Military Abortions** (S 2514) Provide access to abortion services for U.S. military personnel and their dependents stationed overseas. June 21, 2002. (52-40) (D: 46-2; R: 5-38; I: 1-0)

9. **Bar Coop. With Intl. Court** (HR 3338) Prohibit U.S. cooperation with the planned International Criminal Court. Dec. 7, 2001. (78-21) (D: 32-19; R: 46-2)

10. **Trade Promotion Authority** (S 3009) Extend "trade promotion authority" for the president to negotiate trade agreements. May 23, 2002. (66-30) (D: 24-25; R: 41-5; I: 1-0)

11. **Authorize Force in Iraq** (HJRes 114) Authorize the use of U.S. military force against Iraq. Oct. 11, 2002. (77-23) (D: 29-21; R: 48-1; I: 0-1)

12. **Homeland Sec. Dept. Union** (HR 5005) Cloture motion on proposal to limit debate on proposal for Homeland Security Department, excluding presidential authority to bar employees from union membership for national security reasons. Oct. 1, 2002. (45-52) (D: 42-6; R: 2-46; I: 1-0)

LIFE, LIBERTY AND PROPERTY

By Michael Barone

September 11 changed everything. How often have we heard or thought that since that awful morning? Yet for 14 months, September 11 seemed to have changed very little in America's politics. The nation's electorate still seemed split evenly between the parties. Voters still seemed to be divided along cultural lines, with traditionally religious Americans heavily Republican, less religious and unreligious Americans heavily Democratic. The results of the November 2001 state elections were not much out of line with the results of November 2000. Polls during most of the 2002 campaign showed the two parties winning about the same percentages, results that were not different, given the statistical limits of polling, from the 48%–48% tie in the 2000 presidential race and the 49%–48% margin for Republicans in House races that year. That last margin was almost identical to the Republicans' 49%–48% and 49%–48.5% margins in House races in 1998 and 1996. And the Democratic percentage of House vote in 1996 was almost identical to the 49% Bill Clinton won in his campaign for reelection. Until the polls closed November 5, 2002, we still seemed to be the 49% nation as described in the Introduction to the 2002 *Almanac*.

But as the results of the 2002 elections came in, it was clear that something—some things— had changed. It is highly unusual in American politics for a president's party to gain House seats in its first off-year election; the last time it happened was in 1934, when Franklin Roosevelt was assembling what would become the New Deal Democratic majority. But George W. Bush's Republicans—and they *are* George W. Bush's Republicans—gained seats in the House. Likewise, it is highly unusual in American politics for a president's party facing an opposition majority in the Senate to gain a Senate majority in an off-year election; in fact, it had never happened since passage of the 17th Amendment to the Constitution, which provides for popular election of senators. But George W. Bush's Republicans, facing a 51–49 Democratic Senate (counting the former Republican and self-proclaimed Independent Jim Jeffords as a Democrat), emerged from election night with 51 Republican senators.

The popular vote for the House of Representatives turned out to be 51% Republican and 46% Democratic. The popular vote for senator and governor were almost exactly the same; these numbers have less significance, since there was no election for senator in 17 states and no election for governor in 13 states. Contrary to expectations, Republicans ended up with 26 governorships— just one less than before—and they gained 105 seats in state Houses and 36 seats in state Senates. For the first time since 1952, there were more Republican than Democratic state legislators.

These down-the-line gains for Republicans are politically significant. The difference between poll results of 51%–46% and 49%–48% is not statistically significant. But that difference in election results is politically significant. The Republicans' 51%–46% margin in the House vote in 2002 is significantly different from the 49%–48% margins of 2000 and 1998. It is closer to the 52%–45% popular vote margin by which the Republicans won control of the House in 1994 and to the 53%–46% margin by which the first President George Bush was elected in 1988.

What changed? What changed to make the 49% nation into a Bush Republican nation, if only by a small margin? What were the effects of September 11, or of other developments between November 2000 and November 2002 that produced this different result? The changes can be summed up according to the words—they belonged to John Locke—that inspired Jefferson while he was writing the Declaration of Independence; namely that by nature all free people have a right to Life, Liberty and Property. Life, liberty and property have all been changed by September 11 and by other recent developments in ways that reshaped our political alignment and produced the results of the election of 2002.

But before we examine how life, liberty and property have been changed, let us look more closely at the results of the 2002 election and how they compare with the results of the elections of 1996, 1998 and 2000, the elections of the 49% nation. To do so, let us divide the country into three parts with roughly equal population. One is the Coast, which includes the Northeastern states except for Pennsylvania, the three West Coast states and Hawaii. The second is the Heartland, including Pennsylvania, the Midwest, the Rocky Mountain states and Alaska—the great interior of the United States. The third is the South, the 11 Confederate states plus West Virginia, Kentucky and Oklahoma. Each contains about one-third of the nation's population, but turnout in the Heartland is higher and it casts between 37% and 41% of the nation's votes. The Coast, dominated by its large metropolitan areas, is economically the richest part of the country and culturally the most liberal. The Heartland, a mixture of industrial metropolises and small town and rural America, is economically a little less well-off and culturally less liberal. The South, increasingly metropolitan but with strong rural traditions, is growing more prosperous and is culturally very conservative.

Not surprisingly, in the last five elections, the Coast has been consistently the most Democratic of the three regions and the South consistently the most Republican in both presidential and congressional elections. This was not always so. As recently as 1992, the South voted 52%–46% Democratic for the House, a higher percentage than in the rest of the nation, even while it was giving a slight plurality to the beleaguered incumbent George Bush. By 2002, the South voted 56%–41% Republican for the House, a higher percentage than in the rest of the nation—and very much like George W. Bush's 55%–43% lead in the South in 2000.

This similarity is just one instance of a trend that has generally gone unnoticed by political journalists and political scientists: the move toward straight-ticket voting in the 1990s. This was a sharp reversal of a trend from the 1940s to the 1980s toward more split-ticket voting. Presidential and congressional candidates often appealed to voters across party lines. But in the 1990s voters, while still giving lip service to the idea of ticket-splitting, actually split their tickets much less often. The result was a convergence between party preference in presidential elections and party preference in House elections. That convergence is apparent in the following table:

Republican and Democratic percentages
for President and House 1988–2002

Year	President	House
2002		51–46
2000	48–48	49–48
1998		49–48
1996	41–49	49–49
1994		52–45
1992	37–43	46–51
1990		45–53
1988	53–46	46–53

In 1988 and earlier, Democrats held the House for three reasons. First, they started off with most of the incumbents, and incumbents almost always have an advantage in House elections. Second, they had many candidates, usually conservatives, who won large majorities in House seats that regularly voted Republican for president. Third, Democrats had many more politically talented incumbents and challengers than the Republicans—candidates who were able to win in seats that leaned to the other party in presidential voting.

By the 1990s, these strengths started to wear thin. Democrats did not have as many incumbents as they once had, and incumbents did not enjoy their normal advantage in 1990, because of the House bank scandal, and in 1992, the year of the Perot uprising and the peak of the term limits movement. Politically talented Democrats who held Republican-leaning seats started to retire or to lose to Republicans, and were not replaced by others. And as conservative Democrats retired, their seats were often won by Republicans. The convergence began in 1992, when Perot voters were about equally split between Bill Clinton and George Bush as their second choice, Democrats won the presidency by 6% and the House popular vote by 5%. In 1994, when Bill

Clinton's job rating was low, Republicans won a majority of the House vote. In 1995, we entered the period of parity between the parties, and in 1996, Clinton was reelected with 49% of the vote while Democrats won 48% of the House vote. In 1996, most Perot voters were anti-Clinton; if their votes are allocated to their second choices, Clinton would have beaten Dole by about 51%–45%. In 2000, the parties' percentages for president and the House were virtually identical. Southern conservative seats were electing Republican congressmen, and both parties had about the same number of talented politicians able to win and hold seats leaning to the other party.

Preference for president and Congress has converged, not just at the national level, but also in each of our three regions, as the following table shows:

Republican and Democratic percentages for President and the House, by region

Year, region	President	House
2002		
U.S.		**51–46**
Coast		42–54
Heartland		54–44
South		56–41
2000		
U.S.	**48–48**	**49–48**
Coast	40–55	41–56
Heartland	50–47	51–46
South	55–43	54–42
1998		
U.S.		**49–48**
Coast		42–54
Heartland		53–45
South		53–44
1996		
U.S.	**41–49**	**49–49**
Coast	35–54	44–53
Heartland	42–47	49–48
South	46–46	54–45
1994		
U.S.		**52–45**
Coast		47–50
Heartland		55–43
South		55–43
1992		
U.S.	**37–43**	**46–51**
Coast	34–46	43–52
Heartland	37–42	48–49
South	42–41	46–52

In 1996, the Democratic percentage for the House in each region and nationally was within 1% of the Clinton percentage. In 2000, the Republican and Democratic percentages for the House in each region and nationally were within 1% of the Bush and Gore percentages. This is not to say that there is straight-ticket voting in every district. Some House incumbents of both parties run ahead of party, but within large regions and nationally they tend to balance each other out. The vote for the House can now be taken as a good working proxy for the presidential strength of both parties—something that was not true in 1992 or for many years before.

That enables us to write a brief psephological history of the last decade from the presidential and House voting figures. The 1994 election shows us that Bill Clinton was widely unpopular—unpopular enough to squander his party's historic advantage in House elections in his native South. The 1996 election showed that Clinton and Democrats rallied, but unevenly. Republicans retained their strong standing in the South, where Clinton got 46% and House Democrats 45%. Clinton and Democrats did better in the Heartland, but were still stuck under 50%, with Clinton at 47% and House Democrats at 48%. They did better in the Coast, where voters in large metropolitan areas reacted against Newt Gingrich and Christian conservatives. There, Clinton won 54% and House Democrats 53%. In the impeachment year of 1998, Clinton's job rating was higher than in 1996 and his personal ratings lower, but there seems to have been no difference in his overall standing.

In 2000, Al Gore maintained much of Clinton's strength, but in a race without Ross Perot 48% was not enough to guarantee victory. Gore got 43% in his native South, (3% less than Clinton), and lost the region 55%–43%; House Republicans won there 54%–42%, substantially the same as their 1994 showing. In the Heartland, Gore won the same 47% as Clinton, but lost the region 50%–47%; House Republicans carried it 51%–46%. Most of the closely contested states were in this region; the Heartland includes nine of the 18 states decided by margins of 6% or less, with 110 of their 183 electoral votes (Bush won 62 of those electoral votes and Gore 121). In the Coast, Gore ran even better than Clinton, with 55% of the vote, carrying the region 55%–40% (it had a larger Nader vote than the other two regions). House Democrats won there by the nearly identical margin of 56%–41%.

House Republicans improved their standing in all three regions in 2002. They carried the South 56%–41%—even better than in 1994. They carried the Heartland 54%–44%, running 1% behind their 1994 score. And in the Coast, they reduced the Democrats' lead from 56%–41% to 54%–42%, still a decisive margin and a better result for Democrats than in 1994. It seems clear that some part of the Republican improvement in 2002 reflects changes of mind: We are no longer the 49% nation we were between 1995 and 2001.

Over the past decade and a half, Republicans have won more than 50% of the vote in both presidential and House elections—in the presidential race in 1988 and in House races in 1994 and 2002. During the same period, Democrats failed to win more than 50% of the vote in any presidential race, and they have not won 50% in House races since 1992, when they had advantages which they are not likely to have again soon. Democrats no longer have most of the incumbents. They have not had, for whatever reasons, an edge in the number of politically adept candidates that they had in the 1970s and 1980s, and such candidates are less likely to arise and persevere when their party is in the minority. And conservative politicians in the South and conservative parts of the Heartland are much more likely to make their way forward in the Republican party than in a party whose national stands will always be a political liability locally. Bill Clinton in 1996 and Al Gore in 2000, as the nominees of the president's party in a time of apparent peace and prosperity—the most favorable posture to run—won no more than 49% and 48% of the vote. George W. Bush's Republicans, as the nominees of the president's party in a time of national peril and sluggish economic growth, won 51% in 2002. Political scientists' formulas which try to explain election results by economic trends suggested that Republicans would lose votes and seats in 2002. The Republicans in unfavorable circumstances did better than the Democrats did in the most favorable of circumstances. Instead they gained.

That is not a guarantee that there will be a permanent Republican majority; it is not necessarily a harbinger of a Bush victory in 2004. It is not proof positive of conservative activist Grover Norquist's prediction that Republicans will hold the House for the next decade. With an uncertain outlook for the war on terrorism and for the economy, many things are possible. But it does suggest that all those things are lively possibilities. And it does make it clear that we are no longer in the 49% nation and that we are on our way to somewhere else.

Now let us turn to the changes in life, liberty and property that helped produce the outcome of 2002.

Life.   A nation in peril is different from a nation that believes it is safe. On September 11, 2001, the United States changed from a nation that believed it was safe to a nation that knew it was in peril. A nation in peril expects the leaders of its government to confront the danger and defeat its enemies. It does not expect instant deliverance, nor does it flinch at heavy casualties if it is clear that progress is being made against its enemies. Americans sustained the Cold War effort for 42 years, from 1947 to 1989, though the end was never clearly in sight. Americans reelected their presidents in 1864 and 1944, two of the four years of highest American military casualties, because they had confidence that their leaders had put the nation on the road to victory. But even amid these costly and long years of peril, Americans still talked of other things. Everyday life went on. Domestic issues continued to play a part in politics and previous political alignments were not totally altered.

But when choosing their presidents, voters were careful to reward those who waged war on the results of their decisions. Harry Truman was reelected in 1948, to almost everyone's surprise, after he rallied the nation to wage the Cold War and ordered the airlift to isolated West Berlin. Democrats lost in 1952 and 1968 after their presidents embarked on wars but failed to put us on the road to victory. Richard Nixon was reelected in 1972 because he seemed to have brought about American withdrawal from Vietnam without defeat. Jimmy Carter was defeated for reelection in 1980 because he seemed unable to prevent advances by the Soviets and attacks by the Iranian mullahs. From 1968 to 1988, Democrats won only one presidential election—and that by only a narrow margin— when large parts of their party seemed uninterested in protecting and advancing America in time of peril. Democrats won in 1992 and 1996 and nearly won in 2000, when the nation seemed to be safe.

Now, when it is clear once again that the nation is in peril, voters have responded positively to the leadership of George W. Bush. His job ratings in the 14 months after September 11 remained very high, and for a longer sustained period than for any other president since polling began in 1935. He was viewed in 2002 as a strong leader, dedicated to prosecuting the war on terrorism.

Many Democrats seemed to take the war on terrorism seriously: House Minority Leader Dick Gephardt and Senator Joe Lieberman were two prominent examples. But in 2002 some seemed more interested in scoring political points and seeking political advantage. After Bush's speech to the United Nations September 12, 2002, it was clear that Congress would have to debate a resolution supporting military action in Iraq. Senate Majority Leader Tom Daschle at first said that such a debate would have to be extensive, so extensive that it might not be possible to vote on a resolution until after the election. When it became clear that Daschle could not use his scheduling and obstructive powers to produce such a delay, he switched to saying that debate and a vote could take place quickly. It appeared he was seeking political advantage both times—at first to prevent Democratic senators from having to cast a vote before Election Day, then to try to switch the spotlight from Iraq to issues like the economy and prescription drugs. Similarly, on the homeland security bill Daschle persisted in backing provisions protecting public employee unions opposed by Bush and so prevented passage of the bill before the election; this gave Bush and the Republicans an opening to make the argument that Democrats were less interested in homeland security than in protecting a constituency that provides lots of money for Democratic campaigns. Republicans ran tough ads on homeland security that helped defeat Democratic Senators Max Cleland and Jean Carnahan and deprive Democrats of their Senate majority.

On the question of military action against Iraq, the Republicans were almost completely united behind the president, while the Democrats were deeply divided. In the Senate, 29 Democrats voted for the resolution and 21 Democrats and Jeffords voted against; 48 of 49 Republicans voted for it. In the House, 81 Democrats voted for the resolution and 126 against; Republicans voted for it by a 215 to 6 margin. Gephardt voted for it but his Whip and successor as Minority Leader Nancy Pelosi voted against it and lobbied actively to get other Democrats to do so. The Iraq issue also splits Democratic voters and Democratic fundraisers—a serious problem for the party as it chooses its 2004 presidential nominee. Many vocal Democratic caucusgoers and primary voters in early 2003 opposed military action in Iraq even as it was favored by large majorities of Democratic voters. That means that the eventual Democratic nominee may be either unacceptable to much of his party's base or unacceptable to most voters on what could still be an important issue. A party divided when the nation is in peril has grave difficulty getting its citizens' votes.

It was often said during the campaign that voters were more concerned about domestic or economic issues than they were about the war on terrorism. Polls asking voters which issues they were more concerned about—a foolish question in a poll—or which issues they would prefer to hear candidates talk about, often showed more voters choosing domestic or economic issues. But polls often elicited such answers during the Cold War and might even have done so at some stages of World War II. People naturally don't like to contemplate another September 11 or a chemical or biological warfare attack. They prefer to dwell on familiar, quotidian, relatively unthreatening domestic issues. But that doesn't mean that they ever entirely forget that the nation is in peril. And it doesn't mean that some critical number of voters decided to switch to the party of a president who seemed to take that peril seriously from a party many of whose leaders and members did not. "This was an election about security—or, more accurately, about insecurity," Democratic pollster Allan Rivlin wrote two days after the election. "When you think about it, these [domestic] issues seem minor when people want to harm us."

It is true that only one House Democrat who voted against the Iraq military action resolution October 10 was defeated November 5, Jim Maloney of Connecticut, whom redistricting placed in a contest with Republican incumbent Nancy Johnson. And only one Democratic seat in the Senate was put in immediate jeopardy, that of Minnesota's Paul Wellstone, who died in a plane crash October 25. No one can know whether he would have won, but his Democratic replacement, Walter Mondale, who said he would have voted against the resolution, was defeated by Republican Norm Coleman. Most Democrats who voted against the resolution represent safe Democratic seats or seats that are not up until 2004 or 2006. But as a party, Democrats were hurt by this vote, as they were hurt by the votes of most Democrats against the Gulf War resolution in January 1991. It is generally thought that no Democrats lost their seats because of that vote, which was 22 months before the next election. Yet it may have contributed to the defeats of Senators Terry Sanford of North Carolina and Wyche Fowler of Georgia and the near-defeat of Senator Ernest Hollings in South Carolina in 1992, and it almost surely played a role in the decision of some of the party's leading political figures—notably Dick Gephardt, Joseph Biden, Sam Nunn, John Kerry, Mario Cuomo, Lloyd Bentsen, Jay Rockefeller—not to run for president in 1992.

Liberty.   For more than 200 years, indeed for more than 300 years since there are many continuities between colonial and constitutional America, this country has been dedicated to the proposition that people of great variety—of different ethnic origins, different racial classifications, different religions, different opinions on government policy—can live together in liberty. Over that time, the happily elastic definitions of liberty set down by the Founding Fathers have been expanded to include people not covered by them in 1776 or 1787. During much of that time Americans, in the words of historian Robert Wiebe, could live together because Americans lived apart. People of different religions, different moral beliefs, different ethnic origins and racial classifications could pursue their own happiness without bothering each other. But on occasion government has had to address issues that split people along cultural lines, and much of American politics has centered on such cultural issues. The most serious was slavery: the nation split apart and fought a civil war. Others include the place of religion in education, prohibition of liquor and drugs, women's rights, racial segregation and racial quotas and preferences, immigration, abortion, gun control, whether America should go to war and whether it should have conscription. Some are a matter of history now, many are recurring and some are still matters of lively dispute. Often these issues have been seen as battles between liberty and moral principle. Do I have a right to consume alcohol, to have an abortion, to keep and bear arms? Or does moral principle require the government to ban liquor or abortions or handguns? Large numbers of Americans have had very different convictions on such issues and, when the question is raised whether a representative government should take action, such issues inevitably become the stuff–often the central stuff—of democratic politics.

In the America of 2000 such cultural issues—issues that amount to conflicts between principles of liberty and morality—were central to the division between the parties. In the achingly close election between George W. Bush and Al Gore, or between Republicans and Democrats for the House of Representatives, it was not income that divided the voters: if the only thing you knew about a person was his income and from that guessed how he would vote, you would have been wrong almost half the time. Party preference was much more closely related to cultural factors—level of education, racial or ethnic identification and, most of all, religion. Strongly religious voters were very likely to vote Republican. Unreligious or not very religious voters were very likely to vote Democratic. If the only thing you knew about a person was his religious beliefs and from that guessed how he would have voted, you would have been right a very high percentage of the time. And if you knew the person's views on abortion and gun control, you would have been right almost always.

Practically everyone is familiar now with the 2000 election map showing the states Bush carried and the states Gore carried, the red states and the blue states. "The red states and the blue states" became shorthand for the idea that Americans were roughly equally divided between two blocs of people with very different beliefs, with both sides openly hostile to the beliefs of the other. This is reminiscent of Benjamin Disraeli's description of the "two nations" of Britain in the 1840s. The hostility between the red states and the blue states, these two nations, grew more and more bitter during the 36-day controversy over the Florida vote count in November and December 2000.

But on September 11, the red states and the blue states became red, white and blue America. When the World Trade Center and the Pentagon and United Flight 93 were attacked, we realized instantly that we were all attacked. We realized that the differences that had so bitterly divided us were less important than what we shared in common. We realized that the conflicts between claims of liberty and claims of morality were just arguments at the margin, and that they were less important than our common commitment to liberty and morality.

In his State of the Union speech January 29, 2002, Bush put into words what binds us together, our belief in what he called the "seven non-negotiable demands of human freedom." They are the rule of law, limits on the power of the state, respect for women, private property, free speech, equal justice and religious tolerance. Bush was self-consciously echoing Franklin Roosevelt's proclamation of the four freedoms in 1941, "freedom of speech, freedom of religion, freedom from want, freedom from fear." Roosevelt's formulation was the work of a New Deal Democrat, but there was nothing in it that his Republican opponents did not also believe, though they would not have put it that way. Bush's formulation was the work of a conservative Republican, but there is nothing in it in which liberal Democrats do not believe, though they would not have put it that way either.

In this changed atmosphere, it seems likely that for many voters the hard edges of the cultural issues have turned softer. When the nation is in peril, people are less eager to fight culture wars. An October 2002 Ipsos-Reid poll reported that 56% of Americans said they had become more likely over the past year—that is, since September 11—to respect cultures that do not share their values. Our cultural divisions still persist and still account more than anything else for our political divisions. But voters may be willing to cross cultural lines and support the party that does not reflect their own cultural views. Some significant number of voters who rejected George W. Bush in 2000 for his association with religious conservatives and his opposition to abortion and gun control may have voted for his party in the changed atmosphere of 2002.

And there are some signs that opinion has been moving Bush's way on key cultural issues. Most national polls ask whether voters want "stricter [presumably federal] gun control laws," and usually most respondents say they do. But that percentage has been falling in some polls, from 67% in May 2000 to 57% in May 2002 in the ABCNews.com poll, for example. And when presented with the choice of new restrictions on gun ownership or stricter enforcement of current laws, respondents in polls have favored stricter enforcement, by 35% to 11% in an April 2000 NBC/Wall Street Journal poll (45% chose both) and 53%–45% margin in a September 2000 Gallup poll. Congress resisted cries for new gun control laws after the April 1999 Columbine killings and it is generally conceded that his support of gun control laws cost Al Gore critical votes from traditional Democrats in states like West Virginia and his native Tennessee.

Moreover, there are two tracks to the gun issue. At the federal level, there is discussion, widely aired in the overwhelmingly pro-gun control national press, for more restrictions on gun ownership. In the 1990s, it produced some modest increases in regulation that have not significantly reduced the numbers of guns. But at the state level, since 1987, 33 states— with more than half the nation's population— have passed laws requiring that law-abiding citizens who can demonstrate they know how to use guns can get permits to carry concealed weapons.

On abortion, opinion continues to be divided. But there is a large middle ground of voters who believe some abortions should be allowed, but that some abortions now allowed should be prohibited. A September 2002 Gallup poll showed that 26% of adults say abortions should be "always legal," 18% say "always illegal" and 54% say "sometimes legal"—numbers similar to those obtained since 1996. That picture is very different from the one usually found in the overwhelmingly pro-abortion rights national press. There is strong majority support for outlawing partial-birth abortion, which is the issue on the floor in Congress and state legislatures, and strong majority opposition to banning all abortions, which is not.

It is an article of faith among many political analysts that opposition to abortion is a huge liability in national elections. But it is a fact that in five of the seven presidential elections since *Roe v. Wade* was decided in 1972, the more anti-abortion candidate has won. It is true that many women are strongly in favor of "choice," the brilliant euphemism for abortion used by abortion rights supporters. But the number of women choosing to have abortions has been steadily declining since 1990. And, interestingly, an in-depth Kaiser Family Foundation-*Washington Post* poll in spring 2002 found that the gender gap—the tendency of women to vote more Democratic than men, apparent in every election since 1980—scarcely exists among voters under 30. They are the most likely of any age group to favor Republicans, though most have not yet committed to either party. For women in this age group, "choice" may not be so strong an issue as it is for so many Baby Boomer women. These are women who were told that they had a moral duty to stay home with their children, and the "choice" for them is not only about abortion but also about all those other choices they have made which they were trained to think were wrong and which they themselves often have doubts about. Most women under 30 did not receive such training; they were raised to think it was normal and O.K. for mothers to work outside the home and for wives to get divorced; they lived with the consequences, and feel capable of making their own choices without risking disapproval. In fact, more young women today than a decade ago are choosing to stay home with young children. The assumption that American women would always embrace 1970s feminism may turn out to be wrong.

One other non-economic issue that splits voters along red state\blue state lines is the environment. In national polls, and in the states which contain the nation's largest metropolitan areas, there is widespread support for the goals of environment groups, and this issue favors Democrats—particularly if the national press succeeds in characterizing George W. Bush as a despoiler of the environment acting at the behest of big corporate contributors. But in states where environmental restrictions actually have an economic impact, the positions of environmental groups are widely unpopular and the issue is a political liability for Democrats. Al Gore came within 1% of losing Oregon and 6% of losing Washington because of his refusal to oppose breaching the Snake River dams, which is almost unanimously opposed in the eastern parts of those states. He did lose West Virginia, in large part because he backed a ban on mountaintop mining. Clinton administration support of lowering the level of the Missouri River cost Gore support in traditionally Democratic counties in central Missouri, which he lost narrowly. Threats that a Gore EPA would regulate non-point-source pollution—in laymen's terms, agricultural runoff—helped insure that Gore got record low percentages in the Great Plains states. His opposition to oil drilling in the Arctic National Wildlife Refuge did the same in Alaska.

So there are costs as well as benefits for Democrats who take liberal positions on cultural issues like gun control, abortion and the environment, just as there is a cost as well as a benefit for Republicans who take conservative positions on these issues, which pit claims of liberty against claims of morality (and for many environmentalists their issues are issues of morality). The liberal stands which helped Democrats make gains in the largest metropolitan areas in the 1990s also helped Republicans make at least partially offsetting gains in rural areas and the exurban fringe. What impact issues will have in the 2004 election is unclear—but it seems likely to be less of an impact than in 2000. If George W. Bush in fall 2004 is seen as a strong leader who has made gains in the war on terrorism and has prevented an economic collapse, he is likely to win the votes of some of those who oppose his positions on these issues, and make inroads in the blue states. If he is seen as a leader who has faltered on the war and the economy, he is likely to lose some voters who share his views on these issues, and will be hard-pressed to prevent the Democratic nominee from making inroads in the red states.

One final thing should be said about liberty—the liberty, honored through most of American history, of foreigners to come to our land and become citizens. Many of the 22 million immigrants who entered the United States in the last 30-some years have become citizens and are entering the voting stream. They will affect American politics, just as the millions of immigrants who came here from 1840 to 1924 affected American politics from the 1840s to the 1930s. Some believe that because immigrants are relatively poor, they will vote for the Democrats because they will seek government assistance. But it was never as simple as that with the 1840–1924 immigrants (the Democratic party in the 19th century was a party of *laissez faire* and small government), and it is not so simple now. The great mass of today's new Americans fall within two Census-defined categories, Latinos and Asians. Asians are a greatly heterogeneous group and there are few rigorous studies of their political behavior. Many are highly skilled and far from poor; the median household income of people born in India and living in the United States in 2000 was $85,000, double the national average. The VNS exit poll in 2000 reported that Asians voted 55%–41% for Al Gore. But this was skewed by Hawaii, where most people are classified as Asian, though almost all are not recent immigrants but the descendants of immigrants who arrived before 1930. VNS reported that Asians in California voted for Gore by only 49%–48%, about the same as the nation as a whole and more Republican than average in California. The *Los Angeles Times* exit poll shows quite different results, with Gore carrying Asians nationally by 62%–37% and in California by 63%–33%. In 2002 the *Los Angeles Times* California exit poll showed Democrat Gray Davis leading Republican Bill Simon among Asians 54%–37%. With such divergent data about such an ill-defined group, it is hard to draw any firm conclusions, much less predict the future. But it can be said that there is not a self-conscious Asian voting bloc that can be organized and turned out to produce reliable large majorities for either party. In the short and medium term it is unlikely that Asians will shift the partisan balance in American politics appreciably.

Latinos—or Hispanics, as the Census Bureau calls them—are another matter. One out of six people under 18 living in the United States in 2000 was Hispanic, and the large majority of them were U.S. citizens or youngsters on the way to becoming citizens. Those who argue that we should close the gates now lest Latino immigrants make this a permanently Democratic country miss the point: these young people are a very large part of the future of America and of American politics. In 2000, VNS reported that Hispanics voted for Gore over Bush by a 62%–35% margin, a result that is in line with Latino voting behavior in the various states in the 1990s. But unlike blacks—a group that our civil rights laws and most of our journalists tend to analogize them to—Latinos are not a single bloc, voting just about the same way in every state and locality. Their voting behavior seems to be related to the politics of where they came from and the politics of where they moved to, and varies widely from state to state, and from nation of origin to nation of origin. Thus Cubans are strongly Republican, Mexicans from the states of Michoacan and Guerrero (the two states carried by the leftist Cuahtemoc Cardenas in the July 2000 Mexican election) are heavily Democratic: thus Latinos in Miami are heavily Republican, Latinos in Los Angeles heavily Democratic.

The 2002 election showed that the Latino vote is moveable, even volatile—in other words, an appropriate target group for both political parties. In California, where Republican Governor Pete Wilson's ads in 1994 suggested that Latino immigrants were only interested in welfare, Latinos voted 65%–24% for Democratic Governor Gray Davis according to the *Los Angeles Times* exit poll, providing almost all his margin of victory. Latinos in Illinois voted overwhelmingly Democratic. But in other states, it was another story. In Florida, Republican Governor Jeb Bush (whose Spanish is probably the best of any major American politician, so good that he can modulate his accent) won 56% of the Latino vote, according to the Fox News Channel Election Day poll; not surprisingly, he won a huge majority among Cuban-Americans, but he also won 51% among non-

Cuban Hispanics. In New York, Republican Governor George Pataki came close to carrying Hispanics; New York City's Republican Mayor Michael Bloomberg apparently also ran well among Hispanics in 2001—even though Puerto Ricans, historically the largest Latino group in New York, and Dominicans, who are coming to outnumber them, were the most Democratic Hispanic voters in the 2000 presidential election. Pataki and Bloomberg took more liberal positions on many issues than most Republicans nationally, but their performance suggests that Latinos are fluid in the political preferences. Colorado's Republican Governor Bill Owens, on his way to a landslide victory, carried the Hispanic vote. Texas's Republican Governor Rick Perry, running against Rio Grande Valley businessman Tony Sanchez who spent $60 million on his campaign, carried 35% of the Hispanic votes—not a bad showing in those circumstances.

The prediction that Latino voters would be overwhelmingly Democratic is based on two theories, both false. The first is that as people of color they would meet unyielding discrimination by racist white Americans: this is theory undergirding the decision to include Hispanics among the groups entitled to racial quotas and preferences, even though "Hispanic" is not a racial category under either the U.S. definition of race or the various Latin American definitions of race. But Latinos in recent decades have encountered nothing like the discrimination blacks faced in the segregated South or that Latinos faced in Texas until the 1960s, and most Latinos in America today do not have parents or grandparents who encountered that kind of discrimination; it is not part of their family lore, as it is for most American blacks. Nor do Latino immigrants see themselves as rebels against an unjust society, or soldiers in a fight for the *reconquista* of the U.S. Southwest. The large majority come here because they want to be part of the United States and partake of its bounty.

The second theory is that politics is all about economics, and Latinos will vote to redistribute income from the government to themselves. But contrary to what Wilson's ad implied, Latino immigrants are interested not in welfare but in work. Their experience in Latin America is that unless you are well connected it is foolish to rely on the usually corrupt and unreliable state for a living, and if they were well connected they would have stayed at home. On cultural issues, Latinos are a bit more conservative than the average American voter; many are strong Catholics and a growing number are Protestant evangelicals (which is the case in Latin America as well). Nor are Latinos moored to either American political party. This is not a group that has voted Democratic for generation after generation; most Latino voters in the United States in 2000 and 2002 didn't vote in the United States in 1988 or 1990.

Property.   Politics, the political scientist Harold Lasswell wrote in the 1930s, is about who gets what, when and how. In other words, politics is about economics. Lasswell was writing when political scientists were heavily influenced by Marxist theories and when it seemed possible that the New Deal Democrats would become something like European social democratic parties. American politics seemed to be a struggle between New Deal Democrats and *laissez faire* Republicans, between those who wanted to use government to redistribute income and those who wanted it to leave well enough alone, between a party backed by rapidly growing labor unions and a party with almost unanimous backing from corporate and financial leaders. We do not live in such a country today.

The thesis here is that economic issues affect American politics differently from how they affected it in the decades after the depression and the New Deal. The important economic focus for most voters now is not on short-term income but on long-term wealth, not on whether a slowdown in the economy threatens voters with unemployment or reduced income but on whether there is a framework in which voters can make progress in their lifelong project of accumulating wealth. For the fact is that the large majority of Americans do accumulate significant wealth over the course of their lifetimes. Media accounts of statistical data on wealth provided by the Federal Reserve Board always stress that most Americans do not have significant wealth. They overlook the fact that something like 70% of Americans age 55 to 64 have wealth, mostly in the form of housing equity and financial investments, totaling $300,000 or more. That may not sound like much next to Bill Gates's billions, but it is enough, when coupled with Social Security entitlements and private pensions, to provide for a comfortable retirement. Of course very few young people have significant wealth yet; with debts from student loans and little mortgage equity, many have negative net worth; and so at any given time most American adults do not have significant wealth. But a sensible society does not want its young people to have significant wealth; it wants them to have a chance to accumulate significant wealth over the working life. In our society, they do.

American voters who remember the 1930s were, for many years after, exquisitely sensitive to increases in the unemployment rate and signs of an impending recession. They could remember how a one-year economic decline led to economic collapse and personal disaster. In times of recession they were quick to vote for the party out of power, especially if that was the Democrats: look at the election figures for 1958 or 1970, years when most voters remembered the 1930s. But in 2002, only 8% of voters were old enough to remember the 1930s. The memory of voters under 30 in 2002 does not go back before the years 1983–2001—18 years in which the nation experienced low-inflation economic growth 97% of the time. And today unemployment is not the personal disaster it was in the 1930s, 1940s or 1950s. Then, people who lost their jobs had little wealth and small unemployment checks to rely on; without that weekly paycheck or packet of cash and with little wealth to draw on, they had a hard time buying groceries and paying rent or making mortgage payments. Over the last 20 years America has generated more than 41.5 million new jobs, and Americans who lose their jobs today can meet immediate expenses with credit cards until they find a new job; they can get ready cash by taking out a home equity loan. They don't respond to recession or economic sluggishness the way voters who remembered the 1930s did.

So how do voters respond to economic issues when the focus is not on short-term income but long-term wealth? The 2002 elections provide some useful clues to the answers to that question. They can be subsumed under three headings: the investor majority, the Social Security issue and taxes.

The investor majority.   The last decade has seen a spectacular increase in the number of Americans who are investors, who own stocks, bonds or mutual funds. According to surveys conducted by Democratic pollster Peter Hart, it increased from 21% in 1992 to 43% in 1997. In 2002 it was significantly higher. Pollster John Zogby reported that 66% of 2002 voters had a 401(k) or IRA plan and that 52% identified themselves as members of the investor class. Pollster Scott Rasmussen reported that 59% of 2002 voters were investors. Of course some of these people had only small investments. But most were Americans hoping to make progress in their lifelong project of accumulating wealth. In just 10 years time the electorate has changed from one in which a huge majority of voters were non-investors to one in which a substantial majority were investors.

The Founding Fathers believed that representative government could work in America because an overwhelming majority of (white male) Americans were property-holders: in most cases, farmers who owned land. In industrial era America it seemed that we had been transformed into a country where most Americans were not property owners. Before World War II, most non-farmers did not own their homes, and many farmers (one-quarter of the total population) were tenants rather than owners. The large majority of Americans did not have significant savings or own stock, bonds or mutual funds, which in the 1930s weren't worth much anyway. The Founders would have been concerned that a non-property-owning majority would use their votes to effect a redistribution of income and wealth, and that is indeed what happened, to some extent, though much less so than in Europe. The redistributionist impulse was disciplined also by the fact that, thanks to the New Deal's FHA and VA programs, we became in the post-World War II years a nation in which most people owned their own homes. Now, in post-industrial, information age America, we are once again a nation of property-owners, with a financial stake in the country; the large majority of voters own land and financial instruments.

From 1992 to 2000, as most Americans became stockowners, prices on the financial markets rose giddily; from 2000 to 2002, they fell. So 2002 was the first year in which we would see how a majority-investor electorate would respond politically to sharply falling stock prices. Some predicted that when voters got their October 2002 401(k) reports, they would react against the party in power, since stock prices had dropped 18% in the third quarter of 2002—the biggest drop in 15 years. Others predicted that investor-voters would tend to vote for Republicans as the party more likely to provide a framework in which stock prices could increase. One such was Republican National Committee pollster Matthew Dowd, who said that RNC polling actually showed Republicans increasing their support from investors, despite falling stock prices and reports of corporate misdeeds, from 40%–32% in January 2002 to 45%–32% in June 2002. This occurred even while support for Republicans from the non-investor minority decreased.

It appears from the election results that the majority of investor-voters did in fact vote more Republican than the minority of non-investor voters. Rasmussen reported that investors voted 56%–42% Republican, while non-investors voted 52%–45% Democratic. Because about six in 10 voters were investors, this meant that Republicans won 52%–46%; if the proportion of investors had been the same as in 1992, and the percentages in each group the same, the total vote would have been 50%–46% Democratic. Rasmussen also noted that within every measured subgroup of the electorate investors were more Republican than non-investors. Male investors were 18% more Republican than non-investors, female investors 16% more Republican, black investors 6% more Republican, elderly investors 29% more Republican. Zogby found a similar pattern among union members, voters with incomes under $35,000. Union members and low-income voters were the Democrats' core economic groups in the New Deal years and long after; now it appears that stock ownership is moving some of these voters to the Republicans. And the sharp difference among investors and non-investors among the elderly suggests that many elderly voters identify as their chief economic interest not their Social Security entitlements but their investments. In future years, an increasing percentage of elderly voters will be investors, given the spread of 401(k) and IRA plans over the last 20 years. That suggests that the saliency of the Social Security issue among the elderly will continue to decline.

It is seldom that an election provides a clear-cut test of an entirely new question. But the 2002 election provided the first test of how an investor majority would respond to a sharp drop in stock market prices. The results show that they did not react against the party in power. Investor-voters evidently took the long view when they considered their economic interest, voting not on their short-term losses but on their expectations of long-term gain. Investors, Dowd explains, are optimistic simply by virtue of being investors: they have money in the market. Surveys of investors in 2002 showed that they expected stock prices to be higher in two and five years; they seemed to understand that over time the stock market has always proved to be a good long-term investment. In addition, Dowd argues, "The investing voters see the government playing a reduced role in the very large historic economic cycles." That leads investor-voters toward support of tax cuts, free trade, measures to insure corporate accountability—policies which produce economic growth and increase the transparency and fairness of financial markets. Over the long run, there is likely to be a much larger constituency with a vested interest in checking the growth of government and limiting economic redistribution.

It should be noted that even while stock prices were falling, prices of the other major component of investor-voters' wealth, housing, sharply increased in most parts of the country. In 1992, at a time when many fewer voters owned stock and voters' wealth was concentrated in housing, George H.W. Bush's percentage of the vote as compared to 1988 dropped most sharply in New Hampshire and southern California, the two areas where housing prices had dropped most abruptly in 1990–92. The first President Bush was punished by voters in 1992 for seeming disengaged and uninterested in economic and domestic issues; the second President Bush in 2002 could argue that he had produced policies—the 2001 tax cut—to spur economic growth and proposed some other ideas—increasing the deductions for stock losses, cutting the capital gains and dividend taxes, speeding up increases in contribution limits for IRAs—which would arguably help investors.

In contrast, Democrats in 2002 had little to say about how they would improve the economy. It was as if they thought that sluggish economic growth and the brief recession would trigger a reflex in voters to vote for the opposition, as so many voters did in the decades after the 1930s. But that reflex evidently no longer exists. Senate Majority Leader Tom Daschle and former Vice President Al Gore delivered widely-covered speeches describing vitriolically the condition of the economy but providing little or nothing in the way of substantive alternate policies. Many Democrats privately wanted to repeal the Bush tax cuts. But they hesitated to say so publicly, because several Democrats in close Senate and House races had voted for them.

Democrats also thought that news stories about corporate misconduct at Enron, Arthur Andersen and WorldCom would win them votes. Republicans are associated with big corporations, they argued, and so revelations of corporate misconduct would swing voters toward Democrats. But the identification of corporation leaders with Republicans is much weaker than it was in the 1950s, when nearly all top executives were Republicans, nearly 40% of private sector employees outside the South belonged to labor unions and when union members tended to see their interests as adversary to management's. Much of American politics then revolved around labor-management conflicts. But today, only 9% of private sector employees are members of unions, and relatively few employees see their interests as adversary to management's; instead, they want to see management perform profitably and honestly. Voters responded to the stories of corporate misdeeds not as union-member-employees but as investors, and as investors they wanted to see corporate wrongdoers prosecuted and new laws passed to require better accounting standards.

After the election, Gephardt stepped down as minority leader and mused that Democrats should try to come up with proposals to protect investors and enable Americans to invest more. The Bush administration was considering tax changes to benefit investors and in January 2003 proposed to end the double taxation of dividends. These are the kinds of responses a majority-investor electorate will tend to elicit from shrewd politicians. Some Democrats' impulse is to attack such proposals as giveaways to the rich. But that is riskier than it used to be in a nation where a large majority of voters are investors.

The Social Security issue. Much of the dialogue in the 2002 campaign was about Social Security. In many states and districts, Democrats attacked Republicans for supporting "privatization" of Social Security, by which they meant George W. Bush's proposals for voluntary individual investment accounts for young workers. In some states and districts Republicans attacked Democrats for supporting "privatization" of Social Security, by which they meant Bill Clinton's proposal in January 1999, never seriously considered in Congress, to have government invest part of the Social Security taxes of young workers. A few Republicans—notably Elizabeth Dole and John Sununu, running for the Senate in North Carolina and New Hampshire, and Congressmen Pat Toomey of Pennsylvania and Clay Shaw of Florida articulately defended individual investment accounts and won. Other Republicans, like John Thune and Bill Janklow in South Dakota, promised to vote against "privatization"; Thune lost narrowly and Janklow won.

The campaign dialogue seemed to many to signal that proposals for individual investment accounts were doomed. The time when the political stars were in alignment for their passage was in 1999, when prominent Democrats—Daniel Patrick Moynihan, Bob Kerrey, Charles Stenholm—joined most Republicans in supporting them, and when Bill Clinton was making statements intellectually consistent with supporting them. But in early 1999, Clinton came out against the idea. Clinton instead proposed government investment, a nonstarter politically. Moynihan, for one, dismissed it with contempt. In the 2000 campaign, Gore opposed individual investment accounts vehemently, and in 2001 and 2002, just about every Democrat in Congress and running for Congress attacked them scornfully. With some Republicans playing defense on the issue and making commitments to vote against "privatization," and with virtually all Democrats opposed, it was hard to see how individual investment accounts could ever pass Congress.

Until the election results came in. Not only did Republicans gain seats in both houses of Congress against historic precedent, the polls all indicated that elderly voters—long the primary constituent for Social Security as-is—mostly voted for Republicans. This is evidently a result of the fact that an increasing percentage of the elderly get more income from their investments than from Social Security. Not many had noticed during the campaign, but support for voluntary individual investment accounts—the formulation Bush uses—remained well over 50% during all the Democrats' attacks; it was when they were asked about "privatization" that voters disapproved. In June, a CNN/USA Today/Gallup Poll reported that 57% favored a proposal that would "allow people to put a portion of their Social Security payroll taxes into personal retirement accounts that would be invested in private stocks and bonds." That figure dipped to 52% as the campaign season heated up in September, but returned to 57% when the question was asked again after the election. That result mirrors a post-election poll taken by Republican pollster David Winston for the United Seniors Association that found 59% supported a system where you own and control how part of your Social Security retirement money is invested while 35% favored a system where the federal government has complete control over Social Security retirement money. It begins to look as if there are fewer seniors voting to keep Social Security as-is than there are younger people voting to give themselves the option of Social Security accounts.

Some will argue that this gets public opinion wrong because the issue is framed Bush's way. But Bush has the presidential megaphone. If Democrats cannot win a plurality of votes cast on the issue in a year when they are on the attack and Republicans' responses were in many cases confused and muddled, how do they expect to win a plurality of votes cast on the issue if it is framed clearly by a popular president? Of course, Bush may not be popular in 2004, or as popular as he was in November 2002. But he seems determined to raise the issue again in 2004 as he did in 2000 and on the campaign trail in 2002, if, as seems likely, Congress doesn't act on it over the next two years. The fact is that the G.I. generation—the prime supporters of Social Security as-is for many years—will never again cast as high a proportion of the total vote as they did in 2002. Casting higher proportions will be the young voters who believe they have more to gain by investing some of their Social Security taxes than by relying on the promised government return. The argument made by some Democrats in 2002 that there is no problem because the system will be in good shape until 2037 is not appealing to a voter born in 1972 who will turn 65 that year—and there will be an increasing number of voters born in the 1970s in the years ahead.

It used to be said that Social Security was the third rail of American politics: propose changes in the system and you die. Now it seems that the third rail is moving to the other side of the track: oppose changes in the system and you die. Most Democratic politicians do not believe this and believe that opposition to any change in Social Security is a winning issue for them. The results of the 2002 election ought to give them some pause.

Taxes.   There was little argument about taxes in the 2002 elections. Prominent Democrats like Edward Kennedy and Hillary Rodham Clinton called for repeal of the 2001 Bush tax cut, but they weren't out on the campaign trail much, for the critical Senate races took place in states Bush carried or ran well in 2000. Senate Majority Leader Tom Daschle declined to call for repeal of the tax cut, apparently in deference to senators in tough races who voted for it. In speeches decrying the state of the economy, Democrats often blamed it on the Bush tax cut. But they did not explain how a tax cut taking effect mostly in 2004 and after had hurt the economy in 2001 and 2002 (some took a stab at it, arguing that the prospect of higher deficits would produce higher interest rates, but interest rates in fall 2002 were at a record low). At least one part of the tax cut, the rebate, which was the Democrats' idea originally and which they were entitled to take credit for, probably did stimulate the economy a bit. The fact is that most Democrats oppose the tax cut not because of its fiscal effect—who really knows what the fiscal situation will be in 2010?—but because, as one Democrat put it, "I want the government to have the money." They understand that Bush pushed the tax cut because he wanted to reduce the size of government; they want it to be larger, because they believe a larger government can pay for programs that will help people and be good for the country.

That is a principled position, and one in which many reasonable and decent people can and do believe. The problem is that it is hard to sell. The best way to make the case for bigger government is not to argue the abstract case for big government but to make the case for specific, concrete programs which are attractive to most voters or to voters strategically positioned within the electorate. But it is hard to win elections today by promising you are going to be able to enact attractive programs in 2006 or 2010. And the Democrats may have missed the best opportunity to attack the Bush tax cut, which is before it takes effect.

For the tax issue will be in a different posture if and when the significant tax cuts take effect in 2004. In 2000, the posture of the issue was this: Bush was promising a tax cut, which voters were skeptical about; Democrats promised to leave taxes where they were, which voters tended to believe, since they knew that the Democrats remembered how they had been clobbered in 1994 after raising taxes the year before. But in 2004 and even more so in 2006 and 2008, the posture will be what it was in 1988, when the senior George Bush said, "Read my lips, no new taxes": Bush will be promising to keep taxes low, Democrats will be suspected of wanting to raise them. We know what happened to Walter Mondale when he promised to raise taxes in 1984 and to Michael Dukakis when he declined to promise he would not raise them in 1988. The Republican nominees in 1984 carried and in 1988 ran even in the nation's biggest metropolitan areas— Boston, New York, Philadelphia, Detroit, Chicago, Los Angeles. In 2000, when the tax issue was in a different posture, George W. Bush ran weakly in the suburbs and Al Gore carried all of those metropolitan areas by wide margins; suburban women's liberal positions on cultural issues outweighed Bush's promise to cut their taxes. It is possible, though by no means certain, that when the choice is between asserting liberal positions on cultural issues and paying higher taxes, the decision may go, as it did in 1984 and 1988, the other way.

Life, liberty, property: our lives are different since September 11, our politics different from what it was in 2000. How are the parties responding? It is easier to answer that question about the Republicans. George W. Bush is in clear control of his party, and Karl Rove, his chief political strategist in Texas and now in the White House, occupies a position that no one has ever held in American history. Few if any political strategists and operatives have ever had the confidence of a president that Rove has; no political strategist has ever played as big a part in helping the president set public policy. Harry Hopkins, who lived in Franklin Roosevelt's White House for long periods, played a major role in policy, but only occasionally dipped into electoral politics, as when he went to the Chicago convention to engineer FDR's draft for a third term in 1940. Robert Kennedy was enormously powerful in making policy when his brother was president, but as attorney general he properly stayed out of electoral politics. Hamilton Jordan in the West Wing played a major role in making policy and in Jimmy Carter's reelection campaign, but took little part in intramural Democratic politics or the off-year campaigns. Lee Atwater in his tragically brief career had the senior George Bush's confidence in political matters but, headquartered at the Republican National Committee, took little or no part in making policy. Karl Rove does politics and does policy; he helps George W. Bush plan ahead and schedule policy decisions and political moves not just weeks but months ahead. He helps to set the strategic themes of the administration and he steps in and settles local political disputes.

To all this Rove brings a knowledge and understanding of history and political demography of a high level which if not unique has only rarely been found in White House aides and political operatives. Even before he became politically involved with Bush, he had a vision of how Texas could become a solid Republican-majority state. Now it is. For some years now he has had a vision of how to build a Republican majority in America, and the 2002 election results suggest he has made at least a little progress toward that goal. His model is a politician underrated in his own time and remembered later only as a personification of out-of-date thinking, 20th century America's first president, William McKinley. McKinley ran for president in 1896 as governor of Ohio, opposed by the eloquent populist William Jennings Bryan. His Republican party had been defeated four years before, after years of equal division between the parties. Its most loyal voters, Civil War veterans, were dying out. Part of the country, the South, was unremittingly hostile. The plains were filled with angry farmers and the cities with teeming immigrants, seemingly the ingredients of a new Democratic majority.

Yet McKinley built a Republican majority instead—indeed, the only lasting Republican majority at all levels of office the nation has seen. His party gained seats in the Senate but lost some in the House in 1898. In 1900, McKinley won reelection and Republicans gained seats in both houses. Over the 36 years from 1896 to 1932, Republicans held the presidency for 28 and held majorities in the Congress for 26. Their national majority came apart only because of the depression of the 1930s.

What was the McKinley formula for success? Public policies like hard money, limited government, toleration of labor unions and immigration, the vigorous assertion of American military power and moral principles in the world.

There is some resemblance between McKinley's formula and George W. Bush's. Both are less about tactical positioning on short-term issues and more about strategic responses on long-term public policy. In 2000, Bush ran a disciplined campaign on five major issues—tax cuts, education, Medicare reform, individual investment accounts in Social Security and strengthening our defense. Education has usually been a Democratic issue; Bush has changed that by relentlessly shifting the focus from the amount of spending to the quality of results. The tax cut, a favorite of Republican primary voters, wasn't a great asset in the general election; Bush went ahead and made it his priority anyway, because a long-term tax cut sets limits to the size of government over the long term. In his time McKinley and even the learned Teddy Roosevelt were scorned by elite intellectuals like Henry Adams, just as Bush is scorned by their equivalent today; McKinley and his Republicans were always opposed by the South, as Bush seems likely to be always opposed by New England and much of the Northeast and California. But the McKinley Republicans created a majority for a party that believed in market economics, a limited but compassionate government, a vigorous foreign policy, and George W. Bush has made some progress toward creating a majority for his party today.

The Democrats in the wake of the 2002 election began to look much like the Democrats of 1896–1912. The Democratic party, throughout its long history, has been a fissiparous party, a collection of out-groups who at their best unite to become the in-party and at their worst become a brawling mob. They were deeply split on some issues in 2001–02—the Bush tax cut and the Iraq military action resolution were the two most prominent. On many others, they have moved far to the left of the Clinton-Gore formula that won them 49% of the votes in 1996 and 48% in 2000. Clinton backed NAFTA and, less successfully, other free trade measures; House Democrats voted by wide margins against trade promotion authority in 2001–02. This will likely hurt them among young and college-educated voters; one thing you learn in Economics 101, no matter how far left or how far right the professor, is that free trade is good. Clinton at least considered giving young workers some chance to get market returns on a portion of their Social Security taxes; today, Democrats are obdurately opposed. Most Democrats backed Clinton rhetorically when he said we must take action against Saddam Hussein in 1998; some of them cavilled and orated against taking military action against Saddam Hussein in 2002. Their complaints about the economy in 2001 and 2002 were loud, but the critique was incoherent. Bill Clinton's "little things" strategy of proposing lots of little programs—family leave, children's health insurance, school uniforms—to help working families worked for him because he was able to use the presidential megaphone to make each program known and also to create the impression he was working hard and creatively to use government to help people in their daily lives. But "little things" programs, however worthy and attractive, can't do the same for today's Democrats who don't have the presidential megaphone—no one will ever hear about them.

There are no obviously good strategies for a party in opposition to a popular president. They can wait for disaster, but Democrats in their hearts do not want to see failure in the war on terrorism or the collapse of the economy, and they certainly do not want to be seen appearing to want such things. They can try to energize their base by espousing left-wing policies, but this risks antagonizing voters in the center. Or they can appeal with moderate policies to the voters in the center and risk low turnout by their base and breakaways to the Green party. They can wait until demographic trends make them a majority again, though this seems unlikely to happen soon, if ever, as young men and women trend Republican and George W. Bush romances Latinos and Asians as Theodore Roosevelt once romanced Italians and Jews.

History gives a party in such a position two pieces of advice. The first is that you should step back and analyze where the nation is today and what government can do to put it in a better place, and then encourage your local and state officeholders to act on those analyses. The New York Democratic party in the 1920s under Al Smith and Franklin Roosevelt acted on the advice of social workers, ethnic leaders, policy theorists and shrewd political bosses and developed policies which provided much of the substance of the New Deal. Republicans in the 1970s listened to the musings of neoconservative intellectuals and Christian conservatives and under Republican National Chairman Bill Brock developed ideas that became policies in the administration of Ronald Reagan. The Democratic Leadership Council and Democratic governors and mayors in the 1980s and early 1990s developed policy positions and political formulas that became the basis for the successful campaigns and successful governance of Bill Clinton. Democrats today risk appearing to be clinging to policies—the Social Security program of 1935 cannot be improved on, protectionism is better than free trade, no limits should be put on the extent to which a few hundred trial lawyers can transfer the assets of millions of stockholders to themselves. They must take a fresh look at the country, and think, and then act on their ideas.

The second lesson is that you should not show—or feel—contempt for the popular president you oppose, because in doing so you show contempt for the people who elected and support him, the people whose votes you need to win. Democrats in the 1950s and 1980s and 2000s made jokes about the mindlessness of Dwight Eisenhower, Ronald Reagan and George W. Bush, jokes that oozed contempt and condescension. They were idiots, they didn't read books, and they were Manchurian candidates manipulated by behind-the-scenes advisers: the litany is familiar. John Kennedy did not win in 1960 by making Mort Sahl jokes about Ike, and Bill Clinton did not win in 1992 by requiring voters to admit they were wrong in voting for Reagan before they could apply for grace by voting for him. Republicans seethed with hatred for Franklin Roosevelt during all his three full terms as president; that did not prevent him from winning a fourth, or prevent Harry Truman from winning in 1948. Republicans seethed with hatred for Bill Clinton. But voters who had decided that they wanted Clinton to remain in office regardless, because of his professional ability and policies, punished Republicans at the polls in 1998. George W. Bush did not win in 2000 by requiring voters to admit they were wrong in supporting Clinton during the impeachment controversy.

One aspect of the Clinton-Gore era that Democrats do seem to have clung to is the war room mentality—non-stop political spin, constant smash-mouth criticism of the opposition, a willingness to change the rules in order to win at all costs. That approach was apparent in Minnesota, when Democrats turned the memorial service for Paul Wellstone into a campaign rally. The reaction was furious, in Minnesota where most voters were watching the event live and, to a surprising extent across the nation. The highly able and personally decent Walter Mondale lost his home state for the first time in his career. Contrast the 1994 race for governor of Texas. The incumbent Democrat, Ann Richards, who had a positive job rating, felt free to make contemptuous remarks about her opponent and to refer to him as "Shrub." The opponent, George W. Bush, always referred to her as Governor Richards and when in a debate she paid tribute to relief workers in an emergency, he began his response by saying, "Well spoken, Governor." Karl Rove hasn't forgotten. Neither should Democrats.

It may be that history will record the years 1995–2001, when there was parity between the two parties and when Clinton was reelected and Al Gore came so close to being elected, as a Clinton detour within a long period of Republican majority, something like the Eisenhower detour in majority-Democratic America. That's certainly what it will look like if the Republican presidential majorities of 1980, 1984 and 1988 and the Republican congressional majorities of 1994 and 2002 are followed by Republican presidential and House majorities in 2004. We are a long way from there yet, and those who remember the 1992 cycle—when it was widely believed that Republicans had a lock on the presidency and that George H.W. Bush with his 91% job rating in March 1991 could not be defeated—understand that many things can happen in American politics.

But there is some reason to believe that this is the way history will record our as yet unfinished era. In the first two-thirds of the 20th century, this country was industrial America, a country that was moving toward standardization and centralization. This was an America of ever bigger corporations, a bigger and more bureaucratized government, standardized professions and scientific communities, assimilation of immigrants and conformity, common social experiences like the comprehensive high school and the draft military. It was a society temperamentally inclined toward centralization, normalization, standardization. That America had a natural tendency to vote for Democrats, at least starting in the 1930s, when the depression enabled FDR's Democrats to outflank McKinley's and his cousin's TR Republicans and emerge as the party favoring vigorous and active government.

In the last third of the 20th century and now in the first third of the 21st, we are living in post-industrial, information age America. The economy is increasingly decentralized, and market-driven rather than regulated by government or manipulated by oligopolies; the culture is increasingly variegated, as people feel free to choose different lifestyles and as new peoples come from other lands; affluence and surging economic growth enables the emergence of many economic and cultural niches in which Americans can choose to live comfortably. It is a society temperamentally inclined toward decentralization, away from bureaucracies and toward markets, for individual choice rather than standardization. This America has a natural tendency to vote for Republicans, although it is willing to vote for Democrats like Clinton who fashion their public policies and political tactics to suit its predispositions. George W. Bush seems to understand the character of this society: a common theme in his 2000 platform—tax cuts, education, Medicare, Social Security—was allowing more individual choice rather than requiring everyone to fit into the same bureaucratically defined template.

There is a similar contrast in how Americans fight their wars. Industrial America fought its wars by using its centralized industrial strength. Large draft militaries, mass-produced unsophisticated weapons and materiel—these are what we brought to World War I and what enabled us to win World War II and prevented our losing in Korea. But as industrial America became postindustrial America, industrial war-fighting worked less well in Vietnam. Now post-industrial, information age America is winning its wars with a volunteer military and special forces, tactics that put a premium on high skills and personal initiative, with highly sophisticated equipment far beyond the capacity of any other country's military forces. We saw this in the Gulf War, we saw it even more in Afghanistan, we saw it in Iraq. This military is an institution that reflects the basic character of the nation led by George W. Bush, a leader who understands his nation's basic character far better than those who seethe with contempt for him. On the performance of this military, and of this president, much depends—including the course of American politics for the next several years, perhaps the next two decades. But it is clear that this nation at peril, alike though it is in its basic character, is importantly different in its politics, from the 49% nation that we thought we knew so well until the 2002 election returns started coming in.

The Political Government

The Founding Fathers did not intend to make American government easy. They set up three branches of government, with powers intertwined with each other. The president would be Commander-in-Chief, but Congress would declare war; the state's electors would choose the president, but the House could do so when no one got an electoral majority; the president would administer, but the Congress would appropriate, and only the House could initiate taxation; the president would conduct foreign policy, but the Senate must approve treaties. All voters would choose members of the House, but state legislatures, originally, chose members of the Senate, and the method of electing the president was left to the state legislatures. Where exactly the Supreme Court would fit into all this the Founders left ambiguous; and it remains ambiguous still, even as the Supreme Court effectively determined who would become president in January 2001.

The political branches of the United States government are now, technically, in the hands of the Republican Party, but by narrow margins. George W. Bush was chosen by an Electoral College majority of 271–266 (which would have been 278–259 if the states had the number of electoral votes as they will in 2004). The House of Representatives is Republican by a 229–206 margin. The Senate is Republican by a 51–49 margin. (In each house there is a nominal Independent, both from Vermont, who votes with the Democrats to organize the chamber). But it is a mistake to say that the Republican Party is in control of a government which in any circumstances is difficult to control and when the Republican control is so tenuous.

This is not control. But it is incumbency, and incumbents ordinarily have one great power in government and politics, the power to set the agenda. That power can move from one branch of the government to another, as it did from Bill Clinton's White House to Newt Gingrich's House of Representatives in November 1994; and it can move back again. It can move outside government altogether: in the spring of 1992 Ross Perot and his cries for cutting deficits and reforming government eclipsed the incumbent president and the man who would be elected his successor. In early 2001, despite the narrowness of his margin and the bitterness of the Florida contest, the power to set the agenda for government was solidly in the hands of George W. Bush. Senate Democrats gained the power to obstruct some of that agenda after Jim Jeffords left the Republican party and gave Democrats a 51–49 edge. But their attempts to set out an agenda of their own foundered. Bush's campaigning and shrewd use of issues enabled Republicans to pick up two seats in the November 2002 election and they now have a 51–49 margin. In early 2003 Bush was once again in position, more firmly than in early 2001, to set the agenda. So it is with the presidency that we begin.

The Presidency   "An institution is the lengthened shadow of one man," wrote Ralph Waldo Emerson, and the presidency has been the lengthened shadows of the 43 men who have held the office. This presidency is the lengthened shadow of George W. Bush, a man Washington had difficulty understanding during the 2000 campaign but who, when observed over his not overlong political career, is a comprehensible and coherent figure.

Bush's 1993–94 campaign for governor was methodical, dogged, clearly focused on issues, and underestimated by the opposition—a campaign that was very much the model for his 1999–2000 campaign for president.

Once in office, Bush acted like a president with a mandate to govern. He pushed his tax cut through in May, just before Democrats became the majority party in the Senate thanks to the defection of Jim Jeffords. He was unphased when 42 of the 50 Senate Democrats voted against the confirmation of their former colleague John Ashcroft as attorney general. He worked with Edward Kennedy and George Miller to pass a bipartisan education bill. He pressed Defense Secretary Donald Rumsfeld to transform the military establishment, while he backed OMB Director Mitch Daniels who gave Rumsfeld far less money than he wanted. Up through early September, his job ratings hovered just above 50%. The nation was still as closely divided as it was on Election Day 2000.

Through all this Bush operated the way he had in Texas and in his campaigns—and very differently from Bill Clinton. The difference between Bush and Clinton is the difference between the quantum and wave theories of light. Clinton was all wave theory, forever oscillating, forever in motion, never focusing on one fixed place, always adapting skillfully to circumstances and settings, never really changing the way others see things. Bush is all quantum theory: no motion for what seems an agonizingly long time, then a sudden pulse of energy that puts everything in a new light. Bush the candidate did no campaigning until May 1999, then emerged within weeks with a campaign organization and set of issues he stuck to for the duration. Bush the nominee stayed mostly out of sight during the 36 days of the Florida controversy, then when it was settled emerged within days with a staffed government and issue agenda. This is a disciplined, methodical man who gets up early in the morning, keeps to his schedule, makes judgments about personnel and decisions about issues quickly and crisply, and sticks mostly to his long-set-out plans. Deadlines are set and met, speech texts reviewed and speeches given, meetings proceed as scheduled, and public appearances go off as planned. George W. Bush is the first business school graduate to become president. His operating style resembles most closely, among former presidents, that of Dwight Eisenhower, who had been more of a manager than a warrior as a general. Like Eisenhower, he has appointed people of great accomplishment outside politics, including some with views which seem different from his own; like Eisenhower, he seems confident he can manage them to produce the results he wants.

Also like Eisenhower, he is often underestimated—misunderestimated, as he puts it. His lack of fluency, especially in comparison to Clinton, is striking and, to the press, suggests that he is dumb: the chattering class likes people who are good at chattering. But his crisp four- and five-point programs are based on more than polls and focus groups. His convention speech showed a sense of history; it spun out a narrative in which Republican presidents have rescued the nation from the consequences of weakness abroad and have reformed its institutions at home, a narrative which places him in a line with Eisenhower, Nixon, Ford, Reagan and his father. His inaugural speech was suffused with a sense of the importance of religion in helping the nation set its course. It is said by his critics that Bush has no understanding of the complexity of issues, that he cannot match Clinton in the exegesis of detail. But he has the kind of intelligence that can get through the fog and confusion of a complicated world and identify the central issue and prepare a response to it.

Those are qualities that became apparent on September 11. Immediately he recognized that the nation had been attacked, and that it was in danger from terrorists and—of critical importance in the months ahead—states that sponsor terrorism. This was a problem he had not prepared for, and yet he was prepared to deal with it. Three days later he spoke movingly at the National Cathedral and declared that the terrorists would be dealt with "at a time and place of our choosing." That afternoon he went to Ground Zero in New York. There were no plans for him to speak to the rescue workers there. But they wanted to hear him. A bullhorn was found and Bush stood next to a retired firefighter on the rubble. Someone in the crowd yelled that he couldn't hear him. Bush said, "I can hear you. The world can hear you. And the people who knocked down these buildings will hear from all of us soon." The rescue workers started chanting, "U.S.A.! U.S.A.! U.S.A.!" It was a climactic moment, entirely unrehearsed. Then on September 20 he spoke to Congress. "Our war on terror begins with al Qaeda, but it does not end there. It will not end until every terrorist group of global reach has been found, stopped and defeated." He announced that, "From this day forward, any nation that continues to harbor or support terrorism will be regarded by the United States as a hostile regime." The issue had been framed: the United States would fight a worldwide war against terrorism and regimes that harbor terrorists. This was not an inevitable response to the attacks, yet it was George W. Bush's, and became America's.

Over the course of the next year, Bush made in quantum leaps the greatest reorientation of American foreign policy since Harry Truman set America's course in the Cold War in 1947–48. In October military action in Afghanistan began; in November the Taliban government fell. In his State of the Union speech in January 2002 he identified Iraq, Iran and North Korea as an "axis of evil, arming to threaten the peace of the world." He went on, "The United States of America will not permit the world's most dangerous regimes to threaten us with the world's most destructive weapons." Military action against Iraq, seemingly unthinkable before, now seemed likely. At West Point on June 1, 2002, Bush said that deterrence and containment no longer were sufficient against the asymmetric threats of terrorists. "Deterrence — the promise of massive retaliation against nations — means nothing against shadowy terrorist networks with no nation or citizens to defend. Containment is not possible when unbalanced dictators with weapons of mass destruction can deliver those weapons on missiles or secretly provide them to terrorist allies. . . . We must take the battle to the enemy, disrupt his plans, and confront the worst threats before they emerge. In the world we have entered, the only path to safety is the path of action. And this nation will act." On June 24 in the Rose Garden he made a sharp break with previous policy on the Palestinians. The United States would support an independent Palestinian state, but only when Palestinians created "entirely new political and economic institutions, based on democracy, market economics and action against terrorism" and after "its leaders engage in a sustained fight against the terrorists and dismantle their infrastructure." On September 12 he spoke to the United Nations, coolly listing the Security Council resolutions that Iraq had violated or ignored and challenged the U.N. to take action. This led to the adoption of a resolution November 8 demanding immediate compliance by Iraq and authorizing member states to take action ("serious consequences") if it did not. This led proximately to American military action in Iraq in March 2003.

When Bush became president, many thought he would be overshadowed by the far more experienced and knowledgeable foreign and defense policy advisers he appointed—Dick Cheney, Colin Powell, Donald Rumsfeld, Condoleezza Rice. He has certainly drawn on their expertise and experience, but all accounts—notably, Bob Woodward's *Bush at War*—indicate that in this administration, as in most others, it is the president who is the real commander-in-chief. During many of the months after September 11 Bush seemed to be taking what was widely regarded as Rumsfeld's advice—in prosecuting the war in Afghanistan, in identifying Iraq as part of the axis of evil, in ordering military action against Iraq with a force about half the size of that in the 1991 Gulf War. But at other times, he seemed to be taking what was widely regarded as Powell's advice— in encouraging Middle East peace negotiations in spring 2002, in going to the United Nations and seeking support for military action in Iraq in September 2002. The picture one gets is of a president who runs an unusually organized White House, after the manner of Eisenhower and Gerald Ford, who identifies issues and sets timetables to address them, who is respectful of his appointees but who leaves no doubt about who is in charge. Newspaper stories based on leaks by disgruntled appointees do appear from time to time, but much less frequently than in many other administrations.

Bush has accepted defeats on issues which he did not consider central, and signed legislation inconsistent with previous statements he had made—the campaign finance regulation bill which passed the Senate in April, the farm bill passed in May 2002. After the collapse of WorldCom he quickly accepted the bipartisan corporate accountability bill sponsored by Senator Paul Sarbanes though it included many provisions Republicans had opposed in the House. In June he called for creation of a Department of Homeland Security, something previously supported mostly by Democrats. After Bush's speech at the United Nations, Bush made it clear he wanted Congress to vote on a resolution authorizing military action in Iraq. At first Daschle said there would have to be long deliberations, probably until after the November election. When it became clear that that was not acceptable to many, he then said that the Senate would deliberate and vote very quickly, presumably so that Democrats could raise other issues that might help them in the election.

It was not clear in 2001 that Bush would campaign hard for Republicans to retake the Senate in 2002. In Texas he had not opposed Democratic legislators who voted for his program. But at some point, perhaps when the Democrats got a majority in the Senate in June 2001 and certainly by early 2002, he seems to have decided that Daschle and the Senate Democrats were using their majority to obstruct too many of his programs, and he decided to fight. White House political adviser Karl Rove and Bush himself were involved in selecting candidates in key races. Clinton had set the record for presidential appearances at political fundraisers and campaign events; Bush far exceeded that record. In that campaigning he consistently emphasized one issue that Democrats evidently thought would have little impact: homeland security. Senate Democrats had provisions in their homeland security bill for civil service protections for employees that Bush argued would tie his hands in the fight against terrorism. Joe Lieberman, chief sponsor of the bill, who had called for a separate homeland security department long before Bush, seemed incredulous that Bush would persist in opposing these provisions. But he did. In September the homeland security bill was held up by a series of discursive speeches by Robert Byrd. In October Republicans prevented Senate Democrats from passing their version of the bill. On the stump Bush argued that Democrats were blocking an effective homeland security bill; ads attacking Democratic senators took up the theme. The issue did not register much in polls. But when combined with the Democrats' divided stand on military action against Iraq, it made the party and its candidates seem less than fully committed to the war on terrorism. Senate Democrats stayed true to their supporters and contributors, the public employee unions. But Bush made sure they paid a political price.

In early 2003, even amid preparations for military action in Iraq, Bush announced an ambitious legislative agenda—$726 billion in tax cuts, including an end to the double taxation of dividends and an acceleration of the 2001 tax cuts, and major changes in Medicare. It was by no means clear at first that these would pass in the Republican-controlled House; Ways and Means Chairman Bill Thomas indicated that there would have to be modifications. But Bush had accepted modifications of his 2001 tax and education proposals. Certainly the Republican majority in the Senate does not guarantee that Bush will get his entire legislative program through that chamber. Democrats' filibuster of the judicial nomination of Miguel Estrada—the first filibuster of a lower court nomination ever—showed that Senate Democrats were in a mood to obstruct much of his program any way they could. The defection of three Republicans on the budget resolution that halved the tax cut showed that the Republican majority in the Senate was by no means as amenable to discipline as Republicans in the House. So did the failure of Republicans to get the full Bush tax cut into the Senate version of the budget resolution. But an image of obstruction will not necessarily help the Democrats in 2004.

The course of the 2004 presidential campaign cannot be known at this writing. While the outcome of military action in Iraq was favorable, the course of postwar Iraq is not known. Further progress or setbacks in the war on terrorism are possible. It is not clear whether voters in November 2004 will still believe that we are a nation in peril. It is utterly uncertain who will be the Democratic nominee and what will be the posture of the Democratic party. In the months before military action in Iraq, Democratic activists and primary voters seemed to be deeply split. Many were strong and vocal opponents of military action in Iraq; many were quieter and less articulate supporters. If that split continues, the contest for the Democratic nomination will be a battle between hawks and doves, a battle that will make it harder, whichever side wins, for the nominee in the general election: a nominee identified as a dove will have trouble appealing to the center of the electorate; a nominee identified as a hawk will be faced with defections to the Green party or some other leftish alternative and with low morale and possibly low turnout among party doves. In contrast to all these unknowns, it seems pretty clear how George W. Bush will conduct his campaign. He will raise enormous amounts of money and will be able, as Clinton was in 1996, to deliver a political message in spring and summer 2004 when the opposition is likely to be out of money and out of the spotlight. He will be able to campaign as a leader in time of war—how strong and effective a leader the voters, of course, will decide. He will campaign as a president who has sought major changes in taxes, Medicare, Social Security, education and other basic programs—changes that typically provide a broader array of choices to individuals and less centralized command and control. The large numbers of Americans still arrayed on both sides of the culture wars make it unlikely that he can win a majority as high as the 61% of Franklin Roosevelt in 1936, Lyndon Johnson in 1964 or Richard Nixon in 1972 or the 59% of Ronald Reagan in 1984. The uncertainty of the course of the war and the economy mean that it is possible that he will win less than the 48% he won in 2000 and will become, as his father was, a one-term president. But for the moment he remains a president with strength far greater than his electoral vote majority and his party's majorities in Congress would suggest.

The House of Representatives   The Framers expected that the House of Representatives would be the prime moving force of the federal government except in time of war. Article I of the Constitution is not about the president, it is about Congress, and the House of Representatives, not the Senate, comes first. The Framers took care to require that all tax laws originate in the House, and by custom appropriations bills originate there too. But in the 20th century's decades of world war and Depression, Cold War and welfare state, Congress became used to waiting for the president's program and then responding, usually with changes at the margins. Then, after the Cold War ended and the Republican won majorities in the 1994 elections, the House took on something of its old role. Led by Speaker Newt Gingrich, armed with the Contract with America that almost all Republican candidates had signed, it started to set the national agenda. Its moment was relatively brief. Bill Clinton's maneuverings during the 1995–96 budget struggle left the president popular and Gingrich a political liability. Even so, the Republican House made its imprint on public policy. The one-year spending freeze led to the balanced budget at the end of the decade. The welfare act passed in 1996 and signed by a reluctant Clinton built on initiatives in the states and settled an issue that had been bedeviling the nation for three decades.

The Republicans are headed to a full decade of majorities in the House, the longest period of Republican control since the years between the 1918 and 1930 elections. Between 1930 and 1994 Republicans won a majority of seats in only two elections, 1946 and 1952. Now they have won a majority in five straight elections—though by narrow margins. The Republican margins peaked at 235–198 (if independents are counted with the party they vote with) in December 1995 after party switches and special election victories and has been as narrow as 219–212 in September 2001. Now it is 229–206. But these small majorities have made a considerable difference. The Republicans prevented Clinton from expanding spending as much as many Democrats would have liked. And they provided George W. Bush with a political leverage that his father, elected by a wider margin, never had.

That is because in the House, as it has operated for the last quarter century, having a majority almost always means having control. That has been true since the speakership of Tip O'Neill. Since O'Neill's time in office, the House has become a more partisan and confrontational institution—whichever party is in control. The partisan atmosphere has been increased by the increasing homogeneity of the parties in the House. The House Republican Conference has become more uniformly conservative and the House Democratic Caucus has become more uniformly liberal. There are exceptions, enough to make a difference on some issues in a closely divided

House. But Speaker Dennis Hastert has spent much time holding together his party, and succeeded far more often in doing so than not.

Hastert is not much known to the general public; he seldom appears on interview programs and is most visible when he introduces the president to joint sessions. He came to the office suddenly, in December 1998, when Speaker-designate Bob Livingston withdrew on the day of the impeachment vote; he was chosen because Majority Leader Dick Armey was distrusted after the July 1997 coup against Newt Gingrich and because Majority Whip Tom DeLay was seen, by himself as well as others, as too partisan a figure for the job. But Hastert exerted his authority over Armey and DeLay and has done a fine job in keeping in touch with and keeping faith with all Republican members. DeLay, known as "the Hammer," proved to be an exceedingly able whip, counting votes accurately and putting together majorities before issues get to the floor—and occasionally while the roll call is going on.

In 2001 the initiative passed to the new Republican president. When Bush came to office, he said he wanted to work with members of both parties, and on one of his key issues, education, he did. A bill was developed by Education Committee Chairman John Boehner and ranking Democrat George Miller and passed with a solid majority, with some conservative Republicans and liberal Democrats opposed. But other legislation took a more partisan path. A prime example was the tax cut. In quick order the leadership and Budget Chairman Jim Nussle and Ways and Means Chairman Bill Thomas passed a reasonable facsimile of the Bush proposal and sent it over to the Senate. On issue after issue, the House, though closely divided, was a rock of strength for the Bush administration—prescription drugs for seniors, HMO regulation, trade promotion authority. On a couple of issues the leadership position did not prevail. The farm bill was in the hands of Agriculture Chairman Larry Combest, from a cotton-growing district in west Texas; it heavily favored Southern farmers and could not be stopped. The leadership kept campaign finance regulation off the floor after losing a rules vote in July 2001. But after the Enron scandal broke, there was no stopping it; advocates of the bill got 218 signatures on a discharge petition, and it came to the floor and was passed. The leadership and George W. Bush acquiesced in these defeats; Bush is not a politician who battles for his position on second-line issues when it might fracture his party's majority on others. For the most part the leadership kept Appropriations subcommittee chairmen inside the limits set by the Bush administration—a source of much friction. In 2002 Armey did not run for reelection. DeLay moved up to Majority Leader and his Chief Deputy Whip Roy Blunt became Whip; appointed to succeed Blunt was sophomore Eric Cantor. It is not widely appreciated, even in Washington, what a competent job Hastert, DeLay and their team have done.

House Republicans have seen continuity in leadership since 1998; House Democrats had an abrupt change in leadership in 2002. At the beginning of 2001, the Democrats' top leaders were veterans: Minority Leader Dick Gephardt had been part of the leadership since 1984 and Minority Whip David Bonior since 1991. But Bonior faced an unfavorable redistricting and decided to run for governor of Michigan; his successor was chosen in a caucus election in October 2001. And Gephardt, after Democrats failed to win back a majority in November 2002, decided to resign the minority leadership and run for president; his successor was chosen in a caucus election in November 2002. The winner of both elections was Nancy Pelosi, heretofore ranking Democrat on the Intelligence Committee. Pelosi's elevation was a break with the tradition: since the 1930s Democrats had chosen as leaders members who had held positions in the leadership. This tradition produced leaders who had generally but not entirely liberal voting records. Pelosi, in contrast, has a voting record among the leftmost in the House and represents a district entirely within the city of San Francisco that in 2000 voted 77% for Al Gore, with 15% for George W. Bush and 8% for Ralph Nader. Pelosi began campaigning for a leadership position in 2000, when it seemed likely that Gephardt and Bonior would be leaving their positions soon and when she and other Democrats were looking forward to regaining the majority, which would give them an additional leadership position. Her base of support was mostly on the left of the party—the large California delegation, women members, black and Hispanic members. Her opponent was Steny Hoyer of Maryland, an able politician with a somewhat more moderate voting record who had long been on the leadership track. In 2000 he too started campaigning hard for whatever leadership position came open.

Democrats failed to win a majority in the House in 2000, but in 2001 it became clear that Bonior would run for governor and would at some point be unable to be on the House floor all day; he resigned the position effective January 2002. In October 2001 there was an election to replace him, and Pelosi beat Hoyer 118–95. This seemed to reflect the liberal cast of the Democratic Caucus. That was apparent too in the October 2002 vote authorizing military force in Iraq. Gephardt, still minority leader, supported the resolution but did not lobby other members. Pelosi supported it and lobbied other Democrats actively. To the surprise of many, Democrats voted against the resolution by 126–81. In November 2002, after the Democrats lost seats to the Republicans, Gephardt quickly announced that he would step down as minority leader; soon he started running for president. The race to succeed him was quickly settled. Caucus Chairman Martin Frost ran against Pelosi and argued that the party should have a moderate leader. But he counted votes and withdrew from the race. In the last days Harold Ford, a junior member with a moderate record, ran on the same platform. But Pelosi won 177–29.

Pelosi obviously understands that not every House Democrat comes from a district or has a voting record as liberal as hers. But her job is not to hold together a narrow majority but to rally a minority dismayed that it has lost four consecutive House elections by agonizingly narrow margins. Many Democrats emerged from the 2002 election with the conviction that they lost not because they opposed and were seen as obstructing the Bush administration but because they did not oppose it more vociferously. This is probably the most liberal Democratic Caucus ever, and the moderates are split. The Blue Dog Democrats tend to be conservative on cultural issues and liberal on economics; the New Democrat Coalition tends to be conservative on economics and liberal on cultural issues. The likelihood is that Pelosi's Democrats will be a party of vigorous and vociferous opposition—the way the House minority party has operated since the days of Tip O'Neill.

It is a minority party that, in early 2003, seemed to have less reason to believe that it could become the majority at the next election. Most Democrats surely believed that their party would win majorities in the 1996 and 2000 elections, and not without good cause: they were close run defeats. In 2002 again there was optimism; it was an off-year election and parties out of power usually gain seats in off-years. But in 2002, for the first time since 1952, redistricting worked against Democrats, in two ways. First, it gave the Republicans about a seven-seat pickup; that number is an estimate, and some Democratic experts say that redistricting was of no net benefit to Republicans, but no one says it helped Democrats. Partisan Republican redistricting plans in Michigan, Pennsylvania and Florida resulted in Democrats losing 7 seats and Republicans gaining 6 seats. That outweighed the Democratic redistricting plans in Maryland, North Carolina and Georgia that resulted in Democrats gaining 5 seats and Republicans losing 2 seats. Republicans were prevented from making major gains in Texas by a court that ruled that the contours of the 1992 partisan Democratic plan should be followed. But Republicans did pick up the 2 new seats there, and the court left it open for the legislature, now controlled by Republicans, to adopt a new plan for 2004. The second way in which redistricting hurt the Democrats was that there were many bipartisan incumbent protection plans that left few seats at risk for either party. California (though Democrats had control), New York, Illinois and Ohio (though Republicans had such control) adopted such plans. So in these four states with 119 seats—more than one-quarter of the House—there were only a handful of seriously contested elections, and there are not likely to be many more in 2004.

There are not a lot of obvious targets for either party elsewhere. Only 32[1] of the 206 Democrats represent districts carried by George W. Bush in 2000; this is down from 46 in 2001. Of

---

1. The list is as follows.

1. Cramer AL 5	6. Moore KS 3	11. Peterson MN 7 veteran
2. Boyd FL 2	7. Lucas KY 4	[i.e., carried district during
3. Bishop GA 2	8. Alexander LA 5	time of popular Republican
4. Marshall GA 3	9. John LA 7	president]
5. Hill IN 9	10. Stupak MI 1	12. Taylor MS 4 veteran

these, 23 seats are in the South and 6 in Texas alone; some may fall to Republicans when longtime incumbents retire and some of the Texas incumbents may be endangered if there is a new redistricting. Only 10 of these Democrats have had experience holding their seats with a popular Republican president in office. Republicans are even less vulnerable. Only 26[2] of the 229 Republicans represent districts carried by Al Gore in 2000; this is down from 40 in 2001. Of these, 16 seats are in the Northeast and 8 in New York and New Jersey. All but 3 of these Republicans had the experience of running while a popular Democratic president is in office. Pelosi's choice as campaign committee chairman, Bob Matsui, has talked of targeting districts which by most standard criteria would seem hard to win; and in the circumstances this is probably a smart strategy. Regaining the majority may turn out to be a four- or six-year project for House Democrats; their prospects for winning control in early 2003 seemed the worst at this stage of the cycle since 1927. But the Republicans' lead is not huge. And prophecy is a risky business. Few observers in early 1993 thought the Republicans would win a majority of House seats in 1994, but they did. No one should rule out the possibility that events that have not yet happened or events that have not yet been foreseen could produce a Democratic majority in the House once again.

The Senate   In November 2002 the Republicans won control of the House and won a majority of seats in the Senate. The choice of words is deliberate. Journalists speak glibly about who controls the Senate. But no one controls the Senate. It is a body of 100 men and women, most of whom think or thought that he or she should be president. It is a legislative chamber which conducts much of its business under rules that require unanimous consent for many matters and in which a supermajority of 60 votes is required for much that used to be routine business. The Framers created the Senate as a balance wheel, a cooling saucer for hot coffee, a place where superior experience and wisdom could prevent unwise and rash mistakes. With only one-third of its members elected every two years, with a fair number of its members free from political pressures because of their personal relationship with young voters in small or one-party states, with its rules allowing even the weakest and personally least regarded of its members to stop the forward motion of legislation for some precious period of time, with its allowance of unlimited discussion and non-germane amendments and its rules that require a 60% supermajority for passage of strongly-opposed legislation, the Senate supplies some caution to the enthusiasm of the House.

Before the ratification in 1913 of the 17th Amendment providing for popular election of senators, the members of the Senate were elected by state legislatures and were something in the nature of ambassadors from the state governments to the federal government—in some cases, very high-ranking ambassadors. In the early republic they were great landowners and lawyers who

---

13. Skelton MO 4 veteran
14. Etheridge NC 2
15. McIntyre NC 7
16. Miller NC 13
17. Pomeroy ND AL
18. Strickland OH 6
19. Carson OK 2

20. DeFazio OR 4 veteran
21. Davis TN 4
22. Gordon TN 6 veteran
23. Tanner TN 8 veteran
24. Sandlin TX 1
25. Turner TX 2
26. Hall TX 4 veteran

27. Lampson TX 9
28. Edwards TX 11 veteran
29. Stenholm TX 17 veteran
30. Matheson UT 2
31. Boucher VA 9 veteran
32. Mollohan WV 1 veteran

2.

1. Beauprez CO 7 non-veteran [i.e., elected 2002 when there was no popular Democratic president]
2. Simmons CT 2
3. Johnson CT 5
4. Castle DE AL
5. Young FL 10
6. Shaw FL 22
7. Burns GA 12 non-veteran

8. Kirk IL 10
9. Nussle IA 1
10. Leach IA 2
11. Northup KY 3
12. Porter NV 3 non-veteran
13. Bass NH 2
14. LoBiondo NJ 2
15. Saxton NJ 3
16. Smith NJ 4
17. King NY 3

18. Fossella NY 13
19. Kelly NY 19
20. Walsh NY 25
21. Quinn NY 27
22. Gerlach PA 6 non-veteran
23. Weldon PA 7
24. Greenwood PA 8
25. Toomey PA 15
26. Dunn WA 8

were also political philosophers—Henry Clay, Daniel Webster and John C. Calhoun. In the late 19th and the early 20th century, they were often wealthy industrialists of considerable intellect—Marcus Hanna, Boies Penrose, Leland Stanford, George Hearst, William A. Clark. After 1913 they were increasingly professional politicians—Republicans and Democrats who alternated in the Northern states with two-party politics and Democrats of great political skill and legislative acumen from the South. This is the Senate described by Robert Caro in *Master of the Senate*, his account of Lyndon Johnson as Senate majority leader from 1955 to 1961. Before Johnson became majority leader, the post was of little importance. There was no majority leader at all until 1911. You will search through many histories of the Republican 80th Congress of 1947–49, a Congress which produced major partisan domestic legislation and supported a bipartisan Cold War policy, before you find the name of the majority leader, Wallace White of Maine; the focus was all on committee chairmen like Robert Taft and Arthur Vandenberg. Johnson, operating in his first four years in a Senate closely divided between the parties, exercised extraordinary skills to produce an extraordinary flow of legislation, including the first civil rights act passed since the 1870s. But after Democrats gained 13 seats in the 1958 election, Johnson's power was diminished because liberal Democrats insisted on pressing for measures that, under Senate rules, could not be passed. Johnson's achievements between 1955 and 1959 created the idea, still lively, that the majority leader runs the Senate. A better understanding of the position's power came from the man who held it longest, Mike Mansfield, in a speech intended to be delivered on the day John F. Kennedy was murdered and which he only delivered in 1997 at the first Leader's Lecture, in which he argued that the majority leader was the servant, not the master, of the senators. Many people assume that the majority leader runs the Senate; what he does in fact is schedule business, and his schedule is usually subject to unanimous consent: He can stop things from happening, but he can't get things going if some significant body of opinion wants them stopped.

The Senate in which Mansfield worked and the Senate in which Robert Byrd, Howard Baker and Bob Dole were majority leader was a Senate which was an incubator of presidential ambitions and a legislative arena for legislative entrepreneurship, far less partisan than the House. Many senators crossed party lines on many issues, and the Senate's rules allowed senators of both parties plenty of leeway for legislative achievement—and for frustration of legislative achievement. But by the late 1990s and in 2000 and 2001, the Senate suddenly became a strikingly more partisan place. One reason was the performance of the two party leaders. Trent Lott, who succeeded Dole as majority leader in June 1996, led an increasingly fractious Republican majority, its fractiousness symbolized by the mistrust between Lott and the majority whip, Don Nickles. Tom Daschle, elected minority leader by the Democratic Caucus by one vote in December 1994, did a superb job of welding Democrats together, keeping in close touch with each Democratic senator and getting them to work together and avoid embarrassing their colleagues. Democratic senators, unlike Republicans, also contributed generously to each other's campaigns.

In House races both parties tend to win about the same number of close races. But there are many fewer Senate races, so there is a tremendous premium for the party that wins most of the close ones. Republicans won a majority in the Senate in 1980 because they won 11 of the 13 closest races. They lost that majority, with the same seats up, in 1986 when they lost six of the eight closest races. After Republicans won a majority in 1994, some combination of skill and luck worked for the Democrats. In 1996 they won five of the eight races decided by less than 5.0% (that includes the January 1996 special election in Oregon). In 1998 they won three of the five closest races. In 2000 they won six of the closest races, including the race in Washington in which the counting was not over until mid-December. Democrats also picked up a seat in July 2000 when Georgia Republican Paul Coverdell died at 61 and was replaced by Democrat Zell Miller. That left the count at 50–50 in the Senate beginning January 3, 2001. For 17 days, while Al Gore was still Vice President, Democrats were committee chairmen; on January 20, when Dick Cheney became Vice President, Republicans were the majority. Then in May 2001 Vermont Republican Jim Jeffords announced he was becoming an Independent and would vote with Democrats to organize the Senate. A new organizing resolution was adopted in June, giving Democrats the chairmanships and a larger number of seats on committees and larger staffs.

The Democrats were able to block quite a bit of legislation but not to pass very much. They failed to pass a budget resolution—the first time since the budget process went into effect in 1974 that the Senate failed to pass a budget resolution—and that made it impossible for them to pass a prescription drug bill, because money had not been set aside for it in the 2001 budget resolution and it had to win 60 votes to pass. They managed to obstruct judicial nominations and block the administration's energy bill. But they were not able to manage issues in a way for political benefit. Democrats kept alive the homeland security bill, but Bush refused to accept its personnel provisions, which were strongly supported by public employee unions. Republicans were able to prevent the bill from coming to a vote in September and October and had an opening to argue, as Bush did on the stump, that Democrats were holding up the homeland security bill to protect favored special interests. This proved to be a losing issue for the Democrats and perhaps cost them their majority in the Senate.

In the House, the leader of the party that won the election stayed in office while the leader of the party that lost resigned. In the Senate it was the other way around. Daschle, seemingly stunned by the result, remained the party leader and seemed determined to step up opposition to and obstruction of the Republican majority. Trent Lott, set to become majority leader again, then uttered his famous words at Strom Thurmond's 100th birthday party December 5. Initially, there was little reaction, and Daschle said mollifying words. But soon there was furor among both liberals and conservatives, and on December 20 Lott stepped down. He was immediately replaced by Bill Frist, who as campaign committee chairmen had done much to produce the victories that made the Republicans the majority again. Frist, the only physician in the Senate, had little experience leading the party on the floor, but had been heavily involved in both monopartisan and bipartisan health care issues. But in his first days and weeks he was met with a barrage of partisan attacks. Democrats rejected Republicans' organizing resolution, which favored the majority in much the same way organizing resolutions before 2001 had. And Democrats filibustered the nomination of Miguel Estrada to the D.C. Circuit Court of Appeals—apparently the first ever filibuster of a lower court judicial nomination. This was the parliamentary equivalent of a declaration of war. This may be the most partisanly divisive Senate in American history.

What accounts for the harsh partisan atmosphere? Sharp differences in the way senators of the two parties see recent political history. In the Democratic cloakroom the history of the last few presidential elections has been one in which Democrats have won great victories from the voters but have been cheated, in the Senate and the Electoral College, out of majorities that should have been theirs. Senate Democrats with their smashing victory in 2000, when they gained five Senate seats, were evidence that they are the nation's choice. The fact that 2000 campaign committee chairman Bob Torricelli's political skill plus a lot of luck produced that majority, with Democrats winning 14 of the 21 closest races in the years in which the senators of 2001 were elected, is overlooked. Polls showing voters backing Democrats' positions on health care, prescription drugs and other domestic issues is only further evidence of their popularity. Polls showing voters backing Republicans' positions on foreign and defense issues are overlooked. Overhanging all this is the controversy over Florida's electoral votes. Many Democratic senators believe that the U.S. Supreme Court's decision awarding the state's electoral votes to Bush was deeply illegitimate and amounted to something like a hijacking of the executive branch. They understand that continued complaints about the result are not politically helpful. But they believe that they are entitled to use their powers under the Senate's rules to prevent what they regard as illegitimate one-party rule.

The view is quite different in the Republican cloakroom. There recent political history looks like one in which Republicans have mostly prevailed by wide margins, in the presidential elections of the 1980s and in congressional elections starting in 1994. The fact that Bill Clinton did win twice and that Al Gore won a plurality of the popular vote is overlooked. Republicans think the Democrats attained their 2001–03 majority of seats by personal tragedy (the death of Paul Coverdell) and good luck in close elections. In this era of increased straight ticket voting, the natural tendency should be for states to favor in Senate elections the party that carried them in the 2000 presidential election; since George W. Bush carried 30 states, Republicans should naturally expect their numbers in the Senate to rise up toward 60. The fact that Democrats have shown skills in winning both seats in Florida and Arkansas and both Dakotas is overlooked. For Republicans the

Supreme Court's decision in *Bush v. Gore* was the only right course and Bush's election entirely legitimate; what was illegitimate was the attempt to thwart him. The fact that so many of their colleagues have a deep and burning conviction that Bush is illegitimate is overlooked. They believe the Democrats, chastised by the voters, have escalated their obstructive tactics, in ways that go far beyond Senate precedent or tradition.

Nothing can dispel this poisonous atmosphere except time and new elections. Presumably the 2004 presidential election will produce a clear and unambiguous margin for the winning candidate, as most presidential elections have. In time, one party or the other will likely have a majority in the Senate larger than 51–49 or 50–50.

Democrats of course hope to regain a Senate majority in 2004. But in early 2003 it seemed more likely that they would be lucky to avoid losses. In 2004, 19 Democratic seats are up and 14 Republican seats. Moreover, more of the Republican senators appeared to have safe seats, leaving 10 Democratic seats looking in early 2003 like they could be seriously contested versus only 3 Republican seats. The likelihood is that Democrats will have more seats to defend than Republicans and will have significantly less money, since they have raised about as much as the Republicans in soft money, now prohibited by the 2002 campaign finance regulation act, but have lagged far behind Republicans in hard money, which is still legal. Moreover, none of the races that seem likely to be seriously contested are in states that were carried by a wide margin by Al Gore, while six of these races are in states that were carried heavily by George W. Bush.

In the meantime, there is always the possibility of a switch in the Senate majority by party switches or by a sudden vacancy in one or two Senate seats. Party switches are not likely so long as the Republicans have a 51–49 majority; the switcher could not be rewarded, as Jim Jeffords was, by a committee chairmanship. But vacancies can change the balance of the Senate. They tend to occur where no one expects them: Georgia Republican Paul Coverdell died suddenly at 61 in July 2000; Minnesota Democrat Paul Wellstone died in a plane crash at 58 in October 2002, 11 days before Election Day. In the 108th Congress the likelihood is that any vacancy will result in a party switch: 29 of the Democratic senators (counting Jeffords) represent states with Republican governors; 28 of the 51 Republican senators represent states with Democratic governors. In some states statutes bar the governor from appointing a successor, but in most states governors can, and presumably will appoint someone of their own party. So sudden fatal illness or tragic accident could shift the balance of the Senate at any time. So remember that no party reliably controls, or can control, the United States Senate.

President

George W. Bush (R)

Elected 2000, seat up Jan. 2005, 1st term; b. July 6, 1946, New Haven, CT; home, Austin, TX; Yale U., B.A. 1968, Harvard U., M.B.A. 1975; Methodist; married (Laura).

Military Career: TX Air Natl. Guard, 1968–73.

Elected Office: TX Gov., 1994–2000.

Professional Career: Founder & CEO, Bush Exploration Oil & Gas Co., 1975–87; Sr. Adviser, Bush Presidential Camp., 1988; Managing Gen. Partner, Texas Rangers baseball org., 1989–98.

Vice President

Richard (Dick) B. Cheney (R)

Elected 2000, seat up Jan. 2005, 1st term; b. Jan. 30, 1941, Lincoln, NE; home, Casper, WY; U. of WY, B.A. 1965, M.A. 1966; United Methodist; married (Lynne).

Elected Office: U.S. House of Reps., 1978–89.

Professional Career: Spec. Asst. to the Dir. of OEO, 1969–70; White House Staff Asst., 1971; Asst. Dir., Cost of Living Cncl., 1971–73; V.P., Bradley, Woods & Co., 1973–74; Dep. Asst. to Pres. Gerald Ford, 1974–75; White House Chief of Staff, 1975–77; U.S. Secy. of Defense, 1989–93; Sr. Fellow, American Enterprise Inst., 1993–95; Chmn. & CEO, Halliburton Co., 1993–2000.

The People

Pop. 2000:	281,421,906
Pop. 1990:	248,709,873
Change 1990–2000:	Up 13.2%
Change 1980–1990:	Up 9.8%
% of U.S. total:	100.0%
Area size:	3,794,083 sq. mi.
State Native:	60.0%
Non-citizen:	6.6%

Language
English: 81.1%
Spanish: 10.2%
Other Eur.: 5.2%

Race/Ethnic Origin

194,552,774	69.1%	White
33,947,837	12.1%	Black
10,123,169	3.6%	Asian
2,068,883	0.7%	Native Am.
353,509	0.1%	Hawaiian
4,602,146	1.6%	Two + races
467,770	0.2%	Other
35,305,818	12.5%	Hisp. Origin

Ancestry
German: 12.0%   Irish: 8.5%
English: 6.8%   USA: 5.7%
Italian: 4.4%

Military veterans: 26,403,703 (12.6%)
WWII: 20.5%   Korea: 13.6%
Vietnam: 31.7%   Gulf War: 10.2%

Most populous cities:
1. New York   8,008,278
2. Los Angeles   3,694,820
3. Chicago   2,896,016
4. Houston   1,953,631
5. Philadelphia   1,517,550

Urban population: 79.0%
Rural population: 21.0%

Education
H.S. Grad: 80.4%
College Grad: 24.4%

Industry

Agri: 1.9%	Con: 6.8%
Fin: 6.9%	Info: 3.1%
Mfg: 19.3%	Prof: 29.2%
Public: 4.8%	Trade: 15.3%
Other: 12.7%	

Occupation
Blue collar: 24.1%   White collar: 60.3%
Gray collar: 15.6%

Work Sector
Private: 78.5%   Govt: 14.6%
Self: 6.6%   Family: 0.3%
Unemployment: 5.7%

Household Income
<15k: 15.8%   15-35k: 25.6%   35-50k: 16.5%   50-100k: 29.7%
100-150k: 7.7%   >150k: 4.6%   Median: $41,994
Poverty status: 12.4%

Home Value
<50k: 14.9%   50-100k: 29.6%
100-200k: 35.2%   200-300k: 11.2%
300-500k: 6.1%   >500k: 2.9%
Median: $111,800

2000 Presidential Vote

George W. Bush (R)	50,456,169	(47.8%)
Al Gore (D)	50,996,116	(48.4%)
Ralph Nader (Green)	2,831,066	(2.7%)

1996 Presidential Vote

Clinton (D)	47,401,185	(49%)
Dole (R)	39,197,469	(41%)
Perot (I)	8,085,294	(8%)

★ ALABAMA ★

In 21st century Alabama you can still see the monuments that symbolize the cultural and historical history of 20th and 19th century Alabama. On a hill in downtown Montgomery, Dexter Avenue connects two buildings that capture much of southern history. Atop the hill is the restored Greek Revival Alabama Capitol, where the first Confederate Congress convened and Jefferson Davis took the oath of office as president of the Confederacy in February 1861. A few blocks down the hill is the Dexter Avenue Baptist Church, where in December 1956 the 27-year-old Martin Luther King Jr. led the boycott that began when Montgomery seamstress Rosa Parks refused to move to the back of the bus. One building symbolizes the breakout of fiery defiance that led to the tragedy of the Civil War, the other the dignified resistance that produced the success of the civil rights revolution. Today, both the Confederacy and the civil rights movement are celebrated, though as time goes on with less emphasis on the first and more on the latter: Maya Lin's circular Civil Rights Memorial in Montgomery, the Civil Rights Institute across the street from the 16th Street Baptist Church in Birmingham's Civil Rights District, the Pettus Bridge in Selma and the Dexter Avenue Baptist Church are among the many sites of civil rights and black history preserved and promoted by the state.

Yet for all the classic symmetry of the Capitol and the calm simplicity of the black churches, nature still seems untamed in Alabama, and the raw passions of the first settlers that gave life to these serene buildings often seem ready to break into anger—even as its politics moves beyond the struggles of past centuries. There has been a raucous tone to Alabama's history since the first Jacksonian farmers pushed the Indians west and plowed the steeply inclined red clay hills of northern Alabama, and the first plantation owners shipped in hundreds of slaves to grow cotton in the dark Black Belt soil. It was the violent reactions of white Alabamans that led to the greatest triumphs of civil rights: The police dogs and fire hoses of Birmingham in 1963 motivated President John F. Kennedy to endorse what would become the Civil Rights Act of 1964, and the beatings on the bridge to Selma spurred President Lyndon B. Johnson to propose the Voting Rights Act of 1965. Even in Alabama's peaceful economic development is a story of the clang of metal on rock: Miners hacking away in the 1880s at the solid-iron Red Mountain to feed newly cast steel mills glaring in the valley of Birmingham below; motorists today speeding past exposed red earth of gouged-out hillsides towards the factories and Wal-Mart shopping centers that have sprouted up in the past two decades.

There is a similar rawness to Alabama's politics, as it has shifted from one of the nation's most Democratic to one of its more Republican states. Alabama politics in the first half of the 20th century was a struggle between angry populists who favored New Deal government spending to help the little guy—Senator and Supreme Court Justice Hugo Black, Senators Lister Hill and John Sparkman, Governor "Kissin' Jim" Folsom—and the local economic potentates they called the "Big Mules" and the plantation owners of the Black Belt (named for its rich soil, not its numerous slaves and sharecroppers). Then, as the civil rights movement was sparked when Rosa Parks refused to leave a front seat in a city bus, Alabama politics became focused on blacks' peaceable protests against legally enforced racial segregation and whites' angry and sometimes violent opposition to desegregation.

The key figure here was George Wallace, first elected governor in 1962, and who retired as governor in 1986, a changed man in a changed state. While Martin Luther King Jr. was leading what turned out to be a civil rights revolution whose moral force he was among the first to comprehend, Wallace was an opportunistic politician who decided that he would never again be "out-segged," as he believed he had been in the 1958 Democratic gubernatorial primary. Wallace in June 1963 made a symbolic stand in the schoolhouse door after a federal court desegregation order, a charade that encouraged violent resistance. The acts of Alabama officials—Birmingham Police Commissioner Bull Connor (then Alabama's Democratic National Committeeman) ordered police dogs and fire hoses to be turned on peaceful demonstrators in May 1963; Sheriff Jim Clark's cordon tried to prevent the Selma-to-Montgomery march in March 1965—sanctioned and fostered this climate of violence, like the bombing of the 16th Street Baptist Church that killed four

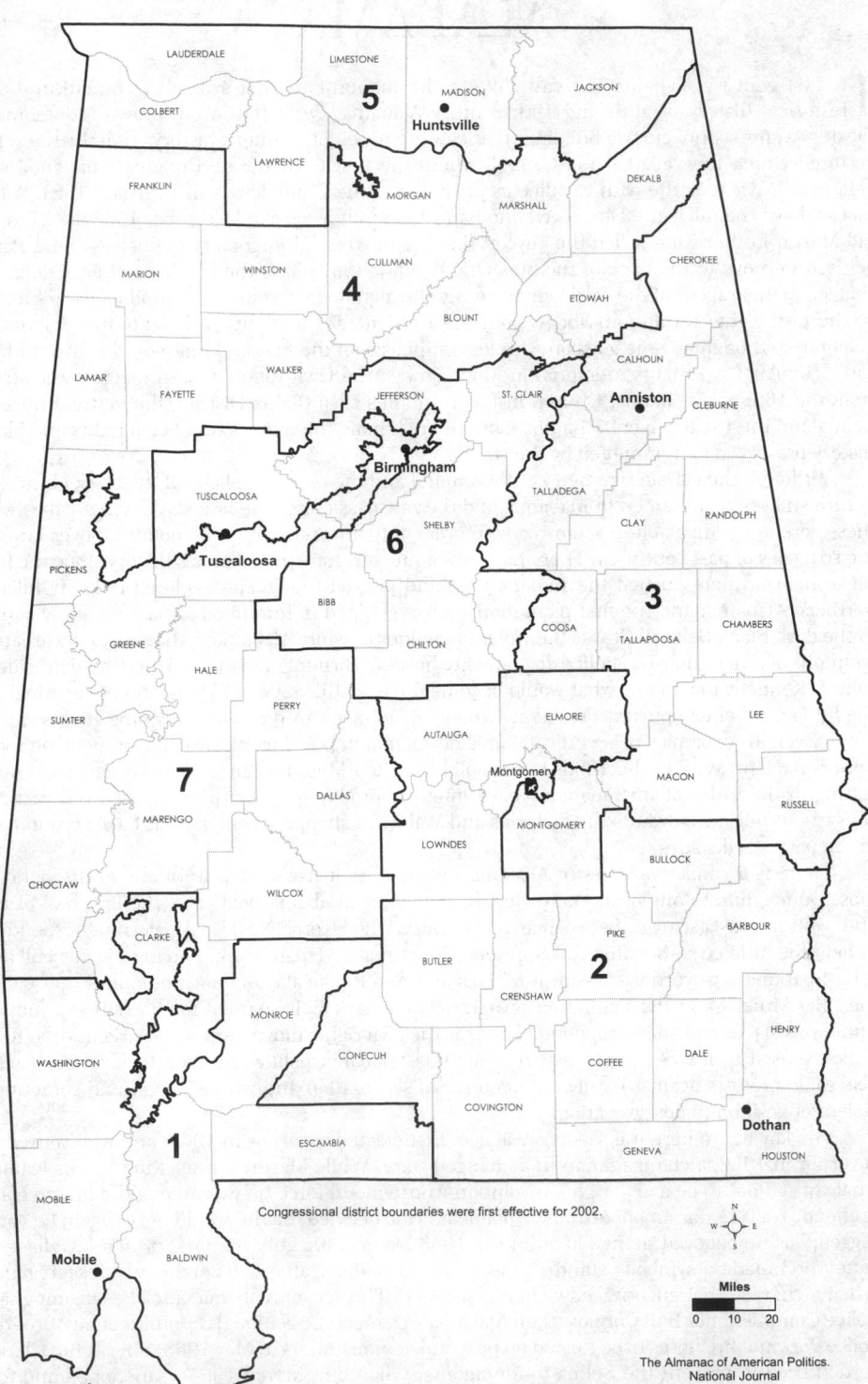

LAUDERDALE
COLBERT
LIMESTONE
5
MADISON
• **Huntsville**
JACKSON
LAWRENCE
FRANKLIN
MORGAN
DEKALB
MARSHALL
MARION
WINSTON
CULLMAN
4
CHEROKEE
ETOWAH
BLOUNT
LAMAR
FAYETTE
WALKER
JEFFERSON
ST. CLAIR
CALHOUN
Anniston •
CLEBURNE
TUSCALOOSA
Birmingham •
SHELBY
TALLADEGA
CLAY
RANDOLPH
PICKENS
Tuscaloosa •
6
BIBB
CHILTON
COOSA
TALLAPOOSA
CHAMBERS
3
GREENE
HALE
PERRY
AUTAUGA
ELMORE
LEE
SUMTER
7
DALLAS
Montgomery •
MACON
RUSSELL
MARENGO
LOWNDES
MONTGOMERY
BULLOCK
CHOCTAW
WILCOX
PIKE
BARBOUR
CLARKE
BUTLER
2
MONROE
CRENSHAW
HENRY
WASHINGTON
CONECUH
COFFEE
DALE
Dothan •
1
ESCAMBIA
COVINGTON
GENEVA
HOUSTON
MOBILE
Congressional district boundaries were first effective for 2002.
Mobile •
BALDWIN

Miles
0   10   20

The Almanac of American Politics.
National Journal

little girls and the murder of two civil rights demonstrators by snipers in Lowndes County. The North was no longer able to turn its eyes away from the South's legally imposed segregation, and most Americans decided it must end.

Despite his defeat, Wallace went national. With a shrewd sense of ordinary voters' resentment at elites' cultural liberalism, Wallace ran well in the 1964 and 1972 northern Democratic presidential primaries, and as a third-party candidate in the 1968 presidential race won 13.5% of the vote. He was partially paralyzed by a gunshot wound while campaigning in May 1972, and lost all force as a national politician when he lost to Jimmy Carter in the March 1976 Florida primary. But he remained the key figure in Alabama for a decade, retiring as governor in 1978 but returning to office in 1982 until his final retirement in 1986. He spent his last sad years apologizing for his acts, meeting with the student he tried to block in the schoolhouse door, and proclaiming, "The South has changed, and for the better," until his death in September 1998.

In the Wallace years, Alabama lost important ground. While Atlanta was peacefully desegregating and beginning three decades of vibrant white-collar growth, Birmingham was violently resisting the civil rights movement, only to see the shrinkage of its once substantial blue-collar base—the steel industry—and an outflow of talented people of all races. The state's economy, regarded as progressive when manufacturing was the leading edge of growth, seemed backward at the end of the Wallace era.

Wallace delayed for a generation the rise of the Republicans in Alabama and the non-metropolitan South. But post-Wallace Alabama has developed a two-party politics in which the Republicans have been more successful than the Democrats—and also more volatile. On one side of this political conflict are the Democrats: Their voting base is Alabama's large black minority and the institutional base is the state's well organized teachers' unions and trial lawyers. On the other side are the Republicans: Their voting base is white evangelical Protestants and their institutional base is small businessmen and the affluent young families filling the fast-growing suburban areas outside Birmingham, Montgomery, Mobile and Huntsville—groups that are fractious and not well organized. The Republicans have tended to prevail, by large margins in presidential and Senate and state Supreme Court elections and by narrow margins in races for governor and statewide downballot offices. But the Democrats have fought back hard, holding onto the legislature and, since Wallace left office, ousting one Republican governor from office (Guy Hunt in 1993), defeating another (Fob James in 1998) and twice contesting election results with dubious legal arguments (the Democratic runoff in 1986 and the general election in 2002).

The 2000 and 2002 elections were examples of these trends. George W. Bush carried Alabama (56%–42%) without difficulty, and so did Republican Senator Jeff Sessions in 2002 (59%–40%). But the 2002 race for governor was much closer, and heatedly contested.

Slowly, a new Alabama is growing along the state's Interstate highways—Alabama ranks number one in the percentage of workers who drive to work—and in the suburban sprawl beyond Birmingham, Montgomery, Mobile and Huntsville. The state's Hispanic population tripled in the 1990s, to 75,000. The Mercedes Benz plant built in 1993 near Tuscaloosa has been expanded; Honda is building a big plant in Talladega County, off I-20 east of Birmingham. The exceedingly close race for governor between Democrat Don Siegelman and Republican Bob Riley showed the close division between the two Alabamas. Siegelman carried the central cities, the Black Belt and the poor-white rural counties in the north. This was the coalition of blacks and poor whites the political scientist V.O. Key, Jr., longed for in his mid-century classic *Southern Politics*. But it was not enough to win. Riley carried prospering small counties along the Interstates near the Georgia and Florida borders and the area around the space-high-tech center of Huntsville. By an even greater margin, he carried the fast-growing suburban counties. Eight counties grew by more than 25% in the 1990s, and Riley carried seven of them 62%–35%, with a 59,000-vote margin, although they cast only 14% of total votes. The other 59 counties went 51%–47% for Siegelman, enough for a 55,000-vote margin, but not quite enough to win. Alabama has seen a future, and it is not what V.O. Key hoped for or George Wallace sought.

The People		Race/Ethnic Origin			Military veterans: 447,397 (13.5%)	
Pop. 2000:	4,447,100	3,125,819	70.3%	White	WWII: 17.5%	Korea: 14.0%
Pop. 1990:	4,040,587	1,150,076	25.9%	Black	Vietnam: 32.9%	Gulf War: 11.6%
Change 1990–2000:	Up 10.1%	30,989	0.7%	Asian	**Most populous cities:**	
Change 1980–1990:	Up 3.8%	21,618	0.5%	Native Am.	1. Birmingham	242,820
% of U.S. total:	1.6%	1,059	0.0%	Hawaiian	2. Montgomery	201,568
Pop. rank:	23d of 50	39,086	0.9%	Two+ races	3. Mobile	198,915
Area size:	52,419 sq. mi.	2,623	0.1%	Other	4. Huntsville	158,216
State Native:	73.4%	75,830	1.7%	Hisp. Origin	5. Tuscaloosa	77,906
Non-citizen:	1.2%	**Ancestry**			Urban population: 55.4%	
Language		USA: 14.8%		English: 6.8%	Rural population: 44.6%	
English: 94.2%	Spanish: 3.1%	Irish: 6.7%		German: 5.0%		
Other Eur.: 1.8%		Scotch-Irish: 1.7%				

Education		Work Sector		Legislature	
H.S. Grad:	75.3%	Private: 77.9%	Govt: 15.5%	Senate	25 D 10 R
College Grad:	19.0%	Self: 6.2%	Family: 0.3%	House	63 D 42 R
Industry		Unemployment: 6.2%		Legislative Term Limits: No	
Agri: 1.9%	Con: 7.6%	**Household Income**		**Registered Voters**	
Fin: 5.8%	Info: 2.2%	<15k: 22.5%	15-35k: 28.4%	No party registration	
Mfg: 23.7%	Prof: 26.4%	35-50k: 16.5%	50-100k: 24.9%		
Public: 5.2%	Trade: 15.8%	100-150k: 4.9%	>150k: 2.7%		
Other: 11.4%		Median: $34,135			
Occupation		Poverty status: 16.1%			
Blue collar: 30.3%	White collar: 55.4%	**Home Value**			
Gray collar: 14.3%		<50k: 28.4%	50-100k: 38.3%	100-200k: 24.7%	200-300k: 5.2%
		300-500k: 2.3%	>500k: 1.1%	Median: $76,700	

Presidential politics   Alabama is one of the most Republican states in presidential elections. In 2000, Alabama whites voted 73%–25% for George W. Bush and Alabama blacks voted 91%–8% for Al Gore; Gore's best county in the nation was one of the nation's poorest, heavily black Macon County, where he won 86% of the vote. As head of the Alabama Democratic Conference Joe Reed has said, "Blacks are the base of the Democratic Party"; blacks sometimes cast most of the votes in Democratic primaries. But overall the state went 56%–42% for Bush.

Alabama's presidential primary is in June—too late to count for much. An attempt to change the date failed in 1999.

Congressional districting   The Democrats in control of redistricting in Alabama in 2002 did a pretty good job of helping their party in drawing the boundaries of the state's

108th Congress Lineup
5 R   2 D

107th Congress Lineup
5 R   2 D

2000 Presidential Vote
Bush (R)	941,173	(56%)
Gore (D)	692,611	(42%)
Nader (Green)	18,323	(1%)
Other	14,165	(1%)

2000 Republican Presidential Primary
Bush (R)	171,077	(84%)
Keyes (R)	23,394	(12%)
Uncommitted	8,608	(4%)

2000 Democratic Presidential Primary
Gore (D)	214,541	(77%)
Uncommitted	48,521	(17%)
LaRouche (D)	15,465	(6%)

1996 Presidential Vote
Dole (R)	768,826	(50%)
Clinton (D)	662,066	(43%)
Perot (I)	92,628	(6%)

seven congressional districts, but not quite good enough of a job to add to the two seats they have held since 1994. They marginally strengthened Democrat Bud Cramer in the 5th District and reduced the black percentage in the majority-black 7th District. The biggest change was to the 3d District, where incumbent Republican Bob Riley left to run for governor. The 3d was made significantly more Democratic by the subtraction of fast-growing St. Clair County east of Birmingham and the addition of part of Montgomery County, including the area around the Capitol. The black percentage was raised from 25% to 32%, the second highest in the state. But these changes were not quite enough to elect former Democratic state Chairman Joe Turnham, who lost narrowly to Republican Mike Rogers.

Governor

Bob Riley (R)

Elected 2002, term expires Jan. 2007, 1st term; b. Oct. 3, 1944, Ashland; home, Ashland; U. of AL, B.A. 1965; Baptist; married (Patsy).

Elected Office: Ashland City Cncl., 1972–76; U.S. House of Reps., 1996–02.

Professional Career: Owner, egg & poultry co.; Rancher; Owner, Midway Transit, 1965–present.

Office: Alabama State Capitol, 600 Dexter Ave., Montgomery, 36130, 334-242-7100; Fax: 334-353-0004; Web site: www.governor.state.al.us.

Election Results

2002 general	Bob Riley (R)	672,225	(49%)
	Don Siegelman (D)	669,105	(49%)
	Other	25,273	(2%)
2002 primary	Bob Riley (R)	262,851	(74%)
	Steve Windom (R)	63,775	(18%)
	Tim James (R)	30,871	(9%)
1998 general	Don Siegelman (D)	760,155	(58%)
	Fob James (R)	554,746	(42%)

Bob Riley, elected governor of Alabama by a 3,120-vote margin in 2002, grew up in Clay County, off the beaten track east of Birmingham, where his father had lived for seven generations. Riley was a University of Alabama student, watching when George Wallace stood in the schoolhouse door in 1963. Two years later, he returned home with a business degree; he and his brother started selling eggs door-to-door. Eventually, that became a large egg and poultry company; he also ran a grocery store, owned an airport, a pharmacy and sold real estate. He ended up with a car dealership (Midway Ford and Chrysler), a trucking company (Midway Transit), half a shopping center and a cattle farm, and served on the city council in Ashland. In 1996, when the 3d District's Democratic congressman ran unsuccessfully for the Senate, Riley ran for the House. He started off little known outside Clay County, but he was a strong and energetic campaigner, a supporter of school prayer, term limits, tax cuts and a balanced budget amendment and an opponent of abortion, gun control and racial quotas. Riley won 50%–47%—a key victory in keeping the House Republican.

In the House, Riley had a solidly conservative voting record; he said he came to Washington intending to be bipartisan, but his first three months made him "become the most partisan person on Capitol Hill." After Fort McClellan was shut down under the 1995 base closings, he fought to save 3,600 jobs at the adjacent Anniston Army Depot, which refurbishes tanks. The Anniston depot was revived with a $4 billion armored vehicle repair project and an $800 million incinerator for destruction of military gases. Riley had serious competition in 1998 from former Democratic state Chairman Joe Turnham, but he spent $845,000 of his own money and won 58%–42%. He was unopposed in 2000 and, eager to return to Alabama, ran for governor in 2002.

It was an audacious decision: Riley was taking on not only Democratic Governor Don Siegelman but also, in the Republican primary, Lieutenant Governor Steve Windom. Siegelman was in an embattled position. A longtime statewide officeholder, he beat incumbent Republican Fob James 58%–42% in 1998, after James had only narrowly won his primary. He won by supporting a lottery to fund education, but voters later rejected the lottery 54%–46% in an October 1999 referendum. "I have no Plan B," Siegelman said, and state spending on education was cut, with universities and K-12 lobbies fighting over shares of a shrinking pie. Siegelman had success in attracting automakers Honda and Hyundai to the state, got a compromise between trial lawyers and business leaders on limits to jury awards, and installed the CHIP children's health care program. He convinced voters to approve Amendment One for $425 million in bonds to fund road and bridge building. But he continued to have trouble on education funding. A special session in mid-2001 rejected his entire proposal; another in December 2001 passed $140 million in business and telephone taxes. Siegelman was also troubled by scandal. In September 1999, he was embarrassed when two young aides were revealed to have been getting tickets fixed. A 1998 campaign contributor and adviser pleaded guilty in October 2001 to Medicaid fraud. That same month, a Montgomery engineer and adviser was indicted for involvement in a deal to build a state warehouse without competitive bidding. Republicans charged that Siegelman got about $900,000 in legal fees for a tobacco case he brought when out of office in 1997 after he pledged $20 million of public funds to settle the case; in July 2001, the Alabama Ethics Commission voted to drop the case. In 2002, it was revealed that Siegelman's personal finances were under investigation by a joint state-federal task force—not the kind of news you want in an election year.

In the June primary, Siegelman beat Agriculture Commissioner Charles Bishop by a 76%–18% margin, but Riley also won, and by the unexpected margin of 74%–18% over Windom, whom he called part of the problem in Montgomery. Riley was further strengthened when George W. Bush came to Alabama in July 2002 for a fundraiser that raised $4 million for his campaign; overall he outspent the incumbent. The issues were pretty squarely posed. Siegelman said in May that he still favored a lottery, but his Plan B appeared to be raising taxes on business; in October 2002, anticipating victory, he called for a special session for that purpose. Siegelman said he had made progress on replacing portable classrooms and raising test scores; he took credit for new roads built thanks to Amendment One and for the new Honda and Hyundai plants. He attacked Riley for liens on his houses in Alabama and Florida and for missing many votes in the House.

Riley charged that state government was "sinking into a quicksand of corruption and fraud." He called the lottery "the return of a bad idea." He opposed tax increases and called for limiting spending to the prior year's revenues. He called for a new model for economic development, aimed at using the University of Alabama at Birmingham and other universities as magnets for biotech, high-tech and research industries and creating incentives for small business. He called for a commission to recommend changes in the 1901 Constitution to give local governments more power to pass local laws that do not require approval by the legislature. In late summer, Riley was running ahead in polls, but in September he made several blunders and his standing fell. He stumped one day with National Rifle Association president Charlton Heston; the next day it was revealed that the NRA endorsed Siegelman (as it does all incumbents who oppose gun control). Then Riley aides hinted that Heston might have been affected by Alzheimer's disease. And contrary to a promise Riley made during a debate, his campaign finance disclosure did not list the names of those who paid $50,000 to get their pictures taken with President Bush.

This turned out to be the closest gubernatorial race in the nation in 2002. Siegelman won overwhelmingly among black voters and his denunciations of corporations who opposed his business tax increase probably helped him carry heavily white rural counties in northwestern Alabama. He carried Birmingham's Jefferson County and Montgomery County, but by narrower margins than in 1998. Riley won by big margins in fast-growing suburban counties—he won Shelby County by more than 2–1. He ran far ahead of the 1998 Republican showing in his old congressional district, and around three widely separated cities—Huntsville in the north, Dothan in the southeast and Mobile, Siegelman's hometown, in the south.

On election night, it was unclear for a time who had won. A clerical error in rapidly-growing and heavily Republican Baldwin County on the Gulf coast credited Siegelman with 7,000 more votes than he actually received; a tally with that number showed him ahead, though it was quickly corrected. Both Riley and Siegelman proclaimed themselves winners. Siegelman refused to recognize that the Baldwin County tally that put him over the top was an error, even though it was absurd to think that 7,000 more votes were cast for governor than for other offices (that would mean that 51,000 people voted for governor and 44,000 for lieutenant governor and other offices).

Siegelman called for a statewide recount which could take months and indicated he would not relinquish the governor's office. Only after two weeks, on November 18, did he concede.

Governing may not be any easier for Riley, the first congressman to be elected governor of Alabama since 1894. The legislature still has Democratic majorities, and Democrats retained some downballot offices. The state still faces revenue shortfalls and demands from many that it spend more on education and jails.

Senior Senator

Richard Shelby (R)

Elected 1986, seat up 2004, 3d term; b. May 6, 1934, Birmingham; home, Tuscaloosa; U. of AL, B.A. 1957, LL.B. 1963; Presbyterian; married (Annette).

Elected Office: AL Senate, 1970–78; U.S. House of Reps., 1978–86.

Professional Career: Practicing atty., 1963–78; City Prosecutor, Tuscaloosa, 1963–71; U.S. Magistrate 1966–70; Spec. Asst. to U.S. Atty. Gen., 1969–71.

DC Office: 110 HSOB, 20510, 202-224-5744; Fax: 202-224-3416; Web site: shelby.senate.gov.

State Offices: Birmingham, 256-731-1384; Huntsville, 256-772-0460; Mobile, 251-694-4164; Montgomery, 334-223-7303; Tuscaloosa, 205-759-5047.

Committees: *Aging (Special). Appropriations*: Defense; Foreign Operations; Homeland Security; Labor, HHS & Education; Transportation, Treasury & General Government (Chmn.); VA, HUD & Independent Agencies. *Banking, Housing & Urban Affairs* (Chmn.): Economic Policy; Housing & Transportation. *Governmental Affairs*: Financial Management, Budget & International Security; Investigations (Permanent).

Group Ratings

	ADA	ACLU	AFS	LCV	CON	ITIC	NTU	COC	ACU	NTLC	CHC
2002	10	20	38	6	51	38	51	85	89	88	—
2001	5	—	0	0	—	—	77	93	100	—	100

National Journal Ratings

	2001 LIB —	2001 CONS		2002 LIB —	2002 CONS
Economic	7%	86%		37%	62%
Social	0%	79%		0%	62%
Foreign	36%	54%		40%	59%

Key Votes of the 107th Congress

1. Approve Bush Tax Cuts	Y	5. Confirm Ashcroft as AG	Y	9. Bar Coop. with Intl. Court	Y
2. Expand Patients' Rights	N	6. Bar Gays in the Boy Scouts	Y	10. Trade Promotion Authority	*
3. Campaign Finance Reform	N	7. $ for Hate Crime Prosecution	N	11. Authorize Force in Iraq	Y
4. Permit ANWR Development	Y	8. Overseas Military Abortions	N	12. Homeland Sec. Dept. Union	N

Election Results

1998 general	Richard Shelby (R)	817,973	(63%)	($1,890,484)
	Clayton Suddith (D)	474,568	(37%)	($15,723)
1998 primary	Richard Shelby (R)	unopposed		
1992 general	Richard Shelby (D)	1,022,698	(65%)	($2,807,764)
	Richard Sellers (R)	522,015	(33%)	($149,578)
	Other	31,811	(2%)	

Prior Winning Percentages: 1986 (50%); 1984 House (97%); 1982 House (97%); 1980 House (73%); 1978 House (94%)

Richard Shelby grew up in Birmingham, the son of a steelworker. After earning two degrees from the University of Alabama, he stayed in Tuscaloosa and went into law practice with Walter Flowers, who was later a conservative Democratic congressman; Shelby was well enough politically connected to be elected state senator in 1970, at 36. When Flowers ran for the Senate in 1978—he lost the Democratic primary to Howell Heflin—Shelby ran for his House seat. The critical contest was the Democratic runoff against Chris McNair, a black legislator whose daughter had been killed in the 1963 Birmingham church bombing; the district had the highest black percentage in Alabama at the time. Once in office, Shelby had a conservative voting record, opposing the Voting Rights Act extension and the Martin Luther King Holiday. In the 1986 Senate race, he won the primary with 51% after getting then-Secretary of State Don Siegelman to withdraw, then ran TV ads attacking incumbent Jeremiah Denton, a retired admiral who had been a prisoner of war in Vietnam, for voting to cut Social Security and owning two Mercedes (not a likely negative now, with the Mercedes plant in Tuscaloosa County). Shelby won by 7,000 votes.

As one of half a dozen or so conservative southern Democrats in the Senate, Shelby at first attracted little notice. He voted for the confirmation of Clarence Thomas and for the Gulf War resolution. He voted against the campaign finance bill supported by almost all Democrats and he voted for the Strategic Defense Initiative. In 1992, he was re-elected 65%–33%; this broke the jinx on a seat which, before Shelby's election in 1986, had four occupants in 10 years.

Shelby's break with the Democratic Party came soon after Bill Clinton took office. In February 1993, angered by Shelby's criticism of the president's just-released economic plan—"the taxman cometh"—Clinton strategists ostentatiously decided to make an example of him and Shelby ostentatiously decided to make a display of his independence. At a meeting in which Vice President Al Gore tried to persuade Shelby to support the plan, Shelby turned to 19 Alabama TV cameras and, embarrassing Gore, further denounced the Clinton program as "high on taxes, low on spending cuts." As punishment, it was announced that a multi-million dollar space facility would be built not in Alabama but in Texas (it eventually went up in Alabama). But, as Clinton's ratings slid downward, this only raised Shelby's popularity ratings to the highest level in the state, making a politician previously known more for his suppleness of maneuver now appear an embattled defender of principle. Relentlessly, Shelby voted against the administration again and again and lined up with Republicans on almost every partisan issue, criticizing the Democrats' health care plan as "ill-conceived, unworkable and unwanted by the American people." The day after Republicans regained control of the Senate in 1994, Shelby announced he was switching parties and increased the Republican majority to 53–47. Republicans happily allowed him to keep his seniority on the Banking Committee and gave him seats on Appropriations and its Defense Subcommittee and on Intelligence as well.

This is the path that led Shelby to the chairmanship of the Intelligence Committee in 1997 and which made him, as ranking minority member on the committee, an important policymaker after September 11. Shelby took an adversarial posture toward the intelligence agencies during the Clinton years and in the Bush years as well. He criticized and helped kill Anthony Lake's nomination as CIA director in 1997. He called the Wye River Memorandum's use of CIA officers to monitor compliance "troubling," and promised to investigate the use of American-made satellites by the Chinese to gather military intelligence. In the November 2000 intelligence reauthorization he included a provision making it a crime for a government official to disclose "properly" classified information. This was supported by the Justice Department, the CIA and by House Intelligence Chairman Porter Goss. But it was opposed by news organizations, many liberals, and by conservatives like Henry Hyde and Bob Barr, and Clinton vetoed the bill.

Soon after September 11, Shelby stopped just short of calling for the resignation of CIA Director George Tenet, who was appointed by Clinton and retained by Bush. "If he's doing such a good job, why so many failures?" he said on *CBS Morning News*, "I'm not sure he has the skills" needed to manage the intelligence committee. He told reporters that he was first disillusioned with Tenet after India conducted three underground nuclear tests and Tenet told him, "We didn't have a clue. I got to thinking, 'I wonder what else they're missing big time.'" He argues that U.S. intelligence was clueless about the February 1993 World Trade Center bombing, the 1996 bombing of Khobar Towers, the 1998 attacks on the embassies in Kenya and Tanzania and the 2000 attack on the U.S.S. Cole. He said he had felt Tenet was insufficiently cooperative on investigations of technology transfer to China and into former CIA Director John Deutsch's downloading of classified material into his personal laptop. Shelby was mostly supportive of the Bush administration's conduct of the war on terrorism, however. In December 2001, he was one of ten senators signing a letter saying, "it is imperative that we plan to eliminate the threat from Iraq."

There was clearly some tension between Shelby's views and those of the two chairmen, Bob Graham and Porter Goss, in the joint Senate and House Intelligence Committees' investigations of the intelligence community pre-September 11. First, Shelby prodded the chairmen to hire more staff, and he was dubious about their choice for staff director, former Tenet aide Britt Snider. When an anonymous leaker revealed that Snider had hired a staffer who flunked a CIA polygraph, Shelby leaped and got him replaced by his original choice, former Defense Department Inspector General Eleanor Hill. Then the joint committee's investigation turned out to be more far-reaching than some advocates of an independent commission expected. Shelby had opposed such a commission as unnecessary, but in September 2002, as the end of the 107th Congress (and his tenure on the Intelligence Committee) loomed, he changed his mind. The organization of the families of September 11 victims insisted that Shelby and John McCain be given veto power over Republican Leader Trent Lott's two nominations to the independent commission. In September 2002, Shelby believed that another such attack remained possible. "Absolutely. To think otherwise would be folly. We've made some adjustments, but the cultures have not changed between all the intelligence agencies. . . . I don't believe they're sharing information. There's no fusion, no central place yet to do it." In December 2002, as he was leaving the committee, he called for separating the Director of Central Intelligence from the CIA and making him responsible for overseeing the entire intelligence community. He also called for recruitment of more agents from America's ethnically diverse population.

On domestic issues, Shelby has compiled a mostly conservative record. But he is not a free market purist. Despite his party switch he has remained friendly with trial lawyers, who usually support Democrats in Alabama. He opposed his colleague Jeff Sessions' amendment to cap lawyers' fees in tobacco cases, and insists tort reform should be only a state issue. He wants to enlarge investors' rights to sue companies, lawyers and accountants—rights limited in the securities reform measure that was the only law Congress passed over Bill Clinton's veto. His opinion on many such issues is more important now that he is chairman of the Banking Committee. He was the only Senate Republican to vote against financial services deregulation in November 1999, and wants to hold hearings on the effect of allowing commercial banks to get into investment banking. He opposes allowing federally-insured banks to sell real estate or insurance. One of his great causes on the committee is privacy. He opposed the 1999 law barring one branch of a financial services company from sharing personal data with another only if a client affirmatively opts out; he favors an opt in provision, which would allow sharing of information only for those clients who affirmatively authorize it. He opposes federal preemption of stricter state privacy laws. He has worked for repeal of the Public Utility Holding Company Act and opposes the current Community Reinvestment Act. He cast the lone committee vote against reauthorization of the Export Administration Act in March 2001and has called for a commission to examine export control policy.

Shelby is the chairman of the Transportation Appropriations Subcommittee. From that perch, he authored a law allowing airliners to fly from Alabama to Dallas's in-town Love Field and, with Washington Sen. Patty Murray, fashioned a compromise on Mexican trucks. The House wanted to keep them inside a zone within 20 miles of the border; the Bush administration wanted to let them in, subject to inspections, as required under NAFTA. Shelby and Murray won agreement that they can come in only at entry points where inspectors are on duty, that their drivers' licenses must be subject to electronic verification and that they must be insured by a company licensed in the U.S. Shelby also has used his Appropriations seat to fund Alabama projects.

Shelby was re-elected easily in 1998. He raised over $5 million, and no serious Democrat ran. The state AFL-CIO even discouraged Democrats from running, fearing Shelby would turn out Republican voters. The Democratic nominee, Clayton Suddith, a retired ironworker and former Franklin County commissioner, mortgaged his pickup truck to pay the $2,672 filing fee and was arrested for public intoxication at 11 a.m. one August morning. Shelby won 63%–37%, with most of the $5 million unspent. Few doubt that he will be reelected in 2004.

Junior Senator

Jeff Sessions (R)

Elected 1996, seat up 2008, 2d term; b. Dec. 24, 1946, Hybart; home, Mobile; Huntingdon Col., B.A. 1969, U. of AL, J.D. 1973; Methodist; married (Mary).

Military Career: Army Reserves, 1973–86.

Elected Office: AL Atty. Gen., 1994–96.

Professional Career: Practicing atty., 1973–75, 1977–81, 1993–94; Asst. U.S. Atty., 1975–77; U.S. Atty., 1981–93.

DC Office: 335 RSOB, 20510, 202-224-4124; Fax: 202-224-3149; Web site: sessions.senate.gov.

State Offices: Birmingham, 205-731-1500; Huntsville, 256-533-0979; Mobile, 251-414-3083; Montgomery, 334-244-7017.

Committees: *Armed Services*: Airland (Chmn.); Readiness & Management Support; Strategic Forces. *Budget. Health, Education, Labor & Pensions*: Children & Families; Employment, Safety & Training; Substance Abuse & Mental Health Services. *Judiciary*: Administrative Oversight & the Courts (Chmn.); Crime, Corrections & Victims' Rights; Immigration, Border Security & Citizenship; Terrorism, Technology & Homeland Security. *Joint Economic Committee* (3d of 10 Sens.).

Group Ratings

	ADA	ACLU	AFS	LCV	CON	ITIC	NTU	COC	ACU	NTLC	CHC
2002	10	20	38	6	47	50	61	84	90	94	—
2001	5	—	0	0	—	—	81	86	96	—	100

National Journal Ratings

	2001 LIB — 2001 CONS	2002 LIB — 2002 CONS
Economic	0% — 94%	26% — 73%
Social	22% — 73%	0% — 62%
Foreign	30% — 65%	42% — 56%

Key Votes of the 107th Congress

1. Approve Bush Tax Cuts	Y	5. Confirm Ashcroft as AG	Y	9. Bar Coop. with Intl. Court	Y
2. Expand Patients' Rights	N	6. Bar Gays in the Boy Scouts	Y	10. Trade Promotion Authority	N
3. Campaign Finance Reform	N	7. $ for Hate Crime Prosecution	N	11. Authorize Force in Iraq	Y
4. Permit ANWR Development	Y	8. Overseas Military Abortions	N	12. Homeland Sec. Dept. Union	N

Election Results

2002 general	Jeff Sessions (R)	792,561	(59%)	($5,115,730)
	Susan Parker (D)	538,878	(40%)	($1,185,718)
	Other	21,584	(2%)	
2002 primary	Jeff Sessions (R)	unopposed		
1996 general	Jeff Sessions (R)	786,436	(52%)	($3,862,359)
	Roger Bedford (D)	681,651	(45%)	($2,284,801)
	Other	31,306	(2%)	

Jeff Sessions grew up in Alabama's Black Belt, walked to school barefoot and is the son of a country store owner. He graduated from Huntingdon College and the University of Alabama Law School, practiced law in a small town near the Tennessee Valley, became a federal prosecutor and then practiced law in Mobile. He was appointed U.S. Attorney in 1981, at 35, where he became known as a tough, aggressive prosecutor, and served for 12 years. In 1985, he was nominated for federal judge, but was attacked by liberals for "gross insensitivity" in racial matters, and defended by conservatives. Alabama's Senator Howell Heflin voted against him in the Judiciary Committee; his nomination never went to the floor. In 1994, Sessions won 57%–43% against state Attorney General Jimmy Evans, who had successfully prosecuted Governor Guy Hunt the year before. When Heflin announced his retirement in March 1995, Sessions started running and became the favorite among the seven Republicans and four Democrats who ran.

Sessions started early, avoiding debates and controversy, and relying on his base in southern Alabama—territory that not long ago cast almost no Republican primary votes. Long-distance carrier executive Sid McDonald spent more than $1 million and attacked Sessions. From Birmingham north, it was a close race: McDonald led in the June 4 primary by 30%–29%. But in the rest of the state, Sessions led 48%–12%, for a 38%–22% statewide margin. In the runoff, McDonald remained on the offensive and Sessions ducked debates. McDonald extended his lead north from Birmingham, 54%–46%, but almost half the votes were cast to the south, and there Sessions led 73%–27%, for a 59%–41% win.

The Democratic nominee, trial lawyer Roger Bedford, was financed by trial lawyers and endorsed by key public employee unions and black organizations—the heart of today's Alabama Democratic Party. In the past, Democratic primaries had turnouts of nearly 1 million, with the advantage going to moderate or conservative candidates, like Glen Browder, the 3d District congressman. But only 315,000 voted in the June 4 Democratic primary in 1996, about half of them black; Bedford led Browder 45%–29%. In the June 25 runoff, Browder attacked Bedford for supporting NAFTA and gambling, and for being backed by trial lawyers, but Bedford had more money. With a low turnout of 230,000, Bedford won 62%–38%.

Bedford also proved the better campaigner in the general. He was competitive in fundraising, and ran close in the polls. "The old liberal days of tax and spend are over," he insisted, and opposed abortion, gun control, and gays in the military. Sessions avoided debates, at which Bedford excelled, and attacked the Democrat as a Ted Kennedy backer and for leading the battle against tort reform in the Alabama Senate in January 1996. Sessions won 52%–45%, running best in the suburbanizing counties around Alabama's cities; Bedford carried the Black Belt and many rural counties in the north.

In the Senate, Sessions has a very conservative voting record. He has proved himself a stickler for details that many senators ignore; he has been known to read GAO reports during the congressional recess. He serves on the Judiciary Committee, where he held up several Clinton administration judicial nominations. Many businesses like to require aggrieved consumers to submit to arbitration; Sessions has sponsored bills to make arbitration more favorable to consumers. In October 2000, by proposing 17 amendments he killed a non-controversial bill ending the requirement that franchised auto dealers must submit to binding arbitration in disputes with auto companies. He also co-sponsored a bill with Edward Kennedy to combat sexual assault in prisons.

Sessions surprised many by co-sponsoring in December 2002 a bill to reduce the ratio between the amount of powder cocaine and the amount of crack cocaine required to justify a five-year sentence. Since 1986 it has been 500–1: 500 grams of powder cocaine and 5 grams of crack will get you five years. Sessions and co-sponsor Orrin Hatch proposed reducing this to 20–1: 400 grams of powder cocaine and 20 grams of crack. The federal Sentencing Commission in 1995 called for eliminating the difference altogether; organizations opposing mandatory drug sentences and civil rights organizations have argued that the discrepancies are unfair to blacks since powder cocaine offenders are mostly white and crack cocaine offenders mostly black. Sessions stops before saying that this is a civil rights issue, but argues that the current discrepancy is unfair. His bill would also reduce mandatory minimum sentences for minor players in drug offenses.

On economic issues, Sessions was one of the co-sponsors of the Bush approach to welfare reform, shoved aside by Finance Chairman Max Baucus under pressure from Majority Leader Tom Daschle. Sessions also has a bill to help the working poor by frontloading the Earned Income Tax Credit. With Bob Graham and Mitch McConnell, Sessions succeeded in putting into the May 2001 tax cut a provision expanding Section 529 plans. It would allow parents and grandparents to contribute up to $250,000 for college expenses into investment accounts if authorized by states. In the 1980s, some states passed prepaid tuition plans and sought such tax advantage for contributions; now many states have authorized general portfolio investment accounts, which under Sessions's provision would not be taxed in the donors' estates. Sessions has also worked to change Alabama's wage index under Medicare to provide a higher Medicare reimbursement rate.

Going into the 2002 election cycle, there was some question whether Sessions would get serious opposition. Chances were lessened when in May 2001 Democratic Congressman Bud Cramer from northern Alabama announced he would not run and after June 2001, when George W. Bush came to Alabama and raised $1 million for Sessions—only the second event in what turned out to be a record-breaking cycle of presidential fundraising. Sessions was worried most about competition from Democrat Julian McPhillips, a trial lawyer who had made a fortune in civil rights cases; he was also opposed by state Auditor Susan Parker, a fundraiser for colleges. These two split the Alabama Democratic constituencies: Trial lawyers were for McPhillips; teachers' unions were for Parker, an education Ph.D. Black organizations—the Alabama Democratic Conference and Alabama New South Coalition endorsed both in the June 5 primary. Perhaps those endorsements, perhaps Parker's evocations of her upbringing on a Morgan County cotton farm were decisive: Parker led McPhillips 48%–43%. In the June 25 runoff, McPhillips made a mistake that was astounding in a man who made a fortune off his ability to affect juries: He argued that he could handle issues of importance to women and children because he was the father of three and Parker had no children. Parker replied that she had had a miscarriage and her doctor advised her not to have children. McPhillips apologized, but Parker won the runoff 65%–35%.

The general election was an anticlimax. Sessions outspent Parker by 4–1, but Parker persevered gamely. In October, she took note of the travails of New Jersey's Democratic Senator Bob Torricelli and attacked Sessions for seeking a provision, not passed, which would allow a group of investors to escape a $15 million debt owed to Lloyds of London. "Just like the Torch [Torricelli's nickname], Sessions tried to sneak in a bailout for millionaires who gave him money," she said, and then proceeded to dump thousands of dollars onto the floor at a press conference. Whoever thought of this deserves a prize, but not a Senate seat. Sessions won 59%–40%, even as Republican Bob Riley was being elected governor by just a narrow margin. Parker carried two Tennessee River counties in the north and 12 Black Belt counties in the center of the state but Sessions carried everything else, sometimes by overwhelming majorities.

FIRST DISTRICT

Rep. Jo Bonner (R)

Elected 2002, 1st term; b. Nov. 19, 1959, Selma; home, Mobile; U. of AL, B.A. 1982, U. of AL Law Schl. 1988; Episcopalian; married (Janee).

Professional Career: Sr. Aide, U.S. Rep. Sonny Callahan, 1984–02.

DC Office: 315 CHOB 20515, 202-225-4931; Fax: 202-225-0562; Web site: www.house.gov/bonner.

District Office: Mobile, 251-690-2811.

Committees: *Agriculture* (21st of 27 R): Conservation, Credit, Rural Development & Research; Department Operations, Oversight, Nutrition & Forestry. *Budget* (17th of 24 R). *Science* (23d of 25 R): Energy; Space & Aeronautics.

Group Ratings and Key Votes: Newly Elected

Election Results

2002 general	Jo Bonner (R)	108,102	(60%)	($1,713,019)
	Judy McCain Belk (D)	67,507	(38%)	($472,383)
	Other	3,078	(2%)	
2002 runoff	Jo Bonner (R)	32,421	(62%)	
	Tom Young (R)	19,501	(38%)	
2002 primary	Jo Bonner (R)	29,857	(40%)	
	Tom Young (R)	15,087	(20%)	
	David Whitstine (R)	10,997	(15%)	
	Albert Lipscomb (R)	7,429	(10%)	
	Chris Pringle (R)	6,001	(8%)	
	Rusty Glover (R)	4,374	(6%)	
2000 general	Sonny Callahan (R)	151,188	(91%)	($344,493)
	Dick Coffee (Lib)	14,031	(8%)	

The People		Race/Ethnic Origin	Ancestry	
Area size:	7,182 sq. mi.	67.8% White	USA: 12.4%	Irish: 6.7%
Urban population:	64.4%	28.0% Black	English: 6.6%	
Rural population:	35.6%	1.0% Asian	**2000 Presidential Vote**	
Pop. 2000:	635,300	1.0% Native Am.	Bush (R)..............138,938	(60%)
Median income:	$34,739	0.0% Hawaiian	Gore (D)...............86,142	(37%)
Poverty status:	16.9%	0.9% Two+ races	Other....................4,798	(2%)
Military veterans:	14.3%	0.1% Other	**Cook Partisan Voting Index:** R + 12	
		1.3% Hispanic Origin		

Occupation	Blue collar: 29.7%	White collar: 54.7%	Gray collar: 15.6%

Mobile, the port where the Tombigbee and Alabama rivers flow into the Gulf of Mexico, was long a key point on the American frontier. Spanish after the Revolutionary War, it was wrested away by threats of war from Secretary of State John Quincy Adams. During the Civil War, it was one of the major Confederate ports; here in 1864 Admiral David Farragut, while steaming into the harbor lashed to his mast, cried, "Damn the torpedoes! Full speed ahead." Today, Mobile is full of graceful signs of its slightly exotic past: Behind the docks and rail lines are downtown buildings and old houses with Spanish motifs, French accents, or tropical Art Deco lines. Further inland are neighborhoods with spacious houses, often with double porches, overhung by huge live oaks, graced with Spanish moss. Mobile is a Gulf Coast version of Charleston or a smaller, more comfortable New Orleans, with a taste for shellfish and spicy food and an even older Mardi Gras, which the locals have been celebrating since 1703. As befits a frontier city with a martial past, Mobile is bristling with arms: One of the city's proudest possessions is the battleship *U.S.S. Alabama*, moored at the head of Mobile Bay, with its guns aimed out toward the Gulf. Mobile's economy was based originally on docks and shipyards, factories and terminals, but with a determination to impose touches of beauty on its hot, flat landscape. For years, this southern seaboard of the Confederacy and the Union has been one of the most hawkish parts of America, and today it is solidly Republican in national elections. Although it continues to lose manufacturing jobs, its economy has been thriving at the shipyards and chemical plants. The capital improvements include Mobile's State Docks, which will promote Alabama's booming Mercedes, Honda, and Hyundai auto-production factories.

Mobile is the focus of Alabama's 1st Congressional District, which extends north along the lazily flowing Tombigbee and Alabama Rivers, near the old forts and mansions. Monroeville was the home of great writers—Truman Capote and his childhood playmate, Harper Lee, whose *To Kill a Mockingbird* is set here; and Winston Groom, author of *Forrest Gump*. Also here are surviving back-country settlements of blacks and Cajans (who may or may not be descended from Louisiana Cajuns) and Creek Indians. To the south, along the shores of the Gulf of Mexico, are the fast-growing condominium communities in Baldwin County, one of the two fastest-growing counties in Alabama; the glorious Gulf beaches are one of the South's best-kept secrets. This is one of the most Republican parts of Alabama. Redistricting made only slight changes in the boundaries in rural Clarke County.

The congressman from the 1st District is Jo Bonner, a Republican elected in 2002. Bonner had not previously run for office, but he had plenty of political experience on Capitol Hill and in southern Alabama. He spent nearly all of his working career as an aide to his predecessor, Sonny Callahan, a gregarious nine-term Republican with a rags-to-riches biography, who rose to become one of the Appropriations Committee's "cardinals" (subcommittee chairman). Bonner grew up in Selma and is just a little too young to remember the days when it was the focus of the civil rights movement; his father, who died when he was 13, was a probate judge appointed by the relatively moderate Governor Albert Brewer. Bonner graduated from the University of Alabama in 1982 and two years later started working for Callahan as a campaign press secretary. In 1989, he was promoted to chief of staff and later moved his family back to Mobile, where he became the rare top aide permanently stationed in the district. That background left Bonner well positioned when Callahan announced his retirement in March 2002, just three months before the June 4 primary.

Bonner's strongest opponent in the in the seven-candidate Republican primary turned out to be a candidate with a similar background, Tom Young, for 12 years the chief of staff to Senator Richard Shelby. Like Bonner, Young had his former boss's endorsement and showed a knack for campaign fundraising. The two candidates raised more than $2 million between them, making this one of the nation's most expensive primaries. With help from their well-connected bosses, each raised lots of money from Washington lobbyists; some complained about the pressure to choose sides. Young contrasted his experience on intelligence and defense policy with Bonner's focus on more mundane constituent-service work. Bonner responded by arguing that the Washington-based Young had more connections in Washington than in southern Alabama; he jibed that Young should have been welcomed at a luncheon for "new Mobilians." Young outspent Bonner by $300,000 and was helped by ads from the pro-tax cut Club for Growth, but Bonner led on June 4 by 40%–20%. Bonner later won endorsements from the Republicans who ran third, fourth and fifth and carried the June 25 runoff 62%–38%. In a district held by Republicans since 1964, when Barry Goldwater swept Alabama, Bonner easily beat Democratic businesswoman Judy McCain Belk, who contributed more than $300,000 to her campaign, by 60%–38% —almost the same districtwide margin posted here by George W. Bush in 2000.

Bonner bills himself as a "conservative with a big heart" and says he plans to focus on health care and local economic development. He called for a strong defense, limited taxation and he opposes abortion; his voting record is likely to be similar to Callahan's. As a freshman, he was unable to get Callahan's seat on Appropriations, but he may in some future Congress. In this safely Republican seat, he can look forward to a lengthy career in the House.

SECOND DISTRICT

Rep. Terry Everett (R)

Elected 1992, 6th term; b. Feb. 15, 1937, Dothan; home, Enterprise; Baptist; married (Barbara).

Military Career: Air Force, 1955–59.

Professional Career: Newspaper reporter, 1959–61, 1966–68; Businessman, 1961–64; Editor & Publisher, 1968–88; Real estate developer, 1988–92; Owner & Pres., *Union Springs Herald*, 1988-present.

DC Office: 2312 RHOB 20515, 202-225-2901; Fax: 202-225-8913; Web site: www.house.gov/everett.

District Offices: Dothan, 334-794-9680; Montgomery, 334-277-9113; Opp, 334-493-9253.

Committees: *Agriculture* (5th of 27 R): General Farm Commodities & Risk Management; Specialty Crops & Foreign Agriculture Programs (Vice Chmn.). *Armed Services* (6th of 33 R): Strategic Forces (Chmn.); Tactical Air & Land Forces. *Permanent Select Committee on Intelligence* (9th of 11 R): Human Intelligence, Analysis & Counterintelligence; Technical & Tactical Intelligence; Terrorism and Homeland Security. *Veterans' Affairs* (3d of 17 R): Oversight & Investigations.

Group Ratings

	ADA	ACLU	AFS	LCV	CON	ITIC	NTU	COC	ACU	NTLC	CHC
2002	0	7	0	0	25	88	58	84	100	89	100
2001	5	—	0	0	—	—	67	87	100	—	—

National Journal Ratings

	2001 LIB	—	2001 CONS		2002 LIB	—	2002 CONS
Economic	19%	—	81%		13%	—	85%
Social	0%	—	81%		0%	—	75%
Foreign	0%	—	97%		24%	—	72%

Key Votes of the 107th Congress

1. Approve Bush Tax Cuts	Y	5. Faith-Based Charities	Y	9. Trade Promotion Authority	Y
2. Limit Patients' Bill of Rights	Y	6. Bar Gays in the Boy Scouts	Y	10. Bar Funds for Intl. Court	Y
3. Campaign Finance Reform	N	7. Ban Partial-Birth Abortion	Y	11. Authorize Force in Iraq	Y
4. Ban ANWR Development	N	8. Arm Commercial Pilots	Y	12. Deny Home. Sec. Dept. Union	Y

Election Results

2002 general	Terry Everett (R)	129,233	(69%)	($1,076,731)
	Charles Woods (D)	55,495	(30%)	
	Other	3,237	(2%)	
2002 primary	Terry Everett (R)	unopposed		
2000 general	Terry Everett (R)	151,830	(68%)	($304,981)
	Charles Woods (D)	64,958	(29%)	
	Other	5,848	(3%)	

Prior Winning Percentages: 1998 (69%); 1996 (63%); 1994 (74%); 1992 (49%)

The People		Race/Ethnic Origin	Ancestry	
Area size:	10,608 sq. mi.	67.0% White	USA: 15.7%	English: 6.2%
Urban population:	50.1%	29.4% Black	Irish: 5.9%	
Rural population:	49.9%	0.6% Asian	**2000 Presidential Vote**	
Pop. 2000:	635,300	0.4% Native Am.	Bush (R) 137,168 (61%)	
Median income:	$32,460	0.0% Hawaiian	Gore (D) 84,435 (38%)	
Poverty status:	17.2%	0.9% Two + races	Other 3,061 (1%)	
Military veterans:	15.1%	0.1% Other	**Cook Partisan Voting Index:** R + 12	
		1.5% Hispanic Origin		

Occupation Blue collar: 29.5% White collar: 55.1% Gray collar: 15.4%

The thick green countryside is everywhere in southern Alabama. Even in Montgomery the stone and brick buildings that rise in the irregular downtown grid do not mask the contours of the hills or hide the lush foliage. You can look downhill from the restored Greek Revival Capitol toward Dexter Avenue Baptist Church where Martin Luther King Jr. was pastor, or out past the impressive Carolyn Blount Theater where the Alabama Shakespeare Festival is held toward new subdivisions and shopping malls, and you can easily imagine when this land was covered with pine trees and cotton fields. The atmosphere is even more rural in southeast Alabama's Wiregrass region, named for the stiff native grass, in the fishing town of Eufaula along the Chattahoochee River, around the town of Dothan, past Daleville and the Army's Fort Rucker (the home of Army aviation) to Enterprise, site of the Boll Weevil Monument that commemorates the insect that destroyed two-thirds of the cotton crop here in 1915 and then spread throughout the South. Peanuts are now the main crop in the area surrounding Dothan, with an estimated 1200 peanut farmers and a $500 million business for the district.

The 2d Congressional District covers the southeast corner of the state. It includes most of the city of Montgomery, but only a small part of Montgomery County; Democratic redistricters put the rest (which includes the Capitol and many black precincts), into the 3d District in an attempt to make that seat more Democrat-friendly. The result left the 2d heavily Republican. The northwest corner of Montgomery County plus Elmore and Autauga Counties voted more than 60% for Republican Governor Bob Riley in the close 2002 race; so did Dothan's Houston County in the Wiregrass region. Republican margins here are larger than Democratic margins in the district's Black Belt counties—Lowndes, the site of a new Hyundai plant, Bullock and Barbour on the Georgia border, George Wallace's home base. It would be a mistake to see these preferences as purely racial, however. The civil rights laws of the 1960s have long since been accepted. Blacks here tend to support a larger and more generous government, and hence vote Democratic. Alabama whites tend to take a hard line on defense and crime, want government to promote traditional cultural values and hence vote Republican.

The congressman from the 2d District is Terry Everett, a businessman from the Wiregrass first elected in 1992. He served in Air Force Intelligence in Germany in the 1950s, learned Russian, worked as a sports and police beat reporter and circulation manager for southern Alabama newspapers. He bought some newspapers himself and sold them for far more, and ended up heading a S&L and owning a large farm and real estate development firm. In 1992, when he decided to run for the seat being vacated by 28-year incumbent Republican Bill Dickinson, he was far from the favorite. But he beat two career politicians: A Montgomery legislator in the Republican primary and, in the general, state Treasurer George Wallace III, son of the former governor (Wallace, now a Republican, is an elected Public Service Commissioner). Everett spent $600,000 of his own money and, echoing an old George Wallace slogan, called on voters to "Send them a message, not a politician." Everett carried the Montgomery area and the Wiregrass but lost the Black Belt and rural areas.

Everett's voting record is mostly conservative; he shows a practical-minded concern about local issues and demonstrates a real impact on some issues. A prime example is peanuts: In 1995, he formed a Peanut Caucus and on the Agriculture Committee held out against the Freedom to Farm Act until he got the peanut program continued, though with a 10% cut in the support price and a lower national quota. On the 2002 farm bill, Everett chaired the Specialty Crops and Foreign Agriculture Programs Subcommittee, which placed him in a strong position to advocate the interests of peanut farmers. When he concluded that Congress would no longer support the 30 cents per pound peanut subsidy, Everett worked with Saxby Chambliss and Sanford Bishop of Georgia on a compromise that guaranteed quota farmers 10 cents per pound, with new farmers receiving a fallback option of government purchase at 18 cents. That Everett was able to get the House to accept a $3.5 billion (over 10 years) program shows his skill in protecting the interests of local farmers. Everett, himself a holder of a peanut quota, estimated that he would get $30,000 over five years from the new program.

Everett has also worked on veterans' issues. As a Veterans Affairs subcommittee chairman in 1999, he took credit for a $1.7 billion increase for veterans' health care spending plus the opening of four new national cemeteries. Following his subcommittee's report on Clinton administration waivers allowing burials of non-veterans in Arlington National Cemetery, he won House passage of a bill to tighten the waiver process. In 2003, Everett moved up the House power structure when departure of several senior members at the Armed Services Committee gave him chairmanship of the new Strategic Forces Subcommittee. In addition to his committee work, Everett has encouraged his wife Barbara, a breast-cancer survivor, in her campaign to educate others on self-awareness.

Everett has been reelected easily. In 2000 and 2002, he faced Democrat Charles Woods, a man with a vivid personal history and a peripatetic and so far unsuccessful career as a candidate. His face and hands were badly burned in a World War II airplane crash in which his doctors gave him up for dead; he later became a wealthy developer of media companies based in Alabama and Nevada. He has run for office several times in Alabama and won 39% of the vote in Nevada against Senator Harry Reid in 1992. But he spent little money against Everett, who won easily as usual.

THIRD DISTRICT

Rep. Mike Rogers (R)

Elected 2002, 1st term; b. July 16, 1958, Hammond, IN; home, Anniston; Jacksonville St. U., B.A. 1981, M.P.A. 1984, Birmingham Schl. of Law, J.D. 1991; Baptist; married (Beth).

Elected Office: Calhoun Cnty. Commission, 1986–90; AL House of Reps., 1994–02, Min. Ldr., 1998–00.

Professional Career: Practicing atty., 1991–02; Owner, auto lot.

DC Office: 514 CHOB 20515, 202-225-3261; Fax: 202-226-8485; Web site: www.house.gov/mike-rogers.

District Offices: Anniston, 256-236-5655; Montgomery, 334-277-4210; Opelika, 334-745-6221.

Committees: *Agriculture* (22d of 27 R): Conservation, Credit, Rural Development & Research; Livestock & Horticulture; Specialty Crops & Foreign Agriculture Programs. *Armed Services* (32d of 33 R): Readiness; Strategic Forces.

Group Ratings and Key Votes: Newly Elected

Election Results

2002 general	Mike Rogers (R)	91,169	(50%)	($1,638,145)
	Joe Turnham (D)	87,351	(48%)	($1,010,933)
	Other	2,703	(2%)	
2002 primary	Mike Rogers (R)	28,113	(76%)	
	Jason Dial (R)	4,681	(13%)	
	Jeff Fink (R)	4,134	(11%)	
2000 general	Bob Riley (R)	147,317	(87%)	($527,222)
	John Sophocleus (Lib)	21,119	(12%)	

The People		Race/Ethnic Origin	Ancestry	
Area size:	7,988 sq. mi.	64.9% White	USA: 15.9%	Irish: 6.0%
Urban population:	53.3%	32.2% Black	English: 5.8%	
Rural population:	46.7%	0.6% Asian	**2000 Presidential Vote**	
Pop. 2000:	635,300	0.3% Native Am.	Bush (R)............112,320 (52%)	
Median income:	$30,806	0.0% Hawaiian	Gore (D)............101,431 (47%)	
Poverty status:	18.8%	0.7% Two+ races	Other..................3,769 (2%)	
Military veterans:	13.4%	0.1% Other	**Cook Partisan Voting Index:** R + 3	
		1.2% Hispanic Origin		
Occupation	Blue collar: 33.1%	White collar: 51.7%	Gray collar: 15.2%	

Forty years ago, Lineville, Alabama, in the red hills of Clay County, was Ku Klux Klan country, with whites determined to resist race-mixing and blacks intimidated by threats of violence. More recently in Lineville, integrated crowds regularly cheer integrated high school teams, and people of all races work amicably together, though they tend to pray separately on Sundays. Lineville's progress perhaps echoes that of America's most integrated institution, the military; for the small town produced more men and women per capita for Operation Desert Storm than any other community in the nation.

The 3d Congressional District is centered geographically and perhaps spiritually in Lineville. The military presence is unmistakable: Calhoun County is home to the Anniston Army Depot and formerly home to Fort McClellan, which survived several rounds of base closings but couldn't escape the last one. Horseshoe Bend is where Andrew Jackson won a climactic battle against the Upper Creek Indians; Fort Mitchell, a 19th century frontier military outpost, is the site of a national military cemetery sometimes referred to as the "Arlington of the South." Phenix City, across the Chattahoochie River from Georgia's Fort Benning, served as a "sin city" in the 1940s and 1950s for pleasure-seeking soldiers; today, the military installation continues to play an important role in the local economy, though in a more positive way. There are other places of distinction in the 3d: Tuskegee, home of Booker T. Washington's Tuskegee Institute; Auburn, home of Auburn University and its renowned sports teams and veterinary school; Talladega, home of the Alabama Institute for the Deaf and Blind, which is perhaps America's most user-friendly city for the disabled. NASCAR fans know it as the home of a famed speedway and for the International Motorsports Hall of Fame—the Cooperstown of auto racing. This looks and feels like rural country, though few people here make a living off their farms. Instead, they drive to work at Tyson Foods or Wal-Mart or in dozens of small- or medium-sized factories. Politically, this was long one of the heartlands of the Democratic Party, the home of populist white Democrats—patriotic supporters of the military, cautious supporters of some domestic programs—who won power so often in the House and Senate. But the cotton mills have closed, and interstates have brought in new businesses, including a huge Honda assembly plant in Talladega County. The area has become Republican, though Democrats remain competitive in state elections. Democratic redistricters in 2002 added much of Montgomery County, including black precincts downtown, and increased the black percentage from 25% to 32%.

Democrats hoped redistricting would help them capture this seat in 2002, when Republican incumbent Bob Riley of Clay County was running for governor. But the new congressman is Republican Mike Rogers—the second Republican Mike Rogers in the House (the other is from the 8th District of Michigan). The Alabama Mike Rogers is a fifth generation resident of Calhoun County who, at the age of 28 in 1986, was the first Republican elected to the county commission. In 1994, he won a seat in the Alabama House and in his second term, he became Minority Leader.

He is an abortion opponent who supports a constitutional amendment for prayer in public school. In 2002, he won the 3d District Republican nomination by winning 76% in the June 4 Republican primary. But he had tough competition from Joe Turnham, Jr., who served three years as Democratic state chairman and then challenged Riley unsuccessfully in 1998. (Riley outspent him by 4–1 and won by a solid 58%–42% margin). Turnout in the 3d District 2002 Democratic primary was almost twice that in the Republican contest—tradition lingers on in many rural counties—and Turnham won his three-candidate primary with 53% of the vote. In an effort to appeal to rural voters, both Turnham and Rogers made concerted efforts to try to "out-Bubba" each other. Turnham called for a congressional auto racing caucus and demanded that Rogers prove he had hunting and fishing licenses. Rogers touted his working class values and support from the National Rifle Association. He promised to focus on education and local economic development, notably for shuttered Fort McClellan, which was officially closed in 1999. Turnham attacked Rogers for supporting free trade and called him a "career politician."

Though both national parties targeted the district, Turnham could not risk bringing in national Democrats to campaign for him in this socially conservative district. Rogers, on the other hand, got frequent visits from national Republican leaders; Speaker Dennis Hastert promised him a seat on the Armed Services Committee, where he could protect the interests of the Anniston Army Depot. The contrast in national party support was evident in Rogers's big fundraising advantage.

Still, the election was close: Rogers won by a 50%–48% margin. Rogers did well in his base, Calhoun County, where he got 60% of the vote and a margin of more than 7,000 votes. In contrast, Turnham lost Lee County, his home, by a 52%–46% margin, and carried the district's portion of Montgomery County by only 57%–42% and a margin of some 4,000 votes. Macon County, 84.6% black, delivered 84.7% of its vote to Turnham, but the county is too small to make much difference. A conservative Democrat can win here, so Rogers will have to hope that, with the advantages of incumbency and his Armed Services seat, he attracts weaker opposition in 2004.

FOURTH DISTRICT

Rep. Robert Aderholt (R)

Elected 1996, 4th term; b. July 22, 1965, Haleyville; home, Haleyville; Birmingham Southern U., B.A. 1987, Samford U., J.D. 1990; Congregationalist; married (Caroline).

Professional Career: Haleyville Municipal Judge, 1992–96; Asst. Legal Advisor, Gov. Fob James, 1995–96.

DC Office: 1433 LHOB 20515, 202-225-4876; Fax: 202-225-5587; Web site: www.house.gov/aderholt.

District Offices: Cullman, 256-734-6043; Gadsden, 256-546-0201; Jasper, 205-221-2310.

Committees: *Appropriations* (22d of 36 R): Military Construction (Vice Chmn.); Transportation, Treasury, & Independent Agencies; VA, HUD & Independent Agencies.

Group Ratings

	ADA	ACLU	AFS	LCV	CON	ITIC	NTU	COC	ACU	NTLC	CHC
2002	0	13	11	0	8	75	54	90	92	89	100
2001	10	—	10	7	—	—	60	87	91	—	

National Journal Ratings

	2001 LIB — 2001 CONS		2002 LIB — 2002 CONS	
Economic	27%	— 74%	9%	— 87%
Social	0%	— 81%	32%	— 63%
Foreign	29%	— 69%	28%	— 72%

Key Votes of the 107th Congress

1. Approve Bush Tax Cuts	Y	5. Faith-Based Charities	Y	9. Trade Promotion Authority	N
2. Limit Patients' Bill of Rights	Y	6. Bar Gays in the Boy Scouts	Y	10. Bar Funds for Intl. Court	Y
3. Campaign Finance Reform	N	7. Ban Partial-Birth Abortion	Y	11. Authorize Force in Iraq	Y
4. Ban ANWR Development	N	8. Arm Commercial Pilots	Y	12. Deny Home. Sec. Dept. Union	Y

Election Results

2002 general	Robert Aderholt (R)	139,705	(87%)	($662,595)
	Tony Hughes McLendon (Lib)	20,858	(13%)	
2002 primary	Robert Aderholt (R)	unopposed		
2000 general	Robert Aderholt (R)	140,009	(61%)	($1,583,278)
	Marsha Folsom (D)	86,400	(37%)	($1,134,694)
	Other	4,697	(2%)	

Prior Winning Percentages: 1998 (56%); 1996 (50%)

The People		Race/Ethnic Origin	Ancestry	
Area size:	8,524 sq. mi.	90.4% White	USA: 21.3%	Irish: 8.2%
Urban population:	26.5%	5.1% Black	English: 6.8%	
Rural population:	73.5%	0.2% Asian	**2000 Presidential Vote**	
Pop. 2000:	635,300	0.4% Native Am.	Bush (R)...............141,285	(61%)
Median income:	$31,344	0.0% Hawaiian	Gore (D)................87,062	(37%)
Poverty status:	14.7%	0.8% Two+ races	Other....................4,240	(2%)
Military veterans:	12.9%	0.0% Other	**Cook Partisan Voting Index:** R +12	
		3.0% Hispanic Origin		

Occupation	Blue collar: 40.8%	White collar: 46.0%	Gray collar: 13.2%

The Appalachians' corduroy ridges, dividing the Atlantic coast from the interior, are America's coal-and-steel industrial spine, from the black coal country of western Pennsylvania to the red hill country of northern Alabama. Here rose America's two premier steel cities, Pittsburgh and Birmingham. Around both, and for many miles in between them, is the country settled by feisty Scots-Irish farmers in the years between the Revolution and the Civil War. In valley land accessible to railroads are the great steel factories built in the 80 years after the Civil War and smaller factories that produce underwear and tires, glass and chemicals, socks and chickens. Politically, the two regions were separated by the Civil War: Western Pennsylvania was overwhelmingly Republican until the 1930s, while northern Alabama was solidly Democratic through the 1950s. But they shared the same political impulses—populist on economics, conservative on culture—which made them both Democratic heartlands during the New Deal and in congressional politics for years afterwards. Now they seem to have traded partisan allegiances: Western Pennsylvania is Democratic, though less solidly so when the Democrats emphasize cultural liberalism; northern Alabama has moved toward the Republicans, even though it has benefited from massive federal public works programs, and the movement is most pronounced in counties close to Birmingham and along the interstates.

Alabama's 4th Congressional District is a collection of small towns—Cullman, Jasper, Russellville, Fort Payne, Albertville—where gritty Gadsden, population 39,000, qualifies as the biggest city. Sandwiched between Huntsville to the north and Birmingham to the south, the 4th crosses the state and the Appalachian ridges, from the Georgia line to the Mississippi line near lightly populated rural counties. Redistricting made this swing district slightly more Republican; it has the lowest black percentage of Alabama's seven congressional districts.

The congressman from the 4th District is Robert Aderholt (pronounced *ADD-er-holt*) , a Republican first elected in 1996 to replace 30-year Democrat Tom Bevill, a senior Appropriations member and benefactor of great federal projects, including the Tennessee-Tombigbee Waterway project. Aderholt is from Winston County, the one ancestrally Republican county in north Alabama, which opposed secession in the Civil War and declared itself the Free State of Winston. His father was a circuit judge for over 30 years; his wife's father was a state senator and state commissioner of Agriculture and Industry. In 1992, Aderholt was appointed Haleyville municipal judge; in 1995, he became a top aide to Governor Fob James. With that pedigree, he decided to run for Congress when Bevill retired. As Republican nominee, he faced Democratic state Senator Bob Wilson Jr., who called himself a Democrat "in the Tom Bevill tradition," and said he supported family values. Aderholt recognized that Bevill did a lot for the district: To his proposed five-year moratorium on federal highway construction he made an exception for Corridor X, Bevill's idea for an interstate-quality road from Birmingham to Memphis, which has not yet been completed. But in this culturally conservative district, Aderholt didn't hedge on cultural issues. Against abortion, gun control and same-sex marriage, and for school prayer, he said, "We want to go to Washington to deliver a message, and that is, don't mess with our traditional family values." He attacked Wilson for his support from unions and trial lawyers, and invited Newt Gingrich to the district. This was a nationally targeted race, seriously contested, and Aderholt won 50%–48%.

Recognizing Aderholt's electoral vulnerability, Republican leaders put him on Appropriations; he has brought home more highway and sewer money than most Republicans. And he didn't forget the social issues. After Judge Roy Moore in DeKalb County (who in 2000 was elected Alabama's Chief Justice) was ordered to remove a copy of the Ten Commandments from his courtroom, Aderholt sponsored legislation permitting the states to display the Ten Commandments in public buildings, including courthouses. "Our nation was founded on basic principles such as those included in the Ten Commandments," he said. But to that, Barry Lynn, who lobbies to keep church and state separate, responded: "Aderholt isn't Moses, and Capitol Hill isn't Mt. Sinai. Americans don't need politicians giving us instruction about religion." Aderholt's voting record is conservative, but he is not a reliable free trade vote—he supported quotas on steel imports and sponsored a bill assessing additional antidumping duties on foreign steel in 1999. At the time, cheap foreign steel was pummeling local producer Gulf States Steel in Gadsden (the steel mill went bankrupt later that year and eventually shut down in 2000). Although he reached out further to industrial unions with his vote against PNTR with China, after George W. Bush was elected—and after he got protection for the local sock industry—he voted for trade promotion authority in 2002.

In his first two re-election campaigns, Aderholt fared surprisingly well against familiar names in Alabama politics. In 1998, he won 56% against Don Bevill, son of the former congressman. Two years later, Democrats enthused about Marsha Folsom, the state's former First Lady when her husband was Acting Governor in 1993–94. She had more than $1 million to fund an aggressive advertising campaign, which included inaccurate accusations that Aderholt supported Internet gambling. This time, Aderholt increased his vote to 61%.

In 2002, Aderholt had no Democratic opponent. He appears to have entrenched himself in what used to be a swing seat.

FIFTH DISTRICT

Rep. Bud Cramer (D)

Elected 1990, 7th term; b. Aug. 22, 1947, Huntsville; home, Huntsville; U. of AL, B.A. 1969, J.D. 1972; Methodist; widowed.

Military Career: Army, 1972; Army Reserves, 1976–78.

Professional Career: Instructor, U. of AL Law Schl., Dir., Clinical Studies Program, 1972–73; Madison Cnty. Asst. Dist. Atty., 1973–75; Practicing atty., 1975–80; Madison Cnty. Dist. Atty., 1981–90; Founder, Natl. Children's Advocacy Ctr., 1985.

DC Office: 2368 RHOB 20515, 202-225-4801; Fax: 202-225-4392; Web site: www.house.gov/cramer.

District Offices: Decatur, 256-355-9400; Huntsville, 256-551-0190; Tuscumbia, 256-381-3450.

Committees: *Appropriations* (17th of 29 D): Commerce, Justice, State & Judiciary; District of Columbia; VA, HUD & Independent Agencies. *Permanent Select Committee on Intelligence* (6th of 9 D): Human Intelligence, Analysis & Counterintelligence; Technical & Tactical Intelligence (RMM); Terrorism and Homeland Security.

Group Ratings

	ADA	ACLU	AFS	LCV	CON	ITIC	NTU	COC	ACU	NTLC	CHC
2002	45	20	67	50	0	62	36	80	56	47	67
2001	45	—	40	29	—	—	40	82	65	—	—

National Journal Ratings

	2001 LIB —	2001 CONS	2002 LIB —	2002 CONS
Economic	52%	48%	51%	48%
Social	46%	55%	49%	50%
Foreign	56%	41%	51%	49%

Key Votes of the 107th Congress

1. Approve Bush Tax Cuts	Y	5. Faith-Based Charities	Y	9. Trade Promotion Authority	N
2. Limit Patients' Bill of Rights	N	6. Bar Gays in the Boy Scouts	Y	10. Bar Funds for Intl. Court	Y
3. Campaign Finance Reform	Y	7. Ban Partial-Birth Abortion	Y	11. Authorize Force in Iraq	Y
4. Ban ANWR Development	N	8. Arm Commercial Pilots	Y	12. Deny Home. Sec. Dept. Union	Y

Election Results

2002 general	Bud Cramer (D)	143,029	(73%)	($770,032)
	Stephen Engel (R)	48,226	(25%)	($13,593)
	Other	3,916	(2%)	
2002 primary	Bud Cramer (D)	unopposed		
2000 general	Bud Cramer (D)	186,059	(89%)	($512,728)
	Alan Barksdale (Lib)	22,110	(11%)	

Prior Winning Percentages: 1998 (70%); 1996 (56%); 1994 (50%); 1992 (66%); 1990 (67%)

The People		Race/Ethnic Origin	Ancestry	
Area size:	4,689 sq. mi.	77.7% White	USA: 16.1%	Irish: 8.0%
Urban population:	59.4%	16.9% Black	English: 7.6%	
Rural population:	40.6%	1.0% Asian	**2000 Presidential Vote**	
Pop. 2000:	635,300	0.9% Native Am.	Bush (R) 131,608	(54%)
Median income:	$38,054	0.0% Hawaiian	Gore (D) 106,685	(44%)
Poverty status:	12.5%	1.4% Two+ races	Other 5,241	(2%)
Military veterans:	14.0%	0.1% Other	**Cook Partisan Voting Index:** R + 6	
		2.0% Hispanic Origin		

Occupation	Blue collar: 29.6%	White collar: 57.1%	Gray collar: 13.3%

Twice this century, the federal government has transformed the northern Alabama counties along the Tennessee River. The first time was when it created the Tennessee Valley Authority in 1933. Proposed by Nebraska Senator George Norris, a favorite of President Franklin Roosevelt, TVA took the World War I federal munitions plant at Muscle Shoals on the unnavigable Tennessee River, and built a series of dams to control flooding and produce cheap hydroelectric power. This was backwards country then: Poor white farmers scratched an existence out of hardscrabble land, were housed in shacks without electricity or running water, and lived off a diet that produced pellagra and rickets. The TVA was intended to showcase what an enlightened, generous federal government could do. The second major federal project here was the space program. After the Soviets put up Sputnik in 1957, the Redstone Arsenal in Huntsville became the nation's major missile development center—the first of the large U.S. ballistic missiles were developed here. NASA built its Marshall Space Flight Center nearby in the 1960s and the Huntsville-Decatur area achieved high-tech critical mass. The Boeing research center here has been a prime contractor for the space station, which—after surviving a legislative funding battle by one vote in 1993—has remained a major project of NASA. Boeing also produces its Delta IV booster out of its local factory in Decatur. With the formation of the U.S. Army Aviation and Missile Command in 1997, recent years also have seen the growth of the Army's Redstone Arsenal. All of this helps to explain why

Huntsville-centered Madison County has been booming and is the third-largest in Alabama; the population of several suburbs nearly doubled in the 1990s.

The 5th Congressional District takes in most of the state's TVA and space counties. TVA and the space program were primarily Democratic projects, and for years most voters here were staunch New Deal Democrats, liberal on economics and not much interested in race, like the longtime Senator John Sparkman, the party's vice presidential nominee in 1952. But professional and technical people in the space business tend to combine high-tech and traditional values, and this has made much of northern Alabama marginal-to-Republican country in the 1990s. This district has never elected a Republican to Congress, but it has voted Republican for president since the departure of Jimmy Carter, and in the mid-1990s, it had seriously contested congressional elections. Fenced in by borders on three states, the district was barely changed by redistricting.

The congressman from the 5th District is Bud Cramer, a Democrat first elected in 1990. He was born in Huntsville, served as an Army tank officer after law school, and beat the incumbent district attorney in 1980, at 33. In 1985, he set up the Child Advocacy Center, a child-friendly environment for abused children; as congressman, he set up a $5 million federal program to encourage such centers across the country in more than 500 programs across the nation in what is known as the National Children's Alliance. "We are the Mayo Clinic there in Huntsville of child abuse," he boasted. When Congressman Ronnie Flippo ran unsuccessfully for governor in 1990, Cramer ran for Congress. He won the general election by a 2–1 margin.

In the House, Cramer has been a tireless booster of the beleaguered Space Station and a leading advocate of a spending boost for missile defense. In the TVA tradition, he supported the Democratic leadership on key issues. But his votes for the Clinton budget and tax package in 1993 and for the Clinton crime bill with its gun control provisions were unpopular locally, and were seized upon by Republican Wayne Parker in 1994. Cramer outspent Parker, and he had support from the local media. But the issues worked against him, and he barely won, 50%–49%. Since then, Cramer has avoided liberal votes on visible issues. He won a 56%–42% rematch against Parker in 1996, and his reelection problems have disappeared since then. With his seat on Appropriations, he has successfully pursued a nonpartisan approach of federal dollars and contracts. In 2001, the 5th District received $7.9 billion from Washington, among the top 60 districts nationwide. The September 11 attacks provided an additional financial boost: Cramer got $23 million for bomb squad training at the Redstone Arsenal.

Cramer's overall voting record remains in the middle of the House. But he has voted conservative on key issues, ranging from the Republicans' impeachment inquiry of Bill Clinton to the ban on partial-birth abortions and needle exchanges. In 2001, he was one of only four Democrats voting both to repeal the Clinton ergonomic standards and to approve George W. Bush's income tax cuts.

After the 2000 election, Cramer was said to be under consideration for a job in the Bush administration. But he also was touted as a possible challenger to Jeff Sessions in the 2002 Senate campaign. In May 2001, he said he wouldn't run for the Senate. Cramer has been strikingly coy about persistent rumors that he might switch parties. Both before and after the 2002 election, his standard response has been, "I don't plan on switching parties right now," or, "at this time." Amid this speculation, Democratic leadership gave him a seat on the Intelligence Committee. So far, Cramer has skillfully played off the two parties to the benefit of both his district and his own political career.

SIXTH DISTRICT

Rep. Spencer Bachus (R)

Elected 1992, 6th term; b. Dec. 28, 1947, Birmingham; home, Birmingham; Auburn U., B.A. 1969, U. of AL, J.D. 1972; Baptist; married (Linda).

Military Career: Natl. Guard, 1969–71.

Elected Office: AL Senate, 1983–84; AL House of Reps., 1984–87.

Professional Career: Owner, Lumber Co.; Practicing atty., 1972–92; AL Repub. Party Chmn., 1991–92.

DC Office: 442 CHOB 20515, 202-225-4921; Fax: 202-225-2082; Web site: www.house.gov/bachus.

District Offices: Birmingham, 205-969-2296; Northport, 205-333-9894.

Committees: *Financial Services* (5th of 37 R): Capital Markets, Insurance & Government Sponsored Enterprises; Financial Institutions & Consumer Credit (Chmn.). *Judiciary* (10th of 21 R): Courts, the Internet & Intellectual Property; The Constitution. *Transportation & Infrastructure* (11th of 41 R): Aviation; Railroads.

Group Ratings

	ADA	ACLU	AFS	LCV	CON	ITIC	NTU	COC	ACU	NTLC	CHC
2002	0	7	0	0	50	88	57	100	100	91	100
2001	0	—	0	7	—	—	67	95	96	—	—

National Journal Ratings

	2001 LIB —	2001 CONS	2002 LIB —	2002 CONS
Economic	19%	81%	28%	69%
Social	32%	67%	0%	75%
Foreign	33%	60%	0%	85%

Key Votes of the 107th Congress

1. Approve Bush Tax Cuts	Y	5. Faith-Based Charities	Y	9. Trade Promotion Authority	Y
2. Limit Patients' Bill of Rights	Y	6. Bar Gays in the Boy Scouts	Y	10. Bar Funds for Intl. Court	Y
3. Campaign Finance Reform	N	7. Ban Partial-Birth Abortion	Y	11. Authorize Force in Iraq	Y
4. Ban ANWR Development	N	8. Arm Commercial Pilots	Y	12. Deny Home. Sec. Dept. Union	Y

Election Results

2002 general	Spencer Bachus (R)	178,171	(90%)	($747,977)
	J. Holden McAllister (Lib)	19,639	(10%)	
2002 primary	Spencer Bachus (R)	79,509	(88%)	
	Terry Reagin (R)	11,042	(12%)	
2000 general	Spencer Bachus (R)	212,751	(88%)	($577,565)
	Terry Reagin (Lib)	28,189	(12%)	

Prior Winning Percentages: 1998 (72%); 1996 (71%); 1994 (79%); 1992 (52%)

The People		Race/Ethnic Origin	Ancestry	
Area size:	4,649 sq. mi.	88.8% White	USA: 14.5%	English: 10.1%
Urban population:	62.1%	7.7% Black	Irish: 8.1%	
Rural population:	37.9%	0.9% Asian	**2000 Presidential Vote**	
Pop. 2000:	635,300	0.3% Native Am.	Bush (R)	200,818 (74%)
Median income:	$46,946	0.0% Hawaiian	Gore (D)	67,975 (25%)
Poverty status:	8.1%	0.7% Two+ races	Other	3,997 (1%)
Military veterans:	12.9%	0.0% Other	**Cook Partisan Voting Index:** R +25	
		1.6% Hispanic Origin		
Occupation	Blue collar: 22.1%	White collar: 67.7%	Gray collar: 10.2%	

Birmingham, once one of America's booming industrial cities, then the site of violence in the civil rights revolution, now has future prospects far more hopeful than seemed possible not long ago. This is a new city by southern standards: Before the Civil War there was nothing here but a few creeks running below Red Mountain. But Red Mountain is almost pure iron ore, and by 1890,

Birmingham had the South's largest steel mills. In the early 20th century, as the statue of Vulcan, Roman god of fire and metalworking, looked out over the smokestack-rich valley, Birmingham seemed the most up-to-date and progressive city in the South. But the worldwide overcapacity in steel and technological obsolescence at home sent the American steel industry into long-term decline starting in the 1950s. Industrial Birmingham's political leaders plotted to avoid desegregation, and the city's violent reaction to civil rights—Police Commissioner (and Democratic National Committeeman at the time) Bull Connor set dogs and fire hoses against peaceful demonstrators, and Ku Klux Klansmen bombed the 16th Street Baptist Church, killing four young girls in 1963—made a vivid impression over the new medium of television news, spurring the Civil Rights Act of 1964, and created a reputation from which Birmingham still suffered a generation later. The convictions in May 2001 and May 2002 of the last surviving suspects in the 16th Street Baptist Church bombing triggered renewed criticism of J. Edgar Hoover's FBI for its lack of vigilance in the case; that incident became the topic of *Four Little Girls*, a film documentary by Spike Lee. More bad publicity resulted two months later when the Vulcan statue fell apart, a victim of age and the icon of a deteriorating industry.

But in recent years, Birmingham has worked to improve race relations and has developed a new economic base to generate growth. Health care is one major industry: Birmingham has some of the largest and most advanced medical care centers in the South, and is especially renowned for its sports medicine facilities and specialists who have treated such athletic greats as Michael Jordan. Banking is the other: While Atlanta's banks foundered and were acquired by outsiders, Birmingham became the largest southern banking center after Charlotte, North Carolina, with headquarters of SouthTrust, AmSouth Bancorp, Regions Financial, and Compass Bancshares. Still, city leaders openly lament that downtown may become "irrelevant" in the next generation. If anything, residential trends have shown an increase in racial polarization. As the city's population has declined by 100,000 since 1960, the black share continues to increase, to 74% in 2000. Whites have been moving out of Birmingham's Jefferson County southeast to Shelby County, which grew 44% in the 1990s—the fastest growth in the state—and is now 90% white. As a result, Jefferson County, once more Republican than most of Alabama, is now almost always Democratic, while Shelby County is one of the two most Republican counties in the state.

The 6th Congressional District, which once included all of Birmingham and most of Jefferson County, is now the suburban Birmingham-area district and strongly Republican. It includes parts of Jefferson County (such as prosperous Mountain Brook), and stretches southwest to Tuscaloosa and south along Interstate 65 halfway to Montgomery. In 2002, the Democratic line-drawers made it even more Republican, removing the last part of Birmingham and some black precincts in Tuscaloosa, and adding most of fast-growing St. Clair County north of Shelby County. Today, this is one of the most Republican districts in the nation: it voted 74% for George W. Bush in 2000—his second best district (the first was the Nebraska 3d) outside of Texas.

The congressman from the 6th District is Republican Spencer Bachus (pronounced *BACK-us*). A Birmingham native, he owned a sawmill company and practiced law; he boasts that he was a good enough trial lawyer to have produced four straight acquittals in murder trials. Elected to the state legislature in 1982, he was an activist—though one of very few Republicans. After running unsuccessfully for attorney general in 1990, he became Republican state chairman. When the 6th District was radically redrawn in 1992, he won a Republican runoff and defeated incumbent Ben Erdreich, a moderate Democrat.

Bachus has a mostly, though not totally, conservative voting record and has been an aggressive lawmaker and investigator. As chairman of Banking's oversight subcommittee, he discovered that the Community Development Financial Institute, which Bill Clinton established in 1994, directed $11 million in loans (one-third of its funds) to four banks with ties to Hillary Rodham Clinton without proper documentation; the two top CDFI officials resigned as a consequence. With George W. Bush in the White House, Bachus has had a less adversarial role as chairman of the Financial Institutions and Consumer Credit Subcommittee, although he was an early critic of then-Securities and Exchange Commission chairman Harvey Pitt. He has been something of a maverick on foreign policy. In the 1990s, Bachus became an unlikely crusader for international debt relief for poor Third World nations. He joined a broad coalition of domestic and international activists in a one-day fast to demand action, which ultimately proved successful. In early 2002, he criticized the Bush administration's dealings with the genocidal regime in Sudan, where Osama bin Laden once lived openly. Later in the year, Congress approved a Sudan Peace Act, which threatens diplomatic reprisals and supports rebel groups.

Bachus has not faced a competitive challenge for re-election, and Democrats have not run a challenger in the past two campaigns. He was an early supporter of Bob Riley's 2002 campaign for governor and has voiced interest in a statewide race, most likely in the event of a Senate vacancy. He is fifth in seniority among Republicans on the Financial Services Committee, and could some day be chairman.

SEVENTH DISTRICT

Rep. Artur Davis (D)

Elected 2002, 1st term; b. Oct. 9, 1967, Montgomery; home, Birmingham; Harvard U., B.A. 1990, J.D. 1993; Lutheran; single.

Professional Career: Asst. U.S. atty., 1994–1998, Practicing atty., 1998–2002.

DC Office: 208 CHOB 20515, 202-225-2665; Fax: 202-226-9567; Web site: www.house.gov/arturdavis.

District Offices: Birmingham, 205-254-1960; Demopolis, 334-287-0860; Livingston, 205-652-5834; Selma, 334-877-4414; Tuscaloosa, 205-752-5380.

Committees: *Budget* (17th of 19 D). *Financial Services* (32d of 32 D): Financial Institutions & Consumer Credit; Housing & Community Opportunity.

Group Ratings and Key Votes: Newly Elected

Election Results

2002 general	Artur Davis (D)	153,735	(92%)	($1,441,878)
	Lauren Orth McCay (Lib)	12,100	(7%)	
2002 runoff	Artur Davis (D)	52,394	(56%)	
	Earl Hilliard (D)	41,162	(44%)	
2002 primary	Earl Hilliard (D)	46,224	(46%)	
	Artur Davis (D)	43,519	(43%)	
	Sam Wiggins (D)	11,315	(11%)	
2000 general	Earl Hilliard (D)	148,243	(75%)	($432,730)
	Ed Martin (R)	46,134	(23%)	($18,431)
	Other	4,256	(2%)	

The People		Race/Ethnic Origin	Ancestry	
Area size:	8,780 sq. mi.	35.5% White	USA: 7.1%	English: 3.7%
Urban population:	72.2%	61.7% Black	Irish: 3.5%	
Rural population:	27.8%	0.6% Asian	**2000 Presidential Vote**	
Pop. 2000:	635,300	0.2% Native Am.	Gore (D) 158,580 (66%)	
Median income:	$26,672	0.0% Hawaiian	Bush (R) 78,670 (33%)	
Poverty status:	24.7%	0.6% Two + races	Other 1,827 (1%)	
Military veterans:	11.6%	0.1% Other	**Cook Partisan Voting Index:** D +17	
		1.3% Hispanic Origin		

Occupation	Blue collar: 28.6%	White collar: 53.4%	Gray collar: 18.0%

Alabama celebrates its black heritage more than any other state, building striking memorials to the civil rights movement in Montgomery and Birmingham, commemorating with dignified restraint a history that was full of raucous hatred and moving sacrifice. Blacks first came here as slaves; the last slave ship to the United States, the *Clotilde*, docked in Mobile in 1859, where its cargo was then set free. Blacks were part of the great migration into the cottonlands after the Jacksonians swept the Indians out of the Southeast and sent them on their Trail of Tears to what is now Oklahoma. Today, Alabama's rural blacks are still clustered in the Black Belt of fertile dark soil across the center of the state: Around Montgomery, where Rosa Parks refused to move to the back of a city bus in 1955 and a young minister named Martin Luther King Jr. led a bus boycott. Around Selma, founded by Alabama's one vice president, William Rufus King, where Sheriff Jim Clark's troops beat up peaceful marchers on the Edmund Pettus Bridge in demonstrations that led to the march on Montgomery and the 1965 Voting Rights Act. All 10 of Alabama's majority-black counties are in the rich farm country of the Black Belt, though not all are contained within the 7th. Most Alabama blacks, however, now live in urban areas—one-quarter in metropolitan Birmingham.

The 7th Congressional District was created in 1992 as a black-majority district. A decade later, the borders had to be changed in redistricting, because the old district was nearly 100,000 below the population standard. Its portion of Montgomery County and black-majority Lowndes County were removed from the 7th and parts of Birmingham and suburban Jefferson County were added. The rest of the district includes Black Belt counties where the Alabama and Tombigbee Rivers flow past old plantations, plus part of Tuscaloosa, home of the University of Alabama, and nearby Vance, site of a much sought-after new Mercedes factory. The district thus combines the remnants of Alabama's old cotton economy with neighborhoods built in the shadows of Birmingham's once booming steel mills. Of its 12 counties, 5 are among the 100 poorest in the nation. Although the district's black population dropped from 70% to 62%, it remained solidly Democratic. Even so, Birmingham-based incumbent Earl Hilliard claimed the new plan "hurts me tremendously," and blamed "white racists" among the Democrats' redistricters for his predicament. Whether racism figured into the equation is arguable; either way, more than 40% of the residents were new to Hilliard.

The new congressman from the 7th District is Artur Davis, who was elected at age 35 in 2002. He grew up in Montgomery and was raised by his mother and grandmother. He graduated from Harvard and Harvard Law School, then returned to Alabama. After working as an intern in the Southern Poverty Law Center and as a clerk to federal Judge Myron Thompson, he served four years as an assistant U.S. attorney. Later, he practiced law in Birmingham. In 2000, he decided to challenge Hilliard in the Democratic primary. Davis ran a vigorous campaign, but lost 58%–34%. In that contest, Davis cited Hilliard's controversial trip to Libya, which ignored a State Department ban on travel there because of its designation as a terrorist state, and contended that Hilliard failed to aid his financially pressed district.

In the 2002 rematch between a 28-year political veteran and a young Harvard-trained lawyer, much of the dialogue focused on the Middle East politics and race. Campaign surrogates for Hilliard questioned whether Davis was "black enough" to represent the district. Referring to Davis' background as a federal prosecutor, Hilliard claimed that, "the only thing [Davis] has done for black people is put them in jail." A pro-Hilliard pamphlet contended that, "Asking blacks to vote for [Davis] is like asking a chicken to vote for Colonel Sanders." Davis framed the debate as a generational battle between old-style black machine politics and a fresher, more effective approach—presumably one that didn't involve the diversion of campaign funds, a maneuver for which Hilliard received a letter of reproval from the House Ethics Committee in 2001. But the key to Davis' victory appeared to be strong financial backing from supporters of Israel. In 2000, Davis was unable to match Hilliard's fundraising. But in 2002, by highlighting his strong support for Israel and contrasting it with Hilliard's record, Davis made successful fundraising visits to New York and Washington where he attracted considerable financing from donors sympathetic to his stands on these issues. Support for Davis was spurred when, on May 2, Hilliard was one of only 21 House members to vote against a resolution supporting Israel's fight against terrorism, a vote coming after weeks when Palestinian suicide bombers killed hundreds of Israelis. Members of the Congressional Black Caucus criticized the Democratic leadership for their perceived lack of support for Hilliard; some black members suggested that party leaders were hesitant to confront supporters of Israel and they threatened retaliation.

In the June 4 primary, Hilliard led Davis by only 46%–43% and was forced into a runoff three weeks later. Several House Democratic leaders sent in checks to the incumbent, although not Democratic campaign committee Chairman Nita Lowey. Hilliard took the offensive with an unsubstantiated charge that Davis had been the target of a date-rape accusation and ran an ad that depicted Davis as "for sale" to cigar-smoking fat cats. Several Black Caucus members, plus Al Sharpton, came in to campaign for Hilliard. Davis accused Hilliard of being divisive and called for "healing." Otherwise, the two candidates had relatively few differences on major legislative policy issues. Davis outspent Hilliard by nearly $180,000 and on June 25 won by a 56%–44% margin. Davis, who had no trouble in the general election, quickly reached out to other Black Caucus members; Black Caucus Chairman Elijah Cummings said Davis was welcomed "into the fold. Our members have moved on from that election."

★ ALASKA ★

With 16% of the nation's land area and 0.22% of the nation's population, Alaska is America in the Arctic, a state that was the creation of a federal government which it now often resents and an individualistic society that has responded to its unique situation in creative ways that commend themselves to the attention of what Alaskans call the Lower 48 or, more simply, Outside. Alaska would not be American at all but for the expansive dream of Secretary of State William Seward, who took advantage of a fleeting opportunity to create an American Pacific empire by purchasing it from Russia in 1867 for $7.2 million. The Alaska Territory owed most of its early growth to decisions made by the federal government. It started growing feverishly with the Klondike gold rush in 1897, just as William McKinley reaffirmed the gold standard. Anchorage, the major city here, had its beginnings in 1913 as the chief worksite of the federal government's Alaska Railroad. The Alcan Highway, connecting Alaska to the Lower 48, was built by the Army in the grim war days of 1942, when the Aleutian island of Attu was held by the Japanese, the only part of the United States occupied by a foreign enemy since the War of 1812. During the Cold War, Alaska was the only state abutting the Soviet Union, across the Bering Strait and over the North Pole. Even today Alaska remains militarily strategic, and the military remains a major presence at Elmendorf Air Force Base near Anchorage and Fort Wainwright near Fairbanks. Alaska's giant size remains hard for Americans to comprehend: If superimposed on the Lower 48, it would stretch from Florida to southern California to Lake Superior. One-third of Alaskans have no access to the state's roads and are reachable only by boat or airplane; Alaska has, per capita, six times the number of pilots and 14 times the number of airplanes as the rest of the nation, and 663 registered airports. Yet only 627,000 of 284.7 million Americans live here, more than 40% in the Anchorage area, the rest in Fairbanks in the interior and Juneau in the Panhandle and scattered in small towns and Native settlements over millions of acres of stunning scenery and bleak tundra.

Statehood was won in 1959, after a valiant campaign. But statehood did not end federal decision-making power over Alaska—or the widespread resentment of it. Alaska's economy at statehood depended on fishing, oil production in Cook Inlet around Anchorage and the military—all federally regulated or controlled. Less than a decade later, however, Alaska's economy and public life were reshaped by the discovery of North Slope oil. It began suddenly, accidentally: On the day after Christmas 1967, at Prudhoe Bay on the Arctic coast, an undulating roar as loud as four jumbo jets directly overhead drew a crowd of 40 men, heavily clothed against the 30-below weather, to an oil rig. Suddenly a natural gas flare shot 30 feet straight up: This was the great 12 billion barrel North Slope oil field. Earlier oil companies had drilled seven dry wells on Prudhoe Bay, and Arco chief executive Robert Anderson wouldn't have ordered this last try, except that he had a drilling rig nearby. This was the greatest oil strike ever in the United States and the beginning of much of today's Alaska.

Finding oil in Prudhoe Bay was something like finding it on the moon. It was not clear in 1967 who owned the oil or how it could be taken out. The Statehood Act of 1959 provided for the state to choose its own public lands, but only after settling Native land claims. Congress, not

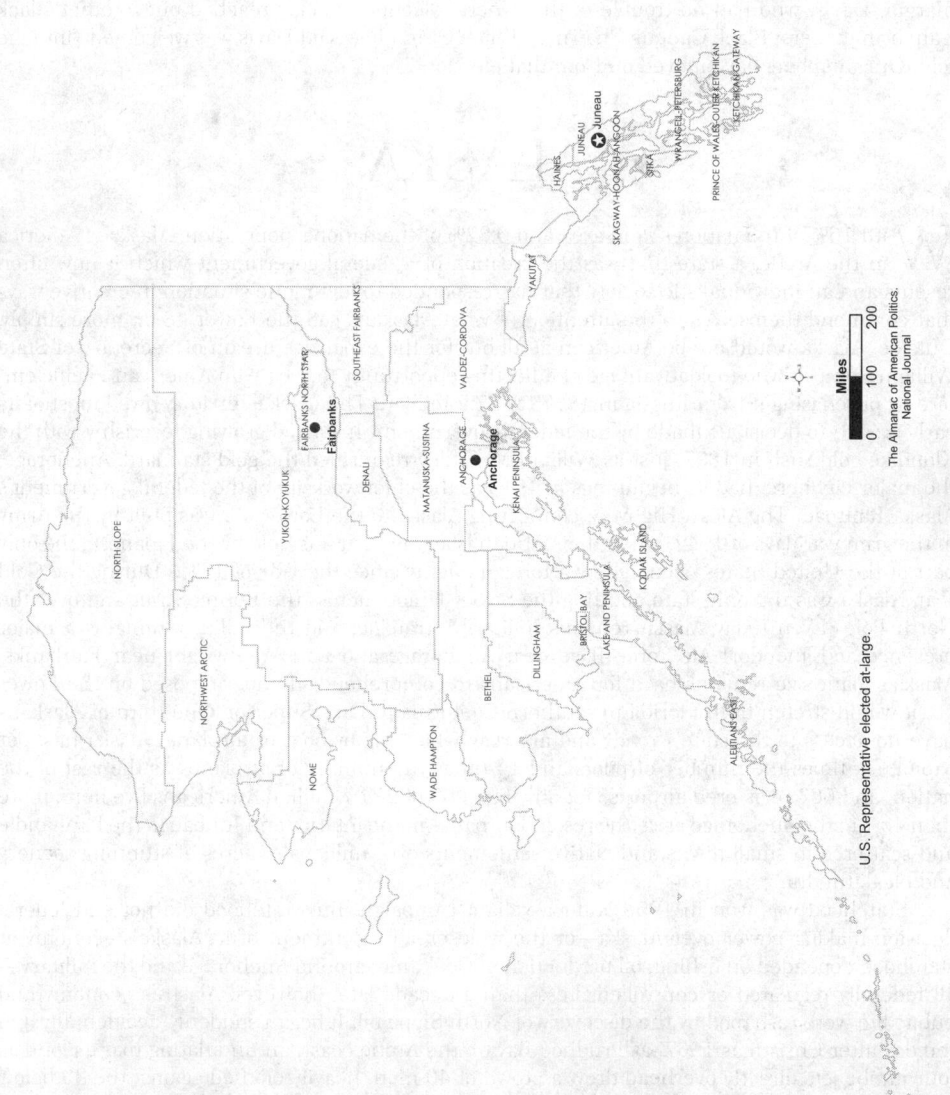

JUNEAU

★ Juneau

HAINES

SKAGWAY-HOONAH-ANGOON

SITKA

WRANGELL-PETERSBURG

PRINCE OF WALES-OUTER KETCHIKAN

KETCHIKAN GATEWAY

YAKUTAT

SOUTHEAST FAIRBANKS

VALDEZ-CORDOVA

FAIRBANKS NORTH STAR

● Fairbanks

DENALI

MATANUSKA-SUSITNA

ANCHORAGE

● Anchorage

KENAI PENINSULA

YUKON-KOYUKUK

KODIAK ISLAND

NORTH SLOPE

BRISTOL BAY

LAKE AND PENINSULA

DILLINGHAM

NORTHWEST ARCTIC

BETHEL

WADE HAMPTON

NOME

ALEUTIANS EAST

Miles

0   100   200

The Almanac of American Politics.
National Journal

U.S. Representative elected at-large.

Alaska, settled such claims in the 1971 Alaska Native Claims Act which set up 12 regional and 220 village Native corporations, gave them $962 million and time to select their own 44 million acres, and ended the Interior Department's freeze that enabled the state to stake claims to mineral-rich acreage. The only feasible way to get the oil out—the Arctic Ocean ice only breaks up in late July for six weeks of the year—was a pipeline. But that was opposed by environmentalists for fear it would destroy the delicate permafrost and interfere with caribou migrations. Development-minded Alaskans got a pipeline bill through Congress in 1973, by just a one-vote margin in the Senate, but the pipeline had to be built on stilts and wasn't opened until 1977, and Congress banned oil exports to Japan and other obvious East Asian markets. Then in 1980, after brilliant lobbying by environmentalists, Congress passed—over the objections of Alaska's two senators and in the face of tears from its Congressman-at-Large Don Young—the Alaska Lands Act, which set aside 159 million acres as national parks, national monuments or wilderness: One-third of the state was protected from development. Much, if not all, of this was for the best. The pipeline came on line just as oil prices were approaching their peak, thus generating maximum revenues to the state, which gets 100% of the royalties. The environment was protected much better than it would have been without the environmentalists' goadings— while there have been complaints about pipeline and oil field safety, operations are good by industrial standards. The caribou herd has risen from 3,000 animals to 32,000 and the Natives got more autonomy than the non-Native majority of Alaskans would have given them. With oil providing more than 80% of its revenue, the state abolished its income tax in 1980 and created a low-tax regime that has helped Alaska to grow even as oil revenues and military spending declined.

Wisely, Alaska did not squander its windfall. In 1976, Governor Jay Hammond persuaded the legislature to establish a Permanent Fund for most of the oil revenues. Each year it presents every one-year resident with a dividend of 20% of the average of profits for the preceding five years—$1,850 in 2001, $1,540 in 2002. More important, even though $12 billion has been paid in dividends, most of the money is invested. The North Slope is producing only half as much oil as in the late 1980s, but the Permanent Fund was worth $21.8 billion in 2002 (down from a $27.8 billion peak in 2000), and most of its income comes now from investments rather than oil. Some speculated that Alaska voters would pressure legislators for bigger payouts. But Alaskans have acted like investors: They want their dividend checks not just now, but in the future. In September 1999, after Governor Tony Knowles proposed tapping the Permanent Fund, voters rejected the change by an 83%–17% margin. Permanent Fund checks are especially valuable to Natives who live on subsistence fishing and hunting, and help account for the fact that Alaska has the smallest income gap between rich and poor of any state.

Similarly, the 12 regional Native Corporations created by the Alaska Native Claims Act have proved to be successful, not just in providing income for Natives, but in helping them preserve Native traditions and adapt to Alaska's market economy at their own pace. On Indian reservations in the Lower 48, all land is held by the tribe and supervised by the government; elections held on the political model have produced a winner-take-all politics that is too often corrupt and incapable of pursuing long-range strategies. The corporate model, on the other hand, allows the Alaska Native corporations' management more continuity in office—though some have made bad decisions and been thrown out. But the cumulative voting method, by which a minority can get a seat on the board, has produced management that is sensitive to all opinions. Huge windfalls are avoided because 70% of profits from mineral sales are shared by all corporations. But the corporation itself, not a distant federal bureaucracy, is left with the choice of how much ancestral land to retain and how much to exploit economically. Individual Natives can make the transition from their traditional communal economy, living on subsistence fishing and hunting, or make their way in the market economy in Anchorage or Fairbanks or the North Slope oil fields, as many have.

Not all is rosy here. Native villages in the bush have essentially no private sector economy, and rates of alcoholism and suicide are agonizingly high. In the solemn mien so typical of Natives, one may be seeing the memory of great kill-offs by disease, which struck Native villages as recently as the 1920s. And the issue of subsistence hunting has been simmering in Alaska politics since the state Supreme Court in 1989 struck down the subsistence preference for fishing and hunting by rural residents. Efforts by Governor Tony Knowles and Senator Ted Stevens to get the legislature to approve a constitutional amendment to allow rural preference failed because conservatives feared Native commercial sales and overfishing. In October 1999, the U.S. Interior Department took control of fisheries (it has managed hunting since 1990), and in 2001, shut down commercial and sports fishing for a time to protect Natives' subsistence. Salmon runs have been declining for a decade, and the salmon industry is ailing. Alaska used to produce half the world's salmon, but most are now produced by salmon farms in foreign markets. To keep Alaska's fishermen employed, the state in 1959 banned fish traps like the ocean pen nets used in Chile, Norway, Scotland and Canada, and it now limits boat and net sizes and the number of commercial fishing permits. Salmon prices are far below their late 1980s peaks, and it's not clear whether Alaska's heavily manned and tightly regularly fishing business can survive in its current form.

One of Alaska's economic assets has been its three-member congressional delegation which, in November 2002, when Senator Frank Murkowski was elected governor, had 86 years of seniority and key committee posts with which to fight for Alaska's economic interests against the stands of environmental restriction groups. Not all their fights have been successful. They have failed to get approval of oil drilling in a small sliver of the Arctic National Wildlife Refuge—an area the size of Washington-area Dulles International Airport in an area the size of Delaware—although it was on the verge of being approved in 1989 when the Exxon *Valdez* ran aground in Prince William Sound in March 1989. Environmental groups have made ANWR oil drilling one of their main issues in their direct-mail fundraising even though ANWR is estimated to have between 9 and 16 billion barrels of oil, the most by far in any untapped U.S. oil field. George W. Bush backed it in his 2000 presidential campaign and put it into his energy bill; it passed the House, with strong support from the Teamsters Union, by a 223–206 margin in August 2001, but was blocked in the Senate in 2002. Other energy development may be going ahead—in the Copper River Delta on Prince William Sound, in the Cook Inlet, on the man-made Northstar Island in the Beaufort Sea—but these are small potatoes in comparison.

Another contentious issue is logging in the dense Tongass National Forest in the Panhandle—the economic mainstay of Ketchikan, where Murkowski grew up. In 2001, the Clinton administration banned logging in roadless areas in national forests, which applied to 9.7 million acres in Alaska. Once loggers cut 600 million board-feet a year; the Clinton ban reduced that to 50 million board-feet, enough for one or two sawmills; the Bush administration seems inclined to allow 155 million board-feet. Frustration over ANWR and Tongass may be one reason Murkowski ran for governor.

Alaska remains heavily dependent on oil and on the federal government, so there is some reason for unease about its economy. The state government benefited when oil prices were high in 2000, but was strapped when they fell in 2001 and 2002. The state receives hundreds of millions of dollars every year in "Stevens money"— construction, highway, sewer and harbor projects shepherded by Senator Ted Stevens, chairman of the Appropriations Committee and the most senior Republican in the Senate. But Stevens, though he was reelected at 78 in 2002 by a 78%–11% margin, will not remain in the Senate forever. There are some promising signs of private sector development, more than in the nation's other offshore state, Hawaii. One is tourism, with more than 1.4 million visitors spending over $1.8 billion a year—some arrive on cruise ships and others head to Denali National Park and Mount McKinley. Tourism is the mainstay of the old Russian-settled capital of Sitka and of the private sector economy in Juneau. Another spur is the air freight business. The Anchorage airport, near the top of the world, is seven hours from New York, Tokyo and London, and is a major transfer point for UPS and FedEx. More all-cargo, wide-bodied aircraft move through Anchorage International than any other U.S. airport. A third reason is that this is a low-tax, low-regulation state, which has been attracting independent-spirited, entrepreneurial-minded young families; Alaska has the nation's third-youngest population, although its small elderly population is growing (up from 4% to 6% in the 1990s). Big institutions don't run things here: Unions, politically pivotal 25 years ago, are much less so now, and the oil companies, while not unpopular, weren't able to stop higher state oil taxes. The biggest private employers now are not the oil companies, but Safeway and Providence Alaska Medical Center: This is an economy that buzzes with small business success.

Politically, Alaska is heavily Republican, with a libertarian streak. In national politics, it has been solidly Republican since the 1970s because national Democrats have favored locking up natural resources. In 2000, George W. Bush carried Alaska 59%–28%, carrying even the traditionally Democratic Panhandle and the Native-majority bush country beyond Anchorage and Fairbanks. No Democrat has been elected to Congress since 1974, though some contests have been close. Oddly, Republicans were shut out of the governorship from 1982 to 2002, until Frank Murkowski finally recaptured the office in 2002. The legislature is not only solidly Republican, but solidly conservative. Referendums show Alaskans to be increasingly conservative, though with a libertarian tinge: In 1998, they voted for medical marijuana, English-only and a ban on same-sex marriage, though a ban on wolf snaring was defeated. In 2000, they rejected an initiative that would not only have legalized marijuana but would have paid restitution to those convicted of marijuana offenses.

Some regional differences persist. Anchorage is much like a prosperous Rocky Mountains' metropolis with longer summer days and winter nights; it is affluent and booming, with an unusually high percentage of working women. Politically, it is solidly Republican. So are the smaller settlements in a 200-mile arc around Anchorage, which have been growing even more rapidly: The Matanuska Valley (one of the few places in Alaska where farming is possible), Seward, the Kenai peninsula and the little port of Valdez at the southern terminus of the pipeline. Fairbanks, Alaska's second-largest city, is a pipeline and mineral service center deep in the interior, unprotected from Arctic winds in winter and crowds of mosquitoes in the brief but hot summer. It tends to vote Republican, too.

The old Alaska, first settled by Russians, can be seen in the towns of the Panhandle and in the capital of Juneau, located on an inlet of the Pacific up against a steep mountain. These are historically Democratic, but variable these days; in the 2002 gubernatorial election, Ketchikan voted for Murkowski, champion of logging in the Tongass, while Juneau, the capital, voted for Ulmer, the city's former mayor. Juneau is a remote site for most Alaskans, reachable only by harrowing and often-cancelled plane rides through the fjords, and there have been efforts to move the capital to a site near Anchorage. Alaskans voted to do so in 1974, but rejected proposals to pay for it in 1978 and 1982. Juneau, threatened with the loss of 40% of its economy, has had no trouble raising up to $1 million to keep state government there. Juneau defeated a proposal to move all state government by 55%–45% in 1994 and a proposal to move the legislature by 67%–33% in 2002. Mostly Democratic is the bush, the villages where Natives—Athabaskans, Aleuts, Yupiks, Inupiats—are the large majority. Natives make up 15% of Alaska's population and nearly 50% in the vast lands north and west of Anchorage and Fairbanks. They are greatly outnumbered and outvoted on many issues, and yet are the object of awed respect for their achievement in building civilizations in such a forbidding environment.

The People		**Race/Ethnic Origin**			**Military veterans:** 71,552 (16.4%)	
Pop. 2000:	626,932	423,788	67.6%	White	WWII: 7.9%	Korea: 6.9%
Pop. 1990:	550,043	21,073	3.4%	Black	Vietnam: 41.2%	Gulf War: 18.4%
Change 1990–2000:	Up 14.0%	24,741	3.9%	Asian	**Most populous cities:**	
Change 1980–1990:	Up 36.9%	96,505	15.4%	Native Am.	1. Juneau	30,711
% of U.S. total:	0.2%	3,181	0.5%	Hawaiian	2. Fairbanks	30,224
Pop. rank:	48th of 50	30,454	4.9%	Two+ races	3. Sitka	8,835
Area size:	663,267 sq. mi.	1,338	0.2%	Other	4. Ketchikan	7,922
State Native:	38.1%	25,852	4.1%	Hisp. Origin	5. Kenai	6,942
Non-citizen:	2.7%	**Ancestry**			Urban population: 65.7%	
Language		German: 12.5%		Irish: 8.1%	Rural population: 34.3%	
English: 82.6%	Asian: 3.9%	English: 7.2%		USA: 4.3%		
Spanish: 3.9%		Norwegian: 3.2%				

Education		Work Sector		Legislature	
H.S. Grad:	88.3%	Private: 64.9%	Govt: 26.8%	Senate	11 R 8 D 1 I
College Grad:	24.7%	Self: 8.0%	Family: 0.3%	House	27 R 13 D
Industry		Unemployment: 8.6%		Legislative Term Limits: No	
Agri: 4.9%	Con: 7.3%	**Household Income**		**Registered Voters**	
Fin: 4.6%	Info: 2.7%	<15k: 10.6%	15-35k: 21.6%	D: 71,073	(15.5%)
Mfg: 12.2%	Prof: 29.3%	35-50k: 16.0%	50-100k: 35.7%	R: 116,435	(25.5%)
Public: 10.7%	Trade: 14.2%	100-150k: 11.4%	>150k: 4.6%	I: 270,054	(59.0%)
Other: 14.2%		Median: $51,571			
Occupation		Poverty status: 9.4%			
Blue collar: 22.4%	White collar: 60.5%	**Home Value**			
Gray collar: 17.1%		<50k: 12.1% 50-100k: 17.7% 100-200k: 51.4% 200-300k: 13.7%			
		300-500k: 4.0% >500k: 1.2% Median: $137,400			

Presidential politics   In presidential elections, Alaska votes Alaska issues, but this was not always so: In 1960 and 1968, its votes came eerily close to the national average. Since then it has voted against the national Democrats: In the year of the Alaska Lands Act, it gave only 26% of its votes to Jimmy Carter, who in some places ran behind Libertarian Ed Clark. In 1992, Ross Perot won 28% here, his second-best showing in the country. In 2000, George W. Bush won 59%–28%, but Ralph Nader got 10% of the vote—his best showing in the country. There was a big gender gap: men voted 65%–24% for Bush, which recalls the plaint of Alaskan women who are outnumbered by men: "The odds are good but the goods are odd."

Alaska has no presidential primary. Party true believers tend to dominate the caucuses. In

2000 Presidential Vote		
Bush (R)	167,398	(59%)
Gore (D)	79,004	(28%)
Nader (Green)	28,747	(10%)
Other	10,411	(4%)

1996 Presidential Vote		
Dole (R)	122,746	(51%)
Clinton (D)	80,380	(33%)
Perot (I)	26,333	(11%)
Other	12,161	(5%)

the January 1996 straw poll or "beauty contest," Alaska Republicans voted 33% for Pat Buchanan, 31% for Steve Forbes, and 17% for Bob Dole. This gave Buchanan the confidence and verve he showed weeks later in Louisiana, where he beat Phil Gramm, and in other early contests climaxed by his win in New Hampshire on February 20. But Buchanan got only 2% here in November 2000. In November 1999, the Republican Party committee voted 39–36 to hold precinct caucuses and a straw poll on January 24, 2000. About 4,000 Alaskans voted, and George W. Bush led Forbes by 5 votes. Alaska, unlike Florida, didn't have a recount.

Governor

Frank Murkowski (R)

Elected 2002, term expires Jan. 2007, 1st term; b. Mar. 28, 1933, Seattle, WA; home, Fairbanks; U. of Santa Clara, 1951–53, Seattle U., B.A. 1955; Catholic; married (Nancy).

Military Career: Coast Guard, 1955–56.

Elected Office: U.S. Senate, 1980–02.

Professional Career: Pacific Natl. Bank of Seattle, 1957–58; Natl. Bank of AK, 1959–67; Commissioner, AK Dept. of Econ. Devel., 1966–70; Pres., AK Natl. Bank of the North, 1971–80.

Office: P.O. Box 110001, Juneau, 99811, 907-465-3500; Fax: 907-465-3532; Web site: www.gov.state.ak.us.

Election Results

2002 general	Frank Murkowski (R)	129,279	(56%)
	Fran Ulmer (D)	94,216	(41%)
	Other	7,989	(3%)
2002 primary	Frank Murkowski (R)	50,838	(70%)
	Wayne Ross (R)	18,852	(26%)
	Other	2,558	(4%)
1998 general	Tony Knowles (D)	112,879	(51%)
	Robin Taylor (write-in)	43,571	(20%)
	John Lindauer (R)	39,331	(18%)
	Ray Metcalfe (RP)	13,540	(6%)
	Other	10,856	(5%)

Frank Murkowski, elected governor in 2002, grew up in Seattle and Ketchikan, the logging town in the Panhandle, where his father was a banker. He went to college in California and Seattle, served in the Coast Guard, worked in a Seattle bank, then returned to Alaska while it was still a territory. He worked for a bank in Wrangell and Anchorage, then at 32 was appointed Commissioner of Economic Development by Governor Walter Hickel. He ran for Congress and lost 55%–45% to incumbent Democrat Nick Begich in 1970, then was president of a bank in Fairbanks for 9 years. In 1980, he ran for the Senate and won a six-candidate primary with 59% of the vote. Meanwhile, in the Democratic primary, incumbent Mike Gravel was beaten by liberal Clark Gruening, grandson of one of Alaska's first two senators. Murkowski campaigned against environmental restriction groups and called Gruening a "no growther"—not a popular position: Jimmy Carter, who signed the Alaska Lands Act that year, got only 26% of Alaskans' votes. Murkowski won 54%–46%.

In the Senate, Murkowski won a seat on the Energy and Natural Resources Committee, which he chaired from 1995 to June 2001. In 1991, he helped secure a ban on drift net fishing in international waters and the lifting of the ban on exports of Alaska oil in 1995. Usually he worked in tandem with senior colleague Ted Stevens, though they differed on a few issues—commercial fishing in Glacier Bay National Park and subsistence hunting and fishing.

Murkowski's great frustrations came on issues involving opposite ends of Alaska—logging in the Tongass National Forest and oil drilling in the Arctic National Wildlife Reserve. Murkowski opposed Clinton administration attempts to stamp out logging in the Tongass, but the amount of timber taken there declined 75% in the 1990s. He managed to get enough logging for one sawmill in Ketchikan, and more logging was allowed by the Bush administration. Clinton vetoed a bill allowing ANWR drilling in 1995, and Murkowski's attempts to pass it as part of an energy bill in 2001 and 2002 were unsuccessful. In April 2002, he was able to get only 46 votes to stop the filibuster threatened by several Democrats, far short of the needed 60; Murkowski and Stevens said that they would have had 51 votes for passage had it come to the floor. A ploy to win votes by using some of the revenues for health benefits for retired steel workers fell even farther short. Murkowski proved more successful getting into the energy bill tax credits estimated at $20 billion for a natural gas pipeline from the North Slope (where the gas brought up now is pumped back into the ground) to Fairbanks and then east through Canada to the Lower 48. But despite Murkowski's yeoman efforts, the energy bill did not pass in the 107th Congress.

Murkowski was reelected to the Senate in 1998 by 74%–20%. There is little doubt that he could have won reelection in 2004. But he evidently found his Senate career frustrating. He had devoted thousands of hours to the ANWR and Tongass issues, with little success. Democrats had a Senate majority in 2001, when he was making his decision to run for governor, so he was no longer a chairman, and term limits would have forced him out of either the ranking position or the Energy chairmanship in January 2003; on Finance, his other major committee, he ranked behind Charles Grassley and Orrin Hatch and figured he wouldn't have a shot at that chair for eight more years, when he would be 77. He had seriously considered running against Democratic Governor Tony Knowles in 1998, and in 2002 Knowles was prevented from running by term limits. So in October 2001, by a press release from his Senate office, he ran for governor.

Knowles, who was mayor of Anchorage from 1982–87, ran for governor unsuccessfully in

1990, was elected by a 536-vote margin in 1994 and was reelected with 51% of the vote in 1998 against a besmirched Republican nominee and a conservative Republican write-in supported by the Republican party. Throughout his two terms he clashed repeatedly with the conservative Republican legislature, and in much of his term, especially at the end, was faced with serious fiscal problems. Alaska gets 80% of its state revenues from royalties on oil, and Prudhoe Bay production is running at about half the levels of the mid-1980s. As oil prices fell, the state faced unpalatable choices: Cut spending on services, institute a state income or sales tax or spend some of the income of the Permanent Fund, thereby reducing Alaskans' annual dividends. The voters strongly rejected the third alternative, 83%–17%, in a September 1999 referendum, and were obviously hostile to the second. So the legislature imposed stringent cuts and the budget was balanced by drawing on the Constitutional Budget Reserve. In April 2002, the state budget was facing an $865 million shortfall; by Election Day, it was routinely described as $1 billion. It was widely predicted that the $2.1 billion Constitutional Budget Reserve would be drawn down to zero during the next governor's four-year term.

The race quickly boiled down to a contest between Murkowski and Democratic Lieutenant Governor Fran Ulmer. Several Republicans who had been considering running for governor ran for lieutenant governor instead; Murkowski ended up defeating Anchorage lawyer Wayne Ross 70%–26%. Ulmer had a career in Alaska politics almost as long as Murkowski's. She moved from Wisconsin to Juneau in the early 1970s and, while still in her 20s, was a policy adviser to Governor Jay Hammond, in the years when he established the Permanent Fund. She was Mayor of Juneau from 1983–85, won election to the state House in 1986 and, as a two-term lieutenant governor, worked closely with Knowles.

Murkowski and Ulmer took diametrically opposed positions on Alaska's future. Murkowski said that Alaska should look to greater production of oil and natural gas for economic growth. Ulmer said the state should try to diversify its economy. Murkowski opposed new taxes and talked about cutting spending in some areas. Ulmer called for caps on spending, plus a "parachute plan" to institute a statewide tax when the Constitutional Budget Reserve fell below $1 billion. "My commitment is to protect the dividend, control spending and get this state moving," Murkowski said; he counseled against "gloom and doom" about the $1 billion shortfall. He called for building roads and other transportation infrastructure—roads from Skagway to Juneau, along the Bradfield Canal near Wrangell, from Anchorage to Bristol Bay, to Cordova, from King Cove to Cold Bay and to remote mining prospect towns like Donlin Creek and Pogo, plus a bridge over Knik Arm near Anchorage and an Alaska-Canada Railroad. Ulmer questioned how Murkowski could pay for these projects and said his approach to the budget was "don't worry, be happy."

Jay Hammond, though a Republican, cut spots for Ulmer in which he charged that Murkowski's reliance on unproven oil and gas revenues would leave state government with no choice but to take money from the Permanent Fund dividend. Murkowski countered that Ulmer had sponsored two amendments to use Permanent Fund earnings for ongoing state government. Commentators chided both for lack of specificity: Murkowski for not saying how much he'd cut and where he would get needed revenue, and Ulmer for not saying what kind of tax would be triggered in her parachute plan. They did agree on some things: Both opposed moving the legislature from Juneau and both promised not to tap the Permanent Fund without a referendum. Through ads, they attacked each other. Murkowski showed Ulmer gleefully casting Alaska's votes for Bill Clinton at the Democratic National Convention; Ulmer chided Murkowski for giving up 22 years of seniority in the Senate.

Polls showed a close race, but Murkowski won by a solid 56%–41% margin. The margin was just about the same in greater Anchorage, which cast 39% of the state's votes (55%–42%), although Anchorage used to be the state's Republican stronghold. Now, the greatest Republican strength is in fast-growing areas around Anchorage—the Kenai Peninsula and Valdez (65%–31% Murkowski) and the Matanuska Valley (68%–28%), where voters have a strong libertarian, anti-tax streak. Greater Fairbanks also went for the Republican (57%–39%), and he carried the Kodiak-Bristol Bay area (54%–43%). The Bush, as usual, was heavily Democratic (66%–29% Ulmer), but in the formerly Democratic Panhandle the race was even (49%–49%). Murkowski's big margin in Ketchikan neutralized Ulmer's big margin in Juneau. In a race in which issues of taxation and the direction of the economy were squarely posed, Alaska's Republican sentiments prevailed. Ulmer won more than 50% of the vote in only 7 of the state's 40 state House districts (two around Juneau, two in central Anchorage and three in the Bush), while Murkowski won more than 50% in 27.

Murkowski took office December 2; under a law passed by the legislature over Knowles's veto, he was permitted to appoint his successor in the Senate—on December 20, he chose his daughter, Lisa.

Senior Senator

Ted Stevens (R)

Appointed Dec. 1968, seat up 2008, 6th term; b. Nov. 18, 1923, Indianapolis, IN; home, Girdwood; U.C.L.A., B.A. 1947, Harvard, LL.B. 1950; Episcopalian; married (Catherine).

Military Career: Army Air Corps, 1943–46 (WWII).

Elected Office: AK House of Reps., 1964–68.

Professional Career: Practicing atty., 1950–53, 1961–68; U.S. Atty., 1953–56; U.S. Dept. of Interior, Legis. Cnsl., 1956–58, Asst. to Secy., 1958–60, Solicitor, 1960–61.

DC Office: 522 HSOB, 20510, 202-224-3004; Fax: 202-224-2354; Web site: stevens.senate.gov.

State Offices: Anchorage, 907-271-5915; Fairbanks, 907-456-0261; Juneau, 907-586-7400; Kenai, 907-283-5808; Ketchikan, 907-225-6880; Wasilla, 907-376-7665.

Committees: *President Pro Tempore. Aging (Special). Appropriations* (Chmn.): Commerce, Justice, State & Judiciary; Defense (Chmn.); Homeland Security; Interior; Labor, HHS & Education; Legislative Branch. *Commerce, Science & Transportation*: Aviation; Communications; Oceans, Fisheries & Coast Guard; Science, Technology & Space; Surface Transportation & Merchant Marine. *Governmental Affairs*: Financial Management, Budget & International Security; Government Management, Federal Workforce & the District of Columbia; Investigations (Permanent). *Rules & Administration*.

Group Ratings

	ADA	ACLU	AFS	LCV	CON	ITIC	NTU	COC	ACU	NTLC	CHC
2002	10	20	13	6	14	100	53	100	83	77	—
2001	20	—	0	13	—	—	73	86	92	—	80

National Journal Ratings

	2001 LIB	—	2001 CONS		2002 LIB	—	2002 CONS
Economic	40%	—	60%		17%	—	82%
Social	22%	—	73%		44%	—	55%
Foreign	36%	—	54%		0%	—	76%

Key Votes of the 107th Congress

1. Approve Bush Tax Cuts	Y	5. Confirm Ashcroft as AG	Y	9. Bar Coop. with Intl. Court	Y
2. Expand Patients' Rights	N	6. Bar Gays in the Boy Scouts	Y	10. Trade Promotion Authority	Y
3. Campaign Finance Reform	N	7. $ for Hate Crime Prosecution	N	11. Authorize Force in Iraq	Y
4. Permit ANWR Development	Y	8. Overseas Military Abortions	Y	12. Homeland Sec. Dept. Union	N

Election Results

2002 general	Ted Stevens (R)	179,438	(78%)	($2,295,429)
	Frank Vondersaar (D)	24,133	(11%)	($1,049)
	Jim Sykes (Green)	16,608	(7%)	
	Other	9,369	(4%)	
2002 primary	Ted Stevens (R)	64,315	(89%)	
	Mike Aubrey (R)	7,997	(11%)	
1996 general	Ted Stevens (R)	177,893	(77%)	($2,711,710)
	Jed Whittaker (Green)	29,037	(13%)	
	Theresa Obermeyer (D)	23,977	(10%)	

Prior Winning Percentages: 1990 (66%); 1984 (71%); 1978 (76%); 1972 (77%); 1970 (60%)

No other senator fills so central a place in his state's public and economic life as Ted Stevens of Alaska; quite possibly no other senator ever has. "They sent me here," Stevens said in one impassioned debate, "to stand up for the state of Alaska." Stevens is now President Pro Tempore of the Senate, and thus third in line for the presidency. He is the chairman of the Appropriations Committee and of its Defense subcommittee; he has also been for two decades the leading public policymaker for and about Alaska. He is a major economic asset for Alaska, because the capitalized value of the money he brings into the state every year would range into the billions. "We ask for special consideration," Stevens is not too shy to say, "because no one else is that far away, no one else has the problems that we have or the potential that we have, and no one else deals with the federal government day in and day out the way we do." Probably more than any other senator, Stevens has shaped the public institutions and private economy of his state.

He has had plenty of training. Stevens grew up in Indiana and California in very modest surroundings, served in World War II flying C-46s and C-47s, graduated from UCLA and Harvard Law, then moved to Alaska in 1950, driving up the Alaska Highway with his new bride. He was U.S. attorney in Fairbanks and worked in the Interior Department in Washington. In 1962, he ran for the Senate and lost to Democrat Ernest Gruening by a 58–42% margin. He then served in the legislature in Juneau and was appointed to the Senate by Governor Walter Hickel in December 1968, at 45. He quickly gained a seat on Appropriations and worked on Alaska issues of all description. He has not been entirely successful. He could not stop the Alaska Lands Act in 1980 and could not win approval of Arctic National Wildlife Refuge oil drilling in 1991 or 1995 or 2002. But he played a major role on the Native Claims Act in 1971 and got the oil pipeline through by one vote in 1973. In 1995, he and Frank Murkowski finally secured the repeal of the 1977 law forbidding exports of Alaskan oil, thus opening up the obvious East Asian markets.

When he succeeded Mark Hatfield as chairman of the Appropriations Committee in 1997, Stevens told colleagues, "Senator Hatfield had the patience of Job and the disposition of a saint. I don't. The watch has changed. I'm a mean, miserable SOB." But if he is terrible-tempered (or wants others to think so), he is also hard-working. And while he chafed under the spending limits set by Senate budget resolutions and by Bush OMB director Mitch Daniels, he has generally, if grudgingly, observed them—though in October 2001, he did get Daniels's $679 billion spending limit for FY2002 stretched to $686 billion. Stevens works closely with his fellow appropriators—West Virginia Senator Robert Byrd, House Republican Bill Young and House Democrat David Obey—to reach consensus decisions on overall spending limits and specific bills. Amid these negotiations there was a flash of the Stevens temper: He threatened to hold up the defense appropriation after George W. Bush limited classified military and investigative briefings to the eight members in the leadership and the head of the Intelligence committees. In late 2002, he complained about the $749 billion spending limit imposed by Daniels; since 11 of the 13 appropriations were not passed in the 107th Congress, the struggle carried over to the 108th.

As chairman of the Defense subcommittee, Stevens has generally supported robust defense spending and has been an advocate of missile defense. He works in tandem with Hawaii's Daniel Inouye; these two senators from America's two offshore states, both decorated World War II veterans, have held the chairmanship or ranking minority positions on this subcommittee since 1989. He works hard to fund the National Guard, to raise military salaries and to keep troops in readiness. When House Defense Appropriations Subcommittee Chairman Jerry Lewis moved to cut off the F-22 jet fighter, Stevens was its great champion and produced a compromise that allowed development to proceed if the jet could pass flight tests.

Since he became Appropriations chairman, Alaskans have started referring matter-of-factly to "Stevens money" for projects he has been able to fund. Stevens sees his work in a broader context: "Congress has not awakened to the fact that we've got a state with one-fifth the land in this country. My mission is to try to make Congress understand that the promise of statehood is that we should have the ability to establish a workable private-enterprise economy in the areas of Alaska that want it. And that's basically 90% of the state." His prowess is legendary. In 1998, Stevens sought a land trade for a seven-mile road through the Izembeck National Wildlife Refuge—which the Clinton Interior Department wanted to declare off-limits—so that the tiny Aleutian village of King Cove would have access to medical facilities. The administration offered three alternatives; Stevens took all three: $37.7 million for an airport road, medical clinic and doctor and nurse. In 1998, he also succeeded in setting up the Denali Commission (Denali is the Native name of Mount McKinley), which funds infrastructure projects—water and sewer, electricity—in central Alaska, to the tune of $38 million in 2001, $45 million in 2002 and $48 million in 2003.

In 2002, Stevens put into appropriations bills what his staff termed a small amount of $115 million for Alaska projects that saw their way to passage in early 2003. They included $11 million to build an Indian health service clinic in St. Paul, $6 million to prevent wildfires in Anchorage and Matanuska-Susitna, $4 million for Alaska's telemedicine program (a longtime Stevens project), $2 million to develop steel technologies for an Alaska natural gas pipeline, $1 million to study coal-bed methane in Alaska, $1 million for North Slope eider duck recovery and the Alaska Sealife Center, $2 million for a land transfer for the Kake tribal council, $3 million for a Kodiak National Wildlife Refuge visitor center, $5 million for volcano monitoring, $1 million for foam-containing devices that can be dragged behind four-wheelers or snowmobiles to fight fires in rural Alaska, $575,000 for seabird bycatch reduction, $500,000 for sonar fish counters, $100,000 to study the feasibility of a causeway to Fire Island, $1 million for dredging in Cook Inlet, $3.3 million to buy land for the Togiak National Wildlife Refuge, $4 million for a Coast Guard dock in Cordova. When a Stevens aide read an *Anchorage Daily News* article about a volunteer group that had raised $6,000 to promote a string of public-use huts linked by hiking trails, she showed it to Stevens. He thought it was a good idea and, without consulting the group, put in $500,000 for a backcountry hut network at Snow River near Seward. "That's crazy!" exulted the group's vice president. "There's, like, tears in my eyes." It could be argued that Stevens is less a legislator than he is a philanthropist in the mode of John D. Rockefeller or Andrew Carnegie, although of course he is not spending his own money.

Citizens Against Government Waste has constantly attacked Stevens and says that Alaska is the number one state in "pork per capita." They singled out for criticism grants of $1 million for a dust abatement study in Kotzebue, $2.25 million for winter recreation opportunities at a recreation area in Fairbanks, $990,000 for an adult day care center in Anchorage, $1 million each to Alaska Native Heritage Center in Anchorage and Inupiat Heritage Center in Barrow. Stevens, however, is unapologetic. When asked by an *Anchorage Daily News* reporter how Alaska had made out in the 2001 defense appropriation, Stevens replied, "Like a bandit."

Even his critics must concede that he does not shovel money into projects willy-nilly; his knowledge of detail is astonishing, and he is prepared to defend every single project on the merits. Issues involving tiny villages or just a few fishermen get his attention. Stevens has worked tirelessly to help Alaska Natives, who vote heavily Democratic in most elections. They have voted overwhelmingly for Stevens in recent elections, but he could win without their support easily. He skillfully elicits consensus with Native leaders when opinion is divided, getting more health and sanitation aid to bush villages and funding for health research on fetal alcohol syndrome and cancers common among Natives, and to allow the CIRI Native corporation to raise capital by reselling its wireless licenses earlier than allowed under FCC small business rules. He steers something like $500 million a year to Native organizations and passed a bill to allow Native contractors to win lucrative sole-source federal contracts. At the same time, Stevens is not uncritical of Native leaders. In October 2002, he urged the Alaska Federation of Natives not to funnel their requests for federal money through the 229 individual village-based tribes granted official status by the Clinton administration, but to consolidate federal requests so that "the very, very poor communities that don't have that ability to hire consultants, to hire grantsmen, people to write applications," get assistance.

After surgery for prostate cancer in 1991, Stevens pushed for more funding for breast, cervical and prostate cancer research, plus telemedicine projects to connect rural Alaskans to hospitals and specialists. He is a big booster of exercise and physical education programs; he says he saw value of exercise as he looked over his classmates at his 50th reunion at Harvard Law School. He supports the Corporation for Public Broadcasting: Alaska's public TV and radio stations have the nation's largest audience shares. And, with the large government work force in high-cost

Alaska, he supports increased salaries and benefits for federal workers and argues volubly for higher salaries for senators and Senate staffers.

Stevens's work has not gone unappreciated. In January 2000, he was named Alaskan of the Century. In July 2000, Anchorage Airport was named the Ted Stevens International Airport and the Challenger Center in Kenai became the Ted and Catherine Stevens Center for Space Science Technology. Stevens has been re-elected easily. His toughest competition recently came in the August 1996 primary when a banker and former legislator spent $1.3 million of his own money and charged that Stevens was insufficiently conservative. Stevens won 59%–27%. The Democratic nominee that fall, former Anchorage school board member Theresa Obermeyer, blamed Stevens for her husband's failure to pass the Alaska bar on 22 separate tries; she sometimes wore black-and-white prisoner stripes and a ball-and-chain to his public events. Democratic Governor Tony Knowles announced he was voting for Stevens, who won 77%.

In 2002, Stevens raised $2.4 million and said, "I'm going to run like there is someone there." There wasn't. Obermeyer lost the Democratic primary to Frank Vondersaar, a denizen of the hip town of Homer, who said that Stevens is part of a government conspiracy to keep him under constant surveillance. He was reelected by a 78%–11% margin, carrying all but three precincts. He campaigned actively for his 22-year colleague Frank Murkowski's successful candidacy for governor. In the 108th Congress, he will have to shoulder the work Murkowski did in the 107th, when he unsuccessfully sought permission for oil drilling in the Arctic National Wildlife Refuge. In April 2002, when Murkowski was able to get only 46 votes against cloture on the issue, Stevens called it "a severe defeat," and declined to offer compromises aimed at making oil drilling more acceptable to opponents. On this issue he will have the support of the Bush administration, but will face filibuster threats from Democrats who are thinking of running for president and who seek support from environmental restriction groups— for whom opposition to ANWR is a great asset in the direct-mail fundraising. Stevens has said that his own number one goal is approval of a natural gas pipeline in Alaska—a provision that Murkowski got into the energy bill, which did not pass—and that his number two goal is funding projects in Alaska. For that he will still have the Appropriations chairmanship. Senate Republicans decided not to count the five months Stevens served as chairman from January to May 2001 under their six-year term limit on chairmanships, and so Stevens will have another two years in which to shower Stevens money on the people of Alaska.

Junior Senator

Lisa Murkowski (R)

Appointed Dec. 2002, seat up 2004, 1st term; b. May 22, 1957, Ketchikan; home, Anchorage; Willamette U., 1975–77, Georgetown U., B.A. 1980, Willamette U., J.D. 1985; Catholic; married (Verne Martell).

Elected Office: AK House of Reps., 1998–02.

Professional Career: Anchorage Dist. Court Clerk's Office, atty., 1987–89; Practicing atty., 1989–98.

DC Office: 322 HSOB, 20515, 202-224-6665; Fax: 202-224-5301; Web site: murkowski.senate.gov.

State Offices: Anchorage, 907-271-3735; Fairbanks, 907-456-0233; Juneau, 907-586-7400; Kenai, 907-283-5808; Ketchikan, 907-225-6880; Wasilla, 907-376-7665.

Committees: *Energy & Natural Resources*: Energy; Public Lands & Forests; Water & Power (Chmn.). *Environment & Public Works*: Fisheries, Wildlife & Water; Transportation & Infrastructure. *Indian Affairs. Veterans' Affairs.*

Group Ratings and Key Votes: Newly Appointed

Election Results

1998 general	Frank Murkowski (R)	165,227	(74%)	($911,926)
	Joseph Sonneman (D)	43,743	(20%)	($26,091)
	Other	12,837	(6%)	
1998 primary	Frank Murkowski (R)	76,635	(72%)	
	Joseph Sonneman (D)	10,716	(10%)	
	Frank Vondersaar (D)	6,343	(6%)	
	William L. Hale (R)	6,312	(6%)	
	Jeffrey Gottlieb (Green)	4,793	(4%)	
	Other	1,986	(2%)	

Lisa Murkowski became Alaska's sixth U.S. senator when Governor Frank Murkowski, her father, appointed her in December 2002 to fill the vacancy caused by his resignation from the Senate. Lisa Murkowski grew up in Ketchikan on Alaska's Panhandle and in Fairbanks, the second of six children. In her senior year of high school she worked five weeks as an intern in Senator Ted Stevens's Washington office. She attended Willamette University in Salem, Oregon, and graduated from Georgetown in 1980, the year her father was first elected to the Senate, and graduated from Willamette law school in 1985. She served as an Anchorage District Court attorney and worked for an Anchorage law firm for eight years, then established her own law practice. In 1998 she was elected to the state House from a north Anchorage district including her neighborhood of Government Hill.

Alaska's state government depends heavily on revenues from North Slope oil, and in early 2002 was facing a budget shortfall of $1.1 billion. Murkowski was one of the leaders of a bipartisan Fiscal Policy Caucus that sought tax increases—a position opposite to that of her father, who was running for governor on a platform of no new taxes. In March 2002 the House Finance Committee passed a package that included spending $900 million from the Permanent Fund, the first such spending since the Fund was created in 1977; that was eventually defeated. But Murkowski pushed hard for increasing the alcohol tax from 3 cents a drink to 10 cents. She fought fiercely—when another legislator proposed an amendment with a much smaller increase, she said, "I'm gonna kill somebody!"—and the tax was passed in May, giving Alaska the nation's highest alcohol tax. Some conservatives referred to her and her allies as RIMs, "Republican invertebrate moderates." She also angered conservatives when she was one of five Republicans to vote against a bill restricting publicly funded abortions. At the time she said, "I may have a very short-lived political future here. But you know, I've got great kids and a great husband, and I'm going to have a good heart, and I'm going to stand up for the women of the state of Alaska, and I'm going to vote no." But she has also said that abortion should be legal only when a mother's life is in danger or in cases of rape and incest, and in March 2003 said she was against partial-birth abortion. Nonetheless, Alaska Right to Life opposed her in 1998, claiming, "She is not pro-life."

Conservatives opposed her reelection in 2002. Redistricting put her in the same district with incumbent Republican Eldon Mulder, co-chairman of the House Finance Committee. But Mulder decided not to run for reelection. She did have primary opposition from conservative Nancy Dahlstrom, who attacked her for favoring tax increases and tapping the Permanent Fund. This was a close contest and Murkowski won by only 486–429 — a margin of 57 votes. During this period she evidently stayed at arm's length from her father, who easily won the nomination for governor. "We have always maintained very separate identities at least for the time I have been in the legislature," Lisa Murkowski said. "I haven't called him for counseling and typically he doesn't offer." During and after the primary, she ran for House speaker. In November 2002, Republican House members chose the more conservative Pete Kott of Eagle River for that post and Murkowski for House Majority Leader.

That was just two days after Frank Murkowski had been elected governor. There were two years left in the Senate term to which he had been elected, and Republican legislators had seen to it that he, and not outgoing Democratic Governor Tony Knowles, would appoint his successor. Earlier in the year, they passed over Knowles's veto a law barring a governor from appointing a successor until five days after the vacancy occurred. After Senator Bob Bartlett died in December 1968, Governor Walter Hickel appointed a 45-year-old Anchorage lawyer named Ted Stevens to fill his place; today Stevens is chairman of the Appropriations Committee and President Pro Tempore of the Senate and thus third in line for the presidency. Alaska has only a three-member congressional delegation, but in 2002 it was one with 86 years of seniority: Congressman-at-Large Don Young first won in a special election in 1973 at 39 and Murkowski won his first term in 1980 at 47. Murkowski said he wanted to appoint someone who had legislative experience, was young enough and reelectable enough to serve for many years, who knew and shared his views on Alaska issues. On November 15 he unveiled a short list of 26 potential nominees, not all of whom met all his criteria. Many were experienced politicians, but some had different backgrounds—General Joseph Ralston, NATO Supreme Commander who had served in Alaska and was registered to vote there, as an Independent; retired General Mark Hamilton, President of the University of Alaska; Jerry Hood, secretary-treasurer of Teamsters Local 959 and a former Democrat who had become a Republican (and supported Murkowski for governor in 2002); Francis Hurley, the retired Catholic Archbishop of Anchorage; John Troxel, an Anchorage plastic surgeon; incoming state Senate Majority Leader Ben Stevens, son of Ted Stevens. Also on the list was House Majority Leader Lisa Murkowski. As she later recalled, "We had a conversation and he said, 'Your name keeps coming up. Are you interested in going back to Washington? I confirmed that that was one of those things that everyone in Alaska office would think to as kind of the highlight of a political career. So basically he asked if I wanted to have my name continue on the list, and I said yes." Frank Murkowski interviewed some of those on the short list and promised a decision by December 10. But he had not yet made up his mind when he left for a 10-day trip to Washington that day. On December 17, he said the short list had been narrowed down.

On December 20, Governor Murkowski appointed state Representative Murkowski as senator. "Above all, I felt the person I appoint to the remaining two years of my term should be someone who shares my basic philosophy, my values, but particularly one who shares on the issues of Alaska matters that are before us," he said. "Someone whose judgment I trust in representing the state and all of its people." This was the first time a governor had appointed his daughter, or for that matter his child, to the Senate. Most Republicans and many Democrats said nice things about the new senator. But there was some disapproval—even from the Republican side. Jim Whitaker, an ally of Murkowski in the Alaska House, said her appointment "is nepotism and therefore contrary to the democratic principles of representative government. An action of this type undermines the public trust and is therefore of great concern."

Lisa Murkowski made it clear that she would work for approval of oil drilling in the Arctic National Wildlife Refuge and for construction of a gas pipeline from the North Slope; she backs a state constitutional amendment allowing a rural priority for subsistence hunting (the federal government has taken over regulation of hunting and fishing on federal land in Alaska) and favors Alaska Native hiring requirements. She noted that as a Republican she was well positioned to help the state. Her first three bills were to increase the authorization for the Denali Commission to $450 million ($97 million was the most recent amount), to extend permanently the Medicaid formula under which the federal government pays about 60% of the cost rather than the 50% in other states and to provide tax deductions for Eskimo whaling captains for the costs of outfitting their boats and crew.

Among those unhappy with the appointment were Alaska conservatives unhappy with her record on taxes and abortion in the state House. Whether they would remain opposed if she should support tax cuts and abortion restrictions in the Senate was unclear. Murkowski said that she expected primary opposition. Mentioned as possible candidates in early 2003 were Alaska Railroad board chairman Johne Binkley, former Anchorage Mayor Rick Mystrom (who made an unsuccessful mayoral return bid in 2003), former lieutenant governor candidate Sarah Palin, Teamsters leader Jerry Hood and Drue Pearce, an aide to Interior Secretary Gale Norton. In February 2003, the White House indicated she would get George W. Bush's support against any opponent. As for the general election, the big question in mid-2003 was whether former Governor Tony Knowles would run. A Democrat who strongly supports oil drilling in ANWR and the gas pipeline, Knowles was elected with 41% in a four-way race in 1994 and with 51% in another four-way race in 1998; he is far and away the most successful Alaska Democrat of his generation. But Knowles was not disclosing his plan; with Alaska's late filing deadline and his universal name identification, he could afford to wait a long time. Also mentioned as possible Democratic candidates if Knowles doesn't run were former Lieutenant Governor Fran Ulmer, who ran a respectable race against Frank Murkowski in 2002, and state House Minority Leader Ethan Berkowitz.

Representative-At-Large

Don Young (R)

Elected Mar. 1973, 15th term; b. June 9, 1933, Meridian, CA; home, Fort Yukon; Yuba Jr. Col., A.A. 1952, Chico St. Col., B.A. 1958; Episcopalian; married (Lu).

Military Career: Army, 1955–57.

Elected Office: Fort Yukon City Cncl., 1960–64; Fort Yukon Mayor, 1964–68; AK House of Reps., 1966–70; AK Senate, 1970–73.

Professional Career: School teacher, Fort Yukon, 1960–68; Riverboat captain, 1960–68.

DC Office: 2111 RHOB, 20515, 202-225-5765; Fax: 202-225-0425; Web site: www.house.gov/donyoung.

District Offices: Anchorage, 907-271-5978; Fairbanks, 907-456-0210; Juneau, 907-586-7400; Kenai, 907-283-5808; Ketchikan, 907-225-6880; Mat-Su, 907-376-7665.

Committees: *Resources* (2d of 28 R): Fisheries Conservation, Wildlife & Oceans. *Select Committee on Homeland Security* (4th of 27 R): Infrastructure & Border Security. *Transportation & Infrastructure* (Chmn. of 41 R).

Group Ratings

	ADA	ACLU	AFS	LCV	CON	ITIC	NTU	COC	ACU	NTLC	CHC
2002	10	8	11	25	14	62	53	90	86	82	100
2001	5	—	0	0	—	—	65	89	91	—	—

National Journal Ratings

	2001 LIB — 2001 CONS			2002 LIB — 2002 CONS		
Economic	20%	—	80%	21%	—	73%
Social	20%	—	69%	0%	—	75%
Foreign	20%	—	80%	29%	—	71%

Key Votes of the 107th Congress

1. Approve Bush Tax Cuts	Y	5. Faith-Based Charities	Y	9. Trade Promotion Authority	*
2. Limit Patients' Bill of Rights	Y	6. Bar Gays in the Boy Scouts	Y	10. Bar Funds for Intl. Court	Y
3. Campaign Finance Reform	N	7. Ban Partial-Birth Abortion	Y	11. Authorize Force in Iraq	Y
4. Ban ANWR Development	N	8. Arm Commercial Pilots	Y	12. Deny Home. Sec. Dept. Union	Y

Election Results

2002 general	Don Young (R)	169,685	(75%)	($1,378,269)
	Clifford Greene (D)	39,357	(17%)	($980)
	Russell DeForest (Green)	14,435	(6%)	
2002 primary	Don Young (R)	unopposed		
2000 general	Don Young (R)	190,862	(70%)	($1,030,168)
	Clifford Greene (D)	45,372	(17%)	($412)
	Anna C. Young (Green)	22,440	(8%)	
	Jim Dore (AI)	10,085	(4%)	
	Other	5,634	(2%)	

Prior Winning Percentages: 1998 (63%); 1996 (59%); 1994 (57%); 1992 (47%); 1990 (52%); 1988 (63%); 1986 (57%); 1984 (55%); 1982 (71%); 1980 (74%); 1978 (55%); 1976 (71%); 1974 (54%); 1973 (51%)

Don Young has been Alaska's congressman-at-large since 1973. He was once tugboat captain on the Yukon and is the only licensed mariner in Congress—in his words, "not one of these smooth, namby-pamby politicians." He is a hot-tempered, salty-tongued true believer, given to malapropisms ("Pribilof's dog" and "bladderdash") and tough talk (when a Texas congressman blocked a motion for unanimous consent on an airline bill, Young replied, "Those in Texas will not fly; may you walk and may you die in the desert"). Young grew up in rural California, served in the Army and graduated from college, then moved to Alaska, captained his tugboat and was elected mayor of Fort Yukon. He was elected to the legislature in 1966 and ran for Congress in 1972. His opponent, incumbent Nick Begich, was killed in a plane crash in October and was reelected posthumously; Young won the March 1973 special election to succeed him. Young is not a free-market conservative—he casts many liberal economic votes—but he is a cultural and foreign policy conservative, and an unceasing advocate of what he considers Alaska's interests.

Young has done most of his legislating from the Resources and the Transportation committees. He was ranking minority member on Resources from 1985 to 1995 and chairman from 1995 to 2001. In 2001, he became chairman of Transportation. He summarizes his career, "On the Resources Committee I like to say I was in charge of everything God made, and now on Transportation I'm in charge of everything man made." Resources was more of a battleground, with supporters of environmental restriction groups having solid majorities (including some Republicans) when Democrats had control. Their numbers were trimmed after the Republican victory of 1994, but environmental groups still have great sway on the floor of the House, where many Republicans from the Northeast, Florida and Arizona are eager to score high on the groups' scoresheets. Often, that came at Alaska's, or Young's, expense. Alaska's two senators can use the Senate's dilatory rules to get their way; in the tightly controlled House, Young can be efficiently steamrollered, as he was often when in the minority—most notably when the Alaska Lands Act passed in 1980. He was stymied as well by Bill Clinton's vetoes, particularly after the House finally approved oil drilling in Arctic National Wildlife Refuge in 1995 and when Congress rallied to maintain logging in the Tongass National Forest. But he did succeed in allowing gambling on Alaska cruise ships inside the three-mile limit.

Young has also shown a talent for consensus. In 1997, he passed, by 419–1, the National Wildlife Improvement Act, which sets new guidelines for the nation's 500-plus wildlife refuges. The bill, endorsed by Clinton and environmental groups, allows for recreational activities that are compatible with the refuges' conservation mission. Another major issue for Young is missile defense. He vigorously and persistently opposed the 1995 Clinton National Intelligence Estimate that asked whether the U.S. would be safe from a hostile missile force for the next 15 years. Alaska and Hawaii, Young argued persuasively, are not excluded from the constitutional requirement that the federal government provide for the common defense.

Young's principal focus in 2000 was on the Conservation and Reinvestment Act, to dedicate royalties from offshore oil and gas wells to provide federal dollars for state purchases of land. His original version would require that $3 billion be spent every year, independent of the appropriations process, for 15 years; Alaska would be guaranteed $163 million a year in compensation for the environmental costs of oil drilling, more than all but two other states. Other money was directed to urban parks, to increase support in the House. Many conservative Republicans opposed this as a federal power grab, but Young pushed it through the House 315–102 in May 2000— "the crowning achievement" of his career, said the *Anchorage Daily News*. But it was not a popular cause in the Senate, where Rocky Mountain Republicans carry greater weight and others thought the money should be subject to the appropriations process, and the Clinton administration moved toward opposing it. Finally, in October 2000, a scaled-down version—CARA lite, Frank Murkowski called it—was passed as part of the Interior appropriation; it authorized $12 billion over six years, subject to appropriators, with about $50 million a year authorized for Alaska.

Even after he left the chairmanship, Young continued to work on Resources issues. He helped build support for oil drilling in the Arctic National Wildlife Refuge by getting unions to support it as a jobs bill; it was approved by the House 223–206 in August 2001, but never came to a vote in the Senate. Young resisted efforts by Louisiana Rep. Billy Tauzin to make it more attractive to opponents by granting wilderness status to parts of ANWR not so designated. Young has long worked to help Alaska's Natives, and he fought the Bush administration Interior Department to allow Natives who served in the military from 1969 to 1971 to get 160-acre allotments on federal lands (they were eligible under a 1906 law, but lost this right under the Alaska Native Claims Act of 1971); this was approved by the committee on voice vote in September 2002. He also fought for a bill to allow Native management of federal lands in Alaska.

From the sharp partisanship of Resources, Young passed to the bipartisan coziness of the huge Transportation Committee—the most popular assignment in the House under his predecessor, former Pennsylvania Rep. Bud Shuster, who made sure every cooperating member received plenty of highway (or mass transit) projects and who fought ruthlessly to keep transportation money flowing directly from the gasoline and airplane fuel taxes without any review by the Appropriations Committees. But Young also had to deal with contentious issues after September 11. There was sharp conflict over the details of emergency aid for Amtrak, over provisions for federal aid to the airlines and over whether airport security personnel should be federal workers. Even after the Senate voted 100–0 for federalization, Young and the Republican leadership held out for federal supervision of private contractors—the system used in Israel and Europe. But the pressure for action was too great, and when the Bush White House made it clear there would be no presidential veto, federalization prevailed. Young also fought the Bush administration on arming airline pilots. He and Florida Rep. John Mica introduced a bill to do so in April 2002, and watered it down by limiting it to 2% of pilots and making it a two-year test program. But in July 2002, Oregon Democrat Peter DeFazio passed an amendment gutting those provisions, and the bill passed by the veto-proof margin of 310–113. The Senate did the same by 87–6 in September, and the administration was overruled.

The fights between Transportation and the appropriators continued. In November 2001, appropriators raided $423 million from the Highway Trust Fund for other spending. In spring 2002, Young worked to get $4.4 billion from the trust fund for current projects. Observers were surprised that Young was as bipartisan as Shuster, but some thought he was not as ruthless in protecting and expanding the committee's jurisdiction. Looming in 2003 is the need to reauthorize Shuster's masterpieces, the $218 billion TEA-21 surface transportation law and the $40 billion AIR-21 airport construction act, both financed by dedicated fuel taxes. With gas and air fuel revenues running below expectations, it may be hard to put together such big packages. He is also expected to work on funding for the Coast Guard and fisheries issues.

Young has had his ups and downs with Alaska voters over the years, with significant opposition in 1978, 1984, 1986, 1990 and 1992. For years, the *Anchorage Daily News'* criticisms hurt him in that usually Republican city, and his reputation for abrasiveness and arrogance became such a problem that he cut an apology spot in 1992, when he was trailing in the polls. It worked—he has not had electoral trouble since. His work over the years on Native causes (he has pushed constantly for more federal jobs for Natives, as promised in the Alaska Native Claims Act) have enabled him to win by large margins even in the usually heavily Democratic bush. In 2000 and 2002, against weak opposition, he was reelected by 70%–17% and 75%–17% margins.

★ ARIZONA ★

Youth and age, new and old: Arizona is home to America's oldest continuous community and is one of America's fastest-growing and most rapidly changing states. The Hopi Indians, living as shepherds on plateaus east of the Grand Canyon, have not changed much in perhaps 500 years. In 1680 they killed the local Franciscan priests and burned their churches and have spurned Christianity since; more recently they have been involved in land disputes with the far more numerous Navajo. The Hopi are the oldest Arizonans; the newest are moving in every day, into subdivisions rising up out of the empty desert east, north, and west of Phoenix, hemmed in only by dry river beds, upcroppings of mountains, and Indian reservation boundaries.

For Arizona was one of the boom states of the 1990s, when its population rose by 40%, the highest except for next-door Nevada, a state with an economy now sophisticated and decentralized enough that there is no easy explanation, as there once was, of how and why Arizona grows. The first explanation was copper: The dome of the state Capitol dome is encased in copper; one of Arizona's leading public figures was Lewis Douglas, copper heir and congressman, Franklin Roosevelt's first budget director and Harry Truman's ambassador to Britain. In those years Arizona depended heavily on the federal government, and on politicians like Carl Hayden, Democratic congressman from statehood in 1912 and senator from 1927–69, whose public works projects watered Arizona's cotton, citrus and cattle farms. Then, in the decades after World War II, businessmen, lawyers, developers and water companies, notably the Salt River Project, built an Arizona based on something like the opposite of New Deal principles: With minimal government and precious little regulation of business, a welcoming of new technological ideas and shunning of new cultural liberalism; like Disneyland, a more gleaming and spotless embodiment of old values than America had ever been. Their political champion was Barry Goldwater, city council member and senator and the nation's Mr. Conservative for much of the 1950s and 1960s. He helped to make Arizona Republican, the only state to vote Republican for president in every election from 1952 to 1992.

This Arizona has grown phenomenally, from 700,000 people at the end of World War II to 3.6 million in 1990 and then to 5.1 million in 2000—an increase in 10 years larger than twice its whole population in 1945. It is growth based on high-tech and low taxes. It is not growth based on an influx of elderly retirees—Arizona may have Sun City, but just 13% of its residents are over 65, compared to 12% nationally. Nor is it based on farming subsidized by cheap water, since thirsty cotton farms are being phased out for urban users who can easily outbid them; the Valley around Phoenix lost nearly half its farmland between 1975 and 2000. It is not based on, though it is helped by, immigration: Arizona has attracted immigrants from Mexico and Latin America eager for entry-level jobs, so eager that many cross the lightly guarded border in the desert even at the risk of death. In 2000, 25% of its population was Hispanic (another 5% is Indian). More than anything else, the engine of Arizona's growth has been technology: Phoenix has been attracting high-tech industries since Motorola built a research center for military electronics there in 1948. Big employers Honeywell (aircraft engines, avionics, industrial control systems), Raytheon (missile systems), Motorola (computer boards), Intel (computer chips) and Avnet (semiconductors, electromechanical components). Landlocked Arizona is a major exporter—nearly $3.5 billion to Mexico and $1.3 billion to Canada in 2002.

Arizona is a place where the private sector is expanding and the public sector, if not shriveling away, is yielding ground. Arizona cut state taxes sharply in the 1990s, though voters did approve a sales tax increase for education and a hotel and rental car increase for stadiums and tourism promotion in 2000. It has pioneered in providing choice in education, with America's largest proportion of charter schools (some 20% of the total) and the for-profit University of Phoenix, based here but with branches in many states, which leases space and hires working-age adults to teach job-related skills to working-age adults. Local choice prevails: The inaptly named Youngtown, near Phoenix, bars children from living there; so does Superstition Heights. Where government once used to allocate precious water, now "shadow governments" (Joel Garreau's term) like

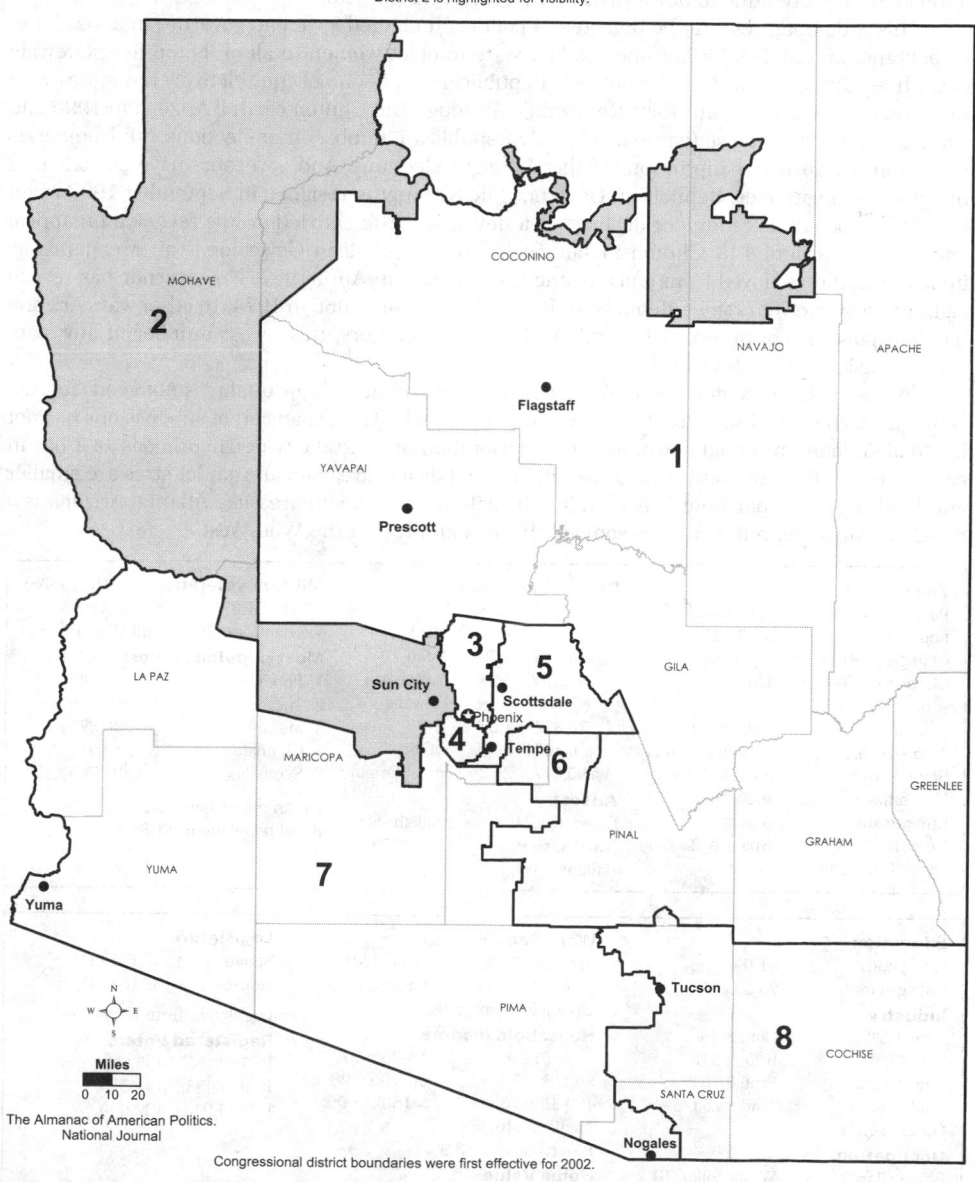

District 2 is highlighted for visibility.

The Almanac of American Politics.
National Journal

Congressional district boundaries were first effective for 2002.

the Salt River District do so, heeding the market signals that say urban users will pay more than farmers. It is a place wide open for entrepreneurs, some of them perhaps a bit shady, others at times wildly overoptimistic, many crossing traditional barriers. Phoenix is the number three metro area for women business owners per capita, and there are a burgeoning number of Latino-owned businesses. But there is a downside. Arizona also has one of the highest percentages of those without health insurance, and its state government was squeezed in 2002 as revenues came in lower than expected due to downturns in high-tech and tourism.

This wide-openness can be reflected in politics. It elected a woman governor in 2002, Janet Napolitano, and in 1998 it became the first state to elect women to all of its top five statewide executive offices; all but Napolitano were Republicans. It is one of the relatively few states with more registered Republicans than Democrats. Although Bill Clinton carried Arizona in 1996 and came close in 1992, the state remains heavily Republican in most other elections, but Democrats have won the governorship in four of the last eight elections. And governors have left office in unusual circumstances. Republican Governor Fife Symington resigned in September 1997 when he was convicted of fraudulent dealings as a developer (the conviction was reversed on appeal and he was pardoned by Clinton in January 2001). Republican Governor Evan Mecham was impeached and removed from office by the state Senate in April 1987. No governor has served eight consecutive years since Republican Jack Williams from 1966 to 1974. In other ways Arizona has had political continuity. It has only had 10 U.S. senators, the lowest number of any state except Alaska (6) and Hawaii (5).

In the exuberance of growth, mistakes are made—Phoenix's air quality is not good. Yet Arizona has been spared some of the worst effects of growth. The expansion of subdivisions has not led to abandonment of old downtowns or deterioration of central city neighborhoods as it has in eastern cities; the imperatives of growth in parched desert areas mean that lot sizes are smaller and land use more parsimonious than in a heavily-watered boom area like Atlanta. Arizona is a mostly urban state, but it still has some of the look and feel of the Wild West.

The People

Pop. 2000:	5,130,632
Pop. 1990:	3,665,228
Change 1990–2000:	Up 40.0%
Change 1980–1990:	Up 34.8%
% of U.S. total:	1.8%
Pop. rank:	20th of 50
Area size:	113,998 sq. mi.
State Native:	34.7%
Non-citizen:	9.0%

Language

English: 73.6%	Spanish: 18.5%
Other Eur.: 3.4%	

Race/Ethnic Origin

3,274,258	63.8%	White
149,941	2.9%	Black
89,315	1.7%	Asian
233,370	4.5%	Native Am.
5,639	0.1%	Hawaiian
76,372	1.5%	Two + races
6,120	0.1%	Other
1,295,617	25.3%	Hisp. Origin

Ancestry

German: 12.2%	English: 8.1%
Irish: 8.0%	USA: 3.7%
Italian: 3.4%	

Military veterans: 562,916 (14.9%)

WWII: 21.3%	Korea: 14.7%
Vietnam: 30.7%	Gulf War: 10.4%

Most populous cities:

1. Phoenix	1,321,045
2. Tucson	486,699
3. Mesa	396,375
4. Glendale	218,812
5. Scottsdale	202,705

Urban population: 88.2%
Rural population: 11.8%

Education

H.S. Grad:	81.0%
College Grad:	23.5%

Industry

Agri: 1.5%	Con: 8.7%
Fin: 7.9%	Info: 2.8%
Mfg: 15.2%	Prof: 28.3%
Public: 5.4%	Trade: 15.6%
Other: 14.7%	

Occupation

Blue collar: 21.9%	White collar: 61.2%
Gray collar: 16.9%	

Work Sector

Private: 78.1%	Govt: 15.2%
Self: 6.4%	Family: 0.3%
Unemployment: 5.6%	

Household Income

<15k: 14.9%	15-35k: 27.9%
35-50k: 17.5%	50-100k: 28.9%
100-150k: 6.9%	>150k: 3.9%
Median: $40,558	
Poverty status: 13.9%	

Home Value

<50k: 13.0%	50-100k: 31.4%	100-200k: 39.7%	200-300k: 9.5%
300-500k: 4.5%	>500k: 1.9%	Median: $109,400	

Legislature

Senate	17 R 13 D
House	39 R 21 D

Legislative Term Limits: Yes

Registered Voters

D: 799,653	(35.9%)
R: 925,485	(41.5%)
I: 504,042	(22.6%)

Presidential politics Far from the media centers of the East Coast, Arizona has tried to make itself another Iowa or New Hampshire in presidential primary politics, with little success. In 1972 it had an early Democratic primary, the improbable winner of which was Republican-turned-Democrat New York Mayor John Lindsay. But he went nowhere anyplace else. In 1996 Arizona tried again. It attempted to set its primary for the same date as New Hampshire; when that failed it set it one week later. The intended beneficiary was Republican Phil Gramm, running with the support of Arizona's John McCain. But Gramm pulled out of the race a week before New Hampshire, and Arizona became a battleground between Bob Dole, who now had McCain's support; Pat Buchanan, who urged his followers to "mount up and ride" after his narrow victory in New Hampshire; and Steve Forbes, who peppered the state with ads boosting his flat tax and attacking Washington politicians. Buchanan's campaigning in gunslinger costume wearing a black hat was a bit too much, and he finished third, with 27%; it was clear he had no

2000 Presidential Vote		
Bush (R)	781,652	(51%)
Gore (D)	685,341	(45%)
Nader (Green)	45,645	(3%)
Other	19,268	(1%)

2000 Republican Presidential Primary		
McCain (R)	193,708	(60%)
Bush (R)	115,115	(36%)
Keyes (R)	11,500	(4%)

2000 Democratic Presidential Primary		
Gore (D)	67,582	(78%)
Bradley (D)	16,383	(19%)
Other	2,797	(3%)

1996 Presidential Vote		
Clinton (D)	653,288	(47%)
Dole (R)	622,073	(44%)
Perot (I)	112,074	(8%)

chance to win the nomination. Dole finished second with 30%; Forbes won 33% and all the delegates, after which his campaign, like that of his fellow easterner Lindsay a quarter-century before, went nowhere.

In 2000, Arizona tried other innovations. McCain had irritated local Republicans enough that Governor Jane Hull and other party leaders endorsed George W. Bush. McCain, however, won a solid victory in his home state in the February primary, but it was overshadowed by his misleading triumph in Michigan the same day—misleading since he won that open-primary state because 20% of Republican primary voters were self-identified Democrats, double the percentage in any other contest that year. As for Arizona's Democrats, they ran and paid for their own primary in March, because the state's February date was outside the "window" allowed by national Democratic Party rules. They allowed voting by Internet, and about 35,000 Arizonans typed in their choices; another 20,000 voted by mail; still others voted by computer or paper ballot at the polls. But the Internet voting was not flawless and the primary was trivial since Al Gore had already clinched the nomination. In February 2003 Governor Janet Napolitano signed a proclamation to hold the 2004 primary on the first Tuesday in February, the same day as South Carolina, and the first primary after New Hampshire. That would mean the Democratic nomination might be decided, or taken some distance toward being decided, by states with Democratic electorates far more heavily black and far more heavily Hispanic than the national average—but then Iowa and New Hampshire Democrats are almost all white.

In the 1990s, Arizona suddenly became competitive in presidential general elections. The national trend toward Clinton-Gore Democrats in the very largest metropolitan areas was felt in Phoenix and Maricopa County; once very heavily Republican, it was closely divided in 1996 and 2000. In 1996 Bill Clinton won by a 47%–44% margin—the first Democrat to carry the state since Harry Truman in 1948. The winning issue was not Medicare—Arizona does not have an especially large elderly population, and the air seemed to go out of the Medicare issue in mid-October. Rather, it was the environment. Arizona has a much lower percentage of rural and small town voters than other Rocky Mountain states: Nearly 80% of Arizonans live in metro Phoenix and Tucson, and they want to preserve the environment that is so visibly being transformed by their own success. Clinton's staging of the announcement of a Utah land preserve at the Grand Canyon may have carried Arizona single-handedly (it may also have defeated the only Democratic congressman in Utah at the time). Clinton went on to create new National Monuments in Arizona—four in 2000 alone—over the opposition of local elected officials, and perhaps in the hope of aiding

Al Gore. If so, it was in vain. Gore won 45% here, a good showing for a national Democrat, but George W. Bush won 51%, carrying not only Phoenix and Maricopa County, as Republican nominees had in 1992 and 1996, but also the smaller counties outside the Phoenix and Tucson metro areas, which they had not. The non-metropolitan backlash against Clinton-Gore environmental policies worked for Bush in Arizona as it did in Colorado and other Rocky Mountain states.

Congressional districting   Arizona gained two House seats in the 2000 Census, after gaining one each in the Censuses of 1960, 1970, 1980 and 1990: In 40 years it has moved from two districts to eight. This time redistricting was done not by the legislature but by a five-member Arizona Independent Redistricting Commission created by Proposition 106 passed in November 2000. Two Republican and two Democratic legislators appoint four members, and the fifth, to be neither a Democrat nor a Republican, is picked by the other four. The commission held 66 hearings and meetings and in October 2001 approved a plan closing resembling a suggestion made in *The Almanac of American Politics* 2002. Democrats were disappointed because it didn't create a competitive seat in the Phoenix area; commissioners said such a district could be created only by drawing grotesque lines that, in their view, would be gerrymandering. Actually, the Democrats came off fairly well, especially in a state in which, absent Proposition 106, Republicans would have controlled redistricting: One new district was heavily Democratic and the other evenly split between the parties. Three Democrats filed a lawsuit against the plan in March 2002, but in May 2002 a judge set it aside on the grounds that trial could not be held before the filing deadline; the trial was scheduled for July 2003.

108th Congress Lineup
6 R   2 D
107th Congress Lineup
5 R   1 D

The competitive seat is the new 1st District, which includes most of northern and east central Arizona, a rural area that includes the Navajo Indian Reservation. The new Democratic seat is the 7th District, which includes about half of Tucson and Pima County and stretches west to Yuma and Parker on the Colorado River. The other half of Tucson and Pima County were put into the new, closely-divided 8th District in the southeast corner of the state. Four districts were established in Phoenix and central Maricopa County (one includes part of Pinal County). There is only one district that is grotesquely shaped, and that arguably for good reason. The 2d District, which begins in the western part of Maricopa County, is connected by a thin strip of La Paz County (9 voters showed up there on Election Day) with Mohave County and then follows the Colorado River eastward through the Grand Canyon (220 voters showed up in this stretch) to include the Hopi Indian Reservation. The justification for this: Mohave County demographically and politically is much like western Maricopa County, and the Hopi have had disputes for many years with the much more numerous Navajo, whose reservation surrounds theirs, and want a congressman who will take their side. The Navajo Nation, which is quite receptive to the idea of a congressional district where they would be the dominant political power over the Hopi, argues that the bizarre shape of the 2d is unconstitutional and has filed suit; the case will be heard along with the Democrats' lawsuit in July.

Governor

Janet Napolitano (D)

Elected 2002, term expires Jan. 2007, 1st term; b. Nov. 29, 1957, New York City; home, Phoenix; Santa Clara U., B.A. 1979, U. of VA, J.D. 1983; Methodist; single.

Elected Office: AZ Atty. Gen., 1998–02.

Professional Career: Clerk, U.S. Appeals Ct. Judge Mary Schroder, 1983–84; Practicing atty., 1984–93; AZ U.S. atty., 1994–98.

Office: 1700 W. Washington, Phoenix, 85007, 602-542-4331; Fax: 602-542-7601; Web site: www.state.az.us.

Election Results

2002 general	Janet Napolitano (D)	566,284	(46%)
	Matt Salmon (R)	554,465	(45%)
	Richard Mahoney (I)	84,947	(7%)
	Other	20,415	(2%)
2002 primary	Janet Napolitano (D)	128,702	(57%)
	Alfredo Gutierrez (D)	50,377	(22%)
	Mark Osterloh (D)	31,422	(14%)
	Mike Newcomb (D)	14,373	(6%)
1998 general	Jane Dee Hull (R)	620,188	(61%)
	Paul Johnson (D)	361,552	(36%)
	Other	35,876	(4%)

Janet Napolitano, a Democrat, in 2002 became the second woman in a row to be elected governor of Arizona. Napolitano was born in New York City and grew up in Pittsburgh and Albuquerque, where her father helped establish the University of New Mexico medical school. She graduated from Santa Clara University and the University of Virginia law school, and moved to Phoenix in 1983 to clerk for Judge Mary Schroeder, currently the chief judge on the 9th Circuit Court of Appeals. She practiced corporate law, volunteered as an attorney for the state Democratic party and later joined the team of lawyers representing Anita Hill at the hearings on the confirmation of Clarence Thomas in October 1991. In 1993 she was appointed U.S. Attorney for Arizona where she served until she ran for attorney general in 1998; she was elected by a 50%–47% margin in a year in which the top 5 statewide offices were won by women of which Napolitano was the only Democrat. As Attorney General, she got plenty of good publicity. She pursued Qwest for its bad telephone service on charges of consumer fraud. She negotiated a $217 million settlement with Arthur Andersen on behalf of investors. She sued Ford for explosions in Crown Victoria police cars. She reduced the number of open child abuse and neglect cases from 6,000 to 700.

By October 2001 Napolitano's work as attorney general had earned her a 55% positive job rating, and she was obviously running for governor (Hull was term limited). She was motivated, she said, after she was diagnosed with breast cancer in 2000 and after having a successful mastectomy; she wanted to work on health care. She announced in January 2002 and in April 2002 presented the 6,000 nominating petitions and 6,000 $5 contributions that qualified her for financing under the Clean Elections Act passed by voters in 1998. She received public financing of $409,000 for the September primary and $615,000 for the general election. She campaigned as a "conservative Democrat" and was criticized as "too Republican" by one primary opponent. But she was able to enlist the help of the fire fighters' union and the United Food and Commercial Workers to amass her nominating petitions and $5 contributions.

The leading Republican candidate was former Congressman Matt Salmon, who was first elected in 1994 and retired in 2000 pursuant to his term limit promise. His high point in the House came in November 1998 when he announced he would not vote for Newt Gingrich for speaker—a move that prompted Gingrich's resignation three days after the election. Salmon is a Mormon who did missionary work in Taiwan, speaks Mandarin Chinese, rides a Harley Davidson and fronts an Elvis cover band. Both candidates won their primaries by wide margins. Napolitano led former state Senator Alfredo Gutierrez 57%–22% and Salmon led Secretary of State Betsey Bayless 56%–30%. In the race as an Independent was Richard Mahoney, a Democrat elected Secretary of State in 1990, who qualified for the Clean Elections Act money. He attacked both nominees. "Are Matt and Janet going to take on the oil companies or the special interests? Tweedledum and Tweedledee, Salmon and Napolitano." He portrayed himself as more conservative on fiscal issues than Salmon and more liberal on cultural issues than Napolitano.

In the general election, Napolitano relied on her record as Attorney General and called for closing loopholes and cutting spending to make up the budget shortfalls; she supported the death penalty. Salmon opposed tax increases—"I will not raise taxes, go after shared revenues or make cuts in the classroom"—and announced a Workforce 2010 plan to create 500,000 jobs paying more than $40,000. The tone of their campaigns was different. Napolitano was businesslike and stressed her experience. Salmon said he wanted to bring God back into government and his ads showed him with his wife and four children (Napolitano is unmarried). The Clean Elections Act played a role: Salmon declined the Clean Elections money, and raised his own, more slowly than he had hoped. But the proceeds he got from a George W. Bush fundraiser were a mixed blessing: The law requires the state to pay candidates who have accepted the Clean Elections funding (and the concomitant limitations on spending) an amount equal to what candidates who decline the Clean Elections Act money raise above its limits. So every dollar Bush raised for Salmon above that amount put a dollar in Napolitano's campaign treasury.

This proved to be a very close election. On election night and Wednesday, Napolitano had a 25,000-vote lead, but there were 200,000 ballots uncounted—mostly early ballots from Phoenix's Maricopa County and Tucson's Pima County, conceivably enough to overcome Napolitano's lead. Counting went on, and by Sunday Napolitano led by 11,000 votes, with only 11,000 left to count; Salmon conceded. Salmon carried Maricopa County, which cast 57% of the state's votes, but by only 48%–44%. Napolitano won Pima County 52%–39%. In the smaller counties, the "conservative Democrat" led 46%–44%. Overall, Napolitano won 46%–45%, with 7% for Mahoney—from which candidate his votes had come was anyone's guess. This was the first orderly transition from one governor to another since 1986, and Napolitano pledged to, as she had done as Attorney General, not to sweep out everybody. "We'll keep some who are already there. I don't plan to take a big broom in." But the broom may turn out to be needed. Estimates for the budget shortfall were in the magnitude of $1 billion.

Senior Senator

John McCain (R)

Elected 1986, seat up 2004, 3d term; b. Aug. 29, 1936, Panama Canal Zone; home, Phoenix; U.S. Naval Acad., B.S. 1958, Natl. War Col., 1973–74; Episcopalian; married (Cindy).

Military Career: Navy, 1958–80 (Vietnam).

Elected Office: U.S. House of Reps., 1982–1986.

Professional Career: Dir., Navy Senate Liaison Ofc., 1977–81.

DC Office: 241 RSOB, 20510, 202-224-2235; Fax: 202-228-2862; Web site: mccain.senate.gov.

State Offices: Phoenix, 602-952-2410; Tempe, 480-897-6289; Tucson, 520-670-6334.

Committees: *Armed Services*: Airland; Readiness & Management Support; Seapower. *Commerce, Science & Transportation* (Chmn.). *Indian Affairs*.

Group Ratings

	ADA	ACLU	AFS	LCV	CON	ITIC	NTU	COC	ACU	NTLC	CHC
2002	20	0	29	41	95	75	64	79	78	67	—
2001	40	—	36	25	—	—	66	50	68	—	60

National Journal Ratings

	2001 LIB —	2001 CONS		2002 LIB —	2002 CONS
Economic	45%	55%		42%	57%
Social	33%	59%		40%	58%
Foreign	7%	72%		35%	61%

Key Votes of the 107th Congress

1. Approve Bush Tax Cuts	Y	5. Confirm Ashcroft as AG	Y	9. Bar Coop. with Intl. Court	Y
2. Expand Patients' Rights	Y	6. Bar Gays in the Boy Scouts	Y	10. Trade Promotion Authority	Y
3. Campaign Finance Reform	Y	7. $ for Hate Crime Prosecution	N	11. Authorize Force in Iraq	Y
4. Permit ANWR Development	N	8. Overseas Military Abortions	N	12. Homeland Sec. Dept. Union	N

Election Results

1998 general	John McCain (R)	696,577	(69%)	($2,461,900)
	Ed Ranger (D)	275,224	(27%)	($371,439)
	Other	41,479	(4%)	
1998 primary	John McCain (R)	unopposed		
1992 general	John McCain (R)	771,395	(56%)	($3,766,588)
	Claire Sargent (D)	436,321	(32%)	($287,682)
	Evan Mecham (I)	145,361	(11%)	($86,433)
	Other	28,974	(2%)	

Prior Winning Percentages: 1986 (60%); 1984 House (78%); 1982 House (66%)

For many Americans John McCain is the closest thing our politics has to a national hero, a presidential candidate widely admired in 2000 and an independent leader of great force in the years after. His personal story is a dramatic one, told beautifully by Robert Timberg in *The Nightingale's Song* and by McCain himself and Mark Salter in the 1999 bestseller *Faith of My Fathers*. McCain is the son and grandson of Navy admirals, a decorated Navy pilot himself who was shot down over Vietnam and who spent five years, most of it in pain and torture, in Communist prisoner of war camps. He refused to be let out ahead of those who had been in longer when he was offered release because of his father's rank. McCain returned to the United States in March 1973. His final assignment in the Navy was as Senate liaison. In 1980 he retired and moved to Arizona, his wife's home state; in 1982 he ran for an open House seat. Attacked as an outsider, he responded, "The longest place I ever lived in was Hanoi." He led 32%–26% in a four-way primary, and won the 1982 and 1984 general elections and then the 1986 Senate contest easily.

In his first years in the Senate he had a low profile. His first major issue was one on which he had great expertise: Vietnam. In the early 1990s McCain worked hard with Massachusetts' John Kerry, also a decorated Vietnam veteran, on the special committee investigating charges that American POWs or MIAs remained in Vietnam; they found no evidence of any. With Kerry he supported ending the trade embargo on, and pressed for, establishing diplomatic relations with Vietnam. But his support for reconciliation with our former enemies has not dimmed his memories of how his captors treated his fellow prisoners of war. On other defense issues, McCain has called for more defense spending and insisted military interventions be designed to achieve victory; he criticized the Clinton administration for using air power alone and ruling out ground troops in Bosnia and for not using "all necessary force" in Kosovo. He strongly supported George W. Bush in the war on terrorism after September 11. In October 2001 he urged more ground troops in Afghanistan, and in December 2001 he was one of 10 members of Congress to sign a letter urging that Iraq be the next target. After North Korea declared it had nuclear weapons in October 2002 he opposed negotiations and warned, "There is scant moral refuge for those accommodationists who believe even today that we can concede our way out of the crisis."

McCain has been chairman or ranking minority member of the Commerce Committee since 1997. But he is anything but a member of the Senate club; his crusades for campaign finance regulation and against pork-barrel spending have provided plenty of material for his self-deprecating jokes about how unpopular he is with many colleagues. He brings to his work a sense of righteousness and a conviction that what have become the normal workings of the political process—campaign contributions, backing local projects—are deeply corrupt. He has worked on difficult and complex legislation but has had, as he concedes, less than complete success in his efforts. He tends to favor deregulation. He took little part in shaping the compromise Telecommunications Act of 1996, and voted against it, arguing that it did not effectively ensure competition. He supports free airtime for political candidates—anathema to the networks—and broadband access for rural areas. He supported FCC Chairman Michael Powell's policy of removing limits on media ownership, but has been critical of cable TV rate increases. When Republicans regained their majority in November 2002, he said, "The whole Telecommunications Act was a disaster. Everybody realizes it. We need to review that."

A pilot in the Navy, McCain has worked on aviation issues. He authored the law banning small airplanes from flying over the Grand Canyon. McCain served as chairman of the Indian

Affairs Committee in 1995–96. Arizona has one of the nation's largest percentages of Indians, and McCain, like Barry Goldwater and Morris Udall, obviously feels sympathy for them. "They have been deceived too many times in the last 200 years," he says. Generally, McCain has supported the tribal agenda.

The issue McCain is most closely identified with is campaign finance regulation. His interest came from his experience as one of the "Keating Five" senators investigated for meeting in 1987 with regulators on behalf of Charles Keating's Arizona savings and loan. Democrats kept McCain in the case, though he had done nothing for Keating; as the one Republican involved, he thus made the scandal bipartisan. Ultimately he was cited for nothing more than bad judgment. Vindicated by reelection in 1992, in the majority after the election of 1994, he sought out Democrat Russ Feingold, whose campaign finance bill had gotten nowhere that year. The McCain-Feingold bills went through several transformations. The 1998 bill purported to ban soft money contributions to political parties and to limit "issue ads" run by independent organizations within 60 days of an election. It was fiercely opposed as an infringement of free speech and as a threat to the Republican Party by Mitch McConnell of Kentucky. Majority Leader Trent Lott yanked the bill from the Senate floor in February 1998; it returned in September, after the House passed a similar bill, but could summon up no more than 52 votes and died. In September 1999, after the House passed a similar bill again, McCain and Feingold introduced a new version that attacked soft money but did not address issue ads. The obvious intent was to get a bill to conference and generate enough public support that McConnell and other Republican opponents would have to back down. But in October McConnell, noting that McCain had charged that the current campaign finance system produces corruption, challenged McCain to name senators who had been corrupted. McCain refused to name names and said the system was corrupt in general. Against McConnell's filibuster a few days later, McCain and Feingold were able to summon up only 55 votes for cloture, five short of the 60 needed, and the bill was taken off the floor.

After his presidential campaign, McCain returned to the closely divided Senate determined to pass his campaign finance bill. In January 2001 he threatened to tie up the Senate unless Lott set aside two weeks of debate on the issue. In March 2001, after two weeks of remarkably civilized but spirited debate, during which McCain and Feingold fended off several poison-pill amendments, the legislation passed April 2 by a 59–41 vote. An amendment by Fred Thompson and Dianne Feinstein was passed to raise limits on individual contributions from $1,000 to $2,000, but the bill retained the soft-money ban and limit on issue ads prior to the election, which some senators fear will be struck down by the courts as an unconstitutional ban of free speech. The House, which twice had passed similar bills, took up the issue in June 2001. But after the Republican leadership's rule was defeated—a very rare event indeed—Speaker Dennis Hastert pulled the bill from the floor. Supporters tried to get the 218 signatures needed for a discharge petition. For months the number hovered just under 218, but in January 2002 the signatures were obtained. The House passed its version of the bill in February 2002 by a 240–189 vote, and the bill became law in March 2002. (In May 2003 a three-judge federal court, deeply divided, issued 1,700 pages of opinions and upheld some of the provisions but not others). But McCain didn't rest on his victory. He was furious that the Bush administration didn't appoint a Democrat designated by Tom Daschle to a seat on the Federal Election Commission; the holdover Democrat was voting with the Republicans and passing regulations which McCain argued undercut the bill; one was to define the word "solicitation" as "ask" rather than as "request, suggest or recommend." In June he threatened to block all nominations until Bush made the appointment, but some nominations were approved anyway in August. In October 2002 he invoked the Congressional Review Act to try to overturn the new regulations and also filed a lawsuit against the FEC. In December the appointment had not yet been made and McCain was furious; finally, in March 2003, the appointment was made.

In 1999, McCain embarked on his presidential campaign. He wisely decided to avoid the Iowa caucuses (McCain had long campaigned against ethanol subsidies as pork) and concentrated on New Hampshire, where he traveled around the state in his 'Straight Talk Express' bus. At first only a few reporters traveled with him and crowds were sparse. But it soon became clear McCain was striking a chord. To increasingly large and fervent crowds he told his personal story in self-deprecating terms, and pledged, "I will never tell you a lie." He was asked to autograph hundreds of copies of *Faith of My Fathers*. He talked about defense and foreign policy issues—the only candidate to do so much—and invariably called for campaign finance reform. On the campaign bus, McCain was always available to answer reporters' questions and banter with the press, while making fun of his aides and consultant Mike Murphy (who later called the press "our constituency"). McCain did not have much support from politicians. Only four fellow senators endorsed him (Jon Kyl, Chuck Hagel, Fred Thompson and Mike DeWine). Back home, Arizona Governor Jane Hull, apparently because of abrasive treatment by McCain, endorsed George W. Bush; *The Arizona Republic* wrote editorials warning of McCain's "volcanic" temper. But the strength of feeling among his ever-larger crowds was palpable. Bush predicted victory in New Hampshire, but on February 1 McCain beat him by an impressive 49%–31% margin. Suddenly he became, if not the frontrunner, at least the most admired of either party's presidential candidates.

From there the 'Straight Talk Express' had mixed success. It went down to South Carolina, where both the Republican establishment and Christian conservatives supported George W. Bush in 2000. The campaigning got negative but what hurt even more was his failure to win over self-identified Republicans. His emphasis on campaign finance reform and his criticisms of Bush's tax plan for giving too much to the rich helped with independents, but sounded like enemy talk to Republicans. On February 18 Bush won 53%–42% in South Carolina, in what turned out to be as decisive a victory as his father's there had been 12 years before. The New Hampshire and South Carolina results were templates for what happened elsewhere; in New Hampshire and other Northeastern states McCain ran about even with Bush among self-identified Republicans and way ahead among self-identified independents and self-identified Democrats; in South Carolina and other states outside the Northeast, Bush ran way ahead among Republicans and behind among independents and Democrats. On February 22 McCain won in Arizona and, in a big 50%–43% upset, in Michigan.

McCain might have done better if he had emphasized other issues on which he had consistently taken stands in line with most Republicans' thinking—defense, tax cuts (he had an interesting tax cut plan himself, but he spent less time on it than on attacking Bush's), abortion, Social Security individual investment accounts. Instead, after South Carolina, he gave a speech in Virginia Beach attacking the religious right and in an offhand comment on the bus called Pat Robertson and Jerry Falwell "forces of evil." As he explained the next day, this was sarcastic "Luke Skywalker talk," which reporters often heard on the bus but which rarely appeared in their reports. But to many Christian conservatives, a large segment of the Republican primary vote, it sounded like angry hostility; McCain lost in Virginia and Washington on February 29. On Super Tuesday, March 7, McCain won in Massachusetts, Connecticut, Rhode Island and Vermont. But he lost decisively in New York, Ohio and California and "suspended" his campaign on March 9. Much attention was focused on the fact that he did not "endorse" Bush; when they finally met in Pittsburgh in May reporters practically had to extract the word from his mouth. He made it clear he did not want to be nominated for vice president and said he wanted no cabinet post, making the plausible argument that he operated better as his own man than as someone else's appointee. He insisted on having his wife Cindy McCain, not Jane Hull, head the Arizona delegation to the convention, and he gave a moving, elegiac speech that ended as if in a minor key.

Some defeated presidential candidates sulk in their tents; McCain became more legislatively active than ever—and increasingly likely to ally himself with Democrats and oppose most Republicans, as he had on campaign finance and the tobacco bill. He voted with the Democrats in July on HMO regulation. He was the only Republican to vote against the water projects bill in October, charging that it contained $1.2 billion of special projects earmarked for districts. He appeared in ads in Colorado and Oregon for ballot propositions requiring background checks for sales at gun shows. But he also campaigned tirelessly for Republican House candidates and tried, with some success, to get them to support his campaign finance bill. In 2002, after campaign finance regulation passed the Senate, he worked with many Democrats again. He, John Edwards and Edward Kennedy sponsored an HMO regulation bill. He supported embryonic stem-cell research. In January 2003 he and Joe Lieberman sponsored a bill to require power plants and factories to reduce carbon dioxide and other emissions. With John Kerry he proposed CAFE standards for all cars and light trucks of 36 miles per gallon by 2015. He was one of two Republicans to vote against the conference report on the tax cut in May and, after Jim Jeffords switched parties, he invited Tom Daschle to a friendly visit to his vacation home near Sedona; speculation abounded that McCain would switch parties too, and liberals writing in *The Washington Monthly* and *The New Republic* argued that he would be the strongest Democratic nominee for president. But he turned that talk aside. And he did take strong stands with George W. Bush and most Republicans on some issues—the nomination of his tobacco adversary John Ashcroft, repeal of ergonomics regulations, the May 2001 budget resolution, and allowing Mexican trucks into the United States.

He took a serious part in legislation after September 11. He called for the government to run airline security and he co-sponsored a bill with Ernest Hollings that effectively decided the issue; it passed 97–0 in October 2001. But he also proposed that screeners be fireable without regard to civil service rules—the position Bush insisted on and Democrats, to their political detriment, opposed on the homeland security bill in 2002. He called for a special commission to investigate intelligence failures before September 11, a proposal opposed for months by the Bush administration, and said that former Senators Gary Hart and Warren Rudman should serve on it. The final version of the law provided, at the insistence of relatives of September 11 casualties, that McCain and Richard Shelby get a veto over Trent Lott's appointees to the commission; but McCain's attempts to get Lott to appoint Rudman failed. In September he appeared with Richard Gephardt in support of the generic drug bill and said it was "very, very likely" that Republicans would lose their majority in the House. He did much less campaigning for Republicans than in 2000, making appearances in tandem with promotion of his latest book *Worth the Fighting For* and only on behalf of Republicans who had supported his brand of campaign finance regulation.

McCain has irritated some Arizona Republican politicians and some conservative activists, but his standing with the state's voters has been very strong. He won the Senate seat in 1986 by 60%–40%. In 1992, after the Keating Five investigation, he was re-elected 56%–32%. In 1998 McCain won by an impressive 69%–27%, carrying the heavily Navajo and Democratic Apache County 54%–42% and winning the Hispanic vote 52%–42%. McCain's seat comes up in 2004, when he turns 68. In 2001 some Arizona conservatives tried to get 349,000 registered voters' signatures to petition for a recall, but a vote would not have been binding and the drive fizzled out. In late 2002 and early 2003 the Club for Growth was encouraging Representative Jeff Flake to challenge McCain in the Republican primary; Flake confirmed he was considering running. But registered Republicans are a broader segment of the electorate in most states, and it was not at all clear that any politician with a reputation would dare to take on McCain. Nor is it clear whether a prominent Democrat would. If McCain does not run, possible candidates include former congressman and nearly successful 2002 governor candidate Matt Salmon and just about any of the state's six Republican congressmen. Will McCain run? "Most likely," he told *National Journal* in February 2003.

Will he run for president again? In *Worth the Fighting For* he wrote, "I did not get to be President of the United States. And I doubt I shall have reason or opportunity to try again . . . I could leave [Congress] now satisfied that I have accomplished enough things that I believe are useful to the country to compensate for the disappointment of my mistakes." This has the same elegiac sound of the last words of his 2000 National Convention speech. At the least it seems highly unlikely that in the middle of a war on terrorism he would run against a commander-in-chief whose conduct of that war he, at this writing, strongly approves. But run or not, Citizen McCain (the title of Elizabeth Drew's admiring book) remains an important figure in American life.

Junior Senator

Jon Kyl (R)

Elected 1994, seat up 2006, 2d term; b. Apr. 25, 1942, Oakland, NE; home, Phoenix; U. of AZ, B.A. 1964, L.L.B. 1966; Presbyterian; married (Caryll).

Elected Office: U.S. House of Reps., 1986–94.

Professional Career: Practicing atty., 1966–86; Chmn., Phoenix Chamber of Commerce, 1984–85.

DC Office: 730 HSOB, 20510, 202-224-4521; Fax: 202-224-2207; Web site: kyl.senate.gov.

State Offices: Phoenix, 602-840-1891; Tucson, 520-575-8633.

Committees: *Republican Policy Committee Chairman. Energy & Natural Resources*: National Parks; Public Lands & Forests; Water & Power. *Finance*: Health Care (Chmn.); Long-Term Growth & Debt Reduction; Social Security & Family Policy. *Judiciary*: Constitution, Civil Rights & Property Rights; Immigration, Border Security & Citizenship; Terrorism, Technology & Homeland Security (Chmn.).

Group Ratings

	ADA	ACLU	AFS	LCV	CON	ITIC	NTU	COC	ACU	NTLC	CHC
2002	0	20	0	12	92	50	82	90	100	100	—
2001	5	—	0	0	—	—	88	100	100	—	100

National Journal Ratings

	2001 LIB	—	2001 CONS		2002 LIB	—	2002 CONS
Economic	7%	—	86%		0%	—	94%
Social	0%	—	79%		0%	—	62%
Foreign	7%	—	72%		0%	—	76%

Key Votes of the 107th Congress

1. Approve Bush Tax Cuts	Y	5. Confirm Ashcroft as AG	Y	9. Bar Coop. with Intl. Court	Y
2. Expand Patients' Rights	N	6. Bar Gays in the Boy Scouts	Y	10. Trade Promotion Authority	Y
3. Campaign Finance Reform	N	7. $ for Hate Crime Prosecution	N	11. Authorize Force in Iraq	Y
4. Permit ANWR Development	Y	8. Overseas Military Abortions	N	12. Homeland Sec. Dept. Union	N

Election Results

2000 general	Jon Kyl (R)	1,108,196	(79%)	($2,503,674)
	William Toel (I)	109,230	(8%)	($21,491)
	Vance Hansen (Green)	108,926	(8%)	
	Barry J. Hess, II (Lib)	70,724	(5%)	
2000 primary	Jon Kyl (R)	unopposed		
1994 general	Jon Kyl (R)	600,999	(54%)	($4,138,203)
	Sam Coppersmith (D)	442,510	(40%)	($1,577,556)
	Scott Grainger (Lib)	75,493	(7%)	

Prior Winning Percentages: 1992 House (59%); 1990 House (61%); 1988 House (87%); 1986 House (65%)

Jon Kyl is a Republican first elected in 1994. His father John Kyl was a Republican congressman from Iowa (1959–65, 1967–73), who eventually lost his seat in redistricting; Jon Kyl moved to a state that, in effect, was gaining the Republican seats that Great Plains states like Iowa were losing. Kyl went to college and law school in Arizona, practiced law in Phoenix, worked on Republican campaigns and headed the Phoenix Chamber of Commerce; he won the heavily Republican 4th District seat in 1986 by beating former (1973–77) Congressman John Conlan, who had support from the religious right, 60%–28%.

In the House, Kyl was a leader among Republicans on missile defense, the balanced budget amendment, and for disclosing the names of House members with overdrafts on the House bank—one of the causes that destabilized Democrats' control of the House in the years running up to 1994. By that time, Kyl was running for the Senate seat held for three terms by Democrat

Dennis DeConcini, whose reputation was stained by his involvement in the Keating Five scandal. Kyl had no primary opposition and the further good fortune that one-term Congressman Sam Coppersmith won the September 13 Democratic primary by only 59 votes of 255,000 cast after a two-week recount. Kyl, with far more money, ran ads with home movie texture showing him traveling through the desert countryside, dressed in jeans and working on ranches, while talking about how he and his wife first fell in love with the state (he has climbed Camelback Mountain "more than 1,000 times"). Coppersmith stressed his pro-choice stand on abortion and said he would welcome a campaign visit from President Clinton. Kyl won easily, 54%–40%.

Kyl has a solidly conservative record. Quietly, he has become a major force on defense policy. He is perhaps the Senate's biggest champion of a missile defense system. A 1996 speech he made in Europe on the future of NATO impressed Margaret Thatcher and Henry Kissinger, who accepted his invitation to a conference at the Arizona Biltmore. In 1997 he led, with Jesse Helms, the losing fight against the Chemical Weapons Convention. Learning from that experience, he organized the winning fight to reject the Comprehensive Test Ban Treaty, submitted by Bill Clinton to the Senate in September 1997. Starting in 1998, Kyl studied the details and worked to persuade Republican colleagues to oppose the treaty. In May 1999 he told Majority Leader Trent Lott that he had 34 solid votes against, enough to prevent ratification, but Helms, the Foreign Relations chairman, insisted that Kyl get more before he would let the treaty come to the floor. All 45 Democrats, unaware in the increasingly partisan Senate of Kyl's efforts, wrote Helms in July demanding the treaty be brought forward by September. Helms replied dismissively that he would not do so until he got action on the Kyoto treaty and amendments to the ABM treaty. In September North Dakota Democrat Byron Dorgan promised to "plant myself on the floor like a potted plant" until the CTBT was considered. The ranking Foreign Relations Democrat still thought that 25 Republicans could be persuaded to vote for the treaty, and concurred when Lott promised to bring it up in October. Only then did Senate Democrats and the Clinton White House begin to discover that they had conspired to defeat their own treaty. Kyl had done his work well: The CTBT did not even get a majority, much less the required two-thirds, as it was defeated 48–51. "Our success," Kyl said, "depended on being quiet about what we did." Kyl continues to press forward on missile defense. He urged George W. Bush to abrogate the treaty, and when Senate Democrats on the Armed Services Committee tried to cut missile defense funds in May 2002 he was quick to respond, pointing out that Iran had just successfully tested an 800-mile-range missile.

Kyl serves on Judiciary and is sponsor, with Dianne Feinstein, of a constitutional amendment on victims' rights. It had 40 co-sponsors but was shelved in April 2000 because it lacked the necessary two-thirds. Before September 11 he and Feinstein co-sponsored a bill to prepare defenses for attacks by terrorists with chemical and biological weapons, and in November 2001 they introduced a bill to establish a comprehensive lookout database, which would combine information from the CIA, the FBI and the State Department and make it available to border and consular personnel. He was a lead Senate sponsor of the bill to ban racial quotas and preferences. He has worked to beef up the Border Patrol and to track legal immigrants who overstay their visas. He supports cuts in legal immigration and new rules for family-based immigration. He sponsored an amendment to the energy bill, defeated 58–40, to eliminate the requirement that utilities generate 10% of their electricity from renewable sources by 2020 (it's now 2%). He has worked for more federal reimbursement of states and localities for the costs of hospitalizing and incarcerating illegal aliens.

Kyl was the Senate leader on the move to change the Clinton administration's barring of doctors who take Medicare patients from contracting with patients for more services or higher fees. He was the prime sponsor of a 1999 law setting up a semiautonomous division of the Energy Department to oversee nuclear weapons research and production. He has worked patiently to settle the water rights claims of Arizona Indian tribes. He and John McCain introduced a bill in September 2002 to codify an intricate compromise that would allow the Gila River Community and the Tohono O'odham Nation to nearly half the water running through the Central Arizona Project Canal and additional water from the Salt, Verde and Gila Rivers—enough water for more than 3.5 million people. The tribes are entitled, under a 1908 Supreme Court decision, to enough water to carry out the purposes of their reservations; this would extinguish the claims of tribes whose large reservations might give them greater claims and would authorize them to lease water to cities and communities, but only in Arizona. Kyl and McCain also introduced a bill codifying the water rights settlement between the Zuni Indian Tribe and the federal government. In 2002, after the vast Rodeo-Chediski fire, he pushed for legislation to increase short-term and long-term salvage operations and forest thinning.

Kyl is not an active seeker of publicity, and is far less well known in Arizona and Washington than his colleague McCain. He often volunteers to take on tasks—objecting, for example, to appropriations in summer 2001, in order to get Tom Daschle to bring more nominations to the floor—and promotes causes he believes in, like missile defense, behind the scenes. He is pleasant and unassuming, but can surprise: He is a big fan of race cars and has been seen driving the lead car around the track in a warm-up lap at the Phoenix International Raceway. He is the chairman of the Republican Steering Committee since 2001 and in November 2002 he was elected chairman of the Republican Policy Committee; he followed Idaho's Larry Craig in both posts.

In June 2000 Kyl was interviewed by Dick Cheney, whom he had chosen as a kind of model when he came to the House, as a possible vice-presidential candidate; he was interviewed a second time in July but recommended against his own selection. In Arizona he had no difficulty winning reelection: No Democrat filed to run against him and he won 79% of the vote against an Independent, a Green Party candidate and a Libertarian. His seat comes up in 2006. In 1994 he said he probably would serve no more than two terms, and in July 2001 he said, "It was my intention then, and it's probably still my intention, although I'm not going to make any decisions for another three or four years."

FIRST DISTRICT

Rep. Rick Renzi (R)

Elected 2002, 1st term; b. June 11, 1958, Ft. Monmouth, NJ; home, Flagstaff; N. AZ. U., B.S. 1980, Catholic U., J.D. 2002; Catholic; married (Roberta).

Professional Career: Admin., Defense Dept, 1984–89; Owner, Patriot Insurance Co., 1989–02; Owner, Renzi & Campbell Dev. Inc., 1994–02; Owner, Renzi Vino vineyard, 1998-present.

DC Office: 418 CHOB 20515, 202-225-2315; Fax: 202-226-9739; Web site: www.house.gov/renzi.

District Offices: Casa Grande, 520-705-2181; Flagstaff, 928-213-3434; Prescott, 928-708-9120; Show Low, 928-537-2800.

Committees: *Financial Services* (37th of 37 R): Capital Markets, Insurance & Government Sponsored Enterprises; Financial Institutions & Consumer Credit; Housing & Community Opportunity. *Resources* (23d of 28 R): Forests & Forest Health; Water & Power. *Veterans' Affairs* (16th of 17 R): Health.

Group Ratings and Key Votes: Newly Elected

Election Results

2002 general	Rick Renzi (R)	85,967	(49%)	($1,557,104)
	George Cordova (D)	79,730	(46%)	($606,443)
	Edwin Porr (Lib)	8,990	(5%)	
2002 primary	Rick Renzi (R)	11,379	(24%)	
	Lewis Noble Tenney (R)	9,569	(20%)	
	Sydney Hay (R)	9,550	(20%)	
	Alan Everett (R)	7,321	(16%)	
	Bruce Whiting (R)	6,872	(15%)	
	David Stafford (R)	1,894	(4%)	

The People		Race/Ethnic Origin	Ancestry	
Area size:	58,714 sq. mi.	58.4% White	German: 10.3%	English: 8.7%
Urban population:	55.5%	1.2% Black	Irish: 7.1%	
Rural population:	44.5%	0.5% Asian	**2000 Presidential Vote**	
Pop. 2000:	641,329	22.1% Native Am.	Bush (R)..............102,068	(51%)
Median income:	$32,979	0.1% Hawaiian	Gore (D)...............91,920	(46%)
Poverty status:	20.3%	1.2% Two+ races	Other....................7,931	(4%)
Military veterans:	15.7%	0.1% Other	**Cook Partisan Voting Index:** R + 3	
		16.4% Hispanic Origin		

Occupation	Blue collar: 25.6%	White collar: 53.5%	Gray collar: 20.9%

Beyond Phoenix and the Valley of the Sun, Arizona is a vast state of stunning beauty: The awe-inspiring Grand Canyon, the subtle pastel hues of the Painted Desert, the sheer cliff walls of Canyon de Chelly, the still waters of Lake Powell, the mountainous pine forests around Flagstaff, the rust-red rocks of Sedona. It is also the home of man-made landmarks: The celebrated U.S. 66, now mostly superseded by Interstate 40, but you can still take the exit ramp and ride on the old 66 in Holbrook and Winslow and Williams; the old gold mining camp of Prescott, home since 1888 of America's oldest annual rodeo; Jerome, a mining town built improbably on hillside stilts, now reborn as an artist colony; and old copper mining towns like Globe.

All of these places are in the 1st Congressional District, which covers over half the state's area and is larger than Pennsylvania. It covers most of northern Arizona, except for Mohave County and the Hopi Indian Reservation and a narrow band of land connecting them; and it covers the central part of eastern Arizona. It reaches south to the northern edges of the Phoenix and Tucson metro areas. The 1st is the home of the nation's largest and fastest-growing Indian population: 22% of its residents identify themselves as American Indians, the highest percentage in any congressional district in America. There are many reservations here—Fort Apache, San Carlos, Zuni—but by far the largest is the Navajo Nation in the northeast. (The Hopi are excluded because they have a long and angry boundary dispute with the Navajo and have been asked to be put in another district. The Hualapai and Havasupai are also carefully excluded.) Most of the Navajo are in (oddly) Apache County, with the rest in Navajo and Coconino counties. They have a history of fiercely contested tribal elections and, alas, considerable corruption; this winner-take-all political governance does not seem to have served the community well: Unemployment runs around 36% and nearly 30% live without running water or electricity.

Environmental stewardship is an everyday issue for residents of this part of Arizona. Near Flagstaff firefighters thin forests by tree-cutting and controlled burns. In Page, north of the Grand Canyon, townspeople making money off Lake Powell oppose the Sierra Club's proposal to get rid of Glen Canyon Dam and the lake. Mexican wolves were released in 1998 in the mountains of the Apache National Forest, and environmental restriction advocates rejoiced when the federal government in 2000 paid $1 million to stop pumice mining operations on the San Francisco Peaks. But the biggest story in recent years was the Rodeo-Chediski fires near Show Low in east central Arizona. Two separate blazes in the summer of 2002 merged into the largest wildfire in Arizona history and consumed 470,000 acres and destroyed 467 homes.

The 1st District was designed to be closely divided between the two parties, and it is. But there are sharp divisions within the district itself. The copper mining counties (Greenlee, Graham, Gila) are historically Democratic and still register that way, but tend to vote Republican. Apache County, with its Navajo majority, is heavily Democratic; Coconino County, which includes Flagstaff, part of the Navajo Reservation and Sedona, is increasingly Democratic. Prescott and Yavapai County are heavily Republican; Prescott is where Barry Goldwater always began his Arizona campaigns. In 2002 this was an open seat, with no incumbent; it is one of three new, closely divided western districts—the others are the Colorado 7th and the Nevada 3d—which were fiercely contested by the two national parties in 2002.

The congressman from the 1st District is Rick Renzi, a Republican elected in 2002 in his first bid for elective office. Renzi grew up in Sierra Vista, Arizona, near Fort Huachuca and the Mexican border, and graduated from Northern Arizona University in Flagstaff. His curriculum vitae became a source of controversy in the campaign. He billed himself as a "hometown, Flagstaff boy," but he has spent most of his life outside the district. In 1986 he moved to Virginia to work for the Defense Department and in 1989 he started an insurance business in Virginia. In 2002, he received a law degree from Catholic University in Washington. Since 1991, he and his family lived in a $765,000 house with five acres in Burke, Virginia, where he was a registered voter. In 1999 he declared himself an Arizona resident; he registered to vote as an independent in Santa Cruz County, near the Mexican border, where he owned a vineyard that has produced small quantities of sauvignon blanc, pinot noir and cabernet sauvignon. In October 2001 the Arizona Independent Redistricting Commission announced the new congressional map; shortly afterward, Renzi bought a $216,000 house in Flagstaff, where he owned a real estate investment firm, and registered to vote there, this time as a Republican.

This new open seat attracted plenty of candidates—six Republicans, seven Democrats and two Libertarians—some, like Renzi, with only weak links to the district. Renzi quickly established himself as the frontrunner among Republicans by spending more than $500,000 of his own money for an early advertising blitz, which the *Arizona Daily Sun* described as "light on issues, heavy on pretty images." He claimed to have worked on legislation for Congressman Jim Kolbe and Senator Jon Kyl; he was an unpaid intern for two months in his office in 1999, an annoyed Kyl said; a Kolbe staffer said that as an intern he did research on the Las Cienegas conservation area bill. The father of 12 children (each of whose names begin with "R"), Renzi opposed abortion and supported gun rights and a flat tax. But these were not the main issues during his campaign; he spent much time discussing local issues such as preserving the Colorado River water supply. Renzi won the Republican primary with 24% of the vote, carrying Yavapai and Coconino Counties— Prescott, Sedona, Flagstaff—plus Pinal County in the south. Next were former Navajo County supervisor Lewis Tenney and talk show host Sydney Hay, with 20% each; former Sedona Mayor Alan Everett won 16% and Payson attorney Bruce Whiting 15%.

Two of the Democratic primary candidates were familiar in Washington. Stephen Udall, a former Apache County Attorney, is a cousin of Congressmen Mark Udall of Colorado and Tom Udall of New Mexico and of Senator Gordon Smith of Oregon. Fred Duval was a longtime aide to Interior Secretary Bruce Babbitt when he was Governor of Arizona (1978–87) and during his 1988 presidential campaign; he was a State Department official in the Clinton administration. But the Democratic nominee was George Cordova, a venture capitalist and political neophyte who did grass roots campaigning on the Indian reservations. He won the primary with 22% of the vote, carrying Navajo County where he had family ties, plus Gila and Pinal Counties to the south. Udall was second with 20%, carrying Greenlee County, an area with little growth once represented by his cousins' fathers Stewart and Morris Udall. Diane Prescott was third with 18%; she carried Prescott and Yavapai County. Duval finished fourth with 16%; he carried Flagstaff, Babbitt's home-town and Coconino County. Derrick Watchman, a Navajo, carried Apache County and was competitive in Navajo and Coconino Counties but won few votes anywhere else and finished fifth with 14%. So in this district with 641,000 people, 100,000 voted in the primaries, and the winners each won 11,000 votes.

Cordova supported abortion rights, a prescription drug benefit, and environmental protection; Renzi was a stronger supporter of using force against Iraq. But the key to the outcome was skillful opposition research by the NRCC. After the September primary, the NRCC quickly launched an intensive attack on Cordova for four failed ventures in the 1980s that left behind a trail of lawsuits, tax liens and court-adjudicated debts. "I've been involved in over 200 companies and three have had problems," he responded. But more than $2 million of Republican ads and a total of $4 million spent on Renzi's behalf clearly weakened Cordova, on whose behalf national Democrats spent about $1 million. Renzi won 49%–46%. Cordova carried the three counties with large Navajo populations, but Renzi led 61%–33% in Yavapai, which cast one-third of the votes, and led in the southern part of the district. The day after the election, Renzi called for the replacement of NRCC chairman Tom Davis because of the "negative campaign" that it ran on his behalf—ingratitude, to say the least. This seat is likely to be seriously contested again in 2004, if not in the Republican primary, then certainly in the general election.

SECOND DISTRICT

Rep. Trent Franks (R)

Elected 2002, 1st term; b. June 19, 1957, Uravan, CO; home, Glendale; Ottawa University, 1989–90; Baptist; married (Josie).

Elected Office: AZ House of Reps., 1984–86.

Professional Career: Director, AZ Governor's Office for Children, 1987–88; Exec. Director, AZ Family Research Institute, 1989–93; Writer-commentator, AZ radio station KTKP; Co-owner, Franks Brothers Independent Drilling; Pres.-CEO, Liberty Petroleum Corp.

DC Office: 1237 LHOB 20515, 202-225-4576; Fax: 202-225-6328; Web site: www.house.gov/franks.

District Office: Glendale, 623-776-7911.

Committees: *Armed Services* (33d of 33 R): Readiness; Strategic Forces. *Budget* (18th of 24 R). *Small Business* (13th of 18 R): Regulatory Reform & Oversight; Tax, Finance & Exports.

Group Ratings and Key Votes: Newly Elected

Election Results

2002 general	Trent Franks (R)	100,359	(60%)	($555,648)
	Randy Camacho (D)	61,217	(37%)	($40,206)
	Edward Carlson (Lib)	5,919	(4%)	
2002 primary	Trent Franks (R)	14,749	(28%)	
	Lisa Atkins (R)	13,952	(26%)	
	John Keegan (R)	10,560	(20%)	
	Scott Bundgaard (R)	8,701	(16%)	
	Dusko Jovicic (R)	3,805	(7%)	
	Other	1,551	(3%)	
2000 general (AZ 3)	Bob Stump (R)	198,367	(66%)	($377,426)
	Gene Scharer (D)	94,676	(31%)	($6,993)
	Other	8,927	(3%)	

The People		Race/Ethnic Origin	Ancestry	
Area size:	20,391 sq. mi.	78.4% White	German: 14.6%	English: 9.4%
Urban population:	89.0%	2.1% Black	Irish: 9.3%	
Rural population:	11.0%	1.7% Asian	**2000 Presidential Vote**	
Pop. 2000:	641,329	2.0% Native Am.	Bush (R)	119,386 (56%)
Median income:	$42,432	0.1% Hawaiian	Gore (D)	86,251 (41%)
Poverty status:	8.9%	1.4% Two+ races	Other	5,760 (3%)
Military veterans:	19.6%	0.1% Other	**Cook Partisan Voting Index:** R + 8	
		14.2% Hispanic Origin		

Occupation	Blue collar: 22.2%	White collar: 60.3%	Gray collar: 17.5%

Beyond the reach of metropolitan Phoenix and Tucson, much of Arizona looks as it did a century ago. Some is intentionally preserved in its natural state, such at the sere uplands of the Hopi Indian Reservation; other places maintain a timeless western look, like Wickenburg, the oldest Arizona town north of Tucson. Still others preserve antiquated ways of life, such as the polygamist community of Colorado City, just south of Utah, which prosecutes open polygamists. In some cases, nature and settlement juxtapose jarringly: the real London Bridge has been transplanted to Lake Havasu City, a retirement community on the Colorado River; or Bullhead City, one-third of whose residents work in "family gambler" casinos in Laughlin, Nevada, just across the bridge over the rock-lined, piping-hot river.

All these areas are part of the 2d Congressional District, which stretches from the west side of Phoenix to cover most of the northwest quadrant of the state, from Hoover Dam and Lake Mead to the western suburbs of Phoenix, where 80% of its voters live. Astride Grand Avenue, the only diagonal street in the rigorous grid of metro Phoenix, is the mushrooming suburb of Glendale, not so long ago just a crossroads but with 219,000 people in 2000. Just west are Peoria, as Middle American as its namesake in Illinois, and the huge retirement community of Sun City, where locals obsessively prune their Seussian hedges. The 2d also includes the fast-growing corridor along the westbound I-10 Papago Freeway, past Luke Air Force Base—the largest fighter training wing in the Air Force and the only active duty F-16 training base in the U.S.—to the once open spaces of Goodyear and Buckeye. The 2d also includes the Hopi Indian Reservation, connected by a narrow, oddly-shaped corridor to the rest of the district.

This is heavily Republican territory: The retirees here remember—and the upwardly-striving, family-oriented young migrants who have populated these new towns in the desert still try to live—the culturally conservative, Ozzie-and-Harriet lifestyle of the 1950s. Culture, more than affluence, which by national standards is not all that striking here, accounts for their political conservatism. Similarly Republican are the new cities along the Colorado River.

The congressman from the 2d District is Trent Franks, a Republican first elected in 2002. He grew up in Colorado, attended college only briefly and started his own oil and gas exploration business. His political career began when he won a single term in the Arizona House in 1984; he was known for wearing a tie tack in the shape of the feet of a fetus. In 1987 he was the director of the Governor's Office for Children under Governor Evan Mecham, a conservative Republican who was impeached and removed from office in April 1988. He was a consultant in 1995–96 to Pat Buchanan's presidential campaign and in 1989 became executive director of the Arizona Family Research Institute, an organization associated with James Dobson's Focus on the Family. Franks led the campaign for an unsuccessful 1992 ballot initiative to limit abortion rights and designed the state's 1997 scholarship tax credit legislation, a much-litigated measure that ultimately was upheld by the U.S. Supreme Court. The plan provides tax credits for donations to non-profits to help families pay for private education. He was a school-choice advocate and an abortion opponent on Family Life radio. In 1994, he ran for the open 4th District seat and finished second in the Republican primary, to John Shadegg, 43%–30% (Shadegg's district is now the 3d).

In April 2002, Republican Congressman Bob Stump, first elected in 1976, announced he was retiring and endorsed Lisa Atkins, his chief of staff throughout his congressional career. When the campaign started, Franks was not considered in the top tier of candidates—Atkins, state Senator Scott Bundgaard and Peoria Mayor John Keegan. But Franks' base of Christian conservatives and abortion opponents (plus more than $300,000 of his own money) made him a contender. Franks spent heavily on radio ads; he also benefited from the distribution of a voter guide by the religious conservative Center for Arizona Policy, which describes itself as "the only organization in Arizona actively fighting in the legislature and media for conservative, traditional views on gambling, homosexuality and pornography." Franks called for the overturning of *Roe v. Wade* and constitutional protection to fetuses. He endorsed a flat income tax as a step toward eliminating the federal income tax, individual investment accounts under Social Security, tougher enforcement of immigration laws and minimal federal involvement in health care.

In a contest that operated mostly under the political radar, Franks' base of Christian conservatives and abortion opponents made the difference. He finished first with 28% of the vote, only 797 votes ahead of Atkins, who got 26%; Keegan and Bundgaard won 20% and 16% of the vote. In November Franks won 60%–37%. Franks said that he will concentrate on abortion and on child and family issues.

THIRD DISTRICT

Rep. John Shadegg (R)

Elected 1994, 5th term; b. Oct. 22, 1949, Phoenix; home, Phoenix; U. of AZ, B.A. 1972, J.D. 1975; Episcopalian; married (Shirley).

Military Career: Air Natl. Guard, 1969–75.

Professional Career: Practicing atty., 1975–94; US Spec. Asst. Atty. Gen., 1983–90; Spec. Cnsl., AZ House Republican Caucus, 1991–92; Cnsl., AZ Wildlife Conservation, 1992.

DC Office: 306 CHOB 20515, 202-225-3361; Fax: 202-225-3462; Web site: www.house.gov/shadegg.

District Office: Phoenix, 602-263-5300.

Committees: *Energy & Commerce* (16th of 31 R): Commerce, Trade & Consumer Protection (Vice Chmn.); Energy & Air Quality; Health. *Financial Services* (23d of 37 R): Capital Markets, Insurance & Government Sponsored Enterprises; Domestic and International Monetary Policy, Trade & Technology; Oversight & Investigations. *Select Committee on Homeland Security* (21st of 27 R): Emergency Preparedness & Response (Chmn.); Infrastructure & Border Security; Intelligence & Counterterrorism.

Group Ratings

	ADA	ACLU	AFS	LCV	CON	ITIC	NTU	COC	ACU	NTLC	CHC
2002	0	13	0	0	99	88	67	90	100	100	100
2001	5	—	0	0	—	—	80	96	96	—	—

National Journal Ratings

	2001 LIB	—	2001 CONS		2002 LIB	—	2002 CONS
Economic	0%	—	94%		16%	—	81%
Social	34%	—	66%		0%	—	75%
Foreign	4%	—	87%		0%	—	85%

Key Votes of the 107th Congress

1. Approve Bush Tax Cuts	Y	5. Faith-Based Charities	Y	9. Trade Promotion Authority	Y
2. Limit Patients' Bill of Rights	Y	6. Bar Gays in the Boy Scouts	Y	10. Bar Funds for Intl. Court	Y
3. Campaign Finance Reform	N	7. Ban Partial-Birth Abortion	Y	11. Authorize Force in Iraq	Y
4. Ban ANWR Development	N	8. Arm Commercial Pilots	Y	12. Deny Home. Sec. Dept. Union	Y

Election Results

2002 general	John Shadegg (R)	104,847	(67%)	($814,461)
	Charles Hill (D)	47,173	(30%)	($11,694)
	Other	3,731	(2%)	
2002 primary	John Shadegg (R)	unopposed		
2000 general (AZ 4)	John Shadegg (R)	140,396	(64%)	($572,248)
	Ben Jankowski (D)	71,803	(33%)	($1,250)
	Other	7,298	(3%)	

Prior Winning Percentages: 1998 (65%); 1996 (67%); 1994 (60%)

The People		Race/Ethnic Origin	Ancestry	
Area size:	599 sq. mi.	78.5% White	German: 14.5%	Irish: 10.0%
Urban population:	96.5%	2.3% Black	English: 8.6%	
Rural population:	3.5%	2.1% Asian	**2000 Presidential Vote**	
Pop. 2000:	641,329	1.2% Native Am.	Bush (R) 114,259	(54%)
Median income:	$48,108	0.1% Hawaiian	Gore (D) 89,308	(43%)
Poverty status:	8.7%	1.6% Two+ races	Other 6,140	(3%)
Military veterans:	13.4%	0.1% Other	**Cook Partisan Voting Index:** R + 6	
		14.1% Hispanic Origin		

Occupation	Blue collar: 17.7%	White collar: 68.2%	Gray collar: 14.1%

In May 1998 Barry Goldwater died at his home in the Phoenix suburb of Paradise Valley. His life had spanned almost the whole history of Arizona. He was born on New Year's Day 1909, when Arizona was still a territory, and could remember when it was the "baby state," with fewer people than every other state but Delaware, Wyoming and Nevada. When he returned from World War II, Paradise Valley was still empty land and Phoenix—founded after the Civil War as a hay market for cavalry horses at Fort McDowell 40 miles away—was not much more than a tiny outpost of American civilization in a sizzling desert. Today Arizona has 5.1 million people, with 3.3 million in metropolitan Phoenix; the city has been transformed from a frontier outpost to a diversified high-tech center, an example of how creativity and ingenuity can build a sophisticated city with relatively minimalist government and low taxes.

Like Los Angeles and San Francisco, Phoenix is dotted with mountains that rise grandly from the plains and are kept as undeveloped parkland. Some, such as Shaw Butte in the shadow of I-17, contain archeological evidence that Indians used them as a base for sophisticated astronomical observations. From Camelback Mountain, 1,800 feet above Phoenix and Paradise Valley, you can with equal awe get a sense of what this land was originally like and an understanding of how impressively Phoenix has grown. East of Camelback, subdivisions were often built with grass and greenery; in the affluent areas north of Camelback and spreading out Scottsdale Road and the Black Canyon Freeway, the natural desert look is more common. In 1999, the master-planned community of Anthem opened 35 miles north of downtown; it is expected to grow to 50,000 within a decade. Grass is discouraged, and often banned by subdivision covenant; planting anything but desert flora is frowned upon. The architecture of the houses tends toward unadorned stucco with picture windows facing away from the sun; the idea is to suggest that there is a horse corral over in the next lot and sometimes, especially in the northern edges of Phoenix, there is.

The 3d Congressional District includes the northern part of Phoenix plus Paradise Valley, bounded on the south by a zigzag line that approximates the Arizona Canal. The 3d also includes, 20 miles north of downtown Phoenix, the communities of New River, Cave Creek and Carefree (so named in 1955 by developers who hoped to lure retirees). Here the stores are more likely to feature horse feed than designer clothes—but that is changing fast, as metro Phoenix moves inexorably north, bringing with it more upscale malls in the adobe vernacular. This is an affluent, and comfortably Republican, district.

The congressman from the 3d District is John Shadegg (pronounced *SHAD-egg*), elected in 1994, with a fine Arizona Republican pedigree. His father, Stephen Shadegg, managed Barry Goldwater's first campaign for the Senate in 1952, when he upset Senate Majority Leader Ernest McFarland; in those pre-fax, pre-email days, the older Shadegg helped deliver campaign press releases. The younger Shadegg is a lawyer who served as special assistant to the state attorney general and a special counsel to the Arizona House Republican Caucus. When Jon Kyl ran for the Senate in 1994, Shadegg ran for his House seat and won 43% in the Republican primary, to 30% for Trent Franks (now the 2d District congressman), and 21% for a county supervisor. He won the general election easily, 60%–36%.

In the House, Shadegg has been a consistent conservative vote. As one of the firebrand 1994 Republican freshmen, he has held firm as a rebel against Democratic policies and often against his own party's leadership. He refused to back the balanced budget amendment without a three-fifths supermajority for tax increases, in defiance of Speaker Newt Gingrich and Majority Leader Dick Armey. He was one of 15 freshmen to vote against a keep-the-government-open compromise in January 1996 and he voted against the Clinton-Gingrich budget deal in 1997, saying its claims of budget balance and tax relief were "overblown and exaggerated." On the Budget Committee, he proposed in 1998 a budget with more domestic spending cuts, more defense increases and more tax cuts than Chairman John Kasich's. When he chaired the House's Republican Study Committee for three years, Shadegg and his group agreed to support the annual budget resolution but they insisted—with occasional success—that appropriators strictly comply with budget limits; when he gave up the post in January 2003, he contended that the RSC's influence had grown and its membership had increased to about 70. In November 2001 he was one of nine members to oppose the airline security bill, arguing that it couldn't be carried out. In 2002, a *Washingtonian* magazine poll of House staffers placed him high on the list of members with the "strongest backbone." But his anti-leadership stands cost him a seat on Ways and Means in 1997; it went to the 5th District's J.D. Hayworth instead.

On the Commerce Committee Shadegg, at the request of Speaker Dennis Hastert, worked to write an alternative HMO bill which would allow some lawsuits against HMOs, but with limits on recovery and a provision requiring losing litigants to pay costs. When House Republicans were pressured to support the more sweeping Norwood-Dingell alternative, Shadegg's version gave them some cover, though it exposed him to attack from both insurance companies and trial lawyers. In 2001, that approach helped to broker Norwood's split from Dingell and his return as a party regular. *The Arizona Republic* editorialized that Shadegg's handling of the issue "has provided real leadership toward middle-ground solutions."

Shadegg has won re-election each time with at least 64% of the vote against weak opposition. His interest in running for the Senate if John McCain retires in 2004 may have caused tension with Hayworth, a potential rival. During Hayworth's unsuccessful bid in 2002 for Republican Conference chairman, Hayworth sent Shadegg a campaign check for $1,000. The frugal Shadegg returned it, saying it could be better used in a more competitive contest—but his staff did not deny that he had kept contributions from other House Republicans.

FOURTH DISTRICT

Rep. Ed Pastor (D)

Elected Sept. 1991, 6th term; b. June 28, 1943, Claypool; home, Phoenix; AZ St. U., B.A. 1966, J.D. 1974; Catholic; married (Verma).

Elected Office: Maricopa Cnty. Bd. of Supervisors, 1976–91.

Professional Career: High schl. teacher, 1966–69; Asst., AZ Gov. Castro, 1975.

DC Office: 2465 RHOB 20515, 202-225-4065; Fax: 202-225-1655; Web site: www.house.gov/pastor.

District Office: Phoenix, 602-256-0551.

Committees: *Chief Deputy Minority Whip. Appropriations* (14th of 29 D): District of Columbia; Energy & Water Development; Transportation, Treasury, & Independent Agencies.

Group Ratings

	ADA	ACLU	AFS	LCV	CON	ITIC	NTU	COC	ACU	NTLC	CHC
2002	95	93	89	75	43	38	18	40	0	3	0
2001	100	—	100	86	—	—	12	39	8	—	—

National Journal Ratings

	2001 LIB	—	2001 CONS		2002 LIB	—	2002 CONS
Economic	72%	—	27%		82%	—	17%
Social	90%	—	0%		84%	—	8%
Foreign	77%	—	22%		77%	—	19%

Key Votes of the 107th Congress

1. Approve Bush Tax Cuts	N	5. Faith-Based Charities	N	9. Trade Promotion Authority	N
2. Limit Patients' Bill of Rights	N	6. Bar Gays in the Boy Scouts	N	10. Bar Funds for Intl. Court	N
3. Campaign Finance Reform	Y	7. Ban Partial-Birth Abortion	N	11. Authorize Force in Iraq	N
4. Ban ANWR Development	Y	8. Arm Commercial Pilots	N	12. Deny Home. Sec. Dept. Union	N

Election Results

2002 general	Ed Pastor (D)	44,517	(67%)	($679,772)
	Jonathon Barnert (R)	18,381	(28%)	($3,112)
	Amy Gibbons (Lib)	3,167	(5%)	
2002 primary	Ed Pastor (D)	unopposed		
2000 general (AZ 2)	Ed Pastor (D)	84,034	(69%)	($569,648)
	Bill Barenholtz (R)	32,990	(27%)	($80,566)
	Other	5,581	(5%)	

Prior Winning Percentages: 1998 (68%); 1996 (65%); 1994 (62%); 1992 (66%); 1991 (56%)

The People		Race/Ethnic Origin	Ancestry	
Area size:	199 sq. mi.	29.3% White	German: 5.8%	Irish: 4.0%
Urban population:	99.5%	7.5% Black	English: 3.4%	
Rural population:	0.5%	1.3% Asian	**2000 Presidential Vote**	
Pop. 2000:	641,329	2.4% Native Am.	Gore (D)................57,198	(63%)
Median income:	$30,624	0.1% Hawaiian	Bush (R)................31,542	(35%)
Poverty status:	25.6%	1.5% Two+ races	Other....................2,598	(3%)
Military veterans:	9.6%	0.1% Other	**Cook Partisan Voting Index:** D +14	
		58.0% Hispanic Origin		

Occupation   Blue collar: 35.7%   White collar: 43.8%   Gray collar: 20.5%

Phoenix is a new American metropolis, grown to huge metropolitan size within most Americans' lifetimes. Yet it is also an ancient city, or built on top of one. The Arizona Canal, several miles north of downtown Phoenix, runs along the route of a canal built about 600 years ago by the Hohokam people. They distributed irrigated water diverted from the Salt River in its wet moments to farmers in what Phoenicians today call the Valley of the Sun and made sophisticated astronomical observations from the mountains that jut up from the plains. This society disappeared, for reasons that are not known, less than half a century before the Spaniards arrived in North America. So today's Phoenix is the second civilization to grow in this desert. Its growth is recent. Phoenix and Maricopa County had 331,000 people in 1950 and 3.2 million in 2000. Half a century ago, Phoenix only spread half a dozen miles north, west and east of the downtown and only a few miles south. Downtown was its single office and main shopping district, and people blew fans over boxes of ice to keep cool. Today from Phoenix's downtown office towers the city seems to spread as far as the eye can see, and you can see other clumps of office towers to the north and northwest.

The 4th Congressional District is centered on downtown Phoenix. It includes downtown, the Capitol in a rundown neighborhood a couple of miles west and Sky Harbor International Airport in an industrial corridor several miles east. It includes most of southern Phoenix and its boundaries follow approximately the southern and western city limits; it extends as far north as Bethany Home Road and Northern Avenue. Geographically it covers most of the land between South Mountain and Camelback Mountain.

The 4th District was designed to be one of Arizona's two Hispanic districts; its population is 58% Hispanic. The typical Latino neighborhood here is a collection of 1940s and 1950s bungalows, spaced out by empty lots. Here Habitat for Humanity recently built South Ranch, the largest low-income subdivision the organization has ever built in the U.S.; the idea was to cluster poor home-owners together and encourage them to stave off neighborhood decline collectively. Politically this is a solidly Democratic district; George W. Bush won just 35% here in 2000, his poorest showing in the state.

The congressman from the 4th District is Ed Pastor, a Democrat who won a September 1991 special election to replace Morris Udall at a time when the district's boundaries were quite different. Pastor grew up in Claypool, a mining town in Gila County, where his parents "taught me the value of education, the need of tolerance and the responsibility of community service. But especially they taught me the reward of a hard day's work." Pastor is a career politician: After teaching high school, he got a law degree at Arizona State, worked as an assistant to Governor Raul Castro in 1975, then was elected in 1976 to the Maricopa County Board of Supervisors, where he served until elected to Congress. In the 1991 special, he beat Republican Pat Connor 56%–44%. He has not faced stiff competition since then.

From 1995 until January 2003 Pastor was the only Arizona Democrat in Congress; he has been a faithful follower of the Democratic leadership and has a mostly liberal voting record. He supported NAFTA, despite strong labor opposition, but he opposed PNTR with China. He vigorously opposed Arizona's English Only law and supports bilingual ballots, but says, "everyone acknowledges that English is the common language of our country." In June 2002 he sponsored legislation to provide amnesty to immigrants who have lived in the U.S. prior to January 2000. During the Clinton years, he proudly sponsored the nation's only Hispanic U.S. Attorney and Arizona's first Hispanic woman federal judge. In August 2002, after a trip to Cuba where he met with Fidel Castro for 3 hours, he urged the immediate end of the trade embargo.

Much of Pastor's work has been on the Appropriations Committee, where he often delivers projects of the kind that John McCain labels "pork." But home state demands on him and Republican Jim Kolbe have been great because neither Arizona senator is an appropriator. Now that he sits on the Energy and Water Development and the Transportation Subcommittees, he truly brings home the bacon—$10 million for a light-rail transit project in Phoenix, $26.3 million for air traffic control facilities at the city airport, $6.6 million for buses in Phoenix and $3 million for improvements to a visitors facility at the Grand Canyon. In 2000 he won enactment of his proposal to authorize a new international port of entry at the border in Yuma, with conveyance of 330 acres to the Greater Yuma Port Authority; the project was designed to relieve congestion that often caused delays of several hours for commercial vehicles at San Luis five miles to the west. Pastor is "not a headline maker," editorialized *The Arizona Republic*. "He is a congressman from the old school, congenial, collaborative, attuned to the needs of his district, with no grand ambitions other than helping his constituents."

Before 2001 redistricting, Pastor's district stretched from Phoenix to Tucson. Much of his old territory is in the 7th District now, but as an appropriator he will still probably look after its needs.

FIFTH DISTRICT

Rep. J.D. Hayworth (R)

Elected 1994, 5th term; b. July 12, 1958, High Point, NC; home, Scottsdale; NC St. U., B.A. 1980; Baptist; married (Mary).

Professional Career: Sports Reporter/Anchor: WPTF–TV Raleigh, NC, 1980–81; WTFF–TV Greenville, SC, 1981–86; WLWT–TV, Cincinnati, OH, 1986–87; KTSP–TV Phoenix, AZ, 1987–94; Insurance agent & PR consultant, 1994.

DC Office: 2434 RHOB 20515, 202-225-2190; Fax: 202-225-3263; Web site: www.house.gov/hayworth.

District Office: Scottsdale, 480-926-4151.

Committees: *Resources* (19th of 28 R): Forests & Forest Health; Water & Power. *Ways & Means* (16th of 24 R): Select Revenue Measures; Social Security.

Group Ratings

	ADA	ACLU	AFS	LCV	CON	ITIC	NTU	COC	ACU	NTLC	CHC
2002	0	7	0	0	87	88	61	85	100	97	100
2001	5	—	0	0	—	—	72	87	100	—	—

National Journal Ratings

	2001 LIB	—	2001 CONS		2002 LIB	—	2002 CONS
Economic	7%	—	89%		0%	—	91%
Social	0%	—	81%		0%	—	75%
Foreign	0%	—	97%		0%	—	85%

Key Votes of the 107th Congress

1. Approve Bush Tax Cuts	Y	5. Faith-Based Charities	Y	9. Trade Promotion Authority	Y
2. Limit Patients' Bill of Rights	Y	6. Bar Gays in the Boy Scouts	Y	10. Bar Funds for Intl. Court	Y
3. Campaign Finance Reform	N	7. Ban Partial-Birth Abortion	Y	11. Authorize Force in Iraq	Y
4. Ban ANWR Development	N	8. Arm Commercial Pilots	Y	12. Deny Home. Sec. Dept. Union	Y

Election Results

2002 general	J.D. Hayworth (R)	103,870	(61%)	($1,482,389)
	Craig Columbus (D)	61,559	(36%)	($351,955)
	Other	4,383	(3%)	
2002 primary	J.D. Hayworth (R)	unopposed		
2000 general (AZ 6)	J.D. Hayworth (R)	186,687	(61%)	($1,183,832)
	Larry Nelson (D)	108,317	(36%)	($39,522)
	Other	9,000	(3%)	

Prior Winning Percentages: 1998 (53%); 1996 (48%); 1994 (55%)

The People		Race/Ethnic Origin	Ancestry	
Area size:	1,423 sq. mi.	76.8% White	German: 14.3% Irish: 9.5%	
Urban population:	97.2%	2.7% Black	English: 9.0%	
Rural population:	2.8%	3.3% Asian	**2000 Presidential Vote**	
Pop. 2000:	641,329	1.8% Native Am.	Bush (R)	121,462 (54%)
Median income:	$51,780	0.2% Hawaiian	Gore (D)	97,604 (43%)
Poverty status:	8.4%	1.7% Two+ races	Other	7,635 (3%)
Military veterans:	12.4%	0.2% Other	**Cook Partisan Voting Index:** R + 6	
		13.3% Hispanic Origin		

Occupation   Blue collar: 14.2%   White collar: 73.1%   Gray collar: 12.7%

As metropolitan Phoenix grows over the expanse of the Valley of the Sun, around and beyond the mountains that block the passage of the grid streets from the plains below, it has encompassed and absorbed the crossroads towns that were separate and distinct—and much smaller—communities 50 years ago. Two such are Tempe and Scottsdale. Tempe is east of downtown Phoenix, south of the Arizona Canal. It was founded in 1871 as Hayden's Ferry, by the father of the future Senator (1927–69) Carl Hayden and was renamed in 1879 for an ancient Greek vale. The old town nucleus centered on Arizona State University; both town and the university have expanded greatly in the last 50 years. The University is home of the Fiesta Bowl, which sits astride a rise with a fine view of much of metropolitan Phoenix; the town is relatively affluent, with 158,000 people in 2000, as compared to 7,600 in 1950. Then there is Scottsdale, east of the affluent part of Phoenix and north of the Salt River Indian Reservation; it now juts far north and encompasses Frank Lloyd Wright's Taliesin West, which was beyond the reach of electricity and telephone lines when it was built in the 1940s. Scottsdale is one of the most affluent parts of Phoenix, with luxury shopping malls. But it tries to retain an Old Western look, with hitching posts for SUVs and Mercedes. Scottsdale now has 202,000 people, as compared to, well, zero in 1940; it shows up first in the 1950 Census, with 2,000.

The 5th Congressional District includes Tempe, Scottsdale and the northeast corner of Maricopa County—Fountain Hills, the Salt River and Fort McDowell Indian Reservations and part of the Tonto National Forest. Before the 2001 redistricting northern Scottsdale was connected to all of northeastern Arizona, up to and including the Navajo Indian Reservation, in the old 6th District, while southern Scottsdale and Tempe were in the old 1st District. Politically, this is a Republican district, though not quite as much as it was a dozen years ago; some affluent people here, like so many in coastal metropolises, have been attracted to the Democrats by their stands on cultural issues.

The congressman from the 5th District is J.D. Hayworth, a conservative Republican who grew up in North Carolina and made his way upward in the hierarchy of local TV stations as a sportscaster, from Raleigh to Greenville to Cincinnati and then, in 1987, to Phoenix. Hayworth is 6'5", weighs 290, speaks with a booming voice and has a certain resemblance—a help in some quarters, a hindrance in others—to Rush Limbaugh. Certainly he was well known when he ran in the old 6th District in 1994 and won the five-way Republican primary with 45%. In the general he attacked first-term Democrat Karan English for voting for the Clinton tax increase and framed the race as "between a citizen who pays taxes and a career politician who raises them." He carried Maricopa County 65%–32%, enough to overcome English's support on the Indian reservations and around Flagstaff, and won 55%–41%.

Hayworth became a strong voice and a solid vote in the new majority. He seems to irritate Democrats more than just about any other Republican. Veteran Democrat David Obey told him, "You are one of the most impolite members I have ever seen in my service in this House." Hayworth usually has supported the Republican leadership, even as other 1994 colleagues have led rebellions. One exception has been his vigorous advocacy of Indians and their needs, from health services to their freedom to operate casinos. He reaped his reward for loyalty when Newt Gingrich gave him a seat on Ways and Means, bypassing colleague John Shadegg. On that committee Hayworth organized a bipartisan coalition to defeat by 22–16 a $1.9 billion proposed tax on Indian gambling. He was also a lead sponsor of the successful $500 per child tax credit. When Bill Clinton line-item vetoed funds for the experimental Case Grande copper mine, Hayworth got commitments for funds from Budget Director Jacob Lew and Interior Secretary Bruce Babbitt. He got the House to pass a bill giving the DEA control over the GBL dietary supplement that nearly killed Phoenix Suns basketball player Tom Gugliotta. In fall 2001, he was a year ahead of George W. Bush in calling for Treasury Secretary Paul O'Neill to resign, arguing that he wasn't sufficiently supportive of the economic stimulus proposal. *The Arizona Republic* still referred to Haywood's "infamous bluster," and a *Washingtonian* survey of Hill staffers named him number one in Congress in the "no rocket scientist" category and number two in "biggest windbag."

As he gained seniority, Hayworth continued to speak his mind. He attacked the "controlled burns" that got out of control at Los Alamos and the North Rim of the Grand Canyon as "misguided management," calling instead for thinning and timber harvesting. He infuriated Democrats during the February 2002 debate on campaign-finance reform when he backed campaign restrictions on "enemies of the state," an apparent reference to legal permanent residents. He became a prominent spokesman for the party on the talk-show circuit and had frequent ribald exchanges with radio personality Don Imus in the morning. In November 2002 he ran for chairman of the Republican Conference, touting his skill as a communicator. He said he had toned down his combative image and that his wife had persuaded him to listen more and talk less. "Righteous indignation can come across at times as a snarl. You have to have a positive image to focus on." But Deborah Pryce defeated Hayworth in a three-candidate contest 133–61, with Jim Ryun finishing a distant third.

Hayworth had some strenuous opposition in the old 6th District; the Navajo Nation, for all Hayworth's work on Indian issues, was a solid Democratic base. In 1996 he won by only 48%–47% and in 1998 by 53%–44%. By 2000 he was winning even outside Maricopa County and won overall 61%–36%. In the new district, he won by the same margin in 2002 despite the fact that he represented only 19% of his old district. Hayworth has said he regrets losing northeast Arizona and will continue to take an interest in Indian issues. One reason is that he may find himself running statewide. He voiced some interest in running for governor in 2002, but did not do so. If Senator John McCain retires in 2004, Hayworth might very well run for the Senate. There would likely be a competitive Republican primary, and quite possibly a seriously contested general election as well.

SIXTH DISTRICT

Rep. Jeff Flake (R)

Elected 2000, 2d term; b. Dec. 31, 1962, Snowflake; home, Mesa; Brigham Young U., B.A. 1986, M.A. 1987; Mormon; married (Cheryl).

Professional Career: Pub. Plcy. Exec., Shipley, Smoak & Henry, 1987–89; Exec. Dir., Fndt. for Democracy (Namibia), 1989–90; Owner, Interface Pub. Affairs, 1990–92; Exec. Dir., The Goldwater Inst., 1992–99.

DC Office: 424 CHOB 20515, 202-225-2635; Fax: 202-226-4386; Web site: www.house.gov/flake.

District Office: Mesa, 480-833-0092.

Committees: *International Relations* (19th of 26 R): Africa; Asia & the Pacific. *Judiciary* (15th of 21 R): Commercial & Administrative Law; Immigration, Border Security & Claims. *Resources* (21st of 28 R): Forests & Forest Health.

Group Ratings

	ADA	ACLU	AFS	LCV	CON	ITIC	NTU	COC	ACU	NTLC	CHC
2002	5	27	22	25	100	88	84	65	96	100	100
2001	5	—	0	7	—	—	87	74	92	—	—

National Journal Ratings

	2001 LIB — 2001 CONS		2002 LIB — 2002 CONS	
Economic	28%	— 69%	40%	— 59%
Social	34%	— 66%	32%	— 63%
Foreign	54%	— 47%	50%	— 49%

Key Votes of the 107th Congress

1. Approve Bush Tax Cuts	Y	5. Faith-Based Charities	Y
2. Limit Patients' Bill of Rights	Y	6. Bar Gays in the Boy Scouts	Y
3. Campaign Finance Reform	N	7. Ban Partial-Birth Abortion	Y
4. Ban ANWR Development	N	8. Arm Commercial Pilots	Y

9. Trade Promotion Authority	Y
10. Bar Funds for Intl. Court	Y
11. Authorize Force in Iraq	Y
12. Deny Home. Sec. Dept. Union	Y

Election Results

2002 general	Jeff Flake (R)	103,094	(66%)	($265,350)
	Deborah Thomas (D)	49,355	(32%)	($22,209)
	Other	3,888	(2%)	
2002 primary	Jeff Flake (R)	unopposed		
2000 general (AZ 1)	Jeff Flake (R)	123,289	(54%)	($505,210)
	David Mendoza (D)	97,455	(42%)	($74,451)
	Jon Burroughs (Lib)	9,227	(4%)	

The People		Race/Ethnic Origin	Ancestry	
Area size:	724 sq. mi.	76.6% White	German: 14.1%	English: 10.2%
Urban population:	96.8%	1.9% Black	Irish: 8.6%	
Rural population:	3.2%	1.8% Asian	**2000 Presidential Vote**	
Pop. 2000:	641,329	0.8% Native Am.	Bush (R)	118,278 (61%)
Median income:	$47,976	0.2% Hawaiian	Gore (D)	72,093 (37%)
Poverty status:	7.7%	1.4% Two+ races	Other	3,942 (2%)
Military veterans:	15.8%	0.1% Other	**Cook Partisan Voting Index:** R +12	
		17.2% Hispanic Origin		

Occupation	Blue collar: 22.6%	White collar: 63.3%	Gray collar: 14.2%

The metropolis of Phoenix is exceedingly young. Barry Goldwater, born in 1909 and living until 1998, grew up knowing people who remembered when the Valley of the Sun—or the Valley, as most people say—was virtually empty, with a few parched settlements set above the dry river bed. As late as 1950, only 106,000 people lived in Phoenix and 331,000 in all of Maricopa County. But in the years after World War II the air conditioner and military technology transformed Phoenix from a sleepy whistlestop to today's high-rise-studded metropolis, with 1.3 million people in Phoenix and 3.3 million in Maricopa County. This is not, as some people think, a giant retirement village, nor is it overrun by crooked land salesmen and fast-buck artists, though Phoenix has attracted its share of both.

The second largest city in Maricopa County is Mesa, south of the Salt River and east of Phoenix. It was founded by Mormons in 1878 on a square mile; it was laid out Salt Lake City-style with broad streets with huge blocks holding just four homesites, using Indian canals built 1,100 years before. A gleaming white Mormon Temple was built there in 1927, one of the few in the United States then. In 1950 Mesa had 17,000 people, enough to make it Arizona's third largest city. In 2000 it had 396,000 people, more than Minneapolis or Pittsburgh, though few people back east have ever heard of it

The 6th Congressional District is made up of Mesa and Chandler, Gilbert and Queen Creek to the south; it crosses the Pinal County line and includes fast-growing bedroom communities such as Apache Junction, Gold Camp and Sun Lakes. Growth has been constant here: In the 1990s Gilbert zoomed from a dot on the map to 110,000 people. The 6th includes some high-income precincts (interestingly, Asians lead whites in income in Chandler and Gilbert) but the district's cultural tone is resolutely middle class, hard-working and churchgoing. It is the most heavily Republican district in a Republican state—61% for George W. Bush in 2000.

The congressman from the 6th District is Jeff Flake, a Republican elected in 2000, and something of a maverick—or, to some in House leadership, a "flake." A fifth-generation Arizonan, he is a practicing Mormon who was born and raised on a ranch in Snowflake; the town was named, in part, after his great-great grandfather. The fifth of 11 children, Flake served a Mormon mission in South Africa and Zimbabwe before he attended Brigham Young University. In 1987 he moved to Washington, D.C., and worked in a lobbying firm. He returned to southern Africa to serve as executive director of the Foundation for Democracy, which monitored democratic progress in Namibia. Following Namibian independence in 1990 and two more years in Washington representing Namibian companies, he returned to Arizona and became executive director of the Goldwater Institute, where he led the fight for Arizona's charter school law.

In 2000, when Congressman Matt Salmon kept his pledge to serve only three terms (he lost narrowly for governor in 2002), he handpicked Flake to succeed him. Flake faced four opponents in a hard-fought September primary, in which he was the most conservative candidate. Flake had the support of several prominent Republican state leaders and was bolstered by more than $200,000 from the Club for Growth, a PAC of Wall Street financiers that promotes conservative economic policies. Flake won with 32%, an unexpectedly large margin over the runner-up, Phoenix Councilman Sal DiCiccio, who had 24%. In the general, Flake won 54%–42% over Democrat David Mendoza, a longtime lobbyist for public employees.

Flake promised to serve no more than three terms and "continue to rock the boat," much as Salmon had for six years (his refusal to vote for Newt Gingrich for speaker in 1998 contributed to Gingrich's retirement). Less than a month after he took office, Flake—who favors replacing the income tax with a national sales tax—said that it would be a mistake for George W. Bush to limit his proposed tax cut to the "easy things," such as repeal of the marriage penalty, and estate and gift taxes. After less than six months, he scored an initial success when the House passed, 240–186, his amendment to lift restrictions on travel by U.S. citizens to Cuba. But House Republican leaders and the Bush administration strongly opposed his proposal and removed it in negotiations with the Senate. In early 2002, Flake organized the bipartisan Cuba Working Group to review the U.S. embargo of Cuba. That summer, the House again passed his proposal to lift the travel ban; this time, despite pressure by Bush senior aide Karl Rove on Flake to back off, it passed 262–167. But in February 2003, all legislative provisions on Cuba were stricken from the FY2003 appropriations bill. On another foreign policy issue, he was one of two members who voted in June 2001 against a bill to punish Sudan for its human right abuses; Flake said he had seen in Africa the adverse impact of economic sanctions on poor nations. Later in 2001, he was one of 33 Republicans who voted against final approval of the Bush education bill.

Back home, Flake formed a political committee to call for a 2004 voter referendum to repeal Arizona's publicly-financed elections. He criticized the new law as "nothing more than welfare for politicians," and said that taxpayer money should not finance attack ads. In his solidly Republican district, he was reelected 66%–32% in 2002; encouraged by the Club for Growth, in 2003 he considered a bid to challenge Senator John McCain in the 2004 Republican primary.

SEVENTH DISTRICT

Rep. Raul Grijalva (D)

Elected 2002, 1st term; b. Feb. 19, 1948, Tucson; home, Tucson; U. of AZ, B.A. 1985; Catholic; married (Ramona).

Elected Office: Tucson Unified Schl. Dist. Governing Bd., 1974–86; Pima Cnty. Bd. of Supervisors, 1988–02.

Professional Career: Assistant Dean of Hisp. Affairs, U. of AZ., 1987.

DC Office: 1440 LHOB 20515, 202-225-2435; Fax: 202-225-1541; Web site: www.house.gov/grijalva.

District Offices: Tucson, 520-622-6788; Yuma, 928-343-7933.

Committees: *Education & the Workforce* (18th of 22 D): Education Reform; Employer-Employee Relations. *Resources* (16th of 24 D): National Parks, Recreation & Public Lands; Water & Power.

Group Ratings and Key Votes: Newly Elected

Election Results

2002 general	Raul Grijalva (D)	61,256	(59%)	($544,081)
	Ross Hieb (R)	38,474	(37%)	($131,282)
	John Nemeth (Lib)	4,088	(4%)	
2002 primary	Raul Grijalva (D)	14,835	(41%)	
	Elaine Richardson (D)	7,589	(21%)	
	Jaime Gutierrez (D)	5,401	(15%)	
	Lisa Otondo (D)	2,302	(6%)	
	Luis Armando Gonzales (D)	2,105	(6%)	
	Mark Fleisher (D)	2,022	(6%)	
	Other	2,066	(6%)	

The People		Race/Ethnic Origin	Ancestry	
Area size:	22,891 sq. mi.	38.6% White	German: 7.8%	Irish: 5.4%
Urban population:	83.6%	2.8% Black	English: 4.8%	
Rural population:	16.4%	1.3% Asian	**2000 Presidential Vote**	
Pop. 2000:	641,329	5.3% Native Am.	Gore (D) 74,176 (58%)	
Median income:	$30,828	0.1% Hawaiian	Bush (R) 49,343 (38%)	
Poverty status:	21.8%	1.3% Two+ races	Other 5,271 (4%)	
Military veterans:	13.3%	0.1% Other	**Cook Partisan Voting Index:** D +10	
		50.6% Hispanic Origin		

Occupation	Blue collar: 26.8%	White collar: 51.4%	Gray collar: 21.8%

Southern Arizona, though technically part of Mexico for hundreds of years, was never a home to Hispanic civilization like northern New Mexico. Here the hot desert land was inhabited mainly by Indians who kept their native ways and language until English-speaking whites came in on cavalry horses, miners' wagons and railroad cars in the late 19th century. This was after the 1854 Gadsden Purchase—$10 million to Mexico for 30,000 square miles of desert—cleared the way for a southern transcontinental railroad. Today's Hispanic Arizonans are mostly descendants of later immigrants from Mexico, some who came over the border in the sleepier days before World War II, when *la frontera* was scarcely patrolled, and many more who came in the 1980s and 1990s and since to partake in the dazzling economic growth which has served as both an attraction and an example to so many *norteno* Mexicans.

The 7th Congressional District was designed to be the state's second Hispanic district; its population is 51% Hispanic. It is a collection of four distant communities connected by many square miles of uninhabited Sonoran desert. One is the suburb of Tolleson just west of downtown Phoenix. The second is the heavily Latino west side of Tucson. The third is Yuma, located at a Colorado River crossing in an irrigated agricultural valley, often the hottest place in the country, with a desalination plant to protect the farmlands as well as extensive recreational facilities. The fourth is the Mexican border town of Nogales, 94% Hispanic and near many maquiladora plants, long an entry point for illegal drugs and the scene of many illegal border crossings until the Border Patrol was beefed up. The twin smuggling tides—drugs and people—have inflicted damage on the fragile desert ecosystem. In an interesting example of international cooperation the sister cities of Nogales, Arizona and Nogales, Sonora have signed an agreement to respond jointly to fire and hazardous material emergencies. Out in the desert there is the Organ Pipe Cactus National Monument, the Tohono O'odham Indian Reservation and the Barry M. Goldwater Air Force Range (the largest aerial gunnery range after Nevada's Nellis Air Force Range), which is twice the size of Delaware; 95% of it is not used for target practice but is home to the endangered Sonoran pronghorn antelope. The 7th is one of two solidly Democratic districts in Arizona.

The new congressman from the 7th District is Raul Grijalva, a Democrat who was elected in 2002. He began the campaign with a decided edge. He grew up in Tucson and graduated from the University of Arizona; he has lived in the city all his life and has deep roots are in the immigrant community on the city's southwest side. He was the director of El Pueblo Neighborhood Center, and an assistant dean for Hispanic student affairs at the University of Arizona. In 1974 he was elected to the Tucson school board and served 12 years. In 1988 he was elected a Pima County Supervisor and served 14 years. As supervisor he backed an effort to extend medical and dental benefits to the same-sex domestic partners of county employees and focused on affordable health-care, family and children services and growth. Developers and builders helped elect him to office in 1988, but his support for planned growth and impact fees quickly alienated them.

In the 7th, the Democratic primary would obviously determine who would be the new congressman, and Grijalva entered with a home court advantage: 64% of the primary votes were cast in Pima County. His chief opponent was state Senator Elaine Richardson, who was endorsed by EMILY's List and spent more than $500,000 on ads. She criticized him for wasting taxpayer money on a $3.8 million contract to survey all the manholes in Pima County. Although outspent nearly 3-to-1, Grijalva had a well-organized grassroots effort and influential endorsements from labor unions, the teachers' unions and the Sierra Club. Mocking his opponent's national funding, Grijalva said that he created "Adelita's List," a homegrown allusion to the independent women who fought in the Mexican Revolution. He opposed any "privatization" of Social Security or increase in the retirement age. His proposals for immigration reform included an amnesty provision plus a comprehensive border policy with legalization, economic development, cost recovery, infrastructure enhancement and environmental protection. He won the primary with 41% to Richardson's 21%, and 15% for Jaime Gutierrez, a University of Arizona official. In Pima County, Grijalva got 54% of the vote. Using the campaign slogan, "It's all about the love," he won easily in November and his daughter Adelita won a seat on the school board on which he had served.

In Washington, *The New York Times* occasionally chronicled the lives of Grijalva and Michigan Republican Candice Miller, as typical House newcomers. In one account, Grijalva is told to return another day during freshman orientation for his official photograph because he was not wearing a necktie. "I knew I was going to need one of those. I just didn't know that it was going to be that soon." Immigration and border policy will inevitably be one of his concerns; his district covers 275 miles of the U.S.-Mexico border.

EIGHTH DISTRICT

Rep. Jim Kolbe (R)

Elected 1984, 10th term; b. June 28, 1942, Evanston, IL; home, Tucson; Northwestern U., B.A. 1965, Stanford U., M.B.A. 1967; United Methodist; divorced.

Military Career: Navy, 1968–69 (Vietnam), Naval Reserves, 1970–77.

Elected Office: AZ Senate, 1976–82.

Professional Career: Asst., IL Bldg. Authority Architect, 1970–72; Asst., IL Gov. Ogilvie, 1972–73; Vice Pres., land planning firm; Real estate consultant.

DC Office: 2266 RHOB 20515, 202-225-2542; Fax: 202-225-0378; Web site: www.house.gov/kolbe.

District Offices: Sierra Vista, 520-459-3115; Tucson, 520-881-3588.

Committees: *Appropriations* (6th of 36 R): Commerce, Justice, State & Judiciary; Foreign Operations & Export Financing (Chmn.); Interior.

Group Ratings

	ADA	ACLU	AFS	LCV	CON	ITIC	NTU	COC	ACU	NTLC	CHC
2002	20	50	0	0	92	100	57	100	80	85	75
2001	20	—	0	14	—	—	62	96	60	—	—

National Journal Ratings

	2001 LIB	—	2001 CONS		2002 LIB	—	2002 CONS
Economic	15%	—	82%		0%	—	91%
Social	56%	—	44%		56%	—	42%
Foreign	33%	—	60%		44%	—	55%

Key Votes of the 107th Congress

1. Approve Bush Tax Cuts	Y	5. Faith-Based Charities	Y	9. Trade Promotion Authority	Y
2. Limit Patients' Bill of Rights	Y	6. Bar Gays in the Boy Scouts	N	10. Bar Funds for Intl. Court	Y
3. Campaign Finance Reform	N	7. Ban Partial-Birth Abortion	N	11. Authorize Force in Iraq	Y
4. Ban ANWR Development	N	8. Arm Commercial Pilots	Y	12. Deny Home. Sec. Dept. Union	Y

Election Results

2002 general	Jim Kolbe (R)	126,930	(63%)	($865,996)
	Mary Ryan (D)	67,328	(34%)	($292,398)
	Other	6,170	(3%)	
2002 primary	Jim Kolbe (R)	35,546	(72%)	
	James Behnke (R)	13,502	(28%)	
2000 general (AZ 5)	Jim Kolbe (R)	172,986	(60%)	($1,541,478)
	George Cunningham (D)	101,564	(35%)	($552,735)
	Other	13,059	(5%)	

Prior Winning Percentages: 1998 (52%); 1996 (69%); 1994 (68%); 1992 (67%); 1990 (65%); 1988 (68%); 1986 (65%); 1984 (51%)

The People		Race/Ethnic Origin	Ancestry	
Area size:	9,057 sq. mi.	73.9% White	German: 14.4%	English: 9.7%
Urban population:	87.3%	3.0% Black	Irish: 9.1%	
Rural population:	12.7%	2.1% Asian	**2000 Presidential Vote**	
Pop. 2000:	641,329	0.8% Native Am.	Bush (R)..............123,585	(50%)
Median income:	$40,656	0.1% Hawaiian	Gore (D)..............114,055	(46%)
Poverty status:	10.5%	1.8% Two+ races	Other....................10,814	(4%)
Military veterans:	19.1%	0.1% Other	**Cook Partisan Voting Index:** R + 2	
		18.2% Hispanic Origin		

| **Occupation** | Blue collar: 16.5% | White collar: 66.7% | Gray collar: 16.8% |

Arizona's first frontier was just south of today's Tucson, where Franciscan friars built San Xavier del Bac mission in the 18th century. To the east the late 19th century mining towns of Tombstone and Bisbee sprang up on desert mountainsides, where miners dug up gold and silver and, for many years, much of America's copper; Cochise County, which includes those two towns, was the most populous county when Arizona became the 48th state in 1912. Here the white man last subdued the Indians, when the Apache leader Geronimo faced the U.S. Army in 1900. In the late 1990s, Cochise County became an active frontier again. After the Border Patrol reduced illegal crossings in California and Texas, Mexicans wishing to enter the United States came to Agua Prieta, just across the border from the town of Douglas. Every night they fan out east and west and then, often with guides, cross the barbed wire and enter the United States. In 2001, the Border Patrol's Tucson sector apprehended 450,000 illegal aliens; in July 2002 alone, 52 of these immigrants died while trying to cross the border.

One of their destinations is Tucson, Arizona's second metropolis, much smaller, more rough-hewn and politically less conservative than Phoenix. Tucson is a high-tech city and home of the University of Arizona. It is also a tourist destination, with famed resorts. For nearly 40 years, Tucson was the political base of the brothers Udall: Stewart, congressman in the 1950s, Interior secretary in the 1960s, now an Arizona lawyer again; Morris, congressman for 30 years and Interior Committee chairman, who retired in 1991 because of Parkinson's disease and died in 1998. Now their sons, Tom and Mark Udall, represent New Mexico and Colorado districts; a cousin, Stephen Udall, finished second in the 2002 primary in Arizona's new 1st District.

The 8th Congressional District includes all of Tucson except the Latino west side that is in the 7th District. The 8th also includes the eastern half of surrounding Pima County and much southeastern Arizona desert real estate: All of Cochise County (including Tombstone and Bisbee), Douglas and Sierra Vista near Fort Huachuca, site of the Army Military Intelligence Center; and very small portions of Santa Cruz and Pinal Counties. Politically it is closely divided. It voted for George W. Bush by 50%–46% in 2000.

The congressman from the 8th District is Jim Kolbe, a Republican first elected in 1984. He was born in Evanston, Illinois, moved to Arizona at age 5 and grew up on a cattle ranch in Sonoita. He graduated from Northwestern and Stanford Business School, served in the Navy in Vietnam, became an assistant to Illinois' Republican Governor Richard Ogilvie in 1972, and moved back to Arizona shortly thereafter and went into real estate. In 1976 he was elected to the Arizona Senate. In 1982 he ran in the 5th District and lost to Democrat Jim McNulty 50%–48%. In 1984 he ran again and beat him 51%–48%.

Kolbe's voting record on economics has been mostly conservative; he ranks near the middle of the House on cultural and foreign issues. He is a strong booster of free trade and of the maquiladora program, in which U.S.-made components shipped to Mexico for assembly can reenter the U.S. without paying full duty. He was one of the Republican leaders in the successful fight to pass NAFTA in the House in November 1993. He supported GATT, trade promotion authority and the WTO and has called for a free-trade zone covering Central America. He attended the Seattle WTO meeting and chairs the Inter-Parliamentary Group for Mexico. In 2000, he was one of the leading House spokesmen for PNTR for China; in 2002, he opposed steel import quotas. In response to the surge in illegal immigration in his district, he worked for more Border Patrol officers and got $2 million to address border problems in June 2000. Looking farther ahead, he has called for a guest worker program, to provide a legal way for Mexicans and others to work in tight-labor markets like Arizona. In April 2002 he called for using more military troops, including National Guard units, on the border. In May 2002 he proposed that the INS be split into three parts, with function-specific units to be folded into the Justice, State and Labor Departments.

Another Kolbe cause is individual investment accounts in Social Security. In May 2002, he said the debate was moving backward, and when Republican candidates in the 2002 cycle, on the advice of NRCC chairman Tom Davis, attacked "privatization" (by which they meant Bill Clinton's 1999 proposal for government investment of Social Security payroll taxes), he said, "A plague on all of them. We ought to be focused on acknowledging the long-term problem and the options that we might look at that would save Social Security. One has to look at the debate and say this will be a tough thing to do in the next several years."

From 1997–2000, Kolbe was Appropriations subcommittee chairman with jurisdiction over the Treasury, the White House and Postal Service. In 2001 he switched to the chairmanship of the Foreign Operations Subcommittee. He devoted particular attention to Pakistan, where he visited Afghan refugee camps in May 2001. After September 11 he called for lifting sanctions on Pakistan and setting it specific tasks in the war on terrorism; he also called for lifting the restrictions on imports of Pakistani textiles and other products. He was disturbed in November 2002 when it became clear that Pakistan had shipped nuclear technology to North Korea, and said that the 1994 Agreed Framework with North Korea was "effectively ended." In May 2002 he inserted $200 million additional aid to Israel into a supplemental; at Colin Powell's suggestion he added $50 million for Palestinian relief. Appropriators like Kolbe resent limits set on them by OMB, the Budget Committee and the House: he was one of three Republicans to vote in May 2002 against the rule on a supplemental appropriation which committed the House to abide by the Bush budget spending ceiling; the rule passed 216–209, and had the effect of preventing passage of most of the 13 appropriations bills in 2002.

On cultural issues Kolbe is often liberal. He angered many Republicans by supporting funding for the National Endowment for the Arts and was one of the few Republicans to vote against the partial-birth abortion ban. He voted for the Defense of Marriage Act and in July 1996, pressured by an impending article in *The Advocate*, announced that he is gay. This had little apparent impact on the 1996 election, in which he beat Morris Udall's chiropractor 69%–26%. He supported hate crimes legislation before the Matthew Shepard slaying and said afterward, "Thank God Wyoming has the death penalty." In July 1998 he opposed Joel Hefley's amendment to overturn Clinton's order banning discrimination against homosexuals in federal employment. Republican leaders got Hefley to agree not to offer his amendment to Kolbe's appropriation; when it came up later, Kolbe helped persuade 63 Republicans to vote against it.

In 1998 Kolbe had an unexpectedly close race for re-election. His opponent was Tom Volgy, Tucson councilman for 10 years and mayor from 1987–91. His biggest issue was campaign finance: He limited his campaign to $250,000 and championed the plan he instituted in Tuscon, which limits total contributions and bans PAC money. Although Kolbe spent nearly three times as much money, he won by only 52%–45%, and many wondered whether his sexual orientation was a hidden liability. In August 2000 Kolbe was the first openly gay speaker at a Republican National Convention. As he spoke about the importance of free trade, his assigned topic and one on which he had a strong record, several members of the Texas delegation in the front took off their cowboy hats and bowed their heads in prayer. Kolbe said he didn't notice. In September he easily dispatched a primary opponent by 79%–21%. In November he had what some considered his strongest opponent, George Cunningham, a former state senator. Kolbe spent much more money and won by a solid 60%–35%. In November 2000 he was disinvited to work at the Gospel Rescue Mission homeless shelter on Thanksgiving because he is gay; later the mission apologized and invited him back on Thanksgiving 2001, where he was greeted warmly.

Redistricting could have hurt Kolbe. But the Arizona Independent Redistricting Commission, determined to produce two Hispanic-majority districts, put the west side of Tucson into the new 7th District and kept Kolbe's district pretty much as it was. He was reelected by a 63%–34% margin against Democrat Mary Judge Ryan, a chief deputy prosecutor for Pima County.

★ ARKANSAS ★

Arkansas, like America, is in the post-Clinton era, but perhaps more poignantly than anywhere else. For Bill Clinton is the ninth former president (the others were Grant, Cleveland, Taft, Wilson, Hoover, Eisenhower, Nixon and Ford) to spend little time back in his home state, and Arkansas' feelings about him are full of ambivalence. Arkansans interviewed by national reporters evoked varied responses. "He didn't start with much. He wasn't born rich. Look where he got. He did us proud," said carpenter Robert Keeling, "Proud enough." Retired Little Rock banker Edward Penick sounded another note: "In Arkansas he's remembered as a great embarrassment." An anonymous Arkansan said that when Clinton left Little Rock for Washington in January 1993, "I distinctly remember thinking that this was finally going to wipe away the stain left by Faubus"— the governor whose disobedience of an order desegregating Little Rock's Central High School prompted President Eisenhower to dispatch federal troops to enforce it in 1957. Arkansas is justly proud of Clinton's great talents, but was abashed that he didn't return here for presidential vacations, and that the scandals associated with him, if they did not bring him down, tarnished the reputations of many other Arkansans. Independent counsel Kenneth Starr, much reviled here, successfully prosecuted 14 Arkansans, including Governor Jim Guy Tucker, who was forced to resign in July 1996. In his final full day in office, Clinton publicly admitted to giving misleading (but not false) testimony about his affair with Monica Lewinsky and agreed to a five-year suspension of his Arkansas law license in a settlement with Independent Counsel Robert Ray that ended the Whitewater criminal probe.

Nevertheless, four blocks of Little Rock's Markham Street have been renamed President Clinton Avenue—but not the 21 blocks originally proposed. The $110 million President Clinton Library and Museum is scheduled to rise near the Old State House along the Arkansas River; it has sparked the building of a $50 million office tower and $30 million charity headquarters nearby. "The controversy," said Clinton Library head Skip Rutherford, "will make our library much more interesting, much more attractive. It's the dull libraries you worry about."

Arkansas, like Clinton, began life without many advantages. In area, it's the smallest state between the Mississippi River and the Pacific; in population, it's the smallest state in the South; it has not been blessed with any great natural resource—unless you count flame-retarding bromine, of which it produces half the world supply—or any growing major industry. Arkansas is the land left over when Louisiana and Missouri were carved out of the Louisiana Purchase and what is now Oklahoma was fenced off as Indian Territory. Settled by poor farmers with large families, few slaves, and little cash, it has had no Atlanta or Dallas or even Memphis to be a focus of growth. Arkansas has the third lowest income levels of any state, the second lowest percentage of college graduates and its economy, increasingly centered on small manufacturing, faltered in the 2001–02 recession. Some national trends of the 1990s touched Arkansas: Its Hispanic population grew 337%, to 3% of the total; it has more visitors from foreign countries, some 78,000 in 2000; it has had some venture capital investment, but less than any other state except for the six that had none at all. Growth is concentrated in the booming northwest corner of the state, in Little Rock and in counties along the Interstate highways. Arkansas prides itself on being a traditional values state—58% of adults are married, higher than any other state except Idaho and Utah. But the divorce rate has also been higher than average, and Governor Mike Huckabee declared "a state of marital emergency."

As the late Arkansas political scientist Diane Blair noted, Arkansas never had a power elite of great plantation owners or economic robber barons. That has left it a heritage without honored traditions or tight standards, but has also made Arkansas a land of great opportunities, where talented people can move up fast—like Blair and her husband Jim, the former house counsel at Tyson Foods, who guided Hillary Rodham Clinton's commodities trading that netted her a quick $100,000. Other more well-known examples are men who have made huge fortunes by taking break-through ideas and making them work. Sam Walton believed that rural and small town America would support a chain of giant discount stores which, through tough bargaining with vendors and ultra-quick distribution, could undersell competitors, but through demanding man-

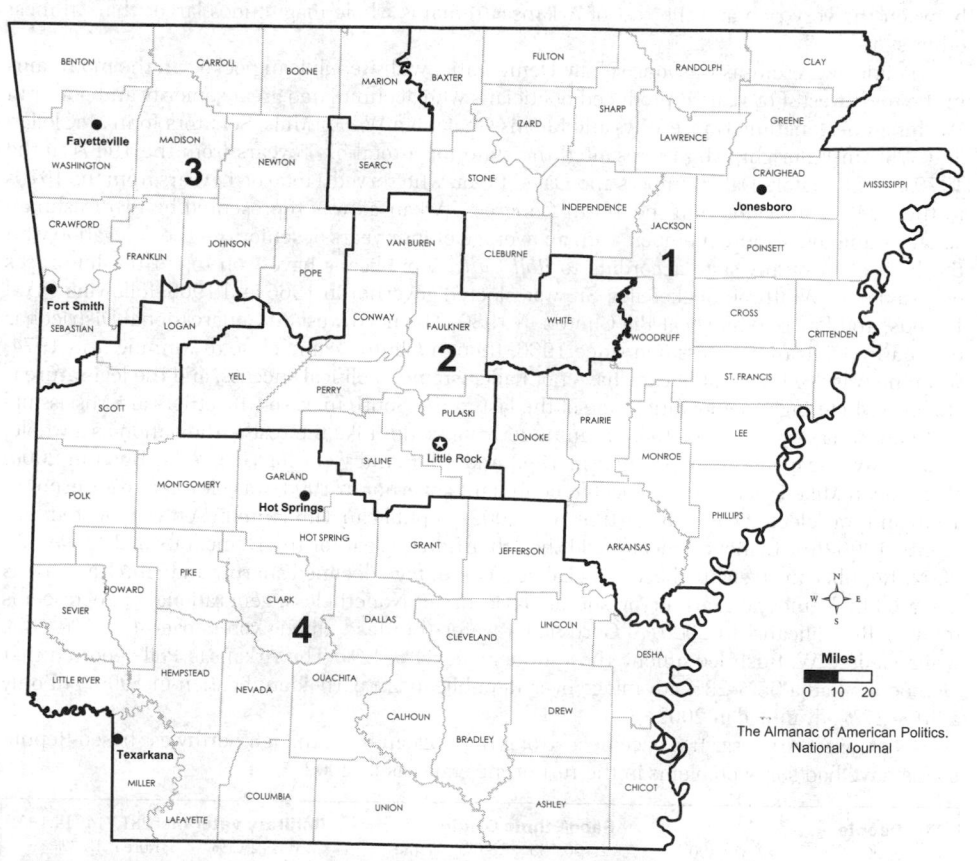

Congressional district boundaries were first effective for 2002.

The Almanac of American Politics.
National Journal

agement and employee profit-sharing, could embody small town friendliness and service; Walton was the richest American when he died in April 1992. Jack Stephens and his late brother Witt started an investment banking house in Little Rock specializing in underwriting municipal bonds and investing in businesses that are a mix of private enterprise, government subsidies and public regulation; their success—and political connections in Arkansas and elsewhere—amassed a billion dollar fortune. Don Tyson took his father's chicken business and made it one of the biggest food producers in America. Other big Arkansas operations include TCBY (The Country's Best Yogurt) and J.B. Hunt's trucking empire. These business giants have cultivated a down-home, laid-back style. But they have also skillfully united their interests with those of the state's politicians—especially Bill Clinton. But even as Arkansas produced in Clinton and in businessmen like Walton, the Stephenses, and Tyson, leaders of unusual ability and outsized personality, the gulf between the very rich and the rest of Arkansas remains whole magnitudes larger than in most other states.

Politically, Arkansas was long solidly Democratic, with Republican pockets in the mountains in the northwest. For years it produced politicians who accumulated great seniority and power in Washington—longtime House Ways and Means Chairman Wilbur Mills, Senators John McClellan and William Fulbright, who represented the state for a total of 65 years from the 1940s to the 1970s, and Senators Dale Bumpers and David Pryor, who served a total of 42 years from the 1970s to the 1990s. But going into the 108th Congress, Arkansas was represented by two freshman senators and four House members with an average of four years of seniority—the delegation with the least clout of any state according to *Roll Call*. Republicans have won top of the line races occasionally—Winthrop Rockefeller, Sr., was elected governor in 1966 and 1968, following Orval Faubus, and Frank White beat Bill Clinton in 1980. The northwest 3d Congressional District has elected Republican congressmen since 1966, though Clinton came close to winning it in 1974, when he was 28. But Republicans have not had sustained political success, and the legislature is still overwhelmingly Democratic—one of the last in the South to be so (the others are Mississippi and Louisiana). Nonetheless there is an underlying trend: Like the rest of the nation as a whole, Arkansas was carried by Bill Clinton in 1992 and 1996 and went for George W. Bush in 2000. Republican Mike Huckabee was elected lieutenant governor in 1993, was elevated to governor in 1996 and was elected governor in 1998 and 2002. Republican Tim Hutchinson was elected senator in 1996. But Blanche Lincoln held the other Senate seat for the Democrats in 1998 and in 2002, Republican strength ebbed: Huckabee's percentage declined sharply and Hutchinson was defeated by Democrat Mark Pryor, son of David Pryor. Nonetheless, generational change seems to favor Republicans. In 2000, Al Gore had a wafer-thin lead among voters over 45, 49%–48%, while George W. Bush led among those under 45, 54%–42%. The Arkansas Poll reported that Democrats had a 35%–23% advantage over Republicans in party identification in 1999, but only a 30%–27% advantage in 2002.

Northwest Arkansas has become a strong Republican base, though northwest-based Republicans have had some problems in the rest of the state, as in 2002.

The People		Race/Ethnic Origin			Military veterans: 281,714 (14.1%)	
Pop. 2000:	2,673,400	2,100,135	78.6%	White	WWII: 20.1%	Korea: 13.3%
Pop. 1990:	2,350,725	416,615	15.6%	Black	Vietnam: 32.0%	Gulf War: 10.5%
Change 1990–2000:	Up 13.7%	19,892	0.7%	Asian	**Most populous cities:**	
Change 1980–1990:	Up 2.8%	16,702	0.6%	Native Am.	1. Little Rock	183,133
% of U.S. total:	1.0%	1,494	0.1%	Hawaiian	2. Fort Smith	80,268
Pop. rank:	33d of 50	30,364	1.1%	Two+ races	3. North Little Rock	60,433
Area size:	53,179 sq. mi.	1,332	0.0%	Other	4. Fayetteville	58,047
State Native:	63.9%	86,866	3.2%	Hisp. Origin	5. Jonesboro	55,515
Non-citizen:	1.9%	**Ancestry**			Urban population: 52.4%	
Language		USA: 13.2%		Irish: 7.9%	Rural population: 47.6%	
English: 93.5%	Spanish: 4.0%	German: 7.7%		English: 6.5%		
Other Eur.: 1.6%		French: 1.6%				

Education		Work Sector		General Assembly	
H.S. Grad:	75.3%	Private: 76.8%	Govt: 14.9%	Senate	27 D 8 R
College Grad:	16.7%	Self: 7.8%	Family: 0.4%	House	70 D 30 R
Industry		Unemployment: 6.1%		Legislative Term Limits: Yes	
Agri: 3.7%	Con: 7.0%	**Household Income**		**Registered Voters**	
Fin: 4.8%	Info: 2.2%	<15k: 22.0%	15-35k: 31.7%		
Mfg: 25.3%	Prof: 25.0%	35-50k: 17.5%	50-100k: 22.8%	No party registration	
Public: 4.3%	Trade: 16.3%	100-150k: 3.8%	>150k: 2.2%		
Other: 11.3%		Median: $32,182			
Occupation		Poverty status: 15.8%			
Blue collar: 31.6%	White collar: 52.8%	**Home Value**			
Gray collar: 15.6%		<50k: 34.1%	50-100k: 40.2%	100-200k: 19.8%	200-300k: 3.6%
		300-500k: 1.6%	>500k: 0.7%	Median: $67,400	

Presidential politics Arkansas voted 53% for Bill Clinton in 1992 and 54% in 1996; these were his best and eighth-best percentages those years. In 2000, it voted only 46% for Al Gore, his 29th-best state. George W. Bush, who targeted the state and appeared in Northwest Arkansas on election eve, won 51% here, his lowest percentage in the South except of course for Florida. But with Clinton out of office and out of state, Arkansas seems unlikely to be a target state for a Democrat, except for one with special appeal in the South.

The Arkansas presidential primary, held in May, attracts little attention; nor did it in 1992 when it was held on Super Tuesday. There is no party registration requirement and Republican turnout has typically been very low; 85% of those voting in the May 2000 primary voted Democratic.

2000 Presidential Vote
Bush (R)	472,940	(51%)
Gore (D)	422,768	(46%)
Nader (Green)	13,421	(1%)
Other	12,652	(1%)

2000 Republican Presidential Primary
Bush (R)	35,759	(80%)
Keyes (R)	8,814	(20%)

2000 Democratic Presidential Primary
Gore (D)	193,750	(78%)
LaRouche (D)	53,150	(22%)

1996 Presidential Vote
Clinton (D)	475,171	(54%)
Dole (R)	325,416	(37%)
Perot (I)	69,884	(8%)
Other	13,791	(2%)

Congressional districting In April 2001, the boundaries of Arkansas's four congressional districts

108th Congress Lineup
3 D   1 R
107th Congress Lineup
3 D   1 R

were adjusted slightly by the Democratic legislature to meet the equal-population standard. The legislature's plan had the highest population difference in the nation between the districts—6,698 people—but it also contained a backup provision that if a court found the plan invalid, it would be repealed and 4,400 voters would be shifted between districts; a court challenge did not materialize. Governor Mike Huckabee, lacking the votes to prevent an override of his veto, let the plan become law without his signature.

Governor

Mike Huckabee (R)

Assumed office, July 1996, term expires Jan. 2007, 2d term; b. Aug. 24, 1955, Hope; home, Little Rock; Ouachita Baptist U., B.A. 1975, Southwestern Baptist Theological Seminary, 1976–80; Baptist; married (Janet).

Elected Office: AR Lt. Gov., 1993–96.

Professional Career: Advertising Dir., Focus, 1976–80; Baptist Minister, 1980–92; Pres., ACTS–TV, 1983–86; Pres., KBSC–TV, 1987–92; Pres., Cambridge Comm., 1992–96.

Office: State Capitol, Rm. 250, Little Rock, 72201, 501-682-2345; Fax: 501-682-3597; Web site: www.state.ar.us/governor.

Election Results

2002 general	Mike Huckabee (R)	427,082	(53%)
	Jimmie Lou Fisher (D)	378,250	(47%)
2002 primary	Mike Huckabee (R)	78,803	(85%)
	Doyle Cannady (R)	13,434	(15%)
1998 general	Mike Huckabee (R)	421,989	(60%)
	Bill Bristow (D)	272,923	(39%)
	Other	11,099	(2%)

Mike Huckabee has been governor of Arkansas since July 1996. Like Bill Clinton, Huckabee was born in Hope; unlike Clinton, he grew up there. Clinton was elected governor of Arkansas Boys State in 1963, Huckabee in 1972. Clinton went off to Georgetown and Yale Law School; Huckabee graduated from Ouachita Baptist University at 19 and attended Southwestern Baptist Theological Seminary in Fort Worth for four years. He had a profound spiritual experience at 15, while on a two-week youth fellowship program at Cape Kennedy—the first time he had been outside Arkansas. In the 1980s, Huckabee was a Baptist minister in Pine Bluff and then Texarkana; in both towns he started a 24-hour television station, where he produced documentaries and hosted a program called *Positive Alternatives*. In 1989, he became president of the Arkansas Baptist Convention, with a membership of 490,000.

Huckabee's first stab at politics was running against Senator Dale Bumpers in 1992; he lost 60%–40%. Then, after Jim Guy Tucker replaced Bill Clinton as governor, Huckabee ran in a special election for lieutenant governor. It was July 1993, the Clinton tax plan and gays in the military had been in the headlines, and Huckabee beat pro-Clinton Democrat Nate Coulter 51%–49%. He was re-elected 59%–41% in November 1994. In October 1995, after David Pryor said he was retiring from the Senate, Huckabee announced for the seat and was ahead in the polls. But in May 1996, Tucker was convicted on one count of arranging nearly $3 million in fraudulent loans. Tucker promised to resign July 15; on that day, claiming he had a good case on appeal, he hesitated, then finally in the early evening he resigned. Huckabee, who had already bowed out of the Senate race, had insisted Tucker resign and handled the transition gracefully but firmly.

Despite facing a heavily Democratic legislature, Huckabee has had passed some significant programs as governor. He is most proud of the ARKids First plan providing health insurance for parents of children above the Medicaid income limits. It requires a small co-payment, to avoid the stigma of being a handout; Huckabee wanted to offer parents the choice of ARKids First or Medicaid, which the Clinton administration overruled in July 2000, so he rolled the two plans into one. Huckabee boasts that the program has given insurance to 50,000 kids who didn't have it and that Arkansas ranks number one in the decrease of percentage of residents without health insurance. In his first years, he cut income taxes and passed a taxpayer's bill of rights for property owners; he supported a successful ballot measure to raise the sales tax 0.5% to fund a $300 homestead property tax credit. The gas tax was raised for a major highway construction program. Huckabee implemented the AASIS (Arkansas Administrative Statewide Information System) program that put all state departments on the same state-of-the-art computer system. He signed a law requiring women to receive information about abortion 24 hours before the procedure and mailed a letter to school superintendents reminding them of children's right to engage in "personal or group prayer." Budget cuts in 2001 cut out most of a promised $3,000 increase for teachers and cut health services programs, but Huckabee, at the time, remained opposed to tax increases.

In 1998, he faced Democrat Bill Bristow, an attorney representing state trooper Danny Ferguson in the case Paula Jones brought against Bill Clinton. Bristow charged that Huckabee spent Governor's Mansion funds on personal items and called for a bond issue for road repairs similar to one beaten 87%–13% in 1996. Huckabee outspent Bristow and won 60%–39%, carrying all but eight lightly populated counties in eastern Arkansas. Through most of his first full term his job ratings remained high, and at the end of 2001, he had raised almost $1 million for his reelection campaign and prominent Democrats declined to run—former FEMA Director Jamie Lee Witt, former Transportation Secretary Rodney Slater, Secretary of State Sharon Priest. Finally, in March 2001, Democrats came up with a candidate, state Treasurer Jimmie Lou Fisher. In 2001, she announced she would retire from this minor office after 22 years and return home to Paragould, where her mother was in bad health. A onetime staffer for freshman Governor Bill Clinton, she was regarded as an exceedingly nice person, always welcome at Democratic get-togethers; she introduced Clinton when he announced for president in 1991. But, wrote local political columnist John Brummett, she "stumbles in her articulation" and her "policy pronouncements are comically evasive or vacuous."

Fisher, however, turned out to be a strong candidate and came close to winning. And the reason was that Mike Huckabee started making astonishing mistakes; his job rating plummeted from 70% to 50%. Huckabee had a penchant for granting pardons; one felon he paroled in 1996 committed a murder in Missouri. In July 2001, he commuted the sentence of the stepson of an administrative aide in the governor's office whose criminal record went back to 1972. That same month, he also granted clemency on state charges to David Hale, who had pleaded guilty in the Whitewater scandal and then testified against Jim Guy Tucker and James and Susan McDougal (even though Hale's sentence in this case was only 21 days). In June 2002, he fired the head of the AASIS project, who promptly told reporters he and other employees had been pressured for campaign contributions and that Huckabee had tried to stifle news of cost overruns—nearly 100%—during the election year. Huckabee aides barraged Arkansas Educational TV with complaints after a business reporter was quoted as saying he could "stomach" four more years of Huckabee, and the state police investigated when a weekly newspaper reported that AASIS couldn't protect the privacy of Social Security numbers. Huckabee had been in the practice of receiving large gifts; he reported a total of $112,000 in 1999, which included $23,000 in clothes from one state appointee. He also accepted $60,000 in speaking fees from a group he helped found. Huckabee responded—in an election year!—with a lawsuit to allow him to receive more gifts and another lawsuit to stop the Ethics Commission from investigating him.

Another self-inflicted wound came in March 2002, when Huckabee's wife announced she was running for Secretary of State. This was the first time ever that a husband and wife ran simultaneously for statewide office. Janet Huckabee was known for her daredevil antics—bungee jumping, skydiving, jet skiing, kayaking—and for her oversight of the two-year renovation of the Governor's Mansion, a time when the Huckabees lived in a triple-wide on the mansion grounds. She insisted on a 24-hour state police detail while campaigning across the state; when that was challenged, she at first said she had no control over it, then promised to pay the cost, then said she would pay only up to $500. Criticism rained in; her reply was, "If it wasn't for the grace of God, I would have shot a few people already."

Meanwhile, Jimmie Lou Fisher, with teachers' union support, called for spending $133 million more for education; she said she would find the money from waste, fraud and abuse, or perhaps from a lottery (though she opposed one). She got more mileage by attacking AASIS and criticizing Huckabee's grants of clemency and acceptance of gifts. By late October, polls showed an even race. On election night there was a victory—a narrow one—for one Huckabee and a defeat for the other: Janet Huckabee lost 62%–38% while Mike Huckabee won 53%–47%, a far lower margin than four years before. Huckabee called the campaign "a kidney stone that takes six months to pass." There may be more stones: On November 14, Huckabee proposed an increase in the sales tax, from 5.125% to 5.75%. Fiscal problems were looming: Revenues were coming in lower than projected, and a Little Rock judge had ruled that Arkansas's education funding system was inequitable, a ruling that, if affirmed by the state Supreme Court, seemed likely to cost an additional $800 million.

Senior Senator

Blanche Lincoln (D)

Elected 1998, seat up 2004, 1st term; b. Sept. 30, 1960, Helena; home, Horseshoe Lake; U. of AR, 1979–80, Randolph Macon Col., B.S. 1982; Episcopalian; married (Steve).

Elected Office: US House of Reps., 1992–96.

Professional Career: Staff Asst., U.S. Rep. Bill Alexander, 1982–84; Lobbyist & govt. affairs rep., 1985–91.

DC Office: 355 DSOB, 20510, 202-224-4843; Fax: 202-228-1371; Web site: lincoln.senate.gov.

State Office: Little Rock, 501-375-2993.

Committees: *Aging (Special)*. *Agriculture, Nutrition & Forestry*: Forestry, Conservation & Rural Revitalization (RMM); Production & Price Competitiveness. *Ethics (Select)*. *Finance*: Health Care; Social Security & Family Policy; Taxation & IRS Oversight.

Group Ratings

	ADA	ACLU	AFS	LCV	CON	ITIC	NTU	COC	ACU	NTLC	CHC
2002	70	60	75	24	8	75	36	75	40	17	—
2001	85	—	75	50	—	—	29	79	28	—	20

National Journal Ratings

	2001 LIB —	2001 CONS	2002 LIB —	2002 CONS
Economic	54%	46%	52%	47%
Social	60%	36%	52%	46%
Foreign	58%	41%	54%	45%

Key Votes of the 107th Congress

1. Approve Bush Tax Cuts	Y	5. Confirm Ashcroft as AG	N
2. Expand Patients' Rights	Y	6. Bar Gays in the Boy Scouts	N
3. Campaign Finance Reform	Y	7. $ for Hate Crime Prosecution	Y
4. Permit ANWR Development	N	8. Overseas Military Abortions	Y

9. Bar Coop. with Intl. Court	Y
10. Trade Promotion Authority	Y
11. Authorize Force in Iraq	Y
12. Homeland Sec. Dept. Union	Y

Election Results

1998 general	Blanche Lincoln (D)	385,878	(55%)	($3,122,776)
	Fay Boozman (R)	292,906	(42%)	($1,093,007)
	Other	21,860	(3%)	
1998 runoff	Blanche Lincoln (D)	134,203	(62%)	
	Winston Bryant (D)	80,889	(38%)	
1998 primary	Blanche Lincoln (D)	145,009	(45%)	
	Winston Bryant (D)	87,183	(27%)	
	Scott Ferguson (D)	44,761	(14%)	
	Nate Coulter (D)	41,848	(13%)	
1992 general	Dale Bumpers (D)	553,635	(60%)	
	Mike Huckabee (R)	366,373	(40%)	

Prior Winning Percentages: 1994 House (53%); 1992 House (70%)

Blanche Lambert Lincoln was elected to the Senate in 1998 after showing something close to perfect political pitch in her 1990s electoral career. She grew up in Helena, on the flat rice lands of eastern Arkansas, where her father and brother are the sixth and seventh generations running a farm raising rice, wheat, soybeans, and cotton, and where she stayed in public schools after they were integrated. Cheerful, active, endowed with good political sense, she lists her hobbies as duck hunting, fishing and yard sales. After college, in 1982, she worked as a staffer for 1st District Congressman Bill Alexander, then after two years worked as a lobbyist for, among others, Billy Broadhurst—Gary Hart's host on the 1987 *Monkey Business* cruise. In 1992, she moved back to Arkansas and, as Blanche Lambert (she was married in 1993) ran against Alexander, sensing he was in trouble. He had lost a leadership race in 1986, was named in a lawsuit for a $308,000 debt, and had 487 overdrafts totaling $208,000 on the House bank. "I'll promise you one thing," the 31-year-old challenger said, "I can sure enough balance my checkbook." She won the primary 61%–39%, carrying 23 of 25 counties.

In the House, Lincoln compiled a moderate voting record and got a seat on the Commerce Committee. She saw Japan open its market to Arkansas rice and denounced the Supplemental Security Income program that provided disability checks to kids who act up in school. She supported much of the Contract with America in 1995. But when the moratorium on regulations threatened duck hunting season and national wildlife refuges were closed, she got laws changed to ensure it wouldn't happen again. Her re-election margin in 1994 was only 53%–47%, but she seemed well positioned to hold the seat when, in January 1996, she announced that she was pregnant with twin boys and would not run for reelection because of the strain of campaigning in an Arkansas summer during a difficult pregnancy.

When Senator Dale Bumpers announced he would not run for reelection in 1998, Lincoln got into the race. She flashed snapshots of her twins and ran ads showing her overseeing mealtime, balancing one twin on her lap, bouncing the other on her knee, laying her head on her husband's shoulder. "Daughter, wife, mother, congresswoman . . . Living our rock-solid Arkansas values." In the primary, she faced Attorney General Winston Bryant, the Democratic nominee in the 1996 Senate race. She led by an impressive 45%–27% in the May primary, with 64% in her old 1st District, which cast nearly one-third of the votes. She won the June runoff 62%–38%.

In the general election, Lincoln stanched the Republican tide that had been running since Bill Clinton left the state, and then some. The Republican nominee was Fay Boozman, an ophthalmologist from Rogers in northwest Arkansas who attended the same church as Republican Senator Tim Hutchinson. Boozman had a profound religious experience in 1992, sold his medical practice, and ran for the state Senate; there he was the champion of the partial-birth abortion ban. Boozman called on Bill Clinton to resign and ran tough comparative ads on Lincoln. He said the Bible dictated his anti-tax philosophy and made a serious gaffe when he said it is rare for women to get pregnant by rape because fear triggers a hormonal change that blocks conception. Lincoln won 55%–42%, a more solid win than Hutchinson's in 1996; Boozman carried the northwest corner of the state and little else. She was the youngest woman ever elected to the Senate.

Lincoln's voting record has been a bit to the left of the midpoint of the Senate; she was one of nine Democrats to form a moderate caucus, similar to the House's Blue Dogs, in February 2000. Working with her 1st District successor, Marion Berry, she promoted farm exports, joining the WTO caucus in October 1999 and in May 2000 visiting Cuba, which, before Fidel Castro, purchased much of Arkansas's rice. She described Castro as "very cordial" and "still very much in command and in control," accepted two boxes of cigars, worth $1,250, and strongly supported ending the embargo on trade in Cuba. She voted for the partial-birth abortion ban, saying it was "always a difficult vote." In February 2001, Lincoln got a seat on the Finance Committee and played an important role in some key votes in the closely divided Senate. In March 2001, she was one of six Democrats to vote to kill the Clinton ergonomics regulations and one of six Democrats to vote for non-severability on campaign finance (which threatened to get the whole bill declared unconstitutional). On the Finance Committee, she and other moderates negotiated with Chairman Charles Grassley and ranking member Max Baucus to get two provisions into the committee bill: One was to make the child care tax refundable to those who pay no income tax and the other was to create a new 10% income bracket. She was one of 12 Democrats to vote for the tax cut in May 2001, but she voted against the Bush budget also in May 2001. She voted against oil drilling in the Arctic National Wildlife Refuge in April 2002. Lincoln has also worked with Republican

Congressman Dan Burton to aid U.S. citizens who have been kidnapped and held in Saudi Arabia (primarily the issue involves children illegally abducted by one of their parents).

On two major issues she struggled unsuccessfully to find middle ground. She and Louisiana Sen. John Breaux supported a welfare reform authorization different from the Bush administration version, with 30 hours of work required each week instead of 40 and giving states more leeway to meet the requirement that 70% of recipients leave the rolls (Lincoln and Breaux would let the states count those who had already left); but no welfare legislation emerged. From June to September 2002, she spent much time and effort trying to come up with a compromise on prescription drugs for seniors but, as on welfare, no bill was passed. In September 2002, Lincoln held up the faith-based services bill until she got agreement on a provision allowing corporations to donate a greater share of their stock to charity while still counting it as stock on the books in determining corporate control.

Never far from her mind are the rice farmers of Arkansas's Delta. She was one of two Democrats to vote against the farm bill in February 2002, because she said it was not generous enough to cotton and rice farmers; she also worked with Olympia Snowe of Maine to change the softwood lumber agreement with Canada. She fought unsuccessfully against limits on farm subsidies. Three rice farms in Stuttgart and Helena were among the top five recipients of farm subsidies in the country, with $106 million from 1996–2001, the largest concentration of subsidies in the United States. In September 2002, Lincoln pushed for extending beyond 2010 scheduled reductions in the estate tax and allowing family farms to treat as a non-taxable "carryover business interest" transfers of interests to family members so long as they don't sell them. She has supported the $16 million Grand Prairie irrigation project, to replace water that rice farmers get from the nearly depleted alluvial aquifer.

Lincoln comes up for reelection in 2004. There are many signs that Arkansas has been trending Republican, but Republican candidates at the top of the ticket have not been faring well lately. Hutchinson was defeated by Democrat Mark Pryor in 2002 and Governor Mike Huckabee was reelected with only 53% of the vote against a weak candidate. In early 2003, neither seemed likely to be a strong opponent for Lincoln in 2004. One possibility is Asa Hutchinson, Tim's brother, a former congressman and head of the Drug Enforcement Administration and most recently a high-level appointee in the Homeland Security Department. It's not clear that he will return to Arkansas to make the race. Another possibility is Arkansas's one Republican congressman, John Boozman, brother of Lincoln's 1998 opponent. But Arkansas is likely to vote for George W. Bush in 2002, and this could be a seriously contested race. And more may be possible for Lincoln: In June 2002, she appeared on *National Journal's* website as a possible vice presidential nominee.

Junior Senator

Mark Pryor (D)

Elected 2002, seat up 2008, 1st term; b. Jan. 10, 1963, Fayetteville; home, Little Rock; U. of AR, B.A. 1985, J.D. 1988; Christian; married (Jill).

Elected Office: AR House of Reps., 1990–94; AR Atty. Gen., 1998–02.

Professional Career: Practicing atty., 1988–96.

DC Office: 217 RSOB, 20510, 202-224-2353; Fax: 202-228-0908; Web site: pryor.senate.gov.

State Office: Little Rock, 501-324-6336.

Committees: *Armed Services*: Airland; Personnel; Readiness & Management Support. *Governmental Affairs*: Financial Management, Budget & International Security; Government Management, Federal Workforce & the District of Columbia; Investigations (Permanent). *Small Business & Entrepreneurship*.

Group Ratings and Key Votes: Newly Elected

Election Results

2002 general	Mark Pryor (D)	434,890	(54%)	($4,414,148)
	Tim Hutchinson (R)	369,069	(46%)	($5,063,923)
2002 primary	Mark Pryor (D)	unopposed		
1996 general	Tim Hutchinson (R)	445,942	(53%)	($1,604,014)
	Winston Bryant (D)	400,241	(47%)	($1,577,838)

Mark Pryor, the junior senator from Arkansas elected in 2002, is one of six children of former senators now serving in the Senate; the others are Christopher Dodd of Connecticut, Robert Bennett of Utah, Evan Bayh of Indiana, Lincoln Chafee of Rhode Island and Lisa Murkowski of Alaska (Jon Kyl of Arizona is the son of a congressman; Edward Kennedy's two brothers and Elizabeth Dole's husband were senators). His grandmother, Susie Newton Pryor, was the first woman in Arkansas to run for office when women got their vote. Mark Pryor grew up in southern Arkansas, the Washington area and Little Rock: His father, David Pryor, was elected to the House in 1966, lost a Senate race in 1972 and was elected governor in 1974 and 1976 and senator in 1978. Mark Pryor graduated from the University of Arkansas and its law school in the 1980s. He practiced law in Little Rock and was elected to the Arkansas House in 1990 and 1992; in 1998, he was elected state attorney general, at 35 the youngest attorney general in the nation (but not in Arkansas history: Bill Clinton won the office at 30). In 1995 he was diagnosed with clear-cell sarcoma, a rare form of cancer. He underwent tendon transplant surgery in his left heel in 1996; the cancer has not returned.

As attorney general, he tried to curb telemarketing and worked for "Do Not Call" legislation. He claimed to save the state $243 million in attorneys' fees in the tobacco settlement. He pushed for legislation to increase penalties for single-incident nursing home accidents (regulating nursing homes was a big issue for young Congressman David Pryor in the 1960s) and to strengthen background checks for long-term care employees. He worked to reduce utility rates and to remove unsafe baby products from licensed day care centers. In July 2002, he filed a brief in the state Supreme Court defending Arkansas's school financing system as constitutional and urging the court to overturn a lower court ruling that some said would cost the state $800 million a year.

In July 2001, Pryor announced that he would run against Senator Tim Hutchinson—the first Republican to win an Arkansas Senate seat since 1879— who was elected in 1996 to replace the retiring David Pryor. Hutchinson is a Baptist minister, owner of a radio station and founder of a Christian school in Rogers, in northwest Arkansas. He had had a successful career representing that conservative area, both in the legislature from 1984 and then as 3d District congressman, elected in 1992 and 1994. Hutchinson's conservative voting record would ordinarily have made him a favorite for reelection in a state that voted 51%–46% for George W. Bush. But in June 1999, Hutchinson filed for divorce from his wife of 29 years, and in August 2000, he married Randi Fredholm, a former member of his House staff. For some senators, this would not have hurt politically. But for a Christian conservative, who criticized Bill Clinton strongly during the impeachment crisis, it was a severe handicap.

Pryor never mentioned Hutchinson's divorce and remarriage and instructed his pollster not to ask questions about them. When asked about Hutchinson's marital problems, he said, "They are what they are. Let the voters decide." But one recurrent theme in his campaign was "Tim Hutchinson has changed"—even though Hutchinson's positions on issues had not changed much, if at all. "Pryor isn't dishonest, he's just sly," Will Saletan wrote in *Slate*. Of the two candidates, he wrote, "Pryor is the more natural aggressor." Pryor campaigned as a supporter of Second Amendment rights, repeal of the estate tax, increased military spending and, in October, of the Iraq war resolution. In 1998, he ran as a "pro-choice" candidate, but in 2002, he emphasized his belief that abortion was wrong except in cases of rape, incest or saving the life of the mother. But he avoided saying whether or not *Roe v. Wade* should be overturned. As *National Journal* put it, "He tempered his previous support for abortion rights, muddling the issue to the point where his stand is unclear; it appears that he supports abortion rights, but with limitations." He attacked Hutchinson for working for special interests, especially the pharmaceutical companies, and for supporting plans that would risk Social Security benefits; he said he was "way too conservative" for Arkansas. But he carefully avoided identification with the national Democratic party, and he made a point of being unavailable and elsewhere when Bill Clinton paid visits to the state.

Pryor's ads were some of the most artful of the 2002 cycle. One showed him, his wife and their two children saying grace before a meal. Then Pryor, holding a Bible, said "The most important lessons in life are in this book right here." The impression was apparently not misleading: The Pryors belong to an evangelical church in Little Rock and sent their children to a private Christian school. He turned down an invitation to appear with Hutchinson on *Meet the Press*, explaining that voters wouldn't be able to watch "because they're in church Sunday morning." In another ad, Jill Pryor says laughingly, "I love my husband, but he's cheap." "You know me as Arkansas Attorney General, but I'm also my father's son," said Pryor, in one ad showing him with his father. He explained that not every Democratic idea is good and not every Republican idea is bad. He asked a meeting of municipal leaders in June to pray for George W. Bush. "I think he has done a pretty good job on the war on terrorism. He has a tremendous burden, an inhuman burden."

Against these ads, the Hutchinson ads showing his walking the halls on Capitol Hill or even those showing him playing with his three-year-old grandson were no match. George W. Bush's visits to Arkansas to campaign for Hutchinson did not succeed, as they did in other southern states, in nationalizing the race. During the campaign Randi Hutchinson said, "I just think when a person goes into the voting booth, they look at issues that affect them and not someone else's personal life." But Pryor pulled ahead in polls in mid-year and never really fell behind. On the Sunday before the election, a story broke that the Pryors had employed an illegal immigrant. Pryor campaign aides found the woman that night; they persuaded her to sign an affidavit that she had been asked whether she was a legal immigrant and had said she was, and provided documents proving that. They went over to her house and photocopied a Social Security and regular resident card and provided them to the press. Two days after the election, the woman told Little Rock's *El Latino* that she had signed the affidavit under pressure and denied that she had provided documents to the Pryors when she was hired. The story seems to have had little effect, and the generally anti-Democratic *Arkansas Democrat-Gazette* treated it lightly. In any case, Pryor won 54%–46%, a solid victory in a year when Democrats lost their majority in the Senate. A survey by pollster John Zogby showed that 12% said Hutchinson's divorce affected their vote—enough by itself to explain his drop from 53% in 1996 to 46% in 2002. Hutchinson's losses were particularly great in his home area. In 1996, he had won 65%–35% in the current 3d Congressional District, with nearly a 61,000-vote majority, more than the 45,000 by which he carried the state. In 2002, he carried the 3d District by only 56%–44%, with a 24,000-vote majority (even though the off-year turnout in 2002 was nearly as high as the presidential year turnout in 1996), while losing the state by a 62,000-vote majority. Similarly, Hutchinson carried the Little Rock metro area by 9,000 in 1996 and lost it by 19,000 in 2002. Pryor won by making inroads in Hutchinson's base—or Hutchinson lost by squandering his home-base advantage.

FIRST DISTRICT

Rep. Marion Berry (D)

Elected 1996, 4th term; b. Aug. 27, 1942, Bayou Meto; home, Gillett; U. of AR, B.S. 1965; Methodist; married (Carolyn).

Professional Career: Pharmacist, 1965–67; farmer, 1968–present; AR Soil & Water Conservation Comm., 1986–94, Chmn. 1992; Special Asst. to the Pres., Domestic Policy Cncl., White House, 1993–96.

DC Office: 1113 LHOB 20515, 202-225-4076; Fax: 202-225-5602; Web site: www.house.gov/berry.

District Offices: Cabot, 501-843-3043; Jonesboro, 870-972-4600; Mountain Home, 870-425-3510.

Committees: *Appropriations* (29th of 29 D): Energy & Water Development; Homeland Security.

Group Ratings

	ADA	ACLU	AFS	LCV	CON	ITIC	NTU	COC	ACU	NTLC	CHC
2002	70	40	89	25	63	62	27	50	32	31	58
2001	60	—	100	50	—	—	31	43	52	—	—

National Journal Ratings

	2001 LIB	—	2001 CONS	2002 LIB	—	2002 CONS
Economic	57%	—	44%	57%	—	42%
Social	47%	—	53%	53%	—	46%
Foreign	56%	—	41%	60%	—	39%

Key Votes of the 107th Congress

1. Approve Bush Tax Cuts	N	5. Faith-Based Charities	N	9. Trade Promotion Authority	N
2. Limit Patients' Bill of Rights	N	6. Bar Gays in the Boy Scouts	Y	10. Bar Funds for Intl. Court	Y
3. Campaign Finance Reform	Y	7. Ban Partial-Birth Abortion	Y	11. Authorize Force in Iraq	Y
4. Ban ANWR Development	N	8. Arm Commercial Pilots	Y	12. Deny Home. Sec. Dept. Union	N

Election Results

2002 general	Marion Berry (D)	129,701	(67%)	($1,315,408)
	Tommy Robinson (R)	64,357	(33%)	($142,244)
2002 primary	Marion Berry (D)	unopposed		
2000 general	Marion Berry (D)	120,266	(60%)	($1,169,274)
	Susan Myshka (R)	79,437	(40%)	($298,491)

Prior Winning Percentages: 1998 (100%); 1996 (53%)

The People		Race/Ethnic Origin	Ancestry	
Area size:	17,521 sq. mi.	80.2% White	USA: 15.3%	Irish: 7.5%
Urban population:	44.5%	16.6% Black	German: 6.8%	
Rural population:	55.5%	0.3% Asian	**2000 Presidential Vote**	
Pop. 2000:	668,360	0.4% Native Am.	Gore (D)...............109,160	(50%)
Median income:	$28,940	0.0% Hawaiian	Bush (R)...............105,547	(48%)
Poverty status:	18.5%	0.9% Two+ races	Other....................5,482	(2%)
Military veterans:	13.8%	0.0% Other	**Cook Partisan Voting Index:** D + 1	
		1.6% Hispanic Origin		

Occupation	Blue collar: 35.0%	White collar: 48.8%	Gray collar: 16.2%

The Mississippi Delta, the flat, mushy, river-crossed lowland on both sides of the great river, was some of the country's first industrial farmland. This land was uncultivated in most of the 19th Century, when plows were still pulled by mules and muddy flatlands were impassable. Then, about a century ago, big landowners used machines to drain the marshlands and persuaded poor blacks to move here to tend fields of cotton, rice, and later, soybeans. The results were bountiful agriculture and impoverished people. Around 1940, the Delta began to change slowly: the first minimum wage and war industry jobs up North drew young people out of the Delta and the mechanical cotton picker forced many off the farms. But this land—stretching flat as far as the eye can see, past rows of telephone poles and ribbons of asphalt that shimmer in the heat—remains poor by national standards and the people are undereducated and underemployed. Local rice farmers are among the largest recipients of federal farm subsidies: three farms in Arkansas and Phillips County were among the top five subsidy farms in the country received $105 million from 1996–2001. The local rice fields also attract enough ducks to make Arkansas the nation's most productive for mallard hunters.

The 1st Congressional District includes most of Arkansas's Delta lands and stretches west to the cool green Ozarks. The largest city in the district is Jonesboro, whose cheap labor and flat land has made it an industrial hub for food-processing companies like Nestle and Frito-Lay. The Delta started off heavily Democratic, while some of the hill counties are ancestrally Republican. That changed as partisan preferences oscillated wildly just after the civil rights revolution, but the district returned to its historical norm by the late 1980s. In 1992, Delta counties voted up to

69% for Bill Clinton, among his best county percentages in the country. But Al Gore narrowly won the 1st District, as this rural area, like so many others, moved away from Democrats and toward George W. Bush.

The congressman from the 1st District is Marion Berry, a Democrat who was first elected in 1996. Berry grew up in Bayou Meto in Arkansas County in the Delta. He earned a pharmacy degree in Little Rock, then ran a pharmacy for two years, and has been a family farmer since 1968, with a net worth of more than $1 million; he and his family have received roughly $1 million in federal farm subsides since 1996. Governor Clinton appointed him to the Arkansas Soil & Water Conservation Commission in 1986, and President Clinton appointed him White House liaison to the Agriculture Department in 1993. Berry returned to Arkansas in 1996, after Congresswoman Blanche Lincoln announced she would not run for re-election because she was pregnant with twins. (In 1998, after a safe delivery, she ran for the Senate and won.) Berry had tough opposition for the seat. Against Tom Donaldson, a 28-year-old deputy prosecutor in Crittenden County who spent little money but ran rural radio ads criticizing Berry for accepting farm subsidies, Berry won the primary runoff by only 52%–48%. In the general, Berry faced Republican Warren Dupwe, a former Jonesboro city attorney. They sparred over Medicare; both candidates opposed abortion rights and gun control and favored a balanced budget. Berry's Washington contacts proved more generous than Dupwe's; Berry outspent him nearly 2–1. In a district that has never elected a Republican, Berry won 53%–44%.

Berry has held seats on the Agriculture and Transportation committees—good spots for a constituency-oriented member in a farming district in a state with notoriously bad roads; in the 108th Congress he attained a much sought-after slot on Appropriations. His voting record is moderate to liberal; a Blue Dog Democrat, he supported the balanced budget amendment and said he wanted to pay off the national debt and save Social Security and Medicare. With his background, Berry was a natural as co-founder of the Prescription Drug Task Force and he has pursued his interest in health care. He complained that Republicans put in loopholes to his proposal to allow the re-importation of prescription drugs from other nations. He criticized the Republicans' plan to cover prescription drugs for seniors though, like other Democrats, he failed to offer a complete alternative of his own. And he lambasted his former co-sponsor Charlie Norwood for abandoning their proposal for HMO regulation under pressure from the Bush White House. On behalf of local catfish farmers, he charged that catfish from Vietnam are contaminated by the defoliant Agent Orange and he tried unsuccessfully to limit Vietnamese imports. Berry voted for PNTR with China in 2000, but he voted against trade promotion authority in 2001 and 2002. He visited Cuba with Lincoln to promote an end to the trade embargo, so that Arkansas farmers could sell rice and feed products there. He actively supported the nuclear waste depository in Yucca Mountain in Nevada, and argued that otherwise nuclear waste from two local Entergy reactors could be dumped into the Arkansas River.

Berry declined to oppose Senator Tim Hutchinson after Mark Pryor got into the race in 2001 and declined to run against Governor Mike Huckabee; health and family responsibilities were factors, he said. Instead, he was challenged for reelection by former Congressman Tommy Robinson, once the controversial Sheriff in Little Rock's Pulaski County, who served three terms in the House from the 2d District before losing in the 1990 Republican primary for governor. Robinson attacked Berry for not supporting George W. Bush in the war on terrorism and for trying to buy black votes, but his candidacy fell flat. He was little known in the 1st District, and Clinton campaigned for Berry, who largely ignored Robinson's vituperative attacks. Robinson was competitive only in the western part of the district; Berry won 67%–33%, carrying all but two counties.

SECOND DISTRICT

Rep. Vic Snyder (D)

Elected 1996, 4th term; b. Sept. 27, 1947, Medford, OR; home, Little Rock; Willamette U., B.A. 1975, U. of OR, M.D. 1979, U. of AR, J.D. 1988; Methodist; single.

Military Career: Marine Corps, 1967–69 (Vietnam).

Elected Office: AR Senate, 1990–96.

Professional Career: Practicing physician, 1982–present.

DC Office: 1330 LHOB 20515, 202-225-2506; Fax: 202-225-5903; Web site: www.house.gov/snyder.

District Office: Little Rock, 501-324-5941.

Committees: *Armed Services* (9th of 29 D): Readiness; Total Force (RMM). *Veterans' Affairs* (5th of 14 D): Health.

Group Ratings

	ADA	ACLU	AFS	LCV	CON	ITIC	NTU	COC	ACU	NTLC	CHC
2002	80	71	89	38	43	88	24	60	12	17	8
2001	85	—	90	79	—	—	19	38	13	—	—

National Journal Ratings

	2001 LIB	—	2001 CONS		2002 LIB	—	2002 CONS
Economic	68%	—	33%		59%	—	40%
Social	62%	—	39%		63%	—	35%
Foreign	60%	—	41%		66%	—	33%

Key Votes of the 107th Congress

1. Approve Bush Tax Cuts	N	5. Faith-Based Charities	N	9. Trade Promotion Authority	Y
2. Limit Patients' Bill of Rights	N	6. Bar Gays in the Boy Scouts	Y	10. Bar Funds for Intl. Court	N
3. Campaign Finance Reform	Y	7. Ban Partial-Birth Abortion	N	11. Authorize Force in Iraq	N
4. Ban ANWR Development	Y	8. Arm Commercial Pilots	N	12. Deny Home. Sec. Dept. Union	N

Election Results

2002 general	Vic Snyder (D)	142,752	(93%)	($440,566)
	Ed Garner (Write-in)	10,874	(7%)	
2002 primary	Vic Snyder (D)	55,098	(72%)	
	Jim Baker (D)	21,033	(28%)	
2000 general	Vic Snyder (D)	126,957	(58%)	($623,489)
	Bob Thomas (R)	93,692	(42%)	($261,200)

Prior Winning Percentages: 1998 (58%); 1996 (52%)

The People		Race/Ethnic Origin	Ancestry	
Area size:	6,045 sq. mi.	75.6% White	USA: 11.7%	German: 8.4%
Urban population:	66.2%	19.4% Black	Irish: 7.9%	
Rural population:	33.8%	0.9% Asian	**2000 Presidential Vote**	
Pop. 2000:	666,058	0.4% Native Am.	Bush (R) ... 116,075 (49%)	
Median income:	$37,221	0.0% Hawaiian	Gore (D) ... 112,720 (48%)	
Poverty status:	12.7%	1.1% Two+ races	Other ... 6,817 (3%)	
Military veterans:	14.5%	0.1% Other	**Cook Partisan Voting Index:** R + 1	
		2.4% Hispanic Origin		

Occupation	Blue collar: 25.0%	White collar: 60.5%	Gray collar: 14.5%

Little Rock has been the capital, largest city and central focus of Arkansas for more than a century. It is one of those capitals located at its state's geographical center and, in a state that has no other metropolis, it stands out. For a long moment, Little Rock became internationally famous. That was in September 1957, when Governor Orval Faubus, eager for a third term, sent in the National Guard to block a desegregation order at Central High School. President Eisenhower sent in U.S.

troops and federalized the National Guard to enforce the order, and Little Rock became a synonym for bigotry around the world. Forty years later, the Little Rock Nine who had integrated the high school returned for an anniversary commemoration with President Bill Clinton. "It was Little Rock that made racial equality a driving obsession in my life," he said, and added that American life still was in too many ways segregated. Also speaking was Republican Governor Mike Huckabee, who said, "Today we come to say once and for all that what happened here 40 years ago was simply wrong." Most impressive were the Little Rock Nine themselves and what these graying adults had achieved: Their occupations included writer, managing director of an investment bank, real estate broker, chairman of a university psychology department, magazine publisher, financial specialist for the Department of Defense, teacher, public relations specialist and journalist.

Little Rock is also the political center of Arkansas. It sets the tone of the public life of its state as do only a few other state capitals—Boston, Providence, Atlanta, Denver, Honolulu. Little Rock is home to the *Arkansas Democrat-Gazette*, the feisty, conservative paper whose editor Paul Greenberg christened Clinton "Slick Willie." It is home to the state government, to Jack Stephens' Worthen Bank investment firm, Dillards department stores, the TCBY yogurt chain, Excelsior Hotel, and the now long-defunct Madison Guaranty Savings & Loan. Little Rock may not be upscale by national standards, but it is in Arkansas.

The 2d Congressional District includes Little Rock, with its large black and affluent white neighborhoods, and North Little Rock, a kind of industrial suburb across the Arkansas River known informally for years as Dog Town. It also includes surrounding counties that have grown rapidly as people move farther out on the freeways, and a couple of small hill counties. On the east bank of the Arkansas River is the site of the President William J. Clinton Presidential Library Complex, which will include an apartment for Clinton; conflicts over the location plus fundraising problems delayed the scheduled completion date until late 2004, but local interests expect a commercial boon. In the 1990s, the Little Rock area was trending Republican, and fast-growing Saline County to the southwest was heavily Republican. But in 2000, Pulaski County voted for Al Gore, and in 2002, it voted for Democrats Mark Pryor and Jimmie Lou Fisher for senator and governor. This makes for a closely divided congressional district: In 2000, Bill Clinton's old home district voted for George W. Bush by 49%–48%.

The congressman from the 2d District is Vic Snyder, a Democrat first elected in 1996. He has held the seat longer than any member since legendary Ways and Means chairman Wilbur Mills, who served 38 years and retired in 1976. Snyder is an unusual politician, "an inveterately private man in a public profession, quite content to be all alone," wrote the *Arkansas Democrat-Gazette*'s Michael Leahy. He grew up fatherless in Medford, Oregon, dropped out of Willamette University, and at 20 signed up in the Marine Corps and served in Vietnam. Then he returned to Oregon for college and medical school, became a practicing physician, and went on medical missions in Thailand, Honduras, Sierra Leone and Sudan. He got a law degree, but never practiced law. In 1990, he was elected to the state Senate and made news when he called for repeal of Arkansas's anti-sodomy law and when he refused to accept a pension.

When the incumbent retired in 1996, Snyder, consulting no one, decided to run for Congress. He campaigned as a reformer, promising not to accept a congressional pension until the establishment of an equitable system for federal employees. His main Democratic opponents had more political backgrounds, but in a 51%–49% upset, Snyder won the June runoff over Pulaski County prosecutor Mark Stodola, who was a strong Clinton supporter. Against Republican lawyer Bud Cummins, Snyder continued to sound reform themes while outspending him. Snyder won narrowly, 52%–48%.

Snyder's voting record is close to the center of the House Democrats, which is liberal for this district. He voted against the partial-birth abortion ban and for needle exchanges. But Snyder has bragged of supporting more moderate measures—the balanced budget, tax cuts, a strong education system—and has stressed his military record and service on the Armed Services Committee. He helped to organize the bipartisan Cuba working group to push the House to end the trade embargo of Cuba and the ban on travel there; he was the only Democrat from Arkansas to vote for trade promotion authority in 2001 and 2002. He criticized the Bush administration for failure to provide increased security for embassies overseas and was the only Arkansas member to vote against authorizing Bush to use military force against Iraq. Snyder has been active on internal House issues: He unsuccessfully sought changes in Democratic rules to spread committee assignments more equitably among members. In July 2002, he challenged as a possible violation of the House's anti-bribery rule the practice of interest groups that notify members that they will include an upcoming vote in their legislative scorecard. And he spoke out against members who wanted to give governors power to appoint new House members in the event of a catastrophic attack on the Capitol.

Snyder's initial election was followed by two reelections by 58%–42% margins. Although the *Democrat-Gazette* editorially disparages him as "Saint Vic" because of his sometimes iconoclastic views, no Republican filed to run against him in 2002; he easily won his primary. He seems to have made this marginal district a safe seat.

THIRD DISTRICT

Rep. John Boozman (R)

Elected Nov. 2001, 1st term; b. Dec. 10, 1950, Shreveport, LA; home, Rogers; U. of AR, 1969–72, Southern Col. of Optometry, O.D. 1977; Baptist; married (Cathy).

Professional Career: Optometrist, 1977–01.

DC Office: 1708 LHOB 20515, 202-225-4301; Fax: 202-225-5713; Web site: www.house.gov/boozman/.

District Offices: Fayetteville, 479-442-5258; Ft. Smith, 479-782-7787; Harrison, 870-741-6900.

Committees: *Transportation & Infrastructure* (32d of 41 R): Aviation; Highways, Transit & Pipelines; Water Resources & Environment. *Veterans' Affairs* (12th of 17 R): Health; Oversight & Investigations.

Group Ratings (Only Served Partial Term)

	ADA	ACLU	AFS	LCV	CON	ITIC	NTU	COC	ACU	NTLC	CHC
2002	0	14	0	0	—	100	56	95	96	100	100
2001	—	—	0	0	—	—	—	100	—	—	—

National Journal Ratings (Only Served Partial Term)

	2001 LIB	—	2001 CONS		2002 LIB	—	2002 CONS
Economic	*	—	*		9%	—	87%
Social	*	—	*		0%	—	75%
Foreign	*	—	*		35%	—	60%

Key Votes of the 107th Congress (Only Served Partial Term)

1. Approve Bush Tax Cuts	*	5. Faith-Based Charities	*	9. Trade Promotion Authority	Y
2. Limit Patients' Bill of Rights	*	6. Bar Gays in the Boy Scouts	*	10. Bar Funds for Intl. Court	Y
3. Campaign Finance Reform	N	7. Ban Partial-Birth Abortion	Y	11. Authorize Force in Iraq	Y
4. Ban ANWR Development	*	8. Arm Commercial Pilots	Y	12. Deny Home. Sec. Dept. Union	Y

Election Results

2002 general	John Boozman (R)	141,478	(99%)	($651,062)
2002 primary	John Boozman (R)	unopposed		
2001 special	John Boozman (R)	53,308	(56%)	($460,665)
	Mike Hathorn (D)	40,237	(42%)	($584,090)
2001 spec. runoff	John Boozman (R)	19,583	(57%)	
	Gunner DeLay (R)	15,029	(43%)	

The People		Race/Ethnic Origin	Ancestry	
Area size:	8,661 sq. mi.	87.3% White	USA: 11.8%	German: 10.0%
Urban population:	54.4%	2.0% Black	Irish: 8.8%	
Rural population:	45.6%	1.4% Asian	**2000 Presidential Vote**	
Pop. 2000:	672,756	1.2% Native Am.	Bush (R).............138,977 (60%)	
Median income:	$33,915	0.2% Hawaiian	Gore (D)..............86,739 (37%)	
Poverty status:	13.7%	1.6% Two+ races	Other....................7,691 (3%)	
Military veterans:	14.3%	0.1% Other	**Cook Partisan Voting Index:** R +12	
		6.3% Hispanic Origin		

Occupation	Blue collar: 32.0%	White collar: 53.0%	Gray collar: 14.9%

The northwest corner of Arkansas has become one of America's boom areas, with major corporate headquarters and dozens of small factories, tourist attractions and retirement developments in the Ozarks, some of America's richest families and growing numbers of hard-working Hispanic immigrants—about 20% of the population of Springdale and Rogers in 2000. It is home to the handsome University of Arkansas in Fayetteville, the mountain-bound resort town of Eureka Springs and the Northwest Arkansas Regional Airport, opened in 1998, only the second major new airport in the country since 1972. All this would have seemed unlikely during most of the 20th century, when these rounded green mountains and pleasant wide valleys, farmhouses and small towns seemed left behind. But the friendly atmosphere and strong religious faith of these communities have proved to be assets, not liabilities, conducive to economic creativity and personal serenity. There have also been touches of genius. Sam Walton, who opened his first Wal-Mart on the town square of Bentonville (it's now a small museum), had the inspiration to build a retail chain in tradition-minded small towns and rural areas using sophisticated computerized management; it made him the richest man in America, though he still drove a pickup truck and kept the corporate headquarters in Bentonville. Don Tyson took his family chicken business and made Tyson Foods, in its sparkling headquarters outside Springdale, the nation's leading chicken producer and processor.

The 3d Congressional District covers Northwest Arkansas, including Bentonville, Fayetteville and Springdale, plus Fort Smith on the Oklahoma line. It extends as far east as Marion County, home to Ranger Boats, the renowned manufacturer of tournament-quality fishing boats. Its 30% population increase in the 1990s far exceeded the state's other districts; with Wal-Mart serving as a corporate magnet, Bentonville was among the nation's six fastest-growing metropolitan areas in the 1990s. Some of these mountain counties have been Republican since the Civil War, for there were few slaves here and much suspicion of planters; others started leaning Republican in the 1950s, and a Republican congressman, John Paul Hammerschmidt, was elected here in 1966. He was strong enough even in Democratic 1974 to beat Bill Clinton, then 28, in his first election, though Clinton did get an impressive 48%. Lately this area has become even more Republican, as Christian conservatives have entered politics and new migrants and millionaires have voted heavily Republican. After voting narrowly for Clinton in 1992 and narrowly against him in 1996, the 3d voted for George W. Bush 60%–37% in 2000.

The congressman from the 3d District is John Boozman (it's pronounced like Bozeman, Montana), a Republican who won a special election in November 2001. He replaced Asa Hutchinson, who had resigned in August to head the Drug Enforcement Administration and later was named by George W. Bush to a top post in the Department of Homeland Security. A graduate of the University of Arkansas, where he was an offensive guard for the football team, Boozman became an optometrist in Rogers, part of rapidly-growing Benton County. He served two terms on the local school board, and he worked for his brother Fay's unsuccessful campaign for the U.S. Senate in 1998.

To win the House seat, Boozman prevailed in three close contests in two months. In the wide-open primary, Boozman had the endorsement of Governor Mike Huckabee and was the only Republican to support George W. Bush's decision to permit limited federal funding of stem-cell research. His chief opponent initially, former state Representative Jim Hendren, was damaged by revelations that he had a lengthy extramarital affair; Boozman ended up in a runoff against state

Senator Gunner DeLay, who raised little funds and had little support from local politicians (but is the cousin of then-House Majority Whip Tom DeLay, who stayed neutral). In the three-week runoff, neither candidate spent heavily and turnout remained low. With a stronger grass-roots organization, Boozman won 57%–43%. The winner of the Democratic runoff was state Representative Mike Hathorn, a 28-year-old lawyer who, local Democrats hoped, could prevail with his Clinton-like personality. But House Democrats did little to help his campaign and only in the closing days of the campaign ran TV and radio ads that criticized Boozman's support for Social Security "privatization" and, despite his endorsement by the NRA, his allegedly weak support of the right to bear arms. Boozman ran ads emphasizing his "guarantee" of Social Security benefits. He won 56%–42%, with help from a sophisticated Republican voter-turnout operation.

Boozman won seats on Transportation and the Veterans' Affairs Committee; he was appointed to the Republican task force that prepared a bill for prescription drugs for seniors. With Roy Blunt of Missouri, he created a water quality committee to get money from the Environmental Protection Agency for the White and Elk Rivers, both vital to local tourism and economic development. He showed his independence of the White House by voting to remove the embargo on trade with Cuba. He also sponsored bills to abolish the tax code and to display the Ten Commandments in the House and Senate chambers.

No Democrat filed to run against Boozman in 2002. After the defeat of Senator Tim Hutchinson, he remained the only Republican in the Arkansas delegation, ensconced in a safe seat.

FOURTH DISTRICT

Rep. Mike Ross (D)

Elected 2000, 2d term; b. Aug. 2, 1961, Texarkana; home, Prescott; U. of AR, B.A. 1987; Methodist; married (Holly).

Elected Office: AR Senate, 1990–2000.

Professional Career: Chief of Staff, AR Lt. Gov. Winston Bryant, 1984–89; Owner, Holly's Health Mart, 1993-present.

DC Office: 314 CHOB 20515, 202-225-3772; Fax: 202-225-1314; Web site: www.house.gov/ross.

District Offices: El Dorado, 870-881-0681; Hot Springs, 501-520-5892; Pine Bluff, 870-536-3376; Prescott, 870-887-6787.

Committees: *Agriculture* (10th of 24 D): General Farm Commodities & Risk Management; Livestock & Horticulture (RMM). *Financial Services* (24th of 32 D): Capital Markets, Insurance & Government Sponsored Enterprises; Financial Institutions & Consumer Credit.

Group Ratings

	ADA	ACLU	AFS	LCV	CON	ITIC	NTU	COC	ACU	NTLC	CHC
2002	65	60	89	38	8	38	27	55	32	22	42
2001	65	—	90	43	—	—	23	48	36	—	—

National Journal Ratings

	2001 LIB	—	2001 CONS		2002 LIB	—	2002 CONS
Economic	56%	—	45%		55%	—	45%
Social	54%	—	45%		49%	—	50%
Foreign	56%	—	41%		64%	—	36%

Key Votes of the 107th Congress

1. Approve Bush Tax Cuts	Y	5. Faith-Based Charities	N	9. Trade Promotion Authority	N
2. Limit Patients' Bill of Rights	N	6. Bar Gays in the Boy Scouts	Y	10. Bar Funds for Intl. Court	Y
3. Campaign Finance Reform	Y	7. Ban Partial-Birth Abortion	Y	11. Authorize Force in Iraq	Y
4. Ban ANWR Development	N	8. Arm Commercial Pilots	Y	12. Deny Home. Sec. Dept. Union	N

Election Results

2002 general	Mike Ross (D)	119,633	(61%)	($2,050,221)
	Jay Dickey (R)	77,904	(39%)	($2,029,545)
2002 primary	Mike Ross (D)	unopposed		
2000 general	Mike Ross (D)	108,143	(51%)	($1,626,164)
	Jay Dickey (R)	104,017	(49%)	($1,786,307)

The People		Race/Ethnic Origin	Ancestry	
Area size:	20,951 sq. mi.	71.0% White	USA: 14.0%	Irish: 7.3%
Urban population:	44.7%	24.4% Black	English: 5.7%	
Rural population:	55.3%	0.4% Asian	**2000 Presidential Vote**	
Pop. 2000:	666,226	0.5% Native Am.	Gore (D)..............114,149	(49%)
Median income:	$29,675	0.0% Hawaiian	Bush (R)..............112,341	(48%)
Poverty status:	18.5%	0.9% Two + races	Other....................6,083	(3%)
Military veterans:	13.9%	0.0% Other	**Cook Partisan Voting Index:** D + 0	
		2.7% Hispanic Origin		

Occupation	Blue collar: 34.9%	White collar: 47.8%	Gray collar: 17.2%

West from the Delta flatlands along the Mississippi River, where the water-soaked fields produce America's largest rice crop, across small cities with antique pasts like Pine Bluff and El Dorado, southern Arkansas runs west to the Ouachita Mountains and the border town of Texarkana, where the main street divides two states and Texan Ross Perot grew up five blocks west of Arkansas. This is the northwestern corner of the Deep South. It includes the state's largest black population, a reminder that parts of southern Arkansas were once plantation country; there is also oil production, a reminder that this is the beginning of the Southwest. The broiler chicken industry looms large in these parts, and the accent is clearly Arkansan: El Dorado, Nevada and Lafayette are all pronounced with long *A*s and penultimate syllable accents, and Ouachita is, with a bow to the original French rendition of the Indian name, *waSHEEta*. The district also includes the little railroad-crossing, county seat town of Hope, where President Bill Clinton and his first White House Chief of Staff Mack McLarty were classmates at Miss Mary's kindergarten, and where Governor Mike Huckabee grew up a decade later; and Hot Springs, the spa resort and gambling haven where Clinton's stepfather sold Buicks, his mother bet on the horses, and he excelled in high school as he began his climb from southern Arkansas obscurity to world prominence.

The 4th Congressional District occupies almost all of the southern geographical half of Arkansas, from the Mississippi River to the Ouachita Mountains, the Delta to Texarkana. Redistricting in 2002 added three mountainous counties in the northwest corner. It is historically a Democratic district, and one that for most of the 20th century elected young men to the House and kept them there for years, to cut deals with the Democratic leadership and bring home the bacon. During the 1990s, it had a very different congressional politics: Bipartisan, with rancorous debates on national issues followed by narrow election victories. But this may be one part of the South returning to its heritage.

The congressman from the 4th District is Mike Ross, a Democrat who in 2000 defeated four-term Republican Jay Dickey, the only House Republican outside California who was defeated that year. A fifth-generation Arkansan, Ross was born in Texarkana. He graduated from Hope High School and from the University of Arkansas at Little Rock. He got his start in local politics in 1982 as a travel aide for Bill Clinton's successful bid to recover from his 1980 loss and recapture the governorship. Then, while in college, he served on the staff of Lieutenant Governor Winston Bryant and was executive director of the Arkansas Youth Suicide Prevention Commission. Ross also sold insurance and worked as a sales manager for a pharmaceutical company. He owns Holly's Health Mart in rural Prescott, where he lives with his wife Holly, who is the store's pharmacist. He was elected to the state Senate in 1990 and served for a decade until term limits forced him out; then he ran for Congress.

This was perhaps the only district in the nation where impeachment played a pivotal role in 2000. Dickey, representing Bill Clinton's boyhood homes, had voted for impeachment, and Clinton vowed to get back at him. Both candidates raised more than $1 million; Republicans criticized

Ross for raising nearly half of his money from political action committees. Ross portrayed himself as a small-town guy who found himself pitted against his own pharmaceutical industry in his fight to lower prescription drug prices and stop telemarketing harassment. Although Dickey often was a thorn in the Republican leadership's side, Ross hitched him to the Republican leadership and argued that "the real Jay Dickey" voted to cut Medicare and Social Security to fund tax cuts for the rich. Dickey responded that Ross was getting his script from "his liberal masters in Washington." Clinton had an impact: He helped raise $300,000 for Ross at fundraisers, orchestrated endorsements from administration officials with Arkansas roots, and campaigned for Ross in Pine Bluff on the Sunday before the election. There were plenty of independent expenditures as well, by pharmaceutical groups against Ross and by labor unions against Dickey. Ross won, 51%–49%, with an especially big 58%–42% margin in Pine Bluff and Jefferson County. Dickey ran best in El Dorado and Hot Springs.

In the House, Ross joined the Blue Dogs and he became a vocal proponent of prescription drug legislation, often citing his experiences as a small-town pharmacist. On the Financial Services Committee, he got approval in 2002 of his proposal to remove Arkansas's constitutional limit on interest rates, which local bankers and consumer groups agreed had made financing difficult. His action won wide support from political leaders in Arkansas, which is the only remaining state to mandate such terms. But national banking interests voiced concerns about separate aspects of his measure, and it died when Congress adjourned. Early in his first term, Ross found himself in the middle of the intense competition for Minority Whip between Nancy Pelosi and Steny Hoyer. As reported by *The Washington Post*, he backed off an initial pledge to back Hoyer and simply told him, "This is awful tough for me." The next day, Ross sent a handwritten note to Hoyer that said, "I'm going to be voting for Nancy Pelosi. I'm sorry." Back home, Ross accused Huckabee of running the Delta Regional Authority as a "slush fund", but refrained from criticizing specific local projects. A Huckabee aide responded that Ross was a "jackleg first-term congressman."

Dickey decided to run again in 2002 and Ross seemed to face a serious challenge. Both candidates again raised substantial sums, but the Republican's campaign stumbled from the start. Dickey refused, as he had in the past, to accept funds from political action committees, but the Republicans' campaign committee got him to back down. Dickey constantly reminded voters that he had delivered federal money to them from his Appropriations Committee seat and carried a pledge from Speaker Dennis Hastert that he would get his seat back. Ross criticized Republican leaders for reversing after the 2000 election the appropriators' tentative decision to send $4 million to the district. Hastert defended the action, in an interview with the *Arkansas Democrat-Gazette*: "If we had a Republican in there, we could deliver the money. Jay is the one who worked for it. Ross wasn't even on the committee." In another embarrassing incident, Dickey complained to his friend Warren Stephens about news coverage in the publisher's *Pine Bluff Commercial*. The publisher's sympathetic response led the editor to resign in a well-publicized protest. National Republicans eventually lost interest in the contest.

Ross won by a convincing 61%–39% margin; Dickey carried only one county, and said that he would not run again. This seat looks unlikely to be seriously contested again any time soon.

★ CALIFORNIA ★

California is America's largest state, a nation-state really, with an economy larger than all but four nations (it passed France in 2000). It is the site of the world's most advanced cutting-edge technology, yet it is a place with plenty of Third World neighborhoods and it greeted the 21st century with Third World-like rolling blackouts of electricity. Its growth has been awesome: The 2000 Census counted 33.9 million Californians, far ahead of second-place Texas's 20.8 million; metro Los Angeles had 16.4 million people, second only to metro New York's 21.2 million, and the San Francisco Bay area had 7 million, not so far behind Chicagoland's 9.2 million. The Central Valley and mountain counties had 6.2 million people; if this were a separate state it would rank 14th in population, yet it has only 18% of the population of California. San Diego County, with 2.8 million people the seventh largest county in the United States, contains only 8% of Californians. California owes this preeminence not to natural advantage but to human ingenuity. Los Angeles, with little in the way of natural resources and no natural harbor, is the nation's leading port and second-biggest manufacturer, as well as the world's entertainment center. The Bay area, which once lived by exporting food, is now the world's leader in computers and high tech. California has grown not because it had to but because people wanted it to. It has not grown without contradictions. California loves its physical environment, but also has the largest urban sprawl in the United States; it likes to think of itself as the America of the future, even as it watches the electricity flicker out; it likes to see itself as the political leader of the nation, but lives now with a president who did not come close to winning here and has a public sector that in important ways—in its public schools, fiscal condition, electricity regulation—has been deeply dysfunctional. California today is solidly Democratic, well off to the left on cultural issues, secular more than religious. If it could imagine itself leading the nation when Bill Clinton was president, it is all too conscious that the nation is not following its lead now that George W. Bush has succeeded Clinton.

Most of all California has been a state that is always transforming itself, whose economy has been transformed several times over, whose population has been transformed by one group of newcomers after another and whose politics is periodically transformed with the suddenness of an earthquake. If other states have changed gradually on an analog scale over the years, California has changed sharply on a digital scale: this is quantum theory physics, not wave theory. So it has been from its American beginning. In 1848, when California passed from Mexico to the United States by the Treaty of Guadalupe Hidalgo, this was an almost entirely empty land, inhabited by a few thousand Indians and Mexicans and by a few hundred American soldiers and men on the make. Then in 1849 gold was found in Sutter's Mill and thousands arrived in the Gold Rush; within months San Francisco became one of America's 25 largest cities. The big money was made not by the miners but by the grocers and dry goods merchants who provisioned them, like the Big Four—Crocker, Hopkins, Huntington, Stanford—who built the Central and Southern Pacific Railroads. The railroads sold off vast chunks of the Central Valley to large farming operations and enticed settlers with low fares to newly-platted suburbs in the Los Angeles Basin. Engineers built great aqueducts that stretched hundreds of miles, from the Hetch Hetchy Valley in Yosemite to San Francisco and from the Owens River to Los Angeles, without which these metropolises with 23.4 million people could not exist. Early 20th century California was affluent and cultured, with great universities already, Berkeley and Stanford, and fine museums and libraries; it was America's window on the Pacific, alert to developments in China and Japan, Hawaii and the Philippines, eager to extend America's economic reach and military strength, but still, as Carey McWilliams wrote, an "island" separated from the rest of the country. Then in World War II California became one of the great defense industry states, building ships and airplanes by the thousands. Millions of Americans came here and millions stayed: The population rose from 7 million in 1940 to 17 million in 1963, when California passed New York and became the nation's most populous state.

California's future was planned by the heads of the big units of government and business—Franklin Roosevelt and Henry J. Kaiser, who built vast shipyards and steel and aluminum factories; Governor Earl Warren, who husbanded tax monies to build schools and freeways in the years after the war; Robert Sproul and Clark Kerr, who built the University of California into what Kerr

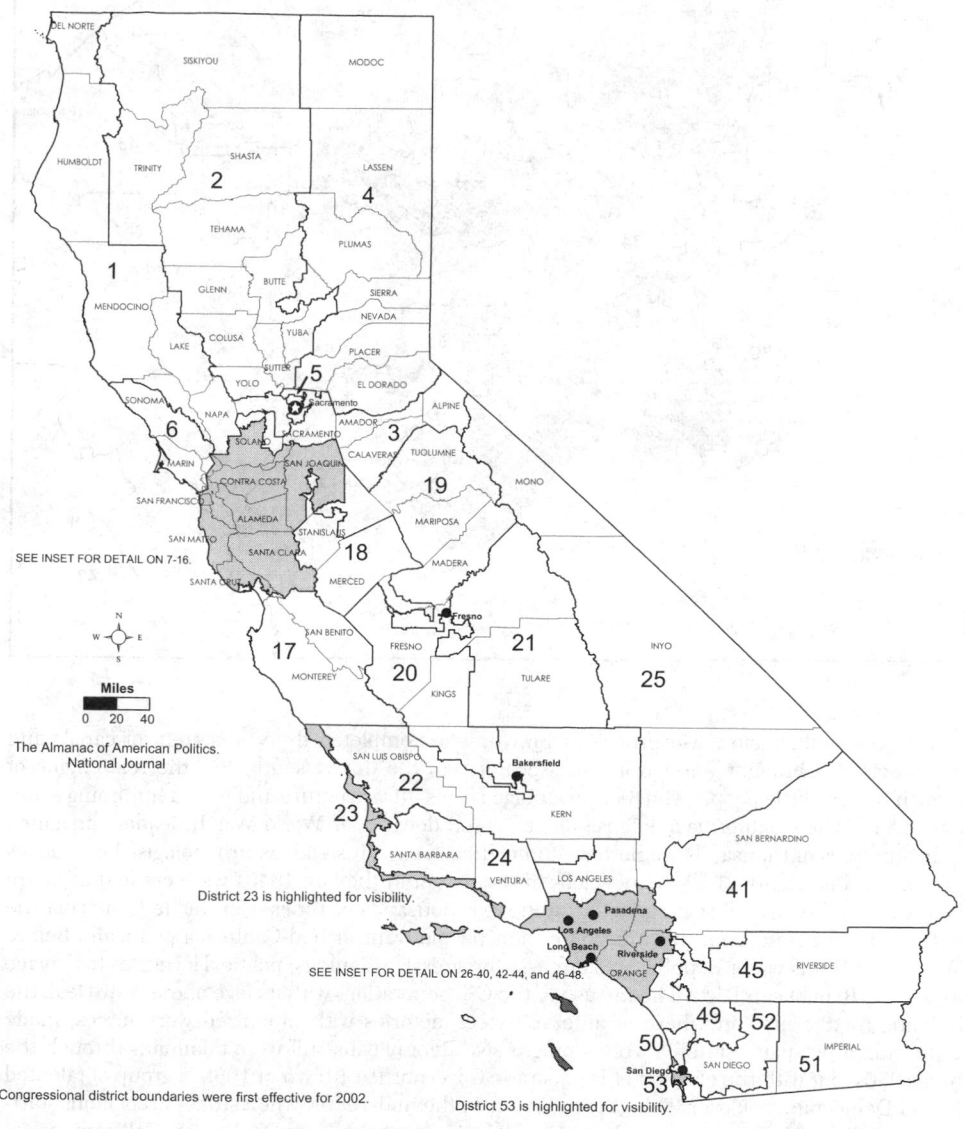

SEE INSET FOR DETAIL ON 7-16.

The Almanac of American Politics.
National Journal

District 23 is highlighted for visibility.

SEE INSET FOR DETAIL ON 26-40, 42-44, and 46-48.

Congressional district boundaries were first effective for 2002.

District 53 is highlighted for visibility.

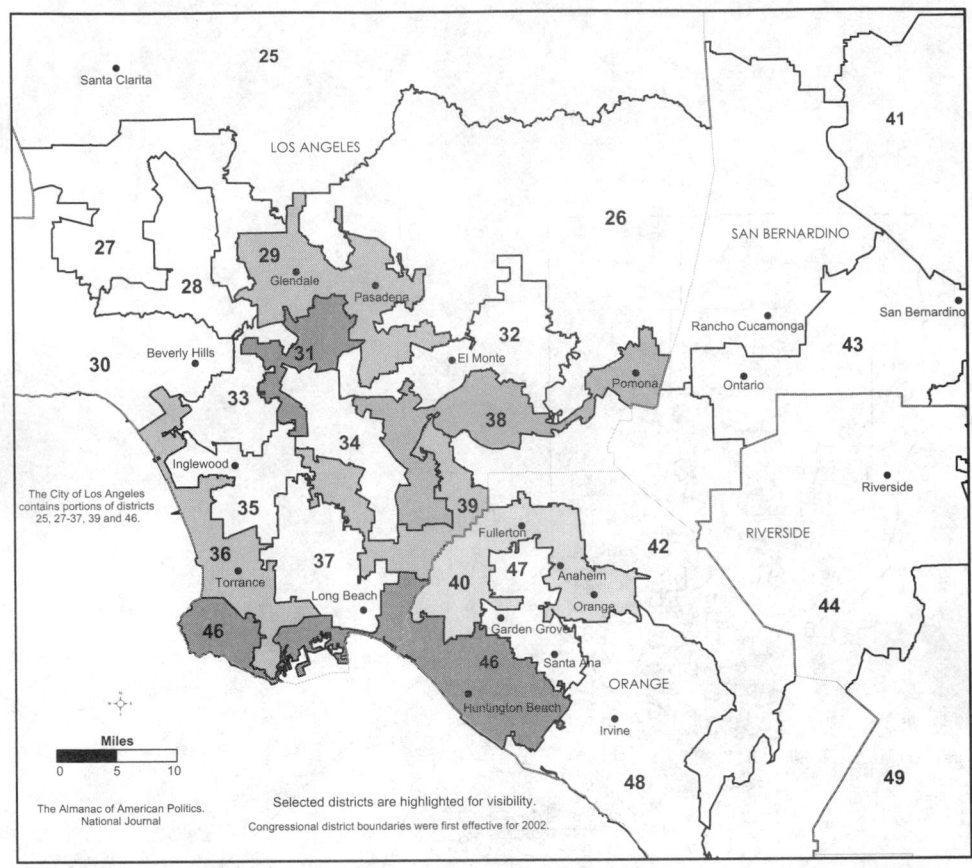

The City of Los Angeles
contains portions of districts
25, 27-37, 39 and 46.

Miles
0   5   10

The Almanac of American Politics.
National Journal

Selected districts are highlighted for visibility.
Congressional district boundaries were first effective for 2002.

called "the multiversity;" Governor Pat Brown, who completed the vast system of canals and aqueducts that brought water from the wet north to the thirsty south. But the real engine of growth was the little people who took advantage of this infrastructure and built a humming economy on it. When California's defense plants closed down after World War II, leaders imagined that hundreds of thousands would have to head back east. Instead, as urbanologist Jane Jacobs points out, one-eighth of all the new jobs in the nation in the late 1940s were created in metro Los Angeles. This small scale growth, multiplied thousands of times over, made California the nation's largest state. And this infusion of new people transformed California politically. Before World War II this was a Republican state, with progressive leanings; political struggles took place inside the Republican Party. The in-rush of the G.I. generation, with its love of the New Deal, the building for the first time here of auto and steel factories with unionized work forces, made California a two-party state. Warren's progressive Republicans still were dominant through the mid-1950s, but with the election of Democratic Governor Pat Brown in 1958, a group of talented liberal Democrats took over. Things turned sour in the mid-1960s, when student rebellions starting in Berkeley in 1964 and the Watts riot of 1965 upset the New Deal order. Californians responded by calling in a disillusioned New Dealer espousing the conformist cultural conservatism of the G.I. generation, Ronald Reagan, who presaged the course the nation would follow in the 1980s.

California veered off on a different path in the 1970s, electing Jerry Brown as governor, entranced for a time by his idiosyncratic version of Baby Boomer liberalism (though he was too old to be a Boomer himself), as the World War II generation started to die out and California

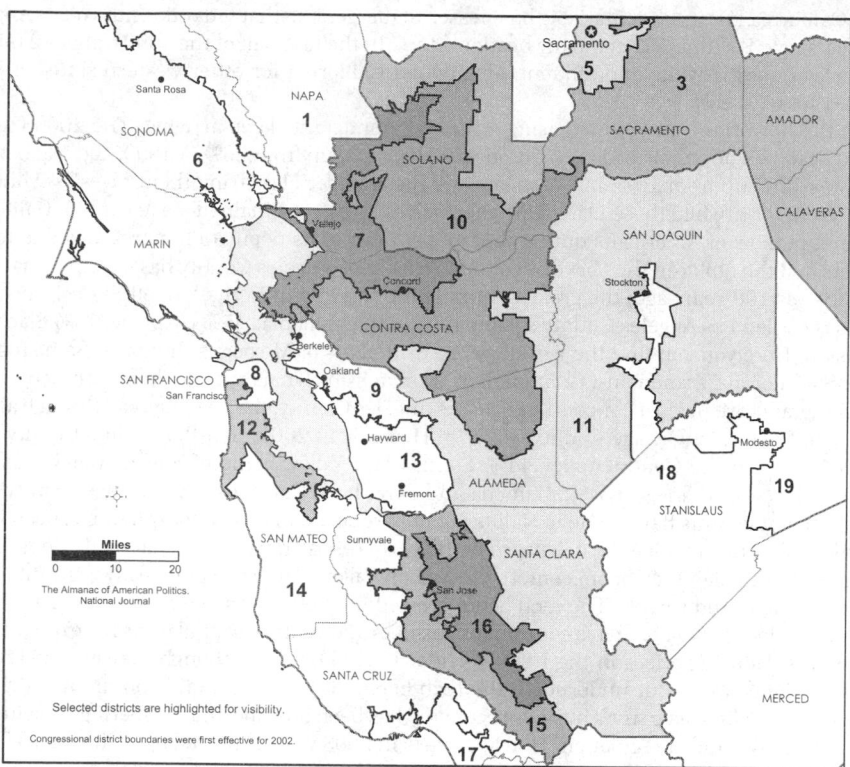

received a new infusion of migrants, well-educated whites attracted to the state's groovy lifestyle and, little noticed at first, Mexicans and other Latin Americans looking for work. Voters soon soured on Brown's liberalism: They passed Proposition 13 in 1978, banning property tax increases in a state where rapidly rising housing values were the chief source of people's wealth; they decried his spraying of Medfly-infested crops with an overly-effective insecticide that peeled paint on houses; they ousted, after he left office, three of his Supreme Court nominees who had overturned death penalty verdicts and struck down tough-on-crime laws.

With Brown gone, politics and government more or less disappeared from TV stations' newscasts and voters' minds. In the 1980s, with Reagan as president and quiet Republican George Deukmejian as governor, California's defense industry boomed and Silicon Valley flowered off I-280 south of San Francisco. Public policy was mostly set by Willie Brown, speaker of the California Assembly from 1980 to 1995 and now mayor of San Francisco, and the Democratic legislature furthered the causes of their clients—teachers' unions, trial lawyers and the criminal defense bar. The response was government by referendum, usually a clumsy matter but sometimes effective, on criminal justice, aid to immigrants, racial quotas and preferences.

In the 1990s California went through another transformation, as a series of natural disasters and a massive economic downturn drained the state of confidence and set it off in a new political direction. Defense industry cutbacks hit metropolitan Los Angeles hard, costing hundreds of thousands of jobs and sending housing values that had skyrocketed in the 1980s plummeting downward in the early 1990s. Television screens were absorbed by disasters both natural and manmade—from floods and earthquakes to riots and O.J. Simpson. Long proud of its efficient and incorruptible government, California saw it grow larger and increasingly dysfunctional, as documented by California's greatest reporter, Lou Cannon, in his book *Official Negligence*, the definitive story of the Rodney King beating, the Los Angeles riot and the trials that followed. In the

1990s California lost its trademark big businesses to mergers, so that today downtown Los Angeles has not a single Fortune 500 company headquarters. In the first half of the 1990s, about 2 million Californians, mostly white and affluent, abandoned California for other western states or went even farther back east.

In the meantime, and in increasing numbers, immigrants keep arriving. The 2000 Census showed that 32% of California's population was Hispanic, up from 26% in 1990; the Asian population was 11%, up from 10%; in the meantime the number classifying themselves as white fell to 47% from 69%, while those classifying themselves as black remained steady at 6%. California had a net outflow of Americans during the 1990s; most of its population increase is due to immigrants and the children they have once they arrive. Los Angeles County has become what New York City was 100 years ago, the greatest immigrant entry point in the United States. The 2000 Census recorded Los Angeles County's population of 9.5 million as 45% Hispanic, 10% Black and 12% Asian. Here you can find the world's largest numbers of Mexicans, Iranians, Samoans, Filipinos, Salvadorans, Armenians, Guatemalans, Koreans and Thais outside their native countries. And immigrants are not just concentrated in Los Angeles County; they have spread through almost all parts of California. Orange County was 31% Hispanic in 2000, San Bernardino County 39%, Fresno County in the Central Valley 44%. Santa Clara Valley, home of Silicon Valley, was 26% Asian in 2000, San Francisco 31%, Alameda and San Mateo Counties 20%, Orange County 14%.

These immigrants have come to California to participate in an economy that has been humming along very nicely since the downturn of the early 1990s ended. Much national attention has been given to the high-tech boom centered in Silicon Valley that for several heady years produced enormous profits and wealth. The tech boom crested in 2000, and since then share prices have plummeted, dot.coms galore have gone out of business and venture capital firms have quit making investments. Housing prices in the I-280 corridor have shot down, though they may still be the highest in the country. But underneath the tech boom, little noticed, and continuing now after the tech bust, California's small business economy has been growing and prospering, despite high taxes and heavy-handed regulation. Housing starts in 2003 were expected to be the highest since 1989. In some senses, this is a two-tier economy. California imports high-skill Americans and some foreigners—especially from Taiwan, China and India—and exports low-skill and retired Americans, and it imports very large numbers of low-skill Latinos and Asians to work in a rapidly growing service economy. This leaves a population with an income and education gap: California has more high-income people and more in poverty than anywhere else in the country; it has a higher than average percentage of people who have college degrees and people who haven't graduated from high school. But low-income people are not just hovering at the bottom; they are working their way up, or their children's. Latinos or Asians own four in ten small businesses in Los Angeles County. Statistics which show the lowest quintile of earners with barely increased incomes are misleading; today's lowest quintile of earners in California 10 years ago were living in some other country, making far less than they do now. California's population and economy are continuing to grow faster than the nation's.

How do these new Californians fit into, and affect, California politics? In the hard economic times of the early 1990s Governor Pete Wilson discovered that the state was spending billions on illegal immigrants and their children—for welfare (though Latinos in poverty apply for welfare much less than anyone else), for schools and for prison spaces. In 1994, uncertain of re-election against state Treasurer Kathleen Brown, Jerry Brown's sister, he supported Proposition 187, which denied non-emergency state government spending on illegal aliens and their children. In speeches Wilson was careful to differentiate between legal and illegal immigrants, and voters did too; at least one-third of Hispanic voters voted for 187, which passed by a wide margin. But campaign ads make a much greater impression than politicians' careful statements in a state where TV news coverage of politics and government is miniscule. Wilson's ad showing Mexicans running across the border, with the announcer proclaiming ominously, "They just keep coming," was taken by many as a slur, suggesting that all Latinos were more interested in welfare than work, which stung all the more because it is simply not true—Hispanic males have the highest work force participation rate of any measured group.

The result was that Latino turnout increased and Latinos increasingly turned to the Democratic Party. The Latino vote increased from 10% of the vote in 1994 to 14% in 1998, and Gray Davis beat Republican Dan Lungren among Hispanics by 78%–16%—a huge drop for Republicans, since Wilson got almost 40% of the Latino vote in 1990. In 2000 Hispanics again cast 14% of California's votes, and voted 68%–29% for Al Gore. The 2002 election was a different story. Hispanics cast only 10% of the votes, and voted for Davis by a reduced 65%–24% margin. The SEIU and the left-wing Organization of Los Angeles Workers registered many Latinos in 2001 to vote for Anthony Villaraigosa for Los Angeles mayor that year and Democrats thereafter; their hope is to transform Latinos into a permanent left-wing voting bloc. But Villaraigosa lost to James Hahn, who had 80% support among blacks and 60% among whites, and Hispanics in 2002 formed no larger a segment of the electorate than in 1994. Much of the political future of California rests on the Hispanics who have never voted in the United States, and something other than the 1994 Wilson campaign may be the defining experience. No one knows what that will be, but White House political strategist Karl Rove has some ideas.

Asian immigrants are even more of a political puzzle. In the early 1990s Asians cast Republican margins, perhaps out of recoil from the 1992 riot, after the establishment showed great solicitude for the needs of the rioters but little sympathy for the Korean shopkeepers who were their victims. Later in the decade, Asians seemed to move toward Democrats, as Bill Clinton and Al Gore (remember his visit to the Buddhist temple in Hacienda Heights) courted them assiduously. There was conflicting information in the 2000 exit polls; the VNS exit poll showed Asians for Gore by only 48%–47% while the *Los Angeles Times* exit poll showed them giving Gore a 63%–33% margin. Some of the problem may be definitional. Most people of Asian descent don't think of themselves as "Asians" and both the Census and exit polls depend on respondents' self-classification. In 2002 the *Los Angeles Times* exit poll showed Asians 54%–37% for Gray Davis—a bigger margin than among voters generally, but not hugely so.

This Democratic trend among Latinos and the increasing prominence of cultural issues like abortion and gun control on which most affluent Californians have liberal views has made this once Republican state into a solidly Democratic one. Between 1980 and 1990 Republicans won seven of nine contests for president, senator and governor and nearly won another. Since 1990 Democrats have won nine of ten such contests, the one exception being Wilson's reelection in 1994. In 2000 California voted 53%–42% for Al Gore over George W. Bush, although Bush spent $20 million on California media and Gore not a penny, and 56%–37% for Democratic Senator Dianne Feinstein, who now has twice won more votes, by far, than any other senator in American history. One key factor was Bill Clinton. After winning California in 1992 with 46% of the vote, Clinton understood that if he could lock up California's 54 electoral votes (it now has 55) he would be a long way toward being assured of re-election. He courted the state with dozens of appearances, with special attention to California issues and projects, with assiduous cultivation of Hollywood celebrities and Silicon Valley cybermillionaires. Clinton's combination of moderation on economic issues and liberalism on cultural issues was a perfect fit for a critical block of California voters, the affluent professionals and techies who support abortion rights and gun control and who are increasingly fearful of the prominence of Christian conservatives in the national and to some extent the state Republican party. Affluent Americans increasingly are not moored to any one locality, but can choose where they live, from an array of places with widely different cultural atmospheres. Those who espouse traditional values and have traditional religious views tend to pick metropolises like Denver, Atlanta, Dallas and Houston; those with liberation-minded values and secular or non-Christian religious attitudes tend to pick Los Angeles and the San Francisco Bay area. The quantum of all these personal decisions over the last decade made Colorado, Georgia and Texas more Republican and made California more Democratic.

In 2002, with Clinton far less prominent, the Democrats' fortunes ebbed a bit in California— but not enough to make the state really competitive. Gray Davis, with low job ratings after the 2001 electricity crisis, was reelected by only a 47%–42% margin. Democrats won every statewide downballot office for the first time since 1882, but not by overwhelming margins: their candidates' percentages varied from 45% to 51%, while Republicans' percentages varied from 40% to 45%, and conservative firebrand Tom McClintock came within 17,000 votes of being elected controller. The popular vote for the U.S. House, a good proxy for opinion on national issues, was 51%–44%

Democratic, about the same as 2000's 52%–43%. Republicans gained two seats in the Assembly, but are still heavily outnumbered in both houses and in the House delegation (33 Democrats, 20 Republicans), and incumbent-friendly redistricting seems to guarantee that there will be no big changes absent a major shift in partisan balance.

The political balance, among officeholders and among the voters, has remained pretty much the same in California since 1996. The key division is along cultural lines; economic status matters much less. George W. Bush and Bill Simon carried voters over $100,000 income, but by only 51%–45% and 47%–42%. The least educated and the most educated, those without high school diplomas and those with graduate degrees (many of them teachers and educators), are the most Democratic. White men voted for Bush and Simon, white women for Gore and Davis. Religiously observant whites voted heavily for Republicans; religiously observant blacks, mostly secular Jews and those with no religious beliefs voted heavily Democratic. This is in line with the national pattern; the difference is that California has fewer observant white Christians and more seculars than the national average. Blacks voted 86% and 79% for Gore and Davis, Hispanics 68% and 65%, Asians 48% or 63%, depending on which exit poll you believe, and 54%. It doesn't appear that there are permanent alliances between different ethnic groups—witness Los Angeles city politics. Businessman and Catholic philanthropist Richard Riordan won the office in 1993 with majority support from whites and Latinos; his liberal opponent Michael Woo had majority support from blacks and Asians. In 2001 the winner was James Hahn, son of 40-year County Supervisor Kenneth Hahn, a white politician beloved (not too strong a word) in the black community; he won with majority support from whites and blacks; his liberal opponent Antonio Villaraigosa had big majorities from Latinos.

There is another way to look at California politics and political divisions, by geography. The pertinent division is not between northern and southern California, for San Francisco has little in common politically with the Central Valley and Los Angeles County is a political world away from Orange County or the Inland Empire east of Los Angeles. The pertinent division is between Coastal California and Heartland California, each of which casts about half the votes in the state. Coastal California, for purposes of political analysis, consists of Los Angeles County, the San Francisco Bay area and the coastal counties from Santa Barbara north to the Oregon border. All but two small counties in this region voted for Al Gore in 2000 and all but three for Gray Davis in 2002. Heartland California is defined all of southern California except for Los Angeles County plus the counties of the Central Valley and the mountains to the north. All but four small counties here voted for George W. Bush in 2000 and Bill Simon in 2002. When personal decisions and politics tended to revolve around economics—you had to live where you could make a living and you tended to vote your economic interests—the political differences between these regions were not very pronounced. In 1980 Coastal California gave Ronald Reagan a 48%–40% margin over Jimmy Carter and Heartland California 59%–31%. Today, when Americans—and foreigners—can move from one metropolitan area to another, or to a non-metropolitan area, and when political choices are highly correlated with cultural attitudes, great regional differences emerge. In 2000 Al Gore carried coastal California 61%–33% and George W. Bush carried Interior California 50%–46%. That means that Coastal California gave Gore a bigger margin than New York or Massachusetts. In 2002 the results were much the same. Coastal California voted 56%–32% for Gray Davis. Interior California voted 51%–40% for Bill Simon.

Since 1996, the Democrats' big lead in Coastal California has made California seem a safe Democratic state. For the moment, California Republicans seem clueless about how to take advantage of their opportunities. Their state conventions have been dominated by conservatives whose insistence on opposition to abortion and gun control makes the party hopelessly weak in Coastal California. They have no statewide elected officials and their leaders in the legislature (like the Democrats' leaders) are unknown to the public. Demography is working in one respect for the Republicans. Coastal California believes in limits on growth; its liberal white voters have few children. Heartland California is growing more rapidly: the leading growth areas in the 1990s were the Inland Empire (San Bernardino and Riverside counties) and the Central Valley. Heartland California cast only 31% of California's votes in 1960. In 1980 it cast 43%. In 2000 it cast 47% and in 2002 it cast 48%. The time may come when Democrats may rue their weakness in

Heartland California as much as today's Republicans should rue their weakness in Coastal California.

There is another danger for Democrats: the leftward tilt of their party. Term-limited statewide elected officials are looking to run for governor in 2006—Lieutenant Governor Cruz Bustamante, Attorney General Bill Lockyer, Treasurer Phil Angelides—and will be preparing to face a left-leaning primary electorate. Term-limited Democratic legislators, most from safe Coastal California districts, will be pushing their pet projects, with less fear of a Davis veto given his weakened political position. And Republicans have a candidate available. Actor Arnold Schwarzenegger spent fall 2002 campaigning for his own Proposition 49, which called for after-school programs to keep kids busy in those hours from 3:00 to 6:00 when so many of their parents are not home; it passed 57%–43%. Schwarzenegger is a pro-choice, pro-gun control, pro-gay rights Republican and so surely will be opposed by conservative activists. But he has what none of their possible candidates has—universal name recognition—and Californians have learned from experience that it is not a bad thing to have an actor as governor.

California at the beginning of the 21st century is very much like New York at the beginning of the 20th: the nation's largest state, its greatest immigrant magnet, with its most productive and creative economy. But it seems to lack two things which enabled New York over the first half of the 20th century to develop its full potential and become a national leader, to create an image of itself as an "empire state" in which every citizen could take pride. One is a coherent and competent civic and political elite. The other is a pattern to interweave the newcomers into the American fabric. California's loss of corporate headquarters has deprived it of many business leaders, although others—real estate billionaire Eli Broad, entrepreneur and former Los Angeles Mayor Richard Riordan—have sometimes stepped in. But Hollywood leaders are transfixed by their own narcissism and by their preoccupation with the censure of the tradition-minded right, and Silicon Valley leaders have been too busy building their own businesses or protecting them from downturns to take much part in civic affairs. The political elite includes many competent and dedicated people. But too often they have been unable or unwilling to break deadlocks, and they are hampered by media that leave the public woefully underinformed.

The other thing California lacks is rooted in the dominant *laissez faire* cultural style in California: letting people do pretty much anything they want (except smoke, that is). But tolerance can segue into indifference, and it does not necessarily translate into a sense of common identity and purpose. The California of Earl Warren, Pat Brown and Ronald Reagan had a kind of nationalism, a shared vision of itself, like the New York of Theodore Roosevelt, Al Smith, Franklin Roosevelt, Fiorello LaGuardia and Thomas Dewey. That seems to be missing in California today. Instead, articulate elites, focusing on changing demography, paint a vision of California as a "multicultural" polity, with a Third World majority (or approaching it) of "people of color." But the immigrants of today's California are no more a single united mass striving to overthrow the system than were the immigrants of New York 100 years ago; they came to the United States not to change this country but to become part of it. California businesses and political elites, like those in the United States generally, have responded to these newcomers with racial quotas and preferences, which cast doubt on their achievements, and with bilingual education, which consigns them to low-wage jobs. Policies designed to address the problems faced by blacks in the 1960s and 1970s are ill-suited to the needs of immigrants in the 1990s and 2000s. They need to learn the lessons taught by the New York elites of a century ago: to help immigrants move forward to become Americans.

The People		**Race/Ethnic Origin**			**Military veterans:** 2,569,340 (10.4%)	
Pop. 2000:	33,871,648	15,816,790	46.7%	White	WWII: 20.5%	Korea: 13.7%
Pop. 1990:	29,760,021	2,181,926	6.4%	Black	Vietnam: 32.4%	Gulf War: 9.8%
Change 1990–2000:	Up 13.6%	3,648,860	10.8%	Asian	**Most populous cities:**	
Change 1980–1990:	Up 25.7%	178,984	0.5%	Native Am.	1. Los Angeles	3,694,820
% of U.S. total:	12.0%	103,736	0.3%	Hawaiian	2. San Diego	1,223,400
Pop. rank:	1st of 50	903,115	2.7%	Two+ races	3. San Jose	894,943
Area size:	163,696 sq. mi.	71,681	0.2%	Other	4. San Francisco	776,733
State Native:	50.2%	10,966,556	32.4%	Hisp. Origin	5. Long Beach	461,522
Non-citizen:	15.9%	**Ancestry**			Urban population: 94.5%	
Language		German: 8.0%		Irish: 6.3%	Rural population: 5.5%	
English: 62.2%	Spanish: 22.4%	English: 6.1%		Italian: 3.5%		
Asian: 8.6%		USA: 2.7%				

Education		**Work Sector**		**Legislature**	
H.S. Grad:	76.8%	Private: 76.5%	Govt: 14.7%	Senate	25 D 15 R
College Grad:	26.6%	Self: 8.5%	Family: 0.4%	Assembly	48 D 32 R
Industry		Unemployment: 6.9%		Legislative Term Limits: Yes	
Agri: 1.9%	Con: 6.2%	**Household Income**		**Registered Voters**	
Fin: 6.9%	Info: 3.9%	<15k: 14.0%	15-35k: 22.9%	D: 6,733,858 (44.4%)	
Mfg: 17.8%	Prof: 30.1%	35-50k: 15.2%	50-100k: 30.7%	R: 5,341,974 (35.2%)	
Public: 4.5%	Trade: 15.2%	100-150k: 10.4%	>150k: 6.9%	I: 3,092,431 (20.4%)	
Other: 13.4%		Median: $47,493			
Occupation		Poverty status: 14.2%			
Blue collar: 21.2%	White collar: 62.7%	**Home Value**			
Gray collar: 16.1%		<50k: 5.1% 50-100k: 11.3% 100-200k: 34.0% 200-300k: 20.8%			
		300-500k: 17.8% >500k: 11.0% Median: $198,900			

Presidential politics   California, which in the 1970s and 1980s was said to have established a lock on the presidency for the Republicans, now seems heavily Democratic in presidential politics. Actually, California was not that heavily Republican: Republicans won handily when they nominated Californians—Richard Nixon in 1972 and Ronald Reagan in 1980 and 1984—but they won only narrowly in 1976 and 1988 when they didn't. Then, in the 1990s it was the Democrats who seemed to have a lock on California and the presidency. Now, after the 2000 election, it is apparent that you can win the presidency without California—indeed, if George W. Bush's percentages rise uniformly in every state in 2004, he could win the presidency with 373 electoral votes without carrying California. California's solid Democratic status owes something to its increasing number of Latino voters and their distaste, rooted in California politics, for Republicans; it owes much to Californians' affection for and assiduous cultivation by Bill Clinton; it owes much as well to the liberal attitude on cultural issues here—abortion and gun control and the environment—which has trumped any desire for lower taxes. In the 1990s Americans in the nation's largest metropolitan areas trended toward Clinton-Gore Democrats, and three-quarters of California voters live in the large metropolitan areas centered on Los Angeles, San Francisco and San Diego.

2000 Presidential Vote
Gore (D) 5,861,203   (53%)
Bush (R) 4,567,429   (42%)
Nader (Green) 418,707   (4%)
Other 118,517   (1%)

2000 Republican Presidential Primary
Bush (R) 2,168,466   (52%)
McCain (R) 1,780,570   (43%)
Keyes (R) 170,442   (4%)

2000 Democratic Presidential Primary
Gore (D) 2,609,950   (80%)
Bradley (D) 642,654   (20%)

1996 Presidential Vote
Clinton (D) 5,119,815   (51%)
Dole (R) 3,828,368   (38%)
Perot (I) 697,845   (7%)
Other 372,553   (4%)

Still, California seems just too big to ignore. In 2000 it cast 54 electoral votes; in 2004 it will cast 55, 20% of those necessary to win. Despite the Democrats' sweep here in 1998, despite Clinton's and Al Gore's cultivation of the state, despite daunting polls, George W. Bush made a serious attempt to carry California. California Republicans had been tired of raising money only to see it spent elsewhere. So Bush enlisted businessman Gerald Parsky to raise $20 million and kept his promise to spend it all in California. On top of that, Bush spent two days in the last two weeks in California, precious time which, if spent in Wisconsin, Iowa, Oregon and New Mexico, all of which he lost by 1%, might have made the controversy over the vote in Florida irrelevant. It mattered not. The Gore campaign coolly assessed its prospects here, and spent nothing; and Gore carried the state by the unambiguous margin of 54%–42%, with another 4% for Ralph Nader. Will the Bush campaign target California in 2004? It is daunting to leave 55 votes uncontested, and the Democratic nominee will not be the candidate of the incumbent party, or a popular incumbent president, in a time of apparent peace and apparent prosperity. Bush strategists have some reason to believe that their candidate will be significantly stronger among California Hispanics than he was in 2000. And he seems likely to be more popular among Jews, who cast 5% of the votes, only 15% of whom voted for him in 2000. He could probably improve his 50%–46% showing in Heartland California. But the strong opposition to military action in Iraq in Coastal California in early 2003 suggests that his chances in California may not be good. The Bush campaign seems sure to be very well financed and the Bush campaign may choose to spend money here in the hope of forcing Democrats to spend their scarcer money on defending what is in effect their home base. No Democrat can win the presidency without carrying California; Bush has and can.

Some can still recall when California's June primary was the national tie-breaker. This state was the center of national attention when Nelson Rockefeller lost here to Barry Goldwater in 1964, when Robert Kennedy and Eugene McCarthy slugged it out in 1968—Kennedy won and was murdered by a Palestinian terrorist on primary night—and when George McGovern edged Hubert Humphrey in 1972. California was all the more important because it was winner-take-all: Voters chose between slates pledged to each candidate, and whoever won a plurality won every vote in the largest delegation in each party's convention. But since the 1980s nominations have been sewed up a lot earlier than June, and California for some time was an irrelevancy.

For 1996 California moved its presidential primary from the first week in June to March 26; that was still too late to make any difference. So in 2000 it moved it to March 7. That was still a problem. California's all-party primary, adopted by referendum, allowed anyone, not just registered Democrats or Republicans, to vote for a Democrat or a Republican. But Secretary of State Bill Jones, a Republican, came up with a computer-assisted double counting procedure, which would allow a total of just registered Democrats' votes to be counted for Democratic delegates. Under those rules, Al Gore won 34% of all votes and 80% of those cast for a Democrat; George W. Bush won 29% and John McCain 23% of all votes. Among those voting for Republicans, Bush led McCain 52%–43%. This is not a result that mattered, as it turned out, and it was conducted under a system that is now extinct: The Supreme Court, in response to a challenge from four of California's political parties, outlawed the all-party primary (a longstanding institution in Washington and Alaska) in June 2000.

Congressional districting

108th Congress Lineup	
33 D	20 R
107th Congress Lineup	
32 D	20 R

California has gained House seats in every Census going back to 1850, when it became a state; over that century and a half it has grown from 2 seats to 53, the most of any state in history. But California grew less rapidly in the early 1990s, and so it gained only 1 seat from the 2000 Census, the first time in a century it has not gained 2 or more. The tradition of partisan redistricting goes way back: Republicans drew the lines to their advantage in the 1940s and 1950s, Democrats in the 1960s, 1970s and 1980s, as the California House delegation grew from 23 in the 1940s to 30, 38, 43, 45 and 52. The great genius of redistricting here was Democratic Congressman Phillip Burton, who dominated the line-drawing for House seats and for the state Senate and Assembly as well (and intervened behind the scenes in other states too); his 1982 plan, slightly revised for 1984–90, left Democrats in secure control of the delegation even though he died in 1983. In the 1990s neither party had full control. Governor Pete Wilson, after hard-nosed bargaining with the Democratic legislature, persuaded the state Supreme Court to adopt a plan drawn up by his appointed commission in 1992. This was a relatively evenhanded plan, with generally regular boundaries; the fact that Democrats had a 32–20 margin in the delegation after the 2000 election reflected the party's strength in most parts of the state, not any acuity in drawing district lines.

The assumption after the 2000 election was that California would produce a Democratic redistricting plan. Democrats held the governorship and controlled the state Senate 26–14 and the Assembly 50–30. But that is not what happened; for the second decade in a row California ended up with a plan that gave neither party any great advantage. Democrats picked up four California seats from Republicans in 2000 and entered the process with a 32–20 edge in the delegation. They could have weakened several Republican incumbents, but that would have made it harder to safeguard the four incumbents who won in 2000. And they had to do something about the Central Valley seat held by Gary Condit, world-famous for his affair with the slain intern Chandra Levy in 2001. With his moderate record, Condit had held a seat that leaned Republican in other races. It would have to be made more Democratic if Democrats hoped to keep it. The key player for Democrats was Michael Berman, brother of Congressman Howard Berman and a redistricting expert who had worked with Phil Burton on redistricting in the 1970s and 1980s. He came out of retirement and was hired as a redistricting consultant by House and state Senate Democrats, at $20,000 per incumbent. As Congresswoman Loretta Sanchez said, "Twenty thousand is nothing to keep your seat. I spend $2 million every election. If my colleagues are smart, they'll pay their $20,000 and Michael will draw the district they can win in."

Term limits played a role in convincing Berman and the Democrats not to maximize the number of Democratic seats. Assemblymen are limited to six years in office, state senators to eight; incumbents, especially assemblymen, spend much of their time plotting to run for other offices. As a result, it was not at all clear that there were 41 Democratic votes in the Assembly for plans that would protect incumbent congressmen and state senators, most of whom feared competition in the primary much more than in the general election. In February 2001 Berman met with five House Republicans, including David Dreier, who spoke for most of his California colleagues, and NRCC Chairman Tom Davis, who is also a redistricting buff. They agreed on the outline of a deal: Democrats would protect all incumbents, strengthen the Condit seat and take the new seat created by reapportionment; Republicans would get 20 seats for 19 of their incumbents in which the Bush 2000 percentage was at least 50%. It was understood that Long Beach Republican Steve Horn, nearly beaten in 2000 and surrounded by mostly Democratic territory, would have to be sacrificed to create a new Hispanic Democratic seat, and that Republicans would get a new seat in the Central Valley. In turn, Republicans would get Republican legislators to vote for the plan, with a view toward getting the two-thirds vote necessary to block a ballot initiative on the subject in 2002. This angered some Sacramento Republicans, who wanted to take their chances in court or with an initiative, and it angered Ways and Means Chairman Bill Thomas, who argued that a plan that put most Latino voters in safe Democratic districts would not give Republicans an incentive to develop ties to Latinos which would be necessary if the party is ever to be a majority in the state again.

While Berman was busy drawing the lines in his Beverly Hills office, Republicans were busy building support for the deal. Howard Berman, who spoke for other delegation Democrats on redistricting, of course favored the deal. The NRCC chartered a private plane to fly Berman to Washington, where he met with at the White House with Karl Rove, who endorsed the plan. Davis secretly flew to Sacramento and lobbied Assembly Republicans. In August 2001 the plan was unveiled; Berman sent out copies to all incumbents, Republicans as well as Democrats, with personal notes. There was never much chance that it would not be approved. In the Assembly only 28 of the 50 Democrats voted for it initially, but some switched their votes and with Republican help it was passed with a two-thirds margin. In the Senate 24 of the 26 Democrats voted for it and it easily got the two-thirds. The plan was signed by Gray Davis September 27. To criticism by Republicans that they should have tried to undermine Democrats via the courts or the ballot box, Tom Davis said, "Our view is that we are trying to control the House in 2002. A bird in the hand is worth two in the bush. Democrats were in control, and they were generous in giving us a 20th District." To national Democrats who hoped for redistricting gains in California, Howard

Berman said, "Sometimes the cautious move is the smart move. Time will tell. But I'm convinced we made the right decision, given the vagaries of politics and unanticipated decisions. . . . We will have a massive Democratic majority in the delegation for the rest of the decade." California Democrats had already done enough for the national party, they said, converting the 26–26 delegation elected in 1994 to 33–20. It was time for Democrats to pick up seats in the rest of the country.

The plan itself has the elegance one would expect of the nation's foremost redistricter. Where the district shapes are contorted, there is often a demographic as well as political rationale: the 23d District, which connects a thin band of Pacific coast in Ventura, Santa Barbara and San Luis Obispo counties, collects a constituency with common interests and proclivities, quite different from those of the voters in the interior of those counties who were placed in the 22d and 24th districts. Naturally there were some complaints. Moderate Democrat Ellen Tauscher complained that she was given a too Democratic district; she wanted one that matched her moderate record. Latino groups complained that only one additional Hispanic district was created. The Mexican American Legal Defense and Educational Fund, a group funded largely by East Coast liberal foundations, filed a lawsuit against the plan, honing in on the fact that it reduced the Hispanic percentages in the districts held by Howard Berman and Bob Filner. In all, 23 of the 26 Latino legislators backed the plan; weighing in against MALDEF also was former Speaker and Los Angeles mayor candidate Antonio Villaraigosa. The suit was dismissed in June 2002.

The plan was condemned by many journalists and political scientists for protecting incumbents and reducing competition. And in 2002 in these 53 seats—12% of the nation's total—only one was seriously contested, the Condit seat. But political trends over the course of a decade can make uncompetitive seats competitive: the political divisions of 2002 will not necessarily stay locked in place forever. Would Phil Burton have accepted a 33–20 split? Probably. He used to make the argument that California members of both parties should have safe seats because it was inhumane to make congressmen take the red-eye, the overnight plane from Los Angeles or San Francisco to Washington, every week.

Governor

Gray Davis (D)

Elected 1998, term expires Jan. 2007, 2d term; b. Dec. 26, 1942, New York, NY; home, Los Angeles; Stanford U., B.A. 1964, Columbia U., J.D. 1967; Catholic; married (Sharon).

Military Career: Army, 1967–69 (Vietnam).

Elected Office: CA Assembly, 1982–86; CA Controller, 1986–94; CA Lt. Gov., 1995–98.

Professional Career: Finance Dir., Tom Bradley mayoral campaign, 1972–74; Chief of Staff, Gov. Jerry Brown Jr., 1974–82.

Office: State Capitol Bldg., Sacramento, 95814, 916-445-2841; Fax: 916-445-4633; Web site: www.governor.ca.gov.

Election Results

2002 general	Gray Davis (D)	3,533,490	(47%)
	Bill Simon (R)	3,169,801	(42%)
	Peter Camejo (Green)	393,036	(5%)
	Other	379,984	(5%)
2002 primary	Gray Davis (D)	1,755,276	(81%)
	Anselmo Chavez (D)	179,301	(8%)
	Charles Pineda, Jr. (D)	139,121	(6%)
	Mosemarie Boyd (D)	95,857	(4%)
1998 general	Gray Davis (D)	4,858,817	(58%)
	Dan Lungren (R)	3,216,749	(38%)
	Other	306,305	(4%)

Gray Davis, the governor of California, was elected in 1998 and 2002—only the fourth Democratic governor of California in the 20th century (and only the second not named Brown). Davis grew up in Connecticut and, after age 11, in Los Angeles; he graduated from Stanford and Columbia Law School, then served in the Army in Vietnam, where he earned a Bronze Star. In 1969 he returned to California and almost immediately plunged into politics. In 1973 he worked on Tom Bradley's first successful campaign for mayor; in 1974, at 31, he ran for state treasurer, and lost the primary to former Speaker Jess Unruh. Later that year he worked on Jerry Brown's successful campaign for governor, and in 1975 he became Brown's chief of staff. To the always improvisatory and provocative Brown, Davis was a balance wheel: well-organized, unflappable, propitiating conventional politicians and bureaucrats, learning the ways of the powers-that-be not only in Sacramento but across the state. When Brown launched into the 1982 Senate campaign that he lost to Pete Wilson, Davis moved to Westside Los Angeles and, preempting serious primary opposition, won a safe Democratic seat in the Assembly. There he served two terms as a conventional California liberal. No other state legislative seat in the country had as many big Democratic contributors, and Davis cultivated them tirelessly.

That enabled him to move from top-level staffer and Assembly insider to statewide office. In 1986 he ran for controller, the one statewide position with significant patronage, and won; in 1990, Davis cruised to reelection. In 1992 he made his one false step, running against Feinstein for the nomination for the last two years of Wilson's Senate term; he ran ads comparing Feinstein to convicted tax evader Leona Helmsley and enraged her and many feminists in the "year of the woman." He lost the primary 57%–33%. But in 1994 he recovered and ran for lieutenant governor. As in 1986, he chose his spot well. His fundraising capacity deterred other potentially strong candidates; his base in the liberal Westside was strong enough to allow him to take moderate positions on some issues, like supporting the death penalty; his knowledge of state government made him an eminently respectable choice for editorial writers and endorsement groups. He won the primary easily and, while Wilson was beating Democrat Kathleen Brown by 55%–40%, Davis was elected by 52%–40% over a poorly financed Republican.

It was no secret that Davis was aiming to run to succeed the term-limited Wilson, with whom he had almost no relationship. Politics and government are everything to Davis: he and his wife live in a tiny West Hollywood apartment; he has never made large amounts of money and his taste for California social life is undetectable. It was widely thought also that he was unelectable—too boring and uncharismatic, many said, too gray. Two self-financed candidates entered the Democratic primary. Former Northwest Airlines Co-Chairman Al Checchi, with a net worth around $550 million, called for striking education reforms; he spent more than $38 million on his campaign. Congresswoman Jane Harman, after three terms representing the Los Angeles beachfront, decided to enter the race in March 1998. She argued that as a woman, she was better able to listen to and understand Californians; she also spent freely of her own money and raised more to spend $20 million.

But Davis was able to take advantage of mistakes made by the big money candidates. In March Harman surged momentarily into a lead in the polls, and Checchi ran negative ads against her. The result was that both sank in the polls. If Davis was heavily outspent by his rivals, he was able to use his Westside contacts to raise $10 million, an impressive amount in any context except this one. The result was a blowout victory for Davis: of the votes cast for Democrats, he won 58%, to 21% for Checchi and 20% for Harman.

In the general election Davis positioned himself shrewdly. Sensing the mood of the voters, he called for an end to the confrontations promoted by Republicans over issues like capital punishment, welfare for immigrants and racial quotas and preferences. The Republican nominee was Attorney General Dan Lungren. In polls until midyear he ran roughly even with Davis and the other Democrats. Until well into October he emphasized the crime issue, and tried to argue that Davis was a closet liberal. But Davis's long record supporting capital punishment gave him no opening. Lungren ran few ads and talked little about education, which polls showed to be far and away the number one issue; Davis, whose party had mostly run the public schools, was able to establish himself as the candidate who would reform them. When Davis battered him for his opposition to abortion, Lungren could only say that as a believing Catholic he opposed abortion—

not a good excuse for many voters in this increasingly secular state—and that the only relevant issues were parental consent and partial-birth abortions.

Davis won by the landslide margin of 58%–38%—a margin of the magnitude of George Deukmejian's 61%–37% in 1986, Jerry Brown's 56%–36% in 1978, Ronald Reagan's 58%–42% in 1966 and Pat Brown's 60%–40% in 1958. California became only the second state (Hawaii was the other) with a Democratic governor, two Democratic senators, a Democratic House delegation and a Democratic legislature. It was a victory as sweeping as that of Tony Blair's New Labour party in Britain in May 1997 and left Davis, like Blair, with a mandate to pursue conciliatory moderate policies not so far out of line as one might think with the confrontational policies of his more conservative predecessors. He also came into office at a time when California's surging economy was producing budget surpluses—very different from the early 1990s, when Pete Wilson announced a $14 billion deficit.

Davis pledged to "govern neither from the left nor the right, but from the center," and in his first two years kept his word. Education he proclaimed as his "first, second and third" priorities. Davis called a special session of the legislature and presented four bills—for peer review for teachers, enhanced reading instruction, a school-rating system and a standardized test for high schools. Democratic legislators watered them down, but in March 1999 versions of all four were passed, and Davis claimed victory. He vetoed laws that would have undone Proposition 227 by restoring bilingual education and Proposition 209 by reimposing racial quotas and preferences; but he declined to appeal a federal judge's ruling against Proposition 187. He vetoed liberals' bills that would have banned racial profiling (though he signed a study of whether it was occurring a year later) and revised the "three strikes and you're out" law. He negotiated an HMO regulation bill that stopped short of what liberals wanted. He opposed trial lawyers' proposal to raise the cap on medical malpractice awards. He signed several gun control bills in 1999, but said he would veto any others until he saw how those worked. He negotiated an agreement that allowed Indian casinos, but barred other casinos from the state. He opposed gay marriage and a bill to give rights to live-in partners, but signed a bill banning harassment of gays in schools and one setting up a domestic partners registry. Working with the legislature, he produced on-time budgets with big spending increases and some tax cuts, as revenues came gushing in.

By the end of 2000 Davis was the colossus of California government. Of Democratic legislators he said, "Their job is to implement my vision." Then in 2001 came two crises that Davis had not anticipated and which voters came to believe he handled poorly. The first was about electricity. In 1996 California passed electricity deregulation, in a bill embraced by the utilities and praised by just about every civic voice; Davis had no responsibility for it. Importantly, the bill was not actually deregulation. Consumers were guaranteed no rate increase until 2002, and the electric utilities were required to buy all their electricity in a state-run spot market and could not, as businesses usually do, hedge against higher prices by entering into long-term contracts. In summer 2000 energy prices spiked up, for not totally unpredictable reasons—natural gas prices rose, low rainfall held hydroelectric power production down, no new power plant has been built in California with its tight environmental laws and nitpicking regulators for more than 10 years. Rolling blackouts started in January 2001. California, with the most advanced economy anywhere, was suddenly living in the Third World.

Davis's initial response was to allow higher rates briefly and promise to avoid them hereafter, and he once said that he could solve the problem in 20 minutes if he raised rates; he evidently feared that so-called consumer advocates would resort to ballot initiatives that would wreck the system. In January, Davis asked George W. Bush to continue a Clinton administration order requiring suppliers to sell power to California utilities; Bush said he would extend it for two weeks, but that California would have to fix its own deregulation law. In February Davis persuaded the legislature to approve a bill to let the state buy power through long-term contracts with revenue bonds and to pass it along to the utilities; the measure also included higher rates for consumers who exceeded baseline usage, a measure that could have much greater impact in Republican-leaning Heartland California, where air conditioning is a must for comfortable living, than in mostly Democratic Coastal California, where air conditioning is usually optional. And Davis ordered 20% rebates to consumers who cut their usage 20% from the previous year. Later that month, Davis agreed to buy Southern California Edison's transmission grid and to guarantee its bonds to pay off its debts. But Davis had difficulty obtaining electricity at rates that would prevent increases to consumers. In March the Public Utilities Commission ordered a $5 billion a year rate increase; Davis said he had no part in the decision. In April Pacific Gas & Electric announced it was going into bankruptcy. Three days later, Davis and Southern California Edison announced that the company would sell its transmission lines. Over the next months Davis got the legislature to authorize state purchase of the transmission lines, to be funded by $12 billion in bonds. The state went out into the marketplace and purchased electricity for $6 billion at what was inevitably a peak price, since California is such a large purchaser. California consumers sharply curtailed their use of electricity, and federal regulators agreed to temporary limits on electricity prices. The predicted summer blackouts failed to materialize, and the crisis passed—but the state had undertaken huge new obligations, one major company was bankrupt, the other deep in debt and electricity rates had risen.

Davis's other unanticipated problem was the budget crisis. Until the beginning of 2001 revenues had come gushing into the state. Davis and the legislature responded by increasing spending, from $74 billion to $101 billion in four years. Spending rose 13% in the 1999–2000 fiscal year and 14% in 2000–01. The state payroll increased from 282,000 to 325,000. California has a progressive income tax, and in 2000, 25% of general fund revenues came from the capital gains tax—Silicon Valley money recycled to Sacramento. But the high-tech stock bubble reached its peak in March 2000. In 2001, revenues came in under estimates by as much as $1 million a day. In May 2001 Davis proposed $3.2 billion in budget cuts. In October 2001 he imposed a state hiring freeze. In January 2002 he said, "I will not advocate raising taxes. That would further burden individuals and businesses struggling to stay afloat in these difficult economic times." But in May 2002, with revenues coming in $19 billion less than expected and an estimated shortfall of $23 billion, he called for increases in license plate fees and the cigarette tax and cuts in Medi-Cal (California's name for Medicaid) and aid to local governments. Davis left the legislature to work out the details and signed a $99 billion budget in September.

In 2000 Davis's job rating was above 50%. It fell to 38% in fall 2001. It began to seem that he was vulnerable even in Democratic California. Liberal Democrats in the legislature saw him as more an adversary than an advocate; Republicans admired his skills, but had no investment in his success. His reputation for competence was undermined by the electricity and budget crises. His strategy from the beginning was, as usual, to disqualify his opponent. Davis was determined to see that he determined who that opponent was. In November 2001, Republican Bill Simon, Jr., son of the former Treasury Secretary and an investor and businessman, announced his candidacy. An opponent of abortion and some gun control measures, Simon preferred to emphasize his platform—cuts in capital gains and property taxes, a 15% cut in state operational spending, using private firms to build new freeways and operate schools. Then, a few days later, former Los Angeles Mayor Richard Riordan entered the race. A nominal Republican who supported abortion rights, gay rights and gun control, he was encouraged to run by none less than White House political strategist Karl Rove. Riordan, universally known in the Los Angeles media market (where 44% of California Republicans live), led in the initial polls. But he also was anathema to conservatives for his stands on issues and his support of Bill Clinton. Riordan, a wealthy entrepreneur and philanthropist, did not take instruction from political advisers. He repeatedly said that the Republican party had to become more "inclusive' or that it would become an "extinct species." This helped Simon appeal to conservatives, a majority in most Republican primaries. Gray Davis also helped: in the seven weeks before the March 2002 primary, he spent $7 million on ads attacking Riordan for inconsistencies on abortion and other issues. It was money well spent. Simon started to surge in the polls in February and in March won by a stunning 49%–31% margin.

Simon led in some polls after the primary and no poll showed Davis with more than 45% of the vote—a danger sign for an incumbent. And Davis's great strength—his fundraising ability—threatened to be his undoing. In May 2002 it was revealed that Oracle had contributed $25,000 to Davis two weeks after it signed a $95 million deal to provide software to the state. There was no competitive bidding and an audit said that the state was overcharged by $41 million. An official of the major teachers' union said that Davis, in the Capitol, had demanded a contribution of $1 million. The state prison guards' union was one of Davis's biggest contributors; the prison guards had been given unusually generous pay increases.

Davis moved to disqualify Simon. He attacked him as "a true blue think tank conservative"; Simon had been on the board of the Heritage Foundation. He ran ads pointing out that Simon opposed abortion and gun control. He also profited from Simon's missteps. For months Simon refused to disclose his income tax returns. Then in July his campaign allowed reporters to come into a room and examine them there. In San Francisco, Simon said that he would not make an official proclamation of Gay Pride Day, but his campaign had sent a questionnaire back to a gay rights group saying he would. In October Simon revealed an ad with a photograph that he said showed Davis accepting a contribution in the lieutenant governor's office. But the campaign had not done its homework; the room in the photo was in a Los Angeles home. These mistakes cost Simon any chance of spotlighting his own issues. And he didn't have much money to project that message; the $5 million of his own money he spent before the primary and the $6 million he spent during the fall were a substantial percentage of his whole campaign budget. Davis raised a total of $68 million and blanketed the airwaves with ads from July to November. By September both candidates had unfavorable ratings from the voters, and some Republicans were talking about conducting a write-in campaign for Arnold Schwarzenegger. California law allows potential write-ins to register by October 22 with the signatures of 100 voters; fortunately for Schwarzenegger it counts write-ins that misspell the candidate's name. South was alarmed enough to send out negative articles about the actor to the press. But Schwarzenegger, who was busy campaigning for his Proposition 49 to provide after-school programs for children, declined to run.

In May Davis predicted that he would be reelected by "double digits." But in November neither candidate won a majority of the vote. Davis was reelected 47%–42%, with 5% for the Green party candidate. Simon's percentages statewide and in both Coastal and Heartland California were almost identical to George W. Bush's in 2000. Davis won only 59% in the San Francisco Bay area and 56% in Los Angeles County, far below his showings in 1998 and Al Gore's in 2000. Simon carried Heartland California 51%–40% while Davis carried Coastal California 56%–32%. After the election Davis said the looming budget shortfall was not $24 billion but $34 billion, and proposed benefit cuts for state employees, layoffs of 3% of the state work force and cuts in aid to localities and education. The legislature seemed headed for deadlock. Davis's job approval rating in early 2003 fell to 27%.

And his hold on the governorship seemed threatened in February 2003 when two groups of Californians started drives to recall Gray Davis. California law requires some 897,000 signatures, usually readily obtainable through the state's signature collection industry, to put the recall of a governor on a special election ballots. Voters decide on whether to recall the governor and then they vote for a replacement from a list of candidates who file to run. If the governor is recalled, the candidate with a plurality of votes wins. But in March 2003, one firm that had been interested refused, on the ground that it would lose other business, and organizers had nothing like the $2 million needed for a signature drive. A few politicians endorsed the recall effort, notably conservative Republican state Senator Tom McClintock, who came within 17,000 votes of being elected controller in November 2002, and former Secretary of State Bill Jones, who finished third in the March 2002 Republican primary for governor, said that he would file to run if recall were put on the ballot. But Gerald Parsky, the Bush White House's lead man on California politics said that a recall could distract the party and drain away money from the Bush 2004 effort. An April poll showed voters opposed to recall by a 62%–33% vote, so the likelihood was that the recall movement would fizzle out, as have recall movements against other governors. But if the organizers succeed in putting it on the ballot some time in fall 2003, Davis will be in some jeopardy if his poll numbers remain low. The outcome may depend on the palatability of the alternatives on the ballot. Jones and McClintock may run, but Republican leaders will want to have just one serious candidate, if that, so as not to split the Republican vote. Davis will undoubtedly try to keep any serious Democrat off the ballot so that he can campaign, as he has throughout his career, by disqualifying the alternative. But in early 2003 political insiders were saying that State Treasurer Phil Angelides might well file. If so that would present a dilemma for the other Democrats considering running for governor in 2006. But a candidate elected in a 2003 recall will still be eligible to seek two full terms as governor. If a Democrat wins, that would mean that the next time the Democratic nomination would come open would be 2014, a political lifetime away. The same consideration might prompt Arnold Schwarzenegger to file. But he had big-money commitments to make movies over the next few years. Davis is generally known as a dull politician. But California politics will not be dull if the recall organizers succeed.

Senior Senator

Dianne Feinstein (D)

Elected 1992, seat up 2006, 2d term; b. June 22, 1933, San Francisco; home, San Francisco; Stanford U., B.A. 1955; Jewish; married (Richard C. Blum).

Elected Office: San Francisco Bd. of Supervisors, 1970–78, Pres., 1970–71, 1974–75, 1978; San Francisco Mayor, 1978–88.

Professional Career: CA Women's Parole Bd., 1960–66.

DC Office: 331 HSOB, 20510, 202-224-3841; Fax: 202-228-3954; Web site: feinstein.senate.gov.

State Offices: Fresno, 559-485-7430; Los Angeles, 310-914-7300; San Diego, 619-231-9712; San Francisco, 415-393-0707.

Committees: *Appropriations*: Agriculture & Rural Development; Defense; Energy & Water Development; Interior; Military Construction (RMM). *Energy & Natural Resources*: Public Lands & Forests; Water & Power. *Intelligence (Select)*. *Judiciary*: Crime, Corrections & Victims' Rights; Immigration, Border Security & Citizenship; Terrorism, Technology & Homeland Security (RMM). *Rules & Administration*.

Group Ratings

	ADA	ACLU	AFS	LCV	CON	ITIC	NTU	COC	ACU	NTLC	CHC
2002	80	60	88	82	21	88	20	55	20	9	—
2001	85	—	92	75	—	—	18	71	12	—	20

National Journal Ratings

	2001 LIB — 2001 CONS	2002 LIB — 2002 CONS
Economic	59% — 40%	80% — 15%
Social	70% — 20%	68% — 28%
Foreign	74% — 14%	64% — 33%

Key Votes of the 107th Congress

1. Approve Bush Tax Cuts	Y	5. Confirm Ashcroft as AG	N
2. Expand Patients' Rights	Y	6. Bar Gays in the Boy Scouts	N
3. Campaign Finance Reform	Y	7. $ for Hate Crime Prosecution	Y
4. Permit ANWR Development	N	8. Overseas Military Abortions	Y

9. Bar Coop. with Intl. Court	Y
10. Trade Promotion Authority	Y
11. Authorize Force in Iraq	Y
12. Homeland Sec. Dept. Union	Y

Election Results

2000 general	Dianne Feinstein (D)	5,932,522	(56%)	($10,346,170)
	Tom Campbell (R)	3,886,853	(37%)	($4,378,283)
	Other	804,233	(8%)	
2000 primary	Dianne Feinstein (D)	3,759,560	(52%)	
	Tom Campbell (R)	1,697,208	(23%)	
	Ray Haynes (R)	679,034	(9%)	
	Bill Horn (R)	453,630	(6%)	
	Other	759,405	(10%)	
1994 general	Dianne Feinstein (D)	3,977,063	(47%)	($14,407,179)
	Michael Huffington (R)	3,811,501	(45%)	($29,969,695)
	Other	714,500	(8%)	

Prior Winning Percentages: 1992 (54%)

Dianne Feinstein, California's senior senator, has twice won far more popular votes than any other senator in American history. Feinstein grew up in San Francisco, in lush Presidio Heights, graduated from Stanford and later studied criminology. She was appointed by Governor Pat Brown to the women's parole board in 1960, at 27. In 1969 she was elected to the San Francisco County Board of Supervisors—the city's council—and twice ran for mayor and lost. As president of the board, she became mayor in 1978 when Mayor George Moscone and Supervisor Harvey Milk were murdered by former Supervisor Dan White; she discovered Moscone's body and showed steadiness and a sense of command that calmed the city. She was elected to full terms in 1979 and 1983. In 1984, Walter Mondale seriously considered her for vice president, but passed over her for Geraldine Ferraro because of qualms about the business dealings of her husband, Richard Blum. Feinstein presided gracefully that year over the Democratic National Convention in San Francisco—while Ferraro juggled questions about *her* family's business. In fact, Feinstein and Blum's investments have thrived; the Capitol Hill newspaper *Roll Call* estimated their net worth in 2002 at $50 million, the tenth highest in Congress. Some of Blum's investments were in businesses in China, which sparked attacks on Feinstein, a strong supporter of trade ties with China; in 1997, Blum offered to give his profits from China to charity and in the 2000 campaign he said that he had divested all his China investments.

Feinstein left the mayor's office in 1987, ineligible for a third full term, and ran for governor in 1990. She won the Democratic primary impressively, then lost 49%–46% to Pete Wilson. When Wilson appointed Orange County state Senator John Seymour—an unknown and bland choice—to replace him in the Senate, Feinstein quickly announced for the seat, even though the 1992 race was for only the last two years of Wilson's term, and she could have run for the seat being vacated by Alan Cranston the same year. She had primary competition from Gray Davis, then state Controller, who ran an ad against her campaign finance practices comparing her to Leona Helmsley. Feinstein won 58%–33% and one can assume that relations between her and Davis, now governor, have not always been warm, though Davis appointed Blum to the University of California Board of Regents in 2002. In the 1992 general election, nothing worked for the hapless Seymour—not his switches to pro-choice on abortion and anti-offshore oil drilling, not his attacks on Feinstein's arguably tricky financing of her 1990 gubernatorial campaign (which resulted in a $190,000 fine), not fears of immigration, not Seymour's tending to agricultural interests. Feinstein won 54%–38%, coming close even in Seymour's southern California base.

In the Senate, she kept a certain distance from the Clinton administration, negotiating for changes before voting for the 1993 budget, voting against NAFTA, withdrawing her support of the Clinton health care plan in May 1994, condemning Bill Clinton's "I did not have sexual relations with that woman, Miss Lewinsky" comment which she had heard in person. She had two significant legislative achievements in her first two years. One was the attachment of the assault weapons ban to the 1994 crime bill. When Idaho's Larry Craig argued that her definition of assault weapons was not rigorous enough and challenged her knowledge of firearms, she responded by saying: "I know something about what firearms can do; I came to be mayor of San Francisco as a product of assassination." Her other major achievement was a California Desert Protection Act. Similar measures had been stymied by the state's Republican senators as too restrictive, but now that there was no Republican senator, Feinstein managed it through enactment.

Feinstein surely hoped that she would face weak competition in 1994 and that her early and hard work raising money would enable her to win essentially unopposed. But then came Michael Huffington, with the determination and the cash to be the biggest spending Senate candidate, as of then. Huffington moved to Santa Barbara in 1991 and in 1992 beat an 18-year Republican congressman in the primary by spending over $3 million. His Senate campaign was lavishly financed—with nearly $30 million of his own money. Huffington pulled even in polls in September, and Feinstein was clearly flustered and angry that she could not count on heavily outspending him. Huffington slipped when it was revealed that he and his wife employed an illegal alien as a nanny. On the Thursday before the election, it was revealed that Feinstein, despite her earlier denials, had employed a woman whose work permit had expired; but the news media ran stories saying that federal officials cast doubt on whether the woman was an illegal. That probably made the difference. Feinstein won 47%–45%, carrying Coastal California—Los Angeles County, the San Francisco Bay area and the coastal counties from Santa Barbara north to the Oregon line—by 56%–36% while Huffington carried Heartland California—the rest of the state—by 54%–36%.

Feinstein has a moderate to liberal voting record, and has differed on some issues from her colleague and Bay area neighbor Barbara Boxer; she sponsored the Y2K liability act opposed by trial lawyers, for example, and voted to repeal the marriage penalty and the estate tax. She has continued to push for gun control measures, like a ban on the import of high-capacity ammunition clips, with less success than in 1994; in 2000 she introduced a bill to require licensing of all guns—something gun control opponents argue would lead to confiscation. She has supported the treaty, opposed by the Bush administration, for international control of light weapons trading.

Starting in 2001 Feinstein has taken a more partisan attitude on the Judiciary Committee. She voted against the confirmation of John Ashcroft. She and Boxer prevented the nomination of Orange County Congressman Christopher Cox to the Ninth Circuit Court of Appeals, currently the most left-wing in the country, routinely reversed by unanimous vote in the Supreme Court. She and Boxer made it clear that they would stop the appointment of Bush judges in California unless they were consulted. With the White House's designated California political leader Gerald Parsky, they set up six-member panels for each of four districts in the state to decide on the merits of potential judges; three members were appointed by each side, and four votes is required for approval of a nominee (and the White House has veto power over all selections). This bypasses the two senior Republicans in the House delegation, Bill Thomas and Jerry Lewis, to whom the White House customarily looks when both state's senators are of the opposition party. Feinstein was the first Judiciary Democrat to come out against the nomination of Charles Pickering in March 2002 and, despite the entreaties of Kay Bailey Hutchison, voted against Priscilla Owen in September.

Before September 11, Feinstein and Jon Kyl co-sponsored a bill to prepare defenses for attacks by terrorists with chemical and biological weapons. After the attacks, she proposed a six-month moratorium on new student visas. College and university presidents squawked; there were 548,000 foreign students in the country in 2000–01, pumping $11 billion into the economy, much of it directly into universities. In October she said she was willing to drop the moratorium if colleges and universities would verify compliance with the visas. She and Kyl came forward with a bill to establish a central database of visa holders and other aliens in the country, to bar entry for people from nations that sponsor terrorism, to require the INS and the State Department to create biometric visa cards and passports, to require foreign nations to supply airlines with passenger manifest lists and to lift the 45-minute deadline for INS inspection of incoming foreigners. This was more stringent than a similar measure sponsored by Edward Kennedy and Sam Brownback. In December the two versions were melded and it was signed into law by Bush in May 2002.

Like others on the feminist left, she opposed impeachment of Bill Clinton, but wrote a proposal to censure Clinton for "immoral and reckless behavior." That did not come to the floor, and she dropped it after the Senate voted for acquittal. She supported various versions of the McCain-Feingold campaign finance legislation, with reservations.

When San Francisco and Shanghai became sister cities in 1979, Feinstein got to know Mayor Jiang Zemin, who subsequently became president of China. She has been one of the most vocal supporters of renewing normal trade relations with China every year and of PNTR in 2000. In 2002 she sponsored a bill to ban reproductive cloning but allow embryonic stem cell research. She struggled to get it to the floor and claimed it had more votes than Sam Brownback's bill to ban research on embryonic stem cells, but both were blocked from the floor in June 2002. Feinstein voted for the Iraq war resolution in October 2002—an act unpopular with many California Democrats. In Jaunary 2003 she said U.S. troop deployments in the area were "deeply disturbing" in what she said was the absence of proof that Iraq had weapons of mass destruction. "Iraq is effectively contained and prevented from developing weapons of mass destruction. It is not an imminent threat either to its neighbors or to the United States. And there is no need for precipitous military action under these circumstances." Hours after Colin Powell spoke at the United Nations in Ferbruary 2003 she took a different view: "I no longer think inspections are going to work."

California has a long tradition of having one senator who expresses ideological views and another who works hard to represent the state's economic interests. Feinstein chose the latter role, as did her predecessors Wilson, Cranston and Thomas Kuchel. She got a seat on Appropriations, where she could funnel money to California, and on Energy and Natural Resources, where she works on water issues. As California faced rolling blackouts of electricity, she and Boxer called for controls on wholesale electricity prices; this seemed unlikely to pass, and Feinstein and Oregon Republican Gordon Smith sponsored a bill giving FERC the choice between imposing price controls or setting cost-based rates to be passed along to consumers. In 2001 and 2002 she worked to revive the CALFED water program, whose authorization had lapsed. This is the label given to a series of projects—raising Shasta Dam, building a new reservoir in Colusa County, buying up and flooding islands in the Sacramento River Delta and providing fish screens there. In May 2001 she introduced a reauthorization with a $3 billion price tag. In May 2002 she scaled it down to $1 billion, but it was still rejected in committee; Republicans from other western states blocked it as overly expensive and perhaps out of pique that California would continue to draw more than what they considered its share of Colorado River water until a January 2003 change. In October Feinstein was struggling for a $30 million authorization. After the November election, she got the Senate to agree to a bill authorizing any project that could get an appropriation over the next three years; the House balked because of opposition from northern California Republicans and the leadership's insistence on waiving Davis-Bacon rules on the projects. In January 2003 she convened a meeting of the chief players in California water policy and sought to work with the northern California House Republicans to revive CALFED.

Since 1994 Feinstein has gotten pretty solid ratings in the polls. In late 1997 she gave thought to running for governor, and delivered a speech stingingly criticizing California's public school system. In 2000 she came up for reelection—her fourth statewide race in 10 years. The first Republicans to announce were Ron Unz, the Silicon Valley entrepreneur whose 1998 Proposition 227 ended the state's bilingual education program, state Senator Ray Haynes and San Diego County Supervisor Bill Horn—none of them well-known. Then in October 1999 Congressman Tom Campbell got into the race, at which point Unz dropped out. Campbell was elected to the House in 1988 and 1990, when Silicon Valley was much more hospitable country for Republicans, and then again in 1995; he ran for the Senate in 1992 and lost the Republican primary 38%–36% to conservative Bruce Herschensohn (many observers believe Campbell would have beaten Barbara Boxer in the fall). He took a conservative line on economics and supported abortion rights. In 1999 and 2000, his big issue was drugs: he favored more treatment and less imprisonment, and called for use of heroin in drug treatments. Campbell won the Republican nomination handily, but was outspent by $10.3 million to $4.4 million. His stand on the drug issue failed to make inroads among Democrats. Feinstein won 56%–37%. She has made it plain that she will run for reelection in 2006.

Junior Senator

Barbara Boxer (D)

Elected 1992, seat up 2004, 2d term; b. Nov. 11, 1940, Brooklyn, NY; home, Greenbrae; Brooklyn Col., B.A. 1962; Jewish; married (Stewart).

Elected Office: Marin Cnty. Bd. of Supervisors, 1976–82; U.S. House of Reps., 1982–92.

Professional Career: Stockbroker & researcher, 1962–65; Journalist, *Pacific Sun*, 1972–74; Dist. aide, U.S. Rep. John Burton, 1974–76.

DC Office: 112 HSOB, 20510, 202-224-3553; Fax: 202-228-4056; Web site: boxer.senate.gov.

State Offices: Fresno, 559-497-5109; Los Angeles, 213-894-5000; Sacramento, 916-448-2787; San Bernardino, 909-888-8525; San Diego, 619-239-3884; San Francisco, 415-403-0100.

Committees: *Commerce, Science & Transportation*: Aviation; Communications; Competition, Foreign Commerce & Infrastructure; Surface Transportation & Merchant Marine. *Environment & Public Works*: Superfund

& Waste Management (RMM); Transportation & Infrastructure. *Foreign Relations*: International Operations & Terrorism; Near Eastern & South Asian Affairs (RMM); Western Hemisphere, Peace Corps, Narcotics Affairs.

Group Ratings

	ADA	ACLU	AFS	LCV	CON	ITIC	NTU	COC	ACU	NTLC	CHC
2002	90	60	100	94	31	50	14	40	5	0	—
2001	95	—	100	100	—	—	6	42	0	—	0

National Journal Ratings

	2001 LIB —	2001 CONS		2002 LIB —	2002 CONS
Economic	93%	0%		95%	0%
Social	93%	7%		82%	0%
Foreign	98%	0%		90%	8%

Key Votes of the 107th Congress

1. Approve Bush Tax Cuts	N	5. Confirm Ashcroft as AG	N
2. Expand Patients' Rights	Y	6. Bar Gays in the Boy Scouts	N
3. Campaign Finance Reform	Y	7. $ for Hate Crime Prosecution	Y
4. Permit ANWR Development	N	8. Overseas Military Abortions	Y

9. Bar Coop. with Intl. Court	N
10. Trade Promotion Authority	N
11. Authorize Force in Iraq	N
12. Homeland Sec. Dept. Union	N

Election Results

1998 general	Barbara Boxer (D)	4,410,056	(53%)	($13,737,548)
	Matt Fong (R)	3,575,078	(43%)	($10,764,892)
	Other	326,771	(4%)	
1998 primary	Barbara Boxer (D)	2,574,264	(41%)	
	Matt Fong (R)	1,292,662	(21%)	
	Darrell Issa (R)	1,142,567	(18%)	
	John M. Brown (R)	489,741	(8%)	
	Frank D. Riggs (R)	295,886	(5%)	
	Other	507,257	(8%)	
1992 general	Barbara Boxer (D)	5,173,443	(48%)	($10,415,811)
	Bruce Herschensohn (R)	4,644,139	(43%)	($7,649,072)
	Other	981,781	(9%)	

Prior Winning Percentages: 1990 House (68%); 1988 House (73%); 1986 House (74%); 1984 House (68%); 1982 House (52%)

Barbara Boxer, California's junior senator, was first elected in 1992 and reelected in 1998. She grew up in Brooklyn, where she was a victim of sexual harassment by a college professor and was refused work as a stockbroker; she moved to California in 1965. In Marin County, the ultra-trendy suburbs nestled between Mount Tamalpais and the Bay, north of the Golden Gate Bridge, she worked on civic affairs and political campaigns and ultimately for Democratic Congressman (and now state Senate President pro tem) John Burton. In 1972 she ran for the Marin County Board of Supervisors. She lost, but in 1976, when women candidates were more accepted, she won a seat on the board. Boxer is energetic, usually good-humored, unafraid to challenge authority, voluble in support of her issue positions but not always candid about her goals. When Burton retired unexpectedly in 1982, she ran for the House and was easily elected. She made many splashes in the House, unearthing the Air Force's $7,622 coffee pot in 1984, denouncing the Persian Gulf War with more ardor than anyone, and leading a march of women on the Senate when Anita Hill was testifying against Clarence Thomas. She also compiled the highest-dollar voting record in the House on spending in 1992.

In the 1980s it seemed improbable that anyone as liberal as Boxer could be elected senator from California, which had after all voted Republican for president in all but one election from 1952 to 1988. But in the 1990s Boxer was elected twice, by decisive and rising margins. In 1992 she started off as neither the best-known nor the best-financed candidate, but this turned out to be the year of the woman, in which the enthusiasm of the feminist left produced important victories for Democratic women. Boxer won the June 1992 Democratic primary with 44% of the vote, to 31% for Lieutenant Governor Leo McCarthy, and 22% for Congressman Mel Levine. Her general election opponent was Bruce Herschensohn, a Los Angeles TV and radio commentator, backer of a flat tax and offshore oil drilling and opponent of abortion. Herschensohn had edged Silicon Valley moderate Congressman Tom Campbell 38%–36% in the primary, with the help of then-Palm Springs Mayor Sonny Bono, who won 17%. The Boxer-Herschensohn race was a battle of opposites, the far left versus the far right of the American electoral spectrum. Boxer was helped by the collapse of the Bush candidacy in California, by hearty support from Feinstein and by the revelation by state Democratic political director Bob Mulholland during the last week of the campaign that Herschensohn attended nude dancer nightclubs.

Boxer's voting record has been strongly liberal, the most liberal in the Senate in 1999, 2000 and second only to Paul Wellstone in 2001 and 2002 in *National Journal's* ratings. She is perhaps the personification of the feminist left, and is one of the strongest proponents of abortion rights in the Senate; she has vehemently opposed the partial-birth abortion ban. But she was also a staunch defender of Bill Clinton. In 1998, the senator who had marched across the Capitol to protest the cross-examination of Anita Hill, found little to believe in the charges against Clinton until he admitted their truth, and even then limited her condemnation to a perfunctory statement combined with a total commitment to defeat impeachment. And in 1999 the crusader against the Gulf War resolution solidly backed the bombing campaign against Serbia. In September 2001 she supported the use of force in Afghanistan. But in October 2002 she voted against the use of force in Iraq, and in 2003 she told Secretary of State Colin Powell that administration policy toward North Korea was "designed neglect."

Gun control is also one of Boxer's causes. She was one of the first to sponsor a bill to require child-proof safety locks on all handguns, and has come forward with provocative proposals embarrassing gun control opponents, like her amendment to ban sales of guns to people who are intoxicated. She has been a critic of the oil industry. For all her partisanship, on some issues Boxer has worked with Republicans. With Phil Gramm she proposed in March 2001 to exempt Mexico from annual drug certification. In June 2001, when Jesse Helms amended the education bill to bar funds for school districts that exclude the Boy Scouts, she successfully pressed a substitute which requires equal access to all youth groups; this would allow San Francisco and other California districts to keep excluding the Boy Scouts, which ban gays from the organization. In 2002 she and Jon Corzine sponsored a bill to limit to 20% the amount of their employers' stock workers could hold in their 401(k) accounts and to limit to 90 days the time an employee could be required to hold employers' stock. But Banking Chairman Paul Sarbanes did not include this in the corporate accountability bill. She has sponsored a bill to make the Environmental Protection Agency a Cabinet agency; for once she got support from the Bush administration.

Boxer was frustrated when Republicans during the Clinton years held up nominations to the Ninth Circuit Court of Appeals, currently the most liberal in the country. In January 2001 she was the first senator to oppose the nomination for attorney general of her former colleague John Ashcroft. In spring 2001 she opposed the nomination of Orange County Congressman Christopher Cox to the Ninth Circuit; when Dianne Feinstein said she might oppose him too, Cox withdrew. She and Feinstein made it clear that they would stop the appointment of Bush judges in California unless they were consulted.

Boxer has weighed in on all manner of California issues. As California was hit by rolling blackouts of electricity in early 2001, she proposed a windfall profits tax on energy producers and, with Feinstein, sponsored a bill to impose temporary price controls on wholesale electric power suppliers. But she split with Feinstein by backing the two Oregon senators' unsuccessful amendment to the bankruptcy reform bill that would have barred PG&E and Southern California Edison from discharging their debts in bankruptcy; a few weeks later PG&E sought bankruptcy protection. She and Anna Eshoo sponsored similar bills to require FERC to order refunds of up to $9 billion to California consumers. In 2002 she introduced a new California wilderness bill to protect 2.5 million acres; her staffers negotiated limits on use with mountain bikers. She has worked for funding of greater port security.

During her first three years in the Senate Boxer's job ratings were among the Senate's lowest. But California with its large metro areas trended sharply toward the Democrats by 1996, and in early 1997 Boxer's job rating was up to 50%. Prominent Republicans—Congressman Tom Campbell, San Diego Mayor Susan Golding, 1994 Senate nominee Michael Huffington—decided not to run against her. In the all-party primary, state Treasurer Matt Fong edged businessman (and now Congressman) Darrell Issa. On paper Fong was a strong candidate, with an Asian heritage and a moderate record on issues; his mother March Fong Eu, a Democrat, was California's Secretary of State from 1974 to 1994. But Boxer raised $15 million and campaigned long and hard. She launched an ad campaign attacking Fong for his ambiguous stances on issues like abortion. She guarded herself from contact with reporters so she would not have to answer questions about Bill Clinton; the president's brother-in-law Tony Rodham was then married to her daughter Nicole. Fong attacked her for the hypocrisy of her stand on the Clinton scandals. But he spoke hesitantly and unconvincingly in the sound bites that are the staple of California politics and never succeeded in raising much money. For much of September and October he was off the air, while Boxer was pounding the airwaves mercilessly. Boxer won 53%–43%. She won 61%–35% in Coastal California and lost by only 49%–47% in Heartland California. This was a gender gap race, an even 48%–48% among men and 57%–39% for Boxer among women.

In April 2003, Boxer's favorability ratings were just 44%, but the state remains Democratic; she must be considered a favorite for reelection. As Boxer conducted extensive fundraising—in February 2003, she had 70 fundraisers scheduled for the year—several Republicans went around the state testing the waters. The list of those mentioned as possible candidates is long: Fresno Mayor Alan Autry, Congresswoman Mary Bono, Congressmen George Radanovich, Orange County Sheriff Mike Corona, Assemblyman Abel Maldonado, lawyer Gary Mendoza, U.S. Treasurer Rosario Marin, talk show host Dennis Prager, former Los Angeles Mayor Richard Riordan, former Baseball Commissioner Peter Ueberroth. Actor Arnold Schwarzenegger seemed much more interested in running for governor in 2006. If Republicans can make this a competitive race, they can force Democrats to spend a lot of their scarcer dollars defending California rather than in other states.

FIRST DISTRICT

Rep. Mike Thompson (D)

Elected 1998, 3d term; b. Jan. 24, 1951, St. Helena; home, St. Helena; CA St. U., B. A. 1982, M. A. 1996.; Catholic; married (Janet).

Military Career: Army, 1969–73 (Vietnam).

Elected Office: CA Senate, 1990–98.

Professional Career: Supervisor, Beringer Winery; CA Assembly fellow, 1982–83; Chief of Staff, CA Assemblyman Lou Papan, 1984–87; Chief of Staff, CA Assemblywoman Jacqueline Speier, 1987–90.

DC Office: 119 CHOB 20515, 202-225-3311; Fax: 202-225-4335; Web site: www.house.gov/mthompson.

District Offices: Eureka, 707-269-9595; Fort Bragg, 707-962-0933; Napa, 707-226-9898; Yolo, 530-662-5272.

Committees: *Agriculture* (21st of 24 D): Department Operations, Oversight, Nutrition & Forestry. *Budget* (13th of 19 D). *Transportation & Infrastructure* (31st of 34 D): Coast Guard & Maritime Transportation; Highways, Transit & Pipelines; Water Resources & Environment.

Group Ratings

	ADA	ACLU	AFS	LCV	CON	ITIC	NTU	COC	ACU	NTLC	CHC
2002	90	87	89	75	43	50	22	53	8	17	8
2001	95	—	100	100	—	—	17	50	8	—	—

National Journal Ratings

	2001 LIB	—	2001 CONS		2002 LIB	—	2002 CONS
Economic	70%	—	29%		71%	—	29%
Social	68%	—	32%		74%	—	19%
Foreign	81%	—	18%		83%	—	17%

Key Votes of the 107th Congress

1. Approve Bush Tax Cuts	N	5. Faith-Based Charities	N	9. Trade Promotion Authority	N
2. Limit Patients' Bill of Rights	N	6. Bar Gays in the Boy Scouts	N	10. Bar Funds for Intl. Court	N
3. Campaign Finance Reform	Y	7. Ban Partial-Birth Abortion	N	11. Authorize Force in Iraq	N
4. Ban ANWR Development	Y	8. Arm Commercial Pilots	Y	12. Deny Home. Sec. Dept. Union	N

Election Results

2002 general	Mike Thompson (D)	118,669	(64%)	($1,037,781)
	Lawrence Wiesner (R)	60,013	(32%)	($85,419)
	Kevin Bastian (Lib)	6,534	(4%)	
2002 primary	Mike Thompson (D)	unopposed		
2000 general	Mike Thompson (D)	155,638	(65%)	($851,612)
	Russel J. Chase (R)	66,987	(28%)	($11,730)
	Other	16,710	(7%)	

Prior Winning Percentages: 1998 (62%)

The People		Race/Ethnic Origin	Ancestry	
Area size:	12,195 sq. mi.	71.2% White	German: 11.3%	Irish: 9.0%
Urban population:	76.0%	1.3% Black	English: 8.9%	
Rural population:	24.0%	3.9% Asian	**2000 Presidential Vote**	
Pop. 2000:	639,087	2.4% Native Am.	Gore (D)	131,376 (52%)
Median income:	$38,918	0.2% Hawaiian	Bush (R)	98,506 (39%)
Poverty status:	15.3%	2.9% Two+ races	Other	24,220 (10%)
Military veterans:	13.4%	0.2% Other	**Cook Partisan Voting Index:** D + 7	
		17.9% Hispanic Origin		

Occupation	Blue collar: 20.9%	White collar: 58.3%	Gray collar: 20.8%

The North Coast of California is unlike any other place in America. It is the only part of the Lower 48 states first settled by Russians, who built Fort Ross in 1812; they sold it in 1841 to a Swiss named John Augustus Sutter, whose discovery of gold near Sacramento started the Gold Rush eight years later. It is the only part of the world with large numbers of redwood trees, shooting up in the moist and drizzly air hundreds of feet toward the sky. It is wet country, and for years it has been one of America's prime lumbering areas: Eureka and smaller lumber towns are filled with filigreed Victorian houses and old lumber mills, saloons and waterfront hotels. It has moved on to other crops: in sunny valleys sealed off from the Coast Range, some of the nation's premium wine grapes grow on ridges, and Mendocino County has been known since the late 1960s for its premier marijuana fields. Thirty years ago, there were only 20 wineries in Napa Valley. Today, there are several hundred, with more just west of the ridges in Sonoma County; wineries were a favorite investment for Silicon Valley millionaires. Some of the land here has been planted in olive trees, and local olive production has grown to more than $100 million annually. These valleys claim some of California's earliest literary haunts: Robert Louis Stevenson took his honeymoon near Calistoga in Napa, and Jack London owned a giant house in Sonoma that mysteriously burned down in 1913.

The 1st Congressional District consists of most of the North Coast from Mendocino County on north and Napa County and the eastern edge of Sonoma County—Healdsburg and the Alexander Valley and part of Sonoma Valley—plus part of the Yolo County flatlands to the east, including the University of California at Davis and industrial West Sacramento. The North Coast lumbering area from Mendocino on north, once filled with rough-hewn working men, was historically Democratic country; but their business became hostage to concern about the northern spotted owl, and the area backlashed toward the Republicans on environmental issues. But as the timber industry waned, veterans of the counterculture settled in Mendocino County and along the coast, and the area became Democratic again. Inland, the wine-growing country around Healdsburg and in Napa County was Republican in the 1970s, but now partakes of the San Francisco Bay area's liberal consensus. The 2001 redistricting removed Fairfield and Travis Air Force Base from the district and added the Davis and gritty West Sacramento, both heavily Democratic. This district changed partisan hands four times during the 1990s, thanks largely to splits among Democrats. But it is heavily Democratic now.

The congressman from the 1st District is Mike Thompson, a Democrat elected in 1998. Thompson grew up in the Napa Valley town of St. Helena, dropped out of high school, served in the Army in Vietnam and earned a Purple Heart. Later, he got a bachelor and master's degree from what has become California State University-Chico, owned a vineyard and worked as a maintenance supervisor for Beringer, a big winery in the valley. In 1982 he was chosen an Assembly Fellow, and from 1984–90 was chief of staff to two Bay Area Assembly members. In 1990, he was elected to the first of two terms in the state Senate, where he chaired the Budget Committee.

In 1998, facing California's legislative term limits, Thompson decided to run for the House seat held, precariously, by Republican Frank Riggs, who had been elected in 1990, 1994 and 1996. Thompson looked like a serious challenger who could unite Democrats, and in January 1998 Riggs announced he was running for Barbara Boxer's Senate seat; with no name identification beyond the district and little money, he withdrew in April. Thompson faced weak opposition and won support from almost every interest group that matters in the 1st: unions, medical providers, vintners, oil and timber interests, environmental restriction advocates, law enforcement groups, fishermen. His issue stands—opposition to oil drilling off the California coast, support of abortion rights and the death penalty—were broadly popular. He won the June primary easily, 78%–22%, and won the general by 62%–33%.

In the House, Thompson has voted and styled himself as a moderate Democrat. He joined both the New Democrats and the Blue Dogs, and pledged bipartisanship. With Republican George Radanovich, he started the House Wine Caucus; in May 2002 they visited Europe to focus on trade issues affecting the industry. On behalf of the wine industry, he lost a battle with conservative senators and beer and alcohol wholesalers to a bill giving states new power to restrict sales over the Internet. He joined Jerry Lewis on a proposal to create a $1 billion pool to help pay for making buildings more resistant to earthquakes. Mindful of local businesses, he voted to override Bill Clinton's veto of the estate tax repeal. Before deciding to vote for PNTR with China, he got the White House's agreement to resolve a nine-year battle over a new local ZIP code; he opposed trade promotion authority though. He proposed a $10 fee on every desktop and laptop computer to finance a mandatory recycling program. In June 2001, the House passed his bill to finance salmon habitat restoration projects. Following the massive fish kill caused by flooding of the Klamath River in late 2002, he proposed emergency aid to local communities plus a long-term water conservation program to end local controversy.

A close ally of Nancy Pelosi, Thompson was seen as a rising star among House Democrats and a possible DCCC chairman. But his ambitions were jolted in September 2002, after he joined David Bonior and Jim McDermott in a visit to Baghdad, where his more liberal and outspoken colleagues sharply criticized George W. Bush and opposed the use of force in Iraq. Thompson, who did not appear on television, said that he went to get first-hand information on the consequences of war and to urge Iraq to comply with demands for inspections. Bonior's and McDermott's comments were strongly criticized by many Republicans (the trio was mocked as "The Baghdad Boys"), and polling evidence suggests they moved many voters away from the Democratic party. They also angered many Democrats who supported Bush's stand against Saddam Hussein. In an opinion article in the *Washington Post,* Thompson wrote, "I never expected conservative partisans to try to use my State Department-licensed trip to fuel their own propaganda machine." He won reelection easily, but it was obvious that making Thompson chairman of House Democrats' campaign committee would give Republican candidates in every close race in the country a talking point, and no more was heard about his candidacy for that position.

Still, with his local seat secured for a longer tenure than his immediate predecessors and with support from Pelosi, Thompson got a consolation prize, a seat on the Budget Committee. He likely will be more cautious on his choice of companions on future overseas missions.

SECOND DISTRICT

Rep. Wally Herger (R)

Elected 1986, 9th term; b. May 20, 1945, Yuba City; home, Marysville; American River Comm. Col., A.A. 1967, CA St. U., 1968–69; Mormon; married (Pamela).

Elected Office: CA Assembly, 1980–86.

Professional Career: Rancher; Owner, Herger Gas Inc., 1969–80.

DC Office: 2268 RHOB 20515, 202-225-3076; Web site: www.house.gov/herger.

District Offices: Chico, 530-893-8363; Redding, 530-223-5898.

Committees: *Ways & Means* (6th of 24 R): Human Resources (Chmn.); Trade.

Group Ratings

	ADA	ACLU	AFS	LCV	CON	ITIC	NTU	COC	ACU	NTLC	CHC
2002	0	13	0	0	61	88	60	100	100	94	100
2001	0	—	0	0	—	—	72	96	96	—	—

National Journal Ratings

	2001 LIB —	2001 CONS		2002 LIB —	2002 CONS
Economic	0%	— 94%		0%	— 91%
Social	20%	— 69%		0%	— 75%
Foreign	41%	— 60%		35%	— 60%

Key Votes of the 107th Congress

1. Approve Bush Tax Cuts	Y	5. Faith-Based Charities	Y	9. Trade Promotion Authority	Y
2. Limit Patients' Bill of Rights	Y	6. Bar Gays in the Boy Scouts	Y	10. Bar Funds for Intl. Court	Y
3. Campaign Finance Reform	N	7. Ban Partial-Birth Abortion	Y	11. Authorize Force in Iraq	Y
4. Ban ANWR Development	N	8. Arm Commercial Pilots	Y	12. Deny Home. Sec. Dept. Union	Y

Election Results

2002 general	Wally Herger (R)	117,747	(66%)	($719,053)
	Mike Johnson (D)	52,455	(29%)	($9,422)
	Other	8,783	(5%)	
2002 primary	Wally Herger (R)	71,028	(89%)	
	Al Thompson (R)	6,616	(8%)	
	Other	2,370	(3%)	
2000 general	Wally Herger (R)	168,172	(66%)	($664,374)
	Stan Morgan (D)	72,075	(28%)	
	Other	15,609	(6%)	

Prior Winning Percentages: 1998 (63%); 1996 (61%); 1994 (64%); 1992 (65%); 1990 (64%); 1988 (59%); 1986 (58%)

The People		Race/Ethnic Origin	Ancestry	
Area size:	21,977 sq. mi.	76.2% White	German: 11.8%	English: 9.0%
Urban population:	67.7%	1.2% Black	Irish: 8.9%	
Rural population:	32.3%	3.6% Asian	**2000 Presidential Vote**	
Pop. 2000:	639,087	1.9% Native Am.	Bush (R)..............150,196	(61%)
Median income:	$33,559	0.1% Hawaiian	Gore (D)...............81,861	(33%)
Poverty status:	17.0%	2.8% Two+ races	Other..................13,609	(6%)
Military veterans:	15.7%	0.2% Other	**Cook Partisan Voting Index:** R + 15	
		14.0% Hispanic Origin		

Occupation	Blue collar: 23.2%	White collar: 54.9%	Gray collar: 21.9%

Rising 14,000 feet over low foothills and the Central Valley, visible for 100 miles, is the snow-capped volcanic cone of Mount Shasta, one of a string of (supposedly) burnt-out volcanoes that march up and down the Pacific Coast states. This is the far northern end of California, where truck traffic on Interstate 5 is the only reminder of the choked metropolitan areas where most of the state's people live. This is lumber country mostly, where the mountains that rise on all sides—the Coast Range to the east, the Sierra Nevada to the west, the scattered mountains sealing off the Central Valley north of Redding—are carpeted with trees: rough flannel-shirt, two-lane-road country that was left behind economically when Los Angeles and San Francisco boomed after World War II. Further south are the flat farm fields of the Sacramento Valley, spread the 50 miles between the Sierra Nevada and the Coast Range. In the last dozen years, however, this northern end of California has been attracting people, mostly young families who come here to raise their children in a small town atmosphere, but also retirees looking for a calm atmosphere and low cost of living. This is one part of California with relatively few Latino or Asian immigrants.

The 2d Congressional District covers most of this area. The district has three major population areas: one around Redding, south of Mount Shasta. The second is further south, at the edge of the Sierra foothills, around the Butte County communities of Paradise and Chico, home to a state university campus and Sierra Nevada Pale Ale. Still further south are the farm counties of Colusa (the leading rice-producing county in the nation), Yuba and Sutter not far north of Sacramento. The region has a Democratic heritage, but is culturally conservative, angry at the diktats of urban environmentalists. Until 1980, it elected rough-and-ready Democrats who pulled strings in Sacramento and Washington to build roads and dams. Now it elects abstemious Republicans who have solidly conservative voting records and tend to local needs. George W. Bush won 61% of the vote here in 2000, his second best showing in California's 53 districts.

The congressman from the 2d District is Republican Wally Herger, an ardent economic conservative but more centrist on foreign issues. He grew up in the farm country north of Sacramento and worked as a rancher and propane gas company owner. In 1980 he was elected to the California Assembly. In 1986 he was elected to the House after winning solid margins over the mayor of Redding in the primary and a Shasta County supervisor in the general. He has served rather quietly on the Ways and Means Committee, favoring balanced budgets and lower taxes. When federal budget deficits disappeared in the late 1990s, Herger was a leader of the rhetorical battle to create lock boxes for the surpluses in the Social Security and Medicare trust funds; that discussion appeared to become moot with the return of big deficits. In 2001 he took over as chairman of the Human Resources Subcommittee, which gave him responsibility for reauthorizing the 1996 welfare act. In May 2002, the House passed the bill that he and other Ways and Means Republicans wrote to increase work requirements for recipients; it included provisions to encourage marriage and other Bush administration recommendations. Only 14 House Democrats voted for this version; it died in the Senate, where Democrats demanded more money for the states. The issue is likely to be revisited in 2003.

On local issues, Herger tends to local water projects, lamenting the failure to shore up levees to prevent local floods, and opposing the Central Valley Project for legislating "a permanent drought." He called for exemption of flood control programs from the Endangered Species Act. One of his most significant efforts was providing clout for the Quincy Library Group, a collection of loggers and (some) local environmentalists in Plumas County in the Sierras who hammered out a plan that permitted the logging of smaller, more crowded trees in national forests as a way to reduce wildfires and provide a steady supply of timber for local mills. Although the Clinton administration initially backed the proposal, national environmental groups came out strongly against it, fearing it would set a precedent for greater local control of federal lands. But Herger worked with others to include language into the October 1998 spending package; the plan remains mired in litigation. With Greg Walden of Oregon, he proposed full compensation of farmers and related businesses that suffered damages from the Klamath River flooding.

In the 2002 primary, Herger won 89% of the vote against two opponents who criticized him for failing to support the gold standard and for backing free trade. Since 1990, Herger has been consistently reelected with more than 60% of the vote against weak Democratic opponents, in what has become one of the safest Republican districts in the nation.

THIRD DISTRICT

Rep. Doug Ose (R)

Elected 1998, 3d term; b. June 27, 1955, Sacramento; home, Sacramento; U. of CA at Berkeley, B.S. 1977; Lutheran; married (Lynnda).

Professional Career: Project mgr., Ose Properties, 1977–85; Real estate developer, 1985-present.

DC Office: 236 CHOB 20515, 202-225-5716; Fax: 202-226-1298; Web site: www.house.gov/ose.

District Office: Sacramento, 916-489-3684.

Committees: *Agriculture* (10th of 27 R): Department Operations, Oversight, Nutrition & Forestry; Livestock & Horticulture (Vice Chmn.). *Financial Services* (18th of 37 R): Capital Markets, Insurance & Government Sponsored Enterprises (Vice Chmn.); Domestic and International Monetary Policy, Trade & Technology; Housing & Community Opportunity. *Government Reform* (9th of 24 R): Criminal Justice, Drug Policy & Human Resources; Energy Policy, Natural Resources and Regulatory Affairs (Chmn.); Technology, Information Policy, Intergovernmental Relations & Census.

Group Ratings

	ADA	ACLU	AFS	LCV	CON	ITIC	NTU	COC	ACU	NTLC	CHC
2002	20	27	0	13	8	100	54	89	84	75	42
2001	20	—	10	21	—	—	60	100	64	—	—

National Journal Ratings

	2001 LIB —	2001 CONS		2002 LIB —	2002 CONS
Economic	36%	63%		41%	58%
Social	52%	47%		51%	49%
Foreign	4%	87%		23%	76%

Key Votes of the 107th Congress

1. Approve Bush Tax Cuts	Y	5. Faith-Based Charities	9. Trade Promotion Authority	Y
2. Limit Patients' Bill of Rights	Y	6. Bar Gays in the Boy Scouts	10. Bar Funds for Intl. Court	*
3. Campaign Finance Reform	Y	7. Ban Partial-Birth Abortion	11. Authorize Force in Iraq	Y
4. Ban ANWR Development	N	8. Arm Commercial Pilots	12. Deny Home. Sec. Dept. Union	Y

Election Results

2002 general	Doug Ose (R)	121,732	(62%)	($659,095)
	Howard Beeman (D)	67,136	(34%)	($63,747)
	Other	6,050	(3%)	
2002 primary	Doug Ose (R)	unopposed		
2000 general	Doug Ose (R)	129,254	(56%)	($593,164)
	Bob Kent (D)	93,067	(40%)	($258,524)
	Other	7,861	(3%)	

Prior Winning Percentages: 1998 (52%)

The People		Race/Ethnic Origin	Ancestry	
Area size:	3,422 sq. mi.	74.4% White	German: 12.4%	Irish: 9.0%
Urban population:	86.4%	4.3% Black	English: 8.9%	
Rural population:	13.6%	5.9% Asian	**2000 Presidential Vote**	
Pop. 2000:	639,088	0.8% Native Am.	Bush (R) 142,946	(55%)
Median income:	$51,313	0.3% Hawaiian	Gore (D) 107,690	(41%)
Poverty status:	8.5%	3.5% Two+ races	Other 9,820	(4%)
Military veterans:	15.7%	0.2% Other	**Cook Partisan Voting Index:** R + 7	
		10.7% Hispanic Origin		

Occupation   Blue collar: 18.4%   White collar: 67.8%   Gray collar: 13.8%

Until recently, Sacramento was chiefly the metropolis of a fertile valley that produced a marvelous variety of crops: rice, plums, almonds, olives, asparagus, pears, hops, beans, celery, onions, potatoes, plus caviar-yielding sturgeon in pools of filtered water. The farmlands remain, and the capital city flourishes as a center of government; greater Sacramento is one of the fastest-growing metro areas in the country. Almost all the growth has been away from the flood plain of the Sacramento River, in the higher land east of the city that eventually turns into hills rising toward the Sierra Nevadas. Here is the Mother Lode country in Amador and Calaveras Counties, which filled up with people in the Gold Rush days, when Mark Twain was inspired to write his story about the famous jumping frog of Calaveras County. Only in recent decades has Calaveras County had more than the 16,000 people who lived there in Twain's time, but some things have not changed. When an animal-rights group called for cancellation of the annual Jumping Frog Jubilee, a local official said that the frogs are not tortured and that the jubilee will continue.

The 3d Congressional District includes much of suburban Sacramento, some territory to the west and some of the Mother Lode country in Amador and Calaveras Counties to the east, where it reaches over the Sierras to Alpine County, the smallest county in California (1,208 people in 2000) and the Nevada line. Its ungainly shape contains only a little territory—northern Sacramento suburbs that have 32% of the district's population—that was in the old district before 2001 redistricting. But more than 80% of the people in the district live in Sacramento County, in suburbs like Carmichael, Citrus Heights and Arden-Arcade (which is shared with the 5th) and the old town of Folsom. Historically Sacramento was Democratic, like the Central Valley. But in the 1980s and 1990s, Sacramento County, with its rapid private-sector growth, became more Republican, like the Central Valley; it voted in 2002 to evict Gray Davis from the governorship and install Republican Bill Simon. The 3d District voted 55% for George W. Bush in 2000 and seems to be a safe Republican seat.

The congressman from the 3d District is Doug Ose, a Republican elected in 1998 to a seat that had elected only Democrats since it was created in 1962. Ose grew up in Sacramento and went into the family real estate development business after graduating from Berkeley in 1977. In 1985, he struck out on his own, mainly to build mini-storage units. This is a booming business in a fast-growing metropolitan area filling up with subdivision houses on narrow lots and garden apartments with little room to store a lifetime's paraphernalia; Ose accumulated enough of a fortune to self-finance a House campaign. The occasion came when Vic Fazio, congressman and chairman of the Democratic Caucus, announced he would not seek re-election after 20 years in the House. The 1992 redistricting had made this a Republican-leaning district, and Fazio had to work hard to hold it. His retirement made Republicans the clear favorite for the district. Their two leading candidates were Ose, who had not run for office before, and Assemblywoman Barbara Alby, a strong conservative. Spending freely, Ose ran a stream of attacks against Alby; one ad asserted that Alby had missed two of every 10 legislative votes in 1997 (some of them due to a "junket to Hawaii," a charge that was accompanied in the ad by dancing hula dolls). The attacks worked. In the nine-candidate all-party June primary, Ose finished first, with 30%, to Alby's 19%. Sandie Dunn, a water and land-use attorney endorsed by Fazio, won the Democratic nomination with 23%. In the general, both candidates showed strengths. Dunn campaigned as a moderate, with special expertise in water law and experience in the Sacramento Valley on this issue. Ose campaigned for tax cuts and giving local governments control over environmental regulation. Ose spent $1.43 million of his own money. In a low-turnout year, he won 52%–45%.

In Washington, Ose has been a moderate on cultural issues and more conservative on economic and foreign issues. The 4th District's John Doolittle helped to scuttle Ose's plan for improvement of Sacramento River levees in the Natomas area. In 2001, he became chairman of the Energy Policy, Natural Resources and Regulatory Affairs Subcommittee of Government Reform, from which he oversaw California's electricity crisis plus water problems that Republicans contend the Clinton administration exacerbated. In February 2002 he chaired a hearing on the gifts that Hillary Rodham Clinton accepted at the White House before she was sworn in as Senator in January 2001 and was covered by its gift rules. He said that the current system for presidential gifts "is broken and needs to be fixed." He demanded more specifics from the Bush administration on the costs and benefits of its regulatory policies. Ose took the lead in a bipartisan effort to curtail production of methamphetamine.

Redistricting provided Ose with a safe though mostly unfamiliar district, and he was reelected 62%–34%. In 1998 he signed a pledge to serve only three terms in the House. By summer 2002, he was traveling around the state attending political forums and exploring a race against Senator Barbara Boxer in 2004. But in May 2003, Ose announced he would not run for the Senate and that he would honor his term limits pledge and not seek reelection. Possible Republican candidates for Ose's open House seat include state Senator Rico Oller and former Congressman and Attorney General Dan Lungren.

FOURTH DISTRICT

Rep. John Doolittle (R)

Elected 1990, 7th term; b. Oct. 30, 1950, Glendale; home, Rocklin; U. of CA at Santa Cruz, B.A. 1972, U. of the Pacific, J.D. 1978; Mormon; married (Julia).

Elected Office: CA Senate, 1980–90, Repub. Caucus Chmn., 1987–90.

Professional Career: Practicing atty., 1978–80.

DC Office: 2410 RHOB 20515, 202-225-2511; Fax: 202-225-5444; Web site: www.house.gov/doolittle.

District Office: Granite Bay, 916-786-5560.

Committees: *Republican Conference Secretary. Appropriations* (27th of 36 R): District of Columbia; Energy & Water Development. *House Administration* (5th of 6 R).

Group Ratings

	ADA	ACLU	AFS	LCV	CON	ITIC	NTU	COC	ACU	NTLC	CHC
2002	5	7	0	0	36	88	60	84	91	94	100
2001	0	—	0	7	—	—	73	91	100	—	—

National Journal Ratings

	2001 LIB	—	2001 CONS		2002 LIB	—	2002 CONS
Economic	7%	—	89%		31%	—	68%
Social	0%	—	81%		0%	—	75%
Foreign	29%	—	69%		0%	—	85%

Key Votes of the 107th Congress

1. Approve Bush Tax Cuts	Y	5. Faith-Based Charities	Y	9. Trade Promotion Authority	Y
2. Limit Patients' Bill of Rights	Y	6. Bar Gays in the Boy Scouts	Y	10. Bar Funds for Intl. Court	Y
3. Campaign Finance Reform	N	7. Ban Partial-Birth Abortion	Y	11. Authorize Force in Iraq	Y
4. Ban ANWR Development	N	8. Arm Commercial Pilots	Y	12. Deny Home. Sec. Dept. Union	Y

Election Results

2002 general	John Doolittle (R)	147,997	(65%)	($979,438)
	Mark Norberg (D)	72,860	(32%)	($7,548)
	Other	7,649	(3%)	
2002 primary	John Doolittle (R)	79,575	(78%)	
	Bill Kirby (R)	23,083	(22%)	
2000 general	John Doolittle (R)	197,503	(63%)	($587,722)
	Mark A. Norberg (D)	97,974	(31%)	($14,540)
	Other	15,946	(5%)	

Prior Winning Percentages: 1998 (63%); 1996 (60%); 1994 (61%); 1992 (50%); 1990 (50%)

The People		Race/Ethnic Origin	Ancestry	
Area size:	17,159 sq. mi.	83.8% White	German: 13.1%	English: 11.2%
Urban population:	67.4%	1.2% Black	Irish: 10.1%	
Rural population:	32.6%	2.3% Asian	**2000 Presidential Vote**	
Pop. 2000:	639,088	1.1% Native Am.	Bush (R)..............172,169 (59%)	
Median income:	$49,387	0.1% Hawaiian	Gore (D)..............104,437 (36%)	
Poverty status:	8.7%	2.4% Two+ races	Other..................15,633 (5%)	
Military veterans:	16.6%	0.2% Other	**Cook Partisan Voting Index:** R +13	
		8.9% Hispanic Origin		

Occupation	Blue collar: 19.6%	White collar: 63.1%	Gray collar: 17.3%

California sprang suddenly into existence: The Gold Rush of 1849 was followed by statehood and the creation of the first 27 counties in 1850. The new state's first boom area was the Mother Lode country in the foothills of the Sierras above Sacramento. Mining camps the size of eastern cities grew up in vacant valleys locked amid steep hills, with thousands of would-be millionaires gathered to find gold—though most of those who actually got rich did so by catering to miners' needs. In Placerville, John Studebaker had a buggy shop, Phillip Armour ran a butcher shop and Mark Hopkins had a dry goods store. The biggest mine in California was sunk in Grass Valley in 1857 and worked for half a century. But long before that, most of the Mother Lode country emptied out, leaving ghost towns and villages with hundreds of deserted houses: an antique vacation country left behind in time.

As they celebrated the sesquicentennial, local residents sought to resurrect their area into a booming ex-urban and tourist mecca. "The American River near Coloma becomes a virtual free-way of whooping rafters on summer weekends," reported *USA Today*. "The Mother Lode also offers modern-day prospectors an intriguing pastiche of bed-and-breakfast inns, musty antique stores and such blink-and-you'll-miss-'em outposts as Volcano, Fiddletown, Rough and Ready"–named after President Zachary Taylor. Thousands of Californians—many of them families from smog-filled, middle-class suburbs of the Los Angeles Basin and the San Francisco Bay area—looking for a more pleasant, small-town, orderly environment, have found it here along fast-flowing creeks where the '49ers camped. For the first time since the 1860 Census, populations of these counties rose sharply in the past three decades. The population of Placer County, which includes Sacramento suburbs and part of the Mother Lode country, rose 44% in the 1990s. Politically, this migration has changed the Mother Lode country from Democratic to Republican. In 1976, nine Mother Lode counties from Sierra to Mariposa cast 118,000 votes and voted 50%–47% for Jimmy Carter over Gerald Ford: close to the California average. In 2000 they cast 286,000 votes and voted 60% for George W. Bush— results closer to Idaho's than California's.

The 4th Congressional District consists of the northern half of the Mother Lode country and the Placer County suburbs of Sacramento, plus a small portion of Sacramento County. It extends northward through thinly populated mountain counties to the Oregon line. Most of its residents live within the I-80 corridor, clustered near the Sacramento County line in places like Roseville (the district's most populous city), Rocklin or in the Mother Lode country from Placerville to Nevada City. Of the state's 53 districts, this has the highest percentage of rural population with 33%. Before redistricting, it extended south along the Nevada border and included Yosemite. Now, it instead shifts north through the Sierras to the Oregon border.

The congressman from the 4th District is John Doolittle, first elected in 1990. Doolittle grew up in the Los Angeles area and went to high school in Cupertino, in what now is Silicon Valley. His conservatism was annealed in the fires of adversity: He graduated from the University of California at Santa Cruz in 1972, when the campus was 97% for George McGovern. After law school he moved to the edge of the Sacramento metro area where the foothills begin, and in 1980 was elected at 30 to the state Senate from a district that stretched north to the Oregon border. When the incumbent retired in 1990 in a district that then stretched from the Mother Lode country to Stockton, Doolittle ran for the seat. He had tougher competition than expected from Democrat Patricia Malberg, who was pro-choice on abortion, against nuclear power and for defense spending cuts; Doolittle won by just 50%–46%.

As a freshman, Doolittle was one of the Republicans' Gang of Seven, who were the advance guard for Newt Gingrich's 1994 revolution. In the Republican House, Doolittle was given a sub-committee chair the old Democrats who represented this area would have relished: Water and Power. But his agenda resembled theirs only in his support for the Auburn Dam, which he and other Sacramento area congressmen for decades have wanted to build on the American River, 35 miles east of Sacramento. Doolittle insisted on a design that could supply water to the Mother Lode. But in 1996 the dam was rejected in committee, 35–28, by a combination of environmentalists and spending opponents. The deadlock has continued between Doolittle and the 5th District's Robert Matsui, who favors raising Folsom Dam seven feet instead. In July 2002, Doolittle contended that plans by the Army Corps of Engineers to repair and strengthen the Folsom Dam, which was completed in 1955, would be a waste of money; Transportation and Infrastructure Committee chairman Don Young agreed with Doolittle, but the dam extension has yet to be authorized. In 2001, Doolittle gave up the subcommittee to take a long-desired seat on the Appropriations Committee, where he soon claimed credit for nearly $20 million in projects for his district, including land acquisition, wastewater treatment facilities, and restoration projects in the Lake Tahoe basin. In October 2002 he introduced with Rick Boucher a bill to permit fair use copying of certain communications software; it would weaken the anti-circumvention rules of a 1998 copyright law.

Doolittle has worked closely with Tom DeLay on several issues, including opposing the Shays-Meehan campaign finance bill as "an abomination" and as unconstitutional; they have offered an alternative to remove restrictions on fundraising but provide daily disclosure of contributions. During the February 2002 debate in which the House passed Shays-Meehan, he described its partisan impact in apocalyptic terms. "If this passes, we lose the House. We may not lose it this time. . . . This is literally the survival of the Republican Party that is going on right now." In 2000, a California PAC controlled by Doolittle made a soft-money contribution of $50,000 to an unsuccessful candidate for Placer County supervisor. As a leader of House conservatives, he was a co-founder of the Conservative Action Team, now renamed the Republican Study Committee, which has become a force in attempting to limit domestic spending.

Back home he defeated Malberg in a close rematch in 1992 and has won more than 60% of the vote since. In 2002, against a primary opponent who called the Auburn dam a "boondoggle" and favored Shays-Meehan, Doolittle won 78%–22%.

After the 2002 election, Doolittle was elected without opposition as secretary of the House Republican Conference; this is the lowest ranking position in the party leadership, but gives him a seat at leadership meetings.

FIFTH DISTRICT

Rep. Robert Matsui (D)

Elected 1978, 13th term; b. Sept. 17, 1941, Sacramento; home, Sacramento; U. of CA at Berkeley, A.B. 1963, J.D. 1966; United Methodist; married (Doris).

Elected Office: Sacramento City Cncl., 1971–78.

Professional Career: Practicing atty., 1967–78.

DC Office: 2310 RHOB 20515, 202-225-7163; Fax: 202-225-0566; Web site: www.house.gov/matsui.

District Office: Sacramento, 916-498-5600.

Committees: *DCCC Chairman. Ways & Means* (3d of 17 D): Social Security (RMM).

Group Ratings

	ADA	ACLU	AFS	LCV	CON	ITIC	NTU	COC	ACU	NTLC	CHC
2002	100	87	89	100	70	50	20	35	0	0	0
2001	95	—	100	100	—	—	7	35	0	—	—

National Journal Ratings

	2001 LIB	—	2001 CONS		2002 LIB	—	2002 CONS
Economic	88%	—	11%		77%	—	20%
Social	83%	—	11%		84%	—	8%
Foreign	77%	—	22%		77%	—	19%

Key Votes of the 107th Congress

1. Approve Bush Tax Cuts	N	5. Faith-Based Charities		9. Trade Promotion Authority	N
2. Limit Patients' Bill of Rights	N	6. Bar Gays in the Boy Scouts	N	10. Bar Funds for Intl. Court	N
3. Campaign Finance Reform	Y	7. Ban Partial-Birth Abortion	N	11. Authorize Force in Iraq	N
4. Ban ANWR Development	Y	8. Arm Commercial Pilots	N	12. Deny Home. Sec. Dept. Union	N

Election Results

2002 general	Robert Matsui (D)	92,726	(70%)	($867,352)
	Richard Frankhuizen (R)	34,749	(26%)	($5,692)
	Other	4,103	(3%)	
2002 primary	Robert Matsui (D)	unopposed		
2000 general	Robert Matsui (D)	147,025	(69%)	($769,342)
	Ken Payne (R)	55,945	(26%)	($44,395)
	Other	11,089	(5%)	

Prior Winning Percentages: 1998 (72%); 1996 (70%); 1994 (68%); 1992 (69%); 1990 (60%); 1988 (71%); 1986 (76%); 1984 (100%); 1982 (90%); 1980 (71%); 1978 (53%)

The People		Race/Ethnic Origin	Ancestry	
Area size:	150 sq. mi.	43.4% White	German: 7.5%	Irish: 5.9%
Urban population:	99.7%	14.4% Black	English: 5.3%	
Rural population:	0.3%	14.9% Asian	**2000 Presidential Vote**	
Pop. 2000:	639,088	0.8% Native Am.	Gore (D) 113,987	(60%)
Median income:	$36,719	0.8% Hawaiian	Bush (R)................66,011	(35%)
Poverty status:	19.7%	4.7% Two+ races	Other....................9,239	(5%)
Military veterans:	12.2%	0.3% Other	**Cook Partisan Voting Index:** D +13	
		20.8% Hispanic Origin		

Occupation	Blue collar: 20.1%	White collar: 62.9%	Gray collar: 17.0%

Sacramento, capital of the nation's largest state, focus of California's third-largest media market (19th in the nation), home of a national sports franchise (the NBA's Sacramento Kings) and an 18-mile light rail system, is no longer just a small city with a lot of civil servants and a vegetable-packing economy. It is a vibrant American metropolis, with some of the nation's highest job growth. Sacramento started as a river port on the sluggish waters of the Sacramento and American rivers. It was the destination of many overland migrants, the site of Sutter's Fort, where John Augustus Sutter found the gold that set off the Gold Rush of 1849, and the western terminus of the Pony Express in 1860. This was the natural choice to be California's capital, halfway between the San Francisco Bay and the Mother Lode country in the foothills of the Sierras, and in the middle of California's vast valley. Agriculture continues to be important today in Sacra-tomato (as some call it): it has the world's largest almond processing plant.

In the old days, government was not a big business. Just a few lobbyists hung out in saloons on K or J streets, the governor's mansion was a musty antique, and the 100-plus degree summers emptied out what there was of the city. But air conditioning has replaced awnings, freeways and shopping malls have followed the city's growth east and north toward the Sierra foothills, and affluence has made this one of America's higher income metropolitan areas. In the 1980s metropolitan Sacramento grew 35% and in the 1990s by 22%, so that it now has 1.8 million people, about the same as metro Cincinnati or Kansas City. The high-tech growth has moved east from Silicon Valley, with Intel and Hewlett-Packard housing large campuses, as Bay Area refugees have welcomed less expensive and more comfortable living standards. Government expanded, too, and the platoons of lobbyists, lawyers and consultants have set up permanent shop here. There's little hostility toward government here; the legislature was the model for the professional legislature. Today, nearly 1,000 registered lobbyists prowl the halls of the Capitol. As Sacramento has grown, this once Democratic, pro-government, working-class bastion has become closer to an upscale Sun Belt boomtown. A long generation ago, in 1966, Sacramento was just about the only part of California beyond the Bay Area that stuck with Pat Brown over challenger Ronald Reagan. When Al Gore swept California 53%–42% in 2000, he carried Sacramento County by only 49%–45%, and George W. Bush carried the four-county metro area by 48%–46%. In 2002 Sacramento County voted 47%–41% for Republican Bill Simon over Democratic Governor Gray Davis.

The 5th Congressional District consists of the center of metropolitan Sacramento, all of the city of Sacramento and some of its close-in suburbs. In contrast to surrounding districts, redistricting left it relatively unchanged. The 5th contains affluent neighborhoods on older grid streets and scattered low-income black, Mexican-American and Hmong neighborhoods, plus new condominiums north of the American River and middle-class subdivisions south of downtown. Sacramento's neighborhoods are more ethnically diverse than those of any other big city in California, according to the Public Policy Institute of California. This is the solidly Democratic part of metro Sacramento, and the 5th is the most Democratic district in the great valley from Bakersfield north to Oregon. Its boundaries were little changed in the 2001 redistricting.

The congressman from the 5th is Robert Matsui, a Democrat first elected in 1978, third-ranking Democrat on the Ways and Means Committee and Minority Leader Nancy Pelosi's choice to chair the DCCC. Born in 1941, the infant Matsui and his family were among the West Coast Japanese Americans forced into internment camps in 1942, and although he has no memory of the experience himself, he does remember the silence his family and others maintained about it. It was Asian shame, when none of the victims had anything to be ashamed about. He was one of the lead sponsors of the 1988 Japanese American redress law that apologized for the internment policy and provided monetary compensation for every survivor of the camps and for so-called "voluntary evacuees."

Matsui has been dependably liberal and has taken a lead role in the Democratic party's movement away from free trade measures. In 1993 he took the lead in seeking House approval of the NAFTA, at a time when the Clinton administration seemed lukewarm and Majority Leader Dick Gephardt was opposed. Working with Republican Jim Kolbe of Arizona, he rallied support and let the White House know that NAFTA was foundering and would not pass without a major push. Both the White House and Newt Gingrich went all out, and NAFTA passed 234–200. Matsui hoped for a similar outcome on fast-track negotiating authority (since renamed trade promotion authority) in 1997. But he found himself isolated as one of very few Democrats strongly supporting fast track; when he and the White House were unable to produce the number of Democratic votes they had promised, Gingrich pulled the measure at the last minute. The Republicans brought it back up for a vote in September 1998, even though it was apparent it had lost rather than gained votes; Matsui was incensed at what he considered a partisan maneuver. When George W. Bush called for trade promotion authority, Matsui opposed it and echoed other Democrats in backing stringent provisions on labor and environmental terms of trade deals.

Matsui is ranking minority member on the Social Security Subcommittee, and by 2001 he had shifted his focus to that issue. He strongly opposes individual investment accounts—the traditional Democratic position, though one fitfully abandoned by the Clinton administration. In the 2002 campaign, he took the lead in attacking Republican plans for "privatization" of Social Security. House Democrats hoped this issue would turn the tide in the election. It didn't, but Matsui was not a target of criticism. At Ways and Means, he has also become a party leader on tax issues, opposing what he considers excessive Republican cuts. But he has sponsored more narrow tax provisions, including repeal of the 3% telephone excise tax and a new tax credit for the deployment of broadband services. Matsui would undoubtedly like to be ranking minority member or, better yet, chairman of Ways and Means; he is a decade younger than the two more senior Democrats, Charles Rangel and Pete Stark.

Matsui has been active in Democratic fundraising, as treasurer of the Democratic National

Committee from 1991–95 and deputy chairman in 1995 and 1996; his wife Doris Matsui was deputy director of public liaison in the Clinton White House until 1998. Soon after Nancy Pelosi was elected Minority Leader in November 2002, she called her northern California friend of nearly 30 years to explore his interest in chairing the DCCC. Initially he said no. But the more they talked about the challenges that Democrats faced in winning back the majority and her aggressive approach as party leader, the more comfortable each became with the idea of Matsui chairing the DCCC. He believed that she needed a loyalist in that job; she evidently did not want to name Bill Jefferson of Louisiana, who was the choice of the Congressional Black Caucus but who had little experience in closely contested general elections. Matsui's selection was announced December 23. Matsui said that Democrats must run competitive challengers in more House seats, including some that look forbidding, and that the party needed to raise more money and create a firmer financial base. That would not be an easy task. Bipartisan redistricting plans in states like California, New York, Illinois and Ohio have reduced the number of competitive seats.

For many years the Sacramento delegation worked together for years to build the Auburn Dam to provide greater flood protection for Sacramento, but the delegation split after losing to a coalition of environmentalists and fiscal conservatives in 1996. Matsui argued that the Auburn Dam would never be built and introduced a plan, endorsed by the Clinton administration, to raise the height of downstream American River levees. As 2002 ended, neither plan had been approved, and the deadlock over Sacramento's flood control system continued.

In the past, Matsui has flirted with running for statewide office—against then-Senator Pete Wilson in 1988, for attorney general in 1990, for the vacant Senate seat in 1992—but decided against it each time. He once contemplated a challenge to Charles Rangel for the ranking minority position on Ways and Means, but the two of them lately have gotten along well. Matsui likely will continue to win reelection easily every two years.

SIXTH DISTRICT

Rep. Lynn Woolsey (D)

Elected 1992, 6th term; b. Nov. 3, 1937, Seattle, WA; home, Petaluma; U. of San Francisco, B.S. 1981; Presbyterian; divorced.

Elected Office: Petaluma City Cncl., 1985–92, Vice Mayor, 1986, 1991.

Professional Career: Human Resources Mgr., Harris Digital Telephone, 1969–80; Owner, Woolsey Personnel Svc., 1980–92.

DC Office: 2263 RHOB 20515, 202-225-5161; Fax: 202-225-5163; Web site: www.house.gov/woolsey.

District Offices: San Rafael, 415-507-9554; Santa Rosa, 707-542-7182.

Committees: *Education & the Workforce* (6th of 22 D): Education Reform (RMM); Workforce Protections. *Science* (5th of 22 D): Energy.

Group Ratings

	ADA	ACLU	AFS	LCV	CON	ITIC	NTU	COC	ACU	NTLC	CHC
2002	95	93	100	88	43	38	24	35	0	0	0
2001	100	—	100	100	—	—	11	26	0	—	—

National Journal Ratings

	2001 LIB	—	2001 CONS		2002 LIB	—	2002 CONS
Economic	95%	—	0%		95%	—	0%
Social	90%	—	0%		84%	—	8%
Foreign	96%	—	0%		94%	—	0%

Key Votes of the 107th Congress

1. Approve Bush Tax Cuts	N	5. Faith-Based Charities	N	9. Trade Promotion Authority	N
2. Limit Patients' Bill of Rights	N	6. Bar Gays in the Boy Scouts	N	10. Bar Funds for Intl. Court	N
3. Campaign Finance Reform	Y	7. Ban Partial-Birth Abortion	N	11. Authorize Force in Iraq	N
4. Ban ANWR Development	Y	8. Arm Commercial Pilots	N	12. Deny Home. Sec. Dept. Union	N

Election Results

2002 general	Lynn Woolsey (D)	139,750	(67%)	($803,235)
	Paul Erickson (R)	62,052	(30%)	($10,187)
	Other	7,761	(4%)	
2002 primary	Lynn Woolsey (D)	69,158	(80%)	
	Mike Martini (D)	16,770	(20%)	
2000 general	Lynn Woolsey (D)	182,116	(64%)	($576,539)
	Ken McAuliffe (R)	80,169	(28%)	($17,979)
	Justin Moscoso (Green)	13,248	(5%)	
	Other	7,585	(3%)	

Prior Winning Percentages: 1998 (68%); 1996 (62%); 1994 (58%); 1992 (65%)

The People		Race/Ethnic Origin	Ancestry	
Area size:	2,119 sq. mi.	76.1% White	German: 11.1%	Irish: 10.6%
Urban population:	89.8%	2.0% Black	English: 9.8%	
Rural population:	10.2%	3.7% Asian	**2000 Presidential Vote**	
Pop. 2000:	639,087	0.6% Native Am.	Gore (D)	178,746 (62%)
Median income:	$59,115	0.2% Hawaiian	Bush (R)	87,082 (30%)
Poverty status:	7.7%	2.7% Two+ races	Other	21,514 (7%)
Military veterans:	12.2%	0.2% Other	**Cook Partisan Voting Index:** D +17	
		14.5% Hispanic Origin		

Occupation	Blue collar: 17.2%	White collar: 68.0%	Gray collar: 14.8%

When the Golden Gate Bridge was opened in 1937, San Francisco was one of the nation's best-known cities, but few knew much about the land beyond the bridge's north pierhead. There were fewer than 50,000 people in Marin County then and another 65,000 just to the north in Sonoma County. For San Franciscans, Marin was known for the ferry terminus in Sausalito, a fishing village and art colony, and as the beginning of the Redwood Empire, with its giant trees in Muir Woods, which has a dense concentration of spotted owls; near the Bay was the state prison at San Quentin, with its infamous gas chamber. Farther north is the Point Reyes peninsula for many recreational outdoor activities, and the wine country of Sonoma County, sunny valleys protected from the fog by the Coast Range. In one such valley was Santa Rosa, site of agronomist Luther Burbank's laboratory, a town that looked Middle American enough to be the set for dozens of movies. Politically, the area was then typical of the nation: traditionally Republican, but favoring Franklin Roosevelt in the 1930s.

Today this part of California is far more populous, with 247,000 people in Marin and 458,000 in the faster-growing Sonoma, affluent beyond the dreams of Americans of 50 years ago and extreme in its cultural attitudes, but with relatively few racial minorities compared to other counties in the San Francisco Bay Area. Santa Rosa (Sonoma County), the largest city in the district, is growing rapidly, thanks to thriving wine and telecommunications industries. Trendy Marin, with its hot tubs and its fashionable people getting in touch with themselves, became a national caricature: economically affluent, culturally liberationist; this was the home of "American Taliban" John Walker Lindh. Until it was surpassed by the Silicon Valley in the late 1990s, it was the nation's most expensive housing market. After a while such an image feeds on itself; a place like Marin attracts affluent people who share its values, while those who don't, go elsewhere—in the Bay Area to the more conservative San Ramon Valley, beyond the mountains east of Oakland. Indeed the Bay Area as a whole seems to attract liberals and repel conservatives, just as Dallas does the opposite. And Marin and Sonoma are attracting the most liberal of the liberal—averse to traditional religion, derisive of traditional sexual and marriage mores, viscerally anti-military.

The 6th Congressional District includes all of Marin County and Sonoma except for its rural eastern border. Marin and Sonoma Counties have been transformed politically over the last generation. In 1980 they voted for Ronald Reagan over Jimmy Carter by a 47%–36% margin. In the Reagan years they moved left and in 1988 voted for Michael Dukakis over George Bush by a 57%–41% margin. Now Republicans seem almost an endangered species here: in 2000 Marin voted for Al Gore over George W. Bush by a 61%–31% margin. The public dialogue here is increasingly monopartisan, and, in this community priding itself on its tolerance, nary a dissenting word is heard.

The congresswoman from the 6th District is Lynn Woolsey, a Democrat first elected in 1992 when Barbara Boxer was elected to the Senate. Woolsey grew up in the Pacific Northwest, moved to Marin and was a housewife with three children under 6 when her marriage ended in 1968. She went on welfare, got a low-paying job and left her children with 13 different babysitters in a year. Deliverance appeared in the form of a job with a high-tech startup firm where she rose to become a top executive. She remarried and moved to a house in Petaluma where her mother could live and look after the kids. She put herself through business school at night, earned a degree in human resources and started her own personnel service. In 1984 Woolsey won a seat on the Petaluma Council. In 1992 she won the House seat in a nine-candidate primary with 26%, well ahead of the next candidate's 19%. In the general she faced liberal Republican Assemblyman Bill Filante. But he had surgery for a brain tumor and stopped campaigning; she won 65%–34%.

An apt representative of her district, Woolsey has one of the most liberal voting records in the House. As the only known former welfare recipient in Congress, she co-chaired the Democrats' task force on welfare. She opposed the 1996 welfare act and calls for easing work requirements and providing more child care; she wants mothers to be able to stay at home until their children are 11. She lobbied against banning gays in the military, accompanied by her son who is gay. When the child-nutrition program was renewed, she took credit for a pilot program to expand school breakfast to all children regardless of income and for opening eligibility to teenagers in after-school snack programs. Republicans sought to embarrass Democrats by calling for a vote in September 2000 on Woolsey's bill to revoke the federal charter for the Boy Scouts because the group excludes gays; her bill was defeated 362–12. On the education bill in 2001, she sought to make improved teacher quality as a top priority, but she voted against the final House-Senate agreement. She introduced a "Go Girl" bill to bridge the digital divide between the genders. As the senior Democrat on the Energy Subcommittee at the Science panel, she worked to increase federal support for alternative energy sources. During debate on the Homeland Security Department, the House passed her amendment to create an independent Homeland Security Institute to provide technological guidance.

Her big local project has been to expand the protected area around the Point Reyes National Seashore by purchasing easements from nearby farmers and barring them from selling their land to nonagricultural users. Many farmers complained about a federal "land grab" and the proposal languished. She has called for export subsidies for winemakers.

Woolsey has been easily reelected. She had a rare challenge in the 2002 primary from Santa Rosa Mayor Mike Martini, the founder of a winery in Sebastopol, who criticized Woolsey's lack of leadership, her excessively liberal votes, and her failure to bring sufficient funds to the district. Woolsey responded that she has delivered $430 million since 1997, and defended on civil-liberties grounds her October 2001 vote against increased federal powers to track down terrorists. Even though he was mayor of the largest city in the district, Martini lost 80%–20% with a relatively high turnout. After the 2002 election, she wanted the Appropriations seat that her Bay Area neighbor Nancy Pelosi relinquished. But Pelosi decided to award the two vacancies on the committee to members from the South.

SEVENTH DISTRICT

Rep. George Miller (D)

Elected 1974, 15th term; b. May 17, 1945, Richmond; home, Martinez; San Francisco St. U., B.A. 1968, U. of CA at Davis, J.D. 1972; Catholic; married (Cynthia).

Professional Career: Legis. aide, CA Senate Majority Ldr., 1969–74; Practicing atty., 1972–74.

DC Office: 2205 RHOB 20515, 202-225-2095; Fax: 202-225-5609; Web site: www.house.gov/georgemiller.

District Offices: Concord, 925-602-1880; Richmond, 510-262-6500; Vallejo, 707-645-1888.

Committees: *Education & the Workforce* (RMM of 22 D). *Resources* (19th of 24 D).

Group Ratings

	ADA	ACLU	AFS	LCV	CON	ITIC	NTU	COC	ACU	NTLC	CHC
2002	100	93	100	100	84	25	27	30	4	6	0
2001	100	—	100	100	—	—	15	27	0	—	—

National Journal Ratings

	2001 LIB —	2001 CONS		2002 LIB —	2002 CONS
Economic	95% —	0%		93% —	5%
Social	90% —	0%		81% —	19%
Foreign	96% —	0%		94% —	0%

Key Votes of the 107th Congress

1. Approve Bush Tax Cuts	N	5. Faith-Based Charities	N	9. Trade Promotion Authority	N
2. Limit Patients' Bill of Rights	N	6. Bar Gays in the Boy Scouts	N	10. Bar Funds for Intl. Court	N
3. Campaign Finance Reform	Y	7. Ban Partial-Birth Abortion	N	11. Authorize Force in Iraq	N
4. Ban ANWR Development	Y	8. Arm Commercial Pilots	Y	12. Deny Home. Sec. Dept. Union	N

Election Results

2002 general	George Miller (D)	97,849	(71%)	($402,021)
	Charles Hargrave (R)	36,584	(26%)	
	Other	3,943	(3%)	
2002 primary	George Miller (D)	unopposed		
2000 general	George Miller (D)	159,692	(76%)	($443,578)
	Christopher A. Hoffman (R)	44,154	(21%)	($5,188)
	Other	4,943	(2%)	

Prior Winning Percentages: 1998 (77%); 1996 (72%); 1994 (70%); 1992 (70%); 1990 (61%); 1988 (68%); 1986 (67%); 1984 (66%); 1982 (67%); 1980 (63%); 1978 (63%); 1976 (75%); 1974 (56%)

The People		Race/Ethnic Origin	Ancestry	
Area size:	443 sq. mi.	43.2% White	German: 7.5%	Irish: 6.7%
Urban population:	98.7%	16.8% Black	English: 5.6%	
Rural population:	1.3%	13.3% Asian	**2000 Presidential Vote**	
Pop. 2000:	639,088	0.5% Native Am.	Gore (D) 139,421	(66%)
Median income:	$52,778	0.6% Hawaiian	Bush (R) 64,477	(31%)
Poverty status:	10.0%	3.9% Two+ races	Other 6,824	(3%)
Military veterans:	12.5%	0.3% Other	**Cook Partisan Voting Index:** D +18	
		21.4% Hispanic Origin		

Occupation	Blue collar: 22.7%	White collar: 60.1%	Gray collar: 17.1%

The journey inward from the Pacific Ocean to the vast flatness of California's Central Valley passes through a wondrous variety of terrain. The traveler starts at the Golden Gate, with the lush green Presidio on one side and the bluff of the Marin mountains on the other; through the waters of San Francisco Bay, looked down upon by ridges above the East Bay on one side and the cone of

Mount Tamalpais on the other; through the narrow Carquinez Strait to Suisun Bay, with its sloughs and marshes, fed by the sluggish waters of the Sacramento and San Joaquin Delta; and finally past the mountains and waters, to the flat, fertile expanse of California's great interior. This is not a journey most tourists make, but it was a familiar route to the first Americans in California and it passes by much of the industrial base of the Bay Area. On the east side of the bay is Richmond, developed almost instantaneously during World War II when Henry J. Kaiser built a shipyard in its deep-water port and 91,000 people from all over the country were put to work building ships for the Pacific theater; what became known as Rosie the Riveter Memorial Park is now a national park, and the city now has a 36% black population and is attracting high-tech spinoffs. Across Carquinez Strait is Vallejo, named for a Mexican general and member of the first California Senate, the site from 1853 to 1996 of the giant Mare Island Naval Shipyard, now being redeveloped, where 41,000 worked during World War II. These shores are the industrial part of the Bay area, with tank farms and refineries. The towns are among the most ethnically diverse in the country, with large percentages of blacks, Hispanics and Asians, with large numbers of Filipinos in Vallejo and other towns.

The 7th Congressional District includes most of this passage, from Richmond to Vallejo (the 7th's largest city), Hercules, Martinez and Pittsburg. It also proceeds inland through the inter-mountain interstices of Contra Costa County to include part of Concord and northeast from Vallejo over the sloughs and up I-80 to include Vacaville, on flat land beneath Vaca Mountain. Politically, this industrial area was blue-collar, labor-union Democratic back in the days when San Francisco, with its larger white-collar population, often voted Republican. Today housing values have risen, as they have just about everywhere in the Bay area, but it remains heavily Democratic, liberal on most issues.

The congressman from the 7th District is George Miller, one of three remaining Democrats of the Watergate class of 1974 (the others are James Oberstar and Henry Waxman), the first baby-boom liberal to chair a House committee. He is heir to a tradition of Bay Area working-class politics. His father was chairman of the state Senate Finance Committee; when he died in 1969, Miller lost the race to succeed him, but became a staffer for Senate Leader (and later San Francisco Mayor) George Moscone. Miller was a protege of San Francisco Congressman Phillip Burton, who did so much to establish liberal hegemony in the House in the 1970s. To his work Miller brings an aggressiveness and zest for political combat reminiscent of Burton. He is a strong backer of protecting the environment against what he sees as greedy private sector operators and of furthering the causes of labor unions. Like Burton, Miller has grasped for top party leadership posts but hasn't made it. But he has learned a legislator's virtues of patience, timing and creativity.

Miller began the 1990s in a position of power, able to advance his causes forward; in the mid-1990s he found himself defending yesterday's gains and trying to prevent losses; in 2001 he found himself working with a Republican president on one of his top priorities. In 1991 he became chairman of Interior (he renamed it Natural Resources in 1993 and Republicans renamed it Resources in 1995) and proceeded, in his words, "to kick ass and take names." He had long crusaded against water reclamation projects that provided cheap water to farmers. In 1992, amid a California drought, he passed a Central Valley Project law that raised farmers' prices closer to those of urban users and imposed environmental restrictions, over the fierce opposition of Central Valley politicians and Governor Pete Wilson. The victory was sealed when Bill Clinton in 1993 appointed a top Miller aide as head of the Bureau of Reclamation. He passed the California desert bill, with Senator Dianne Feinstein, in October 1994; it was the last major legislation of the Democratic Congress.

For several years in the minority he worked more to prevent change than to make change. He helped to stymie John Doolittle's attempt to revise the Central Valley Project and was part of the coalition opposing the Auburn Dam sought by Doolittle and others from the Sacramento area. He harshly criticized Republicans for trying to change the Endangered Species Act, EPA regulations, Arctic National Wildlife Refuge oil drilling, Tongass Forest logging and for commercial sponsorship of national parks; for the most part, he was successful, with help from the Clinton administration. He won with Republican Don Young in 2000 a major expansion of the Land and Water Conservation Fund, although the Senate scuttled a more sweeping version. He successfully moved to award Congressional Medals of Honor to black World War II veterans who were unfairly overlooked and to reopen the mutiny verdicts of black sailors who refused to report for duty after munitions explosions at Port Chicago in 1944. He showed open-mindedness by working with Republican Senator Mike DeWine to change the focus of the Family Reunification Act, which Miller sponsored in 1980, to the best interests of children.

From time to time Miller's short fuse has been on display. In 1997 he and Tom DeLay had a red-faced confrontation over Miller's charge that DeLay let lobbyists write legislation in his office. Later, he obstructed the House by objecting to routine procedures in order to force a vote on the campaign finance bill. Miller mocked what he considered the Republicans' obsession with Monica Lewinsky, speculating they would take her blue dress "through their districts like the Olympic torch or something and see if that helps." But he was the one member who did not vote on impeachment in December 1998, for a good reason: he had just had hip-replacement surgery and his California doctor advised against air travel. In January 2000, he took on the unlikely cause of his old friend Bill Bradley's campaign for President, spending five days campaigning in Iowa before the caucuses.

The election of George W. Bush unexpectedly returned Miller to the center ring. He replaced the retired Bill Clay as ranking Democrat on the Education and the Workforce Committee. The incoming chairman, John Boehner, recommended that Bush include Miller and other Democrats in a pre-inauguration meeting in Austin. They struck up a cordial relationship; Bush started calling Miller "Big George." Miller is a Democrat who doesn't always follow the dictates of the teacher's unions; he seems genuinely concerned that too many American children are getting a rotten education. "My first concern has always been children. I look at the number of poor children who have been denied a chance at a real educational opportunity. This has to rank first and foremost." He came to believe that Bush shared that concern. Miller wanted more spending on education, but he also wanted more rigorous standards, with consequences. Boehner and Miller worked on a bipartisan basis on a committee that has usually had bitter partisan divisions. The committee bill provided more money and required uniform standards, though not the NAEP tests favored by Miller. The bill passed the House in May 2001 384–45. A different version passed the Senate in June 2001. At the bill signing in January 2002 Bush took care to praise Miller for his contributions. Miller was not entirely happy with the way the administration implemented the law, however. In February 2002 he said the Bush budget did not provide enough money, and in December 2002 he complained that the administration was not providing information on dropout rates among minority students.

Miller has routinely been reelected by wide margins. Redistricting added Vacaville and shed El Cerrito, but the alterations did not make any significant political difference.

EIGHTH DISTRICT

Rep. Nancy Pelosi (D)

Elected June 1987, 8th term; b. Mar. 26, 1940, Baltimore, MD; home, San Francisco; Trinity Col., B.A. 1962; Catholic; married (Paul).

Professional Career: CA Dem. Party, Northern Chmn., 1977–81, St. Chmn., 1981–83; DSCC Finance Chmn., 1985–87; PR exec., Ogilvy & Mather, 1986–87.

DC Office: 2371 RHOB 20515, 202-225-4965; Fax: 202-225-8259; Web site: www.house.gov/pelosi.

District Office: San Francisco, 415-556-4862.

Committees: *Minority Leader.*

Group Ratings

	ADA	ACLU	AFS	LCV	CON	ITIC	NTU	COC	ACU	NTLC	CHC
2002	100	87	100	100	70	25	21	37	0	0	0
2001	100	—	100	93	—	—	8	35	0	—	—

National Journal Ratings

	2001 LIB	—	2001 CONS		2002 LIB	—	2002 CONS
Economic	94%	—	6%		88%	—	10%
Social	83%	—	11%		84%	—	8%
Foreign	93%	—	7%		90%	—	8%

Key Votes of the 107th Congress

1. Approve Bush Tax Cuts	N	5. Faith-Based Charities	N	9. Trade Promotion Authority	N
2. Limit Patients' Bill of Rights	N	6. Bar Gays in the Boy Scouts	N	10. Bar Funds for Intl. Court	N
3. Campaign Finance Reform	Y	7. Ban Partial-Birth Abortion	N	11. Authorize Force in Iraq	N
4. Ban ANWR Development	Y	8. Arm Commercial Pilots	N	12. Deny Home. Sec. Dept. Union	N

Election Results

2002 general	Nancy Pelosi (D)	127,684	(80%)	($966,946)
	G. German (R)	20,063	(13%)	($7,130)
	Jay Pond (Green)	10,033	(6%)	
	Other	2,661	(2%)	
2002 primary	Nancy Pelosi (D)	65,949	(93%)	
	Paul McConnell (D)	4,898	(7%)	
2000 general	Nancy Pelosi (D)	181,847	(85%)	($608,318)
	Adam Sparks (R)	25,298	(12%)	
	Other	8,283	(4%)	

Prior Winning Percentages: 1998 (86%); 1996 (84%); 1994 (82%); 1992 (82%); 1990 (77%); 1988 (76%); 1987 (63%)

The People		Race/Ethnic Origin	Ancestry	
Area size:	114 sq. mi.	42.9% White	Irish: 6.9%	German: 6.4%
Urban population:	100.0%	8.6% Black	English: 5.1%	
Rural population:	0.0%	28.7% Asian	**2000 Presidential Vote**	
Pop. 2000:	639,088	0.3% Native Am.	Gore (D) 196,878 (77%)	
Median income:	$52,322	0.5% Hawaiian	Bush (R)................37,737 (15%)	
Poverty status:	12.2%	2.9% Two+ races	Other 20,869 (8%)	
Military veterans:	6.8%	0.3% Other	**Cook Partisan Voting Index:** D +34	
		15.7% Hispanic Origin		

Occupation   Blue collar: 11.9%   White collar: 72.9%   Gray collar: 15.1%

On February 20, 1915, Governor Hiram Johnson and Mayor James Rolph led 150,000 people onto the grounds of the Panama-Pacific International Exposition to see the Spanish-Italian baroque style building built on reclaimed land in what became San Francisco's Marina district. The Exposition ostensibly celebrated the completion of the Panama Canal, but it was clearly intended to show off San Francisco's recovery from the 1906 earthquake. It also spotlighted San Francisco as the central focus of an America that was becoming, with its acquisition of Hawaii and the Philippines and its interest in an open-door policy with China and trade with Japan, a power in the Pacific. The Exposition set the physical style of San Francisco: It encouraged the use of Mediterranean color, accent and detail that characterizes most post-Victorian houses and commercial structures in The City (as the *San Francisco Examiner* called it for years). It created the picturesque Marina district, whose old buildings were among those damaged in the 1989 earthquake, and today's tourist waterfront around Fisherman's Wharf and Ghirardelli Square. This San Francisco has many facets: On a sunny day it looks almost tropical, with brown mountains baking in the sun and light shining off the pastel stucco buildings; when the clouds scud in from the Pacific, it can look sinister, full of dark corners where a private detective's partner might be ambushed by a pretty girl. The buildings can be majestic, like the monumental Beaux Arts City

Hall, or tawdry, like the hotels of the Tenderloin; it is a city that looks exotic at first but, when you look closely, can only be American.

San Francisco has been a dynamic city, capable of great growth, carrying the American tradition of tolerance of diversity to new lengths; it grew from nothing to a major city in the single year of 1850; its American origins are obvious from the regular grids of streets named after politicians and local developers. The San Francisco of 1915 was proud of the writers who had flourished there—Jack London, Ambrose Bierce, Frank Norris—and of the home-town traditions of the arts and crafts movement, just as San Francisco later would have a Herb Caen-ish pride in the beats of the 1950s North Beach, the hippies who thronged Haight-Ashbury in 1967, and the gays of Castro in the 1970s and since. Over the years, the city's booming economy, based initially on food processing, but now on finance, high-tech and clothing (Levi Strauss, The Gap) attracted talented newcomers, weighted increasingly toward those who find its liberation-minded cultural attitudes congenial.

Politically, San Francisco was a progressive Republican town, like the two men who led the way into the Exposition. The sour-tempered Hiram Johnson made his name as a reformer throwing out crooked city politicians; his administration gave California primary elections, referenda and recall, and strong civil service laws. "Sunny Jim" Rolph, mayor from 1911–30 and then governor, built the civic center, parks, schools, streetcars and the Hetch Hetchy aqueduct—the antique infrastructure of San Francisco today. Sympathetic to the conservation movement, willing to deal with organized labor in a union town that had America's only general strike in 1934, tolerant of the diversity of California, these progressive Republicans were the recognizable ancestors of, though certainly not identical to, the San Franciscans who in the 1970s and 1980s became increasingly liberal and even radical.

But San Francisco's hipness can be overstated. For if its distinctive style attracted liberal singles and gays in increasing numbers, its economic dynamism on the Pacific Rim has attracted Asians—as indeed San Francisco did from 1850 until immigration was shut off by the Chinese Exclusion Act in 1882. The city has elected strong liberal politicians—notably, Mayor George Moscone and openly gay Supervisor Harvey Milk, who were shot to death in 1978 by a political opponent who was acquitted of murder by a liberal jury on the bizarre theory that he had been crazed by junk food. Over the next decade, the city's cultural liberalism was tempered by Mayor Dianne Feinstein, who vetoed a gay marriage ordinance and opposed commercial rent control. In 1995, Willie Brown, ousted after 15 years as speaker of the Assembly, returned home and was elected mayor. After reaping admiring publicity following his takeover of the office, Brown's record turned dismal. While the affluent neighborhoods were enriched with new Silicon Valley millionaires, the Chinese, Filipino and other Asian immigrants in the southern and western parts of the city were beleaguered by high taxes that supported the pampered public employee unions. After winning praise for Operation Scrub Down to clean the downtown streets but sparking protests in 2002 for his crackdown on the homeless, he was not eligible for reelection in 2003.

The 8th Congressional District takes in four-fifths of San Francisco, all but the southwest corner. It is the smallest in the state in land area and the most densely packed. It has all of San Francisco's high-rise downtown, the crowded and bustling Chinatown, Telegraph, Nob and Russian Hills, North Beach (which was once really a beach), Pacific Heights (which is still on heights) and the Marina District (which does not have a very big marina). In the valleys are the mostly black Fillmore and Western Addition areas; the 8th is 9% black, 16% Hispanic and 29% Asian—the second highest Asian percentage of any district outside Hawaii. The 8th also has the gay Castro district and Noe Valley, Haight-Ashbury, once the bedraggled center of hippiedom and now another yup-and-coming San Francisco neighborhood, and Portrero Hill with its restored houses overlooking downtown. Farther south are the old residential areas overlooking I-280, with pastel houses strewn along grid streets that hug the steep hills. The district is overwhelmingly Democratic: George W. Bush won an anemic 15 % here in 2000.

The 8th District is represented by Nancy Pelosi, a Democrat with deep political roots and enormous ambition, who was elected in June 1987. She has the energy and shrewdness of one who has handled the most delicate political chores and the charm and unflappability of one who is the mother of five children. Pelosi grew up in Maryland; her father, Thomas D'Alessandro, served in the House from 1939–47 and was mayor of Baltimore for 12 years after that, and her brother, Thomas D'Alessandro Jr., was mayor from 1967–71. Married to a successful San Francisco businessman, she was California Democratic Party chairman in the early 1980s. Since the 1960s, San Francisco's congressional politics were dominated by Phillip Burton, an old-fashioned labor-liberal Democrat. But Burton died in 1983 and his widow Sala, elected to succeed him, died in 1987. With death-bed encouragement from Sala, Pelosi ran and won 35%–31% in the special against gay supervisor Harry Britt.

Pelosi has taken the lead on important issues of local sensitivity. One is human rights, especially in China. After the Tiananmen Square massacre, she sponsored an amendment to give Chinese students the right to remain in the United States; George Bush vetoed it. In 1991 she became the lead sponsor of the bill to condition China's Most Favored Nation status on human rights reforms; the House overrode Bush's veto but it was upheld in the Senate. After that, Pelosi led the annual fight against PNTR and sharply criticized China. "I don't believe in the concept of trickle-down liberty. Economic reform does not necessarily lead to political reform," she said, arguing that the Chinese make concessions not when the U.S. bows to their wishes but when it threatens to walk away. She said that Bill Clinton was either in denial or ill-informed about what's going on in China. When President Jiang Zemin visited Washington in 1997, she termed the White House state dinner shameful and attended a stateless dinner hosted by actor and pro-Tibet activist Richard Gere. When Clinton two years later agreed to terms for China's entry into the World Trade Organization, Pelosi led even more furious opposition to PNTR. Although bitter about the setbacks, she vowed to maintain her human rights vigil. She has done all this at some political risk: Pelosi's position is by no means universally popular with Asian Americans in her district; many think the U.S. should trade and negotiate quietly with China. One of her chief adversaries on the issue is her San Francisco neighbor, Senator Dianne Feinstein; their houses are just a few blocks apart. In addition to working with some Republicans on China, she usually cooperated with chairman Porter Goss as the senior Democrat on the Intelligence Committee, especially after the September 11 attacks. She joined in the committee's final report that, while the intelligence community did not have specific evidence in advance, it did have information that was clearly relevant to the attacks, particularly when considered for its collective significance.

On other issues Pelosi has an almost perfectly liberal voting record. She has used her Appropriations seat to get money for victims of AIDS. She has worked to restore welfare for legal immigrants, and has supported needle exchanges. She has been a leader in encouraging family planning and environmental protection overseas. In 2001, when California suffered an energy shortage, she unsuccessfully sought to force federal regulators to impose temporary price caps on wholesale electricity prices. At home, Pelosi has been re-elected by huge margins.

Although she turned down Dick Gephardt's entreaties to lead the DCCC, Pelosi remained a strong partisan. In hopes that Democrats would regain House control in 2000, she ran a vigorous campaign against Steny Hoyer to become majority whip—raising more than $3 million for her party's candidates and agreeing to head a major fundraising push among non-members. Although she was not running "as a woman," she said, "the fact that I am a woman is an enhancement because we absolutely must have diversity in the leadership." Unfortunately for Democrats and Pelosi, who stood a good chance to win, Republicans kept control and Tom DeLay remained majority whip. When David Bonior decided in 2001 to run for governor of Michigan, she and Hoyer revved up their leadership bids again—this time in a contest to succeed him as minority whip. Pelosi, who was a close ally of Bonior, criticized the party's handling of the 2000 campaign, and said that Democrats needed to refocus on grassroots organization, money and message. Supporters played up her potential to become a celebrity—"a glamorous grandmother who knocks people off their feet," as Representative Neil Abercrombie put it. With nearly unanimous support from the 32 California Democrats, and showing that she knew how to whip and count her supporters, Pelosi won the October 10 vote by a convincing 118–95.

As whip, Pelosi moved quickly to assert herself, sometimes independently from Gephardt. She sparked controversy when she contributed $10,000 to Lynn Rivers in a redistricting-forced Michigan primary against John Dingell—the ranking Democrat on Energy and Commerce who had been a strong supporter of Hoyer for whip. Normally, party leaders do not take sides in such elections. Dingell, who tends to seek retribution for slights against him, handily won the primary. Her biggest conflict came in fall 2002 when she actively encouraged opponents of the resolution authorizing the use of force in Iraq, which Gephardt had enthusiastically endorsed with President Bush at the White House. Pelosi contended that supporters had not made the case for using force, and that she had seen no evidence that Iraq "poses an imminent threat to our nation." To the surprise of many, her efforts helped to secure 126 Democratic votes against the resolution, while only 81 backed the position of Gephardt, which also was endorsed by Democratic Caucus chairman Martin Frost. In retrospect, that split was a compelling signal of the transition underway in the Caucus.

Even before the Election Day votes were counted, Pelosi began making telephone calls to members seeking support to replace Gephardt as Minority Leader if he stepped down. Once the disappointing results were in, Pelosi had all but locked up the support of a majority of the caucus. After Gephardt said that he was stepping down two days after the election, Frost announced his candidacy with warnings that the selection of Pelosi might create a "permanent minority party;" he withdrew from the contest a day later, conceding that he could not win. Harold Ford made a belated, quixotic bid designed to appeal to a combination of blacks and New Democrats, but in the November 14 vote, Pelosi won 177–29.

Following an election that left most Democrats dispirited, she brought a burst of energy—and favorable press coverage—to a party that badly needed it. She quickly settled into the Minority Leader position, showing hands-on management to the initial tasks of selecting members for House committee vacancies and developing a Democratic message designed to highlight the shortcomings of the Bush agenda. There were bruised feelings over some committee assignments but even allies of Hoyer and Frost credited her with bringing a breath of fresh air and enthusiasm to party deliberations after eight years of Gephardt's control.

NINTH DISTRICT

Rep. Barbara Lee (D)

Elected April 1998, 3d term; b. July 16, 1946, El Paso, TX; home, Oakland; Mills Col., B.A. 1973, U. of CA at Berkeley, M.A. 1975; no religious affiliation; divorced.

Elected Office: CA Assembly, 1990–96; CA Senate, 1996–98.

Professional Career: Chief of Staff, U.S. Rep. Ron Dellums, 1975–87.

DC Office: 1724 LHOB 20515, 202-225-2661; Fax: 202-225-9817; Web site: www.house.gov/lee.

District Office: Oakland, 510-763-0370.

Committees: *Financial Services* (13th of 32 D): Domestic and International Monetary Policy, Trade & Technology; Housing & Community Opportunity. *International Relations* (13th of 23 D): Africa; Europe.

Group Ratings

	ADA	ACLU	AFS	LCV	CON	ITIC	NTU	COC	ACU	NTLC	CHC
2002	90	93	100	100	95	38	32	30	0	11	0
2001	95	—	100	100	—	—	18	22	0	—	—

National Journal Ratings

	2001 LIB	—	2001 CONS		2002 LIB	—	2002 CONS
Economic	88%	—	11%		95%	—	0%
Social	90%	—	0%		94%	—	3%
Foreign	96%	—	0%		94%	—	0%

Key Votes of the 107th Congress

1. Approve Bush Tax Cuts	N	5. Faith-Based Charities	N	9. Trade Promotion Authority	N
2. Limit Patients' Bill of Rights	N	6. Bar Gays in the Boy Scouts	*	10. Bar Funds for Intl. Court	N
3. Campaign Finance Reform	Y	7. Ban Partial-Birth Abortion	N	11. Authorize Force in Iraq	N
4. Ban ANWR Development	Y	8. Arm Commercial Pilots	N	12. Deny Home. Sec. Dept. Union	N

Election Results

2002 general	Barbara Lee (D)	135,893	(81%)	($911,962)
	Jerald Udinsky (R)	25,333	(15%)	
	Other	5,691	(3%)	
2002 primary	Barbara Lee (D)	68,550	(85%)	
	Kevin Greene (D)	12,257	(15%)	
2000 general	Barbara Lee (D)	182,352	(85%)	($452,812)
	Arneze Washington (R)	21,033	(10%)	
	Other	11,265	(5%)	

Prior Winning Percentages: 1998 (83%); 1998 (67%)

The People		Race/Ethnic Origin	Ancestry	
Area size:	152 sq. mi.	35.2% White	German: 5.9%	English: 5.1%
Urban population:	99.9%	26.0% Black	Irish: 5.0%	
Rural population:	0.1%	15.4% Asian	**2000 Presidential Vote**	
Pop. 2000:	639,088	0.4% Native Am.	Gore (D) 184,030	(79%)
Median income:	$44,314	0.4% Hawaiian	Bush (R) 31,464	(13%)
Poverty status:	16.9%	3.6% Two+ races	Other 18,868	(8%)
Military veterans:	8.4%	0.4% Other	**Cook Partisan Voting Index:** D +35	
		18.7% Hispanic Origin		

Occupation   Blue collar: 17.3%   White collar: 69.0%   Gray collar: 13.7%

Oakland and Berkeley, on the East Bay opposite San Francisco, stand today on one of the lushest sites in America, overlooking the Bay Bridge and the Golden Gate, basking in the sunshine that is more common here than across the Bay. Both cities are the homes of great institutions, but in different ways they are also museum pieces, antiques from a moment in the 1960s when both, especially Berkeley, gained identities that became hard to shake. Berkeley was founded as a university town, named after the 18th century Irish philosopher Bishop George Berkeley, for his proclamation, "Westward the course of empire takes its way." Famous for years as the home of first-rate scholarship at the University of California, Berkeley became famous politically in 1964 as the home of student rebellion when the Free Speech Movement, protesting an administrator's refusal to let students set up a card table to sign up volunteers for Lyndon Johnson's campaign, led to months of riots, student strikes and classroom confrontation. In 1969, students led protests at "People's Park," a lot owned by the university, and Governor Ronald Reagan sent in the National Guard to protect state property from conversion to a playground: an episode in which both sides relished the confrontation. Berkeley in the 1960s gave birth to a street culture that still exists. Its denizens made common cause with the Black Panthers, a violent quasi-political gang from nearby Oakland, and smoked marijuana with the Hell's Angels motorcycle gang, also once based in Oakland. Berkeley's city council features bizarre political wars in which Democrats who are very liberal by national standards are the right wing. Berkeley is the epicenter of the campus culture that proclaims its diversity and openness, but in fact routinely suppresses non-left speech through university speech codes, shouting down visiting speakers, destruction of campus newspapers that attack the left-wing line; in 2002, Mayor-elect Tom Bates was seen putting piles of a critical newspaper into the trash. Berkeley may pride itself on its tolerance, but it is arguably the least tolerant part of America. The Berkeley campus, with its view of the Bay, remains beautiful, and old buildings like the shingled Claremont Hotel are grand. But Berkeley has had little commercial development, and its public facilities have a low-maintenance, almost Third World look.

Oakland has a different history, centered around commerce and building its own civic institutions (Gertrude Stein was wrong: there is a there there). It became the western terminus of the transcontinental railroad in 1870 and was connected by ferry to San Francisco; it has always had heavy industry, and its port today is the busiest on the bay. The docks attracted young roust-abouts like the writer Jack London, after whom a downtown square is named; civic affairs were run by the local elite, like the Knowland family who owned the *Oakland Tribune*. With the Bay Area's largest black community, Oakland spawned the Black Panthers in the 1960s; blacks took control of city government in the 1970s and the *Tribune* in the 1980s. But Oakland was anything but thriving, with high crime rates, poor public schools and little economic development. Onto the scene came Jerry Brown, governor of California 20 years earlier, unsuccessful presidential candidate in 1976, 1980 and 1992; in 1998, he ran an unorthodox campaign for mayor, and won. Brown irritated local politicos by firing department heads and ignoring long-standing alliances, but he seemed to take seriously his mission of propelling Oakland to the prominence its geographic position suggests it can occupy. He sounded like a conservative, with his tough talk on crime and advocacy of big commercial development projects that drove up rents; he set up a military high school. The local economy thrived, partly with the growth of dot.com businesses and with middle-class refugees from the exorbitant housing costs of San Francisco. In 2002, Brown was easily reelected against a former black councilman.

The 9th Congressional District consists of Oakland and Berkeley, plus Castro Valley. The 2001 redistricting removed Alameda, site of an old Navy base. It still has the largest black percentage of any northern California district (26% in 2000, down from 32% in 1990); almost as high were its percentages of Hispanics (19%) and Asians (15%). Politically, it may be the most left-wing district in the United States.

The congresswoman from the 9th District is Barbara Lee, a Democrat chosen in an April 1998 special election. She grew up in Texas and the San Fernando Valley, graduated from Mills College in Oakland, got a degree in social work at Berkeley, and has brought that training to her work since then. She started a community mental health center in Berkeley and then worked as a staffer for 12 years for Congressman Ronald Dellums, elected in 1970 as a left Democrat and, in time, chairman of the Armed Services Committee. In 1990 Lee was elected to the California Assembly; in 1996, she was elected to the California Senate. After Dellums announced he was resigning, he endorsed Lee as his successor, and she won the special election with 67% of the vote.

In the House, Lee stands at the far left of the ideological spectrum. She wants to reduce the nation's weapons stockpiles and cut Pentagon spending sharply. She won enactment of her bill to require that federal cancer data collection include information on benign brain tumors in order to assist research by health professionals. In May 2001, the International Relations Committee passed her amendment to reverse the Bush policy on denying funding to international groups who offer abortion counseling of services, but later that month the House voted 218–210 to strike the language from the State Department authorization bill. In later negotiations with chairman Henry Hyde, she increased from $469 million to $535 million support for international HIV-AIDS programs. She became co-chair of the Progressive Caucus. After a visit to Cuba, she called for steps to end the 40-year embargo of Castro's island.

Lee has consistently opposed military action. She criticized Bill Clinton's bombing of Iraq in December 1998. As most Democrats voted to authorize bombing of Serbia in March 1999, Lee was the only House member to oppose a resolution supporting U.S. troops. In September 2001 she was the only member of Congress to vote against the resolution authorizing the use of force in response to the terrorist attacks. Her vote brought a torrent of national attention and protest, but there were supportive rallies in her district. She received threats of violence and the Capitol police provided her with 24-hour protection. During debate in October 2002 on whether to authorize the use of force in Iraq, Lee offered an alternative calling for diplomatic rather than military action; it was defeated 355–72.

She has been reelected easily. In late 2001 former Assemblywoman Audie Bock said she would run in the Democratic primary, but changed her mind. She won the March 2002 primary 85%–15% over an opponent who criticized her vote against military force. After the election, she became the whip for the Congressional Black Caucus.

TENTH DISTRICT

Rep. Ellen Tauscher (D)

Elected 1996, 4th term; b. Nov. 15, 1951, Newark, NJ; home, Alamo; Seton Hall U., B.A. 1973; Catholic; divorced.

Professional Career: Wall Street Invest. Banker, 1974–88, NYSE member, 1977–79; Founder & CEO, Registry Cos., 1992–96.

DC Office: 1034 LHOB 20515, 202-225-1880; Fax: 202-225-5914; Web site: www.house.gov/tauscher.

District Offices: Antioch, 925-757-7187; Fairfield, 707-428-7792; Walnut Creek, 925-932-8899.

Committees: *Armed Services* (15th of 29 D): Projection Forces; Strategic Forces; Total Force. *Transportation & Infrastructure* (16th of 34 D): Aviation; Highways, Transit & Pipelines; Water Resources & Environment.

Group Ratings

	ADA	ACLU	AFS	LCV	CON	ITIC	NTU	COC	ACU	NTLC	CHC
2002	85	87	78	75	34	62	22	65	8	19	17
2001	85	—	90	93	—	—	20	48	4	—	—

National Journal Ratings

	2001 LIB	—	2001 CONS		2002 LIB	—	2002 CONS
Economic	58%	—	43%		68%	—	32%
Social	83%	—	11%		67%	—	29%
Foreign	61%	—	36%		60%	—	39%

Key Votes of the 107th Congress

1. Approve Bush Tax Cuts	Y	5. Faith-Based Charities	N	9. Trade Promotion Authority	N
2. Limit Patients' Bill of Rights	N	6. Bar Gays in the Boy Scouts	N	10. Bar Funds for Intl. Court	N
3. Campaign Finance Reform	Y	7. Ban Partial-Birth Abortion	N	11. Authorize Force in Iraq	Y
4. Ban ANWR Development	Y	8. Arm Commercial Pilots	Y	12. Deny Home. Sec. Dept. Union	Y

Election Results

2002 general	Ellen Tauscher (D)	126,390	(76%)	($860,031)
	Sonia Harden (Lib)	40,807	(24%)	
2002 primary	Ellen Tauscher (D)	49,612	(83%)	
	Kurt Rasmussen (D)	9,867	(17%)	
2000 general	Ellen Tauscher (D)	160,429	(53%)	($1,540,830)
	Claude B. Hutchison Jr. (R)	134,863	(44%)	($1,127,901)
	Other	9,527	(3%)	

Prior Winning Percentages: 1998 (53%); 1996 (49%)

The People		Race/Ethnic Origin	Ancestry	
Area size:	1,085 sq. mi.	65.4% White	German: 10.7% Irish: 9.1%	
Urban population:	96.5%	5.7% Black	English: 8.2%	
Rural population:	3.5%	9.1% Asian	**2000 Presidential Vote**	
Pop. 2000:	639,088	0.4% Native Am.	Gore (D)	145,996 (55%)
Median income:	$65,245	0.4% Hawaiian	Bush (R)	109,149 (41%)
Poverty status:	6.3%	3.7% Two+ races	Other	9,273 (4%)
Military veterans:	13.4%	0.2% Other	**Cook Partisan Voting Index:** D + 7	
		15.0% Hispanic Origin		
Occupation	Blue collar: 17.8%	White collar: 69.0% Gray collar: 13.2%		

In the 1950s, when the streets of San Francisco and Oakland were already crowded, the rolling grasslands on the east of the mountain ridges, over the hill and through the tunnel from Oakland, were still mostly empty. In the years since, they have filled up. Freeways took the first commuters through the Caldecott Tunnel to the woodsy trail-like roads of Orinda and Lafayette; I-580 brought people east from the southern East Bay towns to the Amador Valley and Livermore, site of one of the nation's nuclear laboratories; I-680 running north-south provided a spine for businesses and shopping centers up and down the San Ramon Valley, from burgeoning Concord through Walnut Creek and points south; BART stations in Walnut Creek and Orinda took commuters to downtown San Francisco. Not all this area is filled in yet, and there is resistance to overdevelopment. But what has evolved in this sunny land, shielded by the mountains from the ocean fogs and rains, is an advanced civilization of highly skilled and educated people. Affluent and generally tolerant of—if a little put off by—what happens in San Francisco, they are respectful of economic markets and wary of government, but concerned about preserving a physical environment that is one of America's most pleasant. Voters in Livermore, where 8,000 employees of the Lawrence Livermore Lab perform national defense research, passed in 2000 a growth control initiative.

This remains the heart of the 10th Congressional District, which was reshaped by redistricting. The 2001 redistricting removed the San Ramon Valley south of Walnut Creek, the last Republican-leaning part of the San Francisco Bay area, and added part of the Sacramento River Delta and part of Solano County to the north—Fairfield (now the largest city in the 10th) and nearby Travis Air Force Base and Suisun City. This made the district more working-class and more Democratic. Al Gore received 55% of the vote here in 2000.

The congresswoman from the 10th District is Ellen Tauscher, a Democrat elected in 1996. Tauscher grew up in New Jersey, where her father ran a grocery store; at 25, she won a seat on the New York Stock Exchange, where she was a stock trader and investment banker. In 1989, she and her then-husband, owner of Vanstar (formerly ComputerLand), moved to California. After a difficult childbirth plus trouble finding quality childcare for her daughter, Tauscher started the ChildCare Registry, the first company to offer (for $140) background information on child-care providers. In 1996 she ran against two-term Republican Congressman Bill Baker, a fiscal conservative who was also a tart-tongued conservative on cultural issues. She ran as a moderate Democrat and spent liberally of her own money, some $1.7 million in all. Baker ran ads comparing her to a lottery winner buying a congressional seat. Tauscher's ads called Baker an "extremist" on gun control, abortion and the environment. This proved a winning combination, though only barely. Tauscher won 49%–47%.

In the House, Tauscher has a more moderate and bipartisan voting record than other Bay Area Democrats—"Tauscherism," as *Time* called it. She joined the moderate Blue Dog Democrats and the New Democrat Coalition and chaired its entitlement reform task force. In 1998, she took the lead for the region on behalf of both highway projects in her district and Bay Area transit plans. She voted for the Republicans' impeachment inquiry resolution and called on Bill Clinton to stop "legal hairsplitting and speak plain English to the American people." Though a junior member of the minority party, she said she had the ability to make bipartisan deals: "I feel like I'm back on Wall Street. If you have a sensory touch that can tell there's a deal in the room—and I have a great one—you can get things done." Alone among Bay Area Democrats, she voted to override Clinton vetoes of the marriage penalty and estate tax repeals, and she favored PNTR with China. On the Armed Services Committee, she was an early advocate of improving America's homeland security and the nation's ability to deal with the threat of terrorism, which led her to join a bipartisan group urging creation of the Homeland Security Department. After initially opposing trade promotion authority, which disappointed the high-tech industry, she voted for the House-Senate agreement. She supported the use of force in Iraq.

Among Democrats, Tauscher showed her centrism and independence with early support for Steny Hoyer against San Francisco's Nancy Pelosi in the 2001 contest for majority whip. That did not please many local colleagues and may have been one reason the redistricters removed the San Ramon Valley from her district (it was also needed to provide Republican votes for the 11th District's Richard Pombo). While most Democrats would welcome getting a more Democratic district, Tauscher complained and accused other Democrats of giving her a district where her moderate voting record would be a liability; she got some small changes but did not recover the San Ramon Valley.

In the old 10th District, Tauscher had competitive re-election contests. In 1998, Charles Ball, a national-security analyst at the Lawrence Livermore National Laboratory, put together a serious platform and raised $1 million to Tauscher's $1.3 million. The national Republican Party spent another $500,000 on ads attacking Tauscher on taxes. Ball argued that Tauscher's record in Washington was more liberal than she advertised. She won 53%–43%. In 2000 she won 53%–44% against community banker Claude Hutchison, who favored abortion rights and argued that she neglected local transportation. In 2002 she was the only California Democrat without Republican opposition. Tauscher does not discourage speculation that she might run if either of California's Democratic senators steps down, but neither has shown any inclination to do so.

ELEVENTH DISTRICT

Rep. Richard Pombo (R)

Elected 1992, 6th term; b. Jan. 8, 1961, Tracy; home, Tracy; CA Polytechnic Inst., 1979–82; Catholic; married (Annette).

Elected Office: Tracy City Cncl., 1990–92.

Professional Career: Cattle rancher; Co–founder, Citizens Land Alliance, 1986.

DC Office: 2411 RHOB 20515, 202-225-1947; Fax: 202-226-0861; Web site: www.house.gov/pombo.

District Offices: San Ramon, 925-866-7040; Stockton, 209-951-3091.

Committees: *Agriculture* (3d of 27 R): Department Operations, Oversight, Nutrition & Forestry; Livestock & Horticulture. *Resources* (Chmn. of 28 R).

Group Ratings

	ADA	ACLU	AFS	LCV	CON	ITIC	NTU	COC	ACU	NTLC	CHC
2002	5	7	0	13	2	62	55	85	96	91	92
2001	10	—	10	7	—	—	71	87	96	—	—

National Journal Ratings

	2001 LIB —	2001 CONS		2002 LIB —	2002 CONS
Economic	22%	74%		9%	87%
Social	0%	81%		0%	75%
Foreign	16%	82%		0%	85%

Key Votes of the 107th Congress

1. Approve Bush Tax Cuts	Y	5. Faith-Based Charities	Y	9. Trade Promotion Authority	Y
2. Limit Patients' Bill of Rights	Y	6. Bar Gays in the Boy Scouts	Y	10. Bar Funds for Intl. Court	Y
3. Campaign Finance Reform	N	7. Ban Partial-Birth Abortion	Y	11. Authorize Force in Iraq	Y
4. Ban ANWR Development	N	8. Arm Commercial Pilots	Y	12. Deny Home. Sec. Dept. Union	Y

Election Results

2002 general	Richard Pombo (R)	104,921	(60%)	($1,471,650)
	Elaine Shaw (D)	69,035	(40%)	($595,298)
2002 primary	Richard Pombo (R)	53,525	(87%)	
	Tom Benigno (R)	7,982	(13%)	
2000 general	Richard Pombo (R)	120,635	(58%)	($451,956)
	Tom Y. Santos (D)	79,539	(38%)	($12,510)
	Other	8,433	(4%)	

Prior Winning Percentages: 1998 (61%); 1996 (59%); 1994 (62%); 1992 (48%)

The People		Race/Ethnic Origin	Ancestry	
Area size:	2,316 sq. mi.	64.1% White	German: 11.4%	Irish: 8.3%
Urban population:	90.1%	3.4% Black	English: 7.5%	
Rural population:	9.9%	8.7% Asian	**2000 Presidential Vote**	
Pop. 2000:	639,088	0.5% Native Am.	Bush (R) 125,876 (53%)	
Median income:	$61,996	0.2% Hawaiian	Gore (D) 106,354 (45%)	
Poverty status:	8.8%	3.2% Two+ races	Other 5,882 (2%)	
Military veterans:	12.0%	0.2% Other	**Cook Partisan Voting Index: R + 5**	
		19.7% Hispanic Origin		

Occupation	Blue collar: 19.1%	White collar: 67.6%	Gray collar: 13.3%

People from back East looking for clues about California might consider avoiding Beverly Hills and Nob Hill and taking a look at the Central Valley directly east of San Francisco. This is an old part of California with much recent growth. Stockton on the San Joaquin River was a Gold Rush trading town founded in 1847, named after Robert Stockton, the second U.S. military governor of Calfornia, who captured Santa Barbara and Los Angeles from Mexico and proclaimed California U.S. territory. The Central Valley around Stockton, criss-crossed with railroads and canals, became one of the world's greatest agriculture areas; the San Joaquin River channel was deepened to 37 feet and Stockton today is the Central Valley's ocean port. The rich farming attracted immigrants from all over: Mexicans coming up Route 99 joined North Dakotans flocking to the town of Lodi; Italian and Yugoslav immigrants bringing their Old World crops; Yankees and Okies bringing their distinct churches and systems of belief; and now Southeast Asian refugees crowd into the older streets of Stockton. In the 1990s, Stockton positioned itself to take advantage of the region's economic strength by turning into a warehouse and distribution center for northern California. This growth came even though the farm economy was threatened by moves toward reducing water subsidies, the difficulty of attracting migrant workers for harvests and declines in crop prices. And the Central Valley has also become a suburb: with the high cost of living in San Francisco, Bay Area workers with modest incomes are increasingly buying cheaper houses around Tracy and Stockton and commuting to work past the windmills of Altamont on I-580.

The 11th Congressional District includes much of this area plus the San Ramon Valley. The central part of Stockton is not in the district; rather, it is connected by a thin corridor to the 18th District further south in the valley. But the 11th does include northwest Stockton and most of the rest of San Joaquin County—Tracy, Lodi, Manteca. Connected to this is the adjacent town of Brentwood in Contra Costa County, the fastest-growing city in the Bay area in the 1990s. The farm town of Morgan Hill anchors the far southern edge of the 11th in Santa Clara County. The San Ramon Valley towns—Danville and San Ramon in Contra Costa County and Dublin and Pleasanton in Alameda County, are much more affluent than the Central Valley parts of the district. Politically, both parts are Republican. The political heritage of the Central Valley is Democratic, and it produced two House Democratic whips, John McFall in the late 1970s and Tony Coelho in the late 1980s. But it has been moving toward the Republicans since 1980 on cultural issues and on farm interests' hostility to environmental restrictions. The San Ramon Valley is the most Republican part of the Bay area, but not very Republican by national standards, fairly liberal on cultural issues but conservative on economics. Redistricting accounts for the odd geographic shape and bifurcated character of the district. In the interest of creating a more Democratic 18th District (because of the problems of Gary Condit), the solution was to append most of San Joaquin County to the most Republican parts of the Bay area; this district voted 53% for Bush in 2000.

The congressman from the 11th District is Richard Pombo, a Republican elected in 1992, a leader of the property rights movement in Congress and now the chairman of the House Resources Committee. Pombo grew up in Tracy, studied agricultural business at Cal Poly Pomona, worked on the family ranch and served on the Tracy city council for two years. Tracy is Pombo country. He is the second of five sons of his father Ralph; each has a first name beginning with "R" so that they could share the family cattle brand, "RP." The large Pombo Real Estate firm was founded by his uncle. Joe Pombo Parkway was named after his grandfather, who was a dairyman. Richard Pombo got interested in politics during a dispute over a railroad right of way. He was elected to the House by defeating a pro-choice moderate in the Republican primary and then beating the wife of state Senator (now Insurance Commissioner) John Garamendi 48%–46% in the general. Even in his official photos, he often wears a cowboy hat and boots, some of which are eel and ostrich skin. "I'm not going to fit in too well, because I'm anything but politically correct," Pombo predicted.

With a solidly conservative voting record, he tilted with environmentalists on the Resources Committee and with subsidy advocates on Agriculture (most Valley crops are not subsidized). Once in the majority, he took charge of the unsuccessful effort to rewrite the Endangered Species Act; he held hearings with stories of absurd regulations (one Fish and Wildlife Service official wanted to reduce the speed limit on a section of I-10 to 15 miles per hour to avoid disturbing a rare fly) and produced a bill to compensate landowners whose property values declined greatly. His suit to have the American Heritage Rivers program declared unconstitutional was rejected by the Supreme Court. He opposed Don Young's annual $3 billion conservation fund proposal, viewing government as "not a welcome neighbor." The Sierra Club called Pombo an "eco-thug." Environmentalists complained that a chemical industry lobbyist wrote his pesticide bill, but Pombo denied any ethical impropriety. He chaired the Western Caucus, which sought to speak with a unified conservative voice on water and property rights issues. In July 2002, the House passed his resolution in support of the western governors' strategy to reduce wildfire risks. Pombo found common ground with Barney Frank on one issue: winning $24 million for a military base in Portugal's Azores. Pombo's grandparents came from the islands, as have many of Frank's constituents.

Redistricting became a factor in the 2002 election—nearly half the district was new to him—which was Pombo's first serious reelection challenge. Democrats nominated Elaine Shaw, a corporate lawyer and political newcomer who hired several of 10th District Congresswoman Ellen Tauscher's political aides and described herself as a moderate like Tauscher, who had represented the San Ramon Valley since 1996. She called him "a conservative without the compassion," and said Pombo's opposition to abortion rights and environmental protection were too extreme for the new district. But she received little assistance from national Democrats; she self-financed half of her spending. Pombo won 60%–40%. In San Joaquin, which cast 56% of the vote, he won 65% of the vote. He got 57% in Contra Costa, 53% in Santa Clara, and 51% in Alameda.

In January 2003, the Republican Steering Committee, to the surprise of many, elected Pombo chairman of the Resources Committee. The previous chairman, Jim Hansen, retired from Congress. The next two Republicans in seniority were already chairmen of other committees; Pombo was 11th in seniority. But after Hansen announced his retirement in January 2002, Pombo was the first to start running for the post; he worked the hardest and he had the vital support of Majority Leader Tom DeLay plus the backing of the Californians on the Steering Committee. Jim Saxton, the most senior member of the panel who wanted the job, was ruled out; he was perceived as too sympathetic to environmentalists. Elton Gallegly of California also sought the post, but he had been less active on the panel. Pombo was temporarily distracted by the possibility of the Agriculture Committee chairmanship, but Bob Goodlatte quickly wrapped up the contest and shut off that option for Pombo. As is their practice, Steering Committee members did not disclose the vote. But Pombo's victory left some hard feelings among senior committee members who sought the chairmanship, including John Duncan and Joel Hefley.

The combination of a sharply revised district and an unexpected chairmanship poses a challenge to Pombo, as he seeks to deliver on his conservative philosophy that may not be especially popular in the new parts of his district.

TWELFTH DISTRICT

Rep. Tom Lantos (D)

Elected 1980, 12th term; b. Feb. 1, 1928, Budapest, Hungary; home, San Mateo; U. of WA, B.A. 1949, M.A. 1950, U. of CA, Ph.D. 1953; Jewish; married (Annette).

Professional Career: Economist, Bank of America, 1952–53; TV Commentator, San Francisco, 1955–63; Dir. of Intl. Programs, CA St. U., 1962–71; Advisor, U.S. Sen. Joseph R. Biden Jr., 1978–79; Mbr., Pres. Task Force on Defense & Foreign Policy, 1976; Prof., San Francisco St. U., 1950–80.

DC Office: 2413 RHOB 20515, 202-225-3531; Fax: 202-226-9789; Web site: www.house.gov/lantos.

District Office: San Mateo, 650-342-0300.

Committees: *Government Reform* (2d of 19 D): Energy Policy, Natural Resources and Regulatory Affairs; National Security, Emerging Threats & Intl. Relations. *International Relations* (RMM of 23 D).

Group Ratings

	ADA	ACLU	AFS	LCV	CON	ITIC	NTU	COC	ACU	NTLC	CHC
2002	95	79	100	75	84	25	21	30	4	3	0
2001	95	—	100	100	—	—	9	30	8	—	—

National Journal Ratings

	2001 LIB	—	2001 CONS		2002 LIB	—	2002 CONS
Economic	91%	—	9%		75%	—	24%
Social	74%	—	27%		74%	—	19%
Foreign	77%	—	22%		68%	—	31%

Key Votes of the 107th Congress

1. Approve Bush Tax Cuts	N	5. Faith-Based Charities		
2. Limit Patients' Bill of Rights	N	6. Bar Gays in the Boy Scouts	N	
3. Campaign Finance Reform	Y	7. Ban Partial-Birth Abortion	N	
4. Ban ANWR Development	Y	8. Arm Commercial Pilots	Y	

1. Approve Bush Tax Cuts — N
2. Limit Patients' Bill of Rights — N
3. Campaign Finance Reform — Y
4. Ban ANWR Development — Y
5. Faith-Based Charities — N
6. Bar Gays in the Boy Scouts — N
7. Ban Partial-Birth Abortion — N
8. Arm Commercial Pilots — Y
9. Trade Promotion Authority — N
10. Bar Funds for Intl. Court — N
11. Authorize Force in Iraq — Y
12. Deny Home. Sec. Dept. Union — N

Election Results

2002 general	Tom Lantos (D)	105,597	(68%)	($937,721)
	Michael Moloney (R)	38,381	(25%)	
	Maad Abu-Ghazalah (Lib)	11,006	(7%)	($165,522)
2002 primary	Tom Lantos (D)	unopposed		
2000 general	Tom Lantos (D)	158,404	(75%)	($310,957)
	Mike Garza (R)	44,162	(21%)	
	Other	9,990	(5%)	

Prior Winning Percentages: 1998 (74%); 1996 (72%); 1994 (67%); 1992 (69%); 1990 (66%); 1988 (71%); 1986 (74%); 1984 (70%); 1982 (57%); 1980 (46%)

The People		Race/Ethnic Origin	Ancestry	
Area size:	363 sq. mi.	48.2% White	Irish: 8.2%	German: 7.4%
Urban population:	99.9%	2.5% Black	Italian: 6.4%	
Rural population:	0.1%	28.5% Asian	**2000 Presidential Vote**	
Pop. 2000:	639,088	0.2% Native Am.	Gore (D) 164,490 (67%)	
Median income:	$70,307	0.9% Hawaiian	Bush (R) 70,468 (29%)	
Poverty status:	5.4%	3.6% Two+ races	Other 11,103 (5%)	
Military veterans:	8.9%	0.3% Other	**Cook Partisan Voting Index:** D +20	
		15.7% Hispanic Origin		

Occupation	Blue collar: 14.6%	White collar: 72.8%	Gray collar: 12.6%

Running south from San Francisco is the Peninsula, which connects the city with the mainland of the United States. This is geologically interesting, and active, country: The San Andreas Fault runs just east of the Coast Range, underneath the reservoirs that store San Francisco's water supply. To the west are green mountains running down into the foggy ocean. To the east is a zone of flat land between mountain and bay, an unbroken chain of suburbs and urban settlement, with light industry and salt flats along the bay front, and residential neighborhoods and some commercial strips from the Bayshore Freeway up through the Junipero Serra Freeway atop the mountain ridge. Historically, the Peninsula has seemed separate from San Francisco. But Daly City and Pacifica on the ocean are a kind of extension of San Francisco's old working class districts, with boxy houses on streets looking out on the ocean or the freeway; now they are the home of many of the Bay Area's Asian immigrants. Pacific Islanders, too: the mainland's biggest concentration of Samoans is in Daly City and the biggest concentration of Tongans in San Bruno; King Taufa'ahau Tupou IV of Tonga has a house in the high-income suburb of Hillsborough. On the Bay side is South San Francisco which, a sign on the side of San Bruno Mountain proclaims, is "the Industrial City." Actually, these days it is post-industrial, for it is here that Herb Boyer and Bob Swanson sketched on a napkin their plans for the first biotechnology company, Genentech; they bought space in an old warehouse on the waterfront near a Bethlehem Steel plant; today the area is one large biotech campus, with lawns, parkways and earth-tone office complexes, the center of the biotech industry. Further south, between the Bayshore Freeway and I-280, there are middle-class suburbs that are now also cities with office complexes—Millbrae, Burlingame, San Mateo, San Carlos.

The 12th Congressional District consists of these northern Peninsula suburbs plus the southwest quadrant of San Francisco—the city's middle-income Sunset district, with older houses amid unburied telephone and electric wires, lying on curving hills that were once sand dunes, and affluent St. Francis's Wood and West Portal. It is an ethnically and racially diverse, economically productive part of America; 29% of its residents are Asian—the third highest of any district outside Hawaii—and another 16% are Hispanic. The economic orientation here was historically toward San Francisco, then south toward the Silicon Valley, now to its own burgeoning biotech industries. Income levels are among the highest in the state, very far above average. Politically, the Peninsula historically was a bastion of progressive Republicanism, a lively force in California from the election of Governor Hiram Johnson in 1910 until the liberal Democratic breakthrough in 1958. But that tradition is only a memory now, if that. In national and California elections the 12th District is now overwhelmingly Democratic.

The congressman from the 12th District, Tom Lantos, has several distinctions, but none more important than the fact that he is the only Holocaust survivor ever to serve in Congress. Lantos was born in Hungary and as a teenager fought in the underground against the Nazis; he was imprisoned and was one of the Jews saved by Swedish diplomat Raoul Wallenberg. So was his wife Annette, his childhood sweetheart and now his unpaid assistant; these two Holocaust survivors have two daughters and 17 grandchildren. Lantos has shown energy and competence throughout his career. He immigrated to the United States and graduated from the University of Washington and got a Ph.D. in economics at Berkeley. He taught economics at San Francisco State, made money as an investor and appeared on television as a foreign policy expert. He had the political insight to challenge a Republican incumbent in the Peninsula in 1980, a Republican year nationally though not so much here; he has shown great capacity for publicizing his crusades in congressional hearings and on television. In early 1999, he was featured in the release of a documentary by Steven Spielberg, *The Last Days*, which recounts the Nazis' 1944 destruction of Hungary's Jewish community.

Lantos has spent much of his time in the House on foreign policy and is now ranking minority member on the International Relations Committee. Unlike other Bay Area Democrats, he has not brought to his work an instinctive mistrust of American policy or doubts of American good intentions. He founded the Congressional Human Rights Caucus, focusing on Communist regimes as well as the right-wing dictatorships other liberal Democrats denounced. He is among the most enthusiastic supporters of Israel and called for economic sanctions against Iraq back in 1988 for its gassing of the Kurds; he continued to support sanctions against Iraq in 2000 when other Bay area members tried to end them. He helped lead the debate in favor of the Iraq war resolution in October 2002, although he had urged that it be debated after the election. During the collapse of Communism, Lantos stayed in close touch with Eastern Europe, especially Hungary, as new democracies rose up; in 1990 he was the first American official to visit Albania since 1946. He sponsored the first U.S. aid to the newly free countries of Eastern Europe and strongly backed NATO expansion. He advocated a more active American role in Bosnia and other parts of the former Yugoslavia. He has attacked human rights violations in China, opposes normalizing of Chinese trade status and in September 2000 sponsored a resolution urging that Beijing not be selected as the site of the 2008 Olympics.

Lantos has been part of the U.S. delegations to the European Parliament and the United Nations; he became friends with Secretary General Kofi Annan, whose wife Nane Annan is Raoul Wallenberg's niece. He also worked with Hyde to get approval of $1.3 billion to fight AIDS around the world in December 2001 and to give more power to the president to restrict exports for national security reasons. He opposed U.S. participation in the United Nation conference on racism in Durban in 2001. "We have a group of countries hell-bent on hijacking a noble and worthwhile event into yet another forum for Israel-bashing and for the most extreme form of antisemitism to gain global notoriety." In May 2001 he got the House to pass 216–210 an amendment withholding $625,000 in aid to Lebanon and requiring the administration to terminate millions more if Lebanon did not secure its border with Israel and get rid of the Hezbollah terrorists operating there. In April 2002 he introduced a resolution expressing "solidarity with Israel in its fight against terrorism," co-sponsored by Majority Whip Tom DeLay. They delayed it at the request of the White House, but it passed 352–21 in May 2002.

Lantos spent $1.7 million on his 1980 and 1982 campaigns and has won easily ever since. Later his fundraising was targeted to his son-in-law Dick Swett, who was elected congressman from New Hampshire in 1990 and 1992, was defeated by Charles Bass in 1994 and lost for the Senate in 1996. In 2002, Katrina Swett, Lantos' daughter, ran against Bass with extensive assistance from her father. He helped her to raise an impressive $149,000 from congressional leadership PACs, plus money from California contributors such as Steven Spielberg and San Francisco financiers; altogether she raised and spent $1.4 million. Though outspent, Bass still won by a solid 57%–41% margin—his best showing ever.

THIRTEENTH DISTRICT

Rep. Pete Stark (D)

Elected 1972, 16th term; b. Nov. 11, 1931, Milwaukee, WI; home, Fremont; MIT, B.S. 1953, U. of CA at Berkeley, M.B.A. 1960; Unitarian; married (Deborah).

Military Career: Air Force, 1955–57.

Professional Career: Founder, Beacon Savings & Loan Assn., 1961; Founder & Pres., Security Natl. Bank, Walnut Creek, 1963–72.

DC Office: 239 CHOB 20515, 202-225-5065; Fax: 202-226-3805; Web site: www.house.gov/stark.

District Office: Fremont, 510-494-1388.

Committees: *Ways & Means* (2d of 17 D): Health (RMM); Human Resources. *Joint Committee on Taxation* (5th of 5 Reps.). *Joint Economic Committee* (7th of 10 Reps.).

Group Ratings

	ADA	ACLU	AFS	LCV	CON	ITIC	NTU	COC	ACU	NTLC	CHC
2002	100	93	100	100	99	25	31	26	0	3	0
2001	95	—	100	71	—	—	16	26	0	—	—

National Journal Ratings

	2001 LIB —	2001 CONS	2002 LIB —	2002 CONS
Economic	95%	0%	95%	0%
Social	90%	0%	98%	0%
Foreign	96%	0%	94%	0%

Key Votes of the 107th Congress

1. Approve Bush Tax Cuts	N	5. Faith-Based Charities	N	9. Trade Promotion Authority	N
2. Limit Patients' Bill of Rights	N	6. Bar Gays in the Boy Scouts	N	10. Bar Funds for Intl. Court	N
3. Campaign Finance Reform	Y	7. Ban Partial-Birth Abortion	N	11. Authorize Force in Iraq	N
4. Ban ANWR Development	*	8. Arm Commercial Pilots	N	12. Deny Home. Sec. Dept. Union	N

Election Results

2002 general	Pete Stark (D)	86,495	(71%)	($438,055)
	Syed Mahmood (R)	26,852	(22%)	($51,307)
	Other	8,376	(7%)	
2002 primary	Pete Stark (D)	unopposed		
2000 general	Pete Stark (D)	129,012	(70%)	($414,879)
	James R. Goetz (R)	44,499	(24%)	
	Other	9,635	(5%)	

Prior Winning Percentages: 1998 (71%); 1996 (65%); 1994 (65%); 1992 (60%); 1990 (58%); 1988 (73%); 1986 (70%); 1984 (70%); 1982 (61%); 1980 (55%); 1978 (65%); 1976 (71%); 1974 (71%); 1972 (53%)

The People		Race/Ethnic Origin	Ancestry	
Area size:	281 sq. mi.	38.4% White	German: 6.9%	Irish: 5.7%
Urban population:	99.3%	6.3% Black	English: 4.8%	
Rural population:	0.7%	28.2% Asian	**2000 Presidential Vote**	
Pop. 2000:	639,088	0.4% Native Am.	Gore (D)	126,477 (67%)
Median income:	$62,415	0.8% Hawaiian	Bush (R)	55,803 (30%)
Poverty status:	7.1%	4.5% Two + races	Other	6,472 (3%)
Military veterans:	9.6%	0.3% Other	**Cook Partisan Voting Index:** D +19	
		21.1% Hispanic Origin		

Occupation   Blue collar: 22.3%   White collar: 66.8%   Gray collar: 10.9%

The East Bay is the workaday, unglamorous side of metropolitan San Francisco—a narrow strip of land between San Francisco Bay and the surprisingly high mountains that rise just to the east. The shoreline is not picturesque, with its closed-down Navy bases, docks, airports and salt evaporators; the Bay Bridge, bisected by Yerba Buena Island, cuts an inspiring figure, but the San Mateo Bridge to the south is at best utilitarian. Sixty years ago, when the shipyards of Richmond and the Navy yard in Oakland were buzzing, the East Bay south of Oakland was still largely uninhabited farm fields. In the postwar years, it filled up, south along the old Route 17: San Leandro, originally settled by Portuguese; Hayward with its Cal State University campus; Union City with its rail yards; Fremont, home of the famous NUMMI auto plant where Chevrolets and Toyotas are produced together; and Newark, with more than 40 manufacturing plants that range from salt processing to computer network servers. Underneath is the Hayward Fault, not as famous as the San Andreas, but equally if not more hazardous.

The 13th Congressional District is made up of this string of East Bay towns in Alameda County, with lower income than the Peninsula towns across the Bay. The district is racially and ethnically mixed in the California manner. Koreans and other Asians have moved in large numbers to Fremont, Hayward and other East Bay towns; the district is 28% Asian—the fourth highest Asian percentage in any district outside Hawaii—21% Hispanic and 6% black. This has long been a Democratic area, and in the 1990s it became more Democratic than ever: in 2000, Al Gore got 67% of the vote here.

The congressman from the 13th District is Pete Stark, a consistently liberal Democrat and product of the peace movement of the 1960s, first elected in 1972. Stark grew up in Wisconsin, served in the Air Force, got an engineering degree at MIT and an M.B.A. at Berkeley, and in 1961 started a bank in Walnut Creek. He attracted attention, and accounts, all over the Bay Area when he put a giant peace symbol atop the bank headquarters and peace symbols on all checks. In 1972 he ran for Congress, spending his own money freely; he beat an 81-year-old incumbent in the primary 56%–22% and held on in the McGovern undertow to win the general with 53%. By his third term he had a safe seat back home and was on Ways and Means, on which he now is the second ranking Democrat; he chaired its Health Subcommittee from 1985 to 1995.

Stark brought to that post a desire to use government powers to make health care more available. He has not always been successful on policy. He did expand Medicare benefits and provided COBRA benefit continuation to younger workers. But his major achievement was the Catastrophic Health Care Act of 1988, which created a new benefit for Medicare recipients, then was repealed by an overwhelming vote in 1989 after an outpouring of public protest: the problem was that its tax on the high-income elderly was very unpopular while benefits seemed puny. He has supported universal health insurance in various forms.

In the minority, Stark has mostly criticized and found few areas of agreement with Republicans. He was one of two votes against the 1996 Kennedy-Kassebaum bill, on the grounds it did not include mental health coverage and extended patent protection for a drug. When George W. Bush presented a plan for prescription drug coverage for seniors, Stark countered with a plan that would guarantee affordable and comprehensive coverage for all seniors under Medicare. "Our legislation will not be cheap," he conceded.

As senior Democrat on the Joint Economic Committee, he has produced reports that have criticized various Republican policies. He was one of two House members to vote against repeal of the 3% telephone excise tax, and one of three who opposed the resolution expressing outrage at the federal appeals court decision in California declaring that the Pledge of Allegiance is an unconstitutional violation of the First Amendment. In January 2003, he cosponsored a proposal to reinstate the military draft; in previous years he had sought to abolish stand-by registration for the draft, calling it a waste of money.

Stark has been reelected by wide margins, which perhaps explains his often intemperate partisan remarks. After Stark incorrectly stated at a committee hearing in May 2001 that all children of Republican Conference chairman J.C. Watts had been born out of wedlock, Watts confronted him in the House chamber and Stark reportedly gave a flippant response that further angered Watts. At a hearing on prescription-drug coverage in February 2003, he said that President Bush did not have to pay a penny when he went to Alcoholics Anonymous to quit drinking. Bush has never said that he attended AA, or that he was an alcoholic. During a March 2003 speech on the House floor, Stark referred to House leaders as Bush's "Republican henchmen"; earlier that month, he told the *Oakland Tribune* that if terrorists directed another September 11-type attack on the U.S., there would be "blood on Bush's hands."

If senior Ways and Means Democrat Charles Rangel should retire, House Democrats could face a choice between Stark and fellow Californian Bob Matsui for the position.

FOURTEENTH DISTRICT

Rep. Anna Eshoo (D)

Elected 1992, 6th term; b. Dec. 13, 1942, New Britain, CT; home, Atherton; Canada Col., A.A. 1975; Catholic; divorced.

Elected Office: San Mateo Cnty. Bd. of Supervisors, 1982–92, Pres., 1986.

Professional Career: Chmn., San Mateo Cnty Dem. Party, 1980; Chief of Staff, CA Assembly Speaker, 1981.

DC Office: 205 CHOB 20515, 202-225-8104; Fax: 202-225-8890; Web site: www.eshoo.house.gov.

District Office: Palo Alto, 650-323-2984.

Committees: *Energy & Commerce* (12th of 26 D): Health; Telecommunications & The Internet. *Permanent Select Committee on Intelligence* (7th of 9 D): Intelligence Policy & National Security (RMM); Technical & Tactical Intelligence.

Group Ratings

	ADA	ACLU	AFS	LCV	CON	ITIC	NTU	COC	ACU	NTLC	CHC
2002	100	87	100	100	70	50	22	42	0	0	0
2001	95	—	100	100	—	—	15	39	0	—	—

National Journal Ratings

	2001 LIB —	2001 CONS	2002 LIB —	2002 CONS
Economic	83%	15%	76%	23%
Social	72%	27%	72%	28%
Foreign	86%	12%	87%	13%

Key Votes of the 107th Congress

1. Approve Bush Tax Cuts	N	5. Faith-Based Charities	N	9. Trade Promotion Authority	N
2. Limit Patients' Bill of Rights	N	6. Bar Gays in the Boy Scouts	N	10. Bar Funds for Intl. Court	N
3. Campaign Finance Reform	Y	7. Ban Partial-Birth Abortion	N	11. Authorize Force in Iraq	N
4. Ban ANWR Development	Y	8. Arm Commercial Pilots	Y	12. Deny Home. Sec. Dept. Union	N

Election Results

2002 general	Anna Eshoo (D)	117,055	(68%)	($863,431)
	Joseph Nixon (R)	48,346	(28%)	($45,158)
	Andrew Carver (Lib)	6,277	(4%)	
2002 primary	Anna Eshoo (D)	unopposed		
2000 general	Anna Eshoo (D)	161,720	(70%)	($642,146)
	Bill Quraishi (R)	59,338	(26%)	
	Other	9,204	(4%)	

Prior Winning Percentages: 1998 (69%); 1996 (65%); 1994 (61%); 1992 (57%)

The People		Race/Ethnic Origin	Ancestry	
Area size:	1,030 sq. mi.	59.6% White	German: 9.7%	English: 8.3%
Urban population:	93.6%	3.0% Black	Irish: 7.2%	
Rural population:	6.4%	16.0% Asian	**2000 Presidential Vote**	
Pop. 2000:	639,088	0.3% Native Am.	Gore (D) 155,165	(62%)
Median income:	$77,985	0.7% Hawaiian	Bush (R) 84,637	(34%)
Poverty status:	6.4%	2.7% Two + races	Other 12,451	(5%)
Military veterans:	9.5%	0.3% Other	**Cook Partisan Voting Index:** D +14	
		17.5% Hispanic Origin		

Occupation	Blue collar: 12.1%	White collar: 77.1%	Gray collar: 10.8%

Silicon Valley is a place and a state of mind, an area that had no distinctive identity two decades ago but which people all over the world have recognized, admired and tried to imitate. For Silicon Valley has been the center of America's computer industry, a place where creative minds have developed products that large corporations never thought would sell. Its beginnings can be traced back to 1939, when William Hewlett and David Packard started their electronics firm in a Palo Alto garage, or perhaps to 1891, when Stanford University was founded on the estate of a California governor and senator. Not every aspect of the computer business is centered here. Microsoft, routinely disparaged in every Palo Alto espresso shop and bar, is up in Redmond, Washington, and IBM is off in Armonk, New York. But Silicon Valley is where most of the giants, and very much of the creativity, of the high-tech business—as well as the ghosts of dot-coms whose stock has melted down to zero—have been based.

Rapidly growing businesses are inherently unstable, but the Valley's enduring advantages have made it amazingly adaptable. One advantage is Stanford, the students it attracts and produces, and fact that it has always encouraged profit-making activity by faculty. Another is venture capital, widely available from innovation-minded old San Francisco money, dispensed mostly from nondescript office buildings on Sand Hill Road off I-280. A third, perhaps the greatest, is that Silicon Valley is the kind of place where smart young innovators like to live. Elite law and medical school graduates head to the prestigious, high-salary jobs of central cities; but techies are free to live in this pleasant, healthy environment. Sheltered by hills from coastal fogs and rains, Silicon Valley boasts a sunny climate with perceptible but gentle seasons, perfect for year-round outdoor sports; there may well be more jogging trails and bicycle paths here than anywhere else in the country. There is a sort of pure Americana here: these communities were rustic but never poor, rural but never bigoted, country-like but still easily accessible to the luxuries of civilization. People here were ahead of the rest of the nation in fighting for the environment, in favoring natural over processed foods, and in indulging in regular exercise. And they have been quick to adapt to change. In the 1970s Silicon Valley thrived when the semiconductor business took off. In the 1980s, when Japanese firms threatened to monopolize semiconductors, Silicon Valley shifted to microprocessors and personal computers. In the 1990s, when PCs became a low-profit commodity business, Silicon Valley shifted to the Internet. The Internet bubble burst in 2000, and Silicon Valley has since fallen on hard times. By one estimate, it has lost 127,000 jobs since 2000, more than half that were created between 1998 and 2000. Stock prices have plummeted and real estate prices have too, though they are still the highest in the nation. Billions in paper wealth has disappeared, and technology exports from California fell from $61 billion in 2000 down toward $40 billion in 2002. The question now is whether Silicon Valley still has the ability to adapt. No one knows what the next big thing in high-tech will be, but there are still lots of people working in Silicon Valley's bland office parks or in someone's garage who think they're on the way to it, and may be.

The 14th Congressional District includes much of Silicon Valley. It includes Menlo Park, Palo Alto, home of Stanford, and most of Redwood City, where tech office parks went up on the old salt flats. Further south along El Camino Real are Mountain View, Los Altos and Sunnyvale (the district's largest city). There are a few ultra-wealthy enclaves, with real estate prices pushed skyward into the multiple millions by entrepreneurs' paper profits: Atherton, with its stone-walled lots; Woodside, with its 1850s country store and mansions dotting the hills; Portola Valley and Los Altos Hills, with stark contemporary homes overlooking the Bay. Over the mountains it includes the little town of Half Moon Bay, with its pumpkin farms rising over the ocean, and most of the land area but not the population of Santa Cruz County, where imposing redwoods grow to within five miles of spectacular beaches. The 14th's political heritage is progressive: a sort of environmentalist, dovish, healthy-lifestyle, but entrepreneurial Republicanism, typified by former Congressmen Pete McCloskey, Ed Zschau and Tom Campbell, each of whom quit the House to run unsuccessfully for the Senate between 1982 and 2002. But this kind of Republican has become an endangered species, and Silicon Valley has become heavily Democratic. It is liberal on cultural issues and was enchanted by the attention it received from Bill Clinton and Al Gore, and was forgiving even when Clinton, at the behest of trial lawyer William Lerach, vetoed the securities litigation bill that high-tech entrepreneurs wanted; it was one of two bills passed over his veto. In 2000 George W. Bush got only 34% of the vote here.

The congresswoman from the 14th District is Anna Eshoo, a Democrat elected in 1992. Born back East, she is the only member of Congress of Assyrian descent. She was a full time homemaker, then chaired the San Mateo County Democratic Party and was elected to the San Mateo Board of Supervisors in 1982. In 1988, she ran for the House, facing Tom Campbell. The two spent a total of $2.5 million, and Eshoo was the first congressional candidate to distribute videotapes to voters. Campbell won 52%–46%. But in 1992 he ran for the Senate and Eshoo ran for the House again. In the primary she beat an assemblyman redistricted out of his seat at age 30, by 40%–36%. In the general, Eshoo outspent her Republican opponent and won 57%–39%.

In the House, Eshoo's voting record has been mostly liberal and occasionally moderate. She was a bit nervous in 1993 about supporting the Clinton budget and tax package, which hit this high-income area hard, and hesitated before supporting NAFTA and fast track. She joined Republicans on securities litigation, liability relief for Y2K computer problems, changes in the FDA to get quicker regulatory approval for new medical devices, PNTR with China and electronic signatures. She initially supported estate-tax repeal, but switched and voted against overriding Clinton's veto; she voted against the repeal again in 2001. She sought looser controls on high-tech exports and opposed the FASB accounting board proposal to charge stock options against earnings. In March 2003 Eshoo and David Dreier sponsored a bill to provide transparency and information about corporations' issuance of stock options but which did not require expensing of options. Despite local pressure, she voted against trade promotion authority. During the sniper killings in the Washington area, she filed a bill to require ballistics testing of all new firearms to establish a "ballistics fingerprint" to assist law-enforcement investigators.

Eshoo has not been seriously challenged for reelection. In January 2003, she got a seat on the Intelligence Committee. She has been a close friend and confidant of Nancy Pelosi since they first met at a Democratic event in the Bay Area in the early 1970s, and their families have spent time together.

FIFTEENTH DISTRICT

Rep. Mike Honda (D)

Elected 2000, 2d term; b. June 27, 1941, Walnut Creek; home, San Jose; San Jose St. U., B.S. 1969, B.A. 1970, M.A. 1973; Protestant; married (Jeanne).

Elected Office: San Jose Unified Sch. Bd., 1981–90; Santa Clara Cnty. Bd. of Supervisors, 1990–96; CA Assembly, 1996–2000.

Professional Career: Peace Corps, 1965–67; Elem. sch. principal, 1978–90.

DC Office: 1713 LHOB 20515, 202-225-2631; Fax: 202-225-2699; Web site: www.house.gov/honda.

District Office: Campbell, 408-558-8085.

Committees: *Science* (10th of 22 D): Energy; Research. *Transportation & Infrastructure* (25th of 34 D): Aviation; Highways, Transit & Pipelines.

Group Ratings

	ADA	ACLU	AFS	LCV	CON	ITIC	NTU	COC	ACU	NTLC	CHC
2002	95	93	100	100	47	50	26	30	0	0	8
2001	95	—	100	100	—	—	13	39	0	—	—

National Journal Ratings

	2001 LIB	—	2001 CONS		2002 LIB	—	2002 CONS
Economic	86%	—	14%		92%	—	8%
Social	90%	—	0%		98%	—	0%
Foreign	91%	—	8%		94%	—	0%

Key Votes of the 107th Congress

1. Approve Bush Tax Cuts	*	5. Faith-Based Charities	N
2. Limit Patients' Bill of Rights	N	6. Bar Gays in the Boy Scouts	N
3. Campaign Finance Reform	Y	7. Ban Partial-Birth Abortion	N
4. Ban ANWR Development	Y	8. Arm Commercial Pilots	N

9. Trade Promotion Authority	N
10. Bar Funds for Intl. Court	N
11. Authorize Force in Iraq	N
12. Deny Home. Sec. Dept. Union	N

Election Results

2002 general	Mike Honda (D)	87,482	(66%)	($840,384)
	Linda Hermann (R)	41,251	(31%)	($30,470)
	Other	4,289	(3%)	
2002 primary	Mike Honda (D)	unopposed		
2000 general	Mike Honda (D)	128,545	(54%)	($2,125,541)
	Jim Cunneen (R)	99,866	(42%)	($1,429,904)
	Other	8,493	(4%)	

The People		Race/Ethnic Origin	Ancestry	
Area size:	289 sq. mi.	47.1% White	German: 8.0%	Irish: 6.3%
Urban population:	99.3%	2.4% Black	English: 6.1%	
Rural population:	0.7%	29.2% Asian	**2000 Presidential Vote**	
Pop. 2000:	639,088	0.3% Native Am.	Gore (D)..............124,880	(60%)
Median income:	$74,947	0.3% Hawaiian	Bush (R)...............74,974	(36%)
Poverty status:	6.6%	3.2% Two+ races	Other....................7,108	(3%)
Military veterans:	8.4%	0.2% Other	**Cook Partisan Voting Index:** D +12	
		17.2% Hispanic Origin		

Occupation	Blue collar: 16.9%	White collar: 73.6%	Gray collar: 9.6%

The broad valley of Santa Clara County around San Jose a few decades ago was mostly orchards and vineyards. Sheltered by mountains from the chilly ocean fogs, with soil incredibly fertile once it was irrigated, this valley produced peaches, plums, prunes, apricots and grapes and made San Jose half a century ago the nation's biggest fruit-packing center. Today, subdivisions, shopping centers and office buildings have replaced almost all the orchards, and San Jose and Santa Clara County have a population of 1.7 million people. San Jose, with a growing downtown, an arena for its National Hockey League team, and a population of 895,000, has become a major American city. San Jose and some of the towns to the west like Santa Clara and Cupertino are part of Silicon Valley, which has no official boundaries.

The 15th Congressional District consists of the central slice of Santa Clara County. It includes 295,000 people in San Jose, about one-third of the city's population and nearly half of the district's; for the most part these are San Jose's affluent neighborhoods. West of San Jose, the district includes the city of Santa Clara and Cupertino, where Steve Jobs started Apple in a garage in the 1970s and where the company is still headquartered, Los Gatos and Campbell. The district also includes the salt flats of San Jose, site of the Great America theme park not far from where a huge Lockheed plant was once the nation's largest defense contractor, the working class town of Milpitas and, far to the south, connected by a swat of mountains, Gilroy, the garlic capital of the United States. Outside of Hawaii, this district has the highest percentage of Asians in the nation (29.2%). Politically, this area was once marginal territory but is now heavily Democratic. Al Gore got 60% of the vote here in 2000.

The congressman from the 15th District is Democrat Mike Honda, elected in 2000. A Japanese American, Honda was born in Walnut Creek, and he spent his early childhood in a World War II internment camp in Colorado. He received bachelor's and master's degrees from San Jose State University, as an undergraduate, and served two years in the Peace Corps in El Salvador. In 1971, San Jose Mayor Norm Mineta appointed him to the city Planning Commission. From 1978 to 1986, Honda was a principal at two area elementary schools; during these years he was elected to the San Jose Unified School Board and later to the Santa Clara County Board of Supervisors. In 1996, he was elected to the first of two terms in the California Assembly. He worked to reduce classroom sizes and increase teacher benefits, and to secure an apology from Japan for its wartime atrocities against other Asian nations.

In 2000 iconoclastic Republican 15th District Congressman Tom Campbell decided to run against Senator Dianne Feinstein. At first Honda was reluctant to run for the House, even though California's term limits meant that a third term in the Assembly would be his last. Days before the filing deadline, he told supporters that he would not run for the open seat. But persuasive telephone calls from several leading House Democrats and, finally, from Bill Clinton changed his mind. One reason for his initial reluctance was the prospect of running against former Carter administration Pentagon official Bill Peacock, a venture capitalist who was ready to spend $1 million of his own money and had gotten significant endorsements, including that of the mayor of San Jose. But the primary was no contest: Honda won 67% to 24% for Peacock. His Republican opponent was Republican Assemblyman Jim Cunneen. Cunneen was a Campbell protege and was strongly supported by national Republican leaders; the contest shaped up as one of the year's most competitive. Cunneen favored liberal positions on cultural issues; as a former global corporate affairs manager for Applied Materials he was able to get support from many Silicon Valley capitalists. He tried to depict the contest as a referendum on the old economy versus the new economy. After the primary, despite his close ties to organized labor, Honda supported PNTR with China—a politically shrewd move to connect with the high-tech industry. Honda won 54%–42%.

Honda has been among the most liberal members of the House. With Senator John Ensign, he formed the Wireless Task Force to encourage better understanding of spectrum issues and support for innovative technologies. He publicized the cause of American POWs from World War Two who were taken on "hell ships" as slave laborers in Japan, and sought apologies from Japan and its companies that profited from them; the 1951 peace treaty with Japan waived the rights of Americans to file such suits. He signed on to an amendment with Dana Rohrabacher to prevent the State Department from opposing the POWs in court, but the amendment mysteriously disappeared in conference committee after it passed both the House and Senate. He helped to enact the Cyber Security Research and Development bill, which supports training and programs to protect computer data and networks. He was one of three votes against the resolution condemning the Ninth Circuit decision that found the words "under God" in the Pledge of Allegiance unconstitutional. He accused conservative commentator Anne Coulter of spreading "another form of terrorism" with her support for racial profiling of airline passengers.

Honda breezed to reelection in 2002. In February 2003, he demanded an apology from North Carolina's Howard Coble, who said the internment of Japanese Americans in World War II was necessary to protect them.

SIXTEENTH DISTRICT

Rep. Zoe Lofgren (D)

Elected 1994, 5th term; b. Dec. 21, 1947, San Mateo; home, San Jose; Stanford U., B.A. 1970, U. of Santa Clara Law Schl., J.D. 1975; Protestant; married (John Collins).

Elected Office: Santa Clara Bd. of Supervisors, 1980–94.

Professional Career: Staff Asst., U.S. Rep. Don Edwards, 1970–78; Practicing atty., 1978–80; Prof., U. of Santa Clara Law Schl., 1981–94.

DC Office: 102 CHOB 20515, 202-225-3072; Fax: 202-225-3336; Web site: www.house.gov/lofgren.

District Office: San Jose, 408-271-8700.

Committees: *Judiciary* (7th of 16 D): Courts, the Internet & Intellectual Property; Immigration, Border Security & Claims. *Science* (15th of 22 D): Environment, Technology and Standards; Research. *Select Committee on Homeland Security* (14th of 23 D): Cybersecurity, Science and Research & Development (RMM); Rules.

Group Ratings

	ADA	ACLU	AFS	LCV	CON	ITIC	NTU	COC	ACU	NTLC	CHC
2002	100	87	89	100	90	38	25	26	0	3	0
2001	90	—	100	93	—	—	13	35	0	—	—

National Journal Ratings

	2001 LIB —	2001 CONS		2002 LIB —	2002 CONS
Economic	83% —	15%		70% —	29%
Social	83% —	11%		74% —	19%
Foreign	77% —	22%		90% —	8%

Key Votes of the 107th Congress

1. Approve Bush Tax Cuts	N	5. Faith-Based Charities	N	9. Trade Promotion Authority	N
2. Limit Patients' Bill of Rights	N	6. Bar Gays in the Boy Scouts	N	10. Bar Funds for Intl. Court	N
3. Campaign Finance Reform	Y	7. Ban Partial-Birth Abortion	N	11. Authorize Force in Iraq	N
4. Ban ANWR Development	Y	8. Arm Commercial Pilots	Y	12. Deny Home. Sec. Dept. Union	N

Election Results

2002 general	Zoe Lofgren (D)	72,370	(67%)	($524,128)
	Douglas McNea (R)	32,182	(30%)	($1,826)
	Other	3,434	(3%)	
2002 primary	Zoe Lofgren (D)	unopposed		
2000 general	Zoe Lofgren (D)	115,118	(72%)	($486,365)
	Horace (Gene) Thayn (R)	37,213	(23%)	
	Other	7,415	(5%)	

Prior Winning Percentages: 1998 (73%); 1996 (66%); 1994 (65%)

The People		Race/Ethnic Origin	Ancestry	
Area size:	232 sq. mi.	31.9% White	German: 5.7%	Irish: 4.6%
Urban population:	98.7%	3.4% Black	English: 4.2%	
Rural population:	1.3%	23.4% Asian	**2000 Presidential Vote**	
Pop. 2000:	639,088	0.4% Native Am.	Gore (D) 109,632 (64%)	
Median income:	$67,689	0.4% Hawaiian	Bush (R) 57,160 (33%)	
Poverty status:	9.8%	2.8% Two+ races	Other 4,832 (3%)	
Military veterans:	7.6%	0.2% Other	**Cook Partisan Voting Index:** D +15	
		37.6% Hispanic Origin		

Occupation	Blue collar: 24.7%	White collar: 60.9%	Gray collar: 14.4%

With more people than San Francisco, a tradition of high-tech innovation that rivals any on earth, and a major league sports team, San Jose has great claims on national attention and respect. Yet San Jose does not bulk as large in the national consciousness as it should. At the southern end of the Bay, it remains in the shadow of the city on the Golden Gate. San Francisco is every tourist's idea of a city: geographically compact, with picturesque public transportation, old-time and new immigrant groups, an economy historically based on heavy industry and sea trade, a large city bureaucracy symbolized by a monumental city hall. San Jose is quite different. It got its start as a farm-market town, with canneries and fruit-packing operations for the produce from the surrounding fertile plains. It sits not on the Bay, but on the Southern Pacific line above the marshes and salt evaporators; its major transportation arteries are the freeways—U.S. 101, Interstates 280, 680 and 880, California 17—that encircle its revitalized downtown. Starting in the 1950s, San Jose has grown out in every direction, developers hip-hopping across the farmland, putting up subdivisions faster sometimes than the few city employees could update the street map. Economically, San Jose has been sustained by everything from its traditional agriculture to manufacturing to the high-tech businesses that are centered in Silicon Valley towns just to the west but are omnipresent here: an American city, 21st century style. For many years there were Mexican-Americans here, originally farm workers; now there is a major immigrant presence, with large numbers from Latin America and East and South Asia. Nearly half of all Santa Clara County residents speak a language other than English at home, mostly Spanish, Vietnamese or Chinese; one in three are foreign-born.

The 16th Congressional District consists of about two-thirds of San Jose, plus nearby unincorporated area to the south; 92% of its residents live inside the jagged city limits of San Jose. It includes the old and new downtowns and the heavily Mexican-American areas to the east. This is the most heavily Hispanic district in the Bay Area (38%); it is also heavily Asian (23%), with the largest concentration of Vietnamese in the U.S. Politically, it is solidly Democratic. Its future leanings depend on the trends among Latinos and Asians, who are family-oriented and not necessarily as favorable to big government as black voters.

The congresswoman from the 16th District is Zoe Lofgren, a Democrat elected in 1994. Lofgren grew up in the Bay Area, where her father was a Teamster truck driver and her mother worked for the Machinists Union. She went to Stanford and Santa Clara law school, worked for eight years as a staffer to Congressman Don Edwards; as a law student, she worked for him while he served on the Judiciary Committee that voted to impeach Richard Nixon. In 1980 she was elected to the Santa Clara County Board of Supervisors. In 1994, when Edwards retired after 32 years in the House, Lofgren ran for the seat. Her chief Democratic opponent, former San Jose

Mayor Tom McEnery, started off better known. But Lofgren raised almost twice as much money, with the support of the national women's organizations and female lawmakers in the California delegation. She won the primary 45%–42%. She easily won the general election.

Edwards, her predecessor, never saw a day in the minority in over three decades in the House. To Lofgren's surprise, that's where she found herself. Nonetheless she has had some impact, and her voting record, while mostly liberal, includes some free-market positions responsive to local businesses. Working with California Republican David Dreier, she won expanded allotments in the H-1B visa program for high-tech workers. She pushed for looser controls on encryption exports, securities litigation limitation and relaxation of trade restraints on supercomputers: all big Silicon Valley causes. The Clinton impeachment inquiry put Lofgren in the national spotlight. As the only Judiciary member to have served as a staffer during the Nixon proceedings, she attempted to put her experience to use. She brought forward the 1974 committee staff report that had set forth grounds for impeachment, and insisted the committee members vote on what is an impeachable offense, though Judiciary did not have such a vote 24 years before. This argument suited Democrats' partisan purposes, and they included it in their impeachment resolution; this was not acceptable to Chairman Henry Hyde and the Republicans.

After backing PNTR with China, she opposed trade promotion authority. She voted to repeal the estate tax but her position changed when enactment became a possibility. In 2001, she was pleased that the Republicans' energy bill included her proposal to accelerate the development of fusion as an energy source, but she voted against the overall bill. When Republicans brought up a bill to make it a separate offense to injure or kill a fetus while committing a crime against a pregnant woman, she offered an alternative simply to make it a crime to attack a pregnant woman, without conferring rights to the fetus; that was defeated 229–196. In response to bipartisan proposals to make it easier for consumers to download copyrighted works for fair use, she countered with a bill to make it legal to make back-up copies of digital content.

Lofgren has had no trouble winning reelection. After the 2002 election, she ran for vice chairman of the Democratic Caucus. But Nancy Pelosi, also from the Bay Area, had already been elected minority leader, and the Congressional Black Caucus was pressing to have one of its members in the leadership. Lofgren ran third with 53 votes to 95 for James Clyburn and 56 for Gregory Meeks.

SEVENTEENTH DISTRICT

Rep. Sam Farr (D)

Elected June 1993, 5th term; b. July 4, 1941, San Francisco; home, Carmel; Willamette U., B.S. 1963; Episcopalian; married (Shary).

Elected Office: Monterey Cnty. Bd. of Supervisors, 1975–80, Chmn., 1979; CA Assembly, 1980–93.

Professional Career: Peace Corps, Colombia, 1963–65; Staff, CA Assembly, 1965–75.

DC Office: 1221 LHOB 20515, 202-225-2861; Fax: 202-225-6791; Web site: www.house.gov/farr.

District Offices: Salinas, 831-424-2229; Santa Cruz, 831-429-1976.

Committees: *Appropriations* (22d of 29 D): Agriculture, Rural Development, & FDA; Military Construction.

Group Ratings

	ADA	ACLU	AFS	LCV	CON	ITIC	NTU	COC	ACU	NTLC	CHC
2002	95	93	100	100	70	50	25	35	0	0	8
2001	95	—	100	100	—	—	10	43	0	—	—

National Journal Ratings

	2001 LIB	—	2001 CONS		2002 LIB	—	2002 CONS
Economic	83%	—	15%		82%	—	17%
Social	90%	—	0%		94%	—	3%
Foreign	94%	—	7%		87%	—	10%

Key Votes of the 107th Congress

1. Approve Bush Tax Cuts	N	5. Faith-Based Charities	N	9. Trade Promotion Authority	N
2. Limit Patients' Bill of Rights	N	6. Bar Gays in the Boy Scouts	N	10. Bar Funds for Intl. Court	N
3. Campaign Finance Reform	Y	7. Ban Partial-Birth Abortion	N	11. Authorize Force in Iraq	N
4. Ban ANWR Development	Y	8. Arm Commercial Pilots	N	12. Deny Home. Sec. Dept. Union	N

Election Results

2002 general	Sam Farr (D)	101,632	(68%)	($565,220)
	Clint Engler (R)	40,334	(27%)	($1,532)
	Other	7,330	(5%)	
2002 primary	Sam Farr (D)	51,251	(91%)	
	Art Dunn (D)	5,008	(9%)	
2000 general	Sam Farr (D)	143,219	(69%)	($692,932)
	Clint Engler (R)	51,557	(25%)	($29,951)
	E. Craig Coffin (Green)	8,215	(4%)	
	Other	5,769	(3%)	

Prior Winning Percentages: 1998 (65%); 1996 (59%); 1994 (52%); 1993 (52%)

The People		Race/Ethnic Origin	Ancestry	
Area size:	5,386 sq. mi.	46.3% White	German: 7.6%	English: 6.3%
Urban population:	90.0%	2.6% Black	Irish: 6.3%	
Rural population:	10.0%	4.8% Asian	**2000 Presidential Vote**	
Pop. 2000:	639,088	0.4% Native Am.	Gore (D)	124,580 (60%)
Median income:	$49,234	0.3% Hawaiian	Bush (R)	68,717 (33%)
Poverty status:	13.3%	2.5% Two+ races	Other	14,819 (7%)
Military veterans:	10.4%	0.3% Other	**Cook Partisan Voting Index:** D +14	
		42.9% Hispanic Origin		

Occupation	Blue collar: 19.7%	White collar: 55.4%	Gray collar: 24.9%

The California coast around Monterey Bay is for many a working definition of paradise. This kernel of California, where Spanish and then Mexicans governed a virtually empty land and Californians set up their first state capital, still makes a fine living off the land and sea, as it has for 150 years. The locale for *The Grapes of Wrath* and many other John Steinbeck novels, the fields around Salinas supply much of the nation's lettuce and cauliflower. Nearby, the fields around Castroville supply almost all of its artichokes, and the vast greenhouses around Watsonville supply a goodly portion of its roses. The fishing fleet and 18 now-closed canneries of Monterey are no longer a major industry, but they have generated a new industry: Cannery Row is refurbished with upscale shops and hotels, and the magnificent Monterey Bay Aquarium is one of California's top tourist destinations. Monterey Bay has become the nation's language learning capital, with the Defense Language Institute, the AT&T Language Line and Cal State's Monterey Bay Center for Intensive Language and Culture on the site of Fort Ord, the Army's old language school, which was closed in the early 1990s. There are other attractions on the Monterey peninsula: the Pebble Beach golf courses, Del Monte Lodge, and Carmel, whose restrictive laws—no house numbers, no door-to-door mail delivery, no live entertainment, no stop lights, no cutting trees without city council permission—reflect an effort to maintain the atmosphere of 80 years ago, when it really was an artists' colony.

The 17th Congressional District includes all the coast of Monterey Bay and then follows the Big Sur coastline south almost to William Randolph Hearst's castle, San Simeon, past some of the most beautiful scenery in America; to the north along Monterey Bay, it extends past Watsonville to Santa Cruz and the last boardwalk amusement park on the West Coast. The district extends inland, into sunny valleys sheltered from ocean mists, and covers some of the nation's richest farmland. In San Benito County is Hollister, where tens of thousands of motorcyclists assemble annually at an oval dirt racetrack for the Independence Rally. Most of the farm workers are Latino (mainly Mexican), and in the 1990s the district's Latino population rose from 31% to 43%—the largest increase in any northern California district. The Census showed that the gap between rich and poor in Monterey County widened in the 1990s: More than 2,000 homes were valued at more than $1 million, while the county ranked seventh statewide in the share of households below the poverty line; of course many of these people were living in much greater poverty in other countries 10 years ago. This area is a prime example of how the California coast has trended Democratic. Thirty years ago this was a solidly Republican area, dominated politically by the landowners in Salinas and the townspeople who sympathize with them, plus retirees in Santa Cruz and the Monterey peninsula. But an influx of liberation-minded young people, attracted less by the economy than by the atmosphere, moved the coast to the left. Also, the University of California branch at Santa Cruz is so liberal (97% for George McGovern in 1972) that it has changed the political balance of the whole county. In 2002, Santa Cruz officials in front of City Hall gave away medical marijuana in defiance of a law-enforcement crackdown. As late as 1980, Monterey and Santa Cruz counties were voting less Democratic than the nation. But since 1984 they have been 6% to 10% more Democratic than the nation. In 2000 Al Gore won by 60%–33% a district that was carried four times by Ronald Reagan.

The congressman from the 17th is Sam Farr, a Democrat elected in June 1993. A fifth-generation Californian, he grew up in the area, where his father was a state senator for many years. Farr signed up for the Peace Corps after college, learned Spanish at the Monterey Institute of International Studies and served two years in Colombia. He was a California Assembly staffer for a decade, became a Monterey County supervisor in 1975, and was elected to the Assembly in 1980. There he wrote one of the nation's strictest oil spill liability laws. In 1993 Leon Panetta resigned to become Office of Management and Budget director, and Farr ran for the House. He entered the race as the overwhelming favorite, and in the all-party primary won 26% to beat two other Democrats who had 19% and 14%. But in the runoff, after the Clinton budget and tax increase had been introduced, he had trouble against Republican Bill McCampbell, who had been beaten 72%–24% by Panetta seven months before. Farr won, but by just 52%–43%.

In the House, Farr has a solidly liberal voting record. In voting against the trade promotion authority, Farr cited the Clinton administration's failure to restrict imports of cut flowers from Colombia, which have harmed a major local industry; the flowers are allowed across the border with no tariff as an incentive for Colombia to grow crops other than narcotics.

On the Appropriations Committee, Farr has focused on two major local concerns: farming and military bases. He helped to negotiate the final agreement that conveyed the former Fort Ord to civilian hands, and he took the lead in refusing to permit the Navy to establish a practice bombing range near Big Sur. He unsuccessfully attempted to add $350 million in loan guarantees for utilities to address bottlenecks in the Western power grid. George W. Bush signed his bill to add 55,000 acres to Big Sur wilderness area. He co-chaired with Representative Mark Foley the Travel and Tourism Caucus, which urged Bush to establish an advisory commission on tourism development. And he co-chaired the Oceans Caucus to improve oceans-related policy making, including job-protection in the fishing industry.

Farr was elected to a full term in 1994 against McCampbell by only 52%–44%. Since then California has moved to the Democrats and Farr has been reelected easily. His ability to work well with diverse interests has made Farr an effective chairman of the influential California Democratic delegation; he has been a close ally of Nancy Pelosi.

EIGHTEENTH DISTRICT

Rep. Dennis Cardoza (D)

Elected 2002, 1st term; b. March 31, 1959, Merced; home, Atwater; U. of MD, B.A. 1982, CA St. U. Stanislaus; Catholic; married (Kathleen McLoughlin).

Elected Office: Atwater City Cncl., 1984–86; Merced City Cncl., 1994–95; CA Assembly, 1996–02.

Professional Career: Agribusiness owner.

DC Office: 503 CHOB 20515, 202-225-6131; Fax: 202-225-0819; Web site: www.house.gov/cardoza.

District Offices: Merced, 209-383-4455; Modesto, 209-527-1914; Stockton, 209-946-0361.

Committees: *Agriculture* (15th of 24 D): Department Operations, Oversight, Nutrition & Forestry; General Farm Commodities & Risk Management; Livestock & Horticulture. *Resources* (17th of 24 D): National Parks, Recreation & Public Lands; Water & Power. *Science* (21st of 22 D): Research.

Group Ratings and Key Votes: Newly Elected

Election Results

2002 general	Dennis Cardoza (D)	56,181	(51%)	($1,648,539)
	Dick Monteith (R)	47,528	(43%)	($1,042,288)
	Other	5,884	(5%)	
2002 primary	Dennis Cardoza (D)	22,879	(53%)	
	Gary Condit (D)	16,618	(39%)	
	Other	3,487	(8%)	
2000 general	Gary Condit (D)	121,003	(67%)	($686,683)
	Steve R. Wilson (R)	56,465	(31%)	($31,087)
	Other	2,860	(2%)	

The People		Race/Ethnic Origin	Ancestry	
Area size:	3,101 sq. mi.	39.1% White	German: 6.2%	Irish: 4.8%
Urban population:	91.3%	5.6% Black	English: 4.0%	
Rural population:	8.7%	8.9% Asian	**2000 Presidential Vote**	
Pop. 2000:	639,088	0.7% Native Am.	Gore (D) 77,908	(53%)
Median income:	$34,211	0.3% Hawaiian	Bush (R) 65,105	(44%)
Poverty status:	22.7%	3.2% Two+ races	Other 3,690	(3%)
Military veterans:	10.1%	0.2% Other	**Cook Partisan Voting Index:** D + 4	
		41.9% Hispanic Origin		

Occupation	Blue collar: 31.0%	White collar: 46.0%	Gray collar: 23.1%

The Central Valley of California is a miraculous man-made landscape, an outdoor factory stretching as far as the eye can see. Nature created the vast flatlands, rimmed by mountains rising surreally in the distant haze. But man in the last century has disciplined the land with a remorseless mile-square grid of roads, and the sluggish-flowing California Aqueduct and dozens of arrow-straight canals; pipes fitted with valves and gauges to pump water and fertilizer and pesticides to the fields in measured quantities give an air of industrial precision. The crops grow in carefully spaced rows, filling the fields, for the rich soil and the irrigated water are too precious to waste on decoration or flower gardens. Farming here has never been a way of life, but a business; in the 19th century the land was not given to 160-acre homesteaders but sold to thousands-of-acres capitalist enterprises.

The Central Valley in recent years has become one of California's surprise boom areas, growing not just crops but people. Middle-wage employees in the San Francisco Bay area drive east at the end of the day on I-580, past surreal windmills whirling on the bare hills of the Altamont pass, across the Westlands fields to modestly priced homes in Modesto, the town immortalized (when it was much smaller) in *American Graffiti*. Warehouses and factories have sprung up on land that, for all its farming value, is cheaper than industrial land in the Bay Area, and some croplands have been given over to pasture, as subsidized water was cut off from cultivators of cotton, and water prices are moving slowly toward market levels far above those of government subsidy. The result is not stagnation but growth, and a more well-rounded economy. But there are costs. Traffic is a problem, air pollution on bad days approaches coastal metropolitan levels, and the pace of life is getting more hectic.

The 18th Congressional District includes a large chunk of the Central Valley from Stockton, south to Modesto and through Merced County to the fringes of Fresno. The political tradition here had been Democratic: Democrats in Washington and Democratic Governor Pat Brown built the irrigation canals and authorized the water subsidies; Democrats owned the McClatchy newspapers, the predominant Valley chain; Democrats staffed the Bank of America, long the dominant financial force here; on the walls of insider law firms were signed pictures of Franklin Roosevelt and Pat Brown, not Ronald Reagan and Pete Wilson. But the Central Valley is the part of California with the highest proportion of families and children, and there is a natural cultural conservatism here, shared by successful local Democratic politicians. In the 1980s and 1990s the Central Valley trended Republican, and even Latinos here are less heavily Democratic than in Los Angeles.

Yet the 18th District is still Democratic, because of very careful redistricting. The problem was the district held by conservative Democrat Gary Condit, who was weakened by publicity of his involvement with missing intern Chandra Levy. Condit's old Central Valley district had voted 53% for George W. Bush in 2000; Condit held it only because of his conservative record and local popularity, and the latter seemed damaged beyond repair. The solution was to remove much of Condit's old area and to add Democratic territory he had not previously represented. Condit's home town of Ceres and most of Modesto were retained in the new district, but northern and eastern Stanislaus County, Republican-leaning areas where Condit had long been well-known, were removed. Added was a corridor along I-5 in San Joaquin County, including the central part of Stockton, a heavily Hispanic and Democratic area. Retained was Merced County and a small, almost uninhabited portion of Madera and Fresno Counties. Within the boundaries of the new district, the Bush 2000 percentage was only 44%.

The congressman from the 18th District is Dennis Cardoza, a Democrat elected in a 2002 contest that drew international attention because of the notoriety of his predecessor, Gary Condit. Cardoza grew up in Merced and Stanislaus Counties and graduated from the University of Maryland; he is, by the way, not of Latin American but of Portuguese descent (like Devin Nunes of the nearby 21st District and Richard Pombo of the 11th). In the mid-1980s Cardoza worked as an aide to Condit, then an assemblyman, assisted Condit's 1989 special election campaign and served on his Washington staff. In 1997 Cardoza was elected to the Assembly; Condit's son and sister later worked on his staff. Cardoza was one of several Central Valley Democrats who had built their careers around Condit's, and he undoubtedly would have continued to do so had Chandra Levy, a Modesto resident who was working as an intern in the executive branch, not disappeared in Washington in April 2001. Her disappearance generated saturation media coverage; it was revealed that Condit had a relationship with her, though he steadfastly denied it was sexual in nature. D.C. policemen's delay in interviewing Condit led reporters to ask whether Condit had been fully cooperative with police. In those pre-September 11 days, the Levy case suddenly became top news; Condit was harried by reporters and cameramen as he left his Adams-Morgan apartment or walked from the Capitol to the Rayburn Building. For constituents, the case was a revelation. Condit had always portrayed himself as a family man, the son of a preacher; his wife was well known and beloved in the Modesto area. Now it appeared that Condit had been living another life in Washington, dating young women and acting decidedly unlike a family man.

After September 11 Condit disappeared from the cable news networks, but the question remained whether he would seek reelection. Despite a *San Jose Mercury News* poll finding that 60% of his constituents would not vote for him again, in October 2001 Condit began collecting signatures to qualify for the election ballot. Cardoza was careful not to criticize Condit or question his actions at a time when his conduct with Levy generated worldwide speculation. But national and local Democrats urged him to enter the contest because they feared that the badly tarnished Condit could not hold the seat in a general election. To Condit, though, Cardoza's decision to challenge him was a betrayal. Senators Dianne Feinstein and Barbara Boxer endorsed Cardoza, as did many members of the House delegation. In the March primary, Cardoza won 53%–39%. Condit led 48%–46% in his base of Stanislaus County, but Cardoza clobbered him in San Joaquin County, 60%–25%, and in Merced, which Condit had represented, Cardoza won 57%–38%. In his final 10 months in Congress, the embittered Condit all but disappeared. He had few financial assets and his only profession was politics; he was first elected to public office at 23. He said that he might work in construction.

For Cardoza the election was not over. Republicans nominated state Senator Dick Monteith, whose seat included 73% of the congressional district; he claimed Cardoza was too liberal for an agriculture-oriented constituency. Cardoza allies responded by citing his business-oriented reputation in the Legislature. Cardoza tried to mollify Condit supporters, but Condit would not speak to him and predicted that Monteith would win in November. Monteith pledged to oppose "privatizing" Social Security, but Cardoza replied that Monteith had supported personal retirement accounts.

In October, Condit's children released a letter that harshly criticized Cardoza and urged citizens to vote against him; Cardoza won anyway, 51%–43%. Stockton made the difference. Monteith led 49%–47% in Merced, and 48%–44% in Stanislaus. But Cardoza led 67%–27% in San Joaquin County, a 10,000-vote margin that wiped out Monteith's 2,000-vote lead elsewhere.

NINETEENTH DISTRICT

Rep. George Radanovich (R)

Elected 1994, 5th term; b. June 20, 1955, Mariposa; home, Mariposa; CA Polytechnic U., B.S. 1978; Catholic; married (Ethie).

Elected Office: Mariposa Cnty. Planning Comm., 1982–86, Chmn., 1985–86; Mariposa Cnty. Bd. of Supervisors, 1989–92.

Professional Career: Farmer; Founder & Owner, Radanovich Winery, 1986–03.

DC Office: 438 CHOB 20515, 202-225-4540; Fax: 202-225-3402; Web site: www.house.gov/radanovich.

District Offices: Fresno, 559-449-2490; Turlock, 209-656-8660.

Committees: *Energy & Commerce* (21st of 31 R): Commerce, Trade & Consumer Protection; Energy & Air Quality; Environment & Hazardous Materials. *Resources* (11th of 28 R): National Parks, Recreation & Public Lands (Chmn.); Water & Power.

Group Ratings

	ADA	ACLU	AFS	LCV	CON	ITIC	NTU	COC	ACU	NTLC	CHC
2002	5	7	0	13	60	88	56	95	88	89	100
2001	5	—	0	0	—	—	63	95	92	—	—

National Journal Ratings

	2001 LIB	—	2001 CONS		2002 LIB	—	2002 CONS
Economic	7%	—	89%		21%	—	73%
Social	0%	—	81%		25%	—	71%
Foreign	19%	—	81%		40%	—	60%

Key Votes of the 107th Congress

1. Approve Bush Tax Cuts	Y	5. Faith-Based Charities	Y	9. Trade Promotion Authority	Y
2. Limit Patients' Bill of Rights	Y	6. Bar Gays in the Boy Scouts	Y	10. Bar Funds for Intl. Court	Y
3. Campaign Finance Reform	N	7. Ban Partial-Birth Abortion	Y	11. Authorize Force in Iraq	Y
4. Ban ANWR Development	N	8. Arm Commercial Pilots	Y	12. Deny Home. Sec. Dept. Union	Y

Election Results

2002 general	George Radanovich (R)	106,209	(67%)	($646,981)
	John Veen (D)	47,403	(30%)	
	Other	4,190	(3%)	
2002 primary	George Radanovich (R)	unopposed		
2000 general	George Radanovich (R)	144,517	(65%)	($659,104)
	Dan Rosenberg (D)	70,578	(32%)	($179,555)
	Other	7,520	(3%)	

Prior Winning Percentages: 1998 (79%); 1996 (67%); 1994 (57%)

The People		**Race/Ethnic Origin**	**Ancestry**	
Area size:	6,781 sq. mi.	59.9% White	German: 10.0%	English: 7.3%
Urban population:	80.6%	3.4% Black	Irish: 6.9%	
Rural population:	19.4%	4.4% Asian	**2000 Presidential Vote**	
Pop. 2000:	639,088	1.0% Native Am.	Bush (R) 125,465	(58%)
Median income:	$41,225	0.1% Hawaiian	Gore (D) 84,559	(39%)
Poverty status:	14.8%	2.8% Two+ races	Other 6,823	(3%)
Military veterans:	12.4%	0.2% Other	**Cook Partisan Voting Index:** R +10	
		28.2% Hispanic Origin		

Occupation   Blue collar: 22.0%   White collar: 59.3%   Gray collar: 18.8%

The city of Fresno started as a farm-marketing center—one high-income neighborhood is called Fig Garden because that's what it used to be—and as a tourists' stop-off point on the way to Yosemite National Park. But it has long since grown out north, east and west from its old downtown, and its economy has diversified. Like all the Central Valley, Fresno has always been ethnically diverse, with a telephone book that reads like the United Nations; it has America's second largest Armenian community, after Los Angeles. Its already large Latino population has more than doubled in the last 20 years, and Fresno County was 44% Hispanic in 2000; Asians, including Chinese, Filipinos, Vietnamese and Hmong, were 8% of the county's population. The city grew a lusty 17% in the 1990s, despite high unemployment rates, violent teenage gangs and air pollution that made the Sierra Nevada invisible on many days. Historically, Fresno was a Democratic town, the prime Democratic bastion in the Central Valley south of Sacramento. But in the 1990s it moved toward the Republicans. It voted for Bob Dole in 1996 and George W. Bush in 2000, Republican governor candidates Dan Lungren in 1998 and Bill Simon in 2002, all of whom lost statewide. This is one part of California that has trended toward Republicans, when most of the state was moving the other way.

The 19th Congressional District includes nearly half of Fresno, the relatively affluent north side of the city, and the farm towns of Madera County to the northeast. This is one of the two heavily populated parts of the district. The other is the north and eastern half of Stanislaus County, including the northern edge of Modesto and towns like Turlock, Riverbank and Oakdale. These two areas are connected not by land in the Central Valley but by mountainous Mariposa and Tuolumne counties, including Sierra foothills, the peaks of the Sierra Nevada and Yosemite National Park. Gold was once prospected in these butterfly-filled hills and a chain of mining camps ran along what is now Highway 49. Considerable changes were made in the 2001 redistricting. Removed from the district was much of rural Fresno and Tulare Counties, which are now in the new 21st District. Added was the Stanislaus County portion, once represented by Gary Condit, the conservative Democrat who carried this Republican area. Redistricters wanted to remove it to weaken him in the Democratic party and to make the district more Democratic in the general election. That left the 19th as a heavily Republican district.

The congressman from the 19th District is George Radanovich, a Republican elected in 1994. Radanovich is the son of Croatian immigrants, with relatives all over the Valley. He worked on the family farm, served on the Mariposa County Planning Commission in the 1980s and won a seat on the Board of Supervisors in 1989. In 1986, after studying local microclimates, he opened the first winery in Mariposa County and made it work; the Radanovich Winery shipped 4,000 cases annually of sauvignon blanc, merlot, zinfandel and cabernet sauvignon. In 1992 he ran for Congress, losing the primary 33%–30% to 28-year-old Tal Cloud, who lost to incumbent Democrat Richard Lehman 47%–46%. Lehman was an adept politician, but all his fundraising and skills could not avail him in 1994 as Radanovich, an easy winner in this primary, attacked him for supporting the Clinton administration and California Democrat George Miller's efforts to raise the price of Valley water. Radanovich won 57%–40% in the widest defeat of a non-freshman incumbent in 1994. He became the first full-time professional winemaker to serve in the House.

In the House, where Radanovich was elected president of his 74-member freshmen Republican class, he has a mostly conservative voting record recently turned a bit moderate as his ambition began to spread outside his district. In 1996 he passed with David Bonior an amendment to require Turkey to acknowledge the Armenian genocide of 1915; Turkey spurned aid under such conditions. In 2000, Radanovich secured $90 million in aid for Armenia—one of the largest recipients of U.S. aid; but Speaker Dennis Hastert acceded to Bill Clinton's personal appeal to abandon another resolution on Armenian genocide. He held out on trade promotion authority, agreeing to support it only after the Clinton administration agreed to address Mexican wine tariffs; he was more enthusiastic about supporting it after George W. Bush became president. As co-chairman with Mike Thompson of the Congressional Wine Caucus, he sought to educate members on the industry's issues.

In 2001, he joined the Energy and Commerce Committee, and pledged to deal with hydro-electric problems in the Sierra Nevadas. He urged the Bush administration to postpone the Clinton administration ban on road building in national forests. Later in 2001, Radanovich became chairman of the National Parks, Recreation and Public Lands Subcommittee at Resources—a useful assignment for the representative of Yosemite; he pledged a greater local voice in planning for the parks. He enacted his proposal to improve the remote schools serving families that work at the park. Radanovich's criticism of the plan to overhaul operations at Yosemite led its superintendent to resign. He ran into opposition from John Doolittle and Wally Herger to his proposal designating the 318-mile Highway 49 as a national heritage corridor; property rights advocates worried that private landowners would lose their rights and Radanovich backed off.

Back home, Radanovich has won reelection easily. Although redistricting gave him a nearly 50% new constituency, he was not seriously challenged. In 1994 Radanovich pledged to serve only 10 years in the House. More recently Radanovich has said that he might want "some flexibility" to accomplish his priorities. In 2002 and early 2003, he explored a race against Senator Barbara Boxer in 2004. If he decides to move on, Republicans would be strongly favored to hold the seat. Assemblyman Dave Cogdill of Modesto has been mentioned as a possible successor, but he might face a primary challenger from the Fresno area.

TWENTIETH DISTRICT

Rep. Cal Dooley (D)

Elected 1990, 7th term; b. Jan. 11, 1954, Visalia; home, Visalia; U. of CA at Davis, B.S. 1977, Stanford U., M.A. 1987; Methodist; married (Linda).

Professional Career: Farmer, 1978–91; A.A., CA Sen. Rose Ann Vuich, 1987–89.

DC Office: 1201 LHOB 20515, 202-225-3341; Fax: 202-225-9308; Web site: www.house.gov/dooley.

District Office: Fresno, 559-441-7496.

Committees: *Agriculture* (3d of 24 D): Conservation, Credit, Rural Development & Research; Department Operations, Oversight, Nutrition & Forestry (RMM); General Farm Commodities & Risk Management. *Resources* (7th of 24 D): Water & Power.

Group Ratings

	ADA	ACLU	AFS	LCV	CON	ITIC	NTU	COC	ACU	NTLC	CHC
2002	65	71	67	25	55	75	32	85	24	29	8
2001	65	—	70	43	—	—	22	77	32	—	—

National Journal Ratings

	2001 LIB —	2001 CONS		2002 LIB —	2002 CONS
Economic	53%	47%		54%	46%
Social	69%	31%		74%	19%
Foreign	61%	36%		58%	42%

Key Votes of the 107th Congress

1. Approve Bush Tax Cuts	Y	5. Faith-Based Charities	N	9. Trade Promotion Authority	Y
2. Limit Patients' Bill of Rights	N	6. Bar Gays in the Boy Scouts	N	10. Bar Funds for Intl. Court	N
3. Campaign Finance Reform	Y	7. Ban Partial-Birth Abortion	N	11. Authorize Force in Iraq	Y
4. Ban ANWR Development	N	8. Arm Commercial Pilots	N	12. Deny Home. Sec. Dept. Union	Y

Election Results

2002 general	Cal Dooley (D)	47,627	(64%)	($642,724)
	Andre Minuth (R)	25,628	(34%)	($503,230)
	Other	1,515	(2%)	
2002 primary	Cal Dooley (D)	unopposed		
2000 general	Cal Dooley (D)	66,235	(52%)	($1,775,089)
	Rich Rodriguez (R)	57,563	(45%)	($1,257,145)
	Other	2,736	(2%)	

Prior Winning Percentages: 1998 (61%); 1996 (57%); 1994 (57%); 1992 (65%); 1990 (55%)

The People		Race/Ethnic Origin	Ancestry	
Area size:	4,989 sq. mi.	21.4% White	German: 3.2%	Irish: 2.7%
Urban population:	91.2%	7.2% Black	USA: 2.3%	
Rural population:	8.8%	5.6% Asian	**2000 Presidential Vote**	
Pop. 2000:	639,088	0.7% Native Am.	Gore (D) 57,790 (55%)	
Median income:	$26,800	0.1% Hawaiian	Bush (R) 46,058 (44%)	
Poverty status:	32.2%	1.7% Two+ races	Other 1,844 (2%)	
Military veterans:	8.1%	0.2% Other	**Cook Partisan Voting Index:** D + 5	
		63.1% Hispanic Origin		

Occupation   Blue collar: 27.2%   White collar: 37.8%   Gray collar: 35.0%

California's Central Valley by car seems a monotonous landscape: mile after mile of farmland with mile-square grid roads, cut across by diagonal railroads and canals, with an occasional cluster town. The land is hilly and gets more water near the Sierra Nevada, and this is where the larger cities cluster. On the other side is the Westlands, where the land is flatter and the water scarcer. Here the land was always developed and sold in large plots, and it has some of the world's largest farming operations today. And it produces plenty: alfalfa, cantaloupes, cotton, grapes, lima beans, olives, peaches, plums, raisins, sugar beets, tomatoes, walnuts, wheat. The owners are a hardy lot, but like most entrepreneurs they have been happy to have government help: crop price supports (in the case of cotton), agricultural research, exceptions to the immigration laws, irrigation systems and (most important) subsidized water. They have fought hard against liberals' efforts at change, from Governor Jerry Brown's attempts to encourage Cesar Chavez's United Farm Workers in the 1970s to former House Natural Resources Committee Chairman George Miller's 1992 law to draw off more water to the Sacramento delta and charge higher prices for it in the Valley. But the greatest threats may come from conservatives: In a free market for water, Los Angeles users may outbid the farmers. And Congress has declined to approve guest worker programs pushed by Valley members.

The 20th Congressional District includes most of the Westlands of the Central Valley, from Bakersfield to a point northwest of Fresno. Its irregular boundaries were drawn to maximize the Hispanic population and Democratic percentage, so the 20th includes the old downtown neighborhoods of both Bakersfield and Fresno, but not their more affluent neighborhoods; it includes heavily Latino towns like Delano, long Chavez's headquarters and recently the site of a potentially large natural gas discovery, but the 20th does not include more Anglo places like Tulare. Just 36% of Fresno's population is included within the 20th and just 18% of Bakersfield; the district's Hispanic population is 63%, about double that in other Central Valley districts, but the share of voters who are Latino is lower, about 59%. This is the most Democratic Valley seat between Sacramento and Los Angeles; the Valley has been trending Republican, but redistricting reduced the Bush 2000 percentage from 49% to 44%.

The congressman from the 20th District is Cal Dooley, a Democrat first elected in 1990. He is a farmer, growing cotton, alfalfa and walnuts, as his great-grandfather did before him. In 1987 he became a staffer for Tulare state Senator Rose Ann Vuich. In 1990, he ran for Congress in a more Republican-leaning district. Luck was with him: The incumbent had accepted contributions from S&L operator Charles Keating and interceded on his behalf with regulators. Dooley won with a solid 55%. When new district lines were announced in 1992, Dooley and 10-year incumbent Democrat Richard Lehman both eyed the 20th, but Dooley staked it out quickly and Lehman ran in the more Republican 19th, where he lost in 1994.

Dooley's endurance has been partly a testimonial to his moderate voting record, which is the most conservative of California Democrats. On the Agriculture and Resources committees, he tended to district interests. He was one of three committee Democrats to vote for Richard Pombo's guest worker bill, and he supported lifting the ban on food sales to Cuba. He has co-chaired the Congressional Beef Caucus, the Western Water Caucus and the Biotechnology Caucus. He strongly backed PNTR with China and he worked closely with neighboring Congressman and Ways and Means Committee chairman Bill Thomas to get Democratic votes for trade promotion authority in 2001 and 2002. In 2001, he was one of 36 Democrats who voted for the Republican energy bill, including its provision to open the Arctic National Wildlife Refuge to oil drilling. His independence caused some ill will among Democrats. In May 2002, he voted against the farm bill, which he criticized for putting "taxpayers on the hook for billions in questionable subsidies," especially for dairy and peanut farmers; most Central Valley crops are unsubsidized. He sided with most Democrats in opposing the increased work requirements in the Republicans' welfare bill.

Dooley is active on local issues, including flood control projects, increased dam capacity, and additional funds for farm workers. He supported the bill to waive the English language requirement for citizenship for Hmong and Lao veterans who were recruited by the U.S. military in the 1960s and 1970s. He organized in Fresno a bipartisan summit to seek solutions to the methamphetamine crisis, and in 2002 got the Drug Enforcement Administration to reassign four agents to Fresno.

Within his party, Dooley is a founder and past co-chairman of the New Democrat Coalition, a group of moderate House Democrats. After the 1998 election, he ran for vice-chairman of the House Democratic Caucus and tried to assemble a coalition of conservatives and Californians. But he failed to lock up either group and lost 124–81 on the second ballot to Robert Menendez of New Jersey. He reportedly voted for Steny Hoyer against Nancy Pelosi in the October 2001 contest for Minority Whip. A year later, he supported her for Minority Leader, with the caveat that, "Nancy has a perception problem that she has to overcome." Dooley helped lead the New Democratic Network, a well-funded political action committee that promotes moderate Democrats.

Before redistricting made this seat more comfortably Democratic, Dooley had well-financed and competitive reelection challenges. The most serious came in 2000 from Rich Rodriguez, a former Fresno TV news anchorman, who was wooed by national Republicans especially keen that he is Latino, although he does not speak Spanish. Rodriguez made mistakes common for political newcomers; he was not always familiar with the issues. But he had high name recognition and won the endorsement from the California Farm Bureau Federation, whose members griped that Dooley appeared to give as much attention to Silicon Valley as to the Central Valley and had failed to establish a guest worker program. Dooley raised considerably more money than the challenger, much of it from leaders of agricultural enterprises like Sunkist and Blue Diamond and won 52%–45%. In 2002 he faced a Fresno physician and who had escaped from Latvia in World War

II and who was now successful enough to spend $500,000 on his campaign. It was a great American success story, but Dooley won 64%–34%.

A greater threat to Dooley could come in the Democratic primary from a Latino challenger as more Latinos become registered voters. But for the moment Dooley seems safe.

TWENTY-FIRST DISTRICT

Rep. Devin Nunes (R)

Elected 2002, 1st term; b. Oct. 1, 1973, Tulare; home, Visalia; Col. of the Sequoias, A.D. 1993, CA Poly. U., B.S. 1995, M.A. 1996; Catholic; single.

Elected Office: Col. of the Sequoias Governing Bd., 1996–02.

Professional Career: State Dir., USDA Rural Dev., 2001.

DC Office: 1017 LHOB 20515, 202-225-2523; Fax: 202-225-3404; Web site: www.house.gov/nunes.

District Offices: Clovis, 559-323-5235; Visalia, 559-733-3861.

Committees: *Agriculture* (26th of 27 R): Department Operations, Oversight, Nutrition & Forestry; Specialty Crops & Foreign Agriculture Programs. *Resources* (27th of 28 R): Energy & Mineral Resources; Water & Power.

Group Ratings and Key Votes: Newly Elected

Election Results

2002 general	Devin Nunes (R)		87,544	(70%)	($1,213,781)
	David LaPere (D)		32,584	(26%)	($19,827)
	Other		4,070	(3%)	
2002 primary	Devin Nunes (R)		21,438	(37%)	
	Jim Patterson (R)		19,099	(33%)	
	Mike Briggs (R)		14,864	(26%)	
	Other		2,476	(4%)	

The People		Race/Ethnic Origin	Ancestry	
Area size:	8,090 sq. mi.	46.4% White	German: 7.7%	English: 5.6%
Urban population:	79.9%	2.1% Black	Irish: 5.5%	
Rural population:	20.1%	4.9% Asian	**2000 Presidential Vote**	
Pop. 2000:	639,088	0.9% Native Am.	Bush (R)............107,645	(60%)
Median income:	$36,047	0.1% Hawaiian	Gore (D)............65,268	(37%)
Poverty status:	20.7%	2.2% Two+ races	Other..................5,120	(3%)
Military veterans:	10.6%	0.2% Other	**Cook Partisan Voting Index:** R +13	
		43.4% Hispanic Origin		

Occupation	Blue collar: 22.0%	White collar: 52.8%	Gray collar: 25.2%

Fresno, in California's Central Valley, between the flat Westlands and the Sierras, is a city agricultural and industrial, middle American and ethnically diverse. It is a creation of the industrial age, founded by the Central Pacific Railroad; its city fathers bred the local wine grape, developed the raisin industry and introduced the Smyrna fig. These are not all of Fresno's crops, which include cotton, lima beans, tomatoes, cantaloupes, plums, peaches and alfalfa. Fresno County produces more farm products in dollar value than any other county in the United States. Central Valley agriculture is industrial in its precision, its thoroughness and its ownership by large corporations: the vineyards outside Fresno radiate in mechanical precision, with vines just 10 feet apart and exposed to the relentless summer sun: nothing romantic or quaint here. The city of Fresno started as a farm-marketing center and as a tourists' stop-off point on the way to Yosemite National Park. But it has long since grown out north, east and west from its old downtown, and its economy has diversified.

The 21st Congressional District covers most of Fresno County east of Fresno and Tulare County to the south; 42% of the population is in Fresno County (the 21st also includes part of the city of Fresno) and 58% in Tulare. Here and there amid the farm fields are small cities—Visalia (the largest in the district), Tulare, Clovis, Reedley, Porterville. Past Kings Canyon and Sequoia National Parks loom the giant peaks of the Sierra Nevada, including Mount Whitney, at 14,494 feet, the highest point in California and in the lower 48 states. This part of the Central Valley had vigorous growth in the 1990s; the district is 43% Hispanic. The 21st is the new district created by the 2001 redistricting after California gained one seat in the 2000 Census and it is strongly Republican. It may seem surprising that Democratic redistricters gave the new seat to the other party, but they compensated by making one Republican-held seat in Los Angeles safely Democratic. Within the bounds of the 21st District George W. Bush got 60% of the vote in 2000, his third highest percentage in a California district.

The congressman from the 21st District is Devin Nunes, a Republican elected in 2002 and the youngest member of the freshman class. He grew up in Tulare County, on a dairy farm that has been in his family for three generations now. He graduated from Cal Poly in San Luis Obispo with degrees in agriculture and worked on the dairy farm. He is politically well connected. In 1998, at 25, he ran for the House in the 20th District and finished second in the primary, losing by just 52%–48%. In 2000 he was Tulare County campaign chairman for 22d District Congressman Bill Thomas, chairman of the Ways and Means Committee. In 2001, with help from Thomas, he was appointed California director of rural development for the Agriculture Department.

When the redistricting plan was unveiled in September 2001, Nunes moved quickly to demonstrate his support. He was supported by Thomas and in time by nine other California Republican incumbents—half the state Republican delegation. His $5,000 contribution from Thomas opened doors in Washington, and many in the pharmaceutical and insurance industries supported him. At home he won the endorsement of the California Farm Bureau, the state's largest farm organization and a powerful voice in Central Valley politics. But Nunes had serious primary competition. The best known candidate was Jim Patterson, the conservative former mayor of Fresno, who was endorsed and well-financed by the Club for Growth. Another serious candidate was Assemblyman Mike Briggs, who worked on agriculture issues in Sacramento and expected the Farm Bureau's support. Briggs was criticized by other Republicans for being one of only four Republicans to cross the aisle and vote for the state budget in 2001; he defended his vote by saying he got large tax breaks for farmers. Nunes had help in Fresno County, Patterson's and Briggs's home base, when he won the endorsement of *The Fresno Bee*. In the closing days of the campaign, Nunes criticized Patterson because his northwest Fresno home wasn't actually in the new district; Patterson responded that the contest "isn't about ZIP code." There were few differences on policy. All three said that agriculture was their top priority and promised to seek new water sources. All called for cuts in taxes and government regulations. All endorsed expanded guest worker programs.

In the March 2002 primary Nunes won with 37% of the vote, to 33% for Patterson and 26% for Briggs. In Tulare County, which cast 49% of the Republican votes, he had a big lead with 46% of the vote, to 27% for Patterson and 20% for Briggs. In Fresno County Nunes finished third with 27%, but his two opponents divided the vote: Patterson got 37% and Briggs 30%. The primary determined who would be the new congressman; Nunes won in November 70%–26%. Nunes began what could be a lengthy House career with seats on Agriculture and Resources, both well-suited for the new district, plus a very good friend as chairman of the Ways and Means Committee.

TWENTY-SECOND DISTRICT

Rep. Bill Thomas (R)

Elected 1978, 13th term; b. Dec. 6, 1941, Wallace, ID; home, Bakersfield; San Francisco St. U., B.A. 1963, M.A. 1965; Baptist; married (Sharon).

Elected Office: CA Assembly, 1974–78.

Professional Career: Prof., Bakersfield Commun. Col., 1965–74.

DC Office: 2208 RHOB 20515, 202-225-2915; Fax: 202-225-8798; Web site: www.house.gov/billthomas.

District Offices: Bakersfield, 661-327-3611; San Luis Obispo, 805-549-0390.

Committees: *Ways & Means* (Chmn. of 24 R). *Joint Committee on Taxation* (Chmn. of 5 Reps.).

Group Ratings

	ADA	ACLU	AFS	LCV	CON	ITIC	NTU	COC	ACU	NTLC	CHC
2002	10	27	0	0	34	100	52	100	80	81	75
2001	15	—	0	7	—	—	57	100	68	—	—

National Journal Ratings

	2001 LIB —	2001 CONS	2002 LIB —	2002 CONS
Economic	35%	65%	36%	61%
Social	52%	47%	52%	48%
Foreign	14%	85%	34%	65%

Key Votes of the 107th Congress

1. Approve Bush Tax Cuts	Y	5. Faith-Based Charities	Y	9. Trade Promotion Authority	Y
2. Limit Patients' Bill of Rights	Y	6. Bar Gays in the Boy Scouts	Y	10. Bar Funds for Intl. Court	Y
3. Campaign Finance Reform	N	7. Ban Partial-Birth Abortion	Y	11. Authorize Force in Iraq	Y
4. Ban ANWR Development	N	8. Arm Commercial Pilots	N	12. Deny Home. Sec. Dept. Union	Y

Election Results

2002 general	Bill Thomas (R)	120,473	(73%)	($1,591,853)
	Jaime Corvera (D)	38,988	(24%)	($10,426)
	Other	4,824	(3%)	
2002 primary	Bill Thomas (R)	unopposed		
2000 general (CA 21)	Bill Thomas (R)	142,539	(72%)	($1,529,664)
	Pedro Martinez Jr. (D)	49,318	(25%)	
	James Manion (Lib)	7,243	(4%)	

Prior Winning Percentages: 1998 (79%); 1996 (66%); 1994 (68%); 1992 (65%); 1990 (60%); 1988 (71%); 1986 (73%); 1984 (71%); 1982 (68%); 1980 (71%); 1978 (59%)

The People		Race/Ethnic Origin	Ancestry	
Area size:	10,454 sq. mi.	66.8% White	German: 10.7%	Irish: 8.1%
Urban population:	82.5%	5.6% Black	English: 7.8%	
Rural population:	17.5%	2.9% Asian	**2000 Presidential Vote**	
Pop. 2000:	639,088	0.9% Native Am.	Bush (R)	141,156 (64%)
Median income:	$41,801	0.1% Hawaiian	Gore (D)	73,338 (33%)
Poverty status:	13.7%	2.5% Two+ races	Other	5,043 (2%)
Military veterans:	14.8%	0.2% Other	**Cook Partisan Voting Index:** R +16	
		21.0% Hispanic Origin		

Occupation	Blue collar: 23.1%	White collar: 57.8%	Gray collar: 19.1%

Bakersfield, at the apex of the southern end of California's Central Valley, has been the focus of great migrations four times—in a gold rush in 1885, when oil was discovered here in 1899, during the 1930s when the Okies drove their jalopies from the Dust Bowl of Oklahoma and Kansas and Texas across the Southwest on U.S. 66, and again in the 1980s and 1990s, when Bakersfield and

Kern County grew more rapidly than California's biggest metro areas. Bakersfield's oil rigs pump more oil than is produced annually in Oklahoma, but the migration that made the deepest imprint was in the 1930s. The Okies drove over one thousand miles of brown landscape, then through the Tehachapi Pass, and found this vast green valley, with its irrigated fields and its eucalyptus-shaded towns, the richest farming country in the world. The story is told vividly in John Steinbeck's *The Grapes of Wrath*, though his vision of the Okies as workers eager to join together with their fellow proletarians and rise up against their bosses did not get the picture quite right. More accurate is Dan Morgan's *Rising in the West*, which shows the strong Pentecostal beliefs that drove many migrants and, unlike Steinbeck, explains how they prospered in California.

The area around Bakersfield has become the one Southern-accented part of California, the home of country singers Buck Owens and Merle Haggard and a thriving contemporary country music scene, culturally conservative with a strong drive toward discipline and little empathy for the therapy that is so common in Los Angeles, 110 miles south. But Bakersfield's uniqueness may be diluted as southern California spreads north: developers are planning a town of 70,000 on valley land where I-5 plunges downhill from the Tejon Pass.

The 22d Congressional District, the southernmost district in the Central Valley, includes most of Bakersfield and Kern, most of the land area of San Luis Obispo County, over the mountains to the west, and a slice of northern Los Angeles County including half the desert town of Lancaster. At the eastern end in the desert is Edwards Air Force Base where Chuck Yeager flew the X-1 and where the Space Shuttle has frequently landed; not far away is Mojave, the end of the Twenty Mule Team Trail where borate from Death Valley was loaded onto trains. The district's boundaries are designed to maximize the Hispanic percentage of the next-door 20th District, but the population of the 22d is still 21% Hispanic. The 22d includes most of Bakersfield and its surroundings, oil fields and high-income subdivisions, and Kern County desert and mountain communities. The rich farmland produces most of the olives grown in the United States and is the nation's largest dairy-producing region. Politically, Kern County was Democratic territory in the early 1960s—when, for that matter, so was Oklahoma. By the late 1960s, both had become solidly Republican in national politics, and today both seem Republican up and down the ticket. The inland portion of San Luis Obispo County has always been Republican. In 2000 George W. Bush won 64% of the vote here, his best performance in any California district.

The congressman from the 22d District is Bill Thomas, first elected in 1978 and now chairman of the House Ways and Means Committee. Thomas grew up in Orange County; his father was a union plumber and his parents never graduated from high school; he lived for a time in public housing. He graduated from San Francisco State and taught political science from 1965 to 1974 in the community college in Bakersfield. In 1974 he was elected to the Assembly, a conservative in a liberal-run legislature; when Congressman Bill Ketchum died after the 1978 primary, Thomas ran as the relative moderate at the party convention and won the seat. In his first year in Washington he roomed with another young professor just elected to the House, Newt Gingrich. He is bright and testy; he has, wrote Faye Fiore in the *Los Angeles Times*, "an intellect so sharp he is considered one of the brightest members of the House and a temper so mercurial some say he may be one of the meanest." In *Washingtonian's* 2002 poll of congressional staffers, Thomas was number one on the "meanest" list and number three on "brainiest." Thomas says, "Other people have other skills, interpersonal maybe, or [they're] backslappers, or whatever they do. My stock in trade has always been knowledge." Some of that may have come from being beaten again and again by Democrats on elections issues. On the House Administration Committee he was the Republicans' point man on the challenge to Indiana's 8th District result in 1985, in which the Democrats voted in their man though the state authorities said the Republican had won—"rape," said Thomas, who added that if Republicans ever got a majority, "We will not be civilized. We will not assume it's business as usual. We will not go back to playing the lackey." He was also attacked by conservatives for being too moderate, and in December 1992 Gingrich and others ran Paul Gillmor of Ohio against him for ranking-member on House Administration; Thomas won by only 12 votes. "That particular event changed his life. It taught him, in a very serious way, that leadership in the House is a team sport," said Gingrich later.

Now things are different. After Republicans won the majority in 1994, Thomas received two tough assignments from Gingrich. As chairman of House Administration, Thomas managed the Republicans' bills reducing the House budget by $50 million, reducing committee staffs by one-third, providing an independent audit of the House and applying to Congress the laws it applies to others. He opposed Democratic campaign finance measures and proposed his own.

On Ways and Means, and as chairman of its Health Subcommittee, Thomas has been the majority Republicans' lead man on Medicare. He studied the issue intensively, rising at 4:00 a.m. to crack the books, and reflected on the situation of his parents (his mother was killed and his father gravely injured in a Kern County car crash). Thomas played a lead role in the Medicare changes and spending cuts—including steps to give senior citizens additional private-insurance options—that were enacted as part of the Clinton-Republican Congress budget agreement of May 1997. Thomas was co-chairman, with Senator John Breaux, of the National Bipartisan Commission on the Future of Medicare set up under the 1997 law. In June 2000 and again in 2002 he pushed to passage bills to provide a stand-alone prescription drug benefit for seniors; this allowed Republican House members to say they had passed a bill while the Senate Democrats hadn't. In January 2003, Thomas responded skeptically to George W. Bush's words on prescription drugs in his State of the Union address.

Throughout 2000 Thomas was running, quietly, for Ways and Means chairman. Chairman Bill Archer, limited to six years by Republicans' term limits, was retiring from Congress. The next committee Republican in seniority was Philip Crane, who had not been nearly as productive legislatively; in March 2000 Crane admitted he had a problem with alcohol, and spent some weeks in treatment. But in June Thomas was hit with a *Bakersfield Californian* story charging that he had an "intensely personal relationship" with health care lobbyist Deborah Steelman; Thomas denied any professional impropriety, and the story had relatively little impact. His greater problem was his temper. He takes pride in his knowledge, and has shown contempt for those with less. Even his hobbies are unsociable: he likes to disassemble and reassemble old cars and take apart computers. Thomas recognized the problem and assured Republican leaders that he would contain his temper. Crane had backing from some economic and religious conservatives, but Thomas got the backing of Speaker Dennis Hastert, even though both he and Crane are from Illinois. Thomas was the choice of the Republican Steering Committee, a choice ratified by the Republican Conference.

As chairman, Thomas moved first on taxes. Noting the signs that the economy was weakening and taking note of Federal Reserve Chairman Alan Greenspan's testimony favoring a tax cut, he decided in late January 2001 to advance the income tax cut in George W. Bush's $1.6 trillion package. It passed in committee in February and was passed by the House, with a few Democratic votes, in early March. In the next month, Thomas gained bipartisan support, although the cut was scaled down by the Senate. Immediately after the September 11 attacks, Thomas began talking about a cut in capital gains tax to stimulate the economy. In October he put together a $100 billion stimulus package that passed the House in October 216–214. In November and December Thomas denounced Tom Daschle and Trent Lott when they insisted that Thomas's negotiating guidelines would violate Senate rules; the package did not pass the Senate until March 2002. In June 2002, after the World Trade Organization declared the Extraterritorial Income Exclusion an illegal export subsidy, Thomas started working on a bill to replace it with a tax credit for multinational corporations and other changes in the tax code, including higher taxes on U.S. subsidiaries of foreign corporations. In October, under pressure from the House Republican leadership to do something to aid investors, he brought forward two tax bills advanced by other members, one by Zoe Lofgren to increase the deduction for stock market losses from $3,000 to $8,250 and one by Rob Portman and Ben Cardin raising the contribution cap and the age for withdrawals on 401(k) and IRA plans; the Portman-Cardin measure passed the committee on party-line votes but did not come to the floor.

While Thomas was working on the 2001 economic stimulus package, he was also working to renew trade promotion authority, which had lapsed in 1994. He was criticized for not negotiating with Democrats Charles Rangel and Sander Levin, the ranking members on the committee and its Trade Subcommittee, who wanted to require labor and environmental provisions in trade agreements. Instead he negotiated with junior committee Democrats Bill Jefferson and John

Tanner. The bill was passed by a 26–13 vote in committee in October. During the next two months, he struggled to get the Democratic votes necessary for passage even while trying to hold Republicans together on the stimulus package; he got some Democratic votes by supporting more Trade Adjustment Assistance health care spending. Trade promotion authority passed the House December 6 by a 215–214 as Speaker Dennis Hastert kept the roll call on past the usual time limit so that Thomas and Tom DeLay could round up a majority. In all, 23 Republicans voted against, 21 Democrats for: a very small number from a party that from the 1830s through the 1970s had free trade as one of its major causes. In May 2002 the Senate passed a trade package including trade promotion authority, approval of an Andean trade agreement and Trade Adjustment Assistance; the House had passed separate bills on each; the Senate bill also included the Dayton-Craig amendment barring any trade agreements that repealed trade retaliation laws. Thomas again scuffled with the Senate over the rules for the conference committee and pressed for a rule for consideration in the House which many opposed as overly constricting. The leadership pulled the rule from the floor June 20 for lack of votes; it was approved June 26 by 215–214. The conference committee was settled in a late night meeting between Thomas and Senate Finance Chairman Max Baucus; the Senate got $12 billion in Trade Adjustment Assistance and health care provisions opposed by Thomas, the House got rid of Dayton-Craig. The conference report passed the House 215–212 on July 26 and the Senate 64–34 on August 1.

Thomas was active on other issues. He has not been as active on welfare as on taxes and trade, but he did lead debate as the House passed a reauthorization of the 1996 welfare law in May 2002; the Senate did not act on the issue. In 2002 he got the staff of the Joint Economic Committee to prepare an economic model for estimating the effect of tax cuts and increases on the economy; such dynamic scoring has long been a goal of conservatives, who argue that tax cuts tend to stimulate the economy and that current scoring inevitably overstates their cost.

Through all this furious activity Thomas depended largely on Republican support and had little contact with Ways and Means ranking Democrat Charles Rangel. The narrow margins by which Thomas's tax and trade measures passed led many to say that his combative style and strong partisanship nearly cost Republicans these major victories. But on such complex issues it is always possible for the House to pass no bill at all: opposition can aggregate and support splinter. Thomas's proven prowess at building majorities in committee and the House floor, no matter how narrow they sometimes are, is impressive. When Thomas expressed doubts about George W. Bush's proposals for tax cuts and Medicare changes in January 2003, White House strategists and House Republican leaders saw no alternative to letting him take the lead on those issues. His substantive knowledge of the issues and his political skills at accumulating support left them no choice.

Thomas has been reelected easily every two years in his heavily Republican district. In the 1990s he was California House Republicans' point man on redistricting issues. After the November 1998 election, when it became clear that Democrats would control redistricting, Thomas concocted a ballot proposition in 1999 that would turn redistricting over to the California Supreme Court (most of whose justices were appointed by Republicans) and also cut legislators' salaries. The House Republicans' campaign committee, fearful that it could lose eight seats in redistricting, put up $1.3 million to get it on the ballot. But in December 1999 the state Supreme Court ruled it was invalid because it included two subjects. Thomas then split the proposal into two separate initiatives, but in March 2000 the campaign committee declined to put up any more money to get it on the ballot. In 2001 NRCC chairman Tom Davis, acting with the approval of White House political strategist Karl Rove, and David Dreier met directly with California Democratic redistricting consultant Michael Berman and made a deal: Berman would draw a plan with safe seats for all but one of California's Republican incumbents and would make the state's one new seat safely Republican in return for Republican support in the legislature for the plan, which would also provide safe seats for 33 California Democrats. Thomas was the lone member of the delegation who argued against the deal: he feared it would put most of the state's Latinos in Democratic districts, where Republicans would have no incentives to win them over, and he preferred to take his chances on a court challenge to a Democratic plan. But his advice wasn't followed.

TWENTY-THIRD DISTRICT

Rep. Lois Capps (D)

Elected March 1998, 3d term; b. Jan. 10, 1938, Ladysmith, WI; home, Santa Barbara; Pacific Lutheran U., B.S. 1959, Yale U., M.A. 1964, U. of CA at Santa Barbara, M.A. 1990; Lutheran; widowed.

Professional Career: Staff nurse, Visiting Nurses Assn., 1963–64; Head nurse, Yale New Haven Hospital, 1960–63; Instructor, Santa Barbara City Col., 1983–95; Nurse, Santa Barbara Schl. Dist., 1979–96.

DC Office: 1707 LHOB 20515, 202-225-3601; Fax: 202-225-5632; Web site: www.house.gov/capps.

District Offices: Oxnard, 805-385-3440; San Luis Obispo, 805-546-8348; Santa Barbara, 805-730-1710.

Committees: *Budget* (12th of 19 D). *Energy & Commerce* (20th of 26 D): Energy & Air Quality; Health.

Group Ratings

	ADA	ACLU	AFS	LCV	CON	ITIC	NTU	COC	ACU	NTLC	CHC
2002	90	79	89	100	34	50	25	45	12	6	17
2001	85	—	90	93	—	—	15	43	4	—	—

National Journal Ratings

	2001 LIB	—	2001 CONS		2002 LIB	—	2002 CONS
Economic	65%	—	35%		62%	—	38%
Social	74%	—	27%		67%	—	29%
Foreign	77%	—	22%		84%	—	14%

Key Votes of the 107th Congress

1. Approve Bush Tax Cuts	Y	5. Faith-Based Charities	N	9. Trade Promotion Authority	N
2. Limit Patients' Bill of Rights	N	6. Bar Gays in the Boy Scouts	N	10. Bar Funds for Intl. Court	N
3. Campaign Finance Reform	Y	7. Ban Partial-Birth Abortion	N	11. Authorize Force in Iraq	N
4. Ban ANWR Development	Y	8. Arm Commercial Pilots	Y	12. Deny Home. Sec. Dept. Union	N

Election Results

2002 general	Lois Capps (D)	95,752	(59%)	($1,461,132)
	Beth Rogers (R)	62,604	(39%)	($1,844,444)
	Other	3,866	(2%)	
2002 primary	Lois Capps (D)	unopposed		
2000 general (CA 22)	Lois Capps (D)	135,538	(53%)	($1,498,955)
	Mike Stoker (R)	113,094	(44%)	($770,000)
	Other	6,438	(3%)	

Prior Winning Percentages: 1998 (55%); 1998 (53%)

The People		Race/Ethnic Origin	Ancestry
Area size:	2,479 sq. mi.	48.7% White	German: 8.3% English: 7.2%
Urban population:	98.0%	1.9% Black	Irish: 6.5%
Rural population:	2.0%	4.9% Asian	**2000 Presidential Vote**
Pop. 2000:	639,088	0.5% Native Am.	Gore (D) 119,795 (53%)
Median income:	$44,874	0.2% Hawaiian	Bush (R) 90,550 (40%)
Poverty status:	15.7%	2.0% Two+ races	Other 13,574 (6%)
Military veterans:	11.0%	0.1% Other	**Cook Partisan Voting Index:** D + 7
		41.7% Hispanic Origin	

Occupation   Blue collar: 20.3%   White collar: 57.3%   Gray collar: 22.4%

Santa Barbara is one of California's most paradisical places, a collection of red tile roofs and leafy live oaks, sheltered by towering mountains just above the sea. The impression is a bit misleading, for Santa Barbara has its problems, and its Spanish style is a creation not of 18th century Mission culture, but of the 20th century. Most of its white stucco buildings were put up after a 1925 earthquake leveled much of the town and the most distinguished of the Spanish Revival buildings were designed by an architect with the marvelously un-Latin name of George Washington Smith. Santa Barbara, like Disneyland, does not reproduce the past but presents a bigger, more attractive, cleaner version of it, maintained not by a company but by an architectural review board. But Santa Barbara's affluence isn't ersatz. This has long been one of the nation's richest retirement communities, and one determined to preserve its environment and serenity. Both features came under threat spectacularly in 1969, when an underwater oil well ruptured, coating the beach with oil; pictures of the oil slick in the channel and of volunteers trying to wash oil off grounded birds, helped to launch the environmental movement. Almost all the wells are closed now (though some old 19th century wells still send globs of oil to the beach at nearby Summerland), but the oil spill did leave a residue in Santa Barbara's politics—and has helped attract high-tech businesses to replace defense jobs lost in the early 1990s. This was once a mostly Republican community, uninterested in redistribution of wealth, but very concerned about the environment (it has built the nation's largest desalination plant) and moderate to liberal on cultural issues. Like most of coastal California, it moved decisively to the Left in the past decade. But some of those changes have not gone smoothly, as pressures grow to split Santa Barbara into two counties of roughly equal population: a proposed Mission County to the west and north, which would be more conservative; and the residue in the more liberal Santa Barbara County.

The 23d Congressional District is a thin strip of Pacific coastline, from two to 12 miles deep, from the industrial ports of Oxnard and Port Hueneme southeast of Santa Barbara to the north end of San Luis Obispo County on the Big Sur coast, just north of William Randolph Hearst's San Simeon. There are nodes of populated territory. The largest city is Oxnard, in Ventura County, which is anything but upscale, with large number of immigrants; overall the district is 42% Hispanic. Santa Barbara and nearby Montecito are far more upscale. Much of the Santa Barbara coastline is occupied by Vandenberg Air Force Base, which launches unmanned government and commercial satellites into polar orbit. The largest towns in northern Santa Barbara County, like San Luis Obispo to the north, are pleasant, comfortable places, as untrendy as you can find in Coastal California. Before the 2001 redistricting, the district (formerly the 22d) included almost all of Santa Barbara and all of San Luis Obispo Counties; the interior parts of these counties, more Republican than the coast, were removed and put into Republican districts. Added to the district was the Ventura County coastline, which is much more Democratic than the areas removed. As a result, the Bush 2000 percentage in the district dropped from 49% to 40%—the second largest change in any California district. This was a marginal district, seriously contested several times in the 1990s. Now it is safely Democratic.

The congresswoman from the 23d District is Lois Capps, a Democrat chosen in a March 1998 special election to replace her late husband Walter Capps. Lois Capps grew up in Wyoming and Montana, the daughter of a Lutheran minister; she graduated from college with a nursing degree and was head nurse at Yale New Haven Hospital where she met Walter Capps, a student at Yale Divinity School. In 1964 he became a professor at the University of California at Santa Barbara. Lois Capps became the head elementary school nurse for the Santa Barbara school system, director of the county's teenage pregnancy and parenting project, and a part-time instructor at Santa Barbara City Community College.

In 1994, when Michael Huffington gave up the seat after one term to run for the Senate, Walter Capps ran and lost 49.3%–48.5% to Andrea Seastrand, a conservative Republican assemblywoman from San Luis Obispo County. Capps ran again in 1996 and won 48%–44%, but died of a heart attack in October 1997. Speaker Newt Gingrich encouraged the candidacy of Assemblyman Brooks Firestone—an heir to the Firestone tire fortune and successful winemaker, and a centrist in favor of abortion rights and gun control. But also running was Assemblyman Tom Bordonaro, the favorite of Christian conservatives. Bordonaro, a paraplegic since a car accident in college, emphasized his "blue-collar roots and common values" and attacked Firestone's wealthy status. House conservatives were angered by Gingrich's support of Firestone; Majority Whip Tom DeLay steered about $30,000 to Bordonaro during the primary. Meanwhile, Lois Capps announced her candidacy, with support from many of Walter Capps's admirers as well as from labor and environmental groups. In the January 1998 all-party primary, Capps finished first with 45%, Bordonaro was second with 29% and Firestone had 25%. In the runoff, Capps ran a better-organized campaign, including a superior absentee ballot effort, and Bordonaro suffered from lingering animosity of Firestone supporters plus voter backlash against the outside groups' advertising. Capps won by a surprisingly large 53%–45% margin. The same two candidates were on the ballot in November. But national Republicans had few hopes of winning this time, and it was not a priority race. Capps won 55%–43%, carrying San Luis Obispo narrowly and winning Santa Barbara 58%–40%.

With her seat on Energy and Commerce and background as a health-care professional, Capps has focused on HMO regulation and protecting the privacy of medical records, including genetic tests. She passed an amendment, 252–172, in July 2002 to bar offshore oil drilling off the Santa Barbara and San Luis Obispo coasts. But she was less of a down-the-line liberal than her husband, and she has scored more legislative successes in recent years than the typical California Democrat. Following her vote to support PNTR with China, the Teamsters claimed that Capps betrayed them and withdrew their endorsement. When George W. Bush took over, she patched things up with labor by opposing trade promotion authority. In April 2002 she worked with Jim Leach to request former Presidents Carter, Bush and Clinton to collaborate on a peace mission to the Middle East. She stood by Bush's side during a White House signing ceremony of her bill to attract more students into the nursing profession. She gained some unwanted national attention after getting funds for a gang-related tattoo-removal program in San Luis Obispo. The $50,000 program initially received little attention at home, but it became the butt of jokes and criticism from national conservative and anti-pork groups. Capps defended the program for working with "people in our community to help erase this social stigma."

In 2000, Capps had serious competition from moderate Republican Mike Stoker, a former Santa Barbara County Supervisor and California Agricultural Labor Relations Board Chairman. Stoker hoped for the local Farm Bureau's endorsement but the group deadlocked. Capps had a big fundraising edge and won 53%–44%. In 2002, she faced another well-financed challenger in Beth Rogers, who described herself as an "independent thinker" and criticized Capps for opposing the Republicans' prescription drug bill. But in a significantly more Democratic district, Capps won 59%–39%. In the 1998 special election campaign Capps promised to serve only 3 terms, but in March 2003 she announced she would break her pledge and run again in 2004.

TWENTY-FOURTH DISTRICT

Rep. Elton Gallegly (R)

Elected 1986, 9th term; b. Mar. 7, 1944, Huntington Park; home, Simi Valley; Los Angeles St. Col., 1962–63; Protestant; married (Janice).

Elected Office: Simi Valley City Cncl., 1979–80; Simi Valley Mayor, 1980–86.

Professional Career: Owner, real estate firm.

DC Office: 2427 RHOB 20515, 202-225-5811; Fax: 202-225-1100; Web site: www.house.gov/gallegly.

District Offices: Solvang, 805-686-2525; Thousand Oaks, 805-497-2224.

Committees: *International Relations* (6th of 26 R): Europe; International Terrorism, Nonproliferation and Human Rights (Chmn.). *Judiciary* (5th of 21 R): Courts, the Internet & Intellectual Property; Immigration, Border Security & Claims. *Permanent Select Committee on Intelligence* (10th of 11 R): Intelligence Policy & National Security; Technical & Tactical Intelligence; Terrorism and Homeland Security. *Resources* (5th of 28 R): National Parks, Recreation & Public Lands.

Group Ratings

	ADA	ACLU	AFS	LCV	CON	ITIC	NTU	COC	ACU	NTLC	CHC
2002	5	13	0	38	66	88	57	95	100	86	100
2001	0	—	0	7	—	—	62	100	88	—	—

National Journal Ratings

	2001 LIB — 2001 CONS		2002 LIB — 2002 CONS	
Economic	32%	— 68%	33%	— 67%
Social	20%	— 69%	25%	— 71%
Foreign	43%	— 53%	24%	— 72%

Key Votes of the 107th Congress

1. Approve Bush Tax Cuts	Y	5. Faith-Based Charities	Y	9. Trade Promotion Authority	Y
2. Limit Patients' Bill of Rights	Y	6. Bar Gays in the Boy Scouts	Y	10. Bar Funds for Intl. Court	Y
3. Campaign Finance Reform	N	7. Ban Partial-Birth Abortion	Y	11. Authorize Force in Iraq	Y
4. Ban ANWR Development	N	8. Arm Commercial Pilots	Y	12. Deny Home. Sec. Dept. Union	Y

Election Results

2002 general	Elton Gallegly (R)	120,585	(65%)	($427,481)
	Fern Rudin (D)	58,755	(32%)	
	Other	5,666	(3%)	
2002 primary	Elton Gallegly (R)	unopposed		
2000 general (CA 23)	Elton Gallegly (R)	119,479	(54%)	($1,022,565)
	Michael Case (D)	89,918	(41%)	($726,953)
	Other	11,637	(5%)	

Prior Winning Percentages: 1998 (60%); 1996 (60%); 1994 (66%); 1992 (54%); 1990 (58%); 1988 (69%); 1986 (68%)

The People		Race/Ethnic Origin	Ancestry	
Area size:	4,157 sq. mi.	68.6% White	German: 11.7%	English: 9.0%
Urban population:	94.2%	1.6% Black	Irish: 8.8%	
Rural population:	5.8%	4.4% Asian	**2000 Presidential Vote**	
Pop. 2000:	639,088	0.5% Native Am.	Bush (R)..............140,755	(54%)
Median income:	$61,453	0.1% Hawaiian	Gore (D)..............112,436	(43%)
Poverty status:	7.2%	2.2% Two + races	Other...................9,220	(4%)
Military veterans:	13.1%	0.2% Other	**Cook Partisan Voting Index:** R + 6	
		22.3% Hispanic Origin		

Occupation	Blue collar: 17.1%	White collar: 67.8%	Gray collar: 15.1%

On a golden mountainside, looking westward over a valley hemmed in by mountains north and south, five United States presidents gathered in November 1991 to dedicate the Ronald Reagan Library. This was the first time in 202 years that five presidents stood together in one place—one which the Founding Fathers surely did not imagine would ever be American and yet today seems quintessentially so. Simi Valley, famous a few months later as the site of the trial of police officers accused of assaulting Rodney King, is a product of the 1960s, the expansive and still optimistic postwar years when the vast stream of migrants who had come from all over the United States to Los Angeles spread beyond city and county limits to fill up barren valleys between golden mountains. They brought a willingness to work hard, high competence and high tech, an appreciation of the local environment and a distaste for crime and rioting that seemed all too common in the Los Angeles basin they left behind. Simi Valley is just one of several communities in the valleys of Ventura County, west of Los Angeles, that have been filling up with people leaving Los Angeles and the San Fernando Valley and building new communities in what had been orange and lemon groves. To the south, in another valley, is Thousand Oaks (the largest city in the 24th); farther west in Pleasant Valley is Camarillo; in inland valleys still farther west are Santa Paula and Ojai. Looking out toward these valleys and to the Pacific beyond at the Reagan Library is a large piece of the Berlin Wall, which Reagan urged Mikhail Gorbachev to tear down and which fell two years later.

The 24th Congressional District includes all of the interior of Ventura County and of Santa Barbara County to the west, plus a stretch of the Ventura County coastline including the Santa Monica Mountains and Point Mugu Naval Weapons Test Center. The Santa Barbara County interior is lightly inhabited; it includes the small towns of Lompoc, Solvang and Santa Ynez, near Reagan's beloved cabin in the mountains. It shares both Vandenberg Air Force Base and the

Channel Islands with the 23d District; the largest of the islands are in the 23d. Most of the population is in eastern Ventura County. Politically, these areas are solidly Republican. Overall the district cast 54% of its votes for George W. Bush in 2000.

The congressman from the 24th District is Elton Gallegly. He grew up in the working class suburb of Huntington Park, dropped out of college and became a real estate broker. In 1979 he was elected to the Simi Valley city council, became mayor in 1980, then was elected to Congress in 1986. In 1992, when redistricting moved much of Republican Robert Lagomarsino's district into the new Ventura County-based seat, Gallegly moved fast to push Lagomarsino into running in the 22d District to the north, where he lost the primary to Michael Huffington's $3 million campaign.

Gallegly has a moderate-to-conservative voting record and has played a role on major issues. Foremost among them is illegal immigration. He called for a constitutional amendment to deny citizenship to babies of illegal immigrants, a tougher Border Patrol, an end to welfare for illegal immigrants and a tamperproof identification card for legal aliens. He criticized the INS IDs as easily forgeable, carrying one around himself as evidence. "One of the reasons that I am such a strong opponent of illegal immigration, other than the fact that it's illegal, is because it poses the greatest threat to legal immigration," he said. In 1996, he got the House to pass his amendment allowing states to deny education to children who are illegal immigrants. This was heartily supported by Bob Dole, campaigning in California, and opposed by Bill Clinton. After a filibuster threat in the Senate, Republicans agreed to drop it.

On other issues, he sought to minimize labeling requirements on vitamins and dietary supplements issued by the Food and Drug Administration in response to a 1990 law sponsored by Henry Waxman. He passed a law to identify criminal aliens in U.S. prison, with a view toward deportation, and another to allow government agencies to give away their dogs—superannuated drug-sniffers and guard dogs—to their handlers. After pressure from local citrus growers, he decided in the final hours to support PNTR with China. Locally, he worked hard to save the Point Mugu Navy base, threatened with closure and with 18,000 related jobs, Ventura County's largest employer; he worked to get a wing of 16 E-2 radar planes assigned there, plus two new C-130s to fight forest fires.

Gallegly, a non-lawyer, has passed up several opportunities to chair a Judiciary subcommittee and declined to serve as a House manager during the Senate impeachment trial of Clinton. In January 2003 he became chairman of the International Terrorism Subcommittee of International Relations. His strongest recent reelection challenge came in 2000; Gallegly won 54%–41%. Gallegly was one Republican who could have been hurt by redistricting, which was controlled by Democrats; but in 2001 Democrats agreed to pass an incumbent protection plan, and Gallegly was easily reelected in 2002.

TWENTY-FIFTH DISTRICT

Rep. Buck McKeon (R)

Elected 1992, 6th term; b. Sept. 9, 1938, Los Angeles; home, Santa Clarita; Brigham Young U., B.S. 1985; Mormon; married (Patricia).

Elected Office: William S. Hart Schl. District Bd., 1979–87; Santa Clarita Mayor, 1987–88; Santa Clarita City Cncl., 1988–92.

Professional Career: Small businessman; Owner, Howard & Phil's Western Wear, 1973–00; Chmn., Valencia Natl. Bank, 1987–88.

DC Office: 2351 RHOB 20515, 202-225-1956; Fax: 202-226-0683; Web site: www.house.gov/mckeon.

District Offices: Palmdale, 661-274-9688; Santa Clarita, 661-254-2111.

Committees: *Armed Services* (8th of 33 R): Readiness; Tactical Air & Land Forces. *Education & the Workforce* (5th of 27 R): 21st Century Competitiveness (Chmn.); Employer-Employee Relations.

Group Ratings

	ADA	ACLU	AFS	LCV	CON	ITIC	NTU	COC	ACU	NTLC	CHC
2002	5	7	0	13	34	100	57	90	88	81	100
2001	0	—	0	0	—	—	61	100	88	—	—

National Journal Ratings

	2001 LIB	—	2001 CONS		2002 LIB	—	2002 CONS
Economic	19%	—	81%		13%	—	85%
Social	35%	—	63%		32%	—	63%
Foreign	4%	—	87%		15%	—	78%

Key Votes of the 107th Congress

1. Approve Bush Tax Cuts	Y	5. Faith-Based Charities	Y	9. Trade Promotion Authority	Y
2. Limit Patients' Bill of Rights	Y	6. Bar Gays in the Boy Scouts	Y	10. Bar Funds for Intl. Court	Y
3. Campaign Finance Reform	N	7. Ban Partial-Birth Abortion	Y	11. Authorize Force in Iraq	Y
4. Ban ANWR Development	N	8. Arm Commercial Pilots	Y	12. Deny Home. Sec. Dept. Union	Y

Election Results

2002 general	Buck McKeon (R)	80,775	(65%)	($757,256)
	Bob Conaway (D)	38,674	(31%)	($6,995)
	Frank Consolo (Lib)	4,887	(4%)	
2002 primary	Buck McKeon (R)	37,000	(84%)	
	James Aldrich (R)	6,810	(16%)	
2000 general	Buck McKeon (R)	138,628	(62%)	($674,238)
	Sid Gold (D)	73,921	(33%)	($34,112)
	Other	10,229	(5%)	

Prior Winning Percentages: 1998 (75%); 1996 (62%); 1994 (65%); 1992 (52%)

The People		Race/Ethnic Origin	Ancestry	
Area size:	21,622 sq. mi.	57.2% White	German: 10.3%	Irish: 7.6%
Urban population:	88.2%	7.9% Black	English: 7.1%	
Rural population:	11.8%	3.7% Asian	**2000 Presidential Vote**	
Pop. 2000:	639,087	0.9% Native Am.	Bush (R)	108,627 (56%)
Median income:	$49,002	0.2% Hawaiian	Gore (D)	81,893 (42%)
Poverty status:	12.6%	2.7% Two + races	Other	5,055 (3%)
Military veterans:	12.7%	0.2% Other	**Cook Partisan Voting Index:** R + 7	
		27.1% Hispanic Origin		

Occupation   Blue collar: 23.6%   White collar: 60.3%   Gray collar: 16.1%

One tragedy of the 1994 Northridge earthquake was at the intersection of the I-5 and Route 14 freeways at the north edge of the San Fernando Valley, where an overpass collapsed and a motorcycle patrolman hurtled to his death. Destruction of the interchange had an economic and personal impact for months afterwards, for the settled area of Los Angeles County no longer ends at the mountains at the northern rim of the San Fernando Valley. It continues along Route 14 past the mountain-surrounded city of Santa Clarita, with 151,000 people in 2000 and home of the Six Flags Magic Mountain theme park, and 25 miles beyond, where the mountains stop at the San Andreas Fault and the desert stretches out low and flat. This is the Antelope Valley, with huge aerospace plants and military bases around the fast-growing towns of Palmdale and Lancaster, where more than 235,000 people live. Beyond the Antelope Valley the desert stretches for miles, with clumps of human settlement—Edwards Air Force Base, where Chuck Yeager flew the X-1 and where the Space Shuttle has frequently landed, and the desert towns of Victorville and Barstow on I-15.

The 25th Congressional District covers all of these areas (though it shares Edwards AFB with the 22d). It is enormous, geographically the largest in the state, extending far to the north, across almost uninhabited desert and mountains, to include Death Valley and the Owens Valley, where the Los Angeles Aqueduct, one of the glories of early 20th century engineering, begins. The military occupies hundreds of thousands of acres with its China Lake Naval Air Weapons Station and the battlefield training center at Fort Irwin. But less than 10% of the district's people live in this vast expanse. This district was created by the 1992 redistricting, and the 2001 redistricting altered it by removing the northwest portion of Los Angeles's San Fernando Valley and the northwest corner of Los Angeles County and adding the desert and mountain country in San Bernardino, Inyo and Mono Counties. Politically, this is a solidly Republican district.

The congressman from the 25th District is Howard "Buck" McKeon, a Republican first elected in 1992. He grew up in Southern California, graduated from Brigham Young University and was a co-owner of Howard and Phil's Western Wear, a family business that expanded to 52 stores in California, Arizona, Nevada and Utah in the early 1990s, but closed in 2000. McKeon was the first mayor of Santa Clarita, when it was incorporated in 1987 and served five years on the council. He ran for the new House seat in 1992 and won the crucial primary 40%–38% over Assemblyman Phil Wyman, who once proposed to ban the allegedly satanic practice of recording certain words into songs backwards.

McKeon became Republican freshman class president and helped abolish four select committees in 1993. With a seat on the Armed Services Committee, he worked to save local defense jobs—this was the production base for the B-1 and B-2 bombers and the SR-71 fighter. He helped get new contracts for the X-33, the next generation Space Shuttle and the Joint Strike Fighter; in 2000, he enacted a requirement that the Pentagon study building the fighter in the Antelope Valley, instead of the chief competing sites in St. Louis or Fort Worth. He tried to authorize more B-2s and got NASA to perform Space Shuttle modifications to Air Force Base Plant 42 in Palmdale, and criticized the Clinton administration for failing to maintain military readiness.

He has been a leader at the Education and the Workforce Committee. In 1998, his subcommittee reauthorized the Higher Education act, brokering a truce with the Clinton administration over student loan programs; bank-based and government-run programs would continue to coexist. He fought an Equal Employment Opportunity Commission religious harassment guideline that, he felt, would bar people from keeping a Bible on their desk or wearing religious symbols like the Star of David at work. After the 1998 election, he briefly considered a challenge to Majority Leader Dick Armey, but concluded that Armey would prevail. Instead, he moved into the inner circle of Speaker-designate Bob Livingston, who named McKeon one of his top lieutenants. But that assignment disappeared when Livingston surprised everyone by announcing in December 1998 that he would retire. In 2001 McKeon lost out to John Doolittle for an Appropriations seat; instead he became chairman of the 21st Century Competitiveness Subcommittee, which deals mostly with higher education issues.

McKeon has been re-elected without serious opposition. Redistricting caused him no political problems, but now he must travel long distances to keep in touch with all his constituents.

TWENTY-SIXTH DISTRICT

Rep. David Dreier (R)

Elected 1980, 12th term; b. July 5, 1952, Kansas City, MO; home, San Dimas; Claremont McKenna Col., B.A. 1975, Claremont Grad. Schl., M.A. 1976; Christian Scientist; single.

Professional Career: Corp. Relations Dir., Claremont McKenna Col., 1976–78; Mktg. Dir., Industrial Hydrocarbons, 1978–80; V.P., Dreier Development Co., 1985–present.

DC Office: 237 CHOB 20515, 202-225-2305; Fax: 202-225-7018; Web site: www.house.gov/dreier.

District Office: Glendora, 626-852-2626.

Committees: *Chairman, Committee on Rules. Rules* (Chmn. of 9 R): Technology & the House; The Legislative & Budget Process. *Select Committee on Homeland Security* (7th of 27 R): Rules.

Group Ratings

	ADA	ACLU	AFS	LCV	CON	ITIC	NTU	COC	ACU	NTLC	CHC
2002	5	27	0	13	34	100	52	100	84	89	92
2001	10	—	0	0	—	—	63	100	84	—	—

National Journal Ratings

	2001 LIB	—	2001 CONS		2002 LIB	—	2002 CONS
Economic	28%	—	69%		40%	—	59%
Social	46%	—	54%		39%	—	57%
Foreign	4%	—	87%		35%	—	60%

Key Votes of the 107th Congress

1. Approve Bush Tax Cuts	Y	5. Faith-Based Charities	Y	9. Trade Promotion Authority	Y
2. Limit Patients' Bill of Rights	Y	6. Bar Gays in the Boy Scouts	Y	10. Bar Funds for Intl. Court	Y
3. Campaign Finance Reform	N	7. Ban Partial-Birth Abortion	Y	11. Authorize Force in Iraq	Y
4. Ban ANWR Development	N	8. Arm Commercial Pilots	Y	12. Deny Home. Sec. Dept. Union	Y

Election Results

2002 general	David Dreier (R)	95,360	(64%)	($637,925)
	Marjorie Mikels (D)	50,081	(33%)	($64,363)
	Other	4,089	(3%)	
2002 primary	David Dreier (R)	unopposed		
2000 general (CA 28)	David Dreier (R)	116,557	(57%)	($1,130,755)
	Janice M. Nelson (D)	81,804	(40%)	($188,122)
	Other	6,838	(3%)	

Prior Winning Percentages: 1998 (58%); 1996 (61%); 1994 (67%); 1992 (58%); 1990 (64%); 1988 (69%); 1986 (72%); 1984 (71%); 1982 (65%); 1980 (52%)

The People		Race/Ethnic Origin	Ancestry	
Area size:	755 sq. mi.	52.7% White	German: 9.6%	English: 7.5%
Urban population:	98.8%	4.4% Black	Irish: 6.9%	
Rural population:	1.2%	15.2% Asian	**2000 Presidential Vote**	
Pop. 2000:	639,088	0.3% Native Am.	Bush (R)	127,468 (53%)
Median income:	$58,968	0.1% Hawaiian	Gore (D)	105,023 (44%)
Poverty status:	8.4%	2.6% Two+ races	Other	7,044 (3%)
Military veterans:	10.5%	0.2% Other	**Cook Partisan Voting Index:** R + 5	
		24.4% Hispanic Origin		

Occupation   Blue collar: 17.3%   White collar: 70.7%   Gray collar: 12.0%

It was the great route west to California in the first half of the 20th century: Passengers on the Santa Fe railroad's *Super Chief* or motorists on U.S. 66 (John Steinbeck's "Mother Road"), after hours and days in barren desert, descended through the Cajon Pass into the Los Angeles Basin, moving in a stately procession beneath the 10,000-foot snow-capped San Gabriel Mountains, marveling at orange groves and exotic plants. The railroad and highway ran through a line of towns built by Midwestern Protestants as independent communities and now mostly high-income suburbs with their own civic institutions: Claremont, home of the academically strong Claremont Colleges; La Verne and Glendora; Monrovia and Arcadia, site of the Santa Anita race track and the Los Angeles County Arboretum; and, a few miles from the tracks, luxurious San Marino, home of the Huntington Library, one of the world's great museums and scholarly institutions. Today, the traveler arriving in Los Angeles can see the same sights, if the air is clear, much more quickly as the jet glides down the flight path to LAX.

The 26th Congressional District covers this territory in the San Gabriel Valley. It includes, east of Claremont, the newer San Bernardino cities of Upland, Montclair and Rancho Cuca-monga, home of the minor league baseball team the Quakes who play at a stadium called the Epicenter. It also includes the new suburb of Walnut to the south and, far to the west, connected by the San Gabriel Mountains, the mountain-enclosed suburb of La Canada-Flintridge, home of NASA's Jet Propulsion Laboratory. Historically, the towns running east from Los Angeles have been heavily Republican. But many of these towns now have large Hispanic and Asian populations—Arcadia, San Dimas and Walnut have sizable Chinese populations—and have become Democratic. The communities in the 26th District, however, have remained pretty heavily Republican, even San Marino, whose population was 49% Asian in 2000. The 2001 redistricting increased the Bush 2000 percentage in the district from 47% to 53%.

The congressman from the 26th District is David Dreier, a Republican first elected in 1980 and chairman of the House Rules Committee. Dreier grew up in Kansas City, Missouri, then spent a decade mostly on the Claremont McKenna campus, as a student and administrator, before he was elected to Congress in 1980. Dreier first ran in 1978, at 25, and lost to Democratic incumbent Jim Lloyd. He beat Lloyd in 1980 and in 1982 beat fellow Republican Wayne Grisham after they were redistricted together. At that point, Dreier evidently decided never to be pressed for funds again; he raised plenty and spent little, which takes more self-discipline than one might think. After the 2002 campaign he had $2.5 million cash on hand, the highest in the House.

Dreier personifies the intellectually rigorous conservatism and free market economics that has thrived at Claremont and maintains a California cheerfulness and good humor characteristic of California—even after serving for 14 years in the minority, chiefly on the Rules Committee, where Republicans were outnumbered 9–4 and lost almost every vote. Now Dreier is on the long end of the 9–4 split, and the complaints are coming from the Democrats.

The Rules chairman, once upon a time an independent operator, has become an operating member of the House leadership since Democrats instituted election of committee chairmen in 1974. Rules sets the terms for debate and limits the amendments that can be offered—an essential procedural function in a legislature with 435 members, and one which can be and often is used to shape substantive outcome. The 9–4 ratio and the careful selection of members guarantee the chairman control over committee votes, but over time it must be tempered by a sense of fairness: An outraged minority party can store up grievances and wait for a chance to overturn a rule on the floor. In 1999 and 2000, Dreier's Rules Committee produced 229 rules, and not one was defeated on the floor; in 2001 and 2002, the committee produced 155 rules, only two of which were defeated on the floor, one on campaign finance in July 2001, one on bankruptcy reform in November 2002. He also led a bipartisan process that reduced the number of standing House rules from 51 to 27, and expanded the Subcommittee on Technology and the House. After September 11, he opposed conducting congressional sessions electronically and helped establish the Select Committee on Homeland Security for the 108th Congress.

Dreier also has a policy agenda: free trade, high-tech and San Gabriel Valley water. He was one of the leading advocates of PNTR with China, and led the fight for many months when it seemed short of votes. Days before the vote, to counter complaints about China's suppression of religious freedom, he circulated a carefully worded letter from Billy Graham seeming to favor open trade ties; PNTR passed 237–197 in May 2000. In 2001 and 2002 he worked to pass trade promotion authority, which had lapsed in 1994. On high-tech, he was one of the chief sponsors, with the Silicon Valley's Zoe Lofgren, of increasing the number of H1-B visas. He has pushed for changing the Export Administration Act by changing the standard that determines whether high-performance computers can be exported; he argues that the MTOPS standard is obsolete. Dreier has threatened to use his chairmanship to strip from bills measures he opposes, such as an Internet gambling ban (he is against all Internet regulation) and the Northeast Dairy Compact. In January 2003 he announced his own tax cut proposal: a cut in the capital gains tax to 10% on investments made in the next two years; he got support from Majority Leader Tom DeLay and several members of the Ways and Means Committee. In March 2003 he and Anna Eshoo sponsored a bill to provide transparency and information about corporations' issuance of stock options but which did not require expensing of options. In response to France's opposition to the United States on Iraq, Dreier in March 2003 suggested increasing the number of immigration slots to citizens of France, so that more of its most talented citizens can come to the United States.

The San Gabriel Valley's water supply is threatened by perchlorates that have contaminated the groundwater; apparently they came from emissions from defense plants in the 1950s and 1960s. In March 2000 Dreier got the House to authorize an $85 million, multi-year cleanup, plus $25 million more for research on perchlorates; since then the House has appropriated more than $20 million a year for the project. He led the bipartisan California delegation to get full funding of the State Criminal Alien Assistance Program. He worked with Democrat Howard Berman in 2001 and 2002 for a tax credit for TV and movie production to limit runaway production in other countries which subsidize the activity; in 2001 Fox filmed the script for *Pasadena* in Vancouver, British Columbia. He discouraged unions from filing a countervailing duty petition against Canada.

Dreier has taken a role in Republican party politics. He serves on the Republican Steering Committee and was Parliamentarian at the 2000 Republican National Convention, in which capacity he produced the rationale for the three-day "rolling roll call." He supported George W. Bush early in the 2000 race for president; they have been acquainted since Dreier sat next to Bush at a training school for Republican congressional candidates in 1978. That year neither won; 22 years later they were elected and became Rules Committee Chairman and President. He took the lead for the Republican delegation on redistricting in 2001, and played a part in reaching agreement with Democratic redistricter Michael Berman under which 19 of the 20 Republican incumbents got safe districts in return for Republican support in the California legislature. That helped Dreier, whose district was becoming more Hispanic and more Democratic; he was re-elected by 57%–40% in 2000, his closest margin since 1980. He has often been mentioned as a candidate for senator, but has never run. In July 2002 he said that he would be unlikely to run for the Senate unless Republicans lost control of the House in November. "Running for statewide office in California is the closest thing to running for president. You almost have to be obsessed." In early 2003 he showed little interest in running against Senator Barbara Boxer in 2004. But under the six-year term limit he pushed through, he must give up the Rules Committee chairmanship after the 2004 election. He won reelection easily in 2002.

TWENTY-SEVENTH DISTRICT

Rep. Brad Sherman (D)

Elected 1996, 4th term; b. Oct. 24, 1954, Los Angeles; home, Sherman Oaks; U.C.L.A., B.A. 1974, Harvard U., J.D. 1979; Jewish; single.

Elected Office: CA St. Board of Equalization, 1990–95, Chmn., 1991–95.

Professional Career: Accountant, 1980–90.

DC Office: 1030 LHOB 20515, 202-225-5911; Fax: 202-225-5879; Web site: www.house.gov/sherman.

District Office: Sherman Oaks, 818-501-9200.

Committees: *Financial Services* (11th of 32 D): Capital Markets, Insurance & Government Sponsored Enterprises; Domestic and International Monetary Policy, Trade & Technology; Financial Institutions & Consumer Credit. *International Relations* (8th of 23 D): Asia & the Pacific; International Terrorism, Nonproliferation and Human Rights (RMM). *Science* (16th of 22 D): Research; Space & Aeronautics.

Group Ratings

	ADA	ACLU	AFS	LCV	CON	ITIC	NTU	COC	ACU	NTLC	CHC
2002	100	73	100	100	84	38	20	35	4	11	0
2001	95	—	100	93	—	—	15	39	12	—	—

National Journal Ratings

	2001 LIB — 2001 CONS		2002 LIB — 2002 CONS	
Economic	68% —	32%	72% —	27%
Social	74% —	27%	67% —	29%
Foreign	66% —	34%	72% —	26%

Key Votes of the 107th Congress

1. Approve Bush Tax Cuts	N	5. Faith-Based Charities	N	9. Trade Promotion Authority	N
2. Limit Patients' Bill of Rights	N	6. Bar Gays in the Boy Scouts	N	10. Bar Funds for Intl. Court	N
3. Campaign Finance Reform	Y	7. Ban Partial-Birth Abortion	N	11. Authorize Force in Iraq	Y
4. Ban ANWR Development	Y	8. Arm Commercial Pilots	Y	12. Deny Home. Sec. Dept. Union	N

Election Results

2002 general	Brad Sherman (D)	79,815	(62%)	($713,658)
	Robert Levy (R)	48,996	(38%)	($20,104)
2002 primary	Brad Sherman (D)	unopposed		
2000 general (CA 24)	Brad Sherman (D)	155,398	(66%)	($539,122)
	Jerry Doyle (R)	70,169	(30%)	($126,148)
	Other	9,877	(4%)	

Prior Winning Percentages: 1998 (57%); 1996 (49%)

The People		Race/Ethnic Origin	Ancestry	
Area size:	152 sq. mi.	44.9% White	German: 6.3%	Irish: 5.0%
Urban population:	99.7%	4.5% Black	English: 4.6%	
Rural population:	0.3%	10.5% Asian	**2000 Presidential Vote**	
Pop. 2000:	639,088	0.3% Native Am.	Gore (D) 117,120	(60%)
Median income:	$46,781	0.1% Hawaiian	Bush (R) 70,557	(36%)
Poverty status:	13.4%	3.1% Two+ races	Other 6,568	(3%)
Military veterans:	8.4%	0.2% Other	**Cook Partisan Voting Index:** D +12	
		36.5% Hispanic Origin		
Occupation	Blue collar: 19.9%	White collar: 66.2%	Gray collar: 13.9%	

The San Fernando Valley, in the early 20th century when the movie business was young, was a vast expanse of empty land, annexed to Los Angeles in 1915; moviemakers, looking for filming sites for a western, drove past the vacant lots of Westwood, up narrow roads through the Santa Monica Mountains and over into the vast Valley, sheltered from ocean breezes and rain-bearing clouds by the mountains. Since then this vast bowl of land has been transformed, first into 1950s suburbia, then into a postmodern city of its own, economically vital and yeastily ethnic. Even in its suburban years, the San Fernando Valley was not entirely residential: big factories—the General Motors Van Nuys assembly plant, the Anheuser Busch brewery, Rockwell (now, Boeing) and Litton (now, Northrop Grumman) defense plants—provided jobs. In those years this was fast-growing, family-friendly territory; politically, it was turf fought over hard by Republicans and Democrats. By the 1970s young white Anglo families were fleeing, as the Los Angeles Unified School District was hit by a busing order. There is plenty of upscale territory left in the uplands in the rims of the Valley, in Granada Hills and Tarzana; the office blocks and mini-malls show unmistakable signs of affluence. In the inner lowlands of the Valley, new immigrants have moved in to Reseda and Van Nuys. Some old neighborhoods have become rough enclaves, with youth gangs and boarded-up houses and apartments weakened by the Northridge earthquake; Iranians and Chinese, Mexicans and Koreans, Israelis and Filipinos are keeping other neighborhoods solidly middle-class. Even this multiethnic Valley has been unhappy to be linked with the city of Los Angeles, whose liberal-dominated Council imposes high taxes and irksome regulations that have stopped in the Valley the kind of vibrant economic growth seen in independent municipalities like Burbank and Glendale; a Valley secession movement arose and the issue was put on the November 2002 ballot, and the Valley voted 51%–49% for it. But it needed a majority in all of Los Angeles to pass, and failed.

The 27th Congressional District on the map looks like an inverted "U" over the San Fernando Valley, between the Santa Monica and San Gabriel mountains. On the east it includes part of Burbank, famous as the home of the NBC studios and Disney's headquarters. Just to the north are the Sunland and Tujunga neighborhoods at the base of the San Gabriel Mountains, and the Foothill Freeway on which Rodney King was driving 110 miles per hour when police stopped and beat him in 1992. The larger part of the district is on the western side of the Valley, including most of Granada Hills, Northridge, Van Nuys and Tarzana. This is a diverse district indeed, 37%

Hispanic and 11% Asian, roughly half of whom are Filipino or Korean. The 2001 redistricting made major changes in the boundaries of this district. Thousand Oaks and Malibu were removed and the northern and eastern edges of the Valley added. This made the district slightly more Democratic and far more ethnically diverse.

The congressman from the 27th District is Brad Sherman, a Democrat first elected in 1996. Sherman grew up in Monterey Park, in the San Gabriel Valley east of Los Angeles; he started working on Democratic campaigns at age 6, licking stamps and stuffing envelopes, and set up his own stamp-wholesaling firm at 14. He graduated with high honors from UCLA, worked as an accountant, then went to Harvard Law School and practiced tax law in L.A. He always had the political bug, and in 1990 was elected to the state Board of Equalization. This four-member body is a sort of tax court; Sherman's district was most of Los Angeles County. He was known as a stickler for detail, a "tax nerd," as one former staffer said, who used the office with a keen scent for political advantage. He led the fight against Pete Wilson's snack tax in 1991, and got Bill Clinton to side with his opinion on taxing foreign-owned businesses, which he says saved California $2 billion. But he irritated cartoonists with a ruling that exempted them from the state tax on artwork but not on illustrations; they set up a website, the Sherman Gallery, in which they vied in caricaturing the balding and bespectacled Sherman.

Sherman decided to run for Congress, and moved his residence from Santa Monica to Sherman Oaks, when Anthony Beilenson announced he would retire in 1996 after 20 years in the House. Sherman had an active Republican opponent, businessman Rich Sybert, who had lost to Beilenson by 49%–48% in 1994. Both of these self-financers (Sherman spent $578,000 of his own money) stressed their moderation. Sherman ran against Newt Gingrich and the Republican Congress, but he also supported the death penalty, wanted racial quotas and preferences phased out and favored tough measures on illegal immigration. Sybert stressed his independence of Gingrich, favoring abortion rights and environmental protections. Sybert was intense, Sherman a bit humorous (he handed out combs to voters, saying "You'll be able to use it more than I can"). Sherman won 49%–44%.

In the House, Sherman's voting record has been notably more moderate than those of other Los Angeles County Democrats. One of the few CPAs in Congress, he serves on the Financial Services Committee. During debate on corporate accountability, he offered an amendment to require accounting firms that audit publicly held companies to carry liability insurance to cover investor losses caused by their errors; the amendment was defeated. Sherman was one of the few Los Angeles politicians who said that the Valley was not getting its fair share of spending from the city of Los Angeles, but he did not take a position on Valley secession.

On the International Relations Committee, in 2003, he became ranking Democrat of the new International Terrorism, Nonproliferation and Human Rights Subcommittee; subcommittee chairman Elton Gallegly represents the adjacent 24th District. Sherman said he wanted to focus on the threat of rogue states obtaining nuclear weapons. In October 2002 he voted for the use of force in Iraq, after initially backing language to urge more support from the United Nations.

Sherman has won reelection by increasing margins. Redistricting gave him a district that was two-thirds new to him. The first lines, drawn by Michael Berman, brother of 28th District Congressman Howard Berman, were objected to by Sherman. Howard Berman's old district was 65% Hispanic, and the initial plan reduced that percentage by putting many Valley Hispanics into Sherman's new district. The Bermans made some accommodations, and Sherman ended up with district that was 37% Hispanic and Berman with one that was 56% Hispanic. The Mexican American Legal Defense Fund challenged the boundaries of these districts in court; their case was dismissed. It is possible that Sherman may get serious Latino opposition within the decade, but he did not in 2002.

TWENTY-EIGHTH DISTRICT

Rep. Howard Berman (D)

Elected 1982, 11th term; b. Apr. 15, 1941, Los Angeles; home, N. Hollywood; U.C.L.A., B.A. 1962, LL.B. 1965; Jewish; married (Janis).

Elected Office: CA Assembly, 1973–82, Maj. Ldr., 1974–79.

Professional Career: Practicing atty., 1967–72.

DC Office: 2221 RHOB 20515, 202-225-4695; Fax: 202-225-3196; Web site: www.house.gov/berman.

District Office: Van Nuys, 818-994-7200.

Committees: *International Relations* (2d of 23 D): Middle East & Central Asia. *Judiciary* (2d of 16 D): Courts, the Internet & Intellectual Property (RMM); Immigration, Border Security & Claims.

Group Ratings

	ADA	ACLU	AFS	LCV	CON	ITIC	NTU	COC	ACU	NTLC	CHC
2002	90	87	89	100	84	50	23	37	10	3	0
2001	95	—	100	79	—	—	12	36	4	—	—

National Journal Ratings

	2001 LIB	—	2001 CONS		2002 LIB	—	2002 CONS
Economic	91%	—	10%		83%	—	16%
Social	83%	—	11%		98%	—	0%
Foreign	75%	—	25%		68%	—	31%

Key Votes of the 107th Congress

1. Approve Bush Tax Cuts	N	5. Faith-Based Charities	N	9. Trade Promotion Authority	N
2. Limit Patients' Bill of Rights	N	6. Bar Gays in the Boy Scouts	N	10. Bar Funds for Intl. Court	N
3. Campaign Finance Reform	Y	7. Ban Partial-Birth Abortion	N	11. Authorize Force in Iraq	Y
4. Ban ANWR Development	Y	8. Arm Commercial Pilots	N	12. Deny Home. Sec. Dept. Union	N

Election Results

2002 general	Howard Berman (D)	73,771	(71%)	($758,236)
	David Hernandez (R)	23,926	(23%)	($8,953)
	Kelley Ross (Lib)	5,629	(5%)	
2002 primary	Howard Berman (D)	unopposed		
2000 general (CA 26)	Howard Berman (D)	96,500	(84%)	($521,478)
	Bill Farley (Lib)	13,052	(11%)	($38)
	David L. Cossak (NL)	5,229	(5%)	

Prior Winning Percentages: 1998 (82%); 1996 (66%); 1994 (63%); 1992 (61%); 1990 (61%); 1988 (70%); 1986 (65%); 1984 (63%); 1982 (60%)

The People		Race/Ethnic Origin	Ancestry	
Area size:	78 sq. mi.	31.4% White	German: 3.7%	Irish: 3.2%
Urban population:	99.9%	4.1% Black	English: 2.9%	
Rural population:	0.1%	5.9% Asian	**2000 Presidential Vote**	
Pop. 2000:	639,087	0.2% Native Am.	Gore (D) 112,332	(73%)
Median income:	$40,439	0.1% Hawaiian	Bush (R) 36,762	(24%)
Poverty status:	19.1%	2.4% Two+ races	Other 5,021	(3%)
Military veterans:	5.9%	0.2% Other	**Cook Partisan Voting Index:** D +25	
		55.6% Hispanic Origin		
Occupation	Blue collar: 26.2%	White collar: 58.0%	Gray collar: 15.8%	

A hiker looking north from the crest of the Santa Monica Mountains in 1910 would have seen spread out, almost totally empty and barren, 20 miles wide and 12 miles deep, the San Fernando Valley. Separated by the Cahuenga Pass from rapidly growing Los Angeles and Hollywood, the

Valley was bought up in massive tracts by civic leaders even as they were urging city engineer William Mulholland to build a huge 250-mile aqueduct from the Owens Valley to give Los Angeles water and persuading the city in 1915 to annex 200 square miles of the Valley. In the years after World War II, this was modern suburbia, filled with *Leave It to Beaver* families. Today the San Fernando Valley is postmodern urban, with a look you can see in exaggerated form in Disney headquarters buildings in Burbank or Universal City's CityWalk shopping mall: The driver topping the crest today sees office towers looming out over slightly hazy air, shopping centers, occasional palm trees, lines of grid streets stretching out into the distance beyond stucco subdivisions and the squat factory and warehouse buildings that make Los Angeles County a top manufacturing locale.

The people in the Valley have also changed. The white Anglo families with stay-at-home moms in the 1950s have been replaced by hard-working Latino families, with children waiting at the bus stops for schools and parents juggling two jobs. But there is continuity: These remain places where people work hard and try to raise children who will have better chances and make better livings than they have. Pacoima, at the northern end of the Valley, where Rodney King was pulled over and beaten and arrested, is mostly Latino. Farther south, in Canoga Park, Van Nuys and Burbank, are the big aerospace plants; the GM assembly plants were shut down in the late 1980s, with thousands of jobs lost. Less visible are the hundreds of small factories and multimedia plants where thousands of jobs have been created. The lower income areas here are farther from the central city; the southern rim of the Valley, around Studio City and North Hollywood, is still heavily Jewish and is attracting new families who often send their kids to religious schools; there is a trendy and lively shopping strip along Ventura Boulevard. People with money cluster near the rims of the mountains around the Valley; those less well off settle on the flatlands beyond.

The 28th Congressional District consists of about half of the San Fernando Valley and some of the mountains in the south. It includes parts of Van Nuys and several miles of land on either side of the Hollywood Freeway from where it comes through the Cahuenga Pass from Hollywood up to the junction with the Golden State Freeway; much of the northern end of the Valley around the Golden State, including Pacoima and the small city of San Fernando, is in the district. Mulholland Drive, which runs along the crest of the Santa Monica Mountains and the Ventura Freeway, forms the southern border until the district dips south to Hollywood Boulevard. Within these borders are affluent North Hollywood, Studio City, Sherman Oaks and Encino, with big houses on twisting streets overlooking the Valley and just above the shops of Ventura Boulevard. The population of the district is 56% Hispanic; the central and northern parts are much more Hispanic, while the southern end has a large Jewish population. But Hispanics are still not the majority voting bloc here; many are not citizens, many are children or young people not yet in the voting stream; and the tradition among Hispanics today, as among Italians 100 years ago, is to trust family and hard work, not politics and government, to get ahead. The high Democratic percentages here are due as much to Jewish as to Latino voters, who have both trended Democratic in the late 1990s, one group in response to the emergence of the Christian right, the other in response to the campaign for cutting off aid to illegal aliens which suggested, incorrectly, that Latinos are interested more in welfare than hard work.

The congressman from the 28th District is Howard Berman, one of the most aggressive and creative members of the House—and one of the most clear-sighted operators in American politics. He grew up in Los Angeles in modest circumstances, got interested in politics in high school and went to UCLA where he became friends with Henry Waxman, his ally in politics ever since. At UCLA law school he got an internship at the California Assembly. "I was assigned to the Assembly Agriculture Committee. It was dealing with farm labor issues and Cesar Chavez's movement. From then on, I was hooked." Just a few years later he and Waxman were elected to the Assembly, Waxman in 1968 from the Westside, Berman in 1972 by beating the Assembly Republican leader in a Hollywood Hills district. This was the beginning of the so-called Berman-Waxman political machine—not so much a precinct organization as a group of consultants who raised money, redrew district lines and endorsed candidates through direct mail; a key player was Berman's brother Michael Berman, who became an expert on redistricting and who drew the new lines in 2001. Their core constituency was liberal Westside Jews. Berman became Assembly Majority

Leader in his first term. In 1980 he tried to unseat Speaker Leo McCarthy; ultimately both lost to Willie Brown, who served 15 years. Berman's consolation prize was a Valley-based congressional seat in 1982. The machine fell on hard times in the 1990s, as Republicans wrested away control of redistricting and the feminist left became the Democratic Party's driving force. Since then, Berman has been a political force on his own, with a record that is mostly but not always liberal.

Berman has been an active legislator even more than a political operator, and on all manner of issues, but not one who gets much publicity. On foreign policy, he started off less as a Vietnam War dove than as a backer of Israel. For a decade he floor-managed foreign aid authorization bills, defending aid to many countries as well as Israel. With Henry Hyde he wrote the law authorizing embargoes on nations that condone terrorism; in April 1990 he called for sanctions on Iraq, four months before Saddam Hussein invaded Kuwait. Berman voted for the Gulf War resolution, but was understandably critical of the Bush administration—if it had followed his advice there might well have been no need for war. Berman has worked to stop the export of missile and nuclear weapons technology—an uphill battle in the Clinton years. He has been supportive of organized labor and opposed trade promotion authority.

Berman passed a law banning the double-issuing of U.S. passports to coddle Arab countries that refuse to honor passports with Israeli marks. He offered an amendment to revoke PNTR with China if it attacks, invades or blockades Taiwan and, when that was rejected, voted against PNTR. Berman played a critical role in winning passage by a wide margin of the Iraq war resolution in October 2002. He strongly supported military action against Iraq, and in September he came out from behind the scenes and organized a group of Democrats who shared his views. They broke off from the negotiations between Republicans and John Spratt, who ended up offering an alternative to the administration's resolution and talked directly to the Bush administration. He didn't seek the permission of Minority Leader Richard Gephardt but Berman's discussions led to Gephardt's agreement with the administration on the terms of the resolution—talks that undercut the demands of Spratt, Minority Whip Nancy Pelosi and Senate Foreign Relations Chairman Joseph Biden. As Berman describes the process, "the White House always knew they would be making changes. Now they will be able to say they did it because of input from the House Democrats. It's a win-win."

Immigration is another issue on which Berman has been a major legislator. In 1988 he sponsored the provision allowing 20,000 immigrant visas for migrants without close relatives here, to be selected randomly by computer—"Berman visa applications," they are called. He secured in 1990 more family reunification slots, expediting the immigration of Soviet Jews (a vivid presence in L.A.), and gaining amnesty provisions for more family members to remain in this country. In May 2000, as support grew for guest worker legislation, Berman entered negotiations with their sponsors to get provisions to protect incoming farm workers. He pushed especially for legal status for farm workers who have worked in this country for 150 days a year. The measure was killed in the Senate in December 2000, but will undoubtedly be revisited. In 2001 Berman, Lucille Roybal-Allard and Chris Cannon sponsored a bill to offer legal status to illegal immigrants 18 to 21 who had graduated from American high schools and enrolled in college.

In 1999 Berman took the ranking position on the Courts and Intellectual Property Subcommittee of Judiciary, one of vital importance to Hollywood interests. There he passed an anti-cybersquatting law to discourage pouncing on website names. In 2002 he filed a bill to enable copyright owners—primarily the record companies—to use technology to stop people from using peer-to-peer services to copy music; compact discs could contain software that would hack into people's P2P software. It was supported by subcommittee Chairman Howard Coble, but opposed vigorously by tech companies and music users as "vigilante legislation."

In January 1997 Minority Leader Dick Gephardt prevailed on Berman to become ranking minority member of the ethics committee, which had become badly scarred by partisanship during the investigation of Newt Gingrich. With his tacit encouragement, few ethics complaints have been filed for partisan reasons; he was released from this duty in January 2003. Though not the most senior member of the California delegation, he is the go-to guy on many state issues. One California Assembly lobbyist said of him, "He's the conscience and dad of the delegation. In this era of term limits and turnover, Howard Berman is the constant. He has a vast institutional knowledge of issues in both Congress and the legislature that is rare these days."

One issue on which he was the dad of the delegation was redistricting. California gained one seat in the 2000 Census and Democrats controlled the process. Michael Berman was hired as redistricting consultant by all U.S. House and state Senate Democrats at $20,000 per member. Because Assembly members are limited to three two-year terms, these other Democrats couldn't count on Assembly Democrats to draw them favorable districts. The Bermans and Republican David Dreier and House Republican campaign chairman Tom Davis, an expert on redistricting himself, made a deal: 19 of the 20 House Republicans would get safe Republican districts and a new Republican district would be created in return for Republican votes for the plan in the state legislature. National Democrats were angry that Democrats didn't pick up more than one district. But Howard Berman defended the deal. "Sometimes the cautious move is the smart move. Time will tell. But I'm convinced that we made the right decision, given the vagaries of politics and unanticipated decisions," he said. When the lines were unveiled in August 2001, the biggest controversy came over the San Fernando Valley. Brad Sherman, the Democrat from the 27th District, claimed that Howard Berman had been given too much of his territory south of Ventura Boulevard, while Sherman would be given too many Hispanics to have a secure seat over the decade. "Howard Berman stabbed me in the back," Sherman said. At first Berman was dismissive but agreed to negotiate. Adjustments were made in the lines, and Sherman's district ended up 37% Hispanic and Berman's 56%. The Mexican American Legal Defense Fund immediately took the plan to court, arguing that seats in the San Fernando Valley and San Diego tended to reduce Hispanic representation. The court approved the plan in June 2002.

In any case, Hispanics are not a majority of voters in this district and are not likely to be before 2010, and Berman has in fact worked on issues like farm labor and immigration long before he had any significant number of Hispanic constituents. In 1998 he had primary competition from San Fernando Mayor Raul Godinez and won 67%–33%. In November 2002, against Republican David Hernandez, a proponent of Valley secession, he won 71%–23%.

TWENTY-NINTH DISTRICT

Rep. Adam Schiff (D)

Elected 2000, 2d term; b. June 22, 1960, Framingham, MA; home, Burbank; Stanford U., B.A. 1982; Harvard U., J.D. 1985; Jewish; married (Eve).

Elected Office: CA Senate, 1996–00.

Professional Career: Prosecutor, U.S. Atty. Gen. Ofc., L.A., CA 1987–93; Practicing atty. 1986–87, 1995–96.

DC Office: 326 CHOB 20515, 202-225-4176; Fax: 202-225-5828; Web site: www.house.gov/schiff.

District Office: Pasadena, 626-304-2727.

Committees: *International Relations* (19th of 23 D): International Terrorism, Nonproliferation and Human Rights; Middle East & Central Asia. *Judiciary* (15th of 16 D): Crime, Terrorism & Homeland Security; The Constitution.

Group Ratings

	ADA	ACLU	AFS	LCV	CON	ITIC	NTU	COC	ACU	NTLC	CHC
2002	95	86	89	100	34	50	19	45	8	14	17
2001	85	—	90	93	—	—	20	39	13	—	—

National Journal Ratings

	2001 LIB —	2001 CONS		2002 LIB —	2002 CONS
Economic	60% —	40%		77% —	20%
Social	72% —	29%		67% —	29%
Foreign	60% —	40%		61% —	38%

Key Votes of the 107th Congress

1. Approve Bush Tax Cuts	Y	5. Faith-Based Charities	N	9. Trade Promotion Authority	N
2. Limit Patients' Bill of Rights	N	6. Bar Gays in the Boy Scouts	N	10. Bar Funds for Intl. Court	N
3. Campaign Finance Reform	Y	7. Ban Partial-Birth Abortion	N	11. Authorize Force in Iraq	Y
4. Ban ANWR Development	Y	8. Arm Commercial Pilots	Y	12. Deny Home. Sec. Dept. Union	Y

Election Results

2002 general	Adam Schiff (D)	76,036	(63%)	($712,072)
	Jim Scileppi (R)	40,616	(33%)	
	Ted Brown (Lib)	4,889	(4%)	
2002 primary	Adam Schiff (D)	unopposed		
2000 general (CA 27)	Adam Schiff (D)	113,708	(53%)	($4,351,025)
	James E. Rogan (R)	94,518	(44%)	($6,889,947)
	Other	7,548	(3%)	

The People		Race/Ethnic Origin	Ancestry	
Area size:	102 sq. mi.	39.1% White	Armenian: 10.6%	German: 6.2%
Urban population:	99.4%	5.9% Black	English: 5.5%	
Rural population:	0.6%	23.7% Asian	**2000 Presidential Vote**	
Pop. 2000:	639,088	0.2% Native Am.	Gore (D) 119,396 (58%)	
Median income:	$43,895	0.1% Hawaiian	Bush (R) 79,210 (38%)	
Poverty status:	14.5%	4.7% Two + races	Other 7,671 (4%)	
Military veterans:	6.8%	0.2% Other	**Cook Partisan Voting Index:** D +10	
		26.1% Hispanic Origin		

Occupation	Blue collar: 16.0%	White collar: 70.2%	Gray collar: 13.8%

In the early years of the 20th century, when Los Angeles was growing to become one of America's major cities, its richest citizens settled not on the beach (too clammy and cold) or on the west side (too dusty and remote), but in communities they built at the base of the San Gabriel Mountains that rise 10,000 feet above the city, their snow-capped peaks visible most of the year. The premier such community was Pasadena, with its institutions of national stature—the Rose Bowl and the Rose Parade, Cal Tech—and its premier structure is its baroque-domed City Hall. Pasadena and South Pasadena have proudly preserved their bungalow neighborhoods, and Pasadena preserved and rebuilt the 80-year old curving Colorado Boulevard Bridge over Arroyo Seco. More middle class is Glendale, north of downtown Los Angeles, site of Forest Lawn Cemetery; just west, beneath the Verdugo Mountains, is Burbank (named not for botanist Luther Burbank but for a local dentist-developer), famous now for the NBC Studios, ABC Studios, Warner Brothers, Disney and Dreamworks Animation, plus many small entertainment multimedia companies as well. With their lower taxes and business-friendly attitude, and despite earlier loss of aerospace jobs, Glendale and Burbank are booming while inside the city limits of high-tax and high-regulation Los Angeles, Hollywood has become seedy and plagued by commercial buildings with huge vacancy rates.

The 29th Congressional District includes Pasadena, South Pasadena, Glendale and the eastern half of Burbank. Historically, these were solidly Republican cities, but they have become more Democratic in recent years, for various reasons—Pasadena because of affluent voters' cultural liberalism and a growing black community; Glendale because of its large communities of Armenians (the nation's largest), Iranians, Koreans and Filipinos; Burbank from the trendiness of show business. The district also includes a chunk of Los Angeles with a population of 143 (it consists primarily of freeways and Forest Lawn Memorial Park). The district also includes, south of South Pasadena, cities with large Asian populations: Vietnamese in San Gabriel, Chinese in Alhambra, Temple City and the northern edge of Monterey Park (which calls itself the nation's first Chinese suburb). This is one of California's polyglot districts—26% Hispanic, 24% Asian, 11% Armenian and 6% black. Once mostly Republican country, it is now solidly Democratic, casting only 38% of its votes for George W. Bush in 2000.

The congressman from the 29th District is Adam Schiff, a Democrat elected in 2000 over Republican James Rogan in what was the most expensive House race ever. Schiff grew up throughout the country, graduating from high school in northern California, and went on to Stanford and

Harvard Law School. From 1987 to 1993, he worked in the U.S. attorney's office in Los Angeles. He ran for the Assembly and lost three times, twice to Rogan. But in 1996 he was elected to the state Senate, where he became its youngest member. In his first two years, he authored dozens of measures that Governor Pete Wilson signed into law, including landmark textbook legislation. Schiff also taught political science at Glendale Community College. As a state senator, Schiff was limited to two four-year terms; rather than seeking a second term, he ran for the House. This was one of the few House races in which the impeachment of Bill Clinton was an important issue. Rogan was a leading player in the Judiciary Committee's deliberations, and a persuasive voice for the case against Clinton. He obviously knew that supporting impeachment carried political risks; while most impeachment managers had safe seats, Rogan's was anything but: he had won re-election in 1998 by just 51%–46%. Hollywood Democrats were almost hysterical in attacking him. Entertainment mogul—and Clinton pal—David Geffen promised to raise millions to oppose him. After exploring the possibility of running against Senator Dianne Feinstein, Rogan decided to seek reelection, despite the obvious difficulty. The Schiff-Rogan race became a fundraising contest; the candidates, buoyed by responses to direct mail, raised more than $10 million combined, and more was spent by Clinton lovers and Clinton haters. Rogan had no apologies for his work on impeachment. The candidates disagreed on health care, abortion, gun control and taxes. Rogan branded his opponent as a traditional tax-and-spend liberal, who would "run naked through the Treasury, spending everything he can." Schiff attacked Rogan for calling abortion a "Holocaust" for the African-American community and saying that the Ku Klux Klan "couldn't do a better job on committing genocide on African Americans." They also battled for the support of more than 67,000 local Armenians. Rogan was a lead sponsor of a House resolution commemorating their genocide from 1915 to 1923 by the Ottoman Turks; he was promised a floor vote in October 2000 by Speaker Dennis Hastert, but Hastert reneged after phone calls from Clinton and his foreign policy appointees. Schiff cosponsored a state Senate resolution declaring "a day of remembrance of Armenian genocide," and got $400,000 from state taxpayers to produce a documentary about Armenian issues. Schiff said that Rogan's focus on Washington led him to ignore local problems.

Schiff won by a surprisingly large 53%–44% margin. He said he was ready to work across party lines, though few of his issue positions offered much opportunity to cooperate with the Bush administration. In the Judiciary Committee debate on whether to ban human cloning, his substitute proposal to permit therapeutic cloning was defeated. On local issues, Schiff was a big booster of a 22 mile light-rail extension from Los Angeles to Pasadena. With neighboring Republican David Dreier, he restored $50 million to preserve the Mars surveyor program, which is based at the Jet Propulsion Lab in La Canada Flintridge, just north of Pasadena.

Schiff was reelected 63%–33% in 2002; he spent $712,000 against an opponent who did not raise the $5,000 that would require him to file a report with the Federal Election Commission. Schiff's biblical moment came when he and his wife Eve had their first son in July 2002. Helpful constituents urged them to name him Cain or Abel; the parents named him Elijah instead.

THIRTIETH DISTRICT

Rep. Henry Waxman (D)

Elected 1974, 15th term; b. Sept. 12, 1939, Los Angeles; home, Los Angeles; U.C.L.A., B.A. 1961, J.D. 1964; Jewish; married (Janet).

Elected Office: CA Assembly, 1968–74.

Professional Career: Practicing atty., 1965–68.

DC Office: 2204 RHOB 20515, 202-225-3976; Fax: 202-225-4099; Web site: www.house.gov/waxman.

District Office: Los Angeles, 323-651-1040.

Committees: *Energy & Commerce* (2d of 26 D): Energy & Air Quality; Health; Oversight & Investigations. *Government Reform* (RMM of 19 D).

Group Ratings

	ADA	ACLU	AFS	LCV	CON	ITIC	NTU	COC	ACU	NTLC	CHC
2002	80	87	100	75	68	38	22	33	5	3	0
2001	90	—	100	100	—	—	10	36	0	—	—

National Journal Ratings

	2001 LIB	—	2001 CONS		2002 LIB	—	2002 CONS
Economic	95%	—	0%		84%	—	16%
Social	83%	—	11%		92%	—	6%
Foreign	77%	—	22%		75%	—	24%

Key Votes of the 107th Congress

1. Approve Bush Tax Cuts	*	5. Faith-Based Charities	N	9. Trade Promotion Authority	N
2. Limit Patients' Bill of Rights	N	6. Bar Gays in the Boy Scouts	N	10. Bar Funds for Intl. Court	*
3. Campaign Finance Reform	Y	7. Ban Partial-Birth Abortion	N	11. Authorize Force in Iraq	Y
4. Ban ANWR Development	Y	8. Arm Commercial Pilots	N	12. Deny Home. Sec. Dept. Union	N

Election Results

2002 general	Henry Waxman (D)	130,604	(70%)	($509,690)
	Tony Goss (R)	54,989	(30%)	
2002 primary	Henry Waxman (D)	52,785	(90%)	
	Kevin Feldman (D)	6,146	(10%)	
2000 general (CA 29)	Henry Waxman (D)	180,295	(76%)	($389,766)
	Jim Scileppi (R)	45,784	(19%)	
	Other	12,122	(5%)	

Prior Winning Percentages: 1998 (74%); 1996 (68%); 1994 (68%); 1992 (61%); 1990 (69%); 1988 (72%); 1986 (88%); 1984 (63%); 1982 (65%); 1980 (64%); 1978 (63%); 1976 (68%); 1974 (64%)

The People		Race/Ethnic Origin	Ancestry	
Area size:	388 sq. mi.	76.4% White	German: 8.4%	English: 6.8%
Urban population:	97.5%	2.6% Black	Irish: 6.8%	
Rural population:	2.5%	8.8% Asian	**2000 Presidential Vote**	
Pop. 2000:	639,088	0.2% Native Am.	Gore (D) 199,282 (68%)	
Median income:	$60,713	0.1% Hawaiian	Bush (R) 81,336 (28%)	
Poverty status:	9.0%	3.3% Two+ races	Other 11,464 (4%)	
Military veterans:	8.3%	0.3% Other	**Cook Partisan Voting Index:** D +21	
		8.3% Hispanic Origin		

Occupation	Blue collar: 6.9%	White collar: 84.4%	Gray collar: 8.7%

The Westside: The term was not much used 20 years ago, but is now shorthand for what might be the biggest and flashiest concentration of affluence in the world. It is the heartland of one of America's most productive and creative industries and one of the nation's major exports, show business. The first moviemakers came here earlier in the century, looking for a place to shoot silent films where the sunlight was more dependable than in Astoria, Queens, or Englewood, New Jersey. They found it in Hollywood, a suburb just annexed by burgeoning Los Angeles when the first movie studio was built in 1911. In 1923 came the Hollywood sign, overlooking the soon-famous intersection of Hollywood and Vine. By the 1930s, big studio lots were scattered around town, over the mountains in Burbank or out toward the ocean in Westwood and Culver City. Miraculously, the studio bosses of that era—most of them Jewish immigrants with little ancestral experience of America—created a popular culture that was universally accessible and embodied the American spirit in a way that still captures the imagination.

Showbiz still sets the tone for the Westside. It remains tremendously profitable, and not just for the big studios which are owned by large conglomerates; there are thousands of entrepreneurs, actors, writers and craftsmen who are the best in the world at what they do and who tend to cluster on the Westside because so many of the others they do business with are here. Many people on the Westside like to portray themselves as artists in a garret, willing to risk starving to make art and speak truth to bourgeois society. But their yen for fashionable new moral standards often make them disdainful of the ordinary people who are the market of mass entertainment. Showbiz rejoiced in the election of Bill Clinton and in his frequent forays into California and obvious fascination with entertainers; it rejected with fury the notion that there was something wrong about his affair with a White House intern (from the Westside, it turns out) or with lying under oath in a sexual harassment case in a federal court.

Not everyone on the Westside is in show business, of course. The 30th ranks first in the nation in percentage of people who work at home and this is a place where thousands of small entrepreneurs, manufacturers, and inventors and marketers of everything imaginable helped spark the huge growth of the Los Angeles Basin, and there are even traces of pre-show business Los Angeles money, which is also plentiful. There are large numbers of singles and gays here. The Fairfax neighborhood remains solidly middle-class Jewish—though many of its Jews today are recent Russian immigrants. The Westside has been the home of a former president who does not at all exemplify its politics, Ronald Reagan; before his Alzheimer's disease worsened, he kept his office on the former Fox lot that is now Century City. It is the center of the second-largest Jewish community in the United States, as well as the focus of the 1980s immigration of Iranians to the United States (6% of the district population is of Iranian ancestry). It is also the locus of some of America's most expensive residential real estate, where people buy houses for multiples of $1 million, knock down the structure and build something new for more millions, and of one of the world's premier high-priced shopping areas—Rodeo Drive, once a quite ordinary shopping street.

The 30th Congressional District contains most of Westside Los Angeles plus territory to the west. It includes the Fairfax neighborhood east to La Brea Avenue, heavily gay West Hollywood, Beverly Hills and the heavily Jewish Los Angeles neighborhoods to the south, Westwood and UCLA, Bel Air and Brentwood, Santa Monica and the whole 27 miles of Malibu on the ocean; most of the workload of the California Coastal Commission comes from Malibu. The district also includes the western end of the San Fernando Valley, the high-income neighborhoods of Woodland Hills and Chatsworth up against the mountains that rim the Valley. And it includes the high-income suburbs of Hidden Hills, Calabasas, Agoura Hills and Westlake Village, nestled amid mountains along the Ventura Freeway west of the San Fernando Valley. This is a mostly high-income district with a large number of Jews and immigrants from Russia and Iran, but by today's definitions it is the least diverse district in metro Los Angeles. Only 3% of its residents are black; no L.A. County district has a lower percentage. Only 8% of its residents are Hispanic, by a considerable margin the lowest percentage in southern California. Many Latinos work in the district, but few are interested in paying the prices for housing that has been bid up by rich people who can't imagine living anywhere else.

The congressman from the 30th District is Henry Waxman, a Democrat first elected in 1974, one of the ablest members of the House, a shrewd political operator who is a skilled and idealistic policy entrepreneur. There is no Westside glitz about him: He grew up over his family's store in Watts, his personal demeanor is quiet, and he has never attended the Oscars ceremony. He graduated from UCLA and its law school, where he met Howard Berman, his longtime political ally and colleague. He moved up rapidly in politics by spying openings before others did and taking advantage of them. He ran against Assemblyman Lester McMillan in the mostly Jewish Fairfax area in 1968, at 28, and won 64% in the primary. From 1971–72 he chaired the redistricting committee, a good place to make friends, but he went to Congress in 1974 in a district designed, he points out, not by his committee but by a court. Waxman's biggest break came after the 1978 election, when he was elected chairman of the Commerce Committee's Health and Environment Subcommittee. This was one of the first times House Democrats decided to ignore seniority in handing out subcommittee chairs. Nevertheless, Waxman argued his case on the issues and—in a move quite unprecedented at the time, though common in Sacramento and now also in Washington—made campaign contributions to other Democrats on the full committee, and won the post, 15–12, over the widely respected Richardson Preyer of North Carolina.

The campaign contributions were no accident. In the 1970s and 1980s Waxman and Berman built their own political machine in Los Angeles. Its power came not from patronage but from fundraising and savvy. They raised huge sums on the Westside for favored candidates. For them they put out carefully targeted direct mail, with hundreds of customized letters and endorsement slates sent out to different lists of people. In the apolitical commonwealth of California, where television advertising is exceedingly expensive and people seem to avoid politics, this made them critical though not always successful players. But in 1992 their machine foundered; since then, Waxman has rarely taken an active role in Los Angeles area politics.

As part of the Democratic majority and chairman of a key subcommittee from 1978 to 1994, Waxman was a major national policymaker, usually from behind the scenes. In 1981 and 1982 he prevented the Reagan Administration and Commerce Committee Chairman John Dingell from revising the Clean Air Act; biding his time, he worked to strengthen the law in its 1990 revision. Another great Waxman project was expanding Medicaid for the poor. Between 1984 and 1990, he got coverage for all poor children up to 18, all children under seven and pregnant women in families under 133% of poverty income. This helped raise Medicaid from 9% to 14% of state spending in the 1980s, and helps to explain why Waxman was so disliked by many governors because many of these mandates were unfunded.

Waxman had less success on reforming national health care. He wanted to move to something like a single-payer program and supported the Clinton plan but to no avail. He has secured more funding for AIDS research, important in the 30th District with its large gay population. In early 1994, in widely publicized hearings, he lined up the chief executive officers of leading tobacco companies and accused them of adding nicotine and other substances to cigarettes and of lying in their testimony. All this had no immediate legislative result, and when Thomas Bliley of Virginia became Commerce Committee chair, the hearings stopped. But Waxman brought the tobacco issue into public view, and he helped to inspire the lawsuits against tobacco companies which have resulted in the biggest redistribution of corporate assets—from the tobacco companies to state governments and trial lawyers—in history.

Waxman reacted with dismay to the Republican takeover of Congress, but with no slackening of effort. He led the fight against Republicans' regulatory reform and Medicare and Medicaid changes. He and Lincoln Diaz-Balart sought to establish nationally the California practice of not barring immigrants from Medicaid.

In 1997 Waxman gave up the ranking position on Health to become ranking Democrat on the Government Reform Committee. There he sharply attacked Chairman Dan Burton's investigation of Clinton campaign misdeeds, arguing that Burton had given himself unprecedented subpoena power and was misusing it, and he emerged as perhaps the House's most articulate defender of Clinton against scandal charges. In 2001, Waxman switched from being a defender of the administration to being a critic, frequently writing letters to Burton calling for investigations. There is an apologetic note in his comment about this course. "I'm doing what I think I ought to be doing. It's not what I'd like to be doing." In a February 2001 hearing he got NBC president Andrew Lack to promise to hand over an internal videotape of the NBC election desk on election night in 2000; Waxman was concerned about reports that Jack Welch, CEO of NBC's parent company GE, had urged the network's election desk to call the election for George W. Bush. Lack changed his mind a week later; Waxman threatened a subpoena in August (though it seems unlikely that the House would vote for one) and the two had talks in September; but the tapes were never released. In May 2001 he and 15 other members sued the Commerce Department to get release of adjusted population totals for the 2000 Census; Census Bureau professionals had determined that the adjusted totals were too inaccurate to be relied on. In January 2002 a federal court in California ruled in Waxman's favor. The Commerce Department appealed to the Ninth Circuit; the case was later settled.

In May 2001 he and John Dingell asked the GAO for the names of company executives who had been consulted by Vice President Dick Cheney's energy task force. In June he asked Burton to seek the names. In July the GAO sent a letter to Cheney asking for the names, the first such demand letter the GAO had ever sent; Cheney declined. In February 2002 the GAO brought a lawsuit against Cheney. In December 2002 a federal judge ruled against the GAO, and the agency declined to appeal.

Waxman was roused to action by the collapse of Enron. "Whenever I feel I can't be outraged about anything any more something like Enron comes along." In January 2002 he released a copy of the optimistic email Enron Chairman Kenneth Lay sent out to employees in August 2001. In February 2002 he wrote to Burton demanding an investigation of Enron's political activities. He identified issues relating to the Clinton administration (the company's support of the Kyoto Protocol, the administration's actions to help Enron's Dabhol electricity plant in India) as well as the Bush administration (the energy task force, FERC appointments, the company's position on the corporate Alternative Minimum Tax). He looked for evidence that the administration had tried to help the company out of its financial difficulties; no such evidence turned up. On foreign policy, Waxman has always been a strong supporter of Israel. Many Arab countries, in his view, "don't want to reconcile with Israel, they want to destroy Israel."

Waxman has always won re-election easily, and has contributed generously to other Democrats' campaigns. Redistricting added Malibu and the San Fernando Valley to his district but it is still very heavily Democratic; the lines were drawn by Howard Berman's brother, Michael Berman.

THIRTY-FIRST DISTRICT

Rep. Xavier Becerra (D)

Elected 1992, 6th term; b. Jan. 26, 1958, Sacramento; home, Eagle Rock; Stanford U., B.A. 1980, J.D. 1984; Catholic; married (Carolina Reyes).

Elected Office: CA Assembly, 1990–92.

Professional Career: Staff Atty., Legal Assistance Corp. of Central MA; Dist. Dir., CA Sen. Art Torres, 1986; CA Dep. Atty. Gen., 1987–90.

DC Office: 1119 LHOB 20515, 202-225-6235; Fax: 202-225-2202; Web site: www.house.gov/becerra.

District Office: Los Angeles, 213-483-1425.

Committees: *Ways & Means* (13th of 17 D): Social Security; Trade.

Group Ratings

	ADA	ACLU	AFS	LCV	CON	ITIC	NTU	COC	ACU	NTLC	CHC
2002	100	87	100	100	19	38	25	32	0	0	0
2001	95	—	100	93	—	—	11	40	0	—	—

National Journal Ratings

	2001 LIB — 2001 CONS		2002 LIB — 2002 CONS	
Economic	95%	0%	91%	8%
Social	90%	0%	84%	8%
Foreign	80%	20%	94%	0%

Key Votes of the 107th Congress

1. Approve Bush Tax Cuts	*	5. Faith-Based Charities	N	9. Trade Promotion Authority	N
2. Limit Patients' Bill of Rights	N	6. Bar Gays in the Boy Scouts	N	10. Bar Funds for Intl. Court	N
3. Campaign Finance Reform	Y	7. Ban Partial-Birth Abortion	N	11. Authorize Force in Iraq	N
4. Ban ANWR Development	Y	8. Arm Commercial Pilots	N	12. Deny Home. Sec. Dept. Union	N

Election Results

2002 general	Xavier Becerra (D)	54,569	(81%)	($441,254)
	Luis Vega (R)	12,674	(19%)	
2002 primary	Xavier Becerra (D)	unopposed		
2000 general (CA 30)	Xavier Becerra (D)	83,223	(83%)	($1,046,470)
	Tony Goss (R)	11,788	(12%)	
	Other	4,909	(5%)	

Prior Winning Percentages: 1998 (81%); 1996 (72%); 1994 (66%); 1992 (58%)

The People		Race/Ethnic Origin	Ancestry	
Area size:	40 sq. mi.	9.8% White	USA: 1.6%	German: 1.5%
Urban population:	100.0%	4.2% Black	Irish: 1.3%	
Rural population:	0.0%	13.8% Asian	**2000 Presidential Vote**	
Pop. 2000:	639,088	0.3% Native Am.	Gore (D) 79,560 (77%)	
Median income:	$26,093	0.1% Hawaiian	Bush (R) 19,400 (19%)	
Poverty status:	30.1%	1.5% Two + races	Other 4,156 (4%)	
Military veterans:	3.7%	0.2% Other	**Cook Partisan Voting Index:** D +30	
		70.2% Hispanic Origin		
Occupation	Blue collar: 33.7%	White collar: 44.1%	Gray collar: 22.2%	

Surrounding downtown Los Angeles are neighborhoods just now becoming antique, as mid-20th century buildings stop looking familiar and start taking on the patina of the historic. Downtown LA, with its 1980s marble slabs and pink cylinders jutting up to 70 stories from what was once a low-rise business district, seems soulless and detached from its neighborhoods, which change character with every new immigration flow. South of downtown is the garment district, with factories in nondescript buildings, an economically vibrant area and one of the reasons Los Angeles is the second largest manufacturing city in America today. To the north is Lincoln Heights, a heavily Hispanic area centering on the busy shopping street of North Broadway, plus the neighborhoods of Highland Park and Eagle Rock, white middle-class 30 years ago, now mostly Latino but with Asians as well. West of downtown are University Park, which surrounds the University of Southern California campus; Pico Union, an entry point for new immigrants; lower Sunset Boulevard; Thai Town along Hollywood Boulevard between Normandie and Western. Lower Sunset Boulevard has become a more lively shopping strip filled with that rare L.A. commodity: pedestrians. Hollywood has a seedy look: it has not sprouted the office buildings you can see in Burbank or Glendale, because of Los Angeles's high taxes and daffy regulations. Central Americans rioted in Hollywood in 1992, and the Hollywood Boulevard subway line caved in during the 1994 earthquake.

Almost all of these areas, centering geographically on Dodger Stadium, are part of California's 31st Congressional District. In Los Angeles's booming 1980s these neighborhoods were suddenly thronged with immigrants, more thickly populated than a quarter-century before, with small houses and garden apartments full of large families and many children. In the 1990s, the population surge stopped and this became the slowest-growing district in California, as the newcomers of the decade before moved out to more middle class neighborhoods and as incoming immigrants spread more evenly around the Los Angeles Basin. This remains a district of immigrants though: It ranks first in the nation in percentage of non-citizens (41%) and last in the nation in percentage of homes where English is spoken (21%). The population here is 70% Hispanic and 14% Asian.

The congressman from the 31st District is Xavier Becerra, a Democrat first elected in 1992. He grew up in Sacramento, went to college and law school at Stanford, worked for legal services, then worked for state Senator (and current state Democratic chairman) Art Torres and Attorney General John Van de Kamp, and married a Harvard Medical School graduate who became vice president of California's largest health-care foundation. In 1990 he was elected to the Assembly. In 1992, when Edward Roybal, California's first Latino congressman, announced late in the game that he was retiring, Becerra jumped into the race. His main Latino competitor, Leticia Quezada, was a member of the Los Angeles school board, a powerful engine for publicity. But Becerra had the endorsements of Roybal, Congressman Esteban Torres and County Supervisor Gloria Molina. In a primary in which only 33,000 voters turned out, Becerra won with 32% to 22% for Quezada. His 10,417 votes effectively made him the representative of more than half a million people; he won the general in this heavily Democratic district 58%–24%.

In the House, he has been among the most liberal members. His pleasant and businesslike manner combined with his obvious ambition could make him a force in the House, but his views have left him not very effective in a Republican majority. He said declaring English as the official language "sends a message of intolerance for those trying to learn English." He opposed a law to allow local law enforcement agents to enter pacts with the Department of Justice to enforce immigration laws. He opposed restrictions on bilingual education and Republican efforts to stop census sampling techniques. When Becerra visited Cuba and met with Fidel Castro in 1996, he did not denounce his regime or demand free elections as other members have done on such visits. In January 1997 he was elected chairman of the Hispanic Caucus by 12–7 and immediately found himself on the defensive when Republicans Ileana Ros-Lehtinen and Lincoln Diaz-Balart resigned from the Caucus. This partisanized the Hispanic Caucus: in March 2003, six Hispanic Republicans set up their own Hispanic Conference.

On the Ways and Means Committee since 1997, Becerra advocated tax changes to prevent the overseas exodus of jobs in the entertainment industry, including a tax credit for labor costs of independent film producers. He supported PNTR with China and won House approval in 2001 of his resolution supporting reunification efforts between North and South Korea. He opposed expansion of Los Angeles International Airport and favors development of outlying airports. He enacted a bill in 2002 renaming a Western Avenue post office for the late singer Nat King Cole.

Becerra ran for mayor of Los Angeles in 2001. But he did not raise enough money to establish name recognition outside his district and was overshadowed by former Assembly Speaker Antonio Villaraigosa. Villaraigosa reportedly said he would drop out if Becerra agreed not to run again for the House even if he lost the Mayor's race; Becerra was not interested in such a deal. Villaraigosa won the endorsements of several labor unions and, to the surprise of many, Governor Gray Davis, and spent nearly $3 million on ads; Becerra was scarcely a presence in the ad wars. In the primary he finished fifth, with 6% of the vote, far behind Villaraigosa's 30% and James Hahn's 25%; Hahn won the runoff. Among the 21% of voters who were Hispanic, Villaraigosa led Becerra 62%–17%. Post-election analyses noted that Becerra damaged his standing among Latino leaders with negative campaign telephone calls. In March 2003, he backed City Councilman Nick Pacheco, who sought unsuccessfully to retain his seat against a challenge from Villaraigosa.

THIRTY-SECOND DISTRICT

Rep. Hilda Solis (D)

Elected 2000, 2d term; b. Oct. 20, 1957, Los Angeles; home, El Monte; CA St. Polytechnic U., B.A. 1979; U. of S. CA, M.A. 1981; Catholic; married (Sam Sayyad).

Elected Office: CA Assembly, 1992–94; CA Senate 1994–00.

Professional Career: Editor, White House Ofc. of Hispanic Affairs, 1980–81; Management Analyst, Ofc. of Management & Budget, 1981.

DC Office: 1725 LHOB 20515, 202-225-5464; Fax: 202-225-5467; Web site: www.house.gov/solis.

District Offices: East Los Angeles, 323-307-9904; El Monte, 626-448-1271.

Committees: *Energy & Commerce* (26th of 26 D): Commerce, Trade & Consumer Protection; Environment & Hazardous Materials (RMM).

Group Ratings

	ADA	ACLU	AFS	LCV	CON	ITIC	NTU	COC	ACU	NTLC	CHC
2002	100	87	100	100	73	25	18	28	0	0	0
2001	100	—	100	100	—	—	9	30	0	—	—

National Journal Ratings

	2001 LIB	—	2001 CONS		2002 LIB	—	2002 CONS
Economic	91%	—	9%		95%	—	0%
Social	90%	—	0%		97%	—	2%
Foreign	84%	—	16%		90%	—	8%

Key Votes of the 107th Congress

1. Approve Bush Tax Cuts N	5. Faith-Based Charities N	9. Trade Promotion Authority N
2. Limit Patients' Bill of Rights N	6. Bar Gays in the Boy Scouts N	10. Bar Funds for Intl. Court N
3. Campaign Finance Reform Y	7. Ban Partial-Birth Abortion N	11. Authorize Force in Iraq N
4. Ban ANWR Development Y	8. Arm Commercial Pilots N	12. Deny Home. Sec. Dept. Union N

Election Results

2002 general	Hilda Solis (D)	58,530	(69%)	($450,512)
	Emma Fischbeck (R)	23,366	(27%)	($20,031)
	Michael McGuire (Lib)	3,183	(4%)	
2002 primary	Hilda Solis (D)	unopposed		
2000 general (CA 31)	Hilda Solis (D)	89,600	(79%)	($978,263)
	Krista Lieberg-Wong (Green)	10,294	(9%)	
	Michael McGuire (Lib)	7,138	(6%)	
	Richard D. Griffin (NL)	5,882	(5%)	

The People		**Race/Ethnic Origin**	**Ancestry**	
Area size:	93 sq. mi.	14.8% White	German: 3.1%	Irish: 2.5%
Urban population:	100.0%	2.6% Black	English: 2.2%	
Rural population:	0.0%	18.4% Asian	**2000 Presidential Vote**	
Pop. 2000:	639,087	0.3% Native Am.	Gore (D)	96,217 (67%)
Median income:	$41,394	0.1% Hawaiian	Bush (R)	45,018 (31%)
Poverty status:	18.0%	1.4% Two+ races	Other	3,057 (2%)
Military veterans:	6.3%	0.1% Other	**Cook Partisan Voting Index:** D +18	
		62.3% Hispanic Origin		

Occupation　Blue collar: 32.7%　White collar: 51.3%　Gray collar: 16.0%

Anyone interested in the future of America and today's immigrants should drive straight east from downtown Los Angeles on the San Bernardino Freeway, through the string of suburbs that grew up in the 1940s and 1950s. These were once white middle-class communities, with grid streets of stucco houses above the dry riverbeds; they were filled with Midwest and East Coast migrants who discovered California during World War II and decided to stay, or who learned of its golden reputation from the new medium of television in the days before smog became part of the language. The atmosphere then was Midwestern, cheerful, busy, with children always underfoot. Over the next generation, there was almost a complete population turnover here, but some things remained the same. Mexican-Americans spread out from their original East Los Angeles base to become majorities in blue-collar suburbs like El Monte, Baldwin Park, Azusa and West Covina, all with many more residents than in their Anglo days. Chinese and other Asians are the majority in Monterey Park and 49% of the population in Rosemead. *New York Times* food maven R.W. Apple Jr. described "a memorable week in the gastronomic trenches" of the local Asian restaurant scene, and reported that "it is easier to buy bok choy than iceberg" in Monterey Park. Almost every neighborhood here is mixed, with people whose origins are in different continents and cultures. The new people here have upgraded the neighborhoods, bringing in energy and money, the enthusiasm of the young and the community-spiritedness of the homeowner. There are busy shops with new signs, newly painted homes with carefully tended gardens, neighborhoods still filled with children whose parents believe in traditional values. When blacks and Latinos were rioting in South Central and Hollywood in 1992, East Los Angeles and the San Gabriel Valley were quiet and orderly. Some time later in this century, novels will be written about these immigrant suburbs, which will surely tell more about the human condition than a TV series about the clueless youth of Beverly Hills.

The 32d Congressional District covers much of this territory. It includes part of East Los Angeles and a small part of Los Angeles, most of Monterey Park and all of Rosemead, El Monte, Baldwin Park, Irwindale, Azusa, West Covina and Covina. It is 62% Hispanic and 18% Asian—the second-highest Asian percentage and one of the lowest percentages of non-Hispanic whites in southern California. Politically, the new Latinos and Asians have been up for grabs. In the early 1990s Asians, dismayed that the civic elite seemed more interested in ministering to the complaints of rioters than compensating the store owners whose property was ruined and lives threatened, moved toward the Republicans. In the middle 1990s Latinos, because of Republican immigration and welfare laws removing aid to legal immigrants—and because Republican campaign ads suggested Latinos were more interested in welfare than work—moved heavily toward the Democrats; Asians moved a bit in the same direction. This is a heavily Democratic district, but one in which George W. Bush hopes to make inroads in 2004.

The congresswoman from the 32d District is Hilda Solis, a Democrat first elected in 2000. She is the daughter of a Teamsters Union shop steward from Mexico and an assembly-line worker from Nicaragua who met while taking citizenship courses in Los Angeles. She graduated from California State Polytechnic University in 1979 and from the University of Southern California. She worked in the Carter White House's Office of Hispanic Affairs. Solis began her career as an elected official in 1984 when she won a seat on the Rio Hondo Community College Board of Trustees. She was elected to the Assembly in 1992, and in 1994 became the first Latina elected to the state Senate. Her work for environmental justice led the John F. Kennedy Library Foundation to give her a Profiles in Courage Award.

In 2000, she ran against Congressman Matthew Martinez. He was originally elected in 1982 with the support of the Berman-Waxman machine; he lost support among feminist and labor activists by voting for a ban on late-term abortions and fast-track trade authority and helping to stall gun control. Solis was endorsed by organized labor, EMILY's List, the Sierra Club, Senator Barbara Boxer and Congresswoman Loretta Sanchez. Martinez was supported by colleagues Lucille Roybal-Allard and Grace Napolitano; Berman and Waxman, no longer much involved in local politics, were neutral. Solis raised four times as much money as Martinez and had hundreds of volunteers from reinvigorated unions and grass-roots organizations in the Los Angeles area. The contest was caustic. Before conceding defeat, Martinez called Solis "obnoxious" and accused her of putting "a lot of things in her fliers that are absolute untruths." She won 62%–29%, and had no Republican opposition. After the primary, a bitter Martinez switched parties, but his efforts to urge Latinos to vote Republican fell flat.

In the House, Solis has been among the most liberal members. Viewing her role in Republican-controlled Washington as mostly defensive, she opposed the Bush administration's fiscal policy and fought proposals to weaken worker safety regulations. She sought unsuccessfully to move control of a proposed federal-state water-security board to the Interior Department out of concern that it would evade federal rules. The House Resources Committee reported her bill to study the possible creation of a national urban park in the San Gabriel River watershed. With Henry Waxman, she called for an EPA study of the environmental and health effects of the area's extensive gravel pit operations.

She broke her earlier alliance and engaged in bitter arguments with Loretta Sanchez when she backed Hector de la Torre against Sanchez's sister Linda Sanchez in the 2002 primary for the new 39th District. Solis showed her good standing with Nancy Pelosi by becoming the fourth California Democrat to gain a highly-sought seat on the Energy and Commerce Committee. In an unusual move for a new committee member, she became ranking Democrat on its Environment and Hazardous Materials Subcommittee—a good fit with her career work.

THIRTY-THIRD DISTRICT

Rep. Diane Watson (D)

Elected June 2001, 1st term; b. Nov. 12, 1933, Los Angeles; home, Los Angeles; U.C.L.A., B.A. 1954, CA State L.A., M.A. 1968, Claremont U., Ph.D. 1987; Catholic; single.

Elected Office: L.A. Bd. of Education, 1975–78; CA Senate, 1978–98.

Professional Career: Teacher & school psychologist, 1954–75; lecturer, CA State L.A. & CA State Long Beach; U.S. Ambassador, Micronesia 1999–01.

DC Office: 125 CHOB 20515, 202-225-7084; Fax: 202-225-2422; Web site: www.house.gov/watson.

District Office: Los Angeles, 323-965-1422.

Committees: *Government Reform* (12th of 19 D): Technology, Information Policy, Intergovernmental Relations & Census; Wellness & Human Rights (RMM). *International Relations* (20th of 23 D): Asia & the Pacific; International Terrorism, Nonproliferation and Human Rights.

Group Ratings (Only Served Partial Term)

	ADA	ACLU	AFS	LCV	CON	ITIC	NTU	COC	ACU	NTLC	CHC
2002	85	91	89	88	4	29	26	26	0	3	0
2001	50	—	100	100	—	—	—	25	0	—	—

National Journal Ratings (Only Served Partial Term)

	2001 LIB —	2001 CONS	2002 LIB —	2002 CONS
Economic	*	*	95%	0%
Social	90%	0%	83%	17%
Foreign	83%	17%	94%	0%

Key Votes of the 107th Congress (Only Served Partial Term)

1. Approve Bush Tax Cuts	*	5. Faith-Based Charities	N	9. Trade Promotion Authority	N
2. Limit Patients' Bill of Rights	N	6. Bar Gays in the Boy Scouts	*	10. Bar Funds for Intl. Court	*
3. Campaign Finance Reform	Y	7. Ban Partial-Birth Abortion	N	11. Authorize Force in Iraq	N
4. Ban ANWR Development	Y	8. Arm Commercial Pilots	N	12. Deny Home. Sec. Dept. Union	N

Election Results

2002 general	Diane Watson (D)	97,779	(83%)	($1,481,123)
	Andrew Kim (R)	16,699	(14%)	
	Other	3,971	(3%)	
2002 primary	Diane Watson (D)	unopposed		
2001 special (CA 32)	Diane Watson (D)	72,955	(75%)	($103,832)
	Noel I. Hentschel (R)	19,403	(20%)	($709,138)
	Donna Warren (Green)	3,661	(4%)	
	Other	1,512	(2%)	

The People		Race/Ethnic Origin	Ancestry	
Area size:	48 sq. mi.	19.9% White	German: 2.8%	Irish: 2.4%
Urban population:	100.0%	29.9% Black	English: 2.1%	
Rural population:	0.0%	12.1% Asian	**2000 Presidential Vote**	
Pop. 2000:	639,088	0.2% Native Am.	Gore (D) 148,978	(83%)
Median income:	$31,655	0.1% Hawaiian	Bush (R)................24,214	(14%)
Poverty status:	23.5%	2.8% Two+ races	Other 6,067	(3%)
Military veterans:	6.5%	0.4% Other	**Cook Partisan Voting Index:** D +36	
		34.6% Hispanic Origin		

Occupation	Blue collar: 17.8%	White collar: 63.9%	Gray collar: 18.4%

One of the myths of the Los Angeles riots of 1992 and 1965 is that black Angelenos live in conditions of isolation and poverty. Some do, but in levels of income and in degree of residential integration with non-blacks, Los Angeles blacks rank among the top in the United States. Its black-owned businesses have the highest revenues of any city in the nation. Californians have historically shown less prejudice toward blacks than most Americans, and job opportunities in Los Angeles—up to and including the office of mayor for 20 years—have been plenteous for blacks. This is apparent in the hills just west of Crenshaw, an Art Deco neighborhood built in the 1920s and 1930s in vacant flat land southwest of downtown LA and the birthplace of West Coast hip-hop music. Here, in Baldwin Hills, where on clear days you can see the towers of downtown and the snow-capped San Gabriel Mountains beyond, is a high-income black neighborhood, one of the strongest in the country. Near Windsor Hills along Slauson Avenue, other comfortable black-majority neighborhoods have been built. In the more rundown Crenshaw area, former L.A. Laker Magic Johnson built his successful multiplex theaters. With Olympic Boulevard as its main street, Koreatown has become a center for the city's cultural and business life. To the north at Hollywood Boulevard, near the tourist mecca of the famed Grauman's Chinese Theatre, a huge new complex includes the Kodak Theater, which hosts the Oscars plus many live entertainment shows.

This part of Los Angeles is the heart of the 33d Congressional District, which runs from the Golden State Freeway southwest to Culver City and almost to the Pacific Ocean. It includes most of Koreatown, centered on Western Avenue and Olympic Boulevard, and includes some of Hollywood and the affluent Los Feliz neighborhoods to the east. It is 35% Hispanic, 30% black and 12% Asian, with a sizable Korean population. But many Latinos are not citizens or registered voters, and most likely a majority of Democratic primary voters here are black, though that may not be true in 2010. Politically, this is one of the most Democratic districts in the state, as well as in the nation: Al Gore got 83% of the vote here in 2000. Affluent, well-educated blacks seem if anything to be culturally more liberal than low-income black voters who may have closer ties to church and tradition. Many have profited on the way up from some form of government intervention—a student loan, a public sector job, racial quotas and preferences—and many still hold public sector jobs.

The congresswoman from the 33d District is Diane Watson, elected officially in the June 2001 special election runoff but effectively chosen in the April primary. She grew up in Los Angeles and graduated from UCLA. She worked as an elementary school teacher, school psychologist and lecturer at Cal State Los Angeles. Watson began her political career in 1975 as the first black woman elected to the Los Angeles Board of Education, where she worked on school desegregation issues. Three years later, she ran for the state Senate, again becoming the first black woman in that body. She served as chairman of the Health and Human Services Committee for 17 years before term limits forced her to retire in 1998. She stirred controversy in 1989 when she defended legislative perks that have since been outlawed; she argued that legislators deserved special treatment because they were not "ordinary people." In October 1999, Watson was confirmed as U.S. Ambassador to Micronesia, where she replaced former California Secretary of State March Fong Eu; she returned home to run in the special election to replace Julian Dixon, who died in December 2000.

In that contest her chief opponents were state Senator Kevin Murray and Councilman Nate Holden, who lost a 1978 primary to Dixon. Watson's theme was familiarity: "People have trusted me, and I have not let them down. People have read my name on the ballot for 25 years. They have been born, grown up and gotten married in that time. That means a great deal." Murray argued that, at 41 and 26 years younger than Watson and 30 years younger than Holden, he could build seniority; Watson countered by campaigning with her 91-year-old mother. The race was, among other things, a battle of endorsements. Watson was endorsed and funded by EMILY's List; in the waning days of the race, she got the endorsement of Magic Johnson. Murray was endorsed by Dixon's widow Bettye, Maxine Waters, Henry Waxman and Howard Berman. Holden was endorsed by outgoing Mayor Richard Riordan. Turnout was high, spurred by the simultaneous primary for mayor of Los Angeles. Watson won 33% of the vote, to 26% for Murray and 17% for Holden. On her victory night, she angrily attacked the party establishment that opposed her. In June she won 75%–20% over a Republican who spent $709,000 of his own money on his campaign.

Watson has a solidly liberal voting record. She drew protests from California dentists by filing a bill to prohibit the use of mercury amalgams in dental fillings; Watson responded that the California legislature had banned mercury thermometers and was reviewing the use of dental amalgams. To counter a similar Republican task force, she organized the Democratic Entertainment Caucus to advocate the interests of Hollywood and related industries. In 2003, she became ranking Democrat on the Government Reform Subcommittee on Human Rights and Wellness, chaired by Dan Burton.

THIRTY-FOURTH DISTRICT

Rep. Lucille Roybal-Allard (D)

Elected 1992, 6th term; b. June 12, 1941, Los Angeles; home, Los Angeles; CA State L.A., B.A. 1965; Catholic; married (Edward Allard).

Elected Office: CA Assembly, 1986–92.

DC Office: 2330 RHOB 20515, 202-225-1766; Fax: 202-226-0350; Web site: www.house.gov/roybal-allard.

District Office: Los Angeles, 213-628-9230.

Committees: *Appropriations* (21st of 29 D): Homeland Security; Labor, HHS & Education. *Standards of Official Conduct* (4th of 5 D).

Group Ratings

	ADA	ACLU	AFS	LCV	CON	ITIC	NTU	COC	ACU	NTLC	CHC
2002	100	86	100	100	43	38	18	35	0	0	0
2001	100	—	100	93	—	—	6	30	0	—	—

National Journal Ratings

	2001 LIB	—	2001 CONS		2002 LIB	—	2002 CONS
Economic	93%	—	7%		95%	—	0%
Social	90%	—	0%		84%	—	8%
Foreign	75%	—	25%		87%	—	10%

Key Votes of the 107th Congress

1. Approve Bush Tax Cuts	N	5. Faith-Based Charities	N	9. Trade Promotion Authority	N
2. Limit Patients' Bill of Rights	N	6. Bar Gays in the Boy Scouts	N	10. Bar Funds for Intl. Court	N
3. Campaign Finance Reform	Y	7. Ban Partial-Birth Abortion	N	11. Authorize Force in Iraq	N
4. Ban ANWR Development	Y	8. Arm Commercial Pilots	N	12. Deny Home. Sec. Dept. Union	N

Election Results

2002 general	Lucille Roybal-Allard (D)	48,734	(74%)	($449,244)
	Wayne Miller (R)	17,090	(26%)	
2002 primary	Lucille Roybal-Allard (D)	unopposed		
2000 general (CA 33)	Lucille Roybal-Allard (D)	60,510	(85%)	($292,932)
	Wayne Miller (R)	8,260	(12%)	
	Other	2,801	(4%)	

Prior Winning Percentages: 1998 (87%); 1996 (82%); 1994 (81%); 1992 (63%)

The People		Race/Ethnic Origin	Ancestry	
Area size:	59 sq. mi.	11.4% White	German: 2.0%	USA: 1.9%
Urban population:	100.0%	4.4% Black	Irish: 1.5%	
Rural population:	0.0%	5.5% Asian	**2000 Presidential Vote**	
Pop. 2000:	639,088	0.3% Native Am.	Gore (D) 76,876	(72%)
Median income:	$29,863	0.1% Hawaiian	Bush (R) 27,384	(26%)
Poverty status:	26.0%	0.9% Two+ races	Other 1,901	(2%)
Military veterans:	4.8%	0.1% Other	**Cook Partisan Voting Index:** D +23	
		77.2% Hispanic Origin		

Occupation   Blue collar: 40.0%   White collar: 43.7%   Gray collar: 16.4%

A block from the 452-foot white tower of Los Angeles's "modern architecture" City Hall—long the symbol of the city, but now dwarfed by 60- and 70-story postmodern marble slabs and pink cylinders a few blocks away—is the huge retail shopping street of Broadway. The sidewalks are thronged with Latinos, the signs are mostly in Spanish, the merchandise is often strewn on tables: this could be Mexico City or Lima. It is Latin America transplanted a block from a gleaming symbol of Yankee propriety and gaudy emblems of North American prosperity. Broadway, now somewhat in decline from its retail heyday, is neither the geographical nor spiritual center of Los Angeles's Latino communities and it is just one of many shopping areas. But it is an emblem of the entry-level Latino neighborhoods of the nation's second-largest city, the places where many immigrants, not only from Mexico but from Central and South America, come to find a cheap place to live—doubling and tripling up with other families and single newcomers, close enough to drive an old car to work in factories and warehouses that fill so much of the acreage south and east of down-town.

Broadway and many of these entry-level neighborhoods are part of the 34th Congressional District. It includes downtown and Boyle Heights, once an entry neighborhood for Irish and Jewish immigrants and for the last 40 years predominantly Mexican-American. Near the Hollywood Free-way is the newly constructed Cathedral of Our Lady of the Angels, the $190 million center of the nation's largest and most ethnically diverse Roman Catholic archdiocese, which Cardinal Roger Mahony dedicated as an "anchor for the ages." Another landmark will be the Walt Disney Concert Hall, new home of the Los Angeles Philharmonic. The 34th also includes the giant factories south of downtown along the Southern Pacific Railroad and Santa Ana Freeway and it takes in part of East Los Angeles. To the south it includes the garment factories of Vernon and the 1940s working-class suburbs: Huntington Park—with its vibrant shopping strip on the wide Pacific Boulevard and with a youthful population that has more than doubled since 1980—Bell and Bell Gardens, Commerce, Maywood and Cudahy, all of which are now heavily Latino. Added in the 2001 redistricting were the more affluent suburbs of Bellflower and Downey, home of the Boeing (formerly Rockwell) plant that built the space shuttle. Bisecting much of the district is the concrete-lined Los Angeles River, which civic activists want to convert to an artificial lake with giant rubber dams.

The 34th District is 77% Hispanic, the highest percentage in any California district. Politically, this area is heavily Democratic, but with relatively few black residents (just 4%) the 34th is less Democratic than some neighboring districts. In 2002, the district voted 63%–27% for Democratic Governor Gray Davis, while the nearby 35th gave him a 74%–19% margin. It is not clear what the future political preferences of people here will be, for the large majority of adults here do not vote. In 2002, in a constituency of 639,000 people, only 25,000 voted in the Democratic primary and only 66,000 in the general election, not much more than one-third of the 186,000 who voted in the Westside 30th District.

The congresswoman from the 34th District is Lucille Roybal-Allard, first elected in 1992, the daughter of 30-year Congressman Edward Roybal. His roots were in New Mexico, not Mexico, and in 1949 he was the first Latino elected to the Los Angeles city council. Lucille Roybal-Allard dreamed of a show business career as a teenager and later worked as a department store clerk and for non-profit organizations. After raising a family—her two children are both lawyers—she entered politics at age 45, at the encouragement of local activists. She was elected to the Assembly in 1986. She entered the 1992 House race before her father announced his retirement in the adjacent district, and she won without difficulty, with 75% in the Democratic primary and 63% in the general election.

The first Mexican-American woman elected to Congress, Roybal-Allard has compiled a solidly liberal voting record over the past decade. On the Appropriations Committee, where her father had been a subcommittee chairman, she has worked on immigration issues. As chairman of the Hispanic Caucus, she challenged the "East Coast mentality in Washington" and sought to move beyond internal divisions over Cuba and Fidel Castro. She proposed to give immigrants from all of Central America and the Caribbean the same right to permanent resident status as those from Cuba and Nicaragua and called for incentives for undocumented immigrant students who remain in school. On other issues, she won House passage of an amendment to allow breastfeeding in national parks and museums. She has worked on reducing teenage pregnancy by encouraging parents to discuss the issue with their children.

Back home, in her office at the Edward R. Roybal Federal Building, Roybal-Allard sponsors health fairs and workshops on home buying and U.S. citizenship. She wants to revive downtown's former Red Car trolley line, a nine-mile loop from USC to Chinatown. She has been reelected without difficulty.

THIRTY-FIFTH DISTRICT

Rep. Maxine Waters (D)

Elected 1990, 7th term; b. Aug. 15, 1938, St. Louis, MO; home, Los Angeles; CA State L.A., B.A. 1970; Christian; married (Sidney Williams).

Elected Office: CA Assembly, 1976–90.

Professional Career: Head Start teacher, 1966; Dpty., City Councilman David Cunningham, 1973–76.

DC Office: 2344 RHOB 20515, 202-225-2201; Fax: 202-225-7854; Web site: www.house.gov/waters.

District Office: Los Angeles, 323-757-8900.

Committees: *Chief Deputy Minority Whip. Financial Services* (3d of 32 D): Domestic and International Monetary Policy, Trade & Technology; Financial Institutions & Consumer Credit; Housing & Community Opportunity (RMM). *Judiciary* (9th of 16 D): Courts, the Internet & Intellectual Property; Crime, Terrorism & Homeland Security.

Group Ratings

	ADA	ACLU	AFS	LCV	CON	ITIC	NTU	COC	ACU	NTLC	CHC
2002	95	93	100	100	73	25	30	22	0	3	0
2001	95	—	100	100	—	—	13	23	0	—	—

National Journal Ratings

	2001 LIB —	2001 CONS		2002 LIB —	2002 CONS
Economic	76%	25%		95%	0%
Social	79%	21%		94%	3%
Foreign	94%	7%		90%	8%

Key Votes of the 107th Congress

1. Approve Bush Tax Cuts	*	5. Faith-Based Charities	N	9. Trade Promotion Authority	N
2. Limit Patients' Bill of Rights	N	6. Bar Gays in the Boy Scouts	Y	10. Bar Funds for Intl. Court	N
3. Campaign Finance Reform	Y	7. Ban Partial-Birth Abortion	N	11. Authorize Force in Iraq	N
4. Ban ANWR Development	Y	8. Arm Commercial Pilots	N	12. Deny Home. Sec. Dept. Union	N

Election Results

2002 general	Maxine Waters (D)	72,401	(78%)	($262,943)
	Ross Moen (R)	18,094	(19%)	($75,114)
	Other	2,912	(3%)	
2002 primary	Maxine Waters (D)	unopposed		
2000 general	Maxine Waters (D)	100,569	(87%)	($266,309)
	Carl McGill (R)	12,582	(11%)	($7,671)
	Other	3,064	(3%)	

Prior Winning Percentages: 1998 (89%); 1996 (86%); 1994 (78%); 1992 (83%); 1990 (79%)

The People		Race/Ethnic Origin	Ancestry	
Area size:	55 sq. mi.	10.4% White	German: 2.0%	Irish: 1.7%
Urban population:	100.0%	34.1% Black	Subsaharan: 1.6%	
Rural population:	0.0%	5.6% Asian	**2000 Presidential Vote**	
Pop. 2000:	639,088	0.2% Native Am.	Gore (D)..............118,450	(82%)
Median income:	$32,156	0.3% Hawaiian	Bush (R)................24,495	(17%)
Poverty status:	26.4%	1.8% Two+ races	Other....................2,262	(2%)
Military veterans:	7.2%	0.2% Other	**Cook Partisan Voting Index:** D +33	
		47.4% Hispanic Origin		
Occupation	Blue collar: 28.3%	White collar: 53.0%	Gray collar: 18.7%	

Los Angeles in the years just after World War II was the fastest growing metropolitan area in America. If a traveler deplaning today at LAX could suddenly put himself in the postwar Los Angeles of 50 years ago, he would see quite a different city. LAX, today the nation's third-busiest airport, with eight central terminals, was then a small airfield, standing amid open country. The mile-square grids east, north and south of the airport were filling up with rapidly built subdivisions. North of the airport on open fields you would find the spanking new middle class Westchester subdivision; just beyond you would see the wetlands along Ballona Creek, where Howard Hughes took his Spruce Goose, the largest airplane ever built, up for its one and only flight. Inglewood, the rapidly growing suburb just east of the airport around the Hollywood Park Race Track, was filling up with the young families of people who had moved to Los Angeles during or after the war—workers in the giant aircraft factories or in the small factories built by entrepreneurs manufacturing products that Californians got from factories back East before the war. Inglewood would become a focus of sports fans when the Forum opened in 1967, the home of the Los Angeles Lakers for 32 years. In Hawthorne, just to the south, home of a big Northrop Grumman plant, future celebrities were growing up—Sonny Bono and the Beach Boys. Gardena, east of Hawthorne, was famous for its legal poker clubs and its Japanese American residents, back from the wartime internment camps. East of Gardena is the part of Los Angeles called South Central or, more recently, South Los Angeles, after the city council in 2003 officially renamed this community to rid it of the stigma as a place of gang wars and race riots. In the days of residential segregation, much of this area was the home of Los Angeles's black community, its numbers greatly expanded by migration from the South during and after the war. Here you could find the Central Avenue entertainment district, at whose clubs and theaters you could see the likes of Ella Fitzgerald, Sarah Vaughn, Billy Eckstine, Duke Ellington, Louis Armstrong, Count Basie, Dizzy Gillespie and Charlie Parker. Later, it was the epicenter of L.A.'s two postwar riots, in the Watts district of Los Angeles in 1965 and at the corner of Florence and Normandie in 1992. In recent years, South Central was popularized in several violent films: *Training Day, Colors* and *Boyz in the Hood*.

The 35th Congressional District today is made up of all these areas, with a landscape and populations very different from what you would have found 50 years ago. At its west and east ends are two of the Los Angeles area's great transportation facilities. One is LAX and the cluster of hotels and office buildings all around; the swooping arches of LAX's theme building, intended in 1961 to symbolize the jet era, are now an historic landmark, like Disneyland's Tomorrowland or the *Jetsons*, an antique version of a surpassed future. The other is the Alameda Corridor, the 20-mile rail express line connecting the ports of Los Angeles and Long Beach with rail distribution points near downtown Los Angeles in a trench 33 feet below ground, built between 1997 and 2002 at a cost of $2.4 billion. Westchester, once all white, now is home to many blacks and Latinos. Inglewood, once all white, later mostly black, is now 46% Hispanic; it also has a school system that is producing some of the state's highest test scores. Hawthorne, with more Hispanics than whites or blacks, is home of the Western Museum of Flight. Gardena still has its poker clubs and a large Asian population. South Central Los Angeles, an almost entirely black neighborhood at the time of the Watts riot, now is home to more Hispanics than blacks. Since the 1992 riot, local businesses have revived though it still has high crime rates. Politically, this is a very heavily Democratic district; 82% of voters here voted for Al Gore in 2000.

The congresswoman from the 35th District is Maxine Waters, a Democrat first elected in

1990. She grew up in St. Louis, one of 13 children; she has said, "I know all about welfare. I remember the social workers peeking in the refrigerator and under the beds." She moved to California in 1961; she worked in a garment factory and raised two children, got a sociology degree at California State University in Los Angeles and became an assistant Head Start teacher after the Watts riot of 1965. She also got involved in politics and from 1973 to 1976 she worked on the staff of a Los Angeles councilman. In 1976 she won a seat in the California Assembly. She became a Democratic national committeewoman in 1980 and Phil Burton consulted her on the 1982 redistricting. When Augustus Hawkins retired in 1990 after 28 years in the House and 28 years in the California Assembly, Waters was the obvious choice for the seat and won it easily.

Waters comes from a background of poverty and believes with fervor in federal aid for the poor and for racial preferences to help blacks overcome years of slavery, segregation and discrimination; she has favored drastic reductions in defense spending. She was one of six members who voted against supporting the Gulf War once it started, asking how urban gang members could be expected to stop fighting when America's own leaders were waging battles. In March 2003 she was one of 11 members who voted against the resolution to support the troops in Iraq after battle began. She brings to her work a fury that is almost palpable, and an insistence that she will assert herself regardless of protocol, partly perhaps a result of anger but also a weapon she uses shrewdly to get both publicity and results. "I don't have time to be polite," she says, beginning her career by getting herself included in a post-riot White House meeting with George H. W. Bush. The Los Angeles riot was occasion for both Waters' best and worst moments. She flew home immediately and roused the Department of Water and Power to restore water to the riot area, and was effective in gaining provisions to the post-riot emergency act that eventually made it through Congress and was signed into law. But she also suggested rioters were morally justified and claimed ominously, "Los Angeles is under siege," she said. "The violence could spill over to many other cities in this country."

She has produced specific legislation and pushed Section 108 loan guarantees to cities for economic and infrastructure development. To the terrorism insurance bill she added an amendment for a 50% discount on deposit insurance premiums for low-income people with lifeline bank accounts. In a rare legislative success in the Republican House, Waters sponsored an amendment to triple spending for the erasure of the debts of poor nations, mostly in Africa; many Republicans crossed over, and it passed 216–211. She has sponsored bills to repeal mandatory minimum sentences for drug crimes, and charges that the war on drugs has created "apartheid."

Waters isn't afraid to step on toes in pursuit of her legislative agenda. She is a chief deputy Democratic whip. Her husband, a former professional football player and Mercedes Benz salesman, became Bill Clinton's ambassador to the Bahamas. Even so, she voted against the crime bill rule in August 1994 when the administration desperately needed votes, because she said she "could not vote for a crime bill that sweepingly expands the death penalty to include sixty new crimes." In 1996 and 1997, she attracted attention for pushing the theory, supported in a story in the *San Jose Mercury News* (later repudiated by the paper), that the CIA had worked with Nicaraguan Contras to import crack cocaine into South Central Los Angeles. Waters gained her greatest national publicity during the Judiciary Committee's Clinton impeachment inquiry, where she assailed "trumped-up charges,' and termed Kenneth Starr "guilty" of "raw, unmasked, unbridled hatred and meanness that drives this impeachment *coup d'etat*." She waded into the Elian Gonzalez case, meeting with Elian's father in Cuba and with the boy's grandmothers in Washington, arguing that he should be returned to his father in Cuba. At the Los Angeles Democratic Convention she announced she was not prepared to endorse the Gore-Lieberman ticket until Lieberman appeared before the convention's Black Caucus and explained his stands on education, criminal justice and racial quotas and preferences. Lieberman appeared and began by leading a chorus of "Happy Birthday" for Waters (she was 62) and explained that he had never supported Proposition 209 and that he had voted in 1995 and 1998 for racial set-asides in transportation contracts; this brought loud applause, and Waters endorsed him.

Waters is a force to be reckoned with in L.A. politics as well. Other politicians are eager to be included on her Progressive Connections slates that are mailed out to many thousand black voters. Politicians pay to be included—a common California practice. In the April 2001 primary for city attorney Councilman Mike Feuer paid $10,000 to be on the slate and ran even in black areas with Deputy Mayor Rocky Delgadillo. But Feuer wouldn't pay $25,000 to be on the slate for the June runoff; Delgadillo paid $35,000 and got 65% in black areas. For mayor she strongly supported City Attorney James Hahn over former Assembly Speaker Antonio Villaraigosa. Hahn is the son of Kenneth Hahn, Los Angeles County Supervisor for 40 years, whose work for black constituents made him beloved among black voters. Hahn won with the support of 80% of black voters and 60% of white voters; Hispanics heavily favored Villaraigosa. After Hahn won, Waters approached banker and *LA Focus* owner Jheryl Busby and insisted he fire columnist Najee Ali, who had backed Villaraigosa. Busby fired Ali in July 2001. Ali sued Busby, and Busby's attorney said Busby "told me he needs a positive relationship with Waters because of her ability to help him with his bank and other business interests." (Waters is on the Financial Services Committee). But Waters sharply opposed Hahn in February 2002 when he urged the 10-member Police Commission not to reappoint Chief Bernard Parks. Waters wrote an opinion article strongly criticizing Hahn. "The mayor, whom I strongly supported, has failed to be fair and open with the African-American community. His political advisors and kitchen cabinet are all white. He has two inexperienced, unconnected African-American aides who are not consulted on important decisions and lack the experience to represent African-American affairs." Her dismissal was crushing. "The city of Los Angeles deserves better leadership than he has shown. His father would not be proud of that. . . . Mr. Mayor it is you—not Chief Parks—who has failed to earn the right to serve a second term."

Waters has been reelected without difficulty. The 2001 redistricting removed some black areas from the district and added Westchester, LAX and Lawndale, which do not have large black percentages. The one threat to her tenure is the rising Hispanic percentage in the district; blacks are still a majority of Democratic primary voters, but that may no longer be true in 2010. Her strong support of James Hahn over Antonio Villaraigosa in the 2001 Los Angeles mayor race risked angering Latino voters; labor leader Miguel Contreras said that many Latinos in her district felt that she "played the race card against the Latino candidate." She is one of many Democrats who has sought a seat on the Appropriations, but with Republicans in control open seats have been scarce, and she has not been successful yet.

THIRTY-SIXTH DISTRICT

Rep. Jane Harman (D)

Elected 2000, 2d term; b. June 28, 1945, New York, NY; home, Venice; Smith Col., B.A. 1966, Harvard U., J.D. 1969; Jewish; married (Sidney).

Elected Office: U.S. House of Reps., 1992–98.

Professional Career: Legis. Dir., U.S. Sen. John Tunney, 1972–73; Chief Cnsl. & Staff Dir., Senate Judiciary Subcmtee., 1973–77; Dep. Cabinet Secy., White House, 1977; Defense Dept. Special Cnsl., 1979; Harman Intl. Industries, Corp. Secy., 1985–92, Dir., 1990–92; Practicing atty., 1970–72, 1982–92; Regents Prof., U.C.L.A., 1999.

DC Office: 2400 RHOB 20515, 202-225-8220; Fax: 202-226-7290; Web site: www.house.gov/harman.

District Offices: El Segundo, 310-643-3636; Wilmington, 310-549-8282.

Committees: *Permanent Select Committee on Intelligence* (RMM of 9 D). *Select Committee on Homeland Security* (7th of 23 D): Emergency Preparedness & Response; Intelligence & Counterterrorism.

Group Ratings

	ADA	ACLU	AFS	LCV	CON	ITIC	NTU	COC	ACU	NTLC	CHC
2002	60	73	67	75	84	62	37	65	36	29	17
2001	90	—	90	100	—	—	24	52	20	—	—

National Journal Ratings

	2001 LIB —	2001 CONS	2002 LIB —	2002 CONS
Economic	57% —	43%	53% —	47%
Social	72% —	29%	67% —	29%
Foreign	73% —	28%	55% —	44%

Key Votes of the 107th Congress

1. Approve Bush Tax Cuts	N	5. Faith-Based Charities	N	9. Trade Promotion Authority	N
2. Limit Patients' Bill of Rights	N	6. Bar Gays in the Boy Scouts	N	10. Bar Funds for Intl. Court	N
3. Campaign Finance Reform	Y	7. Ban Partial-Birth Abortion	N	11. Authorize Force in Iraq	Y
4. Ban ANWR Development	Y	8. Arm Commercial Pilots	Y	12. Deny Home. Sec. Dept. Union	Y

Election Results

2002 general	Jane Harman (D)	88,198	(61%)	($1,206,046)
	Stuart Johnson (R)	50,328	(35%)	($158,318)
	Mark McSpadden (Lib)	5,225	(4%)	
2002 primary	Jane Harman (D)	unopposed		
2000 general	Jane Harman (D)	115,651	(48%)	($1,998,739)
	Steven T. Kuykendall (R)	111,199	(47%)	($1,988,938)
	Other	12,281	(5%)	

Prior Winning Percentages: 1996 (52%); 1994 (48%); 1992 (48%)

The People		**Race/Ethnic Origin**	**Ancestry**	
Area size:	122 sq. mi.	48.4% White	German: 8.0%	Irish: 6.6%
Urban population:	100.0%	4.1% Black	English: 6.2%	
Rural population:	0.0%	13.4% Asian	**2000 Presidential Vote**	
Pop. 2000:	639,087	0.3% Native Am.	Gore (D)	130,752 (57%)
Median income:	$51,633	0.4% Hawaiian	Bush (R)	88,619 (39%)
Poverty status:	12.7%	2.9% Two+ races	Other	9,423 (4%)
Military veterans:	8.8%	0.3% Other	**Cook Partisan Voting Index:** D + 9	
		30.3% Hispanic Origin		

Occupation	Blue collar: 16.1%	White collar: 71.1%	Gray collar: 12.8%

For many southern Californians, there is no better place to be than the beach. It is not a perfect environment: In the morning there may be mists, the winter air is damp and clammy, even in summer the weather can be chilly, the water is never very warm and is sometimes polluted. But for many this is echt-California, and in this democratic polity, there is a beach to suit the taste of just about everyone. The funkiest of all is Venice, with its beach houses plus some expensive new mansions jammed together, its long-stagnant canals dug by a developer in 1904 and paved over in the late 1920s to make way for cars, and the boardwalk where skateboarding got its start and roller blade sports are *de rigueur*. To the south is Marina Del Rey, with sleek modern apartment complexes and expensive yacht moorings, and El Segundo, named for Chevron's second oil refinery; now it has big office buildings. Next are Manhattan Beach, one of the favorites four decades ago of the Beach Boys who grew up a couple of miles inland in Hawthorne, and tiny Hermosa Beach, with tightly packed frame houses originally the homes of elderly retirees, now filled with the young and would-be young. Farther south are the flower-planted rises of Redondo Beach and the larger city of Torrance, whose vast inland expanse is the home of the North American headquarters of both Honda and Toyota (and to large Korean and Japanese communities). Just to the east, above the harbor, are Wilmington and San Pedro, once working-class, but moving up as well; it is the home of Mayor James Hahn and overlooks L.A.'s eerily modern container port.

The 36th Congressional District includes most of this beach territory, from Venice south to San Pedro (both of which are within the Los Angeles city limits, though the area in between is not). California today is mostly multiethnic, but the beach communities are still, as if in the 1950s, filled mostly with white Anglos. Redistricting increased Hispanic percentage from 19% to 30% by removing the affluent Palos Verdes Peninsula and adding Wilmington. The changes reduced the Bush 2000 percentage from 45% to 39%; this is one of four California districts that were made more Democratic to accommodate a Democrat who narrowly replaced a Republican in 2000. This area is still leery of taxes, but culturally it is libertarian—against restrictions or even aspersions on its various lifestyles. This has been one of America's leading defense and aerospace areas, where Howard Hughes built planes half a century ago and where so much of the 1980s defense buildup took place.

The congresswoman from the 36th District is Democrat Jane Harman, who regained the seat in 2000 that she held for six years before running for governor in 1998. Born in New York City, she grew up in Los Angeles as the daughter of a Westside physician and was in the gallery as a volunteer usher when John F. Kennedy was nominated at the 1960 Democratic National Convention in Los Angeles. She graduated from Smith College and Harvard Law School, when women were still rare there. In the 1970s, she worked for California Senator John Tunney and the Senate Judiciary Committee. She later served in the Carter White House and as a special counsel in the Defense Department. After her stints in government, Harman practiced law and worked as a lobbyist in Washington. When she saw the new 1992 district lines, she returned to California and ran for Congress. Harman is one of the richest members of Congress; her husband Sidney Harman is founder of audio-equipment maker Harman International Industries, and she has spent large amounts of her own money on her campaigns.

In 1992, the "year of the woman," she campaigned as "pro-choice and pro-change," defeating a pro-life Republican woman 48%–42%; she was narrowly reelected in 1994 and 1996. She decided late to run for governor, getting into the race only after Senator Dianne Feinstein announced in January 1998 that she would not run. Harman spent more than $20 million, including $15 million of her own, but finished a disappointing third among Democrats. In 1999 she was appointed as a Regents' professor at UCLA. Congressional and state Democrats lobbied her hard to seek her former House seat, which Republican Steven Kuykendall narrowly won in 1998. Kuykendall supported abortion rights and took liberal stands on environmental issues; many Democrats believed that only Harman could defeat him. She attacked Kuykendall for failing to support the Democrats' proposal for a prescription drug benefit in Medicare and for voting to repeal the estate tax, and tried to tie him to House Republican leaders. She stressed her earlier House record, economically somewhat conservative and culturally liberal. Her assiduous work on defense issues in the 1990s was still a political asset, and Democratic House leadership promised to restore her seniority. Kuykendall may have been hurt by the deadlock between the Republican leadership and the Clinton White House that kept Congress in session through October, and he was certainly hurt by the lack of appeal of George W. Bush in Coastal California. This was a race targeted by both parties, with each candidate spending nearly $2 million. After more than a week of absentee ballot counting following Election Day, Kuykendall conceded; Harman won 48%–47%.

On her return to the House, Harman joined Energy and Commerce, where she urged limits on growth at LAX, including a passenger cap. Other than Gary Condit, she had the most conservative voting record of any Democrat from California. Harman disappointed many Democrats by voting for the final version of trade promotion authority after initially opposing it; she was one of five House Democrats who switched, and cited improved worker training provisions. After September 11, her focus turned to national security. On the Intelligence Committee, she became ranking Democrat of the new Terrorism and Homeland Security Subcommittee. Working closely with chairman Saxby Chambliss, she criticized the CIA, FBI and National Security Agency for moving too slowly to share information and respond to terrorism threats. She was an early supporter of a Department of Homeland Security and she voted for the use of force in Iraq. Nancy Pelosi, who was ranking Democrat on Intelligence, chose Harman to replace her after the 2002 election, despite a strong campaign by Sanford Bishop. At Pelosi's request, Harman took a leave of absence from Energy and Commerce; she now also serves on the Select Homeland Security Committee.

In 2002, she was reelected easily, by a 61%–35% margin. Despite her disappointing bid for governor, she has not ruled out another run for statewide office.

THIRTY-SEVENTH DISTRICT

Rep. Juanita Millender-McDonald (D)

Elected March 1996, 4th term; b. Sept. 7, 1938, Birmingham, AL; home, Carson; U. of Redlands, B.S. 1979, CA State L.A., M.Ed. 1981; Baptist; married (James).

Elected Office: Carson City Cncl., 1990–92; Carson Mayor Pro–Tem, 1991–92; CA Assembly, 1992–96.

Professional Career: Teacher & Schl. Admin., 1981–90.

DC Office: 1514 LHOB 20515, 202-225-7924; Fax: 202-225-7926; Web site: www.house.gov/millender-mcdonald.

District Office: Torrance, 310-538-1190.

Committees: *House Administration* (2d of 3 D). *Small Business* (2d of 17 D): Tax, Finance & Exports (RMM). *Transportation & Infrastructure* (13th of 34 D): Aviation; Coast Guard & Maritime Transportation; Highways, Transit & Pipelines.

Group Ratings

	ADA	ACLU	AFS	LCV	CON	ITIC	NTU	COC	ACU	NTLC	CHC
2002	85	80	100	88	55	38	18	44	0	0	0
2001	90	—	100	100	—	—	8	35	4	—	—

National Journal Ratings

	2001 LIB —	2001 CONS		2002 LIB —	2002 CONS
Economic	93% —	7%		71% —	28%
Social	81% —	19%		83% —	17%
Foreign	76% —	24%		81% —	19%

Key Votes of the 107th Congress

1. Approve Bush Tax Cuts	*	5. Faith-Based Charities	9. Trade Promotion Authority	N
2. Limit Patients' Bill of Rights	N	6. Bar Gays in the Boy Scouts	N	10. Bar Funds for Intl. Court	*
3. Campaign Finance Reform	Y	7. Ban Partial-Birth Abortion	N	11. Authorize Force in Iraq	N
4. Ban ANWR Development	Y	8. Arm Commercial Pilots	N	12. Deny Home. Sec. Dept. Union	N

Election Results

2002 general	Juanita Millender-McDonald (D)	63,445	(73%)	($244,632)
	Oscar Velasco (R)	20,154	(23%)	($14,093)
	Herb Peters (Lib)	3,413	(4%)	
2002 primary	Juanita Millender-McDonald (D)	25,302	(78%)	
	Peter Mathews (D)	7,269	(22%)	
2000 general	Juanita Millender-McDonald (D)	93,269	(82%)	($169,214)
	Vernon Van (R)	12,762	(11%)	
	Margaret Glazer (NL)	4,094	(4%)	
	Other	3,150	(3%)	

Prior Winning Percentages: 1998 (85%); 1996 (85%); 1996 (27%)

The People		Race/Ethnic Origin	Ancestry	
Area size:	75 sq. mi.	16.6% White	German: 3.2%	Irish: 2.7%
Urban population:	100.0%	24.8% Black	English: 2.4%	
Rural population:	0.0%	11.1% Asian	**2000 Presidential Vote**	
Pop. 2000:	639,088	0.3% Native Am.	Gore (D) 112,235	(76%)
Median income:	$34,006	1.4% Hawaiian	Bush (R) 31,832	(22%)
Poverty status:	25.2%	2.4% Two+ races	Other 3,712	(3%)
Military veterans:	8.1%	0.2% Other	**Cook Partisan Voting Index:** D +28	
		43.2% Hispanic Origin		

Occupation   Blue collar: 29.0%   White collar: 53.5%   Gray collar: 17.5%

Long Beach, founded in 1888, with 461,000 people in 2000, would be a major metropolis almost anywhere but in Los Angeles County, where it seems just the largest of many suburbs. But it has an identity of its own. Started as a beach resort, it soon became a port when Los Angeles civic leaders decided that if their town were to be a world-class city it must have a world-class harbor; nature not having provided one, they built it where the Los Angeles River flows into the ocean at the western edge of Long Beach. By 1909, Los Angeles had annexed the harbor towns of San Pedro and Wilmington on the other side of the river; over the next decades the two cities persuaded federal government to dredge channels and build a breakwater and turning basins. Long Beach was developing other businesses as well. It sprouted oil derricks in the 1920s and briefly became one of the nation's big oil producers; it was the site of major aircraft plants in the 1940s and after. By the 1980s the Los Angeles-Long Beach port was the nation's largest, the fastest-growing major cargo center in the world, with huge steel-gray container ships pulling quietly up to enormous automated loading facilities—a 21st century contrast to the rotting docks of New York and San Francisco. Long Beach's downtown, once full of rundown 1920s buildings and pawnshops, now has an array of glittering high-rises and the area has become a favorite for Japanese and Asian companies' American headquarters. In the 1990s, Long Beach was hurt by closure of its naval station and shipyard and by cutbacks at its huge McDonnell Douglas plant before Boeing purchased the company; but small businesses have grown, many of which serve the port. The *Queen Mary,* converted into a floating hotel, has become a major tourist attraction.

The 37th Congressional District includes 80% of the city of Long Beach (but not the harbor), and Signal Hill, surrounded by Long Beach, where the oil rigs are still pumping. It includes two industrial suburbs—Compton, which switched from all-white to all-black in the 1960s and in the 1980s became heavily Latino, and Carson, with recent subdivisions amid freeway interchanges and tank farms. And it includes the south end of South Central Los Angeles, including the Watts tower near which the riot of 1965 broke out. In 2000 the district's population was 25% black and 43% Hispanic, but many of the Hispanics are not U.S. citizens and do not vote here. It is heavily Democratic.

The congresswoman from the 37th District is Juanita Millender-McDonald, chosen in a March 1996 special election. She was born in Alabama, raised a family in Carson, and earned a bachelor's degree in 1979, at 40. She worked as a teacher and editor/writer for the Los Angeles Unified School District and was manuscript editor for *IMAGES,* a state textbook designed for young women to enhance self-esteem. She later became director of gender equity programs for the district and was appointed to the National Commission on Teaching and America's Future. In 1990 she was elected to the Carson City Council. In 1992 she ran for the Assembly and beat an incumbent in the primary. She chaired the Insurance and the Revenue and Taxation Committees for a year each, and sponsored the bill qualifying for designation as a National Transportation Artery the Alameda Corridor—a $2.4 billion combination of underground rail and freeway lanes connecting the port to major east-west rail lines and freeways.

Her opening to run for Congress came in December 1995, when two-term Congressman Walter Tucker was convicted of extortion and tax fraud as mayor of Compton and sentenced to 27 months in federal prison. A special election was set for the following March, the same day as the regular primary; since no Republican ran, it determined the winner. Already running and better-known was Assemblyman Willard Murray, who had been chief of staff to former (1981–93) Congressman Mervyn Dymally. But with help from EMILY's List, Millender-McDonald raised much more money. Murray had other problems, including his support for building a prison for Compton, which voters there turned down 87%–13%. Millender-McDonald won the nine-candidate special with 27% to 20% for Murray.

In the House, Millender-McDonald has a liberal voting record. She got a seat on the Transportation and Infrastructure Committee, where she made the Alameda Corridor her chief priority. She quickly made national news. The *San Jose Mercury News* (in a story it later repudiated) charged that the CIA aided Nicaraguan Contras in smuggling crack cocaine to Los Angeles; and Millender-McDonald invited CIA Director John Deutsch to a public meeting in her district. Astonishingly, he accepted, and was denounced by dozens of speakers and booed and interrupted with obscenities by many others despite Millender-McDonald's pleas for order. She backed the Chinese-government-owned China Ocean Shipping Company's bid to build a container terminal at the former Long Beach Naval Air Station. But despite its likely benefits for the port, she voted against PNTR with China because of its human rights abuses. She co-chaired the Caucus on Women's Issues, where she focused on the impact of proposed Social Security reform and led opposition to the bill making it a crime to harm a fetus during an assault on a pregnant woman. As the second-ranking Democrat on the Small Business Committee, she strongly opposed George W. Bush's proposed cuts in the Small Business Administration.

Millender-McDonald has easily won re-election. Despite the fact that 40% of the district was new to her in 2002, she had modest competition. Peter Mathews, who got 44% of the vote in 1998 against Representative Steve Horn in the old 38th District, challenged her in the Democratic primary. But he raised only $45,000, and Millender-McDonald won 78%–22%. She won the general 73%–23%. Millender-McDonald may face a Latino challenger before the decade is out.

THIRTY-EIGHTH DISTRICT

Rep. Grace Napolitano (D)

Elected 1998, 3d term; b. Dec. 4, 1936, Brownsville, TX; home, Norwalk; Catholic; married (Frank).

Elected Office: Norwalk City Cncl., 1986–92; Norwalk Mayor, 1989–92; CA Assembly, 1992–98.

Professional Career: Employee, Ford Motor Co., 1970–1992.

DC Office: 1609 LHOB 20515, 202-225-5256; Fax: 202-225-0027; Web site: www.house.gov/napolitano.

District Office: Santa Fe Springs, 562-801-2134.

Committees: *International Relations* (18th of 23 D): International Terrorism, Nonproliferation and Human Rights; Western Hemisphere. *Resources* (11th of 24 D): Energy & Mineral Resources; Water & Power (RMM). *Small Business* (9th of 17 D): Workforce, Empowerment & Government Programs.

Group Ratings

	ADA	ACLU	AFS	LCV	CON	ITIC	NTU	COC	ACU	NTLC	CHC
2002	100	80	100	88	43	50	21	40	0	0	0
2001	90	—	100	100	—	—	8	35	4	—	—

National Journal Ratings

	2001 LIB	—	2001 CONS		2002 LIB	—	2002 CONS
Economic	94%	—	6%		72%	—	27%
Social	82%	—	18%		81%	—	18%
Foreign	80%	—	20%		84%	—	14%

Key Votes of the 107th Congress

1. Approve Bush Tax Cuts	N	5. Faith-Based Charities	N	9. Trade Promotion Authority	N
2. Limit Patients' Bill of Rights	N	6. Bar Gays in the Boy Scouts	N	10. Bar Funds for Intl. Court	N
3. Campaign Finance Reform	Y	7. Ban Partial-Birth Abortion	N	11. Authorize Force in Iraq	N
4. Ban ANWR Development	Y	8. Arm Commercial Pilots	Y	12. Deny Home. Sec. Dept. Union	N

Election Results

2002 general	Grace Napolitano (D)	62,600	(71%)	($283,868)
	Alex Burrola (R)	23,126	(26%)	
	Other	2,301	(3%)	
2002 primary	Grace Napolitano (D)	21,815	(65%)	
	Gregory Salcido (D)	11,755	(35%)	
2000 general (CA 34)	Grace Napolitano (D)	105,980	(71%)	($298,484)
	Robert Arthur Canales (R)	33,445	(22%)	($1,689)
	Julia F. Simon (NL)	9,262	(6%)	

Prior Winning Percentages: 1998 (68%)

The People		Race/Ethnic Origin	Ancestry	
Area size:	105 sq. mi.	13.6% White	German: 2.7%	Irish: 1.8%
Urban population:	100.0%	3.6% Black	English: 1.8%	
Rural population:	0.0%	10.2% Asian	**2000 Presidential Vote**	
Pop. 2000:	639,088	0.3% Native Am.	Gore (D)..............104,612 (70%)	
Median income:	$42,488	0.1% Hawaiian	Bush (R)..............41,706 (28%)	
Poverty status:	16.3%	1.4% Two+ races	Other...................2,929 (2%)	
Military veterans:	6.8%	0.1% Other	**Cook Partisan Voting Index:** D +21	
		70.6% Hispanic Origin		

Occupation Blue collar: 34.1% White collar: 50.7% Gray collar: 15.2%

One of the great population surges in the United States is the upward social movement of the hundreds of thousands of immigrants in the Los Angeles Basin, from crowded entry-level neighborhoods out on freeways to the suburbs. It is visible east and southeast of Los Angeles, in suburbs that over a generation have changed from solidly white Anglo to largely Latino. Many people here have made their way up working in small smokeless factories along railroad tracks and near river beds, beneath roaring freeways and on grid streets near stucco garden apartment blocks and in small business offices and stores; these have made Los Angeles the nation's number-two manufacturing metro area. Their values resemble those of working-class Americans of the 1960s: pro-family and respectful of traditional personal morals (L.A.-area Latinos have lower than average divorce rates), patriotic and hard-working (Latino males have the highest work force participation of any measured group and the incomes of U.S.-born Los Angeles County Latinos are at the county average).

Vast numbers of these new residents live in the 38th Congressional District, where the percentage of Hispanics is 71%, the second highest of any California district. This is a swath of Los Angeles County anchored by four primarily Hispanic suburbs. To the northwest is Montebello, a working-class suburb just beyond 97% Hispanic East Los Angeles. To the east is La Puente, a center of the light manufacturing economy that created hundreds of thousands of jobs in the Los Angeles Basin in the 1980s, and in which increasing numbers of small businesses are owned by Asians, Latinos and blacks. Farther east is the old town of Pomona, the district's largest city, now much expanded and site of the Los Angeles County Fair. To the south is Norwalk, a rail crossroad astride the Santa Ana Freeway, 63% Hispanic, and Santa Fe Springs.

The congresswoman from the 38th District is Grace Napolitano, a Democrat first elected in 1998. Napolitano grew up in the Lower Rio Grande Valley of Texas, married at 18, and had five children and moved to California by the time she was 23. She worked as a secretary at Ford Motor Company for 22 years. After her first husband died, she married Frank Napolitano and in 1980 they started a pizzeria business. She served on the city council in Norwalk from 1986 to 1992 and served one term as mayor, becoming the first Latino to hold either position. In 1992 she was elected to the California Assembly from a seat that covered much of this congressional district. She chaired the International Trade and Development Committee and got a 100% rating from the AFL-CIO.

Term-limited in 1998, she got the opportunity to run for Congress when 16-year incumbent Esteban Torres announced three days before the filing deadline that he was retiring. Torres's surprise move seemed designed to promote the election of Jamie Casso, his son-in-law and chief of staff, who immediately announced his candidacy. But Napolitano was not deterred. She convinced the state AFL-CIO to vote an "open endorsement," although the executive board had backed Casso and Torres had been a senior United Auto Workers official under Walter Reuther in the 1960s. Napolitano and Casso waged a fierce campaign. She criticized him for not living in the district; he criticized her $180,000 loan to her campaign at an unusual 18% interest rate, which he said left her little reason to repay the principal. Torres was featured prominently in Casso's campaign literature and appearances. Napolitano had the financial backing of national women's organizations, including EMILY's List, plus the benefit of higher name identification. The two candidates had few differences on major issues; Napolitano signed a pledge to serve only three terms. Napolitano won the primary by 618 votes, 51%–49% among Democratic voters. Her victory in November was routine.

In the House, she has a moderate-to-liberal voting record. She won enactment of a $300 million authorization to remove a leaking 10-million ton pile of radioactive uranium tailings from the defunct mill of Atlas Corporation at Moab, Utah—600 feet from the Colorado River, a prime source of Southern California's drinking water. She has voted against automatic pay increases for members of Congress; she opposes the secret process and says she is adequately compensated. During the Resources Committee debate on reauthorizing the California Bay-Delta (CALFED) water allocation program, Napolitano successfully removed the 25% limit on how much of the federal total for new water conservation projects can go to California; she later sponsored her own version of the bill that removed approval of additional projects outside California. In October 2002 she was the only one of four southern California Democrats on the International Relations Committee to vote against authorizing the use of force in Iraq.

Napolitano has not been seriously challenged for reelection. In 1998 she pledged to serve just three terms in the House, but in February 2003 Napolitano announced she plans to run for reelection two more times and then retire after serving five terms.

THIRTY-NINTH DISTRICT

Rep. Linda Sanchez (D)

Elected 2002, 1st term; b. Jan. 28, 1969, Orange; home, Lakewood; U. of CA, B.A. 1991, U.C.L.A., J.D. 1995; Catholic; married (Mark Valentine).

Professional Career: Practicing atty., 1995–98; Exec. Secy. Treas. of Orange Cnty. AFL-CIO, 2000–02.

DC Office: 1007 LHOB 20515, 202-225-1012; Fax: 202-226-1012; Web site: www.house.gov/lindasanchez.

District Office: Lakewood, 562-429-8499.

Committees: *Government Reform* (15th of 19 D): Criminal Justice, Drug Policy & Human Resources; National Security, Emerging Threats & Intl. Relations. *Judiciary* (16th of 16 D): Immigration, Border Security & Claims. *Small Business* (17th of 17 D).

Group Ratings and Key Votes: Newly Elected

Election Results

2002 general	Linda Sanchez (D)	52,256	(55%)	($1,074,253)
	Tim Escobar (R)	38,925	(41%)	($218,239)
	Richard Newhouse (Lib)	4,165	(4%)	
2002 primary	Linda Sanchez (D)	10,804	(33%)	
	Hector De La Torre (D)	9,450	(29%)	
	Sally Havice (D)	6,223	(19%)	
	Helen Rahder (D)	2,698	(8%)	
	Ken Graham (D)	1,879	(6%)	
	Cecy Groom (D)	1,230	(4%)	

The People		Race/Ethnic Origin	Ancestry	
Area size:	65 sq. mi.	21.0% White	German: 4.3%	Irish: 3.3%
Urban population:	100.0%	6.1% Black	English: 3.0%	
Rural population:	0.0%	9.5% Asian	**2000 Presidential Vote**	
Pop. 2000:	639,088	0.3% Native Am.	Gore (D)...............98,478 (62%)	
Median income:	$45,307	0.3% Hawaiian	Bush (R)...............56,067 (36%)	
Poverty status:	15.7%	1.5% Two+ races	Other....................3,390 (2%)	
Military veterans:	7.1%	0.1% Other	**Cook Partisan Voting Index:** D +13	
		61.2% Hispanic Origin		

Occupation	Blue collar: 31.2%	White collar: 55.0%	Gray collar: 13.9%

In the years just after World War II much of southeast Los Angeles County was farmland—citrus groves, dairy farms. Then in the next two decades subdivisions were built and new cities incorporated so that what had been a few separate towns separated by farmland became one continuous swatch of suburbia. The separate towns were different in character. Whittier, founded by Quakers, was the home town of Richard Nixon, who was a young lawyer thinking about running for Congress in early 1946 was inaugurated as vice president of the United States seven years later. South Gate and Lynwood, with new auto and other factories, filled up with newcomers from the South. Lakewood, just north of Long Beach, was built up so rapidly in the 1950s that it was featured in *Life* magazine. Other towns were built up later; there were still dairy farms in Cerritos in the 1970s.

The 39th Congressional District is made up of a heterogeneous and oddly shaped collection of these suburbs. It is shaped like a U. On the east end of the U are two-thirds of Whittier, a town founded by Midwestern Quakers, where Richard Nixon grew up and went to Whittier College, all of South and West Whittier and La Mirada. The bottom end of the U includes Cerritos, Artesia, Hawaiian Gardens and Lakewood. The west end of the U includes Southgate, Lynwood, Paramount and the eastern fringe of South Central Los Angeles. The district's population is 61% Hispanic and 10% Asian. As this area grew in the postwar years it was pretty closely divided between the parties. But in the 1990s it trended Democratic. This is essentially a new district created by the 2001 redistricting, replacing the old 38th District represented by Republican Steve Horn. Redistricting was controlled by Democrats, but they made a deal to create 20 Republican districts, the same number as they won in 2000, in return for Republican votes for the plan in the legislature. But it was apparent that it would have been hard to draw a safe seat for Horn as well as the other 19 incumbent Republicans, and Horn was not included in the deal; instead a new Republican district was created in the Central Valley and this new Democratic Hispanic-majority district was created.

The congresswoman from the new 39th District is Linda Sanchez, a Democrat elected in 2002, and the junior and younger member of the first pair of sisters ever elected to Congress. They are the oldest and youngest of seven children of Ignacio Sanchez, a machinist, and Maria Macias. Loretta Sanchez, who is nine years older, was elected to the House in 1996 when she unseated Republican Robert Dornan in an Orange County district. Linda Sanchez graduated from Berkeley and UCLA law school. She became a civil rights lawyer and was executive secretary-treasurer of the Orange County Federation of Labor. "She's definitely the more liberal one," Loretta explained.

Even before the district lines were unveiled in August 2001, it was apparent that there would be a new Democratic district in this part of Los Angeles County; when the lines were unveiled, Horn announced that he would not run for reelection. Linda Sanchez was one of six Democrats who filed to run. Her most important asset was her sister's support. Linda Sanchez tapped Loretta's extensive fundraising network, walked precincts with her and appeared in a television commercial with her. In the Spanish language ad, their mother urged voters to send both of her daughters to Capitol Hill. All this gave Linda Sanchez an advantage over her two chief opponents, who started off better known—two-term Assemblywoman Sally Havice and South Gate Councilman Hector De La Torre, who had worked several years in Washington as a legislative aide and Labor Department official. There were few differences between them on major issues, but the campaign turned negative in the closing weeks. Sanchez ran an ad on cable criticizing Havice for allegedly failing to pay property taxes and homeowners dues and attacked De La Torre for receiving a campaign contribution from a trash hauler in Los Angeles who owed franchise fees to the city. Sanchez's labor ties helped her build a strong voter turnout operation; the L.A. County AFL-CIO endorsed both Sanchez and Havice.

With help from her sister, Sanchez won endorsements from then-Minority Whip Nancy Pelosi and aid from Ruben Hinojosa. Her opponents replied that Sanchez had received no endorsements from other Latino members of Congress; Hilda Solis, whom Loretta Sanchez backed in her first House race in 1998, endorsed De La Torre. They charged that Linda Sanchez was a political opportunist who changed her name and residence to run in the newly-created district; like her sister, Sanchez had used her non-Latino married name until she started to run for the House. Sanchez won with 33% of the vote, to 29% for De La Torre and 19% for Havice. Afterwards the Long Beach *Press-Telegram* attacked Sanchez's tactics: "It may have been the only way for Sanchez to win, as an unemployed labor activist with little political experience, but the tactics were deceptive, dishonest and mean."

This district is not as Democratic as the Hispanic-majority 31st, 32d, 34th and 38th Districts, and Sanchez's negative primary campaign may have hurt her. Republican Tim Escobar, a financial adviser and former Army helicopter pilot, said Sanchez was an inexperienced liberal extremist; he quoted the bitter remarks of her primary opponents. But Sanchez won 55%–41%. For a freshman, Sanchez received an unusual greeting upon her arrival on Capitol Hill: The election of the two sisters generated abundant and largely flattering national press coverage.

FORTIETH DISTRICT

Rep. Ed Royce (R)

Elected 1992, 6th term; b. Oct. 12, 1951, Los Angeles; home, Fullerton; CA State Fullerton, B.A. 1977; Catholic; married (Marie).

Elected Office: CA Senate, 1982–92.

Professional Career: Tax Mgr., 1979–82.

DC Office: 2202 RHOB 20515, 202-225-4111; Fax: 202-226-0335; Web site: www.house.gov/royce.

District Office: Fullerton, 714-992-8081.

Committees: *Financial Services* (8th of 37 R): Capital Markets, Insurance & Government Sponsored Enterprises; Financial Institutions & Consumer Credit. *International Relations* (10th of 26 R): Africa (Chmn.); Asia & the Pacific.

Group Ratings

	ADA	ACLU	AFS	LCV	CON	ITIC	NTU	COC	ACU	NTLC	CHC
2002	0	7	0	25	99	88	70	85	100	100	100
2001	5	—	0	0	—	—	81	74	100	—	—

National Journal Ratings

	2001 LIB —	2001 CONS	2002 LIB —	2002 CONS
Economic	13%	86%	28%	69%
Social	0%	81%	0%	75%
Foreign	41%	58%	0%	85%

Key Votes of the 107th Congress

1. Approve Bush Tax Cuts	Y	5. Faith-Based Charities	Y	9. Trade Promotion Authority	Y
2. Limit Patients' Bill of Rights	Y	6. Bar Gays in the Boy Scouts	Y	10. Bar Funds for Intl. Court	Y
3. Campaign Finance Reform	N	7. Ban Partial-Birth Abortion	Y	11. Authorize Force in Iraq	Y
4. Ban ANWR Development	N	8. Arm Commercial Pilots	Y	12. Deny Home. Sec. Dept. Union	Y

Election Results

2002 general	Ed Royce (R)	92,422	(68%)	($845,661)
	Christina Avalos (D)	40,265	(29%)	($10,452)
	Other	3,955	(3%)	
2002 primary	Ed Royce (R)	unopposed		
2000 general (CA 39)	Ed Royce (R)	129,294	(63%)	($327,284)
	Gill G. Kanel (D)	64,938	(32%)	($24,805)
	Other	11,872	(6%)	

Prior Winning Percentages: 1998 (63%); 1996 (63%); 1994 (66%); 1992 (57%)

The People		Race/Ethnic Origin	Ancestry	
Area size:	102 sq. mi.	49.3% White	German: 9.3%	English: 6.8%
Urban population:	100.0%	2.2% Black	Irish: 6.8%	
Rural population:	0.0%	15.6% Asian	**2000 Presidential Vote**	
Pop. 2000:	639,088	0.3% Native Am.	Bush (R)	119,443 (56%)
Median income:	$54,356	0.4% Hawaiian	Gore (D)	86,460 (41%)
Poverty status:	10.2%	2.4% Two+ races	Other	5,886 (3%)
Military veterans:	10.1%	0.2% Other	**Cook Partisan Voting Index:** R + 8	
		29.6% Hispanic Origin		

Occupation   Blue collar: 22.1%   White collar: 64.5%   Gray collar: 13.4%

Orange County is the fifth most populous county in the United States, having grown steadily from 130,000 in 1940 to 703,000 in 1960, 1.9 million in 1980, and 2.8 million in 2000. It is now a community with the patina of maturity—in some places an aging community, fraying around the edges. The county can no longer double its population, as it did in the 1950s and 1960s, when Disneyland sprung up on empty land and mile-square grids of orange groves and bean fields were transformed into one suburban subdivision, shopping center or office tower after another. A distinctive civilization was implanted here: mostly white and middle-class, confident of its traditional values and its market capitalism, proud of American principles and American military might. Orange County has been transformed in the years since by its openness to economic and ethnic change. Its economy was constantly reshaped by the inevitable upheavals of capitalism. There is no single industry here, not even defense, that is totally responsible for the prosperity of Orange County. It was hit hard by the defense cutbacks and recession of the early 1990s but it bounced back, pitched forward by new startups and small entrepreneurial successes not anticipated by government or corporate planners.

Always Republican, Orange County became a symbol of conservatism first in California and then nationally. In 1988 its 317,000-vote plurality for George H. W. Bush was the largest of any county in the country. Orange County's conservatism reflected a belief in technological progress and traditional values as unyielding as the mile-square grid the county's founders imposed on most of its land, a belief in the market economies that had produced such local wonders as Disneyland and the area's advanced military technologies. But problems developed. In 1994, the county government declared bankruptcy because of the county treasurer's sloppy investment and bookkeeping practices; shortly afterwards, the Disney company shelved plans for a $2 billion resort development that would have doubled the size of Disneyland. Orange County has rebounded, and so has Disney, which in 2001 opened its California Adventure amusement park in the neighboring 47th District. Orange County, like the rest of the Los Angeles metropolitan area, has trended toward the Democrats. In 2000 it still voted Republican, but gave George W. Bush only a 149,000-vote margin.

The 40th Congressional District consists of acreage that was mostly farmland when Disneyland was being laid out. At the geographic center is Fullerton, with its own branch of Cal State University; to the southwest are Buena Park, home of Knott's Berry Farm, the earliest theme park (1940), plus Cypress, Los Alamitos, La Palma, Stanton, and parts of Garden Grove and Westminster. Southeast of Fullerton the district includes most of Placentia, a part of eastern Anaheim and all of Villa Park and Orange, the district's largest city. Overall the 40th District is

30% Hispanic, 16% Asian (primarily Korean, Vietnamese and Filipino) and 2% black—the all-white Orange County stereotype is out of date.

The congressman from the 40th District is Ed Royce, whose life almost precisely covers the area's growth. Like Orange County, he has long been conservative. He was in the Young Americans for Freedom at Cal State Fullerton; he worked several years as a tax and capital projects manager for a cement company. In 1982, a bunch of conservative legislators known as "the Cave Men" took him to a Black Angus restaurant—no avocado and sprout sandwiches for them—and persuaded him to run for the state Senate. He won at age 31. When the legislature refused to pass his bill allowing crime victims to object to trial delays, giving grand juries more power and ending shopping for juries, he put it on the ballot as an initiative and it passed by a wide margin.

In 1992 Royce ran for the House. With the blessing of Orange County Republican leaders, he was unopposed in the crucial primary and easily won the general. In the House, Royce has a conservative voting record, though a bit less so on foreign issues. He co-sponsored the nationwide AMBER alert plan to recover abducted children, approved by the House in March 2003. He co-chairs the House "porkbusters," risking others' wrath by opposing appropriations bills with dubious projects. He advocated a breakup of the Energy Department and the abolition of the Overseas Private Investment Corporation, which guarantees foreign investments, as a form of corporate welfare. With John McCain, he estimated that spending bills following the September 11 attacks had $14 billion in pork. His proposal to ensure that nonprofit religious organizations have access to all necessary financial resources was a forerunner of George W. Bush's faith-based initiative.

As chairman of the International Relations Subcommittee on Africa and an ardent free-trader, Royce backed an Africa free trade bill with ranking Ways and Means Democrat Charles Rangel; it came at a time when, after three decades of economic stagnation and dictatorship, several African countries were moving toward market economics and democracy. Despite Rangel's sponsorship, the issue divided the Black Caucus; Jesse Jackson Jr. called for forgiving of African nations' foreign debts instead. But Royce helped steer the bill to enactment in 2000. In 2002, when Congress passed trade promotion authority, it revised the earlier bill to raise the cap on duty-free apparel imports from Africa. Although he had never set foot in Africa before he became chairman, he was widely praised for learning about the continent and was the only Republican on Bill Clinton's 1998 visit to Africa. Royce also has a strong interest in Asia; he co-chairs the Congressional Caucus on India and Indian Americans and urges stronger strategic and trade relationships between the United States and India. In December 2001 George W. Bush signed his bill establishing Radio Free Afghanistan as a tool in the fight against terrorism. In the juggling of subcommittee chairmanships after the 2002 election, Royce expressed interest in taking the Middle East panel; but it went to the more senior Ileana Ros-Lehtinen.

Royce has been reelected by wide margins. After redistricting, half of the district was new to him in 2002, but he still won reelection with 68%.

FORTY-FIRST DISTRICT

Rep. Jerry Lewis (R)

Elected 1978, 13th term; b. Oct. 21, 1934, Seattle, WA; home, Redlands; U.C.L.A., B.A. 1956; Presbyterian; married (Arlene).

Elected Office: CA Assembly, 1968–78.

Professional Career: Insurance exec., 1959–78; Field rep., U.S. Rep. Jerry Pettis, 1968.

DC Office: 2112 RHOB 20515, 202-225-5861; Fax: 202-225-6498; Web site: www.house.gov/jerrylewis.

District Office: Redlands, 909-862-6030.

Committees: *Appropriations* (3d of 36 R): Defense (Chmn.); Foreign Operations & Export Financing; Transportation, Treasury, & Independent Agencies.

Group Ratings

	ADA	ACLU	AFS	LCV	CON	ITIC	NTU	COC	ACU	NTLC	CHC
2002	10	20	0	38	49	100	56	84	88	80	92
2001	5	—	0	0	—	—	62	100	80	—	—

National Journal Ratings

	2001 LIB —	2001 CONS	2002 LIB —	2002 CONS
Economic	13%	86%	36%	61%
Social	40%	60%	37%	63%
Foreign	4%	87%	15%	78%

Key Votes of the 107th Congress

1. Approve Bush Tax Cuts	Y	5. Faith-Based Charities	Y	9. Trade Promotion Authority	Y
2. Limit Patients' Bill of Rights	Y	6. Bar Gays in the Boy Scouts	Y	10. Bar Funds for Intl. Court	Y
3. Campaign Finance Reform	N	7. Ban Partial-Birth Abortion	Y	11. Authorize Force in Iraq	Y
4. Ban ANWR Development	N	8. Arm Commercial Pilots	Y	12. Deny Home. Sec. Dept. Union	Y

Election Results

2002 general	Jerry Lewis (R)	91,326	(67%)	($645,070)
	Keith Johnson (D)	40,155	(30%)	
	Other	4,052	(3%)	
2002 primary	Jerry Lewis (R)	unopposed		
2000 general (CA 40)	Jerry Lewis (R)	151,069	(80%)	($805,526)
	Frank N. Schmit (NL)	19,029	(10%)	
	Jay Lindberg (Lib)	18,924	(10%)	

Prior Winning Percentages: 1998 (65%); 1996 (65%); 1994 (71%); 1992 (63%); 1990 (61%); 1988 (70%); 1986 (77%); 1984 (85%); 1982 (68%); 1980 (72%); 1978 (61%)

The People		Race/Ethnic Origin	Ancestry	
Area size:	13,350 sq. mi.	63.5% White	German: 11.7%	English: 8.4%
Urban population:	89.4%	5.3% Black	Irish: 8.3%	
Rural population:	10.6%	3.7% Asian	**2000 Presidential Vote**	
Pop. 2000:	639,087	1.0% Native Am.	Bush (R) ... 114,498	(56%)
Median income:	$38,721	0.2% Hawaiian	Gore (D) ... 83,584	(41%)
Poverty status:	15.2%	2.7% Two+ races	Other ... 5,116	(3%)
Military veterans:	16.1%	0.2% Other	**Cook Partisan Voting Index:** R + 8	
		23.4% Hispanic Origin		

Occupation	Blue collar: 25.0%	White collar: 57.3%	Gray collar: 17.8%

Over the last two decades the great American movement west has turned back east, at least in California. As settlement reached the Pacific Coast, young families looking for affordable houses, neighborhoods and schools, where traditional values are respected, moved away from the liberation-minded and high-crime coast and toward the sunny, often hot, valleys inland. This impulse has resulted in rapid growth in the Central Valley, the repopulation of the Mother Lode country in the foothills of the Sierras and the startling growth in the Inland Empire at the eastern end of the Los Angeles Basin, around San Bernardino and Riverside, and east and north past the mountain rims into the desert. This Inland Empire grew from 1.6 million in 1980 to 3.2 million in 2000.

The 41st Congressional District covers much of the Inland Empire and the desert beyond the mountains. It includes much of the land area of San Bernardino County, which with 20,052 square miles is the largest county in the United States and is more than twice the size of New Jersey. Nearly half its population is concentrated in its southwest corner, in the Inland Empire, including the northern and eastern edges of San Bernardino and all of Loma Linda, Redlands, Highland, Yucaipa—small towns founded by pious Midwesterners at the base of 10,000-foot mountains. It also includes towns in Riverside County just to the south—Calimesa, Beaumont, Banning, San Jacinto. East of the mountains is the vast Mojave Desert, mostly uninhabited, but with small clusters of population. In the Victor Valley are Hesperia and Apple Valley, new towns in the desert with 117,000 people between them. Roy Rogers and Dale Evans lived for years on a ranch here, with their stuffed Trigger, Buttermilk and Bullet in a nearby museum. The district includes the mountain country around Lake Arrowhead and Big Bear Lake, Desert Hot Springs, the rustic town north of posh Palm Springs, and Twentynine Palms and the huge Twentynine Palms Marine Corps Base, the largest Marine base in the country. This has always been Republican territory and is still Republican today—56% for George W. Bush in 2000.

The congressman from the 41st District is Jerry Lewis, a Republican first elected in 1978 and now chairman of the Defense Appropriations Subcommittee. Lewis grew up in San Bernardino, worked as a lifeguard and graduated from UCLA. (He maintains his swimming skills, and once saved former Speaker Jim Wright off the shore of Hawaii.) He was an insurance agent in Redlands, a joiner in civic causes, and was elected to the California Assembly in 1968, at 34. In 1978, the incumbent congressman retired and Lewis was elected to the House. In 1980, he got a seat on the Appropriations Committee, where bipartisan cooperation was the norm, enabling even minority members to confer favors on their districts. With a small city background and an accommodationist attitude toward Democrats, he steadily won leadership positions—chairman of the Republican Research Committee in 1984, chairman of the Republican Policy Committee in 1986, Republican Conference chairman in 1988, and seemed headed towards the minority leader post. But a small group of young conservatives around Newt Gingrich resented Lewis's cooperation with Democrats and believed that Republicans could break out of the minority if they confronted Democrats more. In March 1989 the minority whip position came open when Dick Cheney was appointed secretary of Defense. Lewis considered running, but declined; Gingrich won by an 87–85 vote. In December 1992 Dick Armey, with support from Gingrich, challenged Lewis for the Conference chairmanship and won 88–84. Those two votes put in place the two top leaders of the Republican majority that emerged after November 1994.

Lewis recovered from that setback, and when Republicans won their majority in 1994, he became chairman of the VA-HUD Appropriations Subcommittee—a member of the "college of cardinals," as Appropriations subcommittee chairmen are known. Here he got his agencies' attention by reporting a bill making deep cuts in NASA, including closing the Goddard space center in Greenbelt, Maryland. Goddard was saved, but Lewis forced other cuts at NASA. He supported Gingrich against the July 1997 coup.

In 1999 Lewis became chairman of the Defense Subcommittee, with the largest share of federal spending of any of the 13 subcommittees. He attracted attention when the subcommittee voted unanimously to cut $1.8 billion for building the first six of the Air Force's F-22s. This was a bolt out of the blue, and something that would not have happened had Gingrich still been speaker—the F-22 is produced in a Lockheed Martin plant in Gingrich's former district. Lewis was disturbed by a report that the Air Force had been spending money on programs Congress never authorized, including an $800 million military communications satellite and updates to the C-5. He argued that the F-22 was a Cold War super weapon, whose high cost left the Air Force as "very close to a broken branch" of the military, and he pointed out that the old F-15 did just fine in the spring 1999 bombing of Kosovo, while the Air Force was short of tankers and radar-jamming aircraft there. Funds were restored by the Senate, but the program was cut by $500 million and the Pentagon's attention was gained. In May 2000 the subcommittee cut $150 million from money requested for the Joint Strike Fighter. In August 2001 Lewis said that he would press for the $18.4 billion George W. Bush had requested over the original $310.5 billion. On the morning of September 11, the subcommittee was debating an increase in funding for counter-terrorism when news of the attacks came; members quickly left the Capitol. In November a $317 billion defense appropriation was passed. It did not include funding for transformation of defense programs; Lewis said that appropriations bills should not be the vehicle for major policy changes, although he had arguably used the process for that on the F-22. In June 2002 Lewis steered a $354.7 billion defense appropriation to passage in the House. "The war on terrorism is very real," he said. "The Afghanistan experience has made it a lot easier for me to fend off those who would like to take a pretty sizeable chunk of our money." In October the final $355.4 billion appropriation was passed.

Lewis generally does not buck the Bush administration, but he operates with the traditional appropriators' bipartisanship when it comes to appropriations bills. In the process he has pressed his own pet projects. One was the Predator unmanned air vehicle, which has been tested on the Mojave Desert. Lewis learned about the Predator in the early 1990s, while serving on the Intelligence Committee. He continues to promote the Predator on the subcommittee.

As an appropriator, Lewis has been unapologetic about channeling funds into his district. One special beneficiary has been Loma Linda University, whose medical center got $26 million for medical research in 2000. He has worked for the Santa Ana River flood control, for reimbursement to state governments for aliens held in prison (California gets 41% of the $565 million), for the Redlands Trolley. Some are sentimental projects. Lewis got $1 million to rebuild the Perris Hill Plunge, a WPA-built pool where he was a lifeguard and taught dozens of children to swim; he helped to get another $1 million for the Jerry Lewis Community Center in his home town of Highland; he helped provide funding for the $20 million Lewis Center for Educational Research in Apple Valley.

Lewis has been reelected easily in this solidly Republican and fast-growing district. But Lewis has noticed that the Hispanic percentage here has been rising, from 16% in 1990 to 23% in 2000, and he has been taking Spanish lessons, including time spent with a family in Mexico City. Appropriations Chairman Bill Young is limited to three terms, which will expire at the end of 2004. Lewis, third Republican in seniority on the panel, has been mentioned as a possible chairman after the 2004 election.

FORTY-SECOND DISTRICT

Rep. Gary Miller (R)

Elected 1998, 3d term; b. Oct. 16, 1948, Huntsville, AR; home, Diamond Bar; Mt. San Antonio Col. 1971, 1988–89; Christian; married (Cathy).

Military Career: Army, 1967–1968.

Elected Office: Diamond Bar City Cncl., 1989–95; Diamond Bar Mayor, 1992; CA Assembly, 1995–98.

Professional Career: Businessman, real estate developer, G. Miller Development Co., 1971–98.

DC Office: 1037 LHOB 20515, 202-225-3201; Fax: 202-226-6962; Web site: www.house.gov/garymiller.

District Offices: Brea, 714-257-1142; Mission Viejo, 949-470-8484.

Committees: *Financial Services* (25th of 37 R): Capital Markets, Insurance & Government Sponsored Enterprises; Housing & Community Opportunity. *Transportation & Infrastructure* (18th of 41 R): Railroads; Water Resources & Environment.

Group Ratings

	ADA	ACLU	AFS	LCV	CON	ITIC	NTU	COC	ACU	NTLC	CHC
2002	0	7	0	13	93	100	64	95	100	91	100
2001	0	—	0	0	—	—	71	100	100	—	—

National Journal Ratings

	2001 LIB — 2001 CONS		2002 LIB — 2002 CONS	
Economic	0% —	94%	0% —	91%
Social	0% —	81%	0% —	75%
Foreign	4% —	87%	0% —	85%

Key Votes of the 107th Congress

1. Approve Bush Tax Cuts	Y	5. Faith-Based Charities	Y	9. Trade Promotion Authority	Y
2. Limit Patients' Bill of Rights	Y	6. Bar Gays in the Boy Scouts	Y	10. Bar Funds for Intl. Court	Y
3. Campaign Finance Reform	N	7. Ban Partial-Birth Abortion	Y	11. Authorize Force in Iraq	Y
4. Ban ANWR Development	N	8. Arm Commercial Pilots	Y	12. Deny Home. Sec. Dept. Union	Y

Election Results

2002 general	Gary Miller (R)	98,476	(68%)	($443,707)
	Richard Waldron (D)	42,090	(29%)	
	Other	4,680	(3%)	
2002 primary	Gary Miller (R)	unopposed		
2000 general (CA 41)	Gary Miller (R)	104,695	(59%)	($482,491)
	Rodolfo Favila (D)	66,361	(37%)	($81,937)
	David Kramer (NL)	6,560	(4%)	

Prior Winning Percentages: 1998 (53%)

The People		Race/Ethnic Origin	Ancestry	
Area size:	317 sq. mi.	54.4% White	German: 10.2% Irish: 7.4%	
Urban population:	98.7%	2.9% Black	English: 7.4%	
Rural population:	1.3%	15.9% Asian	**2000 Presidential Vote**	
Pop. 2000:	639,088	0.3% Native Am.	Bush (R)..............139,655	(59%)
Median income:	$70,463	0.2% Hawaiian	Gore (D)...............92,169	(39%)
Poverty status:	6.0%	2.4% Two+ races	Other....................5,157	(2%)
Military veterans:	9.6%	0.2% Other	**Cook Partisan Voting Index:** R +11	
		23.8% Hispanic Origin		

Occupation	Blue collar: 15.2%	White collar: 74.1%	Gray collar: 10.7%

The fastest growth in the Los Angeles metropolitan area over the last 20 years has been in the Inland Empire at eastern end of the Los Angeles Basin. Mostly orange groves and dairy farms a few decades ago, this territory now is the site of a booming economy, personal upward mobility, and ethnic and cultural harmony. The main ingredient of this economic growth has been small entrepreneurial businesses, usually started by people with no particular connections or advantages—often, of Asian or Latino immigrant background. California has never been a land of leisure, as stereotype would have it, but rather a place for hard work, where the fertility of the soil and the productivity of the people have prospered with considerable effort and tolerance toward newcomers. California hasn't always welcomed people from distant places: anti-Asian sentiment expressed itself in the Chinese Exclusion Act of 1882 and the Japanese American internment camps of 1942–44. But since World War II this has been one of the least prejudiced and most welcoming places on earth, which helps to explain why it has received more immigrants than any other state.

The 42d Congressional District is one place where such trends are visible. It is centered in the Inland Empire on the point where Los Angeles, San Bernardino and Orange Counties come together. In San Bernardino County it includes Chino, site of a low-security prison, and Chino Hills, full of new subdivisions. In Los Angeles County it includes Diamond Bar, La Habra Heights and the eastern part of Whittier. More than half the district's population is in Orange County. Here it includes Yorba Linda, site of the birthplace of Richard Nixon in 1913 (when Orange County had only 40,000 residents) and now his presidential library; Brea and La Habra to the west; the eastern part of Anaheim; and, connected only by uninhabited mountains, the newer condominium communities of Mission Viejo and Rancho Santa Margarita. Ethnically diverse, its residents are 24% Hispanic and 16% Asian, believers still in traditional values (the 42d has the highest percentage of married people in the state), working their way up through the private sector—and leaning toward Republicans. The 2001 redistricting made significant changes to the district, removing Pomona in Los Angeles County and Ontario in San Bernardino County and added territory in Orange County; it raised the Bush 2000 vote from 51% to 59%.

The congressman from the 42d District is Gary Miller, a Republican first elected in 1998. He was born in Arkansas but grew up in Whittier. In his early 20s he became a homebuilder and developed planned communities. He began his public service in 1988 when he was appointed to the Diamond Bar Municipal Advisory Council. A year later, after Diamond Bar was incorporated, Miller was elected to the city council and served as mayor. In May 1995 he was elected to the Assembly in a special election to replace Republican Paul Horcher, who was recalled after he supported Democrat Willie Brown for Assembly speaker. In Sacramento, Miller became chairman of the Budget Committee in his freshman year.

In 1997 he decided to run for the House against scandal-tarred incumbent Jay Kim, who lived just two blocks away in Diamond Bar. Kim and his wife had pleaded guilty to accepting and concealing $230,000 in illegal campaign contributions between 1992 and 1996. In March 1998 he was sentenced to house arrest, confined to the House and his apartment in suburban Virginia, and was required to wear an electronic bracelet around his ankle for two months. As a result, he could not campaign back home for the June primary. Local leaders appealed to Miller to run; he was endorsed by Governor Pete Wilson; the NRCC, which normally endorses incumbents, remained neutral. Miller emphasized standard Republican themes—lower taxes, tougher penalties for crime, improved local education—and largely financed his own campaign. The result was unambiguous. Two-thirds of the votes in the all-party primary were cast for Republican candidates, and Miller won 48% of Republican votes to 26% for Kim. This was not a seriously contested race in November; Miller won 53%–41%.

Miller has a very conservative voting record in the House and advanced some original proposals. He was sponsoring anti-spam legislation in the California Assembly well before it became a notorious problem; in Congress, he sponsored a bill to allow Internet Service Providers to decide whether they want to allow spamming and, if not, to give them a cause of action against spammers, with $500 per message in damages. The House passed this measure, combined with other anti-spam provisions to encourage the FCC to regulate spammers, but it died in the Senate. A Civil War buff who discovered that nearly 20% of the major battle sites have been lost, he successfully sponsored in 2002 a bill to preserve Civil War battlefields by authorizing matching grants to local governments and nonprofits for unprotected sites. In 2003, he became the only California Republican on the Transportation and Infrastructure Committee, which gave him the daunting task of representing the state's diverse interests on the highway bill. Miller shares his Virginia apartment with his daughter Elizabeth, an activist with Witness for Peace; he reports, "We have some very interesting discussions at the dinner table."

Miller has been easily reelected against token opposition.

FORTY-THIRD DISTRICT

Rep. Joe Baca (D)

Elected Nov. 1999, 2d term; b. Jan. 23, 1947, Belen, NM; home, Rialto; CA State L.A., B.A., 1971; Catholic; married (Barbara).

Military Career: Army, 1966–68.

Elected Office: CA Assembly, 1992–98; CA Senate, 1998–99.

Professional Career: Community affairs rep., General Telephone and Electric, 1974–89; Co-owner, Interstate World Travel, 1989-present.

DC Office: 328 CHOB 20515, 202-225-6161; Fax: 202-225-8671; Web site: www.house.gov/baca.

District Office: San Bernardino, 909-885-2222.

Committees: *Agriculture* (9th of 24 D): Department Operations, Oversight, Nutrition & Forestry; Livestock & Horticulture. *Financial Services* (26th of 32 D): Capital Markets, Insurance & Government Sponsored Enterprises; Domestic and International Monetary Policy, Trade & Technology. *Resources* (23d of 24 D).

Group Ratings

	ADA	ACLU	AFS	LCV	CON	ITIC	NTU	COC	ACU	NTLC	CHC
2002	95	73	100	75	17	38	16	42	13	0	8
2001	85	—	100	64	—	—	13	48	24	—	—

National Journal Ratings

	2001 LIB	—	2001 CONS		2002 LIB	—	2002 CONS
Economic	74%	—	27%		67%	—	33%
Social	69%	—	31%		74%	—	19%
Foreign	56%	—	41%		72%	—	26%

Key Votes of the 107th Congress

1. Approve Bush Tax Cuts	*	5. Faith-Based Charities	N	9. Trade Promotion Authority	N
2. Limit Patients' Bill of Rights	N	6. Bar Gays in the Boy Scouts	N	10. Bar Funds for Intl. Court	Y
3. Campaign Finance Reform	Y	7. Ban Partial-Birth Abortion	N	11. Authorize Force in Iraq	N
4. Ban ANWR Development	N	8. Arm Commercial Pilots	Y	12. Deny Home. Sec. Dept. Union	N

Election Results

2002 general	Joe Baca (D)	45,374	(66%)	($511,550)
	Wendy Neighbor (R)	20,821	(30%)	($6,379)
	Other	2,145	(3%)	
2002 primary	Joe Baca (D)	unopposed		
2000 general (CA 42)	Joe Baca (D)	90,585	(60%)	($1,347,431)
	Elia Pirozzi (R)	53,239	(35%)	($831,552)
	Other	7,753	(5%)	

Prior Winning Percentages: 1999 (51%)

The People		Race/Ethnic Origin	Ancestry	
Area size:	193 sq. mi.	23.4% White	German: 4.6%	Irish: 3.4%
Urban population:	99.3%	12.4% Black	English: 3.0%	
Rural population:	0.7%	3.1% Asian	**2000 Presidential Vote**	
Pop. 2000:	639,087	0.4% Native Am.	Gore (D) 76,710	(64%)
Median income:	$37,390	0.3% Hawaiian	Bush (R) 41,272	(34%)
Poverty status:	20.7%	1.9% Two+ races	Other 2,293	(2%)
Military veterans:	8.9%	0.2% Other	**Cook Partisan Voting Index:** D +15	
		58.3% Hispanic Origin		
Occupation	Blue collar: 36.2%	White collar: 46.4%	Gray collar: 17.4%	

The gateway to the Los Angeles Basin for decades was San Bernardino, situated on flat land where the route through the twisting, windy Cajon Pass took passengers on the Santa Fe Railroad and motorists on U.S. 66 from the hot and dusty desert to the greener, tree-lined Los Angeles basin. There were orange groves around the little railroad towns and vineyards to the west; this was an agricultural zone until World War II, when Henry J. Kaiser built the West Coast's first major steel mill between the Santa Fe and Southern Pacific lines in Fontana, just west of San Bernardino. Today, these lands have largely filled up. This Inland Empire, as it is called, may be where the smog piles up against the mountains, but it also has some of the lowest real estate prices in the Los Angeles Basin and an energetic small business economy.

The 43d Congressional District includes most of San Bernardino and Colton and the towns running west—Rialto, Fontana, where many new businesses supplanted the steel mill closed in 1994 (and reassembled in China), and Ontario, with its recently expanded airport. Every year Ontario celebrates the 4th of July at the longest picnic table in the world. Politically this area—and San Bernardino County, in general—trended Republican in the 1980s, as the cultural liberalism of California Democrats repelled family-oriented residents. But as the economy slowed in the early 1990s, and California's growing Latino population and its continuing aversion to Republicans shifted it farther to the left, the district trended to the Democrats. The 2001 redistricting made the district even more Democratic by removing Rancho Cucamonga. The population of the district is now 77% minority and solidly Democratic.

The congressman from the 43d District is Joe Baca, a Democrat who won a November 1999 special election. Baca was born in Belen, New Mexico, the youngest of 15 children. His family moved to Barstow, California, in the desert, when he was four years old. His father worked as a laborer for the Santa Fe Railroad; Baca shined shoes at age 10 and later sold newspapers and worked as a janitor. He served in the Army as a paratrooper during the Vietnam War, but did not see combat. After graduating from California State University at Los Angeles, Baca moved to the San Bernardino area, where he spent 15 years as a community affairs representative for General Telephone and Electric and was elected four times to the San Bernardino Community College board. After two unsuccessful campaigns, he was elected to the Assembly in 1992. Baca was quickly elected speaker pro tempore of the Assembly, becoming the first Latino to serve in this capacity in California. He earned a reputation as a hard worker, introducing more bills than any other member in his first year, but his aggressiveness rubbed some colleagues the wrong way. A moderate to conservative Democrat, he worked to reduce welfare rolls, lower taxes on middle-income earners, and increase penalties for drug dealers. Facing term limits in 1998, he threatened to run in the primary against veteran Congressman George Brown. Instead he ran for the state Senate, spending $2 million to raise his local profile.

His opportunity came in July 1999, when Brown died at age 79 and in his 18th term. His widow Marta Macias Brown ran for the seat. Widows of members had won in 35 of the last 36 such races, but Minority Leader Richard Gephardt refused her request to clear the field, and Baca ran. Baca won the endorsement of organized labor and had a base among Latino voters. Brown attacked Baca for his endorsement by the National Rifle Association. Baca won the all-party primary with 32% of the vote; Brown got 30%, losing by 518 votes. The Republican nominee was real estate developer Elia Pirozzi, who in 1998 lost to Brown 55%–40%. Baca emphasized his centrist voting record and his support for targeted tax cuts, a minimum wage increase and abortion rights. Brown did not endorse Baca. In a light turnout, Baca won 51%–45%.

In the House, Baca had the most conservative voting record of any Latino from California and one of the more conservative voting records of California Democrats. He lobbied for a seat on the Rules Committee, and complained that he had been "bypassed" after Gephardt filled openings there with an African-American from Florida and a white from Massachusetts. He claimed credit for a provision in the 2002 farm bill that restored food stamp benefits to legal immigrants. After extensive review, he opposed the resolution authorizing the use of force in Iraq.

In 2000, former Congressman Jay Kim said he was interested in running for this seat: Kim had pleaded guilty to three misdemeanor charges of accepting illegal campaign contributions in 1997, and was beaten in an adjacent district in the 1998 primary by Gary Miller. Republican party officials urged a reluctant Pirozzi to run a third time. Pirozzi beat Kim 80%–20% in the March primary, and Baca beat Pirozzi 60%–35%. In November 2001, Pirozzi received limited satisfaction when the Federal Election Commission ruled Baca guilty of five violations of campaign financing in his 1999 campaign. The 2001 redistricting made the district significantly more Democratic, and it is unlikely to be seriously contested as it was in the 1990s. In 2002, Baca won 66% against a nurse who spent just $6,400 on the campaign.

FORTY-FOURTH DISTRICT

Rep. Ken Calvert (R)

Elected 1992, 6th term; b. June 8, 1953, Corona; home, Corona; Chaffey Col., 1972–73; San Diego St. U., B.A. 1975; Protestant; divorced.

Professional Career: Restaurant owner, 1975–80; Real estate broker, 1980–92; Chmn., Riverside Cnty. Repub. Party, 1984–88.

DC Office: 2201 RHOB 20515, 202-225-1986; Fax: 202-225-2004; Web site: www.house.gov/calvert.

District Offices: Riverside, 909-784-4300; San Clemente, 949-496-2343.

Committees: *Armed Services* (16th of 33 R): Projection Forces; Readiness. *Resources* (8th of 28 R): Water & Power (Chmn.). *Science* (6th of 25 R): Space & Aeronautics.

Group Ratings

	ADA	ACLU	AFS	LCV	CON	ITIC	NTU	COC	ACU	NTLC	CHC
2002	0	7	0	25	53	88	58	100	92	83	100
2001	0	—	0	0	—	—	62	100	91	—	—

National Journal Ratings

	2001 LIB	—	2001 CONS	2002 LIB	—	2002 CONS
Economic	19%	—	81%	16%	—	81%
Social	20%	—	69%	0%	—	75%
Foreign	33%	—	60%	15%	—	78%

Key Votes of the 107th Congress

1. Approve Bush Tax Cuts	Y	5. Faith-Based Charities	Y	9. Trade Promotion Authority	Y
2. Limit Patients' Bill of Rights	Y	6. Bar Gays in the Boy Scouts	Y	10. Bar Funds for Intl. Court	Y
3. Campaign Finance Reform	N	7. Ban Partial-Birth Abortion	Y	11. Authorize Force in Iraq	Y
4. Ban ANWR Development	N	8. Arm Commercial Pilots	Y	12. Deny Home. Sec. Dept. Union	Y

Election Results

2002 general	Ken Calvert (R)	76,686	(64%)	($643,408)
	Louis Vandenberg (D)	38,021	(32%)	
	Phill Courtney (Green)	5,756	(5%)	
2002 primary	Ken Calvert (R)	30,967	(70%)	
	Martin Collen (R)	11,106	(25%)	
	Khalid Jafri (R)	2,087	(5%)	
2000 general (CA 43)	Ken Calvert (R)	140,201	(74%)	($421,029)
	Bill Reed (Lib)	29,755	(16%)	
	Nat Adam (NL)	20,376	(11%)	

Prior Winning Percentages: 1998 (56%); 1996 (55%); 1994 (55%); 1992 (47%)

The People		Race/Ethnic Origin	Ancestry	
Area size:	549 sq. mi.	51.3% White	German: 9.5%	Irish: 7.0%
Urban population:	97.7%	5.5% Black	English: 6.8%	
Rural population:	2.3%	4.8% Asian	**2000 Presidential Vote**	
Pop. 2000:	639,088	0.5% Native Am.	Bush (R)..............101,897	(53%)
Median income:	$51,578	0.3% Hawaiian	Gore (D)................84,048	(44%)
Poverty status:	12.1%	2.4% Two+ races	Other....................5,143	(3%)
Military veterans:	11.2%	0.2% Other	**Cook Partisan Voting Index:** R + 5	
		35.0% Hispanic Origin		

Occupation	Blue collar: 26.0%	White collar: 59.3%	Gray collar: 14.6%

Riverside was a sleepy town of 34,000, a couple hours' drive from Los Angeles, when Richard and Pat Nixon were married in 1940 in the gaudy Mission Inn, with its bell towers, altars, fountains, rotunda, stained-glass windows and wrought-iron grilles. Riverside was not much larger, with 46,000 people, when Ronald and Nancy Reagan spent their honeymoon at the Mission Inn a dozen years later, in 1952. Riverside then was a citrus center, a market town amid orange groves, where the local agricultural college developed among other things the navel orange. Today the Mission Inn is still doing business, but Riverside has changed completely. The city has expanded to some 255,000 people, and Riverside County, which had 105,000 people in 1940, now has 1.6 million people, more than doubling since 1980. Much of that growth came in the Inland Empire around Riverside, where the flat Los Angeles Basin plains are interrupted by oddly shaped hills and ridges, and the vegetation has an other-worldly air. This has been a boom part of California since the 1980s, where modest-income families found new houses in inexpensive developments and small businesses expanded mightily; it was hit hard by the recession of the early 1990s but rebounded with strong growth.

The 44th Congressional District, which covers this area, has been one of the fastest-growing congressional districts in the nation in the past two decades. This was a newly created district in 1992. Some 40% of its residents live in the city of Riverside and most others in nearby towns like Corona and Norco. The 2001 redistricting removed the Riverside County area around Lake Elsinore and added the eastern edge of Orange County all the way to the ocean, much of it uninhabited mountainsides but also including San Clemente, where Richard Nixon lived after he resigned the presidency, and half of San Juan Capistrano, to which the swallows famously return on the same day each spring. Overall this is a Republican district.

The congressman from the 44th District is Ken Calvert, a Republican first elected in 1992. Calvert grew up in Corona; during college, he was a congressional intern at the Senate Watergate hearings of 1973. Later, he ran the family restaurant back home and in 1980 entered the commercial real estate business. In 1982, at 29, he ran for Congress in a district that included almost all the geographic expanse of Riverside County and lost a nine-candidate primary to Al McCandless by 868 votes. In 1992 he ran in a new district and won the primary with 28% of the vote. His Democratic opponent was Mark Takano, an eighth grade teacher with institutional support from teachers' unions and financial support from Japanese Americans. In a district where George H.W. Bush beat Bill Clinton by 797 votes, Calvert beat Takano by 519 votes.

In the House, Calvert has compiled a conservative voting record. But he ran into trouble back home soon after he was elected, when the Riverside *Press-Enterprise* reported that he had been stopped by police with a convicted prostitute in his car; Calvert apologized, and said that he was upset because his wife had divorced him the month before and his father had recently committed suicide. It was, as he said, "an extremely embarrassing situation," of which his opponents rushed to take advantage. Calvert won the 1994 primary 51%–49%, with only an 884-vote margin, against business professor Joseph Khoury. Takano, running again in the general, ran an ad with the song "The Liar" and accused him of "flagrant womanizing." But the Republican tide of the year showed up in the election results, with Calvert winning by a thumping 55%–38%.

Since 1995, Calvert has been a subcommittee chairman. In 1997, as chairman of the Energy and Environment Subcommittee of Science, he opposed the Clinton administration's support of the global warming protocol then being negotiated in Kyoto, Japan. Since 2001, Calvert has chaired the Water and Power Subcommittee at Resources, which distributes public works projects. He spent many months in committee building support for reauthorization of the vital water supply program (CALFED) for California's Central Valley, as part of a broader water resources package. He got committee approval, but had difficulty amassing a majority: many states were demanding more local projects; environmental restriction advocates complained that the bill was too favorable to farmers. The Republican leadership refused to bring the bill to the floor. Calvert was one of several contenders seeking to chair the Resources Committee in 2003, but he lost to fellow Californian Richard Pombo, who was backed by Tom DeLay; he kept the Water and Power chairmanship.

Calvert got passage in 2000 of a bill barring the Treasury Department from displaying Social Security numbers on checks. In 2001 he joined the Armed Services Committee, where he advocated the interests of local defense contractors and March Air Reserve Base in Riverside. He voted against the 2002 farm bill as too costly and tilted toward the Midwest and South.

Calvert has had opposition in the last three primaries. In 1998 he again faced Khoury, who argued that both Calvert and Bill Clinton "have shown they lack the common decency, sense of right and wrong, concern for the truth and respect for women that the rest of us learned as children." Calvert won 56%–35%. In 2000 and 2002 he was opposed in the primary by Riverside physician Martin Collen, who touted his family values and loaned his 2002 campaign $280,000. Calvert won 58%–25% in 2000 and 70%–25% in 2002. In early 2003 he said he would not keep his 1992 pledge to serve only 12 years.

FORTY-FIFTH DISTRICT

Rep. Mary Bono (R)

Elected April 1998, 3d term; b. Oct. 24, 1961, Cleveland, OH; home, Palm Springs; U. of S. CA, B.F.A. 1984; Protestant; married (Glenn Baxley).

Professional Career: Gen. Mgr., Bono restaurant, 1986–90.

DC Office: 404 CHOB 20515, 202-225-5330; Fax: 202-225-2961; Web site: www.house.gov/bono.

District Offices: Hemet, 909-658-2312; Palm Springs, 760-320-1076.

Committees: *Energy & Commerce* (24th of 31 R): Commerce, Trade & Consumer Protection; Energy & Air Quality; Environment & Hazardous Materials; Telecommunications & The Internet.

Group Ratings

	ADA	ACLU	AFS	LCV	CON	ITIC	NTU	COC	ACU	NTLC	CHC
2002	10	27	0	25	8	100	48	95	71	78	75
2001	15	—	0	0	—	—	63	100	68	—	—

National Journal Ratings

	2001 LIB	—	2001 CONS		2002 LIB	—	2002 CONS
Economic	7%	—	89%		39%	—	61%
Social	49%	—	51%		49%	—	51%
Foreign	49%	—	47%		41%	—	56%

Key Votes of the 107th Congress

1. Approve Bush Tax Cuts	Y	5. Faith-Based Charities	Y	9. Trade Promotion Authority	Y
2. Limit Patients' Bill of Rights	Y	6. Bar Gays in the Boy Scouts	Y	10. Bar Funds for Intl. Court	Y
3. Campaign Finance Reform	Y	7. Ban Partial-Birth Abortion	Y	11. Authorize Force in Iraq	Y
4. Ban ANWR Development	N	8. Arm Commercial Pilots	Y	12. Deny Home. Sec. Dept. Union	Y

Election Results

2002 general	Mary Bono (R)	87,101	(65%)	($582,769)
	Elle Kurpiewski (D)	43,692	(33%)	($312,387)
	Other	2,740	(2%)	
2002 primary	Mary Bono (R)	unopposed		
2000 general (CA 44)	Mary Bono (R)	123,738	(59%)	($582,684)
	Ron Oden (D)	79,302	(38%)	($124,866)
	Other	6,147	(3%)	

Prior Winning Percentages: 1998 (60%); 1998 (64%)

The People		**Race/Ethnic Origin**	**Ancestry**	
Area size:	6,062 sq. mi.	50.1% White	German: 8.9%	English: 7.1%
Urban population:	89.9%	6.3% Black	Irish: 6.6%	
Rural population:	10.1%	2.8% Asian	**2000 Presidential Vote**	
Pop. 2000:	639,088	0.6% Native Am.	Bush (R) 93,802 (51%)	
Median income:	$40,468	0.2% Hawaiian	Gore (D) 85,427 (47%)	
Poverty status:	15.0%	1.9% Two+ races	Other 4,029 (2%)	
Military veterans:	14.5%	0.1% Other	**Cook Partisan Voting Index:** R + 3	
		38.0% Hispanic Origin		

Occupation	Blue collar: 23.1%	White collar: 53.2%	Gray collar: 23.7%

From the air two decades ago, a night flight east from Los Angeles showed the lights of 10 million persons' streets and houses and then almost perfect darkness: a vast metropolis surrounded by almost uninhabited territory. Today the sprinkled pattern of white lights has spread into the Inland Empire around Riverside and San Bernardino and is multiplying outward into the desert. The

Inland Empire has filled up with instant towns like family-oriented Moreno Valley, which did not exist in 1980 and had 142,000 people in 2000. Over the 10,000-foot San Jacinto Mountains, desert communities have boomed: Palm Springs, once the lone winter resort for the stars, is now one of a string of communities along Highway 111 and Frank Sinatra and Bob Hope Drives. Among rich retirees, the vogue for the coast lessened as beach cities filled up with roller bladers and rent control crusaders; the clean, dry, roomy desert, where the days are almost always crystal clear and the sky usually blue and cloudless, became more attractive, and, with everything air-conditioned, a comfortable year-round home. The population is about 240,000 for the entire corridor if you count Indio and Coachella, the heavily Latino cities in the agricultural Coachella Valley, which has 75% of the country's date palms and features camel races at its annual date festival. Two presidents retired to the desert here: Dwight Eisenhower in Palm Desert for the winters and Gerald Ford in nearby Rancho Mirage.

The 45th Congressional District covers almost all the desert in Riverside County from Blythe on the Nevada border to Palm Springs. But about half its population lives west of the 10,000 foot peak that looms above Palm Springs, in fast-growing Moreno Valley and Murrieta and in the old town of Hemet surrounded by surreal landscape. This area tends to vote Republican, but not by large margins; George W. Bush won 51% of the vote here in 2000.

The congresswoman from the 45th District is Mary Bono, who won the seat in April 1998 after the death by her husband Sonny Bono, onetime showbiz celebrity and mayor of Palm Springs. He was on a family vacation when he died in a skiing accident in South Lake Tahoe, California. Mary Bono was strongly encouraged to run for the seat by House Republican leaders who believed that only she could avert a divisive Republican primary and that she had the best chance to hold the seat. She grew up as Mary Whitaker in South Pasadena, where she was an accomplished gymnast; she remains a fitness buff, a certified personal fitness instructor who has studied karate and Tae Kwan Do. They met when she was celebrating her college graduation at his Los Angeles restaurant in 1984; they were married two years later. Before her campaign, she had no political experience and was little known in Washington. In the special election, she faced actor Ralph Waite, best known as "Pa" Walton in *The Waltons*. Waite was hurt during the brief campaign because he kept a commitment to play Willy Loman in *Death of a Salesman* six times a week in a New Jersey theater. The campaign's biggest controversy came when Sonny's 83-year-old mother said that her son would have opposed Mary's candidacy, preferring that she care for their children. But it was no contest. Bono won 64%–29%, a bigger margin than Sonny's two victories.

Bono has a moderate voting record, especially on social and foreign issues; the least conservative voting record of California Republicans. Her initial legislative priority was passage of Sonny's bill to restore the Salton Sea, an artificial body of water in the desert created when a canal burst in 1905; it has been shrinking in recent decades, increasing the salinity of the water and the pollution from agricultural runoff. Although some Democrats objected to taking funds from other California projects, Mary Bono secured $13.4 million for what became the Sonny Bono Salton Sea National Wildlife Refuge. As the only female Republican on the Judiciary Committee and the panel's most junior member, this non-lawyer played a visible role in the impeachment inquiry. *Newsweek* said, "Bono was citizen Jane—the everywoman in a room of blowhards." She voted for impeachment. In 2001 she won a seat on the Energy and Commerce Committee, where she worked on a bill to require companies to expense their employee stock options. To the 2002 farm bill she added a provision requiring that imported fruits and vegetables must have country-of-origin labels. She won $14.2 million for the Torres-Martinez Desert Cahuilla Indians, a tribe that lost much of its land after the Salton Sea flooded much of its reservation; the tribe also got 11,000 acres in the desert plus prime location for a casino.

Bono has been easily reelected. In 2002 she won 65%–33% against a Democrat who spent $312,000. She has been mentioned as a possible candidate for Barbara Boxer's Senate seat in 2004. There would be a certain piquancy to that: Sonny Bono ran for the seat in 1992, and finished third in the Republican primary. But in mid 2003 there were no signs she was interested in running.

FORTY-SIXTH DISTRICT

Rep. Dana Rohrabacher (R)

Elected 1988, 8th term; b. June 21, 1947, Coronado; home, Huntington Beach; Long Beach St. Col. B.A. 1969, U. of S. CA, M.A. 1975; Baptist; married (Rhonda).

Professional Career: Radio & print journalist, 1970–80; Sr. Speechwriter, Special Asst. to Pres. Reagan, 1981–88.

DC Office: 2338 RHOB 20515, 202-225-2415; Fax: 202-225-0145; Web site: www.house.gov/rohrabacher.

District Office: Huntington Beach, 714-960-6483.

Committees: *International Relations* (9th of 26 R): Asia & the Pacific; International Terrorism, Nonproliferation and Human Rights. *Science* (4th of 25 R): Research; Space & Aeronautics (Chmn.).

Group Ratings

	ADA	ACLU	AFS	LCV	CON	ITIC	NTU	COC	ACU	NTLC	CHC
2002	5	13	11	25	97	62	64	85	96	86	92
2001	10	—	0	7	—	—	79	78	96	—	—

National Journal Ratings

	2001 LIB	—	2001 CONS		2002 LIB	—	2002 CONS
Economic	7%	—	89%		21%	—	73%
Social	42%	—	58%		39%	—	57%
Foreign	33%	—	60%		47%	—	51%

Key Votes of the 107th Congress

1. Approve Bush Tax Cuts	Y	5. Faith-Based Charities	Y	9. Trade Promotion Authority	Y
2. Limit Patients' Bill of Rights	Y	6. Bar Gays in the Boy Scouts	Y	10. Bar Funds for Intl. Court	Y
3. Campaign Finance Reform	N	7. Ban Partial-Birth Abortion	Y	11. Authorize Force in Iraq	Y
4. Ban ANWR Development	N	8. Arm Commercial Pilots	Y	12. Deny Home. Sec. Dept. Union	Y

Election Results

2002 general	Dana Rohrabacher (R)	108,807	(62%)	($380,008)
	Gerrie Schipske (D)	60,890	(35%)	($228,084)
	Keith Gann (Lib)	6,488	(4%)	
2002 primary	Dana Rohrabacher (R)	unopposed		
2000 general (CA 45)	Dana Rohrabacher (R)	136,275	(62%)	($300,724)
	Ted Crisell (D)	71,066	(32%)	($52,674)
	Don Hull (Lib)	8,409	(4%)	
	Other	3,635	(2%)	

Prior Winning Percentages: 1998 (59%); 1996 (61%); 1994 (69%); 1992 (55%); 1990 (59%); 1988 (64%)

The People		Race/Ethnic Origin	Ancestry	
Area size:	825 sq. mi.	62.8% White	German: 10.7%	English: 8.5%
Urban population:	99.9%	1.4% Black	Irish: 8.4%	
Rural population:	0.1%	15.4% Asian	**2000 Presidential Vote**	
Pop. 2000:	639,088	0.3% Native Am.	Bush (R)..............145,729 (55%)	
Median income:	$61,567	0.3% Hawaiian	Gore (D)..............110,984 (42%)	
Poverty status:	7.8%	2.6% Two+ races	Other....................9,413 (4%)	
Military veterans:	11.3%	0.2% Other	**Cook Partisan Voting Index:** R + 7	
		16.9% Hispanic Origin		

Occupation	Blue collar: 15.4%	White collar: 72.7%	Gray collar: 11.9%

In the 1950s, when the Beach Boys were at Hawthorne High School, surfers would drive far down the coast to the vast expanse of Huntington Beach in Orange County to catch a wave. This was empty country then, vegetable fields and orange groves, with nary a freeway or shopping center in sight. Today a long stretch of the beach itself is eerily empty, with swampland across the highway where surfers' pickups are parked, but the rest of Orange County is pretty much filled in. Huntington Beach is a city of 190,000, a mixture of family subdivisions and garden apartments and home of the International Surfing Museum. To the north is Westminster, the center of the nation's largest Vietnamese-American community, with miles of malls where all the shops have Vietnamese names and the area has its own Vietnamese-language daily newspaper. Southeast along San Diego Freeway is Fountain Valley, the central focus of many Asian-owned high-tech businesses, an engine of Southern California growth. Near the coast is Costa Mesa, site of South Coast Plaza's luxury stores. Out on the beach in Huntington Beach you can see the curving coastline to the west, past the port of Los Angeles and Long Beach to where the mountains of the seismically active and economically upscale Palos Verdes Peninsula rise above the water.

The 46th Congressional District includes all this beachfront plus the Long Beach Harbor area and the Palos Verdes Peninsula. It also includes territory inland: the eastern end of Long Beach and next-door Seal Beach, areas settled by many retirees, most of Westminster, all of Fountain Valley, Costa Mesa, the southwest corner of Santa Ana and a tiny slice of Los Angeles. Over most of the distance the eastern part of the district is connected to the Palos Verdes Peninsula by just a thin strip of beach or the port area. Politically, the two ends of the district connected by this narrow corridor are solidly Republican. The most competitive areas are in Long Beach and Westminster. But the Vietnamese here are mostly conservative, angry at America—not for going into Vietnam but for leaving it. This is no longer the monoracial Orange County of the 1960s: the district's population is 17% Hispanic and 15% Asian.

The congressman from the 46th District is Dana Rohrabacher, a Republican first elected in 1988. Rohrabacher calls himself a surfer Republican and sports an American flag surfboard. He grew up in southern California, went to college and experimented with drugs, and once had a folk band called the Goldwaters. He was a press aide in the 1976 and 1980 Reagan presidential campaigns, wrote editorials for the *Orange County Register* and was a speechwriter in the Reagan White House. He returned to Southern California in 1988 when Long Beach-based Congressman Dan Lungren decided not to run again (Lungren was elected attorney general in 1990 but lost for governor in 1998). Rohrabacher, with fundraising help from Oliver North, won the primary with 35% of the vote, to 22% for an Orange County supervisor and 20% for Steve Horn, who later represented a Long Beach-based district from 1992 to 2002. After redistricting in 1992, Rohrabacher tussled with Robert Dornan and won, running in this heavily Republican district while Dornan ran and later lost in the marginal district inland.

A self-styled free spirit, Rohrabacher likes to make waves in the House. His Web site once featured the motto: "Fighting for freedom and having fun." His voting record can be unpredictable, especially on cultural issues. That helps to explain why he remains assigned to second-level committees, but he has made the most of his opportunities. As chairman of the Science Subcommittee on Space and Aeronautics, he worked for the single-stage-to-orbit vehicle. After the *Columbia* disaster in February 2003, he quickly noted that he had raised questions about the safety of the aging space shuttle. He strongly opposes illegal immigration, which he says is "going to bankrupt America," and he sharply criticized as "a betrayal of American workers" the policy of giving 600,000 skilled foreign workers temporary visas in the United States.

Rohrabacher has often, but not always, supported restrictions on trade. Opposition to international trade has been a frequent theme. He has been a long-time critic of China's rulers and strongly opposed PNTR. In 2001, the House soundly defeated his attempts to block expanded trade with China and Vietnam. Despite the Bush administration's criticism that it would violate the peace treaty, he won House passage of his amendment to allow World War II prisoners of war to sue Japanese companies for enslaving them. In July 2002, after a lengthy delay while he paced the House floor, he cast one of the final votes that secured the passage by one vote of trade promotion authority. Soon after the September 11 attacks, Rohrabacher, who worked closely with Afghan rebels when he was a White House aide, met the exiled King of Afghanistan in Rome, encouraged him to return to Kabul and promised that the United States would oust the Taliban and help rebuild Afghanistan. He visited liberated Afghanistan in April 2002 and complained that the Pentagon imposed too many limits on his visit. This was not his first visit to the war-torn country. In November 1988, he traveled with a mujahedeen militia unit for one week; "Half of our group was napalmed," he says. With Barney Frank, he unsuccessfully sought to change the House rule that restricts members from discussing or characterizing actions in the Senate.

Rohrabacher has been routinely reelected by wide margins. The 2001 redistricting removed territory in Orange County, including very affluent and Republican Newport Beach, and added Long Beach and the Palos Verdes Peninsula, the latter just as affluent but not quite so Republican. In 2002 his Democratic opponent was Gerrie Schipske, a nurse-practitioner and attorney who lost to Republican Steve Horn in 2000 in the old 38th District by only 48%–47%. But this was a much less Democratic district; Schipske raised only one-third as much money as in 2000, and Rohrabacher won 62%–35%.

FORTY-SEVENTH DISTRICT

Rep. Loretta Sanchez (D)

Elected 1996, 4th term; b. Jan. 7, 1960, Lynwood; home, Santa Ana; Chapman U., B.A. 1982, American U., M.B.A. 1984; Catholic; married (Stephen Brixey).

Professional Career: Mgr. & Financial Analyst, Orange Cnty. Transp. Auth., 1984–87; Asst. Vice Pres., Fieldman, Rolapp & Assoc., 1987–90; Assoc., Booz, Allen & Hamilton, 1990–93; Principal, Amiga Advisors.

DC Office: 1230 LHOB 20515, 202-225-2965; Fax: 202-225-5859; Web site: www.house.gov/sanchez.

District Office: Garden Grove, 714-621-0102.

Committees: *Armed Services* (12th of 29 D): Strategic Forces; Total Force. *Select Committee on Homeland Security* (3d of 23 D): Cybersecurity, Science and Research & Development; Infrastructure & Border Security (RMM); Rules.

Group Ratings

	ADA	ACLU	AFS	LCV	CON	ITIC	NTU	COC	ACU	NTLC	CHC
2002	100	87	100	100	79	25	25	32	4	20	8
2001	90	—	100	100	—	—	21	32	12	—	—

National Journal Ratings

	2001 LIB — 2001 CONS		2002 LIB — 2002 CONS	
Economic	62%	— 39%	69%	— 30%
Social	74%	— 23%	71%	— 28%
Foreign	67%	— 32%	77%	— 19%

Key Votes of the 107th Congress

1. Approve Bush Tax Cuts	N	5. Faith-Based Charities	N	9. Trade Promotion Authority	N
2. Limit Patients' Bill of Rights	N	6. Bar Gays in the Boy Scouts	N	10. Bar Funds for Intl. Court	N
3. Campaign Finance Reform	Y	7. Ban Partial-Birth Abortion	N	11. Authorize Force in Iraq	N
4. Ban ANWR Development	Y	8. Arm Commercial Pilots	Y	12. Deny Home. Sec. Dept. Union	N

Election Results

2002 general	Loretta Sanchez (D)	42,501	(61%)	($1,290,368)
	Jeff Chavez (R)	24,346	(35%)	($47,054)
	Paul Marsden (Lib)	2,944	(4%)	
2002 primary	Loretta Sanchez (D)	unopposed		
2000 general (CA 46)	Loretta Sanchez (D)	70,381	(60%)	($1,640,175)
	Gloria Matta Tuchman (R)	40,928	(35%)	($296,060)
	Other	5,599	(5%)	

Prior Winning Percentages: 1998 (56%); 1996 (47%)

The People		Race/Ethnic Origin	Ancestry	
Area size:	55 sq. mi.	17.3% White	German: 3.5%	Irish: 2.5%
Urban population:	100.0%	1.5% Black	English: 2.3%	
Rural population:	0.0%	13.9% Asian	**2000 Presidential Vote**	
Pop. 2000:	639,087	0.3% Native Am.	Gore (D) 59,515	(56%)
Median income:	$41,618	0.4% Hawaiian	Bush (R) 43,752	(41%)
Poverty status:	19.1%	1.3% Two + races	Other 2,257	(2%)
Military veterans:	5.2%	0.1% Other	**Cook Partisan Voting Index:** D + 7	
		65.3% Hispanic Origin		

Occupation	Blue collar: 37.9%	White collar: 40.9%	Gray collar: 21.2%

When Walt Disney began planning Disneyland in the late 1940s, he did not have to drive far from downtown Los Angeles before arriving at agricultural land. Dairy farms and orange groves covered most of southeast Los Angeles County and adjacent Orange County, which had only 216,000 people in 1950. As Disneyland opened there in 1955 and became a vast success, the area around it—a mass of flat land surrounded by mountains and sea—found itself directly in the path of the most explosively growing metropolitan area in the United States. Orange County's population rose to 703,000 in 1960, 1.4 million in 1970, 1.9 million in 1980, 2.4 million in 1990, 2.8 million in 2000. It is now the nation's fifth-largest county, just a bit ahead of San Diego County.

Just as Orange County was once transformed by newcomers from Los Angeles County and the Midwest, so it is again being transformed by immigrants, from Mexico and other parts of Latin America, and from Vietnam, Taiwan, Korea and other parts of East Asia. By 1990 the county's population was 23% Hispanic and 10% Asian; in 2000, the figures are 31% Hispanic and 14% Asian. Some of these new Orange County residents are direct migrants: Santa Ana, the county seat, is a major arrival point for immigrants from Mexico, and its population 76% Hispanic. Others have moved out along the freeways, like so many southern Californians before them, working hard at jobs, commuting on freeways and living in stucco subdivisions like anyone else. There are concentrations in various places—Latinos in Santa Ana and much of Anaheim, Vietnamese in Westminster and Garden Grove—but many of these new Californians are just speckled through the county. These changes have made for some political wobble, but until the mid-1990s not very much: Asians were split between the parties and few Latinos were registered to vote. Between 1994 and 2000, many more Latinos have been voting, and voting increasingly Democratic, while the fragmentary available evidence suggests Asians have voted increasingly for Democrats too. Latino turnout apparently dipped in 2002, when many Democrats were disillusioned with Governor Gray Davis and the legislature's Democratic Hispanic caucus declined to endorse him.

The 47th Congressional District is the geographic heart of Orange County. About half its people live in Santa Ana, in neighborhoods full of large families and many workers. The district includes most of Garden Grove, with many Latinos and Vietnamese, and most of Anaheim, with many Latinos. It includes many Orange County landmarks—Anaheim Stadium, Disneyland and Disney's California Adventure, opened in 2001. The population of the district is 65% Hispanic and 14% Asian (primarily Vietnamese). This core area has always been the most Democratic part of Orange County; the movement of Latinos to Democrats has made it more Democratic. But it is not overwhelmingly Democratic like most majority-Hispanic districts in Los Angeles County; George W. Bush got 41% of the vote here in 2000 and in 2002 the district gave Governor Gray Davis only a 51%–40% margin.

The congresswoman from the 47th District is Loretta Sanchez, a Democrat first elected in 1996. Sanchez was raised in Anaheim by Mexican immigrant parents and graduated from Chapman University in Orange. She worked as a financial analyst, providing advice to public agencies and private businesses; she established her own firm in the early 1990s. For a time she and her husband lived in affluent Palos Verdes Estates, far from Orange County, but in 1994 she ran for the city council in Anaheim under her married name, Loretta Sanchez-Brixey, and lost. In 1996, she ran for the House against one of the loudest voices of American conservatism, Robert Dornan. In the primary against three Anglo male Democrats, she won with 35% of the vote.

Her primary victory attracted little attention, not even from Dornan. But she shrewdly counted on increasing Latino turnout. Sanchez calculated that she could attract contributions from the many enemies that Dornan had made over a political career that went back to 1976 and included a quixotic presidential campaign that took him far from Orange County during 1995 and 1996. The campaign was acrimonious: Dornan would not debate Sanchez; Sanchez's husband tore down two Dornan signs and was fined $640. Bill Clinton came to Santa Ana late in the campaign to stump for Sanchez, and may have made the difference. She won by 984 votes, 47%–46%. In reply to great cheering in the White House and many liberal precincts came bellows of rage from Dornan and charges of vote fraud. Dornan brought his case to the House Contested Elections Task Force, which issued many subpoenas. Using the privileges afforded to former members, he regularly appeared on the House floor trying to convince his former colleagues to call for a special election; Democrats charged that he was abusing his privileges by promoting a personal agenda and the House voted to bar him from the floor after a heated discussion between Dornan and New Jersey Democrat Bob Menendez. Finally, in February 1998 the House Administration Committee upheld Sanchez's victory.

When Dornan sought vindication in the 1998 election, dubious Republican leaders sought a less controversial candidate and backed lawyer Lisa Hughes. But Dornan won the primary by 49%–27%. He did not have a chance against Sanchez: Latino registration was up, and she had become a Spanish language media celebrity and the third-biggest fundraiser in the House that year. She won by 56%–39%, and Dornan retired to talk radio.

After the election Sanchez was named general co-chairwoman of the Democratic National Committee to lead a Hispanic voter registration drive, and Al Gore tapped her as honorary chair of his political action committee. But that proved a mixed blessing for both Sanchez and her party. She scheduled a fundraiser during the 2000 Democratic National Convention at Hugh Hefner's Playboy Mansion. Gore and many House Democrats—including other Latinos, from whom she has kept her distance—were not amused and said that she was undermining the party's image. At first quietly, then more bluntly, she was urged to choose a new site and warned that she was jeopardizing her rise up the party ladder. Belatedly she relented and moved the event to Universal Studio's City Walk. "In her self-absorption and her unpredictable and at times even loopy behavior," the *Orange County Register* noted, Sanchez had become "eerily akin" to Dornan.

In the House, Sanchez's voting record leaned to the middle. Accompanying Clinton on his November 2000 visit to Vietnam, she met with dissidents to discuss human rights. Along with James Sensenbrenner, she filed the first resolutions calling for the expulsion of James Traficant after his criminal conviction. Sanchez's independence seemed to play well at home; she was reelected by wide margins in 2000 and 2002. In 2002 she angered some Latino Democrats when she worked hard to elect her sister Linda Sanchez in the new 39th District. That may not be her only foray into politics beyond the 47th District; ever ambitious, Sanchez has said that she might like to be a senator some day.

FORTY-EIGHTH DISTRICT

Rep. Christopher Cox (R)

Elected 1988, 8th term; b. Oct. 16, 1952, St. Paul, MN; home, Newport Beach; U. of S. CA, B.A. 1973, Harvard U., M.B.A., J.D., 1977; Catholic; married (Rebecca).

Professional Career: Clerk, U.S. Court of Appeals, Judge Herbert Choy, 1977–78; Practicing atty., 1978–86; Lecturer, Harvard Bus. Schl., 1982–83; Sr. Assoc. Cnsl., White House, 1986–88.

DC Office: 2402 RHOB 20515, 202-225-5611; Fax: 202-225-9177; Web site: www.house.gov/cox.

District Office: Newport Beach, 949-756-2244.

Committees: *Republican Policy Committee Chairman. Energy & Commerce* (8th of 31 R): Energy & Air Quality; Telecommunications & The Internet. *Select Committee on Homeland Security* (Chmn. of 27 R).

Group Ratings

	ADA	ACLU	AFS	LCV	CON	ITIC	NTU	COC	ACU	NTLC	CHC
2002	0	7	0	38	97	88	64	89	96	100	100
2001	5	—	0	0	—	—	74	91	96	—	—

National Journal Ratings

	2001 LIB	—	2001 CONS		2002 LIB	—	2002 CONS
Economic	0%	—	94%		34%	—	66%
Social	32%	—	67%		30%	—	68%
Foreign	27%	—	74%		34%	—	65%

Key Votes of the 107th Congress

1. Approve Bush Tax Cuts	Y	5. Faith-Based Charities	Y	9. Trade Promotion Authority	Y
2. Limit Patients' Bill of Rights	Y	6. Bar Gays in the Boy Scouts	Y	10. Bar Funds for Intl. Court	Y
3. Campaign Finance Reform	N	7. Ban Partial-Birth Abortion	Y	11. Authorize Force in Iraq	Y
4. Ban ANWR Development	N	8. Arm Commercial Pilots	Y	12. Deny Home. Sec. Dept. Union	Y

Election Results

2002 general	Christopher Cox (R)	122,884	(68%)	($736,225)
	John Graham (D)	51,058	(28%)	($10,030)
	Other	5,607	(3%)	
2002 primary	Christopher Cox (R)	84,229	(89%)	
	David Cobert (R)	6,367	(7%)	
	Dave Forman (R)	3,654	(4%)	
2000 general (CA 47)	Christopher Cox (R)	181,365	(66%)	($1,171,803)
	John Graham (D)	83,186	(30%)	($17,922)
	Other	11,850	(4%)	

Prior Winning Percentages: 1998 (68%); 1996 (66%); 1994 (72%); 1992 (65%); 1990 (68%); 1988 (67%)

The People		Race/Ethnic Origin	Ancestry	
Area size:	301 sq. mi.	68.0% White	German: 11.3%	English: 9.3%
Urban population:	99.9%	1.4% Black	Irish: 8.3%	
Rural population:	0.1%	12.7% Asian	**2000 Presidential Vote**	
Pop. 2000:	639,087	0.2% Native Am.	Bush (R) 156,340	(58%)
Median income:	$69,663	0.2% Hawaiian	Gore (D) 106,809	(39%)
Poverty status:	6.3%	2.7% Two+ races	Other 7,421	(3%)
Military veterans:	10.3%	0.2% Other	**Cook Partisan Voting Index:** R +10	
		14.7% Hispanic Origin		
Occupation	Blue collar: 10.1%	White collar: 79.8%	Gray collar: 10.1%	

If you drove south on the Santa Ana and San Diego Freeways in Orange County 30 years ago, once you got past Santa Ana and John Wayne Airport you would have found yourself in open land for the next 25 miles, a vacant landscape of flat plains and low mountains, all beneath the 4,600-foot Trabuco Peak in the distance. This was the land of the Irvine Ranch, purchased by Gold Rush merchant James Irvine from the Sepulveda and Yorba families and maintained as a ranch until the early 1970s, the last large plot of vacant land in metro Los Angeles. Irvine sold some of it to create the cities of Santa Ana and Tustin, but in the 1970s there was still this great swath of land, 10 miles along the Pacific Coast and 22 miles inland to the mountains, where the freeway traveler could see what the California the first American settlers saw looked like. But as Orange County grew up to the limits of the Irvine Ranch, the Irvine family realized that they owned immensely valuable land. In 1959 they donated a site for the University of California at Irvine and in the 1970s they sold the rest of the property to developers. The resulting city of Irvine was a planned community, with eight-lane parkways, huge office parks and shopping malls and attractive subdivisions and condominiums. Irvine has attracted high-tech and high-growth businesses, highly educated and affluent people, including Asian immigrants; in 2000, 10% of its 143,000 residents were Chinese, enough to support a Chinese supermarket and a Chinese-language library. Irvine is one planned city that respects free market economics; the new expressways on the Irvine Ranch land were built by private companies and paid for by tolls. Now Irvine is deciding what to do with its last piece of undeveloped territory, the El Toro Marine Corps Air Station that closed in 1999. In March 2002 Orange County voted against using it as an airport and instead to develop it as a Great Park.

Irvine is set amid a raft of affluent communities, except for low-income and 76% Hispanic Santa Ana (the 48th has a small portion of the city). To the north is Tustin, an older town built on Irvine land. To the south is Newport Beach, one of California's richest cities; Newport Harbor is chock full of expensive boats. To the east is Lake Forest; the name used to be El Toro, although now some residents complain that it has few lakes or forests. To the southeast, on the Ocean is Laguna Beach with its art galleries and cute shops, and more conventionally affluent Dana Point. Inland are new affluent communities—Laguna Niguel, Laguna Hills, Laguna Woods.

The 48th Congressional District is centered geographically on the Irvine Ranch lands and includes all of these communities. Politically, this is a conservative area, and for a long time it was one of the most Republican districts in the United States. In the 1990s, like most of metro Los Angeles, it trended to the Democrats, but it is still very Republican. In 2000, 58% of its votes were cast for George W. Bush.

The congressman from the 48th District is Christopher Cox, a Republican first elected in 1988. Cox grew up in St. Paul, Minnesota, graduated from the University of Southern California in three years, went to Harvard Law and Business Schools jointly, clerked for a Ninth Circuit judge in Hawaii, practiced law at a big firm in Orange County, then was part of the Reagan White House counsel's staff. In fall 1987 he had lunch in the White House Mess with Dana Rohrabacher, then a speechwriter. Cox told him that Orange County Congressman Robert Badham had announced he was retiring; Rohrabacher said Dan Lungren was vacating his Long Beach seat. That day they decided to run for the seats. Cox was one of 14 Republican candidates for the safe Republican seat. With the support of Oliver North, Robert Bork and members of the Irvine family, he won the primary with 31% of the vote. He has since won primary and general elections without difficulty. Cox's intellect and range of interests are impressive: from the former Soviet Union (he and his father published an English translation of *Pravda* from 1984–88) to lobbying for more local control of highway funds.

With the Republican victory in 1994, Cox came into his own, becoming chairman of the Republican Policy Committee and a leading legislator on many fronts. On the first day of the new Congress, he led the move to end baseline budgeting, which typically had given each agency and department either an inflation increase or the previous year's increase, whichever was higher, and an opportunity to argue for even more: this practically insured that government grew faster than the private economy. His radical idea was to state budget totals in dollar terms, so that an increase is an increase and a cut is a cut. Another specialty is tort reform. He wrote the securities litigation reform to prevent predatory suits against high-tech and other companies, which got two-thirds support in both houses and was the only bill passed over Bill Clinton's veto in his first term. His bill to limit appeals of death penalties became law in April 1995. With Democratic Senator Ron Wyden of Oregon, he won enactment in 1998 of an important proposal for the emerging marketplace— the Internet Tax Freedom Act, which placed a three-year moratorium on state and local governments from imposing special taxes on electronic commerce. It was renewed for two years in November 2001. In January 2003 Cox and Wyden sponsored a bill to make it permanent. Cox has sponsored another Internet-related bill, to create an Office of Global Internet Freedom in the Board of International Broadcasting, to monitor state censorship of the Internet, to deploy technology to defeat efforts to block access to sites and to keep track of companies which sell China and other dictatorships technology to block sites.

He also chaired the special committee investigating technology transfers from U.S. companies to China. Thanks to Cox and ranking Democrat Norman Dicks, this investigation was conducted on a bipartisan basis, without leaks, and produced a unanimous report documenting an extensive operation by China to acquire military technology, including nuclear weapons design, by groups with links to the Chinese military or state intelligence service. It faulted the policies of the Reagan, Bush and Clinton administrations; Cox won much bipartisan praise over his handling of the report.

Cox wrote a thesis at Harvard in 1977 on double taxation of corporate dividends, and beginning in 1992 he has sponsored bills to end double taxation. He welcomed George W. Bush's proposal to do just that in January 2003. He has called on Bush to index the capital gains tax, which he argues can be done administratively. In 2002 he and Barbara Boxer sponsored a bill to allow parents to deduct unpaid child support payments from their income and would force parents who don't pay child support to declare the unpaid child support as income.

After the September 11 attacks, some members and scholar Norman Ornstein speculated about what would have happened if United flight 93 had not been downed in Pennsylvania but had struck the Capitol: hundreds of congressmen and senators might have been killed or disabled. Vacancies in the Senate can be filled by gubernatorial appointments of successors, but under the Constitution vacancies in the House can be filled only by elections, which usually takes several months. Cox took the lead among Republicans on the issue. Cox co-chaired the bipartisan Continuity of Government Commission which started meeting in September. Speaker Dennis Hastert did not consider the issue a priority and wanted members to consider solutions which could be achieved by changing House rules and passing statutes before considering a constitutional amendment. In January 2003 Cox proposed three changes in House rules which were adopted with bipartisan support. The first would allow the speaker to designate successors in the event of a vacancy; that would allow the new speaker to convene the House. The second provided that the speaker could adjourn the House at any time of imminent danger; this overrode the rule that the speaker could not adjourn the House when a measure was being considered. The third allowed the House to adjust the number of its members after a catastrophic attack; the House cannot go into session without a majority of members, and so if many members were disabled, it could not act.

Cox has often been mentioned as a candidate for statewide office, but has never run. George Will suggested he would be a good choice for vice president. During the House Republican turmoil in late 1998, Cox twice showed interest in running for speaker but he backed off each time. In early 2001 Cox was on the verge of being nominated to be a judge on the Ninth Circuit Court of Appeals. But Senator Barbara Boxer opposed him and in May 2001, after Jim Jeffords announced he was switching parties, he withdrew his name from consideration even as other Republicans were running active campaigns for what they assumed would soon be a vacant seat.

In January 2003 Cox sought the chairmanship of the Government Reform Committee. He was less senior than Christopher Shays, but Shays seemed unlikely to be picked because of his leadership on the campaign finance regulation bill passed over the leadership's opposition. The Republican Steering Committee passed over both of them and picked Tom Davis. Instead, Cox was named chairman of the Select Committee on Homeland Security. Cox emphasized that "This committee is intended to have all the authority of a standing committee and will exist indefinitely." Cox said he expected it to become a standing committee in 2005.

FORTY-NINTH DISTRICT

Rep. Darrell Issa (R)

Elected 2000, 2d term; b. Nov. 1, 1953, Cleveland, OH; home, Vista; Sienna Heights U., B.A. 1976; Protestant; married (Kathy).

Military Career: Army, 1970–80.

Professional Career: Founder & Pres., Directed Electronics, 1982–99.

DC Office: 211 CHOB 20515, 202-225-3906; Fax: 202-225-3303; Web site: www.house.gov/issa.

District Offices: Temecula, 909-693-2447; Vista, 760-599-5000.

Committees: *Energy & Commerce* (30th of 31 R): Commerce, Trade & Consumer Protection; Energy & Air Quality; Environment & Hazardous Materials.

Group Ratings

	ADA	ACLU	AFS	LCV	CON	ITIC	NTU	COC	ACU	NTLC	CHC
2002	0	20	0	13	58	100	61	100	96	86	83
2001	10	—	10	0	—	—	61	100	84	—	—

National Journal Ratings

	2001 LIB —	2001 CONS	2002 LIB —	2002 CONS
Economic	22%	74%	28%	69%
Social	38%	61%	0%	75%
Foreign	43%	53%	34%	65%

Key Votes of the 107th Congress

1. Approve Bush Tax Cuts	Y	5. Faith-Based Charities	Y	9. Trade Promotion Authority	Y
2. Limit Patients' Bill of Rights	Y	6. Bar Gays in the Boy Scouts	Y	10. Bar Funds for Intl. Court	Y
3. Campaign Finance Reform	N	7. Ban Partial-Birth Abortion	Y	11. Authorize Force in Iraq	Y
4. Ban ANWR Development	N	8. Arm Commercial Pilots	Y	12. Deny Home. Sec. Dept. Union	Y

Election Results

2002 general	Darrell Issa (R)	94,594	(77%)	($326,416)
	Karl Dietrich (Lib)	26,891	(22%)	($27,792)
	Other	1,012	(1%)	
2002 primary	Darrell Issa (R)	unopposed		
2000 general (CA 48)	Darrell Issa (R)	160,627	(61%)	($2,300,907)
	Peter Kouvelis (D)	74,073	(28%)	($17,069)
	Eddie Rose (Ref)	11,240	(4%)	
	Other	15,538	(6%)	

The People		Race/Ethnic Origin	Ancestry	
Area size:	1,778 sq. mi.	57.9% White	German: 10.7%	Irish: 7.9%
Urban population:	90.3%	5.0% Black	English: 7.8%	
Rural population:	9.7%	3.5% Asian	**2000 Presidential Vote**	
Pop. 2000:	639,087	0.9% Native Am.	Bush (R) 114,193	(59%)
Median income:	$46,445	0.5% Hawaiian	Gore (D) 75,561	(39%)
Poverty status:	11.9%	2.5% Two+ races	Other 5,217	(3%)
Military veterans:	15.3%	0.2% Other	**Cook Partisan Voting Index:** R +11	
		29.5% Hispanic Origin		

Occupation	Blue collar: 24.4%	White collar: 58.1%	Gray collar: 17.5%

The California coast between Los Angeles and San Diego has never entirely filled up with development and never will as long as the Marine Corps retains custody of Camp Pendleton, the giant training base just south of the Orange-San Diego County line. The land along the coast and inland in northern San Diego County, usually referred to as North County, this was largely empty territory a quarter century ago—never fertile enough to produce a large farm community, never endowed with much manufacturing, never actively promoted as a retirement community. But North County has been growing rapidly these last 20 years. Today about one million people live here, and who can blame them? For this is one of America's most beautiful and comfortable environments, with ocean and mountain scenery, sunny and warm weather, no rural poverty and low crime. Here, amid dry but not desert landscape, you can see miles of rolling hills, with occasional surrealistic trees and sagebrush-like bushes; mountains clump up not in ridges, but here and there, seemingly at random. This land has attracted thousands of new migrants—many, but by no means all, retirees.

The 49th Congressional District occupies the northern part of San Diego County and the southwestern corner of Riverside County. It was the fastest-growing California district in the 1990s, with a population increase of 35%. On the coast next to Camp Pendleton is Oceanside, a lower-middle-income town heavily dependent on the base; local business declined in early 2003 when thousands of residents went off to war. Inland is Vista, a higher-income community. About

40% of the district's population is in these two areas. About 30% are in small communities in North County, including a small portion of San Diego. Another 30% are in Riverside County. Here is the instant city of Temecula: a corner-grocery town serving a vineyard district in the mid-1980s, it is now the center of an area with more than 100,000 people, mostly commuters attracted by low-priced homes and traditional values. To the north are the older communities of Lake Elsinore, Canyon Lake and Perris. Politically, this is a heavily Republican area, 59% for George W. Bush in 2000. People here are affluent enough to identify with the party of property, conventional enough in their personal lives to identify with what describes itself as the party of traditional values.

The congressman from the 49th District is Darrell Issa (pronounced *EYE-sah*), a Republican first elected in 2000. He grew up in Cleveland and graduated from Sienna Heights University in Adrian, Michigan. After a 10-year career in the Army, Issa started the Viper car alarm company in Cleveland, moved the business to North County and renamed it Directed Electronics, where it became the world's largest manufacturer of vehicle security systems, with the industry's largest R&D budget. The firm, the first with a programmable personal computer system, made him a fortune estimated at $200 million as he found a way to capitalize legally on America's high crime rates. He became active in the high-tech industry, serving as chairman of the Consumer Electronics Association. In the early 1990s he turned to politics, contributing to Republicans and chairing the 1996 campaign to pass Proposition 209, which banned state use of racial quotas and preferences. In 1998 he ran for the Senate seat of Barbara Boxer and spent $12 million of his own money. But he lost the Republican primary 45%–40% to Matt Fong.

In November 1999, when North County incumbent Ron Packard announced his retirement, it was obvious that his successor would be chosen in the March 2000 Republican primary. Although there were 10 candidates, the race turned into a bruising two-man contest between Issa and state Senator Bill Morrow; former Congressman Robert Dornan expressed interest in a comeback attempt, but he deferred to his son, Mark Dornan, who ended up trailing well behind. Morrow questioned Issa's business practices. Issa raised questions about his opponent's honesty. On most issues, the candidates took similar positions; they supported streamlining government, opposed abortion and favored rebuilding the military. Issa spent $1.5 million of his own money on the primary, and beat Morrow 46%–30%. In the fall the Democratic nominee disconnected his phone and abandoned his campaign because his party, predictably, gave him little support. Issa won 61%–28%.

In the House, Issa's voting record was relatively moderate, especially on foreign issues. Probably aided by his prior lobbying and political contacts, he quickly learned his way. "It's a cool job," he told a local reporter after a few months. He became unusually active on overseas issues. On the eve of George W. Bush's decision to start the war in Afghanistan, Issa, who is of Lebanese descent, joined Democrat Robert Wexler, who is Jewish, in a visit to several Middle East nations to build support for the United States. During that trip, he suggested that he was the victim of racial profiling when he was kept off an Air France flight to Paris; the airline claimed that he was late. On the Israeli-Palestinian conflict, Issa urged colleagues to pursue contacts with Palestinians who seek peace. After he hesitatingly voted for a House resolution expressing solidarity with Israel, he voiced reservations about its lack of even-handedness. In December 2001, the issue of terrorism hit especially close to home: Two members of the militant Jewish Defense League were charged with plotting to blow up Issa's office in San Clemente and a Culver City mosque. At the start of his second term, he won a seat on Energy and Commerce that he had sought as a freshman. He has said he may run against Boxer again in 2004. In May 2003, he announced he would at least partially bankroll the ongoing effort to recall Governor Gray Davis; he may run for governor if a recall is on the statewide ballot in October or November 2003.

FIFTIETH DISTRICT

Rep. Randy (Duke) Cunningham (R)

Elected 1990, 7th term; b. Dec. 8, 1941, Los Angeles; home, San Diego; U. of MO, B.A. 1964, M.S. 1965, National U., M.B.A. 1985; Christian; married (Nancy).

Military Career: Navy, 1966–87 (Vietnam).

Professional Career: Teacher, Hinsdale H.S., 1965–66; Businessman, 1987–90.

DC Office: 2350 RHOB 20515, 202-225-5452; Fax: 202-225-2558; Web site: www.house.gov/cunningham.

District Office: Escondido, 760-737-8438.

Committees: *Appropriations* (17th of 36 R): Defense; District of Columbia (Vice Chmn.); Labor, HHS & Education. *Permanent Select Committee on Intelligence* (6th of 11 R): Human Intelligence, Analysis & Counter-intelligence; Intelligence Policy & National Security; Technical & Tactical Intelligence.

Group Ratings

	ADA	ACLU	AFS	LCV	CON	ITIC	NTU	COC	ACU	NTLC	CHC
2002	0	7	0	13	52	100	53	89	96	89	100
2001	5	—	0	0	—	—	61	96	96	—	—

National Journal Ratings

	2001 LIB — 2001 CONS	2002 LIB — 2002 CONS
Economic	15% — 82%	34% — 65%
Social	20% — 69%	0% — 75%
Foreign	27% — 72%	15% — 78%

Key Votes of the 107th Congress

1. Approve Bush Tax Cuts	Y	5. Faith-Based Charities	Y	9. Trade Promotion Authority	Y
2. Limit Patients' Bill of Rights	Y	6. Bar Gays in the Boy Scouts	Y	10. Bar Funds for Intl. Court	Y
3. Campaign Finance Reform	N	7. Ban Partial-Birth Abortion	*	11. Authorize Force in Iraq	Y
4. Ban ANWR Development	N	8. Arm Commercial Pilots	Y	12. Deny Home. Sec. Dept. Union	Y

Election Results

2002 general	Randy (Duke) Cunningham (R)	111,095	(64%)	($770,722)
	Del Stewart (D)	55,855	(32%)	($19,713)
	Other	5,751	(3%)	
2002 primary	Randy (Duke) Cunningham (R)	54,491	(87%)	
	James Hart (R)	8,354	(13%)	
2000 general (CA 51)	Randy (Duke) Cunningham (R)	172,291	(64%)	($572,440)
	George Barraza (D)	81,408	(30%)	
	Other	14,100	(5%)	

Prior Winning Percentages: 1998 (61%); 1996 (65%); 1994 (67%); 1992 (56%); 1990 (46%)

The People		Race/Ethnic Origin	Ancestry	
Area size:	365 sq. mi.	65.8% White	German: 11.5%	English: 8.8%
Urban population:	97.8%	1.8% Black	Irish: 8.6%	
Rural population:	2.2%	10.3% Asian	**2000 Presidential Vote**	
Pop. 2000:	639,087	0.3% Native Am.	Bush (R)	136,311 (54%)
Median income:	$59,813	0.2% Hawaiian	Gore (D)	107,436 (43%)
Poverty status:	8.1%	2.6% Two+ races	Other	8,996 (4%)
Military veterans:	13.4%	0.2% Other	**Cook Partisan Voting Index:** R + 6	
		18.8% Hispanic Origin		

Occupation	Blue collar: 15.7%	White collar: 70.8%	Gray collar: 13.5%

Soledad Mountain looms over La Jolla, the affluent San Diego neighborhood, overlooking the Pacific Ocean to the west, the hills of San Diego and, past them, the flat expanse of Miramar

Marine Corps Air Station. Here a visitor to San Diego the week of the 1996 Republican National Convention could stand in the sunshine and see the Blue Angels perform aerial stunts. It was a sight no one could have seen half a century before: Miramar then was a small airfield, military planes could do nothing like those stunts and San Diego, even after heavy activity in its Navy bases in World War II, was still a small center well to the south. Most of the land you would see looking east and north from Soledad Mountain was empty landscape. Since then San Diego has grown to become the nation's seventh-largest city. Development has jumped over Miramar to the inland communities of Escondido and San Marcos and over the old Del Mar race track on the coast to Encinitas and Carlsbad. These are pleasant and affluent communities, attractively planned, many with red tile roofs which contrast with the tan hillsides.

The 50th Congressional District covers much of this part of San Diego County. About 40% of its population is in the city of San Diego, including most of scenic La Jolla, hillside Clairemont, Carmel Valley and University City to the west and, north of Miramar, Mira Mesa, Rancho Penasquitos and part of Rancho Bernardo. About 25% are on or near the coast, from Del Mar to Encinitas to Carlsbad, home of the La Costa resort. Just inland is affluent Rancho Santa Fe, with its multi-million dollar mansions set amid rolling hills and lush greenery. About 30% of the people are in Escondido and San Marcos. Politically, this is Republican territory, more so as one gets away from the coast, 54% for George W. Bush in 2000.

The congressman from the 50th District is Randy (Duke) Cunningham, a Republican first elected in 1990. Born the day after Pearl Harbor, he taught and coached swimming in Hinsdale, Illinois, and San Diego; in 1966, at 25, he joined the Navy and became one of the most decorated pilots in the Vietnam War. He then trained pilots at Miramar in the Top Gun program; he retired from the Navy in 1987 and started a business in San Diego. In 1990 he ran in a Democratic district against Congressman Jim Bates, who had been charged with sexual harassment. Cunningham beat a former ambassador to Qatar in the Republican primary 46%–30% and in the general beat Bates 46%–45%. In 1992, faced with a choice of districts to run in, he passed up the marginal and culturally more liberal area on the coast and ran here. Incumbent Bill Lowery, a Republican who had 300 overdrafts at the House bank, withdrew from the race, and Cunningham comfortably won the primary and general. He has not been seriously challenged since then.

Cunningham has a generally conservative voting record. He arrived just in time for the Gulf War debate and in his first years worked to make Filipino Gulf war veterans eligible to apply for U.S. citizenship (San Diego is home to a sizable Filipino community) and to prevent base closings in the San Diego area. He was one of four congressmen who in October 1992 met with George H.W. Bush and prompted him to ask questions about Bill Clinton's student trip to Moscow and Eastern Europe, an issue that hurt the Republican ticket. After Republicans gained the majority in 1994, he switched to the Appropriations Committee and has assignments on its two subcommittees with the largest budgets: Defense and Labor-HHS-Education. He has been a forceful advocate of more defense spending. Cunningham has pressed for stricter enforcement of immigration laws and sponsored a "no frills prison act." He successfully opposed efforts to terminate registration with the Selective Service, is a leading advocate of the constitutional amendment to bar flag desecration, and co-sponsored legislation to ensure that military overseas ballots are counted. During the October 2002 debate on authorizing the use of force in Iraq, which he strongly supported, he broke down in tears as he recounted the sacrifices that members of the armed services make during war.

Cunningham has a gift for pungent comments. He said that Bill Clinton's anti-war past would result in being "tried as a traitor and even shot" if he had lived in another country. After he said Jim Moran "switched his vote and turned his back on Desert Storm," Moran pushed him in the hall, then apologized. In 1998 he dressed down an Army official at a subcommittee hearing about "B.S." efforts to combat sexual harassment and discrimination in the military. "Our kids don't like that. They don't like the political correctness," Cunningham lectured. And in 2000, his critique of "our liberal and socialist friends" in the House drew a complaint from Progressive Caucus head Peter DeFazio about the "bizarre and inaccurate accusations." When he ran for Republican Conference secretary in 1997, Cunningham was winnowed out on the second ballot.

FIFTY-FIRST DISTRICT

Rep. Bob Filner (D)

Elected 1992, 6th term; b. Sept. 4, 1942, Pittsburgh, PA; home, San Diego; Cornell U., B.A. 1963, Ph.D. 1973, U. of DE, M.A. 1969; Jewish; married (Jane Merrill).

Elected Office: San Diego Schl. Bd., 1979–83, Pres., 1982–83; San Diego City Cncl., 1987–92, Dpty. Mayor, 1991.

Professional Career: Prof., San Diego St. U., 1970–92; Legis. Asst., U.S. Sen. Hubert Humphrey, 1974; Legis. Asst., U.S. Rep. Don Fraser, 1975.

DC Office: 2428 RHOB 20515, 202-225-8045; Fax: 202-225-9073; Web site: www.house.gov/filner.

District Offices: Chula Vista, 619-422-5963; Imperial, 760-355-8800.

Committees: *Transportation & Infrastructure* (10th of 34 D): Aviation; Coast Guard & Maritime Transportation (RMM); Railroads. *Veterans' Affairs* (2d of 14 D): Health; Oversight & Investigations.

Group Ratings

	ADA	ACLU	AFS	LCV	CON	ITIC	NTU	COC	ACU	NTLC	CHC
2002	100	93	100	88	79	25	25	25	0	0	0
2001	95	—	100	100	—	—	18	22	0	—	—

National Journal Ratings

	2001 LIB —	2001 CONS		2002 LIB —	2002 CONS
Economic	95%	0%		95%	0%
Social	90%	0%		94%	3%
Foreign	96%	0%		94%	0%

Key Votes of the 107th Congress

1. Approve Bush Tax Cuts	N	5. Faith-Based Charities	N	9. Trade Promotion Authority	N
2. Limit Patients' Bill of Rights	N	6. Bar Gays in the Boy Scouts	N	10. Bar Funds for Intl. Court	N
3. Campaign Finance Reform	Y	7. Ban Partial-Birth Abortion	N	11. Authorize Force in Iraq	N
4. Ban ANWR Development	Y	8. Arm Commercial Pilots	N	12. Deny Home. Sec. Dept. Union	N

Election Results

2002 general	Bob Filner (D)	59,541	(58%)	($905,137)
	Maria Garcia (R)	40,430	(39%)	($113,569)
	Other	2,816	(3%)	
2002 primary	Bob Filner (D)	25,179	(70%)	
	Daniel Ramirez (D)	10,584	(30%)	
2000 general (CA 50)	Bob Filner (D)	95,191	(68%)	($357,015)
	Bob Divine (R)	38,526	(28%)	($11,002)
	Other	5,755	(4%)	

Prior Winning Percentages: 1998 (99%); 1996 (62%); 1994 (57%); 1992 (57%)

The People		Race/Ethnic Origin	Ancestry	
Area size:	4,896 sq. mi.	21.3% White	German: 4.2%	Irish: 3.3%
Urban population:	95.6%	9.4% Black	English: 2.9%	
Rural population:	4.4%	12.4% Asian	**2000 Presidential Vote**	
Pop. 2000:	639,087	0.5% Native Am.	Gore (D)..............85,561 (57%)	
Median income:	$39,243	0.6% Hawaiian	Bush (R)..............61,008 (41%)	
Poverty status:	16.3%	2.4% Two+ races	Other....................3,819 (3%)	
Military veterans:	12.2%	0.2% Other	**Cook Partisan Voting Index:** D + 8	
		53.3% Hispanic Origin		

Occupation Blue collar: 23.5% White collar: 54.7% Gray collar: 21.8%

San Diego, at one corner of the continental United States, not so long ago a small Navy town known for its good harbor and splendid weather, is now a major metropolis, a city of 1.2 million people and the center of a metro area of 2.8 million. It is also, to its sometime discomfort, one of the largest cities anywhere directly on an international border and between countries with strikingly different economic conditions, political systems and cultural traditions. Not many other Americans think about it, but Mexican presidential candidate Luis Donaldo Colosio was murdered in March 1994 just a few blocks from the border in Tijuana.

This is, in fact, the busiest border crossing in the world, but most of San Diego seems to look away, toward the ocean. Tijuana looks to the United States, to the lower-income part of San Diego—the industrial zone on brown hills in Otay Mesa and San Ysidro, the industrial suburbs of Chula Vista and National City and the grid streets south of downtown and behind the harbor in San Diego itself. Latinos are scattered in various parts of the city, in the southern corridor and in Encanto and Chollas Park in the east. Oddly, there is not much evidence of Mexican style in San Diego—less even than in Los Angeles, as if the border city was insisting on its Yanqui origins, just as San Diego's civic leaders bridled at the idea of a bi-national airport on the border. Even the city's favorite symbol, the red Tijuana Trolley that takes tourists from downtown to the San Ysidro-Tijuana border station, is as resolutely Yanqui as Main Street in Disneyland.

The 51st Congressional District covers all of California's border with Mexico, including the southeast corner of San Diego, National City and Chula Vista on San Diego Bay, and San Ysidro and Otay Mesa, which are part of the city of San Diego, connected to the rest by lines running down the harbor. The 51st also extends as far east as the Arizona border to include all of Imperial County, with its string of farms and towns running south from the Salton Sea to Mexicali, Mexico. The water comes from the Colorado River through the All-American Canal; the Salton Sea was created when the canal burst in 1905 and water flowed into the lowest part of the desert. In 2000 Imperial County had 142,000 people, 72% Hispanic; Mexicali has 790,000. The 2001 redistricting added Imperial County and a thin, very lightly inhabited strip of San Diego County along the Mexican border: 73% of the people here live in San Diego, National City and Chula Vista, 19% in Imperial County and only 8% in the rest of the district. Overall, minorities make up 80% of the population: 53% Hispanic, 12% Asian (mainly Filipino) and 9% black. This is a Democratic district that gave 57% to Al Gore in 2000.

The congressman from the 51st District is Bob Filner, a Democrat elected in 1992 in what was then a new seat. Filner grew up in New York City and was a Freedom Rider in 1961, imprisoned for two months in Mississippi. He earned a Ph.D. at Cornell, taught history at San Diego State and directed the Lipinsky Institute for Judaic Studies; he took time off to work on Senator Hubert Humphrey's staff in the 1970s, was elected to the San Diego school board in 1979 and to the city council in 1987. The 1992 redistricting created a new Democratic seat in San Diego County, and Filner decided to run for Congress. He was strongly backed by local activists although he had two better-known rivals. Filner won with 26%, to 23% for Waddie Deddeh, state senator and assemblyman since 1966; 20% for Jim Bates, four-term congressman beaten in 1990 after being disciplined for sexual harassment; and 19% for Juan Carlos Vargas, who succeeded Filner on the council in 1993.

Filner is politically savvy, with some original ideas about policy, aggressive in articulating his views, and he has one of the most liberal voting records in the House. In July 2001, he forced a House vote on a Social Security issue, to prohibit spending to implement the final report of Bush's Commission to Strengthen Social Security which proposed various forms of individual investment accounts; the vote was almost entirely on party lines, and Democrats hoped it could be used against Republicans in campaigns.

As the number two Democrat on the Veterans' Affairs Committee, Filner has become a vocal advocate of veterans' rights, a popular cause in a district of many military retirees. He has paid particular attention to restoring benefits denied to Filipino veterans who fought for the U.S. in World War II; he and 15 of the veterans were arrested after they chained themselves to a White House fence. In 1999, he was one of two members to vote against further restrictions on burials at Arlington Cemetery. On other issues, he was one of only five House members to vote against both parties' impeachment inquiries, and one of two who opposed the Medicare lockbox proposal in 2001. In 2002, Filner voted against the use of force in Iraq; in September, in a joint appearance on C-SPAN's *Washington Journal*, Filner and Joe Wilson of South Carolina engaged in a heated argument after Filner stated that the U.S. had supplied biological and chemical weapons to Saddam Hussein in the past. Wilson angrily accused Filner of being "viscerally anti-American." Filner, citing his experience as a Freedom Rider, later said, "I've been beaten up and thrown in jail by better people than Joe Wilson."

In the March 1996 primary, Filner was again challenged by Juan Carlos Vargas, by then on the San Diego Council. Filner won, but by just 55%–45%. Filner had no primary opposition in 1998. The 2001 redistricting plan removed heavily Latino parts of San Diego but the addition of Imperial County resulted in an increase in Hispanic percentage from 51% to 53%; but the Imperial County Hispanics know nothing of Vargas, now a member of the Assembly and eager to run for the House again. Vargas joined in the protests against the plan and the Mexican American Legal Defense and Educational Fund filed a lawsuit claiming that the plan was biased against Hispanics, citing the 51st District and the 27th and 28th in the San Fernando Valley. But the lawsuit was dismissed. In the 2002 primary, Filner was challenged by Danny Ramirez, an Imperial County businessman. Filner won 70%–30%. One-quarter of the vote was cast in Imperial County, which Ramirez carried 60%–40%. But Filner won 70%–30% in San Diego County. Filner won the general election 58%–39%. Many expect Vargas, who is term-limited in the Assembly, to run again, but Filner will have time to get better known in Imperial County and his 2002 showing there suggests he is already well on the way.

FIFTY-SECOND DISTRICT

Rep. Duncan Hunter (R)

Elected 1980, 12th term; b. May 31, 1948, Riverside; home, Alpine; U. of MT, U. of CA, Western St. U., B.S.L & J.D. 1976; Baptist; married (Lynne).

Military Career: Army, 1969–71 (Vietnam).

Professional Career: Practicing atty., 1976–80.

DC Office: 2265 RHOB 20515, 202-225-5672; Fax: 202-225-0235; Web site: www.house.gov/hunter.

District Office: El Cajon, 619-579-3001.

Committees: *Armed Services* (Chmn. of 33 R). *Select Committee on Homeland Security* (8th of 27 R): Infrastructure & Border Security.

Group Ratings

	ADA	ACLU	AFS	LCV	CON	ITIC	NTU	COC	ACU	NTLC	CHC
2002	10	7	22	38	8	75	52	75	88	86	100
2001	5	—	0	0	—	—	68	91	100	—	—

National Journal Ratings

	2001 LIB —	2001 CONS		2002 LIB —	2002 CONS
Economic	7%	89%		34%	65%
Social	0%	81%		0%	75%
Foreign	33%	60%		41%	56%

Key Votes of the 107th Congress

1. Approve Bush Tax Cuts	Y	5. Faith-Based Charities	Y	9. Trade Promotion Authority	Y
2. Limit Patients' Bill of Rights	Y	6. Bar Gays in the Boy Scouts	*	10. Bar Funds for Intl. Court	Y
3. Campaign Finance Reform	N	7. Ban Partial-Birth Abortion	Y	11. Authorize Force in Iraq	Y
4. Ban ANWR Development	N	8. Arm Commercial Pilots	Y	12. Deny Home. Sec. Dept. Union	N

Election Results

2002 general	Duncan Hunter (R)	118,561	(70%)	($761,970)
	Peter Moore-Kochlacs (D)	43,526	(26%)	
	Michael Benoit (Lib)	6,923	(4%)	
2002 primary	Duncan Hunter (R)	unopposed		
2000 general	Duncan Hunter (R)	131,345	(65%)	($856,691)
	Craig Barkacs (D)	63,537	(31%)	($270,663)
	Other	8,112	(4%)	

Prior Winning Percentages: 1998 (76%); 1996 (65%); 1994 (64%); 1992 (53%); 1990 (73%); 1988 (74%); 1986 (77%); 1984 (75%); 1982 (69%); 1980 (53%)

The People		Race/Ethnic Origin	Ancestry	
Area size:	2,129 sq. mi.	72.9% White	German: 12.5%	Irish: 9.1%
Urban population:	93.6%	3.7% Black	English: 8.5%	
Rural population:	6.4%	5.4% Asian	**2000 Presidential Vote**	
Pop. 2000:	639,087	0.7% Native Am.	Bush (R)	143,081 (57%)
Median income:	$52,940	0.3% Hawaiian	Gore (D)	98,633 (40%)
Poverty status:	8.1%	3.2% Two+ races	Other	7,833 (3%)
Military veterans:	16.0%	0.2% Other	**Cook Partisan Voting Index:** R +10	
		13.7% Hispanic Origin		

Occupation	Blue collar: 18.2%	White collar: 67.7%	Gray collar: 14.1%

San Diego began as a port, but today most metropolitan area residents live out of sight of the sea, in hilltop neighborhoods inland that look out over distant ridges and freeways or in warm, sunny valleys amid the mountains which become denser and higher as one travels east from the Pacific. There is a discernible difference in attitudes and values between those who have settled inland and those nearer the ocean, part of the split that became critical in California's political struggles and culture wars since the 1980s. In San Diego, both groups tend to identify as Republicans, and coastal people may be more affluent. But those who settle inland are more likely to be conventionally religious and to have traditional moral values; they tend to be more supportive of the military and assertive foreign policy; they are more dubious about the ability of government to shape poor citizens' lives. They are more conservative on most of the cultural and foreign issues of recent times, and therefore more reliably Republican: When oceanfront voters in San Diego shifted sharply toward Democrats in the 1990s, the movement was much less among voters inland.

The 52d Congressional District takes in many of the inland San Diego suburbs and most of the mountain and desert interior of San Diego County. It includes the part of San Diego north of I-8 and east of I-15; Santee, an East County city of 53,000; El Cajon, which has the nation's second largest (after the Detroit area) community of Chaldeans, Catholic Arabs from Iraq, who own 50% of San Diego County's independent retail convenience stores and are known for their toughness—it was not easy being a Christian in Saddam Hussein's Iraq. It includes high-income Poway, north of San Diego, and more modest La Mesa, east of San Diego. The mountains and the desert to the east are lightly inhabited. In the mountains is tiny Alpine with one Indian casino and another sought by a tribe with a membership of seven adults and one child. In the desert is the town of Borrego Springs amid the giant Anza-Borrego Desert State Park. Politically, this is a solidly Republican district.

The congressman from the 52d District is Duncan Hunter, a Republican first elected in 1980, an upset winner in the Reagan landslide who is now chairman of the Armed Services Committee. He grew up on a ranch outside Riverside, where his father was a real estate developer. He dropped out of college to serve in the Army, and was awarded a Bronze Star for his service in 24 helicopter combat assaults in Vietnam. He graduated from Western State University law school in 1976 and started a legal practice in San Diego's Barrio Logan. In 1980 his father urged him to run against Democratic Congressman Lionel Van Deerlin in what had been a safe Democratic district. But it was a Republican year in southern California and Hunter won 53%–47%. "Your real campaign is just starting," his father told him. "You've got to get on Armed Services." He did, and redistricting gave him a safe Republican seat. In the 1980s he was part of the group of young conservative Republicans around Newt Gingrich, but he concentrated on military issues; he was recently named to the Select Committee on Homeland Security.

On the committee, Hunter supported the Reagan defense buildup and was ardent backer of the Strategic Defense Initiative, which had few backers in the services or among senior members of the committee, and of the 600-ship Navy. He worked to block relaxation of export controls on high-tech products. After the 1994 election he failed in his attempt to get into the Republican leadership when he lost the Conference chairmanship to John Boehner by a 122–102 vote. But he became chairman of the Military Procurement Subcommittee. He worked to accelerate development of the F-22, arguing that the Navy needed a stealth-equipped carrier plane. He argued for building more B-2s and against reducing the number of B-1s. He has tried to push the Pentagon to build more nuclear submarines and match apparent Russian gains in quiet technology. He argued that the Pentagon had too many procurement officials who held up weapons development, and he inserts in each year's defense authorization amendments requiring that their numbers be reduced by 25,000; by 2002 the number had been reduced from 300,000 to 190,000.

Hunter argued for many years that the Clinton administration cut defense spending far too much, and he was willing to buck the Republican leadership and the incoming Bush administration to get more spending. In March 2000 he and six other ranking members of Armed Services threatened to withhold their votes for the budget resolution unless Speaker Dennis Hastert added $4 billion in defense spending to the supplemental spending bill; the threat worked. Included were funds for repairing ships in San Diego. He was disappointed with the increase in the first Bush budget, and in November 2001 called for a $32 billion increase in current spending, and said the administration was trying to "conduct an aggressive Ronald Reagan foreign policy with a Jimmy Carter defense budget." By January 2002 he was asking the Bush administration for a $50 billion increase in the next fiscal year; later, when the administration called for a $45 billion increase, he said he wanted $30 billion more than that.

In 2000 Hunter passed up a chance to run for the committee chairmanship but got the position two years later. In 2000 Chairman Floyd Spence was rotated off as chairman because of House Republicans' six-year term limit. Hunter supported the next most senior member, Bob Stump, over Curt Weldon. Hunter said that he would be a candidate if Stump lost in the Republican Steering Committee; Stump won by one vote. On April 26, 2002, Stump announced that he was retiring because of poor health; that day Hunter said, "I'll be working hard for the chairmanship position." Weldon was considering running, but on May 20 withdrew and endorsed Hunter. During much of the rest of the year Stump was absent and Hunter was chairing committee meetings. In January 2003 he revised the subcommittee structure, establishing a new subcommittee on emerging threats and giving the other subcommittees jurisdiction based on service activities rather than Pentagon procedures.

On some issues Hunter has been at odds with the Bush administration. He said that the campaign in Afghanistan, fought with no area air bases, showed the need for more B-2s and B-1s. He called for more F-22s than the Pentagon wanted and was an enthusiastic supporter of the Joint Strike Fighter. He said there was a danger that the military was no longer capable of fighting two wars at the same time and he argued that Defense Secretary Donald Rumsfeld's plans for transforming the military should be accompanied by a buildup in troops. In November 2002 he argued that the administration's budget request still left the military $30 billion behind on modernization projects. In November 2002 he got the administration to back down on the issue of full retirement and disability benefits for veterans with Purple Hearts or injured during training or hazardous duty. Hunter has also frustrated the Senate; Senator Richard Lugar charged that he and Weldon took money away from the Nunn-Lugar program to dismantle Russian weapons of mass destruction to pay for weapons programs. "It is not the House," said Lugar, "it is two people."

Hunter has taken positions on trade and immigration similar to those of Patrick Buchanan, whom he endorsed in the 1996 primaries (in 2000 he backed John McCain). Hunter ardently opposed NAFTA, opposed GATT in 1994, the Mexico bailout in 1995, fast track in 1997, PNTR for China in 2000 and trade promotion authority in 2002. He was angered by the large number of illegal immigrants in the early 1990s, and at one point he called for using military aircraft for "deep deportation" of illegal immigrants. He wrote the 1997 law requiring the 14-mile, 15-foot high fence along the Mexican border from the Pacific Ocean to Otay Mountain; it was built despite the threat to the endangered California gnat catcher and Least Bell's vireo. The fence reduced illegal immigration in the San Diego area but, critics charged, led to more immigration further east in the desert. Hundreds of illegal immigrants died of thirst in the desert or by drowning in the All-American Canal. In 2000 Poway resident John Hunter, Duncan Hunter's younger brother, organized volunteers to put bottles of water in the desert to keep illegal immigrants from dying of thirst. Duncan Hunter thought it was a good idea—"When people are dying of thirst in the desert, you don't step over their bodies"—and got Bureau of Land Management permits for his brother's project.

Much of Hunter's other legislative efforts reflect a San Diego-centric view of issues. In 1999 he urged huge tax breaks—tax credits for shipbuilders, exemption from corporate income tax, halving the depreciation period, additional tax credits for U.S.-made engines—for builders and operators of cruise ships, a growing industry in San Diego. In June 2002 he and Dianne Feinstein introduced a bill to prohibit export of natural gas to any facility within 50 miles of the border that doesn't meet the standards of the nearest U.S. air quality district.

Hunter has been routinely reelected by wide margins. The 2001 redistricting removed Imperial County from the district and made it a bit more Republican.

FIFTY-THIRD DISTRICT

Rep. Susan Davis (D)

Elected 2000, 2d term; b. Apr. 13, 1944, Cambridge, MA; home, San Diego; U.of CA at Berkeley, B.A. 1964, U. of NC, M.A. 1968; Jewish; married (Steven).

Elected Office: San Diego School Bd., 1983–92; CA Assembly, 1994–00.

Professional Career: Devel. Assoc., KPBS Radio, 1980–82.; Exec. Dir., Aaron Price Fellows, 1990–94.

DC Office: 1224 LHOB 20515, 202-225-2040; Fax: 202-225-2948; Web site: www.house.gov/susandavis.

District Office: San Diego, 619-280-5353.

Committees: *Armed Services* (19th of 29 D): Readiness; Terrorism, Unconventional Threats & Capabilities. *Education & the Workforce* (14th of 22 D): Education Reform; Select Education. *Veterans' Affairs* (13th of 14 D): Benefits.

Group Ratings

	ADA	ACLU	AFS	LCV	CON	ITIC	NTU	COC	ACU	NTLC	CHC
2002	90	87	89	88	70	75	24	50	8	9	17
2001	90	—	90	93	—	—	18	48	12	—	—

National Journal Ratings

	2001 LIB	—	2001 CONS		2002 LIB	—	2002 CONS
Economic	67%	—	33%		70%	—	29%
Social	83%	—	11%		74%	—	19%
Foreign	56%	—	41%		71%	—	29%

Key Votes of the 107th Congress

1. Approve Bush Tax Cuts	N	5. Faith-Based Charities	N	9. Trade Promotion Authority	Y
2. Limit Patients' Bill of Rights	N	6. Bar Gays in the Boy Scouts	N	10. Bar Funds for Intl. Court	N
3. Campaign Finance Reform	Y	7. Ban Partial-Birth Abortion	N	11. Authorize Force in Iraq	N
4. Ban ANWR Development	Y	8. Arm Commercial Pilots	N	12. Deny Home. Sec. Dept. Union	N

Election Results

2002 general	Susan Davis (D)	72,252	(62%)	($582,445)
	Bill VanDeWeghe (R)	43,891	(38%)	($742,535)
2002 primary	Susan Davis (D)	unopposed		
2000 general (CA 49)	Susan Davis (D)	113,400	(50%)	($1,926,497)
	Brian P. Bilbray (R)	105,515	(46%)	($1,846,574)
	Other	9,574	(4%)	

The People		Race/Ethnic Origin	Ancestry	
Area size:	251 sq. mi.	51.0% White	German: 8.8%	Irish: 7.4%
Urban population:	99.9%	7.2% Black	English: 6.3%	
Rural population:	0.1%	8.3% Asian	**2000 Presidential Vote**	
Pop. 2000:	639,087	0.5% Native Am.	Gore (D) 114,435	(58%)
Median income:	$36,637	0.4% Hawaiian	Bush (R) 74,526	(37%)
Poverty status:	20.2%	3.1% Two + races	Other 9,944	(5%)
Military veterans:	12.1%	0.3% Other	**Cook Partisan Voting Index:** D +10	
		29.4% Hispanic Origin		

Occupation	Blue collar: 16.3%	White collar: 64.6%	Gray collar: 19.1%

When the United States was dictating the terms of the Treaty of Guadalupe Hidalgo in 1848, after its successful war with Mexico, it made sure the southern boundary of its new California territory was just south of the port of San Diego. This is one of three splendid natural harbors on the Pacific Coast and the major West Coast U.S. Navy base for more than 50 years. The port and Navy base in the sheltered harbor remain the central focus of a metropolis that has grown tenfold over that time and now stretches far inland and to the north. On one side is downtown, booming with post-modern buildings like the Horton Plaza amid a few well-preserved early 20th century relics like the Spreckels Theatre. Across the harbor, on the sand spit that guards it against the ocean, is the white frame castle of the Hotel Del Coronado, with its surprisingly dark wooden interior—the U.S.'s largest wooden structure and a favored resort of past American presidents; the town of Coronado has long been a favorite retirement place for Navy admirals and captains. But San Diego is not all harbor and Navy. To the north, the Pacific waves pound against the beach beneath erose cliffs of unique rock formations that stride up and down the coast on which stand some of San Diego's great cultural institutions: the Scripps Institute of Oceanography, the University of California San Diego campus, the Salk Institute and the Torrey Pines reserve, home of this unique, wide-spreading pine tree. To the south are raffish Mission Beach, Ocean Beach, with its strong rip currents, and Point Loma, overlooking the entrance to the harbor. The weather—a sunny 70 degrees most of the time—has lured tourists and new residents to San Diego. But this is a working town as well, a sophisticated high-tech center with around 200,000 full and part-time students at its colleges and universities and growing biotech, electronics, software and telecommunications industries. It is a manufacturing center as well, with maquiladora factories clustering near the Mexican border.

The 53d Congressional District—the first 53d District in American history—consists of the center of San Diego, the San Diego beaches from Blacks Beach to Ocean Beach, La Jolla beach (but not its interior) and Balboa Park. It includes the heavily Latino neighborhoods south and east of downtown, the Gaslamp District, the older neighborhoods of University Heights and East San Diego. Altogether, 85% of the district population is inside the San Diego city limits. It also includes Coronado and Imperial Beach, just north of the Mexican border, and the inland suburbs of Lemon Grove and La Presa. The 2001 redistricting increased the district's Hispanic percentage from 17% to 29% and reduced its Bush 2000 percentage from 42% to 37%. Historically, this was a Republican district, but after Coastal California's trend toward cultural liberalism in the 1990s and the 2001 redistricting, it is now a solidly Democratic district.

The congresswoman from the 53d District is Susan Davis, a Democrat first elected in 2000. She grew up in Richmond, California, graduated from the University of California at Berkeley and got a degree in social work at the University of North Carolina. Her father and husband have both been physicians. She moved to San Diego in 1973 and became president of the local League of Women Voters and a community producer for the local public television station. In 1983 she was elected to the San Diego school board. In 1990, she became the executive director of the Aaron Price Fellows Program, which helps teach leadership and citizen skills to high school students. She returned to politics in 1994, winning the first of three terms in the California Assembly.

In 2000 term limits prevented Davis from running for the Assembly again, and she ran against Republican Congressman Brian Bilbray, who had won three close elections. She portrayed him as a conservative, even though he took liberal positions on abortion and the environment and made a point of not attending the Republican convention in Philadelphia. He supported John McCain's campaign finance regulation bill and said that he was comfortable with votes for impeachment for a president he called "a perpetual liar." "He talks moderate in San Diego but votes conservative in Washington," Davis said. She attacked Bilbray for supporting bills that would deny citizenship to U.S. born children of illegal immigrants and that would allow private insurers to provide prescription drug benefits to seniors; she called for coverage under Medicare. Davis also said that Bilbray had failed to deliver federal dollars to the district. The AFL-CIO ran so much advertising on her behalf that Davis requested it stop. Bilbray criticized Davis for her handling of utility deregulation but Davis won 50%–46%.

In the House, she has a moderate-to-liberal voting record. As a freshman, she won plum assignments to the Armed Services and Education and the Workforce committees; her priorities included higher military pay, increased aid for school districts with a large military presence and incentives for better teachers. She angered organized labor and some Democratic activists by voting for trade promotion authority, one of only 21 House Democrats to do so. She called the vote "agonizing," but in the interests of a city that has been built on trade; organized labor rescinded its endorsement. But she was in no trouble in the redrawn district and was reelected 62%–38%.

★ COLORADO ★

At the Front Range of the Rocky Mountains, Colorado is also at the front edge of economic, cultural and political change. Colorado is an island of 4.3 million people surrounded by the sea of the Great Plains and the ramparts of the Rockies. With vistas of vast emptiness, it is mostly an urban state: More than half its people live in metropolitan Denver and four-fifths in the urban strip paralleling the Front Range, where the Rockies rise suddenly from the mile-high plateau. And its very ruggedness is inviting more settlement: As the eastern plains continue to lose population, the valley-crevices between the mountains are being filled with second-home condominiums and ranchettes. It's a beautiful environment, but it can be a dangerous one, as some homeowners found when huge forest fires swept across the state in summer 2002.

Colorado started off with a boom, and its recent history has been punctuated by booms—and then by pauses of slow growth. The first boom came with the discovery of gold and silver in the crevasses of the Rockies. Evidence of this mining boom still can be seen in the opera houses and storefronts of Cripple Creek and Central City, Aspen and Telluride, built when Denver was just a village on the creek that is the South Platte River. Then Denver grew, as a meatpacking, banking and manufacturing center, and also as the state capital and regional headquarters of the federal government. After that came the boom of the high-energy-price 1970s, when the Denver skyline sprouted new buildings overlooking the Capitol's golden dome and entrepreneurs built ever more ski resorts and year-round mountain condominiums.

Colorado's economy sagged during the low-energy-price 1980s but, based more on telecommunications than energy, boomed again in the 1990s. The visible signs of this boom are still all around—in the skyscrapers of downtown Denver, bearing at various times, the names of Qwest and TCI and other telecommunications and high-tech companies; in the retro Coors Field baseball park set amid Denver's LoDo, where warehouses have been renovated into restaurants and clubs; in the startling architecture of the new Denver International Airport far out in the plains; in the

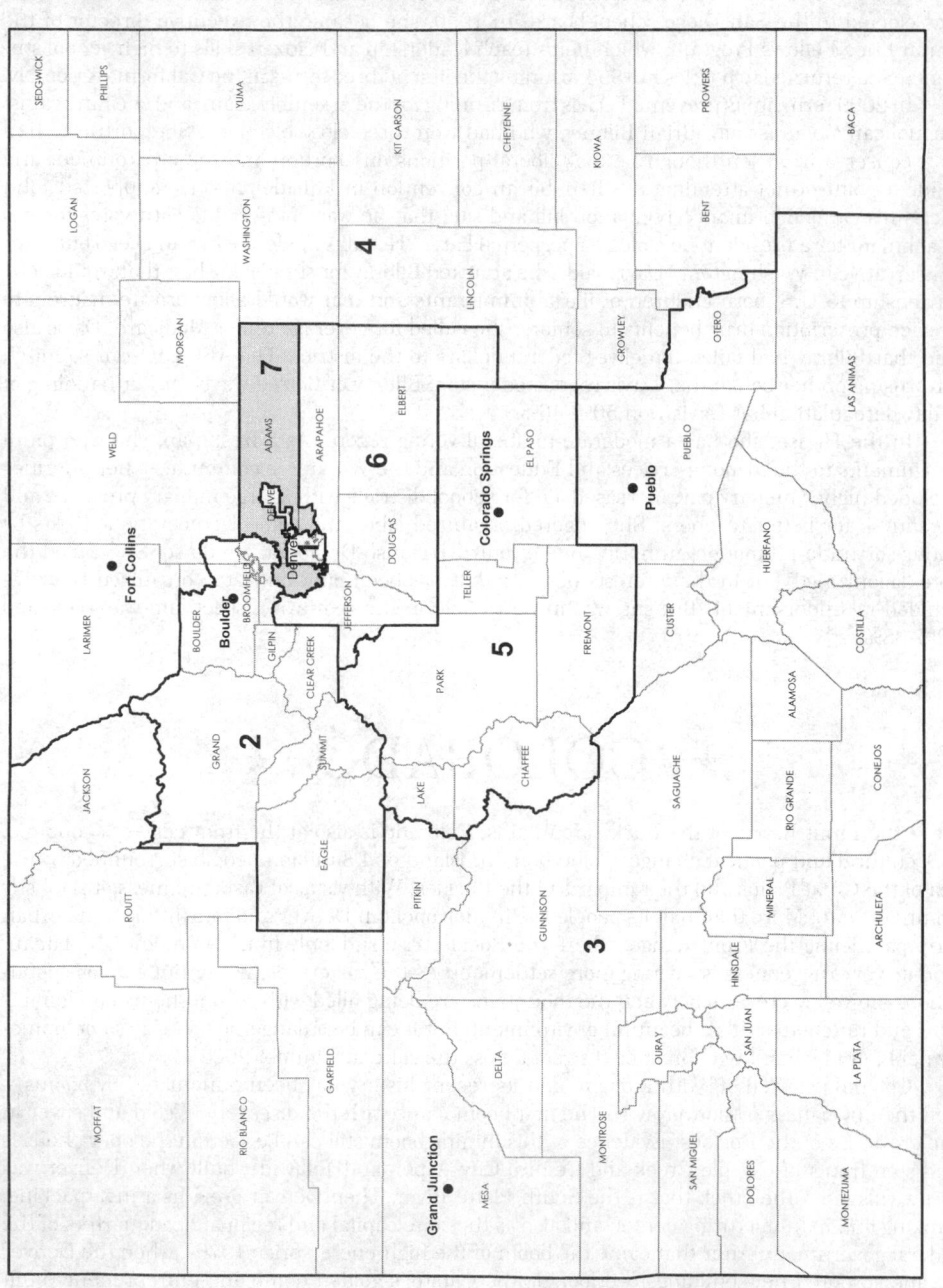

SEDGWICK

PHILLIPS

YUMA

KIT CARSON

CHEYENNE

KIOWA

PROWERS

BACA

LOGAN

WASHINGTON

4

BENT

MORGAN

LINCOLN

CROWLEY

OTERO

LAS ANIMAS

WELD

7

ADAMS

ELBERT

6

PUEBLO

Fort Collins

ARAPAHOE

Colorado Springs

El PASO

Pueblo

LARIMER

BROOMFIELD

DOUGLAS

HUERFANO

BOULDER

DENVER

1

TELLER

COSTILLA

Boulder

GILPIN

Denver

JEFFERSON

GRAND

CLEAR CREEK

5

FREMONT

CUSTER

ALAMOSA

JACKSON

PARK

SAGUACHE

RIO GRANDE

CONEJOS

SUMMIT

2

LAKE

CHAFFEE

MINERAL

EAGLE

ARCHULETA

ROUT

PITKIN

GUNNISON

HINSDALE

SAN JUAN

GARFIELD

DELTA

OURAY

LA PLATA

MOFFAT

RIO BLANCO

3

MONTROSE

SAN MIGUEL

DOLORES

MONTEZUMA

Grand Junction

MESA

Congressional district boundaries were first effective for 2002.

District 7 is highlighted for visibility.

Miles

0   20   40

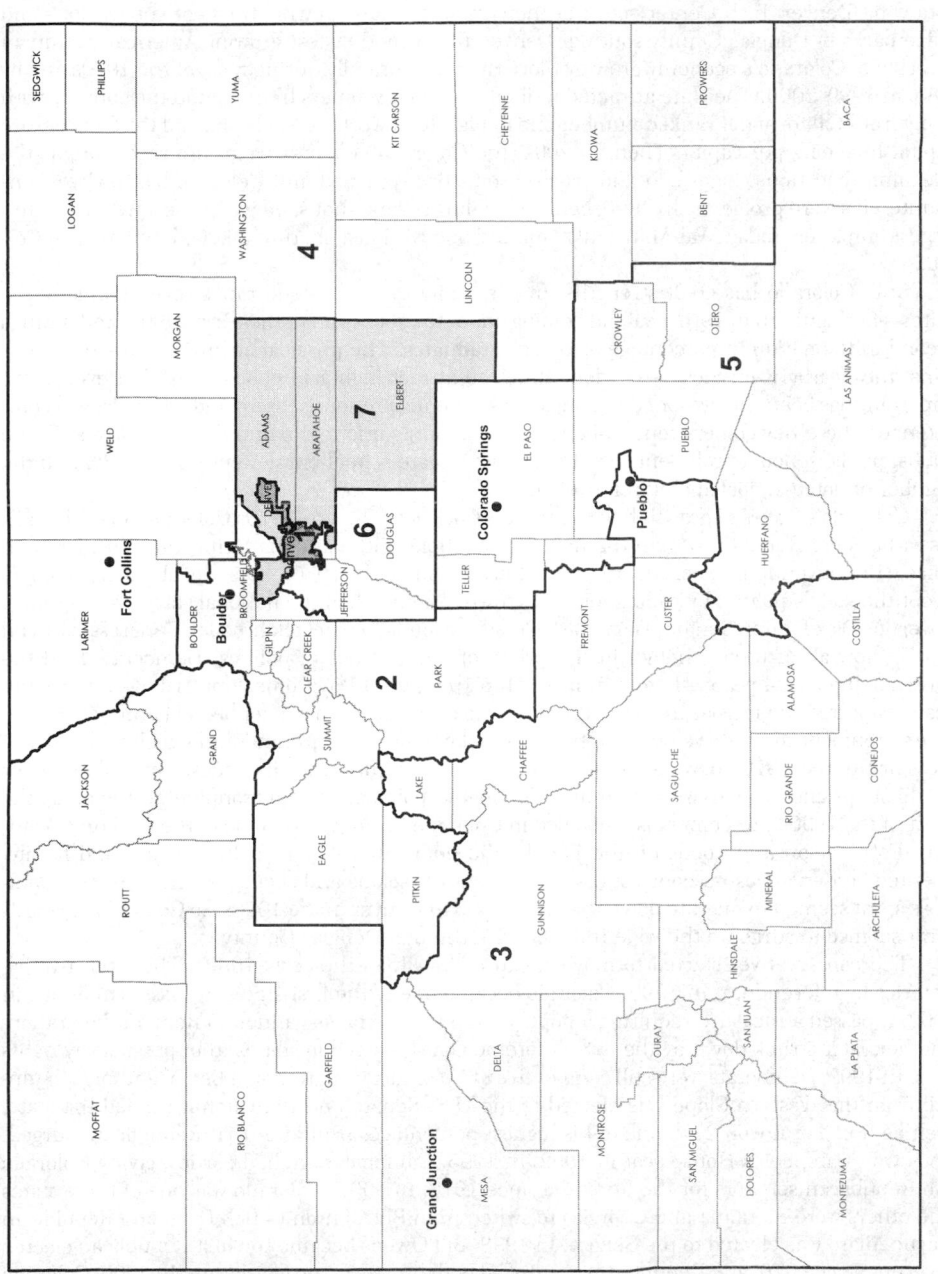

Congressional district boundaries are scheduled to take effect for 2004; subject to court challenge.

Districts 1 and 7 are highlighted for visibility.

The Almanac of American Politics.
National Journal

Miles

0 20 40

sprawling Denver Tech Center south of the city; in the fast-growing tracts of subdivisions and office parks in Douglas County south of Denver, the second fastest-growing American county in the 1990s. Colorado's economy grew by more than 6% annually during most of the 1990s and by 8.8% in 1999–2000. The state attracted well-educated newcomers from around the country, with many from California; it ranked number one in high-tech workers per capita and third in venture capital financing per capita. Then, in 2001, the Colorado economy went into recession, as the telecommunications, high-tech and tourism industries crashed and Colorado-based Qwest encountered severe problems. In 2000, before shedding several thousand jobs, Qwest was the state's largest employer. Today, Wal-Mart ranks number one with just short of 20,000 employees in Colorado.

Still, Colorado has great strengths. In per capita income, it still ranks seventh among the states—far higher than 19th, as it did coming out of the recession of the early 1990s. And it ranks second in the nation in percentage of college graduates. The physical environment—the mountains, the nearby wilderness—has done much to attract high-skill people here, but even more important has been the presence of critical mass of entrepreneurial spirit and technological competence. These newcomers tend to be tech-savvy, family-oriented cultural conservatives: In the 1990s, public school enrollment rose 14%, while private school enrollment was up 33% and the number of home-schooled children tripled.

Colorado's waves of growth have changed its politics. The pre-1970s Colorado was politically just a bit more Republican than the nation as a whole, with cautious Democrats alternating in office with conventionally conservative Republicans. But in the 1970s, a wave of liberal newcomers swept the state's politics by calling for slow growth and reached the national stage—slow-growth Governor Dick Lamm, Senator Gary Hart, Congresswoman Patricia Schroeder, Congressman Tim Wirth. Now all of them, though in the prime of life, are out of politics. Democrats held the governorship for 24 years—Lamm from 1974 to 1986, then Roy Romer until 1998—but Republicans captured the legislature. The new migrants of the 1990s have not been liberals looking for an environment to preserve but conservatives looking for an environment in which to prosper. If the spirit of the 1970s newcomers was embodied in Boulder, with its pedestrian mall, outdoor sports shops and vegetarian restaurants, dominated politically by environmentalist liberals, the spirit of the 1990s newcomers is embodied in Colorado Springs, the home of the Air Force Academy, Fort Carson and Focus on the Family, and dominated politically by religious and family-oriented conservatives—a contrast to environment-conscious and secular Boulder. Just as Boulder's spirit seemed to migrate down the old U.S. 36 to Denver in the 1970s, so Colorado Springs's spirit seemed to surge up the wide Interstate 25, through Douglas County.

The conservatives started to move ahead politically in the early 1990s. They won two big victories by referendum. In 1990, Colorado became one of the first states to pass term limits; in 1992, it passed a measure requiring a popular vote to raise taxes—much to Romer's frustration. Another, later struck down by the U.S. Supreme Court, barred localities from passing gay rights laws. In 1992, Democrats were still competitive in Colorado: Congressman Ben Nighthorse Campbell from the Western Slope was elected to the U.S. Senate and Bill Clinton carried the state, even as Ross Perot won 23%, one of his highest percentages. But after that Republicans surged. They won Campbell's House seat in 1992. In 1995, Campbell switched parties, giving Colorado two Republican senators for the first time since 1972. In 1996, Colorado was one of three states (the others were Montana and Georgia) to switch from Bill Clinton to Bob Dole, and Republican Wayne Allard was elected to the Senate. In 1998, Bill Owens became the first Republican elected governor since 1970, and Republicans controlled both houses of the legislature. In 2000, Colorado seemed conservative enough that it was not targeted by either presidential campaign. It voted 51%–42% for George W. Bush; the central city of Denver (62%–31% for Al Gore) and Boulder County (50%–36% Gore) were outvoted by Colorado Springs's El Paso County (64%–31% Bush) and Douglas County (65%–31% Bush).

In 2002, Republicans did even better. They put new emphasis on their ground game, registering Republican newcomers and producing a flood of absentee Republican votes—so many that the VNS exit poll did not reflect the results. Owens was reelected 63%–34% and Allard won 51%–46%—the same margin against the same candidate as in 1996. Republicans retained the state House, regained a majority in the state Senate and picked up Colorado's new 7th Congressional District, designed to be competitive for both parties, by 121 votes. The only odd result was the defeat of Amendment 31, which would have limited Spanish-language "bilingual" education to one year. Similar initiatives have passed in California in 1998, Arizona in 2000 and Massachusetts in 2002. But in Colorado, a local heiress spent $3 million on a campaign against 31, running ads that raised fears that schools would be flooded with Latino children—a case of liberals using appeals to bigotry to protect the economic interests of unionized Spanish language instructors and the apparat of bilingual consultants.

The People				
Pop. 2000:	4,301,261	3,202,880	74.5%	White
Pop. 1990:	3,294,394	158,443	3.7%	Black
Change 1990–2000:	Up 30.6%	93,277	2.2%	Asian
Change 1980–1990:	Up 14.0%	28,982	0.7%	Native Am.
% of U.S. total:	1.5%	3,845	0.1%	Hawaiian
Pop. rank:	24th of 50	72,721	1.7%	Two+ races
Area size:	104,094 sq. mi.	5,512	0.1%	Other
State Native:	41.1%	735,601	17.1%	Hisp. Origin
Non-citizen:	5.9%			

Race/Ethnic Origin

Ancestry

German: 16.3%		Irish: 9.0%	
English: 8.8%		USA: 3.8%	
Italian: 3.5%			

Language
English: 82.5%   Spanish: 11.3%
Other Eur.: 3.9%

Military veterans: 446,385 (13.9%)
WWII: 15.0%   Korea: 11.3%
Vietnam: 36.3%   Gulf War: 13.1%

Most populous cities:
1. Denver   554,636
2. Colorado Springs   360,890
3. Aurora   276,393
4. Lakewood   144,126
5. Fort Collins   118,652

Urban population: 84.5%
Rural population: 15.5%

Education
H.S. Grad: 86.9%
College Grad: 32.7%

Industry
Agri: 2.0%	Con: 9.1%
Fin: 7.7%	Info: 4.9%
Mfg: 14.0%	Prof: 28.7%
Public: 4.6%	Trade: 15.2%
Other: 13.8%	

Occupation
Blue collar: 21.0%   White collar: 64.5%
Gray collar: 14.5%

Work Sector
Private: 78.1%	Govt: 13.9%
Self: 7.7%	Family: 0.3%

Unemployment: 4.3%

Household Income
<15k: 11.9%	15-35k: 23.8%
35-50k: 17.0%	50-100k: 33.1%
100-150k: 9.1%	>150k: 5.2%

Median: $47,203
Poverty status: 9.3%

Home Value
<50k: 6.0%   50-100k: 13.4%   100-200k: 48.1%   200-300k: 19.3%
300-500k: 9.4%   >500k: 3.8%   Median: $160,100

General Assembly
Senate   18 R 17 D
House   37 R 28 D

Legislative Term Limits: Yes

Registered Voters
D: 841,997   (30.1%)
R: 1,012,518   (36.1%)
I: 946,826   (33.8%)

Presidential politics   Colorado was a three-way battleground in the 1992 presidential race, when it was one of Ross Perot's best states; a two-way battleground in 1996, when Bill Clinton tried to repeat his 1992 victory here and fell short; and not much of a battleground at all in 2000.

Colorado has had an early March presidential primary since 1992, when it was won by Jerry Brown. The 2000 primary came just after Super Tuesday, which ended the campaigns of Bill Bradley and John McCain.

Congressional districting   Colorado gained a House seat from the 2000 Census, just as it did from the Censuses of 1970

108th Congress Lineup
5 R   2 D

107th Congress Lineup
4 R   2 D

2000 Presidential Vote
Bush (R)	883,748	(51%)
Gore (D)	738,227	(42%)
Nader (Green)	91,434	(5%)
Other	27,959	(2%)

2000 Republican Presidential Primary
Bush (R)	116,897	(65%)
McCain (R)	48,996	(27%)
Keyes (R)	11,871	(7%)

2000 Democratic Presidential Primary
Gore (D)	63,384	(75%)
Bradley (D)	20,663	(24%)
Other	821	(1%)

1996 Presidential Vote
Dole (R)	691,846	(46%)
Clinton (D)	671,150	(44%)
Perot (I)	99,628	(7%)
Other	45,646	(3%)

and 1980. Republicans would have controlled the redistricting process, except that they lost control of the state Senate in 2000. When the legislature proved unable to reach a compromise, a state court judge selected a Democrat-designed plan. The judge did not make major changes in the existing districts, but Republicans still responded angrily—they wanted the new district drawn in the fast-growing Republican counties on the south side of Denver. Instead, the newly-created 7th District was anchored in the inner Denver suburbs to the north of the city—making it highly competitive for both parties.

But the Republicans' one-seat takeover of the Senate in 2002 gave them another opportunity to take a crack at the congressional map. They prepared a new map, then introduced and passed it in late May 2003, in the final days of the legislative session. The new Republican map significantly strengthened their control of the 7th District, which Republican Bob Beauprez won in 2002 with the closest margin of any House contest in the nation. They also increased the Republican base of the 3d District to thwart a possible Democratic challenge in the event of an open seat. In exchange, small numbers of Democratic voters were added to the 1st and 2d Districts, which Democrats already held, and to the heavily Republican 5th and 6th Districts south of Denver. With encouragement from national party leaders, Democrats prepared a federal-court challenge that claimed the state lacked authority to redraw its lines after the federal judge had implemented the initial plan for the 2002 election.

Governor

Bill Owens (R)

Elected 1998, term expires Jan. 2007, 2d term; b. Oct. 22, 1950, Ft. Worth, TX; home, Aurora; Austin St. U., B.S. 1973; U. of TX, M.P.A. 1975; Catholic; married (Frances).

Elected Office: CO House of Reps., 1982–88; CO Senate, 1988–94; CO Treasurer, 1994–98.

Professional Career: Consultant, Touche Ross & Co., 1975–77; Project Mgr., Gates Corp., 1977–80, Assoc. Dir., 1980–82; Exec. Dir., CO trade assn., 1982–95.

Office: 136 State Capitol, Denver, 80203, 303-866-2471; Fax: 303-866-2003; Web site: www.state.co.us.

Election Results

2002 general	Bill Owens (R)	884,583	(63%)
	Rollie Heath (D)	475,373	(34%)
	Other	52,646	(4%)
2002 primary	Bill Owens (R)	unopposed	
1998 general	Bill Owens (R)	648,202	(49%)
	Gail Schoettler (D)	639,905	(48%)
	Other	33,200	(3%)

Bill Owens grew up in Fort Worth, Texas and was appointed a congressional page by Congressman Jim Wright, whom Owens's father had supported in his first victory in 1954. He went to Austin State University, where he demonstrated with a red-white-and-blue armband against anti-Vietnam war demonstrators, and to the University of Texas's Lyndon B. Johnson School, where he was one of the few Republicans during the Watergate scandal. He moved to Colorado and went to work for an oil producers association. In 1982, he was elected to the state House and in 1988 to the state Senate. There, he sponsored a successful charter schools law in 1993 and public school choice in 1994. He opposed Governor Roy Romer's 1% tax for education and was one of only nine legislators who supported the 1992 ballot initiative that limited increases in state government spending to the rates of population growth and inflation. In 1994, he was elected state treasurer.

Colorado in 1998 had had only two governors over the past 24 years, both of them Democrats, liberal environmentalist Dick Lamm and the more moderate Roy Romer; 1998 seemed like a good year for a change. Owens won the Republican nomination, leading in the convention and beating Senate President Tom Norton in the primary 59%–41%. On the Democratic side, Lieutenant Governor Gail Schoettler beat state Senate Minority Leader Mike Feeley, who was endorsed by labor, by 53%–45%. Owens called for change; Schoettler for more of the same. Owens said he wanted to cut the state income tax and eliminate the property tax on business property like computers and machines; he called for tort reform; he called for holding teachers and students accountable for results, while reducing education regulation. Schoettler, who had worked for Lamm before being elected Treasurer and Lieutenant Governor, rode across the state on a Tennessee walking horse named Sam. Romer, the outgoing governor, argued that it would be dangerous to turn over control to "an increasingly conservative legislature and a very conservative governor." Schoettler cut into the usual Republican vote among high-earning and high-education voters; Owens depended heavily on the support of the elderly. It was a close election, but Owens won 49%–48%.

In his first two years, Owens delivered on many of his promises, though not always as some Republicans liked. He tried to get voters to pass referenda for transportation bond issues, which were rejected in 1997 and 1998. But in 1999, with a big campaign treasury and support from Romer and Denver Mayor Wellington Webb, he got voters to back a $1.7 billion bond issue, which he claimed would finance $4.4 billion of transportation projects. Much of that money is being spent on rebuilding Interstate 25, the main street of the Front Range, where you can find terrible traffic jams even in rural areas on weekends. Owens's greatest crisis in 1999 was, of course, Columbine, to which he responded with much attention and state aid. Later, reflecting on the tragedy, he called for changes in police tactics and longer school hours for teenagers. Owens and the legislature sidetracked a pending concealed-carry law, and Owens backed a referendum that passed in 2000 requiring background checks for all sales at gun shows.

Owens's major effort in 2000 was education reform. His proposal to expand the use of state assessment tests and to issue and send to parents performance-based report cards for each school was loudly opposed by Democrats and teachers' unions but was passed by the Republican legislature. After insisting on letter grades, Owens changed his mind and instead they rate schools as excellent, high, average, low or unsatisfactory. Owens secured full funding for K-12 schools for four years in a row, after 10 years of lower levels. He was enabled to do this by a tight fiscal policy caused partly by the 1992 referendum and partly by his willingness to use the line-item veto in ways that irritated legislators. He got the legislature to cut the income tax from 5% to 4.75%, and later to 4.63%. As revenues started coming in lower than expected in 2001 and 2002, he imposed across-the-board spending cuts and froze construction budgets. In March 2002, he line-item vetoed the "head notes" of bills, in which legislators defined how departments can spend money, so that department heads would have more flexibility to make cuts. In September 2002, the libertarian Cato Institute gave Owens an A in fiscal policy and ranked him number one among all 50 governors.

On cultural issues Owens has taken conservative stands. His administration cut off Planned Parenthood from state funding in December 2001, because the state Constitution prohibits state funding of abortions; that decision was later reversed, but a woman's health center in Boulder was also cut off. He vetoed a law granting $2 million to libraries and librarians that refused to install Internet filters. He signed a bill banning same-sex marriage that had twice been vetoed by Romer. He passed paycheck protection for state employees, so that union leaders had to get positive authorization of dues payments every year. In January 2002, to make health insurance more affordable, he called for elimination of state mandates of coverage; some who can't afford Cadillac coverage, he said, would be better off with Chevy coverage than no insurance at all.

Owens approached election year 2002 with high job ratings and raised big money early—$4.7 million by April 2002. Democrats couldn't come close to matching this, and in early 2002, two well-known state legislators dropped out of the gubernatorial race to run for Congress. The Democratic nominee was Rollie Heath, a strong liberal and retired executive who had been president of asbestos-maker Johns Manville when it declared bankruptcy in 1982. It was no contest—Owens won 63%–34%. Heath carried Denver, Boulder, San Miguel and Pueblo counties but

Owens carried the other 60, some by huge margins—79%–19% in fast-growing Douglas County, 75%–21% in Colorado Springs's El Paso County. Owens carried metro Denver 59%–37% and the rest of the state 67%–29%. Owens attracted national attention during the campaign. He was called "America's Best Governor" in a cover story in *National Review*, got favorable coverage on the *Wall Street Journal* editorial page and appeared on Fox News and CNN. He was elected chairman of the Republican Governors Association just after the election. Senator Ben Nighthorse Campbell's seat is up in 2004, and some have speculated that Owens might run for it if Campbell retires. Owens's response: "I fully expect to serve out my term, but I don't want to break a promise. I don't expect anything to come up. This could be my final election in Colorado." Either way, Colorado has an array of Republican women in high office who are well-qualified to succeed him: Lieutenant Governor Jane Norton, whom Owens gave responsibility for health insurance, family and volunteerism issues, House Speaker Lola Spradley and Senate Co-Majority Leader Norma Anderson. This may be fitting: Colorado was the first state to allow women to serve in the legislature, and three women were elected to the state House in 1894.

Senior Senator

Ben Nighthorse Campbell (R)

Elected 1992, seat up 2004, 2d term; b. Apr. 13, 1933, Auburn, CA; home, Ignacio; San Jose St. U., B.A. 1957, Meiji U., Japan, 1960–64; no religious affiliation; married (Linda).

Military Career: Air Force, 1951–53 (Korea).

Elected Office: CO House of Reps., 1982–86; U.S. House of Reps, 1986–92.

Professional Career: Rancher; Horse trainer; Jewelry designer.

DC Office: 380 RSOB, 20510, 202-224-5852; Fax: 202-228-4609; Web site: campbell.senate.gov.

State Offices: Colorado Springs, 719-636-9092; Durango, 970-385-9877; Ft. Collins, 970-206-1788; Grand Junction, 970-241-6631; Greenwood Village, 303-843-4100; Pueblo, 719-542-6987.

Committees: *Appropriations*: Commerce, Justice, State & Judiciary; Foreign Operations; Homeland Security; Interior; Legislative Branch (Chmn.); Transportation, Treasury & General Government. *Energy & Natural Resources*: National Parks; Public Lands & Forests; Water & Power (Vice Chmn.). *Indian Affairs* (Chmn.). *Veterans' Affairs*.

Group Ratings

	ADA	ACLU	AFS	LCV	CON	ITIC	NTU	COC	ACU	NTLC	CHC
2002	30	20	38	12	5	62	52	85	88	91	—
2001	15	—	0	0	—	—	79	85	92	—	100

National Journal Ratings

	2001 LIB	—	2001 CONS		2002 LIB	—	2002 CONS
Economic	24%	—	75%		27%	—	71%
Social	33%	—	59%		0%	—	62%
Foreign	30%	—	65%		46%	—	53%

Key Votes of the 107th Congress

1. Approve Bush Tax Cuts	Y	5. Confirm Ashcroft as AG	Y	9. Bar Coop. with Intl. Court	Y
2. Expand Patients' Rights	*	6. Bar Gays in the Boy Scouts	Y	10. Trade Promotion Authority	N
3. Campaign Finance Reform	N	7. $ for Hate Crime Prosecution	N	11. Authorize Force in Iraq	Y
4. Permit ANWR Development	Y	8. Overseas Military Abortions	N	12. Homeland Sec. Dept. Union	N

Election Results

1998 general	Ben Nighthorse Campbell (R)	829,370	(62%)	($3,045,982)
	Dottie Lamm (D)	464,754	(35%)	($1,818,801)
	Other	33,111	(3%)	
1998 primary	Ben Nighthorse Campbell (R)	154,702	(71%)	
	Bill Eggert (R)	64,347	(29%)	
1992 general	Ben Nighthorse Campbell (D)	803,725	(52%)	($1,561,347)
	Terry Considine (R)	662,893	(43%)	($2,215,791)
	Other	85,671	(6%)	

Prior Winning Percentages: 1990 House (70%); 1988 House (78%); 1986 House (52%)

Ben Nighthorse Campbell is the only Native American in the Senate—only the eighth to serve in Congress, and a former Democrat who switched to the Republican Party in March 1995. Campbell had a rough early life: He was placed in an orphanage, dropped out of high school, joined the Air Force and served in the Korean War. He studied judo for four years in Japan and was captain of the 1964 U.S. Olympic judo team; he carried the American flag in the opening ceremonies. He settled not in a trendy ski resort but in the small town of Ignacio, on the plain below Durango, near the New Mexico border, where he bred horses and built a successful jewelry-making business. He is one of the 44 chiefs of the Northern Cheyenne tribe and attends tribal ceremonies; in November 2002, he reburied in the Northern Cheyenne lands in Montana remains of his great-grandfather Black Horse, a chief who in the 1870s escaped twice from federal custody in Okla-homa and returned to Montana—this was made possible by the Native American Graves Protec-tion and Repatriation Act of 1990, which he himself sponsored. "The guy was flat tough," Campbell said. "Sometimes that's where I think I get my saltiness."

Campbell is a distinctive figure on Capitol Hill, with his neck scarves, pony tail, Western-cut sport coats and Levi's Sta-Prest pants, riding a motorcycle (he owns eight of them) as he did in a parade at the 1996 Republican National Convention, or riding a horse wearing full Indian headdress as he did at the 1993 Presidential Inaugural Parade. He worked his way through college driving trucks, and renewed his trucker's license in time to truck in the 2000 Capitol Christmas tree. There are medicine bags on the walls of his Senate office, a carved gourd rattle on the coffee table, a ceremonial pipe on the desk, a shovel used in the groundbreaking of the National Museum of the American Indian leaning against a wall. His Indian headdress has 75 feathers, one for each of his wins in judo.

Campbell got into politics serendipitously. One day in 1982 his plane was grounded and he attended a Democratic Party meeting for a friend being nominated for sheriff; Campbell spoke briefly and was soon drafted to run for the legislature. He spent $13,000 of his own money and won. In 1986, he ran for Congress and beat a Republican incumbent who had personal financial problems. In the House, he had a moderate record, showing more interest in economic growth than in preserving the environment. In 1992, when Senator Tim Wirth retired, Campbell plunged into the race. In the primary, he faced former Governor Dick Lamm, an environmentalist and opponent of immigration, who once said the terminally ill have a "duty to die." Campbell, with backing from the Western Slope and other non-upscale areas, beat the Denver-based Lamm 46%–36%. In the general election, Campbell faced former state Senator Terry Considine, who started the national term limits movement in Colorado. In the weeks before his election, Campbell kept with him a ceremonial eagle feather tuft and Northern Cheyennes held a series of ritual ceremonies and prayer meetings on his behalf. With support from the active Colorado Perot organization, and with the help of his moderate record, Campbell won 52%–43%—even as Bill Clinton was carrying Colorado.

In the Senate, Campbell criticized Clinton's stands on grazing fees and Mining Act revision. Then, in March 1995, the day after the balanced budget amendment failed in the Senate by one vote, he switched parties. He acted partly out of irritation with Denver area liberals, for their environmental stands and also maybe their penchant for reform: He was upset when he was denied an exemption from congressional income limits on his jewelry making, even though book royalties and investment income are exempted. As a Republican, he switched on some issues—

the partial-birth abortion ban, oil-drilling in the Arctic National Wildlife Reserve (ANWR), the assault weapons ban. But he continued to support labor unions' positions on many issues, and his voting record on economic and cultural issues has been near the middle of the Senate.

Campbell has chaired or been ranking member on the Indian Affairs Committee since 1997, and started legislating on Indian issues before that. He co-sponsored the 1989 law authorizing the National Museum of the American Indian on the Mall in Washington, and in 1999 broke ground for the building. But he insists that "I'm Colorado's senator, not the Indian senator-at-large," and opposes changing the name of Columbus Day. He says that high unemployment is the Indians' top problem, and says gaming (gambling) is a major part of the answer. He defends Indian gaming as not being infiltrated by organized crime, as being sufficiently regulated and notes that federal authorities approve contracts. Citing author Hernando de Soto's argument that property rights have to be secure for Third World citizens to work their way out of poverty, he has called for an updating of Indian property laws and has sponsored bills to scale back requirements of approval by the Secretary of the Interior for contracts and mineral leases by tribes and to exempt tribes from the Davis-Bacon Act. In 2000, he passed laws setting up a Indian Tribal Regulatory Reform and Development on Indian Land Commission, providing for Indian land consolidation, addressing probate leasing and transfer of fractionated allotments, and reforming Indian probate law with a uniform national rule. He has worked to develop the Strategic Plan required by the 1994 Indian Trust Fund Reform Act and to establish a Tribal Leaders Trust Fund Task Force so that tribal leaders will be consulted on an issue that has generated lengthy and acrimonious litigation. In 2001, he secured a memorial designation for the site of the 1864 Sand Creek massacre in Colorado.

Campbell has often found himself at odds with environmental restriction groups. "Environmental fanaticism is at the top of my list of concerns," he once wrote. He has worked for years to create the Animas-LaPlata water project in his home area. This, the last major western dam under consideration, has been scaled back and repackaged as an attempt to settle the water rights claims for the Southern Ute tribe and appears to be moving ahead. He has strongly backed oil drilling in ANWR; he traveled there and talked with the Inupiat in Kaktovik, who favored it too. He criticized Denver regional EPA officials for badmouthing the Bush administration's Clear Skies Initiative. He has long backed logging to thin national forests and warned in May 2002 that failure to do so could lead to devastating forest fires, just a month before the catastrophic Colorado fires. But he also worked to upgrade the Black Canyon of the Gunnison to National Park status. He voted against storage of nuclear waste in Nevada's Yucca Mountain, saying he was concerned about waste-laden trucks on Colorado roads. He passed a law setting up a task force on catastrophic cattle diseases like hoof and mouth. After Colorado Republican Rep. Tom Tancredo called for an INS investigation of Jesus Apodaca, a straight-A student who was featured in an article about the eligibility of illegal aliens for in-state tuition, Campbell introduced a bill for amnesty for Apodaca and his family.

Campbell was re-elected in 1998, the first Colorado senator to seek re-election since 1984 and the first Coloradan to have been elected in two different parties since Henry Teller in 1903. It was a little bumpy along the way. Western Slope Congressman Scott McInnis, who believed Campbell would run for governor, had raised $850,000 for a Senate race, and vowed to run anyway; national Republican leaders, eager to protect a party-switcher, persuaded him to withdraw in October 1999. A conservative got 43% against Campbell in the Republican state convention, but national Republicans backed him and he won the primary 71%–29%. In the general election, Campbell received spirited opposition from Dottie Lamm, wife of his 1992 primary opponent and for 17 years a *Denver Post* columnist. Lamm ran an ingenious ad campaign hitting Campbell for his flip-flops on issues from gay rights to campaign finance reform to ANWR. Campbell countered with radio ads of a clock repairman discussing Lamm's columns—17 years of potentially controversial material!—with his wife. As he read words questioning organ transplants to seniors and life support for the smallest premature babies, the listener suddenly heard, "Cuckoo, cuckoo." Lamm carried little more than the liberal base in a state mostly trending conservative—Denver, Boulder, Aspen, Telluride—and not by wide margins. Campbell swamped her in rural areas and in the Denver suburbs, and won 62%–35%.

Campbell comes up for reelection in 2004; amid speculation that he was angling to become chief executive officer of the U.S. Olympic Committee, he said, "Hell, everybody knows I'm running for reelection." Campbell had already bought a $160,000 50-foot tractor-trailer to use as a mobile campaign office. One small drawback: In 1999, he decided to invest $240,000 of campaign money in the stock market; he pulled out two years later, with half of it gone. Possible Democratic opponents include 2d District Rep. Mark Udall and Denver Mayor Wellington Webb (both mulled running against Senator Wayne Allard in 2002), and state Attorney General Ken Salazar and Denver District Attorney Bill Ritter. All may run if Campbell does not, and in that case, possible Republicans include 3d District Rep. Scott McInnis, 6th District Rep. Tom Tancredo and Governor Bill Owens. Footnote: Campbell's son Colin is married to his colleague Wayne Allard's niece Karen.

Junior Senator

Wayne Allard (R)

Elected 1996, seat up 2008, 2d term; b. Dec. 2, 1943, Fort Collins; home, Loveland; CO St. U., D.V.M. 1968; Protestant; married (Joan).

Elected Office: CO Senate, 1982–90; US House of Reps., 1990–96.

Professional Career: Veterinarian, 1968–present; Loveland City Health Officer, 1970–78; Owner, Allard Animal Hosp., 1970–90.

DC Office: 525 DSOB, 20510, 202-224-5941; Fax: 202-224-6471; Web site: allard.senate.gov.

State Offices: Colorado Springs, 719-634-6071; Denver, 303-220-7414; Grand Junction, 970-245-9553; Loveland, 970-461-3530; Pueblo, 719-545-9751.

Committees: *Armed Services:* Emerging Threats & Capabilities; Readiness & Management Support; Strategic Forces (Chmn.). *Banking, Housing & Urban Affairs:* Financial Institutions; Housing & Transportation (Chmn.); Securities & Investment. *Budget. Environment & Public Works:* Fisheries, Wildlife & Water; Superfund & Waste Management.

Group Ratings

	ADA	ACLU	AFS	LCV	CON	ITIC	NTU	COC	ACU	NTLC	CHC
2002	5	20	13	6	43	88	66	100	100	100	—
2001	5	—	0	13	—	—	88	100	100	—	100

National Journal Ratings

	2001 LIB	—	2001 CONS		2002 LIB	—	2002 CONS
Economic	30%	—	66%		14%	—	84%
Social	0%	—	79%		0%	—	62%
Foreign	7%	—	72%		0%	—	76%

Key Votes of the 107th Congress

1. Approve Bush Tax Cuts	Y	5. Confirm Ashcroft as AG	Y	9. Bar Coop. with Intl. Court	Y
2. Expand Patients' Rights	N	6. Bar Gays in the Boy Scouts	Y	10. Trade Promotion Authority	Y
3. Campaign Finance Reform	N	7. $ for Hate Crime Prosecution	N	11. Authorize Force in Iraq	Y
4. Permit ANWR Development	Y	8. Overseas Military Abortions	N	12. Homeland Sec. Dept. Union	*

Election Results

2002 general	Wayne Allard (R)	717,893	(51%)	($5,223,592)
	Tom Strickland (D)	648,130	(46%)	($5,160,517)
	Other	50,059	(3%)	
2002 primary	Wayne Allard (R)	unopposed		
1996 general	Wayne Allard (R)	750,325	(51%)	($2,233,429)
	Tom Strickland (D)	677,600	(46%)	($2,894,916)
	Other	41,686	(3%)	

Prior Winning Percentages: 1994 House (72%); 1992 House (58%); 1990 House (54%)

Wayne Allard is a Republican senator elected in 1996. He grew up in the northern end of the Front Range, the son of a cattle rancher and developer, attended veterinary school, then in 1970 started a veterinary practice in Loveland—a lively business in an area with vast feedlots. His father was a Democrat and a friend of conservative Democratic Congressman Wayne Aspinall, but both father and son switched parties after Aspinall was defeated by a liberal in the 1972 primary. In 1982, Allard was elected to the state Senate, where he succeeded in limiting the length of legislative sessions to 120 days, so legislators would be more in touch with their constituents. In 1990, when Congressman Hank Brown ran for the Senate, Allard ran for the House in the 4th District, which covered much of the High Plains and the northern end of the Front Range. Against a former local university president and legislator, Allard won a 54% victory. He was easily re-elected in 1992 and 1994 and, when Brown retired from the Senate after just one term, Allard ran for the seat.

Allard's voting record was one of the most conservative in the House. He was scarcely the most prominent candidate going into 1996, but others better known declined to run—former Senator Gary Hart, Governor Roy Romer, former Governor Dick Lamm. His primary opponent, Attorney General Gale Norton—now Bush's Interior secretary—lost in the Supreme Court defending Colorado's anti-gay rights Amendment 2 a month before the June 1996 nominating convention, and her support of abortion rights rankled many Republican activists and voters. With strong support from religious conservatives, Allard led 40%–31% at the convention. With more money, he ran a blitz of ads before the primary, stressing his background as a veterinarian: "Four candidates for the U.S. Senate. Three more lawyers and Wayne Allard." In the August 13 primary, Allard won 57%–43%.

The Democratic nominee was Tom Strickland, law partner of Phil Brownstein, one of the state's key fundraisers and political insiders. Strickland had more money and sophistication, but Allard ended up with more votes. Strickland held fundraisers with Robert Redford and Gloria Steinem and attacked Allard's "Neanderthal" positions on the environment; Allard said he was interested in "sound science" rather than emotional appeals, more local decision-making and less bureaucracy. Allard ran ads attacking Strickland for defending clients with environmental problems, including one company trying to build a medical waste incinerator in a poor Denver neighborhood. Allard won 51%–46%.

Allard has a very conservative voting record in the Senate and has often been part of small minorities taking conservative stands—on the Chemical Weapons convention and the May 1997 budget deal, for instance. As ranking member and chairman of the Armed Services Strategic Forces Subcommittee, he has strongly supported missile defense and pushed to develop space-based radar and defenses for space-based assets.

Allard gets low ratings from national environmental groups, but has done much work on his own environmental causes. With 2d District Democrat Mark Udall, he has worked successfully to create a wildlife refuge at Rocky Flats, a much-polluted nuclear plant near Denver that closed in 1989; this was modeled on his action as a House member, when he joined with Democrat Patricia Schroeder to make the Rocky Mountain Arsenal site a wildlife refuge. He won a 15% increase for the National Renewable Energy Laboratory in Golden.

One of Allard's most interesting proposals is a ban on the interstate shipment of roosters for cockfighting. He explains: "I'm a veterinarian. I've never supported the idea of animal fighting. My training is not to encourage that kind of treatment of animals with no purpose other than fighting." By summer 2000, Allard had rounded up a majority of senators as co-sponsors. Cockfighting is illegal in every state but Louisiana and New Mexico; Oklahoma voters voted to ban it in November 2002.

Allard promised in 1996 to hold town meetings in all 63 counties. Every year he has kept that promise, recently adding to his schedule the state's 64th and newest county, Broomfield, which was carved out of several Denver-area counties in November 2001. By fall 2002, he claimed to have held 601 public meetings. Yet as the election approached, he remained relatively little known. Perhaps one-quarter of 2002 voters did not vote in Colorado in 1996 and had never seen Allard's name on a ballot. The county meetings may not have helped much. Some 79% of Colorado voters live in 10 large counties, where a public meeting is likely to have little impact, and the time

Allard and his wife spent driving to meetings in the other 53 or 54 counties every year might have been more profitably spent setting up events likely to be covered by Denver TV stations. Allard, analyst Charlie Cook has written, "always manages to avoid the publicity that some of his colleagues crave so dearly." To such charges Allard responded, "At the end of the day, there are work horses, and there are show horses. As a veterinarian, I know the difference."

Allard's 2002 opponent was again Tom Strickland, who served as Colorado's U.S. Attorney from 1999 to 2001. Early polls showed Allard ahead, but well under 50%, with as many as 30% undecided. There was a vast contrast in style between the rural and stolid Allard and the urban and urbane Strickland: The candidate of the simple rural areas versus the candidate of the sophisticated urban core in a mostly suburban state. Strickland said his favorite food (in landlocked Colorado) was sushi; Allard said his was his wife's Crisco cherry pie. Allard boasted that he handed $2.5 million back to the treasury because he kept a small staff, and pointed out that Strickland passed out a $250,000 surplus in the U.S. Attorney's office to employees as bonuses. Allard constantly called Strickland a lawyer-lobbyist; Strickland called Allard a far right winger and ran ads saying he lived in a right-wing "Wayne's World." Strickland described himself as a conservative Democrat, ready and able to work with senators in both parties; he called for broader access to health care and a $12,000 per year deduction for college tuition. Though he had called for new gun control laws in 1996, in 2002 he said he only wanted current gun laws enforced—a suggestion of how public opinion on gun control had changed in Colorado.

Much of the campaign dialogue focused on corporate wrongdoing and the candidates' involvement in it. Some of the accusations came in the candidates' 13 debates, but voters saw it more in the independent expenditure ads. Over the summer, the bulk were run by liberal groups against Allard; the Club for Growth and the NRA chimed in with ads against Strickland later. Strickland accused Allard of promoting the 1999 acquisition by Qwest of USWest, which had turned out badly, and criticized him for buying 50 shares of Qwest one day after the acquisition was announced. Allard responded that in 1998 Strickland made a profit of $25,000 in one day because he was let in to the IPO of Global Crossing (which later failed). Allard called Strickland a liberal "elitist" who had worked for a company that wanted to build a medical waste incinerator in north Denver in the late 1980s.

The two candidates' campaigns spent about the same, though Allard charged that far more independent spending was made on Strickland's behalf. But Allard had a countervailing advantage. Colorado's newcomers have been heavily Republican, and in 2002, the Republican party made a major ground effort to register them and to get them to vote absentee. In 1996, Colorado Republicans' registration advantage was 102,000; in 2002, it was 171,000. There was a stark and unusual difference in polls in this race: In late October, Democrats' tracking polls and most public polls showed Strickland even or ahead, while Republican tracking polls showed Allard leading. Evidently the Republicans' polls were right: Allard won 51%–46%, the exact same percentages for both candidates as in 1996. Allard was shellacked in Denver and Boulder and carried the old-line suburban Jefferson and Arapahoe Counties with only 51% and 52% of the vote. But he won 65% in fast-growing Douglas County, where the turnout was up 40% from the last off-year election, and 66% in Colorado Springs's El Paso County. Strickland carried some fashionable resort areas in the Western Slope and a few Hispanic counties in the south; Allard won large margins in most of the Western Slope and most of the Eastern Plains counties. Strickland carried metro Denver 51%–45%, but Allard carried the rest of the state 57%–39%.

Allard had long said that he intended to serve only two terms. But after 6th District Rep. Tom Tancredo renounced his term limit pledge in September 2002, Allard, asked whether he would run again, said, "I may or may not. I don't want to talk about what I'll be doing six years from now. I don't see me running again."

FIRST DISTRICT

Rep. Diana DeGette (D)

Elected 1996, 4th term; b. July 29, 1957, Tachikawa, Japan; home, Denver; CO Col., B.A. 1979, N.Y.U., J.D. 1982; Presbyterian; married (Lino Lipinsky).

Elected Office: CO House of Reps., 1992–96, Asst. Min. Ldr., 1994–95.

Professional Career: Practicing atty., 1982–96.

DC Office: 1530 LHOB 20515, 202-225-4431; Fax: 202-225-5657; Web site: www.house.gov/degette.

District Office: Denver, 303-844-4988.

Committees: *Energy & Commerce* (19th of 26 D): Commerce, Trade & Consumer Protection; Environment & Hazardous Materials; Health; Oversight & Investigations.

Group Ratings

	ADA	ACLU	AFS	LCV	CON	ITIC	NTU	COC	ACU	NTLC	CHC
2002	95	93	100	100	75	50	26	35	0	36	0
2001	95	—	100	100	—	—	10	39	0	—	—

National Journal Ratings

	2001 LIB	—	2001 CONS		2002 LIB	—	2002 CONS
Economic	87%	—	13%		95%	—	0%
Social	90%	—	0%		94%	—	3%
Foreign	90%	—	10%		90%	—	8%

Key Votes of the 107th Congress

1. Approve Bush Tax Cuts	N	5. Faith-Based Charities	N
2. Limit Patients' Bill of Rights	N	6. Bar Gays in the Boy Scouts	N
3. Campaign Finance Reform	Y	7. Ban Partial-Birth Abortion	N
4. Ban ANWR Development	Y	8. Arm Commercial Pilots	N

9. Trade Promotion Authority	N
10. Bar Funds for Intl. Court	N
11. Authorize Force in Iraq	N
12. Deny Home. Sec. Dept. Union	N

Election Results

2002 general	Diana DeGette (D)	111,718	(66%)	($787,840)
	Ken Chlouber (R)	49,884	(30%)	($114,832)
	Other	6,962	(3%)	
2002 primary	Diana DeGette (D)	24,526	(73%)	
	Ramona Martinez (D)	8,853	(27%)	
2000 general	Diana DeGette (D)	141,831	(69%)	($542,495)
	Jesse L. Thomas (R)	56,291	(27%)	($63,514)
	Other	8,312	(4%)	

Prior Winning Percentages: 1998 (67%); 1996 (57%)

The People		Race/Ethnic Origin	Ancestry	
Area size:	173 sq. mi.	54.3% White	German: 11.6%	Irish: 7.8%
Urban population:	100.0%	10.1% Black	English: 6.9%	
Rural population:	0.0%	2.7% Asian	**2000 Presidential Vote**	
Pop. 2000:	614,465	0.7% Native Am.	Gore (D) 134,187	(61%)
Median income:	$39,658	0.1% Hawaiian	Bush (R) 72,455	(33%)
Poverty status:	13.7%	1.9% Two + races	Other 14,430	(7%)
Military veterans:	11.3%	0.2% Other	**Cook Partisan Voting Index:** D +15	
		30.0% Hispanic Origin		

Occupation	Blue collar: 20.4%	White collar: 64.3%	Gray collar: 15.3%

The mile high city: One mile above sea level (as the plaque on the 14th step of the gold-domed Capitol reads), a few miles from where the High Plains yield to the sharp peaks of the Front Range of the Rockies, on no historic trade route and with a fresh water supply adequate for a town one-tenth of its size, stands the great metropolitan center of Denver. With 555,000 people, the city has been the economic and cultural capital for 100 years of the whole Rocky Mountain region. On top of its Old West heritage and early 20th Century elegance, Denver has developed an exuberant postmodern style. The National Western Stock Show held here every year and the LoDo entertainment district redeveloped near the railyards along the South Platte evoke the Old West; the Capitol, the spacious parks, the aspens which line so many streets, give the city a lush, burnished air, in contrast to the dry high plains and the stark Rocky peaks. Amid its downtown grid, slanted on a 45-degree angle to align with the South Platte and the railroads, are the skyscrapers of the 1970s energy and 1990s high-tech booms, plus the new-old Coors Stadium and Elitch Gardens amusement park. Rather than losing population as many central cities have, it gained 19% in the 1990s; most of its neighborhoods have vitality, including the black neighborhoods of northeastern Denver, filled with well-maintained 1950s bungalows, and the Hispanic quarter northwest of downtown. But three-quarters of the metro area's people now live in the suburbs, and Denver has disproportionate numbers of singles and cultural liberals who value an urban lifestyle, in the gentrified areas south of the Capitol and the rich neighborhood where the Tattered Cover, among the nation's premier independent book stores, sits opposite posh Cherry Creek Shopping Center.

Denver has become the liberal heart of Colorado, heavily Democratic as the state mostly votes Republican, strongly liberation-minded on cultural issues, cautiously liberal on economic issues. Though it remains majority Anglo, it has elected Hispanic and black mayors for the past two decades. In the early 1970s, Denver liberals were hostile to growth and boosterism; today's Denver has shown that growth can improve a city. Twenty years ago Denver's winters were palled by "brown cloud" air pollution. But the city has cut down on wood fires and used non-polluting deicing agents and oxygenated gasoline, and now boasts of brown-cloudless winters. From Cherry Creek to LoDo, Denver has shown that growth can produce more of the distinctiveness that people here appreciate, and the downturn of 2001–02 has shown that there are things worse than growth. Civic pride is rampant: At the start of the 21st century, boosters noted that Denver was ranked among the nation's top 10 cities in its business climate, livability, libraries, and bikeways. In the lower downtown near Coors Field, dilapidated bars have been replaced by art galleries over the past decade. The down side is apparent if you are stalled in traffic on still-being-widened I-25 and its horrendous interchange with I-70.

The 1st Congressional District includes all of Denver and extends northeast to take in Denver International Airport, encompassing places with warehouses and trucking terminals on main streets and curved-street subdivisions behind. The 2002 redistricting added affluent suburbs, long-settled Englewood and newly-settled Cherry Hills Village, in Arapahoe County (the district includes just a fraction of Arapahoe). This remains a heavily Democratic district, and counts most of metro Denver's blacks and Hispanics, singles and gays: The percentage of households with married couples and children has been among the lowest in America, and was lower in 2000 than in 1990. In an era when cultural attitudes are a better clue to voting behavior than economic status, this district, politically marginal quarter-century ago, is solidly Democratic.

The congresswoman from the 1st District is Diana DeGette, a Democrat elected in 1996. DeGette is a fourth-generation Denverite (though she was born on a military base in Japan) who went away to law school, returned to practice employment law and became involved in politics. In 1992, at 35, she was elected to the Colorado House, where she was surprisingly productive for a member of the minority. She sponsored a "bubble" bill placing a zone of protection around abortion clinics and their clients, which the Supreme Court upheld in 2000; she passed a bill protecting families of accident victims from being contacted by lawyers within 30 days.

In 1995, Congresswoman Patricia Schroeder announced she was retiring after 24 years in the House; she was a pioneer of the feminist left, who gave serious consideration in 1987 to running for president and whose persistence on the Armed Services Committee helped change the military culture. Today, in a place like Denver, the feminist left is the heart of the Democratic Party (as the religious right is the heart of the Republican Party in Colorado Springs) and DeGette—feminist, organizationally adept and legislatively creative—has become a worthy successor to Schroeder. DeGette has a very liberal voting record. And she has shown on the Commerce

Committee, as she did in Denver, some legislative successes even though in the minority. She has focused especially on health-care issues. One victory was an amendment creating "presumptive eligibility" for Medicaid for poor families with children. The idea is to let hospitals and care-givers initiate the application for government aid, so that they get paid rather than provide their services for free. She won House passage of an amendment to ensure that organ-transplant legislation recognizes the needs of children; the House passed the controversial measure with bipartisan support. She angered her labor supporters, but pleased local business groups, by supporting PNTR with China. But she returned to labor's graces by opposing trade promotion authority for President Bush, and she criticized Commerce Committee Republicans for spending excessive time investigating Martha Stewart. In 2001, she supported Maryland Rep. Steny Hoyer in the contest for Minority Whip against California Rep. Nancy Pelosi.

In 2002, DeGette fared impressively against credible primary and general election opponents. Ramona Martinez, a 15-year term-limited member of the Denver City Council and a Democratic National Committeewoman, criticized DeGette for having lost touch with the district. While denying the charge, DeGette moved her family back to Denver from the Maryland suburbs in June 2001. She lamented that Schroeder was a tough act to follow. Although Martinez ran a competitive campaign, DeGette won by an unexpectedly large 73%–27%. Next came Republican Ken Chlouber, a rural state senator known for folksy humor and a flame-painted pickup truck, and relatively liberal views on labor and abortion. Chlouber won the Teamsters' endorsement and argued that the biggest difference between them was his outgoing personality. It was not nearly outgoing enough, apparently, in this Democratic district: DeGette won 66%–30%. The new redistricting map that Republicans approved in May 2003 makes this district even more strongly Democratic, by shifting its Arapahoe County boundaries to pull in more blacks and Hispanics from adjacent Republican districts.

SECOND DISTRICT

Rep. Mark Udall (D)

Elected 1998, 3d term; b. July 18, 1950, Tucson, AZ; home, Boulder; Williams Col., B.A. 1972; no religious affiliation; married (Maggie L. Fox).

Elected Office: CO House of Reps., 1996–98.

Professional Career: CO Outward Bound Course Dir., 1975–85, Exec. Dir., 1985–95.

DC Office: 115 CHOB 20515, 202-225-2161; Fax: 202-226-7840; Web site: www.house.gov/markudall.

District Office: Westminster, 303-650-7820.

Committees: *Agriculture* (22d of 24 D): Livestock & Horticulture. *Resources* (13th of 24 D): Forests & Forest Health; National Parks, Recreation & Public Lands. *Science* (8th of 22 D): Environment, Technology and Standards (RMM); Space & Aeronautics.

Group Ratings

	ADA	ACLU	AFS	LCV	CON	ITIC	NTU	COC	ACU	NTLC	CHC
2002	95	93	89	100	70	25	23	40	4	0	8
2001	100	—	100	100	—	—	14	35	0	—	—

National Journal Ratings

	2001 LIB	—	2001 CONS		2002 LIB	—	2002 CONS
Economic	74%	—	25%		66%	—	33%
Social	90%	—	0%		94%	—	6%
Foreign	90%	—	10%		76%	—	23%

Key Votes of the 107th Congress

1. Approve Bush Tax Cuts	N	5. Faith-Based Charities	N	9. Trade Promotion Authority	N
2. Limit Patients' Bill of Rights	N	6. Bar Gays in the Boy Scouts	N	10. Bar Funds for Intl. Court	N
3. Campaign Finance Reform	Y	7. Ban Partial-Birth Abortion	N	11. Authorize Force in Iraq	N
4. Ban ANWR Development	Y	8. Arm Commercial Pilots	N	12. Deny Home. Sec. Dept. Union	N

Election Results

2002 general	Mark Udall (D)	123,504	(60%)	($776,268)
	Sandy Hume (R)	75,564	(37%)	($34,430)
	Other	6,454	(3%)	
2002 primary	Mark Udall (D)	unopposed		
2000 general	Mark Udall (D)	155,725	(55%)	($1,330,529)
	Carolyn Cox (R)	109,338	(39%)	($512,085)
	Ronald N. Forthofer (Green)	12,398	(4%)	($37,912)
	Other	5,655	(2%)	

Prior Winning Percentages: 1998 (50%)

The People		Race/Ethnic Origin	Ancestry	
Area size:	5,664 sq. mi.	78.9% White	German: 16.9%	Irish: 9.8%
Urban population:	87.3%	1.0% Black	English: 9.1%	
Rural population:	12.7%	3.2% Asian	**2000 Presidential Vote**	
Pop. 2000:	614,465	0.5% Native Am.	Gore (D)	126,607 (52%)
Median income:	$55,204	0.1% Hawaiian	Bush (R)	103,518 (43%)
Poverty status:	7.4%	1.5% Two+ races	Other	13,107 (5%)
Military veterans:	11.2%	0.1% Other	**Cook Partisan Voting Index:** D + 5	
		14.7% Hispanic Origin		

Occupation   Blue collar: 20.2%   White collar: 66.3%   Gray collar: 13.5%

Nestled right up against the Front Range of the Rockies, Boulder, the home of the 28,000-student University of Colorado, once billed by its convention bureau as "a combination of lycra-clad athletes, New Age artists, and thoughtful intellectuals sipping cappuccinos." It has been called the nation's number one town for outdoor sports by *Outdoor* magazine, and an "international mecca for people who thrive on physical challenge and risk" by journalist Clifford May. Boulder, dubbed the "adventure capital of the U.S.," is one of the nation's leading centers for bungee jumping, mountain biking, snowshoe running, rock and ice climbing, downhill skiing, land surfing and hot-air ballooning. It is also the home of the Buddhist Naropa Institute and the Boulder School of Massage Therapy. All of which is suggested by the terrain: The grid streets of Boulder literally look up at erose peaks rising to 14,000 feet from a mile-high plain stretching farther than the eye can see. But not all is pleasant in this paradise: Boulder is where child model JonBenet Ramsey was murdered in 1996, and the supermarket tabloids are still full of the story though the Ramseys have long since moved away.

The 2d Congressional District is centered on Boulder. It includes most of Boulder County and extends west along Interstate 70 on its awesome course through the mountains as it takes in some lightly-populated but picturesque Rocky Mountains acreage, including the old mining town of Central City and the lodges and resorts of Vail. The district contains some of the northwest suburbs of Denver—Northglenn, Federal Heights, Lafayette and most of Westminster and Thornton—and the old Rocky Flats nuclear weapons plant, now being converted to a national wildlife refuge. The plant, where plutonium triggers were once manufactured, was home to the notorious Building 771—once known as the "most dangerous building in America" because of its immeasurably high levels of radioactive contamination. Also in the district is Broomfield County, which separated from Boulder County to become Colorado's 64th and newest county in November 2001. Greater Boulder has grappled with the effects of commercial and residential "growth management," as development is restricted to just 1% annually and open space is protected by a "blue line" barrier, causing housing prices to soar. Politically, the Metro North area is marginal while

Boulder is heavily Democratic. Overall, this remains one of half a dozen Democratic districts in the Rocky Mountain states.

The congressman from the 2d District is Mark Udall, a Democrat elected in a close race in 1998. Udall is the son of longtime (1961–91) Arizona Congressman Morris Udall, who ran for president in 1976 and died in December 1998, and the nephew of Stewart Udall, who served in the House before his brother and was Interior secretary from 1961–68. "I can remember the excitement I felt sitting in a corner of Stewart's kitchen listening to my father, Stewart, Bob McNamara, Bobby Kennedy and Justice Douglas talk about the issues of the day, and there was a sense of optimism and sense of involvement and sense of meaning," Mark has said. He is also a cousin of Oregon Senator Gordon Smith, a Republican, and of New Mexico Congressman Tom Udall, a Democrat also elected in 1998. Another Udall ran in 2002, but lost in the new Arizona 1st District. "Vote for the Udall nearest you," as Mark put it.

Soon after college, Udall moved to Boulder to work for the Colorado Outward Bound School and headed it for 10 years. He is an accomplished mountaineer (though he didn't quite make it to the top of Mount Everest), rock climber and kayaker. In 1996, he ran for the state House, and with his family and ideological connections raised 40% of his money out of state and won. In October 1997, Udall was one of several candidates spurred to run when incumbent Democratic Congressman David Skaggs retired. Republicans nominated Bob Greenlee, mayor of Boulder, who put more than $1 million of his own money into his campaign; Udall stressed environmental protection, growth management and education. Greenlee ran well in the Metro North suburbs, but even with all his involvement in local government and charities in Boulder, he still lost Boulder County, where nearly half the votes were cast, 56%–41%. That gave Udall a 50%–47% victory.

With seats on the Resources and Science Committees and his co-chairmanship of the Renewable Energy Caucus, Udall focuses on the West and environmental issues. Three months after George W. Bush took office, Udall called his energy policy a "war on the West." While the huge Hayman wildfire—the largest in state history—burned close to 138,000 acres in June-July 2002, he urged greater cooperation among key players to reduce the risk of future disasters. In response to complaints from seniors, he filed a bill to separate from the U.S. gross domestic product the reimbursement rate for Medicare payments to physicians. He cited his father's regret over supporting the Tonkin Gulf resolution in 1964, as he explained his October 2002 opposition to the resolution authorizing force against Iraq.

Udall has had relatively easy re-elections. His 2000 challenger spent $450,000 of her own money, but national Republicans did not target the district, and Udall won 55%–39%. Redistricting made the district a bit more Democratic, and Udall's 2002 challenger, Boulder County Treasurer—and Sierra Club member—Sandy Hume ran a campaign that *The Denver Post* reported was "marked by uncommon civility." Udall won 60%–37%. During the fall campaign, he complained when a TV commercial for Senator Wayne Allard showed Udall standing next to him; they had worked together on making Rocky Flats a national wildlife refuge. Udall is often mentioned as a contender for statewide office, perhaps for Senator Ben Nighthorse Campbell's seat in 2004, though he seems much more likely to run if Campbell retires than if he runs for reelection. The redistricting plan passed in May 2003 added several thousand more Democrats to the district by swapping small parts of the Denver suburbs, further entrenching the seat's Democratic trend.

THIRD DISTRICT

Rep. Scott McInnis (R)

Elected 1992, 6th term; b. May 9, 1953, Glenwood Springs; home, Grand Junction; Ft. Lewis Col., B.A. 1975, St. Mary's U., J.D. 1980; Catholic; married (Lori).

Elected Office: CO House of Reps., 1982–92, Maj. Ldr., 1990–92.

Professional Career: Glenwood Springs Police Officer, 1976; Practicing atty., 1980–92.

DC Office: 320 CHOB 20515, 202-225-4761; Fax: 202-226-0622; Web site: www.house.gov/mcinnis.

District Offices: Durango, 970-259-2754; Glenwood Springs, 970-928-0637; Grand Junction, 970-245-7107; Pueblo, 719-543-8200.

Committees: *Resources* (9th of 28 R): Forests & Forest Health (Chmn.). *Ways & Means* (19th of 24 R): Human Resources; Oversight.

Group Ratings

	ADA	ACLU	AFS	LCV	CON	ITIC	NTU	COC	ACU	NTLC	CHC
2002	0	7	13	25	77	100	61	95	100	91	100
2001	0	—	0	14	—	—	69	83	86	—	—

National Journal Ratings

	2001 LIB	—	2001 CONS		2002 LIB	—	2002 CONS
Economic	38%	—	62%		39%	—	60%
Social	34%	—	67%		0%	—	75%
Foreign	27%	—	72%		0%	—	85%

Key Votes of the 107th Congress

1. Approve Bush Tax Cuts	Y	5. Faith-Based Charities	Y	9. Trade Promotion Authority	Y
2. Limit Patients' Bill of Rights	Y	6. Bar Gays in the Boy Scouts	Y	10. Bar Funds for Intl. Court	Y
3. Campaign Finance Reform	N	7. Ban Partial-Birth Abortion	Y	11. Authorize Force in Iraq	Y
4. Ban ANWR Development	N	8. Arm Commercial Pilots	Y	12. Deny Home. Sec. Dept. Union	Y

Election Results

2002 general	Scott McInnis (R)	143,433	(66%)	($567,940)
	Denis Berckefeldt (D)	68,160	(31%)	
	Other	6,379	(3%)	
2002 primary	Scott McInnis (R)	unopposed		
2000 general	Scott McInnis (R)	199,204	(66%)	($545,836)
	Curtis Imrie (D)	87,921	(29%)	
	Other	15,415	(5%)	

Prior Winning Percentages: 1998 (66%); 1996 (69%); 1994 (70%); 1992 (55%)

The People		Race/Ethnic Origin	Ancestry	
Area size:	54,100 sq. mi.	74.6% White	German: 13.6%	English: 9.0%
Urban population:	61.0%	0.7% Black	Irish: 8.1%	
Rural population:	39.0%	0.5% Asian	**2000 Presidential Vote**	
Pop. 2000:	614,467	1.4% Native Am.	Bush (R)	140,191 (54%)
Median income:	$35,970	0.1% Hawaiian	Gore (D)	102,100 (39%)
Poverty status:	12.8%	1.2% Two+ races	Other	19,585 (7%)
Military veterans:	15.3%	0.1% Other	**Cook Partisan Voting Index:** R + 8	
		21.5% Hispanic Origin		

Occupation	Blue collar: 25.0%	White collar: 56.1%	Gray collar: 18.9%

On a clear night from the air, they look like tiny mottled veins with small clots here and there, thicker near Denver but never very bright: The lights of the civilization Americans have built on the Western Slope of the Rockies in Colorado. The lights follow the trails of valley roads and mountainside switchbacks. The nodes mark the dozens of little towns built during mining boom years: The gold rush of the 1870s, the uranium boom of the 1950s, and the oil shale boomlet of the 1970s. The Western Slope—everything west of the Front Range, with dozens of peaks over 14,000 feet—has always blocked east-west movement; except for mining and now skiing, no one would have followed the Ute Indians and settled here. The miners who tracked gold and silver and lead ores also built Victorian towns with opera houses and gingerbread storefronts in Aspen and Telluride in valleys and defiles scarcely accessible to the outside world. Now, many of these towns have been restored by ski resort operators and joined by dozens of new condominiums and shopping malls. Cries of overdevelopment have followed, and stimulated different responses. One is extreme: The "Earth Liberation Front" announced it burned $12 million of Vail's resort expansion facilities "on behalf of the lynx," whose reintroduction to the area began in February 1999. But there is also consensus between former adversaries: Cattlemen and environmentalists are using land trusts to preserve open land in pastures around Steamboat Springs.

The political map of the Western Slope is as diverse as its history. Aspen and Telluride, with Victorian houses and counter-cultural substrata, are liberal and Democratic. Crested Butte and Steamboat Springs, with contemporary condominiums, formerly Republican, are trending left. The rough-handed mining area around Grand Junction, where piles of tailings still crackle with radioactivity, Glenwood Springs, with its old hot springs hotel once visited by President Taft, and the northwest corner of the state, where people remember the oil shale boom with nostalgia, are hostile to environmentalists and heavily Republican.

The 3d Congressional District is the state's largest and includes most of the Western Slope. Redistricters in 2002 removed some of the resort and mining towns like Vail and Leadville. But the southern end of the district continues to move east of the Front Range to include the small industrial city of Pueblo. There, on the banks of the Arkansas River, the Rockefellers built large steel factories before World War I to make barbed wire and rails; now, this blue-collar town has attracted large medical centers and some industrial plants. Pueblo is heavily Democratic and so are Hispanic Conejos and Costilla counties just to the south. These inhabitants are Hispanic, not Mexican-American: Spanish-speaking people have been living here, as in northern New Mexico, for 350 years. Politically, the 3d District has been moving to the right, voting for Bill Clinton in 1992 but for Bob Dole in 1996 and George W. Bush in 2000. On balance, it is a Republican district.

The congressman from the 3d District is Scott McInnis, a Republican elected in 1992, when then-Democratic Congressman Ben Nighthorse Campbell was elected senator. McInnis grew up in Glenwood Springs, in a valley so deeply crevassed that Interstate 70 running into the town is double-decked. He worked as a local policeman and went to law school, practiced law and was elected to the legislature in 1982, at 29. Colorado was one of the few states in the 1980s with a Republican legislature, and McInnis became House majority leader in 1990. In 1992, he won the 3d District Republican nomination unopposed; he outworked and outcampaigned Lieutenant Governor Mike Callihan to win 55%–44%.

McInnis has a moderate-to-conservative voting record, with some maverick tendencies; he supports funding for the National Endowment for the Arts and Denver's light rail, for example. He has followed in the footsteps of members from Henry Gonzalez to Newt Gingrich with frequent late-night "special orders" on the House floor, during which he often speaks for an hour about his party's or his own latest ideas. He has criticized such local sacred cows as the Air Force Academy (for allowing its graduates to cut short their active duty so they can play professional football) and United Airlines (for its poor service in Denver). During the Gary Condit furor, he sparked complaints from both sides of the aisle for requesting an ethics committee rule banning sexual relationships between interns and House members. But McInnis was enough of a party regular to win a seat on Ways and Means.

As chairman of the Forests and Forest Health Subcommittee, he held hearings on eco-terrorist groups that destroy property to "save" the environment. With Democrat George Miller, he pushed legislation to remove obstacles to the thinning of overgrown forests, which he said was designed to reduce the West's massive wildfires; his alternative imposed more limits on new forest roads than did a Bush administration plan, but environmentalists still objected. The willingness of the liberal Miller to cooperate with McInnis was unusual, but Democrats were sensitive to being portrayed as obstructionists; western Republicans like McInnis were blaming the environmental lobby for clogging the courts with lawsuits blocking federal attempts to thin combustible forest undergrowth. According to McInnis, "It is clear the Wilderness Society and Sierra Club did not strike the match but they certainly contributed." With Miller, McInnis sought to relax requirements of the National Environmental Policy Act and in early October 2002, Miller said they were "very close" to an agreement. But the Resources Committee later that month approved a modified version of McInnis' bill on a mostly party-line vote of 23–14; Democrats and environmentalists contended that the proposal "emasculates" environmental laws. Miller ultimately voted against the alternative plan in committee; the bill died at the end of the 107th Congress.

The wildfire issue has cut both ways for McInnis. He was ubiquitous as western Colorado's forests burned in 2002, showing up at fire command centers and shelters, and drew statewide attention. Yet in hard-hit La Plata County, his candor made him some enemies. In a letter, county commissioners requested additional federal assistance; McInnis replied that more aid was unlikely and that, given budget constraints, "there is not enough funding available to make whole every Colorado community, business, and individual hit by fire, drought, chronic wasting disease and other unexpected events." The *Durango Herald* ran this headline: "McInnis to County: Help? Hah!"

Still, McInnis remains upwardly mobile. In the House, he voiced interest in chairing the Resources Committee in 2003, even though eight Republicans had more seniority; California's Richard Pombo won the post instead. His plan to run for the Senate in 1998 was foiled when Campbell dropped plans to run for governor following his 1995 party switch and ran for re-election. McInnis grudgingly dropped out under pressure from national Republicans who were eager not to penalize a party-switcher. But his campaign war chest exceeds $1 million and he has been mentioned as a future statewide candidate. His focus on lands issues could help him: *The Denver Post* called McInnis "a surprisingly strong conservationist." McInnis's switch on his 1992 pledge to limit himself to four terms didn't bother his constituents much. Although the district is safe so long as McInnis wants it, Democrats had some hope of winning it if it became open. But the redistricting plan passed in May 2003 strengthened Republicans here—and McInnis's interest in a statewide bid—by adding new rural areas and removing Hispanic neighborhoods in Pueblo.

FOURTH DISTRICT

Rep. Marilyn Musgrave (R)

Elected 2002, 1st term; b. Jan. 27, 1949, Greeley; home, Ft. Morgan; CO St. U., B.A. 1972; First Assembly of God; married (Steve).

Elected Office: Ft. Morgan Schl. Bd., 1990–94; CO House of Reps., 1994–98; CO Senate, 1998–02.

DC Office: 1208 LHOB 20515, 202-225-4676; Fax: 202-225-5870; Web site: www.house.gov/musgrave.

District Offices: Greeley, 970-352-4037; Las Animas, 719-456-0925; Loveland, 970-663-3536; Sterling, 970-522-1788.

Committees: *Agriculture* (25th of 27 R): General Farm Commodities & Risk Management; Livestock & Horticulture. *Education & the Workforce* (24th of 27 R): Education Reform; Employer-Employee Relations. *Small Business* (12th of 18 R): Rural Enterprises, Agriculture and Technology; Tax, Finance & Exports.

Group Ratings and Key Votes: Newly Elected

Election Results

2002 general	Marilyn Musgrave (R)	115,359	(55%)	($1,249,564)
	Stan Matsunaka (D)	87,499	(42%)	($959,962)
	Other	7,097	(3%)	
2002 primary	Marilyn Musgrave (R)	28,683	(65%)	
	Jeff Bedingfield (R)	15,743	(35%)	
2000 general	Bob Schaffer (R)	209,078	(79%)	($248,736)
	Dan Sewell Ward (NL)	19,721	(7%)	($4,444)
	Kordon L. Baker (Lib)	19,713	(7%)	
	Leslie J. Hanks (AC)	9,955	(4%)	
	Other	4,539	(2%)	

The People		Race/Ethnic Origin	Ancestry	
Area size:	31,048 sq. mi.	79.4% White	German: 20.3%	English: 8.7%
Urban population:	75.1%	0.7% Black	Irish: 8.4%	
Rural population:	24.9%	1.1% Asian	**2000 Presidential Vote**	
Pop. 2000:	614,466	0.5% Native Am.	Bush (R) 145,056 (57%)	
Median income:	$43,389	0.1% Hawaiian	Gore (D) 92,602 (36%)	
Poverty status:	10.9%	1.2% Two+ races	Other 16,271 (6%)	
Military veterans:	12.3%	0.1% Other	**Cook Partisan Voting Index:** R +11	
		17.0% Hispanic Origin		

Occupation	Blue collar: 24.0%	White collar: 59.8%	Gray collar: 16.2%

The High Plains of eastern Colorado are dusty brown, gently rolling grasslands that seem flat but actually slope imperceptibly up toward the Rocky Mountains. The land is fertile, but dry: Rainfall is rare, the rivers are just a trickle most of the year, and in many places groundwater is equally scarce. It is fine wheat country when irrigated and one of the foremost beef cattle regions. But it has been squeezed in recent decades between declining prices for wheat and declining demand for beef and increased prices for water because of high demand in Denver and along the Front Range. Bitter confrontations continue over who gets access to the South Platte River. Local farmers are now finding that the value of their water rights to metro Denver far exceeds what they hope to gain by farming; their neighbors condemn them for selling out and betraying a way of life that seems destined to decline. The prairie lands and small towns of the High Plains have small reminders of their past: The Pawnee National Grasslands, where antelope, coyotes and prairie dogs still roam, and Burlington's 1905 carousel, one of the few with the original paint. But the free market that once peopled the High Plains with farmers and ranchers and made it the scene of farm protests and revolts is now causing it to empty out and revert to untamed land, ready again for now increasingly numerous buffalo. The 2.4 male-female ratio in Crowley County is the nation's highest and reminiscent of frontier days—the main reason is more than one-third of the residents are in prison.

The 4th Congressional District contains almost all of the High Plains plus the medium-sized and fast-growing area around Greeley, Fort Collins and Loveland—the northern end of the densely populated Front Range, off I-25 toward Cheyenne, Wyoming. It includes all of Larimer County (which grew by 35% in the 1990s), and reaches into Boulder County to pick up the city of Longmont. Fort Collins became a center for California transplants seeking a different lifestyle at startup telecommunications firms, and appeared to survive the dot.com bust by spending its money on infrastructure instead of corporate incentives. Fort Collins also is home to a Centers for Disease Control and Prevention lab that conducts cutting-edge research in the war against bio-terrorism. By heritage and usually by inclination, this is Republican territory: It was evenly split in 1992, but later gave solid margins to Bob Dole and George W. Bush. Redistricting removed Denver suburban areas and Hispanic Las Animas County on the New Mexico border. The result is a district whose population is based north of Denver, though its land is mostly to the east.

The congresswoman from the 4th District is Marilyn Musgrave, elected in 2002; she replaced Bob Schaffer, a fellow Republican who reluctantly abided by his pledge to limit himself to three terms. Musgrave grew up in rural Weld County, where she worked as a waitress, cleaned houses and cared for children. She first became interested in politics when a liberal teacher in her high school government class inspired her with his interest in issues. She pursued her interest in social studies at Colorado State, where she found herself increasingly disturbed by socialist ideas. She and her husband Steve, whom she married at college, started a hay-stacking business. Musgrave was first elected to public office in 1990 as a member of the Fort Morgan school board and in 1994, she was elected to the state House. In 1998, she successfully challenged a popular Democratic state senator. In the statehouse, she earned a reputation as an honest, but uncompromising social conservative. She was one of the legislature's strongest Second Amendment supporters, an advocate of tax cuts and a sponsor of bills opposing abortion, same-sex marriage and adoptions by same-sex parents.

When Schaffer announced in November 2001 he would honor his term limits pledge and retire, Musgrave became the immediate front-runner to replace him. In the Republican primary, she was challenged by Greeley lawyer and former Weld County Republican Chairman Jeff Bedingfield, who criticized her focus on cultural issues, pointed to her support from a splinter group of gun owners and to her ardent opposition to abortion and gay rights. Some Republicans feared a bitter conservative-versus-moderate clash. But Musgrave won Schaffer's backing, and easily won the primary 65%–35%. In the general, she faced state Senator Stan Matsunaka of Loveland who, after the Democrats won a one-seat majority in the Senate in 2000, thwarted many of her legislative initiatives. Matsunaka had considered running for governor, but decided not to take on popular incumbent Bill Owens; national Democrats recruited him because of history of winning over Republican voters in Larimer County. Matsunaka emphasized his fiscal conservatism and his support for gun ownership rights. At every opportunity, he depicted Musgrave as an ineffective extremist and as a zealot on cultural issues. But Musgrave raised more money, which enabled her to pick apart Matsunaka's record on tax issues. At the end of the campaign, voters could be excused for thinking that Matsunaka's name was "Stan Taxsunaka" or "Stan the Tax Man." Musgrave's 55%–42% victory was easier than many had expected—she won all 18 counties. In Larimer County, which cast about 45% of the vote, Musgrave won 50%–47%. In Weld and Morgan Counties, she led Matsunaka by 3–2 margins. In the eastern plains, she won overwhelmingly.

FIFTH DISTRICT

Rep. Joel Hefley (R)

Elected 1986, 9th term; b. Apr. 18, 1935, Ardmore, OK; home, Colorado Springs; OK Baptist U., B.A. 1957; OK St. U., M.S. 1962; Baptist; married (Lynn).

Elected Office: CO House of Reps., 1976–78; CO Senate, 1978–86.

Professional Career: Exec. Dir., Community Planning & Research Cncl., 1966–86.

DC Office: 2372 RHOB 20515, 202-225-4422; Fax: 202-225-1942; Web site: www.house.gov/hefley.

District Office: Colorado Springs, 719-520-0055.

Committees: *Armed Services* (3d of 33 R): Readiness (Chmn.); Tactical Air & Land Forces; Terrorism, Unconventional Threats & Capabilities. *Standards of Official Conduct* (Chmn. of 5 R).

Group Ratings

	ADA	ACLU	AFS	LCV	CON	ITIC	NTU	COC	ACU	NTLC	CHC
2002	0	0	0	25	89	75	65	78	100	97	100
2001	5	—	11	7	—	—	78	74	96	—	—

National Journal Ratings

	2001 LIB —	2001 CONS	2002 LIB —	2002 CONS
Economic	39%	61%	31%	69%
Social	0%	81%	0%	75%
Foreign	33%	60%	0%	85%

Key Votes of the 107th Congress

1. Approve Bush Tax Cuts	Y	5. Faith-Based Charities	Y	9. Trade Promotion Authority	Y
2. Limit Patients' Bill of Rights	Y	6. Bar Gays in the Boy Scouts	Y	10. Bar Funds for Intl. Court	Y
3. Campaign Finance Reform	*	7. Ban Partial-Birth Abortion	Y	11. Authorize Force in Iraq	Y
4. Ban ANWR Development	N	8. Arm Commercial Pilots	Y	12. Deny Home. Sec. Dept. Union	Y

Election Results

2002 general	Joel Hefley (R)	128,118	(69%)	($100,786)
	Curtis Imrie (D)	45,587	(25%)	
	Biff Baker (Lib)	10,972	(6%)	($32,333)
2002 primary	Joel Hefley (R)	unopposed		
2000 general	Joel Hefley (R)	253,330	(83%)	($127,282)
	Kerry Kantor (Lib)	37,719	(12%)	
	Randy MacKenzie (NL)	15,260	(5%)	

Prior Winning Percentages: 1998 (73%); 1996 (72%); 1994 (100%); 1992 (71%); 1990 (66%); 1988 (75%); 1986 (70%)

The People		Race/Ethnic Origin	Ancestry	
Area size:	7,732 sq. mi.	77.4% White	German: 16.1%	Irish: 9.1%
Urban population:	85.7%	5.7% Black	English: 8.9%	
Rural population:	14.3%	2.2% Asian	**2000 Presidential Vote**	
Pop. 2000:	614,467	0.7% Native Am.	Bush (R)	151,751	(63%)
Median income:	$45,454	0.2% Hawaiian	Gore (D)	74,940	(31%)
Poverty status:	8.3%	2.5% Two + races	Other	13,116	(5%)
Military veterans:	19.9%	0.2% Other	**Cook Partisan Voting Index:** R +17	
		11.1% Hispanic Origin		

Occupation	Blue collar: 21.3%	White collar: 63.2%	Gray collar: 15.5%

In 1893, Katherine Lee Bates took the cog railway up from Colorado Springs to the top of 14,110-foot Pikes Peak and, looking out at the purple mountain's majesty above amber waves of grain, wrote the lines of "America the Beautiful." Pike's Peak, espied by Zebulon Pike in 1806, and Colorado Springs, with the Garden of the Gods and the Broadmoor Hotel, have been tourist attractions for more than 100 years. In the second half of the 20th century, Colorado Springs, safe in the fastness of North America, has also become a great American military fortress, the home of Fort Carson, the site of the Air Force Academy, and, most recently, at Falcon Air Force Base, site of space-based defense research.

Around them, Colorado Springs has built a high-tech, innovative economy—"silicon mountain." And with the arrival of Dr. James Dobson's Focus on the Family in 1994 and other Christian organizations, it has been a center of conservative Christianity, the home of Colorado's young conservatism, the counterpoint to Denver's aging liberalism. This was the birthplace of Colorado's anti-tax initiatives and of Amendment 2, which in 1992 repealed city gay rights ordinances but was overturned by the U.S. Supreme Court. More recently, Colorado Springs conservative activists have had some local opposition; the city even passed a tax increase to fund purchases of open land. But overall, this is one of America's most Republican metropolitan areas: Colorado Springs's El Paso County in 2000 cast more votes than Denver County, and its 64%–31% margin for George W. Bush gave him a bigger popular vote margin than Denver's 62%–31% margin for Al Gore.

The 5th Congressional District consists of Colorado Springs and El Paso County, plus all or most of four mountain counties to the west. One of them, Lake County, includes the old mining town of Leadville and votes Democratic in many races. But 87% of the district's population is in El Paso County, and to all intents and purposes, this is the Colorado Springs congressional district. Before 2002, the 5th also included fast-growing Douglas County south of Denver; Douglas County is now in the 6th District. The 5th District is the most Republican district in Colorado and one of the most Republican in the nation.

The congressman from the 5th District is Joel Hefley, a Republican first elected in 1986. Hefley grew up in Oklahoma, received his college and graduate degrees there and originally came to Colorado seeking work as a cowboy. He moved to Colorado Springs in 1965, became a professional civic leader, and was elected to the legislature in 1976; he served two years in the state House and eight in the Senate. In 1986, he was elected to the U.S. House when incumbent Ken Kramer ran unsuccessfully for the Senate; he won a two-candidate primary with 57% and the general election with 70%. He is now the third ranking Republican on the Armed Services Committee; in 2003, he resigned from Resources in protest after the less senior Richard Pombo received the chairmanship.

Hefley is one of Congress's artists, making sketches of life on Capitol Hill, drawing political cartoons, and sculpting bronze statues depicting Western scenes. He came to Congress just as defense cutbacks were beginning; he has always backed spending more on defense, and has been a particularly staunch supporter of missile defense. As chairman of the Armed Services Subcommittee on Military Installations and Facilities, which has jurisdiction over base closings, he opposed the Clinton administration's request for new rounds of closings. Since September 2001, Hefley has been chairman of the Readiness Subcommittee. "If we're talking about readiness, we're not ready," he said on taking the post just days after September 11. But he voiced confidence in the war against terrorism. "We can respond to it. We will need to have patience. It's going to be a long and different kind of war. I think we're going to be relentless in trying to root it out."

Between January and September 2001, Hefley was chairman of the Resources subcommittee on the national parks. He held hearings on whether Bill Clinton's designations of new national monuments were legal, and argued that Clinton preserved too much land and did not leave enough for "public enjoyment." He opposed the upgrading of the Great Sand Dunes National Monument to a national park ("a pile of sand") but the Colorado representative of the Sierra Club said that he had worked constructively to reduce forest fires even before the Hayman Fire of June 2002 and that he supported the designation of some, but not all, wilderness areas in Colorado.

Not afraid to take lonely positions, Hefley was one of three Republicans to vote against the budget resolution in May 2001. He favors abolishing the income tax and the IRS and moving to a flat or sales tax. He has backed a number of other so-far lost causes—blocking the Clinton administration ban on discrimination against gay federal workers, passing a federal law like Colorado's grant of immunity to polluters who voluntarily disclose their violations, setting a 10-year term for federal judges. But he also has had some successes.

Prior to 2003, Hefley's greatest time in the spotlight may have come in the course of doing a job he never wanted—chairing the House ethics committee hearings on the expulsion of Ohio Rep. James Traficant. For two days in July 2002, Hefley presided over hearings in which Traficant bullied the committee's lawyers, shouted out objections and requested frequent bathroom breaks. Hefley warned against "unruly, inappropriate language or breach of decorum" and at one point threatened to hold the hearings behind closed doors unless Traficant stopped shouting; he did. The committee voted unanimously to expel Traficant for a "continuing pattern and practice of official misconduct." Hefley and ranking Democrat Howard Berman presented the committee's case on the floor and members voted to expel their boisterous colleague by a 420–1 vote (the 1 was Gary Condit).

The only threat to Hefley's tenure in 2002 came from redistricting. Democrats wanted to divide El Paso County, but his wife, State Rep. Lynn Hefley, successfully advocated keeping the entire county in one district. In a column in the *Colorado Springs Gazette,* she argued that Colorado Springs needed a single member of Congress because it would guarantee the district a seat on the House Armed Services Committee—a key consideration in a district that, in addition to its military installations, is home to many veterans and defense contractors. The court, in its redistricting ruling, concurred with her that the community interest surrounding the military made it "imperative that El Paso County" not be split. Hefley was then routinely elected, as he has been since November 1986. The redistricting plan passed in May 2003 shifted a few rural counties and added a Hispanic portion of Pueblo; the district remains heavily Republican.

In 2003, Hefley's apparent estrangement from Republican House leadership sparked rumors that he would not seek reelection; he voted against the Republican budget resolution and criticized House leaders for awarding chairmanships based on fundraising and for diluting ethics standards.

Whether he runs again or not, Democrats are highly unlikely to be competitive in this Republican stronghold.

SIXTH DISTRICT

Rep. Tom Tancredo (R)

Elected 1998, 3d term; b. Dec. 20, 1945, Denver; home, Littleton; U. of N. CO, B.A. 1968; Presbyterian; married (Jackie).

Elected Office: CO House of Reps., 1976–81.

Professional Career: Jr. high teacher, 1968–81; Regional rep., U.S. Dept. of Education, 1981–93; Pres., Independence Inst., 1993–98.

DC Office: 1130 LHOB 20515, 202-225-7882; Fax: 202-226-4623; Web site: www.house.gov/tancredo.

District Office: Centennial, 720-283-9772.

Committees: *Budget* (15th of 24 R). *International Relations* (15th of 26 R); Africa; Asia & the Pacific; International Terrorism, Nonproliferation and Human Rights. *Resources* (18th of 28 R): Forests & Forest Health; Water & Power.

Group Ratings

	ADA	ACLU	AFS	LCV	CON	ITIC	NTU	COC	ACU	NTLC	CHC
2002	5	7	0	38	95	75	71	79	100	100	100
2001	5	—	0	0	—	—	86	70	100	—	—

National Journal Ratings

	2001 LIB	—	2001 CONS		2002 LIB	—	2002 CONS
Economic	28%	—	69%		13%	—	87%
Social	0%	—	81%		25%	—	71%
Foreign	16%	—	82%		41%	—	56%

Key Votes of the 107th Congress

1. Approve Bush Tax Cuts	Y	5. Faith-Based Charities	Y
2. Limit Patients' Bill of Rights	Y	6. Bar Gays in the Boy Scouts	Y
3. Campaign Finance Reform	N	7. Ban Partial-Birth Abortion	Y
4. Ban ANWR Development	N	8. Arm Commercial Pilots	Y

9. Trade Promotion Authority	Y
10. Bar Funds for Intl. Court	Y
11. Authorize Force in Iraq	Y
12. Deny Home. Sec. Dept. Union	Y

Election Results

2002 general	Tom Tancredo (R)	158,851	(67%)	($475,451)
	Lance Wright (D)	71,327	(30%)	($6,476)
	Other	7,323	(3%)	
2002 primary	Tom Tancredo (R)	unopposed		
2000 general	Tom Tancredo (R)	141,410	(54%)	($1,123,854)
	Kenneth A. Toltz (D)	110,568	(42%)	($994,094)
	Other	10,499	(4%)	

Prior Winning Percentages: 1998 (56%)

The People		Race/Ethnic Origin	Ancestry	
Area size:	4,111 sq. mi.	87.7% White	German: 18.9%	Irish: 10.9%
Urban population:	84.7%	1.9% Black	English: 10.5%	
Rural population:	15.3%	2.6% Asian	**2000 Presidential Vote**	
Pop. 2000:	614,466	0.4% Native Am.	Bush (R) 169,205	(60%)
Median income:	$73,393	0.1% Hawaiian	Gore (D) 104,126	(37%)
Poverty status:	2.7%	1.5% Two+ races	Other 7,580	(3%)
Military veterans:	13.6%	0.1% Other	**Cook Partisan Voting Index:** R +12	
		5.8% Hispanic Origin		

Occupation	Blue collar: 13.2%	White collar: 77.4%	Gray collar: 9.4%

Two generations ago, most people in metro Denver lived in the city itself; at the city limits, the tree-shaded sidewalks gave way to the empty High Plains. Today, three-quarters of metro Denver residents live outside the city, some in long-settled suburbs, some in huge new subdivisions raised up in the 1990s and 2000s on bare rolling land with magnificent views of the Rockies. You can see the boundaries to these areas in Littleton, originally a small, long-settled suburb just south of Denver, but now extending to vast new tracts; this is of course the site of the massacre at Columbine High School in April 1999. Just south of Littleton is Douglas County, which until the 1970s was a sparsely-populated patch of the High Plains just east of the Front Range. In the 1990s, it was the fastest-growing county in the United States, as young families moved into 35-acre "ranchettes" or huge subdivisions around Castle Rock and Parker just south of the Denver Tech Center, and took high-paying telecommunications jobs at local employers Echo Star and AT&T Broadband. And the growth continues: 14% from April 2000 to July 2001, the highest in the nation. It is the nation's most affluent county in median household income ($84,645) and has smallest percentage of people living in poverty (1.8%). This is Patio Land, as David Brooks called it in *The Weekly Standard*, with a high-tech economy, a highly educated population with relatively conservative cultural values, family men and women who want to create a safe, comfortable environment for their children with the serenity if not the close personal ties of the traditional small town and the economic vibrancy and creativity of the great metropolis.

The 6th Congressional District is centered on Littleton and Douglas County. To the west, it includes much of Jefferson County, including part of affluent Evergreen in the mountains. To the east, it goes through much of Arapahoe County and to lightly-settled Elbert County. Most of this area now is empty, and development has slowed as the high-tech economy falters. But most likely the next decade will see acres of new subdivisions here, the expansion of Patio Land across a wider terrain. Redistricting in 2002 changed the 6th District more than any previously existing district in Colorado. The subtraction of suburbs closer in to Denver in Jefferson and Arapahoe Counties and the addition of Douglas County has made the 6th much more Republican. The old 6th voted 53% for George W. Bush in 2000; the new 6th voted 60% for Bush.

The congressman from the 6th District is Tom Tancredo (pronounced *tan-CRAY-doe*), a self-described religious right Republican, who was elected after a turbulent 1998 campaign. Tancredo grew up on the north side of Denver, taught junior high school civics, and in 1976, at 30, was elected to the state House. He was part of a group called "the Crazies," who zeroed out the sales tax on food and utilities, the inheritance tax and the auto safety inspection tax. In 1981, he became head of the regional office of the Education Department, and cut its staff by two-thirds. A lapsed Catholic who began attending an evangelical Presbyterian church in 1990, he became in 1993 head of the Independence Institute, a libertarian think tank in Golden.

When the 6th District incumbent retired in 1998, Tancredo, an energetic and voluble speaker, jumped into the race. He had four opponents in the Republican primary, spanning the ideological spectrum. Tancredo campaigned by walking the district and running radio ads the last 10 days; his big break was an endorsement by former Senator Bill Armstrong (1979–91), a religious conservative who stayed politically active. Armstrong's endorsement was worth 5% of the vote, Tancredo said, and he needed it: He defeated moderate Bill Schroeder 25%–22%. In the general election, Tancredo was smeared by a self-financing 70-year-old Democrat, who ran a TV ad that said in ominous tones, "Gathering at night to lash out at our government—a militia group with featured speaker, Tom Tancredo. A militia linked to white supremacists and the racist Aryan Nation . . . and called 'dangerous' by the FBI." Then, "Tom Tancredo admits he's met with groups even more extreme than this militia." But Tancredo had spoken to many groups and the "more extreme" groups he mentioned were forums with liberal Denver Congresswoman Patricia Schroeder. The *Rocky Mountain News* called this ad a smear; Tancredo won comfortably, 56%–42%.

Tancredo drew attention from the start. He declined to attend a Clinton White House reception for new members. Then came the shootings at Columbine High School, six blocks from Tancredo's house. An outcry arose for new gun controls. Tancredo, a Second Amendment supporter, pointed out that Colorado has stronger gun-control laws than the federal government. When District of Columbia delegate Eleanor Holmes Norton said months later, "The shadow of Columbine [is] hanging over the Congress," he exploded. "I don't know why I think I can ever get near a microphone" without hearing about Columbine, he told the House. "I need no one to remind me how it happened or what happened." Gun control measures failed to pass; Tancredo was the only Colorado House member to vote for the National Rifle Association's bill. In addition, he won passage by voice vote of a bill to establish school violence hotlines across the nation.

Immigration is the other cause that has exercised Tancredo. He favors a "time out," a vast reduction in legal immigration, lest the character of the country be changed. He opposed proposals to grant regularized status to illegal immigrants who entered the country illegally or overstayed visas. After September 11, he crusaded for stricter border controls to keep out terrorists. In April 2002, in an editorial meeting with *The Washington Times,* Tancredo earned the enmity of the White House by stating that George W. Bush was an obstacle to immigration reform and that Bush's "open door" border policy was a threat to national security. According to Tancredo, he received a phone call from Bush aide Karl Rove the next morning, accusing him of disloyalty; Tancredo contends that Rove told him, "Don't ever darken the doorstep of the White House." Six months later, though, Tancredo must have returned to the president's good graces: He was invited to the White House in October for Bush's ceremonial signing of the Sudan Peace Act, which Tancredo sponsored. Democratic National Chairman Terry McAuliffe has attempted to seize on Tancredo's immigration positions, calling him "the true Republican voice on immigration policy." About the same time, Tancredo called for an INS investigation of a straight-A student whose family is in the country illegally and was quoted by name in a newspaper article about whether in-state tuition should be available for illegals. Tancredo said this was an example of how brazen illegal immigrants have become, and evidently wanted the family deported. Republican Senator Ben Nighthorse Campbell sponsored a bill to grant the family legal immigrant status.

Tancredo's views obviously have made him controversial, and in 2000 he was reelected by the not overwhelming margin of 54%–42%. Redistricting made reelection in 2002 much easier; he won 67%–30%. But he may have problems in 2004. In September 2002, he announced that he was renouncing his 1996 pledge to serve only three terms. Armstrong said that he hoped Tancredo would change his mind. Tancredo apologized to leaders of the national term-limits movement, but said he would run again, to pursue his campaign to change immigration laws. State Treasurer Mike Coffman predicted that another Republican would challenge Tancredo in the 2004 primary on "credibility issues." In 2004, there may be an electoral duel in this part of the New West—a duel in which the Bush White House might not be an uninterested bystander. The redistricting plan passed in May 2003 considerably altered the shape of the 6th District by removing much of Arapahoe County and adding more of Jefferson County. As a result, the district will be centered in Jefferson, though it remains safely Republican.

SEVENTH DISTRICT

Rep. Bob Beauprez (R)

Elected 2002, 1st term; b. Sept. 22, 1948, Lafayette; home, Arvada; U. of CO, B.S. 1970; Catholic; married (Claudia).

Professional Career: Dairy farmer, 1970–90; Banker, 1990–02; Chair, CO Rep. Party, 1999–02.

DC Office: 511 CHOB 20515, 202-225-2645; Fax: 202-225-5278; Web site: www.house.gov/beauprez.

District Office: Wheat Ridge, 303-940-5821.

Committees: *Small Business* (16th of 18 R): Tax, Finance & Exports. *Transportation & Infrastructure* (35th of 41 R): Aviation; Highways, Transit & Pipelines (Vice Chmn.). *Veterans' Affairs* (14th of 17 R): Health.

Group Ratings and Key Votes: Newly Elected

Election Results

2002 general	Bob Beauprez (R)	81,789	(47%)	($1,827,119)
	Mike Feeley (D)	81,668	(47%)	($1,147,759)
	Other	9,422	(3%)	
2002 primary	Bob Beauprez (R)	10,172	(38%)	
	Rick O'Donnell (R)	8,213	(31%)	
	Sam Zakhem (R)	4,848	(18%)	
	Joe Rogers (R)	3,430	(13%)	

The People		Race/Ethnic Origin	Ancestry	
Area size:	1,265 sq. mi.	68.9% White	German: 16.0%	Irish: 8.9%
Urban population:	97.7%	5.8% Black	English: 8.4%	
Rural population:	2.3%	2.9% Asian	**2000 Presidential Vote**	
Pop. 2000:	614,465	0.6% Native Am.	Gore (D) 103,592	(50%)
Median income:	$46,149	0.1% Hawaiian	Bush (R) 101,632	(49%)
Poverty status:	8.9%	1.9% Two+ races	Other 2,783	(1%)
Military veterans:	14.1%	0.1% Other	**Cook Partisan Voting Index:** D + 0	
		19.6% Hispanic Origin		

Occupation	Blue collar: 23.8%	White collar: 62.6%	Gray collar: 13.6%

The inner circle of suburbs around Denver were developed in the 1950s, 1960s and 1970s—a bright new time then, but now a good long time ago. West of Denver, on broad avenues running toward the mountains, is Lakewood, where growth was sparked by the Denver Federal Center; affluent in the south, more marginal near the Denver city limits, a place not of uniformity but of suburban diversity. Out to the west is the town of Golden, with the old Colorado School of Mines and the newer Coors brewery. To the north are Arvada (which is shared with the 2d District) and Wheat Ridge, middle-income suburbs with an increasing number of Latinos. On the other side of Denver, to the east of the now-closed Stapleton Airport, is Aurora, as vast as Lakewood, and somewhat newer, with its huge regional mall and an increasing number of middle class blacks. North of Aurora is the sparkling new Denver International Airport, on rolling, empty plains that stretch east to the Kansas line. While the new airport is carefully excluded from the 7th, adjoining Rocky Mountain Arsenal National Wildlife Refuge is encompassed within its borders.

The 7th Congressional District, newly created for the 2002 elections, covers parts of three counties and most of the inner Denver suburbs. The bulk of its land area, but only 15% of its voters, are in Adams County, which includes the industrial zone along the South Platte River. Adams County has long been the most Democratic of the suburban Denver counties, but its political future cannot be predicted safely: This empty area is likely to fill up with new subdivisions some time in the next decade. Aurora, partly in Adams County with a larger part in Arapahoe County, has long been Republican; it is the home base of former Senator Bill Armstrong (1979–91), a Christian conservative who remains an important force in Colorado Republican politics. But with more black and Latino residents, Aurora is becoming more Democratic. Lakewood and the other towns in Jefferson County (or Jeffco, as people call it) is perhaps Colorado's premier political battleground. Long solidly Republican, it is now more marginal; it was the target of 2002 Democratic Senate candidate Tom Strickland, though he failed to carry it. And it is crucial here: Jeffco has 65% of the 7th District's voters.

How did this inner suburb district come to be assembled? The judge who handed down the redistricting decision in January 2002 weighed competing plans and picked the Democratic one, which divided the new 7th between the parties, in terms of voter registration: It is one-third Democratic, one-third Republican and one-third unaffiliated. The vote in the 2000 presidential election was roughly even. And the vote in the 2002 House race was even closer—the closest in the nation.

The congressman from the 7th District is Bob Beauprez, who won the last congressional election in 2002 to be officially decided by exactly 121 votes out of 173,000 cast. Beauprez is a third-generation Coloradoan, whose Belgian-born grandfather immigrated and earned the money to bring the rest of his family to America by shoveling coal into the giant furnaces at a local power plant. When that work destroyed his eyesight, he bought 80 acres of land and became a Colorado farmer. Beauprez's father became a nationally recognized breeder of registered Hereford beef cattle, and later diversified into dairy cattle. Beauprez graduated from the University of Colorado and, after the family sold the dairy farm, Beauprez in 1990 purchased a small community bank wavering on the verge of collapse. By 2001, he was chairman and CEO of Heritage Bank, with a dozen locations in Denver's northern suburbs and more than $300 million in assets. Beauprez also turned the state Republican Party around. When he became state chairman in 1999, the party had a $130,000 debt; when he resigned to run for the House in 2002, it was $700,000 in the black.

Despite his record for the party and his close ties to Governor Bill Owens, Beauprez faced a crowded Republican primary. He had not run for office before and began with low name recognition. One opponent was Lieutenant Governor Joe Rogers, who had publicly feuded with Owens. Another was Owens's former policy chief, Rick O'Donnell, who won the most straw polls. A fourth was former state senator and former ambassador to Bahrain, Sam Zakhem. Zakhem eventually faded and Rogers was hurt when state auditors probed his finances. O'Donnell accused Beauprez of "trying to buy" the contest with $350,000 of his own money; Beauprez claimed the most individual contributions and had the strongest support from state and national party leaders. In light voting, Beauprez defeated O'Donnell 38%–31%, with 18% for Zakhem and 13% for Rogers. In the less negative Democratic primary, former state senate Minority Leader Mike Feeley defeated Jeffco District Attorney Dave Thomas 56%–44%.

The fall campaign dialogue revolved around economic issues—Social Security reform, health care, corporate responsibility. On most issues, each candidate reflected the mainstream of his national party. Feeley argued that his background as a lawmaker would make him far more effective in Congress than Beauprez; Beauprez responded by touting his experience in the private sector. With both national parties actively engaged, the contest remained exceedingly close to the very end. A visit from George W. Bush in the final days surely helped Beauprez—and anything that helped him was enough to make the difference. Feeley won by narrow margins in Adams and Arapahoe Counties. But Jeffco cast 65% of the vote, and Beauprez won there 49%–46%. After Election Day, the official vote tally gave Beauprez a 386-vote lead, though 2,000 provisional ballots (those set aside because of some question about the eligibility of the voter) had not yet been counted. Feeley objected to the three counties' different standards for determining the validity of those ballots; he sued and a court agreed, ordering the counting of all disputed ballots. In the end, Beauprez won by 121 votes. In the meantime, both Beauprez and Feeley attended their party organizing conferences in November. (Feeley had some impact as a member of Congress, even though he turned out not to be one: His vote for Bob Menendez was crucial in Menendez's one-vote victory for Democratic Caucus chairman.) During orientation sessions, they sat on opposite sides of the room to learn about the job that only one of them could hold.

Arguably the most politically competitive district in the nation in 2002, this seat was altered significantly by the controversial May 2003 redistricting plan. The changes moved Lakewood and much of Jefferson County to the 6th District, and added heavily Republican areas of Arapahoe County to the 7th. That increased George W. Bush's vote here from 49.5% to 54.1%, removed Feeley's home, and reduced the Hispanic share of the district from 20% to 14%, to the consternation of national and local Latino advocates. Beauprez claimed unconvincingly that he knew nothing about the changes and would have gladly run in the existing lines. Although he cannot take reelection for granted, the changes should make his reelection bid far smoother.

★ CONNECTICUT ★

Connecticut is by many measures the nation's highest-income state and quite likely the wealthiest, not through any natural advantage but by virtue of its own pluck. Through most of its
history this small chunk of rocky terrain has been isolated and insular, while politically Connecticut has been an odd duck of a state: One of the last to renounce an established church (in 1818)
and one of the last to impose an income tax (in 1991), one of the last to back the Federalist Party
(1816) and one of the few to vote to re-elect Herbert Hoover (1932). Life here still bears the
imprint of the original 17th century settlers, even though most Connecticut residents today are
descendants of Catholic immigrants who arrived here between 1840 and 1924. Connecticut was
founded by Puritans who found Massachusetts too lenient and backsliding; Connecticut Yankees
for years have been flintier and more unyielding, more tight-fisted and set in their ways, than
their Bay State brethren.

These characteristics have yielded economic advantage. For Connecticut's affluence has come
not from any windfall but from a knack for tinkering and making good use of savings. In 1831, Alexis
de Tocqueville was struck by how this spot on the map gave America "the clock-peddler, the schoolmaster, and the senator. The first gives you time, the second tells you what to do with it, and the third
makes your law and civilization." Connecticut made clocks of wood and metal and hats of felt; it produced combs, cigars, clocks, silk thread, pins, matches, furniture; it invented and still manufactures
Pez candy in Orange, Pepperidge Farm bread and Nivea cream in Norwalk, the Stanley Powerlock
tape measure in New Britain and the Wiffle Ball in Shelton. Connecticut—one of the least violent
parts of America—has always specialized in arms. The quintessential Connecticut Yankee, Eli Whitney, was the inventor not only of the cotton gin—which may have been the proximate cause of the
Civil War—but also of the rifles with interchangeable parts. Connecticut has been an arms maker
ever since Samuel Colt won a War Department contract to manufacture guns for the Mexican-
American War; during the Reagan defense buildup of the 1980s it produced Air Force jets and Army
helicopters and, in the Electric Boat Shipyard in New London, most of the Navy's nuclear submarines. But it is hostile to guns: The attorney general subpoenaed records from gun companies when
Smith & Wesson charged its competitors with harassment after it agreed to voluntary restrictions on
selling its guns.

These arms industries, like Connecticut's civilian manufacturers, depend heavily on meticu-
lous work. For years, the state was the center of the brass industry, the nation's main producer of precision instruments. Over the last quarter century, manufacturing productivity has risen as output
went up 33% while manufacturing jobs declined by 33%. Through decades of immigration Connecticut workers never lost the Yankee knack: Connecticut ranks second in new patents per capita,
and a Milken Institute study ranked Connecticut number three among states in its ability to excel in
the information economy. Over the years Connecticut has accumulated capital and invested
shrewdly, with great skill at assessing risk; it is the home of several of the nation's great insurance
companies, and its laws are uniquely friendly to creditors and harsh on bankrupts.

For all its skills, Connecticut has fallen on hard times during recessions. In the early 1990s insurance companies were hit by huge casualty losses; cuts in defense spending cost Connecticut
nearly 150,000 manufacturing jobs. Connecticut's small central cities—New Haven, Hartford,
Bridgeport, Waterbury—have been plagued by crime and have lost manufacturing jobs and people
(to the point that Hartford now casts fewer votes than super-rich Greenwich). After the recession
Connecticut started growing again, but its trajectory was different. The state's biggest employer and
taxpayer is the Foxwoods Resort Casino, opened in 1992, run by a battery of lawyers and lobbyists
and developers working for the 650-member Mashantucket Pequot tribe; its big competitor is Mohegan Sun, owned by the 1,600-member Mohegans. This is big business: In August 2002 the monthly
revenue of Foxwoods was $73.3 million and Mohegan Sun $72.5 million. Rich Connecticut, with its
3 million people, is siphoning off for its taxpayers and its favored 2,250 Indians and their handlers
large amounts of the incomes of the mostly downscale and economically irrational segments of an
area from Massachusetts down to New Jersey, with 27 million people. But there are great disparities
in income, and not just between the few people certified as members of favored Indian tribes and the

CONNECTICUT

Congressional district boundaries were first effective for 2002.

The Almanac of American Politics
National Journal

rest of the state. Connecticut's median household income fell behind that of New Jersey in 2001, but its per capita income remains the highest, buoyed upward by the earnings of the wealthiest. Highways such as I-95, I-91 and I-84 are choked with traffic. Housing values are booming, most spectacularly in wealthy Greenwich, in the state's southwest corner. There has been an influx of immigrants from Mexico, Peru, the Dominican Republic and other parts of Latin America, who fill jobs others let go begging; Hispanics are now the state's largest minority group.

For most of the 20th century, Connecticut politics was an ethnic struggle between Yankee Republicans and Catholic Democrats. Slowly, as Catholic birthrates exceeded Protestant, Democrats gained ground; their great leader was John Bailey, state Democratic chairman from 1946–75, a master legislative strategist and ticket-balancer, who was one of the first to endorse John Kennedy for president. Traces of the old Protestant-Catholic divide are apparent today in geographic voting patterns, but not much in political rhetoric; splitting tickets is now common in a state where the straight-party lever dominated politics a generation ago. Connecticut voters with their high incomes endure high taxes—the nation's highest, by some measures, including a 32-cent gas tax—but bristle at what they consider the imposition of old moral codes. The rigorous Congregationalism of the Federalists and the censoriousness of mid-20th century Catholicism are just memories now, and the whiff of political correctness is in the air: In March 2000 *The Hartford Courant*, founded in 1764 and the oldest continuously published newspaper in the United States, apologized for having run ads for sales of slaves from 1765 to 1823.

These days Connecticut is a mostly Democratic state, and in 2000 voters here backed native son Joe Lieberman twice, voting 63%–34% to re-elect him as U.S. senator and 56%–38% to elect him vice president and, incidentally, Al Gore as president. Democrats ran well ahead among all age groups except the elderly—good news for them in the long term. Senator Christopher Dodd has been re-elected by wide margins. But Republicans sometimes prevail. After independent Governor Lowell Weicker forced through an income tax in the early 1990s, he was replaced by Republican John Rowland, who promised to hold taxes down; he was reelected in 1998 and 2002. But in early 2003 he called for higher taxes, thus squandering the Republicans' one advantage. And it is by no means clear that George W. Bush, born in New Haven in 1946 when his father was a G.I. Bill student at Yale, would carry his native state in 2004.

The People		Race/Ethnic Origin			Military veterans: 310,069 (12.1%)	
Pop. 2000:	3,405,565	2,638,845	77.5%	White	WWII: 25.4%	Korea: 15.3%
Pop. 1990:	3,287,116	295,571	8.7%	Black	Vietnam: 29.6%	Gulf War: 6.3%
Change 1990–2000:	Up 3.6%	81,564	2.4%	Asian	**Most populous cities:**	
Change 1980–1990:	Up 5.8%	7,267	0.2%	Native Am.	1. Bridgeport	139,529
% of U.S. total:	1.2%	958	0.0%	Hawaiian	2. New Haven	123,626
Pop. rank:	29th of 50	52,896	1.6%	Two+ races	3. Hartford	121,578
Area size:	5,543 sq. mi.	8,141	0.2%	Other	4. Stamford	117,083
State Native:	57.0%	320,323	9.4%	Hisp. Origin	5. Waterbury	107,271
Non-citizen:	5.6%	**Ancestry**			Urban population: 87.7%	
Language		Italian: 13.7%		Irish: 12.2%	Rural population: 12.3%	
English: 78.8%	Other Eur.: 10.6%	English: 7.6%		German: 7.3%		
Spanish: 8.4%		Polish: 6.2%				

Education		Work Sector		General Assembly	
H.S. Grad:	84.0%	Private: 79.9%	Govt: 13.3%	Senate	21 D 15 R
College Grad:	31.4%	Self: 6.5%	Family: 0.2%	House	94 D 57 R
Industry		Unemployment: 5.2%		Legislative Term Limits: No	
Agri: 0.4%	Con: 6.0%	**Household Income**		**Registered Voters**	
Fin: 9.8%	Info: 3.3%	<15k: 12.0%	15-35k: 19.7%	D: 682,478	(34.2%)
Mfg: 18.7%	Prof: 32.1%	35-50k: 14.4%	50-100k: 33.6%	R: 462,338	(23.2%)
Public: 4.0%	Trade: 14.4%	100-150k: 11.7%	>150k: 8.5%	I: 850,868	(42.6%)
Other: 11.2%		Median: $53,935			
Occupation		Poverty status: 7.9%			
Blue collar: 19.9%	White collar: 65.6%	**Home Value**			
Gray collar: 14.5%		<50k: 2.5%	50-100k: 14.2%	100-200k: 48.6%	200-300k: 17.7%
		300-500k: 10.2%	>500k: 6.7%	Median: $160,600	

Presidential politics Why does the nation's highest income state vote Democratic for president? Because liberal stands on cultural issues have trumped the hunger for tax cuts among most of these often cynical voters; because most people here regard themselves as members of ethnic groups with a historic Democratic heritage; because, in 2000, Connecticut's own Joe Lieberman was on the Democratic ticket. Here, the Gore-Lieberman ticket ran well ahead of Clinton-Gore. Over the years Connecticut has oscillated between the parties, moving toward Republicans in the 1970s and 1980s as cultural conflicts split the old Democratic majority, moving toward Democrats in the 1990s in response to the 1990–91 recession and also out of increasing distaste for Southern-accented Republican conservatism. Connecticut has had little appetite for either Jimmy Carter or George W. Bush.

Connecticut's presidential primary, though held fairly early in the process, has not been quite early enough and has made little difference. Gary Hart won here in 1984, Jerry Brown in 1992; but they fared no better than the Federalists Connecticut favored in 1816. In 2000 the pattern continued: John McCain won here, as elsewhere in New England, and Al Gore beat Bill Bradley by a comparatively close 56%–41%. But the results helped the McCain and Bradley campaigns not at all.

2000 Presidential Vote		
Gore (D)	816,015	(56%)
Bush (R)	561,094	(38%)
Nader (Green)	64,452	(4%)
Other	17,920	(1%)

2000 Republican Presidential Primary		
McCain (R)	87,270	(49%)
Bush (R)	82,871	(46%)
Other	8,920	(5%)

2000 Democratic Presidential Primary		
Gore (D)	99,563	(56%)
Bradley (D)	74,075	(41%)
Other	5,418	(3%)

1996 Presidential Vote		
Clinton (D)	735,740	(53%)
Dole (R)	483,109	(35%)
Perot (I)	139,523	(10%)
Other	34,237	(2%)

Congressional districting Connecticut has devised a bipartisan process for redistricting. Two Republicans and two Democrats from each house of the legislature meet and try to draw lines; if they are approved by a two-thirds vote in both chambers, they become law. Otherwise, a ninth member is chosen by the other eight, and they try to reach consensus. It worked in 1991, when a plan that made minimal changes in the congressional district lines was approved. And it worked in 2001, with a nudge from the state Supreme Court, when the task was much harder: Connecticut lost one of its six seats in the 2000 Census, and two incumbents had to be put together in one district. Legislators of both parties said they wanted a "fair fight" between a Republican and a Democrat. Some Democrats called for dividing the 2d District in eastern Connecticut, which Republican Rob Simmons won from veteran incumbent Democrat Sam Gejdenson in 2000. But Simmons argued that eastern Connecticut had been a single district since 1843, and the commission moved in another direction.

108th Congress Lineup	
3 R	2 D

107th Congress Lineup	
3 D	3 R

The commission decided to create a new seat out of the 5th District represented by Democrat Jim Maloney and the 6th District represented by Republican Nancy Johnson. The narrow and elongated 5th, the only district to have boundaries with all the others, seemed to many the obvious district to eliminate. But the commissioners haggled over precisely what boundaries would set up a fair fight. Maloney wanted to keep the three biggest cities in the 5th in the new district: Danbury, his hometown, and Waterbury and Meriden had a community of interest, because they were linked by I-84, had a common labor market and had been in the same district for 37 years. But some Republicans tried to put Danbury into the heavily Republican 4th District. Johnson insisted on keeping her hometown of New Britain, even though it is heavily Democratic and she had not always carried it. As she put it, "My towns are my immediate family, and the border towns are my cousins." The four-member commission failed to come up with a plan by the September 2001 deadline, and it appointed as its tie-breaker 79-year-old former Speaker Nelson Brown, a Republican, who had served in the same capacity 10 years before (some hope he may do so again in

2011). The commission tried out various plans, but couldn't reach agreement by a November 30 deadline. Then the issue went to the state Supreme Court, but the commissioners asked for an extension and the court granted one to December 21. Ninety minutes before the deadline the commission reached unanimous agreement. Some 27,000 of Waterbury's residents were put into the 3d District, but otherwise Maloney kept his three cities. Johnson kept New Britain. Both incumbents said they were happy: The Gore 2000 percentage in the new district was lower than in Johnson's old district and the Bush 2000 percentage in the new district was lower than in Maloney's old district. Johnson ended up winning 54%–43%, drawing on personal strength after 20 years of incumbency; this is a seat a Democrat could certainly win some time in the next decade.

Governor

John Rowland (R)

Elected 1994, term expires Jan. 2007, 3d term; b. May 24, 1957, Waterbury; home, Hartford; Villanova U., B.S. 1979; Catholic; married (Patricia).

Elected Office: CT House of Reps., 1980–84; U.S. House of Reps., 1984–90.

Professional Career: Insurance Agent, 1979–84.

Office: 210 Capitol Ave., Hartford, 06106, 860-566-4840; Fax: 860-566-4677; Web site: www.state.ct.us/governor.

Election Results

2002 general	John Rowland (R)	573,958	(56%)
	Bill Curry (D)	448,984	(44%)
2002 primary	John Rowland (R)	unopposed	
1998 general	John Rowland (R)	628,707	(63%)
	Barbara Kennelly (D)	354,187	(35%)
	Other	16,641	(2%)

Prior Winning Percentages: 1994 (36%)

John Rowland was elected in 2002 to a third term that positions him to be the longest-serving governor of Connecticut since 1784. He grew up in Waterbury, a high-skill factory town with its own tough politics; his family has owned an insurance agency for four generations and his father and grandfather were city comptrollers. He graduated from Villanova and in the next election year, 1980, he was elected to the state House from a Democratic district at 23. He ran for Congress in 1984, upsetting a Democratic incumbent to become the youngest member of the House. He has run for governor in the last four elections, losing with 37% in 1990 (to former Republican Senator Lowell Weicker's 40%), winning with 36% in 1994 (to Democrat Bill Curry's 33%) and winning reelection against Barbara Kennelly with 63% in 1998 and against Curry with 56% in 2002.

When Rowland was first elected governor, the dominant issue was the state's income tax, driven through by Lowell Weicker in 1991; Rowland promised to repeal it. But in his three terms he has made no serious move to do so. In his first term he got the legislature to pass a "tough love" welfare bill limiting payments to 21 months and encouraging recipients to get a job and work their way up; the income tax was cut marginally. Business taxes were lowered and unemployment and workmen's comp were made more business-friendly. A new death penalty law and Megan's law to inform communities of released sex offenders were passed. The state workforce was cut by 2,500; the lottery was privatized. State spending increases were minimal. Although

Democrats captured the state Senate in 1996 and held the House throughout, Rowland was able to push through tax cuts every year, as the state's economy revived and revenues rose.

In fall 1997 and spring 1998, Rowland unveiled plans for big projects to spur redevelopment of Connecticut's central cities. Hartford, New Haven, Bridgeport, even small cities like New London, with high crime rates and crumbling housing and empty lots, high poverty rates and empty downtowns, stand out like sore thumbs in affluent Connecticut, and are a vivid contrast with the bustling growth of Manhattan, Boston and even Providence. Over the years the state has issued $1.7 billion worth of bonds for Adriaen's Landing and projects in other cities and issued tax breaks to attract the Pfizer Research Center to New London, but some projects—the New Haven regional mall, Steel Point on the Bridgeport waterfront—fell through. Rowland's urban revival policies, on top of his tax cuts and Connecticut's booming economy enabled him to win reelection by 63%–35%, carrying all but eight of Connecticut's cities and towns. Soon after, he faced a setback. In 1997 Rowland had unveiled his plan for Adriaen's Landing on the Hartford waterfront, with a convention center, restaurants, hotels and shopping centers, capped by a stadium for the New England Patriots to be financed with $375 million in state bonds. But in April 1999 Patriots owner Robert Kraft accepted a $70 million subsidy to stay in Massachusetts. Rowland eventually got a $2.4 million check from the National Football League for Connecticut's out-of-pocket expenses.

Flush times continued for a while. In 1999 the legislature passed Rowland's sales tax rebate and a 7-cent cut in the state's 32-cent gas tax. Rowland approved several liberal bills: Allowing felons to vote, requiring expanded benefits in health insurance, keeping teacher's salaries among the highest in the nation. Rowland was capable of changing policies and, when criticized, to reply, "That was then and this is now." In 1999 nursing home employees threatened to strike, to get $200 million more in state payments, and Rowland gave them an increase. In May 2001 they actually went out on strike; Rowland supplied the owners with money to hire replacements, and the strike collapsed. In spring 2001 he vetoed a bill placing tighter emissions limits on the state's old power plants; he signed a similar bill in spring 2002. In January 2002 he reversed another policy—no tax increases—and proposed a 61 cent increase in the cigarette tax; the state was said to face a $350 million shortfall in the current budget and a prospective $1 billion deficit in the 2003–05 budget. In February Rowland proposed a budget under what he and Democratic legislative leaders had agreed on the year before, and in April he vetoed the Democrats' millionaire's tax, literally: A 1% increase in the tax on income over $1 million (some 6,000 taxpayers were said to be affected) in April 2002.

Scandal touched Rowland employees and formed the background of the 2002 campaign. In September 1999 former state Treasurer Paul Silvester, a Republican appointed by Rowland but defeated in 1998, pleaded guilty to federal charges arising out of a scheme to steer state pension funds to conspiring investment firms in return for campaign contributions. Rowland had attended some of the fundraisers, but an October 2000 indictment of Silvester aides and investment firm executives did not implicate Rowland. In December 2000 Rowland met with Enron executives and their consultant, a big contributor, and a few days later the Connecticut Resources Recovery Authority (the state trash agency) agreed to pay Enron $220 million for a fuel cell facility which would buy energy from CRRA's trash-to-energy facility for $2 million a month for 11 years. That might have seemed a good return on the state's money, but it turned out to be a poor one when Enron went bankrupt in December 2001: The state was out $220 million with no prospect of getting its money back, and municipal trash collection fees had to be raised. Attorney General Richard Blumenthal, well known for his work on the tobacco and Microsoft cases, said the contract was an illegal disguised loan. When it became known that the Enron consultant held a fundraiser for Rowland in October 2001 and that Enron gave $80,000 to the Republican Governors Association, which Rowland headed from October 2001 to November 2002, Democrats demanded that Peter Ellef , CRRA head and Rowland's co-chief of staff, resign. Criticism also focused on the other co-chief of Staff, who had a long-term relationship with a woman who lobbied for CRRA and raised money for Rowland. At first, Rowland stood by his aides. Then in March 2002 he fired both co-chiefs of staff. A year later, scandal again touched the administration: In March 2003, Rowland's former deputy chief of staff pleaded guilty to accepting bribes.

But as he entered the 2002 campaign season, Rowland's job rating remained high. In early

2002, two Democrats were running—Bill Curry, who returned to Connecticut after a stint as a high-level staffer in the Clinton White House, and state Senate Majority Leader George Jepsen. But Jepsen agreed to be Curry's running mate; there was no primary. The campaign provided an interesting debate on how to aid Connecticut's ailing cities. Rowland said in February that was why he was running. "If I thought Hartford was finished, if I thought Bridgeport was finished, I would just go away. If I didn't think there was anything to do, what the hell would I run for?" Curry said, "The governor has made a decision to pursue casinos, convention centers, football stadiums and tourism. This was the governor's urban dream. We will heal our cities by fixing the broken systems on which they depend." He added, "The governor has spent billions of dollars on programs that have resulted in more criminal indictments than jobs. You can't graft prosperity onto a city from the top down."

Curry's plan—similar to what he advocated in 1994—was to lower property taxes by providing $730 million of state aid on condition that cities and towns lower their property tax rates. He said he would "pull the plug" on Rowland's projects which were still on the drawing board. Rowland's lead in the polls persisted and never got below 9% and was usually much more; Curry raised $1 million less than in 1994 and didn't have enough money for positive ads. Rowland won 56%–44%, losing the central cities by smaller margins than most Republicans and carrying all but a few towns. Rowland only barely led, 52%–48%, in the four counties of eastern Connecticut, and won by not much more, 54%–46%, in Hartford and New Haven counties in the center of the state. But he had a huge 62%–38% lead in the two western counties, Fairfield and Litchfield. These are in the most affluent part of the state and are mostly in the New York media market; a Connecticut political analyst calls them the Rudy belt, on the theory that their readiness to vote Republican has been influence by the popularity of Rudolph Giuliani.

In December 2002, Rowland laid off 2,800 state workers. He called a special session of the legislature to consider a $200 million package of spending cuts and $200 million in increased taxes—now he accepted the Democrats' millionaire tax—and $100 million in union concessions. Republicans opposed the higher taxes; Democrats opposed the spending cuts. Will Rowland run again in 2006, when he will not yet be 50? He said in April 2003 that he might run again; but he's not likely to run against one of Connecticut's two Democratic senators. "I'd rather get my teeth drilled than serve in the Senate," he told a reporter in November 2002.

Senior Senator

Christopher Dodd (D)

Elected 1980, seat up 2004, 4th term; b. May 27, 1944, Willimantic; home, East Haddam; Providence Col., B.A. 1966, U. of Louisville, J.D. 1972; Catholic; married (Jackie Clegg).

Military Career: Army Reserves, 1969–75.

Elected Office: U.S. House of Reps., 1974–80.

Professional Career: Peace Corps, Dominican Republic, 1966–68; Practicing atty., 1972–74.

DC Office: 448 RSOB, 20510, 202-224-2823; Fax: 202-228-1683; Web site: dodd.senate.gov.

State Office: Wethersfield, 860-258-6940.

Committees: *Banking, Housing & Urban Affairs*: Financial Institutions; Housing & Transportation; Securities & Investment (RMM). *Foreign Relations*: African Affairs; European Affairs; International Economic Policy, Export & Trade Promotion; Western Hemisphere, Peace Corps, Narcotics Affairs (RMM). *Health, Education, Labor & Pensions*: Children & Families (RMM); Employment, Safety & Training. *Rules & Administration* (RMM).

Group Ratings

	ADA	ACLU	AFS	LCV	CON	ITIC	NTU	COC	ACU	NTLC	CHC
2002	80	60	100	76	74	38	8	40	5	0	—
2001	95	—	92	88	—	—	6	36	16	—	20

National Journal Ratings

	2001 LIB	—	2001 CONS		2002 LIB	—	2002 CONS
Economic	88%	—	9%		89%	—	10%
Social	70%	—	20%		68%	—	28%
Foreign	74%	—	14%		81%	—	15%

Key Votes of the 107th Congress

1. Approve Bush Tax Cuts	N	5. Confirm Ashcroft as AG	Y	9. Bar Coop. with Intl. Court	N
2. Expand Patients' Rights	Y	6. Bar Gays in the Boy Scouts	N	10. Trade Promotion Authority	N
3. Campaign Finance Reform	Y	7. $ for Hate Crime Prosecution	Y	11. Authorize Force in Iraq	Y
4. Permit ANWR Development	N	8. Overseas Military Abortions	Y	12. Homeland Sec. Dept. Union	Y

Election Results

1998 general	Christopher Dodd (D)	628,306	(65%)	($4,442,567)
	Gary A. Franks (R)	312,177	(32%)	($1,478,307)
	Other	23,974	(2%)	
1998 primary	Christopher Dodd (D) .... nominated by convention			
1992 general	Christopher Dodd (D-ACP)	882,569	(59%)	($4,553,792)
	Brook Johnson (R)	572,036	(38%)	($2,395,262)
	Other	46,104	(3%)	

Prior Winning Percentages: 1986 (65%); 1980 (56%); 1978 House (70%); 1976 House (65%); 1974 House (59%)

Christopher Dodd was almost born into politics, one of six senators who are children of former senators (Lisa Murkowski, Mark Pryor, Evan Bayh, Lincoln Chafee and Bob Bennett are the others). His father Thomas Dodd, a prosecutor at the Nuremberg trials, was elected to the House in 1952, when Chris was eight; he lost a Senate race to Prescott Bush, George W. Bush's grandfather, in 1956, then won in 1958. Chris Dodd served in the Peace Corps in the Dominican Republic from 1966–68. In 1967 the older Dodd was censured by the Senate for misuse of funds; he ran as an independent in 1970 and Chris Dodd managed his campaign, in which he finished behind Republican Lowell Weicker and Democrat Joseph Duffey, for whom Yale Law School student Bill Clinton was working as a volunteer. Almost immediately after law school, Christopher Dodd ran for the House in the open-seat eastern Connecticut 2d District and, in the Watergate year of 1974, won comfortably. He was re-elected easily and in 1980 outmaneuvered fellow Watergate Democrat Toby Moffett to get the Democratic nomination to succeed Senator Abraham Ribicoff; he won that race by a wide margin.

Dodd, who speaks fluent Spanish, has often played a role on Latin American issues. On the Western Hemisphere Subcommittee in the 1980s he took the lead in opposing U.S. military aid to El Salvador's government and aid to the Nicaraguan contras. He has long backed freer travel to Fidel Castro's Cuba and an end to the embargo on trade with Cuba. But he opposed the language in the House Republicans' June 2000 bill on lifting the embargo on food and medicine, which he said would restrict the president's ability to open up travel to Cuba. Dodd threatened a filibuster on the issue, and prevented it from being passed in June 2000 with the aid package that included the Clinton administration's $1 billion-plus Plan Colombia. In October, with some grumbling, he voted for the bill lifting the embargo, which passed by a wide margin. In contrast to his wariness of U.S. military aid in Central America in the 1980s, he supported Plan Colombia, to provide equipment and military training to Colombians fighting the FARC guerrillas. In 2001 and 2002 he blocked the confirmation of the Cuban-born Otto Reich as Assistant Secretary of State for Latin American Affairs and even refused to hold a hearing on the nomination. Dodd and his staff had tangled with Reich in the 1980s when he was head of the State Department's Office of Public Diplomacy and supported aid to the contras while Dodd insisted the Sandinistas had no Communist connections and that they were the choice of the Nicaraguan people; when elections were held the Sandinistas lost. Reich served through 2002 under a recess appointment and Dodd claimed that he had signaled support for the abortive coup that in May 2002 threatened the rule of Venezuela's Hugo Chavez; Reich was not renominated in January 2003. On other areas of foreign policy, Dodd does not take such a leftish position. In September 2002 he called for international cooperation to disarm Saddam Hussein but said that lacking that, "I don't think we have any choice but to act alone." He voted for the Iraq war resolution in October 2002.

Connecticut, with its big insurance companies, has long been a creditor state, and one that is leery of trial lawyers. In 1995 Dodd was the chief Democratic sponsor of the securities litigation bill sought by high-tech companies and fought by trial lawyers. "People shouldn't make a business out of ambulance chasing when a stock simply fluctuates on the market," he said. When Bill Clinton vetoed it, Dodd immediately started lobbying Senate and House Democrats, and both houses in December 1995 voted to override. In 1996 and 1998 he worked with Phil Gramm and Alfonse D'Amato to successfully pass a law barring class-action securities litigation suits from state courts, requiring them to be heard in federal court where the rules are stricter. He was a lead sponsor of the product liability bill vetoed by Clinton in May 1996. In March 2002 he and Jon Corzine sponsored a bill to prohibit accountants performing audits from providing many consulting and non-audit services and to allow them to provide tax consulting only if approved by the audit committee.

Dodd was the lead Democratic sponsor of the terrorism bill, which passed the Senate in June 2002. His original version would have had the government pay for the first $10 billion of terrorism claims each year and then 90% of the rest. The House version, passed in December 2001, required insurers to repay the government and provided full coverage of only the first $1 billion of damage. In lengthy negotiations, Dodd managed to get a bill limiting claims to a sliding scale of percentages of premiums and placing a surcharge on all commercial insurance if companies' claims exceeded a sliding scale of limits. But there was intense argument over the House's provision shielding property owners from pain and suffering damages in lawsuits. Finally Dodd's compromise was accepted by the Republicans, consolidating lawsuits in a single federal court and setting up rigid tests for holding property owners liable.

Dodd has a pleasant, friendly manner and seems unfazed by opposition and approaches debates with an affable air, deflating opponents' indignation and suggesting that they are all in this game together. In November 1994 he made an attempt to get a position in the national spotlighted after Jim Sasser, who had expected to run for Senate majority leader, was defeated for reelection by Bill Frist. Dodd spent a month campaigning among colleagues for the minority leadership and lost to Tom Daschle by just 24–23. Dodd was promptly asked by Bill Clinton to be Democratic National Committee chairman. Dodd performed ably in public debates and set-tos with Republican Chairman Haley Barbour, but was embarrassed in October 1996 when he followed White House orders to stonewall on charges that DNC top-level fundraiser John Huang raised millions in illegal foreign contributions. Dodd plausibly denied that he knew much about Huang, who was placed at the committee personally by Clinton; he was less plausible when he said he never thought the White House coffees, some of which he attended, were fundraisers. Dodd dropped the chairmanship in January 1997, and mostly avoided investigations of the DNC thereafter. In 2000 he lobbied hard to get his junior colleague Joe Lieberman nominated for vice president, assuring Jesse Jackson, NEA head Bob Chase, and AFL-CIO President John Sweeney that Lieberman was a good Democrat.

His ambitions for a leadership post may have subsided for a while, but they have not completely disappeared. In December 2002, when many thought that Daschle would step down from the leadership to run for president, Dodd began calling on senators and seemed likely to run against Daschle's favorite, Whip Harry Reid. But in January 2003 Daschle announced that he was not running for president and would stay as Minority Leader. There was another position, of course, that opens up every four years: The presidency. Dodd mulled a run for president, but in March 2003 announced he would remain in the Senate; he then endorsed Lieberman's candidacy.

Presidential elections are not an unfamiliar subject to Dodd. As ranking member on and then as chairman of the Senate Rules Committee, he worked with Mitch McConnell on the elections procedure bill that just about everyone thought was necessary after the Florida controversy. Both sides accepted many provisions, but there were significant differences between the House bill passed in December 2001 and the Senate bill passed in April 2002. Most matters were agreed on: Provisional voting, computerized voter lists, improved access to the polls for the disabled, $3.9 billion to help states upgrade their equipment. Approval was delayed over disagreement over whether first-time voters who register by mail should have to show driver's licenses. Finally it was agreed that they could use utility bills, bank statements, paychecks, government documents with their names and addresses instead, and the bill was signed in October 2002. Other Dodd causes include children's medicine. With Ohio Republican Mike DeWine, Dodd has worked to promote testing of psychiatric drugs prescribed for young children, and they have pressed for continuation of the provision extending the patent life of drugs for pharmaceutical companies that conduct studies of their effects on children.

In June 2002, when the Bureau of Indian Affairs approved tribal designation for Connecticut's Eastern Pequots, Dodd joined other Connecticut elected officials in opposing a new casino in the state. Dodd and Lieberman tried to get the Senate to agree to a one-year moratorium on recognition of new Indian tribes and lost 80–15. In September Dodd met with tribal leaders and said that BIA's designation process had to be fixed. On another state issue, Dodd has worked to preserve the old Colt complex in Hartford, where the Colt .45 was made, the telegraph first conceptualized and jet engine technology first developed.

Dodd was easily re-elected in 1998. His Republican opponent was Gary Franks, elected congressman in 1990 and defeated in 1996 in the often marginal 5th District, and one of the few black Republicans to serve in Congress. Franks' attacks on Dodd's closeness to Bill Clinton and his attendance record struck no sparks, especially since Franks was outspent by $3 million. He won 65%–32%, carrying all but six of the state's cities and towns. In February 2001 Dodd said he would run for re-election in 2004; mentioned as a possible Republican opponent is state Republican Chairman Chris DePino.

Junior Senator

Joe Lieberman (D)

Elected 1988, seat up 2006, 3d term; b. Feb. 24, 1942, Stamford; home, New Haven; Yale U., B.A. 1964, LL.B. 1967; Jewish; married (Hadassah).

Elected Office: CT Senate, 1970–80, Maj. Ldr., 1974–80; CT Atty. Gen., 1982–88.

Professional Career: Practicing atty., 1967–70, 1980–82.

DC Office: 706 HSOB, 20510, 202-224-4041; Fax: 202-224-9750; Web site: www.lieberman.senate.gov.

State Office: Hartford, 860-549-8463.

Committees: *Armed Services*: Airland (RMM); Emerging Threats & Capabilities; Seapower. *Environment & Public Works*: Clean Air, Climate Change & Nuclear Safety; Transportation & Infrastructure. *Governmental Affairs* (RMM). *Small Business & Entrepreneurship*.

Group Ratings

	ADA	ACLU	AFS	LCV	CON	ITIC	NTU	COC	ACU	NTLC	CHC
2002	85	40	88	82	77	75	20	60	20	12	—
2001	95	—	92	100	—	—	7	43	28	—	20

National Journal Ratings

	2001 LIB	—	2001 CONS		2002 LIB	—	2002 CONS
Economic	71%	—	27%		87%	—	11%
Social	70%	—	20%		82%	—	0%
Foreign	51%	—	43%		55%	—	44%

Key Votes of the 107th Congress

1. Approve Bush Tax Cuts	N	5. Confirm Ashcroft as AG	N	9. Bar Coop. with Intl. Court	Y
2. Expand Patients' Rights	Y	6. Bar Gays in the Boy Scouts	N	10. Trade Promotion Authority	Y
3. Campaign Finance Reform	Y	7. $ for Hate Crime Prosecution	Y	11. Authorize Force in Iraq	Y
4. Permit ANWR Development	N	8. Overseas Military Abortions	Y	12. Homeland Sec. Dept. Union	Y

Election Results

2000 general	Joe Lieberman (D)	828,902	(63%)	($3,786,665)
	Phil Giordano (R)	448,077	(34%)	($1,080,020)
	Other	34,282	(3%)	
2000 primary	Joe Lieberman (D)	unopposed		
1994 general	Joe Lieberman (D)	723,842	(67%)	($4,017,520)
	Jerry Labriola (R)	334,833	(31%)	($166,064)
	Other	20,989	(2%)	

Prior Winning Percentages: 1988 (50%)

Joe Lieberman is now a national figure of some eminence after his candidacy for vice president in 2000. He has been admired for some time for his independence of mind, civility of spirit and fidelity to causes in which he believes; if this reputation was not enhanced by the 2000 campaign, which after all was an inevitably partisan enterprise, it was not badly damaged. Lieberman has always been an intensely political person, balancing a solid allegiance to the Democratic Party with a commitment to intellectual rigor and honesty—a balancing act that is never easy and occasionally impossible. Lieberman grew up in Stamford, the son of a liquor store owner, and was interested in politics early on; he remembers coming home from school at age nine eager to watch the televised Kefauver hearings. He went to Yale College and Yale Law School, became chairman of the *Yale Daily News* and worked summers for Senator Abraham Ribicoff and the Democratic National Committee. His political ambitions were no secret— other students called him "the Senator." In college he wrote an admiring yet revealing biography of that quintessential political boss John Bailey, Connecticut Democratic chairman from 1946–1975. Writing a book that was intellectually honest enough to pass academic scrutiny but tactful enough not to displease a man who could make or break his political career was a challenge, and Lieberman met it. At the same time, he was not afraid to challenge the political establishment. He helped found a reform and antiwar Caucus of Connecticut Democrats; in 1970 he ran for state Senate in New Haven against state Senate Majority Leader Edward Marcus, and won with help from, among others, a Yale Law student volunteer named Bill Clinton. In 1980 he ran for an open House seat and lost 52%–46%; in 1982 he was elected attorney general, where he took action against fake charities, crooked car dealers and gouging merchants.

In 1988 Lieberman challenged Senator Lowell Weicker, another maverick, but of a different sort. Weicker was well to the left of most Republicans on economic and cultural issues; Lieberman was more conservative than most Democrats on cultural issues and foreign policy. Lieberman is an Orthodox Jew—he didn't attend the convention that nominated him because it was held on Saturday, and sent in a videotape instead—and a believer that "we in government should look to religion as a partner, as I think the Founders of our country did." He favored the death penalty and a moment of silence in schools, and opposed Weicker's proposed 30-cent gas tax increase. He ran witty ads, one showing a bear sleeping through work—a nice take-off on the growling but erratic Weicker. Lieberman won 50%–49%; the contest cut across party lines, with Lieberman running well in industrial towns and Weicker in Hartford, college towns and tony towns in Litch-field County.

Lieberman has made a distinctive mark in foreign policy. He was one of the leaders in the fight for the Gulf War resolution in January 1991, and without his earnest but vehement support it might not have passed. Presciently, he called for "final victory" over Saddam Hussein. He is a strong supporter of Israel but favored F-15 sales to Saudi Arabia in 1992. He favored U.S. ground troops in Bosnia and action against Bosnian Serb war criminals. He backed NATO expansion in Eastern Europe. In 1998 he led a fight for sanctions to stop Russia from exporting missile technology to Iran. In 1999 hearings, he said there was "a shocking lack of thoroughness, competence and urgency" in government investigations of the leaking of nuclear secrets to China. He has strongly opposed Fidel Castro's regime in Cuba—a glaring difference between him and his colleague Christopher Dodd—and in May 2001 sponsored with Jesse Helms a bill to give $100 million to Cuban opposition groups. After September 11 he strongly supported the war against terrorism in Afghanistan and in December 2001 was one of 10 members who signed a letter urging George

W. Bush to target Iraq next. And his vision is broader: in January 2002 he urged the administration to move its putative allies in the Arab world toward political freedom to prevent a "theological iron curtain" behind which terrorism can build. In May 2002, when Tom DeLay introduced a resolution supporting Israel in the House, Lieberman introduced one in the Senate, but with fewer condemnations of Palestinian leaders.

On economic issues, Lieberman has backed capital gains tax cuts for small business ("you can't be pro-jobs and anti-business") and urged Bill Clinton to sign the 1996 welfare reform bill— both stands opposed by many Democrats. He opposed the Bush tax cut in May 2002 and the post-September 11 stimulus package in January 2002. He preferred instead cuts in depreciation and a 10-day sales tax holiday. In May 2002 he called for delay of scheduled future tax cuts. As chairman of the Governmental Affairs Committee, he presided over hearings on Enron in early 2002. Some critics on the left said he was part of the problem, for having urged delay in Clinton SEC Chairman Arthur Levitt's proposals to bar accounting firms from doing both audits and consulting work for companies and for having opposed the expensing of stock options. He said that he only sought time to think about Levitt's proposal and that expensing stock options fairly was impossible because it was not clear what they were worth. In April 2002 Lieberman presented his own recommendations: Aggressive enforcement, more funding for the SEC, new authority for the SEC to remove corporate board members, increased independence for stock analysts, limiting the non-audit work of accounting firms.

From the platform of the Governmental Affairs Committee, Lieberman also made points on environmental issues. He attacked the Bush administration for refusing to cap wholesale electricity prices during California's electricity crisis. He subpoenaed documents from the Bush Interior and Agriculture departments and EPA on scalebacks of Clinton environmental regulations. With John McCain, increasingly a legislative partner, he sponsored a bill to reduce carbon dioxide and other emissions with an economy-wide cap and to sanction emissions trading. He called Bush's leadership on emissions "feeble" and said his energy policy was "mired in crude oil." In November 2001 he threatened to filibuster against oil drilling in the Arctic National Wildlife Refuge.

Lieberman has spoken out eloquently on moral issues. In 1995 he joined with *Book of Virtues* author William Bennett and criticized gangsta rap records, and shamed Time Warner into selling their Interscope label; in 1998 they said the purchaser, Seagram, failed to keep its promises to clean up the words, and gave it a Silver Sewer award. In highly publicized Commerce Committee hearings in September 2000 he denounced the marketing of violent movies, music and video games with children. But during that fall campaign, after he attended a Hollywood fundraiser and spoke of being a "noodge" to the industry, Bennett criticized him for abandoning their fight against obscenity and violence. One thing that made Lieberman an attractive running mate for Al Gore was the fact that he was one of the few Democrats who was not a lockstep defender of Bill Clinton. He was dismayed by Clinton's August 17, 1998, speech in which he grudgingly admitted lying about the Lewinsky affair for seven months. When the Senate resumed in September, Lieberman took the floor and said, "Such behavior is . . . wrong and unacceptable and should be followed by some measure of public rebuke and accountability." But he was persuaded by Senate Minority Leader Tom Daschle not to call for censure, and he stopped well short of backing impeachment or resignation. In 2001 he proposed that entertainment companies marketing adult content to children should be disciplined by the FTC and fined up to $11,000 a day. Lieberman has long believed, as he said in 2002, that "faith-based groups can help government solve pressing social problems." But he opposed the faith-based charities bill the House passed in July 2001, and with Rick Santorum developed a different approach, based on tax incentives for corporate giving, for matching by banks of poor people's "development accounts," plus charitable deductions of up to $400 a year for taxpayers who take the standard deduction. He has supported gun-control measures, but worked to get a gun produced by Connecticut-based Colt removed from the 1994 assault weapon ban and voted against making lawsuits against gunmakers non-dischargeable in bankruptcy.

Lieberman played a key—and frustrating—role on the issue of homeland security. He became convinced well before George W. Bush that there should be a cabinet department combining the government agencies involved in homeland security, and in October 2001 he sponsored a bill to create one. Then, in June 2002, Bush came out with his proposal for such a department. Lieberman said, with good reason, that Bush's plan resembled his own, and drafted a bill in July 2002. But in late August Bush said that the personnel provisions of Lieberman's bill would not give him sufficient flexibility to manage the department. The main issue was whether the president could get rid of unions in divisions of the department. Lieberman argued that his version allowed removal on a case-by-case basis if there was a showing that union rights were a threat to national security. Bush administration spokesmen said that such civil service procedures were too cumbersome and that Lieberman's version actually reduced the president's ability to move employees out of unions. For most of September there was a standoff in the Senate; in October, the bill was pulled for a while for consideration of the Iraq war resolution and other issues. Lieberman evidently had a 51-vote majority for his version, but Republicans were able to keep it from coming to the floor. Democrats, in refusing to give in to Bush's demands, were being faithful to their longtime supporters, the government employee unions. But the issue played a major role in the defeats of Senators Max Cleland in Georgia and Jean Carnahan in Missouri. After the election, Democrats meekly conceded most of the issue.

Al Gore's selection of Lieberman as his vice presidential nominee in 2000 was history-making: He was the first Jew on a major party ticket in American history. Gore knew Lieberman from the Senate, where they were friends—Gore did not have many close personal relationships with colleagues. But two things probably pushed Gore toward his choice: Lieberman's reputation for probity and denunciation of Clinton, which gave the ticket some insulation from the Clinton scandals, and Lieberman's moderate record on many issues and undoubted ability. Another asset proved to be Lieberman's fervent avowals of religious faith and that it has a rightful place in politics; what might have been resented from a Christian conservative seemed attractive coming from an Orthodox Jew. Some Democrats criticized him for running for vice president and for re-election as senator at the same time; if he won both, Connecticut's Republican Governor John Rowland could have appointed a Republican replacement.

Overall, Lieberman was clearly an asset to the ticket. His poll ratings were high, and if there was general agreement that Dick Cheney excelled at the October 6 vice presidential debate, Lieberman also performed well; some observers wondered whether the order of the tickets should be reversed. Lieberman's Judaism seems not to have hurt the ticket anywhere, and it probably helped in crucial Florida; he made memorable campaign appearances in heavily Jewish Broward and Palm Beach Counties, which voted nearly 2–1 for Gore (the exact margin, of course, turned out to be in some dispute). But there was some tension between positions Lieberman had taken before August 2000 and what he said during the campaign. He had questioned racial quotas and preferences, and refused to oppose Proposition 209 in California in 1996, which banned racial quotas and preferences by paraphrasing the Civil Rights Act of 1964. Lieberman told the Black Caucus at the Democratic convention, to great applause, that he had voted against abolishing racial set asides in transportation contracts. Lieberman had supported vouchers for students in the failing District of Columbia schools; he told teachers' union leaders that he was for demonstration vouchers, but overall wanted to put money into public schools. He had said that Social Security was headed on a disastrous course and needed an injection of funds from private markets; in the campaign he said that the transition costs for George W. Bush's plan were too high. In the Florida controversy, Lieberman took what to some was a surprisingly partisan role—though of course this was a quintessentially partisan issue. On Sunday interview shows he said that he and Gore would never challenge legitimately cast military absentee ballots. But on the preceding Friday night, lawyers working for the Gore-Lieberman ticket did precisely that.

On Election Day, the Gore-Lieberman ticket carried Connecticut 56%–38% and Lieberman was re-elected to the Senate by a 63%–34% margin over Waterbury Mayor Phil Giordano. Governor Rowland tried to keep Giordano from running, on the theory that a contest would only bring out Democratic votes; the result of the race was never in doubt, and Lieberman did not bother to show up at one debate. The margin was a slight downtick from Lieberman's 67%–31% victory in 1994, but his position in Connecticut seems rock-solid.

He returned to the Senate as a major national figure—and one self-evidently eager to run for president in 2004. He made numerous trips to Iowa, New Hampshire and South Carolina and campaigned for many candidates in 2002. He made a series of 11 intellectually hefty policy speeches in 2002 and helpfully bound them into a pamphlet. He even got into a post-mortem argument with Gore over campaign strategy. In August 2002 he said, "Al said some things in the campaign that were not the logical continuation of things—his voting record in the Senate and his career in public service. The people versus the powerful unfortunately left that track and gave a different message, which may have been caused by the pressure that the Nader campaign was giving us. But I think it was not the New Democratic approach." Gore responded in a *New York Times* opinion article that people versus the powerful was "the right choice." Lieberman responded that it was "not expressive of the fiscally responsible, pro-growth, grow-the-middle-class campaign we were running." But one thing could stop his candidacy: He pledged in 2000 that he would not run in 2004 if Gore did, and he kept that pledge. John McCain and other friends gave him advice how to get around it, and Gore himself said that Lieberman shouldn't feel bound by it. But Lieberman said he did. Then in December 2002 Gore surprised just about everyone by saying he wouldn't run. Lieberman was on the phone right away, calling former Gore aides and asking for their support.

The question raised by the Lieberman candidacy was whether a candidate out of line with most politicians of his party on some key issues could be nominated. On some issues Lieberman had changed or at least adjusted his position in the 2000 campaign, and in early 2003 he seemed to stick with his 2000 adjustments. He did not come out for individual investment accounts in Social Security, which he had once considered favorably, but which now almost all Democratic members of Congress opposed. He did not revert to his 1996 comments that looked favorably on California's Proposition 209 that prohibited racial quotas and preferences in state government. Yet there was at least one issue on which he took a position most fervently which was out of line with many, though by no means all, Democrats: The war on terrorism. Lieberman supported George W. Bush on going into Afghanistan and going into Iraq, and he supported him not just perfunctorily or after the fact, but was in fact urging these actions, fervently and cogently, before Bush acted. He has been one of the most prominent voices calling for the remaking of the Middle East and the encouragement of democracy and human rights in the region. These are not, to put it mildly, things valued in the left portion of the Democratic party. But it seems plain that on these issues, unlike some others, Lieberman will not change his views to help his electoral chances, and the 2004 caucuses and primaries will reveal what price he pays.

FIRST DISTRICT

Rep. John Larson (D)

Elected 1998, 3d term; b. July 22, 1948, Hartford; home, E. Hartford; Central CT St. U., B.S. 1971; Catholic; married (Leslie).

Elected Office: E. Hartford Bd. of Ed., 1977–79; E. Hartford Town Cncl., 1979–83; CT Senate, 1983–95, Pres. Pro-Tem 1986–95.

Professional Career: H.S. teacher, 1972–77; Insurance broker, 1977–98; Sr. Fellow, Yale Bush Ctr., 1995-present.

DC Office: 1005 LHOB 20515, 202-225-2265; Fax: 202-225-1031; Web site: www.house.gov/larson.

District Office: Hartford, 860-278-8888.

Committees: *Armed Services* (18th of 29 D): Readiness; Tactical Air & Land Forces. *House Administration* (RMM of 3 D). *Science* (7th of 22 D): Space & Aeronautics.

Group Ratings

	ADA	ACLU	AFS	LCV	CON	ITIC	NTU	COC	ACU	NTLC	CHC
2002	95	80	100	75	70	38	23	50	0	8	0
2001	90	—	100	93	—	—	11	45	8	—	—

National Journal Ratings

	2001 LIB —	2001 CONS	2002 LIB —	2002 CONS
Economic	66% —	35%	72% —	27%
Social	74% —	23%	83% —	16%
Foreign	80% —	20%	77% —	19%

Key Votes of the 107th Congress

1. Approve Bush Tax Cuts	N	5. Faith-Based Charities	N	9. Trade Promotion Authority	N
2. Limit Patients' Bill of Rights	N	6. Bar Gays in the Boy Scouts	N	10. Bar Funds for Intl. Court	N
3. Campaign Finance Reform	Y	7. Ban Partial-Birth Abortion	N	11. Authorize Force in Iraq	N
4. Ban ANWR Development	Y	8. Arm Commercial Pilots	N	12. Deny Home. Sec. Dept. Union	N

Election Results

2002 general	John Larson (D)	134,698	(67%)	($565,840)
	Phil Steele (R)	66,968	(33%)	
2002 primary	John Larson (D)	unopposed		
2000 general	John Larson (D)	151,932	(72%)	($715,753)
	Bob Backlund (R)	59,331	(28%)	($69,042)

Prior Winning Percentages: 1998 (58%)

The People		Race/Ethnic Origin	Ancestry	
Area size:	673 sq. mi.	71.6% White	Italian: 12.1%	Irish: 11.1%
Urban population:	93.4%	12.6% Black	English: 6.9%	
Rural population:	6.6%	2.4% Asian	**2000 Presidential Vote**	
Pop. 2000:	681,113	0.2% Native Am.	Gore (D) 178,977	(62%)
Median income:	$50,227	0.0% Hawaiian	Bush (R) 96,411	(33%)
Poverty status:	9.6%	1.7% Two + races	Other 13,731	(5%)
Military veterans:	12.0%	0.2% Other	**Cook Partisan Voting Index:** D +15	
		11.4% Hispanic Origin		

Occupation	Blue collar: 19.7%	White collar: 65.8%	Gray collar: 14.5%

In 1871, Mark Twain moved to Hartford to become director of an insurance company, and in time became the Connecticut capital's most famous citizen. Hartford, already more than two centuries old, home of the nation's longest circulating newspaper (since 1764), *The Hartford Courant*, boyhood home of the financier J. P. Morgan, was becoming the nation's best-known insurance center. This was not what the harsh Puritans who founded Hartford had in mind, but Connecticut's Yankees turned out to be shrewd businessmen. Thanks to the broad Connecticut River, Hartford also became a seaport; its merchants, prevented from trading and writing marine insurance by Thomas Jefferson's Embargo Act of 1807, turned to writing fire insurance and using the capital they had accumulated in the Napoleonic Wars to finance their ventures. One was Samuel Colt's gun factory just south of downtown Hartford, which became one of the nation's great arms plants—and whose dome and antique buildings Connecticut officials are now trying to preserve as an historic monument.

Insurance and arms are still economic mainstays of Hartford, Connecticut's capital and the center of its largest metropolitan area. Though affected by downsizing and mergers, Aetna and Travelers are still big employers; across the river is the Pratt & Whitney jet engine plant in East Hartford, cornerstone of Connecticut-based United Technologies—even though its local work force is less than one-fourth its size in 1980, it still builds engines for more than 7,400 airlines around the world. The small central city of Hartford is otherwise in bad shape, its high-crime neighborhoods abandoned and bedraggled, its school system deeply troubled. Many words have been written about the sad decline of this once rich city, but a few numbers make the case: Hartford suffered a 11% population decline in the 1990s; where 177,000 people had lived in 1950 there were 124,000 50 years later. Today, its population is 41% Hispanic and 38% black. Yet beyond Hartford, the metropolitan area is mostly affluent and growing slowly, spread out over pleasant hills, and the vast majority of people in the area live outside the central city.

The 1st Congressional District is centered on Hartford. Its shape was considerably altered in the 2001 redistricting, so that it is no longer compact; rather, it resembles a lobster claw. The claw extends west, excluding some affluent suburbs from the district while including small towns toward Torrington in the north; in the south, the district includes the industrial town of Bristol, where along a two-lane country road is the sprawling headquarters of ESPN, the 24-hour cable network that revolutionized sports broadcasting. East of the Connecticut River is East Hartford, home of the Pratt & Whitney plant, and a few other suburbs. Politically, the Hartford area has long been more Democratic than the rest of Connecticut: Hartford is something like Boston, a commercial metropolis more statist than its surroundings. It owes some of its Democratic character to longtime state (1946–75) and national (1961–68) Democratic chairman John Bailey, an old-fashioned political boss with a scandal-free career who promoted a raft of first-class candidates.

The congressman from the 1st District is John Larson, a Democrat elected in 1998 to replace Barbara Kennelly (Bailey's daughter), who ran unsuccessfully for governor after 16 years in the House. Larson grew up in the Mayberry Village public housing project in East Hartford, one of eight children; his father was a fireman at Pratt & Whitney, and his mother worked at the state Capitol. He graduated from Central Connecticut State, taught high school and coached athletics; he then became an insurance agent. He comes from a political family—his brother Timothy became Mayor of East Hartford—and in 1982, at 34, John Larson was elected to the state Senate. Four years later he was Senate President. There Larson sponsored one of the nation's first family medical leave laws, a prototype for the law sponsored by Senator Christopher Dodd and signed by Bill Clinton in 1993. He created neighborhood resource centers for preschoolers, where parents could receive a variety of services. He seemed headed for the governorship, and in 1994 he won the party designation at the state convention. But Comptroller Bill Curry built an organization of unionists and liberal activists, and beat him 55%–45% in the primary. Larson then returned to private life and promoted a volunteer Connect '96 project to hook up libraries and schoolrooms to the information superhighway.

When Kennelly announced her retirement in 1997, Larson ran against Secretary of State Miles Rapoport, from more affluent West Hartford, who had the support of unions, the Sierra Club, and the Connecticut Citizens Action group. Rapoport led in polls and fundraising. But Larson raised impressive sums as well, built a local organization, did lots of door-to-door campaigning, and benefited from the support of Hartford Mayor Mike Peters. Larson ended up with a surprise 46%–43% win. Rapoport won in the northwest part of the district, including Hartford, West Hartford, and heavily Jewish Bloomfield; Larson carried most of the rest, with a big vote in East Hartford. The general election was vigorously contested by Kevin O'Connor, a 31-year-old former law clerk and SEC lawyer, who was endorsed by the *Hartford Courant*, but Larson won 58%–41%.

In the House, Larson prepared a package of bills to close the digital divide between technology haves and have-nots; he called for a Technology Corps of volunteers to train students how to use the Internet. He worked to reverse the Appropriations Committee's decision in 1999 to stop funding for F-22 fighter jets. He voted against PNTR with China, he said, because of a promise he had made to labor unions. The former history teacher took an unusual interest in the institution—pushing successfully for the Library of Congress to write an illustrated, narrative history of the House, to match the fine history of the Senate written by Senator Robert Byrd. In October 2002, he actively opposed authorizing the use of force in Iraq; he worried that unilateral action would unite the Arab world against the United States.

In 2000 Larson faced a celebrity challenger in former World Wrestling Federation champion Bob Backlund, but this was to be no repeat of the Jesse Ventura phenomenon. Backlund had little experience in public life, raised little money, and lost every town as he was defeated 72%–28%. Two years later, Larson won with 67% against the brother of Robert Steele, who won two terms in the eastern Connecticut 2d District in the 1970s.

SECOND DISTRICT

Rep. Rob Simmons (R)

Elected 2000, 2d term; b. Feb. 11, 1943, New York, NY; home, Stonington; Haverford Col., B.A. 1965, Harvard U., M.A. 1979; Episcopalian; married (Heidi Paffard).

Military Career: Army, 1965–69 (Vietnam); Army Reserves, 1969–00.

Elected Office: CT House of Reps., 1990–00.

Professional Career: Operations Ofcr., CIA, 1969–79; Staff, Sen. John Chafee, 1979–81; Staff Dir., Sel. Cmte. on Intelligence, 1981–85; Visiting Lecturer, Yale U., 1985–95; Teaching asst., U. of CT, 1988–91.

DC Office: 215 CHOB 20515, 202-225-2076; Fax: 202-225-4977; Web site: www.house.gov/simmons.

District Office: Norwich, 860-886-0139.

Committees: *Armed Services* (17th of 33 R): Projection Forces; Tactical Air & Land Forces. *Transportation & Infrastructure* (23d of 41 R): Coast Guard & Maritime Transportation; Highways, Transit & Pipelines; Railroads. *Veterans' Affairs* (9th of 17 R): Health (Chmn.).

Group Ratings

	ADA	ACLU	AFS	LCV	CON	ITIC	NTU	COC	ACU	NTLC	CHC
2002	35	47	22	50	25	75	49	90	68	75	33
2001	35	—	20	71	—	—	58	91	44	—	—

National Journal Ratings

	2001 LIB	—	2001 CONS		2002 LIB	—	2002 CONS
Economic	43%	—	56%		48%	—	51%
Social	60%	—	40%		59%	—	40%
Foreign	33%	—	60%		47%	—	51%

Key Votes of the 107th Congress

1. Approve Bush Tax Cuts	Y	5. Faith-Based Charities	Y	9. Trade Promotion Authority	N
2. Limit Patients' Bill of Rights	Y	6. Bar Gays in the Boy Scouts	N	10. Bar Funds for Intl. Court	Y
3. Campaign Finance Reform	Y	7. Ban Partial-Birth Abortion	N	11. Authorize Force in Iraq	Y
4. Ban ANWR Development	Y	8. Arm Commercial Pilots	Y	12. Deny Home. Sec. Dept. Union	Y

Election Results

2002 general	Rob Simmons (R)	117,434	(54%)	($1,861,492)
	Joe Courtney (D)	99,674	(46%)	($1,233,222)
2002 primary	Rob Simmons (R)	unopposed		
2000 general	Robert Simmons (R)	114,380	(51%)	($1,060,197)
	Sam Gejdenson (D)	111,520	(49%)	($1,616,863)

The People		Race/Ethnic Origin	Ancestry	
Area size:	2,143 sq. mi.	88.6% White	Irish: 13.3%	Italian: 10.2%
Urban population:	66.7%	3.3% Black	English: 10.2%	
Rural population:	33.3%	1.7% Asian	**2000 Presidential Vote**	
Pop. 2000:	681,113	0.5% Native Am.	Gore (D) 162,762	(54%)
Median income:	$54,498	0.0% Hawaiian	Bush (R) 119,184	(40%)
Poverty status:	5.8%	1.5% Two + races	Other 19,587	(6%)
Military veterans:	14.6%	0.1% Other	**Cook Partisan Voting Index:** D + 7	
		4.3% Hispanic Origin		

Occupation	Blue collar: 20.9%	White collar: 62.9%	Gray collar: 16.2%

Eastern Connecticut, one of the longest-settled parts of the United States, had great, and sometimes painful, change in the 1990s—a change comparable to those of the 1640s or 1810s or 1950s. When the Puritan settlers from Massachusetts and England arrived, these flinty hills were the home of small Indian tribes, whose numbers were decimated by warfare and even more by disease. This was never fertile farming country, but New London and Norwich were among the 13 colonies' leading workshops and ports. Not long after, factories developed around mills in little villages on the fast-flowing Quinebaug and Shetucket Rivers. Sandbars kept oceangoing ships out of the rivers, but they docked at New London. In the mid-20th century new technology shaped the area. Four nuclear power plants were built here, more than in any similarly populated part of the United States. In Groton, the "Submarine Capital of the World" across the Thames River from New London and downriver from the Coast Guard Academy, is General Dynamics' Electric Boat Company, which built the nuclear submarines that may very well have deterred nuclear war.

By the 1990s, that high-tech economy was in trouble. Nuclear plants were wearing out and being shut down across the country. And with the end of the Cold War, much of the Electric Boat work force was laid off, though some remained to work on the next-generation Virginia-class submarine; the base is home port to more than 20 subs, still the nation's most active submarine port, and about 10,000 employees. Suddenly the area's economic base shifted to entertainment. Some of that was tourism—Mystic Seaport and the Coast Guard Academy. Much more important was the Foxwoods Casino, built by the 650-member Mashantucket Pequot tribe and opened in 1992. Foxwoods is now the largest casino in the world, and with hotels, golf courses and a convention center, it is the largest employer in Connecticut. With the Mohegan Sun casino (the 2d largest casino in the world), opened near Norwich in 1996, gambling establishments now provide more tax dollars to the state than any insurance or defense company. The Mashantucket Pequots, 650 strong, have donated $10 million to the National Museum of the American Indian, and have become a major national political contributor.

The 2d Congressional District includes most of the eastern part of the state, centering on the small cities of New London and Norwich, including mill towns and the University of Connecticut town of Storrs nestled in the rocky hills to the north. The 2d also stretches west to the outskirts of Hartford, and to antique-filled small towns like Essex and Old Lyme on Long Island Sound, but after the 2001 redistricting it no longer includes the heavily Democratic college town of Middletown. For many years this was a politically marginal district, with close battles between Yankee Republicans and Catholic Democrats. But as its politics trended Democratic, they also became more volatile during the past decade, with substantial votes for Ross Perot and Ralph Nader.

The congressman from the 2d District is Rob Simmons, a Republican elected in 2000. Simmons grew up in New York City and enlisted in the Army after graduating from Haverford College in 1965; he spent 19 months in Vietnam, where he earned two Bronze Stars. In 1969 he joined the CIA, working as an operations officer for a decade, including five years on assignment in East Asia. Simmons joined the staff of Senator John Chafee in 1979 and was staff director for the Senate Intelligence Committee from 1981–85. When he left Washington, he said that he never expected to return. He earned a master's in public policy administration from the Kennedy School of Government and was a doctoral candidate in political science at the University of Connecticut. He was an associate fellow of Yale's Berkeley College, where he taught military intelligence; he also chaired the Stonington Police Commission. Simmons served five terms in a Democratic-leaning district in the General Assembly, voting against the state's new income tax. He remained in the Army Reserve, with the rank of colonel.

In 2000, Simmons ran against 20-year Democratic Congressman Sam Gejdenson. Simmons began the race with little recognition. Gejdenson portrayed him as too conservative for the district and criticized his support for individual investment accounts for Social Security. Simmons said Gejdenson was too entrenched in Washington, where he was ranking minority member of the International Relations Committee, and was out of touch with the district—living in his wife's home in a gated community in the 3d District. Simmons also made an issue of the Mashantucket Pequot Indian tribe land claims. In 1983, Gejdenson voted to give the tribe, whose connection to the original Pequots seemed to many questionable, federal recognition and settlement land for a reservation within the state: All essential to the development of Foxwoods. But by 2000 the towns around Foxwoods were complaining about traffic and were fighting the Pequots' claims to more lands. In the campaign's closing days, Gejdenson fired two aides who admitted planting with reporters a story critical of Simmons's service in Vietnam. When House Democratic strategists realized in October that Gejdenson was in trouble, they sent money in, but it was too late. Simmons won by 2,860 votes—51%–49%. He ran strongly in his home base in the district's southeast corner and won 34 of 54 towns, while Gejdenson ran best in the college towns of Middletown, Storrs and Willimantic. Simmons was one of only two successful Republican challengers that year.

In the House, Simmons has had a moderate voting record, a bit more liberal on cultural issues than on defense. He serves on the Armed Services Committee, where he sought to protect workers at Electric Boat. After September 11, he used his background in Army intelligence to advise colleagues on how the military and Congress might have avoided the attacks. He has avidly sought, but has not won, a seat on the Intelligence Committee; still, he is permitted to attend classified briefings and receive classified materials. Since the Cold War ended, he said, terrorists have been able to roam more freely and intelligence agencies have relied more on technical data than on human expertise. He added an amendment to the intelligence bill permitting the CIA to reimburse overseas agents for personal liability insurance. On trade promotion authority, he delayed long before casting his vote and then voted against because, he said, it had inadequate labor and environmental protections. He was one of nine House Republicans who opposed the partial-birth abortion ban.

In 2002, House Democrats targeted him. He survived his first battle when he persuaded the state redistricting commission to keep the 2d District largely intact in redistricting. But the commission, perhaps influenced by Simmons's argument that eastern Connecticut had formed a single district since 1843, decided to put 5th District Democrat Jim Maloney in the same district with 6th District Republican Nancy Johnson, and did Simmons the additional favor of removing Middletown from the 2d. The Democratic candidate was former state Representative Joseph Courtney, the unsuccessful 1998 nominee for lieutenant governor. Courtney ran on the standard Democratic themes of Social Security, prescription drug coverage for seniors and against the Bush tax cut. Friends of the Earth endorsed Simmons, saying that he had the most pro-environment record of the freshmen Republicans. Courtney gained ground late in the campaign, but Simmons won 54%–46%.

THIRD DISTRICT

Rep. Rosa DeLauro (D)

Elected 1990, 7th term; b. Mar. 2, 1943, New Haven; home, New Haven; Marymount Col., B.A. 1964, London Sch. of Econ., 1962–63, Columbia U., M.A. 1966; Catholic; married (Stanley Greenberg).

Professional Career: Exec. Asst., New Haven Mayor Frank Logue, 1976–77; Exec. Asst. & Develop. Admin., City of New Haven, 1977–79; Chief of Staff, U.S. Sen. Christopher Dodd, 1980–87; Exec. Dir., Countdown '87, 1987–88; Exec. Dir., EMILY's List, 1989.

DC Office: 2262 RHOB 20515, 202-225-3661; Fax: 202-225-4890; Web site: www.house.gov/delauro.

District Office: New Haven, 203-562-3718.

Committees: *Democratic Steering Committee Chairwoman. Appropriations* (11th of 29 D): Agriculture, Rural Development, & FDA; Labor, HHS & Education. *Budget* (8th of 19 D).

Group Ratings

	ADA	ACLU	AFS	LCV	CON	ITIC	NTU	COC	ACU	NTLC	CHC
2002	100	87	100	88	43	50	18	35	0	3	0
2001	95	—	100	93	—	—	10	35	0	—	—

National Journal Ratings

	2001 LIB	—	2001 CONS		2002 LIB	—	2002 CONS
Economic	88%	—	11%		88%	—	10%
Social	83%	—	11%		84%	—	8%
Foreign	77%	—	22%		77%	—	19%

Key Votes of the 107th Congress

1. Approve Bush Tax Cuts	N	5. Faith-Based Charities	N	9. Trade Promotion Authority	N
2. Limit Patients' Bill of Rights	N	6. Bar Gays in the Boy Scouts	N	10. Bar Funds for Intl. Court	N
3. Campaign Finance Reform	Y	7. Ban Partial-Birth Abortion	N	11. Authorize Force in Iraq	N
4. Ban ANWR Development	Y	8. Arm Commercial Pilots	N	12. Deny Home. Sec. Dept. Union	N

Election Results

2002 general	Rosa DeLauro (D)	121,557	(66%)	($686,768)
	Richter Elser (R)	54,757	(30%)	($81,050)
	Charles Pillsbury (Green)	9,050	(5%)	($102,890)
2002 primary	Rosa DeLauro (D)	unopposed		
2000 general	Rosa DeLauro (D)	156,910	(72%)	($680,778)
	June M. Gold (R)	60,037	(28%)	($73,864)
	Other	1,258	(1%)	

Prior Winning Percentages: 1998 (71%); 1996 (71%); 1994 (63%); 1992 (66%); 1990 (52%)

The People		Race/Ethnic Origin	Ancestry	
Area size:	485 sq. mi.	76.1% White	Italian: 18.7%	Irish: 12.5%
Urban population:	96.6%	11.5% Black	German: 6.7%	
Rural population:	3.4%	2.5% Asian	**2000 Presidential Vote**	
Pop. 2000:	681,113	0.2% Native Am.	Gore (D) 168,196	(60%)
Median income:	$49,752	0.0% Hawaiian	Bush (R) 96,446	(34%)
Poverty status:	8.8%	1.5% Two + races	Other 15,455	(6%)
Military veterans:	11.8%	0.2% Other	**Cook Partisan Voting Index:** D + 13	
		8.0% Hispanic Origin		

Occupation   Blue collar: 21.1%   White collar: 64.7%   Gray collar: 14.2%

The beginnings of Connecticut's defense industry came two centuries ago, in 1798, when Eli Whitney, a young Yale graduate, won an order from the federal government to produce 10,000 muskets at $13.40 each. Six years before, Whitney had invented the cotton gin, which revolutionized the South but for years only embroiled him in a patent suit. On the musket contract, he was determined to make a profit right off, so he set up a system of interchangeable parts and invented a milling machine and gauges: The beginning of standardized American manufacturing. It was also the beginning of New Haven as a manufacturing center, for Whitney set up his factory along a small, rapidly flowing river just north of this town established more than 150 years before as a religious haven for strict Puritans. For the next 150 years or so, the town mass-produced rifles, clocks, locks, hardware and toys—anything its tinkerers and entrepreneurs could fashion. Today there are few factories left in New Haven and Connecticut's defense contracts have been cut way back, though Sikorsky Aircraft manufactures helicopters in Stratford. Southern Connecticut around New Haven is mostly prosperous with scores of mostly small technology and biomedical firms. But the city itself, with significant crime rates and many neighborhoods scarred by abandoned homes, has been to a considerable extent abandoned: it had 164,000 people in 1950 and 124,000 in 2002. Yale, with its Gothic spires and redbrick halls has always been the visual focus of the city; now it is New Haven's largest employer. There has been some revival in recent years, sparked by Yale's homebuyers' program of incentives to faculty and staff and by $1 billion in local investments by biotech firms. But the economic vitality of the region is centered outside the city limits. New Haven, however, has a new historic claim. It was the birthplace of George W. Bush in 1946, and he lived for two years on Hillhouse Avenue in a building that now houses the economics department.

The 3d Congressional District covers the New Haven metropolitan area, which has long since spread beyond the narrow city limits over the hills of what were once Yankee villages and countryside; New Haven cast only 11% of its votes in 2002. For many years the 3d was a marginal district, changing partisan hands in the 1980s as well as the 1940s and 1950s. But it has moved to the Democratic side: Al Gore won 60% here in 2000.

The congresswoman from the 3d District, Rosa DeLauro, is well connected in New Haven and Washington. She grew up in New Haven's Wooster Square. Both her parents were elected as New Haven aldermen; her mother, Luisa DeLauro, retired in 1999 after 35 years as New Haven's longest-serving alderman. Rosa's husband Stanley Greenberg was Bill Clinton's chief pollster from 1991–94 and worked for Al Gore in 2000. Rosa DeLauro has been in politics nearly all of her life. She was a development administrator in New Haven in the 1970s, chief of staff to Senator Christopher Dodd from 1980–87, then spent a year working to stop U.S. military aid to Nicaraguan contras before going on to become director of EMILY's List, the feminist fundraising group. In 1990, when 3d District incumbent Bruce Morrison ran for governor, DeLauro ran for Congress and won 52%–48% over anti-tax and anti-abortion legislator Tom Scott, after spending an impressive $957,000.

DeLauro has had the most liberal voting record in the Connecticut delegation, and became one of the Democratic leadership's loudest champions on the floor. Like most House Democratic leaders, she voted against NAFTA and PNTR with China. She has been an active and enthusiastic supporter of feminist issues. A cancer survivor, she sponsored the law to require 48-hour hospital stays for mastectomies and argued for insurance coverage of early-detection tests of cervical cancer. She has sought unsuccessfully to remove abortion restrictions on federal employees' health benefits. In 2000, she helped to crystallize House Democrats' attacks on George W. Bush and organized pre-election bus tours for women members in battleground states. As a member of the committee that drafted in 2002 the bill creating the Homeland Security Department, she embarrassed House Republican leaders by winning a vote to restrict federal contracts to companies that move overseas for tax purposes; the House-Senate conference committee later watered down that provision.

She remains an active and intense political strategist, "a live wire whose words rush out like sparks," wrote Frank Bruni of *The New York Times*. She has run twice for chairman of the Democratic Caucus and suffered two painfully close losses. In 1998, she lost 108–97 to Martin Frost, but Dick Gephardt then named her an assistant to the leader to work on the party message. In 2002 she lost by 104–103 to Bob Menendez after an intense year-long contest. The deciding vote was cast for Menendez by Mike Feeley of Colorado, whose election was in question at the time; as it later turned out, he lost his race and was never a member of Congress. DeLauro was an active and early supporter of Nancy Pelosi in her races for minority whip and minority leader, and she was probably hurt in her own race by the reluctance of some Democrats to put so many liberal women in the party leadership. Pelosi subsequently named her as co-chair of the Democratic Steering Committee, which assigns members to House committees.

DeLauro's last serious competition in the 3d District came in 1992, when she won a rematch against Scott 66%–34%. She has been reelected easily since then. When Joe Lieberman's vice presidential candidacy raised the possibility that his Senate seat would become open, she expressed interest in running for it. In 2002, against an openly gay restaurateur, she won 66%–30%.

FOURTH DISTRICT

Rep. Christopher Shays (R)

Elected Aug. 1987, 8th term; b. Oct. 18, 1945, Darien; home, Bridgeport; Principia Col., B.A. 1968, NYU, M.B.A. 1974, M.P.A. 1978; Christian Scientist; married (Betsi).

Elected Office: CT House of Reps., 1974–87.

Professional Career: Peace Corps, Fiji, 1968–70; Aide, Trumbull Mayor, 1971–72.

DC Office: 1126 LHOB 20515, 202-225-5541; Fax: 202-225-9629; Web site: www.house.gov/shays.

District Offices: Bridgeport, 203-579-5870; Norwalk, 203-866-6469; Stamford, 203-357-8277.

Committees: *Budget* (Vice Chmn. of 24 R). *Financial Services* (22d of 37 R): Capital Markets, Insurance & Government Sponsored Enterprises; Housing & Community Opportunity. *Government Reform* (Vice Chmn. of 24

R): Energy Policy, Natural Resources and Regulatory Affairs; National Security, Emerging Threats & Intl. Relations (Chmn.); Wellness & Human Rights. *Select Committee on Homeland Security* (13th of 27 R): Emergency Preparedness & Response; Intelligence & Counterterrorism.

Group Ratings

	ADA	ACLU	AFS	LCV	CON	ITIC	NTU	COC	ACU	NTLC	CHC
2002	20	53	0	50	97	100	58	95	76	83	42
2001	35	—	0	86	—	—	66	83	32	—	—

National Journal Ratings

	2001 LIB	—	2001 CONS		2002 LIB	—	2002 CONS
Economic	45%	—	56%		45%	—	54%
Social	63%	—	37%		59%	—	40%
Foreign	61%	—	40%		47%	—	51%

Key Votes of the 107th Congress

1. Approve Bush Tax Cuts	Y	5. Faith-Based Charities	Y	9. Trade Promotion Authority	Y
2. Limit Patients' Bill of Rights	Y	6. Bar Gays in the Boy Scouts	N	10. Bar Funds for Intl. Court	Y
3. Campaign Finance Reform	Y	7. Ban Partial-Birth Abortion	Y	11. Authorize Force in Iraq	Y
4. Ban ANWR Development	Y	8. Arm Commercial Pilots	Y	12. Deny Home. Sec. Dept. Union	Y

Election Results

2002 general	Christopher Shays (R)	113,197	(64%)	($919,160)
	Stephanie Sanchez (D)	62,491	(36%)	($110,699)
2002 primary	Christopher Shays (R)	unopposed		
2000 general	Christopher Shays (R)	119,155	(58%)	($1,039,573)
	Stephanie Sanchez (D)	84,472	(41%)	($172,155)
	Other	3,131	(2%)	

Prior Winning Percentages: 1998 (69%); 1996 (60%); 1994 (74%); 1992 (67%); 1990 (77%); 1988 (72%); 1987 (57%)

The People		Race/Ethnic Origin	Ancestry	
Area size:	539 sq. mi.	70.9% White	Italian: 13.5%	Irish: 11.6%
Urban population:	95.9%	10.9% Black	German: 7.1%	
Rural population:	4.1%	3.2% Asian	**2000 Presidential Vote**	
Pop. 2000:	681,113	0.1% Native Am.	Gore (D) 148,022	(53%)
Median income:	$66,598	0.0% Hawaiian	Bush (R) 120,140	(43%)
Poverty status:	7.4%	1.7% Two+ races	Other 10,219	(4%)
Military veterans:	10.0%	0.3% Other	**Cook Partisan Voting Index:** D + 5	
		12.8% Hispanic Origin		

Occupation	Blue collar: 15.5%	White collar: 71.8%	Gray collar: 12.7%

No one in colonial America imagined that the rocky shore of southern Connecticut on Long Island Sound would some day lodge one of the largest concentrations of wealth in the world. The soil was stony, the terrain unaccommodating, the harbors not as convenient as those in New York and Rhode Island and Massachusetts. Yet that is what has happened. For 200 years this was the home of unnoticed Yankee farmers, sailors and tinkerers; then, factories were built on its fast-running stream. In the 19th century, Bridgeport became famous as the home of P.T. Barnum, and around that same time rich New Yorkers began taking the train north to country houses in Connecticut. In the 20th century, Greenwich and other Yankee villages clustered around commuter railroad stations became the home of some of New York's elite. Greenwich has beautifully manicured hills, elaborately simple boat docks, carefully casual roads, good manners and dull haircuts, over a dozen private clubs and 12 private schools—and houses which are routinely sold for more than $2 million and then torn down to make way for grander mansions. Starting in the 1950s, New York-based CEOs, eager to minimize their own commutes and avoid New York income taxes, moved their headquarters out to Greenwich and further, and today there are more than a dozen corporations with sales over $1 billion headquartered here, including General Electric in Fairfield. Greenwich, sometimes referred to as "Wall Street by the Sea" for its proliferation of hedge fund offices and financial firms, commands the highest commercial rents of all these places.

The 4th Congressional District covers Connecticut along Long Island Sound, from industrial Bridgeport to affluent Greenwich, plus a row of inland towns from New Canaan to Oxford. It includes bustling Stamford, woodsy Darien, modest Norwalk, artsy-craftsy Westport, Fairfield and then Bridgeport, an odd duck, an industrial and low-income town, though spruced up when the state-financed Ballpark at Harbor Yard opened for minor league baseball. The basic political balance has been the same since the 1940s, when the heavily affluent suburbs out-voted Bridgeport and elected Republican Claire Boothe Luce to the House. More than the rest of Connecticut, the 4th is oriented to New York rather than Hartford or Boston. People here watch New York TV stations: They are Yankee, not Red Sox, fans; their political attitudes are shaped by what is happening in the City as much as in Hartford. Hatred of higher taxes has enabled Republican Governor John Rowland to win by big margins here. But the specter of the religious right eroded the Episcopalian Republican vote and helped Al Gore, with help from Stamford-born Joseph Lieberman, to beat George W. Bush here in 2000.

The 4th District's congressman, Christopher Shays, is a product of the upscale towns and he has been a pivotal Republican in the House. Shays grew up in Darien. After college he and his wife volunteered for the Peace Corps and served in Fiji; after graduate school he was elected to the Connecticut House in 1974, at 29, and served for 12 years, working with Common Cause on rules reform. He was elected to Congress in a 1987 special election by beating a culturally conservative Democrat from Bridgeport. Shays is a pleasant man with a stubborn streak and considerable legislative savvy; his voting record is near the middle of the House on most issues, a bit left on cultural issues. When he feels strongly, he will risk everything: He registered for conscientious objector status during the Vietnam War, and says he would not have served if drafted; as a legislator, he went to jail for seven days in 1986 to protest judicial system corruption.

Despite his dissent from many Republicans' views—on campaign finance reform, abortion, gun control, subsidies to the arts, gay rights, the minimum wage, defense spending, Census sampling—he was a partisan Republican from the time he was ignored by the House's Democratic leaders and impressed by a speech in Connecticut by a backbencher named Newt Gingrich. The first major bill of the Republican Congress was managed by Shays: the Congressional Accountability Act, imposing on Congress the laws it imposes on others, passed unanimously on the first day. Shays was also chief sponsor of the gift ban law and the Lobby Disclosure Act. "I am very much a part of the Republican revolution—and I do think it is a revolution—but I am still an independent person," he said. Shays supported Gingrich on ethics charges and warned him of the other leaders' coup in 1997; he soured on other Republicans in 1998 as Gingrich went to great lengths to sink his campaign finance reform bill. On some big issues he was solidly with George W. Bush: He voted for trade promotion authority and to authorize the use of force in Iraq. After the September 11 attacks that killed members of 70 families in his district, many of whose funerals he attended, he wore a red-white-and-blue cloth bracelet with the words, "God bless America."

As chairman of a Government Reform subcommittee, Shays zeroed in on Gulf War illnesses. A large number of veterans have reported various symptoms, some of which may be related to exposure to chemical weapons, and the Pentagon failed to reveal for years the use of some gas by Iraq or contact with it by American troops. Shays became convinced that the Pentagon and the Veterans' Affairs Departments were "plagued by arrogant incuriosity and a pervasive myopia that sees lack of evidence as proof." In December 2001, the two agencies finally conceded that Gulf War veterans were twice as likely as other soldiers to suffer a fatal neurological illness, and they agreed to pay disability and survivor benefits. In June 2002, he became a leading supporter on the committee of Bush's proposal for a Homeland Security Department and he helped to defeat an amendment to permit its employees to join unions.

Shays's great cause has been campaign finance regulation. As enacted in March 2002, his Shays-Meehan bill—or McCain-Feingold, as it was known in the Senate and more widely—banned in federal elections soft money from corporations, labor unions and wealthy individuals and prohibited issue advocacy ads within 60 days of an election. Although the House passed the bill 240–189, all but 41 House Republicans voted against it, with many contending it was harmful to their party. The conflict caused bitter divisions and anger by Republicans toward Shays. Tom

Davis of Virginia, who chaired the NRCC, said that the bill would drive money from the two parties to interest groups, both right and left. Anne Northup of Kentucky said that Shays's constant criticism of opponents of the legislation as corrupt was "making it very hard to vote your conscience." Still, Shays would not give up the fight. He was an active participant in defending the new law against the federal court suit; in May 2003, a deeply divided three-judge federal court upheld some of the provisions but not others.

After the November 2002 election, the chairmanship of the Government Reform Committee was open, and Shays was next in line in seniority. He actively sought the post; he argued that it was best suited for him and that his work on campaign finance ought not to be held against him. But he clearly was not popular with the Republican leadership, and the Steering Committee chose Davis, who had done a brilliant job maintaining the Republican majority in 2000 and 2002.

Back home, Shays has had opposition from Democrats who have attacked him for supporting Gingrich and, in 2000, from a Republican who said he was too independent and too liberal. But none caused him serious difficulty. There continues to be talk that he might run for governor, once John Rowland steps down.

FIFTH DISTRICT

Rep. Nancy Johnson (R)

Elected 1982, 11th term; b. Jan. 5, 1935, Chicago, IL; home, New Britain; U. of Chicago, 1951–53, Radcliffe Col., B.A. 1957, U. of London, 1957–58; Unitarian; married (Theodore).

Elected Office: CT Senate, 1976–82.

Professional Career: Pres., Sheldon Community Guidance Clinic; Adjunct Prof., Central CT St. Col., 1968–71.

DC Office: 2113 RHOB 20515, 202-225-4476; Fax: 202-225-4488; Web site: www.house.gov/nancyjohnson.

District Offices: New Britain, 860-223-8412; Waterbury, 203-573-1418.

Committees: *Ways & Means* (4th of 24 R): Health (Chmn.); Human Resources.

Group Ratings

	ADA	ACLU	AFS	LCV	CON	ITIC	NTU	COC	ACU	NTLC	CHC
2002	30	53	11	63	58	100	49	90	56	66	33
2001	30	—	10	79	—	—	52	87	32	—	—

National Journal Ratings

	2001 LIB	—	2001 CONS		2002 LIB	—	2002 CONS
Economic	49%	—	51%		51%	—	49%
Social	60%	—	40%		61%	—	39%
Foreign	54%	—	46%		51%	—	48%

Key Votes of the 107th Congress

1. Approve Bush Tax Cuts	Y	5. Faith-Based Charities	Y	9. Trade Promotion Authority	Y
2. Limit Patients' Bill of Rights	Y	6. Bar Gays in the Boy Scouts	Y	10. Bar Funds for Intl. Court	N
3. Campaign Finance Reform	Y	7. Ban Partial-Birth Abortion	N	11. Authorize Force in Iraq	Y
4. Ban ANWR Development	Y	8. Arm Commercial Pilots	Y	12. Deny Home. Sec. Dept. Union	Y

Election Results

2002 general	Nancy Johnson (R)	113,626	(54%)	($3,752,161)
	Jim Maloney (D)	90,616	(43%)	($2,075,621)
	Other	5,212	(3%)	
2002 primary	Nancy Johnson (R)	unopposed		
2000 general (CT 6)	Nancy Johnson (R)	143,698	(63%)	($1,163,610)
	Paul Valenti (D)	75,471	(33%)	($11,142)
	Other	10,374	(5%)	

The People		Race/Ethnic Origin	Ancestry	
Area size:	1,282 sq. mi.	80.2% White	Italian: 14.5%	Irish: 12.7%
Urban population:	85.9%	5.2% Black	German: 8.2%	
Rural population:	14.1%	2.1% Asian	**2000 Presidential Vote**	
Pop. 2000:	681,113	0.2% Native Am.	Gore (D) 146,599	(52%)
Median income:	$53,118	0.0% Hawaiian	Bush (R) 121,424	(43%)
Poverty status:	7.7%	1.5% Two + races	Other 13,887	(5%)
Military veterans:	11.9%	0.3% Other	**Cook Partisan Voting Index:** D + 4	
		10.5% Hispanic Origin		

Occupation	Blue collar: 22.4%	White collar: 62.9%	Gray collar: 14.6%

Over the years, Connecticut's stony soil has become the home of some of the most affluent people in the nation and the world. This is true even in the hills of northwest Connecticut, off the interstates and far from Connecticut's small urban capital of Hartford and its sometime booming edge city of Stamford. Here are exquisite Yankee towns like Washington and Kent, prosperous once in the post-Revolutionary era when Connecticut's ship owners accumulated capital and invested it in factories and mills, and now the "anti-Hamptons," a country-home mecca for ultra-rich New Yorkers seeking to avoid the glitz of Southampton and Easthampton. Not far away are small industrial cities like New Britain, America's ball bearing capital for years; Meriden, which turned from ivory combs, clocks, cutlery, and silver, to producing electrical signaling equipment, jewelry, biotech filters, and nuclear instruments; Waterbury, once the nation's largest producer of brass, where political corruption and economic malaise resulted in the state taking over its finances in 2001; and Danbury, once the nation's leading producer of hats, but now a growing corporate headquarters with an eclectic mix of recent immigrants from South America, the Caribbean and Southeast Asia. Over the hills from Hartford are Avon and Simsbury, booming towns that have become comfortable bedroom communities and the home of champion international ice-skaters and facilities.

The 5th Congressional District covers much of the western side of the state, dipping down to include the northern towns of Fairfield County. It has two arms that reach into the hills of central Connecticut—one to Democratic Meriden, and the other to the affluent and Republican-leaning Farmington Valley suburbs of Hartford. This district merged the surviving pieces of the old 5th and 6th Districts, and was carefully drawn by a bipartisan redistricting commission to provide a "fair fight" between two incumbents forced into the same district because Connecticut lost a House seat in the 2000 Census. As measured by the 2000 presidential election, it was a bit more Republican than the old 6th and a bit more Democratic than the old 5th; in state elections, it has voted by wide margins for Republican Governor John Rowland and Democratic Senators Christopher Dodd and Joe Lieberman.

The congresswoman from the new 5th District is Nancy Johnson, a Republican first elected in 1982. She grew up in Chicago, the daughter of a Republican state legislator, came east to school, then lived in New Britain as a doctor's wife and a teacher, raising three children while active in charitable and community affairs. She was elected to the Connecticut Senate in 1976 from a heavily Democratic district. When 6th District Congressman Toby Moffett ran against Senator Lowell Weicker in 1982, Johnson won the House seat, defeating Bill Curry, then a 30-year-old nuclear freeze organizer and later a Clinton White House aide and unsuccessful Democratic candidate for governor in 1994 and 2002.

Johnson is now a high-ranking member of Ways and Means and chair of its Health Subcommittee. Her record has been fairly liberal on cultural issues and consciously moderate elsewhere, but market-oriented on much of her committee work. For some years, she has been one of the most active and productive legislators in the House. She welcomed George W. Bush's initiative for Medicare reform as an opportunity to push her long-time priorities of a prescription drug benefit for seniors and making long-term care more affordable. She has worked on reshaping Medicare, sponsoring the first preventive health care benefits for seniors, measures to strengthen community hospitals, nursing homes and Medicare Choice plans. She helped to make premiums for long-term health insurance deductible from income taxes and sought a tax credit for families' spending on long-term care. She got funding to conduct training for children's health care and more mammograms to detect breast cancer. In June 2002, she worked with Ways and Means chairman Bill Thomas to craft the House Republicans' voluntary plan for prescription coverage, which would be financed through subsidies to the elderly and provided by private firms, not the government. Democrat John Dingell said that it was "not a drug benefit at all, [but] a host of subsidies to provide to private insurers in the hope that they will offer a drug-only benefit to seniors." The House passed the bill 221–208, with eight members from each party switching sides. Earlier, she opposed the Clinton health care plan, enduring gratuitous and sexist insults from then-Chairman Pete Stark in hearings, and her efforts contributed to its demise. She was the lead Republican sponsor of the 1997 CHIP program for health insurance for uninsured children.

Also on Ways and Means, Johnson worked to increase the Independent Living program for older foster care children and to help fathers on welfare get jobs and develop parental skills. In 2002, the House passed her resolution urging Major League Baseball to implement a mandatory program to test for steroid use. And she responded to constituent unhappiness over the decision of New Britain-based Stanley Works to reincorporate in Bermuda to save $30 million annually in federal taxes, by introducing a bill imposing a moratorium on such actions.

She has often bucked the House Republican leadership. She voted against the Contract with America crime package, has supported abortion rights (Johnson harshly criticized George W. Bush's executive order reimposing a ban on federal aid to international organizations that discuss abortion), was one of the first Republicans to sign a discharge petition for the Shays-Meehan campaign finance bill and introduced legislation to prevent oil drilling in the Arctic National Wildlife Refuge. But her cooperation with Speaker Newt Gingrich ended up causing her electoral trouble in 1996, when she chaired the House ethics committee during its investigation of charges brought by Democrats against him. Her opponent called her "an enabler and participant in the right-wing Republican agenda," and national liberal groups targeted the district. Johnson readily admitted that her role on the ethics committee "absolutely hurt me" in the election, which she won 50%–49%. After that election, the House voted 395–28 to reprimand and fine Gingrich an unprecedented $300,000; Johnson, her term up, immediately left the committee.

Governor John Rowland said just before the November 2000 election that he would appoint Johnson to the Senate if Joe Lieberman were elected vice president. But that became moot once the recount in Florida was finally completed. Instead, this senior lawmaker was faced with redistricting and the unpleasant task of running against her feisty Democratic colleague Jim Maloney. He had been elected three times in competitive contests and compiled a moderate voting record, but Maloney was dogged by campaign finance charges. Although the new district was drawn evenly—in both geographic and partisan terms—from the old districts, Johnson entered the contest with some clear-cut advantages: She was a more experienced legislator, with a longer record of performance; she was a better fundraiser, including the most funds received from the pharmaceutical and hospital industries by any House candidate. In addition, Maloney didn't help his cause by reaffirming a pledge not to seek another term in 2004. Neither contender held anything back, with *The Hartford Courant* describing Johnson as "a pit bull in pearls," and Maloney as "the bulky junkyard dog of Connecticut politics." Maloney depicted Johnson as an ally of the powerful who failed to defend the weak. Johnson stressed her ability to cross party lines and the respect accorded her in Washington. Although Maloney had the active endorsement of the AFL-CIO, Johnson picked up a few local unions.

Johnson came though this contest with a comfortable 54%–43% victory, winning 37 of the 41 cities and towns. So complete was Johnson's victory that she led Maloney 50%–48% in his old district; in her old district, she won 59%–39%, with 2-to-1 margins in Avon, Simsbury and many of the hill towns. She likely will hold this seat as long as she wants it, but it should be a competitive district if she does not run.

★ DELAWARE ★

Delaware, the first state to ratify the Constitution, the second smallest state in area, sixth smallest in population, is a small corner of America, with some considerable claims on the national attention. The mouth of the Delaware River was explored by Henry Hudson, and the Dutch and Swedes built settlements on the west bank in the 1630s. But the three counties of Delaware owe their separate existence to the politics of the proprietors of William Penn's colony of Pennsylvania, and to Delawareans' own speed in ratifying the Constitution which made it literally the "First State."

Through most of its history, Delaware has been unusually affluent. It had the nation's highest income levels during the early 20th century and high incomes in the prosperous 1990s. It houses, in beautiful cobblestone mansions in its chateau country, many members of the most numerous wealthy family in America, the du Ponts. Delaware's ethnic and racial mixture is much like that along the rest of the East Coast and not that much different than the nation's, though with fewer than average Hispanics and Asians; there is a mixture here of suburbs, old immigrant neighborhoods, urban black neighborhoods, attractive beach towns and farmlands. Sussex County in southern Delaware is a world of its own, one of the centers of the nation's chicken industry, producing 800 million pounds of chicken a year (it also processes 96,000 tons of the chicken dung euphemistically called "broiler litter"). If not all parts of the nation can follow Delaware's exact path to continued prosperity, perhaps they can get an idea of the direction to travel.

The central focus of Delaware's economy for two centuries was the business started when Eleuthere Irenee du Pont, the practical, business-minded son of a dreamy, idealistic French immigrant, built a gunpowder mill on the banks of Brandywine Creek in 1802. This was the first enterprise of the family du Pont, and it expanded to become one of America's great munitions and chemical companies. It grew especially rapidly during World War I, generating so much capital that the company bought a huge block of stock in General Motors in the 1920s and controlled GM for thirty years while it was America's largest corporation. DuPont capital also financed what was arguably the world's finest research and development program. In the years during and after World War II, DuPont prospered by bringing to the consumer and industrial market new synthetics and plastics like rayon, nylon, cellophane, polyethylene, lucite and teflon: "Better Living Through Chemistry." Delaware continues to be a high-tech state today, although DuPont has shifted its focus from plastics to biotechnology; the state boasts that it ranks number one in scientists and engineers with Ph.D.s per capita and highest in patents per capita.

Delaware has used its ability to pass laws to set national economic policy. In the late 19th century, it passed pioneering liberal laws of incorporation, giving more flexibility and power to managers and owners. A large share of the nation's big companies are incorporated in Delaware—their legal births take place in a federal-style building near the Capitol in Dover—which means that much of the nation's corporate law, especially on mergers and acquisitions and unfriendly takeovers, is made in Delaware's Chancery Court. In 1981 Governor Pete du Pont pushed through a law abolishing Delaware's usury laws and lowering its bank franchise tax. Inflation was high, and banks were looking for a state with no limit on interest to locate their credit card operations. South Dakota abolished its usury law in 1980, but didn't have a labor force large enough to support many banks; Delaware did. Today 7 of the 10 biggest credit card companies do business in Delaware; they employ 32,000 people, more than any other industry and issue 60% of the nation's credit cards. Charles Cawley, head of MBNA, the largest credit card issuer, has emerged as Delaware's leading civic and business leader, overshadowing every du Pont.

Some critics charge that Delaware lives off out-of-staters. "The organizing principle of Delaware government is to subsidize its people at the rest of the country's expense," wrote the *New Republic's* Jonathan Chait, irritated at the $2 toll and traffic jams at the tollbooths on the Delaware Turnpike. "It is a rapacious parasite state with a long history of disloyalty and avarice." State government gets 3% of its operating budget from the tolls and 20% from corporate fees and franchise taxes. He might have added that slot machines at Delaware race tracks, legalized in 1996, produce $189 million for the state, most of it from out-of-staters, another 8% of revenues. But these taxes have allowed Delaware to levy no sales tax and, first under du Pont and then under Republican Mike Castle

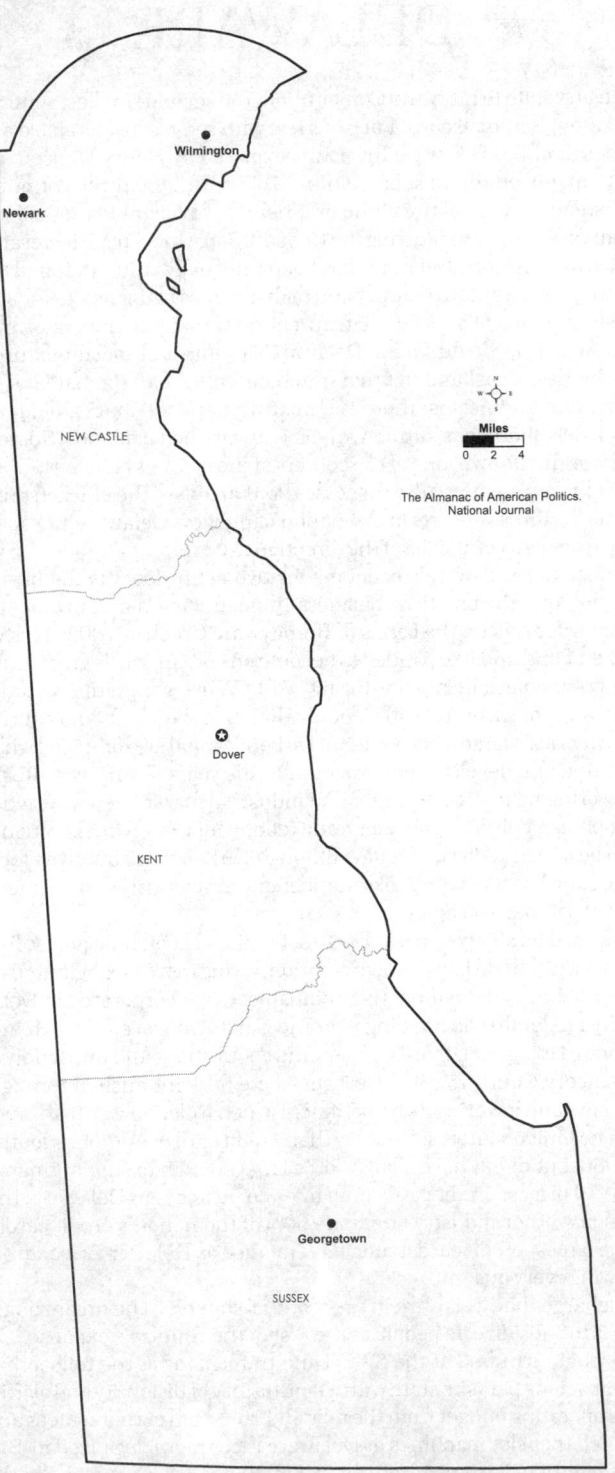

Wilmington

Newark

NEW CASTLE

Miles
0 2 4

The Almanac of American Politics.
National Journal

Dover

KENT

Georgetown

SUSSEX

U.S. Representative elected at-large.

and Democrat Thomas Carper, to lower its income tax several times. Delaware boosters can argue that its state policies have enabled America's industrial economy to grow robustly and have provided easy credit to millions of Americans and have led the nation in a virtuous cycle of lowering taxes. Certainly Delaware has done well: Its economy grew robustly in the 1980s, paused only a little in the recessions of 1990–91 and 2001; its population grew more in the 1990s than any other Northeastern or Midwestern state.

Delaware is on both sides of the Mason and Dixon line; it has immigrant communities in Wilmington and southern-accented farmers in Kent and Sussex Counties (plus Latino migrants working in chicken plants); its suburbs range from very affluent to not-so-affluent in New Castle County. Well-preserved 18th century buildings line the streets of New Castle, the state capital in 1776–77, while mansions gaze out over rolling countryside in the chateau country in Centreville, north of Wilmington. Newark has grown from a country crossroads to a small city as the University of Delaware has expanded; new housing has sprung up along U.S. 40 west of Wilmington while country towns seem little changed from the 1950s. Delaware's considerable variety has produced a robust two-party politics in which tiny Delaware has often voted very much like the nation as a whole. But in the 1990s Delaware, like so many of America's largest metro areas, trended toward the Democrats, and now Democrats hold both the governorship and both Senate seats, while popular former Republican Governor Mike Castle has held onto the state's single seat in the U.S. House. In 2000 Al Gore carried the state 55%–42%, five-term Republican Senator William Roth was defeated by Democratic Governor Tom Carper by a wider than expected 56%–44%, and Democrat Ruth Ann Minner was elected governor by 59%–40%.

But these were not bitter contests. Thanks to Delaware's small size there is still an intimacy to politics here. Most of Delaware is reached (though politically ignored) by Philadelphia TV, so personal campaigning is still important. The candidates for governor in 2000 made the rounds of 33 scheduled joint appearances, starting at the Jewish Community Center in Talleyville. Roth campaigned, as always, with his trademark St. Bernards. The day after the election is "Return Day," when winning and losing candidates—opponents ride in the same car—come back to the Sussex County seat of Georgetown to receive the bipartisan cheers of the voters and, literally, bury a hatchet.

The People		Race/Ethnic Origin			Military veterans: 84,289 (14.3%)	
Pop. 2000:	783,600	567,973	72.5%	White	WWII: 19.2%	Korea: 13.7%
Pop. 1990:	666,168	148,435	18.9%	Black	Vietnam: 31.7%	Gulf War: 10.1%
Change 1990–2000:	Up 17.6%	16,110	2.1%	Asian	**Most populous cities:**	
Change 1980–1990:	Up 12.1%	2,324	0.3%	Native Am.	1. Wilmington	72,664
% of U.S. total:	0.3%	234	0.0%	Hawaiian	2. Dover	32,135
Pop. rank:	45th of 50	10,222	1.3%	Two + races	3. Newark	28,547
Area size:	2,489 sq. mi.	1,025	0.1%	Other	4. Milford	6,732
State Native:	48.3%	37,277	4.8%	Hisp. Origin	5. Seaford	6,699
Non-citizen:	3.3%	**Ancestry**			Urban population: 80.0%	
Language		Irish: 12.6%		German: 10.9%	Rural population: 20.0%	
English: 88.1%	Spanish: 5.4%	English: 9.2%		Italian: 7.1%		
Other Eur.: 4.6%		USA: 4.6%				

Education		Work Sector		General Assembly	
H.S. Grad:	82.6%	Private: 81.1%	Govt: 13.8%	Senate	13 D 8 R
College Grad:	25.0%	Self: 5.0%	Family: 0.2%	House	29 R 12 D
Industry		Unemployment: 5.1%		Legislative Term Limits: No	
Agri: 1.1%	Con: 7.4%	**Household Income**		**Registered Voters**	
Fin: 11.6%	Info: 1.9%	<15k: 12.2%	15-35k: 23.5%	D: 224,130	(43.1%)
Mfg: 18.0%	Prof: 28.6%	35-50k: 16.9%	50-100k: 33.3%	R: 175,326	(33.7%)
Public: 5.2%	Trade: 14.3%	100-150k: 9.4%	>150k: 4.6%	I: 120,360	(23.2%)
Other: 11.9%		Median: $47,381			
Occupation		Poverty status: 9.2%			
Blue collar: 22.0%	White collar: 62.9%	**Home Value**			
Gray collar: 15.1%		<50k: 9.7% 50-100k: 26.0% 100-200k: 47.9% 200-300k: 11.3%			
		300-500k: 3.7% >500k: 1.4% Median: $122,000			

Presidential politics   Delaware has been competitive in presidential elections since the Federalists were battling the Jeffersonians. Until 2000, it could claim to be the nation's presidential bellwether: It had voted for every winner since 1952, the longest winning streak of any state. Wilmington is heavily Democratic but casts relatively few votes, the two lower counties lean Republican and the balance is struck by the New Castle County suburbs, which cast 56% of the votes in 2002. In 2000 these suburbs, like the suburban Philadelphia counties to the north, trended heavily to the Democrats, and Al Gore, though losing the two southern counties, carried the state by 55%–42%. The result was presaged by the Recycled Paperboard Presidential Poll in Sussex County, in which backers of both candidates heaved pumpkins as far as they could, the Gore pumpkins were propelled 13% farther than the Bush pumpkins, and, perhaps coincidentally, Al Gore carried Delaware 55%–42%.

In 1996 Delaware vied for attention by holding its presidential primary February 24, just four days after New Hampshire. But New Hampshire Republicans put pressure on candidates to ignore Delaware, and only Steve Forbes and Alan Keyes showed up here. Forbes advertised heavily on Philadelphia TV and won the contest with 33% of the vote, to 27% for Bob Dole, 19% for Pat Buchanan, and 13% for Lamar Alexander. For 2000 Republicans decided to hold a primary on February 9, nine days after New Hampshire. George W. Bush, who spent two full days in Delaware, led with 51%, well ahead of John McCain (25%) and the still-remembered Forbes (20%). Democrats held a primary February 4, but its result was not recognized under party rules, and neither candidate campaigned. Only 5% of registered voters turned out; Gore led Bill Bradley 57%–40%.

2000 Presidential Vote		
Gore (D)	180,638	(55%)
Bush (R)	137,081	(42%)
Nader (Green)	8,288	(3%)
Other	1,863	(1%)

2000 Republican Presidential Primary		
Bush (R)	15,250	(51%)
McCain (R)	7,638	(25%)
Forbes (R)	5,883	(20%)
Keyes (R)	1,148	(4%)

2000 Democratic Presidential Primary		
Gore (D)	6,377	(57%)
Bradley (D)	4,476	(40%)
LaRouche (D)	288	(3%)

1996 Presidential Vote		
Clinton (D)	140,355	(52%)
Dole (R)	99,062	(37%)
Perot (I)	28,719	(11%)

Governor

Ruth Ann Minner (D)

Elected 2000, term expires Jan. 2005, 1st term; b. Jan. 17, 1935, Milford; home, Dover; G.E.D. 1968; Methodist; widowed.

Elected Office: DE House of Reps., 1974–82; DE Senate, 1982–92; DE Lt. Gov. 1992–00.

Professional Career: Owner, Roger Minner Towing, 1969-present; Receptionist, Gov. Sherman Tribbitt, 1973.

Office: Legislative Hall, Dover, 19901, 302-744-4101; Fax: 302-739-2775; Web site: www.state.de.us/governor.

Election Results

2000 general	Ruth Ann Minner (D)	191,484	(59%)
	John M. Burris (R)	128,436	(40%)
	Other	3,263	(1%)
2000 primary	Ruth Ann Minner (D)	unopposed	
1996 general	Thomas Carper (D)	188,300	(70%)
	Janet C. Rzewnicki (R)	82,654	(30%)

Ruth Ann Minner, a Democrat, was elected governor in 2000. She grew up in southern Delaware, the daughter of a sharecropper; she dropped out of high school to work on the farm, and got married at 17. In 1967, her husband died; at 32, she was left with three sons and no high school diploma. She worked as an agricultural worker and a librarian, got her GED, and in 1972 landed a job as a receptionist in the office of Governor Sherman Tribbitt. "I never had any intention of getting deeply involved in politics," she says, but she had done political volunteer work as a teen and she obviously found politics congenial. In 1974 she ran for the state House and, in one of Delaware's small districts (they average 19,000 residents today), won. In 1982 she was elected to the state Senate. In the legislature, she helped build the state's open space protection program, worked on education and public safety and chaired a commission that reorganized state agencies. She also married again, and she and her husband started a car-towing business; he died in 1991, but her sons still run the business. In 1992 she ran for lieutenant governor as Democratic Congressman-at-Large Tom Carper's running mate, but the offices are elected separately. So when Minner ran for governor in 2000, she had already won two statewide elections.

Minner, the favorite in the election, was unopposed in the Democratic primary. The Republicans had a close primary between former state Senate Majority Leader John Burris and former Judge Bill Lee. Burris was backed by MBNA Chairman Charles Cawley, and company executives contributed $147,000 to his campaign. Lee attacked Burris for being too close to MBNA, and that apparently had some resonance. Some 27,000 voters voted in the Republican primary; Burris won by exactly 46 votes.

Both nominees were from southern Delaware, and both were generally counted as moderates. Minner ran as a successor to Carper, who had continued former Governor Pete du Pont's policy of cutting income taxes even as, helped by the state's surging economy, he increased state spending by 40%. Burris called for addressing the state's high rates of cancer and drug abuse, and for addressing environmental problems by smart planning. Burris attacked the state's education testing program, which produced high fail rates among students; Minner said it was an improvement over the past, but called for extra classes for failing students on afternoons and Saturdays, rather than summer school.

Minner was ahead in polls all along; she won 59%–40%. At first the state's fiscal situation looked good enough that she backed a 2% pay increase in May 2001. But by December she was cutting back. She imposed a hiring freeze in March 2002, lifted it in June, and then reimposed it in November. In fall 2002 she started making $35 million in cuts and asked school districts to give back $10 million; in January 2003 that turned out to be unnecessary when windfall revenue— a $47 million abandoned property settlement, a $4 million fee from Goldman Sachs—came in. When Delaware's big employers laid off 4,000 workers, she worked to attract 2,000 new jobs. She failed to get the legislature to increase the cigarette tax, but did get it to pass a law banning smoking in public buildings, including restaurants and bars. It took effect in November 2002, and Minner was picketed by bar owners with signs saying, "Ban Ruth Ann." She faced controversies about the state police—a demand in 2001 from the state NAACP for the firing of the agency's superintendent, a lawsuit in 2002 brought by white troopers who claimed there were racial quotas.

Minner comes up for reelection in 2004. On Return Day (that's the day after the election, when all candidates meet in Georgetown) 2002, "Ruth Ann '04" bumper stickers were being handed out, as well as others for Republicans—2000 candidate Lee, state House Speaker Terry Spence and Attorney General Jane Brady. The next day Lee announced he was running. In December 2002, at a fundraising dinner with Connecticut Senator Joseph Lieberman, Minner announced she would seek reelection.

Senior Senator

Joseph Biden (D)

Elected 1972, seat up 2008, 6th term; b. Nov. 20, 1942, Scranton, PA; home, Wilmington; U. of DE, B.A. 1965, Syracuse U., J.D. 1968; Catholic; married (Jill).

Elected Office: New Castle Cnty. Cncl., 1970–72.

Professional Career: Practicing atty., 1968–72.

DC Office: 201 RSOB, 20510, 202-224-5042; Fax: 202-224-0139; Web site: biden.senate.gov.

State Offices: Milford, 302-424-8090; Wilmington, 302-573-6345.

Committees: *Foreign Relations* (RMM): European Affairs (RMM); International Operations & Terrorism; Western Hemisphere, Peace Corps, Narcotics Affairs. *Judiciary*: Crime, Corrections & Victims' Rights (RMM); Terrorism, Technology & Homeland Security.

Group Ratings

	ADA	ACLU	AFS	LCV	CON	ITIC	NTU	COC	ACU	NTLC	CHC
2002	80	60	100	94	58	75	15	50	10	0	—
2001	100	—	100	100	—	—	7	38	12	—	0

National Journal Ratings

	2001 LIB —	2001 CONS		2002 LIB —	2002 CONS
Economic	82%	15%		90%	5%
Social	81%	8%		64%	34%
Foreign	87%	3%		67%	30%

Key Votes of the 107th Congress

1. Approve Bush Tax Cuts	N	5. Confirm Ashcroft as AG	N	9. Bar Coop. with Intl. Court	N
2. Expand Patients' Rights	Y	6. Bar Gays in the Boy Scouts	N	10. Trade Promotion Authority	Y
3. Campaign Finance Reform	Y	7. $ for Hate Crime Prosecution	Y	11. Authorize Force in Iraq	Y
4. Permit ANWR Development	N	8. Overseas Military Abortions	Y	12. Homeland Sec. Dept. Union	Y

Election Results

2002 general	Joseph Biden (D)	135,253	(58%)	($3,152,762)
	Raymond Clatworthy (R)	94,793	(41%)	($1,983,141)
2002 primary	Joseph Biden (D)	unopposed		
1996 general	Joseph Biden (D)	165,465	(60%)	($2,466,499)
	Raymond Clatworthy (R)	105,088	(38%)	($1,126,427)
	Other	5,038	(2%)	

Prior Winning Percentages: 1990 (63%); 1984 (60%); 1978 (58%); 1972 (51%)

Joseph Biden, Delaware's longest-serving senator, was first elected in 1972, at age 29 (he reached the constitutional age of 30 by the time he took office); he has spent most of his life as a senator. Biden grew up in the suburbs of Wilmington in a middle class home; his father was a car salesman and one grandfather was a state senator in Pennsylvania. As a teenager he had a stutter, but taught himself to deliver a speech to his whole school; he is now one of the Senate's most fluent orators. He married and started a family while still in law school. After school he moved back to the Wilmington suburbs, practiced law, and in 1970, at 27, was elected to the New Castle County Council. In 1972 he ran for the Senate, against a popular incumbent who seemed ready to retire, while this young challenger had energy, an attractive extended family and an ability to connect with voters' emotions. He won 51%–49%. A month later his wife and daughter were killed in an auto accident; his two young sons were injured. He thought about resigning, but was persuaded to serve, and began his practice, kept to this day, of commuting from his home near Wilmington on Amtrak, 80 minutes to and from Washington every day. He remains a familiar figure in, and one familiar with, his constituency.

In the Senate, Biden has a moderate-to-liberal voting record. For many years he did much of his most visible work on the Judiciary Committee, which he chaired from 1987–95 and served as ranking Democrat on from 1981–87 and 1995–97. The issues that arise here—abortion, flag-burning, capital punishment, crime control—cut deeply, and for years the cultural liberals in the Democratic Party differed sharply on most of them from the constituents Biden saw in Delaware every day. As chairman, Biden presided over the most contentious Supreme Court confirmation hearings in history. In his 1987 hearings, nominee Robert Bork set a high standard for intellectual seriousness, but some of his opponents used his candor to vote against him for disgracefully dishonest reasons, from which Biden's attempts to construct an honestly based, anti-Bork rationale proved politically indistinguishable; no other nominee since has testified so frankly. The 1991 hearings on Clarence Thomas exploded when someone leaked charges of sexual harassment by Anita Hill against the nominee. Biden was bitterly criticized for covering up this information, but he had shared it with committee members, who agreed that Hill's initial unwillingness to testify publicly meant that any reference to it would be unfair to Thomas. Once the story was out though, Hill and then Thomas testified to fascinated television audiences; Thomas was confirmed, over Biden's opposition. In 2001 and 2002 he usually, but not always, sided with Chairman Patrick Leahy in opposing targeted Bush judicial nominees. But he voted for Brooks Smith, despite Smith's 1993 criticism of Biden's views on federalism, and pledged to vote for Dennis Shedd, a former staffer to Strom Thurmond, and was conveniently absent when Shedd was approved for want of a 10th Democratic vote against him.

In the middle of the Bork hearings came a climactic moment for Biden, who in 1987 started running for president. He hoped to inspire a new generation as John Kennedy had inspired his. But Biden decided to leave the race when a Michael Dukakis staffer leaked an "attack video" showing similarities between Biden's stump speech about his background and a speech by British Labour Party leader Neil Kinnock. Paraphrasing someone else's words is not a political crime— most political discourse is conducted in familiar shorthand terms—but Biden in dramatizing his background actually distorted it, for unlike Kinnock he did not rise from working class roots, and unlike in Britain, upward social mobility is a common experience in the United States. In 1988, Biden nearly died of an aneurysm, but recovered fully.

After the Thomas hearings, Biden seemed defensive about attacks from the feminist left, the greatest source of activism in the Democratic Party, just as the religious right is in the Republican Party. He sought out women to serve on Judiciary and worked hard on the 1994 Violence Against Women Act; he helped renew it in 2000, although the Supreme Court declared part of it unconstitutional. He has been the sponsor in Judiciary of the bankruptcy bill, backed strongly by Delaware's MBNA and other credit card issuers, which was vetoed by Bill Clinton in 2000. It was brought up again in 2001 with a president ready to sign it, and versions passed both the Senate and the House. But there were two contentious issues blocking final passage. One was the homestead exemption; the Senate voted to limit it to $125,000, but the House version allowed unlimited exemptions once a home had been owned for two years (Florida and Texas have unlimited exemptions, and some bankrupts hold onto $5 million houses). Biden agreed to accept the House version. The other issue was Charles Schumer's amendment making fines incurred by anti-abortion protesters undischargeable in bankruptcy. On this, Biden would not yield. In November 2002 the bill, with a version of the Schumer provision was defeated in the House when 87 anti-abortion Republicans spurned the leadership's pleas and defeated the bill. In 2003 Biden will presumably try again. He had more success in July 2002 when he moved with Orrin Hatch to require chief executive officers to verify the accuracy of their quarterly financial statements, with violations punishable by 10 years in prison. The law was quickly enacted, and within months CEOs were signing the statements.

Biden became ranking Democrat on the Foreign Relations Committee in 1997 and chairman in June 2001. To the surprise of many, he entered into a constructive working relationship with Chairman Jesse Helms. When democracy in the former Yugoslavia was thwarted by state-led terrorism and when multilateral instrumentalities proved ineffective, Biden was among the strongest voices to call for lifting the arms embargo on Bosnia and training Bosnian Muslims, demanding that the United States and NATO investigate war crimes there, and arguing for NATO air strikes. He once called Slobodan Milosevic a "war criminal" to his face, and in 1999 pushed the Senate to approve the use of U.S. air power in Kosovo. He supported the Comprehensive Test Ban Treaty in 1999, and was one of the Democrats who called for it to be reported to the floor, where to his surprise it was defeated. He opposed national missile defense.

To the incoming Bush administration he was friendly but sometimes critical. He opposed candidate Bush's call for withdrawing troops from the Balkans. In April 2001 he paternalistically criticized George W. Bush when he apparently renounced the long-held policy of strategic ambiguity and stated clearly that the United States would come to the aid of Taiwan if China attacked. "China is not our enemy," he said. "There's nothing inevitable about China and the United States not being as cooperative as other nations." Then Biden became chairman of Foreign Relations in June 2001 and America was attacked on September 11. In the weeks following the attack Biden praised Bush for being "patient, resolute and cautious." In October some Republicans attacked him when he told the Council on Foreign Relations that the bombing campaign in Afghanistan "plays into every stereotypical criticism of us that we're this high-tech bully that thinks from the air we can do whatever we want to do." But Biden was not endorsing that criticism, rather he was calling for ground troops to be sent in soon, as indeed they were. In July and August 2002 he held two days of hearings on Iraq, with administration witnesses. In August he said the United States has "no choice but to eliminate" Saddam Hussein and that "probably" it means war with Iraq. He conferred frequently with Secretary of State Colin Powell and pushed for the U.S. to bring the issue to the United Nations; he said a unilateral attack would be the "single worst option." In late September 2002, he and ranking Republican Richard Lugar were working to bring forward a resolution that would authorize the president to take action to remove weapons of mass destruction, but not Saddam Hussein himself, only after exhausting diplomatic options. Bush opposed this, and forestalled Biden and Lugar by getting agreement on terms of a resolution from Trent Lott, Dennis Hastert and Richard Gephardt. Biden voted for it in October 2002.

Biden continued to campaign against missile defense and opposed abrogation of the ABM Treaty. But Bush's withdrawal from the treaty did not prevent the May 2002 nuclear disarmament treaty, which Biden hailed as "an important step forward." On Israel and the Palestinians, Biden endorsed the "Quartet" mediators' December 2002 proposal for a road map of reciprocal steps to jump-start negotiations. Biden traveled widely as chairman—to China in August 2001, to Kashmir in January 2002, to northern Iraq to confer with Kurdish leaders in December 2002—and seems to have been taken into the confidence of the administration: Condoleezza Rice encouraged him to sound out Iranian diplomats at the United Nations when they requested a meeting. As ranking minority member he does not, of course, have as much power as he did as chairman. But he has worked closely with the new chairman, Richard Lugar, and has said that he and Lugar are in agreement on a great many issues.

Biden remains an everyday figure in Delaware and has tended to its most local needs. He has worked to protect Dover Air Force Base and its C-5s and C-17s against closing. Sussex County is America's number one chicken-producing county, and he held up a bill for favorable trade status for Russia when that country blocked the import of U.S. chickens. And naturally he has supported Amtrak funding. On his daily commutes, he has come to know the Amtrak crew members personally and hosts an annual Christmas dinner for the crews; crew members in turn keep track of his seniority—he was 7th in seniority among senators in early 2001, but only about 65th among the Amtrak crew. In February 2002 he put holds on two administration appointees—the first time he had ever done so—because Republicans were blocking a vote on a bill, passed unanimously in the Commerce Committee, to spend $1.8 billion on railroad safety. In fall 2002, he dropped the holds with the understanding that the bill would be brought to a vote in the 108th Congress.

Biden's most visible gift is an articulateness that can verge on the mellifluous; he can inspire, but can also drone on at great length (being elected a senator at 29 does not curb a tendency to verbosity). But this has not reduced the appreciation most Delawareans have for his admirable personal qualities. He was re-elected by wide margins in 1984, 1990 and 1996. His 1996 opponent Raymond Clatworthy was a Naval Academy graduate, Marine aviator and businessman who walked, rode a bicycle and rollerbladed through the state, raised $1 million and questioned the sale of Biden's house to an executive of MBNA, the big credit card company whose top executives gave generously to Biden's campaign. But Biden won 60%–38%. In 2002 Clatworthy ran again and raised $1.8 million: Evidently Biden has raised the hackles of many Republicans across the country, and you can raise money by direct mail against him. Clatworthy argued that he would support George W. Bush more fully on defense and foreign policy and called for $1,500 child tax credits and individual investment accounts in Social Security. This time the result was a little closer: Biden won 58%–41%, the same margin he had in 1978. He actually lost Kent County, which includes Dover, and only narrowly carried Sussex County; together the two counties cast 37% of the state's votes, up from 33% in 1996.

Will Biden run for president again? In August 2000, when he was asked if he would run if Al Gore lost, he said, "Would I consider running for president again? Yes. Am I going to run for president again? I don't know." In January 2003 he said he would feel compelled to run if Bush doesn't handle Iraq and North Korea well and if no Democrat offers a viable foreign policy alternative, and would decide by fall 2003. "If it's too late, it's too late," he replied in May to those who thought the fall might be too late to begin a campaign. "I don't know how you can go out and do all the things you need to do to run for president and still try to shape—or in some cases, impede—the president's agenda."

Junior Senator

Thomas Carper (D)

Elected 2000, seat up 2006, 1st term; b. Jan. 23, 1947, Beckley, WV; home, Wilmington; OH St. U., B.A. 1968, U. of DE, M.B.A. 1975; Presbyterian; married (Martha).

Military Career: Navy, 1968–73 (Vietnam); Naval Reserves, 1973–91.

Elected Office: DE Treas., 1976–82; U.S. House of Reps., 1982–92; DE Gov. 1992–2000.

Professional Career: Industrial Devel. Specialist, DE Div. of Econ. Devel., 1975–76.

DC Office: 513 HSOB, 20510, 202-224-2441; Fax: 202-228-2190; Web site: carper.senate.gov.

State Offices: Dover, 302-674-3308; Georgetown, 302-856-7690; Wilmington, 302-573-6291.

Committees: *Aging (Special). Banking, Housing & Urban Affairs:* Financial Institutions; Housing & Transportation; International Trade & Finance. *Environment & Public Works:* Clean Air, Climate Change & Nuclear Safety (RMM); Superfund & Waste Management. *Governmental Affairs:* Financial Management, Budget & International Security; Government Management, Federal Workforce & the District of Columbia; Investigations (Permanent).

Group Ratings

	ADA	ACLU	AFS	LCV	CON	ITIC	NTU	COC	ACU	NTLC	CHC
2002	80	40	75	59	98	62	26	50	25	15	—
2001	90	—	92	63	—	—	21	58	24	—	20

National Journal Ratings

	2001 LIB	—	2001 CONS		2002 LIB	—	2002 CONS
Economic	59%	—	40%		73%	—	20%
Social	81%	—	8%		56%	—	38%
Foreign	61%	—	27%		59%	—	38%

Key Votes of the 107th Congress

1. Approve Bush Tax Cuts	N	5. Confirm Ashcroft as AG	N	9. Bar Coop. with Intl. Court	Y
2. Expand Patients' Rights	Y	6. Bar Gays in the Boy Scouts	N	10. Trade Promotion Authority	Y
3. Campaign Finance Reform	Y	7. $ for Hate Crime Prosecution	Y	11. Authorize Force in Iraq	Y
4. Permit ANWR Development	N	8. Overseas Military Abortions	Y	12. Homeland Sec. Dept. Union	Y

Prior Winning Percentages: 1990 House (66%); 1988 House (68%); 1986 House (66%); 1984 House (59%); 1982 House (52%)

Democrat Thomas Carper was elected Delaware's junior senator in 2000, after already serving 24 years in statewide elective office. His election meant that Delaware has two Democratic senators for the first time since January 1943. He grew up in southside Virginia and Ohio and went to college in Ohio. He first came to Delaware as an ensign in the Navy, then returned to get his M.B.A after service in Southeast Asia, where he served as a mission commander piloting submarine-hunting planes. In 1976, he was elected state treasurer, at 29; he ran for Congress in 1982 and beat a scandal-tarred incumbent. In the House, Carper had a moderate voting record and worked to let banks into the securities business and to prevent ocean sludge dumping, both causes supported by Delaware constituencies. In 1992, when Republican Governor Mike Castle had served his two allotted terms and ran for Congress, Carper ran for governor and won the general with 65%.

As governor, Carper pursued an agenda in many ways more conservative than liberal. He continued his Republican predecessor Pete du Pont's policy of cutting taxes, reducing income tax rates about 10% and also cutting small business and utility taxes. Revenues kept gushing in from Delaware's strong economy, and he increased the "rainy day" fund and boosted the state's credit rating to an historic high even as state spending rose 40% in eight years. He inherited Castle's standard-based education reform, raised standards, started testing students in 1998 and provided public school choice, utilized by 8% of students, tried to raise teacher salaries, instituted charter schools and passed a teacher accountability bill in 2000. He has tried to take action against chicken waste, a major problem in southern Delaware and called for a business-friendly "new environmentalism." His major defeats came when the legislature voted in 1996 to allow slot machines at harness racing tracks over his opposition. He was re-elected by 70%–30% over then-Treasurer Janet Rzewnicki. Barred from a third term, he was an obvious candidate for the Senate seat held by Republican William Roth since 1970.

This was a battle of positives. Both candidates had very high approval ratings, and both were familiar figures to many voters; they brought a combined total of 58 years in statewide office to the race. Roth had a record of achievements that paid direct benefits to people in this generally affluent state: The Kemp-Roth tax cut of 1981, the Roth IRAs enacted in 1997, the reform of the Internal Revenue Service passed in 1998, $2.3 billion for capital improvements in Amtrak in 1998 and $10 billion in bonds in 2000. Roth's main problem was that he was 79 in 2000. After serving as head of the National Governors Association, Carper announced that he was running for the Senate in September 1999. A poll that month showed him ahead 48%–38%. Carper was careful not to campaign negatively against Roth or to attack him for his age, but his slogan "A Senator for Our Future" spotlighted the contrast between their ages and his 16-hour days of campaigning at factories, bowling alleys and parades was a contrast with Roth, who stayed in Washington legislating much of the time and made many fewer campaign appearances with his trademark St. Bernards. "People can be too old, or senior, at 59. The question is whether people are effective. I think that his effectiveness has waned," Carper said. As Roth unveiled initiatives—Amtrak funding, a program to aid states to pay for prescription drugs for low-income seniors—Carper suggested that Roth's tax cuts were too large and his prescription drug plan too stingy. Roth, able to raise large sums as Finance chairman, outspent Carper by $4.3 million to $2.5 million, but the Democratic Party spent some $4 million of soft money in Delaware, more than evening the score. In October, Roth fainted twice on the campaign trail, once in full view of cameras. Polls showed the race close to even in September and October, but on November 7 Carper won by a solid 56%–44% margin. This was nearly a carbon copy of Al Gore's 55%–42% margin in the state; Carper ran especially well with younger voters, and with those who were married with children.

In the Senate, Carper has a moderate voting record and supports centrist proposals. He voted with Republicans on farm spending and the tax cut in budget resolution votes in April 2001. With five Republicans and five other Democrats he moved unsuccessfully to condition the Bush tax cut on deficit reduction. In June 2001 he and Judd Gregg got $125 million for public school choice programs and $400 million for charter schools. In June 2001 he got a seat on the Energy Committee and urged the big automakers to develop fuel cells; he lost the seat when Democrats lost their majority. With Arlen Specter, he sponsored a bill to require the Transportation Department to reduce oil consumption by 1 million barrels per day by 2015. He voted with Jim Jeffords to impose on old power plants the standards of the Clean Air Act. But he also put forward, with Lincoln Chafee, John Breaux and Max Baucus, a milder bill that would not impose those standards on old plants when remodeled and require 2001 levels of carbon dioxide by 2012. With Evan Bayh he backed reauthorization of the 1996 welfare act with the work or school requirement raised from 50% to 70% of caseload; the Senate bill approved by the Finance Committee, but never passed, included some provisions he sought—funding transitional jobs, funding for abstinence programs and revocation of passports for those delinquent in child support payments. On homeland security, he sought unsuccessfully to get $1.2 billion for rail security.

Carper said he was "bitterly disappointed" when Democrats lost their majority and because moderate Democrats lost in North Carolina, South Carolina, Texas and New Hampshire. In December 2002 he was one of those starting a group of Senate New Democrats chaired by Bob Graham.

Representative-At-Large

Michael Castle (R)

Elected 1992, 6th term; b. July 2, 1939, Wilmington; home, Wilmington; Hamilton Col., B.A. 1961, Georgetown U., LL.B. 1964; Catholic; married (Jane).

Elected Office: DE House of Reps., 1966–68; DE Senate, 1968–76, Minority Ldr., 1975–76; DE Lt. Gov., 1980–84; DE Gov., 1984–92.

Professional Career: Practicing atty., 1964–80; DE Dep. Atty. Gen., 1965–66.

DC Office: 1233 LHOB, 20515, 202-225-4165; Fax: 202-225-2291; Web site: www.house.gov/castle.

District Offices: Dover, 302-736-1666; Georgetown, 302-856-3334; Wilmington, 302-428-1902.

Committees: *Education & the Workforce* (6th of 27 R): 21st Century Competitiveness; Education Reform (Chmn.). *Financial Services* (6th of 37 R): Capital Markets, Insurance & Government Sponsored Enterprises; Domestic and International Monetary Policy, Trade & Technology; Financial Institutions & Consumer Credit.

Group Ratings

	ADA	ACLU	AFS	LCV	CON	ITIC	NTU	COC	ACU	NTLC	CHC
2002	25	40	0	38	87	100	58	95	76	72	33
2001	30	—	10	79	—	—	56	83	48	—	—

National Journal Ratings

	2001 LIB —	2001 CONS	2002 LIB —	2002 CONS
Economic	49%	52%	45%	54%
Social	54%	45%	58%	42%
Foreign	48%	53%	29%	67%

Key Votes of the 107th Congress

1. Approve Bush Tax Cuts	Y	5. Faith-Based Charities	Y	9. Trade Promotion Authority	Y
2. Limit Patients' Bill of Rights	Y	6. Bar Gays in the Boy Scouts	Y	10. Bar Funds for Intl. Court	Y
3. Campaign Finance Reform	Y	7. Ban Partial-Birth Abortion	Y	11. Authorize Force in Iraq	Y
4. Ban ANWR Development	Y	8. Arm Commercial Pilots	Y	12. Deny Home. Sec. Dept. Union	Y

Election Results

2002 general	Michael Castle (R)	164,605	(72%)	($760,161)
	Michael Miller (D)	61,011	(27%)	($13,202)
	Other	2,789	(1%)	
2002 primary	Michael Castle (R)	unopposed		
2000 general	Michael Castle (R)	211,546	(68%)	($588,911)
	Michael Miller (D)	96,538	(31%)	($28,831)
	Other	4,832	(2%)	

Prior Winning Percentages: 1998 (66%); 1996 (70%); 1994 (71%); 1992 (55%)

Michael Castle, a Republican first elected in 1992, has been in public office for most of his adult life. A direct descendant of Benjamin Franklin, he grew up in Delaware, the son of a DuPont lawyer. After college and law school, he returned to be a deputy attorney general. In 1966, at 27, local Republicans urged him to run for the state House in a Democratic seat; the competitive Castle was elected. Two years later he was elected to the state Senate, and in time became minority leader; he left the legislature in 1976 to practice law. In 1980 Governor Pete du Pont asked him to run for lieutenant governor; he did and won. He was elected governor in 1984 and 1988. In 1992, barred from running for re-election by term limits, he traded jobs with Democratic Congressman-at-Large Thomas Carper. Castle won the Republican primary for Congress by 56%–30% over state Treasurer Janet Rzewnicki, and won the general 55%–43% over former Senate candidate and Lieutenant Governor S. B. Woo.

At that point it seemed unlikely that Castle, as a moderate member of a conservative minority party, could be influential; yet he was. He was a leader of the bipartisan freshmen who offered their own budget cuts. In August 1994 he withdrew his support from the crime bill when he thought Democrats overreached; then, at Newt Gingrich's suggestion, he led a group of moderate Republicans to negotiate with the Clinton administration. This delivered a stinging rebuke to Democrats—it broke their majority apart, in fact—and yet ultimately produced a crime bill with less spending on prevention but with the gun control provisions that Castle, unlike most Republicans, supported.

Castle has a voting record at the middle of the House; he was one of the 10 Republicans to support Clinton administration positions on most issues and is a leader of the informal Tuesday Group of moderate Republicans, 30 or 40 of whom meet for lunches every Wednesday (don't ask). In July 1999 he opposed the Republican leadership's tax cut as overlarge, and was one of a group of moderates who got the leadership to agree to make the income tax cut contingent on progress in reducing the national debt; then he was one of four Republicans who voted against the tax cut anyway. He voted for the 2001 Bush tax cut with some ambivalence; he had voted against repeal of the estate tax and wanted the tax cuts made contingent. In September 2002 he said moderate Republicans would vote against the Labor-HHS appropriations unless more money were available for all the appropriations. After Republicans gained seats in the 2002 elections, he was asked if he was worried that the party would go too far to the right. "I actually am very worried about that. It's the role of moderates to try to rein that in. If the conservatives go too far on issues like the environment or education, I believe we'll have sufficient votes to block them."

Castle is on the Financial Services Committee, which is of great importance to Delaware. Castle sponsored the bill for the commemorative quarter, with different designs for each state. He was present when the first such coin was issued, which shows Delaware Revolutionary leader Caesar Rodney, atop a galloping horse, rushing to Philadelphia in 1776 to sign the Declaration of Independence. He was pleased to announce in 2002 that Dover Air Force Base was to get new C-17s and that its aged C-5s were being refitted with new avionics and engines. He is interested in local land use issues. In August 2002 he went on CNN's *Crossfire* to defend the honor of his state against Jonathan Chait who had written in the *New Republic* that Delaware is "a rapacious parasite state with a long history of disloyalty and avarice." To Chait's criticism of Delaware's management-friendly incorporation laws, Castle said, "The reason [corporations] like to come to Delaware is because the court system is so good, and they know what the laws are, and they know that they will be treated fairly. I understand you didn't do as much research as you might."

Castle serves on the Intelligence Committee and was part of the joint Senate-House hearings on intelligence failures before September 11, and he endorsed the joint report. In May 2002, a month before George W. Bush called for a Department of Homeland Security, Castle advocated giving homeland security adviser Tom Ridge authority over the budgets of the FBI and CIA. He also called for biometric identification of all foreigners entering the United States and for biometric identification for Americans who choose it. He was one of the first four members of Congress to visit in January 2002 Camp X-ray in Guantanamo Bay where foreign terrorists were held. Castle chairs the Education Reform Subcommittee, and while he may support higher spending than some other Republicans, he also questions the worth of programs mostly fashioned by Democrats. "Eliminating the Department of Education is not the answer. But neither is simply spending more for programs that fail to give our children the education they deserve." Castle has strongly supported the Shays-Meehan campaign finance legislation. He was one of the first four Republicans to sign a discharge petition on it in May 1999, and worked on the successful July 2000 bill to require disclosure of Section 527 committees. When advocates of Shays-Meehan finally got 218 signatures on their discharge petition in January 2002, the bill was promptly passed.

Castle played a role in the elevation of Speaker Dennis Hastert. In November 1998, after Newt Gingrich announced his resignation, Castle and Thomas Ewing of Illinois moved to draft Hastert to run for majority leader; Hastert demurred, because he had committed to Dick Armey. But when Bob Livingston renounced the speakership December 19, Hastert was quickly selected to be speaker. Castle has been re-elected by wide margins in Delaware, 68%–31% in 2000 and 72%–27% in 2002. He has often been mentioned as a candidate for the Senate in this small state, and said that he would have run if Republican Senator William Roth had retired in 1994. But Roth chose to run again then and, at 79, in 2000, when he lost. But even if Roth had not run, Castle might not have; he said in 1998, "as time has evolved, I have grown to like my role in the House." Still, it is interesting that both of Delaware's Democratic senators won their seats by beating older incumbents who chose to run despite the fact that younger popular Republicans (Pete du Pont in 1972, Castle in 2000) were waiting in the wings.

★ DISTRICT OF COLUMBIA ★

The District of Columbia is on the way up. For most of the last 25 years, Washington, D.C., the capital of the most successful democracy in the history of the world, was a dysfunctional polity, a city with above-average incomes and a vibrant commercial property base, but with a local government so bloated with employees yet so indifferent to its duties that it destroyed one marginal neighborhood after another. Now things are different. Marion Barry, mayor for 16 of the 20 years from 1978–98, is long out of office. A financial control board installed by Congress, the current mayor, Anthony Williams, and the city council have cut the bloated payroll and improved services. The District's population has stabilized after a long decline; crime is sharply down; affluent professionals and eager immigrants are flowing in, gentrifying and giving vitality to neighborhoods long given up to decline—Columbia Heights, Logan Circle, Shaw. There are still problems: Most of metropolitan Washington's large middle class lives in the suburbs now, in Prince George's County, Maryland, and every other local jurisdiction, and an increasing percentage of the District's blacks live in or near poverty. Some neighborhoods continue to be plagued by crime and flight. But most of the city is safer and more prosperous than it was a decade ago.

The problem of how to govern the nation's capital is not new. In 1787 the framers of the Constitution, familiar with contemporary London and Paris mobs and remembering how crowds had threatened Congress in Philadelphia, purposely gave the new federal government control of the 10-mile-square enclave that came to be called the District of Columbia. Over the years Congress kept control, for its own advantage and, later, out of distrust of the city's large black population. Blacks have consistently made up one-quarter of the population of Washington and surrounding counties since the 1790s, and the city was a center for free blacks even before the Civil War and Emancipation. Radical Republicans gave the District self-government in the era of Reconstruction in 1871, but Governor Alexander "Boss" Shepherd in building great public works spent the District into bankruptcy, and the experiment ended in 1874. Later, Washington's vast growth, starting with the New Deal and World War II, resulted in the growth of large, mostly white suburbs, and blacks became a larger percentage of the city's population—a majority in the 1960 Census. During the 1960s civil rights revolution, it began to seem absurd to deny the vote to Washington. So in 1964, District residents began to cast three electoral votes for president, in 1968 they were allowed to vote for school board, in 1971 they finally got to elect a non-voting delegate to Congress, and in 1974, they got home rule and could vote for a mayor and city council.

The results were tragic. Barry, a man of great ability and charm, a leader of protest organizations with few connections to Washington's established black middle class, was elected narrowly in 1978. He inherited a government that was already overlarge and undermanaged, and over the years made it more so. He raised money from public employee unions and real estate developers and increasingly won votes from poor blacks by attacking any critic as racist. Then, in January 1990, Barry was arrested in a D.C. hotel using crack cocaine, a crime for which he was eventually convicted and imprisoned. A reform-minded mayor, Sharon Pratt Kelly, was elected, but flinched when it came time to cut the payroll. Barry, out of prison and elected to the council in 1992, ran for mayor in 1994 and won the Democratic primary with 47% to 37% for Councilman John Ray and only 13% for Kelly. In the general, Republican Carol Schwartz, a longtime council member, ran a gallant campaign, but Barry won 56%–42%.

In the meantime, the District had changed. Even as the District payroll was peaking—at 51,300 in 1992—the District's population was falling, and becoming more white. Washington's population fell from 802,000 in 1950 to 572,000 in 2000. In the 1950s and 1960s, the District saw white flight; in the Barry years, it saw black flight. The District lost 6% of its population in the 1990s, as blacks headed to majority-black Prince George's County and other suburbs, where three-quarters of Washington-area blacks live. At the same time, Ward 3 and gentrifying neighborhoods near downtown grew in population, so that the black percentage of the population has declined from a peak of 71% in 1970 to 60% in 2000. In some elections, whites account for nearly half the vote. In the 2002 general election, some 43% of the voters were from affluent areas.

After Barry returned to office in 1995, the District faced a fiscal crisis and Congress took most of the government out from under Barry's control. This was not a hostile takeover: House Speaker Newt Gingrich appointed as chairman of the D.C. subcommittee Tom Davis, a Republican congressman from Northern Virginia long sympathetic to the District, and he worked closely with the District's elected delegate, Eleanor Holmes Norton. They got Congress to establish a five-member financial control board in April 1995, which demanded cuts in spending and payroll. The control board took over the public schools in November 1996; in August 1997, Congress stripped Barry of power over nine city departments (Barry kept the libraries and parks). The control board's chief financial officer, Anthony Williams, hacked away at the payroll, reformed management practices and literally cleaned up messes in District offices. Today, he is the mayor.

The electorate changed as well. It remains overwhelmingly Democratic: In 2000, Al Gore carried the District over George W. Bush 85%–9%, with 5% for Ralph Nader; whites voted for Gore 67%–20%—a higher percentage than in any state. In May 1998, Barry announced he would not run again; four council members joined the race, Schwartz and three Democrats. Then there was a move, encouraged by *The Washington Post*, to draft Anthony Williams.

Williams was an unlikely candidate. He was not from Washington at all: He grew up in Los Angeles, a speechless foster child adopted when he was 3. He was once an alderman in New Haven, Connecticut; when he took the CFO job in 1995, he moved first to Virginia and only later to Washington's Foggy Bottom. Williams had a history of changing course: He participated in anti-Vietnam war demonstrations, enlisted in the Air Force and served, then applied for conscientious objector status and got an honorable discharge. After seven years he graduated with honors from

Yale, started an antique map business, then got degrees from Harvard Law and the Kennedy School and worked in Connecticut, Boston and St. Louis. Always dressed in a bow tie, diffident in crowds, he did not seem to have a political touch. But that may have been an asset. As CFO, Williams had moved the District from huge deficits to a $185 million surplus in February 1998. He had cut payrolls deeply, provoking many squawks; he had changed the way many departments were managed. His leading primary opponent, Kevin Chavous, emphasized the need for a compassionate government and called Williams a bean counter. But Williams won the September Democratic primary by 50% to 35%, carrying five of the eight wards; in Ward 3, he beat Chavous 77%–9%. In the general, Schwartz attacked Williams as an interloper and a heartless bureaucrat who fired too many people. But Williams, endorsed by the conservative *Washington Times* as well as *The Washington Post*, won 66%–30%.

The control board immediately delegated power to the new mayor. In fall 2000, judges returned control of most District departments to the city, and in fall 2001, the control board went out of existence. In June 2000, voters narrowly approved a new, partly appointed school board. There were still problems. Williams did not get along well with the Council, and Catania and other members pushed successfully for reforms and for big tax cuts over Williams's opposition. Some city departments still performed abysmally. The Police Department's homicide division was a mess, with dozens of unsolved and uninvestigated cases, and the child welfare agency seemed to do little to help neglected children. In May 2001 the Mayor and Council contracted out operation of the inefficient D.C. General Hospital, on which the very poor depend for care; the contractor failed to perform up to specification, as opponents predicted and in November 2002 filed for bankruptcy. After September 11, tourism declined sharply and thousands of hotel and restaurant workers were laid off; revenues came in below projections, and the city again faced budget problems.

But on balance, progress was being made. The District budget was in surplus and was approved by Congress. The culture of the city bureaucracy seemed to be changing. In spring 2002, Williams seemed headed to easy reelection without serious opposition. Then an officer of the Board of Elections and Ethics began looking over the 10,000 petition signatures Williams's campaign had filed to get on the ballot. Most seemed to be in the same handwriting, with names like Tony Blair and Donald Rumsfeld. The people Williams had entrusted with signature gathering had apparently filled out the forms themselves and pocketed his campaign's money. The Board found that 54% of the signatures were fraudulent and barred Williams from the ballot. On August 14, the D.C. Court of Appeals upheld that decision and fined William's campaign $250,000. All this might have defeated candidates in many other cities. But Washington wanted Williams to stay. He launched an embarrassing write-in campaign. His major opponent was another write-in, Willie Wilson, pastor of a 7,000-member church in Anacostia and a spiritual counselor to Marion Barry. Barry's support turned out to be a dead weight. Wilson carried only Ward 8 in Anacostia, the lowest-voting ward in the city, and Williams won the September 10 primary 66%–22%. In the general, he again faced Schwartz, also nominated by write-ins. But Williams won 61%–34%, with even support in every part of the city; he carried Ward 3, the heaviest-voting ward, with 63% of the vote, and got his lowest percentages in Wards 7 and 8 in Anacostia.

District license plates carry the legend, "Taxation without representation" (you can get a license plate without the slogan, as the Bush White House did for the presidential limousine). The District is not going to get voting representation in Congress or the right to tax suburbanites who work in the city any time soon, but it is at least showing a capacity to build a reasonably competent government.

The People
Pop. 2000:	572,059
Pop. 1990:	606,900
Change 1990–2000:	Down 5.7%
Change 1980–1990:	Down 4.9%
% of U.S. total:	0.2%
Area size:	68 sq. mi.
State Native:	39.2%
Non-citizen:	9.0%

Language
English: 81.0%　Spanish: 9.1%
Other Eur.: 6.2%

Race/Ethnic Origin
159,178	27.8%	White
340,088	59.4%	Black
15,039	2.6%	Asian
1,274	0.2%	Native Am.
273	0.0%	Hawaiian
9,584	1.7%	Two+ races
1,670	0.3%	Other
44,953	7.9%	Hisp. Origin

Ancestry
Irish: 4.3%　German: 4.2%
English: 3.9%　Subsaharan: 2.5%
Italian: 1.9%

Military veterans: 44,484 (9.7%)
WWII: 22.1%	Korea: 14.4%
Vietnam: 29.5%	Gulf War: 10.4%

Most populous cities:
1. Washington　　572,059

Urban population: 100.0%
Rural population: 0.0%

Education
H.S. Grad:	77.8%
College Grad:	39.1%

Industry
Agri: 0.1%	Con: 3.9%
Fin: 7.4%	Info: 6.4%
Mfg: 5.1%	Prof: 36.8%
Public: 15.0%	Trade: 6.9%
Other: 18.4%	

Occupation
Blue collar: 10.0%　White collar: 73.9%
Gray collar: 16.1%

Work Sector
Private: 68.7%	Govt: 25.9%
Self: 5.2%	Family: 0.1%
Unemployment: 10.7%	

Household Income
<15k: 20.7%	15-35k: 23.7%
35-50k: 14.2%	50-100k: 24.9%
100-150k: 8.4%	>150k: 8.0%
Median: $40,127	

Poverty status: 20.2%

Home Value
<50k: 1.9%	50-100k: 19.4%	100-200k: 42.4%	200-300k: 12.0%
300-500k: 14.5%	>500k: 9.7%	Median: $153,500	

Registered Voters
D: 254,628 (76.6%)
R: 24,850　(7.5%)
I: 52,880　(15.9%)

2000 Presidential Vote
Gore (D)	171,923	(85%)
Bush (R)	18,073	(9%)
Nader (Green)	10,576	(5%)
Other	1,322	(1%)

2000 Democratic Presidential Primary
Gore (D)	18,621	(96%)
LaRouche (D)	796	(4%)

2000 Republican Presidential Primary
Bush (R)	1,771	(73%)
McCain (R)	593	(24%)
Other	69	(3%)

1996 Presidential Vote
Clinton (D)	158,220	(85%)
Dole (R)	17,339	(9%)
Perot (I)	3,611	(2%)
Other	6,566	(4%)

Delegate

Eleanor Holmes Norton (D)

Elected 1990; 7th term; b. June 13, 1937, Washington, D.C.; home, Washington, D.C.; Antioch Col., B.A. 1960, Yale, M.A. 1963, LL.B. 1964; Episcopalian; divorced.

Professional Career: Asst. Legal Dir., ACLU, 1965–70; New York City Human Rights Comm., 1970–77; Equal Empl. Oppor. Comm., 1977–81; Sr. Fellow, The Urban Inst., 1981–82; Prof., Georgetown U. Law Ctr., 1982–present.

DC Office:　2136 RHOB, 20515, 202-225-8050; Fax: 202-225-3002; Web site: www.house.gov/norton.

District Offices: Washington, D.C., 202-678-8900; Washington, D.C., 202-783-5065.

Committees: *Government Reform* (17th of 19 D): Civil Service & Agency Organization; Criminal Justice, Drug Policy & Human Resources. *Select Committee on Homeland Security* (13th of 23 D): Emergency Preparedness & Response; Intelligence & Counterterrorism. *Transportation & Infrastructure* (6th of 34 D): Aviation; Economic Development, Public Buildings & Emergency Management (RMM); Water Resources & Environment.

Election Results

2002 general	Eleanor Holmes Norton (D)	119,268	(93%)	($168,650)
	Patricia Kidd (I)	7,733	(6%)	
2002 primary	Eleanor Holmes Norton (D)	unopposed		
2000 general	Eleanor Holmes Norton (D)	158,824	(90%)	($162,346)
	Edward H. Wolterbeek (R)	10,258	(6%)	
	Other	6,549	(4%)	

Prior Winning Percentages: 1998 (90%); 1996 (90%); 1994 (89%); 1992 (85%); 1990 (62%)

Eleanor Holmes Norton, first elected delegate from the District of Columbia in 1990, is a Washington native. She graduated from Antioch and Yale Law School, worked for the ACLU and the New York City Commission on Human Rights, and was head of the Equal Employment Opportunity Commission in the Carter administration. Afterward, she taught law at Georgetown. When the delegate seat came open in 1990, she ran and drew criticism because her husband hadn't filed their income taxes for several years. But in the primary she edged past city Councilwoman Betty Anne Kane, 39%–33%. Norton has been re-elected easily since.

In the House, she had the difficult and sometimes vexing task of responding to the fiscal collapse of the District government just as Republicans took over Congress. She has been hard-working, competent, intellectually honest, able to get along with opponents as well as fellow partisans and willing to take personal and political risks. She established good relations with Republicans active on District matters before 1994, even though she led the drive, much resented by Republicans in 1993 and repealed by them in 1995, to give her and the four territorial delegates to the House—all of whom were then Democrats—votes on most legislation in the House. In March 2001, she and Connecticut Sen. Joseph Lieberman introduced legislation to exempt D.C. residents from federal income taxes until they are represented in Congress. In 1995, she worked with Tom Davis and Newt Gingrich to create the fiscal control board to superintend District finances; in 1997, she and Davis came up with the package that rescued District finances and removed control over most of the District government from Marion Barry. She initially hailed it as "a great day for the District," and with some cause. It also included tax breaks for downtown and some other areas. In return, the District gave up the $660 million federal payment for a $198 million "contribution," which, Norton argues, should in the long run remove the District from the close superintendency of Congress. Norton changed her tone momentarily after Barry criticized the measure for stripping the mayor of effective power over most of the District government. But the powers were restored after Anthony Williams was elected mayor in 1998.

Norton has spoken out effectively for District interests even though she doesn't have a vote on the floor. She got the District borrowing authority for a new convention center. In 1999, she co-sponsored the bill to provide in-state tuition rates for District students at state colleges in Maryland and Virginia and, she argues, other states. She criticized then-Attorney General Janet Reno for seeking the death penalty for the Starbucks killer, because the District repealed its death penalty in 1981 and voted against it in referendum in 1992. She protested when the House passed an amendment repealing the District's ban on handguns; it was quickly reversed. She got the District of Columbia included in the state quarter program.

Norton has opposed the closure of Pennsylvania Avenue and E Street near the White House, and has favored plans to reopen Pennsylvania or to build a tunnel. In early 2002 she called for reopening the White House to tours, at least of schoolchildren and families with children, and for fully reopening Ronald Reagan Washington National Airport and ending the full-throttle take-offs that raise noise levels in northwest Washington. She has vocally opposed vouchers and school choice for D.C. students, speaking out against Dick Armey's plan in July 2002 and against Jeff Flake's proposal in February 2003. She strongly backs full voting rights for D.C. residents.

Norton was reelected in 2002 by a 93%–6% margin over an Independent.

★ FLORIDA ★

Florida: For 36 days it was the cynosure of all eyes, the state that would determine who would become president of the United States, the most evenly balanced political state in the nation. To many this seemed astonishing. Sixty years before, Florida was the smallest Southern state, with just 5 congressional districts and 7 electoral votes, overwhelmingly Democratic. In 2000 it was the fourth-largest state in the nation, with 23 congressional districts and 25 electoral votes—and about to get 2 more from the 2000 Census. Only 12 years earlier, Florida had voted 61% for then-Vice President George Bush; he carried 66 of its 67 counties. Military-minded Southerners in the northern part of the state, affluent retirees on the Gulf Coast, middle-class conservatives in Tampa Bay and Orlando and around Disney World, Cubans in Miami and Dade County—all voted Republican, easily outnumbering the state's scattered black communities and its Jewish voters concentrated in Broward and Palm Beach Counties on the Gold Coast. But by 2000 Florida had become a state with political divisions as deep and political preferences as starkly different as any in the nation. Broward and Palm Beach on the Gold Coast voted 65%–33% for Al Gore; Escambia, Santa Rosa and Okaloosa Counties, on the western end of the Panhandle around what is called, perhaps unkindly, the Redneck Riviera, voted 68%–30% for George W. Bush. How Florida came to be the pivot of American politics is a story of growth and change, and over the past 60 years Florida has grown more rapidly and changed more vividly than just about any other part of the United States.

Florida has an exotic past. It is the only Atlantic Coast state that was not part of the colonial United States; through the exertions of John Quincy Adams and Andrew Jackson it was acquired from Spain in 1819. Starting off as a forgotten swamp and semitropical resort, Florida has emerged as almost an empire of its own, a prototype in many ways of America's future, with an international flavor and sometimes almost with its own foreign policy. Pivotal has been the rise of air conditioning: in 1950 only 20% of Florida houses had it, in 2000, 95% did. For many years, Florida was the place which millions of retirees looked forward to: the sunny, year-round warmth after eternal gray skies over winter factories and dark offices. But in the 1980s and 1990s Florida's population of children grew rapidly as young couples, from the South, from various points north and from Latin America, chose to raise their families and make their livings in a booming economy, with jobs and opportunities in communities that did not exist a generation ago. For refugees from Cuba and Haiti and immigrants from all over the Caribbean and Latin America, Florida has been a land of freedom and security from authoritarian regimes and totalitarian police states. For Americans and foreigners of all kinds—76 million of them in 2002—Florida is the place to visit, with lively attractions, year-round swimming, restaurants and rooms to suit every taste and pocketbook. Yet all is not sunny: crime is down, but still a threat; the economic future is, as always, uncertain; the melting pot seems to work slowly, and Florida's Hispanic population seems often to live in a world apart.

Florida is a creation not of America's elite—though a few millionaires like Henry Flagler and Marcus Plant pioneered tourism here—but a place for which ordinary people have voted with their feet. Before World War II it was the least populous state in the South, with 1.4 million people, isolated, disease-ridden, bigoted, with phosphate mines but no mineral resources, not much agriculture outside its citrus groves, and hardly any manufacturing at all. Today, Florida has 16 million people. It is a state one-fifth of whose economy is based on tourism in a country where tourism is one of the great growth industries; a state with an economy based on services in a country increasingly service-oriented; the state with the largest proportion of elderly and retired citizens in a country where an increasing percentage will live many years in retirement; a state also with a growing number of school children in a country which, replenished by immigration, is growing faster and more robustly than any other advanced nation. It is a state continually replenished with people from out of state, two-thirds of them from the United States, one-third from foreign countries: enough that Florida may replace New York as the third largest state some time in the next decade.

Florida in the 1990s had one of America's most buoyant economies, though its economic

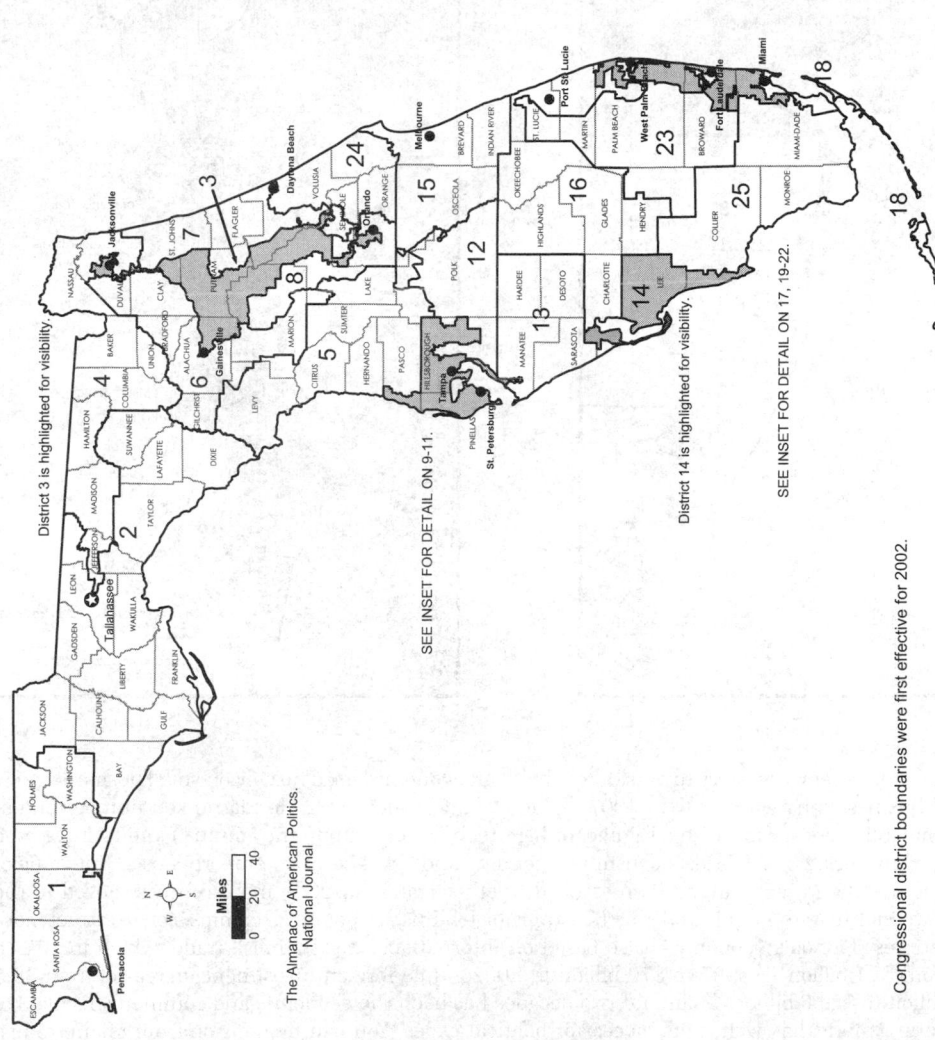

District 3 is highlighted for visibility.

The Almanac of American Politics.
National Journal

SEE INSET FOR DETAIL ON 9-11.

District 14 is highlighted for visibility.

SEE INSET FOR DETAIL ON 17, 19-22.

Congressional district boundaries were first effective for 2002.

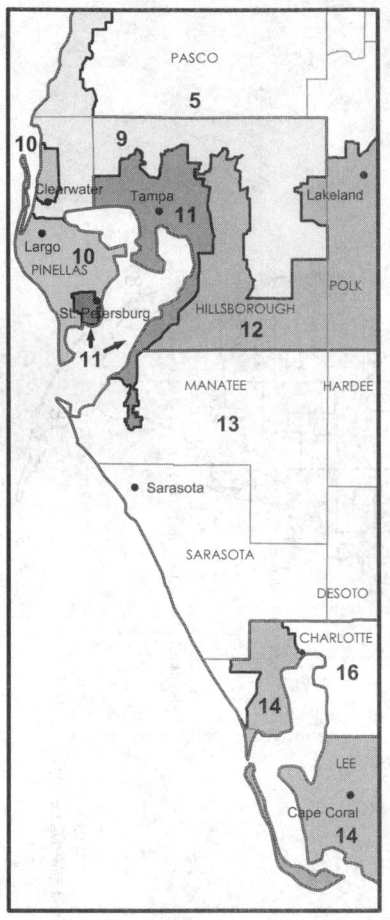

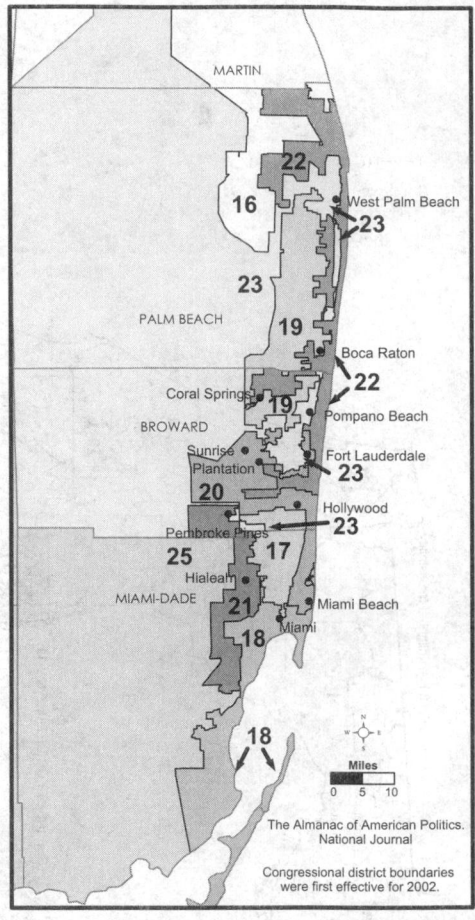

base may seem a mystery to outsiders. This is an economy based heavily on small business—98% of businesses have fewer than 100 employees and in the 1990s Florida ranked number one in small business starts—with a significant high-tech sector (fifth in the country) and retirees, who account for 52% of Florida's consumer spending and pay 47% of its property taxes. But some of this may be in jeopardy, as retirees head to other states: in 2001 more retirees moved to the Carolinas than to Florida and in 2002 Governor Jeb Bush appointed a commission to attract more retirees. Florida's economy is also based on international merchandise trade, which increased from $24 billion in 1987 to $70 billion in 2002; while foreign investment increased from $9.5 billion to $29.6 billion. Miami for two decades has been the economic and commercial capital of Latin America, as well as its mecca for political exiles. You can fly nonstop from Miami to just about any place in Latin America, both English and Spanish are commonly understood, and it has been the one place where Latins could be sure their money and their persons were safe from government takeover. Recent ructions in their countries have brought thousands of Argentinians, Venezuelans and Colombians, some very affluent and some struggling, to south Florida; Puerto Ricans and other Latinos have also been moving into Florida, and Cubans now account for less than half of Florida's Hispanics. And other immigrants have come in as well, especially to the Gold Coast: Russians, Arabs, Haitians, Jamaicans and others from the Caribbean.

What may be fragile in Florida is civil society; Florida can be disorderly and chaotic. Most people here do not have deep roots in the state, most communities sprang into existence within living memory and, if Florida gives people more freedom and options than they may ever have imagined, it has also given them more disruption and crime than they surely anticipated. Many of Florida's great fortunes were made elsewhere, and brought here partly because the state has no income or inheritance taxes. Government is not a major presence: one Census study reported that Florida pays less per capita in taxes than any other states, and as much as one-third of sales tax revenues are paid by non-residents. Even in fighting crime Florida has let citizens take the lead. This was the first major state with a law allowing law-abiding citizens to routinely be licensed to carry guns.

This new Florida, like today's America, has no real center. Its largest urban focus, Miami, is geographically off to one corner and culturally uniquely Cuban, with its eyes increasingly on Latin America. Even before the 2000 imbroglio, Miami's politics held it up to ridicule, as in March 1998 when the Miami city elections were voided because of absentee ballot fraud; in the September 2002 primary only Miami-Dade County (the name was changed from Dade County in 1997) and Broward County just to the north had difficulties with their voting machines. But Miami holds only 362,000 of the 2.25 million people in the renamed Miami-Dade County, which has among other accomplishments developed one of the largest and best community college systems in the country. The rest of the Gold Coast, Broward and Palm Beach counties, with one-sixth of Florida's population, is also atypical, with a population drawn heavily from New York (the largest migration between any two states is from New York to Florida) and other Northeastern metro areas, plus non-Latino migrants from Miami-Dade, with large numbers of Jews, and huge retiree condos lining the ocean front. Then there is Central Florida, the I-4 corridor from Tampa-St. Petersburg through citrus and tourist country and Orlando. This is mostly family, not retiree, country, living off high-tech industries as much as tourism. A year-round rather than seasonal civilization, this area has seen so much growth in the 1990s that it is becoming its own megalopolis—a "Tamplando" or "Orlampa," as the *Orlando Sentinel* called it. There is also the Gulf Coast, the affluent and burgeoning communities south of Tampa Bay and the more modest retirement counties to the north. Growing even more rapidly is the area along the hard-sand-beach Atlantic Coast around Jacksonville and Daytona Beach. Very Southern culturally is the western Panhandle, the Redneck Riviera around Pensacola and Panama City, which has Florida's most luxuriant white sand beaches.

Politically, this all adds up to a Florida that is uniquely balanced between the parties and politically volatile. As Democratic pollster Geoff Garin has pointed out, "There's an enormous amount of churning in the electorate. A lot of people on the voter rolls today weren't on the voter rolls five years ago. As a result, Florida politics are much more related to the tides of events and personalities." In the 1990s the Republicans slowly captured control of state offices, winning the state House in 1994, the state Senate in 1996, and the governorship in 1998, even as the Democratic Party increased its strength in presidential elections so that in 2000 Florida came achingly close to electing Al Gore (48.85%–48.84%) and elected its second Democratic U.S. senator. Republicans have won solid majorities in the legislature—26–14 in the Senate, 81–39 in the House—by organizing intensively and patiently capturing one marginal district after another; they have been helped by term limits, which keeps politically adept Democrats from holding onto Republican-leaning districts forever. Republicans have established a 18–7 margin in the U.S. House delegation in the same way, and by adapting shrewdly to local terrain. Redistricting, which Republicans influenced in 1992 and controlled in 2002, helped: heavily black and Jewish areas are concentrated in a few districts, to the point that two-thirds of Democrats holding legislative and House seats are black or Jewish.

But Republicans have not been able to prevent Democrats from transforming Florida from a solidly Republican state in presidential politics—the elder George Bush carried the state 61%–39% in 1988—to one which has become exquisitely closely divided. Most of the change was due to movement toward Democrats on the Gold Coast and in the I-4 corridor from Tampa-St. Petersburg to Orlando. Drops in crime and welfare rolls deprived Republicans of issues in these metro areas as they did in the big metro areas of the Northeast, industrial Midwest and West Coast, and after 1995 the tax issue was taken off the table; cultural issues like abortion and gun control favored Democrats. Ross Perot detached many voters from the elder Bush in 1992, and most of them voted for Bill Clinton and Al Gore in 1996 and 2000. Also, the increasing Jewish population in Broward and Palm Beach counties moved the Gold Coast toward Democrats; Joseph Lieberman campaigned there and drew enthusiastic crowds in 2000. In the I-4 corridor, what had been a big Republican margin for Bush in 1988 was transformed to a Clinton margin in 1996 and a standoff in 2000. The biggest drop in the Republican percentage in any county in Florida between 1988 and 2000 was in Osceola County, which contains part of Disney World and the Disney-sponsored "new town" of Celebration. In the 1980s, Disney World was still an epitome of traditional conservative values; by 2000, Disney was hosting Gay Day. As compared with 1988, the Bush 2000 percentage fell significantly in counties with large in-migration from the North or from immigrants from abroad, and fell much less—in some cases rose a bit—in counties with a Southern cultural tone or large military installations. This mild change was similar to that in other Southern states, all of which Bush carried easily. But in Florida it was just enough to—barely—win.

After the U.S. Supreme Court made its decision in December 2000, Florida Democrats promised that voters' rage would redound against Jeb Bush in 2002, when he ran for reelection as governor, and in fall 2002 DNC Chairman Terry McAuliffe said that the Florida governor race was the national party's number one priority. Yet his job approval rating remained around 55% throughout the campaign and he won by a 56%–43% margin. At the same time, Republican Charlie Crist was elected attorney general, replacing the last Democrat holding a non-federal statewide office, and Republican margins in the U.S. House delegation and the state Senate and House were increased. The careers of the successful Florida Democrats of the past generation— Lawton Chiles, Reubin Askew, Bob Graham, Bill Nelson—have followed a similar patterns: they were all little-known legislators from conservative middle-sized counties (except Graham, who is from Miami-Dade County) with moderate records who ran for statewide office and managed to finish second in the first primary and then beat a more liberal candidate in the runoff (Nelson's career path was a little different). The problem for Democrats is that there are almost no Democratic officeholders left who fit this template. Florida looks increasingly like a safe Republican state, in state if not in national politics.

Two more things are worth noting about Florida politics. The first is that politics here is not driven by an elderly population terrified of losing government benefits. To be sure, the elderly are a larger percentage of the electorate here than in any other state, but the difference is not overwhelming; most new residents come here to work, not to retire. Republican congressmen with elderly districts who have supported changes in the Social Security system have been reelected in all but one case by wide margins. In 2000 George W. Bush called for individual investment accounts as a part of Social Security and according to VNS carried the over 65 vote in Florida by a 52%–46% margin. The elderly tend to vote in line with long-established partisan preferences, not in panicky response to the latest proposal on Social Security.

The second point is that the environment is an increasingly important issue in Florida, but one that may not cut in a partisan way. People come to Florida partly because of the kind of place it is; migrants from New York or Illinois may not have cared much about environmental issues when they lived there, but they came to Florida in large part because of the climate and setting, and don't want to see oil drilled on the Gulf coast or the Everglades paved over. This is a change from history. The Everglades were seen as a nuisance for years. In 1845, when Florida was admitted to the Union, the legislature called for "reclaiming" the Everglades, and in 1850 Congress passed the Swamp and Overflowed Lands Act. The Army Corps of Engineers started building a dike across Lake Okeechobee in 1930 and for nearly 50 years worked to straighten the Kissimmee River and build dikes and channels to reclaim land for farming. But with the 1947 publication of *The Everglades: River of Grass* by Marjory Stoneman Douglas, who died in 1998 at 108, Floridians began to appreciate the Everglades, which is essentially a flow of water south, from the Kissimmee River near Disney World, through Lake Okeechobee down to Florida Bay and the Gulf of Mexico. In the 1990s Congress ordered the Corps to restore the original flow of the Kissimmee River and in 1996 voters approved an amendment for cleaning up the Everglades (though disapproving a one-cent sugar tax to pay for it). Then both parties came together to call for restoring the Everglades. The Clinton administration package was announced in October 1998 by Al Gore (White House strategists were targeting Florida even then): a $7.8 billion Central and Southern Florida

Project to build huge reservoirs above and under ground, a vast plant to recycle Miami waste water and a system of 70 massive pumps in the Everglades and to make the Tamiami Trail a causeway, like Alligator Alley 25 miles to the north. It was promptly supported by Governor Jeb Bush, who persuaded the Republican legislature to set aside $2 billion over 10 years for the project. Both houses of Congress approved the Everglades project before the 2000 election. It is not clear that it will work and it may well turn out to be more expensive than predicted. But it does appear that the Florida of the mid-21st century will, for all its development, be closer in one important way to the natural Florida of the Seminoles than the Florida of today.

The People

Pop. 2000:	15,982,378
Pop. 1990:	12,937,926
Change 1990–2000:	Up 23.5%
Change 1980–1990:	Up 32.7%
% of U.S. total:	5.7%
Pop. rank:	4th of 50
Area size:	65,755 sq. mi.
State Native:	32.7%
Non-citizen:	9.2%

Language

English: 76.2%   Spanish: 15.7%
Other Eur.: 6.3%

Race/Ethnic Origin

10,458,509	65.4%	White
2,264,268	14.2%	Black
261,693	1.6%	Asian
42,358	0.3%	Native Am.
6,887	0.0%	Hawaiian
236,954	1.5%	Two+ races
28,994	0.2%	Other
2,682,715	16.8%	Hisp. Origin

Ancestry

German: 9.5%   Irish: 8.3%
English: 7.4%   USA: 6.4%
Italian: 5.0%

Military veterans: 1,875,597 (15.2%)
WWII: 25.6%   Korea: 15.0%
Vietnam: 28.0%   Gulf War: 9.2%

Most populous cities:
1. Jacksonville   735,617
2. Miami   362,470
3. Tampa   303,447
4. St. Petersburg   248,232
5. Hialeah   226,419

Urban population: 89.3%
Rural population: 10.7%

Education

H.S. Grad: 79.9%
College Grad: 22.3%

Industry

Agri: 1.3%   Con: 8.0%
Fin: 8.1%   Info: 3.1%
Mfg: 12.6%   Prof: 28.7%
Public: 5.2%   Trade: 17.5%
Other: 15.6%

Occupation

Blue collar: 21.1%   White collar: 61.1%
Gray collar: 17.8%

Work Sector

Private: 79.8%   Govt: 13.7%
Self: 6.2%   Family: 0.3%
Unemployment: 5.5%

Household Income

<15k: 16.3%   15-35k: 28.7%
35-50k: 17.4%   50-100k: 27.2%
100-150k: 6.3%   >150k: 4.1%
Median: $38,819
Poverty status: 12.5%

Home Value

<50k: 16.5%   50-100k: 38.7%   100-200k: 32.1%   200-300k: 7.1%
300-500k: 3.6%   >500k: 2.1%   Median: $93,200

Legislature

Senate   26 R 14 D
House   81 R 39 D

Legislative Term Limits: Yes

Registered Voters

D: 3,958,910 (42.6%)
R: 3,599,053 (38.7%)
I: 1,744,397 (18.8%)

Presidential politics   Political pundits may not have predicted that Florida would be the most closely contested state in the 2000 presidential campaign, but the candidates foresaw it. Al Gore targeted it early and visited it often, even conducting his debate prep sessions in Sarasota County; this was the one close state where Joe Lieberman's Jewish faith paid political dividends. George W. Bush for a time seemed to believe that the state where his brother was governor would fall into his column without too much prodding, and his campaign was outspent here by Gore's. But Bush ended up devoting lots of time and money to Florida as well. Gore's position on Elian Gonzalez—that his custody should be determined by a state court—was widely taken as a turnabout and a bid for Miami-Dade County's Cuban-American vote; in fact it was consistent with Gore's longstanding views on Cuban policy and availed him little since the violent seizure of

2000 Presidential Vote
Bush (R) 2,912,790   (49%)
Gore (D) 2,912,253   (49%)
Nader (Green) 97,488   (2%)
Other 40,579   (1%)

2000 Republican Presidential Primary
Bush (R) 516,161   (74%)
McCain (R) 139,397   (20%)
Keyes (R) 32,343   (5%)

2000 Democratic Presidential Primary
Gore (D) 451,657   (82%)
Bradley (D) 100,259   (18%)

1996 Presidential Vote
Clinton (D) 2,545,690   (48%)
Dole (R) 2,242,951   (43%)
Perot (I) 483,761   (9%)

the 6-year-old boy by armed agents of the Clinton administration put the Cuban vote solidly in favor of Bush.

Indeed, the Cuban vote was so heavily for Bush that he carried Hispanics overall by a 50%–48% margin: this Spanish-speaking president owes his election to Latinos. Blacks voted heavily for Gore, 93%–7%. Despite breathless charges, there was no organized effort to bar black voters from the polls, nor any significant incidents where they were barred. There were other differences between groups of voters that are worth noting. Jewish voters voted overwhelmingly for the Clinton-Gore ticket, and those with no religion voted 68%–24% for Gore; white Protestants voted 65%–33% and white Catholics 54%–42% for Bush. Voters with incomes under $30,000 voted more heavily for Gore and voters with incomes over $100,000 voted more heavily for Bush than in the nation generally: there was more economic polarization in Florida. Voters over 65 voted 52%–46% for Bush, a sign that Social Security individual investment accounts are not abhorrent to the elderly. But voters under 30 voted 56%–38% for Gore, a good omen for Democrats in the future.

The story of the Florida recount will not be fully told here. The Gore campaign was first off the mark, at first claiming that the butterfly ballot in Palm Beach County (designed by a Democratic official and approved by both parties) had been so unfair that it required a county-wide revote, then settling on a two-pronged strategy of disqualifying military absentee ballots sent in without a postmark, and qualifying as votes dimpled chads and bumps on punch card ballots in four carefully selected heavily Democratic counties. The Bush strategy was to oppose hand counts of punch card ballots, on the grounds that counting was inevitably subjective and subject to political manipulation.

The official 537-vote margin, by the way, still includes the Broward and Palm Beach hand counts, which gained Gore votes by counting dimpled chads. The best guess, fortified by post-election press examinations, is that Bush actually won Florida by a little more than 1,000 votes—a paper thin margin, out of 5,963,100 recorded. To charges that the Palm Beach ballot changed the outcome of the election, perhaps the final word should go to Palm Beach County Democratic Chairman Monte Friedkin, speaking in March 2001: "Frankly the system is bad, the machines are not user-friendly, but at the end of the day it's as much the fault of the voters as the process. We can make all the excuses we want, but the facts are the facts and George Bush is president."

Florida has had a presidential primary in March for many years; since 1988 it has been part of Southern Super Tuesday. It was once a pivotal contest: Jimmy Carter's victory here in 1976 tossed George Wallace out of national politics and helped put Carter in the White House. In recent years, as one of many states voting on a single day, it has attracted less attention. In 2004, however, it could be a critical contest for two Democratic candidates, Joseph Lieberman and Florida's own Bob Graham. Before Graham entered the race, Lieberman had high hopes for carrying the state; he had reason to hope that his strong base among Jewish voters in the Gold Coast and his appeal to hawkish voters in north Florida might enable him to carry the state in a multicandidate field. Graham has been on statewide ballots since 1978 and is greatly admired by Florida Democrats, and his candidacy hinges on carrying his own state. His task will be to make a strong enough showing in earlier contests to seem a viable candidate when he gets to Florida. It should be noted that Florida's Democratic electorate differs markedly from what it was the last time the Florida primary was the center of national attention, in 1976. Then, 67% of Florida's voters were registered Democrats; voters in north Florida, segregationist in the 1960s and hawkish in the 1970s were still almost all registered Democrats. That is why George Wallace won the 1972 Florida presidential primary and why he was still a strong candidate in 1976. In 2003 only 42% of Florida's voters were registered Democrats. This is a much smaller and much more liberal pool. There are still some north Florida counties where many who vote Republican in general elections are still registered as Democrats, but the large mass of urban Democrats—in 2002, 31% of registered Democrats were in the three Gold Coast counties and 23% in the I-4 corridor—are not that much different from registered Democrats in big northern states.

Congressional districting   Florida has gained congressional districts from every Census

since 1930, when it was still the smallest state in the South: in 1930 it elected four House members; in the 2000 Census it gained two seats, for a total of 25. In 1992, when the state gained four seats, Democrats controlled the redistricting process, but they were so conflicted they could not produce a plan. The lines were instead drawn by a federal court in May 1992, and the 3d and adjacent districts redrawn after another court ruling in April 1996. Three black Democrats were elected for the first time in 1992; the delegation went from 10–9 Republican in 1992 to 15–8 Republican after the 1994 election.

In 2002 the redistricting process was controlled by Republicans, who unlike the Democrats in 1992 were able to agree on a plan and passed it in March 2002. Disagreement between the House and Senate was resolved when senators agreed to create a district tailor-made for House Speaker Tom Feeney; the other new district was tailor-made for Mario Diaz-Balart, chairman of the House Congressional Districting Committee and brother of 21st District Congressman Lincoln Diaz-Balart. (This was in line with previous practice: the two chairmen of the 1992 Senate and House redistricting committees, Karen Thurman and Peter Deutsch, both ended up with seats in the U.S. House). When Democratic Attorney General Bob Butterworth failed to pass it along to the Department of Justice for Voting Rights Act review, Governor Jeb Bush sent it there in May 2002. Democrats filed lawsuits against the plan in state and federal courts. The Justice Department approved the plan on June 7. The state court on June 17 dismissed the suit and said the federal court had jurisdiction. On July 9, in time for the filing deadline, a three-judge federal court approved the plan.

This was one of the most successful partisan redistrictings of the 2002 cycle. Feeney and Diaz-Balart were both elected to the House by wide margins. Karen Thurman was defeated by Republican state Senator Ginny Brown-Waite. Two senior Republicans, Bill Young of St. Petersburg and Clay Shaw of Fort Lauderdale, were strengthened; both represented areas which were among the first in Florida to elect Republican congressmen, but which had become more Democratic in the 1980s and 1990s. Democrat Allen Boyd of the 2d District was weakened. The seats of the three black Democrats and two Latino Republicans were protected, although the black percentage in Alcee Hastings's 23d District was reduced. The 2002 plan produced a delegation of 18 Republicans and 7 Democrats, a lopsided Republican majority in a state that was evenly divided in the 2000 presidential election. Florida now has the second largest Republican delegation in the House; its 18 Republican congressmen are almost as numerous as California's 20.

Governor

Jeb Bush (R)

Elected 1998, term expires Jan. 2007, 2d term; b. Feb. 11, 1953, Midland, TX; home, Miami; U. of TX, B.A. 1974; Catholic; married (Columba).

Elected Office: FL Commerce Secy., 1987–88; Candidate for FL Gov., 1994.

Professional Career: Pres. & COO, Codina Group, 1981–94; Founder & Chmn., Foundation for Florida's Future, 1995–98.

Office: The Capitol, Tallahassee, 32399, 850-488-4441; Fax: 850-487-0801; Web site: www.state.fl.us.

Election Results

2002 general	Jeb Bush (R)	2,856,845	(56%)
	Bill McBride (D)	2,201,427	(43%)
2002 primary	Jeb Bush (R)	unopposed	
1998 general	Jeb Bush (R)	2,192,105	(55%)
	Buddy MacKay (D)	1,773,054	(45%)

Jeb Bush, son of President George H. W. Bush and brother of President George W. Bush, was elected governor of Florida in 1998 and 2002. Jeb grew up in Midland and Houston, Texas. He majored in Latin American studies at the University of Texas and there met his wife, Columba, who is originally from Mexico. He speaks Spanish fluently—but with more of a Mexican than Cuban accent, he notes. In 1981 he moved to Miami and started a real estate development company. For a year or so, he was Commerce secretary under Republican Governor Bob Martinez. With a well-known name and strong convictions on issues, he decided to run against Governor Lawton Chiles in 1994, vanquishing competition in the Republican primary and leading in polls during most of the fall. He called for fewer appeals for death row inmates and speedier executions, said Florida should withdraw from Aid to Families with Dependent Children and replace it with limited temporary assistance, and called for school choice and demanded voter approval of all state and local tax increases. There was a rigid tone to Bush's campaign; when one black man asked him what he would do to help him, Bush replied, "Probably nothing." Chiles started emphasizing his "cracker" roots and called himself "the he-coon [who] always walks before the light of day." The result was a 51%–49% Chiles victory.

Bush immediately started running again. He set up a foundation that produced intellectually serious proposals for changing government and visited shelters for abused women and children in foster care. Challenged by the teachers' union head to spend more time in classrooms, he visited more than 200 schools and, with the Urban League of Miami, founded and taught at a charter school in Miami's Liberty City neighborhood. While his positions on issues did not change much, his approach and his tone did. The consensus in Florida had been moving for some time toward Bush—Chiles had produced welfare and reinventing government reforms—and now Bush came some distance toward the consensus.

Bush entered 1998 as the heavy favorite for governor while Democrats inflicted damage on themselves. Democrats noisily looked for alternatives to the likely nominee, Lieutenant Governor Buddy MacKay, though MacKay had received good press for his work in office and nearly beat Connie Mack for senator in 1988. Bush won 55%–45%.

With a Republican legislature, Bush got off to a fast start. But in mid-1999 Bush was alarmed when Ward Connerly, sponsor of California's 1996 Proposition 209 which outlawed state government racial quotas and preferences, moved to put a similar proposition on the Florida ballot. Bush said Connerly would start a "war" and in November 1999 put forward his own One Florida proposal, to curtail quotas and set-asides in state contracts, get rid of quotas and preferences in state colleges and universities and replace them by guaranteeing places in the state's 10 public colleges to the top 20% of every high school graduating class. In 2000 Bush continued to have success with the legislature, cutting taxes by $500 million, spending $6 billion on roads and getting a $2 billion, 10-year commitment to the bipartisan program to restore the Everglades.

Jeb Bush did not take a highly visible role in the 2000 presidential campaign. He seldom traveled outside Florida and spoke only every week or so with his brother George W. Bush. A more visible role was played by Jeb Bush's 24-year-old son, George P. Bush, who made appearances before Hispanic audiences, cut a TV spot in Spanish and English and spoke at the podium of the Republican National Convention. In the controversy over Florida's vote, Jeb Bush recused himself from the three-member board of elections, substituting Agriculture Commissioner Bob Crawford, a Democrat who had endorsed George W. Bush; charges that he orchestrated Secretary of State Katherine Harris' decisions to certify George W. Bush as the winner have foundered for lack of evidence. He did say that he would sign a proclamation by the Florida legislature that the Republican electors had won, but there was nothing to back the charges that somehow the governor of Florida had stolen the election for his brother. The day after the election was decided, he appeared with officials of both parties and announced the formation of a bipartisan commission to study Florida's election procedures. In March 2001 it came forward with its recommendations, including getting rid of punch card ballots, leasing optical scanning equipment for all counties for the 2002 election and setting a uniform standard for recounts; an election reform bill was signed by Governor Bush in May 2001.

In 2001 Bush persisted in pushing tax cuts even though the amount of unallocated funds was falling. In January 2001 he attracted national attention when he called on the Interior Department to cancel planned oil leases in the Gulf of Mexico off the Alabama coast. Florida politicians of both parties have long opposed oil drilling in the Gulf off the Florida coast, and Bush claimed that drilling nearby would endanger Florida beaches and threaten the tourism industry; in May, Dick Cheney said the administration favored drilling. In January 2002 the Bushes signed an agreement to implement the Everglades restoration plan approved by Congress by spending $7.8 billion over 30 years to restore 2.4 million acres and provide an extra 1.7 billion gallons of fresh water yearly to south Florida. In October 2001 Bush summoned a special session of the legislature to cut spending to account for a $1.3 billion shortfall in a $51 billion budget; the result was $450 million in spending cuts and a delay in the intangibles tax cut. In January 2002 he presented a budget with just a 1% increase in spending, higher tuition at universities and community colleges, elimination of 3,000 state jobs and continuation of 2001 spending cuts. Still, Florida's fiscal problems were not as great as those in some states; at the end of a year it was one of 10 states seen as expecting revenue increases.

On other issues, Bush in 2001 negotiated rebates with pharmaceutical companies saving 15% on the Medicaid budget and signed an end to the death penalty for the retarded. In July 2002 he named his first nominee to the Florida Supreme Court, Raoul Cantero, a grandson of Cuban dictator Fulgencio Batista. In the summer of 2002 he faced two unhappy incidents, both with likely negative impact on his reelection campaign. In 1998 he had criticized the performance of the state Department of Children and Families and promised to change the agency's supervision of foster parents. Over the next three years the agency's budget was doubled, it reduced the amount of time children spent in foster care and it promoted a hotline for reporting child abuse. But in April 2002 it turned out that the department had lost track of a Miami girl, Rilya Wilson; in the next four months, three children under its supervision were found dead. The agency admitted in July 2002 that it could not account for the whereabouts of 500 children under its supervision; the *Fort Lauderdale Sun-Sentinel* set about finding some of them and found nine, including two in three hours. In August 2002 agency head Kathleen Kearney resigned.

The other incident was personal. In January 2002 Bush's adult daughter Noelle Bush was arrested in Tallahassee for trying to buy Xanax, an anti-anxiety agent, without a prescription. She was ordered to a drug treatment center in Orlando. In July 2002 she was sent to the Orange County jail when she was found in possession of stolen prescription drugs, though she tested negative. This was big news nationally and of course in Florida. Bush went on the *Today* show in mid-October and discussed the painful ordeal. Noelle Bush attended her father's inaugural ceremonies in January 2003 on a one-day pass, and he spoke movingly of the need for strong families to solve problems government cannot fix.

During the December 2000 controversy over Florida's presidential vote and for months after, angry Democrats predicted that Florida voters would defeat Jeb Bush in 2002 in revenge for what happened. But Democrats needed a candidate. Senators Bob Graham and Bill Nelson worked to recruit former 2d District Congressman Pete Peterson, a POW for six years during the Vietnam war. He was the kind of Democrat who had carried Florida in the past—from a rural and small town area, with a moderate voting record, not visibly connected to the teachers' unions and trial lawyers who are the organizational and financial bulwark of the Florida Democratic party. On September 4, 2001, another kind of candidate announced: former Attorney General Janet Reno, from Miami-Dade County, with a liberal record and well positioned to win primary votes from blacks and women. But Reno also had high negatives ratings from general election voters and seemed poorly positioned to carry voters Democrats need to win in November. On September 22, Peterson announced he was not running. Two legislators, state Senator Darryl Jones and state

Representative Lois Frankel, were also looking to run; they seemed unlikely to raise enough money to beat Reno and their liberal records would be a problem in the general election.

So, as Reno drove her red pickup truck around the state, Democratic insiders looked for another candidate and found him in Bill McBride, from 1992 to 2001 managing partner of Tampa's Holland & Knight, the largest law firm in Florida. McBride was unknown to the voting public, but had an interesting biography and plenty of politically useful connections. He grew up in the small town of Leesburg, the son of a TV repairman; he gave up a football scholarship after his knee was injured and worked his way through school; he left law school to enlist in the Marine Corps and was awarded a Bronze Star for his service in Vietnam. The driving force behind McBride's candidacy was the state's teacher's unions, who resented Bush's A-plus program for highlighting teacher performance and providing private school alternatives for children in failing schools. He announced his candidacy in June 2001 and was endorsed by the state AFL-CIO in April 2002.

Neither McBride nor Reno advanced platforms with much in the way of specifics. Darryl Jones did, with a $3.5 billion plan for education, but he had little backing outside the black community and did not raise much money; Lois Frankel withdrew from the race, unable to make headway against Reno. Reno called for health care and schooling for preschoolers; McBride called for a 50-cent increase in the cigarette tax to increase spending on education. The universally known Reno led in early primary polls, and she much free publicity driving her red truck around: appearing on the *Tonight* show with Jay Leno, at an Oscar party with Elton John, appearing late in the campaign on *Saturday Night Live*. But she raised little money and, unlike McBride, took little advantage of the state party's offer of money for administrative expenses. McBride did raise a lot of money, some $3 million by the primary. His obvious strategy was to concede the Gold Coast to Reno and advertise heavily in the I-4 corridor and north Florida media markets. It proved effective. In the weeks before the September 10 primary McBride was running even with Reno in the polls.

The primary turned out to be, Florida fashion, nearly a tie. McBride led in the first count by 8,196 votes out of 1.3 million cast, and was certified as the winner September 12. But Miami-Dade County, where Reno led by a wide margin, had not prepared to handle the new voting equipment, and was still counting votes. Florida's revised election laws require a recount if the margin is less than 0.5% of the vote, and Reno demanded a recount as the vote hovered just outside that. On September 17 Miami-Dade votes came in; Reno, still behind by 4,794 votes, 44.4%–44.0% conceded and endorsed McBride. But his campaign had lost a week of an already short general election campaign. Florida law usually requires a runoff when no candidate gets 50%, but Bush and the Republican legislature passed a law suspending the runoff for 2002 only, presumably because they hoped Reno would win a plurality and did not want to see McBride overtake her in an early October runoff and obtain momentum for November.

The early 2001 talk that this election would be a referendum on the Bush presidency was obviously wrong after September 11, when it was clear that George W. Bush's performance was much more important than and quite different from the issues raised in the Florida governor's race. The chief issue turned out to be one pushed by McBride's teachers' union allies: Amendment 9, which would put into Florida's constitution a requirement that class size would be reduced to 18 in grades K-3, 22 in grades 4–8 and 25 in grades 9–12 by 2010. Proponents said it would cost only $4 billion over seven years; Bush cited a state government study saying that it would cost $27 billion—a huge amount in a state whose budgets have been hovering around $50 billion. When it qualified for the November ballot, Bush strongly opposed it, and proposed his own program for $2.8 billion over five years to build 12,000 new classrooms. McBride, who called Bush's A-plus program a "mirage" and an "illusion" and his testing program "foolish," strongly supported it. Under state law the estimated cost of a ballot proposition has to be put on the ballot; but a Florida judge, in a move that would not surprise those who remember the 2000 Florida ballot controversy, ruled it unnecessary.

At first, Bush seemed to stumble on the issue. On October 3, in a Capitol conversation with three Pensacola area legislators witnessed by a Gannett News Service reporter, Bush talked about how he would respond if Amendment 9 passed. "We're going to have to cut nursing homes. So

I've got a couple of devious plans if this thing passes. . . . We might want to have another look at it." He suggested that taxes might have to be raised and talked about getting the voters to repeal the amendment in 2004. The next day his words were in Gannett's *Pensacola News Journal* and a tape of him speaking them was on the paper's website.

McBride's primary win had provided him enough momentum, and had given him enough of a moderate image; in one October poll, after the "devious plans" story, he trailed by only 48%–43%. But Bush proceeded to bombard television viewers with ads citing his accomplishments and attacking McBride for saying different things to different audiences, hinting that he was a hidden liberal indebted to the teachers' unions and charging that his proposal to eliminate Bush's testing would cost the state $2.5 billion in federal aid. On October 22 the candidates held a debate moderated by *Meet the Press* host Tim Russert. Bush answered questions with mastery of knowledge of state government. McBride was charmingly talkative but unspecific. When Russert asked him whether Amendment 9 would cost $3 billion as some proponents claimed or $27 billion as Bush claimed, McBride conceded it could cost as much as $15 billion. His response gave credence to Bush ads that charged that McBride's overexpansion at Holland & Knight showed that as an executive he was overoptimistic and inclined to overspending.

In late October Bush surged farther ahead in polls; on Election Day, he won by the impressive margin of 56%–43%. Bush appears to have carried Hispanic precincts throughout the state and had huge margins in Cuban areas in Miami-Dade County. He lost ground compared to 1998 in Tallahassee and in small north Florida counties with universities, prisons or other state facilities: his Service First overhauls of the state personnel system and privatization of non-core functions of state agencies made him unpopular with public employee unions. Bush lost the Gold Coast by only 54%–46%; he carried the I-4 corridor by a solid 58%–41% and carried the other counties in the south 62%–37% and in the north 59%–40%. Republican Charlie Crist was elected attorney general over Democrat Buddy Dwyer 53%–47%, completing the Republican sweep of statewide offices. Republican margins were increased in the state Senate to 26–14 and the state House to 81–39. Moreover, those margins seem firm: only three Senate races and 12 House races were won with less than 55% of the vote. McBride said he would not run again.

After the election, Bush said his goals for his second term were higher reading scores, a more diverse economy, a renewal of a spirit of community and strengthening of families, "BHAGs," as he put it, "big, hairy, audacious goals." But he was faced with one big problem: Amendment 9 passed by a 52%–48% margin, far less than it had in polls, but enough to impose unknown new obligations on state government. The text of the amendment left unanswered how class size should be calculated. In January 2003 Bush and incoming Speaker Johnnie Byrd said they would support a tax increase; incoming state Senate President Jim King said, "An increase in taxes, though certainly not what any of us wants, will have to be considered." In his inaugural address, Bush sounded a note that irritated many Democrats, when he said he looked forward to the day when state buildings in Tallahassee will lie empty as "silent monuments to a time when government played a larger role than it deserved or could adequately fill." More than most governors, he seems guided by a philosophy that makes him willing to risk political confrontation and more than most governors, he has shown an ability to prevail.

As the son and brother of presidents, a distinction he shares with only his own brothers and John Quincy Adams's, he has often been mentioned as a candidate for president himself in 2008. He has professed to find the notion incredible. "It's like talking about whatever that group is from outer space. Raelians."

Senior Senator

Bob Graham (D)

Elected 1986, seat up 2004, 3d term; b. Nov. 9, 1936, Coral Gables; home, Miami Lakes; U. of FL, B.A. 1959, Harvard, J.D. 1962; United Church of Christ; married (Adele).

Elected Office: FL House of Reps., 1966–70; FL Senate, 1970–78; FL Gov., 1978–1986.

Professional Career: The Graham Cos., Sengra Development Corp., 1962–66.

DC Office: 524 HSOB, 20510, 202-224-3041; Fax: 202-224-2237; Web site: www.graham.senate.gov.

State Offices: Miami, 305-536-7293; Tallahassee, 850-907-1100; Tampa, 813-228-2476.

Committees: *Energy & Natural Resources*: Energy (RMM); National Parks; Water & Power. *Environment & Public Works*: Fisheries, Wildlife & Water (RMM); Transportation & Infrastructure. *Finance*: Health Care; International Trade; Long-Term Growth & Debt Reduction (RMM). *Veterans' Affairs* (RMM).

Group Ratings

	ADA	ACLU	AFS	LCV	CON	ITIC	NTU	COC	ACU	NTLC	CHC
2002	75	60	88	59	95	62	24	60	20	6	—
2001	100	—	100	75	—	—	8	36	16	—	0

National Journal Ratings

	2001 LIB	—	2001 CONS		2002 LIB	—	2002 CONS
Economic	74%	—	23%		73%	—	20%
Social	70%	—	20%		50%	—	48%
Foreign	61%	—	27%		58%	—	41%

Key Votes of the 107th Congress

1. Approve Bush Tax Cuts	N	5. Confirm Ashcroft as AG	N	9. Bar Coop. with Intl. Court	Y
2. Expand Patients' Rights	Y	6. Bar Gays in the Boy Scouts	N	10. Trade Promotion Authority	Y
3. Campaign Finance Reform	Y	7. $ for Hate Crime Prosecution	Y	11. Authorize Force in Iraq	N
4. Permit ANWR Development	N	8. Overseas Military Abortions	Y	12. Homeland Sec. Dept. Union	Y

Election Results

1998 general	Bob Graham (D)	2,436,402	(62%)	($5,094,581)
	Charlie Crist (R)	1,463,749	(38%)	($1,487,498)
1998 primary	Bob Graham (D)	unopposed		
1992 general	Bob Graham (D)	3,245,565	(65%)	($3,318,473)
	Bill Grant (R)	1,716,505	(35%)	($242,251)

Prior Winning Percentages: 1986 (55%)

Bob Graham, senior Senator from Florida, was first elected governor in 1978 and senator in 1986. He comes from a prominent Florida family and grew up outside Miami on a dairy farm. His father Ernest Graham was a state senator from 1936 to 1944 and in 1944 ran unsuccessfully for governor; his much older half-brother was the publisher of the *Washington Post*. He graduated from the University of Florida and Harvard Law School, then with his brothers developed the dairy farm as the planned city of Miami Lakes. He has been in politics almost all his adult life. He was elected to the state House in 1966, at 30, and to the state Senate in 1970. In 1978 he ran for governor. After a come-from-behind win in the Democratic runoff, he won the general with a solid 56%. He was highly popular and easily won reelection in 1982. In 1986 he ran against Republican Senator Paula Hawkins, and after a spirited campaign won 55%–45%. His trademark campaign device since 1978 has been work days (invented by Senator Tom Harkin for his 1974 House race): Graham worked one day a week at some local job, from bagging groceries to construction, weighing and tagging Gulf sturgeon on the Apalachicola River on a hot August Monday or building an elementary school in Miami Lakes. He keeps it up still, once a month, and in December 2002 logged his 385th work day as a disc jockey at a Miami Haitian radio station. After

September 11 he worked on jobs related to homeland security, as an airport police officer in Jacksonville and a security officer at Port Everglades. He is a careful and methodical man. He wears only ties with an outline of Florida and makes percentage estimates of just about everything. He has a habit of recording every meeting and meal in notebooks he has kept—more than 2,500 now—and on one occasion, noted down a pilot's crash landing instruction. This was ridiculed when mentioned in *Time* in 2000; but as political scientist Larry Sabato pointed out, Thomas Jefferson did the same things.

On domestic issues, Graham's Senate voting record has been moderate. He has been a hardliner on crime legislation, supporting capital punishment, seeking federal reimbursement to states which jail criminal aliens. He serves on the Finance Committee and has called for means-testing Medicare and reducing cost-of-living increases in Social Security—not Democratic orthodoxy and risky in Florida. He called for Medicare to use managed care techniques, like negotiating contracts with competitive bidding, to hold down costs. He has fashioned several bills for prescription drugs for seniors. In June 2000 he sponsored the Senate Democrats' bill, with premiums of $40 a month and a deductible of $250 and full payment of costs over $4,000 for those below a certain income level; it was rejected on party lines. In May 2002 he and Zell Miller introduced a bill with a $25 per month premium, government payment of half of costs up to $4,000 and full payment of costs over that; it was costed out as $425 billion over eight years. At first it attracted no support from either Republicans or Democrats. Then, after the House passed its own different version in June 2002, he began refashioning it to pick up support. In June 2002 Senate Democrats, led by Tom Daschle and Edward Kennedy, embraced a version that eventually used Medicaid as a vehicle and was costed at $390 billion over 10 years. In July 2002, it came to the floor and was beaten 50–49. Since it exceeded the 2001 budget resolution, it required 60 votes for passage; no bill passed.

But by that point Graham was spending most of his time on intelligence matters. He became a member of the Intelligence Committee in 1993 and chairman in June 2001 when Democrats gained their majority in the Senate. Graham had generally taken hard line stands on foreign policy. He voted for the Gulf War resolution. A staunch opponent of Fidel Castro, Graham has strongly backed the embargo on Cuba. He wanted to stem the flow of Haitian refugees to Florida, and backed the dispatch of U.S. troops to Haiti. In late 2000 and early 2001 he argued that the Elian Gonzalez case should be settled in state court; he co-sponsored the bill to make the boy a U.S. citizen. He got a commitment from Bill Clinton not to seize Elian at night, which Clinton violated. On Intelligence he was generally supportive of CIA Director George Tenet, who had been a staffer on the Senate Intelligence Committee before he was appointed CIA Director by Bill Clinton in 1997. Graham developed a good working relationship with fellow Floridian Porter Goss (whom he had appointed to the Lee County Commission in 1982), chairman of the House Intelligence Committee and a former CIA agent who was also supportive of Tenet and had urged his continuation in office in the Bush administration. On the morning of September 11, 2001, Graham and Goss were having breakfast in the Capitol with General Mehmood Ahmed, the chief of Pakistani intelligence, asking him about Osama bin Laden when they were informed of the attacks on the World Trade Center towers. They quickly left the Capitol. Graham held a press conference that afternoon in front of Florida House on Capitol Hill and appeared on three cable news networks that evening; he compared the attacks to Pearl Harbor and said the United States could and should respond with force. The next day he called for an "intelligence czar," to gather information; the day after he said other attacks might be imminent. Working with Goss, he got authorization of an 8% increase in intelligence spending.

In February 2002 the joint inquiry into intelligence failures by the Senate and House Intelligence committees began; the two Floridians were co-chairmen. This was a rocky process. The first chief counsel was forced out in April 2002, by Richard Shelby, the ranking Republican on the Senate committee, who had called for Tenet's resignation. Graham publicly complained of difficulty in getting information from the FBI in May and of CIA "obstructionism" in October. As information came out, Graham concluded that there was information available to various parts of government that, if acted upon, could conceivably have prevented the September 11 attacks if only someone had been able to "connect the dots." By December, the joint inquiry issued a report that Graham said should be a guide to the presidential commission appointed to study the question.

On the Iraq war resolution in October 2002, Graham took a unique stand. He introduced an amendment authorizing action not only against Saddam Hussein's Iraq but also against Hezbollah and four other terrorist organizations. He argued that Hezbollah had even more agents in the United States than Al Qaeda and that they all stood ready to take terrorist action in this country should the United States move against Iraq, and that the U.S. military should "absolutely" attack Hezbollah camps in Syria, Lebanon and Iran. The amendment was rejected 88–10; the Bush administration argued against it on the grounds that it would detract from support to act against Iraq. Graham argued that this was the wrong priority. He voted against the Iraq war resolution, but did not argue, as some other Democrats did, that the United States needed to get United Nations approval first. Rather, he said, "Because I thought it was too limited, too weak and too timid. I take a different lesson out of what happened September 11. That is, as we look at foreign involvements, we need also to ask what are going to be the consequences of our actions there, here at home. Our best analysts say that the prospects of us accomplishing our objective in Iraq, which is regime change, increase to the level of 75% or more the chances of attacks inside the United States. That does not cause me to come to the conclusion we should cower from using force against Saddam Hussein. Rather, it causes me to feel we need to set the table before we start to use force—setting it in such a way as to reduce the vulnerability of the American people." In his view, the fight against Al Qaeda and Hezbollah took priority.

On a related issue, in November 2002 the Senate and House both passed Graham's bill on port security. His original measure would have authorized $3.2 billion in spending; this was pared down to $90 million for research and $33 million for training personnel, with a view toward requiring the 361 U.S. seaports to develop antiterrorism plans and bolster security, setting new standards to make shipping containers tamperproof and to screen cargo; the Senate, however, declined to levy a fee on shippers to pay for it. Graham drew on the experience of Florida, which passed a port security bill in July 2001 aimed at narcotics.

As a former governor, Graham has kept a close eye on Florida issues. He has worked hard on restoring the Everglades, starting with returning the Kissimmee River to its natural state and culminating in the November 2000 Everglades Act, which authorized $1.4 billion toward an eventual $7.8 billion for the dozens of projects to restore the natural flow of water through the Everglades. He sought to amend the welfare reauthorization to allow health care benefits for legal immigrants. And he sought unsuccessfully to prevent oil drilling in the Gulf of Mexico off Florida by allowing oil companies to exchange the value in their leases in the area for payments of fees owed the federal government for drilling elsewhere. In 2002 he intervened directly in state politics. In May 2000 Governor Jeb Bush had signed a law abolishing the Board of Regents for the 11 state universities and replacing it with a seven-member board responsible for education from kindergarten through graduate schools and vesting most power in governor-appointed boards at the 11 universities. To Graham, this was an "extreme politicization" of the state university system, which he believes needs beefing up if the state is to develop economically, and a reversal of the policy he established when as governor he vetoed abolition of the Board of Regents in 1980. The 11 state university presidents all supported the new policy, but Graham decided to put the issue on the ballot in November 2002. His Amendment 11 would establish a 14-member board of governors for the state university system, with terms overlapping the governor's term, with power to spend money, whatever the wishes of the legislature and governor and to establish state university policy, while leaving the 11 university boards in place. Amendment 11 did not get much publicity during the 2002 campaign, but Graham funded a campaign for it, and it passed 61%–39%, winning in all parts of the state. It was a victory for Graham and the Democrats against an otherwise all-triumphant Jeb Bush.

Graham's own prospects for reelection in 2004 looked good. But Graham, rotating off the Intelligence Committee but used to national attention as its chairman, said in December 2002, "I'm seriously thinking about options, including the option of running for president." Graham had already been considered for national office before, in 2000, when he was on Al Gore's short list for the vice presidency; others asked later whether he could have swung Florida safely into the Democratic column. He planned to announce on February 3, but instead had heart surgery that day; it was an operation routine these days, and he formally announced his candidacy on February 27. A Graham candidacy cast a pall over the candidacies of John Edwards, who would have another arguably moderate Southerner in the race, Joseph Lieberman, who would have serious competition for fundraising and votes in Florida's Gold Coast and the members of Congress—Lieberman, Richard Gephardt, John Kerry—who had voted for the Iraq war resolution.

The prospect of a Graham presidential candidacy left many Florida politicians hungry for his Senate seat—at least seven members of the congressional delegation were mentioned as possible aspirants. Republican Congressman Mark Foley was making contacts around the state and was obviously interested in running, as was former Congressman Bill McCollum, who lost to Senator Bill Nelson in 2000. Other Republicans mentioned as possible candidates were HUD Secretary Mel Martinez; former Lieutenant Governor Frank Brogan; state Chief Financial Officer Tom Gallagher, a frequent statewide candidate; and Crist. Andy Martin, a conservative radio broadcaster in West Palm Beach, said in February 2003 he would run. On the Democratic side, Congressman Alcee Hastings said he would run if Graham didn't; in April, Miami-Dade Mayor Alex Penelas filed with the FEC to begin raising funds. But Democrats' prospects if Graham were not the candidate do not look good. In December 2002 former Democratic state Chairman Charles Whitehead said, "If Senator Graham decides to retire, the Democratic party in the state of Florida is in a pitiful condition. I don't think we can get our act together in time to run for a statewide race if he doesn't stay." The bad news for Democrats is that Florida law prohibits a candidate's name from appearing on the ballot twice. The good news for them is that Florida's deadline is not until May 2004, so that if Graham runs for president and loses in the primary he can still run for reelection; it is inconceivable that another Democrat could beat him in the primary, and probably none would try. But if another Democratic nominee, desperate to win Florida, picks Graham as his vice presidential nominee, the Republican nominee would be the favorite to pick up what otherwise would be, if Graham runs again, a safe Democratic seat.

Junior Senator

Bill Nelson (D)

Elected 2000, seat up 2006, 1st term; b. Sept. 29, 1942. Miami; home, Melbourne; Yale U., B.A. 1965; U. of VA, J.D. 1968; Protestant; married (Grace Cavert).

Military Career: U.S. Army, 1968–70; U.S. Army Reserves, 1965–71.

Elected Office: FL House of Reps., 1972–78; U.S. House of Reps., 1978–90; FL Treasurer, Insurance Comm. & Fire Marshal, 1994–2000.

Professional Career: Practicing atty., 1970–79, 1991–94; Legis. asst., FL Gov. Reubin Askew, 1971; Crew member, Space Shuttle Columbia, 1986.

DC Office: 716 HSOB, 20510, 202-224-5274; Fax: 202-228-2183; Web site: billnelson.senate.gov.

State Offices: Ft. Lauderdale, 954-693-4851; Jacksonville, 904-346-4500; Miami, 305-536-5999; Orlando, 407-872-7161; Tallahassee, 850-942-8415; Tampa, 813-225-7040; W. Palm Beach, 561-514-0189.

Committees: *Armed Services:* Emerging Threats & Capabilities; Readiness & Management Support; Strategic Forces (RMM). *Budget. Commerce, Science & Transportation:* Aviation; Communications; Competition, Foreign Commerce & Infrastructure; Science, Technology & Space. *Foreign Relations:* African Affairs; International Operations & Terrorism (RMM); Western Hemisphere, Peace Corps, Narcotics Affairs.

Group Ratings

	ADA	ACLU	AFS	LCV	CON	ITIC	NTU	COC	ACU	NTLC	CHC
2002	70	60	75	59	92	88	24	70	30	40	—
2001	95	—	100	88	—	—	10	43	16	—	0

National Journal Ratings

	2001 LIB	—	2001 CONS		2002 LIB	—	2002 CONS
Economic	71%	—	27%		59%	—	36%
Social	70%	—	20%		56%	—	38%
Foreign	61%	—	27%		56%	—	42%

Key Votes of the 107th Congress

1. Approve Bush Tax Cuts	N	5. Confirm Ashcroft as AG	N	9. Bar Coop. with Intl. Court	Y
2. Expand Patients' Rights	Y	6. Bar Gays in the Boy Scouts	N	10. Trade Promotion Authority	Y
3. Campaign Finance Reform	Y	7. $ for Hate Crime Prosecution	Y	11. Authorize Force in Iraq	Y
4. Permit ANWR Development	N	8. Overseas Military Abortions	Y	12. Homeland Sec. Dept. Union	Y

Election Results

2000 general	Bill Nelson (D)	2,989,487	(51%)	($6,535,832)
	Bill McCollum (R)	2,705,348	(46%)	($8,664,112)
	Other	161,896	(3%)	
2000 primary	Bill Nelson (D)	692,147	(78%)	
	Newall J. Daughtrey (D)	105,650	(12%)	
	David B. Higginbottom (D)	95,492	(11%)	

Prior Winning Percentages: 1988 House (61%); 1986 House (73%); 1984 House (61%); 1982 House (71%); 1980 House (70%); 1978 House (61%)

Bill Nelson was elected Florida's junior senator in 2000, after nearly 30 years in politics. He grew up in Melbourne, on what is now the Space Coast, the son of a developer and real estate investor who died when he was 14; Nelson likes to recall that his great-grandfather arrived in Florida on boat as a stowaway. From his family home, Rock Point, he could see rockets blast off from what is now the Kennedy Space Center in the 1950s and 1960s. Nelson was active in student government and has always been something of a straight arrow; he doesn't drink, smoke or swear. He went to the University of Florida for two years, then graduated from Yale and the University of Virginia Law School. He served two years in the Army, then returned to Melbourne and briefly practiced law and worked on the staff of Governor Reubin Askew. In 1972, at 30, he was elected to the state House of Representatives.

In 1978, when Republican Congressmen Louis Frey retired, Nelson ran for Congress, from a seat that then included the Space Coast's Brevard County and most of Orlando's Orange County. His religious faith and traditional values, his indefatigable campaigning and folksy manner helped make him popular in an area that was trending heavily Republican. He won the seat 61%–39% and in five succeeding elections won between 61% and 73% of the vote, in a district that voted 29% for Michael Dukakis in 1988. In Congress, he was not entirely sure-footed. He got a seat on the Budget Committee in his freshman year, where he wobbled on the Reagan budget and tax cuts. But on the Science Committee he got his fellow Democrats to vote him rather than the more liberal George Brown chairman of the Space Subcommittee—obviously of prime importance to the district. Nelson not only boosted the space program in every possible way, he also rode the space shuttle *Columbia* himself, in early January 1986. Less than two weeks later the *Challenger* exploded. Nelson pressed successfully for funding of the space shuttle and space station, institutionalizing, he said, the manned space program for some time to come. After the *Columbia* was lost in February 2003, he called for continued manned space flight despite the risks. "Americans are explorers and adventurers by nature," he said. "We never want to give that up."

In 1989, with the support of leading Florida Democrats, Nelson set out to run against Republican Governor Bob Martinez, who was not faring well in polls. But in early 1990, some Democrats became antsy about Nelson's prospects, and persuaded Lawton Chiles, who had retired from the Senate in 1988 after three terms, to run. Nelson stayed in the race and attacked Chiles for land deals and his use of Prozac. Chiles charged that Nelson's votes on the Banking Committee may have worsened the savings and loan crisis. Chiles was always far ahead, and won the September primary 69%–31%. Nelson returned to his 77-acre oceanfront home in Melbourne, his political career seemingly over. But in 1994 he found an opening when state Insurance Commissioner Tom Gallagher, a Republican, ran for governor. Nelson was elected in November to an office whose full title was Treasurer, Insurance Commissioner and State Fire Marshal, and proceeded to make a highly publicized activist record. He helped to rebuild the homeowners insurance market, devastated since Hurricane Andrew in 1992. He ordered auto insurers to decrease rates for good drivers, fined big insurers for "churning" life insurance policies on the elderly, investigated insurers who targeted blacks with "junk burial" policies, cracked down on insurance fraud (staged auto accidents, padded medical bills) enough to allow rates to be lowered, and helped get European insurers to honor unpaid Holocaust-related claims.

Nelson was obviously setting himself up to run for higher statewide office, and his opening came in March 1999, when Republican Senator Connie Mack said he would not run for reelection in 2000. His retirement left a seat up for grabs in a state that, as election night viewers learned in November 2000, was very closely divided between the parties. And Republicans had a rough primary contest—always a problem in a state with a late September primary and an even later October runoff if no candidate gets a majority. The contestants were 20-year, Orlando-based Congressman Bill McCollum, one of the House's impeachment managers, and Tom Gallagher, then Florida Education Commissioner. Not until June 2000, after a meeting with Governor Jeb Bush and state Republican Chairman Al Cardenas, did Gallagher take himself out of the race, to run for Insurance Commissioner, the office he had relinquished to Nelson in 1994. A possible problem for Nelson was the independent candidacy of Willie Logan, a veteran African-American legislator whom Democrats had ousted as Speaker-designate in January 1998 on the grounds that he wasn't raising enough money. But Logan, who was getting 5% in many polls, ended up winning just 1.4% in November.

Washington observers considered the race a contest over the wisdom of impeachment but mostly it was a battle of competing styles. Nelson, running his fourth statewide race in 10 years, always led in polls. His easygoing, folksy manner contrasted favorably with McCollum's stiff, often aggressive manner. McCollum, with a long conservative record on abortion and gun control, attempted to modulate his positions, but only succeeded in antagonizing his base; his charge that Nelson was a "liberal" and a proponent of "class warfare" proved unconvincing.

This was the most expensive Senate race in Florida history, with the two candidates spending over $15 million between them; Nelson won 51%–46%. Nelson won 60%–37% in the Gold Coast, almost exactly the same margin as in the presidential race. In the I-4 corridor, which included McCollum's district and most of the district Nelson had represented in the House, Nelson won 51%–46%; superior name identification was not Nelson's only advantage. In the rest of the state Nelson lost by only 52%–46%, compared to the 55%–42% margin by which Al Gore lost there. Folksiness and Florida roots counted.

In the Senate, Nelson voted on the Budget Committee to limit the Bush tax cut, then voted against it on the floor in May 2001. After heavy publicity for a Boca Raton medical practice that charged seniors a $1,500 access fee, he sponsored in 2001 a bill to ban doctors from charging seniors more than Medicare pays. His amendment to delay the sale of land for offshore drilling in the Gulf of Mexico was defeated 67–33 in July 2001. He called for investigations of chemical and biological weapons tests conducted on Navy sailors in the Shipboard Hazard and Defense program in the 1960s and tests of wheat disease weapons at the now closed Boca Raton Army Air Field in the 1950s after the Veterans Affairs Department sent notices to some 4,000 affected veterans. In 2001 and 2002 he tried to amend the terrorism insurance bill to put limits on insurance rate increase and to guarantee continued coverage; in June 2002 he was defeated 70–24. He lamented that his experience as an insurance regulator was unappreciated. "Nobody understands anything about insurance here at the federal level, so there's a big education effort that has got to be made." Meanwhile, he was criticized in a lawsuit against viatical insurance companies which turned out to be Ponzi schemes run by Nelson campaign contributors; the office, now headed by a Republican, said that it had pursued the case as hard as it could.

On the Foreign Relations and Armed Services committees, Nelson traveled to Pakistan, Afghanistan and Central Asia in January 2002. He and Pat Roberts kept pushing to get Iraq to provide information about Scott Speicher, the Navy pilot shot down in 1991 who was classified as Missing In Action; Speicher's family lives in Orange Park, near Jacksonville. With other Florida politicians, he protested the detention of 200 Haitians at the Turner Guilford Knight Stockade near Miami and got INS Commissioner Jim Ziglar to visit. "We cannot have a double standard as a policy that treats Haitians one way and other groups another way."

In 2001 Nelson was named vice-chairman of the Democratic Senatorial Campaign Committee. He was widely regarded as the likely successor to Chairman Patty Murray, but in September 2002 said he didn't want the job. The strongest opponent he could face in 2006 is probably Jeb Bush, who will be ineligible to run for a third term as governor. It is not clear that Bush wants the job, but Florida has plenty of other ambitious Republican politicians.

FIRST DISTRICT

Rep. Jeff Miller (R)

Elected Oct. 2001, 1st term; b. June 27, 1959, St. Petersburg; home, Chumuckla; U. of FL, B.A. 1984; Methodist; married (Vicki).

Elected Office: FL House of Reps., 1998–01.

Professional Career: Real estate broker, Henry Co. homes; Owner, Jeff Miller Real Estate; deputy sheriff.

DC Office: 331 CHOB 20515, 202-225-4136; Fax: 202-225-3414; Web site: www.house.gov/jeffmiller.

District Offices: Ft. Walton Beach, 850-664-1266; Pensacola, 850-479-1183.

Committees: *Armed Services* (22d of 33 R): Readiness; Terrorism, Unconventional Threats & Capabilities. *Veterans' Affairs* (11th of 17 R): Benefits; Health.

Group Ratings (Only Served Partial Term)

	ADA	ACLU	AFS	LCV	CON	ITIC	NTU	COC	ACU	NTLC	CHC
2002	0	12	0	25	—	83	66	84	100	100	100
2001	—	—	0	0	—	—	—	78	—	—	—

National Journal Ratings (Only Served Partial Term)

	2001 LIB — 2001 CONS		2002 LIB — 2002 CONS	
Economic	* — *		21% — 73%	
Social	* — *		0% — 75%	
Foreign	* — *		0% — 85%	

Key Votes of the 107th Congress (Only Served Partial Term)

1. Approve Bush Tax Cuts	*	5. Faith-Based Charities	*	9. Trade Promotion Authority	Y
2. Limit Patients' Bill of Rights	*	6. Bar Gays in the Boy Scouts	*	10. Bar Funds for Intl. Court	Y
3. Campaign Finance Reform	N	7. Ban Partial-Birth Abortion	Y	11. Authorize Force in Iraq	Y
4. Ban ANWR Development	*	8. Arm Commercial Pilots	Y	12. Deny Home. Sec. Dept. Union	Y

Election Results

2002 general	Jeff Miller (R)	152,635	(75%)	($956,353)
	Bert Oram (D)	51,972	(25%)	($13,951)
2002 primary	Jeff Miller (R)	41,990	(64%)	
	Michael Francisco (R)	23,164	(36%)	
2001 special	Jeff Miller (R)	53,247	(66%)	($624,799)
	Steve Briese (D)	22,695	(28%)	($57,925)
	John Ralls Jr. (NPA)	5,115	(6%)	

The People		Race/Ethnic Origin	Ancestry	
Area size:	5,241 sq. mi.	78.0% White	USA: 10.7%	German: 8.8%
Urban population:	77.5%	14.0% Black	Irish: 8.5%	
Rural population:	22.5%	1.9% Asian	**2000 Presidential Vote**	
Pop. 2000:	639,295	0.9% Native Am.	Bush (R)...............173,896	(69%)
Median income:	$36,738	0.1% Hawaiian	Gore (D)................78,469	(31%)
Poverty status:	13.1%	2.0% Two + races	**Cook Partisan Voting Index:** R + 19	
Military veterans:	21.7%	0.2% Other		
		3.0% Hispanic Origin		

Occupation   Blue collar: 24.4%   White collar: 57.1%   Gray collar: 18.6%

The "Redneck Riviera" is the affectionate local name for the Gulf Coast beaches of Florida's Panhandle, stretching from Pensacola east to Destin. This has been military country ever since John Quincy Adams persuaded Spain to sell Florida to the U.S. in 1819 to get the port of Pensacola. In October 1861, the Union defeated the Confederates in a battle to control Santa Rosa Island, the outermost spit of land protecting Pensacola Bay. A quarter century later, the site of that clash, Fort Pickens, became Apache warrior Geronimo's prison. In the 20th century, the Pensacola Naval Air Station was turned into the nation's first naval aviation training base, giving birth to carrier aviation itself. Today, almost 14,000 people are employed at Eglin Air Force Base, which spreads over three counties and, with approximately 100,000 square miles of airspace stretching over the Gulf of Mexico to the Florida Keys, is considered the largest air base in the free world. Eglin developed the "bunker-buster" BLU-82 bomb that would later be used in Afghanistan and in March 2003, this was the test site for the largest conventional bomb in the U.S. arsenal, the 21,000 pound ordnance referred to as the "Mother of All Bombs." Eglin is also home to the minimum-security federal prison camp that is the original "Club Fed;" it was there that former Maryland Governor Marvin Mandel, Watergate burglar E. Howard Hunt and Florida Congressman Richard Kelly served time.

The western panhandle, closer to Memphis than to Miami, is culturally part of Dixie. Until recently, it was economically backward and heavily dependent on the military. As the South has become more prosperous, however, the shore has attracted vacationing and retiring Southerners to its vast, fine-grained white sand beaches, perhaps the finest in the Lower 48, and its pleasant inlet-filled bays; it also has become a leading spring break destination for college students. The region has long been culturally and economically conservative, with a strong pro-military bent.

The 1st Congressional District is so far west that it's in the Central time zone. Pensacola's Escambia County, where about half the district's people live, is the state's westernmost county. The time zone issue became a sore point in 2000, when TV networks announced that Florida's polls had closed at 7 p.m. Eastern time, though they were still open in the Panhandle, and then declared Al Gore the winner of Florida's electoral votes 10 minutes before the Panhandle's polls had closed; without that misinformation, a few thousand votes might have been cast for George W. Bush here and made the whole Florida controversy unnecessary. The district's shoreline runs from Pensacola, adjoining the Alabama border, through Fort Walton Beach and all the way to the west side of Destin; from there, a string of more affluent beach towns is in the 2d District. Inland, the 1st stretches further east, taking in rural Walton, Holmes and Washington Counties. The population here grew almost 20% during the 1990s, with younger people, not just military retirees, moving in and shifting attention towards education and quality-of-life issues. With the highest percentage of military veterans of any district in the nation, the 1st District is strongly Republican. The 1st voted 69%–31% for George W. Bush in 2000; it was one of only two districts in Florida carried by the last two Republican Senate candidates, Charlie Crist in 1998 and Bill McCollum in 2000.

The congressman from the 1st District is Jeff Miller, a Republican who won a special election in October 2001. The son of a pioneering farm family that settled in central Florida in the mid-1800s, Miller grew up in Levy County, where his parents raised cattle. He graduated from the University of Florida and became an aide to the state's long-time agriculture commissioner, Democrat Doyle Conner. He moved in 1988 to Santa Rosa County, his wife's family's home and began to sell real estate. In 1998, a year after he switched to the Republican Party, he ran his first campaign, challenging a Republican incumbent state representative who had received some negative press after an altercation with a state trooper. Miller won 53%–47% out of only 6,000 votes cast (a lot of people here still are registered Democrats though they almost always vote Republican). He chaired the state House Utilities and Telecommunications Committee.

The 1st District House seat came open when incumbent Joe Scarborough, one of the most outspoken members of the Republican Class of 1994 and a leader of the unsuccessful coup attempt against Speaker Newt Gingrich, announced in May 2001 that he would resign in September. Miller was one of the first candidates to declare and he quickly became the favorite of national party leaders. There was only a brief campaign before the July 24 primary; the candidates claimed to be ardent environmentalists, an unusual twist in a Republican primary. Miller's best-known opponent was state Representative Randy Knepper, chief of staff to the district's former Democratic Congressman Earl Hutto, who retired in 1994. On the weekend before the primary, Scarborough endorsed Miller as "a strong voice for northwest Florida." In the six-candidate contest, Miller got 54% to only 15% for Knepper, just behind the 16% for businessman Michael Francisco, a decorated combat pilot. National Democrats made no perceptible effort to win this seat, and in the October general election, Miller won by 66%–28% over a former Republican. Miller's swearing in was delayed because the anthrax scare had closed the Capitol.

In the House, Miller has compiled a conservative record. In contrast to the vocal Scarborough, he gained a reputation for being soft-spoken and a good listener. He won seats on the Armed Services and Veterans' Affairs committees, obvious assignments for this district. He worked quickly to establish a reputation for good constituent service and for focusing on the war against terrorism. He joined a delegation of members to Afghanistan to visit U.S. troops, and accompanied Bush cabinet officials to visit military and veterans' facilities in northwest Florida. Miller claimed credit for winning approval of $30 million for the air training system at the Pensacola Naval Air Station.

In the 2002 primary, Miller faced a rematch with special primary election runner-up Francisco, who criticized his lack of military experience. Miller won 64%–36%. In the general election, he won 75%–25%.

SECOND DISTRICT

Rep. Allen Boyd (D)

Elected 1996, 4th term; b. June 6, 1945, Valdosta, GA; home, Monticello; N. FL Jr. Col., A.A. 1966, FL St. U., B.S. 1969; Methodist; married (Cissy).

Military Career: Army 1969–71 (Vietnam).

Elected Office: FL House of Reps., 1989–96.

Professional Career: Farmer.

DC Office: 107 CHOB 20515, 202-225-5235; Fax: 202-225-5615; Web site: www.house.gov/boyd.

District Offices: Panama City, 850-785-0812; Tallahassee, 850-561-3979.

Committees: *Appropriations* (25th of 29 D): Agriculture, Rural Development, & FDA; Military Construction.

Group Ratings

	ADA	ACLU	AFS	LCV	CON	ITIC	NTU	COC	ACU	NTLC	CHC
2002	70	47	78	38	51	50	16	58	40	17	33
2001	70	—	89	71	—	—	20	52	32	—	—

National Journal Ratings

	2001 LIB — 2001 CONS		2002 LIB — 2002 CONS	
Economic	57%	— 44%	54%	— 45%
Social	56%	— 44%	54%	— 45%
Foreign	54%	— 46%	49%	— 50%

Key Votes of the 107th Congress

1. Approve Bush Tax Cuts	*	5. Faith-Based Charities	N	9. Trade Promotion Authority	N
2. Limit Patients' Bill of Rights	N	6. Bar Gays in the Boy Scouts	Y	10. Bar Funds for Intl. Court	Y
3. Campaign Finance Reform	Y	7. Ban Partial-Birth Abortion	Y	11. Authorize Force in Iraq	Y
4. Ban ANWR Development	N	8. Arm Commercial Pilots	Y	12. Deny Home. Sec. Dept. Union	Y

Election Results

2002 general	Allen Boyd (D)	152,164	(67%)	($588,785)
	Tom McGurk (R)	75,275	(33%)	($35,916)
2002 primary	Allen Boyd (D)	unopposed		
2000 general	Allen Boyd (D)	185,579	(72%)	($378,202)
	Doug Dodd (R)	71,754	(28%)	($16,227)

Prior Winning Percentages: 1998 (100%); 1996 (59%)

The People		Race/Ethnic Origin	Ancestry	
Area size:	11,141 sq. mi.	71.5% White	USA: 10.3%	English: 8.0%
Urban population:	62.1%	22.1% Black	Irish: 7.9%	
Rural population:	37.9%	1.2% Asian	**2000 Presidential Vote**	
Pop. 2000:	639,295	0.5% Native Am.	Bush (R)	132,275 (53%)
Median income:	$34,718	0.0% Hawaiian	Gore (D)	118,758 (47%)
Poverty status:	16.5%	1.3% Two+ races	**Cook Partisan Voting Index:** R + 3	
Military veterans:	15.3%	0.1% Other		
		3.3% Hispanic Origin		

Occupation	Blue collar: 19.3%	White collar: 61.7%	Gray collar: 19.1%

For most of the 36 days from November 7 to December 12, 2000, Tallahassee was the center of the political universe. Reporters covering the aftermath of Election Night 2000 complained about it, especially when they were evicted from their motels on the weekend of the Florida State-University of Florida football game. Many wondered why this small city, in the middle of swampy lowlands and far from Florida's booming cities and beachfronts, should be the capital of the nation's fourth-largest state. The answer is that it was chosen back when Florida's modest population lived mostly along the state's northern tier, placing Tallahassee, more or less, at the state's center of gravity. Ralph Waldo Emerson, visiting Tallahassee in the 19th century, called it a "grotesque place, rapidly settled by public officers, land speculators and desperadoes." Today the countryside around Tallahassee is distinctly Dixie: Cotton fields, soft pine stands, catfish farms, large families, small towns with big churches. Until recently, Tallahassee was little more than a Spanish-mossed county seat with a handsome Creole capitol, built in 1845 and preserved opposite its 1977 skyscraper replacement, and a pair of state universities. In the past 20 years, however, Tallahassee has spread out and become a middling-sized city, with a tight-knit and sometimes fractious political and legal elite, bringing a taste of newly urbanized Florida to the state's north. Tallahassee has not yet attained the critical mass of Sacramento, Austin, or Albany, but perhaps it is on its way as the state legislature inches closer to professionalized status.

The 2d Congressional District is centered on Tallahassee, but it extends along the Gulf coast west to Destin and east to the Suwanee River, which empties into the Gulf in the only part of Florida where the beach is still undeveloped. Inland, the 2d runs north to the Alabama and Georgia borders, and far enough east to be within an hour's drive of downtown Jacksonville. Historically, this was Democratic country, Jeffersonian and segregationist. Today, it is still mostly Democratic, though for different reasons: More than one in three Tallahassee area jobs are in city and state government, three times the statewide level. The district, 22% black, includes Gadsden County, the state's only black-majority county. But growth is spreading south into Wakulla County, which was third among Florida in percentage growth in the 1990s; the beach areas near Destin have attracted affluent families to "new urbanist" communities like Seaside and Rosemary Beach (Seaside is where *The Truman Show* was filmed). The 2d district's population grew by 22% in the 1990s, though there was little growth in many rural areas. This is the part of Florida with the highest percentage of native Floridians.

With state government, two universities and many public employee union members, Tallahassee and Leon County voted solidly for Bill Clinton and Al Gore; the Florida law that establishes Leon County as the venue for election cases clearly favors Democrats. Beyond Leon County, the vote is less predictable. Gadsden County, the state's only black-majority county, is heavily Democratic; the Gulf beach areas tend to be Republican. In 2000, the 2d voted 53%–47% for George W. Bush but two years later, the 2d gave a hefty margin to Democrat Bill McBride over Governor Jeb Bush, who is disliked by most public employee unions.

The congressman from the 2d District is Allen Boyd, a Democrat elected in 1996. A lifelong farmer, Boyd grew up in Monticello in Jefferson County just east of Tallahassee. He served in Vietnam and graduated from Florida State. His political career began when he won a special election to the state House in 1989. There he was majority whip, chairman of two committees and helped form the Conservative Democratic Caucus. Boyd decided to run for the House when incumbent Pete Peterson, a moderate Democrat and Vietnam prisoner-of-war, retired after three terms, saying he believed in term limits. In a high-turnout Democratic primary, Boyd won 48% of the vote to 26% for Leon County Commissioner Anita Davis and 25% for retired Gulf County Judge David Taunton. Boyd easily won the runoff 64%–36%. In the general, Boyd campaigned with Blue Dog conservative Democrats and outspent the Republican by 2–1 to win a solid 59%–40% victory.

In the House, Boyd works as a behind the scenes consensus builder; he lobbied for the 1997 balanced budget agreement and for a campaign finance bill. With one of the House's most centrist voting records, he called himself a "moderate Democrat with a social conscience." In 1998 he was head of the Blue Dogs' PAC and worked with House Democrats' campaign committee to elect more Blue Dogs. He backed a bill to allow private timber harvesters to enter national forests and remove trees damaged in fires or floods and later backed a bill for increased payments for schools and roads in counties with national forests. He was unperturbed when animal rights advocates picketed the Annual Boyd Family Dove Hunt in 1998, and was the only Florida Democrat to vote for an amendment that helped kill the 1999 gun control bill. He criticized the Environmental Protection Agency for "unrealistic" enforcement of pesticide rules for products long used by farmers, and sought a statutory change requiring more detailed justification by EPA. He voted to sustain Clinton's vetoes of the marriage-penalty and estate-tax repeals, and favored PNTR with China. In 1999 he got a seat on Appropriations. After the 2000 election, he was a supporter of the ill-fated centrist coalition in the House. In 2001, he opposed the Bush tax cut but voted to repeal the Clinton administration's ergonomics regulation. Later, he opposed trade promotion authority, but he voted to authorize the use of force in Iraq. With Republican John Peterson of Pennsylvania, Boyd chairs the Rural Caucus in the 108th Congress.

Boyd has been easily re-elected. The Republican redistricting plan in 2002 made the district a bit less Democratic by adding the beach area to the west; Republicans hoped that state Comptroller Bob Milligan would run, but he didn't. Boyd won 67%–33% in 2002, despite losing the two westernmost counties. In 2003, Boyd considered running for the Senate, in the event Bob Graham did not run for reelection. Republican state Representative Bev Kilmer announced in April she would run in the 2d whether or not Boyd runs for the Senate.

THIRD DISTRICT

Rep. Corrine Brown (D)

Elected 1992, 6th term; b. Nov. 11, 1946, Jacksonville; home, Jacksonville; FL A&M, B.S. 1969, M.S., 1971; Baptist; single.

Elected Office: FL House of Reps., 1982–92.

Professional Career: Prof., FL Commun. Col., 1977–82, Guidance Counselor, 1982–92.

DC Office: 2444 RHOB 20515, 202-225-0123; Fax: 202-225-2256; Web site: www.house.gov/corrinebrown.

District Offices: Jacksonville, 904-354-1652; Orlando, 407-872-0656.

Committees: *Transportation & Infrastructure* (9th of 34 D): Aviation; Coast Guard & Maritime Transportation; Railroads (RMM). *Veterans' Affairs* (4th of 14 D): Benefits; Health.

Group Ratings

	ADA	ACLU	AFS	LCV	CON	ITIC	NTU	COC	ACU	NTLC	CHC
2002	95	80	100	63	43	38	19	42	0	3	0
2001	95	—	100	79	—	—	11	43	8	—	—

National Journal Ratings

	2001 LIB — 2001 CONS		2002 LIB — 2002 CONS	
Economic	83%	— 15%	76%	— 23%
Social	74%	— 23%	84%	— 8%
Foreign	85%	— 15%	83%	— 17%

Key Votes of the 107th Congress

1. Approve Bush Tax Cuts	N	5. Faith-Based Charities	N	9. Trade Promotion Authority	N
2. Limit Patients' Bill of Rights	N	6. Bar Gays in the Boy Scouts	N	10. Bar Funds for Intl. Court	N
3. Campaign Finance Reform	Y	7. Ban Partial-Birth Abortion	N	11. Authorize Force in Iraq	N
4. Ban ANWR Development	Y	8. Arm Commercial Pilots	N	12. Deny Home. Sec. Dept. Union	N

Election Results

2002 general	Corrine Brown (D)	88,462	(59%)	($438,810)
	Jennifer Carroll (R)	60,747	(41%)	($229,103)
2002 primary	Corrine Brown (D)	unopposed		
2000 general	Corrine Brown (D)	102,143	(58%)	($479,828)
	Jennifer Carroll (R)	75,228	(42%)	($1,035,709)

Prior Winning Percentages: 1998 (55%); 1996 (61%); 1994 (58%); 1992 (59%)

The People		Race/Ethnic Origin	Ancestry	
Area size:	2,097 sq. mi.	38.4% White	USA: 6.4%	German: 5.2%
Urban population:	89.7%	49.3% Black	Irish: 4.9%	
Rural population:	10.3%	1.6% Asian	**2000 Presidential Vote**	
Pop. 2000:	639,295	0.3% Native Am.	Gore (D)	110,501 (65%)
Median income:	$29,785	0.0% Hawaiian	Bush (R)	59,144 (35%)
Poverty status:	21.5%	2.1% Two+ races	**Cook Partisan Voting Index:** D +15	
Military veterans:	14.2%	0.2% Other		
		8.0% Hispanic Origin		

Occupation	Blue collar: 26.6%	White collar: 51.8%	Gray collar: 21.6%

Before the Civil War, most of Florida was still an uncharted watery wilderness, festooned with exotic greenery, inhabited by unusual animals: a part of the United States so far out of the experience of most Americans as to seem foreign. As late as 1940, Florida had the smallest population of any southern state, and most of the people here lived in classic Dixie rural counties with small courthouse towns, where civic affairs were run by the richest white men; blacks lived in poorly constructed, unpainted shotgun shacks propped up on blocks, with little money and no vote. This was a land of swamps, lakes and orange groves, of Marjorie Kinnan Rawlings's Cross Creek, where she wrote the great children's classic *The Yearling*, and the Florida of the broad St. Johns River, one of the few North American rivers that flows (if only sluggishly) north, through orange grove country to the port of Jacksonville, which was for many years Florida's largest city.

The 3d Congressional District occupies much of this swampy terrain. The district was created in 1992 to be north Florida's black majority seat; it follows the St. Johns River upstream from center city Jacksonville to downtown Orlando, reaching out to pluck additional minority voters from Sanford, where Amtrak's Auto Train unloads its Florida-bound travelers, and Gainesville, home of the University of Florida. The district's boundaries were altered in 1996 after a court rejected the lines and again in the 2002 redistricting. Along the way, the district takes in smaller black settlements, such as lettuce-producing Zellwood, and Eatonville, home of author Zora Neale Hurston. In time, this relatively unpopulated, lake-filled region may see itself become Florida's next development frontier but for now, the 3d District is growing more slowly than the rest of the state. The district is 49% black—the third-highest percentage of any Florida district—and 8% Hispanic. It is solidly Democratic; Republicans seldom get more than one-third of the vote. The district borders five Republican-held districts, each of which was designed to shift as many Democrats as possible to the 3d to strengthen Republicans elsewhere.

The congresswoman from the 3d District is Corrine Brown, a Democrat elected in 1992. She grew up in Jacksonville, taught at the community college, was a guidance counselor and in 1982 was elected to the Florida House. With her Jacksonville base, she was the obvious favorite in 1992. In the Democratic primary, she faced white talk radio host Andy Johnson, who called himself "the blackest candidate in the race." Brown led 43%–31% in the primary and won 64%–36% in the runoff; she won the general 59%–41%. Johnson brought the lawsuit challenging the district boundaries, but was not pleased with the result.

Brown has compiled a liberal record on most issues, though in this district where many voters work at military bases she tends to support high defense; she argues that the military can be a source of opportunity. On the Veterans Committee she sought additional veterans cemeteries for Florida, which is the home to more veterans than any other state except California. She fought to preserve the Medicaid payments for disproportionate share hospitals (those with lots of low-income patients). She reluctantly signed the discharge petition for the Shays-Meehan campaign reform bill, after its sponsors agreed to allow more spending for voter education. On the Coast Guard and Maritime Transportation Subcommittee, she was active on legislation to strengthen security at the ports. In 2003, she became ranking member on the Railroads Subcommittee.

Brown has had spirited campaign opposition, which is unusual for Florida incumbents. Her most difficult contest came in 1998, with her problems largely of her own making. That April the *St. Petersburg Times* reported that she received $10,000 from Baptist minister Henry Lyons, who had since been indicted on theft charges; she said the money was for his help in a rally protesting the redistricting case. In June the same paper reported that her daughter, attorney and EPA employee Shantrel Brown, was given a $50,000 Lexus by agents of African millionaire Foutanga Sissoko; he had been imprisoned in Miami on federal charges of paying an illegal gratuity to a Customs Service officer, and Brown worked furiously to get him released, lobbying Attorney General Janet Reno to have him deported to Africa to continue his humanitarian work. A third charge was that she kept a jazz singer on her payroll as a "congressional outreach specialist," who occasionally visited the district from her New York City home. Brown reacted with fury: she filed a criminal contempt charge against the *Times* reporters with the Capitol Police, claiming they "accosted" her and their questions made her cry. A federal prosecutor said there was not enough to indict them for impeding a member of Congress. These charges attracted national Republican attention. They had a presentable candidate: Bill Randall, also black, a former General Motors manager who had become a minister and worked as a sales manager for a cable company; he opposed abortion, favored local control of schools and school vouchers. As Randall admitted, "I think this race has gotten on the radar screen based on what this candidate has done to herself. It's not so much that I'm all that great a candidate or anything." The charges hurt Brown: she won by only 55%–45%. Randall made inroads among white Democrats and got 77% in heavily Republican Clay County.

But the ramifications were not finished. The Congressional Accountability Project requested that the House ethics committee investigate the $10,000 contribution and the Lexus gift, which her daughter later sold and gave the proceeds to charity. In September 2000 the committee concluded that Brown "demonstrated, at the least, poor judgment and created substantial concerns regarding both the appearance of impropriety and the reputation of the House," but dropped the case because it was unable to question key witnesses, including Sissoko. She faced a vigorous reelection challenge from Republican Jennifer Carroll, a retired Navy officer with 20 years of service, who criticized Brown's lack of vision and her inability to work with people. Brown, who called Carroll "a zero" and "a Republican puppet," was outspent by Carroll, who is also black. But Brown had help from an October campaign rally with Bill Clinton and a strong grass-roots organization. Brown won 58%–42%. During the presidential recount, Brown was insistent that voting irregularities discriminated against black voters.

After redistricting, Brown joined other Democrats in filing a lawsuit contending that the plan was racially biased; the case was dismissed. In 2002 Carroll again challenged her. House Republicans encouraged her because the retirement of J.C. Watts would leave them with no black members. But local Republicans were not enthusiastic about Carroll's candidacy in this heavily Democratic district. "I would rather not give Corrine Brown an excuse to go through another massive voter turnout exercise, in which she is very talented," Duval County Republican chairman Tom Slade told *The Jacksonville Free Press*. Carroll raised only $180,000, two-tenths of what she raised in 2000: a message that her party has given up on this seat. Brown won 59%–41%, again with huge leads in the Jacksonville and Orlando; Carroll led in four counties with small turnout. Barring unexpected problems, Brown appears secure until the next redistricting.

FOURTH DISTRICT

Rep. Ander Crenshaw (R)

Elected 2000, 2d term; b. Sept. 1, 1944, Jacksonville; home, Jacksonville; U. of GA, B.A. 1966, U. of FL, J.D. 1969; Episcopalian; married (Kitty).

Elected Office: FL House of Reps., 1972–78; FL Senate 1986–93.

Professional Career: Investment banker, 1980–2000.

DC Office: 127 CHOB 20515, 202-225-2501; Fax: 202-225-2504; Web site: www.house.gov/crenshaw.

District Offices: Jacksonville, 904-598-0481; Lake City, 386-365-3316.

Committees: *Appropriations* (36th of 36 R): Foreign Operations & Export Financing; Interior; Military Construction. *Budget* (11th of 24 R).

Group Ratings

	ADA	ACLU	AFS	LCV	CON	ITIC	NTU	COC	ACU	NTLC	CHC
2002	0	7	0	0	8	100	55	100	96	83	100
2001	0	—	0	7	—	—	62	100	92	—	—

National Journal Ratings

	2001 LIB	—	2001 CONS		2002 LIB	—	2002 CONS
Economic	22%	—	74%		0%	—	91%
Social	0%	—	81%		0%	—	75%
Foreign	21%	—	74%		0%	—	85%

Key Votes of the 107th Congress

1. Approve Bush Tax Cuts	Y	5. Faith-Based Charities	Y	9. Trade Promotion Authority	Y
2. Limit Patients' Bill of Rights	Y	6. Bar Gays in the Boy Scouts	Y	10. Bar Funds for Intl. Court	Y
3. Campaign Finance Reform	N	7. Ban Partial-Birth Abortion	Y	11. Authorize Force in Iraq	Y
4. Ban ANWR Development	N	8. Arm Commercial Pilots	Y	12. Deny Home. Sec. Dept. Union	Y

Election Results

2002 general	Ander Crenshaw (R)	unopposed		($311,183)
2002 primary	Ander Crenshaw (R)	39,303	(88%)	
	Deborah Katz Pueschel (R)	5,409	(12%)	
2000 general	Ander Crenshaw (R)	203,090	(67%)	($863,422)
	Tom Sullivan (D)	94,587	(31%)	($143,241)
	Other	5,609	(2%)	

The People		Race/Ethnic Origin	Ancestry	
Area size:	4,368 sq. mi.	77.8% White	USA: 9.7%	German: 9.0%
Urban population:	78.2%	13.5% Black	Irish: 8.7%	
Rural population:	21.8%	2.4% Asian	**2000 Presidential Vote**	
Pop. 2000:	639,295	0.3% Native Am.	Bush (R)	154,615 (66%)
Median income:	$43,947	0.1% Hawaiian	Gore (D)	80,227 (34%)
Poverty status:	9.1%	1.5% Two+ races	**Cook Partisan Voting Index:** R +16	
Military veterans:	17.1%	0.1% Other		
		4.2% Hispanic Origin		

Occupation Blue collar: 20.6% White collar: 64.8% Gray collar: 14.7%

With a metropolitan area of more than 1 million people, Jacksonville is beginning to overcome its reputation as Florida's overlooked city. Not long ago, Jacksonville was considered a backwater, dominated by insurance and smelly paper mills. It now boasts a National Football League franchise, the Jaguars; an agreement to host the 2005 Super Bowl; bold new skyscrapers looming above a wide river; and a shopping mall that overshadows gridded streets and tiny shotgun houses. The wide freeways sidestep primeval wetlands on their way to huge beachfront subdivisions. With the Mayport Naval Station and the Naval Air Station Jacksonville has a significant military-employment base (they are two of the top three metro area employers), while shrewd marketing has lured big-name private sector companies; and Jacksonville has the headquarters of Winn-Dixie supermarkets and railway giant CSX and has big operations of Publix supermarkets, UPS and Bank of America. The metro area grew 21% in the 1990s; with bipartisan support, Jacksonville voters agreed in 2000 to a half-penny sales tax increase to finance growth management.

The 4th Congressional District includes much of Jacksonville (minus the mostly black neighborhoods, which are in the 3d District) as well as a northern tier of counties along the Georgia border that runs all the way west to Tallahassee. This northern tier, added in the 2002 redistricting, is sleepy territory punctuated by small towns like White Springs, Lake City, and Raiford (home to a big state prison); it is criss-crossed by Interstates 10 and 75. Some 70% of the population is in Jacksonville and Nassau County, just to the north. The boosterish Jacksonville civic culture and significant military presence make the 4th a pro-business, pro-military and pro-Republican district. In 2000 George W. Bush won 66% of the vote here, his highest percentage in any Florida district.

The congressman from the 4th District is Ander Crenshaw, a Republican elected in 2000. He grew up in Jacksonville and attended the University of Georgia on a basketball scholarship, then graduated from the University of Florida law school. His wife's father, Claude Kirk, was elected governor, the first Republican since Reconstruction, in 1966, then defeated in 1970. Crenshaw was elected to the state House in 1972 and served for six years until he ran unsuccessfully for secretary of state, and left to become an investment banker. In 1980 he ran for the Senate and finished third of six in the 1980 Republican primary won by Paula Hawkins. From 1986 until 1993 he served in the state Senate, and in 1992 became the first Republican state Senate president in 118 years; in that post he helped to kill a tax increase proposed by Governor Lawton Chiles. He ran for governor in 1994 but ran fourth in the primary, far behind Jeb Bush, who narrowly lost to Chiles in November. Crenshaw's opportunity to run for the House came when Republican Tillie Fowler announced in January 2000 that she would honor her promise to serve only four terms. Crenshaw was promptly endorsed by local Republican leaders, which discouraged several other potential candidates. His campaign focused on lowering taxes and a "government that does more for less." He was opposed in the primary by a 31-year-old newcomer who moved to the district only four months before he declared his candidacy and had served as an intern in Ronald Reagan's post-presidential office in California. Crenshaw won the primary 70%–30% and the general election 67%–31%.

In the House, Crenshaw is a reliable conservative. He displayed his political savvy by becoming freshman class liaison to the Republican leadership, which admitted him to weekly leadership meetings. In his second term he won a seat on Appropriations. His top priorities were the district's large military and veterans' facilities. He claimed credit for $2 million for enhanced security at Mayport and $4 million more for new helicopter equipment at the base. He called for a new veterans' cemetery in north Florida and expanded disability coverage for Gulf War veterans. Crenshaw proposed a new "Project Exile" grant program to direct money to states that get tough on people who use guns to commit crimes.

Crenshaw was reelected without general election opposition in 2002. He obviously has a safe seat, but he may be tempted to run for governor or against Senator Bill Nelson in 2006.

FIFTH DISTRICT

Rep. Ginny Brown-Waite (R)

Elected 2002, 1st term; b. Oct. 5, 1943, Albany, NY; home, Brooksville; S.U.N.Y. Albany, B.S. 1976, Russell Sage Col., M.S. 1984; Catholic; married (Harvey).

Elected Office: Hernando Cnty. Commissioner, 1990–92; FL Senate, 1992–2002.

Professional Career: Small business owner; Legis. Dir., NY Senate, 1972–90.

DC Office: 1516 LHOB 20515, 202-225-1002; Web site: www.house.gov/brown-waite.

District Offices: Brooksville, 352-799-8354; Dade City, 352-567-6707.

Committees: *Budget* (24th of 24 R). *Financial Services* (34th of 37 R): Capital Markets, Insurance & Government Sponsored Enterprises; Financial Institutions & Consumer Credit; Oversight & Investigations. *Veterans' Affairs* (15th of 17 R): Benefits; Health.

Group Ratings and Key Votes: Newly Elected

Election Results

2002 general	Ginny Brown-Waite (R)	121,998	(48%)	($922,944)
	Karen Thurman (D)	117,758	(46%)	($1,907,181)
	Other	14,915	(6%)	
2002 primary	Ginny Brown-Waite (R)	31,242	(58%)	
	Don Gessner (R)	23,008	(42%)	
2000 general	Karen Thurman (D)	180,338	(64%)	($643,355)
	Pete Enwall (R)	100,244	(36%)	($274,771)

The People		Race/Ethnic Origin	Ancestry	
Area size:	4,801 sq. mi.	87.7% White	German: 13.0%	Irish: 10.5%
Urban population:	64.5%	4.5% Black	English: 10.1%	
Rural population:	35.5%	0.8% Asian	**2000 Presidential Vote**	
Pop. 2000:	639,295	0.3% Native Am.	Bush (R) 147,231	(54%)
Median income:	$34,815	0.0% Hawaiian	Gore (D) 124,982	(46%)
Poverty status:	10.6%	0.9% Two+ races	**Cook Partisan Voting Index:** R + 4	
Military veterans:	21.5%	0.1% Other		
		5.6% Hispanic Origin		

Occupation	Blue collar: 26.1%	White collar: 55.2%	Gray collar: 18.7%

Over the past quarter century, Florida's urban areas have grown in almost every direction, occupying the high ground between the swamps that still take up much of the state's peninsula. The pattern of development is evident in counties to the north and east of St. Petersburg and Tampa, where subdivisions, trailer parks and shopping centers with Eckerd drug stores and Publix and Winn-Dixie supermarkets sprang up in what previously were sleepy little towns and farm areas with low brick buildings baking in the Florida sun. This area—a haven for manatees, the unusual and beloved sea mammal—has seen suburban development run up the spines of U.S. 19, just off the Gulf Coast, and U.S. 41 and I-75 inland alongside orange groves. Though there are plenty of working people here, this is mainly retirement country. One of every four residents is over 65, and Citrus and Hernando County have a higher percentage of military veterans than any other Florida county but one; Citrus County has the second-highest percentage of retirees, 33% of the total population. Drawn by plenteous lakes, green scenery and a pleasant climate, retirees from Michigan, Indiana and Ohio flocked here by taking Interstate 75 south—a pattern distinct from the retirees who drove Interstate 95 from the Boston-Washington corridor to such destinations as Palm Beach, Fort Lauderdale and Miami. People are comfortable though not usually affluent here, and if the existence of such communities is taken for granted by most Americans, their construction—the creation of an infrastructure of water and sewer lines, underground electricity, and phone and TV cables—is an example of the miracles of modern technology.

The 5th Congressional District occupies much of this fast-growing area. The beach areas in Levy, Citrus and Hernando counties are largely undeveloped; the bulk of the population lives inland, in such places as Citrus Springs in Citrus County, Brooksville in Hernando County, Zephyrhills and Land o' Lakes in Pasco County, and Clermont in Lake County. More than two-thirds of the population is in Pasco, Hernando and Citrus Counties; Sumter County is growing rapidly in part due to a massive retirement community known as the "Villages," which is split between the 5th and 6th Districts. Politically, this is marginal territory. In 2002 Florida's redistricting was controlled by Republicans, for the first time in history. The old 5th included Gainesville, home of the University of Florida, and Alachua County, one of Florida's most Democratic counties, which cast big margins for Democratic Congresswoman Karen Thurman. Redistricters removed Alachua and added new counties, so that 53% of the current 5th District was new to Thurman. The Bush 2000 percentage rose from 46% to 54%.

The congresswoman from the 5th District is Ginny Brown-Waite, a Republican who beat Thurman in 2002. She grew up in Albany, New York, and graduated from State University of New York at Albany and from Russell Sage College. She worked for two decades as a Republican staffer for the state Senate. She moved to Spring Hill in 1987, worked as a health care consultant and became active in politics. In 1990 she was elected to the Hernando County Commission. In 1992 she was elected to the state Senate, after attracting attention for her successful efforts to block a local mining company's controversial plan to burn hazardous waste. In the Senate she backed the state's lawsuit against tobacco companies and frequently championed environmental protection initiatives. As a member of the Senate congressional redistricting committee, Brown-Waite was well positioned to shape the 5th District boundaries. Republican leaders had asked her to run for the House in 1996, but she didn't think it was winnable; here was her chance to draw a district that was.

In the primary, she faced health care consultant Don Gessner, who said he was the only "true conservative" running; he criticized her willingness to vote across party lines. His attacks had some resonance, but she won 58%–42%; Gessner carried only Levy County, which had the smallest turnout of any county. On her home ground in Hernando County, she won 68%–32%.

In the general, she faced Democratic Representative Karen Thurman, who won the district in 1992 after serving as chairman of the state Senate congressional redistricting committee. Thurman worked hard at constituent service, compiled a moderate-to-liberal voting record and served on the Ways and Means Committee. This was one of the most competitive contests in the country, targeted by both national parties: To boost her profile, Thurman was asked to deliver a Democratic response to the president's weekly radio address. House Republican leaders stumped the district for Brown-Waite. Abortion was a key area of disagreement. Both said they supported abortion rights, but Brown-Waite highlighted Thurman's vote against the partial-birth abortion ban as evidence of Thurman's fealty to the Democratic party line. Brown-Waite criticized Thurman for voting against the Republicans' prescription drug bill; Thurman called it a "sham." Brown-Waite received some negative publicity when her husband stole some of Thurman's yard signs, for which she apologized. Thurman outspent Brown-Waite 2-to-1 but Brown-Waite benefited from a late visit by George W. Bush and the strong showing of Governor Jeb Bush, who carried every county in the district. Brown-Waite won 48%–46%. Third-party candidate Jack Gargan, a supporter of Ross Perot's presidential campaigns and his choice for national chairman of his Reform party, had won 34% against Thurman as the Reform Party nominee in 1998, when there was no Republican nominee. This time he won just 3% of the vote. This was an election decided by redistricting: Thurman carried the parts of the district she had previously represented, which cast 49% of the votes, by a 52%–43% margin. But Brown-Waite carried the new parts of the district by 53%–41%.

Brown-Waite, who was one of only four challengers nationwide to defeat an incumbent in 2002, could be a prime Democratic target in 2004; Thurman has been mentioned as a potential challenger.

SIXTH DISTRICT

Rep. Cliff Stearns (R)

Elected 1988, 8th term; b. Apr. 16, 1941, Washington, DC; home, Ocala; George Washington U., B.S. 1963; Presbyterian; married (Joan).

Military Career: Air Force, 1963–67.

Professional Career: Data Control Systems Inc., 1967–68; Negotiator, CBS, 1969–70; Pres., Stearns House Inc., 1972–present.

DC Office: 2370 RHOB 20515, 202-225-5744; Fax: 202-225-3973; Web site: www.house.gov/stearns.

District Offices: Gainesville, 352-337-0003; Ocala, 352-351-8777; Orange Park, 904-269-3203.

Committees: *Energy & Commerce* (5th of 31 R): Commerce, Trade & Consumer Protection (Chmn.); Oversight & Investigations; Telecommunications & The Internet (Vice Chmn.). *Veterans' Affairs* (6th of 17 R): Health.

Group Ratings

	ADA	ACLU	AFS	LCV	CON	ITIC	NTU	COC	ACU	NTLC	CHC
2002	5	7	22	50	94	62	65	82	96	97	100
2001	5	—	0	14	—	—	74	91	96	—	—

National Journal Ratings

	2001 LIB	—	2001 CONS		2002 LIB	—	2002 CONS
Economic	36%	—	63%		27%	—	72%
Social	0%	—	81%		0%	—	75%
Foreign	29%	—	69%		29%	—	71%

Key Votes of the 107th Congress

1. Approve Bush Tax Cuts	Y	5. Faith-Based Charities	Y	9. Trade Promotion Authority	Y
2. Limit Patients' Bill of Rights	Y	6. Bar Gays in the Boy Scouts	Y	10. Bar Funds for Intl. Court	Y
3. Campaign Finance Reform	N	7. Ban Partial-Birth Abortion	*	11. Authorize Force in Iraq	Y
4. Ban ANWR Development	N	8. Arm Commercial Pilots	Y	12. Deny Home. Sec. Dept. Union	Y

Election Results

2002 general	Cliff Stearns (R)	141,570	(65%)	($332,419)
	David Bruderly (D)	75,046	(35%)	($58,524)
2002 primary	Cliff Stearns (R)	unopposed		
2000 general	Cliff Stearns (R)	unopposed		($213,747)

Prior Winning Percentages: 1998 (100%); 1996 (67%); 1994 (100%); 1992 (65%); 1990 (59%); 1988 (54%)

The People		Race/Ethnic Origin	Ancestry	
Area size:	3,026 sq. mi.	78.9% White	German: 10.7%	Irish: 9.1%
Urban population:	69.4%	11.9% Black	English: 8.9%	
Rural population:	30.6%	2.2% Asian	**2000 Presidential Vote**	
Pop. 2000:	639,295	0.3% Native Am.	Bush (R)...............142,489	(58%)
Median income:	$36,846	0.0% Hawaiian	Gore (D)...............102,179	(42%)
Poverty status:	13.4%	1.4% Two + races	**Cook Partisan Voting Index:** R + 9	
Military veterans:	18.3%	0.1% Other		
		5.2% Hispanic Origin		

Occupation   Blue collar: 21.7%   White collar: 61.4%   Gray collar: 16.9%

The flat grasslands of central Florida, once bypassed by southbound tourists heading for the coast, has over the past two decades become a prime growth area in this high-growth state. Central Florida's economy once depended on farming, on tourists getting off the interstate, and on state institutions, most notably the University of Florida in Gainesville. Then retirees began settling in places like the bluegrass country around Ocala, one of America's prime horse-breeding grounds, and Leesburg, perched on a narrow spit of land between Lake Griffin and Lake Harris. Initially, these areas were studded with trailer parks and mobile home developments, but the 1990s brought more upscale development, albeit nothing approaching the high-rise apartments and gated communities that line the coasts further south. Some of this development is at the intersection of Lake, Marion and Sumter counties in the rapidly expanding "Villages" retirement community. This part of central Florida grew by nearly 30 percent during the 1990s, with persons 65 and over accounting for roughly one of every six residents.

The 6th Congressional District includes much of central Florida and also part of the Jacksonville metropolitan area, connected by a thin strip of lightly populated counties. In the south it includes parts of Marion and Sumter Counties, around Ocala, and a corner of Lake County. In the north it includes the western part of Jacksonville's Duval County and most of Clay County just to the south. In between it includes most of Alachua County and Gainesville, home of the University of Florida, where students from wealthier parts of Florida study in a town with many flimsy houses from the impoverished South of 50 years ago; here they can become part of a Florida elite bonded by shared memories of the Gator Growl festivities. On balance, this is a Republican district. The Gainesville area is the exception: Alachua is one of the few Florida counties to vote Democratic in virtually all elections, but the most heavily Democratic precincts were placed by Republican redistricters in the 3d District. The country around Ocala and the Villages in the south is pretty heavily Republican; western Jacksonville and Clay County are solidly Republican. In 2002 Governor Jeb Bush won 77% of the vote in Clay County, his highest percentage in any of Florida's 67 counties. Overall the 6th District voted 58% for George W. Bush in 2000.

The congressman from the 6th District is Cliff Stearns, a Republican elected in 1988. Stearns grew up and attended public schools in Washington, D.C. and served in the Air Force. In 1972 he went into Florida real estate and ended up owning five motels, three restaurants and other property. He was "someone who works in the community, goes to church with his neighbors, and doesn't live in Tallahassee," as he put it in his 1988 campaign, when he beat the favorite, state House Speaker Jon Mills, 54%–46%. "I was elected to put the federal government on a diet,"

Stearns said, and went on to compile a conservative voting record. He was first noticed on Capitol Hill for cutting staff pay raises. In 1994 he penned the letter signed by 87 Republicans calling for the resignation of then-Surgeon General Joycelyn Elders. Since losing a low-level leadership contest in 1994, he has shown independence of the leadership. He opposed IMF funding, trade promotion authority and PNTR with China. In the cliffhanger vote in December 2001 on trade promotion authority, Stearns was among a handful of Republicans who paced the House floor and delayed casting their vote until it became clear that their party needed them. In 2001 he lost on House floor amendments to reduce spending for the National Endowment for the Arts and the Corporation for Public Broadcasting.

Stearns has become an active legislator. On the Veterans Committee, he sponsored a research center on Gulf War syndrome and won new medical facilities and benefits for disabled vets. On Energy and Commerce, he has worked for privacy for health care and genetic records. In 2000 he helped pass the Cardiac Arrest Survival Act, which encourages the use of defibrillators and installs them in all federal buildings. He has been a leader in letting the states take the lead in utility deregulation and wants to drop the requirement that utilities purchase power from renewable and non-traditional energy sources. As chairman of the revamped Commerce, Trade and Consumer Protection Subcommittee, he focused on the widely varying state laws regulating Internet content and wanted to make sure that they do not obstruct e-commerce. With Rick Boucher, he filed a broadly-backed bipartisan bill on consumer privacy issues that permitted businesses to collect and share personal financial information unless consumers opt out. Stearns helped to prepare the post-Enron bill to set stricter standards in accounting. He enacted a bill amending the Consumer Product Safety Act to cover low-speed electric bicycles.

Stearns has not suffered from breaking a 1988 promise to serve only six terms. He was unopposed in 1998 and 2000. The addition of the Gainesville area to the district may have sparked opposition in 2002. But Stearns carried Alachua County 51%–49% and won by much bigger margins in other counties—65%–35% in Marion and 77%–23% in Clay—for a 65%–35% victory.

SEVENTH DISTRICT

Rep. John Mica (R)

Elected 1992, 6th term; b. Jan. 27, 1943, Binghamton, NY; home, Winter Park; Miami-Dade Commun. Col., A.A. 1965, U. of FL, B.A. 1967; Episcopalian; married (Patricia).

Elected Office: FL House of Reps., 1976–80.

Professional Career: Exec. Dir., Palm Beach & Orange Cnty. Govt. Charter Study Commissions, 1970–74; Pres., MK Development, 1975–92; A.A., U.S. Sen. Paula Hawkins, 1981–85; Partner, Mica, Dudinsky & Assoc., 1985–92.

DC Office: 2445 RHOB 20515, 202-225-4035; Fax: 202-226-0821; Web site: www.house.gov/mica.

District Offices: Deltona, 386-860-1499; Maitland, 407-657-8080; Ormond Beach, 386-676-7750; St. Augustine, 904-810-5048.

Committees: *Government Reform* (6th of 24 R): Civil Service & Agency Organization; Criminal Justice, Drug Policy & Human Resources. *House Administration* (3d of 6 R). *Transportation & Infrastructure* (7th of 41 R): Aviation (Chmn.); Highways, Transit & Pipelines; Railroads.

Group Ratings

	ADA	ACLU	AFS	LCV	CON	ITIC	NTU	COC	ACU	NTLC	CHC
2002	0	7	0	13	58	100	60	95	96	86	100
2001	0	—	0	0	—	—	64	96	92	—	—

National Journal Ratings

	2001 LIB —	2001 CONS		2002 LIB —	2002 CONS
Economic	7% —	89%		9% —	87%
Social	0% —	81%		0% —	75%
Foreign	21% —	74%		0% —	85%

Key Votes of the 107th Congress

1. Approve Bush Tax Cuts	Y	5. Faith-Based Charities	Y	9. Trade Promotion Authority	Y
2. Limit Patients' Bill of Rights	Y	6. Bar Gays in the Boy Scouts	Y	10. Bar Funds for Intl. Court	Y
3. Campaign Finance Reform	N	7. Ban Partial-Birth Abortion	Y	11. Authorize Force in Iraq	Y
4. Ban ANWR Development	N	8. Arm Commercial Pilots	Y	12. Deny Home. Sec. Dept. Union	Y

Election Results

2002 general	John Mica (R)	142,147	(60%)	($1,756,115)
	Wayne Hogan (D)	96,444	(40%)	($4,659,352)
2002 primary	John Mica (R)	unopposed		
2000 general	John Mica (R)	171,018	(63%)	($206,125)
	Dan Vaughen (D)	99,531	(37%)	($40,088)

Prior Winning Percentages: 1998 (100%); 1996 (62%); 1994 (73%); 1992 (56%)

The People		**Race/Ethnic Origin**	**Ancestry**
Area size:	2,221 sq. mi.	81.3% White	German: 11.7% Irish: 10.6%
Urban population:	86.7%	8.8% Black	English: 9.9%
Rural population:	13.3%	1.4% Asian	**2000 Presidential Vote**
Pop. 2000:	639,295	0.3% Native Am.	Bush (R)..............143,672 (54%)
Median income:	$40,525	0.0% Hawaiian	Gore (D)...............122,818 (46%)
Poverty status:	10.1%	1.1% Two+ races	**Cook Partisan Voting Index:** R + 4
Military veterans:	17.6%	0.1% Other	
		6.9% Hispanic Origin	

Occupation	Blue collar: 20.3%	White collar: 63.2%	Gray collar: 16.4%

In 1513, Spanish explorer Ponce de Leon headed to Florida, hoping to discover the Fountain of Youth; instead, he found Ponte Vedra Beach, located just south of modern-day Jacksonville. A few decades later and a little further south, Spanish colonists founded St. Augustine, the oldest permanent European settlement in North America—42 years older than Jamestown, Virginia, and 55 years older than the Plymouth colony in Massachusetts. But near long-settled St. Augustine are a Northrop Grumman aircraft plant and some of the newest communities in America. The coastal region from metro Jacksonville to Daytona Beach—including St. Johns, Flagler and Volusia counties—grew 26% in the 1990s; Flagler grew 71%, the most of any county in Florida. Some of the communities here are old: John D. Rockefeller used to winter in Ormond Beach, and cars have been zooming on Daytona's rock-hard beach for decades before Dale Earnhardt died on its NASCAR track in February 2001. Nearby DeLand is a mecca for skydivers, while Heathrow, just off Interstate 4, serves as the home base of the American Automobile Association. Other places are much newer, instant cities: the Palm Coast development on the beach in Flagler County and Deltona, built inland on a drained swamp in Volusia County.

The 7th Congressional District covers the Atlantic coast for nearly 100 miles, from Ponte Vedra Beach to Daytona Beach. Inland it includes Deltona and affluent Seminole County suburbs of Orlando as well as the timber center of Palatka. Nearly two-thirds of the population is in the south, around Orlando, Deltona and Daytona Beach. The political tendencies in this area are mixed. Seminole County and St. Augustine's St. Johns County are affluent and heavily Republican. Palm Coast's Flagler County often votes Democratic. So does Volusia County, which includes Daytona Beach, DeLand and Deltona, but about 40% of it is in the 24th District. On balance, the 7th District is Republican, but not heavily so: in 2000 it voted 54% for George W. Bush.

The congressman from the 7th District is John Mica, a Republican first elected in 1992. He grew up in south Florida, in a bipartisan political family: His younger brother Dan Mica was a Democratic congressman from Palm Beach County from 1978–88, when he lost a primary for U.S. Senate; another brother David Mica worked for Democratic Governor Lawton Chiles and became executive director for the Florida Petroleum Association. John Mica made a small fortune by turning 360 feet of New Smyrna beachfront into a real estate business. He was elected to the state House in 1976 and served four years, then worked on Senator Paula Hawkins's staff from 1981 to 1985; after that he worked as a lobbyist. He ran for the House when this district was created in 1992. After he was attacked in the 1992 Republican primary as an insider representing special interests, he said, "Some of the finest folks I've met are lobbyists." He won the primary 53%–34%. In the general election, against an opponent he attacked as a liberal backed by trial lawyers and labor unions, he won 56%–44%. He has since been reelected easily.

Mica started off as a consistent conservative and a brash reformer, leading the charge to abolish House select committees and to make public the names of those signing petitions to discharge legislation. He also pushed a plan to require the EPA to subject new regulations to a cost-benefit analysis, versions of which ultimately passed. When Republicans took control of the House, Mica became chairman of Government Reform's Civil Service Subcommittee. There he helped pass the White House Accountability Act of 1996, imposing on the White House, just as a Republican-pushed law imposed on Congress, the laws that are imposed on the private sector. He has said that his biggest issue is fighting drugs. He criticized Mexico as a continuing safe haven for drug traffickers, and later said that the Clinton White House had "sabotaged" the war on drugs by sharply reducing Pentagon interdiction. After he held a hearing in Sioux City, Iowa, to examine the spread of methamphetamines in the Midwest and the "mind-boggling" foothold by Mexican traffickers, Clinton's drug policy adviser Barry McCaffrey criticized Mica for "unprecedented oversight and interference."

When Mica took over in 2001 as chairman of the Aviation Subcommittee at Transportation and Infrastructure, he pledged faster building of runways across the nation. But after the September 11 attacks he focused on security. After congressional leaders moved within days to pass a bill to aid the airlines, Mica played a major role in designing the next legislation: improved screening at all airports. The Senate, by 100–0, approved a bill that federalized the screeners. Mica and House Republicans objected to a complete federal takeover and sought to preserve some role for the private sector. In November 2001 Mica and others reached a deal that that allows airports to "opt out" of the federal system after three years if they meet certain standards. A few months later Mica found himself in the middle of another post-September 11 conflict. With Transportation Committee chairman Don Young, Mica introduced a bill to permit commercial airline pilots to carry guns in the cockpit. The bill was initially opposed by the Bush administration and the Senate; airlines worried about the risks of having firearms aboard planes. In July 2002 Mica brought to the floor a bill permitting a few pilots to carry the weapons during a two-year demonstration period. But the House, to his surprise, voted 310–113 voted to allow all pilots to carry guns. The Senate agreed by a 87–6 margin. The Bush administration acquiesced to what was obviously the popular will. In October 2002 beleaguered airline executives came in and pleaded for direct cash assistance. Mica objected to that, but worked with senators on a measure to subsidize the industry's insurance costs, and it was included in the homeland security bill.

Mica takes an interest in local transportation issues, notably controlling the sprawl around Orlando. Mica has fought for mass transit and commuter rail systems for the area. On another local issue, he worked to keep simulation training command for all four branches of the military in Orlando, where it has spawned many local businesses. Mica was the only Florida congressman who opposed a ban on all oil drilling in the Gulf of Mexico, and he helped to broker the compromise that banned drilling only within 100 miles of shore; his actions were unrelated to his brother David's work with oil companies, he insisted.

Amid all this legislative work in October 2002, Mica faced an unexpectedly serious challenge at home from Democrat Wayne Hogan, a Jacksonville trial lawyer who spent $2.7 million of his own money on his campaign. Redistricting had made the district a bit more Republican, but more than half of the voters were new to Mica. Hogan, part of the legal team that won Florida's settlement with the tobacco industry, from which he netted $54 million, said that he would fight for "ordinary families against powerful interests." Mica responded that Hogan was trying to buy the seat, and that his pledge not to take contributions from political action committees was like "Rockefeller saying he won't take food stamps." He won comfortably, 60%–40%, carrying all six counties. He carried Flagler and Volusia counties narrowly, but won more than 60% in Seminole and St. Johns counties.

EIGHTH DISTRICT

Rep. Ric Keller (R)

Elected 2000, 2d term; b. Sept. 5, 1964, Johnson City, TN; home, Orlando; E. TN St. U., B.S. 1986, Vanderbilt U., J.D. 1992; Methodist; divorced.

Professional Career: Practicing atty., 1992–00.

DC Office: 419 CHOB 20515, 202-225-2176; Fax: 202-225-0999; Web site: www.house.gov/keller.

District Offices: Eustis, 352-589-9909; Ocala, 352-624-9994; Orlando, 407-872-1962.

Committees: *Education & the Workforce* (17th of 27 R): 21st Century Competitiveness; Education Reform; Workforce Protections. *Judiciary* (13th of 21 R): Courts, the Internet & Intellectual Property; Crime, Terrorism & Homeland Security.

Group Ratings

	ADA	ACLU	AFS	LCV	CON	ITIC	NTU	COC	ACU	NTLC	CHC
2002	0	7	0	13	67	100	57	100	100	100	100
2001	0	—	0	7	—	—	66	100	96	—	—

National Journal Ratings

	2001 LIB	—	2001 CONS		2002 LIB	—	2002 CONS
Economic	27%	—	73%		13%	—	85%
Social	0%	—	81%		0%	—	75%
Foreign	0%	—	97%		0%	—	85%

Key Votes of the 107th Congress

1. Approve Bush Tax Cuts	Y	5. Faith-Based Charities	Y	9. Trade Promotion Authority	Y
2. Limit Patients' Bill of Rights	Y	6. Bar Gays in the Boy Scouts	Y	10. Bar Funds for Intl. Court	Y
3. Campaign Finance Reform	N	7. Ban Partial-Birth Abortion	Y	11. Authorize Force in Iraq	Y
4. Ban ANWR Development	N	8. Arm Commercial Pilots	Y	12. Deny Home. Sec. Dept. Union	Y

Election Results

2002 general	Ric Keller (R)	123,497	(65%)	($1,038,656)
	Eddie Diaz (D)	66,099	(35%)	($218,651)
2002 primary	Ric Keller (R)	unopposed		
2000 general	Ric Keller (R)	125,253	(51%)	($1,318,044)
	Linda W. Chapin (D)	121,295	(49%)	($1,669,191)

The People		Race/Ethnic Origin	Ancestry	
Area size:	1,158 sq. mi.	69.9% White	German: 10.7%	Irish: 9.0%
Urban population:	91.7%	7.2% Black	English: 8.6%	
Rural population:	8.3%	3.0% Asian	**2000 Presidential Vote**	
Pop. 2000:	639,295	0.3% Native Am.	Bush (R)...............119,139 (54%)	
Median income:	$41,568	0.1% Hawaiian	Gore (D)...............102,538 (46%)	
Poverty status:	9.4%	1.6% Two+ races	**Cook Partisan Voting Index:** R + 4	
Military veterans:	14.9%	0.3% Other		
		17.6% Hispanic Origin		

Occupation	Blue collar: 19.3%	White collar: 63.6%	Gray collar: 17.2%

Who would have supposed 40 years ago that the most popular tourist destination in the world would rise amid the swamps and orange groves of central Florida? The answer: Walt Disney, and just about no one else. In the mid-1960s, Disney looked at the map and decided that the inter-section of I-4 and Florida's Turnpike, the "crossroads of Florida," just a few miles southwest of Orlando, was the perfect place for the vast theme park he was planning. The spirit of this place was set by a man who never lived here but created something now taken for granted. Disney conceived the first theme park in the flatlands of Orange County, California, in 1955, but he perfected it in the 17,000 acres of swamp and lakes in Florida's Orange County that his associates had stealthily snapped up and where Disney World opened in 1971. With the invention of the theme park, Disney also pioneered sophisticated communications, utility, and waste-disposal methods—all out of sight and underground. Yet Disney World is not just an engineering marvel; it requires some 56,000 people with know-how and earnest cheerfulness to entertain its 40 mil-lion-plus visitors. Disney's vision was of a future that was high-tech, labor-intensive, and geared towards the provision of services—in retrospect, an accurate forecast of today's American econ-omy. Walt Disney World also set the model for the private corporation handling functions his-torically run by cities—a model that would be followed, on a much smaller scale, by countless gated developments nationwide. Greater Orlando itself has an increasingly high-tech economy; defense contractor Martin Marietta has a big facility here.

The 8th Congressional District includes parts of Orlando and surrounding Orange County and most of the enormous Walt Disney World complex, including the Disney new urbanist town of Celebration. It includes most of the southeast and southwest parts of Orlando and adjoining suburbs; the heavily black areas of central Orlando are in the 3d District, which stretches all the way to Jacksonville. More than three-quarters of the district's residents live in Orange County. The rest live in a ribbon of territory to the northwest, past Lake Apopka to little market towns like Mount Dora and Umatilla in Lake County that seem insulated by distance from the booming metro area; around here, turtles, alligators and river otters go about their lives underneath cypress trees draped with Spanish moss. Nearby is Silver Springs, where tourists can view the world's largest formation of clear artesian springs from glass-bottomed boats—a theme park from an earlier era. Beyond that is the horse farm country of Marion County, around Ocala, part of which is in the 8th. The 2002 redistricting changed the district's boundaries considerably; much of Orange County was removed and put in the new 24th District. In the 1980s the Orlando area was heavily Republican, but in the 1990s it moved perceptibly toward national Democrats. The 8th District was designed to be a Republican district, and voted 54% for George W. Bush in 2000. Some 18% of the district's residents are Hispanic, most of them not Cuban Republicans, but Puerto Ricans in growing numbers and people with roots in other parts of Latin America; many work in the tourism industry. Politically, they have voted Democratic, but do not seem to have a strong allegiance to the party; they favored Governor Jeb Bush, who speaks fluent Spanish, in 2002.

The congressman from the 8th District is Ric Keller, a Republican elected in 2000 in one of the closest races in the country. A political newcomer, he was born in Tennessee but grew up mostly in Orlando, in a one-bedroom house with his brother, sister, mother and grandmother. With financial help from Pell grants, he graduated first in his class at East Tennessee State Uni-versity, then graduated from Vanderbilt Law School. In 1992 he moved to Orlando and practiced law, and quickly earned conservative credentials. His firm served as general counsel to a business coalition that won passage of changes in tort law in the Florida legislature. He chaired a successful mentoring program for local students at risk of dropping out of high school in Orange County.

When Congressman Bill McCollum, who had held the seat for 20 years, decided to run for the Senate in 2000, Keller ran for the House. He had tough primary competition from state Representative Bill Sublette, who boasted of delivering state funds to the area and was supported by most local Republican leaders. With greater name recognition, Sublette led in most polls. Keller focused on issues like abortion and gun owners' rights. Sublette led Keller in the September primary 43%–31%; since neither had a majority, the nomination would be decided in the October 3 runoff. The Democrats already had a nominee, Linda Chapin, former Orange County Com-mission chairman, who was seen by national party leaders as one of their strongest candidates in a Republican-held seat. The NRCC, fearing that there would not be enough time to campaign against her after the runoff, began running negative ads against her even as Keller and Sublette attacked each other. Keller was helped by $400,000 in contributions and issue ads by the conservative Club for Growth. Keller won the runoff 52%–48%; he had prepared a concession speech and admitted that he was surprised.

Keller again was considered the underdog against Chapin, who argued that her moderate views plus her experience as a county official put her more in line with district voters. Keller played up his anti-tax views and outsider status, while Republican ads lampooned Chapin for providing frills for the county jail and other local facilities, including $150,000 for palm trees. Chapin objected that the ads were inaccurate; some were pulled. Keller generated additional controversy when he called Palestinians "lower than pond scum." Keller's 50.8%–49.2% win was a great disappointment to House Democratic leaders, who had long expected to Chapin to win. But it may have been decided by the personal touch: Keller's folksy, self-deprecating style made him "an easy man to like," wrote the *Orlando Sentinel*.

In the House, Keller has been a reliable conservative. His strong support for tax cuts plus his advocacy of increased education funding for the disadvantaged made him "a bootstrap conservative," in the *Orlando Sentinel's* words. On oil drilling in the Gulf of Mexico and the Clinton administration's proposed regulations on arsenic in drinking water, he surprised many by voting against the Republican leadership. Redistricting made the district a bit more Republican in 2002, but national Democrats were enthusiastic about their nominee, Eddie Diaz, a Puerto Rican-born former Orlando policeman who had been gravely wounded while his partner was killed in a shootout. Diaz's lack of campaign experience and his modest fundraising skills hampered his effort; his campaign never caught fire. Keller, a relentless campaigner and fundraiser, reached out to the Hispanic community. In a major disappointment for Democrats, Keller won 65%–35%. He has pledged to serve only four terms.

NINTH DISTRICT

Rep. Michael Bilirakis (R)

Elected 1982; 11th term; b. July 16, 1930, Tarpon Springs; home, Palm Harbor; U. of Pittsburgh, B.S. 1959, U. of FL, J.D. 1963; Greek Orthodox; married (Evelyn).

Military Career: Air Force, 1951–55.

Professional Career: Steelworker, 1955–59; Govt. contract negotiator, 1959–60; Petroleum engineer, 1960–63; Aerospace Industries admin., 1963–1969; Practicing atty., 1969–82.

DC Office: 2269 RHOB 20515, 202-225-5755; Fax: 202-225-4085; Web site: www.house.gov/bilirakis.

District Offices: Palm Harbor, 727-773-2871; Tampa, 813-960-8173.

Committees: *Energy & Commerce* (2d of 31 R): Health (Chmn.); Oversight & Investigations; Telecommunications & The Internet. *Veterans' Affairs* (Vice Chmn. of 17 R): Oversight & Investigations (Vice Chmn.).

Group Ratings

	ADA	ACLU	AFS	LCV	CON	ITIC	NTU	COC	ACU	NTLC	CHC
2002	0	7	0	38	58	88	60	89	100	85	92
2001	10	—	10	36	—	—	59	91	84	—	—

National Journal Ratings

	2001 LIB	—	2001 CONS	2002 LIB	—	2002 CONS
Economic	43%	—	56%	35%	—	64%
Social	20%	—	69%	0%	—	75%
Foreign	16%	—	82%	0%	—	85%

Key Votes of the 107th Congress

1. Approve Bush Tax Cuts	Y	5. Faith-Based Charities	Y	9. Trade Promotion Authority	Y
2. Limit Patients' Bill of Rights	Y	6. Bar Gays in the Boy Scouts	Y	10. Bar Funds for Intl. Court	Y
3. Campaign Finance Reform	N	7. Ban Partial-Birth Abortion	Y	11. Authorize Force in Iraq	Y
4. Ban ANWR Development	N	8. Arm Commercial Pilots	Y	12. Deny Home. Sec. Dept. Union	Y

Election Results

2002 general	Michael Bilirakis (R)	169,369	(71%)	($816,932)
	Chuck Kalogianis (D)	67,623	(29%)	($307,568)
2002 primary	Michael Bilirakis (R)	unopposed		
2000 general	Michael Bilirakis (R)	210,318	(82%)	($518,118)
	Jon Duffey (Ref)	46,474	(18%)	($12,775)

Prior Winning Percentages: 1998 (100%); 1996 (69%); 1994 (100%); 1992 (59%); 1990 (58%); 1988 (100%); 1986 (71%); 1984 (79%); 1982 (51%)

The People		Race/Ethnic Origin	Ancestry	
Area size:	800 sq. mi.	85.2% White	German: 13.3%	Irish: 11.2%
Urban population:	93.8%	3.5% Black	English: 9.2%	
Rural population:	6.2%	1.8% Asian	**2000 Presidential Vote**	
Pop. 2000:	639,296	0.2% Native Am.	Bush (R) 146,735	(54%)
Median income:	$40,742	0.0% Hawaiian	Gore (D) 124,242	(46%)
Poverty status:	8.6%	1.1% Two+ races	**Cook Partisan Voting Index:** R + 5	
Military veterans:	17.2%	0.1% Other		
		7.9% Hispanic Origin		

Occupation   Blue collar: 17.6%   White collar: 68.0%   Gray collar: 14.4%

Half a century ago, the land north of St. Petersburg and Tampa was scarcely inhabited. Behind the barrier island of beaches, the land along the Gulf shore was swampy; further inland was dense, semitropical forest spotted with lakes. Over the years, development has moved up the coast and inland via the major highways, first to Clearwater and Tarpon Springs in Pinellas County and then up the once-empty coast of Pasco County. Much of this area originally was designed for retirees, offering everything from condominiums to garden apartments to trailer parks. But while Clearwater still has a higher percentage of senior citizens than any other city over 100,000, these communities got slightly younger during the 1990s. Businesses have sprouted in northern Pinellas County and inland off the I-75 corridor; nearly half of Pasco County's workers commute to jobs in other counties. The people who settled here in recent decades brought their ancestral political beliefs with them: In the 1950s and 1960s, only white-collar retirees could afford to buy new places in Florida, and they were heavily Republican. As Florida retirements became more feasible for people with modest incomes in the 1970s and 1980s, the partisan balance shifted toward Democrats. In the 1990s, young in-migrants with professional and technical backgrounds flooded the area; their political independence has turned this into one of Florida's most politically marginal areas.

The 9th Congressional District covers part of the area north of St. Petersburg and north and east of Tampa. It includes the string of towns on the coast of Pasco County—Holiday, New Port Richey, Bayonet Point, Hudson. In Pinellas County to the south, the 9th includes Tarpon Springs, an old resort first settled by Greek sponge divers a century ago, the affluent neighborhoods of mid- and upper-level managers in East Lake, the young commuter families of Oldsmar, the bayside community of Safety Harbor and Clearwater. Sleepy Clearwater is the spiritual headquarters for the Church of Scientology; its downtown is being transformed by the $50 million Mediterranean Revival Scientology religious center, scheduled for late 2003 completion. The district also includes the northern Tampa suburbs in Hillsborough County and much of the eastern part of the county, including part of strawberry-growing Plant City (named not for plants but for Tampa pioneer Henry B. Plant). The borders were drawn by Republican redistricters to produce a district that would elect a Republican. The district gave Jeb Bush a big margin in 2002, but voted just 54% for brother George W. Bush in 2000.

The congressman from the 9th District is Michael Bilirakis, a Republican who grew up near Pittsburgh; he served in the Air Force, and then worked his way through college, toiling in a steel mill. He also worked for the government in Washington and an aerospace contractor in Florida, then practiced law. He believes strongly that Americans can work their way up, with occasional government assistance (like the G.I. Bill that helped him through school). Originally a Democrat, he switched to the Republican Party in 1980, and in 1982, when this district was created, he won though it had been designed for a Democrat.

Bilirakis has a moderate record on economics and is more conservative on other issues. He has made something of an environmental record, opposing Western water subsidies and offshore oil drilling on the Gulf Coast. Early in his career, Bilirakis won a seat on the Commerce Committee, and starting in 1995 he held one of the most potentially powerful chairmanships in Congress, that of the Health and Environment Subcommittee; he managed to retain it in 2001, despite House Republicans' six-year term limit, by arguing that it had been reconfigured to merely the Health Subcommittee and thus wasn't the same subcommittee any more.

In 1993 and 1995, Bilirakis sponsored a bill which tried to make health insurance portable and to stop insurers from denying coverage for pre-existing conditions; it was put aside in 1994 in the debate over the Clinton health care plan, but something very like it was passed in 1996, known from its Senate sponsors as Kennedy-Kassebaum. He served on the Medicare Commission and was part of the majority that supported the Breaux-Thomas premium support plan; a version of that has been supported by George W. Bush and Bilirakis may play a role in Medicare legislation. Bilirakis also sponsored a bill to provide a state-based prescription drug benefit for the poorest and sickest Medicare beneficiaries. This became the Republican party's plan, and again Bush supported something quite similar. Bilirakis supported the Dingell-Norwood HMO regulation bill, and was its only supporter placed on the conference committee by Speaker Dennis Hastert. Bilirakis sponsored the November 1999 law to establish a pediatric research institute at NIH. In March 2003, he won House approval of his bill to increase public education programs on organ sharing and reimbursing travel and subsistence expenses for individuals who make living organ donations.

Bilirakis is also vice-chairman of the Veterans Committee. He sponsored a 1997 law to provide "forgotten widows" of veterans with a minimum annuity of $165 a month, and a 1999 law to enable severely disabled military retirees to collect retirement as well as disability benefits. For most of his congressional career, Bilirakis has backed a center to treat veterans with spinal cord injuries; the $17 million Tampa facility opened in February 2002.

Bilirakis had no Democratic opponent in 1998 or 2000. In 2000 he was opposed by the Reform Party's Jon Duffey, who took Bilirakis aside and offered to withdraw if he would contribute $600,000 to a health care trust fund for residents near the Stauffer site, refuse to accept PAC money, and hire Duffey as an unpaid "ethical adviser." Bilirakis responded, "Silly boy." In October 1999, Bilirakis said, "I don't intend to stay there much longer. I think one more term." But he ran in 2002 and was reelected 71%–29%. Despite the wide margin, Bilirakis got an Election Day scare: While he and his son, state Representative Gus Bilirakis, were waving to passing vehicles at a local intersection, a car went careening out of control and came barreling toward them. The car narrowly missed the elder Bilirakis and struck his son; Gus suffered no serious injuries though, and returned from the hospital in time to make it to the joint father-son victory party that evening.

TENTH DISTRICT

Rep. Bill Young (R)

Elected 1970, 17th term; b. Dec. 16, 1930, Harmarville, PA; home, Largo; Baptist; married (Beverly).

Military Career: Army Natl. Guard, 1948–57.

Elected Office: FL Senate, 1960–70, Min. Ldr., 1966–70.

Professional Career: Aide, U.S. Rep. William Cramer, 1957–60.

DC Office: 2407 RHOB 20515, 202-225-5961; Fax: 202-225-9764; Web site: www.house.gov/young.

District Offices: Largo, 727-581-0980; St. Petersburg, 727-893-3191.

Committees: *Appropriations* (Chmn. of 36 R): Defense; Homeland Security (Vice Chmn.). *Select Committee on Homeland Security* (3d of 27 R): Intelligence & Counterterrorism.

Group Ratings

	ADA	ACLU	AFS	LCV	CON	ITIC	NTU	COC	ACU	NTLC	CHC
2002	0	7	0	38	36	100	58	85	96	83	92
2001	5	—	10	21	—	—	60	91	80	—	—

National Journal Ratings

	2001 LIB	—	2001 CONS		2002 LIB	—	2002 CONS
Economic	39%	—	61%		36%	—	64%
Social	20%	—	69%		0%	—	75%
Foreign	4%	—	87%		0%	—	85%

Key Votes of the 107th Congress

1. Approve Bush Tax Cuts	Y	5. Faith-Based Charities	Y
2. Limit Patients' Bill of Rights	Y	6. Bar Gays in the Boy Scouts	Y
3. Campaign Finance Reform	N	7. Ban Partial-Birth Abortion	Y
4. Ban ANWR Development	N	8. Arm Commercial Pilots	Y

9. Trade Promotion Authority	Y
10. Bar Funds for Intl. Court	Y
11. Authorize Force in Iraq	Y
12. Deny Home. Sec. Dept. Union	Y

Election Results

2002 general	Bill Young (R)	unopposed		($487,592)
2002 primary	Bill Young (R)	unopposed		
2000 general	Bill Young (R)	146,799	(76%)	($336,372)
	Josette Green (NL)	26,908	(14%)	($11,938)
	Randy Heine (I)	20,296	(11%)	

Prior Winning Percentages: 1998 (100%); 1996 (67%); 1994 (100%); 1992 (57%); 1990 (100%); 1988 (73%); 1986 (100%); 1984 (80%); 1982 (100%); 1980 (100%); 1978 (79%); 1976 (65%); 1974 (76%); 1972 (76%); 1970 (67%)

The People		Race/Ethnic Origin	Ancestry	
Area size:	448 sq. mi.	88.0% White	German: 14.0%	Irish: 11.6%
Urban population:	100.0%	3.6% Black	English: 10.2%	
Rural population:	0.0%	2.3% Asian	**2000 Presidential Vote**	
Pop. 2000:	639,295	0.3% Native Am.	Gore (D) 137,286	(51%)
Median income:	$37,168	0.0% Hawaiian	Bush (R) 133,004	(49%)
Poverty status:	8.9%	1.3% Two+ races	**Cook Partisan Voting Index:** D + 1	
Military veterans:	18.3%	0.1% Other		
		4.4% Hispanic Origin		

Occupation	Blue collar: 19.9%	White collar: 64.9%	Gray collar: 15.2%

St. Petersburg was first settled in the 1870s, reached by railroad in 1888 and named for the then-Russian capital. For decades, it was known as the American city with the largest percentage of elderly residents, no doubt due to its 361 days of sunshine per year. In the early 1900s, *St. Petersburg Times* editor W. L. Straub sought to reverse the industrialization of the waterfront, establishing the parks and benches that continue to define the city's character. By the 1950s, St. Petersburg had become a national cliche, bringing to mind old folks trying to drum up a game of shuffleboard. Starting out on the grid streets facing Tampa Bay, St. Petersburg later spread toward the Gulf Coast as the migration of retirees accelerated. Mostly from the North and modestly affluent, the newcomers adapted easily to a city whose civic tone was set by the *St. Petersburg Times* and its longtime owners Nelson and Henrietta Poynter: Sober, good-humored, supportive of clean government and civil rights. More recently, retirees have come to prefer homes in less urbanized settings, and St. Petersburg has become a more conventional central city, with a larger working population, more families and minorities, and more office buildings and civic attractions—the Salvador Dali Museum, the Florida International Museum, the Museum of Fine Arts. The new balance has brought new politics. White-collar Yankee retirees in the 1940s and 1950s made St. Petersburg and surrounding Pinellas County the first Republican county in ancestrally Democratic Florida. Then, as more workers came to afford a Florida retirement and the affluent moved farther down the Gulf Coast, St. Petersburg trended Democratic in the 1970s and 1980s.

The 10th Congressional District is the only Florida district entirely within one county. It includes all of Pinellas County south of Clearwater except for heavily black precincts in south St. Petersburg, which are part of the Tampa-based 11th District. It also includes all the Pinellas County beach communities on the barrier islands facing the Gulf from Belleair Beach to Mullet Key and, north of Clearwater, includes middle-class Dunedin and pricey Palm Harbor in the north to the new subdivisions of Largo in the center of the peninsula. The removal of the south St. Petersburg precincts reduced the district's black percentage from 11% to 4% and increased its Bush 2000 percentage from 44% to 49%.

The congressman from the 10th District is Bill Young, a Republican first elected in 1970, second in seniority among House Republicans and chairman of the Appropriations Committee. Young grew up in a dirt-poor Pennsylvania coal town. His first home was a shotgun shack that was swept down a river when he was 6; at 16 he was shot in a hunting accident. The family moved to Florida, and Young dropped out of high school to support his ill mother by hauling concrete blocks and mixing mortar; at 25 he applied for a job as an insurance salesman, and ultimately ran a successful insurance agency. In the 1950s he worked for St. Petersburg's first Republican congressman, William Cramer. Young was elected to the state Senate in 1960, at 29; when Cramer ran for the Senate in 1970, Young ran for his House seat and won. In the early 1970s Social Security was vastly increased and indexed to inflation and St. Petersburg basked in prosperity.

Young has a moderate to conservative voting record. Early on, Young got a seat on Appropriations, where he, like many Republicans, worked closely with the Democratic chairmen. Young's special project has been the bone marrow donor program, originated by Dr. Robert Good of All Children's Hospital in St. Petersburg. Working from his seat on the Defense Subcommittee, he originally placed the program in the Pentagon; in 1987 it started off with $2.1 million; by 2002 it had matched nearly 15,000 patients with one of 4.8 million volunteers.

Despite his seniority, Young did not become full committee chairman after Republicans won their majority in 1994. Speaker-designate Newt Gingrich passed over him and two more senior Republicans for being too accommodating to Democrats. Young says that Gingrich offered him the job, but that he preferred to chair the Defense Subcommittee, on which he had done much of his work. In that post he worked to produce bipartisan appropriations out of the spotlight; he has said he knew every dime that goes into secret "black" military and intelligence operations. Young sharply criticized the Clinton administration for stretching the military too thin. His philosophy, he says, goes back to his memories of hearing about Pearl Harbor as a child. In his office he has kept a "horseshoe nail" list ("for want of the nail, the shoe was lost") of small items the military needs; on a scroll, it stretched across the room and included items like more training hours for pilots, barracks repair and more bullets, compasses, tents and flashlights.

In 1998 Young considered retiring, but at the end of the year he was suddenly catapulted into the Appropriations chairmanship. It happened three days after the November election, when Gingrich decided to resign; Appropriations Chairman Bob Livingston quickly became the Speaker-designate, and Young became chairman. In the fall 2000 appropriations crunch, he was upbraided by Tom DeLay for his concessions to Clinton administration negotiators on education spending, the ergonomics rule and a rule that prevented dispensing of the morning-after pill in schools; Young wanted to avoid a veto and a protracted dispute like that in 1995–96.

In 2001 and 2002 Young was caught between demands by OMB Director Mitch Daniels that spending be held down to Bush administration limits and demands by appropriators for more spending. For the most part he came down on Bush's side. On the antiterrorism supplemental in November 2001 he reluctantly backed the administration and the Republican leadership, but warned that committee members might vote for more. When the administration proposed an end to earmarking money for members' projects (there were 7,803 earmarks in 2001, totaling $15 billion), Young demurred. "Unless the Constitution is amended, Congress will continue to exercise its discretion over federal funds and will earmark those funds for purposes we deem appropriate." In early May 2002 he proposed to add $2.5 billion to the $27.3 billion emergency spending bill, but after a meeting where George W. Bush expressed his "disappointment" and stormier sessions with Daniels and Speaker Dennis Hastert, Young held to the $27.3 level, partly through accounting legerdemain—$1.8 billion of defense spending was put on a contingency basis. Later $383 million of airline bailout money that seemed unlikely to be used was put into the next fiscal year. In September he tried to get Hastert to move the $130 billion Labor-HHS appropriation to the floor under an open rule, to see if the Bush limits would be accepted by the House; Hastert declined, and work on appropriations was not completed until early 2003. After the November election, House Republicans adopted a new rule requiring Appropriations subcommittee chairmen—the college of cardinals—to be approved by the Republican Steering Committee. This was seen as a move to rein in appropriators; when it passed by a close voice vote, Young did not call for a roll call vote. "I could not let that meeting conclude with the Speaker having lost."

Like other appropriators, Young has worked on projects in his district. The 2002 defense bill had $80 million for the Tampa Bay area, including $10 million for the Moffitt Cancer Center in Tampa, $20 million for research at the University of South Florida on rapid responses to bioterrorism, underwater sensors to detect explosives and microelectromechanical systems weapons. In February 2002 the USF marine science complex was named for Young. He plays a key role in distributing sand money to rebuild beaches; the committee voted to appropriate $142 million in 2002, 60% more than the administration requested; $30 million of it is for Florida.

The trend toward Democrats in Pinellas County has not posed any political threat to Young. But Republican redistricters wanted to make it more Republican anyway, so that the party will have a good chance to hold it if Young is not a candidate. Young said he simply wanted a compact district. He seemed disappointed when redistricters removed a heavily black part of south St. Petersburg and put it in the 11th District and said he would keep working for those voters. He was reelected unopposed in 2002. He may choose to retire in 2004, which will be the last year of his chairmanship if House Republicans continue to enforce their six-year term limit on chairmanships. If he does, there could a seriously contested race in the 10th District.

ELEVENTH DISTRICT

Rep. Jim Davis (D)

Elected 1996, 4th term; b. Oct. 11, 1957, Tampa; home, Tampa; Wash. & Lee U., B.A. 1979, U. of FL, J.D. 1982; Episcopalian; married (Peggy).

Elected Office: FL House of Reps., 1988–96, Maj. Ldr. 1994–96.

Professional Career: Practicing atty., 1982–96.

DC Office: 409 CHOB 20515, 202-225-3376; Fax: 202-225-5652; Web site: www.house.gov/jimdavis.

District Office: Tampa, 813-354-9217.

Committees: *Energy & Commerce* (24th of 26 D): Commerce, Trade & Consumer Protection; Environment & Hazardous Materials; Oversight & Investigations; Telecommunications & The Internet.

Group Ratings

	ADA	ACLU	AFS	LCV	CON	ITIC	NTU	COC	ACU	NTLC	CHC
2002	75	60	89	63	84	75	28	65	24	8	25
2001	80	—	90	86	—	—	18	48	12	—	—

National Journal Ratings

	2001 LIB	—	2001 CONS		2002 LIB	—	2002 CONS
Economic	62%	—	38%		63%	—	36%
Social	65%	—	34%		63%	—	35%
Foreign	54%	—	46%		55%	—	45%

Key Votes of the 107th Congress

1. Approve Bush Tax Cuts	N	5. Faith-Based Charities	N	9. Trade Promotion Authority	Y
2. Limit Patients' Bill of Rights	N	6. Bar Gays in the Boy Scouts	Y	10. Bar Funds for Intl. Court	N
3. Campaign Finance Reform	Y	7. Ban Partial-Birth Abortion	Y	11. Authorize Force in Iraq	Y
4. Ban ANWR Development	Y	8. Arm Commercial Pilots	N	12. Deny Home. Sec. Dept. Union	N

Election Results

2002 general	Jim Davis (D)	unopposed		($385,272)
2002 primary	Jim Davis (D)	unopposed		
2000 general	Jim Davis (D)	149,465	(85%)	($447,707)
	Charlie Westlake (Lib)	27,197	(15%)	($14,604)

Prior Winning Percentages: 1998 (65%); 1996 (58%)

The People		Race/Ethnic Origin	Ancestry	
Area size:	460 sq. mi.	48.3% White	German: 7.6%	Irish: 6.6%
Urban population:	99.6%	27.4% Black	English: 5.8%	
Rural population:	0.4%	2.0% Asian	**2000 Presidential Vote**	
Pop. 2000:	639,295	0.3% Native Am.	Gore (D).............120,926	(61%)
Median income:	$33,559	0.1% Hawaiian	Bush (R)..............77,367	(39%)
Poverty status:	17.5%	1.7% Two + races	**Cook Partisan Voting Index:** D +11	
Military veterans:	13.1%	0.2% Other		
		20.0% Hispanic Origin		

Occupation	Blue collar: 21.2%	White collar: 61.4%	Gray collar: 17.4%

Tampa, one of America's boomtowns, has a history that goes back just over a century. Its industrial past can be traced to 1886, when Cuban cigarmakers left Key West for what became the Ybor City neighborhood. Then Tampa became the major embarkation port for U.S. troops in the Spanish-American War of 1898. It also became a major citrus distribution center. The old industrial city developed along the waterfront, where today you can find what is billed as the world's longest sidewalk (6.5 miles along Bayshore Boulevard); you can also see the 13 minarets on the Arabian-style Tampa Bay Hotel built by railroad and real-estate tycoon Henry B. Plant in the 1890s (now part of the University of Tampa). For a time, Tampa was Florida's one industrial city. Now, it has a diversified economy: A healthy service sector, the University of Tampa and the University of South Florida, and tourist attractions led by Busch Gardens. Tampa's subdivisions and condominiums, office towers and low-rise commercial buildings have spread inland across swamps and lowlands.

Through all of this, and in contrast to St. Petersburg with its many retirees, Tampa has remained a city of families and young people; seniors account for only about one in eight residents here, an unusually low percentage for Florida. As Tampa expands, its blue-collar character is quickly moving upscale: Tampa was the nation's number one area for job growth in 1999, the city got a pro hockey team in 1990, a major league baseball franchise in 1995 and the Super Bowl at Raymond James Stadium in 2001. Tampa is also an important military center. The Central Command, which ran the Persian Gulf War and the campaigns in Afghanistan and Iraq, is headquartered at MacDill Air Force Base on the south side of Tampa.

The 11th Congressional District is centered on Tampa, but since the 2002 redistricting has rather irregular boundaries. It now includes most of the city of Tampa and close-in suburbs and the east shore of Tampa Bay. But the northern Hillsborough County suburbs are in the 9th District and the suburbs just to the east are in the 12th District. The current 11th District also includes two areas across Tampa Bay. One is the heavily black and lower-income neighborhoods south of Central Avenue in St. Petersburg. The other is a strip of Manatee County that includes working-class neighborhoods in Memphis, Palmetto and Bradenton, as well as the world headquarters of the Tropicana juice company. Connecting them is the distinctive Sunshine Skyway Bridge, a four-mile span completed in 1987 that has come to symbolize the Tampa Bay area. Before 2002, the 11th was entirely within Hillsborough County. But Republican redistricters removed Republican areas and placed them in the 9th and 12th Districts and removed heavily Democratic areas from St. Petersburg and Manatee County to make the 10th and 13th districts more Republican. The result is an 11th District with a population that is 27% black and 20% Hispanic—the most heavily minority district in Florida outside the Gold Coast and the Jacksonville-to-Orlando 3d District. While Hillsborough County as a whole voted for George W. Bush in 2000, the 11th District voted by a wide margin for Al Gore.

The congressman from the 11th District is Jim Davis, a Democrat elected in 1996. Davis grew up in Tampa as the grandson of a former mayor, returned after law school, and was elected in 1988, at 31, to the state House. There he showed insider skills and interests; after the 1994 election, he was elected state House Majority Leader—the last Democrat to hold that job, since Republicans won a majority in 1996. That year, Congressman Sam Gibbons decided to retire after 34 years, including a frustrating final two years in the minority. Davis was far from the best-known candidate, but he showed great skill at raising money and was the only one running TV ads for the September primary. Sandy Freedman, Tampa's mayor from 1986–95, led Davis in that contest 35%–25%. Both supported the balanced budget amendment, the 1996 welfare reform and called for more managed care. Davis won the runoff 56%–44% and in the general faced Republican Mark Sharpe, who had given Gibbons two close contests. He attacked Davis as a fan of higher taxes and a career politician. Davis insisted he was a New Democrat, supporting the Defense of Marriage Act and opposing the penny-per-pound sugar tax on the Florida ballot; he also called for more education spending. Davis won by a solid 58%–42%.

Davis's record has moved toward the center of the House. He was elected the Democratic freshman class president and got a seat on the Budget Committee. He favored a number of New Democrat causes: federal funding of charter schools, and the partial-birth abortion ban. After securing a deal to liberalize trade in manufactured fertilizers, whose chief U.S. shipping port is Tampa, Davis voted for PNTR with China. With most Florida Republicans siding with him, he won House passage in 2001 of his amendment to prevent a final lease agreement on a prime oil-development site in the Gulf. And he voted for trade promotion authority after he got protection for Florida citrus. In 2003, he became one of the three co-chairmen of the House's New Democrat Coalition.

Davis has entrenched himself in the seat. His expected Republican opponent in 2002 failed to submit his nominating petitions on time. In 2003, he got a seat on the Energy and Commerce Committee after being "deeply, deeply disappointed" over his failure to win it in 2001. He has expressed interest in running statewide in the past, including the 2002 race for governor, but he has failed to step up to the starting line. Still, he is one of the few Democratic officeholders in Florida with a relatively moderate record of the sort that enabled Reubin Askew, Lawton Chiles and Bob Graham to win statewide office; if Graham does not run for reelection in 2004 he might give up this safe seat to run for the Senate.

TWELFTH DISTRICT

Rep. Adam Putnam (R)

Elected 2000, 2d term; b. July 31, 1974, Bartow; home, Bartow; U. of FL, B.S. 1995; Episcopalian; married (Melissa).

Elected Office: FL House of Reps., 1996–00.

Professional Career: Rancher, Putnam Groves, Inc.

DC Office: 506 CHOB 20515, 202-225-1252; Fax: 202-226-0585; Web site: www.house.gov/putnam.

District Office: Bartow, 863-534-3530.

Committees: *Agriculture* (18th of 27 R): Conservation, Credit, Rural Development & Research; Department Operations, Oversight, Nutrition & Forestry; Livestock & Horticulture. *Budget* (12th of 24 R). *Government Reform* (14th of 24 R): Civil Service & Agency Organization; National Security, Emerging Threats & Intl. Relations;

Technology, Information Policy, Intergovernmental Relations & Census (Chmn.). *Joint Economic Committee* (5th of 10 Reps.).

Group Ratings

	ADA	ACLU	AFS	LCV	CON	ITIC	NTU	COC	ACU	NTLC	CHC
2002	0	7	0	0	8	88	57	95	96	89	100
2001	5	—	10	14	—	—	61	96	88	—	—

National Journal Ratings

	2001 LIB —	2001 CONS		2002 LIB —	2002 CONS
Economic	28% —	69%		0% —	91%
Social	20% —	69%		0% —	75%
Foreign	20% —	80%		0% —	85%

Key Votes of the 107th Congress

1. Approve Bush Tax Cuts	Y	5. Faith-Based Charities	Y	9. Trade Promotion Authority	N
2. Limit Patients' Bill of Rights	Y	6. Bar Gays in the Boy Scouts	Y	10. Bar Funds for Intl. Court	Y
3. Campaign Finance Reform	N	7. Ban Partial-Birth Abortion	Y	11. Authorize Force in Iraq	Y
4. Ban ANWR Development	N	8. Arm Commercial Pilots	Y	12. Deny Home. Sec. Dept. Union	Y

Election Results

2002 general	Adam Putnam (R)	unopposed		($350,343)
2002 primary	Adam Putnam (R)	unopposed		
2000 general	Adam Putnam (R)	125,224	(57%)	($1,047,257)
	Mike Stedem (D)	94,395	(43%)	($650,578)

The People		Race/Ethnic Origin	Ancestry	
Area size:	2,096 sq. mi.	72.1% White	German: 9.9%	USA: 9.8%
Urban population:	84.3%	13.0% Black	Irish: 8.4%	
Rural population:	15.7%	1.1% Asian	**2000 Presidential Vote**	
Pop. 2000:	639,296	0.3% Native Am.	Bush (R)	121,083 (55%)
Median income:	$37,769	0.0% Hawaiian	Gore (D)	99,826 (45%)
Poverty status:	12.4%	1.3% Two+ races	**Cook Partisan Voting Index:** R + 5	
Military veterans:	17.0%	0.1% Other		
		12.0% Hispanic Origin		

Occupation　Blue collar: 26.1%　White collar: 55.9%　Gray collar: 18.0%

With their skyscrapers rising over bays and rivers, the great gleaming cities of Florida are found near the Atlantic or Gulf coasts. But the most expansive inland county in the state, billed as the heart of central Florida, is Polk County. It is filled with modest lakes and small and medium-sized cities: Lakeland, Bartow, Lake Wales, Winter Haven, Frostproof and Haines City. It is the part of Florida most dependent on agriculture: strawberries, cattle and citrus remain economic mainstays, though periodic freezes have convinced some orange growers to move south or to produce tomatoes instead. Turpentine distilleries, dependent on the big stands of pine, and phosphate mining businesses can be found as well; there are more manufacturing jobs here proportionately than almost anywhere else in Florida (though still not very many). Retired *Ladies Home Journal* editor Edward Bok built the most prominent landmarks here: the gothic Bok Tower and the surrounding Mountain Lake Sanctuary and gardens. But the area has not become a major retiree haven; it grew by 20% percent during the 1990s—rapid growth in most of the country, but not in Florida. About half the growth here has been an influx of Latinos; Polk County's Hispanic population expanded by 176% between 1990 and 2000.

The 12th Congressional District includes most of Polk County. This was the home of Spessard Holland and Lawton Chiles, two legendary Democrats who each served as governor and senator. Even today, there are more registered Democrats than Republicans, but Polk County, like most of the Deep South, increasingly votes Republican, and Chiles lost Polk County in his last race in 1994 to Jeb Bush. The 12th District also includes a sliver of Osceola County and the rapidly growing suburbs just east of Tampa in Hillsborough County—places like Brandon, home to strip malls and younger, pro-business families. Overall this district, historically Democratic, is becoming reliably Republican. It voted 55% for George W. Bush in 2000 and by a wide margin for Jeb Bush in 2002.

The congressman from the 12th District is Adam Putnam, a Republican elected in 2000 who entered the House as its youngest member, at 26; he was still the youngest member after the 2002 election. A fifth-generation member of a Bartow family, he graduated from the University of Florida and worked in his family's citrus and cattle business. In 1996 he was elected to the state House, where as Agriculture Committee Chairman he supported controversial legislation, including a "sovereign lands" bill that would have given shoreline property on inland waters to adjacent property owners and was strongly opposed by environmentalists. When Congressman Charles Canady retired at age 46, keeping his pledge to serve only four terms, Putnam was unopposed in the Republican primary. He became the clear frontrunner when former Democratic state Senator Rick Dantzler decided not to run. Putnam supported most parts of the Republican agenda. He opposes abortion and gun control, wants to lower the capital gains tax and allow workers to invest part of their Social Security tax in private investments, and favors a missile defense system. In his first election, Putnam had a tougher than expected challenge from auto-dealer and first-time candidate Michael Stedem; he said that Putnam did not have enough life experience for the job. Stedem's message gained some traction. "Putnam is 26 and looks as if he's going on 13," wrote Daniel Ruth of *The Tampa Tribune* in October 2000, in a story headlined, "Opie runs for Congress." But Putnam won the seat 57%–43%.

With one notable exception, Putnam was a reliable conservative vote. That one case was the December 2001 vote on trade promotion authority, where an evidently conflicted Putnam sided with the citrus industry, despite considerable pressure from party leaders, including during a ride to Florida with George W. Bush on Air Force One a week before the vote. "The pressure was unbelievable," he recounted, but the administration would not agree to legislative language that Putnam said was essential. When the bill returned to the House a few months later to resolve final details, Putnam voted in favor after he got what he viewed as a stronger commitment to protect citrus interests. Putnam had another memorable ride with Bush three months earlier. On the morning of September 11, 2001 he was with Bush during a visit to an elementary school in Sarasota when word came of the attacks on the World Trade Center towers. After their rapid and steeply-banking exit and before they landed at Barksdale Air Force Base in Louisiana, Bush called in Putnam and the 13th District's Dan Miller for a briefing of his options that morning. The two congressmen returned to Washington on another plane. On the farm bill, Putnam took some credit for killing an amendment by environmentalists that would have required increased conservation. He called the final version more "Florida friendly" because it increased conservation funds to protect the state's waterways.

Redistricting made the district more suburban but didn't affect the party balance. Putnam was reelected without opposition. In 2003, he became chairman of the Technology, Information Policy, Intergovernmental Relations and the Census Subcommittee on Government Reform, making him the youngest subcommittee chairman since the post-World War II era. In his early months in the House, there were many jokes about his youth; some people refused to believe he was a congressman. Putnam was nonplussed. In March 2003, when Pete Stark (who was elected to Congress before Putnam was born) took to the House floor and called Bush "a liar" who was going to war "to cover up his failed diplomatic, social and economic agenda," an angry Putnam retorted that Stark "should take his tongue-in-cheek comments back to Baghdad."

THIRTEENTH DISTRICT

Rep. Katherine Harris (R)

Elected 2002, 1st term; b. April 5, 1957, Key West; home, Sarasota; Agnes Scott Col., B.A. 1979, Harvard U. Kennedy Schl. of Gov., M.P.A. 1996; Presbyterian; married (Anders).

Elected Office: FL Senate, 1994–98; FL Secy. of State, 1998–02.

DC Office: 116 CHOB 20515, 202-225-5015; Fax: 202-226-0828; Web site: www.house.gov/harris.

District Offices: Bradenton, 941-747-9081; Sarasota, 941-951-6643.

Committees: *Financial Services* (36th of 37 R): Capital Markets, Insurance & Government Sponsored Enterprises; Domestic and International Monetary Policy, Trade & Technology; Housing & Community Opportunity. *International Relations* (26th of 26 R): Middle East & Central Asia; Western Hemisphere.

Group Ratings and Key Votes: Newly Elected

Election Results

2002 general	Katherine Harris (R)	139,048	(55%)	($3,298,146)
	Jan Schneider (D)	114,739	(45%)	($336,796)
2002 primary	Katherine Harris (R)	47,761	(68%)	
	John Hill (R)	22,144	(32%)	
2000 general	Dan Miller (R)	175,918	(64%)	($369,407)
	Daniel E. Dunn (D)	99,568	(36%)	($40,948)

The People		Race/Ethnic Origin	Ancestry	
Area size:	2,948 sq. mi.	86.0% White	German: 14.1%	English: 10.8%
Urban population:	89.4%	4.4% Black	Irish: 10.2%	
Rural population:	10.6%	0.8% Asian	**2000 Presidential Vote**	
Pop. 2000:	639,295	0.2% Native Am.	Bush (R)..............152,725	(54%)
Median income:	$40,187	0.0% Hawaiian	Gore (D)..............127,751	(46%)
Poverty status:	9.4%	0.8% Two+ races	**Cook Partisan Voting Index:** R + 5	
Military veterans:	19.2%	0.1% Other		
		7.7% Hispanic Origin		

Occupation	Blue collar: 21.0%	White collar: 58.5%	Gray collar: 20.5%

When the Ringling Brothers made a success of the circus they founded in the 1880s, they needed a place for performers and animals to rest during the winter months. They settled on the bayfront village of Sarasota, located behind a barrier island on the Gulf of Mexico. It was just far enough north to be reachable by railroad, just far enough south to be semitropical so the elephants would not get sick and die. Here, on the calm Sarasota Bay, John Ringling established the Ringling Museum of Art, a huge sculpture garden and his own Venetian palace, the Ca'd'Zan; next door, his brother Charles built a pair of neoclassical revival mansions made of pink Georgia marble, now owned and used by New College of Florida. After World War II, the balmy Gulf Coast attracted new settlers—affluent, well-educated Republicans from WASPy, upper-crust suburbs in the north. The population exploded, with Manatee and Sarasota Counties leaping from 63,000 in 1950 to 590,000 in 2000.

The 13th Congressional District runs from just below Tampa Bay to Charlotte Harbor, north of Fort Myers. It includes all of Sarasota County (which accounts for just over half the district's population) and all of lightly populated, rural DeSoto and Hardee Counties, most of Manatee County to the north and an adjoining sliver of Charlotte County to the south. The barrier islands include much idyllic beachfront, from sleepy Anna Maria down through pricey Longboat Key and Lido Key to more casual Siesta Key. The bayfront area, along the Intracoastal Waterway, is lined with high rises and often clogged with traffic, running from Bradenton south to Sarasota. Below that, Venice—established in 1920 as a speculative land venture by the Brotherhood of Locomotive Engineers and, since 1960, the winter quarters for the circus—sits directly on the ocean. Though some high-tech firms diversify the economy, this remains a place of tourists and well-off retirees: 29% of the population is over 65, the 2d highest percentage of all 435 congressional districts (Florida's 19th ranked first). For many years, the 13th District was heavily Republican, and it remains that way in registration, but like the affluent northern suburbs from which so many of its voters came it trended toward the Democrats in the 1990s. George W. Bush carried this district in 2000, but with only 54% of the vote.

The congresswoman from the 13th District is Katherine Harris, a Republican first elected in 2002 and a political figure of renown before her election to the House. She grew up in Bartow in Polk County, where her grandfather Ben Hill Griffin Jr. was one of Florida's largest landowners, with thousands of acres of citrus grove and cattle range; he was also politically influential, and the University of Florida football stadium is named for him. Harris interned for Porter Goss in college, graduated from Agnes Scott College in Georgia, and studied art and other courses in Europe. She moved to Sarasota and worked as a real estate executive and in marketing for IBM and became a patron of the arts. In 1994, she was elected to the state Senate in what was then the costliest legislative race in state history. In the Senate she sponsored a contentious bill requiring minors to get parental consent for abortions, but it was vetoed by Governor Lawton Chiles. In 1998 she ran against the incumbent secretary of state, who was backed by Jeb Bush, and won the primary 61%–39% and the general election 54%–46%. In 1999, the legislature voted to remove the office from the Cabinet and make it an appointed position rather than elected. So Harris was something of a lame duck on election night 2000, as the votes coming in showed that the presidential race in Florida was going to be extremely close.

Florida law gave Harris the responsibility of certifying the election and declaring the winner of the state's 25 electoral votes (now it has 27). When she vowed to certify the results one week after Election Day, as state law required, lawyers for Al Gore sued for more time. Two weeks later, when Harris did certify Bush as the winner, Gore sued her again, claiming she acted before all the recounts were complete. Democratic critics charged that her actions were biased; Republicans hailed her for adhering to the letter of the law and for ultimately certifying Bush, by 537 votes, as winner in accordance with state law.

There was an obvious political opening for Harris, when 13th District Congressman Dan Miller, a crusader against the sugar program and the Republicans' point man on the Census, kept his promise to retire after serving 10 years. In October 2001 Harris announced she was running and immediately got into trouble; her Republican primary opponent, former local TV anchor John Hill, filed a lawsuit arguing that under Florida law she could not run until she resigned as secretary of state. She quickly did resign, and the court eventually ruled that her action was "statutorily forgiven," but not until the day after the September 10 primary. Even with that cloud over her candidacy, Harris beat Hill 68%–32%.

Although the general election was mostly treated as a coronation, it actually featured elements of political interest. The Democratic nominee was Jan Schneider, who graduated from Yale Law School in the same class as Bill and Hillary Clinton. She worked in Washington as a lawyer and lobbyist for 25 years, and played a bit role in the 2000 election aftermath by interviewing allegedly disenfranchised voters in Palm Beach County. She reiterated Democrats' charges that Harris had not followed the law in November and December 2000, and she questioned whether the nation was "adopting a 'might is right' policy" in dealing with Iraq. Harris opposed oil drilling in the Gulf of Mexico, supported private Social Security investment accounts, and supports the current law on abortion—although she calls herself pro-life. She made the case for her Election 2000 conduct in her book, *Center of the Storm,* which was released in October. She then departed for a national publicity tour; Schneider criticized her for leaving the district. Harris said she had pleaded with the publisher to release the book much later.

Harris won 55%–45%, but given her name identification and money advantage, this was not a huge margin; basically it was a along party lines. Harris has been mentioned as a possible candidate for the Senate if Bob Graham does not seek reelection in 2004.

FOURTEENTH DISTRICT

Rep. Porter Goss (R)

Elected 1988, 8th term; b. Nov. 26, 1938, Waterbury, CT; home, Sanibel; Yale U., B.A. 1960; Presbyterian; married (Mariel).

Military Career: Army Intelligence, 1960–62.

Elected Office: Sanibel City Cncl., 1974–82; Sanibel Mayor, 1974–77, 1980; Lee Cnty. Commissioner 1982–88.

Professional Career: CIA Clandestine Svcs. 1960–71; Businessman & newspaper publ., 1973–78.

DC Office: 108 CHOB 20515, 202-225-2536; Fax: 202-225-6820; Web site: www.house.gov/goss.

District Offices: Ft. Myers, 239-332-4677; Naples, 239-774-8060.

Committees: *Permanent Select Committee on Intelligence* (Chmn. of 11 R). *Rules* (Vice Chmn. of 9 R): The Legislative & Budget Process. *Select Committee on Homeland Security* (14th of 27 R): Intelligence & Counter-terrorism; Rules.

Group Ratings

	ADA	ACLU	AFS	LCV	CON	ITIC	NTU	COC	ACU	NTLC	CHC
2002	0	7	0	38	25	100	57	100	84	86	100
2001	0	—	0	21	—	—	62	100	80	—	—

National Journal Ratings

	2001 LIB	—	2001 CONS		2002 LIB	—	2002 CONS
Economic	28%	—	69%		33%	—	67%
Social	20%	—	69%		32%	—	63%
Foreign	21%	—	74%		15%	—	78%

Key Votes of the 107th Congress

1. Approve Bush Tax Cuts	Y	5. Faith-Based Charities	Y	9. Trade Promotion Authority	Y
2. Limit Patients' Bill of Rights	Y	6. Bar Gays in the Boy Scouts	Y	10. Bar Funds for Intl. Court	Y
3. Campaign Finance Reform	N	7. Ban Partial-Birth Abortion	Y	11. Authorize Force in Iraq	Y
4. Ban ANWR Development	N	8. Arm Commercial Pilots	Y	12. Deny Home. Sec. Dept. Union	Y

Election Results

2002 general	Porter Goss (R)	.... unopposed		($90,189)
2002 primary	Porter Goss (R)	.... unopposed		
2000 general	Porter Goss (R)	 242,614	(85%)	($259,684)
	Sam Farling (NL)	 41,988	(15%)	($7,215)

Prior Winning Percentages: 1998 (100%); 1996 (73%); 1994 (100%); 1992 (82%); 1990 (100%); 1988 (71%)

The People		Race/Ethnic Origin	Ancestry	
Area size:	1,718 sq. mi.	83.8% White	German: 14.5%	Irish: 11.0%
Urban population:	90.7%	5.1% Black	English: 10.2%	
Rural population:	9.3%	0.7% Asian	**2000 Presidential Vote**	
Pop. 2000:	639,295	0.2% Native Am.	Bush (R) 163,750 (61%)	
Median income:	$42,541	0.0% Hawaiian	Gore (D) 103,118 (39%)	
Poverty status:	8.8%	1.0% Two+ races	**Cook Partisan Voting Index:** R +12	
Military veterans:	19.8%	0.1% Other		
		9.0% Hispanic Origin		
Occupation	Blue collar: 21.1%	White collar: 59.6%	Gray collar: 19.3%	

On the edge of the Tropics, in a physical environment once teeming with diseases and inhospitable to advanced civilization three generations ago, Florida's Gulf Coast has sprung up as a model for retirement living. Early on, there were few white settlements here; one was Fort Myers, built in

1850 as an Army base to help get rid of the Seminole Indians. The fort achieved its goal: In 1858, the last Seminoles were sent west on boats. For another century after that, this corner of Florida was mostly deserted. But in time, it became resort country, thanks to its wide, white-sand beaches with gentle breakers; the inlets and broad estuaries that are perfect for boating; and the wetlands graced with exotic birds. Thomas Edison had his winter home in Fort Myers, Henry Ford used to visit here, Tourists came to a beach thick with sea shells on nearby Sanibel and Captiva islands. But the local economy could not support many permanent residents, and at the beginning of World War II, there were only 68,000 people living on the Gulf Coast from Bradenton south to Naples.

By 2000, there were 1.4 million: The climate and environment had attracted waves of afflu-ent suburbanites from the Midwest and Northeast, with the added lure of no state income or inheritance taxes. Developers like Barron Collier, who built the Tamiami Trail across the soggy Everglades and designed Naples with the wealthy in mind (and gave his name to Collier County, the richest and in the 1990s the second fastest-growing in Florida), were determined to avoid the high-rise canyons that line the Atlantic from Palm Beach to Miami. Their alternative was to construct low-rise, city-style developments, such as Cape Coral, with canals in most backyards, and thinly paved roads along the sand spits next to the sultry, lapping waves of the Gulf, and luxurious boutique towns like Naples, set amidst preserved coastal islands, St. Augustine grass and banyan trees. This is very much retirement country, for those who can afford it.

The 14th Congressional District occupies the southern half of the habitable Gulf Coast below Tampa Bay; it grew by almost 40% in the 1990s, largely from retirees, who account for more than one of every four residents. The 14th includes a small part of Port Charlotte and Charlotte County, all of Fort Myers and Lee County and the coastal strip of Collier County including Naples and Marco Island. Two-thirds of the district's residents live in Lee County, in places like Fort Myers, Bonita Springs and the idyllic resorts of Sanibel and Captiva. In a state where Republican regis-tration rates often understate Republican voting strength, the 14th District counts 52% of its electorate as registered Republicans. In 2000 George W. Bush won 61% of the vote here; in 1998 this was one of only two districts not carried by Democratic Senator Bob Graham.

The congressman from the 14th District is Porter Goss, a Republican first elected in 1988. After graduating from Yale, where he majored in Greek, he worked 10 years in the CIA's Clan-destine Services in Latin America, the Caribbean and Europe. He retired from the agency in 1971 after he nearly died from blood poisoning and a heart infection and moved to Sanibel Island. There he founded the prize-winning *Island Reporter*, served on the city council and as mayor and passed growth management laws. In 1982 he was appointed to the Lee County Commission by then-Governor Bob Graham and was elected in 1984. Even then, he was worried about terrorism; he saw to it that the airport police at the Southwest Florida Regional Airport were armed with Uzi submachine guns. When incumbent Congressman Connie Mack ran for the Senate in 1988, Goss ran for this seat and effectively won it in the Republican primary, leading 38%–29%–19% over former Congressman Skip Bafalis and retired General James Dozier.

Goss has been chairman of the Intelligence Committee since 1997. Some have been critical of having a CIA veteran head the committee and have charged that Goss is too easy on the agency. "I've got to be harsher than the next guy because I was in the business," is one of Goss's replies. "I think I'm a pretty good watchdog, because I know what to look for." As chairman he led efforts to increase intelligence spending in the October 1998 omnibus budget bill. He wanted more spending to enable intelligence agencies to recapitalize technological intelligence collection, re-build espionage capabilities, develop the ability to respond with covert action to transnational threats and hostile states and to increase analytic depth and breadth.

Goss's concern for security is balanced by a realization that there can be too much secrecy. In October 1999 he and Senator Daniel Patrick Moynihan sponsored a bill to create a Public Interest Declassification Board to declassify old documents, especially those relating to historical controversies. When the NSA said it couldn't divulge to Congress details on its Echelon global spying operation, he threatened to cut off funds and the agency changed its stand. Goss has opposed loosening export controls on encryption. After the 2000 election, he urged George W.

Bush to keep George Tenet as CIA director, and has generally supported him, despite former Senate Intelligence Chairman Richard Shelby's harsh criticism of Tenet. Goss got on much better with Florida Democrat Bob Graham, who replaced Shelby as Senate Intelligence Chairman in June 2001. On the morning of September 11, 2001, Goss and Graham were having breakfast in the Capitol with General Mehmood Ahmed, the chief of Pakistani intelligence, asking him about Osama bin Laden when they were informed of the attacks on the World Trade Center towers. They quickly left the Capitol, but Goss, as Speaker pro tem for the day, hastily convened the House for a one-minute session. Within weeks Goss and Graham got authorization of an 8% increase in intelligence spending.

In February 2002 the House and Senate Intelligence committees began a joint inquiry into intelligence failures before September 11; the two Floridians were co-chairmen. This was a rocky process. The first chief counsel was forced out by Shelby in April 2002. In June he and Graham asked the Justice Department to investigate possible leaks after Dick Cheney called them to complain about a newspaper story about an intercepted phone call in Arabic. In October he and Graham agreed to support an independent commission to go over the same questions; they stressed that their inquiry was only a beginning and not an end. The task, Goss said, was to develop agencies able to assemble and interpret information about terrorist threats. He was critical of the CIA for not having the human intelligence capacity it had in his time. "We are being too namby-pamby about taking risks to get the good penetrations of the hard targets in denied areas." In May 2002 he said the FBI was not prepared to do intelligence work. By December the joint inquiry issued its report. Goss said in March 2002 that the war on terrorism would not be over until the U.S. dealt with Saddam Hussein, but said that we weren't yet prepared militarily; he strongly supported the Iraq war resolution in October 2002.

Goss is the second-ranking Republican on the Rules Committee and has reliably supported the Republican leadership. On most issues he has taken conservative stands. In line with Gulf Coast opinion, he has supported and worked to extend the 1982 moratorium on oil drilling in the Gulf of Mexico off the Florida shore.

Goss has always been reelected easily. In May 2000 he said he would serve only one more term in the House. In July 2001 he said he was reconsidering because of redistricting: Republican redistricters were talking about putting some of his territory into a district that extended east to the Gold Coast. After September 11 many tried to persuade him to run again, including George W. Bush and Dick Cheney. At the end of a meeting on Capitol Hill in the winter, as people were getting up to leave, Cheney said, "Not so fast, Goss. My instructions are not to open that door until you say yes." In February 2002 he announced he would run again and apologized to his constituents for "taking so long to come to my decision." There was no question that House Republicans would again waive their three-term limit on chairmanships for Goss; the Republican next in line on the committee, Doug Bereuter said immediately after Goss's announcement, "I think absolutely that Porter Goss is the person best qualified by knowledge and experience to lead the Intelligence Committee."

When Goss announced he was running, several Republicans had already filed to run; it was obvious that in this district the Republican nomination would be tantamount to election. But all immediately withdrew and Goss was reelected without opposition. Goss has again said this term will be his last. Possible candidates if he retires in 2004: Lee County Commissioners John Albion and Andrew Coy; physician Page Kreegel; Wayne Daltry, longtime head of the Southwest Florida Regional Planning Council; state Representative Carole Green; state Senator Burt Saunders.

FIFTEENTH DISTRICT

Rep. Dave Weldon (R)

Elected 1994, 5th term; b. Aug. 31, 1953, Amityville, NY; home, Palm Bay; S.U.N.Y. Stony Brook, B.A. 1978, S.U.N.Y. Buffalo, M.D. 1981; Christian; married (Nancy).

Military Career: Army Medical Corps, 1981–87, Army Reserves, 1987–92.

Professional Career: Practicing physician, 1987–94.

DC Office: 2347 RHOB 20515, 202-225-3671; Fax: 202-225-3516; Web site: www.house.gov/weldon.

District Office: Melbourne, 321-632-1776.

Committees: *Appropriations* (32d of 36 R): District of Columbia; Labor, HHS & Education; VA, HUD & Independent Agencies.

Group Ratings

	ADA	ACLU	AFS	LCV	CON	ITIC	NTU	COC	ACU	NTLC	CHC
2002	0	7	0	38	77	75	60	90	100	91	100
2001	5	—	0	14	—	—	71	87	92	—	—

National Journal Ratings

	2001 LIB	—	2001 CONS		2002 LIB	—	2002 CONS
Economic	22%	—	74%		28%	—	69%
Social	0%	—	81%		0%	—	75%
Foreign	33%	—	60%		0%	—	85%

Key Votes of the 107th Congress

1. Approve Bush Tax Cuts	Y	5. Faith-Based Charities	Y	9. Trade Promotion Authority	Y
2. Limit Patients' Bill of Rights	Y	6. Bar Gays in the Boy Scouts	Y	10. Bar Funds for Intl. Court	Y
3. Campaign Finance Reform	N	7. Ban Partial-Birth Abortion	Y	11. Authorize Force in Iraq	Y
4. Ban ANWR Development	N	8. Arm Commercial Pilots	Y	12. Deny Home. Sec. Dept. Union	Y

Election Results

2002 general	Dave Weldon (R)	146,414	(63%)	($721,859)
	Jim Tso (D)	85,433	(37%)	($51,697)
2002 primary	Dave Weldon (R)	46,086	(83%)	
	Gerry Newby (R)	9,126	(17%)	
2000 general	Dave Weldon (R)	176,189	(59%)	($910,906)
	Patsy Ann Kurth (D)	117,511	(39%)	($698,292)
	Other	5,745	(2%)	

Prior Winning Percentages: 1998 (63%); 1996 (51%); 1994 (54%)

The People		Race/Ethnic Origin	Ancestry	
Area size:	3,253 sq. mi.	77.8% White	German: 12.2%	Irish: 10.6%
Urban population:	89.6%	7.3% Black	English: 9.7%	
Rural population:	10.4%	1.6% Asian	**2000 Presidential Vote**	
Pop. 2000:	639,295	0.3% Native Am.	Bush (R)	141,242 (54%)
Median income:	$39,397	0.0% Hawaiian	Gore (D)	121,611 (46%)
Poverty status:	9.8%	1.4% Two+ races	**Cook Partisan Voting Index:** R + 4	
Military veterans:	19.4%	0.2% Other		
		11.3% Hispanic Origin		
Occupation	Blue collar: 21.5%	White collar: 58.4%	Gray collar: 20.1%	

When Cape Canaveral was chosen as the nation's rocket testing site in the 1940s, there were only 20,000 people in all of Brevard County, which stretches along 63 miles of the coast north and south of the Cape. It was a backward place reliant on fishing and citrus-growing, chosen because it was on the sunny Atlantic coast: rockets here have to be launched eastward so that spent parts fall into the ocean. The Brooklyn Dodgers' spring-training home of Vero Beach, located 60 miles south of Canaveral in Indian River County, remained segregationist through the mid-1950s, until Dodger executives used an ingenious method to flex their economic muscle in the service of integration: They stamped the team's name on 20,000 dollar bills and told players and reporters to spend them freely at local establishments. Local officials got the message, easing off on Jim Crow, at least when Jackie Robinson and his teammates were in town. Today, the region has come a long way. Brevard is home to nearly half a million people, and the Kennedy Space Center alone attracts 2.5 million visitors annually. Brevard is a prototype of America's future, with no city center but plenty of shopping centers along strip highways, with a white-collar, service economy, knitted together by interest in the space program. Its proximity to Disney World has spawned growth in the local cruise business, including Disney's own mega-ships.

The 15th Congressional District includes much, but not all, of the Space Coast, which grew by almost 30% in the 1990s. Its northern end is at Cape Canaveral itself, but most of the Space Center facilities, including the visitors' center are in the 24th District just to the north. It runs south along the Atlantic Coast and includes all of Indian River County; among the bigger towns are Cocoa Beach, Melbourne, Palm Bay and Vero Beach. The district also includes all but a small piece of Osceola County to the west; the population here is concentrated around Kissimmee and just south of Disney World. The district also includes the northern tip of Polk County further west. In between are trackless swamp and ranch lands traversed by Florida's Turnpike. Yeehaw Junction, home to the historic Desert Inn and not much else, got its start as a watering hole for cowboys driving cattle south from the Orlando area and the Kissimmee River. The Army Corps of Engineers, which straightened out the Kissimmee in the early 1970s, continues to restore it to its natural snake-like course, just as it will do to the Everglades further south. The population here is a mixture of young workers and retirees, plus military families stationed at Patrick Air Force Base, home of the 45th Space Wing. Politically, the district leans Republican. In 2000 it voted narrowly for George W. Bush, but was carried narrowly by Democratic Senator Bill Nelson, who is from Melbourne and represented most of the district in the House from 1978 to 1990.

The congressman from the 15th District is Dave Weldon, a Republican elected in 1994. Weldon grew up on Long Island, went to medical school in Buffalo, and served in the Army as a Major at Fort Stewart, Georgia. In 1987, he joined Melbourne Internal Medicine Associates in Florida; two years later, he founded the Space Coast Family Forum "to promote family-friendly issues and positions." When Weldon ran for the House in 1994 after moderate Democrat Jim Bacchus retired, he was considered a weak candidate because of his strong conservative views on cultural issues. But he led the seven-candidate Republican primary with 24% of the vote, and in the runoff won 54%–46% over moderate Carole Jordan. Democrats ran Sue Munsey, a former Republican and Space Coast Chamber of Commerce head who supported abortion rights. Weldon called for phasing out welfare and banning abortion; he won 54%–46%. Speaker Newt Gingrich, whom Weldon called an "idol," gave him a seat on the Science Committee and made him vice chairman of the Space and Aeronautics Subcommittee.

Weldon started off defending the Kennedy Space Center and promoting the Space Shuttle, protecting their funding even when NASA funding was going down. But in time he moved from defending an existing program to transforming it. With Senator Bob Graham, he passed a bill in 1998 to move toward commercialization of space. The idea was to increase U.S. commercial launching capacity, by using antiquated (and disposable) ballistic missiles. Still, commercial competition and the response to the loss of the space shuttle *Columbia* in February 2003, may bring long-term challenges to the Cape Canaveral area. Even before the shuttle blew up over Texas, Weldon complained that budget cuts were "slowly killing space exploration"; he has cited reduced spending as a factor in the failure of two Mars missions. With Dennis Kucinich, he formed and co-chaired the Aerospace Caucus to respond to international challengers in the global market; he wants to increase federal support for research and development. In 2002, he co-authored with writer William Proctor *Moongate,* a sci-fi novel about a Brevard County congressman who chairs the House Space Committee and gains the power to cure many ills through genetic engineering; Weldon called it an opportunity to explore several topics that interest him.

Weldon has a conservative voting record; he favors increased defense spending, a 17% flat tax, school vouchers and education IRAs. Citing labor and human rights abuses plus undercutting of the U.S. space launch industry, he voted against PNTR with China; but he voted for trade promotion authority. In late September 2001, the House defeated his amendment to prohibit the District of Columbia from providing benefits under its domestic partner law; when opponents criticized him for jeopardizing the spirit of national unity after the September 11 attacks, he attacked their "name calling" during the nation's time of healing. Weldon became a leader in the campaign to ban cloning, including embryonic stem cell research. When the House passed his anti-cloning bill, Weldon noted that it does not restrict research on adult stem cells. The Senate failed to act on the measure. On a more practical matter, he won a change in House rules to drop the restrictions on members who are physicians from earning income from their medical practice.

Weldon, who home-schools his children, has a reputation for outspoken conservatism. It has inspired strong electoral opposition, but he has survived with comfortable margins. In 2000 he had a well-financed opponent, Patsy Kurth, a state Senator and cousin of Dick Gephardt. She criticized Weldon's failure to prevent NASA cutbacks and supported abortion rights; Weldon won 59%–39%. Redistricting in 2002 removed northern Brevard County, but did not change the leanings of the district much. Weldon beat a primary opponent who criticized him for violating his term-limit pledge by 83%–17% and won the general election 63%–37%. After the election, Weldon won a seat on the Appropriations Committee. Although that forced him to leave the Science Committee, he gained an opportunity to have more direct impact on NASA's budget.

SIXTEENTH DISTRICT

Rep. Mark Foley (R)

Elected 1994, 5th term; b. Sept. 8, 1954, Newton, MA; home, West Palm Beach; Palm Beach Commun. Col., 1974; Catholic; single.

Elected Office: Lake Worth City Commissioner, 1977–83; Vice Mayor, 1983–84; FL House of Reps., 1990–92; FL Senate, 1992–94.

Professional Career: Restaurateur, 1974–84; Real estate broker, 1984–90.

DC Office: 104 CHOB 20515, 202-225-5792; Fax: 202-225-3132; Web site: www.house.gov/foley.

District Offices: Palm Beach Gardens, 561-627-6192; Port St. Lucie, 772-878-3181.

Committees: *Ways & Means* (21st of 24 R): Oversight; Select Revenue Measures.

Group Ratings

	ADA	ACLU	AFS	LCV	CON	ITIC	NTU	COC	ACU	NTLC	CHC
2002	15	33	0	0	25	88	56	95	92	81	50
2001	30	—	10	36	—	—	60	91	64	—	—

National Journal Ratings

	2001 LIB —	2001 CONS		2002 LIB —	2002 CONS
Economic	36%	63%		40%	59%
Social	52%	47%		47%	53%
Foreign	43%	53%		15%	78%

Key Votes of the 107th Congress

1. Approve Bush Tax Cuts	Y	5. Faith-Based Charities	Y	9. Trade Promotion Authority	N
2. Limit Patients' Bill of Rights	Y	6. Bar Gays in the Boy Scouts	Y	10. Bar Funds for Intl. Court	Y
3. Campaign Finance Reform	Y	7. Ban Partial-Birth Abortion	Y	11. Authorize Force in Iraq	Y
4. Ban ANWR Development	Y	8. Arm Commercial Pilots	Y	12. Deny Home. Sec. Dept. Union	Y

Election Results

2002 general	Mark Foley (R) 176,171	(79%)	($902,644)
	Jack McLain (CPF) 47,169	(21%)	($2,587)
2002 primary	Mark Foley (R) .... unopposed		
2000 general	Mark Foley (R) 176,153	(60%)	($1,544,903)
	Jean Elliott Brown (D) 108,782	(37%)	($559,210)
	Other 7,565	(3%)	

Prior Winning Percentages: 1998 (100%); 1996 (64%); 1994 (58%)

The People		Race/Ethnic Origin	Ancestry	
Area size:	5,249 sq. mi.	81.8% White	German: 12.3%	Irish: 11.3%
Urban population:	84.5%	5.8% Black	English: 9.7%	
Rural population:	15.5%	1.0% Asian	**2000 Presidential Vote**	
Pop. 2000:	639,295	0.3% Native Am.	Bush (R)...............141,029	(53%)
Median income:	$39,408	0.0% Hawaiian	Gore (D)...............124,752	(47%)
Poverty status:	10.0%	1.0% Two + races	**Cook Partisan Voting Index:** R + 3	
Military veterans:	18.9%	0.1% Other		
		10.1% Hispanic Origin		

Occupation   Blue collar: 21.8%   White collar: 57.5%   Gray collar: 20.6%

Urban Florida has fanned far across the swamplands from its original nuclei in beachfront resort communities. Once, metro Palm Beach was a narrow stretch along Lake Worth; now it runs inland almost halfway to Lake Okeechobee. Thus Palm Beach has spread out from its original locus around the posh Breakers Hotel and the Addison Mizner villas, across Lake Worth and well beyond West Palm Beach: These are now just neighborhoods within a vast metropolitan area. Old beach towns, such as Hobe Sound, located northward along the ocean, have become the the hub of extremely affluent developments that stretch all the way to Stuart in Martin County. Farther north, near the old town of Fort Pierce, are larger but more modest developments like Port St. Lucie. Here, spring training sites compete for baseball franchises that direct millions of dollars to local economies.

The 16th Congressional District stretches from the Atlantic almost to the Gulf of Mexico; it is one of the most oddly shaped districts in the nation. In 2000, prior to redistricting, 44% of the 16th District's vote was cast in Palm Beach County; after redistricting, just 15% was cast there in 2002. On the Atlantic Coast it includes most of Martin County, with its very affluent towns of Stuart and Hobe Sound; much of St. Lucie County, where it includes the new developments of Port St. Lucie and Hutchinson Island and the white neighborhoods of Fort Pierce; and just a bit of Palm Beach County—Tequesta, its northernmost beach town, inland Royal Palm Beach and Wellington, a town for rich horse fanciers. By a thin corridor of land this Atlantic Coast area is connected to rural territory north and west of Lake Okeechobee: here huge farms produce citrus, tomatoes and other vegetable or support large dairy herds; the only population cluster is around Sebring, with its car racing track. This area is connected by the swamps of eastern Charlotte County with the Gulf Coast towns of Port Charlotte and Punta Gorda, on the wide Peace River where it empties into Port Charlotte and the Gulf of Mexico. There was, of course, a political motive for this configuration. The Republican redistricters wanted to create Republican-leaning districts for two Republican incumbents whose political bases are on the Atlantic Coast. But Palm Beach County has been voting Democratic by increasing margins: few other counties in America which are classified as largely suburban voted as heavily for Al Gore in 2000 as Palm Beach County did (62%–35%); perhaps the only one is Broward County just to the south, which voted 67%–31% for Gore. At the same time, the heavily Republican Gulf Coast districts had increased greatly in population, and some of their territory had to be placed elsewhere. Where better to put it than in the 16th District, to which it after all is geographically contiguous? Locals in Port Charlotte and Punta Gorda complained when they saw the district lines, but the Republican redistricters had bigger things on their minds. They raised the Bush 2000 percentage in the 16th District from 47% to 53%.

The congressman from the 16th District is Mark Foley, a Republican first elected in 1994. Foley was born in Massachusetts, moved to Florida at age 3, dropped out of Palm Beach Community College and opened The Lettuce Patch restaurant in Lake Worth at 20. He was active in politics, working for Democratic Congressman Paul Rogers; he was a real estate broker and served on civic boards. Foley was elected to the Lake Worth City Commission in 1977, at 23, to the state House as a Republican in 1990, and to the state Senate from a Democratic district in 1992. When Republican Congressman Tom Lewis decided to retire after 12 years, he and the local Republican organization supported Foley, who won a three-way primary with 61% of the vote. In the general, he outraised the Democrat and outpolled him 58%–42%.

In the House, Foley's political skills caught the eye of leadership; he was named a deputy whip and a member of task forces to abolish government departments. But Foley also displayed an independent streak, with a record on cultural issues that leans to the left. He has concentrated on issues with particular local resonance, including immigration and agriculture. He pushed to deport imprisoned illegal immigrants, and to amend the Constitution so that children born here are not automatically citizens; he also worked to increase the number of immigrants admitted as farmworkers. He proved capable of shifting on issues, voting in 1995 to cut EPA monies and in 1996 against such cuts; his vote to repeal the assault weapons ban contrasted with his support of some gun control measures in Florida. In July 2001, he temporarily delayed George W. Bush's faith-based initiative to demand language that religious groups covered by the proposal not discriminate against gays.

On the Ways and Means Committee since 1999, he worked with Sander Levin to give additional preventive screening tests to Medicare beneficiaries. Initially, Foley was one of only 23 House Republicans—and the only one on Ways and Means—to oppose trade promotion authority. He cited opposition from local citrus farmers; the leadership was angry because Foley's stand forced them to seek votes from members who had much weaker holds on their districts. (Citrus farmers had little national political clout in 1940 when their industry was very important to the state but Florida had only four House members; now they have much more clout, though the industry has little bearing on the vast majority of Floridians, because the state has 25 House members). But in 2002 Foley voted in favor of trade promotion authority. Speaker Dennis Hastert tapped Foley to lead an entertainment task force for House Republicans to sell themselves to Hollywood; his work extended from escorting actors across Capitol Hill to shepherding a treaty that protects creative work from Internet piracy and opposing legislative limits on "violent" material. He passed a bill to increase federal support for researchers who are developing cures and treatments for the estimated 6,000 rare diseases that affect 25 million Americans.

In 2000 Foley was reelected 60%–37%; in 2002 he had no Democratic opponent. He did complain about the new shape of the district, but used it as an opportunity to become better known outside the West Palm Beach media market; he has often been available to speak to local stations or cable news networks. By June 2003 he was preparing to run for Bob Graham's Senate seat in 2004. His liberal stands on some issues will likely antagonize some Republican primary voters; if Graham does run again, he will be very hard to beat. But in mid 2003 Graham had embarked on a presidential campaign; if he is nominated for president, state law prevents him from running for reelection. Since Florida has a May filing deadline, Graham could easily run for reelection if his presidential campaign fizzles out in the primary. But if another Democratic nominee chooses him as a vice presidential candidate—which is certainly possible, because he is the only Democrat who could help a ticket in crucial Florida—he would not be able to run for reelection, and the Republican nominee chosen in the September primary would probably be the favorite to win. In May 2003, rumors that Foley is gay surfaced in several newspaper stories; in response, he held a news conference where he said he will not discuss his sexual orientation.

SEVENTEENTH DISTRICT

Rep. Kendrick Meek (D)

Elected 2002, 1st term; b. Sept. 6, 1966, Miami; home, Miami; FL A&M U., B.S. 1989; Baptist; married (Leslie).

Elected Office: FL House of Reps., 1994–98; FL Senate, 1998–02.

DC Office: 1039 LHOB 20515, 202-225-4506; Fax: 202-226-0777; Web site: www.house.gov/kenmeek.

District Offices: Miami, 305-690-5905; Pembroke Pines, 954-450-6767.

Committees: *Armed Services* (25th of 29 D): Strategic Forces; Tactical Air & Land Forces. *Select Committee on Homeland Security* (23d of 23 D): Cybersecurity, Science and Research & Development; Intelligence & Counterterrorism; Rules.

Group Ratings and Key Votes: Newly Elected

Election Results

2002 general	Kendrick Meek (D)	.... unopposed	($286,738)
2002 primary	Kendrick Meek (D)	.... unopposed	
2000 general	Carrie P. Meek (D)	.... unopposed	($298,389)

The People		Race/Ethnic Origin	Ancestry	
Area size:	99 sq. mi.	18.4% White	West Indian: 20.3%	USA: 4.7%
Urban population:	100.0%	55.2% Black	Italian: 2.4%	
Rural population:	0.0%	1.5% Asian	**2000 Presidential Vote**	
Pop. 2000:	639,296	0.2% Native Am.	Gore (D)...............145,341 (85%)	
Median income:	$30,426	0.0% Hawaiian	Bush (R)................26,081 (15%)	
Poverty status:	23.3%	3.1% Two+ races	**Cook Partisan Voting Index:** D +35	
Military veterans:	7.2%	0.3% Other		
		21.2% Hispanic Origin		
Occupation	Blue collar: 24.0%	White collar: 52.5%	Gray collar: 23.5%	

North from downtown Miami, alongside the railroad tracks that Henry Flagler built shortly after Miami was founded in 1896, and alongside Interstate 95, Miami's main north-south artery, is the city's largest black community, stretching from the Miami Arena in downtown Miami north through Allapattah and Liberty City, to the brightly painted minarets and Moorish arches of Opa-Locka. This has been a kind of frontierland in Miami, the scene where hostilities between Miami's blacks and its Cuban-American majority have played out. In 1980, 18 people died in a riot after the acquittal of a police officer charged with killing a black insurance salesman. Many Miami blacks have resented the economic upward mobility and political strength of the Cubans, the first generation of which rose while still speaking mostly Spanish, and of other Latins—including the Haitians in Little Haiti, the Creole-speaking community whose heart is in N.E. 54th Street, north of downtown—who have been moving upward as well. The Elian Gonzalez affair reminded many local blacks of the refugee status granted to Cubans even as many black Haitians were deported without notice or turned away at the shore. This animosity is reflected in partisan politics: Blacks in Miami-Dade County vote more than 90% Democratic, while Cuban Americans vote 70% to 80% Republican.

The 17th Congressional District covers much of northeast Miami-Dade County right up to Biscayne Boulevard; it does not include the affluent enclaves facing Biscayne Bay or the beach towns north of Miami Beach nor does it include heavily Hispanic Hialeah to the west. Within its borders is the historic, socially active Greater Bethel AME Church in Overtown; the district also includes part of Hollywood and other communities in southern Broward County, with fewer blacks, but still very heavily Democratic. Some 55% of the 17th District's residents are black, the highest percentage of any Florida district. It is also 21% Hispanic—a large enough presence to have created more black-Hispanic tensions than in the state's other two predominantly black districts.

The congressman from the 17th is Kendrick Meek, a Democrat first elected in 2002. He is the son of his predecessor, Carrie Meek, who was first elected when the district was created in something like its present form in 1992. She is the granddaughter of a slave and was elected to the state Legislature in 1978, when Kendrick Meek was 12. In July 2002, just two weeks before the filing deadline, Carrie Meek announced that she would not run again and promised to work "24 hours a day, seven days a week" to elect her son. It turned out not to require that much effort: no Democrat or Republican filed to run against him. T. Willard Fair, president of the Urban League of Greater Miami, was among the few who complained about the succession scheme: "In a democracy, people should have a right to choose the candidate of their choice. . . . I've been denied the right to participate in the process to elect the person I think is best to serve me."

But Kendrick Meek would have been a formidable candidate in any case. He served as a page in the Florida legislature when his mother was elected. At Florida A&M in Tallahassee he was president of state College Young Democrats. After college he worked as a state trooper and became security aide to Lieutenant Governor Buddy MacKay. He was elected to the Florida House in 1994, at 28, and the Florida Senate in 1998; in each case he took on longtime respected incumbents and waged contentious campaigns to oust them. He attracted nationwide attention in January 2000 for staging a 25-hour sit-in at the lieutenant governor's office to protest Bush's "One Florida" executive orders, which called for ending the use of racial preferences in state contracting and university admissions. Meek failed to change Bush's mind, but his act of political theater helped spark the largest-ever protest march on the state Capitol two months later. In 2002 he was well known as the chief proponent of the class size initiative which qualified for the November 2002 ballot and which, despite the opposition of Governor Jeb Bush, was approved 52%–48%; after the election, Bush met with Meek and said he would cooperate with him on implementing the measure. The Meeks are not the first mother-son combination in the House. In 1952 Oliver Bolton, an Ohio Republican, was elected to the House from a district adjoining the one which had been represented by his mother Frances Bolton since 1940 and by his father Chester Bolton before that. The Boltons were Republican, white and very rich, the Meeks are Democratic, black and come from a background of poverty: Only in America.

In Washington, Democratic leaders were openly impressed by Meek's political and fundraising skills and predicted a bright future for him. He failed to win his mother's seat on Appropriations, but freshmen seldom do.

EIGHTEENTH DISTRICT

Rep. Ileana Ros-Lehtinen (R)

Elected Aug. 1989, 7th term; b. July 12, 1952, Havana, Cuba; home, Miami; Miami-Dade Commun. Col., A.A. 1972, FL Intl. U., B.A. 1975, M.S. 1986; Catholic; married (Dexter).

Elected Office: FL House of Reps., 1982–86; FL Senate, 1986–89.

Professional Career: Teacher, Principal & Owner, Eastern Academy Elem. Schl., 1978–85.

DC Office: 2160 RHOB 20515, 202-225-3931; Fax: 202-225-5620; Web site: www.house.gov/ros-lehtinen.

District Office: Miami, 305-275-1800.

Committees: *Government Reform* (4th of 24 R): Wellness & Human Rights. *International Relations* (7th of 26 R): Middle East & Central Asia (Chmn.); Western Hemisphere.

Group Ratings

	ADA	ACLU	AFS	LCV	CON	ITIC	NTU	COC	ACU	NTLC	CHC
2002	10	14	0	25	13	88	56	75	88	71	58
2001	10	—	0	14	—	—	62	86	71	—	—

National Journal Ratings

	2001 LIB	—	2001 CONS			2002 LIB	—	2002 CONS
Economic	40%	—	60%			44%	—	56%
Social	48%	—	52%			29%	—	70%
Foreign	32%	—	69%			35%	—	60%

Key Votes of the 107th Congress

1. Approve Bush Tax Cuts	Y	5. Faith-Based Charities	Y	9. Trade Promotion Authority	Y
2. Limit Patients' Bill of Rights	Y	6. Bar Gays in the Boy Scouts	Y	10. Bar Funds for Intl. Court	N
3. Campaign Finance Reform	Y	7. Ban Partial-Birth Abortion	Y	11. Authorize Force in Iraq	Y
4. Ban ANWR Development	N	8. Arm Commercial Pilots	Y	12. Deny Home. Sec. Dept. Union	Y

Election Results

2002 general	Ileana Ros-Lehtinen (R)	103,512	(69%)	($446,561)
	Ray Chote (D)	42,852	(29%)	
	Other	3,423	(2%)	
2002 primary	Ileana Ros-Lehtinen (R)	38,885	(88%)	
	May Chote (R)	5,327	(12%)	
2000 general	Ileana Ros-Lehtinen (R)	unopposed		($192,368)

Prior Winning Percentages: 1998 (100%); 1996 (100%); 1994 (100%); 1992 (67%); 1990 (60%); 1989 (53%)

The People		Race/Ethnic Origin	Ancestry	
Area size:	3,196 sq. mi.	29.7% White	German: 4.0%	English: 3.5%
Urban population:	99.1%	5.7% Black	Irish: 3.3%	
Rural population:	0.9%	0.9% Asian	**2000 Presidential Vote**	
Pop. 2000:	639,295	0.1% Native Am.	Bush (R)..............109,596	(57%)
Median income:	$32,298	0.0% Hawaiian	Gore (D)...............83,524	(43%)
Poverty status:	19.3%	0.7% Two+ races	**Cook Partisan Voting Index:** R + 7	
Military veterans:	6.6%	0.1% Other		
		62.7% Hispanic Origin		

Occupation	Blue collar: 20.6%	White collar: 60.1%	Gray collar: 19.3%

A century ago it was a tiny tropical village where the Miami River empties into Biscayne Bay. Today it is a world-city, not just America's "Gateway to Latin America" but the "Capital of the Americas," as welcoming signs proclaim. The surrealistic high-rises of Brickell Boulevard, the reminders of the 1920s in the pseudo-Spanish Villa Vizcaya and the winding lanes of Coral Gables, the shimmer of orange and pink neon signs in the hot night air: the lights of the grid streets stretching for miles and then abruptly turning to darkness at the bayfront or the Everglades: This is Miami today. It lives on the cusp of two civilizations, North American and Latin American, with different traditions, styles and sensibilities converging in this one place, despite some friction, toward an amalgam with the strengths of both. Miami has become commercially and economically the capital of Latin America, the one place from which it is easiest to fly directly to any other part of Latin America, where top business and banking services are available to a sophisticated Spanish-speaking (and usually also English-speaking) clientele.

The 1980s TV program *Miami Vice* showed the underside of Miami, the air of menace in streets where many are armed and vast quantities of drugs and cash regularly change hands and killings are not at all unusual. The news columns have focused on violence: The riots in 1980 and 1989; the late 1990s shenanigans of the city's politicians, when corruption charges were lodged at several officeholders (and the mayor thrown out after the courts ruled that vote fraud produced his winning margin); and on the controversy over six-year-old Elian Gonzalez in 1999 and 2000. But the negatives are often exaggerated. What is striking about Miami is less its vices than its virtues—the vitality and creativity of entrepreneurs and artists, the cosmopolitan sophistication of people living and prospering in two (or more) cultures, the successful Americanization of Cubans and other Latinos who make up more than half of Miami-Dade County's population, together with the retention of a cultural flavor that is linked to the past but headed fast into the future.

John Quincy Adams believed that Cuba must inevitably become a part of the United States. That never happened, but many of Cuba's people have become Americans, and the focus of Cuban America has been Miami, ever since the first refugees fled Fidel Castro in 1959. That caused some resentment among the previous majority. In the 1960s, as the Cuban population grew, the tone of Miami civic life was set by the large Jewish community and the liberal voice of the *Miami Herald*: Dade County was the one liberal bastion in a state dominated by George Wallace Democrats and rising conservative Republicans. But the Cubans, implacably opposed to the totalitarian Castro and estranged by John Kennedy's betrayal of their cause at the Bay of Pigs, entered the voting stream heavily Republican. Liberals bristled at the late Cuban activist Jorge Mas Canosa's charges that the *Miami Herald* "manipulates information just like *Granma*," Castro's mouthpiece newspaper in Havana.

In the early 1960s, Cubans were a noisy minority in the Miami area; now they are dominant in a Latino majority in Miami-Dade County (as Dade County was renamed in 1997). In 2000, the population of Miami-Dade was 57% Hispanic and 19% black, leaving Anglo whites a fading minority. South Florida's Jewish community has mostly moved north to Broward and Palm Beach counties. Little Havana around Calle Ocho (Southwest 8th Street in English) is now home to many Nicaraguans, Hondurans and Peruvians; its annual spring carnival has featured the world's largest paella (serving 300,000 people) and the longest conga line (four miles). Latinos in Miami-Dade tend to go to school at Miami-Dade Community College (one of the nation's largest) and Florida International University and start businesses or join the professions in Miami's vibrant economy.

Politically, Miami-Dade is trending Republican. It voted 57%–38% for Bill Clinton in 1996, after he signed the Helms-Burton Act and responded angrily to the shooting down of two Brothers to the Rescue planes. But it soured on him after he suspended Helms-Burton and clashed with the community during the Elian Gonzalez affair, which culminated in April 2000 when immigration agents seized the 6-year-old from his relatives' home in an armed, pre-dawn raid and returned him to his father and, ultimately, Cuba. The Elian case soured Cuban Americans on anything connected with the Clinton administration, and Al Gore, despite overwhelming support from Miami-Dade's blacks and Jews, carried the county by only 53%–46%. While the constituency for ending the embargo on Cuba is growing outside of Miami, it remains a small minority here.

The 18th Congressional District is one of Miami-Dade County's three Hispanic-majority districts. It is 63% Hispanic, mostly Cuban-American, and only 6% black. The district includes most of the city of Miami, which is the home of only 16% of Miami-Dade County's residents. It follows Calle Ocho west to heavily Hispanic West Miami and Westchester. It includes most of metro Miami's high-income residential areas—Coral Gables, with streets laid out in the 1920s with Spanish, French country and even Chinese style houses; Cocoplum, the gated community with huge houses of rich Cuban-Americans with docks for their boats; the postmodern apartment buildings along Brickell Bouelvard; and Key Biscayne, with its high-rise apartments mostly owned by Latin Americans in need of a safe harbor if their countries are threatened with revolution or confiscation. The district also includes parts of Miami Beach—South Beach, where old art deco hotels that used to house elderly retirees and have become a home to the glitziest celebrities of North America, Latin America and Europe, the high-rises along Collins Avenue facing the ocean, and the increasingly Latino neighborhoods around 63d Street to the north. South of Miami, the district is connected to the Florida Keys by U.S. 1, the sturdier successor to Henry Flagler's "folly" of a railway that was built on an archipelago of calcified outcroppings and destroyed, two decades after its construction, by a hurricane in 1935. The highway ends in bustling, tropical Key West, the southernmost city in the continental United States. Key West was long accessible only by sea, and treasures from shipwrecks along the miles of coral reefs once provided its residents the highest per capita income in the nation. Key West has attracted famous residents—Ernest Hemingway, Tennessee Williams, Jimmy Buffett—and a large gay population, many living in quaint clapboard bungalows called "conch houses." The sizable gay communities in Key West and Miami Beach are solidly Democratic, and they have begun to exercise some clout: Gay leaders in Miami-Dade spearheaded a successful effort to reject a countywide gay-rights repeal ordinance in 2002. Overall, though, the 18th is Republican. The huge Republican margins from heavily Cuban precincts inland overcome the Democratic margins from glitzier neighborhoods in sight of the water, and in 2000 the district voted 57% for George W. Bush.

The congresswoman from the 18th District is Ileana Ros-Lehtinen, the first Cuban-American elected to Congress, in August 1989. She was born in Cuba, came to Miami at 7, graduated from Miami-Dade Community College and Florida International University. She became a teacher, then was the owner of a private school. She was elected to the Florida House in 1982, at 30, and to the state Senate in 1986; her husband Dexter Lehtinen also served in both houses of the legislature and served as U.S. attorney in Miami during the first Bush administration. Ros-Lehtinen ran for the House in the special election after the death in 1989 of Claude Pepper, one of the most enduring liberals in American politics and a staunch opponent of Castro. It was an acrimonious contest, with voting almost entirely on ethnic lines: exit polls showed that 96% of blacks and 88% of non-Hispanic whites voted for Democrat Gerald Richman, while 90% of Hispanics voted for Ros-Lehtinen. Overall, Ros-Lehtinen won with 53% of the vote. With a much more heavily Latino district since 1992, she has won without serious opposition.

Ros-Lehtinen has a mixed voting record: moderate on economics and cultural policy, more conservative on foreign issues. She refused to sign the Contract with America, and was a harsh critic of Republican attempts to pass English-only legislation, to cut off welfare for legal immigrants and to reduce the immigration quota for relatives of U.S. citizens. She has been the chief sponsor of the Child Custody Protection Act, to bar the transport of minors across state lines for abortions; the House passed it in 1999 and 2002, but it died each time in the Senate because, she said, the chamber is "controlled by the abortion lobby." In 2001 she sought to scuttle the House Republicans' term limits on committee chairmen because she said it was causing a "brain drain," but was resoundingly defeated.

Ros-Lehtinen serves on the International Relations Committee, where much of her energy has been devoted to Cuban and Latin issues. She strongly backed the Cuban Democracy Act and the 1996 Helms-Burton law that tightened sanctions against Fidel Castro. In 2000 she opposed an amendment by farm state Republicans to relax the trade embargo on Cuba, which passed in a diluted version. She gained added leverage over many of these and other issues when she became chairwoman of the International Operations and Human Rights Subcommittee. In response to reports that Chinese doctors were using their U.S. training to gain expertise on potential organ recipients, she filed a bill to bar visas to Chinese doctors seeking such training. But Ros-Lehtinen and her Cuban-American allies have been losing ground on their overriding cause: the U.S. embargo of Cuba that has been in effect since 1961. Even though George W. Bush firmly supports the embargo, its opponent—a coalition liberal Democrats, farm state Republicans and foreign policy left-wingers—has been gaining strength.

Ros-Lehtinen was re-elected without opposition from 1994 through 2000. In 2002, an elderly couple opposed Ros-Lehtinen. She beat the wife in the Republican primary 88%–12% and the husband in the general by 69%–29%.

NINETEENTH DISTRICT

Rep. Robert Wexler (D)

Elected 1996, 4th term; b. Jan. 2, 1961, Queens, NY; home, Boca Raton; U. of FL, B.A. 1982, George Washington U., J.D. 1985; Jewish; married (Laurie).

Elected Office: FL Senate, 1990–96.

Professional Career: Practicing atty., 1985–96.

DC Office: 213 CHOB 20515, 202-225-3001; Fax: 202-225-5974; Web site: www.house.gov/wexler.

District Offices: Boca Raton, 561-988-6302; Margate, 954-972-6454.

Committees: *International Relations* (9th of 23 D): Asia & the Pacific; Europe (RMM). *Judiciary* (12th of 16 D): Courts, the Internet & Intellectual Property.

Group Ratings

	ADA	ACLU	AFS	LCV	CON	ITIC	NTU	COC	ACU	NTLC	CHC
2002	100	80	100	100	53	25	17	32	9	6	0
2001	100	—	100	100	—	—	7	30	4	—	—

National Journal Ratings

	2001 LIB	—	2001 CONS		2002 LIB	—	2002 CONS
Economic	95%	—	0%		86%	—	12%
Social	83%	—	11%		74%	—	19%
Foreign	66%	—	34%		57%	—	43%

Key Votes of the 107th Congress

1. Approve Bush Tax Cuts	N	5. Faith-Based Charities	N	9. Trade Promotion Authority	N
2. Limit Patients' Bill of Rights	N	6. Bar Gays in the Boy Scouts	N	10. Bar Funds for Intl. Court	N
3. Campaign Finance Reform	Y	7. Ban Partial-Birth Abortion	N	11. Authorize Force in Iraq	Y
4. Ban ANWR Development	Y	8. Arm Commercial Pilots	Y	12. Deny Home. Sec. Dept. Union	N

Election Results

2002 general	Robert Wexler (D)	156,747	(72%)	($650,528)
	Jack Merkl (R)	60,477	(28%)	($25,784)
2002 primary	Robert Wexler (D)	unopposed		
2000 general	Robert Wexler (D)	171,080	(72%)	($447,274)
	Morris Kent Thompson (R)	67,789	(28%)	($10,620)

Prior Winning Percentages: 1998 (100%); 1996 (66%)

The People		Race/Ethnic Origin	Ancestry	
Area size:	234 sq. mi.	77.5% White	Italian: 9.0%	German: 8.4%
Urban population:	99.6%	6.1% Black	Irish: 7.6%	
Rural population:	0.4%	2.0% Asian	**2000 Presidential Vote**	
Pop. 2000:	639,295	0.1% Native Am.	Gore (D) 191,382 (73%)	
Median income:	$42,237	0.0% Hawaiian	Bush (R) 71,544 (27%)	
Poverty status:	7.7%	1.4% Two+ races	**Cook Partisan Voting Index:** D +23	
Military veterans:	16.6%	0.3% Other		
		12.7% Hispanic Origin		
Occupation	Blue collar: 17.1%	White collar: 67.1%	Gray collar: 15.7%	

When the first millionaires came to Palm Beach in the 1920s to winter in their new Addison Mizner pseudo-Mediterranean mansions, and as the first real estate speculators arrived in Miami, there was virtually nothing man-made between these two cites. In 1920, Dade, Broward and Palm Beach counties boasted a mere 66,000 residents. Now, 5 million people live in the 5- to 15-mile strip between the Atlantic Ocean and the protected Everglades—a number that increased by 1 million during the 1990s. The contrast between the 1920s and today is especially striking in Boca Raton, where Mizner built in 1926 what is now the Boca Raton Hotel and Club. Its azure fountains and red-tiled roofs, its pseudo-Moorish columns and pink stucco walls bespeak a vision of a holiday Florida, a bit mannered and antique to today's eye, but still exuberant. Boca Raton has grown inland and is still solidly affluent, but it has become more functional and workaday. Affluent retirees from the Northeast and Canada ("snowbirds") live in unadorned high-rise towers, enjoying the weather and the lack of a state income tax.

The 19th Congressional District includes former swampland and citrus groves in Palm Beach and Broward counties. It does not touch the ocean at all, kept inland by the majority-black 23d District, which collects poorer black neighborhoods just behind the Intracoastal Waterway, and the 22d District, which ties together more affluent (and more Republican) oceanside precincts. The boundaries of the 19th District are erose and irregular, obviously drawn with an eye to political advantage (The Republicans who controlled the redistricting process were happy to pack in heavily Democratic precincts into the already Democratic 19th). It extends north from Fort Lauderdale to Okeechobee Boulevard in West Palm Beach, taking in the towns of Margate, Mission Bay and Boca Raton; what ties these communities together is that they have large Jewish populations and vote heavily Democratic. Senior citizens are an especially important voting bloc here: the 19th ranks first among all 435 congressional districts in percentage of residents who are over the age of 65. Politically, aside from Florida's two black majority districts, this is the most Democratic district in the state.

The congressman from the 19th is Robert Wexler, a Democrat elected in 1996. Wexler grew up in Florida from age 10, and after law school went into practice in Boca Raton. In 1990, at 29, he was elected to the state Senate. When Democrat Harry Johnston retired in 1996, Wexler was one of three Democratic legislators who jumped into the race. He led with 47% to 29% for state Senator Peter Weinstein. The October 1 runoff was bitter. Wexler won 65%–35%; afterwards Weinstein filed a $10 million defamation suit against him, citing an unflattering picture of Weinstein in a Wexler TV ad (the suit soon was dropped). In this heavily Democratic district, Wexler won the general 66%–34%.

Wexler has a fairly liberal voting record in the House and a flare for gaining attention. On the International Relations Committee, he traveled to the Middle East with Madeleine Albright; he was the only member of the House in attendance at the Wye River accords. An orthodox Jew, he later said Yasir Arafat needed to do more to prepare Palestinians for peace. By December 2002, he said that Israel was engaged in full-scale war, and that it was time for the United States to force the ouster of terrorist leaders in the Mideast, including Arafat and Saddam Hussein. On the Judiciary Committee, he was the only Democrat to favor a three-year pilot program giving temporary visas to an unlimited number of foreign workers for seasonal farm work. He vociferously objected when Major League Baseball threatened to move or close down the Miami-based Florida Marlins.

Wexler made his greatest mark as an ardent defender of Bill Clinton. Producers of cable shows are always looking for someone who can be relied on to take one side of an issue and to bring energy to the broadcast: one look at Wexler convinced bookers that he would fill the bill, and he seemed to turn down few invitations. He denounced Clinton's personal conduct to be sure, but then bellowed with rage over the acts of Independent Counsel Kenneth Starr, House Judiciary Committee Republicans and everyone who was preventing him from working on issues like health care, education and Social Security. One typical plaint: "The president betrayed his wife; he did not betray his country. God help this nation if we fail to recognize the difference." Two years later, Wexler found another opportunity to hit the cable circuit during the Florida vote controversy. As the deadlock continued, he received death threats; but that didn't keep him from appearing on *Rivera Live*. Once the Clinton and Florida sagas faded, so too did Wexler's shooting star. Like many other Washington media celebrities, he discovered that someone who lives by the sword of sound bites can also die by that sword. To make things worse, it was revealed in October 2002 that Wexler had a complex financial arrangement involving a loan and stock ownership with an airline security investor who was charged with stock fraud. Wexler voiced regret about his corporate dealings.

Wexler has frequently been rumored to be a potential statewide candidate. In the latest variation on that theme, in 2003 he drew mention as a possible 2004 Senate candidate if Bob Graham does not run for reelection. Wexler was reelected 72%–28% in 2002.

TWENTIETH DISTRICT

Rep. Peter Deutsch (D)

Elected 1992, 6th term; b. Apr. 1, 1957, New York, NY; home, Lauderhill; Swarthmore Col., B.A. 1979, Yale Law Schl., J.D. 1982; Jewish; married (Lori).

Elected Office: FL House of Reps., 1982–92.

Professional Career: Practicing atty., 1983–92.

DC Office: 2303 RHOB 20515, 202-225-7931; Fax: 202-225-8456; Web site: www.house.gov/deutsch.

District Offices: Aventura, 305-936-5724; Pembroke Pines, 954-437-3936.

Committees: *Energy & Commerce* (10th of 26 D): Commerce, Trade & Consumer Protection; Environment & Hazardous Materials; Oversight & Investigations (RMM); Telecommunications & The Internet.

Group Ratings

	ADA	ACLU	AFS	LCV	CON	ITIC	NTU	COC	ACU	NTLC	CHC
2002	85	73	89	88	84	50	19	45	12	9	8
2001	90	—	100	100	—	—	15	43	8	—	—

National Journal Ratings

	2001 LIB	—	2001 CONS		2002 LIB	—	2002 CONS
Economic	77%	—	23%		67%	—	32%
Social	74%	—	23%		73%	—	27%
Foreign	70%	—	28%		58%	—	42%

Key Votes of the 107th Congress

1. Approve Bush Tax Cuts	N	5. Faith-Based Charities	N
2. Limit Patients' Bill of Rights	N	6. Bar Gays in the Boy Scouts	N
3. Campaign Finance Reform	Y	7. Ban Partial-Birth Abortion	N
4. Ban ANWR Development	Y	8. Arm Commercial Pilots	Y

9. Trade Promotion Authority	N
10. Bar Funds for Intl. Court	N
11. Authorize Force in Iraq	Y
12. Deny Home. Sec. Dept. Union	N

Election Results

2002 general	Peter Deutsch (D) .... unopposed		($683,827)
2002 primary	Peter Deutsch (D) .... unopposed		
2000 general	Peter Deutsch (D) .... unopposed		($558,259)

Prior Winning Percentages: 1998 (100%); 1996 (65%); 1994 (61%); 1992 (55%)

The People		Race/Ethnic Origin	Ancestry	
Area size:	218 sq. mi.	66.9% White	Italian: 7.9%	German: 7.7%
Urban population:	99.7%	7.9% Black	Irish: 7.5%	
Rural population:	0.3%	2.3% Asian	**2000 Presidential Vote**	
Pop. 2000:	639,295	0.2% Native Am.	Gore (D)...............161,154	(69%)
Median income:	$44,034	0.0% Hawaiian	Bush (R)...............72,553	(31%)
Poverty status:	9.6%	1.6% Two + races	**Cook Partisan Voting Index:** D +19	
Military veterans:	11.3%	0.3% Other		
		20.6% Hispanic Origin		

Occupation	Blue collar: 16.0%	White collar: 69.4%	Gray collar: 14.6%

Fort Lauderdale, back when Connie Francis made it famous in the 1960 spring break movie *Where the Boys Are*, was just a small town with a strip of motels along the beach and some nice houses fronting canals. Now it is the center of a sprawling metropolitan area. In 1950, Fort Lauderdale and Broward County had fewer than 100,000 people; now they have more than 1.6 million. The land from the strip of beach along the Atlantic Ocean west to the Sawgrass Expressway and the Everglades Wildlife Management Area has filled up with subdivisions, shopping centers, office complexes, warehouses and trucking terminals. Broward County is no longer just vacation country; it is also a major port and business center with high-tech companies and startups that have become national giants, including Blockbuster Video.

As it has grown, the ethnic composition of Broward County has changed. In the 1950s, it was understood that Jews couldn't buy houses or rent hotel rooms this far north of Miami. Today, after four decades of Cubans moving into the Miami area and many Jews moving out, Broward County is the most heavily Jewish part of Florida, indeed one of the most heavily Jewish parts of the United States. Nearer the coast, especially in the huge high-rises of Hollywood and Hallandale, most of Broward's Jews are retirees from New York and other Northeastern metro areas. But inland, in towns like booming Davie, Plantation and Sunrise that didn't exist a few decades ago, there are many young Jewish parents raising families in communities that pride themselves on fine schools and high property values. Places like Weston, a 15,000-home development built in the mid-1980s over 16 square miles beyond the Sawgrass Expressway on the edge of the Everglades, drew affluent transplants to its gated communities, including, in Weston's case, many from Venezuela. This is one reason that in the 1990s the number of children in Florida rose more rapidly than the number of seniors, with school enrollment rising more than 35% in Broward alone.

The 20th Congressional District includes much of southeastern Broward County and the northern Biscayne Bay shoreline in Miami-Dade. Precinct by precinct, its computer generated borders are drawn to exclude relatively Republican areas and to include heavily Jewish areas and also most of Fort Lauderdale's large gay community. It includes much of Fort Lauderdale, Hollywood and Dania Beach on the coast, but its biggest blocks of territory are inland, around Davie, Plantation, Sunrise and Weston. It also includes part of Miami-Dade County, the shores of Biscayne Bay both on the Miami and Miami Beach side, with expensive homes and huge high-rises, the homes of most of the Jews still living south of Broward County. This is a strongly Democratic district. It cast only 31% of its votes for George W. Bush in 2000, and in 2002, as Floridians were reelecting Governor Jeb Bush to office by a solid margin, it voted heavily for Democrat Bill McBride.

The congressman from the 20th District is Peter Deutsch, a Democrat elected in 1992. Deutsch grew up in New York, graduated from Yale Law School in 1982, moved to Florida and five months later was elected to the legislature. Two years later, he was reelected with the largest percentage in Florida; he was unopposed in the next three elections. A *Miami Herald* reporter said that, in Tallahassee, Deutsch was "viewed by colleagues as bright but abrasive, and an expert at using procedural rules to advance or torpedo legislation." In 1992 a new 20th District, centered mostly in Broward, seemed tailor-made for Deutsch. Most of its voters were unfamiliar to Dante Fascell, chairman of the Foreign Affairs Committee and a 38-year veteran of the House; he decided to retire, and Deutsch won the primary by nearly 2–1 and the general election 55%–39%.

Deutsch has a moderate-leaning voting record and is a member of the New Democrat Coalition. In 1998, the strongly pro-Israel Deutsch charged that a United Nations agency was funding antisemitic textbooks in Palestinian schools, and got language in the State Department appropriation to end it. He supported the Helms-Burton Act, plus Radio and TV Marti, and criticized Fidel Castro for the burdens he has placed on his people. As ranking Democrat on the Oversight and Investigations Subcommittee on Energy and Commerce, he was a junior partner in the Republican investigation of Enron and introduced a bill to protect employees' retirement funds in the future. During the House debate in July 2001 on whether to ban cloning, he teamed with Republican Jim Greenwood on an alternative to permit restricted research and therapy, but they lost to proponents of an outright ban.

Deutsch has spent much time on Everglades restoration and water quality in the Keys (the Keys and much of the Everglades were in the 20th District before the 2002 redistricting), with considerable progress. On the eve of the 2000 election he helped to enact the Everglades Restoration Plan, which he calls the "largest ecosystem restoration project in the world." On the Florida Keys, he won House passage of a bill to improve water quality, and the Senate provided the requisite funding. Deutsch faced protests from a Conch Coalition of fishermen, real estate agents and treasure hunters opposed to government bureaucrats declaring, despite previous assurances, no-fishing zones in the Florida Keys National Marine Sanctuary.

With no worries about reelection—he has not had Republican opposition since 1996—Deutsch has operated his campaign fund like a business. He invested $700,000 in January 1997 and it grew to $1.1 million 15 months later. Even after he contributed $250,000 to the Gore campaign—which he called "the largest hard-dollar contribution in U.S. history"—he had $2.5 million in the bank during the 2002 cycle. When party campaign strategists pressured him to increase his contribution to the DCCC, he wrote an angry letter to Minority Leader Richard Gephardt. During the Florida recount, Deutsch served as an official observer in Broward and an ever-ready voice for the Democratic party line on cable TV. He was the first member to protest on the House floor during the formal certification of the Electoral College vote. Like Robert Wexler in the neighboring 19th, he has talked about a statewide bid while waiting for the right opportunity. It may come if Senator Bob Graham chooses not to run for reelection in 2004.

TWENTY-FIRST DISTRICT

Rep. Lincoln Diaz-Balart (R)

Elected 1992, 6th term; b. Aug. 13, 1954, Havana, Cuba; home, Miami; U. of S. FL, B.S. 1977, Case Western Reserve U., J.D. 1979; Catholic; married (Cristina).

Elected Office: FL House of Reps., 1986–89; FL Senate 1989–92.

Professional Career: Practicing atty., 1979–92; Asst. FL Atty., 1983–84.

DC Office: 2244 RHOB 20515, 202-225-4211; Fax: 202-225-8576; Web site: www.house.gov/diaz-balart.

District Office: Miami, 305-470-8555.

Committees: *Rules* (5th of 9 R): The Legislative & Budget Process (Vice Chmn.). *Select Committee on Homeland Security* (16th of 27 R): Emergency Preparedness & Response; Infrastructure & Border Security; Rules (Chmn.).

Group Ratings

	ADA	ACLU	AFS	LCV	CON	ITIC	NTU	COC	ACU	NTLC	CHC
2002	15	13	0	25	14	88	55	83	88	80	100
2001	5	—	0	14	—	—	61	86	84	—	—

National Journal Ratings

	2001 LIB — 2001 CONS		2002 LIB — 2002 CONS	
Economic	33%	— 66%	43%	— 57%
Social	43%	— 55%	29%	— 70%
Foreign	16%	— 85%	35%	— 60%

Key Votes of the 107th Congress

1. Approve Bush Tax Cuts	Y	5. Faith-Based Charities	Y	9. Trade Promotion Authority	Y
2. Limit Patients' Bill of Rights	Y	6. Bar Gays in the Boy Scouts	Y	10. Bar Funds for Intl. Court	N
3. Campaign Finance Reform	N	7. Ban Partial-Birth Abortion	Y	11. Authorize Force in Iraq	Y
4. Ban ANWR Development	N	8. Arm Commercial Pilots	Y	12. Deny Home. Sec. Dept. Union	Y

Election Results

2002 general	Lincoln Diaz-Balart (R) .... unopposed		($404,300)
2002 primary	Lincoln Diaz-Balart (R) .... unopposed		
2000 general	Lincoln Diaz-Balart (R) .... unopposed		($294,122)

Prior Winning Percentages: 1998 (75%); 1996 (100%); 1994 (100%); 1992 (100%)

The People		Race/Ethnic Origin	Ancestry	
Area size:	140 sq. mi.	21.0% White	USA: 3.2%	German: 2.6%
Urban population:	99.9%	6.5% Black	West Indian: 2.6%	
Rural population:	0.1%	1.8% Asian	**2000 Presidential Vote**	
Pop. 2000:	639,295	0.1% Native Am.	Bush (R)..............104,888 (58%)	
Median income:	$41,426	0.0% Hawaiian	Gore (D)................76,322 (42%)	
Poverty status:	13.0%	0.8% Two+ races	**Cook Partisan Voting Index:** R + 8	
Military veterans:	4.8%	0.2% Other		
		69.7% Hispanic Origin		

Occupation	Blue collar: 22.6%	White collar: 63.6%	Gray collar: 13.9%

Miami's Cuban-American community has been one of America's most dynamic over the last 40 years (see 18th District), growing from 50,000 in 1960, the year after Fidel Castro took over Cuba, to well over 1 million today. Over those years, the Cuban-American neighborhoods centered along 8th Street—Calle Ocho—expanded to the southwest, west and northwest. Development first filled the land all the way to the Palmetto Expressway; in the 1980s, development reached outward to the Homestead extension of Florida's Turnpike; in the 1990s it went out beyond. Cuban-Americans moved out and beyond Hialeah, whose now-closed racetrack was constructed in the 1920s beyond the edge of urban development; its 90% Hispanic population is the highest in the Miami area. The suburbs of Miami have spread through former swampland, with planned communities and subdivisions often built with just one guarded entrance, leading to streets that fan out around lakes and golf courses.

The 21st Congressional District is an irregular rectangle about 20 miles long and two to six miles wide on the western side of settled territory in Miami-Dade County and southern Broward County. In Miami-Dade it includes Kendall and Cutler, southwest of Miami, and Westwood Lakes and Sweetwater, directly to the west. It includes low-income Hialeah and not far north Miami Lakes, developed in the 1960s by Senator Bob Graham and his brothers. In Broward County the 21st District includes much of Miramar and Pembroke Pines. It includes such landmarks as Florida International University and Miami International Airport. The population of the district is 70% Hispanic, the highest of any Florida district, but only 58% of these are of Cuban origin. Cuban voters continue to be very heavily Republican; other Latino voters are much less so, but by no means overwhelmingly Democratic. There are relatively few Hispanics in the Broward County portion of the district, which tends to vote Democratic. Overall, this is a Republican district, but one that has voted for Senator Bob Graham, who is very popular in the Cuban community.

The congressman from the 21st District is Lincoln Diaz-Balart, a Republican first elected when the district was created in 1992. Diaz-Balart was born in Cuba where his grandfather and father served in the Cuban Congress; the family left Cuba in 1959, shortly after Castro took over and after their house was looted and burned while they were vacationing in Paris. His aunt was the former wife of Fidel Castro and the mother of Castro's only recognized child. Diaz-Balart started off as a poverty lawyer and a Democrat, but switched parties. He was elected to the state House as a Republican in 1986 with 78% of the vote and to the state Senate in 1989 with 82%, a year after his younger brother Mario was elected to the state House; Mario Diaz-Balart is now the congressman from the 25th District just west of the 21st. There is another reason the Diaz-Balarts are called the "Cuban Kennedys": Aside from the two congressmen, they have one brother who is a TV anchorman on Telemundo and another who is an investment banker. In 1989 Jorge Mas Canosa's Cuban American National Foundation convinced Diaz-Balart not to run against Ileana Ros-Lehtinen in the then-18th District special election to replace Claude Pepper. In 1992 the organization endorsed Diaz-Balart to run in the new 21st. But fellow state Senator Javier Souto, also Cuban-born, opposed him in the primary, charging that Diaz-Balart was backed by wealthy contributors and was not a lifelong Republican. Diaz-Balart won 69%–31%.

Diaz-Balart has a voting record that is rather liberal on economics, veering far from market principles on issues from the minimum wage to NAFTA, though he has said he believes a hemispheric common market is inevitable. He was one of three Republican incumbents who refused to sign the Contract with America in 1994, and he voted against the Republican welfare bills because of their provisions denying welfare to legal immigrants. Many older Cubans who have not taken U.S. citizenship because they hoped some day to return to Cuba are dependent on Supplemental Security Income and other aid. He persevered, and his bill to restore SSI benefits to legal immigrants passed. In 2000 he led a bipartisan group that sought to reduce from five years to two the ban on legal immigrants from receiving federal or state health care insurance. The continuing push by House Republicans to include anti-immigrant provisions in their welfare-reform initiative, he feared, might permit Democrats to "California-ize this country."

Diaz-Balart, who shares a birthday with Castro, hopes that he will return some day to his freed homeland (Castro, on the other hand, refers to the Diaz-Balarts as "his most repulsive enemies" and "miserable Judases"). Naturally he has favored sanctions against Cuba, and when the Clinton administration announced in 1995 that it would no longer give automatic safe haven to Cuban refugees and instead would return them to Cuba, Diaz-Balart was arrested while protesting this switch. Diaz-Balart wrote the section of the Helms-Burton Act codifying the embargo against Cuba. During the Elian Gonzalez affair, Diaz-Balart closely advised the Miami family—he gave the six-year-old a black Labrador puppy—and he was a prominent spokesman for the local community. Although farm state Republicans—working with Democrats—have been able to win House passage of steps to relax the trade embargo, Diaz-Balart has worked to assure the Bush administration's unyielding opposition to significant trade openings to Cuba.

After a lengthy investigation, the Federal Election Commission announced in July 2001 a $30,000 fine of the Diaz-Balart campaign for accepting contributions in excess of the legal limits; earlier in the year, the FEC announced a separate $5,500 fine for filing late reports. Diaz-Balart acknowledged some mistakes but said that they had been corrected. In 2001, his campaign hired a new treasurer and refunded some excess contributions. The final agreement left unresolved an earlier FEC statement that a "discrepancy remains unexplained" about $114,000 in cash that could not be found in the campaign's accounts; representatives for Diaz-Balart disputed that charge and said that it resulted from arithmetic errors. Diaz-Balart has had no problem winning reelection; in 2002, it didn't hurt that his brother, Mario, was chairman of the state Senate congressional redistricting committee.

TWENTY-SECOND DISTRICT

Rep. Clay Shaw (R)

Elected 1980, 12th term; b. Apr. 19, 1939, Miami; home, Ft. Lauderdale; Stetson U., B.S. 1961, U. of AL, M.B.A. 1963, Stetson U., J.D. 1966; Catholic; married (Emilie).

Elected Office: Ft. Lauderdale City Commissioner., 1971–73; Ft. Lauderdale Vice Mayor, 1973–75, Mayor, 1975–80.

Professional Career: Practicing atty., 1966–68; Ft. Lauderdale Chief Prosecutor, 1968–69; Assoc. Municipal Judge, 1969–71.

DC Office: 2408 RHOB 20515, 202-225-3026; Fax: 202-225-8398; Web site: www.house.gov/shaw.

District Offices: Ft. Lauderdale, 954-522-1800; West Palm Beach, 561-832-3007.

Committees: *Ways & Means* (3d of 24 R): Social Security (Chmn.); Trade. *Joint Committee on Taxation* (3d of 5 Reps.).

Group Ratings

	ADA	ACLU	AFS	LCV	CON	ITIC	NTU	COC	ACU	NTLC	CHC
2002	10	20	0	38	82	100	52	95	88	78	92
2001	10	—	0	21	—	—	56	100	76	—	—

National Journal Ratings

	2001 LIB	—	2001 CONS		2002 LIB	—	2002 CONS
Economic	41%	—	60%		40%	—	60%
Social	43%	—	55%		32%	—	63%
Foreign	4%	—	87%		15%	—	78%

Key Votes of the 107th Congress

1. Approve Bush Tax Cuts	Y	5. Faith-Based Charities	Y	9. Trade Promotion Authority	Y
2. Limit Patients' Bill of Rights	Y	6. Bar Gays in the Boy Scouts	Y	10. Bar Funds for Intl. Court	Y
3. Campaign Finance Reform	N	7. Ban Partial-Birth Abortion	Y	11. Authorize Force in Iraq	Y
4. Ban ANWR Development	N	8. Arm Commercial Pilots	Y	12. Deny Home. Sec. Dept. Union	Y

Election Results

2002 general	Clay Shaw (R)	131,930	(61%)	($1,968,153)
	Carol Roberts (D)	83,265	(38%)	($1,138,776)
2002 primary	Clay Shaw (R)	unopposed		
2000 general	Clay Shaw (R)	105,855	(50%)	($3,086,708)
	Elaine Bloom (D)	105,256	(50%)	($2,378,327)

Prior Winning Percentages: 1998 (100%); 1996 (62%); 1994 (63%); 1992 (52%); 1990 (98%); 1988 (66%); 1986 (100%); 1984 (66%); 1982 (57%); 1980 (55%)

The People		**Race/Ethnic Origin**	**Ancestry**	
Area size:	500 sq. mi.	82.3% White	German: 11.7%	Irish: 11.0%
Urban population:	99.2%	3.8% Black	Italian: 9.5%	
Rural population:	0.8%	1.7% Asian	**2000 Presidential Vote**	
Pop. 2000:	639,295	0.1% Native Am.	Gore (D) 135,868	(52%)
Median income:	$51,200	0.0% Hawaiian	Bush (R) 123,302	(48%)
Poverty status:	7.1%	1.2% Two + races	**Cook Partisan Voting Index:** D + 2	
Military veterans:	14.9%	0.2% Other		
		10.7% Hispanic Origin		

Occupation	Blue collar: 16.0%	White collar: 69.4%	Gray collar: 14.7%

The barrier islands of Florida's Gold Coast have been developed in spasms of speculative frenzy, not just as vacation places and retirement homes but as embodiments of dreams and fantasies. Consider Palm Beach, the great beach resort of the 1920s, where rich WASPs would leave their snow-covered Tudor or Georgian mansions and live in Addison Mizner's pseudo-Mediterranean confections. Or think of the 1970s and 1980s, as high-rise condos sprouted all along the coastline of Broward and Palm Beach counties—a promised land for retirees, free from winter frost and state and city income taxes. South Florida has been so transient for so long that people hardly gave its fluidity a second thought, until it was revealed that the suicide terrorists who attacked the World Trade Center and the Pentagon on September 11 had used this part of Florida as their base of operations: Several hijackers lived in Delray Beach, they exercised in a Boynton Beach gym, and they practiced flying at a Lantana airport.

The 22d Congressional District covers most of the Atlantic oceanfront in Palm Beach and Broward counties, from Juno Beach in Palm Beach County to Fort Lauderdale in Broward County. It is rarely more than a few miles wide and in some places it is not much wider than the barrier islands separated from the mainland by the Indian River and Lake Worth. But it also has jagged salients that extend several miles inland. The district, a testament to the advances made in redistricting software, was drawn by Republican redistricters to provide a safe seat for Republican Congressman Clay Shaw after he barely won reelection in 2000. The Miami-Dade County portion of the district was removed, as was heavily Democratic Hollywood in Broward County. Inland salients in Broward County brought in Republican precincts in Plantation and Coral Springs. Much new territory was added in Palm Beach County—an inland finger in wealthy Boca Raton, a long strand parallel to the oceanfront of affluent areas from Delray Beach to Glen Ridge (here the 22d surrounds the heavily black 23d district on three sides) and an inland slice in north Palm Beach County including parts of Palm Beach Gardens and Jupiter. Redistricting raised the Bush 2000 percentage in the 22d District from 39% to 48%—the biggest increase in any Florida district.

The resulting district is affluent, elderly, with a large Jewish population politically very active in condominium groups.

The congressman from the 22d District is Clay Shaw, first elected in 1980. Shaw grew up in Fort Lauderdale, practiced law and served as a judge and councilman; in 1975, at 36, he became the city's mayor. In 1980 he ran for the House in a very differently shaped district, and had the good fortune of seeing the Democratic incumbent lose his primary. Shaw won the seat handily and held it despite the Fort Lauderdale area's increasing Democratic tilt. For eight years he served on the Judiciary Committee, working on drug and crime bills. In July 1988 he switched to Ways and Means.

In the Republican Congress Shaw has taken on the really big issues—first welfare, then Social Security. After Republicans won control in 1994, Shaw became chairman of the Way and Means subcommittee handling welfare. His little-noticed 1993 bill, to end the federal entitlement to welfare and take most recipients off the rolls and require them to work after two years, was part of the Contract with America and became one of House Republicans' major priorities. Shaw's bills were passed twice in 1995, in somewhat different form, and vetoed twice by Bill Clinton. In early 1996 House Republicans hoped that Bob Dole could use the welfare issue against Clinton. By July 1996 they decided that Dole was likely to lose anyway, and so decided to pass welfare reform a third time, giving Dole an issue if Clinton vetoed it again and giving House Republicans an accomplishment if Clinton signed it. They had no idea what he would do, but in the end he signed, and a major change in American public policy was made.

After the 1998 election, Shaw, then representing the House district with the nation's highest percentage of those 65 and over, became chairman of the Social Security Subcommittee. He said he wanted to reform the system and preserve it for baby boomers' retirements. In April 1999, Shaw and Ways and Means Chairman Bill Archer introduced a bill to give workers income tax credits to fund personal retirement accounts. But the Republican leadership did not want to go forward, and the effort foundered in summer 1999. In the next year Shaw focused on the earnings tax on Social Security recipients; he managed to pass a bill repealing it for Social Security recipients age 65 to 69. Shaw had other accomplishments in that Congress. Shaw had worked for many years on restoring the Everglades, and was lauded as the $7.8 billion Everglades Restoration Act was passed just before the November 2000 election.

This could not have hurt politically, for in 2000 Shaw had the strongest opposition since he first won the seat. It came from state Representative Elaine Bloom, who had a base in the condominiums and raised large sums from national liberal and feminist groups. Bloom ran an ad saying that Shaw had "voted" for privatization of Social Security, though he never had (there were no votes on the issue), and she had to pull the spot. With both candidates buying Miami and West Palm Beach television, this was one of the most expensive House races in the country: Bloom spent $2.4 million and Shaw $3 million. Bloom campaigned on her support for abortion and gun control, and on her support of Al Gore and Joe Lieberman, who were running far ahead in the district. Bloom called for lower prescription drug prices for seniors. In mid-October Shaw attacked Bloom for keeping seniors from buying drugs at lower prices; she owned $5 million of stock in and served on the board of generic drugmaker Andrx, which in June 2000 had been found guilty in federal court of violating the antitrust laws by taking $89 million from the maker of Cardizem CD in return for keeping its cheaper generic drug, Cartia XT off the market. She was further embarrassed when it was revealed that her personal physician wrote a prescription to her campaign manager for Cardizem CD and Cartia XT so the candidate could use them as props in a debate—a prescription that could under Florida law trigger disciplinary action. This turned out to be one of the closest races in the country. The initial count showed Shaw ahead by 599 votes; the mechanical recount required by Florida law didn't change the margin. Bloom sought a hand count, but the three county boards of canvassers, willing to order hand counts for Al Gore, declined to do so in this race (Miami-Dade did hand count six precincts, three chosen by each candidate). Shaw ran far ahead, 58%–42%, in Palm Beach County and carried his home base in Broward County by 55%–45%. He lost in the Miami-Dade County portion 67%–33%.

It was against this background that the Republican redistricters removed portions of the district and added interior territory to balance off some of the Democratic oceanfront condominiums. In February 2002, a month before the redistricting plan was unveiled, Shaw got a well-known opponent in Palm Beach County Commissioner Carol Roberts. Roberts had served 16 years on the County Commission and had also been mayor of West Palm Beach, but she was chiefly known as one of the three members of the board of canvassers in November and December 2000 who sought to count dimpled chads as votes for Al Gore. Roberts was a heroine to many local and national Democrats and managed to raise $1.1 million. With her trademark combat boots, she attacked Shaw fiercely. Her chief issue was prescription drugs for seniors; she set up a toll-free hotline for voters to obtain prescription drugs from foreign countries—which, the *Palm Beach Post* pointed out, is illegal. When Shaw voted for the Republican prescription drug bill that passed the House in June 2002, she said, "I believe that what he voted for today is really a payoff to the pharmaceutical industry for over $100,000 in contributions, including more than $50,000 since the 2000 campaign." She also criticized him for supporting "privatization" of Social Security. He continued to support individual investment accounts in Social Security and called his bill Social Security Guarantee Plus Act. Shaw ran ads attacking Roberts as developer-friendly; the *Palm Beach Post* chided her for changing the rules for a housing development in the Agricultural Reserve Area for a developer who gave her campaign $7,000.

The Roberts candidacy turned out to be less successful than national Democrats hoped. She had not had serious electoral competition since 1990, and anger over the Florida controversy worked both ways. Shaw campaigned more vigorously than in 2000, calling bingo at senior centers, attending chamber of commerce breakfasts, holding coffees in condominium party rooms. He raised and spent $1.9 million; his long years of constituency service helped him win endorsements from the Democratic mayors of Fort Lauderdale, Plantation and six towns in Palm Beach County. Shaw won 61%–38%. In Palm Beach County, where 60% of the votes were cast, Shaw won 59%–40%; in Broward County he won 64%–35%.

TWENTY-THIRD DISTRICT

Rep. Alcee Hastings (D)

Elected 1992, 6th term; b. Sept. 5, 1936, Altamonte Springs; home, Miramar; Fisk U., B.A. 1958, Howard U., 1958–60, FL A&M, J.D. 1963; Methodist; single.

Elected Office: Broward Cnty. Circuit Court Judge, 1977–79.

Professional Career: Practicing atty., 1964–77; Federal Judge, U.S. District Court, 1979–89.

DC Office: 2235 RHOB 20515, 202-225-1313; Fax: 202-225-1171; Web site: www.house.gov/alceehastings.

District Offices: Ft. Lauderdale, 954-733-2800; West Palm Beach, 561-684-0565.

Committees: *Permanent Select Committee on Intelligence* (2d of 9 D): Intelligence Policy & National Security; Terrorism and Homeland Security (RMM). *Rules* (4th of 4 D): Technology & the House.

Group Ratings

	ADA	ACLU	AFS	LCV	CON	ITIC	NTU	COC	ACU	NTLC	CHC
2002	95	86	100	63	38	25	22	42	0	0	0
2001	100	—	100	79	—	—	11	29	8	—	—

National Journal Ratings

	2001 LIB	—	2001 CONS		2002 LIB	—	2002 CONS
Economic	83%	—	15%		91%	—	8%
Social	90%	—	0%		97%	—	3%
Foreign	70%	—	28%		77%	—	19%

Key Votes of the 107th Congress

1. Approve Bush Tax Cuts	N	5. Faith-Based Charities	N	9. Trade Promotion Authority	N
2. Limit Patients' Bill of Rights	N	6. Bar Gays in the Boy Scouts	N	10. Bar Funds for Intl. Court	N
3. Campaign Finance Reform	Y	7. Ban Partial-Birth Abortion	N	11. Authorize Force in Iraq	N
4. Ban ANWR Development	Y	8. Arm Commercial Pilots	*	12. Deny Home. Sec. Dept. Union	N

Election Results

2002 general	Alcee Hastings (D)	96,347	(77%)	($325,685)
	Charles Laurie (R)	27,986	(23%)	($13,501)
2002 primary	Alcee Hastings (D)	unopposed		
2000 general	Alcee Hastings (D)	89,179	(76%)	($375,037)
	Bill Lambert (R)	27,630	(24%)	

Prior Winning Percentages: 1998 (100%); 1996 (73%); 1994 (100%); 1992 (59%)

The People		Race/Ethnic Origin	Ancestry	
Area size:	3,703 sq. mi.	29.4% White	West Indian: 16.2% USA: 5.0%	
Urban population:	97.9%	51.2% Black	German: 4.1%	
Rural population:	2.1%	1.2% Asian	**2000 Presidential Vote**	
Pop. 2000:	639,295	0.2% Native Am.	Gore (D)	130,518 (80%)
Median income:	$31,309	0.1% Hawaiian	Bush (R)	33,034 (20%)
Poverty status:	21.9%	3.9% Two + races	**Cook Partisan Voting Index:** D +30	
Military veterans:	9.1%	0.4% Other		
		13.7% Hispanic Origin		

Occupation	Blue collar: 25.8%	White collar: 48.0%	Gray collar: 26.2%

In the morning shadow of the high-rise condominiums that line the Atlantic Ocean, behind the quiet waters that separate the barrier islands from the mainland, usually a few blocks off of old U.S. 1 and behind the railroad lines, are the black neighborhoods of South Florida's Gold Coast. They are gatherings of older stucco homes and commercial storefronts, ranging from enclaves of upper-middle-class residents to rundown slums. These neighborhoods, populated by the working poor and with relatively few seniors, are overlooked by most tourists.

The 23d Congressional District gathers together many of South Florida's black neighborhoods in a geographically contrived, but demographically coherent, constituency. Geographically most of the district is in the Everglades, east and south of Lake Okeechobee. This is a land of swamps and drainage canals, with some farms and citrus groves—and very few people, some in migrant worker camps, some on the Miccosukee Indian Reservation. Almost all of the people in the district live within four narrow tentacles that extend east from the Everglades and get close to but never reach the Atlantic Ocean. The northernmost reaches into St. Lucie County and takes in black neighborhoods in Fort Pierce. In northern Palm Beach County a tentacle reaches past high-income Wellington into West Palm Beach and then continues south along the railroad tracks and U.S. 1 to Delray Beach, which has a big Haitian community (16% of the district claims West Indian ancestry). The most heavily populated tentacle reaches east into Broward County to take in heavily black areas in Lauderhill, Fort Lauderdale, Pompano Beach and Deerfield Beach plus the gay area in Wilton Manor. Farther south in Broward County there is a much smaller tentacle that reaches into parts of Pembroke Pines and Miramar. The district's population is 51% black and 14% Hispanic (primarily non-Cuban though)—lower figures than before the 2002 redistricting, which added Century Village, the retirement development in Pembroke Pines known for its politically powerful, liberal associations led by "condo commandos." (The Del Boca Vista subdivision in *Seinfeld* tweaked such places for their neighborhood busybodies and early-bird dinner deals.) This is a very heavily Democratic district.

The congressman from the 23d District is Alcee Hastings, a Democrat elected in 1992, the only member of Congress ever to have been impeached and removed from office as a federal judge. Hastings is charming but hard-edged, the son of a hotel maid from Orlando; he practiced law, finished fourth in the five-candidate Democratic primary when he ran for the U.S. Senate in 1970, and was confirmed as a federal judge in 1979. He was impeached by the House of

Representatives by a vote of 413–3 in 1988 and convicted by the Senate by a vote of 69–26. Hastings was charged with conspiring with a friend to take a $150,000 bribe and give two convicted swindlers light sentences. A Miami jury acquitted Hastings in 1983, but the friend was convicted. The 11th Circuit Court of Appeals called for impeachment in 1987 and referred the case to Congress. In the House, John Conyers, senior member of the Congressional Black Caucus, made the case for impeachment; a panel of 12 senators heard the case, and Hastings was removed in 1989. Footnote: In 1997 the Department of Justice in investigating the FBI crime lab found that an agent falsely testified against Hastings, and he and Conyers moved to reopen the case. Nothing came of that, raising a question: Can a removed federal judge be restored to office?

After his removal Hastings was unapologetic. In 1990 he ran an abortive campaign for governor, then lost the primary for secretary of state. When the 23d District was created, he sprang into that race and led the primary 28%–27%. In the October runoff he faced Palm Beach County legislator Lois Frankel, who later became a national figure as state House Minority Leader during the November-December 2000 Florida presidential controversy. He was helped by a ruling by federal Judge Stanley Sporkin that his removal from office was invalid since the full Senate did not hear the charges; the Supreme Court ruled to the contrary in a case involving another federal judge in January 1993, but by that time Hastings was in Congress. Frankel blasted Hastings for his record; Hastings responded, "The bitch is a racist." He won the runoff 58%–42%, with voting closely following racial lines. He won the general election 59%–31%.

"I sort of came back like gangbusters, didn't I?" he said later, but in the House he treated colleagues pleasantly and respectfully. His voting record has been the most liberal in the Florida delegation. He focused on international issues, and won a seat on the Intelligence Committee. He strongly supported the U.S. intervention in Kosovo but opposed the use of force in Iraq. He teamed with Republican Melissa Hart on an economic assistance bill for individuals who lost their jobs as a result of September 11. Fearful of terrorism even before the attacks, he wanted to establish a uniform communications technology among "first response" groups. In 2001, he was given a seat on the House Rules Committee, an influential assignment though less so for those in the minority party.

Naturally, Hastings's opinion was sought when the subject of impeachment arose, and it was exuberantly given. He saw Bill Clinton's impeachment as being driven by prosecutors as his own was, in his view, by judges—in both cases abusing their powers: "In my case, they nullified a jury. In this case, they are nullifying an election." In September 1998 he moved to impeach Independent Counsel Kenneth Starr; his motion was voted down 340–71. When one senator estimated that a trial would take just three weeks, Hastings replied, "Hello? I don't think so. Over on Ego Mountain they don't have a clue."

At home, Hastings criticized Governor Jeb Bush's One Florida plan to end race and gender preferences in state colleges and universities, contending that white men have developed a "good old boy system . . . and a whole bunch of other things that are preferences." He called the presidential election recount in Florida "a stain on democracy." In 2002, he objected to the final redistricting as "retrogression" because he would not have won within those lines in 1992, but a federal court rejected his claim. After the 2002 election, he said that he would run for the Senate if Bob Graham did not seek reelection and predicted that he would probably lose, but said that it would be the "capstone" of his long career, 34 years after his first Senate race.

TWENTY-FOURTH DISTRICT

Rep. Tom Feeney (R)

Elected 2002, 1st term; b. May 21, 1958, Abington, PA; home, Oviedo; PA St. U., B.A. 1980, U. of Pittsburgh, J.D. 1983; Presbyterian; married (Ellen).

Elected Office: FL House of Reps., 1990–94, 1996–02, Speaker, 2000–02.

Professional Career: Practicing atty., 1983–02.

DC Office: 323 CHOB 20515, 202-225-2706; Fax: 202-226-6299; Web site: www.house.gov/feeney.

District Offices: Orlando, 407-208-1106; Port Orange, 386-756-9798; Titusville, 321-264-6113.

Committees: *Financial Services* (30th of 37 R): Domestic and International Monetary Policy, Trade & Technology; Financial Institutions & Consumer Credit. *Judiciary* (20th of 21 R): Commercial & Administrative Law; Crime, Terrorism & Homeland Security; The Constitution. *Science* (24th of 25 R): Space & Aeronautics.

Group Ratings and Key Votes: Newly Elected

Election Results

2002 general	Tom Feeney (R)	135,576	(62%)	($1,853,423)
	Harry Jacobs (D)	83,667	(38%)	($3,989,408)
2002 primary	Tom Feeney (R)	unopposed		

The People		Race/Ethnic Origin	Ancestry	
Area size:	1,915 sq. mi.	80.0% White	German: 12.4%	Irish: 10.5%
Urban population:	91.2%	6.3% Black	English: 9.3%	
Rural population:	8.8%	2.0% Asian	**2000 Presidential Vote**	
Pop. 2000:	639,295	0.3% Native Am.	Bush (R)..............133,531	(53%)
Median income:	$43,954	0.0% Hawaiian	Gore (D)..............116,502	(47%)
Poverty status:	8.7%	1.4% Two+ races	**Cook Partisan Voting Index:** R + 4	
Military veterans:	17.1%	0.2% Other		
		9.8% Hispanic Origin		

Occupation	Blue collar: 19.4%	White collar: 65.3%	Gray collar: 15.3%

In 1960, central Florida was a sleepy place: Orlando was a small city surrounded by citrus groves; the Atlantic Coast from Cape Canaveral north was a quiet winter vacation spot, with small motels lining U.S. 1 or along the beach on Highway A1A. Then two outsiders transformed this part of America, and made it in two different ways a leader in the world: John F. Kennedy and Walt Disney. Kennedy promised in 1960 to put a man on the moon before the end of the decade, and the Kennedy Space Center was built on an island near Cape Canaveral. This part of Florida suddenly became the Space Coast, from which Americans traveled directly to the moon. Disney in 1971 opened Disney World southwest of Orlando, near the intersection of I-4 and Florida's Turnpike. Other theme parks followed, and metro Orlando became the number one tourist destination in the world. In the process, the populations of metro Orlando and the Space Coast have more than tripled since the 1960s. People from all over the United States and, more recently, immigrants from Latin America and elsewhere, have come here in large numbers and, with the aid of ubiquitous air conditioning, have transformed sleepy backwaters into vibrant metropolitan areas. This is a part of Florida that has attracted many more young families and people in their working years than retirees: people who have built all-American communities where there used to be orange groves and swamps.

The 24th Congressional District has about half its population in the Orlando area, much of it in affluent Orange and Seminole County suburbs north and northeast of Orlando— all of Oviedo and parts of Maitland and Altamonte Springs. The other half is on the coast. The 24th includes the northern half of Brevard County, including the main grounds of the Space Center itself, the Canaveral National Seashore and the county seat of Titusville. It also contains the southern half of Volusia County, including part of Daytona Beach, where NASCAR is a big employer and Bike Week and Speed Weeks are held every year, and New Smyrna Beach, founded as a colony by Andrew Turnbull, a Scotch doctor, where you can see the ruins of an 1820s sugar mill. In between is Ponce de Leon Inlet, near which 20 people were bitten by sharks in the summer of 2001: the sort of thing that made national news before September 11. This is as close as Florida gets to a typical suburban district: There are higher than average numbers of homeowners, families with children, working women and white-collar employees. Most of this district tends to vote Republican, though Al Gore carried Volusia County in 2000; overall the 24th District voted 53% for George W. Bush.

The congressman from the new 24th District is Tom Feeney, a Republican elected in 2002 who was a prominent political player in the 2000 Florida presidential recount. His political career has been marked by ambition, impulsiveness and a lightning-quick rise through the ranks. He grew up Pennsylvania, the son of school teachers, and moved to Florida after graduating from Penn State and University of Pittsburgh law school and practiced real estate law. Within seven years, in 1990 he was elected to the state House, where his early focus was on education. In 1993 he was named the Christian Coalition's legislator of the year. In 1994 Jeb Bush picked him as his lieutenant governor candidate. The statewide race was a sobering experience. Democrats zeroed in on Feeney's conservative voting record—he opposed abortion rights and favored school prayer and vouchers—and pounded him as an extremist bent on injecting religion into the public schools. Bush and Feeney lost to Lawton Chiles and Buddy MacKay 51%–49%. In an April 1996 special election, Feeney was returned to the state House, in which Republicans won a majority in 1996.

In November 2000, he became Speaker and suddenly found himself in the national spotlight. During the 36-day presidential recount he aggressively challenged the rulings of the Florida Supreme Court and supported Secretary of State Katherine Harris. When it was unclear whether the U.S. Supreme Court would review the Florida court's second decision, Feeney called a special session of the House to appoint presidential electors for Bush; that became moot with the U.S. Supreme Court decision December 12. In 2001 he concentrated on more typical state issues— tort law, education, welfare. He blocked Republican state Senate President John McKay's ambitious attempt to overhaul the sales tax, although Feeney ultimately agreed to a watered-down version; that stance earned him the campaign backing and the considerable financial support of the anti-tax Club for Growth.

In 2001 and 2002 Feeney also concentrated on congressional redistricting. Florida imposes term limits on state legislators, and Feeney could not run for the state House again in 2002. Central Florida's population had increased robustly in the 1990s, and it was the part of the state most obviously entitled to one of the two additional seats Florida had picked up in the 2000 Census. Feeney's problem is that he had to accommodate three Republican House incumbents in the area, none of them eager to lose Republican territory they represented. In 2001 Senate Republicans delayed agreement on redistricting to gain leverage on other legislative issues. But the plans were passed in March 2002, in plenty of time for court challenges before the July filing deadline; Feeney immediately started to run in the new 24th District and was unopposed in the Republican primary.

The general election featured one of the most aggressively negative campaigns in the nation. The Democratic nominee was Harry Jacobs, a wealthy trial lawyer who in November 2000 filed a lawsuit challenging the validity of some 16,000 absentee ballots in Seminole County. The weakness of the lawsuit was that even Jacobs conceded that the overwhelming majority of the ballots were valid, and there was no way to distinguish those that weren't from those that were. The Gore campaign refused to endorse the suit, though Jacobs did seem to get from nudges and winks from Gore supporters; a trial judge appointed by a Democratic governor dismissed it December 8. Jacobs spent $3.2 million of his own money on his 2002 campaign. He boasted about his work as a public school teacher and attacked Feeney's "questionable ethics." At one point it was revealed that one of Feeney's senior aides in Tallahassee used her official computer for campaign purposes; Feeney denied any impropriety. A Democratic operative also filed an ethics complaint accusing Feeney of using his influence to protect one of his clients from an investigation; a week before the election, the Florida Ethics Commission cleared Feeney of the charges.

Feeney won 62%–38%. The race was closest in Volusia County, where he won 55% of the vote; he won 63% in Brevard, 65% in Orange and 66% in Seminole.

TWENTY-FIFTH DISTRICT

Rep. Mario Diaz-Balart (R)

Elected 2002, 1st term; b. Sept. 25, 1961, Ft. Lauderdale; home, Miami; U. of S. FL; Catholic; single.

Elected Office: FL House of Reps., 1988–92, 2000–02; FL Senate, 1992–00.

Professional Career: A.A., Miami Mayor Xavier Suarez, 1985–88; Public relations executive.

DC Office: 313 CHOB 20515, 202-225-2778; Fax: 202-226-0346; Web site: www.house.gov/mariodiaz-balart.

District Offices: Miami, 305-225-6866; Naples, 239-348-1620.

Committees: *Budget* (22d of 24 R). *Transportation & Infrastructure* (40th of 41 R): Aviation; Coast Guard & Maritime Transportation (Vice Chmn.); Water Resources & Environment.

Group Ratings and Key Votes: Newly Elected

Election Results

2002 general	Mario Diaz-Balart (R)	81,845	(65%)	($999,322)
	Annie Betancourt (D)	44,757	(35%)	($155,450)
2002 primary	Mario Diaz-Balart (R)	unopposed		

The People		Race/Ethnic Origin	Ancestry	
Area size:	4,724 sq. mi.	24.3% White	USA: 3.8%	West Indian: 3.7%
Urban population:	94.4%	10.0% Black	German: 3.2%	
Rural population:	5.6%	1.6% Asian	**2000 Presidential Vote**	
Pop. 2000:	639,295	0.1% Native Am.	Bush (R) 88,308	(55%)
Median income:	$44,489	0.0% Hawaiian	Gore (D) 72,050	(45%)
Poverty status:	13.7%	1.4% Two + races	**Cook Partisan Voting Index:** R + 5	
Military veterans:	6.0%	0.2% Other		
		62.4% Hispanic Origin		

Occupation	Blue collar: 20.8%	White collar: 61.7%	Gray collar: 17.5%

An interconnected sea of wetlands once covered 8.9 million acres of southern Florida, stretching from present-day Orlando down to the peninsula's southern tip. Initially, it was a coherent ecosystem, a "river of grass" in which water moved slowly down a gentle slope to the ocean, buffering plants and animals from meteorological extremes, and providing different microenvironments for flora and fauna based on an inch or two gained or lost in elevation. It was long a dream of Florida's white settlers to control this land and make it more useful, but for decades, this goal proved elusive. It took three attempts between 1915 and the late 1920s to build the Tamiami Trail from Miami to Tampa; to this day, it is one of only two roads that cross the South Florida interior from coast to coast. Over time, however, man managed to reshape the Everglades. In 1948, Congress approved the Central and South Florida Project, which authorized the construction of 1,000 miles of canals and 720 miles of levees to channel and drain the Everglades. Since that time, about half of the original ecosystem has been turned over to agriculture and housing, and the amount of water discharged into the ocean has fallen by 70%. Floridians began to question the wisdom of government policy and call for restoration of the Everglades. Florida politicians of both parties began to take notice, and called for change. So did officials of the Clinton administration. In 2000 they all came together in agreement, and Congress passed a law to restore the Everglades, authorizing $7.8 billion over 30 years. Now comes the hard part: no one is actually sure how to accomplish the goals, but in 2002 the President and his brother signed an agreement to proceed and the Army Corps of Engineers was set to work.

A century of meddling has produced an often-surreal landscape. In her book *The Orchid Thief*, journalist Susan Orlean relates the tortured history of the Fakahatchee Strand, a swampy stretch east of Naples. "What is compelling about Florida is not just its ever-expanding quantity of land—it's the qualities that the land has come to represent," she writes. "Florida was to Americans what America had always been to the rest of the world—a fresh, free, unspoiled start." Farmers came to the Fakahatchee in the early 20th century, but they found that crops would not grow reliably, and livestock often escaped, leaving a legacy of feral, mean-spirited swamp pigs. Timbering came next, until there were no more trees to chop down. Then the timber barons sold their land to real estate speculators who made hundreds of millions of dollars duping customers into buying wretched plots for $10 a month, using patently false promises, spying on their customers' private conversations in their hotel rooms, and driving potential buyers out to remote areas of the site and threatening to let them walk home if they did not sign a contract. Much of the landholdings became an untamed state park.

The 25th Congressional District sprawls almost all the way across this uninhabitable portion of South Florida, connecting population centers near (but not on) each of Florida's two coasts. About 13% of its residents live in Collier County, in new housing wedged between decidedly upscale Naples and the wild Everglades and in the farm town of Immokalee. The large majority live in western and southern edges of metropolitan Miami, never very far from the swamps. Here you can drive out on roads past the subdivisions and find strawberry, tomato and citrus farms; the trees thin out and then the road just ends, and the Everglades begin. This was the fastest-growing district in Florida during the 1990s, when its population grew by 52%. The towns in the northern part of the district are heavily Cuban and Latino—Hialeah Gardens, Tamiami, Kendale Lakes, South Miami Heights, Cutler Ridge. Farther south the 25th takes in low-income agricultural areas along South Dixie Highway (U.S. 1), like Princeton and Naranja, as well as a few older tourist attractions, like the Metrozoo, Monkey Jungle and Coral Castle. Even further south is what was once the country town of Homestead. Before 1992, Homestead Air Force Base was a major employer here. But in August 1992 Hurricane Andrew hit Homestead, causing 14 deaths and leaving massive property destruction; Homestead was leveled and the Air Force Base closed. In one of his last acts as president, Bill Clinton rejected a plan to convert the base to a commercial airport, citing environmental concerns; instead, 700 acres were transferred to the county for likely use by developers. Politically, this area leans Republican, thanks to the strong Republican allegiance of its many Cuban Americans (though this is the least Cuban of the three South Florida Hispanic majority districts).

The congressman from the 25th District is Mario Diaz-Balart, a Republican elected in 2002. His father, Rafael Lincoln Diaz-Balart, served as Majority Leader in Cuba's House of Representatives. His uncle and grandfather also served in the Cuban House. His aunt was once married to Fidel Castro. He comes from a prominent family sometimes called "the Cuban Kennedys" which seems to have politics in its blood. One of his three older brothers is Lincoln Diaz-Balart, congressman since 1992 from the 21st District just to the east. Mario Diaz-Balart, unlike his brother, was born in the United States after his family fled Cuba.

Even for a scion of one of Miami's most prominent political families, Mario Diaz-Balart's ascent has been unusually rapid. He dropped out of the University of South Florida at 24 to work for former Miami Mayor Xavier Suarez and was elected in 1988 to the Florida House. In 1992, at 31, he became the youngest person ever elected to the Florida Senate. Soon after that, Diaz-Balart was named chairman of the Senate Ways and Means Committee, where he quickly established a reputation as a budget hawk. His 1995 order calling for state agencies to cut spending by 25% earned him the nickname "The Slasher"—a moniker he wore with pride. The eight-year term limit forced him from the state Senate in 2000, so he again ran for the Florida House and was elected. He was no ordinary freshman, though. As a veteran of the state's 1992 round of redistricting, Diaz-Balart requested and received the chairmanship of the congressional redistricting committee. Republicans controlled redistricting; the resulting plan included a central

Florida district tailored to Speaker Tom Feeney and this western Miami-Dade district tailored for Diaz-Balart.

The election proved anticlimactic. Diaz-Balart went to court and eliminated all his opponents in the Republican primary. In the general election he coasted to victory over Democratic state Representative Annie Betancourt, a former social worker and the widow of a Bay of Pigs veteran. Betancourt's campaign was underfinanced and she remained largely unknown; Diaz-Balart was well financed and had support from teachers' unions and other unions. Probably the biggest news in the campaign was Betancourt's call to end the "failed" embargo of Cuba in a way "that doesn't pander to the Cuban regime but likewise doesn't punish the Cuban people." This was a bold move in a strongly anti-Castro constituency. But Diaz-Balart did not pursue the issue vigorously, perhaps because he sensed that the growing population of non-Cuban Latinos in south Florida are less concerned about Castro.

Diaz-Balart won 65%-35%. In the House he quickly showed that he would be a player by getting on the Budget and Transportation and Infrastructure committees. In the battle for influence among the new pairs of siblings in the House, Florida's Diaz-Balart brothers were well ahead of California's Sanchez sisters.

★ GEORGIA ★

G eorgia and Atlanta—the megacity whose metropolitan area spreads out over the red clay hills of 20 of Georgia's 159 counties—have been one of the great boom areas of America over the last dozen years and were the site of the biggest political upset and upheaval of election year 2002. Georgia's population grew by 26% in the 1990s, the sixth highest rate of population growth among states, the highest east of Colorado, and the highest rate of growth for Georgia since the 1870s, when Atlanta rose literally from the ashes of the Civil War and Henry Grady's New South sprang into being. Atlanta and Georgia have been in many ways, for many years, the center of the South, at least since William Tecumseh Sherman marched here in 1864. This is where John Stith Pemberton invented Coca-Cola, where Margaret Mitchell wrote *Gone With the Wind,* where Martin Luther King Jr. grew up, and where most of the civil rights organizations that changed America were headquartered. But in growth and flamboyance, Georgia for decades was outdazzled by other parts of the South—by Texas with its oil wells and high-tech industries, by Florida with Miami Beach and Disney World, even by North Carolina with its Research Triangle and college basketball champions.

In the 1990s, however, Georgia grew faster than any of them, and by 2000 was the tenth-largest state—the first time it has been in the top 10 since the Census of 1850. Most of this growth has come in the booming Atlanta metropolitan area, not in the core city, but amid the hills of suburban counties for almost 100 miles around. Atlanta, long a regional capital, has become a world city, a status suitably memorialized when it hosted the 1996 Summer Olympics, and re-emphasized every day as travelers all over the world watch the news from the CNN Broadcast Center. Atlanta in the 1990s was the central focus of Tom Wolfe's 1998 novel *A Man in Full*, with scenes ranging from a developer's mansion in Buckhead and 29,000-acre hunting estate in south Georgia to a phony Ku Klux Klan rally.

Neither Atlanta's rise to world eminence nor its role as the capital of the South was inevitable. This was only a small, though well located, railroad crossroads when it was burned by General William Tecumseh Sherman's troops on their "march to the sea." Richmond, Charleston and New Orleans all had stronger claims to being the central focus of the South a century ago. But in the 20th century two figures imprinted Atlanta on the national imagination. One was Margaret Mitchell, whose 1936 novel *Gone with the Wind* inspired the 1939 movie. The other was Martin Luther King Jr., reared in Atlanta and based there during most of his career, as a leader and ultimately the national symbol of the civil rights revolution that changed the South and the nation. Linking the two was Atlanta's business community, notably Robert Woodruff, who headed Coca-Cola from 1932–60 and made Coke a worldwide enterprise. Perhaps aware that a world company

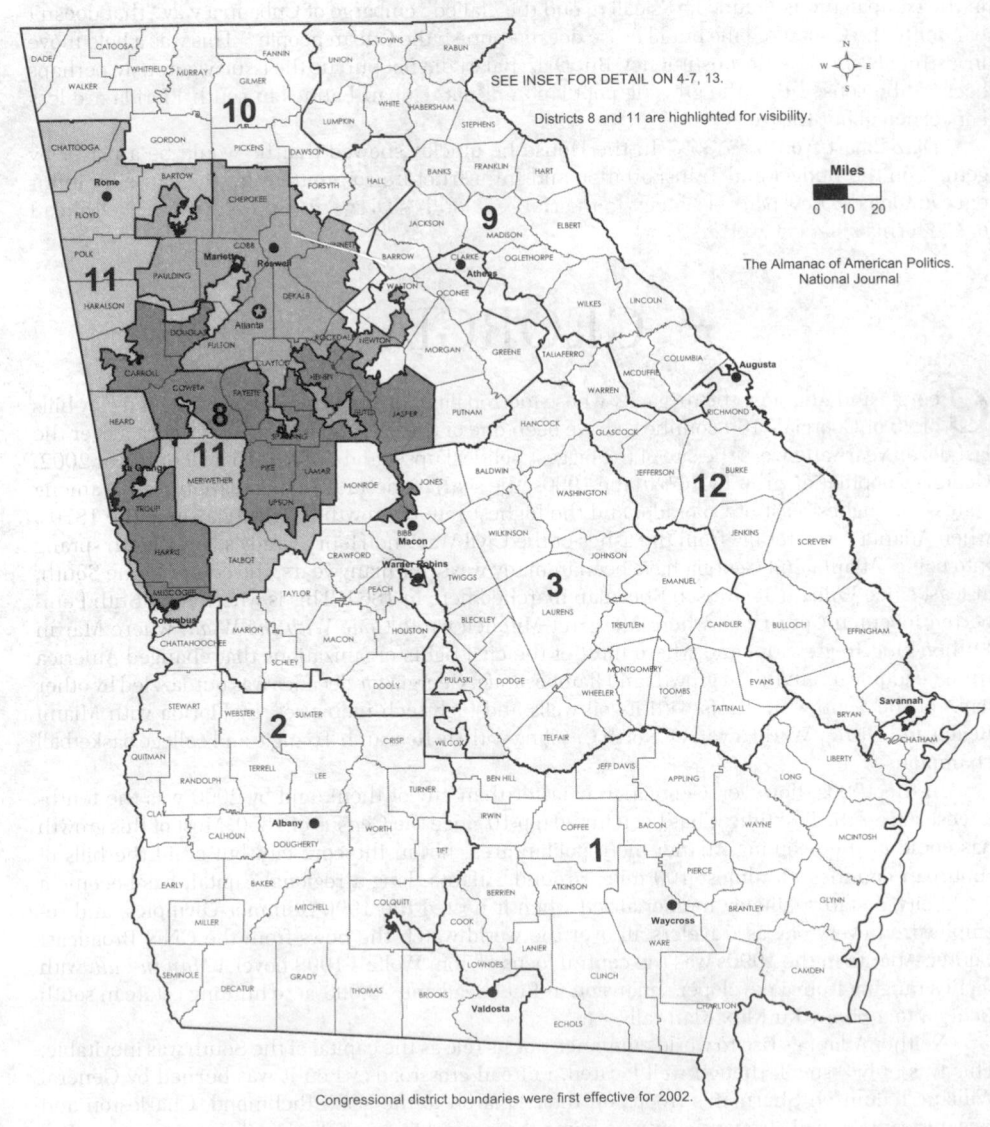

SEE INSET FOR DETAIL ON 4-7, 13.

Districts 8 and 11 are highlighted for visibility.

Miles
0   10   20

The Almanac of American Politics.
National Journal

Congressional district boundaries were first effective for 2002.

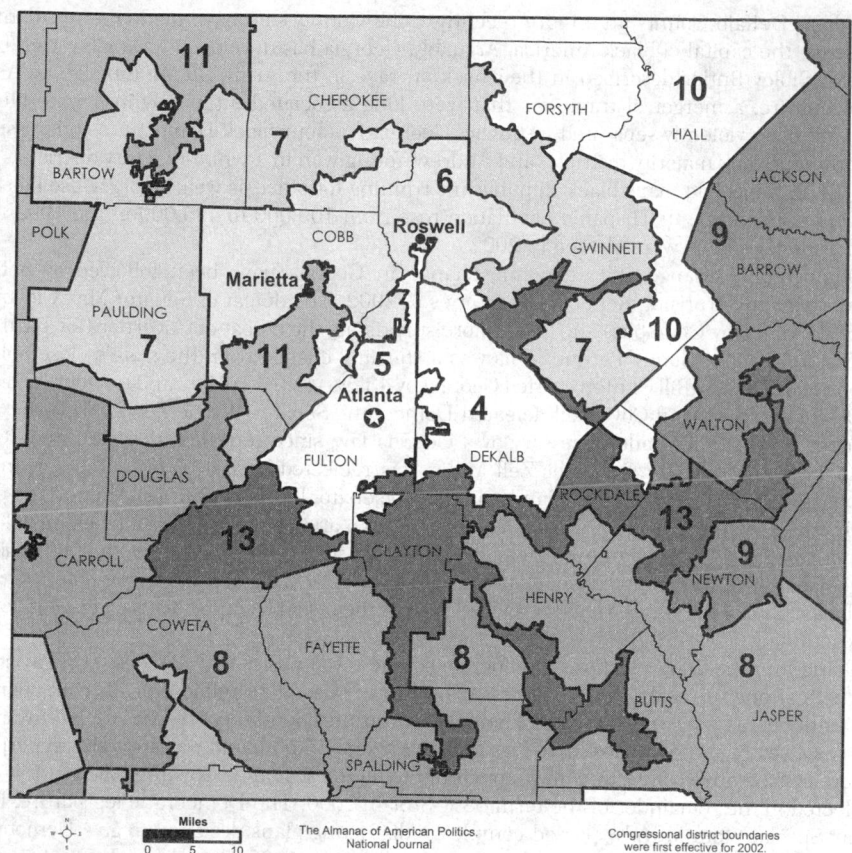

could not indefinitely be associated with racial segregation, Woodruff and William Hartsfield, mayor from 1937–61, cooperated with blacks and promoted Atlanta as "the city too busy to hate." Hartsfield's successor, Ivan Allen, elected in 1961 and 1965, supported the Civil Rights Act of 1964, as Peachtree Center and the first atriumed Hyatt Regency were going up in downtown Atlanta.

This new Atlanta was growing up amid a mostly rural, deeply segregationist Georgia that as late as 1960 cast the second-highest Democratic percentage of any state for president: Hatred of Sherman was still strong. Political contests typically matched Atlanta-supported moderates against rural-supported segregationists, and the latter invariably won: Georgia's electoral votes were cast for Barry Goldwater in 1964 and George Wallace in 1968. Then came change in the person of Jimmy Carter, a former nuclear submarine officer and one-term state senator who was elected governor in 1970 with a rural base as well as conspicuous black support. On taking office he proclaimed a reconciliation of the races and installed a portrait of Martin Luther King Jr. in the Capitol. Carter thus became one of the first politicians from the rural South to celebrate and honor the civil rights revolution and in the process set himself on the road to being elected president in 1976.

Since then, Georgia and Atlanta have seen an in-migration of black Americans. The state's population was 29% black in 2000, the highest figure since 1950; the state has more blacks than any other state except New York and Texas, and will surpass them soon if present trends continue. The presence of 9 historically black colleges, of large numbers of prominent black public officials and businessmen, the growth of middle- and upper-income predominantly black suburban neighborhoods in DeKalb County and, more recently, Cobb County—all have made metro Atlanta in some sense the capital of black America. Arguably, Georgia has developed what Charles Moskos and John Sibley Butler described in their book on race in the Army, *All We Can Be*, an Anglo-African culture, a merger of traditions that were long associated intimately in private life but rigidly and even violently separated in public. Georgia has four black Democratic congressmen, two from non-black majority districts, and Andrew Young won in a white-majority district as long ago as 1972; it has had many black Republicans running for office as well. Georgia also has been attracting immigrants: Its Hispanic population rose from 109,000 to 435,000 in the 1990s, and three Latino legislators were elected in 2002.

Demographic change and economic change in Georgia have been followed by political change—big and surprising Republican victories of 2002: The defeat of Senator Max Cleland by Congressman Saxby Chambliss and, even more surprising, the defeat of Governor Roy Barnes by former state Senator Sonny Perdue. This was a startling change from the state's close political divisions of the 1990s. Bill Clinton carried Georgia by 43.5%–42.9% in 1992 and lost it by 47%–46% in 1996. Republican Paul Coverdell defeated Democratic Senator Wyche Fowler 51%–49% in a November 1992 runoff made necessary by a Georgia law, since repealed, that required 50% to win. In 1994, Democratic Governor Zell Miller was reelected 51%–49% over Republican Guy Millner. In 1996, Democrat Max Cleland was elected senator by 49%–48% over Millner. In heavily pro-incumbent 1998, Coverdell was reelected 52%–45% and Democrat Roy Barnes was elected governor by 52%–44% over Millner—not a breakthrough for either party. Then, in 2000, a sign of change: George W. Bush carried Georgia by a solid 55%–43% margin. Bush carried metro Atlanta (which cast 53% of the state's votes) by 52%–45% and the rest of Georgia, historically Democratic, by a resounding 57%–41%.

Going into the 2002 elections Democrats seemed well-positioned. Barnes, an activist governor with strong ties to Atlanta's business community, raised $19 million for his campaign and was mentioned as a possible vice presidential or even presidential candidate. Cleland was well known as a veteran who had lost both legs and an arm in Vietnam and was strongly supported by his more conservative colleague Miller, appointed to fill the seat after Coverdell died in July 2000 and elected to the remainder of the term 58%–38% in 2000. The Democratic legislature, led by 28-year Speaker Tom Murphy passed complex redistricting plans designed to give Democrats a majority of the state's 13 House seats (up from 11 thanks to 1990s growth) and to lock in Democratic majorities in the legislature.

Arrayed against this juggernaut was Ralph Reed, former head of the Christian Coalition and later a campaign consultant, who was elected Republican state chairman in May 2001. His Democratic counterpart said he was "a leading indicator of how extreme Georgia Republicans have become." But Reed believed that the state was demographically Republican, and becoming more so: Republican national tickets went from 43% in 1992 to 47% in 1996 and 55% in 2000. He knew he could not match Barnes in dollars, so he created an on-the-ground organization that ultimately deployed 3,000 volunteers and 500 paid workers to knock on 150,000 doors in 600 precincts. He ran registration drives in fast-growing heavily Republican counties in metro Atlanta. He helped the party find strong candidates—Perdue, a party-switcher, for governor; Chambliss, head of a congressional anti-terrorism task force, for senator. (It helped that Barnes's Democrats redistricted Chambliss out of his seat.) Perdue beat Barnes 51%–46%, losing the Atlanta area 48%–49% but carrying the rest of the state 55%–43%. Chambliss beat Cleland 53%–46%, carrying the Atlanta area 52%–47% and the rest of the state 54%–45%. Turnout rose robustly in central Atlanta and in black counties, but it rose even more in the fast-growing suburbs: Demographic growth translated into votes. Speaker Tom Murphy, after 42 years in the legislature, and state Senate Majority Leader Charles Walker were defeated by Republicans. In the week after the election, four state senators switched parties and gave Republicans control of the state Senate for the first time since Reconstruction. Conservative Democrat Terry Coleman won the speakership with a coalition of rural Democrats and two Republican crossover votes.

This was a political revolution of a sort that seldom occurs in a state. Smart, aggressive, relatively conservative Democrats like Miller and Barnes had kept their party on top with the help of Atlanta's business establishment and by the perception among ambitious politicos that the only way to win high office was to stay a Democrat. Now the business interests are likely to have little reason to support Democrats and many reasons to back Republicans. The politically ambitious could ponder the careers of Barnes and Perdue. Both started in politics as canny young legislators with ambitions to be governor. Barnes chose to remain a Democrat and was elected governor, then couldn't hold the office. Now Perdue, by winning against a well-financed incumbent, has shown that it is easier to win as a Republican. Georgia Democrats had a long run in power and compiled records in which they can reasonably take pride. Georgia Republicans may or may not do as well. But Georgia Democrats aren't likely to have another such run any time soon.

The People		Race/Ethnic Origin			Military veterans: 768,675 (12.8%)	
Pop. 2000:	8,186,453	5,128,661	62.6%	White	WWII: 13.5%	Korea: 10.8%
Pop. 1990:	6,478,216	2,331,465	28.5%	Black	Vietnam: 34.4%	Gulf War: 15.4%
Change 1990–2000:	Up 26.4%	171,513	2.1%	Asian	**Most populous cities:**	
Change 1980–1990:	Up 18.6%	17,670	0.2%	Native Am.	1. Atlanta	416,474
% of U.S. total:	2.9%	3,278	0.0%	Hawaiian	2. Columbus	185,781
Pop. rank:	10th of 50	87,364	1.1%	Two+ races	3. Savannah	131,510
Area size:	59,425 sq. mi.	11,275	0.1%	Other	4. Macon	97,255
State Native:	57.8%	435,227	5.3%	Hisp. Origin	5. Roswell	79,334
Non-citizen:	5.0%	**Ancestry**			Urban population: 71.7%	
Language		USA: 11.6%		English: 7.0%	Rural population: 28.3%	
English: 88.6%	Spanish: 6.0%	Irish: 6.7%		German: 6.0%		
Other Eur.: 3.2%		Italian: 1.7%				

Education		Work Sector			General Assembly	
H.S. Grad:	78.6%	Private: 78.9%		Govt: 15.0%	Senate	30 R 26 D
College Grad:	24.3%	Self: 5.9%		Family: 0.3%	House	106 D 73 R 1 I
Industry		Unemployment: 5.4%			Legislative Term Limits: No	
Agri: 1.4%	Con: 7.9%	**Household Income**			**Registered Voters**	
Fin: 6.5%	Info: 3.5%	<15k: 16.0%		15-35k: 24.9%	No party registration	
Mfg: 20.8%	Prof: 27.0%	35-50k: 16.7%		50-100k: 30.1%		
Public: 5.0%	Trade: 15.8%	100-150k: 7.8%		>150k: 4.6%		
Other: 11.9%		Median: $42,433				
Occupation		Poverty status: 13.0%				
Blue collar: 26.5%	White collar: 59.5%	**Home Value**				
Gray collar: 14.0%		<50k: 16.9%	50-100k: 32.8%	100-200k: 34.4%	200-300k: 9.3%	
		300-500k: 4.7%	>500k: 1.9%	Median: $100,600		

Presidential politics For many years Georgia seemed to vote against General Sherman, shunning Republican presidential candidates even when states less ravaged by Sherman's troops, like next-door South Carolina and Alabama, embraced them. It was the second most Democratic state for John Kennedy in 1960, voted for opponents of the Civil Rights Act of 1964 Barry Goldwater in 1964 and George Wallace in 1968, delivered big margins for Jimmy Carter in both 1976 and 1980 and voted heavily Republican only in 1972, 1984 and 1988. A residual anti-Sherman vote in rural Georgia can perhaps explain why Bill Clinton carried the state outside metro Atlanta in 1992 and lost it by only 2% in 1996. But no more. George W. Bush carried Georgia 55%–43% in 2000, and won outside metro Atlanta by 57%–41%. This poses a serious problem for Democratic strategists: A candidate who can't run better than Al Gore in the rural South is going to have a hard time carrying Georgia's 15 electoral votes.

2000 Presidential Vote
Bush (R) 1,419,720 (55%)
Gore (D) 1,116,230 (43%)
Other 47,258 (2%)

2000 Republican Presidential Primary
Bush (R) 430,480 (67%)
McCain (R) 179,046 (28%)
Keyes (R) 29,640 (5%)

2000 Democratic Presidential Primary
Gore (D) 238,396 (84%)
Bradley (D) 46,035 (16%)

1996 Presidential Vote
Dole (R) 1,080,840 (47%)
Clinton (D) 1,053,848 (46%)
Perot (I) 146,337 (6%)

Georgia's 1992 presidential primary was scheduled one week before Super Tuesday at the insistence of Governor Zell Miller, who wanted to help Bill Clinton, and did: Clinton won smartly to balance losses in Maryland and Colorado the same day. George Bush's 64%–36% victory here over Pat Buchanan showed the Buchanan brigades were not about to overrun the South. Since then, Georgia's primary has been of little consequence, except as a measure of its Republican presidential trend since voters are free to mark the ballot for either party. In 1988, when both parties had contests, 622,000 voted Democratic and 400,000 voted Republican; in 1992, 454,631 voted Democratic and 453,990 voted Republican; in 2000, 284,000 voted Democratic and 643,000 Republican.

Congressional districting After the 1990 and 2000 Censuses, Georgia Democrats, led by Speaker Thomas Murphy, pushed through convoluted redistricting plans—arguably the most convoluted in the nation each time—to guarantee majorities for their party in the state's House delegation. Both times they failed. In the 1990s Murphy tried to end the career of Newt Gingrich and strengthen incumbent Democrats. Instead, what was a 9–1 Democratic delegation in October 1992 was 8–3 Republican in April 1995, and Gingrich was Speaker of the House. A court-ordered redistricting in 1995 left virtually all incumbents with safe seats, and the balance remained 8–3. In 2001 the Democrats tried again, drawing several plans and negotiating among themselves. This time the boundaries were even more convoluted, and Democrats had a bit more success. But only a bit—plus some unintended consequences. Congressman Saxby Chambliss, placed in the new 1st District with fellow Republican Jack Kingston, ran for the Senate and beat incumbent Max Cleland. The new 11th and 12th Districts, created to elect Democrats, elected Republicans instead, and Democrats only narrowly won the new 3d District. The new 13th District did elect a black Democrat, Georgia's fourth, but the delegation remains Republican by an 8–5 margin. And Georgia's plan prompted the House Republicans' campaign committee head Tom Davis to push successfully for a similarly convoluted Republican gerrymander in Pennsylvania, one which netted the Republicans more gains than the Democrats achieved in Georgia.

108th Congress Lineup
8 R   5 D
107th Congress Lineup
8 R   3 D

Still, the Democrats' plan must be admired for its creativity. The new 13th District sends narrow tentacles into 11 metro Atlanta counties to unite black neighborhoods along strip highways or in town centers with majority-black Clayton County just south of Atlanta. The new 11th District made a stab, though unsuccessful in 2002, at creating a Democratic district in Republican north-west Georgia by excluding fast-growing mostly white areas and sending in tentacles to south Cobb County with its increasing population; this district could remain seriously contested throughout the decade. The new 12th District for the most part has a regular shape and yet connects black neighborhoods in cities as distant as Savannah, Augusta and Athens. Heavily Republican areas are packed into five districts—the 6th and 7th on the north side of metro Atlanta, the 8th on the south side, the 9th and 10th in north Georgia—which voted 68% to 70% for George W. Bush in 2000 and are among the most Republican in America.

But this work of art may not endure. After winning the governorship on November 5, 2002, and securing a majority in the state Senate within the next week by party switches, Georgia Republicans began drawing new redistricting plans for congressional and legislative districts. Those plans failed to pass the legislature in 2003, but a group of Republican plaintiffs filed suit in federal court in March 2003 challenging both the legislative and congressional districts.

Governor

Sonny Perdue (R)

Elected 2002, term expires Jan. 2007, 1st term; b. Dec. 20, 1946, Perry; home, Bonaire; U. of GA, D.V.M 1971; Baptist; married (Mary).

Military Career: Air Force, 1971–74 (Vietnam).

Elected Office: GA Senate, 1990–01; Maj. Ldr. 1994–97.

Professional Career: Veterinarian; owner, Houston Fertilizer and Grain; owner, Perdue Inc.; owner, AgroStar.

Office: 203 State Capitol, Atlanta, 30334, 404-656-1776; Fax: 404-657-7332; Web site: www.gov.state.ga.us.

Election Results

2002 general	Sonny Perdue (R)	1,041,677	(51%)
	Roy Barnes (D)	937,062	(46%)
	Other	47,122	(2%)
2002 primary	Sonny Perdue (R)	259,966	(51%)
	Linda Schrenko (R)	142,911	(28%)
	Bill Byrne (R)	108,586	(21%)
1998 general	Roy Barnes (D)	941,076	(52%)
	Guy Millner (R)	790,201	(44%)
	Other	61,531	(3%)

Sonny Perdue, the first Republican governor of Georgia since Reconstruction, grew up near Warner Robins in central Georgia, site of Warner Robins Air Force Base; he was the quarterback in high school football. He earned a veterinarian degree at the University of Georgia, where he was a walk-on football player, and served in the Air Force from 1971 to 1974. He practiced as a veterinarian briefly in North Carolina, then returned to Georgia and started a fertilier and grain business and a trucking firm near Warner Robins. In the 1980s he served on Houston County zoning boards. In 1990 he was elected to the state Senate as a Democrat; he was easily reelected and was elected Senate Majority Leader in 1994 and Senate President Pro Tem in 1997. His major legislative success was a law to deregulate natural gas; he voted against Governor Zell Miller's lottery to fund Hope scholarships and opposed a moment of silence bill because he favored prayer in schools. In 1998 he announced that he was switching parties and running for reelection as a Republican; he said his values were not the same as Bill Clinton's and those of other Democrats and that his efforts to change the party had not worked. He was stripped of his leadership posts and staff, but was reelected as a Republican with 70% of the vote. In December 2001, after his Senate seat had been hacked up in redistricting, he resigned his seat and announced he was running for governor.

He had taken on the daunting task of running against Governor Roy Barnes, elected in 1998 after a 22-year legislative career and an unsuccessful 1990 run for governor. Barnes, a conservative-sounding Democrat from suburban Cobb County, won the office by a 52%–44% margin over businessman Guy Millner and had pushed through an ambitious program. In 1999 he persuaded the legislature to create the Georgia Regional Transportation Authority that gave him control over transportation and development in the 20-county metro Atlanta area, with $300 million to allow local governments to purchase land and maintain it as open space. He pushed hard for a Northern Arc highway in fast-growing Cherokee and Forsyth Counties north of Atlanta. He got a $640 million property tax cut and HMO regulation. In 2000 he produced an education reform plan that required annual testing and held teachers accountable for results, with bonuses for some and adverse consequences for others; it also ended tenure for newly-hired teachers. In January 2001 Barnes addressed the issue of the state flag. Since 1956, back when Georgia politicians were resisting desegregation, it had featured the Confederate stars and bars; many blacks, liberals and businessmen wanted it changed. Governor Zell Miller tried to change it in 1993, in anticipation of the 1996 Atlanta Olympics, but the legislature resisted. In January 2001 Barnes unveiled a new design, in which the state seal would occupy most of the flag and it would include at the bottom small depictions of five flags that have flown over the state, including the Confederate flag. He quickly amassed majorities for it in both houses of the legislature made up of black Democrats, suburban Republicans and a few Democrats from non-metro areas.

But in the process of achieving all these successes, Barnes antagonized many voters and pressure groups. The Georgia Association of Educators bitterly opposed his education reforms, as did Republican state School Superintendent Linda Schrenko. Many voters were bitter about the change of flags, or at least the slick way it was brought about. Local activists opposed the Northern Arc. Barnes got the legislature to outlaw video poker: Operators of the games were furious. People began referring to Barnes as King Roy and said the GRTA stood for Give Roy Total Authority. It was this sentiment that Perdue, a legislative ally of Barnes in the 1990s, set out to tap. In May 2002 he put out a video for supporters showing Barnes as a giant rat named King Roy, with crown and necklace. He called for dismantling the Office of Education Accountability, and relying less on yearly tests and state standards and more on local teachers and parents to enforce standards. He called for a constitutional amendment to require 2/3 supermajorities of legislators to use surplus revenue for anything but tax cuts or paying down state debt. He attacked Barnes for the Democrats' highly partisan redistricting of state legislative and U.S. House seats.

Coming from south (or at least central) Georgia, Perdue employed a rural strategy. "We're trying to capture the basic voting instincts of the non-metro voter," he said. The state flag issue, which he did not talk about much, was just part of that strategy. This worked in tandem with state Republican Chairman Ralph Reed's program of building Republican organizations and volunteer corps not just in heavily Republican metro Atlanta counties, but also in 70 target counties outside the metro area, which had voted in 1998 for Barnes and for the late Republican Senator Paul Coverdell. This increasing Republican activity helped Perdue win 51% in the August primary against Schrenko and former Cobb County Commissioner Bill Byrne. In 1998, 64% of Republican primary votes were cast in the metro area, but in 2002 only 57% were. Perdue won only 45% in metro Atlanta but got 58% in the rest of the state, just enough to get over the 50% mark and avoid a runoff.

Still, the progress of his campaign was largely invisible. Barnes had a 50% job approval rating in an August poll and in a late October poll still led Perdue 51%–40%. Barnes spent $19 million, almost all on TV advertising; Perdue spent $3 million, some of it on on-the-ground organization. Barnes was put on the defensive when the GAE refused to endorse anyone for governor and endorsed Kathy Cox, another opponent of the Barnes education reform, for School Superintendent. Barnes put a hold on the Northern Arc and, curiously, said that Augusta National Golf Club should admit women as members. Then, in the biggest shock of election night 2002, Perdue beat Barnes 51%–46%. Barnes led very narrowly in metro Atlanta, 49%–48%, but Perdue won the rest of the state 55%–43%—just 2% below George W. Bush's 2000 showing there.

There were really two electoral keys to Perdue's victory. One was the rural strategy. Barnes carried only 41 of the 159 counties, most of them either central city or very small rural counties, down from 118 in 1998. The other factor was increased turnout in the fast-growing suburbs. Turnout was up 13% statewide and 15% in metro Atlanta. It was up only between 5% and 8% in the three black-majority counties in the center of metro Atlanta—Fulton, DeKalb and Clayton. But it was up far more in the heavily Republican fast-growing counties—up 60% in Forsyth, 49% in Paulding, 40% in Henry, 34% in Cherokee, 32% in Walton, 28% in Newton, 25% in Fayette, 19% in Gwinnett, 13% in Cobb. These counties gave Perdue a 116,000-vote margin, more than his statewide margin of 104,000 votes.

It turned out to be a Republican victory up and down the line. Congressman Saxby Chambliss beat Senator Max Cleland, with a bigger margin than Perdue's. Kathy Cox was elected too, although Democrats won most of the other downballot offices. Democrats had evidently held control of the state legislature, but Speaker Tom Murphy, Speaker since 1974 (and as a state representative since 1960, the nation's senior state legislator), and state Senate Majority Leader Charles Walker were beaten by Republicans. Within a week of the election four Democratic state senators switched parties and gave Republicans a 30–26 margin in the Senate. In the House, where Democrats had a 106–73 margin, Democrat Larry Walker, Perdue's "coalition" candidate, ran for speaker against the Democratic caucus's choice Terry Coleman; Coleman prevailed 109–70.

Perdue's first legislative session achieved little. His redistricting and ethics bills passed the Senate but failed in the House, as did his proposed tobacco tax increase. The flag issue dominated news coverage. After extended debate, a temporary flag, without the Confederate battle emblem, was established; in March 2004, the issue will be put to a referendum where voters will choose between two alternate flag designs.

Senior Senator

Zell Miller (D)

Appointed July 2000, seat up 2004, 1st term; b. Feb. 24, 1932, Young Harris; home, Young Harris; U. of GA, A.B. 1957, M.A. 1958; Methodist; married (Shirley).

Military Career: Marine Corps, 1953–56.

Elected Office: Mayor, Young Harris, 1959; GA Senate, 1960–64; GA Lt. Gov., 1976–90; GA Gov. 1990–98.

Professional Career: Professor, Young Harris College, 1956–66; Dir., St. Board of Probation, Personnel Officer, GA Dept. of Corrections, 1965–66; Exec. Secy., Gov. Lester Maddox, 1969–71; Exec. Dir., GA Dem. Party, 1971–73; Professor, Young Harris College, Emory U. & U. of GA, 1999–00.

DC Office: 257 DSOB, 20510, 202-224-3643; Fax: 202-228-2090; Web site: miller.senate.gov.

State Offices: Atlanta, 404-347-2202; Macon, 478-745-6025; Moultrie, 229-985-8113; Savannah, 912-238-3244; Young Harris, 706-379-9950.

Committees: *Agriculture, Nutrition & Forestry*: Production & Price Competitiveness; Research, Nutrition & General Legislation. *Banking, Housing & Urban Affairs*: Economic Policy; Financial Institutions; International Trade & Finance. *Veterans' Affairs*.

Group Ratings

	ADA	ACLU	AFS	LCV	CON	ITIC	NTU	COC	ACU	NTLC	CHC
2002	30	25	75	6	3	75	41	79	47	58	—
2001	35	—	42	38	—	—	63	85	60	—	60

National Journal Ratings

	2001 LIB — 2001 CONS		2002 LIB — 2002 CONS	
Economic	43%	57%	45%	54%
Social	33%	59%	54%	45%
Foreign	36%	54%	0%	76%

Key Votes of the 107th Congress

1. Approve Bush Tax Cuts	Y	5. Confirm Ashcroft as AG	Y	9. Bar Coop. with Intl. Court	Y
2. Expand Patients' Rights	Y	6. Bar Gays in the Boy Scouts	Y	10. Trade Promotion Authority	Y
3. Campaign Finance Reform	Y	7. $ for Hate Crime Prosecution	Y	11. Authorize Force in Iraq	Y
4. Permit ANWR Development	Y	8. Overseas Military Abortions	*	12. Homeland Sec. Dept. Union	N

Election Results

2000 special	Zell Miller (D)	1,413,224	(58%)	($2,533,746)
	Mack Mattingly (R)	920,478	(38%)	($1,093,408)
	Other	94,540	(4%)	
1998 general	Paul Coverdell (R)	918,540	(52%)	($6,936,745)
	Michael Coles (D)	791,904	(45%)	($5,275,419)
	Other	43,467	(2%)	
1998 primary	Paul Coverdell (R)	unopposed		

Zell Miller, a Democrat, was appointed to the Senate to replace Paul Coverdell after his death in July 2000 and was elected to fill out the remainder of his term in November. Miller grew up in the mountains of north Georgia in the town of Young Harris, in a house his widowed mother built of stones and in a town of which she was elected Mayor. This is the sort of country that produced Andrew Jackson and Miller, more than any other active politician, brings a Jacksonian spirit to his work. He joined the Marines Corps after dropping out of Emory University; his 1997 book is entitled *Corps Values: Everything You Need to Know, I Learned in the Marines*. He returned home, graduated from the University of Georgia, and taught political science at Young Harris College, and was elected Mayor as well. He was elected to the Georgia Senate in 1960, at 28, and ran unsuccessfully for the U.S. House in 1964 and 1966; he worked for Lester Maddox in his last two years as governor, and ran the state Democratic Party when Jimmy Carter was governor. He ran against Senator Herman Talmadge in 1980, and lost 59%–41% in the runoff. Miller was elected lieutenant governor in 1974 and held the office, whose occupant tends to run the state Senate, for 16 years. In 1990, he finally ran for governor. In the Democratic primary he led with 41% of the vote to 29% for Andrew Young, longtime Atlanta mayor, congressman and ambassador to the United Nations, and 21% for Roy Barnes, then a state senator and later Miller's successor as governor. In the runoff he beat Young 62%–38%. In the general he beat Johnny Isakson, now 6th District congressman, 53%–45%.

Miller's main issue in his 1990 campaign was a lottery, with revenues to go to education. The lottery passed, and the money went to fund pre-kindergarten for four-year-olds and to fund HOPE scholarships—free tuition at any Georgia college, public or private, for freshmen who maintain B averages in high school. Miller had occasional defeats: In 1993 he tried to get the Confederate stars and bars removed from the Georgia flag (it was placed there in 1956, when politicians were opposing school desegregation) but the legislature resisted.

Miller was an early supporter of Bill Clinton for president and in 1992 got the Georgia primary rescheduled a week earlier, on March 3. Clinton's victory there was a key step in his nomination, and Miller's support helped him carry Georgia in November by 13,000 votes. But his association with Clinton hurt in 1994 when Miller was opposed by Guy Millner, founder of the Norrell temporary employee firm. Miller won by only 51%–49% in this heavily Republican year, and took tougher stands on welfare and taxes in his second term. His job approval rating rose to as high as 85%. Term-limited, he decided to retire and teach at Young Harris College and Emory University, declaring, "I will never be a candidate ever again, and we might as well go further and say that I will not take a job or an appointment in Washington."

Coverdell had been re-elected in 1998 by 52%–45% and became an important part of the Republican leadership. Then, entirely unexpectedly, in three days in July 2000 Coverdell was hospitalized, underwent surgery and died of a stroke. The appointment to fill his seat was in the hands of Governor Roy Barnes. He asked Miller, who refused. Barnes flew up to Young Harris and tried again, and Miller finally agreed: he had, after all, tried to keep his promise by turning down this Senate seat twice. The appointment lasted only until November, when under Georgia law voters would choose among candidates listed without party affiliation for the remaining four years of Coverdell's term; if no candidate received 50%, there would be a runoff. Miller, with his high job ratings, was the immediate favorite, and Georgia's eight Republican congressmen, most interested in the race, quickly dropped out. Two Republicans remained. One was Lewis Jordan, founder of ValuJet, who promised to put $3 million of his own into the race. The other was Mack Mattingly, who won the seat against troubled veteran Herman Talmadge in 1980 by 51%–49% and then lost it to Democrat Wyche Fowler in 1986 by 51%–49%. (In 1992 Coverdell beat Fowler by, you guessed it, 51%–49%.) Concerned that having two Republicans in the race would cost the party any chance of winning, Jordan bowed out in early August 2000.

Miller was far ahead in the polls; his appointment, *National Journal*'s Charlie Cook wrote at the time, "effectively puts control of the Senate into play for the first time in this election cycle." Miller started off his career by joining Republicans and voting for repeal of estate tax and marriage penalty, a measure Clinton vowed to veto. Mattingly based much of his campaign on the Republican label. In debates and ads, Miller reached back to Mattingly's Senate record and accused him of voting to increase the retirement age and limit Social Security inflation increases and of "voting no" on education 14 times. He admitted that he supported Al Gore for president, but only, he said, because Gore helped with the Atlanta Olympics and with recovery from natural disasters.

Mattingly ran a spot showing Coverdell's widow saying, "If Paul were here, he'd wish Zell well, but he'd work day and night to elect Mack to follow in his true conservative footsteps." A Miller ad—there were more of them, for he had more funding—signed off, "Zell Miller—the man who brought HOPE to Georgia." Even as George W. Bush carried the state 55%–43%, Miller whipped Mattingly 58%–38%. Bush carried 125 of Georgia's 159 counties; Mattingly carried only 10.

Miller carried out a promise to be bipartisan early in the 107th Congress. Soon after former Senator John Ashcroft was nominated to be attorney general, Miller said he would support him—the first Democrat to do so. In George W. Bush's first week in office, Miller joined Texas Republican Phil Gramm, a Georgia native, in co-sponsoring Bush's tax cut. Miller supported oil drilling in the Arctic National Wildlife Refuge and voted to kill the Clinton administration's ergonomics regulations. In 2002 he was a lead sponsor, with Edward Kennedy and Bob Graham, of the Democrats' prescription drug bill, which got 52 votes but failed because it was short of the 60 required to exceed the budget resolution. In April 2002 he was the keynote speaker at the National Rifle Association convention. But in September 2002 he wrote in *The Washington Post* a list of 10 questions George W. Bush should answer about war in Iraq.

As the most popular politician in Georgia, he weighed in on state politics. In October 2001 he criticized Congresswoman Cynthia McKinney's letter to Saudi Prince Alwaleed, which apologized for Mayor Rudy Giuliani's rejection of his contribution, as "disgraceful"; in the August 2002 primary he endorsed her successful opponent Denise Majette. He gave the strongest possible backing to his colleague Max Cleland, in his tough race against Congressman Saxby Chambliss, appearing in TV spots for him. But at the same time he criticized the Democrats' opposition to Bush on the homeland security bill and joined with Gramm in sponsoring an amendment, rejected by other Democrats including Cleland, that would have given the president the right to waive work rules provided he notified Congress in advance. "We are not doing our party any good by feeding the perception that Democrats are undermining the President of the United States on the war on terrorism. The purpose of homeland security should be to protect lives, not jobs." He also cut TV spots for Governor Roy Barnes, Lieutenant Governor Mark Taylor and Attorney General Thurbert Baker and radio spots for Speaker Thomas Murphy (a frequent adversary when they ran the two houses of the legislature from 1974 to 1990) and Democratic candidates for labor commissioner and school superintendent. Watching an attack ad against Tennessee Democrat Bob Clement, an old friend, he got mad—"I stood up so fast, I scared my dogs"—and made his only campaign appearance outside Georgia for him. Chambliss consultant Tom Perdue tartly noted, "They use him like a cleaning fluid to remove the stain of Bill Clinton and Al Gore from a candidate."

After the election that was so disastrous for his party in his state, he said, "It is a heck of a note when you have the chairman, the leader and the titular leader of the national party who can't go into the South because they would do more harm than good. We have got to become a national party not just in name, but in fact." Of the Senate Democrats' stand on homeland security, he said, "It will go down as one of the major political blunders of our time. I could not believe what I was seeing and hearing. It was the chief reason for the defeat of some of our best people." Miller's votes and outspoken statements naturally prompted questions about whether he would switch parties. After Jim Jeffords announced his switch in May 2001, he said, "I am not going to switch to the Republican party, but neither am I going to march in lockstep with these Democrats up here blindly off a cliff, and that's where they sometimes try to lead me."

Then, in January 2003, Miller announced he would not seek reelection. He also said he would not campaign for any candidate for the seat. Within a week, Republican Congressman Johnny Isakson announced his candidacy; in May, Republican Congressman Mac Collins also said he would run. Possible Democratic candidates included Lieutenant Governor Mark Taylor, Attorney General Thurbert Baker, former Secretary of State Lewis Massey and Atlanta Mayor Shirley Franklin. Republicans will have a good chance of winning this seat, as they did in 1980, 1992 and 1998.

Junior Senator

Saxby Chambliss (R)

Elected 2002, seat up 2008, 1st term; b. Nov. 10, 1943, Warrenton, NC; home, Moultrie; U. of GA, B.A. 1966, U. of TN, J.D. 1968; Episcopalian; married (Julianne).

Elected Office: U.S. House of Reps., 1994–02.

Professional Career: Practicing atty., 1968–94.

DC Office: 416 RSOB, 20510, 202-224-3521; Fax: 202-224-0103.

State Offices: Atlanta, 404-763-9090; Macon, 478-476-0788; Moultrie, 229-985-2112.

Committees: *Agriculture, Nutrition & Forestry*: Marketing, Inspection & Product Promotion; Production & Price Competitiveness. *Armed Services*: Airland; Emerging Threats & Capabilities; Personnel (Chmn.); Readiness & Management Support. *Intelligence (Select)*. *Judiciary*: Antitrust, Competition Policy & Consumer Rights; Constitution, Civil Rights & Property Rights; Immigration, Border Security & Citizenship (Chmn.); Terrorism, Technology & Homeland Security. *Rules & Administration*.

Group Ratings (as Member of U.S. House of Representatives)

	ADA	ACLU	AFS	LCV	CON	ITIC	NTU	COC	ACU	NTLC	CHC
2002	0	7	0	0	25	88	53	90	100	89	100
2001	0	—	0	0	—	—	65	95	100	—	—

National Journal Ratings (as Member of U.S. House of Representatives)

	2001 LIB	—	2001 CONS		2002 LIB	—	2002 CONS
Economic	13%	—	86%		13%	—	85%
Social	32%	—	67%		0%	—	75%
Foreign	21%	—	74%		0%	—	85%

Key Votes of the 107th Congress (as Member of U.S. House of Representatives)

1. Approve Bush Tax Cuts	Y	5. Faith-Based Charities	Y	9. Trade Promotion Authority	Y
2. Limit Patients' Bill of Rights	Y	6. Bar Gays in the Boy Scouts	*	10. Bar Funds for Intl. Court	Y
3. Campaign Finance Reform	N	7. Ban Partial-Birth Abortion	Y	11. Authorize Force in Iraq	Y
4. Ban ANWR Development	N	8. Arm Commercial Pilots	*	12. Deny Home. Sec. Dept. Union	Y

Election Results

2002 general	Saxby Chambliss (R)	1,071,153	(53%)	($7,743,004)
	Max Cleland (D)	931,857	(46%)	($9,116,775)
	Other	26,981	(1%)	
2002 primary	Saxby Chambliss (R)	300,371	(61%)	
	Bob Irvin (R)	132,132	(27%)	
	Robert Brown (R)	59,109	(12%)	

Prior Winning Percentages: 2000 House (59%); 1998 House (62%); 1996 House (53%); 1994 House (63%)

Saxby Chambliss, the junior Senator from Georgia, was elected in 2002 after serving four terms in the House. Chambliss grew up in Shreveport, Louisiana, the son of an Episcopalian minister, went to college in Georgia, and practiced business and agriculture law in Moultrie starting in 1968. In 1992 he ran for the House and lost the Republican primary; in 1994 he was the sole Republican candidate, while Democrats, as in days of yore, had a multi-candidate contest. The winner was Craig Mathis, the 32-year-old son of Congressman (1971–81) Dawson Mathis and a former House staffer. Chambliss called for targeting repeat offenders and reducing the deficit; he opposed Dick Armey's proposal to zero out peanut subsidies. Chambliss won 63%–37%.

In the House, Speaker Newt Gingrich saw that Chambliss got the committee assignments he needed most—Armed Services, to look after Warner Robins Air Force Base near Macon, and Agriculture, to protect subsidies for peanut farmers in the counties to the south. In his first term Chambliss toured every military base in Georgia and worked with locals to remove Warner Robins, an air logistics center, from the final Base Closing Commission list in 1995. To protect the peanut and cotton programs, Chambliss and four other Republicans voted against the Freedom to Farm Act in committee, which defeated it temporarily; when the leadership folded the farm bill into the budget, Chambliss threatened to oppose it but backed down under pressure. In 2001 he helped draft the farm bill provisions that phased out the peanut quota program—evidently he concluded there was just not enough support to maintain it—but to compensate quota holders.

In November 1998, Speaker-designate Bob Livingston put Chambliss on the Budget Committee and named him Vice Chairman; in July 1999 Budget Chairman John Kasich announced his retirement and Chambliss started a campaign for the post. In July 2000, after Senator Paul Coverdell died suddenly, Chambliss considered running in the November election to replace him; he had also considered running for governor in 1998. But Speaker Dennis Hastert persuaded him to stay in the House, and Chambliss came away feeling he would get the Budget chair. But he had competition from Jim Nussle, who was supported by Majority Leader Dick Armey. The Republican Steering Committee interviewed both candidates and in December 2000 picked Nussle. Chambliss got an Agriculture subcommittee chairmanship and Hastert made him head of a working group on terrorism. After September 11, Hastert made that into an Intelligence Subcommittee on Terrorism and Homeland Security.

These were obviously good political credentials for a Senate candidacy, and Chambliss had two other reasons to consider challenging Democratic Senator Max Cleland in 2002. One was Cleland's narrow 49%–48% margin of victory in 1996 and Georgia's Republican trend, evident in George W. Bush's 55%–43% margin there in 2000. The other was the uncertainty of his House seat. Democratic redistricters passed a plan in September 2001 that left him with two unpleasant options: run in a primary against Savannah-based 1st District Republican incumbent Jack Kingston or in the new Democratic-leaning 3d District. The Bush White House and campaign committee Chairman Bill Frist urged Chambliss to run for the Senate, and in October 2001 he announced he would.

Chambliss was not an initial favorite to win. Cleland had a compelling biography. After college he volunteered for the Army and went to Vietnam in 1967; he lost both legs and his right arm when a loose grenade exploded. In 1982 he was elected Georgia Secretary of State and was reelected three times by wide margins. In October 1995, after Senator Sam Nunn announced his retirement after four terms, he ran for the Senate and had no primary opposition. Against Republican businessman Guy Millner, Cleland won 49%–48%. He served on the Armed Services Committee and had a moderate voting record by the standards of some Democratic senators, but in 2001 and 2002 he tended to stick with the close-knit Democratic Caucus while his new colleague, Zell Miller, dissented vociferously on issues from the tax cut to the Department of Homeland Security personnel rules.

In the weeks after announcing Chambliss made one embarrassing mistake. To a crowd in Valdosta he said in November 2001 that the way to improve homeland security was to "just turn loose Lowndes County Sheriff Ashley Paulk loose and let him arrest every Muslim that comes across the state line," and then tried to get the *Valdosta Daily Times* not to print the remark; he said he was just joking. But he retained the support of the Bush White House and Georgia Republican insiders, and was able to win an easy victory over state Representative Bob Irvin in the August 2002 primary, 61%–27%, carrying all but two of Georgia's 159 counties and every one in metro Atlanta. "From Rabun Gap to Tybee Light, voters continue to tell me that Max Cleland is too liberal for Georgia," he said on primary election night.

Cleland's two major strengths—his sacrifice in Vietnam and his support from the highly popular Zell Miller—seemed formidable. In ads and speeches Cleland referred often to his service in Vietnam and of course the sacrifice he made was visible to everyone. Cleland supporters noted that Chambliss had received four student deferments in the 1960s and then was found ineligible for service because of a bad knee. Moreover, Cleland pointed out, he voted for the use of military force in Iraq in 1998, in Kosovo in 1999 and in the war on terrorism in September 2001, and he voted for the use of force against Iraq in October 2002. Miller, in ads, told voters of Cleland's "rock solid Georgia values" and said, "Don't let them fool you." But that did not deter Chambliss from launching sharp attacks. He ran a series of 10-second spots, mentioning Cleland's opposition to an amendment banning aid for schools that barred the Boy Scouts, his votes against the partial-birth abortion ban, his support of school clinics passing out morning-after pills without parental permission, his vote against confirming Attorney General John Ashcroft, his vote against speeding elimination of the marriage penalty—all ending with an apparently astounded announcer asking, "Why would he do that?" Chambliss burnished his own national security issues by talking of his work on Armed Services and the Terrorism Subcommittee, and in October 2002 he was endorsed by the Veterans of Foreign Wars, which was evidently still unhappy with Cleland's support of VA budget cuts in 1979. A late September poll showed Cleland still ahead 51%–42%, but only barely over 50%.

But probably the most important issue was homeland security. Cleland stood with other Senate Democrats in opposing the degree of flexibility over work rules in the new department. The dispute occupied the Senate for much of October; it prevented passage of the bill. On the other side, standing loudly in his support of Bush and his opposition to the other Senate Democrats was Zell Miller. Chambliss ran an ad, much attacked in the press, showing pictures of Osama Bin Laden, Saddam Hussein and Max Cleland, and saying that Cleland "voted against the President's vital homeland security efforts 11 times." Against this, Cleland's ads attacking Chambliss for opposing an increase in the minimum wage and financing children's health insurance, for cutting student loans and school aid for the disabled, were weak stuff. In an October 27 debate, Cleland, echoing John Randolph of Roanoke on Henry Clay, said that the Osama Bin Laden ad was "like a mackerel in the moonlight—it both shines and stinks at the same time." But Cleland's record in Vietnam did not inoculate him against charges that he had given short shrift to homeland security.

The tide of opinion, as measured by very late polls, was moving toward Chambliss. George W. Bush visited the state three times in his behalf, with visits to Atlanta and Savannah the Saturday before the election. On Election Day Chambliss won 53%–46%, a much bigger margin than just about anyone expected for either candidate. Chambliss, though from south Georgia, carried metro Atlanta 52%–47%, running ahead of Republican governor candidate Sonny Perdue, and he carried the rest of Georgia 54%–45%. It was a slightly stronger showing than Paul Coverdell made running for reelection to the Senate four years before, primarily because of increased turnout and increasing Republican percentages in the outer counties of metro Atlanta. In the three black-majority counties of 20-county metro Atlanta (Fulton, DeKalb and Clayton), turnout was up 26,000 from 1998 and the Democratic margin up 34,000. But in the other 17 counties, turnout was up 123,000 and the Republican margin was up 40,000.

FIRST DISTRICT

Rep. Jack Kingston (R)

Elected 1992, 6th term; b. Apr. 24, 1955, Bryan, TX; home, Savannah; U. of GA, B.S. 1977; Episcopalian; married (Libby).

Elected Office: GA House of Reps., 1984–92.

Professional Career: Insurance agent, 1979–92.

DC Office: 2242 RHOB 20515, 202-225-5831; Fax: 202-226-2269; Web site: www.house.gov/kingston.

District Offices: Baxley, 912-367-7403; Brunswick, 912-265-9010; Savannah, 912-352-0101; Warner Robins, 912-923-3764.

Committees: *Republican Conference Vice Chairman. Appropriations* (13th of 36 R): Agriculture, Rural Development, & FDA; Military Construction; The Legislative Branch (Chmn.).

Group Ratings

	ADA	ACLU	AFS	LCV	CON	ITIC	NTU	COC	ACU	NTLC	CHC
2002	0	7	0	0	8	88	55	85	96	94	100
2001	5	—	0	0	—	—	68	95	100	—	—

National Journal Ratings

	2001 LIB	—	2001 CONS		2002 LIB	—	2002 CONS
Economic	0%	—	94%		21%	—	73%
Social	0%	—	81%		0%	—	75%
Foreign	0%	—	97%		0%	—	85%

Key Votes of the 107th Congress

1. Approve Bush Tax Cuts	Y	5. Faith-Based Charities	Y	9. Trade Promotion Authority	Y
2. Limit Patients' Bill of Rights	Y	6. Bar Gays in the Boy Scouts	Y	10. Bar Funds for Intl. Court	Y
3. Campaign Finance Reform	N	7. Ban Partial-Birth Abortion	Y	11. Authorize Force in Iraq	Y
4. Ban ANWR Development	N	8. Arm Commercial Pilots	Y	12. Deny Home. Sec. Dept. Union	Y

Election Results

2002 general	Jack Kingston (R)	103,661	(72%)	($819,954)
	Don Smart (D)	40,026	(28%)	($21,768)
2002 primary	Jack Kingston (R)	unopposed		
2000 general	Jack Kingston (R)	131,684	(69%)	($652,186)
	Joyce Marie Griggs (D)	58,776	(31%)	($70,119)

Prior Winning Percentages: 1998 (100%); 1996 (68%); 1994 (77%); 1992 (58%)

The People		Race/Ethnic Origin	Ancestry	
Area size:	12,071 sq. mi.	71.0% White	USA: 15.3%	English: 7.2%
Urban population:	57.9%	22.5% Black	Irish: 7.0%	
Rural population:	42.1%	0.9% Asian	**2000 Presidential Vote**	
Pop. 2000:	629,761	0.3% Native Am.	Bush (R)............119,133	(64%)
Median income:	$36,158	0.1% Hawaiian	Gore (D)...............65,744	(35%)
Poverty status:	14.8%	1.0% Two + races	Other....................1,524	(1%)
Military veterans:	15.8%	0.1% Other	**Cook Partisan Voting Index:** R +15	
		4.1% Hispanic Origin		

Occupation	Blue collar: 30.2%	White collar: 53.3%	Gray collar: 16.5%

Georgia's South Atlantic coast, long one of the poorest parts of the country, has been booming in recent years. The area was settled in the 1730s by James Oglethorpe as Britain's 13th coastal colony as a refuge and reformatory for convicts. It did not take long for the sea islands and lowlands along the wide rivers and inlets to become plantation country. It is here where General William Tecumseh Sherman and his troops famously set their sights when they marched from Atlanta in 1864. Without supplies or lines of communication, they burned plantation houses, destroyed crops and captured the Confederacy's leader (the Jefferson Davis Memorial in Ocilla marks the spot where Union troops nabbed him in May 1865); when their march was complete, they let behind memories of slaves freed, which were handed down as family lore for more than a century.

The 1st Congressional District includes much of southeast and south central Georgia. It includes the whole Atlantic coast of the state and runs approximately to Interstate 75 and from the Ocmulgee and Altamaha Rivers in the north to the Florida border in the south. It takes in a sliver of Savannah, most of which is now in the 12th District, and all of the Sea Islands, which are now housing a vibrant resort economy with efforts to preserve the African-American Gullah culture and its eponymous West African-originated language. One of those coastal communities is the historic black settlement of Pin Point, nine miles southeast of Savannah. Its 300 citizens are mostly descendants of the first slaves here and its most famous son is Supreme Court Justice Clarence Thomas. In central Georgia, a salient of the 1st District thrusts north near enough to Macon to take in part of Warner Robins, adjoining Warner Robins Air Force Base; another salient thrusts west to include Moultrie, the home town of Senator Saxby Chambliss. There are a few modest-sized cities like Brunswick, a World War II shipbuilding center on the coast and Waycross, a railroad junction town and gateway to the Okefenokee Swamp. But much of the district is rural, with cotton and tobacco fields and softwood forests inhabited by wild hogs and bears. Appling County and Berrien County are known for turpentine and bell peppers, respectively. This was Democratic country for many years after General Sherman's troops marched through Georgia, but voters here are solidly conservative on cultural and military issues and many economic issues as well. For two decades this part of south Georgia voted for national Republicans but Georgia Democrats; in 2002 it voted solidly Republican for governor and senator.

The congressman from the 1st District is Jack Kingston, a Republican first elected in 1992. Kingston grew up in Texas, Ethiopia, and Athens, Georgia, the son of a professor. After college he moved to Savannah and became a commercial insurance agent. In 1984 he was elected to the Georgia House, at 29, and served eight years. In 1992, when incumbent Democrat Lindsay Thomas retired to work on the Atlanta Summer Olympics, Kingston ran for Congress. Against Democrat Barbara Christmas, a school principal, he won decisively—58%–42%, with a 2–1 margin in his home base of Savannah and Chatham County. He has not been seriously challenged since then.

In the House, Kingston has a mostly conservative voting record and has tended to district interests. He parted company with Bill Clinton on trade issues, notably NAFTA, GATT and PNTR for China, and he decries the World Trade Organization; but he voted for trade promotion authority. He serves on the Agriculture Subcommittee of Appropriations, where he has used his vote and lobbied his colleagues for district interests; in 2003 he became chairman of the Appropriations Legislative Branch Subcommittee. In July 2002, he worked for House passage of the proposal permitting commercial airline pilots to carry firearms in the cockpit; sponsors assured him that the Federal Law Enforcement Training Center in Brunswick would give the pilots safety lessons. He took some credit when the Bush administration announced a plan to speed generic prescription drugs to the market.

Kingston has pursued leadership activities. As leader of the Republicans' "theme team," which coordinates the party's national message on the House floor and at home, he became a spokesman on late-night television shows. For the 108th Congress, he defeated Melissa Hart of Pennsylvania to win election as vice-chairman of the Republican Conference—the party's fifth-highest leadership post—and planned to increase his role in setting the party's message.

On local issues, Kingston has fought for historic preservation and looked after Fort Stewart, a major local employer. As an appropriator, he has brought millions of dollars to improve the water flow of the Savannah River and complete the Sidney Lanier drawbridge in Brunswick; he has pushed for $230 million to dredge the Savannah harbor, despite criticism from environmentalists and from South Carolina port interests. With the addition of the Warner Robins base, he now represents several major defense facilities. At Kingston's request, the Air Force studied the potential threat posed by a nuclear bomb that had been dumped in the Atlantic Ocean near Savannah in 1958 but concluded in 2001 that there was no jeopardy. He reached out to the black community with $450,000 from the Interior Department to preserve the remnants of slave cabins on Cumberland Island.

When Senator Paul Coverdell died in July 2000, Kingston gave serious thought to running in the special election; but, like other Georgia House Republicans, he backed out when Democrat Zell Miller agreed to take the seat. The September 2001 redistricting, which removed most of Savannah and moved the district well to the west, had him contemplating the race against Max Cleland. But the redistricting plan was even more discommoding to Saxby Chambliss, whose home town of Moultrie, but not the majority of his old district, was included in the 1st. Kingston decided that he wanted to spend more time with his four children and Chambliss ran for the Senate and won. Redistricting made this a heavily Republican district—64% for George W. Bush in 2000—and Kingston can be confident he holds a safe seat. But in 2003 Kingston was again weighing a Senate bid, after Miller announced in January that he would not seek reelection.

SECOND DISTRICT

Rep. Sanford Bishop (D)

Elected 1992, 6th term; b. Feb. 4, 1947, Mobile, AL; home, Albany; Morehouse Col., B.A. 1968, Emory U., J.D. 1971; Baptist; divorced.

Military Career: Army, 1970–71.

Elected Office: GA House of Reps., 1976–90; GA Senate, 1990–92.

Professional Career: Practicing atty., 1971–92.

DC Office: 2429 RHOB 20515, 202-225-3631; Fax: 202-225-2203; Web site: www.house.gov/bishop.

District Offices: Albany, 229-439-8067; Dawson, 229-995-3991; Valdosta, 229-247-9705.

Committees: *Appropriations* (28th of 29 D): Military Construction; VA, HUD & Independent Agencies.

Group Ratings

	ADA	ACLU	AFS	LCV	CON	ITIC	NTU	COC	ACU	NTLC	CHC
2002	75	57	89	25	17	62	25	55	40	25	50
2001	70	—	89	57	—	—	30	65	39	—	—

National Journal Ratings

	2001 LIB	—	2001 CONS		2002 LIB	—	2002 CONS
Economic	55%	—	46%		58%	—	41%
Social	60%	—	41%		59%	—	40%
Foreign	70%	—	31%		55%	—	45%

Key Votes of the 107th Congress

1. Approve Bush Tax Cuts	*	5. Faith-Based Charities	N	9. Trade Promotion Authority	N
2. Limit Patients' Bill of Rights	N	6. Bar Gays in the Boy Scouts	Y	10. Bar Funds for Intl. Court	Y
3. Campaign Finance Reform	Y	7. Ban Partial-Birth Abortion	Y	11. Authorize Force in Iraq	Y
4. Ban ANWR Development	N	8. Arm Commercial Pilots	Y	12. Deny Home. Sec. Dept. Union	N

Election Results

2002 general	Sanford Bishop (D)	....	unopposed	($306,022)
2002 primary	Sanford Bishop (D)	....	unopposed	
2000 general	Sanford Bishop (D)	....	96,430	(54%)	($1,069,838)
	Dylan Glenn (R)	....	83,870	(47%)	($953,867)

Prior Winning Percentages: 1998 (57%); 1996 (54%); 1994 (66%); 1992 (64%)

The People		Race/Ethnic Origin	Ancestry	
Area size:	9,887 sq. mi.	50.3% White	USA: 12.2%	English: 5.0%
Urban population:	58.6%	44.5% Black	Irish: 4.7%	
Rural population:	41.4%	0.6% Asian	**2000 Presidential Vote**	
Pop. 2000:	629,735	0.3% Native Am.	Bush (R)...............84,854	(51%)
Median income:	$29,354	0.1% Hawaiian	Gore (D)...............81,684	(49%)
Poverty status:	22.5%	0.8% Two+ races	Other....................1,160	(1%)
Military veterans:	12.7%	0.1% Other	**Cook Partisan Voting Index:** R + 1	
		3.5% Hispanic Origin		
Occupation	Blue collar: 31.1%	White collar: 50.2%	Gray collar: 18.7%	

Before the Civil War, the southwest corner of Georgia was plantation country; it was in this part of Georgia that Confederates ran the Andersonville military prison, which within 14 months killed more than 13,000 of the 45,000 Union soldiers confined there, through disease, poor sanitation, malnutrition, overcrowding and exposure; they are remembered at the National Prisoner of War Museum at Andersonville, dedicated to all Americans who have endured wartime captivity. The military is still a presence here, most notably at Fort Benning, the Army's third largest installation and home of the Army Infantry School. But today the region is mostly farmland: Cotton fields, peanut acreage, pecan groves, pine lands. In the south, near the Florida border, is the Plantation Trace area around Thomasville, where rich Northerners have come to shoot quail and ducks in winters since the 1880s—a part of Georgia memorialized in Tom Wolfe's *A Man in Full*. A bit to the north is Albany, with several factories, a civil rights museum and the site of Martin Luther King Jr.'s least successful civil rights protests in the 1960s. Not far from Albany, between upland pine stands and bottomland habitats, lies the Chickasawatchee Swamp, one of the Southeast's largest freshwater swamps and home to rare plant species such as the needle palm and the green fly orchid. Two counties north is the village of Plains, the home since childhood of Jimmy Carter. This is hardscrabble country: As recently as World War II most rural residents lived in clapboard cabins without power or running water, eking a living out of over-tilled soil. Today this remains one of the low-income quarters of America. But rural electrification and then air-conditioning made homes and workplaces comfortable; automobiles and good roads have given people options they never had before (such as outlet malls); racial desegregation has given dignity to all in a way few dreamed possible thirty-some years ago.

This is the land of Georgia's 2d Congressional District. The 2d came out of the radical redistricting of September 2001 with the least changed boundaries of any district in the state—in contrast to the 1990s, when it was the focus of a Supreme Court case which resulted in a smoothing out of its boundaries in 1995. There is some splitting of cities at the edges: The 2d includes about two-thirds of Valdosta and nearly a third of Columbus and Muscogee County. Redistricting raised the black percentage of the district from 40% to 45% and thus made it more Democratic. But it cast a bare majority of its votes for George W. Bush in 2000.

The congressman from the 2d District is Sanford Bishop, a Democrat first elected in 1992. Bishop grew up in Mobile, Alabama, where his father was a state college president. He went to Morehouse College in Atlanta, where he was student body president in 1968 and sang at Martin Luther King Jr.'s funeral. He was an award-winning student at Emory Law School, then served in the Army. After a year in New York he settled in Columbus, practiced law, joined the church choir and many civic organizations, and was elected to the state legislature in 1976, at 29. He served there until 1990, when he was elected to the Georgia Senate. In 1992 he ran for the House against Democratic incumbent Charles Hatcher, who gained his greatest public notice when it was revealed he had 819 overdrafts on the House bank. Bishop defeated Hatcher in the runoff 53%–47%, and won the general election 64%–36%.

Bishop describes himself as "a moderate conservative on fiscal issues and a 'traditionalist' on so-called family issues." His style is not confrontational, and his voting record is far more moderate than that of most Democrats of any race. After first voting for the assault weapons ban, he switched, joined the NRA and started hunting doves. He joined the conservative Blue Dog Democrats, and supported the balanced budget, school prayer, partial-birth abortion ban, and anti-flag burning amendments. He was one of 10 House Democrats to vote for George W. Bush's tax cuts in March 2001. He works to protect local military bases, like the School of the Americas that trains Latin American soldiers at Fort Benning, which was renamed the Western Hemisphere Institute for Security Cooperation. In 2002, the NAACP gave him a "C" on its report card for House votes.

Bishop has served on the Agriculture Committee and on its Specialty Crops Subcommittee, which has jurisdiction over peanuts and tobacco. On the 1996 Freedom to Farm Act, he worked with Republicans to fashion a "market-oriented, no-net cost" program for peanuts. He delivered more help to peanut farmers in 2000 when Congress passed a $35 million bailout for their previous year's losses resulting from a surplus harvest. When the farm bill was renewed in 2002, Bishop worked on the Agriculture Committee with Terry Everett of Alabama for a scaled-back program for peanut support, which was based on a combination of phasing out quotas and price guarantees. He also visited Cuba to promote new markets for U.S. farm products. Bishop served on the Intelligence Committee, where he urged the appointment of additional minorities to intelligence and diplomatic agencies. He sought the position of ranking Democrat for the 108th Congress; Minority Leader Nancy Pelosi awarded it to Jane Harman but gave Bishop a slot on the Appropriations Committee.

Bishop had serious competition in 1998 and especially 2000. The Republican candidate that year was Dylan Glenn, a black 31-year-old former Bush White House and Republican National Committee staffer. The unprecedented contest between two African-Americans in a rural, majority-white district was strikingly lacking in racial notes. Instead, Bishop largely ignored the challenger and ran on his record, while Glenn offered the perspective of a new generation focusing on economic growth; at the Republican convention in Philadelphia, MTV followed him around for a "young candidates" special. Bishop won 54%–47%, carrying heavily black rural counties by wide margins. The 2001 redistricting made the district more Democratic and Bishop had no opposition in 2002.

THIRD DISTRICT

Rep. Jim Marshall (D)

Elected 2002, 1st term; b. March 31, 1948, Ithaca, NY; home, Macon; Princeton U., B.A. 1972, Boston U., J.D. 1977; Catholic; married (Camille).

Military Career: Army, 1968–70 (Vietnam).

Elected Office: Macon Mayor, 1995–99.

Professional Career: Mercer U. Law Professor, 1979–95, 1999–02.

DC Office: 502 CHOB 20515, 202-225-6531; Fax: 202-225-3013; Web site: www.house.gov/marshall.

District Offices: Dublin, 478-296-2023; Macon, 478-464-0255.

Committees: *Agriculture* (17th of 24 D): Conservation, Credit, Rural Development & Research; General Farm Commodities & Risk Management; Specialty Crops & Foreign Agriculture Programs. *Armed Services* (24th of 29 D): Projection Forces; Readiness. *Small Business* (14th of 17 D): Tax, Finance & Exports.

Group Ratings and Key Votes: Newly Elected

Election Results

2002 general	Jim Marshall (D)	75,394	(51%)	($1,006,764)
	Calder Clay (R)	73,866	(49%)	($2,014,777)
2002 primary	Jim Marshall (D)	26,614	(54%)	
	Chuck Byrd (D)	16,542	(33%)	
	Joe Lester (D)	5,663	(11%)	
	Other	851	(2%)	
2000 general (GA 8)	Saxby Chambliss (R)	113,380	(59%)	($1,841,653)
	Jim Marshall (D)	79,051	(41%)	($846,565)

The People		Race/Ethnic Origin	Ancestry	
Area size:	11,003 sq. mi.	56.2% White	USA: 15.2%	English: 5.4%
Urban population:	48.8%	39.8% Black	Irish: 4.8%	
Rural population:	51.2%	0.5% Asian	**2000 Presidential Vote**	
Pop. 2000:	629,748	0.2% Native Am.	Bush (R) 98,100 (52%)	
Median income:	$31,433	0.0% Hawaiian	Gore (D) 89,374 (47%)	
Poverty status:	19.9%	0.7% Two+ races	Other 1,766 (1%)	
Military veterans:	13.1%	0.1% Other	**Cook Partisan Voting Index:** R + 3	
		2.6% Hispanic Origin		

Occupation	Blue collar: 32.5%	White collar: 48.9%	Gray collar: 18.7%

Macon, the hub of central Georgia, is a city proud of its restored houses and its Japanese cherry trees, of which it has 20 times as many as Washington, D.C. It is the home of music legends Otis Redding, Little Richard and the Allman Brothers, and of the Harriet Tubman Historical and Cultural Museum. A short drive up Interstate 75 is Juliette, an old mill town that's too small for most maps; it is the place where many scenes in the movie *Fried Green Tomatoes* were filmed.

The 3d Congressional District, newly created by the Democrats' 2001 redistricting, includes almost all of Macon and Bibb County and is bookended by two military reservations, both just outside the district boundaries—Fort Benning in the west near the Alabama border and Fort Stewart in the east near Savannah. Fort Benning is the home of the Army Infantry School, famous for training generals and troops since before World War II; Fort Stewart, with 18,000 troops on 280,000 acres is the home of the 3d Infantry Division (Mechanized). But these are not the only military landmarks: Much of this land was the site of General William Tecumseh Sherman's 1864 march from Atlanta to the sea. Macon is the population center of the 3d, casting 20 percent of the vote, but a good deal of the district is rural: Toombs County is the home of the fragrant Vidalia onions that folks say are so sweet you can eat 'em like an apple; Claxton in tiny Evans County has for nearly a century been home to two of the nation's prime fruitcake makers. Twiggs, Wilkinson and Washington Counties are among the world's major sources of kaolin, a clay used for china and ceramics. Politically, the large majority of whites here vote Republican, at least in national contests; an even larger percentage of blacks vote Democratic. Since the district is 40% black, it is basically evenly divided between the parties. George W. Bush won a narrow majority here in 2000, but the Democratic candidate for the House won an even narrower margin in 2002, as the Democratic redistricters hoped.

The congressman from the 3d District is Jim Marshall, elected in 2002. The son and grandson of Army generals, he grew up at several Army posts. He graduated from high school in Mobile, Alabama, and went on to Princeton but interrupted his education to enlist in the Army and volunteer for infantry combat in Vietnam. He served there in the elite Airborne Ranger reconnaissance platoon, was wounded in combat and awarded two Bronze Stars and a Purple Heart. After his military service, he graduated from Princeton and Boston University law school. He joined the faculty of Mercer University law school in Macon, practiced business law and became active in Democratic politics. His wife Camille is a federal bankruptcy trustee. In his first political contest, Marshall was elected mayor of Macon in 1995. During his term, the city balanced its budget for the first time since 1982. He made his first run for Congress in 2000 against Saxby Chambliss in the old 8th District, which covers much of the same territory as the current 3d. He campaigned almost exclusively on prescription drugs for seniors, and lost 59%–41%.

When Democrats drew the new 3d District, Marshall quickly entered the contest and made his military experience the centerpiece of his campaign. He announced his candidacy in front of the veterans memorial at the Macon Coliseum and featured his endorsement by the Veterans of Foreign Wars. He had three opponents in the Democratic primary. His toughest competitor was politically-connected attorney Chuck Byrd, whose father Garland Byrd was lieutenant governor from 1959–63. Byrd campaigned in the Sam Nunn tradition and ran as a conservative and an opponent of abortion. He ran well in the rural counties outside Macon, but Marshall carried Bibb County solid and won 54% of the total vote—enough to avoid a runoff. In the general election, Marshall faced Bibb County Commissioner Calder Clay, an energetic fundraiser who said Marshall was too liberal for the district. Marshall kept emphasizing his military record; Clay had not served in the military. Both supported George W. Bush on Iraq, but they differed on abortion and Social Security. Clay criticized the Social Security "scare tactics" of national Democrats and focused on the need to save Warner Robins Air Force Base from closing. Each candidate got a pledge of a seat on the House Armed Services Committee. In one of 2002's closest contests, Clay carried most of the eastern counties and the Warner Robins area. But Marshall won 61%–39% in Bibb County and 50.5%–49.5% overall. It didn't take long for him to get noticed within the Democratic Caucus. In March 2003, on the day after hostilities began in Iraq, Marshall showed up, uninvited, to a press conference convened by a group of anti-war House Democrats. "The time for debate is past," he announced. He then invoked an obscure House rule to cancel a Democratic Caucus meeting organized to debate war alternatives. While the members he upstaged did not appreciate the maneuver, it is likely to play well back home where it's possible that Republicans will seriously contest this district in 2004.

FOURTH DISTRICT

Rep. Denise Majette (D)

Elected 2002, 1st term; b. May 18, 1955, Brooklyn, NY; home, Stone Mountain; Yale U., B.A. 1976, Duke U., J.D. 1979; African Methodist Episcopal; married (Rogers).

Elected Office: DeKalb Cnty. State Ct. judge, 1993–02.

Professional Career: Practicing atty., Legal Aid Soc. of Winston-Salem, 1981–83; Law Asst., GA Ct. of Appeals, 1984–89; Spec. Asst. Atty. Gen. of GA, 1991–92.

DC Office: 1517 LHOB 20515, 202-225-1605; Fax: 202-226-0691; Web site: www.house.gov/majette.

District Office: Decatur, 404-633-0927.

Committees: *Budget* (18th of 19 D). *Education & the Workforce* (19th of 22 D): Education Reform; Workforce Protections. *Small Business* (13th of 17 D): Regulatory Reform & Oversight; Tax, Finance & Exports.

Group Ratings and Key Votes: Newly Elected

Election Results

2002 general	Denise Majette (D)	118,045	(77%)	($1,917,879)
	Cynthia Van Auken (R)	35,202	(23%)	($69,681)
2002 primary	Denise Majette (D)	68,612	(58%)	
	Cynthia McKinney (D)	49,058	(42%)	
2000 general	Cynthia McKinney (D)	139,579	(61%)	($410,270)
	Sunny Warren (R)	90,277	(39%)	($302,012)

The People		Race/Ethnic Origin	Ancestry	
Area size:	254 sq. mi.	32.0% White	English: 5.4%	German: 4.6%
Urban population:	99.6%	53.1% Black	Irish: 4.2%	
Rural population:	0.4%	4.2% Asian	**2000 Presidential Vote**	
Pop. 2000:	629,690	0.2% Native Am.	Gore (D) 140,767	(69%)
Median income:	$49,307	0.0% Hawaiian	Bush (R) 58,338	(29%)
Poverty status:	10.5%	1.7% Two+ races	Other 4,107	(2%)
Military veterans:	10.7%	0.2% Other	**Cook Partisan Voting Index:** D +20	
		8.5% Hispanic Origin		

Occupation	Blue collar: 19.6%	White collar: 67.4%	Gray collar: 13.0%

In 1920, when Gutzom Borglum began sculpting Jefferson Davis, Robert E. Lee and Stonewall Jackson into the side of Stone Mountain, the huge outcropping of granite was a day's drive into the country from central Atlanta. Even when the memorial (the largest single piece of sculpture in the world) was completed in 1972, suburban development barely reached this far. But today, after two decades of some of the most explosive metropolitan growth in the country, DeKalb County, which Stone Mountain overlooks, is part of the core of the Atlanta metropolitan area, and this monument to the Confederacy sits in one of the most cosmopolitan and liberal constituencies in the South. Not far from Stone Mountain is Emory University, just beyond the old mansions of Druid Hills. A few miles away are the Centers for Disease Control and Prevention, one of the federal government's superb research institutions. All around in north DeKalb County are affluent suburbs, including much of Atlanta's Jewish community, with voting habits much more liberal than in other suburbs. South DeKalb is being transformed from mostly rural territory 25 years ago to one of the nation's largest collections of affluent black neighborhoods, rivaled only by Prince George's County, Maryland. This has pushed DeKalb County's politics well to the left: It was a Republican county when rural Georgia was almost all Democratic in the 1960s, now it is the most heavily Democratic major county in Georgia, considerably more so than next-door Fulton County which includes central Atlanta; in 2000 DeKalb voted 71%–27% for Al Gore, his best percentage except for one tiny rural county in all the 159 counties of Georgia.

The 4th Congressional District consists of almost all of DeKalb County plus a small slice of the more Republican Gwinnett County to the northeast. It is one of the most regularly shaped districts in Georgia, and one of those least changed from the previous redistricting. The 4th and next-door 5th districts are the most Democratic districts in Georgia: They voted 69% and 70% for Al Gore in 2000.

The congresswoman from the 4th District is Denise Majette, a Democrat elected in 2002. She grew up in Brooklyn and graduated from Yale University and Duke University law school. She worked as a staff attorney for the Legal Aid Society in Winston Salem, North Carolina, where she also was an adjunct law professor at Wake Forest. In 1983 she moved to Georgia and worked as a law clerk, a special assistant attorney general, and a partner in the Atlanta law firm of Jenkins, Nelson & Welch. In 1992, Majette was sworn in as an administrative law judge for Georgia's workers compensation board. In June 1993, then-Governor Zell Miller appointed her to the state court in DeKalb County; she later won two elections to the post. She resigned as judge in February 2002 to run for Congress against incumbent Democrat Cynthia McKinney.

McKinney was a 10-year incumbent with a left-wing voting record and a flair for controversy. In October 2001, after New York Mayor Rudolph Giuliani turned down a $10 million gift from Saudi Prince Alwaleed because of Alwaleed's urging that the United States "reexamine its policies in the Middle East and adopt a more balanced stance toward the Palestinian cause." On October 12, McKinney wrote Alwaleed a letter saying that "there are a growing number of people in the United States who recognize, like you, that U.S. policy in the Middle East needs serious examination." She added, "Although your offer was not accepted by Mayor Giuliani, I would like to ask you to consider assisting Americans who are in dire need right now. I believe we can guide your generosity to help improve the state of black America and build better lives." Senator Zell Miller called her letter "disgraceful" and said it "crossed the line" in agreeing with the position of our enemy." In an October 29 opinion piece in *The Washington Post* McKinney defended herself and said, "I believe that when it comes to major foreign policy issues, many prefer to have black people seen and not heard."

McKinney attracted even more attention in April 2002 when she charged that George W. Bush "may" have had prior knowledge of the September 11 attacks and did not act on it because the war on terrorism would boost the defense stocks of associates of his father. Miller immediately called her comments "loony" and sent a $1,000 check to Majette. An April 2002 poll showed Majette leading McKinney 41%–37%—a highly unusual result, since incumbents rarely trail lesser-known challengers in primary races, and an indication that McKinney may already have been headed for defeat. But the race only began to receive national attention in June 2002 when Congressman Earl Hilliard of Alabama, another critic of U.S. policy in the Middle East, was defeated in the Democratic runoff by Artur Davis. At that point, by the end of June, McKinney had raised $269,000 in the previous quarter and had $463,000 cash on hand, while Majette had raised $246,000 (a larger percentage of it from Georgia) and had $99,000 cash on hand. Between the end of June and the August 22 primary, it became known that one-third of McKinney's contributions over the past five years had come from donors with apparently Arab-American or Muslim names and that at least 18 of her donors were officers of Muslim foundations under investigation by the FBI or people who had voiced support for Palestinian and Lebanese terrorist organizations or had made inflammatory statements about Jews. McKinney's own father, longtime Atlanta state Representative Billy McKinney, in October 1996 called her Republican opponent a "racist Jew." After July 1, Majette herself raised a lot of money from contributors outside Georgia, most presumably from supporters of Israel or those appalled by some of McKinney's statements: By the end of the primary, Majette had raised $1.12 million to McKinney's $618,000.

The national media treated the contest as a proxy battle on Middle East policy; it was also a contest between conflicting styles of black leadership. McKinney attacked Majette as "a Democrat in name only" and a tool of white interests. She accused her of "flip-flopping" on affirmative action because Majette did not support reparations for descendants of slaves. Majette, for the most part, declined to return fire, preferring instead to focus on domestic issues and criticism of McKinney's constituent service record. McKinney was endorsed by civil rights leader Joseph Lowery, state Representative Tyrone Brooks, Martin Luther King III, Jesse Jackson and the Nation of Islam's Louis Farrakhan. Former Atlanta Mayor and Congressman Andrew Young, listed as a

McKinney supporter, said he had been in a previous campaign but wasn't this time. Billy McKinney, asked about Young by a television interviewer the night before the primary, said, "That ain't nothing. That's nothing. Jews have bought everybody. Jews. J-E-W-S." (He was forced into a runoff, which he lost after serving in the legislature for 30 years). Majette beat Cynthia McKinney 58%–42% a resounding margin in a primary against an incumbent. "I may be five foot one, but I'm ten feet tall tonight," Majette said on election night. "We united this district. My opponent had divided it for 10 long years."

McKinney seemed to think that the outcome was produced by a Republican crossover, made easy because Georgia does not have party registration. "It seems like the Republicans wanted to beat me more than the Democrats wanted to keep me." But this is, to judge from the 2000 presidential election results, a 69% Democratic district; there are not that many Republicans who could cross over. In the much lower-turnout 2000 primary, 82% of primary votes had been cast in the Democratic primary; in this much higher-turnout contest, 95% of primary votes were cast in the Democratic primary. If 13% of Democratic primary votes were cast by behavioral Republicans, they could not have made the difference, because Majette's margin was 17% of the vote. A post-election review of the vote by the *Atlanta Journal-Constitution* found that Majette's strongest black-majority precincts were those with the highest median incomes, mostly near Stone Mountain, while McKinney won poorer neighborhoods by margins exceeding 4-to-1; overall it appears that blacks voted about 2–1 for McKinney and whites 9–1 for Majette.

In this strongly Democratic district, Majette won the general election easily.

FIFTH DISTRICT

Rep. John Lewis (D)

Elected 1986, 9th term; b. Feb. 21, 1940, Troy, AL; home, Atlanta; Amer. Baptist Theol. Seminary, B.A. 1961, Fisk U., B.A. 1963; Baptist; married (Lillian).

Elected Office: Atlanta City Cncl., 1981–86.

Professional Career: Chmn., Student Nonviolent Coord. Cmte., 1963–66; Field Foundation, 1966–67; Community Organization Dir., Southern Regional Cncl., 1967–70; Exec. Dir., Voter Educ. Project, 1970–76; Assoc. Dir., ACTION, 1977–80; Community Affairs Dir., Natl. Coop. Bank, 1980–82.

DC Office: 343 CHOB 20515, 202-225-3801; Fax: 202-225-0351; Web site: www.house.gov/johnlewis.

District Office: Atlanta, 404-659-0116.

Committees: *Senior Chief Deputy Minority Whip. Budget* (6th of 19 D). *Ways & Means* (8th of 17 D): Health.

Group Ratings

	ADA	ACLU	AFS	LCV	CON	ITIC	NTU	COC	ACU	NTLC	CHC
2002	80	93	88	88	69	38	22	31	0	0	0
2001	100	—	100	71	—	—	10	26	0	—	—

National Journal Ratings

	2001 LIB	—	2001 CONS		2002 LIB	—	2002 CONS
Economic	95%	—	0%		95%	—	0%
Social	90%	—	0%		97%	—	2%
Foreign	86%	—	12%		94%	—	0%

Key Votes of the 107th Congress

1. Approve Bush Tax Cuts	N	5. Faith-Based Charities	N	9. Trade Promotion Authority	N
2. Limit Patients' Bill of Rights	N	6. Bar Gays in the Boy Scouts	*	10. Bar Funds for Intl. Court	*
3. Campaign Finance Reform	Y	7. Ban Partial-Birth Abortion	N	11. Authorize Force in Iraq	N
4. Ban ANWR Development	Y	8. Arm Commercial Pilots	N	12. Deny Home. Sec. Dept. Union	N

Election Results

2002 general	John Lewis (D) .... unopposed		($537,597)
2002 primary	John Lewis (D) .... unopposed		
2000 general	John Lewis (D) 137,333	(77%)	($811,850)
	Hank Schwab (R) 40,606	(23%)	($25,836)

Prior Winning Percentages: 1998 (79%); 1996 (100%); 1994 (69%); 1992 (72%); 1990 (76%); 1988 (78%); 1986 (75%)

The People		Race/Ethnic Origin	Ancestry	
Area size:	254 sq. mi.	34.4% White	English: 5.4%	German: 4.5%
Urban population:	99.5%	55.7% Black	Irish: 4.4%	
Rural population:	0.5%	2.2% Asian	**2000 Presidential Vote**	
Pop. 2000:	629,727	0.2% Native Am.	Gore (D) 136,606	(70%)
Median income:	$39,725	0.0% Hawaiian	Bush (R) 55,605	(28%)
Poverty status:	19.7%	1.2% Two+ races	Other 3,232	(2%)
Military veterans:	9.5%	0.2% Other	**Cook Partisan Voting Index:** D +21	
		6.1% Hispanic Origin		

Occupation   Blue collar: 16.7%   White collar: 68.1%   Gray collar: 15.2%

Venture out of the quiet of the Ebenezer Baptist Church or the shade of Martin Luther King Jr.'s boyhood home two blocks away and into the steamy heat of the sun on Auburn Avenue—Sweet Auburn—and you can see, a mile away, downtown Atlanta's atrium-skyscrapers towering in their glory. They are evidence of the wealth and vibrant growth of the commercial capital of the South, the metropolis that has grown up where there was little more than a railroad junction at the time of the War Between the States. But the awesome achievement that is downtown Atlanta is over-shadowed by the revolution made in very large part by a man who grew up on Auburn Avenue, where people who never felt air-conditioning moved slowly in the sweltering heat, and around Morehouse and Spelman colleges, where proud professionals struggled and worked hard and raised their families. Atlanta's white establishment, led by Mayors William Hartsfield and Ivan Allen and Coca-Cola's Robert Woodruff, deserve credit for abandoning segregation, but it was King and other civil rights leaders who took the risks that led them to do so. Atlanta's city fathers acted out of good will, but also with an eye for the economic growth of their city, which they knew would be hurt by violent resistance.

Yet, sadly, not all is entirely well in Atlanta. Downtown Atlanta's primacy in office buildings is being eclipsed by north-side edge cities in Buckhead and along I-285. Many of Atlanta's black neighborhoods today have been abandoned by families who have headed to subdivisions in DeKalb County, leaving the central city with vacant housing and street crime. But Atlanta also has its glories: The headquarters of world-girdling Coca-Cola and CNN, the gigantic Hartsfield Inter-national Airport, the modern Martin Luther King Jr. Center that depicts the triumphs of the civil rights movement, the Jimmy Carter Presidential Center, the antique Cyclorama that shows Atlanta burning during the Civil War, and the stadiums and sports facilities built for the 1996 Summer Olympics.

The 5th Congressional District includes most of Atlanta (the other parts are in the 4th and 13th districts), including the posh and Republican Buckhead neighborhood in the north, plus the suburbs of East Point to the south; it also extends a tentacle north along Route 400 to include a part of Roswell and another northwest to include a small part of Cobb County. Redistricting did not make substantial changes, though it did reduce the black percentage from 62% to 56%. It remains overwhelmingly Democratic—70% for Al Gore in 2000, the highest percentage in any Georgia district.

The congressman from the 5th District is John Lewis, who made history a generation ago as a hero of the civil rights movement, as he recounts in his 1998 autobiography, *Walking With the Wind*. A sharecropper's son from Troy, Alabama, he was seized by religious fervor as a child, preaching in the barnyard, determined to be a minister. Lewis was the first in his family to finish high school; he wrote to Ralph Abernathy for help in suing for the right to enter Troy State College;

he met Martin Luther King Jr. when he was 18. In 1959, at 19, he helped organize the first lunch-counter sit-in, which was received with open hostility hard to imagine today. In 1960, the day after John Kennedy was elected, Lewis sat in the Krystal Diner in Nashville while a waitress poured cleansing powder down his back and water over his food; he went to talk to the manager, who turned a fumigating machine on him. In May 1961, he was on the first of the Freedom Rides, riding buses as they were attacked and burned; he was viciously beaten in Rock Hill, South Carolina and Montgomery, Alabama. He spoke at the 1963 March on Washington, criticizing Kennedy liberals for inaction on civil rights and calling for massive help for the poor. In 1964, he helped coordinate the Mississippi Freedom Project. In 1965, he led the Selma-to-Montgomery march to petition for voting rights and was beaten by policemen who fractured his skull. Modestly, quietly, maintaining his poise and good judgment under harsh circumstances, Lewis was one of the people who risked their lives many times to make the civil rights revolution happen. He worked for Robert Kennedy for president in 1968, and was with him in Indianapolis when they heard King was killed, and in Los Angeles just before Kennedy himself was shot. Forty years to the day he was beaten on the Freedom Rides, he received the John F. Kennedy Library's Profiles in Courage award for "steadfast devotion to the dream of an integrated society."

Lewis's first foray into electoral politics was unsuccessful: He ran in 1977 to replace Andrew Young in the House and was soundly beaten by Wyche Fowler (but ran ahead of Republican Paul Coverdell, who beat Fowler in the 1992 Senate election). After winning a seat on the Atlanta Council in 1981, Lewis ran for Congress in 1986, and trailed Julian Bond 47%–35% in the primary. But even though Bond won more than 60% of the black vote, Lewis won the runoff by assembling a coalition of poor blacks and affluent whites: "Vote for the tugboat, not the showboat" was his slogan, stressing his hard work on local issues. He has been re-elected easily since.

Lewis has been a strong partisan, with one of the most liberal voting records in the House, and an impassioned supporter of Bill Clinton on issues and amid scandal. Usually quiet, he can speak in the cadences of black preachers, as he did on the Gulf War resolution in January 1991 and impeachment in November 1998. He is the Democrats' senior chief deputy whip, an integral part of the leadership, and has a seat on Ways and Means. Only occasionally does he defect from his party, as when he opposed the 1994 crime bill because of his disapproval of capital punishment. He furiously voiced his disappointment when Republicans captured the House in 1994. Lewis argued passionately against the Republican welfare bills: "They're coming for the children. They're coming for the poor. They're coming for the sick, the elderly and the disabled"—implicitly comparing the Republicans to Nazis by paraphrasing an anti-Nazi German theologian against them. In October 2002 he spoke against the Iraq war resolution: "For those who argue that war is a necessary evil, I say you are half right. War is evil. But it is not necessary. War cannot be a necessary evil because nonviolence is a necessary good. The two cannot coexist."

Lewis has worked to commemorate the civil rights revolution in which he played such a large part. He got a federal building in Atlanta named for Martin Luther King Jr. and got the route from Selma to Montgomery designated a National Historic Trail. He has said affirmative action should move from race to class as a criterion, but he has stoutly defended racial quotas and preferences and opposed school vouchers for low-income children in Washington, D.C. He passed a Minority Health and Health Disparities Research and Education Act, setting up a research center at the National Institutes of Health. He spotlighted what he thought was racial profiling in Customs searches. In 2002 he co-sponsored with J.C. Watts a bill that passed creating a commission to set up an African-American history museum on the Mall.

In August 1999, Lewis declared that he was running for majority whip should Democrats win a House majority; Nancy Pelosi and Steny Hoyer had already started lining up support. But not all Congressional Black Caucus members supported him, and Lewis left the race (which turned out to be academic) in July 2000. At the same time he said he would "gladly" accept appointment to the Senate seat vacated by the death of Coverdell, but Governor Roy Barnes appointed former Governor Zell Miller instead. Lewis supported Al Gore for president in 1999, and noted that the Georgia primary would be held on the 35th anniversary of the Selma march. At the Los Angeles Democratic National Convention, Lewis took to the podium to give testimony for vice presidential nominee Joe Lieberman, who was suspect by some blacks for having voiced doubts about racial quotas and preferences.

Lewis was unopposed in 2002.

SIXTH DISTRICT

Rep. Johnny Isakson (R)

Elected Feb. 1999, 2d term; b. Dec. 28, 1944, Atlanta; home, Marietta; U. of GA, B.B.A. 1966; Methodist; married (Dianne).

Military Career: GA Air Natl. Guard, 1966–72.

Elected Office: GA House of Reps., 1976–90, Repub. Ldr., 1983–90; GA gubernatorial candidate, 1990; GA Senate, 1993–96; U.S. Senate candidate, 1996.

Professional Career: Northside Realty, 1967–99, Pres., 1979–99; Co-chair, Dole GA presidential campaign, 1988, 1996; Chmn., GA Board of Ed., 1997.

DC Office: 132 CHOB 20515, 202-225-4501; Fax: 202-225-4656; Web site: www.house.gov/isakson.

District Office: Atlanta, 404-252-5239.

Committees: *Education & the Workforce* (13th of 27 R): 21st Century Competitiveness (Vice Chmn.); Workforce Protections. *Transportation & Infrastructure* (21st of 41 R): Aviation; Highways, Transit & Pipelines; Water Resources & Environment.

Group Ratings

	ADA	ACLU	AFS	LCV	CON	ITIC	NTU	COC	ACU	NTLC	CHC
2002	5	20	0	13	17	100	54	100	96	83	92
2001	5	—	0	14	—	—	60	100	88	—	—

National Journal Ratings

	2001 LIB	—	2001 CONS		2002 LIB	—	2002 CONS
Economic	20%	—	80%		21%	—	73%
Social	43%	—	55%		39%	—	57%
Foreign	33%	—	60%		24%	—	72%

Key Votes of the 107th Congress

1. Approve Bush Tax Cuts	*	5. Faith-Based Charities	Y	9. Trade Promotion Authority	Y
2. Limit Patients' Bill of Rights	Y	6. Bar Gays in the Boy Scouts	Y	10. Bar Funds for Intl. Court	Y
3. Campaign Finance Reform	N	7. Ban Partial-Birth Abortion	Y	11. Authorize Force in Iraq	Y
4. Ban ANWR Development	N	8. Arm Commercial Pilots	Y	12. Deny Home. Sec. Dept. Union	Y

Election Results

2002 general	Johnny Isakson (R)	163,203	(80%)	($541,913)
	Jeff Weisberger (D)	41,043	(20%)	
2002 primary	Johnny Isakson (R)	unopposed		
2000 general	Johnny Isakson (R)	256,595	(75%)	($1,601,856)
	Brett DeHart (D)	86,666	(25%)	($35,168)

Prior Winning Percentages: 1999 (65%)

The People		Race/Ethnic Origin	Ancestry	
Area size:	441 sq. mi.	83.0% White	German: 11.1%	English: 11.0%
Urban population:	97.8%	6.9% Black	Irish: 10.1%	
Rural population:	2.2%	4.0% Asian	**2000 Presidential Vote**	
Pop. 2000:	629,725	0.2% Native Am.	Bush (R)...............174,414	(68%)
Median income:	$75,611	0.0% Hawaiian	Gore (D)................77,646	(30%)
Poverty status:	3.7%	1.2% Two+ races	Other....................6,303	(2%)
Military veterans:	12.1%	0.2% Other	**Cook Partisan Voting Index:** R +20	
		4.5% Hispanic Origin		

Occupation	Blue collar: 11.2%	White collar: 79.7%	Gray collar: 9.1%

In the red clay hills north of Atlanta, over the last three decades an almost wholly new metropolitan quarter has grown up as affluent Atlanta has spread out past the I-285 Perimeter into territory that was once just farms, small towns and little factory cities. Where there were perhaps 100,000 people in the 1950s, there are more than 1 million today. No longer is downtown Atlanta the only focus: The edge cities of Perimeter Center and the area near Cumberland Mall are now not just shopping; they are major office centers, rivaling downtown Atlanta in square footage. Cobb County is the headquarters of Home Depot and the Weather Channel. Farther out, in the fast-growing northern part of Fulton County, are the affluent suburbs of Alpharetta and Roswell (Roswell was once a county seat before its county was consolidated into Fulton, and was the girlhood home of the mother of Theodore Roosevelt). Yet for all this economic and demographic change, this Golden Crescent north of the Perimeter and between I-75 in Cobb County and I-85 in Gwinnett County outwardly does not seem to have changed greatly: The buildings are tree-shaded, and lush foliage and large-lot requirements have given most of the communities a woodsy look.

The 6th Congressional District occupies a large portion of this Golden Crescent north of Atlanta, including the bulk of north and west Cobb County, almost all of Fulton County north of the Perimeter and a slice of Cherokee County including Woodstock. This seat owes its existence to Georgia's growth during the 1980s; it was in effect the seat Georgia gained after the 1990 Census, and its boundaries were contracted in the 2001 redistricting to accommodate the population growth of the 1990s. It would surely surprise Georgians a generation or two ago to learn that one of their congressional districts would rank among the nation's richest and most educated: Now the 6th and the 7th, which surrounds it on the north, east and west, both do. It is one of several heavily Republican Georgia districts, and the political tension here tends to be between economic and cultural conservatives.

The congressman from the 6th District is Republican Johnny Isakson, who won a 1999 special election to replace Newt Gingrich, who had resigned after serving as the 50th speaker of the House. A real estate agent, Isakson in 1979 became president of Sandy Springs-based Northside Realty, which became one of the nation's largest residential brokerage firms. He was elected to the Georgia House in 1976, serving as Republican leader from 1983 until 1990, when he lost the gubernatorial election to Zell Miller, 53%–45%. In the state House, Isakson authored and passed legislation on growth policy and regional planning, major issues in the sprawling Atlanta metro region. He was elected to the state Senate in 1993 and served until 1996, when he sought the Republican nomination to succeed Senator Sam Nunn. But Isakson had tough competition from Guy Millner, the millionaire founder of the Norrell temporary employee firm, and Clint Day of the Days Inn family. In a primary overshadowed by the Summer Olympics, Millner led with 42% of the vote, with 35% for Isakson and 19% for Day; Millner won the runoff 53%–47% and then lost the general 49%–48% to Max Cleland. That December, Governor Miller appointed Isakson chairman of the state Board of Education.

In the six-candidate, nonpartisan February 1999 contest in to replace Gingrich, the question was whether the moderate, pro-choice Isakson, Gingrich's handpicked successor and by far the best-known and best-financed candidate, would win a majority of the vote and thus avoid a runoff. The one Democrat was attorney Gary "Bats" Pelphrey, who had lost to Gingrich in 1998, 71%–29%. The only other candidate with significant name recognition was Kennesaw State University professor Christina Jeffrey, whom Gingrich hired and then dismissed as House historian in 1995 after Democrats attacked her criticism of a high school Holocaust course for not describing the views of the Nazis. Jeffrey ran as a conservative, pro-life alternative to Isakson. But no one could compete with the $1 million Isakson had raised and the additional $500,000 he contributed of his own money, which allowed him to maintain a steady advertising presence for weeks. Isakson won 65% of the vote and carried all four counties then in the district; Jeffrey finished second with 25%.

Isakson won a seat on the Transportation Committee, where he pushed for a rapid-transit line for the overburdened Georgia 400 corridor on the north side and he talked up high-speed rail service from Atlanta to Richmond. Isakson also got a seat on the Education Committee, where he was named to the Web-Based Education Commission to examine education technology issues. When Bill Clinton pushed Congress to fund 100,000 new teachers, Isakson objected that there wasn't a large enough supply of available teachers and got Republican leaders to substitute a block grant allowing the states discretion to hire teachers. In 2001, he took a leading role in the negotiations on President Bush's No Child Left Behind Act, and was instrumental in giving elementary and secondary schools more control of how they use federal funds. Education and Workforce Committee chairman John Boehner credited Isakson for the provision requiring that 25% of technology funds be used for teacher classroom training. Serving as a link between speakers, he became friendly with Gingrich's successor Dennis Hastert and was invited to the Speaker's delegation visiting the Pacific Rim in November 1999.

Isakson was easily re-elected in 2000 and 2002. He was mentioned as a possible statewide candidate, but in March 2001 said it would be "irresponsible" of him to consider a statewide race while trying to pass the Bush education proposal. With his safe district, easygoing style, and well-placed friends, he settled into what looked like an influential role in the House. But in January 2003, one week after Senator Zell Miller said he would not seek reelection, Isakson announced he would seek the open Senate seat.

In February 2003, former Congressman Bob Barr announced he would run to replace Isakson in the 6th District; two months later, he announced he had changed his mind and would not run. State Senator Robert Lamutt announced his candidacy in April; through May, a handful of other Republican state legislators were still considering bids.

SEVENTH DISTRICT

Rep. John Linder (R)

Elected 1992, 6th term; b. Sept. 9, 1942, Deer River, MN; home, Duluth; U. of MN, B.S. 1964, D.D.S., 1967; Presbyterian; married (Lynne).

Military Career: Air Force, 1967–69.

Elected Office: GA House of Reps., 1974–80, 1982–90.

Professional Career: Practicing dentist, 1969–82; Founder & Pres., Linder Financial Corp., 1977–92.

DC Office: 1727 LHOB 20515, 202-225-4272; Fax: 202-225-4696; Web site: linder.house.gov.

District Offices: Canton, 770-499-1888; Duluth, 770-232-3005.

Committees: *House Administration* (4th of 6 R). *Rules* (3d of 9 R): Technology & the House (Chmn.). *Select Committee on Homeland Security* (20th of 27 R): Cybersecurity, Science and Research & Development; Intelligence & Counterterrorism; Rules.

Group Ratings

	ADA	ACLU	AFS	LCV	CON	ITIC	NTU	COC	ACU	NTLC	CHC
2002	0	7	0	13	87	100	60	100	100	92	100
2001	0	—	0	0	—	—	64	100	96	—	—

National Journal Ratings

	2001 LIB	—	2001 CONS		2002 LIB	—	2002 CONS
Economic	15%	—	86%		0%	—	91%
Social	0%	—	81%		0%	—	75%
Foreign	4%	—	87%		0%	—	85%

Key Votes of the 107th Congress

1. Approve Bush Tax Cuts	Y	5. Faith-Based Charities	Y	9. Trade Promotion Authority	Y
2. Limit Patients' Bill of Rights	Y	6. Bar Gays in the Boy Scouts	Y	10. Bar Funds for Intl. Court	Y
3. Campaign Finance Reform	N	7. Ban Partial-Birth Abortion	Y	11. Authorize Force in Iraq	Y
4. Ban ANWR Development	N	8. Arm Commercial Pilots	Y	12. Deny Home. Sec. Dept. Union	Y

Election Results

2002 general	John Linder (R)	138,997	(79%)	($2,214,265)
	Michael Berlon (D)	37,124	(21%)	
2002 primary	John Linder (R)	56,892	(64%)	
	Bob Barr (R)	31,374	(36%)	
2000 general (GA 11)	John Linder (R)	unopposed		($418,105)

Prior Winning Percentages: 1998 (69%); 1996 (64%); 1994 (58%); 1992 (51%)

The People		Race/Ethnic Origin	Ancestry	
Area size:	1,220 sq. mi.	82.4% White	USA: 11.9%	English: 9.5%
Urban population:	85.9%	6.9% Black	German: 9.4%	
Rural population:	14.1%	3.8% Asian	**2000 Presidential Vote**	
Pop. 2000:	629,706	0.2% Native Am.	Bush (R) 154,575	(70%)
Median income:	$63,455	0.0% Hawaiian	Gore (D) 60,082	(27%)
Poverty status:	4.5%	1.1% Two+ races	Other 6,694	(3%)
Military veterans:	12.1%	0.1% Other	**Cook Partisan Voting Index:** R +22	
		5.4% Hispanic Origin		

Occupation	Blue collar: 20.6%	White collar: 69.1%	Gray collar: 10.3%

In the last two decades, greater Atlanta has grown out in every direction, south past the airport, west over the Chattahoochee, north past far Buckhead and the Perimeter Mall, and east and northeast past Stone Mountain. The outer suburbs north of Atlanta have grown fastest of all: A semi-circular ring that stretches from Paulding County in the west, with its starter homes for young families, to Gwinnett County to the east, with its more mature neighborhoods of affluent professionals and entrepreneurs. The closer-in portion of Gwinnett, near I-85, with their older shopping districts, have been attracting Georgia's largest concentration of Hispanics and also middle class blacks; recently, several of Atlanta's outer counties decided to link up with urban bus lines for the first time, after shunning them for years. But further out, downtown Atlanta seems very far away, both physically—it is 30 to 50 miles, and more than an hour of clogged rush-hour driving, to Peachtree Street—and in state of mind. For many, Atlanta is something that whizzes by on the way to Hartsfield International Airport.

The growth here is hard to overstate. Gwinnett County cast 21,000 votes in 1972 and 190,000 in 2000, not so far behind Fulton County, which includes central Atlanta, or DeKalb County just to the east. Forsyth County, with golf courses and expensive subdivisions, was the 3d fastest growing county in the United States in the 1990s; it grew another 12% between 2000 and 2001. Paulding County was the 10th fastest growing county during that period. These counties were once rural, low-income and heavily Democratic; now they are full of strivers and achievers, with many religious conservatives and many economic conservatives, but very, very few liberals. The big local issue has been the Northern Arc highway proposed by Governor Roy Barnes; commuters between Forsyth and Cherokee Counties ached for relief, but others opposed the new highway, and Barnes was defeated not least by Forsyth and Cherokee, which voted a combined 71%–25% for his Republican opponent Sonny Perdue.

The 7th Congressional District owes its existence to the rapid growth here in the 1990s; it was a new district created by Democratic redistricters to cordon off Republican votes away from districts they hoped to win. It includes almost all of Paulding County and Cherokee County, plus large parts of Bartow, Forsyth and Gwinnett Counties. The last is most important: Gwinnett casts well over half the district's votes. This is one of the Atlanta area districts into which Democratic redistricters packed fast-growing, heavily Republican areas, in hopes of capturing districts denuded of such Republican support. The result is a very heavily Republican district—70% for George W. Bush in 2000.

The congressman from the 7th District is John Linder, a Republican first elected in 1992 in the 4th District (which combined north DeKalb County and half of Gwinnett) and, after a court-ordered redistricting, elected in 1996, 1998 and 2000 in the 11th District (which stretched from Gwinnett to Athens and the South Carolina border). Like many in the Georgia House delegation, Linder grew up elsewhere, in his case Minnesota, where he went to college and dental school. After two years in the Air Force he moved to greater Atlanta and practiced dentistry for 13 years. In 1977 he started Linder Financial Corporation, a lending institution for entrepreneurial ventures in the South. In 1974, at 32, he was elected to the Georgia House, where he served all but two of the next 16 years. In 1990 he challenged 4th District Democratic Congressman Ben Jones and lost 52%–48%. Following the 1992 redistricting, Linder ran again in the 4th, where he ran first in a six-candidate primary and won the runoff with 62% of the vote. In the general, he faced Democratic state Senator Cathey Steinberg and, in a race that went along national party lines, won by just 51%–49%.

From this tenuous beginning Linder quickly became an important congressman. For a time he was a close ally to Newt Gingrich. They went back a ways: In 1975 Linder, Gingrich and Paul Coverdell began meeting to try to build a strong Georgia Republican Party, surely not imagining that within 20 years they would be Congressman, Speaker and Senator. In 1984 they developed an Operation Breakthrough for electing Republicans in conservative-leaning Georgia legislative districts which had never been seriously contested before. A decade later, they were setting political strategy for congressional Republicans.

Linder has a calm, usually humorous demeanor; his views are solidly conservative—though a bit more Wall Street than Main Street. After Republicans won control, Gingrich gave Linder a seat on the House Rules Committee and called on him often to preside over contentious debates; he floor-managed rules on complex bills like the 1996 Telecommunications Act. After the 1996 election, Gingrich chose Linder to replace Bill Paxon as chairman of the NRCC. He excelled at fundraising, and relentlessly prevailed on incumbents to contribute to Republican challengers. He did a good job at recruiting candidates. He shared the assumption of most observers that Republicans would gain seats as the out party in a presidential off-year election. His targeting was good, but one of his ads misfired: At the behest of Gingrich, it raised the trust and impeachment issues against Bill Clinton. While run in only a few districts, the ad was publicized nationally; it yielded a minimum of gain and a maximum of pain. When the Republicans actually lost five seats, Linder was obviously in deep trouble. Linder said the problem was the lack of a "strong message," which "was not my responsibility"—an obvious reference to Gingrich, who paid a far bigger price for the election outcome. Gingrich, already under attack before resigning, said that the next NRCC head would be elected by the conference rather than appointed by the speaker. Tom Davis of Virginia, a highly competent election buff, started running for the job, with the support of Whip Tom DeLay. Linder reacted bitterly: "I remember when Newt Gingrich's wife left a press conference in tears when he blamed her. So I don't think he has any compunction about blaming me." That was Thursday, two days after the election. Gingrich announced his resignation late on Friday; 12 days later, Linder lost to Davis 130–77.

Taking a far lower profile, Linder resumed his legislative work and got on well with the new Republican leadership; Rules is not a good committee for a party rebel. He turned his long-term attention toward the fight for fundamental tax reform. If Republicans continue to limit the terms of their committee chairmen, and if they retain their House majority, and if Porter Goss retires in 2004 as he nearly did in 2002, Linder could be chairman of Rules in January 2005.

Linder is a redistricting buff, and was named the NRCC's vice chairman for redistricting by Davis. But he had no say in redistricting in Georgia, which was controlled by Democrats. They placed two pairs of Republican incumbents in the same seats and created four new districts which they hoped would elect Democrats. Some of their ideas backfired. Saxby Chambliss, placed in the same district with Jack Kingston, decided to run for the Senate and won. Two of the four districts targeted by Democrats elected Republicans. But the 7th District did end up with a primary contest between two Republican incumbents, Linder and Bob Barr. Barr angered many Republicans when he decided to run in the new 7th, only a little of which he had represented; that was only 18% of his old district. They hoped he would run in the new 11th, which contained more of his old seat and which in fact ended up electing a Republican, albeit by a very narrow margin. Linder had represented, at one time or another, most of Gwinnett County, and one-third of his old 11th District was in the new 7th.

The race was a contrast of styles, not of voting records. Barr had raised serious civil liberties questions about the USA Patriot Act and other legislation coming through the Judiciary Committee, but otherwise their records were much the same. Linder campaigned as a political insider and an experienced representative who quietly got things done. Barr, an early advocate of the impeachment of Bill Clinton, campaigned as a champion of conservative principle. Linder had more local financial support; Barr had financial supporters from across the nation. The campaign grew bitter after a while, and there were some odd moments. Two weeks before the primary Barr, long an advocate of Second Amendment rights, was handling a gun at a supporter's house when it went off and shattered a glass door. But the final result was unambiguous. On August 20, Linder won 64%–36%. Barr won 60% and 61% in Bartow and Paulding Counties, but they cast only 14% of the primary votes. Linder won 74% in Gwinnett County, which cast 57% of the primary votes.

EIGHTH DISTRICT

Rep. Mac Collins (R)

Elected 1992, 6th term; b. Oct. 15, 1944, Jackson; home, Hampton; Methodist; married (Julie).

Military Career: Army Natl. Guard, 1964–70.

Elected Office: Chmn., Butts Cnty. Commission, 1977–80; GA Senate, 1988–92.

Professional Career: Founder & Pres., Collins Trucking Co., 1962–92; Chmn., Butts Cnty. Repub. Party, 1981–82.

DC Office: 1131 LHOB 20515, 202-225-5901; Fax: 202-225-2515; Web site: www.house.gov/maccollins.

District Offices: Columbus, 706-327-7228; McDonough, 678-583-6500; Newnan, 770-683-4622.

Committees: *Permanent Select Committee on Intelligence* (11th of 11 R): Human Intelligence, Analysis & Counterintelligence; Technical & Tactical Intelligence; Terrorism and Homeland Security. *Ways & Means* (13th of 24 R): Select Revenue Measures; Social Security.

Group Ratings

	ADA	ACLU	AFS	LCV	CON	ITIC	NTU	COC	ACU	NTLC	CHC
2002	0	13	11	25	75	88	73	85	100	92	100
2001	5	—	0	0	—	—	64	91	96	—	—

National Journal Ratings

	2001 LIB	—	2001 CONS		2002 LIB	—	2002 CONS
Economic	33%	—	68%		21%	—	73%
Social	20%	—	69%		0%	—	75%
Foreign	33%	—	60%		24%	—	72%

Key Votes of the 107th Congress

1. Approve Bush Tax Cuts	Y	5. Faith-Based Charities	Y	9. Trade Promotion Authority	Y
2. Limit Patients' Bill of Rights	Y	6. Bar Gays in the Boy Scouts	Y	10. Bar Funds for Intl. Court	Y
3. Campaign Finance Reform	N	7. Ban Partial-Birth Abortion	Y	11. Authorize Force in Iraq	Y
4. Ban ANWR Development	N	8. Arm Commercial Pilots	Y	12. Deny Home. Sec. Dept. Union	Y

Election Results

2002 general	Mac Collins (R)	142,505	(78%)	($781,503)
	Angelos Petrakopoulos (D)	39,422	(22%)	
2002 primary	Mac Collins (R)	unopposed		
2000 general (GA 3)	Mac Collins (R)	150,200	(64%)	($697,766)
	Gail Notti (D)	86,309	(37%)	($131,447)

Prior Winning Percentages: 1998 (100%); 1996 (61%); 1994 (66%); 1992 (55%)

The People		Race/Ethnic Origin	Ancestry	
Area size:	3,553 sq. mi.	82.8% White	USA: 15.6%	English: 8.8%
Urban population:	58.5%	12.5% Black	Irish: 8.7%	
Rural population:	41.5%	1.3% Asian	**2000 Presidential Vote**	
Pop. 2000:	629,700	0.2% Native Am.	Bush (R)...............157,703	(69%)
Median income:	$52,406	0.0% Hawaiian	Gore (D)...............67,192	(29%)
Poverty status:	6.3%	0.9% Two+ races	Other....................4,098	(2%)
Military veterans:	15.4%	0.1% Other	**Cook Partisan Voting Index:** R +20	
		2.1% Hispanic Origin		

Occupation   Blue collar: 27.5%   White collar: 60.7%   Gray collar: 11.8%

Running south from Atlanta, within an hour or so by car, you leave behind the newest parts of Georgia—like Henry County, the sixth-fastest growing county in America in 2000–01—and come upon some of the most traditional. Henry County's flourishing residential, commercial and industrial development has risen near its seven I-75 interchanges and has benefited from its proximity to Hartsfield International Airport. To the west is the old courthouse town of Fayetteville, now surrounded by new suburbs, whose Holliday-Dorsey-Fife House is thought to have inspired the columned architecture of Tara in Margaret Mitchell's *Gone With the Wind*. Further west metro Atlanta is spreading through the countryside to Newnan and Carrollton, further east to Jasper County, further south past Barnesville to Thomaston. Even farther to the southwest is yet another Georgia, the small industrial city of Columbus and next-door Fort Benning, long the home of the Army's Infantry School; it is the place where General George Marshall's talents were first noted and where he kept his little black book with a list of gifted officers whom he would make generals in World War II.

Much of this territory is within the 8th Congressional District. On the map it looks like an unsightly splatter. In metro Atlanta, it is divided by tentacles of territory in the new, heavily black 13th District. One way to think of it is that it contains most of the white areas of a ring around the southern edge of metro Atlanta, with tentacles reaching down to include heavily white portions of Columbus and Macon. Politically, this is conservative country, with young tradition-minded families with busy breadwinners and with a heavy military background. People here are upwardly mobile, but not necessarily at the upper end of the income scale. The ancestral politics of most of this area was Democratic, but that is as much a part of history—or legend—now as Tara; this is one of the most heavily Republican congressional districts in Georgia, and in the country.

The congressman from the 8th District is Mac Collins, first elected in 1992. Collins grew up in Jackson and started his trucking company at age 18, hauling logs for Georgia-Pacific; he is known, a local paper said, for "his lumbering stature and signature boots." He served as a Democrat on the Butts County Commission in the late 1970s, lost in 1980, then became Butts County Republican chairman. In 1988, he was elected to the state Senate; in 1992, he ran for Congress in a newly fashioned district. Collins capitalized on a fierce Democratic primary battle between incumbent Congressman Richard Ray and David Worley, who had come close to beating Newt Gingrich in the old 6th District in 1990. Ray won 51%–32%. Collins, like Worley, attacked Ray as an insider; Ray spent $1.1 million, but Collins won 55%–45%.

Collins has a mostly conservative voting record. Hartsfield International Airport, now a few miles outside the district but still a major local employer, is a chief concern; he is a cosponsor of a bill that would impose a two-year moratorium on the excise tax on jet fuel and has introduced legislation to reimburse airlines for all security costs—and suspend security fees— imposed by the 2002 Aviation Security Act for two years. He voted to pare spending at almost every opportunity, except for defense and his district's projects. He made a point of opting out of the congressional pension plan. He won House approval in June 2000 to delay EPA enforcement of strict air quality standards until a new president took office (although George W. Bush later upheld the standards). When the Pentagon decided in 2002 to move its Army South command from Puerto Rico to Fort Sam Houston in Texas, he criticized it for failing to give members information on other options, including Fort Benning. On Ways and Means since his second term, Collins backed welfare reform, a lower tax on earnings by Social Security recipients, and temporary repeal of the federal gasoline tax. On trade issues, he voted against NAFTA, GATT and PNTR with China when each was proposed by Bill Clinton. But he voted for trade promotion authority, saying that he believed the Bush administration would look after the interests of the textile industry. Collins is not afraid to go against the tide. In July 2002, he was one of three House members to vote against the corporate accountability bill, referring to the bill as "politics, pure and simple."

Collins has not faced a serious challenge since 1992. In May 2003, he announced that he would run for the Senate in 2004 to succeed retiring Democratic Senator Zell Miller.

NINTH DISTRICT

Rep. Charlie Norwood (R)

Elected 1994, 5th term; b. July 27, 1941, Valdosta; home, Evans; GA S. U., B.S. 1964, Georgetown U., D.D.S. 1967; Methodist; married (Gloria).

Military Career: Army, 1967–69 (Vietnam).

Professional Career: Small businessman, 1969–present; Practicing dentist, 1969–93; Pres., GA Dental Assn., 1983.

DC Office: 2452 RHOB 20515, 202-225-4101; Fax: 202-226-0776; Web site: www.house.gov/norwood.

District Offices: Augusta, 706-733-7066; Toccoa, 706-886-2776.

Committees: *Education & the Workforce* (9th of 27 R): Select Education; Workforce Protections (Chmn.). *Energy & Commerce* (12th of 31 R): Energy & Air Quality; Health (Vice Chmn.).

Group Ratings

	ADA	ACLU	AFS	LCV	CON	ITIC	NTU	COC	ACU	NTLC	CHC
2002	5	7	11	13	12	62	59	68	96	91	100
2001	10	—	10	7	—	—	64	81	96	—	—

National Journal Ratings

	2001 LIB	—	2001 CONS		2002 LIB	—	2002 CONS
Economic	0%	—	94%		13%	—	85%
Social	20%	—	69%		0%	—	75%
Foreign	41%	—	58%		24%	—	72%

Key Votes of the 107th Congress

1. Approve Bush Tax Cuts	Y	5. Faith-Based Charities	Y	9. Trade Promotion Authority	N
2. Limit Patients' Bill of Rights	Y	6. Bar Gays in the Boy Scouts	Y	10. Bar Funds for Intl. Court	Y
3. Campaign Finance Reform	N	7. Ban Partial-Birth Abortion	Y	11. Authorize Force in Iraq	Y
4. Ban ANWR Development	N	8. Arm Commercial Pilots	*	12. Deny Home. Sec. Dept. Union	Y

Election Results

2002 general	Charlie Norwood (R)	123,313	(73%)	($1,143,213)
	Barry Irwin (D)	45,974	(27%)	($14,404)
2002 primary	Charlie Norwood (R)	42,452	(82%)	
	Lee Dickerson (R)	9,522	(18%)	
2000 general (GA 10)	Charlie Norwood (R)	122,590	(63%)	($787,855)
	Marion Spencer Freeman (D)	71,309	(37%)	($26,713)

Prior Winning Percentages: 1998 (60%); 1996 (52%); 1994 (65%)

The People		Race/Ethnic Origin	Ancestry	
Area size:	7,124 sq. mi.	81.2% White	USA: 16.8%	English: 8.1%
Urban population:	34.1%	13.6% Black	Irish: 7.8%	
Rural population:	65.9%	1.2% Asian	**2000 Presidential Vote**	
Pop. 2000:	629,762	0.3% Native Am.	Bush (R)..............141,065 (66%)	
Median income:	$39,987	0.0% Hawaiian	Gore (D)...............67,451 (32%)	
Poverty status:	11.2%	0.9% Two+ races	Other....................4,025 (2%)	
Military veterans:	13.9%	0.1% Other	**Cook Partisan Voting Index:** R +18	
		2.6% Hispanic Origin		

Occupation	Blue collar: 32.8%	White collar: 53.5%	Gray collar: 13.7%

Northeastern Georgia is a land where the coastal plains and cotton fields yield first to gently rolling hills, then finally near the North Carolina border to the Appalachian Mountains. For most of its history, this has been quiet rural country, with courthouse towns and a few small cities, mostly forgotten by national elites, bypassed even by General Sherman on his march to the sea. But in the last two decades, economic growth has radiated outward from Atlanta and has spread across much of the region, including northwest Georgia. The effects can be seen as far away as the old city of Augusta, on the Savannah River across from South Carolina. Founded in 1735, with a medical college that dates back to 1835, with an old Cotton Exchange and mansions untouched by Sherman, it is rich in history. It is also a center for newer industries, for the paper industry and for the nuclear industry at the old Savannah River site over the border in South Carolina. Augusta is also known as the home of the Augusta National Golf Club, the site of the Masters tournament every year, its entrance barely visible off four-lane Washington Road.

The 9th Congressional District includes most of the northeast corner of the state, with a few prominent exceptions. It includes most of the Augusta area but not heavily black precincts in Augusta itself and it excludes Athens, the home of the University of Georgia—both were included in the 12th District by Democratic redistricters in the hope, vain it turned out, of creating a new Democratic seat. There are new retiree communities and second-home development in the mountains in the northern part of the district, and there is rapid growth in its west end, in Walton and Barrow Counties, now part of metro Atlanta. Barrow was once a sleepy rural county, notable mainly as the home of longtime (1933–71) Senator Richard Russell. Elberton, to the east, centers a granite-producing region; Columbia County, next to Augusta, and Oconee County, next to Athens, are particularly affluent and rapidly growing. Voters here prefer traditional values over liberal values; several counties have consistently rejected ballot propositions to end prohibition of alcohol. There are relatively few blacks here this far north in Georgia, at least within the boundaries of the 9th. This is an overwhelmingly Republican district, in national politics and, since 2002, in state elections as well. George W. Bush won 66% here in 2000.

The congressman from the 9th District is Charlie Norwood, a Republican first elected in 1994. Norwood grew up in Valdosta, went to college and dental school, served in the Army in Vietnam and at Fort Gordon, then practiced dentistry in Augusta. He was president of the Georgia Dental Association and also started small businesses—Northwood Tree Nursery and Park Avenue Fabrics. In 1993 he decided to sell his dental practice and run against Congressman Don Johnson, a freshman elected in 1992. Johnson came under scathing criticism when he broke a campaign promise to vote against any tax increase and supported the Clinton budget and tax package in 1993. Norwood's toughest race in 1994 turned out to be the primary; he came from behind to beat Ralph Hudgens in the runoff 51%–49%. When Johnson said he wanted Bill Clinton or Al Gore to visit the 10th District only if "they are coming down to endorse my opponent," Norwood invited Clinton and offered to pay his plane fare. Norwood won 65%–35%, as Johnson took one of the worst lickings of a non-scandal-tarred incumbent in recent history.

Norwood generally has had a conservative voting record. That made it all the more remarkable when he suddenly emerged from obscurity in 1997 to become one of the House's most influential members. The reason was PARCA, the Patient Access to Responsible Care Act, regulating health maintenance organizations, which Norwood sponsored and pushed with great vehemence: "This is something that has been festering in my soul for a long time. People are trying to deny our patients treatment." In his dental practice, Norwood was in an HMO for three years and decided, "This was no way to go." To some critics, PARCA looked like "provider protection." But Norwood insisted, "This is not about money for physicians. It is about them losing control of their ability to practice medicine." He assembled 230 co-sponsors, including 90 Republicans. PARCA provided that patients could sue HMOs when they overrule doctors and refuse to pay for treatments that turn out to have been needed; that patients can visit emergency rooms without the permission of the insurer; that doctors couldn't be prohibited from discussing alternative treatments (the gag rule); that patients have free selection of doctors, hospitals and treatments; and that patients can see specialists on a doctor's recommendation. PARCA produced new political alliances and results. Large businesses and the Chamber of Commerce were appalled, and predicted it would raise insurance costs by 35%. HMOs and the Blues also opposed it. The American Medical Association, American Dental Association and American College of Emergency Physicians came out in favor, as did most Democrats. In January 1998, as momentum grew, Newt Gingrich appointed a Republican working group headed by then-Chief Deputy Whip Dennis Hastert. Norwood judged that he couldn't pass his full bill, and so was ready to compromise. The working group's bill did not include the right to sue, but did include a ban on the gag rule, emergency room visits without previous approval, and allowing patients to appeal decisions to an outside arbitrator. The Patient Protection Act passed 216–210 after a Democratic "Patient Bill of Rights" failed 212–217; but the Senate did not act.

When the issue returned in the 106th Congress, Hastert had become speaker but he could no longer stop the tide once Norwood signed on with senior Democrat John Dingell on the patients' bill of rights. In October 1999, Norwood-Dingell passed 275–151. Norwood was now many Democrats' favorite Republican, and Clinton embraced the bill as "a major victory for every family." Then something unexpected happened. For the next year, all sorts of negotiations took place: Republican-Democratic, House-Senate, Congress-White House. But the bill remained logjammed. Unwilling to add further burdens to the courts, Republicans gambled that momentum for HMO regulation had waned. And many Democrats moved on to their new health-care issue *du jour*: Prescription-drug coverage for seniors. Then, in August 2001, his former allies were miffed when Norwood, to their surprise, went to the White House and agreed to a deal with George W. Bush on a new version of the bill that permitted employers to limit their liability. House Republicans passed that plan amid cries from Democrats that Norwood had sold out his principles; the Senate Democratic majority had no interest in reaching a compromise.

Norwood's standing has remained strong among leadership Republicans. He hosted Hastert at a fundraiser in Augusta in April 2000, and was named chairman of the Workforce Protections panel on the Education and the Workforce Committee in 2001. He used that position to press for tougher enforcement by the Labor Department of union disclosure forms. But in December 2001 he showed his independence when he was the only Georgia Republican to vote against trade promotion authority.

Norwood faced tough electoral competition in 1996 after a court-ordered redistricting made the district 38% black; he won by only 52%–48%. But as the champion of PARCA and as an excellent fundraiser, he did not attract such strong competition in 1998 and 2000. Democratic redistricters in 2001 gave up on beating him and created the 9th District in its current, overwhelmingly Republican form. "We've got this great new district," he told reporters in early 2003. "It's so Republican, it's boring."

TENTH DISTRICT

Rep. Nathan Deal (R)

Elected 1992, 6th term; b. Aug. 25, 1942, Millen; home, Clermont; Mercer U., B.A. 1964, J.D. 1966; Baptist; married (Sandra).

Military Career: Army, 1966–68.

Elected Office: Hall Cnty. Juvenile Court Judge, 1971–72; GA Senate, 1980–92, Pres. Pro-Tem, 1989–90, 1991–92.

Professional Career: Hall Cnty. Atty., 1966–70; Asst. Dist. Atty., NE Judicial Circuit, 1970–71; Practicing atty., 1971–92.

DC Office: 2437 RHOB 20515, 202-225-5211; Fax: 202-225-8272; Web site: www.house.gov/deal.

District Offices: Dalton, 706-226-5320; Gainesville, 770-535-2592; Lafayette, 706-638-7042.

Committees: *Energy & Commerce* (9th of 31 R): Health; Telecommunications & The Internet. *Government Reform* (18th of 24 R): Civil Service & Agency Organization; Criminal Justice, Drug Policy & Human Resources (Vice Chmn.); Energy Policy, Natural Resources and Regulatory Affairs.

Group Ratings

	ADA	ACLU	AFS	LCV	CON	ITIC	NTU	COC	ACU	NTLC	CHC
2002	0	7	0	13	25	88	63	90	100	89	100
2001	5	—	0	0	—	—	67	90	100	—	—

National Journal Ratings

	2001 LIB	—	2001 CONS		2002 LIB	—	2002 CONS
Economic	0%	—	94%		9%	—	87%
Social	20%	—	69%		32%	—	68%
Foreign	33%	—	60%		0%	—	85%

Key Votes of the 107th Congress

1. Approve Bush Tax Cuts	Y	5. Faith-Based Charities	Y	9. Trade Promotion Authority	Y
2. Limit Patients' Bill of Rights	Y	6. Bar Gays in the Boy Scouts	Y	10. Bar Funds for Intl. Court	Y
3. Campaign Finance Reform	N	7. Ban Partial-Birth Abortion	Y	11. Authorize Force in Iraq	Y
4. Ban ANWR Development	N	8. Arm Commercial Pilots	Y	12. Deny Home. Sec. Dept. Union	Y

Election Results

2002 general	Nathan Deal (R)	unopposed		($307,161)
2002 primary	Nathan Deal (R)	unopposed		
2000 general (GA 9)	Nathan Deal (R)	183,171	(75%)	($429,979)
	James Harrington (D)	60,360	(25%)	($69,884)

Prior Winning Percentages: 1998 (100%); 1996 (66%); 1994 (58%); 1992 (59%)

The People		Race/Ethnic Origin	Ancestry	
Area size:	3,820 sq. mi.	85.4% White	USA: 17.8%	Irish: 8.3%
Urban population:	52.0%	3.3% Black	English: 7.8%	
Rural population:	48.0%	0.7% Asian	**2000 Presidential Vote**	
Pop. 2000:	629,702	0.3% Native Am.	Bush (R) 134,619	(69%)
Median income:	$42,037	0.0% Hawaiian	Gore (D) 54,633	(28%)
Poverty status:	10.3%	0.8% Two+ races	Other 4,614	(2%)
Military veterans:	12.2%	0.1% Other	**Cook Partisan Voting Index:** R +21	
		9.4% Hispanic Origin		

Occupation	Blue collar: 36.9%	White collar: 51.4%	Gray collar: 11.7%

In the last years of the 20th century, the hills and mountains of north Georgia have suddenly become one of the boom areas of the South. This is a sharp turn in their history: Since the Cherokee were driven out early in the 19th century this has been poor country, where small farmers scratched a living off rocky land. It was devastated by the Civil War, by General Sherman's troops and because so many young men who left to fight for the Confederacy (and a few who left from mountain counties to fight for the Union) never returned. After the war, not much changed for a while. Most communities lived in isolation; roads with hairpin curves led to remote hills where until very recently moonshine stills were more common than summer cabins (the novel *Deliverance* was a thinly-disguised portrait of life along the Coosawatee River in Gilmer and Murray Counties, though the subsequent movie was filmed on the Chattooga River in Rabun County). In time, textile mills began springing up along the railroads, around Gainesville poultry production became a big business, and in Dalton the craft tradition of tufted bedspread handiwork was transformed into the world's largest carpet industry, producing 60% of the world's tufted carpet. But these were low-wage industries and all white; there had never been many slaves here.

In the 1980s and especially the 1990s there has been a rush of change. Interstate highways have brought north Georgia in easy range of the world-city of Atlanta; the carpet industry has become more high-tech; small manufacturing is booming, with higher-skill work replacing low-tech mills; vacation and retirement communities have been built in mountains and around lakes. Agribusiness remains important, with huge poultry processors in Hall County around Gainesville. The carpet industry still plays a key economic role, too: The area economy is vulnerable to fluctuations in new construction activity. Once rural counties are now part of the booming ring around Atlanta, and Lake Sidney Lanier, named for the 19th century poet who wrote *Song of the Chattahoochee*, is the most visited lake served by the Army Corps of Engineers. So tight are the labor markets that tens of thousands of Latinos from Texas, Mexico and other Latin countries have come to Dalton, Gainesville and the area around to snap up the jobs the boom is creating; this area now has nearly four times as many Hispanics as blacks.

The 10th Congressional District covers most of northwest Georgia, snaking far enough south to take parts of counties in metro Atlanta—Forsyth, Gwinnett, Walton, Rockdale. Its northern tier of counties borders North Carolina, Tennessee and Alabama, much of it in the Chattanooga—not the Atlanta—media market. Here are some of the few mountainous parts of Georgia, where within living memory the major product was moonshine whiskey and which in the days of the Democratic Solid South had a robust and ornery two-party politics. Today the Democratic history of most of this region is forgotten, and this is a solidly Republican area in national and state elections; in 2000, this district gave George W. Bush his second-highest percentage in the state with 69%. The only Democrat with a chance of winning here is north Georgia native Senator Zell Miller.

The congressman from the 10th District is Nathan Deal, first elected in 1992 as a Democrat, who switched parties and became a Republican in April 1995. Deal grew up in Gainesville, went to Mercer University, then served in the Army from 1966–68; he returned home to practice "street level law," with offices always on the ground floor, and public offices a young lawyer takes as civic duty: Assistant district attorney, juvenile court judge, county attorney. In 1980, at 38, he was elected to the state senate as a Democrat. Jimmy Carter was still president, the legislature was overwhelmingly Democratic, and it would have been quixotic to run as a Republican. He proved a capable legislator and was elected Senate president pro tem in 1989 and 1991. In 1992, incumbent Ed Jenkins retired; Deal ran, defeating a Republican abortion opponent with 59% of the vote.

In the House, Deal opposed the new Clinton administration's economic policies, voting against the 1993 budget, for the line-item veto and balanced budget amendment. He helped found a 26-Democrat Fiscal Caucus. Many saw Deal as a potential party-switcher, but while campaigning in 1994 he said, "If I choose to switch during the term, I think the honest thing to do is resign and have a special election." He beat an underfunded Republican, but with only 58%—a sign of increasing Republican sentiment. In early 1995, he worked with other Democrats to offer an alternative to the Republicans' welfare reform package. On Monday, April 3, Deal said how pleased he was by Democrats' support for that plan. Two days later, he was unhappy with Democrats' opposition to tax cuts and with senior Democrats' criticisms of Clean Water Act revisions he had won on a bipartisan committee vote. On April 10, back home in Gainesville, Deal announced he was a Republican—but he did not resign and run in a special election. He said the national Democratic Party was unwilling to admit it was "out of touch with mainstream America," and "I think that it is important that at some point you get away from the schizophrenia I have had to deal with." Democrats were stunned, and Newt Gingrich was clearly delighted; Deal was rewarded with a seat on the Commerce Committee.

Deal's voting record is mostly conservative, but he has not been a totally party line Republican. He supported early versions of the Shays-Meehan campaign finance bill, though not its final passage in February 2002. He held local meetings to discuss the problems faced by Lake Lanier because of heavy use and Georgia's water shortage, and he filed a bill to make public recreation a priority in the management of federal lakes. He sponsored higher penalties for illegal aliens and smugglers of aliens, and he opposed the Bush administration's study of legalization of immigrants from Mexico. Such actions might some day hurt Deal politically in a district with a rapidly growing Hispanic population, but he said, "We're a nation of laws. It's our responsibility to forge support for the concept of law."

Deal has not faced serious opposition from either party since 1995, and he was unopposed in 2002. In 1992, Deal pledged to limit his service in the House to 12 years; he has since made clear that he never actually signed a term limits pledge and intends to run for reelection in 2004.

ELEVENTH DISTRICT

Rep. Phil Gingrey (R)

Elected 2002, 1st term; b. July 10, 1942, Augusta; home, Marietta; GA Inst. of Tech., B.S. 1965, Med. Col. of GA, M.D. 1969; Catholic; married (Billie).

Elected Office: Marietta Schl. Bd., 1993–97; GA Senate, 1998–02.

Professional Career: Practicing obstetrician, 1976-present.

DC Office: 1118 LHOB 20515, 202-225-2931; Fax: 202-225-2944; Web site: www.house.gov/gingrey.

District Offices: Carrollton, 770-836-8130; Marietta, 770-429-1776.

Committees: *Armed Services* (31st of 33 R): Tactical Air & Land Forces; Total Force. *Education & the Workforce* (26th of 27 R): 21st Century Competitiveness; Select Education. *Science* (20th of 25 R): Energy; Research.

Group Ratings and Key Votes: Newly Elected

Election Results

2002 general	Phil Gingrey (R)	69,260	(52%)	($1,819,423)
	Roger Kahn (D)	64,922	(48%)	($3,683,359)
2002 runoff	Phil Gingrey (R)	9,930	(64%)	
	Cecil Staton (R)	5,692	(36%)	
2002 primary	Phil Gingrey (R)	12,377	(40%)	
	Cecil Staton (R)	9,750	(32%)	
	Bob Herriott (R)	8,717	(28%)	
2000 general (GA 7)	Bob Barr (R)	126,312	(55%)	($3,495,641)
	Roger Kahn (D)	102,272	(45%)	($3,859,860)

The People		Race/Ethnic Origin	Ancestry	
Area size:	3,750 sq. mi.	61.7% White	USA: 13.7%	Irish: 6.3%
Urban population:	72.3%	28.2% Black	English: 5.7%	
Rural population:	27.7%	1.2% Asian	**2000 Presidential Vote**	
Pop. 2000:	629,730	0.2% Native Am.	Bush (R)	93,359 (51%)
Median income:	$37,582	0.0% Hawaiian	Gore (D)	85,542 (47%)
Poverty status:	13.8%	1.1% Two+ races	Other	2,632 (1%)
Military veterans:	12.8%	0.2% Other	**Cook Partisan Voting Index:** R + 3	
		7.2% Hispanic Origin		

Occupation	Blue collar: 33.4%	White collar: 52.3%	Gray collar: 14.3%

Northwest Georgia, home of the Cherokee Nation before they were sent west in the 1830s on the Trail of Tears, has been manufacturing country for the last century. There were once hundreds of textile mills and dozens of carpet mills located near the supply of natural cotton and along the railroad lines heading southwest at the base of the southern Appalachian chain. The late 19th century propagandists of the New South hailed factories as the vanguard of technological progress, and in fact the factories produced a higher standard of living than farms on this stubborn land. But mill work put scant premium on education or the cultivation of civic virtues and did little to bring in higher-skill white-collar work. All-white hiring practices maintained racial segregation in mostly white north Georgia. Today, north Georgia is developing a different kind of economy, as metro Atlanta spreads out over highways north into what used to be mill towns. Floyd County is home to an auto-parts manufacturing cluster; places like the textile mill town of LaGrange or the carpet mill town of Rome are seeing change as well, as Latino immigrants have become a major part of the mill work force.

The 11th Congressional District includes much of this part of the state, taking in small industrial towns and rural cotton, poultry and cattle-producing areas and a cluster of older suburbs around Atlanta. It stretches from Rome in the north to the outer reaches of Columbus in the south (which, like Augusta, Macon, Savannah and Valdosta, is divided among districts). The 11th includes part of Bartow County, enough to include the Democratic stronghold of Cartersville, and has a tentacle that extends past fast-growing subdivisions into parts of central and south Cobb County just west of Atlanta that have a rapidly increasing number of black residents. The slice of the district includes most of Marietta, where Lockheed Martin builds the F-22A Raptor and the C-130J cargo plane. Directly west of Atlanta is Carrollton, once the home of an untenured West Georgia College professor who in his third try became a Republican congressman: Newt Gingrich. The 11th also includes heavily black Meriwether County, home of Hot Springs, where Franklin Roosevelt recuperated from polio in the 1920s and died in April 1945. The boundaries here are contorted, drawn with an eye to political advantage by Democratic redistricters, and an affront to the notions of compactness or communities of interest. Northwest Georgia generally is Republican, but the redistricters were careful to exclude the most heavily Republican areas, including fast-growing metro Atlanta suburbs, and to add on to the district Democratic areas, like south Cobb County and Meriwether County. The result is a district that is not Democratic, but competitive between the parties. George W. Bush carried it with 51% in 2000; before that it mostly voted Democratic in state elections. The obvious target of this redistricting was Cobb County-based Republican Congressman Bob Barr, who had represented most of this area since 1994. The controversial Barr decided to run instead in the new 7th District, very little of which he had represented, and lost in the Republican primary to fellow incumbent John Linder.

The congressman, however, is not a Democrat but a Republican, Phil Gingrey, a physician elected in his party's sweep of Georgia in 2002. He grew up in Augusta, graduated from Georgia Tech, and returned home to attend the Medical College of Georgia. After his medical training in Georgia hospitals, he settled in Marietta, where he set up an obstetrics and gynecology practice, in which he delivered more than 5,200 babies. During his spare time, he served on the local school board, and was chosen as chairman. In 1998, he was elected to the state Senate, where he had a reputation as a staunch social conservative but one who could work with Democrats on other issues. When Barr decided not to run in the 11th, Gingrey got into the race, and faced tough competition in both the primary and general election. The issue differences were small among the three candidates in the Republican primary. Gingrey, who is Catholic, styled himself as the only native Georgian. Cecil Staton, an ordained Baptist minister, vowed to view all legislation from the perspective of the traditional family. Barr supported Bob Herriott, a pilot for Delta Airlines. In the primary, Gingrey won 40% of the vote to 32% for Staton and 28% for Herriott; Gingrey's greatest strength was in Cobb County, which cast 31% of the vote. The bitter September runoff revolved around their respective religions and allegations by Staton that Gingrey supported homosexual causes. Voters who knew Gingrey from his state Senate tenure didn't buy it; he won 64%-36%, carrying every county. The Democrats, meanwhile, had their own brawl featuring former Congressman (1983-1995) Buddy Darden, who had served on the Armed Services Committee, and Roger Kahn, a millionaire beer distributor who in 2000 lost to Barr 55%-45%. Kahn was a good friend of House Speaker Tom Murphy, and Darden was close to Governor Roy Barnes, for whom he once worked; by the end of 2002, all four had been defeated. Darden was the first one out, losing 52%–48%.

The general election was another negative contest that with aspersions cast on both candidates. Kahn accused Gingrey of seeking special favors for cocaine-dealing felons and violent criminals who had assaulted police officers. He spent $2.8 million from his own pocket, on top of the $2.9 million he spent against Barr two years earlier, and complained that national Democrats did not give him more help; Gingrey spent $1.2 million in the primary, runoff and general. Gingrey portrayed Kahn as a wealthy liquor distributor posing as a modest farmer. He urged voters not to be "Kahned" on Election Day. "He looks benign," said Gingrey. "He's got a nice smile. But we need to let the people of this district know the character of this man." The campaign grew ugly enough that both candidates ultimately signed a "clean election pledge," but they were at each other's throats again within 36 hours. Kahn prevailed in six of the 17 counties, but Gingrey won 52%–48%. He credited the Georgia Republican tide and the Republicans' House campaign committee, which—though slow to place the contest on its radar screen—eventually "got behind us in a way that I never really understood was possible."

Gingrey, who had heart bypass surgery shortly after the election, sought seats on the Armed Services and Education Committees and got them both. This seat could be seriously contested again in 2004.

TWELFTH DISTRICT

Rep. Max Burns (R)

Elected 2002, 1st term; b. Nov. 8, 1948, Millen; home, Sylvania; GA Tech. U., B.S. 1973, GA St. U., M.B.A. 1977, Ph.D. 1987; Baptist; married (Lora).

Military Career: Army Reserve, 1973–81.

Elected Office: Screven Cnty. Commission, 1993–98.

Professional Career: College prof.; Info. mgmt. exec., 1977–02.

DC Office: 512 CHOB 20515, 202-225-2823; Fax: 202-225-3377; Web site: burns.house.gov.

District Offices: Augusta, 706-854-4595; Savannah, 912-352-1736; Statesboro, 912-764-4589.

Committees: *Agriculture* (20th of 27 R): Conservation, Credit, Rural Development & Research; General Farm Commodities & Risk Management. *Education & the Workforce* (27th of 27 R): 21st Century Competitiveness; Select Education. *Transportation & Infrastructure* (37th of 41 R): Economic Development, Public Buildings & Emergency Management; Highways, Transit & Pipelines.

Group Ratings and Key Votes: Newly Elected

Election Results

2002 general	Max Burns (R)	77,479	(55%)	($925,706)
	Charles Walker (D)	62,904	(45%)	($1,120,201)
2002 primary	Max Burns (R)	13,956	(50%)	
	Barbara Dooley (R)	13,700	(50%)	

The People		Race/Ethnic Origin	Ancestry	
Area size:	5,265 sq. mi.	51.9% White	USA: 8.8%	Irish: 5.8%
Urban population:	74.5%	42.3% Black	English: 5.8%	
Rural population:	25.5%	1.4% Asian	**2000 Presidential Vote**	
Pop. 2000:	629,735	0.2% Native Am.	Gore (D) 95,845 (54%)	
Median income:	$31,108	0.1% Hawaiian	Bush (R) 80,665 (45%)	
Poverty status:	21.7%	1.1% Two + races	Other 2,636 (1%)	
Military veterans:	13.5%	0.1% Other	**Cook Partisan Voting Index:** D + 4	
		2.9% Hispanic Origin		

Occupation	Blue collar: 28.0%	White collar: 53.6%	Gray collar: 18.4%

In Georgia, the focus is usually on Atlanta. But Georgia also has some gracious smaller cities, with roots deep in the past. One is Savannah, the state's first capital, which by the 1830s was one of America's booming cotton ports; it languished after the Civil War, living off paper mills and chemical plants in the 20th century, while impoverished blacks on the islands a few miles away still spoke Gullah dialects. Then, a few decades ago, preservationists started restoring houses and churches on the grid punctuated by 24 squares that James Oglethorpe had laid out more than 200 years before. Today Savannah is one of the most graciously preserved cities in the country, and a major tourism mecca thanks to the popularity of John Berendt's *Midnight in the Garden of Good and Evil*, a somewhat-based-on-facts story of eccentricity and murder on the bestseller lists for four years in the 1990s. The city actively competes with neighboring—and equally well-preserved—Charleston, South Carolina, not only for tourists but for shipping. Another such city is Augusta, upriver on the Savannah River, founded in 1735 as a fur-trading post, home of the Medical College of Georgia since 1835 and boyhood home of President Woodrow Wilson, with its own Cotton Exchange and Riverwalk. A third such city is Athens, on the smaller Oconee River, site of the gracious campus of the University of Georgia since 1801 and home to the rock bands R.E.M. and the B-52s, with graceful Greek Revival mansions, boxwood gardens and magnolias.

The 12th Congressional District, newly created by the Democratic redistricting of 2001, combines almost all of Savannah (but only some of its suburbs), four-fifths of Augusta (but not much of its suburbs) and all of Athens into a long slim district that extends some 230 miles. The 12th is sometimes referred to as Georgia's "higher education district"—because nearly a dozen universities and colleges are concentrated within its boundaries. It is one or two counties deep along the Savannah River from Savannah to Augusta, then runs northwest in a narrowing finger from Augusta to Athens. There is, of course, a political explanation for the shape of the district. The district carefully excludes the heavily Republican suburbs of Savannah's Chatham County (in the 1st District), the heavily Republican suburbs of Augusta in Columbia County and heavily Republican Oconee County outside Athens (in the 9th District). It also carefully excludes most of Hunter Army Airfield near Savannah and Fort Gordon near Augusta. It contains the Depression-wracked farm country near Augusta that Erskine Caldwell chronicled in his scandalous bestseller, *Tobacco Road*; the titular dirt thoroughfare, which led to a small port on the Savannah River, is now paved and passes a nondescript mix of residential and commercial areas. The 12th District is one of Georgia's two new House districts and was intended to be safely Democratic.

But the congressman from this new district is a Republican, Max Burns, who won a terrific upset in the 2002 election. Burns grew up in Screven County, where he continues to live on his family's beef and timber farm. He graduated from Georgia Tech with a degree in industrial engineering, and received a Ph.D. from Georgia State University. During his more than 10 years of graduate study, he held information management positions with Oxford Industries and the North American Mission Board of the Southern Baptist Convention. A former Senior Fulbright Scholar, he was a professor of information systems at Georgia Southern University's College of Business Administration in Statesboro. From 1993 to 1998, he served on the Screven County Commission.

Burns entered the race as a long shot. He was from a small county and was largely unknown beyond. He was the underdog in the Republican primary against radio talk show host Barbara Dooley, the wife of revered former University of Georgia head football coach Vince Dooley, who had been encouraged by state and national Republican leaders. Initial press reports declared her the winner with 51%, but a recount gave Burns the win by 256 votes. Dooley carried Savannah and Athens by wide margins, but Burns, with assiduous campaigning, carried most of the small counties, plus fast-growing Effingham County outside Savannah and won his home county, 92%–8%, with 1,408 votes of 1,530 cast. The district had been designed by state Senate Majority Leader Charles Walker to elect his son, Charles "Champ" Walker Jr., from Augusta. But Champ Walker faltered at every turn. In the seven-candidate Democratic primary, he won 33% of the vote; only in Savannah's Chatham County did he win over 50% of the vote. Walker won the lower-turnout runoff by only 54%–46% over state Representative Ben Allen; again, Savannah was his one stronghold, and this time he lost Richmond County, his home base.

As the campaign progressed, Walker's credibility eroded after local newspapers reported a past littered with failed business ventures and run-ins with the law. *The Augusta Chronicle* found that he had been arrested at least four times on charges including disorderly conduct, shoplifting, and driving with a suspended license. Burns ran ads highlighting Walker's arrests for shoplifting and leaving the scene of an accident. Walker avoided debating Burns, saying that one major debate conflicted with a campaign office opening, and showed up late to one debate claiming that he had been held up by traffic in Washington, D.C. A local newspaper wrote that Walker "had neither the backbone nor the preparation to tackle the tough issues in Congress." Walker said that Burns lacked integrity in "using racial politics to attempt to divide this district." Burns said that the district needed "honest and ethical representation;" he called for improving math and science education, making distance learning more accessible and improving English fluency programs for immigrants. By campaign's end, both Walker and his father were in trouble. Burns was making inroads among black voters in rural and urban counties, and the president of Augusta's Concerned Black Clergy endorsed Walker Sr.'s Republican opponent. On Election Day, Charles Walker Sr. was defeated and Burns beat Champ Walker 55%–45%. In Chatham and Richmond counties, both with substantial black majorities, Walker won only 53% and 52% of the vote; Burns carried usually Democratic Clarke County (Athens) 52%–48%. Of the 11 rural counties, Burns carried 10, most by large majorities—87%–13% in tiny Glascock County, 80%–20% in Effingham County.

In Washington, the 33 Republican freshmen elected Burns as their class president. Still, Burns is likely to be a Democratic target in 2004. But he will also have two years to provide constituency services and build personal relationships with his constituents, in the hope of running as far ahead of his party as an incumbent as he did against a deeply flawed opponent in 2002.

THIRTEENTH DISTRICT

Rep. David Scott (D)

Elected 2002, 1st term; b. June 27, 1946, Aynor, SC; home, Atlanta; FL A&M U., B.A. 1967, U. of PA, M.B.A. 1969; Baptist; married (Alfredia).

Elected Office: GA House of Reps., 1974–82; GA Senate, 1982–02.

Professional Career: Founder and Pres., Dayn-Mark Advertising, 1977-present.

DC Office: 417 CHOB 20515, 202-225-2939; Fax: 202-225-4628; Web site: davidscott.house.gov.

District Office: Jonesboro, 770-210-5073.

Committees: *Agriculture* (16th of 24 D): Livestock & Horticulture; Specialty Crops & Foreign Agriculture Programs. *Financial Services* (31st of 32 D): Capital Markets, Insurance & Government Sponsored Enterprises; Housing & Community Opportunity.

Group Ratings and Key Votes: Newly Elected

Election Results

2002 general	David Scott (D)	70,011	(60%)	($1,505,191)
	Clay Cox (R)	47,405	(40%)	($639,841)
2002 primary	David Scott (D)	22,624	(54%)	
	Greg Hecht (D)	8,384	(20%)	
	David Worley (D)	5,568	(13%)	
	Donzella James (D)	4,703	(11%)	
	Other	762	(2%)	

The People		Race/Ethnic Origin	Ancestry	
Area size:	784 sq. mi.	42.1% White	USA: 8.2%	Irish: 5.1%
Urban population:	92.1%	40.7% Black	English: 4.6%	
Rural population:	7.9%	5.1% Asian	**2000 Presidential Vote**	
Pop. 2000:	629,732	0.2% Native Am.	Gore (D) 91,895	(57%)
Median income:	$43,429	0.0% Hawaiian	Bush (R) 66,576	(41%)
Poverty status:	11.2%	1.5% Two+ races	Other 3,392	(2%)
Military veterans:	12.4%	0.2% Other	**Cook Partisan Voting Index:** D + 8	
		10.2% Hispanic Origin		

Occupation	Blue collar: 29.6%	White collar: 55.9%	Gray collar: 14.5%

Many of the great landmarks of the civil rights movements, the headquarters of major civil rights organizations and the campuses of six historically black colleges are all in the central city of Atlanta. The city's cohesive and talented black community, more than any other, provided the leadership of and inspiration for the civil rights movement which changed America so much for the better. In the 1960s, Atlanta's blacks were clustered in ghetto neighborhoods on the south and west side of the city; the north side of Atlanta and the suburbs in every direction were heavily or entirely white. Today, a long generation after the great days of the civil rights movement, blacks have moved outward from Atlanta in almost all directions in one of the nation's fastest-growing metro areas. The central city of Atlanta has had an increasing white percentage, as whites move into affluent Buckhead and the thriving communities of Midtown Atlanta, while the crime-ridden ghettoes in south and west Atlanta lose population. But this is a story not of failure but of success: members of metro Atlanta's thriving middle class have been moving out to many other parts of the Atlanta metro area—to south DeKalb County to the east and south Cobb County to the west, to Clayton County directly south of the city and Hartsfield Airport, to southwest Fulton County outside Atlanta and out radial highways in heretofore heavily white suburban counties.

The 13th Congressional District, newly created in the 2001 redistricting, can rightfully be depicted as the most geographically grotesque district in the country. Yet it can be defended as a collection of areas into which Atlanta area blacks have been moving or are likely to be moving in the next 10 years—Sweet Auburn marching out to the suburbs. Its nucleus is Clayton County, almost all of which is in the district: a county that voted for George Wallace in 1968 and that now has a black majority. It also includes southwest Fulton County and small portions of south Fulton and DeKalb Counties. Then there are the tentacles that thrash out in several directions. One extends south from Clayton County into Spalding County to black neighborhoods in the old county seat of Griffin. Another extends southeast along I-75 into the middle of Henry and Butts Counties. To the east, another tentacle moves to include most of Rockdale County and east into Newton County and northward to Walton County. From Rockdale, another particularly tenuous tentacle hugs the Gwinnett County line and then heads northeast along the I-85 and Buford Highway low-income corridor in high-income Gwinnett County. The result is a district whose perimeter might well be as long as the combined boundaries of the state of Georgia and whose lines an area freeway driver may cross over a dozen times a day. In 2000, the population of this district was 41% black and 10% Hispanic, the latter the highest figure of any Georgia district. In 2000 the precincts now in the 13th voted 57%–41% for Al Gore over George W. Bush.

The congressman from the new 13th District is David Scott, a Democrat elected in 2002. Born in rural South Carolina, he grew up around the country—in Scranton, Pennsylvania, Scarsdale, New York, and Daytona Beach, Florida. He graduated from Florida A&M and the Wharton

School of Finance. He was elected to the Georgia House in 1974 and to the Georgia Senate in 1982; there he chaired the Rules Committee. He sponsored a state law requiring a moment of silence for reflection and prayer at the start of each school day and a law requiring background checks before gun purchases. Since 1979 he has owned the Dayn-Mark Advertising Company, which creates and places radio, television and print advertising. He has also has produced television programs and received four Emmys for the PBS production of "Langston!", a tribute to the poetry of Langston Hughes.

In 2002, Scott decided to run for the new 13th District seat, though he lives in Inman Park, near Midtown Atlanta. It seemed obvious that in this heavily Democratic district the Democratic primary would be decisive. Four other Democrats ran, the best known of whom was former Democratic state Chairman David Worley, whom some remembered as the candidate who nearly defeated Newt Gingrich in the old 6th District in 1990. Scott, however, was far more familiar to most voters, after more than a quarter-century in the legislature. He is also the brother-in-law of baseball's home run king Hank Aaron, who was co-chairman of his campaign. Scott brought his advertising expertise to the campaign, plastering the Interstates with eye-catching billboards. His chief competitors, Worley and state Senator Greg Hecht of Clayton County, were both white, and ran ads against each other; racial appeals seem to have played little part in the campaign. Scott won the August 20 primary without a runoff, with 54% of the vote and at least 50% in every county but one. The son of a minister and grandson of a deacon, Scott credited God and said that "a divine hand worked with us." He won the general election 60%–40%—not a huge margin, but a decisive one. He lost five counties in the eastern part of the district by narrow margins, while carrying Clayton County, which cast 36% of the votes, by a 67%–31%.

Scott has had more than two decades' experience in business and nearly three decades' experience in representing multiracial, multiethnic constituencies—interesting credentials to bring to the Congressional Black Caucus and the House. He joined the Blue Dogs group of moderate Democrats.

★ HAWAII ★

Trouble in paradise was the story of Hawaii in the 1990s. Change in paradise was the story of Hawaii in 2002. Hawaii missed out on the economic boom of the 1990s, falling behind while the rest of the nation surged ahead. Gross state product declined from 1992 to 1998, and the number of jobs peaked in 1991, then fell 4% by 1997, and rose only because of government jobs. Hawaii's population grew 9% in the decade, but the number of private sector jobs declined 1%. Foreign investment plummeted, bankruptcies zoomed, home sales dropped and welfare caseloads increased. Labor force participation declined as the number of young adults fell and the number of elderly rose: Hawaii seems to be getting old and tired. The early 1990s recession in California and the decade-long recession in Japan had a devastating effect on the mainstay of Hawaii's economy— tourism. The number of visitors peaked at 7 million in 1990, dropped to 6.1 million in 1993, and did not reach 7 million again until 2000: it was 6.9 million in 2001 and estimated at 6.4 million in 2002: September 11 really hurt. Sugar plantations closed down—Wailua Sugar in Oahu, Hamakua Sugar on the Big Island, the McBryde plantation in Kauai, plus the Dole pineapple plantation in Lanai. Agriculture, Hawaii's economic mainstay before tourism, employed just 12,000 Hawaiians in 2000. The military and the federal government have also been important to Hawaii's economy, but the number of military personnel and civilian federal employees fell from 97,800 in 1988 to 67,750 in 2000. State government remained expensive—Hawaii has by far the largest number of state employees per capita—and dominated by public employee unions. Hawaii has been strongly Democratic since just after statehood in 1960, and since 1962 elected a series of Democratic governors of the same Democratic machine. But hard times led to voter rebellion. In 1998 Republican Linda Lingle lost to Governor Ben Cayetano by just 50%–49%, and in 2002 Lingle beat Lieutenant Governor Mazie Hirono by 52%–47%. The question now is whether Lingle, facing a still heavily Democratic legislature, can turn around Hawaii's sluggish economy

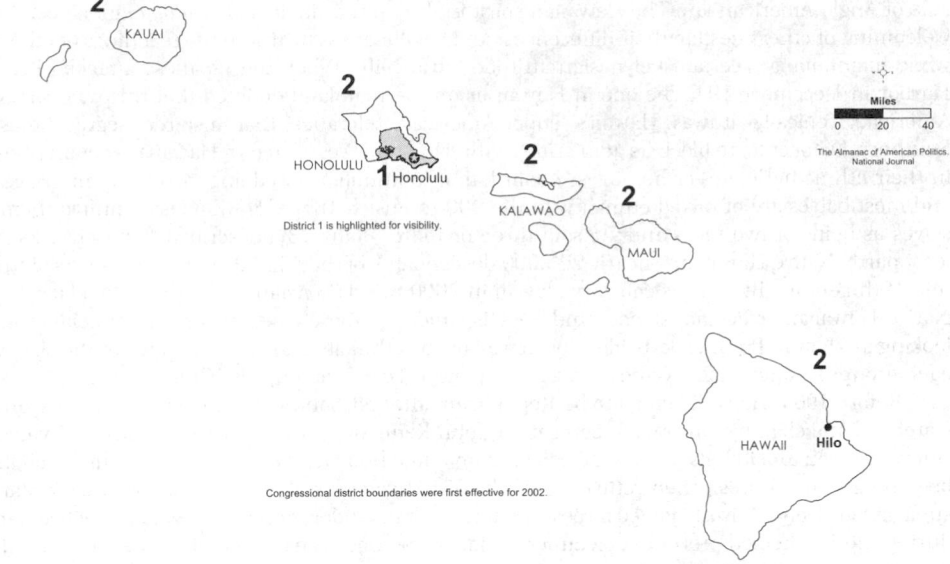

2 KAUAI

2

HONOLULU **1** Honolulu

District 1 is highlighted for visibility.

2 KALAWAO

2

MAUI

Miles
0   20   40

The Almanac of American Politics,
National Journal

2

HAWAII   Hilo

Congressional district boundaries were first effective for 2002.

and at the same time preserve the defining characteristics that have made Hawaii strong and tolerant in the six decades after Pearl Harbor.

Hawaii was settled only about a thousand years ago by Polynesians who paddled across vast Pacific expanses in small outrigger canoes; when Captain Cook came here in 1776, he found his Maori interpreter from New Zealand could understand Hawaiian. On these geologically young islands, teeming with food and seldom inconvenienced by bad weather, Hawaiians built a fierce civilization, with harsh taboos and cannibalism as well as alluring music and dance. The islands were united politically in 1779 by King Kamehameha I, who ate one of his rivals and maintained the old culture. In 1819, within a year of his death, his consort Kaahumanu outlawed the Hawaiian religious taboos and welcomed the American missionary Hiram Bingham. New England missionaries and their trader cousins came—while British and Russian ships occasionally put into port—and established the predominant culture. By the 1850s, laborers from China, Japan, Portugal and the Philippines streamed in to work the sugar and pineapple plantations. American planters and businessmen bridled at the caprices of the royal family and, in January 1893, with the help of U.S. Marines, ousted Queen Liliuokalani from the Iolani Palace and called on the United States to annex Hawaii. President Grover Cleveland demurred, and Hawaii for five years was a republic; President William McKinley annexed it in July 1898.

This history is a source of regret for some; an *Onipa'a* ceremony remembering Liliuokalani's overthrow was staged by John Waihee, the first governor of native Hawaiian descent, in January 1993, with the American flag conspicuously absent; in 1998, native Hawaiians staged a protest demonstration on the Mall in Washington. Yet Hawaii is a civilization both American and Pacific, which has created a better life for its citizens than almost any island or native commonwealth. Its ethnic mixing began a century ago when disease reduced the native Hawaiians to 45,000; they shared Liliuokalani's Hawaii with 3,000 Americans, 20,000 Chinese and 25,000 Japanese. Hawaii was well on it way to being "the gathering place of peoples," as Walter McDougall called it in his history of the North Pacific, *Let the Sea Make a Noise*.

To that Americana, each group has made a positive contribution. The Asian migrant laborers brought traditions of hard work, family loyalty and group solidarity that found expression most vividly in the performance of the 442d "Go for Broke" Regimental Combat Team, made up mostly of sons of Japanese immigrants, which became the most decorated unit in U.S. military history. The Yankee spirit has been evident in Hawaii's commercial success and in its attachment to the rule of Anglo-American law. The Hawaiian spirit is alive in the vitality of the *aloha* ambience, the welcoming of others despite their differences, and a willingness to absorb the teachings of others while maintaining a certain Polynesian attitude toward life. When the Japanese attacked Pearl Harbor in December 1941, no one in Hawaii or on the mainland doubted that this was part of America. Ironically, it was Hawaii's super-American tolerance that inspired segregationist Southern Democrats to block its admission to the Union for years. Today, Hawaiians retain pride in their ethnic heritage—or heritages: About half of non-military weddings are "out" marriages and most babies are of mixed ethnicity. In the 2000 Census, 18% of Hawaiians identified themselves as being of two races and 7% said three or more. Some 23% described themselves as at least partly Native Hawaiian—nearly 225,000 descendants of the 45,000 Native Hawaiians of the mid 19th century. By Census category Hawaii in 2000 was 41% Asian, 23% white, 2% black, 9% Native Hawaiian or Pacific Islander and 7% Hispanic. But those categories seem artificial when looking at Hawaii. Local experts identify Hawaiians by ethnicity and give estimates of the size of each group: Hawaiian 22%, Caucasian 21%, Japanese 18%, Filipino 12%, Chinese 5%.

Before 1960, Hawaii seemed to be Republican; after all, southern Democrats were blocking statehood and championing racial segregation. John Kennedy carried it in 1960 by just 115 votes. But from 1962 to 2002, its politics have been dominated by a Democratic machine which had its beginning in the 1950s, when returning World War II veterans like Daniel Inouye, Spark Matsunaga and George Ariyoshi joined forces with former mainlander John Burns, who as a policeman during the war helped prevent persecution of Japanese Americans. They allied themselves with the then-powerful International Longshoremen's and Warehousemen's Union, and cemented the allegiance of Japanese American voters. The Burns-Inouye machine built on the grievances against the *haole* (a pejorative word for white) owners of the big companies and triumphed. Inouye was elected as a Democrat to the House in 1959 and to the Senate in 1962; Burns was elected governor in 1962, and for 40 years the office was passed down in lineal succession to George Ariyoshi, John Waihee and Benjamin Cayetano—a balanced ticket, of Japanese, native Hawaiian and Filipino descent. As agriculture and the docks became less important, the ILWU's power waned; it has been replaced by the public employee unions that are strongly Democratic. Voting has long tended to run along ethnic lines. Japanese Americans, used to working in organizations in unions and government, have tended to be the heart of the Democratic Party; whites, with relatively high incomes, tend toward Republicans; Filipinos, often in menial jobs, are heavily Democratic; Chinese, somewhat less so; Native Hawaiians, are heavily Democratic but not as likely to be active in politics.

Over the years this machine has built a large government. Despite some 1990s tax cuts, Hawaii had the third highest per capita tax burden in the nation in 2000 and by far the highest number of state and local employees per capita. This is centralized government: Hawaii has five counties (with one, Honolulu, covering 72% of the population), one school district, and one state-wide health care plan. And it is thick with regulations; as *Forbes* put it, "Doing business in Honolulu becomes nearly equivalent to suicide." It can be ridiculously generous: For a while, Hawaii paid workmen's comp to workers who were traumatized by being laid off. The culture created by one-party control and a large state apparatus seems to be characterized in a phrase of Cayetano's, "You've got to support your friends and you have to punish your enemies."

Eight public and private entities own 69% of Hawaii's land: The federal government 16%, the state 29%, and six private landowners 24%. The Bishop Estate (Mrs. Bishop was the last surviving descendant of Kamehameha I) owns 9%. A 1984 U.S. Supreme Court decision upheld a Hawaii law forcing the estate to sell land held in 99-year leaseholds when they expire, and with the resulting cash the estate has made vast investments. Its total net worth is some $10 billion, and its purpose is to fund the Kamehameha Schools for Native Hawaiians. Until 1999 its five trustees were appointed by the state Supreme Court, which is to say the Democratic machine, and paid more than $900,000 a year. But in 1998 the five trustees were embroiled in lawsuits: A criminal charge of breach of fiduciary duty was brought against one; an ouster suit was brought against four; one trustee sought the ouster of two others. Meanwhile, students at the schools charged that one trustee undermined the headmaster's authority and created an oppressive atmosphere on campus with her arbitrary and intimidating actions. All five ultimately had to settle a lawsuit, brought by the state attorney general's office, for $20.1 million for excessive compensation and mismanagement of the estate. For 2000, a probate judge picked the five trustees from seven nominees found by a court appointed committee. Salaries were slashed to $97,000, terms are limited, and the 116-year-old Bishop Estate is now called the Kamehameha Schools Estate.

The sluggish economy, high taxes and insider control all worked to undermine the hold of the Democratic machine on voters. The opposition to the machine, often carried on in primaries or in the form of third party candidacies by longtime Honolulu Mayor Frank Fasi, coalesced in 1998 in the person of Republican Linda Lingle.

Lingle, then mayor of Maui, ran a vigorous campaign calling for reform of Hawaii's swollen government and led for a while in polls but Cayetano, the incumbent who had already cut taxes and government payrolls somewhat, hung on for a 50%–49% victory. Two years later Republicans made gains in state legislative races; in 2002, Lingle ran again. This time the Democrats were in some disarray. Term limits prevented Cayetano from running again and the desire for change was too great: Lingle won 52%–47%. Yet union-backed Democrats made gains in both the primary and general elections. It was unclear whether Lingle could carry out her detailed platform or get Hawaii out of its economic stagnation.

Hawaii still has great potential. It is still the favorite tourist destination of the Japanese, who throng to the King Kamehameha Hula Competition every June. It still has great potential as a central Pacific emporium—the stability of the American flag and dollar, the heritage of tolerance and openness to diversity that is second to none, the wondrous climate and physical beauty of these islands. The last is almost too good: Hawaii's island ecology means there were few species here when Captain Cook landed and that many of them were vulnerable to predators and pests. It has been estimated that Hawaii has lost 80% of its original bird species and one-third of its plants; it has 317 species listed as endangered, more than any other state. To preserve those that are left, Hawaiians have been chopping down miconia trees, whose dense cover prevents native trees from growing, shooting wild goats, poisoning ants (pre-Cook Hawaii had no social insects or snakes), shooing away tiny coqui frogs whose croaking can reach 100 decibels and rappelling down cliffs to get pollen to pollinate trees now scarce. A special threat is the brown tree snake that has infested Guam and destroyed many native plants and animals there; after a typhoon in Guam, Hawaiians carefully examined every incoming plane from the island and killed brown tree snakes found in the landing gear.

Hawaii may face problems also from the native Hawaiian sovereignty movement. Consciousness of native ancestry grew in the 1990s: Many more Hawaiians claimed Native Hawaiian ancestry in the 2000 Census than before, partly because of the new option of claiming multiple races. More people are learning the Hawaiian language. The centennials of the overthrow of Queen Liliuokalani (1993) and of U.S. annexation of Hawaii (1998) inspired demonstrations and expressions of bitterness over the end of the Hawaiian kingdom; a Hawaiian who claims he is still living under the pre-1893 constitution has brought a case in the World Court. A state sovereignty commission met for two years and in 1996 sponsored a referendum of native Hawaiians; 73% of those eligible (with some native blood) voted yes on the question, "Shall the Hawaiian people elect delegates to propose a native Hawaiian government?" The problem is that no one is quite sure what sovereignty means. A few activists have called for independence; others seek a commonwealth status something like Puerto Rico's (though in Puerto Rico support for statehood has been rising). Some want Native Hawaiians to be a "nation within a nation," like various North American Indian tribes. But Native Hawaiians live scattered all over the Islands, and few if any Native Hawaiians live in aboriginal communities.

Hawaii's officeholders take a typically tolerant view. Cayetano said sovereignty will be fine if it is "acceptable to the non-Hawaiians, as well as the United States government"; the four-member Hawaiian congressional delegation promised to abide by the results of the referendum, and in the 106th Congress introduced a bill which would give Native Hawaiians the same status as most mainland Indian tribes and a "government-to-government" relation with the federal government. The U.S. Supreme Court took another view. In a case argued by Theodore Olson, who later became George W. Bush's solicitor general, the Court in February 2000 declared unconstitutional the 1978 Hawaii constitutional amendment setting up Native-Hawaiian-only elections for the Office of Hawaiian Affairs, which administers a $400 million trust fund. "It demeans the dignity and worth of a person to be judged by ancestry instead of by his or her own merit," the Court wrote. That decision casts doubt on other provisions of the 1978 amendment, including the Hawaiian Homes Commission and the recognition of native gathering rights on private property. The bill granting Native Hawaiians Indian status was passed in the U.S. House in September 2000, but was not acted on by the Senate when it adjourned in December 2000; its advocates considered it effectively killed by the election of George W. Bush, though it was reintroduced in the 108th Congress.

The People

Pop. 2000:	1,211,537
Pop. 1990:	1,108,229
Change 1990–2000:	Up 9.3%
Change 1980–1990:	Up 14.9%
% of U.S. total:	0.4%
Pop. rank:	42d of 50
Area size:	10,931 sq. mi.
State Native:	56.9%
Non-citizen:	7.0%

Language

English: 65.7%	Asian: 29.1%
Spanish: 2.7%	

Race/Ethnic Origin

277,091	22.9%	White
20,829	1.7%	Black
494,149	40.8%	Asian
2,539	0.2%	Native Am.
108,441	9.0%	Hawaiian
218,700	18.1%	Two + races
2,089	0.2%	Other
87,699	7.2%	Hisp. Origin

Ancestry

German: 4.6%	Irish: 3.5%
English: 3.4%	Portuguese: 3.2%
Italian: 1.4%	

Military veterans: 120,587 (13.1%)

WWII: 17.6%	Korea: 12.0%
Vietnam: 34.5%	Gulf War: 13.2%

Most populous cities:

1. Honolulu CDP	371,657
2. Hilo CDP	40,759
3. Kailua CDP	36,513
4. Kaneohe CDP	34,970
5. Waipahu CDP	33,108

Urban population: 91.6%
Rural population: 8.4%

Education

H.S. Grad:	84.6%
College Grad:	26.2%

Industry

Agri: 2.3%		Con: 6.0%
Fin: 7.0%		Info: 2.5%
Mfg: 9.8%		Prof: 28.5%
Public: 8.1%		Trade: 15.4%
Other: 20.5%		

Occupation

Blue collar: 17.5%	White collar: 60.3%
Gray collar: 22.2%	

Work Sector

Private: 70.9%		Govt: 21.0%
Self: 7.6%		Family: 0.4%

Unemployment: 5.9%

Household Income

<15k: 12.5%	15-35k: 21.9%
35-50k: 15.7%	50-100k: 33.3%
100-150k: 11.1%	>150k: 5.4%

Median: $49,820
Poverty status: 10.7%

Home Value

<50k: 2.3%	50-100k: 7.4%	100-200k: 26.8%	200-300k: 27.6%
300-500k: 26.3%	>500k: 9.6%	Median: $249,300	

Legislature

Senate	20 D 5 R
House	36 D 15 R

Legislative Term Limits: No

Registered Voters

No party registration

Presidential politics   Hawaii's presidential voting over the years has been the product of two, sometimes countervailing, forces. One is the Islands' historic preference for the Democratic party. This helps explain why Hawaii voted Democratic when few other states did in 1980 and 1988. The other is an inclination to support incumbents in a state that takes patriotism very seriously, in part because the patriotism of so many of its citizens was once unjustly questioned and in part because, in these heavily fortified Pacific islands, foreign threats may seem more menacing. This helps explain why Hawaii supported Ronald Reagan solidly in 1984 and came close to voting for Gerald Ford in 1976, though it wasn't nearly enough to help George H. W. Bush in 1992: Ross Perot's military background, and the presence of Hawaiian Orson Swindle

2000 Presidential Vote

Gore (D)	205,286	(56%)
Bush (R)	137,845	(37%)
Nader (Green)	21,623	(6%)
Other	3,197	(1%)

1996 Presidential Vote

Clinton (D)	205,012	(57%)
Dole (R)	113,943	(32%)
Perot (I)	27,362	(8%)
Other	13,807	(4%)

among his top leaders, gave him 14% and helped Bill Clinton carry Hawaii 48%–37%. In 1996 and 2000, as in 1968 and 1980, both those forces were moving in the same direction, and Hawaii voted 57%–32% for Clinton and a nearly identical 56%–37% for Al Gore. In 2004, they will be in tension, and at a time when Hawaii has just elected a Republican governor, though few observers of national politics expect Hawaii to vote for George W. Bush.

Hawaii chooses presidential delegates by caucus. Sometimes insurgent candidates have been able to swamp thinly-attended meetings and win, as Jesse Jackson and Pat Robertson did in 1988. Since then Hawaii's caucusgoers have gone for the frontrunners.

Congressional districting Hawaii has two congressional districts: The 1st includes urban Honolulu (city elections now cover all of Oahu) and extends westward to Pearl Harbor and the rural area beyond; the 2d includes the rest of Oahu and the Neighbor Islands. Both districts have long elected Democrats and, despite the death of the 2d District's Patsy Mink in September 2002, both continued to do so in 2002 and 2003. The Democratic legislature made minor and politically insignificant changes for 2002.

108th Congress Lineup
2 D
107th Congress Lineup
2 D

Governor

Linda Lingle (R)

Elected 2002, term expires Dec. 2006, 1st term; b. June 4, 1953, St. Louis, MO; home, Honolulu; CA St. U. at Northridge, B.A. 1975; Jewish; divorced.

Elected Office: Maui Cnty. Cncl., 1980–90; Mayor, Maui Cnty., 1990–98.

Professional Career: Founder and editor, *Moloka'i Free Press*, 1977–80.

Office: State Capitol, Executive Chambers, Honolulu, 96813, 808-586-0034; Fax: 808-586-0006; Web site: www.hawaii.gov/gov.

Election Results

2002 general	Linda Lingle (R)	197,009	(52%)
	Mazie Hirono (D)	179,647	(47%)
2002 primary	Linda Lingle (R)	70,808	(90%)
	John Carroll (R)	7,616	(10%)
1998 general	Benjamin J. Cayetano (D)	204,206	(50%)
	Linda Lingle (R)	198,952	(49%)
	Other	4,398	(1%)

Linda Lingle, governor of Hawaii, is the first Republican elected since 1959 and the first woman ever. She grew up in the St. Louis area and Los Angeles's San Fernando Valley; after graduating from California State University at Northridge in 1975, she moved to Hawaii, where her father owned a Ford dealership. She worked for the Teamsters and Hotel Workers unions in Honolulu and then founded the *Moloka'i Free Press* on that island, which is part of Maui County. In 1980 she was elected to the Maui Council and for six years represented Molokai and for four more held an at-large seat. She was elected mayor of Maui in 1990 over former Mayor and House Speaker Elmer Carvalho and reelected in 1994 over a 40-year member of the Council. There she worked to implement performance-based budgeting; in her years as mayor, Maui gained jobs while the rest of Hawaii lost them.

In 1998 she ran for governor. She hailed what she called "the Maui miracle"—job growth in at least one part of Hawaii—and said, "It's time for a change, and change is about joining the other 49 states with economic revitalization that is taking place across the country." Lingle led in polls throughout the campaign, but incumbent Ben Cayetano appealed to Hawaii's ethnic groups and Democratic tradition. In August, Lingle accused the Cayetano campaign of spreading the false rumor that she is gay (she has been divorced twice). Senator Daniel Inouye said later, "I would prefer to have a governor who's had a family. Ben's my man." The outcome may have been determined by Lingle's decision to take state matching funds and abide by a $2.7 million spending limit; she was heavily outspent by Cayetano in the last two weeks. Cayetano won 50%–49%. He carried heavily Filipino and Japanese American areas, while Lingle carried 21 of the 29 state House districts where whites are the largest ethnic group.

Lingle immediately set out to run again. She became Republican state chairman, traveled around the state and built an organization much stronger than what she had in 1998. In 2000 Republicans made notable gains in state House seats. She raised plenty of money, much of it from the mainland and changed the mindset in Hawaii that Democratic victories were inevitable. In the meantime, Cayetano struggled with budget problems and in April 2001 teachers in the state's single public school district went out on strike seeking a 22% raise. More Democrats were caught up in scandals. Members of the Honolulu Council were accused of theft and other Democrats appeared to be involved in a kickback scheme at Honolulu International Airport. Critics of Cayetano were intimidated: A flea market owner had his land condemned for a stadium, the head of the state's Tax Foundation was kicked off a state commission, a Republican state senator was put through an ethics investigation for issuing a critical press release on his personal stationery and a reporter for *Pacific Business News* was fired after Cayetano complained about an accurate story about a leaked governor's task force report that found a pattern of retribution and intimidation of business owners by state agencies.

Lingle led in the polls from the start. She set out a detailed platform with specific pledges: Distribution of land to Native Hawaiians entitled to Hawaiian homelands leases; a 50% cut in education bureaucracy expenses; allowing special education parents to use vouchers in private schools; dividing the state into seven school districts, with seven locally elected school boards; ending the 4% tax on medical services; tax credits to partially offset the 4% tax on food (tourists, you see, would still pay it). She was by no means conservative on all issues; she called for 20% of energy to come from renewable sources by 2020 and backed Native Hawaiian groups' claims for some form of sovereignty. She favored parental consent for abortions and a partial-birth abortion ban, but was not against abortion altogether. She called for a financial audit of state government and for performance-based budgeting. But the chief theme of her campaign was change. "We've got to break our reputation as a place where you've got to know someone to get things done."

Democrats were in disarray. The initial party insider favorite, Honolulu Mayor Jeremy Harris, was accused of violating fundraising laws and was ruled by a court to be ineligible to run until he resigned as mayor in March 2002. He suspended his campaign for two months, and then withdrew from the race in May. Lieutenant Governor Mazie Hirono, who had been running for mayor, immediately entered the race for governor. She was part of the ruling Democratic machine, and there were two candidates who were running as outsiders. Then-state Representative Ed Case, a cousin of Steve Case, then head of AOL Time Warner (the Cases are an old Hawaii family), ran as "an independent, moderate, clean candidate who is change-oriented." He called for changes in public schools, privatization of some services and changes in collective bargaining with public employee unions. He said that Hirono was a spear-carrier for the status quo with no plan for meaningful change. Also running was Andy Anderson, a former Republican who lost two previous races for governor and who had also served 20 years in the legislature. Both Case and Anderson were regarded as archenemies by the Democratic machine and the public employees union, and they campaigned furiously for Hirono. It was just barely enough. She won the September 21 primary with 41% of the vote to 39% for Case and 18% for Anderson. Democratic turnout was down 8% from 1994, the last year with seriously contested primaries, while Republican turnout, even though Lingle did not have a strong opponent, was up 44%.

Hirono had an appealing life story. She was born in Japan and raised by a single mother who came to Hawaii to escape an abusive husband. She did well at the University of Hawaii and Georgetown law school and soon went into politics: She was elected to the state House in 1980 and served there until elected Lieutenant Governor in 1994. As a legislator she worked for the law that forced big landowners like the Bishop Estate to sell land rather than lease it; as Lieutenant Governor she worked to set up a state-owned workmen's comp insurer. When Lingle ran an ad highlighting Hawaii's poor test scores, low rate of job creation and growing poverty, Hirono said that Lingle was "always putting our people down." But it was the Democrats who stayed on the defensive on corruption. And Hirono was far behind Lingle in fundraising. With the Democrats no longer seen as inevitable winners, and after the Harris fundraising charges, many business interests were no longer ponying up for the party that had held the governorship for 40 years. Ethnic balance for once helped Republicans; they had a ticket with a white Caucasian and a Native Hawaiian, Lingle and retired Judge James "Duke" Aiona, while the Democrats had a ticket with two Japanese Americans, Hirono and former state Senator Matt Matsunaga.

Hirono did manage to narrow the gap by appealing to the party loyalties and by now ancient memories that had rallied late victories for Cayetano in 1998 and Waihee in 1986. Senator Daniel Inouye told the Democratic State Convention, "We're fighting for our political lives!" But it all wasn't quite enough. Lingle brought in a heavy supporter in October, when she ran an ad showing her endorsement by 600-pound Hawaiian sumo wrestler Konishiki; she won 52%–47%. She carried Oahu, which cast 70% of the vote, 53%–46% and ran only narrowly ahead in Maui, 50%–47%, and the Big Island, 51%–47%; she lost only in Kauai, which cast only 6% of the votes, by 58%–41%.

Lingle has a daunting task as governor. The legislature seems likely to be hostile; public employee unions had beaten Democrats who did not vote their way in the primary and Republicans in the general. But not all of her program required legislative action, and she promised to proceed immediately with her financial audit. And the momentum she had after ending 40 years of Democratic rule could impose some restraint on her opponents. Moreover, she appoints almost all top state officials, including the attorney general, and she can promote Republicans to positions of high visibility and crack down on corruption.

Senior Senator

Daniel Inouye (D)

Elected 1962, seat up 2004, 7th term; b. Sept. 7, 1924, Honolulu; home, Honolulu; U. of HI, B.A. 1950, George Washington U., J.D. 1952; United Methodist; married (Margaret).

Military Career: Army, 1943–47 (WWII).

Elected Office: HI House of Reps., 1954–58; HI Senate, 1958–59; U.S. House of Reps., 1959–62.

Professional Career: Honolulu Dpty. Public Prosecutor, 1953–54.

DC Office: 722 HSOB, 20510, 202-224-3934; Fax: 202-224-6747; Web site: inouye.senate.gov.

State Offices: Hilo, 808-935-0844; Honolulu, 808-541-2542; Kauai, 808-245-4611; Kona, 808-935-0844; Maui, 808-242-9702; Molokai, 808-642-0203.

Committees: *Appropriations*: Commerce, Justice, State & Judiciary; Defense (RMM); Foreign Operations; Homeland Security; Labor, HHS & Education; Military Construction. *Commerce, Science & Transportation*: Aviation; Communications; Oceans, Fisheries & Coast Guard; Surface Transportation & Merchant Marine (RMM). *Indian Affairs* (RMM). *Rules & Administration*.

Group Ratings

	ADA	ACLU	AFS	LCV	CON	ITIC	NTU	COC	ACU	NTLC	CHC
2002	80	50	100	71	45	38	15	41	0	0	—
2001	90	—	100	88	—	—	6	43	9	—	0

National Journal Ratings

	2001 LIB	—	2001 CONS		2002 LIB	—	2002 CONS
Economic	78%	—	22%		70%	—	29%
Social	81%	—	8%		67%	—	32%
Foreign	74%	—	14%		79%	—	19%

Key Votes of the 107th Congress

1. Approve Bush Tax Cuts	N	5. Confirm Ashcroft as AG	N	9. Bar Coop. with Intl. Court	N
2. Expand Patients' Rights	Y	6. Bar Gays in the Boy Scouts	N	10. Trade Promotion Authority	*
3. Campaign Finance Reform	Y	7. $ for Hate Crime Prosecution	Y	11. Authorize Force in Iraq	N
4. Permit ANWR Development	Y	8. Overseas Military Abortions	Y	12. Homeland Sec. Dept. Union	Y

Election Results

1998 general	Daniel Inouye (D)	315,252	(79%)	($1,375,601)
	Crystal Young (R)	70,964	(18%)	
	Other	11,908	(3%)	
1998 primary	Daniel Inouye (D)	108,891	(93%)	
	Richard Thompson (D)	8,468	(7%)	
1992 general	Daniel Inouye (D)	208,266	(57%)	($3,515,722)
	Rick Reed (R)	97,928	(27%)	($438,851)
	Linda B. Martin (Green)	49,921	(14%)	($6,687)
	Other	7,547	(2%)	

Prior Winning Percentages: 1986 (74%); 1980 (78%); 1974 (83%); 1968 (83%); 1962 (69%); 1960 House (74%); 1959 House (68%)

The largest figure in Hawaii's public life remains Senator Daniel K. Inouye, who has held elective office here since Hawaii attained statehood in 1959, and before. Inouye (pronounced *in-NO-ay*) grew up in Honolulu, the son of Japanese immigrants; his ambition was to become a surgeon. He served in the 442d Regimental Combat Team in World War II, in which capacity he earned 15 medals and citations and, in the last days of the war, lost his right arm. Unsure of what to do, recovering in a Michigan veterans' hospital, he asked a Kansas veteran whose right arm had been shattered what his plans were; the man said he was going to law school, would run for the legislature and "when the opportunity presents itself, I am going to Congress": It was Bob Dole. They served together two years in the House and 28 in the Senate. Inouye graduated from the University of Hawaii and George Washington University Law School, then became a leader of a group of young veterans who took over Hawaii's creaking Democratic party. He was elected to the territorial legislature in 1954, the House in 1959, and the Senate in 1962. He was keynoter at the turbulent 1968 Democratic National Convention, a tenacious member of the Senate Watergate Committee in 1973–74 and the first chairman of the Senate Intelligence Committee, in 1976. Inouye believes in the Senate, the Democratic Party, Hawaii, the armed services, and Native Americans—among other things. He is the third most senior member of the Senate, after Robert Byrd and Edward Kennedy. In June 2000 he was awarded the Congressional Medal of Honor.

Inouye is chairman of the Appropriations Defense Subcommittee and the second ranking Democrat on Appropriations; the committee's ranking Republican is Ted Stevens of Alaska, which gives enormous clout to two senators in office since the 1960s from the two states most recently admitted to the Union, both with their own special claims on the federal government. Inouye's voting record has generally been very liberal, but not always. On foreign and defense issues he is close to the center of the Senate. He and Hawaii colleague Daniel Akaka were two of the four Democrats who joined all Republicans in 1998 in seeking to deploy a ballistic missile defense system; the Clinton administration's opposition to deployment was based in part on an intelligence estimate that there will be no missile threat within the next 10 years to the continental 48 states—which seems to exclude Hawaii and Alaska from the "common defense" the Constitution promises. He has opposed the Bush administration also on occasion, as when in January 2003 he and Stevens characterized Defense Secretary Donald Rumsfeld's decision to defer funding for two Army Stryker combat brigades as contrary to laws passed by Congress. He took great umbrage in September 2002 when George W. Bush, speaking about the homeland security bill while campaigning in New Jersey, said, "The House responded, but the Senate is more interested in special interests in Washington and not interested in the security of the people." Perhaps taking this as a comment about those who opposed military action in Iraq, Inouye said, "This is a time when we should be working together, debating this issue. It is American to question the president. It is American to debate the issue."

Inouye has long used his seat on Appropriations to fund projects he finds worthy, from his alma mater of George Washington University to native Hawaiian education. In 1999 Hawaii received $800 million in federal spending, and in 2000, $1.25 billion, most of it from the military budget, which is to say it passes through Inouye's subcommittee. In 2002 the defense appropriation included $257 million for projects in Hawaii, including $202 million to refurbish Pearl

Harbor. That year also saw the opening of a $56 million FAA Honolulu Control Facility which gathered together facilities scattered over the metropolitan area. He helped to persuade the Navy that the *U.S.S. Missouri's* final berth would be at Pearl Harbor and got $4.5 million for the Smithsonian Astrophysical Observatory at Hilo.

He has proudly earmarked projects for Hawaii in the defense appropriations bill; the December 2000 bill included $41 million for ocean resources and marine research—$1 million to the Pacific Coastal Services Cooperative Center, $8 million to convert the Adventurous, a mothballed Navy vessel, to a high-endurance fisheries and oceanographic research vessel, $13.5 million for the East-West Center at University of Hawaii. Like his colleague and friend Ted Stevens, Inouye takes a kind of proprietary interest in the public policy of his home area, with a sense of responsibility for its long-term development and character. Seemingly small matters can get Inouye's attention: in 2001 he sponsored a bill to exempt from the airline ticket tax the fees charged to shuttle military personnel on helicopters to cleanup on Kahoolawe.

Inouye chaired the Indian Affairs Committee from 1989–94 and again in 2001, and was moved by their tragic history. He described his reaction: "By God, did we do all these things? We should be embarrassed and ashamed of ourselves." After the BIA gave tribal recognition to the Eastern Pequots of Connecticut, Christopher Dodd and Joe Lieberman tried to get a one-year moratorium on recognition of new tribes. Inouye vigorously opposed them and prevailed 80–15; one newspaper noted that Inouye's counsel was married to the chief counsel of the Eastern Pequots. Inouye evidently sees many analogies between the condition of mainland Indians and Native Hawaiians. He was a co-sponsor of the 1993 law in which the United States apologized for overthrowing the Hawaiian monarchy. He supported the Hawaiian Homes Commission Act and in 2000 finally secured funding for Native Hawaiians purchasing property in the Home Lands, the 200,000 acres set aside in 1920 for a permanent homeland for Native Hawaiians. He secured reauthorization of Native Hawaiian health care programs in 2000, but did not succeed in giving it entitlement status. On the heated issue of Native Hawaiian sovereignty, some Native Hawaiian activists consider him lukewarm. In October 1999, Office of Hawaiian Affairs Trustee Mililani Trask attacked him with vile insults; Inouye said he was saddened. In 2000 and 2002, he and colleague Daniel Akaka did not succeed in getting through the Senate Akaka's bill granting Indian tribe status to Native Hawaiians and a "government-to-government" relation with the federal government. Some Republican senators objected, and its prospects seem dim while George W. Bush is president; the measure was reintroduced again in February 2003.

On the Commerce Committee, Inouye was long involved in communications issues and tends to favor government regulation over markets. He backed cable reregulation and was pleased that the Telecommunications Act of 1996 imposed a competition checklist for local services on the Regional Bells before they could enter the long-distance market. In June 2001 Inouye substituted for Harry Reid (who recused himself) in the uncongenial post of chairman of the Ethics Committee and presided over the hearings on Bob Torricelli's acceptance of gifts and loans from David Chang. In July 2002 the committee "severely admonished" Torricelli, but declined to make public the testimony. Inouye acted well before the election, taking the unexceptionable view that action just before an election would be unfair. But the testimony was made public in September in a separate lawsuit and had a devastating effect on Torricelli's political fortunes.

Honolulu is a long two flights from Washington, and Inouye's local influence has varied, but is generally great. He is part of the faction of Hawaii's Democratic party that held the governorship from 1962 to 2002. In 2002 he vigorously supported Lieutenant Governor Mazie Hirono in her nearly successful attempt to extend this 40-year string. "We are fighting for our political lives!" he bellowed to the state Democratic convention. And he seemed to be criticizing her primary rivals, including Ed Case who is now 2d District congressman, who campaigned for change in state government, when he said, "We cannot allow stupid and self-serving members of our party to tarnish our accomplishments." He has complained that the Bush administration was not consulting him on Hawaii judicial nominations. Inouye has always been re-elected by wide margins. His greatest trouble came in 1992, when Republican Rick Reed ran an ad with tapes of a woman who was long Inouye's barber making charges about events many years before. On Election Day, Inouye won with a much reduced percentage, 57%, to 27% for Reed and 14% for the Green

Party's Linda Martin. In 1998 he faced less controversy. In October, Republican Crystal Young alleged that actress Shirley MacLaine implanted electromagnetic needles in her. Inouye won 79%–18%. He seems likely to win re-election again, if he runs, in 2004; if Inouye does not run again, Army Chief of Staff Eric Shinseki has been mentioned as a possible candidate for the seat.

Junior Senator

Daniel Akaka (D)

Appointed May 1990, seat up 2006, 2d term; b. Sept. 11, 1924, Honolulu; home, Honolulu; U. of HI, B.Ed. 1952, M.A. 1966; Congregationalist; married (Mary Mildred).

Military Career: Army Corps of Engineers, 1945–47 (WWII).

Elected Office: U.S. House of Reps., 1976–90.

Professional Career: Public schl. teacher, principal & admin., 1953–71; Dir., HI Office of Econ. Oppor., 1971–74; Asst., HI Gov. Ariyoshi, 1975–76; Dir., Progressive Neighborhoods Program, 1975–76.

DC Office: 141 HSOB, 20510, 202-224-6361; Fax: 202-224-2126; Web site: akaka.senate.gov.

State Offices: Hilo, 808-935-1114; Honolulu, 808-522-8970.

Committees: *Armed Services*: Airland; Emerging Threats & Capabilities; Readiness & Management Support (RMM). *Energy & Natural Resources*: Energy; National Parks (RMM); Public Lands & Forests. *Ethics (Select)*. *Governmental Affairs*: Financial Management, Budget & International Security (RMM); Government Management, Federal Workforce & the District of Columbia; Investigations (Permanent). *Indian Affairs*. *Veterans' Affairs*.

Group Ratings

	ADA	ACLU	AFS	LCV	CON	ITIC	NTU	COC	ACU	NTLC	CHC
2002	80	60	100	59	20	38	17	53	0	0	—
2001	95	—	100	75	—	—	6	54	13	—	0

National Journal Ratings

	2001 LIB	—	2001 CONS		2002 LIB	—	2002 CONS
Economic	71%	—	27%		68%	—	31%
Social	81%	—	8%		82%	—	0%
Foreign	74%	—	14%		92%	—	7%

Key Votes of the 107th Congress

1. Approve Bush Tax Cuts	N	5. Confirm Ashcroft as AG	N
2. Expand Patients' Rights	Y	6. Bar Gays in the Boy Scouts	N
3. Campaign Finance Reform	Y	7. $ for Hate Crime Prosecution	Y
4. Permit ANWR Development	Y	8. Overseas Military Abortions	Y

9. Bar Coop. with Intl. Court	N
10. Trade Promotion Authority	N
11. Authorize Force in Iraq	N
12. Homeland Sec. Dept. Union	Y

Election Results

2000 general	Daniel Akaka (D)	251,215	(73%)	($428,516)
	John Carroll (R)	84,701	(25%)	($97,407)
	Other	9,707	(3%)	
2000 primary	Daniel Akaka (D)	13,857	(91%)	
	Art P. Reyes (D)	1,317	(9%)	
1994 general	Daniel Akaka (D)	256,189	(72%)	($1,017,872)
	Maria M. Hustace (R)	86,320	(24%)	($29,293)
	Richard O. Rowland (Lib)	14,393	(4%)	

Prior Winning Percentages: 1990 (54%); 1988 House (89%); 1986 House (76%); 1984 House (82%); 1982 House (89%); 1980 House (90%); 1978 House (86%); 1976 House (80%)

Daniel Akaka is the first senator of Native Hawaiian descent and the only senator of Chinese descent. Born four days after Daniel Inouye, he served in the Army Corps of Engineers in the

1940s, went to college, taught school and became a principal. As he tells it, "People have asked me, 'When did you plan to run for the Senate?' I say, 'I never did.' As an educator, my goal was to be superintendent. That's it." In 1971, at 47, he became director of the Hawaii antipoverty program; in 1975, he became an assistant to Governor George Ariyoshi. The next year, when both of Hawaii's congressmen ran for the Senate, he was elected to the House, where he served quietly on the Appropriations Committee. In May 1990, after the death of Senator Spark Matsunaga, Governor John Waihee appointed Akaka to the Senate. He has thus been an integral part of the dominant Democratic organization and a quiet but diligent worker on Hawaii issues for nearly 30 years.

Akaka, though a member of Congress since 1976, is not well known in Washington. "I do much of my work with members in committees," he said. "I do it that way because it works, it's where you find out whether you have heavy opposition, which could cause you to change tactics or not even bring [the issue] up." In 1997, as a member of the Governmental Affairs Committee investigating Clinton-Gore campaign finances, Akaka charged that Clinton had dropped Asian-Americans from consideration for Cabinet posts because of the controversy and criticized the Democratic National Committee for having auditors ask Asian-Americans about "whether they were citizens, how they earn their money, if they would provide their tax returns, and other intrusive questions."

Akaka has a mostly liberal voting record, somewhat less so on foreign and defense issues; he and Inouye were two of the four Democrats supporting deployment of a ballistic missile defense system in 1998. Hawaii, out in the Pacific, is much more vulnerable to North Korean missiles than the U.S. mainland. Akaka also worked for a 1991 ban on German chemical weapons dumping on Johnston Island, 700 miles southwest of Hawaii, and in 1996 he opposed a proposed nuclear waste dump on Palmyra Island, 1,000 miles southwest. He vehemently opposed French nuclear testing in the South Pacific. He has sponsored bills to discourage sex trafficking and assure enforcement of immigration laws in the Commonwealth of the Northern Marianas. He wrote a law giving home loan benefits for veterans of Chamorro, other Pacific Islander, Native Hawaiian or American Indian ancestry in the U.S. Pacific islands.

Much of Akaka's time has been spent on the issue of Native Hawaiian sovereignty. He was the sponsor of the 1993 Apology Resolution, signed by Bill Clinton, in which the United States acknowledged as illegal the overthrow of the Kingdom of Hawaii in 1893 and the denial of Native Hawaiians' right to self-determination. In 1998 and 1999 he pushed the Clinton administration to recognize Native Hawaiians as an aboriginal people with whom the U.S. has a special relationship, as it does with Indian tribes. But in February 2000 the U.S. Supreme Court ruled that the Hawaii Constitution provision limiting voting for the Office of Hawaiian Affairs to those of Native Hawaiian descent was unconstitutional racial discrimination; the Clinton administration assertion of a special relationship was rejected. Other lawsuits were brought against OHA activities. In response, in July 2000 Akaka introduced a native recognition bill, which would recognize Native Hawaiians as an indigenous people with a right to self-determination and set up a process for formation of a Native Hawaiian governing body to have, as many Indian tribes do, a government-to-government relationship with the United States. Thanks to the energetic efforts of Congressman Neil Abercrombie, this passed the House in September 2000. But in the Senate some Republicans objected to unanimous consent, and it died there in December. Akaka brought the bill up again in 2001 and it was passed by Inouye's Indian Affairs Committee in July. It had passed the House committee in May 2001, but House Republican leaders refused to bring it to the floor. In the Senate, Akaka had lobbying help from Alaska Native and American Indian groups, but a hold was placed on the bill by a Republican perhaps influenced by the opposition of some Native Hawaiians, who argue that it would make them wards of the government. In August 2002 Inouye said it would not come to the floor during the rest of the year, and Akaka promised to try again and reintroduced the bill in 2003.

Other Akaka causes include the 1995 law for a review of service records in World War II with a view to awarding higher medals to deserving Asian Americans (under this, Senator Daniel Inouye was awarded the Congressional Medal of Honor in 2000), a law making permanent the waiver of visa requirements from certain countries including Japan (2 million Japanese visit Hawaii every year), laws expanding (and renaming) the Hawaii Volcanoes National Park and requiring the FAA and the National Park Service to negotiate limits on air tours over Haleakala and a five-year study of the energy potential of methane hydrates. He pushed through a doubling of Puluhonua O Honaunay National Historical Park on the Big Island. He has taken a lead role on the 1989 and 1994 laws to protect whistleblowers in government and in June 2001 co-sponsored another to overturn what he thought were incorrect court decisions. He was one of the nine senators (Inouye was another) voting against the homeland security bill in November 2002, arguing that it gave the government too much power to compile information about citizens and failed to protect the rights of whistleblowers. "The threat of a Big Brother new department cannot be overemphasized." He supported oil drilling in the Arctic National Wildlife Refuge, perhaps out of solidarity with colleagues from Alaska, who like Hawaiians often feel resentment that policy is made for their states by mainlanders who have little knowledge and understanding of their needs. On becoming a subcommittee chairman in June 2001 he started working before September 11 to strengthen responses to bioterrorism.

Akaka had one tough election in 1990—indeed the only Senate election in Hawaii that has generated any suspense since 1976. His opponent, Republican Congresswoman Pat Saiki, conceded that Akaka was congenial, but suggested he was ineffective and not too bright. Akaka struck back with ads attacking drugs and his work to end the use of the island of Kahoolawe as a target range. The Democratic organization worked hard and Akaka won 54%–45%, carrying not just the Democratic Neighbor Islands and poorer areas of Honolulu, but most of Oahu as well. In 1994 Akaka was easily re-elected, 72%–24%. In 2000, his Republican opponent campaigned against the native recognition bill, and lost 73%–25%. Akaka has not said whether he will run again in 2006, when he turns 82.

FIRST DISTRICT

Rep. Neil Abercrombie (D)

Elected 1990, 7th term; b. June 26, 1938, Buffalo, NY; home, Honolulu; Union Col., B.A. 1959, U. of HI, M.A.1964, Ph.D. 1974; no religious affiliation; married (Nancie Caraway).

Elected Office: HI House of Reps., 1974–78; HI Senate, 1978–86; U.S. House of Reps., 1986–87; Honolulu City Cncl., 1988–90.

Professional Career: College prof., 1959–63; Probation Officer, Marin Cnty., CA, 1964–67; Sociologist, 1967–74; Asst. prof., HI Loa Col., 1979–80; Consultant, 1983–87, 1989–90; Asst., HI Superintendent of Educ., 1987–88.

DC Office: 1502 LHOB 20515, 202-225-2726; Fax: 202-225-4580; Web site: www.house.gov/abercrombie.

District Office: Honolulu, 808-541-2570.

Committees: *Armed Services* (6th of 29 D): Projection Forces; Readiness; Tactical Air & Land Forces (RMM). *Resources* (4th of 24 D): Fisheries Conservation, Wildlife & Oceans.

Group Ratings

	ADA	ACLU	AFS	LCV	CON	ITIC	NTU	COC	ACU	NTLC	CHC
2002	85	93	78	75	8	38	24	45	12	8	17
2001	90	—	90	93	—	—	19	39	8	—	—

National Journal Ratings

	2001 LIB	—	2001 CONS		2002 LIB	—	2002 CONS
Economic	68%	—	32%		72%	—	27%
Social	78%	—	23%		82%	—	18%
Foreign	70%	—	28%		87%	—	10%

Key Votes of the 107th Congress

1. Approve Bush Tax Cuts	Y	5. Faith-Based Charities	N	9. Trade Promotion Authority	N
2. Limit Patients' Bill of Rights	N	6. Bar Gays in the Boy Scouts	*	10. Bar Funds for Intl. Court	N
3. Campaign Finance Reform	Y	7. Ban Partial-Birth Abortion	N	11. Authorize Force in Iraq	N
4. Ban ANWR Development	Y	8. Arm Commercial Pilots	N	12. Deny Home. Sec. Dept. Union	N

Election Results

2002 general	Neil Abercrombie (D)	131,673	(73%)	($673,054)
	Mark Terry (R)	45,032	(25%)	
	Other	4,028	(2%)	
2002 primary	Neil Abercrombie (D)	unopposed		
2000 general	Neil Abercrombie (D)	108,517	(69%)	($722,133)
	Phil Meyers (R)	44,989	(29%)	($22,042)
	Other	3,688	(2%)	

Prior Winning Percentages: 1998 (62%); 1996 (50%); 1994 (54%); 1992 (73%); 1990 (60%); 1986 (30%)

The People		Race/Ethnic Origin	Ancestry	
Area size:	326 sq. mi.	17.7% White	German: 3.8%	English: 2.9%
Urban population:	99.3%	1.9% Black	Irish: 2.8%	
Rural population:	0.7%	53.6% Asian	**2000 Presidential Vote**	
Pop. 2000:	606,718	0.1% Native Am.	Gore (D)	100,403 (55%)
Median income:	$50,798	6.6% Hawaiian	Bush (R)	70,674 (39%)
Poverty status:	9.7%	14.4% Two+ races	Other	10,211 (6%)
Military veterans:	13.0%	0.2% Other	**Cook Partisan Voting Index:** D + 8	
		5.4% Hispanic Origin		

Occupation	Blue collar: 15.7%	White collar: 63.8%	Gray collar: 20.5%

Tourists in Honolulu see the airport and adjacent Hickam Air Force Base, the *Arizona* monument in Pearl Harbor, perhaps the downtown with its wondrously Victorian Iolani Palace, and of course Waikiki, with its 40-story hotels rising within a few feet of one another. This is tight-packed Hawaii, between the 3,000-foot Koolau Range and the beaches and harbor, where tropical bungalows and garden apartments house Hawaiians of all incomes. Here are Hawaii's largest shopping centers and its state university; here are neighborhoods where the rich overlook the ocean and neighborhoods where the relatively poor are packed into people-clogged streets. Hawaii's topography also jams cars into just a few freeways and avenues, where traffic slows during rush hour and the *aloha* spirit is sorely tested.

Politically, the neighborhoods around Honolulu's downtown and the university campus are middle and lower income and usually Democratic. To the west, around the harbor, are many military families in modest neighborhoods who may vote for Democrats but can be attracted to Republicans. To the east, past Waikiki, around Diamond Head and out to the Kahala and Koko Head beach areas, is higher-income territory, voting for Republicans when they seriously contest a race. Oahu remains home to 72% of Hawaiians, but it grew only 5% in the 1990s, far less than Maui or the Big Island of Hawaii. Redistricting made only the slightest of changes in the district lines.

The congressman from the 1st District is Neil Abercrombie, a Democrat with a graying beard who used to sport a ponytail (he cut it off because "it was getting in the way of getting things done"). He has been called an aging hippie but he bench-presses 260 pounds in the House gym; he debates with an aggressiveness and bombast tempered by enthusiasm and good humor. After college in upstate New York, he taught school, moved to Hawaii, earned a Ph.D. in American studies; he was elected to the Hawaii legislature in 1974 and served 12 years. Abercrombie first came to the House in 1986, when he won a special election, and served only three months; he lost a primary for the full term to a Democrat who then lost to Republican Pat Saiki. When she ran for the Senate, Abercrombie won a three-way primary in 1990 for the House seat and won the general election easily.

Abercrombie is one of the distinctive and often delightful figures in the House. His voting record is mostly, but not entirely, liberal. He serves on the Armed Services Committee and sees no contradiction between his protests of the Vietnam War and votes for military spending in Hawaii and elsewhere. "I see my work on Armed Services as a fulfillment of my principles and the motivating force of my life. I never opposed the military. . . . It's not about pro-war or anti-war, but how do you keep the peace." He voted against military intervention in Bosnia and Kosovo and, in October 2002, in Iraq, because he believed diplomatic options had not been exhausted. But he still gets things done on Armed Services. As ranking Democrat on the Military Installations Subcommittee, he helped to get $268 million in military construction for Hawaii in 2002. He got a Navy admiral to commit to keeping nuclear submarine jobs in Hawaii, but endorsed a later plan to move some subs to Guam. "By building up Guam, we build up Hawaii. The logistical tail that runs from Guam runs right through Hawaii."

On other issues Abercrombie is not always predictable. He joined Resources Committee Republicans in voting for a contempt citation opposed by other Democrats. He co-sponsored repeal of the estate tax—there are a lot of small businesses in Hawaii, he said. Despite Hawaii's trade interests, he voted against PNTR with China and opposed trade promotion authority. He filed a tourism business-friendly bill to allow businesses to write off the travel costs of spouses on business trips. And he showed his union credentials by warning that a labor dispute at a factory that produces bulletproof vests for the military could jeopardize the safety of U.S. soldiers. In September 2000, he won a signal and surprising victory as House sponsor of a bill to recognize Native Hawaiians as an indigenous people with a right to self-determination. It was brought to the floor as a noncontroversial matter and passed there. But Senator Daniel Akaka was not able to do the same. The Indian Affairs Committee, chaired by Daniel Inouye, approved the bill, but when it was brought to the floor in October 2000 some Republicans objected, and the bill died. In the next Congress, the House Republican leadership did not allow the bill to come to the floor, and the full Senate never considered it either. After his 2d District colleague Patsy Mink died in September 2002, Abercrombie passed a resolution renaming her trademark "Title IX" provision for equal opportunity in college sports in her name.

The 1st District is usually solidly Democratic, but in 1994 Abercrombie had serious competition from Orson Swindle, Marine Corps pilot and Vietnam POW, a national leader of Ross Perot's United We Stand America, and later member of the Federal Communications Commission. Swindle charged that Abercrombie was too dovish, but Abercrombie raised more money and won 54%–43%. In 1996 Swindle labeled Abercrombie a far left hippie and called for big spending cuts. Abercrombie narrowly outspent him, and won by only 50%–46%. Since then, he has won comfortably.

SECOND DISTRICT

Rep. Ed Case (D)

Elected Nov. 2002, 1st term; b. Sept. 27, 1952, Hilo; home, Honolulu; Williams Col., B.A. 1975, U. of CA Hastings Col. of Law, J.D. 1981; Protestant; married (Audrey).

Elected Office: Manoa Neighborhood Bd., 1985–89; HI House of Reps., 1999–02, Maj. Ldr., 1999–00.

Professional Career: Practicing atty., 1983–02; L.A., Sen. Spark Matsunaga, 1975–78; Clerk, HI Supreme Ct. Chief Justice William Richardson, 1981–82.

DC Office: 128 CHOB 20515, 202-225-4906; Fax: 202-225-4987; Web site: www.house.gov/case.

District Office: Honolulu, 808-541-1986.

Committees: *Agriculture* (12th of 24 D): Conservation, Credit, Rural Development & Research; General Farm Commodities & Risk Management. *Education & the Workforce* (17th of 22 D): Education Reform; Employer-Employee Relations. *Small Business* (11th of 17 D): Rural Enterprises, Agriculture and Technology; Workforce, Empowerment & Government Programs.

Group Ratings and Key Votes: Newly Elected

Election Results

2003 special	Ed Case (D)	33,002	(44%)	($124,973)
	Matt Matsunaga (D)	23,050	(30%)	
	Colleen Hanabusa (D)	6,046	(8%)	
	Barbara Marumoto (R)	4,497	(6%)	
	Bob McDermott (R)	4,298	(6%)	
	Other	4,681	(6%)	
2002 special	Ed Case (D)	23,576	(51%)	
	John Mink (D)	16,624	(36%)	
	John Carroll (R)	1,933	(4%)	
	Other	2,754	(6%)	
2002 general	Patsy Mink (D)	100,671	(56%)	($320,130)
	Bob McDermott (R)	71,661	(40%)	($85,813)

The People		Race/Ethnic Origin	Ancestry	
Area size:	10,605 sq. mi.	28.0% White	German: 5.4%	Portuguese: 4.2%
Urban population:	83.8%	1.5% Black	Irish: 4.0%	
Rural population:	16.2%	28.0% Asian	**2000 Presidential Vote**	
Pop. 2000:	604,819	0.3% Native Am.	Gore (D)..............104,830	(56%)
Median income:	$48,686	11.3% Hawaiian	Bush (R)................67,118	(36%)
Poverty status:	11.7%	21.7% Two+ races	Other..................14,577	(8%)
Military veterans:	13.3%	0.2% Other	**Cook Partisan Voting Index:** D +11	
		9.0% Hispanic Origin		
Occupation	Blue collar: 19.3%	White collar: 56.7%	Gray collar: 24.0%	

The 2d District of Hawaii includes not only the Neighbor Islands but most of Oahu's acreage beyond what is generally regarded as the city of Honolulu (juridically, it includes all of Oahu). It has Wheeler Air Force Base, still looking much as it did in December 1941, and the farmlands north of Pearl Harbor, between two jagged chains of mountains that lift the island out of the sea. Over the mountains to the west is the Leeward Coast—calm, sultry and lightly populated; over the mountains to the northeast is the Windward Coast with many prosperous and Republican subdivisions in and around Kaneohe and Kailua. The Neighbor Islands have distinct personalities. Hawaii, the Big Island, is the size of Connecticut and boasts huge cattle ranches, the active volcano of Kilauea (which erupted most recently in 1984), and Mauna Kea, the highest mountain in the world if you count from its base far under the ocean to the peak; tourists are told that it is bad luck to take pieces of lava home, and many send them back. On the north shore, with heavy rainfall and tropical foliage, is the old port of Hilo and Hawaii's macadamia nut industry; this is a blue-collar Democratic area. On the Kona Coast, where there is little rainfall and the landscape is dominated by lava flows, there are retirement condominiums and a higher-income, more Republican population. Maui, favored more by North American than Asian tourists, has dozens of luxury condominiums and vast upscale resorts. But there is risk in paradise: Many of Hawaii's native plants are facing extinction due to the pigs, goats and diseases introduced to the islands since Captain Cook arrived in 1776. Kauai, much of which was devastated by Hurricane Iniki in 1992, is the least-developed and most agricultural of the main islands; parts of it have the nation's highest rainfall, while others seldom get wet. Its large farm work force—a reminder of what most of Hawaii was like a century ago—makes it the most Democratic of the islands.

The congressman from the 2d District is Ed Case, a Democrat who managed to win two special elections after the November 2002 general election and still get sworn in with the other members of the 108th Congress in January 2003. A fourth-generation Hawaiian, his father founded the local chapter of the Association for Retarded Citizens; his mother was a librarian and was elected to the Hawaii School Advisory Council. He is a cousin of former AOL Time-Warner chairman Steve Case. Ed Case attended local schools before venturing to the Mainland, where he graduated from Williams College and Hastings Law School in San Francisco. He spent three years on Capitol Hill as an aide to Senator Spark Matsunaga. After returning home, he became a partner in a Honolulu law firm, where he specialized in land and commercial law. He narrowly lost each of his first two bids for public office: for the state House in 1986 and the state Senate in 1988. Finally he was elected to the state House in 1994, where he was majority leader in 1999 and 2000.

The year 2002 was an extraordinarily busy campaign year for Case by any measure. On September 21 he lost the gubernatorial primary to Lieutenant Governor Mazie Hirono by a 41%–39% margin. He ran as a reformer in a state where the dominant Democratic machine had held the governorship for 40 years and was buffeted by criticism for overspending and corruption. Then 2d District Congresswoman Patsy Mink, first elected in 1964, defeated in a Senate primary in 1976 and elected again to the House in 1990, died on September 28; she had been hospitalized since August 30 with viral pneumonia that resulted from a case of chicken pox and her family had given no information on her condition. State law prohibited changes in the general election ballot after September 26, and so Mink's name remained on the ballot. On November 5 she was posthumously reelected 56%–40% against Republican state Representative Bob McDermott.

This was the first of three elections in three months for this district. Outgoing Governor Ben Cayetano called a special election for November 30 to fill the rest of the term, even though Congress had adjourned and seemed highly unlikely to reconvene. It was a winner-take-all contest, in which 12 Democrats, 13 Republicans and 16 candidates of other parties filed to run. The initial favorite was John Mink, Patsy Mink's widower, who said that he wanted to honor the work of his former wife and keep her office together. Case entered the race soon after losing the primary for governor, running as a reformer with more moderate views on economic and labor issues than other Hawaii Democrats. Only 45,000 voters turned out in a district of more than 600,000 people; Case won a surprising 51% of the votes to John Mink's 36%. Case never took the oath of office for the 107th Congress, but he did accrue seniority over freshmen in the 108th Congress. And he was able to run as the incumbent in the January 4 special election to fill the seat in the 108th Congress that was empty because of Patsy Mink's death. In all, 44 candidates filed to run in this winner-take-all contest—12 Democrats, 16 Republicans, 13 from the Natural Law party, one Libertarian and two Greens. McDermott ran again, but the Republican party remained neutral. Case's chief opponent was former Democratic state Senator Matt Matsunaga, a son of the late Spark Matsunaga and the Democratic nominee for lieutenant governor in November 2002. Matsunaga had the endorsement of the AFL-CIO and was the candidate of the Democratic machine that had held the governorship from 1962 to 2002; Case ran as the reform candidate. Case said that he could support unilateral military action against Iraq only if there was "a clear and present danger" against the United States; Matsunaga ran election-eve ads claiming that Case supported the legalization of marijuana and lower pay for teachers. On January 4, 75,000 voted, more than on November 30 but far less than the 179,000 who voted November 5. Case led Matsunaga 44%–30%. He won decisively in Kauai, where the Case family has roots, and on the Big Island; he led by a wide margin in Oahu, where Matsunaga may have lost votes to state Senator Colleen Hanabusa. Democratic candidates won 82% of the votes and Republicans only 16%, but Case's critique of the long-ruling Democrats was similar to that of incoming Republican Governor Linda Lingle: This was another repudiation of Hawaii's Democratic machine.

★ IDAHO ★

I daho, with just 1.3 million people, tucked off near the northwest edge of the country, has been an American success story of late. Since the early 1990s it has been one of the nation's leading states in population growth, technological progress and economic creativity. Idaho's growth has tapered off a bit after 2000, but it still has a robust economy. Its biggest businesses are big: J.R. Simplot is the nation's largest potato processor; Micron Technology, the state's number one employer, is a leader in semiconductors; Albertson's is the nation's second largest supermarket chain. And dozens of smaller high-tech and service businesses have sprung up. From California, a few highly publicized liberal entertainment personalities and a much larger number of conservative engineers and entrepreneurs have come to Idaho for a fresh environment and fresh start, clean air and few crowds, and no cumbersome or expensive regulations, where family lifestyles are still prevalent, traditional values respected, and traditional rules enforced.

The wilderness is never far away in Idaho, nor is the experience of the first settlers. Towering over the state Capitol in Boise is the vast peak of Shafer Butte, and not far away are impassable mountains of the Frank Church River of No Return Wilderness: Idaho ranks third in National Wilderness lands, behind California and Alaska. This was the last North American area European pioneers—fur traders—set eyes on. In the 1840s, New England Yankees led by ministers made their way west on the Oregon Trail through southern Idaho. Idaho's northern panhandle, an extension of Washington's Columbia Valley, was first settled by miners seeking gold and silver, then by loggers seeking timber. Mormons moved north from Utah and settled eastern Idaho. But federal water reclamation projects first authorized in 1894 brought the most settlers, and they transformed the barren Snake River Valley into some of the nation's best volcanic soil-enriched farmland. Fresh in family lore are the people who pioneered this state, built the first towns and farms, established the first churches and schools and became its community leaders. Yet Idaho is also cosmopolitan. It exports potatoes—mostly frozen french fries—across the Pacific Rim, and its high-tech companies have competitors all over the world. If Idaho politicians used to concentrate on water and maintaining irrigation, now they also work to curb Canadian potato imports and South Korean semiconductor subsidies.

Not so long ago Idaho was a state of farms and small towns; Boise, the pleasant state capital, was just the largest of the small towns. Today Idaho is increasingly urbanized. Most of its people live in just five counties, in and around Boise, Idaho Falls, Pocatello and Coeur d'Alene. One-third live in the Boise's Treasure Valley, which has been growing rapidly, with big increases in the towns west of Boise—Eagle, Meridian, Middleton, Nampa. There have been large influxes from California (53% of people turning in other states' driver's licenses in the 1990s were from California) and from Mexico and other parts of Latin America. Idaho's Hispanic population grew by 92% in the 1990s and is now 8% of the total; driver's license exams are given in English, Spanish, Serbo-Croatian, Russian, Arabic and Vietnamese. Here the political trend has been very much toward the Republicans: The newcomers are from Orange County, not San Francisco, and they seek not cultural liberation, but an environment in which they can raise their children in traditional lifestyles.

At the same time, small counties that have depended on mining and grazing have been hurting. But they think of themselves not as downtrodden employees of absentee corporations needing a protective federal government, but as pioneering entrepreneurs who need to get a bloated, bossy federal government off their backs. The federal government owns 62% of Idaho's land, and most Idahoans were furious at how Clinton appointees managed it. The Clinton administration's proposal to stop roadbuilding in about one-third of national forest land was bitterly opposed. Federal limitations on grazing on public lands have squeezed cattle ranchers already hurt by declining beef consumption and lower prices. Similarly, potato farmers dependent on irrigated water were enraged when the *Idaho Statesman* and local environment restriction advocates called for breaching dams on the Snake River to protect salmon. Even more fury was aroused by the Clinton administration proposal to reintroduce 25 grizzly bears into the Bitterroot Range on the border with Montana.

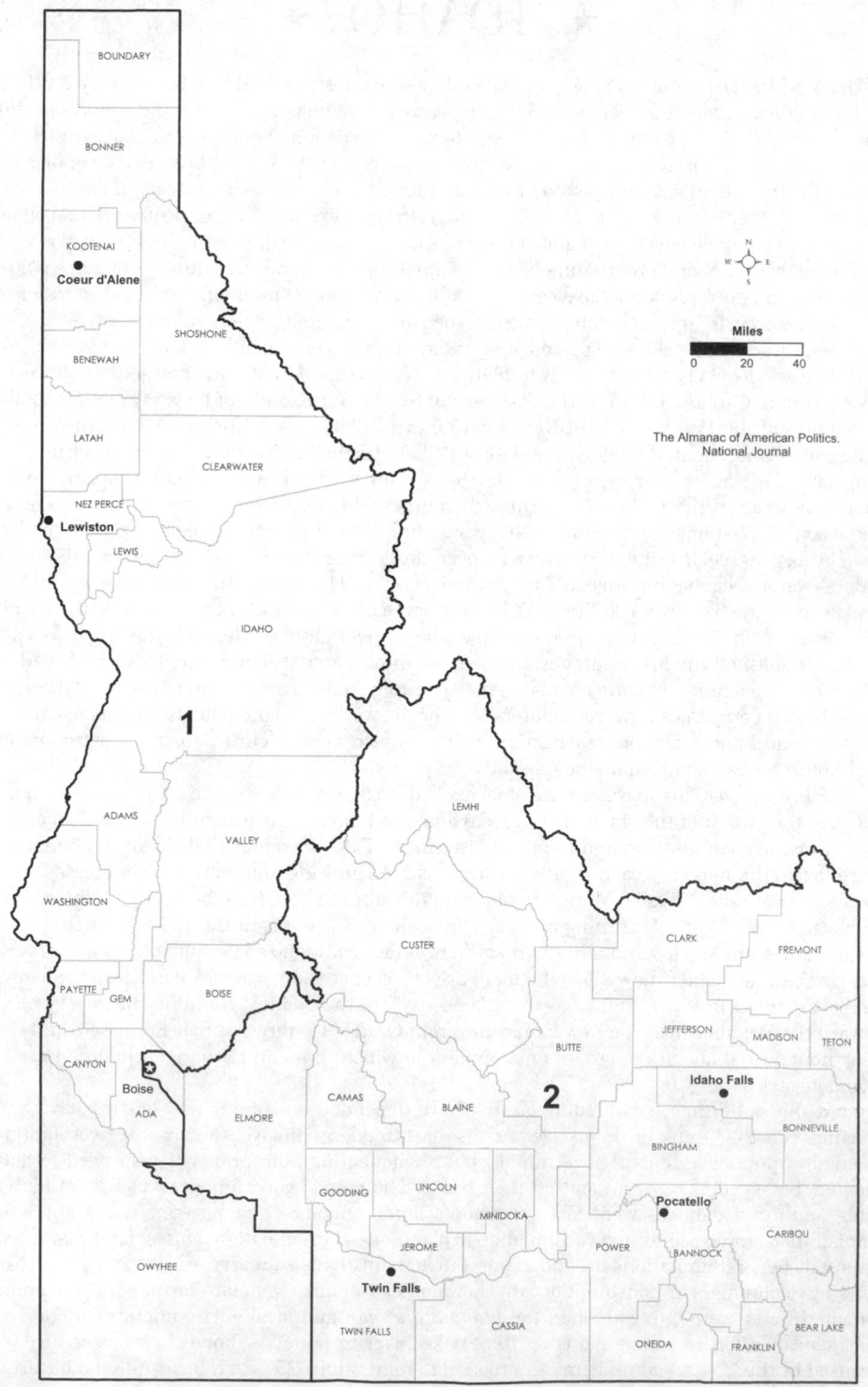

Congressional district boundaries were first effective for 2002.

The political result of all these things was to produce a Republican trend that seems to have peaked in 2000. George W. Bush—against breaching the Snake River dams, dubious about the reintroduction of grizzlies and the prohibition of roadbuilding in the national forests, eager to cut taxes on entrepreneurs—carried Idaho by a 67%–28% margin, his third best in the country; he lost only Blaine County, with Sun Valley and its trendy newcomers, and by only 220 votes. (It's interesting that Al Gore, who campaigned for "the people versus the powerful," carried only the state's wealthiest county.) In 2000 House races, the two Republican candidates carried every county and won with 65% and 71% of the vote. Two years before, Senator Dirk Kempthorne won 68% of the votes for governor and Congressman Mike Crapo won 70% for the Senate. Republicans controlled the state House by 61–9 and the state Senate by 32–3.

Idaho's members of Congress hailed the Bush administration's November 2002 proposal to give national forest regional managers more flexibility in approving commercial use and its December Healthy Forest Initiative to streamline approval of forest thinning; the huge forest fires of summer 2002, they argued, showed the need to clear away combustible timber. But the slowdown in the economy produced problems for state government. Revenues came in lower than expected, and Kempthorne found himself cutting spending below projected levels and refused to rule out a tax increase. Republican legislators overturned, over Kempthorne's veto, the term limits initiative approved by voters in 1994 and 1998; term limits advocates put the issue on the ballot again, and voters went along with their repeal by a 50.2%–49.8% margin (1,889 votes) in November 2002. Democrat Jerry Brady waged a vigorous campaign against Kempthorne and, though coming far from victory, held him to a 56%–42% margin—pretty modest for a Republican in Idaho these days. On election night, Democrats had smiles on their faces because they reduced the Republican margins in the state House to 54–16 and the state Senate to 28–7. They made their biggest gains, and Kempthorne suffered his biggest losses, in the high-education areas of the state, in Boise and always Democratic Sun Valley, but also in the college towns of Pocatello, Moscow, Lewiston and Coeur d'Alene. The small counties, threatened economically, remained staunchly Republican. But Idaho in early 2003 seemed just a bit less monopartisan than it had been a few months before.

The People		Race/Ethnic Origin			Military veterans: 136,584 (14.8%)	
Pop. 2000:	1,293,953	1,139,291	88.0%	White	WWII: 18.6%	Korea: 12.6%
Pop. 1990:	1,006,749	4,889	0.4%	Black	Vietnam: 32.3%	Gulf War: 13.5%
Change 1990–2000:	Up 28.5%	11,641	0.9%	Asian	**Most populous cities:**	
Change 1980–1990:	Up 6.7%	15,789	1.2%	Native Am.	1. Boise	185,787
% of U.S. total:	0.5%	1,200	0.1%	Hawaiian	2. Nampa	51,867
Pop. rank:	39th of 50	18,261	1.4%	Two + races	3. Pocatello	51,466
Area size:	83,570 sq. mi.	1,192	0.1%	Other	4. Idaho Falls	50,730
State Native:	47.2%	101,690	7.9%	Hisp. Origin	5. Meridian	34,919
Non-citizen:	3.3%	**Ancestry**			Urban population: 66.4%	
Language		German: 13.8%		English: 13.3%	Rural population: 33.6%	
English: 88.4%	Spanish: 7.4%	Irish: 7.3%		USA: 6.1%		
Other Eur.: 2.7%		Norwegian: 2.6%				

Education		Work Sector		Legislature	
H.S. Grad:	84.7%	Private: 73.8%	Govt: 16.4%	Senate	28 R 7 D
College Grad:	21.7%	Self: 9.3%	Family: 0.5%	House	54 R 16 D
Industry		Unemployment: 5.7%		Legislative Term Limits: No	
Agri: 5.8%	Con: 8.1%	**Household Income**		**Registered Voters**	
Fin: 5.1%	Info: 2.3%	<15k: 15.8%	15-35k: 30.3%	No party registration	
Mfg: 17.8%	Prof: 27.2%	35-50k: 19.1%	50-100k: 27.6%		
Public: 5.1%	Trade: 16.2%	100-150k: 4.8%	>150k: 2.5%		
Other: 12.5%		Median: $37,572			
Occupation		Poverty status: 11.8%			
Blue collar: 25.0%	White collar: 56.7%	**Home Value**			
Gray collar: 18.3%		<50k: 12.3%	50-100k: 36.3%	100-200k: 39.5%	200-300k: 7.5%
		300-500k: 2.8%	>500k: 1.6%	Median: $102,100	

Presidential politics   Idaho is one of the most Republican states in national politics. George W. Bush and Bob Dole carried it easily; in 1992 Bill Clinton only narrowly beat out Ross Perot for second place, 28%–27%. From 1988–96, Idaho's presidential primary was held in late May, but was not binding for Democrats, who select their presidential nominee in the early March caucus. Idaho considered joining other Rocky Mountain states voting in an early March 2000 primary, but the state House voted it down in March 1999.

Congressional districting   Idaho has two congressional districts, which split Boise between them. After the 2000 Census, a bipartisan commission drew new boundaries. It moved the boundary of the districts in Boise about a mile to the west, along Cole Road—a minor and uncontroversial change.

108th Congress Lineup
2 R
107th Congress Lineup
2 R

2000 Presidential Vote		
Bush (R)	336,937	(67%)
Gore (D)	138,637	(28%)
Nader (Green)	12,292	(2%)
Other	13,749	(3%)

2000 Republican Presidential Primary		
Bush (R)	116,385	(73%)
Keyes (R)	30,263	(19%)
None Shown	11,798	(7%)

2000 Democratic Presidential Primary		
Gore (D)	27,025	(76%)
None Shown	5,722	(16%)
LaRouche (D)	2,941	(8%)

1996 Presidential Vote		
Dole (R)	256,595	(52%)
Clinton (D)	165,443	(34%)
Perot (I)	62,518	(13%)

Governor

Dirk Kempthorne (R)

Elected 1998, term expires Jan. 2007, 2d term; b. Oct. 29, 1951, San Diego, CA; home, Boise; U. of ID, B.A. 1975; Methodist; married (Patricia).

Elected Office: Boise Mayor, 1986–93; U.S. Senate, 1992–98.

Professional Career: Exec. Asst. to Dir., ID Dept. of Public Lands, 1976–78; Exec. V.P., ID Home Builders Assn., 1978–81; Campaign Mgr., Phil Batt for Gov., 1982; ID Public Affairs Mgr., FMC Corp, 1983–86.

Office: P.O. Box 83720, Boise, 83720, 208-334-2100; Fax: 208-334-2175; Web site: www.state.id.us/gov.

Election Results

2002 general	Dirk Kempthorne (R)	231,566	(56%)
	Jerry Brady (D)	171,711	(42%)
	Other	8,200	(2%)
2002 primary	Dirk Kempthorne (R)	95,882	(66%)
	Milt Erhart (R)	37,523	(26%)
	Walter Bayes (R)	6,873	(5%)
	Raynelle George (R)	5,271	(4%)
1998 general	Dirk Kempthorne (R)	258,095	(68%)
	Robert C. Huntley (D)	110,815	(29%)
	Other	12,338	(3%)

Dirk Kempthorne was elected governor of Idaho in 1998 after six years in the U.S. Senate. He was born in San Diego, grew up in Spokane, Washington, and graduated from the University of Idaho. He has spent most of his adult life in the political arena, starting in state government, then working for the Idaho Home Builders Association and FMC Corporation. He managed Phil Batt's unsuccessful gubernatorial campaign in 1982 (Batt finally won in 1994) and was mayor of Boise for seven boom years from 1986–93. Kempthorne was elected to the Senate seat vacated in 1992 by two-term incumbent Republican Steve Symms and over tough competition from Democratic Congressman Richard Stallings. A Mormon and a conservative on abortion and gun control, Stallings was a three-time congressman from the eastern Idaho 2d District. Kempthorne won with 57%, barely carrying the northern panhandle, but running far ahead in the Boise market and carrying the Mormon areas in the east.

Kempthorne started off 100th in seniority in a Democratic Senate, concentrating on the nonstarter issue of unfunded mandates. But after the 1994 Republican victory, Majority Leader Bob Dole made Kempthorne's unfunded mandates bill S.1, the first order of legislative business. Kempthorne impressed colleagues with his knowledge of detail and his willingness to face off with West Virginia Senator Robert Byrd, who fought mightily against the bill as an infringement of congressional prerogatives; it passed the Senate easily with bipartisan support.

But Idaho beckoned. Phil Batt, elected at 67, decided to retire after a long career in state politics and one successful four-year term as governor. Welfare rolls were cut more than 75%, crime was sharply down, taxes and state payrolls were cut, and in 1996, voters had endorsed by 63%–37% the 40-year compact with the federal government Batt negotiated on nuclear waste disposal. In September 1997, Batt announced his decision to retire; in October 1997, Kempthorne announced he was running. He was willing to give up what easily could have been a lifetime Senate seat for, at most, two term-limited terms as governor. "I truly do believe power now is irreversibly returning to the states, and that is where the important action will be," he said. Once Kempthorne was in, the race was essentially over. Former state Supreme Court Justice Robert Huntley ran, he said, to maintain two-party competition. Kempthorne won 68%–29%, carrying every county but the one including Sun Valley.

In 1999 he proclaimed "the Generation of the Child" and got the legislature to pass a $5.5 million Idaho Reading Initiative and scholarships for 3.0 high school graduates at in-state colleges. He passed a voluntary immunization registry bill. Criticized for aloofness, he held an open house in his office for legislators in 2000. He got $5 million in federal funds to crack down on methamphetamine labs that have flourished across the state. He opposed the November 2000 decision of the Fish and Wildlife Service to reintroduce grizzly bears into the Bitterroot Range, and filed a lawsuit; the Bush administration withdrew the proposal in June 2001. He worked on a four-state salmon recovery program and entered a Memorandum of Understanding with Indian tribes as part of the Northwest Power Planning Council's sub-basin planning process. He got funding for a Rural Idaho Initiative, with state money for projects in the non-booming parts of Idaho—a strawboard plant in Benewah County, a new plant site away from North Idaho College in Coeur d'Alene, sewers and streets in Rupert, extension of a sewer line in Shoshone, rail lines for malting barley operations in Bonneville County.

In his first three years, Kempthorne and the legislature cut taxes several times. But by late 2001 revenues came in under expectations, and there were rounds of cuts in planned increases in public schools and actual cuts in higher education. The state tapped the Budget Stabilization Fund and tobacco settlement money and state employees were laid off. He opposed giving state businesses the benefit of George W. Bush's 30% immediate depreciation allowance, over the opposition of the Idaho Association of Commerce and Industry. Many members of the overwhelmingly Republican legislature complained that Kempthorne was aloof and uninvolved. They were unhappy when in early 2002 Kempthorne vetoed their repeal of term limits; the voters upheld the law by the narrowest of margins in November. Kempthorne had articulate opposition from Democrat Jerry Brady, owner of the *Idaho Falls Post Register*, the state's second largest newspaper, whose great-grandfather James Brady had been elected governor as a Republican in 1908. (Brady didn't tell his reporters he was running and the managing editor said, "We were nearly scooped!") Brady spent $320,000 of his own money and attacked Kempthorne for cutting education spending in a "formulaic" and "lazy" way. He criticized Kempthorne for ousting Fish and Game Commissioner Rod Sando and said the commission was subservient to farmers and ranchers, and said he would appoint new members nominated by sportsmen. Kempthorne protested that he had only cut planned increases in school spending and that he would permit no further education cuts. He appointed a Blue Ribbon Task Force to examine the budget and report after the election.

Kempthorne won by the reduced margin of 56%–42%. He lost the counties containing Sun

Valley and Pocatello, three northern panhandle counties and, surprisingly, Boise's Ada County, where voters presumably know him best. Facing a budget crisis in January 2003, Kempthorne proposed the largest tax increase in state history. "I have done something that is absolutely not part of my fiber," he explained to *The Washington Post*. "But I'm not going to dismantle this state, and I'm not going to jeopardize our bond rating, and I'm not going to reduce my emphasis on education."

Senior Senator

Larry Craig (R)

Elected 1990, seat up 2008, 3d term; b. July 20, 1945, Midvale; home, Payette; U. of ID, B.A. 1969; United Methodist; married (Suzanne).

Military Career: Army Natl. Guard, 1970–74.

Elected Office: ID Senate, 1974–80; U.S. House of Reps., 1980–90.

Professional Career: Rancher, farmer.

DC Office: 520 HSOB, 20510, 202-224-2752; Fax: 202-228-1067; Web site: craig.senate.gov.

State Offices: Boise, 208-342-7985; Coeur d'Alene, 208-667-6130; Idaho Falls, 208-523-5541; Lewiston, 208-743-0792; Pocatello, 208-236-6817; Twin Falls, 208-734-6780.

Committees: *Aging (Special)* (Chmn.). *Appropriations*: Agriculture & Rural Development; Energy & Water Development; Homeland Security; Labor, HHS & Education; Military Construction; VA, HUD & Independent Agencies. *Energy & Natural Resources*: Energy; Public Lands & Forests (Chmn.); Water & Power. *Judiciary*: Administrative Oversight & the Courts; Constitution, Civil Rights & Property Rights; Crime, Corrections & Victims' Rights; Immigration, Border Security & Citizenship. *Veterans' Affairs*.

Group Ratings

	ADA	ACLU	AFS	LCV	CON	ITIC	NTU	COC	ACU	NTLC	CHC
2002	5	25	0	6	43	100	60	90	100	94	—
2001	0	—	0	0	—	—	82	100	96	—	100

National Journal Ratings

	2001 LIB	—	2001 CONS		2002 LIB	—	2002 CONS
Economic	0%	—	94%		0%	—	94%
Social	0%	—	79%		0%	—	62%
Foreign	7%	—	72%		24%	—	67%

Key Votes of the 107th Congress

1. Approve Bush Tax Cuts	Y	5. Confirm Ashcroft as AG	Y	9. Bar Coop. with Intl. Court	Y
2. Expand Patients' Rights	N	6. Bar Gays in the Boy Scouts	Y	10. Trade Promotion Authority	Y
3. Campaign Finance Reform	N	7. $ for Hate Crime Prosecution	N	11. Authorize Force in Iraq	Y
4. Permit ANWR Development	Y	8. Overseas Military Abortions	*	12. Homeland Sec. Dept. Union	N

Election Results

2002 general	Larry Craig (R)	266,215	(65%)	($3,045,521)
	Alan Blinken (D)	132,975	(33%)	($2,170,928)
	Other	9,354	(2%)	
2002 primary	Larry Craig (R)	unopposed		
1996 general	Larry Craig (R)	283,532	(57%)	($2,992,451)
	Walt Minnick (D)	198,422	(40%)	($2,140,878)
	Other	15,279	(3%)	

Prior Winning Percentages: 1990 (61%); 1988 House (66%); 1986 House (65%); 1984 House (69%); 1982 House (54%); 1980 House (54%)

Larry Craig was first elected to the Senate in 1990. Born on a ranch homesteaded by his grandfather in 1899, he was first elected to the state Senate in 1974, at 29, and to the U.S. House in

1980, at 35. In 1990, when Senator James McClure retired, he was elected to the Senate. Throughout his career he has had a very conservative voting record and has been a well-informed and persistent critic of Western lands policies favored by environmentalists or, as he says, "environmental extremism." In the Senate he became chairman of the informal conservative Steering Committee, whose members seemed to win most of the leadership positions. After Kansas Senator Bob Dole's resignation in June 1996, Craig became chairman of the Republican Policy Committee, the number four leadership position. He was, Idaho reporter Dan Popkey wrote, "poised to become the fourth face on Idaho's Mount Rushmore, joining Senators William Borah, Frank Church, and Jim McClure."

Craig has used his seats on the Appropriations, Agriculture and Energy committees to fight for what he considers sensible environmental policies. He opposed Bill Clinton's efforts to revise the Mining Act of 1872 and increase grazing fees and the Clinton proposal to introduce grizzly bears into Idaho's Bitterroot Range. He opposed expansion of the Craters of the Moon National Monument, and sponsored a bill to create certain requirements for presidents to declare national monuments, as Clinton frequently did. He is against breaching the Snake River dams to allow salmon to swim more easily upstream and sponsored a bill to require the Fish and Wildlife Service to consider many factors, including the effect on farming, when it makes decisions on salmon protection programs.

Craig is chairman of the Public Lands and Forests Subcommittee and seems engaged in a long-term battle to change the policies and institutional culture of the Forest Service. In the wake of the summer 2000 wildfires that raged in Idaho, he strongly criticized the Clinton administration for failing to fund fire prevention and, with New Mexico Senator Pete Domenici, called for $240 million for federal agencies to remove timber and brush. He sponsored a reorganization bill to streamline planning procedures, limit court challenges to local people who commented during the planning process, and forbid deviations from the plan once adopted. It would allow states and private organizations, with congressional approval, to take over management of National Forest and Bureau of Land Management lands. He opposed the Clinton proposal to ban construction of roads in national forests and supported the Bush administration's 2002 proposal to give regional managers power to approve commercial or recreational use without protracted environmental impact statements. He favored the Bush Healthy Forest Initiative streamlining approval of forest thinning. Craig keeps up with even the most arcane of resource issues. In October 2002 he sponsored a bill to authorize the Forest Service to study silver-based biocides as wood preservatives. In November 2002, following up on his 1996 Plant Protection Act, which blocks the importation of noxious weeds and plant pests, he introduced a bill to create a noxious weed office in the Interior Department; he says that some scientists believe that noxious weeds are the second greatest threat to endangered species.

Another Craig cause is nuclear waste. He has been pushing relentlessly for the government to meet its commitment to establish a permanent nuclear waste repository at Yucca Mountain in Nevada. Opposition came from Nevada's two senators and from Clinton, who carried Nevada twice by narrow margins after promising to veto bills to establish a temporary waste facility there. In July 2002, Craig's efforts came to fruition: George W. Bush signed a resolution establishing the repository. In March 2002 he inserted into the energy bill a Nuclear Power 2010 program for the Energy Department; noting the lead role of Idaho in nuclear power, he said that the U.S. should consider moving toward more use of nuclear power.

Craig has taken on a variety of national issues. He was a lead sponsor of the constitutional amendment to require a balanced budget in the House in 1982 and in the Senate in 1995. The high-water mark for this measure came in early 1995, when it passed the House with 300 votes and came within one vote of the required two-thirds margin in the Senate. He has supported free trade measures but was co-sponsor with Minnesota Senator Mark Dayton in May 2002 of the amendment to trade promotion authority which would allow Congress to separately examine provisions of any trade agreement that affect trade remedy laws; in effect this would block the president from negotiating such changes. Craig has opposed what he considers dumping of Korean microchips (Micron is Idaho's biggest employer) and Canadian softwood lumber, particularly after the expiration of the Canadian Softwood Lumber Agreement in March 2001. Craig-Dayton passed

61–38, but George W. Bush indicated he would veto the bill if it stayed in, and it was dropped in conference committee. He was one of the leaders in the gun control debate in the Senate in 1999, sponsoring a measure to allow (but not force) unlicensed sellers at gun shows to conduct background checks. In July 2002 he, John McCain, Edward Kennedy and Charles Schumer were an "odd duck" coalition sponsoring a bill to improve the National Instant Check background check system; they want to make sure that it includes all those convicted of crimes or otherwise ineligible to buy guns.

Craig has been part of a group of conservatives who took over party leadership positions in the 1990s. He was elected chairman of the Republican Policy Committee, the number four position, in June 1996. He was often a conduit between Majority Leader Trent Lott and Republican conservatives. In December 2000 Craig was challenged for the Policy Committee leadership by the more senior and more conciliation-minded Pete Domenici—one of two serious leadership challenges after Senate Republicans had seen their 54–46 majority converted by the 2000 elections to a 50–50 tie. Craig just barely prevailed, by a 26–24 margin. The Policy chairmanship is term limited, and Craig had to leave the position after the 2002 election; he considered running for whip in the fall, but evidently became convinced that Kentucky Senator Mitch McConnell had the votes and did not run. He was always a strong supporter of Lott, and after his remarks at Senator Strom Thurmond's 100th birthday party he talked often with him. "In the beginning, I said, 'I accept Trent Lott's apology and I think it's time we move on,'" he told a reporter after Lott stepped down. "But I was saying to Trent all along as this developed, 'Trent, this is rapidly not about you. It's become about our party, leadership, the United States Senate and, ultimately, the presidency."

On Idaho issues, he sponsored a bill to transfer 10 acres of land in the Sand Mountain Wilderness Study Area to the Sand Hills Resort with Congressman Mike Simpson; with Congressman Butch Otter, he sponsored a bill to correct an erroneous 1880 public land survey that put a cloud on the titles of owners of land around Spirit Lake and Twin Lakes in Kootenai County.

Craig won the seat relatively easily in 1990, with 59% in the primary against Attorney General Jim Jones and with 61% in the general. In 1996 and 2002, self-financing millionaires opposed him. In 1996 building materials tycoon Walt Minnick spent $945,000 of his own money and attacked Craig sharply for backing Governor Phil Batt's nuclear waste compact. Craig responded by rafting down the river with his family and running ads predicting toxic desolation if the nuclear waste compact was not carried out. Craig won 57%–40%, losing only three counties. In 2002 he was opposed by retired investment banker Alan Blinken, who owned a house in Sun Valley for 10 years and registered to vote there in 2001. Clinton had appointed Blinken Ambassador to Belgium and so he had many points against him: Former investment banker, Clinton appointee, recent New Yorker. Some thought it a liability that he is Jewish, but Idaho can not easily be tarred as anti-Semitic: This was the first state to elect a Jewish governor, Moses Alexander, in 1914, and when Idaho was embarrassed by the doings of an Aryan Nations compound near Coeur d'Alene, citizens responded with a $6.3 million jury verdict for the assault of two people. Blinken did not shy away from such criticism. He boasted that he owned eight pistols, eight rifles and eight shotguns, "and I use them all. I'm a gun-totin' Idaho Democrat."

Blinken said he could bring "good paying" jobs to Idaho and attacked Craig for voting in favor of certain interests shortly after receiving campaign contributions from them. He took umbrage at a Craig press release hailing a new business coming to Idaho that Blinken said he had recruited. Craig defended his votes as being in line with long-held principles and on many issues said that Blinken's stands showed he doesn't understand life in Idaho. Blinken spent over $1.5 million of his own money plus $650,000 contributed by others, but Craig spent more than $3 million and Idaho did not drift far from its usual voting habits. Craig won 65%–33%; he carried 43 counties and Blinken carried the county that includes Sun Valley.

Junior Senator

Mike Crapo (R)

Elected 1998, seat up 2004, 1st term; b. May 20, 1951, Idaho Falls; home, Idaho Falls; Brigham Young U., B.A. 1973, Harvard U., J.D. 1977; Mormon; married (Susan).

Elected Office: ID Senate, 1984–92, Senate Ldr., 1988–92; U.S. House of Reps., 1992–98.

Professional Career: Practicing atty., 1977–92.

DC Office: 239 DSOB, 20510, 202-224-6142; Web site: crapo.senate.gov.

State Offices: Boise, 208-334-1776; Caldwell, 208-455-0360; Coeur D'Alene, 208-664-5490; Idaho Falls, 208-522-9779; Pocatello, 208-236-6775; Twin Falls, 208-734-2515.

Committees: *Agriculture, Nutrition & Forestry:* Forestry, Conservation & Rural Revitalization (Chmn.); Research, Nutrition & General Legislation. *Banking, Housing & Urban Affairs:* Financial Institutions; International Trade & Finance; Securities & Investment. *Budget. Environment & Public Works:* Clean Air, Climate Change & Nuclear Safety; Fisheries, Wildlife & Water (Chmn.). *Small Business & Entrepreneurship.*

Group Ratings

	ADA	ACLU	AFS	LCV	CON	ITIC	NTU	COC	ACU	NTLC	CHC
2002	10	40	0	6	43	100	54	94	94	87	—
2001	10	—	8	0	—	—	79	100	92	—	80

National Journal Ratings

	2001 LIB	—	2001 CONS		2002 LIB	—	2002 CONS
Economic	28%	—	71%		24%	—	75%
Social	31%	—	68%		0%	—	62%
Foreign	7%	—	72%		24%	—	67%

Key Votes of the 107th Congress

1. Approve Bush Tax Cuts	Y	5. Confirm Ashcroft as AG	Y	9. Bar Coop. with Intl. Court	Y
2. Expand Patients' Rights	N	6. Bar Gays in the Boy Scouts	Y	10. Trade Promotion Authority	Y
3. Campaign Finance Reform	N	7. $ for Hate Crime Prosecution	*	11. Authorize Force in Iraq	Y
4. Permit ANWR Development	Y	8. Overseas Military Abortions	N	12. Homeland Sec. Dept. Union	N

Election Results

1998 general	Mike Crapo (R)	262,966	(70%)	($1,563,811)
	Bill Mauk (D)	107,375	(28%)	($241,443)
	Other	7,833	(2%)	
1998 primary	Mike Crapo (R)	unopposed		
1992 general	Dirk Kempthorne (R)	270,468	(57%)	
	Richard Stallings (D)	208,036	(43%)	

Prior Winning Percentages: 1996 House (69%); 1994 House (75%); 1992 House (61%)

Mike Crapo (pronounced *CRAY-poe*) is a Republican elected to the House in 1992 and the Senate in 1998. He grew up in Idaho Falls, went to Brigham Young University and Harvard Law School, is a faithful Mormon who was named a bishop in the church at 31. He was elected to the state Senate in 1984, at 33, and became state Senate leader in 1988. Crapo ran for the House in 1992 and campaigned against all tax increases, for spending cuts, a balanced budget amendment and the line-item veto—the Contract with America two years early. He won the primary 68%–32%. "Cowboy Democrat" J. D. Williams, the state controller, ran on a "put America first" stand on industrial policy and trade. Crapo won 61%–35%.

With a self-professed "passion for reform," Crapo became Republican freshman class leader and championed institutional reforms—on discharge petitions, select committees, closed rules, closed committee meetings, open voting—many of which were adopted after Republicans won control in 1994. Like many Republicans, he favored simple, hard-and-fast rules—a balanced budget, term limits, across-the-board discretionary spending cuts (excluding Social Security)—

to force tough decisions. He sponsored the deficit reduction lock box bill that passed the House in 1995; he served on Agriculture as it passed the Freedom To Farm Act. He was a founding member of the Congressional Water Caucus and a member of the fabled Congressional Boot Caucus, an informal group of Western lawmakers who wear boots; he is co-chairman of the Congressional Sportsman's Caucus and the Senate Nuclear Cleanup Caucus. His overall voting record has been very conservative, with some exceptions on economics. He opposed NAFTA in 1993 but supported PNTR for China in 2000; he said that opening markets would help China's citizens "realize that there are other ways of governing." In 2002, he voted in favor of trade promotion authority. At the WTO meeting in Seattle, he worked to get China to agree to imports of 1.5 million metric tons of wheat from the Pacific Northwest.

In 1997 Crapo, who prides himself on returning to Idaho Falls to be with his family every weekend, faced a career choice that many House members would like to face. In September Governor Phil Batt announced his retirement and in October Senator Dirk Kempthorne said he would run for governor. Within days Crapo announced he would run for the Senate. His opponent was former Democratic chairman and Boise trial lawyer Bill Mauk. He attacked Crapo for accepting tobacco PAC money; Crapo replied he had stopped taking it some time ago. Idaho, one-quarter Mormon, had never elected a Mormon senator—this time it did. Crapo led in polls by a wide margin and won 70%–28%, carrying every county.

In his first years in the Senate, Crapo became chairman of the subcommittee with jurisdiction over the troubled Superfund program and many EPA programs. In March 2001 he was one of three voting against the brownfields bill in committee, on the grounds that it did not give state governments enough authority over cleanups. On the Agriculture Committee he worked on the farm bill in 2001 and 2002. He was particularly concerned about the provision that would require farmers taking advantage of the conservation program to agree to be bound by federal water standards; he saw this as undermining state water law, and he and Larry Craig introduced an amendment that would not require surrendering of water rights. He was troubled with the bill's dairy provisions, which he said would take money away from Western producers and give it to Eastern dairies. But he favored the more equal treatment of specialty crops, the tripling of the environmental quality incentives program, the increased funding for private grazing land and Craig's Grasslands Reserve Program; ultimately he voted in favor of the bill. In October 2002 he was one of 10 senators protesting the Agriculture Department's use of differential crop loan rates for different oilseeds and the elimination of loans for crambe and sesame seeds. With North Dakota Senator Kent Conrad, he sponsored a bill to pay for telehealth networks.

Much of his legislative work has an Idaho angle. In 1999 he developed Project SEARCH, a $1.3 million program to help cities with less than 2,500 people to apply for federal grants and comply with federal mandates; it was inspired by difficulties encountered by the town of Stanley in Custer County. He opposed reintroduction of grizzly bears to the Bitterroot Mountains and breaching the Snake River dams. He opposed spring drawdowns on lower Snake River dams and wrote a bill to compensate businesses around the Dworshak Reservoir for summer drawdowns to help migrating salmon. He rounded up support from California and Oregon colleagues for a plan that would give Idaho funding for salmon recovery proportionate to that of the Pacific Coast states, but Ted Stevens of Alaska remained resolutely opposed because it gave priority to stocks listed under the Endangered Species Act. He opposed fees at national forests and persuaded his colleague Larry Craig to switch and stand with him. "The grades are in, and the recreation fee demonstration project has flunked in Idaho. We have seen the Forest Service aggressively grow the user fees beyond the original intent of the program." With Harry Reid of Nevada he got the Senate in June 2002 to pass unanimously a bill providing for continuous producton of the American Eagle Silver Bullion Coin by having the Treasury replenish its silver supply on the open market. Blanks for coins are manufactured at the Sunshine Minting in Coeur d'Alene and Idaho's Silver Valley mines produce $70 million of silver per year. He got the Secretaries of the Interior and Agriculture to agree that they would not close grass airstrips on government land without consulting the state.

Crapo announced in April 2001 that he would seek reelection in 2004; he had expressed interest in a federal district judgeship. There is no reason to think he will have serious competition.

FIRST DISTRICT

Rep. Butch Otter (R)

Elected 2000, 2d term; b. May 3, 1942, Caldwell; home, Star; Col. of ID, B.A. 1967; Catholic; divorced.

Military Career: ID Natl. Guard, 1967–73.

Elected Office: ID House of Reps., 1972–76; ID Lt. Gov., 1986–2000.

Professional Career: Rancher; Dir., Food Products Div., Pres., Simplot Livestock, Pres., Simplot Intl., 1963–1993.

DC Office: 1711 LHOB 20515, 202-225-6611; Fax: 202-225-3029; Web site: www.house.gov/otter.

District Offices: Boise, 208-336-9831; Coeur d'Alene, 208-667-0127; Lewiston, 208-298-0030; Nampa, 208-466-4503.

Committees: *Energy & Commerce* (31st of 31 R): Commerce, Trade & Consumer Protection; Energy & Air Quality; Environment & Hazardous Materials.

Group Ratings

	ADA	ACLU	AFS	LCV	CON	ITIC	NTU	COC	ACU	NTLC	CHC
2002	0	20	11	0	25	100	60	90	96	97	100
2001	0	—	0	7	—	—	73	87	96	—	—

National Journal Ratings

	2001 LIB	—	2001 CONS		2002 LIB	—	2002 CONS
Economic	0%	—	94%		0%	—	91%
Social	35%	—	63%		32%	—	63%
Foreign	29%	—	69%		49%	—	51%

Key Votes of the 107th Congress

1. Approve Bush Tax Cuts	Y	5. Faith-Based Charities	Y	9. Trade Promotion Authority	Y
2. Limit Patients' Bill of Rights	Y	6. Bar Gays in the Boy Scouts	Y	10. Bar Funds for Intl. Court	Y
3. Campaign Finance Reform	N	7. Ban Partial-Birth Abortion	Y	11. Authorize Force in Iraq	Y
4. Ban ANWR Development	N	8. Arm Commercial Pilots	Y	12. Deny Home. Sec. Dept. Union	Y

Election Results

2002 general	Butch Otter (R)	120,743	(59%)	($997,441)
	Betty Richardson (D)	80,269	(39%)	($476,354)
	Other	5,129	(2%)	
2002 primary	Butch Otter (R)	unopposed		
2000 general	Butch Otter (R)	173,743	(65%)	($1,005,580)
	Linda Pall (D)	84,080	(31%)	($72,061)
	Other	10,293	(4%)	

The People		Race/Ethnic Origin	Ancestry	
Area size:	39,972 sq. mi.	89.0% White	German: 15.4%	English: 10.6%
Urban population:	65.8%	0.3% Black	Irish: 8.2%	
Rural population:	34.2%	0.9% Asian	**2000 Presidential Vote**	
Pop. 2000:	648,774	1.2% Native Am.	Bush (R) 171,364	(68%)
Median income:	$38,364	0.1% Hawaiian	Gore (D) 70,523	(28%)
Poverty status:	11.0%	1.5% Two+ races	Other 11,983	(5%)
Military veterans:	15.5%	0.1% Other	**Cook Partisan Voting Index:** R +21	
		6.8% Hispanic Origin		

Occupation	Blue collar: 26.2%	White collar: 56.1%	Gray collar: 17.7%

The 1st District of Idaho stretches from the Nevada border to Canada, including some of usually Republican Boise and all of the panhandle, historically Democratic but more recently leaning Republican. It includes two of Idaho's big growth areas, the western suburbs of Boise and the Coeur d'Alene area to the north in Kootenai County; high-tech and tourism have fueled the economy. In Nampa, which nearly doubled its population in the 1990s and replaced Pocatello as

Idaho's second-largest city, commercial developers have taken over land that not long ago grew wheat and alfalfa. Subdivisions with as many as 1,000 homes are being constructed in Meridian, the fastest-growing city in Idaho, as city planners struggle to upgrade their infrastructure. Some old-timers worry that their areas may become a new version of San Jose or Orange County, but support for property rights remain strong here. Politically, the 1st District has become just as Republican as the 2d: Al Gore won just 28% here in 2000. Northern mining counties were once the district's Democratic base; now it is the university town of Moscow.

The congressman from the 1st District is C.L. "Butch" Otter, a Republican first elected in 2000 and something of a free spirit. His father was a journeyman electrician and lifelong Democrat. He entered an abbey to pursue the priesthood but quickly decided that was not his calling; in 1967, he graduated from the College of Idaho. He went to work for his then father-in-law, billionaire J.R. Simplot, at the J.R. Simplot Company, the largest potato processor in the world, owner of the largest feedlot in the nation, and an early investor in Micron Technology. In 1972 he was elected to the state House. Otter ran for governor in 1978, finishing third in the Republican primary. In 1986, he was elected lieutenant governor, and served under three governors until he was elected to Congress. Otter, who became a wealthy independent ranch owner after his 1993 divorce, believes strongly in gun ownership and property rights. But he is not the social conservative that other Idaho Republicans have been. In 1992, he won the "Mr. Tight Jeans" contest at the Rockin' Rodeo bar in Boise. While he opposes abortion, he believes that the government should stay out of people's lives. He wants to check the power of the Environmental Protection Agency. This isn't a surprise: As a ranch owner, Otter has been charged three times by the EPA for violating the Clean Water Act; in 2001, he paid a fine of $50,000 for dredging and filling wetlands without a permit. But violating federal environmental regulations is not necessarily the worst offense in Idaho. Otter, who said that his pond digging was designed to improve the wetlands, responded that he showed he's willing to "stand up for folks in Idaho against a government that is arrogant, intransigent."

In 2000, when Helen Chenoweth-Hage kept her pledge to limit herself to three terms, a venomous Republican primary ensued between Otter and Dennis Mansfield, who founded the Christian conservative group Idaho Family Forum. Mansfield's supporters highlighted Otter's 1993 drunk-driving conviction, following which he agreed to perform 72 hours of community service and attend 16 hours of an alcohol treatment program; he apologized and went on a speaking tour to youngsters across Idaho. One of Mansfield's ads stated: "Just what we need in Washington—another bad example for our children." But Otter had the support of most Republican insiders, including Governor Dirk Kempthorne and 29 of 31 state senators. He argued that Washington had usurped the power of local governments, and that states can better make decisions that affect people's lives. He supported individual investment accounts in Social Security but declined to take a term limits pledge. Mansfield, running as a political outsider, backed term limits and was endorsed by the Wall Street-based Club for Growth. With help from a late get-out-the-vote campaign by the National Rifle Association and local farming and ranching interests—plus a more than 3–1 fundraising advantage—Otter won all 19 counties and defeated Mansfield 48%–27%; former state Republican chairman Ron McMurray took 17%. Otter won the general election 65%–31%.

In the House, Otter occasionally broke with conservatives on cultural and foreign-policy issues. He worked with others in the Idaho delegation to enact a bill that enables the Treasury to replenish its supply of silver on the open market for the first time in four decades. He took some local heat when he called for a 10-year study of how to control development in the state's vast wilderness areas, rather than follow other elected officials who have sought to work with competing interests; Idaho is one of two states without a statewide wilderness law. He sought $50 million to restore salmon habitat in Idaho rivers. He showed independence by abstaining during the House vote to expel Ohio Rep. Jim Traficant, and he was one of three Republicans to vote against the additional law-enforcement authority that Attorney General John Ashcroft sought in the USA Patriot Act.

Otter faced a competitive re-election challenge from Betty Richardson, who was U.S. Attorney for Idaho during the Clinton administration. She called Otter too conservative for his constituents, but conceded that national Democrats were too liberal for Idaho. Richardson took a term-limits pledge, and said that she would push for a constitutional amendment to impose term limits on members of Congress. Otter modified his earlier position on Social Security, and said that investment in private accounts should be for amounts above the payroll deduction. He softened some earlier rhetoric in favor of decriminalization of drugs and other libertarian positions. Richardson spent plenty of money and carried two counties surrounding the University of Idaho, but Otter won 59%–39%.

SECOND DISTRICT

Rep. Mike Simpson (R)

Elected 1998, 3d term; b. Sept. 8, 1950, Burley; home, Blackfoot; UT St. U., 1968–72; WA U. Dental Schl., D.D.S. 1977; Mormon; married (Kathy).

Elected Office: Blackfoot City Cncl., 1980–84; ID House of Reps., 1984–98, Speaker, 1993–98.

Professional Career: Practicing dentist, 1977-98.

DC Office: 1339 LHOB 20515, 202-225-5531; Fax: 202-225-8216; Web site: www.house.gov/simpson.

District Offices: Boise, 208-334-1953; Idaho Falls, 208-523-6701; Pocatello, 208-478-4160; Twin Falls, 208-734-7219.

Committees: *Appropriations* (33d of 36 R): Energy & Water Development; Labor, HHS & Education; VA, HUD & Independent Agencies.

Group Ratings

	ADA	ACLU	AFS	LCV	CON	ITIC	NTU	COC	ACU	NTLC	CHC
2002	0	13	0	0	8	100	56	100	92	81	92
2001	5	—	10	0	—	—	61	100	84	—	—

National Journal Ratings

	2001 LIB	—	2001 CONS		2002 LIB	—	2002 CONS
Economic	28%	—	69%		0%	—	91%
Social	20%	—	69%		0%	—	75%
Foreign	33%	—	60%		15%	—	78%

Key Votes of the 107th Congress

1. Approve Bush Tax Cuts	Y	5. Faith-Based Charities	Y	9. Trade Promotion Authority	Y
2. Limit Patients' Bill of Rights	Y	6. Bar Gays in the Boy Scouts	Y	10. Bar Funds for Intl. Court	Y
3. Campaign Finance Reform	N	7. Ban Partial-Birth Abortion	Y	11. Authorize Force in Iraq	Y
4. Ban ANWR Development	N	8. Arm Commercial Pilots	Y	12. Deny Home. Sec. Dept. Union	Y

Election Results

2002 general	Mike Simpson (R)	135,605	(68%)	($320,236)
	Edward Kinghorn (D)	57,769	(29%)	($12,467)
	Other	5,508	(3%)	
2002 primary	Mike Simpson (R)	unopposed		
2000 general	Mike Simpson (R)	158,912	(71%)	($532,746)
	Craig Williams (D)	58,265	(26%)	
	Other	7,542	(3%)	

Prior Winning Percentages: 1998 (53%)

The People		Race/Ethnic Origin	Ancestry	
Area size:	43,598 sq. mi.	87.1% White	English: 16.0%	German: 12.2%
Urban population:	67.0%	0.5% Black	Irish: 6.4%	
Rural population:	33.0%	0.9% Asian	**2000 Presidential Vote**	
Pop. 2000:	645,179	1.2% Native Am.	Bush (R)..............165,559 (67%)	
Median income:	$36,934	0.1% Hawaiian	Gore (D)...............68,055 (28%)	
Poverty status:	12.6%	1.3% Two+ races	Other....................12,319 (5%)	
Military veterans:	14.0%	0.1% Other	**Cook Partisan Voting Index:** R +21	
		8.9% Hispanic Origin		

Occupation	Blue collar: 23.8%	White collar: 57.3%	Gray collar: 18.9%

The 2d District of Idaho, from central Boise east to the Utah and Wyoming borders, is one of America's most Republican districts in presidential elections. It's also one of the most picturesque. The thick forests, mountain ranges and river valleys close by the Montana border are strongly Republican and suspicious of government (scenic and untamed Lemhi County is the only one Democrat Cecil Andrus never carried). Southeast Idaho is part of the Mormon heartland, and the LDS presence runs deep; eastern Idaho's first Mormon settlements were in Franklin, Bear Lake and Caribou Counties. The old frontier and railroad town of Pocatello was once a Democratic outpost, home to unionized rail workers, a liberal college campus and a far more diverse population than the surrounding parts (Idaho State University used to be known as the place where Mormon kids went to lose their religion). But in recent years, Pocatello has moved in a Republican direction—particularly in national elections—as union strength declined and the conservative Mormon influence increased. Fifty miles north on I-15, Idaho Falls serves as the metropolis for a vast region stretching from West Yellowstone, Wyoming to the Salmon River Mountains. The nearby Idaho National Engineering and Environmental Laboratory, a massive facility that occupies 890 square miles and employs more than 8,000 workers, is located on a windswept, desolate range—exactly why the federal government selected the site in the 1940s to test nuclear reactors. West of INEEL, in the year-round resort community of Sun Valley (Blaine County), celebrities from Bill Gates to Arnold Schwarzenegger have spurred rapid development with soaring costs, which has led to calls for restrictions on growth. Blaine is in the one Idaho county that voted for Al Gore—by 220 votes. Elsewhere, most of the farm counties and towns, including those in the Magic Valley (the Twin Falls area), are Republican; the 2d's portion of Boise includes the city's few Denverish-liberal neighborhoods, however. The other counties in the 2d District gave between 69% and 89% of their votes to George W. Bush.

The congressman from the 2d District is Mike Simpson, a Republican elected in 1998 when incumbent Mike Crapo was elected to the Senate. He grew up in Blackfoot, became a dentist and joined his father's practice there; he returned to Utah State University in 2002 to get his bachelor's degree, after having completed some much-delayed paperwork. Simpson was elected to the city council in 1980 and the state House in 1984; he didn't declare himself as a Republican until then and was opposed by the local party organization. In 1993 he became Speaker, but kept up his dental practice as well. In the legislature he was known as a moderate in a conservative House, affable and able to get differing sides together. When Governor Phil Batt announced he would retire in 1998, Simpson wanted to run for his office; Senator Dirk Kempthorne's decision to run for governor closed that option. Then 2d District Congressman Mike Crapo ran for Kempthorne's Senate seat, and Simpson entered that race.

His elevation to the House required some work. In the Republican primary, Simpson was opposed by state Representative Mark Stubbs and two former state senators. Simpson called for tax reform, Stubbs for lower payroll taxes; Stubbs had opposed nuclear programs at the Idaho National Engineering and Environmental Laboratory in the 1980s, while Simpson wanted more work at the facility. But the big issue was term limits. Simpson refused to take a pledge to serve only three terms; the other three did. Term limits advocates spent large sums to run TV ads against Simpson. Enraged by these ads, Batt endorsed Simpson five days before the election. Simpson ran ads against "outsiders" and "out-of-state folk;" Batt recorded a message which was delivered to 47,000 households by telemarketing. Simpson beat Stubbs, 47%–41%. The Democratic nominee was Richard Stallings, a former history professor elected to the House in 1984 and re-elected three times; in 1992 he ran against Kempthorne for the Senate and lost 57%–43%. Stallings talked about his conservative voting record in the House, called for more education spending and pointed with anxiety at falling farm commodity prices. Simpson wanted a smaller federal role in education; he favored tax cuts and individual investment accounts in Social Security. As farm prices plummeted, Simpson called for trade talks to open markets, with possible tariffs if others didn't go along, and renegotiating NAFTA. Simpson won 53%–45%, losing the most visible parts of the district—Pocatello, Sun Valley, Boise—but carrying just about everything else, and in the Mormon southeast and ultraconservative northeast by considerable margins.

In the House, Simpson has been relatively moderate for a western Republican. He dedicated much of his first two years to building relationships with each of his 434 colleagues—preferably, he said, in one-on-one informal conversations. But he did not get to know all of them—the House is a big place—and that reinforced his opposition to term limits. More than most western Republicans, he has reached out to Democrats on economic and social issues. He helped to establish a bipartisan caucus to talk about the trade-related needs of farmers and ranchers. Despite his call for a middle ground on resource issues, he endorsed a prohibition on breaching dams along the Columbia and Snake Rivers. He criticized the Clinton administration for acting unilaterally to expand the Craters of the Moon National Monument and filed a bill to prevent similar actions. Simpson advocates a renewed commitment to research and development of nuclear energy, and expanded use of nuclear power. He took credit for $2.8 million in airport improvement projects in Arco, Burley, Pocatello and Idaho Falls, and a $1 million loan for an alcoholism and drug abuse center in Gooding. George W. Bush signed two of his bills; one, to protect hunting rights in the expanded portions of the Craters of the Moon monument, and the other to overhaul a job-training program for veterans.

Simpson has had an easy time winning reelection. In 2000 his Democratic opponent refused campaign contributions and relied on the Internet to get his message out; Simpson won 71%–26%. In 2002 he won almost as easily. In the meantime, he raised $100,000 for the NRCC as he lobbied for a seat on the Appropriations Committee; he got it.

★ ILLINOIS ★

At the beginning of the 20th century Chicago seemed destined to be the center of America. This brash new city on the lake had grown from 112,000 residents in 1860, when it was host to the Republican Convention that nominated Illinois' Abraham Lincoln, to 1.4 million when it hosted the Columbian Exposition in 1893 and 1.7 million in 1900. "Make no little plans," Chicago architect Daniel Burnham exhorted. And Chicago was making vast plans: building grand parks on the lakefront, erecting America's first downtown of skyscrapers, building expansive retail palaces, becoming the headquarters of the new American Medical and American Bar associations, creating a great university from scratch on the Exposition's Midway Plaisance, housing the union agitators and their liberal advocate Clarence Darrow as well as the corporate leaders and attorneys who bested them, hosting the Democratic Convention of 1896 that nominated 36-year-old William Jennings Bryan after his "cross of gold" speech, and becoming the headquarters of the brilliant campaign Marcus Hanna waged for William McKinley that beat Bryan in the fall. Chicago started with the advantage of a great location, where the Great Lakes meet the prairies of the vast Mississippi Valley, and Chicago's entrepreneurs made it the hub of the nation's railroad network and the center of the nation's trade in lumber, grain and meat, as William Cronon describes in *Nature's Metropolis*.

A century later, Chicago is the nation's third-largest metropolis, sometimes overshadowed by and often ignored by the media of coastal New York and Los Angeles, but it is still a productive and creative world-city. Illinois, after near-zero population growth in the 1970s and 1980s, saw its population rise 9% in the 1990s, more than any decade since the 1960s. In commerce, Chicago remains a prime producer and processor of food products, the nation's number one manufactur-

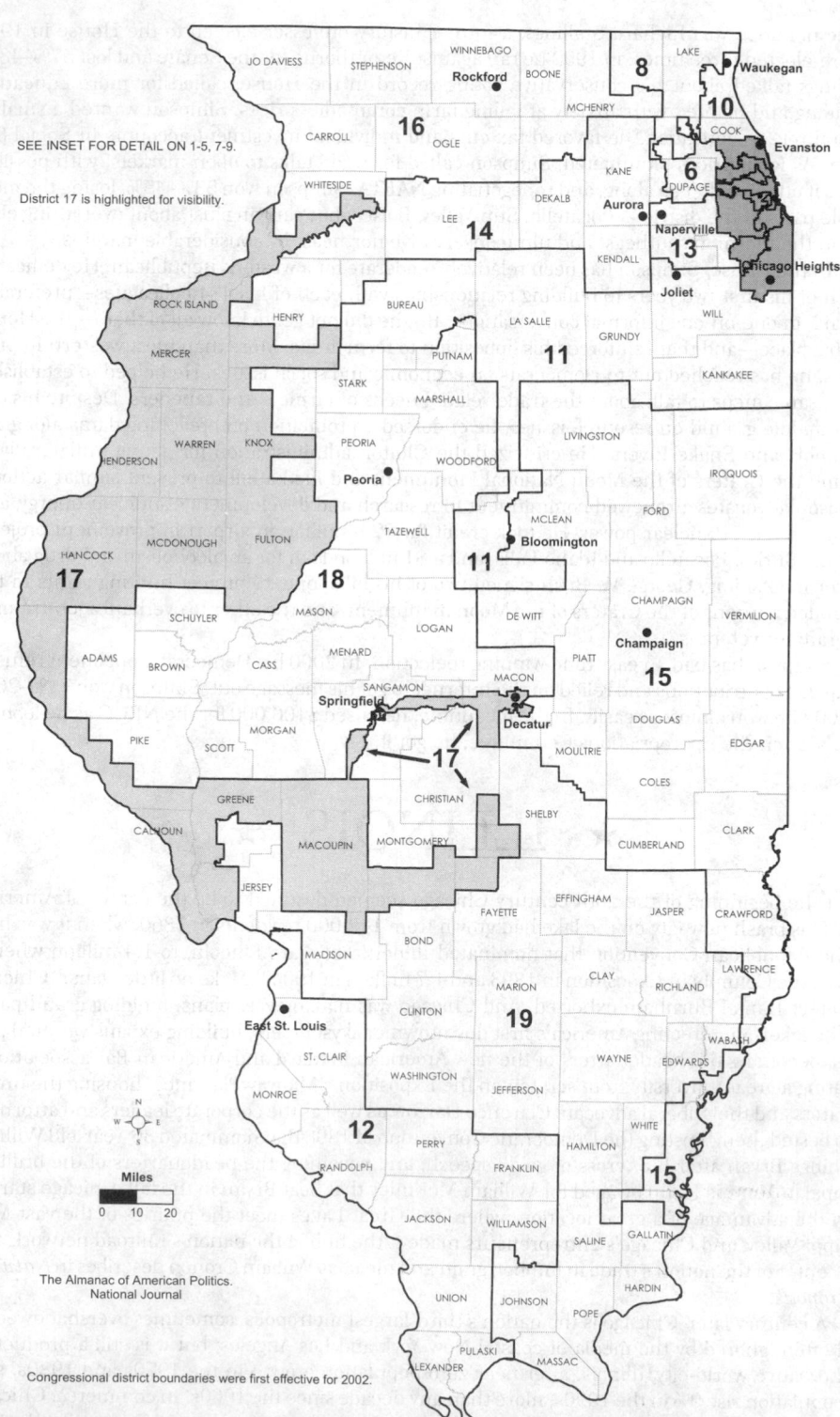

SEE INSET FOR DETAIL ON 1-5, 7-9.

District 17 is highlighted for visibility.

The Almanac of American Politics.
National Journal

Congressional district boundaries were first effective for 2002.

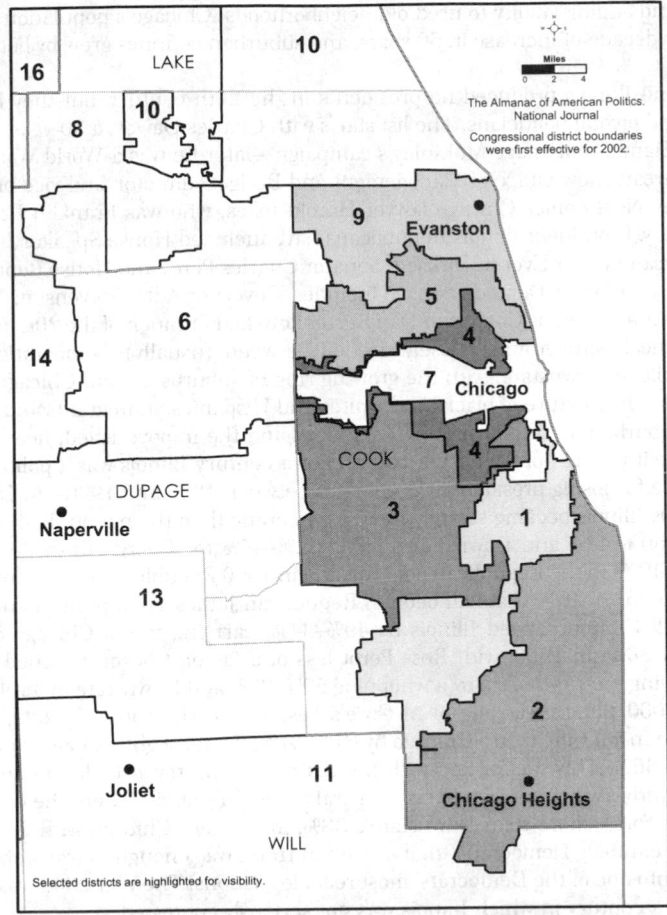

ing center with the strongest white-collar and service economy between the coasts, the home of the world's greatest commodities exchanges and futures markets. O'Hare Airport, promoted and nurtured by longtime (1955–76) Mayor Richard J. Daley and long one of the world's busiest airports is one of its great hubs of commerce. But for the most part Chicago was established not by government but by markets; it has always been a free enterprise city, settled by pioneers from New England and Kentucky, by immigrant Irishmen who dug the first canal connecting Lake Michigan and the Illinois River, and by railroad promoters who saw its potential as the great connecting point between East and West, the Great Lakes and the Mississippi Valley. Its factories, built where iron ore from Great Lakes freighters and coal from inland hills came together, attracted migrants from near and far. Today many of the old factories have been closed or demolished, and some of the Chicago area's biggest corporations have had problems. Sears, which moved out of the Sears Tower to suburban Schaumburg, is no longer the nation's leading retailer; McDonald's, headquartered in suburban Oak Brook, has suffered its first-ever quarterly loss in 2002; Boeing, which moved its headquarters from Seattle to downtown Chicago in 2001, is struggling to compete against Europe's Airbus Industrie; United Airlines, headquartered next to O'Hare in Elk Grove Village, filed for bankruptcy in December 2002. But Chicago's economy, based on finance and commodities, manufacturing and food, and undergirded by thousands of small firms, continues to thrive. The O'Hare area rivals downtown Chicago in number of jobs; central city neighborhoods north and south of the Loop are attracting new affluent residents; Latinos are thronging to the

Chicago area and adding vitality to tired old neighborhoods. Chicago's population rose 4% in the 1990s, the first decade of increase in 50 years, and suburban counties grew by between 16% and 42%

Chicago and Illinois produced no presidents in the 20th century, but they have produced crucial votes and pivotal politicians. The list starts with Charles Dawes, a 30-year-old lawyer sent to Chicago by Hanna to manage McKinley's campaign—later he was a World War I general, the first Budget Bureau (now Office of Management and Budget) director, and vice president under Calvin Coolidge. Next comes Chicago lawyer Harold Ickes, who was Franklin Roosevelt's great Interior secretary. Prominent Illinois Republicans have included House Speaker Joseph Cannon, Senate Republican Leader Everett Dirksen, Senator Charles Percy and House Republican Leader Robert Michel; prominent Democrats have included Governor Adlai Stevenson, Mayor Richard J. Daley and Ways and Means Chairman Dan Rostenkowski. For much of the 20th century, Illinois was a key political battleground, closely divided between (usually) Democratic Chicago and (mostly) Republican Downstate, with the growing ring of suburbs around Chicago becoming increasingly pivotal. Its mixture of blacks and whites and Hispanics, immigrants and pioneers, city-dwellers and suburbanites and farmers, the affluent and the impoverished, heavy industry and high-tech, make it a rough proxy for the nation. For a century Illinois was a political bellwether, voting only twice for losing presidential candidates between 1896 and 1996—in 1916 and 1976. But in the 1990s Illinois became steadily more Democratic than the nation. Back in 1988 metro Chicago voted 50%–49% and Downstate Illinois 52%–47% for George Bush, leaving the state narrowly (51%–49%) in the Republican column, and in 1990 Republican Jim Edgar narrowly held the governorship, 51%–48%, that had been in Republican James Thompson's hands since 1976. But in 1992 Bill Clinton carried Illinois by 49%–34%, carrying metro Chicago 50%–34% and Downstate 45%–36%. In 1996, with Ross Perot less of a factor, Clinton widened his margin to 54%–37%, carrying metro Chicago by a whopping 59%–33% and Downstate by a relatively narrow 47%–42%. In 2000 Illinois was one of Al Gore's best states. He won 55%–43%, running even ahead of Clinton in winning metro Chicago by 61%–37%; he did slightly worse Downstate, which Bush won 51%–46%. This was in line with the national trend toward Clinton and Gore in the suburbs and slightly away from Democrats in rural areas. In Illinois, where the Chicago suburbs cast 42% of the votes, more than Downstate's 38%, and where Chicago with 20% of the votes remains overwhelmingly Democratic, that suburban trend was enough to transform a classically marginal state into one of the Democrats' most reliable bastions. The year 2000 was the first close election year in a century in which Illinois was not seriously contested.

It may seem strange that a state whose politics since Abraham Lincoln's time has mostly been run by political machines should be transformed by a change of opinion in the suburbs. Illinois's party machines were already up and going when they rallied thousands of partisans to cheer and boo at the debates between Lincoln and Stephen Douglas in 1858. Machine politics continued through the Gilded Age as politicians in a closely divided state competed for public jobs and as politicians of both parties courted the immigrants who came streaming into Chicago. Both Chicago and Downstate had a thriving two-party politics in the early 20th century; it was not until the Depression of the 1930s that Chicago became reliably Democratic. In the decades that followed, the suburbs, wary of Chicago, became Republican and developed machines of their own. Starting in 1950, Illinois's political trends were set by reactions to the political officeholder most visible to the voters, who was not the governor off in remote Springfield and certainly not the senators who have to work "out of town" in Washington, but the mayor of Chicago. It was only through the herculean efforts of Mayor and party boss Richard J. Daley that John F. Kennedy was able to win Illinois by exactly (or so it was certified) 8,858 votes out of 4.7 million cast—a turnout that has been exceeded since only in 1960 and 1980. In the 1970s, reaction against Daley was key to the rise of James Thompson, who as U.S. Attorney successfully prosecuted machine denizens. For most of the 1980s the dominant figure was Mayor Harold Washington, the able black mayor who was vociferously opposed by white politicians in the "council wars." Suburbanites, repelled by the hubbub and out of fear that Chicago's demands might increase their taxes, voted heavily Republican.

The dominant figure since his election in 1989 has been Mayor Richard M. Daley. Like his father, he seems to know the city block by block, and has worked to beautify it—planting thousands of trees and encouraging handsome wrought-iron fences. He has sought and obtained racial reconciliation, even while rallying to his side the new immigrant voters and the old Lakefront liberals. In just about every poll Daley is the most popular political figure not just in Chicago, but in all of Illinois. The old political machine which his father so ably led is no more, but Daley has used the powers of office to propitiate the black politicians who at first seemed to be obdurate opponents, and in February 1999 won reelection 72%–28%, with nearly 45% of the black vote against a serious black candidate, Congressman Bobby Rush. His luster has extended to his party. His example as the state's leading Democrat undoubtedly helped ease the way for suburbanites to move toward Clinton and Gore in 1996 and 2000.

And Daley surely had something to do with the fact that Illinois was the Democrats' number one success story politically in 2002. He provided an example of competent, corruption-free Democratic government that contrasted vividly with the corruption and disarray among the state's machine Republicans. Governor George Ryan, elected in 1998 after a lifetime in politics, had terrible scandal problems; Ryan, with abysmally low job ratings, prudently decided not to seek a second term. The Republican nominee, Jim Ryan, was no relation but bearing the handicap of the same last name, in July 2002 called on George Ryan to resign—an off-putting sign of intraparty strife, to say the least. In July 2002 longtime state House Republican leader Lee Daniels was forced to resign as state party chairman after his staff was accused of making hundreds of campaign trips on state time. In the meantime, the Democrats in their March 2002 primary produced a candidate who seemed to have the Daley imprimatur, Congressman Rod Blagojevich. Democrats had not won the governorship for 30 years, when maverick Democrat Daniel Walker won, and Blagojevich had no trouble running as the candidate of change. He won by a solid, though lower than expected, 52%–45% margin, carrying metro Chicago 57%–40% while losing Downstate 52%–46%: the key was the suburbs. In addition, Democrats increased their margin in the state House and won control of the state Senate for the first time in 10 years. So Illinois will now have a state government controlled by Democrats on friendly terms with the mayor of Chicago, for the first time since 1968.

The People		Race/Ethnic Origin			Military veterans: 1,003,572 (10.9%)	
Pop. 2000:	12,419,293	8,424,140	67.8%	White	WWII: 22.7%	Korea: 14.4%
Pop. 1990:	11,430,602	1,856,152	14.9%	Black	Vietnam: 30.1%	Gulf War: 9.0%
Change 1990–2000:	Up 8.6%	419,916	3.4%	Asian	**Most populous cities:**	
Change 1980–1990:	Down 0.0%	18,232	0.1%	Native Am.	1. Chicago	2,896,016
% of U.S. total:	4.4%	3,116	0.0%	Hawaiian	2. Rockford	150,115
Pop. rank:	5th of 50	153,996	1.2%	Two+ races	3. Aurora	142,990
Area size:	57,914 sq. mi.	13,479	0.1%	Other	4. Naperville	128,358
State Native:	67.1%	1,530,262	12.3%	Hisp. Origin	5. Peoria	112,936
Non-citizen:	7.5%	**Ancestry**			Urban population: 87.8%	
Language		German: 15.1%		Irish: 9.3%	Rural population: 12.2%	
English: 80.3%	Spanish: 9.6%	Polish: 5.8%		English: 5.1%		
Other Eur.: 7.1%		Italian: 4.6%				

Education		Work Sector		General Assembly		
H.S. Grad:	81.4%	Private: 81.8%	Govt: 12.7%	Senate	32 D 27 R	
College Grad:	26.1%	Self: 5.3%	Family: 0.3%	House	66 D 52 R	
Industry		Unemployment: 6.0%		Legislative Term Limits: No		
Agri: 1.1%	Con: 5.7%	**Household Income**		**Registered Voters**		
Fin: 7.9%	Info: 3.0%	<15k: 13.8%	15-35k: 23.2%	No party registration		
Mfg: 22.0%	Prof: 29.5%	35-50k: 16.2%	50-100k: 32.3%			
Public: 4.0%	Trade: 14.9%	100-150k: 9.0%	>150k: 5.4%			
Other: 11.9%		Median: $46,590				
Occupation		Poverty status: 10.7%				
Blue collar: 24.0%	White collar: 61.8%	**Home Value**				
Gray collar: 14.3%		<50k: 11.2%	50-100k: 26.1%	100-200k: 39.7%	200-300k: 13.6%	
		300-500k: 6.6%	>500k: 2.8%	Median: $127,800		

Presidential politics Illinois's presidential primary, for years held fittingly on or around St. Patrick's Day, clinched the nominations for Republican victors Gerald Ford in 1976, Ronald Reagan in 1980 and George Bush in 1988, and Democratic victors Jimmy Carter in 1980, Walter Mondale in 1984 and Bill Clinton in 1992. In 1988 the Democratic nomination would probably have been clinched here for Michael Dukakis, except for the dominance of two Illinois candidates, Paul Simon and Jesse Jackson. But in the 1990s and 2000, as more states voted earlier, Illinois was too late to decide any nomination. Illinois' Republican primary voters are about evenly split between the suburbs, with their affluent free-market dislike for taxes, and Downstate, with their old-fashioned, practical-minded Midwestern politics. More than 60% of Illinois' Democratic primary votes are cast in Cook County, most of them in Chicago.

By 2000 Illinois had become as solidly a Democratic state in presidential elections as California, a development that has not attracted as much national notice because California in 2004 will cast 55 electoral votes and Illinois 21. Only a major move in the suburbs away from Democrats and toward George W. Bush will make Illinois competitive in 2004. Otherwise, it remains the Democrats' strongest state between the District of Columbia and California.

2000 Presidential Vote		
Gore (D)	2,589,026	(55%)
Bush (R)	2,019,421	(43%)
Nader (Green)	103,759	(2%)
Other	29,902	(1%)

2000 Republican Presidential Primary		
Bush (R)	496,646	(67%)
McCain (R)	158,752	(22%)
Keyes (R)	66,057	(9%)
Other	15,402	(2%)

2000 Democratic Presidential Primary		
Gore (D)	682,916	(84%)
Bradley (D)	115,317	(14%)

1996 Presidential Vote		
Clinton (D)	2,341,744	(54%)
Dole (R)	1,587,021	(37%)
Perot (I)	346,408	(8%)

Congressional districting Illinois lost one of its 20 House seats in the 2000 Census, and control of redistricting was split between the Democratic state House and the then-Republican state Senate and governor. In similar circumstances, the 1980s and 1990s redistricting plans had been drawn by courts, with results that were politically unpredictable and unpalatable to incumbents: in 1992, four incumbents lost their primaries. Things worked differently in 2001.

108th Congress Lineup
10 R   9 D

107th Congress Lineup
10 D   10 R

Speaker Dennis Hastert and 3d District Democrat William Lipinski started negotiating early, to produce an incumbent-protection plan that would pass both houses of the legislature. Before the Census data came in, it was assumed that the 5th District would be eliminated, since Democratic incumbent Rod Blagojevich had announced that he was running for governor. But the Census figures showed that the 5th District and adjacent districts in Chicago, swelled with new immigrants, had gained population, while rural southern Illinois had lost population. Mayor Richard M. Daley let it be known that he would not like to see Chicago lose a seat.

So Hastert and Lipinski concocted a new plan taking a district away from southern Illinois. The victim was 19th District Democratic Congressman David Phelps, a former professional gospel singer with little seniority and a somewhat conservative voting record. His hometown was connected by a narrow band of land on the eastern edge of the state with the central Illinois 15th district held by Republican Tim Johnson. Phelps had no clout in the legislature, and the Hastert-Lipinski plan became law in May 2001. Phelps sued unsuccessfully and then ran, also unsuccessfully, against Republican incumbent John Shimkus in the new 19th District. Why were Lipinski, Daley and Speaker Michael Madigan willing to sacrifice a fellow Democrat and lose their party's 10–10 parity in the House delegation? Because the low-seniority Phelps could do little for them in the House, while Hastert had been generous in using his powers as Speaker to aid Daley, Lipinski and other Chicago Democrats on Chicago issues and projects. Maintaining a Republican majority that would keep Hastert in the speakership was in the interests of Chicago Democrats.

The resulting map is a nightmare for those who believe redistricting plans should have compact and competitive districts. Aside from Phelps and perhaps Shimkus, every other incumbent was strengthened. And the resulting district lines are grotesque. The 17th District, long confined to west central Illinois, now has a narrow finger extending to downtown Springfield and Decatur. The 15th District in central Illinois has a long narrow tentacle along the eastern border of the state, then snakes south to the Kentucky border. Hastert's 14th District extends from the Chicago suburbs to a point six miles from the Iowa border. Incumbents were accommodated in the most minute fashion. A small portion of Livingston County was added to Jerry Weller's 11th District so his parents could vote for him. Complicated boundaries were drawn to Philip Crane's 8th District so that his Palatine office would still be in his district. Jesse Jackson Jr.'s 2d district was extended southward to be nearer to Peotone, the site for the proposed third Chicago airport that he has been tirelessly promoting. Lipinski lost a heavily black ward in Chicago and majority-Hispanic Cicero and in return got the white Bridgeport neighborhood that is the homeland of the Daleys and some heavily white suburbs.

Governor

Rod Blagojevich (D)

Elected 2002, term expires Jan. 2007, 1st term; b. Dec. 10, 1956, Chicago; home, Chicago; Northwestern U., B.A. 1979, Pepperdine U., J.D. 1983; Eastern Orthodox; married (Patti).

Elected Office: IL House of Reps., 1992–96; U.S. House of Reps., 1996–02.

Professional Career: Practicing atty., 1984–96; Asst. Cook County Atty., 1986–88.

Office: State Capitol, 207 Statehouse, Springfield, 62706, 217-782-6830; Fax: 217-524-1676; Web site: www.illinois.gov/gov.

Election Results

2002 general	Rod Blagojevich (D)	1,847,040	(52%)
	Jim Ryan (R)	1,594,960	(45%)
	Other	96,883	(3%)
2002 primary	Rod Blagojevich (D)	457,197	(37%)
	Paul Vallas (D)	431,728	(34%)
	Roland Burris (D)	363,591	(29%)
1998 general	George H. Ryan (R)	1,714,094	(51%)
	Glenn Poshard (D)	1,594,191	(47%)
	Other	50,420	(2%)

Rod Blagojevich was elected governor of Illinois in 2002, the first Democrat elected to the office since 1972. He grew up in Chicago, the son of a Serbian immigrant who worked at the A. Finkl & Sons steel works on the North Side; his mother worked as a ticket-taker for the Chicago Transit Authority. He lived in a five-room walkup near Cicero and Armitage and worked as a shoeshine boy and a dishwasher on the Alaskan pipeline. Blagojevich (pronounced *blah-GOY-eh-vich*) graduated from Northwestern and Pepperdine Law School and was a Golden Gloves boxer. A fine athlete, he runs marathons, climbs perilous mountains and played on the House Democrats' baseball team. He practiced law and worked two years in State's Attorney Richard M. Daley's office. But he got his start in politics through his father-in-law, 33d Ward Alderman and Democratic Ward Committeeman Richard Mell. Mell was first elected alderman in 1975; he delivered the highest ward percentage for Mayor Jane Byrne in 1983, against Harold Washington and Richard M. Daley, and was a foe of Washington in the 1980s "council wars"; he is currently chairman of the Council's Rules Committee. In 1988 Blagojevich met Mell's daughter Patti at a Mell fundraiser, and in 1990 they were married. In 1988 he got a job on Mell's staff and in 1992 he was elected to the Illinois House. His opportunity to run for the U.S. House came after Republican Michael Flanagan upset Ways and Means Chairman Dan Rostenkowski in 1994. Flanagan, who had little backing, was obviously a one-termer. Blagojevich outspent Flanagan and won 64%–36%. In the House he opposed free trade measures and the B-2 bomber. In 1999 he traveled to Serbia with Jesse Jackson and, as translator and chief negotiator, secured the release of three American POWs despite lack of cooperation from the Clinton administration.

The initial impulse for Blagojevich's gubernatorial candidacy may have come from uncertainty about redistricting. It was fairly clear early on that Illinois would lose a seat in the 2000 Census, and most politicians assumed one of the Chicago districts would have to go—and Blagojevich's 5th District was vulnerable because it could easily be sliced up by its neighbors and was not represented by a black or Hispanic. Moreover, it was apparent that unpopular incumbent Republican George Ryan would be hard put to win a second term. Ryan was Secretary of State from 1990 to 1998; even before he was elected governor by a 51%–47% margin in November 1998, evidence started coming out that employees in the secretary of state's office had taken bribes for issuing large numbers of commercial driver's licenses to unqualified applicants and had funneled some of the money to Ryan's campaign accounts. One of the unqualified drivers was responsible for an expressway accident that killed six children. In early 2000 a former top Ryan aide was indicted for covering up information about these charges (he pleaded guilty in January 2001). In January 2000 Ryan apologized for the corruption that existed in that department and said he had not been aware of it. But evidence came out that whistleblowers in the department had been fired and had tried to get information to Ryan and others close to him. In May 2001 another former high-ranking official in the secretary of state's office admitted to trading coveted low-number license plates for campaign contributions. A February 2001 poll found that 45% of Illinois residents thought he should resign. Ryan generated some positive press by proclaiming a moratorium on executions in January 2000 after a *Chicago Tribune* series on flaws in death penalty cases and by leading a trade mission to Cuba, but these were issues that appealed more to elites than to the mass of voters. Against this background, Blagojevich in July 2001 announced that he was running for governor. He plunged ahead, although the redistricting plan passed two months earlier had preserved his 5th District in almost identical form.

There were crowded races in both parties' March 2002 primaries. In the Democratic primary, Blagojevich faced former Chicago schools CEO Paul Vallas and former Attorney General Roland Burris. Burris was relying on his appeal to black voters, Vallas on his record in improving Chicago's public schools, although he had left office at odds with his original patron, Mayor Richard M. Daley. In metro Chicago Vallas led with 38% of the vote to 32% for Burris and 29% for Blagojevich. But Blagojevich won 56% of the vote Downstate, for a 37%–34%–29% victory over Vallas and Burris. There was more acrimony on the Republican side. All three candidates vied to distance themselves from George Ryan. State Senator Patrick O'Malley campaigned as an outspoken conservative. Lieutenant Governor Corinne Wood, a supporter of abortion rights, said her two rivals were "too extreme" because they opposed abortion. Ryan, well known from his years as DuPage County State's Attorney and state Attorney General, was pummeled from both sides. But he won convincingly, with 45% of the vote to 28% for O'Malley and 27% for Wood.

Ordinarily in Illinois politics it is an advantage to have an Irish name shared by other successful politicians. Candidates named Ryan, Hynes or Hines, or Cullerton are often elected to downballot state and Cook County offices without much difficulty and can easily become serious contenders for the top positions. Being mistaken for another politician of the same name can be a plus. But in 2002 it was not an advantage to be a Ryan. Jim Ryan, no relation to or friend of the incumbent governor, was at pains to distinguish himself from George Ryan, to the point that he had campaign signs that said simply "Jim." Jim Ryan lamented that Blagojevich was not being hurt by his ties to machine politicians. But Richard Mell was not a political liability in 2002 and Daley was a decided political asset. In July 2002 Jim Ryan called on George Ryan to resign—about as strong a repudiation of one's own party's governor as one can imagine. In September 2002 George Ryan called Jim Ryan "a lousy candidate," and Jim Ryan said that the governor was "a bitter man" who "ran the worst administration in the history of Illinois." But it was not much help.

Meanwhile, Blagojevich was not hurt by minor mistakes—stating that his truth-in-sentencing law had passed the legislature when it hadn't, claiming that he had never supported banning handguns when he had said on a 1996 questionnaire that he did. Big lobby groups which usually back Republicans—the Illinois State Medical Society, the Illinois Retail Merchants Association—backed Blagojevich. Altogether Blagojevich raised $25 million, far more than Jim Ryan. He called Ryan "a different kind of Republican, out of step with the mainstream values of Illinois" and a member of "the radical right." In October Republicans charged that Blagojevich had been a "ghost payroller" when he worked on Mell's aldermanic staff.

The only surprise about the outcome was that it was a bit closer than expected. Blagojevich won 52%–45%, a showing a couple of points under Gore's in 2000. He carried metro Chicago by a solid 57%–40% and lost Downstate by only a 52%–46%—a good return on the time and money he spent there. On election night, held at the A. Finkl & Sons steel works, Blagojevich, a big Elvis Presley fan, said he was "all shook up" and full of "a whole bunch of hunk o', hunk o' burnin' love for each one of you." Democrats picked up the state Senate, and Chicagoan Emil Jones succeeded longtime Republican leader Pate Philip as Senate Majority Leader; Democratic State Chairman Michael Madigan remained in charge of the Chicago House. In December 2002 federal prosecutors announced that George Ryan had been present when his chief aide, under indictment and scheduled to be tried in January 2003, ordered a secretary of state employee to destroy evidence he suspected federal prosecutors would seek. Amid the good publicity Ryan received for considering commuting all death sentences and calling for reforms in the death penalty, there was also speculation that he would be indicted; by 2003 nearly 60 workers in Ryan's old office had been indicted, but Ryan still had not been charged. "Illinois has voted for change," Blagojevich proclaimed on election night and some Democratic measures long blocked by Republicans—gay rights, reopening of some state facilities, a special Chicago casino, new runways at O'Hare—seemed likely to pass. But Blagojevich also faced a $5 billion budget deficit and a depleted state rainy day fund; the $52 billion budget he proposed in April 2003 called for increasing business taxes and selling some state-owned buildings, although he continued to oppose raising state income or personal property taxes.

But Blagojevich is an optimist. He gave up a safe House seat for what many thought was a very risky race for governor, and won—the first House member to be elected governor of Illinois since 1834—and that may not be the limit of his ambition. In November 2002 Blagojevich was already talking with Democratic allies about a six-year plan to run for president in 2008. That seemed improbable—but so did Blagojevich's talk about running for governor of Illinois in 1999.

Senior Senator

Richard Durbin (D)

Elected 1996, seat up 2008, 2d term; b. Nov. 21, 1944, E. St. Louis; home, Springfield; Georgetown U., B.S. 1966, J.D. 1969; Catholic; married (Loretta).

Elected Office: U.S. House of Reps., 1982–96.

Professional Career: Staff, Lt. Gov. Paul Simon, 1969–72; Legal Cnsl., IL Sen. Judiciary Cmte., 1972–82; Prof., S. IL Schl. of Medicine, 1978–82.

DC Office: 332 DSOB, 20510, 202-224-2152; Fax: 202-228-0400; Web site: www.durbin.senate.gov.

State Offices: Chicago, 312-353-4952; Marion, 618-998-8812; Springfield, 217-492-4062.

Committees: *Appropriations*: Agriculture & Rural Development; Defense; District of Columbia; Foreign Operations; Legislative Branch (RMM); Transportation, Treasury & General Government. *Governmental Affairs*: Government Management, Federal Workforce & the District of Columbia (RMM); Investigations (Permanent). *Intelligence (Select). Judiciary*: Administrative Oversight & the Courts; Constitution, Civil Rights & Property Rights; Crime, Corrections & Victims' Rights; Immigration, Border Security & Citizenship. *Rules & Administration*.

Group Ratings

	ADA	ACLU	AFS	LCV	CON	ITIC	NTU	COC	ACU	NTLC	CHC
2002	95	60	100	88	58	50	9	50	0	0	—
2001	95	—	100	100	—	—	7	31	0	—	0

National Journal Ratings

	2001 LIB —	2001 CONS	2002 LIB —	2002 CONS
Economic	88%	9%	80%	15%
Social	60%	36%	82%	0%
Foreign	87%	3%	96%	0%

Key Votes of the 107th Congress

1. Approve Bush Tax Cuts	N	5. Confirm Ashcroft as AG	N	9. Bar Coop. with Intl. Court	Y
2. Expand Patients' Rights	Y	6. Bar Gays in the Boy Scouts	N	10. Trade Promotion Authority	N
3. Campaign Finance Reform	Y	7. $ for Hate Crime Prosecution	Y	11. Authorize Force in Iraq	N
4. Permit ANWR Development	N	8. Overseas Military Abortions	Y	12. Homeland Sec. Dept. Union	Y

Election Results

2002 general	Richard Durbin (D)	2,103,766	(60%)	($4,979,865)
	Jim Durkin (R)	1,325,703	(38%)	($794,634)
	Other	57,382	(2%)	
2002 primary	Richard Durbin (D)	unopposed		
1996 general	Richard Durbin (D)	2,384,028	(56%)	($4,966,804)
	Al Salvi (R)	1,728,824	(41%)	($4,696,065)
	Other	137,870	(3%)	

Prior Winning Percentages: 1994 House (55%); 1992 House (57%); 1990 House (66%); 1988 House (69%); 1986 House (68%); 1984 House (61%); 1982 House (50%)

Richard Durbin, a Democrat, was first elected to the Senate in 1996. Durbin grew up in East St. Louis, and for almost all his adult life has been in politics: Right out of law school he joined Paul Simon's staff when he was lieutenant governor (1969–73), then was a state Senate staffer in the 1970s. He lost two races for office in the 1970s, but in 1982 won the nomination to oppose Republican Congressman Paul Findley, who had characterized himself as Yasir Arafat's best friend in Congress; that helped Durbin raise large sums from Israel supporters. Durbin won that race, got a seat on the Agriculture Committee and then moved to Appropriations, where in 1993 he became chairman of the Agriculture Subcommittee. He worked to promote ethanol and soybean-based ink in government documents—big causes in the homeland of Archer Daniels Midland. Durbin's father died of lung cancer when he was 14, and Durbin's most prominent achievement was the 1988 ban on smoking on domestic airline flights; he followed that up by trying to limit tobacco subsidies and in 1994 moved unsuccessfully to direct the FDA to regulate tobacco as a health hazard.

In the Senate, Durbin has compiled a liberal voting record, though he has supported welfare reform and the death penalty; he has been a dependable Democratic partisan on the floor and on cable news networks. He got a seat on Appropriations in 1998. He defended the Clinton-Gore campaign resolutely in Fred Thompson's 1997 investigation of campaign finance irregularities and staunchly opposed impeachment in 1999, but did criticize Clinton in February 2001 for pardoning Marc Rich.

On tobacco, Durbin opposed provisions to limit FDA regulation of tobacco or "any additive ingredient of a tobacco product" and in July 1998 moved to ban smoking on international flights. In the House, Durbin favored restrictions on abortion, including the Hyde amendment and the Human Life Amendment; in the Senate, he has backed abortion rights and introduced a bill to ban abortions once the fetus can survive outside the womb, except where two physicians certify that a woman's life is at risk or she faces "grievous injury" to physical health. Durbin has tried to move his goal of gun control incrementally forward, calling for a ban on gun possession by foreigners on non-immigrant visas, a ban on certain cheap handguns, criminal penalties for parents whose children get hold of guns, and a permanent extension of the Brady bill's five-day waiting requirement (the original bill had it lapse to be replaced by an instant criminal background check). Durbin has a very strong pro-union voting record, but split with them on trade, supporting NAFTA in the House and PNTR for China in the Senate: Illinois is a big exporter. He sponsored a bill to give the FDA power to approve genetically modified foods but would not require labeling. He opposed the Gulf War resolution in January 1991 and the Iraq war resolution in October 2002, but voted to authorize the use of force in Iraq when Bill Clinton was president in February 1998. In the wake of September 11, Durbin proposed $1.8 billion for more security on trains and on rail bridges and tunnels and for national standards for state-issued driver's licenses. In July 2002 Durbin switched from his previous position and voted for storage of nuclear waste at Yucca Mountain in Nevada, saying that radiation standards were much tougher than in previous bills; Illinois depends more than most states on nuclear power and has much waste it would like to transport elsewhere.

On one local issue of great moment, Durbin was not able to deliver in 2002. This was the expansion of O'Hare Airport, whose supporters wanted federal law to codify an agreement between Mayor Richard M. Daley and Governor George Ryan so that no future governor could undo it. In May 2002 Durbin, previously uncertain on the question, said he was for it and had the 60 votes needed to overcome a filibuster threatened by his Illinois colleague Peter Fitzgerald. But he did not bring it to the floor that spring nor in the fall, even though Speaker Dennis Hastert and 3d District Congressman William Lipinski managed to rally a two-thirds majority for it in the House in July 2002. Fitzgerald at one point used Senate procedure to frustrate Durbin, and Durbin was unable to get Majority Leader Tom Daschle to call the issue up. All of which prompted Hastert to say, "We moved the bill out of the House and—I'm not trying to talk in a prejudicial way here—but I'm disappointed that Durbin hasn't carried out his side of the bargain." The *Chicago Sun-Times's* Steve Neal wrote that Durbin "is better at settling scores than passing legislation."

The O'Hare issue was simmering while Durbin was seeking reelection, but it wasn't much of a fight. Durbin had won the seat in 1996 after his onetime employer Senator Paul Simon announced his retirement; the race may have looked more attractive because his margins in the 1992 and 1994 House races were fairly close. Raising more than $1 million, he outspent former state Treasurer (and current Lieutenant Governor) Pat Quinn in the March 1996 primary and won 65%–30%. In the general he faced trial lawyer and abortion opponent Al Salvi. In some states, Senate races often pit two candidates who are known in-depth by the voters; this race in this megastate pitted two candidates with low name identification in a year when Bill Clinton carried the state by a wide margin. The hottest issue may have been gun control. Durbin was endorsed in October by gun control activists Jim and Sarah Brady, at which point Salvi made an astonishing mistake: someone he met at a rally told him that Jim Brady used to sell machine guns and, without checking out the story, Salvi repeated it in a radio interview. It was totally untrue and Salvi had to apologize, but any chance of his overtaking Durbin was gone. Durbin won 56%–41%, carrying both metro Chicago and, narrowly, Downstate. In 2002 Durbin had a more politically adept opponent, but one who raised very little money, and it was no contest. Durbin won 60%–38%, leading 64%–35% in metro Chicago and 56%–42% Downstate. Durbin was mentioned briefly in 2000 as a possible vice presidential nominee (he quickly leaked it to the press when it became apparent he was under consideration); he said that he had been contacted by Warren Christopher in June and asked for information, but had called back four days later to say they he did not want to be considered. He chaired the Democrats' 2000 platform committee and aroused some criticism when he insisted on being one of three white males to announce the Illinois vote on the roll call at the Democratic Convention in Los Angeles.

Junior Senator

Peter Fitzgerald (R)

Elected 1998, seat up 2004, 1st term; b. Oct. 20, 1960, Elgin; home, Inverness; Dartmouth Col., A.B. 1982, U. of MI Law Schl., J.D. 1986; Catholic; married (Nina).

Elected Office: IL Senate, 1992–98.

Professional Career: Practicing atty., 1986–96.

DC Office: 555 DSOB, 20510, 202-224-2854; Fax: 202-228-1372; Web site: www.fitzgerald.senate.gov.

State Offices: Chicago, 312-886-3506; Dixon, 815-288-3140; Glen Carbon, 618-692-0364; Springfield, 217-492-5089.

Committees: *Aging (Special). Agriculture, Nutrition & Forestry*: Marketing, Inspection & Product Promotion; Research, Nutrition & General Legislation (Chmn.). *Commerce, Science & Transportation*: Aviation; Communications; Competition, Foreign Commerce & Infrastructure; Consumer Affairs & Product Safety (Chmn.). *Governmental Affairs*: Financial Management, Budget & International Security (Chmn.); Government Management, Federal Workforce & the District of Columbia; Investigations (Permanent). *Small Business & Entrepreneurship.*

Group Ratings

	ADA	ACLU	AFS	LCV	CON	ITIC	NTU	COC	ACU	NTLC	CHC
2002	20	0	25	59	27	88	55	90	85	88	—
2001	15	—	25	38	—	—	77	77	78	—	80

National Journal Ratings

	2001 LIB — 2001 CONS	2002 LIB — 2002 CONS
Economic	44% — 56%	41% — 58%
Social	33% — 59%	0% — 62%
Foreign	7% — 72%	35% — 61%

Key Votes of the 107th Congress

1. Approve Bush Tax Cuts	Y	5. Confirm Ashcroft as AG	Y	9. Bar Coop. with Intl. Court	Y
2. Expand Patients' Rights	Y	6. Bar Gays in the Boy Scouts	Y	10. Trade Promotion Authority	Y
3. Campaign Finance Reform	Y	7. $ for Hate Crime Prosecution	N	11. Authorize Force in Iraq	Y
4. Permit ANWR Development	N	8. Overseas Military Abortions	N	12. Homeland Sec. Dept. Union	N

Election Results

1998 general	Peter Fitzgerald (R)	1,709,041	(50%)	($17,678,198)
	Carol Moseley-Braun (D)	1,610,496	(47%)	($7,200,895)
	Other	74,984	(2%)	
1998 primary	Peter Fitzgerald (R)	372,916	(52%)	
	Loleta Didrickson (R)	346,606	(48%)	
1992 general	Carol Moseley-Braun (D)	2,631,229	(53%)	($6,699,942)
	Richard S. Williamson (R)	2,126,833	(43%)	($2,300,924)
	Other	181,496	(4%)	

Peter Fitzgerald, a Republican born in 1960 and elected to the Senate in 1998, is the third-youngest member of the Senate. He grew up in the affluent northwest suburb of Inverness—as Republican as Chicago is Democratic. His father started a suburban bank chain and sold it to the Bank of Montreal in 1994 for $246 million, netting his son some $40 million in stock. Fitzgerald went to Catholic schools and majored in Latin and Greek at Dartmouth; after a year in Greece he went to Michigan Law School. In his college years he was an intern for Congressman Philip Crane—now the senior Republican in the House—and organized a New Hampshire rally for Crane's 1980 presidential campaign. In 1988 Fitzgerald lost a close primary for the state House; in 1992 he was elected to the state Senate. There he opposed tax increases and was known as one of the "Fab Five" conservatives. In 1994 he spent more than $700,000 of his own money challenging Crane in a primary, and lost by only 40%–33%.

Fitzgerald won his Senate seat by beating incumbent Democrat Carol Moseley-Braun, who had become the first black woman senator in 1992. She had a mostly liberal record but tended closely to Chicago and Downstate business interests. But she had terrible problems, including a report that she had split among herself and siblings a $28,750 inheritance owed to her mother, a nursing home resident who was supposed to have reimbursed Medicaid with the money; a month-long trip to Africa after her election with her South African campaign manager and ex-fiance Kgosie Matthews, where they allegedly spent some $281,000 in campaign funds; and a "private" visit to Nigeria with Matthews, a former registered agent of the Nigerian government, where they met with now-deceased dictator General Sani Abacha without the normal checking-in with the State Department. As a result, Moseley-Braun's poll numbers dropped to near-record lows. But Democrats shied away from challenging the only black senator, and the best-known Republicans declined to run. Fitzgerald announced in April 1997, but Edgar and other Republican leaders, fresh from watching abortion opponent Al Salvi lose the 1996 Senate race, did not want an abortion opponent as the nominee. They encouraged Comptroller Loleta Didrickson, though she was reluctant to run. Fitzgerald spent some $7 million in the primary, starting off with warm ads showing him as a basic suburban father, then calling for lower taxes. Fitzgerald attacked Didrickson as a tax-raiser; Didrickson called him "the trust fund kid" and argued that he would lose the general election. She was heavily outspent, but Fitzgerald won by only 52%–48%, losing the suburbs narrowly but carrying Downstate 59%–41%.

In the general, Fitzgerald attacked "six years of scandal and controversy" and said that Moseley-Braun had "been to Nigeria more than she's been to Rockford." Moseley-Braun fought back. In ads she conceded, "I know I've made some mistakes and disappointed some people. But I want you to know that I've always tried to do what's best for Illinois." Moseley-Braun accused Fitzgerald of running a stealth campaign and relying on ads, and she performed credibly in debate. But Fitzgerald, with more than $14 million of his own money, outspent her 2–1. Fitzgerald won by just 50%–47%, losing Cook and four small Downstate counties and carrying the other 97. Moseley-Braun carried Cook County heavily, but Fitzgerald was ahead in the suburbs and he carried the rest of the state 60%–36%.

In the Senate, Fitzgerald has set his own course, opposing fellow Republicans on key issues while compiling a mostly conservative record. He surprised colleagues by voting for the Democrats' HMO regulation bills, for background checks at gun shows, for the Democrats' prescription drug bill and for a Democratic lockbox proposal for Medicare in March 2001. He got into the 2001 tax bill a provision exempting from income tax compensation payments to Holocaust survivors. He voted for the McCain-Feingold campaign finance regulation bill. He has not put his holdings into a blind trust, but has refrained from voting on bills with impact on banking, like the financial services deregulation bill.

Fitzgerald and colleague Richard Durbin continued a previous practice of holding weekly breakfasts for Illinois constituents and worked together to promote ethanol. But his relations with Durbin and with other Illinois Republicans were frayed by Fitzgerald's lonely stands on Illinois issues. He refused to sign an Illinois delegation letter supporting Illinois projects, instead writing, "The mere fact that a project is located somewhere in Illinois does not mean that it is inherently meritorious and necessarily worthy of support." One such project was the Abraham Lincoln Library project in Springfield. In October 2000 he conducted a two-day filibuster insisting on federal standards and charging that the state's bidding process would result in a sweetheart contract for a crony of Republican Governor George Ryan. This was a head-on attack on Speaker Dennis Hastert, who had supported the Illinois competitive-bidding system in the House. "I find Senator Fitzgerald's political grandstanding on the Abraham Lincoln Library outrageous," Hastert wrote. Fitzgerald called Hastert's position "morally and ethically wrong," but his filibuster did not prevail.

Another cause that sets Fitzgerald apart from his colleagues was expansion of O'Hare Airport. In December 2001 George Ryan and Mayor Richard M. Daley reached agreement on its terms. Fitzgerald opposes expansion and, with House members Henry Hyde and Jesse Jackson, Jr., backs a third Chicago area airport in Peotone, south of the city. In October 1999 he filed 304 amendments against a bill by John McCain that would have increased the number of slots at O'Hare; McCain accused him of jeopardizing the safety of airline passengers and Fitzgerald withdrew the amendments and agreed to 30 more slots at O'Hare—far fewer than in New York's LaGuardia. In October 2001 he cast the lone vote in the Senate against the airline aid bill ("a gift of billions of taxpayer dollars, the ultimate effect of which will be to enrich sophisticated investors in these airlines") and in November 2002 he declined to sign a delegation letter supporting aid for United Airlines, one of O'Hare's major tenants. In December 2001 he filibustered an O'Hare expansion bill that would have put the Daley-Ryan agreement into federal law, and throughout 2002 threatened to filibuster it again. Speaker Dennis Hastert and 3d District Congressman William Lipinski got the House to pass a similar measure by a two-thirds vote, but Durbin was unwilling or unable to put the measure on the floor in the face of Fitzgerald's filibuster threat. In October 2002 Fitzgerald placed a hold on all aviation legislation, which held up approval of allowing pilots to carry guns in cockpits. By this time, his relations with Durbin had cooled greatly.

By late 2002 Fitzgerald was highly unpopular with Illinois politicians of both parties. In November 2002 18th District Republican Ray LaHood told the *Chicago Sun-Times*, "I'm thinking about trying to make sure that Peter has an opponent" in the Republican primary. "I think we can do better than him." LaHood said that Fitzgerald did nothing to help Republican candidates south of I-80 in 2002 and didn't show up at a rally in Springfield two days before the election. "I've been disenchanted with Fitzgerald for a long time, but when he really trashed Denny Hastert that was just the straw that broke the camel's back for me." Fitzgerald's response: "I am single-minded, and I have single-mindedly tried to do everything in my power to clean up the rot in Springfield with measures like competitive bidding for the Lincoln Library to protect against George Ryan's cronies. That doesn't sit well with Mr. LaHood, who apparently comes from another school." In November 2002 the Republican state committee met and declined to support Fitzgerald for reelection. Two businessmen capable of self-financing were mentioned as primary opponents: Andy McKenna of Schwartz Paper Company in Morton Grove and Jack Ryan, who considered running against Durbin in 2002.

Fitzgerald was certainly the national Democrats' number one target in the 2004 Senate races. He won in 1998 by only 50%–47%, against a candidate with grave problems and, as he points out, he represents a state more Democratic in recent presidential elections than any other Republican senator except Lincoln Chafee of Rhode Island. Even before the 2002 election, many Democrats were lining up to run against him. But in April 2003 Fitzgerald announced he would not seek reelection; he cited as reasons a desire to spent time with his family and the high costs of a competitive campaign. Republicans immediately looked to popular former Governor Jim Edgar as the party's best chance to hold the seat; President George W. Bush made a personal call to persuade him to run. But in May, Edgar announced he would not seek the seat.

Aside from McKenna and Jack Ryan, a handful of other Republicans drew mention as possible candidates after Edgar declined to run; state Treasurer Judy Baar Topinka, the only Republican to win statewide in 2002, declined to run. On the Democratic side, former Chicago School Board president (and former chief of staff to Mayor Daley) Gerry Chico raised $1 million by the end of 2002; he would have a head start on Illinois's growing number of Hispanic voters. Chicago insiders seemed convinced that Daley would back investment banker Blair Hull, who sold his firm to Goldman Sachs in 1999 for $531 million and said he would spend $40 million on the race. State Senator Barack Obama, an accomplished legislator and the first black president of the *Harvard Law Review*, formally announced his candidacy in January 2003; about one-quarter of Illinois's Democratic primary voters are black, and his appeal could cross racial lines. State Comptroller Dan Hynes would be the youngest candidate; he was first elected to his statewide office in 1998 at age 30. And Cook County Treasurer Maria Pappas, in the middle of a four-year term, said she might run, because "there is absolutely nothing for me to lose."

Illinois's filing date is in December and its primary in March, one of the nation's earliest.

FIRST DISTRICT

Rep. Bobby Rush (D)

Elected 1992, 6th term; b. Nov. 23, 1946, Albany, GA; home, Chicago; Roosevelt U., B.A. 1973, U. of IL, M.A. 1994, McCormick Seminary, M.A. 1998; Baptist; married (Carolyn).

Military Career: Army, 1963–68.

Elected Office: Chicago City Alderman, 1983–92; 2d Ward Committeeman, 1984–present.

Professional Career: Member, Student Non–Violent Coord. Cmte., 1966–68; Co–founder, IL Black Panther Party, 1968; Med. Clinic Dir., 1970–1973; insurance agent, 1978–83.

DC Office: 2416 RHOB 20515, 202-225-4372; Fax: 202-226-0333; Web site: www.house.gov/rush.

District Office: Chicago, 773-224-6500.

Committees: *Energy & Commerce* (11th of 26 D): Energy & Air Quality; Environment & Hazardous Materials; Oversight & Investigations; Telecommunications & The Internet.

Group Ratings

	ADA	ACLU	AFS	LCV	CON	ITIC	NTU	COC	ACU	NTLC	CHC
2002	85	85	100	75	37	38	19	50	0	9	0
2001	75	—	100	57	—	—	8	35	10	—	—

National Journal Ratings

	2001 LIB —	2001 CONS		2002 LIB —	2002 CONS
Economic	82%	18%		81%	18%
Social	80%	20%		92%	6%
Foreign	96%	0%		84%	14%

Key Votes of the 107th Congress

1. Approve Bush Tax Cuts	*	5. Faith-Based Charities	N	9. Trade Promotion Authority	N
2. Limit Patients' Bill of Rights	N	6. Bar Gays in the Boy Scouts	*	10. Bar Funds for Intl. Court	N
3. Campaign Finance Reform	Y	7. Ban Partial-Birth Abortion	N	11. Authorize Force in Iraq	N
4. Ban ANWR Development	Y	8. Arm Commercial Pilots	N	12. Deny Home. Sec. Dept. Union	N

Election Results

2002 general	Bobby Rush (D)	149,068	(81%)	($299,460)
	Raymond Wardingley (R)	29,776	(16%)	
	Other	4,812	(3%)	
2002 primary	Bobby Rush (D)	unopposed		
2000 general	Bobby Rush (D)	172,271	(88%)	($656,599)
	Raymond Wardingley (R)	23,915	(12%)	

Prior Winning Percentages: 1998 (87%); 1996 (86%); 1994 (76%); 1992 (83%)

The People		Race/Ethnic Origin	Ancestry	
Area size:	99 sq. mi.	27.3% White	Irish: 7.1%	German: 6.2%
Urban population:	100.0%	65.2% Black	Polish: 4.5%	
Rural population:	0.0%	1.4% Asian	**2000 Presidential Vote**	
Pop. 2000:	653,647	0.1% Native Am.	Gore (D) 213,244	(84%)
Median income:	$37,222	0.0% Hawaiian	Bush (R) 39,400	(15%)
Poverty status:	19.7%	1.0% Two+ races	Other 2,097	(1%)
Military veterans:	10.8%	0.1% Other	**Cook Partisan Voting Index:** D +34	
		4.8% Hispanic Origin		

Occupation	Blue collar: 21.6%	White collar: 61.3%	Gray collar: 17.1%

The South Side of Chicago has been the nation's largest urban black community for nearly a century now. A hundred years ago there were just a few blocks where black families from the South could settle; this ghetto grew rapidly with the first influx of blacks from the Mississippi

Delta in the 1910s. By the 1920s the South Side was well established, a center of blues music in America and of black-owned businesses. Politically, the South Side was a heavily Republican constituency throughout those years; the comfortable white Protestants who settled in solid brick houses here believed in the party of Yankee propriety, and the blacks had faith in the party of Lincoln. This was one of the heartlands of the Republican Party, represented in Congress by Appropriations Chairman Martin Madden. After Madden died in the Appropriations Committee room in 1928, the 1st District elected Oscar DePriest, the first black elected to the House in the 20th century. Blacks remained faithful to the party of Lincoln even during the Depression, voting for Herbert Hoover and DePriest in 1932.

The New Deal and the racial liberalism of New Dealers like Eleanor Roosevelt and Interior Secretary Harold Ickes (both former Republicans themselves) attracted blacks to the Democratic Party, and a black Democrat beat DePriest in 1934. The South Side has been Democratic ever since. For 40 years it was a cooperative part of Chicago's Democratic machine; then, after the death of longtime Congressman William Dawson, it rebelled against Mayor Richard J. Daley. The South Side seemed to take over the city when Congressman Harold Washington was elected mayor in 1983 and 1987. After Washington died in November 1987, other black South Side politicians flailed at each other, even though Chicago's electorate peaked at about 40% black (because so many blacks have been moving to the suburbs) and black candidates need non-black voters to win.

The 1st Congressional District includes about half of Chicago's black South Side community plus many suburbs beyond. The lines were sharply redrawn by the 2001 redistricting—only 54% of the new district was in the old 1st—since the 1st and adjacent 2d Districts each needed to add about 100,000 people. The 1st has a northern salient that includes some of Chicago's first black neighborhoods and includes include the Gothic spires of the University of Chicago and the mansions of Kenwood, once the home of Chicago's Jewish aristocracy and more recently the headquarters of the Nation of Islam and home to its leader, Louis Farrakhan. It includes most of the South Side from Stony Island west almost to the city limit and from 60th Street to 95th—miles and miles of bungalow neighborhoods, with single-family houses lining arrow-straight streets. The 1st added the heavily black 18th Ward and gave up the mostly white 19th Ward to the 3d District. From there a narrow neck connects the 1st with a still mostly white collection of suburbs, starting with Blue Island and fanning southwest to Palos Heights, Orland Park and Oak Forest. Redistricting reduced the district's black percentage from 70% to 65%, but it remains overwhelmingly Democratic: Only 15% for George W. Bush in 2000, his weakest district in Illinois.

The congressman from the 1st District is Bobby Rush, a man who has gone through several transformations. He grew up on the North Side, a Boy Scout whose mother was a Republican precinct captain. In the Army he became involved in the Student Non-Violent Coordinating Committee in the South, then went AWOL and founded the Illinois Black Panthers, where he recruited Fred Hampton, later killed in a raid by police in 1969. Rush served six months in prison for illegal possession of firearms, but also during his time with the Black Panthers he had run a medical clinic that developed the nation's first mass sickle cell anemia testing program. "I don't repudiate any of my involvement in the Panther party—it was part of my maturing," Rush later said. Lately, he has commemorated the anniversary of the raid by holding a job fair to promote the future. In 1983 he was elected 2d Ward alderman and became a strong Harold Washington supporter. In 1992, he challenged Congressman Charles Hayes, an older generation politician with a union background. Just before the primary it was revealed that Hayes had 716 overdrafts on the House bank. Rush beat Hayes 42%–39%, carrying eight of 12 black wards.

In the House, Rush has had a liberal voting record and has a seat on the Energy and Commerce Committee. Rush's rhetoric has toned down over the years, and his more deliberate style contrasts sharply with his days as a Panther. "Most African-Americans just want a comfortable, middle-class lifestyle," he said in 1992. "Twenty-five years ago, I didn't know that." Gun violence caused great pain to Rush in October 1999, when his son Huey Rich—who was born three weeks before the 1969 police raid, and, although raised by an aunt, had recently grown close to his father—was murdered by a man wielding a handgun as he returned to his South Side home with his fiancee. "My son's death was a senseless death," Rush told supporters a day later at Jesse

Jackson's PUSH headquarters. "We've got to rid our communities of guns." In March 2002, two men were convicted of murder and robbery in the case. In that same month, Rush's 17-year-old nephew Dennis Rush was charged with murder and attempted robbery on the South Side, during what police said was a drug transaction. Seeking a constructive approach to dealing with social maladies, Rush has filed a bill to finance research and counseling to combat postpartum depression and psychosis.

Rush waged a quixotic mayoral campaign in 1999 against Richard M. Daley, of whom he has sometimes been a harsh critic. During the campaign, he attacked the mayor for tolerating police brutality, inadequate mass-transit service and "cronyism." House colleagues Jesse Jackson Jr. and Danny Davis were at his side, but only three of the 50 aldermen endorsed him—many had been appointed by Daley to fill vacancies and he worked with almost all of them on local projects. Rush insisted that he wanted to build a multiracial coalition, but for practical purposes his only chance was with black voters. Daley's record was too popular and his financial advantage overwhelming. Daley won the February election by 72%–28%, with nearly 45% of the black vote and the support of many prominent black ministers, an achievement that reflects more on his record than on Rush.

After that pounding, Rush found himself challenged in the primary for his own re-election in 2000 by two state senators—Donne Trotter and Barack Obama. Obama, a civil rights lawyer who was the first black president of the *Harvard Law Review*, made the more spirited campaign. But he missed a gun control vote in the state Senate two months before the election. With an additional boost from a primary-eve endorsement from Bill Clinton, Rush ran well in both the city and suburbs, and won an unexpectedly strong 61%. Surely not by coincidence, redistricting shifted Obama's Hyde Park home two blocks outside the new lines and removed the 19th Ward that he had carried. Rush was routinely renominated and reelected in 2002. His most newsworthy action was to support state Treasurer Judy Baar Topinka for reelection; she was the only successful statewide Republican candidate. This was sweet revenge: her Democratic opponent Thomas Dart managed Daley's 1999 campaign. In the House, Rush ran for chairman of the Congressional Black Caucus, but he was defeated by Elijah Cummings of Maryland; this suggests that Rush is a serious player, but that he has not moved into the top echelon of Democratic politics.

SECOND DISTRICT

Rep. Jesse Jackson Jr. (D)

Elected Dec. 1995, 4th term; b. Mar. 11, 1965, Greenville, SC; home, Chicago; NC A&T, B.S. 1987, Chicago Theological Seminary, M.A. 1990, U. of IL, J.D. 1993; Baptist; married (Sandra).

Professional Career: Civil rights activist; Pres., Keep Hope Alive PAC, 1989–90; V.P., Operation PUSH, 1991–95; Field Dir., Natl. Rainbow Coalition, 1993–95.

DC Office: 313 CHOB 20515, 202-225-0773; Fax: 202-225-0899; Web site: www.jessejacksonjr.org.

District Office: Homewood, 708-798-6000.

Committees: *Appropriations* (23d of 29 D): Foreign Operations & Export Financing; Labor, HHS & Education.

Group Ratings

	ADA	ACLU	AFS	LCV	CON	ITIC	NTU	COC	ACU	NTLC	CHC
2002	90	93	100	100	36	38	24	25	0	14	0
2001	95	—	100	100	—	—	18	23	0	—	—

National Journal Ratings

	2001 LIB	—	2001 CONS		2002 LIB	—	2002 CONS
Economic	76%	—	24%		95%	—	0%
Social	90%	—	0%		84%	—	8%
Foreign	96%	—	0%		87%	—	10%

Key Votes of the 107th Congress

1. Approve Bush Tax Cuts	N	5. Faith-Based Charities	N	9. Trade Promotion Authority	N
2. Limit Patients' Bill of Rights	N	6. Bar Gays in the Boy Scouts	N	10. Bar Funds for Intl. Court	N
3. Campaign Finance Reform	Y	7. Ban Partial-Birth Abortion	N	11. Authorize Force in Iraq	N
4. Ban ANWR Development	Y	8. Arm Commercial Pilots	N	12. Deny Home. Sec. Dept. Union	N

Election Results

2002 general	Jesse Jackson Jr. (D)	151,443	(82%)	($749,704)
	Doug Nelson (R)	32,567	(18%)	($9,249)
2002 primary	Jesse Jackson Jr. (D)	100,370	(85%)	
	Yvonne Christian-Williams (D)	11,757	(10%)	
	Anthony Williams (D)	5,501	(5%)	
2000 general	Jesse Jackson Jr. (D)	175,995	(90%)	($304,619)
	Robert Gordon III (R)	19,906	(10%)	

Prior Winning Percentages: 1998 (89%); 1996 (94%); 1995 (76%)

The People		**Race/Ethnic Origin**	**Ancestry**	
Area size:	192 sq. mi.	25.6% White	German: 5.8%	Polish: 4.4%
Urban population:	99.9%	62.0% Black	Irish: 4.4%	
Rural population:	0.1%	0.6% Asian	**2000 Presidential Vote**	
Pop. 2000:	653,647	0.1% Native Am.	Gore (D) 204,372	(82%)
Median income:	$41,330	0.0% Hawaiian	Bush (R) 41,005	(17%)
Poverty status:	15.2%	1.2% Two+ races	Other 2,455	(1%)
Military veterans:	11.7%	0.1% Other	**Cook Partisan Voting Index:** D +33	
		10.4% Hispanic Origin		

Occupation	Blue collar: 23.8%	White collar: 60.1%	Gray collar: 16.1%

Chicago is a great center of both commerce and industry, and if its white-collar offices are heavily concentrated in the Loop, its blue-collar heavy industries are most visible on the far South Side. This Chicago, diminished in importance economically today, is historically significant and, with the remnants of its great hulking factories around Lake Calumet and the nearby rail yards, has a certain undeniable majesty. Thomas Geoghegan, who writes more poetically than a lawyer ought to be able to, has told in his book, *Which Side Are You On?* , of the fights to wrest severance benefits and pension rights for the workers whose steel mills shut down, of the decline in the labor movement in a place where it got much of its inspiration. This is where the Pullman strike of 1894 was broken by federal troops and where policemen killed 10 union supporters in the Little Steel strike of 1937. Over the years, Chicago grew around the tight ethnic neighborhoods where workers went home at shift break each afternoon or midnight; today they are mostly empty buildings that suburbanites speed past on the Calumet and Dan Ryan Expressways.

The 2d Congressional District includes much of Chicago's old South Side industrial area, Comiskey Park and many Cook County suburbs to the south. The district reaches north to include Jackson Park, where the Columbian Exposition of 1893 was held, and the South Shore neighborhood to the south, once heavily Jewish and now home to middle-class blacks. The district includes all of Chicago south of 95th Street and east of I-57—including the old industrial area around Lake Calumet. The Chicago portion of the 2d is overwhelmingly black, though many blacks, especially young parents fleeing Chicago public schools, are moving into suburbs directly to the south—Harvey, Dolton, Markham. Farther south are Homewood and Flossmoor, with significant Jewish populations, high-income Olympia Fields, the planned town of Park Forest, and Chicago Heights, home town of America's premier political reporter for more than four decades, David Broder. In the south is Ford Heights; once a steel-industry hub known as East Chicago Heights, it is now the nation's leader in single mothers per capita, the vast majority of whom live in public housing. Redistricting removed Jerry Weller's 11th District from the far southern tier of Cook County, and moved Jackson into those communities. The 2d District now has more people in the suburbs than in Chicago; the district spills over the southern border of Cook County and into Will County, to include Governors State University in University Park. These extensions reduced the black percentage from 76% to 62%, but the district remains middle class and still one of the most Democratic in the nation.

The congressman from the 2d District is Jesse Jackson Jr., a Democrat first elected in December 1995, son of civil rights activist and 1984 and 1988 presidential candidate Jesse Jackson. Jesse Jackson Jr. was born in Greenville, South Carolina, while his father was marching to Selma; he went to the St. Albans School in Washington, then to North Carolina A&T (as did his father), and got a masters degree at Chicago Theological Seminary and a law degree at the University of Illinois. He worked for his father's Rainbow Coalition and did not run for office until the spectacular rise and fall of Congressman Mel Reynolds, who was hailed nationally when he defeated the anti-Semitic Gus Savage in the 1992 primary and then disgraced when he was convicted and sentenced to five years in prison for having sexual relations with a teenage campaign worker. Jackson had serious competition in the 1995 special election from Emil Jones, then a legislator for 23 years and now the state Senate President, who had the support of Mayor Richard M. Daley. Jones emphasized his clout and political experience; Jackson said being his father's son was a lifetime of political experience. He talked of bringing dollars to the South Side and, echoing the argument Dan Rostenkowski made to Mayor Richard J. Daley in 1957, said, "The only way one grows into leadership in Congress is to get elected young enough that you become speaker of the House or chairman of the Ways and Means Committee." Jackson won the primary 46%–37% and easily won the special general election.

In the House, Jackson has combined liberal advocacy with careful attention to the interests of his district and a steady advancement of his own influence. He called for a single-payer universal health care system and a constitutional amendment to ensure quality public education and health care for every citizen—all would be nonstarters even in a Democratic Congress. He waged unexpectedly fierce opposition to the Crane-Rangel bill to relax trade restrictions on Africa, saying that he feared exploitation of African workers. Charles Rangel, a long-time ally of the senior Jackson, was furious—calling the attack on his bill "unprofessional." The bill was enacted, but the dispute badly split the Congressional Black Caucus.

Jackson has worked on local projects, notably on the building of a third Chicago area airport in Peotone, 45 miles south of the Loop and just south of the 2d District along Interstate 57. This fight has pitted him against fellow Democrats, including Congressman William Lipinski, the great protector of Midway Airport in his 3d District, and Daley, the great protector of O'Hare. Jackson's allies have been Congressman Henry Hyde, who is worried about O'Hare noise over his suburban 6th District, and Senator Peter Fitzgerald, who has filibustered to prevent O'Hare expansion. Consequently, Jackson opposes expansion at O'Hare.

Jackson has been mentioned as a candidate for higher office—including mayor, the only office that matters for Chicago pols. With his seat on the Appropriations Committee, he seems content to remain in the House. "His ultimate goal is to become the first black speaker of the House," reported the *Chicago Daily Herald*. In December 2002, Jackson seemed to finally close the door on mayoral speculation. "I'm not interested in the job of mayor of Chicago," he told the *Chicago Tribune*. "I'm not interested in it today, I'm not interested in it tomorrow. I'm not ever going to be interested in being the mayor of the city of Chicago." Jackson has been careful not to exploit his huge name recognition or to be seen as exclusively the "black issues" congressman. In October 2001, his new book *A More Perfect Union* vigorously argued for steps to promote equal opportunity and protection under the law for all citizens. "The history of race is central to understanding America and may be even more profound than the federal-state relationship," Jackson wrote. It's been the Democratic Party, he continued, that has frequently stymied the interests of blacks.

The movement of middle-class blacks to the suburbs reduces his core constituency but Jackson's advocacy of the Peotone airport suggests he has anticipated this and is set on representing a mostly suburban, mostly black district for some time. In the 2002 campaign, an unknown candidate promoted by a Jackson rival, state Senator William Shaw, filed nominating petitions in the name of "Jesse L. Jackson." The state elections board rejected them; Congressman Jackson won the primary 85%–10% over another candidate backed by Shaw. Despite their disagreement on O'Hare, Jackson and Rod Blagojevich were close pals when they served together in the House, and Jackson was an early supporter of Blagojevich's successful candidacy for governor. In Illinois, where clout and connections are highly valued, that can't hurt.

THIRD DISTRICT

Rep. William Lipinski (D)

Elected 1982, 11th term; b. Dec. 22, 1937, Chicago; home, Chicago; Loras Col., 1956–57; Catholic; married (Rose Marie).

Military Career: Army Reserves, 1961–67.

Elected Office: Chicago City Alderman, 1975–83; Committeeman, 23d Ward, 1975–present.

Professional Career: Chicago Parks & Recreation Dept., 1958–75.

DC Office: 2188 RHOB 20515, 202-225-5701; Fax: 202-225-1012; Web site: www.house.gov/lipinski.

District Offices: Chicago, 312-886-0481; LaGrange, 708-352-0524; Oak Lawn, 708-952-0860.

Committees: *Transportation & Infrastructure* (3d of 34 D): Aviation; Highways, Transit & Pipelines (RMM); Railroads.

Group Ratings

	ADA	ACLU	AFS	LCV	CON	ITIC	NTU	COC	ACU	NTLC	CHC
2002	55	36	100	38	51	38	21	53	32	30	75
2001	40	—	63	36	—	—	29	50	55	—	—

National Journal Ratings

	2001 LIB —	2001 CONS	2002 LIB —	2002 CONS
Economic	55%	46%	59%	41%
Social	51%	50%	48%	52%
Foreign	48%	52%	52%	48%

Key Votes of the 107th Congress

1. Approve Bush Tax Cuts	*	5. Faith-Based Charities	Y	9. Trade Promotion Authority	N
2. Limit Patients' Bill of Rights	*	6. Bar Gays in the Boy Scouts	Y	10. Bar Funds for Intl. Court	Y
3. Campaign Finance Reform	N	7. Ban Partial-Birth Abortion	Y	11. Authorize Force in Iraq	N
4. Ban ANWR Development	*	8. Arm Commercial Pilots	N	12. Deny Home. Sec. Dept. Union	N

Election Results

2002 general	William Lipinski (D)	.... unopposed		($419,270)
2002 primary	William Lipinski (D)	.... unopposed		
2000 general	William Lipinski (D)	 145,498	(76%)	($387,674)
	Karl Groth (R)	 47,005	(24%)	($18,073)

Prior Winning Percentages: 1998 (72%); 1996 (65%); 1994 (54%); 1992 (64%); 1990 (66%); 1988 (61%); 1986 (70%); 1984 (64%); 1982 (75%)

The People		Race/Ethnic Origin	Ancestry	
Area size:	126 sq. mi.	68.2% White	Irish: 14.2%	Polish: 13.5%
Urban population:	100.0%	5.8% Black	German: 11.0%	
Rural population:	0.0%	2.8% Asian	**2000 Presidential Vote**	
Pop. 2000:	653,647	0.1% Native Am.	Gore (D) 131,650	(58%)
Median income:	$48,048	0.0% Hawaiian	Bush (R) 91,471	(40%)
Poverty status:	8.3%	1.7% Two+ races	Other 4,913	(2%)
Military veterans:	10.9%	0.1% Other	**Cook Partisan Voting Index:** D + 9	
		21.3% Hispanic Origin		

Occupation	Blue collar: 27.6%	White collar: 58.1%	Gray collar: 14.3%

A century ago, Finley Peter Dunne's fictional Mr. Dooley pontificated on matters political in a saloon on Archer Avenue. This was, and is, Archer Avenue on the South Side of Chicago, one of the radial streets that cut across what was once open prairie near the Loop and out the Chicago River and the Chicago and Sanitary Ship Canal. Archer Avenue was one of the paths of outward migration and upward mobility for the children and grandchildren of Chicago's ethnic and cultural groups, and still is. (Even today, in Archer Heights, you can scarcely go a block without hearing someone speaking Polish). Italians from the river wards along the Canal moved west; the South Side Irish moved west and south along Cicero Avenue toward Oak Lawn; the Bohemians (as they were called then; now Czechs) were heavily concentrated in the neat bungalows of industrial suburbs like Berwyn. Today, Latinos are driving these same avenues, up before dawn to arrive at large factories and small, or heading to the Loop on the CTA or to "edge city" jobs out the expressways or the Tollway, then home past storefronts with Spanish signs to carefully refurbished old bungalows. Midway Airport, Chicago's main airport before O'Hare opened in 1955, has been expanding its terminals and parking lots in the heart of a busy commercial area on the southwest side.

The 3d Congressional District consists of much of this territory, crisscrossed by the Canal, the radial streets and the railroad lines and switching yards so common in this, the center of the nation's rail network. It includes much of the Bungalow Belt; in his book, *The Lost City*, Alan Ehrenhalt describes the houses as "so close together that one had to make a special effort even to notice the side of the building. Driving down the street, what you saw was one front after another, and the fronts, clean and well-laid in dark-brown brick by Swedish and Italian immigrant masons, always looked good." The 3d also includes the far southwest edge of Chicago and most of Berwyn; Riverside, with its early 20th century prairie-style houses; a few older affluent suburbs like Western Springs and the more recent and middle-income expanses of Oak Lawn and Palos Hills. The 3d was one of the Illinois districts least changed by the 2001 redistricting, which is no coincidence—the lead negotiator of the bipartisan deal was the 3d District's William Lipinski. Pared off from the old district were most of Cicero, now heavily Hispanic, the black-majority 18th Ward of Chicago and the heavily Hispanic neighborhoods along Archer Avenue. Retained were the Archer Avenue neighborhoods where Poles defiantly cling to their heritage with more than 20 weekend schools teaching Polish to local kids and adults. Added were the integrated Beverly-Morgan Park 19th Ward of Chicago and, connected by a narrow corridor, the famed Bridgeport neighborhood, the lifetime home of the late Mayor Richard J. Daley and the storied Irish stronghold that produced four other Chicago mayors. Politically, this is marginal territory: ancestrally Democratic, culturally conservative, multiethnic and viscerally patriotic. Of the seven districts based primarily in Cook County, this was the best—or least bad—for George W. Bush, who won 40% of the vote here in 2000.

The congressman from the 3d District is William Lipinski, a Democrat who grew up in southwest Chicago, started off as a patronage employee with the Parks District and was elected 23d Ward alderman and ward committeeman in 1975. He still holds the latter position in the ward that includes Midway Airport and Chicago's westernmost stretch of Archer Avenue. He ran for Congress and beat an aging incumbent in the 1982 primary 61%–36%.

Lipinski is by some margin the most conservative Democrat in the Chicago delegation. His views seem in line with his constituents, if not with the majority of the Democratic Caucus. He opposes abortion rights and gays in the military and voted for the Defense of Marriage Act. He favors the death penalty and opposed NAFTA, GATT and PNTR with China. He was one of the few Democrats to favor education vouchers for poor children in Washington, D.C., and tax-free education savings accounts.

Lipinski is on the Transportation and Infrastructure Committee and is the ranking Democrat on its Aviation Subcommittee. He is a staunch advocate of Midway Airport, which generates more jobs than any other site in the 3d District. He is frequently at odds with Jesse Jackson Jr., a strong backer of a proposed third airport in Peotone, 45 miles south of Chicago, for that reason. He sponsored the controversial proposal, which the House passed by a two-thirds vote on its second attempt, to codify into federal law the agreement of Mayor Richard M. Daley and Governor George Ryan to expand O'Hare Airport. He has also pushed a provision allowing local communities to regulate train whistles; it may not sound like much, but when your district has (probably) the largest number of freight yards and surface crossings in the nation and whistle-blowing is mandatory, you will hear about it.

Lipinski is often out of line with the Democratic Party, but is a close ally of Michael Madigan, who is speaker of the Illinois House, but, perhaps more important, 13th Ward committeeman, just south of the 23d. Lipinski took a stern attitude toward Bill Clinton. He was one of 31 Democrats to vote for the Republican impeachment inquiry; on the day before the vote, Lipinski said Clinton should resign but that he "unfortunately" would not vote for impeachment. He has become a close friend of Speaker Dennis Hastert, whose district starts about 18 miles to the west and who helped Lipinski win $832 million for the CTA; they were the two brokers who produced Illinois's bipartisan incumbent-friendly congressional redistricting plan in May 2001. He also has worked closely, in the House and back home, with Governor Rod Blagojevich. The two of them plus Hastert have demanded fairer treatment for Illinois when Congress writes the spending formula in its new highway bill. Lipinski filed a bill increasing the gasoline tax by ten cents a gallon.

Lipinski comes naturally to his interest in redistricting. Illinois lost a district after the 1990 Census, and Lipinski was placed in the same district with fellow Democratic incumbent Marty Russo. Russo had more money but Lipinski had support from Mayor Daley and the *Chicago Tribune* and won 58%–37%. After the 2000 Census, when Illinois lost another seat, Lipinski was trusted by his fellow Democrats to negotiate the new lines with Hastert. Some Democrats grumbled when he agreed to a plan that resulted in the defeat of Downstate Democrat David Phelps. But junior Downstate Democrats can do much less for Chicago's interests than the Republican Speaker of the House; in this American city, party is less important than clout.

FOURTH DISTRICT

Rep. Luis Gutierrez (D)

Elected 1992, 6th term; b. Dec. 10, 1953, Chicago; home, Chicago; NE IL U., B.A. 1975; Catholic; married (Soraida).

Elected Office: Chicago City Alderman, 1986–92, Pres. Pro Tem, 1989–92.

Professional Career: Teacher, Puerto Rico, 1977–78; Social Wkr., Chicago Dept. of Children & Family Svcs., 1979–83; Advisor, Chicago Mayor Harold Washington, 1984–86.

DC Office: 2367 RHOB 20515, 202-225-8203; Fax: 202-225-7810; Web site: www.house.gov/gutierrez.

District Offices: Northside Chicago, 773-384-1655; Southside Chicago, 312-666-3882.

Committees: *Financial Services* (5th of 32 D): Domestic and International Monetary Policy, Trade & Technology; Financial Institutions & Consumer Credit; Oversight & Investigations (RMM). *Veterans' Affairs* (3d of 14 D): Health.

Group Ratings

	ADA	ACLU	AFS	LCV	CON	ITIC	NTU	COC	ACU	NTLC	CHC
2002	95	80	88	75	76	25	17	42	0	6	0
2001	95	—	100	93	—	—	10	35	16	—	—

National Journal Ratings

	2001 LIB	—	2001 CONS		2002 LIB	—	2002 CONS
Economic	90%	—	10%		80%	—	19%
Social	74%	—	23%		84%	—	8%
Foreign	79%	—	21%		76%	—	24%

Key Votes of the 107th Congress

1. Approve Bush Tax Cuts	N	5. Faith-Based Charities	N	9. Trade Promotion Authority	N
2. Limit Patients' Bill of Rights	N	6. Bar Gays in the Boy Scouts	N	10. Bar Funds for Intl. Court	N
3. Campaign Finance Reform	Y	7. Ban Partial-Birth Abortion	N	11. Authorize Force in Iraq	N
4. Ban ANWR Development	Y	8. Arm Commercial Pilots	N	12. Deny Home. Sec. Dept. Union	N

Election Results

2002 general	Luis Gutierrez (D)	67,339	(80%)	($805,574)
	Anthony Lopez-Cisneros (R)	12,778	(15%)	
	Maggie Kohls (Lib)	4,396	(5%)	
2002 primary	Luis Gutierrez (D)	38,338	(68%)	
	Martin Castro (D)	12,008	(21%)	
	John Joseph Holowinski (D)	5,849	(10%)	
2000 general	Luis Gutierrez (D)	89,487	(89%)	($454,558)
	Stephanie Sailor (Lib)	11,476	(11%)	

Prior Winning Percentages: 1998 (82%); 1996 (94%); 1994 (75%); 1992 (78%)

The People		Race/Ethnic Origin	Ancestry	
Area size:	39 sq. mi.	18.4% White	Polish: 5.0%	German: 3.4%
Urban population:	100.0%	3.7% Black	Irish: 3.1%	
Rural population:	0.0%	1.7% Asian	**2000 Presidential Vote**	
Pop. 2000:	653,647	0.1% Native Am.	Gore (D)	93,266 (79%)
Median income:	$35,935	0.0% Hawaiian	Bush (R)	23,809 (20%)
Poverty status:	20.2%	1.4% Two+ races	**Cook Partisan Voting Index:** D +29	
Military veterans:	4.3%	0.1% Other		
		74.5% Hispanic Origin		
Occupation	Blue collar: 39.2%	White collar: 43.5%	Gray collar: 17.3%	

Just west of the Loop, the Chicago River splits into North and South branches, both penetrating the heart of old neighborhoods where immigrants fresh off the boat first got their start in Chicago. The South Branch is the guts of Chicago, the site of one of Western civilization's astonishing engineering feats: in 1900 the course of the river was reversed so that sewage flowed Downstate through a canal rather than out into Lake Michigan. Just blocks away was Maxwell Street, then thronged with market stalls, long the arrival neighborhood for Chicago's Jews; not far away, in an Italian-American neighborhood on Halsted Street, was Jane Addams's Hull House, the original settlement house, where social workers told new immigrants not how to rebel against middle-class American mores but how to live up to them. To the south were Pilsen, arrival neighborhood for the Bohemians (Czechs), and the Irish neighborhoods along Archer Avenue. To the north was Milwaukee Avenue, the main street of Polish-Americans and Ukrainian-Americans for a century now.

Today, many of these places are arrival neighborhoods again, mostly for Chicago's wide variety of Hispanic immigrants. On the South Side, in the old river wards, is Chicago's Mexican-American community, extending west into the once Bohemian suburb of Cicero (famous as a haven for Al Capone's mobsters in the 1920s) and to Pilsen; this is the largest community of Mexican-Americans in the nation outside California. On the North Side are many Puerto Ricans and other Hispanics. In the 1990s, Chicago's Hispanic population increased from 545,000 to 754,000, by far the largest Latino concentration north of Texas and Florida and between the two coasts, and not all that much less than the 1.1 million blacks in Chicago.

The 4th Congressional District is the Hispanic-majority district created in 1992 and altered somewhat by the 2001 redistricting. The problem was that the South Side Mexican-American and the North Side Puerto Rican communities were separated by the West Side black ghetto. The solution was the creation of one of the most bizarrely-shaped congressional districts in the country. Essentially these two Latino communities, defined by careful boundaries to maximize the Hispanic percentage, are connected by a thin line of territory stretching around the West Side black-majority 7th District to meet at the Cook-DuPage County line. The district is sandwiched between the 5th District to the north and the 3d District to the south; it is shaped something like a pair of earmuffs. Most of this salient consists of parkland, railroad yards and cemeteries; more than 95% of the votes are in Chicago or Cicero. The latest redistricting raised the Hispanic share of the district population to 75% (75% of these Hispanics are Mexican; 10% are Puerto Rican). Even so, because many have not become citizens and some who have do not vote, Latinos may be only a bare majority of the electorate.

The congressman from the 4th District is Luis Gutierrez, a Democrat who has held the seat since its creation in 1992. He is of Puerto Rican descent, grew up in Chicago and returned for two years to Puerto Rico as a teacher after college. Back in Chicago, he worked as a cab driver and social worker. In 1983 he ran for 32d Ward committeeman against Dan Rostenkowski, and lost decisively. Then he became a staffer for Mayor Harold Washington, ran for alderman in 1984 and lost; in 1986 he ran again and won in one of two new Hispanic-majority aldermanic seats. After Washington died, Gutierrez backed Richard M. Daley in the 1989 election to succeed him. For that, Gutierrez was rewarded: He became chairman of the Housing Committee and pushed through his "New Homes for Chicago" affordable housing plan. In the 1992 primary race for the new 4th Congressional District seat, rival alderman Juan Solis called Gutierrez a machine candidate; Gutierrez won anyway, 60%–40%. After easily winning a rematch in 1994, Gutierrez has not had serious competition since.

In the House, Gutierrez's in-your-face style has produced mixed results. As a freshman, his outspoken opposition to congressional pay raises and his appearance on a *60 Minutes* broadcast— in which he called the House "the belly of the beast" and charged that the Democratic leadership stifled reform and that some freshmen Democrats "sold out"— was not well received. "I've gotten my rear end kicked around here," Gutierrez told *The Washington Post*; a leadership staffer said Gutierrez "will never get a choice committee" and "will always end up on the Banking Committee." He's still there, though he's moved into the senior ranks of what is now the Financial Services Committee. In a 1999 return visit to *60 Minutes*, he was not repentant but he did say, "I'm more careful" in speaking out. Gutierrez has staked out liberal positions and has been more a commentator than a legislative craftsman. As a leader of the Hispanic Caucus, he has cheered on efforts to restore food stamp eligibility and other benefits to legal immigrants. He filed a sweeping amnesty bill that would grant legal status by 2007 to illegal immigrants who entered the country by February 6, 2001. Gutierrez has been passionate about giving independence to Puerto Rico. He vehemently opposed the Navy's bombing exercises on the island of Vieques off Puerto Rico's coast. He was arrested with others in May 2000 for protesting at a makeshift chapel on Vieques inside the bombing range and again a year later when the Navy resumed its exercises, after which he complained of "inhumane" treatment.

Gutierrez often takes the posture of the political rebel, but he is also capable of making accommodations with the powerful—as his first race for alderman and then his endorsement of Daley showed. Similarly, he endorsed Bill Bradley over Al Gore in 2000 but also endorsed his then-5th District colleague Rod Blagojevich for governor in the 2002 primary, despite his many local battles with Blagojevich's father-in-law Alderman Richard Mell. Blagojevich, who ran third in Chicago, swept seven Hispanic wards. Locally, Gutierrez has consolidated Chicago's previously fractious Democratic politicians so as to maximize Latino influence. "Everyone likes to win, and with Gutierrez, everyone does," Juan Andrade, president of the U.S. Hispanic Leadership Institute, wrote after the 2002 primary. Gutierrez himself easily defeated well-funded primary challenger Marty Castro, a Mexican-American attorney who criticized him as ineffective and soft on terrorism.

FIFTH DISTRICT

Rep. Rahm Emanuel (D)

Elected 2002, 1st term; b. Nov. 29, 1959, Chicago; home, Chicago; Sarah Lawrence Col., B.A. 1981; Northwestern U., M.A. 1985; Jewish; married (Amy).

Professional Career: Natl. Campaign Dir., DCCC, 1988; Sr. White House adviser, 1993–99; Investment bank dir., 1999–02.

DC Office: 1319 LHOB 20515, 202-225-4061; Fax: 202-225-5603; Web site: www.house.gov/emanuel.

District Office: Chicago, 773-267-5926.

Committees: *Budget* (16th of 19 D). *Financial Services* (30th of 32 D): Capital Markets, Insurance & Government Sponsored Enterprises; Domestic and International Monetary Policy, Trade & Technology.

Group Ratings and Key Votes: Newly Elected

Election Results

2002 general	Rahm Emanuel (D)	106,514	(67%)	($2,971,514)
	Mark Augusti (R)	46,008	(29%)	($217,731)
	Frank Gonzalez (Lib)	6,913	(4%)	
2002 primary	Rahm Emanuel (D)	46,774	(50%)	
	Nancy Kaszak (D)	35,716	(39%)	
	Peter Dagher (D)	4,145	(4%)	
	Other	5,990	(6%)	
2000 general	Rod R. Blagojevich (D)	142,161	(87%)	($277,035)
	Matt Beauchamp (Lib)	20,728	(13%)	($28,231)

The People		Race/Ethnic Origin	Ancestry	
Area size:	58 sq. mi.	65.9% White	Polish: 13.5%	German: 11.5%
Urban population:	100.0%	2.2% Black	Irish: 9.9%	
Rural population:	0.0%	6.5% Asian	**2000 Presidential Vote**	
Pop. 2000:	653,647	0.2% Native Am.	Gore (D)	143,106 (66%)
Median income:	$48,531	0.0% Hawaiian	Bush (R)	73,793 (34%)
Poverty status:	8.5%	2.2% Two+ races	**Cook Partisan Voting Index:** D +16	
Military veterans:	6.7%	0.2% Other		
		23.0% Hispanic Origin		

Occupation	Blue collar: 21.5%	White collar: 64.9%	Gray collar: 13.6%

Few places in America today have more variety—ethnic and cultural—than the North Side of Chicago. This has been the homeland of one immigrant group after another and the chosen neighborhoods of all manner of successful middle-class people. Wooden workingman's cottages from the late 19th century give way to sturdy huge brick houses of the early 1900s and then to the prairie bungalows of the 1920s and white-shuttered, orange-brick colonials of the 1950s. Chicago was America's number one immigrant destination for Poles, Lithuanians, Czechs, Slovaks, Ukrainians and Romanians; something about the heavy dull clouds of the long winters, the short hot summers, a climate suited to potatoes and cabbage and other hardy vegetables, may have reminded them of central and eastern Europe. By the late 1980s new upwardly mobile immigrants from Mexico and Guatemala, Korea and the Philippines moved in; the 1990s witnessed immigrants from Poland and Ukraine, Pakistan and India. Family ties, webs of acquaintance that reach back to ancestral villages, have made the North Side of Chicago a natural port of entry for Eastern bloc migrants, even as newcomers establish new family ties and webs of relationships extending to Latin America and Southeast Asia.

The 5th Congressional District covers an oddly shaped slice of Chicago's North Side, running from the lakefront to the suburbs directly south of O'Hare Airport. Its boundaries were carefully drawn to put most Hispanics in the 4th District just to the south, but otherwise it reflects the full variety of the North Side. It includes Chicago's most glamorous lakefront apartments facing the Oak Street beach and the gentrified neighborhoods of Old Town, where old houses and factories are being converted into upscale condominiums, and nearby Lincoln Park, which has the highest median household income of Chicago's 77 community areas. It takes in baseball's famed Wrigley Field, the Polish-American and Ukrainian-American neighborhoods around Milwaukee Avenue, and the old Italian neighborhoods running west on Grand Avenue. It includes, a couple of blocks from the Chicago River, the grand old church of St. Stanislaus Kostka—a traditional center of the Polish community since the 19th century but now with Masses in Spanish—and the residence across Pulaski Park of Dan Rostenkowski, chairman of the House Ways and Means Committee from 1981 to 1994, for whom the district was originally designed. It reaches the Cook County suburbs, beyond River Grove and Franklin Park into Schiller Park and Northlake. This is a solidly Democratic district; in 2000, Al Gore won here by 66%–34%.

The congressman from the 5th District is Rahm Emanuel, a Democrat elected in 2002 when Rod Blagojevich gave up the seat and ran successfully for governor. It was not apparent in early 2001 that there would be another 5th District: with Blagojevich running for governor, it seemed convenient for the bipartisan redistricters, Speaker Dennis Hastert and 3d District Democrat William Lipinski, to slice up the district. But when the 2000 Census came in, it showed a big population increase in Chicago's immigrant neighborhoods. Mayor Richard M. Daley insisted that Chicago should retain all its districts; the May 2001 plan left the boundaries of the 5th District mostly undisturbed. Emanuel grew up in Chicago, the son of an Israeli immigrant; he graduated from Sarah Lawrence and from Northwestern. He worked on the 1992 Clinton campaign and was a high-level staffer in the Clinton White House, where he gained wide respect for his political savvy but drew criticism, even from allies, for an arrogant and abrasive style. In 1999 he left the White House and returned to Chicago where he made millions as an investment banker. His decision to seek Blagojevich's seat was greeted with disdain by those who had toiled for years in the vineyards of local Chicago politics. His strongest opponent was former state Representative Nancy Kaszak, who lost the 1996 primary to Blagojevich; she portrayed him as an interloper with few ties to the district. But Emanuel had his own local connections. He was endorsed by Daley and by labor unions (despite his support of NAFTA), and he raised large sums—nearly $2 million for the primary—from his extensive Chicago and national Democratic fundraising networks.

Emanuel benefited from controversy two weeks before the primary, when a local Polish-American leader supporting Kaszak charged that Emanuel served in the Israeli army in 1991 during the Gulf War and suggested he had dual loyalties. But the charge was false—Emanuel is a U.S. citizen who volunteered as a civilian at an Israeli supply base—and Kaszak's campaign was thrown off-stride. Emanuel won large majorities on the Lakefront and in Lincoln Park; he won 50%–39%. He carried all of the 13 wards in the district, except for the heavily Polish 30th. In the general election, Emanuel faced a feisty challenger who attacked him as overly ambitious, but Emanuel won 67%–29%. Even before winning the election, he cut an unusually high-profile figure: He strategized for the national party, met with the national media and sought a prime committee assignment. His aggressiveness, political skills and fundraising prowess make him a freshman congressman to watch.

SIXTH DISTRICT

Rep. Henry Hyde (R)

Elected 1974, 15th term; b. Apr. 18, 1924, Chicago; home, Wood Dale; Georgetown U., B.S. 1947, Loyola U., J.D. 1949; Catholic; widowed.

Military Career: Navy, 1944–46 (WWII); Naval Reserves, 1946–68.

Elected Office: IL House of Reps., 1966–74, Maj. Ldr., 1971–72.

Professional Career: Practicing atty., 1950–75.

DC Office: 2110 RHOB 20515, 202-225-4561; Fax: 202-225-1166; Web site: www.house.gov/hyde.

District Office: Addison, 630-832-5950.

Committees: *International Relations* (Chmn. of 26 R). *Judiciary* (2d of 21 R): Courts, the Internet & Intellectual Property.

Group Ratings

	ADA	ACLU	AFS	LCV	CON	ITIC	NTU	COC	ACU	NTLC	CHC
2002	0	7	0	13	32	88	53	100	88	83	100
2001	5	—	0	14	—	—	56	96	92	—	—

National Journal Ratings

	2001 LIB —	2001 CONS		2002 LIB —	2002 CONS
Economic	33%	66%		31%	69%
Social	0%	81%		0%	75%
Foreign	21%	74%		15%	78%

Key Votes of the 107th Congress

1. Approve Bush Tax Cuts	Y	5. Faith-Based Charities	Y
2. Limit Patients' Bill of Rights	Y	6. Bar Gays in the Boy Scouts	Y
3. Campaign Finance Reform	N	7. Ban Partial-Birth Abortion	Y
4. Ban ANWR Development	N	8. Arm Commercial Pilots	Y

9. Trade Promotion Authority	Y
10. Bar Funds for Intl. Court	Y
11. Authorize Force in Iraq	Y
12. Deny Home. Sec. Dept. Union	Y

Election Results

2002 general	Henry Hyde (R)	113,174	(65%)	($839,199)
	Tom Berry (D)	60,698	(35%)	
2002 primary	Henry Hyde (R)	unopposed		
2000 general	Henry Hyde (R)	133,327	(59%)	($2,436,839)
	Brent Christensen (D)	92,880	(41%)	($234,608)

Prior Winning Percentages: 1998 (67%); 1996 (64%); 1994 (73%); 1992 (66%); 1990 (67%); 1988 (74%); 1986 (75%); 1984 (75%); 1982 (68%); 1980 (67%); 1978 (66%); 1976 (61%); 1974 (53%)

The People		Race/Ethnic Origin	Ancestry	
Area size:	215 sq. mi.	75.3% White	German: 16.7%	Irish: 11.0%
Urban population:	100.0%	2.7% Black	Polish: 9.4%	
Rural population:	0.0%	8.1% Asian	**2000 Presidential Vote**	
Pop. 2000:	653,647	0.1% Native Am.	Bush (R)	126,254 (53%)
Median income:	$62,640	0.0% Hawaiian	Gore (D)	103,616 (44%)
Poverty status:	4.3%	1.3% Two+ races	Other	6,945 (3%)
Military veterans:	9.6%	0.1% Other	**Cook Partisan Voting Index:** R + 5	
		12.5% Hispanic Origin		

Occupation	Blue collar: 20.2%	White collar: 69.5%	Gray collar: 10.3%

In World War II, what is now the nation's second-busiest airport was an apple orchard on which a defense plant was built (hence its current three-letter code: ORD); to the east was the Forest Preserve along the Des Plaines River, to the west little suburban villages strung along rail lines, separated by cornfields. But in the 1940s, Chicago politicians, in search of a new airport site, annexed the orchard and named it after a World War II airman awarded the Medal of Honor, who got a military appointment from the feds after his father gave state's evidence against Al Capone and was gunned down. Mayor Richard J. Daley opened O'Hare in 1955 and promoted its development, correctly concluding that a great airport could maintain in the 20th century the economic strength Chicago gained from railroad stations and rail yards in the 19th century. Today, O'Hare is surrounded on all sides by suburbs almost as densely settled as the bungalow wards of the city. Politically, these suburbs were for many years solidly Republican, convinced that civic virtues could best be realized by opposing the party of City Hall in Chicago and that economic growth could best be assured by opposing the party that backed stifling government regulation.

The 6th Congressional District includes O'Hare and much of the suburban area to its west. Most of the district is in DuPage County, the second largest county in the state. It includes the string of long-settled suburbs due west of the Loop: Elmhurst, Villa Park, Lombard, Glen Ellyn, Wheaton, plus the newer suburbs along I-290 and Lake Street: Bensenville, Addison, Wood Dale, Bloomingdale. Over the years growth has brought some changes, with many former Chicagoans of ethnically diverse backgrounds. Economically, this remains high-income territory; culturally, it is now cautiously moderate or even liberal. Politically, it has become less overwhelmingly Republican. In 1988 George Bush carried DuPage by 124,000 votes, with 68% of the vote, but in 2000 George W. Bush carried the county by only 48,000, with 55% of the vote—which tells you in a nutshell why the elder Bush carried Illinois and the younger Bush lost it.

The congressman from the 6th District is Henry Hyde, former chairman of the House Judiciary Committee, chief manager of the impeachment of Bill Clinton and one of the most respected and intellectually honest members of the House. Hyde springs from Chicago earth, was raised a Catholic and a Democrat; he was an all-city basketball center and played against basketball great George Mikan; he went off to college at Georgetown and enlisted in the Navy and served at Lingayen Gulf. After the war, he finished college and law school, practiced law in Chicago, and in 1958 switched parties, convinced that Republicans were more in line with his anti-Communist beliefs. He ran for the House in 1962 in northwest Chicago and lost 53%–47% to incumbent Roman Pucinski. He was elected to the Illinois House in 1966 and in the Democratic year of 1974 was elected, as one of only 144 Republicans, to the U.S. House.

There he first made his name as an abortion opponent, attaching to Appropriations subcommittee bills his Hyde amendments prohibiting the use of federal funds to pay for abortions in various circumstances. "I look for the common thread in slavery, the Holocaust and abortion," he said in 1998. "To me, the common thread is dehumanizing people." In 1976 he passed the first Hyde amendment to an appropriation bill, banning abortions financed by Medicaid. It has remained in force ever since, though states can spend their own money on abortions, and some do; exceptions for saving the life of the mother, and victims of rape and incest were added in 1993. Hyde is concerned about born as well as unborn children. He was one of the few Republicans who supported the family leave bill, and has sponsored bills to expand the number of women eligible for pregnancy benefits under the children's health insurance program. He opposes assisted suicide as part of a "culture of death" and sponsored the bill passed by the House to criminalize the prescription of lethal drugs to terminally ill patients contemplating ending their lives.

On many occasions, Hyde has proven himself one of the most eloquent members of the House. His speeches against term limits and in favor of the flag-burning amendment are classics; his evisceration of the nuclear freeze resolution helped turn the tide on foreign policy in the House in the 1980s. He defended the Reagan administration on Iran-Contra and in the process said, somewhat to his embarrassment in the impeachment debate, that to condemn all lying "seems to me too simplistic. In the murkier grayness of the real world, choices must often be made." Three major Hyde measures passed both houses but were vetoed by Clinton: the partial-birth abortion ban, product liability and tort reform.

None of these challenges he had faced before was as great or as public as the challenge of impeachment. From the first, Hyde had little taste for the subject, yet realized he had the responsibility to handle it. Early on he said that any impeachment resolution must be bipartisan if it were to be credible, but it became clear by September that many Democrats were determined to defend Clinton at every turn. Democrats resisted his resolution for an impeachment inquiry but felt obliged to advance one of their own, with time limits and with Zoe Lofgren's requirement that members vote first on the definition of an impeachable offense. All Republicans and 31 Democrats voted for the Republican resolution. Clinton defenders tried to put Hyde on the defensive. In September, an online publication, *Salon*, reported that Hyde had had an affair 30 years before; "youthful indiscretions," Hyde responded. As the facts of Clinton's conduct became known, Hyde obviously decided that the president had lied under oath in a United States District Court proceeding, and that that could not be forgiven. He ran the fractious hearings with scrupulous fairness, and even with occasional humor. His summation to the House was genuinely eloquent, and impeachment was voted on two of four counts.

Then came the historic march of Hyde and the 12 other House managers to the Senate presided over by Chief Justice William Rehnquist. The managers were pitted against Clinton's professional litigators, and the discomfort of almost all senators was obvious. (In 1996, Hyde rebuffed requests that he run for the Senate, adding "I'd be a great senator—God, I'd be so arrogant.") Remembering his own experience in combat, he summoned up memories of Americans who had fallen in battle and urged the senators to uphold the rule of law. But Democrats did not waver, and the articles of impeachment were rejected.

After the 2000 election he tried to get the House Republican leadership to waive the six-year term limit on chairmanships, arguing that he had lost one year of chairing Judiciary to impeachment. But they declined, and instead Hyde got the chairmanship of the International Relations Committee. This was a far less partisan assignment for Hyde, who agreed with committee senior Democrat Tom Lantos on many foreign-policy issues, including firmness toward Iraq, support for Israel, door-opening to Vietnam, economic aid to Afghanistan, and increased federal dollars for "public diplomacy" overseas following September 11.

Hyde has continued to work on other issues. Much of his district lies under O'Hare flight paths, and he has been a champion of building a third Chicago-area airport in Peotone in Will County; in this, his chief ally has been the 2d District's Jesse Jackson Jr. He was the only House Republican from Illinois not to endorse a federal bailout for United Airlines. He supported bankruptcy reform, passed by the House in March 2001 and in July 2001 by the Senate, and unexpectedly found himself on the other side of the issue from the House's pro-life movement that he had been instrumental in creating. When he painstakingly negotiated in the summer of 2002 a deal with Senator Charles Schumer on the Democrat's amendment to the bankruptcy bill to make it more difficult for abortion-clinic protestors from declaring bankruptcy to avoid paying court fines or damages, many conservative colleagues said that Hyde had been too accommodating, and the bankruptcy bill did not pass.

Hyde considered not running for re-election in 2000, but decided to do so after Democrats' threatened to target the House impeachment managers. In 2002, he improved on his showing in 2000, when evidently he paid some political price for his stand. Now the second-oldest member of Congress (Ralph Hall is older) and the fifth most-senior House Republican, he enjoys a more bipartisan respect accorded to an icon.

SEVENTH DISTRICT

Rep. Danny Davis (D)

Elected 1996, 4th term; b. Sept. 6, 1941, Parkdale, AR; home, Chicago; AR AM&N Col., B.A. 1961, Chicago St. U., M.S. 1968, Union Inst., Ph.D. 1977; Baptist; married (Vera).

Elected Office: Chicago City Alderman, 1979–90; Cook Cnty. Commissioner, 1990–96.

Professional Career: Teacher, Chicago Public Schls., 1962–69; Health Care Planner, 1969–79.

DC Office: 1222 LHOB 20515, 202-225-5006; Fax: 202-225-5641; Web site: www.house.gov/davis.

District Office: Chicago, 773-533-7520.

Committees: *Education & the Workforce* (16th of 22 D): Education Reform; Select Education. *Government Reform* (9th of 19 D): Civil Service & Agency Organization (RMM); Criminal Justice, Drug Policy & Human Resources. *Small Business* (7th of 17 D): Tax, Finance & Exports; Workforce, Empowerment & Government Programs.

Group Ratings

	ADA	ACLU	AFS	LCV	CON	ITIC	NTU	COC	ACU	NTLC	CHC
2002	90	93	100	88	70	38	22	42	0	6	0
2001	100	—	100	93	—	—	9	35	4	—	—

National Journal Ratings

	2001 LIB — 2001 CONS		2002 LIB — 2002 CONS	
Economic	83% —	15%	86% —	12%
Social	90% —	0%	92% —	6%
Foreign	96% —	0%	87% —	13%

Key Votes of the 107th Congress

1. Approve Bush Tax Cuts	N	5. Faith-Based Charities	N	9. Trade Promotion Authority	N
2. Limit Patients' Bill of Rights	N	6. Bar Gays in the Boy Scouts	N	10. Bar Funds for Intl. Court	N
3. Campaign Finance Reform	Y	7. Ban Partial-Birth Abortion	N	11. Authorize Force in Iraq	N
4. Ban ANWR Development	Y	8. Arm Commercial Pilots	N	12. Deny Home. Sec. Dept. Union	N

Election Results

2002 general	Danny Davis (D)	137,933	(83%)	($215,233)
	Mark Tunney (R)	25,280	(15%)	($51,387)
	Other	2,543	(2%)	
2002 primary	Danny Davis (D)	unopposed		
2000 general	Danny Davis (D)	164,155	(86%)	($196,566)
	Robert Dallas (R)	26,872	(14%)	

Prior Winning Percentages: 1998 (93%); 1996 (83%)

The People		Race/Ethnic Origin	Ancestry	
Area size:	59 sq. mi.	27.3% White	German: 5.6%	Irish: 5.2%
Urban population:	100.0%	61.6% Black	Italian: 2.9%	
Rural population:	0.0%	3.8% Asian	**2000 Presidential Vote**	
Pop. 2000:	653,647	0.1% Native Am.	Gore (D)	199,064 (83%)
Median income:	$40,361	0.0% Hawaiian	Bush (R)	38,196 (16%)
Poverty status:	24.0%	1.2% Two+ races	Other	1,985 (1%)
Military veterans:	8.0%	0.1% Other	**Cook Partisan Voting Index:** D +34	
		5.8% Hispanic Origin		

Occupation	Blue collar: 15.5%	White collar: 70.6%	Gray collar: 13.9%

The cross-country flyer on a lucky day can get a clear view of the biggest man-made cityscape between the Atlantic and Pacific Oceans: Chicago's Loop. High-rise buildings were pioneered a century ago in the Loop—named in 1897 for the circle the elevated train forms around the city's center—by architects like Louis Sullivan and Daniel Burnham. International School modernists built their most impressive collection of buildings here and along Lake Shore Drive in the years after World War II; in recent years, postmodernists have decorated the Chicago River and reinvented the skyscraper. The Loop now spreads beyond the El, up the wondrous shopping street of North Michigan Avenue with a peak at the John Hancock Tower, and west beyond the commodities exchanges to the Sears Tower on the Chicago River. This is the face Chicago likes to present to the world: giant structures rising where the prairies meet the inland sea, a vast concentration of brains and muscle, the nerve center of the markets of the nation and the world.

Behind the lakefront, where the air traveler sees the grid spread out below with occasional radials, are the muscle and sinew, gristle and fat of the city. There also are parts that do not work so well: houses and apartment buildings are abandoned; commercial space stands empty and vandalized; giant, crime-racked housing projects, like the Robert Taylor Homes off the Dan Ryan Expressway, built by Mayor Richard J. Daley in the 1960s (he preferred low-rise projects, but the feds wouldn't finance them) and now torn down by another Daley. The West Side of Chicago, the vast acres directly west of the Loop, for years was a dreadful slum, with some areas almost emptied out; the decay spread west to the Austin neighborhood, just before the border of upper-income—and for decades racially integrated—Oak Park. In the 1990s, there was some revival. The United Center, the erstwhile home court of Michael Jordan and site of the 1996 Democratic convention, sparked commercial development of the West Side, and lower crime rates have raised the value of land once again.

The 7th Congressional District contains the Loop and most of the North Michigan corridor and the Near North Side, where the infamous Cabrini-Green housing project is being replaced by new, mixed-market housing. It also goes south, past 19th century Prairie Avenue mansions to take in a few of the heavily black South Side neighborhoods chronicled in the groundbreaking 1945 book, *Black Metropolis*. Its heart, demographically and spiritually, is the black ghetto of the West Side, more depopulated and socially disorganized than the South Side. To the west, just outside city limits, are Oak Park, the boyhood home of Ernest Hemingway and location of the Frank Lloyd Wright home and museum and many of his prairie-style houses; River Forest; and the much more modest Maywood, which is black-majority; and Broadview and Hillside, site of a one-lane bottleneck on the Chicago expressway system known as the Hillside Strangler. As with the 1st and 2d Districts on the South Side, redistricting in 2001 added nearly 100,000 people to the 7th and reduced slightly the share of black population, but it did not change the basic contours. A bit less than two-thirds of the people here are black; there are relatively few Hispanics, since Latino neighborhoods were carefully placed in the 4th District.

The congressman from the 7th District is Danny Davis, a Democrat first elected in 1996 after two unsuccessful tries in the 1980s. Davis grew up on a cotton farm in Arkansas, graduated from college there, then moved to Chicago and worked as a teacher, assistant principal and guidance counselor in Chicago public schools. For 10 years, he ran a community health project on the West Side. He was elected alderman in the 29th Ward on the boundary of Oak Park in 1979 and supported Mayor Harold Washington in the council wars of the 1980s. In 1990 he was elected a Cook County commissioner; in 1991 he made a quixotic run for mayor against Richard M. Daley; he lost his 29th Ward committeeman post to a Daley-backed challenger in 2000.

In 1996, when Cardiss Collins retired after nearly 24 years in the House, Davis decided to run. His major opponents were 3d Ward Alderman Dorothy Tillman, a Daley ally, and 37th Ward Alderman Ed Smith. Davis campaigned as a big-government liberal, calling for a $7.60 minimum wage, affirmative action, and a national health care plan. Davis won with 33%, followed by Tillman with 20% and Smith with 12%. He won the general with ease and has not faced a serious challenge since then.

In the House, Davis has a very liberal voting record. He has opposed tax cuts, even when advocated by Bill Clinton. He opposed the sugar program as corporate welfare (Chicago is the nation's leading candy manufacturer). Davis has worked with Republicans, co-sponsoring with Jim Talent and J.C. Watts the American Community Renewal Act, to provide tax cuts and credits for businesses locating in troubled central city neighborhoods. Aspects of that proposal were embraced by Clinton and Speaker Dennis Hastert as the "new markets" tax incentive and enacted into law. He was the only member to get Transportation Chairman Bud Shuster not to oppose an amendment to the 1998 highway bill: an increase from $42 million to $150 million in a pilot program to provide transportation for low-income central city residents to get to work sites in the suburbs; this was supported by UPS and United Airlines. With his wife Vera, who is president of the West Side NAACP, Davis advocated a local program to increase from its existing 28% the share of black home ownership in his district by offering credit counseling and innovative forms of mortgage financing. Davis also created a 7th District task force on ex-offenders to assist 1,000 paroled men in the state's Crossroads program, as they return to their communities.

Davis speaks in an impressive sepulchral tone, and his self-evident sincerity and concern for the poor has helped him achieve additional success in a mostly conservative House. But he stirred controversy within the Chicago delegation when he asked colleagues to support him for a seat on Ways and Means after freshman Rahm Emanuel already had lined up support for his own bid. As it turned out, Democrats' failure to regain a majority in the House meant that there was not a slot for either one; since 1995, Illinois has been represented on the committee only by Republicans.

Davis's hold on the district seems secure, but there are plenty of local black politicians eager for his seat.

EIGHTH DISTRICT

Rep. Phil Crane (R)

Elected Nov. 1969, 17th term; b. Nov. 3, 1930, Chicago; home, Wauconda; Hillsdale Col., B.A. 1952, IN U., M.A. 1961, Ph.D. 1963; Protestant; married (Arlene).

Military Career: Army, 1954–56.

Professional Career: Instructor, IN U., 1960–63; Asst. Prof., Bradley U., 1963–67; Dir., Westminster Academy, 1967–68.

DC Office: 233 CHOB 20515, 202-225-3711; Fax: 202-225-7830; Web site: www.house.gov/crane.

District Offices: Lake Villa, 847-265-9000; Palatine, 847-358-9160.

Committees: *Ways & Means* (2d of 24 R): Health; Trade (Chmn.). *Joint Committee on Taxation* (2d of 5 Reps.).

Group Ratings

	ADA	ACLU	AFS	LCV	CON	ITIC	NTU	COC	ACU	NTLC	CHC
2002	0	7	0	13	76	88	67	94	100	100	100
2001	0	—	0	0	—	—	79	96	100	—	—

National Journal Ratings

	2001 LIB	—	2001 CONS		2002 LIB	—	2002 CONS
Economic	0%	—	94%		0%	—	91%
Social	20%	—	69%		30%	—	68%
Foreign	0%	—	97%		0%	—	85%

Key Votes of the 107th Congress

1. Approve Bush Tax Cuts	Y	5. Faith-Based Charities	Y	9. Trade Promotion Authority	Y
2. Limit Patients' Bill of Rights	Y	6. Bar Gays in the Boy Scouts	Y	10. Bar Funds for Intl. Court	*
3. Campaign Finance Reform	N	7. Ban Partial-Birth Abortion	Y	11. Authorize Force in Iraq	Y
4. Ban ANWR Development	N	8. Arm Commercial Pilots	Y	12. Deny Home. Sec. Dept. Union	Y

Election Results

2002 general	Phil Crane (R)	95,275	(57%)	($834,585)
	Melissa Bean (D)	70,626	(43%)	($320,956)
2002 primary	Phil Crane (R)	unopposed		
2000 general	Phil Crane (R)	141,918	(61%)	($970,024)
	Lance Pressl (D)	90,777	(39%)	($280,791)

Prior Winning Percentages: 1998 (69%); 1996 (62%); 1994 (65%); 1992 (56%); 1990 (82%); 1988 (75%); 1986 (78%); 1984 (78%); 1982 (66%); 1980 (74%); 1978 (80%); 1976 (73%); 1974 (61%); 1972 (74%); 1970 (58%); 1969 (58%)

The People

Area size:	646 sq. mi.	**Race/Ethnic Origin**		**Ancestry**	
Urban population:	96.1%	78.8% White		German: 19.5% Irish: 11.0%	
Rural population:	3.9%	3.2% Black		Polish: 8.3%	
Pop. 2000:	653,647	5.6% Asian		**2000 Presidential Vote**	
Median income:	$62,762	0.1% Native Am.		Bush (R)...............131,967 (56%)	
Poverty status:	4.4%	0.0% Hawaiian		Gore (D)...............98,664 (42%)	
Military veterans:	10.6%	1.2% Two + races		Other...................6,954 (3%)	
		0.1% Other		**Cook Partisan Voting Index:** R + 8	
		10.8% Hispanic Origin			

Occupation   Blue collar: 21.8%   White collar: 67.3%   Gray collar: 10.9%

Schaumburg may not be nationally known, but it is one of America's major corporate headquarters cities and one of several edge cities northwest of Chicago. Sixty years ago this was farmland, half a dozen miles beyond the orchard that is now O'Hare Airport. Today, Schaumburg—near the intersection of the Northwest Tollway and I-290, with lots of office space and Woodfield Mall and miles of subdivisions, with some moderately priced apartments—is the site of the headquarters of Motorola and Zurich American Life Insurance; nearby are the headquarters of Sears and Kemper Insurance. Yet Schaumburg yearns for traditions. It has built a performing arts center, formed an orchestra for young people, and has built from scratch a traditional downtown.

The 8th Congressional District is made up of Schaumburg and dozens of similar communities to the north, on the hilly lakelands north and northwest of Chicago. Just to the north are Palatine and Barrington Hills (in-between Inverness is connected by a narrow corridor to the 10th District). The district includes the rapidly-growing western half of Lake County, with little lake communities being surrounded by new suburbs, and also includes the Lake Michigan town of Zion. To the west, the 8th includes about half of fast-growing McHenry County. The tone of life here is not elite, but people here are affluent; culturally, this is part of the great rural Midwest as much as—perhaps more than—it is of yeasty, lusty Chicago. Economically, it is suspicious of government spending, which it associates with the corrupt big city of yore. Historically, this area was one of the most Republican places in the nation. In the 1990s, like other suburban Chicago areas, it moved toward the Democrats, and if the 8th is still one of Illinois's most Republican districts, as measured by its support of George W. Bush in 2000, it is far less Republican than districts with similar demographics in Texas or Georgia.

The congressman from the 8th District is Philip Crane, the senior Republican in the House of Representatives. Crane grew up in Indiana, one of several sons of a doctor who had his own radio program; he went to Hillsdale College, got a Ph.D. at Indiana University, and was a conservative intellectual when that seemed an oxymoron. He moved to the Chicago area in 1967 and, at 39, won a November 1969 special election to the House, replacing Donald Rumsfeld, then Richard Nixon's poverty program director, and now Defense Secretary for George W. Bush. Crane supported a set of ideas which then seemed backward-looking but which have been on the ascendant in the nation and the world since: free market economics, a strong national defense, traditional values.

In his first years in the House, Crane sat largely unnoticed on the back benches and had meager influence. In 1980 he ran for president, hoping, as the truer libertarian, to cut in on the elderly Ronald Reagan's support and then take it over when the Reagan candidacy faded. But his strategy failed and through the 1980s he seemed embittered and unfocused; he was not part of the young conservative movement in the House led by Jack Kemp, Newt Gingrich and Trent Lott. By the early 1990s, Crane was in trouble back home. In the anti-incumbent year of 1992, in a redistricted seat with unfamiliar territory, he beat Gary Skoien, a former aide to Governor James Thompson, by only 55%–45% in the Republican primary and won the general by only 56%–40%. In the 1994 primary, he faced Skoien and then-state Senator Peter Fitzgerald, who spent $700,000 of his own money; Crane won with 40% of the vote to Fitzgerald's 33% and Skoien's 21%.

After those close scrapes, Crane suddenly found himself part of a Republican majority. He was not a committee chairman—Bill Archer had seniority over him on Ways and Means—but he did become chairman of its Trade subcommittee. Crane is as much of a pure free trader as anyone who has ever served in Congress: He supported NAFTA, GATT, fast track, and often chided the Clinton administration for not lobbying for bipartisan support of free trade measures it nominally supported. Crane shepherded through Most Favored Nation status for Bulgaria, Romania and Cambodia. Then in 1999 and 2000 he had quite spectacular success. He worked hard to pass the Africa trade bill originated in the Black Caucus and co-sponsored by Ways and Means ranking Democrat Charles Rangel. This was a thankless task: There is not much constituency for it in the 8th District or in Republican circles, and it was fiercely opposed by textile interests, unions, Jesse Jackson Jr. and several other Black Caucus members. But Crane and Rangel managed to strike a House-Senate deal in May 2000 and it became law. That agreement also lowered trade barriers with nations in the Caribbean Basin. Starting in early 1999 he pushed for action on PNTR with China. The House passed PNTR in May 2000 and the Senate did likewise in September.

At the same time, Crane was campaigning for the Ways and Means chairmanship; Republican rules limit chairmen to six-year terms and Bill Archer had announced that he would retire in 2000. But in November 1994 Newt Gingrich had established the precedent that Republicans would not always honor seniority, and Crane had serious competition from the next most senior member, Bill Thomas. While Crane had long been a supporter of the flat tax, he had played little part in tax legislation; in the July 1999 sessions considering the tax cut, Archer and Thomas had taken lead roles while Crane was mostly silent. Nor was he a factor on health care issues, on which Thomas, as chairman of the Health Subcommittee, took the lead. In the 105th Congress, Crane had scorned Gingrich's demand that members seeking chairmanships raise money to elect other Republicans; in October 1998, in a response to requests for funds, he sent in a desultory $25,000 with a tart note: "I understand, however, that a career of service to our party and our candidates means little today, and the only question that now apparently matters, at least when it comes to 'properly securing' a chairmanship, is 'what have you done for me lately?' "

Gingrich's downfall in November 1998 and his replacement by Crane's fellow Illinoisan Dennis Hastert in January 1999 gave heart to Crane's campaign for the chairmanship. His attitude toward fundraising changed, but there was a widespread feeling that Thomas would be a more competent and active leader; one member in early March 2000 said, "There aren't five votes in the Conference" for Crane. Then in mid-March 2000, eight friends and family members confronted Crane in an intervention and demanded that he seek treatment for alcoholism; he had fallen into the habit, exacerbated by his daughter's death from cancer around Christmas 1997, of drinking 10 Heinekens a night. Crane asked for a 30-day leave of absence for treatment. He returned to the House a month later, the object of many warm remarks, and stepped up his legislative work—and his fundraising. With help from friends—one of whom, Silicon Valley executive Tom Siebel, gave $500,000—Crane raised some $2.5 million for the National Republican Congressional Committee and Republican candidates, plus $251,000 from his campaign committee and $816,000 for Battleground 2000. But Thomas was raising money in similar magnitudes and Hastert, despite his friendliness, would not commit to observing seniority. In January 2001 the Republican Steering Committee voted overwhelmingly to give the chairmanship to Thomas; the Republican Conference ratified the decision.

This surely was a great disappointment to Crane, but he continued as chairman of the Trade Subcommittee and took the lead in sponsoring trade promotion authority for the president in 2001. Crane's package included legislation to expand duty-free trade with the Andean nations—Bolivia, Peru, Ecuador, Colombia. Opposed by almost all Democrats, trade promotion authority survived two breathtakingly close votes on the floor—215–214 in December 2001 and 215–212 in July 2002. But for the first time in eight years, a president had trade promotion authority—a major achievement. After being reelected routinely, Crane immediately started working on a substitute for an export subsidy law likely to be repealed, because it has been ruled an unfair trade practice; his proposal, supported by ranking Democrat Charles Rangel, was to cut the corporate income tax rate by 1%.

NINTH DISTRICT

Rep. Jan Schakowsky (D)

Elected 1998, 3d term; b. May 26, 1944, Chicago; home, Evanston; U. of IL, B.S. 1965; Jewish; married (Robert Creamer).

Elected Office: IL House of Reps., 1990–98.

Professional Career: Founder, Natl. Consumers Unite, 1969–73; Prog. Dir., IL Public Action, 1976–85; Exec. Dir., IL State Cncl. of Sr. Citizens, 1985–90.

DC Office: 515 CHOB 20515, 202-225-2111; Fax: 202-226-6890; Web site: www.house.gov/schakowsky.

District Offices: Chicago, 773-506-7100; Evanston, 847-328-3399.

Committees: *Chief Deputy Minority Whip. Energy & Commerce* (25th of 26 D): Commerce, Trade & Consumer Protection (RMM); Environment & Hazardous Materials; Oversight & Investigations.

Group Ratings

	ADA	ACLU	AFS	LCV	CON	ITIC	NTU	COC	ACU	NTLC	CHC
2002	100	93	100	100	63	38	23	30	0	8	0
2001	100	—	100	100	—	—	14	27	0	—	—

National Journal Ratings

	2001 LIB	—	2001 CONS	2002 LIB	—	2002 CONS
Economic	88%	—	11%	95%	—	0%
Social	90%	—	0%	84%	—	8%
Foreign	96%	—	0%	94%	—	0%

Key Votes of the 107th Congress

1. Approve Bush Tax Cuts	N	5. Faith-Based Charities	N
2. Limit Patients' Bill of Rights	N	6. Bar Gays in the Boy Scouts	N
3. Campaign Finance Reform	Y	7. Ban Partial-Birth Abortion	N
4. Ban ANWR Development	Y	8. Arm Commercial Pilots	N

9. Trade Promotion Authority	N
10. Bar Funds for Intl. Court	N
11. Authorize Force in Iraq	N
12. Deny Home. Sec. Dept. Union	N

Election Results

2002 general	Jan Schakowsky (D)	118,642	(70%)	($864,506)
	Nicholas Duric (R)	45,307	(27%)	($32,750)
	Other	4,887	(3%)	
2002 primary	Jan Schakowsky (D)	unopposed		
2000 general	Jan Schakowsky (D)	147,002	(76%)	($694,724)
	Dennis J. Driscoll (R)	45,344	(24%)	($98,852)

Prior Winning Percentages: 1998 (75%)

The People		Race/Ethnic Origin	Ancestry	
Area size:	78 sq. mi.	62.5% White	German: 10.5%	Polish: 8.4%
Urban population:	100.0%	10.7% Black	Irish: 8.2%	
Rural population:	0.0%	12.3% Asian	**2000 Presidential Vote**	
Pop. 2000:	653,647	0.2% Native Am.	Gore (D) 155,529	(67%)
Median income:	$46,531	0.1% Hawaiian	Bush (R) 71,064	(31%)
Poverty status:	11.0%	2.6% Two+ races	Other 4,331	(2%)
Military veterans:	8.0%	0.3% Other	**Cook Partisan Voting Index:** D +18	
		11.5% Hispanic Origin		

Occupation	Blue collar: 16.1%	White collar: 69.8%	Gray collar: 14.0%

"Make no little plans," commanded architect Daniel Burnham, who made no little plans for the Chicago lakefront. The glorious parks he designed are among America's urban jewels, and the row of high-rise apartment buildings—some austere works of masters of the International style, some in traditional styles evocative of some other place and time, some sleek Art Deco works of the 1920s and 1930s—are a splendid accompaniment. Behind the lakefront is all the diversity of Chicago. In sturdy brick houses, with scarcely a shoehorn's space between them, or in stubby apartment buildings, are ethnic and racial groups of all sorts, from Argentineans to Slavs, Plains Indians to Indian plainsmen. In the 1970s the neighborhoods behind the lakefront seemed to be getting grimier and heading downhill. Since the late 1980s, they have been busy gentrifying, as young couples and gays, professionals and entrepreneurs renovate old houses and open new businesses. Today this part of Chicago has as much urban energy and lively diversity as any place in America.

The lakefront has long been the most heavily Jewish part of Chicago. Chicago's Jewish community, prominent for more than a century, has never been as much a force for big government as in New York, nor is it connected as much to a glamorous industry as in Los Angeles. Yet these Jewish voters' liberal impulses have been strong: the 19th century impulse to resist state authority and imposition of cultural uniformity and the 20th century impulse to increase state responsibility for individuals' lives. Chicago's North Side Jews, on the lakefront or in neighborhoods like Rogers Park and nearby suburbs like Skokie and Niles, have been a solidly Democratic voting bloc, involved with—but skeptical of—the old Democratic machine. In the racial city politics of the 1980s, as in state politics, Jewish voters and lakefront liberals of all backgrounds were a key swing group.

The 9th Congressional District covers most of Chicago's lakefront, from just north of Diversey Harbor past the thriving Asian and orthodox Jewish communities in West Rogers Park and on to Evanston, the home of Northwestern University and a city that has moved gracefully from historic Yankee Republican-ness to trendy post-graduate Democratic-ness. From Evanston and nearby Wilmette (which is shared with the 10th), the 9th presses inland through heavily Jewish Skokie to Morton Grove and Niles and includes most of Des Plaines. In 2001, redistricting added once rock-solid Republican territory to the west—Park Ridge, with its characteristic Chicago brick houses in orderly rows, where Hillary Rodham Clinton grew up at 235 Wisner, and the cluster of office buildings and interchanges in Rosemont, next to O'Hare Airport; also added was the far northwest corner of the city of Chicago. This new territory, much less Republican than it was before the 1990s, nevertheless lowered the district's Democratic percentage, but not in a way that makes any practical difference: This is an overwhelmingly Democratic district.

The congresswoman from the 9th District is Jan Schakowsky, a Democrat elected in 1998 and an outspoken progressive, one of the leftmost members of the Democratic Caucus. She grew up in Rogers Park, and worked two years as a teacher; in 1969 she formed National Consumers Unite and worked for date-of-freshness labels on dairy products and other food. Later she joined Illinois Public Action, a consumer group; in 1985 she became executive director of the Illinois State Council of Senior Citizens. She organized the 1989 protest to Dan Rostenkowski's prescription-drug plan for seniors because of its financing, which resulted in televised pictures of him fleeing from elderly protestors and led Congress to repeal the benefit. In 1990 she was elected to the state House from Evanston and Skokie.

Schakowsky was selected in the Democratic primary to replace Sidney Yates, who had represented the lakefront in Congress for all but two of the preceding 50 years, chiefly as chairman of the Interior Appropriations Subcommittee. Her strategy was to run from the left—"I don't think I can be defined as too far left in a district like this"—and to build a volunteer organization. With ads in college papers, she got 400 young people to apply for 20 field organizer jobs; they set about identifying Schakowsky voters. She also raised plenty of money, $1.4 million, with help from EMILY's List; she survived attacks based on the fact that her husband Robert Creamer had resigned as head of Citizens Action of Illinois because of a federal investigation. Longtime state Senator Howard Carroll, with roots in the heavily Jewish 50th Ward, had the support of most Democratic ward committeemen. He attacked Schakowsky for her opposition to the death penalty. J. B. Pritzker, a member of the billionaire family that started Hyatt hotels, put $1.5 million into his own campaign. On primary day, Schakowsky's campaign fielded 1,500 workers, 250 from unions; they helped to give her a 45%–34% win over Carroll. Of course, she easily won the general election; the Republican nominee was once her physician.

In the House, Schakowsky has sought to expand Medicare to cover everybody—single payer government health insurance, in effect—and has advanced a proposal to have a government-run investment fund that taxpayers could use to supplement Social Security. When the House voted to create the Homeland Security Department, she objected to exemptions from the Freedom of Information Act that were granted to corporate disclosures to the new agency. Back home, when her support for expansion of O'Hare caused problems with voters in her district's new towns near the airport, she called for soundproofing and quieter airplanes to help people adversely affected.

Schakowsky has worked with party leaders on electoral strategy, gaining their support to expand her training program for political organizers. In 2001, she was tapped to head the DCCC's Women LEAD fundraising program, which raised more than $25 million. She promised to be "the skunk at the garden party" in criticizing George W. Bush's agenda and called on Democrats to be bolder. Schakowsky was an early supporter of Nancy Pelosi for party whip, and Pelosi rewarded her with one of two additional chief deputy whip slots. Pelosi's elevation to Democratic leader positioned Schakowsky for additional leadership influence, including membership on the party Steering Committee that makes House committee assignments.

Schakowsky was reelected by a 70%–27% margin in 2002. Afterwards, she said she was considering challenging Senator Peter Fitzgerald in 2004 but in January 2003 she announced that she would seek reelection to the House.

TENTH DISTRICT

Rep. Mark Kirk (R)

Elected 2000, 2d term; b. Sept. 15, 1959, Champaign; home, Kenilworth; Universidad Nacional Autonoma de Mexico, 1977–78, Cornell U., B.A. 1981, London Sch. of Econ., M.Sc. 1982; Georgetown U., J.D. 1992; Congregationalist; married (Kimberly Vertolli).

Military Career: U.S. Naval Reserve, 1989-present.

Professional Career: Parliamentary aide, British House of Commons, 1981–83; A.A., U.S. Rep. John E. Porter, 1984–89; Staffer, World Bank, 1990–91; Spec. Asst., U.S. Dept. of State, 1991–93; Practicing atty., 1993–95; Counsel, U.S. House Cmte. on Intl. Relations, 1995–2000.

DC Office: 1531 LHOB 20515, 202-225-4835; Fax: 202-225-0837; Web site: www.house.gov/kirk.

District Offices: Deerfield, 847-940-0202; Waukegan, 847-662-0101.

Committees: *Appropriations* (35th of 36 R): Commerce, Justice, State & Judiciary; Foreign Operations & Export Financing; The Legislative Branch.

Group Ratings

	ADA	ACLU	AFS	LCV	CON	ITIC	NTU	COC	ACU	NTLC	CHC
2002	20	47	0	38	77	100	59	95	76	83	42
2001	25	—	10	71	—	—	57	83	48	—	—

National Journal Ratings

	2001 LIB	—	2001 CONS	2002 LIB	—	2002 CONS
Economic	46%	—	54%	42%	—	57%
Social	58%	—	42%	59%	—	40%
Foreign	33%	—	60%	15%	—	78%

Key Votes of the 107th Congress

1. Approve Bush Tax Cuts	Y	5. Faith-Based Charities	Y	9. Trade Promotion Authority	Y
2. Limit Patients' Bill of Rights	Y	6. Bar Gays in the Boy Scouts	Y	10. Bar Funds for Intl. Court	Y
3. Campaign Finance Reform	Y	7. Ban Partial-Birth Abortion	N	11. Authorize Force in Iraq	Y
4. Ban ANWR Development	Y	8. Arm Commercial Pilots	Y	12. Deny Home. Sec. Dept. Union	Y

Election Results

2002 general	Mark Kirk (R)	128,611	(69%)	($1,436,056)
	Henry Perritt (D)	58,300	(31%)	($473,270)
2002 primary	Mark Kirk (R)	unopposed		
2000 general	Mark Kirk (R)	121,582	(51%)	($2,015,292)
	Lauren Beth Gash (D)	115,924	(49%)	($1,967,426)

The People		Race/Ethnic Origin	Ancestry	
Area size:	252 sq. mi.	75.2% White	German: 14.4%	Irish: 9.9%
Urban population:	99.6%	5.3% Black	Polish: 7.3%	
Rural population:	0.4%	5.9% Asian	**2000 Presidential Vote**	
Pop. 2000:	653,647	0.1% Native Am.	Gore (D) 134,149	(51%)
Median income:	$71,663	0.0% Hawaiian	Bush (R) 123,982	(47%)
Poverty status:	4.8%	1.1% Two + races	Other 6,097	(2%)
Military veterans:	10.5%	0.2% Other	**Cook Partisan Voting Index:** D + 2	
		12.3% Hispanic Origin		

Occupation   Blue collar: 14.4%   White collar: 75.9%   Gray collar: 9.7%

Since 1855, when the first Chicago & Northwestern opened the railroad line from downtown Chicago north along the lakeshore, the North Shore suburbs along Lake Michigan have been the favorite residence for Chicago's elite. The North Shore starts in Evanston, founded by Methodists to promote temperance (a cause that has never prospered in Chicago), and goes on to Wilmette and Winnetka and Glencoe, then crossing into the Lake County towns of Highland Park and Lake Forest—each with a slightly different personality, each long established, mightily prosperous and with a patina of age. Not far from the gritty, monosyllabic city, these are communities of pleasant, affluent, well-educated people living in an environment whose natural beauty—the long water vista and blue light off the lake, the gentle hills and fine trees—is kept carefully disciplined.

The 10th Congressional District is the North Shore district, starting on the Wilmette lake-front, just north of Evanston, to the city of Waukegan (once famous as the home of comedian Jack Benny) and almost to the Wisconsin border beyond. The district also goes inland to what for many years was just cornfields to Northbrook and Deerfield, just west of Glencoe and Highland Park. Farther inland are suburbs like Arlington Heights, developed in the 1950s and 1960s on the Northwestern railroad line, and Wheeling, developed in the 1960s and 1970s near I-294. To the north is Libertyville, near where the Adlai Stevensons, the late presidential candidate and his son the former senator, have owned what is now one of the last farms only a few miles from Lake Michigan. With the big movement toward Democrats in the Chicago suburbs in the 1990s, this historically establishment Republican district still voted narrowly for Al Gore.

The congressman from the 10th District is Mark Kirk, a Republican first elected in 2000. Kirk was born in Downstate Illinois but grew up mostly in Kenilworth, on the Lake between Wilmette and Winnetka. Kirk graduated from Cornell in 1981 and the London School of Economics in 1982, and worked as a staffer in Congressman John Porter's Washington office and became the chief of staff after just three years. Kirk left Capitol Hill in 1990 and moved on to a number of Washington jobs, first at the World Bank, then as a State Department aide working on the Central American peace process. After two years of international law practice, he served four years as counsel to the House International Relations Committee; he is also a lieutenant commander in the Naval Reserves, serving as an aviator with tours of duty in Turkey, Serbia, Bosnia, Haiti, and Panama. In flights during the Persian Gulf War, he was a frequent target of Iraqi guns; for the past nine years, he has continued to work one weekend each month at the Pentagon's "war room," monitoring intelligence reports. During one such weekend in 1994, Kirk was on hand as North Korea lobbed a missile toward the Pacific Ocean without warning. For nearly 30 minutes, no one had any idea where it would land. "It was a tough half hour," Kirk recounted to *Roll Call.* "Everyone was pretty much drenched in sweat."

In 1999, when Porter announced his retirement, Kirk returned home to the 10th District, where he was one of no fewer than 11 competitors in the Republican primary. This contest included six millionaires who spent nearly $4 million of their own money. Kirk did not spend nearly as much, but he had great advantages: the endorsement of the highly popular Porter, the fact that he was the only candidate with moderate views on cultural issues and his greater experience in government. His 31% in the March primary was enough to put him well ahead of the 15% for R.R. Donnelley & Sons printing company heiress Shawn Margaret Donnelley, who ran an astonishing number of radio ads, and the 14% for Northbrook Mayor Mark Damisch. The Democratic nominee was state Representative Lauren Beth Gash, who won the nomination without opposition after Chris Kennedy, son of Robert F. Kennedy and an executive of Chicago's Merchandise Mart, decided not to run. Both Kirk and Gash campaigned as candidates in the Porter mold, promising to carry on his fiscally conservative, culturally moderate record. Gash, an attorney, tried to downplay Kirk's years in Washington, touting her own legislative experience while talking about Social Security and prescription drugs. But Kirk won a 51%–49% victory.

In the House, Kirk compiled a centrist voting record and said that he wanted to strengthen moderate Republicans with a libertarian approach. His familiarity with the workings of the House and the aid of Speaker Dennis Hastert enabled him to get seats on the Armed Services, Budget, and Transportation Committees but in January 2003 Kirk gave up his committee seats for a slot on Appropriations. His explanation for the assignment: "Three words—J. Dennis Hastert."

On Armed Services, he cited his experience in the Naval Reserve to demonstrate his familiarity with military operations. But when he raised questions about Iraq at a September 2002 hearing with Defense Secretary Donald Rumsfeld, who represented the North Shore in the House from 1963 to 1969, Rumsfeld dismissed his suggestion that Saddam Hussein would grant unconditional inspections. "Come on," Rumsfeld scorned. On the Transportation Committee, he pushed for O'Hare expansion and full funding for rail service to the northern suburbs. Kirk also teamed with Democrat Adam Schiff of California to form a bipartisan coalition of freshmen to promote campaign finance reform.

Winning reelection proved relatively easy for Kirk. Democrat Hank Perritt, dean of the Chicago-Kent College of Law, earned some notice as an openly gay candidate; he also attracted national attention for a September 2002 opinion article in *The Washington Post* in which he criticized party colleagues for their approach to the use of force in Iraq. Democratic leaders "seem tongue-tied when it comes to matters of war and peace," he wrote. But the Human Rights Campaign backed Kirk for his support of gay rights, and the Sierra Club and Planned Parenthood also endorsed him. Kirk seems headed for a lengthy career like Porter's, though like Porter he could face a serious primary challenge from a conservative.

ELEVENTH DISTRICT

Rep. Jerry Weller (R)

Elected 1994, 5th term; b. July 7, 1957, Streator; home, Morris; U. of IL, B.S. 1979; Christian; divorced.

Elected Office: IL House of Reps., 1988–94.

Professional Career: Farmer; Aide, U.S. Rep. Tom Corcoran, 1980–81; Aide, U.S. Agriculture Secy. John Block, 1981–85.

DC Office: 1210 LHOB 20515, 202-225-3635; Fax: 202-225-3521; Web site: www.house.gov/weller.

District Office: Joliet, 815-740-2028.

Committees: *International Relations* (22d of 26 R): Asia & the Pacific; Western Hemisphere. *Ways & Means* (17th of 24 R): Oversight; Select Revenue Measures.

Group Ratings

	ADA	ACLU	AFS	LCV	CON	ITIC	NTU	COC	ACU	NTLC	CHC
2002	5	13	0	0	25	100	56	95	92	86	100
2001	0	—	0	29	—	—	60	100	92	—	—

National Journal Ratings

	2001 LIB	—	2001 CONS		2002 LIB	—	2002 CONS
Economic	28%	—	69%		0%	—	91%
Social	20%	—	69%		0%	—	75%
Foreign	21%	—	74%		15%	—	78%

Key Votes of the 107th Congress

1. Approve Bush Tax Cuts	Y	5. Faith-Based Charities	Y	9. Trade Promotion Authority	Y
2. Limit Patients' Bill of Rights	Y	6. Bar Gays in the Boy Scouts	Y	10. Bar Funds for Intl. Court	Y
3. Campaign Finance Reform	N	7. Ban Partial-Birth Abortion	Y	11. Authorize Force in Iraq	Y
4. Ban ANWR Development	N	8. Arm Commercial Pilots	Y	12. Deny Home. Sec. Dept. Union	Y

Election Results

2002 general	Jerry Weller (R)	124,192	(64%)	($1,600,389)
	Keith Van Duyne (D)	68,893	(36%)	($30,233)
2002 primary	Jerry Weller (R)	unopposed		
2000 general	Jerry Weller (R)	132,384	(56%)	($976,795)
	James P. Stevenson (D)	102,485	(44%)	($144,916)

Prior Winning Percentages: 1998 (59%); 1996 (52%); 1994 (61%)

The People		Race/Ethnic Origin	Ancestry	
Area size:	4,284 sq. mi.	83.7% White	German: 18.4%	Irish: 11.8%
Urban population:	78.2%	7.8% Black	Italian: 6.0%	
Rural population:	21.8%	0.8% Asian	**2000 Presidential Vote**	
Pop. 2000:	653,647	0.1% Native Am.	Bush (R)................128,280	(50%)
Median income:	$47,800	0.0% Hawaiian	Gore (D)...............122,979	(48%)
Poverty status:	8.4%	0.9% Two+ races	Other....................7,269	(3%)
Military veterans:	12.5%	0.1% Other	**Cook Partisan Voting Index:** R + 1	
		6.7% Hispanic Origin		

Occupation	Blue collar: 29.4%	White collar: 55.3%	Gray collar: 15.3%

The low-lying land west and south of Chicago, where sluggishly flowing rivers run circles around industrial sites, is a great divide over which French explorers portaged the easiest path from the inland oceans of the Great Lakes to the Mississippi River valley. Today there is still a kind of borderland here, as the factories and shopping centers and subdivisions stop somewhere past the Cook County line and downstate prairies begin, cornfields bisected by highways and railroads radiating out from the Loop and the rail yards of the nation's transportation hub. Politically, this is a borderland as well, between the traditionally Democratic Chicago metropolitan area, with its hard-bitten machine politics, and heavily Republican Downstate Illinois, with its tradition of governance by local civic leaders that stretches back to the days of Abraham Lincoln.

The 11th Congressional District covers much of this borderland. It includes Joliet in Will County, whose 38% growth in the 1990s was the third fastest in Illinois. Once a canal boat town, and later the producer of one-third of America's wallpaper, Joliet now has two big prisons and a 75,000-seat NASCAR racetrack; it owes its current prosperity in part to two riverboat casinos built in the last decade. To the south is Kankakee, a county seat amid rich prairie earth on the Illinois Central main line; this is Republican territory. Farther west, on bluffs above the Illinois River heading down to the Mississippi, are the factory towns of Ottawa and LaSalle and, to the south, Streator; this is LaSalle County, the politically marginal area in the district. Redistricting in 2001 removed the southernmost townships of Cook County, which were increasingly Democratic, and added two ungainly-looking appendages. One goes west to rural Bureau County; the other heads south at the intersection of I-80 and I-39 and includes most of Bloomington in McLean County, the fastest-growing county in Downstate Illinois in the 1990s. Another addition was a small corner of Livingston County, which includes the home of the parents of 11th District Congressman Jerry Weller. The redistricting significantly helped the Republican Weller: it raised the Bush 2000 percentage in his district from 45% to 50%. As one Joliet councilman said, "It's going to be difficult to elect a Democrat to the 11th Congressional District."

The congressman from the 11th District is Jerry Weller, a hard-working, politically savvy Republican who won the seat in 1994. Weller grew up on a farm, where his family still raises hogs. Out of college, he was a staffer to Congressman Tom Corcoran and Agriculture Secretary John Block; in the mid-1980s he returned to Illinois and was elected to the state House in 1988. In 1994, when Democratic Congressman George Sangmeister retired, Weller was one of six Republicans and seven Democrats to run for the seat. He called for reforming health care via market-based principles and promoting markets for ethanol fuels and soybean inks; he was proud of replacing the "granny tax" on nursing home residents with a cigarette tax as a way to pay for health care. Against Democrat Frank Giglio, a 20-year state legislator, who said of Congress, "Wouldn't this be a nice way to finish my career?" Weller won 61%–39%.

In the House, Weller quickly showed impressive insider skills. In 1996, Weller ran hard for a seat on the Ways and Means Committee, arguing that no one there represented Chicago. With help from Dennis Hastert, then Chief Deputy Whip, he succeeded. He became a prime sponsor of ending the marriage penalty. And he backed several other tax cuts, including the end of the Social Security earnings limit on seniors, which Bill Clinton signed; and elimination of the estate tax, which Clinton opposed and George W. Bush signed. Later, he was an early advocate of making the 2001 tax cuts permanent. On behalf of Republicans, Weller reached out to the motion picture and casino industries with a favorable tax policy, and now chairs the House Gaming Caucus. And he led the fight for elimination of the 3% telephone excise tax, first passed to pay for the Spanish-American War.

Weller did not neglect local concerns. On Transportation, he promoted the third Chicago-area airport proposed for Peotone, 45 miles south of Chicago and a few miles north of Kankakee, while also supporting improvements at O'Hare. He won enactment of his provision to bar the deposit of garbage from outside Will County at a landfill there. But his attempt to name a new Joliet veterans' cemetery after Abraham Lincoln was foiled by Ray LaHood, who feared confusion with the cemetery in Springfield where Lincoln is buried.

Weller has been active in internal House Republican politics. He lost a race for Republican Conference secretary in July 1997, after some bad publicity when he held a breakfast and promised $1,500 contributions to each member who attended; he withdrew from a race for chairman of the Policy Committee in November 1998. In December 1998, when Speaker-designate Bob Livingston stunned everyone by announcing his retirement, Weller worked the phones for Hastert, along with Tom DeLay and Tom Davis, and helped Hastert win the speakership within hours. In early 2001, Weller was named finance chairman of the NRCC; among his fundraising tools was creation of the high-tech "New Economy Republicans," but its tax-exempt status raised ethical concerns. In 2002, he returned $110,000 in illegal contributions uncovered by the Federal Election Commission, but he did not admit violating any laws. Weller suffered another setback to his leadership ambitions in November 2002, when Tom Reynolds defeated him for NRCC chairman, 119–90.

In 1998 and 2000, Weller spent about $1 million against lightly funded opponents, but was held below 60% each time. In 2002, in a more Republican district, he won with 64%.

TWELFTH DISTRICT

Rep. Jerry Costello (D)

Elected Aug. 1988, 8th term; b. Sept. 25, 1949, E. St. Louis; home, Belleville; Belleville Area Col., A.A. 1971, Maryville Col., B.A. 1973; Catholic; married (Georgia).

Elected Office: Chmn., St. Clair Cnty. Bd. of Supervisors, 1980–88.

Professional Career: Dir., IL Court Svcs. & Probation, 1973–80; Chmn., Region's Cncl. of Govts., 1980–84.

DC Office: 2454 RHOB 20515, 202-225-5661; Fax: 202-225-0285; Web site: www.house.gov/costello.

District Offices: Belleville, 618-233-8026; Carbondale, 618-529-3791; Chester, 618-826-3043; E. St. Louis, 618-397-8833; Granite City, 618-451-7065; West Frankfort, 618-937-6402.

Committees: *Science* (3d of 22 D): Energy. *Transportation & Infrastructure* (5th of 34 D): Aviation; Railroads; Water Resources & Environment (RMM).

Group Ratings

	ADA	ACLU	AFS	LCV	CON	ITIC	NTU	COC	ACU	NTLC	CHC
2002	70	47	78	50	87	38	28	50	36	8	58
2001	80	—	100	64	—	—	19	48	44	—	—

National Journal Ratings

	2001 LIB —	2001 CONS		2002 LIB —	2002 CONS
Economic	63%	37%		62%	38%
Social	49%	52%		50%	49%
Foreign	56%	41%		56%	43%

Key Votes of the 107th Congress

1. Approve Bush Tax Cuts	N	5. Faith-Based Charities	N	9. Trade Promotion Authority	N
2. Limit Patients' Bill of Rights	N	6. Bar Gays in the Boy Scouts	Y	10. Bar Funds for Intl. Court	Y
3. Campaign Finance Reform	Y	7. Ban Partial-Birth Abortion	Y	11. Authorize Force in Iraq	N
4. Ban ANWR Development	Y	8. Arm Commercial Pilots	Y	12. Deny Home. Sec. Dept. Union	N

Election Results

2002 general	Jerry Costello (D) 131,580	(69%)	($466,184)
	David Sadler (R) 58,440	(31%)	
2002 primary	Jerry Costello (D) .... unopposed		
2000 general	Jerry Costello (D) .... unopposed		($373,057)

Prior Winning Percentages: 1998 (60%); 1996 (72%); 1994 (66%); 1992 (71%); 1990 (66%); 1988 (53%); 1988 (51%)

The People		Race/Ethnic Origin	Ancestry	
Area size:	4,556 sq. mi.	79.7% White	German: 18.6%	Irish: 8.7%
Urban population:	76.7%	16.3% Black	English: 6.6%	
Rural population:	23.3%	0.8% Asian	**2000 Presidential Vote**	
Pop. 2000:	653,647	0.2% Native Am.	Gore (D) 144,548	(54%)
Median income:	$35,198	0.0% Hawaiian	Bush (R) 116,724	(43%)
Poverty status:	15.0%	1.0% Two+ races	Other 7,634	(3%)
Military veterans:	15.3%	0.1% Other	**Cook Partisan Voting Index:** D + 5	
		1.8% Hispanic Origin		
Occupation	Blue collar: 26.2%	White collar: 55.1%	Gray collar: 18.7%	

The nation's two mightiest rivers, the Mississippi and Missouri, their waters roiling together, join just a few miles above St. Louis and just a few miles below Alton, Illinois. Most views of this center of the Mississippi Valley focus on the Gateway Arch and the buildings of downtown St. Louis. But the Mississippi shoreline of Illinois is worthy of attention as well. Alton's 19th century buildings recall its turbulent history, when it was the home of the anti-slavery agitator Elijah Lovejoy, who was murdered by a mob; more recently it was the longtime home of conservative crusader and columnist Phyllis Schlafly. Nearby in Hartford, Lewis and Clark spent five months preparing their team and collecting supplies for their journey westward. Just across from the Gateway Arch is East St. Louis, where dozens of rail lines and highways funnel into bridges over the river. Once a rail and stockyards center second only to Chicago, East St. Louis is now almost entirely black and one of America's poorest and most troubled cities, a half-abandoned slum with one of the nation's highest crime rates and a rapidly declining tax base, almost entirely dependent on a riverboat casino and an adjacent waterfront hotel for its tax revenue. After peaking at 82,000 in 1960, its population is now less than 32,000—down 9,000 in the 1990s.

South of East St. Louis and the industrial area around Belleville, the river counties are lightly inhabited, but they were not always unimportant. This was the site of the French Kaskaskia settlement that became Illinois's first capital in 1818, but repeated flooding turned it into an island and reduced its population to 9 people and many more egrets. Farther south, the river abuts coal country and is not far from Carbondale, once a coal center but now, as the home of Southern Illinois University, bustling with students from Downstate Illinois and Chicago and the retirement base of former Senator Paul Simon. The land here is sometimes known as Egypt, the southern end of Illinois where the Ohio River meets the Mississippi: flat, fertile farmland, protected by giant man-made levees because it is susceptible to yearly floods. There is more than a touch of Dixie here: The unofficial capital of Egypt, Cairo (pronounced *KAY-roh*), is a declining town closer to Mississippi than to Chicago. In his 1842 work, *American Notes*, Charles Dickens described the town in these unflattering terms: "The hateful Mississippi circling and eddying before it, and turning off upon its southern course a slimy monster hideous to behold; a hotbed of disease, an ugly sepulchre, a grave uncheered by any gleam of promise: a place without one single quality, in earth or air or water, to commend it: such is this dismal Cairo."

The 12th District covers all of this riverfront from Alton south to Cairo, with some inland territory as well. Most of its population is in the Metro East area in St. Clair (East St. Louis and Belleville) and Madison (Alton) Counties. For a time in 2003, Madison County was the epicenter of tobacco-related litigation and gained renown as a plaintiffs paradise when a local judge awarded $12 billion in compensatory and punitive damages against Philip Morris; the company said it might have to seek protection from its creditors, which stunned the market for securitized state tobacco settlement bonds.

The congressman from the 12th District is Jerry Costello, a Democrat first elected in 1988. He grew up in a St. Clair County political family, worked for the courts after college, then became chairman of the St. Clair County Board of Supervisors. He waited with some impatience for the retirement of Congressman Mel Price, first elected in 1944, who was re-elected by only 943 votes in 1986 and announced his retirement not long after; Price died in office in April 1988. Experienced, well connected, supported by organized labor, Costello was the obvious successor. Yet he received only 51% of the votes in the special election and 53% for a full term.

Costello is a practical-minded politician with a seat on the Transportation and Infrastructure Committee and a voting record more liberal on economics than on cultural and foreign issues. He opposed the first George Bush's Clean Air Act and Bill Clinton's NAFTA, bucked Clinton on the balanced budget amendment and House Republicans on public works votes, and voted against authorizing George W. Bush to use force against Iraq. He trumpets his accomplishments without subtlety. Bridges are important in a river district: Costello has worked to replace the Clark Bridge in Alton and, with the late Congressman Bill Emerson of Missouri, to build a new bridge to Cape Girardeau now named after Emerson. His biggest ongoing project has been creating the Mid-America Airport at Scott Air Force Base near Belleville; it opened in 1997 but, alas, has no scheduled airline service.

For a while a cloud hung over Costello. In September 1996 federal prosecutors indicted Amiel Cueto, Costello's longtime friend and business partner, for trying to stop an investigation of a gambling operation run by a client and for conspiring to get himself installed as St. Clair County state's attorney. In May 1997 a federal judge ruled that Costello was an "unindicted co-conspirator;" prosecutors said he was a silent partner in a plan to build an Indian casino and that he worked in Congress to get recognition of an Indian tribe to sponsor it. Costello denied all in June 1997, arguing that he had no interest in the casino, his role in the Indian designation was minimal, and he had tried to get a rival to vacate the state's attorney job only to avoid the political fuss of a primary. Cueto was convicted and Costello was never indicted.

Costello put aside plans to run for secretary of state and found himself opposed in 1998 by Bill Price, an orthopedic surgeon and son of Mel Price, who switched parties and ran as a Republican. Price said Costello was taking credit for projects that were his father's and that he allowed southern Illinois highway money to be shifted to Chicago projects. Price came close to equaling Costello's $1 million in spending, but Costello won by a solid 60%–40%. Interestingly, Costello ran weakest in his home territory, where knowledge of the Cueto case was presumably greatest, with just 55% in St. Clair County, and lost fast-growing Monroe County just to the south. Later, it was revealed that Costello made prison visits in South Dakota to see Cueto, who was fighting disbarment. But he was re-elected in 2000 and 2002 without significant opposition. Those results suggest that Costello is safe in this basically Democratic district. He is likely to be bolstered as well by his early support for Governor Rod Blagojevich in the 2002 primary; in the three-way race, Blagojevich won 59% in St. Clair and 69% in Madison County. On Capitol Hill, Costello moved up the ranks of the Transportation Committee to become the ranking Democrat on the Water Resources and Environment Subcommittee.

THIRTEENTH DISTRICT

Rep. Judy Biggert (R)

Elected 1998, 3d term; b. Aug. 15, 1937, Chicago; home, Hinsdale; Stanford U., B.A. 1959, Northwestern U., J.D. 1963; Episcopalian; married (Rody).

Elected Office: IL House of Reps., 1992–98.

Professional Career: Clerk, U.S. Ct. of Appeals, 1963–64; Practicing atty., 1975–98.

DC Office: 1213 LHOB 20515, 202-225-3515; Fax: 202-225-9420; Web site: www.house.gov/biggert.

District Office: Clarendon Hills, 630-655-2052.

Committees: *Education & the Workforce* (14th of 27 R): Education Reform; Workforce Protections (Vice Chmn.). *Financial Services* (19th of 37 R): Capital Markets, Insurance & Government Sponsored Enterprises; Domestic and International Monetary Policy, Trade & Technology (Vice Chmn.); Financial Institutions & Consumer Credit. *Science* (13th of 25 R): Energy (Chmn.); Environment, Technology and Standards. *Standards of Official Conduct* (3d of 5 R).

Group Ratings

	ADA	ACLU	AFS	LCV	CON	ITIC	NTU	COC	ACU	NTLC	CHC
2002	15	53	0	38	58	100	59	100	84	83	50
2001	20	—	10	21	—	—	61	100	56	—	—

National Journal Ratings

	2001 LIB — 2001 CONS		2002 LIB — 2002 CONS	
Economic	28%	— 69%	0%	— 91%
Social	58%	— 42%	56%	— 42%
Foreign	43%	— 53%	41%	— 56%

Key Votes of the 107th Congress

1. Approve Bush Tax Cuts	Y	5. Faith-Based Charities	Y	9. Trade Promotion Authority	Y
2. Limit Patients' Bill of Rights	Y	6. Bar Gays in the Boy Scouts	Y	10. Bar Funds for Intl. Court	Y
3. Campaign Finance Reform	N	7. Ban Partial-Birth Abortion	Y	11. Authorize Force in Iraq	Y
4. Ban ANWR Development	N	8. Arm Commercial Pilots	Y	12. Deny Home. Sec. Dept. Union	Y

Election Results

2002 general	Judy Biggert (R)	139,546	(70%)	($464,054)
	Thomas Mason (D)	59,069	(30%)	
2002 primary	Judy Biggert (R)	unopposed		
2000 general	Judy Biggert (R)	193,250	(66%)	($381,623)
	Thomas Mason (D)	98,768	(34%)	

Prior Winning Percentages: 1998 (61%)

The People

Area size:	362 sq. mi.
Urban population:	98.8%
Rural population:	1.2%
Pop. 2000:	653,647
Median income:	$71,686
Poverty status:	2.9%
Military veterans:	9.9%

Race/Ethnic Origin

81.6% White
4.9% Black
6.6% Asian
0.1% Native Am.
0.0% Hawaiian
1.2% Two+ races
0.1% Other
5.5% Hispanic Origin

Ancestry

German: 16.5%   Irish: 13.1%
Polish: 10.0%

2000 Presidential Vote

Bush (R)	148,621	(55%)
Gore (D)	113,450	(42%)
Other	7,166	(3%)

Cook Partisan Voting Index: R + 7

Occupation   Blue collar: 15.8%   White collar: 74.9%   Gray collar: 9.4%

Most residents of Chicagoland now live not in the city but in the suburbs, and increasingly not even in Cook County but in the Collar Counties all around. DuPage County, straight west of Chicago, had 103,000 residents in 1940; in 2000, there were 904,000—a 16% increase from the previous decade—with new subdivisions still springing up at the outer edges. Nor are these just bedroom communities. Here in Oak Brook are the headquarters of Ace Hardware, Federal Signal, the Spiegel catalog, Molex and, most prominently, McDonald's and its Hamburger University, an 80-acre campus where more than 70,000 trainees have received Bachelor of Hamburgerology degrees since it was founded in 1961. Nearby are gracefully older railroad commuter towns like Hinsdale and Downers Grove, but also Naperville, once a country village, now an edge city, with a school district ranked number one in the world in science in an international exam. The Argonne National Laboratory has sparked numerous private research firms along the Sanitary and Ship Canal, the Des Plaines River and the Illinois and Michigan Canal, built way back in 1848.

The 13th Congressional District includes the southern part of DuPage County (including Oak Brook, Downers Grove and Naperville), a small section of southwest corner of Cook County and the northern slice of Will County (including Bolingbrook, Romeoville and Lockport). Politically, this has been a heavily Republican area, suspicious of the motives and operations of Chicago Democrats, devoted to free enterprise and hostile to higher taxes. Republican margins shrunk in DuPage County as the Chicago suburbs became more Democratic in the 1990s, but the 13th District has not been in danger of going Democratic.

The congresswoman from the 13th District is Judy Biggert, a Republican elected in 1998. She grew up in Kenilworth, on the affluent North Shore (as did Mark Kirk of the 10th District), graduated from New Trier Township High School, Stanford and Northwestern Law School and clerked for a federal appeals judge. She raised four children in Hinsdale, practicing estate and real estate law out of her home, served on the Hinsdale Township Board of Education, was chairman of the Visiting Nurses Association of Chicago—a "former car pool mom and assistant soccer coach," as her campaign put it. In 1992 she was elected to the state House, and was soon part of the leadership.

Biggert started running for the House in 1997 when incumbent Republican Harris Fawell announced his retirement; he endorsed her in November 1997. She said she supported abortion rights and opposed most gun control measures for constitutional reasons, though she had campaigned for gun control in 1992. She had primary opposition from state Representative Peter Roskam, who moved into the district to run. He attacked her on abortion and criticized her for voting for a $485 million school funding bill that included tax increases on cigarettes, casino gambling and telephones. Gary Bauer's Campaign for Working Families ran ads against Biggert, but Biggert raised far more money, including $402,000 of her own funds and contributions from Planned Parenthood and the Human Rights Campaign (she has voted for gay rights bills). Biggert won the March 1998 primary by 45%–40% and the November the general election 61%–39%.

In the House, Biggert supported the Violence Against Women Act and a 24-hour, but not 72-hour, background check for gun sales at gun shows in June 1999. A supporter of free trade, she attended the Seattle WTO conference in 1999 but could not leave her hotel due to the protests; she criticized Bill Clinton: "Labor isn't a trade issue. He was only trying to placate the unions, and it undercut our negotiations." In 2002 she gathered 64 cosponsors, including others with national laboratories in their districts, for her bill to reorganize the Energy Department's Office of Science in line with the American Physical Society's recommendations to emphasize energy research. Working with Democrats Barney Frank and Carolyn Maloney and Republican Christopher Shays, she sought to make it clear that the Gramm-Leach-Bliley Act's privacy provisions do not cover lawyers, who are subject to stricter confidentiality regarding their clients. In 2002, she was co-chairman of the Congressional Caucus for Women's Issues, "a forum for women members." She has paid heed to local issues, seeking a study of breast cancer in DuPage County when the *Daily Herald* revealed that breast cancer rates are very high there and getting grants for the creation of a Juvenile Drug Court in Joliet and for housing in Lockport Township for sufferers from chronic depression.

Biggert's attempts to move into the Republican leadership have been less successful. In November 2000 she ran for secretary of the Republican Conference and lost to Barbara Cubin of Wyoming, 122–73. In July 2002, when Cubin was moving up to another position, she ran for one day for the same post, but withdrew when it became clear that John Doolittle of California, who had been campaigning for a week when Biggert entered the race, had the votes. In October 1999 Biggert abandoned her pledge to serve only three terms. "If I knew what I know now, I wouldn't have signed," she said. "I didn't realize how important seniority was." She was reelected easily in 2000 and 2002.

FOURTEENTH DISTRICT

Rep. Dennis Hastert (R)

Elected 1986, 9th term; b. Jan. 2, 1942, Aurora; home, Yorkville; Wheaton Col., B.A. 1964, N. IL U., M.A. 1967; Protestant; married (Jean).

Elected Office: IL House of Reps., 1980–86.

Professional Career: H.S. teacher & coach, 1965–80.

DC Office: 235 CHOB 20515, 202-225-2976; Fax: 202-225-0697; Web site: www.house.gov/hastert.

District Offices: Batavia, 630-406-1114; Dixon, 815-288-0680.

Committees: *Speaker of the House.*

Group Ratings and Key Votes: Speaker does not usually vote.

Election Results

2002 general	Dennis Hastert (R)	135,198	(74%)	($2,970,554)
	Laurence Quick (D)	47,165	(26%)	($18,136)
2002 primary	Dennis Hastert (R)	unopposed		
2000 general	Dennis Hastert (R)	188,597	(74%)	($2,299,072)
	Vern Deljonson (D)	66,309	(26%)	

Prior Winning Percentages: 1998 (70%); 1996 (64%); 1994 (76%); 1992 (67%); 1990 (67%); 1988 (74%); 1986 (52%)

The People		Race/Ethnic Origin	Ancestry	
Area size:	2,866 sq. mi.	74.0% White	German: 18.9% Irish: 9.9%	
Urban population:	86.2%	4.6% Black	English: 6.0%	
Rural population:	13.8%	1.8% Asian	**2000 Presidential Vote**	
Pop. 2000:	653,647	0.1% Native Am.	Bush (R)...............129,745	(54%)
Median income:	$56,314	0.0% Hawaiian	Gore (D)...............101,369	(42%)
Poverty status:	7.0%	1.0% Two + races	Other...................7,428	(3%)
Military veterans:	10.3%	0.1% Other	**Cook Partisan Voting Index:** R + 6	
		18.5% Hispanic Origin		

Occupation	Blue collar: 26.8%	White collar: 59.9%	Gray collar: 13.3%

A few dozen miles beyond the Loop there is an invisible line marking two different Chicagos. One is the Chicago dominated by blacks and descendants of the vast immigrations of 1840–1924 and 1970–2000, a Chicago where certain loyalties are taken for granted: loyalty to ethnic group, to church (usually the Catholic Church, often with an ethnic prefix), and to party (almost always the Democrats). This Chicago is a gritty city, where personal cheerfulness and courtesy lighten up days otherwise as cold and impersonal as the gray winter sky. The other Chicago is the beginning of the Great Plains, originally a white Anglo-Saxon Protestant Chicago, a place whose residents are products of the first great wave of immigration to America. The tone of this Chicago is lighter, its streets and highways cleaner and neater, its daily life generally free from evidence of unpleasantness and deprivation. Ronald Reagan grew up in Downstate Illinois within the orbit of this Chicago (though he did live in the city briefly), and its spirit helped to characterize his presidency. His migration to southern California, incidentally, is not atypical: You can see in the geometric grids and Republican voting patterns of Orange County or Phoenix almost exact replicas of the grids and patterns in Chicago's suburban Collar Counties, transported to the once-empty Southwest on the Atchison, Topeka & Santa Fe or out the old U.S. 66 from their beginnings in Chicago's Loop.

The 14th Congressional District straddles this line between metropolitan Chicago and Downstate Illinois. It gets as close as 30 miles to Chicago's Loop, in western DuPage County, with two great Chicagoland landmarks—Cantigny, the estate of Colonel Robert McCormick, longtime publisher of the *Chicago Tribune*, and FermiLab, the world's fastest energy particle accelerator and employer of some 2,500 people—icons of political conservatism and high technology within two miles of each other. The 14th also contains the Fox River Valley and its industrial cities of Elgin and resurgent Aurora—which grew to the third-largest city in Illinois in 2000—plus antique St. Charles in the heart of the Collar Counties. Farther west, amid what may be the world's richest cornfields, the 14th passes through DeKalb, long the world's leading manufacturer of barbed wire, and goes on to Kendall and Lee Counties, including Reagan's boyhood home in Dixon. Since the 2001 redistricting, the 14th moves farther west, almost to the Mississippi River, to include farmlands in parts of Whiteside, Bureau and Henry Counties. This was traditionally some of the most heavily Republican territory in the country. Northern Illinois was settled when Chicago was just a frontier village by Yankees from Ohio, Indiana, Upstate New York and New England, and by Germans emigrating after the failed revolutions of 1848: people who formed the heart of the Republican Party from its founding in 1854 and who would form the core of the Grand Army of the Republic a few years later. Their descendants, in this extension of Chicagoland, remain mostly Republican today.

The congressman from the 14th District is Dennis Hastert, a Republican first elected in 1986, and today the 51st Speaker of the House of Representatives. He comes from the Fox River Valley, outside the Chicago metro orbit when he was growing up, but now part of its booming outer edge. His great-grandfather emigrated from Luxembourg to Aurora, on the Fox River, in the 19th century, to work on the railroads. His father, originally an embalmer, opened a feed supply business in Oswego, and Denny and his two younger brothers hoisted 100-pound bags and delivered milk in the early morning; his parents also had a restaurant where he worked as a fry cook. At high school in Oswego—then a rural town, now exploding with subdivisions—he wrestled and played football. He graduated from Wheaton College, a religious school in nearby DuPage County, and then he became a high school teacher at Yorkville High School, a few miles south of Oswego. There he taught history and coached wrestling for 16 years and met his wife, a physical education teacher. But his experience was not entirely local. In summers he traveled as a teacher for the YMCA or other groups to Japan, Colombia, Venezuela, Europe and the Soviet Union. And as a wrestling coach he excelled. His team won the state championship and he was named the national coach of the year in 1976, and he can still remember the names and records of all of his wrestlers. He tries to attend the NCAA wrestling tournament every year. He owns nine antique vehicles, including two fire engines and a pickup truck; he likes to carve duck decoys and fish for walleye in the Fox River.

After a trip to Washington in 1978, when Democrats had a 2–1 majority in the House, Hastert got involved in politics, interning with state Senator John Grotberg. In 1980 he finished third in an Illinois House primary; then the incumbent became fatally ill and Hastert was chosen to take his place on the November ballot. After the March 1986 primary, Grotberg, at that point a member of Congress, was fatally stricken with cancer and Hastert again was chosen by the party as a replacement. The election was unusually close, but Hastert won 52%–48%.

In his early years in the House, Hastert had a conservative voting record and made few waves. But he gained valuable experience. He got a seat on the Commerce Committee and on the subcommittees handling health, energy and telecommunications issues. He built a relationship with Minority Leader Robert Michel, from the 18th District of Illinois. He worked together with Tom DeLay of Texas for Illinois's Ed Madigan in the race for minority whip in March 1989; Madigan lost by just two votes to an upstart from Georgia named Newt Gingrich. In 1994 he was chief organizer for DeLay's campaign for whip, the one leadership post won by a non-Gingrichite after the big Republican gains that fall. Afterwards Hastert was named Chief Deputy Whip and shared an office and staff with DeLay. If he had not stopped in the hall to answer a reporter's question, he would have been in the line of fire when a crazed killer stormed into DeLay's office in July 1998.

To his work Hastert brought the habits of a coach, listening long to colleagues' goals and complaints, sizing up their character and capacity, then insisting firmly on a course of action when he reached a judgment. He operated with minimal ego and a bear-like friendliness, putting his arm around a colleague when asking advice or seeking intelligence; increasingly he was looked to by other leaders to help Republicans reach consensus and to negotiate difficult issues with Democrats, particularly health care. In 1997 he helped put together the Republicans' Medicare bill. Gingrich made him head of a task force that hammered out a patients' rights bill, which was passed by the House in August 1998. Hastert was active in negotiations on the 1996 telecommunications bill and on repealing the Social Security "earnings tax"—the deduction of benefits among senior citizens who earn over a certain figure—in the 1995 Contract With America. Over the years, Hastert has continued his trips abroad, including to Japan, and has been supportive of free trade; central Illinois, where the largest company is Caterpillar, produces more exports than just about anywhere else in the country.

Then suddenly one day in December 1998 he was chosen Speaker of the House. Speaker Newt Gingrich announced his retirement three days after the November election. Members scrambled for leadership positions, and Hastert was urged to run against Majority Leader Dick Armey. But Hastert had pledged to support him and, when he asked to be released from the pledge, Armey said no; so he kept his word and didn't run for a position he probably could have won. Then on December 19, just before the House voted on impeachment, Speaker-designate Bob Livingston announced his retirement too. Gingrich told Hastert, "You are the only one in this conference who could pull this body together. You are going to have to be the next speaker of the House." At 1 p.m. he announced; by the end of the day he had more than 100 votes, and the speakership.

Some called him "the accidental Speaker," but when he finishes this term Hastert will have served as Speaker longer than anyone since Tip O'Neill and his fitness for the job has long since ceased to be in question. In many ways he resembles O'Neill, who likely would never have been Speaker but for the death of Hale Boggs in a plane crash in 1972. Like O'Neill, Hastert is tall and heavy, is from a modest background, speaks in a rough and tumble manner but has a sophisticated understanding of politics and a more than sufficient command of policy; and like O'Neill he is a tough partisan and a man of his word. He is a backslapper who continually listens to other members—in the words of the *Wall Street Journal's* Paul Gigot, "the rumpled, enormous Speaker who doesn't approach members so much as engulf them." As Mark Leibovich wrote in the *Washington Post*, "He does much of his communicating without words. He fidgets with his glasses, clears his throat and stretches his eyebrows into weird positions to evince surprise, frustration, boredom or wryness. When others are talking, he often purses and unpurses his lips slowly. If necessary, Hastert will wrap this thick arm around a shoulder and land a THWAPP to emphasize his point."

As Speaker, Hastert has been good at tactics. In his first four years, working with Majority Leader Dick Armey and Majority Whip Tom DeLay, Hastert's leadership team brought to the floor 387 rules—the resolutions that set the terms and conditions of debate—and with never more than 223 Republicans, just five more than a 218-vote majority, lost on only two. But Hastert, though he has none of the grandiose vision of Newt Gingrich, has also been good at strategy. "It's my job that we keep the majority," he said in September 2002, and during the last two years of the Clinton administration and the first two years of the Bush administration, Hastert has steered House Republicans to compile a record that has enabled them to keep their majorities in the elections of 2000 and 2002. In 1999, when Republicans were in opposition, he got the House to pass an "EdFlex" bill, block grants for the states supported by all 50 governors, and a "lockbox" on Social Security, so that they could say they had not tapped the trust fund. When Republicans rebelled at the 1999 appropriations bills, he brought them together; he got them to pass a $792 billion tax cut that was vetoed by Bill Clinton; facing a large number of defections, he allowed the Shays-Meehan campaign finance bill to come to the floor and pass, confident that it would be killed by filibuster in the Senate. The House passed financial services deregulation and, after negotiations with White House Chief of Staff John Podesta (whom Hastert had known in college), an appropriations bill. He backed Clinton's Plan Colombia in June 2000 and agreed in August 2000 to allow a minimum wage increase in return for tax relief for small business; in October 2000 he canceled a vote on a resolution condemning Turkey's 1915–23 massacres of Armenians in response to pleas from the White House. His bitterest moment came in November 1999, when he and Armey passed over a Catholic priest recommended by a plurality of a special committee for the post of House chaplain; Democrats quickly accused the Republican leaders of anti-Catholic prejudice. The controversy ended when Hastert in March 2000 abruptly announced the appointment of another Catholic priest recommended by Chicago's Cardinal George. Hastert took special umbrage at Minority Leader Dick Gephardt, and relations between them were chilly to nonexistent until September 11, 2001.

All the while, Hastert kept his eye on the 2000 elections. He effectively lobbied some Republicans in marginal seats, like Upstate New York's Amo Houghton, to stay on rather than retire; he allowed members with Democratic-leaning districts to cast votes against the leadership that would be useful at home; he used the tool of the Republicans' six-year term-limit on chairmanships to get those competing for spots opening up to raise money for Republican candidates; he helped the Battleground 2000 program raise some $21 million; he went fly-fishing with contributors during the Republican convention at $5,000 a head. His quiet pursuit of a modest legislative strategy let Republican candidates emphasize their own local issues—a far cry from Gingrich's nationalized Contract With America campaign in 1994. As the election approached, Republican chances improved, and by late October Hastert sent an appropriation to the White House knowing that Clinton would veto it because it overrode the administration's proposed ergonomics regulations; he evidently thought that he could negotiate on better terms after the election if House Republicans and George W. Bush won. His Republicans did hold their majority, narrowly, on November 7 and when the House came back after settlement of the Florida controversy in December the negotiations mostly went Hastert's way.

With a Republican president, Hastert's role changed. Legislative priorities would be set mainly by the White House; the House's job was to pass administration-backed legislation so that the President could put pressure on the always shaky Senate. Hastert's relations with Bush were good (his nickname is "Speak") but not subservient: he was careful to protect his members and wary lest the White House water down legislation too much in negotiations with the Senate. In spring 2001 the House quickly passed the Bush tax cut and education bill. On campaign finance, passed by the Senate in March 2001, Bush refused to threaten a veto; in July 2001 Hastert lost a rule vote and then yanked the measure from the floor. When the measure's supporters got 218 signatures on a discharge petition, the bill passed the House in February 2002. But on other issues in July and August 2001—when Bush's job rating was hovering around 50% and there were only 222 House Republicans, four more than a majority—Hastert had a spectacular record otherwise. The House passed the Bush energy program, including drilling in the Arctic National Wildlife Refuge and not including an increase in auto mileage standards. In 2000, Republican Charlie Norwood had gotten 68 Republicans to join him and almost all Democrats on his HMO regulation bill. In July 2001 Hastert developed and gathered votes for a Republican alternative and in the meantime the White House negotiated with Norwood, who agreed to George W. Bush's terms, much to the dismay of many of his allies. A Bush veto threat—and the existence of a plausible alternative that might pass—persuaded Norwood to compromise; the House passed an HMO regulation bill acceptable to Republicans and for which they could claim credit.

On September 11, the mood of the House changed. Hastert and Gephardt, together with Senate leaders Tom Daschle and Trent Lott were taken to a secure location far from the Capitol and emerged with much closer bonds. But Hastert also continued to forge a record that Republicans could run on in 2002. He got the House to pass a Republican bill providing prescription drugs for seniors; the Senate never passed a bill on the issue. Republicans went to the floor to give the president trade promotion authority with fewer than 218 commitments and, with little Democratic help, prevailed by 215–214 in December 2001 and then again by 215–212 in July 2002. When the corporate misdeeds of Enron, WorldCom and other companies filled the headlines, Hastert saw that the issue could be political poison for Republicans. The House passed a corporate accountability bill fashioned by Financial Services Chairman Michael Oxley in April 2002, but it was attacked in the press and by Democrats as too lenient. In July, Hastert pressed Oxley and other Republicans to pass the bill sponsored by Senator Paul Sarbanes and passed 97–0 by the Senate, to put in place legislation and take off the calendar a political issue; Oxley and others resisted, but Hastert prevailed, and House Republicans could go home in the August recess and say they had acted against corporate misconduct. Hastert's power increased when he got the

Republican Conference to require Appropriations subcommittee chairmen to be approved by the party's Steering Committee—additional leverage for the leadership interested in holding spending within limits in its continuing institutional battle against appropriators interested in controlling the level of spending themselves.

Amid all this work on legislation and national politics, Hastert has become a power in Illinois politics—a far more important factor in his state's politics than any speaker in living memory. He has worked closely with Mayor Richard M. Daley on any number of projects and Daley obviously appreciates having a Chicago area Speaker of the House. In May 2001, Hastert and 3d District Democrat William Lipinski reached agreement on a congressional redistricting plan which strengthened almost all of the state's incumbents; the loser—and there had to be one, because the state lost one of its 20 seats in the 2000 Census—was Downstate Democrat David Phelps, a low seniority member in a position to do little for Chicago. Hastert has strongly supported the plan Daley in December 2001 negotiated with Governor George Ryan to expand O'Hare Airport, and in July 2002 brought to the House floor a bill which would have frozen it into federal law, so that it couldn't be rejected by a future governor; on the first vote Hastert failed to get the necessary two-thirds, thanks to opposition from Henry Hyde and Jesse Jackson Jr., but Hastert brought it to the floor three days later and lobbied for it furiously and successfully. He was disappointed that Senator Richard Durbin was never able to do the same in the Senate. In November 2002 Hastert lobbied the Bush administration to approve a loan application from United Airlines, which has 19,000 employees in the Chicago area; when that was turned down by the Air Transportation Stabilization Board, with the crucial vote cast by Treasury official Peter Fisher, he indicated his displeasure with Treasury Secretary Paul O'Neill, who was told to resign in December. After Illinois Republicans' debacle in the 2002 elections, he in effect chose a new state party chairman, Treasurer Judy Baar Topinka, and had much to say in the choice of the new Illinois House Minority Leader, his Kendall County neighbor Tom Cross.

Hastert has told friends that he yearns to retire from the hectic pace of the speakership; he has sold his house on the Fox River and lives on a farm nearby in Kendall County. But there is no demand from House Republicans that he move on. On the contrary, at the motion of the new Majority Whip, Roy Blunt, House Republicans voted in January 2003 to repeal their eight-year term-limit on the party's leader. The accidental Speaker, it seems, has become the indispensable Speaker. But Hastert may choose to retire in 2004 or 2006, at the height of his powers, as Tip O'Neill did in 1986.

FIFTEENTH DISTRICT

Rep. Tim Johnson (R)

Elected 2000, 2d term; b. July 23, 1946, Champaign; home, Sidney; U. of IL, B.A. 1969, U. of IL, J.D. 1972; Assembly of God; divorced.

Elected Office: Urbana City Council, 1971–76; IL House of Reps., 1976–00.

Professional Career: Practicing atty., Johnson, Frank, Frederick & Walsh.

DC Office: 1229 LHOB 20515, 202-225-2371; Fax: 202-226-0791; Web site: www.house.gov/timjohnson.

District Offices: Bloomington, 309-663-7049; Champaign, 217-403-4690.

Committees: *Agriculture* (13th of 27 R): General Farm Commodities & Risk Management. *Science* (16th of 25 R): Environment, Technology and Standards; Research. *Transportation & Infrastructure* (26th of 41 R): Aviation; Highways, Transit & Pipelines.

Group Ratings

	ADA	ACLU	AFS	LCV	CON	ITIC	NTU	COC	ACU	NTLC	CHC
2002	15	20	11	25	8	100	51	85	76	72	75
2001	15	—	20	64	—	—	56	74	68	—	—

National Journal Ratings

	2001 LIB — 2001 CONS	2002 LIB — 2002 CONS
Economic	47% — 53%	45% — 54%
Social	41% — 59%	44% — 54%
Foreign	43% — 53%	41% — 56%

Key Votes of the 107th Congress

1. Approve Bush Tax Cuts	Y	5. Faith-Based Charities	Y	9. Trade Promotion Authority	Y
2. Limit Patients' Bill of Rights	N	6. Bar Gays in the Boy Scouts	Y	10. Bar Funds for Intl. Court	Y
3. Campaign Finance Reform	Y	7. Ban Partial-Birth Abortion	Y	11. Authorize Force in Iraq	Y
4. Ban ANWR Development	Y	8. Arm Commercial Pilots	Y	12. Deny Home. Sec. Dept. Union	Y

Election Results

2002 general	Tim Johnson (R)	134,650	(65%)	($398,949)
	Joshua Hartke (D)	64,131	(31%)	
	Carl Estabrook (Green)	7,836	(4%)	($25,004)
2002 primary	Tim Johnson (R)	unopposed		
2000 general	Tim Johnson (R)	125,943	(53%)	($1,760,128)
	Mike Kelleher Jr. (D)	110,679	(47%)	($953,233)

The People		Race/Ethnic Origin	Ancestry	
Area size:	10,122 sq. mi.	88.5% White	German: 18.8%	Irish: 9.2%
Urban population:	64.2%	5.7% Black	English: 8.4%	
Rural population:	35.8%	2.3% Asian	**2000 Presidential Vote**	
Pop. 2000:	653,647	0.2% Native Am.	Bush (R) 148,176	(54%)
Median income:	$38,583	0.0% Hawaiian	Gore (D) 116,436	(42%)
Poverty status:	11.7%	1.0% Two+ races	Other 9,616	(4%)
Military veterans:	12.4%	0.1% Other	**Cook Partisan Voting Index:** R + 6	
		2.2% Hispanic Origin		

Occupation	Blue collar: 26.3%	White collar: 57.7%	Gray collar: 16.0%

South from Chicago, the Illinois Central Railroad heads to the city of New Orleans on a railbed elevated a few feet above the rich black soil of the Illinois prairie, topsoil reaching down not just inches but feet. This land dazzled its first settlers, who were used to land that had to be cleared of trees and stumps before it could be plowed; this treeless prairie could be cultivated almost immediately, and with bounteous results. Today this remains farming country, made up not of small family farms but of large commercial operations, typically of 1,000 acres or more. Cultivating this soil is a business, requiring informed decisions about crop selection, maximizing yields, proper pesticides, marketing decisions, watching farm export prospects and, except for the early years of the 1996 Freedom to Farm Act, taking advantage of government programs. The prairie landscape of eastern Illinois is marked by only a few towns, the largest of which are the sites of universities (the University of Illinois in Champaign-Urbana and Illinois Wesleyan and Illinois State in Bloomington-Normal). Politically, these prairie lands have been Republican, often very Republican; they incline much more to the party of former House Speaker Joseph Cannon, a Republican from the manufacturing city of Danville east of Urbana, than to that of Vice President Adlai Stevenson, a Democrat from Bloomington, who served under *laissez-faire* Democrat Grover Cleveland and was the grandfather of the Adlai Stevenson nominated by Democrats for president in 1952 and 1956.

The 15th Congressional District occupies much of this prairie, beginning 60 miles from Chicago, where the Illinois Central heads south into Iroquois County and covering some 130 miles south to the old National Road and U.S. 40, traditionally the line between northern Republican and southern Democratic Downstate Illinois. The biggest city here is Champaign-Urbana and the district also includes Normal, though next-door Bloomington was removed by the 2001 redistricting. Redistricting also added, south of the prairie, a narrow corridor of land extending more than 100 miles along the Wabash River border with Indiana as far south as the Ohio River, with an extension to the town of Eldorado. The university towns are somewhat liberal but the prairie counties have long been Republican, and this on balance is a Republican district.

The congressman from the 15th District is Tim Johnson, a Republican elected in 2000. Johnson grew up in Champaign and graduated from the University of Illinois and its law school. He was elected to the Urbana City Council while still in law school and served there four years before winning election to the state House in 1976. In the legislature, Johnson worked his way up to Deputy Majority Leader (when Republicans had a majority after the 1994 election). He worked to eliminate the sales tax on food and medicine and to devise tougher drunk-driving laws and played an important roles in passing welfare reform, educational improvements and truth-in-sentencing laws. He is a trial lawyer and manages a small local farm operation.

Johnson's chance to run for Congress came after incumbent Republican Tom Ewing announced his retirement in October 1999, just two months before the filing deadline. Ewing and Speaker Dennis Hastert had been close friends in Congress and previously in the state House, and Ewing was part of the team that backed Hastert for speaker and then closely advised him in his early months in that office. But Hastert was evidently unhappy that Ewing delayed his retirement announcement until his 29-year-old son Sam could move back to the district from Texas to launch his own candidacy. The Speaker endorsed state Representative Bill Brady, the scion of a prominent real estate family from Bloomington. But Johnson had more political experience than either and was a ferocious campaigner: "I've been a precinct committeeman involved in the affairs of my party more years than [Sam Ewing has] been alive." He also had the support of Governor George Ryan of Kankakee, who remained influential in party affairs despite a dismal job rating. The primary results broke along regional lines. Brady won his base of McLean County, 62%–20% over Johnson. In Champaign, Johnson led Brady, 61%–28%. Johnson rolled up the vote elsewhere, carrying seven of the 11 counties; he won 44% of the vote, while Brady finished second with 36% and Ewing was third with 17%.

In the general, Johnson faced Illinois State University instructor Mike Kelleher, who with union support won the Democratic primary, 53%–47%. Kelleher dredged up a 1980 photo of a paper clip-rigged device Johnson had used to hold down the "yes" button on his desk in the legislature, enabling him to be recorded as voting when he was absent off the floor. Johnson said such tactics were "accepted practice" at the time and called it a "silly little red herring" raised by a desperate candidate. The voting pattern was similar to the primary: Kelleher narrowly won his home of McLean County, while Johnson again took Champaign and nine of the 11 counties, winning 53%–47% overall. Johnson outperformed George W. Bush in the district's population centers.

In the House, Johnson compiled a moderate voting record. He voted against opening the Alaska National Wildlife Refuge to oil drilling, winning him a reelection endorsement from the League of Conservation Voters. He supported the Shays-Meehan campaign-finance bill because, while it was "imperfect," it was a step toward reducing the influence of "big money" in politics. He called his vote in favor of the use of force in Iraq "the most difficult decision of my political career." To discourage efforts by Miami Indians to build a casino in Paxton, Johnson filed a bill that would exempt local property owners from tribal land disputes.

The May 2001 redistricting placed Eldorado, the hometown of 19th District Democratic incumbent David Phelps, into the 15th District; for a time, it seemed that Phelps would run against Johnson. But the bulk of his old district was parceled into other districts, and Phelps decided to run against Republican John Shimkus in the new 19th, where he was at a lesser disadvantage (Phelps lost anyway). Otherwise, redistricting was good to Johnson, raising the district's Bush percentage and peeling off the home bases of his 2000 rival Mark Kelleher and of state Representative Julie Curry, who was considered a likely candidate. Johnson had weak opposition and was reelected 65%–31%. In October 2002 he announced that he had changed his mind and renounced the term-limit pledge he made during his first campaign. In March 2003 he was hospitalized after a car accident near a church where he was scheduled to speak; he suffered a fractured rib and punctured lung but delivered the speech anyway—before seeking medical treatment.

SIXTEENTH DISTRICT

Rep. Don Manzullo (R)

Elected 1992, 6th term; b. Mar. 24, 1944, Rockford; home, Egan; American U., B.A. 1967, Marquette U., J.D. 1970; Baptist; married (Freda).

Professional Career: Practicing atty., 1970–92; author.

DC Office: 2228 RHOB 20515, 202-225-5676; Fax: 202-225-5284; Web site: www.house.gov/manzullo.

District Offices: Crystal Lake, 815-356-9800; Rockford, 815-394-1231.

Committees: *Financial Services* (16th of 37 R): Capital Markets, Insurance & Government Sponsored Enterprises; Domestic and International Monetary Policy, Trade & Technology. *Small Business* (Chmn. of 18 R).

Group Ratings

	ADA	ACLU	AFS	LCV	CON	ITIC	NTU	COC	ACU	NTLC	CHC
2002	5	27	11	13	56	75	64	95	100	100	92
2001	0	—	10	7	—	—	70	96	92	—	—

National Journal Ratings

	2001 LIB	—	2001 CONS		2002 LIB	—	2002 CONS
Economic	15%	—	82%		39%	—	61%
Social	41%	—	59%		0%	—	75%
Foreign	41%	—	58%		35%	—	60%

Key Votes of the 107th Congress

1. Approve Bush Tax Cuts	Y	5. Faith-Based Charities	N	9. Trade Promotion Authority	Y
2. Limit Patients' Bill of Rights	Y	6. Bar Gays in the Boy Scouts	Y	10. Bar Funds for Intl. Court	Y
3. Campaign Finance Reform	N	7. Ban Partial-Birth Abortion	Y	11. Authorize Force in Iraq	Y
4. Ban ANWR Development	N	8. Arm Commercial Pilots	Y	12. Deny Home. Sec. Dept. Union	Y

Election Results

2002 general	Don Manzullo (R)	133,339	(71%)	($945,291)
	John Kutsch (D)	55,488	(29%)	($45,808)
2002 primary	Don Manzullo (R)	unopposed		
2000 general	Don Manzullo (R)	178,174	(67%)	($674,125)
	Charles W. Hendrickson (D)	88,781	(33%)	($54,882)

Prior Winning Percentages: 1998 (100%); 1996 (60%); 1994 (71%); 1992 (56%)

The People		Race/Ethnic Origin	Ancestry	
Area size:	4,158 sq. mi.	85.7% White	German: 21.8%	Irish: 10.0%
Urban population:	78.4%	5.3% Black	English: 6.7%	
Rural population:	21.6%	1.3% Asian	**2000 Presidential Vote**	
Pop. 2000:	653,647	0.2% Native Am.	Bush (R) 141,878	(54%)
Median income:	$48,960	0.0% Hawaiian	Gore (D) 113,020	(43%)
Poverty status:	7.3%	1.0% Two + races	Other 8,163	(3%)
Military veterans:	12.8%	0.1% Other	**Cook Partisan Voting Index:** R + 6	
		6.5% Hispanic Origin		

Occupation	Blue collar: 29.7%	White collar: 57.2%	Gray collar: 13.0%

The far northwest corner of Illinois is one of the heartlands of the Republican Party. Here in the town square of Freeport, some 15,000 people came to hear Abraham Lincoln and Stephen Douglas in one of their seven debates in 1858, and on the terrain most partial to Lincoln. Settled by New England Yankees, northern Illinois was one of the strongest Republican constituencies in 1860 and for years after. Not far away, on a little river once navigable by Mississippi River steamboats, is Galena, one of the earliest settlements in northern Illinois, the home of Ulysses S. Grant before he became general and then president. The largest city here is Rockford, on the Rock River, settled by Swedes as well as Yankees, one of America's leading furniture manufacturers at one time, then a major center for machine tools. Politically, northern Illinois, perhaps inspired by Democratic Chicago, remained steadfastly Republican for many years; it backed Herbert Hoover in 1932, Barry Goldwater in 1964 and George H.W. Bush in 1992 when most of America and Illinois were going the other way.

The 16th Congressional District consists of much of the northwest part of the state. It includes the hilly, almost mountainous country around Galena and the Mississippi River, and the flatter plains in the farming counties to the east and south. Rockford remains the biggest city, but the fastest-growing part of the district is in the east, where it contains part of McHenry County and all of Boone County, the two fastest-growing counties in Illinois in the 1990s. They are full of new subdivisions surrounding old towns, where Motorola has been opening new cellular phone plants to supply Japan, and affluent young families make their way up through free enterprise and have conservative cultural values.

The congressman from the 16th District is Donald Manzullo, a Republican first elected in 1992. He grew up in Rockford, where his father ran a grocery store, and his brother owns Manzullo's Famous Italian Restaurant. While in college in Washington in the mid-1960s he worked for Republican candidates and he started practicing law in Illinois in 1970. He lives on a cattle-breeding farm, writes poetry and books on constitutional law, and ran a radio talk show; he and his wife home-schooled their three children until high school and started the Northern Illinois Crisis Pregnancy Center. Manzullo ran for Congress in 1990 and lost the primary 54%–46% to a moderate, who after revelations of personal problems then lost the general to Democrat John Cox. Cox favored increased taxes, opposed capital punishment and was hurt when heavily Republican McHenry County was added in redistricting. Manzullo ran again and, with support from conservative Christians, beat a moderate 56%–44% in the primary. In the general election, Cox campaigned for higher taxes; Manzullo for a 10% across-the-board income tax cut. Manzullo won with 56% of the vote.

Manzullo is now chairman of the Small Business Committee, a post he won over New York's Sue Kelly after the 2000 campaign. He has used the committee to hold hearings on all manner of issues, in Washington and around the country. In April 2002 he demanded that Thomas Scully resign as head of the Centers for Medicare and Medicaid Services (formerly HCFA) when Scully declined to testify in a hearing on Medicare payments to providers of portable X-ray machines. He was critical of Federal Prison Industries, which is alleged to use non-prison subcontractors to produce goods that then are eligible for preference in federal purchasing. He journeyed to West Yellowstone, Montana, in January 2002, to hold a hearing in which he encouraged allowing snowmobiles in Yellowstone National Park; several Rockford-area factories produce snowmobile parts. Manzullo is a market conservative and a strong supporter of free trade. He supported NAFTA, GATT, the WTO and PNTR for China. But he joined many protectionists in arguing against an FTC proposal to reduce the percentage of U.S. content to 75% in goods labeled "Made in U.S.A." He criticized the Bush administration's imposition of steel tariffs in March 2002 and cited Rockford manufacturers' increased costs; he has worked to exclude products like tool-grade steel from the tariffs. He has also complained about strict export controls. His free market principles have limits: He voted for the farm bill in May 2002. He has taken up eclectic causes. He amended the Clean Air Act to make its carpooling provisions voluntary. Some conservatives were surprised that Manzullo was the co-sponsor of the Mychal Judge Law, signed in June 2002, which allows gay partners to receive federal police and firefighter death benefits and applies to Judge and other victims of the September 11 attacks. But, as Manzullo points out, the act simply allows benefits to go to any beneficiary designated on a life insurance policy by the decedent; he drafted a similar measure at the request of the Rockford Police Department, and saw the bill as a pro-police measure. "I'm in zero contact with the gay community," Manzullo said.

Manzullo has worked on local projects, and sponsored a $300,000 study of a rail-to-truck facility in Rochelle, then introduced Union Pacific officials to the town where they are now building a $180 million facility. He entered Illinois's airport wars by arguing that any third Chicago-area airport should be based in Rockford. He supported the O'Hare Airport expansion agreement of Mayor Richard M. Daley and Governor George Ryan and the attempt to enact it into federal law in 2002; he wanted to name Greater Rockford Airport as the official reliever airport for O'Hare during the five years of construction, but settled for Senator Richard Durbin's proposal to name Gary-Chicago and Greater Rockford as possible reliever airports. Manzullo has been easily re-elected every two years and, once a fan of term limits, says he has no intention of retiring.

SEVENTEENTH DISTRICT

Rep. Lane Evans (D)

Elected 1982, 11th term; b. Aug. 4, 1951, Rock Island; home, Rock Island; Augustana Col., B.A. 1974, Georgetown U., J.D. 1978; Catholic; single.

Military Career: Marine Corps, 1969–71.

Professional Career: Practicing atty., 1978–82.

DC Office: 2211 RHOB 20515, 202-225-5905; Fax: 202-225-5396; Web site: www.house.gov/evans.

District Offices: Decatur, 217-422-9150; Galesburg, 309-342-4411; Moline, 309-793-5760.

Committees: *Armed Services* (4th of 29 D): Readiness; Tactical Air & Land Forces. *Veterans' Affairs* (RMM of 14 D): Oversight & Investigations.

Group Ratings

	ADA	ACLU	AFS	LCV	CON	ITIC	NTU	COC	ACU	NTLC	CHC
2002	100	86	100	88	34	38	18	40	0	0	0
2001	100	—	100	86	—	—	10	27	0	—	—

National Journal Ratings

	2001 LIB	—	2001 CONS		2002 LIB	—	2002 CONS
Economic	77%	—	23%		95%	—	0%
Social	83%	—	11%		84%	—	8%
Foreign	81%	—	18%		84%	—	14%

Key Votes of the 107th Congress

1. Approve Bush Tax Cuts	N	5. Faith-Based Charities	N	9. Trade Promotion Authority	N
2. Limit Patients' Bill of Rights	N	6. Bar Gays in the Boy Scouts	N	10. Bar Funds for Intl. Court	N
3. Campaign Finance Reform	Y	7. Ban Partial-Birth Abortion	N	11. Authorize Force in Iraq	N
4. Ban ANWR Development	Y	8. Arm Commercial Pilots	N	12. Deny Home. Sec. Dept. Union	N

Election Results

2002 general	Lane Evans (D)	127,093	(62%)	($774,108)
	Peter Calderone (R)	76,519	(38%)	($45,275)
2002 primary	Lane Evans (D)	unopposed		
2000 general	Lane Evans (D)	132,494	(55%)	($1,230,267)
	Mark Baker (R)	108,853	(45%)	($984,857)

Prior Winning Percentages: 1998 (52%); 1996 (52%); 1994 (55%); 1992 (60%); 1990 (67%); 1988 (65%); 1986 (56%); 1984 (57%); 1982 (53%)

The People		Race/Ethnic Origin	Ancestry	
Area size:	8,289 sq. mi.	87.3% White	German: 18.2%	Irish: 9.0%
Urban population:	71.1%	7.2% Black	English: 7.7%	
Rural population:	28.9%	0.6% Asian	**2000 Presidential Vote**	
Pop. 2000:	653,647	0.2% Native Am.	Gore (D) 146,548 (54%)	
Median income:	$35,066	0.0% Hawaiian	Bush (R) 119,563 (44%)	
Poverty status:	12.5%	1.0% Two+ races	Other 7,807 (3%)	
Military veterans:	14.4%	0.1% Other	**Cook Partisan Voting Index:** D + 5	
		3.7% Hispanic Origin		

Occupation   Blue collar: 29.9%   White collar: 51.7%   Gray collar: 18.4%

Illinois's western prairies are some of America's richest agricultural land. They were first settled by Yankees coming overland from northern Indiana and Ohio and Upstate New York. After 1848, Germans left their homeland in search of better opportunities and settled this land that in so many ways resembles the flat, orderly plains of northern Germany. All these migrants farmed quarter-sections and built small towns, with banks and stores, community churches and libraries. As farming expanded, so did the need for agricultural equipment. Investors built farm machinery factories, and the Quad Cities of the Mississippi—Davenport and Bettendorf, Iowa, and Rock Island and Moline, Illinois—became one of the nation's biggest agricultural equipment manufacturing centers. These plants were unionized in the 1930s and 1940s, and in post-World War II America their wages went up as the demand for ever more sophisticated machines rose among the Midwest's government-subsidized farmers. But eventually the cost of subsidies rose too high and the market had its revenge. In the early 1980s farm profits vanished, land values declined and orders for new machinery and equipment dried up. The result was a depression in western Illinois and neighboring Iowa, and a political swing toward the Democrats and away from the Republicans who had been the ancestral party in most of this area. In the 1990s the Democratic tide receded a bit, but this was still one of the few parts of rural America carried by Al Gore in 2000.

The 17th Congressional District includes the Illinois portion of the Quad Cities plus several rural counties to the south: All of the Mississippi River border with Iowa and south almost to St. Louis. But that is not the entire district, for redistricting in 2001 changed its shape considerably. Removed were counties north and directly east of Rock Island and Moline. Added was a thin strip of land along the Mississippi River and the lower Illinois River. Connected to that was an extension that includes rural Macoupin County and a tentacle heading east, plus a very thin strip of land that includes central Springfield (but not the state Capitol building) and, some miles further east, a portion of Decatur. Decatur is home to Archer Daniels Midland, the largest agricultural processor in the world. It would be fairly easy to drive directly from any part of the 17th District to another, but only if you crossed over into the 18th or 19th Districts. To drive from one end of the 17th to the other while remaining entirely inside the district would take many more miles and many, many more hours than to drive from Chicago to the southern tip of Illinois in Cairo. There is, of course, a good political explanation for this weird configuration. Illinois's redistricting was largely a bipartisan, incumbent protection enterprise, negotiated by Speaker Dennis Hastert and 3d District Democrat William Lipinski. For many years Republicans hoped that the Republican counties outlying Rock Island and Moline in the 17th District would outvote those Democratic towns and oust local Democratic Congressman Lane Evans, who was first elected in something of a fluke in 1982 and then was helped by the Democratic trend in the Farm Belt in the 1980s; he later survived several serious challenges. So the current 17th was drawn to help Evans. He lost the Republican counties east and north of the Quad Cities. The Mississippi River corridor casts few votes. Macoupin County has always been Democratic. Central Springfield and Decatur are solidly Democratic.

Evans, first elected in 1982, is now the ranking minority member on the Veterans Affairs Committee. He grew up in Rock Island, the son of a union firefighter. He joined the Marine Corps in 1969 after high school and served two years, then went to college and law school and worked as a legal services lawyer. In 1982, he ran for Congress—a seemingly quixotic race against longtime incumbent Republican Tom Railsback. But Railsback lost his primary to a conservative and the economically hard-pressed district voted 53% for Evans. He calls himself a "populist" rather than a liberal; by most standards, his voting record is solidly liberal and one of the most pro-union in the House. He was a strong opponent of NAFTA, GATT and PNTR with China. He fervently favored higher agricultural subsidies during his five-year tenure on the Agriculture Committee, but left that post to take a seat on Armed Services in 1988, even as farm subsidies were cut back in 1985, 1990 and 1996. He was one of 31 Democrats who voted for the Republicans' impeachment inquiry in October 1998, though he later voted against impeachment.

Evans has devoted much time to veterans' issues. He worked hard for years to get compensation for veterans who claimed they were harmed by exposure to Agent Orange, and ultimately succeeded. In 1994 he began to investigate what he and others have characterized as Gulf War syndrome. In 1996 Evans passed a bill providing benefits to children of Vietnam veterans exposed to Agent Orange who were born with spina bifida—the first entitlement for children of veterans. In 2000 he helped pass a law providing VA benefits for children with birth defects born to women who served in Vietnam; he expressed anger in 2002 that only one child had been found eligible for benefits by the VA, even though a doctor testifying on the 2000 law said 200 such children existed.

On Armed Services, Evans worked to find alternatives to tritium production; he also questioned how much export controls should be relaxed on critical weapons materials. His major cause on the committee has been a ban on land mines, which continue to injure thousands of people years after wars are over. In 1996 he passed a one-year moratorium, to begin in 1999, but Congress repealed it in 1998. In 1997 he co-sponsored, with Republican Jack Quinn, a total ban along the lines championed by Canada and agreed to by many other nations; his ban would include "smart" mines, those which remain explosive for only a limited time and, after a 12-year exemption, all mines in South Korea. This approach was rejected by the Clinton administration, which wanted to keep mines in South Korea to repel any attack by North Korea.

In the years of agricultural unrest and high unemployment in western Illinois, Evans was re-elected by wide margins. But in the 1990s he had closer calls. He won with 55% in 1994, and in the next three elections faced Republican Mark Baker, a former TV anchor in Quincy, a town on the Mississippi, one of the smallest media markets in America. In 1996 Evans won 52%–47%, in 1998 by 52%–48%, in 2000 by 55%–45%—each candidate spent $1 million or more in the last two contests. In May 1998 Evans announced he had Parkinson's disease, which was diagnosed in 1995; he said he could not stand long without pain or smile easily, but could still jog and that he had lost weight under doctor's orders. In 2000 Evans spent much of his ad budget talking about his Parkinson's disease; one showed him jogging and saying, "If you hear someone say they're worried about Lane Evans, tell them you saw him running today and he's doing just fine." After redistricting, Evans did not have serious competition in 2002, and does not seem likely to have any in future elections.

EIGHTEENTH DISTRICT

Rep. Ray LaHood (R)

Elected 1994, 5th term; b. Dec. 6, 1945, Peoria; home, Peoria; Canton Jr. Col., 1963–65, Bradley U., B.S. 1971; Catholic; married (Kathy).

Elected Office: IL House of Reps., 1982.

Professional Career: Jr. High Schl. Teacher, 1971–77; Dir., Rock Island Youth Svcs., 1972–74; Chief Planner, Bi–state Planning Comm., 1974–76; Dist. A.A., U.S. Rep. Tom Railsback, 1977–82; Dist. A.A., U.S. Rep. Bob Michel, 1983–90, Chief of Staff, 1990–94.

DC Office: 1424 LHOB 20515, 202-225-6201; Fax: 202-225-9249; Web site: www.house.gov/lahood.

District Offices: Jacksonville, 217-245-1431; Peoria, 309-671-7027; Springfield, 217-793-0808.

Committees: *Appropriations* (28th of 36 R): Agriculture, Rural Development, & FDA; The Legislative Branch (Vice Chmn.); VA, HUD & Independent Agencies. *Permanent Select Committee on Intelligence* (5th of 11 R): Intelligence Policy & National Security (Vice Chmn.); Terrorism and Homeland Security (Chmn.).

Group Ratings

	ADA	ACLU	AFS	LCV	CON	ITIC	NTU	COC	ACU	NTLC	CHC
2002	0	13	0	13	8	88	53	89	92	71	92
2001	15	—	20	50	—	—	57	86	72	—	—

National Journal Ratings

	2001 LIB —	2001 CONS	2002 LIB —	2002 CONS
Economic	48%	52%	34%	66%
Social	46%	55%	32%	63%
Foreign	43%	53%	35%	60%

Key Votes of the 107th Congress

1. Approve Bush Tax Cuts	Y	5. Faith-Based Charities	Y	9. Trade Promotion Authority	Y
2. Limit Patients' Bill of Rights	Y	6. Bar Gays in the Boy Scouts	Y	10. Bar Funds for Intl. Court	Y
3. Campaign Finance Reform	N	7. Ban Partial-Birth Abortion	Y	11. Authorize Force in Iraq	Y
4. Ban ANWR Development	Y	8. Arm Commercial Pilots	Y	12. Deny Home. Sec. Dept. Union	Y

Election Results

2002 general	Ray LaHood (R)	unopposed		($1,051,220)
2002 primary	Ray LaHood (R)	unopposed		
2000 general	Ray LaHood (R)	173,706	(67%)	($974,251)
	Joyce Harant (D)	85,317	(33%)	($86,262)

Prior Winning Percentages: 1998 (100%); 1996 (59%); 1994 (60%)

The People		Race/Ethnic Origin	Ancestry	
Area size:	8,302 sq. mi.	90.0% White	German: 21.2%	Irish: 9.7%
Urban population:	68.0%	6.4% Black	English: 8.8%	
Rural population:	32.0%	0.9% Asian	**2000 Presidential Vote**	
Pop. 2000:	653,647	0.2% Native Am.	Bush (R) 159,475	(54%)
Median income:	$41,934	0.0% Hawaiian	Gore (D) 128,411	(43%)
Poverty status:	8.9%	0.9% Two+ races	Other 7,464	(3%)
Military veterans:	14.2%	0.1% Other	**Cook Partisan Voting Index:** R + 6	
		1.5% Hispanic Origin		

Occupation	Blue collar: 24.7%	White collar: 59.1%	Gray collar: 16.2%

Old vaudeville bookers, presented with a new act, used to ask, "Will it play in Peoria?" The implication was that if an act went over in this small city on the bluffs above the Illinois River, 154 miles from Chicago and 171 miles from St. Louis, it would go over just about anywhere. In the first half of this century, Peoria did seem pretty typical of America. If its citizens were mostly of British or German descent, with a small percentage of blacks, that was the image of ordinary America that prevailed up through the 1960s, despite the great immigrations of 1880–1924 and the northward urban migrations of southern rural blacks of 1940–1965. But Peoria's economy, arguably typical at mid-century, is less so today. This is still a heavy manufacturing town, dominated by big plants that produce farm machinery and earth-moving equipment. Its biggest employer is Caterpillar, the world's leading producer of earth-moving and construction equipment, and one of America's major exporters. There are more than just memories here of the sharp divide between blue collar and white collar, union and management, Democrat and Republican— the basis of the class warfare politics that was the norm in the heavy industrial metropolises of the Great Lakes region for three or four decades starting with the sit-down strikes of the late 1930s. But the blue-collar workers now are not as numerous and the unions not as strong. The Peoria area went through terrible times in the 1980s, as big farm machinery plants laid off workers and even closed down. Then Caterpillar, struck by the United Auto Workers in 1992, hired replacement workers and continued to operate—not without some friction and inefficiency, but profitably—something unheard of a dozen or more years before. Not until March 1998 did union members approve a settlement, pretty much on the company's terms. There was no population growth here in the 1990s, and Peoria slipped from 3d to 5th among the largest cities in Illinois.

The 18th Congressional District, variously configured, has been the Peoria district since the 1940s. It has been represented by two national Republican leaders: from 1933–49 by Everett McKinley Dirksen, who was elected senator in 1950 and was Senate Republican leader from 1959–69, and Robert Michel, congressman from 1957–95 and Republican House leader from 1981–95. The 18th's boundaries have changed considerably over that time; currently they extend south along the Illinois River and east to include half of Springfield (including the state Capitol) and west within a few miles of Iowa, away from historically Republican Peoria toward the historically marginal counties of central Illinois. It is the home of Eureka College, which dedicated the Ronald Reagan Peace Garden in honor of its 1933 graduate and the end of the Cold War that he helped to achieve.

The congressman from the 18th District is Ray LaHood, a Republican elected in 1994. LaHood grew up in Peoria, the grandson of an immigrant from Lebanon and son of a restaurant manager. He worked his way through school, spent six years teaching in Catholic schools, then moved to Rock Island, where he worked with delinquent teens and became a staffer for Congressman Tom Railsback. He served in the Illinois House in 1982, then worked for Congressman Michel in Peoria and, from 1990–94, was his chief of staff in Washington. When Newt Gingrich pointedly declined to rule out running against Michel for Republican leader after the 1994 election, Michel decided to retire. LaHood ran to replace his boss, and in the Republican primary beat state Representative Judy Koehler, 50%–40%, carrying the Peoria area but running behind in the rest of the district. LaHood's Democratic opponent was Douglas Stephens, a labor lawyer and small businessmen, who held Michel to 52% in 1982 and 55% in 1988. Stephens favored school prayer, term limits and abortion restrictions, and put on an energetic campaign, but in this Republican year LaHood carried all but one county and won 60%–39%.

LaHood's voting record has been toward the middle of the House. An odd man out under Speaker Gingrich, LaHood became one of its most visible members in Gingrich's final days as speaker. He was one of only three Republicans who did not sign the Contract with America; he had reservations about voting for tax cuts until the budget was balanced. And he disliked the Republicans' confrontational strategy in the 1995–96 budget crisis. During those years, decrying the angry tone of House debate, LaHood and Democrat David Skaggs started the Bipartisan Retreat at Hershey, Pennsylvania, "to foster a Congress that is more civil and to create better communication among members." He also gained a niche by frequently presiding over the House. With his experience in monitoring the floor for Michel, LaHood's evenhanded rulings, his surefooted mastery of parliamentary procedure and his determination to maintain decorum were widely appreciated. Most famously, he was called on often to preside over the impeachment of Bill Clinton.

When Speaker Dennis Hastert replaced Gingrich, LaHood suddenly was well placed with House leaders. With Hastert's support, he has won seats on the Appropriations, Budget and Intelligence committees. As a self-styled deficit hawk, he supports a freeze in federal spending. He seized on the disputed 2000 count in Florida as an opportunity to advance his longtime cause of abolishing the Electoral College and replacing it with a national popular vote count. But the moment passed without action. After September 11, he refused to join critics who complained that the government was targeting people of Middle Eastern descent and he voted for the use of force against Iraq. He was the only House member to speak out against the creation of the commission to investigate the causes of the September 11 attacks.

LaHood has worked for district interests. He says that he has supported Caterpillar 90% of the time and worked to lift duties off four chemicals used to produce herbicides at DuPont's request. He has been willing to tangle with colleagues on behalf of local interests. And when the 11th District's Jerry Weller got Joliet's new veterans' cemetery named after Abraham Lincoln, LaHood got a sentence in an appropriations bill revoking that, for fear of confusion with Springfield's Oak Ridge Cemetery, where Lincoln is buried.

LaHood has been re-elected by wide margins throughout his district, and was unopposed in 2002. When Republican Senator Peter Fitzgerald in October 2000 attacked Speaker Dennis Hastert for not imposing federal bidding requirements on the Abraham Lincoln Library project and called his position "morally and ethically wrong," LaHood took umbrage. In November 2002, LaHood told the *Chicago Sun-Times*, "I'm thinking about trying to make sure that Peter has an opponent" in the Republican primary. "I think we can do better than him." He said that Fitzgerald did nothing to help Republican candidates south of I-80 in 2002 and didn't show up at a rally in Springfield two days before the election. "I've been disenchanted with Fitzgerald for a long time, but when he trashed Denny Hastert that was just the straw that broke the camel's back for me." But when Fitzgerald announced in April 2003 that he would not seek another term, LaHood said he would not run for the open Senate seat. He did consider running for Majority Whip after Dick Armey retired in 2002, but he decided not to when it became clear that Roy Blunt had locked up the votes.

NINETEENTH DISTRICT

Rep. John Shimkus (R)

Elected 1996, 4th term; b. Feb. 21, 1958, Collinsville; home, Collinsville; West Point Military Acad., B.S. 1980, Christ Col., Teaching Cert., 1990, S. IL U., M.B.A. 1997; Lutheran; married (Karen).

Military Career: Army 1980–85; Army Reserves, 1985-present.

Elected Office: Collinsville Township Trustee, 1989–93; Madison Cnty. Tres., 1990–96.

Professional Career: High schl. teacher, 1986–90.

DC Office: 513 CHOB 20515, 202-225-5271; Fax: 202-225-5880; Web site: www.house.gov/shimkus.

District Offices: Centralia, 618-532-9676; Collinsville, 618-344-3065; Harrisburg, 618-252-8271; Olney, 618-392-7737; Springfield, 217-492-5090.

Committees: *Energy & Commerce* (14th of 31 R): Commerce, Trade & Consumer Protection; Energy & Air Quality (Vice Chmn.); Environment & Hazardous Materials; Telecommunications & The Internet.

Group Ratings

	ADA	ACLU	AFS	LCV	CON	ITIC	NTU	COC	ACU	NTLC	CHC
2002	0	13	0	0	77	100	58	90	100	89	92
2001	5	—	10	0	—	—	65	100	92	—	—

National Journal Ratings

	2001 LIB —	2001 CONS		2002 LIB —	2002 CONS
Economic	36%	— 63%		21%	— 73%
Social	0%	— 81%		0%	— 75%
Foreign	49%	— 47%		35%	— 60%

Key Votes of the 107th Congress

1. Approve Bush Tax Cuts	Y	5. Faith-Based Charities	Y	9. Trade Promotion Authority	Y
2. Limit Patients' Bill of Rights	Y	6. Bar Gays in the Boy Scouts	Y	10. Bar Funds for Intl. Court	Y
3. Campaign Finance Reform	N	7. Ban Partial-Birth Abortion	Y	11. Authorize Force in Iraq	Y
4. Ban ANWR Development	N	8. Arm Commercial Pilots	Y	12. Deny Home. Sec. Dept. Union	Y

Election Results

2002 general	John Shimkus (R)	133,956	(55%)	($2,144,611)
	David Phelps (D)	110,517	(45%)	($1,278,758)
2002 primary	John Shimkus (R)	unopposed		
2000 general (IL 20)	John Shimkus (R)	161,393	(63%)	($645,920)
	Jeffrey S. Cooper (D)	94,382	(37%)	($233,699)

Prior Winning Percentages: 1998 (61%); 1996 (50%)

The People		Race/Ethnic Origin	Ancestry	
Area size:	11,646 sq. mi.	94.0% White	German: 21.6%	USA: 8.8%
Urban population:	52.2%	3.5% Black	Irish: 8.6%	
Rural population:	47.8%	0.5% Asian	**2000 Presidential Vote**	
Pop. 2000:	653,647	0.2% Native Am.	Bush (R)..............164,541	(56%)
Median income:	$38,955	0.0% Hawaiian	Gore (D)..............121,210	(41%)
Poverty status:	9.1%	0.7% Two+ races	Other.....................7,621	(3%)
Military veterans:	14.4%	0.1% Other	**Cook Partisan Voting Index:** R + 8	
		1.1% Hispanic Origin		

Occupation	Blue collar: 28.2%	White collar: 55.4%	Gray collar: 16.4%

Southern Illinois is a land of prairies, of flat, treeless land sloping imperceptibly down to the Ohio and Mississippi Rivers. It was settled almost entirely from the south by farmers coming overland from Kentucky, such as Abraham Lincoln's family. Just beyond the Ohio River, they found hilly terrain, some of which turned out to have coal deposits. To the north they must have been astonished, after miles of thick forest, to see the great American prairie stretch before them, a vast sea of empty land extending past the horizon. The prairie lands proved wondrously rich, and were soon crisscrossed by rail lines taking their produce away and bringing in products of industrial civilization from St. Louis, Chicago and points east. About the same time, vast coal deposits were found in southern Illinois, producing one mining town after another: This was, for the most part, the home turf of John L. Lewis, the imperious leader of the United Mine Workers for half a century and, in the late 1930s and early 1940s, one of the most powerful and eloquent figures in American politics.

The 19th Congressional District, which extends more than 200 miles up and down and across, covers much of 30 counties in the rural heartland of southern Illinois—most of the land area of the state south of Springfield. A product of 2001 redistricting, the district is a reconstitution of the old 19th and 20th Districts. Much of it is south of the old National Road, which became U.S. 40 and is paralleled by Interstate 70, the traditional boundary between the part of Downstate Illinois settled by Southerners and that settled by Yankees, and also the boundary between traditional Democrats and traditional Republicans. Its boundaries are jagged, and seemingly without rational basis; yet there is a rational political explanation for them. The biggest voting blocs are in Madison, Clinton and Washington Counties, which are part of the St. Louis metropolitan area, and the Sangamon County suburbs of Springfield, the state capital. About one-third of Springfield itself is also in this district. But the district also includes the coal mining area around Mount Vernon, the sparsely settled counties along the Ohio River and prairie counties along U.S. 40 and south of Springfield.

The congressman from the 19th District is John Shimkus, a Republican first elected in 1996. Shimkus grew up in Collinsville, a county seat in Madison County, on the other side of the Mississippi River from St. Louis. His father was an installer for Illinois Bell, and his mother a township trustee; he is of Lithuanian descent, as is his predecessor in the House, Democratic Senator Richard Durbin. Shimkus graduated from West Point, trained in the Army as a ranger and paratrooper, studied in California, then came back to Collinsville to teach high school. Almost immediately he began running for local office. In 1988 he ran for the Madison County Board, and lost; in 1989 he was elected Collinsville Township Trustee. In 1990, at 32, he beat a 12-year incumbent and was elected Madison County Treasurer, the only Republican countywide officer, and was re-elected in 1994. In 1996, when Durbin ran for the Senate, Shimkus easily won the Republican primary with 51% against seven other candidates. In the general election he faced state Representative Jay Hoffman. Both were anti-abortion, anti-gun control, and pro-balanced budget amendment. Hoffman raised more money and had the benefit of AFL-CIO ads but he refused to take Americans for Tax Reform's pledge not to raise taxes; Shimkus won by 50.3%–49.7%, a margin of 1,238 votes.

In the House, Shimkus got a seat on the Commerce Committee and used it to sponsor one small but locally important piece of legislation. This was his amendment that qualified the soybean-diesel fuel blend B-20 for the alternative fuels program. This would make vehicles able to use B-20 qualify for the federal environmental quotas, and the Clinton administration opposed it, arguing that any standard diesel fuel engine would qualify. But Shimkus, working with Democrat Karen McCarthy, got it enacted. Shimkus seems to enjoy the political rough and tumble. When Governor George Ryan sought federal funding for an Abraham Lincoln presidential library in Springfield, Senator Peter Fitzgerald objected that the state's contracting procedures were inadequate to prevent favoritism and that federal guidelines should be used. That infuriated not only Ryan but also House Republicans, including Speaker Dennis Hastert, who accused Fitzgerald of grandstanding. Shimkus sought to broker a deal by calling for a panel to review contracts for the state project. But that did not satisfy Fitzgerald, who filibustered the appropriation bill for several more days.

Illinois lost one House seat in the 2000 Census, and when the detailed Census figures came in, it was apparent that the loss would come from low-population-growth southern Illinois. The state's redistricting plan was produced by Speaker Dennis Hastert and 3d District Democrat William Lipinski; they decided to eliminate the 19th District seat held since 1998 by David Phelps, a conservative Democrat and former professional gospel singer from far south Illinois. Phelps's hometown, but not much else of his old district, was placed in the safely Republican 15th District. Several other Democratic counties were placed in the 12th District, represented by Democrat Jerry Costello, who had an impregnable base in the Democratic primaries in St. Clair County and part of Madison County directly across the river from St. Louis. Phelps' third alternative was to run against Shimkus in the new 19th, of which Shimkus had been representing 63% of the voters and Phelps 34%. Chicago-based Democrats, interested in colleagues that could help them with O'Hare expansion and other Chicago priorities, did not care much about Phelps. Phelps protested at having his hometown included in the prairie 15th District. "No one can convince me that Iroquois County or McLean County has the same common community interests as southern Illinois. Southern Illinois has Shawnee National Forest issues. It has river communities with unique issues. Oil, coal and gas, along with agriculture, is the main backbone of the economy." He filed a lawsuit in July 2001, which was dismissed in October; without any better alternative, he decided—the decision had to be quick since Illinois has a March primary and a December filing deadline—to run in the new 19th.

The result was a spirited contest. The candidates disagreed on whether the Bush tax cuts should be made permanent, on trade promotion authority, on prescription drugs. The AFL-CIO spent more than $1.5 million attacking Shimkus; Shimkus was helped by campaign ads paid by the pharmaceutical industry. But the numbers were all for Shimkus. In the portions of the district he had represented he won 59%–41%, with a popular vote margin of 29,000. In the portions he had represented, Phelps won by only 53%–47%, with a popular vote margin of 5,000. Overall Shimkus won 55%–45%, and this seat looks pretty safe for Republicans for the rest of the decade.

★ INDIANA ★

On Memorial Day every year the nation's eyes turn to Indianapolis, the center of a state with the nation's most distinctive nickname—Hoosier—and some of its least distinctive borders, for a sports spectacle celebrating the knack for tinkering and the taste for powerful machines that make the Midwest the nation's manufacturing center: The Indianapolis 500. This combination of sports and manufacturing is symbolic of Indiana's strengths and successes. The image of its manufacturing base and sports heritage seems as antique as the bricks with which the Indianapolis Speedway was originally paved, though all but one yard at the start/finish line has long since been asphalted. Throughout the 1990s, Indiana's manufacturing economy was humming and becoming increasingly high-skill, high-employment and high-tech. The Speedway is literally at the center of American manufacturing: Almost precisely half the country's manufacturing jobs are east of Indiana and the other half west, almost half are north and half south. Indiana itself

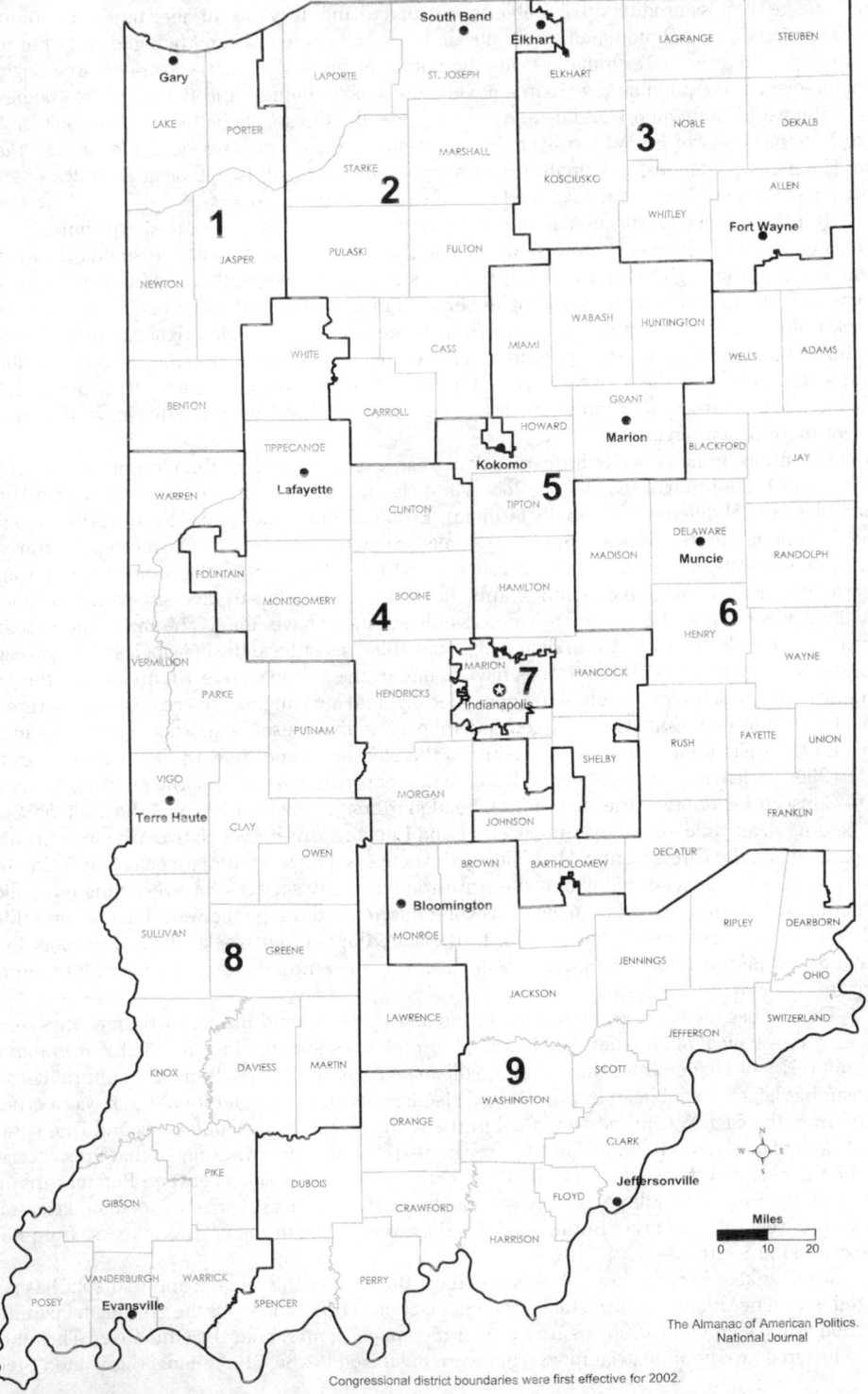

Congressional district boundaries were first effective for 2002.

has the nation's second-highest percentage of workers in manufacturing and is number one in percentage of gross product attributable to manufacturing. It is the number one steel producer with its giant, heavily automated steel mills on the south shore of Lake Michigan and mini-mills scattered across the state. Indiana leads the nation in making elevators, refrigerators, engines, engine-electrical equipment, recreational vehicles, mobile homes, and truck and bus bodies. It gave the world canned pork and beans, tomato juice, the Coca-Cola bottle and Alka-Seltzer. Nor are Indiana's days of innovation over. Just as it has attracted new teams and events to Indianapolis's sports facilities, the small factories set amidst farm landscape or at the edge of small cities have become centers of advanced manufacturing innovation.

But there is one downside to a manufacturing economy: It is subject to sharp contraction in times of recession. The economic slowdown of 2000–02 was not by historic standards a major one. But it was enough to bring to a halt Indiana's growth. Between 2000 and 2002, the state lost some 180,000 jobs; its relative standing in personal income declined and it had large numbers of bankruptcies and foreclosures. State government revenue fell well below expectations; Governor Frank O'Bannon, who earned popularity as a tax-cutter, felt obliged to raise the cigarette, gambling and sales taxes. And the long-term trajectory of the state is unclear. Some of its political and business leaders worry that too many of its high school and college graduates leave Indiana for larger metropolitan areas.

Culturally, Indiana is like an earlier America; it retains some of the old norms that in the 1920s and 1930s brought sociologists Robert and Helen Lynd in their search for the typical American place to "Middletown" (actually Muncie). Ethnically, Indiana seems like an earlier America too: Except for the steel area around Gary—really an extension of the Chicago metropolitan area—Indiana has relatively few descendants from the 1840–1924 wave of immigration and only a small flow of recent Hispanic or Asian immigrants. But it does have religious diversity, with 109 denominations according to the Glenmary Center; only six states have more. The major metropolitan area, Indianapolis, now has 1.5 million people but still doesn't have the big singles and gay neighborhoods of larger cities. What it does have is one of the nation's largest foundations, the Lilly Endowment (which gives much of its money locally) and a willingness to create and innovate. In the 1980s, the Lilly Endowment urged Indianapolis to make itself a sports center. The city attracted the Colts professional football team to the Hoosier Dome (now the RCA Dome). In the late 1990s, Indianapolis's downtown filled with new construction projects: the pro basketball Pacers' Conseco Fieldhouse, the new NCAA headquarters, a conservatory and the Indiana State Museum. Meanwhile, the Convention Center and Eiteljorg Museum of Native American Art were expanded and the Circle Center Mall filled with shoppers. Longtime Indianapolis Mayor Stephen Goldsmith, a Republican, pioneered the privatization of city services for everything but police, fire and zoning. He reduced costs by nearly one-quarter and the public work force by one-third, while taxes were cut some $240 million. In the state Capitol four blocks away, Governors Evan Bayh and O'Bannon, both Democrats, also cut taxes. Government has been not a drain on the private economy, but a booster.

The last decade has seen innovation in Indiana's government. But its partisan politics sometimes seems typical of an older America, with preferences anchored in the Civil War era and a small overlay of change from the union-organizing days of the 1930s. Indiana's cultural conservatism has kept it Republican in presidential elections for the last generation, but it was a crucial state from the Civil War to the New Deal in the struggles between Republicans and Democrats. Party identification was handed down like religious affiliation—the Lynds noted that Presbyterians had little to do with Methodists, but that was nothing next to divisions between Republicans and Democrats—in a state still peopled largely by descendants of its original settlers, Yankees from Ohio and New England and "Butternuts" (as they were called in the Civil War years) from Kentucky and the South.

Most Yankees became Republicans and most Butternuts Democrats, and that split has persisted over generations and can still be seen in election returns today. Of the 26 Indiana counties carried by Bill Clinton in 1996, 18 are south of Indianapolis, most near the Ohio River. The others are clustered around industrial towns that were organized by the CIO unions, the United Steelworkers and the United Auto Workers, in the 1930s. In the 1920s the Lynds, liberal academics influenced by Marx's idea that political beliefs were determined by economic interests, were puzzled why the factory workers in "Middletown" didn't vote against the bosses; in the 1930s and since in some parts of industrial Indiana they have. But this is not so in other cities, including Indianapolis, which is by far the largest. Why not? One answer is that cultural identity and personal values tend to be permanent and so have usually been the critical determinants of political allegiance in an America where economic status can often be changeable. Another is that the economic interests of Indiana's high-skill workers and its small and large factory owners are not nearly as adversarial as academics and Washington liberals suppose.

Indiana's partisan allegiances have remained remarkably steady. There is an historic base here large enough to allow Democrats to win: Evan Bayh broke a 20-year Republican hold on the governorship in 1988, with his strongest support from southern Indiana and the far northwest industrial zone. His successor, Democrat O'Bannon—from a Butternut town near the Ohio River—with similar moderate policies beat Indianapolis' Goldsmith 52%–47% in 1996 and Congressman David McIntosh by 57%–42% in 2000, with voting patterns much the same as in 1988. Some Hoosier politicians have been able to transcend the ancient allegiances. Richard Lugar, the only five-term senator in Indiana's history, was re-elected by 2–1 margins in 1988, 1994 and 2000; Bayh was re-elected governor in 1992 and won election to the Senate in 1998 by margins nearly as large.

The People		Race/Ethnic Origin			Military veterans: 590,476 (13.1%)	
Pop. 2000:	6,080,485	5,219,373	85.8%	White	WWII: 19.7%	Korea: 13.7%
Pop. 1990:	5,544,159	505,462	8.3%	Black	Vietnam: 31.3%	Gulf War: 9.3%
Change 1990–2000:	Up 9.7%	58,424	1.0%	Asian	**Most populous cities:**	
Change 1980–1990:	Up 1.0%	13,654	0.2%	Native Am.	1. Indianapolis	781,870
% of U.S. total:	2.2%	1,573	0.0%	Hawaiian	2. Fort Wayne	205,727
Pop. rank:	14th of 50	61,115	1.0%	Two+ races	3. Evansville	121,582
Area size:	36,418 sq. mi.	6,348	0.1%	Other	4. South Bend	107,789
State Native:	69.3%	214,536	3.5%	Hisp. Origin	5. Gary	102,746
Non-citizen:	1.9%	**Ancestry**			Urban population: 70.8%	
Language		German: 17.6%		USA: 9.3%	Rural population: 29.2%	
English: 91.7%	Spanish: 4.1%	Irish: 8.4%		English: 6.9%		
Other Eur.: 3.1%		Polish: 2.3%				

Education		Work Sector		General Assembly	
H.S. Grad:	82.1%	Private: 83.4%	Govt: 10.9%	Senate	32 R 18 D
College Grad:	19.4%	Self: 5.4%	Family: 0.3%	House	51 D 49 R
Industry		Unemployment: 4.9%		Legislative Term Limits: No	
Agri: 1.4%	Con: 6.6%	**Household Income**		**Registered Voters**	
Fin: 5.7%	Info: 2.1%	<15k: 14.3%	15-35k: 27.2%	No party registration	
Mfg: 28.0%	Prof: 25.6%	35-50k: 17.9%	50-100k: 31.5%		
Public: 3.3%	Trade: 15.2%	100-150k: 6.3%	>150k: 2.8%		
Other: 12.0%		Median: $41,567			
Occupation		Poverty status: 9.5%			
Blue collar: 31.4%	White collar: 54.0%	**Home Value**			
Gray collar: 14.6%		<50k: 15.7% 50-100k: 40.6% 100-200k: 34.5% 200-300k: 6.1%			
		300-500k: 2.2% >500k: 0.9% Median: $92,500			

Presidential politics   Indiana has not voted for a Democratic presidential candidate since 1964. It has been close, though not suspenseful, only in 1976, when Gerald Ford beat Jimmy Carter here by 53%–46%, and in 1996, when Bob Dole beat Bill Clinton 47%–42%. In 2000, George W. Bush won 57%–41%; he lost only 6 of 92 counties and—a bad sign for Democrats— carried voters under 30 by 64%–34%. So Indiana sees little of presidential candidates in election year autumns. Nor does it see much of them in spring or summer: Indiana's May presidential primary has not been influential since 1968. Only if Evan Bayh is on the Democratic ticket is Indiana likely to be seriously contested in 2004.

2000 Presidential Vote		
Bush (R)	1,245,836	(57%)
Gore (D)	901,980	(41%)
Other	51,489	(2%)

2000 Republican Presidential Primary		
Bush (R)	330,095	(81%)
McCain (R)	76,569	(19%)

2000 Democratic Presidential Primary		
Gore (D)	219,604	(75%)
Bradley (D)	64,339	(22%)
LaRouche (D)	9,229	(3%)

1996 Presidential Vote		
Dole (R)	1,006,632	(47%)
Clinton (D)	887,454	(42%)
Perot (I)	224,280	(11%)

Congressional districting   Indiana lost one congressional district in the 2000 Census, and that required significant changes in

108th Congress Lineup
6 R   3 D

107th Congress Lineup
6 R   4 D

district lines that had stayed pretty much the same for 20 years. In charge were Democrats, who had a majority in the state House and the governorship, though Republicans had a majority in the state Senate; Indiana law provides that if the House and Senate cannot agree, the decision goes to a five-member commission, with the tie-breaking member appointed by the governor. In May 2001, the commission adopted a plan largely identical to that passed by the state House. Democrats hoped to retain the four seats they held and improve their chances in at least one more. Eliminated was the central Indiana district represented by Republican Steve Buyer; his home county was placed in the new 4th District that contained no other county from his old 5th District. Republican freshman Brian Kerns, whose home county was placed in the new 8th District (most of which had been represented by Republican John Hostettler), moved to the 4th and ran in the primary against Buyer, which Buyer won. Democrats had to weaken two of their incumbents, because their inner city bases in Gary and Indianapolis had lost population and almost all the adjacent territory that could be added was heavily Republican. Democrats did improve their chances in the new 2d District, though its incumbent, Democrat Tim Roemer, had already announced he would not run again. But Republican Chris Chocola, who had held Roemer to a 52%–47% win in 2000, ran again and beat former Congresswoman Jill Long Thompson. The states' two southernmost districts remain potentially marginal; the two incumbents, Hostettler and Democrat Baron Hill, were each reelected by a 51%–46% margin.

Governor

Frank O'Bannon (D)

Elected 1996, term expires Jan. 2005, 2d term; b. Jan. 30, 1930, Louisville, KY; home, Indianapolis; IN U., B.A. 1952, J.D. 1957; Methodist; married (Judy).

Military Career: Air Force, 1952–54.

Elected Office: IN Senate, 1971–88; IN Lt. Gov., 1989–96.

Professional Career: Practicing atty., 1957–88; Dir. & Chmn., O'Bannon Publishing Co., 1970–88.

Office: 206 State House, Indianapolis, 46204, 317-232-4567; Fax: 317-232-3443; Web site: www.in.gov/gov.

Election Results

2000 general	Frank O'Bannon (D)	1,232,525	(57%)
	David McIntosh (R)	908,285	(42%)
	Other	38,458	(1%)
2000 primary	Frank O'Bannon (D)	unopposed	
1996 general	Frank O'Bannon (D)	1,087,128	(52%)
	Stephen Goldsmith (R)	986,982	(47%)
	Other	35,937	(2%)

Frank O'Bannon, elected governor in 1996, grew up in the old town of Corydon, near the Ohio River, went to Indiana University, served in the Air Force, and then went to law school. He returned to Corydon, practiced law and published weekly newspapers. In 1970, at 40, he was elected to the state Senate from an Ohio River district; from 1979 he was Democratic floor leader. In 1988, he was elected as Evan Bayh's lieutenant governor and was given serious responsibilities as head of the state departments of Agriculture and Commerce. In 1996, Bayh retired after two terms and O'Bannon ran. The early favorite was Republican Mayor Stephen Goldsmith of Indianapolis, one of the nation's leading innovators in privatizing government and cutting spending and taxes. But Goldsmith's call for startling change did not go over as well as O'Bannon's pledge, as a "compassionate conservative," to continue Bayh's highly popular policies at a time when most voters believed Indiana was moving in the right direction. O'Bannon won 52%–47%, carrying Indianapolis.

In his first years as governor O'Bannon had the happy task of dealing with budget surpluses generated by a booming economy. In four years he produced $1.5 billion in tax cuts and set up a new community college system; the welfare rolls continued to fall, though more slowly. He has had some frustrations. He was accused of mismanagement in handling a fish kill in the White River. His campaign finance reform plan was beaten by labor Democrats in 1997, and the Democratic teachers' unions in 1998 opposed his education proposals. In 1999, the Republican state Senate rejected his proposal for full-day kindergarten. But Indiana does have testing, and scores have improved. In 2000, he signed a bill to use tobacco settlement money for anti-smoking measures and a prescription drug benefit for low-income seniors. He signed another bill to allow the Ten Commandments to be displayed in schools, courts and other public buildings. When gas prices spiked in June 2000, O'Bannon declared two 60-day moratoriums on the state gas tax, the first governor to do so. He used some of the surplus for a property tax credit for homeowners, more highway spending and shoring up pension funds. Overall, it was a popular record. In 2000, he was opposed by Republican Congressman David McIntosh. McIntosh's campaign centerpiece was a 25% property tax cut, to be paid for by holding spending increases to inflation levels except for education and law enforcement; he promised not to run for reelection if he failed to put it into effect. But O'Bannon's consensus politics was more appealing to voters than McIntosh's conservatism, and O'Bannon 57%–42%, carrying all but 15 heavily Republican counties.

O'Bannon faced more problems in his second term. As revenues came in lower than expected, O'Bannon ordered large cuts in Medicaid and cut 700 government jobs. In March 2002, he cut off funding for the 21st Century Research and Development Fund he had created in 1999 that awarded $50 million in grants for high-tech projects. In June 2002, he got the legislature to raise the taxes on cigarettes and riverboat casinos. Facing a court decision that would increase property taxes, he convinced the legislature to raise the sales tax to finance a 25% property tax cut. Still, deficits loomed. In August 2002, O'Bannon was embarrassed when the *Indianapolis Star* revealed that his aides had done the background check on a man hired to a top position in the Public Employees' Retirement Fund, with access to 20,000 employees' names and Social Security numbers, and had failed to find out that he had a criminal record for identity theft. O'Bannon's long-high job ratings turned negative. In early December 2002, O'Bannon and Lieutenant Governor Joe Kernan unveiled an 10-year, $1.25 billion Energize Indiana plan, to be funded by bonds secured by the state's future tobacco settlement payments, to encourage the creation of high-wage jobs by improving education, building university research facilities and investing in entrepreneurial companies.

A few days later Kernan—charming, energetic, a pilot in Vietnam and prisoner of war—

stunned the Hoosier political world when he announced that he would not run for governor. He was widely assumed to be the sure Democratic nominee and, despite O'Bannon's recent poor ratings, to have an excellent chance to win. Two other leading Democrats—Indianapolis Mayor Bart Peterson and outgoing Congressman Tim Roemer—said they wouldn't run either. Afterwards, Democrats waited on Senator Evan Bayh. Widely popular, he obviously could have had the nomination if he wanted it, though he would have had to give up his Senate seat to run. Bayh's spokesman said it was "unlikely" he would run, but he refused to say no. In January 2003, however, Bayh ended the speculation by announcing he would not run. By May 2003, former state and national Democratic Chairman Joe Andrew and state Senator Vi Simpson had announced their candidacies.

Republicans, meanwhile, waited on the decision of one man. Several little known candidates were already running—conservative activist Eric Miller, state Senators Luke Kenley and Murray Clark, Petersburg Mayor Randy Harris—and a few days after Kernan bowed out, David McIntosh announced he was running again. But many were urging federal Office of Management and Budget Director and former Lilly Endowment head Mitch Daniels to run. In June 2003, Daniels resigned and filed preliminary campaign committee papers with the state Election Division; Clark then dropped out of the race and announced his support for Daniels.

Senior Senator

Richard Lugar (R)

Elected 1976, seat up 2006, 5th term; b. Apr. 4, 1932, Indianapolis; home, Indianapolis; Denison U., B.A. 1954, Rhodes Scholar, Oxford U., M.A. 1956; Methodist; married (Charlene).

Military Career: Navy, 1957–60.

Elected Office: Indianapolis Bd. of Schl. Commissioners, 1964–67; Indianapolis Mayor, 1968–75.

Professional Career: Mgr., family farm; V.P. & Treas., Thomas L. Green & Co., 1960–67; Prof., U. of Indianapolis, 1976.

DC Office: 306 HSOB, 20510, 202-224-4814; Fax: 202-228-0360; Web site: lugar.senate.gov.

State Offices: Evansville, 812-465-6313; Ft. Wayne, 260-422-1505; Indianapolis, 317-226-5555; Jeffersonville, 812-288-3377; Valparaiso, 219-548-8035.

Committees: *Agriculture, Nutrition & Forestry*: Forestry, Conservation & Rural Revitalization; Research, Nutrition & General Legislation. *Foreign Relations* (Chmn.).

Group Ratings

	ADA	ACLU	AFS	LCV	CON	ITIC	NTU	COC	ACU	NTLC	CHC
2002	5	0	13	12	74	100	70	95	90	94	—
2001	15	—	0	13	—	—	81	100	92	—	80

National Journal Ratings

	2001 LIB	—	2001 CONS		2002 LIB	—	2002 CONS
Economic	26%	—	73%		35%	—	64%
Social	22%	—	73%		0%	—	62%
Foreign	7%	—	72%		0%	—	76%

Key Votes of the 107th Congress

1. Approve Bush Tax Cuts	Y	5. Confirm Ashcroft as AG	Y
2. Expand Patients' Rights	N	6. Bar Gays in the Boy Scouts	Y
3. Campaign Finance Reform	Y	7. $ for Hate Crime Prosecution	N
4. Permit ANWR Development	Y	8. Overseas Military Abortions	N

9. Bar Coop. with Intl. Court	Y
10. Trade Promotion Authority	Y
11. Authorize Force in Iraq	Y
12. Homeland Sec. Dept. Union	N

Election Results

2000 general	Richard Lugar (R)	1,427,944	(67%)	($4,251,603)
	David L. Johnson (D)	683,273	(32%)	($1,179,029)
	Other	33,992	(1%)	
2000 primary	Richard Lugar (R)	unopposed		
1994 general	Richard Lugar (R)	1,039,625	(67%)	($4,688,326)
	James Jontz (D)	470,799	(31%)	($472,788)
	Other	33,144	(2%)	

Prior Winning Percentages: 1988 (68%); 1982 (54%); 1976 (59%)

Richard Lugar, still running 5K races at the annual Dick Lugar Run and Walk in Indianapolis, has a career in public life going back to the late 1950s, when as a young Navy officer he prepared intelligence briefings for Chief of Naval Operations Arleigh Burke and briefed President Eisenhower over closed-circuit television. Now he is the first Indiana senator ever elected to a fourth or fifth term and a powerful voice on foreign policy. Lugar grew up in Indianapolis, near his family's farm and food machinery firm, which was founded in 1893. He was an Eagle Scout, straight-A student and Rhodes scholar. After the service Lugar returned to the family business, was elected to the school board in 1964, then was elected mayor of Indianapolis in 1967, at 35. As mayor, he consolidated the city and county into Unigov, which brought in tax resources and suburban voters, keeping the city both solvent and Republican (until 1999, when a Democrat was finally elected mayor). In the late 1960s, Lugar bucked fashion and called for fewer rather than more federal programs and became known as Richard Nixon's favorite mayor. This was not a political asset in 1974, when Lugar ran against Senator Birch Bayh, father of his current junior colleague, and lost 51%–46%. But in the more favorable climate of 1976 and against a weaker Democratic incumbent, Vance Hartke, Lugar won 59%–40%.

Throughout his public life, Lugar's strength has been that he has followed where his stubborn convictions and his considerable intellect led, regardless of political risk or reward: He has plenty of accomplishments but also some disappointments to show for it. His lone course has served him well in Indiana, but has had mixed results in the Senate and in the national arena. He is a conservative on some, but not all, of the hot-button issues of today's conservative activists; he is solidly anti-abortion but voted for background checks at gun shows in 1999. He was an internationalist even in the mid-1990s when the president's attention to foreign issues was episodic and some Republicans were opposing Bill Clinton's foreign interventions. Lugar started off in the Senate leading the 1978 filibuster to defeat the AFL-CIO's labor law reform bill, although unions were then big in Indiana. He strongly supported NAFTA in 1993, in a Midwest manufacturing state where many thought foreigners were taking their jobs. He ran for president in 1996 on his own platform and without any concessions to the political shorthand or the TV sensibility of the day, but his candidacy made little impact. Lugar based his campaign on "nuclear security and fiscal sanity"—deterring nuclear terrorism and backing a 17% national sales tax. But he got little coverage, and finished 7th in Iowa and 5th in New Hampshire and soon left the race.

Lugar's great interest is foreign policy. In January 2003, he became chairman of the Foreign Relations Committee, a post he also held from January 1985 to January 1987. Then he quickly took command over a committee sharply divided between Jesse Helms and liberal Democrats. Lugar was in the middle, backing Contra aid and favoring sanctions on South Africa. He took the lead on the Philippines, quickly concluding that Ferdinand Marcos's 1986 election "victory" over Corazon Aquino was fraudulent and, at a decisive point, called on Marcos to leave office. Helms had allowed him to become chairman in 1985, despite his lower seniority, because of a campaign promise in 1984 to take the chairmanship of the Agriculture Committee. But after Republicans lost their Senate majority in 1986, Helms said he was no longer bound by his promise and invoked seniority; Lugar took the issue to the Republican Conference, but lost a vote there. So Helms was ranking minority member from 1987 to 1995 and 2001 to 2003 and chairman from 1995 to 2001, while Lugar waited. Helms left Lugar off conference committees and seldom communicated with Lugar; Lugar led the fight to ratify the Chemical Weapons Agreement over Helms' opposition in April 1997, and won. Lugar has favored the arms control treaties about which many conservatives have been skeptical—INF in 1988, START I in 1992, START II in 1996. He supported NATO expansion and U.S. payment of U.N. dues. But in October 1999, he joined other Republicans in voting against the Comprehensive Test Ban Treaty, arguing that the U.S. must keep testing to maintain its nuclear arsenal.

His greatest achievement was passage in 1991 of the Nunn-Lugar Cooperative Threats Reduction program to pay Russia, Ukraine, Belarus and Kazakhstan to dismantle and destroy their nuclear weapons and some chemical and biological weapons as well, to prevent them from falling into the hands of hostile powers or terrorists. Lugar was frustrated in 2001 and 2002 when State Department officials held up some Nunn-Lugar spending because they refused to certify that Russia was being open about its biological weapons; as part of his negotiations with the administration on the Iraq war resolution, Nunn got a provision in the defense authorization bill suspending the certification requirement for three years. Lugar has gotten some notice for this work—he and Nunn have been nominated for the Nobel Peace Prize and an Indianapolis TV station filmed a documentary of him inspecting weapons in Russia—but probably not enough. After September 11, he has called for a Nunn-Lugar approach to prevent chemical and biological weapons throughout the world from falling into the hands of terrorists. "Every nation that has weapons and materials of mass destruction must account for what it has, safely secure what it has (spending its own money or obtaining international technical and financial resources to do so) and pledge that no other nation, cell or cause will be allowed access or use." This is one of his first priorities as Foreign Relations chairman.

In the 1990s, Lugar kept a vigilant eye on Iraq. Starting in August 1990, he called for an end to Saddam Hussein's regime and said that Saddam might have to be killed and U.S. ground troops needed to accomplish that. But he has not necessarily been a team player for the Bush administration. In summer 2002, he and then-Chairman Joseph Biden conducted hearings on Iraq to which the administration declined to send witnesses. In September 2002 he and Biden, unhappy with the White House's broad resolution authorizing military action in Iraq, drafted their own resolution, which limited the authorization geographically and required the administration either to obtain a U.N. resolution or to certify to Congress that its efforts at the U.N. had failed. This was not what Bush wanted, and in early October he circumvented the committee and got agreement on a resolution with geographical limits with House Minority Leader Dick Gephardt and Democratic Senators Joe Lieberman and Evan Bayh. Secretary of State Colin Powell told Lugar that his draft would weaken his negotiating position at the U.N., and Lugar dropped his separate resolution; the agreement on Nunn-Lugar evidently came at this time.

As chairman, Lugar seemed likely to have a similar arms-length relationship with the administration, and he seems much more comfortable with positions taken by Powell than with those taken by Defense Secretary Donald Rumsfeld (whom he dealt with when Rumsfeld was head of the federal poverty program and he was mayor of Indianapolis). "I don't want to alarm the Republican right," said Biden in late 2001, "but there is very little that Dick Lugar and I disagree on. He is the most informed Republican in Congress on foreign affairs, and if I can't be chairman there is no one who I would rather have be chairman." An anonymous conservative took another view: "Lugar will be dreadful. He is a conventionally minded apparatchik of the establishment." Lugar planned to start off as chairman in 2003, as he did in 1985, with three months of wide-ranging hearings on foreign policy problems. But there may come points of conflict. Lugar complained in late 2002 that he had not been briefed on the administration's plans for postwar Iraq. After North Korea announced it had a nuclear bomb, Lugar said the administration should keep up a dialogue with the North Koreans, while Powell was saying just the opposite. He also argued that the administration should engage with the government of Iran. There may be disagreement on Latin America as well: Lugar opposed the appointment of Otto Reich as assistant secretary for Latin America.

To become chairman of Foreign Relations, Lugar gave up the chairmanship of Agriculture, which he had held from 1995 to 2001. He likes to point out that he was the only working farmer on the committee—his 604 acres, thanks to Unigov, is inside the city of Indianapolis—and he played a key role in the 1996 passage of the Freedom to Farm Act, which purported to phase out over seven years the farm subsidies of which he had long been a critic. But low crop prices starting in 1998 resulted in disaster relief payments that kept in place something very much like the old subsidy system. In October 2001 he opposed the House farm bill with its big increases for farmers of historically subsidized crops, and proposed his own bill, guaranteeing up to 80% of income of qualified farmers, but at far less cost. Lugar's argument against traditional farm policy is intellectually strong. "American agricultural policy distorts food prices, frustrates innovatio, limits product diversity and subsidizes a select group of farmers at enormous public cost. Its inherent protectionist qualities confound American efforts to reduce protectionism abroad and gain access to new markets." But with key Senate races in states with historically subsidized farmers, the argument was politically very weak in spring 2002, when the Senate passed a farm bill similar to the House's and George W. Bush signed it. In 2003, Lugar left the chairmanship to Thad Cochran of Mississippi, whose cotton farmers were well taken care of in the 2002 bill and who supports traditional farm legislation.

Lugar has used his Agriculture seat for other causes. With Indianapolis Congresswoman Julia Carson, he passed in May 2000 a law allowing mothers to enroll in the CHIPS health program when they sign up for Women with Infant Children funds. With Vermont Senator Patrick Leahy, he fought in fall 2000 to increase the deduction for donations of food by businesses and farmers to organizations that feed the hungry. He and Ohio Rep. John Boehner sponsored a law to allow farmers to income-average and fully deduct health insurance. Other Lugar causes include opposition to gambling (he co-sponsored the National Gambling Impact Study Commission), free trade, allowing future trading on individual stocks, and deregulating the derivatives markets. On local matters, he wrote on personal stationery a letter opposing a route for I-69 that would go across Mann Road near his farm. "I believe this would be a tragic public policy and environmental error."

In Indiana, Lugar has remained vastly popular. His most recent victory margins have been 68%–32% in 1988, 67%–31% in 1994 and 67%–32% in 2000—pretty monotonous. The last was won against a respectable opponent, who raised little money; Lugar nevertheless agreed to meet in three Lincoln-Douglas style debates.

Junior Senator

Evan Bayh (D)

Elected 1998, seat up 2004, 1st term; b. Dec. 26, 1955, Shirkieville; home, Indianapolis; Indiana U., B.S. 1978, U. of VA, J.D. 1981; Episcopalian; married (Susan).

Elected Office: IN Secy. of State, 1986–88; IN Gov., 1986–96.

Professional Career: Practicing atty., 1981–86, 1997–98; Visiting Prof., Indiana U., 1997–98.

DC Office: 463 RSOB, 20510, 202-224-5623; Fax: 202-228-1377; Web site: bayh.senate.gov.

State Offices: Evansville, 812-465-6500; Fort Wayne, 260-426-3151; Hammond, 219-852-2763; Indianapolis, 317-554-0750; Jeffersonville, 812-218-2317; South Bend, 574-236-8302.

Committees: *Aging (Special). Armed Services*: Airland; Emerging Threats & Capabilities; Readiness & Management Support. *Banking, Housing & Urban Affairs*: Financial Institutions; International Trade & Finance (RMM); Securities & Investment. *Energy & Natural Resources*: Energy; National Parks; Public Lands & Forests. *Intelligence (Select). Small Business & Entrepreneurship.*

Group Ratings

	ADA	ACLU	AFS	LCV	CON	ITIC	NTU	COC	ACU	NTLC	CHC
2002	70	60	75	41	88	75	31	65	30	21	—
2001	100	—	92	88	—	—	20	50	32	—	0

National Journal Ratings

	2001 LIB	—	2001 CONS		2002 LIB	—	2002 CONS
Economic	61%	—	37%		58%	—	41%
Social	60%	—	36%		56%	—	38%
Foreign	51%	—	43%		59%	—	38%

Key Votes of the 107th Congress

1. Approve Bush Tax Cuts	N	5. Confirm Ashcroft as AG	N	9. Bar Coop. with Intl. Court	Y
2. Expand Patients' Rights	Y	6. Bar Gays in the Boy Scouts	N	10. Trade Promotion Authority	Y
3. Campaign Finance Reform	Y	7. $ for Hate Crime Prosecution	Y	11. Authorize Force in Iraq	Y
4. Permit ANWR Development	N	8. Overseas Military Abortions	Y	12. Homeland Sec. Dept. Union	Y

Election Results

1998 general	Evan Bayh (D)	1,012,244	(64%)	($3,914,375)
	Paul Helmke (R)	552,732	(35%)	($642,784)
	Other	23,641	(1%)	
1998 primary	Evan Bayh (D)	unopposed		
1992 general	Daniel R. Coats (R)	1,267,972	(57%)	($3,802,077)
	Joseph H. Hogsett (D)	900,148	(41%)	($1,584,173)
	Other	43,306	(2%)	

Evan Bayh (pronounced *BY*) was elected in 1998 to the Senate seat his father Birch Bayh first won in 1962 when Evan was just 6. He grew up mostly in Washington, graduated from Indiana University and the University of Virginia Law School, then returned to Indiana to practice law—and politics. His father, a charismatic candidate, beat three serious opponents: Incumbent Senator Homer Capehart in 1962, later-Deputy Attorney General William Ruckelshaus in 1968, and future Senator Richard Lugar in 1974. But in 1980, with Evan helping run the campaign, he lost to Dan Quayle. In 1986, at 30, Evan Bayh was elected secretary of state, an office that is often a steppingstone. In 1988, at 32, he ran for governor. Republicans had controlled the office, and most of Indiana state government, for 20 years. However, their smoothly run machine had grown sluggish: The Republican nominee promised innovation, but Bayh was a young and fresh face. Birch Bayh had had a mostly liberal voting record in the Senate; Evan Bayh has been one of the most conservative Democrats. He calls himself "pragmatic" and says he wants to find "the sensible center." As governor, he balanced the budget, cut taxes and piled up a $1.6 billion budget surplus. He trimmed a deficit in state pension plans and sliced Medicaid spending. He claimed credit for the creation of 350,000 jobs, as Indiana's manufacturing economy revived. He did less to reform education and other government services, but he was immensely popular when he left office.

It was widely expected that Bayh would run for the Senate in 1998, and in December 1996, incumbent Republican Dan Coats announced he would not run for reelection; he is now George W. Bush's Ambassador to Germany. Bayh's 1998 opponent was Fort Wayne Mayor Paul Helmke, the moderate in the field, who had backed tax increases in Fort Wayne and who even had kind words for the Clintons, whom he had known since law school. He narrowly won the primary with 35% against two more conservative candidates. Helmke argued that Bayh "still comes across a little the empty suit." But Bayh's platform—a balanced budget, saving Social Security, raising education standards and a "fairer, flatter" tax—preempted the Hoosier political center. He ran ads showing his wife extolling his accomplishments, saying he "cracked down on deadbeat dads, sponsored Indiana's fatherhood initiative . . . worked to make our schools safer and drug-free and to move people from welfare to work." Bayh won 64%–35%, carrying 88 of 92 counties, although it is a victory that probably never would have happened if Birch Bayh had not beaten Homer Capehart by 10,000 votes 36 years before—one election can make a big difference.

In the Senate, Bayh has pursued the issues he campaigned on. He managed to irritate some Democratic constituency groups, voting reluctantly for PNTR for China in 2000 and voting to ban partial-birth abortions in 1999; he says he opposes abortion personally, but in most instances doesn't want to impose his religious beliefs on others; as governor, he vetoed an 18-hour waiting period. He was one of two Democrats and one of only 21 senators to vote against allowing the importing of foreign price-controlled prescription drugs in July 2000. This was portrayed as truckling to Eli Lilly, one of Indiana's biggest employers and on whose board Bayh served in 1997–98, but his stand was vindicated when HHS Secretary Donna Shalala declined to enforce the law later in the year. His first major bill was passed in November 2000, a measure to protect senior citizens from fraud.

In May 2000, Bayh and Connecticut Senator Joe Lieberman sponsored a revision of the basic federal aid to education act, which would increase spending by $35 billion over five years, target poor-performing school districts, foster English proficiency among immigrants, promote public school choice and demand accountability of teachers and students. Many of these measures became part of the Bush education bill, for which Bush gave Bayh some of the credit. Bayh has taken other stands favorable to Bush. He voted against the Bush tax cut and has come out for individual investment accounts as part of Social Security. But he voted against the confirmation of Attorney General John Ashcroft and criticized the Bush energy package. After September 11, he co-sponsored with Arizona Senator John McCain the Call to Service Act that would expand AmeriCorps support from 40,000 to 250,000 volunteers. Since August 2000, he has been chairman of the moderate Democratic Leadership Council, which helped foster the national career of Bill Clinton and which has advanced many innovative policies. "There's a whole cluster of cultural issues or values issues on which we need to make sure that people in Middle America—Iowa, Indiana, the South, the Plains—understand that we are not cultural elitists," Bayh said in a speech in Iowa.

Bayh serves on the Intelligence Committee and has backed the Bush administration in the war on terrorism. After September 11 he said that Congress should "think carefully about a more proactive response to terrorism. We should think carefully about some of the prohibitions that have been put in place the last 30 years." Well into 2002, he opposed the idea of an independent commission to examine what happened before September 11. "The problem was that we couldn't connect the dots because the dots weren't all on the same page. The FBI had some dots, the CIA had some dots, foreign intelligence services had some dots." With Kansas Senator Sam Brownback, he sponsored a bill to cut off aid to countries that permit "state-sponsored" hate propaganda and don't share intelligence on terror. He has called for funding for state stockpiles of drugs that may be needed in the event of a bioterrorism attack. He was one of the Democrats who early on indicated he would support a resolution authorizing military force in Iraq.

Birch Bayh ran for president in 1976 and Evan Bayh has often been mentioned as a candidate for national office. In July 2000, he was on Al Gore's short list of presidential possibilities. But leaders of feminist organizations opposed him because of his vote for a partial-birth abortion ban. In June 2001, he announced he wouldn't run for president in 2004; it would keep him away too much from his young children. But a vice presidential run, which would take only three months, was something else: "Well, that's another issue. That's completely up to whoever the party's nominee is, and only time will tell with regard to that." In late 2002, he seemed sure to run for reelection in 2004. Few Republicans seemed interested in running; names mentioned included Helmke and philanthropist Crystal DeHaan. But Indiana's political landscape changed in December 2002, when Lieutenant Governor Joe Kernan shocked Indiana Democrats by announcing he wouldn't run for governor in 2004. State Democrats immediately looked to Bayh; Bayh's spokesman said it was "unlikely" he would run, but Bayh refused to say no. In January 2003, though, Bayh announced he would not seek the governorship. "To both serve in the Senate and simultaneously run for governor would not be responsible," he told *The Indianapolis Star*.

FIRST DISTRICT

Rep. Peter Visclosky (D)

Elected 1984, 10th term; b. Aug. 13, 1949, Gary; home, Merrillville; IN U. Northwest, B.S. 1970, U. of Notre Dame, J.D. 1973, Georgetown U., LL.M. 1982; Catholic; divorced.

Professional Career: Practicing atty., 1973–76, 1983–84; Aide, U.S. Rep. Adam Benjamin, 1976–82.

DC Office: 2313 RHOB 20515, 202-225-2461; Fax: 202-225-2493; Web site: www.house.gov/visclosky.

District Office: Merrillville, 219-795-1844.

Committees: *Appropriations* (8th of 29 D): Defense; Energy & Water Development (RMM).

Group Ratings

	ADA	ACLU	AFS	LCV	CON	ITIC	NTU	COC	ACU	NTLC	CHC
2002	90	79	100	50	55	25	20	35	12	0	0
2001	85	—	100	64	—	—	17	39	17	—	—

National Journal Ratings

	2001 LIB	—	2001 CONS		2002 LIB	—	2002 CONS
Economic		76%	—	25%	88%	—	10%
Social		70%	—	31%	74%	—	26%
Foreign		56%	—	41%	71%	—	29%

Key Votes of the 107th Congress

1. Approve Bush Tax Cuts	N	5. Faith-Based Charities	N
2. Limit Patients' Bill of Rights	N	6. Bar Gays in the Boy Scouts	N
3. Campaign Finance Reform	Y	7. Ban Partial-Birth Abortion	Y
4. Ban ANWR Development	Y	8. Arm Commercial Pilots	N

9. Trade Promotion Authority	N
10. Bar Funds for Intl. Court	Y
11. Authorize Force in Iraq	N
12. Deny Home. Sec. Dept. Union	N

Election Results

2002 general	Peter Visclosky (D)	90,443	(67%)	($755,668)
	Mark Leyva (R)	41,909	(31%)	($11,956)
	Other	2,759	(2%)	
2002 primary	Peter Visclosky (D)	57,099	(86%)	
	Ralph Spelbring (D)	9,621	(14%)	
2000 general	Peter Visclosky (D)	148,683	(72%)	($390,320)
	Jack Reynolds (R)	56,200	(27%)	($12,457)
	Other	2,907	(1%)	

Prior Winning Percentages: 1998 (73%); 1996 (69%); 1994 (56%); 1992 (69%); 1990 (66%); 1988 (77%); 1986 (73%); 1984 (71%)

The People		Race/Ethnic Origin	Ancestry	
Area size:	2,443 sq. mi.	69.8% White	German: 13.8%	Irish: 8.9%
Urban population:	87.0%	18.2% Black	Polish: 7.3%	
Rural population:	13.0%	0.8% Asian	**2000 Presidential Vote**	
Pop. 2000:	675,562	0.2% Native Am.	Gore (D) 141,163	(56%)
Median income:	$44,087	0.0% Hawaiian	Bush (R)..............104,917	(42%)
Poverty status:	10.5%	1.0% Two+ races	Other 4,759	(2%)
Military veterans:	13.4%	0.1% Other	**Cook Partisan Voting Index:** D + 7	
		10.0% Hispanic Origin		

Occupation	Blue collar: 31.2%	White collar: 53.1%	Gray collar: 15.7%

At the southernmost shore of Lake Michigan is a part of America made by steel. Here, in the northwest corner of Indiana, where the water highway of the Great Lakes comes closest to the rail highway of the transcontinental railroads, America's leading capitalists nearly a century ago recognized an ideal site for manufacturing steel. On empty sand dunes United States Steel, then the nation's largest corporation, founded Gary in 1906 and named it for the company's chairman, Chicago Judge Elbert Gary. For nearly 70 years the steel mills attracted a diverse work force, like Chicago and quite unlike the rest of Indiana: Irish, Poles, Czechs, Ukrainians and blacks from the American South. Politics here has always been turbulent, from the Communist-led long and unsuccessful steel strike of 1919 to the racially polarized politics of the 1960s and 1970s. The tone of public life—the clash between union stewards and management foremen, between blacks and eastern European ethnics, between the stalwarts of different factions vying for control of Gary's massive City Hall—was always abrasive, like the clash of steel on steel.

Steel brought sudden growth and sudden depression to northwest Indiana. The massive storefronts built on Gary's aptly named Broadway bear witness to the confidence and exuberance of the 1920s. But today they stand vacant—vandalized, whole blocks burned down—witness to steel layoffs and crime waves. The steel mills went cold during the Depression of the 1930s, but were thronged with workers during World War II, and in the years afterward their massiveness helped create the illusion that life in the steel towns of Gary, Hammond and East Chicago would go on forever just like it was in the 1950s. But technological advances inevitably replaced increasingly expensive workers with increasingly efficient machines. And the efforts to seal off the U.S. steel market from the world inevitably failed. The oil crunch of 1979 was the catalyst for change, reducing the demand for large-sized autos, the biggest customer for steel. Steel employed 70,000 workers in northwest Indiana in 1979, 35,000 a few years later, 23,000 in 2001. Obsolete mills were closed, old mills modernized and new ones built that cut the number of man-hours needed by two-thirds. Just-in-time methods were introduced, management and high-skill workers cooperated to engineer higher-quality, less expensive steel to meet customers' needs. For the last decade, Indiana has been the number one steel-producing state. But trouble has arisen again, as recession-stricken steel-producing countries—Russia, Japan and others—have sold steel at distress prices, and in March 2002, at the urging of steel producers, George W. Bush imposed tariffs on steel imports.

As the steel industry was changing, Gary was falling almost into ruins. As long ago as 1967, Gary elected a black mayor, Richard Hatcher, who was determined to use city government to cure poverty. But high crime rates produced a flight to the suburbs; for 9 of the past 10 years, Gary has ranked as the nation's murder capital. In 1995, majority-black Gary responded by electing a white Democrat mayor, Scott King. Despite some signs of revival the city's population fell another 12% in the 1990s, to 102,000, far below its historic peak of 170,000. In nearby Hammond, with many Hispanic immigrants, the population loss was much less. Most of northwest Indiana's people have long since scattered out from Gary to its Lake County suburbs and even beyond. Lake County has by far the largest percentage of minorities in Indiana; in 2000, its population was 25% black and 12% Hispanic.

Indiana's 1st Congressional District stretches from Gary and Hammond along the Lake Michigan shore, east almost to Michigan City. It includes Valparaiso, known locally as Valpo, notable for its annual Popcorn Festivals, honoring longtime resident and developer of 300 popcorn hybrids, Orville Redenbacher. The 2001 redistricting added Republican-leaning Newton, Jasper and Benton Counties south of Gary, but nearly three-quarters of the population is in Lake County. This remains the most Democratic district in Republican Indiana, as it has been since the United Steelworkers' organizing drives of the late 1930s.

The congressman from the 1st District is Pete Visclosky, a Democrat first elected in 1984. Visclosky grew up in northwest Indiana (his father was mayor of Gary in the early 1960s), went to college there and law school at Notre Dame, not far away. He practiced law, and then worked for six years for 1st District Congressman Adam Benjamin. Benjamin died suddenly in 1982 and Visclosky returned to Indiana. In 1984 he ran against Katie Hall, a black state senator who had been given the 1982 nomination—and thus the election, in this area—by Mayor Richard Hatcher, then district party chairman. But Hall was able to win only 33% of the 1984 primary vote; Visclosky had 34% and another white candidate 31%. Visclosky beat Hall again 57%–35% in 1986 and 51%–30% in 1990.

Visclosky has a fairly liberal voting record and concentrates much of his effort on projects to help the local economy, notably the steel industry. He has a solid pro-union voting record, as one might expect. He is a leader of the Congressional Steel Caucus and has been vigilant in monitoring surges in steel imports. In 1999, his bill to require the Commerce Department to limit imports to the average monthly levels of 1994–97 passed 289–141. Some may have supported the measure expecting (as indeed happened) that the Senate would take no action; critics charged it would raise steel prices and would save relatively few jobs. In October 2000, he called for an International Trade Commission investigation of steel imports and said the Clinton White House promise of a report the next spring—when a new administration would be in office—was insufficient. Later that month, he and Republican Rep. Ralph Regula inserted an amendment to the State-Commerce-Justice appropriation expanding Commerce's monthly steel import report by requiring breakdowns of carbon, alloy and stainless steel import levels. When George W. Bush was elected with critical help from steel-producing areas, Visclosky had greater leverage, and in March 2002, Bush delivered at least some of what they sought: Tariffs on some imports over the next three years. Bush's decision rankled free traders and steel users domestically and trading partners worldwide. Visclosky, meanwhile, was working for other federal assistance, health benefits for unemployed and retired workers whose steel companies were unable to pay them.

As ranking Democrat on the Appropriations Subcommittee on Energy and Water Development, Visclosky has secured large federal infusions for projects in his district. He pushed through an exception to the Johnson Act, making Lake Michigan waters eligible for gambling and thus allowing riverboat casinos for Gary. He worked to fund a 760-job postal encoding facility in Gary and to stop the FAA from closing its air tower at Gary Regional Airport. After the September 11 attacks, he sought $25 million to move three Indiana National Guard units to Gary.

In heavily Republican 1994, with an opponent who spent more than $100,000, Visclosky lost some conservative suburbs and won by just 56%–44%. Since then he has won without difficulty, by 67%–31% in 2002.

SECOND DISTRICT

Rep. Chris Chocola (R)

Elected 2002, 1st term; b. Feb. 24, 1962, Jackson, MI; home, Bristol; Hillsdale Col., B.L.S. 1984, Thomas Cooley Law Schl., J.D. 1988; Presbyterian; married (Sarah).

Professional Career: Foreign Exchange Trader, 1984–87; Mngr. and CEO, CTB Intl., 1988–02.

DC Office: 510 CHOB 20515, 202-225-3915; Fax: 202-225-6798; Web site: www.house.gov/chocola.

District Offices: Logansport, 574-753-4700; South Bend, 574-251-0596.

Committees: *Agriculture* (24th of 27 R): General Farm Commodities & Risk Management; Livestock & Horticulture. *Small Business* (17th of 18 R): Tax, Finance & Exports; Workforce, Empowerment & Government Programs. *Transportation & Infrastructure* (34th of 41 R): Aviation (Vice Chmn.); Water Resources & Environment.

Group Ratings and Key Votes: Newly Elected

Election Results

2002 general	Chris Chocola (R)	95,081	(50%)	($1,697,816)
	Jill Thompson (D)	86,253	(46%)	($1,535,962)
	Sharon Metheny (Lib)	7,112	(4%)	
2002 primary	Chris Chocola (R)	30,176	(78%)	
	Lewis Hass (R)	8,417	(22%)	
2000 general (IN 3)	Tim Roemer (D)	107,438	(52%)	($734,206)
	Chris Chocola (R)	98,822	(47%)	($1,088,166)
	Other	2,050	(1%)	

The People		Race/Ethnic Origin	Ancestry	
Area size:	3,719 sq. mi.	84.4% White	German: 18.3%	Irish: 8.8%
Urban population:	72.8%	8.1% Black	USA: 6.4%	
Rural population:	27.2%	0.8% Asian	**2000 Presidential Vote**	
Pop. 2000:	675,766	0.3% Native Am.	Bush (R)..............128,803	(53%)
Median income:	$40,381	0.0% Hawaiian	Gore (D)..............107,344	(44%)
Poverty status:	9.5%	1.3% Two + races	Other....................5,276	(2%)
Military veterans:	13.5%	0.1% Other	**Cook Partisan Voting Index:** R + 5	
		5.0% Hispanic Origin		

Occupation	Blue collar: 34.7%	White collar: 50.7%	Gray collar: 14.6%

When Notre Dame University was founded in 1842, Catholics were still a rarity in most of America and certainly rare on the limestone-bottomed plains of northern Indiana. This was still farm country and South Bend no more than a crossroads on the St. Joseph River. But by the 1920s, both had grown. Notre Dame, thanks to its football team, "the Fighting Irish," was the most famous Catholic university in the land, and South Bend was a significant industrial city, home of Studebaker and Bendix and dozens of other factories. In the last 50 years, Notre Dame has grown in size and reputation, but South Bend has had the experience of many Midwestern industrial cities: In the 1960s, Studebaker went out of business, in the early 1980s there were big layoffs at big factories, and in the early 1990s there were well-publicized layoffs in nearby Elkhart. But more important than these high-visibility job losses was the largely invisible creation of jobs in small factories throughout the region. The work here requires more skill than did the old assembly lines, and the products must be more responsive to just-in-time prime contractors or computer-inventory retailers. In the late 1990s, many employers had trouble filling job openings, and the economic base was more secure than when it depended on the fate of two or three big companies; there were still painful layoffs in 2001 and 2002, but nothing like the agony of 20 years before.

The 2d Congressional District is centered on South Bend, which for two decades has seen plenty of close congressional contests. South Bend is an industrial and ethnic city—with perhaps the nation's largest percentage of Hungarian-Americans, plus a growing community of Mexicans—that has long been Democratic; so is LaPorte County around Michigan City. Elkhart County to the east is heavily Republican and conservative—there's a six-foot Ten Commandments monument in front of Elkhart City Hall. The 2d District also covers several counties on the limestone plains to the south down past the Wabash River. This is an area rural in appearance but with much small manufacturing; politically, it has been part of the Republican heartland since the party was created in the 1850s. The 2d District, in its current form, is the descendant of the old South Bend-based 3d District. Moderate Democrat Tim Roemer, who announced his retirement in January 2001, held that district for 12 years. Democrats controlled redistricting, and they drew the lines of the 2d to maximize their chance to hold it—by including Michigan City, which was sought by 1st District Democrat Pete Visclosky; excluding much of heavily Republican Elkhart County; and adding the industrial town of Kokomo at the 2d District's extreme southern edge. All that was not enough, however, to elect a Democrat.

The congressman from the 2d District is Chris Chocola, a Republican elected in the 2002 open-seat contest. Chocola grew up in Williamston, Michigan, graduated from Hillsdale College and Thomas Cooley Law School in Michigan and entered his family's agricultural equipment manufacturing business. In 2000, he ran in the old 3d District and held Tim Roemer to a 52%–47% victory, Roemer's weakest showing since he was first elected in 1990. When Roemer announced that he would not run again, Chocola was the obvious Republican frontrunner—though Democratic redistricters placed his home 1.4 miles outside the district. Democrats rallied around Jill Long Thompson, who as Jill Long served three terms in the old Fort Wayne-based 4th District before losing in 1994 and serving as an undersecretary of the Agriculture Department in the Clinton administration.

The campaign was bitterly contested. Chocola derided career politicians and highlighted his background in business. He called Thompson "a liberal former congresswoman from Fort Wayne": Her old district included none of the territory now in the 2d. Democrats in turn assailed him for living outside the district. Chocola emphasized Thompson support for "Hillary Clinton's health care plan" and her service in the Clinton administration. Thompson struck a populist note against her CEO opponent and walked the 100 miles from Kokomo to South Bend to get acquainted with the district. She criticized Chocola as a threat to Social Security because of his support of personal retirement accounts. "Eventually, I'd like to see the entire system privatized," Chocola had said during his 2000 campaign. In 2002, he said he would "support our president in making sure that 20-year-olds find a way to get Social Security." Democrats mined his record as chairman of CTB International to portray him as the embodiment of corporate greed. In one controversial attack ad, the state Democratic Party claimed that Chocola laid off 500 employees while enjoying an executive pay raise; the ad was ultimately pulled off the air because it was untrue. Chocola said that the Bush tax cuts should be made permanent in 2011. The North American Free Trade Agreement was an especially contentious issue. Chocola, who said his company conducted nearly 40% of its business overseas, defended free trade. Thompson, who voted against NAFTA in 1993, argued that it cost the state 30,000 jobs. Chocola's support for NAFTA resulted in a key endorsement from the Indiana Farm Bureau; this was a blow to Thompson, a farmer's daughter who served on the House Agriculture Committee. Chocola also benefited from two visits by George W. Bush, the first to raise $650,000, the second to rally voters five days before Election Day.

Chocola did not carry St. Joseph or LaPorte Counties, but he made inroads there and held down Thompson's margins; his 60% in the district's portion of Elkhart County produced a 4,000-vote margin that came close to neutralizing her 4,700-vote margin in St. Joseph. Thompson's margins in LaPorte County and tiny Starke County were overwhelmed by Chocola's big percentages—as high as 66%—in the district's southern counties; he won 50%–46%. In Washington, Speaker Dennis Hastert delivered on his pledge to give Chocola a seat on Transportation and Infrastructure, where he promised to seek funding to improve U.S. 31 from South Bend to Indianapolis. This seat could be seriously contested in 2004, although Chocola stands to be helped by the top of the ticket in a presidential year.

THIRD DISTRICT

Rep. Mark Souder (R)

Elected 1994, 5th term; b. July 18, 1950, Ft. Wayne; home, Ft. Wayne; IN U., B.S. 1972, Notre Dame U., M.B.A. 1974; Protestant; married (Diane).

Professional Career: Furniture salesman, 1976–83; Staff Dir., U.S. House Select Cmte. on Children, Youth & Families, 1984–89; Legis. Dir., U.S. Sen. Dan Coats, 1989–91, Dep. Chief of Staff, 1991–93.

DC Office: 1227 LHOB 20515, 202-225-4436; Fax: 202-225-3479; Web site: www.house.gov/souder.

District Office: Ft. Wayne, 260-424-3041.

Committees: *Government Reform* (7th of 24 R): Civil Service & Agency Organization; Criminal Justice, Drug Policy & Human Resources (Chmn.). *Resources* (16th of 28 R): Energy & Mineral Resources; Fisheries Conservation, Wildlife & Oceans; National Parks, Recreation & Public Lands. *Select Committee on Homeland Security* (22d of 27 R): Cybersecurity, Science and Research & Development; Emergency Preparedness & Response; Infrastructure & Border Security.

Group Ratings

	ADA	ACLU	AFS	LCV	CON	ITIC	NTU	COC	ACU	NTLC	CHC
2002	10	13	0	13	25	75	58	85	88	100	92
2001	10	—	0	0	—	—	67	91	96	—	—

National Journal Ratings

	2001 LIB —	2001 CONS	2002 LIB —	2002 CONS
Economic	0% —	94%	21% —	73%
Social	35% —	63%	38% —	61%
Foreign	21% —	74%	35% —	60%

Key Votes of the 107th Congress

1. Approve Bush Tax Cuts	Y	5. Faith-Based Charities	Y	9. Trade Promotion Authority	Y
2. Limit Patients' Bill of Rights	Y	6. Bar Gays in the Boy Scouts	Y	10. Bar Funds for Intl. Court	Y
3. Campaign Finance Reform	N	7. Ban Partial-Birth Abortion	Y	11. Authorize Force in Iraq	Y
4. Ban ANWR Development	N	8. Arm Commercial Pilots	N	12. Deny Home. Sec. Dept. Union	Y

Election Results

2002 general	Mark Souder (R)	92,566	(63%)	($518,717)
	Jay Rigdon (D)	50,509	(34%)	($131,458)
	Other	3,531	(2%)	
2002 primary	Mark Souder (R)	53,186	(60%)	
	Paul Helmke (R)	33,038	(37%)	
	Other	3,079	(3%)	
2000 general (IN 4)	Mark Souder (R)	131,051	(62%)	($288,827)
	Mike D. Foster (D)	74,492	(35%)	($30,285)
	Other	4,887	(3%)	

Prior Winning Percentages: 1998 (63%); 1996 (58%); 1994 (55%)

The People		Race/Ethnic Origin	Ancestry	
Area size:	3,292 sq. mi.	87.6% White	German: 22.8%	USA: 8.4%
Urban population:	65.1%	5.6% Black	Irish: 7.1%	
Rural population:	34.9%	0.9% Asian	**2000 Presidential Vote**	
Pop. 2000:	675,457	0.2% Native Am.	Bush (R) 147,106	(66%)
Median income:	$44,013	0.0% Hawaiian	Gore (D) 73,775	(33%)
Poverty status:	7.8%	1.1% Two+ races	Other 3,682	(2%)
Military veterans:	11.9%	0.1% Other	**Cook Partisan Voting Index:** R +17	
		4.5% Hispanic Origin		

Occupation	Blue collar: 35.9%	White collar: 51.7%	Gray collar: 12.4%

The northeast corner of Indiana, in the center of a flat agricultural and manufacturing area, can claim to be the center of Middle America. Its first settlers were of New England Yankee stock, establishing orderly communities with public schools and even colleges; they were joined by German immigrants, who built tidy farms and their own civic institutions. In the northern part of the state there are hills and lakes, and the strange swamp that is the central focus of Gene Stratton Porter's children's classic, *A Girl of the Limberlost*. The one large city here, Fort Wayne, was built on the flat terrain along the Maumee River that flows to Toledo, Ohio. It grew as a factory town, surging ahead and then falling back as large factories, often tied to the auto industry, opened and closed over the years. As much as anything else, the 3d District is a place where people make things. Northwest of Fort Wayne on U.S. Route 33, Elkhart County is a manufacturing hub where local companies make everything from pharmaceuticals to musical instruments—such as oboes, bassoons, and piccolos. The county is best known as the nation's manufacturing center for recreational vehicles ("I represent the biggest gas guzzling district in the U.S.," says the congressman), a business that flourished after the September 11 attacks as travelers became more self-sufficient and stayed closer to home. Neighboring Kosciusko County is renown for a different industry — medical devices; residents have been making orthopedic devices in Warsaw for at least a century. This is a surprisingly diverse area. Its eclectic population mix includes the largest concentration of Amish outside of central Ohio, plus Bosnians and some of the nation's largest populations of Macedonian-Americans and dissident Burmese.

The 3d Congressional District consists of most of eight counties in northeast Indiana. It is essentially the old 4th District, renumbered, with a few counties added and a few subtracted. Politically, this did not make much difference; all are heavily Republican. Indeed, this part of northern Indiana has been heavily Republican since the Civil War, though since the New Deal it has sometimes veered Democratic in times of economic distress. The seat has had a series of members who have gone on to other positions: Dan Quayle, who was elected here in 1976 and 1978 and went on to be elected senator and vice president; Dan Coats, a Quayle aide who was elected here in 1980 and to the Senate in 1990 and 1992 and is now Ambassador to Germany; and Democrat Jill Long, elected in 1989, 1990 and 1992, who as Jill Long Thompson was the unsuccessful Democratic candidate in the next-door 2d District in 2002.

The congressman from the 3d District is Mark Souder (pronounced *SOW-dur*), a Republican first elected in 1994. Souder grew up in Grabill, 10 miles from Fort Wayne, where his Amish great-great-grandfather's family settled. There the family started Souder's of Grabill in 1907, originally a harness shop and now a furniture store and manufacturer of store fixtures. As an undergraduate at Indiana University, he wore a button, "I'm proud to be a square." Souder worked in the furniture business, returned to Grabill, then went to work in 1984 for Congressman Dan Coats, as staff director of the Select Committee on Children, Youth and Families. He moved with Coats to the Senate in 1989, where he served as his legislative director. In 1993, he returned to Fort Wayne and started running against Jill Long, a Democrat elected to replace Coats. With a moderate record and a farm background, she was not an easy target. But Souder, after winning a six-candidate primary with 40%, raised more money. When the state Republican ticket ran far ahead of the Democrats, Souder won a 55%–45% victory.

Souder says that he is "most defined by the fact that I'm an evangelical Christian." Despite his Washington experience, he has been something of a rebel in the House, even—or especially— against his own party's leaders. His independence frequently leaves Republican leaders muttering. As a one-time leader of the Conservative Action Team, Souder frequently challenged House appropriators for excessive spending—including the close-to-home matter of House members' office allowances. He voted against the balanced budget amendment because it did not require a supermajority to raise taxes. When Souder and John Hostettler cast two of the 17 votes against a continuing resolution in January 1996, Speaker Newt Gingrich announced that he would not appear at fundraisers for them. In December 1998, he voted for the third article of impeachment and against the others. More recently, he has displayed a greater interest in sending money to projects back home, including a windmill museum near Kendallville.

Souder has been active on drug issues and blamed Bill Clinton's "half-hearted" anti-drug message for increased drug use by teens. He proposed a bill pre-empting state laws that allow marijuana for medicinal purposes. He helped manage the drug-free workplace law and sponsored a 1998 amendment to require that students with drug convictions are ineligible for loans for a period of time based on the severity of the offense. When that requirement eventually was fully implemented and students discovered that they were ineligible for aid, universities mounted a campaign to repeal it; Souder said that he supported change to restrict the disqualification to students who committed the offense while receiving the aid. As chairman of the Government Reform subcommittee dealing with criminal justice and drug policy, Souder held hearings on U.S. border security and gained unanimous support for a report on the problems.

Souder opposed PNTR with China because trade should be "a leverage in foreign policy," but he voted for trade promotion authority. Souder has worked for some years to ensure that faith-based programs are eligible for federal funds, a cause taken up by George W. Bush in his 2000 campaign and after.

Souder has been comfortably re-elected since 1994 against poorly funded opponents. In 2002, former Fort Wayne Mayor Paul Helmke, who lost 64%–35% to Senator Evan Bayh in 1998, challenged him in the primary. With support from the League of Conservation Voters, Helmke ran as a moderate and criticized Souder's use of congressional perks. Souder said that Helmke, who attended Yale Law School with Bill Clinton, had been a liberal mayor and called him "a Clinton clone." In a sign of concern from Souder's camp, President Bush issued an endorsement. But Souder carried all eight counties, winning 59%–39% in Fort Wayne's Allen County and 60%–37% overall. He won the general election easily, in the course of which he said that he may not keep his pledge to limit himself to 12 years in the House.

FOURTH DISTRICT

Rep. Steve Buyer (R)

Elected 1992, 6th term; b. Nov. 26, 1958, Rensselaer; home, Monticello; The Citadel, B.S. 1980, Valparaiso U., J.D. 1984; Methodist; married (Joni).

Military Career: Army, 1984–87, 1990–91 (Persian Gulf); Army Reserves, 1980–84, 1987–present.

Professional Career: IN Dep. Atty. Gen., 1987–88; Vice Chmn., White Cnty. Repub. Party, 1988–90; Practicing atty., 1988–92.

DC Office: 2230 RHOB 20515, 202-225-5037; Fax: 202-225-2267; Web site: www.house.gov/buyer.

District Offices: Monticello, 574-583-9819; Plainfield, 317-838-0404.

Committees: *Energy & Commerce* (20th of 31 R): Energy & Air Quality; Environment & Hazardous Materials; Health. *Veterans' Affairs* (4th of 17 R): Oversight & Investigations (Chmn.).

Group Ratings

	ADA	ACLU	AFS	LCV	CON	ITIC	NTU	COC	ACU	NTLC	CHC
2002	0	8	0	0	15	100	54	94	91	85	100
2001	0	—	0	0	—	—	62	96	96	—	—

National Journal Ratings

	2001 LIB	—	2001 CONS		2002 LIB	—	2002 CONS
Economic	22%	—	74%		0%	—	91%
Social	20%	—	69%		38%	—	62%
Foreign	33%	—	60%		35%	—	60%

Key Votes of the 107th Congress

1. Approve Bush Tax Cuts	Y	5. Faith-Based Charities	Y	9. Trade Promotion Authority	Y
2. Limit Patients' Bill of Rights	Y	6. Bar Gays in the Boy Scouts	Y	10. Bar Funds for Intl. Court	Y
3. Campaign Finance Reform	N	7. Ban Partial-Birth Abortion	Y	11. Authorize Force in Iraq	Y
4. Ban ANWR Development	N	8. Arm Commercial Pilots	Y	12. Deny Home. Sec. Dept. Union	Y

Election Results

2002 general	Steve Buyer (R)	112,760	(71%)	($924,869)
	Bill Abbott (D)	41,314	(26%)	($21,634)
	Other	3,934	(2%)	
2002 primary	Steve Buyer (R)	44,608	(55%)	
	Brian Kerns (R)	24,443	(30%)	
	Michael Young (R)	6,605	(8%)	
	Other	6,027	(8%)	
2000 general (IN 5)	Steve Buyer (R)	132,051	(61%)	($720,714)
	Greg Goodnight (D)	81,427	(38%)	($451,647)
	Other	3,507	(2%)	

Prior Winning Percentages: 1998 (63%); 1996 (65%); 1994 (70%); 1992 (51%)

The People		Race/Ethnic Origin	Ancestry	
Area size:	4,033 sq. mi.	93.6% White	German: 17.0%	USA: 11.7%
Urban population:	68.2%	1.3% Black	Irish: 8.9%	
Rural population:	31.8%	1.5% Asian	**2000 Presidential Vote**	
Pop. 2000:	675,617	0.2% Native Am.	Bush (R)	156,747 (66%)
Median income:	$45,947	0.0% Hawaiian	Gore (D)	74,660 (31%)
Poverty status:	8.0%	0.8% Two+ races	Other	5,739 (2%)
Military veterans:	13.0%	0.1% Other	**Cook Partisan Voting Index:** R +18	
		2.6% Hispanic Origin		

Occupation Blue collar: 29.6%   White collar: 56.5%   Gray collar: 13.9%

The landscape of central Indiana is some of the most prosaic in the United States, mostly flat, with neat farms and frame-bungalowed towns, looking mostly unchanged from many years ago. Across this landscape run some of the nation's chief transportation arteries. The earliest was the old National Road, from Baltimore to St. Louis, which was paralleled by U.S. 40 in the 1930s and Interstate 70 in the 1960s. Another are the great east-west rail lines, on which famed railroad passenger trains like the old *Wabash Cannonball* that rumbled along Indiana's Wabash River. Today the *Cannonball* no longer runs: People bounce around the Midwest on commuter airlines from small city to hub, and the National Road and U.S. 40 have been replaced for through traffic by Interstate 70. The landscape still looks rural, and there are some large farms. But the economy here is more industrial, with small factories at crossroads and in courthouse towns. This is a part of America with little immigrant heritage from the early waves of immigration, relatively few blacks, and only a handful of the more recent Latin and Asian immigrants. Basic values have not been shaken so much here as in other parts of the nation.

The 4th Congressional District covers much of this territory, running from Indiana's northern plains to its southern hills. It includes all or part of 12 counties in western Indiana, including the far western edge of Indianapolis and Marion County, and extends south past (but not including) Bloomington to Lawrence County, which was the source of the limestone used to rebuild the Pentagon after the September 11 attacks. The largest city is Lafayette, where the main business is Purdue University, Indiana's land-grant college and the alma mater of C-SPAN founder Brian Lamb. Growing and prosperous, Lafayette tends to vote Republican. Even more Republican are the small counties and the suburban territory outside Indianapolis—places like fast-growing Hendricks County, which gave 72% to George W. Bush in 2000.

The 4th District's congressman is Steve Buyer (pronounced *BOO-yer*), a Republican elected in 1992. Buyer grew up in White County, graduated from The Citadel, served in the Army, worked in Indianapolis and started a family law practice in Monticello, where he joined all the civic organizations. A lieutenant colonel in the Army reserve, he was called to active duty in fall 1990, serving as legal adviser at a prisoner-of-war camp in the Persian Gulf. Buyer was enraged that most House Democrats, including then-5th District Democratic Congressman Jim Jontz, voted against the war. After Buyer returned to Indiana, where he was White County Republican vice chairman, he began making speeches around the Hoosier Heartland attacking Jontz on his Gulf War stand. Jontz was a skilled politician, but Buyer won 51%–49%. He hasn't been below 60% since.

Buyer has made more of a legislative mark than one would have expected back in 1993 for a conservative-to-moderate Republican in a then-Democratic House. On the Veterans' Affairs Committee, he has spent much time on the lingering effects of Gulf War illness—which Buyer says is incorrectly referred to as "Gulf War syndrome." Since his return from the Gulf, Buyer has suffered from flu, pneumonia, spastic colon, kidney infection, bronchitis and a constant cough. In 1994 he successfully co-sponsored legislation that allows the Veterans Administration to compensate Gulf War vets suffering from chronic disabilities resulting from undiagnosed illnesses that became manifest to a degree of 10% or more within a year of the Gulf War—a real departure in veterans' law. When he served as chairman of the Military Personnel Subcommittee on Armed Services, he won enactment of what military officials term the greatest expansion of health care benefits for military retirees in at least three decades. In 2001, Buyer gave up that post for a seat on the Energy and Commerce Committee. He worked on the Dingell-Tauzin broadband bill, successfully sponsoring an amendment with Ed Towns of New York that guarantees access to local exchange customers served by Bell company high-speed networks under FCC-regulated terms and conditions. He also has worked on legislation to expedite market access for new medical devices, which are a growing local industry.

Buyer can be blunt to the point of being cocky. A year after impeachment, he told a statewide radio interviewer that Hillary Rodham Clinton was running for the Senate because it was her best way to avoid a federal indictment and stay out of jail. But he can also be candid about his own party. When John McCain was riding high in Republican presidential primaries, Buyer said, "Clearly I cannot support him" because of their differences on military legislation and because it can be "very exhausting" to work with him. During the post-election recount in Florida, he was so angry about Democrats' attempts to throw out absentee ballots by U.S. soldiers that he flew there to investigate and voice his outrage.

Probably his most self-assured—and politically successful—strategy was his handling of redistricting in 2002. Democratic redistricters sliced up Buyer's old 5th District so that its remains were grafted onto seven of Indiana's nine surviving districts. Left without a seat, Buyer picked the one that happened to be the most heavily Republican, that happened to include his hometown of Monticello (population 5723) and that had the greenest member of the delegation—first-term Democrat Brian Kerns. This district, the new 4th, was 97% new to Buyer (the only part he had represented before was White County). It was solidly Republican, but it included seven of the 13 counties and 68% of the population from Kerns' old 7th District—including Lafayette-based Tippecanoe County. Buyer charged Democrats with trying to end his career because of his work as a manager of Clinton's impeachment and in the Florida recount. He emphasized that Kerns's home in Vigo County was 70 miles outside the new 4th, and argued that he should run against the 8th District's John Hostettler. Kerns said Buyer should run elsewhere, and when he didn't, Kerns seemed dumbfounded. "He has declared his candidacy but hasn't really done anything else," said Brian Howey, publisher of a nonpartisan newsletter on Indiana politics. Kerns, a son-in-law of 30-year incumbent John Myers, who retired in 1996, had won an unimpressive victory in 2000 against weak opposition. His reelection effort moved in fits and starts: During the final quarter of 2001, Kerns sent out more franked mail than any other member of the House. But in a peculiar campaign incident, Kerns initially claimed to witness the September 11 airplane crash into the Pentagon while he was driving to the Capitol. When subsequent inquiry raised questions about whether Kerns had been in the area, he responded, "Who knows?" Buyer outraised Kerns by more than 3–1; a third candidate, Michael Young, who was hoping to benefit from the clash of the two incumbents, spent only $25,000. The result wasn't close. In the six-candidate contest, Buyer bested Kerns 55%–30%, with Young trailing with 8%. Buyer won every county, including 61% in Tippecanoe, which cast one-fifth of the vote. Buyer won easily in November, and should be safe for the rest of the decade.

A lieutenant colonel in the Army Reserves, Buyer was again called to duty in March 2003 during the conflict with Iraq. He returned home, collected his gear and had received a leave of absence from Speaker Dennis Hastert but the Army later notified Buyer that his high-profile status jeopardized both him and his Army colleagues; he was not deployed.

FIFTH DISTRICT

Rep. Dan Burton (R)

Elected 1982, 11th term; b. June 21, 1938, Indianapolis; home, Indianapolis; IN U., 1958–59, Cincinnati Bible Seminary, 1959–60; Protestant; widowed.

Military Career: Army, 1956–57, Army Reserves, 1957–62.

Elected Office: IN House of Reps., 1966–68, 1976–80; IN Senate, 1968–70, 1980–82.

Professional Career: Real estate broker; Founder, Dan Burton Insurance Agency, 1968.

DC Office: 2185 RHOB 20515, 202-225-2276; Fax: 202-225-0016; Web site: www.house.gov/burton.

District Offices: Indianapolis, 317-848-0201; Marion, 765-662-6770.

Committees: *Government Reform* (2d of 24 R): National Security, Emerging Threats & Intl. Relations; Wellness & Human Rights (Chmn.). *International Relations* (5th of 26 R): Asia & the Pacific; Europe.

Group Ratings

	ADA	ACLU	AFS	LCV	CON	ITIC	NTU	COC	ACU	NTLC	CHC
2002	0	7	0	0	66	88	—	80	100	97	100
2001	5	—	0	0	—	—	72	87	100	—	—

National Journal Ratings

	2001 LIB —	2001 CONS		2002 LIB —	2002 CONS
Economic	0% —	94%		15% —	85%
Social	0% —	81%		32% —	68%
Foreign	20% —	81%		44% —	56%

Key Votes of the 107th Congress

1. Approve Bush Tax Cuts	Y	5. Faith-Based Charities	Y	9. Trade Promotion Authority	Y
2. Limit Patients' Bill of Rights	Y	6. Bar Gays in the Boy Scouts	Y	10. Bar Funds for Intl. Court	*
3. Campaign Finance Reform	N	7. Ban Partial-Birth Abortion	Y	11. Authorize Force in Iraq	Y
4. Ban ANWR Development	N	8. Arm Commercial Pilots	Y	12. Deny Home. Sec. Dept. Union	Y

Election Results

2002 general	Dan Burton (R)	129,442	(72%)	($844,159)
	Katherine Carr (D)	45,283	(25%)	($25,551)
	Other	5,130	(3%)	
2002 primary	Dan Burton (R)	65,022	(84%)	
	Thomas George Holland (R)	12,560	(16%)	
2000 general (IN 6)	Dan Burton (R)	199,207	(70%)	($622,401)
	Darin Patrick Griesey (D)	74,881	(26%)	($9,123)
	Joe Hauptmann (Lib)	9,087	(3%)	($13,529)

Prior Winning Percentages: 1998 (72%); 1996 (75%); 1994 (77%); 1992 (72%); 1990 (63%); 1988 (73%); 1986 (68%); 1984 (73%); 1982 (65%)

The People		Race/Ethnic Origin	Ancestry	
Area size:	3,291 sq. mi.	93.2% White	German: 18.7%	USA: 9.6%
Urban population:	74.5%	2.6% Black	Irish: 9.1%	
Rural population:	25.5%	1.3% Asian	**2000 Presidential Vote**	
Pop. 2000:	675,577	0.3% Native Am.	Bush (R)	187,489 (69%)
Median income:	$52,800	0.0% Hawaiian	Gore (D)	80,945 (30%)
Poverty status:	5.2%	0.9% Two+ races	Other	5,110 (2%)
Military veterans:	12.9%	0.1% Other	**Cook Partisan Voting Index:** R +20	
		1.6% Hispanic Origin		
Occupation	Blue collar: 24.4%	White collar: 63.2%	Gray collar: 12.4%	

Indianapolis is one of America's most symmetrical cities, sited in almost the exact center of Indiana, centered on Monument Circle with eight avenues radiating like wheel spokes. A hundred years ago, it was a compact city, with everybody living within walking distance or a buggy ride of the circle in the center of downtown; even Indianapolis's one president, Benjamin Harrison, lived not far away in a mansion on North Meridian Street. But today's Indianapolis is spread out in all directions, and the metropolitan area includes eight counties smack in the center of Indiana. The most explosive growth has been in the most affluent quarter, to the north, where the fields of Carmel and Fishers in Hamilton County have filled with subdivisions, shopping centers and corporate headquarters. Hamilton County, directly north of Indianapolis's Marion County, was the fastest-growing county in the state in the 1990s, when its population rose 68%; it is now the fifth largest county in the state. Hamilton County had five banks in 1969; now there are 21, as many as in Marion County. The affluent establishment of Indianapolis is increasingly located here north of the city limits. The city of Carmel was one of the top zip codes for political donors in 2002; it was the only zip code outside New York, Chicago, California, Texas and the D.C. area that made the top 30. These are not wealthy suburbs with a penchant for Democrats: Hamilton County is the most Republican county in Indiana and voted 74%–24% for George W. Bush in 2000. *Sixty Minutes* once referred to Noblesville, the county seat, as "arguably the most Republican spot on earth."

The 5th Congressional District includes Hamilton County and other prosperous parts of metropolitan Indianapolis—the northern fringes of the city itself, Hancock County just to the east (where the U.S. Lawn Mower Racing Association's championship is held every September), and parts of less affluent but still conservative Shelby and Johnson Counties to the south. It juts northward from Hamilton County to include part of Kokomo and, in the north, Wabash and Huntington Counties, which are a cradle of vice presidents: Thomas Marshall, Woodrow Wilson's vice president, was from North Manchester in Wabash County, and Dan Quayle, the first George Bush's vice president, spent his high school years and later practiced law in Huntington (which was in another district when Quayle represented it in the House).

The congressman from the 5th District is Dan Burton, an active and enthusiastic Republican first elected to the House in 1982. He has been running for office since he was in his 20s. He had a horrific childhood: His father was abusive and left the family, his mother worked as a waitress and bought the kids' clothes at Goodwill, his father ultimately kidnapped his mother and went to jail, and the kids were sent to the county home. "Looking back on my life, I think one of the reasons I'm so aggressive is because all through my childhood we were looked upon as second-class citizens," he has said. Burton earned money as a teenager shining shoes and at 18 enlisted in the Army. He never finished college but made his way up as a real estate broker and insurance salesman. He also ran for public office, often unsuccessfully. He was elected to the Indiana House in 1966, 1976 and 1978 and to the Indiana Senate in 1968 and 1980; he lost races for Congress in 1970 and 1972 and finally won when the Republican legislature created a heavily Republican suburban seat.

For years, Burton was regarded by many Democrats as a nut, excitably pursuing lost causes. He opposed sanctions on South Africa, backed UNITA in Angola and Renamo in Mozambique, offered dozens of spending cuts that were overwhelmingly defeated, and pushed for universal mandatory AIDS testing. He has sometimes challenged health experts: In February 2000, he filed a bill to allow a four-year-old Texas boy to be treated by a Houston doctor using nontoxic drugs not approved by the FDA, and in April 2000, he asked the Health and Human Services Department whether MMR vaccine could cause autism; he has an autistic grandchild, and in December 2002, bitterly criticized the Department of Homeland Security bill provision ending lawsuits against vaccine makers. But he has also been vindicated by events for some stands that were widely scorned, from his hard-line opposition to the Soviet Union to his lonely vote against the later-repealed Catastrophic Health Care Act of 1988.

Burton has had some significant legislative successes but his biggest achievement was the Helms-Burton Act. It was a response to the shooting down of the Brothers to the Rescue planes by the Cuban Air Force and stated that foreign companies could be sued in American courts if, as part of business deals with Fidel Castro's regime, they took over property expropriated from American owners. Helms-Burton passed both houses in fall 1995 and was signed by Bill Clinton, but Clinton then delayed its full implementation.

As chairman of the Government Reform Committee (it dropped "Oversight" from its title in 1999), he conducted tumultuous hearings on the Clinton-Gore campaign finance scandals from 1997 to 2000. Many Republicans were queasy about having Burton conduct the hearing; they felt he was too excitable and vulnerable to attack by Democrats and remembered with dismay his 1994 speech questioning whether White House counsel Vincent Foster had been murdered and his body moved. Burton promised a bipartisan approach but encountered early and fierce opposition; ranking Democrat Henry Waxman, one of the brainiest Democrats in the House, set the tone, calling it "a partisan witch hunt." Burton helped that impression along when, in reference to Clinton, he told *The Indianapolis Star* editorial board in April 1998, "This guy's a scumbag. That's why I'm after him." Burton faced great resistance —some 90 witnesses took the Fifth Amendment or left the country—and perhaps official retaliation: In July 1997, the FBI subpoenaed Burton's finance records of his House campaigns. Burton worked doggedly to get hold of memos to Attorney General Janet Reno with recommendations on dealing with Clinton-Gore campaign fundraising irregularities, or worse; he was still seeking them in 2002, when the Bush administration claimed executive privilege. In May 2000, when it was revealed that White House e-mails from 1996–98 sought in the investigation had been erased, Burton angrily sought an investigation, an independent counsel and he sent a criminal referral to the Justice Department; the e-mail stonewall continued until the end of the Clinton presidency. Burton has also tried to get internal Justice documents about an FBI scandal in which agents covered up evidence of crime by mobster informants in Boston from the 1960s to the 1980s; when his efforts were opposed by the Bush administration, erstwhile critic Barney Frank said, "I see now a genuine intellectual integrity in his approach." Disgusted with the FBI, Burton sponsored a bill in July 2002 to have J. Edgar Hoover's name taken off its headquarters building.

On International Relations, Burton has bucked the tide on several issues. He opposed normalization of relations with Vietnam. He moved to reduce aid to India, because of its treatment of the Sikhs and Kashmiris, whose American counterparts contributed heavily to his 1996 campaign; he has been a steady backer of Pakistan. In June 2002 he held hearings on U.S. citizens who were kidnapped contrary to U.S. law and held in Saudi Arabia—mostly children, but some of them now grown. The Saudis refuse to let women leave their country without permission from a husband or a male relative, and no U.S. citizen abducted there has been allowed to leave. In August 2002 he went to Riyadh with a five-member delegation for talks with Foreign Minister Prince Saud and expecting to see the daughters of Pat Roush, an American whose children were kidnapped 17 years before. But the Saudis whisked the Roush daughters for a "vacation" to London, where they were tended by Saudi minders; they said, supposedly voluntarily, that they did not want to go back to the U.S. When Burton returned, he accused the Saudis of "disinformation and PR stunts" and in November 2002 complained when Saudi lobbyists and public relations agents refused his subpoenas for documents on dubious grounds of diplomatic privilege. Burton also attacked State Department personnel for conniving with the Saudis in this business; State Department e-mails accusing him of McCarthyism and neo-Nazism were made public in June 2002, and Deputy Secretary of State Richard Armitage apologized. Burton had to relinquish the Government Operations chairmanship in January 2003 because of House Republicans' six-year limit on committee chairmen; he was seeking the chairmanship of what was then the Middle East and South Asia Subcommittee of International Relations, but Chairman Henry Hyde was said to have doubts about whether he should get it. Burton ultimately became chairman of the Government Reform Subcommittee on Wellness and Human Rights.

For all the pasting Burton has taken from the national press, he has never been in trouble for re-election—not even when it was revealed in 1998 that he had fathered an illegitimate son some 15 years before. The woman had not notified Burton until her companion, long presumed to be the father, left her five years later. Burton took a blood test and afterward paid child support. Redistricting changed the shape of the district considerably, and changed the number too. But any district that contains Hamilton County will be heavily Republican, and Burton won reelection without difficulty.

SIXTH DISTRICT

Rep. Mike Pence (R)

Elected 2000, 2d term; b. June, 7, 1959, Columbus; home, Elwood; Hanover Col., B.A. 1981, IN U., J.D. 1986; Protestant; married (Karen).

Professional Career: Practicing atty., 1986–91; Pres., IN Policy Review Fndt., 1991–93; Radio broadcaster, Network Indiana, 1992–99; Host, Pub. Affairs TV, UPN-23, 1995–99.

DC Office: 1605 LHOB 20515, 202-225-3021; Fax: 202-225-3382; Web site: www.house.gov/mikepence.

District Office: Anderson, 765-640-2919.

Committees: *Agriculture* (15th of 27 R): General Farm Commodities & Risk Management; Livestock & Horticulture. *International Relations* (23d of 26 R): International Terrorism, Nonproliferation and Human Rights; Middle East & Central Asia. *Judiciary* (16th of 21 R): Courts, the Internet & Intellectual Property; Crime, Terrorism & Homeland Security.

The *Almanac* is on the Web —

······→ *with updates!*

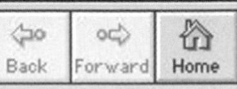   

Your purchase includes free, "buyers-only" access to the *Almanac 2004* on the Web.

Updates — The Web Edition keeps you current with:

* ★ redistricting battles
* ★ important committee changes
* ★ election forecasts
* ★ coverage of special elections
* ★ and much more

Searchable — You also get quick, easy access to the members, districts and issues that are important to you.

Access the Web Edition today! Simply go to:

www.nationaljournal.com/almanac

and enter your registration number (located below). If you have any questions, please call us toll free at **1-800-356-4838**.

Registration Number
630464

Need quick, easy access to the Washington power structure?

Look to *The Capital Source.*

The one resource that puts you in instant contact with the 7,000 most important people and organizations in Washington, D.C.

The Capital Source provides you with contacts, organization names, mailing addresses, phone and fax numbers, and Web addresses. And because it's published twice a year, you can be confident that the information is completely up-to-date and accurate.

If you need to contact:

White House, Cabinet, Congressional Committees, Senate, Senate Staff, House of Representatives, House Staff, Federal & Related Agencies, Foreign Embassies, Courts, State & Local Governments, Corporations, Labor Unions, Think Tanks, Interest Groups, Trade & Professional Associations, Political Consultants, Lobbyists, Advertising & Public Relations, Law Firms, TV, Radio, Talk Shows, Syndicated Columnists, News Services, Publishing Companies, Magazines & Trade Publications, Newspapers, Media Organizations, Political Web sites, Foreign Press, Newsletters, Restaurants and more.

. . . then you need The Capital Source.

The Spring edition is available in early May and the Fall edition is available in late October.

Pricing

You can purchase either the Spring or Fall edition for $29.95. Or you can purchase both editions at once and pay just $49.95—a 15% savings off the combined single-edition price.

Order your copy today

Call us toll free at 1-800-356-4838
www.nationaljournal.com/capitalsource

Group Ratings

	ADA	ACLU	AFS	LCV	CON	ITIC	NTU	COC	ACU	NTLC	CHC
2002	5	7	0	13	58	88	59	84	100	100	100
2001	0	—	0	0	—	—	76	96	100	—	—

National Journal Ratings

	2001 LIB	—	2001 CONS		2002 LIB	—	2002 CONS
Economic	7%	—	89%		20%	—	79%
Social	0%	—	81%		0%	—	75%
Foreign	0%	—	97%		0%	—	85%

Key Votes of the 107th Congress

1. Approve Bush Tax Cuts	Y	5. Faith-Based Charities	Y	9. Trade Promotion Authority	Y
2. Limit Patients' Bill of Rights	Y	6. Bar Gays in the Boy Scouts	Y	10. Bar Funds for Intl. Court	Y
3. Campaign Finance Reform	N	7. Ban Partial-Birth Abortion	Y	11. Authorize Force in Iraq	Y
4. Ban ANWR Development	N	8. Arm Commercial Pilots	Y	12. Deny Home. Sec. Dept. Union	Y

Election Results

2002 general	Mike Pence (R)	118,436	(64%)	($1,214,879)
	Melina Fox (D)	63,871	(34%)	($342,987)
	Other	3,346	(2%)	
2002 primary	Mike Pence (R)	unopposed		
2000 general (IN 2)	Mike Pence (R)	106,023	(51%)	($1,106,140)
	Robert W. Rock (D)	80,885	(39%)	($364,888)
	Bill Frazier (I)	19,077	(9%)	($398,999)
	Other	2,422	(1%)	

The People		Race/Ethnic Origin	Ancestry	
Area size:	5,572 sq. mi.	93.4% White	German: 16.8%	USA: 12.7%
Urban population:	59.3%	3.8% Black	English: 7.7%	
Rural population:	40.7%	0.5% Asian	**2000 Presidential Vote**	
Pop. 2000:	675,669	0.2% Native Am.	Bush (R)	148,415 (58%)
Median income:	$39,002	0.0% Hawaiian	Gore (D)	100,231 (40%)
Poverty status:	9.7%	0.8% Two+ races	Other	5,090 (2%)
Military veterans:	13.6%	0.1% Other	**Cook Partisan Voting Index:** R +10	
		1.3% Hispanic Origin		

Occupation	Blue collar: 35.0%	White collar: 49.7%	Gray collar: 15.3%

Muncie, Indiana, became famous as the "Middletown" that sociologists Robert and Helen Lynd lived in and reported on in 1924–25 and again in 1935, and where a team of sociologists investigated again in 1976–78. The Lynds were attracted to Muncie by its typicalness—"every small city from Maine to California," said *Life* magazine. But it wasn't exactly: It was a factory town in a country still almost half rural, it was almost entirely Protestant and Northern in a country one-quarter Catholic and one-third Southern. Muncie was more typical in being culturally homogeneous but economically riven. In the 1920s Muncie celebrated its common values and was loath to admit its economic disparities; in the 1930s the latter came out into the open when Muncie, like most of the industrial Midwest, was unionized in what were sometimes violent uprisings. Workers who were joining CIO unions and voting for Democrats fiercely opposed the business elite—local bankers, merchants, executives at General Motors and the Ball family's glass company. Partisan politics took on the sharp, bitter tone of a struggle for wealth between two rival classes whose claims seemed irreconcilable. Echoes of this class-warfare politics reverberate only faintly today. They grow louder with local economic distress, as Muncie suffered years ago in layoffs at GM and more recently when the Ball headquarters moved to Colorado in 1998. And there are higher Democratic percentages in towns with union traditions, like Muncie and Anderson, than in others such as Richmond. But Indiana's late 1990s prosperity, based on high-skill manufacturing, brought something like a political consensus here for tax cuts, trimmed budgets and quiet support of traditional values, with strong support for candidates of either party who agree.

The 6th Congressional District covers most of east-central Indiana. It includes Muncie and

Anderson, with their big GM factories, in the north; and Richmond, founded by a major branch of American Quakers and the home of their Earlham College. Suburbs of Fort Wayne and Cincinnati, but none of the cities themselves, are part of the district. Redistricting added some rural counties to the north and south and renumbered the district (it used to be the 2d) and removed parts of Shelby and Johnson Counties outside Indianapolis. The district leans Republican in presidential politics and has been a swing district in some Indiana races.

The congressman from the 6th District is Mike Pence, a Republican first elected in 2000. He grew up in Columbus and graduated from Hanover College and Indiana University Law School, then practiced law; he is an evangelical Christian. Starting before he was 30, he ran as the Republican nominee for this seat in 1988 and 1990 against longtime Democratic Congressman (1975–95) Philip Sharp, then wrote an article after the second contest called "Confessions of a Negative Campaigner," in which he apologized for running negative advertisements. From 1991 to 1993, he was president of the conservative Indiana Policy Review Foundation, a think tank based in Fort Wayne. In 1992, he began broadcasting "The Mike Pence Show," a conservative talk radio program that was syndicated statewide beginning in 1994 until he began his 2000 campaign.

The seat opened up when three-term Republican Congressman David McIntosh challenged Governor Frank O'Bannon. In the six-candidate Republican primary in May 2000, Pence led the second-place finisher, state Representative Jeff Linder, by a solid 44%–24%. Robert Rock, Anderson lawyer and son of former Lieutenant Governor Robert Rock, had a closer contest in the Democratic primary, 30%–23%. The general became complicated when Bill Frazier, a former Republican state Senator and four-time losing nominee against Sharp, entered the race as an independent after the primary. All three candidates opposed abortion rights and gun control and supported increased military spending. But Frazier tried to tap into populist sentiment by attacking free trade agreements, supporting a minimum wage increase, touting American energy independence and offering to donate his congressional salary to fund college scholarships. Rock, a former Marine, attacked Pence for not serving in the military (Pence was 13 when the draft was abolished and U.S. troops left Vietnam) and supported tax cuts for middle-income families. Pence called for across-the-board tax cuts, including repeal of the marriage penalty and estate tax, as well as reform of Medicare financing. Pence won 51% to 39% for Rock and 9% for Frazier.

Pence was the only freshman to get a subcommittee chairmanship in 2001: The Small Business panel on Regulatory Reform Oversight. He quickly made his mark as one of the House's more conservative members. He worked with Tom DeLay and conservative Christian groups to pressure the Bush administration to advocate strong support for Israel. He antagonized the business community by voting against the bankruptcy bill because he objected to a provision on abortion. As the only House member to become a plaintiff in the lawsuit challenging the constitutionality of campaign finance reform, Pence said that Senator John McCain was "so deep in bed with the Democrats that his feet are coming out of the bottom of the sheets." He was one of 33 House Republicans to vote against final action on President Bush's education bill. His first term was marked by some unwanted notoriety: His sixth-floor Longworth building office was one of three in the House that was shut down in October 2001 after inspectors detected slight traces of anthrax.

Pence was easily reelected in 2002.

SEVENTH DISTRICT

Rep. Julia Carson (D)

Elected 1996, 4th term; b. July 8, 1938, Louisville, KY; home, Indianapolis; Baptist; divorced.

Elected Office: IN House of Reps., 1972–76; IN Senate, 1976–90; Marion Cty. Center Township Trustee, 1991–96.

Professional Career: Secy., UAW, 1962–63; Legis. Aide, U.S. Rep. Andy Jacobs, 1965–72.

DC Office: 1535 LHOB 20515, 202-225-4011; Fax: 202-225-5633; Web site: www.house.gov/carson.

District Office: Indianapolis, 317-283-6516.

Committees: *Financial Services* (10th of 32 D): Financial Institutions & Consumer Credit; Housing & Community Opportunity. *Transportation & Infrastructure* (29th of 34 D): Highways, Transit & Pipelines; Railroads.

Group Ratings

	ADA	ACLU	AFS	LCV	CON	ITIC	NTU	COC	ACU	NTLC	CHC
2002	100	87	100	88	43	38	21	37	0	6	8
2001	100	—	100	93	—	—	10	35	4	—	—

National Journal Ratings

	2001 LIB —	2001 CONS		2002 LIB —	2002 CONS
Economic	80% —	21%		91% —	8%
Social	83% —	11%		83% —	16%
Foreign	81% —	18%		90% —	10%

Key Votes of the 107th Congress

1. Approve Bush Tax Cuts	N	5. Faith-Based Charities	N	9. Trade Promotion Authority	N
2. Limit Patients' Bill of Rights	N	6. Bar Gays in the Boy Scouts	N	10. Bar Funds for Intl. Court	N
3. Campaign Finance Reform	Y	7. Ban Partial-Birth Abortion	N	11. Authorize Force in Iraq	N
4. Ban ANWR Development	Y	8. Arm Commercial Pilots	N	12. Deny Home. Sec. Dept. Union	N

Election Results

2002 general	Julia Carson (D)	77,478	(53%)	($1,099,924)
	Brose McVey (R)	64,379	(44%)	($1,105,370)
	Other	3,983	(3%)	
2002 primary	Julia Carson (D)	24,807	(91%)	
	Bob Hidalgo (D)	2,515	(9%)	
2000 general (IN 10)	Julia Carson (D)	91,689	(59%)	($340,203)
	Marvin B. Scott (R)	62,233	(40%)	($82,504)
	Other	2,780	(2%)	

Prior Winning Percentages: 1998 (58%); 1996 (53%)

The People		Race/Ethnic Origin	Ancestry	
Area size:	265 sq. mi.	63.0% White	German: 12.3%	Irish: 7.8%
Urban population:	99.7%	29.4% Black	USA: 7.8%	
Rural population:	0.3%	1.3% Asian	**2000 Presidential Vote**	
Pop. 2000:	675,674	0.2% Native Am.	Gore (D) 109,800	(55%)
Median income:	$36,522	0.0% Hawaiian	Bush (R) 84,362	(43%)
Poverty status:	13.5%	1.5% Two+ races	Other 3,795	(2%)
Military veterans:	12.6%	0.2% Other	**Cook Partisan Voting Index:** D + 6	
		4.4% Hispanic Origin		

Occupation	Blue collar: 26.2%	White collar: 57.7%	Gray collar: 16.1%

Indianapolis, radiating outward from the Soldiers and Sailors statue in Monument Circle, is precisely at the center of Indiana, dominating it as few other cities do a state. It is the political and governmental capital, industrial and financial center, and the intellectual center of Indiana as well. It is symmetrically laid out: Just to the west of the circle is the state Capitol, to the north is the American Legion headquarters, to the east is the City-County building, and to the south is the Circle Center mall, and the RCA Dome (formerly Hoosier Dome). Farther out are some classic and some new Indianapolis institutions: the Indiana University Medical Center, the Convention Center, the Eiteljorg Museum of Native American and Western Art and the new Indiana State Museum, Conseco Fieldhouse and NCAA headquarters. Indianapolis has become the nation's amateur sports capital, especially for basketball, and one of the most popular places for religious conventions. Eli Lilly and Co. has been expanding its already large corporate presence. The city has the world's biggest children's museum and is home to the Hudson Institute, a conservative think tank.

Politically, Indianapolis has long had robust competition in national as well as local races. Republicans held the mayor's office from 1967, when Richard Lugar won it, until 1999, when Stephen Goldsmith retired and became a top adviser to George W. Bush; they made Indianapolis a national innovator in privatization of services. By putting services up for bid, they saved taxpayers money and spurred many incumbent city employees to come up with innovations. Lugar expanded Indianapolis's city limits to include all of Marion County, which made it a solidly Republican constituency then. But more recently, affluent young people have been moving to counties farther out, and Marion County is trending Democratic. That trend was evident in November 1999 when Democrat Bart Peterson, a former chief of staff to Governor Evan Bayh, was elected mayor, and in 2000, when Marion County voted for George W. Bush by only a 50%–48% margin, even as six surrounding suburban counties gave Bush 70% to 75% of their votes.

Indiana's 7th Congressional District includes most but not all of Indianapolis and Marion County. It includes all of Center Township, a Democratic stronghold with a large black population and gentrified middle class, but does not include much of the affluent, Republican northern edge of the county. It extends west to include Speedway, where the Indianapolis 500 has been held on a 2.5 mile track since 1911, and southward and east to modest neighborhoods, including Amtrak's largest repair yard in Beech Grove; Mexicans, who nearly tripled in size during the 1990s, are the newest immigrant group. Within these boundaries, the 7th District leans Democratic, and it gave Bill Clinton and Al Gore solid margins. But even though redistricting was controlled by Democrats, they could not make it more Democratic; they had to add 106,000 people, and the territory all around the old district (then numbered the 10th) was more Republican; so the black population was reduced from 34% to 29% and the Bush 2000 percentage increased from 38% to 43%.

The congresswoman from the 7th District is Julia Carson, a Democrat first elected in 1996. Carson was born to an unmarried teenage mother and grew up in poverty, working as a waitress, newspaper deliverer and summer farm laborer; she can remember going to the welfare office for a ration of cornmeal and lard. As a divorced mother, she raised two children and then two grandchildren. In 1965 she was hired away from her job as a secretary at UAW Local 550 by newly-elected Congressman Andy Jacobs to do casework in his Indianapolis office. When his election prospects looked dim in 1972 (he did lose, but won the seat back two years later), he encouraged Carson to run for the state House; she won, then was elected to the state Senate in 1976. In 1990 she was elected as Center Township trustee, the position responsible for running welfare in central Indianapolis.

In 1996, when Jacobs retired, Carson decided to run. She won Jacobs's endorsement and that of the local Democratic organization. She was outspent by former prosecutor and party chairman Ann DeLaney, but won the primary 49%–31%. The Republican nominee was Virginia Blankenbaker, a stockbroker and state senator from 1980–92. In this race between two grandmothers, both were also more liberal than many in their parties, pro-choice on abortion and against the death penalty. Many commentators wondered whether a black Democrat could beat a white Republican in this district, but Carson raised and spent almost as much as Blankenbaker; she won 53%–45%. As Carson said later, "This is a wonderful city. A lot of people see you beyond the color of your skin. That becomes passe."

Carson, who was sworn into office from her hospital bed after heart surgery in January 1997 and was hospitalized in December 1999 with a serious case of pneumonia, has compiled a liberal voting record. She worked with Senator Richard Lugar to enact a bill wiping away bureaucratic roadblocks to child health insurance. She cried at the Capitol ceremony when President Clinton gave the Congressional Gold Medal to civil-rights pioneer Rosa Parks, pursuant to a bill that Carson authored. One of the last House members to decide how to vote on PNTR with China, she spent the final hours before the vote chatting with Clinton for 45 minutes at the White House (but refusing to tell him how she would vote), listening to union officials, and then talking to CNN. Her vote for PNTR left organized labor steaming, but its Indiana officials supported her reelection because they liked her overall record. Three weeks into the 2000 presidential-vote deadlock in Florida, she became one of the first Democratic defectors when she publicly advised Al Gore to "take the high ground and hand it over," which caused some grumbling among Democrats. In November 2001, human-rights concerns caused her to agonize over the anti-terrorism bill, which she finally supported. "The light next to my name kept going from green to red and back again. I didn't sleep well after that vote," she said. She voted against trade promotion authority and against the use of force in Iraq.

Carson has had fairly serious competition in every election. In 2000, her Republican opponent was Butler University sociology professor Marvin Scott, making his fourth bid for the seat. But Scott received little national party support, and Carson won 59%–40%. Two years later, with a boost from redistricting, public affairs specialist and former Senate Republican aide Brose McVey ran, saying that Indianapolis needs "a congressman with energy and creativity" and that Carson was "out of step with her own constituency." Carson cited the federal funds that she delivered for local development and anti-violence programs; she said that Congress should put "the skids on the tax cuts" until the economy strengthened. McVey raised large amounts from the local business community and received national Republican backing in an ad that accused Carson of not paying her property taxes on time from 1997 to 2001. During their final pre-election debate, Carson walked off the stage to protest "the lowest common denominator" and "racial polarization" campaign run by McVey. Using that message to motivate her strong grass-roots network, Carson won, 53%–44%. With the usually higher turnout in a presidential election, she could face another competitive campaign in 2004.

EIGHTH DISTRICT

Rep. John Hostettler (R)

Elected 1994, 5th term; b. July 19, 1961, Evansville; home, Blairsville; Rose-Hulman Inst. of Tech., B.S. 1983; Baptist; married (Beth).

Professional Career: Mechanical Engineer, S. IN Gas & Electric Co., 1983–94.

DC Office: 1214 LHOB 20515, 202-225-4636; Fax: 202-225-3284; Web site: www.house.gov/hostettler.

District Offices: Evansville, 812-465-6484; Terre Haute, 812-232-0523; Vincennes, 812-882-0632.

Committees: *Armed Services* (10th of 33 R): Projection Forces; Readiness. *Judiciary* (11th of 21 R): Immigration, Border Security & Claims (Chmn.); The Constitution.

Group Ratings

	ADA	ACLU	AFS	LCV	CON	ITIC	NTU	COC	ACU	NTLC	CHC
2002	15	36	33	63	76	38	65	80	84	92	92
2001	15	—	11	0	—	—	74	85	92	—	—

National Journal Ratings

	2001 LIB — 2001 CONS		2002 LIB — 2002 CONS	
Economic	36% —	63%	44% —	56%
Social	0% —	81%	32% —	63%
Foreign	32% —	68%	50% —	49%

Key Votes of the 107th Congress

1. Approve Bush Tax Cuts	Y	5. Faith-Based Charities	Y	9. Trade Promotion Authority	*
2. Limit Patients' Bill of Rights	Y	6. Bar Gays in the Boy Scouts	Y	10. Bar Funds for Intl. Court	Y
3. Campaign Finance Reform	N	7. Ban Partial-Birth Abortion	Y	11. Authorize Force in Iraq	N
4. Ban ANWR Development	N	8. Arm Commercial Pilots	Y	12. Deny Home. Sec. Dept. Union	Y

Election Results

2002 general	John Hostettler (R)	98,952	(51%)	($573,220)
	Bryan Hartke (D)	88,763	(46%)	($395,840)
	Other	5,150	(3%)	
2002 primary	John Hostettler (R)	unopposed		
2000 general	John Hostettler (R)	116,879	(53%)	($743,755)
	Paul E. Perry (D)	100,488	(45%)	($1,543,521)
	Other	4,342	(2%)	

Prior Winning Percentages: 1998 (52%); 1996 (50%); 1994 (52%)

The People		Race/Ethnic Origin	Ancestry	
Area size:	7,132 sq. mi.	93.7% White	German: 18.1%	USA: 11.9%
Urban population:	58.1%	3.7% Black	Irish: 8.1%	
Rural population:	41.9%	0.6% Asian	**2000 Presidential Vote**	
Pop. 2000:	675,564	0.2% Native Am.	Bush (R)..............144,848	(56%)
Median income:	$36,732	0.0% Hawaiian	Gore (D)..............106,850	(42%)
Poverty status:	10.7%	0.8% Two+ races	Other...................4,808	(2%)
Military veterans:	13.9%	0.1% Other	**Cook Partisan Voting Index:** R + 8	
		0.9% Hispanic Origin		

Occupation	Blue collar: 31.9%	White collar: 51.9%	Gray collar: 16.2%

"Evansville," wrote John Bartlow Martin in 1947, "is the capital of a tri-state area comprising the neglected tag ends of Indiana, Kentucky and Illinois." It was a factory town then, building car parts and refrigerators, drawing workers from Kentucky, Tennessee and the picturesque but not very fertile hills of southern Indiana. It has seen hard times, such as the terrible flood of March 1997, but it also has the state's first riverboat casino and claims to have the nation's second largest street festival, second only to New Orleans's Mardi Gras celebration.

Evansville is one of two major focuses of the 8th Congressional District, which covers most of southwest and west central Indiana. The other, in Vigo County, is Terre Haute, an old manu-facturing town and the boyhood home of Socialist Eugene Debs. It hosts a maximum-security penitentiary, which includes the only federal death chamber; as such, Terre Haute was the place where Oklahoma City bomber Timothy McVeigh in June 2001 was administered a deadly injection of drugs through a needle in his right leg. This southwest corner of Indiana was the first part of the state settled by whites. Vincennes, now a small town on the banks of the Wabash River, was once the metropolis of Indiana, and Scottish philanthropist and visionary Robert Owen established the town of New Harmony downstream. Owen's son was the first congressman from the area, elected in 1842 and 1844. Southern Indiana is ancestrally Democratic, just as northern Indiana is ancestrally Republican; these southern counties were hostile to the Civil War and southern Indiana's Senator Jesse Bright was expelled by the Senate for "acknowledging Jefferson Davis as 'President of the Confederate States' and support of the rebellion." In New Deal times, workers in Evansville moved again toward the Democrats.

The result has been a very close political balance, and this district has become known as the "Bloody Eighth" for its close congressional races. At one point in the 1970s it elected four different congressmen in four successive elections. In 1984, the state counted the Republican as the winner by exactly 34 votes, but the Democratic House, in a fight that left many House Republicans bitterly aggrieved, overturned the result. In the 1990s, it was as fiercely contested as ever, and in presidential politics as well: Bill Clinton carried it by 2% in 1992 and 1996. In the latest redistricting, it lost about one-third of its old turf as Democrats made the roughly even partisan switch of Democratic-leaning Bloomington to the 9th District in exchange for Terre Haute from the old 7th District.

The congressman from the 8th District is John Hostettler, a Republican first elected in 1994, an ingenuous and idealistic man who seems miscast in politics. Hostettler is from Posey County, just west of Evansville; he went to Rose-Hulman Institute of Technology in Terre Haute and in 1983 became a Southern Indiana Gas & Electric Company engineer. He had never run for office, but in 1994, at 33, he was one of six Republican candidates vying to run against 12-year incumbent Democrat Frank McCloskey. Hostettler's great strength was his support from anti-abortion and Christian fundamentalist groups; he also had regional strength in the western edge of the district, along the Wabash. Hostettler refused to take PAC money; his biggest fundraiser was a $100-per-family fried chicken dinner with Marilyn Quayle. He attacked McCloskey on taxes, gay rights, gun control, the environment, school prayer, his 65 overdrafts at the House bank, and constantly referred to him as "Frank McClinton." McCloskey accused Hostettler of wanting to outlaw all abortions and called him "John McGingrich." McCloskey carried Evansville and Bloomington by microscopic margins, but Hostettler carried most of the rural counties and won 52%–48%.

In the House, Hostettler has been a conservative willing to buck conventional political wisdom and his party leadership. He and fellow Indiana freshman Mark Souder were the only two Republicans to vote against the balanced budget amendment in 1995 because it did not require a supermajority to raise taxes. He opposed term limits, saying that he was against amending the Constitution unless there is no alternative. In 2000 Hostettler was one of three members to vote against the Violence Against Women Act in September; the other two weren't running for reelection. Also that year, he sponsored a flurry of amendments to stop the Clinton administration accord on gun safety with Smith & Wesson—even though pro-gun forces didn't want to raise the issue. Hastert did not want the amendment on any appropriation bill, lest it be vetoed, and Hostettler's proposals were beaten by narrow margins. He had a similar battle with Republican leaders in 2002, when he unsuccessfully sought to remove a compromise deal permitting only a limited number of airplane pilots to carry guns in the flight deck; but Hostettler later prevailed when the Senate agreed to no restrictions. Opposed to "hate crimes" legislation, he asked, "What crime is motivated out of love? We should not create a federal thought police."

Hostettler has repeatedly faced serious Democratic opposition. Refusing to raise PAC money, he had only a narrow money advantage in 1996; he was outspent in the next two contests. In 1996 he eked out a 50%–48% victory. In 1998 Evansville Councilwoman Gail Riecken, with the support of EMILY's List and other national feminist groups, blamed Hostettler for Congress's failure to pass HMO regulation reform. In a low turnout election, Hostettler won 52%–46%. In 2000, he faced Paul Perry, an Evansville orthopedic surgeon who had never run for office. Perry insisted that he opposed abortion and gun control as stoutly as Hostettler and campaigned vigorously, spending $350,000 of his own money. But the undertow of the Democrats' national ticket in the rural and small town area was strong. As in many rural areas, Al Gore was considerably weaker here than Bill Clinton; George W. Bush carried the Bloody Eighth by 56%–42%. Hostettler won 53%–45%—not a landslide by any means, but his best performance in four races.

In 2002, Hostettler showed once again that he is a politician who goes his own way, and creates good breaks for himself. The Democratic-drawn redistricting placed Republican freshman Brian Kerns in the same district, but Kerns decided to run in the 4th District. Democrats hoped that state House Speaker John Gregg from Vigo County would run in the district he helped draw; Gregg unexpectedly said no, as did Paul Perry and, just before the filing deadline, former Representative McCloskey. That left the inexperienced Brian Hartke, the nephew of Indiana's former three-term Senator (1959–1977) Vance Hartke. Hostettler's biggest problems, it seemed, were himself and the *Evansville Courier & Press*. In September 2002, Hostettler said on a local radio program that he would no longer give interviews to the local newspaper because of what he considered unfair coverage of his August meeting in Washington with breast-cancer survivors; during that session, he offended some by discussing controversial studies that link abortion and

breast cancer. In October 2002 he was one of only six House Republicans to vote against authorizing military force against Iraq; he kept a low profile on the vote, but argued on the House floor
that it would set "an ominous precedent" that the "rest of the world could justifiably follow." On
Election Day, Hostettler won, 51%–46%. As in the past, he lost Evansville's Vanderburgh County
and three others at the southern tip of the district, and he lost Vigo and two nearby counties. But
in other rural counties, bolstered by support in churches, he won between 53% and 69% of the
vote. As always, he is certainly not guaranteed a free ride in 2004.

NINTH DISTRICT

Rep. Baron Hill (D)

Elected 1998, 3d term; b. June 23, 1953, Seymour; home, Seymour; Furman
U., B.A. 1975; Christian; married (Betty).

Elected Office: IN House of Reps., 1982–90.

Professional Career: The Hill Agency (insurance), 1975–90; Exec. Dir.,
IN Student Assistance Comm., 1990–94; Financial analyst, Merrill Lynch,
1994–98.

DC Office: 1024 LHOB 20515, 202-225-5315; Fax: 202-226-6866; Web
site: www.house.gov/baronhill.

District Office: Jeffersonville, 812-288-3999.

Committees: *Chief Deputy Minority Whip. Agriculture* (8th of 24 D): Department Operations, Oversight, Nutrition & Forestry; General Farm Commodities & Risk Management; Specialty Crops & Foreign Agriculture Programs. *Armed Services* (17th of 29 D): Readiness; Terrorism, Unconventional Threats & Capabilities. *Joint Economic Committee* (10th of 10 Reps.).

Group Ratings

	ADA	ACLU	AFS	LCV	CON	ITIC	NTU	COC	ACU	NTLC	CHC
2002	70	64	78	13	75	88	25	65	28	21	33
2001	75	—	89	64	—	—	27	50	32	—	—

National Journal Ratings

	2001 LIB — 2001 CONS		2002 LIB — 2002 CONS	
Economic	64%	— 36%	61%	— 39%
Social	59%	— 41%	62%	— 37%
Foreign	56%	— 41%	61%	— 38%

Key Votes of the 107th Congress

1. Approve Bush Tax Cuts	N	5. Faith-Based Charities	N	9. Trade Promotion Authority	Y
2. Limit Patients' Bill of Rights	N	6. Bar Gays in the Boy Scouts	N	10. Bar Funds for Intl. Court	Y
3. Campaign Finance Reform	Y	7. Ban Partial-Birth Abortion	Y	11. Authorize Force in Iraq	Y
4. Ban ANWR Development	Y	8. Arm Commercial Pilots	Y	12. Deny Home. Sec. Dept. Union	Y

Election Results

2002 general	Baron Hill (D)	96,654	(51%)	($1,144,666)
	Mike Sodrel (R)	87,169	(46%)	($1,626,646)
	Other	5,134	(3%)	
2002 primary	Baron Hill (D)	unopposed		
2000 general	Baron Hill (D)	126,420	(54%)	($981,802)
	Michael E. Bailey (R)	102,219	(44%)	($218,270)
	Other	4,644	(2%)	

Prior Winning Percentages: 1998 (51%)

The People		Race/Ethnic Origin	Ancestry	
Area size:	6,670 sq. mi.	94.0% White	German: 19.9%	USA: 12.2%
Urban population:	52.3%	2.3% Black	Irish: 8.7%	
Rural population:	47.7%	0.9% Asian	**2000 Presidential Vote**	
Pop. 2000:	675,599	0.2% Native Am.	Bush (R).............142,694	(56%)
Median income:	$39,011	0.0% Hawaiian	Gore (D).............106,417	(42%)
Poverty status:	10.5%	0.9% Two+ races	Other...................4,288	(2%)
Military veterans:	13.0%	0.1% Other	**Cook Partisan Voting Index:** R + 8	
		1.5% Hispanic Origin		

Occupation   Blue collar: 34.4%   White collar: 50.6%   Gray collar: 15.0%

The southeastern corner of Indiana was a busy place when settlers rafted down the Ohio River in the early 19th Century. They were mostly Southerners, "Butternuts," from across the river in Kentucky or over the mountains in Virginia, and they built the first large Indiana settlements. Today, you can see their work in the marvelous old buildings of Madison, now quiet but once one of the busiest ports on the Ohio River. Farther down the river is Corydon, from 1816–25 the state capital, now the hometown of Governor Frank O'Bannon. The early 19th century buildings here have been well preserved because these towns were bypassed first by the railroads, then by U.S. routes and interstate highways, and they certainly are remote from major airports. The river is still an artery of commerce, but utilitarian barges have replaced steamers, except for riverboat casinos.

Butternut Indiana retained its affection for things Southern into the Civil War and beyond. Local politician Jesse Bright was expelled from the U.S. Senate in 1862 for "supporting the rebellion." To this day, the hills along the Ohio River typically vote Democratic, as do the Indiana suburbs of Louisville. But to the east, Indiana is now filling up with migrants from Cincinnati—a Yankee and German abolitionist bastion in Jesse Bright's time, an overwhelmingly Republican stronghold in ours—who are moving the southeast corner of Indiana away from its ancestral party.

The 9th Congressional District is made up of most of the state's Ohio River counties. Since 2001 redistricting, it has included the Indiana University campus in Democratic-leaning Bloomington. Most of the district is ancestrally Democratic and culturally conservative; much of it has recently been trending Republican, particularly in the suburbs of Louisville and Cincinnati.

The congressman from the 9th District is Baron Hill, a Democrat elected in 1998. Hill grew up in Seymour, the small town of John Mellencamp's song "Small Town." He played basketball for Furman, which later won him induction into the Indiana Basketball Hall of Fame with the more famous Larry Bird, then returned home to a family insurance business. In 1982, at 29, he was elected to the state House and served eight years. In 1990 he ran against Senator Dan Coats and, despite a huge money disadvantage, held him to a 54%–46% win. Governor Evan Bayh appointed Hill to head the state student assistance agency; then he worked for Merrill Lynch. In 1997, Democratic Congressman Lee Hamilton, who represented the district for 34 years and became chairman of the Foreign Affairs Committee, announced his retirement. Hill plunged into the race. His opponent was Jean Leising, a former state senator who gave Hamilton two competitive challenges. Against Hill, she began the campaign ahead, presumably because she was better known. She featured Charlton Heston in TV ads and called in national Republicans to campaign but Hill raised nearly twice as much money. In his 1990 Senate race he had walked the state, from the Ohio River to Lake Michigan; this time he walked 400 miles through all 21 counties of the district starting in July. Hill was behind in polls in late October, but he unleashed two ads that may have made the difference. In one, he said Leising wanted to abolish federal education funding (she said she wanted the money to go to local schools without strings); in the other, he claimed she wanted to privatize Social Security (Leising said she was looking for ways for young people to invest a portion of Social Security taxes). Helped by last minute campaigning from Hamilton and O'Bannon and a solid get-out-the-vote campaign, Hill won 51%–48%.

In the House, Hill has leaned toward the center and joined the Blue Dogs, to the occasional dismay of the party's interest groups. He has voted for the partial-birth abortion ban. In 2000, he was denounced by a United Steelworkers local for his vote in favor of PNTR with China, which he said would benefit Indiana farmers and autoworkers; still, the Chamber of Commerce refused to support his reelection. As a closely watched swing vote, he held firm to support George W. Bush's request for trade promotion authority. And he bucked organized labor again by opposing the proposal to give collective-bargaining rights to employees of the new Homeland Security Department. He joined a group of deficit-conscious Democrats who said they would consider spending controls.

Hill has remained high among the House Republicans' targets, but they have not nominated a candidate with a strong party background. The district includes counties in the Louisville, Cincinnati, Indianapolis and Evansville television markets and not all can be reached by a single radio station; it is an expensive district to run in. In 2000, Indiana Republicans recruited Kevin Kellems, a former aide to Senator Richard Lugar, whom they were convinced would be a strong challenger. But Kellems met an unexpected obstacle: Michael Bailey, who ran graphic ads showing aborted fetuses. Kellems lost 14 of the district's 21 counties and Bailey won, 51%–49%. A surprised and embarrassed NRCC removed the district from its target list, and Speaker Dennis Hastert called it "a second-tier race." Remaking himself as a populist, Bailey seized on Hill's voting to style himself as an opponent of free trade and sought support from unions, winning a local Teamsters endorsement. Hill was aided by the National Rifle Association's support. He won, 54%–44%, though he lost seven counties in the Cincinnati and Indianapolis metro orbits. In 2002, trucking and bus-company owner Mike Sodrel easily won the Republican primary over two other challengers. As a first-time candidate and without attracting much local or national attention, Sodrel raised more than $1 million (more than $900,000 from his own pocket) and called himself a victim of federal regulations for 30 years. He identified closely with Bush. National Republicans ran an ad criticizing Hill for telling an audience that he liked the idea of government investing Social Security funds. This time, Hill won 51%–46%, again losing seven counties.

Although Sodrel said that he would not likely run again, Hill could have a serious challenge in 2004. In December 2002, Hill drew serious mention as a candidate for governor when Lieutenant Governor Joe Kernan bowed out of the race. But in January 2003, Hill announced he would not seek the governorship.

★ IOWA ★

As Americans were surging westward in the 1840s, Iowa was filling up with Yankee farmers and German immigrants, watching as wagon trains headed to the Oregon Trail and the Mormon thousands mustered by Brigham Young headed from the Mississippi across the rolling hills to Council Bluffs on the Missouri and then west. Iowa was a young state then, proud of its hundreds of schools and dozens of colleges, sending more than its share of young men back east to fight for the cause of the Union. After that war Iowans built a solid civilization based on farming, farm-machine making and meat processing that resisted the blandishments of William Jennings Bryan's populism and cheap money, and Iowa became one of the most solidly Republican states in the nation.

But starting around 1900, Iowa grew old. "If you build it they will come" was the theme from the movie *Field of Dreams*, set in Iowa, and in the 19th century, Iowans built a model society. Yet for most of the 20th century very few people came. Iowa's commercial and financial center remained stuck in the railroad hub of Chicago, its economy failed to diversify and develop the dense manufacturing base of the Great Lakes states, and its young people started to move away to make their fortunes. Iowa's population, up from 674,000 in 1860 to 2.2 million in 1900, increased only slowly, and has not reached 3 million to this day: In 1900, Iowa had 11 congressional districts and California 7; now Iowa has 5 and California 53. Its solid Capitol and courthouses, its sturdy but mostly old housing stock, give testimony to Iowa's strengths but also bespeak its lack of dynamism. Even its great economic achievement—the development of high-tech, ever more productive, but also less labor-intensive agriculture—has made this a state that did not grow much. Iowa is still

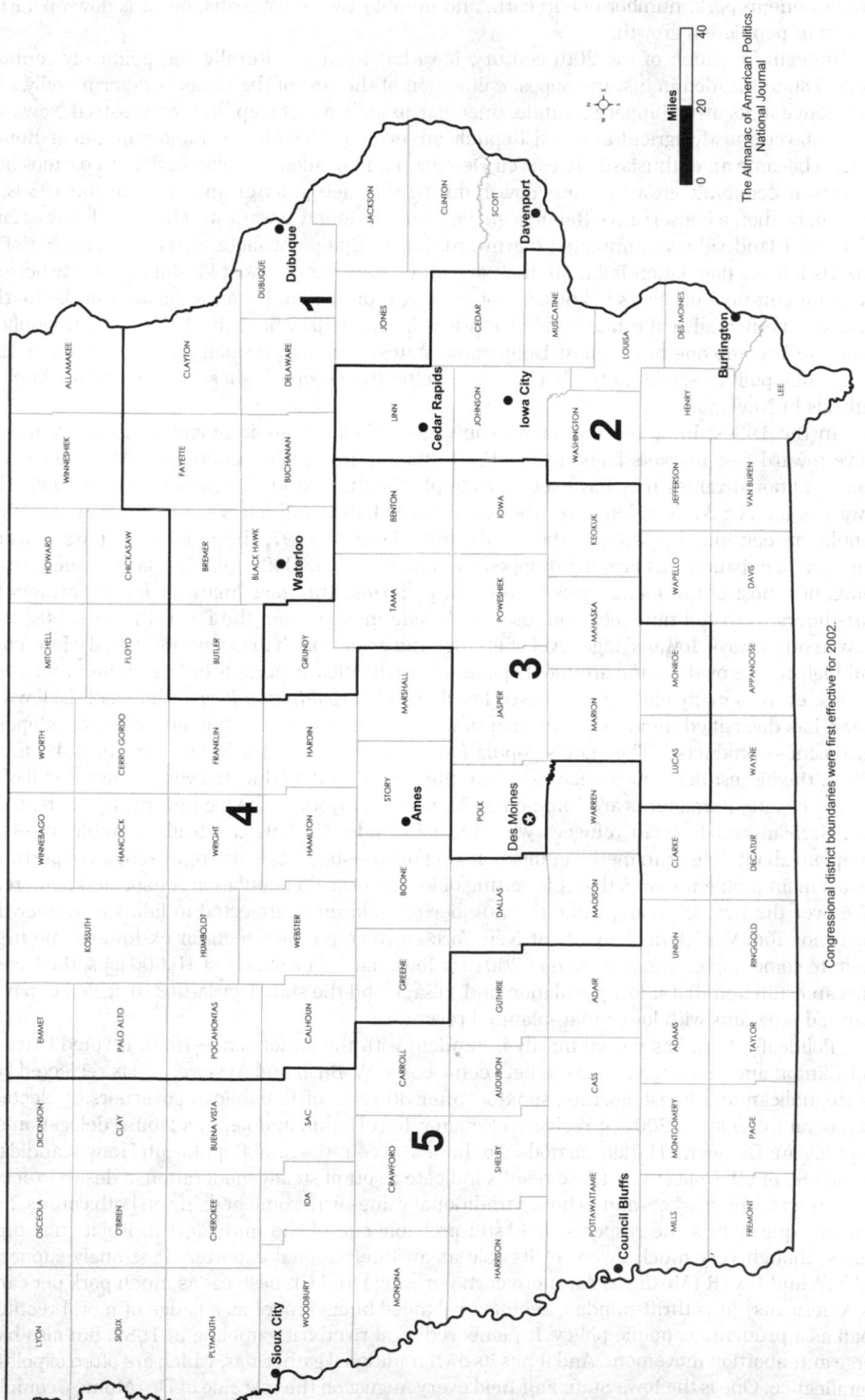

Congressional district boundaries were first effective for 2002.

number one in pork, number one in corn, and number two in soybeans, but it is down near the bottom in population growth.

Indeed, for much of the 20th century, Iowa has been a culturally and politically counter-cyclical state, headed in just the opposite direction of the rest of the nation—determinedly, with confidence in its own chipper rectitude, unembarrassedly out of step. In the industrial New Deal era, it stayed mostly agricultural and Republican, even as Des Moines radio announcer Ronald Reagan became an enthusiastic Roosevelt Democrat and headed to Hollywood. Iowa partook little of postwar economic growth. It was dovish during the Vietnam War and after. In the 1980s, as Reagan, by then a conservative Republican, became president, Iowans watched helplessly as farm prices and land values plummeted downward, farm implement factories closed, and 5% of its citizens left; its population fell more than any other state except West Virginia. Self-pity became the dominant note of Iowa's politics, as voters sought protection from the vagaries of the market even as commercial real estate and stock prices boomed elsewhere. By 1988, once-Republican Iowa had become one of the most Democratic states, sending presidential caucus winner Dick Gephardt's politics solidly to the left and producing the second-highest percentage for Michael Dukakis in November.

In the 1990s, Iowa and the nation converged. If its economic rebellion against America's move toward free markets failed in the 1980s, its cultural qualms about America's move away from traditional values may have set an example for the rest of the country in the 1990s. For Iowa has managed to combine over the years steady habits and tolerance of diversity. The farm population continued to drop in the 1990s; from 1982 to 1997, the number of Iowans whose principal occupation was farming dropped from 86,000 to 56,000. Subsidies keep some farmers going, but most of the money goes to a few large farms, and today many of Iowa's farmers are part-timers, with full-time jobs and just a little side income from the farm. In the 1990s, Iowa grew in other ways. Iowans' high level of literacy and good work habits have produced white-collar and high-tech growth in and around its pleasant small cities, especially in Des Moines and Cedar Rapids, even as many old factories have closed. As *The Washington Post's* Thomas Edsall wrote, "Iowa has diversified into a powerful manufacturing and insurance hub and a key developer of agribusiness products." The state's population fell 4.7% in the 1980s but grew by 5.4% in the 1990s, the biggest percentage increase since the 1910s. And if educated young Iowans still often leave the state, immigrants are coming in—Mexicans to work in the big new meatpacking factories, Serbian and Bosnian refugees who find jobs and stay. This can lead to problems—some complain about "Mexican meth" in meatpacking towns—but it can also represent an opportunity. Iowa's main problem now is that it is getting older: Its over-65 population is expected to increase 47% over the next 20 years, while the number of children is projected to fall. No wonder that Governor Tom Vilsack held a party at New York's Tavern on the Green for ex-Iowans and urged them to come home. The recession of 2001 hit Iowa hard: The state lost 10,000 jobs, the Census Bureau estimated that it lost population and Vilsack and the state legislature struggled to pay for planned programs with lower-than-planned revenue.

Politically, Iowa has moved mostly in tandem with the nation since 1990. It voted twice for Bill Clinton and produced a near-tie between George W. Bush and Al Gore. It has reelected both its Republican and its Democratic senator; after 30 years of Republican governors, it elected a Democrat in 1998. In 2002, it reelected Senator Tom Harkin and kept its House delegation 4–1 Republican: Democrat Harkin carried 79 of Iowa's 99 counties, and Republican House candidates carried 87 of 99. Collectively these results indicate a sort of steady moderation, a desire to accept the verdict of the markets and to honor traditional values with some hedging on both counts. Iowa remains quirky in some respects. It is still probably one of the most dovish, isolationist-prone states, though very much aware of its role as an international exporter: It strongly supported NAFTA and PNTR (Mexicans eat more corn per capita and Chinese eat as much pork per capita as Americans). It is thrift-minded, seeing a balanced budget more as a badge of moral rectitude than as a prudent economic policy. It pioneered legal riverboat gambling in 1989, but also has a large anti-abortion movement. And it has its own traditional gatherings, which are often of political significance. One is the Iowa State Fair held every August on the east side of Des Moines, complete with the traditional 600-pound butter cow and, in 2002, figures from *Peanuts* carved in butter.

And then there are the Iowa precinct caucuses held on a cold night in January in presidential years, the first occasion in which ordinary Americans decide who will be their president.

The People		Race/Ethnic Origin			Military veterans: 292,020 (13.3%)	
Pop. 2000:	2,926,324	2,710,344	92.6%	White	WWII: 22.6%	Korea: 15.6%
Pop. 1990:	2,776,755	60,744	2.1%	Black	Vietnam: 31.4%	Gulf War: 8.3%
Change 1990–2000:	Up 5.4%	36,345	1.2%	Asian	**Most populous cities:**	
Change 1980–1990:	Down 4.7%	7,955	0.3%	Native Am.	1. Des Moines	198,682
% of U.S. total:	1.0%	888	0.0%	Hawaiian	2. Cedar Rapids	120,758
Pop. rank:	30th of 50	25,472	0.9%	Two + races	3. Davenport	98,359
Area size:	56,272 sq. mi.	2,103	0.1%	Other	4. Sioux City	85,013
State Native:	74.8%	82,473	2.8%	Hisp. Origin	5. Waterloo	68,747
Non-citizen:	2.1%	**Ancestry**			Urban population: 61.1%	
Language		German: 26.0%		Irish: 9.8%	Rural population: 38.9%	
English: 92.5%	Spanish: 3.7%	English: 6.9%		USA: 4.9%		
Other Eur.: 2.6%		Norwegian: 4.1%				

Education		Work Sector		General Assembly	
H.S. Grad:	86.1%	Private: 77.8%	Govt: 13.6%	Senate	29 R 21 D
College Grad:	21.2%	Self: 8.2%	Family: 0.4%	House	54 R 46 D
Industry		Unemployment: 4.2%		Legislative Term Limits: No	
Agri: 4.4%	Con: 6.2%	**Household Income**		**Registered Voters**	
Fin: 6.7%	Info: 2.8%	<15k: 14.9%	15-35k: 29.0%	D: 576,725	(29.2%)
Mfg: 21.9%	Prof: 27.8%	35-50k: 19.0%	50-100k: 29.8%	R: 627,520	(31.8%)
Public: 3.4%	Trade: 15.6%	100-150k: 4.9%	>150k: 2.4%	I: 769,188	(39.0%)
Other: 11.1%		Median: $39,469			
Occupation		Poverty status: 9.1%			
Blue collar: 27.0%	White collar: 57.2%	**Home Value**			
Gray collar: 15.8%		<50k: 22.9%	50-100k: 42.2%	100-200k: 27.5%	200-300k: 5.0%
		300-500k: 1.8%	>500k: 0.6%	Median: $82,100	

Presidential politics   On a frosty evening in January every four years, more than 100,000 Iowans troop to caucuses in some 2,131 precincts and begin the process of choosing a president of the United States. The precinct caucuses were scheduled early in the cycle for 1972 by Democratic doves who wanted more leverage for their views, and that year they started George McGovern on his way to the Democratic nomination. But the caucuses have had other, unanticipated consequences. In 1976, Jimmy Carter's strategist Hamilton Jordan determined that intensive campaigning could produce a surprise victory that could make a little-known candidate a national contender: Without Iowa and the next-week New Hampshire primary, Carter would never have become president.

2000 Presidential Vote		
Gore (D)	638,517	(49%)
Bush (R)	634,373	(48%)
Nader (Green)	29,374	(2%)
Other	13,299	(1%)

1996 Presidential Vote		
Clinton (D)	620,258	(50%)
Dole (R)	492,644	(40%)
Perot (I)	105,159	(9%)

Then, for 20 years, the Iowa caucuses were less nomination-determinative. In 1980, George H.W. Bush's intensive campaigning gave him a victory among Republicans, while Carter, still profiting from his 1976 contacts, trounced Senator Edward Kennedy. But Bush lost the nomination to Ronald Reagan, and Carter lost in November. In 1984 Democratic favorite Walter Mondale won 49% of the "delegate strength" (Democrats don't compute the actual number of votes), but the momentum went to the 17% second place finisher Gary Hart, though Mondale did win the nomination. In 1988, Iowa failed to pick the winners on either side: Dick Gephardt, dressed in a warm-up jacket and baseball cap, capitalized on Iowa's economic woes to win among Democrats, while George Bush finished in third place behind Kansas Senator Bob Dole and televangelist Pat Robertson among Republicans—a sign of the rising strength of Christian conservatives here. But Gephardt and Dole lost in New Hampshire, and neither was nominated. In 1992, Iowa went dark: No Democrat challenged Iowa's Tom Harkin here, and Pat Buchanan began his campaign in New Hampshire. In 1996, Dole had the support of leading Republicans, led by Governor Terry Branstad and Senator Charles Grassley, and farm state roots as well: Dole's very narrow victory was an omen of the weakness of his candidacy later, and the negative ads run against him by Steve Forbes and others may have contributed to his weak showing in Iowa in the fall.

But Iowa is determined to maintain its first-in-the-nation status, enshrined in national Democratic (but not Republican) rules. In 2000, Iowa moved its caucus date back to Monday, January 24, when New Hampshire surprised everyone by scheduling its primary for Tuesday, February 1. And in 2000, Iowa turned out to be important again. The Republican favorite, George W. Bush, refused to campaign here (or anywhere else) before the Texas legislature adjourned in May 1999, but he charged into the battle for the Republicans' straw poll at Ames on August 14. Originally designed as a Republican fundraiser, the straw poll had let anyone with $25 vote up through 1996; in 2000, it limited participation to Iowans, and drew much more interest than ever before—25,000 attended, about 30% as many as would vote in the much more convenient precinct caucuses in January. Bush won with 31%, followed by intensive campaigner Steve Forbes, with 21%; Elizabeth Dole, with 14%, and Gary Bauer, with 9%, which kept their campaigns alive for a time. Pat Buchanan, with fewer votes from a larger crowd than in 1996, did not succeed, and not long afterwards left the Republican Party for his ill-fated Reform Party candidacy. In January the standing was not much different. Bush won with 41% of the vote and Forbes got 30%, not the upset victory he needed. Both got a share of religious conservatives, as did Alan Keyes, who was third with 14%. In November 1999, Arizona Senator John McCain announced he was staying out of dovish Iowa.

Democrats had only two candidates, and both Al Gore and Bill Bradley campaigned intensively. In his 1988 campaign, Gore skipped what he called "madness" in "the small state of Iowa"; in June 1997 he was proclaiming, "I love Iowa," and in November 1998, he was on the phone congratulating Tom Vilsack before Vilsack himself realized he had been elected governor. Gore did not get Vilsack's support—he stayed carefully neutral—but Gore did get vigorous support from Vilsack's wife, from Senator Harkin and, perhaps most important, from Iowa's labor unions. Bradley ran ahead in university towns, carrying Johnson County (Iowa City) and running even in Story County (Ames). And with support from professional-class liberals, he did not run far behind in the two biggest counties, Polk (Des Moines) and Linn (Cedar Rapids). But Gore won 70% or more in counties containing heavily unionized factory towns—Waterloo, Mason City, Fort Dodge, Marshalltown, Jasper, Keokuk, Burlington, Council Bluffs. That was dispositive since the Democratic vote is concentrated in urban areas, and Gore won in "delegate strength" with 63% to Bradley's 35%. This big victory undoubtedly gave Gore some momentum in New Hampshire, which he won by just 50%–46%. It would be five weeks until the next Democratic contest and, as eyes turned to George W. Bush's battles with McCain, the race for the Democratic nomination was over.

No one pays close attention to Iowa's seven electoral votes in the fall, though perhaps someone should; this state came very close to the national average in 2000. Al Gore won a 48.5%–48.2% victory, carrying most of the counties east and north of Cedar Rapids plus a narrow margin in the Des Moines area; George W. Bush carried most counties in the west and south. (Bush's campaign strategist Karl Rove later rued that the Bush campaign plane was too big to land in any airport in eastern Iowa.) In some ways, this ran on traditional Iowa divisions: Bush carried Protestants, Gore Catholics. But it was not necessarily a harbinger of future Democratic victories. Iowa has the nation's third-highest percentage of elderly, and Gore carried those over 65 by 51%–48%, according to the VNS exit poll; of those who voted the issue of Social Security, Gore won by a surprisingly narrow 54%–43%. In contrast, Bush carried voters under 45—the future of Iowa—by 52%–45%. This is a state that should be seriously contested in any close race in the future.

Congressional districting

Iowa's congressional district lines are drawn by the nonpartisan Legislative Services Bureau and then approved by the governor and legislature—a process that is praised by many critics of partisan gerrymandering and bipartisan incumbent protection plans. But it is not entirely apolitical. The Legislative Service Bureau is not supposed to take past voting patterns or legislator's place

108th Congress Lineup	
4 R	1 D

107th Congress Lineup	
4 R	1 D

of residence into account, and in good Iowa fashion, they don't. But the governor and legislators can and do. In May 2001, the Iowa Senate rejected the Legislative Service Bureau's first plan; Republicans said the population disparities were too large, but Democrats contended that Republicans thought it was politically damaging to them. So a special session was called in June to consider the Bureau's second plan. That plan placed Republican congressmen Jim Nussle and Jim Leach in the same district—"mathematically defensible, but socially and politically awkward," Leach said—and separated Des Moines from suburban Dallas and Warren Counties, with which it arguably has a community of interests. Indeed, with the exception of the 5th District in western Iowa, all the districts combine very disparate parts of Iowa. Nevertheless Democratic Governor Vilsack and the Republican legislature approved the plan. Two incumbents moved their residences, Leach into the 2d District, most of which he had been representing, and Democrat Leonard Boswell into Des Moines in the new 3d District, whose incumbent, Republican Greg Ganske, was running for the Senate.

The Iowa plan did produce more strenuous competition than was seen in most states. Four of the five districts were contested seriously by both Democrats and Republicans, and the 5th had a spirited Republican primary. Still, no incumbent was defeated, and most are likely to strengthen their position by 2004.

Governor

Tom Vilsack (D)

Elected 1998, term expires Jan. 2007, 2d term; b. Dec. 13, 1950, Pittsburgh, PA; home, Mt. Pleasant; Hamilton Col., B.A. 1972, Albany Law Schl., J.D. 1975; Catholic; married (Christie).

Elected Office: Mt. Pleasant Mayor, 1987–92; IA Senate, 1992–98.

Professional Career: Practicing atty., 1975–98.

Office: State Capitol, Des Moines, 50319, 515-281-5211; Fax: 515-281-6611; Web site: www.governor.state.ia.us.

Election Results

2002 general	Tom Vilsack (D)	540,449	(53%)
	Doug Gross (R)	456,612	(45%)
	Other	28,741	(3%)
2002 primary	Tom Vilsack (D)	unopposed	
1998 general	Tom Vilsack (D)	500,231	(52%)
	Jim Ross Lightfoot (R)	444,787	(47%)
	Other	11,397	(1%)

Tom Vilsack, the only Democratic governor Iowa has had since 1968, was elected in 1998 and reelected in 2002. He grew up in Pennsylvania (and was beaten often by his mother, he revealed in 2000), went to college and law school in Upstate New York, visited Iowa courting his wife and decided to live there. They moved to Mount Pleasant in southeast Iowa where he joined his father-in-law's law firm and won notable verdicts for farmers defrauded in the Prairie Grain Elevator case and in a class action that returned $13 million to 86,000 insurance policyholders (average: $151 each). In 1987, he became mayor of Mount Pleasant and was elected to the state Senate in 1992 with 50% of the vote. He nearly retired from the state Senate in 1996, but decided to stay; now he is governor.

Vilsack was an upset winner in both the Democratic primary and in the general election. Republicans had held the governorship for 30 years; they had just gained control of the state House in 1994 and the state Senate in 1996. The state had a record surplus, unemployment was down to 3% and it was widely assumed Republicans would win again. Governor Terry Branstad had held office for a record 16 years; in March 1997, there was talk first that Republican Senator Charles Grassley might run, then that Democratic Senator Tom Harkin might. Neither did. In the Democratic primary, Vilsack was endorsed by the United Auto Workers and upset a better-known candidate, former state Supreme Court Justice Mark McCormack, who ran as a moderate, 51%–48%. Vilsack carried Cedar Rapids and Davenport, but lost Des Moines and the university towns of Iowa City and Ames, as well as most small counties. In the general election, he faced former Congressman Jim Ross Lightfoot, who had held Harkin to a 52%–47% victory in 1996. Vilsack called for upgrading education and attracting agribusinesses to make Iowa "the Silicon Valley of food." Lightfoot, who even aides admitted disliked campaigning, ran mainly on the tax cut and ended with ham-handed negative ads. Harkin played a key role. He had a grudge against Lightfoot since 1996 and had set up a PAC to beat him if he ran for governor; he insisted that he was against Lightfoot on issues rather than personal grounds. Harkin helped raise $300,000 of Vilsack's $2.3 million treasury and Harkin himself campaigned for the last two weeks all over the state. Vilsack ran a 23-city bus caravan and advanced steadily in polls. On election night, Vice President Al Gore called Vilsack to tell him he'd won; Vilsack was watching *All the President's Men* instead of the televised results. His margin was 52%–47%.

The legislature remained in Republican hands, so Vilsack did not achieve some of his goals—such as an increase in the minimum wage. But he did push through laws to reduce classroom size in the early grades and to crack down on methamphetamine addiction. He also got increases in teacher pay—the teachers' unions are one of his mainstays of support—and greatly increased the number of children in the children's health insurance program. In April 2000, the legislature repealed Vilsack's order banning discrimination in state employment against gays, lesbians and transsexuals; Vilsack vetoed that and in the fall 22 legislators sued, charging he exceeded his powers—a state judge declared Vilsack's order invalid. Vilsack vetoed a waiting period for abortions and signed a health insurance regulation law without the right to sue as he had sought. Perhaps most controversial was the recommendation, embraced by Vilsack, of a bipartisan commission headed by former Republican governor primary candidate David Oman that Iowa needs to recruit 310,000 foreign workers to settle in the state. Vilsack projected that Iowa's elderly population, already the third highest in the country, would increase to 20% by 2010; already Iowa's unemployment rate is one of the lowest in the nation, and more workers are needed to keep its economy growing. Vilsack has gone on trips to New York, Chicago and Los Angeles to encourage former Iowans to return home; he has set up "welcome centers" for Mexicans and others who have come to work in the state's meatpacking factories.

But Iowa's economy stopped growing in 2000, and little more was heard about encouraging immigration. Instead, the focus was on cutting state spending when expected revenues failed to flow in. Cuts began in 2001; in February 2002, Vilsack dipped into the state's rainy day fund. The state seemed unable to afford promise teacher pay increases and class size reduction. State employees were furloughed or given retirement buyouts. Some initiatives continued though. Sales of Vision Iowa bonds, to build museums and arenas, came in better than expected. Vilsack proposed a 10-year $600 yearly tax credit for graduates of Iowa colleges who stayed in the state.

That was the situation as Vilsack sought to be the first Iowa Democratic governor reelected since 1966. Several Republicans stepped forward to challenge him, but not University of Iowa wrestling coach Dan Gable, who turned down party leaders in July 2001. All were little known. State Representative Steve Sukup, owner of a family farm equipment business, called for a $20 million tax cut. Robert VanderPlaats, a Sioux City businessman and head of a children's physical rehabilitation nonprofit, called for thoroughgoing tax reform. Doug Gross, a relatively late entry, had been a staffer for Governor Robert Ray and chief of staff to Branstad; he charged Vilsack with mismanaging the budget. This turned out to be an exceedingly close race. Gross won with 36% of the vote—just above the 35% threshold required to keep the nomination from going to a state party convention—while Sukup and VanderPlaats, with different geographic bases, got 32% each. In the general, Vilsack, as the incumbent and with strong support from labor unions, had more money and attacked Gross for being a $300,000 lawyer-lobbyist whose firm represented hog lot producers who opposed proposals for local regulation of hog lots. This is a sulphurous issue in some communities, and one that gets attention. Polls in late June showed the race even. But

Vilsack's attacks enabled him to pull ahead, and in November, he won by a 53%–45% margin, carrying 68 of Iowa's 99 counties.

But Republicans retained control of both houses of the legislature. Fiscal and personnel problems remained: There were estimates that the state faced a $400 million shortfall on the 2003–04 budget. On the day before Thanksgiving, Vilsack fired six of his commissioners. As he grapples with state problems, Vilsack will have the compensation of the companionship of several Democratic presidential candidates until the Iowa precinct caucuses in January 2004 and at least a moment in the national spotlight. Vilsack said during this campaign, as he had in 1998, that he would seek only two terms.

Senior Senator

Charles Grassley (R)

Elected 1980, seat up 2004, 4th term; b. Sep. 17, 1933, New Hartford; home, New Hartford; U. of N. IA, B.A. 1955, M.A. 1956, U. of IA, 1957–58; Baptist; married (Barbara).

Elected Office: IA House of Reps., 1958–74; U.S. House of Reps., 1974–80.

Professional Career: Farmer.

DC Office: 135 HSOB, 20510, 202-224-3744; Fax: 202-224-6020; Web site: grassley.senate.gov.

State Offices: Cedar Rapids, 319-363-6832; Council Bluffs, 712-322-7103; Davenport, 563-322-4331; Des Moines, 515-284-4890; Sioux City, 712-233-1860; Waterloo, 319-232-6657.

Committees: *Agriculture, Nutrition & Forestry:* Marketing, Inspection & Product Promotion; Production & Price Competitiveness. *Budget. Finance* (Chmn.): International Trade; Social Security & Family Policy. *Judiciary:* Administrative Oversight & the Courts; Crime, Corrections & Victims' Rights (RMM); Immigration, Border Security & Citizenship. *Joint Committee on Taxation* (Vice Chmn. of 5 Sens.).

Group Ratings

	ADA	ACLU	AFS	LCV	CON	ITIC	NTU	COC	ACU	NTLC	CHC
2002	10	20	0	6	69	88	64	95	95	91	—
2001	5	—	0	0	—	—	78	100	92	—	100

National Journal Ratings

	2001 LIB	—	2001 CONS		2002 LIB	—	2002 CONS
Economic	17%	—	77%		32%	—	66%
Social	0%	—	79%		0%	—	62%
Foreign	7%	—	72%		0%	—	76%

Key Votes of the 107th Congress

1. Approve Bush Tax Cuts	Y	5. Confirm Ashcroft as AG	Y	9. Bar Coop. with Intl. Court	Y
2. Expand Patients' Rights	N	6. Bar Gays in the Boy Scouts	Y	10. Trade Promotion Authority	Y
3. Campaign Finance Reform	N	7. $ for Hate Crime Prosecution	N	11. Authorize Force in Iraq	Y
4. Permit ANWR Development	Y	8. Overseas Military Abortions	N	12. Homeland Sec. Dept. Union	N

Election Results

1998 general	Charles Grassley (R)	648,480	(68%)	($2,781,940)
	David Osterberg (D)	289,049	(30%)	($165,429)
	Other	10,378	(1%)	
1998 primary	Charles Grassley (R)	unopposed		
1992 general	Charles Grassley (R)	899,761	(70%)	($2,486,030)
	Jean Lloyd-Jones (D)	351,561	(27%)	($410,894)
	Other	40,879	(3%)	

Prior Winning Percentages: 1986 (66%); 1980 (54%); 1978 House (75%); 1976 House (57%); 1974 House (51%)

Charles Grassley, the senior Senator from Iowa, was first elected to the Senate in 1980. He grew up on a farm in Butler County near Waterloo; his parents switched parties when Franklin Roosevelt ran for a third term in 1940. In 1956, Grassley ran for the state legislature and lost by 70-some votes. While in graduate school, he ran for the state House in the Democratic year of 1958 and was elected, at 25; while in the legislature he worked as a sheet metal shearer and an assembly line worker. He won an U.S. House seat in the Democratic year of 1974 and a Senate seat by beating a strong incumbent, John Culver, in 1980. Grassley combines political shrewdness with a seeming naivete that at some level is surely genuine. He describes himself as "just a hog farmer from New Hartford," and says, "I don't know how you're going to have a strong farm economy if we don't have some farmers in Congress. I can't tell you how many people I have to tell that food doesn't grow on grocery shelves." Starting in 1997, he led the Senate in consecutive roll call votes; the last one he missed came when he was inspecting flood damage in Iowa in 1993. He goes back home to Iowa just about every weekend, helps his son run the 710-acre family farm and holds open meetings in every one of Iowa's 99 counties each year.

Three issues guided Grassley's early record in Congress: Thrift, agriculture and dovishness on defense. He is ever alert for abuse of power. His first major legislation was the 1986 Federal False Claims Act, which authorizes suits for fraud on behalf of the government; he says it has brought in $5.6 billion. He long sponsored the bill to apply to Congress the same laws it applies to others, and was the chief sponsor of the Congressional Accountability Act of 1995. He is a strong supporter of free trade and has worked from Washington to Seattle to open up markets for agricultural products; he strongly supported PNTR with China and managed trade promotion authority to passage in May 2002. Grassley supported both the Freedom to Farm Act of 1996 and subsequent emergency payments and loan provisions for farmers. In 1991, he was one of two Republicans to vote against the Gulf war resolution. He does not echo other Republicans' calls for more defense spending and is quick to seize on Pentagon outrages; in 2002, he was complaining about misuse of Defense Department credit cards.

Grassley is now chairman of the Senate Finance Committee, a position he also held from January to June 2001. There he had worked for the childcare tax credit, enacted in 1997, and to reinstate the deductibility of interest on student loans. He was chief sponsor of the wind energy production tax credit of 1992 and seeks favorable treatment for ethanol and biomass; in 1998, he got the ethanol tax credit extended to 2007. He spent years highlighting abuses by the IRS and helped pass the IRS reforms of 1998. Later he worried that the IRS was not enforcing the law strictly enough; in April 2001 he said, "I'm worried by claims that the IRS is the dog that doesn't bark—or perhaps bark enough—about Internet tax fraud." As chairman in May 2001, he negotiated a bipartisan package that became the largest tax cut in history. He pushed unsuccessfully for the Bush stimulus package in fall 2001 and in summer 2002 was chief sponsor of the "tripartisan" prescription drug plan (it was co-sponsored by John Breaux and Jim Jeffords), one of several that failed to get the required 60 votes. In 2003 he is likely to be a key player on any Medicare/prescription drug bill.

Grassley is likely to seek a change in the Medicare reimbursement formula under which Iowa currently receives the lowest reimbursement per beneficiary of any state ($3,053 per patient versus over $7,000 in Breaux's Louisiana); this became a big issue in Iowa in 2002 thanks to a *Des Moines Register* series and Republican Rep. Greg Ganske, running for the Senate, who put through a formula change in the House. Grassley has called for a less sweeping change than his colleague Tom Harkin, though Harkin also supported Grassley's bill. On the Judiciary Committee, Grassley has been the chief sponsor of bankruptcy reform, not yet passed; he has taken special care to see that Chapter 12, applying to farmers, would allow them to reorganize without creditors' consent. He supported the Freedom to Farm Act in 1996 and later, disaster relief spending. But he opposed the May 2002 farm bill, since the final version lacked his amendment to ban meatpacker ownership of livestock and had higher limits on subsidies than the $275,000 he had persuaded the Senate to vote for. "A number of folks have been saying this is a good bill, and I'd say those folks are part right. It's a good bill if you're a cotton and rice producer. The problem is, we don't grow those commodities in my state of Iowa."

Large issues claim much of Grassley's attention, but he is willing to devote much time to smaller issues as well. He worked on the money-laundering bill after September 11 and said of bank lobbyists, "They are being very unpatriotic in their approach." He has called for the Justice Department to conduct antitrust investigations of mergers that affect Iowa—most recent, Smith-field Foods' proposed purchase of bankrupt Farmland Industries. Since the 1992 Ruby Ridge incident, he has been a frequent critic of the FBI; he has said that Director Robert Mueller needs to change the culture of the agency. He worked to bring airline competition to Iowa and to encourage renewable sources of energy—wind, biomass, soy diesel, animal waste nutrients. With New York Senator Charles Schumer, he has tried to bring television to federal courts. They urged Chief Justice William Rehnquist to let in the cameras when the court was considering the Florida cases in December 2000; the Court said no, but did release audiotapes immediately after oral argument.

For more than 20 years, Grassley has been the most popular politician in Iowa. As he once said, "I think I've established credibility with the people of Iowa that they know I'm going to use a common-sense approach to government." In 1986, he became the first Iowa senator to win re-election in 20 years, with a record 66% of the vote. In 1992, he broke the record when he won 70%–27%, carrying all 99 counties. In 1998, against a Democrat who campaigned by taking trips down Iowa rivers, he fell back to 68%–30%, carrying all 99 counties again, from Johnson County and its college town Iowa City (53%–45%) to heavily Dutch-American Sioux County (91%–9%). In August 1999, he said he expected to run again in 2004 and no one doubts that he will win. At that point, he will have tied Bourke Hickenlooper for the second-longest tenure of an Iowa senator; he will beat the record set by William B. Allison if he serves until June 2016, three months before he turns 83.

Junior Senator

Tom Harkin (D)

Elected 1984, seat up 2008, 4th term; b. Nov. 19, 1939, Cumming; home, Cumming; IA St. U., B.S. 1962, Catholic U., J.D. 1972; Catholic; married (Ruth).

Military Career: Navy, 1962–67; Naval Reserves, 1969–72.

Elected Office: U.S. House of Reps., 1974–84.

Professional Career: Practicing atty., 1972–74; Staff Aide, House Select Cmte. on U.S. Involvement in SE Asia, 1973–74.

DC Office: 731 HSOB, 20510, 202-224-3254; Fax: 202-224-9369; Web site: harkin.senate.gov.

State Offices: Cedar Rapids, 319-365-4504; Davenport, 563-322-1338; Des Moines, 515-284-4574; Dubuque, 563-582-2130; Sioux City, 712-252-1550.

Committees: *Agriculture, Nutrition & Forestry* (RMM). *Appropriations*: Agriculture & Rural Development; Defense; Foreign Operations; Homeland Security; Labor, HHS & Education (RMM); VA, HUD & Independent Agencies. *Health, Education, Labor & Pensions*: Children & Families; Employment, Safety & Training. *Small Business & Entrepreneurship*.

Group Ratings

	ADA	ACLU	AFS	LCV	CON	ITIC	NTU	COC	ACU	NTLC	CHC
2002	80	60	100	76	31	62	19	45	15	0	—
2001	100	—	100	100	—	—	6	38	8	—	0

National Journal Ratings

	2001 LIB	—	2001 CONS		2002 LIB	—	2002 CONS
Economic	93%	—	0%		87%	—	11%
Social	95%	—	0%		76%	—	23%
Foreign	74%	—	14%		81%	—	15%

Key Votes of the 107th Congress

1. Approve Bush Tax Cuts	N	5. Confirm Ashcroft as AG	N	9. Bar Coop. with Intl. Court	Y
2. Expand Patients' Rights	Y	6. Bar Gays in the Boy Scouts	N	10. Trade Promotion Authority	Y
3. Campaign Finance Reform	Y	7. $ for Hate Crime Prosecution	Y	11. Authorize Force in Iraq	Y
4. Permit ANWR Development	N	8. Overseas Military Abortions	Y	12. Homeland Sec. Dept. Union	Y

Election Results

2002 general	Tom Harkin (D)	554,278	(54%)	($6,897,168)
	Greg Ganske (R)	447,892	(44%)	($5,392,510)
	Other	20,905	(2%)	
2002 primary	Tom Harkin (D)	unopposed		
1996 general	Tom Harkin (D)	634,166	(52%)	($6,070,137)
	Jim Ross Lightfoot (R)	571,807	(47%)	($2,439,679)

Prior Winning Percentages: 1990 (54%); 1984 (55%); 1982 House (59%); 1980 House (60%); 1978 House (59%); 1976 House (65%); 1974 House (51%)

Tom Harkin, a Democrat first elected to the Senate in 1984, is an accomplished veteran of Capitol Hill who still brings the attitude of the aggrieved outsider to his work. Harkin grew up poor in a rural town, where his father was a coal miner and his mother, a Slovenian immigrant, died when he was 10. His desire to use government to help those who are struggling comes not from academic theory, but from tough personal experience. He worked his way through college and law school, and spent five years in the Navy during the 1960s, ferrying planes from Vietnam for repair. Returning there in 1970 as an aide to Congressman Neal Smith, he discovered the infamous "tiger cages" prison cells. After a narrow loss in 1972, Harkin ran for Congress again in 1974 and invented "work days," a campaign technique widely imitated since: He spent a day working at each of a dozen or so local jobs. He won solidly and held the seat with good percentages. Well before the 1984 election, he cornered the Democratic nomination to run against Senator Roger Jepsen. In the midst of Iowa's farm depression of the 1980s, Harkin was elected with 55% of the vote.

Harkin served as chairman of the Agriculture Committee from June 2001 to January 2003 and steered to passage the 2002 farm bill. This was a considerable achievement, and one out of line with his previous record. His big initiative was the 1987 Harkin-Gephardt supply management farm bill, which would have raised overall food costs in order to benefit small farmers. But it was a nonstarter even in the 1980s, when Iowa farmers were hurting. In 1996, Harkin opposed the Freedom to Farm Act, which purported to phase out farm subsidies. But starting in 1998, Congress approved disaster relief every year for farmers, which had much the same economic effect. Harkin supported these efforts and worked to make conservation payments an entitlement and to promote the use of ethanol and alcohol fuels. Farm exports are important to Iowa, and Harkin, despite his warm feelings for labor unions, voted, apparently with some reluctance, for NAFTA in 1993 and PNTR for China in 2000. On taking the chairmanship in June 2001, Harkin worked to fashion a farm bill that would restore much of the subsidies (and end the need, supporters said, for annual disaster relief) and that could win bipartisan support, though it was clear that his predecessor as chairman, Richard Lugar, would not go along. His goals were to increase conservation programs, come up with a formula for countercyclical aid and fight concentration in agribusiness. In July 2001, the Agriculture Committee and the Senate voted for a $7.4 billion farm aid package over Lugar's $5.5 billion alternative; but George W. Bush insisted on a $5.5 billion limit and Harkin's side felt obliged to back down in order to pass the bill.

In November 2001, Harkin introduced his bill, with no limit on subsidies (though Harkin had proposed one) and more spending for conservation and food stamps (to secure votes from non-farm states)—a contrast with the bill the House passed in October 2001, with higher subsidies and less for conservation and food stamps. Senate Republicans defeated the bill in December 2001, but it was revived and passed in February 2002, with increased but limited subsidies for grain and cotton and a doubling of conservation money. The total cost was estimated at $73.5 billion over 10 years, with most of that money spent in the near-years. Harkin put in subsidies to discourage the use of irrigated water and added dairy and peanut provisions that won votes from

New England and the Deep South; it passed 58–40. It included a ban on meatpackers owning livestock—a key issue for Iowa Republican Charles Grassley. The bill went to conference committee, in which the House Republicans, led by Larry Combest from cotton-farming west Texas, insisted on higher subsidy limits and deletion of the ban on meatpacker ownership of livestock. Harkin brought the bill back and got the Senate to pass it; it was opposed, however, by his colleague Grassley and by his 2002 opponent, Congressman Greg Ganske, on the subsidy limits and livestock ownership issues.

Apart from agriculture, Harkin's greatest impact has probably been on health policy. Two of his sisters died from breast cancer and one brother of thyroid cancer; another brother became deaf at age nine. He insisted on having a sign language interpreter present for his brother for his swearing-in in 1985, and when he left the 1992 presidential race he spoke partly in sign language at Gallaudet University in Washington, D.C., a noted school for the hearing impaired. Harkin was a key player in shaping the Americans with Disabilities Act of 1990. This was a great achievement, one that required overcoming resistance based on cost and qualms about the real-world effect of regulations, to build a bipartisan coalition with the Bush administration. As chairman and ranking Democrat on the Labor-HHS Appropriations Committee, Harkin worked creatively and determinedly to double the budget for the National Institutes of Health over five years—strengthening one of America's greatest research institutions in a way that may be remembered gratefully 50 or 100 years from now.

On foreign policy, Harkin's views seem to have been shaped by the Vietnam War. He was a vocal opponent of Contra aid in the 1980s and of the Gulf War resolution in 1991, bringing a lawsuit against President Bush to try to prevent him from using force without congressional approval. But he favored the threat of force in Haiti in 1994. He voted to authorize the use of force in Iraq in 1998, when Bill Clinton sought it; in October 2002, he opposed the initial resolution authorizing force for Bush as overbroad, but voted in favor of the final version of the resolution.

In Iowa politics, Harkin has been a figure much like Jesse Helms in North Carolina: His fervent stands on issues and his hard-edged campaigning give him a large base of strong supporters and a large base of strong detractors as well. But, like Helms, he always seems to have more strong supporters: He has never won by a large margin, but he has never lost either, and in his career he has beaten no less than five officeholding Republicans—in his first House race in 1974 and in the Senate races of 1984, 1990, 1996 and 2002—but, like Helms, has never won with more than 56% of the vote. He ran for president in 1992. In angry phrases, with a Truman-esque zest, Harkin preached that George Bush and the Republicans helped only the rich and that government must get involved to help the poor and middle class. But organized labor withheld an early endorsement despite his 90%-plus AFL-CIO voting record—a great tactical victory for Bill Clinton. Harkin's sweep of the Iowa caucuses February 10, actually an impressive testimonial to his home state popularity, was mostly discounted by the media. He finished with only 10% in New Hampshire; though he won the Minnesota and Idaho caucuses March 3, he got only 7% in South Carolina March 7 after campaigning there with Jesse Jackson. In debt and ineligible for matching funds, Harkin quit the race. He supported Clinton fervently during impeachment, calling the House managers' case "a pile of dung" and made the only objection during the trial, arguing that senators should not be called "jurors" because their duties went beyond those of jurors and they were not limited by the Constitution or the Federalist Papers to just a narrow finding of fact; Chief Justice William Rehnquist, presiding over the trial, agreed. In 2000, Harkin endorsed Gore in the Iowa precinct caucuses and appeared with him all over the state—an important factor in Gore's smashing victory. Harkin was mentioned in July 2000 as a possible vice presidential nominee and was interviewed twice by Warren Christopher.

In 2002, Harkin's opponent was Congressman Greg Ganske, a Des Moines plastic surgeon who had upset 36-year incumbent Neal Smith in 1994 and had been one of the lead supporters of HMO regulation in the House. Many Republican leaders thought Ganske's moderate record and base in usually Democratic Des Moines would make him a strong candidate. But first he had to face a primary opponent, 33-year-old farmer Bill Salier, who ran as a strong conservative. The Bush White House backed Ganske, but seemed unimpressed with his fundraising and campaign; George W. Bush came to Iowa for Congressman Tom Latham in March 2002, but pointedly ignored

Ganske, though a month later he appeared at a Ganske fundraiser. Ganske won the June 2002 primary, but by an unimpressive 59%–41% margin.

Against Harkin, Ganske argued that his work on HMO regulation showed that he could work on a bipartisan basis for solutions to problems. Harkin argued that with his seniority he could best serve Iowa's interests. Harkin attacked Ganske for supporting "privatization" of Social Security; Ganske said his plan would not affect workers over 50 and would give younger workers the choice of putting some of their taxes into individual investment accounts. Harkin touted passage of the farm bill; Ganske said it gave too much in subsidies to southern cotton and rice farmers and didn't include a ban on meatpacker ownership of livestock. Polls showed the race fairly close after the June primary. But Harkin had far more money and, for the first time, the endorsement of the Iowa Farm Bureau Federation. Then, in September, scandal struck. A Des Moines Democrat who had worked on Harkin's staff in the 1970s and in 2002 changed his registration to Republican and contributed $50 to Ganske attended a meeting of Ganske fundraisers with a tape recorder in his pocket. After the meeting, he turned it over to a 21-year-old Harkin campaign staffer. A transcript was leaked to a political reporter by "Democratic sources" quoting Ganske as saying, "You've never seen a campaign where anyone will attack him like we're going to. With a smile on our face. Not angry, not growling or scowling." Ganske protested that his meeting had been spied on and called for prosecutors to investigate; Harkin's campaign manager said his campaign had nothing to do with it. That lie was exposed and by the end of the week, the campaign manager resigned and Harkin apologized. At their next debate angry words flowed. It was a foolish incident all round. Ganske's comments were braggadocio (his campaign ran no such ads), the Harkin staff learned nothing useful from the spying (anyone could guess that Ganske might say negative things about Harkin) and Republicans' calls for prosecution were overblown.

Many observers speculated that in squeaky-clean Iowa this caper would cost Harkin votes. Perhaps it did, but not very many. Iowa in 2002 was in a mood to reelect incumbents, Democratic and Republican, and Harkin's work on the farm bill and his endorsement by the Farm Bureau helped him win many rural counties he had never won before. His campaign and the Iowa Democratic party also ran an effective, high-tech voter registration and turnout operation, with volunteers equipped with Palm Pilots and wireless transmission devices; they appear to have maximized the Democratic vote not only in factory towns but in rural counties Democrats usually don't carry. Harkin won 54%–44%. Regional patterns of support evident in Harkin's 1990 and 1996 runs were not evident in 2002. He carried Des Moines, Cedar Rapids and all of Iowa's significant cities except Council Bluffs, but he won in most rural areas as well, carrying 79 of Iowa's 99 counties—far more than the 50 he carried in 1996 or the 63 he carried in 1990.

FIRST DISTRICT

Rep. Jim Nussle (R)

Elected 1990, 7th term; b. June 27, 1960, Des Moines; home, Manchester; Luther Col., B.A. 1983, Drake U., J.D. 1985; Lutheran; married (Karen).

Professional Career: Practicing atty., 1985–86; Delaware Cnty. Atty., 1986–1990.

DC Office: 303 CHOB 20515, 202-225-2911; Fax: 202-225-9129; Web site: www.house.gov/nussle.

District Offices: Davenport, 563-326-1841; Dubuque, 563—557-7740; Manchester, 563-927-5141; Waterloo, 319-235-1109.

Committees: *Budget* (Chmn. of 24 R). *Ways & Means* (10th of 24 R): Trade.

Group Ratings

	ADA	ACLU	AFS	LCV	CON	ITIC	NTU	COC	ACU	NTLC	CHC
2002	0	13	0	25	25	100	57	100	92	92	100
2001	0	—	0	21	—	—	63	100	88	—	—

National Journal Ratings

	2001 LIB —	2001 CONS	2002 LIB —	2002 CONS
Economic	7%	89%	21%	73%
Social	20%	69%	32%	63%
Foreign	49%	47%	41%	56%

Key Votes of the 107th Congress

1. Approve Bush Tax Cuts	Y	5. Faith-Based Charities	Y	9. Trade Promotion Authority	Y
2. Limit Patients' Bill of Rights	Y	6. Bar Gays in the Boy Scouts	Y	10. Bar Funds for Intl. Court	Y
3. Campaign Finance Reform	N	7. Ban Partial-Birth Abortion	Y	11. Authorize Force in Iraq	Y
4. Ban ANWR Development	N	8. Arm Commercial Pilots	Y	12. Deny Home. Sec. Dept. Union	Y

Election Results

2002 general	Jim Nussle (R)	112,280	(57%)	($1,692,794)
	Ann Hutchinson (D)	83,779	(43%)	($1,020,908)
2002 primary	Jim Nussle (R)	unopposed		
2000 general (IA 2)	Jim Nussle (R)	139,906	(55%)	($907,935)
	Donna L. Smith (D)	110,327	(44%)	($92,477)
	Other	2,288	(1%)	

Prior Winning Percentages: 1998 (55%); 1996 (53%); 1994 (56%); 1992 (50%); 1990 (50%)

The People		Race/Ethnic Origin	Ancestry	
Area size:	7,291 sq. mi.	92.1% White	German: 31.5% Irish: 11.1%	
Urban population:	66.3%	3.8% Black	English: 6.0%	
Rural population:	33.7%	0.8% Asian	**2000 Presidential Vote**	
Pop. 2000:	585,302	0.2% Native Am.	Gore (D)	135,856 (52%)
Median income:	$38,727	0.0% Hawaiian	Bush (R)	116,588 (45%)
Poverty status:	10.1%	1.0% Two + races	Other	7,737 (3%)
Military veterans:	13.8%	0.1% Other	**Cook Partisan Voting Index:** D + 4	
		2.0% Hispanic Origin		

Occupation   Blue collar: 28.3%   White collar: 55.7%   Gray collar: 16.0%

Northeast Iowa, along the Mississippi River and westward, has some of the loveliest landscape in America. Here the Mississippi flows past green bluffs, then broadens out in great quiet pools and flows past picturesque towns. A century and a half ago settlers surged west of the Mississippi. Germans stopped at the river bluffs reminiscent of their native land and built neat farmhouses and substantial towns. Inland, on the rolling hills portrayed with surprisingly little exaggeration in the paintings of Iowa's Grant Wood, and in the more open territory to the west, New England and Midwestern Yankees built their characteristic farmhouses, barns, town halls, church spires and small colleges. Railroad builders, headquartered in Chicago, extended their networks of steel rails over the plains and rivers. You can see the stamp of these pioneers today, though the old ethnic folkways have faded and giant barges and riverboat casinos have replaced the old river steamboats. Davenport, on the hills over the Mississippi River still has the look of the city where Ronald Reagan got his first radio job more than 60 years ago; in order to maintain its riverfront heritage, the city has refused to erect flood walls along the Mississippi which brought the ire of FEMA Director Joseph Allbaugh during the April 2001 flood season. German Catholics settled Dubuque, whose giant Victorian courthouse looks down on the Mississippi and up at the Fenelon Place Elevator that rides up the bluff. Farther west is Waterloo, which grew rapidly after 1900 as the John Deere tractor factory expanded and the eight-floor Rath factory became the largest meat-packing plant in the world; Rath closed in 1984 and Deere had thousands of layoffs, but Waterloo has rebounded somewhat with new businesses from a dog track to telemarketing to a high-tech Iowa Beef Processing (IBP) factory.

The 1st Congressional District covers much of northeast Iowa, including the Mississippi riverfront from the antique town of McGregor south to Davenport, Iowa's part of the Quad Cities and heading west 100 miles as far as Butler County. There is considerable political variation here. Davenport and next-door Bettendorf were historically Republican, but in 2000, like much of eastern Iowa, they voted narrowly for Al Gore. Dubuque, heavily German Catholic, was for years Iowa's most Democratic city, and still is sometimes unless abortion is the issue. But the rural counties along the river and farther west—more German Protestant, Scandinavian and Yankee—were traditionally Republican. Waterloo and Cedar Falls, originally Republican, trended sharply Democratic in the troubled 1980s. Overall this district is pretty evenly balanced, though it gave Al Gore a majority in 2000, if only because, as Bush strategist Karl Rove ruefully observed, there was no airport large enough in eastern Iowa to handle the Bush campaign plane.

The congressman from the 1st District is Jim Nussle, first elected in 1990, at 30 the youngest member of the 102d Congress, and now chairman of the House Budget Committee. Nussle grew up in Chicago, then moved back to his native Iowa to attend a Lutheran college (he is Danish-American and speaks Danish; he has a Great Dane PAC) and law school. In the small town way, he soon became Delaware County attorney, known for prosecuting a local day care employee for child abuse. He coupled his anti-abortion stance with support for helping expectant mothers with the expenses of parenthood. When Republican Congressman Tom Tauke ran for the Senate in 1990, Nussle ran for his seat, narrowly winning the Republican primary and then facing a better-financed Democrat. He won 50%–49%, one of the closest margins in the country that year.

Nussle quickly became one of the leaders of the nascent Republican revolution. He was one of the Gang of Seven, a group of freshman Republican reformers who attacked the Democratic leadership. In October 1991 he made national news by donning a paper bag over his head on the House floor to protest Democratic leaders' refusal to make full disclosure of House bank over-drafts. He voted against agricultural appropriations, to the dismay of senior Iowa Democrats, and moved to cut congressional salaries 5% every year the federal budget is not balanced. For 1992, redistricting put Nussle into a district with Democratic incumbent Dave Nagle. Nagle had rep-resented more of the new district's territory, but Nussle won again by 50%–49%. In 1994 Nagle tried again, and Nussle won more easily, 56%–43%.

After the election, Gingrich appointed Nussle chairman of the transition to Republican rule: From paper bag to power in just three years. Nussle froze hiring, demanded detailed accountings, and supervised an overhaul of House administration. He also got a seat on Ways and Means. But Nussle had an unexpectedly tough time of it in the 1996 election. He vastly outspent Democrat Donna Smith, a 17-year Dubuque County supervisor, but she hammered home his closeness to Gingrich, and attacked "Georgia Jim" for supporting big hog feedlots. Nussle won by just 53%–46%.

After that election, Nussle sounded a much less revolutionary note. He was passed over by Gingrich for the chair of the Republicans' campaign committee and in July 1997 he ran for Conference vice chairman against Jennifer Dunn, Gingrich's choice; he lost 129–85. Nussle turned to issues with local appeal. In June 2002, he got Ways and Means to approve an amend-ment raising Iowa's Medicare reimbursement rate, the lowest in the nation, by 5% a year for three years; it passed the House but died in the Senate. One of his children is a special education student, and he wants to increase IDEA funding. He inserted into the energy bill in summer 2001 a provision giving appliance makers $292 million to make the energy-efficient washing machines and refrigerators required by Clinton administration regulations.

When he was just a member of the Budget Committee, he worked with Democrat Ben Cardin to change the budget process. In July 1999, when John Kasich announced his retirement from the House, Nussle said he would run for Budget chairman. His main competitor was Saxby Chambliss of Georgia, who held the leadership spot on the committee and thought he had a commitment from the leadership. But Majority Leader Dick Armey, who tangled with Chambliss on base closings and peanut subsidies, strongly backed Nussle, and the House leadership picked him in January 2001.

As chairman, Nussle vowed not to pass a phony budget resolution with spending figures so low appropriators would ignore them, and he worked closely with Appropriations members and took care to consult committee Democrats. But he was largely guided by the recommendations of the Bush administration. In the May 2001 budget conference committee, he abandoned the emergency reserve fund opposed by appropriators and ruled in violation of the budget law by the Senate parliamentarian (who, however, was fired the next day). In the conference he got a low budget number, while Senate Budget Chairman Pete Domenici got money allotted for a Medicare reserve fund, health insurance for the uninsured and restoration of Medicare cuts. The House passed the conference report 221–207 in May 2001. In 2002, things were different because the Senate, by now with a Democratic majority, never passed a budget resolution. In the post-election session in November 2002, he exerted his power as Budget chairman when others had agreed to allow states to keep $2.7 billion of children's health insurance money they had not spent; Nussle heard about it at 12:30 a.m. and killed it by 2:00.

Nussle was reelected with 55% of the vote in 1998 and 2000—not large margins for an incumbent. The June 2001 redistricting plan removed the western parts of Nussle's old 2d District and added three counties, two of which he had represented in the early 1990s. But the other— Scott County—was the largest in the new, renumbered 1st District, and included Davenport and Bettendorf, Iowa's half of the bistate Quad Cities. Scott County was also the home of incumbent Republican Jim Leach, first elected in 1976; Leach, however, decided to move to Iowa City and run in the new 2d District. Scott County was also the home base of Nussle's 2002 Democratic opponent, Ann Hutchinson. She appeared to be a strong candidate, and this was a first-tier race for both parties. Hutchinson had been mayor of Bettendorf since 1988; she boasted that she turned a $4 million budget deficit into a $4 million surplus. Just before announcing, she switched her party registration from Republican to Democratic; she said she had registered Republican in 1988 to vote for a friend in a state Senate primary. Hutchinson beat Dave Nagle soundly in the primary, and accused Nussle of being a Washington insider who voted for big corporate interests. She attacked Nussle on prescription drugs and said he backed "privatization" of Social Security; he said he was against "privatization" but wanted to add options for savings and investment for younger workers. Speaker Dennis Hastert ventured in from Illinois to support a new I-74 bridge in Davenport, and just about every live Democratic presidential possibility came in for Hutchinson. George W. Bush came in for Nussle in September 2002 and then again just before the election.

The surprise of this election is that it turned out not to be very close. Nussle won 57%–43% and carried every county, including Scott County by a 56%–44% margin. He carried both of the district's two heavily Democratic counties, Dubuque and Black Hawk (Waterloo) with 54% and 53% of the vote, and in rural counties won between 57% and 68% of the vote. Democrats were dumbfounded and Republicans elated. The size of Nussle's majority makes it unclear whether Democrats will seriously contest this district in 2004.

SECOND DISTRICT

Rep. Jim Leach (R)

Elected 1976, 14th term; b. Oct. 15, 1942, Davenport; home, Iowa City; Princeton U., B.A. 1964, Johns Hopkins U., M.A. 1966, London Schl. of Econ., 1966–68; Episcopalian; married (Elisabeth).

Professional Career: Staff Asst., U.S. Rep. Donald Rumsfeld, 1965–66; U.S. Foreign Svc., 1968–69, 1971–72 (Arms Control & Disarmament Agency); A.A. to Dir., U.S. Office of Econ. Opp., 1969–70; Pres., Flamegas Co., 1973–76; Chmn. of the Bd., Adel Wholesalers, Inc., 1973–76; Dir., Fed. Home Loan Bank Bd., Midwest Reg., 1975–76.

DC Office: 2186 RHOB 20515, 202-225-6576; Fax: 202-226-1278; Web site: www.house.gov/leach.

District Offices: Burlington, 319-754-1106; Cedar Rapids, 319-363-4773; Iowa City, 319-351-0789; Ottumwa, 641-684-4024.

Committees: *Financial Services* (2d of 37 R): Domestic and International Monetary Policy, Trade & Technology. *International Relations* (2d of 26 R): Asia & the Pacific (Chmn.); Western Hemisphere.

Group Ratings

	ADA	ACLU	AFS	LCV	CON	ITIC	NTU	COC	ACU	NTLC	CHC
2002	30	43	11	38	15	88	44	85	56	56	42
2001	45	—	30	71	—	—	53	78	25	—	—

National Journal Ratings

	2001 LIB	—	2001 CONS	2002 LIB	—	2002 CONS
Economic	52%	—	49%	51%	—	49%
Social	62%	—	39%	54%	—	45%
Foreign	75%	—	25%	66%	—	33%

Key Votes of the 107th Congress

1. Approve Bush Tax Cuts	Y	5. Faith-Based Charities	Y	9. Trade Promotion Authority	Y
2. Limit Patients' Bill of Rights	N	6. Bar Gays in the Boy Scouts	N	10. Bar Funds for Intl. Court	N
3. Campaign Finance Reform	Y	7. Ban Partial-Birth Abortion	Y	11. Authorize Force in Iraq	N
4. Ban ANWR Development	Y	8. Arm Commercial Pilots	Y	12. Deny Home. Sec. Dept. Union	Y

Election Results

2002 general	Jim Leach (R)	108,130	(52%)	($780,586)
	Julie Thomas (D)	94,767	(46%)	($1,342,801)
	Other	4,274	(2%)	
2002 primary	Jim Leach (R)	unopposed		
2000 general (IA 1)	Jim Leach (R)	164,972	(62%)	($335,143)
	Bob Simpson (D)	96,283	(36%)	($28,536)
	Other	5,564	(2%)	

Prior Winning Percentages: 1998 (57%); 1996 (53%); 1994 (60%); 1992 (68%); 1990 (100%); 1988 (61%); 1986 (66%); 1984 (67%); 1982 (59%); 1980 (64%); 1978 (64%); 1976 (52%)

The People		Race/Ethnic Origin	Ancestry	
Area size:	7,684 sq. mi.	92.4% White	German: 24.0% Irish: 10.4%	
Urban population:	66.0%	2.0% Black	English: 7.3%	
Rural population:	34.0%	1.5% Asian	**2000 Presidential Vote**	
Pop. 2000:	585,241	0.2% Native Am.	Gore (D)	141,487 (53%)
Median income:	$40,121	0.0% Hawaiian	Bush (R)	113,255 (43%)
Poverty status:	9.9%	1.0% Two+ races	Other	11,581 (4%)
Military veterans:	13.0%	0.1% Other	**Cook Partisan Voting Index:** D + 5	
		2.7% Hispanic Origin		

Occupation	Blue collar: 26.5%	White collar: 58.6%	Gray collar: 14.9%

Eastern Iowa is a land little known to outsiders. It is a land of rolling hills and deep river valleys, of undulant farm fields and big skies, of prosperous small towns and grain elevators and factories. Even political writers, who come to Iowa by the thousands for the quadrennial precinct caucuses tend to hang out in Des Moines and to do their reporting there or in small counties within an hour's drive; this is a lot bigger state than New Hampshire, and driving from Des Moines east to the second largest city, Cedar Rapids, takes more than two hours—only worth it for some major event. Eastern Iowa was not accessible even to candidate George W. Bush in 2000, since his campaign plane was too big to land in any of the airports here. So Al Gore ran well in eastern Iowa—it was one of the few parts of the country where he carried most rural counties—and carried the state by 4,000 votes.

But there are things to see in eastern Iowa, and people worth meeting. Cedar Rapids, the metropolis in these parts, has high-tech employers and contemporary office buildings; it boomed in the 1990s, and per capita income, adjusted for the local cost of living, is among the nation's highest. Yet traditional industries still make themselves known: Go down by the river and you can't miss the smell of burnt oats coming from the Quaker Oats factory. Iowa City, just to the south, is a university town complete with trendy bookstores and vegetarian eateries; the University of Iowa is known for its Writer's Workshop. Travel farther afield, and you will come on increasing oddities. Rural Cedar County, the birthplace of Herbert Hoover, reported a tie on election night 2000, the only county in the nation to do so; a recount gave Al Gore a 4,033–4,031 vote lead.

Bentonsport, in Van Buren County near the Missouri border, was mostly bought up by the county's conservation board in the 1970s, and restored; now it is an artists' and craftsmen's colony. Conesville, in Muscatine County near the Mississippi, has an Hispanic majority—the only city in Iowa that does—attracted at first by farm work in the fields and more recently by the IBP plant in nearby Columbus Junction. Anamosa, in Jones County just east of Cedar Rapids, features the house painted by Anamosa native Grant Wood in *American Gothic*—the models for the two figures were his dentist and his sister, who died only in 1990—and you can have your picture taken there too. Or visit the Inn of the Six-Toed Cat in Allerton, in Wayne County, where natives returned from the big city have saved a 1912 round barn and built an International Center for Rural Culture and art in 93 acres. The oddest of all is Iowa's newest city, incorporated in 2001, Vedic City. It's just outside Fairfield, in Jefferson County, where followers of the Maharishi Mahesh Yogi built Maharishi University in 1973, where believers in transcendental meditation study and meditate and practice yogic flying (the first step is hopping around). There's a political angle too: TM followers supported John Hagelin of the Natural Law party for president in 1996, and he won 21% of the vote in Jefferson County in 1996 and 15% in 2000.

All these parts of eastern Iowa are in the state's 2d Congressional District. It is by most measures Iowa's most Democratic congressional district, thanks in large part to big Democratic majorities in Iowa City's Johnson County; Cedar Rapids's Linn County has also been inclined toward the Democrats of late.

The congressman from the 2d District is, however, a Republican, Jim Leach, first elected in 1976, and chairman of the House Banking Committee from 1995 to 2001. Leach grew up in Davenport, where his family owned propane gas and wholesale businesses, attended Princeton, studied Soviet politics at Johns Hopkins and the London School of Economics. He became a Foreign Service officer in 1968, worked for Donald Rumsfeld in the House in 1965 and at the Office of Economic Opportunity (like Rumsfeld he wrestled at Princeton), then was assigned to the Arms Control and Disarmament Agency and served in the United Nations when George Bush was U.S. ambassador there. In 1973, Leach resigned after Richard Nixon fired special prosecutor Archibald Cox and returned to the family businesses in Davenport; in 1976 he ran for the House and beat incumbent Democrat Edward Mezvinsky. A believer in free enterprise with hands-on experience in a regulated business, Leach remains market-oriented on most economic issues. On cultural issues, he looks with favor on international family planning and affirmative action. On foreign policy, like many Iowa Republicans, he has shown caution about asserting U.S. military power, but supported the Gulf War resolution in 1991 and continued deployment of troops in Bosnia in 1997. He voted against the Iraq war resolution in October 2002, one of six House Republicans to do so; he said his major concern was the possible use of Iraq's biological weapons.

On the Banking Committee (now Financial Services), Leach was one of the few who predicted the S&L crisis of the late 1980s: He warned early on that allowing the states to liberate their savings and loans from investment limits while maintaining federal deposit insurance and not increasing capital requirements would lead to trouble. His greatest achievement was the November 1999 passage of financial services deregulation, tearing down the 1933 Glass-Steagall Act wall between commercial and investment banks, authorizing financial holding companies and allowing them to own insurance companies. This bill was the focus of most of his chairmanship; his efforts were blocked by the insurance industry in 1996 and his bill was yanked from the floor by the leadership in March 1998. Despite his reputation for being above partisanship, in July 1995, when he chaired hearings on Whitewater, he was confronted by a barrage of loud partisan objections from Democrats, who then tried to discredit the hearings as partisan.

Leach stuck with his moral principles through this hurricane, and in other contexts. He has been trying to ban Internet gambling with a bill that would bar payment by credit card, check or electronic transfer. His stand was strong enough to inspire a profile in the *Las Vegas Review-Journal*: "It is precisely because of Leach's moderate and cerebral persona that the casino industry has come to regard him as a more formidable foe than fire-breathing Virginia Republican Frank Wolf, a longtime and vocal gambling critic." At a hearing in July 2002 on WorldCom, he told CEO Bernard Ebbers, "The issue of the year is moral clarity. To put it plainly, it is self-dealing for a corporate head to give himself a multi-hundred-million-dollar loan, and it is dereliction of duty for a board to go along."

House Republicans impose a six-year limit on committee chairmanships, and so Leach lost the Banking Committee chair in January 2001. Leach then took the chairmanship of the East Asia Subcommittee, on which he had been ranking minority member from 1985 to 1993. In 2001, he took care to warn Chinese officials that the United States would worry about China's intentions toward Taiwan as long as it kept missiles aimed there. But he and Henry Hyde opposed conservatives who wanted to bring up the Taiwan Security Enhancement Act that passed the House but not the Senate in 2000; they argued that Taiwan could depend on George W. Bush to protect its interests.

At home, Iowa's much-praised nonpartisan redistricting system put Leach in jeopardy of losing his seat in 2002. He had won without difficulty from 1978 to 1994, and his one serious challenge came in 1996, after the Whitewater hearings, when Bill Clinton juiced up a campaign by a former state senator who held Leach to a 53%–46% win. The 2001 redistricting plan sliced up his district and forced Leach to make a tough choice: He could either run in the new 1st District, which included Scott County, his home and the county that supplied almost all of his victory margin in 1996, or he could run in the new 2d District, where over half the votes were cast in Johnson and Linn counties (Iowa City and Cedar Rapids) which Leach lost in 1996. Leach decided to run in the 2d, which contained more of his old district than the new 1st, and, characteristically, sold his house in Davenport and bought one in Iowa City: You don't have to be a resident of the district to run, but he thought it just wouldn't be right.

In these circumstances Leach attracted a formidable opponent, Julie Thomas, a Cedar Rapids pediatrician since 1974 who had lobbied state legislators on laws like the one banning drive-by deliveries. She said she decided to run because Leach wouldn't endorse universal health care coverage for children. Thomas ran an aggressive, politically savvy campaign, on what were standard Democratic themes in 2002: Against "privatization" of Social Security, for a prescription drug benefit under Medicare, for reimportation of drugs from Canada, against trade promotion authority, against tort reform (which earned her the opposition of the American Medical Association PAC). She raised money assiduously and far outraised Leach—ultimately by $1.3 million to $780,000 (Leach refuses to accept contributions from PACs or from contributors outside Iowa). This was Al Gore's best Iowa district, and to Democrats she argued: Vote for a real Democrat.

Lack of money forced Leach to pull ads off the air during the summer, while Thomas was able to keep them coming. "We've almost reversed roles. I'm running the challenger's campaign. I go to all the events. I'm everywhere. She spends most of her time on the telephone, what Democrats call dialing for dollars. It's smart politics. I just happen to be uncomfortable with it. I'm confident I'll be the most outspent Republican incumbent." But Leach was helped by the spending of others, for whom this was a top tier race. The League of Conservation Voters, appreciative of his environmental record, spent $200,000 on ads to help him. He had the endorsements of the Iowa State Education Association, the Iowa Farm Bureau Federation and the Human Rights Campaign—not groups usually found in the same room. In September 2002, Leach took to the floor of the House and denounced the nationalization of campaigns, and went over to NRCC chairman Tom Davis and asked him not to buy ads in his district. "I think he looked at me as if I'm naive," Leach said later; the campaign committee, seeing polls that showed Leach's early wide leads narrowing, spent money on anti-Thomas ads all through October. It turned out to be the closest House race in a state with much more than its national share of close races. Leach won 52%–46%. He carried Linn County, Thomas's home base, by 52%–46% and Johnson County by 51%–48%. Thomas carried industrial Ottumwa and Fort Madison and Keokuk on the lower Mississippi River; Leach carried the three rural counties he had been representing from 1992 with 60% or more of the vote. This may not be the last serious challenge that he, hampered by his self-imposed limits on fundraising, will face in this Democratic-leaning district.

THIRD DISTRICT

Rep. Leonard Boswell (D)

Elected 1996, 4th term; b. Jan. 10, 1934, Harrison Cnty., MO; home, Davis City; Graceland Col., B.A. 1969; Reorganized Latter Day Saints; married (Dody).

Military Career: Army, 1956–76 (Vietnam).

Elected Office: IA Senate, 1984–96, Pres., 1992–96.

Professional Career: Farmer.

DC Office: 1427 LHOB 20515, 202-225-3806; Fax: 202-225-5608; Web site: www.house.gov/boswell.

District Office: Des Moines, 515-282-1909.

Committees: *Agriculture* (19th of 24 D): General Farm Commodities & Risk Management; Livestock & Horticulture. *Permanent Select Committee on Intelligence* (4th of 9 D): Human Intelligence, Analysis & Counterintelligence (RMM); Terrorism and Homeland Security. *Transportation & Infrastructure* (18th of 34 D): Aviation; Railroads.

Group Ratings

	ADA	ACLU	AFS	LCV	CON	ITIC	NTU	COC	ACU	NTLC	CHC
2002	80	67	78	75	63	50	27	55	32	14	25
2001	85	—	100	71	—	—	22	48	24	—	—

National Journal Ratings

	2001 LIB —	2001 CONS		2002 LIB —	2002 CONS
Economic	57%	44%		58%	42%
Social	65%	34%		56%	42%
Foreign	61%	36%		64%	36%

Key Votes of the 107th Congress

1. Approve Bush Tax Cuts	N	5. Faith-Based Charities	N
2. Limit Patients' Bill of Rights	N	6. Bar Gays in the Boy Scouts	N
3. Campaign Finance Reform	Y	7. Ban Partial-Birth Abortion	Y
4. Ban ANWR Development	Y	8. Arm Commercial Pilots	Y

9. Trade Promotion Authority	N
10. Bar Funds for Intl. Court	Y
11. Authorize Force in Iraq	Y
12. Deny Home. Sec. Dept. Union	N

Election Results

2002 general	Leonard Boswell (D)	115,367	(53%)	($1,316,037)
	Stan Thompson (R)	97,285	(45%)	($895,163)
	Other	3,333	(2%)	
2002 primary	Leonard Boswell (D)	unopposed		
2000 general	Leonard Boswell (D)	156,327	(63%)	($710,518)
	Jay Marcus (R)	83,810	(34%)	($198,403)
	Other	8,677	(3%)	

Prior Winning Percentages: 1998 (57%); 1996 (49%)

The People		Race/Ethnic Origin	Ancestry	
Area size:	7,034 sq. mi.	90.1% White	German: 20.7%	Irish: 9.6%
Urban population:	73.1%	3.2% Black	English: 7.7%	
Rural population:	26.9%	1.9% Asian	**2000 Presidential Vote**	
Pop. 2000:	585,305	0.4% Native Am.	Gore (D) 132,890	(49%)
Median income:	$43,176	0.0% Hawaiian	Bush (R) 131,319	(48%)
Poverty status:	8.0%	1.1% Two+ races	Other 7,226	(3%)
Military veterans:	12.7%	0.1% Other	**Cook Partisan Voting Index:** X +00	
		3.2% Hispanic Origin		

Occupation	Blue collar: 23.5%	White collar: 62.0%	Gray collar: 14.5%

Iowa, which today seems very much in the middle of the country, was once part of the West. It was not only the home of sober farmers and pious burghers, but also the eastern terminus of the first Transcontinental Railroad, a waystop for people in a hurry to get across the Great Plains to the Rockies and the Pacific Northwest. Those who stayed behind were determined to use the wealth accumulated by methodical husbandry of their fertile farmlands to implant firmly the glories of Western civilization. You can feel that impulse today in Des Moines when you look across the river from downtown at the Victorian Capitol, its gold dome above a Corinthian pediment, or Terrace Hill, the beautifully restored governor's mansion, atop a hill overlooking the Raccoon River. The nearby Living History Farms, which recreate Indian villages, frontier towns and turn-of-the-century farms, show the effort the new settlers made to put their imprint on the environment.

The 3d Congressional District covers 12 counties in central Iowa, including Des Moines's Polk County and extending to the east. It is the only Iowa district that does not border another state or a mighty river on the east or west. Some 65% of its votes are cast in Polk County, but it does not include Dallas or Warren Counties which are in the Des Moines metropolitan area. Des Moines remains classically Middle America, consuming more Jell-O per capita than anywhere else in the nation. It is now spreading into the countryside even as Iowa farm counties' population continues to decline. Insurance, agricultural supply and printing and service businesses are expanding in office centers downtown and at freeway interchanges; Iowans are driving 100 miles or more to fill the shopping malls at cities' edges. The remainder of the district is largely rural, with no city larger than 30,000. But these small towns continue to house some giant manufacturing plants. Pella (9,800) is the home of the Pella window and door maker, which employs 3,000 workers. The famed Amana colonies, which were founded in 1855 by the Community of True Inspiration, German pietists who have retained many of their old customs, is the home of the Amana appliance business; in 2001, Newton (population 15,000) appliance-maker Maytag acquired Amana in a marriage of two of the state's largest manufacturers. Polk County has historically voted Democratic, but has become more Republican as its white collar businesses grow and its blue collar businesses fade; the rural counties here have mostly been historically Republican. The result is a district split right down the middle, about as evenly divided as the nation in the presidential election of 2000.

The congressman from the 3d District is Leonard Boswell, a Democrat elected in 1996, the only new Iowa Democrat elected to the House since 1986. He is not the stereotypical Democrat, however. Boswell grew up on farms in Ringgold and Decatur Counties, near the Missouri border. He was drafted in 1956, at 22, and was a private in the Army. He re-enlisted, graduated first in his class in both fixed wing and helicopter flying school, served two years in Vietnam, and retired as a lieutenant colonel in 1976. Boswell settled down on his Decatur County farm and became head of the local Farmers' Co-op. He managed to keep it out of bankruptcy during the farm depression of the 1980s and decided to go into politics. He was elected state senator from a six-county Republican district in 1984, served as chairman of Appropriations and, after 1992, Senate president; he was the Democratic nominee for lieutenant governor in 1994.

In 1996, Boswell ran for an open seat in the old 3d District, whose Republican congressman was running against Senator Tom Harkin. The district was largely rural and extended across the southern tier of Iowa from the Mississippi River to within one county of the Missouri. His contest with Poweshiek County attorney Mike Mahaffey was very much a contest of nice guys. Boswell flew his four-seater Piper Comanche 250 around the district and called for balancing the budget, higher education aid and protections against Medicare reductions, all to be financed with Pentagon cuts and elimination of Medicare waste. Mahaffey ran as a moderate Republican. Boswell was endorsed by the Farm Bureau, which usually backs Republicans. He raised more money than Mahaffey and, like other Democrats, ran ads attacking Newt Gingrich and the Republican Medicare plan. The result was a 49%–48% Boswell victory.

Boswell got a seat on Agriculture and, amid dropping farm prices, continued to support the Freedom to Farm Act. Along with all of the delegation's Republicans, he voted for PNTR with China, the world's biggest market for pork. His voting record has consistently placed him in the most conservative quadrant of House Democrats. He helped to form the Mississippi River Caucus to seek consensus on commercial uses of the river and its environmental protection. In 2001, Boswell was assigned to the Intelligence Committee. With his extensive military background and "top secret" clearance, he was well positioned to investigate the nation's response to terrorism. In October 2002, he voted to authorize military action in Iraq.

The 2001 redistricting plan drawn by the Legislative Service Bureau and approved by the legislature and governor left Boswell with a dilemma. Only 7 of the 27 counties and 24% from the population in his former district were moved to the new 3d District. His farmhouse, along with 7 counties, was moved to western Iowa's new, heavily Republican 5th District. The other option was to move to the new 2d District, which leans Democratic but where he probably would have faced a tough contest against Republican Jim Leach. Boswell decided to move to Des Moines and run in the 3d. But he faced an internal challenge from Polk County state Senator Matt McCoy, who had been running for months in whatever district included Polk County. McCoy did not drop out quietly or quickly, but local fundraising events for Boswell by Minority Leader Dick Gephardt eventually convinced him to defer. Republican challenger Stan Thompson was less accommodating. A Des Moines lawyer who worked for George W. Bush in the 2000 Iowa caucuses, Thompson argued that Boswell was out of step with the new district's geography and philosophy. He cited the incumbent's votes against Bush's tax bill and trade promotion authority. Thompson ran a credible campaign and won several endorsements, including a joint designation with Boswell from the Farm Bureau. Iowa Republicans, preoccupied with bolstering three House incumbents who were facing spirited challenges, were unable to provide significant financial support; on Election Day Boswell won by a 53%–45% margin. Thompson won four rural counties, but Boswell carried Polk County 55%–44%.

When he was first elected, Boswell said that he would limit himself to four terms, which expire in 2004. But in March 2003, Boswell said he would break his pledge and run again. "I made a mistake," he explained to the *Des Moines Register*. "It seemed like sort of the popular thing, and I was ok with it." This could be a competitive district again in 2004.

FOURTH DISTRICT

Rep. Tom Latham (R)

Elected 1994, 5th term; b. July 14, 1948, Hampton; home, Alexander; Wartburg Col., 1966–67, IA St. U., 1967–70; Lutheran; married (Kathy).

Professional Career: Farmer; Bank Teller/Bookkeeper, 1970–72; Independent Insurance Agent, 1972–74; Hartford Insurance Mktg. Rep., 1974–76; Co-Owner, Latham Seed Co., 1976–present.

DC Office: 440 CHOB 20515, 202-225-5476; Fax: 202-225-3301; Web site: www.house.gov/latham.

District Offices: Ames, 515-232-2885; Clear Lake, 641-357-5225; Fort Dodge, 515-573-2738.

Committees: *Appropriations* (20th of 36 R): Agriculture, Rural Development, & FDA (Vice Chmn.); Energy & Water Development; Homeland Security.

Group Ratings

	ADA	ACLU	AFS	LCV	CON	ITIC	NTU	COC	ACU	NTLC	CHC
2002	5	20	0	25	34	100	56	100	88	83	100
2001	0	—	0	7	—	—	59	86	91	—	—

National Journal Ratings

	2001 LIB	—	2001 CONS		2002 LIB	—	2002 CONS
Economic	20%	—	80%		21%	—	73%
Social	20%	—	69%		39%	—	57%
Foreign	43%	—	58%		41%	—	56%

Key Votes of the 107th Congress

1. Approve Bush Tax Cuts	Y	5. Faith-Based Charities	Y	9. Trade Promotion Authority	Y
2. Limit Patients' Bill of Rights	Y	6. Bar Gays in the Boy Scouts	Y	10. Bar Funds for Intl. Court	Y
3. Campaign Finance Reform	N	7. Ban Partial-Birth Abortion	Y	11. Authorize Force in Iraq	Y
4. Ban ANWR Development	N	8. Arm Commercial Pilots	Y	12. Deny Home. Sec. Dept. Union	Y

Election Results

2002 general	Tom Latham (R)	115,430	(55%)	($1,546,043)
	John Norris (D)	90,784	(43%)	($1,258,631)
	Other	7,512	(3%)	
2002 primary	Tom Latham (R)	38,321	(89%)	
	Gail Boliver (R)	4,956	(11%)	
2000 general (IA 5)	Tom Latham (R)	159,367	(69%)	($375,152)
	Mike Palecek (D)	67,593	(29%)	($5,933)
	Other	4,792	(2%)	

Prior Winning Percentages: 1998 (100%); 1996 (65%); 1994 (61%)

The People		Race/Ethnic Origin	Ancestry	
Area size:	15,833 sq. mi.	94.7% White	German: 27.1%	Norwegian: 9.1%
Urban population:	50.5%	0.8% Black	Irish: 8.9%	
Rural population:	49.5%	1.1% Asian	**2000 Presidential Vote**	
Pop. 2000:	585,305	0.2% Native Am.	Bush (R).............131,391	(49%)
Median income:	$38,242	0.0% Hawaiian	Gore (D)..............129,280	(48%)
Poverty status:	8.9%	0.6% Two+ races	Other...................8,506	(3%)
Military veterans:	13.1%	0.1% Other	**Cook Partisan Voting Index:** R + 1	
		2.5% Hispanic Origin		
Occupation	Blue collar: 27.2%	White collar: 56.2%	Gray collar: 16.6%	

Central Iowa is where the Great Plains begin—a land of farm fields marked off by straight roads every mile and rolling slightly upward to the west, punctuated by occasional crossroads towns and grain elevators, with a sky that seems to fill the eyes. Pioneers coming here in the 1840s and 1850s found prairie grass whose roots were two feet thick and girded trees with grubbing machines that cut off their roots below ground. Central Iowa has some of the world's most productive soil, and it has also had some of its most productive and creative agricultural scientists and farmers. A monument to one of them is the 12-foot statue of Norman Borlaug in his home town of Cresco, in Howard County near the Minnesota border, by Karen Novak, another Cresco native. This is long-settled land now, and Iowans' productivity means that there are fewer people living here on farms than there were 50 and 100 years ago. But its towns and small cities remain centers of creativity. One is Ames, in Story County, home of Iowa State University, and home of Iowa Republicans' straw poll that has started off the Republican presidential contest in August 1987, 1991, 1995 and 1999—though it is likely to be only an academic exercise in August 2003. Ames is part of the growth zone around Des Moines, 30 miles south; so is Boone County to the west. Directly west of Des Moines and its most affluent suburbs is Dallas County, the fastest-growing county in Iowa in the 1990s. To the south is Madison County, famous for the wooden covered bridges that gave their name to a best-selling novel and movie; in September 2002 one of the bridges caught fire and burned, and so now there are only five left. Toward the north is Mason City, the boyhood home of *Music Man* author Meredith Wilson. In nearby Winnebago County is Winnebago Industries, which manufactures motor homes and recreation vehicles on computer-controlled assembly lines with robotic equipment; the main factory in Forest City employs more than 3,000 workers.

The 4th Congressional District includes all these parts of central Iowa. Drawn by the Legislative Service Bureau and approved by the legislature and governor, the 4th District covers 28 counties. It does not include Des Moines, but counties around Des Moines cast more than one-third of its votes. Like Iowa, the 4th District is closely divided politically: George W. Bush won 49% here in 2000.

The congressman from the 4th District is Tom Latham, a Republican first elected in 1994.

Latham grew up on a farm in Franklin County, near Alexander (population 165) where his family has owned a seed company—a very Iowa business—since 1947. For years Latham was active in Republican politics, attending the national convention and serving as a farm adviser to Congressman Fred Grandy. In 1994 Grandy ran against Governor Terry Branstad and lost a close primary, and Latham ran for the House. His Democratic opponent Sheila McGuire had been one of 47 health care professionals to sit on an advisory panel for Hillary Rodham Clinton's health care plan; Latham opposed it. He won 61%–39%.

In the House, Latham has a solidly conservative record. In 1997 he got a seat on the Appropriations Committee and its Agriculture Subcommittee. With the support of independent producers seeking fair pricing, he won a requirement that packers report prices they pay for livestock. He has usually been a quiet member who avoids the national spotlight, but in 2000 he took the lead on an amendment lifting the sanctions on food sales to Cuba, which is seen by some as a bonanza market for American farm products. He strongly opposed legislation to permit states to allow physician-assisted suicide. He talked of his 87-year-old father who has Alzheimer's disease and said, "We could question what the value of that life is, but to my mother . . . that is her life every day, is to go to the home, visit my father, and there is extraordinary quality there." Latham has generally supported the Bush administration. He was a lead sponsor of the bill to raise to $2,000 the annual ceiling for contributions to education individual retirement accounts, which was enacted as part of the 2001 tax cuts. When the House passed the defense spending bill in 2002, it included $2.5 million to develop evaluation tools for the nation's aging Air Force fleet, plus $5.4 million for work by a company in Ames on the Navy's new hull-mounted sonar systems.

Redistricting split Latham's old 5th District between the new 4th and 5th, and he chose to run in the 4th, which includes his home in Franklin County, rather than in the 5th, which is much more Republican. The result was his first competitive campaign since he was first elected. Latham had not been an active fundraiser and Democrats targeted the race. Their nominee was John Norris, former chief of staff to Governor Tom Vilsack, who had been thinking about running in the 3d District in Des Moines, but decided not to when his onetime boss, incumbent Democrat Leonard Boswell, moved there. Norris talked about jobs, education and Social Security and sounded the theme of working hard for "Iowa's working families;" he attacked Latham for supporting Republican positions on taxes and health care. He was an aggressive campaigner and raised more than $1 million. But in a year in which voters were more consumed by war and terror threats to the nation, the two candidates generally agreed on international issues and Norris failed to find a clear vulnerability in Latham. Latham won by a relatively comfortable 55%–43%, winning all 28 counties—though, only by 9 votes in Story County, which cast the most votes.

Angry at Latham's negative ads, Norris refused to make the customary election-night concession call to Latham. "He called me a phony and a hypocrite and made personal attacks on my character, and I don't intend to talk to him at all." Latham responded that Norris attacked him from the start, and forced him to respond. Latham has been mentioned as a possible statewide candidate; if he does not run for reelection, the 4th District will likely be seriously contested again.

FIFTH DISTRICT

Rep. Steve King (R)

Elected 2002, 1st term; b. May 28, 1949, Storm Lake; home, Kiron; NW MO St. U., 1967–70; Catholic; married (Marilyn).

Elected Office: IA Senate, 1996–02.

Professional Career: Construction co. owner, 1975–02.

DC Office: 1432 LHOB 20515, 202-225-4426; Fax: 202-225-3193; Web site: www.house.gov/steveking.

District Offices: Council Bluffs, 712-325-1404; Sioux City, 712-224-4692; Storm Lake, 712-732-4197.

Committees: *Agriculture* (23d of 27 R): Conservation, Credit, Rural Development & Research; Department Operations, Oversight, Nutrition & Forestry. *Judiciary* (18th of 21 R): Immigration, Border Security & Claims; The Constitution. *Small Business* (18th of 18 R): Regulatory Reform & Oversight; Workforce, Empowerment & Government Programs.

Group Ratings and Key Votes: Newly Elected

Election Results

2002 general	Steve King (R)	113,257	(62%)	($650,612)
	Paul Shomshor (D)	68,853	(38%)	($91,855)
2002 primary	Steve King (R)	16,503	(30%)	
	John Redwine (R)	13,428	(25%)	
	Brent Siegrist (R)	12,978	(24%)	
	Jeff Ballenger (R)	11,563	(21%)	

The People		Race/Ethnic Origin	Ancestry	
Area size:	18,429 sq. mi.	93.7% White	German: 26.8%	Irish: 9.2%
Urban population:	49.4%	0.6% Black	English: 6.7%	
Rural population:	50.6%	0.9% Asian	**2000 Presidential Vote**	
Pop. 2000:	585,171	0.4% Native Am.	Bush (R) 141,820	(57%)
Median income:	$36,773	0.0% Hawaiian	Gore (D) 99,004	(40%)
Poverty status:	8.9%	0.7% Two+ races	Other 7,623	(3%)
Military veterans:	14.0%	0.0% Other	**Cook Partisan Voting Index:** R + 9	
		3.6% Hispanic Origin		
Occupation	Blue collar: 29.5%	White collar: 53.3%	Gray collar: 17.2%	

Sioux City, one of the oldest market towns on the Great Plains, is situated picturesquely, nestled below and running up the loess bluffs above the Missouri River. Although still the largest city on the Plains west of Des Moines and north of Omaha, Sioux City has not grown much in the past five decades. Its original economic base has become obsolete, and so has some of the city itself: The waterfront, once raucous with boatmen and stockyard workers, is now quiet; the stockyards—which employed thousands and slaughtered millions of hogs during their peak years in the 1920s—have closed and many workers have relocated to IBP's modern (and low-wage) beef factory across the river in Dakota City, Nebraska; downtown stores have been replaced by shopping malls at the edge of town where people will still drive for hours to spend a day doing a season's shopping.

Sioux City is the largest city in the 5th Congressional District, which covers western Iowa from the Minnesota border to the Missouri line. The old 5th District before the June 2001 redistricting covered the northwestern corner of the state and moved east; redistricting removed 15 counties centered around Fort Dodge and added 17 counties centered around Council Bluffs. That city houses the mansion of General Grenville Dodge, who in 1859 lobbied Illinois lawyer Abraham Lincoln on the need for a transcontinental railroad; Lincoln got it through Congress in 1863, Dodge became its chief engineer, and Council Bluffs became its eastern terminus when it was completed in 1869. Surrounded by beef grazing territory, where federal intrusion has long been resented, Council Bluffs looks west across the Missouri River to Omaha, taking on the culturally more conservative tone of Nebraska and the conservative politics of the *Omaha World-Herald*. Farther south is Stanton, home of "The World's Largest Swedish Coffee Pot," a 125-foot water tower with a handle, spout and colorful design that has made the town a tourist attraction. By far the most Republican area in Iowa, this is the only district in the state where George W. Bush won an absolute majority of the votes in 2000. The relocated district includes 56% of the old 5th District, which was represented by Tom Latham. But Latham's home was shifted to the new 4th District, and he decided to run there.

The congressman from the 5th District is Steve King, a Republican who won the open seat in 2002. He was born in Storm Lake in western Iowa and attended Northwest Missouri State University. As a businessman, he operated King Construction Company, which he founded in 1975. He began his political career in 1996, at 47, when he was elected to the state Senate where he quickly gained a reputation as a conservative's conservative. He opposed abortion, racial quotas and preferences and gay marriage. He sponsored Iowa's "God and Country" bill, which would require Iowa schools to recognize that the United States "has derived its strength from biblical values," and was a driving force behind the state's English-only law. In 2000, King filed suit to repeal Governor Tom Vilsack's executive order banning workplace discrimination based on sexual orientation. On economic matters, King was just as resolute. He supported repeal of the state's inheritance tax, backed a 15% state income tax reduction and a national right-to-work law.

In 2002, it was clear that the Republican nominee would be the new congressman in this open seat. But the result was not determined in the June 2002 primary because of Iowa's law requiring candidates to receive 35% of the primary vote to be nominated; otherwise, the nomination is determined by a special party convention. There were four main contenders. King ran as a strong conservative and the only rural candidate. House Speaker Brent Siegrist of Council Bluffs called for limiting federal control over local schools. State Senator John Redwine from the Sioux City area, was a family physician whose "pro-life" principles led him to oppose capital punishment as well as abortion. Council Bluffs car-wash owner Jeff Ballenger loaned more than $400,000 to his own campaign (there must be a lot of clean cars in Council Bluffs). King got a boost from endorsements by 2000 presidential candidates Steve Forbes and Gary Bauer, and the Club for Growth raised money for him. He led in the June primary with 30% of the vote, followed by Siegrist and Redwine with 24% each and Ballenger with 21%. At the convention three weeks later (by coincidence, at the high school in Denison from which King had graduated), the 533 voting delegates needed three ballots to select a winner. King led on each ballot and defeated Siegrist 272–253 in the final round, marking the first time in 38 years that Iowans used a convention to select a congressional nominee. The general election outcome was never in doubt. Democrat Paul Shomshor attempted to paint King as too conservative for the district, and won the endorsement of the *Omaha World-Herald*—perhaps because his home city of Council Bluffs had not elected a member to Congress since the 1920s—but he fell far short, 62%–38%. He carried Council Bluffs's Pottawattamie County by 350 votes, but King did especially well in northwest Iowa—87% in Sioux County and 81% in Lyon County, both with large numbers of Dutch-Americans, the nation's most Republican ethnic group.

The *Des Moines Register*'s David Yepsen wrote that King could easily become a "right-wing nut" like Bob Dornan of California. "Or he could be a thoughtful conservative who works hard to build the economy of western Iowa." *National Review* called him the "Great Right Hope." He seems likely to be the most conservative member of the Iowa delegation, if not his freshman class, and one with great political security.

★ KANSAS ★

"Like everyone else, she was taught that the earth and the other planets circled the sun, but deep down she had the feeling that the sun and the rest of the cosmos really revolved around western Kansas," James Dickenson writes of his grandmother Mary Phipps, who lived her 91 years in Kansas. "She took as the First Principle that bread, the staff of life, was one of the bases of existence itself, along with air and water. From this flowed the inescapable conclusion that wheat farmers were truly engaged in the Lord's work." These words open the book *Home on the Range*, in which Dickenson, for three decades a top national political reporter, starts with his own family and boyhood in Rawlins County to explain how Kansas came to be what it was, and how it is ceasing to be that and becoming something else.

But Kansas has always been quintessentially American, which is not to say entirely placid or entirely unflavorful. In 1989, when Russia's Yevgeny Primakov wanted to see "real Americans," he flew out with Bob Dole to Dodge City, to visit Boot Hill Museum and the Long Branch Saloon. Kansas, like so much of Russia, may look quiet, full of solid farmers who work hard and have deep roots in the soil, the place around which the cosmos revolves. But Kansas's history, like Russia's, has also been punctuated by uprisings, intellectual and violent, by moments of anger and rage sweeping through the tall sheaves like a tornado wind. The difference, of course, is that

Miles
0 10 20

The Almanac of American Politics.
National Journal

DONIPHAN
ATCHISON
LEAVENWORTH
WYANDOTTE
Kansas City
Overland Park
JOHNSON
MIAMI
LINN
BOURBON
CRAWFORD
CHEROKEE
BROWN
JEFFERSON
Lawrence
DOUGLAS
FRANKLIN
ANDERSON
ALLEN
NEOSHO
LABETTE
NEMAHA
JACKSON
Topeka
SHAWNEE
OSAGE
COFFEY
WOODSON
WILSON
MONTGOMERY
2
MARSHALL
POTTAWATOMIE
WABAUNSEE
LYON
GREENWOOD
ELK
CHAUTAUQUA
WASHINGTON
RILEY
Manhattan
GEARY
MORRIS
CHASE
BUTLER
COWLEY
CLAY
DICKINSON
MARION
4
REPUBLIC
CLOUD
OTTAWA
SALINE
Salina
MCPHERSON
HARVEY
SEDGWICK
Wichita
SUMNER
JEWELL
MITCHELL
LINCOLN
ELLSWORTH
RICE
RENO
KINGMAN
HARPER
SMITH
OSBORNE
RUSSELL
BARTON
STAFFORD
PRATT
BARBER
PHILLIPS
ROOKS
ELLIS
RUSH
PAWNEE
EDWARDS
KIOWA
COMANCHE
1
NORTON
GRAHAM
TREGO
NESS
HODGEMAN
FORD
CLARK
DECATUR
SHERIDAN
GOVE
LANE
Dodge City
GRAY
MEADE
RAWLINS
THOMAS
LOGAN
SCOTT
FINNEY
HASKELL
SEWARD
CHEYENNE
SHERMAN
WALLACE
GREELEY
WICHITA
KEARNY
HAMILTON
GRANT
STANTON
STEVENS
MORTON

Congressional district boundaries were first effective for 2002.

Russian traditions of law and liberty, culture and civility are weak, while in Kansas, as in all America, they are remarkably strong.

Kansas literally began in a moment of violence, the Bleeding Kansas of the 1850s that led proximately to the terrible war that split the whole nation. The trigger was the Kansas-Nebraska Act of 1854, which left to local settlers the question of whether this new Kansas Territory would be a free or slave state. Pro-slavery "bushwhackers" rode over the line from Missouri, stealing elections and writing a pro-slavery constitution. But much larger numbers of free-soil "jayhawkers" from New England and the New England-Yankee-settled Great Lakes states put down roots and, despite the massacres of the mad John Brown, prevailed and established their own law and order. The effect on national politics was tumultuous: The Democratic Party was split, the Republican Party was created, and the nation was plunged into Civil War. The effect on Kansas was calming: The anti-slavery majority bent the soil to the plow and built small towns thick with schools, churches and colleges, to the point that in the 1939 color movie, *Wizard of Oz*, the Kansas scenes were shot in dreary black and white as the image of dull, prim, old-fashioned Middle America. But the rebellious impulse did not totally die out. Kansans' livelihoods were always at risk: Hailstorms, grasshopper invasions, dry seasons or a drop in world farm prices could mean disaster for thousands. The high-rainfall 1880s attracted hundreds of thousands of new settlers to Kansas; the low-rainfall 1890s produced a bust and a populist rebellion. "What you farmers should do," said orator Mary Ellen Lease, "is to raise less corn and more hell." For a few years in the 1890s, and then in farm rebellions of the 1930s, 1950s and 1970s, Kansans did, but afterwards always returned to jayhawker Republicanism.

Kansas remains Republican in the 21st century, but not in quite the same old way. Its most famous politician, Bob Dole, still returns occasionally to his small hometown of Russell, out on the plains. But Kansas' population is increasingly metropolitan. Half of Kansans live in just five counties, which include Kansas City, Lawrence, Topeka and Wichita, and in most of the other 100 counties population is declining. A majority of Kansans lives in or within easy reach of metropolitan Kansas City, which has a diverse economy that is by no means dependent on farming. While small towns on the plains see their city halls and post offices padlocked, new office complexes and corporate headquarters are rising amidst the affluent suburbs of Johnson County, which has one of the highest job growth rates in the country. The smaller metropolitan area of Wichita, while less diversified, has an economy built on its role as the world's leading producer of small airplanes: Here Boeing, Cessna, Bombardier, Raytheon and other manufacturers make 69% of the general aviation aircraft in the world, and 60% of its aviation sales are exports. Kansas is wired to the world, its unemployment rate is low. Hispanics are flocking to work in meatpacking factories in towns like Dodge City, Garden City and Liberal, whose populations in 2000 were more than 40% Hispanic; Hispanics accounted for nearly half of Kansas's population growth in the 1990s. There is no warrant today for shooting the Kansas scenes in a movie in black and white.

This transformation has had political consequences. Some 39% of Kansas's votes in 2000 were cast in the mostly suburban counties from Kansas City west to Topeka, and another 15% in Wichita's Sedgwick County. If rural Kansas once produced farm rebellions, these urban and suburban Kansans have produced their own kind of rebellion. In 1992, 27% of Kansans voted for Ross Perot—his fifth best showing in the nation—and his vote was heaviest not in the wheat country but from just at the edge of metropolitan expansion and in the sparsely populated Flint Hills, places where young families live, commuting to jobs and shopping malls 50 or even 100 miles away. Much of the politics of Kansas in the last decade has been a struggle within the Republican party between followers of Governor Bill Graves, elected in 1994 and 1998, who favored abortion rights and gun control, and Christian conservatives who take the opposite stand. Graves beat back a conservative challenge in the 1998 Republican primary by nearly a 3–1 margin, but the conservatives have won legislative leadership posts and control of the party organization. The ultimate beneficiaries have been Kansas Democrats. They captured the 3d Congressional District seat in 1998 by beating a conservative who was hated by Republican moderates and in 2002 they captured the governorship in the same way. This was not completely out of character: Republican Kansas has had Democratic governors for 20 of the preceding 36 years.

But Kansas has not moved toward Democrats in national politics. In 2000 it voted 58%–37%

for George W. Bush. Voters in Kansas's metropolitan areas showed little of the allegiance to Clinton-Gore Democrats seen in the bigger metro areas of the Northeast and West Coast, and voters in rural areas were less interested in getting higher government subsidies than in preventing government interference of the sort threatened by the Clinton EPA plan to regulate the water runoff from farms and to regulate privately owned lakes and farm ponds. The two Republican senators elected in 1996 (there was a special election to replace Bob Dole) have both been reelected by wide margins, Sam Brownback in 1998 and Pat Roberts in 2002; Kansas has not elected a Democratic senator since 1932—the only state that hasn't. Three of the state's four House seats have gone to Republicans essentially uncontested, although Democrats represented two of them in the 1980s and early 1990s.

The People		**Race/Ethnic Origin**			**Military veterans:** 267,452 (13.5%)	
Pop. 2000:	2,688,418	2,233,997	83.1%	White	WWII: 21.2%	Korea: 13.1%
Pop. 1990:	2,477,574	151,407	5.6%	Black	Vietnam: 32.6%	Gulf War: 10.9%
Change 1990–2000:	Up 8.5%	46,301	1.7%	Asian	**Most populous cities:**	
Change 1980–1990:	Up 4.8%	22,322	0.8%	Native Am.	1. Wichita	344,284
% of U.S. total:	1.0%	1,154	0.0%	Hawaiian	2. Overland Park	149,080
Pop. rank:	32d of 50	42,508	1.6%	Two+ races	3. Kansas City	146,866
Area size:	82,277 sq. mi.	2,477	0.1%	Other	4. Topeka	122,377
State Native:	59.5%	188,252	7.0%	Hisp. Origin	5. Olathe	92,962
Non-citizen:	3.3%	**Ancestry**			Urban population: 71.4%	
Language		German: 19.5%		Irish: 8.7%	Rural population: 28.6%	
English: 89.7%	Spanish: 6.0%	English: 8.1%		USA: 6.7%		
Other Eur.: 2.6%		French: 2.3%				

Education		**Work Sector**		**Legislature**	
H.S. Grad:	86.0%	Private: 76.3%	Govt: 15.5%	Senate	30 R 10 D
College Grad:	25.8%	Self: 7.8%	Family: 0.4%	House	80 R 45 D
Industry		Unemployment: 4.2%		Legislative Term Limits: No	
Agri: 3.8%	Con: 6.5%	**Household Income**		**Registered Voters**	
Fin: 6.1%	Info: 3.3%	<15k: 14.9%	15-35k: 27.8%	D: 441,269	(27.3%)
Mfg: 20.3%	Prof: 29.1%	35-50k: 18.1%	50-100k: 29.9%	R: 742,903	(46.0%)
Public: 4.4%	Trade: 14.8%	100-150k: 6.1%	>150k: 3.2%	I: 431,527	(26.7%)
Other: 11.6%		Median: $40,624			
Occupation		Poverty status: 9.9%			
Blue collar: 24.9%	White collar: 59.7%	**Home Value**			
Gray collar: 15.5%		<50k: 27.3%	50-100k: 35.6%	100-200k: 28.6%	200-300k: 5.6%
		300-500k: 2.2%	>500k: 0.7%	Median: $81,000	

Presidential politics   Except for 1964, when it narrowly favored Lyndon Johnson over Barry Goldwater, Kansas has voted Republican for president throughout the last 60 years. It was also one of Ross Perot's best states in 1992. In 2000 George W. Bush carried 103 of its 105 counties, losing only those containing the old industrial city of Kansas City and the university town of Lawrence. Things are only likely to get better for national Republicans. Kansans under 30 voted 68%–28% for Bush according to the VNS exit poll.

In 1996 and 2000 the state legislature voted to cancel the April presidential primary; if Kansans want a look at presidential candidates, they are well advised to look up into the sky as they jet over on their way to more marginal states.

2000 Presidential Vote

Bush (R)	622,332	(58%)
Gore (D)	399,276	(37%)
Nader (Green)	36,086	(3%)
Other	14,522	(1%)

1996 Presidential Vote

Dole (R)	583,245	(54%)
Clinton (D)	387,659	(36%)
Perot (I)	92,639	(9%)

Congressional districting   Republicans had full control of redistricting in Kansas for the first time since the 1960s, but did not use it to partisan advantage.

| 108th Congress Lineup |
| 3 R   1 D |
| 107th Congress Lineup |
| 3 R   1 D |

Why? As one legislator put it, "What's ground zero with reapportionment? I'd say it's Lawrence." Lawrence, midway between Kansas City and Topeka, and home of the University of Kansas, in the previous plan was in the 3d District captured by Democrat Dennis Moore in 1998 and held in 2000. The 3d District had to shed 61,000 people, and the obvious partisan move was to remove Lawrence, which Moore carried by wide margins, and place it in the heavily Republican 2d District, where incumbent Republican Jim Ryun would be unbeatable anyway. But Lawrence civic leaders insisted that Lawrence be kept together in the 3d District—they wanted the university to be in the same district as its hospital in Kansas City—and Republicans in the state House in March 2002 passed a plan splitting the city but keeping most of it, including the university, in the 3d. The state Senate in April 2002 passed a different plan, promoted by national Republicans, which extended the western 1st District all the way to the southeast corner of the state. But the House's plan prevailed and was adopted in June. Attorney General Carla Stovall brought a lawsuit against the plan, making the absurd argument that it was unconstitutional because it put Junction City in one district and nearby Fort Riley in another; it took just one day for a three-judge federal court to slap that down. Moore was reelected in November by 7,213 votes; he carried Lawrence's Douglas County by 5,585.

Governor

Kathleen Sebelius (D)

Elected 2002, term expires Jan. 2007, 1st term; b. May 15, 1948, Cincinnati, OH; home, Topeka; Trinity Col., B.A. 1970, U. of KS, M.P.A. 1977; Catholic; married (Gary).

Elected Office: KS House of Reps., 1986–94; KS Insurance Commissioner 1994–02.

Professional Career: KS Dept. of Corrections, 1975–77; Dir., KS Trial Lawyers Assoc., 1977–87.

Office: State Capitol, 2d Fl., Topeka, 66612, 785-296-3232; Fax: 785-296-7973; Web site: www.ksgovernor.org.

Election Results

2002 general	Kathleen Sebelius (D)	441,858	(53%)
	Tim Shallenburger (R)	376,830	(45%)
2002 primary	Kathleen Sebelius (D)	unopposed	
1998 general	Bill Graves (R)	544,882	(73%)
	Tom Sawyer (D)	168,243	(23%)
	Other	29,540	(4%)

Kathleen Sebelius was elected governor of Kansas in 2002, the second Democratic woman to win the office (the first was Joan Finney in 1990). She grew up in Cincinnati, where her father John Gilligan was elected to the city council in 1953, when she was 5. Campaigns were very much a part of her life. Her father was elected to Congress in a usually Republican district in the very Democratic year of 1964; he was defeated in 1966 by Robert Taft Jr., father of Ohio's current Governor, Bob Taft: They will have something to talk about at governors' conferences. John Gilligan was elected governor of Ohio in 1970 and in 1971 pushed through the state's first income tax. A man of wry humor, he was given to self-deprecating statements; when asked at the Ohio State Fair in 1972 whether he would shear sheep, he said, "I shear taxpayers, not sheep." Comments like this helped defeat him in 1974 by a 49%–48% margin. Still active and a member of the Cincinnati school board, he had the satisfaction in 2002 of being the first governor to see his daughter elected governor.

Kathleen Sebelius graduated from Trinity College in Washington, D.C., where she met her husband, the son of Kansas Republican Congressman (1969–81) Keith Sebelius. After graduation the Sebeliuses moved to Topeka, where they live just 12 blocks from the state Capitol. Kathleen Sebelius worked for the state trial lawyers association and in 1986 was elected to the state House as a Democrat. With a Topeka base and a name well known in western Kansas, she was elected state Insurance Commissioner in 1994. It was a position held since its creation by Republicans, and by just three men over the preceding 50 years. Sebelius won much publicity for setting up anti-fraud and market conduct units; she pruned duplicative regulations, deregulated commercial insurance lines and got tax credits for businesses that provide health insurance to employees. In 2001, she became President of the National Association of Insurance Commissioners and worked for consumer privacy laws.

Sebelius's moderate image and her political savvy made her the obvious Democrat to run for governor in 2002, and she had no primary opposition. Term-limited Governor Bill Graves was a moderate who engaged in fierce feuds with conservatives in the Republican party, and there was a riproaring battle for the Republican nomination. Attorney General Carla Stovall, the choice of the moderate wing, announced in 2001 and raised over $500,000. But in April 2002, while vacationing in Europe with a radio broadcaster with whom she had a relationship, she let it be known that she was leaving the race, just two months before the filing deadline. That left moderates with no candidate against conservative state Treasurer Tim Shallenburger, a strong opponent of abortion who pledged not to increase taxes and said he would cut state spending by 10%. Quickly state Senate President Dave Kerr and Wichita Mayor Bob Knight jumped in. State House Speaker Kent Glasscock, Stovall's running mate, jumped to Knight's ticket and tried to bring Stovall's money with him. But the one conservative beat the two moderates. Shallenburger won the August primary with 41% of the vote to 30% for Kerr and 26% for Knight.

The general election provided a clear contrast on issues. Sebelius promised a top-to-bottom review of state government and refused to pledge she would veto any tax increase. She favored abortion rights, opposed capital punishment and favored banning concealed weapons except for retired law enforcement officers. She picked a Republican, a retired Cessna executive, for her running mate. She called for a $1,000 increase in per pupil spending and said she would institute character education in schools. She proved to be an excellent fundraiser and spent $3.2 million to Shallenburger's $1.5 million. Meanwhile, Graves waited until six weeks after the primary to grudgingly endorse Shallenburger, and the Kansas Farm Bureau in September decided to be neutral. Sebelius made one slip when she said that Missouri's underfunded highways were "much more terrifying to me than the attacks on the World Trade Center," but she quickly apologized. She got some mileage attacking Shallenburger for calling her, in a fundraising letter, "a lying dangerous liberal who will ruin our schools and endanger our children." Polls showed her well ahead all along, and she won 53%–45%. She carried most counties in eastern Kansas and lost heavily Republican Johnson County by only 52%–46%. She ran only about even in the Wichita area, but carried most rural counties west of the 100th meridian, long regarded as the boundary between the fertile Midwest and the arid West. She carried four of the state's five largest counties, which cast almost exactly 50% of the votes, by 54%–44% and the 100 smaller counties by 52%–46%.

Sebelius's victory established that Kansas's conservative Republicans will not control state government, but it was less clear what it would mean for Kansas fiscally. Sebelius appointed task forces to begin her top-to-bottom review in November and December 2002 and withstood criticism and a lawsuit brought by newspapers to open the meetings to the public. She retained Graves's budget director and appointed a Republican as secretary of administration. Graves announced cuts in the budget, but Sebelius seemed likely in early 2003 to face serious budget difficulties. Republicans still had majorities in the legislature and their leaders tried to mend the party split that raged throughout Graves's governorship.

Senior Senator

Sam Brownback (R)

Elected 1996, seat up 2004, 1st term; b. Sept. 12, 1956, Garnett; home, Topeka; KS St. U., B.S. 1978, U. of KS, J.D. 1982; Methodist; married (Mary).

Elected Office: U.S. House of Reps., 1994–96.

Professional Career: Radio broadcaster, KKSU, 1978–79; Practicing atty., 1982–86, 1993; Prof., KS St. U. Law Schl., 1982–86; Ogden & Leonardville City Atty., 1983–86; KS Secy. of Agriculture, 1986–93; White House Fellow, Office of USTR, 1990–91.

DC Office: 303 HSOB, 20510, 202-224-6521; Fax: 202-228-1265; Web site: brownback.senate.gov.

State Offices: Garden City, 316-275-1124; Overland Park, 913-492-6378; Pittsburg, 620-231-6040; Topeka, 785-233-2503; Wichita, 316-264-8066.

Committees: *Appropriations*: Agriculture & Rural Development; Commerce, Justice, State & Judiciary; District of Columbia; Interior; Military Construction; Transportation, Treasury & General Government. *Commerce, Science & Transportation*: Aviation; Communications; Competition, Foreign Commerce & Infrastructure; Science, Technology & Space (Chmn.); Surface Transportation & Merchant Marine. *Foreign Relations*: African Affairs; East Asian & Pacific Affairs (Chmn.); International Operations & Terrorism; Near Eastern & South Asian Affairs. *Joint Economic Committee* (2d of 10 Sens.).

Group Ratings

	ADA	ACLU	AFS	LCV	CON	ITIC	NTU	COC	ACU	NTLC	CHC
2002	5	20	0	6	69	88	67	100	100	94	—
2001	0	—	0	0	—	—	85	93	96	—	100

National Journal Ratings

	2001 LIB	—	2001 CONS		2002 LIB	—	2002 CONS
Economic	7%	—	86%		22%	—	77%
Social	33%	—	59%		0%	—	62%
Foreign	7%	—	72%		0%	—	76%

Key Votes of the 107th Congress

1. Approve Bush Tax Cuts	Y	5. Confirm Ashcroft as AG	Y	9. Bar Coop. with Intl. Court	Y
2. Expand Patients' Rights	N	6. Bar Gays in the Boy Scouts	Y	10. Trade Promotion Authority	*
3. Campaign Finance Reform	N	7. $ for Hate Crime Prosecution	N	11. Authorize Force in Iraq	Y
4. Permit ANWR Development	Y	8. Overseas Military Abortions	N	12. Homeland Sec. Dept. Union	N

Election Results

1998 general	Sam Brownback (R)	474,639	(65%)	($1,719,612)
	Paul Feleciano Jr. (D)	229,718	(32%)	($39,500)
	Other	22,879	(3%)	
1998 primary	Sam Brownback (R)	unopposed		
1996 special	Sam Brownback (R)	574,021	(54%)	($2,269,550)
	Jill Docking (D)	461,344	(43%)	($1,125,844)
	Other	29,351	(3%)	
1996 special	Sam Brownback (R)	187,914	(55%)	
	Sheila Frahm (R)	142,487	(42%)	
	Christina Campbell-Cline (R)	12,378	(4%)	
1992 general	Bob Dole (R)	706,246	(63%)	($3,542,989)
	Gloria O'Dell (D)	349,525	(31%)	($249,359)
	Christina Campbell-Cline (I)	45,423	(4%)	
	Other	25,253	(2%)	

Prior Winning Percentages: 1994 House (66%)

Sam Brownback grew up on a farm in Anderson County, some 50 miles from Kansas City, was student body president at Kansas State University and briefly was a farm broadcaster. After law school, Brownback practiced law for four years in Manhattan, Kansas, in the 1980s; he was appointed secretary of the state Board of Agriculture in 1986 and served until it was abolished in

1993. He claims credit for encouraging the use of wheat to make plastics and cattle hides to make wound dressings. He was a White House Fellow, working from 1990–91 for Special Trade Representative Carla Hills. In March 1994 he announced for Congress, condemning "a welfare system that discourages the work ethic and encourages the disintegration of families and a government that can't say no to spending or yes to reform." Brownback won the three-way House primary; in the general, he faced John Carlin, governor from 1978–86. Brownback won 66%–34%, carrying every county.

Brownback was one of the enthusiastic 1994 freshmen who tried to shake up the House. He was put in charge of selling off a House annex building, which proved harder than expected. He pushed successfully to reduce Congress' own budget. He headed a group of "New Federalists," which sought to abolish three cabinet departments. He backed the McCain-Feingold campaign finance bill and in 1995 spoke at Ross Perot's United We Stand convention denouncing "influence peddling" in Washington. On immigration, he played a key role in separating the legal and illegal immigration issues, which led to passage of a tough measure against illegal immigrants but no major reductions in the number of legal immigrants.

On May 15, 1996, Bob Dole surprised just about everyone when he announced he was resigning from the Senate on June 11. On May 17, Brownback said he would seek the seat, noting, "They are size 25 shoes that even Michael Jordan couldn't fill." Governor Bill Graves' choice to fill the vacancy, Lieutenant Governor Sheila Frahm, delayed ten days before accepting. Though both were labeled conservative, Frahm and Brownback presented a strong contrast in the subsequent primary. She was pro-choice on abortion, he was pro-life. Brownback accused her of voting as a state legislator to raise taxes $500 million; she criticized his "slash and burn" approach to federal spending. Graves and Senator Nancy Kassebaum endorsed Frahm; William Bennett of Empower America and James Dobson of Focus on the Family endorsed Brownback. In the August primary, Brownback won 55%–42%. In the general election for the remaining two years of Dole's term, Brownback faced a Democrat with a great political name, Wichita stockbroker Jill Docking, wife of a former lieutenant governor whose father and grandfather both served as governor. Docking promised "Kansas common sense" and likened herself to Kassebaum. Brownback campaigned on the 3 Rs: "Reduce, reform and return. Reduce the size and scope of the federal government. Reform the Congress. Return to the basic values that built the country: Work and family and the recognition of a higher moral authority." He promised to serve only two terms—presumably two full terms. Both candidates spent liberally, and some fall polls showed the race close. But Brownback won by the convincing though not overwhelming margin of 54%–43%.

Brownback has a very conservative voting record in the Senate but has also made common cause with liberals on some issues. "I think every life is sacred and beautiful, whether it's the unborn or whether it's Ted Kennedy," he has said. "I really try to reach out and work with anybody and everybody I can." After September 11, Brownback and Kennedy co-sponsored a bill to strengthen the nation's borders. It provided for an automatic entry and exit system, the development of biometric identifiers and tracking of foreign students and called for greater sharing of information about potential terrorists by the INS, State Department and intelligence agencies. The bill became law in May 2002. He has had less success in banning human cloning, an issue he became interested in while working as state agriculture secretary. His bill, co-sponsored by Mary Landrieu, would ban reproductive human cloning and the cloning of embryos for use in research; as a fallback, he called for a six-month moratorium on cloning. In November 2001 Majority Leader Tom Daschle promised him a freestanding vote that winter. Then in June 2002 Daschle offered him floor time under rules that required 60 votes for passage and favored the competing bill sponsored by Dianne Feinstein and Arlen Specter which would prohibit only reproductive cloning; Brownback refused the offer and tried, unsuccessfully, to bring up his bill as an amendment to the terrorism insurance bill, but that was voted down 65–31.

Brownback has a seat on Foreign Relations and is chairman of the East Asian and Pacific Affairs Subcommittee. He co-sponsored the Iraq Liberation Act in 1998; he criticized the Clinton administration's handling of UNSCOM inspections in Iraq. He returned from a trip to India in 1999 determined to do something about the international sex trade; working with liberal Paul Wellstone, he sponsored a bill to curb sex trafficking that became law in October 2000. In the process, he focused as well on the continued existence of slavery in Sudan and other countries. He and Kansas colleague Pat Roberts sponsored a law passed in October 1999 authorizing the president to lift the embargo on India; Bill Clinton, determined to get India to sign the Comprehensive Test Ban Treaty that the Senate had rejected that same month, refused. After September 11, he worked to ease sanctions against Pakistan and urged a tough approach on Iraq; he called the Iraqi National Congress, a group shunned by many in the State Department and the CIA, "invaluable in the fight to rid the world of Saddam's threat." He worked with Barbara Boxer on women's rights in Afghanistan.

Brownback has taken interesting initiatives on communications issues. He worked closely with Joseph Lieberman on measures addressing religious persecution in Sudan and other countries. After Lieberman was nominated for vice president, Brownback explained their joint efforts: "Senator Lieberman and I are part of a political alliance that is quite logically emerging between theologically orthodox Christians and Jews. . . . We share a belief in universal Truths, in a moral order ordained by God and discovered, not created, by man." He has tried to get a national policy to make broadband communication universal, which he argues is especially important in rural areas, and he has urged broadcasters to move more quickly to digital television.

He has worked with liberals on other issues. With Congressman John Lewis, he has worked to build an African-American Museum on Washington's Mall; in late 2002, he explored the idea of creating a temporary congressional committee on race relations but dropped the initiative after failing to win support from party leadership.

In 2003, Brownback won an Appropriations Committee seat; he received a waiver that permitted him to serve on two "Super A" committees (the other is Foreign Relations). He was elected to a full six-year term in 1998 by a 65%–32% margin after well-known candidates declined to run. Campaign finance caused him some embarrassment. In March 1997, the *Kansas City Star* ran stories revealing that Brownback's in-laws gave $32,500 to seven PACs which promptly gave his campaign $31,500; in December 2002 the Federal Election Commission fined the in-laws $9,000 and ordered the Brownback campaign to refund $19,000 to the U.S. Treasury. Brownback announced in November 2002 he would run again; Democrats mentioned as possible opponents include Jill Docking, former Congressman Dan Glickman and Congressman Dennis Moore.

Junior Senator

Pat Roberts (R)

Elected 1996, seat up 2008, 2d term; b. Apr. 20, 1936, Topeka; home, Dodge City; KS St. U., B.A. 1958; United Methodist; married (Franki).

Military Career: Marine Corps, 1958–62.

Elected Office: U.S. House of Reps., 1980–96.

Professional Career: Co–owner, editor, *The Westsider* (AZ newspaper) 1962–67; A.A., U.S. Sen. Frank Carlson, 1967–68; A.A., U.S. Rep. Keith Sebelius, 1968–80.

DC Office: 109 HSOB, 20510, 202-224-4774; Fax: 202-224-3514; Web site: roberts.senate.gov.

State Offices: Dodge City, 620-227-2244; Overland Park, 913-451-9343; Topeka, 785-235-3665; Wichita, 316-263-0273.

Committees: *Agriculture, Nutrition & Forestry:* Forestry, Conservation & Rural Revitalization; Marketing, Inspection & Product Promotion; Production & Price Competitiveness. *Armed Services:* Airland; Emerging Threats & Capabilities (Chmn.); Readiness & Management Support. *Ethics (Select). Health, Education, Labor & Pensions:* Aging; Children & Families; Employment, Safety & Training. *Intelligence (Select)* (Chmn.).

Group Ratings

	ADA	ACLU	AFS	LCV	CON	ITIC	NTU	COC	ACU	NTLC	CHC
2002	0	20	0	0	69	88	64	100	100	85	—
2001	0	—	0	0	—	—	81	93	100	—	100

National Journal Ratings

	2001 LIB —	2001 CONS		2002 LIB —	2002 CONS
Economic	7% —	86%		6% —	90%
Social	29% —	70%		0% —	62%
Foreign	7% —	72%		0% —	76%

Key Votes of the 107th Congress

1. Approve Bush Tax Cuts	Y	5. Confirm Ashcroft as AG	Y	9. Bar Coop. with Intl. Court	Y
2. Expand Patients' Rights	N	6. Bar Gays in the Boy Scouts	Y	10. Trade Promotion Authority	Y
3. Campaign Finance Reform	N	7. $ for Hate Crime Prosecution	N	11. Authorize Force in Iraq	Y
4. Permit ANWR Development	Y	8. Overseas Military Abortions	N	12. Homeland Sec. Dept. Union	N

Election Results

2002 general	Pat Roberts (R)	641,075	(83%)	($1,038,984)
	Steven Rosile (Lib)	70,725	(9%)	
	George Cook (Ref)	65,050	(8%)	($3,473)
2002 primary	Pat Roberts (R)	233,642	(84%)	
	Tom Oyler (R)	45,491	(16%)	
1996 general	Pat Roberts (R)	652,677	(62%)	($2,305,898)
	Sally Thompson (D)	362,380	(34%)	($659,066)
	Other	37,243	(4%)	

Prior Winning Percentages: 1994 House (77%); 1992 House (68%); 1990 House (63%); 1988 House (100%); 1986 House (75%); 1984 House (76%); 1982 House (68%); 1980 House (62%)

Pat Roberts is from a fine Kansas Republican background: His abolitionist great-grandfather founded Kansas' second-oldest newspaper, and his father, Wes Roberts, was briefly Republican National Committee chairman during the Eisenhower years. Pat Roberts has spent most of his adult life preparing for the place he is in now. After four years in the Marine Corps and five years running an Arizona newspaper, he worked for two years as an aide to Senator Frank Carlson and 12 years as chief aide to 1st District Congressman Keith Sebelius, Bob Dole's successor in the House and the father-in-law of Democratic Governor Kathleen Sebelius. When Sebelius retired in 1980, Roberts won the seat with 56% in a three-candidate Republican primary. For 14 years, in the minority in the House, he concentrated on farm issues, learning their intricacies and minutiae, traveling in a van to keep in touch with constituents in a district so large that it took two weeks to visit every county seat. His voting record was moderate, and he looked after Kansas interests.

In January 1995 Roberts became chairman of the House Agriculture Committee. He had long believed that the huge subsidies of the early 1980s would never return. Faced with Republican budget parameters, Roberts fashioned a Freedom to Farm bill designed to phase out subsidies over seven years. In September 1995 his bill failed in committee when Southern Republicans eager to protect cotton, rice and peanut subsidies voted against it. But in November 1995, Roberts persuaded Agriculture conferees to include most of his bill in the 1996 budget reconciliation bill, which Bill Clinton vetoed. He agreed to maintain cotton and rice marketing loans and managed to preserve the Conservation Reserve Program, which is popular in Kansas. But overall this was the biggest change in agriculture policy since the New Deal act of 1933. Roberts' new bill passed the Agriculture Committee 29–17 in January 1996, the full House in February, and became law in April. But after the Asian financial collapse in 1997, world crop prices fell and Congress started voting disaster relief to farmers every year—the subsidies in another form.

Amid this furious legislative activity, one of Kansas' Senate seats came open when Nancy Landon Kassebaum announced her retirement in November 1995. At first Roberts said he was too busy working on the farm bill and declined to run. When the bill's fortunes improved, he announced his candidacy in January 1996; the law seemed likely to remove much of the power of the committee, and under new Republican rules he was limited to three terms as chairman. He won the August primary with an overwhelming 78% in a four-way race. In the general election he faced state Treasurer Sally Thompson and won easily, 62%–34%, carrying 104 counties and losing just one (Wyandotte County, which contains Kansas City). Thus Roberts became the first

House member to give up a committee chairmanship to run for the Senate since Lister Hill in 1938 (and Hill got appointed to his Senate seat).

Roberts is on the Senate Agriculture Committee and has spent much time on farm issues. The Freedom to Farm Act worked well in 1997, and farmers seemed pleased to be able to decide what crops to plant without getting government approval. But in 1998 crop prices plunged—in line with the long-run trend of falling prices for basic commodities—and some demanded a return to the old system. Roberts resisted that, and bills were passed to give temporary aid and accelerate $4.5 billion in payments and give farmers an extra $4 billion in disaster assistance. In 1999, with prices still low, federal aid to farmers totaled $23 billion including subsidies to crop insurance, CRP payments, drought relief and direct payments to make up for low world prices and world demand. In 2000 the pattern continued: Roberts argued that increased subsidies for crop insurance would mean less need for yearly assistance and argued that limiting production would not raise prices because the U.S. accounts for less than one-fifth of world production. The problem seems intractable. The number of family farmers continues to fall in places like western Kansas, where farm communities are tending to disappear, yet prices are not sufficient to maintain many operations.

The Freedom to Farm Act came up for reauthorization in 2002, and this time Roberts was not chairman of an Agriculture Committee but the fifth-ranking member of the minority. He admitted the Freedom to Farm Act "didn't work out as anybody would have hoped," and with Thad Cochran pushed for farm savings accounts: The federal government would match farmers up to $10,000 a year in their accounts, which could be drawn on when, for any reason, farm income was below average. But in committee that was rejected in favor of Chairman Tom Harkin's approach: Revival of countercyclical subsidies when crop prices are low, plus a larger conservation reserve program and inclusion of previously uncovered crops. Harkin prevailed on the Senate floor 58–40 in February 2002; Roberts wasn't even on the conference committee. "I've never seen such partisanship in a farm bill," Roberts said. "This policy fails farmers." He argued that it would provide no aid when production was low and crop prices rose, which is exactly what happened when drought struck the Great Plains in summer 2002. Roberts has tried to encourage farm exports in many ways, opposing cargo preferences, urging passage of trade promotion authority and replenishment of IMF funds. He was a lead sponsor of the 2000 law to end the embargo on food to Cuba, and he and Kansas colleague Sam Brownback sponsored the 1999 law allowing the president to lift the embargo on India and Pakistan and in 2000 sought to end food sanctions altogether. He supported PNTR with China and met with Fidel Castro in Cuba in 2000. In October 2002 he got all 100 senators to sign a letter urging the Bush administration to keep the new McGovern-Dole International Food for Education and Child Nutrition Program—school lunches for the world—in the Agriculture Department, not AID.

In 1999 Roberts was named chairman of the new Emerging Threats and Capabilities Subcommittee of Armed Services. He began his first hearing by saying, "I want to know what keeps you awake at night." In hearings that attracted little attention, he probed the nation's vulnerability to terrorists and predicted that targets would be "selected for their symbolic value, like the World Trade Center in the heart of Manhattan." He warned of the dangers of information and biological warfare. When he heard the news on September 11 while driving to work, he thought. "Oh, my God. It's just exactly what we predicted." He was driving in front of the Capitol when United flight 93 would have hit it if that was its intended target. In October 2001 he called for using $3.5 billion of money set aside for farm programs modernizing Agriculture Department research laboratories, to study animal diseases and plants and develop antidotes and vaccines for bioterrorism weapons and to develop rapid response procedures. He has given strong support to the Bush administration on Iraq, although after his annual listening tour of all 105 Kansas counties, he said in early September 2002 that the administration had "to be much more focused and clear" about the reasons for regime change in Iraq. He was focused and clear himself, describing Saddam Hussein's weapons of mass destruction and the likelihood that he would get missiles to deliver them. In spring 2002 he asked Defense Secretary Donald Rumsfeld to change the classification of Navy pilot Michael Speicher, shot down in Iraq in 1991, from Missing In Action to MIA, Captured; the Navy made the change that fall.

In January 2003 Roberts became chairman of the Intelligence Committee, and brought an approach quite different from that of his predecessors: he is an admirer of CIA Director George Tenet, while the previous Republican Chairman, Richard Shelby, was a harsh critic. Some of that difference was apparent in the hearings of the joint Senate-House Intelligence Committee hearings on intelligence failure before September 11. When former CIA counterterrorism head Cofer Black was testifying, Roberts angrily read a note from the committee staff briefing book that said, "Mr. Black will probably dissemble." He apologized to Black, and said that the joint committee was conducting "gotcha" hearings and was "a runaway train." He said committee members were not given enough access to information.

On local issues, Roberts saw to it that when B-1Bs were transferred out of McConnell Air Force Base, KC-135Rs were brought in. In 2002, for the third year in a row, Roberts was voted the funniest member in *Washingtonian's* annual poll of congressional staffers. "I think Kansas is where the humor comes from. Something in the chlorine."

Roberts came up for re-election in 2002. In summer 2001 former Congressman Dan Glickman, who was Bill Clinton's second Secretary of Agriculture, made the political rounds, and the DSCC said it had a poll that showed Roberts and Glickman running about even. But Glickman had had friendly relations with Roberts in their 14 years together on the House Agriculture Committee; a few days after September 11 he announced he would not run. No Democrat filed to run against Roberts and against Libertarian and Reform party candidates he got 83% of the vote.

FIRST DISTRICT

Rep. Jerry Moran (R)

Elected 1996, 4th term; b. May 29, 1954, Great Bend; home, Hays; U. of KS, B.S. 1976, J.D. 1981; Methodist; married (Robba).

Elected Office: KS Senate, 1988–96, Majority Ldr., 1995–97.

Professional Career: Operations Officer, Consolidated State Bank, 1975–77; Mgr., Farmers State Bank & Trust Co., 1977–78; Practicing atty., 1981–96; Instructor, Ft. Hays St. U., 1986.

DC Office: 1519 LHOB 20515, 202-225-2715; Fax: 202-225-5124; Web site: www.house.gov/moranks01.

District Offices: Hays, 785-628-6401; Hutchinson, 620-665-6138.

Committees: *Agriculture* (7th of 27 R): Conservation, Credit, Rural Development & Research; General Farm Commodities & Risk Management (Chmn.). *Transportation & Infrastructure* (17th of 41 R): Aviation; Highways, Transit & Pipelines; Railroads. *Veterans' Affairs* (7th of 17 R): Health (Vice Chmn.).

Group Ratings

	ADA	ACLU	AFS	LCV	CON	ITIC	NTU	COC	ACU	NTLC	CHC
2002	5	27	0	0	25	88	63	90	96	83	92
2001	5	—	10	0	—	—	67	96	88	—	—

National Journal Ratings

	2001 LIB —	2001 CONS	2002 LIB —	2002 CONS
Economic	36%	63%	9%	87%
Social	0%	81%	39%	57%
Foreign	48%	53%	49%	50%

Key Votes of the 107th Congress

1. Approve Bush Tax Cuts	Y	5. Faith-Based Charities	Y	9. Trade Promotion Authority	Y
2. Limit Patients' Bill of Rights	Y	6. Bar Gays in the Boy Scouts	Y	10. Bar Funds for Intl. Court	Y
3. Campaign Finance Reform	N	7. Ban Partial-Birth Abortion	Y	11. Authorize Force in Iraq	Y
4. Ban ANWR Development	N	8. Arm Commercial Pilots	Y	12. Deny Home. Sec. Dept. Union	Y

Election Results

2002 general	Jerry Moran (R)	189,976	(91%)	($393,078)
	Jack Warner (Lib)	18,585	(9%)	
2002 primary	Jerry Moran (R)	unopposed		
2000 general	Jerry Moran (R)	214,328	(89%)	($358,597)
	Jack Warner (Lib)	25,581	(11%)	

Prior Winning Percentages: 1998 (81%); 1996 (73%)

The People		**Race/Ethnic Origin**	**Ancestry**	
Area size:	57,576 sq. mi.	84.5% White	German: 23.2%	English: 7.3%
Urban population:	52.4%	2.1% Black	USA: 7.2%	
Rural population:	47.6%	0.9% Asian	**2000 Presidential Vote**	
Pop. 2000:	672,091	0.4% Native Am.	Bush (R) ... 177,857	(67%)
Median income:	$34,869	0.0% Hawaiian	Gore (D) ... 76,448	(29%)
Poverty status:	11.0%	1.1% Two + races	Other ... 12,514	(5%)
Military veterans:	13.4%	0.1% Other	**Cook Partisan Voting Index:** R +20	
		10.9% Hispanic Origin		

Occupation	Blue collar: 28.5%	White collar: 52.8%	Gray collar: 18.8%

"A prairie is not any old piece of flatland in the Midwest," writes Kansas-born reporter Dennis Farney. "No, a prairie is wine-colored grass, dancing in the wind. A prairie is a sun-splashed hillside, bright with wild flowers. A prairie is a fleeting cloud shadow, the song of the meadowlark. It is the wild land that has never felt the slash of the plow." This prairie once covered almost all of Kansas. Now only a little virgin prairie can still be found, in the Flint Hills region west and south of Topeka, where the waist-deep sea of grass still waves in the wind as it did when the pioneers on the Santa Fe Trail went west through here some 150 years ago; the Tallgrass Prairie National Preserve was created in 1996 to protect this unique landscape. Much of it was grazing land, first for buffalo, then for the cattle driven to Kansas railheads like Abilene and Dodge City in the 1870s and 1880s, a brief moment in history recaptured with varying accuracy in movies over a much longer span, and commemorated in Dodge City's Boot Hill Museum.

Then, after the harsh winter of 1886–87 wiped out the cattle herds, came the plow and barbed wire (commemorated in LaCrosse's Barbed Wire Museum), which enabled farmers to keep livestock out of their wheat fields. The farmers also brought to this vacant landscape Yankee civilization, with its schools and churches, and some foreign traditions as well, like the Cathedral of the Plains built by German Catholics. Now this civilization is threatened. "My great-grandparents and grandparents were part of the stream of settlers who migrated to western Kansas after the Civil War to become wheat farmers," writes James Dickenson in his elegiac *Home on the Range*. "They broke the virgin sod, erected houses, barns, schools, churches and towns, and made the area one of the most agriculturally productive in the world. A little more than a century later, the population has ebbed away from this area and many of the farms, schools, churches and towns lie vacant, dilapidated and boarded up like old boomtowns."

The 1st Congressional District consists of most of this expanse of Kansas, almost everything from the Flint Hills and Abilene west. Its 66 full counties (it also contains parts of three others; only the Nebraska 3d District has more) increased from 76,000 people in 1870 to 570,000 in 1890; then growth slowed to 666,000 in 1940 and dropped to 637,000 in 2000. Since the district's population grew less than the rest of the state in the 1990s, redistricters added parts of Nemaha and Greenwood Counties and almost all of Geary County to the district: It now stretches 350 miles east from the Colorado border. Kansas now has more "frontier counties," with between two and six people per square mile, than it did in 1890. Most of the counties here lost population in the 1990s—by as much as 15%. But there has also been some growth, around Salina and, even more, around Dodge City, Garden City and Liberal (the "Golden Triangle of meatpacking")— where giant non-union meatpacking plants have attracted thousands of Latinos to fill jobs; the counties which contained those towns were 38%, 43% and 42% Hispanic in 2000, and the district is 11% Hispanic—a big change. The demands of the factories and animals have put a strain on the water supply in this arid region. Politically, the 1st District is heavily Republican—67% for

George W. Bush in 2000, though in the 2002 governor's race it voted narrowly for Democrat Kathleen Sebelius, whose late father-in-law, a Republican, represented the district for 14 years.

The congressman from the 1st District is Jerry Moran, a Republican elected in 1996. Moran grew up in Plainville in Rooks County and got his start in politics as an intern for Keith Sebelius, the former congressman. He worked as a banker for four years before attending the University of Kansas law school. He was elected to the state Senate in 1988 where, as chairman of Judiciary, he pushed to give judges greater flexibility on juvenile crime. In 1995 he became state Senate Majority Leader. When Congressman Pat Roberts announced in January 1996 that he would run for the seat of retiring Senator Nancy Kassebaum, Moran stepped into the 1st District race and, with the help of Republican leaders, avoided serious primary competition. He won 76% of the vote in the primary, which was tantamount to election; in November he was elected 73%–24%.

His voting record has been sporadically moderate on economic and foreign issues, and he has pursued district causes. He voted against the November 1999 omnibus spending bill, he said, because it spent too much money and "the process was wrong," including the fact that members had little time to digest the conference report filed at 3 a.m., just hours before the vote. In response to Moran's pressure, the Agriculture Department reversed in April 2002 its earlier decision to end its role in helping rural communities get visas for overseas doctors; at the same time, he called unworkable the Bush administration's failure to increase Medicare reimbursement for rural hospitals. He praised the 2002 farm bill for improving the safety net to farmers. And despite continuing opposition from Republican leaders and the Bush administration, he was a leader in bipartisan efforts to bar the Treasury Department from enforcing sanctions against the sale of food and medicine to Cuba; in August 2002, he called the embargo "a failed policy." "What I do in Congress does not change dramatically from year to year," Moran said once. "It's a goal of keeping Kansas communities and the people who live there viable."

Each year, Moran has logged 5,000 miles around the district (people here expect to see their congressman without driving to the next county over). He was rewarded in 1998 with a record 81% of the vote and has had no Democratic opponent since. He explored the possibility of running for governor in 2002, but said that he changed his mind after the September 11 attacks because of the importance of his job in Congress.

SECOND DISTRICT

Rep. Jim Ryun (R)

Elected 1996, 4th term; b. Apr. 29, 1947, Wichita; home, Lawrence; U. of KS, B.A. 1970; Presbyterian; married (Anne).

Professional Career: U.S. Olympian, Track & Field, 1964, 1968, 1972; Founder & Dir., Jim Ryun Running Camps, 1976–present; Rancher, 1983–present.

DC Office: 2433 RHOB 20515, 202-225-6601; Fax: 202-225-7986; Web site: www.house.gov/ryun.

District Offices: Pittsburg, 316-232-6100; Topeka, 785-232-4500.

Committees: *Armed Services* (12th of 33 R): Readiness; Tactical Air & Land Forces; Total Force. *Budget* (5th of 24 R). *Financial Services* (14th of 37 R): Capital Markets, Insurance & Government Sponsored Enterprises; Financial Institutions & Consumer Credit.

Group Ratings

	ADA	ACLU	AFS	LCV	CON	ITIC	NTU	COC	ACU	NTLC	CHC
2002	0	7	0	0	58	75	63	95	100	97	100
2001	0	—	0	0	—	—	75	96	100	—	—

National Journal Ratings

	2001 LIB —	2001 CONS	2002 LIB —	2002 CONS
Economic	0%	94%	19%	80%
Social	0%	81%	0%	75%
Foreign	0%	97%	0%	85%

Key Votes of the 107th Congress

1. Approve Bush Tax Cuts	Y	5. Faith-Based Charities	Y	9. Trade Promotion Authority	Y
2. Limit Patients' Bill of Rights	Y	6. Bar Gays in the Boy Scouts	Y	10. Bar Funds for Intl. Court	Y
3. Campaign Finance Reform	N	7. Ban Partial-Birth Abortion	Y	11. Authorize Force in Iraq	Y
4. Ban ANWR Development	N	8. Arm Commercial Pilots	Y	12. Deny Home. Sec. Dept. Union	Y

Election Results

2002 general	Jim Ryun (R)	127,477	(60%)	($431,532)
	Dan Lykins (D)	79,160	(38%)	($38,926)
	Other	4,340	(2%)	
2002 primary	Jim Ryun (R)	unopposed		
2000 general	Jim Ryun (R)	164,951	(67%)	($284,064)
	Stanley Wiles (D)	71,709	(29%)	
	Other	8,099	(3%)	

Prior Winning Percentages: 1998 (61%); 1996 (52%)

The People		Race/Ethnic Origin	Ancestry	
Area size:	14,318 sq. mi.	87.3% White	German: 19.3%	Irish: 9.1%
Urban population:	59.8%	4.9% Black	English: 8.2%	
Rural population:	40.2%	1.0% Asian	**2000 Presidential Vote**	
Pop. 2000:	672,102	1.2% Native Am.	Bush (R)	144,721 (54%)
Median income:	$37,855	0.1% Hawaiian	Gore (D)	109,133 (41%)
Poverty status:	11.2%	1.7% Two+ races	Other	13,723 (5%)
Military veterans:	14.6%	0.1% Other	**Cook Partisan Voting Index:** R + 7	
		3.8% Hispanic Origin		

Occupation	Blue collar: 26.1%	White collar: 57.6%	Gray collar: 16.3%

The green plains of eastern Kansas have seen more than their share of American history. Here, on bluffs above the Missouri River, Fort Leavenworth was built in 1827, famous in later years for its war college and military prison and now the oldest U.S. fort west of the Mississippi. In the 1850s, newly founded towns along the Kansas River and along the Missouri line were the centers of Bleeding Kansas, where the pro-slavery bushwhackers set up a state capital in tiny Lecompton and anti-slavery New Englanders set up their stronghold down the river at Lawrence. Farther up the river is Fort Riley, once an outpost against the Indians, now a major Army base often threatened with closure, and Manhattan, home of Kansas State University. Topeka, the state capital, sits here on a low bluff above the river; it was this city whose system of legal segregation was overturned in the 1954 landmark case, *Brown v. Board of Education*. Farther south, on the Missouri border, are the hills called "the Balkans." Here coal miners, often of Eastern European origin, lived in and near towns like Pittsburg and Girard, once a center of American socialism, where Clarence Darrow and Upton Sinclair made pilgrimages; the local paper, *Appeal to Reason*, had circulation of 750,000 across the nation. Population loss is not as great here as in western Kansas. The Topeka area and the Balkans have had slow growth, and Lawrence and the area around have been booming as, in effect, the perimeter of metropolitan Kansas City.

These disparate areas, Topeka and Manhattan, Fort Riley and Fort Leavenworth, the wheat-growing counties and the Balkans—most of eastern Kansas except the Kansas City metropolitan area—make up the 2d Congressional District. Redistricting added Miami County and a part of Lawrence west of Iowa Street, but not the University of Kansas campus. Fort Riley is in the district but next-door Junction City was put into the 1st District. The heritage of most of this area has been Republican ever since the jayhawks defeated the bushwhackers once the votes were counted honestly in the 1850s. Yet Democrats in recent decades have been competitive in state and local races, especially in Topeka. For 20 of the years from 1970–94, Democrats were elected to fill the 2d District seat. Since then, it has voted for strongly conservative Republicans by increasingly solid margins.

The congressman from the 2d District is Jim Ryun, famous more than 30 years before he ran for Congress. He grew up in Wichita, where in 1965 he was the first high-schooler to break the four-minute mile; his 3:55.3 time remained the world record for high schoolers until May 2001. He was a star runner at the University of Kansas, and ran in the Olympics of 1964, 1968 and 1972; he won a silver medal and set world records for the mile, half-mile and 1500-meter runs. After his competitive athletic career, he operated a sports camp, was a motivational speaker for corporations and Christian groups, wrote two books, started a sports management firm and worked with a hearing aid company that produced a "Sounds of Success" program to help hearing-impaired children achieve their potential. His four children all became competitive runners, and one outran her boss—George W. Bush—in the three-mile President's Fitness Challenge race at Fort McNair.

In 1996, when 2d District freshman Sam Brownback ran for the Senate seat suddenly vacated by Bob Dole, Ryun decided to run for the House. He was opposed by former Topeka Mayor Douglas Wright and Cheryl Brown Henderson, whose father was the plaintiff in *Brown v. Board*. Wright called Ryun an "extremist" and predicted that Ryun couldn't win the general. Ryun campaigned for tax cuts and opposed abortion rights. While the press treated Ryun as something of an oddity, Republican primary voters didn't: He won 62% of the vote. In the general, Ryun was outspent by trial lawyer John Frieden. Democrats circulated "Courtship Makes a Comeback," written by Ryun and his wife for Focus on the Family. It told how any young man wanting to date Ryun's daughters has to call him and ask permission. Again there was ridicule, with the press calling Dr. Ruth to mock the Ryuns' practices. However absurd these beliefs may seem to Manhattan or Malibu sophisticates, they were not political poison in Kansas. Ryun lost Topeka and Shawnee County 52%–46%, but won the district 52%–45%.

In the House, Ryun has a very conservative voting record. Unlike former athletes like Jack Kemp and Bill Bradley, he has not sought the spotlight. In 2002, he was a leader of anti-abortion forces who voted against the bankruptcy reform bill because of a provision put in by the Senate which made fines for certain abortion protesters undischargeable in bankruptcy. On the Armed Services Committee, he backed increased military spending. The House passed his amendment designed to protect nuclear secrets by preventing Energy Department safety and security managers from also working for the new National Nuclear Security Administration. In 2001, he helped to defeat an Air Force plan to reduce the number of B-1s and move them from Kansas and Georgia to bases in South Dakota and Texas. He also worked to funnel $500,000 to solve Topeka's red water problem by replacing rusty pipes. Ryun, who suffered 50% hearing loss because of childhood measles, wants to provide hearing aids to those with disabilities.

After his initial close contest, Ryun has breezed to re-election. In 2002 he won 60%–38%. Redistricting made little partisan change to the district; Ryan carried the portion of Lawrence and Douglas County in the district. Following that election, he finished a distant third to Deborah Pryce with 28 of 222 votes cast in his bid to become chairman of the House Republican Conference.

THIRD DISTRICT

Rep. Dennis Moore (D)

Elected 1998, 3d term; b. Nov. 8, 1945, Anthony; home, Lenexa; U. of KS, B.A. 1967; Washburn U. Law Schl., J.D. 1970; Protestant; married (Stephene).

Military Career: Army, 1970; Army Reserves, 1971–73.

Elected Office: Johnson Cnty. Dist. Atty., 1976–88.

Professional Career: Asst. KS Atty. Gen., 1971–73; Practicing atty., 1973–76, 1989–98.

DC Office: 431 CHOB 20515, 202-225-2865; Fax: 202-225-2807; Web site: www.house.gov/moore.

District Offices: Kansas City, 913-621-0832; Lawrence, 785-842-9313; Overland Park, 913-383-2013.

Committees: *Budget* (5th of 19 D). *Financial Services* (15th of 32 D): Capital Markets, Insurance & Government Sponsored Enterprises; Financial Institutions & Consumer Credit; Oversight & Investigations. *Science* (18th of 22 D): Research; Space & Aeronautics.

Group Ratings

	ADA	ACLU	AFS	LCV	CON	ITIC	NTU	COC	ACU	NTLC	CHC
2002	85	87	89	88	25	75	24	60	20	19	17
2001	85	—	80	79	—	—	27	57	20	—	—

National Journal Ratings

	2001 LIB	—	2001 CONS		2002 LIB	—	2002 CONS
Economic	58%	—	43%		62%	—	38%
Social	72%	—	27%		67%	—	29%
Foreign	61%	—	36%		61%	—	38%

Key Votes of the 107th Congress

1. Approve Bush Tax Cuts	Y	5. Faith-Based Charities	N	9. Trade Promotion Authority	Y
2. Limit Patients' Bill of Rights	N	6. Bar Gays in the Boy Scouts	N	10. Bar Funds for Intl. Court	N
3. Campaign Finance Reform	Y	7. Ban Partial-Birth Abortion	N	11. Authorize Force in Iraq	Y
4. Ban ANWR Development	Y	8. Arm Commercial Pilots	Y	12. Deny Home. Sec. Dept. Union	N

Election Results

2002 general	Dennis Moore (D)	110,095	(50%)	($1,871,416)
	Adam Taff (R)	102,882	(47%)	($1,050,226)
	Other	6,412	(3%)	
2002 primary	Dennis Moore (D)	unopposed		
2000 general	Dennis Moore (D)	154,505	(50%)	($1,759,414)
	Phill Kline (R)	144,672	(47%)	($1,054,489)
	Other	9,533	(3%)	

Prior Winning Percentages: 1998 (52%)

The People		Race/Ethnic Origin	Ancestry	
Area size:	787 sq. mi.	79.6% White	German: 18.0%	Irish: 10.5%
Urban population:	94.7%	8.8% Black	English: 9.0%	
Rural population:	5.3%	2.6% Asian	**2000 Presidential Vote**	
Pop. 2000:	672,124	0.6% Native Am.	Bush (R)...............152,832	(53%)
Median income:	$51,118	0.0% Hawaiian	Gore (D)...............122,463	(42%)
Poverty status:	7.8%	1.5% Two+ races	Other...................13,452	(5%)
Military veterans:	12.1%	0.1% Other	**Cook Partisan Voting Index:** R + 6	
		6.8% Hispanic Origin		

Occupation   Blue collar: 17.3%   White collar: 70.4%   Gray collar: 12.3%

Though its central city is in Missouri, 40 percent of metropolitan Kansas City's residents now live west of the state line in Kansas. Some are in Kansas City, Kansas, (or KCK as it is sometimes called) where the low-lying land near the Missouri River used to house one of the nation's largest stockyards. This is still a working-class town with a few dilapidated looking streets and lots of modest frame houses, the largest black neighborhood, new Latino neighborhoods and oldest Catholic ethnic neighborhoods in Kansas. Kansas City's Wyandotte County was 28% black and 16% Hispanic in 2000. South of Kansas City and Wyandotte is Johnson County, very much more affluent and more than three times larger than Wyandotte, separated from the affluent Kansas City, Missouri, neighborhood around the old Country Club Plaza shopping center by just a single small street. The newer neighborhoods are arrayed along the interstates, and have grown to the point that Overland Park, Olathe, Shawnee and Lenexa are among the largest cities in the state. These suburbs are not just residential; Sprint's headquarters is in Johnson County, and a J.C. Penney catalog center, as well as lots of thriving small businesses, are also located there. Politically, Wyandotte County has an old Democratic machine politics, while Johnson County has long been heavily Republican, but with plenty of voters moderate or even liberal on cultural issues.

The 3d Congressional District consists of Johnson County, Wyandotte County and the part of Douglas County to the west, which includes the portion of Lawrence that is home of the University of Kansas campus. Redistricting removed Miami County to the south and part of Douglas County (Lawrence, west of Iowa Street); the district had grown rapidly in the 1990s. More than two-thirds of its people live in Johnson County, which grew by 27% in the 1990s and had a $62,000 median household income. The most hard-fought struggle here has been between conservative and moderate Republicans. In the 1990s, conservatives made great strides, taking over the Republican party organization and leadership positions in the legislature. In 1996 they showed across-the-board strength, electing three conservative freshmen to Congress, plus Senator Sam Brownback. But in 1998 the moderates rebounded. A primary challenge to moderate Governor Bill Graves was beaten nearly 3–1, and in the 3d District, conservative Republican Vince Snowbarger was one of six House incumbents defeated for re-election.

The congressman from the 3d District is Dennis Moore, a Democrat with a long political pedigree first elected in 1998. Moore grew up in Wichita, and his father Warner Moore ran for Congress in the 4th District and lost the general by only 50.3%–49.7% in 1958—the same year in which a Democrat last won in the 3d. Moore went to college and law school in Kansas, served in the Army and practiced law in Johnson County. In 1976, at 31, he was elected Johnson County district attorney and was twice re-elected. He went into private law practice, and was elected to the local community college board in 1997.

His election success made Moore a natural when national Democrats were recruiting a candidate to oppose Snowbarger, whose strong conservative views were off-putting to many Republicans. Moore got the support of a local Mainstream Coalition organized to fight the conservatives in local elections. Snowbarger made "trust" his major theme, but ran few if any ads on what he'd done positively. The contest attracted independent expenditure campaigns, with the Sierra Club and the AFL-CIO spending heavily on TV ads, mailings and phone banks to elect Moore. Moore won 52%–48%, carrying Kansas City and Lawrence by wide margins, but his key wins came in the affluent, long-settled, elderly suburbs in northeast Johnson County. That was enough to hold Snowbarger, to a 53%–47% margin in Johnson County.

In the House, Moore joined the Blue Dogs and emulated earlier moderate Democrats who sought to straddle party lines. To the dismay of organized labor, he voted for PNTR with China and voted for trade promotion authority. He brought federal dollars home, including $22 million for projects in Wyandotte County—compared to only $3.5 million for Johnson County; Moore aides explained the disparity by saying that previous congressmen had shortchanged Wyandotte. He filed legislation to permit the Wyandotte Tribe to build a casino and hotel near the Kansas Speedway in Edwardsville. He sponsored a bill to give millions of dollars to engineers to improve construction and retrofit existing structures against tornados.

All that has not diminished Republican hopes of recapturing this seat. In 2000, the primary was a contest between tax-cutting state Representative Phill Kline and Greg Musil, an Overland Park councilman. Brownback and conservative leaders endorsed Kline. Musil was endorsed by Graves and moderates and had the backing of NRCC Chairman Tom Davis. Kline won the primary 50%–37%. In the general, Kline did a more effective job than Snowbarger had in rallying moderate Republican leaders, but Moore appealed to moderates by portraying himself as a fiscal conservative and a crime-fighter. He said that Kline belonged to the "farthest right of the far right" and that his votes in the legislature weakened education. In a result similar to 1998, Moore won 50%–47%; Kline took Johnson County by only 52%–45%, while it was voting 60%–36% for George W. Bush.

It was much the same in 2002. This time, the NRCC supported reconstructive surgeon Jeff Colyer, the anti-abortion candidate, against United Airlines pilot and former Naval F-18 aviator Adam Taff, who supported abortion rights. Colyer outspent him 2-to-1, but Taff got a late endorsement from Graves and unexpectedly won the primary, 52%–48%. Republicans coalesced behind Taff, who emphasized his military experience and top-secret clearance, but it didn't help that NRCC chairman Davis earlier had said Taff is "a nice kid, but he's got no clue." Moore voted to authorize the use of force in Iraq, and emphasized bipartisanship. Supporters of Taff, who was significantly outspent and did not run negative ads, complained that NRCC support was too little and too late. Moore won again by the same 50%–47% margin. Taff carried Johnson County by 53%–44% but Moore was helped by redistricting, though it was controlled by Republicans. A more aggressively partisan districting plan could have removed Douglas County from the district altogether and added much more Republican counties south of Miami County. Moore carried the district by 7,213 votes and carried Douglas County by 5,585. Substitution of more Republican territory for Douglas County would almost certainly have produced a different result.

Johnson County continues to grow rapidly, while Wyandotte County has been losing population. Moore has shown himself able to appeal to enough Republican voters to win, but not by great margins. This will probably remain a seriously contested district for as long as he runs; Taff kept his campaign office open and has already announced he will run again in 2004. There has been talk that Moore may run against Senator Sam Brownback in 2004 and try to break the jinx: Kansas has not elected a Democratic senator since 1932.

FOURTH DISTRICT

Rep. Todd Tiahrt (R)

Elected 1994, 5th term; b. June 15, 1951, Vermillion, SD; home, Goddard; SD Sch. of Mines, 1969–71; Evangel Col., B.A. 1975; SW MO St. U., M.B.A. 1989; Assembly of God; married (Vicki).

Elected Office: KS Senate, 1992–94.

Professional Career: Project Engineer, Zenith Corp., 1978–81; Proposal Mgr., Boeing Co., 1981–94.

DC Office: 2441 RHOB 20515, 202-225-6216; Fax: 202-225-3489; Web site: www.house.gov/tiahrt.

District Office: Wichita, 316-262-8992.

Committees: *Appropriations* (18th of 36 R): Defense; The Legislative Branch; Transportation, Treasury, & Independent Agencies (Vice Chmn.).

Group Ratings

	ADA	ACLU	AFS	LCV	CON	ITIC	NTU	COC	ACU	NTLC	CHC
2002	5	20	0	0	25	100	56	95	96	94	100
2001	0	—	0	0	—	—	68	96	96	—	—

National Journal Ratings

	2001 LIB — 2001 CONS		2002 LIB — 2002 CONS	
Economic	0%	— 94%	9%	— 87%
Social	0%	— 81%	0%	— 75%
Foreign	29%	— 69%	29%	— 67%

Key Votes of the 107th Congress

1. Approve Bush Tax Cuts	Y	5. Faith-Based Charities	Y	9. Trade Promotion Authority	Y
2. Limit Patients' Bill of Rights	Y	6. Bar Gays in the Boy Scouts	Y	10. Bar Funds for Intl. Court	Y
3. Campaign Finance Reform	N	7. Ban Partial-Birth Abortion	Y	11. Authorize Force in Iraq	Y
4. Ban ANWR Development	N	8. Arm Commercial Pilots	Y	12. Deny Home. Sec. Dept. Union	Y

Election Results

2002 general	Todd Tiahrt (R)	115,691	(61%)	($1,132,104)
	Carlos Nolla (D)	70,656	(37%)	($686,952)
	Other	4,616	(2%)	
2002 primary	Todd Tiahrt (R)	unopposed		
2000 general	Todd Tiahrt (R)	131,871	(54%)	($854,357)
	Carlos Nolla (D)	101,980	(42%)	($313,524)
	Steven A. Rosile (Lib)	8,732	(4%)	

Prior Winning Percentages: 1998 (58%); 1996 (50%); 1994 (53%)

The People		Race/Ethnic Origin	Ancestry	
Area size:	9,596 sq. mi.	81.0% White	German: 17.7%	English: 8.0%
Urban population:	78.8%	6.8% Black	Irish: 7.9%	
Rural population:	21.2%	2.4% Asian	**2000 Presidential Vote**	
Pop. 2000:	672,101	1.1% Native Am.	Bush (R) 146,921	(59%)
Median income:	$40,917	0.0% Hawaiian	Gore (D) 91,232	(37%)
Poverty status:	9.6%	2.0% Two+ races	Other 10,918	(4%)
Military veterans:	14.0%	0.1% Other	**Cook Partisan Voting Index:** R +12	
		6.6% Hispanic Origin		

Occupation	Blue collar: 28.3%	White collar: 57.0%	Gray collar: 14.6%

Wichita is the largest Kansas-only metropolitan area, smaller than million-plus metro Kansas City, but a Great Plains metropolis of the magnitude of Omaha or Tulsa, and still growing. It began as a farm market town and grew with local oil and gas discoveries in the 1920s. But its real impetus came during World War II and the years just after, when aircraft factories sprouted up here on the Kansas plains and Wichita suddenly became the nation's major producer of small planes. Today the big four—Cessna, Raytheon, Boeing, Bombardier—are all located here. In the early 1990s, general aviation was hurt by the recession and by suits which held manufacturers liable for planes they had produced years, even decades, before. Later in the decade, Wichita recovered: The demand for small planes was robust, and a federal limit on liability pushed through by, among others, its former Congressman Dan Glickman, enlivened the industry. But the September 11 attacks were a severe blow to the airline industry—and, therefore, to Wichita and its jobs; in the 18 months ending in December 2002, 14,000 aircraft workers in the area were laid off. Some shifted to health care, as Wichita has become a regional center in the common Great Plains pattern, with rural counties unable to attract new doctors or maintain hospitals, and people from miles around come to the metropolis for treatment.

Kansas' 4th Congressional District is centered around Wichita, covering wheat-growing areas to the east and west, but with most of its people in Wichita and Sedgwick County. Politically, it has voted Republican most of the time; it went 59% for George W. Bush in 2000.

The congressman from the 4th District is Todd Tiahrt (pronounced *TEE-hart*), a Republican first elected in 1994. He grew up on a farm in South Dakota, went to the same high school as South Dakota Senator Tim Johnson, played football for the South Dakota School of Mines and Technology and graduated from Evangel College. In 1976 he moved to the Wichita area to be closer to his wife's family and worked at Zenith as a project engineer and at Boeing as a proposal manager on the Space Station, Air Force One, KC-135, B-52, B-1, B-2, A-67, YF-22 and Comanche helicopter programs. In 1990 he went to the courthouse to file to run for the Kansas House and decided he was a Republican; he lost that race by only 8 votes. His grandfather had raised him to be a Democrat, but he found his strong religious views—"to me, liberty is the freedom to do the right thing, not the freedom to do anything"—were more in line with Republicans. In 1992 he was elected to the Kansas Senate, where his great cause was a concealed weapons law.

In 1994 Tiahrt decided to run against Glickman, a task all the more daunting because Glickman seemed to be having a productive ninth term. Tiahrt ran ads showing Glickman's face morphing into Bill Clinton's, and attacked him for voting for gun control in the 1994 crime bill. With his base among Wichita's numerous religious conservatives, who had taken over the local Republican Party, he assembled a corps of 1,800 volunteers, many from church contacts. Glickman outspent him more than 3-to-1 and continued to run relatively well in high-income Republican precincts, but he suffered serious losses in middle-income areas in Sedgwick County. Tiahrt won a solid 53%–47% victory.

In the House, Tiahrt boasted that he voted with Newt Gingrich 97% of the time; he is an active deputy in Tom DeLay's Whip organization. He proposed eliminating the Department of Energy and transferring nuclear weapons storage and waste disposal to the Pentagon, to no effect. He tried to zero out—and later, to reduce—AmeriCorps, as "largely inefficient and ineffective," but with no success. Tiahrt keeps his eye on the local economy and was a big supporter of the controversial congressional decision to lease dozens of jet-tankers from Boeing for $37 billion.

On Appropriations since 1997, he sponsored the ban on needle exchanges in the District of Columbia and called for a felony investigation of District officials who continued to fund abortions after Congress banned the financing. He kept the pressure on Metro officials in the Capitol region to make sure that their signs recognized the name change at Ronald Reagan Washington National Airport. After Martin and Gracia Burnham from his district were taken hostage in May 2001 by Abu Sayyaf terrorists in the Philippines, Tiahrt traveled to Manila to urge help by government leaders there and he relentlessly pressured the State Department for action; more than a year later, Martin Burnham was murdered but Filipino troops rescued his wife.

Not surprisingly, Democrats have targeted Tiahrt. They have continued to run well-financed opponents against him, but he may finally be locking up the district. In 2000, Wichita attorney and former Glickman aide Carlos Nolla ran a tougher-than-expected challenge against him. Tiahrt won 54%–42%, sweeping all 12 counties, but winning only 52%–45% in Sedgwick County, which cast two-thirds of the vote. In a rematch two years later, Nolla doubled his fundraising with support from national Hispanics, and said that Tiahrt was beholden to pharmaceutical companies, but he lost by 61%–37%. Tiahrt has sought to move up the political ladder. He considered running for governor in 2002, but backed off. In the House, he pushed for Roy Blunt to appoint him as chief deputy whip; following the election, he was disappointed that the job went to the more junior Eric Cantor of Virginia.

★ KENTUCKY ★

K entucky is a state that in many ways remains close to its beginnings. This is, literally, a Jeffersonian commonwealth: It is one of four commonwealths (the others are Virginia, Pennsylvania and Massachusetts) and when the first settlers came here, in the years Thomas Jefferson was writing his *Notes on Virginia*, it was part of Virginia. Kentucky was admitted to the Union in 1792, when Jefferson was secretary of state; when Jefferson was aroused at the Federalists' antisedition acts, he ghostwrote the Kentucky Resolutions in 1798. Kentucky's largest county is named after Jefferson and its largest city after the monarch to whom he was credentialed as ambassador to France, Louis XVI. To this day, Kentucky still has a constitution informed by a Jeffersonian jealousy of power. Its one-term limit on governors was raised to two only in 1995 (the current governor, Paul Patton, was the first eligible for a second consecutive term); it has strict limits on when the legislature can meet, so that much important business gets done in special sessions; every governor must swear that he or she has not participated in a duel (remember what Jefferson thought of Aaron Burr). Kentucky also has long favored the Democratic Party, which can trace its ancestry at least tenuously back to Jefferson; Republicans have made gains recently in federal elections, and George W. Bush carried the state handily in 2000, but in the 1990s Kentucky voted twice, though by diminishing margins, for William Jefferson Clinton.

The agrarian Jefferson would approve of Kentucky's demography, which is still quite rural, with well under half its population in the big metropolitan areas of Louisville, Lexington and the Northern Kentucky area across the Ohio River from Cincinnati; only three counties have populations over 100,000. And the tobacco planters who once presided over what one historian called "the alcoholic republic" might not entirely disapprove of a Kentucky economy that remained for years heavily dependent on century-old industries such as tobacco (Kentucky is the nation's number two producer after North Carolina, and it has the largest number of tobacco farms), whiskey (Bourbon County, where the beverage was invented in the 18th century, is in Kentucky) and coal. Today tobacco makes up a small percentage of the state economy, but according to the U.S. Department of Agriculture, it is still home to 17 of the 20 most tobacco-dependent counties in the nation. In 2000 Kentucky ranked second in percentage of smokers and last in percentage of smoke-free workplaces. But there is some change. Employment is sharply down in coal and tobacco, and Kentucky has big plants producing appliances, Toyotas, Ford trucks and Lexmark printers; it also has big companies that specialize in things not traditionally Kentuckian, such as Humana health services and Ashland Inc. oil company. Still, this is an economy that did not partake much of the bounteous growth of the 1990s.

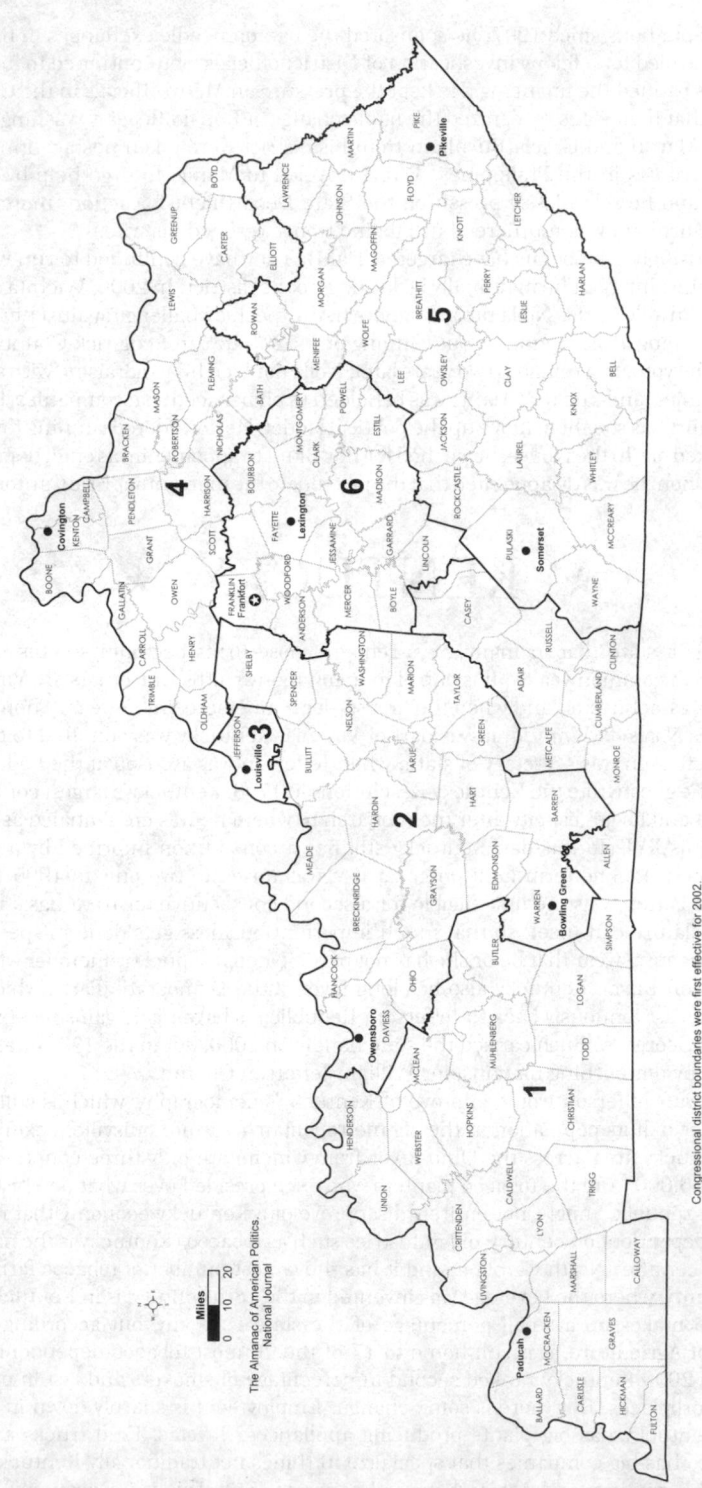

Congressional district boundaries were first effective for 2002.

Many of the buildings here are old: The small-town 19th century courthouses, the cabins in the coal mining Appalachians, the unpainted houses in the soggy lowlands beneath the levees by the Mississippi River. Kentucky is the home of some of the nation's oldest traditions, from bourbon to bluegrass music to religious revivals (the Disciples of Christ got their start in the enormous revival at Cane Ridge in 1801); it was the home of the inventor of Mother's Day in 1887 and a Louisville restaurant claims credit for inventing the cheeseburger. Some things have changed. Satellite dishes and four-lane highways have brought modern civilization into hollows and lowland farms that lacked indoor plumbing and electricity within living memory and farmers have begun to diversify their crops; Eastern Kentucky farmers raise goats for meat production and the state touts its grape vineyards and fruit orchards. But people in this state still have a strong attachment to place and family; the continuity is real. Kentucky's population has grown just 42% over the past 50 years; few outsiders have moved in, though the number increased in the 1990s, so today's Kentuckians are mostly descendants of settlers who poured over the mountains in the 40 years after Daniel Boone made his way through the Cumberland Gap in 1775, when Kentucky's population rose from 73,000 in the Census of 1790 to 564,000 in 1820.

There has long been hearty, though lopsided, political competition here, with most of the 120 counties voting today as they did in the Civil War era. The eastern mountains were pro-Union and remain Republican, except for counties where coal miners were organized by the United Mine Workers in the 1930s; the Bluegrass region and the western end of the state were slave-holding territory and Democratic. In the mountains politics can get downright violent—in spring 2002 the Pulaski County sheriff was shot to death and shots were fired at a candidate for Clay County Clerk—and selling votes for $50 or for a pint of whiskey is not unheard of; in 1998 a Wayne County grand jury declined to indict 54 people who confessed to selling their votes. Louisville, with many German immigrants, was an anti-slavery town, and for years flirted with Republicans, though now it mostly supports Democrats. These patterns, which have more or less prevailed for more than 100 years, were apparent in the returns for governor in 1995, senator in 1996 and 1998, and president in 1992 and 1996. For years, all this meant Democratic party control, with the real battle in the primary. For nearly half a century there was almost a two-party system within the dominant party, with factions going back to the 1938 primary when Senate Majority Leader (and later Vice President) Alben Barkley was challenged by Governor (and later Senator and Baseball Commissioner) Happy Chandler. Barkley's faction was later led by Governor (1959–63) Bert Combs and Chandler's by Governor (1971–74) and Senator (1974–99) Wendell Ford. But as Louisville *Courier-Journal* reporter Al Cross notes, factional gave way to money, with rich candidates elected governor over most of the last 20 years—John Y. Brown Jr. in 1979, Wallace Wilkinson in 1987 and Brereton Jones in 1991. But lineage still has its claims: Ben Chandler, Happy Chandler's grandson, was elected attorney general in 1995 and 1999.

In the last decade there have been some changes in these patterns. Even as Democratic Governor Paul Patton, a narrow winner in 1995, was re-elected by a wide margin over a hapless Republican in 1999, Republicans were winning near-total control of Kentucky's congressional delegation—albeit in some cases by narrow margins initially. Much of this has been the work of Senator Mitch McConnell, first elected in 1984. McConnell helped line up candidates who carried three formerly Democratic congressional districts in 1994 and 1996; he provided key support for Senator Jim Bunning's 6,766-vote win in 1998 and helped capture the 6th District vacated by Bunning's opponent that year as well. Now only the 4th District is represented by a Democrat, a conservative who often votes with Republicans. In July and August 1999 party switches gave Republicans a 20–18 margin in the state Senate, where they were outnumbered 30–8 at the beginning of the decade; the state House is still heavily Democratic. The biggest Republican triumph came in the 2000 presidential race. Al Gore initially targeted Kentucky, which is just north of his home state of Tennessee and which the Clinton-Gore ticket carried twice. But Kentucky was part of the rural trend away from Clinton Democrats and toward Republicans in the 1990s, and Gore had taken stands seen as hostile to the state's leading industries—tobacco, coal and automobiles. Early polls showed Bush far ahead, and Gore took his ads off Kentucky stations and took the state off his schedule. Bush swept the state, 57%–41%; in 50 of the 120 counties he won a higher percentage than Ronald Reagan had in his landslide re-election victory in 1984.

Moreover, the popularity of his issue positions and cultural stance helped defeat Democrats the party had considered itself lucky to recruit in the 1st, 3d and 6th Congressional Districts. If Bush's politics of decentralized government and confident nationalism can be called Jeffersonian, then Kentucky in 2000 voted in line with its Jeffersonian roots. The question now is whether the Republicans will make a serious push for the governorship in 2003 for the first time since 1971.

The People		Race/Ethnic Origin			Military veterans: 380,618 (12.5%)	
Pop. 2000:	4,041,769	3,608,013	89.3%	White	WWII: 18.9%	Korea: 13.5%
Pop. 1990:	3,685,296	293,639	7.3%	Black	Vietnam: 32.6%	Gulf War: 10.8%
Change 1990–2000:	Up 9.6%	29,368	0.7%	Asian	**Most populous cities:**	
Change 1980–1990:	Up 0.7%	7,939	0.2%	Native Am.	1. Louisville	693,604
% of U.S. total:	1.4%	1,275	0.0%	Hawaiian	2. Lexington	260,512
Pop. rank:	25th of 50	37,750	0.9%	Two+ races	3. Owensboro	54,067
Area size:	40,409 sq. mi.	3,846	0.1%	Other	4. Bowling Green	49,296
State Native:	73.7%	59,939	1.5%	Hisp. Origin	5. Covington	43,370
Non-citizen:	1.3%	**Ancestry**			Urban population: 55.7%	
Language		USA: 17.3%		German: 10.5%	Rural population: 44.3%	
English: 94.4%	Spanish: 2.7%	Irish: 8.6%		English: 8.0%		
Other Eur.: 2.0%		Scotch-Irish: 1.4%				

Education		Work Sector		Legislature	
H.S. Grad:	74.1%	Private: 78.5%	Govt: 14.4%	Senate	21 R 17 D
College Grad:	17.1%	Self: 6.7%	Family: 0.4%	House	65 D 35 R
Industry		Unemployment: 5.7%		Legislative Term Limits: No	
Agri: 3.3%	Con: 7.2%	**Household Income**		**Registered Voters**	
Fin: 5.4%	Info: 2.2%	<15k: 22.3%	15-35k: 29.2%	D: 1,582,532 (59.0%)	
Mfg: 23.6%	Prof: 26.6%	35-50k: 16.4%	50-100k: 24.9%	R: 927,528 (34.6%)	
Public: 4.3%	Trade: 15.5%	100-150k: 4.6%	>150k: 2.6%	I: 172,936 (6.4%)	
Other: 12.0%		Median: $33,672			
Occupation		Poverty status: 15.8%			
Blue collar: 30.7%	White collar: 54.1%	**Home Value**			
Gray collar: 15.2%		<50k: 27.3%	50-100k: 38.9%	100-200k: 26.1%	200-300k: 5.1%
		300-500k: 1.9%	>500k: 0.8%	Median: $79,600	

Presidential politics   Kentucky's solid 57%–41% margin for George W. Bush in 2000 was all the more remarkable because Kentucky has usually been a competitive state when Democrats run a Southerner or two on its ticket, as in such widely separated years as 1952, 1976, 1980, 1992 and 1996. But it was a continuation of a trend apparent in 1996, when Bill Clinton carried the state only by increasing his vote in the Lexington and Louisville areas and in Northern Kentucky, while falling behind his 1992 showing in the rural counties. In 2000 Gore carried Louisville's Jefferson County 50%–48% and won the usually Democratic state capital of Frankfort; he lost Lexington's Fayette County 52%–45% and trailed far behind in Northern Kentucky. Otherwise, he won only nine coal counties in the east and four ancestrally Democratic counties in the west. Gore carried only the very lowest income voters (below $15,000), and he was especially weak among younger voters (under 30s went 62%–35% for Bush)—not good signs for national Democrats here.

2000 Presidential Vote
Bush (R)	872,520	(57%)
Gore (D)	638,923	(41%)
Nader (Green)	23,118	(1%)
Other	9,465	(1%)

2000 Republican Presidential Primary
Bush (R)	75,783	(83%)
McCain (R)	5,780	(6%)
Other	5,423	(6%)
Keyes (R)	4,337	(5%)

2000 Democratic Presidential Primary
Gore (D)	156,966	(71%)
Bradley (D)	32,340	(15%)
Uncommitted	26,046	(12%)

1996 Presidential Vote
Clinton (D)	636,614	(46%)
Dole (R)	623,283	(45%)
Perot (I)	120,396	(9%)

Kentucky was part of the Super Tuesday primary in March 1988, but switched back to a May date in 1992, so that state and presidential contests can be held on the same day. It has had no effect on the outcome of the presidential contest.

Congressional districting   Kentucky's 1991 redistricting plan, drawn by Democrats after

108th Congress Lineup
5 R   1 D
107th Congress Lineup
5 R   1 D

the state lost one House seat in the 1990 Census, was intended to protect Democratic incumbents, but instead produced a delegation that has been 5–1 Republican since 1996. Party control of the legislature in 2001 was split, because Republicans held on to their 20–18 majority in the state Senate in the 2000 election— a nice dividend of George W. Bush's strong run here. House Democrats prepared a plan that would have chopped off the east end of the 1st District and added Owensboro to it, making it more difficult for Republican Ed Whitfield. Senate Republicans were prepared to pass the incumbent Republicans' plan that would have added heavily Republican Oldham County to the 3d District to strengthen Anne Northup. The impasse continued through January 2002, delaying the January 29 filing deadline for candidates. On February 1, the legislature finally adopted a compromise plan that changed the lines very little. With one important exception: It removed increasingly Republican suburban Shelby County from the 4th District and added three and one-half traditionally Democratic counties. That change helped the state's one Democratic incumbent, Ken Lucas, to win by a 6,000-vote margin; in the old district, his margin might have been less than 1,000 votes.

Governor

Paul Patton (D)

Elected 1995, term expires Dec. 2003, 2d term; b. May 26, 1937, Fallsburg; home, Pikeville; U. of KY, B.S. 1959; Presbyterian; married (Judi).

Elected Office: Pike Cnty. Judge Exec., 1982–91; KY Lt. Gov., 1991–95.

Professional Career: Coal Co. Exec., 1959–79; KY Dpty. Transportation Secy., 1979–80; KY Dem. Party Chmn., 1981–83; KY Economic Develop. Secy., 1991–95.

Office: State Capitol, 700 Capitol Ave., Frankfort, 40601, 502-564-2611; Fax: 502-564-2517; Web site: gov.state.ky.us.

Election Results

1999 general	Paul Patton (D)	352,099	(61%)
	Peppy Martin (R)	128,788	(22%)
	Gatewood Galbraith (Ref)	88,930	(15%)
	Other	6,934	(1%)
1999 primary	Paul Patton (D)	unopposed	
1995 general	Paul Patton (D)	500,787	(51%)
	Larry Forgy (R)	479,227	(49%)

There is no question who ordinarily stands at the apex of Kentucky politics: The governor. The governor's appointment powers are wide: The legislature meets in regular session for only 60 days in even-numbered years and, since 2001, 30 days in odd-numbered years. After that, the governor can shift around line items in the state budget and call special sessions. But Kentucky's governor, Paul Patton, first elected in 1995, entered his final year as governor in 2003 under a cloud of scandal.

Patton is a Democrat from the eastern Kentucky coal fields. He grew up in Lawrence County on the West Virginia border in a house converted from a silo. He graduated from the University of Kentucky's College of Engineering, and ran a coal company from 1962 to 1978. He was deputy state Transportation secretary from 1979–80, chaired the state Democratic Party and in 1982 was elected judge-executive of Pike County, at the far eastern extremity of the state. In 1991 he was elected lieutenant governor and worked on a law granting tax credits to firms that create jobs. In 1995 he ran for governor and won the Democratic primary with 45% of the vote, with 24% for Secretary of State Bob Babbage and 21% for legislator John "Eck" Rose. In the general, he faced Republican Larry Forgy, who campaigned hard against the Kentucky Education Reform Act, passed in 1990 after the state Supreme Court outlawed school finance laws. Patton won 51%–49%, the Democrats' first major success in stalling Republican advances since Bill Clinton took office; Democrats all over the country took heart.

In his first years as governor, Patton took a conservative tack. When the Clinton administration threatened to regulate tobacco as a drug, Patton supported a lawsuit opposing the FDA rules, lit up a cigarette, and said he wouldn't support Clinton in 1996 if the FDA acted. He got a bipartisan majority to vote to reduce the cost of worker's compensation. This stirred great opposition in Patton's eastern Kentucky base and among the unions who had supported him strongly in 1995, but he refused to call a special session to change the law. In 1997, he called a special session to change the health care law passed in 1994, but no bill was passed. Patton had a high job rating in 1999, the first year in which a Kentucky governor could seek a four-year term. The little-known Republican candidate, publicist Peppy Martin, in an October debate charged that 80% of sheriffs and 30% of state police were "bootlegging hard drugs." Senator Mitch McConnell and state Senate Republican leader David Williams endorsed Patton. He won with 61% of the vote, to 22% for Martin and 15% for Gatewood Galbraith, an independent who backed legalization of marijuana. Patton carried 113 counties; the seven he lost were in eastern Kentucky, evidently because of anger over his worker's comp changes.

In his second term, Patton moved to the left. He tried to get major tax increases in 2000, but was stopped by the state Senate, in which Republicans had a 20–18 majority. Patton signed an early childhood development bill, funded by tobacco settlement money and designed by a commission headed by his daughter Nicki Patton. Worker's comp was liberalized in regards to injury claims, as Patton said he had gone too far in his 1996 law. Republicans held their state Senate majority in the 2000 election amid much bitter partisan dispute.

In early 2002 Patton seemed at the summit of his career; he became head of the National Governors Association in July and he was seen as a likely and formidable candidate against Senator Jim Bunning in 2004. Then, in September 2002, Tina Conner, owner of a nursing home in Hickman County, in the far western end of Kentucky, sued Patton for sexual harassment. She charged that when she had met the governor in 1997, he had fondled her and they began an intimate relationship; he appointed her to the state Institute on Aging and when she came to official meetings they would meet in a Louisville hotel. For two years, she said, that continued, and for two years more they had phone sex. She said she broke off the relationship in October 2001; after that, state inspectors came in and found serious violations, which resulted in the closing of the nursing home and its bankruptcy. At first Patton denied her charges, but when the Louisville *Courier-Journal* obtained phone records showing 440 calls from Patton's office to Conner's home and office, he admitted that they had had an "inappropriate personal relationship," but denied that he had used state government to retaliate. Not surprisingly this was the biggest Kentucky news story of the year. The state's two U.S. attorneys and state Attorney General Ben Chandler announced they were investigating. A few days after his confession Patton said, "I do not anticipate, in the foreseeable fuure, any involvement in the political process, including the U.S. Senate race." Republicans ran ads for the November legislative races urging voters to "stand up to Paul Patton and the scandals in Frankfort"; Patton's chief of staff had been indicted for violating campaign finance laws in the 1995 election. Patton spent the remaining months of 2002 and early 2003 confronting an expected $509 million shortfall between revenues and current spending; he sought an "open dialogue" with legislators of both parties, but in early 2003 Senate Republicans, with a 21–17 majority, seemed determined to oppose a major tax increase.

Meanwhile, candidates were lining up to run in the May 2003 primary. The state's public financing system, passed in 1992 and limiting spending to $1.8 million, was rendered moot when the state Senate refused to fund it. Republicans have not elected a governor since Louie Nunn won in 1967, but this time had hopes of winning. Despite a court challenge that successfully knocked his running mate from the race and another that unsuccessfully sought to keep him off the ballot, 6th District Congressman Ernie Fletcher easily won the Republican nomination with 57% over former Jefferson County Judge-Executive (the county and Louisville city governments were merged in 2003) Rebecca Jackson, state Representative Steve Nunn, Louie Nunn's son, and state Senator Virgil Moore. Chandler (grandson of former Governor and Senator Happy Chandler), who was unpopular with some insiders but popular with voters for his prosecution of Patton's chief of staff and two union leaders, narrowly won the Democratic nomination over state House Speaker Jody Richards. Chandler's running mate Charlie Owen, a businessman who had run self-financed unsuccessful campaigns for the House, the Senate and the governorship, can spend as much of his own money as he wants for the Chandler ticket.

Senior Senator

Mitch McConnell (R)

Elected 1984, seat up 2008, 4th term; b. Feb. 20, 1942, Sheffield, AL; home, Louisville; U. of Louisville, B.A. 1964, U. of KY, J.D. 1967; Baptist; married (Elaine Chao).

Elected Office: Jefferson Cnty. Judge Exec., 1977–84.

Professional Career: Chief Legis. Asst., U.S. Sen. Marlow Cook, 1967–70; Dpty. Asst. U.S. Atty. Gen., 1974–75.

DC Office: 361-A RSOB, 20510, 202-224-2541; Fax: 202-224-2499; Web site: mcconnell.senate.gov.

State Offices: Bowling Green, 270-781-1673; Ft. Wright, 859-578-0188; Lexington, 859-224-8286; London, 606-864-2026; Louisville, 502-582-6304; Paducah, 270-442-4554.

Committees: *Majority Whip. Agriculture, Nutrition & Forestry*: Forestry, Conservation & Rural Revitalization; Production & Price Competitiveness; Research, Nutrition & General Legislation. *Appropriations*: Agriculture & Rural Development; Commerce, Justice, State & Judiciary; Defense; Energy & Water Development; Foreign Operations (Chmn.); Homeland Security. *Rules & Administration*.

Group Ratings

	ADA	ACLU	AFS	LCV	CON	ITIC	NTU	COC	ACU	NTLC	CHC
2002	0	20	13	6	51	88	64	95	100	97	—
2001	5	—	0	0	—	—	81	93	96	—	100

National Journal Ratings

	2001 LIB — 2001 CONS		2002 LIB — 2002 CONS	
Economic	7% —	86%	0% —	94%
Social	22% —	73%	0% —	62%
Foreign	7% —	72%	0% —	76%

Key Votes of the 107th Congress

1. Approve Bush Tax Cuts	Y	5. Confirm Ashcroft as AG	Y	9. Bar Coop. with Intl. Court	Y
2. Expand Patients' Rights	N	6. Bar Gays in the Boy Scouts	Y	10. Trade Promotion Authority	Y
3. Campaign Finance Reform	N	7. $ for Hate Crime Prosecution	N	11. Authorize Force in Iraq	Y
4. Permit ANWR Development	Y	8. Overseas Military Abortions	N	12. Homeland Sec. Dept. Union	N

Election Results

2002 general	Mitch McConnell (R)	731,679	(65%)	($5,336,099)
	Lois Combs Weinberg (D)	399,634	(35%)	($2,244,035)
2002 primary	Mitch McConnell (R)	unopposed		
1996 general	Mitch McConnell (R)	724,794	(55%)	($5,031,293)
	Steven L. Beshear (D)	560,012	(43%)	($2,073,794)
	Other	22,240	(2%)	

Prior Winning Percentages: 1990 (52%); 1984 (50%)

Mitch McConnell is Kentucky's senior senator, the architect of its 7–1 Republican congressional delegation and Senate Majority Whip; his wife is Labor Secretary Elaine Chao. He grew up in Alabama, where he overcame polio, and after age 13 moved to Louisville. He has been in politics almost his whole career. He was an intern for Senator John Sherman Cooper in 1964 and, after finishing law school, became a staffer for Senator Marlow Cook. He moved back to Louisville and in 1977, at 35, won by a narrow margin the office that had been Cook's political stepping stone, Jefferson County judge-executive. In 1981 he was re-elected, again narrowly. In 1984 he ran for the Senate, against incumbent Dee Huddleston. McConnell ran ads showing bloodhounds sniffing for Huddleston in vacation locales where he had collected fees for speeches while the Senate was in session. McConnell won by 5,169 votes of 1.2 million cast.

Many senators go to Washington and over the years become less conservative; McConnell has become more so. As his longtime adversary on campaign finance regulation, John McCain, has said, "There are few things more daunting in politics than the determined opposition of Senator McConnell." He has taken on tough assignments on occasion: As Ethics Committee chairman in 1995, he led the investigation of Bob Packwood for sexual harassment (the committee recommended expulsion, and Packwood ultimately resigned). He has often opposed trial lawyers, backing product liability and medical malpractice laws that would reduce their leverage and sponsoring the auto choice plan that would let car owners pay less for insurance by disclaiming pain and suffering damages. In July 2002 he tried to put a provision requiring lawyers' clients to be informed of the costs of legal services onto the corporate accountability bill, but lost 62–35. He has served as chairman of the Senate Rules Committee, and after the 2000 election he was one of the leading Republicans working on the bill to improve election procedures.

McConnell served on Foreign Relations until 1992, then switched to Appropriations and in 1994 became chairman of the Foreign Operations Subcommittee. In that capacity he has had much to say about foreign aid. He has strongly supported aid to Israel and in July 2001 called for reconsidering aid to Egypt in light of the often vile propaganda its government-supervised media puts out. He has kept close watch on the unsteady condition of Cambodia. McConnell has frequently used his seat on Appropriations to insert riders that help Kentucky and channel aid to the state. He has also worked hard on tobacco issues. In early 2003 he was still working for a buyout of tobacco quotas from farmers, which he said would be "no slam dunk" and would likely have to come as part of a bill allowing the FDA regulation of tobacco.

McConnell's greatest expertise is on campaign finance. He first got interested while teaching a night course at the University of Louisville, and his thinking at first was quite different from what it is now. In 1990 he drafted a bill that would have banned PACs, cut in half out-of-state donations and banned soft money. But in a few years he came to believe that these provisions and those in the various bills sponsored by John McCain and Russ Feingold are unconstitutional infringements of free speech. He disputes the notions that campaign ads are some kind of pollution and that too much is spent on them. In 1994 he spoke all night to filibuster a campaign finance bill, "the only true all-night filibuster in the last 12 years," he said in 1999. In October 1999, with more than 40 senators on his side, he killed a version of the McCain-Feingold campaign finance bill. In 1999 Bill Clinton broke with tradition and refused to nominate Bradley Smith for FEC commissioner, the law professor picked by Senate Republicans, who opposed much campaign finance regulation as a violation of the First Amendment. McConnell got Clinton to nominate Smith by putting a hold on the nomination of Richard Holbrooke to be UN Ambassador. In March 2001, McCain insisted on bringing campaign finance forward again, and despite McConnell's efforts, managed to pass his measure. But as McConnell pointed out, it did not include many provisions in previous McCain-Feingold bills, including public subsidies for candidates and voluntary spending limits. And the sweeping provisions against independent advertising inserted by an amendment by Paul Wellstone (which McConnell voted for) seemed likely to be ruled unconstitutional. McCain's bill was also amended by a doubling of the limit on individual contributions— something McConnell supported.

In 2001 the House Republican leadership blocked consideration of the similar Shays-Meehan bill. But after the implosion of Enron, Shays and Meehan got enough signatures on a discharge petition to bring their bill to the floor, and it passed in February 2002. For more than a month, McConnell put forward 13 "technical corrections," and Majority Leader Tom Daschle refused to bring the issue to the floor until he and McCain settled their differences. The bill passed on March 27, and immediately McConnell filed a lawsuit charging it was unconstitutional. He had an interesting trio of lawyers—First Amendment litigator Floyd Abrams, Stanford Law Dean Kathleen Sullivan and former Solicitor General and Independent Counsel Kenneth Starr. In May 2003 a deeply divided three-judge federal court issued 1,700 pages of opinions and upheld some provisions of the law but not others.

McConnell's interest in elections is not just theoretical. He ran for chairman of the NRSC and lost to Phil Gramm in 1990 and in 1992 by one vote; he won the post in November 1996. But he was unable to get Republican senators to contribute as much to campaigns as Democratic senators did in 1998. He was criticized for contributing heavily to Mark Neumann of Wisconsin, who ran against Russ Feingold, and for skimping on Washington state's Linda Smith, a McCain-Feingold backer; both lost and the party gained no seats. After the election, Chuck Hagel of Nebraska ran for the post, but McConnell won 39–13. In the 2000 cycle, he had tougher sledding; Republicans lost most of the close races, and the result was a 50–50 split.

McConnell has had more success in building up Kentucky's long ailing Republican Party. He helped Ed Whitfield pick up the 1st District and Republican legislative candidates win in western Kentucky in 1994. He backed Anne Northup in her win in Louisville's 3d District in 1996. In 1998 McConnell strongly backed Jim Bunning's candidacy for the Senate. In 2000 McConnell helped the Bush campaign target and carry Kentucky; he backed the ballot proposition to merge the Jefferson County and Louisville city governments. He helped to persuade two Democratic state senators to switch parties in July and August 1999, which gave Republicans a 20–18 margin in the state Senate. In 2000 he helped them hold that majority. In 2002 he brainstormed with Republican senators weekly; encouraged them to or at least did not discourage them from, defunding and thus effectively ending the public financing system in governor elections; recruited candidates; reviewed radio and TV ad scripts and appeared in ads for Republican senators. In November 2002 the Republicans increased their majority to 21–17. But he was not always partisan. In January 2002 he filed papers in the criminal case brought against two aides to Paul Patton and two Teamsters officials for violating campaign finance laws in 1995; McConnell argued that the laws were unconstitutional and the men should not have been prosecuted.

McConnell has now won reelection three times. In 1990 he had spirited competition from former Louisville Mayor Harvey Sloane, and won by only 52%–48%. In 1996 the then new Democratic Governor Patton put his political resources behind the Democratic nominee, former Lieutenant Governor and Attorney General Steve Beshear. He attacked McConnell on campaign finance regulation, the minimum wage and NAFTA. McConnell charged that Beshear was a lobbyist, a political insider and, worst, a fox hunter; on the campaign trail Beshear was followed by a character dressed in fox-hunting regalia. McConnell spent $5 million to Beshear's $2 million and, after early polls showed a close race, won 55%–43%.

In 2002 McConnell's opponent was Lois Combs Weinberg, daughter of former (1959–63) Governor Bert Combs. She had the support of the state's Democratic establishment, but memories of her father, one of the state's most notable governors, had evidently dimmed. She had primary opposition from former 1st District Congressman Tom Barlow, but he spent only $6,000. Weinberg decided to save money and spent only $105,000 on TV before the May primary. In the meantime McConnell was running ads accusing her family's natural gas company of running roughshod over a Knott County landowner. She won, but by only 958 votes out of 461,000 cast— 50.1%–49.9%. She evidently didn't calculate that Barlow would win 74%–26% in his old congressional district, with a 47,000-vote margin; he carried just about every county west and south of Lexington, plus a few more scattered counties. Primary night was effectively the end of Weinberg's campaign; in June, Al Cross of the Louisville *Courier-Journal* wrote, "Now her chances seem almost entirely theoretical," and the chances that national Democrats would put money into this race were nil. McConnell refused to debate and ran ads showing how he had done things for Kentuckians—helping the widow of a police officer killed in the line of duty, getting compensation for the families of workers sickened by radiation poisoning at the Paducah uranium plant. Weinberg said in July she needed $5 million to be competitive; she spent only $2.2 million to McConnell's $5.3 million. McConnell won 65%–35%, carrying 112 of 120 counties, losing only in a few Democratic strongholds in the eastern mountains.

Back in Washington, he won another election a week later, to become majority whip. He had been campaigning for months among colleagues and his only opponent, Larry Craig, dropped out several days before the contest. He planned to spend most of his time on the Senate floor when it was in session. In December, when Trent Lott was criticized for his comments at Strom Thurmond's 100th birthday party, McConnell was at first his strongest public defender, suggesting on December 15 that Lott might resign from the Senate if ousted (which would mean a Democrat would get his seat and the Republicans would no longer have a majority) and threatening that if Democrats moved to censure Lott, he would amend the motion to add censure of some Democrats' comments. But on December 20 he privately recommended to Lott that he "step down as soon as possible"; McConnell did not challenge Bill Frist for the majority leadership, and urged Rick Santorum not to either.

All the while he kept dabbling in Kentucky politics. He was criticized by some for endorsing his former top aide Hunter Bates for the 2004 4th District House seat, after Republican Geoff Davis had come close to beating Democrat Ken Lucas in 2002; Bates later left that race. And he continued jousting with the *Courier-Journal*, the state's dominant newspaper, which has long attacked him for opposing campaign finance regulation and for refusing to divulge the names of contributors to the McConnell Center for Political Leadership at the University of Kentucky. Most senators strive to get favorable coverage, or avoid reading negative press. McConnell seems to relish it. "I enjoy their ire," he says. "I'm proud of my enemies. I wouldn't trade them for anything."

Junior Senator

Jim Bunning (R)

Elected 1998, seat up 2004, 1st term; b. Oct. 23, 1931, Campbell Cnty.; home, Southgate; Xavier U., B.S. 1953; Catholic; married (Mary).

Elected Office: Ft. Thomas City Cncl., 1977–79; KY Senate, 1979–83; U.S. House of Reps., 1986–98.

Professional Career: Pro baseball player, 1950–71; Investment broker & agent, 1960–86.

DC Office: 316 HSOB, 20510, 202-224-4343; Fax: 202-228-1373; Web site: bunning.senate.gov.

State Offices: Ft. Wright, 859-341-2602; Hazard, 606-435-2390; Hopkinsville, 270-885-1212; Lexington, 859-219-2239; Louisville, 502-582-5341; Owensboro, 270-689-9085.

Committees: *Banking, Housing & Urban Affairs*: Economic Policy (Chmn.); Financial Institutions; Securities & Investment. *Budget*. *Energy & Natural Resources*: Energy; Water & Power. *Finance*: Health Care; International Trade; Social Security & Family Policy. *Veterans' Affairs*.

Group Ratings

	ADA	ACLU	AFS	LCV	CON	ITIC	NTU	COC	ACU	NTLC	CHC
2002	0	20	13	0	51	88	65	95	100	100	—
2001	0	—	0	0	—	—	85	93	100	—	100

National Journal Ratings

	2001 LIB	—	2001 CONS	2002 LIB	—	2002 CONS
Economic	7%	—	86%	20%	—	78%
Social	0%	—	79%	0%	—	62%
Foreign	0%	—	94%	24%	—	67%

Key Votes of the 107th Congress

1. Approve Bush Tax Cuts	Y	5. Confirm Ashcroft as AG	Y	9. Bar Coop. with Intl. Court	Y
2. Expand Patients' Rights	N	6. Bar Gays in the Boy Scouts	Y	10. Trade Promotion Authority	Y
3. Campaign Finance Reform	N	7. $ for Hate Crime Prosecution	N	11. Authorize Force in Iraq	Y
4. Permit ANWR Development	Y	8. Overseas Military Abortions	N	12. Homeland Sec. Dept. Union	N

Election Results

1998 general	Jim Bunning (R)	569,817	(50%)	($3,746,540)
	Scotty Baesler (D)	563,051	(49%)	($3,841,950)
	Other	12,546	(1%)	
1998 primary	Jim Bunning (R)	152,493	(74%)	
	Barry Metcalf (R)	52,798	(26%)	
1992 general	Wendell H. Ford (D)	836,888	(63%)	($2,321,131)
	David L. Williams (R)	476,604	(36%)	($335,304)

Prior Winning Percentages: 1996 House (68%); 1994 House (74%); 1992 House (62%); 1990 House (69%); 1988 House (74%); 1986 House (55%)

Jim Bunning, a Republican elected to the Senate in 1998, is the first player elected to the Baseball Hall of Fame to serve in Congress. Bunning grew up in Northern Kentucky, just across the Ohio River from Cincinnati. He started in minor league baseball in 1950, but at his father's insistence finished high school and college. He made the majors in 1956 and the next year became the only pitcher to strike out Ted Williams three times in one game. Bunning threw a no-hitter for the Detroit Tigers in 1958 and pitched a perfect game for the Philadelphia Phillies in 1964; he also played for the Pittsburgh Pirates and the Los Angeles Dodgers. He retired in 1971 with a 224–184 record, a 3.24 ERA and 2,855 strikeouts; he was the second pitcher (Cy Young was the first) to achieve 1,000 strikeouts and 100 wins in both the American and the National Leagues. He was inducted into the Baseball Hall of Fame in August 1996. He is a family man, with nine children (two sets of twins) and at last count 35 grandchildren and 2 great-grandchildren; his son David Bunning, after 10 years as a federal prosecutor, was unanimously confirmed as a federal judge in February 2002 (despite a persnickety report by the American Bar Association that complained he had only 10, not 12 years of experience, and had attended the University of Kentucky Law School). Jim Bunning and fellow pitcher Robin Roberts set up the Major League Baseball Players Association and hired Marvin Miller in 1966, when the minimum player salary was $6,000; in 2002, however, he was criticizing the players for not accepting a salary cap, the big metro area teams for not accepting revenue sharing and the owners for not opening their books. "If they do strike, we'll never recover baseball as you and I know it." He has long been in favor of repealing baseball's exemption from the antitrust laws.

The skill, energy and aggressiveness he showed in baseball—Bunning registered one of the highest totals in baseball history for hitting batters —he brought to politics in his native northern Kentucky. He was elected to the Fort Thomas City Council in 1977, to the state Senate in 1979, and won a respectable 44% against Martha Layne Collins in the 1983 race for governor (the best showing for a Republican gubernatorial candidate between 1971 and 1999). When incumbent 4th District Congressman Gene Snyder retired in 1986, Bunning won the seat with 55% of the vote. Bunning showed great impatience with the ways of doing business in the Democratic House. He served six years on the ethics committee, starting off in March 1992 by leading the charge against the House bank overdraft scandal, and ending in January 1997 by resigning from the committee out of disgust with the partisanship of ranking Democrat Jim McDermott. In September 1993 he called Bill Clinton "the most corrupt, the most amoral, the most despicable person I've ever seen in the presidency."

When Republicans became the majority, Bunning had achievements as a legislator. He chaired the Social Security Subcommittee for two terms, and sponsored two major changes—raising the earnings limit for Social Security recipients up to $30,000 by 2002, and the law making the Social Security Administration an independent agency.

In February 1997, Senator Wendell Ford announced he would retire in 1998, and Bunning, with typical aggressiveness, made plans to run for his seat. Three Democrats ran serious campaigns for the nomination. Louisville cable TV entrepreneur Charlie Owen spent $6.6 million of his own money and ran ads attacking the other two. Lieutenant Governor Steve Henry spent $500,000 of his own money and counted on his Louisville base and Owensboro roots. The third candidate was Lexington Congressman Scotty Baesler, who had less money but other advantages: He was popular in his Republican-leaning 6th District, he is a tobacco farmer and he was still known as a star on one of Adolph Rupp's University of Kentucky basketball teams in the early 1960s. Baesler won the May primary with 34% of the vote, to 29% for Owen and 28% for Henry.

Baesler emerged from the primary ahead of Bunning in the polls but out of money; Bunning, with extensive help from Senator Mitch McConnell, had plenty of money. Bunning ran an ad showing actors thanking Baesler, in Spanish and (with subtitles) Chinese, for voting for NAFTA and for MFN with China. This was perhaps the country's closest race for months. And, despite Kentucky's early poll closing times and rapid count, it was not until late in the evening that Bunning was declared the winner. His margin was 49.7%–49.2%, or 6,766 votes. Baesler carried normally Republican Lexington, but only by 54%–46%. Bunning carried the three counties of Northern Kentucky by 70%–29%; his margin there was 34,791 votes, more than five times his statewide margin, and more than Baesler's Lexington and Louisville margins put together.

Bunning has compiled one of the most conservative voting records in the Senate. His bill allowing disabled people to continue getting Medicaid or Medicare after getting a job was passed. He has long pressed for making foster care stipends exempt from income tax; he got such a provision in the tax bill vetoed by Clinton in 1999 and in the stimulus package George W. Bush signed in March 2002. He cautioned Alan Greenspan against quenching the flames of the economy and when he did lower interest rates in July 2001, Bunning said he was six months too late. In July 2002 he cast lone votes against the confirmation of two Fed members who, he said, hadn't satisfied him they would be independent of Greenspan. On the Armed Services Committee in 2001 and 2002, he expressed admiration for General Tommy Franks's "unbelievable accomplishments in Afghanistan," but then testily asked, "Why were so many people able to flee Afghanistan that were Al Qaeda and/or Taliban?" In December 2002 he gave up the seat on Armed Services for one on Finance.

Bunning has worked on many Kentucky issues, sponsoring a bill to distribute $1.2 billion from the Abandoned Mine Reclamation Fund directly to Kentucky and other coal mining states and passing a bill to compensate TVA for mineral rights transferred to the Daniel Boone National Forest; this prevented coal mining in forest lands.

Bunning's seat comes up in 2004, and for a long time everyone assumed that he would run against Governor Paul Patton, scheduled to leave office after his second term in December 2003. The relationship between the two seemed to resemble those between Henry Clay and some of his rivals that ended up in duels. But in September 2002 Patton admitted that he had had an affair with a nursing home operator who sued him that month for sexual harassment; she accused him of sending in state inspectors to close down her business after she broke off the affair. Patton, after denying the affair, admitted it after the Louisville *Courier-Journal* reported that phone records showed 440 calls from his office to her home or business; a few days later he announced, unsurprisingly, that he would not run for the Senate. That left ace pitcher Bunning running against pinch-hitting Democrats. Mentioned as candidates in early 2003 were Charlie Owen, running that year as Attorney General Ben Chandler's running mate in the 2003 governor primary; Lieutenant Governor Steve Henry, who did not run for governor in part because the federal government was suing him for Medicare overbillings; and state Treasurer Jonathan Miller, a former staffer for Al Gore, who ran sixth out of seven candidates in the 1998 6th District House primary with 11% of the vote. Congressman Ken Lucas in early 2003 said he would renege on his pledge to limit himself to three terms and run for reelection to the House rather than run against Bunning. In January 2003 Bunning had already raised $1 million and seemed a strong favorite for reelection.

FIRST DISTRICT

Rep. Ed Whitfield (R)

Elected 1994, 5th term; b. May 25, 1943, Hopkinsville; home, Hopkinsville; U. of KY, B.S. 1965, J.D. 1969; Methodist; married (Connie).

Military Career: Army Reserves, 1967–73.

Elected Office: KY House of Reps., 1973–75.

Professional Career: Practicing atty., 1969–79; Owner, Rhodes Oil Co., 1975–79; Cnsl., Seaboard System Railroad, 1979–83; V.P., CSX, 1983–91; Cnsl., Interstate Commerce Comm., 1991–93.

DC Office: 301 CHOB 20515, 202-225-3115; Fax: 202-225-3547; Web site: www.house.gov/whitfield.

District Offices: Henderson, 270-826-4180; Hopkinsville, 270-885-8079; Paducah, 270-442-6901; Tompkinsville, 270-487-9509.

Committees: *Energy & Commerce* (11th of 31 R): Commerce, Trade & Consumer Protection; Energy & Air Quality; Health; Telecommunications & The Internet.

Group Ratings

	ADA	ACLU	AFS	LCV	CON	ITIC	NTU	COC	ACU	NTLC	CHC
2002	0	13	11	0	25	100	55	94	100	83	100
2001	0	—	0	0	—	—	60	100	96	—	—

National Journal Ratings

	2001 LIB	—	2001 CONS		2002 LIB	—	2002 CONS
Economic	22%	—	74%		21%	—	73%
Social	0%	—	81%		0%	—	75%
Foreign	21%	—	74%		41%	—	56%

Key Votes of the 107th Congress

1. Approve Bush Tax Cuts	Y	5. Faith-Based Charities	Y	9. Trade Promotion Authority	Y
2. Limit Patients' Bill of Rights	Y	6. Bar Gays in the Boy Scouts	Y	10. Bar Funds for Intl. Court	Y
3. Campaign Finance Reform	N	7. Ban Partial-Birth Abortion	Y	11. Authorize Force in Iraq	Y
4. Ban ANWR Development	N	8. Arm Commercial Pilots	Y	12. Deny Home. Sec. Dept. Union	Y

Election Results

2002 general	Ed Whitfield (R)	117,600	(65%)	($828,894)
	Klint Alexander (D)	62,617	(35%)	($544,511)
2002 primary	Ed Whitfield (R)	unopposed		
2000 general	Ed Whitfield (R)	132,115	(58%)	($1,495,305)
	Brian Roy (D)	95,806	(42%)	($716,066)

Prior Winning Percentages: 1998 (55%); 1996 (54%); 1994 (51%)

The People		Race/Ethnic Origin	Ancestry	
Area size:	12,058 sq. mi.	89.7% White	USA: 19.5%	English: 7.8%
Urban population:	36.5%	7.2% Black	Irish: 7.7%	
Rural population:	63.5%	0.3% Asian	**2000 Presidential Vote**	
Pop. 2000:	673,629	0.2% Native Am.	Bush (R) 147,486	(58%)
Median income:	$30,360	0.0% Hawaiian	Gore (D) 101,551	(40%)
Poverty status:	16.5%	0.9% Two+ races	Other 3,961	(2%)
Military veterans:	12.9%	0.1% Other	**Cook Partisan Voting Index:** R +10	
		1.5% Hispanic Origin		
Occupation	Blue collar: 37.3%	White collar: 46.6%	Gray collar: 16.0%	

The point where the Ohio River flows into the Mississippi—the intersection Huckleberry Finn and Jim missed in the fog—must have struck early settlers as a site for a great city. But no Pittsburgh or St. Louis grew up on this fertile black soil. Instead, the Kentucky land west of the dammed-up Tennessee and Cumberland rivers, bought from the Chickasaw Indians by General

Andrew Jackson and Governor Isaac Shelby in 1818—the Jackson Purchase, it is still called—was settled by farmers. Most people here today are the descendants of these farmers, with memories of earlier generations living in family lore. Just to the east of the Tennessee and the Cumberland rivers is the Pennyrile (after pennyroyal, a common variety of local wild mint), a land of low hills and small farms, where you find the west Kentucky coal fields, the site of much strip mining in recent years. Here is Lyon County, founded by Matthew "Spitting" Lyon, who earned his epithet while a congressman from Vermont, and who later represented western Kentucky from 1803–1811. These areas are separated by the Land Between the Lakes, the boating and recreational haven created by the damming of the Tennessee and Cumberland Rivers just before the debouche into the Ohio; this is the fastest-growing area in these parts, as the Jackson Purchase and the Pennyrile struggle economically.

The 1st Congressional District is made up of the Jackson Purchase and much of the Pennyrile, plus a line of counties stretching some 200 miles east of the Mississippi in the mountains along the Tennessee border and then north toward the center of the state. There is a distinctive Southern atmosphere here—in the crops that are grown, in historically low wage levels, and in the fact that the big city people look to is more often Nashville than Louisville. The Jackson Purchase and the Pennyrile have long been Democratic; Paducah produced one of the most enduring Democratic politicians of this century, Alben Barkley, whose career from 1912–56 included 14 years in the House, 24 in the Senate and four as vice president; he was Senate majority and minority leader, keynoted four Democratic National Conventions, and died while delivering the peroration at Washington and Lee University's mock political convention in 1956. But the hills far from the Mississippi are Republican country and this, combined with the Republican trend that reached north from Dixie to Paducah, have made the 1st District seriously contested territory—and one of the longtime Democratic rural areas solidly (58%) for George W. Bush in 2000.

The congressman from the 1st District is Ed Whitfield, a longtime Democrat who turned Republican. Whitfield grew up in Hopkinsville and Madisonville, in a family with Pennyrile roots going back before 1800. He served in the Army, practiced law in Hopkinsville, and was elected to the legislature in 1973 as a Democrat where he was something of an insider; former Governor (1963–67) Edward Breathitt was best man at his wedding. After one term in Frankfort, Whitfield ran an oil distributorship in the west Kentucky coalfields, then in 1979 moved to Washington to become an executive for the Seaboard and CSX railroads. He was legal counsel to the chairman of the Interstate Commerce Commission from 1991–93, when he returned to west Kentucky and ran for Congress as a Republican. He was returning to a district that since Barkley's time had been represented by quiet, long-serving, conservative Democrats. But the one-term incumbent, Tom Barlow, was a free-spirited supporter of the Clinton administration. Encouraged to run by Senator Mitch McConnell, Whitfield turned aside criticism that he was carpetbagging and concentrated on attacking Barlow's vote for the Clinton budget and tax increase. With help from the mountain counties added by redistricting, and running strongly in the Pennyrile, Whitfield scored a 51%–49% win in the big Republican sweep of 1994.

In the House, Whitfield has a moderate-to-conservative voting record and a seat on the Energy and Commerce Committee. One major concern has been aid to workers exposed to radiation at the nuclear weapons plant in Paducah; overriding appropriators, Whitfield on the eve of the 2000 election won $150,000 lump sum payments and medical benefits for thousands of affected workers. He also overcame objections from the Bush administration to cleaning up the site, which is expected to cost more than $1 billion and take at least a decade. He voted for PNTR with China after the Chinese agreed to lower tariffs on imported tobacco, and he voted for trade promotion authority. In 2001, some local Internet service providers objected when Whitfield co-sponsored the Tauzin-Dingell bill on behalf of the former Bell companies. He has been a big supporter of using clean-coal technology to reduce the cost of electricity. With Hal Rogers, he sponsored a bill designed to reduce prescription drug costs by monitoring abusers.

Whitfield has entrenched himself to the point that he is no longer much of a Democratic target. In 1996, when lawyer Dennis Null opposed him, the AFL-CIO ran TV ads attacking him on tax cuts, pension security, and Medicare. But Whitfield had nearly a 2–1 money advantage and he criticized the Clinton administration proposal for FDA regulation of tobacco. He carried 18 of the district's 31 counties, including Paducah, which he lost in 1994, and won 54%–46%. In 1998, Tom Barlow ran again, this time with a lightly funded "grass roots" campaign. Whitfield won 55%–45%. In 2000, former U.S. Marshall Brian Roy ran a better-funded challenge emphasizing the issues of preserving Social Security and providing a prescription drug Medicare benefit. In many ways Roy, a former county sheriff and federal marshal opposed to gun control and abortion, seemed well-suited to the district. But, curiously for a Republican, Whitfield criticized him for an allegedly poor record of tax collections as sheriff, as well as for having Patrick Kennedy speak at a local fundraiser. With his vote closely tracking Bush's pattern, Whitfield increased his margin to 58%–42%, taking for the first time several counties in the far western corner. In 2001 state House Democrats tried to make the district more Democratic by removing the eastern counties and adding Owensboro, but that was blocked by state Senate Republicans. In 2002 against a Democrat he said was not committed to protect Second Amendment rights, Whitfield won 65%–35%. This longtime Democratic stronghold now seems to be a safe Republican seat.

SECOND DISTRICT

Rep. Ron Lewis (R)

Elected May 1994, 5th term; b. Sept. 14, 1946, South Shore, KY; home, Cecilia; U. of KY, B.A. 1969, Morehead St. U., M.A. 1981; Southern Baptist; married (Kayi).

Military Career: Navy OCS, 1972.

Professional Career: Heavy Equip. Sales Rep., 1975–80; Baptist Minister, 1980–present; Prof., Watterson Col., 1980–85; Owner, Alpha Christian Bookstore, 1985–94.

DC Office: 2418 RHOB 20515, 202-225-3501; Web site: www.house.gov/ronlewis.

District Offices: Bowling Green, 270-842-9896; Elizabethtown, 270-765-4360; Owensboro, 270-688-8858.

Committees: *Government Reform* (10th of 24 R): National Security, Emerging Threats & Intl. Relations. *Ways & Means* (20th of 24 R): Human Resources; Select Revenue Measures; Social Security.

Group Ratings

	ADA	ACLU	AFS	LCV	CON	ITIC	NTU	COC	ACU	NTLC	CHC
2002	0	7	0	0	8	88	55	90	96	86	100
2001	0	—	0	0	—	—	68	96	100	—	—

National Journal Ratings

	2001 LIB	—	2001 CONS		2002 LIB	—	2002 CONS
Economic	0%	—	94%		16%	—	81%
Social	0%	—	81%		0%	—	75%
Foreign	4%	—	87%		0%	—	85%

Key Votes of the 107th Congress

1. Approve Bush Tax Cuts	Y	5. Faith-Based Charities	Y	9. Trade Promotion Authority	Y
2. Limit Patients' Bill of Rights	Y	6. Bar Gays in the Boy Scouts	Y	10. Bar Funds for Intl. Court	Y
3. Campaign Finance Reform	N	7. Ban Partial-Birth Abortion	Y	11. Authorize Force in Iraq	Y
4. Ban ANWR Development	N	8. Arm Commercial Pilots	Y	12. Deny Home. Sec. Dept. Union	Y

Election Results

2002 general	Ron Lewis (R)	122,773	(70%)	($553,116)
	David Williams (D)	51,431	(29%)	
2002 primary	Ron Lewis (R)	unopposed		
2000 general	Ron Lewis (R)	160,800	(68%)	($225,008)
	Brian Pedigo (D)	74,537	(31%)	
	Other	2,125	(1%)	

Prior Winning Percentages: 1998 (64%); 1996 (58%); 1994 (60%); 1994 (55%)

The People		Race/Ethnic Origin	Ancestry	
Area size:	7,669 sq. mi.	90.6% White	USA: 18.7%	German: 9.2%
Urban population:	47.2%	5.7% Black	Irish: 8.5%	
Rural population:	52.8%	0.7% Asian	**2000 Presidential Vote**	
Pop. 2000:	673,224	0.2% Native Am.	Bush (R)..............152,236 (62%)	
Median income:	$35,724	0.1% Hawaiian	Gore (D)................90,086 (37%)	
Poverty status:	13.3%	1.0% Two+ races	Other...................4,288 (2%)	
Military veterans:	13.7%	0.1% Other	**Cook Partisan Voting Index:** R +13	
		1.7% Hispanic Origin		

Occupation	Blue collar: 35.2%	White collar: 49.6%	Gray collar: 15.1%

In the 1770s and 1780s, Americans began settling the limestone-soiled country of central Kentucky, staking out towns like Bardstown and Elizabethtown and starting academies and colleges; they were well-settled when Stephen Foster wrote "My Old Kentucky Home" just before the Civil War. That conflict tore deeply here: This part of Kentucky gave birth to Abraham Lincoln and in the Civil War it lost thousands of soldiers, Union and Confederate; it would suffer disproportionate casualties in the 20th century wars as well. This area is the home of several Kentucky landmarks—Fort Knox, the nation's gold depository; some of the nation's largest bourbon distilleries; and Mammoth Cave, the world's largest accessible cavern, near Bowling Green. And Kentucky culture is more broadly disseminated than one might think: Japanese executives at the five Japanese-owned plants in Bardstown feel at home there because Stephen Foster's songs, apparently well adapted to Japanese tones, are universally known in Japan.

The 2d Congressional District consists of much of the territory south and southwest of Louisville, starting with economically-booming southern Jefferson County suburbs and proceeding south to Bowling Green and west along the Ohio River to Owensboro, the home of the International Bluegrass Music Museum. Much of this is rural and small-town country, where most people have family roots that go back generations and a connection with the past not often found in big metropolitan areas. Civil War loyalties are reflected in the election returns here; Kentucky was deeply split on secession, and a color-coded map of the current 2d District would show various splotches of counties pro-South and splotches pro-Union. But the bits of color would only hint at the deep and often bitter feelings caused by the splits over the War—feelings of which current partisan preferences are a persistent reflection, though growing dimmer. For many years, the balance of opinion here favored the Democrats; in the past decade, opinion moved toward the Republicans, with George W. Bush winning 62% of the vote here in 2000.

The congressman from the 2d District is Ron Lewis, a Republican first elected in a May 1994 special election that had national implications. Lewis was born in a log cabin and raised in eastern Kentucky; he worked his way through Morehead State as a laborer at Armco Steel. He worked in the highway department, at a state hospital, then served in the Navy. In 1980, he became a Baptist minister; in 1985 he started a Christian bookstore in Elizabethtown, two counties south of Louisville; he was the opposite of a political insider. Then, in March 1994, Democratic Congressman William Natcher died. He was chairman of the Appropriations Committee and a politician of a very old school, so hard-working and conscientious that he never missed a roll call vote in 41 years. Though the district voted for George H.W. Bush in 1992, Democratic leaders assumed they would win: They handpicked former state Senate President Joe Prather. Before the election, Prather even flew to Washington to go apartment hunting. But they failed to account for the national and local conservative trend. When the NRCC spent $200,000, Prather raised campaign money belatedly and asserted that he was quite a different sort of Democrat than Bill Clinton. Lewis won a solid 55%–45% victory, carrying Bowling Green heavily and running ahead in Owensboro and outside Louisville.

In the House, Lewis has a solidly conservative voting record and is attentive to local concerns. After a few months in office, he made news when he attended a smokers' rights rally where Hillary Rodham Clinton was burned in effigy. He co-sponsored emergency farm relief and pushed for precision agriculture research. He backed tobacco buyout proposals, phasing out tobacco price supports and providing a mandatory buyout of tobacco farmers' entitlements. He unsuccessfully led the fight against Henry Waxman's amendment to permit the Clinton Justice Department to raise money from other federal agencies to finance its tobacco suit. With a seat on the Ways and Means Committee, Lewis—who doesn't drink—took up the cause of local distillers and got more than 60 cosponsors on his bill to reduce the excise tax on liquor by 26%. But by the time the lobbying campaign was in full gear, the budget surplus had disappeared. He worked with other social conservatives on behalf of Dr. James Dobson's Christian conservative agenda. He was successful in helping pass legislation to double the tax credit for adoption expenses. He cited his own experience as the father of an adopted child to oppose stem-cell research on embryos. Concerned about exposure of Fort Knox to the base-closing commission in 2005, Lewis in 2001 got $200 million for the Army to spend on housing at what has become mostly a training facility.

In 1994, many Democrats assumed that Lewis's special election victory was aberrational and that Democratic Owensboro Mayor David Adkisson would win in November. But Lewis projected sincerity, and his strong religious views and opposition to the Clinton tax increase and health care plan were pluses. Lewis won by a resounding 60%–40% margin, even carrying Owensboro's Daviess County. In 1998, Lewis reversed his 1994 campaign pledge to serve no more than four full terms, announcing he had changed his mind. "I came to believe that if those of us who believe in term limits limit ourselves, then we're a dying breed." But he said he would still vote for term limits. Breaking the pledge caused barely a ripple back home. Since then, he has easily defeated little-known and poorly-funded challengers.

Lewis seems headed for a long career in the House, where he can work from his seat on Ways and Means on his promises to cut the capital gains tax to 15% and fix the long-term financing of Social Security.

THIRD DISTRICT

Rep. Anne Northup (R)

Elected 1996, 4th term; b. Jan. 22, 1948, Louisville; home, Louisville; St. Mary's Col., B.A. 1970; Catholic; married (Robert).

Elected Office: KY House of Reps., 1986–96.

DC Office: 1004 LHOB 20515, 202-225-5401; Fax: 202-225-5776; Web site: www.house.gov/northup.

District Office: Louisville, 502-582-5129.

Committees: *Appropriations* (21st of 36 R): Labor, HHS & Education (Vice Chmn.); Transportation, Treasury, & Independent Agencies; VA, HUD & Independent Agencies.

Group Ratings

	ADA	ACLU	AFS	LCV	CON	ITIC	NTU	COC	ACU	NTLC	CHC
2002	0	7	0	13	34	100	57	100	88	86	100
2001	0	—	0	7	—	—	62	100	96	—	—

National Journal Ratings

	2001 LIB —	2001 CONS		2002 LIB —	2002 CONS
Economic	15% —	82%		13% —	85%
Social	20% —	69%		44% —	54%
Foreign	4% —	87%		23% —	77%

Key Votes of the 107th Congress

1. Approve Bush Tax Cuts	Y	5. Faith-Based Charities		9. Trade Promotion Authority	Y
2. Limit Patients' Bill of Rights	Y	6. Bar Gays in the Boy Scouts	Y	10. Bar Funds for Intl. Court	Y
3. Campaign Finance Reform	N	7. Ban Partial-Birth Abortion	Y	11. Authorize Force in Iraq	Y
4. Ban ANWR Development	N	8. Arm Commercial Pilots	Y	12. Deny Home. Sec. Dept. Union	Y

Election Results

2002 general	Anne Northup (R)	118,228	(52%)	($3,221,714)
	Jack Conway (D)	110,846	(48%)	($1,539,362)
2002 primary	Anne Northup (R)	unopposed		
2000 general	Anne Northup (R)	142,106	(53%)	($2,916,818)
	Eleanor Jordan (D)	118,785	(44%)	($1,700,171)
	Other	7,804	(3%)	

Prior Winning Percentages: 1998 (52%); 1996 (50%)

The People		Race/Ethnic Origin	Ancestry	
Area size:	379 sq. mi.	76.0% White	German: 14.8%	Irish: 10.4%
Urban population:	98.3%	19.1% Black	USA: 8.8%	
Rural population:	·1.7%	1.4% Asian	**2000 Presidential Vote**	
Pop. 2000:	674,032	0.2% Native Am.	Gore (D).............141,337	(50%)
Median income:	$39,468	0.0% Hawaiian	Bush (R).............134,234	(48%)
Poverty status:	12.4%	1.3% Two + races	Other...................5,628	(2%)
Military veterans:	13.7%	0.2% Other	**Cook Partisan Voting Index:** D + 1	
		1.8% Hispanic Origin		

Occupation	Blue collar: 23.7%	White collar: 62.0%	Gray collar: 14.3%

At the falls of the Ohio River, Americans more than 200 years ago founded one of their first inland metropolises, the river port and industrial city of Louisville (pronounced *LOOuhv'l*). The city has always retained an air of the South; when Kentucky decided not to secede in 1861, the decision was not unanimous, and the culture of tidewater Virginia is still visible in the Louisville lawn party. Steamboats are tied up in front of Louisville's downtown, primed to follow the channel around the falls of the Ohio that prompted George Rogers Clark to found the town in 1778. Mint juleps are served on the verandas of mansions, especially (but not only) during Kentucky Derby week in May; horse racing is a preoccupation throughout the year. Although the Ohio River is crossed with many bridges and the accent across the river in Indiana may sound the same to outsiders, Louisville partakes of the cavalier culture that second sons of big landowners from England brought to Virginia in the 17th century and their heirs brought over the Appalachians to the valleys of Kentucky in the 18th century.

Louisville is Kentucky's largest city by far, though in the 2000 Census it was ranked number two, behind Lexington, which includes all of Fayette County. One of the arguments that persuaded voters in November 2000 by a 54%–46% margin to consolidate the city and surrounding Jefferson County is that it would make Louisville number one again; the merger took effect in January 2003. Louisville has not been growing as rapidly as many other Southern and Midwestern cities. Its economy is in many ways pre-postindustrial: It produces cigarettes and whiskey, large appliances and automobiles. But it is also the headquarters of Humana health services and has a new medical services center going up downtown, as well as the Muhammad Ali Center and the Owsley Brown Frazier Historical Arms Museum. After the consolidation vote, local worthies commissioned a study by the Brookings Institution, which warned of the dangers of sprawl and the need to beef up Louisville's historic downtown. But Louisville, with less growth than other metro areas, is not about to become another Atlanta, unless high tax rates or poor schools in Louisville-Jefferson County drive young families into still sparsely-settled outer counties in Kentucky or Indiana, just as a school busing decision led to Jefferson County's losing population in the 1970s. Louisville has not yet attracted large numbers of immigrants, but has an interesting variety—Vietnamese, Cubans, Chinese, Indians, Koreans, Mexicans.

The 3d Congressional District includes all but a dozen or so precincts of Louisville-Jefferson County. There is a large black population on the west side of Louisville and just south of the old city limits and a lower-income white population along the strip highway that leads to Fort Knox. The suburbs to the east tend to be affluent; little elite neighborhoods—Mockingbird Valley, Glenview, Ten Broeck—incorporated long ago to avoid being annexed by the city. Louisville has long been an odd duck in Kentucky politics. If its elite were Virginia cavaliers, many of its burghers were Germans and Pennsylvanians who made this river town a Republican and anti-slavery island in a secessionist and pro-slavery sea. That tradition helps explain why Republican Mitch Mc-Connell was able to get elected Jefferson County judge-executive in the 1970s and 1980s when the state was electing Democrats to most other offices. In the 1990s Louisville, like so many bigger metro areas, trended toward the Democrats, even as the rest of Kentucky trended Republican. The 3d District voted for Al Gore in 2000, while the state's other five districts all voted for George W. Bush.

The congresswoman from the 3d District is Anne Northup. She grew up in a large Catholic family in Louisville—she has nine sisters and one brother—and has raised six children of her own. Her husband is a small business owner; she volunteered and served on the boards of many charities and associations. She was elected to the Kentucky House in a 1987 special election, where she became the number one critic of tobacco in the capital of the nation's number two tobacco state.

In 1996 she decided to run for Congress, against freshman Democrat Mike Ward, an "old Democrat" who won the seat by 425 votes in 1994, when 12% voted for an anti-abortion third candidate. In a year when almost all Democrats and most Republicans ran cookie-cutter campaigns, Northup showed originality in strategy and tactics. First, she outraised the incumbent, with an amazing $868,000 coming from individuals; she spent $1,182,000 to Ward's $880,000. Second, she started TV spots in August—three weeks before Ward got on the air. Third, she used unusual issues, such as Ward's vote against making English the official language. Both candidates opposed FDA regulation of tobacco, but her criticisms of tobacco companies moderated her image. Ward ran behind his party ticket and Northup won 50.3%–49.7%, a margin of 1,299 votes.

In Washington, Northup was singled out by the leadership and was one of two Republican freshmen to get a seat on Appropriations. Her voting record is somewhat moderate on economic and foreign issues and conservative on cultural issues. When the Lewinsky scandal broke, Northup appeared on *Meet the Press* and criticized feminists for their silence on Clinton's behavior. She opposes abortion and claims the district is "more pro-life than pro-choice." She joined most Democrats in supporting the 72-hour check for sales at gun shows. She strongly supported the Republican version of HMO regulation.

Despite her votes against spending generally, Northup has used her seat on Appropriations to bring in what she estimated in 2000 as "approaching $500 million" into her district—a "fair share" she called it. In 2001 she got $25.8 million in earmarked projects. She earmarked $3 million in projects for St. Stephen Baptist Church and New Canaan Baptist Church. In 2000 she set up a group called Louisville Neighborhood Initiative and earmarked $2 million in 2001 and $3 million in 2002 for it, to be distributed by the organization. LNI, on whose board she served, decided to give $600,000 to Cable Missionary Baptist Church for a family center, $350,000 to Mount Olive Missionary Baptist Church to build a neighborhood center and $200,000 to Catholic Charities for senior citizens' housing. In February 2002 the ACLU sued LNI for limiting its grants to faith-based organizations. LNI dropped that limitation in April. Common Cause charged that by steering money to an organization she was connected with, Northup violated House ethics rules. Northup said she had gotten oral clearance from the ethics committee, but in May 2002 stopped LNI disbursal of grants and went back to earmarking to specific organizations. Democrats charged that Northup was seeking favorable political treatment from black ministers and their congregations. Her response: "From the first day I was elected, I have tried to help the disadvantaged and the most distressed areas of my community. I know where to put money if I want political benefit from it. I know where the swing neighborhoods are. It is not the West End."

Northup's biggest project in dollar terms is the building of two new bridges over the Ohio River, one downtown which would also replace the "spaghetti junction" intersection of Interstates 64, 65 and 71, and one in eastern Jefferson County. At $2 billion, this is the second biggest pending highway project in the nation, after metro Washington's Woodrow Wilson Bridge, and she worked with Indiana Democrat Baron Hill to promote it over several years. She favored building both bridges at the same time, lest the eastern bridge be delayed indefinitely, and DOT prioritized the project for accelerated environmental review in October 2002. On another issue, Northup journeyed to China in January 2002 to try to get the Chinese to lift their limit on the number of

Chinese babies that can be adopted by Americans. In August 2001 she complained about the separate, and in her view unequal, gym that the House has for women members.

The 3d District has been seriously contested in every election since 1992. In 1998, former Attorney General and County Commissioner Chris Gorman challenged Northup. Gorman attacked Northup for voting with Newt Gingrich 95% of the time and attacked her vote for the Republican version of HMO regulation. Northup once again showed her fundraising prowess: She raised over $1.6 million, almost three times as much as Gorman. She won 52%–48%. In 2000 Northup was opposed by state Representative Eleanor Jordan, from the heavily black West End of Louisville. Northup campaigned on her "balanced approach" and the projects she had won for the district, but also capitalized deftly on Jordan's mistakes. She ran an ad showing Jordan in Frankfort urging colleagues to finish action quickly because "I have a fundraiser at six o'clock and I want to get out of here." This was a very big-spending race, targeted by both sides. Northup, outdoing previous efforts, spent $2.9 million. Jordan, with help from EMILY's List and other liberal supporters, raised and spent $1.7 million. Northup won 53%–44%, her biggest victory yet.

In 2002 Northup's opponent was Jack Conway, 33, Deputy Cabinet Secretary to Governor Paul Patton. He was her first opponent who had no legislative record she could attack. She had an additional embarrassment: In June 2002 she had sent a letter to the FCC inquiring about the treatment of her husband's company's application for a license to sell radios; she said she didn't know her office sent the letter. This was another race with prodigious fundraising. Northup spent $3.2 million, raising $1.8 million from individuals and $1 million from PACs. Conway, with much help from Patton (who called him "the closest thing I've seen in Kentucky to Jack Kennedy"), raised $508,000 by the end of 2001, more than any other Democrat challenging a Republican incumbent, and $1.5 million in all. Conway's theme was that Northup was more conservative than voters thought: "Anne Northup says one thing in Louisville and votes another way in Washington."

Northup called Conway a state bureaucrat "who has never held a private sector job," and said, "This is no time for fast-talking, inexperienced approaches to the challenges that face this country." They differed on the Ohio River bridges. Conway favored building the downtown bridge first, and also a $551 million light rail system from downtown to the airport and the Gene Snyder Freeway. Northup declined to endorse the light rail and said she feared that if an eastern bridge wasn't built immediately it might never be. Her position was backed up by two trips to Louisville in the last six weeks of the campaign by Federal Highway Administrator Mary Peters. Conway was hurt when, in September 2002, Patton admitted to having an affair with a nursing home operator who sued, claiming he had state inspectors close down her business after she broke off the affair. Patton's job rating in Jefferson County dropped sharply, and Patton withdrew from politicking; Democrats said he otherwise would have raised another $100,000 for Conway. In debate Conway declined to renounce him: "I'm disappointed, deeply. But he's my friend, and I am not gonna pull an Al Gore, and I am not the type of person who runs away from their friends when times are tough."

Northup won 52%–48%, with a 7,382-vote margin. Northup got 20% of the vote in heavily black legislative districts, which suggests that she may have won the 28% of the black vote shown in the final *Courier-Journal* poll. If so, that is one of the best performances among blacks by a Republican anywhere in the country in a seriously contested race. Conway's strong performance led some Democrats to urge him to run again in 2004.

Northup has lost or dropped bids for Republican leadership positions—for vice chairman of the Republican Conference in November 1998 and April 2000, for Conference secretary in November 2000. But in December 2002 she took the lead by being the first House Republican to criticize Trent Lott for his comments on Strom Thurmond's 100th birthday.

FOURTH DISTRICT

Rep. Ken Lucas (D)

Elected 1998, 3d term; b. Aug. 22, 1933, Kenton Cnty.; home, Union; U. of KY, B.S. 1955, Xavier U., M.B.A. 1970; Christian; married (Mary).

Military Career: Air Force, 1955–57; Air Natl. Guard, 1957–67.

Elected Office: Florence City Cncl., 1967–74; Boone Cnty. Commissioner, 1974–82; Boone Cnty. Judge Exec., 1992–98.

Professional Career: Financial planner, Sagemark Consulting, 1967–98; Pres., Boone St. Bank, 1971–86; Dir., Drees Co., 1980-present; Chmn., Fifth Third Bank, 1986–97.

DC Office: 1205 LHOB 20515, 202-225-3465; Fax: 202-225-0003; Web site: www.house.gov/kenlucas.

District Offices: Ashland, 606-324-9898; Ft. Mitchell, 859-426-0080.

Committees: *Agriculture* (20th of 24 D): Livestock & Horticulture. *Financial Services* (20th of 32 D): Capital Markets, Insurance & Government Sponsored Enterprises; Financial Institutions & Consumer Credit. *Select Committee on Homeland Security* (21st of 23 D): Cybersecurity, Science and Research & Development; Emergency Preparedness & Response.

Group Ratings

	ADA	ACLU	AFS	LCV	CON	ITIC	NTU	COC	ACU	NTLC	CHC
2002	10	7	11	13	20	100	43	90	84	72	75
2001	25	—	20	21	—	—	48	91	76	—	—

National Journal Ratings

	2001 LIB	—	2001 CONS		2002 LIB	—	2002 CONS
Economic	48%	—	52%		44%	—	56%
Social	0%	—	81%		0%	—	75%
Foreign	43%	—	53%		35%	—	60%

Key Votes of the 107th Congress

1. Approve Bush Tax Cuts	Y	5. Faith-Based Charities	Y	9. Trade Promotion Authority	Y
2. Limit Patients' Bill of Rights	Y	6. Bar Gays in the Boy Scouts	Y	10. Bar Funds for Intl. Court	Y
3. Campaign Finance Reform	Y	7. Ban Partial-Birth Abortion	Y	11. Authorize Force in Iraq	Y
4. Ban ANWR Development	N	8. Arm Commercial Pilots	Y	12. Deny Home. Sec. Dept. Union	Y

Election Results

2002 general	Ken Lucas (D)	87,776	(51%)	($1,451,062)
	Geoff Davis (R)	81,651	(48%)	($874,453)
	Other	2,308	(1%)	
2002 primary	Ken Lucas (D)	unopposed		
2000 general	Ken Lucas (D)	125,872	(54%)	($779,740)
	Don Bell (R)	100,943	(44%)	($59,994)
	Other	5,148	(2%)	

Prior Winning Percentages: 1998 (53%)

The People		Race/Ethnic Origin	Ancestry	
Area size:	5,770 sq. mi.	95.1% White	German: 17.6%	USA: 13.6%
Urban population:	59.7%	2.2% Black	Irish: 10.4%	
Rural population:	40.3%	0.5% Asian	**2000 Presidential Vote**	
Pop. 2000:	673,588	0.2% Native Am.	Bush (R)	152,856 (61%)
Median income:	$40,150	0.0% Hawaiian	Gore (D)	92,768 (37%)
Poverty status:	11.4%	0.8% Two+ races	Other	6,060 (2%)
Military veterans:	13.0%	0.1% Other	**Cook Partisan Voting Index:** R +13	
		1.1% Hispanic Origin		

Occupation	Blue collar: 29.6%	White collar: 56.0%	Gray collar: 14.3%

The commonwealth of Kentucky has gone to court more than once to assert its claim to all of the Ohio River up to its northern bank: This is one of the northernmost extensions of the South. The Ohio sees many different parts of Kentucky. Ashland, near the West Virginia border, is industrial, the home of ancestral Ashland Inc.; the river here is bound in by tight hills that hold smoke and soot close in the air. Farther down the river, the country is more bucolic: Here Eliza fled across the ice floes in Harriet Beecher Stowe's *Uncle Tom's Cabin.* Farther west, between Louisville and Cincinnati, are counties that still look like they're in the 19th century. But metropolitan growth obtrudes. Oldham County, just upriver from Louisville, has some of Kentucky's oldest homes, though the horse country is also sprouting affluent subdivisions; this is, by far, the most wealthy county in the state. The three Northern Kentucky counties across the river from Cincinnati are urban and suburban. Overlooking the suspension bridge built by John Roebling 16 years before the Brooklyn Bridge, are new buildings on the Covington waterfront while Newport, once known for its gambling, is sprucing up, and office buildings and new subdivisions are rising on the hills in Boone County above the river and near the Cincinnati-Northern Kentucky International Airport.

The 4th Congressional District spans all these variations of Ohio River country; it also includes lightly populated counties just inland. Economically, it runs the gamut from coal mining towns to rich suburbs. Politically, it has some of the most Democratic counties in America, like mountain-bound Elliott County (64%–35% for Al Gore in 2000), and some of the most Republican territory in Kentucky, like Oldham County with its affluent migrants from Louisville (67%–31% for George W. Bush). The three northern Kentucky counties across the river from Cincinnati cast nearly half the district's votes, and they too are heavily Republican; Bush won here, 61%–37%.

The congressman from the 4th District is Ken Lucas, a conservative Democrat elected in 1998. Lucas grew up on a farm in northern Kentucky, worked his way through the University of Kentucky on a tobacco farm, and became a financial planner. In the manner of local businessmen, he served two terms on the Florence Council and two years on the Boone County Board of Commissioners in the 1970s and 1980s. In 1992 he was appointed Boone County judge-executive, and was reelected twice. In 1998 he ran for the House, stressing that he was a very conservative Democrat, "a common sense conservative, pro-life, pro-gun and pro-business." He pledged to limit himself to three terms.

Lucas was not the favorite when the campaign started; it looked like the race would be determined in the Republican primary. The contenders were state Senator Gex (pronounced *jay*) Williams and lawyer Rick Robinson, a longtime supporter of 4th District Congressman Jim Bunning, who was running for the Senate. Williams was backed by Dr. James Dobson; his political consultant was former Christian Coalition head Ralph Reed. Robinson was backed by almost all local Republican politicians and was funded by a host of business PACs. The outsider Williams, a computer consultant, showed the greater political skills. He won the primary 51%–41%, and leaders of the religious right across the nation pointed to him as one of their future leaders. But in the general election, everything went wrong for Williams and right for Lucas. Williams was accused of making campaign phone calls from the Kentucky statehouse; an investigation found no significant violation, but only after the election. Lucas raised more money and ran hard-hitting ads. Staying true to his conservative themes, Lucas refused to appear at the Cincinnati airport when Bill Clinton came there September 27. The result was a stunning 53%–47% victory for Lucas.

In the House, Lucas joined the Blue Dogs and became one of the most conservative Democrats, on issues generally and on abortion, guns and tobacco especially. Early on, Republicans urged him to switch parties, but he said he had no intention of doing so. He took Democratic positions on some domestic issues, notably education. But he was one of 13 Democrats to vote for George W. Bush's tax cuts and one of 25 to vote for trade promotion authority; he was one of only three Democrats who voted for both. When Republicans passed their big domestic spending bill before the 2000 election, he was one of four Democrats in favor. He made a point of skipping the Democratic convention in Los Angeles, and said that he would abstain in the presidential election because of Al Gore's views on abortion, guns and tobacco. In 2002, he was the most conservative House Democrat in the *National Journal* vote ratings. The League of Conservation

Voters put him on their "dirty dozen" list. But he stuck with Democrats, and opposed Senator Mitch McConnell, in supporting the Shays-Meehan campaign finance regulation bill.

In 2000 Gex Williams considered a rematch but decided against it. Instead, Lucas was opposed by Don Bell, a retired Secret Service agent and perennial candidate who called himself the true conservative in the contest. Bell won Oldham and Shelby counties outside of Louisville 56%–41%, but Lucas won the district 54%–44%. In 2002, he faced Geoff Davis, a business consultant and another first-time candidate. Hard-pressed to identify issues where he disagreed with Lucas, Davis focused instead on his lack of "leadership" in Congress. Although Davis was better-financed than Bell in 2000, the national Republican party did not open its coffers very wide for him—a statement, perhaps, of gratitude. Lucas won 51%–48%, carrying 19 of the 24 counties, including margins as high as 3-to-1 in rural areas. Davis won the three counties in the Cincinnati suburbs, 54%–44%, and also took Oldham County in the west and Lewis County in the east. Court-imposed redistricting gave Lucas critical help. It removed Shelby County outside Louisville, which has been trending Republican, and added three and one-half Democratic counties in the Bluegrass region.

His win keeps alive Kentucky's record of electing at least one Democrat every year since Andrew Jackson founded the party in 1828. But it is not clear whether that string will continue after 2004. After the 2002 election, Lucas publicly said that he was considering a party switch, which he earlier had discussed with Speaker Dennis Hastert. But he decided against it, perhaps because he failed to win assurances that local Republicans would not challenge him. At the start of the new Congress, he took the unusual step of voting "present" for Speaker, rather than support the party's nominee of Nancy Pelosi. Lucas was mentioned as a candidate against Senator Jim Bunning in 2004, but announced in January 2003 that he would break his term limits pledge and run for the House again. "These are not ordinary times in America and I cannot in good conscience step away from my work," he said, adding that popular support for term limits had "evaporated." Geoff Davis declared he will run again, and objected when Senator Mitch McConnell endorsed his former aide Hunter Bates for the seat; Bates later withdrew to run for lieutenant governor but was ruled ineligible for that post because he was not a state resident for most of the last 6 years. Geoff Davis could have serious competition in the Republican primary: former Campbell County Judge-Executive Lloyd Rogers and attorney Kevin Murphy both announced in early 2003 they intend to seek the party nomination.

FIFTH DISTRICT

Rep. Harold Rogers (R)

Elected 1980, 12th term; b. Dec. 31, 1937, Barrier; home, Somerset; U. of KY, B.A. 1962, J.D. 1964; Baptist; married (Cynthia).

Military Career: Army Natl. Guard, 1957–64.

Professional Career: Practicing atty., 1964–69; Pulaski–Rockcastle Commonwealth's Atty., 1969–80.

DC Office: 2406 RHOB 20515, 202-225-4601; Fax: 202-225-0940; Web site: www.house.gov/rogers.

District Offices: Hazard, 606-439-0794; Pikeville, 606-432-4388; Somerset, 606-679-8346.

Committees: *Appropriations* (4th of 36 R): Commerce, Justice, State & Judiciary; Homeland Security (Chmn.); Transportation, Treasury, & Independent Agencies. *Select Committee on Homeland Security* (9th of 27 R): Intelligence & Counterterrorism.

Group Ratings

	ADA	ACLU	AFS	LCV	CON	ITIC	NTU	COC	ACU	NTLC	CHC
2002	0	7	0	0	13	75	52	100	88	83	100
2001	10	—	10	7	—	—	59	91	88	—	—

National Journal Ratings

	2001 LIB	—	2001 CONS		2002 LIB	—	2002 CONS
Economic	22%	—	74%		28%	—	69%
Social	20%	—	69%		0%	—	75%
Foreign	21%	—	74%		29%	—	67%

Key Votes of the 107th Congress

1. Approve Bush Tax Cuts	Y	5. Faith-Based Charities	Y	9. Trade Promotion Authority	N
2. Limit Patients' Bill of Rights	Y	6. Bar Gays in the Boy Scouts	Y	10. Bar Funds for Intl. Court	Y
3. Campaign Finance Reform	N	7. Ban Partial-Birth Abortion	Y	11. Authorize Force in Iraq	Y
4. Ban ANWR Development	N	8. Arm Commercial Pilots	Y	12. Deny Home. Sec. Dept. Union	Y

Election Results

2002 general	Harold Rogers (R)	137,986	(78%)	($480,850)
	Sidney Jane Bailey (D)	38,254	(22%)	
2002 primary	Harold Rogers (R)	77,615	(92%)	
	Billy Ray Wilson (R)	6,948	(8%)	
2000 general	Harold Rogers (R)	145,980	(74%)	($459,993)
	Sidney Jane Bailey (D)	52,495	(26%)	

Prior Winning Percentages: 1998 (78%); 1996 (100%); 1994 (79%); 1992 (55%); 1990 (100%); 1988 (100%); 1986 (100%); 1984 (76%); 1982 (65%); 1980 (67%)

The People		Race/Ethnic Origin	Ancestry	
Area size:	10,759 sq. mi.	97.1% White	USA: 29.5%	English: 6.8%
Urban population:	21.3%	1.1% Black	Irish: 5.7%	
Rural population:	78.7%	0.3% Asian	**2000 Presidential Vote**	
Pop. 2000:	673,670	0.2% Native Am.	Bush (R)...............131,494	(57%)
Median income:	$21,915	0.0% Hawaiian	Gore (D)................97,104	(42%)
Poverty status:	28.1%	0.6% Two + races	Other....................3,423	(1%)
Military veterans:	10.0%	0.0% Other	**Cook Partisan Voting Index:** R + 8	
		0.7% Hispanic Origin		

Occupation	Blue collar: 35.3%	White collar: 48.4%	Gray collar: 16.3%

The mountains of eastern Kentucky have been a special place since Daniel Boone came through the Cumberland Gap in 1775. As Virginians poured through and created their version of a Tidewater civilization in the Bluegrass country, the people who settled the mountain counties and the Cumberland Plateau, most of them of Irish Protestant or Border Scot descent, brought different values—an assertive egalitarianism, loyalty to family and community, and passionate willingness to settle differences by feuds or violence. Most of the people in the mountains today are descendants of families who settled there in the two or three generations after Boone. Handed down are living memories of the old ways of doing things from the time not so far distant when there was little contact here with the outside world and the ties to the rest of American civilization were secured mainly by school primers and the King James Bible. Only when people's lives have been changed and uprooted by outside events and institutions have their basic political attitudes been changed—and with a lasting imprint. The first agent of such change here was the Civil War; the second was the great United Mine Workers organizing drives in the coalmines around the 1930s. The Civil War made the mountains and the Cumberland Plateau a stronghold of the Republican Party. This was never slave territory—hardly any blacks have ever lived here, yet communities and families were riven by the rebellion of the South. People have not forgotten: The counties around Somerset and Corbin in south central Kentucky cast some of the highest Republican percentages in the nation, election after election.

Then came coal. Early in the 20th century, vast seams of coal were discovered under the Kentucky mountains; representatives of eastern capitalists (including the young Franklin D. Roosevelt) began prowling through these hills, hiring town lawyers to buy up mineral rights from unsuspecting farmers, building industrial slum towns in hollows and creek beds beneath glowering, heavily forested mountainsides. Coal mining was harsh and deadly work: Mine accidents, black lung disease and simple exhaustion killed tens of thousands of miners, while low wages and company stores kept them poor. Then John L. Lewis's United Mine Workers came in and something like open warfare followed, with neither mine operators nor union organizers loath to use violence and threats. The union mostly won in eastern Kentucky and in the short run raised wages and built hospitals for miners and their families; in the longer run, the UMW phased out many jobs in the mines in return for job security and health benefits, as use of oil expanded. Today there are just over 400 mines in Kentucky, a drop from over 2,000 25 years ago. Politically, the UMW counties in the eastern part of the state became heavily Democratic. In the mid-1960s Lyndon Johnson came to eastern Kentucky and cited the poverty here in pushing for his Appalachian and anti-poverty bills. The high energy prices of the 1970s sparked strip mining, and eastern Kentucky's economy moved upward; the lower energy prices of the 1980s and 1990s were something of a setback. Most eastern coal counties have lost population since 1980, but life here today is much closer to the ordinary American standard of living than it was in Johnson's time. There is less insularity and less defensiveness, and more celebration of heritage, as in the Hillbilly Days Festival that draws 100,000 people every June to Pikeville.

The 5th Congressional District includes much of the Cumberland Plateau and most of the eastern mountains, a mixture of heavily Republican and heavily Democratic territory. There are huge political differences here between counties separated by just a mountain ridge or two, evidence of the depth of Civil War and United Mine Workers political loyalties, and only somewhat modulated by the trend toward George W. Bush in the coal country in 2000. Jackson County, which Bill Clinton visited on his "poverty tour" in 1999, voted 84%–14% for Bush in 2000; a few counties over, Knott County (where 96% of registered voters are Democrats) voted 67%–31% for Al Gore. The 5th District, created in the 1991 redistricting and modified just slightly in 2001, spans these lines and combines most of two former districts, one heavily Democratic and the other heavily Republican. But in 2000 at least this was a solidly Republican district that gave Bush 57%.

The congressman from the 5th District is Harold Rogers, a Republican first elected in 1980. Rogers grew up in Wayne County, went off to the University of Kentucky and served in the National Guard, then practiced law in Somerset; in 1969, at 34, he was elected Pulaski-Rockcastle Commonwealth's Attorney. In 1979 he was the Republican nominee for lieutenant governor. In 1980, when the 5th District congressman retired, Rogers was one of 11 Republicans in the primary; he won 23% in the primary and then easily in November. His toughest race came in 1992, with redistricting. At first his likely opponent was 7th District incumbent Chris Perkins, longtime Congressman Carl Perkins's son; but then Perkins retired at 37, before it was revealed he had 514 overdrafts on the House bank. Rogers ended up facing state Senator John Doug Hays of Pike County, whose grandfather Doug "Sawloggin" Hays was state senator before him. Hays attacked Rogers for supporting trickle-down economics and argued that as a Democrat he could get more money for the district. Rogers countered by pointing to his ongoing efforts to build the $250 million Cumberland Gap twin tunnels and Harlan County flood projects. Rogers won with 55%. He had 71% in his old 5th District, which cast 52% of the new district's votes.

Rogers is now the fourth ranking Republican on the Appropriations Committee; until 2003, he was chairman of its Transportation Subcommittee. In February 2003 he gave up his chairmanship—although he remains a member—to become the first chairman of the Homeland Security Appropriations Subcommittee. His voting record is mostly, but not always, conservative. Representing a low-income district, he is sympathetic to some spending bills; he was one of three Republicans to vote for the Clinton stimulus package in March 1993.

Rogers represents a district that has long been hungry for federal aid, and does not have a uniformly conservative record on economic issues. He supported most of the Contract with America, but prevented the zeroing out of several programs—the Appalachian Regional Commission, the Legal Services Corporation—by straightforwardly negotiating deals, then sticking to them. And of course he has worked on projects for eastern Kentucky. Over the years he has worked to provide $162 million to protect the solvency of the funds for the United Mine Workers Combined Benefit Fund. In January 2001 he switched from the chairmanship of the Commerce-Justice-State Subcommittee to Transportation: a much better position from which to pump money into eastern Kentucky. Suddenly Kentucky became the fourth highest state in transportation funding per capita. The December 2001 transportation appropriation included $30 million for the Appalachian highway corridor development, $22.5 million for I-66 between London and Somerset, $4 million for an industrial park in Clay and Leslie County. Projects in other parts of Kentucky were included, such as $5 million for Louisville's airport (which got the nation's first new system tracking aircraft via satellite) and $2.5 million for planning for two Ohio River bridges in the Louisville area. Rogers's home town of Somerset got $6.6 million for a bypass, $5 million for improvements on U.S. 27, $3 million for an access road and runway at the airport and $2 million for downtown revitalization.

Rogers has gotten involved on other transportation issues. Even before September 11, he was lamenting that most airport screeners were not U.S. citizens. After Congress voted to federalize airport screeners, he kept close watch in the new TSA, insisting that it get rid of the Argenbright firm, objecting when it got around Congress's 45,000-employee cap by classifying 9,000 five-year workers as temporary. In December 2001 Rogers cut the money for executive bonuses at the FAA and NHTSA because they did not meet their targets under the 1993 Government Performance and Results Act, the first time this had been done; he noted with disapproval that 85% of executives at agencies had been given top ratings and hailed FAA administrator Jane Garvey for giving no bonuses because of September 11. In September 2002 he proposed cutting Amtrak's budget from $1.2 billion to $765 million, arguing that anything more would exceed the budget spending cap and could be defeated by a point of order; the funding was ultimately restored to $1.05 billion. He capped subsidies to long distance trains to $150 million and limited them to trains on which the subsidy was less than $200 per passenger. Anything else, he said, "would reward Amtrak for their poor management and poor performance." In 2002 he set the appropriations for highways at $27.7 billion, $4.4 billion less than the previous year but $4.1 billion more than the administration request.

Rogers has been dismayed by the epidemic of people in eastern Kentucky taking the painkiller OxyContin as a narcotic and berated officials of the company that makes it for not tracking overusage. "Your company did nothing and people were dying!" he roared at one hearing.

Since 1992, Rogers has been re-elected by overwhelming margins, carrying even the most Democratic counties. In 2002 he won the Republican primary 92%–8% and the general election by 78%–22%. In the latter election he did lose the one-third of Bath County added to the district by redistricting. That year he set up a leadership PAC and contributed $600,000 to Republican candidates and party organizations. Many Republicans urged him to run for governor in 2003, but in March 2002 he said he could do more for the state from his current position.

SIXTH DISTRICT

Rep. Ernie Fletcher (R)

Elected 1998, 3d term; b. Nov. 12, 1952, Mt. Sterling; home, Lexington; U. of KY, B.S. 1974, M.D. 1984; Baptist; married (Glenna).

Military Career: Air Force, 1974–80.

Elected Office: KY House of Reps., 1994–96.

Professional Career: Practicing physician, 1984-present; CEO, St. Joseph Medical Foundation, 1997–99.

DC Office: 1117 LHOB 20515, 202-225-4706; Fax: 202-225-2122; Web site: www.house.gov/fletcher.

District Office: Lexington, 859-219-1366.

Committees: *Energy & Commerce* (27th of 31 R): Commerce, Trade & Consumer Protection; Environment & Hazardous Materials; Health.

Group Ratings

	ADA	ACLU	AFS	LCV	CON	ITIC	NTU	COC	ACU	NTLC	CHC
2002	0	13	0	0	8	100	53	95	92	83	100
2001	0	—	0	0	—	—	61	100	96	—	—

National Journal Ratings

	2001 LIB —	2001 CONS		2002 LIB —	2002 CONS
Economic	15%	82%		28%	69%
Social	0%	81%		0%	75%
Foreign	21%	74%		15%	78%

Key Votes of the 107th Congress

1. Approve Bush Tax Cuts	Y	5. Faith-Based Charities	Y	9. Trade Promotion Authority	Y
2. Limit Patients' Bill of Rights	Y	6. Bar Gays in the Boy Scouts	Y	10. Bar Funds for Intl. Court	Y
3. Campaign Finance Reform	N	7. Ban Partial-Birth Abortion	Y	11. Authorize Force in Iraq	Y
4. Ban ANWR Development	N	8. Arm Commercial Pilots	Y	12. Deny Home. Sec. Dept. Union	Y

Election Results

2002 general	Ernie Fletcher (R)	115,622	(72%)	($1,238,265)
	Gatewood Galbraith (I)	41,753	(26%)	($18,697)
	Other	3,313	(2%)	
2002 primary	Ernie Fletcher (R)	unopposed		
2000 general	Ernie Fletcher (R)	142,971	(53%)	($2,300,940)
	Scotty Baesler (D)	94,167	(35%)	($1,484,436)
	Gatewood Galbraith (Ref)	32,436	(12%)	($12,094)

Prior Winning Percentages: 1998 (53%)

The People		Race/Ethnic Origin	Ancestry	
Area size:	3,775 sq. mi.	87.1% White	USA: 15.3%	English: 9.5%
Urban population:	71.3%	8.2% Black	German: 9.3%	
Rural population:	28.7%	1.2% Asian	**2000 Presidential Vote**	
Pop. 2000:	673,626	0.2% Native Am.	Bush (R)..............145,606	(55%)
Median income:	$37,544	0.0% Hawaiian	Gore (D)..............109,602	(42%)
Poverty status:	13.2%	1.1% Two + races	Other....................7,282	(3%)
Military veterans:	11.7%	0.1% Other	**Cook Partisan Voting Index:** R + 7	
		2.1% Hispanic Origin		

Occupation	Blue collar: 25.8%	White collar: 58.8%	Gray collar: 15.4%

With its white picket fences, horse farms and Georgian brick house-filled small towns, the rolling plateau of the Bluegrass country almost plumb in the middle of Kentucky is the part of interior America longest settled by English speakers: Lexington was founded in 1775; the town of Hopewell was renamed Paris in 1789 out of gratitude for French help during our Revolution and in a salute to theirs (though the county name remained Bourbon even after Louis XVI was guillotined). Tobacco farming started here in the 1770s, horse racing in 1787, and the first whiskey distillery, in Bourbon County, was built in 1790. Tobacco, whiskey and racehorses remained the staples of the Bluegrass economy for six generations until 1956, when IBM built its typewriter plant and headquarters in Lexington. IBM's arrival "really was the beginning of Lexington's industrial revolution," as University of Kentucky historian Carl Cone put it. But capitalism, as Joseph Schumpeter wrote, is a process of creative destruction. The PC eventually outclassed the typewriter, and the IBM plant put on the block. Now the big employer here is Lexmark International, an independent IBM spinoff that makes inkjet and laser printers. Another mainstay of the local economy is the Toyota plant, built for $2 billion in the 1980s, in Georgetown, a town with early 19th century houses and lush countryside, just one county north of Lexington and west of Paris; auto parts and suppliers have naturally moved in nearby. Lexington, which includes all of Fayette County, grew by a sprightly 16% in the 1990s, and the 2000 Census showed it the largest city in Kentucky, just ahead of Louisville. But Louisville voters decided to merge the city and Jefferson County, and in January 2003 Louisville became number one again.

The 6th Congressional District includes Lexington and the surrounding counties—a natural unit, unlike some other Kentucky districts. Lexington casts about one-third of the votes. It was the home base of the Whig Party's great leader Henry Clay, but in the 150 years after his death, the Bluegrass country was mostly Democratic. In 2000 Al Gore wrote off Kentucky early on, and the 6th District gave George W. Bush 55% of the vote.

The congressman from the 6th District is Ernie Fletcher, a Republican elected in 1998. Fletcher grew up in Mount Sterling, got an engineering degree from the University of Kentucky, was an Air Force pilot for five years, intercepting Soviet aircraft; then he went to medical school, practiced medicine, and was CEO of a company that managed medical practices. He did volunteer medical work in India and was a lay minister. In 1994 he was elected to the Kentucky House. In 1996 he won the Republican primary—by exactly 4 votes—and ran against Democratic Congressman Scotty Baesler, a tobacco farmer and onetime University of Kentucky basketball star. With help from national Republicans, Fletcher raised and spent nearly as much as the incumbent and ran a spirited campaign. He lost 56%–44%, but kept his taste for campaigning. When Baesler ran for the Senate in 1998, Fletcher decided to run for the House again, and this time had no serious primary competition. The Democratic nominee was state Senator Ernesto Scorsone, a criminal defense lawyer who had defended drug dealers. Scorsone claimed credit for managing Governor Paul Patton's tough anti-crime bill and he supported the partial-birth abortion ban; but overall his record was liberal. Scorsone said that Fletcher was carrying water for insurance companies; Fletcher said Scorsone played a key role in Kentucky's health care law that increased insurance premiums and favored trial lawyers, and said that as a physician he could better handle the issue. Fletcher ran one ad showing a woman whose breast cancer he had treated and another featuring a rape victim who said Scorsone represented her assailant and helped him avoid prison time. Fletcher won 53%–46%.

In the House, Fletcher established a conservative record and became an activist legislator. Unlike other recent Republican doctors elected to the House who have taken on HMOs, he worked with Education Committee chairman John Boehner and Democrat Collin Peterson to craft the less sweeping Republican alternative on HMO regulation. They prevailed in the House when Republican Charlie Norwood emerged from an August 2001 meeting with George W. Bush to join them and abandon his co-sponsorship with John Dingell of the Democratic alternative. On the Education Committee, Fletcher advocated the successful ed-flex bill to give the states greater flexibility in education spending. He voted for PNTR with China after presidential candidate George W. Bush called him and assured him of his commitment to human rights in China. On local issues, Fletcher won an amendment to destroy chemical munitions such as those stored in the local Bluegrass Army Depot.

In 2000 Baesler ran for the House again, and Democrats were optimistic they could recapture the seat. The contest became ground zero for interest groups of many persuasions. Pharmaceutical firms spent more than $500,000 on ads against Baesler, and the managed care industry supported Fletcher as well. The American Medical Association, which supported the Democrats' version of HMO regulation, was disappointed with this doctor-congressman and refused to endorse him. But HMO regulation, which national Democrats expected to be a big vote-winner, failed to work for Baesler here. Polls showed Baesler falling behind, and in the final days of the campaign he took the curious step of emphasizing gun control in a district that had never shown much enthusiasm for it. Fletcher won by the impressive margin of 53%–35%, winning all 19 counties, including 48%–37% in Lexington. Perennial third party candidate Gatewood Galbraith took 12%. In 2002, no Democrat filed to run.

In May 2003, Fletcher won the Republican nomination for governor with 57% of the vote. He is seeking to become the first Republican to win the office since 1967. If Fletcher is elected governor in November 2003, he would be sworn in on December 9; Governor Paul Patton would call a special election to fill the seat. The special is likely to be seriously contested.

★ LOUISIANA ★

Louisiana often seems to be America's banana republic, with its charm and inefficiency, its communities interlaced by family ties and its public sector sometimes laced with corruption, with its own indigenous culture and its tradition of fine distinctions of class and caste. It is a state with an economy uncomfortably like that of an underdeveloped country, based on pumping minerals out of soggy ground and shipping grain produced in the vast hinterland drained by its great river, an economy increasingly dependent on businesses typical of picturesque Third World countries—tourism (now the second largest industry, hard hit by September 11) and gambling. Its politics too has a Third World quality, with its own peculiar election laws and a heritage of no-holds-barred conflict and demagoguery no other state can match: what other state has produced a Huey Long or an Edwin Edwards? Louisiana has a hereditary rich class and a large low-wage working class. It has conservative cultural attitudes: Louisiana and Utah have the most restrictive abortion laws in the U.S.—its partial-birth abortion ban and optional "Choose Life" license plates have been ruled illegal by federal courts—and Louisiana in 1997 became the first state to offer covenant marriages, in which spouses would agree not to be covered by no-fault divorce laws. But Louisiana also has a lazy tolerance of rule-breaking, and feels more like the Caribbean or the Mediterranean than the North Atlantic or the Pacific Rim. This is not an entirely original observation. Four decades ago, A. J. Liebling described Louisiana as an outpost of the Levant along the Gulf of Mexico. Most of the United States faces east toward the vast Atlantic Ocean or west toward the vast Pacific; Louisiana faces south, to the Gulf of Mexico and the steamy heat and volatile societies of the Caribbean and Latin America.

New Orleans preserves the look and feel it had as a French and Spanish outpost in the New World. Traditions of centralized control and easygoing corruption, classic traits of colonialism, are part of this heritage. The *dirigiste* tradition comes from the fact that Louisiana is the only state whose law is based not on the common law of England but on the Napoleonic Code of France; the concept of civil liberties has shallower roots in Louisiana than in the other 49 states. Here abstract ideals have been overshadowed by the practical need for centralized action. This Delta land—much of it below sea level, soggy, swampy, laced with tributaries and offshoots of the Mississippi and other major rivers like the Atchafalaya—requires vast capital expenditures for levees and drainage and causeways. Even today, houses in New Orleans don't have basements, people are buried in above-ground cemeteries in grandiose crypts, and swamp lands begin abruptly at the edges of subdivisions and people find alligators in their backyards.

The economy that grew up in these rich Delta lands has always been based on raw materials. Antebellum Louisiana produced and exported sugar, rice and cotton in enough abundance to generate the wealth which built grand plantation houses behind alleys of oaks running in from the Mississippi, and to make New Orleans the nation's fifth largest city by the time of the Civil War. Then came oil, found in the great Spindletop strike just over the Texas line in 1901 and in salt domes in Louisiana not long after, followed by the huge Baton Rouge refinery that became the training ground for generations of top oil executives. When energy prices boomed after the oil shocks of 1973 and 1981, Louisiana, like an oil-rich Third World country, boomed too, reaching up toward national income levels, generating 500,000 new jobs between 1972 and 1981. But it lost 150,000 jobs in the next six years as oil prices crashed and the rig count dropped by two-thirds and energy taxes fell from 41% of state government revenues in 1982 to 9% in 1996. Louisiana's economy has never regained much forward momentum. Gambling, legalized in 1991, has produced less revenue than expected, and nothing like the boom that some promised. People have been leaving the state—116,000 in the 1990s, 47,000, more than any other state, between 2000 and 2002. Louisiana has high rates of cancer, early death rates, a high incidence of AIDS. The 1980s saw almost no population growth in Louisiana, and there are few immigrants; the state's population in 2000 was 32% black and only 2% Hispanic and 1% Asian. It is a population with low incomes and work force participation and low levels of education. Income disparities here are greater than almost anywhere else in the United States. New Orleans's rich are noto-

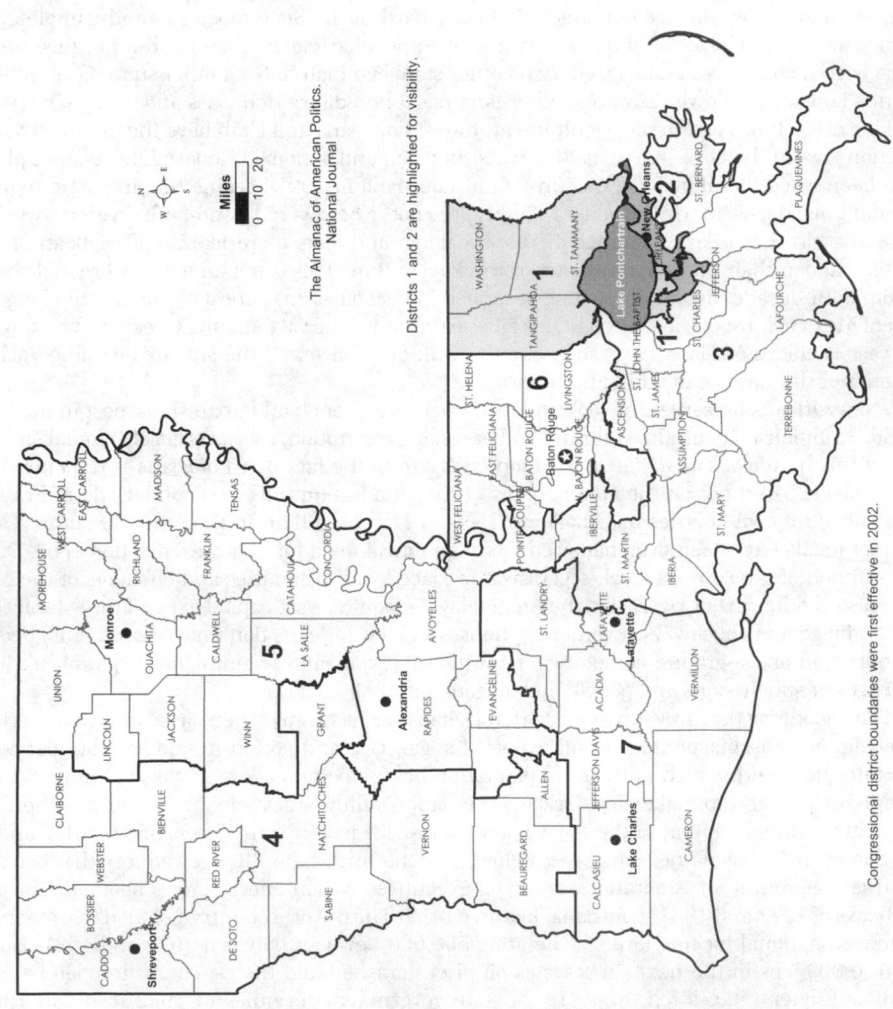

The Almanac of American Politics.
National Journal

Districts 1 and 2 are highlighted for visibility.

Congressional district boundaries were first effective in 2002.

riously unventuresome and tight-knit, determined to hold on to their wealth against the grasp of the impecunious and unlearned masses.

The most enduringly famous politican here, and by far the most talented, was Huey P. Long, who in less than a single term each as governor (1928–32) and senator (1932–35), left an imprint on the state's public life and imposed an organization to its politics that have faded into history only in the last decade. Long's genius was not that he promised to tax the rich to help the poor—hundreds of idealists and demagogues in America have done that—but that, to an amazing extent, he actually delivered. He dominated the legislature so thoroughly that, as governor, he roamed the floors of both chambers at will, bringing to the podium bills he insisted be passed without changing a comma—and they were. He was ready to use bribery, intimidation and physical violence. He built a new skyscraper Capitol, a new Louisiana State University and more miles of roads than any state but rich New York and huge Texas. He also built a national following, and by 1935, he was planning to run for president on the platform of "Share the wealth, every man a king," when he was assassinated at age 42 in the hallway of the Capitol, where the bullet holes can still be seen in the marble walls.

For America, the Long threat may have moved Franklin Roosevelt to embrace the liberal programs—the Wagner Labor Act, social security, steeply graduated taxes—of the second New Deal. For Louisiana, Long delivered a political structure that revolved around him even after he was dead—and a class of political leaders who, lacking his talents, treated the state as Long's incompetent doctors had treated his fatal wound, leaving Louisiana without either a fully developed economy or a fully competent public sector. For 50 years, until Huey's son Senator Russell Long retired in 1986, Longs and Long proteges held high political office in Louisiana and elections were run along pro- and anti-Long lines. The Long experience has strengthened Louisiana's already strong predispositions—tolerance of corruption, disinterest in abstract reform and taste for colorful extremists regardless of their short-term means or long-term ends—in a way that helps explain the rise and fall of such unlikely politicians as the four-term Governor Edwin Edwards and the onetime Ku Klux Klan leader and state legislator David Duke, both of whom in early 2003 were spending time in jail.

Louisiana has natural political divides. One divide is by religion: Catholic Cajun parishes (Louisiana has parishes rather than counties) cast about 30% of the state's vote, the New Orleans area casts around 25% or so, and about 45% are cast in Protestant parishes from Baton Rouge on north. White Protestants for years have wanted nothing to do with national Democrats, while Cajuns tend to mull it over. Another divide is by race: Blacks are overwhelmingly Democratic, whites split in seriously contested elections. A third divide is by income: Low- and high-income whites vote very differently and are much less influenced than voters in most other states by candidates' cultural values, marital status, lifestyles and the like. As a result, Louisiana politics since Huey P. Long's time has often been a struggle between reformist and conservative forces on one side and roguish populists on the other, a struggle waged in lavishly financed campaigns and with grandiloquent rhetoric.

For a quarter century, the lead role was played by Edwin Edwards as the roguish populist, with a number of Republican rivals as reformist conservatives. Edwards was elected governor in 1971 and 1975 and was not eligible to run in 1979. In 1983 he beat incumbent Republican David Treen; in 1987 he lost to Buddy Roemer, a Democratic congressman who later switched parties. For much of this third term, Edwards faced corruption charges, until he was acquitted by a jury in 1986. In 1991 he ran again, and this time an even odder character surfaced. David Duke was an active Nazi sympathizer up through 1989, but he also had a knack for speaking to mainstream political issues in attractive political language. In 1989 he was narrowly elected to the state legislature from a district in suburban Jefferson Parish as a nominal Republican—a victory that got enormous national publicity. Immediately he ran for senator in 1990 against incumbent Bennett Johnston, and lost by the unnervingly narrow margin of 54%–44%, making major inroads into the non-affluent white vote, both Cajun and Protestant. Then in 1991, Duke ran for governor, against Roemer and Edwards. (Louisiana has a unique primary system, invented by Edwards: candidates of all parties run in a single primary; any candidate who gets 50% is elected; otherwise, the top two finishers, regardless of party, have a runoff. In December 1997 the Supreme Court ruled that this system violates a federal law requiring all congressional elections to be held on the same day in November; and since then in federal election years the first primary is held in November and runoffs, if necessary, are held in December; a schedule that may have determined the outcome of the 2002 Senate race.) Edwards received only 34% of the votes, and Duke made the runoff by finishing second with 32%. All articulate opinion in Louisiana moved to Edwards's side, and Republicans from George H.W. Bush on down endorsed Edwards, who won 61%–39%. But Duke won enormous attention, even as his electoral career spun into decline; he ran for president in 1992, and got only 9% in the Louisiana primary.

In 2003 Louisiana will elect a new governor, who will probably set the course for state government for most of a decade; in early 2003 it was by no means clear who it would be. In the meantime Edwin Edwards and David Duke are in public housing. In May 2000 Edwards was convicted of extortion and sentenced to ten years without parole; he entered prison in October 2002. In December 2002 David Duke pleaded guilty in federal court to mail and tax fraud and entered prison in Texas in April 2003 to serve a 15-month sentence.

The People

Pop. 2000:	4,468,976			
Pop. 1990:	4,219,973			
Change 1990–2000:	Up 5.9%			
Change 1980–1990:	Up 0.3%			
% of U.S. total:	1.6%			
Pop. rank:	22d of 50			
Area size:	51,840 sq. mi.			
State Native:	79.4%			
Non-citizen:	1.3%			

Language

English: 85.9%		Other Eur.: 9.3%
Spanish: 3.5%		

Race/Ethnic Origin

2,794,391	62.5%	White
1,443,390	32.3%	Black
54,256	1.2%	Asian
24,129	0.5%	Native Am.
1,076	0.0%	Hawaiian
39,260	0.9%	Two + races
4,736	0.1%	Other
107,738	2.4%	Hisp. Origin

Ancestry

French: 10.2%	USA: 8.4%
German: 5.9%	Irish: 5.9%
English: 4.4%	

Military veterans: 392,486 (12.1%)

WWII: 19.5%	Korea: 12.7%
Vietnam: 32.2%	Gulf War: 12.4%

Most populous cities:

1. New Orleans	484,674
2. Baton Rouge	227,818
3. Shreveport	200,145
4. Lafayette	110,257
5. Lake Charles	71,757

Urban population: 72.7%
Rural population: 27.3%

Education

H.S. Grad:	74.8%
College Grad:	18.7%

Industry

Agri: 4.2%		Con: 7.9%
Fin: 5.7%		Info: 2.0%
Mfg: 15.5%		Prof: 29.3%
Public: 5.8%		Trade: 15.4%
Other: 14.3%		

Occupation

Blue collar: 25.8%	White collar: 56.6%
Gray collar: 17.5%	

Work Sector

Private: 76.2%		Govt: 17.4%
Self: 6.1%		Family: 0.3%
Unemployment: 7.3%		

Household Income

<15k: 24.1%	15-35k: 28.5%
35-50k: 15.7%	50-100k: 24.2%
100-150k: 4.8%	>150k: 2.6%
Median: $32,566	
Poverty status: 19.6%	

Home Value

<50k: 28.3%	50-100k: 38.5%	100-200k: 25.4%	200-300k: 5.0%
300-500k: 2.0%	>500k: 0.9%	Median: $77,500	

Legislature

Senate	26 D 13 R
House	71 D 34 R

Legislative Term Limits: Yes

Registered Voters

D: 1,572,594	(57.6%)
R: 632,430	(23.2%)
I: 524,538	(19.2%)

Presidential politics Louisiana's presidential politics is racially polarized. In 2000 it voted 53%–45% for George W. Bush, with whites voting 72%–26% for Bush and blacks 92%–6% for Al Gore. One reason is that Louisiana's black percentage is the second highest in the country, after Mississippi, and rising: The state's white population increased 1% in the 1990s and its black population increased 12%, as many whites left the state and some blacks in the North and West returned to their southern roots. An estimated 29% of Louisiana voters were black in 2000; if that percentage had been 35%, with the same balance between the candidates, Gore would have carried the state.

Louisiana has never played a significant role in presidential primaries and caucuses, with one odd exception. That was in 1996, when Republican allies of Phil Gramm set up a pre-Iowa-and-New-Hampshire February 6 caucus. The aim was to jump-start Gramm's campaign; instead the caucuses killed it. Gramm, relying on polls of active Republicans, was cocksure that he would win. But Pat Buchanan crisscrossed the bayous and upcountry parishes, meeting with voters, talking on cell-phones with any radio show that would have him. Only 20,000 Republicans showed up at 42 voting sites voted (as compared to 100,000 at 2,000 sites in Iowa), and Buchanan won more votes than Gramm and took 13 of the 21 delegates. Gramm's campaign in Iowa faltered, and he left the race before the vote in New Hampshire.

In January 1999 state Republican chairman Mike Francis got the party to schedule another pre-Iowa caucus. But in December 1999 Governor Mike Foster got the state central committee to cancel the caucus and hold a March primary. He cited the low turnout in 1996 and the fact that only Orrin Hatch, Gary Bauer and Alan Keyes were competing in Louisiana. George W. Bush, Foster's candidate, won in March and Francis lost his seat on the party committee.

2000 Presidential Vote		
Bush (R)	927,871	(53%)
Gore (D)	792,344	(45%)
Nader (Green)	20,473	(1%)
Other	24,968	(1%)
2000 Republican Presidential Primary		
Bush (R)	86,038	(84%)
McCain (R)	9,165	(9%)
Keyes (R)	5,900	(6%)
2000 Democratic Presidential Primary		
Gore (D)	114,942	(73%)
Bradley (D)	31,385	(20%)
LaRouche (D)	6,127	(4%)
Other	5,097	(3%)
1996 Presidential Vote		
Clinton (D)	927,836	(53%)
Dole (R)	712,586	(40%)
Perot (I)	123,292	(7%)

Congressional districting Louisiana redistricted its congressional districts three times in the 1990s. The first two plans created two black-majority districts, one of them in each case highly irregular in shape; they were declared unconstitutional in federal court in December 1993 and July 1994. The first plan was used in the 1992 elections, the second in 1994. In January 1996 a federal court came up with a plan, adopted by the legislature, that cut through few parish boundaries and had much more regular lines, and had only one black-majority district, centered in New Orleans. It was upheld by the Supreme Court in June 1996.

108th Congress Lineup	
4 R	3 D
107th Congress Lineup	
5 R	2 D

In August 2001 six of the seven House incumbents (all except John Cooksey, who was running for the Senate) submitted to the legislature their own plan. Governor Mike Foster called a special session for redistricting in October, and the legislators made minor tweaks in the House incumbents' plan. It was opposed by the Black Legislative Caucus, which drew up a plan with a second black-majority district stretching from Lafayette and Baton Rouge along the Mississippi River to the Arkansas border. But it was rejected by solid margins. Foster signed the new plan in October; it certainly seemed likely to be upheld by the courts, since the Supreme Court had already approved an almost identical plan. It was submitted to the Justice Department in January 2002 and approved in April. Unexpectedly, the plan turned out to have an effect on the results. In the December 2002 runoff, Democrat Rodney Alexander won an upset victory for Cooksey's old seat. His margin of victory came from heavily black areas added to the district.

Governor

Mike Foster (R)

Elected 1995, term expires Jan. 2004, 2d term; b. July 11, 1930, Shreveport; home, Franklin; LA St. U., B.S. 1951; Episcopalian; married (Alice).

Military Career: Air Force, 1952–55 (Korea), Air Force Reserves, 1955–59.

Elected Office: LA Senate, 1987–95.

Professional Career: Farmer; Pres., M.J. Foster Inc.; Pres., Sterling Sugars, Inc.; Partner, Maryland Corp.; Owner, Oaklawn Manor.

Office: State Capitol, P.O. Box 94004, Baton Rouge, 70804, 225-342-0991; Fax: 225-342-7099; Web site: www.gov.state.la.us.

Election Results

1999 primary	Mike Foster (R)	805,203	(62%)
	William Jefferson (D)	382,445	(30%)
	Other	107,557	(8%)
1995 general	Mike Foster (R)	984,499	(64%)
	Cleo Fields (D)	565,861	(36%)
1995 primary	Mike Foster (R)	385,267	(26%)
	Cleo Fields (D)	280,921	(19%)
	Mary Landrieu (D)	271,938	(18%)
	Buddy Roemer (R)	263,330	(18%)
	Phil Preis (D)	133,271	(9%)
	Melinda Schwegmann (D)	71,288	(5%)
	Other	69,881	(5%)

Mike Foster, a Republican, was elected governor of Louisiana in November 1995 and reelected in October 1999. He grew up in Franklin, in St. Mary Parish, in the Cajun country near the Gulf; he served in the Air Force and founded a contracting firm and served as president of Sterling Sugars. He is a large landowner who loves duck hunting, piloting helicopters and riding tractors; a critic of trial lawyers, he started taking law school classes in August 2000, at 70. He was elected to the state Senate in 1987, and in 1991 was appointed chairman of the Commerce Committee. He portrays himself as an amateur in politics, convincingly, given his penchant for blunt, impolitic statements; bald, with a mustache, he campaigned as "not just another pretty face." But he had a political pedigree: His grandfather Murphy Foster was governor from 1892–1900 and played a part in abolishing Louisiana's graft-ridden lottery.

Foster ran in 1995 as a not very well-known candidate in a large field; he switched parties in mid-campaign. A gambling opponent, he pledged to hold a referendum on video poker (operators had been caught bribing legislators), riverboat gambling (allowed in many parishes) and the New Orleans land-based casino. At first he attracted little attention. Former Governor Buddy Roemer seemed to be the leading Republican, brandishing a Contract with Louisiana and criticizing New Orleans as "Cape Fear." Congressman Cleo Fields was the one well-known black candidate, but New Orleans Mayor Marc Morial, who is black, endorsed both Fields and Democratic State Treasurer Mary Landrieu. Landrieu called for cleaning up Louisiana; she was running ahead of Lieutenant Governor Melinda Schwegmann, whose family owned New Orleans's biggest supermarket chain. Foster surged ahead in fall campaigning, and in the October 21 primary led with 26%. There was almost a three-way tie for second place. Fields edged into second place with 19%, to 18.4% for Landrieu and 17.8% for Roemer. In the runoff against Fields, Foster called for a vast consolidation of state agencies and reform of state education and welfare. Fields said he would get tough on juvenile crime and accused Foster of "race baiting" after Foster referred to "that jungle in New Orleans." Foster won 64% to Fields's 36% and took 84% of the white vote, while Fields took 96% of the black vote.

In his first term, Foster pushed through a food tax cut and a $25 per child tax credit; he increased teacher salaries and initiated a school-based accountability system. Foster's job rating for three years hovered around 75%, and he took his own political course at every turn. He pushed for initiatives and referenda, unpopular with just about every other Louisiana official. Endorsed by Patrick Buchanan in October 1995, he announced he was voting for Buchanan just before the February 1996 caucus, in which Buchanan won his upset victory. Foster declined in 1995 to disclaim his endorsement by David Duke; it was revealed in May 1999 that his campaign purchased Duke's mailing list for $150,000, for which it was fined $20,000. Foster's actions do not always produce the results he wants: the gambling referenda he sponsored in November 1996 resulted in approval of all proposed casinos and a big New Orleans turnout which may have elected Landrieu to the Senate.

Foster entered election year 1999 an overwhelming favorite. His only well-known opponent was New Orleans Congressman Bill Jefferson, who raised $2.2 million but who, as an urban black with a liberal voting record, was not well positioned. Foster won the October primary with 62% of the vote, well over the 50% required to win; Jefferson had 30%, carrying New Orleans and one rural parish. In the new year Foster faced fiscal problems, a shortfall in revenue and no apparent way to keep his promises to raise teacher's pay to the regional average and to alleviate poverty with early childhood education and job training. In April 2000 he persuaded the legislature to accept his plans to renew a temporary 3 cent sales tax on food and utilities and to convert the state economic development commission to a private agency, but it was rejected 68%–32% by voters in November. In May he proposed a net $700 million tax increase, with new business taxes; legislative leaders were aghast, and instead passed a fourth cent on the sales tax on food and utilities. In November 2000 voters rejected Foster's two-pronged tax package, which would have eliminated the 4 cent tax and raised most income taxes. Scrambling for revenue to raise pay for teachers, who were refusing to show up for work, Foster made a deal with Harrah's Casino; the state would lower its $100 million minimum tax payment (Harrah's threatened to close down otherwise) combined with a tax on riverboat casinos which would fund a $2,000 raise for teachers and college professors. This passed, and two crises were at least temporarily averted; voters also seemed pleased with the plan, Foster's job approval rating had bounced back to 62% in April 2001. In 2002 he got the legislature to extend for 10 years the temporary food and utility taxes and to put in place a formula that would reduce taxes in line with the growth in the state's general fund. To attract new businesses, he got the legislature to pass tax credits for biotech, technological and customized software investments. In February 2003 he proposed a pilot program of school vouchers and state takeover of failing schools, most of them in New Orleans.

Louisiana elects a new governor in 2003; candidates of all parties compete in the October primary and then, if no one gets 50% of the vote, the top two finishers regardless of party compete in the November runoff. In early 2003 a runoff seemed a certainty, since five Democrats and seven Republicans were running what looked like serious campaigns. Early polls showed that none of them was a frontrunner. They might as well be listed in alphabetical order, Republicans first. Public Service Commissioner Jay Blossman, from St. Tammany Parish, who said, "We can't sell the state until we change how we tax business"; state Senator Hunt Downer; state Senate President John Hainkel, who called for taxing offshore oil; state Senator Ken Hollis, who called for slot machines at racetracks; Bobby Jindal, appointed by Foster at 24 as head of the Department of Health and Hospitals and later as head of the University of Louisiana system, and appointed by George W. Bush as HHS Assistant Secretary; former Congressman Bob Livingston; state Senator Tony Perkins, a Christian conservative who ran for senator in 2002; Auditor Dan Kyle, who criticized other Republican legislators in the race as tax and spenders and said the state was facing "a bottomless pit" of fiscal disaster; and former Governor David Treen. Lieutenant Governor Kathleen Blanco, who led one poll with 14%; former state Senate President Randy Ewing, who argued that programs can be funded without additional taxes; Attorney General Richard Ieyoub, who favored increasing the cigarette tax from 50 cents to $1; Treasurer John Kennedy, who argued that programs can be funded without additional taxes and spent $250,000 of his own money; and former state Representative and one-term (1979–81) Congressman Buddy Leach, who favored new taxes on the oil and gas industry, increased taxes on gambling and a minimum wage increase;

he loaned his campaign $1.39 million by March 2003 and started running TV ads in December 2002.

Senior Senator

John Breaux (D)

Elected 1986, seat up 2004, 3d term; b. Mar. 1, 1944, Crowley; home, Lafayette; U. of SW LA, B.A. 1964, LA St. U., J.D. 1967; Catholic; married (Lois).

Elected Office: U.S. House of Reps., 1972–87.

Professional Career: Practicing atty., 1967–68; Legis. Asst. & Dist. Mgr., U.S. Rep. Edwin W. Edwards, 1968–72.

DC Office: 503 HSOB, 20510, 202-224-4623; Fax: 202-228-2577; Web site: breaux.senate.gov.

State Offices: Baton Rouge, 225-248-0104; Lafayette, 337-262-6871; Monroe, 318-325-3320; New Orleans, 504-589-2531.

Committees: *Aging (Special)* (RMM). *Commerce, Science & Transportation*: Aviation; Communications; Oceans, Fisheries & Coast Guard; Science, Technology & Space (RMM); Surface Transportation & Merchant Marine. *Finance*: Health Care; Social Security & Family Policy (RMM); Taxation & IRS Oversight. *Rules & Administration*.

Group Ratings

	ADA	ACLU	AFS	LCV	CON	ITIC	NTU	COC	ACU	NTLC	CHC
2002	65	50	88	18	1	62	29	79	42	26	—
2001	55	—	50	25	—	—	42	71	48	—	80

National Journal Ratings

	2001 LIB	—	2001 CONS		2002 LIB	—	2002 CONS
Economic	47%	—	49%		46%	—	51%
Social	46%	—	54%		55%	—	44%
Foreign	51%	—	43%		47%	—	52%

Key Votes of the 107th Congress

1. Approve Bush Tax Cuts	Y	5. Confirm Ashcroft as AG	Y
2. Expand Patients' Rights	Y	6. Bar Gays in the Boy Scouts	Y
3. Campaign Finance Reform	N	7. $ for Hate Crime Prosecution	Y
4. Permit ANWR Development	Y	8. Overseas Military Abortions	*

9. Bar Coop. with Intl. Court	Y
10. Trade Promotion Authority	Y
11. Authorize Force in Iraq	Y
12. Homeland Sec. Dept. Union	Y

Election Results

1998 primary	John Breaux (D)	620,502	(64%)	($3,858,472)
	Jim Donelon (R)	306,616	(32%)	($364,073)
	Other	42,047	(4%)	
1992 primary	John Breaux (D)	616,021	(73%)	($2,007,675)
	Jon Khachaturian (I)	74,785	(9%)	($94,919)
	Lyle Stockstill (R)	69,986	(8%)	($34,711)
	Nick Accardo (D)	45,839	(6%)	
	Fred Clegg Strong (R)	36,406	(4%)	

Prior Winning Percentages: 1986 (53%); 1984 House (86%); 1982 House (79%); 1980 House (100%); 1978 House (60%); 1976 House (83%); 1974 House (89%); 1972 House (100%); 1972 House (55%)

John Breaux, once the youngest member of Congress, is a Democrat first elected to the House in 1972 and to the Senate in 1986. He grew up in the politically fertile soil of the Acadia Parish seat of Crowley in Cajun country, the only child of a dressmaker and an oil field worker who spoke French before he spoke English. After graduating from LSU law school, he practiced law for a year, then got a job with a young congressman from Crowley named Edwin Edwards. When Edwards was elected governor in 1972, Breaux ran for Congress and won the seat, at 28. Quietly in the House, more publicly in the Senate, he became a natural dealmaker, with contacts developed everywhere from the tennis court (he is one of Congress's best players) to the Democratic Leadership Council to Mardi Gras in New Orleans (where he performs every year playing a washboard). His views on issues have a Louisiana Cajun accent: market-oriented with populist twists on economics, culturally conservative and strongly anti-abortion in the Louisiana mode. He has encouraged people to think of him as a cynical dealmaker: "I'd always rather have half of something than 100% of nothing," he likes to say. But over time it has become apparent that he does have a core of beliefs and has developed strong principles on issues he has worked hard on.

After serving 14 years in the House, Breaux took the political gamble of his life and ran for the Senate. These were the Reagan years, and Republicans were advancing in the House, and the Republican candidate, Congressman Henson Moore, was ahead in polls and led in the all-party primary. But Breaux held him under 50% and then overtook him in the runoff. In the Senate, Democrats had regained the majority, and Breaux compiled a middle-of-the-road voting record and a bent toward bipartisan coalitions. He was chosen chief deputy whip in 1993 and was mentioned as a candidate for majority leader when George Mitchell retired in 1994; instead he supported Tom Daschle. He was less successful in influencing the Clinton administration. He opposed the 1993 Clinton stimulus package and the Btu tax, and helped defeat both. As the administration moved to the center after the 1994 elections, Breaux had more successes.

In 1998 Breaux became a major force for reform of entitlements and health care. With Judd Gregg he introduced the CSIS Social Security reform, with 2% of income in individual investment accounts. In January 1998 he was named chairman of the bipartisan commission on Medicare, and labored for more than a year with Republican Bill Thomas and others to come up with a bipartisan plan. Breaux modeled his approach on the Federal Employees Health Benefit Plan; he would allow Medicare recipients to choose from an array of choices of competitive health care plans and provide them with a specific amount of "premium support" to buy into a plan; most plans would include prescription drug benefits. He got bipartisan support, from the Republican appointees and Senator Bob Kerrey, but was one vote short of the 11 required for an official recommendation to Congress.

On Medicare, Breaux is at his most uncynical. "The good news is that people are living longer. The bad news is that people are living longer. It's a challenge. And if we don't figure out how to handle it, it becomes a problem." With Republican Bill Frist he prepared two legislative versions of his Medicare Commission proposal, in 1999 and 2000. In January 2000 he proposed a tax credit for the uninsured. Breaux opposed a stand-alone prescription drug benefit as unworkable; in June 2000 he was the only Democratic senator who voted against the Democrats' drug benefit, saying it was "good politics but bad policy." In the 2000 campaign George W. Bush endorsed something much like Breaux-Frist as the centerpiece of his Medicare proposal, but Breaux criticized it, opposing Bush's proposal for aid to state prescription drug benefit plans and arguing that the Bush tax cut would take up funds needed for Medicare changes.

After the November 2000 election, Breaux was the first Democrat who went to Austin to talk with George W. Bush. He urged him not to start off emphasizing Medicare or Social Security, but to start with education reform, on which the parties could get used to working together. He voted with Bush and Republicans on several key issues. In January he was one of eight Democrats to vote to confirm John Ashcroft; in February he was chief co-sponsor with Frank Murkowski of the bill to allow oil drilling in the Arctic National Wildlife Refuge; he was one of three Democrats who opposed the McCain-Feingold campaign finance bill, arguing openly that it would hurt Democratic chances. On taxes he stayed obdurately centrist. With 15 other senators, including a couple of Republicans, he resisted Bush's $1.6 trillion tax cut which failed by one vote; then he and others agreed on a $1.35 trillion cut, which passed 65–35. Some Democrats would have gone higher; Breaux kept the cut down. In November 2001, with several other moderates he proposed a compromise, with both business tax cuts and increased aid to the unemployed, on the post-September 11 stimulus package.

On HMO regulation, Breaux joined Bill Frist and Jim Jeffords on a bill to would expand patient's rights but not the right to sue employers; but a more expansive bill supported by John McCain, Edward Kennedy and John Edwards passed the Senate. On prescription drugs, he and

Olympia Snowe and Jim Jeffords produced a "tripartisan" plan; Breaux opposed the Democrats' version because he wanted broader changes in Medicare, believed it would get Congress micromanaging the prices of drugs and said its cost was indeterminable. Tom Daschle prevented the tripartisan bill from going forward in the Finance Committee, where with Breaux's vote it had a majority; it, like other prescription drug plans, failed to get the 60 votes required to pass in July 2002. On major entitlements, Breaux made little progress. In July 2001 he and Gregg reiterated their support of changes in Social Security. But Democrats soon were busy campaigning against change, and Republicans feared to bring the issue forward. On Medicare, Breaux and other moderates called for a plan that would give recipients three options, including the current program with a prescription drug benefit, a new fee-for-service program with deductibles for hospital and physician services and a Medicare HMO with defined benefits. But in January 2003 Breaux reacted negatively to George W. Bush's rather vague call for major changes in Medicare. And in January 2003 Breaux called for universal health care, going farther than he had before. He proposed that all Americans get a government-defined basic insurance package similar to that provided by the Federal Employee Health Benefit Plan, with subsidies through tax credits for lower- and middle-income recipients. He reacted negatively to the tax cuts George W. Bush proposed in January 2003, and by April had made no move to advance a compromise proposal as he had in 2001.

Breaux has stayed busy on less high-profile issues. One focus is wetlands: the Breaux Act, providing $40 million a year to protect and rebuild wetlands, funded by user fees on small boat engines and motor fuel; he hailed the approval of a Red River National Wildlife Refuge in Louisiana. He serves on the Migratory Bird Commission. In January 2003 he added to the omnibus appropriation $13.5 million for emergency and disaster relief to Louisiana oyster and shrimp producers. With Charles Grassley and John McCain he sponsored a bill in 2002 to increase trade with Turkey.

During summer 2001 Breaux mused aloud about running for governor and noted that if he didn't run in 2003 at 57 he probably never would. In January 2002 he ruled out a race. In early 2003 he said he hadn't decided to run for reelection in 2004. If he runs he is considered sure to win, probably with only weak opposition, as he did in 1992 and 1998. If he should surprise Washington and decide not to run, the race would be wide open. In early 2003 the most likely competitors seemed to be House members, Republican David Vitter and Democrat Chris John. But Louisiana's governor race may produce other contenders: Bennett Johnston was elected to the Senate here in 1972 just after he had narrowly lost the governor's race to Edwin Edwards, and Mary Landrieu was elected in 1996 a year after she ran unsuccessfully for governor.

Junior Senator

Mary Landrieu (D)

Elected 1996, seat up 2008, 2d term; b. Nov. 23, 1955, Arlington, VA; home, New Orleans; LA St. U., B.A. 1977; Catholic; married (Frank Snellings).

Elected Office: LA House of Reps., 1979–88; LA Treasurer, 1987–96.

DC Office: 724 HSOB, 20510, 202-224-5824; Fax: 202-224-9735; Web site: landrieu.senate.gov.

State Offices: Baton Rouge, 225-389-0395; Lake Charles, 337-436-6650; New Orleans, 504-589-2427; Shreveport, 318-676-3085.

Committees: *Appropriations*: Agriculture & Rural Development; District of Columbia (RMM); Foreign Operations; Labor, HHS & Education; Military Construction. *Energy & Natural Resources*: Energy; National Parks; Public Lands & Forests. *Small Business & Entrepreneurship.*

Group Ratings

	ADA	ACLU	AFS	LCV	CON	ITIC	NTU	COC	ACU	NTLC	CHC
2002	70	75	75	12	23	88	26	84	35	15	—
2001	85	—	75	38	—	—	24	69	28	—	20

National Journal Ratings

	2001 LIB — 2001 CONS		2002 LIB — 2002 CONS	
Economic	56%	44%	51%	48%
Social	59%	41%	64%	34%
Foreign	51%	43%	53%	46%

Key Votes of the 107th Congress

1. Approve Bush Tax Cuts	Y	5. Confirm Ashcroft as AG	N	9. Bar Coop. with Intl. Court	Y
2. Expand Patients' Rights	Y	6. Bar Gays in the Boy Scouts	N	10. Trade Promotion Authority	Y
3. Campaign Finance Reform	Y	7. $ for Hate Crime Prosecution	Y	11. Authorize Force in Iraq	Y
4. Permit ANWR Development	Y	8. Overseas Military Abortions	Y	12. Homeland Sec. Dept. Union	Y

Election Results

2002 runoff	Mary Landrieu (D)	638,654	(52%)	($7,384,554)
	Suzanne Haik Terrell (R)	596,642	(48%)	($2,760,276)
2002 primary	Mary Landrieu (D)	573,347	(46%)	
	Suzanne Haik Terrell (R)	339,506	(27%)	
	John Cooksey (R)	171,752	(14%)	
	Tony Perkins (R)	119,776	(10%)	
	Other	41,952	(3%)	
1996 general	Mary Landrieu (D)	852,945	(50%)	($2,504,815)
	Louis (Woody) Jenkins (R)	847,157	(50%)	($1,878,242)
1990 primary	J. Bennett Johnston (D)	752,902	(54%)	($5,389,624)
	David Duke (R)	607,391	(44%)	($2,615,267)
	Other	35,820	(3%)	

Mary Landrieu, a Democrat, was elected to the Senate in 1996 and reelected in 2002. Landrieu grew up in New Orleans, the oldest of nine children of Moon Landrieu (all with names starting with M), mayor of New Orleans in the 1970s. She was educated at Ursuline Academy and LSU and in 1979, at 23, became the youngest woman ever elected to the Louisiana state legislature, where she was sometimes the object of undue ridicule. In 1987 she was elected state Treasurer; she was a sharp critic of Governor Edwin Edwards and opposed gambling as "political cancer." In 1995 she ran for governor, and in the September primary finished third, just 1% and 8,983 votes behind second-place finisher Congressman Cleo Fields. She immediately started running for the Senate seat held by Bennett Johnston, who was retiring 24 years after he was elected to the Senate after a narrow loss in a governor's race.

With a well-known name and a moderate platform—for a balanced budget amendment and capital gains tax cut, promising to make education a top priority—Landrieu shared a lead in the polls with Attorney General Richard Ieyoub, also a Democrat; under Louisiana law if they finished in the top two in the September primary, they would meet in a November runoff, and Democrats would be guaranteed a win no matter what. This was an alarming situation for Republicans, who had no such well-known candidate and who believed that they could win the seat if they could get someone into the runoff. Stepping forward to fill the gap was Woody Jenkins, a 25-year state legislator and strong abortion opponent, who had run twice unsuccessfully for the Senate as a Democrat. In August he claimed the party endorsement; he surged in the polls, and led the September 21 primary with 26%, to 22% for Landrieu and 20% for Ieyoub; David Duke got 12%.

At this point Jenkins looked like the favorite; Republican candidates had won 55% of the total votes and Democrats only 44%. But he had little money left, and Landrieu, who ultimately outspent him, ran ads attacking him as an extremist. Jenkins attacked her for opposing abortion restrictions and supporting gay rights. Landrieu had to spend much time getting support from blacks, since many were unhappy that she had given only nominal support to Cleo Fields for governor in 1995. Gambling interests, who were busy trying to increase black turnout in New Orleans and elsewhere for their gambling referenda, also threw their support to Landrieu.

The result was an exceedingly close election. The official results showed Landrieu ahead by 5,788 votes, 50.2%–49.8%. Jenkins filed a lawsuit claiming vote fraud, but withdrew it, and submitted his case to the Senate. At the behest of Majority Leader Trent Lott, the Senate seated Landrieu "without prejudice" to Jenkins's challenge. To the Senate Rules Committee Jenkins submitted evidence that more votes were counted in many New Orleans precincts than the number of voters who signed in, and that campaign operatives ferried in ineligible voters. But in June, it was revealed that one of Jenkins's witnesses was a convicted felon, and several others retracted their testimony. Democrats protested, and Landrieu was bitter, but Rules Chairman John Warner continued the hearings. Finally in October 1997 the committee voted unanimously to end the inquiry. While concluding that "isolated instances" of voter fraud did occur, Warner said there was no evidence to prove that there was a "widespread effort to illegally affect the outcome of this election," or that Landrieu had any involvement in the violation of election laws.

In the Senate, Landrieu has a generally moderate voting record, a little more liberal than that of colleague John Breaux. Her first bill was for a $5 million block grant for adoption services; her two children are adopted. She backs adoption tax credits and wants higher breaks for those who adopt special needs or foster children. She was the lead co-sponsor of the law providing for speedy citizenship for foreign-born children adopted by U.S. citizens; when it went into effect it created the largest number of new U.S. citizens ever on a single day.

Landrieu was one of four Democrats voting for the $792 billion Republican tax cut in July 1999, and one of eight to vote for marriage penalty repeal in July 2000. She voted for the $1.35 trillion compromise tax cut in May 2001. But she voted against the confirmation of John Ashcroft in February 2001. She was the only Democrat who joined in co-sponsoring Sam Brownback's bill to prohibit human cloning for reproduction or research. In January 2001 Landrieu won a seat on the Appropriations Committee. In 2002 she announced many Louisiana projects, including creation of the Red River National Wildlife Refuge, and $500,000 for museum exhibits commemorating the Louisiana Purchase of 1803. In January 2003 she put into the omnibus appropriation $10 million a year for five years to help historically black colleges and universities renovate their historic buildings.

All the while she was running hard for reelection in 2002. She was an obvious Republican target, because of the closeness of her margin in 1996 and because George W. Bush carried Louisiana in 2000. In early 2001 the only active Republican candidate was 5th District Congressman John Cooksey, a north Louisiana ophthalmologist. But on September 18, 2001, a week after September 11, in a radio interview in Louisiana, he said, "If I see someone comes in that's got a diaper on his head and a fan belt wrapped around the diaper on his head, the guy needs to be pulled over." He acknowledged that this was "racial profiling," but said, "When you've got a group of people who are not American citizens, who are of Arab descent and they were involved in killing 5,000 Americans. . . . I think we can and should scrutinize people that fit that profile until this war on terrorism is over." Cooksey spent $200,000 on radio ads defending his comments.

Cooksey's candidacy was undone by one word, "diaper." It was obvious that the Bush White House did not want to have the president portrayed as supporting a candidate whose remark would be an embarrassment to the United States in the Middle East. For such a candidate no flow of Republican money and no presidential visits would be forthcoming. Louisiana has a late filing deadline, and other Republicans started thinking about running. The NRSC, headed by Bill Frist, started encouraging other Republicans to run. In May 2002 state Representative Tony Perkins, a sponsor of a school prayer bill, met with Frist and decided to run. Perkins telegraphed Frist's strategy. "Republicans' best shot is to get a multiple field of candidates in this race. If we can get Landrieu in a runoff, it will be like the Coverdell runoff [in Georgia] in 1992. This is our seat." Perkins also encouraged Elections Commissioner Suzanne Haik Terrell to run. "I would like to see Suzie Terrell in the race because she would draw votes from Mary in New Orleans." Terrell was elected to the New Orleans Council in 1994 and in 1999 she ousted longtime state Elections Commissioner Jerry Fowler and in the runoff beat none other than Woody Jenkins. There she pushed through legislation to abolish her office. Terrell had been mentioned as a candidate for Senate, but during the spring seemed uninterested; she did not announce until July 9.

In July the NRSC started running what would eventually be $2 million of TV ads against

Landrieu. "There's just something about Mary and higher taxes," said one. "Landrieu voted in favor of higher taxes over 120 times." Landrieu seemed further imperiled in July when Cleo Fields said he was thinking about running and might spend $1 million of his own money. "There is no secret that Mary Landrieu was not respectful to the black community," he said, no doubt referring to the 1995 governor campaign. But Fields bowed out in early August. Playing defense, Landrieu ran ads saying she supported Bush 74% of the time and that only two Democrats, Zell Miller and John Breaux, had voted more often with Bush. At the end of August Frist announced that the NRSC would support Terrell and spend the allowed $464,000 on her behalf. His strategy was obviously to hold Landrieu below 50% in November, and he evidently calculated, as Perkins had, that Terrell, a New Orleans Catholic, was better positioned than the two north Louisiana Protestants to take votes away from Landrieu in the New Orleans area. Other Republicans were angry. Mike Foster, who had considered running himself up to the August 23 filing deadline, endorsed Cooksey. Later Foster said, "I didn't like that the nationals came down here and took over the race and gave all the money to one candidate."

In mid-October Landrieu started running anti-Terrell ads, charging that taxes and spending went up in New Orleans when she was on the Council. Perkins ran ads attacking Landrieu for living in a "Washington mansion"; she said she wanted to be close to her small children. The NRSC ran ads saying that Landrieu's voting record was similar to Hillary Rodham Clinton's. On November 5, as Republicans were gaining a majority in the Senate by picking up seats in Georgia, Minnesota and Missouri, Landrieu failed to clinch a victory. She won 46% of the vote, to 27% for Terrell, 14% for Cooksey and 10% for Perkins. The three Republicans together led Landrieu 51%–46%.

If Republicans had picked up only one seat in November and had lost one seat, as they did, in Arkansas, all eyes would have moved now to Louisiana, for the race would have determined which party would have the majority in the Senate. Now it would just determine whether the Republican majority would be 51–49 or 52–48: important but not world-shaking. On the Democratic side there was discontent among black leaders about Landrieu's ads proclaiming her 74% support of Bush, and there was some indication that black turnout was low. Cleo Fields said, "All that talk about supporting the president turned my stomach."

In debates the two candidates tangled about abortion. In one debate Terrell said, "I'm 100% pro-life. As a practicing Catholic, I did not leave my faith, as did Mary Landrieu." Her reference was to Landrieu's votes for taxpayer funding of abortions. Landrieu replied, "I have a good relationship with my God and my savior. I respect life. At least I'm consistent in my positon, not like Ms. Terrell, who has had four positions on this issue in the past four weeks." After another debate, on leaving the TV studio Landrieu said to Terrell, "This is your last campaign." Terrell, taken aback, said "She threatened me." The candidates continued to argue about tax cuts, personnel rules for the Department of Homeland Security and privatizing government jobs. Then a Democratic opposition researcher made a propitious find—an article in the Mexican center-left newspaper *Reforma* reporting that the Bush administration had agreed with the Mexican government to double the amount of sugar that could be imported from Mexico. The Office of Special Trade Representative and the State Department denied that any such agreement had been made. But Landrieu trumpeted the claim in ads and promised to do everything she could to stop any such agreement. Sugar is a heavily protected crop, with U.S. prices kept at levels three times the world price; Louisiana is the prime cane sugar producing state. Even so, the issue does not affect huge numbers of people—there are perhaps 32,000 Louisianans involved in sugar production or processing.

But it was a fine issue for Landrieu to document her claim that Terrell would be a "rubber stamp" for Bush, even though Terrell said she opposed any such deal as well. It turned out the *Reforma* story was wrong; Landrieu met with trade and State Department officials in January 2003 and reported that there was no deal. But it may have changed enough votes to give Landrieu her 52%–48% victory.

Landrieu also owed her victory to a money advantage and to good turnout efforts. National Republicans spent $6.3 million in Louisiana to national Democrats' $4.6 million, but the Landrieu campaign spent $7.4 million and the late-starting Terrell campaign only $2.8 million.

FIRST DISTRICT

Rep. David Vitter (R)

Elected May 1999, 2d term; b. May 3, 1961, New Orleans; home, Metairie; Harvard U., A.B. 1983, Rhodes Scholar, Oxford U., B.A. 1985, Tulane Law Schl., J.D. 1988; Catholic; married (Wendy).

Elected Office: LA House of Reps., 1991–99.

Professional Career: Practicing atty., 1988–99; Adjunct Law Prof., Tulane U. & Loyola U., 1995–98.

DC Office: 414 CHOB 20515, 202-225-3015; Fax: 202-225-0739; Web site: www.house.gov/vitter.

District Offices: Hammond, 985-542-9616; Metairie, 504-589-2753.

Committees: *Appropriations* (30th of 36 R): Commerce, Justice, State & Judiciary (Vice Chmn.); Foreign Operations & Export Financing; Military Construction. *Budget* (16th of 24 R).

Group Ratings

	ADA	ACLU	AFS	LCV	CON	ITIC	NTU	COC	ACU	NTLC	CHC
2002	0	7	0	0	25	88	59	95	100	94	100
2001	0	—	0	0	—	—	66	100	100	—	—

National Journal Ratings

	2001 LIB —	2001 CONS	2002 LIB —	2002 CONS
Economic	0% —	94%	0% —	91%
Social	0% —	81%	0% —	75%
Foreign	14% —	85%	0% —	85%

Key Votes of the 107th Congress

1. Approve Bush Tax Cuts	Y	5. Faith-Based Charities	Y	9. Trade Promotion Authority	Y
2. Limit Patients' Bill of Rights	Y	6. Bar Gays in the Boy Scouts	Y	10. Bar Funds for Intl. Court	Y
3. Campaign Finance Reform	N	7. Ban Partial-Birth Abortion	Y	11. Authorize Force in Iraq	Y
4. Ban ANWR Development	N	8. Arm Commercial Pilots	Y	12. Deny Home. Sec. Dept. Union	Y

Election Results

2002 primary	David Vitter (R)	147,117	(81%)	($1,703,084)
	Monica Monica (R)	20,268	(11%)	
	Robert Namer (R)	7,229	(4%)	
	Other	5,956	(3%)	
2000 primary	David Vitter (R)	191,379	(80%)	($1,604,204)
	Michael A. Armato (D)	29,935	(13%)	
	Cary J. Deaton (D)	10,982	(5%)	
	Other	5,514	(2%)	
1999 spec. runoff	David Vitter (R)	61,661	(51%)	($807,505)
	David Treen (R)	59,849	(49%)	($494,789)

The People		Race/Ethnic Origin	Ancestry	
Area size:	2,840 sq. mi.	79.6% White	French: 13.3%	German: 10.9%
Urban population:	79.6%	12.8% Black	Irish: 9.4%	
Rural population:	20.4%	1.5% Asian	**2000 Presidential Vote**	
Pop. 2000:	638,355	0.3% Native Am.	Bush (R) 179,196 (66%)	
Median income:	$40,948	0.0% Hawaiian	Gore (D) 83,779 (31%)	
Poverty status:	12.1%	1.0% Two+ races	Other 6,650 (2%)	
Military veterans:	13.1%	0.1% Other	**Cook Partisan Voting Index:** R +18	
		4.7% Hispanic Origin		

Occupation	Blue collar: 20.2%	White collar: 65.3%	Gray collar: 14.5%

New Orleans, founded in 1718, the nation's fifth-largest city at the outbreak of the Civil War, is ancient for an American metropolis; yet it is still closely girded by the peculiar wilderness of the mushy Delta lands of the sluggish Mississippi River. Climb a levee overlooking the Mississippi and you will see an expanse of water with untidy clumps of trees and disorganized-looking, seemingly abandoned docks—what Mark Twain had in his mind's eye while writing *Life on the Mississippi* in the 1870s. Or drive just past the last block of a suburban subdivision, and you are in unreclaimed swamp, vegetation and wetness, thick with herons and alligators, flat as far as the eye can see. For years the river has funneled the products of half a continent down to a single port with an international heritage and flair; the New Orleans metropolitan area is still living off that geography and history, with an inward-looking elite preoccupied with who is in which Mardi Gras krewe and interested more in old families' genealogy than in Oil Patch geology. The old buildings of New Orleans are finely proportioned and its old neighborhoods charming, like those in France; and its early 20th century improvements, like Olmstead's City Park, are grand. But its middle and late 20th century streetscapes and subdivisions, like those of France, are without ornament or charm, utilitarian works of man made to master the below-sea-level environment.

The 1st Congressional District includes much of the newer part of the New Orleans metropolitan area, spread over the soggy lands of the lower Mississippi and Lake Pontchartrain. A bit less than half of its people live in affluent white neighborhoods in New Orleans, in the Uptown area and west of City Park, in mostly white neighborhoods on the West Bank of the Mississippi opposite New Orleans and in the vast suburb of Metairie in Jefferson Parish, divided by slanting grids and elevated only where bridges jut out over the many canals. It also includes part of suburbanizing St. Charles Parish to the west. The boundaries have been drawn so that the next-door 2d District has a black majority; the black percentage in the 1st, 13%, is the lowest of any Louisiana district. The 1st extends across the 26-mile Lake Pontchartrain Causeway to include St. Tammany Parish, the state's fastest-growing areas, with old towns lush with trees and clusters of new growth around giant intersections; it also includes, to the north and west, Washington and Tangipahoa Parishes, still mostly rural country. Altogether 53% of the district's population is north of the Lake: much of New Orleans has moved across Lake Pontchartrain. This is the most upscale, affluent, highly educated district in Louisiana, and by far the most Republican, supportive of political reformers and against economic redistribution. George W. Bush got 66% of the vote here in 2000.

The congressman from the 1st District is David Vitter, a Republican first chosen in a May 1999 special election. He grew up in the New Orleans area, graduated from Harvard and Tulane Law School and was a Rhodes Scholar. He was a business attorney and taught law at Tulane and Loyola. Vitter was elected in 1991 to the state House, where he passed a term-limits bill through a reluctant state legislature. Slim and boyish-looking, he is noted for his ability to irritate other politicians; many were enraged by his crusade for term limits, and a popular sheriff sued him three times after Vitter criticized his ethics.

The chance to run for Congress came suddenly. When Newt Gingrich was forced to retire as speaker three days after the 1998 election, 1st District Congressman and Appropriations Committee Chairman Bob Livingston quickly rounded up the votes and became Speaker-designate. But six weeks later, as the House was debating impeachment, Livingston confessed that he had had affairs and stunned everyone by announcing that he was resigning, even as he called on Bill Clinton to do so. Many Republicans jumped into the race, but the chief preoccupation of the national press, and the chief fear of Louisiana and national Republicans, was that former Ku Klux Klansman David Duke would run and make it into the runoff. This seemed a bit farfetched, since his career peaked almost a decade before, and his 1998 book *My Awakening* that asserted, "belief in racial equality is the modern equivalent of believing the earth is flat," was gathering dust on bookshelves. The establishment choice was David Treen, 70, who won four terms in the House starting in 1972 and was elected governor in 1979. In contrast, Vitter said, "We need a younger congressman like me, so we can start building up the seniority we lost when Bob Livingston resigned." Treen, with 25%, and Vitter, with 22%, advanced to the runoff. Duke, unnervingly close to making the runoff, finished third with 19%. Subtle differences emerged during the runoff: Vitter denounced all forms of gun control; Treen said he supported some restrictions on more sophisticated automatic or semiautomatic weapons and would require dealers at gun shows to perform background checks. Both opposed racial quotas and preferences but Treen also said the federal government should not prevent colleges and universities from deciding their own racial admission policies. Low turnout was probably a factor, as Vitter rallied his troops and won 51%–49%.

In the House, Vitter has compiled the most conservative voting record in the delegation and one of the most conservative in the House. On the Appropriations Committee, like his predecessor he worked on local projects, including $140 million for clean-up of Lake Pontchartrain. After enactment in 2000 of the bill to require more disclosure of political activity by Section 527 tax-exempt groups, Vitter sought to relax the new rules, arguing they were burdensome at the state and local level; a scaled back version was approved in 2002. He enacted easier access to prescription drug coverage for military retirees and advocated aggressive controls of HMOs. When the House debated the education bill in 2001, it passed his amendment to require secondary schools that take federal money to allow military recruiters to visit the school. Vitter became a vigorous advocate of a national missile defense. After the House passed his amendment to block the Chinese government's purchase of land near the Pentagon, which he feared could become a "spy tower," the Chinese dropped their plans. He showed his maverick tendencies when he sought a new regional authority to replace the city's control of the New Orleans International Airport; that caused an angry battle within the Louisiana delegation on the House floor.

Vitter has twice won reelection with at least 80% of the vote. In 2002, one of his opponents was Republican Monica Monica, an ophthalmologist who spent $1.4 million in the 1999 special, including $900,000 of her own money, but only got 16%; this time, she spent far less and got 11%. Vitter considered running for governor in 2003, but decided not to.

SECOND DISTRICT

Rep. William Jefferson (D)

Elected 1990, 7th term; b. Mar. 14, 1947, Lake Providence; home, New Orleans; Southern U., B.A. 1969, Harvard U., J.D. 1972, Georgetown U., LL.M. 1996; Baptist; married (Andrea).

Military Career: Army Reserves, 1969–78, Army Judge Advocate Corps, 1975.

Elected Office: LA Senate, 1979–90.

Professional Career: Law clerk, U.S. Dist. Judge Alvin Rubin, 1972–73; Legis. aide, U.S. Sen. Bennett Johnston, 1973–75; Practicing atty., 1975–90.

DC Office: 240 CHOB 20515, 202-225-6636; Fax: 202-225-1988; Web site: www.house.gov/jefferson.

District Office: New Orleans, 504-589-2274.

Committees: *Ways & Means* (11th of 17 D): Select Revenue Measures; Trade.

Group Ratings

	ADA	ACLU	AFS	LCV	CON	ITIC	NTU	COC	ACU	NTLC	CHC
2002	75	79	75	50	60	75	26	58	20	6	17
2001	80	—	90	57	—	—	16	70	21	—	—

National Journal Ratings

	2001 LIB	—	2001 CONS		2002 LIB	—	2002 CONS
Economic	68%	—	32%		62%	—	37%
Social	79%	—	22%		66%	—	33%
Foreign	83%	—	18%		69%	—	30%

Key Votes of the 107th Congress

1. Approve Bush Tax Cuts	N	5. Faith-Based Charities	N	9. Trade Promotion Authority	Y
2. Limit Patients' Bill of Rights	N	6. Bar Gays in the Boy Scouts	N	10. Bar Funds for Intl. Court	N
3. Campaign Finance Reform	Y	7. Ban Partial-Birth Abortion	Y	11. Authorize Force in Iraq	Y
4. Ban ANWR Development	N	8. Arm Commercial Pilots	Y	12. Deny Home. Sec. Dept. Union	N

Election Results

2002 primary	William Jefferson (D)	90,310	(64%)	($1,049,231)
	Irma Dixon (D)	28,480	(20%)	
	Silky Sullivan (D)	15,440	(11%)	
	Other	7,926	(6%)	
2000 primary	William Jefferson (D)	unopposed		($563,238)
1998 primary	William Jefferson (D)	102,247	(86%)	($495,522)
	David Reed (D)	10,803	(9%)	
	Don-Terry Veal (D)	5,899	(5%)	($1,609)

Prior Winning Percentages: 1996 (100%); 1994 (75%); 1992 (73%); 1990 (52%)

The People		Race/Ethnic Origin	Ancestry	
Area size:	444 sq. mi.	28.3% White	French: 6.3%	German: 4.3%
Urban population:	99.4%	63.7% Black	Irish: 3.6%	
Rural population:	0.6%	2.7% Asian	**2000 Presidential Vote**	
Pop. 2000:	638,562	0.3% Native Am.	Gore (D) 165,587	(76%)
Median income:	$27,514	0.0% Hawaiian	Bush (R) 48,726	(22%)
Poverty status:	26.8%	1.0% Two + races	Other 4,457	(2%)
Military veterans:	10.9%	0.2% Other	**Cook Partisan Voting Index:** D +27	
		3.8% Hispanic Origin		

Occupation	Blue collar: 21.4%	White collar: 56.2%	Gray collar: 22.4%

Founded by the French in 1718, ruled by the Spanish from 1763 to just days before the French took over to sell it to the United States in 1803, New Orleans was a Creole city—part French, a bit Spanish, more than a touch Caribbean—when the American flag was raised over what is now Jackson Square. The statue of Andrew Jackson still seems an alien intrusion in a square set off by a French Market, the Cabildo, the Presbytere, the Pontalba apartments and Cathedral St. Louis. New Orleans was the fifth largest American city from 1840 until the Civil War and the only sizable city in the South; yet even as it was sending southern cotton out to the mills of Lancashire, it was an alien cultural force in both the nation and region. Urbanized, yet poor and in many ways primitive, New Orleans had yellow fever epidemics late in the 19th century, even as it was installing electric lights; it had a riot in which Italian immigrants were massacred, even as it was laying streetcar tracks and telephone lines. This was one of the most corrupt American cities during Reconstruction and the Gilded Age, when its votes were regularly bid for and bought; like other Southern cities, it became rigidly segregated after 1890.

For a time during the 1970s oil boom, New Orleans seemed to be a fast-growing Sun Belt city; in the middle 1980s, it reverted to its rougher traditions and was beset by woes big and small. Its port lost business—oil to Houston, and Latin American trade to Miami—though it still ships large amounts of grain. In the mid-1990s New Orleans took a turn for the better. Crime plummeted and no longer depressed tourism. Incomes went up and home ownership increased among blacks as well as whites. Harrah's Casino opened in 1999, and it got the state to lower its minimum tax payment. But people come to New Orleans for things other than gambling. They want to see the gaudy bars of Bourbon Street and the restored houses there and in the Garden District. They want to see Mardi Gras and the krewes that parade for weeks before. And they want to dine in New Orleans's array of restaurants, with a cuisine all New Orleans's own, spicy and rich and unaffected by today's taste for low-fat food.

The 2d Congressional District includes almost all of the city of New Orleans, everything except a few affluent white neighborhoods, plus nearly half of Jefferson Parish, black neighborhoods in Metairie and Kenner, the West Bank towns of Harvey, Marrero and Westwego, between the levee and the swamp. Here is the French Quarter—the *Vieux Carre*—its 19th century homes still intact because the Americans who moved here after 1803 wanted to stay away from the snobbish Creoles and then built a new downtown across Canal Street. North of the Quarter is the site of Storyville, where prostitution was legal until 1918 and where jazz was probably first played; the old frame houses have long since been torn down and replaced by half-empty and crime-ridden housing projects. But many similar neighborhoods remain, where blacks and some working-class whites live in rickety frame houses which are not always strong enough to keep the rain out and never tight enough to protect against the summer humidity or the damp winter chill, along the vividly named streets—Elysian Fields, Spain, Desire, Arts—that go north from the river wharves. South of the quarter is the downtown flecked with skyscrapers and the ominous Superdome, and to the east is the old slum known as the Irish Channel—a reminder that New Orleans had more foreign immigrants than any other part of the South; a community of more than 10,000 Vietnamese refugees has grown, apparently comfortable in the hot and swampy environs. Up St. Charles Avenue is the Garden District. This was the home of rich early American settlers, and its antebellum homes are still covered with vines and Spanish moss. New Orleans, for many years a speckled black-and-white city, now has a 67% black majority, and the 2d District is overwhelmingly Democratic.

The congressman from the 2d District is Bill Jefferson, a Democrat first elected in 1990. Jefferson grew up in the northeast corner of Louisiana in Lake Providence. He graduated from Southern University and Harvard Law School, clerked for a federal judge, worked for Senator Bennett Johnston and finally settled in New Orleans to set up what became the largest black law firm in the South; he received an LL.M. from Georgetown while serving in Congress. Jefferson was elected to the state Senate in 1979; he twice ran for mayor and lost. In 1990, when Lindy Boggs retired, Jefferson won 25% of the primary vote to 22% for Marc Morial, whose father was New Orleans's first black mayor and who was later elected mayor himself. In the November runoff, charges flew: Jefferson was dogged by reports of defaults on outstanding loans and mortgages, while Morial admitted he was the father of an eight-year-old girl living in the Ivory Coast. Jefferson won with 52% and became the first Louisiana black elected to Congress since Reconstruction.

In the House Jefferson has shown impressive political skills and has a moderate voting record among Democrats. From his seat on Ways and Means, Jefferson has expressed doubts about Social Security individual investment accounts and has also questioned reliance on the payroll tax. He wants to expand the availability of Individual Retirement Accounts. In 2000, he won approval of an amendment requiring health insurers to notify consumers about cheaper generic drug options. Jefferson co-sponsored the Africa free trade bill that was enacted that year. Jefferson bucked senior Democrats on Ways and Means and joined chairman Bill Thomas in support of trade promotion authority, which he said was vital to Louisiana's economy.

Jefferson has not had serious opposition for reelection. But he has also eyed other offices, seeking to become the first black elected statewide since Reconstruction. In 1991, he filed to run for governor, but withdrew; in 1995, he began running for governor again, but withdrew in favor of Cleo Fields, and said he would run for Senate; in May 1996 he bowed out of that race. In January 1999 Republican Mike Foster and other statewide officials met at the Governor's Mansion and promised not to oppose each other regardless of party. Jefferson was evidently peeved and days later circulated a letter of protest and said he was running for governor. Raising more than $2.2 million, he challenged Foster's claims of improving the state's economy and schools; he pledged to raise teacher pay, reduce class sizes, and push for tougher education standards. But voting ran pretty much along racial lines, and Foster won 62%–30%.

After the 2002 election, with support from the Congressional Black Caucus, Jefferson sought the chairmanship of the Democratic Congressional Campaign Committee. He cited his active fundraising for the committee plus his success in helping to elect Rodney Alexander and re-elect Mary Landrieu in December runoffs. Some black members were upset when Nancy Pelosi instead selected fellow Californian Robert Matsui, with whom she had a closer relationship. Jefferson was opposed by some union officials who were unhappy about his free trade views. He said that Matsui's selection was "not in the best interests" of House Democrats.

THIRD DISTRICT

Rep. Billy Tauzin (R)

Elected May 1980, 12th term; b. June 14, 1943, Chackbay; home, Chackbay; Nicholls St. U., B.A. 1964, LA St. U., J.D. 1967; Catholic; married (Cecile).

Elected Office: LA House of Reps., 1971–79.

Professional Career: Practicing atty., 1968–80.

DC Office: 2183 RHOB 20515, 202-225-4031; Fax: 202-225-0563; Web site: www.house.gov/tauzin.

District Offices: Chalmette, 504-271-1707; Gonzales, 225-621-8490; Houma, 985-876-3033; New Iberia, 337-367-8231.

Committees: *Energy & Commerce* (Chmn. of 31 R). *Resources* (3d of 28 R): Energy & Mineral Resources; Fisheries Conservation, Wildlife & Oceans. *Select Committee on Homeland Security* (6th of 27 R): Emergency Preparedness & Response.

Group Ratings

	ADA	ACLU	AFS	LCV	CON	ITIC	NTU	COC	ACU	NTLC	CHC
2002	0	7	0	0	25	100	58	95	96	92	100
2001	0	—	0	0	—	—	61	100	96	—	—

National Journal Ratings

	2001 LIB	—	2001 CONS		2002 LIB	—	2002 CONS
Economic	15%	—	82%		0%	—	91%
Social	20%	—	69%		0%	—	75%
Foreign	21%	—	74%		15%	—	78%

Key Votes of the 107th Congress

1. Approve Bush Tax Cuts	Y	5. Faith-Based Charities	Y	9. Trade Promotion Authority	Y
2. Limit Patients' Bill of Rights	Y	6. Bar Gays in the Boy Scouts	Y	10. Bar Funds for Intl. Court	Y
3. Campaign Finance Reform	N	7. Ban Partial-Birth Abortion	Y	11. Authorize Force in Iraq	Y
4. Ban ANWR Development	N	8. Arm Commercial Pilots	Y	12. Deny Home. Sec. Dept. Union	Y

Election Results

2002 primary	Billy Tauzin (R)	130,323	(87%)	($1,566,897)
	William Beier (I)	12,964	(9%)	
	David Iwancio (I)	7,055	(5%)	
2000 primary	Billy Tauzin (R)	143,446	(78%)	($1,194,679)
	Edwin J. Albares (I)	16,908	(9%)	
	Anita W. Rosenthal (I)	13,488	(7%)	
	Dion Bourque (Lib)	10,118	(6%)	

Prior Winning Percentages: 1998 (100%); 1996 (100%); 1994 (76%); 1992 (82%); 1990 (88%); 1988 (89%); 1986 (100%); 1984 (100%); 1982 (100%); 1980 (85%); 1980 (53%)

The People		Race/Ethnic Origin	Ancestry	
Area size:	12,675 sq. mi.	69.7% White	French: 17.4%	USA: 8.7%
Urban population:	73.0%	24.6% Black	German: 5.9%	
Rural population:	27.0%	1.0% Asian	**2000 Presidential Vote**	
Pop. 2000:	638,322	1.6% Native Am.	Bush (R) 133,749	(52%)
Median income:	$34,463	0.0% Hawaiian	Gore (D) 115,734	(45%)
Poverty status:	18.6%	1.0% Two+ races	Other 7,967	(3%)
Military veterans:	10.8%	0.1% Other	**Cook Partisan Voting Index:** R + 4	
		2.1% Hispanic Origin		

Occupation	Blue collar: 33.6%	White collar: 50.3%	Gray collar: 16.2%

Below sea level, veined with bayous and creeks and wide streams of water, crossed by only an occasional road or railroad, the wetlands of southern Louisiana are one of America's unique landscapes. Technically, most of this waterlogged land rests on islands in a broad river mouth, through which the waters of the Mississippi and its tributaries drain into the Gulf of Mexico. It is rich with animal life, herons and egrets, shrimp and crawfish, muskrats and alligators. Yet it supports more people than one might think, in surprisingly sturdy small towns, with shopping malls on high ground, and in cabins along the bayous and crossroad towns where Cajun French remains the first language and roadside diners feature crawfish etoufee. But the steep-roofed Cajun houses are not the only structures: Here and there, jutting out of the swampy land, are huge elaborate metal sculptures—refineries and petrochemical plants, processing the oil and natural gas trapped under these wetlands and the shallow continental shelf of the Gulf, and released through 20th Century oil rig technology. In the 1960s and 1970s, the oil industry, by providing good jobs for young people here, helped preserve Cajun culture and built a Cajun pride that was seldom articulated a generation ago. Then oil payrolls plummeted and the wetlands were threatened by coastal erosion and battered by Hurricane Andrew in August 1992. The erosion continues, as the wetlands get less water because the Mississippi is not permitted to flood, and the shrimp fishermen, who still sail out in Blessing of the Fleet (La Benediction des Bateaux) ceremonies in April or May, have found their catch declining and their profits threatened by competition from aquaculture-raised Asian and Latin American shrimp. But the petrochemical plants, refineries, aluminum smelters and sugar refineries still provide well-paying jobs in these parts, and most Cajuns have been able to remain in this land of good hunting and good food. The town of Vacherie on the Mississippi River is the most rooted place in the United States: 98% of people here were born in Louisiana and 80% in 2000 lived in the same house as in 1995.

The 3d Congressional District includes about half the Cajun country. It includes most of Louisiana's swamplands, covering Houma, where seven bayous converge; St. Bernard and Plaquemines parishes, downriver from New Orleans; St. Charles, St. John the Baptist, St. James and Ascension parishes on both sides of the Mississippi, once the greatest sugar producers in America, now studded with refineries and petrochemical plants; roughneck Morgan City, which services many offshore oil rigs; and Iberia Parish, the home of McIlhenny's Tabasco sauce. Behind the Mississippi's western levee, hunkered side by side in Vacherie are twin reminders of the region's grandeur and pain: the stately Oak Alley plantation, whose stunning vista stood in for the home of a fictional, aristocratic governor in the 1998 movie *Primary Colors;* and the Laura Plantation, believed to be the original home of the famous Br'er Rabbit stories, and whose current owners are preserving and displaying the plantation's slave cabins to remind visitors of the facts many would prefer to forget. The ancestral language here is French (23% claim French or French Canadian ancestry), mainly Cajun but also Creole; the ancestral religion is Roman Catholic and the ancestral politics Democratic, though very conservative.

The congressman from the 3d District is Billy Tauzin, first elected as a Democrat and now a Republican, who is now chairman of the Energy and Commerce Committee. Tauzin grew up in Chackbay, worked on an oil rig to put himself through Nicholls State University and LSU law school, where he was a roommate of Senator John Breaux. He was first elected to the legislature in 1971, at 28; he won the 3d District seat in a May 1980 special election. Tauzin ran for governor in 1987, but was doomed when Edwin Edwards entered the race, squeezing him out in Cajun country; he finished fourth, with 10%. In 1989, Tauzin inherited a Merchant Marine subcommittee chairmanship just in time to handle legislation inspired by the Exxon *Valdez* oil spill in Alaska. Tauzin is knowledgeable, eloquent and can also be wily. Defeated in the committee and on the House floor, he and Senator Bennett Johnston inserted in conference committee on the Alaska Oil Export Act of 1995 a provision for royalty relief for deep-water oil drilling; that, plus advances in technology, led to a resurgence in offshore drilling in 1996.

Tauzin's party switch was not a complete surprise. He was one of two Democrats who supported all provisions of the Contract with America and in February 1995 he and 22 other Democrats formed The Coalition, a conservative group. In August 1995 he finally became a Republican. He was expected to run for Johnston's Senate seat in 1996, but he bowed out after being promised by the Republican leadership the chairmanship of the Telecommunications and Finance Subcommittee. Mike Oxley, the next Republican in line, objected, and, as a compromise, Telecommunications lost its Finance jurisdiction to Oxley's subcommittee. Tauzin wants to eliminate the long distance tax and wants cable companies to give consumers a wider range of options (including low-cost service with few channels) and has passed an anti-slamming bill through the House. Tauzin opposes auctioning the digital TV spectrum, regulating liquor advertising and any campaign finance bill giving free or discounted air time to candidates (in his view, unconstitutional, unfair and ineffective).

Tauzin supported the Telecommunications Act of 1996 but afterwards criticized the Clinton FCC for blocking the regional Bells from the long-distance business; George W. Bush's FCC chairman, Michael Powell, shares his view. In 1999 and 2000 Tauzin cannily built a coalition to allow the regional Bells to provide broadband Internet connections. He accumulated a "digital divide" coalition of members from rural districts and from poor urban areas, members of the Black and Hispanic caucuses and conservatives wary of federal broadband subsidies. He met with regional Bell lobbyists in weekly sessions and got the endorsement of committee ranking Democrat John Dingell. In June 2000 he announced he had 218 co-sponsors, a majority of the House, but declined to bring the bill forward because of the opposition of Commerce Chairman Thomas Bliley. In January 2001 Tauzin replaced Bliley as chairman; in May Dingell persuaded Tauzin to accept an amendment to force the Bells to build facilities to provide broadband service in rural, inner city and other unprofitable areas. The committee approved the bill 32–23 in May 2001. Judiciary Chairman James Sensenbrenner insisted on hearings in Judiciary, which passed an amendment requiring antitrust oversight by the Justice Department and reporting the bill to the floor unfavorably. It reached the floor of the House in February 2002, where John Conyers and Chris Cannon pushed an amendment barring the Bells from offering broadband until their share of local telephone service fell below 85%. This was defeated on a procedural motion to move the previous question on a motion to recommit, a procedural maneuver last used successfully in 1910, and Dingell-Tauzin passed 273–157. But Senate Commerce Committee Chairman Ernest Hollings was hostile (he called it "blasphemy, a total fraud") and it went nowhere in the Senate. Probably this issue will be revisited in this Congress.

As subcommittee and committee chairman, Tauzin has held memorable hearings. In September 2000 he dominated the hearings on Firestone tires that had blown out on Ford Explorers, and proposed legislation which passed the House under suspension of the rules in October 2000 and was accepted in full by the Senate, without the criminal penalties Senate Commerce Chairman John McCain wanted. In February 2001 he held hearings on network news coverage of the 2000 elections, in which he found no evidence that networks tried to influence the outcome, but concluded that VNS's flawed models produced "a bias that consistently tended to favor Democrats." In July 2002 Tauzin was asking the SEC whether it had investigated Tyco, WorldCom, Global Crossing, Qwest and Xerox from 1998 on and was asking 13 corporations to reveal how and whether their directors oversaw management starting in the early 1990s. "Some of these corporate criminals need to go to jail," he said at the time.

Tauzin's accession to the chairmanship of Energy and Commerce was not automatic. It was contested by Mike Oxley, who had more seniority as a Republican; Tauzin had more seniority if you (as Newt Gingrich agreed to do) count his years as a Democrat. But House Republicans do not necessarily follow seniority, and each raised about $500,000 for Republican colleagues. The contest was settled by an intricate deal, much as the Telecommunications Subcommittee chairmanship had been settled four years before. Tauzin became chairman of what he renamed the Energy and Commerce Committee. Oxley became chairman of the newly-named Financial Services Committee, essentially the old Banking Committee with Oxley's subcommittee jurisdiction added; the loser in this was Marge Roukema, the ranking Republican on Banking, who retired in 2002. As chairman, Bliley had taken tight control of subcommittees but had not aggressively asserted the committee's jurisdiction. Tauzin followed the opposite strategy, as Dingell had during his years as chairman from 1981 to 1995; he fought immediately to keep some jurisdiction over the SEC and to have the budget resolution framed so the committee would have some jurisdiction over Medicare. In September 1995 Tauzin was named Deputy Majority Whip; he is the first American to have been part of the leadership of both parties in the House.

As chairman, Tauzin took a lead role on many pieces of legislation. In July 2001 he and Dingell agreed on an energy bill amendment directing the Department of Transportation to raise

CAFE standards or use other means to reduce SUV energy consumption by 5 billion gallons of gas by 2010. After September 11 he worked with Dingell and with Senators Edward Kennedy and Bill Frist on a bioterrorism bill. They reached a compromise in May 2002, with $1.5 billion for states and $3 billion for hospitals to prepare for a biological attack, increased food inspection and a speedup in approval of generic drugs, assessments of vulnerability to attack by local water systems and $300 million for the Centers for Disease Control. He and Ways and Means Chairman Bill Thomas co-sponsored the Republicans' prescription drug bill, which passed 221–207 in July 2002. That month Tauzin and Dingell asked the FCC to require computer and consumer electronics manufacturers to include anti-piracy technology in their products. In January 2003 Tauzin reversed himself and supported FTC Chairman Tim Muris's requests for funds for a national do-not-call list for telemarketers, though Tauzin said he had doubts about the FTC's authority.

Tauzin has had no difficulty getting reelected; indeed he had no Democratic opposition since 1992. In September 1996 he became the only party-switcher to be reelected without opposition. He was unopposed in 1998. In 2000 and 2002, against minor party candidates, he was reelected with 78% and 87% of the vote.

FOURTH DISTRICT

Rep. Jim McCrery (R)

Elected Apr. 1988, 8th term; b. Sept. 18, 1949, Shreveport; home, Shreveport; LA Tech. U., B.A. 1971, LA St. U., J.D. 1975; Methodist; married (Johnette).

Professional Career: Practicing atty. 1975–78; Asst. Shreveport City Atty., 1979–80; Legis. Dir., U.S. Rep. Buddy Roemer, 1981–84; Regional Mgr., Georgia–Pacific Corp., 1984–88.

DC Office: 2104 RHOB 20515, 202-225-2777; Fax: 202-225-8039; Web site: www.house.gov/mccrery.

District Offices: Leesville, 337-238-0778; Shreveport, 318-798-2254.

Committees: *Ways & Means* (7th of 24 R): Health; Human Resources; Select Revenue Measures (Chmn.).

Group Ratings

	ADA	ACLU	AFS	LCV	CON	ITIC	NTU	COC	ACU	NTLC	CHC
2002	0	13	0	0	8	100	56	100	92	89	92
2001	5	—	0	0	—	—	62	100	92	—	—

National Journal Ratings

	2001 LIB	—	2001 CONS		2002 LIB	—	2002 CONS
Economic	13%	—	86%		28%	—	69%
Social	38%	—	61%		25%	—	71%
Foreign	4%	—	87%		0%	—	85%

Key Votes of the 107th Congress

1. Approve Bush Tax Cuts	Y	5. Faith-Based Charities	Y	9. Trade Promotion Authority	Y
2. Limit Patients' Bill of Rights	Y	6. Bar Gays in the Boy Scouts	Y	10. Bar Funds for Intl. Court	Y
3. Campaign Finance Reform	N	7. Ban Partial-Birth Abortion	Y	11. Authorize Force in Iraq	Y
4. Ban ANWR Development	N	8. Arm Commercial Pilots	Y	12. Deny Home. Sec. Dept. Union	Y

Election Results

2002 primary	Jim McCrery (R)	114,649	(72%)	($1,117,836)
	John Milkovich (D)	42,340	(26%)	
	Other	3,104	(2%)	
2000 primary	Jim McCrery (R)	122,678	(71%)	($574,127)
	Phillip R. Green (D)	43,600	(25%)	
	Other	7,689	(4%)	
1998 primary	Jim McCrery (R)	unopposed		($666,860)

Prior Winning Percentages: 1996 (71%); 1994 (80%); 1992 (63%); 1990 (55%); 1988 (68%); 1988 (51%)

The People		Race/Ethnic Origin	Ancestry	
Area size:	11,151 sq. mi.	62.0% White	USA: 10.2%	Irish: 6.9%
Urban population:	59.3%	33.3% Black	English: 5.6%	
Rural population:	40.7%	0.7% Asian	**2000 Presidential Vote**	
Pop. 2000:	638,466	0.8% Native Am.	Bush (R).............129,908	(55%)
Median income:	$31,085	0.1% Hawaiian	Gore (D).............102,228	(43%)
Poverty status:	20.0%	1.1% Two+ races	Other...................5,466	(2%)
Military veterans:	14.7%	0.1% Other	**Cook Partisan Voting Index:** R + 6	
		2.0% Hispanic Origin		

Occupation	Blue collar: 28.5%	White collar: 52.7%	Gray collar: 18.9%

Northwestern Louisiana, south of Arkansas and just east of Texas, is part of the Deep South. The overwhelming majority of people here are Protestants, not Catholics, often very tradition-minded, with names that are English or Scottish, not French. The tone is set not by wide-open New Orleans—which was not easily accessible by interstate until 1996, when the last chunk of I-49 was completed—but by the much smaller Shreveport, which could be just another East Texas oil town, albeit one which has its own, comparatively sedate, Mardi Gras. The countryside is agricultural, though there are few vestiges of large riverfront plantations and backward farm country. Roots go back here a long way. Natchitoches is the oldest town, founded by Louis Antoine Juchereay de St. Denis in 1714. Shreveport was founded when Captain Henry Miller Shreve, with the Army Corps of Engineers, in the 1830s dispatched a young deputy named Robert E. Lee to break up a 100-mile blockade of logs in the Red River, moving the region's epicenter upriver to a new town, which was named after him. Oil provided the basis for much of the economic growth of the 20th century. Defense facilities also helped, although the Fifth Infantry Division was moved from Louisiana's Fort Polk to Texas's Fort Hood in 1993; but Fort Polk is still operating and so is Barksdale Air Force Base near Shreveport, where George W. Bush landed on September 11, 2001 and spoke briefly to the nation. Politically, northern Louisiana voters, for more than 100 years, have been voting against cosmopolitan New Orleans and the Catholic Cajun south, sometimes for riproaring populists, and more often, as the economy grows more sophisticated, for market-oriented Republicans.

The 4th Congressional District consists of the northwest corner of the state. More than half the votes here are cast in Caddo and Bossier Parishes in the far corner around Shreveport, with the rest scattered around rural areas, like picturesque Natchitoches and strip-highway towns like Leesville near Fort Polk. This area seemed to be trending Republican in the 1980s, but in the middle 1990s it went the other way: Both Bill Clinton and Senator Mary Landrieu carried the district in 1996, a critical factor in her narrow 5,788-vote statewide margin. In 2000 George W. Bush carried the area by a comfortable 55% margin, but in November and December 2002 it voted for Landrieu again.

The congressman from the 4th District is Jim McCrery, a Republican first elected in April 1988. McCrery grew up in Leesville, graduated from Louisiana Tech in Ruston (next door to Grambling, site of the football-famous, historically black college) and LSU law school, and practiced law in Leesville and Shreveport. In 1981 he worked for Congressman Buddy Roemer, then a Democrat; in 1984 he went to work for Georgia Pacific. When Roemer was elected governor in 1987, McCrery ran as a Republican and won the special election 51%–49%. McCrery's toughest reelection race was in 1992, when the creation of the black-majority 4th District put him in the 5th District with 16-year incumbent Jerry Huckaby, a conservative Democrat. But the district, with few black voters, was heavily Republican and Huckaby had 88 overdrafts on the House bank. McCrery weathered some negative personal attacks, led in the October primary 44%–29% and won the November runoff 63%–37%.

McCrery has compiled a mostly conservative voting record and has worked on major legislation from his seat on the Ways and Means Committee. Armed with the intuition that made him one of only 72 House members to vote against the disastrous 1988 catastrophic health care bill, he advanced a Republican alternative to the Clinton health care plan in 1994, capping deductibility of health insurance, opposing the Democrats' cost control measures, limiting medical malpractice and instituting medical savings accounts. Seven years later, he continued his innovative approach when he joined with liberal Democrat Jim McDermott on a sweeping plan to replace employer-provided health insurance with a system for all individuals to find private insurance, coupled with mandatory pay increases to assist them and subsidies for the poor. He worked on the Republicans' Medicare and prescription drug bills and on the party task force on HMO reform. He favors individual investment accounts for Social Security. He sponsored tax breaks for energy companies in the energy bill in 2001 and 2002. He has been chairman of the Select Revenue Measures Subcommittee since 2001 and has worked closely with Ways and Means Chairman Bill Thomas on many issues, including jurisdiction fights with Louisiana's Billy Tauzin, chairman of the Energy and Commerce Committee.

Since 1991 McCrery has been working to create a Red River National Wildlife Refuge. In October 2000 the bill establishing the refuge was signed. The private Conservation Fund has provided some funding and Entergy Corporation donate 180,000 seedlings; the Refuge was dedicated in August 2002 and will be administered by the Fish and Wildlife Service; up to 50,000 acres may be included. McCrery has also worked to extend I-49 north from Shreveport, amid fears that Arkansas may route its portion of the road toward Texas. McCrery opposed the proposal of the Jena Band of Choctaw Indians, from northeast Louisiana, to build a casino in Logansport on the Texas border, which would compete with Shreveport's riverboat casinos.

Since 1994 McCrery has not faced serious competition in elections. In 2002 he faced Democrat John Milkovich, a Shreveport lawyer who won local renown for getting overturned, after nine years, the murder conviction of a Barksdale airman. McCrery won 72%–26%.

FIFTH DISTRICT

Rep. Rodney Alexander (D)

Elected 2002, 1st term; b. Dec. 5, 1946, Quitman; home, Quitman; attended LA Tech. U., 1965; Baptist; married (Nancy).

Military Career: Air Force Reserves, 1965–71.

Elected Office: Jackson Parish Police Jury, 1972–87; President, 1980–87; LA House of Reps., 1988–02.

Professional Career: Insurance agent, 1990–93; contractor, 1993-present.

DC Office: 316 CHOB 20515, 202-225-8490; Fax: 202-225-5639; Web site: www.house.gov/alexander.

District Offices: Alexandria, 318-445-0818; Monroe, 318-322-3500.

Committees: *Agriculture* (13th of 24 D): General Farm Commodities & Risk Management; Livestock & Horticulture; Specialty Crops & Foreign Agriculture Programs. *Armed Services* (27th of 29 D): Projection Forces; Tactical Air & Land Forces.

Group Ratings and Key Votes: Newly Elected

Election Results

2002 runoff	Rodney Alexander (D)	86,718	(50%)	($831,088)
	Lee Fletcher (R)	85,744	(50%)	
2002 primary	Rodney Alexander (D)	52,952	(29%)	
	Lee Fletcher (R)	45,278	(25%)	
	Clyde Holloway (R)	42,573	(23%)	
	Robert Barham (R)	34,533	(19%)	
	Other	9,321	(5%)	
2000 primary	John Cooksey (R)	123,975	(69%)	($508,238)
	Roger Beall (D)	42,977	(24%)	
	Sam Houston Melton Jr. (D)	7,186	(4%)	
	Other	5,335	(3%)	

The People		Race/Ethnic Origin	Ancestry	
Area size:	14,225 sq. mi.	63.4% White	USA: 13.2%	Irish: 6.4%
Urban population:	52.9%	33.7% Black	French: 5.6%	
Rural population:	47.1%	0.5% Asian	**2000 Presidential Vote**	
Pop. 2000:	638,517	0.4% Native Am.	Bush (R).............143,628	(57%)
Median income:	$27,453	0.0% Hawaiian	Gore (D).............100,287	(40%)
Poverty status:	23.6%	0.6% Two+ races	Other...................7,706	(3%)
Military veterans:	12.0%	0.0% Other	**Cook Partisan Voting Index:** R + 9	
		1.3% Hispanic Origin		

Occupation	Blue collar: 26.9%	White collar: 53.5%	Gray collar: 19.5%

Northeast Louisiana is perhaps the least known part of the state. Along the Mississippi River and the Red River and their dozens of tributaries, it was plantation country before the Civil War, with black majorities still in many parishes. Away from the larger rivers, it is hill country, places where small farmers scratched out a living on land connected to parish courthouses by dusty lanes. Such was Winn Parish, where Huey P. Long, the pivotal figure in modern Louisiana politics, was born in 1893, and from which he began his meteoric political career—elected governor in 1928, senator in 1930, a national figure threatening both parties when he was assassinated in 1935 in the new high-rise Capitol he built in Baton Rouge.

The 5th Congressional District contains much of this country, from the river parishes to the hills of Winn Parish. The biggest urban areas here, with about 50,000 people each, are Monroe in the north and Alexandria in the south. Alexandria in Rapides Parish sits at the northernmost extension of Cajun, Catholic Louisiana, and is majority black; Monroe in Ouachita Parish is heavily WASP and Baptist, and is home to one of the world's leading Bible collections, assembled by an heir to an early Coca-Cola bottler. Redistricting added some Cajun areas in Allen and Evangeline Parishes and heavily black precincts in Pointe Coupee and Iberville Parishes, all Democratic areas.

The congressman from the 5th District is Democrat Rodney Alexander, the 435th member of the House elected in 2002. Alexander graduated from Louisiana Tech and won election to the Jackson Parish police jury in 1972 at the age of 25. In 1988 he was elected to the state House, where he chaired the Health and Welfare Committee. He characterized himself as pro-guns, pro-life and pro-prayer.

The district became open when Republican John Cooksey ran unsuccessfully for the Senate after serving three terms in the House. There were four serious candidates in the November primary, three of them Republicans; the top two finishers, of whatever party, would meet in the December 7 runoff if, as seemed certain, no candidate got 50%. The primary turned out to be a regional contest. Alexander led with 29% of the vote, carrying three hill counties in his legislative district and five heavily black parishes along the Mississippi River. Second was Lee Fletcher, chief of staff to Cooksey for five years, was second with 25% of the vote, carrying Monroe's Ouachita Parish and three nearby parishes. Close behind, with 23%, was Clyde Holloway, elected congress-man by narrow margins in 1986, 1988 and 1990 from the old 8th District which Louisiana lost in the 1990 Census. Holloway, a tree farmer from Rapides Parish, carried seven parishes in the southern end of his district. Fourth, with 19%, was Robert Barham, who carried three parishes in the northern end of the district.

It is a common practice for top congressional aides to return home and run to replace their bosses; it is also a common practice for voters to reject them for candidates more familiar with conditions at home. After the primary, Holloway was angry because he thought the House Republicans' campaign committee was steering contributors to Fletcher's campaign despite Holloway's prior service in the House, and he called a press conference to denounce Fletcher as someone who "will do anything to win and he scares me." The Alexander campaign attacked Fletcher as a Washington insider and contrasted Alexander's "blue jeans" supporters with Fletcher's "blue blood" contributors. Turnout in the district was down only 7% from November, and that differential was a problem made up largely of Cooksey supporters who didn't care for Republican Senate candidate Suzanne Haik Terrell. Alexander squeaked by with a 50.3%–49.7% victory. His margin was 974 votes; he carried Pointe Coupee and Iberville Parishes by 3,684.

Alexander carried two hill parishes, all the Mississippi River parishes and all but one of the parishes in the southern end of the district.

In the House, Alexander got seats on Agriculture and Armed Services. National Republicans, who set the district as an early priority for 2004, were not enthusiastic when Fletcher voiced interest in running again.

SIXTH DISTRICT

Rep. Richard Baker (R)

Elected 1986, 9th term; b. May 22, 1948, New Orleans; home, Baton Rouge; LA St. U., B.A. 1971; United Methodist; married (Kay).

Elected Office: LA House of Reps., 1972–86.

Professional Career: Real estate developer, 1972–86.

DC Office: 341 CHOB 20515, 202-225-3901; Fax: 202-225-7313; Web site: www.house.gov/baker.

District Office: Baton Rouge, 225-929-7711.

Committees: *Financial Services* (4th of 37 R): Capital Markets, Insurance & Government Sponsored Enterprises (Chmn.); Financial Institutions & Consumer Credit; Housing & Community Opportunity. *Transportation & Infrastructure* (14th of 41 R): Aviation; Highways, Transit & Pipelines; Water Resources & Environment. *Veterans' Affairs* (8th of 17 R): Health.

Group Ratings

	ADA	ACLU	AFS	LCV	CON	ITIC	NTU	COC	ACU	NTLC	CHC
2002	0	7	11	0	25	100	55	95	100	85	100
2001	0	—	0	0	—	—	64	100	96	—	—

National Journal Ratings

	2001 LIB —	2001 CONS		2002 LIB —	2002 CONS
Economic	7% —	89%		19% —	80%
Social	20% —	69%		0% —	75%
Foreign	4% —	87%		0% —	85%

Key Votes of the 107th Congress

1. Approve Bush Tax Cuts	Y	5. Faith-Based Charities	Y	9. Trade Promotion Authority	Y
2. Limit Patients' Bill of Rights	Y	6. Bar Gays in the Boy Scouts	Y	10. Bar Funds for Intl. Court	Y
3. Campaign Finance Reform	N	7. Ban Partial-Birth Abortion	Y	11. Authorize Force in Iraq	Y
4. Ban ANWR Development	N	8. Arm Commercial Pilots	Y	12. Deny Home. Sec. Dept. Union	Y

Election Results

2002 primary	Richard Baker (R)	146,932	(84%)	($790,953)
	Rick Moscatello (I)	27,898	(16%)	
2000 primary	Richard Baker (R)	165,637	(68%)	($916,205)
	Kathy J. Rogillio (D)	72,192	(30%)	
	Other	5,649	(2%)	
1998 primary	Richard Baker (R)	97,044	(51%)	($1,444,171)
	Marjorie McKeithen (D)	94,201	(49%)	($664,611)

Prior Winning Percentages: 1996 (69%); 1994 (81%); 1992 (51%); 1990 (100%); 1988 (100%); 1986 (51%)

The People		Race/Ethnic Origin	Ancestry	
Area size:	3,210 sq. mi.	62.7% White	French: 10.3%	USA: 7.4%
Urban population:	75.5%	33.2% Black	Irish: 6.3%	
Rural population:	24.5%	1.4% Asian	**2000 Presidential Vote**	
Pop. 2000:	638,324	0.2% Native Am.	Bush (R)..............142,239	(55%)
Median income:	$37,931	0.0% Hawaiian	Gore (D)..............111,602	(43%)
Poverty status:	16.6%	0.7% Two+ races	Other....................5,716	(2%)
Military veterans:	11.2%	0.1% Other	**Cook Partisan Voting Index:** R + 6	
		1.6% Hispanic Origin		

Occupation	Blue collar: 23.6%	White collar: 61.5%	Gray collar: 15.0%

Baton Rouge is the central node of Louisiana, on the boundary between the French-speaking, Catholic Cajun country and the heavily Baptist Deep South, its skyscraper Capitol and Exxon refinery sitting just beyond the levees that line the Mississippi River. Baton Rouge still bears the impress of the man who dominated Louisiana politics for much of the 20th century, Huey P. Long. Here Long became governor at 36 in the old (and still-standing) Gothic Capitol, when Baton Rouge had only 30,000 people, and was assassinated in 1935 in the hallway of the 34-story Art Deco Capitol he built, next door to the Governor's Mansion, which he also built. To the south are the buildings of Louisiana State University, much of which he built, in an amazingly short time. Today Baton Rouge is the center of a metro area of 603,000, almost all on the east bank of the Mississippi, and reaching far inland to Livingston Parish. Baton Rouge tries to maintain all of Louisiana's traditions; according to James Carville, who comes from nearby Carville in Iberville Parish (where three generations of his family served as postmaster), it has "the best restaurants per capita of any city in the United States."

The 6th Congressional District includes just about all of metropolitan Baton Rouge, plus three small mostly rural parishes to the north. The city of Baton Rouge itself in 2000 had a 50% black majority; suburban East Baton Rouge Parish was 40% black and fast-growing Livingston Parish to the east 4% black. Overall the district is 33% black. Historically, all of this territory was Democratic. In the 1980s the Baton Rouge area moved toward the Republicans and in the 1990s it was fairly closely balanced. In 2000 East Baton Rouge Parish voted 53% for George W. Bush and Livingston Parish 68% for Bush; overall the 6th District was 55% for Bush.

The congressman from the 6th District is Richard Baker, a Republican first elected in 1986. Baker has spent most of his adult life in public office. He came to Baton Rouge to attend LSU, then in 1972, at 23, was elected as a Democrat to the Louisiana House from a blue-collar district in Baton Rouge. He became a Republican in 1985, and in 1986, when Baton Rouge Republican Congressman Henson Moore ran for the Senate, Baker ran for the House and beat a Democratic state senator 51%–46%. In 1992 he was redistricted in the same district with Republican Congressman Clyde Holloway and was opposed as well by the Democratic mayor of Alexandria. The new district lines put Baker at a disadvantage, and he trailed 37%–33% in the September primary. But he won the November runoff 51%–49%, with 71% in his home territory of East Baton Rouge and Livingston parishes.

Baker has had a conservative voting record and is chairman of the Capital Markets and Insurance Subcommittee of the Financial Services Committee. He worked on financial services deregulation, one of the most heavily lobbied issues in the 1990s; the issue was how, under what terms and conditions, to dismantle the wall separating banks and other institutions created by the Glass-Steagall Act of 1933. Baker generally favored deregulation, and served on the conference committee that finally reached agreement in November 1999.

Baker's greatest legislative enterprise has been to change the operation of the government-sponsored enterprises (GSEs) Fannie Mae and Freddie Mac, which purchase and securitize home mortgages. These are for-profit enterprises, indeed hugely profitmaking in recent years, yet the fact that they each have $2.25 billion lines of credit with the U.S. Treasury creates an impression in the marketplace that the government will bail them out if they become insolvent. Baker admitted that they were well-managed and not at risk, and argued that that was the best time for reform. In February 2000 Baker introduced legislation to create a new regulatory agency for the

GSEs and terminate their line of credit, increase disclosure requirements, toughen capital mandates and give regulators more say in approving new activities. Fannie Mae and Freddie Mac vigorously opposed the bill and predicted it would never pass. In a March hearing a Treasury undersecretary testified in favor of much of the bill, including repeal of the lines of credit. Sometimes tumultuous negotiations followed. In October they reached agreement. Fannie Mae and Freddie Mac agreed to increase their equity capital and subordinated debt to 4% of assets and to disclose more information to investors. By February 2001 Fannie Mae CEO Franklin Raines was praising Baker, but they still disagreed: Baker still wanted an independent regulator, while Raines was opposed. In summer 2001 Baker introduced a bipartisan bill to require Fannie Mae and Freddie Mac to register their stock with the SEC; they agreed to do so voluntarily, but do not issue SEC prospectuses for the securitized instruments they sell to investors—who are, they say, sophisticated enough to evaluate them. In 2002 the Office of Federal Housing Enterprise Oversight issued long-delayed regulations of Fannie Mae and Freddie Mac and subjected them to "stress tests," to discover how their portfolios would fare in times of economic stress.

In 2000 Banking Chairman Jim Leach reached the end of House Republicans' six-year term limits, and Baker sought the chairmanship over the more senior Marge Roukema. But in the days after the November 2000 election, Baker presented a fallback position to the Republican leadership. An even bigger chairmanship struggle was going on in the Commerce Committee, between Louisiana's Billy Tauzin and Mike Oxley. Baker would support Oxley for the Banking Committee chairmanship, with Commerce's jurisdiction over securities and insurance transferred to Banking. Baker would keep his Financial Services subcommittee chair plus the securities jurisdiction; Roukema would get another subcommittee. And so it happened: Baker was in a position to continue his work on the GSEs, Oxley got a chairmanship and Roukema decided to retire in 2002. On two major bills in the next two years Baker and Oxley worked together. One was terrorism insurance, proposed after the September 11 attacks. Unlike the White House and the Senate bills, Baker and Oxley's bill would require insurers to pay a large deductible before the federal government would pay anything, and the federal government would make loans rather than direct payments to insurers. After much negotiation, agreement was reached in November 2002. The deductible would be a percentage of direct premiums for covered commercial property casualty risk, rising from 7% in 2003 to 15% in 2005, and federal coverage of losses would be capped at $100 billion.

The other big issue was auditor independence. Oxley and Baker avoided flamboyant hearings; they cancelled a hearing after former Enron Chairman Kenneth Lay said he would take the Fifth Amendment. In February 2002 they rolled out a bill which would create an accounting oversight board inside the SEC, require far more disclosure and would bar external auditing firms from doing certain financial systems consulting and internal auditing. Ranking Democrat John LaFalce criticized the bill for not completely separating accounting and consulting and for not placing the oversight board outside the SEC; he also called for CEOs to sign certified financial reports subject to criminal penalties. The committee approved the Oxley-Baker approach in April 2002 and the bill passed the House later that month. Meanwhile, in the Senate, Banking Committee Chairman Paul Sarbanes was preparing a bill with bipartisan support which went farther than Oxley and Baker but not as far as LaFalce. That bill was languishing when disclosure of the WorldCom accounting scandal in June propelled it forward. It passed the Senate by a wide margin and in conference, at the prodding of the Bush White House, Oxley and Baker yielded on most points of disagreement; the bill was passed and signed before the August recess. In the process, Baker proposed a Federal Account for Investor Restitution (FAIR) Fund, with money raised from monetary penalties levied against corporations and funds disgorged from executives guilty of fraud or malfeasance to be paid over to defrauded investors; this was included in what became the Sarbanes-Oxley Act. In November 2002 Baker urged that it be expanded to include money recovered by states; he was critical of New York Attorney General Eliot Spitzer for usurping federal authority in negotiating a $3 billion global settlement with brokerage houses, but was pleased when Spitzer supported a restitution fund.

On other legislation, Baker in December 2002 called for giving life insurers, but not property and casualty and auto insurers, the option of federal chartering: an issue to be much lobbied in 2003 and 2004.

With one major exception, Baker has not had difficulty winning reelection since 1992. That exception was in 1998, when he was challenged then by Democrat Marjorie McKeithen, the granddaughter of former Governor (1964–72) John McKeithen and daughter of Secretary of State Fox McKeithen. Strongly opposed to gun control and abortion, McKeithen knocked on 40,000 doors and charmed voters with her north Louisiana accent. She criticized Baker for voting to raise his own pay $30,000 while voting against increases in the minimum wage. Baker attacked her for being a trial lawyer and for not voting consistently in local elections. Baker raised $1.4 million, McKeithen almost half that. In the end, Baker squeaked by, winning 50.7%–49.3%. McKeithen decided not to run again in 2000, and Baker was reelected easily in that year and in 2002.

SEVENTH DISTRICT

Rep. Chris John (D)

Elected 1996, 4th term; b. Jan. 5, 1960, Crowley; home, Crowley; LA St. U., B.A. 1982; Catholic; married (Payton).

Elected Office: Crowley City Cncl., 1983–87; LA House of Reps., 1987–95.

Professional Career: Co-owner, John N. John Truckline, 1983–96.

DC Office: 403 CHOB 20515, 202-225-2031; Fax: 202-225-5724; Web site: www.house.gov/john.

District Offices: Lafayette, 337-235-6322; Lake Charles, 337-433-1747.

Committees: *Energy & Commerce* (22d of 26 D): Energy & Air Quality; Health.

Group Ratings

	ADA	ACLU	AFS	LCV	CON	ITIC	NTU	COC	ACU	NTLC	CHC
2002	45	40	67	13	2	75	28	74	46	29	58
2001	40	—	44	7	—	—	36	83	63	—	—

National Journal Ratings

	2001 LIB	—	2001 CONS		2002 LIB	—	2002 CONS
Economic	52%	—	49%		53%	—	47%
Social	38%	—	61%		48%	—	51%
Foreign	49%	—	47%		52%	—	47%

Key Votes of the 107th Congress

1. Approve Bush Tax Cuts	Y	5. Faith-Based Charities	N	9. Trade Promotion Authority	Y
2. Limit Patients' Bill of Rights	N	6. Bar Gays in the Boy Scouts	Y	10. Bar Funds for Intl. Court	*
3. Campaign Finance Reform	Y	7. Ban Partial-Birth Abortion	Y	11. Authorize Force in Iraq	Y
4. Ban ANWR Development	N	8. Arm Commercial Pilots	Y	12. Deny Home. Sec. Dept. Union	N

Election Results

2002 primary	Chris John (D)	138,659	(87%)	($525,754)
	Roberto Valletta (I)	21,051	(13%)	
2000 primary	Chris John (D)	152,796	(83%)	($627,685)
	Michael P. Harris (Lib)	30,687	(17%)	
1998 primary	Chris John (D)	unopposed		($287,732)

Prior Winning Percentages: 1996 (53%)

The People		Race/Ethnic Origin	Ancestry	
Area size:	7,294 sq. mi.	72.0% White	French: 14.1%	USA: 11.6%
Urban population:	68.9%	24.8% Black	Fr. Canadian: 6.6%	
Rural population:	31.1%	0.7% Asian	**2000 Presidential Vote**	
Pop. 2000:	638,430	0.2% Native Am.	Bush (R)..............141,378	(55%)
Median income:	$31,453	0.0% Hawaiian	Gore (D)..............107,190	(42%)
Poverty status:	19.9%	0.7% Two+ races	Other....................7,357	(3%)
Military veterans:	11.8%	0.1% Other	**Cook Partisan Voting Index:** R + 7	
		1.4% Hispanic Origin		

Occupation   Blue collar: 27.9%   White collar: 54.9%   Gray collar: 17.2%

More than 200 years ago, French-speaking settlers were forced to leave their land of Acadie, which the British had taken over and renamed Nova Scotia, and make their way to the wetlands of southern Louisiana. Here, without much notice, they built steep-roofed houses to slough off non-existent snow and adapted French cuisine to the crawfish and muskrat they found in abundance in the pelican-tended swamps. The heart of the Cajun country is around Lafayette, just west of the Atchafalaya Basin, where Mississippi waters pour through bayous and canals, with only occasional bits of solid land visible on the 30-mile section of Interstate 10 built on elevated stilts. For half a century the Cajun country thrived, thanks to the oil and gas plentiful here and just off shore in the Gulf of Mexico; oil rigs are common, and every once in a while the swampy foliage parts to reveal a giant refinery or petrochemical plant. In the past two decades, Cajun pride has grown: Cajun French is surviving decades of efforts to eliminate it; Cajun music—and its black-influenced variant, zydeco—are popular here and nationally; spicy Cajun cooking has become a tourist attraction here and, in watered-down form, familiar all over the United States. About 45% of the people in Acadiana speak French as a second language. Lafayette, with its Acadian Village and plethora of oil exploration firms, features its annual *Festivals Acadiens* to celebrate music, food and crafts. Unlike New Orleans, its Mardi Gras reveries do not require anti-discrimination statements; the result has been an all-white parade and an all-black parade.

The oil price crash of the middle 1980s hit the Cajun country hard. Rising expectations, and the giddy sense that the oil industry promised lasting prosperity, suddenly collapsed, leaving borrowers overextended and ordinary homeowners unable to maintain the standard of living they expected. Politically, the Cajun country seemed to move then toward national Democrats, whom it had shunned because their cultural liberalism seemed alien to the Cajun tradition of respecting the authority of Church and state while tolerating a certain amount of *laissez les bons temps rouler* spirit. The Cajun country voted for Bill Clinton in 1992 and 1996, as it had voted for Louisiana's foremost Cajun politician, Edwin Edwards, who was elected governor four times. But George W. Bush also won here, perhaps benefiting from his neighboring-state affinity, or from his opposition to abortion, which is anathema in heavily Catholic Acadiana.

The 7th Congressional District covers much of the Cajun country, from Lafayette and the Atchafalaya west along I-10 to Lake Charles and the Texas border. Here, 21% of the population claims either French or French Canadian ancestry.

The congressman from the 7th District is Chris John, a Democrat first elected in 1996. John grew up in Crowley, which seems to have become an incubator for prominent politicians (such as Edwin Edwards and John Breaux). After graduating from LSU he went into the family trucking business. In 1987, at 27, he was elected to the seat in the Louisiana House his father had once held, and served eight years, chairing the Acadiana delegation. In 1996 the 7th District seat opened when Jimmy Hayes, a 10-year incumbent who had switched to the Republican Party, ran unsuccessfully for the Senate. Eight candidates ran in the open primary to replace Hayes. John's chief opponents were Republican David Thibodaux, an English professor at the University of Southwestern Louisiana who called for abolishing the Internal Revenue Service and the Department of Education, and Democrat Hunter Lundy, a maritime lawyer from Lake Charles and an anti-abortion religious conservative. John campaigned as tough on crime; he led the first round with 26%. Thibodaux seemed to place second, 29 votes ahead of Lundy, but a recount gave the slot to Lundy by 8 votes; Thibodaux protested and filed suit, to no avail. This meant that Democrats knew they had picked up one House seat, even though neither candidate showed much support for national Democratic principles. John was endorsed by the House Blue Dog Democrats, and in the closing days by Jimmy Hayes and Billy Tauzin, both former Democrats. The result came down to geography. Lundy led 63%–37% in the parishes west of the Mermenteau River; and John led 62%–38% in the parishes to the east, for a 53%–47% win.

John joined the Blue Dogs and has been among the more conservative Democrats in the House. He has sought to encourage farm exports and looked after rice farmers (his family owns two rice farms); and he worked to protect estuaries, fishlands and marshlands. John worked with John Dingell—a fellow sportsman—to weaken gun control proposals. He opposed Bill Clinton on trade promotion authority, months after Fruit of the Loom closed some local plants and moved production abroad, but he later voted for PNTR with China in 1999 and for trade promotion authority in 2001 and 2002. He opposed impeachment because he believed Bill Clinton "had not breached national security," and added that "the 7th District is a mixed bag of philosophic thought." In 2001, John won a seat on the Energy and Commerce Committee, where he worked for a national energy policy, and became co-chairman of the Blue Dogs. Later that spring, he opposed George W. Bush's income tax cut but voted for the final agreement in May, calling it a good compromise on both the tax and spending sides. He joined Republicans and business lobbyists to repeal Bill Clinton's ergonomics regulations.

Republicans have not challenged his reelection since he first won the House seat. He has been mentioned as a Senate candidate if John Breaux does not seek reelection in 2004. John actively supported Martin Frost in his campaign for Minority Leader against Nancy Pelosi.

★ MAINE ★

Maine is a state with a distinctive personality—ornery, contrary-minded, almost bullheaded, rough-hewn. It is the state closest geographically to Europe, but it was not heavily settled until the mid-19th century, and then by people coming from the south and west—the opposite of America's usual pattern. In an urbanizing and rapidly changing country, Maine was famous for its pointed firs and steady habits, with a few dozen small factory and mill towns but nothing like a major metropolis. Maine grew in a rush and then mostly stopped: There were 600,000 people here in 1860 but its population did not top 1 million until the 1970s. Then the tremors of the New England high-tech booms of the 1980s and 1990s reverberated up I-95 and shook Maine. The simple, back-to-nature Yankee style came into vogue. The antique dockside buildings on Portland's waterfront were restored and an old-style Public Market was constructed; the Maine Mall expanded and saw office parks spring up nearby, a miniature edge city; real estate prices rose by hundreds of percents, not just in vacation coves, but in Portland and small towns that had never considered themselves picturesque. The L.L. Bean headquarters in Freeport, open 24 hours a day, 365 days a year, symbolized the boom: The two chaste initials and the Anglo-Saxon monosyllable suggesting the dry understatement of Down East Yankees; the 24-hour-a-day schedule recalling the hard work needed to eke out a living from the cold waters of the North Atlantic to the pine-covered north woods; the commercial success of the enterprise a prime example of Maine's unexpected 1980s boom.

In the process, Maine's economy was transformed. It lost jobs in shoes, chicken processing, papermaking and timber, but gained in call centers, tourism and high-tech. By mid-2000 unemployment was down to 3.6%, and 1.7% in Portland's Cumberland County; $8 an hour jobs were going begging. Shoe factory employment fell from 17,000 to 6,000 from 1983 to 1999, while telephone call center employment rose from zero to 10,000. The Grand Banks were overfished, and scratching small Maine boiling potatoes out of the soil of Aroostook County has become harder: The nation's top potato producer 50 years ago, Maine fell to eighth place in the 1990s, even as national consumption rose by 15%. By the late 1990s, biotech outproduced lobster fishing and potato harvesting combined. Paper mill towns like Millinocket now stand half empty, while intersections around Portland are jammed with cars waiting for the green arrow so they can turn

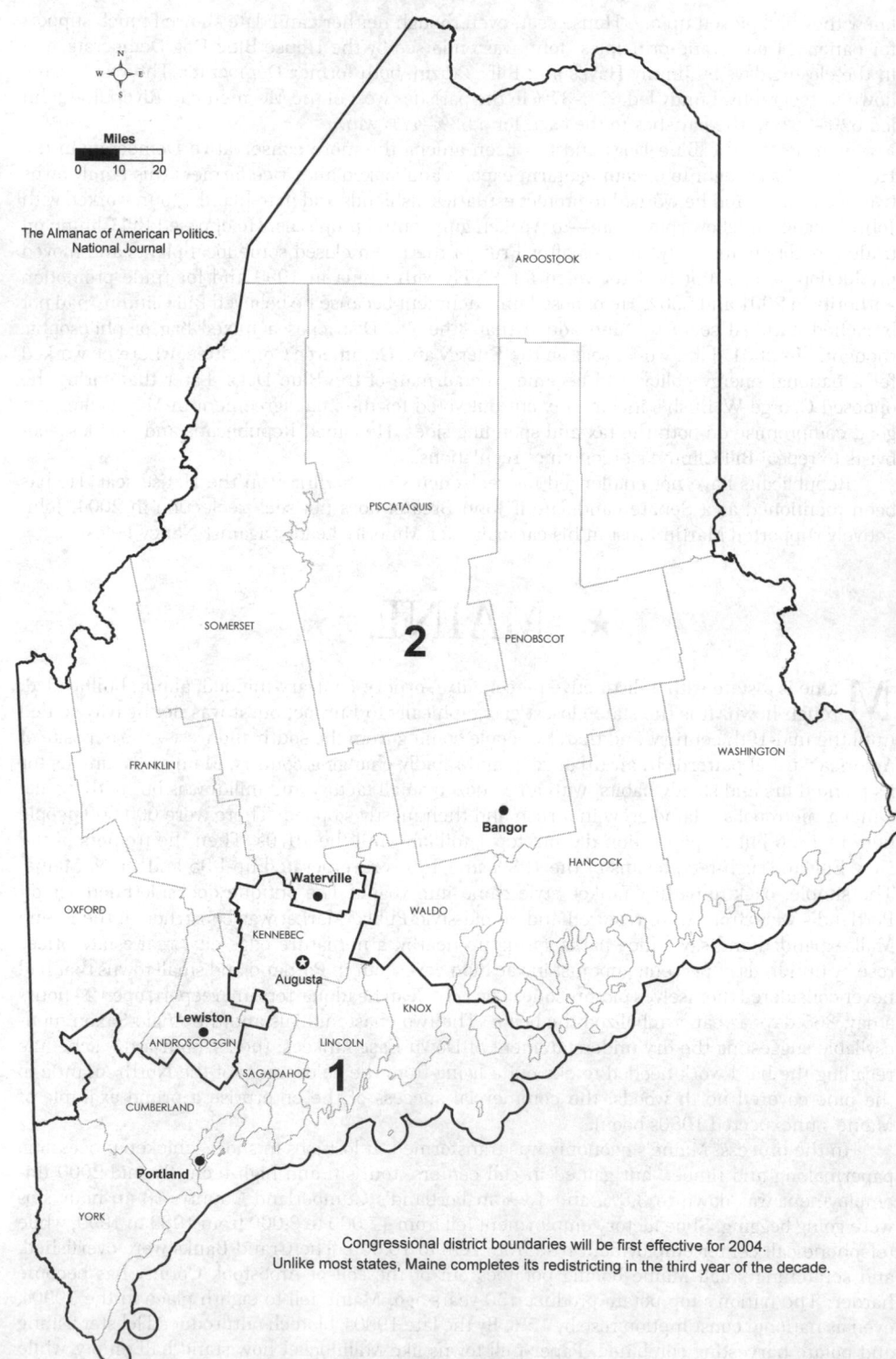

Miles
0   10   20

The Almanac of American Politics.
National Journal

AROOSTOOK

PISCATAQUIS

SOMERSET

2

PENOBSCOT

WASHINGTON

FRANKLIN

Bangor

HANCOCK

Waterville

WALDO

OXFORD

KENNEBEC

Augusta

KNOX

Lewiston

LINCOLN

ANDROSCOGGIN

SAGADAHOC

1

CUMBERLAND

Portland

YORK

Congressional district boundaries will be first effective for 2004.
Unlike most states, Maine completes its redistricting in the third year of the decade.

into the mall. Tourism continues to be the biggest business here, and Bath Iron Works, long the state's largest private employer, has a long-term contract to build 21 *Arleigh Burke* Class Naval destroyers, the work partly of former Senator and Defense Secretary William Cohen. But it is the new economy that undergirds Maine's flannel-shirt lifestyle and its fierce pride.

Now in effect there are two Maines—booming coastal Maine and declining interior Maine. Schools are closing in Aroostook County but they're being built in York County, at the southern end of the state. Loring Air Force Base up north closed in 1994, while Amtrak inaugurated Portland-to-Boston service for the first time in 36 years in 2001. The lobster industry has been thriving, with catches since 2000 near the all-time record, even as lumber mills close down. Maine farmers have switched to specialty crops and market their crops at fruit and vegetable stands or to high-end Boston area markets and restaurants. Demographically, Maine is like Western Europe, with an aging population and the lowest birth rate in the United States; it has attracted few immigrants and in the 1990s, despite low unemployment, was 46th in population growth. An aging population has its advantages (Maine was also 46th on the FBI crime index) and disadvantages (health care costs are high and the percentage with employer-provided health insurance low). Maine has the highest high school graduation rate in the country, but its high schools and colleges have not been providing enough graduates to fill its job openings. Outgoing Governor Angus King in December 2002 estimated that the state's labor force was growing by 2,000 people fewer than its job openings. Immigration "is one way we can make up the gap," he said. But in 2000 Maine was the whitest state in the nation, less than 1% Hispanic or Asian, and the most visible immigrants have been the 1,000 Somalis who have come to the old French Canadian mill town of Lewiston (population 36,000), where they can find cheap housing and low living costs and, in many cases, live on Maine's comparatively generous welfare benefits. Interestingly, many say they come so their children will be insulated from American popular culture and crime; while they have evoked some hostile reaction, they have also been greeted generously.

In politics, Maine is contrary-minded. Until 1958, Maine held state elections in September, a date originally chosen because it followed the state's early harvest; in the days before polls, the results here were taken as a gauge of national partisan movement—hence the saying, "As Maine goes, so goes the nation." However, in September 1936, Maine voted 56% for Republican Governor Lewis Barrows and in November only Maine and Vermont voted for Alf Landon over Franklin Roosevelt, prompting Roosevelt's campaign manager to observe, "As Maine goes, so goes Vermont." Maine's adherence to flinty Yankee Republicanism and Prohibition was echoed almost nowhere else in the nation. Since then, it has voted for the loser in the close presidential elections of 1948, 1960, 1968, 1976 and 2000—a record equaled by no other state. Maine cast the nation's highest percentages for Ross Perot, 30% in 1992 and 14% in 1996. In 1994 and 1998 it elected King, an Independent and former Democrat, as governor, as it had elected Independent and former Republican James Longley in 1974. Thus in the past eight gubernatorial elections Maine voted twice for Republicans, three times for Democrats and three times for Independents.

If Maine's tradition-minded Yankees kept the state Republican long after the nation embraced the New Deal, the sons and daughters of its ethnics—Irish, French Canadian, Greek and Arab immigrants have come to equal the numbers of pure WASPs (though these new Mainers in many ways share traditional Yankee traits and values)—made the Democrats competitive, perhaps even dominant, here in the 1980s as they were losing ground in the rest of the nation. But as the economy changed, these differences became less important. Ticket-splitting is very much the norm here. In 2000 Maine voted 49%–44% for Al Gore, 69%–31% for Republican Senator Olympia Snowe and 66%–32% Democratic in its two House races. In 2002 Maine reelected Republican Senator Susan Collins 58%–42% and elected Democrat John Baldacci as governor by 47%–41%. In the 1990s Maine had more partisan turnover in its state legislative seats than any other state; in its small seats (average population of a state House seat is 8,461) Mainers vote for the person, not the party. In 2000 Protestants gave Bush a 6% margin; Catholics gave Gore a 5% margin: the old religious polarization is gone. Who owns the future? Those with more education voted for Gore, a good sign for Democrats in an increasingly educated country. But voters under 30 were carried by Bush, a good sign for Republicans. Maine is up for grabs.

As the economy changed, Maine moved toward a consensus on how to balance economic growth and preserve the environment. Maine's environment-conscious newcomers have made this a good market for natural toothpaste, organic baby food and canvas bags rather than paper or plastic at the supermarket. It was the first state to ban the juicebox as insufficiently biodegradable and it recycles liquor bottles. On cultural issues, Maine voters have been wary of change. By narrow margins they rejected gay rights initiatives in 1998 and 2000; in 1999 they rejected a partial-birth abortion ban but endorsed medical marijuana; in 2000 they rejected physician-assisted suicide.

The People		Race/Ethnic Origin			Military veterans: 154,590 (15.9%)	
Pop. 2000:	1,274,923	1,230,297	96.5%	White	WWII: 19.8%	Korea: 14.1%
Pop. 1990:	1,227,928	6,440	0.5%	Black	Vietnam: 33.1%	Gulf War: 8.2%
Change 1990–2000:	Up 3.8%	9,014	0.7%	Asian	**Most populous cities:**	
Change 1980–1990:	Up 9.2%	6,911	0.5%	Native Am.	1. Portland	64,249
% of U.S. total:	0.5%	334	0.0%	Hawaiian	2. Lewiston	35,690
Pop. rank:	40th of 50	11,731	0.9%	Two+ races	3. Bangor	31,473
Area size:	35,385 sq. mi.	836	0.1%	Other	4. South Portland	23,324
State Native:	67.3%	9,360	0.7%	Hisp. Origin	5. Auburn	23,203
Non-citizen:	1.3%	**Ancestry**			Urban population: 40.2%	
Language		English: 16.0%		Irish: 11.2%	Rural population: 59.8%	
English: 87.9%	Other Eur.: 10.0%	French: 10.6%		USA: 7.0%		
Spanish: 1.3%		Fr. Canadian: 6.4%				

Education		Work Sector		Legislature	
H.S. Grad:	85.4%	Private: 75.9%	Govt: 14.5%	Senate	18 D 17 R
College Grad:	22.9%	Self: 9.3%	Family: 0.3%	House	80 D 67 R 4 I
Industry		Unemployment: 4.7%		Legislative Term Limits: Yes	
Agri: 2.6%	Con: 6.9%	**Household Income**		**Registered Voters**	
Fin: 6.2%	Info: 2.5%	<15k: 17.8%	15-35k: 29.0%	D: 298,443	(31.4%)
Mfg: 18.5%	Prof: 30.1%	35-50k: 18.3%	50-100k: 27.7%	R: 277,059	(29.2%)
Public: 4.5%	Trade: 17.0%	100-150k: 4.7%	>150k: 2.4%	I: 374,547	(39.4%)
Other: 11.8%		Median: $37,240			
Occupation		Poverty status: 10.9%			
Blue collar: 25.6%	White collar: 57.4%	**Home Value**			
Gray collar: 17.0%		<50k: 15.4%	50-100k: 39.6%	100-200k: 34.6%	200-300k: 6.5%
		300-500k: 2.7%	>500k: 1.2%	Median: $94,300	

Presidential politics   Maine turned out to be a target state in the 2000 presidential election, with the lead see-sawing back and forth in polls. Indeed, Maine has been unstable in recent presidential voting, casting majorities for Republican George Bush in 1988 and Democrat Bill Clinton in 1996 and producing a virtual three-way tie in 1992, with Clinton in first place and Bush, who spent nearly every summer of his life in Maine, finishing third. In 2000, Al Gore won by a 49%–44% margin. Maine is one of two states (Nebraska is the other) which gives one elector to the winner in each congressional district. Bush lost the 2d District by only a 47%–46% margin; with 1% more there he would have won 272 electoral votes instead of 271.

Maine held its first-ever presidential primary on March 5, 1996, in an attempt to generate an early contest to which candidates would pay attention. But they didn't—at least not much. Clinton had no competition and Bob Dole

2000 Presidential Vote

Gore (D)	319,951	(49%)
Bush (R)	286,616	(44%)
Nader (Green)	37,127	(6%)
Other	8,123	(1%)

2000 Republican Presidential Primary

Bush (R)	49,308	(51%)
McCain (R)	42,510	(44%)
Other	4,806	(5%)

2000 Democratic Presidential Primary

Gore (D)	34,725	(54%)
Bradley (D)	26,520	(41%)
Uncommitted	2,634	(4%)

1996 Presidential Vote

Clinton (D)	312,788	(53%)
Dole (R)	186,378	(32%)
Perot (I)	85,970	(15%)

had clinched the Republican nomination three days earlier in South Carolina. In 2000 Maine got lost in the crush of states voting on Super Tuesday, March 7, though the results were close. George W. Bush beat John McCain 51%–44%, the one Bush victory in New England, and Al Gore beat Bill Bradley 54%–41%.

Congressional districting   The lines in Maine are drawn by a 15-member bipartisan Legislative Apportionment Committee; the legislature can amend the plan and must approve it by a two-thirds vote. The governor has a veto, though presumably that's academic since there would be a two-thirds majority to override it. Under state law the committee sends its plan to the legislature in spring 2003. This arguably violates the Constitution, since the 2002 elections were held within lines drawn on the basis of the 1990 Census. But no one has filed a lawsuit for the good reason that it makes no practical difference. There has been little change in the boundary between the two districts since Maine lost its third seat in the 1960 Census. In the 2003 session, however, the legislature failed to adopt a plan. On July 2, 2003, the state supreme court adopted a plan for the 2004 elections.

108th Congress Lineup
2 D
107th Congress Lineup
2 D

Governor

John Baldacci (D)

Elected 2002, term expires Jan. 2007, 1st term; b. Jan. 30, 1955, Bangor; home, Augusta; U. of ME, B.A. 1986; Catholic; married (Karen).

Elected Office: Bangor City Cncl., 1978–81; ME Senate, 1982–94; U.S. House of Reps., 1994–2002.

Professional Career: Restaurateur.

Office: 1 State House Station, Augusta, 04333, 207-287-3531; Fax: 207-287-1034; Web site: www.state.me.us/governor.

Election Results

2002 general	John Baldacci (D)	238,179	(47%)
	Peter Cianchette (R)	209,496	(41%)
	Jonathan Carter (Green)	46,903	(9%)
2002 primary	John Baldacci (D)	unopposed	
1998 general	Angus S. King Jr. (I)	246,772	(59%)
	James B. Longley Jr. (R)	79,716	(19%)
	Thomas J. Connolly (D)	50,506	(12%)
	Patricia H. Lamarche (I)	28,722	(7%)
	Other	15,293	(4%)

John Baldacci (pronounced *ball-DA-chee*) in 2002 became the first Democrat elected Governor of Maine since 1986. Baldacci grew up in Bangor, where until recently he lived across the street from the house he grew up in and still attends the same church where he was christened. His family ran Momma Baldacci's, a restaurant started by his grandparents in 1933. He is of Italian and Lebanese descent, distantly related to former Senator George Mitchell, and the family restaurant used to get a daily delivery of rolls from former Senator William Cohen's father's bakery. Baldacci followed his father on the Bangor City Council in 1978, at 23; in 1982 he was elected to the state Senate, where he often dissented from Democrats and chaired the tax committee. When 2d District Congresswoman Olympia Snowe ran for the Senate in 1994, Baldacci ran for the House and campaigned by holding spaghetti dinners at $2 a head (children under 12 free) around the district. In a seven-candidate primary, with lots of support around Bangor, Baldacci won with 27% to 23% for former Democratic state Chairman James Mitchell, George Mitchell's nephew. Maine's contrary-mindedness came out in the general election: Baldacci opposed the Clinton health care plan and pledged to oppose any new taxes; Republican nominee Richard Bennett was iffy about the Contract With America's defense spending increase. Green Party and Independent candidates pressed both candidates. Baldacci won 46%–41%.

In the House, Baldacci had a mostly liberal voting record and chimed in on Maine issues. He was a leader in passing the law allowing drugs to be reimported from Canada and other foreign countries, which then-HHS Secretary Donna Shalala declined to implement. He pushed to get reclassification of Canadian lumber under the Canadian Softwood Agreement. He opposed PNTR with China because of its alleged apple juice dumping that prompted the shutdown of at least one Maine orchard. He fought a Fish and Wildlife Service proposal to list the Atlantic salmon as an endangered species. He was reelected three times with more than 70% of the vote.

Maine's congressional districts are good springboards to statewide office, for each one is within both the Portland and Bangor television markets; Baldacci's three immediate predecessors in the 2d District were all elected to the Senate. Baldacci's goal was the governorship, and he had pledged to serve only eight years in the House. From the time Independent Angus King was elected to a second and last term, Baldacci was recognized as the frontrunner for 2002. But there was plenty of competition. The issues were framed by a *New York Times* story that said Maine was the most heavily taxed state, with 14% of incomes going to state and local government and by the state's fiscal woes. Baldacci said he was against tax increases; to spur economic development, he wanted to increase aid to public schools (to hold down property taxes), slow down the growth of state spending and eliminate the property tax on business equipment. He called for business tax breaks in distressed areas. He said a single-payer health care finance plan was unworkable and said he would set up an Office of Health Policy to coordinate changes in health care finance. It was not as liberal as some Democrats would have liked, but he had no primary opposition. The leading Republican was former state Representative Peter Cianchette, who promised to cut the state tax burden 20%; he said he would veto any tax increase and "any budget that grows faster than your paychecks." He called for a property tax cap, with no corresponding state aid. There were also Independent candidacies, some of them short-lived. Daniel Wathen resigned as chief justice of the Supreme Judicial Court in November 2001, but quit the gubernatorial race after seven weeks. Former Central Maine Power CEO David Flanagan dropped out of the race in July 2002 citing poor polling numbers and inadequate fundraising. But one Independent, Jonathan Carter, won the Green party nomination (there was actually a primary) and also qualified for the state's public financing system, which gave him $902,000 but limited his spending. Low contribution limits meant that neither Baldacci nor Cianchette, who won the Republican primary 2–1, were able to spend much more than $1.5 million.

Carter called for single-payer health insurance and for a sales tax on professional services; like the others he was for eliminating the property tax on business equipment. Carter got the most attention when he ran an ad accusing Baldacci of supporting casino gambling despite his statements to the contrary; the ad featured ominous music and phrases from *The Sopranos*—ethnic stereotyping, many said. On Election Day, Baldacci won a 47%–41% plurality over Cianchette; Carter got only 9%. Baldacci won absolute majorities only in the counties north and east of Bangor, and they accounted for 26,000 of his 29,000-vote plurality; interestingly, these same counties were the strongest area for Republican Senator Susan Collins, who is from Aroostook County: Hometown, rather than partisan voting. Cianchette narrowly carried his home area, Portland's Cumberland County, though it is usually more Democratic than the rest of the state. Baldacci promised a "balanced economic strategy" with different approaches for rural and urban areas and reiterated his promise to limit spending increases to the rate of inflation. Some speculated that he may encounter friction with his Democratic and union allies, as the state faced a budget shortfall estimated to be as high as $1 billion.

Senior Senator

Olympia Snowe (R)

Elected 1994, seat up 2006, 2d term; b. Feb. 21, 1947, Augusta; home, Auburn; U. of ME, B.A. 1969; Greek Orthodox; married (John McKernan).

Elected Office: ME House of Reps., 1973–76; ME Senate, 1976–78; U.S. House of Reps., 1978–94.

Professional Career: Dir., Superior Concrete Co., 1969–78; Auburn Bd. of Voter Registration, 1971–73.

DC Office: 154 RSOB, 20510, 202-224-5344; Fax: 202-224-1946; Web site: snowe.senate.gov.

State Offices: Auburn, 207-786-2451; Augusta, 207-622-8292; Bangor, 207-945-0432; Biddeford, 207-282-4144; Portland, 207-874-0833; Presque Isle, 207-764-5124.

Committees: *Commerce, Science & Transportation*: Aviation; Communications; Oceans, Fisheries & Coast Guard (Chmn.); Surface Transportation & Merchant Marine. *Finance*: Health Care; International Trade; Social Security & Family Policy; Taxation & IRS Oversight. *Intelligence (Select)*. *Small Business & Entrepreneurship* (Chmn.).

Group Ratings

	ADA	ACLU	AFS	LCV	CON	ITIC	NTU	COC	ACU	NTLC	CHC
2002	30	60	50	82	74	100	41	85	65	59	—
2001	40	—	25	50	—	—	65	79	60	—	40

National Journal Ratings

	2001 LIB —	2001 CONS	2002 LIB —	2002 CONS
Economic	46%	54%	46%	51%
Social	51%	48%	45%	54%
Foreign	36%	54%	41%	58%

Key Votes of the 107th Congress

1. Approve Bush Tax Cuts	Y	5. Confirm Ashcroft as AG	Y	9. Bar Coop. with Intl. Court	Y
2. Expand Patients' Rights	Y	6. Bar Gays in the Boy Scouts	N	10. Trade Promotion Authority	Y
3. Campaign Finance Reform	Y	7. $ for Hate Crime Prosecution	Y	11. Authorize Force in Iraq	Y
4. Permit ANWR Development	N	8. Overseas Military Abortions	Y	12. Homeland Sec. Dept. Union	N

Election Results

2000 general	Olympia Snowe (R)	437,689	(69%)	($1,981,504)
	Mark Lawrence (D)	197,183	(31%)	($727,655)
2000 primary	Olympia Snowe (R)	unopposed		
1994 general	Olympia Snowe (R)	308,244	(60%)	($2,041,834)
	Thomas H. Andrews (D)	186,042	(36%)	($1,482,060)
	Other	17,447	(3%)	

Prior Winning Percentages: 1992 House (49%); 1990 House (51%); 1988 House (66%); 1986 House (77%); 1984 House (76%); 1982 House (67%); 1980 House (79%); 1978 House (51%)

Olympia Snowe is a Republican elected in 1994. Snowe grew up in Auburn and worked as a legislative staffer after college; in 1973, after her husband, state Representative Peter Snowe, died in an auto accident, she was elected to his seat. In 1978, when then-Congressman William Cohen ran for the Senate, she ran for the House in the northern 2d District, and won handily. She had a moderate record and won by large margins in the 1980s but more narrowly in the 1990s; in 1989 she married Governor John McKernan, her former House colleague. When Senator George Mitchell announced his retirement in March 1994, Snowe decided instantly to run. Immediately she went on the attack against her obvious Democratic opponent, 1st District Congressman Tom Andrews, whose winning margin two years before had been 107,000 votes, while hers was only 22,000. Snowe attacked him hard for voting for the bill that closed Loring Air Force Base in northern Maine and for opposing the balanced budget amendment. She won 60%–36%, carrying every county, losing only the cities of Portland and Lewiston and a few mill towns.

In the Senate, she was the least conservative of the 11 freshman Republicans elected in 1994. Her voting record has been around the middle of the Senate; she has voted with Democrats on some economic and many cultural issues and has been more conservative on defense and foreign policy. Since 1999 she and John Breaux have been convening a Centrist Coalition with senators of both parties, and on occasion they have played a key role in shaping legislation. On impeachment, she supported Republican positions on most issues, and worked with Democrats to come up with a compromise; she and Maine colleague Susan Collins proposed that the Senate vote first on a "finding of fact" describing Clinton's conduct and then separately on whether he should be removed from office. It was not successful, and Snowe voted against impeachment. In early 2001, with the Senate equally divided, Snowe played a pivotal role on some issues. In May 2001 she led a group of Finance Committee members who insisted that the child care tax credit would be refundable, so that money would go to those with low incomes who pay no income tax. Many Republicans opposed this as a form of welfare; Snowe argued that these people needed tax relief. The provision went into the Senate bill and while the conference committee was pending Snowe sponsored a nonbinding resolution insisting on it that passed 94–4: so the refundable credit became law. She supported the McCain-Feingold campaign finance bill and did not bring forward, as she had in 1998, a provision, an anathema to Democrats, to ban unions from spending their members' dues money on politics without their permission. After September 11 she was part of the bipartisan group that negotiated with Treasury Secretary Paul O'Neill provisions of the stimulus package; she argued unsuccessfully for a sales tax holiday during the holiday season, with the federal government reimbursing states for lost sales tax revenues. She was one of two Republicans voting with Democrats in July 2001 for a $7.5 billion farm aid bill; that was stopped by George W. Bush's veto threat. She and Collins voted for the 2002 farm bill after insertion of the $2 billion dairy program. In November 2002, the pair threatened to vote against the homeland security bill because of provisions, added quietly in the House, limiting liability of vaccine makers for additives, permitting overseas companies to compete for contracts and targeting one project to Texas A&M. Telephone lines buzzed with negotiations; Speaker Dennis Hastert was tracked down in Istanbul. Snowe and Collins agreed to vote for the bill after Majority Leader Trent Lott gave them a commitment that the three provisions would be revisited early in 2003; in January 2003, new Majority Leader Bill Frist, honored that commitment.

Snowe has taken a lead role on many women's health care issues. In July 2000 she sponsored a $200 million appropriation for women's health research, with $175 million for breast cancer, $12 million for ovarian cancer and $6 million for osteoporosis. In 1999 she pushed a bill to allow mastectomy patients to remain in the hospital as long as a doctor prescribes. In 2000 she sponsored a bill to extend osteoporosis screening to all Medicare recipients. With Edward Kennedy, she worked in 2000 to extend prescription drug coverage to military retirees through the military Tricare program and in 2001 to extend the CHIP program to the parents of eligible children. She supports abortion rights and came out against George W. Bush's reinstatement of the Mexico City policy in 2001. She has sponsored bills to pay for computerized prescription delivery in hospitals and nursing homes and to require gender analysis in FDA clinical trials. On prescription drugs, she was one of the sponsors of the tripartisan plan, developed in the Finance Committee in 2001 and which became the chief alternative to the Democrats' plan in summer 2002. She also has sponsored with Ron Wyden a bill to make Medigap insurance one of five options for seniors, all with coverage of prescription drug expenses over $3,000 a year.

On the Armed Services Committee from 1997 to 2001, she took the lead in opposing the recommendation of the commission headed by former Senator Nancy Kassebaum Baker to end gender-integrated basic training, and she and Mary Landrieu sponsored the March 1999 resolution declaring it U.S. policy to deploy a ballistic missile system as soon as "technologically possible"; it passed 99–0 and spurred a reluctant Clinton administration. She became chairman of the Small Business Committee in January 2003 and promised to work for more affordable health insurance, regulatory relief and access to foreign markets. She and Dianne Feinstein have sought to raise CAFE gas mileage standards for SUVs and light trucks. She has labored on many local issues, establishing a pilot $25 million fishing vessel buyback, passing a "Maine Lights" program to preserve historic Maine lighthouses, and working to ban lobster dragging.

Snowe approached the 2000 campaign with very high job approval ratings. She received vigorous opposition from state Senate President Mark Lawrence, who campaigned in support of Maine's prescription drug law and charged that Snowe had voted against a bill that would have provided $97 million for school construction in Maine. But it was no contest. Snowe was re-elected 69%–31%, this time carrying even Portland and Lewiston, and trailing only in a few small, isolated communities.

Junior Senator

Susan Collins (R)

Elected 1996, seat up 2008, 2d term; b. Dec. 7, 1952, Caribou; home, Bangor; St. Lawrence U., B.A. 1975; Catholic; single.

Professional Career: Legis. Aide, U.S. Sen. Bill Cohen, 1975–87; Staff Dir., Oversight of Gov. Mgmt. Subcmte., 1981–87; Professional & Financial Regulation Comm., 1987–92; New England Regional Dir., U.S. Small Business Admin., 1992; ME Dpty. Treas., 1993; Exec. Dir., Ctr. for Family Business, Husson Col., 1994–96.

DC Office: 172 RSOB, 20510, 202-224-2523; Fax: 202-224-2693; Web site: collins.senate.gov.

State Offices: Augusta, 207-622-8414; Bangor, 207-945-0417; Biddeford, 207-283-1101; Caribou, 207-493-7873; Lewiston, 207-784-6969; Portland, 207-780-3575.

Committees: *Aging (Special)*. *Armed Services*: Emerging Threats & Capabilities; Personnel; Seapower. *Governmental Affairs* (Chmn.). *Joint Economic Committee* (6th of 10 Sens.).

Group Ratings

	ADA	ACLU	AFS	LCV	CON	ITIC	NTU	COC	ACU	NTLC	CHC
2002	35	40	50	76	78	88	40	85	55	62	—
2001	35	—	25	38	—	—	67	79	64	—	60

National Journal Ratings

	2001 LIB —	2001 CONS	2002 LIB —	2002 CONS
Economic	47%	49%	46%	51%
Social	53%	46%	46%	52%
Foreign	36%	54%	44%	54%

Key Votes of the 107th Congress

1. Approve Bush Tax Cuts	Y	5. Confirm Ashcroft as AG	Y	9. Bar Coop. with Intl. Court	Y
2. Expand Patients' Rights	Y	6. Bar Gays in the Boy Scouts	Y	10. Trade Promotion Authority	Y
3. Campaign Finance Reform	Y	7. $ for Hate Crime Prosecution	Y	11. Authorize Force in Iraq	Y
4. Permit ANWR Development	N	8. Overseas Military Abortions	Y	12. Homeland Sec. Dept. Union	N

Election Results

2002 general	Susan Collins (R)	295,041	(58%)	($3,961,167)
	Chellie Pingree (D)	209,858	(42%)	($3,806,798)
2002 primary	Susan Collins (R)	unopposed		
1996 general	Susan Collins (R)	298,422	(49%)	($1,621,475)
	Joseph E. Brennan (D)	266,226	(44%)	($976,805)
	Other	42,129	(7%)	

Susan Collins, Maine's junior Republican senator, was elected in 1996, the first time she won elective office. She grew up in Caribou, in potato-growing Aroostook County, about as far northeast as you can get in the United States, closer to the capitals of New Brunswick and Quebec than to the capital of Maine. Her family is in the lumber business, and also in politics: Her father was a state senator, her mother a mayor and her uncle a state Supreme Court justice. As a high school senior, she went to Washington on a Senate youth program, and Senator Margaret Chase Smith took her into her private office and talked to her for nearly two hours. Right after college, she got a job as an intern with William Cohen, then a congressman on the Judiciary Committee who voted to impeach Richard Nixon. She was a Cohen staffer for 12 years and served as the staff director for the Senate Subcommittee on Oversight of Government Management on Governmental Affairs, which Cohen chaired from 1981–87. After Republicans lost their majority, Collins returned to Maine to work five years for Governor John McKernan as a financial regulation commissioner. In 1992 she was New England administrator of the Small Business Administration, and by 1994 she had announced her candidacy for governor. It was a disastrous campaign: She won the Republican nomination, but was overshadowed by independent Angus King, and ran third, with only 23% of the vote. She then became the executive director of the Husson College Center for Family Business.

Then in January 1996 Cohen surprised almost everybody by announcing he would retire from the Senate—almost as big a surprise as his selection as Defense Secretary by Bill Clinton a year later. But there was a precedent in Maine for a third-place gubernatorial finisher to be elected senator: George Mitchell was similarly humiliated in 1974, then, after being appointed senator in 1980, won smashing victories in 1982 and 1988. In the primary she played up her resemblance to Olympia Snowe and Cohen and called for a balanced budget amendment, line-item veto and term limits (and pledged to serve no more than two terms). She won with 56% of the vote to 31% and 13% for the two others. In the general election she was opposed by Joseph Brennan, a product of working class Portland, elected governor in 1978 and 1982, then to Congress in 1986 and 1988. But he had lost races for governor in 1990 and 1994. Brennan attacked Collins on economic issues and gun control. Collins raised much more money and won 49%–44%.

Collins has compiled a middle-of-the-Senate voting record; she has joined Democrats on issues including the 1999 tax cut, campaign finance regulation and the partial-birth abortion ban. Collins was visible during the impeachment process. She read history and constitutional law, coming up with an obscure article that argued the Senate could vote on findings of fact separately from removal; she and Snowe pushed a plan to have such separate votes, to no avail. She said that much of the evidence weighed against Clinton, but in the end voted against removal. Her first great cause in the Senate was campaign finance reform; she was beaten by a millionaire in 1994, faced two of them in the 1996 primary and had only meager finances herself. She said that limitations on self-financing candidates were a "cornerstone" of any reform for her. But these have not been included because they were held unconstitutional under *Buckley v. Valeo*. In March 2001 she sponsored with Ron Wyden an amendment requiring negative ads to include a picture of the candidate running them or otherwise be ineligible for the lowest discounted advertising rate.

Collins has done much of her work on the Governmental Affairs Committee, on one of whose subcommittees she was once a staffer and of which she has been chairman since January 2003. She insisted that investigations of Clinton-Gore campaign finance violations should look at misdeeds of both parties; she probed deftly at the notorious 1996 Buddhist temple fundraiser. As chairman of the Permanent Subcommittee on Investigations she probed into Medicare fraud, investment scams, unsafe food, Internet ripoffs and fraudulent telephone billing—slamming and cramming—day trading, direct mail sweepstakes, property flipping, lead paint; as ranking minority member she participated in Chairman Carl Levin's careful and apolitical investigation into fraudulent corporate accounting. On homeland security, she worked quietly to preserve the Coast Guard's search-and-rescue missions; with Ted Stevens, her amendment to do so passed 10–7 over the opposition of Chairman Joe Lieberman and ranking minority member Fred Thompson. She also held out for aggrieved department employees to have access to an appeals board. On becoming committee chairman in 2003, she said. "I'm going to take the same aggressive approach I've always had. I don't have a different standard for wasteful spending if it's in a Democratic administration versus a Republican one."

In November 2002 she and Olympia Snowe threatened to vote against the homeland security bill because of provisions, added quietly in the House, limiting liability of vaccine makers for additives, permitting overseas companies to compete for contracts and targeting one project to Texas A&M. Collins and Snowe agreed to vote for the bill after Majority Leader Trent Lott gave them a commitment that the three provisions would be revisited early in 2003; in January 2003, new Majority Leader Bill Frist honored that commitment.

Collins has been active on health care issues. She backed the Republican version of HMO reform, and has sponsored her own version with John Breaux, with internal and external appeals processes to resolve complaints. In April 2001 she got the Senate to vote 99–1 to eliminate the budget provision for a 15% cutback in Medicare home health care providers; she argued that it was a fiction anyway, since the Senate had voted to postpone it three years in a row. The issue on which she spent most effort in 2002 was prescription drugs, which she says she started working on in 1999. This was of great importance, for the chief achievement of her 2002 opponent, former Maine Senate Majority Leader Chellie Pingree, was a law authorizing the state to negotiate with pharmaceutical companies purchases of prescription drugs for the uninsured (it was challenged in court but in May 2003 the Supreme Court ruled that Maine could put the program into effect); Pingree had been taking busloads of Maine seniors to Canada on well-publicized drug-buying trips. Collins was one of the co-sponsors, of the Tripartisan prescription drug plan, designed to help seniors buy insurance prescription drug coverage, which became the chief alternative to the Democrats' plan in summer 2002. At the same time, she co-sponsored with Democrat John Edwards a bill to restrict the automatic 30-month exclusive marketing time pharmaceutical companies get when they sue a generic drug maker for patent infringement; the measure was designed to get drugs out of patent more quickly and thus reduce prices. It passed in committee 16–5 in July 2002, and on the last day of the month, amid the prescription drug debate, it passed the Senate 78–21. Collins voted for the Tripartisan bill and, unlike colleague Olympia Snowe, voted for the Graham-Smith version for a prescription drug within Medicare supported by most Democrats. But no prescription drug benefit had the votes to pass in the Senate and the patent bill was never taken up in the House.

In 2001 she got Snowe's seat on Armed Services, from which she can look after Bath Iron Works. She has worked on local issues—she got fishermen included in Chapter 12 of the Bankruptcy Act, which covers farmers. Maine is a border state, and Collins tends to border issues. She sought a National Weather Service office for her hometown of Caribou, pointing out that since it is surrounded by Canada it does not receive weather warnings from adjacent Weather Service offices as most other American communities do.

To Democratic strategists, Collins looked vulnerable in 2002: She had won the seat with only 49% of the vote in a state where George W. Bush got only 44%. And they thought they had a dynamite candidate: Pingree was energetic and politically creative; she combined leftish stands with a populist flair and emphasis on an issue that touched ordinary people's lives. She was elected to the legislature from a Republican district. She announced in April 2001 and raised $1 million by January 2002, more than Collins did during that period. Not widely known in the state, she ran a series of ads in the first months of 2001—positive spots on herself and tough attacks on Collins. The debate over prescription drugs in July helped Collins: She could say that her amendment to make prescription drugs less expensive had passed the Senate by a wide margin and that she had voted for a couple of different prescription drug benefit programs. Pingree ads insisted that Collins was "siding with the big drug companies." Collins ads replied that Pingree should "get her facts straight." George W. Bush came to Maine in August and said of Collins, "She's kind of an independent thinker, I might add. I don't do everything she says—and she doesn't do everything I say. But she's an ally, and I'm proud to call her friend." National Democrats didn't pour any major money into the race, though Pingree raised and spent over $3 million, nearly as much as Collins.

Collins won by a solid 58%–42% margin. She won 68% in Aroostook County and between 63% and 66% in three adjacent counties, which include Bangor; interestingly these were also the strongest areas for the successful Democratic gubernatorial candidate John Baldacci, who is from Bangor. She won at least 53% in every county.

FIRST DISTRICT

Rep. Tom Allen (D)

Elected 1996, 4th term; b. Apr. 16, 1945, Portland; home, Portland; Bowdoin Col., B.A. 1967, Rhodes Scholar, Oxford U., B. Phil. 1970; Harvard J.D. 1974; Protestant; married (Diana).

Elected Office: Portland City Cncl., 1989–95; Portland Mayor, 1991.

Professional Career: Staffer, U.S. Sen. Edmund Muskie, 1970–71; Practicing atty., 1974–94; Chmn., ME Clinton–Gore Campaign, 1992; Public Policy Consultant, 1995.

DC Office: 1717 LHOB 20515, 202-225-6116; Fax: 202-225-5590; Web site: www.house.gov/allen.

District Office: Portland, 207-774-5019.

Committees: *Energy & Commerce* (23d of 26 D): Energy & Air Quality; Environment & Hazardous Materials.

Group Ratings

	ADA	ACLU	AFS	LCV	CON	ITIC	NTU	COC	ACU	NTLC	CHC
2002	95	87	100	88	70	50	18	53	0	0	0
2001	95	—	100	93	—	—	11	30	0	—	—

National Journal Ratings

	2001 LIB —	2001 CONS	2002 LIB —	2002 CONS
Economic	91%	9%	76%	24%
Social	83%	11%	74%	19%
Foreign	85%	15%	77%	23%

Key Votes of the 107th Congress

1. Approve Bush Tax Cuts	N	5. Faith-Based Charities	N	9. Trade Promotion Authority	N
2. Limit Patients' Bill of Rights	N	6. Bar Gays in the Boy Scouts	N	10. Bar Funds for Intl. Court	N
3. Campaign Finance Reform	Y	7. Ban Partial-Birth Abortion	N	11. Authorize Force in Iraq	N
4. Ban ANWR Development	Y	8. Arm Commercial Pilots	N	12. Deny Home. Sec. Dept. Union	N

Election Results

2002 general	Tom Allen (D)	172,646	(64%)	($521,308)
	Steven Joyce (R)	97,931	(36%)	($172,350)
2002 primary	Tom Allen (D)	unopposed		
2000 general	Tom Allen (D)	202,823	(60%)	($639,119)
	Jane Amero (R)	123,915	(37%)	($478,817)
	J. Frederic Staples (Lib)	12,356	(4%)	

Prior Winning Percentages: 1998 (60%); 1996 (55%)

The People		Race/Ethnic Origin	Ancestry	
Area size:	5,480 sq. mi.	96.3% White	English: 16.1%	Irish: 11.9%
Urban population:	50.4%	0.6% Black	French: 9.7%	
Rural population:	49.6%	0.9% Asian	**2000 Presidential Vote**	
Pop. 2000:	666,936	0.3% Native Am.	Gore (D) 176,293	(51%)
Median income:	$41,585	0.0% Hawaiian	Bush (R) 148,618	(43%)
Poverty status:	8.8%	0.9% Two+ races	Other 23,741	(7%)
Military veterans:	15.8%	0.1% Other	**Cook Partisan Voting Index:** D + 4	
		0.8% Hispanic Origin		

Occupation	Blue collar: 23.0%	White collar: 61.3%	Gray collar: 15.7%

The 1st District of Maine stretches from southernmost Kittery and nearby Kennebunkport to the craggy-shored ancestrally Republican counties to the east. The historic center is Portland, Maine's largest city, home to the yuppies and lawyers that have revived and renovated its downtown landmarks. Portland's antique charm, mostly booming economy and tolerant lifestyle have made it a haven for singles, for lesbians and gays: the 2000 Census reported that Portland has the nation's third-largest concentration of women living together and is tenth in men living together. L.L. Bean, open 24/7/365, is not far away in Freeport. Most voters in the 1st District live within a couple hours drive of the Maine Mall—just off the Maine Turnpike and I-295 and near the airport—the state's heaviest concentration of retail and office space. Lobsters are not just a tradition here but an economic resource: Lobster fishing has been booming, with a 2002 harvest worth $188.5 million. Politically, the 1st votes very much like the state as a whole, quirkily, often for independents, splitting tickets with abandon. From 1968 to 1996 it elected three Democrats and three Republicans to the House, with each party holding the seat for 14 years.

The congressman from the 1st District is Tom Allen, a Democrat elected in 1996. Allen grew up in Portland, where his grandfather and father served on the city council. He was class president in high school and college; at Bowdoin, he was captain of the football team and criticized fraternities because they wouldn't admit blacks. He was a Rhodes Scholar in Oxford the same years as Bill Clinton (who struck him as "one of the nicest, warmest people I ever knew"), Robert Reich and Strobe Talbott, and when he returned, he got a job on the staff of Senator Edmund Muskie. Then he dropped out of politics, went to law school, practiced in Portland, and worked on charities and community service. In 1989 he was elected to the Portland City Council, and in 1991 rotated into the position of mayor. In 1994 he ran for governor, finishing a distant second to former Governor Joseph Brennan in the Democratic primary. The 1st District race in 1996 was an obvious next step, and an attractive opportunity. Freshman Republican James Longley had a well-known name as son of the independent governor elected in 1974, and he had won the 1994 race 52%–48%, though heavily outspent. But Longley's moderate record was overshadowed by his support for the Contract with America and more than $1 million in ads run against him by the AFL-CIO. Allen, with heavy support from Portland, won a 52%–48% primary victory over state Senator Dale McCormick. Allen called for "incremental steps" toward a single-payer health care system. In the general, the candidates disagreed on capital punishment, partial-birth abortions, term limits and the balanced budget amendment. Allen called for scaling back Republicans' $10 billion increase in defense spending. Longley pointed out it included a Navy destroyer to be built at the Bath Iron Works; Allen backtracked and said he would of course support Maine defense contracts. Allen won 55%–45%.

Allen has a liberal voting record. His first major initiative was a bipartisan campaign finance bill, proposed with other freshmen. In April 1998, after Allen launched a discharge petition, Speaker Newt Gingrich switched and allowed the freshman bill to come to the floor as the vehicle for campaign finance bills. Allen was pleased when the more stringent Shays-Meehan bill passed the House later that year; he subsequently became an active proponent. When a revised version was enacted four years later, Common Cause lauded his leadership. When a federal judge before the 2000 election overturned Maine's landmark prescription-drug law, Allen promised to change federal law to reinstate the local law; he failed to gain bipartisan support in the House. In 2001, he was defeated on parliamentary grounds when he sought a House vote on requiring that applications for new pharmaceutical drugs disclose the cost of research and development, including public dollars. He has voiced concern about the inability of small businesses to pay the cost of health insurance for their employees, and has called for federal subsidies to the states to help them.

On other issues, he pushed to require power plants and trash incinerators to cut mercury emissions 95% and sponsored the compact to allow Maine and Vermont to dump nuclear waste in Sierra Blanca, Texas, near the Mexico border, a measure Senator Paul Wellstone called "environmental racism." On the Armed Services Committee, he helped to secure $2.8 billion for three Aegis destroyers with construction work divided by Bath Iron Works in Maine and Ingalls Shipyards in Mississippi, plus funds for projects at Saco Defense, Brunswick Naval Air Station, and Portsmouth Naval Shipyard at Kittery. As an advocate of arms control, he backed the Bush administration's plan to dismantle MX missiles. But he voiced alarm that the decline in shipbuilding could reduce the Navy's aging fleet to 240 ships, which might fall short of the nation's combat needs. He voted against the use of force in Iraq because the resolution gave President Bush "a blank check," and a war might benefit "recruiting for al Qaeda." He launched a House

Ocean Caucus to focus on environmental, fishing and other topics that affect Maine's 4500-mile shoreline.

Bowdoin political scientist Chris Potholm describes the swing voters in this district as "cruel yuppies," attracted to candidates who reflect their trendy values and aversion to taxes. Allen seems to have won their allegiance. In 2000 he won 60%–37%. Against a conservative who attacked him as "anti-defense," he won 64%–36% in 2002. Two years later than other states, redistricting moved a small part of the 1st to the slower-growing 2d District, but left Knox County wholly within the 1st District.

SECOND DISTRICT

Rep. Michael Michaud (D)

Elected 2002, 1st term; b. Jan. 18, 1955, Millinocket; home, East Millinocket; Schenck H.S., 1973; Catholic; single.

Elected Office: ME House, 1980–94; ME Senate, 1994–01, Pres., 2001.

Professional Career: Mill worker, Great Northern Paper, 1973–02.

DC Office: 437 CHOB 20515, 202-225-6306; Web site: www.house.gov/michaud.

District Offices: Bangor, 207-942-6935; Lewiston, 207-782-3704; Presque Isle, 207-764-1036.

Committees: *Small Business* (15th of 17 D): Rural Enterprises, Agriculture and Technology; Tax, Finance & Exports. *Transportation & Infrastructure* (33d of 34 D): Economic Development, Public Buildings & Emergency Management; Highways, Transit & Pipelines; Railroads. *Veterans' Affairs* (7th of 14 D): Benefits (RMM).

Group Ratings and Key Votes: Newly Elected

Election Results

2002 general	Michael Michaud (D)	116,868	(52%)	($1,178,398)
	Kevin Raye (R)	107,849	(48%)	($1,128,820)
2002 primary	Michael Michaud (D)	12,230	(31%)	
	Susan Longley (D)	10,800	(28%)	
	Sean Faircloth (D)	7,829	(20%)	
	John Nutting (D)	4,751	(12%)	
	David Costello (D)	1,773	(5%)	
	Lori Handrahan (D)	1,623	(4%)	
2000 general	John Baldacci (D)	219,783	(73%)	($508,966)
	Richard Campbell (R)	79,522	(27%)	($69,343)

The People		Race/Ethnic Origin	Ancestry	
Area size:	29,904 sq. mi.	96.7% White	English: 15.9%	French: 11.5%
Urban population:	29.0%	0.4% Black	Irish: 10.4%	
Rural population:	71.0%	0.5% Asian	**2000 Presidential Vote**	
Pop. 2000:	607,987	0.8% Native Am.	Gore (D) 143,658	(47%)
Median income:	$32,678	0.0% Hawaiian	Bush (R) 137,998	(46%)
Poverty status:	13.2%	0.9% Two+ races	Other 21,179	(7%)
Military veterans:	16.0%	0.1% Other	**Cook Partisan Voting Index:** D + 1	
		0.7% Hispanic Origin		

Occupation	Blue collar: 28.7%	White collar: 52.8%	Gray collar: 18.5%

The 2d District of Maine is heavily forested, rough-hewn and enormous. It covers the northern three-quarters of the state's acreage; indeed, in size, it is the largest congressional district east of the Mississippi. The population is not evenly distributed, however: The district dips south to include the heavily Democratic mill town of Lewiston—which recently received an influx of 1,000

Somalis—and east to Eastport, just across the bay and the Franklin D. Roosevelt Bridge from the Roosevelt Campobello International Park (Campobello is in New Brunswick, but is connected by bridge to the United States and not Canada). At Belfast on Penobscot Bay, art galleries and boutiques have replaced fish-processing plants. There are several different Maines here: The bays of coastal Maine, with their small fishing towns; the potato fields of far northern Aroostook County (at 6,543 square miles, Aroostook is so big that it covers an area greater than Rhode Island and Connecticut together); the mill towns on the fast-running streams of western Maine, penned in between mountains where there are more moose than people. This was one of America's frontiers in the 1850s, when Bangor on the Penobscot River was the lumber capital of the world; today tiny Bangor is the largest city in the district, planning a $184 million redevelopment of its industrial waterfront. This part of Maine has had its economic troubles, losing 22,000 jobs to neighboring Canada and other foreign markets since the 1993 passage of NAFTA: Potato production is only half what it was in 1980; once-thriving sardine canning is virtually gone; Loring Air Force Base was closed in 1994, though new businesses have sprouted to replace its civilian jobs; logging—though the largest single contributor to Maine's economy—has run into environmental critics and the industry fought a proposed national park in the north woods. (Opponents' bumper stickers read: "If you don't like cutting trees, try using plastic toilet paper.") But Maine now has 24,000 export-dependent manufacturing jobs—50 percent more than a decade ago. And Washington County's sandy soil plains remain responsible for more than 90% of the nation's wild blueberry crop. Politically, this is protest country: This was Ross Perot's strongest congressional district in the United States in 1992 and 1996.

The congressman from the 2d District is Mike Michaud (*me-SHOO*), a Democrat elected in 2002 when John Baldacci gave up the seat and was elected governor. A native of East Millinocket in what natives call the North Woods, he comes from a strong blue-collar background and did not attend college. For 28 years, he was a mill worker at the Great Northern Paper, the dominant employer in the economically depressed area. "I know what it's like to work the day shift, the midnight shift. I've been on strike. I know what it's like to worry about whether you will have a job or not." In 1980 he was elected to the state House and in 1994 to the state Senate, where he chaired the Appropriations Committee and became Senate President. Michaud has an eclectic mix of political views, which would have been popular several decades ago among House Democrats but no longer now. He is staunchly pro-labor, but opposes abortion rights. He opposes drilling for oil in the Arctic National Wildlife Refuge, but strongly supports gun ownership rights.

Baldacci's run for governor produced wide-open primaries in each party and one of the most competitive general election contests in the nation; the seat is something of a political prize since the three incumbents prior to Baldacci were all elected to the U.S. Senate. In the six-way Democratic contest, Michaud's chief opponent was state Senator Susan Longley of Lewiston, the daughter of the state's former Independent Governor James Longley and sister of the 1st District's former Republican Representative James Longley Jr. She emphasized her support for abortion rights in this district that had not elected a pro-life candidate since the *Roe v. Wade* decision in 1973. But with support from organized labor, Michaud won by 1,430 votes; he got 31% of the vote to Longley's 28% and 20% for former state Senator Sean Faircloth. It was a regional contest: Michaud carried the five most rural counties, including 66% in Aroostook; Longley carried six counties chiefly in the southern part of the district, including 59% in trendy Belfast-based Waldo.

Michaud wasn't the only one to eke out a narrow primary win. Republican nominee Kevin Raye, the veteran chief of staff to Senator Olympia Snowe, also had a close race. The result made Michaud look like a landslide winner: Raye wasn't named the official winner of the June 11 primary until June 29, when a recount certified his 319-vote victory former Bangor Mayor Tim Woodcock. Michaud attempted to turn Raye's experience as a Senate staffer into a liability. His campaign slogan was, "I'm One of Us, Working for Us"—an attempt to contrast his blue collar background and union membership with Raye's white collar Washington experience. Raye responded with his own populist pedigree as the son of an electrician and a teacher. He attacked Michaud for a 1999 vote to tax high-income Social Security recipients. Michaud, perhaps to appeal to feminists despite his opposition to abortion, set out a 10-point "women's equity agenda," including family planning, increased child care aid, breast cancer research, and equal pay for equal work; Raye won the support of abortion rights groups. Michaud criticized Raye's support of trade promotion authority.

Polls showed the race was close to the end, and Michaud won 52%–48%. He ran better than most Democrats in rural areas, winning 53% in the seven northern counties, where labor interests helped with a voter turnout drive in the mill towns, while he and Raye split the four counties closest to Penobscot Bay. Redistricting added some territory to the 2d, but the political balance has not been changed significantly.

★ MARYLAND ★

Just south of the Mason-Dixon line and just north of the line between the Union and the Confederacy, the midpoint of the 13 colonies, Maryland has always been betwixt and between. It has a claim to be the typical American state, yet stands out for its particularities. This was the only one of the 13 colonies founded by Roman Catholics—the Calvert family—and its embrace of religious tolerance came less from abstract principle than from the Calverts' desire to protect their property from Protestant monarchs: A harbinger of Maryland's practical-mindedness. Similarly, although hot-blooded Baltimoreans wanted to secede in 1861 ("Maryland, My Maryland" condemns Abraham Lincoln's suppression of pro-Confederate rioters), practical heads prevailed.

The puritan impulse was never lively here: Prohibition was enforced only laxly in Baltimore, to the delight of its great journalist-cum-lexicographer H.L. Mencken; slot machines were legal in the rural counties of the Western Shore; horse-racing has long thrived here. An old state law guaranteeing blacks equal access to public accommodations specifically excluded the Eastern Shore. By not pursuing any one course rigorously, Maryland could be many things at once: Northern as well as Southern, moralistic as well as libertine, industrial as well as rural, leaving people to their own devices yet with a heavy government presence. Perhaps as a result, much of Maryland's political history reads like a chronicle of rogues, from Luther Martin, the drunken haranguer at the Constitutional Convention, to the Annapolis lobbyist convicted of fraud who in 1998 continued to conduct business from the jail pay phone; a judge sentencing another lobbyist in 2000 condemned "a culture of corruption that has been tolerated by lobbyists, legislators, and the citizens of Maryland."

Maryland's genial tolerance may have given it a little too savory a history, but this state cherishes its sense of uniqueness. The Chesapeake Bay, for example, is the nation's largest estuary, with water saltier than a river but fresher than the ocean and with unique watermen and shellfish. The terrapin and Chesapeake oyster are rare today; oystermen harvested 20 million bushels in 1900 but only 100,000 in 1995—and down again in 2002, as the drought made the Bay saltier. Rockfish and Chesapeake Bay blue crabs are much scarcer too. Waste runoff from Eastern Shore and Delaware chicken farms remains a problem; it has polluted the Bay and killed crabs. But countermeasures are being taken. The Maryland, Virginia, and Pennsylvania state governments entered a Chesapeake Bay restoration agreement in June 2000 to increase oyster production tenfold, set harvest goals for crabs, and limit development which produces more runoff.

Maryland also has some reason to be proud of the economy, or economies, it has built over the years. Half a century ago, half the state's population lived in the city of Baltimore and only one-fifth in the suburbs. Now the proportions are the other way around, and then some: 12% Baltimore, 76% in the ever-growing suburbs. The Census Bureau classifies Washington-Baltimore as a single metropolitan area, the nation's fourth largest, with more than 7.6 million people. But Baltimore and Washington are not fraternal twins like Dallas and Fort Worth or Minneapolis and St. Paul; they are two quite separate cities, with different economic bases and different attitudes toward public life. Baltimore started off as a port and an industrial city, and has managed to stay diversified and successful as it spread out into the countryside from its new central core at the Inner Harbor and the solidly built edifices of its downtown grid streets. Baltimore has raised private money to rebuild the 146-year-old *U.S.S. Constellation*; it makes McCormick spices and writes insurance; it is home to the power-tool maker Black & Decker and the investment bank Deutsche

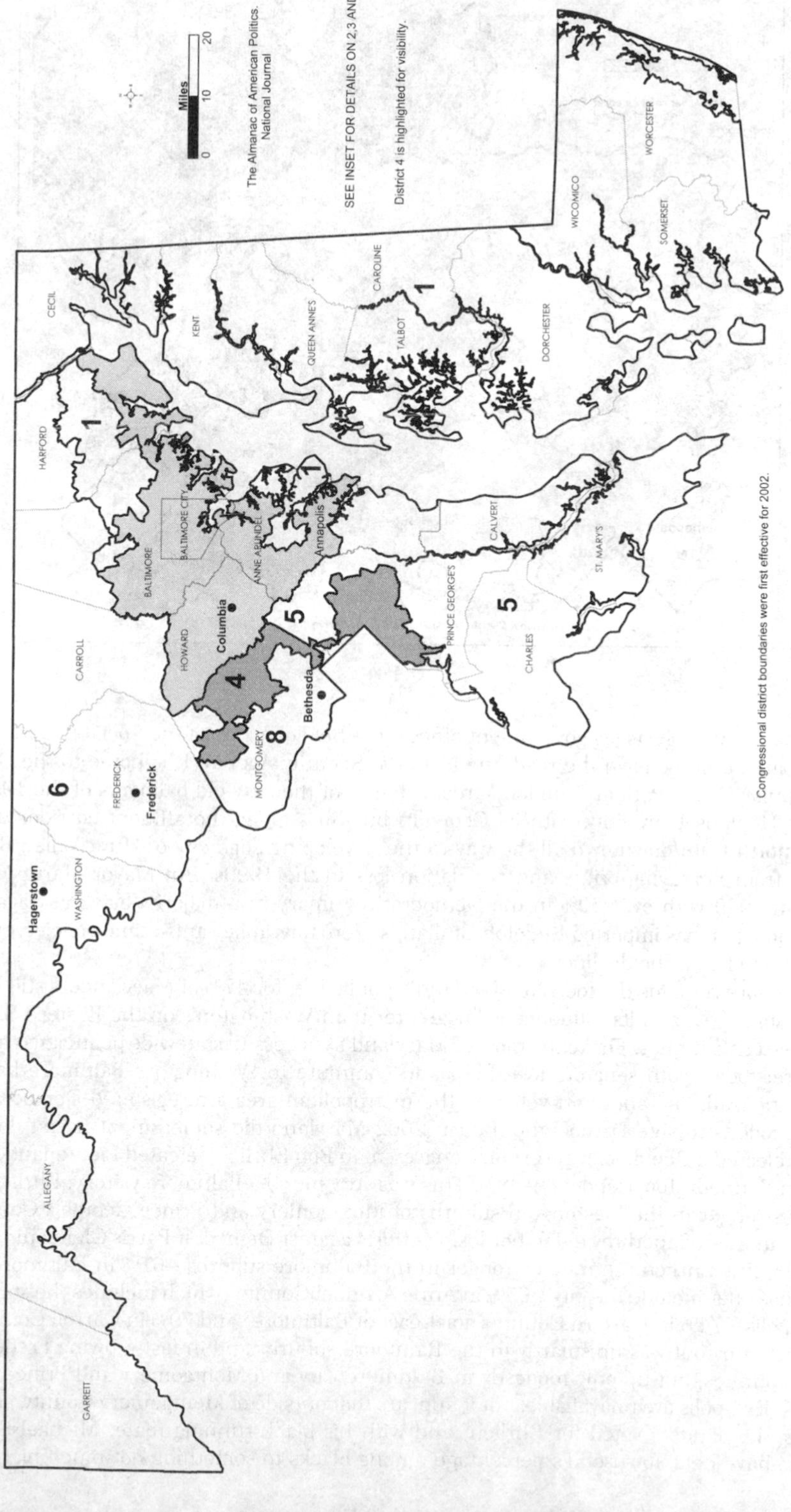
Miles
0 10 20
The Almanac of American Politics.
National Journal
SEE INSET FOR DETAILS ON 2,3 AND 7.
District 4 is highlighted for visibility.
GARRETT
ALLEGANY
WASHINGTON
Hagerstown
FREDERICK
Frederick
6
CARROLL
MONTGOMERY
8
Bethesda
4
HOWARD
Columbia
BALTIMORE
BALTIMORE CITY
ANNE ARUNDEL
Annapolis
5
PRINCE GEORGE'S
CHARLES
5
CALVERT
ST. MARY'S
HARFORD
1
CECIL
KENT
QUEEN ANNE'S
TALBOT
CAROLINE
1
DORCHESTER
WICOMICO
SOMERSET
WORCESTER
Congressional district boundaries were first effective for 2002.

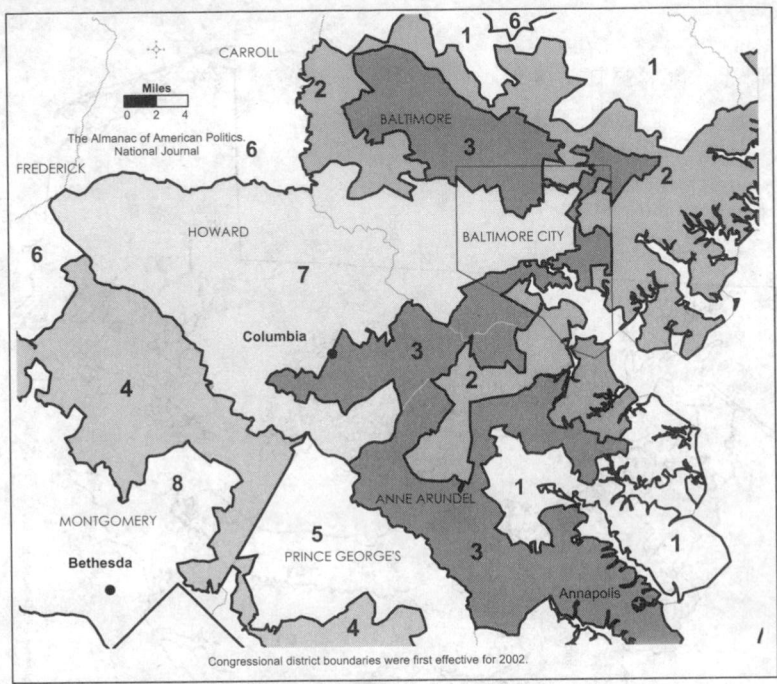

Congressional district boundaries were first effective for 2002.

Banc Alex. Brown. It has big government offices, the headquarters of the Social Security Administration and, quietly down the road, the National Security Agency. It is home to the Orioles in their popular Oriole Park at Camden Yards, the first of the new-old ballparks of the 1990s, and to Johns Hopkins University, with its Georgian buildings along the affluent corridor that runs directly north from downtown all the way to the developing edge city of Hunt Valley. Baltimore suffered from horrifying crime and population loss in the 1990s. But Mayor Martin O'Malley, elected in 1999 with over 50% in the Democratic primary in a majority-black city against two black opponents, has imported Rudolph Giuliani's "zero tolerance" anti-crime policies, and crime rates seem to be on the decline.

Baltimore remains the focus of Maryland's public life, for 47% of Marylanders still live in its metropolitan area, and its influence is far greater than Washington's on the Eastern Shore and in the western counties. For years, most of Maryland's successful statewide politicians came from Baltimore; today, both senators live there and commute to Washington. Baltimore has a long Democratic tradition, and most voters in the metropolitan area are registered Democrats; their default mode is to vote Democratic. But in 2002 Maryland did something it hasn't done since 1966: It elected a Republican governor. Congressman Bob Ehrlich defeated Lieutenant Governor Kathleen Kennedy Townsend 52%–48%. This was very much a Baltimore victory: Ehrlich did not run any stronger in the Washington suburbs of Montgomery and Prince George's County than Republican Ellen Sauerbrey did in her losing efforts against Democrat Parris Glendening in 1994 and 1998. But Ehrlich ran much stronger in the Baltimore suburbs—61% in Baltimore County (which does not include the city), 65% in Anne Arundel County (which includes the state capital of Annapolis), 74% in Harford County (northeast of Baltimore) and 79% in Carroll County to the northwest. Turnout was up smartly in the Baltimore suburbs and in fast-growing Frederick and Calvert counties, but up only modestly in Baltimore City and Montgomery and Prince George's counties. Exit polls are unavailable, but it appears that outside of Montgomery County, about 80% of white Marylanders voted for Ehrlich; and with his black running mate, Michael Steele, he seems to have held Townsend's percentage among blacks to something not much higher. Glen-

Circle coll., etc. :

Circ.

- Ref. (to be kept for -)

    - 5 yrs.

    - 10 yrs.

    - Other _____

    - Move older ed. to Circ.

- Texana

- Sp. Coll.

- TX Sp. Coll.

General Comments:

Keep or withdraw the
2002 ed. ?

                    — mel

It reported 31,600 customers with
the storm. Duke said it would tak
Durham customers.

Carolina Power and Light, which
power to 116,000 customers. The
power today.

About 4,300 utility workers from

On Saturday, Gov. Michael F. Ea
visit shelters.

Today the governor joined Natio
Raleigh. He said they had contac

dening's liberal administration, in which Townsend took an active part, had raised spending sharply and taken liberal stands on all manner of issues. Voters in the suburbs evidently had enough of that, and of an administration that concentrated on Baltimore City, Prince George's and Montgomery. The suburban growth of the 1990s produced a Republican victory in 2002. It helped that Ehrlich is an authentic son of Baltimore, with the characteristic Bawlmer accent and a brio for political conflict not often seen in the Washington suburbs. Indeed, the only Republicans elected governor in the last 60 years—Ehrlich, Spiro Agnew and Theodore McKeldin—all had deep roots in Baltimore. Townsend, though a Baltimore County resident for more than 20 years, speaks in the unregional accent of the Washington suburb of McLean, Virginia, where she grew up; it is hard to think of her (though surely she does this) hammering open blue crabs and getting Chesapeake Bay spices under her fingernails.

Maryland remains by most measures one of the nation's most Democratic states. In 2000, it voted 57%–40% for Al Gore, his fourth-best percentage, after Rhode Island, Massachusetts and New York—although, interestingly, all four elected Republican governors in 2002. Republicans remain heavily outnumbered in the legislature, despite some gains in 2002. Top positions in the big counties' governments remain a near-monopoly of Democrats; Democrats picked up two Republican-held U.S. House seats in 2002, thanks to partisan redistricting—the best such pickup for Democrats in the entire nation. One reason for this Democratic strength is that some 28% of Marylanders are black, the highest percentage in any state outside the Deep South; even the prosperous blacks of Prince George's County still vote overwhelmingly Democratic. Another overlapping reason is that this state and neighboring Virginia have by far the two highest percentages of federal and public employees, natural backers of the party of government. They help to keep the Washington suburbs solidly Democratic.

The People		Race/Ethnic Origin			Military veterans: 524,230 (13.3%)	
Pop. 2000:	5,296,486	3,286,547	62.1%	White	WWII: 17.6%	Korea: 12.1%
Pop. 1990:	4,781,468	1,464,735	27.7%	Black	Vietnam: 32.1% ·	Gulf War: 12.3%
Change 1990–2000:	Up 10.8%	209,738	4.0%	Asian	**Most populous cities:**	
Change 1980–1990:	Up 13.4%	13,312	0.3%	Native Am.	1. Baltimore	651,154
% of U.S. total:	1.9%	1,913	0.0%	Hawaiian	2. Frederick	52,767
Pop. rank:	19th of 50	82,946	1.6%	Two+ races	3. Gaithersburg	52,613
Area size:	12,407 sq. mi.	9,379	0.2%	Other	4. Bowie	50,269
State Native:	49.3%	227,916	4.3%	Hisp. Origin	5. Rockville	47,388
Non-citizen:	5.4%	**Ancestry**				
Language		German: 12.5%		Irish: 9.3%	Urban population: 86.1%	
English: 85.2%	Other Eur.: 5.4%	English: 7.1%		USA: 4.6%	Rural population: 13.9%	
Spanish: 5.2%		Italian: 4.0%				

Education		Work Sector		General Assembly	
H.S. Grad:	83.8%	Private: 72.1%	Govt: 22.3%	Senate	33 D 14 R
College Grad:	31.4%	Self: 5.4%	Family: 0.2%	House of Del.	98 D 43 R
Industry		Unemployment: 4.7%		Legislative Term Limits: No	
Agri: 0.6%	Con: 6.9%	**Household Income**		**Registered Voters**	
Fin: 7.1%	Info: 4.0%	<15k: 11.1%	15-35k: 20.2%	D: 1,555,569	(56.1%)
Mfg: 12.1%	Prof: 33.1%	35-50k: 15.4%	50-100k: 35.1%	R: 832,616	(30.0%)
Public: 10.5%	Trade: 13.3%	100-150k: 11.6%	>150k: 6.5%	I: 386,428	(13.9%)
Other: 12.4%		Median: $52,868			
Occupation		Poverty status: 8.5%			
Blue collar: 18.1%	White collar: 67.7%	**Home Value**			
Gray collar: 14.2%		<50k: 5.2% 50-100k: 20.6% 100-200k: 47.9% 200-300k: 15.5%			
		300-500k: 7.7% >500k: 3.0% Median: $143,300			

Presidential politics   In the 1990s, Maryland became one of the most Democratic states in presidential elections. It was Bill Clinton's third-best state in 1992 and fifth-best in 1996 and Al Gore's fourth-best in 2000. Whites voted 51%–46% for George W. Bush, but blacks, casting one-quarter of the total, voted 92%–7% for Gore.

Since 1992, Maryland has held its presidential primaries a week before Super Tuesday to try to get noticed, with limited success. The one notable result: In 1992, Paul Tsongas beat Bill Clinton 41%–33%, with all his margin and more coming from suburban Baltimore and Montgomery County.

Congressional districting   Maryland was the scene of the Democrats' most successful partisan gerrymandering in the 2002 cycle.

108th Congress Lineup
6 D   2 R
107th Congress Lineup
4 D   4 R

2000 Presidential Vote		
Gore (D)	1,145,782	(57%)
Bush (R)	813,797	(40%)
Nader (Green)	53,768	(3%)
Other	12,133	(1%)

2000 Republican Presidential Primary		
Bush (R)	211,439	(56%)
McCain (R)	135,981	(36%)
Keyes (R)	25,020	(7%)

2000 Democratic Presidential Primary		
Gore (D)	341,630	(67%)
Bradley (D)	144,387	(28%)
Uncommitted	16,935	(3%)

1996 Presidential Vote		
Clinton (D)	966,208	(54%)
Dole (R)	681,530	(39%)
Perot (I)	115,812	(7%)

Gerrymandering is not too harsh a word: The convoluted shapes of the districts in the Baltimore area would have made Elbridge Gerry blush. The goal of the plan, largely concocted by Governor Parris Glendening, was to protect all four of their incumbents and to draw districts that would be impossible to win for 2d District Republican Bob Ehrlich and 8th District Republican Connie Morella. The Bush 2000 percentage in the 2d fell from 55% to 41% and in the 8th from 36% to 31%. Ehrlich ran for governor and had his revenge. The 8th District attracted three Democratic challengers, each arguably a stronger candidate than any Morella had faced before, and she ended up losing narrowly to state Senator Christopher Van Hollen. The four Democratic incumbents had no problems. The two other districts, the 1st, based in the Eastern Shore and the 6th, based in western Maryland, both snake into the Baltimore suburbs to take in heavily Republican precincts; they are safely Republican. The Maryland Court of Appeals in June 2002 struck down Glendening's redistricting of state legislative seats and drew its own plan, but the congressional district lines survived court challenge.

Governor

Robert Ehrlich (R)

Elected 2002, term expires Jan. 2007, 1st term; b. Nov. 25, 1957, Arbutus; home, Annapolis; Princeton U., B.A. 1979, Wake Forest U., J.D. 1982; Methodist; married (Kendel).

Elected Office: MD House of Delegates, 1986–94; U.S. House of Reps., 1994–02.

Professional Career: Practicing atty., 1982–94.

Office: 100 State Circle, Annapolis, 21401, 410-974-3591; Fax: 410-974-2542; Web site: www.gov.state.md.us.

Election Results

2002 general	Robert Ehrlich (R)	879,592	(52%)
	Kathleen Kennedy Townsend (D)	813,422	(48%)
2002 primary	Robert Ehrlich (R)	229,927	(93%)
	James Sheridan (R)	9,181	(4%)
1998 general	Parris N. Glendening (D)	846,972	(55%)
	Ellen Sauerbrey (R)	688,357	(45%)

Robert Ehrlich (pronounced *ER-lick*) is the first Republican to be governor of Maryland since Spiro Agnew resigned in January 1969 to become Vice President of the United States. Ehrlich grew up in a rowhouse in the modest Baltimore suburb of Arbutus, the son of a car salesman. A six-footer at 13, he got a football scholarship to the elite Gilman School in Baltimore and then to Princeton, where he was a linebacker; he went to law school at Wake Forest, working part-time as assistant football coach, then practiced law in Baltimore. Ehrlich volunteered in Republican campaigns and in 1986, at 28, was elected to the Maryland House of Delegates. There he worked on tough sentencing and child pornography laws, but also opposed some bills as unneeded or unconstitutional. When 2d District Congresswoman Helen Delich Bentley ran for governor in 1994 (she lost the Republican primary to anti-tax legislator Ellen Sauerbrey), Ehrlich ran for the House. He campaigned as an opponent of over-regulation, as a military hawk and a libertarian, and beat an anti-abortion candidate in the primary 57%–38%. In the fall, he campaigned against the Democratic leadership and signed the Contract With America, though he opposed term limits. He was enthusiastic about tax cuts. He ran ads showing the rowhouse where he grew up and said the most important lessons he learned were around the dining room table. The result was a solid 63%–37% Ehrlich victory.

In the House, Ehrlich showed a willingness to cast tough votes, as when he opposed the minimum wage and argued that it would cost some workers their jobs. He supported the partial-birth abortion ban. He broke with the Republican leadership on some issues, such as displaying the Ten Commandments in public schools, and he praised the Consumer Product Safety Commission for keeping kids safe. He voted against PNTR with China, siding with local unions. He was reelected easily in 1996, 1998 and 2000. He kept in touch with state politics and during 2001 was often mentioned as a candidate for governor. Speaker Dennis Hastert, fearful of losing the seat, urged him to run for reelection; many Maryland Republicans urged him to run for governor. But he did not commit himself until after he was faced with the redistricting plan announced by Governor Parris Glendening in February 2002. That plan reduced the Bush 2000 percentage in the 2d District from 55% to 41%, and it put Ehrlich's house barely outside the district, in the 1st District represented by Wayne Gilchrest of the Eastern Shore. The new 2d was clearly designed for Democratic Baltimore County Executive Dutch Ruppersberger. A race for reelection would have been risky at best, so Ehrlich decided to run for governor—a risky race also, but one with greater rewards if he won—and announced in March 2002.

At that point, it seemed likely but not certain that his opponent would be Lieutenant Governor Kathleen Kennedy Townsend. Elected on the ticket with Glendening in 1994 and 1998, well known because she was the daughter of the late Senator Robert Kennedy, she had gained notice for her work on law enforcement issues. She spoke in a public service radio ad on vehicle theft that ran 12,000 times, and her name was plastered on almost as many official notices and signs as Glendening's. But her numbers in polls were not spectacular. In 2001, Montgomery County Executive Douglas Duncan thought about running, but in October announced he would not and endorsed Townsend. Baltimore Mayor Martin O'Malley, popular everywhere in the Baltimore media market, left the question open until, without mentioning Townsend, he announced he would not run in June 2002. Townsend started far ahead in money, with $4.4 million raised by January 2002, while Ehrlich had only $600,000 in his state campaign fund. But her association with Glendening was in many ways a liability. His Smart Growth anti-sprawl program got favorable attention (Ehrlich said he was for it), but his high spending policies and his frosty to nonexistent relationships with other Democratic politicians were problems. So was his opposition to the Inter-County Connector highway in Montgomery County and Townsend's own work on criminal justice was smirched by problems with boot camps that had been closed after a critical Baltimore *Sun* series in 1999. Glendening's divorce and marriage to a former staffer, followed by the birth of a child seven months later were not helpful; neither were his public attempts to get hired as chancellor of the University of Maryland at $375,000 a year; neither were the ads he ran in the primary for his friend John Willis against Comptroller William Donald Schaefer, his still very popular predecessor as governor (Schaefer easily won).

Townsend talked about government programs in education and health care; Ehrlich talked about holding down taxes and spending. To solve the state's fiscal woes, Ehrlich advocated legalizing slot machines at race tracks (they're legal in next-door Delaware) and Townsend talked about securitizing the state's future tobacco settlement payments. Gun control became a big issue. Ehrlich voted against many gun control proposals; Townsend strongly favors them. When Ehrlich said in September that he would review gun laws prohibiting certain handguns and using ballistic "fingerprinting" and consider repealing them if they were ineffective, Townsend attacked in shrill rhetoric underpinned by the belief that his positions would be anathema in the suburbs. In October, Republicans were worried that the Beltway sniper murders would spur a demand for new forms of gun control. In June 2002, Townsend picked as her running mate Charles Larson, a retired admiral who was a former superintendent at the Naval Academy—interpreted as an attempt to appeal to moderate whites. In July 2002, Ehrlich picked as his running mate state Republican Chairman Michael Steele, who is black—interpreted an attempt to appeal to blacks. Some black politicians started complaining that Townsend was ignoring black people, as Ehrlich made repeated campaign appearances in black churches and neighborhoods.

In August, many national and Maryland Democrats began complaining about how Townsend and her "CEO" Alan Fleischmann were running her campaign. The complaints were mostly about tactics, but they might better have been about strategy. Townsend's liberal policies and her attacks on Ehrlich as out of the mainstream because of his opposition to some gun control laws and a partial-birth abortion ban may have had the desired effect among Washington area liberals in Montgomery County and blacks in Prince George's County and Baltimore City, but they were not well calculated to appeal to white voters in suburban Baltimore counties. As Townsend continued to stay under 50% in the polls—and even fall behind Ehrlich in some— Ehrlich's fundraising accelerated and exceeded hers. In the end, he raised $10.4 million to her $8.7 million. In November, Ehrlich won 52%–48%. Townsend carried the Democrats' "Big Three"—Baltimore City, Montgomery and Prince George's—by wide margins, but Ehrlich carried everything else, and in most cases by wide margins as well. Baltimore City, which cast only 9% of the state's votes, went 75%–24% for Townsend, but that was an uptick for the Republican. The Washington suburbs, with 29% of the state's votes, voted 67%–32% for Townsend, essentially the same margin as in 1998. But the Baltimore suburbs, casting 37% of the votes, voted 63%–36% for Ehrlich, far better than Sauerbrey's 54%–46% four years before.

So Ehrlich returns to Annapolis as governor to face a new Speaker of the Assembly, Michael Busch, who was a friend of his when they were freshmen delegates in 1987, and the 16-year Senate President Mike Miller; he reached out to blacks by appointing outgoing Prince George's County Executive Wayne Curry to his transition team. Republicans made gains in the legislature, with the help of a court-ordered redistricting, but Ehrlich still faces a heavily Democratic legislature. He faced a budget gap estimated at $550 million for the fiscal year in progress and $1.2 billion in 2003–04. And in this Democratic state Ehrlich must know that he could face a strong opponent in 2006 if he stumbles—perhaps O'Malley, whom he said publicly he could not have beaten in 2002, or Congressman Ben Cardin. Ehrlich got off to an inauspicious start in his first year as governor—the Democrat-controlled legislature failed to approve his plan to legalize slot machines, the centerpiece of his 2003 legislative agenda.

Senior Senator

Paul Sarbanes (D)

Elected 1976, seat up 2006, 5th term; b. Feb. 3, 1933, Salisbury; home, Baltimore; Princeton, A.B. 1954, Rhodes Scholar, Oxford U., B.A. 1957, Harvard, LL.B. 1960; Greek Orthodox; married (Christine).

Elected Office: MD House of Delegates, 1966–70; U.S. House of Reps., 1970–76.

Professional Career: Law Clerk, Judge Morris A. Soper, U.S. 4th Circuit Crt. of Appeals, 1960–61; Practicing atty., 1961–62, 1965–70; A.A., Pres. Kennedy's Cncl. of Econ. Advisers, 1962–63; Exec. Dir., Baltimore Charter Revision Comm., 1963–64.

DC Office: 309 HSOB, 20510, 202-224-4524; Fax: 202-224-1651; Web site: www.senate.gov/~sarbanes.

State Offices: Baltimore, 410-962-4436; Bryans Road, 301-283-0947; Cumberland, 301-724-0695; Salisbury, 410-860-2131; Silver Spring, 301-589-0797.

Committees: *Banking, Housing & Urban Affairs* (RMM). *Budget. Foreign Relations*: European Affairs; International Economic Policy, Export & Trade Promotion (RMM); Near Eastern & South Asian Affairs. *Joint Economic Committee* (9th of 10 Sens.).

Group Ratings

	ADA	ACLU	AFS	LCV	CON	ITIC	NTU	COC	ACU	NTLC	CHC
2002	100	60	100	94	58	38	10	40	0	0	—
2001	95	—	100	100	—	—	5	36	8	—	0

National Journal Ratings

	2001 LIB	—	2001 CONS		2002 LIB	—	2002 CONS
Economic	93%	—	0%		90%	—	5%
Social	81%	—	8%		82%	—	0%
Foreign	74%	—	14%		90%	—	8%

Key Votes of the 107th Congress

1. Approve Bush Tax Cuts	N	5. Confirm Ashcroft as AG	N	9. Bar Coop. with Intl. Court	N
2. Expand Patients' Rights	Y	6. Bar Gays in the Boy Scouts	N	10. Trade Promotion Authority	N
3. Campaign Finance Reform	Y	7. $ for Hate Crime Prosecution	Y	11. Authorize Force in Iraq	N
4. Permit ANWR Development	N	8. Overseas Military Abortions	Y	12. Homeland Sec. Dept. Union	N

Election Results

2000 general	Paul Sarbanes (D)	1,230,013	(63%)	($1,837,286)
	Paul H. Rappaport (R)	715,178	(37%)	($146,866)
2000 primary	Paul Sarbanes (D)	384,748	(83%)	
	George English (D)	45,984	(10%)	
	Sidney Altman (D)	31,502	(7%)	
1994 general	Paul Sarbanes (D)	809,125	(59%)	($2,767,187)
	William Brock (R)	559,908	(41%)	($3,201,650)

Prior Winning Percentages: 1988 (62%); 1982 (64%); 1976 (59%); 1974 House (84%); 1972 House (70%); 1970 House (70%)

Paul Sarbanes, the longest-serving Maryland senator in history, was first elected to the Senate in 1976. His liberalism is rooted in his experience growing up in Salisbury on the Eastern Shore, as the son of a Greek immigrant who owned the Mayflower Grill and taught himself enough on the side to discuss philosophy with his son's Princeton professors. Sarbanes was always interested in politics: As a Princeton student in 1952 he went up to Manhattan with a "Princeton for Adlai" sign and got into the candidate's hotel suite, and as a big firm lawyer in Baltimore he worked on the city Charter Revision Commission. Working with small groups, organizing liberal supporters, he ran for office as an insurgent, and always won. He was first elected to the Maryland House of Delegates in 1966. In 1970, he challenged an incumbent in the primary and was elected to the

U.S. House; another incumbent retired rather than run against him after redistricting in 1972. In 1976, he defeated former Senator Joseph Tydings in the Democratic primary and incumbent Senator Glenn Beall in the general by 59%–41%.

Since then, Sarbanes has been one of the most durable champions of liberal politics: On the Banking Committee, on which he has been ranking Democrat since 1995 and chairman from June 2001 to January 2003, on the Joint Economic Committee, which he chaired from 1991–95, and on Foreign Relations. He was one of just 21 senators who voted against the 1996 Welfare Reform Act. On the financial services deregulation bill, he sponsored an amendment to allow states to issue tougher laws protecting the privacy of depositors and credit card holders than those in the federal bill. On becoming chairman, he worked to promote opt-in clauses, which would prohibit financial institutions from using personal financial information unless the individual affirmatively authorizes it. In October 2001, he got the committee to pass a money laundering bill which was then attached to the anti-terrorism bill which sailed through the Senate with one dissenting vote; he held oversight hearings on the issue in 2002 and called for more aggressive enforcement. He called in October 2000 for investigations of lenders to low-income homeowners who require single-premium credit life insurance. His own approach to investing is conservative: He purchased his first mutual fund in 2000 and since entering Congress has not owned stock.

Sarbanes's first moment in the national spotlight came in 1974 when he served on the House Judiciary Committee and sponsored articles of impeachment against Richard Nixon. Another came in July 2002, when the Senate passed and George W. Bush signed his bill regulating the accounting industry. The issue was raised by the collapse of Enron in late 2001 after the company's accountants approved statements that in retrospect were highly misleading. Sarbanes pursued the issue in his typical fashion. Without seeking publicity and with a minimum of partisan rhetoric, he held 10 hearings on the issue in March 2002, with many points of view represented; despite his liberal reputation, he was careful to listen to arguments made by the accounting industry and large corporations. He postponed a markup in May 2002, when ranking Republican and former Chairman Phil Gramm filed many amendments. But in June he did hold markup hearings, and gained the support on critical issues of Republican Mike Enzi of Wyoming, the only CPA in the Senate. Sarbanes's bill banned accounting firms from selling many, but not all, consulting services to firms for which they did audit work; it limited to five years the time an individual partner could work on one company's books and it set up an accounting regulatory board independent of the SEC. He did not go so far as to require companies to list stock options to executives and employees as expenses. Sarbanes's bill passed the committee 17–4 on June 18. Breaking news about the WorldCom scandal made the bill's prospects on the Senate floor far more favorable, and debate started July 2002. Sarbanes defended his bill and opposed Arizona Senator John McCain's amendment to require expensing of stock options. On July 12, the Senate voted 91–2 to cut off debate and on July 15, the bill passed 97–0. It went to conference committee with a bill passed by the House in April which made lesser changes in the law. With George W. Bush pressing for a bill before the August recess, House Financial Services Chairman Michael Oxley yielded on most provisions, but did get the accounting regulatory board designated as being within the SEC, though independent of its commissioners. Senate Majority Leader Tom Daschle and Democratic campaign strategists probably would have preferred a protracted debate in which they could have portrayed Republicans as defenders of corrupt corporate executives. But Sarbanes preferred to make a law, and did; it was signed July 30.

Sarbanes is the second ranking Democrat on the Foreign Relations Committee, where he has tilted toward aid for Greece and away from Turkey; he has supported the resolution condemning the Turks for genocidal treatment of Armenians in World War I. He backed renewal of sanctions against Iran and Libya in 2001. In June 2000, he was one of 19 senators to vote to cut most of the funding for the Clinton administration's military assistance to Colombia. He was the only senator to vote against the bill authorizing payment of the U.S.'s United Nations dues; he argued that it was wrong to impose conditions on the UN for payment of dues that were owed: "It's simply unacceptable that the richest nation on earth is also the biggest debtor to the United Nations." He and his Maryland colleague Barbara Mikulski were two of the 15 senators who voted against PNTR in September 2000.

Closer to home, Sarbanes sponsored the reauthorization of the Chesapeake Bay Restoration Act in 2000, which doubled federal spending to $40 million. To help drought-stricken Maryland farmers, he sponsored in 2000 an increase in market loss payments from $75,000 to $150,000. In 2000, he also pushed through a bill to roll back federal employee benefit contribution rates to 1998 levels.

Sarbanes is not a senator who courts publicity; he sponsors few bills and sends out few press releases. He enjoys working on the mechanics of government, but returns every night to his home in Baltimore. When one lobbyist cracked that he had sponsored no major law and "the best he could have hoped for was having a Metro stop named after him," Sarbanes said, "Look, my name was on the first article of impeachment on the president of the United States. Having done that, I don't feel any great compulsion to throw out my name. I keep getting these assignments, you know. The Nixon impeachment. I got Iran-contra. I got Whitewater. I had a role in the Clinton impeachment when it was here." Publicity or no, he has been re-elected without great difficulty four times. His smallest margin was in the Republican year of 1994, when he beat former Tennessee Senator Bill Brock (who beat Albert Gore Sr. in 1970) by a solid 59%–41% margin. At one point, it looked like Sarbanes might face Republican Congressman Bob Ehrlich in 2000. But Ehrlich, after seeing how handily Governor Parris Glendening beat Republican Ellen Sauerbrey in 1998, decided not to run; instead he ran for governor in 2002 and won. Sarbanes won in 2000 by a 63%–37%, running 6% ahead of Al Gore's strong showing.

Junior Senator

Barbara Mikulski (D)

Elected 1986, seat up 2004, 3d term; b. July 20, 1936, Baltimore; home, Baltimore; Mt. St. Agnes Col., B.A. 1958, U. of MD, M.S.W. 1965; Catholic; single.

Elected Office: Baltimore City Cncl., 1971–76; U.S. House of Reps., 1976–86.

Professional Career: Social worker, Baltimore Dept. of Social Svcs., 1965–70; Chmn., DNC Delegate Selection Comm., 1972; Adjunct prof., Loyola Col., 1972–76.

DC Office: 709 HSOB, 20510, 202-224-4654; Fax: 202-224-8858; Web site: mikulski.senate.gov.

State Offices: Annapolis, 410-263-1805; Baltimore, 410-962-4510; Greenbelt, 301-345-5517; Hagerstown, 301-797-2826; Salisbury, 410-546-7711.

Committees: *Democratic Conference Secretary. Appropriations*: Commerce, Justice, State & Judiciary; Foreign Operations; Homeland Security; Interior; Transportation, Treasury & General Government; VA, HUD & Independent Agencies (RMM). *Health, Education, Labor & Pensions*: Aging (RMM). *Intelligence (Select)*.

Group Ratings

	ADA	ACLU	AFS	LCV	CON	ITIC	NTU	COC	ACU	NTLC	CHC
2002	100	60	100	82	63	38	9	47	0	3	—
2001	95	—	100	100	—	—	5	43	12	—	0

National Journal Ratings

	2001 LIB	—	2001 CONS		2002 LIB	—	2002 CONS
Economic	82%	—	15%		71%	—	28%
Social	81%	—	8%		82%	—	0%
Foreign	61%	—	27%		96%	—	0%

Key Votes of the 107th Congress

1. Approve Bush Tax Cuts	N	5. Confirm Ashcroft as AG	N	9. Bar Coop. with Intl. Court	Y
2. Expand Patients' Rights	Y	6. Bar Gays in the Boy Scouts	N	10. Trade Promotion Authority	N
3. Campaign Finance Reform	Y	7. $ for Hate Crime Prosecution	Y	11. Authorize Force in Iraq	N
4. Permit ANWR Development	N	8. Overseas Military Abortions	Y	12. Homeland Sec. Dept. Union	Y

Election Results

1998 general	Barbara Mikulski (D)	1,062,810	(71%)	($3,014,312)
	Ross Z. Pierpont (R)	444,637	(30%)	($297,768)
1998 primary	Barbara Mikulski (D)	349,382	(84%)	
	Ann L. Mallory (D)	43,120	(10%)	
	Kauko H. Kokkonen (D)	21,658	(5%)	
1992 general	Barbara Mikulski (D)	1,307,610	(71%)	($3,623,974)
	Alan L. Keyes (R)	533,688	(29%)	($1,175,682)

Prior Winning Percentages: 1986 (61%); 1984 House (68%); 1982 House (74%); 1980 House (76%); 1978 House (100%); 1976 House (75%)

Barbara Mikulski is a senator with deep roots in immigrant, urban America and a fascination for the new technology and jobs growing in edge cities and beyond, a person who doesn't look anything like a traditional politician but who has become a savvy Senate insider. Her roots are in east Baltimore, where her Polish immigrant parents ran a bakery, and she still lives in the city and commutes to Washington; she graduated from Mount St. Agnes College and got a social work degree at the University of Maryland. Mikulski got her start in politics as a social worker, organizing to stop a highway from going through Highlandtown. She won, and in the process was elected to the Baltimore City Council in 1971. She ran for the Senate in 1974, and got a respectable 43% against incumbent Charles Mathias; when Paul Sarbanes ran for the other Senate seat in 1976, Mikulski ran for his 3d District House seat and won. Ten years later, she gave up that seat for what seemed like a chancy Senate race. She won handily, with 50% in the primary to 31% for Montgomery County Congressman Michael Barnes and 14% for Governor Harry Hughes. In the general, she beat Linda Chavez (whom George W. Bush later nominated as Labor secretary in January 2001) 61%–39%.

Mikulski is loud and brash, humorous and warm, brusque and aggressive when she feels it is necessary, curious and thoughtful when encountering another new part of the world. One such world was the Senate. "The House is a scrappy body, and I was scrappy in the body," she explained later. "I knew the Senate was a different institution. I needed to know the rules." In her first term, she won a seat on the Appropriations Committee; within two years, she was chairman of a subcommittee, handling housing, space and veterans' programs; she was elected Democratic Caucus secretary in 1994, and so is a member of the Democratic leadership. She is also the Senate's chief superintendent of the space program and an enthusiast for space exploration. In February 2000, when the Near Earth Asteroid Rendezvous went into orbit around an asteroid, she and NASA Administrator Daniel Goldin high-fived each other. It does not hurt that some NASA facilities are in Maryland—the Goddard Space Center in Greenbelt and the Wallops Island flight facility—but she also keeps an eye on others. In May 2002, she was disappointed by the $15 billion budget for NASA—she wanted at least $17 billion. She has vowed to continue to raise funds for a mission to Pluto, the only unexplored plant in the solar system, stating, "Pluto is a bargain at less than $500 million." She cosponsored a bill in 2001 to see that federal employees who are in the Reserve forces get their full federal salary when called to active duty.

On domestic policy, Mikulski is a liberal who insists that "where there are rights there are responsibilities" and has criticized fellow Democrats for being "angst-addicted." She voted for the Defense of Marriage Act. With Iowa Senator Charles Grassley, she sponsored a 2000 law to extend long-term care insurance for 13 million federal employees, military and their dependents. She passed an amendment in 2001 to spend $100 million over five years on 1,000 community technology centers to teach computer skills. She is capable of righteous indignation: During the hearings on Firestone tires in September 2000, she asked executives, "Where was your sense as a human being, as well as a corporation, to say, 'Look out, America, these tires are coming apart'?" She is not afraid to cast lonely votes. She was one of eight senators to vote against financial deregulation in November 1999, one of 19 to vote to cut most of the money for Plan Colombia in June 2000 and one of 15 to vote against PNTR with China in September 2000.

Mikulski is the senior woman in the Senate and convenes meetings of women senators. She has pushed many of what might be called women's issues—mammography clinic standards and homemaker IRAs, retaining a guaranteed benefit with inflation protection in Social Security reform. She was the chief Senate co-sponsor with John Chafee and his son and successor Lincoln Chafee of the 2000 breast cancer bill, providing Medicaid financing of mammograms and Pap tests; but she was denied a White House signing ceremony because the chief House sponsor was Rick Lazio, Hillary Rodham Clinton's opponent in the New York Senate race. In 2002, she set out to reauthorize her 1992 mammography quality standards law to provide for periodic testing of doctors who examine the X-rays. In 2001, she focused on the nursing shortage. "Nurses tell me they feel undervalued, overworked and underpaid." With Arkansas Sen. Tim Hutchinson, she sponsored a bill to encourage students to go into nursing, to provide scholarships for nurses who promise to work in underserved areas and to train nursing teachers. Mikulski's skills are not just political. She coauthored *Capitol Offense* and *Capitol Venture*, mystery novels featuring freshman Senator Eleanor "Norie" Gorzack of Pennsylvania.

Mikulski's toughest Senate election was her first, which she won fairly easily against strong competition. In 1992 and 1998 she was re-elected with 71%, first against Alan Keyes, a former Reagan appointee who has since run for president twice, and then against Ross Pierpont, a genial 81-year-old physician who had run for office and lost 14 times.

FIRST DISTRICT

Rep. Wayne Gilchrest (R)

Elected 1990, 7th term; b. Apr. 15, 1946, Rahway, NJ; home, Kennedyville; Wesley Col., A.A. 1971, DE St. Col., B.A. 1973, Loyola Col., 1984; Methodist; married (Barbara).

Military Career: Marine Corps, 1964–68 (Vietnam).

Professional Career: High schl. teacher, 1973–86; Natl. Forest Service worker, Bitterroot Natl. Forest, 1986.

DC Office: 2245 RHOB 20515, 202-225-5311; Fax: 202-225-0254; Web site: www.house.gov/gilchrest.

District Offices: Bel Air, 410-838-2517; Chestertown, 410-778-9407; Salisbury, 410-749-3184.

Committees: *Resources* (7th of 28 R): Fisheries Conservation, Wildlife & Oceans (Chmn.); National Parks, Recreation & Public Lands. *Science* (14th of 25 R): Environment, Technology and Standards. *Transportation & Infrastructure* (6th of 41 R): Coast Guard & Maritime Transportation; Water Resources & Environment.

Group Ratings

	ADA	ACLU	AFS	LCV	CON	ITIC	NTU	COC	ACU	NTLC	CHC
2002	10	29	0	13	8	88	51	94	78	72	58
2001	25	—	10	50	—	—	59	87	48	—	—

National Journal Ratings

	2001 LIB —	2001 CONS	2002 LIB —	2002 CONS
Economic	43% —	56%	50% —	50%
Social	51% —	49%	50% —	49%
Foreign	43% —	53%	45% —	54%

Key Votes of the 107th Congress

1. Approve Bush Tax Cuts	Y	5. Faith-Based Charities	Y	9. Trade Promotion Authority	Y
2. Limit Patients' Bill of Rights	Y	6. Bar Gays in the Boy Scouts	Y	10. Bar Funds for Intl. Court	Y
3. Campaign Finance Reform	Y	7. Ban Partial-Birth Abortion	Y	11. Authorize Force in Iraq	Y
4. Ban ANWR Development	Y	8. Arm Commercial Pilots	Y	12. Deny Home. Sec. Dept. Union	Y

Election Results

2002 general	Wayne Gilchrest (R)	192,004	(77%)	($440,605)
	Ann Tamlyn (D)	57,986	(23%)	($36,528)
2002 primary	Wayne Gilchrest (R)	35,599	(60%)	
	Dave Fischer (R)	21,524	(36%)	
	Brad McClanahan (R)	2,185	(4%)	
2000 general	Wayne Gilchrest (R)	165,293	(64%)	($225,166)
	Bennett Bozman (D)	91,022	(35%)	($52,487)

Prior Winning Percentages: 1998 (69%); 1996 (62%); 1994 (68%); 1992 (52%); 1990 (57%)

The People		Race/Ethnic Origin	Ancestry	
Area size:	3,702 sq. mi.	84.7% White	German: 15.5%	Irish: 12.1%
Urban population:	64.2%	11.2% Black	English: 10.7%	
Rural population:	35.8%	1.4% Asian	**2000 Presidential Vote**	
Pop. 2000:	662,062	0.2% Native Am.	Bush (R)..............160,402	(57%)
Median income:	$51,918	0.0% Hawaiian	Gore (D)..............111,807	(40%)
Poverty status:	7.3%	0.9% Two+ races	Other...................8,424	(3%)
Military veterans:	15.2%	0.1% Other	**Cook Partisan Voting Index:** R + 9	
		1.6% Hispanic Origin		

Occupation	Blue collar: 21.9%	White collar: 63.3%	Gray collar: 14.8%

Chesapeake Bay, technically not a bay but an estuary, was the central focus of the most thickly settled of the 13 colonies, and today remains a central focus for much of modern Maryland and a backwater where an older civilization lives on. The first British here were amazed at the Chesapeake's oysters and terrapin turtles and crabs and rockfish; despite pollution and vastly depleted populations of crabs and oysters, watermen still make hardy livings bringing them to shore. This was an estuary civilization in colonial days, with every little hamlet tied together by the highways of bays and creeks and inlets off the Chesapeake. The streets and docks of Chestertown, Oxford, St. Michaels and Cambridge still look something like what they did when George Washington slept there.

In post-colonial times, when most Americans were caught up in the romance of westward movement, these estuaries and peninsulas were mostly forgotten, off the main lines of railroads and highways, left behind by thousands moving west. In the 160 years between 1790 and 1950, the Eastern Shore counties of Maryland only doubled in population, perhaps the slowest growth rate on the Eastern Seaboard. Today much of the Chesapeake has changed beyond recognition, as the Eastern Shore grew vigorously in the 1980s and 1990s with second-home buyers and commuters across the Chesapeake Bay Bridge. This is a land of genteel estates fronting the water and of Frank Perdue's chicken empire around Salisbury, of Easton's Waterfowl Festival and the swarms of motorboats and sailing ships making their way up and down the inlets or under the twin spans of the Bay Bridge. People are attracted by its continuity with the past and closeness to nature. This growth has forced people along the Bay to address modern-day environmental and cultural problems. But it has been accompanied by a continuing loss of blue-collar jobs. Black and Decker began shutting down its Easton plant in 2003, which employed more than 1,000 workers, many of whom were bused in from surrounding counties to assemble power tools.

The 1st Congressional District includes the nine counties of the Eastern Shore. It extends across the Bay and grabs parts of Harford, Baltimore and Anne Arundel counties, where the former countryside is speckled with suburban developments. The incredibly erose boundaries drawn by Democratic redistricters in 2002 bring into the 1st District the Timonium home of Governor Bob Ehrlich, who represented the adjacent 2d District. The Baltimore and Harford County suburbs north of Baltimore are as solidly Republican as any part of Maryland. In Anne Arundel, the 2d no longer includes the state capital in Annapolis, though it does include Arnold and Severna Park on the other side of the Severn River. Although it is hard to avoid thinking of this district as the Eastern Shore district, one-third of the population is on the west side of the Bay. What the portions of the district west of the Bay have in common is that they are heavily Republican; this was 1 of only 2 districts in the state that voted for George W. Bush in 2000.

The congressman from the 1st District is Wayne Gilchrest, a Republican with political views that stamp him as an independent thinker, both on national and local issues. Gilchrest served in the Marine Corps in the Dominican Republic and then in Vietnam, where he was wounded in the chest as a platoon leader and received the Purple Heart and Bronze Star; he returned to study rural poverty in Appalachia, taught history in high school for 13 years and painted houses in the summer. In 1988 he ran for Congress and lost to incumbent Democrat Roy Dyson 50.4%–49.6%; Dyson spent vastly more money but was embarrassed by a *Washington Post* story on his personnel practices. In 1990, Gilchrest was again vastly outspent, but this time defeated Dyson 57%–43%, in part drawing on his genuineness and *Mr. Smith Goes to Washington* demeanor. The 1992 redistricting placed him in the same district with Democratic incumbent Tom McMillen, a former Rhodes Scholar and pro-basketball player. McMillen raised far more money, but Gilchrest won 52%–48%, carrying 60% on the Eastern Shore. Since then, he has not faced a competitive Democratic challenger.

Gilchrest's voting record in recent years has been almost precisely at the midpoint of the House, making him a crucial vote on many issues. His specialty, helpful in a district centered on the Chesapeake Bay, is environmental protection, without sacrificing economic development. His committee assignments—Resources and Transportation, with the chairmanship of the Fisheries and Oceans Panel on Resources—give him some leverage on these issues. He encouraged a federal program to restore oysters in the Bay by expanding their protected areas, and he secured additional funding for farm conservation on the Shore to reduce agricultural runoff into the Bay. He worked to enforce international treaties to conserve migratory fish, plus tigers and African elephants. He took issue with Western Republicans when they sought to relax the Endangered Species Act. He was the chief Republican sponsor in 2001 of an unsuccessful amendment to reduce crop subsidies and increase conservation programs in the farm bill; he also sponsored a conservation amendment to encourage preserving Chesapeake lands from development. He was the only Maryland member to vote for D.C. statehood, and he opposed the National Rifle Association in 1999 on its amendment to weaken restrictions on gun show sales—in a district where many are strongly opposed to gun control.

He also has been a maverick to the point of being courageous—and occasionally effective—in taking on local economic and political powers. He attacked large poultry producers for running roughshod over local chicken growers. And, he opposed efforts backed by the Port of Baltimore to dredge the Chesapeake and Delaware Canal, which links the Chesapeake and Delaware bays; his objections to the pollution risk outraged powerful Marylanders, but the Corps abandoned the plan in 2001.

Gilchrest does not accept PAC contributions, but he has won the endorsements of the Sierra Club and League of Conservation Voters. He had a scare in the 2002 primary, when Baltimore County attorney and political unknown David Fischer loaned his campaign more than $300,000 and attracted support from the National Rifle Association and the Club for Growth. Fischer called Gilchrest out of step with the district's conservative views. He ran a newspaper ad stating "A safe Republican district deserves a congressman who actually votes like a Republican," and he criticized Gilchrest for winning support from abortion rights and gay and lesbian groups. In the final two weeks before the September primary, the moderate Republican Main Street Partnership attacked Fischer's "distorted and negative campaign," which it called a violation of Ronald Reagan's 11th Commandment against attacking other Republicans. Gilchrest spent roughly $400,000 and won, 60%–36%. But he ran much better on the Eastern Shore (67%–30%) than in the suburbs (52%–44%); in Harford County, he won by only 8 votes out of more than 11,000 cast. In the general election, he won against a 78-year-old opponent 77%–23%. Gilchrest is likely to get another primary challenge in 2004. Conservative state Senator Richard Colburn, who ran unsuccessfully in the 1990 primary, announced in May 2003 that he will seek to unseat Gilchrest.

SECOND DISTRICT

Rep. Dutch Ruppersberger (D)

Elected 2002, 1st term; b. Jan. 31, 1946, Baltimore; home, Cockeysville; U. of MD, 1963–67, U of Baltimore, J.D. 1970; Methodist; married (Kay).

Elected Office: Baltimore Cnty. Cncl. 1986–94; Baltimore Cnty. Exec., 1994–02.

Professional Career: Practicing atty.

DC Office: 1630 LHOB 20515, 202-225-3061; Fax: 202-225-3094; Web site: www.house.gov/ruppersberger.

District Office: Timonium, 410-628-2701.

Committees: *Armed Services* (28th of 29 D). *Government Reform* (16th of 19 D): Criminal Justice, Drug Policy & Human Resources; National Security, Emerging Threats & Intl. Relations. *Permanent Select Committee on Intelligence* (9th of 9 D): Human Intelligence, Analysis & Counterintelligence; Intelligence Policy & National Security; Technical & Tactical Intelligence.

Group Ratings and Key Votes: Newly Elected

Election Results

2002 general	Dutch Ruppersberger (D)	105,718	(54%)	($1,219,821)
	Helen Bentley (R)	88,954	(46%)	($1,071,333)
2002 primary	Dutch Ruppersberger (D)	32,974	(50%)	
	Oz Bengur (D)	23,729	(36%)	
	Kenneth Bosley (D)	5,104	(8%)	
	Other	3,793	(6%)	
2000 general	Robert Ehrlich (R)	178,556	(69%)	($871,393)
	Kenneth Bosley (D)	81,591	(31%)	

The People		Race/Ethnic Origin	Ancestry	
Area size:	359 sq. mi.	66.3% White	German: 15.6%	Irish: 10.4%
Urban population:	98.3%	27.1% Black	English: 5.9%	
Rural population:	1.7%	2.4% Asian	**2000 Presidential Vote**	
Pop. 2000:	662,060	0.3% Native Am.	Gore (D) 127,510	(57%)
Median income:	$44,309	0.0% Hawaiian	Bush (R) 91,677	(41%)
Poverty status:	9.8%	1.5% Two+ races	Other 5,285	(2%)
Military veterans:	15.0%	0.2% Other	**Cook Partisan Voting Index:** D + 8	
		2.2% Hispanic Origin		

Occupation	Blue collar: 23.0%	White collar: 61.5%	Gray collar: 15.5%

The spokes of Baltimore's avenues spread out in all directions from the downtown centered on the Inner Harbor, connecting the central city with the suburbs where most residents of metropolitan Baltimore now live. The streets reach east to Dundalk and Essex, industrial suburbs where the tone of life was set for years by the giant Sparrows Point steel mill, long the biggest in the country. Northeastward, they extend to Havre de Grace and the oldest lighthouse in continuous use on the East Coast, plus modest working-class suburbs in Harford County. The locale of the Aberdeen Proving Grounds is now better known for its Ripken Stadium, the home of the Aberdeen Iron Birds, a Class A baseball team owned by home town hero Cal Ripken, the Iron Man who set a baseball record by playing 2,632 consecutive games for the Baltimore Orioles. In an arc north of downtown are middle-income towns from Randallstown to White Marsh. A couple miles northwest of the county seat of Towson is Timonium, the site of the Maryland state fair.

The 2d Congressional District is an irregularly shaped hodgepodge that includes much of this territory. Most of its territory is not far from Chesapeake Bay, running south from Havre de Grace past the Aberdeen Proving Grounds and the bustling Port of Baltimore, with its container facilities and large warehouses, and south toward the increasingly busy Baltimore-Washington

International Airport. It juts inland to include some Baltimore County suburbs, residential neighborhoods in northeast Baltimore and an industrial pocket in far southeast Baltimore. At that point, the district crosses the Harbor Tunnel to capture the rowhomes of Brooklyn and Curtis Bay, whose residents are mainly descendants of German and East European immigrants who arrived there to labor in the industries along the Patapsco River and the harbor. The Democrats who drew the district lines obviously wanted to connect Democratic suburban and city neighborhoods while including as little Republican territory as possible. About half its population is in Baltimore County, with the remainder divided roughly equally between Anne Arundel and Harford Counties and Baltimore City. The district's boundaries are very different from those of the old 2d District, and the inclusion of Baltimore neighborhoods helped raise the district's black percentage from 8% to 27% and lowered the Bush 2000 percentage from 55% to 41%—one of the biggest changes in the nation. Before the redistricting plan became public in February 2002, 2d District Republican Congressman Bob Ehrlich, urged by many Maryland Republicans to run for governor and by Speaker Dennis Hastert to run for reelection, left both options open. But the plan, which went to the trouble of relocating Ehrlich's Timonium home to the 1st District (a majority of whose residents live on the Eastern Shore), helped Ehrlich make up his mind. In March 2002, he announced he was running for governor. That made it easier for the Democrats to achieve their goal of capturing the seat. But to their surprise and dismay, Ehrlich was elected Governor by a 52%–48% margin over Democratic Lieutenant Governor Kathleen Kennedy Townsend (who had run unsuccessfully in the 2d District in 1986).

The congressman from the 2d District is C.A. Dutch Ruppersberger, a Democrat first elected in 2002, for whom this district was drawn. Ruppersberger grew up in Baltimore, attended the University of Maryland and graduated from the University of Baltimore law school, and then served as Baltimore County assistant state's attorney. In 1986, he was elected to the Baltimore County Council; in 1994, he was elected Baltimore County Executive, a position once held by a vice president of the United States, Spiro Agnew. Barred from seeking a third term in 2002, he claimed credit for the county government's high bond rating and for winning national acclaim for economic growth and sound management. He was an advocate for smart growth initiatives and championed extensive land conservation efforts. He calls himself a pro-business Democrat and seriously considered running for governor in 2002, but decided not to challenge Townsend. In fall 2001, he signaled that he would run for the House if Democratic redistricters produced a favorable district; after they did, he announced he was running. He faced some tough obstacles. In 2000, he had backed a property condemnation plan that would give him the power of eminent domain to redevelop large pieces of the county; the proposal was soundly rejected at the polls. In the 2002 Democratic primary, his little-known opponent, investment banker and Princeton graduate Osman "Oz" Bengur, spent more than $500,000 of his own money. Bengur, a former Republican whose political experience had been as an alternate delegate from Maine to the 1980 Democratic convention, said the proposal showed Ruppersberger was too closely tied to developers. But the state's Democratic establishment lined up behind Ruppersberger; Bengur failed to pull off an upset. Ruppersberger won by the surprisingly weak margin of 50%–36%, carrying Baltimore County, which cast 62% of the primary votes, by 52%–36% and the rest of the district by 48%–38%.

The fall campaign was no easier. This open seat centered on the port of Baltimore attracted former Congresswoman Helen Delich Bentley, who had won the 2d District seat in 1984 and held it until she ran, unsuccessfully, for governor in 1994. At 78, Bentley was by far the oldest candidate in a seriously contested House race in the 2002 cycle. But she was still feisty and energetic. She said that Republican leaders promised to restore her seat on Appropriations and that she would concentrate on national security and maritime issues. With a strong record of constituent service, cross-party popularity and a willingness to buck her own party, Bentley seemed to have a chance to overcome the new district's Democratic leanings. Both candidates supported additional dredging of shipping channels in the Bay plus increased port security.

Ruppersberger won by a larger than expected 54%–46%. His popular vote margin was more than 13,000 votes in the small part of the district in Baltimore City, which he carried 79%–21%, and only 3,000 votes in the rest of the district. Bentley did not fare as well as Republicans had hoped in the suburbs, losing Baltimore County 51%–48% and running about even in the other two. The last two members who have held this seat, Bentley and Ehrlich, both ran for governor; Ruppersberger may be the next, in 2006 or 2010.

THIRD DISTRICT

Rep. Ben Cardin (D)

Elected 1986, 9th term; b. Oct. 5, 1943, Baltimore; home, Baltimore; U. of Pittsburgh, B.A. 1964, U. of MD, LL.B., J.D. 1967; Jewish; married (Myrna).

Elected Office: MD House of Delegates, 1966–86, Speaker, 1979–86.

Professional Career: Practicing atty., 1967–86.

DC Office: 2207 RHOB 20515, 202-225-4016; Fax: 202-225-9219; Web site: www.house.gov/cardin.

District Offices: Annapolis, 410-974-9703; Baltimore, 410-433-8886.

Committees: *Select Committee on Homeland Security* (8th of 23 D): Emergency Preparedness & Response; Infrastructure & Border Security. *Ways & Means* (5th of 17 D): Human Resources (RMM); Social Security.

Group Ratings

	ADA	ACLU	AFS	LCV	CON	ITIC	NTU	COC	ACU	NTLC	CHC
2002	95	87	100	88	92	38	21	55	0	6	0
2001	100	—	100	93	—	—	11	35	4	—	—

National Journal Ratings

	2001 LIB —	2001 CONS	2002 LIB —	2002 CONS
Economic	77%	23%	67%	32%
Social	83%	11%	67%	29%
Foreign	70%	28%	74%	25%

Key Votes of the 107th Congress

1. Approve Bush Tax Cuts	N	5. Faith-Based Charities	N	9. Trade Promotion Authority	N
2. Limit Patients' Bill of Rights	N	6. Bar Gays in the Boy Scouts	N	10. Bar Funds for Intl. Court	N
3. Campaign Finance Reform	Y	7. Ban Partial-Birth Abortion	N	11. Authorize Force in Iraq	N
4. Ban ANWR Development	Y	8. Arm Commercial Pilots	Y	12. Deny Home. Sec. Dept. Union	N

Election Results

2002 general	Ben Cardin (D)	145,589	(66%)	($1,050,896)
	Scott Conwell (R)	75,721	(34%)	($27,859)
2002 primary	Ben Cardin (D)	62,938	(90%)	
	John Rea (D)	6,986	(10%)	
2000 general	Ben Cardin (D)	169,347	(76%)	($564,687)
	Colin Harby (R)	53,827	(24%)	

Prior Winning Percentages: 1998 (78%); 1996 (67%); 1994 (71%); 1992 (74%); 1990 (70%); 1988 (73%); 1986 (79%)

The People		Race/Ethnic Origin	Ancestry	
Area size:	293 sq. mi.	75.7% White	German: 14.3%	Irish: 11.1%
Urban population:	98.6%	16.2% Black	English: 7.7%	
Rural population:	1.4%	3.2% Asian	**2000 Presidential Vote**	
Pop. 2000:	662,062	0.3% Native Am.	Gore (D) 143,685	(55%)
Median income:	$52,906	0.0% Hawaiian	Bush (R) 107,481	(41%)
Poverty status:	7.7%	1.5% Two+ races	Other 8,456	(3%)
Military veterans:	13.0%	0.2% Other	**Cook Partisan Voting Index:** D + 7	
		2.9% Hispanic Origin		

Occupation   Blue collar: 15.7%   White collar: 71.7%   Gray collar: 12.5%

Baltimore, one of America's major cities since the Revolution, in the 1980s and early 1990s suddenly became one of America's star cities. Its Inner Harbor and new ballpark at Camden Yards became national models. Its cuisine—steamed crabs with Chesapeake spices, crab cakes—became known beyond the watershed of the Chesapeake Bay. The central city of Baltimore has terrible problems—high crime, abandoned neighborhoods, poor schools—but the greater Baltimore that has grown far beyond the city and county lines retains a distinctive character. This is a city built solidly on commerce, and one that has always known how to reap its pleasures. To the south, Annapolis was laid out as a capital in 1694, with one circle planned for the Statehouse and one for the Church; the marble-halled Statehouse, built in 1772, where the Continental Congress ratified the Treaty of Paris, is the oldest state capitol in continuous use. Annapolis is also the home of the United States Naval Academy and its waterfront, though gentrified, is a waterman's as well as a yachter's port.

The 3d Congressional District consists of three oddly disjointed portions that extend from the locus of the Inner Harbor area. Its boundaries were designed by Democrats with politics in mind: The 3d envelops on three sides the majority-black 7th District and is itself enveloped on three sides by the 2d District, which redistricters made much more Democratic. One spoke extends northeast from black city neighborhoods into mostly white suburbs. Another extends north and west from the city to the Baltimore County seat of Towson and the heavily Jewish suburbs of Pikesville and Owings Mills, past the array of temples and synagogues on Park Heights Avenue in Baltimore city. The largest bloc of voters is in the crooked spoke that extends southwest, past the old rowhouse neighborhoods overlooking Fort McHenry and out past Governor Bob Ehrlich's birthplace in blue-collar Arbutus into Linthicum in Anne Arundel County, and continuing to Annapolis. Just over one-third of the district population resides in Anne Arundel County (including all of Annapolis); a quarter resides within Baltimore city itself, in neighborhoods like Roland Park, and among the restaurants and bars of Little Italy and Fells Point. A small portion of Howard County is also in the 3d, consisting of parts of Elkridge and Columbia in Howard County. Redistricting left the 3d District less Democratic than it had been; the Bush 2000 percentage vote increased from 34% to 41%.

The congressman from the 3d District is Benjamin Cardin, former speaker of the Maryland House of Delegates and one of the many bright politicos produced by the Jewish neighborhoods of northwest Baltimore. He was elected to the House of Delegates in 1966, at 23, the first time he was eligible to run; he became speaker in 1979, at 35; he was easily elected to Congress in 1986 when Barbara Mikulski ran for the Senate. In the House, Cardin got a seat on Ways and Means in his second term and has been a productive and creative legislator. He supported NAFTA despite union opposition, backed a cap on medical malpractice damages despite trial lawyers' opposition, and voted for PNTR with China after securing for local consumption a rider designed to crack down on international dumping of subsidized steel in U.S. markets.

More than any Democrat at Ways and Means—and perhaps more than any Democrat in the House—he has worked skillfully on bipartisan legislation at a time when few were sufficiently clever or independent to pursue such initiatives. Few House members of either party "can match his stature as legislative architect and master of bipartisan lawmaking," the Baltimore *Sun* editorialized. "Being a member of Congress is about working with Democrats and Republicans and crafting legislation. From reforming the IRS to protecting pensions, members need to work together," Cardin has said. Such has been his record, occasionally to the dismay of more partisan Democrats. He was co-sponsor with Ohio Rep. Rob Portman of the 1998 IRS reform law, the first major reform in four decades, which shifted the burden of proof away from the taxpayer and toward the government, established greater oversight of the agency, and encouraged electronic filing and updated technology. Again with Portman, he produced in 2000 major bipartisan legislation to expand 401(k) savings and other retirement plans. In 2001, when Congress enacted the Bush tax cut, it included his and Portman's measure to increase the limits for maximum IRA and 401(k) contributions. At the dawn of the 108th Congress, he and Portman teamed again on a plan to sponsor pension savings and rollovers for low and moderate-income workers. On Social Security, too, he has shown willingness to seek bipartisan reform with retirement accounts, and he could become instrumental if Republicans reach out to moderate Democrats.

Cardin has been a workhorse on health care and welfare, but with less bipartisan success. He concedes frustration that Congress has been "not equal to the sum of our parts" in the legislative results. He helped draft the Democrats' version of HMO reform, including the provision that guarantees patients the right to an external process to appeal adverse health insurance decisions. On prescription drugs for seniors, he opposed Republicans' plans for private insurance coverage. In 2002, the House defeated his Democratic alternative to welfare reform, which he said focused on removing families from poverty rather than pushing them off welfare rolls.

Cardin protested the new redistricting lines that removed more than one-third of his former district and added unfamiliar territory in Anne Arundel County, which now casts more votes in the district than Baltimore County, Baltimore City or Howard County. Some thought he was facing retaliation from the chief map drawer, Governor Parris Glendening, for having considered running against him in 1998, or perhaps Glendening simply wanted to maximize the Democratic vote in the 2d and didn't think Cardin would have trouble winning the new 3d. He didn't in 2002, although he carried Anne Arundel by only 53%–46%; with margins of 2–1 or more in the other jurisdictions, he won districtwide 66%–34%. But this district might be competitive if Cardin retires or, more likely, runs for statewide office.

FOURTH DISTRICT

Rep. Albert Wynn (D)

Elected 1992, 6th term; b. Sept. 10, 1951, Philadelphia, PA; home, Mitchellville; U. of Pittsburgh, B.S. 1973, Howard U., 1973–74, Georgetown U. Law Schl., J.D. 1977; Baptist; married (Gaines).

Elected Office: MD House of Delegates, 1982–87; MD Senate 1987–92.

Professional Career: Exec. Dir., Prince George's Cnty. Consumer Protection Comm., 1977–81; Chmn., Metro Wash. Cncl. of Consumer Agencies, 1980–81; Practicing atty., 1981–92.

DC Office: 434 CHOB 20515, 202-225-8699; Fax: 202-225-8714; Web site: www.house.gov/wynn.

District Offices: Largo, 301-773-4094; Olney, 301-929-3462.

Committees: *Energy & Commerce* (15th of 26 D): Energy & Air Quality; Environment & Hazardous Materials; Telecommunications & The Internet.

Group Ratings

	ADA	ACLU	AFS	LCV	CON	ITIC	NTU	COC	ACU	NTLC	CHC
2002	85	80	89	75	18	38	21	50	8	3	33
2001	90	—	100	93	—	—	10	35	4	—	—

National Journal Ratings

	2001 LIB —	2001 CONS	2002 LIB —	2002 CONS
Economic	68%	33%	69%	30%
Social	65%	34%	67%	29%
Foreign	86%	12%	82%	18%

Key Votes of the 107th Congress

1. Approve Bush Tax Cuts	*	5. Faith-Based Charities		
2. Limit Patients' Bill of Rights	N	6. Bar Gays in the Boy Scouts	N	9. Trade Promotion Authority	N
3. Campaign Finance Reform	Y	7. Ban Partial-Birth Abortion	N	10. Bar Funds for Intl. Court	N
4. Ban ANWR Development	Y	8. Arm Commercial Pilots	Y	11. Authorize Force in Iraq	Y
				12. Deny Home. Sec. Dept. Union	N

Election Results

2002 general	Albert Wynn (D)	131,644	(79%)	($696,244)
	John Kimble (R)	34,890	(21%)	
2002 primary	Albert Wynn (D)	66,225	(83%)	
	Don Williams (D)	13,299	(17%)	
2000 general	Albert Wynn (D)	172,624	(87%)	($465,471)
	John Kimble (R)	24,973	(13%)	

Prior Winning Percentages: 1998 (86%); 1996 (85%); 1994 (75%); 1992 (75%)

The People		Race/Ethnic Origin	Ancestry	
Area size:	318 sq. mi.	27.6% White	German: 5.3%	Irish: 5.0%
Urban population:	97.9%	56.8% Black	English: 4.0%	
Rural population:	2.1%	5.6% Asian	**2000 Presidential Vote**	
Pop. 2000:	662,062	0.2% Native Am.	Gore (D)...............176,780	(77%)
Median income:	$57,727	0.0% Hawaiian	Bush (R)..............:49,202	(21%)
Poverty status:	7.3%	2.0% Two+ races	Other....................4,098	(2%)
Military veterans:	12.2%	0.2% Other	**Cook Partisan Voting Index:** D +28	
		7.5% Hispanic Origin		

Occupation   Blue collar: 15.0%   White collar: 70.7%   Gray collar: 14.3%

In 1696, the proprietors of the colony of Maryland created a new county between the Potomac and Patuxent Rivers and named it after the husband of the heir to the throne, Prince George of Denmark. For 300 years Prince George's County has not often won national fame—maybe briefly when investigators chased the plotters of Abraham Lincoln's murder here—but it should now. Historically, Prince George's was tobacco country, rural and heavily settled, with blacks and Catholics and big property-owners who pretty much ran things. Today Prince George's is—or should be known as—the home of America's largest black middle class, a place that gives a hopeful glimpse of the future; overall, the county is 63% black and 7% Hispanic. Prince George's is affluent by national standards, with over 70% of women working, one of the highest percentages in the nation. With office and shopping mall growth, it has proved itself a far more commercially vibrant and culturally constructive community—including substantial home-schooling—than adjacent parts of the District of Columbia. New economic projects include the building of a 12-lane span across the Potomac (to replace the crumbling Wilson Bridge), plus a huge new hotel and conference center at Oxon Hill near the bridge. Prince George's has always had many black residents, since the first tobacco crop was planted, but that population grew as middle-class blacks moved out of Washington into modest suburbs at the county's edge and affluent subdivisions far to the east. The black percentage here increased from 14% in 1970 to 37% in 1980 to 63% by 2000; the total population grew by 11% in the 1990s. The county's median household income of more than $55,000 compares favorably with the national median of about $43,000 and doubles the national median for black households. But there are problems: Prince George's has a high crime rate and its police force has shot and killed people at a rate higher than just about any other in the nation.

The 4th Congressional District includes most of Prince George's County inside the Capital Beltway. It also includes a large portion of Montgomery County that is mostly outside the Beltway—starting in Silver Spring, heading up Georgia Avenue and covering a sizable rural area all the way to Clarksburg at the Frederick County line. Although the redistricting shifts increased the Montgomery share to well over one-third of the district's voters, this remains the safest Democratic district in Maryland. The biggest industry here is still government: It has the highest percentage of federal government employees of any congressional district in the nation; Suitland is home to the Census Bureau headquarters.

The congressman from the 4th District is Albert Wynn, a Democrat effectively chosen in the 1992 primary. Wynn grew up in Prince George's County, attending all-black schools there until integration began in his sophomore year. He went to the University of Pittsburgh on a debate team scholarship and received a law degree from Georgetown University. He served a decade in the Maryland legislature, first as a member of the House of Delegates and later the Senate. Twenty candidates—13 Democrats and seven Republicans—ran for the seat when it was created in 1992; Wynn was endorsed by the major local newspapers and won the primary with 28% of the vote. He hasn't had a close contest since then.

Wynn is a loyal member of the Democratic Caucus who campaigned heartily for Bill Clinton, Al Gore and Governor Parris Glendening when each was beleaguered. One of his causes has been racial discrimination in the federal government. On behalf of the American Federation of Government Employees and its opposition to privatization, he took the lead in seeking to halt contracting-out of federal jobs until Congress could improve its monitoring. As a member of the

Commerce committee, he has sought to ban automatic dialing systems that send recorded telephone messages. But Wynn was not a team player on campaign finance regulation. Democratic leaders strongly backed the Shays-Meehan bill, but Wynn felt that its ban on soft money would make it much harder to conduct voter registration and turnout drives in black districts. He was the lead Democratic sponsor of an unsuccessful amendment to strip out the soft money ban.

At home, Wynn sponsors an annual jobs fair, bringing together 9,000 jobseekers and over 200 employers. In the 2002 campaign, he became more of a political powerhouse in the county and state: He worked to elect Jack Johnson as the new County Executive and criticized gubernatorial candidate Kathleen Kennedy Townsend for not reaching out sufficiently to black voters. Wynn also blamed the DCCC for failing to work closely with the black community. He has won re-election without difficulty, though he has been the target of four challenges by his Republican opponent, John Kimble, who once offered to pose naked for *Playgirl* magazine, saying "I'll do whatever it takes to win the election." In 2000, Kimble transmitted a 20-second telephone message from Wynn's former wife, which said that the congressman "does not respect black women. He left me for a white woman,"and urged support for Kimble, who is white. The Montgomery County portion of the district is much more Republican than Prince George's—it was included to deprive 8th District Republican Connie Morella of precincts she would be sure to carry, a factor in her 2002 defeat—but Wynn carried Montgomery 65%–35% and won overall 79%–21%.

FIFTH DISTRICT

Rep. Steny Hoyer (D)

Elected May 1981, 11th term; b. June 14, 1939, New York, NY; home, Mechanicsville; U. of MD, B.S. 1963, Georgetown U., J.D. 1966; Baptist; widowed.

Elected Office: MD Senate, 1966–78, Pres., 1975–78.

Professional Career: Practicing atty., 1966–80; MD Bd. of Higher Educ., 1978–81.

DC Office: 1705 LHOB 20515, 202-225-4131; Fax: 202-225-4300; Web site: www.house.gov/hoyer.

District Offices: Greenbelt, 301-474-0119; Waldorf, 301-843-1577.

Committees: *Minority Whip. Appropriations* (5th of 29 D): Labor, HHS & Education; Transportation, Treasury, & Independent Agencies.

Group Ratings

	ADA	ACLU	AFS	LCV	CON	ITIC	NTU	COC	ACU	NTLC	CHC
2002	95	87	100	88	43	38	18	42	4	3	0
2001	95	—	100	86	—	—	10	43	9	—	—

National Journal Ratings

	2001 LIB —	2001 CONS	2002 LIB —	2002 CONS
Economic	72%	27%	74%	25%
Social	81%	19%	74%	19%
Foreign	69%	31%	72%	26%

Key Votes of the 107th Congress

1. Approve Bush Tax Cuts	N	5. Faith-Based Charities	N	9. Trade Promotion Authority	N
2. Limit Patients' Bill of Rights	N	6. Bar Gays in the Boy Scouts	N	10. Bar Funds for Intl. Court	N
3. Campaign Finance Reform	Y	7. Ban Partial-Birth Abortion	N	11. Authorize Force in Iraq	Y
4. Ban ANWR Development	Y	8. Arm Commercial Pilots	N	12. Deny Home. Sec. Dept. Union	N

Election Results

2002 general	Steny Hoyer (D)	137,903	(69%)	($1,236,900)
	Joseph Crawford (R)	60,758	(31%)	
2002 primary	Steny Hoyer (D)	unopposed		
2000 general	Steny Hoyer (D)	166,231	(65%)	($1,268,702)
	Tim Hutchins (R)	89,019	(35%)	($64,208)

Prior Winning Percentages: 1998 (65%); 1996 (57%); 1994 (59%); 1992 (53%); 1990 (81%); 1988 (79%); 1986 (82%); 1984 (72%); 1982 (80%); 1981 (55%)

The People		Race/Ethnic Origin	Ancestry	
Area size:	1,509 sq. mi.	60.4% White	German: 10.5%	Irish: 9.9%
Urban population:	75.2%	30.0% Black	English: 8.1%	
Rural population:	24.8%	3.7% Asian	**2000 Presidential Vote**	
Pop. 2000:	662,060	0.4% Native Am.	Gore (D) 139,068	(57%)
Median income:	$62,661	0.0% Hawaiian	Bush (R) 101,056	(41%)
Poverty status:	5.6%	1.9% Two+ races	Other 5,871	(2%)
Military veterans:	15.4%	0.2% Other	**Cook Partisan Voting Index:** D + 8	
		3.5% Hispanic Origin		

Occupation   Blue collar: 18.8%   White collar: 68.0%   Gray collar: 13.2%

Southern Maryland was first settled by Catholics, the Calvert family of the Lords Baltimore, who founded St. Marys in 1634, not long after Jamestown and Plymouth Rock. Maryland became one of the two great Chesapeake tobacco colonies, and plantation houses were built on every inlet off the broad Potomac and Patuxent Rivers. For years, none of these towns grew much, and even today many people here are directly descended from the old families. This was never puritanical country: Liquor flowed even during Prohibition and slot machines were specifically allowed for years by Maryland law. But tobacco farming is nearing an end here. Still, the area hasn't completely renounced its tobacco heritage: The highlight of the annual Charles County fair remains the crowning of Queen Nicotina. The area's economic base owes much to government installations like the Civil War Point Lookout prisoner-of-war camp and the Patuxent River Naval Complex, where many astronauts got their first training. And now metro Washington and Baltimore are spreading into southern Maryland, with rapid growth in the 1990s in Calvert County south of Annapolis—the fastest growing county in Maryland—and Charles County south of Prince George's County; it is reaching even further south into St. Mary's County, where the first settlers landed in 1634.

The 5th Congressional District of Maryland includes those three counties, plus a large slice of Prince George's—most of the county beyond the Capital Beltway. Its lines were drawn to assure a large black percentage in the adjacent 4th District, but there are also large numbers of blacks in the 5th—30% of the population in 2002—both new suburbanites and descendants of old southern Maryland families. Many of its people live north of Washington, in College Park, home of the University of Maryland, and in Hyattsville, Greenbelt, Beltsville, Laurel and Bowie. The 5th also includes southern Prince George's, from Clinton south, southern Anne Arundel County and all of St. Mary's, Calvert and Charles counties. Historically, this is a Democratic area, but southern Maryland voted heavily for Republican Governor Bob Ehrlich in 2002.

The congressman from the 5th District is Steny Hoyer, a veteran Democrat and now minority whip, who was first elected in 1981. Hoyer was elected to the Maryland Senate in 1966, at 27, just after graduating from law school. He was Senate president from 1975–78, the youngest in Maryland history; he made a misstep running for lieutenant governor on a losing ticket in 1978. But when the 5th District, then entirely in Prince George's, was declared vacant in 1981—after incumbent Gladys Spellman went into an irreversible coma—Hoyer won the special election by edging out Spellman's husband and several other Democrats in the primary and beating a well-financed, competent Republican candidate in the general.

Interestingly, Hoyer is of Danish descent, like the original Prince George. He has fine political instincts, works hard and can speak in an old-fashioned patriotic style that is genuinely moving. A fast riser in Maryland politics, he was also a fast riser in Congress. He excelled at constituency service and soon won a seat on the Appropriations Committee, where he became a key player for the whole D.C. metropolitan area. When Democrats had control, Hoyer chaired the Treasury, Postal Service and General Government Appropriations subcommittee, which oversees several major components of the federal work force and the White House budget. He used the panel to get $6 million for flexiplace telecommuting centers and to roll back benefit contribution rates for federal employees to 1998 levels in 2001. In 2001, he urged the Bush administration to convert 1% of federal pay increase into a "locality pay" adjustment for workers in high cost-of-living areas; Bush declined to do so in 2002.

Hoyer has pushed for funding for Chesapeake Bay cleanup and dredging the Bay for Baltimore harbor; he got into a dispute with Wayne Gilchrest over whether dredging spoils should be dumped near the Bay Bridge. He got the proposed National Harbor resort exempted from further federal review in 1999. Hoyer has worked indefatigably and shrewdly to maintain and increase jobs at the Goddard Space Flight Center in Greenbelt, the Patuxent River Naval Air Station, and the Naval Surface Warfare Center at Indian Head. He uses his Appropriations seat to fund programs and to see that local facilities are suited for them. In summer 2000, he added to the Clinton budget $3 million for the Joint Strike Fighter, $2.5 million for the Force Operational Readiness Combat Simulator, and $7.5 million for a Navy Remote Emitter Simulator. He helped get the Marine Corps chemical and biological warfare team moved to Indian Head in 2000.

Hoyer's voting record is fairly liberal, though less so than when he represented a near-black-majority district in the late 1980s. He broke with party lines by supporting the balanced budget amendment in 1995, but worked hard in 1996 to support Democratic stands on the minimum wage and health insurance portability; he backed NAFTA, GATT, fast track and PNTR with China. He was the chief House sponsor of the Americans with Disabilities Act of 1990; in January 2002, he criticized the Supreme Court for what he considered an overly narrow interpretation of it. He backed the Shays-Meehan campaign finance bill. In June 1999, he helped launch dozens of motions against the legislative appropriation, arguing that the Republican leadership unilaterally rewrote the appropriation bill. He defended raising the president's salary to $400,000 on the ground that the current value of George Washington's salary was $4.6 million. He begged Speaker Dennis Hastert to lobby for the resolution supporting the Bosnia bombing in April 1999, which was defeated 213–213—"one of the most shameful things the House has done since I was a member." In October 2002, he voted to authorize military action in Iraq. As ranking minority member on House Administration, he took the lead in October 2001 in hammering out bipartisan election reform legislation; it passed 362–63 in December 2001. Hoyer and Chairman Bob Ney have worked in a bipartisan manner on other issues as well and especially after September 11. He is a former chairman of the Helsinki commission and has been a champion of human rights around the world. On September 11, 2001, it was Hoyer's idea to have rank and file members stand behind the leadership in front of the Capitol in the evening, when members long-locked in partisan battle sang out together, "God Bless America."

In 1989, Hoyer was elected chairman of the Democratic Caucus, a term-limited position that he left in 1994. When he tried to move up in June 1991, he was beaten for majority whip by David Bonior, who had the support of liberals and committee chairmen, 160–109. He then became chairman of the Democratic Steering Committee and was parliamentarian at the 2000 Democratic National Convention. During much of 2000 he conducted a campaign for majority whip against Nancy Pelosi, all premised on the notion that Democrats would win control of the House. He ran as the candidate with the more moderate voting record, but that contest was mooted by the 2000 election. But in 2001 Bonior, faced with unfavorable redistricting, began running for governor of Michigan; Hoyer and Pelosi both sought to replace him as minority whip. Hoyer argued that he had greater experience in leadership positions and could do a better job of unifying the caucus; he cited his support from such different members as John Dingell, John Lewis and Charles Stenholm. Pelosi had more publicly committed votes going into the October 2001 caucus—100 versus 77—and she won 118–95 (both did less well than predicted, as often happens in secret ballot leadership races).

Looking ahead, it was plain to Hoyer that there might be another whip contest soon. If Democrats failed to win a majority in November 2002, Dick Gephardt might well resign as Minority Leader, which is what happened; if they succeeded in winning a majority, Gephardt would have been in line to be Speaker and Pelosi Majority Leader, leaving the majority whip position open. So Hoyer kept collecting commitments for a race that was likely but not certain to happen. In April 2002 he announced he had 141 pledges of public support from incumbent Democrats; in May he announced he had 19 more. He campaigned widely for Democrats in House races and contributed more than $750,000 to their campaigns. When many Maryland Democrats complained about Kathleen Kennedy Townsend's 2002 gubernatorial campaign, Hoyer in September made an angry speech telling Democrats to "stop apologizing for our candidate." After Gephardt announced his resignation as Leader after the November election, Pelosi was easily elected to replace him; Hoyer was unanimously elected Minority Whip.

Hoyer had no trouble winning reelection in 2002. After the 1992 redistricting, Hoyer had some serious Republican competition; he won by only 53%–44% in 1992. But he increased his margins as the decade went on, and his district was the only one in Maryland substantially unchanged by the 2002 redistricting.

SIXTH DISTRICT

Rep. Roscoe Bartlett (R)

Elected 1992, 6th term; b. June 3, 1926, Moreland, KY; home, Frederick; Columbia Union Col., B.A. 1947, U. of MD, M.S. 1949, Ph.D. 1952; Seventh Day Adventist; married (Ellen).

Professional Career: Farmer; Prof., U. of MD, 1948–52; Asst. Prof., Loma Linda Schl. of Medicine, 1952–54; Asst. Prof., Howard U. Medical Schl., 1954–56; Research scientist, N.I.H., 1956–58; Research scientist, U.S. Naval Aerospace Medical Inst., 1958–62; Research scientist, Johns Hopkins U., 1962–67; Research Mgr., IBM, 1967–74; Pres., Roscoe Bartlett & Assoc., 1974–86.

DC Office: 2412 RHOB 20515, 202-225-2721; Fax: 202-225-2193; Web site: www.house.gov/bartlett.

District Offices: Cumberland, 301-724-3105; Frederick, 301-694-3030; Hagerstown, 301-797-6043; Westminster, 410-857-1115.

Committees: *Armed Services* (7th of 33 R): Projection Forces (Chmn.); Terrorism, Unconventional Threats & Capabilities. *Science* (8th of 25 R): Energy; Space & Aeronautics. *Small Business* (2d of 18 R): Regulatory Reform & Oversight.

Group Ratings

	ADA	ACLU	AFS	LCV	CON	ITIC	NTU	COC	ACU	NTLC	CHC
2002	10	7	11	38	50	50	57	80	96	97	100
2001	15	—	10	36	—	—	70	78	88	—	—

National Journal Ratings

	2001 LIB —	2001 CONS		2002 LIB —	2002 CONS
Economic	28%	69%		36%	61%
Social	0%	81%		0%	75%
Foreign	29%	69%		46%	53%

Key Votes of the 107th Congress

1. Approve Bush Tax Cuts	Y	5. Faith-Based Charities	Y	9. Trade Promotion Authority	N
2. Limit Patients' Bill of Rights	Y	6. Bar Gays in the Boy Scouts	Y	10. Bar Funds for Intl. Court	Y
3. Campaign Finance Reform	N	7. Ban Partial-Birth Abortion	Y	11. Authorize Force in Iraq	Y
4. Ban ANWR Development	Y	8. Arm Commercial Pilots	Y	12. Deny Home. Sec. Dept. Union	Y

Election Results

2002 general	Roscoe Bartlett (R)	147,825	(66%)	($237,991)
	Donald DeArmon (D)	75,575	(34%)	($82,515)
2002 primary	Roscoe Bartlett (R)	unopposed		
2000 general	Roscoe Bartlett (R)	168,624	(61%)	($225,919)
	Donald DeArmon (D)	109,136	(39%)	($397,509)

Prior Winning Percentages: 1998 (63%); 1996 (57%); 1994 (66%); 1992 (54%)

The People		Race/Ethnic Origin	Ancestry	
Area size:	3,094 sq. mi.	91.5% White	German: 20.1%	Irish: 10.6%
Urban population:	60.5%	4.8% Black	English: 8.4%	
Rural population:	39.5%	1.0% Asian	**2000 Presidential Vote**	
Pop. 2000:	662,060	0.2% Native Am.	Bush (R)...............160,263	(61%)
Median income:	$50,957	0.0% Hawaiian	Gore (D)................95,282	(36%)
Poverty status:	6.7%	0.9% Two+ races	Other....................8,029	(3%)
Military veterans:	14.0%	0.1% Other	**Cook Partisan Voting Index:** R +13	
		1.4% Hispanic Origin		

Occupation	Blue collar: 23.9%	White collar: 61.5%	Gray collar: 14.6%

America's first frontier was in western Maryland, where the Appalachian ridges that cross the state diagonally from northeast to southwest cut through the long green sloping fields. These wheat fields were settled first by Pennsylvania Dutch and Scots-Irish hill people, not Chesapeake Bay tobacco growers. Maryland is where the fall line comes closest to an ocean port, where the 19th century's great paths to the interior were staked out: The National Road, and then the nation's first railroad, the Baltimore & Ohio, crossed the wide valleys of bounteous farms and climbed over the Catoctin Mountains. Towns grew up on narrow streets lined with rowhouses that today are overhung with telephone and streetcar wires, overlooking long vistas of cornfields, pastureland and mountains of ancient stone rising above the plains. Across this placid land moved vast armies during the Civil War. In Frederick, city officials paid Confederates $200,000 not to burn down the town, and near Sharpsburg, blue and gray-clad soldiers fought the Battle of Antietam, on the bloodiest day in American military history. Today, there is a new rush of settlement into Carroll County, long part of metro Baltimore, and Frederick County, which is classified as part of metro Washington, both of which grew rapidly in the 1990s.

The 6th Congressional District includes all of western Maryland, runs east through all of Carroll County, takes in a small part of northern Montgomery County and cuts across the northern farmlands and hunt country of Baltimore and Harford Counties all the way to the Susquehanna River. The political tradition in most of this area, unlike the rest of Maryland, is Republican. This was Union country in the Civil War and has been mostly Republican ever since. The new rush of settlement—which made this the fastest growing district in Maryland in the 1990s—is mostly made up of young families of modest incomes seeking respite from metropolitan life, strengthening the area's already conservative leanings. Only 7 of 24 counties in Maryland have more registered Republican voters than Democrats—5 of them are in this district.

The congressman from the 6th District is Roscoe Bartlett, a Republican who matches its current mood. He is an interesting character, a descendant of a signer of the Declaration of Independence and a Seventh Day Adventist with 10 children; he grew up in poverty in Pennsylvania, but his family would not take welfare. He earned a Ph.D. in physiology at the University of Maryland, where he also taught, and he has operated his 145-acre dairy farm. He invented life-support equipment for pilots, astronauts and fire fighters, ran his own business and taught at Frederick Community College. When Bartlett first ran for Congress in 1992, he was a 65-year-old retired University of Maryland physiology professor who seemed to have no chance of winning. Democrat Beverly Byron had represented the district for 14 years and had a conservative voting record. But she was upset in the primary by a liberal who favored national health insurance and abortion rights. Bartlett's conservative views and his attacks on his opponent's legislative perks won him a 54%–46% victory. That unlikely background explains why a colleague once said that Bartlett views his job as "almost like a retirement thing."

Bartlett has proved a surprisingly durable, though iconoclastic, politician. He is the most conservative member of the state's congressional delegation; he has a consistently conservative voting record and was the only Marylander to vote for all 10 provisions of the Contract With America. He carries a copy of the Constitution and consults it frequently. He voted against PNTR with China and he was one of 27 House Republicans to vote against trade promotion authority in 2002. He has voted no on various big-spending budget bills, including George W. Bush's education-reform proposal. But the terrorism threat led him to request $31 million for projects in his districts, including protection of Camp David and Fort Detrick, which is the Army's biological weapons lab.

Bartlett was gratified by the November 2000 passage of his bill to end the Pentagon's practice of euthanizing military working dogs at the end of their useful career. "These military dogs deserve a dignified retirement in loving homes in return for their unique and irreplaceable service to our country," he said. He has been less successful in pushing the recommendation of a commission headed by former Senator Nancy Kassebaum-Baker that men and women should be separated for basic training; he could not even get a roll call on this politically incorrect proposal. His fiscal prudence was reflected in his opposition to expanded federal funds for the local Interstate highway. But he had serious domestic problems resulting from a bad stench caused by wastewater on his property in March 2002; one of the complainants, the Baltimore *Sun* reported, was his stepson.

Bartlett has been re-elected by solid margins. In 2002, he faced a rematch against Donald DeArmon, a veteran House Democratic staffer, who spent only $83,000 after collecting nearly $400,000 in 2000. He campaigned against Bartlett as "a mismatch for the district from the beginning." But Bartlett's share of the vote rose from 61% to 66%.

SEVENTH DISTRICT

Rep. Elijah Cummings (D)

Elected April 1996, 4th term; b. Jan. 18, 1951, Baltimore; home, Baltimore; Howard U., B.S. 1973, U. of MD, J.D. 1976; Baptist; separated.

Elected Office: MD House of Delegates, 1982–96, Speaker Pro–Tem, 1995–96.

Professional Career: Practicing atty., 1976–96.

DC Office: 1632 LHOB 20515, 202-225-4741; Fax: 202-225-3178; Web site: www.house.gov/cummings.

District Office: Baltimore, 410-685-9199.

Committees: *Government Reform* (7th of 19 D): Criminal Justice, Drug Policy & Human Resources (RMM); Wellness & Human Rights. *Transportation & Infrastructure* (14th of 34 D): Highways, Transit & Pipelines; Railroads.

Group Ratings

	ADA	ACLU	AFS	LCV	CON	ITIC	NTU	COC	ACU	NTLC	CHC
2002	95	87	100	75	63	38	20	45	0	0	0
2001	95	—	100	100	—	—	8	27	4	—	—

National Journal Ratings

	2001 LIB —	2001 CONS		2002 LIB —	2002 CONS
Economic	94%	6%		77%	20%
Social	83%	11%		67%	29%
Foreign	86%	12%		84%	14%

Key Votes of the 107th Congress

1. Approve Bush Tax Cuts	N	5. Faith-Based Charities	N	9. Trade Promotion Authority	N
2. Limit Patients' Bill of Rights	N	6. Bar Gays in the Boy Scouts	N	10. Bar Funds for Intl. Court	N
3. Campaign Finance Reform	Y	7. Ban Partial-Birth Abortion	N	11. Authorize Force in Iraq	N
4. Ban ANWR Development	Y	8. Arm Commercial Pilots	Y	12. Deny Home. Sec. Dept. Union	N

Election Results

2002 general	Elijah Cummings (D) 137,047	(74%)	($466,160)
	Joseph Ward (R) 49,172	(26%)	
2002 primary	Elijah Cummings (D) 67,938	(89%)	
	Robert Kaufman (D) 4,905	(6%)	
	Other 3,210	(4%)	
2000 general	Elijah Cummings (D) 134,066	(87%)	($444,442)
	Kenneth Kondner (R) 19,773	(13%)	

Prior Winning Percentages: 1998 (86%); 1996 (83%); 1996 (81%)

The People		**Race/Ethnic Origin**	**Ancestry**	
Area size:	296 sq. mi.	34.2% White	German: 7.9%	Irish: 6.0%
Urban population:	94.9%	58.8% Black	English: 4.6%	
Rural population:	5.1%	3.5% Asian	**2000 Presidential Vote**	
Pop. 2000:	662,060	0.2% Native Am.	Gore (D)..............166,410	(73%)
Median income:	$38,885	0.0% Hawaiian	Bush (R)...............57,262	(25%)
Poverty status:	17.6%	1.3% Two+ races	Other....................5,766	(3%)
Military veterans:	12.0%	0.2% Other	**Cook Partisan Voting Index:** D +24	
		1.7% Hispanic Origin		

Occupation	Blue collar: 16.2%	White collar: 66.7%	Gray collar: 17.1%

At the junction of North and South, terminus of America's first railroad and the East Coast port closest to the great West, Baltimore is one of the few American cities to have had large numbers of both blacks and European immigrants throughout its history. Its black community has a rich and notable history: The *Afro-American* newspaper has been published here for more than 100 years and there was once a black symphony orchestra. Eubie Blake, the famous black musician and one of the founders of ragtime music, grew up here and now has a museum in his honor on Charles Street. Jazz great Billie Holliday was born here; these were the stomping grounds of Thurgood Marshall and Cab Calloway. Near downtown on the west side is the childhood home of Babe Ruth and the home of H.L. Mencken, two great white westside Baltimoreans. For years this side of town had a biracial, bipartisan politics in which Democrats like Governor Albert Ritchie and Republicans like Mayor and Governor Theodore McKeldin competed zestfully for black and white votes.

Baltimore has been a black-majority city since the late 1970s, and most of its westside neighborhoods are heavily black. Black Republicanism has long since died out, though Republican Bob Ehrlich and his running mate Michael Steele campaigned heavily in black areas and made small inroads among black voters in the 2002 race for governor. In the 1990s Baltimore had a terrible crime wave, and with open drug markets on both the west and east sides; this was not suppressed by 12-year Mayor Kurt Schmoke, who called for consideration of drug legalization. Martin O'Malley, the new mayor elected in 1999, has taken a different approach, promising to build "a new Baltimore" with "zero tolerance" of crime.

Maryland's 7th Congressional District includes most of Baltimore city's black neighborhoods and reaches into the heavily black suburbs running west from the city, to Catonsville along the old Baltimore National Pike, and also extends west to include most of suburban Howard County. Democratic redistricters added Howard County in 2002 (and removed some black Baltimore neighborhoods) to strengthen Democrats' chances of capturing the mostly suburban 2d District (which they did). Howard County is quite a different area: It grew 32% in the 1990s and its largest community, Columbia, has been called a planned town, though it differs from most other Baltimore suburbs by attracting a culturally liberal population. In Howard County, 32% of families earned more than $100,000 and 4% of children under five were in poverty status; in Baltimore City, only 6% earned more than $100,000 and 32% of children were poor. But a change in partisan control is not likely. George W. Bush's vote share grew from 14% to only 25%. Redistricting reduced the black percentage of the district from 75% to 59%; essentially the Democratic redistricters decided to reduce the number of blacks and substitute the Baltimore suburbanites least inclined to resent an inner city voting record. Baltimore still anchors the district: Just under half the district's vote is cast in city precincts, largely north of Pratt Street, in places like Druid Heights, Charles Village (home to Johns Hopkins University), Harlem Park and poverty-stricken Sandtown-Winchester.

The congressman from the 7th District is Elijah Cummings, who won a 1996 special election after Kweisi Mfume resigned to become president of the NAACP. Cummings grew up in Baltimore, graduated from Howard University and the University of Maryland law school, practiced law in Baltimore, and in 1982, at 31, was elected to the Maryland House of Delegates. Two years later he was chairman of the Legislative Caucus, the youngest in its history, and he became known as a consensus builder. When Mfume quit, Cummings's main competition came from the Reverend Frank Reid III, stepbrother of Mayor Kurt Schmoke, who raised $255,000. Cummings had support from community development organizations and from businessmen and lobbyists. He raised $450,000, and won 37% of the vote to 24% for Reid. He has not been seriously challenged in a primary or general since then.

Cummings still lives in west Baltimore, where he has witnessed more than his share of personal struggles, with both crime and personal finances. "When you begin slipping financially, it can become like going down a mountain of ice," he told the Baltimore *Sun*. Cummings explained that he spent so much time helping other people that he failed to spend enough time on his own life. Those urban realities have made him a crusader against drug abuse and a death-penalty foe; he favors strict gun control. His voting record is very liberal; he was the only Marylander to oppose the 1996 Welfare Reform Act.

In his committee work, he has been ranking Democrat on the Government Reform Criminal Justice subcommittee, where he also tends to the interests of his many federal employees. The enactment of a bill he introduced has made 20 million federal employees eligible to enroll in a long-term health insurance program, including care at home or in a nursing facility. With his seat on Transportation and Infrastructure, he responded to the summer 2001 derailment in the Howard Street Tunnel of a train carrying hazardous materials by calling for review by the General Accounting Office of the transportation of hazardous materials throughout the nation's urban areas. He has explored getting other committee assignments. For the 108th Congress, he defeated Bobby Rush to become chairman of the Congressional Black Caucus.

Redistricting reduced Cummings's winning percentage to 74%. He carried Howard County by only 50%–49%, but carried Baltimore County 71%–29% and Baltimore city 94%–6%.

EIGHTH DISTRICT

Rep. Chris Van Hollen (D)

Elected 2002, 1st term; b. Jan. 10, 1959, Karachi, Pakistan; home, Kensington; Swarthmore Col., B.A. 1982, Harvard U., M.P.P. 1985, Georgetown U., J.D. 1990; Protestant; married (Katherine).

Elected Office: MD House of Delegates, 1990–94; MD Senate, 1994–02.

DC Office: 1419 LHOB 20515, 202-225-5341; Fax: 202-225-0375; Web site: www.house.gov/vanhollen.

District Office: Rockville, 301-424-3501.

Committees: *Education & the Workforce* (20th of 22 D): 21st Century Competitiveness; Education Reform. *Government Reform* (14th of 19 D): Civil Service & Agency Organization; Energy Policy, Natural Resources and Regulatory Affairs.

Group Ratings and Key Votes: Newly Elected

Election Results

2002 general	Chris Van Hollen (D)	112,788	(52%)	($2,985,329)
	Constance Morella (R)	103,587	(47%)	($2,996,119)
2002 primary	Chris Van Hollen (D)	37,494	(43%)	
	Mark Shriver (D)	35,022	(41%)	
	Ira Shapiro (D)	10,956	(13%)	
	Other	2,809	(3%)	
2000 general	Constance Morella (R)	156,241	(52%)	($1,154,410)
	Terry Lierman (D)	136,840	(46%)	($2,217,488)

The People		Race/Ethnic Origin	Ancestry	
Area size:	307 sq. mi.	56.1% White	German: 8.2%	Irish: 7.9%
Urban population:	98.8%	16.4% Black	English: 6.6%	
Rural population:	1.2%	10.9% Asian	**2000 Presidential Vote**	
Pop. 2000:	662,060	0.2% Native Am.	Gore (D) 177,475	(66%)
Median income:	$68,306	0.0% Hawaiian	Bush (R) 84,088	(31%)
Poverty status:	6.2%	2.4% Two+ races	Other 9,382	(3%)
Military veterans:	9.6%	0.3% Other	**Cook Partisan Voting Index:** D +18	
		13.7% Hispanic Origin		

Occupation	Blue collar: 10.6%	White collar: 77.1%	Gray collar: 12.3%

Along an old road, down which colonial farmers rolled barrels of tobacco to the port of Georgetown 200 years ago, has grown one of America's most affluent and best-educated communities. The old road, now called Wisconsin Avenue and Rockville Pike, is the commercial spine of Montgomery County. And this suburban jurisdiction just northwest of Washington, D.C., has for several decades ranked at or near the top of the list of counties in income and education. Today's Montgomery County is in large part a creation of the federal government, which has put huge facilities there— Bethesda Naval Hospital, the National Institutes of Health, the Food and Drug Administration, the National Institute of Standards and Technology—and it has become the center of America's biotech industry, the home of firms like Celera and Human Genome Sciences which, in parallel with the Human Genome Project, are pioneering the study of the human gene. With the growth of private sector science, the percentage of government workers has been declining. Montgomery County has also become racially diverse: in 2000, it was 15% black, 12% Hispanic and 11% Asian.

Wisconsin Avenue and Rockville Pike have become strip highways, with 1950s commercial development and 1960s shopping centers like so many in the country. But the stores are upscale, some *very* upscale, and the new skyscrapers of downtown Bethesda are genuinely impressive. Author David Brooks mocked Bethesdans as "urban exiles" who frequent "anti-chain chain stores . . . that cater to people who consider themselves too refined and individualistic to shop at the mall or the mass-market big-box stores." Not all of Montgomery County is exclusively high-income: There are some modest neighborhoods in Silver Spring and Wheaton, and one of the nation's largest Asian populations—some, hard-working store owners; others, educated professionals with high incomes. Historically, the typical Montgomery County voter was a high-ranking civil servant. "A candidate knocking on doors in the 8th District can reasonably expect to be questioned about a government regulation by the person who wrote it," explained *The Washington Post*. But as private employment outpaces government work, the picture has changed. The fastest-growing parts of the county, out the I-270 corridor past Rockville in Gaithersburg and Germantown, are filling up with Republicans and conservatives as much as Democrats and liberals.

The 8th Congressional District includes most of the heavily populated parts of Montgomery County, which accounts for more than 90% of the population. Democratic redistricters in 2002 removed most of the fast-growing part of the county, and added a slice of heavily black Democratic territory in Prince George's County. Perhaps its most unique precinct is Leisure World in Silver Spring, whose 6,000-plus senior citizens have one of Maryland's largest, most heavily Democratic and highest turnout precincts; candidates in Democratic primaries practically camp out there. Democrats drew these lines with the avowed purpose of defeating Republican Congresswoman Connie Morella, who was first elected in 1986 and whose winning percentages fell consistently from 61% in 1996 to 52% in 2000. Redistricting reduced the Bush 2000 percentage from an already low 36% to 31%.

The congressman from the 8th District is Chris Van Hollen, who was elected in 2002 in one of the nation's most competitive and closely-watched congressional races. The son of a Foreign Service officer, Van Hollen was born in Pakistan, graduated from Swarthmore, got a masters from Harvard and graduated from Georgetown University law school. He worked on the staff of the Senate Foreign Relations Committee in the late 1980s, and he co-authored a report on Iraq's use of chemical weapons. In 1990 he was elected to the House of Delegates and in 1994 to the state Senate, where he helped win the largest education funding increase for Montgomery County in its history, passed two cigarette tax increases, and worked to protect the Chesapeake Bay from drilling. He also helped win enactment of a first-in-the-nation state law requiring trigger locks on. Wonky and telegenic, Van Hollen's legislative accomplishments earned him the moniker, "Mr. Fix-It" from the *Post*. Van Hollen must have kicked himself for not running for Congress in 2000, when a much less well-known Democrat held Morella to a 52%–46% margin, and he would not have had to give up his Senate seat to run (all Maryland legislators have four-year terms). The 2002 race attracted a field of strong Democratic candidates: Van Hollen; Delegate Mark Shriver, a state representative and Kennedy cousin, who gained extensive labor support; and Ira Shapiro, a former Clinton administration trade official who stressed his familiarity with federal policy issues as a senior Senate aide. The candidates all supported abortion rights and stricter gun control measures; all wanted to repeal the Bush tax cut. Bolstered by a crucial endorsement from the *Post*, Van Hollen defeated Shriver, 43%–41%, with 13% for Shapiro.

Van Hollen had only eight weeks to take on Morella, who was widely viewed as hard working, cooperative with colleagues, congenial with constituents, and with a liberal voting record that was largely out of step with the Republican-controlled House. Morella stressed her independence from her party, and proved it once again by voting against military force in Iraq and by becoming the lead House sponsor of the amendment, opposed by the Bush administration, insisting on strict civil service protections for Department of Homeland Security employees (the House Republican leadership didn't mind; they only wanted to see her reelected). Van Hollen refrained from directly attacking Morella, but argued that her vote to organize the House with Republicans kept in power a conservative leadership out of line with the views of most of the district's voters: She was an enabler of the Republican majority. Morella dared Van Hollen to agree to a ban on soft-money ads, which he rejected, and criticized his record in Annapolis, including his decision to quit a Senate subcommittee over proposed budget cuts. The campaign was overshadowed during the three weeks in October when the Beltway sniper was at large in Montgomery County and other parts of metro Washington. *The Washington Post* and the Baltimore *Sun* endorsed Morella, but it wasn't enough. In a race in which the two candidates together spent over $5 million, Van Hollen won 52%–47%. He carried Montgomery County 51%–48% and Prince George's County 78%–21%; nearly half his popular vote margin came in the small sliver of the district in Prince George's (this portion is 55% black). If the contest had been held in the old district, Morella clearly would have won, and probably by a wider margin than in 2000.

As a junior member of the minority party, Van Hollen—and his district—won't have much influence in the House. But he will surely carry on the same tradition of strong constituency service that helped Morella and her predecessors in both parties.

★ MASSACHUSETTS ★

It would be a city on a hill, John Winthrop wrote of the Massachusetts Bay colony his Puritans were building, an example to the entire world. And Massachusetts, in the nearly four centuries since, has always assumed it has a lot to teach others. The New World Puritans' austere creed taught that only the select would be saved and that they must extirpate the forces of Satan—Indians, Papists, to-lerationists. For 150 years, New England was partial to learning, but also insular, hostile to outsiders and economically stagnant. Then, after the American Revolution, the international war between royal Britain and revolutionary and Napoleonic France allowed New England ship owners to cross enemy lines to become the world's leading merchants. They made vast profits and invested the money into textile mills, then railroads, then coal mining and steel-making, providing much of the capital that made industrial America.

Massachusetts made a new America in other ways. Intellectually, New England flowered in the 19th century: Writers from Boston, Cambridge and Concord—Ralph Waldo Emerson, Henry Wadsworth Longfellow, Henry David Thoreau, John Greenleaf Whittier, Nathaniel Hawthorne—created an American literature and popularized an American philosophy, more than 200 years after Plymouth Rock. Demographically, New England Yankees surged across the continent: Long blocked from Upstate New York by mountains and the British-Iroquois alliance, they only reached Syracuse in the 1820s. By the 1850s, they were in Iowa and Kansas and Oregon's Willamette Valley, and by the 1870s, in Los Angeles. They helped start the Republican Party and did much to start—and win—the Civil War. They planted their economic system and their values, articulated in the *McGuffey Readers*, across the continent.

In the meantime, Massachusetts itself and Boston, the hub of the universe, were being remade. The potato famine of the 1840s and an economy that continued imploding for decades sent Irish immigrants across the Atlantic, and many came to Boston, looking for work in the mills, docks and factories. Yankee Protestants had seen Catholics as their great political and cultural enemy since the 17th century and felt their commonwealth was under siege. As Catholics became a majority, first in Boston and then statewide, Protestants feared the Irish would use their political clout to ladle out government jobs and benefits to their own. And the Irish had a much better flair for politics than instinct for commerce. But they encountered such bigotry and rejection by the Yankees that even as successful an Irish Catholic as Joseph Kennedy felt obliged to move from Boston to New York in 1927. Politics in Massachusetts for years was a kind of culture war between Yankee Republicans and Irish Democrats, an argument not so much over the distribution of income or the provision of services as over whose vision of Massachusetts should be honored, and whose version of history should be taught—not unlike battles being fought between cultural liberals and conservatives today.

Sometimes, the stakes were concrete—control of patronage jobs, command of the Boston Police Department—but more often they were symbolic. Yankee Republicans tended to back activist government programs: Public works and protective tariffs to help business, the Civil War and Reconstruction to help suitably distant oppressed people like Southern blacks, uplifting (and productivity-enhancing) social movements like temperance. The Irish found 19th century Democrats—a party promoting *laissez-faire*—more congenial. The Irish had come from a place where the government was the enemy and didn't want government spending money to help the rich or to stimulate commerce. They also didn't want government to restrict immigration, to advance blacks (who might compete with them in the labor market), or to prohibit liquor.

The Irish and Catholic populations slowly rose over the years. Yankees had smaller families, moved west, intermarried with people of immigrant stock and lost their Yankee identity. The Irish mostly stayed put, raised large families and maintained their Catholic identity. Eventually, Massachusetts moved from being one of the most Republican states to one of the most Democratic. Economically, early 20th century Massachusetts did not make much progress. The descendants of the Yankees who had been so venturesome in the early 19th century became the most cautious investors in the early 20th, while the predominance of the textile mills in their home state meant that for a century beginning in the 1820s, Massachusetts imported low-skill labor and exported high-skill people. As textile mills started moving south in the 1920s, Massachusetts started exporting low-skill peo-

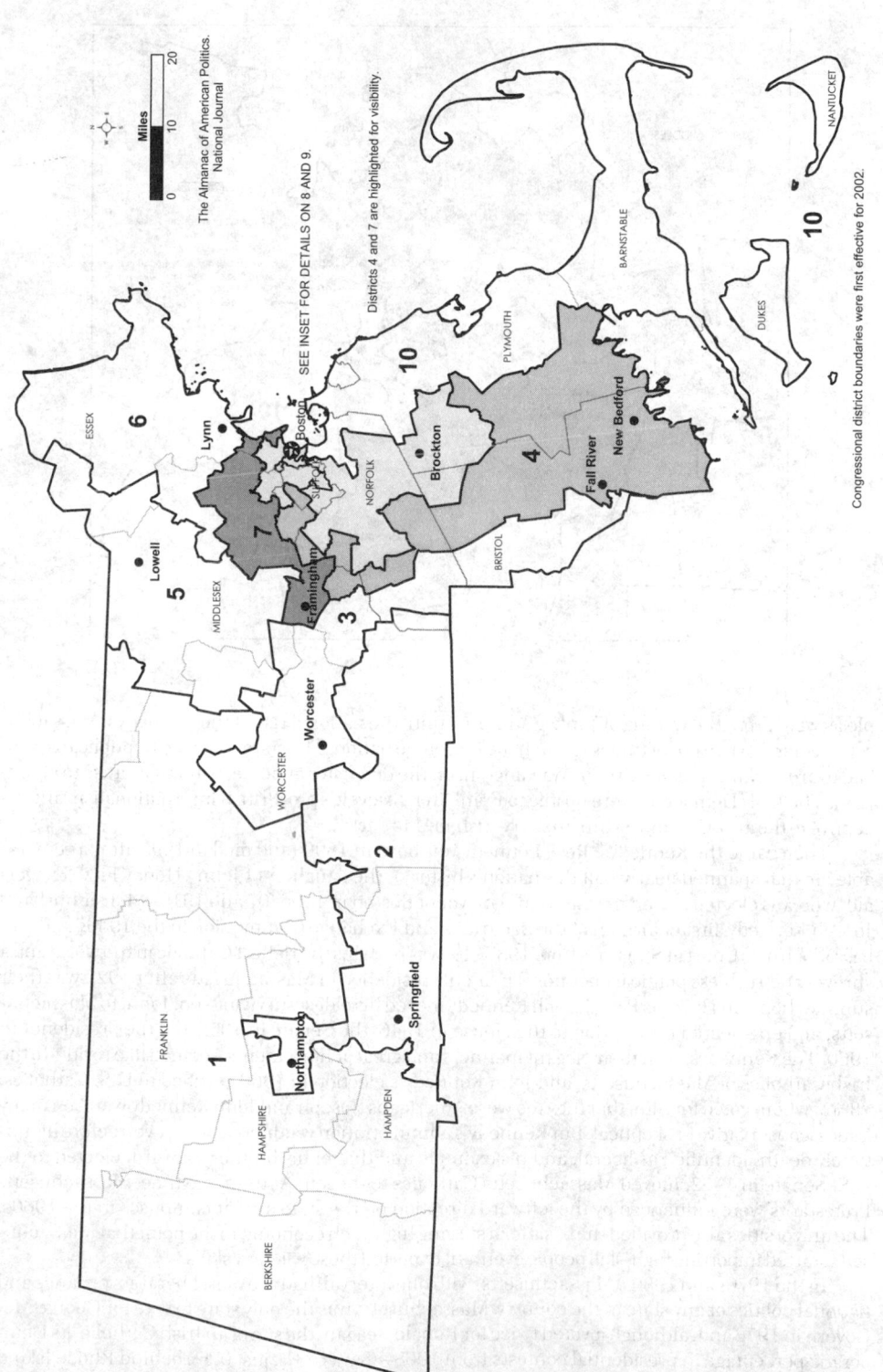

The Almanac of American Politics.
National Journal

SEE INSET FOR DETAILS ON 8 AND 9.

Districts 4 and 7 are highlighted for visibility.

Congressional district boundaries were first effective for 2002.

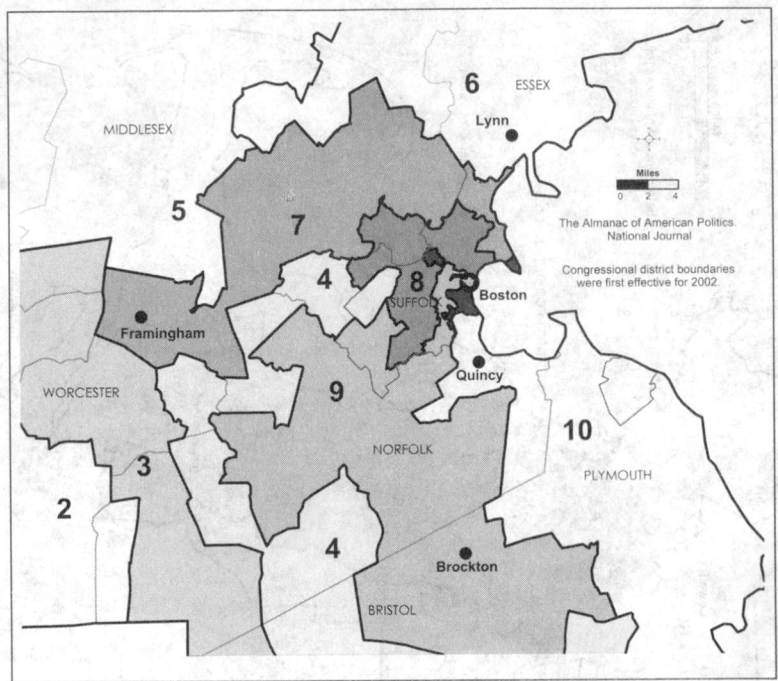

ple as well. From the waning of Yankee authority until the national rise of the Kennedys, Massachusetts seemed to run out of things to teach the rest of the nation. The state's Yankee Republicans were backward-looking, out of power in Washington, on the defensive at home, without a cause to champion. The Irish Democrats were hostile to Franklin Roosevelt's pro-British internationalism and receptive to the anti-Communism of the very Irish Joe McCarthy.

Then came the Kennedys. Rose Kennedy was born in 1890 (and died in 1995 after a remarkable life that spanned nearly half this nation's history), the daughter of John "Honey Fitz" Fitzgerald, who was elected to Congress at 31 and mayor of Boston in 1906–07 and 1910–14. Her husband Joseph Kennedy, first chairman of the Securities and Exchange Commission in the 1930s and ambassador to the Court of St. James from 1937–40, was perhaps the richest Catholic in the world and a shrewd and ruthless political operator. Their only residence in Massachusetts after 1927 was their summer home in Hyannis Port. Joseph Kennedy moved his oldest surviving son, John, to Massachusetts, and engineered his election to the House in 1946, the Senate in 1952 and the presidency in 1960. The Kennedys, with their elegant manners and great achievements, seemed like royalty to the Irish Catholics of Massachusetts, and John Kennedy's election in 1960 certified to U.S. Catholics, 78% of whom voted for him, that they too were Americans. Joseph and John Kennedy were, on many issues, conservative or skeptical. But Kennedy's administration was increasingly, even before his untimely death, identified as liberal, and his example and that of his brother, Edward, elected to the U.S. Senate in 1962, moved Massachusetts Catholics to the left. At the same time, Massachusetts Protestants were influenced by the leftward direction on the state's great campuses in the 1960s. The universities also provided the basis for a surging high-tech economy, to the point that Massachusetts started importing high-skill people even as it exported those with low skills.

In the 1970s and 1980s, Massachusetts, with one interval, had the most liberal governance and national politics of any state in the country. Massachusetts was the only state to vote for George McGovern in 1972 and, although it voted twice for Ronald Reagan, the son of an Irish Catholic, its Democratic percentage in presidential contests from 1968–88 was 53%, just 0.4% behind Rhode Island and well ahead of every other state. The state's senators included Edward Kennedy, liberal Republican Edward Brooke, and Democrats Paul Tsongas and John Kerry. Liberal governors such as Republican Francis Sargent and Democrat Michael Dukakis vastly increased spending and endorsed the inexplicable policies that sunk Dukakis's 1988 presidential campaign, notably the law that granted weekend furloughs to prisoners sentenced to life without parole. As historian David Hackett Fischer points out in *Albion's Seed*, the mindset of the original settlers remains strong even when the ethnic origin of current residents is far different, and the spirit of the Puritans, the faith that they had much to teach the rest of the world, is strong in Massachusetts liberals: In both the quietly smug liberalism of Michael Dukakis and the hearty and combative liberalism of Edward Kennedy. Then, in the early 1990s, Massachusetts had a momentary political revolution. The 1980s "Massachusetts miracle" had turned into a nightmare, as the state's economy sagged badly, as the defense cutbacks long sought by Massachusetts politicians sent unemployment rising and high-tech firms like Wang and Digital withered and Cambridge-based Lotus's software was eclipsed by Redmond, Washington-based Microsoft's. The Northeast real estate bubble burst and Massachusetts banks foundered. The state government essentially went bankrupt. In 1990, as Dukakis retired, voters embraced big tax cuts and elected Republican William Weld in his place.

Republicans have held the governorship ever since. Weld envisioned a government that taxes and spends lightly, that is friendly to feminism and gay rights, that exerts some effort to protect the environment and that is tough on crime. He cut spending and taxes sharply in his first years, and the state's economy began recovering. He was reelected by a resounding 71%–28% in 1994. His policies were generally endorsed by his successors—Paul Cellucci, who took office in 1997, Jane Swift, who took office in 2001 and Mitt Romney, who took office in 2003—and voters seem to have endorsed them too. Much of the coverage of the 2002 campaign concentrated on the rollicking five-candidate Democratic gubernatorial primary, not held until mid-September. But it turned out not to matter much.

But in national politics, Massachusetts has remained overwhelmingly Democratic. The state voted heavily for Bill Clinton in 1992 and 1996; it eliminated Republicans from its congressional delegation in 1996 and voted in veto-proof Democratic majorities in the legislature. Weld lost 52%–45% to John Kerry in 1996, and in 2002, Kerry had no Republican opponent—the first time one of the major parties has not contested a Senate seat here since popular election of senators began. Massachusetts voted 61%–28% for Bill Clinton in 1996, his biggest margin in the nation; in 2000, it voted 60%–33% for Al Gore, his biggest margin except for Rhode Island. And Massachusetts Democrats have produced another presidential candidate, their fourth in a quarter-century: John Kerry hopes to be more successful in the primaries than Edward Kennedy was in 1980 or Paul Tsongas was in 1992 and more successful in the general election than Michael Dukakis was in 1988.

Massachusetts still has lessons to teach the rest of the country, but they are not necessarily those taught by its successful politicians. Massachusetts is the site of the Big Dig, the building of a new underground freeway to replace the tangle of the Central Artery overhead highway and tunnel bottlenecks in downtown Boston, first approved in 1987 and budgeted then at $6.4 billion. It has turned out to cost far more. Lawsuits, contract disputes, the discovery of unforeseen bedrock, and the firing of the project head in April 2000 for concealing $1.4 billion of cost overruns have raised the cost to an estimated $14.6 billion by the expected completion date of July 2004. It's a deadline that Massachusetts will try very hard to meet: Mayor Thomas Menino got the Democratic National Committee to select Boston as the site for the 2004 national convention—the first national convention in this hyperpolitical city ever—and it is scheduled to open July 26.

Massachusetts is one of the few states in the Northeast that allows voters to decide issues by referendum. And when presented with issues, they have not always been as liberal as their congressional delegation. In 2000, they voted to lower the state income tax from 5.85% to 5% over three years, despite opposition from Democrats and teachers' unions; in 2002, they defeated by only a 55%–45% margin a proposal to zero out the income tax altogether. In 2000, voters defeated a proposition that would have established universal health care; it was opposed vigorously by the state's great teaching hospitals. In 2002, they voted 68%–32% to eliminate bilingual education, which the state pioneered in 1971, and to limit Spanish-language instruction to one year. Meanwhile, state politicians struggled with the Clean Elections law voters passed in 1998. The law authorizes public financing for state candidates who limit contributions to $100 and limit spending (in the governor's race) to $6 million, but Speaker Thomas Finneran, an opponent of the measure, refused to pony up the money. A lawsuit followed, and in May 2002, the Supreme Judicial Court ordered that state property be sold to fund the law. Station wagons and SUVs, armories and other state property were auctioned off. In a November 2002 non-binding referendum, voters voted against using taxpayer money to finance campaigns for public office by a 74%–26% margin—a direct repudiation of the law they voted for in 1998. Liberalism governs in Massachusetts, but sometimes messily.

The People		Race/Ethnic Origin			Military veterans: 558,933 (11.5%)	
Pop. 2000:	6,349,097	5,198,359	81.9%	White	WWII: 25.7%	Korea: 15.7%
Pop. 1990:	6,016,425	318,329	5.0%	Black	Vietnam: 28.4%	Gulf War: 6.6%
Change 1990–2000:	Up 5.5%	236,786	3.7%	Asian	**Most populous cities:**	
Change 1980–1990:	Up 4.9%	11,264	0.2%	Native Am.	1. Boston	589,141
% of U.S. total:	2.3%	1,706	0.0%	Hawaiian	2. Worcester	172,648
Pop. rank:	13th of 50	110,338	1.7%	Two+ races	3. Springfield	152,082
Area size:	10,555 sq. mi.	43,586	0.7%	Other	4. Lowell	105,167
State Native:	66.1%	428,729	6.8%	Hisp. Origin	5. Cambridge	101,355
Non-citizen:	6.9%	**Ancestry**			Urban population: 91.4%	
Language		Irish: 16.8%		Italian: 10.1%	Rural population: 8.6%	
English: 78.8%	Other Eur.: 11.4%	English: 8.5%		French: 6.0%		
Spanish: 6.3%		German: 4.4%				

Education		Work Sector		General Court	
H.S. Grad:	84.8%	Private: 80.0%	Govt: 13.5%	Senate	34 D 6 R
College Grad:	33.2%	Self: 6.4%	Family: 0.2%	House	136 D 23 R 1 I
Industry		Unemployment: 4.6%		Legislative Term Limits: No	
Agri: 0.4%	Con: 5.5%	**Household Income**		**Registered Voters**	
Fin: 8.2%	Info: 3.7%	<15k: 14.4%	15-35k: 20.5%	D: 1,442,897 (36.3%)	
Mfg: 17.0%	Prof: 35.3%	35-50k: 14.5%	50-100k: 32.9%	R: 530,512 (13.4%)	
Public: 4.3%	Trade: 14.4%	100-150k: 10.9%	>150k: 6.8%	I: 1,999,242 (50.3%)	
Other: 11.2%		Median: $50,502			
Occupation		Poverty status: 9.3%			
Blue collar: 18.7%	White collar: 67.0%	**Home Value**			
Gray collar: 14.3%		<50k: 1.5% 50-100k: 10.2% 100-200k: 45.1% 200-300k: 23.6%			
		300-500k: 14.0% >500k: 5.6% Median: $182,800			

Presidential politics   Over the last eight presidential elections, Massachusetts has been the most Democratic state, giving Democratic nominees an average margin of 53%–39%, just ahead of next-door Rhode Island's 53%–40%. It was Bill Clinton's best state in 1996 and Al Gore's second best, after Rhode Island, in 2000. There was something approaching unanimity for Al Gore in 2000 among many groups: He carried women 67%–28%, those with graduate school educations 60%–29% (with 9% for Ralph Nader), 62%–32% among Catholics.

Massachusetts's presidential primary has long been held in early March and was once the scene of great commotion. It produced victories for native sons in 1988 and 1992, Democrats Michael Dukakis and Paul Tsongas and Republican George Bush the elder. In 2000, it voted solidly for Al Gore and John McCain, as many independents reregistered as Republicans. Candidates contesting New Hampshire always buy time on Boston TV stations, which reach much of the Granite State (most of the cost of which does not have to be charged against the low limit

2000 Presidential Vote

Gore (D)	1,616,487	(60%)
Bush (R)	878,502	(33%)
Nader (Green)	173,564	(6%)
Other	32,389	(1%)

2000 Republican Presidential Primary

McCain (R)	324,708	(65%)
Bush (R)	159,534	(32%)
Other	17,709	(4%)

2000 Democratic Presidential Primary

Gore (D)	341,586	(60%)
Bradley (D)	212,452	(37%)
Other	16,036	(3%)

1996 Presidential Vote

Clinton (D)	1,571,755	(61%)
Dole (R)	718,104	(28%)
Perot (I)	226,787	(9%)
Other	39,347	(2%)

on spending in New Hampshire), and so their ads are widely seen in Massachusetts. But they don't usually bother campaigning here.

Congressional districting Massachusetts's convoluted congressional district lines deserve

their own biographer, someone with a sure political instinct and a touch of whimsy. This is, after all, the state whose Governor Elbridge Gerry gave name to the term "gerrymander" in the early 19th century. The state lost one seat in the 1980 and 1990 Censuses; it survived the 2000 Census without losing another. The redistricting process was a ruckus this time. Many legislators wanted simply to protect all 10 incumbents, but that was hard to do because the districts were already mind-bogglingly convoluted. In July 2001, House Speaker Thomas Finneran advanced a plan to smooth out the district lines and create a district that would unite southeastern Massachusetts—the congressmen who represent the area live in Boston and next-door Newton and Quincy and far off Worcester—and a Boston-based district with large percentages of blacks and Hispanics and to eliminate the district of Martin Meehan, who was contemplating running for governor. But other politicians complained loudly and Meehan opted out of the race for governor; state senators, helped by senior incumbent Edward Markey, came up with a plan to protect incumbents. Republican Governor Jane Swift came up with her own plan, which of course didn't pass in the heavily Democratic statehouse. In January 2002, both houses agreed on an incumbent protection plan and passed it over Swift's veto.

Governor

Mitt Romney (R)

Elected 2002, term expires Jan. 2007, 1st term; b. March 12, 1947, Detroit, MI; home, Belmont; Brigham Young U., B.A. 1971, Harvard U. M.B.A., J.D. 1975; Mormon; married (Ann).

Professional Career: V.P., Bain & Co., 1978–84, 1990–92; Founder, Bain Capital, 1984–90, 1992–99; CEO, Salt Lake Organizing Cmte. (2002 Winter Olympics), 1999–02.

Office: State House, Rm. 360, Boston, 02133, 617-725-4005; Fax: 617-727-9725; Web site: www.mass.gov/gov.

Election Results

2002 general	Mitt Romney (R)	1,091,988	(50%)
	Shannon O'Brien (D)	985,981	(45%)
	Jill Stein (Green)	76,530	(4%)
	Other	38,379	(2%)
2002 primary	Mitt Romney (R)	unopposed	
1998 general	Paul Cellucci (R)	967,160	(51%)
	Scott Harshbarger (D)	901,843	(47%)
	Other	34,333	(2%)

Mitt Romney, elected governor of Massachusetts in 2002, is the son of George Romney, who was governor of Michigan from 1963 to 1969. The younger Romney grew up in Bloomfield Hills, Michigan, when his father was CEO of American Motors and then embarked on a political career. A devout Mormon, he graduated from Brigham Young University at a time when it was not beset by turmoil as so many other campuses were, and from Harvard Law School and Harvard Business School in 1975, the same year as George W. Bush. Unlike Bush, who was eager to return to Texas, Romney stayed in the Boston area and became vice president of Bain & Company, a management consultant firm. In 1984, he founded Bain Capital, an investment company that provided crucial capital to Staples, Domino's Pizza and Brookstone; he had a considerable ownership stake in some of these companies. In 1990, he returned to Bain & Company as interim CEO and got it out of financial difficulties. In the process, he accumulated a considerable fortune and was active in civic and charitable affairs; for four years he was president of his stake in the Mormon Church—the rough equivalent of bishop. In 1994, he was the Republican nominee against Senator Edward Kennedy, and succeeded in giving him a good scare before losing 58%–41%—Kennedy's closest race since he was first elected in 1962. In February 1999, he was asked to head the Salt Lake City Winter Olympics Organizing Committee, which was in deficit and suffering from charges of misconduct. Romney erased a $379 million deficit, rallied 23,000 volunteers and ran an effective security operation at the February 2002 Winter Games; 87% of Utahns rated his performance positively. There was much speculation over whether Romney would run for public office in Utah.

After the Olympics, Romney immediately began talking about running for governor—of Massachusetts, that is. This was a dicey business: In fall 2001, he had said he wouldn't run, and in October 2001, Republican Governor Jane Swift had announced she would. Swift had been elected Lieutenant Governor in 1998 and became Governor in April 2001, when Paul Cellucci resigned to become Ambassador to Canada. She took office at 36, pregnant with twins. She quickly aroused controversy. She had been criticized before for using a state limousine to commute to her home in Williamstown, 130 miles from the State House. She was criticized after September 11 for the poor security at Boston's Logan Airport, from which the two planes that hit the World Trade Center towers took off. After budget struggles with the legislature, she had exceedingly low job ratings. On March 19, she abruptly left the governor's race; three hours later, Romney announced his candidacy. Financing was no problem: He ultimately spent $6.1 million of his own money and had fundraising help from the Bush White House. He ran as an outsider, a professional manager who wasn't part of the Beacon Hill crowd; in some public appearances he made PowerPoint presentations rather than standard speeches. Romney was embarrassed in March when he couldn't identify the MCAS student exam system (he later said it stood for Mitt Cares About Schools) and in June when it was revealed that he had listed his Utah house as his "primary residence" from 1999 to 2001 and thus got a $54,000 property tax break (he offered to pay the money and said he had intended to return to Massachusetts all along). He said he was against tax increases, but declined to rule them out. He supported aid to faith-based institutions. He worked at various jobs over the summer, riding a garbage truck and cleaning fish.

Meanwhile, Democrats jousted in a primary fight. The leader in most polls was Treasurer Shannon O'Brien, a longtime Beacon Hill insider, even though she was criticized for some money-losing investments. Running close behind was state Senate President Thomas Birmingham, a Rhodes Scholar with a solidly liberal record in the legislature. Attracting much attention was former Clinton Labor Secretary Robert Reich, a provocative writer whose political memoir evidently angered Bill Clinton, who conspicuously did not support him, but instead backed former Democratic National Chairman Steve Grossman, who bowed out before the primary. The one candidate who participated in Clean Elections funding—ultimately some $3.6 million—was former state Senator Warren Tolman. There were upward blips in the polls for Reich and Tolman, but O'Brien won the September 17 primary with 33% of the vote to 25% for Reich, 24% for Birmingham and 18% for Tolman.

Massachusetts has one of the nation's latest primaries, and O'Brien had only six weeks to focus on her differences with Romney. She and other Democrats evidently decided to defeat him by proving he was out of place in Massachusetts. She said he was trying to "mask a very conservative set of belief systems." Although she said she wouldn't criticize his religion, she criticized him for making major contributions to Brigham Young, which bars expressions of homosexuality. Democrats circulated a news story that Romney, at a church meeting, had called homosexuality "perverse"; he denied using the word but said he opposed all extramarital sex. O'Brien herself came out in favor of gay marriage, though she added that she thought the legislature would never vote for it. O'Brien attacked Romney aggressively in debates, and when he referred to her style as "unbecoming," he was accused of being insensitive to women.

Such attitudes may be obligatory at gatherings of Democratic activists, but they evidently did not go over so well with voters in the broad swathes of suburban Massachusetts and in heavily Democratic central cities as well. Romney won 50%–45%, carrying the belt between Route 128 and Interstate 495 by wide margins and holding O'Brien to very small margins in working class towns like Quincy, Worcester, Lynn, Brockton and Lowell. O'Brien's core areas—Boston and the cities immediately adjacent, the New Bedford-Fall River area and the Pioneer Valley and the Berkshires in western Massachusetts—were not enough to produce a statewide majority. For the fourth time in a row, Massachusetts voters declined to put the whole of state government in the control of the Democratic party. Romney has been mentioned as a potential presidential candidate in 2008; if so, he will have run for that office, as he ran for a governorship, exactly 40 years after his father did so. But in the meantime he must tend to the state's problems. Approaching office, he promised to present a balanced budget without a tax increase, to combine the Turnpike Authority and Highway Department, to institute full-day kindergarten in underperforming school districts, to fund the Clean Elections law without public funds and to give merit pay to teachers.

Another task he might want to attend to is building a Republican party. Democrats hold 85% of the seats in the legislature; Republicans fielded no candidates in 62% of the seats. Romney is not likely to be taken seriously as a presidential candidate until his party does better in legislative and downballot races.

Senior Senator

Edward Kennedy (D)

Elected 1962, seat up 2006, 7th term; b. Feb. 22, 1932, Boston; home, Hyannis Port; Harvard U., B.A. 1956, The Hague Intl. Law Schl., 1958, U. of VA, LL.B. 1959; Catholic; married (Vicki).

Military Career: Army, 1951–53.

Professional Career: Western states coord., John F. Kennedy Pres. Campaign, 1960; Asst. Dist. Atty., Suffolk Cnty., 1961–62.

DC Office: 315 RSOB, 20510, 202-224-4543; Fax: 202-224-2417; Web site: kennedy.senate.gov.

State Office: Boston, 617-565-3170.

Committees: *Armed Services*: Emerging Threats & Capabilities; Personnel; Seapower (RMM). *Health, Education, Labor & Pensions* (RMM): Aging; Substance Abuse & Mental Health Services (RMM). *Judiciary*: Constitution, Civil Rights & Property Rights; Immigration, Border Security & Citizenship (RMM); Terrorism, Technology & Homeland Security. *Joint Economic Committee* (8th of 10 Sens.).

Group Ratings

	ADA	ACLU	AFS	LCV	CON	ITIC	NTU	COC	ACU	NTLC	CHC
2002	100	60	100	82	63	38	13	29	0	0	—
2001	100	—	100	88	—	—	9	38	4	—	0

National Journal Ratings

	2001 LIB	—	2001 CONS		2002 LIB	—	2002 CONS
Economic	88%	—	9%		85%	—	13%
Social	81%	—	8%		82%	—	0%
Foreign	87%	—	3%		89%	—	10%

Key Votes of the 107th Congress

1. Approve Bush Tax Cuts	N	5. Confirm Ashcroft as AG	N	9. Bar Coop. with Intl. Court	N
2. Expand Patients' Rights	Y	6. Bar Gays in the Boy Scouts	N	10. Trade Promotion Authority	N
3. Campaign Finance Reform	Y	7. $ for Hate Crime Prosecution	Y	11. Authorize Force in Iraq	N
4. Permit ANWR Development	N	8. Overseas Military Abortions	Y	12. Homeland Sec. Dept. Union	N

Election Results

2000 general	Edward Kennedy (D)	1,889,494	(73%)	($3,662,652)
	Jack E. Robinson III (R)	334,341	(13%)	($150,430)
	Carla A. Howell (Lib)	308,860	(12%)	($1,055,186)
	Other	66,725	(3%)	
2000 primary	Edward Kennedy (D)	unopposed		
1994 general	Edward Kennedy (D)	1,265,997	(58%)	($11,493,735)
	Mitt Romney (R)	894,000	(41%)	($7,624,491)

Prior Winning Percentages: 1988 (65%); 1982 (61%); 1976 (69%); 1970 (62%); 1964 (74%); 1962 (55%)

Edward Kennedy has served 40 years in the Senate—longer than all but four other senators in American history—and he is still going strong. He has had the highs and lows of his personal life followed by millions and criticized vitriolically by many. He has been a presidential candidate and, while still in his 30s, was widely assumed to be the next president. He is second in seniority in the Senate, behind Robert Byrd of West Virginia. His reputation as an idealistic champion of the poor has been burnished by the praise of first-rate celebrators that no American political family has attracted before, and the nation has watched him cope impressively time and again with family tragedy, most recently when his nephew John Kennedy Jr. died in July 1999. To others, he is a symbol of personal immorality and unpunished criminal behavior, a man who has gotten away with things that would have ended the public career of almost anyone else. There is some basis for both views, but neither is an entirely fair picture of this politician, who was re-elected without much fuss in 2000, after a term in which he did much to set national policy even while Republicans controlled the Congress.

The luster of the Kennedys has worn off, in America and even in Massachusetts, and the percentage of Americans who look to the Kennedys for political leadership has grown small. Most voters can't remember, or never knew, what made the Kennedys so exciting. There was little in the early life of this youngest of the Kennedy siblings to suggest he would be a major politician, much less for so long. He grew up in Bronxville, New York, a rich suburb with many other rich Catholics, was thrown out of Harvard for cheating on a Spanish exam and served in the Army, returned to earn degrees at Harvard and Virginia Law School, and married a Bronxville girl who never developed a taste for politics. Then his brother was elected president of the United States at 43, and the 28-year-old Edward Kennedy was a national celebrity. His father insisted that he run for the Senate; a JFK college roommate was found to hold the seat until he reached the constitutional age of 30, in 1962. His family money and the enthusiasm among Massachusetts Catholics for this seeming royalty enabled him to beat strong candidates with good political names: Attorney General Edward McCormack, nephew of Speaker John McCormack, in the Democratic primary; George Cabot Lodge, son and great-grandson of senators, in the general. "He can do more for Massachusetts" was his slogan, as it had been John F. Kennedy's in his first Senate race 10 years before.

After his brothers' assassinations, Edward Kennedy was seen by many as their natural heir, and he could have been nominated for president in 1968, at 36, or in 1972, had he chosen to run. Instead, in the latter year, he gave the first of several stirring convention speeches promoting his trademark liberalism. In 1979, he did run for president, and began the race against incumbent Jimmy Carter far ahead in the polls. But he was unable to articulate his reasons for running, and his candidacy was greeted with adverse reaction to him personally as well as to his policies. It ended in a crushing defeat, relieved only by another stirring convention speech, after which he pointedly refused to raise Carter's hand on the podium. In retrospect, it is plain that Edward Kennedy's presidential chances were ended in July 1969, with the accident at Chappaquiddick. But he has been re-elected with solid margins in Massachusetts, though he received spirited competition in 1994 from Mitt Romney, then a venture capitalist and now governor.

Kennedy has been a hardworking and practical politician who, after his brothers' deaths, took up liberal causes and attention to the poor, which had been the focus of Robert Kennedy in the last years of his life. He has worked hard for a quarter century on their behalf without the friendship of a Democratic administration, until the election of Bill Clinton, and since 1994, for much of the time, without the backing of a Democratic majority. As chairman of the Health, Education, Labor and Pensions Committee from 1987–94, Kennedy supported teachers' unions; on the Judiciary Committee, which he chaired back in 1979–80 (his chief aide was a young lawyer named Stephen Breyer, now on the U.S. Supreme Court), he supported abortion rights and feminist groups with energy and enthusiasm. He immediately pounced on Judge Robert Bork's nomination in 1987, but played a lesser role in the Clarence Thomas hearings, which came shortly after an incident when his nephew William Kennedy Smith was arrested and charged with rape in Palm Beach, Florida.

In 1992, Kennedy supported Bill Clinton happily and basked as Clinton gave repeated homage to the Kennedy family. Legislatively, Kennedy was productive, though not as much as he wished. He worked to pass direct student loans, AmeriCorps, Goals 2000 and the School-to-Work Opportunity Act. He again sponsored the Family and Medical Leave Act which George Bush had vetoed; it was the first law Bill Clinton signed. But he was frustrated on other issues. He sought to prevent states from regulating abortions and to ban the death penalty when imposed disproportionately on criminals of different races; both efforts failed. On health care, a longtime Kennedy cause, he backed a Canadian-style single-payer system. In May 1994, he got a health care bill resembling Clinton's through his committee, but that was as far as it went.

After the hard-fought 1994 election, Kennedy returned to a Republican Senate and shifted his focus from expanding government to protecting it from downsizing. In 1996, he went on the offensive. He pushed the Kassebaum-Kennedy health care bill, an incremental measure to provide portability of health insurance and to limit exclusions for pre-existing conditions; he worked to keep Medical Savings Accounts out, and the bill passed.

Kennedy has continued to be active on health issues, opposing Republican measures and sponsoring some bipartisan initiatives of his own. He supported the Dingell-Norwood bill regulating HMOs and called the Republican version of HMO regulation "a minimalist bill that only the insurance industry could love." Kennedy has continued to press for increases in the minimum wage and in Pell grants. He was a floor manager for the 1965 immigration law, which opened the doors to millions of immigrants, and in 2000, pressed for amnesty for illegal aliens in the United States since 1986 and for giving Central American and Haitian refugees the same refugee status as Cubans.

Kennedy did not quit legislating even when George W. Bush took office with a Republican Senate. Kennedy goes back a long time with the Bushes. Elected to fill his brother's unexpired term in November 1962, he was technically a colleague of George W. Bush's grandfather Prescott Bush, whose last term ended in January 1963. George W. Bush invited Kennedy to the White House three days after his inauguration to talk about education and twice on February 1, to talk about disabilities legislation and to view *Thirteen Days*, the film about the Cuban missile crisis. Kennedy played a major role in producing Bush's first major bipartisan achievement, the education bill passed by the Senate in June 2001 and the conference committee reached agreement in December 2001. It did not include Bush's vouchers for private schools which Republicans wanted (it did include private after-school tutoring) but it did include a pilot program to allow some districts to spend money with virtually no federal conditions which Democrats disliked; its core was requiring annual testing of students and requiring schools to show improvement over the years or face state takeover. But Kennedy kept pressing Bush for more education money, especially for special education.

On several other issues, Kennedy also showed great adeptness at bipartisan legislating. As Chairman of the Immigration Subcommittee, he and Kansas Sen. Sam Brownback in October 2001 wrote a bill to establish automated exit and entry systems at airports, ports and border crossings, develop biometric identifiers and require special scrutiny of student visa applicants from terrorism-sponsoring countries; it passed the Senate in April 2002. In November 2001, he and Tennessee Sen. Bill Frist introduced a bill to strengthen defenses against germ warfare; after negotiations with the House, it became law in May 2002. In February 2001, Kennedy joined with Senators John Edwards and John McCain to sponsor a bill similar to the Dingell-Norwood bill on HMO regulation; a version passed the Senate in June 2001. He co-sponsored with North Carolina Sen. Jesse Helms a bill to pay for colon cancer screening. He was a co-sponsor of the Senate

Democrats' prescription drugs bill in 2002. But on other issues Kennedy held strongly to the liberal position. He opposed the Iraq war resolution in October 2002, saying, "There are realistic alternatives between doing nothing and declaring unilateral or immediate war."

Even his partisan opponents admit that Kennedy has proved to be a superlative legislator, and one as active and energetic in his 70s as he was two or three decades before. Certainly his constituents in Massachusetts have long since reached that conclusion. There used to be speculation that Kennedy might step down, for one of the younger members of his family; that seems unlikely now. After his victory over Mitt Romney in 1994, no serious Republican wanted to run against him in 2000. His opponent was one Jack E. Robinson, who claimed to be a successful entrepreneur and who lived in Greenwich, Connecticut. Governor Paul Cellucci made it clear he would not support Robinson, and his petitions were rejected by the secretary of state for insufficient signatures. The Supreme Judicial Court put him on the ballot in July 2000; his hapless candidacy went nowhere. Kennedy won with 73% of the vote, to 13% for Robinson and 12% for Libertarian Carla Howell. There seems little doubt that Kennedy will run again. He has served with all of the other four senators who served more than 40 years—Strom Thurmond, Robert Byrd, Carl Hayden and John Stennis—and he seems ready to stay longer than any of them. There seems little doubt that he can be reelected in 2006, when he will be 74, and if he serves out that term, he will have served 50 years in the Senate, more than anyone else in history, assuming that Robert Byrd does not reach that milepost before him.

Junior Senator

John Kerry (D)

Elected 1984, seat up 2008, 4th term; b. Dec. 11, 1943, Denver, CO; home, Boston; Yale U., A.B. 1966, Boston Col., LL.B. 1976; Catholic; married (Teresa Heinz).

Military Career: Navy, 1966–70 (Vietnam), Naval Reserves, 1972–78.

Elected Office: MA Lt. Gov., 1982–84.

Professional Career: Organizer, Vietnam Veterans Against the War; Asst. Dist. Atty., Middlesex Cnty., 1976–81; Practicing atty., 1981–82.

DC Office: 304 RSOB, 20510, 202-224-2742; Fax: 202-224-8525; Web site: kerry.senate.gov.

State Offices: Boston, 617-565-8519; Fall River, 508-677-0522; Springfield, 413-785-4610; Worcester, 508-831-7380.

Committees: *Commerce, Science & Transportation*: Communications; Oceans, Fisheries & Coast Guard (RMM); Science, Technology & Space; Surface Transportation & Merchant Marine. *Finance*: Health Care; International Trade; Social Security & Family Policy. *Foreign Relations*: East Asian & Pacific Affairs (RMM); European Affairs; Western Hemisphere, Peace Corps, Narcotics Affairs. *Small Business & Entrepreneurship* (RMM).

Group Ratings

	ADA	ACLU	AFS	LCV	CON	ITIC	NTU	COC	ACU	NTLC	CHC
2002	85	60	88	94	65	75	18	55	20	3	—
2001	95	—	100	88	—	—	7	38	4	—	0

National Journal Ratings

	2001 LIB	—	2001 CONS		2002 LIB	—	2002 CONS
Economic	93%	—	0%		95%	—	0%
Social	81%	—	8%		82%	—	0%
Foreign	74%	—	14%		73%	—	26%

Key Votes of the 107th Congress

1. Approve Bush Tax Cuts	N	5. Confirm Ashcroft as AG	N	9. Bar Coop. with Intl. Court	Y
2. Expand Patients' Rights	Y	6. Bar Gays in the Boy Scouts	N	10. Trade Promotion Authority	Y
3. Campaign Finance Reform	Y	7. $ for Hate Crime Prosecution	Y	11. Authorize Force in Iraq	Y
4. Permit ANWR Development	N	8. Overseas Military Abortions	Y	12. Homeland Sec. Dept. Union	Y

Election Results

2002 general	John Kerry (D)	1,605,976	(80%)	($9,305,860)
	Michael Cloud (Lib)	369,807	(18%)	($207,684)
2002 primary	John Kerry (D)	unopposed		
1996 general	John Kerry (D)	1,334,135	(52%)	($12,619,152)
	William Weld (R)	1,143,120	(45%)	($8,002,123)
	Other	78,687	(3%)	

Prior Winning Percentages: 1990 (57%); 1984 (55%)

John Kerry has been a national political figure since he was one of the organizers of Vietnam Veterans Against the War in 1971. He attracted attention then because of his background, unusual for a Vietnam veteran (he went to Yale, and his mother is from the Brahmin Forbes family) and because of his record of heroism in combat, for which he was awarded a Silver Star and three Purple Hearts. "How do you ask a man to be the last to die for a mistake?" he asked in congressional testimony—a good question, and one that also suggested his future political ambitions. He condemned "war crimes committed in Southeast Asia"; he said they were "not isolated incidents, but crimes committed on a day-to-day basis with the full awareness of officers at all levels of command." Kerry became well enough known to be featured in *Doonesbury* and plunged quickly into politics. He ran for Congress in 1972, after some widely observed district-shopping, and lost in a district carried by George McGovern. Chastened, he went to law school, worked for a prosecutor, was elected lieutenant governor on the Dukakis ticket in 1982, and ran for senator in 1984. In both races, he upset a favored rival for the Democratic nomination. In 1982, Kerry won the general as part of a ticket with Dukakis; in the 1984 general, he beat Raymond Shamie, a businessman and state Republican chairman, 55%-45%.

His toughest race came in 1996, when he was opposed by Republican Governor William Weld, who had been reelected in 1994 with 71% of the vote. Earlier, the two had worked together on some state problems and emphasized the similarity of their views, but the campaign inevitably produced disagreements and some gentlemanly acrimony. Weld called Kerry a "tax-and-spend liberal who is soft on crime." Kerry charged that Weld would vote for budget cuts that would hurt Medicare, Medicaid, education and the environment. They held seven debates altogether, literate rounds of accusations and one-liners. They both spent liberally—Kerry, $12.6 million, the second highest of any Senate candidate that year; Weld, $8 million. It got more coverage than any other Senate race that year, but the outcome in retrospect was unsurprising: Democratic Massachusetts voted 52%-45% for its junior Democratic senator. Kerry got his biggest percentages in Boston and university towns like Cambridge and Amherst, and he carried—but not by large margins—old mill towns like Lowell and Lawrence.

Kerry came to the Senate with a reputation as a strong liberal. He has a similar voting record to fellow Senator Edward Kennedy, but there have been differences of nuance and interest: Kerry has been more respectful of economic free markets and moved earlier than Kennedy toward supporting an expansive U.S. foreign and military policy. In the majority, Kerry made a name as an investigator, spending some time up blind alleys with klieg lights but also producing some important information. He used his Foreign Relations Western Hemisphere, Peace Corps, Narcotics and Terrorism Subcommittee chairmanship to investigate the infamous Bank of Credit & Commerce International scandal. He also brought forward evidence that Manuel Noriega of Panama was involved with drug-dealing. Kerry's other great investigation was as chairman of the Select Committee on POW/MIA Affairs, on whether Americans were left behind in Vietnamese hands in 1973. Kerry and Republican Bob Smith of New Hampshire went to Vietnam and attempted to turn up new evidence. He concluded that there is evidence "that indicates the possibility of survival, at least for a small number," after 1973, but also said, "There is at this time no compelling evidence that any American remains alive in captivity in southeast Asia." By May 1995, Kerry and fellow Vietnam veteran Senator John McCain were convinced that Hanoi was fully cooperating and, aware they had standing on this issue that Bill Clinton conspicuously lacked, they got him to normalize relations with Vietnam. Kerry has traveled a number of times to Vietnam, and he and McCain pushed successfully for the appointment of the first U.S. ambassador there. He was the lead negotiator with the State Department and the United Nations to create an international tribunal to hold hearings on genocide and war crimes in Cambodia.

Kerry has remained close with McCain and other Vietnam veterans in the Senate. Like McCain, he spoke out strongly in favor of the bombing of Bosnia in April 1999. "One of the lessons of Vietnam is: If you are going to send American forces into harm's way, you don't do it in a limited way. You don't do it tying your hands behind your back ahead of time. You don't ask people to give their lives for something less than the prospect of success." He has also spoken out against the constitutional amendment to allow punishment for flag desecration, arguing that only countries like Iran, Iraq, Libya, and North Korea have such laws.

When Bill Clinton was president, Kerry took some interesting positions on issues that put him at odds with Democratic interest groups. In June 1998, he decried the "implosion" of public education and said it was caused not just by overcrowded classrooms but also by the "stifling bureaucracy" of school systems. His list of reforms, co-sponsored with Oregon Republican Gordon Smith, included some strongly opposed by the teachers' unions—important backers of the Democratic Party—ending teacher tenure, changing certification requirements to end the education school monopoly and allow lateral entry into teaching. He worked with Missouri Republican Christopher Bond to allow direct grants to charities, including faith-based organizations, for early childhood education of at-risk children. He opposed unions by supporting expansion of H1-B visas. He urged the Clinton administration to lift export barriers on encryption and high performance computers. He favored PNTR with China and led the floor fight against the Thompson-Torricelli amendment, which would have required review of China's human rights practices.

With George W. Bush in the White House, Kerry has spoken out little about education or faith-based charities and has turned to sharp-edged opposition to administration policy. The Bush tax cut, he said, was "unfair, unaffordable and unquestionably ineffective in growing our economy." He argued in 2002 that it should be replaced by middle-class tax cuts and an expansion of the Earned Income Tax Credit; in December, he called for a tax holiday on payroll tax on the first $10,000 of wages—a $765 tax cut for every worker. "The plan would be paid for out of general revenues, so it wouldn't touch a dime slated for Social Security or Medicare," he said, though the payroll tax is explicitly tied to Social Security and Medicare. On the environment, he has been one of the most outspoken opponents of oil drilling in the Arctic National Wildlife Refuge and has threatened a filibuster on the issue. He has criticized the administration for its rejection of the Kyoto Protocol, although he was one of 95 senators who voted in 1997 to reject Kyoto so long as it exempted developing nations like China and India—a main feature of the document then and now.

A harsh note is often apparent in Kerry's criticism of Bush's foreign policy too. In June 2002, he said it was a "catastrophic mistake" not to press the Israelis to negotiate with the Palestinians; he said at the same time he would not negotiate with Yasir Arafat but would not support the calls that he be removed. He interrupted Secretary of State Colin Powell at a July 2002 Foreign Relations Committee hearing and complained that the administration's nuclear arms agreement with Russia "neutered" previous arms control agreements and contained a "huge contradiction." He criticized the administration for letting Afghan troops take the lead in Tora Bora in late 2001 and said that may have allowed Al Qaeda and Taliban leaders to escape. "In some ways Al Qaeda is more dangerous today because we didn't take advantage of initiative, which is critical in war." Despite considerable criticism of administration policy on Iraq, he voted for the Iraq war resolution in October 2002 but said shortly afterward, "I'm going to keep asking tough questions to hold the President accountable for his promise to insist on arms inspections first, act multilaterally and only go to war as a last resort."

It can be said with reasonable certainty that Kerry has long wanted to run for president. He has been known to speak in private with contempt not only of George W. Bush, but also of Bill Clinton, and if he does not share all of their strengths, he lacks their greatest faults. In February 1999, he announced he would not run for president in 2000, and in July 2000, he was in the running for the vice presidential nomination and must have been disappointed when it went to his fellow New Englander Joseph Lieberman instead. If he comes across as arrogant and aloof to some, he is also intelligent and hard-working. He has an interesting wife, Teresa Heinz, widow of Republican Senator John Heinz of Pennsylvania, who inherited some $600 million when he died in a 1991 plane crash. In the past, Kerry and Heinz have said that he would not spend her money on his campaigns, and so far have not done so. In 1996, when Kerry was hard-pressed by Weld and by his practice of not taking PAC contributions, he borrowed $1.9 million against his own assets. He has said that he would spend her money only if "something dramatic takes place in some sort of underhanded, extraordinary way in which they would attack us personally."

Kerry's liberal positions on most cultural and economic issues would obviously be an asset in most Democratic primaries but might not be in a general election. He would, after all, be the fourth Massachusetts Democrat to run for president in 24 years, and the other three lost. (In 1988, the elder George Bush made a practice of referring to Michael Dukakis as "the Governor of Massachusetts.") Kerry is opposed to gay marriage, but in favor of legal partnership rights for gay couples—a moderate position in Massachusetts, where the 2002 Democratic candidate for governor came out for gay marriage, but not perhaps in many other states. He is opposed to the death penalty in general, though said after September 11 he supported the death penalty for terrorist acts. In 1989, he voted against the death penalty for terrorists who kill Americans abroad. But Kerry was, as he often emphasizes, a decorated soldier in Vietnam and he was a prosecutor. As Massachusetts Congressman Barney Frank puts it, "He's killed people and he's put people in prison. So it's tough for Republicans to say he's too soft somehow to be president. He is a very strong candidate." Yet a record of heroism in Vietnam may not be insulation against all attacks. As Kerry noted with dismay and anger after the election, Georgia Senator Max Cleland, who lost both legs and an arm in Vietnam, was defeated after being attacked for opposing the Bush version of the homeland security bill.

There was no doubt that Kerry would be reelected in 2002: He was the first Massachusetts senator to have no major-party opposition since direct election of senators came in, and he won 80% of the vote against a Libertarian and a nuclear freeze organizer who ran a write-in campaign after Kerry voted for the Iraq resolution. He immediately made it clear that he was running for president and, after Al Gore's withdrawal, led in a poll of New Hampshire Democrats. In February 2003, Kerry underwent surgery for prostate cancer but he quickly returned to the Senate and the campaign trail.

FIRST DISTRICT

Rep. John Olver (D)

Elected June 1991, 6th term; b. Sept. 3, 1936, Honesdale, PA; home, Amherst; Rensselaer Polytechnic Inst., B.S. 1955, Tufts U., M.A. 1956, M.I.T., Ph.D. 1961; no religious affiliation; married (Rose).

Elected Office: MA House of Reps., 1968–72; MA Senate, 1972–91.

Professional Career: Chemistry Prof., U. of MA, Amherst, 1961–69.

DC Office: 1027 LHOB 20515, 202-225-5335; Fax: 202-226-1224; Web site: www.house.gov/olver.

District Offices: Fitchburg, 978-342-8722; Holyoke, 413-532-7010; Pittsfield, 413-442-0946.

Committees: *Appropriations* (13th of 29 D): Interior; Transportation, Treasury, & Independent Agencies (RMM).

Group Ratings

	ADA	ACLU	AFS	LCV	CON	ITIC	NTU	COC	ACU	NTLC	CHC
2002	95	93	100	88	55	38	24	37	0	3	0
2001	100	—	100	93	—	—	8	23	0	—	—

National Journal Ratings

	2001 LIB	—	2001 CONS	2002 LIB	—	2002 CONS
Economic	94%	—	6%	93%	—	5%
Social	90%	—	0%	92%	—	8%
Foreign	94%	—	5%	90%	—	8%

Key Votes of the 107th Congress

1. Approve Bush Tax Cuts	N	5. Faith-Based Charities	N	9. Trade Promotion Authority	N
2. Limit Patients' Bill of Rights	N	6. Bar Gays in the Boy Scouts	N	10. Bar Funds for Intl. Court	N
3. Campaign Finance Reform	Y	7. Ban Partial-Birth Abortion	N	11. Authorize Force in Iraq	N
4. Ban ANWR Development	Y	8. Arm Commercial Pilots	*	12. Deny Home. Sec. Dept. Union	N

Election Results

2002 general	John Olver (D)	137,841	(68%)	($635,460)
	Matthew Kinnaman (R)	66,061	(32%)	($192,969)
2002 primary	John Olver (D)	unopposed		
2000 general	John Olver (D)	169,375	(68%)	($646,363)
	Peter J. Abair (R)	73,580	(30%)	($151,633)
	Other	5,246	(2%)	

Prior Winning Percentages: 1998 (72%); 1996 (53%); 1994 (100%); 1992 (52%); 1991 (50%)

The People		Race/Ethnic Origin	Ancestry	
Area size:	3,192 sq. mi.	88.8% White	Irish: 13.5%	French: 10.7%
Urban population:	69.3%	1.6% Black	English: 9.0%	
Rural population:	30.7%	1.7% Asian	**2000 Presidential Vote**	
Pop. 2000:	634,479	0.2% Native Am.	Gore (D)...............150,418	(56%)
Median income:	$42,570	0.0% Hawaiian	Bush (R)................88,690	(33%)
Poverty status:	10.5%	1.2% Two+ races	Other.....................27,700	(10%)
Military veterans:	13.5%	0.1% Other	**Cook Partisan Voting Index:** D +13	
		6.3% Hispanic Origin		

Occupation	Blue collar: 23.9%	White collar: 59.8%	Gray collar: 16.4%

The stony hills and green-clad mountains of western Massachusetts, with more trees today than when Henry David Thoreau was writing in the 1840s, where stone wall fencing once bounded one working farm from another, probably does not look much different from 300 years ago. This was the frontier in the 17th century, where Puritan preachers founded new towns in the wilderness, farming the stony soil and preaching against declension. This was also the site of the Indian uprising known as King Philip's War in 1676, and the Indian raid, supported by the French from Quebec, at Deerfield in 1704. This was Yankee New England's western frontier for nearly 200 years. In the 19th century, western Massachusetts was the home of writers and artists: Emily Dickinson lived quietly in Amherst, Edith Wharton grandly on her estate in Lenox, "The Mount," and Herman Melville struck a friendship with Nathaniel Hawthorne after purchasing a farm near Hawthorne's Pittsfield home, not far from where the Boston Symphony plays at the Tanglewood Festival each summer. There were mill towns here as well, jammed in mountain crevasses or along the wide Connecticut River; but as the 20th century went on, and trees grew up on stony land once farmed, western Massachusetts came to look less settled, except near giant factories like General Electric's electric transformer plant in Pittsfield and the Crane paper factory in nearby Dalton.

Western Massachusetts has also changed politically. For many years it was one of the heartlands of the Republican Party—flinty, thrifty and chilly just like the area's most famous politician, Calvin Coolidge. But by the end of the 20th century, western Massachusetts contained some of the most left-wing parts of America. Stockbridge attracted liberal artist Norman Rockwell and baby boom radical Arlo Guthrie, whose Alice's Restaurant was there. The concentration of colleges and universities in the Pioneer Valley, around Amherst, Northampton and South Hadley, brought together a critical mass of liberal scholars and an even more leftish graduate student proletariat. The results show up in the election returns: Hampshire County, dominated by those college towns, voted 56%–28% for Al Gore in 2000; he carried Amherst, home of the University of Massachusetts, 60%–14% over George W. Bush; the runner-up, with 25%, was Ralph Nader. Western Massachusetts voted heavily for Democrat Shannon O'Brien for governor in 2002, even as she lost in the rest of Massachusetts to Mitt Romney.

The 1st Congressional District covers most of western Massachusetts—all of Berkshire and Franklin Counties, most of Hampshire County (but not the college towns of Northampton and South Hadley), Holyoke and West Springfield on the Connecticut River, northern Worcester County and goes as far east as the town of Pepperell in Middlesex County, about 40 miles from Boston. It is the state's largest congressional district (it borders four states) and covers about 40% of the land area of Massachusetts. Almost all of the Berkshire and Connecticut River valley towns are solidly Democratic and voted for Shannon O'Brien for governor in 2002. But over time, the Democratic voting base has shifted from low-income mill workers in places like Holyoke and Pittsfield to liberal and radical academics in college towns like Amherst. The recent 20-month tenure of Jane Swift of North Adams as acting governor gave the region unfamiliar influence at the statehouse. As the first western Massachusetts native in the job in 40 years (and the first woman ever), Swift brought attention to local projects and economic needs in the parts of the region that continue to lag economically, though they are now shifting to tourism promotion and publishing.

The congressman from the 1st District is John Olver, a Democrat chosen in a June 1991 special election after longtime Republican Congressman Silvio Conte died. Olver was educated at Tufts and MIT and came to UMass as a chemistry professor in 1961, at 25; his wife Rose is a professor of psychology and women's and gender studies at Amherst College. In 1968, he began a 22-year career in the legislature. In the special election to replace Conte, his Pioneer Valley base helped him win 31% in the fragmented Democratic primary. In the general, he faced Steven Pierce, former state House Republican leader and Governor William Weld's conservative opponent in the 1990 primary. With Massachusetts's liberalism in grave disrepute, the contest was close and Weld scheduled it after students' summer vacation began. But Olver eked out a 50%–48% win, becoming the first Democrat to hold the seat since the Spanish-American War.

Olver has one of the most liberal voting records in the House. He has voted against the kind of international trade deals that decades ago would have added manufacturing jobs in the 1st District, and he favors Canadian-style single-payer health insurance. He filed a bill requiring improved fuel efficiency for SUVs. Olver has worked quietly to fund local projects on the Appropriations Committee. From his unlikely post as the Military Construction Subcommittee's senior Democrat, he sent $14 million to Westover Air Force Base in Chicopee for a Marine reserve training facility and dormitory renovations. Despite local opposition, he pushed ahead with a proposal to make a national scenic trail of the Metacomet-Monadnock trail, an old Indian route that cuts through his district. Olver does not seem a natural politico: He likes to rock climb, a solitary and meticulous business. In a delegation filled with publicity hounds and political schemers, Olver is notably shy. Some Massachusetts Democrats have said that as the state's only Appropriations member, he hasn't done much for their districts. "Everyone kind of works around him," the late Rep. Joe Moakley told *The Boston Herald.* "He's a nice guy, bright enough, but he's not collegial."

For a conscientious Democrat in a basically Democratic district, Olver has not always had dazzling electoral performance. In 1996, he faced Jane Swift, then a state representative, who waged a vigorous campaign; Olver won by only 53%–47%. In 2000 and 2002, Olver won easily with 68% of the vote.

SECOND DISTRICT

Rep. Richard Neal (D)

Elected 1988, 8th term; b. Feb. 14, 1949, Springfield; home, Springfield; Amer. Intl. Col., B.A. 1972, U. of Hartford, M.A. 1976; Catholic; married (Maureen).

Elected Office: Springfield City Cncl., 1978–83; Springfield Mayor, 1984–88.

Professional Career: Staff Asst., Springfield Mayor William C. Sullivan, 1973–78; High Schl. & Col. teacher, 1978–83.

DC Office: 2133 RHOB 20515, 202-225-5601; Fax: 202-225-8112; Web site: www.house.gov/neal.

District Offices: Milford, 508-634-8198; Springfield, 413-785-0325.

Committees: *Budget* (7th of 19 D). *Ways & Means* (9th of 17 D): Trade.

Group Ratings

	ADA	ACLU	AFS	LCV	CON	ITIC	NTU	COC	ACU	NTLC	CHC
2002	90	67	100	88	73	38	19	37	4	3	8
2001	85	—	100	71	—	—	9	27	13	—	—

National Journal Ratings

	2001 LIB	—	2001 CONS		2002 LIB	—	2002 CONS
Economic	78%	—	22%		72%	—	27%
Social	65%	—	34%		66%	—	34%
Foreign	86%	—	12%		86%	—	14%

Key Votes of the 107th Congress

1. Approve Bush Tax Cuts	N	5. Faith-Based Charities	N	9. Trade Promotion Authority	N
2. Limit Patients' Bill of Rights	N	6. Bar Gays in the Boy Scouts	N	10. Bar Funds for Intl. Court	N
3. Campaign Finance Reform	Y	7. Ban Partial-Birth Abortion	Y	11. Authorize Force in Iraq	N
4. Ban ANWR Development	Y	8. Arm Commercial Pilots	N	12. Deny Home. Sec. Dept. Union	N

Election Results

2002 general	Richard Neal (D)	.... unopposed	($441,767)
2002 primary	Richard Neal (D)	.... unopposed	
2000 general	Richard Neal (D)	.... unopposed	($369,098)

Prior Winning Percentages: 1998 (100%); 1996 (72%); 1994 (59%); 1992 (53%); 1990 (100%); 1988 (80%)

The People		Race/Ethnic Origin	Ancestry	
Area size:	952 sq. mi.	82.5% White	Irish: 13.4%	French: 10.8%
Urban population:	84.8%	5.5% Black	Italian: 8.9%	
Rural population:	15.2%	1.3% Asian	**2000 Presidential Vote**	
Pop. 2000:	634,444	0.2% Native Am.	Gore (D)..............150,148	(58%)
Median income:	$44,386	0.0% Hawaiian	Bush (R)...............89,775	(35%)
Poverty status:	10.8%	1.2% Two+ races	Other...................19,588	(8%)
Military veterans:	13.3%	0.1% Other	**Cook Partisan Voting Index:** D +12	
		9.2% Hispanic Origin		
Occupation	Blue collar: 24.1%	White collar: 60.6%	Gray collar: 15.4%	

As American as apple pie, the place where basketball was invented, the city where the Webster's unabridged dictionaries (2d and 3d editions) were edited and published, the site of the armory where M-1 rifles were manufactured during World War II: This is Springfield, Massachusetts. Springfield is the third largest city in the Bay State, but far from Boston; historically overshadowed by Hartford as the center of the Connecticut River Valley; a medium-sized American city built by New England Yankees, where immigrants from a dozen different countries have worked their way up. Like other New England cities, its downtown has emptied; business leaders have tried to revive it, with the opening of the expanded Basketball Hall of Fame. The gun manufacturer Smith

& Wesson in the 1990s embraced the marketing restrictions sought by gun control advocates, and then saw its sales sag, as gun control opponents—its natural market—shunned its products. Now, under new ownership, it has abandoned that stance, and sales are rising again.

Springfield is the largest city in the 2d Congressional District, whose irregular boundaries stretch north to the college towns of South Hadley and Northampton, tourist destinations now with trendy restaurants. To the east across stony hills it includes the antique center of Brimfield and the factory towns of the Blackstone Valley just north of Woonsocket, Rhode Island. Historically, this was a Yankee Republican district for much of the 20th century, then a solidly Catholic Democratic district. Now it is more diverse culturally, but still solidly Democratic.

The congressman from the 2d District is Richard Neal, mayor of Springfield from 1984–88. Neal grew up in Springfield, went to work for the mayor in 1973, and was elected to the Council in 1978, while teaching high school and college history. As mayor, Neal worked to rehabilitate the downtown and revitalize neighborhoods. His predecessor, 36-year incumbent Edward Boland, a longtime friend of Tip O'Neill, essentially bequeathed him the House seat. In 1988, Boland announced his retirement just before the filing deadline, and after Neal had been making the rounds of the district for a year. Unopposed in the Democratic primary, Neal won 80% in the general.

Neal has a generally liberal voting record but has favored enough moderate initiatives to separate himself from more ideological Massachusetts colleagues. He voted for the final version of welfare reform, the partial-birth abortion ban and the Defense of Marriage Act; he refused to support Bill Clinton's health care plan. He voted for NAFTA and GATT and—after considerable hand wringing—for PNTR with China. But he opposed trade promotion authority in 2001 and 2002 and voted against the Iraq war resolution. He serves on Ways and Means, where he decries the complications of the tax code and has a bill that would repeal the alternative minimum tax and eliminate 200 lines from federal tax forms. When other Ways and Means Democrats cut a bipartisan deal to expand pensions and retirement incentives, he filed an alternative targeted more to blue-collar workers.

Neal took the lead for House Democrats on a popular proposal to clamp down on companies that incorporate in Bermuda and other offshore havens to avoid U.S. taxes. He gave the initiative an additional bite when he directed its fire at companies that moved offshore after September 11, terming it "The Corporate Patriot Enforcement Act of 2002." Opponents said that such moves were not illegal, but when Democrats forced a late-night vote on adding Neal's proposal to the bill creating the Homeland Security Department, the Republican leadership decided it could not defeat it; 109 Republicans voted for Neal's proposal. After the November election, in conference committee, the provision was gutted by allowing the Department of Homeland Security to waive the provision when necessary to uphold national security or protect U.S. jobs. Neal resolved to raise the issue again in the 108th Congress.

Like many other Irish Catholic brethren over the years, Neal has encouraged American attempts at reconciliation in Northern Ireland. In 1980, when he was a city council member, he sponsored a plank at the Democratic National Convention for the unification of Ireland. In 1993, he started one-hour special orders sessions on Irish issues; a year later, he personally lobbied Bill Clinton to grant a visa for Gerry Adams of Sinn Fein to visit the U.S. In 2002, the American Ireland Fund gave Neal its International Leadership Award for his years of efforts.

Neal had serious primary challenges in 1990 and 1992, but won by satisfactory margins. Republicans have never mounted credible opposition. He has faced no opposition at all since 1996. With his secure local seat, he is free to wait to rise to the heights of seniority on Ways and Means.

THIRD DISTRICT

Rep. Jim McGovern (D)

Elected 1996, 4th term; b. Nov. 20, 1959, Worcester; home, Worcester; American U., B.A. 1981, M.P.A. 1984; Catholic; married (Lisa).

Professional Career: Aide, U.S. Sen. George McGovern, 1977–80; Sr. Aide, U.S. Rep. Joseph Moakley, 1982–96.

DC Office: 430 CHOB 20515, 202-225-6101; Fax: 202-225-5759; Web site: www.house.gov/mcgovern.

District Offices: Attleboro, 508-431-8025; Fall River, 508-677-0140; Worcester, 508-831-7356.

Committees: *Rules* (3d of 4 D): Technology & the House (RMM).

Group Ratings

	ADA	ACLU	AFS	LCV	CON	ITIC	NTU	COC	ACU	NTLC	CHC
2002	100	87	100	100	43	50	21	30	0	0	0
2001	90	—	100	100	—	—	8	35	4	—	—

National Journal Ratings

	2001 LIB	—	2001 CONS		2002 LIB	—	2002 CONS
Economic	95%	—	0%		93%	—	5%
Social	83%	—	11%		84%	—	8%
Foreign	96%	—	0%		94%	—	0%

Key Votes of the 107th Congress

1. Approve Bush Tax Cuts	N	5. Faith-Based Charities	N
2. Limit Patients' Bill of Rights	N	6. Bar Gays in the Boy Scouts	N
3. Campaign Finance Reform	Y	7. Ban Partial-Birth Abortion	N
4. Ban ANWR Development	Y	8. Arm Commercial Pilots	N

9. Trade Promotion Authority	N
10. Bar Funds for Intl. Court	N
11. Authorize Force in Iraq	N
12. Deny Home. Sec. Dept. Union	N

Election Results

2002 general	Jim McGovern (D)	unopposed	($628,444)
2002 primary	Jim McGovern (D)	unopposed	
2000 general	Jim McGovern (D)	unopposed	($550,240)

Prior Winning Percentages: 1998 (57%); 1996 (53%)

The People		Race/Ethnic Origin	Ancestry	
Area size:	612 sq. mi.	86.2% White	Irish: 16.1%	Italian: 9.5%
Urban population:	93.4%	2.6% Black	English: 8.5%	
Rural population:	6.6%	3.2% Asian	**2000 Presidential Vote**	
Pop. 2000:	634,585	0.2% Native Am.	Gore (D) 153,044 (59%)	
Median income:	$50,223	0.0% Hawaiian	Bush (R) 90,375 (35%)	
Poverty status:	9.0%	1.5% Two+ races	Other 17,711 (7%)	
Military veterans:	11.7%	0.3% Other	**Cook Partisan Voting Index:** D +13	
		6.0% Hispanic Origin		

Occupation	Blue collar: 20.6%	White collar: 65.5%	Gray collar: 13.8%

Worcester (its name still pronounced with a particularly pungent Massachusetts accent making it sound as if it had no *R*s), for more than 200 years has been one of the nation's centers of tinkering, contriving and inventing. In the mid-19th century, the city was renown as the valentine-making capital of the U.S. for its production of lavish valentines and greeting cards. Fifty years ago, Worcester's biggest industries were wire-making, textiles, grinding wheels and envelopes. It is where the birth control pill was invented and where Worcester native and Clark University professor Robert Goddard shot off experimental rockets before relieved locals saw him off to New Mexico. Yet Worcester, the second-largest city in Massachusetts, is one of the few active industrial cities not located on a river, lake or seacoast, and far from a major airport.

In the 1970s and 1980s, electronics and computer firms sprouted along I-495—the circumferential highway 20 miles east of Worcester, as they had earlier around Route 128, closer to Boston. The high-tech boom brought prosperity, labor shortages, new residents and higher housing prices to central Massachusetts. Then, in the early 1990s, the minicomputer industry slumped, bringing recession and a collapse of real estate values. But Worcester's ingenious entrepreneurs and skilled labor force hustled, and local leaders set up a Biotechnology Research Institute to draw on the city's 9 colleges and a state university medical center.

Just as the city's economy has changed, so has its face. Nearly 100% white in 1950, the city is now just 77% white. Between 1990 and 2000, Worcester saw a 78% rise in Asian population, a 55% rise in African-Americans, and a 61% increase in the number of Hispanics (mainly Puerto Rican). Overall, population declined by 20% between 1950 and 1980, but rebounded to increase by almost 7% between 1980 and 2000.

The 3d Congressional District has Worcester as its largest city, though not its geographic center. A little more than half its people live in Worcester and a cluster of adjacent towns. The other population cluster is 60 miles away, in and around the old textile mill town of Fall River, east of Rhode Island. The two are connected by a string of towns, in some places only a few miles wide, that reaches almost to Buzzards Bay. In national elections since 1992 this district has been solidly Democratic. Worcester itself is heavily Democratic; only 12% of city voters are registered as Republicans. In Massachusetts gubernatorial elections, however, the district is mixed. Worcester and Fall River (only a portion of which is in the district) voted by significant margins for Democrat Shannon O'Brien in 2002. But the Interstate 495 corridor and the towns northeast of Rhode Island gave even larger margins to Republican Mitt Romney.

The congressman from the 3d District is Jim McGovern, a Democrat elected in 1996. McGovern grew up in Worcester, where his parents owned a package store on West Boylston Street. He went to American University in Washington, and while in graduate school worked in the office of former South Dakota Senator George McGovern (no relation). He ran McGovern's 1984 campaign in the Massachusetts presidential primary, where he finished third with 21% of the vote, and nominated him at the San Francisco convention. After that he got a job in Boston Rep. Joe Moakley's office and became chief of staff as Moakley became chairman of the Rules Committee. McGovern got into the spotlight himself, leading a 1989 investigation of the murders of six Jesuits and two lay women in El Salvador, which led to a cutoff of aid. In 1994, he ran for the House and lost in the Democratic primary 38%–30%. In 1996 he ran again, this time with no primary opposition. In the general election, two-term Republican Congressman Peter Blute stressed his "independence" from the House leadership and attacked McGovern for liberal stands on abortion and Cuba. The AFL-CIO targeted the district with TV ads, and McGovern ran a humorous spot that asked, "If you wouldn't vote for Newt, why would you ever vote for Blute?" McGovern won 53%–45%.

With deft maneuvers that reflect his Capitol Hill experience, McGovern has positioned himself to become a House power broker when Democrats regain the majority, however many years that might take. The dying Moakley made a personal request to Minority Leader Dick Gephardt that McGovern get a seat on Rules; the next seat went to Florida Rep. Alcee Hastings, a member of the Congressional Black Caucus, but McGovern got a commitment for the next available Democratic seat, with seniority over Hastings. In 2002 McGovern officially moved onto Rules, where he immediately showed familiarity with House procedures.

McGovern has continued to push openings to Cuba and has called for easing sanctions against Fidel Castro's totalitarian regime. When Elian Gonzalez's Miami relatives sought to allow him to grow up in freedom in America, McGovern worked with the boy's father to arrange their return to Cuba. He is a member of the Cuba working group, which won a bipartisan House vote to lift the travel ban to the island. During his own visits to Cuba, he has persuaded authorities there to make available to American scholars Ernest Hemingway's personal papers at his home outside Havana. McGovern has been less successful with other Latin American interests: The House defeated his amendment to reduce military aid to Colombia.

Although Republicans held this seat less than a decade ago, they have given up on it: McGovern ran unopposed in 2000 and 2002.

FOURTH DISTRICT

Rep. Barney Frank (D)

Elected 1980, 12th term; b. Mar. 31, 1940, Bayonne, NJ; home, Newton; Harvard U., B.A. 1962, J.D. 1977; Jewish; companion (Sergio Pombo).

Elected Office: MA House of Reps., 1972–80.

Professional Career: Exec. Asst., Boston Mayor Kevin White, 1967–71; A.A., U.S. Rep. Michael Harrington, 1971–72; Teaching Fellow, Harvard JFK Schl. of Govt., 1978–80.

DC Office: 2252 RHOB 20515, 202-225-5931; Fax: 202-225-0182; Web site: www.house.gov/frank.

District Offices: New Bedford, 508-999-6462; Newton, 617-332-3920; Taunton, 508-822-4796.

Committees: *Financial Services* (RMM of 32 D). *Select Committee on Homeland Security* (6th of 23 D): Infrastructure & Border Security; Intelligence & Counterterrorism.

Group Ratings

	ADA	ACLU	AFS	LCV	CON	ITIC	NTU	COC	ACU	NTLC	CHC
2002	100	93	100	100	84	25	26	26	8	3	0
2001	100	—	100	100	—	—	16	22	0	—	—

National Journal Ratings

	2001 LIB — 2001 CONS		2002 LIB — 2002 CONS	
Economic	95%	0%	93%	5%
Social	90%	0%	84%	8%
Foreign	91%	8%	76%	23%

Key Votes of the 107th Congress

1. Approve Bush Tax Cuts	N	5. Faith-Based Charities	N	9. Trade Promotion Authority	N
2. Limit Patients' Bill of Rights	N	6. Bar Gays in the Boy Scouts	N	10. Bar Funds for Intl. Court	N
3. Campaign Finance Reform	Y	7. Ban Partial-Birth Abortion	N	11. Authorize Force in Iraq	N
4. Ban ANWR Development	Y	8. Arm Commercial Pilots	Y	12. Deny Home. Sec. Dept. Union	N

Election Results

2002 general	Barney Frank (D)	unopposed		($476,688)
2002 primary	Barney Frank (D)	unopposed		
2000 general	Barney Frank (D)	200,638	(75%)	($471,381)
	Martin D. Travis (R)	56,553	(21%)	($24,553)
	David J. Euchner (Lib)	10,553	(4%)	($8,613)

Prior Winning Percentages: 1998 (100%); 1996 (72%); 1994 (100%); 1992 (68%); 1990 (66%); 1988 (70%); 1986 (89%); 1984 (74%); 1982 (60%); 1980 (52%)

The People		Race/Ethnic Origin	Ancestry	
Area size:	844 sq. mi.	87.9% White	Irish: 13.5%	Portuguese: 13.4%
Urban population:	88.2%	2.0% Black	English: 9.0%	
Rural population:	11.8%	3.2% Asian	**2000 Presidential Vote**	
Pop. 2000:	634,624	0.2% Native Am.	Gore (D)	178,354 (65%)
Median income:	$53,169	0.0% Hawaiian	Bush (R)	79,201 (29%)
Poverty status:	8.4%	1.9% Two+ races	Other	18,067 (7%)
Military veterans:	11.0%	1.6% Other	**Cook Partisan Voting Index:** D +19	
		3.3% Hispanic Origin		

Occupation	Blue collar: 19.2%	White collar: 67.6%	Gray collar: 13.2%

The political transformation of Massachusetts is nowhere better illustrated than in the Boston suburbs of Brookline and Newton. These were Yankee enclaves a century ago, with avenues built to resemble the sweep of Haussmann's Grand Boulevards in Paris, and villages of giant clapboard houses clustered within a few blocks of commuter railroad stations. Brookline was where The Country Club (the very first one) was established in 1882, and where Joseph Kennedy, an Irish

Catholic 20-something banker seeking respectability, moved his family in 1914. Brookline and Newton then were solidly Republican in politics, the political base of leading politicians like Christian Herter, governor of Massachusetts and U.S. secretary of state in the 1950s; as late as 1960, Brookline and Newton and adjacent wards of Boston were electing a Republican congressman. Then came the transformation, personified by the election in 1962 of Michael Dukakis at 29 to the Great and General Court (the legislature). As Massachusetts's university-educated classes became more liberal, as Brookline's and Newton's Jewish populations grew, and as young liberal-minded families refurbished the graceful old houses, these towns became Democratic bastions. Brookline and Newton, even more than Boston, are the liberal heart of Massachusetts: They voted 75%–20% for Bill Clinton in 1996 and 73%–19% for Al Gore in 2000—even better than Gore's 72%–20% lead in Boston.

The 4th Congressional District includes Brookline and Newton, which are the political home bases for its congressman, Barney Frank. Anchoring the hook-like northern tip of the district, they account for less than one-quarter of the district's population. The shape results from successive redistrictings: In 1982, Frank's district was extended south to the old textile mill city of Fall River; in 1992, it lost much of Fall River and gained New Bedford, a great 19th century whaling port and still home to one of the largest fishing fleets in the United States, with the largest percentage of Portuguese-Americans in the nation; in 2002, it kept New Bedford and regained most of Fall River. Brookline and Newton are connected to the rest of the district by an attenuated series of towns—Wellesley, Dover, Sherborn, Millis, Norfolk, Sharon—and at some points the district is only a mile wide. This is a Democratic district in national politics, but not as Democratic or as uniformly culturally liberal as Brookline and Newton; in state politics it is more marginal: Brookline and Newton voted for Democrat Shannon O'Brien in 2002, and so did New Bedford and Fall River, but almost all the other towns in the district voted for Republican Governor Mitt Romney. There is a bit of most kinds of America here: high-income WASPy Wellesley, French-Canadian mill-worker Fall River, Foxboro with its football stadium, Sharon with a middle-income Jewish population and countrified Dover.

Frank, elected in 1980, is one of the intellectual and political leaders of the Democratic Party in the House—political theorist and pit bull all at the same time. In *Washingtonian*'s annual polls of House staffers, he is consistently voted the brainiest and the funniest member of the House by wide margins. New York filmmaker Bart Everly, in Washington to shoot a movie about the impeachment controversy, decided to concentrate on Frank instead; the result was a 2001 movie called *Let's Get Frank*. Barney Frank grew up in Bayonne, New Jersey, and went to Harvard, where he got to know local politicians as well as political scientists. In 1967, he went to work for newly elected Boston Mayor Kevin White; in 1971, he went to Washington to work for Congressman Michael Harrington. In 1972, Frank was elected to the Massachusetts House from the Back Bay of Boston, then just starting to be a liberal singles neighborhood. In 1980, when Congressman Robert Drinan retired after Pope John Paul II commanded Jesuits to leave elective office, Frank moved to Brookline and ran in the 4th District. With a strong base in Brookline and Newton, he won. He defeated Republican Margaret Heckler 60%–40% in 1982, and has been re-elected by wide margins since.

In the House, Frank quickly gained a reputation as one of the smartest talkers and best debaters in the chamber—maybe one of the best of all time. Frank listens to others' arguments and engages them in his inimitable rapid-fire delivery. While he stands at the left end of the American electoral spectrum, there is an element of solid small-c conservatism beneath him. More recently he said he is for "capitalism plus," that is, market capitalism with welfare state protections, and he has expressed unease at what he considers increasing isolationism in Congress, though in 2002 he opposed the Iraq war resolution. An invasion of Iraq, he said, would be "disastrously wrong" for Middle East peace.

Frank has worked hard, often behind the scenes, on many substantive issues. He has shaped immigration acts since 1986, working to expand legal immigration, to allow HIV-positive people to enter the country, to bar states from excluding children of illegal aliens from school and, most recently, to change the 1996 law that required mandatory deportation of immigrants convicted of a crime carrying a one-year sentence even if the offense occurred many years ago; this had been hurting Azorean and Cape Verdean immigrants in New Bedford. After the 1998 election, Frank took the ranking position on Banking's Housing Subcommittee. In 2002, he worked cooperatively with Financial Services Chairman Michael Oxley on housing issues, including a program to help teachers, police officers and fire fighters make down payments on houses in the communities where they work. "It could be the beginning of a beautiful relationship," he said, echoing the movie *Casablanca*. "I'm not sure which of us is Humphrey Bogart and which is Claude Rains. We'll have to wait until after the election to find out." But he promised to object if Republicans tried to significantly scale back the Sarbanes-Oxley Act passed in summer 2002 and said he was skeptical about Republican plans for a broad-scale financial regulatory relief bill.

He has had other bipartisan successes. With Banking Committee Republican Spencer Bachus he worked hard for debt relief for very poor countries. With conservatives Henry Hyde and Bob Barr, he worked to modify the harsh federal confiscation laws enacted as part of the war against drugs; the measure passed the House by a wide margin in 1999. He also passed a law, vital for the biotech industry, allowing companies to receive patents for processes for artificially manufacturing substances that exist naturally. In the 107th Congress he got 50 co-sponsors for a bill repealing the 1998 ban on college loan and grant aid to students convicted of drug offenses; he points out that those convicted of much more serious felonies face no such ban. In 2002, he joined with conservative Dana Rohrabacher to seek repeal of the House rule barring members on the floor from "describing and characterizing" any action taken by the Senate, which imposes no similar restriction on its members. It is, Frank argues persuasively, "a dumb rule."

But not until the 1998 impeachment hearings was Frank able to overshadow another aspect of his career. In May 1987, in a seemingly casual answer to a reporter's question, Frank said he is gay. Then in August 1989, the conservative *Washington Times* reported that Frank had employed as a personal aide a male prostitute and convicted drug possessor, Steve Gobie, and let him live in his apartment. When faced with a scandal that threatened to end his career, Frank told the truth. He admitted paying Gobie, but was careful never to use official or campaign funds; he denied that he tolerated prostitution in his apartment and said he had thrown the man out when he suspected it was going on. Frank called on the ethics committee to investigate. It did and dismissed all but two minor charges. The committee recommended a reprimand, but not censure; Frank agreed in a contrite appearance before the House in July 1990 and the House voted 287–141 against censure. The vote for reprimand was 408–18. "I think members will agree that I have always had a reputation for honesty, not always tact or tolerance," Frank said to the House. That reputation was one reason he survived and has thrived in the House; his brains, liberal stands, hard work and constituency service helped him not only survive, but be overwhelmingly popular in the 4th District.

Frank has been the House's leading legislator on gay rights issues. One was the issue, raised in the 1992 campaign by Bill Clinton and not by Frank or by gay advocacy groups, of gays in the military. To the disappointment of many in the gay community, Frank admitted that allowing open homosexuals to serve in the military would not be accepted by most in Congress or the Pentagon. In the years since, Frank has criticized the military because the number of service members discharged for homosexuality has actually increased, and he helped persuade Al Gore to come out against "Don't ask, Don't tell" in 1999. Frank and Republican Christopher Shays have sponsored a bill to prohibit employment discrimination on account of sexuality, and it appears to be heading toward majority support, even in a Republican House. He spoke out against provisions of the faith-based charities act that would allow charities to discriminate against gay people in violation of state or local laws.

After the Republican victory in November 1994, Minority Whip David Bonior asked Frank to be the Democrats' point man in floor debates. During the Contract With America debate, Frank prowled the floor, ready to take up a microphone and deliver stinging attacks on Republicans' hypocrisy. His strong and orderly mind, his ability to argue abstract principles in rapid-fire but comprehensible words, were on display—and made him the most feared adversary by the Republican side.

Frank also emerged, well before the impeachment crisis, as a defender of Bill Clinton against charges of scandal. He came at these issues as a civil libertarian who is attentive to defendants' rights. On the Banking Committee in 1994 he defended Clinton with attack-dog intensity against Whitewater charges. Frank acknowledged that Clinton lied in his deposition in the Paula Jones case, but he also ridiculed the case against him. Yet he was harshly critical of Bill Clinton's last minute pardons and in February 2001 proposed a constitutional amendment to prevent the president from using the pardoning power from a month before the presidential election until inauguration day.

Through all his work on national issues, Frank has not neglected the home front. He has worked especially hard on projects in Fall River and New Bedford, for which he obtained the creation of a national park commemorating the whaling industry. He has worked for the fishing and cranberry industries. He pushed for reregulation of cable TV after hearings complaints from constituents in Fall River about rises in monthly cable charges. Frank campaigned for Al Gore in 2000 and attacked Green Party candidate Ralph Nader for never speaking on abortion rights, gay rights, or gun control. But in December 2002, he said that Gore should not run again in 2004. "His negatives are too high," he explained. "It's unfair and it's not his fault, but it's reality." He recovered smartly from heart surgery in 1999, and in 2000, said he hoped to serve in the House "another 15 years or so."

FIFTH DISTRICT

Rep. Martin Meehan (D)

Elected 1992, 6th term; b. Dec. 30, 1956, Lowell; home, Lowell; U. of MA, B.S. 1978, Suffolk U., M.A. 1981, J.D. 1986; Catholic; married (Ellen Murphy).

Professional Career: Staff Asst., U.S. Rep. James Shannon, 1979–81; Research analyst, MA Legislature's Joint Cmte. on Elections, 1982–84; MA Dpty. Secy. of State for Securities & Corps., 1985–90; Middlesex Cnty. 1st Asst. Dist. Atty., 1990–92.

DC Office: 2229 RHOB 20515, 202-225-3411; Fax: 202-226-0771; Web site: www.house.gov/meehan.

District Offices: Haverhill, 978-521-1845; Lawrence, 978-681-6200; Lowell, 978-459-0101.

Committees: *Armed Services* (7th of 29 D): Terrorism, Unconventional Threats & Capabilities (RMM); Total Force. *Judiciary* (10th of 16 D): Courts, the Internet & Intellectual Property; Crime, Terrorism & Homeland Security.

Group Ratings

	ADA	ACLU	AFS	LCV	CON	ITIC	NTU	COC	ACU	NTLC	CHC
2002	75	86	100	63	79	50	20	44	9	3	0
2001	90	—	100	86	—	—	11	29	0	—	—

National Journal Ratings

	2001 LIB —	2001 CONS	2002 LIB —	2002 CONS
Economic	86%	14%	84%	16%
Social	83%	11%	74%	19%
Foreign	86%	12%	70%	29%

Key Votes of the 107th Congress

1. Approve Bush Tax Cuts	N	5. Faith-Based Charities	N	9. Trade Promotion Authority	N
2. Limit Patients' Bill of Rights	N	6. Bar Gays in the Boy Scouts	N	10. Bar Funds for Intl. Court	N
3. Campaign Finance Reform	Y	7. Ban Partial-Birth Abortion	N	11. Authorize Force in Iraq	Y
4. Ban ANWR Development	Y	8. Arm Commercial Pilots	Y	12. Deny Home. Sec. Dept. Union	*

Election Results

2002 general	Martin Meehan (D)	122,562	(60%)	($897,286)
	Charles McCarthy (R)	69,337	(34%)	($256,212)
	Ilana Freedman (Lib)	11,729	(6%)	($160,640)
2002 primary	Martin Meehan (D)	unopposed		
2000 general	Martin Meehan (D)	unopposed		($508,730)

Prior Winning Percentages: 1998 (71%); 1996 (100%); 1994 (70%); 1992 (52%)

The People		Race/Ethnic Origin	Ancestry	
Area size:	582 sq. mi.	79.7% White	Irish: 16.6%	Italian: 9.8%
Urban population:	93.5%	1.7% Black	English: 8.9%	
Rural population:	6.5%	5.2% Asian	**2000 Presidential Vote**	
Pop. 2000:	635,326	0.1% Native Am.	Gore (D) 145,277	(57%)
Median income:	$56,217	0.0% Hawaiian	Bush (R) 93,406	(36%)
Poverty status:	8.9%	1.4% Two+ races	Other 18,433	(7%)
Military veterans:	10.9%	0.2% Other	**Cook Partisan Voting Index:** D +11	
		11.6% Hispanic Origin		

Occupation   Blue collar: 20.9%   White collar: 66.9%   Gray collar: 12.1%

The Merrimack River Valley at the northern edge of Massachusetts has had an erratic history: High-tech boom, bust, boom, bust, boom. When Massachusetts was a kind of maritime republic in the 19th century, with many farmers struggling to scratch out a living from the stony soil, a few clever Yankees used their profits from the sea trade to try to tame the rapidly flowing Merrimack and build cotton-spinning mills. Creating the cities of Lowell and Lawrence, they built model dormitories and recreation programs for their women workers. This was the center of America's textile industry for more than a century, long after the maritime industry faded. But in the 1920s, the price of labor rose and newly built mills in the Carolinas, much closer to the cotton supply, decimated the industry that Lawrence and Lowell built. Many residents—by then, rather elderly—waited forlornly for an upturn in the local economy.

It came eventually, largely due to an unexpected source. High-tech industry drove the growth, beginning in the 1960s around MIT, then moving out to the Route 128 ring road and then I-495, which passes through Lowell and Lawrence. Wang, headquartered in Lowell, grew spectacularly, and Senator Paul Tsongas spearheaded a national historic restoration of the old mill area. This was the Massachusetts miracle of the early 1980s. Then came the bust: Wang's word processors and minicomputers slumped as businesses purchased personal computers and hooked them together in networks. But Lowell revived again. Its new immigrants—mostly from Cambodia and Puerto Rico—provide vitality and entrepreneurial creativity; the old Wang buildings are filled with health care, banking, telecommunications and Internet companies.

The 5th Congressional District includes Lawrence and Lowell, which along with next-door towns account for about two-thirds of the district's population. The remainder of the district is the high-tech corridor south on circumferential Interstate 495. The district also includes tony suburbs like Concord, the mountains along the New Hampshire state line and the small towns west of Lowell that once hosted Fort Devens, which closed in 1996, though part of the base today survives as a training site for Army Reserve and National Guard soldiers from across New England. Except for Lowell and Lawrence, it is ancestrally Yankee Republican. It is culturally liberal and trended toward the Democrats in the early 1970s. Back then, the 5th produced two Democratic candidates who would later run for president: John Kerry, who lost the general election in 1972, and Paul Tsongas, who won the seat two years later. In the 1980s and 1990s, amid the high-tech boom, it went Republican in national and even statewide elections: A kind of Baja New Hampshire. In 1992, it gave Bill Clinton his lowest percentage in the state, while a big vote went to high-tech pioneer Ross Perot. But in the 1990s, its cultural liberalism moved it toward Democrats, and in 1996 and 2000, it voted solidly for Clinton and Al Gore. This was George W. Bush's second-strongest district in Massachusetts, but that's not saying much: He won only 36% of the vote here.

The congressman from the 5th District is Martin Meehan, a Democrat elected in 1992. Meehan grew up in Lowell, one of seven children of a 43-year Lowell *Sun* typesetter. As a child, he memorized President Kennedy's speeches from long-playing records, kept a scrapbook on Robert Kennedy, and idolized Sen. Edward Kennedy. He is a lifelong politico: He was an aide to Congressman James Shannon while working on his masters degree, worked in the Massachusetts secretary of state's office after law school, and was first assistant district attorney in Middlesex County from 1990 until he ran for Congress in 1992. He took on eight-year incumbent Democrat Chester Atkins, who had grown highly unpopular in the district. Meehan beat Atkins by the astonishing margin of 65%–35%. In the general, Meehan faced former Republican Rep. Paul Cronin, who beat Kerry in 1972 (the only open seat carried by George McGovern to also elect a Republican to the House), but lost to Tsongas in 1974. Meehan won 52%–38%.

Meehan combines a mostly liberal voting record with distinctive stands on issues. One of his crusades is against tobacco; his father, a smoker, had heart surgery when Marty was 11. He sponsored a bipartisan bill with a $1.50 a pack tax and a target of cutting youth smoking by 80%, and later proposed a ban on Internet sale of cigarettes to kids. His other great cause is campaign finance reform. Starting in 1997, with Connecticut Rep. Christopher Shays and Senators Russ Feingold and John McCain, Meehan co-sponsored a series of campaign finance bills, and the law was finally enacted in 2002. It outlawed soft money, subjected non-candidate ads to disclosure and contribution limit requirements, strengthened FEC enforcement powers, required posting of forms on the Internet and created a commission to recommend more reforms. House Republican leaders opposed Shays-Meehan in its various forms, but the House passed the bill in September 1999 when it was clear that it could be stopped in the Senate by the Republican leadership or by filibuster. Then, when John McCain pushed a version of the bill to passage in the Senate in April 2001, Meehan and his allies saw an opportunity to turn it into law. They managed to defeat the House leadership's rule which would have made it difficult for their version to pass in July 2001—the only rule defeated on the House floor during Dennis Hastert's first four years as Speaker—but the House Republican leadership yanked it from the calendar. Meehan and his allies then sought to get the required 218 signatures on a petition to discharge it from committee and bring it to the floor under their own terms of debate. That finally happened in February 2002. Despite the apprehensions of Democratic fundraisers, who were more dependent on soft money than Republicans, Meehan kept most Democrats and many Republicans aboard. George W. Bush signaled that he would not veto it, and it passed with a large bipartisan majority 240–189, with 41 Republicans and 198 Democrats voting in favor.

Meehan serves on the Armed Services Committee and has generally moved to cut defense spending, but he boosts local Raytheon operations and its upgrades of the Patriot missile. Over the years, his voting record seems to have drifted left: He voted for NAFTA in 1993 and against trade promotion authority in 1997 and 2001. Yet he was one of three House Democrats from Massachusetts to vote to authorize President Bush to use force against Iraq.

When Meehan first ran for the House in 1992, he pledged to serve no more than four terms. In 1999, he said he would break his pledge. He roiled some Democrats when he voiced interest in the 2002 race for governor, but then changed his mind when threatened with the loss of his district through redistricting. Against nominal opposition in 2002, he was reelected to his House seat with only 60% of the vote, a sign that he needs to spend more time working his base. But Meehan remains interested in running statewide if an opening should appear.

SIXTH DISTRICT

Rep. John Tierney (D)

Elected 1996, 4th term; b. Sept. 18, 1951, Salem; home, Salem; Salem St. U., B.A. 1973, Suffolk U., J.D. 1976; no religious affiliation; married (Patrice).

Professional Career: Practicing atty., 1976–96.

DC Office: 120 CHOB 20515, 202-225-8020; Fax: 202-225-5915; Web site: www.house.gov/tierney.

District Offices: Lynn, 781-595-7375; Peabody, 978-531-1669.

Committees: *Education & the Workforce* (9th of 22 D): 21st Century Competitiveness; Employer-Employee Relations. *Government Reform* (10th of 19 D): Energy Policy, Natural Resources and Regulatory Affairs (RMM); National Security, Emerging Threats & Intl. Relations.

Group Ratings

	ADA	ACLU	AFS	LCV	CON	ITIC	NTU	COC	ACU	NTLC	CHC
2002	100	93	100	100	92	38	24	32	0	3	0
2001	100	—	100	100	—	—	13	26	0	—	—

National Journal Ratings

	2001 LIB	—	2001 CONS		2002 LIB	—	2002 CONS
Economic	95%	—	0%		93%	—	5%
Social	90%	—	0%		84%	—	8%
Foreign	96%	—	0%		90%	—	8%

Key Votes of the 107th Congress

1. Approve Bush Tax Cuts	N	5. Faith-Based Charities	N	9. Trade Promotion Authority	N
2. Limit Patients' Bill of Rights	N	6. Bar Gays in the Boy Scouts	N	10. Bar Funds for Intl. Court	N
3. Campaign Finance Reform	Y	7. Ban Partial-Birth Abortion	N	11. Authorize Force in Iraq	N
4. Ban ANWR Development	Y	8. Arm Commercial Pilots	N	12. Deny Home. Sec. Dept. Union	N

Election Results

2002 general	John Tierney (D)	162,900	(68%)	($515,113)
	Mark Smith (R)	75,462	(32%)	($30,078)
2002 primary	John Tierney (D)	unopposed		
2000 general	John Tierney (D)	205,234	(71%)	($426,934)
	Paul McCartney (R)	83,501	(29%)	($53,528)

Prior Winning Percentages: 1998 (55%); 1996 (48%)

The People		Race/Ethnic Origin	Ancestry	
Area size:	805 sq. mi.	89.8% White	Irish: 18.6%	Italian: 13.1%
Urban population:	94.9%	1.9% Black	English: 10.6%	
Rural population:	5.1%	2.5% Asian	**2000 Presidential Vote**	
Pop. 2000:	636,554	0.1% Native Am.	Gore (D) 172,840	(57%)
Median income:	$57,826	0.0% Hawaiian	Bush (R) 107,415	(36%)
Poverty status:	6.3%	1.1% Two+ races	Other 20,760	(7%)
Military veterans:	12.6%	0.2% Other	**Cook Partisan Voting Index:** D +11	
		4.4% Hispanic Origin		

Occupation	Blue collar: 17.2%	White collar: 69.7%	Gray collar: 13.1%

The North Shore of Massachusetts Bay has a number of times been at the leading edge of the nation's economy. In 1640, the Saugus Iron Works was built here—the beginning of American heavy industry. When Europe's great powers were convulsed in international war from 1792 to 1815, American ship owners suddenly became the richest in the world and traders from Boston accumulated the capital needed to build textile mills and railroads and to finance much of the American industrial revolution. From the small port of Salem, ships left for China, bringing back porcelain and artifacts, which helped change American styles forever. Salem, first settled in 1626, had the nation's first millionaire, Elias Hasket Derby; in 1900, it was the richest city per capita in the nation. But the North Shore is a quiet place, from Boston Harbor north to the mouth of the Merrimack River, a collection of ethnic factory towns from Lynn on up through next-door Peabody (once one of the world's great leather producers with over 100 tanneries) to the former ship-building Newburyport, alternating with the high-income enclaves of Marblehead with its yachts and Beverly with its estates, and artsy Rockport. Moviegoers will recognize the fishing town of Gloucester as the homeport of the *Andrea Gail*, the 72-foot swordfishing boat whose tragic plight was dramatized in the novel and subsequent film, *The Perfect Storm*. Although the ports were hard hit by overfishing of mackerel and herring in the 1970s and cod in the 1990s, pleasure boating surged in the past decade. Lynn is the largest city and its General Electric jet engine plant is the largest employer, though with far fewer jobs than during the defense buildup of the 1980s and with payrolls threatened by offset deals to produce some engines in the countries purchasing them.

The 6th Congressional District includes the North Shore from Saugus and Lynn northward, plus towns and cities inland west to Burlington. Its high-income Yankee towns were historically liberal Republican, while Lynn, Salem, Peabody and the Merrimack mill towns are still Irish working-class Democratic. Gloucester fishermen struggle with depleted stocks and increased federal controls. The 6th has been a Democratic district on balance since the 1960s, but in the 1980s and in the early 1990s only marginally so. While this district is the site of the original gerrymander—named after Elbridge Gerry—the current 6th District boundaries are hardly grotesque by current national standards; it was barely changed by 2002 redistricting.

The congressman from the 6th District is John Tierney, a Democrat elected in 1996. Tierney grew up in Salem in modest circumstances; he worked his way through Salem State College and Suffolk University Law School as a janitor on the night shift and clerk in a Boston law firm. For nearly 20 years, he practiced law in Salem. In 1994, he spied a political opening and ran for Congress. The incumbent, Peter Torkildsen, was a Republican elected in 1992 by beating veteran Democrat Nicholas Mavroulas, who had been indicted for tax evasion and bribery; the district had been safely Democratic since liberal Michael Harrington won a special election in 1969. But in a Republican year, Torkildsen won 51%–47%. In 1996, Tierney ran again. His ads, along with the AFL-CIO's, assailed Newt Gingrich and Republican Medicare "cuts." He called for greater educational opportunities, health care insurance for children, aid to college students and criticized Torkildsen for not bringing enough defense dollars to the district. Torkildsen raised and spent $1.1 million, while keeping his promise to accept no PAC money. Tierney held his spending—$776,000 in total—mostly until the end. The result was one of the closest races in the country. Tierney led narrowly in initial returns; after several recounts, which stretched into December, he won by 371 votes.

In the House, Tierney has been a solid ally of the unions on Education and the Workforce Committee and has been a consistent liberal in his votes. He has been a leader among Democrats seeking to reduce prescription-drug costs for senior citizens, and he conducted a study showing that seniors in his district pay more than twice what they pay in other countries; the House defeated his amendment to shift $74 million from national missile defense to health programs. But he has worked with Republicans to get appropriations for the district, and he joined with Massachusetts colleague Bill Delahunt and New Jersey Republican Jim Saxton to support a ban on big fishing trawlers from Georges Bank. Tierney is well-connected to Minority Leader Nancy Pelosi: His chief of staff is her daughter, Christine Pelosi.

Torkildsen challenged him in a rubber match in 1998, but even as Republican Governor Paul Cellucci easily carried the district, Tierney won 55%–42%. He has faced token opposition since then.

SEVENTH DISTRICT

Rep. Edward Markey (D)

Elected 1976, 14th term; b. July 11, 1946, Malden; home, Malden; Boston Col., B.A. 1968, J.D. 1972; Catholic; married (Susan Blumenthal).

Military Career: Army Reserves, 1968–73.

Elected Office: MA House of Reps., 1973–76.

DC Office: 2108 RHOB 20515, 202-225-2836; Fax: 202-226-0092; Web site: www.house.gov/markey.

District Offices: Framingham, 508-875-2900; Medford, 781-396-2900.

Committees: *Energy & Commerce* (3d of 26 D): Commerce, Trade & Consumer Protection; Energy & Air Quality; Telecommunications & The Internet (RMM). *Resources* (20th of 24 D). *Select Committee on Homeland Security* (4th of 23 D): Infrastructure & Border Security; Intelligence & Counterterrorism.

Group Ratings

	ADA	ACLU	AFS	LCV	CON	ITIC	NTU	COC	ACU	NTLC	CHC
2002	100	87	100	88	90	38	23	30	4	0	0
2001	100	—	100	100	—	—	11	36	4	—	—

National Journal Ratings

	2001 LIB —	2001 CONS		2002 LIB —	2002 CONS
Economic	95% —	0%		86% —	12%
Social	79% —	21%		84% —	8%
Foreign	84% —	16%		84% —	14%

Key Votes of the 107th Congress

1. Approve Bush Tax Cuts	N	5. Faith-Based Charities		9. Trade Promotion Authority	N
2. Limit Patients' Bill of Rights	N	6. Bar Gays in the Boy Scouts	N	10. Bar Funds for Intl. Court	N
3. Campaign Finance Reform	Y	7. Ban Partial-Birth Abortion	N	11. Authorize Force in Iraq	Y
4. Ban ANWR Development	Y	8. Arm Commercial Pilots	N	12. Deny Home. Sec. Dept. Union	N

Election Results

2002 general	Edward Markey (D)	.... unopposed		($705,775)
2002 primary	Edward Markey (D)	 73,014	(85%)	
	James Hall (D)	 12,964	(15%)	
2000 general	Edward Markey (D)	.... unopposed		($584,630)

Prior Winning Percentages: 1998 (71%); 1996 (70%); 1994 (64%); 1992 (62%); 1990 (100%); 1988 (100%); 1986 (100%); 1984 (71%); 1982 (78%); 1980 (100%); 1978 (85%); 1976 (77%)

The People		**Race/Ethnic Origin**	**Ancestry**	
Area size:	188 sq. mi.	83.5% White	Irish: 18.5%	Italian: 16.9%
Urban population:	99.5%	3.3% Black	English: 7.5%	
Rural population:	0.5%	5.7% Asian	**2000 Presidential Vote**	
Pop. 2000:	634,287	0.1% Native Am.	Gore (D) 181,417	(64%)
Median income:	$56,110	0.0% Hawaiian	Bush (R) 82,250	(29%)
Poverty status:	6.7%	1.9% Two+ races	Other 20,891	(7%)
Military veterans:	10.5%	0.5% Other	**Cook Partisan Voting Index:** D + 19	
		4.8% Hispanic Origin		

Occupation	Blue collar: 14.3%	White collar: 72.9%	Gray collar: 12.8%

The Yankee Protestants and Irish Catholics who settled Massachusetts arrived by boat, the Yankees to a cold stony land with a few Indians, the Irish to a crowded city with Yankees who seemed even less welcoming. The Yankees whose ancestors once farmed the soil had, by the early 20th century, founded suburbs filled with solid brick and white frame houses, furnished in Early American furniture. As the years went on, their local public schools were emptied as young people with children moved out, and attendance at Protestant churches went down. The Irish, for decades heavily concentrated in the crowded wards of Boston, started moving out into the Yankee suburbs 50 years ago. There were other ethnic groups here and there (Jews, Italians, French-Canadians) but the major conflict—fought out in neighborhood playgrounds, in school committee meetings and not least in political campaigns—was between Protestant Yankee Republicans and Catholic Irish Democrats.

The 7th Congressional District is made up of Boston's northern and western suburbs, where vestiges of this conflict can still be seen. Geographically, it forms an arc around Boston, starting with the clapboard beach towns of Winthrop and Revere just beyond Logan Airport, going north as far as working-class Woburn (where Charles Goodyear developed the art of vulcanizing rubber) and west as far as modest-income Natick and Framingham. Framingham is home to many Brazilian immigrants who began arriving after World War II, when Boston-based mining companies began extracting mica from an area near the Brazilian city of Governador Valadares. The 7th also includes the university towns of Medford, home of Tufts University, and Waltham, home of Brandeis University, the patriot town of Lexington and high-income Lincoln and Weston. Many of these towns were Yankee Republican through the 1950s, but by the late 1960s they were solidly Democratic; the high-tech suburbs trended Republican again in the 1980s but swung against Republicans in the 1990s. The highest income areas seem to run across the grain of their ethnic experience: Weston, with many Catholics, often votes Republican, though it went 50%–43% for Al Gore in 2000. Lincoln has been liberal Democratic since it voted for George McGovern in 1972; it voted 60%–29% for Gore in 2000. But in state politics, the suburbanites of the 7th District have been less liberal: This district was even in the gubernatorial elections of 1998 and 2002: Republican Mitt Romney won 11 of the district's 19 towns in 2002.

The congressman in the 7th District is Edward Markey, elected in 1976 at age 30, and now one of the most powerful Democrats in the House. He grew up in Malden, where his father was a milkman; he went to Malden Catholic High, Boston College and Boston College law school, then immediately to the state House, at 26. In 1976, he ran for the House and won a 12-candidate primary with 22% of the vote; he had never been to Washington. Markey first made a name as a fierce opponent of nuclear power. In 1983, he was the leading political crusader for the nuclear freeze.

Seniority and events put Markey in position to be a serious legislator, and he has long since become one of the House's most legislatively productive and creative members. With help from Speaker Tip O'Neill, he got on the Commerce Committee; impressed by the high-tech boom around Route 128, he joined the old Communications Subcommittee early. Then, after only eight years in the House, he became chairman of the Energy Conservation and Power Subcommittee; after the 1986 election, with help from Chairman John Dingell, who liked aggressive and loyal younger Democrats, Markey became chairman of the Telecommunications Subcommittee. This is one of the plum positions in the House, with fabulous possibilities for campaign fundraising, and with subject matter that is intellectually more demanding (and, in lobbying terms, more fiercely contested) than almost anything else in Congress. Markey raised $686,000 in the 2002 cycle and could easily raise four times that if he wanted.

Markey has been a major shaper of public policy, often working with Republicans, often coming up with original initiatives, knowledgeable about the workings of these industries and inclined often toward deregulation, but also casting himself as the defender of consumers. He combined his penchant for regulation with political shrewdness to produce the 1992 cable TV reregulation bill on which both houses overrode President Bush's veto—the only bill passed over his veto in his four-year term. Markey's influence was not greatly reduced when he became ranking minority member; bills in these areas are hard to pass without bipartisan consensus, and he was in a key position to create or withhold it. He was a major player in the passage of the landmark Telecommunications Act of 1996. Markey and then-Commerce Chairman Tom Bliley passed through the House a bill to demonopolize the satellite communications industry, which became law in March 2000. Markey and Republican Mike Oxley moved a bill to stop stock exchanges from denominating prices in 1/8s and to use dollars and cents instead; when it passed, the exchanges decided to do this on their own.

On the major telecom issue before the 107th Congress, Markey was less successful. He opposed the Tauzin-Dingell bill to revise the 1996 act by allowing the Bell phone companies—Verizon, SBC, BellSouth and Qwest—to offer broadband services without opening up their lines to competitors, including the CLECs which came into existence after the 1996 law and first soared and then thudded on the stock market. "We do not have a broadband crisis in America," Markey said, saying that 75% to 80% of Americans already have gotten access to broadband since 1996. He tried to defeat Tauzin-Dingell in committee and, with Utah Republican Rep. Chris Cannon, on the floor, but was defeated in February 2002 when a motion to move the previous question to recommit the bill to committee with instructions was defeated 256–173—the first time such a parliamentary motion had been rejected since 1910. Markey has continued to press for digital television, seeking to force the FCC to require cable companies to carry digital TV before the required date of 2007. He has also pressed for more auctions of currently government-owned spectrum, to allow the emergence of new wireless technologies that he says will boost the economy, with revenues to go into a trust fund to encourage digital TV and advanced wireless services. These are ongoing fights.

Markey has continued to seek tougher regulation of nuclear power plants. In October 2001, he got committee Republicans to go along with his proposal to require the Nuclear Regulatory Commission to force plant owners to come up with plans to defend their plants against terrorist attacks. In November 2001, he sponsored a bill to require that guards at nuclear plants be federal employees; in a March 2002 report, he pointed out that the NRC doesn't require plant guards to be U.S. citizens and limits its background criminal checks to the U.S. In another report, he pointed out that the number of security guards at nuclear facilities declined 40% between 1992 and 2001. Markey has a gift for memorable phrases. "We have a 'loose nuke' problem right here at home," he said in May 2002, because some 1,500 types of radioactive material had been lost in five years and only half traced down; he estimated that the loose material, put together, could create a "dirty bomb." He passed an amendment quadrupling the amount of potassium iodide provided to state and local authorities to protect citizens in case of nuclear accident. He opposed the transfer of nuclear waste to Yucca Mountain in Nevada and said that other states had dealt Nevada the "nuclear queen of spades." In June 2002, he called for a permanent end to the testing of nuclear weapons and in August 2002, he criticized the Bush administration for continuing the Clinton administration's policy of providing support for North Korea's light water reactor.

Other Markey causes include financial privacy—he and Republican Rep. Joe Barton got a provision into the financial services deregulation—and demonopolizing the electric power industry. His moves to raise the miles per gallon standard for automobiles and SUVs were defeated by wide margins in committee and on the floor. He opposes drilling in the Arctic National Wildlife Reserve and sponsored a bill to designate the ANWR coastal area as wilderness. In May 2002, he presented a report showing that eight people have died and 58 people suffered brain injuries on roller coasters and amusement park rides; he wants Consumer Product Safety Commission regulation and an end to the "roller coaster arms race."

In 2001, Markey chose to remain ranking Democrat on the Telecommunications Subcommittee rather than become ranking Democrat on the full Resources Committee—an indication of the importance of this subcommittee. Now the dean of the Massachusetts delegation, he has been reelected easily every two years.

EIGHTH DISTRICT

Rep. Michael Capuano (D)

Elected 1998, 3d term; b. Jan. 9, 1952, Somerville; home, Somerville; Dartmouth Col., B.A. 1973, Boston Col., J.D. 1977; Catholic; married (Barbara).

Elected Office: Somerville Alderman Ward 5, 1977–79; Somerville Alderman-At-Large, 1985–89; Somerville Mayor, 1989–98.

Professional Career: Chief Legal Cnsl., MA Legislature Taxation Cmte., 1978–84; Practicing atty., 1984–90.

DC Office: 1232 LHOB 20515, 202-225-5111; Fax: 202-225-9322; Web site: www.house.gov/capuano.

District Office: Cambridge, 617-621-8628.

Committees: *Financial Services* (17th of 32 D): Capital Markets, Insurance & Government Sponsored Enterprises; Housing & Community Opportunity. *Transportation & Infrastructure* (27th of 34 D): Aviation; Highways, Transit & Pipelines.

Group Ratings

	ADA	ACLU	AFS	LCV	CON	ITIC	NTU	COC	ACU	NTLC	CHC
2002	95	93	100	100	88	38	30	28	4	0	0
2001	95	—	100	93	—	—	13	32	4	—	—

National Journal Ratings

	2001 LIB	—	2001 CONS		2002 LIB	—	2002 CONS
Economic	95%	—	0%		81%	—	18%
Social	79%	—	21%		84%	—	8%
Foreign	80%	—	20%		84%	—	14%

Key Votes of the 107th Congress

1. Approve Bush Tax Cuts	N	5. Faith-Based Charities	N	9. Trade Promotion Authority	N
2. Limit Patients' Bill of Rights	N	6. Bar Gays in the Boy Scouts	N	10. Bar Funds for Intl. Court	N
3. Campaign Finance Reform	Y	7. Ban Partial-Birth Abortion	N	11. Authorize Force in Iraq	N
4. Ban ANWR Development	Y	8. Arm Commercial Pilots	N	12. Deny Home. Sec. Dept. Union	N

Election Results

2002 general	Michael Capuano (D)	unopposed	($448,944)
2002 primary	Michael Capuano (D)	unopposed	
2000 general	Michael Capuano (D)	unopposed	($387,340)

Prior Winning Percentages: 1998 (82%)

The People		Race/Ethnic Origin	Ancestry	
Area size:	92 sq. mi.	48.9% White	Irish: 9.9%	Italian: 7.3%
Urban population:	100.0%	21.9% Black	West Indian: 5.2%	
Rural population:	0.0%	8.1% Asian	**2000 Presidential Vote**	
Pop. 2000:	634,835	0.2% Native Am.	Gore (D) 142,500	(73%)
Median income:	$39,300	0.1% Hawaiian	Bush (R) 28,903	(15%)
Poverty status:	19.9%	3.5% Two+ races	Other 23,374	(12%)
Military veterans:	5.5%	1.5% Other	**Cook Partisan Voting Index:** D +33	
		15.9% Hispanic Origin		

Occupation	Blue collar: 12.4%	White collar: 70.6%	Gray collar: 17.0%

The "Hub of the Solar System" is what the elder Oliver Wendell Holmes called the Massachusetts State House in the 19th century, though over time, his statement has come to be remembered as referring to Boston as the "Hub of the Universe." Either way, this most political of cities often has been the focal point of essential moments in American history. These streets, originally laid out as 17th Century cowpaths, are where Samuel Adams and Paul Revere plotted revolution, where the abolitionist movement helped ignite the Civil War and are the sites of rallies and headquarters of the various Kennedy campaigns. Today's Boston is a different city from the Boston of John Kennedy's time. Boston then was a gray city with no new buildings and dust on every windowsill; the sky was dark with pollution and the air was thick with ancient Yankee and Irish animosity. The old office buildings were full of Yankees seeking safe investments for their antique family fortunes; the State House and City Hall were full of Irishmen, scampering after good patronage jobs and regaling each other with political battle stories. Today that Boston is mostly gone. The new skyscrapers are full of venture capitalists, lawyers and management consultants, many working for high-tech companies radiating from Cambridge out into the countryside. Most of Boston's neighborhoods have changed. Minorities and young singles increasingly populate the central city. The city's population is down from 801,000 in 1950 to 589,000 in 2000, though the latest figure is an increase of 15,000 from 1990; more than 80% of the metropolitan area is in the suburbs.

A long generation ago, students from suburbs across the country who were exploring Boston from their dormitories and campuses felt they were pawing through the living remnants of 1920s America, a quaint place where people called traffic circles "rotaries" and milk shakes "frappes." Massachusetts has since changed, and nowhere more than in Cambridge. As universities and high tech have become driving forces of economic growth, Cambridge has gone glitzy, with trendy restaurants and high-priced hotels, boutiques and upscale condominiums. Greater Boston may well have the heaviest concentration of graduate students and post-graduate hangers-on of any major city, and this graduate student proletariat's world is centered on Cambridge, with outposts in lower-income Somerville, Boston's Back Bay, and Allston and Brighton near the Harvard Business School. Boston will gain the political spotlight when Democrats hold their national convention at the Fleet Center the last week of July 2004. Local officials promise to have nearly completed the Big Dig reconstruction of the ugly Central Artery, the North-South expressway that for decades divided much of the city but has been moved underground, though with huge cost over-runs driving the bill over $14 billion.

These communities are part of Massachusetts's 8th Congressional District, a district with great historic sites, from the Paul Revere house in the North End to the frigate *U.S.S. Constitution* in the Charlestown docks. The district, with MIT and the software concentration in Cambridge's once downscale Lechmere Square, is one of the high-tech capitals of America. The 8th includes all of Cambridge, Somerville and Chelsea and many Boston neighborhoods—East Boston around Logan Airport, Brighton and the Back Bay, Fenway, Mattapan, Mission Hill, the South End. It shares Hyde Park, Roxbury, Dorchester and Jamaica Plain with the neighboring 9th District. For the first time in its history, whites are a minority of Boston's population. As they replace the Irish and Italians, Hispanics have caused a population boom in low-income Chelsea and in Dorchester, which annually celebrates one of the nation's largest Caribbean festivals. This is by far the most Democratic district in Massachusetts, and one of the nation's most reliable.

The congressman from the 8th District is Michael Capuano, the winner of a 10-candidate primary in 1998. It could be said that over the last 50-odd years this district has been represented alternately by townies and Kennedys: James Michael Curley, the scampish five-term mayor of Boston and one-term governor; followed by John F. Kennedy in 1946, then from 1952, Tip O'Neill, the most successful House speaker of this half-century; succeeded on his retirement in 1986 by Joe Kennedy; and now Capuano. He was born and raised in Somerville; his paternal grandfather emigrated from Italy, and his father was the first Italian-American elected official in Somerville; his mother is the granddaughter of Irish immigrants. Capuano graduated from Dartmouth and Boston College Law School. He returned to Somerville to raise his family, practice law and get into politics. By day, he worked for the legislature's Joint Committee on Taxation and practiced law; in off-hours, he served as alderman in the 5th Ward, like his father before him. He was elected alderman-at-large from 1985–89, then won election five times as the city's mayor. For decades an Irish and Italian town, Somerville now attracts many grad students and yuppies. Capuano seems to have been the right politician for this mix, with deep Somerville roots and a penchant for innovation and reform. So he had a solid base to run for the 8th District seat in 1998 when Joe Kennedy announced that he wouldn't seek re-election.

There was no lack of competitors for the Democratic nomination to determine who would represent this safe Democratic seat. Six were far out on the left wing of the Democratic Party, and between them won 49% of the votes. The four more moderate candidates split the remaining 51%, and Capuano got a near-majority of that. His 23% total led the runner-up, former Boston Mayor (1983–93) Ray Flynn, who had 17%.

Capuano is still well to the left on the national political spectrum: For gay marriage, against the partial-birth abortion ban and opposed to the flag-burning amendment. On the Budget Committee, he challenged the Bush administration's budget calculations justifying its tax cut. Reflecting the interests of his local community, he criticized Bush's decision to ban federal funding for most research on embryonic stem cells and he worried that it will force the biomedical industry out of America.

Capuano received unwanted publicity when a *Vanity Fair* article pictured him drinking and singing with colleagues and young female interns in a private room of a restaurant near the Capitol two days after the September 11 terror attacks. Capuano said that the Democratic members met every Thursday to "blow off steam," and that they were singing patriotic songs with the women who had introduced themselves. He acknowledged that his wife of 27 years was not thrilled by the magazine article. That should be his biggest concern, because in this district Capuano has little reason to worry about Republicans.

NINTH DISTRICT

Rep. Stephen Lynch (D)

Elected Oct. 2001, 1st term; b. Mar. 31, 1955, Boston; home, South Boston; Wentworth Inst., B.S. 1988, Boston Col. Schl. of Law, J.D. 1991, Harvard U. JFK Schl. of Gov., M.A. 1998; Catholic; married (Margaret).

Elected Office: MA House of Reps., 1994–96; MA Senate, 1996–01.

Professional Career: Structural ironworker, 1973–91; Practicing atty., 1991–01.

DC Office: 319 CHOB 20515, 202-225-8273; Fax: 202-225-3984; Web site: www.house.gov/lynch/.

District Office: Boston, 617-428-2000.

Committees: *Financial Services* (28th of 32 D): Capital Markets, Insurance & Government Sponsored Enterprises; Housing & Community Opportunity; Oversight & Investigations. *Government Reform* (13th of 19 D): National Security, Emerging Threats & Intl. Relations; Technology, Information Policy, Intergovernmental Relations & Census.

Group Ratings (Only Served Partial Term)

	ADA	ACLU	AFS	LCV	CON	ITIC	NTU	COC	ACU	NTLC	CHC
2002	90	50	100	100	—	33	23	40	13	3	33
2001	—	—	100	100	—	—	—	44	—	—	—

National Journal Ratings (Only Served Partial Term)

	2001 LIB —	2001 CONS	2002 LIB —	2002 CONS
Economic	* —	*	92% —	7%
Social	* —	*	58% —	41%
Foreign	* —	*	71% —	29%

Key Votes of the 107th Congress (Only Served Partial Term)

1. Approve Bush Tax Cuts	*	5. Faith-Based Charities	*	9. Trade Promotion Authority	N
2. Limit Patients' Bill of Rights	*	6. Bar Gays in the Boy Scouts	*	10. Bar Funds for Intl. Court	Y
3. Campaign Finance Reform	Y	7. Ban Partial-Birth Abortion	Y	11. Authorize Force in Iraq	Y
4. Ban ANWR Development	*	8. Arm Commercial Pilots	Y	12. Deny Home. Sec. Dept. Union	N

Election Results

2002 general	Stephen Lynch (D)	unopposed		($2,386,568)
2002 primary	Stephen Lynch (D)	69,244	(81%)	
	William Ferguson (D)	16,643	(19%)	
2001 special	Stephen Lynch (D)	44,943	(66%)	($1,887,960)
	Jo Ann Sprague (R)	22,645	(33%)	($173,565)
2001 spec. prim.	Stephen Lynch (D)	44,105	(39%)	
	Cheryl Jacques (D)	32,933	(29%)	
	Brian Joyce (D)	16,818	(15%)	
	Marc Pacheco (D)	15,009	(13%)	

The People		Race/Ethnic Origin	Ancestry	
Area size:	319 sq. mi.	79.3% White	Irish: 23.2%	Italian: 10.3%
Urban population:	98.4%	8.1% Black	English: 7.0%	
Rural population:	1.6%	3.7% Asian	**2000 Presidential Vote**	
Pop. 2000:	634,062	0.2% Native Am.	Gore (D) 167,059	(60%)
Median income:	$55,407	0.0% Hawaiian	Bush (R) 93,529	(33%)
Poverty status:	7.5%	2.4% Two+ races	Other 19,051	(7%)
Military veterans:	11.6%	1.8% Other	**Cook Partisan Voting Index:** D +14	
		4.6% Hispanic Origin		

Occupation	Blue collar: 17.3%	White collar: 68.9%	Gray collar: 13.7%

The Irish remain the dominant political tribe in Boston and in Massachusetts, though even in South Boston, long the center of Irish Boston, vestiges of the old Irish neighborhoods are starting to gentrify. But Southie's influence endures in the memory of two Irish Democrats who represented the area for all but two years from the Great Depression to the start of the 21st century. The first was John McCormack, an old-style backroom dealmaker who served as House Speaker during the 1960s, when he arguably had passed his political prime; then came Joe Moakley, a close pal of Tip O'Neill, who got his former seat on the Rules Committee and chaired the panel before Democrats lost their House majority.

The 9th Congressional District, historically anchored in Boston, has followed the move of the Irish to the suburbs. Today, less than one-third of its residents are in Boston, mostly in still-Irish areas of South Boston, Hyde Park (shared with the 8th) and West Roxbury; it also includes much of Beacon Hill, including the gold-domed State House facing Boston Common. From there, the 9th heads west to comfortable suburbs of Needham and Medfield and southeast to Braintree, ancestral home of the presidential Adamses, and Brockton, the old shoe manufacturing town, and Bridgewater. Ethnically, it is the nation's second-most heavily Irish congressional district (working-class Southie is home to an annual St. Patrick's Day parade, preceded by a political breakfast/roast that is a must-attend for state politicians). Only the neighboring 10th District has more residents of Irish ancestry—further evidence of the Irish move out of Boston to the far south suburbs.

The congressman from the 9th District is Stephen Lynch, who won a special election in October 2001 to replace Joe Moakley, who had served since 1973 and was beloved by many House Democrats as a link between the party's old and new generations. Lynch came from Boston's housing projects and took pride in succeeding by the old ethnic codes of hard work, family loyalty and personal determination. After graduating from South Boston High School, he joined his father in working full-time as an ironworker while attending Wentworth Institute; eventually, he became the youngest president ever of the 2,000-member Local 7 of the Ironworkers union. After a fall on the job cut short his work on the iron, he graduated from Boston College Law School and opened a legal practice representing working people. In 1994, he was elected to the state House. Fourteen months later, he won a special election for a seat in the state Senate, where he sponsored an increase in the state's minimum wage.

Lynch built a large base in South Boston and had strong union ties, advantages that led him to seek the 9th District seat when Moakley announced in February 2001 that he would not seek reelection; Moakley died of leukemia at the Bethesda Naval Hospital in May 2001. Lynch was one of several Democrats who had expressed interest in the race. The most prominent, however, was Max Kennedy, son of Robert and Ethel Kennedy, but his campaign never gathered any traction. When Kennedy bowed out in June from what became the special election, Lynch became the front-runner. He stumbled following the *Boston Globe*'s revelations of his student loan defaults years earlier, plus a tax lien that was resolved in 1998; he also had been twice arrested two decades earlier, once for striking an anti-American student demonstrator and the other for smoking marijuana at a concert. Three other state senators opposed Lynch: Cheryl Jacques, Brian Joyce, and Marc Pacheco. The strongest foe was Jacques, who is openly gay and had support from EMILY's List and other national feminist groups, which criticized Lynch's anti-abortion views. But her switch to opposing capital punishment stirred controversy. Joyce, who dropped his earlier opposition to abortion, was the most prolific fundraiser of the four; he sought to rally suburban support against Lynch, who was perceived as the South Boston candidate. Pacheco vied with Jacques for the liberal vote, and was endorsed by teachers' unions. Citing her as "the most principled progressive in the race," the *Globe* endorsed Jacques. Moakley's two brothers, however, endorsed Lynch.

Lynch got favorable press coverage in the final days of the campaign from an emotional ad that described how he gave part of his liver months earlier to his ailing brother-in-law. Coincidentally, Lynch was hospitalized several days before the primary because of intense pain caused by complications from his surgery. On the morning of the September 11 primary, Lynch and others thought that the terror attacks—two of the hijacked airplanes had taken off from Boston—would postpone the voting, but Governor Jane Swift asked voters to stare down fear and the voter turnout was higher than expected. Lynch won with 39%, a comfortable margin ahead of Jacques, who had 29%. He credited his large grass-roots organization, which he claimed included 4,000 volunteers. In the anti-climactic general election five weeks later, Lynch defeated another state senator, Jo Ann Sprague. Republican strategists had hoped that her pro-choice views on abortion might give them a chance against Lynch, but polls showed otherwise and the national party gave Sprague little support. Lynch won 66%–33%. His swearing-in was delayed several days because the anthrax scare had closed the Capitol.

Given the circumstances of his election, Lynch not surprisingly turned his attention to security, both at the nation's airports and in the war on terrorism. He also visited each post office in his district to monitor anthrax protection measures. He was one of three Massachusetts House members to vote for the Iraq war resolution. On a personal concern, Lynch filed a bill to streamline research on liver disease at the National Institutes of Health.

Lynch won a full term with no difficulty in 2002. But shortly after the election, he drew unpleasant notice in his home base after University of Massachusetts President William Bulger, the former state Senate President and a favorite son of Southie, was required to appear before the House Government Reform Committee in December. The hearing was part of a congressional inquiry into Bulger's fugitive brother's relationship with the FBI; Lynch voted to deny Bulger's request to close or postpone the hearing. In a well-publicized letter to a local newspaper, Bulger's son Christopher, who was defeated by Lynch in a 1996 bid to succeed his father in the state Senate, harshly attacked Lynch for the vote and for not defending his father.

TENTH DISTRICT

Rep. Bill Delahunt (D)

Elected 1996, 4th term; b. July 18, 1941, Quincy; home, Quincy; Middlebury Col., B.A. 1963, Boston Col., J.D. 1967; Catholic; divorced.

Military Career: Coast Guard, 1963; Coast Guard Reserves, 1963–71.

Elected Office: Quincy City Cncl., 1971; MA House of Reps., 1972–75.

Professional Career: Practicing atty., 1967–75; Asst. Clerk, Norfolk Superior Court, 1969–71; Norfolk Cnty. Dist. Atty., 1975–96.

DC Office: 1317 LHOB 20515, 202-225-3111; Fax: 202-225-5658; Web site: www.house.gov/delahunt.

District Offices: Hyannis, 508-771-0666; Quincy, 617-770-3700.

Committees: *International Relations* (11th of 23 D): Europe; Western Hemisphere. *Judiciary* (11th of 16 D): Commercial & Administrative Law; Courts, the Internet & Intellectual Property.

Group Ratings

	ADA	ACLU	AFS	LCV	CON	ITIC	NTU	COC	ACU	NTLC	CHC
2002	90	85	100	75	81	38	26	39	0	0	0
2001	95	—	100	100	—	—	12	26	4	—	—

National Journal Ratings

	2001 LIB —	2001 CONS	2002 LIB —	2002 CONS
Economic	95%	0%	81%	18%
Social	90%	0%	83%	16%
Foreign	85%	16%	87%	10%

Key Votes of the 107th Congress

1. Approve Bush Tax Cuts	N	5. Faith-Based Charities	N
2. Limit Patients' Bill of Rights	N	6. Bar Gays in the Boy Scouts	N
3. Campaign Finance Reform	Y	7. Ban Partial-Birth Abortion	N
4. Ban ANWR Development	Y	8. Arm Commercial Pilots	*

9. Trade Promotion Authority	N
10. Bar Funds for Intl. Court	N
11. Authorize Force in Iraq	N
12. Deny Home. Sec. Dept. Union	N

Election Results

2002 general	Bill Delahunt (D)	179,238	(69%)	($266,025)
	Luiz Gonzaga (R)	79,624	(31%)	($55,428)
2002 primary	Bill Delahunt (D) .... unopposed			
2000 general	Bill Delahunt (D)	234,675	(74%)	($231,526)
	Eric V. Bleicken (R)	81,192	(26%)	($1,146)

Prior Winning Percentages: 1998 (70%); 1996 (54%)

The People		Race/Ethnic Origin	Ancestry	
Area size:	2,969 sq. mi.	92.2% White	Irish: 23.9%	English: 11.9%
Urban population:	92.2%	1.5% Black	Italian: 9.9%	
Rural population:	7.8%	2.7% Asian	**2000 Presidential Vote**	
Pop. 2000:	635,901	0.3% Native Am.	Gore (D)..............175,426	(54%)
Median income:	$51,928	0.0% Hawaiian	Bush (R)..............124,956	(39%)
Poverty status:	5.9%	1.3% Two+ races	Other...................22,722	(7%)
Military veterans:	15.1%	0.6% Other	**Cook Partisan Voting Index:** D + 8	
		1.3% Hispanic Origin		

Occupation	Blue collar: 18.1%	White collar: 66.7%	Gray collar: 15.2%

The South Shore of Massachusetts Bay, from Boston southward to Plymouth and then down Cape Cod (there is a lot of dispute about which way is up and down on the Cape), is Massachusetts's oldest-settled territory. The Pilgrims landed here at Plymouth Rock in 1620; this stony land was farmed by John Adams's father, who was anything but the aristocrat some later members of the Adams family would have you believe. Daniel Webster lived in the South Shore town of Marshfield, today a high-income suburb of Boston far out on the usually clogged Southeast Expressway. Joseph P. Kennedy used to summer with his young family on Nantasket Beach in Hull, before moving out of Massachusetts when the Yankees wouldn't let them into their beach club in Cohasset in the 1920s; but the Kennedys continue to summer at their Hyannis Port compound on the Cape. Provincetown, at the tip of the Cape, is still a fishing port, and also one of the major gay vacation areas in the country; the islands of Martha's Vineyard and Nantucket, rich whaling ports in the early 19th century, are now favored summer resorts for the trendy liberal rich of New York and Washington. Half the nation's cranberry growers are clustered among the bogs along Cape Cod Bay. But the Cape is also filled increasingly with retirees and, to the dismay of some, is the fastest-growing part of Massachusetts. The Cape's Barnstable County grew 19% in the 1990s, almost four times the state average.

The 10th Congressional District follows the South Shore from Quincy (pronounced *quin-zee*) to the Cape. It juts inland almost, but not quite to Brockton, and includes Martha's Vineyard and Nantucket. The South Shore and the Cape were once exclusively Protestant and Yankee, but in the Massachusetts way they have changed over the years, with Irish and Italian surnames as common as Yankee ones (this is the nation's most heavily Irish congressional district), and the descendants of Portuguese-Azorean fishermen have fanned out into the countryside. Trendy liberal politics, well established on the Vineyard and Nantucket, have spread inland as well. The South Shore is generally Democratic territory, but in 2002 Republican Mitt Romney carried Plymouth and Weymouth in the gubernatorial election –they are two of the district's three South Shore population centers.

The congressman from the 10th District is William Delahunt, a Democrat elected in 1996. Delahunt is a lifelong resident of Quincy at the northern tip of the district, who graduated from Middlebury College and Boston College Law School and served in the Coast Guard. He practiced law and was elected to the Quincy Council. In 1972, he was elected to the state House; Governor Michael Dukakis in 1975 appointed him district attorney of Norfolk County, a job that Delahunt held for two decades. He was prompted to run for the House in 1996 when 24-year incumbent Gerry Studds retired. Delahunt had serious primary competition from former state Representative Philip Johnston and self-financed environmentalist Ian Bowles. The initial results showed 38% each for Delahunt and Johnston, with Johnston ahead by 266 votes; a recount declared Johnston still ahead by 175 votes. But Delahunt sued, and on October 4, a judge ruled that more than 900 punch card votes in Weymouth had not been properly tabulated. In shades of another election challenge four years later, the judge ordered a recount of every ballot with an indentation, dimple or other mark: Only in this district and in 14 counties in Texas had dimpled chads ever been counted as votes in the U.S. until the Broward, Palm Beach and Miami-Dade County canvassing boards started counting them in November 2000. On October 10, Delahunt was declared the winner by 108 votes, even as Johnston was being hailed at a Quincy rally by Ted Kennedy and Hillary Rodham Clinton. (Subsequently, Massachusetts eliminated punch-card voting, and Delahunt voiced support for hand recounts of punch cards elsewhere). Johnston called the result a "travesty," and Delahunt had less than a month to campaign for the general against conservative state House Minority Leader Edward Teague, who had won the Republican primary. Both ran million-dollar campaigns, but Teague had been running ads against Johnston. Eight years earlier, George Bush carried this district over Michael Dukakis, but reaction here to the new Republican majority in the House was hostile; Delahunt won 54%–42%.

Delahunt has been an active legislator, and has kept pledge to wear Cape Cod ties in the House and hand them out to colleagues of both parties. As the father of an adopted daughter who escaped Vietnam in the 1975 Operation Babylift, he has written laws to ease international adoptions. His positions on abortion are part of Massachusetts's move to the left: In 1974 as a state legislator he called *Roe v. Wade* "a tragic decision," but he switched to a pro-abortion rights position before running for the House and has voted against the partial-birth abortion ban. His experience with contested elections later made him an enthusiast for abolishing the Electoral College. On the Judiciary Committee during the Clinton impeachment, he was one of the few members who sat down in bipartisan breakfasts to discuss procedures. But he ended up siding completely with impeachment opponents. He took the lead in framing a Democratic motion to censure Clinton and protested bitterly when Judiciary Chairman Henry Hyde would not allow it to be heard. A former state prosecutor, Delahunt has also explored further steps to rein in the authority of federal prosecutors and to protect defendants' rights. He filed the Innocence Protection Act with Illinois Rep. Ray LaHood, and it was cosponsored by a majority of members in the 107th Congress; it includes federal funding to the states for DNA testing of the accused. On the International Relations Committee, he worked with North Carolina Rep. Cass Ballenger to make several visits with Venezuela president Hugo Chavez to encourage cooperation between the two nations, and he criticized the Bush administration's handling of the failed coup in Caracas in April 2002.

Delahunt also has worked on local projects, including the Cape Cod land bank, the Salt Pond visitors' center at the National Seashore entry in Eastham, and conversion of the former Camp Edwards National Guard training site to a federal wildlife refuge. He wrote a law requiring large ships entering Massachusetts' waters to notify the Coast Guard, so they could be warned away from endangered right whales.

Delahunt has easily won his re-election bids—no need to count dimpled chads. Even with the Cape's population growth, it's not likely to give much hope for a Republican revival. On Capitol Hill, he is the fourth tenant in a long-running apartment rental shared by Senators Chuck Schumer and Richard Durbin and Representative George Miller. He shares the living room with Schumer in conditions best described as ramshackle.

★ MICHIGAN ★

Michigan entered the 21st century much as it entered the 20th: a state transformed in a few years by a creative, dynamic economy and a burst of political reform. Michigan in the 1990s was one of America's premier laboratories of innovation, busy expanding high-skill manufacturing while rethinking and downsizing government programs, just as it was once busy inventing the mass-production factory economy and then developing the giant industrial labor union and its version of the American welfare state. The latest experiment, like the earlier one, seems to be a success: Michigan's economy, which seemed headed for disaster in the early 1980s, has sharply rebounded and for most of a decade it led the nation in the number of new factories and expansions, and the quality of Michigan products and services is vastly better than that of a generation ago. This is a manufacturing state that has transformed itself in line with the nation's movement from an industrial to a post-industrial economy, from domination by big units—big business, big labor, big government—to growth increasingly driven by small units—small businesses, individual workers, flexible government.

Michigan is arguably going back to its roots in the Tocquevillian decade of the 1830s, when Tocqueville visited Michigan and when it achieved statehood. These two peninsulas, explored and named by French explorers (which explains why Mackinac is pronounced with a silent final c and Michigan with a ch pronounced like sh), were settled in a rush by Yankee migrants from Upstate New York, who cut down trees and built farms and neat New Englandish towns complete with schools and colleges. Politically, Michigan was full of reformers who hated slavery, manned the Underground Railroad, promoted temperance and in 1855 gave Michigan a constitution that banned (as it does to this day) capital punishment. Michigan was one of the birthplaces of the Republican Party, which was founded in Jackson in 1854 (Ripon, Wisconsin, also stakes a claim as the party's birthplace) and swept the state in the elections later that year. Until 1929, Michigan was one of the most Republican states in the nation.

Michigan also developed an industrial economy. Its Lower Peninsula was mostly covered with trees, and lumber was the first boom industry on which Michigan overrelied; forests were clear-cut or swept by blazes like the 1881 fire that burned out half the Thumb. In the late 1800s, huge copper deposits were discovered on the Keweenaw Peninsula, which juts from the Upper Peninsula into icy Lake Superior; immigrants from Italy and Finland, Cornwall and Croatia came to work in the mines. Then came the auto industry. A combination of accident and shrewdness, of bankers willing to finance auto startups and the prickly genius of Henry Ford, ensured that America's fastest-growing industry for the first 30 years of the 20th century was centered in Michigan. Detroit became a boomtown—the nation's fastest-growing metropolitan area after Los Angeles—zooming from 426,000 in 1900 to 2.2 million in 1930 (it was 4.2 million in 2000). The auto industry drew labor from the Outstate Michigan, from southern Ontario and from the farms of Ohio and Indiana. During World War II and after, it brought whites from the Kentucky and Tennessee mountains and blacks from Alabama and Mississippi. It attracted Poles and Italians, Hungarians and Belgians, Greeks and Jews. This influx of a polyglot proletariat eventually changed Michigan's politics. The catalyst was the Great Depression of the 1930s and the company managers' desire to use machines efficiently, treating employees as extensions of machines and with great distrust. The results were the 1937 sit-down strikes organized by the new United Auto Workers (UAW); management and labor fought, sometimes literally, for pieces of what both sides feared was a shrinking pie. The UAW won and organized most of the companies after Democratic Governor Frank Murphy refused to send in troops to break the illegal strikes. In the years that followed, autoworkers became a heavily Democratic voting bloc.

Michigan politics became a kind of class warfare, conducted with a bitterness that split families and neighbors. The union mostly won, because demographics benefited the Democrats: autoworkers and post-1900 immigrants produced more children than did Outstate Yankees or management. After Walter Reuther's election as UAW president in 1947, voters elected young, liberal G. Mennen Williams governor in 1948. By 1954, the Democrats, closely tied to the UAW, seemed to have become the natural majority in the state. As growth continued, economic issues

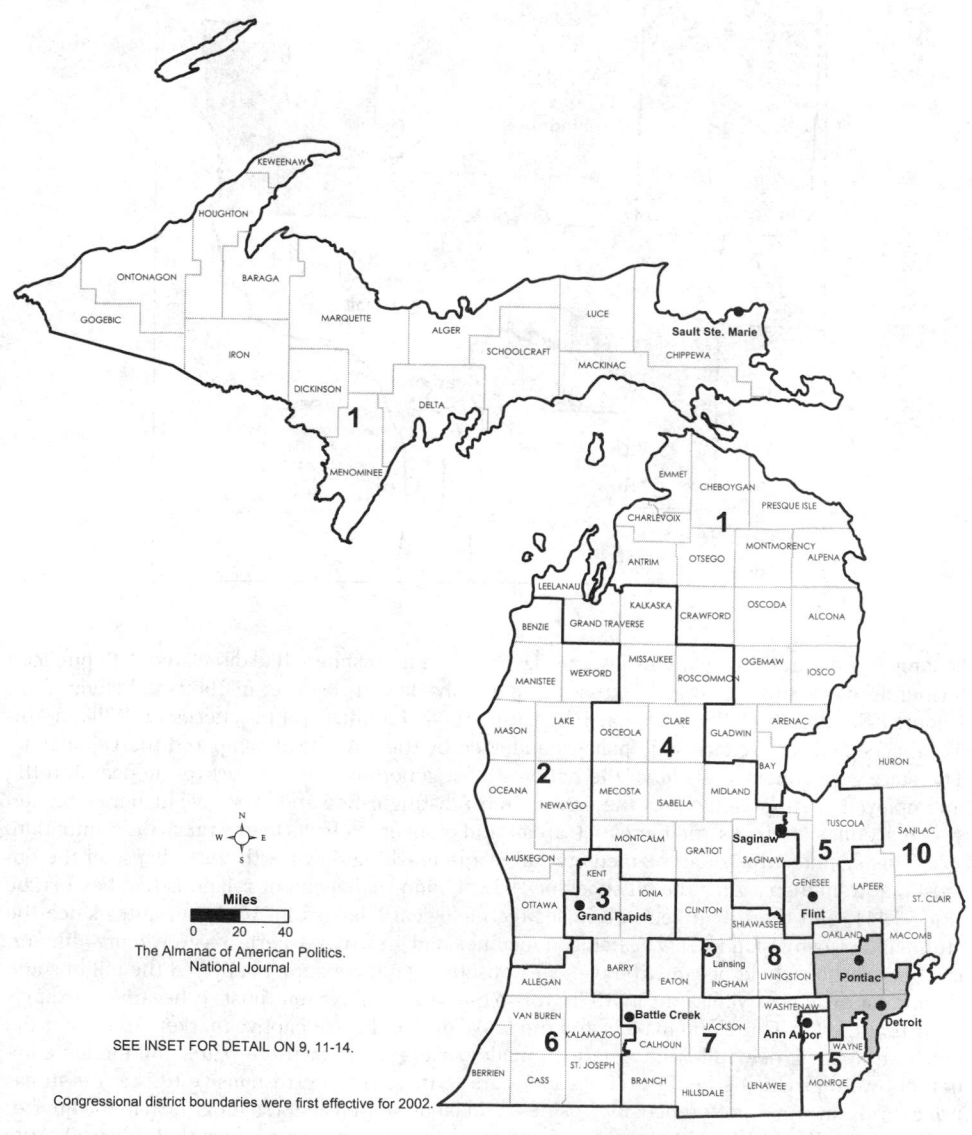

SEE INSET FOR DETAIL ON 9, 11-14.

The Almanac of American Politics.
National Journal

Miles
0   20   40

Congressional district boundaries were first effective for 2002.

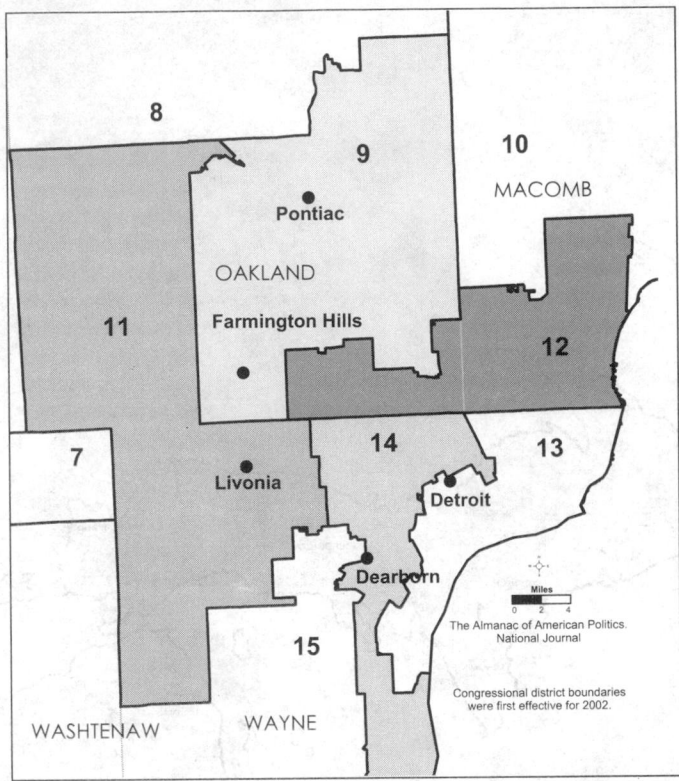

The Almanac of American Politics.
National Journal

Congressional district boundaries
were first effective for 2002.

became less bitter; by the early 1960s, the class-warfare atmosphere had dissipated. A Republican former auto executive, George Romney, was narrowly elected governor in 1962, and Henry Ford II joined Reuther in backing Lyndon Johnson in 1964. Romney and his successor, William Milliken, accepted the welfare-state policies endorsed by the UAW leadership and the Democrats. The state government was one of the nation's most generous, and not just to the poor and the unemployed: it supported one of the nation's most distinguished and extensive higher education systems, built state parks and recreation areas, and pioneered efforts to end racial discrimination.

This system, which had seemed eternal, came crashing down with the collapse of the domestic auto industry after the oil shock of 1973. Union-management relations had been static since 1941, and there had been no major technological changes in American autos since the automatic transmission in 1940. Michigan incomes had grown as Americans grew more affluent; the one-car household became the two-car household, and consumers enjoyed the tail fins and chrome of new car styling. But in 1979, this big-unit economy went bust. It became startlingly clear that the Big Three automakers and the UAW did not have a captive market, Americans did not have to buy a new full-sized American-made car every two or three years, and foreign competitors were producing better and cheaper cars that were more responsive to changes in gas prices and consumer preference. Big business and labor, so well adapted for growth in the quarter century after World War II, proved poorly adapted for the quarter century that followed. Auto employment in Michigan fell from 437,000 in October 1978 to 289,000 in October 1982. Chrysler nearly went bankrupt, Ford was in financial distress, and General Motors posted its first losses in years.

The collapse of the big-unit economy after 1979 forced the state to experiment. The first to try was Governor James Blanchard, a Democrat elected in 1982 with a record of supporting big units. His major achievement in eight years in Congress was managing the Chrysler bailout in the House. Blanchard worked to build a small-unit economy; he was proud of his efforts to stimulate high-skill, capital-intensive, flexible manufacturing, and he used $750 million of state pension funds as venture capital for manufacturers of items from tape drives for microcomputers to fiberglass coffins. Dodging his traditional labor allies, Blanchard made it clear that Michigan must learn how to nurture growth and that workers, instead of seeking more vacation and earlier retirement, would have to hustle and work harder than ever before.

The second experiment came from John Engler, the Republican who beat Blanchard in 1990 and was resoundingly re-elected in 1994 and 1998. Engler believed in less government activism and industrial policy; he cut or held the line on every state program but education. In three terms he cut taxes more than 30 times; welfare rolls were cut by more than two-thirds. Engler pressed for public school choice and charter schools, changing state pensions from defined benefits (which produce huge liabilities for the state and a sense of entitlement in employees) to defined contributions (which reduce the state's future expenses and empower employees to act as investors). Throughout the second half of the 1990s, the economy boomed. The auto industry, once an employer of thousands of low-skill workers, became high-tech; the number of unionized auto workers fell to 250,000 in 2000, but jobs required much higher skills and auto workers' earnings averaged $60,000. With the auto companies requiring high standards and speedy turnaround from subcontractors, Michigan became the home of almost all the nation's auto parts engineering centers and of much of the nation's large-scale manufacturing experts. Michigan's population rose 7% in the 1990s after staying even in the 1980s; median household incomes rose 5% after inflation; housing values in metro Detroit rose 47% after inflation. In the economic slowdown of 2002, Michigan's unemployment rate was no longer below the national average, but it was only about 1% higher—a stark contrast with 1979–83. Large parts of the state—the western and northern suburbs of Detroit, greater Grand Rapids, the northwest corner of the Upper Peninsula— were unmistakably booming. But there was one notable exception: the city of Detroit. Detroit's population fell to 951,000 in 2000, almost exactly half its 1,849,000 in 1950. Starting with the riot of 1967, crime rates in Detroit were enormously high for 25 years, and much of the city simply vanished—houses abandoned or burned down, commercial frontage with nearly 100% vacancy rates, the downtown a beleaguered fortress surrounded by blasted-out square miles. Detroit rebounded in the 1990s and after: crime and welfare rolls were down, new stadiums and a gambling casino were built downtown and old theaters refurbished.

Engler was barred from running in 2002 by term limits, and Michigan took a political turn when it elected Democrat Jennifer Granholm by a 51%–47% margin over Lieutenant Governor Dick Posthumus. She came to office with relatively little experience in public office—she was elected attorney general in 1998—and with great charm and articulateness. Her victory was not part of a Democratic sweep, however. Republicans Mike Cox and Terry Land were elected attorney general and secretary of state. Republicans kept majorities in both the state House and state Senate, but few veteran legislators remain: term limits insured that at least 27 of the 38 state senators were freshmen.

The election results show how Michigan politics has changed. Historically, politics divided Michigan between labor and management, and between the Detroit metro area and Outstate: in 1960, John Kennedy carried three-county metro Detroit 62%–38% and Richard Nixon carried Outstate 60%–39%. In 2002 Granholm carried the three-county metro area 58%–41% and lost Outstate by only 51%–47%. The reason her statewide margin wasn't much larger than Kennedy's 51%–49% is that metro Detroit cast only 40% of the state's votes in 2002 as compared to 49% in 1960. But there are other differences. Outstate Michigan is no longer so heavily Republican. And the Democratic margin in the three-county metro area comes almost entirely from Detroit, which cast 7% of the state's votes and which voted 92%–6% for Granholm. The rest of metro Detroit favored Granholm by only 50%–49%. In the industrial Michigan of 1960, economic status—and more specifically, union membership or non-membership—tended to drive party preference. In the post-industrial Michigan of 2002, economics played some role, but more often cultural attitudes drove voting behavior. Granholm carried affluent Oakland County, where many upscale voters moved toward the Democrats in the 1990s on cultural issues. She lost Macomb County, historically more blue collar and Democratic, though pretty affluent now, which in the 1970s and

1980s trended away from Democrats on cultural issues. The Grand Rapids area, with its large Dutch-American population and many Christian conservatives, voted heavily Republican. The industrial Flint, Saginaw and Bay City areas, where unions remain relatively strong, voted heavily Democratic, as did the area around Lansing, the state capital. Despite Granholm's victory, voter turnout (as compared to the previous peak year of 1994), was down in most heavily Democratic areas—Detroit, Flint, Lansing—and sharply up in heavily Republican areas—Grand Rapids, Livingston County northwest of Detroit, the counties around Traverse City. So Michigan, narrowly Democratic in presidential races, seems even more narrowly Republican in state politics, despite Granholm's victory. Michigan politics, like Michigan's economy, is more complex, with more moving parts and serious players, than it was a generation ago.

The People

Pop. 2000:	9,938,444	7,806,691	78.6%	White
Pop. 1990:	9,295,297	1,402,047	14.1%	Black
Change 1990–2000:	Up 6.9%	175,311	1.8%	Asian
Change 1980–1990:	Up 0.4%	53,421	0.5%	Native Am.
% of U.S. total:	3.5%	2,145	0.0%	Hawaiian
Pop. rank:	8th of 50	163,487	1.6%	Two+ races
Area size:	96,716 sq. mi.	11,465	0.1%	Other
State Native:	75.4%	323,877	3.3%	Hisp. Origin
Non-citizen:	2.9%			

Race/Ethnic Origin

Language
English: 89.2%   Other Eur.: 4.8%
Spanish: 3.5%

Ancestry
German: 14.9%   Irish: 7.9%
English: 7.3%   Polish: 6.3%
USA: 3.8%

Military veterans: 913,573 (12.4%)
WWII: 21.3%   Korea: 14.0%
Vietnam: 31.4%   Gulf War: 8.4%

Most populous cities:
1. Detroit   951,270
2. Grand Rapids   197,800
3. Warren   138,247
4. Flint   124,943
5. Sterling Heights   124,471

Urban population: 74.7%
Rural population: 25.3%

Education
H.S. Grad: 83.4%
College Grad: 21.8%

Industry
Agri: 1.1%   Con: 6.0%
Fin: 5.3%   Info: 2.1%
Mfg: 26.7%   Prof: 27.9%
Public: 3.6%   Trade: 15.2%
Other: 12.2%

Occupation
Blue collar: 27.6%   White collar: 57.1%
Gray collar: 15.3%

Work Sector
Private: 83.1%   Govt: 11.4%
Self: 5.2%   Family: 0.3%
Unemployment: 5.8%

Household Income
<15k: 14.1%   15-35k: 24.8%
35-50k: 16.5%   50-100k: 32.0%
100-150k: 8.6%   >150k: 4.1%
Median: $44,667
Poverty status: 10.5%

Home Value
<50k: 14.3%   50-100k: 30.3%   100-200k: 38.8%   200-300k: 10.6%
300-500k: 4.4%   >500k: 1.5%   Median: $110,300

Legislature
Senate   22 R 16 D
House   63 R 47 D
Legislative Term Limits: Yes

Registered Voters
No party registration

Presidential politics   In 1984, 1988 and 1992 Michigan voted within 1% of the national average for all major presidential candidates. But in 1996 and in 2000, as in most of the 1960s and 1970s, it was a little more Democratic than the nation: 52%–39% for Bill Clinton in 1996 and 51%–46% for Al Gore in 2000. In those two elections, Clinton and Gore carried suburban Oakland and Macomb Counties, the latter a special target for Democrats. Macomb was heavily Democratic in the 1950s and 1960s, then trended Republican in the 1970s, and now has swung back some distance toward the Democrats. Gore's victory owed much to the efforts of labor unions, not just the United Auto Workers (which in bargaining with the Big Three automakers obtained a paid day off on Election Day 2000) but also the Michigan Education Association, whose members are spread more evenly around the state.

2000 Presidential Vote
Gore (D)	2,170,418	(51%)
Bush (R)	1,953,139	(46%)
Nader (Green)	84,165	(2%)
Other	24,779	(1%)

2000 Republican Presidential Primary
McCain (R)	650,805	(51%)
Bush (R)	549,665	(43%)
Keyes (R)	59,032	(5%)

1996 Presidential Vote
Clinton (D)	1,989,683	(52%)
Dole (R)	1,481,572	(39%)
Perot (I)	336,681	(9%)

With 17 electoral votes it will obviously be a target state for George W. Bush and for the Democrats in 2004.

Michigan has had problems setting up a presidential primary. One reason is that it does not have party registration, which is required by Democratic party rules. In 2000, Republicans held their primary February 22. Governor John Engler hoped to deliver the state's delegates to George W. Bush, whose candidacy he had backed early on. But John McCain, aroused after his defeat in South Carolina February 19, contested the state vigorously. In a stinging rebuke to Engler, McCain won 51%–43%. His admirers in the national press hailed this as a great breakthrough, but it turned out to be atypical and an augury of nothing. Turnout was a huge 1.3 million, far higher than the 524,000 of 1996 or the 437,000 of 1992; indeed, even Bush got more votes than were cast for all candidates in those primaries. But the VNS exit poll showed that 18% of the votes were cast by self-identified Democrats (almost double the percentage in any other primary that year) and only 47% by self-identified Republicans. Bush won solidly among Republicans, as he did everywhere except in a few Northeast states, but lost by 2–1 among self-identified Independents and 8–1 among Democrats. Nothing barred Democrats from voting; when Democrats held caucuses in March, only 22,000 bothered to vote or mail in ballots. The McCain vote was really an anti-Engler vote. Many Michigan Democrats hated Engler the way many national Republicans hated Bill Clinton: the man had outsmarted them and beaten them time and again and now there was a way to get back at him. They did so by voting for McCain and by carrying the state for Gore in November; Engler, though able and an early Bush backer, did not get an appointment in the Bush administration.

In 2003, the Michigan Democratic party, led by Senator Carl Levin, attempted to challenge New Hampshire's first-in-the nation status by moving the 2004 Michigan Democratic caucuses to the same January date as the New Hampshire primary; after a noisy debate, the Michigan Democratic State Central Committee backed down and voted to hold their caucuses in February.

Congressional districting   Michigan has now lost four seats in the last three censuses—one after the 1980 Census, two after the 1990 Census, another one after the 2000 Census. In 2001, for the first time since the 1930s, redistricting was controlled by Republicans, with majorities in both houses of the legislature and with Governor John Engler determined to use the power to reverse the Democrats' 9–7 edge to a 9–6 Republican edge: He succeeded. There was no

108th Congress Lineup
9 R   6 D
107th Congress Lineup
9 D   7 R

pretense of bipartisanship: bills were introduced in the House and Senate abruptly in June 2001 and passed on near party-line votes. The plan ended the 26-year congressional career of House Democratic Whip David Bonior, by removing just about every Macomb County precinct he carried heavily and adding the Thumb to the 10th District (it used to be numbered the 12th); he ran for governor and lost in the Democratic primary. It put two pairs of Democratic incumbents in the same districts; Jim Barcia of the 5th District decided to return to the state Senate, where he used to serve, while John Dingell, the dean of the House, slugged it out with liberal Lynn Rivers in the new 15th District. The 1st District, held by Democrat Bart Stupak, seems likely to go Republican if he is not running. A new Republican district was created in western Wayne and Oakland Counties, and shaky Republican incumbents Mike Rogers and Joe Knollenberg were strengthened. This was arguably the most successful partisan redistricting plan in the nation. In a state carried by Bill Clinton and Al Gore, only five of the 15 seats are now safely Democratic.

Governor

Jennifer Granholm (D)

Elected 2002, term expires Jan. 2007, 1st term; b. Feb. 5, 1959, Vancouver, BC; home, Northville; U. of CA, B.A. 1984, Harvard U., J.D. 1987; Catholic; married (Daniel Mulhern).

Elected Office: MI Atty. Gen., 1998–02.

Professional Career: Fed. Prosecutor, U.S. Atty.'s Office, 1991–94; Corporation Cnsl., Wayne Cnty., 1994–98.

Office: P.O. Box 30013, Lansing, 48909, 517-373-3400; Fax: 517-335-6863; Web site: www.michigan.gov/gov.

Election Results

2002 general	Jennifer Granholm (D)	1,633,796	(51%)
	Dick Posthumus (R)	1,506,104	(47%)
	Other	37,665	(1%)
2002 primary	Jennifer Granholm (D)	499,129	(48%)
	David Bonior (D)	292,958	(28%)
	James Blanchard (D)	254,586	(24%)
1998 general	John M. Engler (R)	1,883,005	(62%)
	Geoffrey Fieger (D)	1,143,574	(38%)

Jennifer Granholm, a Democrat, was elected governor of Michigan in 2002. She was born in British Columbia, a Canadian citizen and so not eligible for the presidency—as surely many Democrats wish she was—and moved to California at age 4 when her father's work as a bank teller and branch manager took him there. She lived in Anaheim in the 1960s, where she could watch the fireworks over Disneyland, and then to San Jose and San Carlos, a middle-class suburb on the Peninsula south of San Francisco. She was a popular student in San Carlos High School and won the Miss San Carlos beauty/talent pageant. At 18 she became a U.S. citizen. That year she also moved to Los Angeles to try her luck as an actress even though her parents wanted her to be the first in the family to graduate from college. She graduated from the American Academy of Dramatic Arts with Nick Cassavetes but never got a part; she once was a contestant on *The Dating Game*. She made her living as a tour guide at Universal Studios, taking delivery complaints for the *Los Angeles Times* and was the first female tour guide at Marine World Africa USA in Redwood City, piloting boats with 25 tourists aboard. "I hated it," she told the Detroit *Free Press* of her experiences in LaLaLand. It was "a very selfish place to be. The L.A. scene, the L.A. values . . . just wasn't what I was interested in. To be in an environment where I was not using my intellect, or expected to . . . was very disturbing." She returned to San Carlos and in 1980 won admission to the University of California at Berkeley. There she excelled. She spent her junior year in France, where she worked for Jews trying to emigrate from the Soviet Union; she spent two weeks there during the height of the Cold War. She graduated summa cum laude in French and political science, and in these years showed some interest in politics: in 1980 she worked for the Independent presidential campaign of John Anderson but in 1984 supported the Mondale-Ferraro ticket. In 1984 she went off to Harvard Law School, where she demonstrated in favor of disinvestment in South Africa and edited the Civil Rights and Civil Liberties Law Review. She worked one summer for a big law firm in New York, which she considered a terrible experience. In Cambridge she met her husband, Dan Mulhern, from Inkster, Michigan, a working class suburb near Detroit's Metro Airport. After law school, they moved to Michigan. Thus was a star of Michigan politics born.

Granholm worked as a law clerk for federal appeals court Judge Damon Keith, then got a job in the U.S. Attorney's office in Detroit, where she claims a 98% conviction rate. In 1994 she got what turned out to be her great political break when she was appointed corporation counsel to

Wayne County Executive Ed McNamara. McNamara, who obviously has an eye for political talent, has called Granholm a "child of destiny." In 1998 Frank Kelley, Michigan's Attorney General since January 1962, announced that he was retiring (the "Eternal General," some called him). McNamara pushed Granholm forward to run for the office. She won the Democratic nomination at the state party convention in August 1998 and was elected in November—the only Democrat to win statewide, as Republican Governor John Engler and Secretary of State Candice Miller were re-elected by wide margins. She might not have won except that conservatives at the Republican state convention nominated a little known candidate rather than Engler's choice, Scott Romney, son of former Governor George Romney and brother of Massachusetts Governor Mitt Romney.

Suddenly Granholm was the most visible Democrat in Michigan state government and an obvious candidate to succeed Engler in 2002, when he would be barred from running by term limits. She claimed credit for setting up a high-tech crime unit and prosecuting an on-line seller of the date rape drug and the proprietor of a child pornography site. But what made her an attractive candidate was less his record than her persona. She is articulate, poised, always able to connect with her audience, enthusiastic, almost always striking a note of consensus rather than confrontation.

She was running to replace Engler, for more than a decade the dominant figure in Michigan state politics. Granholm had serious competition in the Democratic primary from Blanchard and Congressman David Bonior. Blanchard had success as governor in reorienting Michigan's economy and was well-liked by Democrats; Bonior had a strong liberal record on union issues, foreign policy and the environment. But Bonior was little known outside his Macomb and St. Clair Counties district, and Blanchard had spent much time outside of Michigan, as Ambassador to Canada and in a Washington law practice. Granholm campaigned as a consensus-minded centrist. Blanchard presented a detailed economic plan and called for repeal of the single business tax, then in the second year of a 22-year phase-out. Bonior campaigned as the champion of the working man and an opponent of big corporate interests. Granholm did not start off ahead in the polls, but her two opponents both targeted her for attacks. Much of the primary was a battle for endorsements. Bonior was endorsed by the state AFL-CIO and the United Auto Workers—endorsements that in the 1960s or 1970s would have cinched the nomination for him. But Granholm was endorsed in 2002 by the Teamsters and the Michigan Education Association—now at least as important a factor in Democratic politics. In December 2001, Granholm was endorsed by EMILY's List, which had raised $1.4 million in bundled contributions for Senator Debbie Stabenow in 2000. The legislature passed a law that month limiting bundled contributions to $34,000, the limit for PACs. But it did not take effect until April 2002, by which time EMILY's List had raised more than $400,000 for Granholm. Blanchard and Bonior decided to take state matching funds and accept a spending limit of $2 million in the primary; Granholm rejected the matching funds and raised and spent $5.7 million.

By early 2002, Granholm was leading in polls both for the primary and the general election against the presumed Republican nominee Lieutenant Governor Dick Posthumus (who won 81%–19% over state Senator John Schwarz, the head of John McCain's 2000 Michigan campaign). Michigan does not have party registration, so voters can vote in either party's primary; in August 2002, 1.8 million voted, 58% of them in the Democratic primary, which was much more seriously contested—a turnout of 1,047,000. Granholm won 48% of the vote, Bonior 28% and Blanchard 24%. Blanchard carried Detroit, with strong support from blacks, and Bonior carried Macomb and St. Clair Counties, parts of which were in his congressional district. But Granholm carried Wayne County, and she won 51% in Oakland County. Outstate Michigan beyond the three-county Detroit area played a pivotal role for the first time in a seriously contested primary; it cast an unusually high 48% of the vote, and Granholm won 56% there.

Posthumus, Granholm's general election opponent, was not well known to voters. A farmer from Grand Rapids's Kent County with solid conservative credentials, he insisted he was a blue-collar candidate. He had a detailed program—a three-fifths requirement to raise taxes, more tax cuts and ending the single business tax, sparing school districts from spending cuts. He split with Engler to oppose slant oil drilling under the Great Lakes and opposed school vouchers, which had been beaten in a 2000 referendum. He attacked Granholm for saying she favored "tweaking"

Proposal A—evidently allowing school districts to raise property taxes more than the measure allowed—and for opposing changes in welfare. But he concentrated much of his fire on her out-of-state origins. He portrayed himself as "raised in Michigan, went to Michigan public schools." "Let's just say I've got different values than come from Hollywood, Berkeley and Harvard." But most voters did not seem to care that Granholm grew up somewhere else; after all, she chose to live in Michigan.

Then on September 20 a reporter for Channel 50 exposed a memo from Detroit Mayor Kwame Kilpatrick in August. It promised Granholm that Kilpatrick would work to turn out 275,000 voters in Detroit if Granholm would agree that 20% of her appointees would be black, that all new state office buildings would be in Detroit, and that Detroiters would be named to head six state departments (including welfare, housing, corrections). Kilpatrick said he never sent the memo and Granholm said she never received it. But Posthumus pounced hard on it. "This memo hands over the ATM card to the state budget and says 'unlimited withdrawals.' It turns Michigan state government into a department store window at Christmas time. But this Christmas Santa will only be filling the stockings of Detroit and Wayne County." Granholm said she called Kilpatrick and told him "the only thing you're getting is good government," and attacked Posthumus for bringing the issue up. A few days later Engler brought up the issue of racial reparations. At a July 2002 NAACP meeting, all three Democratic gubernatorial candidates said they supported reparations; Granholm said, "I support reparations. I support the John Conyers bill," which would set up a commission to study reparations. She later said that reparations to her didn't mean money payments. Michigan and national Democrats said that bringing up the Kilpatrick memo and reparations was appealing to racism. Posthumus said they were legitimate issues and part of a pattern: "she has said one thing to the special interests and another to the voters."

Granholm won by a closer-than-expected 51%–47%. Only 220,000 Detroiters voted, but they cast more than 92% of their votes for Granholm and accounted for all of her popular vote margin and more. Granholm carried Oakland County and suburban Wayne County but lost Macomb County. She carried the Upper Peninsula, the Flint-Saginaw-Bay City corridor and the counties containing Lansing, Battle Creek and Kalamazoo; she lost Outstate by only 51%–47%—a good showing for a Democrat. Posthumus showed great strength only in the Grand Rapids area and the northern Lower Peninsula.

Granholm in any case did not seem interested in overturning most of Engler's achievements. As the state faced budget problems, she called for spending cuts and no increase in taxes. She will surely appoint very different kinds of judges and administrative judges and may change Engler's 1994 law that effectively ended teachers' strikes; she favors ending the state takeover of Detroit schools. But bitter partisan differences may be a thing of the past. Term limits insure that almost no legislators or legislative leaders were part of the angry battles of the early 1990s. The biggest cloud on her horizon is the FBI's investigation of Ed McNamara's top appointees over alleged cash for contracts in the construction of the beautiful new midfield terminal (named the McNamara Terminal) at Metro Airport. On taking office in January 2003, her first official act was to issue a code of ethics, with new disclosure requirements for state contracts, a ban on soliciting campaign contributions from contractors and Internet publication of a list of state vendors.

Senior Senator

Carl Levin (D)

Elected 1978, seat up 2008, 5th term; b. June 28, 1934, Detroit; home, Detroit; Swarthmore Col., B.A. 1956, Harvard U., J.D. 1959; Jewish; married (Barbara).

Elected Office: Detroit City Cncl., 1969–77, Pres., 1973–77.

Professional Career: Practicing atty., 1959–64, 1971–73, 1978–79; MI Asst. Atty. Gen. & Gen. Cnsl., MI Civil Rights Comm., 1964–67; Detroit Chief Appellate Defender, 1967–69.

DC Office: 269 RSOB, 20510, 202-224-6221; Fax: 202-224-1388; Web site: levin.senate.gov.

State Offices: Alpena, 989-354-5520; Detroit, 313-226-6020; Downriver, 734-285-8596; Escanaba, 906-789-0052; Grand Rapids, 616-456-2531; Lansing, 517-377-1508; Saginaw, 989-754-2494; Traverse City, 231-947-9569; Warren, 586-573-9145.

Committees: *Armed Services* (RMM). *Governmental Affairs*: Financial Management, Budget & International Security; Investigations (Permanent) (RMM). *Intelligence (Select)*. *Small Business & Entrepreneurship*.

Group Ratings

	ADA	ACLU	AFS	LCV	CON	ITIC	NTU	COC	ACU	NTLC	CHC
2002	95	60	100	65	88	25	11	40	0	0	—
2001	100	—	100	88	—	—	6	36	8	—	0

National Journal Ratings

	2001 LIB	—	2001 CONS	2002 LIB	—	2002 CONS
Economic	86%	—	14%	64%	—	34%
Social	95%	—	0%	82%	—	0%
Foreign	74%	—	14%	94%	—	4%

Key Votes of the 107th Congress

1. Approve Bush Tax Cuts	N	5. Confirm Ashcroft as AG	N
2. Expand Patients' Rights	Y	6. Bar Gays in the Boy Scouts	N
3. Campaign Finance Reform	Y	7. $ for Hate Crime Prosecution	Y
4. Permit ANWR Development	N	8. Overseas Military Abortions	Y

9. Bar Coop. with Intl. Court	N
10. Trade Promotion Authority	N
11. Authorize Force in Iraq	N
12. Homeland Sec. Dept. Union	Y

Election Results

2002 general	Carl Levin (D)	1,896,614	(61%)	($4,133,866)
	Andrew Raczkowski (R)	1,185,545	(38%)	($849,501)
2002 primary	Carl Levin (D)	unopposed		
1996 general	Carl Levin (D)	2,195,738	(58%)	($6,223,409)
	Ronna Romney (R)	1,500,106	(40%)	($3,208,968)
	Other	66,731	(2%)	

Prior Winning Percentages: 1990 (57%); 1984 (52%); 1978 (52%)

Carl Levin, first elected in 1978, is a durable and likable liberal Democrat, a member of one of Michigan's most respected political families. He is rumpled, unfashionable, speaks articulately but without apparent political artifice and takes unpopular stands on issues he cares about. He grew up in Detroit, graduated from Swarthmore and Harvard Law School, worked for the state Civil Rights Commission and the appellate public defender's office, and was elected to Detroit's city council in 1969 and 1973, with substantial support from both blacks and whites. In 1978 he ran for the Senate and was helped when incumbent Robert Griffin got out of the race and then back in; Levin won 52%–48%. In 1984 he won by a similar margin against a former astronaut who had given a public testimonial for his Japanese car; in 1990, 1996 and 2002 he was re-elected by wide margins. He is the longest serving senator from Michigan in history.

Levin was Armed Services Committee chairman from June 2001 to January 2003. He brought to the Senate the skepticism about defense spending and military involvements common among Democrats in the 1970s, and has built up an impressive expertise in military affairs. For a time he opposed the B-2, he voted against selling AWACS planes to Saudi Arabia in 1981 and he voted against the Gulf War resolution in 1991—on the advice of Colin Powell, he says now, and adds that he was mistaken. On taking the chair, he said he would not concentrate on major weapons systems, but on military pay, health care and housing, plus purchasing systems; unlike his predecessor and successor, John Warner, he favored another round of base closings—one issue on which he agreed with Defense Secretary Donald Rumsfeld, but neither prevailed.

Where he disagreed most strongly with Rumsfeld was on missile defense, of which he has been the Senate's most persistent critic. He led a filibuster on the issue in September 1998, arguing that missile defense would undermine chances of Russian approval of the 1993 START II treaty. In January 2001 he warned that a missile defense system would irritate our allies and provoke countermeasures from Russia and China. In June 2001, on becoming chairman, he said more testing was needed and a system was unlikely to be fielded until after the next presidential election. "There is a serious possibility that if we take the wrong approach, it would decrease our security and increase the risk of nuclear proliferation. I think we could even start a second cold war, Cold War II." He set out his own conditions for the program. "Under the right circumstances—and only under the right circumstances, we ought to deploy it. Those right circumstances include operational effectiveness, cost effectiveness, impact on arms reductions, whether we are more or less secure with such a deployment." When Rumsfeld called the ABM Treaty "a Cold War construct," Levin replied, "I think it would be useful for you to at least attempt to understand" why some people fear abrogation could provoke Russia to boost ballistic missile capacity. On defense bills he worked to freeze any money that might conceivably conflict with ABM Treaty. On September 7, 2001, he got the committee to move $1.3 billion from missile defense to anti-terrorism programs. On September 16 John Warner said he was ready to file his own defense bill. On September 21 Levin backed down, saying he did not wish to "create dissent where we need unity."

In December 2001 Levin was outflanked when George W. Bush invoked the clause in the ABM Treaty allowing him to abrogate it with six month's warning. Russian President Vladmir Putin responded nonchalantly: Levin's fears of a second cold war were not realized. Still, in May 2002 he got the committee to approve a defense authorization bill that cut the Bush administration missile defense request by $812 million; in June, a Senate compromise was struck on the final version that gave Bush the authority to restore the cuts.

Levin was very skeptical about the need for military action in Iraq and argued fervently that any such action must be taken multilaterally. He welcomed Bush's announcement in a White House meeting in September 2002 that he would consult with Congress on military action. He argued that it was not necessary now because Saddam Hussein would be deterred from using weapons of mass destruction. He argued that the United States should not act without first receiving the approval of the United Nations. In October 2002 he offered an alternative resolution on military action in Iraq, calling on the administration to get the UN to vote a more vigorous weapons inspection program, but not authorizing military action until it was approved by the UN. It was defeated 75–24. In February 2003 he continued to argue that the United States should not take military action without another resolution from the United Nations, even if that meant that action could be stopped by a veto from France. He has remained skeptical about the Saudis: in January 2002 he proposed that American troops should be withdrawn from Saudi Arabia and restationed in "a place that is more hospitable," as indeed some of them were.

Working from the Governmental Affairs Committee, Levin was chief sponsor of the Senate gift rule, setting a limit of $50 on gifts to senators and staffers. As ranking member of the Permanent Investigations Subcommittee, he and Chairman Susan Collins held hearings in March 2001 on money laundering. These bore fruit in October 2001, when Levin successfully pushed his money laundering bill forward as an amendment to the anti-terrorism bill. The bill attempted to force banks to give greater scrutiny to transactions involving banks in countries like the Cayman Islands and Antigua with loose banking laws exploited by criminals and terrorism. In June 2001, with Levin now as chairman, the subcommittee held hearings on gasoline prices, after Levin noticed that prices in Michigan had spiked even though oil prices had not moved; the oil companies blamed a shortage of refineries. In July 2002 Levin held hearings on Enron in which Levin carefully avoided political posturing and instead focused on the need to provide accurate information to investors. Levin argued that stock options should be treated as expenses by corporations, and in July 2002 pushed an amendment to the corporate accountability bill to require the Financial Accounting Standards Board to consider the issue and vote on it within a year. The board later decided that options should be treated as an expense.

Levin generally has one of the most liberal records in the Senate, with some Michigan accents. He opposed NAFTA and has complained about Japanese auto-parts and Korean car trade restrictions. When John Kerry and John McCain proposed raising CAFE auto mileage standards to 36 miles per gallon by 2015, Levin and Christopher Bond responded with an amendment requiring NHTSA to raise the standard for light trucks (including SUVs) within 15 months and for cars within two years; it passed 62–38. One issue on which he is passionate is capital punishment (abolished in Michigan in 1855), and he has often led the fight against it, calling for a moratorium on the federal death penalty in 2000. Levin was angry when the Republican majority blocked votes on Michigan appointees to federal judgeships when Clinton was president, and since Bush has become president, has blocked all appeals court nominees for the 6th Circuit, which includes Michigan, Ohio, Kentucky and Tennessee.

Levin's reputation for candor and hard work, and his rumpled persona have given him great political strength in Michigan. Every six years his percentage has crept a little higher. Governor John Engler looked high and low for a candidate to oppose him in 2002, considering at different times his own chief of staff, a pizza heiress and a software publisher who appeared on CBS's *Survivor*. The nominee turned out to be Andrew "Rocky" Raczkowski, a term-limited state representative, who put "Rocky" on his bumper stickers but could not get it on the ballot though it is part of his legal name. Levin won 61%–38%, carrying Outstate Michigan as well as metro Detroit.

Junior Senator

Debbie Stabenow (D)

Elected 2000, seat up 2006, 1st term; b. Apr. 29, 1950, Gladwin; home, Lansing; MI St. U., B.A. 1972, M.S.W. 1975; United Methodist; married (Tom Athans).

Elected Office: Ingham Cnty. Comm., 1975–78, Chair, 1976–78; MI House of Reps., 1978–90; MI Senate, 1990–94; U.S. House of Reps 1996–00.

Professional Career: Consultant & Co–founder, MI Leadership Inst., 1995–96.

DC Office: 702 HSOB, 20510, 202-224-4822; Fax: 202-228-0325; Web site: www.stabenow.senate.gov.

State Offices: Detroit, 313-961-4330; E. Lansing, 517-203-1760; Flint, 810-720-4172; Grand Rapids, 616-975-0052; Marquette, 906-228-8756; Traverse City, 231-929-1031.

Committees: *DSCC Vice Chairman. Aging (Special). Agriculture, Nutrition & Forestry*: Marketing, Inspection & Product Promotion; Research, Nutrition & General Legislation. *Banking, Housing & Urban Affairs*: Financial Institutions; Housing & Transportation; Securities & Investment. *Budget.*

Group Ratings

	ADA	ACLU	AFS	LCV	CON	ITIC	NTU	COC	ACU	NTLC	CHC
2002	95	60	100	71	58	50	12	45	0	0	—
2001	100	—	100	100	—	—	6	43	8	—	0

National Journal Ratings

	2001 LIB —	2001 CONS	2002 LIB —	2002 CONS
Economic	82%	15%	69%	30%
Social	94%	6%	77%	18%
Foreign	87%	3%	94%	4%

Key Votes of the 107th Congress

1. Approve Bush Tax Cuts	N	5. Confirm Ashcroft as AG	N	9. Bar Coop. with Intl. Court	Y
2. Expand Patients' Rights	Y	6. Bar Gays in the Boy Scouts	N	10. Trade Promotion Authority	N
3. Campaign Finance Reform	Y	7. $ for Hate Crime Prosecution	Y	11. Authorize Force in Iraq	N
4. Permit ANWR Development	N	8. Overseas Military Abortions	Y	12. Homeland Sec. Dept. Union	Y

Election Results

2000 general	Debbie Stabenow (D)	2,061,952	(49%)	($7,892,518)
	Spencer Abraham (R)	1,994,693	(48%)	($13,028,636)
	Other	111,040	(3%)	
2000 primary	Debbie Stabenow (D)	unopposed		

Prior Winning Percentages: 1998 House (57%); 1996 House (54%)

Michigan's junior senator is Debbie Stabenow, a Democrat elected in 2000. Stabenow grew up in the small Outstate town of Clare, where her father was an Oldsmobile dealer and her mother a nurse. She went to Michigan State, where she got a master's degree in social work and made money singing folk songs in coffeehouses. She marched in antiwar rallies and volunteered for George McGovern in 1972, when her then-husband ran an unsuccessful race for Ingham County Commissioner. Provoked when the commission closed a nursing home, she ran for the commission two years later and, at 24, beat an incumbent who referred to her as "that young broad." She was elected to the state House in 1978, at 28, and was elected to the state Senate in 1990. In 1994, while running for governor, she was at the storm center of state politics and policy. In response to Republican Governor John Engler's call for education finance reform, she proposed to zero out the property tax and start over, apparently calculating that he would reject such a drastic tax cut. Instead he accepted her proposal and passed a plan reducing property taxes vastly and increasing the sales tax, which was approved by voters 70%–30% in March 1994. In the August 1994 primary for governor, the major forces in the Democratic Party opposed Stabenow: the Michigan Education Association, the UAW and AFL-CIO. She won 30% of the vote, ahead of Larry Owen's 26% but behind former Congressman Howard Wolpe's 35%. Perhaps it is best she lost; she was chosen as Wolpe's running mate, but the ticket lost to Engler by a 61%–38% margin.

Undaunted, Stabenow almost immediately began running for Congress. The 8th District seat, which included Lansing's Democratic Ingham County and heavily Republican Livingston County to the east, was held by Republican Dick Chrysler. For the 1996 race, Stabenow raised more than $1 million in individual contributions, a tribute to her industriousness and the fundraising prowess of the feminist left; overall each spent $1.5 million. On national issues, Stabenow struck a thematic note similar to Bill Clinton, calling for "balancing the budget in a way that does not shift the burden to middle class families," equipping schools with computers, and encouraging job creation by new-tech small businesses. She won impressively, 54%–44%.

In the House, Stabenow had a fairly liberal voting record; she was sought out by the moderate Democratic Blue Dogs but did not join. She opposed trade promotion authority and the partial-birth abortion ban. In March 1999 she announced she was running against Senator Spencer Abraham in 2000; the same day Abraham ran full-page ads calling her a liberal.

This turned out to be one of the critical races in the 2000 Senate cycle. Abraham, a former state Republican chairman and deputy chief of staff to Vice President Dan Quayle, had been elected in 1994 by a 52%–43% margin over Congressman Bob Carr. The grandson of immigrants from Lebanon, his greatest achievement in the Senate was to squelch proposals to reduce the number of legal immigrants allowed in each year; Abraham put together an alliance of conservatives and liberals that beat subcommittee chairman Al Simpson, and the basic immigration laws remained unchanged. In 2000 Abraham secured near-unanimous approval for an increase in H1-B immigration visas for high-tech workers—one of the chief legislative goals of the high-tech industry. Abraham was also a strong supporter of tax cuts, but he kept a relatively low profile in Washington. The good news for Abraham and Stabenow was that neither had primary opposition; the bad news was that neither was known in any depth by most Michigan voters.

The first barrage of ads in the race came not from either candidate or party, but from the Federation for American Immigration Reform, which in early 2000 spent $700,000 attacking

Abraham for his stands on immigration and charging that his stands cost Michigan workers jobs. In 1999 Abraham's voting record became more moderate than before, and in July 2000 he called for a suspension of the federal gas tax until November, a move beaten in the Senate 59–40. In summer 2000 Abraham used his money advantage—he ultimately spent nearly $13 million, to Stabenow's nearly $8 million—to run ads spotlighting his own program for prescription drugs for seniors and attacked Stabenow as a free-spending liberal favoring increased bureaucracy and opposing tax cuts, opposing welfare reform and supporting more lenient sentences for criminals. He set up a liberaldebbie.com website, and faced threats of a lawsuit from the makers of Little Debbie cakes. Stabenow resisted pressure and hoarded her money for an October ad buy.

This proved to be a good strategy: Stabenow was down by 17% in one mid-October poll but, after several weeks of equal advertising by each, wound up winning by 1%. Stabenow answered charges that she was a liberal by citing her votes for a balanced budget and ending the marriage penalty; she kept herself in the good graces of labor by voting against PNTR with China. Stabenow said Abraham was beholden to corporations and special interests and attacked his stands on prescription drug and HMO regulation. He pointed to his votes for a balanced budget, welfare reform and highway funds for Michigan and talked of "the total absence of congressional achievements of Debbie Stabenow." This race was light on debates— the two had just one televised debate—and heavy on ads by outside groups—the Sierra Club, Peace Action and EMILY's List for Stabenow, the Chamber of Commerce, Business Roundtable, Americans for Job Security, National Rifle Association and Michigan Right to Life for Abraham.

This was the most expensive Senate race in Michigan history, and the first since 1942 in which neither candidate won a majority of the vote. Stabenow won 49%–48%; she said that after the campaign Bill Clinton "told me all along that next to Hillary's, mine was the race he was most proud of." Abraham won Outstate Michigan 56%–42%, but in the metro Detroit area, Stabenow led 57%–40%. Stabenow carried only 13 of the state's 83 counties, but she ran essentially even in critical Oakland and Macomb Counties.

Senate Democrats made Stabenow head of the prescription drug task force, and she concentrated on the issue, organizing bus trips of seniors to Canada and pushing for a package of legislation that came to the floor in July 2002. The Senate, unlike the House, was unable to pass a prescription drug benefit. But it did pass a law withdrawing patent protection for pharmaceutical companies pending the outcome of suits brought by generic drug companies by 78–21. And it passed measures allowing reimportation of drugs from Canada—though both Clinton and Bush HHS secretaries found this to be unsafe and did not allow it—and to allow states to continue to negotiate prices with pharmaceutical companies on Medicaid drug purchases. But the House did not act on these. Stabenow objected strongly in December 2002 to the insertion into the homeland security bill of an amendment directing suits against Eli Lilly for its vaccine additive thimerosal to the Vaccine Injury Compensations program; the suits allege that thimerosal causes autism and the VIC handles all other vaccine lawsuits with the federal government compensating victims. Trent Lott promised to bring the measure up in early 2003, and Bill Frist said he would honor that promise; Stabenow and Patrick Leahy sponsored a bill repealing the provision.

In 2001 Stabenow's bill to impose a two-year moratorium on slant oil drilling under the Great Lakes passed the Senate; the House passed a permanent ban but Stabenow compromised to get the support of Pete Domenici. Michigan under Governor Engler was the only state to allow slant drilling; his successor Jennifer Granholm opposed it in her campaign. Stabenow was less successful in getting approval to an agreement between Engler and the Bay Mills Indians to build a gambling casino under the Blue Water Bridge in Port Huron; Harry Reid of Nevada objected to her unanimous request motion. With Republican Kay Bailey Hutchison, Stabenow sponsored a bill for a national AMBER Alert child abduction advisory system; state systems have recovered 27 children. In December 2002, Stabenow was appointed vice-chairman of the Senate Democrats' campaign committee.

FIRST DISTRICT

Rep. Bart Stupak (D)

Elected 1992, 6th term; b. Feb. 29, 1952, Milwaukee, WI; home, Menominee; NW MI Comm. Col., A.A. 1972, Saginaw Valley St. Col., B.S. 1977, Thomas Cooley Law Schl., J.D. 1981; Catholic; married (Laurie).

Elected Office: MI House of Reps., 1988–90.

Professional Career: Escanaba Police Officer, 1972–73; MI St. Trooper, 1974–84; Practicing atty., 1981–92.

DC Office: 2352 RHOB 20515, 202-225-4735; Fax: 202-225-4744; Web site: www.house.gov/stupak.

District Offices: Alpena, 989-356-0690; Crystal Falls, 906-875-3751; Escanaba, 906-786-4504; Houghton, 906-482-1371; Marquette, 906-228-3700; Petoskey, 231-348-0657; West Brance, 989-345-2258.

Committees: *Energy & Commerce* (13th of 26 D): Commerce, Trade & Consumer Protection; Environment & Hazardous Materials; Health; Telecommunications & The Internet.

Group Ratings

	ADA	ACLU	AFS	LCV	CON	ITIC	NTU	COC	ACU	NTLC	CHC
2002	80	53	89	88	63	38	22	45	16	0	33
2001	75	—	100	71	—	—	15	38	38	—	—

National Journal Ratings

	2001 LIB —	2001 CONS		2002 LIB —	2002 CONS
Economic	82%	19%		77%	20%
Social	50%	50%		52%	48%
Foreign	67%	32%		74%	25%

Key Votes of the 107th Congress

1. Approve Bush Tax Cuts	N	5. Faith-Based Charities	N	9. Trade Promotion Authority	N
2. Limit Patients' Bill of Rights	N	6. Bar Gays in the Boy Scouts	Y	10. Bar Funds for Intl. Court	Y
3. Campaign Finance Reform	Y	7. Ban Partial-Birth Abortion	Y	11. Authorize Force in Iraq	N
4. Ban ANWR Development	Y	8. Arm Commercial Pilots	Y	12. Deny Home. Sec. Dept. Union	N

Election Results

2002 general	Bart Stupak (D)	150,701	(68%)	($717,661)
	Don Hooper (R)	69,254	(31%)	($12,952)
	Other	2,732	(1%)	
2002 primary	Bart Stupak (D)	unopposed		
2000 general	Bart Stupak (D)	169,649	(58%)	($971,337)
	Chuck Yob (R)	117,300	(40%)	($691,468)
	Other	3,620	(1%)	

Prior Winning Percentages: 1998 (59%); 1996 (71%); 1994 (57%); 1992 (54%)

The People		Race/Ethnic Origin	Ancestry	
Area size:	27,809 sq. mi.	93.8% White	German: 15.8%	English: 7.7%
Urban population:	33.4%	1.0% Black	Irish: 7.2%	
Rural population:	66.6%	0.4% Asian	**2000 Presidential Vote**	
Pop. 2000:	662,563	2.4% Native Am.	Bush (R)..............154,772	(52%)
Median income:	$34,076	0.0% Hawaiian	Gore (D)..............135,503	(45%)
Poverty status:	11.2%	1.4% Two+ races	Other....................9,371	(3%)
Military veterans:	16.9%	0.0% Other	**Cook Partisan Voting Index:** R + 4	
		0.9% Hispanic Origin		

Occupation	Blue collar: 28.8%	White collar: 50.7%	Gray collar: 20.5%

Michigan's Upper Peninsula, commonly known as the UP, is a land apart. Surrounded on three sides by frigid Lake Superior and Lake Michigan, it has its own flora, including the world's largest known living object, a giant fungus that lives under 37 acres of a forest floor and is 1,500 years old. Although the UP is no farther north than Montreal or Seattle, it has one of the coldest climates in settled parts of North America. "In October, usually, the first snow falls steady on the north-land," writes Dixie Lee Franklin in *A Most Superior Land*, "whispering teasing promises of more to come"—for eight months more. Far away from any major city, with ground too frozen and stony and a growing season too short for most crops, the Upper Peninsula was explored by French voyagers more than 300 years ago but was never thickly settled until prospectors found rich veins of ore here. The mineral veins of the Keweenaw Peninsula produced 13.3 billion pounds of copper; the Marquette, Menominee and Gogebic iron ranges have more than one billion tons of iron ore. Starting in the 1880s, immigrants flocked here to work the mines: Irish, Italians, Swedes, Norwegians, miners' sons from Wales and Cornwall, and most prominently Finns, who must have found this cold land with its lakes and hills much like their home. By 1900, the UP was a northern industrial belt, with a few bosses and some absentee overlords and a work force disposed to radical ideas and union movements.

A major strike in 1913–14 and falling ore prices after World War I—events that would be long forgotten elsewhere—are remembered in the UP as the beginning of its decline: The UP's population peaked at 332,000 in 1920. The copper veins were mostly depleted by then, mining iron ore became less labor-intensive, and lumber and farming provided only a few thousand jobs. In the last half century, there has been great migration to Detroit, Chicago and the West Coast; the UP's population has hovered around 300,000, rising to 318,000 in 2000. But "Yoopers"—who some say have their own dialect, "Yoopanese"—remain devoted to their land.

The 1st Congressional District includes the Upper Peninsula and 16 northern-tier counties in the Lower Peninsula. Nearly half the people live in the UP; the remainder live south of the breathtaking Mackinac Bridge. This is a vast area, in sheer size the second-largest district east of the Mississippi (after Maine's 2d), and it has the most shoreline of any district; it is a 490-mile drive from Ironwood at the western end of the UP to the edge of Bay City on the southern tip of Saginaw Bay. The Lower Peninsula counties have two different personalities. On Lake Huron— the sunrise side—are smaller industrial towns and resorts that grew in the 1990s. On Lake Michigan are affluent resort areas around Petoskey and Charlevoix, long summer places for people from Chicago (this is Ernest Hemingway's "up in Michigan"). Politically, the UP has long been Democratic, some parts more than others; but this is one part of Michigan that did not like Al Gore's environmental stands, and the UP went for George W. Bush in 2000. The Lake Michigan shore of the Lower Peninsula is growing fast and heavily Republican, the sunrise side is growing more slowly and politically marginal. The 1st District voted solidly for Bush in 2000 and narrowly for Republican governor candidate Dick Posthumus in 2002, even as both lost statewide.

The congressman from the 1st District is Bart Stupak, a Democrat and a "Yooper" from Menominee on the Wisconsin border. He was a police officer in Escanaba, then became a Michigan state trooper in 1974 and also earned a law degree; in 1984 he was injured in the line of duty and retired from the force. In 1988 he was elected to the Michigan House; in 1990 he lost a race for the state Senate. Stupak got into the 1992 House race when incumbent Republican Bob Davis, with 878 overdrafts on the House bank, decided to drop out. In the general he beat Republican Philip Ruppe, who had represented the district from 1966–78, by 54%–44%.

In the House, Stupak has paid great attention to local issues. He formed the Law Enforcement Caucus and in 2002 enacted a ban on possession of body armor by felons plus increased penalties for crimes committed by persons wearing body armor; the legislation is named for a policeman from Alabama and another formerly from Stupak's district who were killed in shootouts by criminals wearing armor. When a Sault Ste. Marie, Ontario, firm tried to sell Lake Superior water to China, he sponsored a resolution to prevent sale of any Great Lake water to a foreign country—at least until federal standards were in place. He opposed slant drilling for oil and gas under the Great Lakes and worked on the successful bill to kill it in 2001; both major party candidates for governor in 2002 opposed it. When the Energy Department wanted to transport plutonium fuel rods from Los Alamos to Ontario, he led opposition to the route through Michigan; ultimately, the shipment proceeded, without incident. Worried about the viability of the state's last two iron mines, both in Marquette County, he criticized Bush's tariffs on steel imports because they were not high enough.

Stupak's voting record has been toward the center for House Democrats, though he is more conservative than most of them on cultural issues. He is strongly opposed to abortion, and spoke out against it at the 1996 Democratic National Convention; when invited to speak at the 2000 convention, he talked about his district. In February 2003, the House passed the bill he cosponsored to prohibit cloning, including for the production of embryos intended for research. He has become well known in the House for his unpredictability and for taking his time making decisions on issues.

All this has served him well in elections. Once in office, he had several competitive contests but none serious enough to jeopardize his seat. On Mother's Day 2000, Stupak suffered a personal tragedy, which for a time raised questions about his political future. His 17-year-old son B.J., a high school football player and class president, killed himself on the morning after his prom; more than 60 House members attended the funeral in Menominee. In coping with the aftermath, Bart and his wife Laurie eventually focused on their son's use of Accutane, a prescription-drug for acne treatment; the Food and Drug Administration had issued warnings about adverse psychological effects, including suicide attempts. In October, Stupak went public with his concerns and he later organized a House hearing about Accutane. He and his wife console other grieving families, he devotes part of his Web site to Accutane and he hopes to eventually take legislative action against the drug, whose sales have declined because of news reports about its risks. During the 2000 campaign, there was talk that Stupak was considering retirement. Stupak was facing a vigorous challenge from Chuck Yob, a longtime Republican National committeeman, who criticized Stupak for taking more than 80% of his campaign money from special interest groups; the NRA endorsed Yob. But Stupak argued that voters favored common-sense gun laws, and voters seemed to be in no mood for controversy after the family tragedy. Stupak won 58%–40%, losing only one county.

Republican redistricters made the district a little more Democratic by removing the Republican Traverse City area and adding marginal sunrise side counties and part of Democratic Bay County. They hope a Republican can still win it if Stupak does not run, but there is little chance as long as he does: in 2002, he won 68%–31%.

SECOND DISTRICT

Rep. Pete Hoekstra (R)

Elected 1992, 6th term; b. Oct. 30, 1953, Groningen, Netherlands; home, Holland; Hope Col., B.A. 1975, U. of MI, M.B.A. 1977; Christian Reformed; married (Diane).

Professional Career: Furniture Exec., Herman Miller Co., 1977–92.

DC Office: 2234 RHOB 20515, 202-225-4401; Fax: 202-226-0779; Web site: www.house.gov/hoekstra.

District Offices: Cadillac, 231-775-0050; Holland, 616-395-0030; Muskegon, 231-722-8386.

Committees: *Education & the Workforce* (4th of 27 R): Select Education (Chmn.); Workforce Protections. *Permanent Select Committee on Intelligence* (7th of 11 R): Human Intelligence, Analysis & Counterintelligence; Intelligence Policy & National Security; Technical & Tactical Intelligence (Chmn.). *Transportation & Infrastructure* (8th of 41 R): Coast Guard & Maritime Transportation; Highways, Transit & Pipelines.

Group Ratings

	ADA	ACLU	AFS	LCV	CON	ITIC	NTU	COC	ACU	NTLC	CHC
2002	5	27	11	38	97	62	62	85	92	94	100
2001	10	—	10	29	—	—	74	91	88	—	—

National Journal Ratings

	2001 LIB	—	2001 CONS		2002 LIB	—	2002 CONS
Economic	28%	—	69%		16%	—	81%
Social	35%	—	63%		38%	—	61%
Foreign	56%	—	41%		46%	—	53%

Key Votes of the 107th Congress

1. Approve Bush Tax Cuts	Y	5. Faith-Based Charities	Y	9. Trade Promotion Authority	N
2. Limit Patients' Bill of Rights	Y	6. Bar Gays in the Boy Scouts	Y	10. Bar Funds for Intl. Court	Y
3. Campaign Finance Reform	N	7. Ban Partial-Birth Abortion	Y	11. Authorize Force in Iraq	Y
4. Ban ANWR Development	N	8. Arm Commercial Pilots	N	12. Deny Home. Sec. Dept. Union	Y

Election Results

2002 general	Pete Hoekstra (R)	156,937	(70%)	($272,845)
	Jeffrey Wrisley (D)	61,749	(28%)	($23,316)
	Other	4,221	(2%)	
2002 primary	Pete Hoekstra (R)	unopposed		
2000 general	Pete Hoekstra (R)	186,762	(64%)	($291,642)
	Bob Shrauger (D)	96,370	(33%)	($171,728)
	Other	6,793	(2%)	

Prior Winning Percentages: 1998 (69%); 1996 (65%); 1994 (75%); 1992 (63%)

The People		Race/Ethnic Origin	Ancestry	
Area size:	5,508 sq. mi.	87.5% White	German: 15.3%	Dutch: 14.8%
Urban population:	56.2%	4.5% Black	English: 7.1%	
Rural population:	43.8%	1.0% Asian	**2000 Presidential Vote**	
Pop. 2000:	662,563	0.6% Native Am.	Bush (R)...............172,428	(59%)
Median income:	$42,589	0.0% Hawaiian	Gore (D)...............111,739	(38%)
Poverty status:	8.9%	1.2% Two+ races	Other....................6,550	(2%)
Military veterans:	13.2%	0.1% Other	**Cook Partisan Voting Index:** R +11	
		5.2% Hispanic Origin		
Occupation	Blue collar: 33.1%	White collar: 51.3%	Gray collar: 15.6%	

Lining the eastern shoreline of Lake Michigan, where the lake winds temper the frigid Michigan winters, are some of the nation's longest and highest sand dunes. In the late 19th century, this shoreline was America's greatest lumber country; the ports on the small rivers were choked with logs and full of lumbermen from Norway and Sweden, Ireland and Scotland, Quebec and New England. During the timber boom, the shoreline just to the south was the locus of America's largest migration from the Netherlands and still has the nation's largest concentration of Dutch-Americans. Wooden shoes are now seen only in the Tulip Festival in Holland, but here conscientious Dutch work habits have produced some of the most highly skilled workers in America, and major companies have grown up, like Gerber Foods in Fremont and Herman Miller furniture in Zeeland.

The 2d Congressional District occupies the Lake Michigan shoreline counties, plus a tier of counties inland including part of Grand Rapids's Kent County, from the lumber country around Manistee south to Holland and the resort town of Saugatuck. Some 15% of people here claim Dutch ancestry. Politically, the district is one of Michigan's two most Republican (the other is the Grand Rapids 3d). Its first Yankee settlers were part of the original Republican Party, and Dutch-Americans with their innate conservatism vie with Cuban-Americans for the title of America's most heavily Republican ethnic group (though there is little similarity in their cultural style). Holland and surrounding Ottawa County voted 71% for Republican Dick Posthumus for governor in 2002; despite that, in the nation's first such referendum, the town in 2000 voted against a proposal from Christian conservative groups to bar access to obscene materials on the public library's computers.

The congressman from the 2d District is Pete Hoekstra (pronounced *HOOK-stra*), who emigrated from the Netherlands at 3, graduated from Hope College in Holland (with a semester in Washington during Watergate) and got an MBA at the University of Michigan. Hoekstra went to work at Herman Miller, where he helped develop the "Equa Chair" seat and became a vice president. In 1992, he decided to run what seemed an improbable campaign for Congress against Guy Vander Jagt, 26-year incumbent and chairman of the NRCC since 1975. Hoekstra saved up vacation time and took a county-by-county bicycle tour of the district. With an earnestness that rang true, Hoekstra called for citizen, not career, politicians; refused PAC money and supported abolishing PACs; advocated 12-year term limits; promised to uphold family values and to oppose abortion. Hoekstra spent only $55,600 to Vander Jagt's $725,000. But on primary day, he carried the heavily Dutch Ottawa and Allegan Counties, 53%–31%; they cast 59% of the primary vote, and so Hoekstra won 46%–40%. He won the general election easily and has not been threatened since.

Hoekstra brought to Washington a mistrust of government and a desire to apply the participatory management ideas he had developed at Herman Miller. In early 1994 he was asked by Newt Gingrich to plan how to manage a Republican House, something few others thought they would live to see. After his proposals were stalled in March 1996, he had an angry confrontation with Gingrich. Only a few of his reforms were adopted: the House barred former members from lobbying on the floor, and it passed (though the Senate didn't) a ban on pensions to former members convicted of a felony.

In 1995, Hoekstra got the chair of the Oversight and Investigations Subcommittee of the Education and Workforce Committee. In summer 1997 he started on two major assignments from the leadership, with a special $1.4 million budget. The first was an investigation of labor law. Republican leaders hoped he would investigate the role of unions in the 1996 campaigns, but instead he conducted what he called the American Worker at a Crossroads project. Another assignment was investigating the Teamsters Union. The 1996 election of Teamsters president Ron Carey had to be set aside in 1997 and the union treasury was found depleted of $150 million. But the Teamsters were unforthcoming with evidence and subpoena problems delayed the probe until 1998 when the requirement of subcommittee approval for every deposition and subpoena was dropped. Hoekstra would not hold publicized hearings: "I don't want to grandstand. It's the wrong thing to do." In early 1999 the leadership took the issue away from Hoekstra and gave it to committee chairman Bill Goodling. In May 2001 he was one of 52 Republicans voting against the annual testing provisions in George W. Bush's education bill. He was the only Michigan member to vote against the bill in December 2001, when it passed overwhelmingly; he was unhappy that vouchers had been voted down.

Hoekstra has voted against most Republicans on issues like missile defense and PNTR with China. He got a seat on the Intelligence Committee in 2001 and sponsored the bill to improve intelligence sharing between law enforcement and intelligence agencies that passed overwhelmingly in June 2002. Some of his causes have local angles. He pressed hard for the Competition in Contracting law that ended Federal Prison Industries mandatory source status for federal purchases of office furniture; three of the nation's biggest office furniture manufacturers are located in Holland and Grand Rapids. In August 2002 he got a law authorizing the State Department to pay compensation to the survivors of Veronica Bowers, a western Michiganian whose plane was wrongfully shot down by Peru drug police. In April 2002, after much pressure, the Agriculture Department announced it would purchase processed asparagus; western Michigan produces 90% of American asparagus.

Hoekstra has made several attempts to win Republican leadership positions. In November 1998 he ran for vice chairman of the House Republican Conference but he was eliminated on the second ballot. After the 2000 election, he voiced interest in succeeding John Kasich as Budget chairman. And he sought the chairmanship of the Education and the Workforce Committee, but he lost to John Boehner in the closed-door meetings of the Republican Steering Committee. Hoekstra unsuccessfully urged that the committee be divided into two parts with Hoekstra taking the education panel; party leaders were not keen on creating a new committee and may have known that Hoekstra didn't like Bush's testing proposal. In May 2001 he voiced interest in the chairmanship of the Republican Policy Committee when it was thought that Christopher Cox would be appointed a federal judge; but the appointment never happened. One gets the sense that unity-minded Republican leaders see Hoekstra as too independent-minded and unpredictable for a leadership post. Some of his proposals are indeed quixotic: He has proposed a constitutional amendment to establish recall for members of Congress, nonbinding national referenda on issues and a "none of the above" choice in elections.

In 1992, as term limits passed in Michigan, Hoekstra pledged to serve only 12 years. By 2002 he had changed his mind and announced he would run again in an open letter to his constituents. He also communicates with his district by posting a daily travel diary from his foreign trips. "A five-and-a-half hour flight to Amsterdam, a little more than eight hours to Detroit, another 35 minutes to Grand Rapids, an hour drive, and I will be home," he wrote in January 2003 near the end of a fact-finding trip to England and Kuwait. "For the rest of the week, I will meet with constituents to discuss what I learned on this trip and other issues important to Western Michigan."

THIRD DISTRICT

Rep. Vernon Ehlers (R)

Elected Dec. 1993, 5th term; b. Feb. 6, 1934, Pipestone, MN; home, Grand Rapids; Calvin Col., 1952–55; U. of CA at Berkeley, A.B. 1956, Ph.D. 1960, U. of Heidelberg, Germany, 1961–62; Christian Reformed; married (Johanna).

Elected Office: Kent Cnty. Comm., 1975–82, Chmn., 1978–81; MI House of Reps., 1982–86; MI Senate, 1986–93, Pres. Pro Tem, 1990–93.

Professional Career: Prof., Calvin Col., 1966–82.

DC Office: 1714 LHOB 20515, 202-225-3831; Fax: 202-225-5144; Web site: www.house.gov/ehlers.

District Office: Grand Rapids, 616-451-8383.

Committees: *Education & the Workforce* (11th of 27 R): 21st Century Competitiveness; Education Reform. *House Administration* (2d of 6 R). *Science* (9th of 25 R): Energy; Environment, Technology and Standards (Chmn.). *Transportation & Infrastructure* (10th of 41 R): Aviation; Water Resources & Environment.

Group Ratings

	ADA	ACLU	AFS	LCV	CON	ITIC	NTU	COC	ACU	NTLC	CHC
2002	15	27	0	63	50	100	59	95	80	83	100
2001	10	—	0	57	—	—	60	91	68	—	—

National Journal Ratings

	2001 LIB	—	2001 CONS		2002 LIB	—	2002 CONS
Economic	39%	—	61%		19%	—	80%
Social	41%	—	59%		48%	—	52%
Foreign	49%	—	47%		53%	—	46%

Key Votes of the 107th Congress

1. Approve Bush Tax Cuts	Y	5. Faith-Based Charities	Y	9. Trade Promotion Authority	Y
2. Limit Patients' Bill of Rights	Y	6. Bar Gays in the Boy Scouts	Y	10. Bar Funds for Intl. Court	N
3. Campaign Finance Reform	N	7. Ban Partial-Birth Abortion	Y	11. Authorize Force in Iraq	Y
4. Ban ANWR Development	Y	8. Arm Commercial Pilots	N	12. Deny Home. Sec. Dept. Union	Y

Election Results

2002 general	Vernon Ehlers (R)	153,131	(70%)	($371,513)
	Kathryn Lynnes (D)	61,987	(28%)	($8,290)
	Other	3,737	(2%)	
2002 primary	Vernon Ehlers (R)	unopposed		
2000 general	Vernon Ehlers (R)	179,539	(65%)	($302,826)
	Timothy Steele (D)	91,309	(33%)	($26,024)
	Other	5,415	(2%)	

Prior Winning Percentages: 1998 (73%); 1996 (69%); 1994 (74%); 1993 (67%)

The People		Race/Ethnic Origin	Ancestry	
Area size:	1,897 sq. mi.	82.2% White	German: 14.6%	Dutch: 13.1%
Urban population:	77.1%	7.9% Black	Irish: 7.9%	
Rural population:	22.9%	1.6% Asian	**2000 Presidential Vote**	
Pop. 2000:	662,563	0.4% Native Am.	Bush (R)..............170,622	(60%)
Median income:	$45,936	0.0% Hawaiian	Gore (D)..............110,121	(38%)
Poverty status:	8.6%	1.5% Two+ races	Other......................5,942	(2%)
Military veterans:	11.4%	0.1% Other	**Cook Partisan Voting Index:** R +11	
		6.2% Hispanic Origin		

Occupation	Blue collar: 29.5%	White collar: 56.7%	Gray collar: 13.8%

Grand Rapids is Michigan's second-largest city, the center of its most prosperous and confident metropolitan area. The city's roots are in trees: It grew as a center for processing and turning into furniture the hardwood forests of northern Michigan. By the early 20th century, Grand Rapids was the leading furniture manufacturer in the nation. But the Depression knocked the bottom out of the residential furniture market, and many manufacturers moved to cheaper-labor North Carolina. So Grand Rapids had to reinvent itself, and did. It went into office furniture, and today, three of the nation's largest office furniture manufacturers (Steelcase, Haworth and Herman Miller) are located in or near here. It capitalized also on a knack for sales. Rich DeVos and Jay Van Andel started Amway, the direct sales empire, which now has half of its sales abroad, and Frederik and Hendrik Meijer started Meijer's Thrifty Acres, combining supermarkets with discount stores in a way that even Wal-Mart has not been able to equal. Grand Rapids is also the center of a machine tool empire, the home of Wolverine World Wide, maker of Hush Puppy shoes and the headquarters of Bissell and its carpet sweepers. Fifty years ago Grand Rapids and its up-and-coming businesses were outshined by Detroit and the auto industry. Today, the Grand Rapids region has been growing rapidly and has been a major engine in Michigan's surging economy.

One ingredient in Grand Rapids's success is its unique ethnic mix. It was founded by New England Yankees, but much of its character was set by the Dutch immigrants who began arriving in western Michigan in the 1870s, and are still coming today; 13% of people here claim Dutch ancestry (probably no other American city has such a high proportion of "V" pages in the phone book). The Dutch brought with them a piety witnessed in their Reform and Christian Reform churches, and a culture of hard work and precision craftsmanship; their cultural conservatism and belief in market economics runs deep. Dutch tradition and entrepreneurial success have been the ingredients of a civic activism that has given Grand Rapids a host of creative civic institutions –and an Alexander Calder stabile—that are the match of any city in the country.

Politically, Grand Rapids has been the center of Michigan Republicanism for much of the last century. It has also produced national Republican leaders. Arthur Vandenberg, originally a newspaper editor, was U.S. senator from 1928–51; once an isolationist, he provided key support for the bipartisan internationalist foreign policies of Franklin Roosevelt and Harry Truman. Another was Gerald Ford, who rose to House Republican leader in 1965, vice president in 1973, and then president after Richard Nixon resigned in 1974. Nixon got a bit of a nudge from the Grand Rapids area when, in a February 1974 special election, it voted to replace Ford with a Democrat, a clear sign that the Republican heartland was turning on Nixon. Since then, however, the area became more Republican than ever; in 2000 Grand Rapids and Kent County voted 59% for George W. Bush.

The 3d Congressional District includes Grand Rapids and almost all of Kent County, plus Ionia and Barry Counties to the east and south. It is the most Republican district in Michigan, indeed one of the most Republican in the Midwest.

The congressman from the 3d District is Vern Ehlers, chosen in a December 1993 special election. Ehlers grew up in small-town Minnesota, the son of a Christian Reform minister, attended Calvin College in Grand Rapids, got a Ph.D. in physics at Berkeley and then returned to Calvin to teach for 17 years. In 1974, concerned about local waste management, he was elected Kent County commissioner; in 1982 he won a seat in the state House and in 1986 the state Senate. After Congressman Paul Henry died in July 1993, Ehlers ran to succeed him, as he had in both houses of the legislature. He won the November primary with 33% of the vote; a month later he whipped the Democrat 67%–23%.

Ehlers brought to House Republicans, then entering their 40th year in the minority, a majority mindset. That brought him to the attention of Newt Gingrich, who named him to his transition team after the 1994 election. He assigned Ehlers, the first research physicist in Congress, to lead efforts to revamp the House's computer system. In 1995 Ehlers responded with a system making available vote tallies, public hearing transcripts and texts of amendments and bills. His religious faith and scientific training have left Ehlers with a middle-of-the-House voting record. As co-chairman of the Great Lakes Task Force, he called attention to water loss and diversion threats. As vice chairman of the Science Committee, he produced "Unlocking Our Future," the first major report on federal support of science in half a century, calling for "substantial and stable" science funding. He told Fermi Lab physicists, "It's a real indictment of the physics community that more of us haven't gotten involved."

As chairman of the Science Subcommittee overseeing EPA and NOAA, he has sponsored several laws that have won widespread backing. The House unanimously passed his bill for $100 million for the National Science Foundation to train math and science teachers in July 2001 and his bill to create a new position to improve the use of science in EPA in April 2002—a measure supported both by environmental restriction groups and those decrying EPA regulation. In November 2002 he gained passage of three bills. One provided $250 million over five years to clean up contaminated sediments in the Great Lakes basin. Another reauthorized the Sea Grant College Program, and provided for peer-review of its work and inclusion of the Great Lakes. A third was a cybersecurity bill to enhance computer security. Also that month he sponsored a bill to provide for research on and control of invasive aquatic species, often introduced in ballast water discharge. In November 2001 he became chairman of the Joint Committee on the Library of Congress; he has served on the library boards of Grand Rapids, Kent County and the state of Michigan and helped set up the Lakeland Library Cooperative.

Ehlers has a penchant for compromise. As head of a three-member task force on Robert Dornan's challenge to his 984-vote defeat in 1996, Ehlers looked over the evidence and announced that it showed "a large amount" of vote fraud but not enough to vacate the seat. That may help explain why Speaker Dennis Hastert bypassed him and selected Bob Ney to chair the House Administration Committee after the 2000 election.

Ehlers refuses to take more than 30% of his campaign money from outside the district. He has been re-elected by very wide margins.

FOURTH DISTRICT

Rep. Dave Camp (R)

Elected 1990, 7th term; b. July 9, 1953, Midland; home, Midland; Albion Col., B.A. 1975, U. of San Diego Law Schl., J.D. 1978; Catholic; married (Nancy).

Elected Office: MI House of Reps., 1988–90.

Professional Career: Practicing atty., 1978–90; MI Special Asst. Atty. Gen., 1980–84; A.A., U.S. Rep. Bill Schuette, 1984–87.

DC Office: 137 CHOB 20515, 202-225-3561; Fax: 202-225-9679; Web site: www.house.gov/camp.

District Offices: Midland, 517-631-2552; Traverse City, 231-929-4711.

Committees: *Select Committee on Homeland Security* (15th of 27 R): Cybersecurity, Science and Research & Development; Emergency Preparedness & Response; Infrastructure & Border Security (Chmn.). *Ways & Means* (8th of 24 R): Health; Human Resources; Trade.

Group Ratings

	ADA	ACLU	AFS	LCV	CON	ITIC	NTU	COC	ACU	NTLC	CHC
2002	0	13	0	0	25	100	55	100	96	86	100
2001	0	—	0	14	—	—	66	100	96	—	—

National Journal Ratings

	2001 LIB —	2001 CONS		2002 LIB —	2002 CONS
Economic	15%	82%		0%	91%
Social	20%	69%		0%	75%
Foreign	33%	60%		24%	72%

Key Votes of the 107th Congress

1. Approve Bush Tax Cuts	Y	5. Faith-Based Charities	Y	9. Trade Promotion Authority	Y
2. Limit Patients' Bill of Rights	Y	6. Bar Gays in the Boy Scouts	Y	10. Bar Funds for Intl. Court	Y
3. Campaign Finance Reform	N	7. Ban Partial-Birth Abortion	Y	11. Authorize Force in Iraq	Y
4. Ban ANWR Development	N	8. Arm Commercial Pilots	Y	12. Deny Home. Sec. Dept. Union	Y

Election Results

2002 general	Dave Camp (R)	149,090	(68%)	($697,237)
	Lawrence Hollenbeck (D)	65,950	(30%)	($10,172)
	Other	3,533	(2%)	
2002 primary	Dave Camp (R)	unopposed		
2000 general	Dave Camp (R)	182,128	(68%)	($1,026,361)
	Lawrence Hollenbeck (D)	78,019	(29%)	($6,099)
	Other	7,672	(3%)	

Prior Winning Percentages: 1998 (91%); 1996 (65%); 1994 (73%); 1992 (63%); 1990 (65%)

The People		Race/Ethnic Origin	Ancestry	
Area size:	8,053 sq. mi.	92.8% White	German: 19.5%	English: 8.9%
Urban population:	41.4%	2.1% Black	Irish: 8.2%	
Rural population:	58.6%	0.7% Asian	**2000 Presidential Vote**	
Pop. 2000:	662,563	0.8% Native Am.	Bush (R) 154,539	(54%)
Median income:	$39,020	0.0% Hawaiian	Gore (D) 126,282	(44%)
Poverty status:	10.5%	1.1% Two+ races	Other 7,468	(3%)
Military veterans:	13.6%	0.1% Other	**Cook Partisan Voting Index:** R + 5	
		2.4% Hispanic Origin		

Occupation   Blue collar: 28.7%   White collar: 53.5%   Gray collar: 17.8%

Flat and treeless for miles, the central reaches of Michigan's Lower Peninsula are farm country, exposed to bitter winds and snow drifts in winter and shining sun for precious weeks in summer. Like the steppes of Eastern Europe, these are farmlands that produce hearty crops: potatoes, navy beans, sugar beets. The little cities here are often small factory towns, with neat tree-lined streets on a grid layout that suddenly end and turn to bare fields. Each city has some distinction. Midland in 1891 was a declining lumber town when Herbert Dow perfected an electrolytic process to extract chemicals from northern Michigan's extensive brine wells; that was the start of Dow Chemical, still headquartered in this now upscale town. Owosso in 1902 was the birthplace of Thomas E. Dewey, later New York governor and Republican candidate for president in 1944 and 1948. It was also the home of novelist James Oliver Curwood and his Curwood Castle writing studio; today it hosts the Curwood Festival, lovingly chronicled by Thomas Mallon in *Rockets and Rodeos*, and is the site of Mallon's novel *Dewey Defeats Truman*. Mount Pleasant, to the north, is the site of Central Michigan University; it is the home base of former Governor John Engler.

   The 4th Congressional District includes much of this territory north of Lansing and Grand Rapids and west of Flint and Saginaw. It stretches north up the freeways, hemmed in between U.S. 131 to the west and I-75 to the east, both routes where thousands drive in fall to hunt and in winter to ski, into the rolling country around Houghton Lake, once lumber country and now a retirement and resort area, with trailers and condominiums between knotty-pine cottages clustered around icy green lakes. It has more farms than any other district in Michigan. Redistricting added the boom area around Traverse City, which has the world's largest concentration of red tart cherry orchards and is burgeoning with condominiums, resorts and more than two dozen wineries: this district is the main reason Michigan leads the nation in production of tart cherries, blueberries and dry edible beans. Politically, it remains mostly Republican territory, though some counties vote Democratic on occasion; the most Republican areas are Midland and Traverse City. The district voted for George W. Bush in 2000 and Republican governor candidate Dick Posthumus in 2002.

The congressman from the 4th District is Dave Camp, a Republican first elected in 1990. Camp grew up in Midland and returned there after school to practice law. In 1984 he managed the successful congressional campaign of his boyhood friend Bill Schuette; in 1990 Schuette unsuccessfully ran against Senator Carl Levin, and Camp ran for Congress after having served two years in the state House. His key victory was in the Republican primary, where with 62% in Midland County he beat former legislator and Pat Robertson supporter Al Cropsey, 33%–30%. He has won since without difficulty.

Camp has a generally conservative voting record and is influential on the Ways and Means Committee, where he has been an ally of Chairman Bill Thomas. He played a key role in passing the welfare bill in 1996, helping to write the two bills vetoed by Bill Clinton. At the time, he and John Ensign circulated a letter signed ultimately by about 100 Republicans urging that they separate their welfare and Medicaid changes, which had been passed as one bill, and vote on welfare reform alone, daring Clinton to sign it and make history, or veto it and make it a campaign issue. Newt Gingrich and the Republican leadership decided to do this, essentially disengaging House Republicans from the fate of the flagging Bob Dole presidential campaign. The bill passed, Clinton signed it, and the incumbent president and incumbent congressional Republicans got credit in November.

Camp has worked on other issues. In 2000, he helped win enactment of the Intercountry Adoption Act, which designates the State Department to help adoptive parents in dealing with officials in other nations. "We have a responsibility to establish international standards," said Camp, who handled adoptions and worked with the foster care system as an attorney. He authored the Organ Donor Card Insert Act, under which 70 million taxpayers received organ donor information with their income tax refunds. Medicare reforms have included his provisions to provide permanent drug coverage for transplant recipients and to improve reimbursement for kidney dialysis patients. When House Republicans passed their prescription drug bill in 2002, they included an amendment by Camp to cover cholesterol screening for all beneficiaries. The Water Resources Development Act in 2000 included Camp's provision to ensure that sales of Great Lakes water will remain under state management.

Camp has had minimal opposition in the 4th District. In 2002, his Green Party opponent was a Central Michigan University political science professor who had two criminal convictions since 1990. Camp keeps in close touch with the district by signing every constituent letter that leaves his office, often with a personal note—a total of roughly 30,000 each year. At Ways and Means, he is young enough that if he stays in the House he could some day be chairman.

FIFTH DISTRICT

Rep. Dale Kildee (D)

Elected 1976, 14th term; b. Sept. 16, 1929, Flint; home, Flint; Sacred Heart Seminary, B.A. 1952, U. of MI, M.A. 1961, Rotary Fellow, U. of Peshawar, Pakistan; Catholic; married (Gayle).

Elected Office: MI House of Reps., 1964–74; MI Senate, 1974–75.

Professional Career: H.S. teacher, 1954–64.

DC Office: 2107 RHOB 20515, 202-225-3611; Fax: 202-225-6393; Web site: www.house.gov/kildee.

District Office: Flint, 810-239-1437.

Committees: *Education & the Workforce* (2d of 22 D): 21st Century Competitiveness (RMM); Employer-Employee Relations. *Resources* (2d of 24 D): Forests & Forest Health; National Parks, Recreation & Public Lands.

Group Ratings

	ADA	ACLU	AFS	LCV	CON	ITIC	NTU	COC	ACU	NTLC	CHC
2002	80	53	100	88	43	38	16	40	8	0	33
2001	85	—	100	86	—	—	10	35	32	—	—

National Journal Ratings

	2001 LIB — 2001 CONS		2002 LIB — 2002 CONS	
Economic	80%	— 19%	88%	— 10%
Social	58%	— 42%	53%	— 46%
Foreign	67%	— 32%	66%	— 33%

Key Votes of the 107th Congress

1. Approve Bush Tax Cuts	N	5. Faith-Based Charities	N	9. Trade Promotion Authority	N
2. Limit Patients' Bill of Rights	N	6. Bar Gays in the Boy Scouts	N	10. Bar Funds for Intl. Court	Y
3. Campaign Finance Reform	Y	7. Ban Partial-Birth Abortion	Y	11. Authorize Force in Iraq	N
4. Ban ANWR Development	Y	8. Arm Commercial Pilots	Y	12. Deny Home. Sec. Dept. Union	N

Election Results

2002 general	Dale Kildee (D)	158,709	(92%)	($416,089)
	Clint Foster (Lib)	9,344	(5%)	
	Other	5,286	(3%)	
2002 primary	Dale Kildee (D)	unopposed		
2000 general (MI 9)	Dale Kildee (D)	158,184	(61%)	($307,376)
	Grant Garrett (R)	92,926	(36%)	($104,366)
	Other	7,818	(3%)	

Prior Winning Percentages: 1998 (56%); 1996 (59%); 1994 (51%); 1992 (54%); 1990 (68%); 1988 (76%); 1986 (80%); 1984 (93%); 1982 (75%); 1980 (93%); 1978 (77%); 1976 (70%)

The People		Race/Ethnic Origin	Ancestry	
Area size:	1,780 sq. mi.	75.0% White	German: 15.3%	Irish: 7.6%
Urban population:	79.4%	18.5% Black	English: 7.4%	
Rural population:	20.6%	0.7% Asian	**2000 Presidential Vote**	
Pop. 2000:	662,563	0.5% Native Am.	Gore (D)	174,788 (61%)
Median income:	$39,675	0.0% Hawaiian	Bush (R)	106,445 (37%)
Poverty status:	13.7%	1.7% Two + races	Other	5,811 (2%)
Military veterans:	13.2%	0.1% Other	**Cook Partisan Voting Index:** D + 12	
		3.6% Hispanic Origin		

Occupation	Blue collar: 31.4%	White collar: 51.0%	Gray collar: 17.6%

The flat plains south of Saginaw Bay, the inlet of Lake Huron that separates Michigan's Thumb (people really call it that) from the mitten of the Lower Peninsula, is one of the nation's premier industrial areas. Some 130 years ago it was the nation's premier lumber country, with huge stands of virgin trees being cut down and 36 sawmills in Bay City, with logs piled high along both banks of the Saginaw River in the 15 miles between Bay City and Saginaw. When the land was clear it was sown with beans—the navy beans which are the prime ingredient of Senate bean soup—and sugar beets. A century ago, industry followed. Flint, a small town on a minor branch of the Saginaw River, was the home base of W. C. Durant, the investor who merged several young auto firms and formed General Motors. GM put its Chevrolet and Buick factories in Flint and its power steering facility in Saginaw, chosen because it was already a center of precision machinery manufacturing. From 1910 through the 1960s, Flint grew lustily as it built Chevrolets and Buicks, attracting workers from the mountains of Kentucky and Tennessee and the Black Belt of Alabama; country music, blues and soul and Southern accents became common in an area originally settled by New England Yankees. There was turmoil, too. Flint was the scene in January 1937 of the great sit-down strike that, when Governor Frank Murphy refused to send the National Guard to enforce a court order, forced GM to recognize the United Auto Workers as the bargaining agent for all its workers. Yet in many ways the GM company towns built good lives for their citizens. The UAW-

GM contracts produced the world's highest wages for industrial workers and lavish fringe benefits, including a generous health care plan.

Then disaster struck. Auto sales plummeted with the oil shock of 1979, and imports, especially from Japan, that were higher-quality and lower-price than American cars, were taking an increasing share of the market. GM managers and UAW leaders assumed that increased labor costs could be passed along to consumers, that buyers were indifferent to quality and eager for new models. Those assumptions proved vitally wrong: not even the cleverest advertising could persuade Americans to buy a new American car every two years. In 1979 GM employed more than 70,000 workers in its Flint plants, a huge share of the labor force in a metro area of 430,000 people. Over the years, thousands left Flint as GM closed 12 of its 15 factories; by 2002 the GM payroll was down to less than 22,000. Flint's brave attempts to spruce up its downtown failed; its economic woes forced the state to take control of the city government in July 2002. But there has also been some upturn. American car manufacturers have grown more adaptable and resilient, and small high-skill manufacturing operations in the Saginaw area have grown up in old factory buildings once considered worthless; this is part of southern Michigan's industrial belt with the expertise to sustain just-in-time manufacturing.

The 5th Congressional District includes Flint and surrounding Genesee County, Saginaw and eastern Saginaw County, Bay City and eastern Bay County and rural Tuscola County, which is part of the Thumb. Flint, evenly divided between the parties when the sit-down strikes divided the community in the 1930s, is now heavily Democratic; Saginaw and Bay City somewhat less so. Tuscola County continues to vote Republican. Before the 2001 redistricting, Flint was in a district with northern Oakland County and Saginaw and Bay City were in a district that included all of the Thumb and the sunrise side coast of Lake Huron running 80 miles north of Bay City; both were represented by Democrats. Republican redistricters put the three cities together and used the other parts of the old districts to make adjacent districts more Republican. The current 5th is a district they will never seriously contest.

The congressman from the 5th District is Dale Kildee, a Democrat first elected in 1976 in the old Flint district. Kildee grew up in Flint, studied for the priesthood, taught at a Catholic high school in Detroit and at Flint Central. His door-to-door campaigning got him elected to a state legislative seat in 1964, at 35, and enabled him to beat a 26-year veteran of the state Senate in 1974. He won the House seat in 1976, when it was solidly Democratic, without a primary opponent and held it easily until the 1990s, when the district was redrawn to include a large chunk of Oakland County; Kildee was held below 55% in both 1992 and 1994, but his margins subsequently rebounded. Redistricting put Kildee in the same district with Bay City Democrat Jim Barcia, one of the more conservative Democrats in the House and, like Kildee, an opponent of abortion. Barcia was only 50 and had served 10 years in the House. But evidently he found the prospect of taking on Kildee daunting, and decided to run for the state Senate, where he had served from 1982 to 1992 (After all, from Bay City it's a lot shorter trip to Lansing than to Washington). Kildee was reelected without Republican opposition in 2002.

Kildee has an intensity of conviction derived from the liberal tradition lively in the American Catholic church—a tradition with little regard for market economics, a strong sense of obligation to care for the needy and a cultural conservatism. He is always pro-union, opposes abortion and is something of a stickler on ethics. As a senior member of the Education and the Workforce Committee, he is a strong ally of teachers' unions, a backer of increased federal aid for education and an opponent of school choice; he worked in 2001 on the Democratic alternative to President Bush's "No Child Left Behind" education bill. He joined with Republican Mark Souder to retain separate grants for the Safe and Drug-Free Schools Program.

On other issues, Kildee was the first House member to argue imported minivans should be subject not to the 2.5% tariff for cars but to the 25% tariff for trucks; he was a strong opponent of NAFTA. On the Resources Committee, he has concentrated on Indian issues; he helped set up a Native American Caucus. Kildee can remember as a child traveling to the Grand Traverse reservation, where his grandfather had traded with Indians, and hearing his father talk of the Indians' plight. He took to visiting reservations and noted how the Bureau of Indian Affairs spruced them up for his visits; Kildee carries with his copy of the Constitution a copy of the 1832 Supreme Court decision that recognized Indian sovereignty.

SIXTH DISTRICT

Rep. Fred Upton (R)

Elected 1986, 9th term; b. Apr. 23, 1953, St. Joseph; home, St. Joseph; U. of MI, B.A. 1975; Protestant; married (Amey).

Professional Career: Project coord., U.S. Rep. David Stockman, 1975–80; Legis. Affairs, O.M.B., 1981–83, Dir., 1984–85.

DC Office: 2161 RHOB 20515, 202-225-3761; Fax: 202-225-4986; Web site: www.house.gov/upton.

District Offices: Kalamazoo, 269-385-0039; St. Joseph, 269-982-1986.

Committees: *Education & the Workforce* (10th of 27 R): 21st Century Competitiveness; Education Reform. *Energy & Commerce* (4th of 31 R): Commerce, Trade & Consumer Protection; Health; Telecommunications & The Internet (Chmn.).

Group Ratings

	ADA	ACLU	AFS	LCV	CON	ITIC	NTU	COC	ACU	NTLC	CHC
2002	5	13	0	25	77	100	58	95	92	86	75
2001	10	—	10	43	—	—	60	100	76	—	—

National Journal Ratings

	2001 LIB —	2001 CONS	2002 LIB —	2002 CONS
Economic	45%	56%	36%	61%
Social	43%	55%	39%	57%
Foreign	49%	47%	35%	60%

Key Votes of the 107th Congress

1. Approve Bush Tax Cuts	Y	5. Faith-Based Charities	Y
2. Limit Patients' Bill of Rights	Y	6. Bar Gays in the Boy Scouts	Y
3. Campaign Finance Reform	Y	7. Ban Partial-Birth Abortion	Y
4. Ban ANWR Development	N	8. Arm Commercial Pilots	Y

9. Trade Promotion Authority	Y
10. Bar Funds for Intl. Court	Y
11. Authorize Force in Iraq	Y
12. Deny Home. Sec. Dept. Union	Y

Election Results

2002 general	Fred Upton (R)	126,936	(69%)	($1,573,678)
	Gary Giguere (D)	53,793	(29%)	($18,028)
	Other	2,788	(2%)	
2002 primary	Fred Upton (R)	44,487	(66%)	
	Dale Shugars (R)	21,580	(32%)	
2000 general	Fred Upton (R)	159,373	(68%)	($620,512)
	James Bupp (D)	68,532	(29%)	
	Other	6,735	(3%)	

Prior Winning Percentages: 1998 (70%); 1996 (68%); 1994 (73%); 1992 (62%); 1990 (58%); 1988 (71%); 1986 (62%)

The People		Race/Ethnic Origin	Ancestry	
Area size:	3,420 sq. mi.	84.3% White	German: 17.2%	English: 8.3%
Urban population:	58.3%	8.8% Black	Irish: 8.3%	
Rural population:	41.7%	1.1% Asian	**2000 Presidential Vote**	
Pop. 2000:	662,563	0.5% Native Am.	Bush (R)..............138,658	(52%)
Median income:	$40,943	0.0% Hawaiian	Gore (D)..............119,740	(45%)
Poverty status:	11.4%	1.6% Two+ races	Other...................7,413	(3%)
Military veterans:	12.8%	0.1% Other	**Cook Partisan Voting Index:** R + 4	
		3.6% Hispanic Origin		

Occupation	Blue collar: 31.3%	White collar: 53.0%	Gray collar: 15.7%

The southwest corner of Michigan is at the western end of the overland trail from Detroit, where the state's two southern tiers of counties were settled by New England Yankees and Upstate New Yorkers in the 1830s and 1840s. They built small towns with schools and churches and colleges, supported temperance and opposed capital punishment, and in 1854 started the Republican party. There are towns in southwest Michigan that still recall proudly their past as termini of the Underground Railroad, and black families with ancestors who made their way north out of slavery to freedom. Later, big industries transformed some of the small towns into significant cities. Kalamazoo, started by Dutch-Americans who introduced celery to this country, became the home of what was once Upjohn pharmaceuticals. Predominantly black and struggling Benton Harbor and predominantly white and prosperous St. Joseph, twin towns on Lake Michigan originally known for cherry and peach orchards, became the home of Whirlpool appliances. This southwest corner is where the influence of Michigan recedes: People here watch Chicago television and root for the Cubs or White Sox rather than the Tigers.

The 6th Congressional District occupies this southwest corner of the state, with Kalamazoo and Benton Harbor-St. Joseph its two major urban areas, and three smaller counties and parts of two others besides. It was for many years arch-Republican territory, represented by a succession of congressmen who deplored federal spending and welfare state measures: New Deal opponent Clare Hoffman (1935–63), Nixon defender Edward Hutchinson (1963–77), and pork barrel critic and later Reagan Office of Management and Budget Director David Stockman (1977–81). More recently, Kalamazoo trended toward the Democrats, and the 6th (in only a slightly different form then) cast small pluralities for Bill Clinton in 1992 and 1996. But George W. Bush and Senator Spencer Abraham won here in 2000, despite losing statewide.

The congressman from the 6th District is Fred Upton. The grandson of one of the founders of Whirlpool, Upton grew up in St. Joseph, attended the University of Michigan and worked for David Stockman, first on his House staff, then from 1981–85 at OMB. He returned home and ran in the 1986 Republican primary against Congressman Mark Siljander, a conservative and evangelical Christian and won 55%–45%. Upton is less like the congressional David Stockman, a scourge of federal spending, and more like the OMB Stockman, who rued the Reagan tax cuts.

Upton has a moderate voting record and he has been anything but a team player in the Republican House. He has sought, with limited success, to use his leverage to reduce the size of tax cuts. He called for making Republican tax cuts in 1995 contingent on certification by the Clinton OMB that the budget was on a realistic path toward being balanced in 2002; as it turned out, the budget was balanced four years earlier than that target, at which point Upton based his tax-cutting caution on the need to pay down the national debt. He voted against some Republican environmental bills and called for a lifetime ban on former members' lobbying for foreign governments. Referring to the moderate Republicans' Tuesday Group, he said, "Our group was responsible for the positive agenda" in 1996 on welfare and the Safe Drinking Water Act. After that election, Upton decried the "shut-down, dark ages" approach taken by Republicans and said his party had come to be seen as "narrow" and "intolerant." He spoke out against John Kasich's proposed budget cuts. In December 1998, the Clinton White House hoped Upton would vote against impeachment, but in the final days he decided to vote for it. He has not missed a House vote since 1997.

Seniority increased Upton's prominence at the Energy and Commerce Committee. In 1999 and 2000, he chaired the Oversight and Investigations Subcommittee, where he investigated the funding scandal of the Salt Lake City Olympic games and the dangers of Firestone-Bridgestone tires; on that he worked with Billy Tauzin to pass a modest package of safety reforms. Following the 2000 election, he became chairman of the Telecommunications Subcommittee, though he preferred to take the Health Subcommittee. He endorsed the Tauzin-Dingell bill to allow regional telephone operators to provide broadband service more easily. He opposed a tax on broadcasters who delay converting to digital service, but he did support a revamped e-rate to wire all classrooms. He criticized the recording industry for its inadequate parental advisory labels on music that contains sex, violence or strong language, but he took the view that the First Amendment bars Congress from such regulation. Bush signed his bill to create a "safe playground for kids" on the Internet—a ".kids" space free of pornography and other inappropriate materials. Meanwhile, Upton pressed his efforts at bipartisanship, helping to organize a new House coalition of moderates from each party. Conservatives were unhappy that he opposed the Michigan school-choice referendum in 2000.

Upton considered but rejected running for the Senate in 1994 and 1996. In 2002, he had a primary challenge from term-limited state Senator Dale Shugars, a conservative whose reelection Upton opposed in 1998. Shugars criticized his support of abortion and campaign-finance reform, but Upton said that he remained a Ronald Reagan Republican. Upton spent more than $1 million on the primary and won 66%–32%, carrying every county. Otherwise, he has not been seriously challenged for reelection.

SEVENTH DISTRICT

Rep. Nick Smith (R)

Elected 1992, 6th term; b. Nov. 5, 1934, Addison; home, Addison; MI St. U., B.A. 1957, U. of DE, M.S. 1959; Congregationalist; married (Bonnie).

Military Career: Air Force, 1959–61.

Elected Office: Somerset Township Trustee, 1962–66, Supervisor, 1966–68; Hillsdale Cnty. Bd. of Supervisors, 1966–68; MI House of Reps., 1978–82; MI Senate, 1982–92, Pres. Pro-Tem, 1983–90.

Professional Career: Businessman, farmer; Hillsdale Cnty. Repub. Chmn., 1966–68; MI Chmn., Agricultural Stabilization and Conservation Svc., 1969–72; Natl. Energy Dir., U.S. Dept. of Agriculture, 1972–74; MI Occup. Safety Standards Comm., 1975.

DC Office: 2305 RHOB 20515, 202-225-6276; Fax: 202-225-6281; Web site: www.house.gov/nicksmith.

District Offices: Battle Creek, 269-965-9066; Jackson, 517-783-4486.

Committees: *Agriculture* (4th of 27 R): Department Operations, Oversight, Nutrition & Forestry; General Farm Commodities & Risk Management (Vice Chmn.). *International Relations* (17th of 26 R): International Terrorism, Nonproliferation and Human Rights; Middle East & Central Asia. *Science* (7th of 25 R): Environment, Technology and Standards; Research (Chmn.).

Group Ratings

	ADA	ACLU	AFS	LCV	CON	ITIC	NTU	COC	ACU	NTLC	CHC
2002	5	7	13	25	92	75	67	85	92	86	100
2001	5	—	10	0	—	—	66	87	92	—	—

National Journal Ratings

	2001 LIB	—	2001 CONS		2002 LIB	—	2002 CONS
Economic	41%	—	58%		42%	—	58%
Social	20%	—	69%		39%	—	57%
Foreign	29%	—	69%		44%	—	56%

Key Votes of the 107th Congress

1. Approve Bush Tax Cuts	Y	5. Faith-Based Charities	Y	9. Trade Promotion Authority	Y
2. Limit Patients' Bill of Rights	Y	6. Bar Gays in the Boy Scouts	Y	10. Bar Funds for Intl. Court	Y
3. Campaign Finance Reform	Y	7. Ban Partial-Birth Abortion	Y	11. Authorize Force in Iraq	Y
4. Ban ANWR Development	N	8. Arm Commercial Pilots	N	12. Deny Home. Sec. Dept. Union	Y

Election Results

2002 general	Nick Smith (R)	121,142	(60%)	($155,157)
	Mike Simpson (D)	78,412	(39%)	($48,905)
	Other	3,515	(2%)	
2002 primary	Nick Smith (R)	unopposed		
2000 general	Nick Smith (R)	147,369	(61%)	($112,467)
	Jennie Crittendon (D)	86,080	(36%)	($3,753)
	Other	7,561	(3%)	

Prior Winning Percentages: 1998 (57%); 1996 (55%); 1994 (65%); 1992 (88%)

The People		Race/Ethnic Origin	Ancestry	
Area size:	4,365 sq. mi.	88.5% White	German: 17.4%	English: 9.7%
Urban population:	54.0%	5.6% Black	Irish: 8.3%	
Rural population:	46.0%	0.8% Asian	**2000 Presidential Vote**	
Pop. 2000:	662,563	0.4% Native Am.	Bush (R)	141,647 (51%)
Median income:	$45,181	0.0% Hawaiian	Gore (D)	127,344 (46%)
Poverty status:	7.9%	1.4% Two + races	Other	6,682 (2%)
Military veterans:	13.5%	0.1% Other	**Cook Partisan Voting Index:** R + 3	
		3.2% Hispanic Origin		

Occupation	Blue collar: 31.3%	White collar: 53.6%	Gray collar: 15.1%

The small cities and towns spotting the southern-tier farmland counties of Michigan have been incubators of innovation since they were settled by Yankees from New England 150 years ago. The state's public school system was established by two politicians from Marshall, whose hopes to make it the state capital were dashed. A few miles away, in Battle Creek, sanitarium operator W.K. Kellogg invented corn flakes as a health food; he and his one-time patient, C.W. Post, both established factories in the late 19th century and created the American breakfast cereal industry. To the south is Hillsdale, where conservative Hillsdale College has been proudly admitting blacks and women since the 1850s and refusing all federal aid. Politically, this area has been Republican territory since 1854, when the party was founded in the manufacturing and prison town of Jackson as a kind of reformist institution out of the same activist impulse that produced local support for women's rights and Prohibition and opposition to the death penalty. Southern Michigan mostly rejected New Deal tinkering and was hostile to the UAW, but the people here were receptive to moral claims made by later 20th century reformers challenging racial segregation, the Vietnam War and the Watergate cover-up.

The 7th Congressional District covers all of five counties and parts of two others in Michigan's southern tier. It typically votes Republican, but not always: Bill Clinton carried the district by small pluralities in 1992 and 1996, but it returned to the ancestral fold and voted for George W. Bush in 2000 and Republican governor candidate Dick Posthumus in 2002.

The congressman from the 7th District is Nick Smith, a Republican who won the seat in 1992 after it was greatly altered by redistricting. Smith is a Hillsdale County dairy farmer who was elected to the Somerset Township Board in 1962 after his wife "told me to get involved or stop complaining." He was elected to the state House in 1978 and state Senate in 1982. In 1992, the 7th had a brawling primary between Smith and fellow state Senator John Schwarz of Battle Creek. Smith boasted of his 1992 property tax freeze and anti-abortion record and attacked Schwarz for raising money in Washington and from PACs while he took no PAC money. Smith won 43%–36%.

In the House, Smith has worked on agriculture and local issues but has been most prominent as an advocate of individual investment accounts in Social Security. Back in 1995 he came forward, a self-starter, with a plan to allow workers to put 2.3% of their 12.4% payroll tax into a private account that could be invested in stocks, and to raise the retirement age in steps to 69. Around his district and to anyone in Washington who would listen, Smith showed his Social Security proposal charts. He persevered after Bill Clinton in early 1999 torpedoed efforts at Social Security changes and was buoyed by the availability of budget surpluses to pay for transition costs. When Smith started talking about Social Security, his was a lonely and obscure voice. But others, including for a time some Democrats, took up the cause, and in 2000 George W. Bush made his own similar plan one of his major campaign issues. Now it is possible that Smith's initiative, or something very much like it, could become law.

On most issues Smith has taken a conservative stand, but he sometimes casts lonely votes on principle. He backed the Freedom to Farm Act and supported a bipartisan agriculture research program in 1998. In 2002 he co-sponsored the move to impose a $275,000 limit on farm subsidies. He has sought to make commodities hedging more accessible to farmers. He was one of 10 House Republicans to vote against the Republican prescription drug bill in June 2000 and one of four House members to vote against allowing futures contracts on individual stocks in October 2000. In 2001 he called for suspending the 4.3 cent gas tax increase voted in 1993 till the end of the year.

Smith chairs the Research Subcommittee of the Science Committee. In April 2000 he issued a "Seeds of Technology" report on genetically modified organisms (GMOs), which are hugely controversial in Europe. He pointed out that biotechnology products include insulin, growth factors in bone marrow transplants, products for treating heart attacks, diagnostic tests for AIDS and hepatitis and enzymes used in food production. In 2002 he supported doubling funding of the National Science Foundation over five years; the first tranche became law in December 2002.

Smith has had some serious competition in the 7th District. In 1996 his Democratic opponent outspent him on television, and held him to a 55%–43% victory, much less than expected. In 1998 he was challenged by state Senator Jim Berryman, who attacked Smith's stand on Social Security. Smith won 57%–40% and carried every county. In 2000 and 2002, Smith was reelected 61%–36% and 60%–39%; redistricting altered the district only slightly. In 1992 Smith promised to serve only 12 years. In December 2002 he said he would keep that promise and not run for reelection in 2004, but he held out the possibility of running for the Senate in 2006. In early 2003, two Republican state representatives, Clark Bisbee and Gene DeRossett, announced they would run for the open seat; a handful of other state and local officials were also considering bids.

EIGHTH DISTRICT

Rep. Mike Rogers (R)

Elected 2000, 2d term; b. June 2, 1963, Livingston Cnty.; home, Brighton; Adrian Col., B.A. 1985; Methodist; married (Diane).

Military Career: Army, 1985–88.

Elected Office: MI Senate, 1995–00, Maj. Floor Ldr., 1999–00.

Professional Career: Co-founder, E.B.I. Builders, 1985; FBI Spec. Agent, 1988–94.

DC Office: 133 CHOB 20515, 202-225-4872; Fax: 202-225-5820; Web site: www.house.gov/mikerogers.

District Office: Lansing, 517-702-8000.

Committees: *Energy & Commerce* (29th of 31 R): Energy & Air Quality; Environment & Hazardous Materials; Health; Oversight & Investigations.

Group Ratings

	ADA	ACLU	AFS	LCV	CON	ITIC	NTU	COC	ACU	NTLC	CHC
2002	0	13	0	0	25	100	56	90	92	83	92
2001	5	—	10	7	—	—	61	96	84	—	—

National Journal Ratings

	2001 LIB	—	2001 CONS		2002 LIB	—	2002 CONS
Economic	36%	—	63%		9%	—	87%
Social	38%	—	61%		39%	—	57%
Foreign	4%	—	87%		0%	—	85%

Key Votes of the 107th Congress

1. Approve Bush Tax Cuts	Y	5. Faith-Based Charities	Y	9. Trade Promotion Authority	Y
2. Limit Patients' Bill of Rights	Y	6. Bar Gays in the Boy Scouts	Y	10. Bar Funds for Intl. Court	Y
3. Campaign Finance Reform	N	7. Ban Partial-Birth Abortion	Y	11. Authorize Force in Iraq	Y
4. Ban ANWR Development	N	8. Arm Commercial Pilots	Y	12. Deny Home. Sec. Dept. Union	Y

Election Results

2002 general	Mike Rogers (R)	156,525	(68%)	($1,604,619)
	Frank McAlpine (D)	70,920	(31%)	($11,443)
	Other	3,152	(1%)	
2002 primary	Mike Rogers (R)	unopposed		
2000 general	Mike Rogers (R)	145,190	(49%)	($2,195,500)
	Dianne Byrum (D)	145,079	(49%)	($2,093,216)
	Other	7,335	(2%)	

The People		Race/Ethnic Origin	Ancestry	
Area size:	2,288 sq. mi.	87.7% White	German: 17.3%	English: 9.6%
Urban population:	70.0%	4.8% Black	Irish: 9.2%	
Rural population:	30.0%	1.9% Asian	**2000 Presidential Vote**	
Pop. 2000:	662,563	0.4% Native Am.	Bush (R) 153,798	(51%)
Median income:	$52,510	0.0% Hawaiian	Gore (D) 141,770	(47%)
Poverty status:	8.4%	1.6% Two+ races	Other 8,426	(3%)
Military veterans:	11.0%	0.1% Other	**Cook Partisan Voting Index:** R + 2	
		3.5% Hispanic Origin		

Occupation	Blue collar: 23.0%	White collar: 62.6%	Gray collar: 14.4%

Lansing is Michigan's state capital, chosen in 1847 because of its geographic position halfway between Lake Huron and Lake Michigan and away from the border with Canada and the threat of invasion by British forces, but in ignorance of the fact that it has fewer days with sunshine than any place else in the state. But it is a tidy and pleasant city with more than its share of amenities. It has a beautifully restored Capitol and a fine state history museum and is neighbor to Michigan State University in East Lansing, started in 1855 as America's first land-grant college. Its Oldsmobile plant stimulated growth in the first half of the 20th century, and state government did the same in the second half. GM announced in 2000 that it would close its Olds line, but two new GM assembly plants have been under construction in the Lansing area and the Oldsmobile name will remain alive at two local museums and a baseball stadium for the Lansing Lugnuts. Lansing has tended to go with the party controlling state government. When the legislature was apportioned to stay Republican, as it was until 1964, the Lansing area was usually Republican; Democrats have had majorities in the state House in 28 of the 40 years since and Lansing has voted mostly Democratic.

Just east of Lansing's Ingham County is quite another part of Michigan, Livingston County (most of the counties in these parts were named for members of President Andrew Jackson's Cabinet; Livingston was secretary of state and Ingham secretary of the Treasury). Thirty years ago, Livingston County was mostly rural, known mainly for its many lakes. But in the years since then, thousands of Detroit area residents have driven out I-96 to Brighton and Howell and other Livingston townships, and subdivisions, schools and shopping malls have sprouted up. Most of these people are conservatives, happy to leave the problems of Detroit behind them, angry at high taxes and annoyed by government regulations and hewing to traditional religious faiths. They have made Livingston Michigan's fastest-growing county and one of its most Republican. In 1970 Livingston had 58,000 people to Ingham's 261,000; in 2000 Livingston had 156,000 to Ingham's 279,000. So as Ingham has grown more Democratic, Livingston has been casting bigger Republican margins to partly counterbalance Ingham's Democratic margins. In the close presidential election of 1968, 19,000 people voted in Livingston and gave Richard Nixon a 3,000-vote margin. In the close presidential election of 2000, 75,000 people voted in Livingston and gave George W. Bush a 16,000-vote margin.

The 8th Congressional District includes all of Ingham and Livingston Counties, Shiawassee County south of Owosso, plus Clinton County directly north of Lansing and northern Oakland County. Redistricting in 2001 removed Democratic-leaning parts of Washtenaw County west of Ann Arbor, and adding townships of Oakland County in the Detroit suburbs, including Independence and Oxford. The political balance in the 8th was one of the chief concerns of the Republicans. This district had switched back and forth between the parties in 1994, 1996 and 2000; only one other district saw party control switch three times between 1994 and 2000, the New York 1st, and that was because the incumbent congressman switched to the Democratic party and then was defeated. Now there was a Republican congressman, Mike Rogers, elected by a margin of 111 votes, and the redistricters wanted to protect him. So from the old 8th District they removed Democratic-leaning Genesee County townships outside Flint and rural Washtenaw County townships that they felt might be infected by the adjacent liberal university town of Ann Arbor. They added reliably Republican Clinton County (Bill Clinton carried very few of the nation's many Clinton Counties), southwest Shiawassee County and most of the northern two tiers of townships in Oakland County. These are fast-growing areas, demographically and politically very much like Livingston County. The district's Bush 2000 percentage was increased from 47% to 51%, the best that could be done without putting part of Lansing into the 7th District where it might weaken Republican Nick Smith in 2002 or make the district vulnerable to a Democrat when Smith keeps his term limit promise and steps down in 2004, as he has announced.

The congressman from the 8th District is Mike Rogers, a Republican elected in 2000 (He is one of two Republican Mike Rogers in the House; the other hails from Alabama). He grew up in Brighton, in Livingston County, and graduated from Adrian College in southeastern Michigan. He was commissioned by the ROTC as commander of an Army rapid deployment unit. Next, he graduated from the FBI Academy, and he focused on public-corruption cases as a special agent in Chicago for six years before returning to Michigan in 1994 and winning election to the state Senate. In 1999 he was selected to be majority floor leader, where he handled pieces of Governor John Engler's legislative program. Rogers also co-founded E.B.I. Builders, a family-owned home construction business. When Democrat Debbie Stabenow gave up the 8th District seat to run successfully for the Senate, Rogers and Democrat Dianne Byrum, a fellow state senator, waged one of the tightest and most-watched open seat campaigns in the country: forecaster Charlie Cook predicted that this could be the closest race in the country, and it was. Each candidate raised about $2 million; neither faced primary opposition. It took six weeks to count the final tally, and Rogers won by 111 votes. Byrum carried her base of Ingham County by a 58%–40% margin and Rogers won his base of Livingston County by 64%–34%.

Rogers describes his political philosophy as consistent with Bush's "compassionate conservatism," with a more moderate record on cultural issues than on the economy. He strongly advocated the provision in the Bush tax cut that provides tax-free status to the earnings from college savings accounts. With his military, law-enforcement and legislative backgrounds, Rogers was well-positioned to advise colleagues on policies to respond to the September 11 attacks. He provided expertise on the high-tech tools to track terrorists and on the use of wiretaps, sought federal aid to pay for National Guard troops at Michigan's borders with Canada, and urged that airport screeners have federal supervision. He traveled with congressional delegations on five trips to the Middle East and Afghanistan in just two years; after returning from a March 2003 trip, he said that Iraqi military defectors reported that Saddam Hussein had authorized the use of chemical weapons in the event of war. On local issues, he sought more authority for Michigan to limit its flow of trash from other states and Canada. He opposed higher CAFE standards for the automobile fleet until the industry is in better financial condition. Despite a campaign appearance by John McCain on the eve of the 2000 election, he opposed his campaign finance bill, worried that it might disrupt the Bush agenda and that the measure was full of loopholes. In 2003, he won a seat on the Energy and Commerce Committee.

At home, Democrats accused Rogers of abusing the state's pension law by setting himself up for favorable benefits before he left the state Senate, and they talked up the $10,750 in fines that the Federal Election Commission levied on his campaign in 2000 for illegal contributions. He also received unfavorable publicity when a young woman on his staff resigned after revealing to *Vanity Fair* details of her flirting with congressmen at the Capitol Grille and her one-night stand with a well-connected Republican aide. But none of this caused reelection problems for Rogers. Redistricting discouraged serious Democrats from running. With a $1.6 million fundraising advantage, Rogers won 68%–31%. So the House member with the narrowest margin of victory in 2000 appears to have made his seat safe by 2002. He has a seat on an important committee, and one from which it is easy to raise money. Political insiders in Michigan have speculated that he might make a strong statewide candidate.

NINTH DISTRICT

Rep. Joe Knollenberg (R)

Elected 1992, 6th term; b. Nov. 28, 1933, Mattoon, IL; home, Bloomfield Township; E. IL U., B.S. 1955; Catholic; married (Sandie).

Military Career: Army, 1955–57.

Professional Career: Insurance agent, 1958–92.

DC Office: 2349 RHOB 20515, 202-225-5802; Fax: 202-226-2356; Web site: www.house.gov/knollenberg.

District Office: Farmington Hills, 248-851-1366.

Committees: *Appropriations* (12th of 36 R): Foreign Operations & Export Financing; Military Construction (Chmn.); VA, HUD & Independent Agencies.

Group Ratings

	ADA	ACLU	AFS	LCV	CON	ITIC	NTU	COC	ACU	NTLC	CHC
2002	0	7	0	0	8	100	55	100	88	86	100
2001	0	—	0	0	—	—	62	100	92	—	—

National Journal Ratings

	2001 LIB	—	2001 CONS		2002 LIB	—	2002 CONS
Economic	7%	—	89%		0%	—	91%
Social	20%	—	69%		38%	—	62%
Foreign	4%	—	87%		22%	—	77%

Key Votes of the 107th Congress

1. Approve Bush Tax Cuts	Y	5. Faith-Based Charities	Y
2. Limit Patients' Bill of Rights	Y	6. Bar Gays in the Boy Scouts	Y
3. Campaign Finance Reform	N	7. Ban Partial-Birth Abortion	*
4. Ban ANWR Development	N	8. Arm Commercial Pilots	Y

9. Trade Promotion Authority	Y
10. Bar Funds for Intl. Court	Y
11. Authorize Force in Iraq	Y
12. Deny Home. Sec. Dept. Union	Y

Election Results

2002 general	Joe Knollenberg (R)	141,102	(58%)	($2,524,728)
	David Fink (D)	96,856	(40%)	($2,321,103)
	Other	4,922	(2%)	
2002 primary	Joe Knollenberg (R)	45,696	(87%)	
	Bart Baron (R)	7,044	(13%)	
2000 general (MI 11)	Joe Knollenberg (R)	170,790	(56%)	($1,104,909)
	Matthew Frumin (D)	124,053	(41%)	($207,948)
	Other	11,459	(4%)	

Prior Winning Percentages: 1998 (64%); 1996 (61%); 1994 (68%); 1992 (58%)

The People		Race/Ethnic Origin	Ancestry	
Area size:	323 sq. mi.	81.4% White	German: 13.6%	Irish: 9.2%
Urban population:	99.3%	8.0% Black	English: 8.5%	
Rural population:	0.7%	5.6% Asian	**2000 Presidential Vote**	
Pop. 2000:	662,563	0.2% Native Am.	Bush (R)..............164,149	(51%)
Median income:	$65,358	0.0% Hawaiian	Gore (D)..............151,996	(47%)
Poverty status:	5.4%	1.6% Two+ races	Other...................5,987	(2%)
Military veterans:	10.6%	0.1% Other	**Cook Partisan Voting Index:** R + 2	
		3.0% Hispanic Origin		

Occupation	Blue collar: 14.7%	White collar: 75.2%	Gray collar: 10.1%

Oakland County, Michigan, long considered just a suburban adjunct of Detroit, is now the center of a giant, spread-out, affluent urban area. It is only minutes on the Lodge Freeway from the empty, abandoned blocks of inner-city Detroit; but suddenly, north of the Eight Mile Road boundary, there are giant office buildings and multiplying small businesses, expensive houses on large lots and one shopping mall after another, high education levels and low crime rates. Even physically there is a distinction between the two areas: Detroit is on almost perfectly flat land, while much of Oakland County lies on a line of hills and lakes that marks the southernmost advance of an Ice Age glacier. Like most large suburban counties, Oakland is a mixture of communities, more diverse than the standard critique of suburbs suggest and, in this case, it is the heart of the metropolitan area. I-75 in eastern and northern Oakland County is now the nerve center of tier one and two auto company suppliers, many in the big office centers and near the upscale malls in Troy, others north into Auburn Hills, near Daimler Chrysler's North American headquarters. Near the center of Oakland is Bloomfield Hills, metro Detroit's wealthiest community; just to the north is the old factory town of Pontiac, with a black majority and a fair amount of poverty. Birmingham and Royal Oak, little suburbs set among farm fields half a century ago, are now upscale gentrified nodes amid a vast suburban expanse. Booming growth came in the 1990s to Rochester Hills, north of Troy, and West Bloomfield, west of Bloomfield Hills; the latter is increasingly the focus of metro Detroit's Jewish community and has a large number of Asians, many from India and Pakistan; others are Chaldeans, descended from Iraqi Catholics, who are building a $20 million cultural center and country club. Oakland County has become the population center of metro Detroit. In 1950, the city of Detroit had 1,849,000 million people and Oakland County 396,000. In 2000, Detroit had 951,000 and Oakland 1,194,000.

The 9th Congressional District includes a little more than half the population of Oakland County. It does not include Southfield, Oak Park, Ferndale, Hazel Park or Madison Heights in the southeast—all heavily Democratic and part of the 12th District. It does include almost all of Royal Oak, all of Birmingham and Bloomfield Hills, Rochester Hills and Auburn Hills, Farmington Hills (you begin to see the prestige value of hills to people who grew up in the flatlands of Detroit) and West Bloomfield, Pontiac and Waterford Township. It is Michigan's most affluent congressional district, and also one that trended toward the Democrats because of cultural issues during the 1990s. This has created problems for Republicans, for there is a strong Right to Life movement in Michigan, and in December 2000, in a raucous convention, cultural conservatives won control of the county Republican party. Still, the 9th District is on balance Republican territory, giving small majorities to George W. Bush in 2000 and Republican governor candidate Dick Posthumus in 2002. Redistricting removed Southfield and western Oakland County and part of western Wayne County and added Pontiac, Waterford and Rochester Hills; this raised the Bush 2000 percentage from 49% to 51%.

The congressman from the 9th District is Joe Knollenberg, a Republican first elected in 1992. Knollenberg grew up the fifth child in a family of 13 on a farm in Downstate Illinois, went to college in Illinois and became an insurance agent. He moved to Oakland County in 1967 and became involved in civic affairs and Republican politics. When Republican William Broomfield retired in 1992 after 36 years in office—every one of them in the minority—Knollenberg ran to succeed him. With Broomfield's support and that of Michigan Right To Life, he was able to win the primary with 43% of the vote. He won the general election easily.

Knollenberg entered the House as a junior member of the minority. But in two years, with a change in control, he became a member of Appropriations advancing some cutting-edge ideas. He moved to zero out funding for the statistics required for CAFE standards and managed to zero out funding for implementation of the 1997 Kyoto treaty until the Senate ratifies it. Knollenberg has been a strong supporter of NAFTA, PNTR for China and trade promotion authority; Michigan is the sixth-largest exporter among states. He opposed Bush's tariffs on steel imports in March 2002 and in October called for a review of them; he said auto suppliers were faced with 20% to 50% price increases for steel.

In 2000 he sponsored a bill to repeal the 1992 law which reduced the water flow in toilets from 3.5 to 1.6 gallons per flush; toilet makers, eager for more sales and uniformity among states, supported that law, but Knollenberg points out that the new toilets often do not perform adequately and require extra flushing. But in April 2000 the bill was beaten 13–12 in subcommittee. Later that year Knollenberg objected to the Energy Department's proposed regulations on washing machines, which would outlaw inexpensive top-loading washers. In 2001 he became chairman of the District of Columbia Subcommittee, and hence one of Appropriation's 13 "cardinals." He said the post helped him understand better the problems of central cities. In 2003 he became chairman of the Military Construction Subcommittee.

Oakland County became more Democratic in the 1990s. Knollenberg, easily reelected three times, found himself pressed in 2000 by a light-spending opponent who campaigned for gun control, abortion rights and HMO regulation. He won by only 56%–41%, a sharp decline from other elections. Redistricting made the district slightly more Republican, but it also meant that nearly two-thirds of the district was new territory for Knollenberg. In 2002 he had vigorous and well-financed opposition from politically connected attorney David Fink, who spent $1.2 million of his own money on his campaign. Knollenberg started out with positive ads, extolling the $60 million he said he had gotten to clean up the Rouge River, his efforts to beef up security and keep the traffic flowing at Detroit's two crossings into Canada and his support of prescription drugs for seniors. Fink campaigned for an assault weapons ban and as a supporter of abortion rights. He said the race was "David versus Joe-liath" and that Knollenberg was beholden to the gun and pharmaceutical industries. Knollenberg replied that Fink was a product of Wayne County Executive Ed McNamara's political machine and was a trial lawyer who defended big polluters. Knollenberg said that with his seniority and subcommittee chairmanship he could do more; Fink reminded him that he had promised in 1992 to retire in 2004; Knollenberg replied that he no longer believed in term limits. "I'm just at a point now where I'm in the best position to serve by having a position of power. And we've learned here in Michigan how terrible term limits can be." Knollenberg voted for the Iraq war resolution in October 2002; Fink said he would condition U.S. action on UN approval. This was a big-spending race in an affluent metropolitan district: Knollenberg spent $2.5 million; Fink spent $2.3 million. Fink was one of two Detroit area candidates Democrats hoped would overcome small Republican partisan edges; neither one did. Knollenberg won 58%–40%, an uptick from his 2000 showing against an opponent who spent $16,000; his percentage was 2% higher in a district that was 2% more for George W. Bush in 2000. There is a Democratic base in this district that gives a challenger a chance to win if the national tide turns toward the Democrats. But it did not in 2002, and it is not clear whether Democrats will have a challenger serious enough to take advantage of such a tide in 2004.

TENTH DISTRICT

Rep. Candice Miller (R)

Elected 2002, 1st term; b. May 7, 1954, Detroit; home, Harrison Twnshp.; Macomb Cnty. Community Col., 1973–74, Northwood U.; Presbyterian; married (Donald).

Elected Office: Trustee, Harrison Twnshp. Bd., 1979–80; Harrison Twnshp. Supervisor, 1980–92; Macomb Cnty. Treasurer, 1992–94; MI Secy. of State, 1994–02.

Professional Career: Secy.-Treas., D.B. Snider Inc. marina, 1972–79.

DC Office: 508 CHOB 20515, 202-225-2106; Fax: 202-225-1169; Web site: www.house.gov/candicemiller.

District Office: Shelby Twnshp., 586-997-5010.

Committees: *Armed Services* (30th of 33 R): Readiness; Total Force. *Government Reform* (19th of 24 R): Energy Policy, Natural Resources and Regulatory Affairs; Government Efficiency & Financial Management; Technology, Information Policy, Intergovernmental Relations & Census (Vice Chmn.).

Group Ratings and Key Votes: Newly Elected

Election Results

2002 general	Candice Miller (R)	137,339	(63%)	($1,421,613)
	Carl Marlinga (D)	77,053	(36%)	($970,409)
	Other	2,536	(1%)	
2002 primary	Candice Miller (R)	unopposed		
2000 general	David E. Bonior (D)	181,818	(64%)	($2,312,101)
	Tom Turner (R)	93,713	(33%)	($21,123)
	Other	6,738	(2%)	

The People		Race/Ethnic Origin	Ancestry	
Area size:	3,663 sq. mi.	93.6% White	German: 19.1%	Polish: 10.5%
Urban population:	66.0%	1.5% Black	Irish: 8.2%	
Rural population:	34.0%	1.2% Asian	**2000 Presidential Vote**	
Pop. 2000:	662,562	0.3% Native Am.	Bush (R)..............152,780	(53%)
Median income:	$52,690	0.0% Hawaiian	Gore (D)..............127,640	(45%)
Poverty status:	6.0%	1.2% Two+ races	Other....................6,242	(2%)
Military veterans:	12.6%	0.1% Other	**Cook Partisan Voting Index:** R + 5	
		2.1% Hispanic Origin		

Occupation	Blue collar: 31.5%	White collar: 55.2%	Gray collar: 13.4%

Macomb County, Michigan, on the billiard-table-flat shore of Lake St. Clair just northeast of Detroit, has been one of the nation's most closely watched political battlegrounds, a place where it seemed the electoral fate of Michigan and even the entire country might be determined. But its reputation as blue collar suburbia is no longer quite accurate: more people hold white-collar jobs than blue-collar these days and far fewer work in auto plants than in earlier generations; there are plenty of affluent subdivisions now, and boat ownership is close to the highest in the country. Macomb County is the product of the post-World War II boom: With just over 107,000 people in 1940, many in the old sulphur-water spa town of Mount Clemens, Macomb passed the 400,000 mark in 1960 and 600,000 by 1970; in 2000, it reached 788,000. Many people came here from Detroit: These new suburbanites were heavily Catholic, often blue-collar, at least modestly affluent and ancestrally Democratic. They accepted the New Deal as part of their natural heritage but resented the efforts of Detroit politicians to tax them to pay for welfare, and they were fearful of the high crime rates in Detroit's black neighborhoods.

In 1960, Macomb County was the most Democratic major suburban county in the United States, voting 63% for America's first Catholic president, John F. Kennedy. For three decades afterwards Macomb moved away from the national Democrats—in 1962 because they would let Detroit tax suburbanites, in 1972 because they didn't vehemently oppose a metropolitan school busing plan. From 1976 through 1992, no Democratic presidential candidate got more than 40% of the vote here. In 1996, after great effort and with the advice of pollster Stan Greenberg, who has studied Macomb closely, Bill Clinton carried Macomb County by a 49%–39% margin; in 2000 Al Gore carried it by 50%–48%, nearly the national average. But those gains seem to have been temporary. In 2002 Macomb County voted 52%–47% for Republican governor candidate Dick Posthumus, even as he was losing statewide, and it elected more Republican state legislators than Democrats. Central and northern Macomb County have been filling up with expensive subdivisions not much different or less pricey than those in adjacent Oakland County; these have been growing rapidly—some by more than 40% in the 1990s—and are not as culturally liberal as affluent parts of Oakland County.

The 10th Congressional District includes the northern two-thirds geographically of Macomb County, with nearly half of its voters. It also includes fast-growing Lapeer County, north of Macomb and Oakland and east of Flint, St. Clair County, with Port Huron and its Blue Water Bridge to Canada, and two rural counties in Michigan's Thumb (people really call it that). Northern Macomb has become increasingly Republican, Lapeer and St. Clair have long been pretty Republican and the Thumb has long been very Republican. Overall this is a comfortably Republican district—53% for George W. Bush in 2000. It was created by Republican legislators to elect a Republican—and to end the congressional career of David Bonior, who had been elected from Macomb and Macomb-St. Clair districts since 1976 and had risen to become Democratic party whip in 1989. The plan worked. Bonior decided to run for governor rather than reelection, and finished second to Jennifer Granholm in the Democratic primary.

The congresswoman from the 10th District is Candice Miller, a Republican elected in 2002. Miller grew up in Macomb County. In 1979, at 25, she was elected Harrison Township Trustee. A year later, she was elected as the youngest and first female Supervisor in the township. In 1986 she ran against Bonior and lost 66%–34%. In 1992, she won an upset bid to become Macomb County Treasurer. In 1994, she defeated 24-year incumbent Richard Austin and was elected Michigan secretary of state. In 1998 she carried all of Michigan's counties and set a state record for total votes. In 2000 Governor John Engler urged her to run against Bonior, but she decided not to. As secretary of state, she was credited with sharply increasing participation in the state's organ donation registry, creating fraud-proof driver's licenses and introducing technology into a hidebound agency. In its editorial endorsement, the *Detroit Free-Press* called her performance in that job "innovative, progressive and popular."

Everyone in Michigan sees the secretary of state's name when they renew license plates. Armed with that name recognition but prevented from running for reelection by term limits, Miller entered the House race as the favorite. Democrats hoped that Macomb County Prosecutor Carl Marlinga would be a strong candidate; he had held office 20 years and had been mentioned several times as a candidate for statewide office. But he could not keep pace with her fundraising and wasn't able to do much to increase his name recognition north of Macomb. He called himself a "Hubert Humphrey Democrat"—not a big advantage in this district. Miller called herself a "George W. Bush Republican." She opposed abortion and supported NAFTA, trade promotion authority and favored making the Bush tax cuts permanent—all positions opposite to Marlinga. Both candidates supported gun rights. Citing the fact that her daughter is a member of the United Auto Workers member, Miller reached out to unions, and was endorsed by the Teamsters (but not the AFL-CIO). While Miller was benefiting from years of favorable publicity, Marlinga was hurt by allegations that he accepted campaign contributions from supporters of a convicted rapist who benefited from the prosecutor's handling of his case.

Miller won by a huge 63%–36% margin; she carried Macomb County 61%–37%. Conservatives have been speculating about Miller running in 2006 against either Governor Jennifer Granholm or Senator Debbie Stabenow.

ELEVENTH DISTRICT

Rep. Thaddeus McCotter (R)

Elected 2002, 1st term; b. Aug. 22, 1965, Detroit; home, Livonia; U. of Detroit, B.A. 1987, J.D. 1990; Catholic; married (Rita).

Elected Office: Schoolcraft Community Col. Trustees Bd., 1989–92; Wayne Cnty. Commission, 1992–98; MI Senate, 1998–02.

DC Office: 415 CHOB 20515, 202-225-8171; Fax: 202-225-2667; Web site: www.house.gov/mccotter.

District Office: Livonia, 734-632-0314.

Committees: *Budget* (21st of 24 R). *International Relations* (24th of 26 R): Europe; Middle East & Central Asia.

Group Ratings and Key Votes: Newly Elected

Election Results

2002 general	Thaddeus McCotter (R)	126,050	(57%)	($1,292,928)
	Kevin Kelley (D)	87,402	(40%)	($635,405)
	Other	6,953	(3%)	
2002 primary	Thaddeus McCotter (R)	25,940	(69%)	
	David Hagerty (R)	11,619	(31%)	

The People		Race/Ethnic Origin	Ancestry	
Area size:	413 sq. mi.	89.5% White	German: 15.5%	Irish: 10.8%
Urban population:	97.0%	3.7% Black	Polish: 9.8%	
Rural population:	3.0%	3.0% Asian	**2000 Presidential Vote**	
Pop. 2000:	662,563	0.3% Native Am.	Bush (R) 150,692	(51%)
Median income:	$59,177	0.0% Hawaiian	Gore (D) 138,735	(47%)
Poverty status:	4.3%	1.4% Two+ races	Other 6,022	(2%)
Military veterans:	12.1%	0.1% Other	**Cook Partisan Voting Index: R + 2**	
		2.0% Hispanic Origin		

Occupation	Blue collar: 23.4%	White collar: 64.8%	Gray collar: 11.8%

The inexorable pattern of growth and its consequences is a vivid tale in the western suburbs of Wayne County, 15 and 25 miles from downtown Detroit. Consider the case of Livonia, just west of Northwest Detroit. Half a century ago the 36 square miles of Livonia had 17,000 people; by 1960 there were 66,000 and by 2000 100,000. Similar growth occurred just to the south in Westland, named after a shopping center. To the west, around the old towns of Plymouth and Northville, affluent subdivisions sprang up; to the southwest, Canton Township grew 34% with more modest subdivisions. To the northwest Novi, in Oakland County, was the site of a new upscale shopping mall and emerged as one of the metro area's highest-income suburbs; Lyon Township just to the west looks to be the next boom area. Livonia is aging now—its school-age population was 38,000 in the 1970s and 17,000 in 2002—but these newer places are young, and all have been thriving while much of Detroit is terribly troubled. Tying these areas together was I-275 which runs along the western edge of Livonia and Westland and provides easy access to Metro Airport, the Northwest hub with nonstop flights to just about every big city in the country, as well as major European cities and Tokyo and Beijing. From affluent areas in Oakland County you have to budget an hour to drive to Metro; from I-275 it's more like 15 minutes.

Livonia was originally the political base of longtime Wayne County Executive Ed McNamara (1986–2002), who built the beautiful new midfield terminal at Metro (which is named after him). Northville is the home of his protege, Michigan's new Democratic Governor Jennifer Granholm. Livonia, originally settled by Detroiters, was long closely divided between the two parties, but the most affluent recent influx into western Wayne County and Novi and other Oakland towns to the west and north has made those areas more Republican.

The 11th Congressional District covers much of this territory in western Wayne and Oakland counties—Livonia and Redford Township just to the east, Westland and Canton Township, Northville and Plymouth, Novi and several fast-growing townships to the north and west. This was a new district, created in July 2001 by Republican redistricters, the residence of no incumbent at the time. Redford, most of Livonia and western Oakland County were mostly in the old 9th District represented by Republican Joe Knollenberg; Northville, Plymouth, Canton and Westland were in the old 13th District represented by Ann Arbor Democrat Lynn Rivers. The lines were carefully drawn to produce a district that voted 51% for George W. Bush in 2000 and with the clear intention of electing a Republican congressman.

The congressman from the 11th District is Thaddeus McCotter, a Republican elected in 2002. He grew up in Livonia, where his mother Joan McCotter is city clerk. He graduated from Detroit's Catholic Central High School, where he was a first-team all-Catholic football player, and from the University of Detroit and its law school. He was elected to the Wayne County Commission in 1992, at 27, and became the driving force to change the county's charter to require a new tax to win approval of two-thirds of the commissioners and 60% of the voters in a referendum. He became active in Republican politics, chairing both the Wayne County party committee and the state party's candidate assistance committee. In 1998, he was elected to the state Senate where, critically, he was vice-chairman of the Senate's reapportionment committee. He helped to design the new 11th District, which included his entire senate district, and became the early frontrunner in 2002. He received pre-primary endorsements and contributions from House Republican leaders Tom DeLay and Tom Davis, and he won the primary by 69%–31%.

But McCotter did not win the seat without a contest. Democrat Kevin Kelley, Redford Township Supervisor and son of longtime Detroit Councilman Jack Kelley, entered the race late and was unopposed in the primary. Kelley was encouraged when he won many more votes than both Republicans in the primary, although that was due to the fact that Michigan has no party registration and the spirited contest for governor on the Democratic side attracted many more votes than the pallid contest on the Republican side. Kelley called himself a "centrist Democrat"; both candidates supported the Bush tax cut, authorization of military force in Iraq and opposed individual investment accounts in Social Security. McCotter defined himself as a conservative who opposed abortion and gun control; Kelley supported abortion rights and restrictions on gun ownership. They drew sharp distinctions on trade policy. McCotter favored NAFTA, trade promotion authority and PNTR with China; Kelley opposed all three. National Democrats were impressed by Kelley and sent in money in the hopes of making this second-tier race into a first-tier contest. Kelley hoped to benefit from Granholm's local popularity and hoped that his outgoing personality would be more appealing than McCotter's reserved persona. But McCotter raised more money, much of it at a mid-October fundraiser starring George W. Bush.

McCotter's 57%–40% margin was larger than expected. He won 55% of the vote in Wayne County and 63% in Oakland County. Demography may help him in future elections: new affluent subdivisions are likely to be heavily Republican.

TWELFTH DISTRICT

Rep. Sander Levin (D)

Elected 1982, 11th term; b. Sept. 6, 1931, Detroit; home, Royal Oak; U. of Chicago, B.A. 1952, Columbia U., M.A. 1954, Harvard U., LL.B. 1957; Jewish; married (Vicki).

Elected Office: Oakland Bd. of Supervisors, 1961–64; MI Senate, 1964–70.

Professional Career: Practicing atty., 1957–64, 1970–76; Fellow, Harvard JFK Schl. of Govt., 1975; A.A., Agency for Intl. Devel., 1977–81.

DC Office: 2300 RHOB 20515, 202-225-4961; Fax: 202-226-1033; Web site: www.house.gov/levin.

District Offices: Oak Park, 248-968-2025; Roseville, 586-498-7122.

Committees: *Ways & Means* (4th of 17 D): Human Resources; Trade (RMM).

Group Ratings

	ADA	ACLU	AFS	LCV	CON	ITIC	NTU	COC	ACU	NTLC	CHC
2002	95	87	100	88	43	50	18	40	0	0	0
2001	95	—	100	86	—	—	10	43	4	—	—

National Journal Ratings

	2001 LIB —	2001 CONS	2002 LIB —	2002 CONS
Economic	88%	11%	82%	17%
Social	83%	11%	74%	19%
Foreign	86%	12%	76%	23%

Key Votes of the 107th Congress

1. Approve Bush Tax Cuts	N	5. Faith-Based Charities	N	9. Trade Promotion Authority	N
2. Limit Patients' Bill of Rights	N	6. Bar Gays in the Boy Scouts	N	10. Bar Funds for Intl. Court	N
3. Campaign Finance Reform	Y	7. Ban Partial-Birth Abortion	N	11. Authorize Force in Iraq	N
4. Ban ANWR Development	Y	8. Arm Commercial Pilots	N	12. Deny Home. Sec. Dept. Union	N

Election Results

2002 general	Sander Levin (D)	140,970	(68%)	($1,007,802)
	Harvey Dean (R)	61,502	(30%)	($43,323)
	Other	4,056	(2%)	
2002 primary	Sander Levin (D)	71,881	(79%)	
	William Callahan (D)	16,926	(19%)	
	Other	2,444	(3%)	
2000 general	Sander Levin (D)	157,720	(64%)	($1,054,666)
	Bart Baron (R)	78,795	(32%)	($36,158)
	Other	8,654	(4%)	

Prior Winning Percentages: 1998 (56%); 1996 (57%); 1994 (52%); 1992 (53%); 1990 (70%); 1988 (70%); 1986 (76%); 1984 (100%); 1982 (67%)

The People		Race/Ethnic Origin	Ancestry	
Area size:	160 sq. mi.	81.7% White	German: 14.1%	Polish: 11.4%
Urban population:	100.0%	12.0% Black	Irish: 8.0%	
Rural population:	0.0%	2.3% Asian	**2000 Presidential Vote**	
Pop. 2000:	662,563	0.3% Native Am.	Gore (D) 175,524	(61%)
Median income:	$46,784	0.0% Hawaiian	Bush (R) 106,628	(37%)
Poverty status:	7.3%	2.1% Two+ races	Other 5,940	(2%)
Military veterans:	12.5%	0.2% Other	**Cook Partisan Voting Index:** D +12	
		1.5% Hispanic Origin		
Occupation	Blue collar: 26.7%	White collar: 59.7%	Gray collar: 13.6%	

The flat expanse of land just north of Eight Mile Road, Detroit's northern city limit, was mostly vacant in the years just after World War II. A string of suburbs in Oakland County ran along

Woodward Avenue, Detroit's main street, where Henry Ford drove his first prototype in 1896, and which led to the Shrine of the Little Flower church in Royal Oak. There, in the 1930s, Father Charles Coughlin made his radio broadcasts backing and then opposing Franklin Roosevelt and denouncing bankers and Jews. In the 1950s and 1960s, Woodward was one of America's greatest cruising highways, where teenagers drove big Detroit cars up and down the eight lanes where the lights were timed at 42 miles per hour and zoomed into its drive-in restaurants—an era commemorated since 1994 with the Woodward Dream Cruise of old cars, a mega-celebration that annually draws more than 1 million for the one-day event. To the east in Macomb County was some industrial development along Van Dyke Road, but this was mostly empty land, too. Then Polish-Americans began marching out Van Dyke from Hamtramck to Warren; Italian-Americans headed out Gratiot from Detroit's east side to Roseville and Clinton Township; Belgian-Americans from the Mack corridor moved out farther to St. Clair Shores. Today, these areas are well-settled suburbs, long since built up, a few neighborhoods edging toward seediness, many others continually renovated and restored. Almost half of metro Detroit's population is now north of Eight Mile, in communities drawing on old traditions but crackling with economic creativity. Now Eight Mile, long known to Detroiters, is known to the world, thanks to *8 Mile*, the movie made by the rapper Eminem telling the story of his emergence in Detroit's music scene during the 1990s.

The 12th Congressional District is in this suburban territory, with two-thirds of its population in Macomb. On the Oakland County side are the southern part of Royal Oak and other Woodward Avenue suburbs, now attracting singles and gays as well as families; Oak Park, heavily Jewish in the 1950s and now perhaps the only small city in America with sizable numbers of Jews, Arabs and blacks; Hazel Park and Madison Heights, mostly peopled with descendants of the Appalachian migrants of a few decades ago; Southfield, Michigan's largest office space center (far ahead of Detroit), with a black middle class majority in 2000; and Ferndale, one of the original bedroom communities for autoworkers that has been revived with help from $45 million in bonds to modernize downtown and is now viewed as a model for how to rescue aging suburbs. On the Macomb County side are Warren and the southern part of Sterling Heights, site of the General Motors Technical Center, a big Chrysler plant and the now-privatized M-1 tank plant. Farther east are blue-collar communities of Macomb: Eastpointe (formerly known as East Detroit, it voted to change its name to make it sound less like Detroit and more like Grosse Pointe), Roseville, St. Clair Shores, Clinton Township and Mount Clemens. This district pulls out the strongest Democratic parts of Oakland and Macomb Counties to protect the three Republicans elected in the other districts in the area, now making the 12th safely Democratic.

The congressman from the 12th District is Sander Levin, a Democrat first elected in 1982 and a member of one of Michigan's most respected political families; he is the older brother of Senator Carl Levin. Levin grew up in Detroit and got degrees from the University of Chicago, Columbia and Harvard Law School. He settled in the Woodward Avenue suburb of Berkley after school and was elected state Senator in 1964, after a late redistricting; in 1970 and 1974 he ran for governor and lost narrowly each time to Republican William Milliken. In the Carter administration he was a top appointee at the Agency for International Development. In 1982, a House seat suddenly opened up in redistricting. Levin won a spirited primary and held the seat without difficulty through 1990. The 1992 redistricting moved him east, into Macomb County, and placed him in the same district with Democrat Dennis Hertel, who decided to retire; Levin easily won the Democratic nomination.

Levin is a hard worker, a details man, willing to spend endless hours with others working out solutions. He often seems to be seeking the mean between two extremes; he likes negotiations and dislikes issues that divide opponents on stark lines of principle. On Ways and Means, he has played an important role on major issues. On welfare, Levin opposed the 1995 bills passed by Republicans but helped shape the bill passed in August 1996. He was willing to end the welfare entitlement but insisted on health insurance guarantees and childcare support for welfare recipients who work. Like most Democrats, he split with Republicans when the House extended the welfare law in 2002 and he found little opportunity for bipartisanship on health issues after George W. Bush took office.

Amid great controversy, Levin has been at the center of trade debates—seeking ways, as he often says, to shape globalization. He favored the Free Trade Agreement with Canada, which was designed in large part by auto manufacturers and the United Auto Workers. But he was wary of Japanese trade barriers and pushed unsuccessfully for stringent measures on Japanese minivans. He was a strong opponent of NAFTA in 1993, but supported GATT and PNTR with China. He opposed trade promotion authority in both the Clinton and Bush years. In 2001, he worked across the aisle to pass implementation of the free-trade agreement with Jordan. He wants trade agreements to contain provisions on workers' rights, fair ways of settling workers' disagreements and environmental provisions. Especially on China, his initiative made a major difference in public policy. He opposed George W. Bush's tariffs on steel, which increase costs to automakers and auto suppliers. In opposing the use of force in Iraq, he consulted extensively with his brother Carl, who was then chairman of the Senate Armed Services Committee. Each offered alternatives reflecting what they view as a more internationalist approach, but each was defeated.

Following the 1992 redistricting, which removed much of metro Detroit's Jewish community from Levin's district and added unfamiliar territory in Macomb County, Levin had serious competition from Republican John Pappageorge, a retired Army colonel and M-1 tank executive. In the anti-incumbent atmosphere of 1992, Levin outspent Pappageorge by $1.18 million to $190,000 and won by just 53%–46%. In 1994, when Clinton was affirmatively unpopular and Republican Governor John Engler was running strong, Levin again greatly outspent Pappageorge and won by 52%–47%. But in the more pro-incumbent environment of 1996, Levin won by a larger 57%–41%. Since then Levin has won easily. Redistricting was kind to him in 2002. The 12th became considerably more Democratic, though half the district was new to him. The 2002 primary was marred by an ugly incident. State Representative William Callahan, running against Levin, said to the Associated Press in July, "I mean, that man has never owned a Christmas tree. He's not a Christian. And I'm thinking, 'Jeez, how can he represent me then?'" Levin largely ignored the remarks and won 79%–19%.

Although bipartisanship has not been in vogue much recently, especially at the Ways and Means Committee, Levin seems determined on continuing the legislative career to which he seems so well suited; he has shown no sign of wanting to retire.

THIRTEENTH DISTRICT

Rep. Carolyn Cheeks Kilpatrick (D)

Elected 1996, 4th term; b. June 25, 1945, Detroit; home, Detroit; Ferris St. U., 1968–70, W. MI U., B.S. 1972, U. of MI, M.S. 1977; African Methodist Episcopal; divorced.

Elected Office: MI House of Reps., 1978–96.

Professional Career: Teacher, Detroit public schls., 1970–78.

DC Office: 1610 LHOB 20515, 202-225-2261; Fax: 202-225-5730; Web site: www.house.gov/kilpatrick.

District Office: Detroit, 313-965-9004.

Committees: *Appropriations* (24th of 29 D): Foreign Operations & Export Financing; Transportation, Treasury, & Independent Agencies.

Group Ratings

	ADA	ACLU	AFS	LCV	CON	ITIC	NTU	COC	ACU	NTLC	CHC
2002	95	85	100	88	43	25	23	42	0	0	8
2001	100	—	100	79	—	—	11	39	4	—	—

National Journal Ratings

	2001 LIB —	2001 CONS	2002 LIB —	2002 CONS
Economic	91% —	10%	86% —	12%
Social	90% —	0%	73% —	26%
Foreign	85% —	15%	87% —	10%

Key Votes of the 107th Congress

1. Approve Bush Tax Cuts	N	5. Faith-Based Charities	N
2. Limit Patients' Bill of Rights	N	6. Bar Gays in the Boy Scouts	N
3. Campaign Finance Reform	Y	7. Ban Partial-Birth Abortion	N
4. Ban ANWR Development	Y	8. Arm Commercial Pilots	N

9. Trade Promotion Authority	N
10. Bar Funds for Intl. Court	N
11. Authorize Force in Iraq	N
12. Deny Home. Sec. Dept. Union	N

Election Results

2002 general	Carolyn Cheeks Kilpatrick (D)	120,869	(92%)	($343,173)
	Raymond Warner (Lib)	11,072	(8%)	
2002 primary	Carolyn Cheeks Kilpatrick (D)	unopposed		
2000 general (MI 15)	Carolyn Cheeks Kilpatrick (D)	140,609	(89%)	($357,453)
	Chrysanthea Boyd-Fields (R)	14,336	(9%)	
	Other	3,806	(2%)	

Prior Winning Percentages: 1998 (87%); 1996 (88%)

The People		Race/Ethnic Origin	Ancestry	
Area size:	108 sq. mi.	28.9% White	German: 5.4%	Polish: 4.2%
Urban population:	100.0%	60.5% Black	Irish: 4.2%	
Rural population:	0.0%	1.2% Asian	**2000 Presidential Vote**	
Pop. 2000:	662,563	0.3% Native Am.	Gore (D) 167,830	(80%)
Median income:	$31,165	0.0% Hawaiian	Bush (R) 39,024	(19%)
Poverty status:	24.4%	1.8% Two+ races	Other 1,975	(1%)
Military veterans:	10.7%	0.2% Other	**Cook Partisan Voting Index:** D +31	
		7.2% Hispanic Origin		

Occupation	Blue collar: 29.3%	White collar: 50.7%	Gray collar: 20.1%

Few central cities in America had as vibrant a 20th century history, and as sad a recent past, as Detroit. This was America's first automobile city, not just because it manufactured so many of the nation's cars but also because it was built to automobile scale. Detroit started the century as a second-rank city, no bigger than Milwaukee, with less than half a million people and extending no farther than four or five miles out from the site where the French built Fort Pontchartrain on the Detroit River in 1701. As the Motor City boomed, it grew outward along wide avenues and, starting in the 1950s, freeways; the auto companies put their factories and headquarters near the edge of urban settlement. As early as 1954, the nation's first big suburban shopping center, with parking for 10,000 cars, was drawing retail trade from downtown. Metro Detroit expanded to four million people, each generation moving out the roadways rapidly in many directions, leaving behind the previous generation's neighborhoods and civic institutions.

Today, that rapid movement has left large parts of Detroit literally empty. The central city had nearly 1.9 million people in 1950, but not even the help of a city bureaucracy detailed to round up uncounted residents could keep the total from falling below 1 million in 2000. The reason is obvious: crime. For 30 years Detroit had a murder rate drastically higher than in the suburbs, and naturally those who could afford to leave did so. Downtown, the giant Hudson's department store has been torn down and several skyscrapers are all but empty. There have been some positive developments. GM bought for $72 million the 70-story Renaissance Center, built in the 1970s for $350 million, and the company moved 10,000 employees there. Beyond downtown, some of the city's jewels have been maintained: the Detroit Institute of Arts, the hospital center, the old Fox Theater. New baseball and football stadiums have opened just north of downtown, and three gambling casinos have opened in nearby Greektown; residential and commercial projects have risen and more are planned on the long-neglected riverfront, which has been renamed the Tri-Centennial State Park and Harbor. But beyond these well-policed enclaves lie acres of vacant fields and half-empty blocks where there were once five-story apartments or brick houses; once vital neighborhoods are now home to pheasants.

Detroit's fate is all the more tragic because it comes in a city where liberal reformers hoped to create model anti-poverty and anti-discrimination programs. Coleman Young, Detroit's mayor from 1973 to 1993, spent his energy on courting the Big Three; he bulldozed the viable Poletown neighborhood for a new Cadillac plant. Dennis Archer, who served the next eight years, took a more constructive and intelligent approach, and the city began to turn around, with lower crime, more jobs, new housing permits and a start at a growing private sector. But much of Detroit is still achingly vacant.

The 13th Congressional District includes most of Detroit, plus a few adjacent suburbs, from the affluent Grosse Pointes with nearly 50,000 people looking out toward Lake St. Clair to the Downriver industrial towns of River Rouge, Ecorse, Lincoln Park and Wyandotte. It includes practically all of the east side of Detroit and the west side up to about five miles north of the Detroit River—the entire riverfront and downtown, the old General Motors and Fisher Buildings, most of Detroit's auto factories. At 108 square miles, this is the smallest district in the state, yet it has the biggest problems: the state's highest rates of poverty, unemployment and percentages of residents on public assistance. Politically, the 13th is overwhelmingly Democratic, but voter turnout is low—132,000 in the House race in 2002, barely half the 243,000 in the high-income 9th District. Redistricting reduced the district's black percentage from 70% to 61%, because more people had to be added to meet the population standard, and because Southfield, which became majority-black in the 1990s, was kept in the Oakland-Macomb 12th District. But this remains one of the safest Democratic districts in the nation.

The congresswoman from the 13th District is Carolyn Cheeks Kilpatrick, a Democrat elected in 1996. She was raised in Detroit, attended Ferris State and graduated from Western Michigan University and the University of Michigan. She taught business education in Detroit public schools and was elected to the state House in 1978. There, she got a seat on the Appropriations Committee and worked on local projects, notably the highly successful River Place hotel and office complex in the old Stroh Beer headquarters. Kilpatrick lost a race for the Detroit City Council, but won the 15th District in the 1996 Democratic primary by a solid 51%–31% margin against her one-time political partner, incumbent Barbara-Rose Collins. Collins, an ally of Coleman Young, was accused of campaign finance violations and misuse of campaign and office funds and had the third highest absentee rate in 1995.

In her first term, Kilpatrick had one of the most liberal voting records in the House, but she has moderated slightly. She made a point of visiting the suburbs in her district, meeting local officials and assigning staffers to work with them—a contrast to Collins. She wants to increase the availability of the dependent care tax credit for the elderly. On Appropriations since 1999, she has taken credit for funding Detroit-area projects for pre-college engineering and $20 million for buses and other transportation improvements in the Detroit area. Following visits to Africa, she has sought increased foreign aid funding for needy areas. She chaired the board of the Black Caucus's political action committee, and co-chaired the bipartisan Urban Caucus.

Kilpatrick has had no primary or general-election problems since she was first elected, and had no major party opposition in 2002. She has been an active supporter of her son Kwame Kilpatrick, a former all-American football player who was elected to the state House, quickly rose to be Democratic leader and who was elected mayor of Detroit in 2001, at age 32.

FOURTEENTH DISTRICT

Rep. John Conyers (D)

Elected 1964, 20th term; b. May 16, 1929, Detroit; home, Detroit; Wayne St. U., B.A. 1957, LL.B. 1958; Baptist; married (Monica).

Military Career: National Guard, 1948–50; Army, 1950–54 (Korea), Army Reserves, 1954–57.

Professional Career: Legis. Asst., U.S. Rep. John Dingell, 1958–61; Practicing atty., 1959–61; Referee, MI Workmen's Comp. Dept., 1961–63.

DC Office: 2426 RHOB 20515, 202-225-5126; Fax: 202-225-0072; Web site: www.house.gov/conyers.

District Office: Detroit, 313-961-5670.

Committees: *Judiciary* (RMM of 16 D): Courts, the Internet & Intellectual Property; Immigration, Border Security & Claims; The Constitution.

Group Ratings

	ADA	ACLU	AFS	LCV	CON	ITIC	NTU	COC	ACU	NTLC	CHC
2002	100	93	100	88	80	25	26	21	0	6	0
2001	90	—	100	93	—	—	22	23	4	—	—

National Journal Ratings

	2001 LIB	—	2001 CONS		2002 LIB	—	2002 CONS
Economic	83%	—	15%		95%	—	0%
Social	90%	—	0%		98%	—	0%
Foreign	96%	—	0%		94%	—	0%

Key Votes of the 107th Congress

1. Approve Bush Tax Cuts	N	5. Faith-Based Charities	N	9. Trade Promotion Authority	N
2. Limit Patients' Bill of Rights	N	6. Bar Gays in the Boy Scouts	N	10. Bar Funds for Intl. Court	N
3. Campaign Finance Reform	Y	7. Ban Partial-Birth Abortion	N	11. Authorize Force in Iraq	N
4. Ban ANWR Development	Y	8. Arm Commercial Pilots	N	12. Deny Home. Sec. Dept. Union	N

Election Results

2002 general	John Conyers (D)	145,285	(83%)	($421,346)
	Dave Stone (R)	26,544	(15%)	
2002 primary	John Conyers (D)	unopposed		
2000 general	John Conyers (D)	168,982	(89%)	($554,892)
	William Ashe (R)	17,852	(9%)	
	Other	3,143	(2%)	

Prior Winning Percentages: 1998 (87%); 1996 (86%); 1994 (82%); 1992 (82%); 1990 (89%); 1988 (91%); 1986 (89%); 1984 (89%); 1982 (97%); 1980 (95%); 1978 (93%); 1976 (92%); 1974 (91%); 1972 (88%); 1970 (88%); 1968 (100%); 1966 (84%); 1964 (84%)

The People		Race/Ethnic Origin	Ancestry	
Area size:	123 sq. mi.	32.1% White	German: 5.0%	Polish: 4.8%
Urban population:	100.0%	61.1% Black	Arab: 4.7%	
Rural population:	0.0%	1.2% Asian	**2000 Presidential Vote**	
Pop. 2000:	662,563	0.3% Native Am.	Gore (D) 198,687	(81%)
Median income:	$36,099	0.0% Hawaiian	Bush (R) 44,345	(18%)
Poverty status:	19.7%	3.3% Two+ races	Other 2,449	(1%)
Military veterans:	11.2%	0.2% Other	**Cook Partisan Voting Index:** D +32	
		1.8% Hispanic Origin		

Occupation	Blue collar: 28.4%	White collar: 53.0%	Gray collar: 18.5%

Detroit's early auto factories—Packard, Hudson, Ford Highland Park, Dodge Main, Briggs, Ford Rouge, Cadillac, Kelsey-Hayes, Chrysler, Plymouth, DeSoto—were built between 1905 and 1925 in an arc about five miles from the city's center, in green fields at what was then the edge of urban development. Almost instantly the flat farmlands all around were platted in grid streets and filled with wooden bungalows and brick prairie-style houses, often with a driveway at the side and a single elm in front. Commercial strips lined the mile-square and radial main streets, stretching straight as far as the eye could see. Detroit's neighborhoods filled up with factory workers and civil servants, professionals and maintenance men, corner store owners and management personnel, Catholics and Protestants and Jews: a middle-class melting pot. With one exception: Detroit in those days had few blacks; they did not begin their big migrations here from the South, especially Alabama, until around 1940, when defense plants began hiring in large numbers.

The history of black Detroit is one of conflict and uplift, inspiration and tragedy. The wartime mixture of Appalachian mountain whites and Deep South blacks proved volatile: there was a violent race riot in June 1943. During the war years, blacks were pent up in a few severely overcrowded neighborhoods like the Black Bottom, which is now the Chrysler Freeway. After 1945, when blacks began moving outward, real estate agents played on racial fears, and in the 1950s whole square miles of Detroit changed racial composition in months. In the 1960s there was hope that the civil rights movement, encouraged by Walter Reuther's UAW, and antipoverty programs would improve blacks' lot, and in fact many black Detroiters found good jobs and made good incomes, bought their own homes and built community institutions. Then came the riot of July 1967, followed by extensive white flight and terrible increases in crime. Detroit's first black mayor, Coleman Young, elected in 1973, responded with policies that may have seemed appropriate in the 1960s but had disastrous results in the 1970s and 1980s: He pressured major employers like the Big Three auto companies to build facilities in Detroit, raised taxes to support a vast army of city employees, and attributed city problems to white racism. Violent crime became a part of everyday life and arson became common.

Detroit took on a garrison atmosphere. Crime reduced the value of residential real estate to near zero, and the city's population dropped from 1.7 million in 1960 to 951,000 in 2000. In political dialogue, most black politicians called for, and most black voters seemed to support, an ever-increasing public sector. Yet the existing public sector, which took a larger share of residents' income than almost anywhere else in the country, served citizens very poorly. Turnaround came agonizingly late in the 1990s, as Mayor Dennis Archer, elected in 1993, worked to fight crime and encourage private-sector growth. In 1997 the state legislature agreed to freeze aid to Detroit in return for a phaseout of the city income tax by 2007. General Motors bought the Renaissance Center downtown for its headquarters. More important, incomes rose (the median household income was up 21% in the decade) and the median housing value doubled from $32,000 to $63,000.

The 14th Congressional District consists of nearly half of Detroit (though not the downtown) and some disparate suburbs. Its part of Detroit is north and west of where the old auto plants were built and is mostly residential—square mile after square mile of grid streets, some always working class, some middle class, a few—Palmer Woods, Sherwood Forest, Rosedale Park—upscale. In most of them, abandoned houses and empty lots are commonplace where houses once stood, and yet in many neighborhoods, residents struggle to maintain their houses and patrol their streets. Commercial frontage on Detroit's straight-line avenues is still patchy and often vacant. Politically, the district is heavily Democratic; the city of Detroit even more so, 94% for Al Gore and 5% for George W. Bush in 2000.

The suburbs of the 14th are diverse. Highland Park is like much of Detroit; Hamtramck still retains the flavor of its original Polish immigrants (on Fat Tuesday, this is where to find the best paczki) who made it America's fastest-growing city in 1910–20; it had 56,000 people in 1930 but only 22,000 in 2000. Redistricting considerably altered the district, adding territory to the south from John Dingell's old 16th District. The 14th District now includes most of Dearborn, including the Ford headquarters, the Ford Rouge plant and Henry Ford's Greenfield Village. Dearborn was known from the 1940s to the 1970s as an adamantly all-white town under longtime Mayor Orville Hubbard. Today it still has few blacks, but it has America's largest Arab-American community; you can see signs in Arabic and can find mosques and Arab community centers. From Dearborn, the district extends south, to take in working-class suburbs—Melvindale, Allen Park, Southgate, Riverview, Trenton and Gibraltar. The last three are on the Detroit River, and the district also includes the island of Grosse Ile, a high-income community that works to keep some of its space open. Local political writers speculated that the new communities would change the political character of the district. But the new 14th is 61% black and overwhelmingly Democratic.

The congressman from the 14th District is John Conyers, the second most senior member of the House and its most liberal, according to *National Journal*'s 2002 vote ratings. First elected in 1964, he is a founder of the Congressional Black Caucus, and the ranking Democrat on the House Judiciary Committee. The son of a left-wing UAW operative, he grew up in Detroit, served in the Army in Korea, practiced law and worked as a staffer for a young congressman named John Dingell. Conyers was first elected to Congress in 1964—one of six blacks in the House at the time and the only one to take a militant approach to politics; he won his primary, in which 60,000 votes were cast, by 108 votes. The civil rights heroine Rosa Parks, who had moved to Detroit, worked in his 1964 campaign and then worked in his Detroit office until her retirement in 1988. His response to the 1967 riots was to introduce the first bill for a guaranteed annual income. He first sponsored a Martin Luther King holiday bill days after the civil rights leader was murdered in 1968, and persevered until it passed in 1983. Since 1989 he has sponsored bills to establish a commission to examine slavery and its lingering effects, and for consideration of whether reparations should be paid to descendants of slaves. He opposed most controversial parts of the crime bills of the past three decades and welfare changes in the 1990s and calls for single-payer health plans and massive public works projects.

Conyers remains alert to evidence of racism. He has pushed bills to collect racial statistics on traffic stops, in the belief that many blacks are stopped for DWB (driving while black). He criticizes Republicans bitterly, but not only Republicans; he criticized the Clinton administration on Haiti until it weighed in on the side of Jean-Bertrand Aristide. On some civil liberties issues, he has joined forces with Judiciary Committee conservatives.

After September 11, Conyers worked together with the new Judiciary chairman, James Sensenbrenner, on terrorism legislation. In October 2001 they agreed that the government could detain immigrants suspected of terrorism without bringing charges, but only for seven days, and they introduced the antiterrorism bill together. Conyers also worked on tightening border security. In April 2002 Sensenbrenner got Conyers's support for splitting the INS into two agencies by agreeing to add counsel positions. Conyers has also weighed in on other legislation. He has sought to limit the number of civilian workers in Plan Colombia to 300. Together with Senator Paul Wellstone, he sponsored a bill to repeal Major League Baseball's exemption from the antitrust laws. Conyers opposed the Dingell-Tauzin bill which, in his view, would allow the regional Bells to have a monopoly of broadband communication which they could extend to other services.

Conyers is the only member of Congress ever to have served on two committees handling presidential impeachment. In May 1972, a month before the Watergate burglary, he called for impeaching Richard Nixon because of his conduct of the Vietnam War. As the hearings on Bill Clinton's impeachment opened in 1998, some Democrats were queasy about Conyers, sharing the judgment of Judiciary Committee Republican George Gekas that he was "predictably unpredictable." But Conyers, the ranking Democrat, performed ably. For all his criticisms of Clinton, Conyers rallied behind him; he managed to craft an alternative investigation resolution that Republicans wouldn't accept, the start of partisan divisions on the issue. Interestingly, he did not back reauthorization of the independent counsel law that he strongly supported in 1994.

Over the years, Conyers has mostly been re-elected without difficulty. He made two runs for mayor of Detroit, in 1989 and 1993. But he ran a desultory campaign the first time and almost no campaign the second, and came in far behind. He had two serious primary opponents in 1994, but finished well ahead of both with 51% of the vote. He has not had serious opposition since, and redistricting didn't hurt him in 2002—although it did prompt him to travel to the Downriver communities, which he could not recall ever having visited.

FIFTEENTH DISTRICT

Rep. John Dingell (D)

Elected Dec. 1955, 24th term; b. July 8, 1926, Colorado Springs, CO; home, Dearborn; Georgetown U., B.S. 1949, J.D. 1952; Catholic; married (Deborah).

Military Career: Army, 1944–46 (WWII).

Professional Career: Practicing atty., 1952–55; Wayne Cnty. Asst. Prosecuting Atty., 1953–55.

DC Office: 2328 RHOB 20515, 202-225-4071; Web site: www.house.gov/dingell.

District Offices: Dearborn, 313-278-2936; Monroe, 734-243-1849.

Committees: *Energy & Commerce* (RMM of 26 D).

Group Ratings

	ADA	ACLU	AFS	LCV	CON	ITIC	NTU	COC	ACU	NTLC	CHC
2002	90	79	89	88	43	38	20	42	4	0	8
2001	95	—	100	79	—	—	11	41	24	—	—

National Journal Ratings

	2001 LIB —	2001 CONS	2002 LIB —	2002 CONS
Economic	77%	23%	84%	15%
Social	68%	33%	66%	34%
Foreign	60%	40%	82%	18%

Key Votes of the 107th Congress

1. Approve Bush Tax Cuts	N	5. Faith-Based Charities	N	9. Trade Promotion Authority	N
2. Limit Patients' Bill of Rights	N	6. Bar Gays in the Boy Scouts	N	10. Bar Funds for Intl. Court	N
3. Campaign Finance Reform	Y	7. Ban Partial-Birth Abortion	Y	11. Authorize Force in Iraq	N
4. Ban ANWR Development	Y	8. Arm Commercial Pilots	Y	12. Deny Home. Sec. Dept. Union	N

Election Results

2002 general	John Dingell (D)	136,518	(72%)	($3,461,009)
	Martin Kaltenbach (R)	48,626	(26%)	
	Other	3,919	(2%)	
2002 primary	John Dingell (D)	58,120	(59%)	
	Lynn Rivers (D)	40,832	(41%)	
2000 general (MI 16)	John Dingell (D)	167,142	(71%)	($1,048,787)
	William Morse (R)	62,469	(27%)	
	Other	5,906	(3%)	

Prior Winning Percentages: 1998 (67%); 1996 (62%); 1994 (59%); 1992 (65%); 1990 (67%); 1988 (97%); 1986 (78%); 1984 (64%); 1982 (74%); 1980 (70%); 1978 (77%); 1976 (76%); 1974 (78%); 1972 (68%); 1970 (79%); 1968 (74%); 1966 (63%); 1964 (73%); 1962 (83%); 1960 (79%); 1958 (79%); 1956 (74%); 1955 (76%)

The People		Race/Ethnic Origin	Ancestry	
Area size:	981 sq. mi.	79.2% White	German: 15.0%	Irish: 8.4%
Urban population:	87.7%	11.7% Black	Polish: 6.7%	
Rural population:	12.3%	3.7% Asian	**2000 Presidential Vote**	
Pop. 2000:	662,563	0.4% Native Am.	Gore (D) 161,913	(60%)
Median income:	$48,963	0.0% Hawaiian	Bush (R) 101,607	(38%)
Poverty status:	10.3%	2.0% Two+ races	Other 7,086	(3%)
Military veterans:	11.1%	0.2% Other	**Cook Partisan Voting Index:** D +11	
		2.8% Hispanic Origin		

Occupation	Blue collar: 26.2%	White collar: 59.0%	Gray collar: 14.7%

The southeast corner of Michigan is a part of the country most Americans don't think about much, and it doesn't look very interesting out the plane window as you approach Metro Airport.

The flat marshlands along the shore of Lake Erie give way to flat farm lands, with rivers flowing lazily in summer and flashing with ice in winter. Here and there you see power plants with giant smokestacks and factories. Out on the horizon you can get a glimpse of the sprawl of metro Detroit, of the great auto and steel and chemical plants along the Detroit River; over on the other side is Ann Arbor, home of the University of Michigan.

The 15th Congressional District includes much of this southeastern corner of Michigan. It owes its shape to Republican redistricters, who in July 2001 devised the nation's most successful partisan redistricting plan of the decennial cycle. The 15th was drawn to put two incumbent Democratic congressmen in the same district, John Dingell, the dean of the House, and Lynn Rivers, an Ann Arbor liberal first elected in 1994. Each had represented about half the new district. The district includes industrial parts of Wayne County, all of Monroe County and the Ann Arbor and Ypsilanti areas in Washtenaw County. In Wayne County, the 15th includes the western part of Dearborn and most of Dearborn Heights; the most heavily Arab-American parts of Dearborn were put in the 14th District, and these are more middle class, even affluent areas; the line cuts through Dearborn Heights and put one trailer park in two districts. To the south are working class suburbs: Taylor, Romulus (home of Metro Airport), and Woodhaven, site of a big Ford plant. Flat Rock is home to an automaking plant owned by both Ford and Mazda; in 2003 Ford announced it would move production of the Mustang muscle car here from its Dearborn Assembly Plant. Monroe was the birthplace of General George Armstrong Custer, and in his day agricultural; now it is more industrial, and the southern part is in many ways an extension of Toledo, Ohio. (Michigan and Ohio almost went to war over the Toledo land in the 1830s; Ohio got Toledo and Michigan got the Upper Peninsula as recompense.) Ann Arbor is one of the nation's largest university towns, oriented to the university but also full of people, from auto executives to perennial graduate students, who like the atmosphere of a town with plenty of book stores, coffee houses and liberal neighbors. Ypsilanti, though it also has a university (Eastern Michigan), is less bookish and more industrial. All of these areas tend to vote Democratic, though Monroe is sometimes marginal, but they house very different kinds of Democrats. In Wayne County, union political operatives have dominated Democratic party politics for 50 years. In Ann Arbor, Democratic politics is dominated by leftist peace enthusiasts, environmentalists and, most of all, feminists.

The congressman from the 15th District is John Dingell, the senior member of the House of Representatives. His father, John Dingell, Sr., was elected to the House in 1932, from a district created as a result of the Detroit area's auto boom. The first Congressman Dingell was one of the most productive urban liberals of his day, a sponsor of Social Security and, starting in 1943, of national health insurance. John Dingell Jr. has been around Capitol Hill almost as long. He was a House page from 1938–43 and served in the Army in World War II; he graduated from Georgetown and its law school, paying his way by working as an elevator operator in the Capitol; he practiced law and served as an assistant prosecutor in Wayne County. After his father died in September 1955, Dingell was elected to succeed him in December, at 29, from a district entirely within Detroit with large Polish, black and Jewish populations. He still uses his father's office furniture and every session continues to introduce as H.R. 15 (the number matches the district) the national health insurance bill his father co-sponsored in 1943. He is the only member of the House who served in the 1950s; indeed only three others served in the 1960s (John Conyers, Philip Crane and David Obey); it is a measure of his seniority that the second most senior member of the House, Conyers, once served on his staff. He has an interesting personal life, raising his children after his divorce (his son Christopher was elected to the Michigan Senate in 1986) and marrying in 1981 a granddaughter of one of General Motors' Fisher brothers. Debbie Dingell is head of the General Motors Foundation and a Democratic National committeewoman, and an encourager of bipartisan amity as well; she also headed Al Gore's 2000 presidential campaign in Michigan, and is given much credit for his 51%–46% win there.

From 1981–95 Dingell was chairman of the Energy and Commerce Committee and of its Investigative and Oversight Subcommittee, one of the most powerful and effective chairmen ever. It had wide jurisdiction, handled up to 40% of all House bills, and had the largest budget and staff of any House committee. As institutions will, the committee took on the character of its leader, widely known as "the truck": bright, aggressive, domineering, determined. Dingell and his committee superintended the breakup of AT&T and the sale of Conrail by public offering; Commerce's cable reregulation law of 1992 was the only bill on which Congress overrode George H.W. Bush's presidential veto. After a decade of sparring over clean air legislation, Dingell worked together with Health Subcommittee Chairman Henry Waxman to produce the 1990 Clean Air Act.

On other issues, Dingell backed organized labor's agenda against NAFTA and trade promotion authority. An avid outdoorsman (he hunts deer, elk, caribou and moose), he long opposed gun control but voted for the 1994 crime bill and resigned from the National Rifle Association board. In many ways, he is an old-fashioned Franklin Roosevelt Democrat, supporting big government and strenuous regulation, taking a conservative line on some cultural issues and backing an assertive foreign policy; he was the only Michigan Democrat to vote for the Gulf War resolution in January 1991, although he voted against the Iraq war resolution in October 2002.

When the Republican majority took over, many expected Dingell to sulk or to launch bitter attacks on the other side. But he did neither. As the senior House member, he swore in Newt Gingrich with good grace and proceeded to work with Republicans and produce legislation.

Dingell has also been successful in forging Democratic positions that prevailed in the Republican House. He proposed the health care portability legislation that passed in somewhat different form in August 1996. He introduced a bill to regulate HMOs in February 1998 and then joined with Republican Greg Ganske. It lost 217–212 and a Republican alternative passed 216–210. The Senate never acted. In July 1999 Dingell came back, allied with Ganske and Republican Charlie Norwood, and in October 1999 the renamed Dingell-Norwood bill passed 275–151, with 68 Republicans voting yes. The bill imposed uniform national standards for health insurance, including guaranteed access to emergency care and medical specialists, appeals of coverage decisions to an independent board, a prohibition on HMOs retaliating against doctors and a right to sue HMOs in state courts. Again the Senate didn't act, and Dingell and Norwood tried again in 2001. In the course of negotiations at the White House, George W. Bush joshed Dingell, "You're the biggest pain in the ass on Capitol Hill." Dingell replied, "Thank you for a high compliment. I've worked 47 years for that reputation, and I'd hate to see it dissipate in one afternoon." But in August 2001, Bush managed to convince Norwood to sign onto a bill with less regulation, which passed the House; but the Senate again didn't act. Dingell's goal remains national health insurance; asked what is a desirable system, he says, "Canada's, right across the river."

In January 2001 Dingell strongly opposed stripping the Commerce Committee of jurisdiction over insurance and the securities industry, which was part of a Republican plan to make Mike Oxley the chairman of Banking, a committee Dingell accused of "incompetence and indifference." In July 2001 Dingell and Billy Tauzin reached agreement on CAFE standards for gas mileage: the Department of Transportation would be directed to reduce gas consumption for SUVs and light trucks by 5 miles per gallon by 2010. This was a substitute for mandating the auto companies to meet higher standards and was part of the energy bill that passed the House in August 2001. In 2001 Dingell and Tauzin also pressed for their bill allowing regional Bell companies to provide broadband service. Despite opposition from the Judiciary Committee, this passed 273–157 in February 2002, but got no vote in the Senate. Dingell and Tauzin also urged the FCC to take action against piracy of digital TV.

Since his first election, Dingell has had only two serious challenges, both in Democratic primaries after being redistricted in with another incumbent. In 1964 he ran in a district mostly new to him against another incumbent who had followed him to the House, John Lesinski of Dearborn, who was the only northern Democrat to vote against the Civil Rights Act of 1964. With strong support from the UAW, Dingell won 54%–46%. Then in July 2001 the Republican legislature put him in the same district with Lynn Rivers of Ann Arbor. Rivers was born in 1956, one year after Dingell was first elected to the House, and was first elected herself in 1994. Dingell was elected in the first of 40 consecutive years of Democratic majorities in the House; Rivers never served in a Democratic House. She had a leftish voting record and took no major role on legislation. After redistricting, some Democrats urged her to run in the 11th District, which included some of her old territory. But she decided to stay with Ann Arbor and run against Dingell in what she called a "David vs. Goliath match up."

It was that, and more. Their voting records were similar, though not identical, but their cultural backgrounds were as different as the working class suburbs of Wayne County and the university town of Ann Arbor. Rivers campaigned as a congresswoman who knew what the ordinary person went through and cast her votes accordingly. Dingell campaigned as a congressman who had gotten many things done and was in a position to do much more. Dingell was endorsed by the state AFL-CIO, the UAW and the National Rifle Association. Rivers was endorsed by EMILY's List, the Sierra Club and the Brady Campaign. On September 10, 2001, the day before the redistricting bill was to be signed, Nancy Pelosi, then running for Minority Whip, sent Rivers $10,000—"a minor annoyance," Dingell said, though he later refused to raise any money for the House Democrats' campaign committee. Rivers emphasized their differences on the partial-birth abortion ban, particular gun control proposals and environmental standards; Dingell voted for the first, opposed the second and tended to support the auto companies (and the UAW) on the third. Rivers said, "Clout is a wonderful thing, if you're using it for good. If you're using it to stop gun control legislation, that's not a good thing. If you're using it to limit women's choice, that's not a good thing." Dingell parried by pointing to the women's issues he had been instrumental on— breast and cervical cancer screening, minimum hospital stays after childbirth, children's health insurance. Dingell talked of the work he had done on wildlife refuges and cleaning up the Rouge River; with Carolyn McCarthy, he sponsored a bill making it tougher for felons to buy firearms. Dingell reached into her old district for endorsements, including the 13th District Democratic party and several local Democratic officials.

This was Michigan's most expensive House primary ever. Dingell raised $2.5 million, from unions, the auto industry and regulated industries generally. But Rivers was competitive. With major help from EMILY's List and its bundled contributions she raised $1.5 million, enough to make this a seriously contested race on television. For most of the months before the August 6 primary Dingell led in polls by about 10%. In June, Rivers started running spots in which she recounted her personal struggles and how she understood what working families go through. Her plainspoken, perky manner evidently got through: by late July, two polls showed the race even. Dingell fired back with a spot praising his effectiveness on prescription drugs, HMO regulation, children's health insurance and the Clean Air Act. In contrast, he said, "She's never authored a single piece of legislation that's been signed into law." On the stump, Dingell told reporters that he had had some difficult times in life as well. "I know what it is to sit up at night with sick kids and take care of kids and help with their homework. I know all of these things firsthand, because I've lived them. I got the kids in a terrible divorce because I had no choice. These things do not qualify me for office. They might qualify me for sympathy, but I'm Polish, and Poles don't ask for sympathy. I have the curious view that I should be judged on the basis of what I stand for, what I've done, my ability, my effectiveness, the kind of service I give my constituents, my legislative record, my personal integrity." For him the race came down to the question, "Are you going to replace one of the most effective members of the House of Representatives with one of the least effective members?" Dingell was endorsed by the *Ann Arbor News* as well as the *Detroit Free Press* and *Detroit News*. Bizarrely, John Conyers in July circulated a letter calling on Dingell to drop out and be elected Speaker when Democrats won a majority; Dingell would have none of it.

On August 6, Dingell won 59%–41%. He won 74%–26% in Wayne County, which cast 43% of the votes, even though part of it was in Rivers's old district, and 80%–20% in Monroe County, which cast 19% of the votes. Rivers won Washtenaw County 69%–31%. The general election was anticlimactic; Dingell won easily in this Democratic district. In September 2002 Dingell said he would run again in 2004 and didn't expect another tough fight for 10 years. He stands to become the longest-serving House member in history in February 2009.

★ MINNESOTA ★

Minnesota has long been a distinctive commonwealth, set far in America's frozen North, a state which in commerce, culture and politics has set one example after another for the rest of the nation. It is the node of transcontinental railroads that linked the winter wheat fields of the northern prairies to the greatest grain milling center in the world and the great Pacific ports of Puget Sound. It is also the birthplace of Scotch tape, Betty Crocker, Target and the Mall of America, the home base of dyspeptic chroniclers of small town America from Sinclair Lewis to Garrison Keillor. Politically, Minnesota over the last half century provided the nation with some of its most articulate and honorable leaders—Harold Stassen, Hubert Humphrey, Eugene McCarthy, Walter Mondale—and with traditions of probity, civic-mindedness and innovation which are second to none. Yet while commercially and culturally Minnesota has never been stronger, its recent political history has been unusual and on occasion tragic. For more than a decade, two political parties, the Democratic-Farmer-Labor and the Republican—have been dominated by activists of left and right stubbornly out of touch with ordinary voters. At least partly in response, voters in 1998 elected a former professional wrestler and suburban mayor, Jesse "The Body" Ventura, as governor. The bald, blunt-spoken Ventura, with his strong Midwestern accent and gift for pithy phrases, quickly became a national celebrity, a possible trend-setter as a political libertarian on most cultural issues and market oriented on economics. For three years he was highly popular; in his fourth he faced resistance when he tried to raise taxes and retired without seeking a second term. In the meantime, what had been one of the nation's more heavily Democratic states seemed to be moving to the Republicans. George W. Bush didn't carry Minnesota in 2000, but he lost by only 48%–46%; for the first time in half a century Minnesota cast a lower Democratic percentage for president than the nation as a whole. And in 2002 Republicans won the governorship, a Senate seat, and increased their ranks in the legislature. Their victories were narrow and may have been affected by the death of DFL Senator Paul Wellstone in a plane crash October 25. Still, something seems to be stirring in Minnesota.

Minnesota's distinctive traditions come from a distinctive history. The far northern states were ignored by most Yankee immigrants, who headed straight west into Iowa, Nebraska and Kansas. But others saw opportunity in Minnesota's icy lakes and ferocious winters. James J. Hill, the builder of the Great Northern Railroad ("You can't interest me in any proposition in any place where it doesn't snow"), and others operating out of Minneapolis and St. Paul—already twin cities by 1860—worked to attract Norwegian, Swedish and German migrants who would find the terrain and climate congenial. By 1890, the Twin Cities—rivals that year in a Census competition—were the nerve center of a sprawling and rich agricultural empire stretching west from Minnesota through the Dakotas and into Montana and beyond. Minneapolis and St. Paul became the termini of its rail lines and the site of its grain-milling companies.

The Twin Cities also became the center of a three-party politics and an economic radicalism reminiscent of the politics of Scandinavia. For our American regions seem a mirror image of the geography of Europe, with the East Coast resembling the British Isles and France, the industrial Midwest reminiscent of Germany and Poland, the relatively poor and always hawkish South a Baptist Mediterranean, and the Upper Midwest of Minnesota, Wisconsin and North Dakota as North American versions of Scandinavia. The Scandinavian flavor of life lives on: You can get lutefisk (smelly lye-soaked cod), around Christmastime in Minneapolis restaurants. It extends also to politics. Like Scandinavia, these Upper Midwestern commonwealths pioneered their continent's welfare states, with an effect on public policy far out of proportion to their numbers. Alarmed by the unprecedented concentration of economic power and wealth into the hands of just a few identifiable millionaires who lived on St. Paul's Summit Avenue or the hill above Minneapolis's Hennepin Avenue, the immigrants drew on their native traditions of cooperative activity and bureaucratic socialism.

As in Wisconsin and North Dakota, a strong third party developed here in the years after the Populist era. This Farmer-Labor Party elected senators in the 1920s and dominated state politics in the 1930s. Hurt by their ties to Communists, the Farmer-Laborites were beaten by Harold

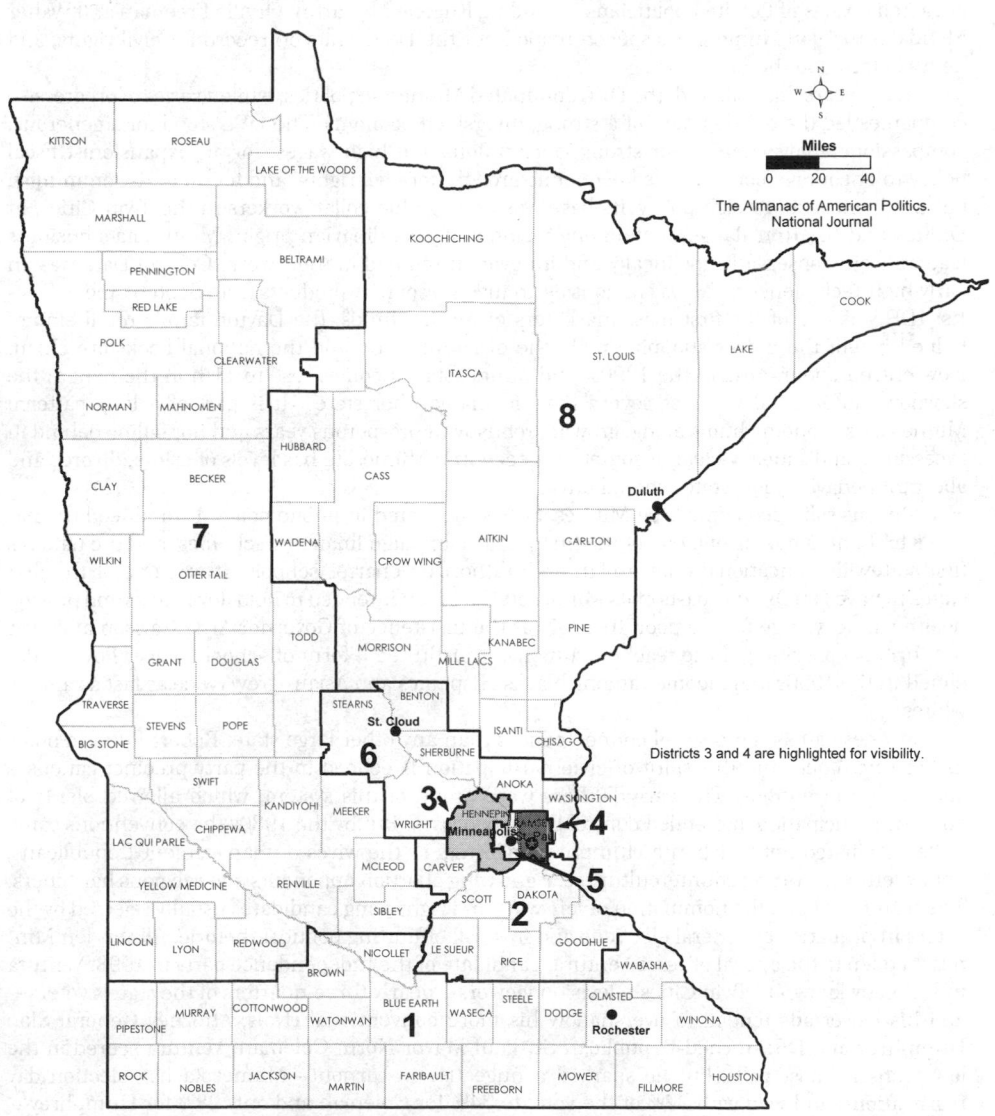

The Almanac of American Politics.
National Journal

Districts 3 and 4 are highlighted for visibility.

Congressional district boundaries were first effective for 2002.

Stassen's Republicans in 1938. But this was still a New Deal state, and by 1944 the bedraggled local Democrats were merged with the anti-Communist faction of Farmer-Laborites to form the Democratic-Farmer-Labor Party. A key role was played by Hubert Humphrey—mayor of Minneapolis in 1945, and the dazzling advocate of the civil rights plank at the 1948 Democratic National Convention. Humphrey's DFL—clean, idealistic, closely tied to labor, backed by many farmers—attracted dozens of talented politicians, including Eugene McCarthy, Orville Freeman and Walter Mondale. In 1948 Humphrey's speech helped put the Democrats on record for civil rights, and he was elected to the Senate at age 37.

In the years that followed, the DFL dominated Minnesota politics, while a series of progressive companies led the development of a strong, diversified economy. The DFL stood for a generous, compassionate government, for strong labor unions and high wages, for an expansionist fiscal policy to encourage consumer-led economic growth, for civil rights, and for an anti-Communist, but not bombastic, foreign policy. Its base was among blue-collar workers in the Twin Cities, in Duluth and the Iron Range, and among farmers of Scandinavian origin. Minnesota's business leaders were conservative politically and innovation-minded in their work: Control Data was an early high-tech pioneer; 3M was famous as an inventor of new products from Scotch tape to Post-Its; IDS was one of the first mass-marketers of mutual funds; the Dayton family retail empire helped invent the indoor shopping mall, the discount store, and the national bookstore chain. New entrepreneurs rose in the 1990s, and Minnesota's incomes rose to 11th in the nation; the slowdown after 2000 was less severe than in many other states. It is part of a long pattern: Minnesota's economy hums along, growing robustly in prosperous years and not falling behind in recessions, and squeaky-clean if sometimes eccentric Minnesota has levels of crime, divorce and aberrant behavior most states should envy.

On this solid economic base Minnesota has innovated in public policy. It produced the nation's first anti-smoking bill, one of the first public campaign financing schemes, and the nation's first statewide educational choice plan and authorized charter schools. It was one of the first states to have HMOs and boasts of its MinnesotaCare plan intended to hold down costs and provide health care coverage for the poor. In 1997, at the insistence of Governor Arne Carlson and over the furious opposition of the teachers' unions, it instituted a form of school choice. Poverty declined in the 1990s and incomes among blacks Hispanics and Asians grew twice as fast as among whites.

Minnesota has more social connectedness than any other large state, Robert Putnam notes in *Bowling Alone*, and this spirit of civic participation is echoed in the party precinct caucuses and party conventions. The early DFLers were proud of this system, which allowed plenty of political participation and ended control by party bosses. But by the 1980s the conventions came to be dominated not by laborite Humphrey followers or the wives of management Republicans, but by left-wingers and counterculturites, right-wing abortion opponents and religious hardliners. The result has been the nomination of left-wing and right-wing candidates usually rejected by the voters in primaries or general elections and in shrill offputting political rhetoric. All this left Minnesota open to the appeal of Jesse Ventura, candidate of the Independence party in 1998. Ventura was already known to Twin Cities television viewers—nearly three-quarters of the state's voters—and his clever ads tended to overshadow his more conventional rivals, Attorney General Skip Humphrey and DFL-turned-Republican St. Paul Mayor Norm Coleman. Ventura scored in the low teens in most polls, but he sparked a huge rise in turnout—Minnesota has election day registration—and won with 37% of the vote, to 34% for Coleman and only 28% for Humphrey—less than half the 60% his father won in his first electrifying election for senator exactly 50 years earlier.

It was, literally, a new Minnesota that elected Ventura. In the Twin Cities core, Hennepin and Ramsey counties, with one-third of the vote, it was an almost even three-way race, with Ventura leading narrowly with 36%, to 32% for Coleman and 31% for Humphrey. In the one-third of Minnesota beyond the range of Minneapolis-St. Paul TV stations on which Ventura concentrated his meager TV buy, Ventura finished third, with 27%, to 38% for Coleman and 35% for Humphrey. Coleman carried the ancestral Republican base—heavily German counties in southern Minnesota and the heavily Norwegian counties north and west of St. Cloud—and Humphrey carried the far north with pluralities plus Austin, site of the bitter Hormel strike. Ventura's breakout came in the counties outside the Twin Cities core but within the Twin Cities media market: Call it the Ventura Belt. In this one-third of the state, turnout was actually up 2% from the presidential year of 1996, and up a whopping 28% from the last off-year of 1994. This is the youngest part of Minnesota, with many young families moving out from the Twin Cities core: the voters less closely connected to traditional politics. Ventura carried these counties with 45% of the vote—a stunning performance for a third-party candidate—to 34% for Coleman and only 21% for Humphrey.

Ventura seems to have detached many young voters from the DFL loyalty of their parents. This is apparent from the results of the elections of 2000 and 2002. George W. Bush, like his father in 1988, got 46% of the vote in Minnesota; but the Democratic percentage declined from 53% for Michael Dukakis in 1988 to 48% for Al Gore in 2000. Almost none of this drop came in the Twin Cities core and a little in the counties beyond Twin Cities TV; most of it came in the Ventura Belt, where the elder Bush ran even, 49%–49%, in 1988 while George W. Bush ran ahead, 50%–44%, in 2000. In 2002 Coleman lost the Twin Cities core and the counties beyond Twin Cities TV. But in the Ventura Belt, Coleman won 56%–41% over Walter Mondale. The last time Mondale ran for the Senate, in 1972, when those counties cast little more than half as many votes, he carried the area 53%–47%. In the 2002 governor race there was a similar pattern. Republican Tim Pawlenty won because he carried the Ventura Belt 51%–30% over the DFL's Roger Moe, with 17% for Independence party candidate Tim Penny. Minnesota's DFL has a long and noble tradition—but one that is perhaps too old for voters in the newest and fastest-growing part of the state. To be sure, these were late-breaking races, and there was strong revulsion against the Democrats after the October 29 memorial service for DFL Senator Paul Wellstone turned into a campaign rally. But the response in the final week also reflected attitudes held during what had been a tumultuous campaign year.

The People

Pop. 2000:	4,919,479
Pop. 1990:	4,375,099
Change 1990–2000:	Up 12.4%
Change 1980–1990:	Up 7.3%
% of U.S. total:	1.8%
Pop. rank:	21st of 50
Area size:	86,939 sq. mi.
State Native:	70.2%
Non-citizen:	3.3%

Language

English: 89.6%	Other Eur.: 3.9%
Spanish: 3.6%	

Race/Ethnic Origin

4,337,143	88.2%	White
168,813	3.4%	Black
141,083	2.9%	Asian
52,009	1.1%	Native Am.
1,714	0.0%	Hawaiian
70,304	1.4%	Two + races
5,031	0.1%	Other
143,382	2.9%	Hisp. Origin

Ancestry

German: 25.2%	Norwegian: 11.8%
Irish: 7.7%	Swedish: 6.8%
English: 4.3%	

Military veterans: 464,968 (12.8%)

WWII: 20.2%	Korea: 14.6%
Vietnam: 32.8%	Gulf War: 7.6%

Most populous cities:

1. Minneapolis	382,618
2. St. Paul	287,151
3. Duluth	86,918
4. Rochester	85,806
5. Bloomington	85,172

Urban population: 70.9%
Rural population: 29.1%

Education

H.S. Grad:	87.9%
College Grad:	27.4%

Industry

Agri: 2.6%	Con: 5.9%
Fin: 7.2%	Info: 2.5%
Mfg: 21.4%	Prof: 29.7%
Public: 3.4%	Trade: 15.5%
Other: 11.8%	

Occupation

Blue collar: 23.3%	White collar: 62.3%
Gray collar: 14.4%	

Work Sector

Private: 80.4%	Govt: 12.4%
Self: 6.9%	Family: 0.3%

Unemployment: 4.1%

Household Income

<15k: 12.1%	15-35k: 23.8%
35-50k: 17.0%	50-100k: 34.5%
100-150k: 8.3%	>150k: 4.4%

Median: $47,111
Poverty status: 7.9%

Legislature

Senate	35 D 31 R 1 I
House	82 R 52 D

Legislative Term Limits: No

Registered Voters

No party registration

Home Value

<50k: 11.1%	50-100k: 27.6%	100-200k: 45.8%	200-300k: 10.1%
300-500k: 4.0%	>500k: 1.3%	Median: $118,100	

Presidential politics   Minnesota has the longest consecutive streak of voting Democratic for president of any state: the last time it voted Republican was in 1972, and even then it gave Richard Nixon his lowest percentage margin over George McGovern. But in 2000 Minnesota was seriously contested, and in the end gave Al Gore only a 48%–46% victory over George W. Bush. It was a vivid contrast to 1988, when Bush's father lost the state to Michael Dukakis by 53%–46%. What changed in the meantime? Ross Perot and Jesse Ventura evidently detached many voters from their ancestral allegiance. Perot won 24% of the vote here in 1992 and 12% in 1996, more in each case than in any other state this large. And in the Ventura Belt counties around the Twin Cities, Bush beat Gore by 50%–44% in an area where his father had only run even. In addition, in the rural west and north, George W. Bush led by wider margins (or trailed by less) than his father had; he carried five of the state's eight congressional districts. In farm country and the north woods he carried many counties that had long voted DFL. If the major metro movement toward Democrats in the 1990s so visible on the East and West Coasts was less visible in Minnesota, the countervailing rural movement toward Republicans was even more prominent. The result is that Minnesota must be counted as competitive in the next close presidential race.

2000 Presidential Vote		
Gore (D)	1,168,266	(48%)
Bush (R)	1,109,659	(46%)
Nader (Green)	126,696	(5%)
Other	34,064	(1%)
1996 Presidential Vote		
Clinton (D)	1,120,279	(51%)
Dole (R)	766,476	(35%)
Perot (I)	257,704	(12%)
Other	48,425	(2%)

Minnesota has a tradition of selecting national convention delegates in caucuses. But caucus turnout has been low: In the 1998 DFL caucuses, an average of 4.4 voters showed up in each precinct, and in one-fourth of the precincts, no one showed up at all. DFL leaders, reeling from their party's third-place finish in 1998, tried to attract more voters to the March 2000 presidential precinct caucuses by moving them from Tuesday night to Saturday and by holding a presidential preference vote, with national convention delegates assigned proportionately. It made little difference: By the time Minnesotans caucused, the nomination was already clinched.

Congressional districting   It never seemed likely that Minnesota's Republican House, DFL Senate and Independence party governor would agree on congressional redistricting, and they didn't—the new plan was drawn by a special panel of five judges appointed by Chief Justice Kathleen Blatz. The Republicans wanted to combine Minneapolis and St. Paul into one heavily Democratic district, in the hope of winning three or four of four suburban districts. Democrats designed a plan that would continue the longstanding practice of having predominantly rural districts anchored in each corner of the state; the result would be four rural districts, two dominated by Minneapolis and St. Paul and two in the suburbs. Governor Jesse Ventura submitted a plan with two urban, three suburban and three rural districts, with one of them stretching along the western side of the state from Iowa to Canada.

108th Congress Lineup	
4 DFL	4 R
107th Congress Lineup	
5 DFL	3 R

The special panel drew its own plan and, when Republicans, Democrats and Ventura couldn't agree by the March 19, 2002, deadline, it was publicly revealed and put into effect. Minneapolis and St. Paul would each continue to dominate a district. Three suburban and three rural districts were created, one running along the southern end of the state from Wisconsin to South Dakota. Republican and Democratic leaders and Ventura all said they were pleased with the plan: It is probably what they might have agreed to if someone had put a gun to their heads. The homes of two incumbents, DFLer Bill Luther and Republican Mark Kennedy were placed in the new 6th District. Luther, after pondering the decision for two months, decided to run in the new 2d District, much of which he had represented; he lost in November.

Governor

Tim Pawlenty (R)

Elected 2002, term expires Jan. 2007, 1st term; b. Nov. 27, 1960, St. Paul; home, Eagan; U. of MN, B.A. 1983, J.D. 1986; Protestant; married (Mary).

Elected Office: Eagan Planning Comm., 1988–89; Eagan City Cncl., 1990–92; MN House of Reps., 1992–02, Maj. Ldr., 1999–02.

Professional Career: Practicing atty., 1986–92.

Office: 130 State Capitol, 75 Rev. Dr. Martin Luther King Blvd., St. Paul, 55155, 651-296-3391; Fax: 651-296-0039; Web site: www.governor. state.mn.us.

Election Results

2002 general	Tim Pawlenty (R)	999,473	(44%)
	Roger Moe (DFL)	821,268	(36%)
	Tim Penny (I)	364,534	(16%)
	Other	67,198	(3%)
2002 primary	Tim Pawlenty (R)	172,927	(89%)
	Leslie Davis (R)	22,172	(11%)
1998 general	Jesse Ventura (Ref)	773,713	(37%)
	Norm Coleman (R)	717,350	(34%)
	Hubert Humphrey III (DFL)	587,528	(28%)
	Other	13,175	(1%)

Tim Pawlenty, a Republican, was elected governor of Minnesota in 2002, but his victory received none of the attention from the national press that greeted the victory of his predecessor, Jesse Ventura, in 1998. Pawlenty grew up in South St. Paul near the stockyards and a meatpacking plant; when he was 16 his mother died and his father lost his job at a trucking company. He worked his way through college and law school at the University of Minnesota, the first college graduate in his family. He first got involved in politics when interning for Senator David Durenberger. He practiced law and in 1992 was elected to the state House from Eagan in suburban Dakota County. Soon he became recognized as one of his party's leaders. Pawlenty started running for governor in 1998, but was persuaded to step aside for Norm Coleman, the mayor of St. Paul, who had switched parties and become a Republican. In 1999 Pawlenty was elected Majority Leader in the state House. With Speaker Steve Sviggum, he helped pass large tax cuts and was a major player, with Sviggum, DFL state Senate President Roger Moe and Independent Governor Jesse Ventura, in Minnesota's tripartisan government. In 2001 he set out to run against Senator Paul Wellstone, but White House political strategist Karl Rove thought Coleman would be a stronger candidate. Dick Cheney then called Pawlenty and said that it would be better if he got out of the Senate race and ran for governor. For the second time, Pawlenty deferred to Coleman.

Running for governor in 2002 was a formidable task. Brian Sullivan, a self-financing businessman, was already running for the Republican nomination and had a set of issue positions well tailored for the conservatives likely to dominate the Republican caucuses and convention. And the incumbent governor was Ventura, universally known and for his first three years highly popular. A former professional wrestler, talk radio host and suburban mayor, Ventura ran for governor in 1998 as the candidate of Ross Perot's Reform party. With his shaved head and plain-spoken talk, Ventura was something of a celebrity in the Twin Cities media market; Minnesota's high-minded public finance system limited major party candidates to $2.1 million, giving Ventura the opportunity to be reasonably competitive in spending. Ventura was a national celebrity but also a serious governor. He pressed for tax cuts and rebates; he backed concealed weapons permits for law-abiding citizens and opposed abortion restrictions.

Pawlenty set his own agenda and put forward his own persona. He talked constantly of his South St. Paul roots and said he wanted Republicans to be "the party of Sam's Club, not the country club." He promised never to raise taxes and took conservative stands on abortion and other cultural issues; he had voted for gay rights as a freshman legislator, but now said that was a mistake. He opposed a gas tax increase and called for $2 billion in bonds for transportation. He opposed the state's Profiles of Learning program and said it should be replaced with more rigorous standards. He called for merit pay for teachers. In effect, he was taking on Minnesota's two most powerful behind-the-scenes groups, the Freedom Club of wealthy entrepreneurs who were backing Brian Sullivan and Education Minnesota, the merged teachers' union which boasted it was the most powerful lobby in St. Paul. Sullivan, with his earlier start, was in the lead; a straw poll of those attending the March 2002 precinct caucuses showed him leading Pawlenty 51%–37%. But Pawlenty's organizational work left him even when the state convention assembled in June. Almost every state House Republican showed up wearing a Pawlenty blue shirt, and he ended up winning 58%–42%.

The DFL nomination had already been settled. It was a three-way race between Roger Moe, the state Senate President since 1981, state Auditor Judi Dutcher, who was elected as a Republican in 1994 and 1998 and switched parties in January 2000, and state Senator Becky Lourey, who criticized Moe for stands on environmental issues and compromises with House Republicans. Moe, first elected to the legislature in 1970, had been poised to run for governor several times, but had always drawn back. Democrats chose him at their May convention after Lourey and Dutcher conceded. For the first time since 1978, no serious candidate challenged the candidate endorsed by either party's nominating convention.

The guiding assumption in both parties was that Ventura would run for another term. But on June 18 Ventura announced he wasn't running. Angry about press coverage of his family, he said, "You have to have your heart and soul into these types of jobs. I feel that it is time to go back to the private sector." Into that void stepped Tim Penny, a former Democratic congressman from a Republican-leaning district who was first elected in 1982 and retired in 1994 disgusted with the partisanship of Washington. Penny had returned to Minnesota, taught at colleges and the Humphrey Institute in Minneapolis; several of his former aides had been appointed to top jobs by Ventura. On June 26 Penny announced that he was switching to the Independence party and running for governor. He chose a Republican state senator as his running mate, and Ventura supported him.

Ventura had not cared about making friends in politics, but the three men running to succeed him had. Just about everyone in Minnesota politics agreed that Pawlenty, Moe and Penny were decent, likeable people: a Minnesota nice campaign. Of course there were differences on issues. Pawlenty pledged no tax increase. "The last thing I want to do is raise your taxes," Moe said. But also: "You pay a high income tax because you have high incomes in this state and we enjoy a higher quality of life." Penny said he "would keep taxes on the table as a last resort," and suggested there would have to be tax increases and spending cuts, and that he was the only candidate leveling with the voters. Pawlenty favored restrictions on abortion; Moe and Penny opposed them. Pawlenty and Penny favored a concealed weapons law; Moe was against. Moe said that Pawlenty's regret at his gay rights vote showed that he had move "incredibly far to the right." Penny said he represented "the sensible center." In October Moe proposed a 6-cent increase in the gasoline tax and a referendum in the Twin Cities area on a sales tax increase for transportation. Pawlenty stirred some fury when he proposed that state driver's licenses for legal aliens with temporary visas should expire on the same date as their visas; this was attacked, curiously, as racist. Pawlenty was unrepentant. "I have never had anyone explain to me why someone who will only be here for another week or two legally should be entitled to a four-year driver's license."

For most of the campaign, polls showed the three in a three-way tie. Then in October it suddenly seemed that Pawlenty might be knocked out of the race. All three had accepted public financing of up to $400,000, which required them to limit spending to $2.2 million. The parties were allowed to spend money for their candidates, but not in "cooperation or concert." The Pawlenty campaign in the summer shot footage of the candidate talking about growing up in South St. Paul and making humorous comments and then sold the footage to the state Republican party. On October 9, the Campaign and Finance Disclosure Board ruled that this violated the law. Board Chairman Doug Kelley, a friend of Pawlenty, said that the cost of those ads had to be counted against Pawlenty's $2.2 million; initial estimates of that cost were $1 million, and Pawlenty had already spent $1 million. On October 12 Pawlenty appeared before cameras and said that while he disagreed with the ruling he would defer to the Board's "higher authority" and not appeal, but would negotiate with the Board on the amount of the fine. (Just before he spoke, a cell phone went off in the room. Pawlenty quipped, "It's not Cheney, is it?") On October 14 the Board fined the campaign $100,000 and charged it with $500,000 in ad spending; that left Pawlenty with about $600,000 to spend.

Pawlenty, who had raised more money than his competitors, remained even with them in polls and in late October pulled ahead. He won with 44% of the vote to 36% for Moe and 16% for Penny. Moe won big margins only in Duluth and the Iron Range and his home area in northwest Minnesota. Pawlenty only narrowly lost the Twin Cities core to Moe, 43%–40%. In counties beyond the Twin Cities media market, Pawlenty led Moe 40%–39%, with 19% for Penny. But in the Ventura Belt, Pawlenty led Moe 51%–30%. Very many of the voters who had elected Ventura in 1998 elected Pawlenty in 2002. After the election Penny speculated that the memorial service for Paul Wellstone moved undecided voters to Republicans. "The way the memorial service turned into a political rally offended your typical undecided voter. I heard it everywhere I campaigned in those final five days. If you are going to protest inappropriate behavior by the Democratic party, you don't vote for an Independent. You send them a message by voting Republican."

Pawlenty may also have been helped by the fact that he was the only candidate committed to opposing a tax increase. For this was a Republican victory up and down the ballot. Walter Mondale failed to carry Minnesota for the first time in his long political career, and Norm Coleman was elected senator. Republicans Mary Kiffmeyer and Patricia Awada were elected, narrowly, secretary of state and auditor. The only statewide DFL winner was Attorney General Mike Hatch, who handled the issue of replacing Paul Wellstone on the ballot calmly and fairly. Republicans increased their majority in the state House to 82–52 and narrowed the DFL margin in the state Senate to 35–31–1.

In the meantime Pawlenty had to deal with a budget shortfall estimated at $4.5 billion; he started in January 2003 with $450 million in cuts in the current budget. He pledged that, unlike Ventura, "I will not bash the public education establishment." But he said that businesses, charities and other institutions must play a role in providing services. His first measures were putting visa expiration dates on drivers' licenses, repealing the Profiles of Learning standards, setting up tax-free zones in distressed rural areas and $1 billion in transportation bonds.

Senior Senator

Mark Dayton (DFL)

Elected 2000, seat up 2006, 1st term; b. Jan. 26, 1947, Minneapolis; home, Minneapolis; Yale U., B.A. 1969; Presbyterian; divorced.

Elected Office: Dem. nominee, U.S. Senate, 1982; MN Auditor, 1990–94.

Professional Career: Teacher, NYC public schools, 1969–71; Counselor & administrator, social service agency, Boston, MA, 1971–75; Legis. asst., U.S. Sen. Walter Mondale, 1975–76; Aide, MN Gov. Rudy Perpich, 1977–78; MN Comm. of Economic Development, 1978–82; MN Comm. of Energy & Economic Development, 1983–86; Founder & Pres., Vermillion Investment Co., 1987–90, 1995–97.

DC Office: 346 RSOB, 20510, 202-224-3244; Fax: 202-228-2186; Web site: dayton.senate.gov.

State Offices: Biwabik, 218-865-4480; E. Grand Forks, 218-773-1110; Fort Snelling, 612-727-5220; Renville, 320-905-3007.

Committees: *Agriculture, Nutrition & Forestry*: Forestry, Conservation & Rural Revitalization; Research, Nutrition & General Legislation. *Armed Services*: Airland; Readiness & Management Support; Strategic Forces. *Governmental Affairs*: Financial Management, Budget & International Security; Investigations (Permanent). *Rules & Administration*.

Group Ratings

	ADA	ACLU	AFS	LCV	CON	ITIC	NTU	COC	ACU	NTLC	CHC
2002	95	60	100	88	74	38	14	45	11	0	—
2001	100	—	100	100	—	—	6	36	4	—	0

National Journal Ratings

	2001 LIB —	2001 CONS	2002 LIB —	2002 CONS
Economic	93%	0%	80%	15%
Social	95%	0%	82%	0%
Foreign	87%	3%	88%	11%

Key Votes of the 107th Congress

1. Approve Bush Tax Cuts	N	5. Confirm Ashcroft as AG	N
2. Expand Patients' Rights	Y	6. Bar Gays in the Boy Scouts	N
3. Campaign Finance Reform	Y	7. $ for Hate Crime Prosecution	Y
4. Permit ANWR Development	N	8. Overseas Military Abortions	Y

9. Bar Coop. with Intl. Court	N
10. Trade Promotion Authority	Y
11. Authorize Force in Iraq	N
12. Homeland Sec. Dept. Union	Y

Election Results

2000 general	Mark Dayton (DFL)	1,181,553	(49%)	($11,957,114)
	Rod Grams (R)	1,047,474	(43%)	($6,024,866)
	Jim Gibson (I)	140,583	(6%)	
	Other	49,910	(2%)	
2000 primary	Mark Dayton (DFL)	178,972	(41%)	
	Mike Ciresi (DFL)	96,874	(22%)	
	Jerry R. Janezich (DFL)	90,074	(21%)	
	Rebecca Yanisch (DFL)	63,289	(15%)	
	Other	4,190	(1%)	
1994 general	Rod Grams (IR)	869,653	(49%)	($2,439,798)
	Ann Wynia (DFL)	781,860	(44%)	($2,659,423)
	Dean M. Barkley (I)	95,400	(5%)	($24,266)

Mark Dayton, elected to the Senate in 2000, grew up in Minnesota, the son of Bruce Dayton, head of Dayton Hudson, one of the nation's major and most innovative retailers (it is now called Target Corporation, and in 2001 changed the name of Dayton's in Minnesota to Marshall Field's). Mark Dayton graduated from Yale in the student-rebellion year of 1969 and taught 9th grade science in a New York public school in the Bowery for two years, then worked as a counselor and administrator for a Boston crisis center for teenage runaways. He was a conscientious objector and was active in the anti-Vietnam War movement and his name found its way—presumably because of his family and that of his then-wife, a Rockefeller—to Richard Nixon's enemies list. In 1975 and 1976 he worked for then-Senator Walter Mondale; in 1977 he returned to Minnesota and worked for Governor Rudy Perpich. In 1979, after Perpich lost, Dayton funded with $400,000 a nonprofit agency to spur development in rural Minnesota.

In 1982 Dayton ran for the Senate, and spent the then enormous sum of $7 million of his own money. He beat former Senator Eugene McCarthy's quixotic campaign by 69%–24% in the DFL primary, but lost 53%–47% to Republican Senator David Durenberger. Between 1983 and 1986 he was Perpich's commissioner of Energy and Economic Development. In 1990 he was elected state auditor; in 1994 he decided not to run for reelection. In 1998 he ran in the Democratic primary for governor, but spent only $2 million of his own money, and finished fourth, far behind the winner, Skip Humphrey, with 18% of the vote. In 1999 and 2000 he was finance chairman for Senator Paul Wellstone.

In 2000 he stepped up to run against Senator Rod Grams. Grams was the most obviously vulnerable Republican senator up that year. A former Minneapolis-St. Paul TV news anchor, he had won in the Republican year of 1994 by only 49%–44% against Ann Wynia, an under-funded, liberal candidate; he had served just one term in the House from a suburban Twin Cities district. Grams' very conservative voting record—as different from his colleague Wellstone's as those of any two senators from the same state have been for more than half a century—was out of line with Minnesota opinion on many issues, and he had no signal legislative accomplishments.

Grams attracted seven DFL opponents before Dayton entered the race. Dayton first gave it thought in January, when he realized his second marriage had broken up. He gave it more thought in March 2000, when former Congressman Tim Penny, a fiscally conservative Democrat, surprised everyone by dropping out of the race. Dayton kept thinking about Penny's withdrawal as he went training that month near Churchill, Manitoba, for a North Pole expedition. "I saw a political vacuum. Politics, like nature, abhors a vacuum," he said later, and decided to forego the North Pole for a Senate race. He announced on April 3. He steered clear of the nominating convention, which chose state Senator Jerry Janezich, owner of a bar in the Iron Range. Instead, Dayton came up with innovative campaign ideas. He borrowed from a Senate candidate from Montana the idea of accompanying busloads of senior citizens to Canada to buy prescription drugs at lower prices than in the United States; this Rx Express got plenty of publicity. He set up a Healthcare Hotline for people having disputes with their HMOs, which are very common in Minnesota. He performed menial jobs across the state—the work days strategy pioneered by Iowa Senator Tom Harkin in 1974. He spent his own money liberally, but so did trial lawyer Mike Ciresi; Ciresi's firm received $427 million for working on Minnesota's $6.1 billion tobacco lawsuit and he spent some $5 million on the primary. But Ciresi went off the air in mid-June while Dayton, who spent $5.2 million on the primary, had the airwaves to himself from June 17 to August 1. In the September 12 primary, Dayton won 41%, to 22% for Ciresi, 21% for Janezich and 15% for construction executive Rebecca Yanisch.

The two major-party nominees presented the voters with a clear contrast on the issues. Dayton was for universal government-run health insurance (a position many of whose ardent backers are millionaires who self-financed their first campaigns: Dayton, Jon Corzine, Jay Rockefeller, Edward Kennedy), while Grams was for medical savings accounts. Grams favored individual investment accounts in Social Security, while Dayton argued that the current system would be sound until 2037. Dayton would have the government lower the price of prescription drugs; Grams' prescription drugs program would cover low-income seniors. Grams called for eliminating the estate tax and the marriage penalty and replacing the income tax with a flat tax; Dayton called for doubling the $500 per child tax credit (co-sponsored by Grams) and expanding the childcare dependent tax credit. But much of the campaign was dominated by negative charges and driven by Dayton's financial advantage. Dayton spent $11.9 million, almost all of it his own money, doubling the previous Minnesota record (set by himself in 1982); Grams spent only $6 million. Grams was hurt by publicity about two arrests of his 22-year-old son. Grams, who was divorced in 1996, was also dogged by rumors of an affair between him and his aide Christine Gunhus (they married the weekend after the election); in September 2000, four e-mails criticizing Ciresi that were sent to 100 DFL officials were traced to Gunhus' home telephone number—she plead no contest in June to a misdemeanor complaint alleging she sent them. In response Grams ran an ad showing his mother saying, "Have you ever had someone spend a million dollars a week telling lies about someone you love?" and dismissing Dayton with the Norwegian expression "Uff-da!"

Given all this, Dayton won by only 49%–43%, with 6% for Jim Gibson, enough to give the Independence party major party status for 2002—a help to Governor Jesse Ventura. Dayton ran best in the Twin Cities core, leading there 54%–36%. In the remainder of the Twin Cities media market, the part of the state that voted heavily for Ventura two years before, Grams led 48%–44%. In Minnesota beyond the Twin Cities media market, Dayton led 50%–45%.

Dayton entered the Senate 100th in seniority. His major focus was on getting a prescription drug benefit for seniors. But that issue was put aside by September 11. As Dayton said, "September 11 derailed everything I wanted to do. I figured there'd be a huge learning curve, but now it's exponential." In March 2002 he pushed successfully for two amendments to the energy bill, one providing a tax credit for diesel producers using soydiesel, the other requiring more ethanol to be used by federal cars and trucks—an idea, he said, that came from talking with a Minnesota farmer. He supported the farm bill in May 2002 which entitled Minnesota farmers to $1.16 billion in crop payments, third highest in the country, and a new national dairy program that got Minnesota dairy producers an extra $225 million. He and Wellstone went to the White House for the signing, their first such trip in the Bush administration. He and Wellstone sponsored a bill to give benefits to same-sex partners of federal employees: no White House signing on that. When Defense Secretary Donald Rumsfeld announced cancellation of the Crusader artillery program, Dayton tried to get Crusader technology and contractors used on its replacement; part of the system was to be made in an 800-employee plant in Fridley, just north of Minneapolis.

The prime legislative achievement of Dayton's first two years was passage in May 2002 by a 61–38 vote of the Dayton-Craig amendment to the trade bill. It gave Congress the right to a separate vote on any provision in a trade agreement weakening U.S. dumping laws. Dayton and co-sponsor Larry Craig have very different ideologies, but both come from states on the Canadian border where many businesses complain about Canadian dumping. But George W. Bush indicated he would veto the trade bill if it contained Dayton-Craig, and it was dropped in conference committee in July. Dayton did get a provision granting unemployment benefits for steelworkers. In July 2002 Dayton participated in the lengthy debate on prescription drugs; no bill was passed. At one point Dayton proposed a 25% tax on the difference in the price of prescription drugs between the United States and Canada.

Dayton voted for the September 2001 resolution authorizing military action against Al Qaeda. After Bush sought a congressional vote on military action in Iraq, Dayton criticized "this rush to vote." He wrote that, "Gaining political advantage in a midterm election is a shameful reason to hurry decisions of this magnitude." He was undecided until three hours before the vote and decided to vote no. On October 23, he embarked on a two-week trip to inspect Europe's NATO facilities, but he returned after Wellstone died in an October 25 plan crash. After the election, he revived his and Wellstone's bill to give wartime benefits to National Guard troops called up to serve; it passed both houses. He was less successful in pressing his and Wellstone's amendment to the homeland security bill barring contracts with companies that incorporate in other countries; it was defeated. In late 2001 he proposed in an open letter a four-step process to build a stadium for the Minnesota Twins with bonds backed by stadium revenues. Despite his baseball background—his stepfather Lee McPhail was once president of the American League—it did not seem to go anywhere.

Dayton's seat comes up in 2006. In the 2002 cycle he gave more than $200,000 to other Democrats. He has said he will not self-finance his next campaign.

Junior Senator

Norm Coleman (R)

Elected 2002, seat up 2008, 1st term; b. Aug. 17, 1949, Brooklyn, NY; home, St. Paul; Hofstra U., B.A. 1971, U. of IA, J.D. 1976; Jewish; married (Laurie).

Elected Office: St. Paul Mayor, 1993–01.

Professional Career: MN Atty. Gen.'s office, 1976–93.

DC Office: 320 HSOB, 20510, 202-224-5641; Fax: 202-224-1152; Web site: coleman.senate.gov.

State Office: St. Paul, 651-645-0323.

Committees: *Agriculture, Nutrition & Forestry*: Forestry, Conservation & Rural Revitalization; Production & Price Competitiveness. *Foreign Relations*: African Affairs; International Economic Policy, Export & Trade Promotion; Near Eastern & South Asian Affairs; Western Hemisphere, Peace Corps, Narcotics Affairs (Chmn.). *Governmental Affairs*: Government Management, Federal Workforce & the District of Columbia; Investigations (Permanent) (Chmn.). *Small Business & Entrepreneurship*.

Group Ratings and Key Votes: Newly Elected

Election Results

2002 general	Norm Coleman (R)	1,116,697	(50%)	($10,035,279)
	Walter Mondale (DFL)	1,067,246	(47%)	($1,833,029)
	Other	70,696	(3%)	
2002 primary	Norm Coleman (R)	195,630	(94%)	
	Jack Shepard (R)	11,678	(6%)	
1996 general	Paul Wellstone (DFL)	1,098,493	(50%)	($7,459,878)
	Rudy Boschwitz (R)	901,282	(41%)	($4,385,982)
	Dean Barkley (Ref)	152,333	(7%)	($37,240)

Norm Coleman, a Republican, was elected to the Senate after a tumultuous and tragic campaign in 2002. Coleman grew up in a modest neighborhood in Brooklyn and graduated from James Madison High School; he shares that alma mater with New York Senator Charles Schumer and Supreme Court Justice Ruth Bader Ginsburg. He graduated from Hofstra University on Long Island and the University of Iowa law school. In 1975 he went to work in the attorney general's office in St. Paul and became chief prosecutor and solicitor general, working closely with DFL Attorney General Skip Humphrey. In 1989 he ran for mayor of St. Paul but withdrew after losing the DFL endorsement. In 1993 he ran again and won by challenging the DFL endorsee in the primary. During his mayoral tenure, Coleman was credited with leading a downtown revitalization that featured the return of a National Hockey League franchise to Minnesota, after persuading city and state officials to finance a new hockey arena. He boasted of attracting 18,000 new jobs and not raising property taxes for his last seven years. Coleman's opposition to abortion and his bargaining stance toward public employee unions made him many enemies among the liberals who dominate DFL precinct caucuses, and in December 1996 he switched to the Republican party; he has the unusual distinction of having served as the 1996 state co-chairman for Bill Clinton and the 2000 state chairman for George W. Bush. In 1997 he ran for reelection and defeated the DFL candidate, and became the first Republican mayor of St. Paul since 1960. In 1998 he ran for governor. He won the Republican nomination but finished second, behind Reform Party nominee Jesse Ventura, by a 37%–34% margin; but he ran ahead of his old boss, DFL nominee Skip Humphrey, who won only 28% of the vote. Coleman did not run for reelection in 2001, and was considering running for governor again. But George W. Bush called and asked him to run for the Senate, and in February 2002 he announced he was running against Senator Paul Wellstone. Coleman was spared serious primary opposition when Dick Cheney in April 2001 called state House Majority Leader Tim Pawlenty, just 90 minutes before he planned to announce his candidacy, and persuaded him to run for governor rather than senator.

Wellstone was first elected in a major upset in 1990, when he was a Carleton College political science professor; he had run unsuccessfully for state auditor and co-chaired Jesse Jackson's 1988 presidential campaign in the state. He had probably the most liberal voting record of any senator and delivered stirring orations on many issues. He characterized much of his work as defensive, blocking items on the conservative agenda. In his first campaign Wellstone promised to accept no PAC money or contributions over $100 and to serve only two terms. In 1996 he dropped the $100 limit and in January 2001 he announced he would run for a third term. Wellstone's greatest political asset was his authenticity: You might not like the positions he took, but you knew he did so sincerely and without regard to political consequences. Going back on his two-term promise evidently made him seem insincere to some voters, and polls showed him under 50% of the vote and with no great advantage against Coleman.

Coleman's strategy was to portray Wellstone as an obstructionist and himself as someone who gets things done; an attempt to make Wellstone's strength, his authenticity, into a weakness. Coleman took care to oppose George W. Bush on some issues: he opposed oil drilling in the Arctic National Wildlife Refuge and favored an increase in the minimum wage. But he also called for making the 2001 tax cuts permanent, opposed Senate Democrats' union provisions in the homeland security bill and called for individual investment accounts for Social Security, though he ran an ad in October opposing "privatization." Wellstone, as always, campaigned as the tribune of the little guy, opposed to "Robin Hood in reverse" tax cuts. Using the fundraising system he had criticized in 1990, he raised more money than Coleman, though both campaigns were well-funded. After George W. Bush's speech to the United Nations September 12, Coleman came out in favor of authorizing military action in Iraq. Wellstone was opposed and favored action only with the approval of the United Nations. Polls showed the race exceedingly close.

On Friday, October 25, 11 days before the election, Wellstone, his wife and daughter and five others died in a plane crash in northern Minnesota. As the news became known about noon, Coleman suspended his campaign. Democrats gathered at Wellstone headquarters, including Edward Kennedy and Walter Mondale, who had been at a DFL fundraiser in Minneapolis and DFL gubernatorial nominee Roger Moe. Coleman after a meeting with supporters decided not to drop out of sight, as Missouri's John Ashcroft had done in October 2000 when his opponent died in a plane crash, but to participate publicly in the mourning process.

But behind the scenes, leaders of both parties were pondering what to do next, and understandably so: A Senate seat and perhaps a majority in the Senate were at stake. Minnesota has a law that allows parties to substitute a new nominee in these circumstances. On Saturday Wellstone's son David, his campaign treasurer Rick Kahn and his campaign manager met with Mondale and asked him to run. Mondale, though 74, was obviously the strongest candidate. He had been elected to the Senate by solid margins in 1966 and 1972 and after serving as Jimmy Carter's vice president had returned to Minnesota, run his 1984 presidential campaign from St. Paul and had been practicing law and serving on civic and charitable boards. He was widely respected by Minnesotans of all parties. Mondale declined to say he would run, and said he would not until after the funeral and memorial service, but let the Wellstone supporters tell reporters he was "highly likely to run."

Coleman and his advisers decided not to resume campaigning until after the memorial service, but to be ready to campaign vigorously beginning the morning after. Coleman would not attack Mondale, but speak respectfully of him, and campaign around the clock across the state as the candidate of 21st century ideas. In the meantime he would appear on TV and talk only about mourning. On Monday the Wellstones were buried after a private funeral. On Tuesday night, one week before the election, the memorial service was held at the Williams Arena at the University of Minnesota. It was broadcast statewide and across the country; most Minnesota voters were watching. Suddenly the memorial service turned into a campaign rally. Kahn spoke about Wellstone, then launched into campaigning. "We are begging you to help us win this election for Paul Wellstone," he thundered. He even called on Republican Congressman Jim Ramstad to endorse the Democrats. Many in the crowd of more than 20,000 booed Republican senators who had come to show their respect. Former Republican Congressman Vin Weber, watching on television, was repelled and e-mailed the *Minneapolis Star Tribune*, "What a complete, total, absolute sham. The DFL clearly intends to exploit Paul Wellstone's memory totally, completely and shamelessly for political gain. To them, Wellstone's death, apparently, was just another campaign event." His words appeared on the front page the next morning; that morning Wellstone's campaign manager apologized for the tone of the memorial.

Coleman boarded a plane at 6:15 the next morning to campaign around the state, while the DFL met and nominated Mondale. Mondale and his staff were amazed when DFL pollster Paul Harstad reported that an overnight survey had shown 73% of voters agreeing that the memorial service went overboard, with 52% agreeing strongly. Mondale's Sunday night lead of 52%–39% had vanished and the race was suddenly at 43%–43%. Seldom has political polling shown such an overnight shift. On Thursday, Coleman continued campaigning across the state while Mondale campaigned in Minneapolis. On Monday morning Mondale and Coleman appeared in their one televised debate. Coleman treated Mondale with great respect, always referring to him as Vice President, but aggressively argued that he was the candidate of the future. Mondale debated aggressively, referring to Coleman as Norman; he may have reflected the contempt DFL insiders have for Coleman as a party-switcher when he asked, "Who do you trust?" On the issues Mondale was clearly well-informed, but he sounded antique and abstract, while Coleman sounded contemporary and concrete. Afterwards, Coleman embarked on an 18-hour bus tour.

Coleman won 50%–47%, with a popular vote margin of 49,000; 11,000 absentee votes were counted for Wellstone. It was the first time Mondale had lost an election in Minnesota. This was a different Minnesota than the one that had reelected him to the Senate in 1972, 30 years before.

In the Twin Cities core, Hennepin and Ramsey Counties, Mondale won 53%–44%. In the counties outside the Twin Cities media market, Mondale won 50%–46%; the city-based Coleman did not have as strong an appeal as George W. Bush had in 2000 in rural areas. But the different was the Ventura Belt, the counties in the Twin Cities media market beyond the core. In 1972 they had cast 481,000; in 2002 they cast 906,000, a rise of 88%. In 1972 Mondale had carried those counties 53%–47%. In 2002 Coleman carried them 56%–41%.

After the organizers of the Coleman-Mondale debate refused to invite the Independence and Green party candidates, Ventura angrily decided to appoint a replacement for Wellstone. He named Dean Barkley, who as the Reform candidate for senator in 1996 had won 7% of the vote, more than the 5% needed to keep the party on the ballot in 1998, when Ventura ran on its line. He was sworn in after the election and decided not to caucus with either party. On the homeland security bill, he cast a decisive vote against Wellstone's and Mark Dayton's amendment to bar agency contracts with companies that reincorporate overseas. He got a bill passed providing $10 million to build a Wellstone Center for Community Building in St. Paul, which provides help for immigrants.

After the election Coleman said he wanted to carry on Wellstone's work for health insurance for mental illness. He did not immediately support George W. Bush's 2003 tax cut proposals in January but eventually displayed his loyalty.

FIRST DISTRICT

Rep. Gil Gutknecht (R)

Elected 1994, 5th term; b. Mar. 20, 1951, Cedar Falls, IA; home, Rochester; U. of N. IA, B.A. 1973; Catholic; married (Mary).

Elected Office: MN House of Reps. 1982–94.

Professional Career: Sales Rep., Latta School Supply Co., 1973–82; Real Estate Auctioneer, 1979–94.

DC Office: 425 CHOB 20515, 202-225-2472; Fax: 202-225-3246; Web site: www.gil.house.gov.

District Offices: Fairmont, 507-238-2835; Rochester, 507-252-9841.

Committees: *Agriculture* (9th of 27 R): Department Operations, Oversight, Nutrition & Forestry (Chmn.); Specialty Crops & Foreign Agriculture Programs. *Budget* (3d of 24 R). *Science* (10th of 25 R): Environment, Technology and Standards; Research.

Group Ratings

	ADA	ACLU	AFS	LCV	CON	ITIC	NTU	COC	ACU	NTLC	CHC
2002	0	7	11	0	25	100	64	85	100	86	100
2001	0	—	0	7	—	—	61	83	96	—	—

National Journal Ratings

	2001 LIB — 2001 CONS		2002 LIB — 2002 CONS	
Economic	33%	— 66%	42%	— 57%
Social	0%	— 81%	25%	— 71%
Foreign	16%	— 82%	44%	— 55%

Key Votes of the 107th Congress

1. Approve Bush Tax Cuts	Y	5. Faith-Based Charities	Y	9. Trade Promotion Authority	Y
2. Limit Patients' Bill of Rights	Y	6. Bar Gays in the Boy Scouts	Y	10. Bar Funds for Intl. Court	Y
3. Campaign Finance Reform	N	7. Ban Partial-Birth Abortion	Y	11. Authorize Force in Iraq	Y
4. Ban ANWR Development	N	8. Arm Commercial Pilots	Y	12. Deny Home. Sec. Dept. Union	Y

Election Results

2002 general	Gil Gutknecht (R)	163,570	(61%)	($770,201)
	Steve Andreasen (DFL)	92,165	(35%)	($123,060)
	Greg Mikkelson (Green)	9,964	(4%)	($16,761)
2002 primary	Gil Gutknecht (R)	unopposed		
2000 general	Gil Gutknecht (R)	159,835	(56%)	($969,598)
	Mary Rieder (DFL)	117,946	(42%)	($372,636)
	Other	5,440	(2%)	

Prior Winning Percentages: 1998 (55%); 1996 (53%); 1994 (55%)

The People		**Race/Ethnic Origin**	**Ancestry**	
Area size:	13,521 sq. mi.	93.2% White	German: 31.7%	Norwegian: 14.3%
Urban population:	56.5%	1.0% Black	Irish: 7.1%	
Rural population:	43.5%	1.7% Asian	**2000 Presidential Vote**	
Pop. 2000:	614,935	0.2% Native Am.	Bush (R)..............146,212	(49%)
Median income:	$40,941	0.0% Hawaiian	Gore (D)..............133,078	(45%)
Poverty status:	8.5%	0.8% Two+ races	Other...................17,501	(6%)
Military veterans:	13.0%	0.1% Other	**Cook Partisan Voting Index:** R + 3	
		3.0% Hispanic Origin		

Occupation	Blue collar: 26.8%	White collar: 56.7%	Gray collar: 16.5%

The Mississippi River runs majestically southeast from Minneapolis and St. Paul, cutting through rolling hills and, where it widens, forming calm lakes lapping at the bottomlands: one of the finest river landscapes of North America, exemplified by the river towns of Wabasha and Winona, with their 19th century stone storefronts and mountain-like rock outcroppings above the river. This far north, the westward tide of Yankee migrants thinned out. After the Civil War, most settlers following the railroads on the flood plains west of the river were Germans and Scandinavians, bringing their families to this terrain so much like the Rhine, and to the rolling uplands beyond, which resemble the northern European plain.

Southern Minnesota is a borderland between Yankee and German settlements. Along the Mississippi River, tourism has spiked upward (from a nonexistent base) after the old St. Paul and Milwaukee Railroad was converted into a hiker-biker nature trail during the 1990s; "Historic Bluff Country" now draws enough visitors to support not one but two former jails that have been converted, with Minnesota practicality, into upscale bed-and-breakfasts. A little to the west is Rochester, home to the Mayo Clinic, founded in 1863 when English-born physician William Mayo set up a practice to examine inductees into the Union Army. Today, Rochester, with its large professional population, is prosperous and growing. Austin, a county away, is headquarters of the Hormel meatpacking firm that beat a bitter strike in the 1980s; its huge plant produces Spam, Hormel chili, Dinty Moore stew and, say critics, too much ammonia-loaded waste; this is one place where class-conscious politics survives. The farther west you go, the more frequently you find communities with a German heritage, like New Ulm, where the Concord Singers—30 men decked out in lederhosen, red vests and white shirts—are described as one of the best male choruses in the nation. Further south is dairy country, with a sprinkling of small industry.

The 1st Congressional District includes the state's two southern tiers of counties, running along Interstate 90 just north of the Iowa border. Historically, this was a political borderland, with Civil War Republicans in the east and Farmer-Laborites more common in the west. Rochester has long been a Republican stronghold; Austin has long been solidly Democratic-Farmer-Labor. Redistricting changed the shape of the district in 2002. Formerly the 1st reached deep into the Twin Cities suburbs. Redistricters put those areas in the new 6th District and extended the 1st west to the South Dakota border. Most of the district is outside the Twin Cities media market, and did not cast large percentages for Jesse Ventura in 1998. In 2002 the district cast a larger percentage for the candidate of Ventura's Independence party, Tim Penny, a former Democrat who was elected to the 1st District seat in 1982 and served until he retired from Congress in 1994.

The congressman from the 1st District is Gil Gutknecht, a Republican elected in 1994. The name, he likes to explain, means "good hired hand," though "good indentured servant" might be closer to the mark. He grew up in Iowa, son of a union machinist, worked nine years as a school supply salesman, then became an auctioneer, eventually handling large real estate auctions. He was elected to the legislature in 1982 from Rochester and became Republican floor leader. Partisan, ebullient, he once told Iron Range DFLers that the state motto *L'etoile du Nord* did not mean "send the money north." When Penny decided to retire, Gutknecht ran for the House. In the Republican primary, he argued that he was the more conservative candidate and beat former two-term Congressman Arlen Erdahl, 57%–36%. In the general against Mankato state Senator John Hottinger, who backed a single-payer health care system, Gutknecht called himself "the Minnesota equivalent of Newt Gingrich." Gutknecht won big in Rochester and in the river counties, for a 55%–45% victory.

Gutknecht was an enthusiastic member of the new Republican majority who proudly talked of listening to Gingrich's lecture tapes, and he has a mostly conservative voting record. But by the end of the Clinton era, he conceded that the hype of a Republican revolution was "greatly exaggerated" and that Gingrich had been "a disappointment to everybody" in thinking he could run the nation as speaker. He calls himself a "Teddy Roosevelt Republican," and has been an occasional maverick as he pays heed to district interests. He has voted to allow reimportation of prescription drugs from Canada (which HHS Secretaries Donna Shalala and Tommy Thompson both blocked for safety reasons) and opposed changes in the sugar program (southern Minnesota is sugar beet country.) He supported trade promotion authority in order to increase farm exports. On the Agriculture Committee, he sponsored a bill to require meatpackers to disclose prices they pay hog farmers and promised to "push for a better 'shock absorber' that protects farm income." He filed another proposal to require that 5% of the nation's fuel come from renewable sources by 2016. When the 1999 spending bill favored dairy farmers in the Northeast at the expense of those from the upper Midwest, Gutknecht angrily sent a letter to Speaker Dennis Hastert resigning his post as a regional Whip rather than continue on a leadership team "that has trampled on the interests of thousands of Minnesota dairy farmers." He sponsored—and went on the talk radio circuit to boost—a 12-year limit on congressional pension accrual. In October 2001, Gutknecht asked the Bureau of Prisons to move convicted 1993 World Trade Center bomber Sheik Omar Abdel-Rahman from the federal medical center in Rochester after an employee there received a white powdery substance in a letter postmarked from a foreign country. About five months later, he was transferred to an undisclosed site.

Gutknecht has attracted active opposition in a district with a strong DFL base and a Democratic trend. In 1996 he was targeted by AFL-CIO ads and had serious competition from Winona State economics professor Mary Rieder. She said she was a fiscal conservative like Penny, and she raised enough money to be competitive. Bill Clinton carried the district with a plurality and Rieder's vote tracked his closely. But that left the Democrat with 47% to Gutknecht's 53%. In 1998, state Senator Tracy Beckman, with Tim Penny as his campaign chairman, focused on Gutknecht's support for the Freedom to Farm Act together with the year's sharp drop in crop prices. Gutknecht wobbled a bit, voting against a Republican tax cut, and running ads saying he "listens to farmers," but he had a big money advantage, and won 55%–45%. In 2000 against Rieder he won with a more comfortable 56%–42%. After redistricting, he did not have a serious challenge in 2002 and won 61%–35%.

SECOND DISTRICT

Rep. John Kline (R)

Elected 2002, 1st term; b. Sept. 6, 1947, Allentown, PA; home, Lakeville; Rice U., B.A. 1969, Shippensburg U., M.P.A. 1988; Christian; married (Vicky).

Military Career: Marine Corps, 1969–94 (Vietnam).

Professional Career: Vice-pres., Cntr. of the American Experiment, 2001–02.

DC Office: 1429 LHOB 20515, 202-225-2271; Fax: 202-225-2595; Web site: www.house.gov/kline.

District Office: Burnsville, 952-808-1213.

Committees: *Armed Services* (29th of 33 R): Projection Forces; Terrorism, Unconventional Threats & Capabilities. *Education & the Workforce* (22d of 27 R): Employer-Employee Relations; Workforce Protections.

Group Ratings and Key Votes: Newly Elected

Election Results

2002 general	John Kline (R)	152,970	(53%)	($1,534,873)
	Bill Luther (DFL)	121,121	(42%)	($2,263,619)
	Samuel Garst (NTX)	12,430	(4%)	
2002 primary	John Kline (R)	unopposed		
2000 general (MN 6)	Bill Luther (DFL)	176,340	(50%)	($2,597,244)
	John Kline (R)	170,900	(48%)	($1,200,309)
	Other	8,584	(2%)	

The People		Race/Ethnic Origin	Ancestry	
Area size:	3,154 sq. mi.	91.8% White	German: 28.4%	Norwegian: 11.3%
Urban population:	80.1%	1.6% Black	Irish: 9.2%	
Rural population:	19.9%	2.3% Asian	**2000 Presidential Vote**	
Pop. 2000:	614,934	0.4% Native Am.	Bush (R)	150,366 (51%)
Median income:	$61,344	0.0% Hawaiian	Gore (D)	131,414 (44%)
Poverty status:	3.9%	1.1% Two+ races	Other	14,526 (5%)
Military veterans:	12.1%	0.1% Other	**Cook Partisan Voting Index:** R + 4	
		2.6% Hispanic Origin		

Occupation	Blue collar: 22.3%	White collar: 65.0%	Gray collar: 12.6%

Drive south from the Twin Cities and you will encounter new housing developments and big-box store parking lots inhabited by youngish families working in managerial, business and technical careers. Many come from elsewhere, attracted by Minnesota's strong economy and pleasant living (if you don't mind winter). They have turned such places as Eagan, Lakeville, Apple Valley, Mendota Heights and Burnsville in Dakota County into fast-growing, "mallified" suburbs. More upscale are the fast-growing suburbs of Scott and Carver Counties. Drive further south—a little further every year—and suddenly you are surrounded by farm country, as well as modest towns such as Northfield, the idyllic home of Carleton College and its late professor-turned-Senator, Paul Wellstone. Northfield is only 40 miles from Minneapolis and St. Paul, and already there are people who commute to the Twin Cities core on Interstate 35.

These places make up the 2d Congressional District. There is almost no overlap with the old 2d District before the 1992 redistricting, which was mostly rural and spread west to the South Dakota border. Historically, Dakota County, just south of St. Paul, which casts nearly half the votes in the district, was marginally Democratic, while the other counties were fairly heavily Republican. But in 1998 this was Jesse Ventura Country: in that three-way race he carried each of the counties in the district, with between 40% and 48% of a sharply increased turnout. In 2000 George W. Bush narrowly carried Dakota County in the district. In 2002 the district voted by big margins for Republican Senator Norm Coleman and Governor Tim Pawlenty; the strongest DFL area was

Rice County, home of Northfield and Carleton College. Tim Penny, the Independence party candidate for governor, who used to represent the southern counties here when they were in the 1st District, carried the southern counties but failed to match Ventura's performance in the more populous suburban counties.

The congressman from the 2d District is John Kline, a Republican elected in 2002 and one of only four challengers to defeat an incumbent that year: Kline's third try at beating DFL incumbent Bill Luther proved a charm. Kline grew up in Corpus Christi, Texas, where his father owned a small hometown newspaper and his mother managed the Corpus Christi Symphony Orchestra for more than 40 years. After graduating from Rice he served 25 years in the Marine Corps. He served in Vietnam, commanded marine aviation forces in Somalia, and his headquarters duties included responsibility for the Corps's $50 billion program objective memorandum. As a colonel he was assigned to the White House when Jimmy Carter was president and carried the nuclear "football"—the package containing the launch codes—for Ronald Reagan: he surely has had more face time with presidents than any other member of Congress. When he retired in 1994, he settled in Lakeville, in Dakota County, where he managed his wife's family farm.

In 1998, Kline challenged Luther, a Democrat who was first elected in 1994 who had a history of expensive and fierce campaigns. Kline favored tax cuts, more military spending and the resignation of Bill Clinton, and opposed abortion. He spent only $283,000; Luther, who raised $1.1 million in the cycle, spent only $412,000. That might have become a mistake. In a turnout swelled with new voters supporting Jesse Ventura, Republicans did well in other races. Luther won by only 50%–46%. Kline hardly stopped running; more experienced and better financed in 2000, he made the rematch one of the nation's high-profile House contests. Unlike some Democrats in marginal districts, Luther did not try to fudge the differences between them: He opposed repeal of the marriage penalty and estate and gift taxes, and individual investment accounts in Social Security. The result was closer across the board than in 1998, but Luther survived 50%–48%. Discouraged, Kline said he was unlikely to run again.

Then the unexpected happened. The redistricting plan ordered into effect by the state supreme court in March 2002 placed Kline's home in a new 2d District that contained the home of no incumbent. Republican leaders in Minnesota and Washington urged Kline to run again, and a few days later he announced his candidacy. Carver and Scott Counties had been in the 2d District represented by freshman Republican Mark Kennedy, but his home was just across the line in the new 6th District, and he said he would run there. Luther, whose home was in the 6th District, a dozen miles north of the 2d, waited two months before announcing which district he would run in, or whether he would retire. About 40% of Luther's old 6th District had been put into the 2d and the 6th, both of which had given winning margins to George W. Bush in 2000. Luther was also coping with the death of his wife in January.

Luther finally decided to run in the 2d and started with some advantages: 28 years of experience in elected office, $1.2 million in cash on hand. The acrimonious campaign resumed where it left off in 2000. Luther called Kline an extremist who held "Texas values." Kline firmly supported Bush on the use of force in Iraq; Luther voted for the Iraq war resolution in October 2002. Luther's campaign manager encouraged Sam Garst, a Sierra Club activist and Luther supporter, to enter the race as a candidate of a new "No New Taxes" party—a purposefully deceptive banner designed to siphon votes from the Republican column. At first the Luther campaign denied all connection with Garst, but the facts came out: Luther had not discouraged the action. Even liberal local media harshly criticized the scheme as "un-Minnesotan" and characterized it as a cynical dirty trick in a hotly contested race where a few votes might make the difference. Kline got further mileage out of the issue by refusing to debate Luther unless Garst was included; Garst ended up leaving town in the weeks before the election.

What was a close race in 1998 and 2000 turned out to be no contest in 2002. Kline won by a comfortable 53%–42%. Luther led in Rice County and the district's small portion of his home county, Washington. Kline led 54%–42% in Dakota County and won more than 60% in Carver and Scott Counties. Luther later said that the controversial memorial service for Paul Wellstone cost him independent and Republican support and conceded that he was hurt by anger over the

Garst candidacy. Kline won a seat on Armed Services, his top priority, plus the Education and Workforce Committee.

THIRD DISTRICT

Rep. Jim Ramstad (R)

Elected 1990, 7th term; b. May 6, 1946, Jamestown, ND; home, Minnetonka; U. of MN, B.A. 1968, George Washington U., J.D. 1973; Protestant; single.

Military Career: Army Reserves, 1968–74.

Elected Office: MN Senate, 1980–90.

Professional Career: Special Asst., U.S. Rep. Tom Kleppe, 1970; Practicing atty., 1973–80; Adjunct Prof., American U., 1975–78.

DC Office: 103 CHOB 20515, 202-225-2871; Fax: 202-225-6351; Web site: www.house.gov/ramstad.

District Office: Minnetonka, 952-738-8200.

Committees: *Ways & Means* (9th of 24 R): Health; Trade.

Group Ratings

	ADA	ACLU	AFS	LCV	CON	ITIC	NTU	COC	ACU	NTLC	CHC
2002	15	27	11	50	87	100	59	95	92	81	58
2001	20	—	10	86	—	—	62	87	52	—	—

National Journal Ratings

	2001 LIB —	2001 CONS	2002 LIB —	2002 CONS
Economic	47% —	53%	42% —	57%
Social	50% —	50%	47% —	53%
Foreign	43% —	53%	35% —	60%

Key Votes of the 107th Congress

1. Approve Bush Tax Cuts　Y	5. Faith-Based Charities　Y	9. Trade Promotion Authority　Y
2. Limit Patients' Bill of Rights　Y	6. Bar Gays in the Boy Scouts　Y	10. Bar Funds for Intl. Court　Y
3. Campaign Finance Reform　Y	7. Ban Partial-Birth Abortion　Y	11. Authorize Force in Iraq　Y
4. Ban ANWR Development　Y	8. Arm Commercial Pilots　Y	12. Deny Home. Sec. Dept. Union　Y

Election Results

2002 general	Jim Ramstad (R)	213,334	(72%)	($794,176)
	Darryl Stanton (DFL)	82,575	(28%)	
2002 primary	Jim Ramstad (R)	unopposed		
2000 general	Jim Ramstad (R)	222,571	(68%)	($747,976)
	Sue Shuff (DFL)	98,219	(30%)	($22,824)
	Other	8,272	(3%)	

Prior Winning Percentages: 1998 (72%); 1996 (70%); 1994 (73%); 1992 (64%); 1990 (67%)

The People		Race/Ethnic Origin	Ancestry	
Area size:	513 sq. mi.	88.6% White	German: 22.8%	Norwegian: 11.3%
Urban population:	95.8%	3.8% Black	Irish: 8.6%	
Rural population:	4.2%	4.0% Asian	**2000 Presidential Vote**	
Pop. 2000:	614,935	0.3% Native Am.	Bush (R) 161,999	(50%)
Median income:	$63,816	0.0% Hawaiian	Gore (D) 149,277	(46%)
Poverty status:	3.5%	1.4% Two+ races	Other 13,483	(4%)
Military veterans:	12.4%	0.1% Other	**Cook Partisan Voting Index:** R + 2	
		1.8% Hispanic Origin		

Occupation	Blue collar: 16.7%	White collar: 73.1%	Gray collar: 10.1%

Over the past half century, Minnesota's great twin metropolis has spread out from the neat streets inside the city limits of Minneapolis and St. Paul into the countryside all around. People have sorted themselves out geographically. In the lower lands along the Mississippi and Minnesota Rivers, where rail lines fan out from the Twin Cities heading toward the great farmlands of America, are the blue-collar suburbs, with neat modest houses on grid streets and warehouses and factories near the tracks. Inland, around the lakes Minnesota is so proud of, in subdivisions with curved streets hugging the hills, are the Twin Cities' more affluent neighborhoods, quiet and unflashy in the Minnesota way, but comfortable whether blanketed with snow or when the lake is glinting in the summer sun. In between are the freeway interchanges where some of the Twin Cities' great innovations can be seen—Southdale Shopping Center in Edina, the first enclosed mall and site of the first B. Dalton store, which begat the national book chains; and now the giant Mall of America, with its 4.2 million square feet, 525 stores, 50 restaurants, 14 theaters, 7 nightclubs and 13,000 employees, plus expansion plans to add 5.6 million square feet, a 5,000 seat performing arts center and a rail connection to downtown Minneapolis. The mall, the nation's number one tourist attraction, is unmatched as a symbol of American consumerism; security was quickly heightened after the September 11 attacks.

The 3d Congressional District takes in Hennepin County suburbs north, south and west of Minneapolis. On the north side of the 3d is working-class Brooklyn Park, long a DFL stronghold but more famous now for its former mayor, Jesse Ventura; on the south is middle-income Bloomington, home of the Mall of America; to the west are Edina, Plymouth, Wayzata and other towns around Lake Minnetonka, all heavily Republican. This is the largest lake and these are the most affluent communities in the Twin Cities area. The area is home to the headquarters of such diverse companies as Cargill and Radisson Hotels. Historically Republican, this area trended Democratic in the 1990s, as Bill Clinton twice won pluralities here. In 2000, George W. Bush carried the district, but with barely 50% of the vote—not a robust showing in what not long ago was the most Republican district in Minnesota. Redistricting made only minor changes in the district's boundaries.

The congressman from the 3d District is Jim Ramstad, a Republican first elected in 1990. He has been in politics since childhood: Raised in North Dakota, he used to go with his grandfather to visit Republican Senator Milton Young. He saw President Eisenhower in 1956 and met President Kennedy in 1963 at the same Rose Garden ceremony where a young Bill Clinton was photographed shaking Kennedy's hand (Ramstad is in the background of the now famous photo). He worked as an intern to Young and a staffer to Congressman Tom Kleppe while in his 20s. He moved to Minnesota and in 1980, at 34, he unseated a Democratic state senator (spending the then record-breaking sum of $77,932).

In 1990, when 3d District Congressman Bill Frenzel retired after 20 years, Ramstad ran for the House. The crucial contest was the Republican convention. Ramstad was pro-choice on abortion while most delegates were anti-abortion, but he had good endorsements, from Senator Rudy Boschwitz and Congressman Vin Weber, both anti-abortion, and won the party convention on the eighth ballot.

Ramstad's voting record has been squarely in the middle of the House. His task force on legal reforms helped produce the securities litigation bill that became law over Clinton's veto, but he worked with the Clinton White House to restore full funding to the Legal Services Corporation. The House passed his Missing Children Tax Fairness Act, which allows families of abducted children to continue to claim a dependency exemption. Ramstad has taken his market economics to the Ways and Means Committee. He worked on the Taxpayer Bill of Rights, on Medicare and hospital funding formulas, and on saving the housing tax exemption for clergy members. He argues that the current tax system is too complex, too costly and too invasive. He has been a strong supporter of free trade.

Ramstad has been a recovering alcoholic since 1981, when he awoke in jail after a night of drinking ended in a brawl, and he has backed measures for both discipline and therapy for substance abusers. He has supported drug tests for released federal prisoners. With Senator Paul Wellstone, he sponsored a bill to require insurance coverage for alcohol and drug addiction programs. He argues that alcoholism costs society $90 billion a year, and that his program would save $7 for every dollar spent; the increase in premiums, he says, would be no more than the price of a cup of coffee. The National Association of Alcoholism and Drug Addiction Counselors named him "Legislator of the Year." But when Ramstad later called for programs to emphasize abstinence and discourage treatment of narcotics, Wellstone disagreed. He has been an enthusiastic backer of Bush's faith-based initiative. He has counseled House colleagues with a drinking problem, including Philip Crane of Ways and Means. On other issues, Ramstad talked about his mother's Alzheimer's disease when he urged George W. Bush to support stem cell research. He split with Republican leaders on campaign finance regulation, federalizing security agents at the airports and the Cuban trade embargo. He called the 2002 farm bill "a horrendous hit on taxpayers."

Ramstad has been easily reelected every two years in this high-turnout district. In April 2001, he publicly chastised Dick Cheney for acting as "king maker" in urging Tim Pawlenty to defer to Norm Coleman in the Senate race and to run instead for governor. Near the end of that Senate contest, he unexpectedly became a player again at the memorial service for Paul Wellstone. There Wellstone's campaign treasurer in a frenzied speech implored Ramstad to "help us win this race" in its closing days; Ramstad continued to back Coleman, and many voters were repelled by the Democrats who turned a memorial service into a political rally. After the election Ramstad persuaded the House to pass a $10 million Wellstone Center for Community Building center for immigrants.

FOURTH DISTRICT

Rep. Betty McCollum (DFL)

Elected 2000, 2d term; b. July 12, 1954, Minneapolis; home, St. Paul; Inver Hills Comm. Col., A.A. 1980, Col. of St. Catherine, B.A. 1987; Catholic; divorced.

Elected Office: N. St. Paul City Cncl., 1986–92; MN House of Reps., 1992–00.

Professional Career: Teacher; Retail sales & management.

DC Office: 1029 LHOB 20515, 202-225-6631; Fax: 202-225-1968; Web site: www.house.gov/mccollum.

District Office: St. Paul, 651-224-9191.

Committees: *Education & the Workforce* (15th of 22 D): 21st Century Competitiveness; Employer-Employee Relations. *International Relations* (22d of 23 D): Africa. *Resources* (24th of 24 D).

Group Ratings

	ADA	ACLU	AFS	LCV	CON	ITIC	NTU	COC	ACU	NTLC	CHC
2002	100	87	100	100	43	38	25	40	4	3	0
2001	100	—	100	93	—	—	10	39	4	—	—

National Journal Ratings

	2001 LIB —	2001 CONS		2002 LIB —	2002 CONS
Economic	88%	— 11%		72%	— 27%
Social	83%	— 11%		84%	— 8%
Foreign	94%	— 7%		84%	— 14%

Key Votes of the 107th Congress

1. Approve Bush Tax Cuts	N	5. Faith-Based Charities	N	9. Trade Promotion Authority	N
2. Limit Patients' Bill of Rights	N	6. Bar Gays in the Boy Scouts	N	10. Bar Funds for Intl. Court	N
3. Campaign Finance Reform	Y	7. Ban Partial-Birth Abortion	N	11. Authorize Force in Iraq	N
4. Ban ANWR Development	Y	8. Arm Commercial Pilots	N	12. Deny Home. Sec. Dept. Union	N

Election Results

2002 general	Betty McCollum (DFL)	164,597	(62%)	($589,276)
	Clyde Billington (R)	89,705	(34%)	($93,250)
	Scott Raskiewicz (Green)	9,919	(4%)	
2002 primary	Betty McCollum (DFL)	unopposed		
2000 general	Betty McCollum (DFL)	130,403	(48%)	($1,090,046)
	Linda Runbeck (R)	83,852	(31%)	($900,795)
	Tom Foley (I)	55,899	(21%)	($267,287)
	Other	1,285	(0%)	

The People		Race/Ethnic Origin	Ancestry	
Area size:	220 sq. mi.	77.7% White	German: 22.0%	Irish: 9.5%
Urban population:	99.9%	6.5% Black	Norwegian: 7.7%	
Rural population:	0.1%	7.5% Asian	**2000 Presidential Vote**	
Pop. 2000:	614,935	0.7% Native Am.	Gore (D) 166,919	(57%)
Median income:	$46,811	0.0% Hawaiian	Bush (R) 109,670	(37%)
Poverty status:	9.6%	2.2% Two+ races	Other 18,146	(6%)
Military veterans:	11.8%	0.1% Other	**Cook Partisan Voting Index:** D +10	
		5.2% Hispanic Origin		

Occupation	Blue collar: 19.2%	White collar: 67.0%	Gray collar: 13.7%

Above the Mississippi River bluffs, forested when the first settlers arrived in the 1850s and one of America's great urban vistas today, stand the two great landmarks of St. Paul: the Minnesota Capitol and Archbishop Ireland's Cathedral. This is the older and smaller of the Twin Cities, settled mainly by Catholic Irish and German immigrants, while Minneapolis was attracting Protestant Swedes and Yankees. St. Paul became a major transportation hub, a railroad center and river port, while Minneapolis, farther up river at the Falls of St. Anthony, became the nation's largest grain milling center; both industries stoked the ire of farmers in the Dakotas who had no choice but to deal with them to make a living. Beneath the Capitol and the cathedral, the city's skywalk-linked downtown is home to the Ordway Music Theater, the headquarters of Minnesota Public Radio and an active pop music industry. Beyond the cathedral is Summit Avenue, on which capitalists like the Great Northern Railway's James J. Hill built grandiose Romanesque houses, and which, with Monument Avenue in Richmond and Meridian Street in Indianapolis, remains one of America's grand 19th century residential boulevards. The parallel Grand Avenue is home to a pleasant commercial strip with a walkable, urban feel; more modest neighborhoods elsewhere are notable for their grid streets lined with sturdy houses.

Minnesota's 4th Congressional District is made up of St. Paul, the Ramsey County suburbs to the north, and the southern suburbs of West St. Paul and South St. Paul. When a special panel of judges drew the new districts in 2002, they rejected a Republican proposal to combine Minneapolis and St. Paul into one district and made only modest changes in the boundaries. St. Paul was one of the most Democratic parts of Minnesota even before the Democratic-Farmer-Labor Party was formed in 1944, and it remained proudly DFL for a half-century; it did reelect Mayor Norm Coleman in 1997 after he switched to the Republican party, but he failed to carry a single precinct in the city when he ran successfully for the Senate in 2002. The area has become home to more than 24,000 Hmong immigrants, the largest concentration in any American city; the Hmong had been recruited by the CIA and U.S. Special Forces during the Vietnam War and resettled here after Laos fell to the Communists in 1975. The 4th District seat has been held by the DFL since it elected Eugene McCarthy in 1948, and the modest changes made in redistricting barely changed the numbers. The 4th remains the second-most Democratic district in the state and voted for losing Democrat candidates Walter Mondale and Roger Moe in 2002.

The congresswoman from the 4th District is Betty McCollum, a Democrat first elected in 2000. She grew up in North St. Paul and graduated from the College of St. Catherine. For 11 years she taught high school social studies and then she was a retail sales manager for 14 years at Dayton's department store. "Retail teaches you to listen to people," she said. After her daughter was hurt on the slide in a city park, McCollum ran and was elected in 1986 to the North St. Paul

City Council. She served on the council until 1992, when she was elected to the state House of Representatives after defeating incumbents in both the primary and general. Although she called herself "a little more conservative than my [state House] caucus sometimes wants," she was assistant majority leader for six years.

The 4th District had been represented since 1976 by Bruce Vento, a Democrat with an almost perfectly liberal voting record. In February 2000 Vento announced he would not seek reelection and that he had malignant mesothelioma; despite surgery to remove one of his lungs, he died on October 10, 2000.

In the September primary, McCollum, who was endorsed by Minnesota's Democratic-Farmer-Labor Party and EMILY's List, faced three opponents. The primary at first appeared wide open, but in this race, unlike some statewide contests, the DFL convention endorsement counted for something, and McCollum won easily with 50% to 23% for state Senator Steve Novak and 19% for St. Paul City Council member Chris Coleman. Republicans nominated state senator Linda Runbeck, a vigorously anti-abortion candidate. McCollum backed prescription drug coverage under Medicare and opposed large tax cuts before Congress paid down the debt. Runbeck, who opposed gun control and took conservative positions on health care and education, attacked McCollum and her Democratic allies for running "hateful, vicious attack ads" that distorted her positions on guns. McCollum conceded at a debate the she was "very disappointed in my own party for sending out distasteful images" on her behalf. This was a three-way race, thanks to the candidacy of former Ramsey County prosecutor Tom Foley, a long-time DFLer now running on the ticket of Governor Jesse Ventura's Independence party. Foley called McCollum and Runbeck "puppets" of their national parties. McCollum supporters feared that she could lose if Foley won 20% of the vote. Once again, McCollum won unexpectedly easily, 48%–31%, with 21% for Foley. She was the first woman elected to the House from Minnesota since Coya Knutson was famously called home by her estranged husband in 1958 (see 7th District).

In the House, McCollum has a liberal voting record, and she worked on the elementary and secondary education bill as a member of the Education and Workforce Committee. In March 2003, she won House passage of her first bill—a resolution condemning stoning of people to death; she prepared the proposal after reading a newspaper article about a Nigerian woman who was sentenced to such a fate after conviction for adultery. She made the national news when Fox News Channel showed footage of her leading the House in the Pledge of Allegiance and omitting the words "under God." She quickly became an ally of Nancy Pelosi, whom she calls a mentor, and delivered the speech formally nominating her as party whip in 2001. In return, McCollum has won some leadership assignments, including a seat on the steering committee. Her reelection was easy and mundane compared to her initial campaign for Congress.

FIFTH DISTRICT

Rep. Martin Olav Sabo (DFL)

Elected 1978, 13th term; b. Feb. 28, 1938, Crosby, ND; home, Minneapolis; Augsburg Col., B.A. 1959; Lutheran; married (Sylvia).

Elected Office: MN House of Reps., 1960–78, Min. Ldr., 1968–72, Speaker, 1972–78.

DC Office: 2336 RHOB 20515, 202-225-4755; Fax: 202-225-4886; Web site: www.house.gov/sabo.

District Office: Minneapolis, 612-664-8000.

Committees: *Appropriations* (4th of 29 D): Commerce, Justice, State & Judiciary; Defense; Homeland Security (RMM).

Group Ratings

	ADA	ACLU	AFS	LCV	CON	ITIC	NTU	COC	ACU	NTLC	CHC
2002	100	93	100	88	43	25	18	35	0	0	0
2001	100	—	100	86	—	—	13	26	0	—	—

National Journal Ratings

	2001 LIB —	2001 CONS	2002 LIB —	2002 CONS
Economic	87%	13%	74%	25%
Social	90%	0%	94%	3%
Foreign	94%	5%	87%	13%

Key Votes of the 107th Congress

1. Approve Bush Tax Cuts	N	5. Faith-Based Charities	N	9. Trade Promotion Authority	N
2. Limit Patients' Bill of Rights	N	6. Bar Gays in the Boy Scouts	N	10. Bar Funds for Intl. Court	N
3. Campaign Finance Reform	Y	7. Ban Partial-Birth Abortion	N	11. Authorize Force in Iraq	N
4. Ban ANWR Development	Y	8. Arm Commercial Pilots	N	12. Deny Home. Sec. Dept. Union	N

Election Results

2002 general	Martin Olav Sabo (DFL)	171,572	(67%)	($507,205)
	Daniel Nielsen Mathias (R)	66,271	(26%)	($9,589)
	Tim Davis (Green)	17,825	(7%)	
2002 primary	Martin Olav Sabo (DFL)	unopposed		
2000 general	Martin Olav Sabo (DFL)	176,629	(69%)	($467,849)
	Frank Taylor (R)	58,191	(23%)	($51,941)
	Rob Tomich (I)	11,323	(4%)	
	Other	9,002	(4%)	

Prior Winning Percentages: 1998 (67%); 1996 (64%); 1994 (62%); 1992 (63%); 1990 (73%); 1988 (72%); 1986 (73%); 1984 (70%); 1982 (66%); 1980 (70%); 1978 (62%)

The People		Race/Ethnic Origin	Ancestry	
Area size:	130 sq. mi.	71.2% White	German: 17.6%	Norwegian: 9.3%
Urban population:	100.0%	12.8% Black	Irish: 7.6%	
Rural population:	0.0%	5.1% Asian	**2000 Presidential Vote**	
Pop. 2000:	614,935	1.5% Native Am.	Gore (D)	185,874 (63%)
Median income:	$41,569	0.1% Hawaiian	Bush (R)	85,447 (29%)
Poverty status:	12.7%	3.0% Two+ races	Other	24,577 (8%)
Military veterans:	10.8%	0.2% Other	**Cook Partisan Voting Index:** D +18	
		6.0% Hispanic Origin		
Occupation	Blue collar: 17.9%	White collar: 67.2%	Gray collar: 14.9%	

From almost nowhere in Minneapolis today can you see the geographic feature that put the city here—the Falls of St. Anthony, the head of navigation on the Mississippi River, where waters rush in rapids beneath low downtown bridges. In olden days, every riverboat had to stop here, and the waterpower generated by the falls was the energy source first for pioneers' grist mills and then for the giant grain mills that processed the wheat of the northern Great Plains into food for the United States and the world. By 1890 Minneapolis and St. Paul made up one of America's largest urban areas, living mainly off grain. Today, Minneapolis is a center of high-tech industry, banking and finance. It is a regional railroad center and the nerve center of an economic region that extends almost 1,000 miles west to the Rocky Mountains in Montana.

The city of Minneapolis, plus a few of its older, adjoining suburbs, comprise the 5th Congressional District. In the southwest corner are the affluent neighborhoods around Lake Calhoun and Lake Harriet—long built-up and proudly maintained, amidst trees that turn beautifully golden in early autumn. Not far are Minneapolis's skywalk-laced downtown skyscrapers, the museum quarter up on the hill above Hennepin Avenue, and the Hubert H. Humphrey Metrodome, nicknamed (inaccurately, say some) the "Homerdome" but still unloved by baseball fans. Straddling the Mississippi River is the University of Minnesota. Most of the 5th District, however, is lower on the income scale. Many of the working-class neighborhoods of small frame houses on grid streets with ample parks are now kept up by elderly homeowners, while new immigrants live in small communities of their own. Minneapolis does not have the endless stretches of abandoned blocks commonly seen in Chicago or Detroit, but all is not well. In August 2002, a violent, race-tinged rampage followed the accidental police shooting of an 11-year-old boy during a drug bust.

For a place often thought of as monochromatically white and Scandinavian, the city is a place of surprising diversity. To the northeast, behind the railroad and warehouse district along the Mississippi, is the home of many Hmongs from Laos. Hennepin County itself is now home to the largest number of African immigrants in the state, following a decade in which the number of African immigrants in Minnesota jumped sevenfold. Ticket machines on the new Hiawatha Avenue light-rail line do business in four languages — English, Spanish, Hmong and Somali.

The 5th is the most reliably Democratic district in the state. Minneapolis's political liberalism is drawn from the Yankee tradition of clean government, the Scandinavian tradition of cooperative enterprise and the industrial-labor tradition of economic redistribution. To this has been added in recent years, by feminists and the graduate student proletariat, a more antic cultural liberalism that is alien to both. George W. Bush got only 29% of the vote here in 2000, his worst performance in the state's eight districts.

The congressman from the 5th District is Martin Olav Sabo, born in North Dakota, the son of Norwegian immigrants, a DFL leader who has spent all his adult life in politics. He was elected to the Minnesota legislature in 1960 at age 22, was the Minority Leader at 30 and Speaker at 34. In 1978 he was elected to the House and in his first year got a seat on the Appropriations Committee. It began as a quiet career: Sabo can be articulate, even humorous, and certainly is knowledgeable and averse to the cheap shot. But he pursued his career with a certain Scandinavian reticence and aversion to national publicity that is unusual in Congress—except perhaps for his role as coach for the Democrats in the annual House baseball game. Sabo also served on the Budget Committee, where he wrote the 1990 budget summit agreement's "firewalls" between defense and domestic spending, intended by liberals as an attempt to save domestic programs and by conservatives as a way of protecting the Pentagon. After Leon Panetta was appointed OMB director in January 1993, Sabo ran for Budget Committee chairman, and won by 149–112 over the more moderate John Spratt of South Carolina. In that position it fell to Sabo to defend the first Clinton budget, which eventually passed by 218–216. Although that budget had untoward political consequences for many Democrats, he takes credit for passing "the largest deficit-reduction package in history." Sabo then fought against the spending cut packages proposed by his Minnesota DFL colleague Tim Penny and his successor as Budget Chairman, Republican John Kasich.

After the 1996 election Sabo rotated off Budget and concentrated on Appropriations, where he is an ally of ranking Democrat David Obey. Sabo is ranking member on the Transportation Subcommittee; he has a penchant for mass transit. He got more than $100 million for construction of the Hiawatha transit line. He has delivered other projects to his district, including the new federal courthouse and improvements to Minnesota's VA hospital.

On other issues, Sabo pursues goals both practical and visionary. He calls himself a "liberal decentrist," which means he supports liberal social causes but believes that the federal government should intervene only when local governments can't or need help. But he has a bill, not likely to pass soon, limiting CEO pay to 25 times the pay of the lowest-paid full-time worker or taxing the corporation at a higher rate. He has another bill for public financing of House general election campaigns. He opposed the moratorium on Internet taxes, calling it "grossly unfair" to Main Street merchants. He opposed PNTR with China, despite the importunings of Minnesota's 3M, Honeywell and Cargill. He sought a congressional Gold Medal for former Senator Eugene McCarthy, who began his career in Washington as the Congressman from St. Paul. In 2001, Sabo filed an amendment to require additional safety inspections of trucks entering the United States from Mexico, which sparked major conflicts within Congress, with the Bush administration and with the Mexican government; the result was a compromise that delayed opening the border until there were systems in place to verify driver's licenses, train inspectors and install truck scales.

Continuing to practice old-fashioned political door-knocking that he began when he campaigned for Adlai Stevenson in 1956, Sabo has been reelected by wide margins of 2–1 or more. The locals concede that his Norwegian habits leave little conversation; it's simply good to be seen, he maintains. His daughter Julie was a state senator who ran unsuccessfully for lieutenant governor on the DFL ticket with Roger Moe in 2002.

SIXTH DISTRICT

Rep. Mark Kennedy (R)

Elected 2000, 2d term; b. Apr. 11, 1957, Benson; home, Watertown; St. John's U. (MN) B.A. 1979, U. of MI, M.B.A. 1983; Catholic; married (Debbie).

Professional Career: CPA, Arthur Anderson, 1978–81; Dir. of Finance, Pillsbury Co., 1983–87; Treas., Federated Dept. Stores, 1987–92; CFO, Shopko Stores, 1992–95; CFO Dept. 56, Inc., 1995–00.

DC Office: 1415 LHOB 20515, 202-225-2331; Fax: 202-225-6475; Web site: www.house.gov/markkennedy.

District Offices: Buffalo, 763-684-1600; Hugo, 651-653-5933; St. Cloud, 320-259-0099.

Committees: *Financial Services* (29th of 37 R): Capital Markets, Insurance & Government Sponsored Enterprises; Domestic and International Monetary Policy, Trade & Technology; Financial Institutions & Consumer Credit. *Transportation & Infrastructure* (30th of 41 R): Aviation; Highways, Transit & Pipelines.

Group Ratings

	ADA	ACLU	AFS	LCV	CON	ITIC	NTU	COC	ACU	NTLC	CHC
2002	0	7	0	38	25	100	59	95	96	92	92
2001	10	—	10	29	—	—	62	91	88	—	—

National Journal Ratings

	2001 LIB	—	2001 CONS		2002 LIB	—	2002 CONS
Economic	39%	—	61%		21%	—	73%
Social	20%	—	69%		0%	—	75%
Foreign	4%	—	87%		23%	—	76%

Key Votes of the 107th Congress

1. Approve Bush Tax Cuts	Y	5. Faith-Based Charities	Y	9. Trade Promotion Authority	Y
2. Limit Patients' Bill of Rights	Y	6. Bar Gays in the Boy Scouts	Y	10. Bar Funds for Intl. Court	*
3. Campaign Finance Reform	N	7. Ban Partial-Birth Abortion	Y	11. Authorize Force in Iraq	Y
4. Ban ANWR Development	Y	8. Arm Commercial Pilots	Y	12. Deny Home. Sec. Dept. Union	Y

Election Results

2002 general	Mark Kennedy (R)	164,747	(57%)	($1,891,653)
	Janet Robert (DFL)	100,738	(35%)	($2,192,965)
	Dan Becker (I)	21,484	(7%)	($22,996)
2002 primary	Mark Kennedy (R)	unopposed		
2000 general (MN 2)	Mark Kennedy (R)	138,957	(48%)	($886,650)
	David Minge (DFL)	138,802	(48%)	($848,795)
	Other	9,212	(3%)	

The People		Race/Ethnic Origin	Ancestry	
Area size:	3,237 sq. mi.	94.9% White	German: 29.9%	Norwegian: 10.0%
Urban population:	63.8%	0.9% Black	Irish: 8.0%	
Rural population:	36.2%	1.4% Asian	**2000 Presidential Vote**	
Pop. 2000:	614,935	0.4% Native Am.	Bush (R).............152,977	(52%)
Median income:	$56,862	0.0% Hawaiian	Gore (D).............123,247	(42%)
Poverty status:	4.7%	1.0% Two+ races	Other..................15,954	(5%)
Military veterans:	12.4%	0.1% Other	**Cook Partisan Voting Index:** R + 6	
		1.3% Hispanic Origin		

Occupation	Blue collar: 26.9%	White collar: 60.3%	Gray collar: 12.8%

The earliest settlers to the Twin Cities of Minneapolis and St. Paul came up the Mississippi River, or up the rail lines that were soon built on the bottomlands beside. They lived within walking distance of the mills and factories and railyards; as the first streetcars and then automobiles allowed them to live farther from work, they spread out in St. Paul and Minneapolis and then all around the lake-strewn countryside. The flatlands are bleak here when the winter sun struggles to shine through gray clouds. The lakes are often surrounded by, and sometimes indistinguishable from, swamps. Stillwater, an old lumber mill town built by pioneers on the hills above the St. Croix River, once nearly became Minnesota's capital, but later turned into an economic backwater, its Victorian structures ill-tended. Even so, the creativity and productivity of Minnesotans have turned this superficially grim countryside into some of the world's most pleasant suburbs. Taking maximum advantage of their lakes, they refurbished old towns and farmhouses and built comfortable homes in new subdivisions.

The 6th Congressional District is primarily a suburban district north of St. Paul and Minneapolis. It dips as far south as Stillwater and spreads north over Washington and Anoka Counties, just north of the Twin Cities, with a mix of upscale and working class suburbs. To the northwest, along the Mississippi River, are Wright, Sherburne and Benton Counties, which in the 1990s were among the fastest-growing counties in Minnesota. These were once rural areas, with here and there a small town and a small city as the county seat. Now this lake country is filling with new subdivisions and shopping centers, young voters usually from ancestrally DFL families who have become the key swing voters in the state recently. In 1998 this was Ventura Country: Thousands of people, many of them young and newly moved in, went to the polls on Election Day and registered to vote, for Ventura. He carried these areas with about 50% of the vote in a four-way race. At the same time, the newcomers tended to vote Republican for other offices and in 2000 to vote for George W. Bush. In 2002 these areas gave big margins to Republican Senator Norm Coleman and Governor Tim Pawlenty. Farther to the northwest, the district also includes the eastern half of Stearns County, a heavily German Catholic area and a stronghold of anti-abortion sentiment. The 1990s saw an influx of Vietnamese, Chinese and Japanese people into St. Cloud, so that by 2000 there were more Asians than either blacks or Hispanics in the 6th District.

The congressman from the 6th District is Mark Kennedy, a Republican elected in 2000 in the old 2d District. He was born in Benson and grew up in Murdock and Pequot Lakes; his great-grandfather was a Swift County commissioner and his grandfather was mayor of Murdock. Kennedy graduated from St. John's University in 1978 and University of Michigan business school in 1983. He was a CPA with Arthur Andersen before becoming financial director of Pillsbury. His path up the corporate ladder led him to Cincinnati as treasurer of Federated Department Stores, to Green Bay as chief financial officer of ShopKo, and finally back to Minneapolis as a senior vice president at Department 56, before he ran for Congress in 2000—his first bid for elected office. During those years he did political work for Senator Rudy Boschwitz and he served in 1998 as state Republican platform co-chairman. With his strong business background and the slogan "Mark Kennedy means business," he said that he could help the district market its farm products abroad and bring more businesses to its small towns.

In 2000, Kennedy challenged incumbent David Minge, a "common sense Democrat," as Minge put it, who was first elected in 1992 by 569 votes in a district stretching west through rural territory to the South Dakota border. Kennedy campaigned on opening foreign markets to Minnesota's farm products, repealing the marriage penalty and the estate tax, and improving the district's roads. The national parties did not focus on this race until the final weeks of the campaign; Minge remained in Washington for much of October while Kennedy was busy campaigning at home. Kennedy was one Republican who benefited from the coattails of George W. Bush, who ran well in rural areas and carried the district with 52% of the vote. The initial count showed Kennedy the winner by 155 votes. Minge dropped his demand for a recount December 12, the day that the Supreme Court ended the presidential recount in Florida, with Kennedy's lead at 148 votes and 300 contested ballots remaining, so the 155-vote margin stood as the official tally. His margin of victory came from the three suburban counties west of Minneapolis, Wright, Carver and Scott, where Kennedy won 51%–45%.

In the House, Kennedy has a conservative-to-moderate voting record. As often is the case with freshmen who have unexpectedly won their seats, he made few waves legislatively and usually was a party loyalist. He took the advice of Republican leaders to build a large campaign war chest and to prepare for the next campaign. The most important decision that he made during his first term came after a panel of five judges issued the redistricting map on March 19, 2002. Kennedy's home was shifted inside the 6th District by 800 yards, but it included only Wright County from his old district, with just 14% of the old district's voters. Nearby Carver and Scott Counties, heavily Republican, were in the new 2d District. Other chunks of his district were divided among the new 1st, 2d, and 7th districts. Republican John Kline, who had twice lost to DFL Congressman Bill Luther in the old 6th District, made the first move by quickly deciding to run in the new 2d. With secure incumbents seeking reelection in the 1st and 7th, that left Kennedy the option of running against Kline in a primary or running in the Republican-leaning but largely new territory of the 6th, which included Luther's home. Kennedy acted more resolutely. The NRCC polled the new 6th District and party leaders pledged to clear the primary field for him, Kennedy decided six days after the court decision to run in the 6th.

Two months later Luther decided to run in the new 2d; he lost to Kline in November. In July, Stillwater attorney Janet Robert announced her candidacy as a Democrat. She was anti-abortion and pro-gun, and had little political experience. But she had one attribute that endeared her to national Democrats: She was willing to spend lavishly on her own campaign. With her heavy advertising barrage, she attacked Kennedy for voting against corporate reforms, and she claimed that he misled shareholders when he was in the private sector. The *St. Paul Pioneer-Press* called her ads "among the dirtiest and most untruthful in the flood of negative ads this year." It turned out that she had her own boardroom controversy: A federal judge ruled that her family squeezed out some minority shareholders from their private company. Robert spent $1.6 million of her own money, which was the total of what Kennedy raised, but she had little to show for it. Kennedy won 57%–35%, far easier than expected, with at least 52% in each county.

Secure in his new district and with seats on the Financial Services and Transportation Committees, Kennedy is now in a good position to make his mark on both national and local issues.

SEVENTH DISTRICT

Rep. Collin Peterson (DFL)

Elected 1990, 7th term; b. June 29, 1944, Fargo, ND; home, Detroit Lakes; Moorhead St. U., B.A. 1966; Lutheran; divorced.

Military Career: Army Natl. Guard, 1963–69.

Elected Office: MN Senate, 1976–86.

Professional Career: Accountant, 1966–90.

DC Office: 2159 RHOB 20515, 202-225-2165; Fax: 202-225-1593; Web site: www.house.gov/collinpeterson.

District Offices: Detroit Lakes, 218-847-5056; Red Lake Falls, 218-253-4356; Willmar, 320-235-1061.

Committees: *Agriculture* (2d of 24 D): Conservation, Credit, Rural Development & Research; General Farm Commodities & Risk Management (RMM); Livestock & Horticulture. *Permanent Select Committee on Intelligence* (5th of 9 D): Human Intelligence, Analysis & Counterintelligence; Technical & Tactical Intelligence; Terrorism and Homeland Security.

Group Ratings

	ADA	ACLU	AFS	LCV	CON	ITIC	NTU	COC	ACU	NTLC	CHC
2002	45	57	56	25	38	50	26	70	48	32	58
2001	50	—	70	57	—	—	34	55	43	—	—

National Journal Ratings

	2001 LIB —	2001 CONS		2002 LIB —	2002 CONS
Economic	61% —	39%		52% —	48%
Social	54% —	47%		44% —	54%
Foreign	56% —	45%		54% —	45%

Key Votes of the 107th Congress

1. Approve Bush Tax Cuts	Y	5. Faith-Based Charities	N	9. Trade Promotion Authority	N
2. Limit Patients' Bill of Rights	Y	6. Bar Gays in the Boy Scouts	*	10. Bar Funds for Intl. Court	Y
3. Campaign Finance Reform	N	7. Ban Partial-Birth Abortion	Y	11. Authorize Force in Iraq	Y
4. Ban ANWR Development	N	8. Arm Commercial Pilots	Y	12. Deny Home. Sec. Dept. Union	N

Election Results

2002 general	Collin Peterson (DFL)	170,234	(65%)	($535,214)
	Dan Stevens (R)	90,342	(35%)	($201,196)
2002 primary	Collin Peterson (DFL)	unopposed		
2000 general	Collin Peterson (DFL)	185,771	(69%)	($207,292)
	Glen Menze (R)	79,175	(29%)	($59,446)
	Other	5,550	(2%)	

Prior Winning Percentages: 1998 (72%); 1996 (68%); 1994 (51%); 1992 (51%); 1990 (54%)

The People		Race/Ethnic Origin	Ancestry	
Area size:	33,745 sq. mi.	93.1% White	German: 28.5%	Norwegian: 20.3%
Urban population:	34.0%	0.3% Black	Swedish: 7.0%	
Rural population:	66.0%	0.5% Asian	**2000 Presidential Vote**	
Pop. 2000:	614,935	2.4% Native Am.	Bush (R)	155,794 (54%)
Median income:	$36,453	0.0% Hawaiian	Gore (D)	116,099 (40%)
Poverty status:	10.3%	0.9% Two+ races	Other	18,706 (6%)
Military veterans:	13.7%	0.0% Other	**Cook Partisan Voting Index:** R + 8	
		2.6% Hispanic Origin		

Occupation	Blue collar: 29.2%	White collar: 53.3%	Gray collar: 17.5%

Mark Twain's fabled Mississippi River begins so modestly in Minnesota's Itasca State Park, 2,552 miles from its destination, that it can be crossed by foot on a series of stones. The lake-strewn country in which the river is born has made its own contributions to American literature: A century ago, Sinclair Lewis grew up in the town of Sauk Centre, which provided grist for his critical but affectionate portrayals of small-town America in *Main Street* and *Babbitt*. In those years, this seemingly placid country was seething with rage, as WASPy nationalists banned German from schools, renamed sauerkraut "liberty cabbage," and boycotted German-American businesses. This fed the bitter isolationism of the 1930s and 1940s, led by Charles Lindbergh, who grew up in Little Falls, just across the border in the 8th, as the son of an isolationist congressman who opposed declaring war on Germany in 1917. This part of Minnesota is probably also the home of Lake Wobegon; Garrison Keillor says he was inspired by small towns in Stearns County that were evenly divided between German Catholics and Norwegian Lutherans. Further south, where the plains rise above the river-cut gorges, is great farming country, settled more than 100 years ago by Yankees, Germans and Scandinavians. Even today, farmers still toil against the elements to make a profitable living, so productively that their lands are slowly but surely depopulating. On the shores of Plum Creek, near Walnut Grove, Minn., is where Laura Ingalls Wilder's family came on the way west to the "Little House on the Prairie" in South Dakota; after all their struggles, Laura's family left the farm for town as soon as they could. Their pain would be all too familiar to contemporary residents along the Red River of the North, which overflowed its banks in April 1997, inundating Grand Forks, North Dakota, and East Grand Forks, Minnesota, and dislocating 50,000 residents of the region—America's largest mass evacuation since the Civil War. With federal disaster relief funds and loads of sweat equity, East Grand Forks managed to rebuild its entire downtown, better than it was before.

The 7th Congressional District covers almost all of the western part of the state. The 7th takes in the wheat-farming plains adjoining North Dakota as well as the German Catholic areas strewn with farm villages named for saints. Many political traditions coexist here: some wheat counties are heavily DFL while heavily Norwegian Otter Tail County leans Republican. The 7th's political history reads like something out of *Lake Wobegon Days*. Back in 1958, Congresswoman Coya Knutson lost re-election when her husband Andy issued a plaintive statement urging her to come home and make his breakfast again; she was the only incumbent Democrat to lose in heavily Democratic 1958. Other Scandinavian names followed, of varying partisan affiliations; for three decades this was one of America's prime marginal districts. In 2000 this traditionally marginal rural area rejected the Democratic party, and the 7th District gave George W. Bush his largest majority of any Minnesota district. The 2002 redistricting adjusted the district's boundaries, removing the St. Cloud area and adding smaller counties to the south.

The congressman from the 7th District is Collin Peterson, a Democrat who after four unsuccessful tries won the seat and now seems safely entrenched even as the district has become more Republican. Peterson was born in Fargo, North Dakota grew up across the Red River of the North on a farm in Baker, went to Moorhead State College, then started a CPA office in Detroit Lakes; all are within 50 miles of each other. In 1976 he was elected to the state Senate, passing a 16% farm property tax reduction in 1985 and starting the Chickadee Checkoff, which raises $900,000 a year for a non-game wildlife fund. He also started running for the House. He lost a DFL caucus in 1982; he lost to Republican Arlan Stangeland in 1984 and 1986 (by only 121 votes the second time; he declared victory and went to Washington to set up an office); he lost the DFL primary again in 1988. But in 1990, when the *St. Cloud Times* reported that Stangeland made 341 credit card calls to a woman not his wife, Peterson won with a robust 54%. In office, he has been known as a free spirit, wearing cowboy boots and playing guitar in a country rock band called the Recess Renegades, acting as his own campaign consultant and pilot on flights within the district, and enjoying a cigar in the Speaker's Lobby off the House floor. He has a small staff, with community economic development professionals rather than Washington policy wonks. He opposes abortion and gun control; backs farm subsidies and labor unions; opposed Bill Clinton on his 1993 budget, NAFTA and PNTR with China. He pulled his freshman colleague Katherine Harris out of a snow bank during an Aspen ski vacation in 1991; the two dated for a while and remain friends.

In the House Peterson has been something of a populist, with conservative leanings on social issues and definitely a maverick. His political fortune has been bolstered by the Republican takeover in 1994, which made him a visibly different kind of Democrat. In 1995, while voting for parts of the Contract with America, he founded with Gary Condit the Blue Dog Democrats for "common sense legislation that embraces the ideas and values of mainstream America." With John Linder, he has cosponsored "FairTax," a national sales tax that would replace all income, payroll, corporate and estate taxes. He sided with Republicans on HMO regulation and was one of eight Democrats to vote for their prescription drug bill in June 2002. He was one of 10 House Democrats to vote for the Bush tax cut and he voted for the use of force in Iraq; but he opposed trade promotion authority. Peterson is the opposite of many middle-of-the-House Republicans, who favor heavy environmental restrictions; he takes the view of his constituents, who hunt and fish as a way of life and see environmentalists' policies as hindrances. Peterson once said, "City people have no understanding of the rural way of life. Still, they always come up there and try to tell us how to live." He has been co-chairman of the Congressional Sportsmen's Caucus and wants to require that federal lands be open to hunting and fishing except when there is a good reason not to (as in national parks). The House attached the proposal as an amendment to the farm bill in October 2001, although Peterson did not offer the proposal himself, out of deference to leaders of the Agriculture Committee (where he is the second-ranking Democrat); the measure became law when Congress completed the farm bill. After expressing reservations that the 1996 Freedom to Farm Act would cause low prices, he joined the bipartisan majority on the committee in restoring market controls when the farm program was renewed.

Peterson's politics have been a smash hit with 7th District voters and an irritant to local DFL activists, while local Republicans typically give him a pass. He has not had a close contest since 1994. He was rumored for a post in the Bush administration and, before that, with Governor Jesse Ventura. But he apparently likes it where he is.

EIGHTH DISTRICT

Rep. James Oberstar (DFL)

Elected 1974, 15th term; b. Sept. 10, 1934, Chisholm; home, Chisholm; St. Thomas Col., B.A. 1956, Col. of Europe, Bruges, Belgium, M.A. 1957; Catholic; married (Jean).

Professional Career: Navy civilian language teacher, Haiti, 1959–63; A.A., U.S. Rep. John Blatnik, 1963–74; A.A., U.S. House Public Works Cmte., 1971–74.

DC Office: 2365 RHOB 20515, 202-225-6211; Fax: 202-225-0699; Web site: www.house.gov/oberstar.

District Offices: Brainerd, 218-828-4400; Chisholm, 218-254-5761; Duluth, 218-727-7474; North Branch, 651-277-1234.

Committees: *Transportation & Infrastructure* (RMM of 34 D).

Group Ratings

	ADA	ACLU	AFS	LCV	CON	ITIC	NTU	COC	ACU	NTLC	CHC
2002	80	67	100	88	3	50	26	26	4	0	33
2001	75	—	100	79	—	—	9	35	24	—	—

National Journal Ratings

	2001 LIB —	2001 CONS	2002 LIB —	2002 CONS
Economic	86%	— 14%	91%	— 8%
Social	57%	— 44%	56%	— 44%
Foreign	96%	— 0%	93%	— 6%

Key Votes of the 107th Congress

1. Approve Bush Tax Cuts	*	5. Faith-Based Charities	N
2. Limit Patients' Bill of Rights	N	6. Bar Gays in the Boy Scouts	Y
3. Campaign Finance Reform	Y	7. Ban Partial-Birth Abortion	Y
4. Ban ANWR Development	N	8. Arm Commercial Pilots	N

9. Trade Promotion Authority	N
10. Bar Funds for Intl. Court	N
11. Authorize Force in Iraq	N
12. Deny Home. Sec. Dept. Union	N

Election Results

2002 general	James Oberstar (DFL)	194,909	(69%)	($1,022,904)
	Bob Lemen (R)	88,673	(31%)	($17,584)
2002 primary	James Oberstar (DFL)	unopposed		
2000 general	James Oberstar (DFL)	210,094	(68%)	($1,032,070)
	Bob Lemen (R)	79,890	(26%)	($22,253)
	Mike Darling (I)	19,667	(6%)	

Prior Winning Percentages: 1998 (66%); 1996 (67%); 1994 (66%); 1992 (59%); 1990 (73%); 1988 (75%); 1986 (73%); 1984 (67%); 1982 (77%); 1980 (70%); 1978 (87%); 1976 (100%); 1974 (62%)

The People		Race/Ethnic Origin	Ancestry	
Area size:	32,419 sq. mi.	94.6% White	German: 20.2%	Norwegian: 10.8%
Urban population:	37.4%	0.5% Black	Swedish: 9.6%	
Rural population:	62.6%	0.4% Asian	**2000 Presidential Vote**	
Pop. 2000:	614,935	2.5% Native Am.	Gore (D) 153,962	(49%)
Median income:	$37,911	0.0% Hawaiian	Bush (R) 136,884	(44%)
Poverty status:	10.4%	1.0% Two+ races	Other 22,302	(7%)
Military veterans:	16.2%	0.0% Other	**Cook Partisan Voting Index:** D + 3	
		0.8% Hispanic Origin		
Occupation	Blue collar: 28.9%	White collar: 52.9%	Gray collar: 18.2%	

In the 1860s, prospectors in the Arrowhead region of the new state of Minnesota, northwest of Lake Superior in the low hills of the Mesabi Range, happened upon the nation's largest veins of iron ore; they moved on, looking for gold. But in the 1880s, Duluth banker George Stone and Philadelphia financier Charlemagne Tower started mining the Iron Range and created the northern end of the lifeline of American heavy industry. South from the Range run rail lines to the port of Duluth, nestled on dramatic bluffs over the always cold and, for long months every winter, frozen waters of Lake Superior—one of the most beautiful settings for a city in North America, and there is similar beauty on the North Shore of Lake Superior for the 150 miles from Duluth to the Canadian border. Duluth was a grain-shipping rival of Chicago and the premier iron ore port. Its city plan was drawn up by Daniel Burnham and its splendid turn-of-the-century buildings still celebrate the triumph of technology and civilization over wilderness and the elements. Millions of tons of ore have been dug out of the Range, loaded into rail cars for the ride to Duluth, and into Great Lakes freighters for shipment to Cleveland, Gary, Detroit, Chicago, Pittsburgh and Buffalo.

For most of the last century, in this land where the Arctic winds blow down over the Canadian Shield's thousands of inland lakes, about 100,000 people have lived on the Iron Range and another 100,000 in Duluth, most of them the products of America's 1880–1924 wave of immigration: Italians, Poles, Serbs and Croats, Jews, Swedes and Finns. In this punishing environment, they worked to the point of exhaustion, built solid houses with staunch central heating, and wore layers of warm clothing to survive the winter. Life was rough: The work was hard, the hours long and the pay low. The churches, a separate one for each ethnic group, were the main community institutions. Living conditions improved vastly in the decades of great economic growth after World War II, but life remains rough-hewn today, and there is still economic distress. As iron mines and steel factories got more efficient they needed fewer workers; employment is well below its 1970s peak. As water fills abandoned open-pit mines and factories close and mines are shut down, the Iron Range looks bleaker. Duluth's population was down to 86,000 in 2000, and the Iron Range's was about the same. But all is not moribund. Northwest Airlines, with an $840 million investment from state government in 1993, has built a repair facility in Duluth and a reservations center in the Iron Range. The port of Duluth still ships large quantities of grain, and in the late 1990s a new taconite and steelmaking factory was built—the first big new plant in more than 20 years. There is a Greyhound Museum in Hibbing, where in 1914 an entrepreneur started transporting people in unsaleable open-air Hupmobiles, an enterprise that eventually became the Greyhound Bus Company. People here have made the best of the frozen climate: Nearby Eveleth boasts the world's longest hockey stick, 107 feet long, carved from aspen and aimed at a 700-pound puck; the severe winters of International Falls in Koochiching County have given rise to a cold weather testing industry—this is where automakers test a car's performance under extreme winter conditions.

The 8th Congressional District includes Duluth and the Iron Range, plus much of the north woods and lake country to the west and south; it moves all the way south to the boundaries of the Twin Cities metro area, to Isanti and Chisago Counties, where young families are building new homes near pleasant old lakeside towns. This district has been a bulwark of Minnesota's Democratic-Farmer-Labor Party since it was formed in 1944, and is ordinarily safe Democratic today; but there are signs of change. In 2000, cultural issues like gun control and environmental restrictions here moved opinion toward the Republicans; George W. Bush lost the 8th District to Al Gore but by a smaller margin than his father's 60%–40% loss 12 years earlier. The 8th did vote for DFLers Walter Mondale and Roger Moe, but again by smaller margins than of yore.

The congressman from the 8th District is Jim Oberstar, a Democrat first elected in 1974—"part scholar and part Iron Range street fighter, part pothole-filling ward healer and part workaholic," in the words of *St. Paul Pioneer Press*. Oberstar grew up in the Iron Range city of Chisholm, where his father was an iron miner and union official, who sent him off to St. Thomas College with $2,500 saved in quarters at the Slovenian National Benefit Society; Oberstar has been known to sing polka songs in Slovenian at a House Democratic retreat. He studied French in college and in Belgium; for four years he was a civilian employee of the U.S. Naval Mission to Haiti, teaching French and Creole to Marines, and French and English to Haitians (he also speaks Serbo-Croatian, Italian and Spanish). Then, in 1963, at 29, he landed a job as chief of staff to Congressman John Blatnik in Washington: he has been working for the 8th District for more than four decades. When Blatnik retired in 1974, Oberstar won a primary over Tony Perpich, brother of Governor Rudy Perpich. He won tough primaries in 1980 and 1984, the latter after briefly running for the Senate.

Oberstar's views are in the liberal Catholic tradition. He believes in an economically active government and has little faith in economic markets. He was long dubious about American military involvement abroad, especially in Central America, but favored the 1994 deployment in Haiti. He voted against the Iraq war resolution in October 2002. He is an opponent of abortion and a backer of adoption, sponsoring bills to insure family and medical leave and dependent deductions for families in the process of adopting; when he first proposed a $1,500 adoption tax deduction in the 1970s he was laughed out of Ways and Means, but now, thanks in large part to his effort, there is a $5,000 tax credit. With Henry Hyde, he sponsored a bill to criminalize prescribing lethal drugs to terminally ill patients.

From this North Country district, Oberstar has been a supporter of local hunting and fishing activities and of the steel industry. When PNTR with China came before the House, he tried to get an amendment of the 1974 trade act that would treat steel slab imports as a direct threat to taconite miners; when the administration wasn't interested, he voted against PNTR. In December 2000, after LTV Steel announced a mine closure, he sought a Section 201 investigation of steel imports. He was disappointed when the Commerce Department said in January 2002 there was not a 201 violation. He was disappointed as well by George W. Bush's steel tariffs in March 2002, because imported semifinished slab steel, which competes with Minnesota's taconite, was not subject to the 30% top duty until imports reached 5.4 million tons, 77% of previous levels.

Since October 1995, Oberstar has been ranking Democrat on Transportation and Infrastructure—a position of real power, even in a Republican Congress. This committee (long known as Public Works) has a long tradition of bipartisanship, and of sponsoring members' roads (and, since 1994, other transportation) projects; it has 75 members, the largest in the House. For six years Oberstar and Chairman Bud Shuster worked to make it more powerful than ever. Their great monument was the May 1998 TEA-21 transportation bill, with $217 billion in spending, including $10 billion in projects earmarked by members. Back when Oberstar's boss John Blatnik was chairman, the committee's power was threatened by an alliance of environmentalists and fiscal conservatives; by 1998 it was carrying all before it. Another reason: the 1991 ISTEA, of which 1998's TEA-21 was the reauthorization, included spending for mass transit, bicycle trails and pollution control research, at the option of states or House members. This has helped win the support of many liberals; Oberstar himself is a bicycling enthusiast, proud of logging 2,000 miles a year in Washington, Duluth, on the Range and in the Tour de Frog in St. Cloud. In December 2002, Oberstar and the new Transportation chairman, Don Young, planned a transportation bill that would raise highway spending from $32 billion to $60 billion by 2009, by raising the gas tax by 2 cents, drawing down interest and balance in the highway trust fund and eliminating the 5.3 cent subsidy on ethanol fuel. Oberstar has opposed plans to let states subsidize many Amtrak lines and wants to reduce train crew hours.

Oberstar once chaired Transportation's Aviation Subcommittee and remains involved in aviation issues. He worked hard for the state investment in Northwest Airlines, but in recent years has criticized the company harshly. As if in response to pressure, the airline instituted jet service from its Detroit hub to Duluth in October 1998. He has been critical of big airline mergers. He was one of the architects of the airline bailout bill in fall 2001 and strongly pushed for federal employees in airport security. Originally opposed to allowing pilots to have guns, he changed his mind by summer 2002. When airlines sought more aid in fall 2002 Oberstar worked on the bill that would save them $1.5 billion by extending subsidies on war risk insurance; it would reopen the federal guarantee program in case of war with Iraq. He sponsored a bill to provide relief for laid-off airline employees.

In July 2002 Oberstar introduced a bill to overturn a Supreme Court decision ruling that "navigable waters" in the wetlands protection law meant waters having some actual nexus with navigation. His bill would substitute the term "the waters of the United States" to include, among other things, sloughs, prairie potholes, wet meadows, playa lakes, natural ponds or impoundments of any of these waters." In October 2002 he sponsored a bill to require the Army Corps of Engineers to obtain outside peer review of its economic projections. He is co-chairman of the reactivated Tilt-Rotor Caucus to support the Marine Corps's Osprey helicopter. In July 2002 he introduced a bill to provide aid for people caring for family members with chronic fatal illness.

Oberstar's one political setback came in 1984, when he ran for the Senate but was denied endorsement by the liberal DFL convention. In the 8th District he has been re-elected by very wide margins; longtime DFL voters may be moving away from Democrats higher up on the ticket, but they have been faithful to Oberstar. In 2000 he won 68%–26%, running nearly 20% ahead of Al Gore; in 2002 he won 69%–31%.

★ MISSISSIPPI ★

M ississippi bears the weight of a tragic history as it takes quickening steps toward the future. This green land was settled in a rush in Jacksonian America, mostly by small farmers heading west from Georgia and south from Tennessee—and also by a few big planters, who made vast gains and great losses, built grand mansions and sent their sons to fight in the Civil War. For a century afterward, even as industrial farmers drained the Delta lands, Mississippi with its racial segregation, subsistence farmers and sharecroppers and low wages, lived apart from most of America. Faulkner's Mississippi never knew the Homestead Act, the giant factories, the rushes of immigration, the rise of suburbs that were the indispensable backdrop of most of 20th century American life. Mississippi never developed great cities—its two commercial metropolises are just outside its borders, Memphis and New Orleans. But if it did not excel at commerce, it did produce great art. Mississippi gave us the music of the blues and Elvis Presley. It gave the world William Faulkner and Eudora Welty, Walker Percy and Shelby Foote. Their work was informed by a sense of the tragic missing or forgotten in most of America, where life is a triumphant sales pitch or a labor-saving invention. The writer Willie Morris, who chronicled his success in New York in *North Toward Home*, returned to live in Mississippi and, when he died in August 1999, lay in rest at the Old Capitol and then was buried in the cemetery in Yazoo City where he walked as a child where "I learned more about the town's past here, the migrations, the epidemics, the old forgotten tragedies, than I could ever have learned in the library. Sometimes we would take our lunch."

Mississippi has made much progress in the last three decades, but the past still hangs heavy. For years no other state had such a painful contrast between image and reality, between an ideal sincerely strived for and the tawdry facts of everyday life. Magnolia trees on the lawns of ante-bellum mansions, golden-haired young women in white dresses on the veranda, faithful black servants and retainers: This was once the ideal. And behind it stood loose-jointed frame houses and unpainted back-country stores, cabins without indoor plumbing and poor white crossroads clustered with askew advertising signs. This is a state, writes David Sansing, with "two souls, two hearts, two minds. We have the highest rate of illiteracy and the largest number of Pulitzer Prize winners in literature. We at one time have the scent of magnolias and the smell of burning crosses." Mississippi for years ranked 50th, and a very low 50th, among states in income, literacy, health and education levels, despite the best efforts of civic, political and business leaders. As Faulkner said of his state, "You don't love because: you love despite."

Today Mississippi still ranks 50th on many scales, but the gulf between Mississippi and the rest of America has narrowed enormously in the last half-century. In 1940, Mississippi had an economy based on low-wage, subsistence or sharecropper agriculture and a system of racial segregation enforced often by violence. If history is, as Sir Henry Maine wrote, the story of the progress from status to contract, then old Mississippi was still at the beginning, for status—race—meant just about everything. In the years since, Mississippi has moved, not always willingly, from status to contract, in its economy and in race relations. Per capita income in Mississippi was 36% of the national average in 1940; in 1999, it was 72%, well below average but, given the lower cost of living here, a level recognizably American. In the 1990s incomes increased smartly and poverty declined. Mississippi is home to the nation's second largest furniture industry, around Tupelo; a $930 million Nissan plant is being built in Canton. Daily life, thanks to cheap gas and air conditioning, national brands and the mechanization of farming, has changed drastically. Most Mississippians of 50 years ago would be astonished by the physical comforts and mechanical marvels

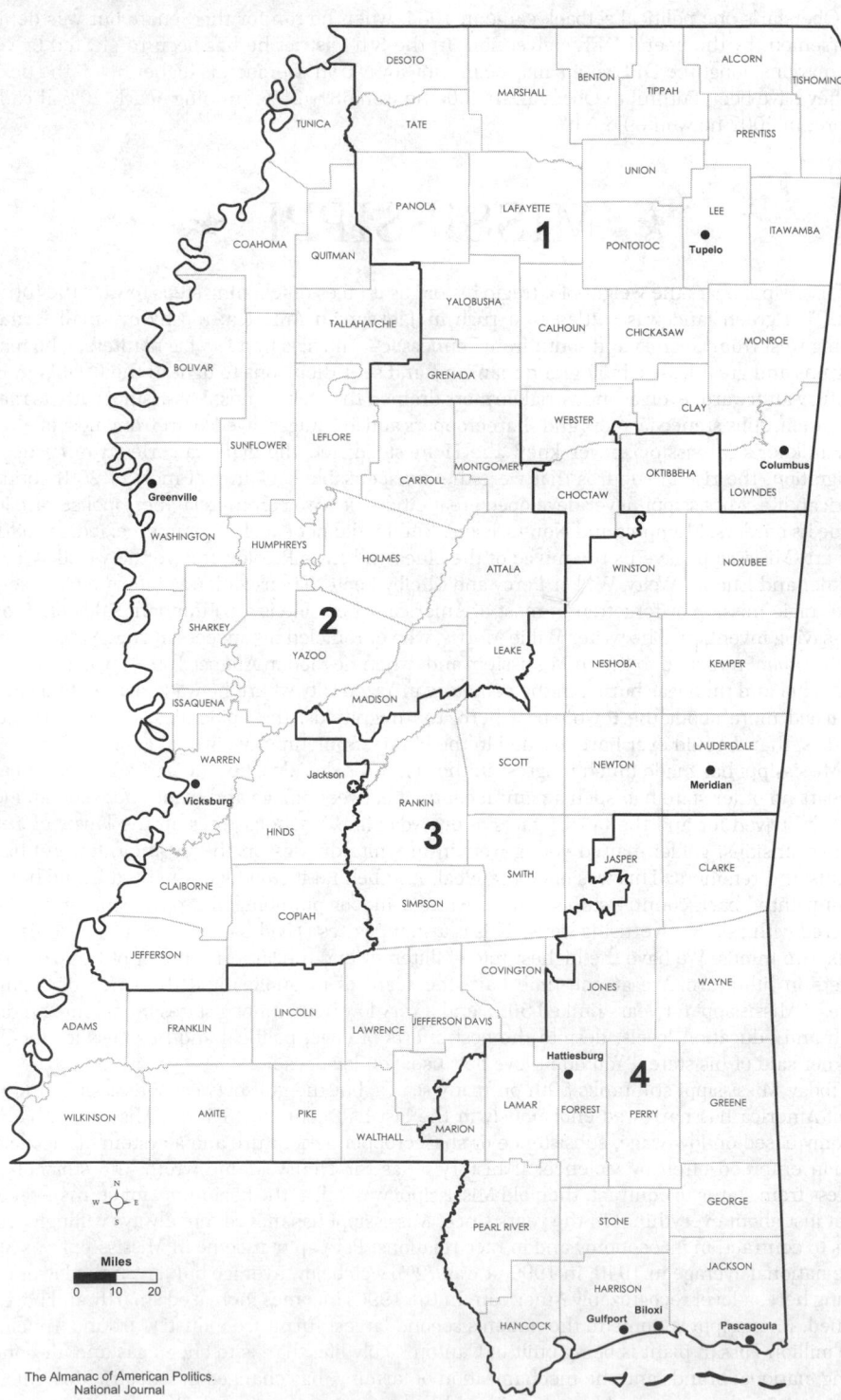

DESOTO

MARSHALL   BENTON   TIPPAH   ALCORN   TISHOMINGO

TUNICA   TATE   PRENTISS

UNION

PANOLA   LAFAYETTE   **1**   LEE   ITAWAMBA

COAHOMA   QUITMAN   PONTOTOC   ● Tupelo

YALOBUSHA

TALLAHATCHIE   CALHOUN   CHICKASAW   MONROE

GRENADA

BOLIVAR   WEBSTER   CLAY

LEFLORE   MONTGOMERY   ● Columbus

SUNFLOWER   CARROLL   CHOCTAW   OKTIBBEHA   LOWNDES

● Greenville

WASHINGTON   HUMPHREYS   ATTALA   WINSTON   NOXUBEE

HOLMES

SHARKEY   **2**   LEAKE

YAZOO   NESHOBA   KEMPER

ISSAQUENA   MADISON

WARREN   LAUDERDALE ●

SCOTT   NEWTON   Meridian ●

● Vicksburg   Jackson ⊗

RANKIN   **3**

HINDS   JASPER   CLARKE

SMITH

CLAIBORNE   SIMPSON

COPIAH   COVINGTON   JONES   WAYNE

JEFFERSON

LINCOLN   JEFFERSON DAVIS

ADAMS   FRANKLIN   LAWRENCE   Hattiesburg ●   **4**   GREENE

LAMAR   FORREST   PERRY

WILKINSON   AMITE   PIKE   WALTHALL   MARION

GEORGE

PEARL RIVER   STONE

JACKSON

HARRISON

HANCOCK   Gulfport ● ● Biloxi   ● Pascagoula

Miles
0   10   20

Congressional district boundaries were first effective for 2002.

their grandchildren take for granted today: Nearly every classroom in the state is air-conditioned and the governor wants to wire them all up to the Internet. They would be astonished as well by relations between blacks and whites. As *The Washington Post's* William Raspberry, a Mississippi native, wrote, "There is an easiness to relationships, a mutual respect and a willingness to move beyond race that, quite frankly, didn't exist during my years in the state. Mississippi is finally a good place to be." Forty years ago, blacks held no public offices in Mississippi; in 2001, 10 of 52 state senators, 35 of 122 state representatives and 116 of 410 county supervisors were black. The Mississippi traditions of friendliness and courtesy seem to be trumping the historical tradition of racism: Mississippi may rank 50th in incomes, but it ranks number one in per capita charitable giving.

One way Mississippi has improved is in education. Governor William Winter, elected in 1979, finally made kindergarten mandatory and raised the dropout age to 14; Governor Ray Mabus, elected in 1987, also made major changes. But the uncomfortable fact is that most high taxpayers are white and most public school children are black, because many white children attend private academies. About 40% of state spending goes to education, but those who oppose higher spending or taxes can point to the fact that there is no demonstrated correlation between higher spending and improved test scores and learning. But test scores are rising and dropout rates are falling. Another way Mississippi has improved is by encouraging small businesses and service industry. In the 1990s the number of manufacturing jobs here dropped, but the number of service jobs increased even more, and the new jobs tended to pay higher wages.

The biggest driver of growth has been gambling. Mississippi approved riverboat gambling in 1989, and Mississippi now has 31 casinos, 11 in Harrison County on the Gulf Coast and 9 in once-impoverished Tunica County, just south of Memphis, and the rest scattered along the Mississippi River with one inland. Mississippi is number three in gambling revenues, behind Nevada and New Jersey; gambling has produced 40,000 service jobs, at above-average wages. But this is not an alloyed good. The original riverboats Mark Twain described in *Life on the Mississippi* were working vehicles, sooty and dangerous, taking chances on the treacherous river, but their captains showed how hard work could get people ahead. Mississippi's riverboat casinos are a form of entertainment, a diversion from gainful economic activity, which teaches the lesson that getting ahead depends on luck rather than talent and hard work. Popular culture hurts in other ways. Greenville, which produced authors Hodding Carter (*Main Street Meets the River*) and William Alexander Percy (*Lanterns on the Levee*) —and where Shelby Foote and Walker Percy went to high school together—not long ago rated as the nation's media market in which people watch television more hours a day than any other.

The get-rich-quick mindset has also been apparent in Mississippi's courtrooms. By 2002 the state had become a trial lawyer's paradise, with seven product liability judgments of $100 million or more in six years; medical malpractice lawsuits raised insurance premiums so much that 73 doctors left the state, an obstetric clinic in the Delta closed down temporarily and there was only one neurosurgeon left on the Gulf Coast. Hundreds of cases were brought in tiny, impoverished Jefferson County where juries awarded huge judgments; there were more plaintiffs in court than the county had people. The U.S. Chamber of Commerce ran full-page ads in Mississippi newspapers calling for change, and Governor Ronnie Musgrove called a special session of the legislature in September 2002. It labored almost three months and enacted caps on pain and suffering damages in medical malpractice cases and on punitive damages in product liability cases; it also limited forum-shopping. In November 2002, a pro-plaintiff Supreme Court justice was ousted by the voters.

Politically, Mississippi is a conservative state, carried by Republicans in the last six presidential elections. But Mississippi Democrats with good old boy personas have become competitive. Democrat Gene Taylor was elected to Senator Trent Lott's old House seat in 1989 and in 1999 Democrat Ronnie Musgrove was elected governor; he failed to win 50% of the popular vote, but under Mississippi law he was installed by the legislature, which remains overwhelmingly Democratic. Nor do Mississippians dislike these old-time politicians: In 1995 and 1999 they rejected term limits for state legislators—the only state that voted them down in the 1990s. The legislators, politically canny, handed the hottest of hot potatoes back to the voters in 2001. Since 1894, the

Mississippi flag has included the Confederate battle cross in the top left corner. But in May 2000 the state Supreme Court ruled it was not the legal flag, since the 1894 law was not included in the full codification of state laws in 1906. Black politicians and many white businessmen wanted to replace it, and Musgrove appointed a commission headed by former Governor Winter, which presented a new design in January 2001 with a circle of 20 white stars (rather like those in the European Union flag) replacing the Confederate cross. Musgrove supported the change, but legislators decided to leave the decision up to the voters in an April 2001 referendum. Many admitted that the legislators would have kept the old flag and many feared—or hoped—that a large majority of white voters would choose that in the privacy of the voting booth. They did, by a 65%–35% margin. The old design won in 64 of 82 counties; turnout was close to the November 2000 level in many rural counties that voted overwhelmingly for the flag, but sharply down in black-majority counties, some of which voted for the old flag too. Apparently the economic argument did not convince Mississippians: Shelby Foote noted, "I think a lot of people like me think that flag represents something they stand for . . . never mind its definitions of slavery. I think the people who want a new flag are worried about tourists. I never cared much for tourists myself."

The People		Race/Ethnic Origin			Military veterans: 249,431 (12.0%)	
Pop. 2000:	2,844,658	1,727,908	60.7%	White	WWII: 18.7%	Korea: 13.5%
Pop. 1990:	2,573,216	1,028,473	36.2%	Black	Vietnam: 31.0%	Gulf War: 13.1%
Change 1990–2000:	Up 10.5%	18,349	0.6%	Asian	**Most populous cities:**	
Change 1980–1990:	Up 2.1%	11,224	0.4%	Native Am.	1. Jackson	184,256
% of U.S. total:	1.0%	569	0.0%	Hawaiian	2. Gulfport	71,127
Pop. rank:	31st of 50	17,272	0.6%	Two+ races	3. Biloxi	50,644
Area size:	48,430 sq. mi.	1,294	0.0%	Other	4. Hattiesburg	44,779
State Native:	74.3%	39,569	1.4%	Hisp. Origin	5. Greenville	41,633
Non-citizen:	0.8%	**Ancestry**			Urban population: 48.8%	
Language		USA: 12.7%		Irish: 6.1%	Rural population: 51.2%	
English: 94.4%	Spanish: 3.1%	English: 5.4%		German: 4.1%		
Other Eur.: 1.6%		French: 2.1%				

Education		Work Sector		Legislature	
H.S. Grad:	72.9%	Private: 75.6%	Govt: 17.6%	Senate	29 D 23 R
College Grad:	16.9%	Self: 6.4%	Family: 0.4%	House	84 D 35 R 3 I
Industry		Unemployment: 7.3%		Legislative Term Limits: No	
Agri: 3.4%	Con: 7.6%	**Household Income**		**Registered Voters**	
Fin: 4.8%	Info: 1.8%	<15k: 24.9%	15-35k: 29.9%	No party registration	
Mfg: 23.7%	Prof: 25.3%	35-50k: 16.4%	50-100k: 22.8%		
Public: 5.1%	Trade: 15.2%	100-150k: 3.9%	>150k: 2.2%		
Other: 13.1%		Median: $31,330			
Occupation		Poverty status: 19.9%			
Blue collar: 31.6%	White collar: 52.3%	**Home Value**			
Gray collar: 16.1%		<50k: 36.4%	50-100k: 38.9%	100-200k: 19.1%	200-300k: 3.7%
		300-500k: 1.3%	>500k: 0.7%	Median: $64,700	

Presidential politics   Mississippi voted 58%–41% for George W. Bush in 2000—almost the same as the 60%–39% margin by which his father carried the state in 1988. There is no way of avoiding the conclusion that this is a racially polarized electorate: Whites voted 82%–17% for Bush, blacks 96%–3% for Gore. Yet it should also be said that few Mississippi whites yearn for a return of racial segregation; they line up with Republicans on a whole raft of other issues— defense, crime, cultural attitudes, taxes—just as most blacks line up with Democrats on the same issues. Mississippi holds a presidential primary on Southern Super Tuesday; in 2000 both parties' contests were effectively over.

2000 Presidential Vote		
Bush (R)	572,844	(58%)
Gore (D)	404,614	(41%)
Nader (Green)	8,122	(1%)
Other	8,604	(1%)

2000 Republican Presidential Primary		
Bush (R)	101,042	(88%)
Keyes (R)	6,478	(6%)
McCain (R)	6,263	(5%)

2000 Democratic Presidential Primary		
Gore (D)	79,408	(90%)
Bradley (D)	7,621	(9%)

1996 Presidential Vote		
Dole (R)	439,833	(49%)
Clinton (D)	394,020	(44%)
Perot (I)	52,221	(6%)

Congressional districting   Mississippi lost one of its five House districts in the 2000 Census; this is the first time Mississippi has

108th Congress Lineup	
2 D	2 R

107th Congress Lineup	
3 D	2 R

had just four congressmen since the 1840s. In 2001 Democrats held the governorship and both houses of the legislature, and one might have expected that they would draw a plan ousting one of the state's two Republican congressmen. But the state House, led by Speaker Tim Ford, and the state Senate, led by Lieutenant Governor Amy Tuck, could not agree on a plan. Ford wanted to draw a plan connecting northeast Mississippi, home of Republican incumbent Roger Wicker, and DeSoto County, just south of Memphis, with part of Rankin County, just east of Jackson and home of Republican incumbent Chip Pickering. Republicans called this the "tornado district" because it was shaped something like a funnel cloud. This plan would leave Pickering with the choice of running against Wicker in a primary where he would be at a great geographic disadvantage or running in a new 3d District against incumbent Democrat Ronnie Shows in a district that was 38% black. Tuck (who in December 2002 switched parties and became a Republican), Republicans and northeast Mississippians in the Senate favored a plan that would combine most of the old 3d and 4th districts, represented by Pickering and Shows and would be 34% black. Governor Ronnie Musgrove called a special session in November 2001, and on the first day, the Senate and House passed versions of Ford's and Tuck's plans. Negotiations for a compromise went nowhere, and Ford moved to adjourn the session.

Action shifted to the courts. Democrats filed a lawsuit in state court and Republicans filed one in federal court. The Mississippi Supreme Court left the Democrats' case to Hinds County Chancery Judge Patricia Wise, elected from a heavily Democratic district. On December 21 she adopted a plan put forward by Democrats with a 38% black 3d District. On December 26 Attorney General Mike Moore forwarded it to the U.S. Justice Department for the preclearance required by the Voting Rights Act. On January 15, the three-judge federal court in the case brought by Republicans took the issue away from the Chancery Court on the ground that the Justice Department might not finish its review by Mississippi's March 1 filing deadline; the federal judges put forward a plan with a 30% black 3d District, similar to the state Senate's. On February 14 the Justice Department sent a five-page letter to Mississippi officials asking them to "explain the state's view of the legal basis for the Mississippi Supreme Court to vest a chancery court with jurisdiction to create and implement a statewide redistricting plan." Democrats complained that that was not an issue pertinent to the Voting Rights Act and that the three federal judges, all appointed by Republican presidents, were improperly trying to impose a plan favoring Pickering, who is the son of federal Judge Charles Pickering, whose nomination to a federal appeals court judgeship was rejected on party lines by the Senate Judiciary Committee in March 2002. On February 25 the federal court ordered its own plan into effect; Supreme Court Justice Antonin

Scalia rejected an emergency appeal by Democrats. "There has been no indication that the chancery court had any legislative authority to draw the state's districts," the court said.

Democrats were furious. They claimed that DOJ dragged its feet during the preclearance process and that Scalia, a friend of the Pickering family, should have recused himself from the case. "The deck is stacked against me," Shows said. "The Justice Department is sticking it to me because of pure partisan politics." Shows was certainly correct in saying that the Justice Department's course, whatever the motivation, hurt him politically. Pickering was certainly correct in saying that the "tornado district" was much more irregular and weirdly shaped than any previous Mississippi district. The districts in the federal court plan were, in contrast, about as compact as possible given the state's geography and the imperative, which everyone agreed on, of creating a black-majority 2d District. Democrats persisted in their appeal of the federal court decision even though it was obvious its lines would be in effect for the November 2002 election. On March 31, the Supreme Court ruled against their claim, holding that a federal court may impose a congressional redistricting plan when a state fails to properly enact its own plan.

Governor

Ronnie Musgrove (D)

Elected 1999, term expires Jan. 2004, 1st term; b. Jul. 29, 1956, Tocowa; home, Batesville; U. of MS, B.A. 1978, J.D. 1981; Southern Baptist; divorced.

Elected Office: MS Senate, 1987–95; MS Lt. Gov., 1995–99.

Professional Career: Atty., Smith, Musgrove & McCord, 1981–99.

Office: State Capitol, P.O. Box 139, Jackson, 39205, 601-359-3100; Fax: 601-359-3741; Web site: www.state.ms.us.

Election Results

1999 general	Ronnie Musgrove (D)	379,034	(50%)
	Mike Parker (R)	370,691	(49%)
	Other	14,213	(2%)
1999 primary	Ronnie Musgrove (D)	309,519	(57%)
	James Roberts Jr. (D)	142,617	(26%)
	Richard Barrett (D)	32,383	(6%)
	Other	61,036	(11%)
1995 general	Kirk Fordice (R)	455,261	(56%)
	Dick Molpus (D)	364,210	(44%)

Ronnie Musgrove was elected governor by the Mississippi House of Representatives in January 2000, after leading the popular vote in November 1999 by a 49.6%–48.5% margin. Musgrove grew up in Tocowa, in Panola County; he can remember political discussions at the dinner table with his father, a state highway worker, who died when he was 7. Musgrove says he wanted to become a lawyer because his father had spoken well of the profession. He is the first Mississippi governor not to have lived as an adult during the searing years of the civil rights revolution: The protests when James Meredith integrated the University of Mississippi in 1962, the murder of Medgar Evers in 1963, the murders of three civil rights workers in 1964—all happened when he was younger than 8. Musgrove went to college and law school at Ole Miss, where he was a classmate and friend of the novelist John Grisham—and where his nickname was "Governor," "because Musgrove knew everybody," Grisham says. He worked his way through school selling encyclopedias. After school he practiced law in Batesville. Musgrove was elected to the state Senate in 1987, at 31, and re-elected in 1991. During legislative sessions he was well known for eschewing whiskey for soft drinks and for refereeing high school and community college basketball games. In 1995 he ventured to run for lieutenant governor, and with his strong Southern drawl, elaborate courtesy and high-pitched laugh, and with his emphasis on education and family values beat Republican incumbent Eddie Briggs. In his second month in office, February 1996, he suffered a mild brain injury in an auto accident; for a time it seemed his life was in danger, but he recovered fully.

Musgrove was obviously on the road to running for governor, and he campaigned hard and effectively. In the August 1999 Democratic primary—still the primary of choice of the large majority of voters—he won with 57% of the vote in an eight-candidate field. The Republican primary was between three former Democrats; former Congressman Mike Parker won by a 51%–28% margin over Musgrove's 1999 opponent Briggs. Polls showed the race about even. Parker ran folksy ads featuring endorsements from his relatives, including a distant cousin named Loretta Musgrove, who was shown shelling peas. Ronnie Musgrove attacked Parker's record in the acrimonious House and spotlighted education. Musgrove pledged to raise teacher pay to the Southeastern state average, to put an Internet-connected computer on the desk of every pupil in every grade and to lower class size in kindergarten through third grade from 24 to 15. He opposed abortion and any new gun control law, but did not abandon the Democratic base entirely; he had lots of support from trial lawyers and accompanied Bill Clinton on his July 1999 tour of the Mississippi Delta.

The election turned out to be the closest in Mississippi history. Musgrove won by 8,343 votes out of 764,000 cast. Musgrove ran far ahead of national Democrats in northeast Mississippi, where he carried most counties, and he held down Republican margins in the Gulf Coast impressively. The Delta and the Jackson area split much as they do in national elections, with huge majorities of blacks voting Democratic and huge majorities of whites Republican. But winning the popular vote was not decisive under a Mississippi law passed in 1890 to prevent blacks from winning statewide elections with pluralities. The law said that if no candidate won a majority of the popular vote the winner would be determined by which candidate won the most state House districts. After the tedious tabulation, it appeared that 61 districts voted for Musgrove and 61 for Parker. Under the 1890 law, the decision then went to the state House of Representatives. Democrats had a big margin there, but Parker refused to concede and Musgrove did not choose agency heads or set the details of his legislative agenda. On January 4, 2000, Musgrove was finally elected by a margin of 86–36.

In his first legislative session, Musgrove achieved his biggest goal, a six-year, $338 million teacher pay raise, up to the Southeastern state average. But he had to make some concessions: The first raise came in the 2001–02 school year, and raises were contingent on 5% growth in state revenues—a provision insisted on by Lieutenant Governor Amy Tuck and the state Senate. To avoid antagonizing legislators, Musgrove let pass into law a bill giving them a better retirement system than any other state employees; voters screamed, and Musgrove called a special session to repeal the law. Musgrove also called an August special session to reshape state job development efforts as the Advantage Mississippi Initiative. Musgrove's program to put computers on every desk in every classroom passed and the first were installed in February 2001. He worked to increase the number of children in the CHIP health care program. The state finally settled for $500 million a suit brought in 1975 regarding higher education desegregation; the settlement will pay for extra spending for its three historically black colleges. Musgrove was pleased to announce that Nissan was building a $930 million plant employing 4,000 in Canton, just north of Jackson.

The issue of the Mississippi flag was kindled in May 2000, when the state Supreme Court ruled that the flag, which features the Confederate battle cross in the upper left corner, was not legally the state flag, because the 1894 law authorizing it was not included in the full codification in state laws in 1906. Musgrove appointed a commission headed by former Governor William Winter to design a new flag which he and four other statewide officials endorsed, but the legislators decided to send the issue to voters in a referendum in April 2001. Most blacks and many business leaders support the new design, but there was vocal opposition from many whites, and many feared—or hoped—that a large majority of white voters would choose that in the privacy of the voting booth. The new flag design was defeated by a resounding 65%–35%. In 2001 Musgrove started scheduling One on One with the Governor; citizens could line up in the Capitol and talk to Musgrove for five minutes. In July 2001 he got the legislature to repeal the 5% revenue growth requirement for the teacher pay increase.

The big issue of 2002 was the civil justice system. Mississippi had become a trial lawyers' paradise, with huge verdicts awarded by juries in tiny impoverished counties. Doctors were leaving the state because they could not afford huge increases in malpractice insurance premiums, and national businesses were being subject to potentially confiscatory verdicts they could not feasibly appeal. The U.S. Chamber of Commerce ran full-page ads in Mississippi newspapers calling for change. Musgrove, though supported by and generally friendly to trial lawyers, called a special session for September 2002. But he insisted that the legislature first pass his private prisons proposal and that it must consider medical malpractice before product liability. In October he signed a bill limiting malpractice pain and suffering damages to $500,000, to rise to $1 million by 2017; cases would have to be brought in the county where the damage occurred. In December he signed a bill capping punitive damages in product liability cases at $20 million for the biggest firms and at 4% of a firm's net worth for those worth less than $50 million; retailers were protected against liability for products they sold; restrictions were put on where cases could be brought. In November 2002, as the legislature was conferring, a pro-trial lawyer state supreme court justice was defeated. Nonetheless, Musgrove vetoed a second time a bill opposed by trial lawyers capping damages from fraudulent lending. Meanwhile, there were newspaper reports that investigators were looking into allegations that prominent trial lawyers Paul Minor and Richard Scruggs paid off debts owed by two judges and were looking into the pattern of Musgrove receiving big contributions from trial lawyers just before he made judicial appointments.

Just before election year 2003, Tuck announced she was switching to the Republican party; as leader of the state Senate she had pushed for a congressional redistricting plan favored by Republicans, had not endorsed Al Gore in 2000 and favored more changes in the civil justice system than Musgrove. He said he was not surprised. "She was obviously going to be challenged in the Democratic primary. I believe it was a matter of political survival." Musgrove's own survival was also in doubt. There was widespread speculation that Musgrove was seeking to be named president of Delta State University, rather than stand for reelection in 2003, but he ultimately filed to run. Trial lawyer John Arthur Eaves also filed to run for governor in the Democratic primary, but later withdrew from the race. Musgrove's Republican opponent seemed certain to be Haley Barbour, Republican National Committee chairman from 1993 to 1997 and a successful Washington lobbyist. He had run against Senator John Stennis in 1982 and lost 64%–36%. In 2002 he traveled to most of the state's counties and said, "We're in a deep hole and nobody in state government is talking about it." The civil justice system seemed likely to be one of his issues.

Senior Senator

Thad Cochran (R)

Elected 1978, seat up 2008, 5th term; b. Dec. 7, 1937, Pontotoc; home, Jackson; U. of MS, B.A. 1959, J.D. 1965, Rotary Fellow, Trinity Col., Ireland, 1963–64; Baptist; married (Rose).

Military Career: Navy, 1959–61.

Elected Office: U.S. House of Reps., 1972–78.

Professional Career: Practicing atty., 1965–72.

DC Office: 113 DSOB, 20510, 202-224-5054; Fax: 202-224-9450; Web site: www.senate.gov/~cochran.

State Offices: Gulfport, 228-867-9710; Jackson, 601-965-4459; Oxford, 662-236-1018.

Committees: *Agriculture, Nutrition & Forestry* (Chmn.). *Appropriations:* Agriculture & Rural Development; Defense; Energy & Water Development; Homeland Security (Chmn.); Interior; Labor, HHS & Education. *Rules & Administration.*

Group Ratings

	ADA	ACLU	AFS	LCV	CON	ITIC	NTU	COC	ACU	NTLC	CHC
2002	25	0	13	6	2	88	52	100	90	82	—
2001	15	—	0	13	—	—	77	86	88	—	80

National Journal Ratings

	2001 LIB	—	2001 CONS		2002 LIB	—	2002 CONS
Economic	30%	—	66%		27%	—	71%
Social	22%	—	73%		0%	—	62%
Foreign	0%	—	94%		0%	—	76%

Key Votes of the 107th Congress

1. Approve Bush Tax Cuts	Y	5. Confirm Ashcroft as AG	Y	9. Bar Coop. with Intl. Court	Y
2. Expand Patients' Rights	N	6. Bar Gays in the Boy Scouts	Y	10. Trade Promotion Authority	Y
3. Campaign Finance Reform	Y	7. $ for Hate Crime Prosecution	N	11. Authorize Force in Iraq	Y
4. Permit ANWR Development	Y	8. Overseas Military Abortions	N	12. Homeland Sec. Dept. Union	N

Election Results

2002 general	Thad Cochran (R)	533,269	(85%)	($1,453,688)
	Shawn O'Hara (Ref)	97,226	(15%)	
2002 primary	Thad Cochran (R)	unopposed		
1996 general	Thad Cochran (R)	624,154	(71%)	($1,305,680)
	James W. Hunt (D)	240,647	(27%)	
	Other	13,861	(2%)	

Prior Winning Percentages: 1990 (100%); 1984 (61%); 1978 (45%); 1976 House (76%); 1974 House (70%); 1972 House (48%)

Thad Cochran was elected to the House in 1972 and the Senate in 1978, where he sits at Jefferson Davis's old desk. He grew up in small towns in northern Mississippi and near Jackson, the son of a principal and a teacher, graduated with high grades from Ole Miss (where he was a cheerleader, which was a very big deal) and its law school, served in the Navy, spent a year abroad and practiced law in Jackson. In 1972, as Richard Nixon was sweeping Mississippi, he was elected as a Republican to the House from the Jackson-area district with a plurality against a white Democrat and black independent. After three terms, he was ready to step down, when Senator James Eastland retired; Cochran ran, and once again won with a plurality over a white Democrat and a black independent. In the House and in the Senate he has managed to amass a generally conservative record with little controversy or acrimony. His pleasant personal demeanor, his refusal to engage in racial politics and his Republican Party label, in a state where most whites have been voting Republican for president for three decades, have made him broadly acceptable to voters. His toughest race came in 1984, when he was opposed by popular former Governor William Winter. Winter could make a case for himself but not against Cochran; Cochran outraised him $2.7 million to $738,000, and won 61%–39%.

Cochran is now the chairman of the Agriculture Committee, the number two Republican on the Appropriations Committee and chairman of its Homeland Security Subcommittee. He played an important role in shaping the very different 1996 and 2002 farm bills. In 1996 he supported the move to phase out most crop subsidies over seven years, but insisted on maintaining the cotton marketing loan plan that he largely wrote in 1985. In 2002 he supported the strategy of reviving annual crop payments through the marketing loan program and the target price mechanism, which was abolished in 1996, and of vastly increasing the Conservation Reserve Program to provide money for producers of non-program crops, thus producing more support for the bill. The bill also required country-of-origin labeling for beef, pork, lamb and fish—the last being very important for Mississippi's big catfish farm industry; Cochran has worked hard to get the Senate to prevent a similar Vietnamese fish from being labeled catfish. Also included was money for biomass research, which means among other things finding uses for Mississippi's chicken waste. After the bill passed Cochran argued that it was weaning farmers from subsidies. He said that government in the U.S. provides 21% of farm income, higher admittedly than in Australia and New Zealand (4% and 1%), but much lower than in Europe (45%). In January 2003 Cochran moved swiftly to fashion a $3.1 billion drought relief measure, about half the size of Tom Daschle's, which spread money not just to the drought-stricken Great Plains but to most of the South, with special aid for tobacco and catfish producers; he got it into the omnibus appropriation with a coalition of all Republicans and seven southern Democrats.

Cochran has used his Appropriations seat to legislate on many other issues. He has been the Senate's leading proponent of missile defense. In March 1999, after the implications of the July 1998 Rumsfeld report and the August 1998 North Korean three-stage missile launching sunk in, his missile defense resolution passed by 97–3. He defended missile defense after the test failure in January 2000. "We test because we expect to find problems and try to solve them. This technology is not just within our reach, but is actually in our grasp now." He has supported the construction of a land-based missile defense system on an Aleutian Island in Alaska, and in January 2001 opposed phasing that out in favor of developing sea-based or space-based systems—a stand that may put him in conflict with the Bush administration. "To change direction at this point . . . would unnecessarily delay deployment and cause us to be vulnerable for a long time." He serves on the Defense Appropriations Subcommittee and, working with Mississippi colleague Trent Lott, has worked to fund projects big and small which are based in Mississippi—the DDG-51 Aegis destroyers, two of them to be built at Ingalls Shipyard in Pascagoula, the LHD-8 helicopter carrier, additional AN/APG-73 radars for the F-18 Hornet, Mississippi State University's research center where superfast computers do undersea modeling of Navy projects, the University of Mississippi computer labs receiving information from orbiting satellites. The 2003 military construction appropriations contained $110 million for Mississippi facilities—a new hangar for the Air National Guard's 172d Airlift Wing at Jackson, new housing at Keesler Air Force Base in Biloxi, a new Navy channel at the Naval Station Pascagoula, and a control tower for the Meridian Naval Air Station.

Timely amendments to appropriations that make major policy are a Cochran specialty. To the bill allowing reimportation of prescription medicines in July 2000 Cochran added an amendment to require the FDA to certify lack of risk to public health and safety; HHS Secretary Donna Shalala was unable to so certify, and the law became a dead letter. An October 2000 amendment delaying the imposition of regulations on the treatment of rats, mice and birds in research laboratories prevented a big increase in the cost of medical research. Smaller issues also attract Cochran's attention: He tried to get the government to pay the legal fees of former Congressman and Agriculture Secretary Mike Espy, he wants to make the Congressional Research Service separate from the Library of Congress, he wants to repay federal employees placed through no fault of their own in the wrong retirement system. He authored the Mississippi Wilderness Act, worked for grants for historically black colleges and for vocational training for the disabled, expanded the Grand Bay National Wildlife Refuge on the Gulf Coast and sought to let the entrepreneurial Choctaw Tribe in Neshoba County add newly purchased land to its reservation. He and Lott have worked to fund the Yazoo Pump Project in the Delta. Over the years he has built up a National Writing Program, to instruct teachers how to teach writing; for only $10 million it sends 100,000 teachers to summer programs on 167 campuses. He has fostered programs to improve arts education.

Going into the 108th Congress, Cochran and Trent Lott have combined congressional service of 60 years; both were first elected to the House in 1972. Their relations have not always been harmonious. They clashed over judgeships and vied for White House favor in the 1980s and mixed it up in leadership fights in the 1990s. In 1990 Cochran challenged the more moderate John Chafee of Rhode Island for the chairmanship of the Senate Republican Conference, the number three leadership position, and won 22–21. When Lott challenged Alan Simpson for majority whip, the number two position, Cochran pointedly endorsed Simpson; Lott won anyway, with the support of junior conservatives, and thus leapfrogged Cochran. When Bob Dole announced in May 1996 that he would resign from the Senate in June, Cochran and Lott both entered the race for majority leader; Lott had the contest sewed up, but Cochran stayed in and lost 44–8. In January 2001, Cochran appeared by John McCain's side as a new co-sponsor of the latest version of the McCain-Feingold campaign finance bill; this had been strongly opposed by Lott, and Cochran's vote made the bill apparently filibuster-proof. It gave McCain leverage in his drive to get it early consideration. But Cochran spoke sympathetically about Lott after he relinquished the majority leadership in December 2002.

Cochran holds what seems to be one of the safest seats in the Senate. In 1990 he was unopposed and in 1996 he was re-elected 71%–27% over a Democrat who spent half of his $4,700 on gas for a borrowed car. In 2002 he beat a Reform party candidate 85%–15%. He has a ways to go, however, before he matches John Stennis's record as Mississippi's longest serving senator: that won't happen until March 2020.

Junior Senator

Trent Lott (R)

Elected 1988, seat up 2006, 3d term; b. Oct. 9, 1941, Grenada; home, Pascagoula; U. of MS, B.A. 1963, J.D. 1967; Baptist; married (Tricia).

Elected Office: U.S. House of Reps., 1972–88.

Professional Career: Practicing atty., 1967–68; A.A., U.S. Rep. William Colmer, 1968–72.

DC Office: 487 RSOB, 20510, 202-224-6253; Fax: 202-224-2262; Web site: lott.senate.gov.

State Offices: Greenwood, 662-453-5681; Gulfport, 228-863-1988; Jackson, 601-965-4644; Oxford, 662-234-3774; Pascagoula, 228-762-5400.

Committees: *Commerce, Science & Transportation*: Aviation (Chmn.); Communications; Oceans, Fisheries & Coast Guard; Science, Technology & Space; Surface Transportation & Merchant Marine. *Finance*: Health Care; International Trade; Long-Term Growth & Debt Reduction; Taxation & IRS Oversight. *Intelligence (Select)*. *Rules & Administration* (Chmn.).

Group Ratings

	ADA	ACLU	AFS	LCV	CON	ITIC	NTU	COC	ACU	NTLC	CHC
2002	0	20	0	0	78	88	69	100	100	97	—
2001	0	—	0	0	—	—	81	85	96	—	100

National Journal Ratings

	2001 LIB —	2001 CONS	2002 LIB —	2002 CONS
Economic	0%	94%	6%	90%
Social	28%	72%	0%	62%
Foreign	0%	94%	0%	76%

Key Votes of the 107th Congress

1. Approve Bush Tax Cuts	Y	5. Confirm Ashcroft as AG	Y	9. Bar Coop. with Intl. Court	Y
2. Expand Patients' Rights	*	6. Bar Gays in the Boy Scouts	Y	10. Trade Promotion Authority	Y
3. Campaign Finance Reform	N	7. $ for Hate Crime Prosecution	N	11. Authorize Force in Iraq	Y
4. Permit ANWR Development	Y	8. Overseas Military Abortions	N	12. Homeland Sec. Dept. Union	N

Election Results

2000 general	Trent Lott (R)	654,941	(66%)	($3,663,052)
	Troy Brown (D)	314,090	(32%)	($40,349)
	Other	25,113	(3%)	
2000 primary	Trent Lott (R)	unopposed		
1994 general	Trent Lott (R)	418,333	(69%)	($2,516,189)
	Ken Harper (D)	189,752	(31%)	($345,379)

Prior Winning Percentages: 1988 (54%); 1986 House (82%); 1984 House (85%); 1982 House (79%); 1980 House (74%); 1978 House (100%); 1976 House (68%); 1974 House (73%); 1972 House (55%)

Trent Lott, Senate Majority Leader from June 1996 until June 2001 and Majority Leader-designate in November and December 2002, was first elected to the House in 1972 and to the Senate in 1988. He grew up in Pascagoula, the son of a shipyard worker and a teacher, went to Ole Miss (where he was a cheerleader, like his Mississippi colleague Thad Cochran) and worked his way through law school by running the Ole Miss alumni affairs office, accumulating good contacts along the way. After a year of law practice, he got a job with Democratic Gulf Coast Congressman William Colmer, chairman of the House Rules Committee. When Colmer retired in 1972, Lott ran for the House seat with Colmer's encouragement and endorsement—as a Republican. He was elected with 55% in what was the strongest Nixon district in the country that year. In 1974, Lott was the youngest member of the Judiciary Committee, loyally defending Richard Nixon in the impeachment hearings. In 1980, he was elected Republican Whip, and he ran the Republican National Convention's platform committees in 1980 and 1984. In the House he was an ally of Jack Kemp and Newt Gingrich. He supported Kemp for president in 1988, and his decision to run for the Senate that year opened the way for Gingrich's rise: Lott was succeeded as whip by Dick Cheney; when Cheney became Defense secretary in March 1989, Gingrich was elected whip 87–85.

There is a discernible hard core of beliefs in Lott's career, and yet he is less the hard-edged ideologue that Washington insiders presumed than he is an instinctive deal-maker, not much interested in quixotic gestures, an orderly and well-organized man who is dismayed by the dilatoriness of others. As one colleague put it in 2001, "After pork, Trent's default position is conservative—but he likes to compromise." His beliefs are reminiscent of the mostly unarticulated beliefs of the coalition of Southern conservative Democrats and small-town conservative Northerners which had controlled the House for most of the 35 years prior to when he arrived there: Against increased taxes, hostile to federal regulation of business and local government, for an assertive foreign policy and strong defense, for the traditional rules of moral conduct. On one issue, civil rights, he has moved from Colmer's support for racial segregation to the small town Republicans' backing for equal rights—although doubts were raised about that by comments he made at Strom Thurmond's 100th birthday party in December 2002, comments that cost him the majority leadership. He can be sharp in debate, aggressively partisan and combative, but he is gregarious and personable, striving to keep on good terms with most other members and careful to cultivate those whose support he needs.

In the Senate, as in the House, Lott seemed less interested in committee work than in moving into a leadership position. After the 1992 election, he ran for Conference secretary, the number four leadership post, and won. In 1994, after he had been reelected 69%–31%, he challenged Republican Whip Al Simpson. Majority Leader Bob Dole and most Republican moderates backed Simpson, but Lott won most of the younger conservatives elected in 1992 and 1994 and won 27–26—the first Republican ever elected whip in both houses. In the process he leapfrogged over his Mississippi colleague Thad Cochran, who held the number three leadership position.

As whip for 17 months, Lott was careful not to usurp the prerogatives of Dole, who kept many decisions close to the chest. Then in May 1996 Dole surprised almost everyone when he announced he would resign from the Senate in June. Lott immediately began canvassing for votes for majority leader and found himself far ahead of Cochran, who ran anyway and lost 44–8. During the summer, Lott moved adroitly, pushing for a vote on welfare reform, disposing of the minimum wage issue, pushing for the compromise health care bill and the Safe Drinking Water Act. He gave Senate Republicans a solid record to run on—but left Dole with fewer issues on which to attack Clinton. He established a smooth working relationship with Democratic Leader Tom Daschle.

After Dole lost and Gingrich faced ethics charges that threatened to topple him, Lott was suddenly the most visible Republican leader in Congress. At times he angered colleagues. His insistence on investigating the Louisiana Senate race results infuriated Democrats. Conservatives were angry when he worked with the Clinton administration, and against Foreign Relations Chairman Jesse Helms, to secure ratification of the Chemical Weapons Treaty in April 1997.

Then came impeachment, which tested both his influence among Republican senators and his close working relationship with Tom Daschle. In December 1998 after the House voted, Lott encouraged the Gorton-Lieberman plan to allow four days of argument in the impeachment trial, to be followed by a vote on whether the charges, if true, would justify impeachment; if that fell short of the two-thirds required for removal, as everyone assumed it would, the trial would be adjourned. House Judiciary Chairman Henry Hyde, the leader of the House managers, wrote an angry letter and Senate conservatives howled; Lott retreated. Democrats remained furious about the prospect of a lengthy, salacious trial, and raised the specter of partisanship which most senators, after the House debate and in line with Senate tradition, wanted to avoid. On January 7, Lott tagged along with Daschle for a scheduled press conference, and they agreed to an all-senators closed caucus the next day. In that extraordinary meeting, senators agreed to a suggestion by Phil Gramm and Edward Kennedy to postpone the issue of calling witnesses and go on with the trial. There was giddy delight at this demonstration of senatorial comity, though the House managers were furious and the Clinton defense team still wary. The trial proceeded in orderly fashion; the verdict went as expected, mostly along partisan lines, with Lott and most Republicans preventing a vote on censure until after the verdict, at which point Democrats weren't much interested.

In 1999 and 2000, Lott tried to bar non-germane amendments on appropriations bills, arguing that Democrats were using them to hurt Republicans in elections and that it was better procedure to have "clean votes" on issues. He took to filing cloture petitions when he brought bills to the floor and filed lots of amendments himself, to preclude others. Democrats were immensely irritated, and in spring 2000 relations between Lott and Daschle turned very sour; Daschle said Lott was resorting to "a Senate version of dictatorship that I think is unacceptable." In June 2000 Nebraska's Chuck Hagel said there could be changes in the leadership if Republicans lost seats in November; Hagel had contemplated running against Lott after the November 1998 elections, and ran unsuccessfully against campaign chairman Mitch McConnell instead. In July 2000 Lott steered estate tax repeal through, but at the cost of allowing votes on many Democratic amendments. In fall 2000 Lott followed a "no veto" strategy and tried to negotiate with the Clinton administration on appropriations; House Republican Whip Tom DeLay, who wanted to set clear conservative markers and get members out of town, opposed this. The result was relatively high spending, and a delay in many appropriations until after the November elections and, as seemed sensible, after the Florida recounts as well.

By late 2000, almost everyone seemed angry with Lott for one reason or another. "I don't feel unappreciated, and I don't feel exceedingly appreciated," he said. But no one—not even Majority Whip Don Nickles, a frequent critic—moved to run against him, though Lott ally Larry Craig was challenged for his leadership position and kept it by only a 26–24 vote. Lott had lost some of his closest confidants in the Senate—Connie Mack retired, Paul Coverdell died in July 2000 and Slade Gorton, after a long recount, was defeated for re-election. That left the Senate divided 50–50. Democrats demanded equal numbers of members on each committee; some Republican conservatives strongly opposed that, though some committee chairmen offered equal membership. On January 5, 2001, after negotiations with Daschle, Lott surprised many by agreeing to equal membership. There was a strong theoretical argument for that—committee membership should reflect the balance on the floor—but even stronger practical arguments; plus not insisting on every ounce of partisan advantage was probably prudent. Lott wanted to make sure that no Democratic senator would challenge the Florida electoral votes on January 6, and thereby trigger debate on that issue. Lott acceded to John McCain's demand for two weeks of debate on campaign finance regulation in March, but in May had still not sent the bill over to the House; McCain got a 61–36 vote for a resolution calling on him to do so, and he did. In early May he abruptly fired Senate Parliamentarian Robert Dove after Dove disagreed with him on whether a provision of the budget resolution would trigger a 60-vote point of order. Yet even as Lott was moving aggressively, there was always the possibility that control could shift to the Democrats. Most observers pointed to 98-year-old Thurmond as one senator who might leave office, but there were 45 senators with governors of a different party, 26 Democrats and 19 Republicans, whose departure could change party control. While there was some hope that Georgia's Zell Miller—much paraded about as a Democratic backer of Bush's tax cut—might cross the aisle and strengthen this fragile majority, it was not much suspected until May 2001 that James Jeffords would defect and unravel it. The visibly angry Lott called it a "coup of one" and said, "The decision of one man has—however else you describe it—trumped the will of the American people."

Even as Minority Leader, Lott had sharp elbows. In July 2001 he decried "an anti-Mexican, anti-Hispanic, anti-NAFTA attitude among Democrats" when they sought to block Mexican trucks from entering the country. He asked for review of the American Medical Association's contract to set Medicare and Medicaid reimbursement rates after the AMA backed the Democrats' HMO regulation bill. In 2002, after the Senate Judiciary Committee voted down his nominee Charles Pickering for a federal appeals court judgeship, he blocked a $1.5 million request from the committee for oversight funds, blocked the nomination of a Daschle staffer to the FCC, derailed an energy bill amendment by Dianne Feinstein and blocked continuation of a Judiciary meeting. When it became clear that Senate Democrats would pass no budget resolution, he said, "The Senate is becoming dysfunctional, the Daschle Democrat dysfunctional process." In the fall things seemed to be going very much his way. In October 2002 Don Nickles announced he would not challenge Lott for the leadership, even though term limits would force him to leave his position as Whip. On election night, Lott, Hastert and Senate and House Republican campaign chairmen Bill Frist and Tom Davis and their wives dined at the White House with George W. and Laura Bush, and exulted as the returns came in. The president's party for the first time in history went from a minority to a majority in the Senate in an off-year election. Lott would be majority leader again.

Then came Thurmond's 100th birthday party. Speaking from notes Lott said, "I want to say this about my state. When Strom Thurmond ran for president, we voted for him. We're proud of it. And if the rest of the country had followed our lead, we wouldn't have had all these problems over the years, either." There were audible gasps and silence, but Lott went on. Major media did not mention the comment over the next 24 hours. Asked about it, Lott's spokesman the next day said, "Senator Lott's remarks were intended to pay tribute to a remarkable man who led a remarkable life. To read anything more into these comments is wrong." But bloggers—people who write weblogs, commenting frequently on various topics—noticed. On December 6, the liberal blogger Joshua Marshall called Lott's comments "just another example of the hubris now reigning among Capitol Hill Republicans," and they were noted in abcnews.com's *The Note*. On December 7, Thomas Edsall wrote a short story about the comments in *The Washington Post*. By Monday, December 9, conservative bloggers were writing about Lott's comments, and not favorably. Former Bush White House speechwriter David Frum in nationalreview.com wrote, "I cannot help thinking that this story is not over—that Republicans will hear Lott's words quoted at them again and again in the months to come." *National Review's* Jonah Goldberg wrote in nationalreview.com's The Corner, "On the facts, Lott's comments were dumb. Morally, they were indefensible."

It was not surprising that liberals like Al Gore and Jesse Jackson called on Lott to resign the majority leadership, but it was noteworthy that demands for his resignation resounded over the conservative weblogs. On December 9 Lott, on vacation in Key West, Florida, three hours' drive from the nearest television studio, issued a statement saying, "A poor choice of words conveyed to some the impression that I embraced the discarded policies of the past. Nothing could be further from the truth, and I apologize to anyone who was offended by my statement." Tom Daschle downplayed the remarks and Lott's sometime adversaries—Jeffords and former Democratic Senator Paul Simon—came forward to testify that he was not a racist. But others poking through old clippings found similar comments. Campaigning with Thurmond for Ronald Reagan in November 1980 Lott said, "You know, if we had elected this man 30 years ago, we wouldn't be in the mess we are today." Lott had voted against the Martin Luther King holiday, and against extension of the Voting Rights Act; he had opposed denial of tax-exempt status for Bob Jones University despite its policy of banning interracial dating. In the early 1960s, former CNN President Tom Johnson noted, Lott had opposed integration of his Sigma Nu fraternity (Johnson, to his embarrassment, had opposed it too). On Thursday, December 12, George W. Bush spoke to an inner city group in Philadelphia. "Any suggestion that the segregated past was acceptable or positive is offensive, and it is wrong. Recent comments by Senator Lott do not reflect the spirit of this country. He has apologized, and rightly so. Every day our nation was segregated was a day that America was unfaithful to our founding ideals."

On December 13 Lott held a press conference in Pascagoula and announced that he would appear on Black Entertainment Television the next week. "I apologize for opening old wounds and hurting many Americans who feel so deeply in this area. I take full responsibility for my remarks. . . . I only hope people will find it in their heart to forgive me for that grievous mistake on that occasion." On December 15 a "senior administration official" was quoted in *The Washington Post* as saying, "He didn't do what he needed to do. People were looking for absolute and total contrition, and I don't think they saw that." The same day, on ABC News's *This Week*, George Stephanopoulos read a statement from Don Nickles questioning whether Lott could continue to serve as majority leader. Lott's hearty endorsement of affirmative action on BET December 16 dismayed some conservatives who opposed racial quotas and preferences precisely because they believe they violate the civil rights laws which Lott's old boss William Colmer strongly opposed. Lott had been elected majority leader at a November 14 Republican Conference meeting, and that could not be reconsidered until the next scheduled meeting January 6, unless five members called for a special meeting. Nickles was one such vote, and it quickly became clear that there would be others. On December 19 Bill Frist stepped forward and said he would accept the job of majority leader if his colleagues voted for him; Mitch McConnell recommended to Lott that he step down immediately. On the same day, John Warner and George Allen publicly supported Frist as Lott's replacement. On the morning of December 20 Lott stepped down. By the end of the day, Frist had the votes to become majority leader, and was elected by a Conference meeting held by conference call. He said later that he had no "vengeance in his heart" but noted a little tartly, "You can't just lay this at the door of the Democrats—some of the Republicans didn't do me any good either. I plan to look to the future, to be very sensitive to everything I say." In January 2003 Lott became chairman of the Senate Rules Committee, which has a limited jurisdiction but affords some prominence; if Republicans retain their majority, he will preside over the Inaugural ceremonies on January 20, 2005.

Lott gave up a safe House seat to run for the Senate in 1988, and was elected over Democratic Congressman Wayne Dowdy. He won by a 61%–39% margin in the Jackson area, the Gulf Coast and other counties where turnout had increased 10% since 1980; in the rest of the state, Dowdy won only 51%–49%, giving Lott a 54%–46% win overall. In 1994 and 2000 Lott did not have serious competition and won easily, 69%–31% and 66%–32%.

FIRST DISTRICT

Rep. Roger Wicker (R)

Elected 1994, 5th term; b. July 5, 1951, Pontotoc; home, Tupelo; U. of MS, B.A. 1973, J.D. 1975; Baptist; married (Gayle).

Military Career: Air Force, 1976–80; Air Force Reserves, 1980–present.

Elected Office: Tupelo City Judge Pro Tem, 1986–87; MS Senate, 1987–94.

Professional Career: Staff, U.S. House Rules Cmte., 1980–82; Practicing atty., 1982–94; Lee Cnty. Public Defender, 1984–87.

DC Office: 2455 RHOB 20515, 202-225-4306; Fax: 202-225-3549; Web site: www.house.gov/wicker.

District Offices: Columbus, 662-327-0748; Grenada, 662-294-1321; Southaven, 662-342-3942; Tupelo, 662-844-5437.

Committees: *Appropriations* (15th of 36 R): Defense; Foreign Operations & Export Financing (Vice Chmn.); Labor, HHS & Education. *Budget* (13th of 24 R).

Group Ratings

	ADA	ACLU	AFS	LCV	CON	ITIC	NTU	COC	ACU	NTLC	CHC
2002	0	7	0	0	25	100	53	90	100	89	100
2001	0	—	0	0	—	—	61	96	96	—	—

National Journal Ratings

	2001 LIB	—	2001 CONS		2002 LIB	—	2002 CONS
Economic	15%	—	82%		9%	—	87%
Social	0%	—	81%		0%	—	75%
Foreign	4%	—	87%		0%	—	85%

Key Votes of the 107th Congress

1. Approve Bush Tax Cuts	Y	5. Faith-Based Charities	Y	9. Trade Promotion Authority	Y
2. Limit Patients' Bill of Rights	Y	6. Bar Gays in the Boy Scouts	Y	10. Bar Funds for Intl. Court	Y
3. Campaign Finance Reform	N	7. Ban Partial-Birth Abortion	Y	11. Authorize Force in Iraq	Y
4. Ban ANWR Development	N	8. Arm Commercial Pilots	Y	12. Deny Home. Sec. Dept. Union	Y

Election Results

2002 general	Roger Wicker (R)	95,404	(71%)	($395,163)
	Rex Weathers (D)	32,318	(24%)	
	Other	5,845	(5%)	
2002 primary	Roger Wicker (R)	unopposed		
2000 general	Roger Wicker (R)	145,967	(70%)	($1,283,515)
	Joey Grist (D)	59,763	(29%)	
	Other	3,310	(2%)	

Prior Winning Percentages: 1998 (67%); 1996 (68%); 1994 (63%)

The People		**Race/Ethnic Origin**	**Ancestry**	
Area size:	11,647 sq. mi.	71.3% White	USA: 16.6%	Irish: 7.1%
Urban population:	38.5%	26.2% Black	English: 6.1%	
Rural population:	61.5%	0.4% Asian	**2000 Presidential Vote**	
Pop. 2000:	711,160	0.2% Native Am.	Bush (R)	146,197 (59%)
Median income:	$32,535	0.0% Hawaiian	Gore (D)	98,350 (40%)
Poverty status:	16.4%	0.5% Two + races	Other	3,690 (1%)
Military veterans:	11.4%	0.0% Other	**Cook Partisan Voting Index:** R +10	
		1.4% Hispanic Origin		

Occupation　　Blue collar: 38.6%　　White collar: 48.5%　　Gray collar: 12.9%

The university town of Oxford, the "Jefferson" of William Faulkner's fictional Yoknapatawpha County, sits on a divide between the hill country of Mississippi and the flat farmlands of the Mississippi Delta. It is the home of the Center for the Study of Southern Culture and of Ole Miss, the University of Mississippi, which saw violence when James Meredith integrated the school in 1962; Senator Thad Cochran was at the law school then and Senator Trent Lott a senior in college. To the west is the Delta, with a large black majority, and also DeSoto County, just south of Memphis, Tennessee, one of Mississippi's fastest-growing and most affluent counties. East of Oxford is the hill country, which stretches up to where the Tennessee River nicks the northeast corner of Tishomingo County. The Tennessee Valley Authority brought electricity here, the Tennessee-Tombigbee Waterway provided construction jobs for years and a new shipping canal when it was completed in 1985. This was traditional farming country, now more engaged in small manufacturing. The biggest town here is Tupelo, a stronghold of private enterprise and traditional values. It is home to an upholstered furniture industry that is the largest manufacturing sector in the state and Donald Wildmon's American Family Association. Elvis Presley was born in Tupelo in 1935, in a two-room house that is open to visitors, as is the Elvis Presley Museum with a modest collection of memorabilia.

The 1st Congressional District includes most of the hill country and DeSoto County. This is the descendant of the district represented by Jamie Whitten, the longest-serving House member in history, from his special election victory in November 1941 until January 1995: 53 years and two months. Historically this was hell-of-a-fellow Democratic territory, almost unanimously; in an April 2001 referendum it voted overwhelmingly to keep the 1894 state flag with the Confederate battle cross. It also voted solidly for Democratic Governor Ronnie Musgrove in 1999. In national politics it is solidly Republican, 59% for George W. Bush in 2000.

The congressman from the 1st District is Roger Wicker, a Republican elected in 1994. He grew up in Pontotoc, 20 miles from Tupelo, the son of a state senator and circuit judge, attended public schools and was a House page in 1967: The first of the 1994 freshmen to get on the floor of the House. Wicker went to college and law school at Ole Miss, where he was student body president, served in the Air Force, and in 1980 became a staffer to Trent Lott on the House Rules Committee. In 1987, at 36, he was the first Republican elected to the state Senate from northern

Mississippi since Reconstruction; he chaired the Elections, and Public Health and Welfare committees, where he sponsored a 24-hour waiting period for abortions, helped write the state's welfare reform law, and led the fight for student-led prayer in school. In 1994, when Whitten retired, Wicker was one of six Republicans and three Democrats to run for the seat. Wicker, carrying his home base around Tupelo, led in the first primary 27%–19% over Grant Fox, former aide to Cochran. In the runoff, Wicker campaigned as a conservative, but Fox, just 27, hit him hard for voting to override Governor Fordice's sales tax increase veto. Wicker won by 53%–47%. The Democratic nominee state Representative Bill Wheeler, had defeated longtime House Speaker Tim Ford in the primary with support from blacks, unions and teachers—an advantage in the primary but not the general. The result wasn't even close: A district held for 53 years by a Democratic titan voted 63%–37% for the Republican.

In the House, Wicker was elected president of the 73-member freshman class, one of the largest in the 20th century, and has compiled a solidly conservative voting record. He also won Whitten's old seat on the Appropriations Committee. Wicker sponsored a "litigation fairness" proposal to specify the rules for government-sponsored lawsuits. He became part of "The Group," an informal network of Speaker Dennis Hastert's close legislative advisers. Yet despite his New South style, in some ways Wicker has acted like an old-style Democrat. He worked on local projects and backed measures which helped local industries. He fought to preserve the Appalachian Regional Commission and the Economic Development Administration to promote local job creation, to support funding of the Natchez Trace Parkway (started in the 1930s, but never completed), and for Yalobusha River flood control. After winning approval of a study of flame-retardant chemicals that blocked further regulation of upholstered furniture companies by the Consumer Product Safety Commission, Wicker claimed complete vindication in 2000 when scientists for the National Research Council found little or no health risk from the chemicals. On health care, he has vigorously advocated heart-disease prevention strategies; Mississippi has the nation's highest death rate from cardiovascular disease. He has sought increased spending for research on cancer survivors and has worked on a global campaign to eradicate polio. In the old style, Wicker has used that focus to bring research dollars to Mississippi universities.

Wicker has consistently been re-elected by better than 2–1 margins. Although he has a far different voting record from his predecessor's, Wicker has shown that the nation's consensus-minded mood has reached even the rebel hills of northern Mississippi. The federal court redistricting maintained the 1st as a solidly Republican district in 2002; Wicker was reelected by a 71%–24% margin.

SECOND DISTRICT

Rep. Bennie Thompson (D)

Elected April 1993, 5th term; b. Jan. 28, 1948, Bolton; home, Bolton; Tougaloo Col., B.A. 1968, Jackson St. U., M.S. 1972; Methodist; married (London).

Elected Office: Bolton Bd. of Aldermen, 1969–73; Bolton Mayor, 1973–79; Hinds Cnty. Supervisor, 1980–93.

DC Office: 2432 RHOB 20515, 202-225-5876; Fax: 202-225-5898; Web site: www.house.gov/thompson.

District Offices: Bolton, 601-866-9003; Greenville, 662-335-9003; Greenwood, 662-455-9003; Marks, 662-326-9003; Mound Bayou, 662-741-9003.

Committees: *Agriculture* (5th of 24 D): General Farm Commodities & Risk Management; Specialty Crops & Foreign Agriculture Programs. *Select Committee on Homeland Security* (2d of 23 D): Emergency Preparedness & Response (RMM); Rules.

Group Ratings

	ADA	ACLU	AFS	LCV	CON	ITIC	NTU	COC	ACU	NTLC	CHC
2002	90	93	100	63	54	38	18	55	8	8	17
2001	85	—	100	64	—	—	16	48	12	—	—

National Journal Ratings

	2001 LIB —	2001 CONS		2002 LIB —	2002 CONS
Economic	72% —	27%		70% —	29%
Social	72% —	27%		74% —	19%
Foreign	81% —	18%		82% —	17%

Key Votes of the 107th Congress

1. Approve Bush Tax Cuts	N	5. Faith-Based Charities	N	9. Trade Promotion Authority	N
2. Limit Patients' Bill of Rights	N	6. Bar Gays in the Boy Scouts	N	10. Bar Funds for Intl. Court	N
3. Campaign Finance Reform	N	7. Ban Partial-Birth Abortion	N	11. Authorize Force in Iraq	N
4. Ban ANWR Development	N	8. Arm Commercial Pilots	Y	12. Deny Home. Sec. Dept. Union	N

Election Results

2002 general	Bennie Thompson (D)	89,913	(55%)	($647,649)
	Clinton LeSueur (R)	69,711	(43%)	($100,342)
	Other	3,426	(2%)	
2002 primary	Bennie Thompson (D)	9,810	(72%)	
	George Irvin (D)	3,835	(28%)	
2000 general	Bennie Thompson (D)	112,777	(65%)	($409,852)
	Hardy Caraway (R)	54,090	(31%)	
	Other	6,440	(4%)	

Prior Winning Percentages: 1998 (71%); 1996 (60%); 1994 (54%); 1993 (55%)

The People		Race/Ethnic Origin	Ancestry	
Area size:	13,937 sq. mi.	34.5% White	USA: 6.8%	Irish: 3.7%
Urban population:	62.8%	63.2% Black	English: 3.3%	
Rural population:	37.2%	0.4% Asian	**2000 Presidential Vote**	
Pop. 2000:	711,164	0.2% Native Am.	Gore (D) 134,513	(57%)
Median income:	$26,894	0.0% Hawaiian	Bush (R) 97,979	(41%)
Poverty status:	27.3%	0.5% Two + races	Other 4,464	(2%)
Military veterans:	10.0%	0.0% Other	**Cook Partisan Voting Index:** D + 8	
		1.2% Hispanic Origin		

Occupation	Blue collar: 28.8%	White collar: 52.2%	Gray collar: 19.0%

"The Mississippi Delta," wrote Delta native David Cohn, "begins in the lobby of the Peabody Hotel in Memphis and ends on Catfish Row in Vicksburg." For centuries, the flooding Mississippi and Yazoo Rivers left their sediments here, producing a fertile dark soil. Ironically, what may well be America's richest agricultural land has been home for more than a century to many of its poorest people. The Delta, criss-crossed by rivers and famously disease-ridden, wasn't much settled until after the Civil War; the tradition here is not of paternal masters and gracious mansions, but of sharp, profit-seeking operators who used late 19th century technology to drain the land, line the river with levees and build railroads on tracks above the rise of the river. Black sharecroppers and field hands worked here in conditions almost of bondage. From this episode of industrial farming came both great misery and great art: Clarksdale in Coahoma County was the home of W.C. Handy and Muddy Waters, the real birthplace of blues music; Greenville on the Mississippi has produced writers of the caliber of Walker Percy and Shelby Foote; Yazoo City produced Willie Morris. Now Vicksburg's antebellum mansions, battlefield monuments and riverboat gambling bring in 1.5 million tourists annually from around the country.

Twentieth century technology changed life in the Delta. The mechanical cotton-picking machine, invented in 1944, came along just as northern factories were seeking low-wage workers; the great exodus to Chicago and Memphis began, and the Delta's population has been declining ever since. Income levels remain very low, poverty is over 50% in some areas and infant mortality is at Third World levels; the crime and drugs of urban Chicago have been brought back by Delta migrants returning home. Yet, there are signs of hope: Soybeans have become a big dollar crop here, although there is more acreage still in cotton; poultry farms have become a major enterprise, and the Delta produces 62% of the nation's catfish. Riverboat gambling was approved in 1992 in Tunica County, by some measures the nation's poorest county, which had been perhaps best known for its Sugar Ditch, the open sewer in the town's black section. In 2002, 12 million people entered Tunica's 9 casinos (which have more square footage than Atlantic City's), and runways at the regional airport have been extended to accommodate Boeing 747s bearing even more tourists. The casinos have led to a local increase in per capita income and a decrease in welfare rolls, but there is still a gulf between the races, culturally and economically, and the Delta has been slow to develop the self-propelling market economy that has brought growth to most of the nation. During his 1999 tour to focus on the nation's poorest communities, Bill Clinton stopped in Clarksdale to listen to local stories of deprivation. At the edge of the Delta there are other economic stories. In early 2003 Nissan was preparing to open a $930 million, 4,000-job factory in Canton, historically a heavily black area but just north of fast-growing affluent suburbs of Jackson. A few miles southwest in Clinton, just west of Jackson, is the former headquarters of WorldCom, which filed the largest bankruptcy in U.S. history in July 2002 and laid off hundreds of local employees.

The 2d Congressional District includes the entire Delta, indeed the whole riverfront of the Mississippi from Tunica almost to Natchez. It includes all of Jackson and surrounding Hinds County except for the affluent Bellehaven neighborhood of Jackson. This is Mississippi's one black-majority district, first created as such in 1984, with boundaries expanded for 2002 to raise the district's population to the one-person-one-vote standard. The 2d includes a few counties in the east that are majority-white and vote Republican, but the political tone of the district is set by the black neighborhoods in Jackson and the black counties of the Delta. Before the Voting Rights Act of 1965, these were run politically by segregationists like Senator James Eastland, Judiciary Committee chairman from 1955 to 1979, and proud Delta landowner. Even after blacks won the right to vote, their registration was low and habits of deference in some places prevailed. In 1986, the district elected its first black congressman since Reconstruction, Mike Espy, whose grandfather and father built a chain of funeral homes and were among the biggest landowners in the state.

The congressman from the 2d District is Bennie Thompson, who grew up in Bolton, in Hinds County outside Jackson, graduated from Tougaloo College and Jackson State. He was elected alderman in Bolton in 1969, at 21, and mayor four years later; he was the first person in Mississippi to get a street named after Martin Luther King Jr. and he got the first fire engine for Bolton. In 1980 he became a Hinds County supervisor. A life-long grass-roots activist and labor organizer, he successfully worked to encourage other blacks to run for office. After Espy resigned in 1993 to become Secretary of Agriculture, Thompson ran for the House, and in a March 1993 all-party primary, he ran ahead of Henry Espy, Mike Espy's brother and mayor of Clarksdale by a 28% to 20% margin. But Republican Hayes Dent, a 31-year-old aide to Governor Kirk Fordice, had 34%. Voting in the runoff was mostly along racial lines, and Thompson won 55%–45%, with most of his margin coming from Hinds County.

Unlike Espy, Thompson made no particular attempt to win white votes and has a solidly liberal voting record, making almost as few concessions across the racial divide as had Eastland in his day. He was a lead plaintiff in the suit against the state in a 26-year-old case to increase funding for black colleges, settled in 2001. In time, he moderated his votes and reached out to the white community, including a meeting with the Clarksdale area Chamber of Commerce and with some large farmers. "Delta planters have gradually warmed up to Thompson, with a few even hosting political fund-raisers on his behalf," the *Clarksdale Press-Register* reported.

Thompson chaired the Congressional Black Caucus's Tobacco Working Group, which worked to make sure minority groups got a share of public health spending in the tobacco settlement. He sponsored the law to award the Congressional Gold Medal to the nine students who integrated Little Rock's Central High School. In late 2000 he ran for chairman of the Black Caucus and pledged to work more closely with business interests, but he lost by one vote to Eddie Bernice Johnson. He complained that the Shays-Meehan campaign finance regulation bill hurt black politicians. He opposed the nomination of Judge Charles Pickering to the federal appeals court despite Pickering's support from many blacks in his home area.

In 2002 Thompson was reelected by a 55%–43% margin; his challenger Clinton LeSueur, a former legislative aide to the District of Columbia city council, claimed that this was unimpressive given the large black majority in the district and Thompson's fundraising advantage, and said he would run again in 2004.

THIRD DISTRICT

Rep. Chip Pickering (R)

Elected 1996, 4th term; b. Aug. 10, 1963, Laurel; home, Hebron; MS Col., 1981–82, U. of MS, B.A. 1986, Baylor U., M.B.A. 1988; Baptist; married (Leisha).

Professional Career: Baptist missionary, Budapest, Hungary, 1986–87; Spec. Asst. to the Admin. & Asst. Coord., East European & Soviet Secretariat, U.S. Dept. of Agriculture, 1989–90; Legis. Aide, U.S. Sen. Trent Lott, 1990–94.

DC Office: 229 CHOB 20515, 202-225-5031; Fax: 202-225-5797; Web site: www.house.gov/pickering.

District Offices: Meridian, 601-693-6681; Pearl, 601-932-2410.

Committees: *Agriculture* (12th of 27 R): General Farm Commodities & Risk Management; Livestock & Horticulture. *Energy & Commerce* (17th of 31 R): Energy & Air Quality; Health; Telecommunications & The Internet.

Group Ratings

	ADA	ACLU	AFS	LCV	CON	ITIC	NTU	COC	ACU	NTLC	CHC
2002	0	13	0	0	25	88	55	90	100	89	100
2001	5	—	0	0	—	—	60	91	96	—	—

National Journal Ratings

	2001 LIB —	2001 CONS	2002 LIB —	2002 CONS
Economic	22%	74%	21%	73%
Social	0%	81%	25%	71%
Foreign	33%	60%	0%	85%

Key Votes of the 107th Congress

1. Approve Bush Tax Cuts Y	5. Faith-Based Charities Y	9. Trade Promotion Authority Y
2. Limit Patients' Bill of Rights Y	6. Bar Gays in the Boy Scouts Y	10. Bar Funds for Intl. Court Y
3. Campaign Finance Reform N	7. Ban Partial-Birth Abortion Y	11. Authorize Force in Iraq Y
4. Ban ANWR Development N	8. Arm Commercial Pilots Y	12. Deny Home. Sec. Dept. Union Y

Election Results

2002 general	Chip Pickering (R)	139,329	(64%)	($3,071,410)
	Ronnie Shows (D)	76,184	(35%)	($1,439,921)
	Other	3,638	(2%)	
2002 primary	Chip Pickering (R)	unopposed		
2000 general	Chip Pickering (R)	153,899	(73%)	($519,957)
	William Thrash (D)	54,151	(26%)	($1,349)
	Other	2,313	(1%)	

Prior Winning Percentages: 1998 (85%); 1996 (61%)

The People		Race/Ethnic Origin	Ancestry	
Area size:	13,310 sq. mi.	63.7% White	USA: 13.5%	Irish: 6.1%
Urban population:	40.3%	33.1% Black	English: 6.0%	
Rural population:	59.7%	0.6% Asian	**2000 Presidential Vote**	
Pop. 2000:	711,115	0.9% Native Am.	Bush (R)...............173,434	(64%)
Median income:	$31,907	0.0% Hawaiian	Gore (D)...............93,454	(35%)
Poverty status:	19.2%	0.5% Two+ races	Other...................2,752	(1%)
Military veterans:	11.5%	0.0% Other	**Cook Partisan Voting Index:** R +15	
		1.2% Hispanic Origin		

Occupation	Blue collar: 28.9%	White collar: 56.7%	Gray collar: 14.5%

Mississippi, old and new: The old Mississippi is the Neshoba County fair, held every August since 1892 in the town of Philadelphia. This is traditionally the place where Mississippi politicians announce their candidacies, with the crowds watching to take their measure. When Ronald Reagan came here in 1980 and Michael Dukakis in 1988, neither mentioned what Philadelphia and Neshoba County are best known for in history, nor is there any memorial except engraved stones at two black churches: It was here during the "Freedom Summer" of 1964 that three civil rights workers, two white and one black, were murdered for the crime of urging black American citizens to register and vote. The new Mississippi is some 80 miles away, in Rankin and Madison County east and north of Jackson, where subdivisions and shopping centers are sprouting up in the countryside, as well as the big new Nissan plant in Canton.

The 3d Congressional District includes the Rankin and south Madison County suburbs of Jackson, plus the affluent neighborhoods of northeast Jackson in Hinds County. It stretches north to Starkville, home of Mississippi State University, and south almost to Laurel. In the southwest it reaches over to include Natchez, where antebellum mansions sits on the bluffs overlooking the Mississippi River. In the middle are Neshoba County and Meridian, a small city that may go down in history as the site of departures of two White House chiefs of staff: Here Richard Nixon informed Bob Haldeman that he was out in April 1973 and here John Sununu penned his letter of resignation to George H. W. Bush in December 1991. The political tradition here was Southern Democratic, but the area's recent preference has been strongly Republican: Mississippi, old and new. The district lines were drawn by a federal court in February 2002 and combined most of the old 3d District represented by Republican Chip Pickering and most of the old 4th District represented by Democrat Ronnie Shows. Democratic leaders wanted to put much of Rankin County in with northeast Mississippi in a new 1st District whose funnel-like shape inspired Republicans to call it the "tornado district;" they would have created a new 3d District that was 38% black. Such a plan was adopted by a Hinds County Chancery Court judge, but the three-judge federal court took over the case and created a district which is instead 33% black. That makes a lot of difference in Mississippi, where large majorities of blacks vote Democratic and large majorities of whites vote Republican.

The congressman from the 3d District is Chip Pickering, a Republican elected in 1996. He grew up in Laurel where he worked on the family dairy and catfish farm and attended public schools. His father, Judge Charles Pickering, was defeated for reelection as prosecutor in the 1968 after testifying against a Ku Klux Klan leader—something that took great courage in those days. He later was a state senator and state Republican chairman, and was nominated by George H. W. Bush to be a federal district judge and then confirmed without controversy by the Democratic-controlled Senate. When George W. Bush nominated him to be a federal appeals court judge, the Senate Judiciary Committee voted him down on party lines in March 2002; Chip Pickering said that Senator John Edwards had "distorted the facts." In January 2003, Charles Pickering was nominated again.

Chip Pickering was more interested in football than politics at college; after that, he spent 17 months as a Southern Baptist missionary in then-Communist Hungary. He was at the Agriculture Department in the administration of Bush the elder and worked on Senator Trent Lott's staff on telecommunications issues. In 1995, Congressman Sonny Montgomery, a Democrat who mostly voted with Republicans, announced that he would retire in 1996 after 30 years in the

House. Chip Pickering returned to Mississippi and ran for the seat. Against nine Republicans and three Democrats, Pickering made use of his party ties: His father's executive director at the state party had been Haley Barbour, Republican National Committee chairman from 1993 to 1997 (and in 2003, Republican candidate for Mississippi governor). In the primary Pickering ran first in 13 of 19 counties, and won 27% of the vote; former state Representative Bill Crawford, with 24%, was second. Pickering won the runoff 56%–44% with big margins in the Jackson suburbs. Against 29-year-old John Arthur Eaves Jr., son of a well-known lawyer and Democratic politician, Pickering spent more than $1 million in the general, which was twice what Eaves spent, and won 61%–36%.

In the House, Pickering has a solidly conservative voting record; his Capitol Hill contacts led to assignment on the Energy and Commerce Committee. He filed a bill limiting the FCC's ability to review telecommunications mergers. As co-chairman of the Congressional Wireless Caucus, he sought increased focus on the industry's concerns: Competition, public safety, privacy and the spectrum. Although an opponent of the Tauzin-Dingell bill to enable the regional Bells to offer broadband service, he backed off when House passage became certain.

Redistricting placed Pickering in the same district with two-term Democrat Ronnie Shows in 2002, on favorable terms. Shows had grown up in Jones County, near Laurel; as he noted, "In Jones County you're either a kin to a Shows or a Pickering. Heck, his district director is a Shows, so we have a lot of family history and a lot of mutual respect." His countrified ways were a political asset in the old 4th District, which was made up of small counties plus heavily black parts of Jackson and Hinds County. Democratic strategists hoped Shows could run as a populist, denouncing the executives of WorldCom, the bankrupt telecommunications giant that was headquartered just outside Jackson. He called for trade protections, attacked Republicans on Social Security, and distanced himself from national Democrats on gun control and abortion. But the new 3d District, though 33% black, had voted 64% for George W. Bush in 2000; 59% of its voters had been represented by Pickering and just 41% by Shows; parts of the Jackson area in the district—in Rankin, Madison and Hinds counties—were heavily white and affluent. Shows understood that the federal court's lines worked against him. "They don't want a fair fight. It's not fair the way they've taken this district. It's not right. It's been a setup deal since day one," was his reaction. Pickering raised twice as much money and ran the more skillful campaign. He voiced sympathy for WorldCom workers and brought in George W. Bush and Dick Cheney. He criticized Shows for taking a contribution from Hillary Rodham Clinton, and said that a vote for Shows was a vote for Dick Gephardt for Speaker. And Pickering wasn't shy about criticizing Shows for his lukewarm support for his father's nomination. In the end, it wasn't close. Pickering won 64%–35%. He won 71%–28% in his old territory and 53%–45% in Shows's. In Rankin, Madison and Hinds counties he won by an astounding 78%–21%.

Pickering's victory put him on the path to a long and influential House career, and opened the door further to an eventual run for the Senate to replace Thad Cochran or Trent Lott. When the controversy over Lott's comments at Strom Thurmond's 100th birthday got people talking about the possibility that Lott might resign from the Senate, Pickering was mentioned prominently as a successor. He would have many factors going for him, including local resentment over the opposition to his father's nomination and his own proven campaign skills.

FOURTH DISTRICT

Rep. Gene Taylor (D)

Elected Oct. 1989, 7th term; b. Sept. 17, 1953, New Orleans, LA; home, Bay St. Louis; Tulane U., B.A. 1974; Catholic; married (Margaret).

Military Career: Coast Guard Reserves, 1971–84.

Elected Office: Bay St. Louis City Cncl., 1981–83; MS Senate, 1983–89.

Professional Career: Sales rep., Stone Container Corp., 1977–89.

DC Office: 2311 RHOB 20515, 202-225-5772; Fax: 202-225-7074; Web site: www.house.gov/genetaylor.

District Offices: Gulfport, 228-864-7670; Hattiesburg, 601-582-3246; Laurel, 601-425-3905; Ocean Springs, 228-872-7950.

Committees: *Armed Services* (5th of 29 D): Projection Forces (RMM); Readiness. *Transportation & Infrastructure* (12th of 34 D): Highways, Transit & Pipelines; Water Resources & Environment.

Group Ratings

	ADA	ACLU	AFS	LCV	CON	ITIC	NTU	COC	ACU	NTLC	CHC
2002	50	20	78	50	100	38	30	45	48	37	58
2001	55	—	89	43	—	—	32	39	64	—	—

National Journal Ratings

	2001 LIB	—	2001 CONS		2002 LIB	—	2002 CONS
Economic	54%	—	47%		53%	—	46%
Social	35%	—	63%		39%	—	57%
Foreign	54%	—	46%		52%	—	48%

Key Votes of the 107th Congress

1. Approve Bush Tax Cuts	N	5. Faith-Based Charities	N	9. Trade Promotion Authority	N
2. Limit Patients' Bill of Rights	N	6. Bar Gays in the Boy Scouts	Y	10. Bar Funds for Intl. Court	Y
3. Campaign Finance Reform	Y	7. Ban Partial-Birth Abortion	Y	11. Authorize Force in Iraq	Y
4. Ban ANWR Development	N	8. Arm Commercial Pilots	Y	12. Deny Home. Sec. Dept. Union	Y

Election Results

2002 general	Gene Taylor (D)	121,742	(75%)	($372,065)
	Karl Mertz (R)	34,373	(21%)	
	Other	5,753	(4%)	
2002 primary	Gene Taylor (D)	unopposed		
2000 general (MS 5)	Gene Taylor (D)	153,264	(79%)	($287,750)
	Randy McDonnell (R)	35,309	(18%)	
	Other	5,822	(3%)	

Prior Winning Percentages: 1998 (78%); 1996 (58%); 1994 (60%); 1992 (63%); 1990 (81%); 1989 (65%)

The People		Race/Ethnic Origin	Ancestry	
Area size:	9,536 sq. mi.	73.5% White	USA: 13.4%	Irish: 7.3%
Urban population:	53.7%	22.1% Black	English: 6.3%	
Rural population:	46.3%	1.2% Asian	**2000 Presidential Vote**	
Pop. 2000:	711,219	0.3% Native Am.	Bush (R)..............154,997	(65%)
Median income:	$33,023	0.0% Hawaiian	Gore (D)................78,224	(33%)
Poverty status:	16.9%	0.9% Two+ races	Other....................4,152	(2%)
Military veterans:	15.3%	0.1% Other	**Cook Partisan Voting Index:** R +17	
		1.8% Hispanic Origin		

Occupation	Blue collar: 29.7%	White collar: 51.9%	Gray collar: 18.4%

The strand where Mississippi faces the Gulf of Mexico has gone through several transformations. French explorers here founded Biloxi in 1699, before New Orleans or St. Louis, and made it the capital of an empire extending to what is now Yellowstone National Park. Two hundred years later, rich people from New Orleans came to this Gulf Coast in summer to get away from yellow fever and to rest on Victorian verandas; six American presidents have vacationed here. More recently the Gulf Coast, with the help of riverboat casinos since 1992, has grown more than any other part of Mississippi; along much of the strand, new 1,000-room hotels rose as part of Mississippi's boom and about 50,000 jobs were created during the past decade. There is a military flavor to the Gulf Coast: Biloxi's Keesler Air Force Base is one of the four largest in the country. Pascagoula, once a small town, is now home of the 11,000-employee Ingalls Shipyard, whose gray hangar-like buildings and skeletons of ships under construction loom over the flat landscape; it is also the home of Senator Trent Lott. To the west is the Stennis Space Center named for longtime (1947–89) Senator John Stennis, where Lockheed Martin has established an advanced propulsion center.

This is the heart of the 4th Congressional District. About half of its people live on the Gulf Coast; the rest are inland, in farm counties or around Hattiesburg and Laurel. This was mostly scrub land, not much good for plantations. With its low black percentage and mostly booming economy, the 4th District has become prime Republican territory. This district, in close to current form, gave Richard Nixon his highest percentage in all 435 districts in 1972, voted five times against fellow Southerners Jimmy Carter, Bill Clinton and Al Gore, and was represented for 16 years in the House by Lott until he was elected to the Senate in 1988.

The congressman from the 4th District is Gene Taylor, a Democrat chosen in a 1989 special election. Taylor graduated from Tulane and served in the Coast Guard Reserves as skipper of a search and rescue boat for 10 years. He was elected to the Bay St. Louis Council in 1981 and in 1983, at 30, was elected to the state Senate. In 1988, when Lott ran for the Senate, Taylor ran for his House seat, won the Democratic primary, but lost to Republican Larkin Smith 55%–45%. When Smith died in an August 1989 plane crash, Lott brushed aside Smith's widow and backed his own longtime aide Tom Anderson, who had spent little time in the district and proved to be an abrasive candidate. Taylor, combining a barely reined-in aggressiveness with a down-home manner, won the special 65%–35%.

In the House, Taylor has a conservative voting record and has bluntly criticized the leadership of both parties. When asked to vote for the October 1998 budget, he characteristically remarked, "One of the people who is asking us to trust him is now being studied to see if he committed perjury. Another of the people who says trust us admitted lying to the ethics committee. That's not a very good place to start." Taylor is a peppery populist with a reasonably consistent view on issues. He is against abortion, gun control, free trade and foreign aid. He is strongly pro-defense and boasts of bringing defense contracts to the area. As a senior Democrat on the Armed Services Committee, and now the ranking Democrat on the Projection Forces Subcommittee, he is a firm believer in improving pay and benefits. He was a leading proponent of the major expansion in 2000 of health benefits for military retirees.

Feisty almost to the point of being belligerent, he opposes any U.S. military commitment that stops short of assured and total victory: He voted against the Gulf War resolution, lifting the arms embargo on Bosnia, and sending troops to Haiti, and favored limits on forces in Colombia. But he seems to have become in recent years more willing to use military power. When faced with apparently ineffective American military involvement in Serbia in April 1999, he called for a declaration of war; he backed the skipper of the USS *Cole*, when it returned to Pascagoula for repairs following its bombing by terrorists in Yemen; in 2002, he voted for the use of force in Iraq. He is a protectionist, loudly opposing NAFTA, GATT and trade with China. If anything holds his record together, it is boats. He promotes Ingalls and other shipyards, succeeded in widening and deepening the Gulfport shipping channel, champions the seafood industry, and wants to prohibit foreign-flag ships from conducting passenger "voyages to nowhere" from U.S. ports. He supports the federal shipbuilding program and revitalizing the Merchant Marine; he objects to waivers to the Jones Act, which requires coastal shipping to be conducted in U.S.-made ships. When American Classic Voyages went bankrupt while building a cruise ship in Pascagoula, Taylor sought to have the government finish construction and use the ship as a floating barracks. He has vigorously opposed the base-closing process scheduled in 2005, for fear that Congress has surrendered its constitutional authority—and out of concern that facilities in his district may be on the chopping block.

He is hardly ever a reliable Democratic vote. Taylor voted "present" for speaker in 1995, and he voted for John Murtha in 2001 and again in 2003, rather than Richard Gephardt or Nancy Pelosi. There was little doubt about his vote for impeachment. When White House chief of staff Erskine Bowles asked a group of Blue Dog Democrats what they thought the president should do, Taylor's hand shot up first. "I think he should resign." He was one of five Democrats to vote for two counts of impeachment. But Taylor has rebuffed all importunings to switch parties. "I personally would feel like a prostitute. I still believe the average working person's best interest is best served by the Democratic Party." When Republican National Chairman Haley Barbour offered a $1 million reward to anyone who could prove Republicans had "cut" Medicare, Taylor laid claim to it. Facing possible House action in the event of an Electoral College deadlock in 2000, he said that he would vote for George W. Bush to reflect the views of his constituents. In April 2001, he said he would vote to retain Mississippi's 1894 flag with the Confederate battle cross.

Taylor seldom has much serious opposition, except in 1996, when Republican Dennis Dollar opposed him. A party-switcher himself in the legislature, Dollar matched Taylor's spending. But Taylor won with a solid 58%–40%, even as Bob Dole was carrying the district by a similar margin. Since then, he has won overwhelmingly. Should Taylor not run for reelection, Republicans would have an excellent chance to capture in this seat.

★ MISSOURI ★

When Meriwether Lewis and William Clark set out on their expedition across the Louisiana Purchase to the Pacific in May 1804, the place they embarked from was St. Louis. On high ground just below the point where the Missouri River swirls into the Mississippi, St. Louis was at the time the one well-established city in America's interior, with an aristocracy of French merchants, a brawling bourgeoisie of Yankee and Southern frontiersmen and fur traders and a proletariat of black slaves. Part of the Louisiana Purchase in 1803, St. Louis by 1821 was part of the new state of Missouri, and for decades St. Louis and Missouri were the gateways to the frontier. In Missouri Daniel Boone finally found elbow room. Here were the eastern termini of the Pony Express, in St. Joseph, and the Santa Fe Trail, in Westport, now part of Kansas City; here were railroads reaching across the continent, connecting the farmers of vast prairies with their markets. Here also were the Mississippi River steamboats, and the boyhood home of their great chronicler, Mark Twain.

For Missouri was not just the gateway to the frontier; it was also a focus of the furious battle over slavery. Missouri was the northernmost slave state in 1850; it was Missouri ruffians crossing the border and killing antislavery settlers in the Kansas Territory that led proximately to the Civil War, and Missouri had its own mini-civil war in the hilly counties along the Missouri River. Throughout the 19th century, both before and after the Civil War, Americans turned away from their oceans and headed inward to settle the great interior of the continent. They found Missouri at its heart, with farmland and mines, rivers and railroads, a major manufacturing state—and in the days before tractors, the nation's leading breeder and trader of mules. In 1874 the Eads Bridge opened, one of very few across the Mississippi, and St. Louis' Cupples Station was the largest rail hub in the world. At the turn of the 20th century, Missouri was the fifth largest state and St. Louis was the fourth largest city, site of the 1904 World's Fair, and one of the few cities with two major league baseball teams, the Cardinals and the Browns; Missouri after the 1900 Census had 16 congressional districts.

Today, Missouri does not loom as large in the national consciousness, yet it is in some ways still central. In the 20th century, Americans—like the Browns who moved to Baltimore in the 1950s and the football Cardinals who moved to Phoenix in the 1980s—increasingly headed toward the coasts, to the big cities of the East and to California, and eventually to Florida and Texas. Missouri has had below average population growth since 1900, and today it is the 17th largest state, with just nine congressional districts. But Missouri was the geographic center of the nation's population in the 2000 Census: an imaginary, flat map of the United States population, if everyone

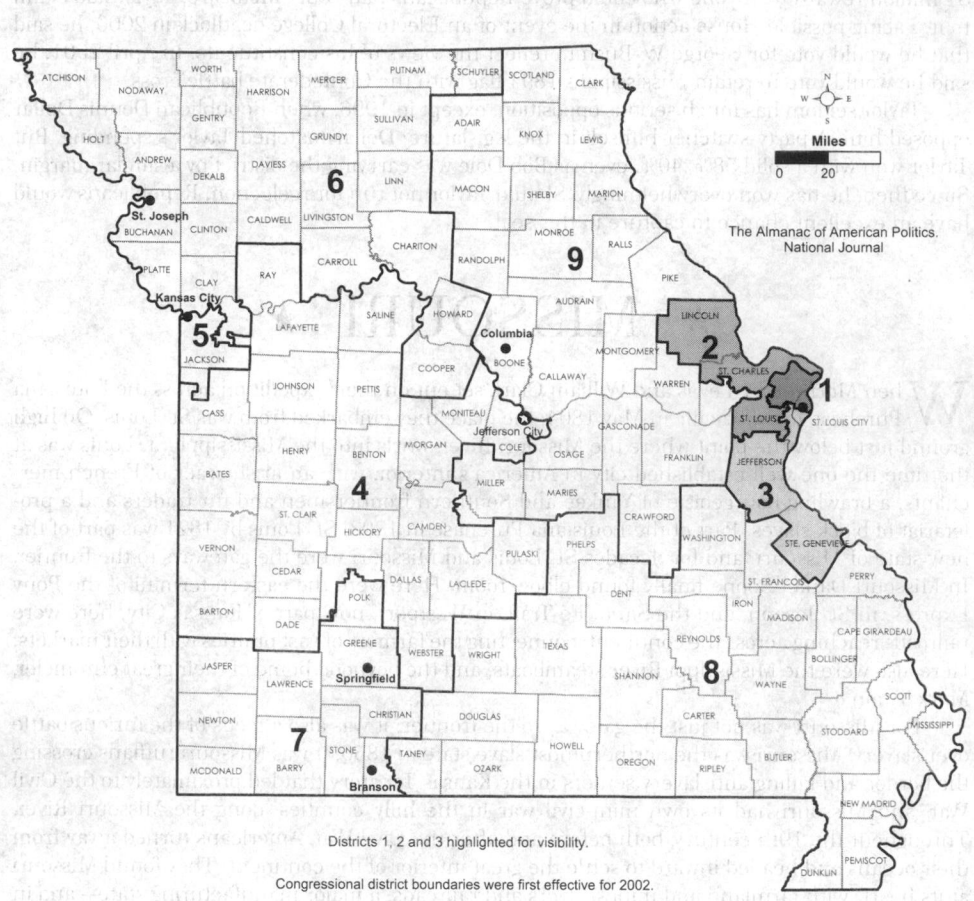

The Almanac of American Politics.
National Journal

Districts 1, 2 and 3 highlighted for visibility.

Congressional district boundaries were first effective for 2002.

weighed the same, would balance near Edgar Springs in Phelps County, Missouri. Missouri started perking up demographically in the 1990s, growing by 9% (its greatest decennial increase in a century); growth was particularly strong in the outer suburbs of St. Louis and Kansas City and in the Ozarks; dozens of rural counties that have been losing population for most of the 20th century started growing again. But the state has not seen only a small influx of immigrants. The state economy, long sluggish, was showing signs of solid growth. And Missouri has again captured Americans' imaginations: if Americans in 1904 flocked to St. Louis on the banks of the Mississippi, in the 1990s their vans and buses were jamming the two-lane road through the Ozarks to Branson, population 6,050, now one of America's top tourist destinations (with 7 million visitors a year), with country music stars and soft rock veterans, country violinist Shoji Tabuchi, nearly 50 theaters and more seats than on Broadway, and more seats for regularly scheduled music concerts than anywhere else in America.

Culturally, Missouri remains more conservative than most bigger states. Its relatively slow-growing metro areas have not overwhelmed the countryside; the biggest growth is at the far edges of the metro areas and in the Ozarks. This rural Missouri is a land of farms and small towns, thick with churches and free of glitzy shopping centers, laced with man-made lakes and boat launches, with only one town over 150,000 (Springfield) and 103 counties where life—and politics—seem not to have changed much over the past half-century.

For most of the 20th century, Missouri was one of America's political bellwethers: it has voted for every presidential winner but one (Eisenhower in 1956) since 1900. From the 1960s to the 1990s it mirrored national trends by moving its congressional politics from pretty solidly Democratic to leaning Republican. In the excruciatingly close presidential year of 2000, the results in Missouri were exquisitely close as well. George W. Bush carried the state by a 50%–47% margin. At the same time Missourians gave Democrats narrow margins for governor and senator—49%–48% for Governor Bob Holden and 51%–48% for the late Mel Carnahan over Senator John Ashcroft. In 2002 the results at the top of the ticket were just as close—Republican Jim Talent beat Senator Jean Carnahan 50%–49%. But the patterns of support were very different from those in the recent past. For most of the 20th century, Missouri's ancient Civil War political divisions still held: Little Dixie in the northeast, first settled by Virginians, and the northwest, settled by Southerners, voted Democratic; the Ozarks in the southwest, which was pro-Union, was unusually Republican; the southeast was split, like next-door Downstate Illinois. But in 2000 and 2002 the real divide was between the state's two big metropolitan areas and the rural remainder of Missouri. The St. Louis metro area voted 53%–45% for Al Gore; metro Kansas City, about half as big, voted 54%–43% for Gore. But the rest of Missouri, casting 44% of the votes, was 58%–39% for George W. Bush. Of the 103 counties outside the two big metro areas, Bush carried 95 and Gore eight. Other Democrats did a little better outside the metro areas but not much: their majorities came almost entirely from big city and close-in suburban precincts. Ancestrally Democratic rural counties have taken to electing Republican legislators. Only one Democrat, Ike Skelton, represents a U.S. House district that is predominantly rural. In January 2001 Republicans won two special elections and won an 18–16 margin in the state Senate; in November 2002 they widened that to 20–14 and gained control of the state House for the first time in 52 years by a 90–73 majority. But it is certainly too early to say that Missouri has become a predominantly Republican state. Democrats here have a structural problem: positions insisted on by black politicians and voters in St. Louis and Kansas City are unpopular elsewhere in the state, and black politcians complain that they are overlooked by white Democrats after elections. But Republicans, nationally and in Missouri, have to grapple with the responsibilities of governing in a time of disappointing economic growth and national peril.

The People

Pop. 2000:	5,595,211
Pop. 1990:	5,117,073
Change 1990–2000:	Up 9.3%
Change 1980–1990:	Up 4.1%
% of U.S. total:	2.0%
Pop. rank:	17th of 50
Area size:	69,704 sq. mi.
State Native:	67.8%
Non-citizen:	1.6%

Language

English: 92.9%	Spanish: 3.1%
Other Eur.: 2.8%	

Race/Ethnic Origin

4,686,474	83.8%	White
625,667	11.2%	Black
61,041	1.1%	Asian
23,302	0.4%	Native Am.
2,939	0.1%	Hawaiian
71,905	1.3%	Two + races
5,291	0.1%	Other
118,592	2.1%	Hisp. Origin

Ancestry

German: 17.9%	Irish: 9.7%
USA: 8.0%	English: 7.2%
French: 2.7%	

Military veterans: 592,271 (14.2%)

WWII: 20.3%	Korea: 14.4%
Vietnam: 31.6%	Gulf War: 9.2%

Most populous cities:

1. Kansas City	441,545
2. St. Louis	348,189
3. Springfield	151,580
4. Independence	113,288
5. Columbia	84,531

Urban population: 69.4%
Rural population: 30.6%

Education

H.S. Grad:	81.3%
College Grad:	21.6%

Industry

Agri: 2.2%	Con: 6.9%
Fin: 6.7%	Info: 3.0%
Mfg: 20.5%	Prof: 27.9%
Public: 4.6%	Trade: 15.5%
Other: 12.8%	

Occupation

Blue collar: 26.0%	White collar: 58.3%
Gray collar: 15.7%	

Work Sector

Private: 80.0%	Govt: 12.8%
Self: 6.9%	Family: 0.4%

Unemployment: 5.3%

Household Income

<15k: 17.1%	15-35k: 28.9%
35-50k: 17.5%	50-100k: 27.7%
100-150k: 5.7%	>150k: 3.0%

Median: $37,934
Poverty status: 11.7%

Home Value

<50k: 21.3%	50-100k: 38.6%	100-200k: 29.9%	200-300k: 6.3%
300-500k: 2.6%	>500k: 1.2%	Median: $86,900	

General Assembly

Senate	20 R 14 D
House	90 R 73 D

Legislative Term Limits: Yes

Registered Voters

No party registration

Presidential politics Missouri's peculiar balance of North and South, urban and rural, has helped to make it a presidential bellwether and explains its one deviation in the 20th century: it voted for Adlai Stevenson in 1956, who capitalized on farmer discontent and whose lukewarmness about civil rights helped him carry traditional Southern Democrats. In the 1990s Missouri saw the two countervailing national trends—toward Democrats in major metropolitan areas, toward Republicans in rural areas—but in different proportions: the rural areas count for more here. Bill Clinton carried Missouri by 10% in 1992 and by 7% in 1996. In 2000 Al Gore could carry only a handful of counties outside Missouri's two big metropolitan areas, and lost by a 3% margin. Issues like gun control and abortion, which worked for him in the largest states, worked against him in Missouri. Blacks voted 84%–14% for Gore—a lesser margin than in many states—while white Protestants voted 59%–39% and white Catholics 56%–43% for Bush. This seems sure to be a seriously contested state in November 2004.

Missouri joined the Super Tuesday primary for 1988, then went back to multi-tiered caucuses to elect delegates in 1992 and 1996. In 2000 Missouri went back to the Super Tuesday primary, in which George W. Bush and Gore won easy victories, even though Gore's rival Bill Bradley grew up in Jefferson County, Missouri. In 2004 St. Louis's Dick Gephardt will be a heavy favorite in the Missouri primary, which may not be seriously contested by other candidates.

2000 Presidential Vote

Bush (R)	1,189,924	(50%)
Gore (D)	1,111,138	(47%)
Nader (Green)	38,515	(2%)
Other	20,315	(1%)

2000 Republican Presidential Primary

Bush (R)	275,366	(58%)
McCain (R)	167,831	(35%)
Keyes (R)	27,282	(6%)

2000 Democratic Presidential Primary

Gore (D)	171,562	(65%)
Bradley (D)	89,092	(34%)

1996 Presidential Vote

Clinton (D)	1,025,935	(48%)
Dole (R)	890,014	(41%)
Perot (I)	217,219	(10%)

Congressional districting   Missouri did not lose any seats in the 2000 Census, and control of redistricting was split between the parties: Democrats held the governorship and had a majority in the state House; Republicans, by winning two special election in January 2001, had an 18–16 margin in the state Senate. The main problem was how to adjust for the declining population of St. Louis. Back in 1950 the city of St. Louis had 856,000 people, enough for almost three congressional districts; in 2000 it had 348,000 people, not enough for half a district. But it is heavily Democratic, and in early 2001 1st District Congressman William Lacy Clay was demanding more of the city, to keep the black percentage in his district well above 50%. That was resisted by 3d District Congressman Dick Gephardt, who didn't want his district moved farther out into Republican suburbs. Privately some Gephardt aides worried that Clay would persuade black House Democrats to make a deal with Republicans. But Gephardt, as House Minority Leader and as onetime boss of Governor Bob Holden, had leverage; Holden could be counted on to veto such a deal. On April 23 Gephardt and Clay met at the St. Louis Labor Central headquarters and made a deal; the city would be divided roughly along I-44. Some black legislators grumbled, but Clay assured them the new 1st District could be counted on to elect a black.

108th Congress Lineup
5 R   4 D
107th Congress Lineup
5 R   4 D

In early May, Democrats passed a plan in the House which protected all incumbents and pretty well followed the Gephardt-Clay deal. In Senate committee Republicans prepared a plan that would have given Gephardt a much more Republican district, but Democrats filibustered to keep it from the floor. A phalanx of Gephardt aides, "the machine," was busy lobbying through all this. On May 11, with "the machine" and representatives of all nine incumbents present, a deal was reached. Gephardt got the agreed on portion of St. Louis and the close-in, increasingly Democratic suburbs of Maplewood, Richmond Heights, Clayton and University City. Clay got the increasingly black northern suburbs of Florissant, Hazelwood, Bridgeton and St. Ann plus affluent Creve Coeur and Ladue. Republican Todd Akin of the 2d District lost all those areas and got Sunset Hills, Sappington and Concord from Gephardt's old district and new territory in suburban St. Charles and rural Lincoln Counties. Akin was the only incumbent who didn't like the plan, and but said he wouldn't challenge it in court. It passed the House 117–37 and the Senate 28–5 in May and was signed by Governor Bob Holden June 1. Some Republicans complained that it did not make the 3d District more Republican. But otherwise it was a success for Republicans, especially considering that their sole leverage was an 18–16 margin in the state Senate. They have a 5–4 lead in the delegation, and it is generally agreed that the 4th District, safe for conservative Democrat Ike Skelton, will probably elect a Republican when he retires.

Governor

Bob Holden (D)

Elected 2000, term expires Jan. 2005, 1st term; b. Aug. 8, 1949, Kansas City; home, Jefferson City; S.W. MO St. U., B.S. 1973.; Disciples of Christ; married (Lori).

Military Career: MO Natl. Guard, 1971–77.

Elected Office: MO House of Reps., 1982–88; MO Treasurer, 1992–00.

Professional Career: Asst., MO Treasurer James Spainhower, 1976–81; St. Louis A.A., U.S. Rep. Richard Gephardt, 1989–91.

Office: State Capitol Bldg., Rm. 216, Jefferson City, 65102, 573-751-3222; Fax: 573-751-1495; Web site: www.gov.state.mo.us.

Election Results

2000 general	Bob Holden (D)	1,152,752	(49%)
	Jim Talent (R)	1,131,307	(48%)
	Other	62,771	(3%)
2000 primary	Bob Holden (D)	unopposed	
1996 general	Mel Carnahan (D)	1,224,801	(57%)
	Margaret Kelly (R)	866,268	(40%)
	Other	51,449	(2%)

Bob Holden, elected governor of Missouri in 2000, was born in Kansas City but grew up outside of Birch Tree in rural Shannon County, where his home was more than a mile from a paved road. Holden graduated from Southwest Missouri State, the first in his father's family to graduate from college, and worked as an assistant to state Treasurer Jim Spainhower. In 1982, at 33, Holden was elected to the state House, beating a Republican incumbent in heavily Republican Springfield. He served for six years and ran for state treasurer in 1988, and lost. For three years he worked for Congressman Dick Gephardt in St. Louis, then ran for treasurer again in 1992, and won. He was reelected in 1996 and soon became a candidate for governor. He avoided primary opposition in March 1998 when Lieutenant Governor Roger Wilson announced that he wouldn't run. The Republican nominee, not seriously challenged in his primary, was suburban St. Louis Congressman Jim Talent, who had also served eight years in the legislature and announced in February 1999. This was the most expensive gubernatorial race in Missouri history, by far; the candidates took advantage of a court ruling overturning the limit on individual contributions to raise some $3 million in over-limit money, until the U.S. Supreme Court upheld the Missouri law in January 2000.

In many ways this race was a referendum on the eight-year governorship of Democrat Mel Carnahan, who was not eligible for a third term and was running against his predecessor, Senator John Ashcroft. Back in 1993, Carnahan passed a $315 million tax increase to pay for a new school funding plan; he pushed through a children's health plan; he helped to defeat a proposal to allow law-abiding citizens to get permits to carry concealed weapons in 1998; his 1999 veto of a partial-birth abortion ban was overturned. Holden promised to use tobacco settlement money to provide prescription drugs for the elderly and health insurance to more low-income people; he said he would raise education spending, provide more accountability and reduce class sizes. Talent called for resuscitating a 1992 rural highway-building program that had been abandoned in 1998; he promised to deliver all gambling revenue to education, and called for school vouchers for parents of children in failing schools.

The race took a tragic turn when Mel Carnahan was killed in a plane crash October 16, the night before the third presidential debate in St. Louis. All candidates agreed to pull negative ads, though some Talent spots still ran—despite his efforts, he said. Carnahan's eulogies naturally recalled his service in positive terms, and probably made Talent's anti-status quo theme less appealing. This was one of the closest races in the country, and one of three top-of-the-ticket races that turned out to be very close in Missouri. On election night, St. Louis Democrats got a state judge to order the polls remain open three extra hours because of alleged shortages of ballots and booths; 45 minutes later the order was reversed on appeal, but Republicans from Senator Christopher Bond on down argued that Democrats got illegitimate votes, and no one defended the competence of St. Louis's election procedures. Holden won by 21,000 votes, 49%–48%. Talent ran ahead of other Republicans in his native St. Louis area, but ran farther behind in the Kansas City area and did not carry rural Missouri by a wide margin.

Holden started off on the wrong foot, holding a $1 million inaugural, the largest in state history, and then confessing that the committee was $417,000 in debt. Then in January 2001 he discovered he needed to cut state spending by $200 million and, thanks to Republican victories in special elections, he had to deal with a Republican state Senate, which killed his plan for a $500 million tax increase for roads. He was criticized for granting collective bargaining rights to 30,000 state employees. He did better with a September special session of the legislature, which agreed on a prescription drugs for low-income seniors program, though by year's end it attracted fewer participants than expected. He got a compromise on a livestock pricing law and a one-time exemption from income tax of federal tax rebates. In the 2002 regular session the legislature resisted his proposal to dip into the rainy day fund and found enough revenue, but for the first time since 1997 did not provide full school funding. A $511 million roads proposal was put on the ballot in August 2002 and defeated 73%–27%. But Holden's proposals for state aid for new stadiums in St. Louis and Kansas City were rejected. In November 2002 Republicans gained seats in the state Senate and had a 20–14 majority and gained control of the state House for the first time since 1948, with a 90–73 margin. Term limits meant that most state House members were freshmen; much power was in the hands of Senate President Peter Kinder and House Speaker Catherine Hanaway.

By midterm Holden had cut state spending by $900 million and in early 2003 seemed likely to cut it more. Holden called for closing what he called business tax loopholes to bring in an extra $100 million and to increase taxes on cigarettes and casinos by $710 million, plus a 5% surcharge on households with incomes over $200,000. He proposed to use money from securitization of tobacco settlement payments; Republicans wanted to limit that tobacco settlement spending to $100 million and to cut spending by $85 million and delay building a $30 million pharmacy building for the University of Missouri at Kansas City.

In early 2003 Holden's prospects for reelection in 2004 looked iffy. The liberal *St. Louis Post-Dispatch* called him "a luckless politician who has encountered one problem after another since taking office." Auditor Claire McCaskill, a Democrat who was reelected 60%–37% in 2002, had in 2001 said, "I would never run against Bob Holden in a Democratic primary and I don't think anyone would be wise to do that." But in November 2002 she was sidestepping questions about a primary challenge. In February 2003 she said, "A lot of people are talking to me, and I'm talking to a lot of people." She said she would not announce a decision until after the legislative session ended in May.

Meanwhile, Republicans seemed to develop consensus on a candidate. In fall 2002 possible candidates included Senate President Peter Kinder, Congressman Kenny Hulshof and Secretary of State Matt Blunt. Kinder decided early on to run for another, unspecified statewide office. Hulshof decided to run the day after the 2002 election, but his father died later that month, leaving his mother to run the family farm, and in January 2003 Hulshof announced he would not run for governor. That left Matt Blunt, the one successful statewide candidate on the 2000 ballot, when he was elected secretary of state at age 29. Blunt is the son of 7th District Congressman Roy Blunt, who was elected Secretary of State himself in 1984 (at 34) and 1988 and narrowly lost a primary for governor in 1992. Matt Blunt served as an officer in the Navy from 1993 to 1998 and as a naval reservist was called up for six months active duty in the United Kingdom after September 11. By late 2002 he was busy canvassing for support and raising money and seemed certain to be the Republican nominee. He does not appear to consider his age a problem; he points out that if elected in November 2004 he will be several months older than Senator Christopher Bond was when he was first elected governor in 1972 and that he will have had more experience in elective office.

Senior Senator

Christopher (Kit) Bond (R)

Elected 1986, seat up 2004, 3d term; b. Mar. 6, 1939, St. Louis; home, Mexico; Princeton U., B.A. 1960, U. of VA, LL.B. 1963; Presbyterian; divorced.

Elected Office: MO Auditor, 1970–72; MO Gov., 1972–76, 1980–84.

Professional Career: Practicing atty., 1964–69, 1977–80; MO Asst. Atty. Gen., 1969–70.

DC Office: 274 RSOB, 20510, 202-224-5721; Fax: 202-224-8149; Web site: bond.senate.gov.

State Offices: Cape Girardeau, 573-334-7044; Jefferson City, 573-634-2488; Kansas City, 816-471-7141; Springfield, 417-864-8258; St. Louis, 314-725-4484.

Committees: *Appropriations*: Agriculture & Rural Development; Defense; Energy & Water Development; Foreign Operations; Transportation, Treasury & General Government; VA, HUD & Independent Agencies (Chmn.). *Environment & Public Works*: Clean Air, Climate Change & Nuclear Safety; Superfund & Waste Management; Transportation & Infrastructure (Chmn.). *Health, Education, Labor & Pensions*: Aging (Chmn.); Children & Families; Employment, Safety & Training. *Intelligence (Select)*. *Small Business & Entrepreneurship*.

Group Ratings

	ADA	ACLU	AFS	LCV	CON	ITIC	NTU	COC	ACU	NTLC	CHC
2002	10	40	0	12	18	88	59	100	84	91	—
2001	10	—	8	0	—	—	83	93	88	—	80

National Journal Ratings

	2001 LIB — 2001 CONS		2002 LIB — 2002 CONS	
Economic	30%	— 66%	14%	— 84%
Social	0%	— 79%	42%	— 57%
Foreign	7%	— 72%	0%	— 76%

Key Votes of the 107th Congress

1. Approve Bush Tax Cuts	Y	5. Confirm Ashcroft as AG	Y	9. Bar Coop. with Intl. Court	Y
2. Expand Patients' Rights	N	6. Bar Gays in the Boy Scouts	Y	10. Trade Promotion Authority	Y
3. Campaign Finance Reform	N	7. $ for Hate Crime Prosecution	*	11. Authorize Force in Iraq	Y
4. Permit ANWR Development	Y	8. Overseas Military Abortions	N	12. Homeland Sec. Dept. Union	N

Election Results

1998 general	Christopher (Kit) Bond (R)	830,625	(53%)	($6,229,649)
	Jay Nixon (D)	690,208	(44%)	($2,568,879)
	Other	56,024	(4%)	
1998 primary	Christopher (Kit) Bond (R)	213,569	(87%)	
	Other	32,274	(13%)	
1992 general	Christopher (Kit) Bond (R)	1,221,901	(52%)	($5,048,333)
	Geri Rothman-Serot (D)	1,057,967	(45%)	($1,112,187)
	Other	75,048	(3%)	

Prior Winning Percentages: 1986 (53%)

Christopher Bond was first elected to statewide office in 1970 and was first elected to the Senate in 1986. Bond grew up in the town of Mexico, Missouri, where his family were part owners of the largest business, A.P. Green, makers of heat-resistant bricks, which was sold to another firm in 1998. He graduated from Princeton and the University of Virginia Law School, then clerked for Judge Elbert Tuttle, one of the great pioneers on civil rights in the Fifth Circuit in Atlanta. He returned to Missouri, practiced law and ran for Congress in 1968, at age 29, and narrowly lost. He was elected state auditor in 1970 and was elected governor at 33 in 1972, and became one of the youngest governors in the nation's history. He lost in an upset to Democrat Joseph Teasdale in 1976 and won a comeback victory against Teasdale in 1980. As governor, Bond pushed reorganization, open meetings, merit hiring and campaign finance in his first term; he wrestled with fiscal problems, crime and early childhood education in his second term. After two years in private life he ran for the Senate against Harriett Woods, who had come close to beating Bond's longtime ally, then-Senator John Danforth, in 1982. Woods ran a three-part ad showing a farmer breaking into tears as he and his wife told Woods about their foreclosure and named Bond as a board member of the insurance company that foreclosed; evidently this struck voters as either demagoguery or an invasion of privacy, and Woods fell in the polls. Bond won, 53%–47%.

Bond has a moderate voting record in the Senate. He has usually worked behind the scenes, trying to forge bipartisan consensus. He was the chief Republican sponsor of the Family and Medical Leave Act, vetoed by George H.W. Bush and signed by Bill Clinton. He has been the lead Republican senator on housing, starting on the Banking Committee and now as chairman of the VA-HUD Appropriations Subcommittee. There he has worked in bipartisan fashion with ranking Democrat Barbara Mikulski, funding the space program in which she takes an interest and projects affecting Missouri. Bond has sponsored many amendments aiding inner city organizations and encouraging small businesses in troubled urban areas and has worked cooperatively with many black community leaders in St. Louis and Kansas City, to the point that Kansas City's mayor declined to endorse his Democratic opponent in 1998. When Citizens Against Government Waste named Bond as the number six promoter of pork barrel projects between 1995 and 2002, a Bond aide replied, "Senator Bond always said pork is a mighty fine diet for Missouri, low in fat and high in jobs." He has opposed companies and European nations which have sought to ban genetically modified food, of which the chief producer is St. Louis-based Monsanto, and has sought tougher FDA regulation of compounded medicines in pharmacies. On the Defense Appropriations Subcommittee, he has worked hard to keep in operation the F-15 production line at Boeing's (formerly McDonnell Douglas's) plant next to the St. Louis airport. Bond objected vigorously when the Air Force said it would quit buying F-15s and looked for other customers. In 1999 and 2000 he got $700 million for the purchase of 10 F-15s over the objections of the Clinton administration. He has made numerous trips to South Korea since 1989 to promote the plane and at one point warned the Koreans that "very unfortunate things could happen" to their relationship with the U.S. if they bought European planes. He was overjoyed in April 2002 when Boeing announced that South Korea would buy 40 F-15s, keeping the production line open at least till 2007, and he was pleased when Boeing won a $42 million contract for the Air Force's Programmable Armament Control Set Production Process.

Other Missouri interests have prompted Bond initiatives. He was the co-sponsor with Carl Levin of the amendment, passed 62–38 in March 2002 that delayed any increase in CAFE auto mileage standards for two years. In January 2003 he became chairman of the Environment and Public Works Subcommittee that has jurisdiction over reauthorization of highway and other transportation spending. He held hearings around Missouri on road issues in 2002. Another important local issue is the level of the Missouri River. Bond opposed Clinton administration proposals to allow a spring rise by releasing water at Gavins Point Dam in South Dakota; the idea was to restore the natural flow of the river to protect endangered species like the least tern and pallid sturgeon. Bond argued that this would cause floods in the spring and low water levels in the summer and fall and destroy Missouri's barge industry. In 2000 Bond inserted a rider in an appropriation preventing the Army Corps of Engineers from spending any money to restore the natural flow; in September 2000 Bill Clinton announced he would veto the bill unless the amendment was removed. So it was, but with political cost: This controversy, invisible nationally, was big news in Missouri and may have had something to do with the fact that Al Gore lost the state to George W. Bush. In 2001 and 2002 his riders stayed in the bill, much to the irritation of South Dakota's senators. An avid fisherman, he sponsored a law to encourage voluntary activity to clean up rivers; it would create watershed councils which would give grants to help farmers establish buffer zones, fence off livestock, and reduce runoff of fertilizers and farm chemicals without onerous regulations. Bond's Senate suite includes Harry Truman's old Senate office.

Bond got his political start as part of a group of young reform-minded Republicans—his former Senate colleague John Danforth was another—working against the Democratic political establishment in Missouri, and he can be a strong partisan on occasion. On election night 2000 he was furious when St. Louis Democrats persuaded a state judge to order the polls opened three extra hours in the city; an appeals court overturned the order within 45 minutes, but Bond, who charged that Democrats tried to keep the St. Louis polls open till midnight to defeat him in 1972, said the election had been stolen, and indeed Republicans Jim Talent and John Ashcroft lost by narrow margins. He was further outraged when 3,000 registration cards were dropped off at the city's election board, filled out in the names of people who were dead or already registered to vote; one carried the name of Ritzy Meckler, a Springer spaniel whom Bond later brought to press conferences. Even Democrats admitted there were irregularities in St. Louis; in April 2001 Governor Bob Holden removed the entire election board. In Washington Bond became heavily involved in the election procedures bill that was an obvious item of business after the 2000 Florida controversy. The centerpiece of the bill was its national standards for voting equipment coupled with $3.5 million in federal aid and statewide voter registries. Bond argued that the motor voter act had installed and kept on the rolls many names of those not entitled to vote, and insisted on a provision requiring mail-in registrants to vote in person the first time they vote and to present a driver's license or photo identification. He negotiated this with lead Democrat Christopher Dodd; "I've told him [Dodd] that I will agree with his concept that we need to make it easier to vote, if he agrees with my concept that we need to make it harder to cheat." But in February 2002 Charles Schumer and Ron Wyden proposed an amendment dropping the photo identification requirement; Schumer said that lots of people in New York don't have driver's licenses and Wyden said the requirement would destroy Oregon's mail-in voting system. The Schumer-Wyden amendment passed 51–46. Bond said it was a deal-breaker and launched a filibuster. A deal was made: Democrats abandoned Schumer-Wyden in return for making the new provisional voting system, setting to one side disputed ballots like those in St. Louis in 2000, effective at the same time in 2004 as Bond's anti-fraud provision. The issue resurfaced in September in conference committee, but the bill was eventually passed in October 2002.

Bond was reelected 52%–45% in 1992, a year in which Missouri Republicans lost every other major race. In 1998, against Attorney General Jay Nixon, he was reelected 53%–44%. This was a raucous race in which Nixon was attacked by black Democrats for arguing the state's case against school busing orders in St. Louis and Kansas City; Bond built on the work he had done in inner cities and won 33% of the black vote. He lost metro St. Louis by only 49%–48% and carried metro Kansas City (where he lived between his two terms as governor) 51%–45%; he carried rural Missouri 57%–39%. He may have lost some of his support among blacks when he joined John Ashcroft in 1999 in opposing the judicial nomination of Justice Ronnie White; in December 2002 he had little to say in public about Trent Lott's comments at Strom Thurmond's 100th birthday party, but in a private meeting told Lott he should resign as majority leader. Bond has naturally been on national Democrats' target list for 2004. In his three Senate races he has not won more than 53% of the vote, and of Republican senators up in 2004 only two won with smaller percentages in 1998. But in mid-2003 no prominent Missouri Democrat had stepped forward to run. Governor Bob Holden was running for reelection and Auditor Claire McCaskill was mulling a race against him. Attorney General Jay Nixon had already lost two Senate races. Lieutenant Governor Joe Maxwell announced he would not run. Congressman Dick Gephardt was running for president. Bond is an indefatigable campaigner and fundraiser and seems well positioned for the race. But Missouri is a closely divided state, and this could be a seriously contested seat.

Junior Senator

Jim Talent (R)

Elected 2002, seat up 2006, 1st term; b. Oct. 18, 1956, Des Peres; home, Chesterfield; Washington U., B.S. 1978, U. of Chicago Law Schl., J.D. 1981; Presbyterian; married (Brenda).

Elected Office: MO House of Reps., 1984–92, Min. Ldr., 1989–92; U.S. House of Reps., 1992–00.

Professional Career: Practicing atty., 1981–92; Law Clerk, 7th Circuit Court of Appeals Judge Richard Posner, 1982–83.

DC Office: 493 RSOB, 20510, 202-224-6154; Fax: 202-228-1518; Web site: www.talent.senate.gov.

State Offices: Cape Girardeau, 573-651-0964; Jefferson City, 573-636-1070; Kansas City, 816-421-1639; Springfield, 417-831-2735; St. Louis, 314-432-5211.

Committees: *Aging (Special). Agriculture, Nutrition & Forestry*: Forestry, Conservation & Rural Revitalization; Marketing, Inspection & Product Promotion (Chmn.). *Armed Services*: Airland; Emerging Threats & Capabilities; Readiness & Management Support; Seapower (Chmn.). *Energy & Natural Resources*: Energy; Public Lands & Forests; Water & Power.

Group Ratings and Key Votes: Newly Elected

Election Results

2002 general	Jim Talent (R)	935,032	(50%)	($8,322,003)
	Jean Carnahan (D)	913,778	(49%)	($12,293,579)
	Other	28,810	(2%)	
2002 primary	Jim Talent (R)	395,994	(90%)	
	Joseph May (R)	18,525	(4%)	
	Other	27,552	(6%)	
2000 general	Mel Carnahan (D)	1,191,812	(51%)	($8,800,864)
	John Ashcroft (R)	1,142,852	(48%)	($9,378,581)
	Other	26,922	(1%)	

Prior Winning Percentages: 1998 House (70%); 1996 House (61%); 1994 House (67%); 1992 House (50%)

Jim Talent, a Republican, was elected Missouri's junior senator in 2002. He grew up in Des Peres and lives in Chesterfield, in western St. Louis County. He graduated from Washington University and the University of Chicago Law School and clerked for Judge Richard Posner, the federal bench's most prolific writer of opinions and books. He returned to St. Louis and practiced business law. In 1984, at 28, he was elected to the state House. He served as House Minority Leader from 1989 to 1992. In 1992 he ran for the 2d District House seat in the St. Louis suburbs and in the primary beat George W. Bush's cousin George Herbert Walker 58%–32%. In the general Talent faced Democratic incumbent Joan Kelly Horn, who in 1990 defeated Republican Jack Buechner by a grand total of 54 votes. Redistricting had made the district more Republican, and Talent won 50%–48%.

In the House he had a solidly conservative record and became a leader on some conservative causes. On the Armed Services Committee he decried the Clinton defense budget cuts and managed to save the F-18, assembled by Boeing (formerly McDonnell Douglas) in St. Louis. In his first term he sponsored a welfare bill much like the one passed in 1996, and in 1996 he teamed with J.C. Watts to sponsor the American Community Renewal Act, to encourage enterprise zones, capital gains tax cuts, reduction of red tape and public-private partnerships in central cities. In 1997 he became chairman of the Small Business Committee where he often worked in tandem with Missouri's Christopher Bond, who chaired the Senate Small Business Committee. In November 1998, when Speaker Newt Gingrich announced he would resign, Talent started running for speaker. But when Majority Whip Tom DeLay endorsed Bob Livingston, Talent withdrew from the race.

Talent was reelected by wide margins and could probably have held the House seat for many years. But in February 1999 he announced he was running for governor. He won the primary without serious competition and was locked in a close race with state Treasurer Bob Holden. The central figure in that contest was Mel Carnahan, incumbent Democratic candidate for governor and candidate against Senator John Ashcroft. Then, on October 16, 22 days before the election, Carnahan was killed in a plane crash. The campaigns were suspended; it was too late to change the ballots. A week later Governor Roger Wilson offered to appoint Jean Carnahan to the seat if her husband got more votes than Ashcroft; on October 30 she agreed and in effect became the candidate. On election night Democrats persuaded a judge to hold the polls in St. Louis open an extra 45 minutes. George W. Bush carried the state 50%–47%, but Mel Carnahan led Ashcroft 51%–48% and Bob Holden edged Talent 49%–48%, with a margin of 21,000 votes. Ashcroft conceded, although some Republicans urged him to contest the result, and Wilson appointed Jean Carnahan to the vacancy in December. Under Missouri law, she would serve two years and an election for what would be the remaining four years of the term was held in November 2002.

In the Senate Carnahan was one of 42 Democrats to vote against the confirmation of Ashcroft to be attorney general and was one of 12 Democrats who voted for the $1.3 trillion tax cut in May 2001. Talent, whose family has always remained in St. Louis County, got a fellowship at Washington University and worked part-time for a law firm in Washington. Talent, with his nearly successful showing and his congressional experience, seemed a likely candidate for the Senate. Carnahan declined to say whether she was running but in the first half of 2001 her campaign committee raised $2.3 million. Hovering over the race, as in November 2000, were the tragic circumstances in which Carnahan had come to office. "It's like the elephant in the room. It's always there," said Talent. "Sympathy is a factor, but I don't know how much of a factor it is in the campaign. I think the people still feel sympathy. I do. I knew Mel for 15 years. But I think people view the election as about what we're going to do in the future rather than what happened in the past." Talent's approach was to stress his experience in office and in-depth knowledge of issues; after all, he had served in elective office for 16 years while Carnahan had never been elected to anything. Carnahan did have some political experience: for 40 years she kept a card catalogue of her husband's political acquaintances and wrote many of his speeches; she had an appealing personality and could speak articulately about issues. But in July 2002 *National Journal's* Charlie Cook wrote of "considerable anecdotal evidence from . . . both parties that Carnahan sometimes seems lost in the Senate."

Carnahan stressed that she had voted with George W. Bush 71% of the time, but also made standard Democratic arguments on issues like Social Security and prescription drugs. She boasted of her role in negotiating the merger of TWA, a big employer in St. Louis, into American Airlines. One Republican ad accused her of "undermining national unity" by opposing the administration stimulus package and she was attacked for opposing Bush's position on homeland security. Talent quoted the Bible readily; raised in a Jewish family, he became a Christian and as an adult had a profound religious experience while listening to evangelist Luis Palau on *Focus on the Family*.

Carnahan led in polls up through the summer, as national Democratic groups and her campaign dominated the airwaves. But Talent seemed to pull ahead in September. In late October the race tightened again; the death of Minnesota Senator Paul Wellstone in a plane crash October 25 may have reminded many voters of Mel Carnahan's death in October 2000. George W. Bush came to Missouri to campaign for Talent no less than five times, including an appearance in St. Charles the day before the election. This may have made the difference. This was a close race: Talent won 50%–49%, with a 21,000-vote margin. He lost the St. Louis area 53%–46% and the Kansas City area 57%–41%, but carried rural Missouri 57%–42%.

Talent became a senator when the results were certified November 23. He said he would concentrate on reauthorization of the 1996 welfare act and on his bill to enable small businesses to buy health care plans through trade associations. On abortion he urged a cautious approach. "Since we now have leadership that is favorable to the whole agenda of protecting life, I hope we will step back and ask ourselves, 'What is the best way of doing that right now?' And then pursue those in a respectful way, in a way where we listen to the other side, where we seek as broad a coalition as we can, but we keep moving forward." He got a seat on the Armed Services Committee, as he had in the House, and called for increased defense spending; he was named chairman of the Seapower Subcommittee, an unusual post for a freshman.

FIRST DISTRICT

Rep. William Lacy Clay (D)

Elected 2000, 2d term; b. July 27, 1956, St. Louis; home, St. Louis; U. of MD, B.S. 1983; Catholic; married (Ivie).

Elected Office: MO House of Reps., 1983–90; MO Senate, 1991–00.

Professional Career: Asst. Doorkeeper, U.S. House of Reps, 1976–83; Paralegal, 1982–00; Real estate agent, 1986–00.

DC Office: 131 CHOB 20515, 202-225-2406; Fax: 202-225-1725; Web site: www.house.gov/clay.

District Offices: St. Louis, 314-367-1970; Vinita Park, 314-890-0349.

Committees: *Financial Services* (22d of 32 D): Capital Markets, Insurance & Government Sponsored Enterprises; Housing & Community Opportunity. *Government Reform* (11th of 19 D): Criminal Justice, Drug Policy & Human Resources; Technology, Information Policy, Intergovernmental Relations & Census (RMM).

Group Ratings

	ADA	ACLU	AFS	LCV	CON	ITIC	NTU	COC	ACU	NTLC	CHC
2002	80	93	88	75	78	38	20	44	4	9	8
2001	100	—	100	86	—	—	11	35	8	—	—

National Journal Ratings

	2001 LIB	—	2001 CONS		2002 LIB	—	2002 CONS
Economic	80%	—	19%		68%	—	31%
Social	83%	—	11%		92%	—	8%
Foreign	84%	—	16%		87%	—	13%

Key Votes of the 107th Congress

1. Approve Bush Tax Cuts	N	5. Faith-Based Charities	N
2. Limit Patients' Bill of Rights	N	6. Bar Gays in the Boy Scouts	N
3. Campaign Finance Reform	Y	7. Ban Partial-Birth Abortion	N
4. Ban ANWR Development	Y	8. Arm Commercial Pilots	N

9. Trade Promotion Authority	N
10. Bar Funds for Intl. Court	*
11. Authorize Force in Iraq	N
12. Deny Home. Sec. Dept. Union	N

Election Results

2002 general	William Lacy Clay (D)	133,946	(70%)	($335,527)
	Richard Schwadron (R)	51,755	(27%)	($12,198)
	Other	5,454	(3%)	
2002 primary	William Lacy Clay (D)	41,405	(74%)	
	Carl Harris (D)	14,322	(26%)	
2000 general	William Lacy Clay (D)	149,173	(75%)	($679,776)
	Dwight Billingsly (R)	42,730	(22%)	($3,787)
	Other	6,444	(3%)	

The People

Area size:	227 sq. mi.
Urban population:	99.2%
Rural population:	0.8%
Pop. 2000:	621,690
Median income:	$36,314
Poverty status:	15.8%
Military veterans:	13.6%

Race/Ethnic Origin

45.8% White
49.7% Black
1.5% Asian
0.2% Native Am.
0.0% Hawaiian
1.3% Two+ races
0.1% Other
1.3% Hispanic Origin

Ancestry

German: 13.6%   Irish: 7.8%
English: 4.3%

2000 Presidential Vote

Gore (D)	182,323	(72%)
Bush (R)	65,686	(26%)
Other	5,022	(2%)

Cook Partisan Voting Index: D +23

Occupation   Blue collar: 20.7%   White collar: 61.9%   Gray collar: 17.4%

For a century or more, St. Louis seemed the center of America: the starting point for the Lewis and Clark expedition in 1804; the locus half a century later of the *Dred Scott* case, a Supreme Court ruling that helped split the nation; the site of the 1904 World's Fair that introduced the hot dog and the ice cream cone and got 19 million people to *Meet Me in St. Louis*. Its 630-foot-high Gateway Arch is just below the point where the waters of the Missouri surge into the Mississippi, about halfway between New Orleans and Lake Superior, the Atlantic and the Pacific. This first major American city west of the Mississippi River was the final resting place of Daniel Boone and for many years was Chicago's rival as the transportation hub of America. In 1904 St. Louis already had the Eads Bridge, one of America's first suspension bridges; the Wainwright Building, one of Louis Sullivan's first skyscrapers; and Union Station, the world's largest passenger train station when it opened in 1894. Some 600,000 people lived then in densely-packed brick houses on old street grids radiating outward from downtown. This was a heavily German city, with a Teutonic solidity and orderliness which distinguished it from the surrounding Southern-ac-cented rural terrain; and from Mitteleuropa came the founders of St. Louis's great businesses—the Anheuser-Busch brewery, May Company department stores, Joseph Pulitzer's *St. Louis Post-Dispatch*—and its first great politician and a friend of Abraham Lincoln, Senator and Interior Secretary Carl Schurz. There is almost a European aura to Forest Park, the site of the 1904 fair, and the dozen mansion-lined private streets nearby, like Portland Place.

St. Louis is still one of the nation's 20 largest metro areas, but today it does not occupy as central a place in the national consciousness, and the central city itself has largely emptied out. The German order that made so many people comfortable living in close quarters and commuting by streetcar seems to have yielded to an American desire for Daniel Boone's wide open (suburban) spaces and the less restrictive automobile. St. Louis' population peaked at 856,000 in 1950; it was down to 348,000 in 2000, less than its 350,000 in 1880 and far less than the 1 million in suburban (and juridically separate) St. Louis County. Indeed, more blacks live in St. Louis County (193,000) than St. Louis City (178,000). Downtown St. Louis has been spruced up admirably: the Gateway Arch was finished in 1965; Union Station has been redeveloped; Laclede's Landing is stocked with shops. But most of St. Louis's old factories have closed and many of its once tight neighborhoods are only a memory.

Missouri's congressional districts have followed the people out of St. Louis. The 1st District, historically based on the north side of the city, now has three-quarters of its residents in suburban St. Louis County. It includes St. Louis City north of I-64 and the northern and some central portions of St. Louis County. The district includes all the predominantly black suburbs to the north of the city, including Bellefontaine Neighbors, Ferguson, Spanish Lake and Black Jack. It also includes along I-70 working-class St. Ann and Bridgeton and, just west of the city, parts of the affluent suburbs of University City, Ladue and Creve Coeur. Originally 1st District Congressman William Lacy Clay wanted all of St. Louis, but that was resisted by the 3d District's Dick Gephardt and in April 2001 the two reached an agreement on the boundaries. Before redistricting, the population of the district was 60% black; now it is 50% black. But blacks undoubtedly account for more than 50% of the votes in Democratic primaries that, in this heavily Democratic district, are the contests that matter.

The congressman from the 1st District is William Lacy Clay, a Democrat elected in 2000 to the seat that his father Bill Clay had held for 32 years. Lacy Clay's whole life bears the imprint of his father's politics. Born in St. Louis, he moved to the Washington, D.C. area after his father's election in 1968 and grew up there as a congressman's son. He attended Silver Spring, Maryland public schools and then the University of Maryland, studying by night for seven years while he worked as a House staffer by day. He had started law classes at Howard University when a special election for the state House in 1983 drew him back to St. Louis, and party leaders appointed him the Democratic nominee. Eight years later, Lacy Clay was again picked by party leaders to run in a special election for a safely Democratic state Senate seat, after the incumbent got a job with a congressional subcommittee.

In 1999 Bill Clay decided to retire after having helped to enact many labor and education laws. Lacy Clay ran and had something of a serious contest. His most credible primary opposition was from St. Louis Councilman Charlie Dooley. Dooley raised nearly $400,000 and, though black, built up a base of support in the mostly white suburbs of St. Louis County. Dooley campaigned that the office should not be "inherited" and he attacked what he called Clay's old-style tactics of political threats and bossism. To make sure voters knew he was not challenging the incumbent, Dooley's billboards said, "Congressman Bill Clay is retiring this year." The St. Louis Labor Council and Missouri AFL-CIO, long allied to Bill Clay, declined to endorse his son, but he won endorsements from more than 30 locals. With many voters still thinking the two Clays were the same person, Lacy Clay played up his father's name and revved up the still reliable machine. He won the six-candidate primary 61%–28% over Dooley, winning the St. Louis City 76%–12% and St. Louis County, where twice as many votes were cast, 49%–39%. The general election was no contest. Lacy Clay won 75%–22%, which was better than his father had done in recent elections. Clay was one of the Democrats who persuaded a state judge to order the polls kept open an extra three hours. An appeals court reversed that order 45 minutes later, but Republicans charged that there were gross irregularities in the voting in St. Louis.

In Washington, Clay was president of the Democrats' freshman class and has had a liberal voting record. He said that he opposed the campaign finance regulation bill because it "only dabbles around the edges," but he voted the final version. He sought to make the point that he was not entirely his father's son. "Call me 'Clay Lite'," he said as he discussed his softer image with the *St. Louis Post-Dispatch*. But the truth inevitably was more complex. Despite his agreement with Gephardt on redistricting, Clay criticized Democrats who "dilute" minority districts and said that judges were fairer to black voters and politicians. Asserting himself in the sharply charged partisanship of St. Louis politics, he criticized Republicans including Senator Christopher

Bond who tied him to allegations of local vote fraud. Thanks to redistricting nearly one-third of the district was new to him but he was reelected 70%–27% in 2002.

SECOND DISTRICT

Rep. Todd Akin (R)

Elected 2000, 2d term; b. July 5, 1947, New York, NY; home, Town and Country; Worcester Polytech Inst. (MA), B.S. 1971, Covenant Theological Seminary (MO), M. Div. 1985; Presbyterian; married (Lulli).

Military Career: Army Reserves 1972–80.

Elected Office: MO House of Reps., 1988–00.

Professional Career: Marketing Mgr., IBM, 1974–78; Mgmt. Dir., Laclede Steel, 1977–80; Instructor, Maryville U.

DC Office: 117 CHOB 20515, 202-225-2561; Fax: 202-225-2563; Web site: www.house.gov/akin.

District Offices: St. Charles, 636-949-6826; St. Louis, 314-590-0029.

Committees: *Armed Services* (20th of 33 R): Tactical Air & Land Forces; Terrorism, Unconventional Threats & Capabilities. *Science* (15th of 25 R): Energy; Research. *Small Business* (9th of 18 R): Workforce, Empowerment & Government Programs (Chmn.).

Group Ratings

	ADA	ACLU	AFS	LCV	CON	ITIC	NTU	COC	ACU	NTLC	CHC
2002	0	7	0	0	87	75	65	85	100	97	100
2001	5	—	0	0	—	—	74	91	100	—	—

National Journal Ratings

	2001 LIB	—	2001 CONS		2002 LIB	—	2002 CONS
Economic	7%	—	89%		0%	—	91%
Social	0%	—	81%		0%	—	75%
Foreign	0%	—	97%		0%	—	85%

Key Votes of the 107th Congress

1. Approve Bush Tax Cuts	Y	5. Faith-Based Charities	Y	9. Trade Promotion Authority	Y
2. Limit Patients' Bill of Rights	Y	6. Bar Gays in the Boy Scouts	Y	10. Bar Funds for Intl. Court	Y
3. Campaign Finance Reform	N	7. Ban Partial-Birth Abortion	Y	11. Authorize Force in Iraq	Y
4. Ban ANWR Development	N	8. Arm Commercial Pilots	Y	12. Deny Home. Sec. Dept. Union	Y

Election Results

2002 general	Todd Akin (R)	167,057	(67%)	($586,796)
	John Hogan (D)	77,223	(31%)	
	Other	4,548	(2%)	
2002 primary	Todd Akin (R)	unopposed		
2000 general	Todd Akin (R)	164,926	(55%)	($1,015,568)
	Ted House (D)	126,441	(42%)	($858,204)
	Other	6,695	(2%)	

The People		Race/Ethnic Origin	Ancestry	
Area size:	1,288 sq. mi.	93.2% White	German: 26.7%	Irish: 12.7%
Urban population:	91.7%	2.2% Black	English: 8.2%	
Rural population:	8.4%	2.0% Asian	**2000 Presidential Vote**	
Pop. 2000:	621,690	0.2% Native Am.	Bush (R)	179,633 (59%)
Median income:	$61,416	0.0% Hawaiian	Gore (D)	119,907 (39%)
Poverty status:	3.6%	0.9% Two+ races	Other	6,744 (2%)
Military veterans:	13.5%	0.1% Other	**Cook Partisan Voting Index:** R + 10	
		1.4% Hispanic Origin		

Occupation	Blue collar: 17.5%	White collar: 71.3%	Gray collar: 11.2%

Just as the U.S. population's geographic center has moved west from the St. Louis area to rural Phelps County, so the center of metropolitan St. Louis area continues to move farther west from the Gateway Arch on the Mississippi River. The fulcrum point now is in St. Louis County, established in 1876 when the city, tired of paying for dusty back roads, separated itself from the sticks. There were then about 350,000 people in the city and 31,000 in the county. In 2000, the city had 348,000 and St. Louis County 1,016,000. By the 1960s, the center of office employment had moved from downtown across the county line to Clayton; now, the focus is fast moving out the Daniel Boone Expressway (U.S. 40) to Chesterfield, west of the I-270 ring road.

The 2d Congressional District is made up of central and western St. Louis County, most of fast-growing St. Charles County northwest across the Missouri River plus rural Lincoln County to the north. In the center of St. Louis County, along the Daniel Boone Expressway, are the long-settled suburbs of Kirkwood, most of high-income Town and Country and Ladue, fast-growing Chesterfield and, to the south, Sunset Hills—all Republican areas, even more so in the newer family-oriented subdivisions than in the leafy precincts of the old rich. St. Charles County now casts more votes than the city of St. Louis and is the most Republican suburban county in Missouri. The 2001 redistricting increased the Bush 2000 percentage in the 2d from 55% to 59%.

The congressman from the 2d District is Todd Akin, a Republican first elected in 2000. He continues to live in his boyhood home, a 50-year-old farmhouse that rests in what has become an upscale neighborhood in Town and Country. He graduated from Worcester Polytechnic Institute and got a divinity degree at Covenant Seminary. After service as an Army combat engineer, he worked for IBM in the Boston area and then at Laclede Steel in Alton, Illinois, the same company where his father once worked. He was elected to the state House in 1988. During the next 12 years, as part of the Republican minority, few of his bills passed. Undaunted, he took to the courts, filing one lawsuit to stop a tax increase for education improvements and another to stop riverboat gambling on barges moored in artificial ponds; the former case failed but the latter succeeded, forcing the gambling industry to spend millions on a referendum that changed the law in its favor. Akin's idealism derives from his avid study of American history and the Constitution, on which he lectures at various public and private institutions. While a state legislator, he sold standardized tests to parents who home school their children; he and his wife have home schooled their six children. State House reporters noted that he sometimes played gospel tunes on his guitar in the Capitol late at night.

When Republican Congressman Jim Talent announced in early 1999 that he was running for governor, Akin ran for the House. He started off as the underdog to Gene McNary, the former Bush Administration INS commissioner and well known from his 15 years as St. Louis County Executive and as a candidate for the Senate in 1980 and for governor in 1972 and 1984. A third candidate, former state Senate Minority Leader Franc Flotron, ran as a conservative. Akin called himself "a conservative with a soft edge," who tries to work as a team player. He emphasized that he had never voted to raise taxes, and he had strong support from religious conservatives; he may have benefited from staying above the personal attacks. In a low-turnout, rainy day Republican primary, Akin rallied his committed cadre to win the five-candidate contest by 56 votes. Akin won St. Louis County by 293 votes over McNary; in St. Charles County, both narrowly trailed Barbara Cooper, who was Talent's former district director, but she was much weaker in St. Louis County and finished fourth overall. In the general election against state Senator Ted House, a former aide to Congressman Ike Skelton, Akin focused on their differences on taxes. House depicted Akin as a narrow ideologue who was an ineffective legislator. House, whose TV ads did not identify himself as a Democrat, cited a report by a liberal activist group that Akin had written a supportive letter read at a militia rally in 1995 that focused on the right to bear arms; Akin responded that he had turned down an invitation to speak. House managed to carry 50%–48% in St. Charles County, his home base, but that was only 21% of the total vote; Akin took St. Louis County 57%–40% and won overall 55%–42%.

In the House, Akin has one of the most strongly conservative voting records. He joined Senator Christopher Bond in successfully urging the Bush administration not to tighten ozone standards for the St. Louis area. He also urged the Navy not to cut back Boeing's production of F/A-18 Super Hornet electronic-warfare aircraft at its St. Louis County plant. On the Republicans' education bill, Akin opposed mandatory school testing because he was concerned about excessive federal involvement. After a federal appeals court in California ruled that the reference to "one nation under God" in the Pledge of Allegiance was unconstitutional, he proposed a bill that would strip the lower courts of jurisdiction over the Pledge.

Back home, Akin was unhappy about losing some of his St. Louis County suburbs to the 1st District of William Lacy Clay and was the only member of the delegation who did not support the redistricting plan. But he declined to challenge it in court. The changes made what had been a competitive district a decade before significantly more Republican. Akin was reelected 67%–31%.

THIRD DISTRICT

Rep. Dick Gephardt (D)

Elected 1976, 14th term; b. Jan. 31, 1941, St. Louis; home, St. Louis; Northwestern U., B.S. 1962, U. of MI, J.D. 1965; Baptist; married (Jane).

Military Career: Air Natl. Guard, 1965–71.

Elected Office: St. Louis City Alderman, 1971–76; Dem. Presidential Candidate, 1988.

Professional Career: Practicing atty., 1965–77.

DC Office: 1236 LHOB 20515, 202-225-2671; Fax: 202-225-7452; Web site: www.house.gov/gephardt.

District Offices: Festus, 636-937-6399; St. Louis, 314-894-3400.

Committees: None.

Group Ratings

	ADA	ACLU	AFS	LCV	CON	ITIC	NTU	COC	ACU	NTLC	CHC
2002	90	71	100	88	43	25	18	35	8	0	0
2001	95	—	100	93	—	—	9	30	13	—	—

National Journal Ratings

	2001 LIB —	2001 CONS	2002 LIB —	2002 CONS
Economic	93%	8%	86%	12%
Social	81%	20%	72%	28%
Foreign	65%	36%	69%	30%

Key Votes of the 107th Congress

1. Approve Bush Tax Cuts	N	5. Faith-Based Charities	N	9. Trade Promotion Authority	N
2. Limit Patients' Bill of Rights	N	6. Bar Gays in the Boy Scouts	N	10. Bar Funds for Intl. Court	N
3. Campaign Finance Reform	Y	7. Ban Partial-Birth Abortion	Y	11. Authorize Force in Iraq	Y
4. Ban ANWR Development	Y	8. Arm Commercial Pilots	N	12. Deny Home. Sec. Dept. Union	N

Election Results

2002 general	Dick Gephardt (D)	122,181	(59%)	($3,389,306)
	Catherine Enz (R)	80,551	(39%)	($114,143)
	Other	4,146	(2%)	
2002 primary	Dick Gephardt (D)	44,535	(74%)	
	Michael Bram (D)	16,014	(26%)	
2000 general	Dick Gephardt (D)	147,222	(58%)	($5,580,964)
	William J. Federer (R)	100,967	(40%)	($2,319,819)
	Other	6,350	(2%)	

Prior Winning Percentages: 1998 (56%); 1996 (59%); 1994 (58%); 1992 (64%); 1990 (57%); 1988 (63%); 1986 (69%); 1984 (100%); 1982 (78%); 1980 (78%); 1978 (82%); 1976 (64%)

The People		Race/Ethnic Origin	Ancestry	
Area size:	1,266 sq. mi.	85.7% White	German: 23.1%	Irish: 11.6%
Urban population:	86.7%	9.1% Black	English: 5.9%	
Rural population:	13.3%	1.6% Asian	**2000 Presidential Vote**	
Pop. 2000:	621,690	0.2% Native Am.	Gore (D) 140,954	(54%)
Median income:	$41,091	0.0% Hawaiian	Bush (R) 112,460	(43%)
Poverty status:	10.1%	1.4% Two + races	Other 7,972	(3%)
Military veterans:	13.2%	0.1% Other	**Cook Partisan Voting Index:** D + 5	
		1.8% Hispanic Origin		
Occupation	Blue collar: 24.2%	White collar: 60.4%	Gray collar: 15.4%	

Middle America, it could be said, lies somewhere on the south side of metropolitan St. Louis. The geographical center of the country's population was here in 1980, just south of St. Louis in once rural and now mostly suburban Jefferson County; while that point has moved about 35 miles southwest, St. Louis is still the metro area nearest the midpoint of a country most of whose people live in million-plus metro areas. Geographically, this is a node where some of the nation's main arteries come together. The Missouri River flows into the Mississippi a few miles north of St. Louis's Gateway Arch; the National Road and its successors, U.S. 40 and Interstate 70, cross the Mississippi just below the Arch. And the great tides of Southerners migrating west up the Mississippi and Germans migrating overland met here to create one of the nation's largest and most bustling cities out of a town founded by the French before the Revolutionary War. The south side of St. Louis is famous for its tight-knit, neat neighborhoods and pleasant parks; its most famous symbols are the Anheuser-Busch brewery just south of downtown and Grant's Farm, where Ulysses S. Grant lived in the 1850s and where Anheuser-Busch now keeps the Budweiser Clydesdales. But many more people now live in the suburbs heading out all directions, well into Jefferson County to the south.

The 3d Congressional District consists of the south side of St. Louis, part of suburban St. Louis County and, to the south, Jefferson County and rural Ste. Genevieve County, the site of Missouri's oldest permanent settlement, founded near a salt mine in 1730. Its St. Louis County portions are mostly suburbs close to the St. Louis City line—Clayton, Maplewood, Richmond Heights, Webster Groves, Affton, Lemay, Oakville. This is the descendant of districts dominated by St. Louis voters, but today the city casts less than 25% of its votes, fewer than Jefferson County; almost half are cast in St. Louis County. Ethnically, this has been a heavily German-American area since the mid-19th century. Politically, it has been Democratic since the New Deal of the 1930s. The 2001 redistricting removed some Republican suburbs in southwest St. Louis County and reduced the Bush 2000 percentage from 46% to 43%.

The congressman from the 3d District is Richard Gephardt, first elected in 1976, a Democratic leader in the House for 18 years, presidential candidate in 1988 and again in 2003. Gephardt grew up on the south side of St. Louis, the son of a milk truck driver who worked himself up into the middle class. A bit too old and cautious to be part of the generation of Vietnam era student rebels, Gephardt returned home from law school in 1965 to work in a large downtown law firm, but was clearly intent on a traditional political career; he moved to the south side of St. Louis and was elected alderman in 1971. In 1976, when 3d District Congresswoman Leonor Sullivan announced her retirement, Gephardt jumped into the race as an anti-establishment candidate. He beat a labor union official in the primary and a former board of aldermen president in the general. Gephardt started off in the House as one of the new breed of Democrats who did not automatically embrace big government and higher taxes. With the help of Missouri's Richard Bolling, Gephardt got a seat on the Ways and Means Committee, rare for a freshman. He voted for the 1981 Reagan tax cut and was the House co-sponsor of New Jersey Senator Bill Bradley's bill that was the basis of the 1986 tax reform. Gephardt was one of the founders of the moderate Democratic Leadership Council and initially opposed many popular Democratic causes such as abortion, busing and raising the minimum wage.

Gephardt was elected caucus chairman over David Obey in 1984, and in the years that followed grew more in sync with the increasingly liberal tenor of the Democratic Caucus. Gephardt was a superb caucus politician and a good listener, a hard-working detail man, eager to absorb information and to sit through endless meetings, with a gift for molding compromises and positions that hold together the often unruly and divisive Democratic Caucus. When he ran for president he had the enthusiastic support of dozens of House colleagues as he spent 144 days in Iowa campaigning for the February 1988 caucuses. But he abandoned legislative work as he shifted to this new arena, sometimes to the dismay of allies, such as Ways and Means Committee chairman Dan Rostenkowski. He played little role in the 1986 tax reform he had originally co-sponsored; he changed his stand on abortion to pro-choice. In Iowa, he supported mandatory agricultural production controls, a non-starter even in a Democratic Congress. Even more prominently, he went on the offensive on trade issues. The United Auto Workers is a major factor in Iowa caucuses, and Gephardt came up with his amendment requiring retaliation against countries (chiefly, Japan) running large trade surpluses with the United States. Gephardt won the Iowa caucuses with 31% of the vote, to 27% for Paul Simon and 22% for Michael Dukakis. In New Hampshire, Gephardt found himself under attack for switching positions in a state that hates taxes and government regulation; he finished second with 20% to Dukakis's 36%. On Super Tuesday, Gephardt had run out of money, won only Missouri and quit the race.

Back in the House, Gephardt quickly rebounded to the ranks of party insider. In June 1989, when Speaker Jim Wright and Majority Whip Tony Coelho resigned and Thomas Foley was elected speaker, Gephardt ran for majority leader and defeated Georgian Ed Jenkins 181–76. Gephardt went to work creating a sense of camaraderie in a dispirited caucus. In the 1990 budget summit talks, Gephardt used OMB Director Richard Darman's desire for agreement to frame the issue as a choice between the Democrats' plan to tax the rich more and Bush's refusal to do so—a contrast that led to Republican losses in the 1990 election. In September 1990 Gephardt supported George Bush's dispatch of troops to the Persian Gulf, but in January 1991 he led House opposition to the Gulf War resolution and uncharacteristically stumbled by threatening to cut off funds for U.S. troops there.

In the early Clinton years, Gephardt combined ardent support for the administration on most issues with carefully calibrated dissent on others. His major dissent was on trade. He delayed opposing NAFTA for several months as he sought more concessions from administration officials but he eventually came out against it. He came up with his own plan to force Japan to meet numerical goals in opening its markets or face retaliation. Gephardt vigorously supported the Clinton health care plan in 1994 and tried to put together his own bill combining the Clinton and Ways and Means plans; but it was tough slogging and no bill came to the floor.

In November 1994, Clinton and House Democrats were stunningly repudiated. Democrats lost 52 seats. Speaker Foley lost his seat, and Gephardt was now minority leader as Democrats lost control of the House for the first time in 40 years. The strategy followed by Speakers Tip O'Neill, Jim Wright and Foley—hold the Democratic Caucus together enough to produce 218 votes—was now obsolete: there weren't 218 Democrats any more. Gephardt pushed aside a challenge by North Carolina's Charlie Rose for the party leadership, 150–58. But the day he handed over the gavel to Speaker Newt Gingrich, Gephardt later said, "was one of the worst days of my life."

In this setting Gephardt saw himself as an independent force. After support for Republicans and Gingrich plummeted during the government shutdown, he and Senate Minority Leader Tom Daschle came up with a united Democratic "Families First" platform, including tax deductions for child care, health insurance and higher education, a balanced budget and tough anti-crime measures. But the surging Clinton-Gore campaign ignored Gephardt and, though campaign polls showed Democrats ahead of Republicans in House races, ignored Democrats' efforts to win a majority in the House. Clinton and Gore each devoted one sentence in their acceptance speeches to the need for Democratic majorities in Congress. Gephardt's hard-fought effort to elect the majority and become speaker came crashing down in November 1996, as Democrats scored a nine-seat net gain but still had only 207 House seats, despite Gingrich's unpopularity, despite the AFL-CIO's $35 million ad campaign and despite Clinton's victory.

Over the next two years Gephardt's fortunes and strategies oscillated widely. Major budget issues were settled in negotiations between House Republicans and the White House, from which

Gephardt was ostentatiously shut out. In December 1997 Gephardt made a speech at Harvard's Kennedy School, celebrating "core Democratic values," calling for the party to reject small-bore ideas and speak boldly to the needs of working people in the United States and around the world: a *cri de coeur* against the Clinton administration. For that Gephardt was criticized by many House Democrats. Still, he continued to receive great applause from AFL-CIO audiences, happy with his opposition to NAFTA and PNTR status with China, and angry at Al Gore's stands in favor.

Then came the Lewinsky scandal. Suddenly Clinton was finding his strongest defenders among the left wing of the congressional party; and he began making concessions to them. After Clinton's televised address to the nation in August when he conceded his inappropriate and "wrong" relationship with the White House intern, Gephardt, whose personal life is exemplary, called the president's conduct "reprehensible" and said impeachment was possible. He said he would decline to take a partisan role in defending Clinton, and began the impeachment inquiry process in a statesmanlike joint appearance with Gingrich. In December, Gephardt assailed Clinton's character and reliance on polls—but said he would vote against impeachment. On the day of the vote, speaking just after Bob Livingston made his breathtaking announcement that he would step down, Gephardt junked his previous draft and made an eloquent speech. "The politics of slash and burn must end," he said. "We need to stop destroying imperfect people at the altar of an unobtainable majority."

One reason for Democratic unity was that the party unexpectedly gained seats in the 1998 election, as Republican core voters were turned off by the tepid budget compromises the party's leaders accepted in October and Democrats were energized by their support of Clinton. Democrats gained five House seats, the first such gain for a president's party in an off-year election since 1934. Sensing that Democrats had a real chance for a majority, and deterred perhaps by the Clinton White House's all-out support of Al Gore, Gephardt in February 1999 announced—at a press conference emblazoned with "Speaker Gephardt" signs—that he would not run for president. As the year went on, the Clinton-Gore team took stands in line with Gephardt's, in rejecting Social Security investment accounts, which had a likely majority in Congress; in rejecting the Medicare changes worked out by Democrats John Breaux and Bob Kerrey; in replacing broad-based tax cuts with the targeted tax cuts favored by Clinton. Democrats demanded votes on issues on which they could amass bipartisan majorities—campaign finance, the minimum wage, education spending increases. In the process, Gephardt's relationship with the mild-mannered Speaker Dennis Hastert frayed. During 2000 they barely spoke, although Hastert was willing to negotiate with Minority Whip David Bonior.

Gephardt concentrated instead—and again—on winning back a majority in the House. He appointed Patrick Kennedy as chairman of the DCCC, not for his electoral skills but for his ability to raise money: Democrats all over the country paid money to see a Kennedy. Gephardt staffers took control of the DCCC, and did a fine job of targeting weak Republicans and fielding good candidates. It is hard to think of what else Gephardt could have done, yet on Election Day Democrats fell heartbreakingly short of their goal, as Republicans won 221 seats—three more than a 218 majority. Al Gore's candidacy did not help much; as Gephardt said later, "In retrospect, if we had a little wind at the top of the ticket, it would have helped some of those close races."

In the House, he reestablished a speaking relationship with Hastert after the election. But for all of George W. Bush's talk of a "new tone," Gephardt saw little bipartisanship from House Republicans. After the party switch by Jim Jeffords gave Democrats a majority in the Senate and made Tom Daschle the premier Democrat on Capitol Hill, Gephardt was even less relevant as Republicans passed bills in the House to pile on the doorstep of the Senate. That changed for a time after September 11, when Gephardt joined a handful of bipartisan leaders who worked closely and speedily to move emergency legislation and respond to further threats of terrorism. But the decision by Gephardt to oppose trade promotion authority mostly ended that cooperation. The one major exception came in September 2002, when—unlike 1991—he worked closely with Bush and independently of most House Democrats to support the use of force in Iraq, a step that angered many in his own party and assured easy passage of the resolution; Gephardt clearly believed that the nation was in peril and that he must act in what he felt were the nation's best interests regardless of partisan effect. But for months he had made clear that his political interest had shifted to the presidency and that the opportunity to become Speaker was no longer his predominant goal. Though few professed to know what Gephardt would do, most colleagues said that they would accept his decision. In the back of his mind were regrets about not challenging George H. W. Bush in 1992.

Back home, the 3d District has trended Republican, and Gephardt, despite spending millions of dollars every campaign year, has not topped 60% since 1992. In 1998 Republican William Federer, operating with only $196,000, held him to a 56%–42% margin. In 2000 Federer ran again; this time George W. Bush's uncle William Bush chaired his finance committee, and Federer spent $2.3 million. He launched sharp attacks on Gephardt on issues like gay rights, and Democrats punched back sharply. A Gephardt worker charged Federer with assault when he tried to prevent videotaping a parade in early October. Gephardt won 58%–40%. In 2002, in a more Democratic district, Gephardt faced term-limited state Representative Catherine Enz, who raised little money; Gephardt won 59%–39%. Gephardt led by only 55%–43% in St. Louis County and 56%–42% in Jefferson County, but carried St. Louis City 69%–28%.

In November 2002 Democrats failed for the fifth time in a row to win a majority of House seats. To the surprise of many, they lost six seats; this was the second consecutive off-year election in which the president's party gained seats, and perhaps it is time to junk the old political rule that it always loses. On Thursday Gephardt announced that he would step down from the position of Minority Leader; perhaps there would have been demands that he do so if he had not acted so quickly, perhaps not.

Gephardt later announced that he would not seek reelection to the House and would run for president in 2004. In the House he refused to take a committee assignment; he is likely to miss many floor votes when he is on the campaign and fundraising trails. He called for repealing the Bush tax cuts and, in April 2003, proposed that the federal government guarantee that all Americans have health insurance. In the 3d District, those named as possible candidates in 2004 included Democrats state Senator Steve Stoll, St. Louis Circuit Court Clerk Mariano Favazza and state Representative Russ Carnahan, son of the late governor Mel Carnahan and former Senator Jean Carnahan. Possible Republican candidates included Federer, former state Representatives Zane Yates and Catherine Enz, the 2002 nominee. The Democratic nominee would obviously be the favorite, but this could be a seriously contested district.

FOURTH DISTRICT

Rep. Ike Skelton (D)

Elected 1976, 14th term; b. Dec. 20, 1931, Lexington; home, Lexington; Wentworth Military Acad. Jr. Col., 1949–51, U. of MO, A.B. 1953, LL.B. 1956; Disciples of Christ; married (Susie).

Elected Office: MO Senate, 1971–76.

Professional Career: Lafayette Cnty. Prosecuting atty., 1957–60; MO Special Asst. Atty. Gen., 1961–63; Practicing atty., 1963–76.

DC Office: 2206 RHOB 20515, 202-225-2876; Web site: www.house.gov/skelton.

District Offices: Blue Springs, 816-228-4242; Jefferson City, 573-635-3499; Lebanon, 417-532-7964; Sedalia, 660-826-2675.

Committees: *Armed Services* (RMM of 29 D): Tactical Air & Land Forces.

Group Ratings

	ADA	ACLU	AFS	LCV	CON	ITIC	NTU	COC	ACU	NTLC	CHC
2002	60	33	78	38	43	75	21	70	32	15	58
2001	50	—	67	43	—	—	25	64	64	—	—

National Journal Ratings

	2001 LIB	—	2001 CONS	2002 LIB	—	2002 CONS
Economic	56%	—	44%	59%	—	40%
Social	38%	—	61%	49%	—	50%
Foreign	43%	—	53%	60%	—	39%

Key Votes of the 107th Congress

1. Approve Bush Tax Cuts	N	5. Faith-Based Charities	Y	9. Trade Promotion Authority	Y
2. Limit Patients' Bill of Rights	N	6. Bar Gays in the Boy Scouts	Y	10. Bar Funds for Intl. Court	Y
3. Campaign Finance Reform	Y	7. Ban Partial-Birth Abortion	Y	11. Authorize Force in Iraq	Y
4. Ban ANWR Development	N	8. Arm Commercial Pilots	Y	12. Deny Home. Sec. Dept. Union	N

Election Results

2002 general	Ike Skelton (D)	142,204	(68%)	($596,705)
	Jim Noland (R)	64,451	(31%)	
	Other	3,583	(2%)	
2002 primary	Ike Skelton (D)	unopposed		
2000 general	Ike Skelton (D)	180,634	(67%)	($624,593)
	Jim Noland (R)	84,406	(31%)	($11,256)
	Other	4,849	(2%)	

Prior Winning Percentages: 1998 (71%); 1996 (64%); 1994 (68%); 1992 (70%); 1990 (62%); 1988 (72%); 1986 (100%); 1984 (67%); 1982 (55%); 1980 (68%); 1978 (73%); 1976 (56%)

The People		Race/Ethnic Origin	Ancestry	
Area size:	14,825 sq. mi.	92.4% White	German: 17.4%	USA: 11.0%
Urban population:	39.9%	3.2% Black	Irish: 8.6%	
Rural population:	60.1%	0.6% Asian	**2000 Presidential Vote**	
Pop. 2000:	621,690	0.5% Native Am.	Bush (R).............147,694	(58%)
Median income:	$34,541	0.1% Hawaiian	Gore (D).............100,171	(39%)
Poverty status:	12.1%	1.3% Two+ races	Other...................6,024	(2%)
Military veterans:	16.1%	0.1% Other	**Cook Partisan Voting Index:** R +10	
		1.9% Hispanic Origin		

Occupation	Blue collar: 31.9%	White collar: 51.4%	Gray collar: 16.7%

Missouri was the first state settled west of the Mississippi, and the folks who settled it were a picture of pioneer diversity. Virginians and other Southerners made their way to counties north of the Missouri River, while Germans settled around the still small capital city of Jefferson City. A taste of that diversity can be found in the Capitol, with its mural by Thomas Hart Benton, great-grandnephew and eponym of Missouri's first senator, who championed hard money and westward expansion for 30 years and lost his seat for opposing the expansion of slavery. The painting shows dance hall girls, black coal miners and a mother diapering an infant—all reminders that pioneer life was less homogeneous than many imagine.

The 4th Congressional District occupies much of this early-settled part of central and western Missouri. It includes Blue Springs and Oak Grove in Jackson County east of Kansas City, but the overall atmosphere here is rural and small-town, with political traditions dating back to the community's early days. The rural counties around Kansas City were full of pro-slavery-expansion Bushwhackers who rode across the Kansas line to thwart the Yankee Jayhawks, and these areas today vote Democratic. The German area around Jefferson City was anti-slavery and remains among the most Republican parts of Missouri, and the new resort areas around Lake of the Ozarks are mixed. The southern portion of the district, near Springfield, was Union country during the Civil War and Republican now. There are some big military bases here: Fort Leonard Wood in Pulaski County and Whiteman Air Force Base, near Knob Noster in Johnson County, from which B-2s took off and flew across the world to drop precision-targeted bombs in Afghanistan.

Much of this region is Truman country: Harry Truman was born in Barton County, at the southern end of the district, and lived in Independence, just a few miles from Blue Springs. He spent much of election night 1948, when just about everyone thought he would lose, in Excelsior Springs, on the border of Ray County, the district's one county north of the Missouri River. In his long life Truman spanned the the gaps between country and city, South and North: his mother could remember her house being attacked by Yankee soldiers, and she remained pro-Confederate even when her son was in the White House; he got his political start in urban Independence and Kansas City and desegregated the military services.

The congressman from the 4th District is Ike Skelton, who in many ways can be called a Truman Democrat; his father met Truman in 1928, when he was Lafayette County prosecutor and the future president was Jackson County judge, and they remained friends for life; his father took 17-year-old Ike to Washington for Truman's inaugural in 1949. Skelton is from a military family: his father served in the Navy, he and his brothers went to military academies and he has sons in the Army and Navy; a teenage bout with polio made him ineligible for military service. He grew up in Lexington, of old Missouri stock; he is a distant cousin through the Boone family of New York Congresswoman Louise Slaughter. Skelton graduated from the University of Missouri and its law school and returned to Lexington to practice law. He became county prosecutor in 1957, at 25, and was elected to the Missouri Senate in 1970. In 1976 he ran for Congress and won rather easily; Bess Truman endorsed him. Skelton looks and votes like an old-fashioned rural Missouri Democrat: his voting record puts him near the midpoint of this Republican House on economics and foreign issues, slightly to the right on cultural issues. He supports the same expansive, assertive foreign and defense policies the preponderance of Democrats supported in the days of Truman.

Skelton is the ranking Democrat on the Armed Services Committee where he has made great contributions to policy. He played a key role in passing the Goldwater-Nichols Act in 1986, which created the joint commands which have proved so successful in Iraq. He has said that the Clinton administration cut the military too much, as did Defense Secretary Dick Cheney in the first Bush administration, and he has criticized the current Bush administration for not seeking higher force levels. "At the present time, we do not have enough people in uniform to adequately protect American interests throughout the world," he wrote in May 2002. He has worked hard to improve housing and facilities for service members and their families and has proposed offering 18-month enlistments plus four years of Reserve duty to get more recruits. He warned the Clinton and Bush administrations that troops could be worn out by multiple deployments. He was reluctant to support sending troops to Bosnia in September 1995, and passed a resolution, 287–141, which called for strict neutrality in the peacekeeping effort. He supported the air war in the former Yugoslavia in March 1999. In 2000 he called for the Navy to supplement the fleet with smaller vessels that could be built in greater numbers. Missile defense is the one issue on which he says he has felt constrained by his party; in May 2001 he joined other Democrats in stressing that the technology doesn't work yet and that it is not sufficiently funded. "I'm not opposed to it at all. I just think we should take a deep breath and treat it like other weapons systems: don't rush to judgment."

But on the whole, Armed Services is one of the House's least partisan committees; most members are strong defense supporters and it usually reports bills with bipartisan support. Skelton is greatly respected by Republicans as well as Democrats on the committee. But the House as a whole is not always of the same opinion on military issues. "I have detected a growing cultural gap between military and civilian America," Skelton noted in 1997. "Fewer people today have direct contact with the military. I can tell you that as fewer sons and daughters wear the uniforms of our country, members of Congress receive less encouragement from voters in their districts to support a substantial military for our nation." In January 2002, after George W. Bush identified Iraq, Iran and North Korea as the axis of evil, Skelton noted, "We're going to go after these regimes. That's clear. Details are not included." He drew a historic parallel with the Barbary Pirates: "The American Navy and Marines stamped them out and stopped them. There are no more Barbary Pirates. That's the lesson that comes out of that." Yet he was cautious after Bush's September 12 speech at the United Nations. On October 9 he announced he would vote for the Iraq war resolution.

Naturally Skelton looks out for the interests of Fort Leonard Wood and Whiteman Air Force Base which, as he points out are both major bases with unique function unlikely to wind up on any base-closing list. He was instrumental in getting Whiteman, with its 12,400-foot runway, designated in 1987 as the home of the first wing of B-2s; the base had been used for the Minuteman II missile which was about to be phased out. His loyalty to Missouri only goes so far: in 1999, when other Missourians were trying to keep the F-15 line open in St. Louis County, Skelton said that he doubted any more F-15s would be built; he opposed ordering them in appropriations bills when they hadn't been authorized by Armed Services. He also worked for 10 years for the aircraft carrier the *U.S.S. Harry S Truman*, commissioned in July 1998, and with Missourian Roy Blunt co-sponsored the 2000 law naming the State Department building after Truman. Skelton chaired the joint session of Congress held on Truman's 100th birthday in 1984 and criticized the Smithsonian's Enola Gay exhibit for unfairly questioning Truman's motives toward the Japanese.

On non-military issues, Skelton tends to stick with other Democrats on taxes and economic issues, though he was one of only 20 Democrats who voted for trade promotion authority in 2001 and 2002: "For me it was the right thing to do. I represent a rural area. We have a lot of farms—a lot of soybeans, wheat and corn. And one-fourth of all that depends on foreign markets." In October 1998 he was one of 31 Democrats who voted for the Republican impeachment inquiry resolution. But he strongly criticized the Republicans for going ahead with the impeachment vote while Clinton's bombing of Iraq was going on, and voted against impeachment after being one of the last Democrats to announce his position.

Skelton's toughest race came in 1982, when he was redistricted in with a Republican incumbent; he won 55%–45%. He has won by very large margins in recent years; in 1999 citizens in Lexington and Lafayette Counties began raising money to build the Ike Skelton Museum of the American Armed Forces. It is widely assumed that when he retires, the 4th District, which voted 58% for George W. Bush in 2000, will elect a Republican to replace him.

FIFTH DISTRICT

Rep. Karen McCarthy (D)

Elected 1994, 5th term; b. Mar. 18, 1947, Haverhill, MA; home, Kansas City; U. of KS, B.A. 1969, M.B.A. 1986, U. of MO, M.S. 1976; Catholic; divorced.

Elected Office: MO House of Reps., 1976–94.

Professional Career: High schl. teacher, 1969–76; Financial analyst, 1984–86; Govt. affairs consultant, Marion Merrill Dow, 1986–94; Pres., Natl. Conf. of State Legislatures, 1994.

DC Office: 1436 LHOB 20515, 202-225-4535; Fax: 202-225-4403; Web site: www.house.gov/karenmccarthy.

District Offices: Independence, 816-833-4545; Kansas City, 816-842-4545.

Committees: *Energy & Commerce* (17th of 26 D): Commerce, Trade & Consumer Protection; Energy & Air Quality; Telecommunications & The Internet. *Select Committee on Homeland Security* (15th of 23 D): Intelligence & Counterterrorism; Rules.

Group Ratings

	ADA	ACLU	AFS	LCV	CON	ITIC	NTU	COC	ACU	NTLC	CHC
2002	95	87	100	100	17	50	19	40	0	8	0
2001	95	—	100	93	—	—	13	48	4	—	—

National Journal Ratings

	2001 LIB —	2001 CONS		2002 LIB —	2002 CONS
Economic	74%	27%		76%	24%
Social	83%	11%		74%	19%
Foreign	86%	12%		77%	23%

Key Votes of the 107th Congress

1. Approve Bush Tax Cuts	*	5. Faith-Based Charities		9. Trade Promotion Authority	N
2. Limit Patients' Bill of Rights	N	6. Bar Gays in the Boy Scouts	N	10. Bar Funds for Intl. Court	N
3. Campaign Finance Reform	Y	7. Ban Partial-Birth Abortion	N	11. Authorize Force in Iraq	N
4. Ban ANWR Development	Y	8. Arm Commercial Pilots	N	12. Deny Home. Sec. Dept. Union	N

Election Results

2002 general	Karen McCarthy (D)	122,645	(66%)	($445,602)
	Steve Gordon (R)	60,245	(32%)	($4,059)
	Other	3,277	(2%)	
2002 primary	Karen McCarthy (D)	40,532	(86%)	
	Charles Lindsey (D)	6,460	(14%)	
2000 general	Karen McCarthy (D)	159,826	(69%)	($331,907)
	Steve Gordon (R)	66,439	(29%)	($10,060)
	Other	5,872	(3%)	

Prior Winning Percentages: 1998 (66%); 1996 (67%); 1994 (57%)

The People		Race/Ethnic Origin	Ancestry	
Area size:	519 sq. mi.	66.3% White	German: 13.5%	Irish: 8.8%
Urban population:	96.1%	24.2% Black	English: 7.5%	
Rural population:	3.9%	1.3% Asian	**2000 Presidential Vote**	
Pop. 2000:	621,691	0.4% Native Am.	Gore (D) 149,621	(60%)
Median income:	$38,311	0.2% Hawaiian	Bush (R) 91,626	(37%)
Poverty status:	12.4%	1.9% Two+ races	Other 6,625	(3%)
Military veterans:	14.0%	0.1% Other	**Cook Partisan Voting Index:** D +12	
		5.6% Hispanic Origin		

Occupation	Blue collar: 22.7%	White collar: 61.8%	Gray collar: 15.4%

Kansas City, named after a state it isn't in and a river it doesn't touch, is the center of one of America's large metro areas, the biggest on the central Great Plains. The first pioneers here started little towns on the bluffs above the Missouri River—Independence, Kansas City, Westport—which coalesced a few decades later. Here traders on the Santa Fe Trail set out to cross the Sand Hills of Kansas and reach Mexican territory; here Jayhawks and Bushwhackers set out to fight for control of Bleeding Kansas. Kansas City was a rail center and, in the 1920s, had one of the largest stockyards in the country, a major commercial center with lean skyscrapers and the Country Club Plaza, the first shopping center in America. It is famous for Harry Truman, who grew up on a farm now in the suburb of Grandview and who lived in his wife's family's house in Independence, the old county seat just to the east. It is famous also for its black community, and jazz musicians like Scott Joplin, Charlie Parker and Count Basie, and for its much-praised barbecue.

The 5th Congressional District includes most of Kansas City, the largest city in Missouri, plus Grandview and the bulk of Independence, and more suburban slices of Jackson County to the east; it also includes fast-growing Belton and Raymore along U.S. 71 in Cass County just to the south; most of the metro area's landmarks, including the Truman home, are here. One-quarter of the district's residents are black, the second highest percentage among Missouri districts. Politically, the seat is solidly Democratic.

The congresswoman from the 5th District is Karen McCarthy, a Democrat first elected in 1994. She moved to Kansas City to teach school, and shortly thereafter, in 1976, at 29, was elected to the Missouri House. She served there 18 years, rising to become chairwoman of Ways and Means in 1983 and president of the National Conference of State Legislators in 1994. In 1994 Congressman Alan Wheat ran for the Senate, and lost to John Ashcroft. McCarthy ran for his House seat and managed the not inconsiderable feat of winning 41% in an 11-candidate primary; the next two finishers were also women. McCarthy was supported by unions, environmentalists, black organizations and Kansas City Mayor Emanuel Cleaver. The Republicans had a serious candidate, Ron Freeman, an African American who played professional football in the short-lived United States Football League and then worked with the Fellowship of Christian Athletes. McCarthy was supported by business leaders and had a $250,000 edge in PAC money. In the face of the Republican tide, she won 57%–43%, carrying Kansas City 2–1 but losing the suburban half of the district. She has not been seriously challenged since.

McCarthy calls herself a New Democrat and her voting record has leaned toward the center of House Democrats. She supported the balanced budget amendment and a capital gains tax cut, and opposed unfunded federal mandates. She has been pro-gun control, pro-choice on abortion, against the flat tax and school vouchers.

On the Energy and Commerce Committee she advocated prescription drug coverage under Medicare. After delaying long enough to include herself in the "anxiety caucus," she opposed PNTR with China because of reservations about the World Trade Organization. McCarthy voted against trade promotion authority and the use of force in Iraq. Backing the interests of an important local company, she urged the Justice Department to abandon its plan to end the tradition of donating Hallmark greeting cards to millions of prison inmates during the Christmas season; the department maintained the tradition.

McCarthy has been reelected by wide margins. She was embarrassed when, during a late night session in March 2003, she fell down an escalator and injured herself in the Rayburn Office Building while she reportedly was drunk; she missed two key votes as a result. The next day, she issued a statement of apology and regret acknowledging her alcoholism, and recognizing "I have hit bottom and I realize I must take action to change." She underwent treatment for addiction at an Arizona clinic; after returning from a month-long stay, she said she was committed to running for reelection. "I tried so hard to be this perfect legislator," she told the *Kansas City Star*. "I don't have to be perfect anymore."

SIXTH DISTRICT

Rep. Sam Graves (R)

Elected 2000, 2d term; b. Nov. 7, 1963, Tarkio; home, Tarkio; U. of MO (Columbia), B.S. 1986; Baptist; married (Lesley).

Elected Office: MO House of Reps., 1992–94; MO Senate 1994–00.

Professional Career: Farmer.

DC Office: 1513 LHOB 20515, 202-225-7041; Fax: 202-225-8221; Web site: www.house.gov/graves.

District Offices: Liberty, 816-792-3976; St. Joseph, 816-233-9818.

Committees: *Agriculture* (17th of 27 R): Conservation, Credit, Rural Development & Research; General Farm Commodities & Risk Management. *Small Business* (7th of 18 R): Rural Enterprises, Agriculture and Technology (Chmn.). *Transportation & Infrastructure* (29th of 41 R): Aviation; Highways, Transit & Pipelines; Railroads.

Group Ratings

	ADA	ACLU	AFS	LCV	CON	ITIC	NTU	COC	ACU	NTLC	CHC
2002	0	20	0	0	25	100	58	95	100	86	92
2001	5	—	10	0	—	—	61	100	88	—	—

National Journal Ratings

	2001 LIB —	2001 CONS		2002 LIB —	2002 CONS
Economic	28%	69%		9%	87%
Social	20%	69%		0%	75%
Foreign	33%	60%		35%	60%

Key Votes of the 107th Congress

1. Approve Bush Tax Cuts	Y	5. Faith-Based Charities	Y	9. Trade Promotion Authority	Y
2. Limit Patients' Bill of Rights	Y	6. Bar Gays in the Boy Scouts	Y	10. Bar Funds for Intl. Court	Y
3. Campaign Finance Reform	N	7. Ban Partial-Birth Abortion	Y	11. Authorize Force in Iraq	Y
4. Ban ANWR Development	N	8. Arm Commercial Pilots	Y	12. Deny Home. Sec. Dept. Union	Y

Election Results

2002 general	Sam Graves (R)	131,151	(63%)	($1,176,557)
	Cathy Rinehart (D)	73,202	(35%)	($240,835)
	Other	3,735	(2%)	
2002 primary	Sam Graves (R)	unopposed		
2000 general	Sam Graves (R)	138,925	(51%)	($1,115,338)
	Steve Danner (D)	127,792	(47%)	($811,060)
	Other	6,484	(2%)	

The People		Race/Ethnic Origin	Ancestry	
Area size:	13,124 sq. mi.	92.4% White	German: 17.1%	Irish: 9.8%
Urban population:	66.3%	2.8% Black	USA: 8.9%	
Rural population:	33.7%	0.8% Asian	**2000 Presidential Vote**	
Pop. 2000:	621,690	0.4% Native Am.	Bush (R) 143,954	(53%)
Median income:	$41,225	0.1% Hawaiian	Gore (D) 119,861	(44%)
Poverty status:	8.7%	1.1% Two+ races	Other 7,380	(3%)
Military veterans:	14.5%	0.1% Other	**Cook Partisan Voting Index:** R + 5	
		2.4% Hispanic Origin		

Occupation   Blue collar: 25.9%   White collar: 58.6%   Gray collar: 15.5%

The rolling, surging fields along the Missouri River in northwest Missouri were settled in a rush in the late 19th century and they lost people most of the 20th century. Fewer hands were needed on farms than half a century ago, far fewer than a century ago. In 1940, this area had one of the largest meatpacking operations in the world, but the meatpacking business for years generated no new jobs. The river town of St. Joseph, which was the starting point for the Pony Express to Sacramento, is the biggest town north of Kansas City with 73,000 people in 2000. The counties of northwest Missouri, aside from those in the Kansas City metro area, had 508,000 people in 1900, 452,000 in 1940 and 318,000 in 1990. But in the 1990s, the local economy began to perk up a little, and the number climbed to 330,000; some counties that had been losing population since 1900 started to gain.

The 6th Congressional District takes in all these counties plus part of metro Kansas City— Clay and Platte Counties and a small portion of Jackson County east of Independence. The Kansas City area casts about half the district's votes. The historic political tradition here was mostly Democratic, but it has been tempered by dislike for national Democrats' cultural liberalism. This was strong Perot country in 1992; Bill Clinton carried it with a plurality in 1992 and 1996. But the rural vote here, as across the nation moved toward Republicans in the 1990s, and in 2000 George W. Bush carried the district with 53%.

The congressman from the 6th District is Sam Graves, a Republican first elected in 2000. A lifelong resident of Tarkio in the northwest corner of the state, he began his career in agriculture, the issue which defines much of his politics. He graduated from the University of Missouri as an agronomist, and soon joined the Farm Bureau. He ran for the state House in 1992 and beat a longtime Democratic incumbent; in 1994 he was elected to the state Senate. He attracted attention in 1998 with a five-hour filibuster, when he nearly derailed the legislature over a school desegregation bill he called slanted against rural areas, though the bill eventually passed.

Graves got his opportunity to run for the House when Congresswoman Pat Danner, 22 minutes before the May withdrawal deadline and without a public announcement, delivered to the secretary of state her withdrawal for reelection. She had surgery for breast cancer in January, but had described her prognosis as excellent. Not by accident, the immediate favorite to succeed her was her son, state Senator Steve Danner. Graves quickly entered the race within the short window provided by state law under such circumstances and drew support from House Republican leaders. This caused tension within the party; Teresa Loar, a moderate Republican on the Kansas City Council, who had already filed for office before Danner's retirement, attacked Graves as the darling of extremist and sexist party leaders. Graves rolled over Loar 68%–17%. Against three weak Democratic alternatives, Steve Danner was held to 56% in the Democratic primary—a bad omen for November. In the general, Danner called himself a conservative Democrat and the candidates agreed on some issues: the death penalty, repeal of the marriage-penalty tax and trade relations with China. But they differed on education funding, abortion rights, gun control and the performance of Bill Clinton. Graves called Danner a "tax and spend liberal" and said that when this acorn fell from the tree (his mother), "it rolled to the left." Surprisingly, Danner made little use of his mother or her record during the campaign. In an editorial in favor of Graves, *The Kansas City Star* said that Danner's campaign switch on abortion showed that he "engaged in raw opportunism at the slightest opportunity," with his central principle of "me first." Graves won 51%–47%, carrying 20 of the 27 counties and keeping Danner's metro Kansas City lead to 192 votes of nearly 135,000 cast.

In the House, Graves showed some moderate instincts, especially on foreign policy, and was usually a party loyalist. He supported the farm bill and tended mostly to local issues. With support from national corn growers, he proposed additional crop insurance for participants who suffer large losses from drought or floods. When Citizens Against Government Waste criticized his $273,000 grant to the Blue Springs Youth Outreach Unit to study how to combat the local Goth culture, in which teenagers dress in black clothing and gravitate toward the occult and occasionally morbid music, Graves responded that the Goth culture had posed an "acute problem" for the community, including drug use, violence and self-mutilation.

In this previously competitive district, Graves had no trouble with reelection. After Steve Danner and other local Democratic officials decided not to run, Clay County Assessor Cathy Rinehart contributed $230,000 to her campaign but raised hardly any other money. She criticized Graves as too conservative for the district, opposed creation of the Homeland Security Department, NAFTA and trade promotion authority; she sought but failed to gain the endorsement of EMILY's List. He was reelected 63%–35%, carrying all 26 counties. In January 2003, Roy Blunt named Graves to his Whip team.

SEVENTH DISTRICT

Rep. Roy Blunt (R)

Elected 1996, 4th term; b. Jan. 10, 1950, Niangua; home, Strafford; SW Baptist U., B.A. 1970, SW MO St. U., M.A. 1972; Baptist; divorced.

Elected Office: MO Secy. of State, 1984–93.

Professional Career: H.S. teacher, 1970–73; Greene Cnty. Clerk, 1973–85; Adjunct Instructor, Drury Col., 1976–82; Pres., SW Baptist U., 1993–96.

DC Office: 217 CHOB 20515, 202-225-6536; Fax: 202-225-5604; Web site: www.house.gov/blunt.

District Offices: Joplin, 417-781-1041; Springfield, 417-889-1800.

Committees: *Majority Whip. Energy & Commerce* (19th of 31 R).

Group Ratings

	ADA	ACLU	AFS	LCV	CON	ITIC	NTU	COC	ACU	NTLC	CHC
2002	0	14	0	0	25	75	56	100	100	91	92
2001	5	—	10	0	—	—	67	95	96	—	—

National Journal Ratings

	2001 LIB	—	2001 CONS		2002 LIB	—	2002 CONS
Economic	15%	—	82%		0%	—	91%
Social	0%	—	81%		0%	—	75%
Foreign	4%	—	87%		0%	—	85%

Key Votes of the 107th Congress

1. Approve Bush Tax Cuts	Y	5. Faith-Based Charities	Y	9. Trade Promotion Authority	Y
2. Limit Patients' Bill of Rights	Y	6. Bar Gays in the Boy Scouts	Y	10. Bar Funds for Intl. Court	Y
3. Campaign Finance Reform	N	7. Ban Partial-Birth Abortion	Y	11. Authorize Force in Iraq	Y
4. Ban ANWR Development	N	8. Arm Commercial Pilots	Y	12. Deny Home. Sec. Dept. Union	*

Election Results

2002 general	Roy Blunt (R)	149,519	(75%)	($1,331,576)
	Ron Lapham (D)	45,964	(23%)	
	Other	4,380	(2%)	
2002 primary	Roy Blunt (R)	unopposed		
2000 general	Roy Blunt (R)	202,305	(74%)	($1,177,456)
	Charles Christup (D)	65,510	(24%)	
	Other	6,122	(2%)	

Prior Winning Percentages: 1998 (73%); 1996 (65%)

The People		Race/Ethnic Origin	Ancestry	
Area size:	5,555 sq. mi.	92.9% White	German: 13.5%	USA: 10.8%
Urban population:	59.1%	1.2% Black	Irish: 9.2%	
Rural population:	40.9%	0.7% Asian	**2000 Presidential Vote**	
Pop. 2000:	621,690	1.0% Native Am.	Bush (R)	153,453 (62%)
Median income:	$32,929	0.1% Hawaiian	Gore (D)	87,663 (35%)
Poverty status:	13.0%	1.5% Two+ races	Other	6,124 (2%)
Military veterans:	14.4%	0.1% Other	**Cook Partisan Voting Index:** R +14	
		2.6% Hispanic Origin		

Occupation	Blue collar: 28.5%	White collar: 55.0%	Gray collar: 16.5%

One of the biggest tourist destinations in America today is Branson, Missouri—something almost no one predicted 25 years ago. Even today Branson has only 6,050 residents, is served by two-lane roads, is nowhere near a major airport; but it thrives, paralleling the surging popularity of country and western music. Branson was put on the map early in the century by Harold Bell Wright's novel, *The Shepherd of the Hills*, about the hardy people of the mountains, hills and meadows of southwest Missouri, just north of Arkansas. More tourists came in with completion of the Ozark Beach Dam that created Bull Shoals Lake in 1913, lured by the native bass and stocked trout. Then in the 1960s, new lakes were formed, a Shepherd of the Hills pageant and Silver Dollar City were started, and entertainers—the five Maybe brothers performing as "The Baldknobbers" and Box Car Willie from the Grand Ole Opry—started performing. Today Branson has 6 million visitors a year and more than two dozen theaters with 61,000 seats—more than Broadway. What do people like about Branson? The non-stop entertainment and fishing and boating; country music and family style entertainment; plenty of shopping and a safe atmosphere. These are also things that have made southwest Missouri the fastest growing part of the state in the last 20 years, generating new businesses and attracting retirees as well as vacationers. Workers come to Branson from as far away as Springfield, the biggest city in southwest Missouri. Springfield is the headquarters of such middle American institutions as the Mid-America Dairymen, the nation's largest milk producers' cooperative; the Bass Pro Shops Outdoor World, probably the nation's largest fishing equipment store; the Assemblies of God, one of the nation's and the world's largest and fastest-growing Protestant denominations; and two of the nation's three largest coach-builders (stretch limousine manufacturers), Springfield Coach and DaBryan Coach Builders, with a third nearby in Seymour, Executive Coach, run by a Nigerian immigrant. Southwest Missouri is also dairy country and has a growing poultry industry; Latinos have been moving into McDonald County to work in chicken plants. The Ozarks, long considered a backwater, are on the cutting edge of many trends in today's America.

The 7th Congressional District includes Branson and Springfield and most of southwest Missouri. Historically, this area has been Republican since it opposed secession in 1861: pro-Union Springfield changed hands several times as Missouri staged its own civil war. Its conservative response to the big-spending government of the 1960s and cultural liberalism of the 1970s reinforced its allegiance, and now this is the most Republican part of Missouri.

The congressman from the 7th District is Roy Blunt, a Republican first elected in 1996. Blunt grew up on a dairy farm near Springfield, in a political family; his father was a state representative. He graduated from Southwest Baptist University, 25 miles north of Springfield, and taught high school and college history and government. He got his start in politics by volunteering for John Ashcroft's unsuccessful campaign for Congress in 1972; the story goes that he showed up at campaign headquarters in his pickup truck, Ashcroft asked, "Have you got gas in this truck?", Blunt said yes and became his driver (another congressman, Democrat Earl Pomeroy of North Dakota, also started his political career driving around a future senator). In 1973, 33-year-old freshman Governor Christopher Bond, in his second appointment, named the 23-year-old Blunt Greene County clerk. In 1984, at 34, Blunt was elected Missouri secretary of state and was re-elected with 60% of the vote in 1988. In 1992 he ran for governor and lost the Republican primary to William Webster, 44%–39%. Blunt became president of Southwest Baptist University. In 1996 Congressman Mel Hancock kept his pledge to serve only four terms and retired. In the primary Blunt faced Gary Nodler, businessman and one-time staffer to Congressman Gene Taylor. Nodler carried his home area around Joplin and Carthage, but Blunt carried everything else and won 56%–44%. There were 75,000 votes cast in the Republican primary and only 16,000 in the Democratic primary: a harbinger of the general election, which Blunt won 65%–32%, running ahead of the Republican ticket and carrying every county with at least 62% of the vote. He has been reelected easily since.

Blunt has shown great political skills and is now Majority Whip. He wanted to run for freshman class president, but at then-Majority Whip Tom DeLay's suggestion ran for the freshman spot on the Republican Steering Committee, on which he worked to get good committee assignments for freshmen. White House political adviser Ken Mehlman was working for freshman Kay Granger then and remembers Blunt, "He was the one person every single member of his class felt like they could go to to solve a problem." In the process he got good committee assignments himself—Agriculture, International Relations, Transportation and Infrastructure. On International Relations, he supported the bill to penalize countries that practice or allow religious persecution—a concern of denominations like the Assemblies of God, which has more members abroad than in the United States. He was part of DeLay's "free speech" team proposing bills to undermine the Shays-Meehan campaign finance bill. Blunt was not inattentive to fellow members. In the 1998 campaign cycle he raised and contributed $250,000 to other incumbent Republicans.

Three weeks after the 1998 election Blunt won a seat on the Commerce Committee. Then in January 1999 Tom DeLay plucked him from the ranks of 48 deputy whips and appointed him Chief Deputy Whip, the position Dennis Hastert held until his astonishing elevation to speaker. Blunt has said that he never lobbied for the job and didn't even know he was being considered until he read it in a newspaper. On a number of issues Blunt was given the job of making more palatable to core Republicans measures that were going through in any case. In September 1999 he brokered a deal to tie business tax cuts to the minimum wage increase. In September 2000 he brokered a deal on food sales to Cuba: Miami's two Cuban-American Republicans got a ban on U.S. credits for sales, but the export-minded George Nethercutt got third-party financing. Blunt endorsed George W. Bush early, in March 1999, and was named the Bush campaign's liaison to House members, a busy position and a sensitive one given Bush's pointed criticisms of House Republicans in 1999.

As chief deputy whip, Blunt spent much time meeting with lobbyists, organizing groups interested in different issues like trade, taxes and energy. He developed a reputation as a good listener and took care to pay attention to party moderates. David Rehr, a lobbyist close to the Republican leadership, describes him thus: "Roy is more of the velvet glove, almost a confessor figure. He's the kind of guy who is able to say, 'That's a really good idea, but maybe it's better to do it this way,' without being confrontational." Speaker Dennis Hastert assigned Blunt to mediate disputes between Republicans and to win over votes on critical issues. Blunt also weighed in on some local issues. Alerted by constituents whose relatives had died in the bombings of U.S. embassies in Kenya and Tanzania, he sponsored a bill to treat relatives of American victims of those attacks the same as relatives of September 11 victims; it passed the House 391–18. And after Democrat Rob Andrews complained that New Jersey-licensed limousines were not allowed into New York without paying a tax, Blunt, representing the number one stretch-limousine-producing district, sponsored a bill limiting local regulation of limousines that cross state lines. It was opposed by New Yorker officials eager for revenue and Nevada limousine drivers, worried about competition from California drivers; but it passed by wide margins and was signed into law in November 2002.

In 2000 Blunt began keeping a list of members who would back him for a higher leadership position. In the 2002 cycle he headed the Battleground 2002 operation, which raised many millions, and contributed $5.6 million to Republican House candidates. In December 2001 Majority Leader Dick Armey announced that he would retire in 2002. Immediately DeLay began to run for majority leader and Blunt said he would run for majority whip. Ray LaHood of Illinois, whose evenhanded presiding over important session has impressed members in both parties, announced he was running for whip too. But in February 2002 he said he would not run and was supporting Blunt; he found that Blunt had the support not only of most Republicans but of most moderates. In November 2002 both DeLay and Blunt were elected to their new positions without opposition; DeLay presented Blunt with a velvet-covered hammer.

As Whip Blunt made two decisions on his own which showed that he was not DeLay's puppet. One was his decision to name as his chief deputy whip Eric Cantor, who had served only one term and who is the only Jewish Republican in the House; Cantor was as astonished as everyone else. And he proposed to change House rules by repealing the eight-year term limit Newt Gingrich had imposed on speakers; that was agreed to by the whole House. Naturally there was speculation that Blunt might some day run for speaker, presumably against DeLay.

Blunt has been reelected by very wide margins. His son Matt Blunt was elected to the state House in 1998 and as Missouri's secretary of state in 2000; an Annapolis graduate, he was called up as a naval reservist and served six months in the United Kingdom after September 11; in early 2003, at 32, he seemed to be the consensus Republican candidate for governor against a Democratic incumbent with low job ratings: moving up as rapidly in Missouri politics as his father has in the House.

EIGHTH DISTRICT

Rep. Jo Ann Emerson (R)

Elected 1996, 4th term; b. Sept. 16, 1950, Washington, D.C.; home, Cape Girardeau; Ohio Wesleyan U., B.A. 1972; Presbyterian; married (Ron Gladney).

Professional Career: Deputy Communications Dir., Natl. Repub. Cong. Cmte., 1984–91; Dir., State Relations & Grassroot Programs, Natl. Restaurant Assn., 1991–94; Sr. Vice Pres., Pub. Affairs, American Insurance Assn., 1994–96.

DC Office: 2440 RHOB 20515, 202-225-4404; Fax: 202-226-0326; Web site: www.house.gov/emerson.

District Offices: Cape Girardeau, 573-335-0101; Farmington, 573-756-9755; Rolla, 573-364-2455.

Committees: *Appropriations* (23d of 36 R): Agriculture, Rural Development, & FDA; Energy & Water Development; Homeland Security.

Group Ratings

	ADA	ACLU	AFS	LCV	CON	ITIC	NTU	COC	ACU	NTLC	CHC
2002	0	21	13	0	34	100	55	95	96	82	92
2001	5	—	10	7	—	—	57	91	83	—	—

National Journal Ratings

	2001 LIB	—	2001 CONS		2002 LIB	—	2002 CONS
Economic	46%	—	54%		33%	—	66%
Social	20%	—	69%		30%	—	68%
Foreign	43%	—	58%		35%	—	60%

Key Votes of the 107th Congress

1. Approve Bush Tax Cuts	Y	5. Faith-Based Charities	Y	9. Trade Promotion Authority	Y
2. Limit Patients' Bill of Rights	Y	6. Bar Gays in the Boy Scouts	Y	10. Bar Funds for Intl. Court	Y
3. Campaign Finance Reform	N	7. Ban Partial-Birth Abortion	Y	11. Authorize Force in Iraq	Y
4. Ban ANWR Development	N	8. Arm Commercial Pilots	Y	12. Deny Home. Sec. Dept. Union	Y

Election Results

2002 general	Jo Ann Emerson (R)	135,144	(72%)	($777,711)
	Gene Curtis (D)	50,686	(27%)	
	Other	2,491	(1%)	
2002 primary	Jo Ann Emerson (R)	50,605	(87%)	
	Allen Kline (R)	7,499	(13%)	
2000 general	Jo Ann Emerson (R)	162,239	(69%)	($794,800)
	Bob Camp (D)	67,760	(29%)	
	Other	4,067	(2%)	

Prior Winning Percentages: 1998 (63%); 1996 (50%); 1996 (63%)

The People		Race/Ethnic Origin	Ancestry	
Area size:	18,818 sq. mi.	92.5% White	USA: 13.7%	German: 12.7%
Urban population:	39.6%	4.3% Black	Irish: 8.5%	
Rural population:	60.4%	0.4% Asian	**2000 Presidential Vote**	
Pop. 2000:	621,690	0.6% Native Am.	Bush (R)..............143,511	(59%)
Median income:	$27,865	0.0% Hawaiian	Gore (D)...............93,244	(38%)
Poverty status:	18.2%	1.1% Two+ races	Other...................5,635	(2%)
Military veterans:	15.1%	0.0% Other	**Cook Partisan Voting Index:** R +11	
		1.0% Hispanic Origin		

Occupation	Blue collar: 34.5%	White collar: 47.7%	Gray collar: 17.8%

Mark Twain might not recognize life on the Mississippi below St. Louis today, where the land flattens out and the river is hidden behind levees, which ordinarily, except during the terrible flood of 1993, screen small towns and river roads from the sight of rows of barges tethered together, full of coal or soybeans. The Mississippi today is an industrial waterway. But it was never really all that romantic. Twain's steamboats, as he was at pains to point out, were dangerous, noisy contraptions, forever blowing up or getting embedded in roots and branches in the swirling river currents. This is one of the older-settled parts of the U.S.: French settlers founded Missouri towns like Cape Girardeau in the late 1700s. The big influx started a few years after the 1811 earthquake centered on New Madrid; the spongy Mississippi valley land is also seismically very active, and this was the site of one of the most devastating earthquakes in U.S. history.

The southeast quadrant of Missouri—the river valley and the hills to the west, with coal and lead mines (the area produces most of the world's lead) with their miles of tunnels, plus the Bootheel that hangs down in the far southeast—has not seemed to change much in 50 years. For years there has been a population outflow from the Bootheel, as machines replaced low-wage farm workers and crops shifted from cotton to corn and soybeans. Dairy cattle, pigs, apples, and berries—plus, some timber—are among the area's other products. The only big growth here has been around Cape Girardeau and along I-44; the poverty rate in the Bootheel is the highest in the state. At a point 20 miles south of Rolla is Edgar Springs, the home to 190 residents and the population center of the nation, according to the 2000 Census; 10 years earlier, that designation was 35 miles to the northwest in Steelville.

The sprawling 8th Congressional District covers this southeast corner of Missouri. The political heritage is mixed. The Bootheel was as solidly Democratic as the Mississippi Valley around Memphis once was, and some mining counties remain Democratic. Cape Girardeau is heavily Republican and an incubator of Republican talent: it is the home town of Rush Limbaugh and his columnist brother David Limbaugh, of state Senate President Peter Kinder and Republican National Committee Deputy Chairman and ace fundraiser Jack Oliver. For many years this district was safely Democratic, but since 1980, it has been represented by Republicans. This was one of the rural areas that trended to Republicans in the Clinton years, and George W. Bush won 59% of the vote here in 2000.

The congresswoman from the 8th District is Jo Ann Emerson, elected in 1996 to replace her late husband Bill Emerson, who died that June. Jo Ann Emerson grew up in Bethesda, Maryland, in a Republican family (her father was executive director of the RNC) but next door to Democrats Hale and Lindy Boggs, who served in Congress over a half-century; their daughter, Cokie Roberts, babysat Jo Ann. In 1975 she married Republican Bill Emerson, then a Washington lobbyist. In 1979, spotting the vulnerability of the Democratic incumbent, he went home to Missouri to run, and won with 55%. In 1995 he was diagnosed with cancer, but missed few votes during radiation therapy. After Bill's death, Jo Ann Emerson decided to run. She had worked for the American Insurance Association and National Restaurant Association, and was a press aide at the NRCC. Her views are conservative, and leading state and national Republicans quickly endorsed her. But she could not seek the party nomination in the August primary: Missouri law bars reopening the filing deadline if an incumbent dies less than 11 weeks before the primary, so she ran as an independent. Democrats nominated Emily Firebaugh, a timber company owner who attacked Emerson as a product of the Washington suburbs. Firebaugh spent $831,000, slightly more than Emerson. The Republican nominee Richard Kline was less trouble: In 1995 he had used pepper spray to try to place a Veterans Administration doctor under citizen's arrest. Bill Emerson's record, Jo Ann Emerson's conservative views, and the poignancy of the situation all worked toward an Emerson victory. She won 50%, with 37% for Firebaugh and 11% for Kline; in the same-day election to fill the remaining two months of her husband's term, Emerson won 63%–34%.

In the House, Emerson has had a moderate-leaning voting record though more conservative on cultural issues. A property rights supporter, she got her portion of the district excluded from Bill Clinton's American Heritage Rivers project, which she opposed as an abuse of executive power to save wetlands. On the Appropriations Committee and its Agriculture Subcommittee, her priority was addressing low prices for farm commodities. She worked with other members from farm districts to open agricultural trade with Cuba and later made visits to Cuba to encourage deals. She chaired the Congressional Hunger Center, which trains young people to help reduce hunger across the nation, and she works to send more farm surpluses to poor countries. After the September 11 attacks, she bucked Attorney General—and former Missouri Senator—John Ashcroft by voting with House Democrats to federalize airport security. She was one of eight Republicans who voted against their party's prescription drug bill in 2002 and, with Democrat Sherrod Brown, she co-sponsored a proposal to make generic drugs more readily available for prescriptions; she complained that her mother-in-law pays $11,000 a year for drug coverage. In 2003, she joined the newly organized Homeland Security subcommittee of Appropriations. She opposed requiring Medicare beneficiaries to enroll in private health care plans if they want prescription drug coverage under President Bush's medicare reform plan.

Emerson has won reelection without difficulty. She turned down the opportunity to run in 2002 against Senator Jean Carnahan.

NINTH DISTRICT

Rep. Kenny Hulshof (R)

Elected 1996, 4th term; b. May 22, 1958, Sikeston; home, Columbia; U. of MO, B.S. 1980, U. of MS, J.D. 1983; Catholic; married (Renee).

Professional Career: Asst. Pub. Defender, 32d Judicial Circuit, 1983–86; Asst. Prosecuting Atty., Cape Girardeau, 1986–89; Spec. Prosecutor, MO Atty. Gen., 1989–96.

DC Office: 412 CHOB 20515, 202-225-2956; Fax: 202-225-5712; Web site: www.house.gov/hulshof.

District Offices: Columbia, 573-449-5111; Hannibal, 573-221-1200; Washington, 636-239-4001.

Committees: *Budget* (14th of 24 R). *Standards of Official Conduct* (4th of 5 R). *Ways & Means* (18th of 24 R): Social Security.

Group Ratings

	ADA	ACLU	AFS	LCV	CON	ITIC	NTU	COC	ACU	NTLC	CHC
2002	10	20	0	0	8	100	56	100	96	86	92
2001	5	—	10	7	—	—	61	100	92	—	—

National Journal Ratings

	2001 LIB	—	2001 CONS		2002 LIB	—	2002 CONS
Economic	28%	—	69%		21%	—	73%
Social	20%	—	69%		25%	—	71%
Foreign	32%	—	69%		29%	—	67%

Key Votes of the 107th Congress

1. Approve Bush Tax Cuts	Y	5. Faith-Based Charities	Y	9. Trade Promotion Authority	Y
2. Limit Patients' Bill of Rights	Y	6. Bar Gays in the Boy Scouts	Y	10. Bar Funds for Intl. Court	Y
3. Campaign Finance Reform	N	7. Ban Partial-Birth Abortion	Y	11. Authorize Force in Iraq	Y
4. Ban ANWR Development	N	8. Arm Commercial Pilots	Y	12. Deny Home. Sec. Dept. Union	Y

Election Results

2002 general	Kenny Hulshof (R)	146,032	(68%)	($879,910)
	Donald Deichman (D)	61,126	(29%)	
	Other	6,967	(3%)	
2002 primary	Kenny Hulshof (R)	unopposed		
2000 general	Kenny Hulshof (R)	172,787	(59%)	($1,202,235)
	Steven R. Carroll (D)	111,662	(38%)	($360,765)
	Other	7,161	(2%)	

Prior Winning Percentages: 1998 (62%); 1996 (49%)

The People		Race/Ethnic Origin	Ancestry	
Area size:	14,082 sq. mi.	92.6% White	German: 21.7%	Irish: 9.3%
Urban population:	45.8%	3.9% Black	USA: 9.2%	
Rural population:	54.2%	0.9% Asian	**2000 Presidential Vote**	
Pop. 2000:	621,690	0.3% Native Am.	Bush (R)	145,604 (55%)
Median income:	$36,693	0.0% Hawaiian	Gore (D)	112,239 (42%)
Poverty status:	11.8%	1.1% Two+ races	Other	7,093 (3%)
Military veterans:	13.5%	0.1% Other	**Cook Partisan Voting Index:** R + 7	
		1.1% Hispanic Origin		

Occupation	Blue collar: 29.7%	White collar: 54.4%	Gray collar: 15.9%

Little Dixie, the swath of northeast Missouri along the Mississippi River, was settled by Southerners from Kentucky and Virginia. Its most famous native son is Mark Twain, born Sam Clemens in Hannibal, then as now a little town on bluffs overlooking the river. Hannibal was the thinly disguised St. Petersburg of Tom Sawyer and Huckleberry Finn, lovingly created years later complete with Pike County and other dialect by Twain, then living in New England. Little Dixie was pro-Confederate during the Civil War; Callaway County declared its independence from the Union. For many years faithfully Democratic, Little Dixie has reared some notable politicians as well. One was Champ Clark, speaker of the House from 1911–19 and presidential candidate in 1912; another was Clarence Cannon, author of the definitive text on the House's parliamentary procedures and chairman of the House Appropriations Committee in 1941–47, 1949–53 and 1955–1964.

The 9th Congressional District is the descendant of the Little Dixie districts that elected Clark and Cannon, but slow population growth has meant that it has had to be expanded far to the south and into the foothills of the Ozarks. It includes Columbia, home of the University of Missouri, and Fulton, home of Westminster College, where in 1946 Winston Churchill, accompanied by President Harry Truman, told the world that "from Stettin on the Baltic to Trieste on the Adriatic, an iron curtain has descended across the continent." The district includes the western edge of the St. Louis metro area, western St. Charles County and Franklin County south of the Missouri River. Despite its Democratic heritage, it votes mostly Republican now; it gave George W. Bush 55% of its votes in 2000.

The congressman from the 9th District is Kenny Hulshof (pronounced *HULLZ-hoff*), a Republican first elected in 1996. He grew up on a farm in far southeast Missouri. After law school he joined the public defender's office in Cape Girardeau. In 1989 he became a special prosecutor for the Missouri attorney general's office and traveled to 53 counties, obtaining 60 violent felony convictions and seven death sentences. In the midst of this, in 1994, he became the Republican nominee in the 9th District. This was a surprise: challenger Rick Hardy had held Democratic Congressman Harold Volkmer to a 48%–46% victory in 1992 and was running again; but after the filing deadline he withdrew from the race due to depression and exhaustion. Party leaders named Hulshof as Hardy's replacement. He was far outspent, but made a respectable showing, carrying Columbia and Boone County, and trailing 50%–45% overall.

In January 1996 Hulshof resigned as special prosecutor and started to run again. Volkmer's combative temperament and irritation with the new Republican majority made him one of its most persistent antagonists on the floor. Hulshof narrowly won his primary; in the general election, Volkmer ran an ad showing Hulshof in a Porsche driven by Newt Gingrich and attacking him for signing away his independence in the Contract with America. Hulshof replied that his Porsche was a used car sitting in his yard, and he charged that Volkmer had voted to raise taxes 20 times in 20 years and had voted for 40% pay raises. The key moment came in October when Volkmer, in response to a question, said voters were not overtaxed and that he would not mind paying $1 million in taxes. Hulshof ran radio ads quoting Volkmer all over the district. Volkmer carried Little Dixie 53%–46%, but Hulshof led elsewhere for a 49%–47% win.

In the House, Hulshof had a voting record near the center of his party. He was elected president of the Republican freshman class and quickly sounded the note of consensus that voters yearned for: he decried "partisan bickering" 15 days after taking office, helped organize the civility retreat in Hershey, backed Shays-Meehan campaign finance regulation and, with Democratic freshman president Jim Davis, supported the 1997 balanced budget agreement. The Republican leadership gave him a prized seat on Ways and Means as a freshman. He used the platform to back proposals like repeal of the estate tax, scaling back taxation of dividend and interest income and preserving favorable tax treatment of ethanol. With a district crisscrossed by many long-distance rail lines, he proposed to cut the excise tax on rail fuel. Hulshof became a leading spokesman for tax cuts proposed by George W. Bush. He kept in touch with the real world of agriculture in August 2002 by helping his father who was undergoing radiation treatments for cancer, harvest corn on the family farm in the Bootheel.

Hulshof was reelected 68%–29%. He said later that on Election Day he had decided to run for governor in 2004. But his father died later that month and, saying that he had to help his mother tend the farm, he announced in January 2003 that he would not run for governor.

★ MONTANA ★

Nearly 200 years ago, in April 1805, Meriwether Lewis and William Clark and their pirogues wended up the Missouri River just past the Yellowstone into what now is Montana. It was wild, open country, under a big sky—and most of it still is. The late historian Stephen Ambrose, who took his family to Lemhi Pass at the other end of Montana, nearly 500 miles west, where Lewis became the first American to cross the Continental Divide, to celebrate July 4, 1976, noted that the land was little different from when Lewis and Clark passed through. Ambrose later retold the Lewis and Clark story in *Undaunted Courage* and he and his family settled in Montana; they are far from the only outsiders who have moved, part-time or full, into the Big Sky State in recent decades.

Yet American civilization has touched down only lightly on Montana. It is still a land of great empty vistas, with mountains in the west and vast expanses of plateaus and plains in the east—the 4th largest state in area and 44th in population. Almost nowhere in the state are wilderness

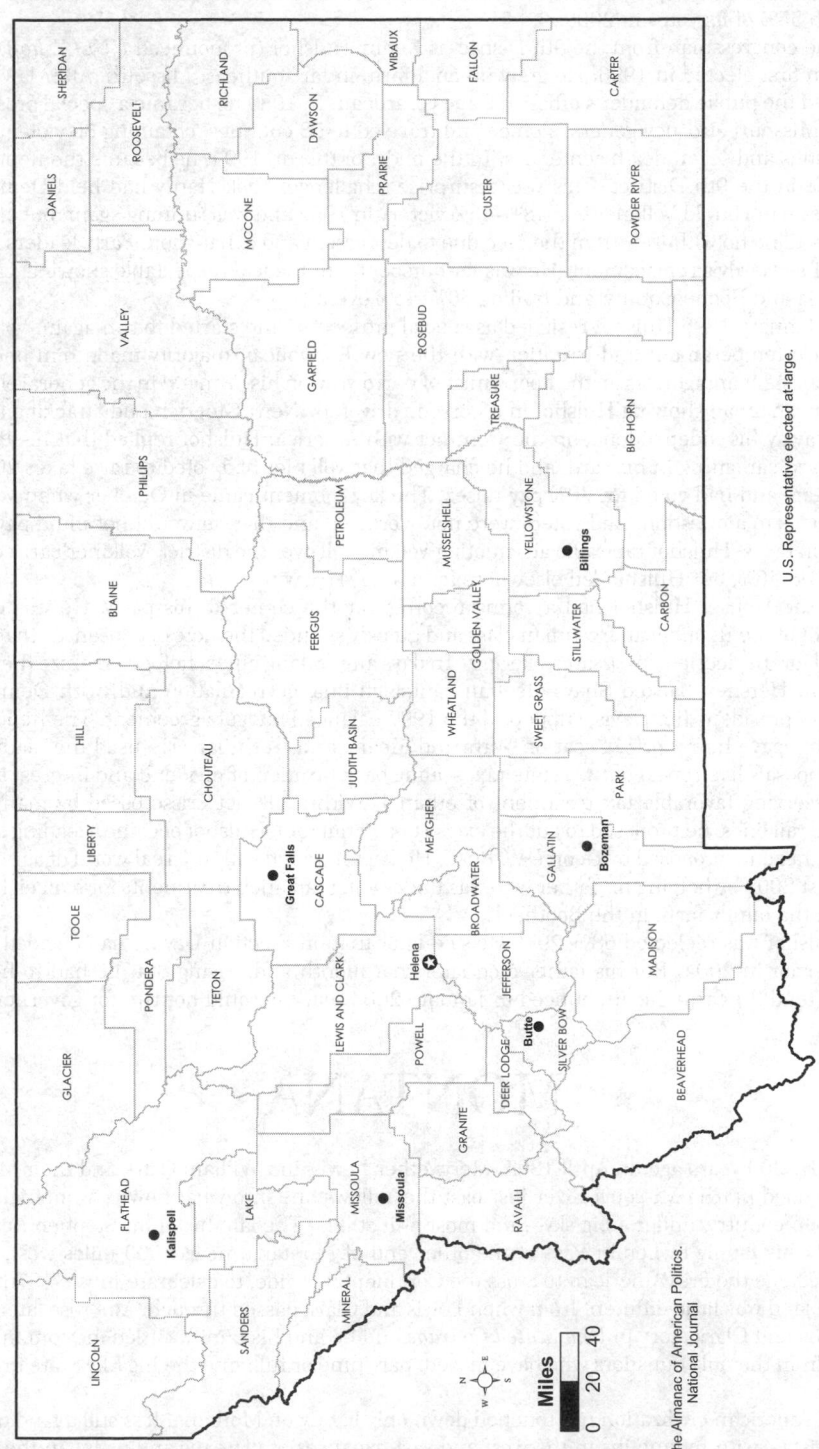

SHERIDAN

RICHLAND

WIBAUX

FALLON

CARTER

ROOSEVELT

DAWSON

DANIELS

PRAIRIE

MCCONE

CUSTER

POWDER RIVER

VALLEY

ROSEBUD

GARFIELD

TREASURE

BIG HORN

PHILLIPS

PETROLEUM

MUSSELSHELL

YELLOWSTONE

Billings

CARBON

BLAINE

FERGUS

GOLDEN VALLEY

STILLWATER

WHEATLAND

SWEET GRASS

HILL

CHOUTEAU

JUDITH BASIN

PARK

MEAGHER

GALLATIN

LIBERTY

Great Falls

CASCADE

Bozeman

TOOLE

BROADWATER

PONDERA

TETON

Helena ✪

MADISON

LEWIS AND CLARK

JEFFERSON

GLACIER

POWELL

Butte

SILVER BOW

BEAVERHEAD

DEER LODGE

FLATHEAD

GRANITE

Kalispell

LAKE

MISSOULA

RAVALLI

Missoula

LINCOLN

SANDERS

MINERAL

N
W ⊕ E
S

Miles

0   20   40

U.S. Representative elected at-large.

The Almanac of American Politics.
National Journal

and empty land out of sight. Montana sits atop America, spanning the Rockies so that on I-15 you can cross the Continental Divide three times. But since the time of Lewis and Clark, it has not been much of a crossroads. The first Americans here were itinerant trappers seeking fur and miners seeking gold, silver and copper, who built ramshackle towns where outlaws battled vigilantes—and, in a few cases gained sudden riches, which would make them kings not of this barren land but of the metropolises back East. Then came the workers who built and serviced the Northern Pacific and Great Northern railroads, followed by wheat farmers and ranchers. Montana's natural history is ancient: At Egg Mountain near Choteau on the Deep Teton River, is the world's most plenteous source of dinosaur remains. But the state's recorded history is recent: At its 1989 centennial, the son of one of its original cattleman-settlers watched 105 cowboys drive 4,000 cattle with 300 covered wagons trailing behind.

Statehood came less than a century after the first white Americans came here as agents of the government—the Lewis and Clark expedition in 1805. The mining economy gave Montana a radical, class warfare politics. On one side was the Anaconda Mining Company, which until 1959 owned five of Montana's six daily newspapers, many of its utilities, and many of its politicians. It had strong allies in the Stockmen's Association and the Farm Bureau. On the other side were progressives like Senators Thomas Walsh, who exposed the Teapot Dome scandal, and Burton Wheeler, a New Dealer who broke with Franklin Roosevelt over court packing and isolationism, the labor unions (Montana has no right-to-work law and is the most pro-union state in the Rockies), and pork barrel beneficiaries (for a while in the 1930s, Montana received more federal money per capita than almost any other state). The locus of all this was Butte, with its gold and copper mines on "The Richest Hill on Earth," with its gamblers and bootleggers, company goons and union thugs, IWW organizers and Socialist mayor, and millionaires who bought seats in the U.S. Senate. Today the mines are closed, the ore depleted, and the stone temples of commerce are grim; looming mineheads are being restored to a cleanliness they never enjoyed in the boom days.

Butte's population peaked in 1920, mines gradually closed all over the state, and agriculture—wheat growing and cattle grazing—became the mainstays of the economy. Class warfare died down. Other towns grew, though none is over 100,000 yet: Billings with its agricultural marketing in the east, the university town of Missoula, Great Falls just east of the Rockies, Kalispell near Flathead Lake, the university and resort town of Bozeman, and the state capital of Helena. The muscular tone of a land settled by ranch hands, miners and railroad workers, of cowboy hats, boots and blue jeans, of men who do hard physical work and relax hard afterwards, remains a link with Montanans going back to the mountain men, miners and cowboys who drove herds of Texas longhorns across the open range. And there is still the sense of space. Hunting and fishing are never far away; development in the small cities and resort areas has not been enough to drive the game away.

Over the past quarter-century, the Big Sky country attracted at first a trickle and then a flood of affluent Americans who purchased second homes here—high-visibility movie stars and billionaires like Ted Turner, but also just ordinary people buying small spreads near Big Sky or McLeod, near Bozeman, or around Flathead Lake or Big Timber or the Big Mountain ski resort in Whitefish, where grizzlies come down to forage and the bars hold mouse races. Many newcomers, from California and other urban states, set down roots here, as computers, modems and fax machines make it possible for small businessmen and entrepreneurs to work in Montana, far from their customers and clients, but in an environment they love. These new Montanans have added a spark of energy and inventiveness to a state much of which consisted of those left behind when others moved elsewhere. In the 1990s, Montana's population grew 13%, despite losses in the eastern plains. Growth was especially vigorous around Bozeman and Big Sky, in Missoula and Ravalli County to the south and around Kalispell and Lake Flathead to the north. In little towns like Seeley Lake, the focus of the economy has switched from logging to recreation. Sometimes there are conflicts between newcomers' expectations and the hardiness of Montana life: Gallatin County issued a 20-page Code of the West, explaining to new residents that they shouldn't expect an immediate response from emergency services and they shouldn't plough their snow onto a county road. The DeLorme Montana Road Atlas gives advice on what you should do if you encounter a bear.

But the 1990s growth was not quite enough for Montana to get back the second congressional district it lost in the 1990 Census; it fell about 8,000 people short. But it may get it back in the 2010 Census: With 21st century electronic telecommunications, you can e-mail clients and co-workers, sell stock or design software within sight of towering mountains and seemingly endless scenery—and still be only minutes away from coffee houses and gambling parlors. Even Butte is turning itself around, restoring 1920s commercial buildings and houses; its population increased in the 1990s, after decades of decline.

With its heritage of class warfare politics, radical miners and angry labor unions, Montana was for many years the most Democratic of the Rocky Mountain states; from 1952 to 1988, it elected only Democratic U.S. senators. As late as 1992, it voted narrowly for Bill Clinton, 38%–35%, as Ross Perot came in a close third with 26%. But since then, Montana has trended heavily to the Republicans. Clinton administration environmental policies, popular in East Coast metropolises, were heartily unpopular—even hated—in Montana. Most voters here seem to be part of what conservative activist Grover Norquist calls the "Leave-Us-Alone Coalition." In the 1990s, the legislature stoutly resisted tax increases, even when proposed by the popular Racicot, and when the state Supreme Court decision ordered the legislature to pass a speed limit, it set it at 75 miles per hour.

In 2000, Montana voted 58%–33% for George W. Bush, with 6% for Ralph Nader. Republicans won elections for senator, congressman-at-large, and governor by narrower margins. In these races Democrats carried old mining towns like Butte and Anaconda, Indian reservations (6% of Montanans are Indians), old railroad towns like Great Falls and Havre, university towns like Missoula and Bozeman, and the state capital of Helena. Republicans carried everything else, including fast-growing Billings, Kalispell, and the Bitterroot Valley. Montana also looks like an ultra-safe state for George W. Bush in 2004.

The People		Race/Ethnic Origin			Military veterans: 108,476 (16.1%)	
Pop. 2000:	902,195	807,823	89.5%	White	WWII: 19.7%	Korea: 13.4%
Pop. 1990:	799,065	2,534	0.3%	Black	Vietnam: 34.2%	Gulf War: 9.5%
Change 1990–2000:	Up 12.9%	4,569	0.5%	Asian	**Most populous cities:**	
Change 1980–1990:	Up 1.6%	54,426	6.0%	Native Am.	1. Billings	89,847
% of U.S. total:	0.3%	425	0.0%	Hawaiian	2. Missoula	57,053
Pop. rank:	44th of 50	13,768	1.5%	Two+ races	3. Great Falls	56,690
Area size:	147,042 sq. mi.	569	0.1%	Other	4. Bozeman	27,509
State Native:	56.1%	18,081	2.0%	Hisp. Origin	5. Helena	25,780
Non-citizen:	0.8%	**Ancestry**			Urban population: 54.0%	
Language		German: 18.8%	Irish: 10.3%		Rural population: 46.0%	
English: 92.0%	Other Eur.: 3.3%	English: 8.8%	Norwegian: 7.4%			
Spanish: 2.6%		USA: 3.6%				

Education		Work Sector		Legislature	
H.S. Grad:	87.2%	Private: 69.2%	Govt: 18.3%	Senate	29 R 21 D
College Grad:	24.4%	Self: 11.8%	Family: 0.7%	House	53 R 47 D
Industry		Unemployment: 6.3%		Legislative Term Limits: Yes	
Agri: 7.9%	Con: 7.4%	**Household Income**		**Registered Voters**	
Fin: 5.5%	Info: 2.2%	<15k: 20.2%	15-35k: 32.5%	No party registration	
Mfg: 11.4%	Prof: 28.2%	35-50k: 18.2%	50-100k: 23.5%		
Public: 5.9%	Trade: 15.8%	100-150k: 3.6%	>150k: 1.9%		
Other: 15.6%		Median: $33,024			
Occupation		Poverty status: 14.6%			
Blue collar: 22.0%	White collar: 58.6%	**Home Value**			
Gray collar: 19.4%		<50k: 19.4%	50-100k: 33.8%	100-200k: 34.5%	200-300k: 7.2%
		300-500k: 3.1%	>500k: 2.0%	Median: $95,800	

Presidential politics   Montana, with its 3 electoral votes, doesn't see much of presidential candidates. Its presidential primary is in early June, far too late to affect any results. But in 1992 and 1996 Montana was closely divided, as Ross Perot got some of his highest percentages here—26% in 1992 and 13.6% in 1996, his second best showing that year, just under Maine's 14.2% for his best showing. Almost all those votes seem to have gone for Bush in 2000, as he carried the state by a wider margin than Ronald Reagan or Richard Nixon in the Republican landslide years of 1984 and 1972.

2000 Presidential Vote		
Bush (R)	240,178	(58%)
Gore (D)	137,126	(33%)
Nader (Green)	24,437	(6%)
Other	9,245	(2%)

2000 Republican Presidential Primary		
Bush (R)	88,194	(78%)
Keyes (R)	20,822	(18%)
No Preference	4,655	(4%)

2000 Democratic Presidential Primary		
Gore (D)	68,420	(78%)
No Preference (D)	19,447	(22%)

1996 Presidential Vote		
Dole (R)	179,652	(44%)
Clinton (D)	167,922	(41%)
Perot (I)	55,229	(14%)

Governor

Judy Martz (R)

Elected 2000, term expires Jan. 2005, 1st term; b. July 28, 1948, Big Timber; home, Helena; E. MT Col.; Christian; married (Harry).

Elected Office: MT Lt. Gov., 1996–00.

Professional Career: Field Ofc. Rep., Sen. Conrad Burns, 1989–95; Owner, Martz Disposal, 1965-present.

Office: State Capitol, Helena, 59620, 406-444-3111; Fax: 406-444-4151; Web site: www.state.mt.us/governor.

Election Results

2000 general	Judy Martz (R)	209,135	(51%)
	Mark O'Keefe (D)	193,131	(47%)
	Other	7,926	(2%)
2000 primary	Judy Martz (R)	64,278	(57%)
	Rob Natelson (R)	48,738	(43%)
1996 general	Marc Racicot (R)	320,768	(79%)
	Judy Jacobson (D)	76,471	(19%)
	Other	7,936	(2%)

Judy Martz, elected governor in 2000, was born in Big Timber, on the plains beneath the Absaroka Range, and has spent most her life in Butte. An amateur athlete, she was crowned Miss Rodeo Montana at 20 and represented the U.S. as a speed skater in the 1964 Winter Olympics. She worked for Republican candidates in the 1960s and in the 1970s became more involved in politics after her husband set up a garbage disposal company in Butte. In 1990, she became a field representative for Senator Conrad Burns. She served on a Butte hospital board, chaired the local Chamber of Commerce, and helped build a high altitude speed skating center in Butte. She worked to clean up mining tailings and build baseball fields on the site.

Martz always wears a turtle pin on her blouse to illustrate a favorite saying: "Behold the turtle. He only goes forward when his neck's stuck out." In 1995, Lieutenant Governor Dennis Rehberg started running for the Senate (he lost in 1996, but was elected congressman-at-large in 2000), and Governor Marc Racicot was looking for a new running mate. Martz stuck out her neck and called him up and asked him for the job. After two extensive interviews, he chose her. Racicot's job approval was around 75%, and the Racicot-Martz ticket won with 79% of the vote.

As lieutenant governor, she chaired a drought advisory council and co-chaired the Montana-Alberta Boundary Advisory Commission (Montana abuts three Canadian provinces, the only state to do so). In 1999, she began running for governor. She said she wanted to make Montana "open for business" and phase out the 3% business equipment tax in 2003. She emphasized a 21-point JOBS program to encourage public-private partnerships and supported Racicot's Vision 2005 program to double agricultural output. She favored five-year tax credits to high-tech companies.

In the primary, Martz faced University of Montana law professor Rob Natelson, an anti-tax crusader who won 24% against Racicot in the 1996 primary and sponsored a 1998 ballot measure to require voter approval for new taxes and fees. Martz won 57%–43%. Three term-limited state-wide officials ran in the Democratic primary. The best known at the start was probably Attorney General Joe Mazurek. But state Auditor Mark O'Keefe organized early and spent $240,000 of his own money; he is married to Dayton-Hudson heir Lucy Dayton, whose brother Mark Dayton spent liberally of his own money and was elected to the U.S. Senate in Minnesota in 2000. O'Keefe won with 48%, to 36% for Mazurek and 16% for Secretary of State Mike Cooney.

O'Keefe argued that the key to economic growth was education and proposed increasing state funding of public schools to 70%. He said scornfully, "I don't think she's prepared to be governor. She doesn't understand the policy implications of her proposals." He said he would retain the 3% business property tax and use the money for property tax relief for homeowners. Martz claimed his policies would require $183 million in new spending and higher taxes.

Polls showed an even race for much of the year. O'Keefe spent $2.2 million of his own money; a group called People for Montana, financed by 10 large corporations, ran ads attacking O'Keefe's policies as harmful to Montana's economy. Racicot appeared in TV spots for Martz, and on November 1, he asked the attorney general to investigate whether O'Keefe improperly helped Montanans to invest in a venture capital fund while he also regulated securities. Martz won 51%–47%, carrying most of the state's counties. O'Keefe carried the mining towns, counties with large Indian populations, plus Missoula, Great Falls, and Helena.

Martz had a rocky first two years as governor. Tragedy struck in August 2001 when state House Majority Leader Paul Sliter, 32, was killed in the crash of a car driven by Martz's chief policy adviser, Shane Hedges, 27. Hedges denied to officers that he had been driving, and Martz took him from the hospital at 4 a.m. and washed his bloodstained clothes, which the police later sought as evidence; when this was made public in January 2002, she admitted she had acted wrongly. Hedges, who was intoxicated, was charged with felony negligent homicide; he resigned in August and was sentenced in October to six months at a pre-release center and a 6-year suspended sentence.

In November 2001, it was revealed that Martz and her husband in September 1999 purchased an 80-acre parcel of land next to their home from Arco for $300 an acre. As governor, Martz is the trustee for the state in litigation against Arco ongoing since the 1980s over the Clark Fork Superfund site near Butte. The Martzes had paid $833 an acre for a nearby parcel; Democrats in spring 2002 charged that Arco made a gift to Martz in violation of the state's ethics law. A two-day hearing was held in June 2002 and in September 2002 the state Political Practices Commissioner ruled that Arco had made no gift (the Martzes argued the Arco land was worth less than the other parcel) and that Martz did not violate the law. Despite the vindication, she had to endure months of unfavorable publicity—to the point where she announced she would not give interviews to some reporters.

On taxes and spending, Martz kept her promises during 2001 and 2002, but with difficulty. She prevented tax increases and kept asserting that she wanted to cut state income taxes by 10%. But as revenue estimates plummeted, she called a special session of the legislature in August 2002, which voted spending cuts of $21 million and $35 million in fund transfers and accounting changes. In November 2002, projections were that revenues would still be short $32 million in June 2003; Martz recommended $12 million in further cuts. Democrats projected a $250 million deficit for the next biennial budget; Martz proposed tapping $93 million in principal in the coal severance tax trust fund. On environmental issues, Martz has said that extractive industry officials are "true environmentalists" and that protesters who tie themselves to logging trucks should "get a job." In September 2002, she hailed Bush administration measures allowing more logging in national forests and she criticized the National Park Service for not doing its part under a 2000 agreement, reached after 10 years of controversy, in rounding up bison roving outside Yellowstone National Park; the Park Service and protesters who monitor the treatment of bison denied her charges.

Martz's job rating declined sharply during her first two years in office. In late 2001, it hovered around 40%— weak, but not dismal. But in October and November 2002, polls showed her with 23% and 20% positive job approval, the lowest of any of the 50 governors. Republicans lost seats in the 2002 legislative elections, but still had majorities in both houses. At the same time voters rejected by 68%–32% an initiative, supported by Democrats and opposed by Martz, which would have authorized the state to buy power dams owned by Montana Power until electricity deregulation was passed in 1997.

In late 2002, Martz said she would decide whether to run again in 2004 after the legislative session. Longtime Billings legislator Thomas Keating, 74, Natelson's running mate in 2000, said he would run on a platform of getting "back to our natural resource industry base." Another possible Republican candidate was Secretary of State Bob Brown. A host of Democrats were seen as possible candidates: rancher Brian Schweitzer, who lost by only 51%–47% to Senator Conrad Burns in 2000; O'Keefe and Mazurek, who ran first and second in the 2000 gubernatorial primary; and Yellowstone County Commissioner Bill Kennedy. Montana voters have not ousted an incumbent governor in a general election since 1968; it could happen again in 2004.

Senior Senator

Max Baucus (D)

Elected 1978, seat up 2008, 5th term; b. Dec. 11, 1941, Helena; home, Helena; Stanford U., B.A. 1964, LL.B. 1967; Protestant; married (Wanda).

Elected Office: MT House of Reps., 1973–74; U.S. House of Reps., 1974–78.

Professional Career: Staff atty., Civil Aeronautics Bd., 1967–69; Legal Asst., Securities & Exchange Comm., 1969–71; Practicing atty., 1971–74.

DC Office: 511 HSOB, 20510, 202-224-2651; Fax: 202-224-4700; Web site: baucus.senate.gov.

State Offices: Billings, 406-657-6790; Bozeman, 406-586-6104; Butte, 406-782-8700; Great Falls, 406-761-1574; Helena, 406-449-5480; Kalispell, 406-756-1150; Missoula, 406-329-3123.

Committees: *Agriculture, Nutrition & Forestry:* Marketing, Inspection & Product Promotion (RMM); Production & Price Competitiveness. *Environment & Public Works:* Fisheries, Wildlife & Water; Transportation & Infrastructure. *Finance* (RMM): Health Care; International Trade (RMM); Taxation & IRS Oversight. *Joint Committee on Taxation* (4th of 5 Sens.).

Group Ratings

	ADA	ACLU	AFS	LCV	CON	ITIC	NTU	COC	ACU	NTLC	CHC
2002	75	60	75	47	0	88	32	70	37	24	—
2001	80	—	58	75	—	—	43	71	28	—	20

National Journal Ratings

	2001 LIB	—	2001 CONS		2002 LIB	—	2002 CONS
Economic	55%	—	45%		54%	—	45%
Social	60%	—	36%		66%	—	33%
Foreign	74%	—	14%		51%	—	47%

Key Votes of the 107th Congress

1. Approve Bush Tax Cuts	Y	5. Confirm Ashcroft as AG	N	9. Bar Coop. with Intl. Court	Y
2. Expand Patients' Rights	Y	6. Bar Gays in the Boy Scouts	N	10. Trade Promotion Authority	Y
3. Campaign Finance Reform	Y	7. $ for Hate Crime Prosecution	Y	11. Authorize Force in Iraq	Y
4. Permit ANWR Development	N	8. Overseas Military Abortions	Y	12. Homeland Sec. Dept. Union	Y

Election Results

2002 general	Max Baucus (D)	204,853	(63%)	($6,189,970)
	Mike Taylor (R)	103,611	(32%)	($1,839,020)
	Other	18,073	(5%)	
2002 primary	Max Baucus (D)	unopposed		
1996 general	Max Baucus (D)	201,935	(50%)	($4,280,747)
	Denny Rehberg (R)	182,111	(45%)	($1,358,165)
	Becky Shaw (Reform)	19,276	(5%)	

Prior Winning Percentages: 1990 (68%); 1984 (57%); 1978 (56%); 1976 House (66%); 1974 House (55%)

Max Baucus is from a well-known Montana ranching family; in 1897 his great-grandfather Henry Sieben started the huge Sieben Ranch, including the land in *A River Runs Through It*. Baucus grew up on a 125,000-acre (195 square miles) ranch near Helena, graduated from college and law school at Stanford, then worked four years at the now-abolished Civil Aeronautics Board and the Securities and Exchange Commission in Washington. He returned to Montana in 1971 and was executive director of the state constitutional convention in 1972. In 1973, he served in the state House. In 1974, at 32, he won the western House seat (Montana had two House seats until 1992) by walking 600 miles along highways through the district and beating three past or future holders of it (Democrats Pat Williams and Arnold Olsen in the primary and Republican Richard Shoup in the general). He won his Senate seat in 1978 by easily beating an appointed senator in the primary and a conservative Republican investment adviser in the general. Reelected easily in 2002, he is set to become (in March 2005) the longest-serving senator from Montana, though he has spent only four years of his adult life living full-time in the state.

For 18 months in 2001 and 2002, he was chairman of the Senate Finance Committee; now he is again, as he was in early 2001 (thanks to the retirement of Daniel Patrick Moynihan), its ranking minority member. He is also the second ranking Democrat on the Environment and Public Works Committee, which he chaired in 1993–94. To these posts he has not brought the philosophic depth of Moynihan nor a reputation of loyalty to the Democratic leadership; he always remembers that he is a Democrat in a mostly Republican state. In the runup to the 1996 election—his closest race ever—he switched positions and supported the balanced budget amendment. In March 2001, he was one of six Democrats to vote to kill the Clinton administration's rule on ergonomics and was one of six to support the Frist-Breaux proposal to remove the soft-money ban from McCain-Feingold.

On Finance, before he got the top Democratic spot, he concentrated on trade issues. He was a leading advocate of normal trade relations with China, a potentially huge market for Montana wheat. In 2000, he led the fight for approval of PNTR with China, in the process opposing the Taiwan Security Enhancement Act and the Thompson-Torricelli amendment to penalize Chinese companies that traffic in nuclear, chemical and biological weapons; the amendment lost 65–32. PNTR was soon approved, and Baucus responded by calling, with Pat Roberts of Kansas, for an end to the trade embargo on Cuba.

In early 2001, as ranking minority member, he worked closely with Chairman Charles Grassley; like Moynihan and William Roth in the early 1990s, or Russell Long and Bob Dole in the 1970s and 1980s, when they occupied the same posts, they were operating independently of their party leaderships. They decided to put aside George W. Bush's Medicare proposals and concentrate on a prescription drug benefit instead. And they decided to produce a bipartisan tax cut similar to Bush's, but different in some important respects that could gain a committee majority. They unveiled their $1.3 trillion package in May; specific provisions were aimed at moderate Republicans Lincoln Chafee and Olympia Snowe and Democrats John Breaux and Bob Torricelli. The bill passed the committee 14–6 on May 15 and the Senate 62–38 (with 12 Democrats, including Baucus) on May 23. Key members of the coalition Grassley and Baucus assembled insisted they would not accept major changes from the Senate bill; so something very much like it came out of the conference committee. So, just as Jim Jeffords was in the process of leaving the Republican party, the biggest domestic priority of the Bush administration was passed into law.

Daschle was reportedly furious that Baucus refused to consult with the Democratic Caucus before markup; he presumably wanted the 50 Democrats to hold out for a much more Democratic tax cut that would have left the government with much more revenue in the out-years. Pressure from Daschle may have reined in Baucus in October 2001, when Baucus introduced a $70 billion stimulus package and Republicans urged him to negotiate a compromise with Grassley; Baucus instead called on Bush to step in; a smaller Baucus plan passed the committee 11–10 in November (with Jeffords as the swing vote). In effect, Daschle had forced Baucus to go along with his strategy for confrontation with Republicans on the floor rather than compromise in committee. Similarly, on welfare, Baucus was unable to come up with a united Democratic position; the 1996 law was not reauthorized in 2002, and became an issue for the 108th Congress. Baucus was more successful on securing trade promotion authority for the president, for which there was a large majority in the Senate; after passage by an excruciatingly narrow margin in the House in December 2001, it was delayed some months by Daschle but became law in July 2002.

In September 2002, Baucus summoned all Finance members and told them that Daschle would allow no prescription drug bill to come out of committee and, according to some reports that Baucus denied, said that Daschle would strip him of his chairmanship if he marked one up; instead Daschle brought his own bill to the floor. That month Baucus also cancelled the markup on a small business tax cut after Daschle, the third-ranking Democrat on Finance, filed 78 amendments—one of four markups cancelled because Baucus could not assemble a majority. Baucus and Daschle fought over whether Baucus would brief the Democratic Caucus on the repeal of a tax law ruled by the WTO as an illegal export subsidy on which the European Union was threatening a $4 billion retaliatory tariff. In December 2002, Baucus proposed a $160 billion economic stimulus package that included $75 billion in block grants to the states, a one-time $300 income tax cut and $16 billion in incentives for businesses to invest in plants and equipment. This time, Baucus first consulted with Daschle, though news reports indicated party leadership was concerned about Baucus' discussions with the White House regarding his proposals and theirs, such as a stock dividends tax cut and an acceleration of income tax cuts. In 2003 and 2004, Daschle will presumably prevent Baucus from making bipartisan deals with Grassley, but the pressure may be less intense because Grassley now has the gavel at Finance and Daschle does not have 50 Democratic votes to pass measures on the floor.

When Baucus came to the Senate, there were six Democratic and eight Republican senators from the Rocky Mountain states. Today, there are three Democrats and 11 Republicans. He was reelected in 1996 by only a 50%–45% margin, despite a huge money advantage, over Dennis Rehberg, then lieutenant governor and since 2000, the state's congressman-at-large. The increasing conservatism of Montana voters and resentment at Clinton environmental policies put him in an uncomfortable position in the runup to the 2002 election. He supported the Clinton administration moratorium on mining in the Rocky Mountain Front north of Helena, but was neutral on the Clinton proposal to give national monument status to the 149-mile Missouri River Breaks area, which Republican Conrad Burns strongly opposed. He was the only Senate Democrat to oppose a resolution calling for gun control legislation by Memorial Day 2000.

Baucus has worked hard to maintain a presence in Montana. In 1995–96 he walked 820 miles across the state and shook thousands of hands. He has a "day in the life" program of working a day a month at an ordinary job, building houses with Great Falls high school students, working at a high-tech aerospace firm in Helena, building a grandstand at the Glendive fairgrounds (for once a politician admits to grandstanding).

In early 2001, Baucus nonetheless seemed vulnerable. One Republican who could clearly beat him was Marc Racicot, who had 75% to 80% positive job ratings during most of his years as governor from 1992 to 2000. But Racicot, having been the lowest-salaried governor in the nation, wanted to make money and refused to run, despite pleas from George W. Bush himself; in December 2001 Bush made him Republican National Committee Chairman. That left the Republican nomination to state Senator Mike Taylor, sponsor of the law that cut the business equipment tax from 6% to 3% by 2003. Taylor had made millions in a hair salon and cosmetology school business and eventually spent $1 million of his own money on the campaign. He won the June 2002 primary with 60% of the vote against three rivals.

But Baucus had much more money. As chairman of the Senate Finance Committee, his fundraising capacity was enormous, and in all he spent over $6 million—almost four times as much as Taylor. Baucus ran ads showing how he helped Montana small businesses and showing George W. Bush thanking him at bill-signing ceremonies. Then, on October 10, Taylor announced he was dropping out of the race, because of an ad run by the Montana Democratic party that slyly suggested he was homosexual. The ad showed 1980s footage of Taylor, with open front shirt and gold chains, massaging a man's face applying facial cream; it stated that Taylor had failed to refund student loan money when students dropped out. Taylor claimed that his wife made paperwork errors and a Taylor aide said, "They're playing off the old stereotype of men who work in the hair-care profession." In any case, the race was already probably over. Taylor had only raised $658,000 from others, almost half of it from a fundraiser featuring Dick Cheney, and he proved unwilling or unable to put more of his own money in; he was still far behind Baucus in public polls, and national Republicans had decided this was not a priority race. In late October, Taylor resumed his campaign. It didn't matter. Baucus won 63%–32%, carrying all but two small counties.

Junior Senator

Conrad Burns (R)

Elected 1988, seat up 2006, 3d term; b. Jan. 25, 1935, Gallatin, MO; home, Billings; U. of MO, 1952–54; Lutheran; married (Phyllis).

Military Career: Marine Corps, 1955–57.

Elected Office: Yellowstone Cnty. Comm., 1986–88.

Professional Career: TWA and Ozark Airlines, 1958–61; Field rep., *Polled Hereford World*, 1962; Mgr., Billings Livestock Show, 1968; Radio & TV broadcaster, 1968–86.

DC Office: 187 DSOB, 20510, 202-224-2644; Fax: 202-224-8594; Web site: burns.senate.gov.

State Offices: Billings, 406-252-0550; Bozeman, 406-586-4450; Butte, 406-723-3277; Glendive, 406-365-2391; Great Falls, 406-452-9585; Helena, 406-449-5401; Kalispell, 406-257-3360; Missoula, 406-329-3528.

Committees: *Appropriations*: Agriculture & Rural Development; Defense; Energy & Water Development; Interior (Chmn.); Military Construction; VA, HUD & Independent Agencies. *Budget. Commerce, Science & Transportation*: Aviation; Communications (Chmn.); Competition, Foreign Commerce & Infrastructure; Consumer Affairs & Product Safety; Science, Technology & Space; Surface Transportation & Merchant Marine. *Energy & Natural Resources*: Energy; National Parks; Public Lands & Forests (Vice Chmn.). *Small Business & Entrepreneurship*.

Group Ratings

	ADA	ACLU	AFS	LCV	CON	ITIC	NTU	COC	ACU	NTLC	CHC
2002	10	40	29	12	25	88	53	90	100	94	—
2001	10	—	8	0	—	—	81	100	96	—	80

National Journal Ratings

	2001 LIB	—	2001 CONS	2002 LIB	—	2002 CONS
Economic	17%	—	77%	11%	—	87%
Social	0%	—	79%	0%	—	62%
Foreign	7%	—	72%	39%	—	60%

Key Votes of the 107th Congress

1. Approve Bush Tax Cuts	Y	5. Confirm Ashcroft as AG	Y	9. Bar Coop. with Intl. Court	Y
2. Expand Patients' Rights	N	6. Bar Gays in the Boy Scouts	Y	10. Trade Promotion Authority	Y
3. Campaign Finance Reform	N	7. $ for Hate Crime Prosecution	N	11. Authorize Force in Iraq	Y
4. Permit ANWR Development	Y	8. Overseas Military Abortions	N	12. Homeland Sec. Dept. Union	N

Election Results

2000 general	Conrad Burns (R)	208,082	(51%)	($4,337,961)
	Brian Schweitzer (D)	194,430	(47%)	($2,033,530)
	Other	9,089	(2%)	
2000 primary	Conrad Burns (R)	unopposed		
1994 general	Conrad Burns (R)	218,542	(62%)	($3,518,574)
	Jack Mudd (D)	131,845	(38%)	($1,107,591)

Prior Winning Percentages: 1988 (52%)

Conrad Burns makes weighty speeches on foreign policy and the future of the Internet even as he cuts the figure of a stereotypical Westerner, picking his teeth with a pocketknife, chewing tobacco, telling deadpan jokes. He grew up in northwest Missouri, joined the Marines after two years of college, worked for two airlines, then became a livestock fieldman and auctioneer and field representative of the *Polled Hereford World* and moved to Billings. When he was reassigned back east (to Des Moines), he quit so he could stay in Montana. He set up the Northern Ag Network, which grew from four radio stations in 1975 to 29 radio and six TV stations in 1988. Piqued at a local politician, Burns ran for Yellowstone County commissioner in 1986 and won; two years later, he ran against Democratic Senator John Melcher. Burns attacked him as "a liberal who is soft on drugs, soft on defense and very high on social programs." Melcher was hurt by public opposition to the "let-it-burn" policy that resulted in the Yellowstone fires of summer 1988. Burns, who ended every speech with a Western "You bet!" won 52%–48%. In 1994, he faced poorly-funded law professor Jack Mudd; Burns won 62%–38%, the first time Montana voters have ever re-elected a Republican senator.

Burns has a solidly conservative voting record in the Senate. In 1997, he became chairman of the Communications Subcommittee, one of the key regulatory posts in Congress. There, this former broadcaster has generally favored deregulation and encouragement of Internet commerce. He wrote Section 706 of the 1996 Telecommunications Act, which provided incentives for broadband data networks. More than one-third of Montana households subscribe to satellite TV; Burns wants commercial network stations to be available on satellite TV. His bill to provide for electronic authentication of online contracts and user identities became law in June 2000. In November 2001, a bill he co-sponsored extended the moratorium enacted by the Internet Tax Freedom Act through November 2003. He got the Commerce Committee to approve a bill co-sponsored by Democrat Ron Wyden to require mass e-mailers to include return addresses to allow recipients to opt out; it awaited action in the 108th Congress.

Burns has weighed in on other issues as well. On the first anniversary of the September 11 attacks, he delivered a National Press Club speech—vetted by the Bush administration, according to the *National Review*—on the future of American foreign and energy policy in the Middle East. In it, Burns argued for diversifying energy sources to increase national security, and called for greater imports of oil from West Africa, Russia and Caspian nations. He decried America's "dependency on rogue oil," and singled out Saudi Arabia for especially harsh criticism. He was a strong advocate of allowing airline pilots to carry guns, and called for shifting airport security from the Transportation Department to Justice. He cast the lone vote against the election procedures bill passed in April 2002, on the grounds that it imposed too many mandates on state and local government.

On Montana issues, Burns is often critical of environmentalists. He opposed reintroduction of grey wolves into Yellowstone National Park, estimating the cost at $1.8 million per wolf. He has blocked Democrats' plans for a Montana wilderness bill and they have blocked his. He opposed Clinton proposals for national monument status for the 149-mile Missouri Breaks region and a ban on snowmobiles in national parks. He joined several Democrats in 2002 in seeking over $5 billion for drought relief for farmers, on the ground that they deserve it as much as victims of hurricanes and floods; this was opposed by George W. Bush, and Burns and others had to settle for $752 million coming out of farm programs. As chairman of the Appropriations Subcommittee on the Interior, he is well-positioned to steer money to Montana projects, like the Minuteman installations at Malmstrom Air Force Base or the Rocky Boy project to bring water to the Chippewa-Cree in north central Montana.

Burns had a surprisingly hard time winning reelection in 2000 in a state that was voting 58%–33% for George W. Bush. One reason was term limits: In February 1999, he announced he would break his pledge to serve only two terms. That same month, speaking before a Montana group, he referred to Arabs as "ragheads" and had to make a quick apology—his penchant for quips had gone too far. The next month, he got a tough opponent when Brian Schweitzer, a Whitefish rancher who raises cattle, mint and dill, and used to export bull semen, got into the race. Schweitzer had some political connections—he was a Clinton appointee to the Farm Service Agency—but, driving a Dodge pickup with a cracked windshield, he effectively portrayed himself as nonpolitical. Schweitzer once worked on irrigation projects in the Middle East, and charged that Montana had a third-world economy, exporting raw materials and exporting educated young people. Schweitzer was the first candidate in the 1999–2000 cycle to call for a prescription drug benefit, and in fall 1999, he organized the first busload of seniors to Canada to buy drugs at lower prices. Burns responded ineptly and did not seem comfortable arguing that pharmaceutical companies set prices in order to fund pathbreaking research. At one point, he said that many Montanans choose to be uninsured and suggested that some seniors like to go to the doctor to have "somebody to visit with. There's nothing wrong with them."

Another issue that played a role was asbestos. There was heavy publicity about the asbestos-related illnesses and deaths in the town of Libby, where children played in tailings from a closed vermiculite plant. In January 2000, a trial lawyer-financed group attacked Burns for supporting a bill that would limit compensation to those who had asbestos-related disease and shut down the giant asbestos tort cases; it showed a Libby resident accusing Burns of "standing up for the people who made me sick and killed my father." In March, Burns withdrew his support of the bill and pushed for $3.5 million for a Libby hospital and $8 million for local economic development. In addition, a group backed by the U.S. Chamber of Commerce and an asbestos company ran ads showing relatives of an asbestos victim blaming "asbestos lawyers" for clogging the courts and preventing them from getting compensation. Later, another group backed by pharmaceutical companies ran ads saying Schweitzer favored "Canadian-style government controls on prescription medicine." On the defensive, Burns in April voted for a Democratic resolution to bar tax cuts until a prescription drug benefit was passed.

Burns outspent Schweitzer by 2–1, and in ads talked about bringing $1 billion of federal money to Montana. He also linked Schweitzer to Al Gore. Polls in the closing weeks showed the race close, and Burns won by only 51%–47%—a margin similar to that by which Republicans won the races for congressman-at-large, governor and secretary of state. After the election, Burns said he did not rule out running for a fourth term in 2006.

Representative-At-Large

Denny Rehberg (R)

Elected 2000, 2d term; b. Oct. 5, 1955, Billings; home, Billings; WA St. U., B.A. 1977; Episcopalian; married (Jan).

Elected Office: MT House of Reps., 1984–90; MT Lt. Gov., 1991–96.

Professional Career: Leg. Asst., U.S. Rep. Ron Marlenee, 1979–82; Rancher, 1982-present.

DC Office: 516 CHOB, 20515, 202-225-3211; Fax: 202-225-5687; Web site: wwww.house.gov/rehberg.

District Offices: Billings, 406-256-1019; Great Falls, 406-454-1066; Helena, 406-443-7878; Missoula, 406-543-9550.

Committees: *Agriculture* (16th of 27 R): Department Operations, Oversight, Nutrition & Forestry (Vice Chmn.); General Farm Commodities & Risk Management; Specialty Crops & Foreign Agriculture Programs.

Resources (22d of 28 R): Energy & Mineral Resources; Forests & Forest Health. *Transportation & Infrastructure* (27th of 41 R): Aviation; Highways, Transit & Pipelines.

Group Ratings

	ADA	ACLU	AFS	LCV	CON	ITIC	NTU	COC	ACU	NTLC	CHC
2002	0	21	0	0	25	100	56	95	100	83	92
2001	5	—	10	0	—	—	59	100	84	—	—

National Journal Ratings

	2001 LIB	—	2001 CONS		2002 LIB	—	2002 CONS
Economic	36%	—	63%		0%	—	91%
Social	32%	—	67%		25%	—	71%
Foreign	33%	—	60%		35%	—	60%

Key Votes of the 107th Congress

1. Approve Bush Tax Cuts	Y	5. Faith-Based Charities	Y	9. Trade Promotion Authority	Y
2. Limit Patients' Bill of Rights	Y	6. Bar Gays in the Boy Scouts	Y	10. Bar Funds for Intl. Court	Y
3. Campaign Finance Reform	N	7. Ban Partial-Birth Abortion	Y	11. Authorize Force in Iraq	Y
4. Ban ANWR Development	N	8. Arm Commercial Pilots	Y	12. Deny Home. Sec. Dept. Union	Y

Election Results

2002 general	Denny Rehberg (R)	214,100	(65%)	($949,631)
	Steve Kelly (D)	108,233	(33%)	($18,757)
	Other	8,988	(3%)	
2002 primary	Denny Rehberg (R)	unopposed		
2000 general	Denny Rehberg (R)	211,418	(51%)	($2,125,364)
	Nancy Keenan (D)	189,971	(46%)	($1,932,099)
	Other	9,132	(2%)	

Dennis Rehberg, a Republican elected in 2000, is a rancher from Billings who raises 500 cattle and 600 cashmere goats on his family ranch and who has been involved in politics most of his adult life. After college, he worked in real estate and then on the Washington staff of Congressman Ron Marlenee. He returned to Montana in 1982 and was elected to the state House in 1984, at 29; he managed Marlenee's campaign in 1986 and Conrad Burns' first campaign for the Senate in 1988. He served as Burns' state director for two years, then was appointed lieutenant governor by Republican Stan Stephens, and was elected to that post on the ticket headed by Marc Racicot in 1992. In 1996, he ran against Senator Max Baucus. Rehberg backed term limits, promised to forego pay increases and attacked Baucus for backing the 1993 tax increase and the assault weapons ban. Baucus called Rehberg a "special interest" candidate backing billions in tax cuts for the rich and argued against Republican Medicare "cuts." Rehberg was outspent by $4.3 million to $1.4 million, but made it a close race: Baucus won 50%–45%.

Rehberg (pronounced *REE-berg*) returned to ranching. The opportunity to run for the House arose in September 1999 when incumbent Republican Rick Hill, reelected by only 53%–44% and facing vigorous opposition from Democratic Superintendent of Public Instruction Nancy Keenan, announced he would not run because of complications from eye surgery which made it impossible for him to read. Rehberg was unopposed for the Republican nomination. The general race against Keenan was a classic contest between a liberal Democrat and a conservative Republican. Both decried Montana's low-wage economy and how it made it difficult for young people to stay in the communities where they were raised. But it was not clear what either would do about it. Rehberg and Keenan also agreed on opposing gun control, repealing the marriage penalty and letting patients sue HMOs.

Naturally there was more discussion of their disagreements—on abortion rights, on inheritance taxes, a prescription drug benefit (Rehberg favored it for the needy, Keenan for all), and individual investment accounts in Social Security. Rehberg favored a minimum wage increase only if it included tax breaks for small business and a ban on soft money only if it covered unions; he opposed taxes on Internet commerce. Keenan emphasized education, opposing vouchers and favoring small class sizes, safe and drug-free schools and more money for special education. The tone got testier, as outside groups—the AFL-CIO, the NEA, the Chamber of Commerce, the NFIB—spent over $100,000 each; something like $20 million was spent in this state with seriously contested races for Senate and House. Rehberg ran ads with strong endorsements from Governor Marc Racicot and often showing his family, especially his two-year-old daughter—an implicit contrast with Keenan, a former copper smelter worker and special education teacher who had never married. By the end of the campaign, Rehberg was accusing Keenan of being a social liberal favoring big government, more taxes and more spending, while Keenan called Rehberg a dirty politician whose positions would hurt education and deny essentials for the elderly. Spending was almost even: $2.1 million for Rehberg, $1.9 million for Keenan. Rehberg won 51%–46%, almost precisely the same margin, with almost the same results county by county, by which Senator Conrad Burns won and by which Republican Judy Martz was elected governor. All the Republicans were surely helped by George W. Bush's 58%–33% margin over Al Gore.

As a freshman, Rehberg concentrated on issues with impact in Montana. He worked with Senator Conrad Burns in 2002 to get $5 billion in drought relief for farmers in addition to the farm bill; they were frustrated by George W. Bush's opposition, and had to settle for $752 million in farm bill funds. He sought repeal of the Clinton administration's restrictions on snowmobiling in Yellowstone National Park; after a hearing Rehberg organized, the Bush administration changed the policy. He persuaded the House to authorize the $200 million Rocky Boy project to provide clean water for the Chippewa-Cree despite the opposition of the Director of the Bureau of Reclamation. When some senators proposed a holiday moratorium on state sales taxes in December 2001, Rehberg responded with a proposal for a tax credit for travel and lodging for out-of-state shoppers who come to shop in states without a sales tax; Montana is one of five such states.

Rehberg declined to run against Senator Max Baucus in 2002, though polls suggested he would be competitive. Democrats could find no well-known candidate to challenge Rehberg; their nominee was an art gallery owner who had previously run for office as a Republican and an Independent and voted for Ralph Nader in 2000. He spent $18,800; Rehberg spent $950,000. Rehberg won 65%–33%; he lost only four counties, two in Indian reservations, the other two containing the mining towns of Butte and Anaconda.

★ NEBRASKA ★

"The sea of Nebraska" is what the first settlers coming west called the Platte River—not actually a single river, but a braid of streams that weaves a silver chain around sandbars and islands, flooding the level floor of the great plain—a mile wide, as the saying goes, and six inches deep. Nebraska was formed in one rush of settlement in the 1880s, when its population increased from 452,000 to 1,062,000; it has increased just a bit more than that (to 1,711,000 in 2000) in the 110 years since. In the 1880s Omaha became a major railroad center, Lincoln the state capital, and farming and food products the main businesses. And for about 100 years, Nebraska remained pretty much that way. This is not what its founders intended: They hoped Nebraska would develop a diversified farming, industrial and commercial economy like Ohio, Illinois, Missouri or Minnesota. But while the 1880s were a time of plentiful rain here, the 1890s were a decade of drought, and Nebraska stopped growing. Many rural counties, and even Omaha, lost population and Nebraska exported people for 100 years: 48% of Nebraskans in 1890 were children; in 2000, only 26% were. For a long time the creative energies in the economy seem to have skipped over the Great Plains and moved far to the West.

The sudden boom of the 1880s and the bust of the 1890s produced the most colorful—and atypical—politics of Nebraska's history: The populist movement and William Jennings Bryan, the "silver tongued orator of the Platte." Bryan was only 36 when he delivered his Cross of Gold speech at the 1896 Democratic National Convention and was swept to the Democratic nomination. He was so radical that Democratic President Grover Cleveland wouldn't support him, but he still won 47% of the popular vote in the first of three attempts at the presidency. Since Bryan's time, Nebraska's most notable politician has been George Norris, who led the House rebellion against Speaker Joseph Cannon in 1911, and in the 1930s championed the state's unicameral legislature and pushed through the Norris-LaGuardia Anti-Injunction Act (the first federal pro-

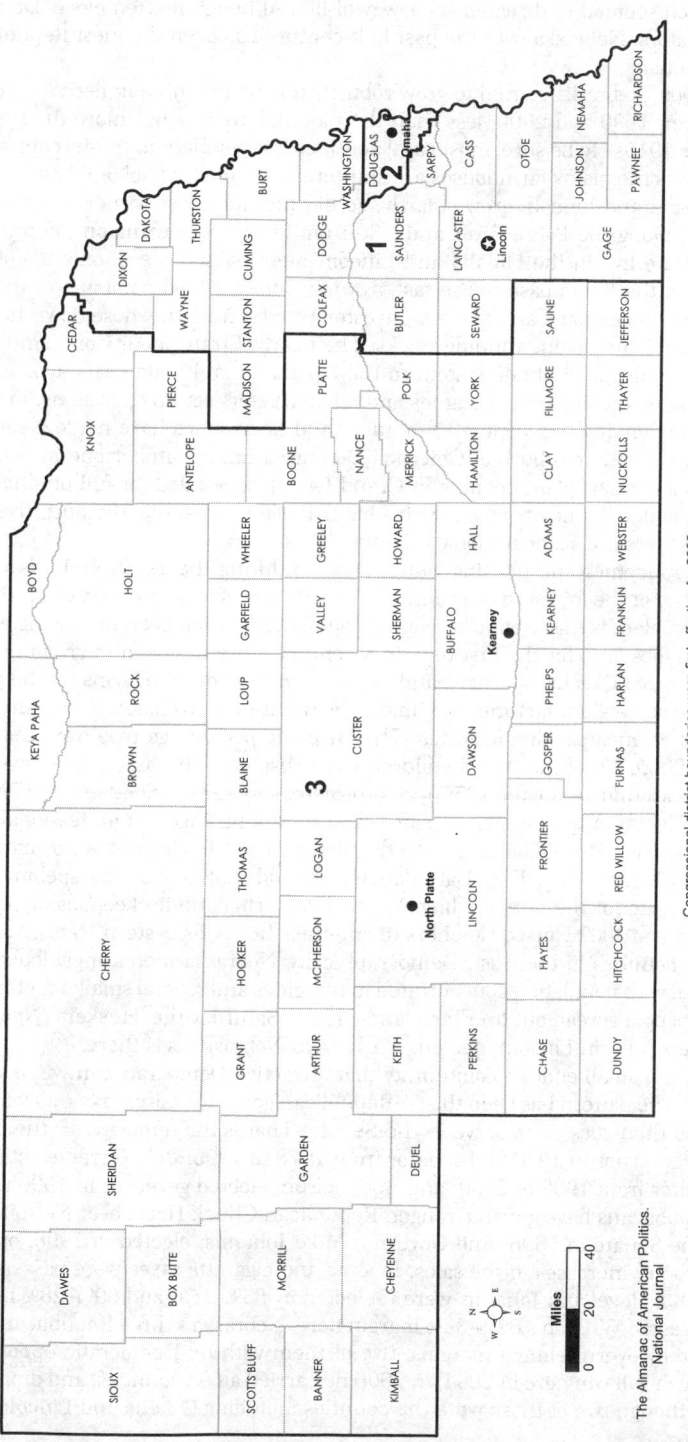

RICHARDSON

NEMAHA

PAWNEE

JOHNSON

OTOE

CASS

SARPY

Omaha

DOUGLAS

WASHINGTON

2

1

SAUNDERS

LANCASTER

Lincoln

GAGE

BURT

DODGE

BUTLER

SEWARD

SALINE

JEFFERSON

CUMING

COLFAX

POLK

YORK

FILLMORE

THAYER

STANTON

PLATTE

MADISON

NANCE

MERRICK

HAMILTON

CLAY

NUCKOLLS

THURSTON

DAKOTA

DIXON

WAYNE

CEDAR

PIERCE

KNOX

ANTELOPE

BOONE

HOWARD

HALL

ADAMS

WEBSTER

WHEELER

GREELEY

SHERMAN

BUFFALO

Kearney

KEARNEY

FRANKLIN

BOYD

HOLT

GARFIELD

VALLEY

Kearney

PHELPS

HARLAN

ROCK

LOUP

CUSTER

DAWSON

GOSPER

FURNAS

KEYA PAHA

BROWN

BLAINE

3

FRONTIER

RED WILLOW

THOMAS

LOGAN

North Platte

LINCOLN

CHERRY

HOOKER

MCPHERSON

HAYES

HITCHCOCK

GRANT

ARTHUR

KEITH

PERKINS

CHASE

DUNDY

SHERIDAN

GARDEN

DEUEL

DAWES

BOX BUTTE

MORRILL

CHEYENNE

SIOUX

SCOTTS BLUFF

BANNER

KIMBALL

Miles
0 20 40

N
W E
S

Congressional district boundaries were first effective for 2002.

The Almanac of American Politics,
National Journal

union legislation) and the Tennessee Valley Authority. But most Nebraskans were repelled by the New Deal, which seemed to threaten their way of life. Although it often elects Democratic governors and senators, Nebraska over the past half-century has been the most Republican state in presidential elections.

In the 1990s, Nebraska started to grow robustly for the first time in decades. Its population grew 8% between 1990 and 2000, less than the national average but more than Nebraska has grown since the 1910s. To be sure, most rural counties lost population: In tiny county seats stores are closing, across the plains farmhouses are shuttered up, small school buildings are half-empty. But metro Omaha and Lincoln grew smartly; so did the northeast corner of the state and the counties strung along the Platte River and I-80 from Omaha to Lexington. More than half the people in the state live in the Omaha and Lincoln metropolitan areas; only 6% of jobs are on farms. Omaha is the home base of the fast-growing ConAgra food combine, of the giant Peter Kiewit construction company and of mega-investor Warren Buffett, whose down-home wit complements his knack for picking winning stocks. The nearby Strategic Air Command base brought the world's most advanced phone system to the Omaha area 40-odd years ago; starting in the 1980s hotel chains, credit card companies and telemarketers set up operations, making this the world's leading telemarketing center. Computers and fiber optics have made Nebraska, as one mayor said, "just another suburb of Chicago." Nebraska ranks number one in combine manufacturing, with a big new plant opening in Grand Island, scheduled for full production in 2005; it is one of the leaders in meatpacking, with a big IBP plant across the Missouri River from Sioux City, Iowa; and there are six operational ethanol plants.

Nebraska's incomes and housing values shot up during the 1990s and its unemployment rate has been one of the lowest in the country. The number of jobs rose 18% when the population rose 8%. The problem is that Nebraska's aging population has not been producing enough young people to fill its jobs, and for the first time in a century there has been migration into the state. A hundred years ago Czechs, Germans and Danes came to work the farms on the plains—Willa Cather tells the story—and factories in Omaha. Now Latinos have been coming from Texas and Mexico to work in meatpacking factories: The Hispanic percentage rose from 2% to 6% in the 1990s, and in 2000, 8% of the state's children were Hispanic. Hispanic percentages are highest in the counties around Lexington (25%), South Sioux City (23%), Scottsbluff (17%) and Grand Island (14%). Nebraska business leaders are even recruiting Nigerian professionals. Businesses and the state spent $70 million to create the Peter Kiewit Institute of Information Sciences, Technology and Engineering; First Data donated the old Ak-Sar-Ben (try spelling it backward) racetrack as the site for the new building. Meanwhile, farm counties keep losing population; the drought of summer 2002 caused ranchers to cull their herds, as eastern Nebraska farmers sent hay to the dry counties in the west. Demographically, Nebraska increasingly looks like a Rocky Mountain state, with population concentrated in two cities and several smaller factory towns, with relatively few people spread out over farmlands. Every Saturday the 'Huskers (Nebraskans don't say Cornhuskers) play in Lincoln, one out of every 25 Nebraskans is there.

Nebraska is a small enough community that attractive Democrats can win even in this Republican state. The pattern has been this: A Republican governor raises taxes, a Democrat defeats him or her and then goes on to serve in the Senate. That is the template for the careers of Jim Exon, elected governor in 1970 and senator from 1978 to 1996; Bob Kerrey, elected governor in 1982 and senator from 1988 to 2000; and Ben Nelson, elected governor in 1990 and senator in 2000. But Republicans have grown stronger. Republican Chuck Hagel beat Nelson when Nelson first ran for the Senate in 1996. And Governor Mike Johanns, elected in 1998, opposed tax increases; temporary increases in the sales, income and cigarette taxes were passed over his veto in 2002. In 2002 Hagel and Johanns were reelected by 83%–15% and 69%–28% margins—even greater than George W. Bush's 62%–33% margin here. Nebraska's three Republican congressmen were reelected by overwhelming margins, two of them with no Democratic opponents. No one doubts that Bush will win here in 2004; in 2000 he carried all 93 counties, and dipped below 60% in just seven, though two of those were the counties including Omaha and Lincoln.

The People		**Race/Ethnic Origin**			**Military veterans:** 173,189 (13.7%)	
Pop. 2000:	1,711,263	1,494,494	87.3%	White	WWII: 20.0%	Korea: 15.0%
Pop. 1990:	1,578,385	67,537	3.9%	Black	Vietnam: 32.3%	Gulf War: 10.8%
Change 1990–2000:	Up 8.4%	21,677	1.3%	Asian	**Most populous cities:**	
Change 1980–1990:	Up 0.5%	13,460	0.8%	Native Am.	1. Omaha	390,007
% of U.S. total:	0.6%	647	0.0%	Hawaiian	2. Lincoln	225,581
Pop. rank:	38th of 50	17,696	1.0%	Two+ races	3. Bellevue	44,382
Area size:	77,354 sq. mi.	1,327	0.1%	Other	4. Grand Island	42,940
State Native:	67.1%	94,425	5.5%	Hisp. Origin	5. Kearney	27,431
Non-citizen:	3.0%	**Ancestry**			Urban population: 69.7%	
Language		German: 27.7%		Irish: 9.6%	Rural population: 30.3%	
English: 90.4%	Spanish: 5.4%	English: 6.9%		Swedish: 3.5%		
Other Eur.: 2.9%		USA: 3.2%				

Education		**Work Sector**		**Unicameral**	
H.S. Grad:	86.6%	Private: 77.1%	Govt: 13.7%	Senate	49 I
College Grad:	23.7%	Self: 8.7%	Family: 0.5%		
Industry		Unemployment: 3.5%		Legislative Term Limits: Yes	
Agri: 5.6%	Con: 6.5%	**Household Income**		**Registered Voters**	
Fin: 7.7%	Info: 2.5%	<15k: 14.9%	15-35k: 29.5%	D: 381,991	(35.3%)
Mfg: 18.4%	Prof: 28.0%	35-50k: 18.4%	50-100k: 29.2%	R: 543,935	(50.2%)
Public: 3.9%	Trade: 15.7%	100-150k: 5.5%	>150k: 2.6%	I: 157,618	(14.5%)
Other: 11.9%		Median: $39,250			
Occupation		Poverty status: 9.7%			
Blue collar: 24.4%	White collar: 59.4%	**Home Value**			
Gray collar: 16.2%		<50k: 21.3%	50-100k: 40.2%	100-200k: 30.4%	200-300k: 5.3%
		300-500k: 2.0%	>500k: 0.7%	Median: $86,900	

Presidential politics Over the last 50 years, Nebraska has voted more Republican in presidential elections than any other state—61.0% to Utah's second-place 60.7%. It was appropriate, perhaps, that this was the last state Bill Clinton visited as president, in December 2000. Greater Omaha usually goes Republican, while Lincoln is more closely divided; rural western counties are heavily Republican— Bush's percentages there ranged up to 86%. In the VNS exit poll, no statistically significant demographic group came close to voting for Al Gore. Nebraska law allows its electoral votes to be split, with one going to the winner of each congressional district and two to the statewide winner. This has never made any difference; in 2000 the closest district was the 2d, which Bush carried 57%–39%.

Nebraska has a presidential primary in May that once attracted attention; the whole national press followed Robert Kennedy and Eugene McCarthy out here in 1968 and took note when Frank Church won in 1976. No more, though: Nominations are now sewn up long before May, and Nebraska votes as unnoticed then as in November.

2000 Presidential Vote		
Bush (R)	433,862	(62%)
Gore (D)	231,780	(33%)
Nader (Green)	24,540	(4%)
Other	6,837	(1%)

2000 Republican Presidential Primary		
Bush (R)	145,176	(78%)
McCain (R)	28,065	(15%)
Keyes (R)	12,073	(7%)

2000 Democratic Presidential Primary		
Gore (D)	73,639	(70%)
Bradley (D)	27,884	(26%)
Other	3,748	(4%)

1996 Presidential Vote		
Dole (R)	363,467	(54%)
Clinton (D)	236,761	(35%)
Perot (I)	71,278	(11%)

Congressional districting

Nebraska has had three congressional districts since the 1960s. Redistricting made only marginal changes for 2002; Democrats were angered when traditionally Democratic Saline County was moved from the 1st to the 3d District. No Democrat has been elected from a Nebraska district since 1992.

Governor

Mike Johanns (R)

Elected 1998, term expires Jan. 2007, 2d term; b. June 18, 1950, Osage, IA; home, Lincoln; St. Mary's Col., B.A. 1971; Creighton U., J.D. 1974; Catholic; married (Stephanie).

Elected Office: Lancaster Cnty. Bd. of Comm., 1982–88; Lincoln City Cncl., 1989–90; Lincoln Mayor, 1991–98.

Professional Career: Law clerk, Hon. Hale McCown, 1974–75; Practicing atty., 1975–91.

Office: P.O. Box 94848, Lincoln, 68509, 402-471-2244; Fax: 402-471-6031; Web site: www.gov.state.ne.us.

Election Results

2002 general	Mike Johanns (R)	330,349	(69%)
	Stormy Dean (D)	132,348	(28%)
	Paul Rosberg (NEB)	18,294	(4%)
2002 primary	Mike Johanns (R)	128,277	(87%)
	Robert Wicht (R)	19,441	(13%)
1998 general	Mike Johanns (R)	293,910	(54%)
	Bill Hoppner (D)	250,678	(46%)

Mike Johanns in 2002 became the first Republican to be reelected governor of Nebraska since 1956. He was born in Iowa and is of Luxembourgois descent (as is U.S. House Speaker Dennis Hastert). He grew up on a dairy farm, went to college in Minnesota, then got a law degree at Creighton University in Omaha and clerked for a judge there for one year. He practiced law in O'Neill, in the vast sand hills of Holt County, then in Lincoln; he was elected to the Lancaster County Board of Commissioners in 1982 and to the Lincoln City Council in 1989. These were nonpartisan offices; Johanns was a Democrat until 1988. He was elected Lincoln mayor in 1991 and re-elected without opposition in 1995; his wife is a former state senator (a nonpartisan office in Nebraska, the only state with a one-house legislature). He helped establish a work empowerment program for Lancaster County inmates and a Handi-Van service for seniors in rural Lancaster County. In 1995 he began his campaign for governor and traveled all over the state, ultimately visiting all 93 counties (some with only a few hundred voters).

There was vigorous competition in the Republican primary. State Auditor John Breslow spent $2.5 million of his own money, and 2d District Congressman Jon Christensen had strong religious conservative support. All supported Initiative 413, which would limit state spending increases based on the rate of inflation plus population growth; all favored property tax relief. A week before the May primary, Christensen's campaign distributed flyers attacking Johanns for allowing obscene and racist broadcasts to air on Lincoln's public access cable channel. In fact, Johanns had tried to stop the broadcasts, but was foiled by the city council. On the Saturday before the primary, Senator Chuck Hagel called the flyer "absolute trash" and said, "Nobody in the Republican Party of Nebraska can be proud of Jon Christensen's conduct." This was a high-spending contest—Breslow spent $3.8 million altogether, Christensen $1.8 million, Johanns $1.7 million—and turnout was up 14% from the last seriously contested Republican primary for governor. Johanns won with 40% of the vote, to 30% for Breslow and 28% for Christensen. Meanwhile, the winner in the much quieter Democratic primary was Bill Hoppner, longtime aide to former Governor and Senator Jim Exon and former Governor and Senator Bob Kerrey, who had lost the 1990 primary to Ben Nelson by only 42 votes.

Hoppner based much of his campaign on the plausible charge that Initiative 413 would make property tax relief impossible. But in early July Johanns switched and came out against 413. Hoppner argued that Johanns couldn't be trusted to keep his word. The campaign was conducted civilly, but with major differences on issues, with Johanns taking crisp conservative positions. Johanns won 54%–46%. Hoppner carried Lancaster County (with the state Capitol and the University of Nebraska, always an opponent of state spending cuts) but Johanns carried the Omaha area and got nearly 60% in central and western Nebraska. At the same time, Initiative 413 lost by a wide margin.

As governor, Johanns proved to be low-key and outgoing; by August 2000 he had traveled to all 93 counties again. Nebraska is the only state with a unicameral legislature, the Senate, often called the Unicam, adopted by referendum at the urging of George Norris in 1934. The Senate is capable of taking the initiative. In March 1999 it overrode a Johanns veto by a 39–7 margin and Johanns agreed to back property tax relief through a school aid increase of $90 million. They also agreed on a $1,000 incentive to adopt state wards and funding for 12 more state troopers. Johanns continued his predecessor Ben Nelson's childcare subsidy, despite a $30 million cost overrun, and approved more money for special education. He vetoed a moratorium on the death penalty. He vetoed 26 bills, the most in 10 years, including a measure raising elected officials' salaries and his own salary from the nation's lowest, $65,000; that veto was overridden 46–1. He got passed a $10 million bill for tax credits and entrepreneurship grants to firms that open businesses in rural areas and a voluntary meatpacking workers' bill of rights, to be published in English and Spanish.

By late 2001 revenues started coming in under estimate, and in a November 2001 special session Johanns got $171 million in cuts of planned spending. "I'm not here to sign tax increases," Johanns said. "Government tends to operate better when it's under pressure." In 2002, revenues were down 4% from 2001, and the Senate passed temporary increases in the sales, income and cigarette taxes over Johanns's veto; school aid was cut and the Rural Development Commission terminated. In July 2002 Johanns proposed cuts in Medicaid and a freeze on higher education. In late 2002 legislators were looking to increase the sales tax; Johanns said, "Raising taxes is the last alternative." In January 2003 he introduced a budget that cut the University of Nebraska and state aid to schools by 10% and imposed a 20-cent increase in the cigarette tax; it did not cut children's health care, nursing homes or early childhood education. Johanns called a special session just after the 2002 election to revise the state's death penalty law to conform to a June U.S. Supreme Court ruling that juries, not judges, must decide whether aggravating factors justifying the death penalty were present. The Senate agreed by a 38–7 margin, but state Senator Ernie Chambers, an opponent of the death penalty, prevented a change from the electric chair to lethal injection. Nebraska is the only state that uses the electric chair as its sole method of execution, and Chambers hopes that a court will rule it cruel and unusual punishment.

There was little serious competition in Nebraska's elections in 2002. Turnout in the May primary was a record low, and turnout in November was the lowest in an off-year election since 1974. Johanns's Democratic opponent was Omaha area businessman Stormy Dean, recruited by Senator Ben Nelson after several other Democrats turned him down. Dean criticized the governor's fiscal management and strongly supported a ballot initiative legalizing video gambling; Johanns has opposed gambling of all kinds. But a judge took the initiative off the ballot. Johanns was endorsed by 20 unions, evidently for his support of the packinghouse workers' bill of rights; the state AFL-CIO and teachers' union were neutral. In November Johanns was reelected 69%–28%; the lowest percentage he received in any county was 59% and the highest 85%. He had raised $2 million and was confident enough to leave $874,000 unspent. Speculation immediately arose that Johanns would run against Senator Ben Nelson in 2006. Possible 2006 candidates for governor include Lieutenant Governor David Heineman (appointed by Johanns in October 2001 when the incumbent quit to become a FEMA regional director) and Attorney General

Jon Bruning, both Republicans, and Democratic state Senators Matt Connealy and Patrick Bourne. But the strongest candidate, if he wanted to run, would probably be 3d District congressman and former University of Nebraska football coach Tom Osborne.

Senior Senator

Chuck Hagel (R)

Elected 1996, seat up 2008, 2d term; b. Oct. 4, 1946, North Platte; home, Omaha; U. of NE, B.A. 1971; Episcopalian; married (Lilibet).

Military Career: Army, 1967–68 (Vietnam).

Professional Career: Newscaster & Talk Show Host, KBON & KLNG Radio, 1969–71; Admin. Asst., U.S. Rep. John Y. McCollister, 1971–77; Mgr., Govt. Affairs, Firestone Tire & Rubber Co., 1977–80; Dpty. Admin., Veterans' Admin., 1981; U.S. Dpty. Commissioner General, World's Fair, 1982; Pres., Collins, Hagel & Clarke Inc., 1983–84; Co–founder, Dir. & Exec. V.P., Vanguard Cellular Systems Inc., 1984–87; Pres. & CEO, World USO, 1987–90; Pres. & CEO, Priv. Sector Cncl., 1990–92; Pres., McCarth & Co., 1992–95.

DC Office: 248 RSOB, 20510, 202-224-4224; Fax: 202-224-5213; Web site: hagel.senate.gov.

State Offices: Kearney, 308-236-7602; Lincoln, 402-476-1400; Omaha, 402-758-8981; Scottsbluff, 308-632-6032.

Committees: *Banking, Housing & Urban Affairs*: Financial Institutions; International Trade & Finance (Chmn.); Securities & Investment. *Foreign Relations*: East Asian & Pacific Affairs; European Affairs; International Economic Policy, Export & Trade Promotion (Chmn.); Near Eastern & South Asian Affairs. *Intelligence (Select)*.

Group Ratings

	ADA	ACLU	AFS	LCV	CON	ITIC	NTU	COC	ACU	NTLC	CHC
2002	10	60	13	0	12	88	69	95	95	85	—
2001	25	—	8	0	—	—	82	100	84	—	60

National Journal Ratings

	2001 LIB	—	2001 CONS		2002 LIB	—	2002 CONS
Economic	30%	—	66%		20%	—	78%
Social	33%	—	59%		0%	—	62%
Foreign	7%	—	72%		0%	—	76%

Key Votes of the 107th Congress

1. Approve Bush Tax Cuts	Y	5. Confirm Ashcroft as AG	Y	9. Bar Coop. with Intl. Court	Y
2. Expand Patients' Rights	N	6. Bar Gays in the Boy Scouts	N	10. Trade Promotion Authority	Y
3. Campaign Finance Reform	N	7. $ for Hate Crime Prosecution	N	11. Authorize Force in Iraq	Y
4. Permit ANWR Development	Y	8. Overseas Military Abortions	N	12. Homeland Sec. Dept. Union	N

Election Results

2002 general	Chuck Hagel (R)	397,438	(83%)	($1,394,770)
	Charlie Matulka (D)	70,290	(15%)	
	Other	12,489	(3%)	
2002 primary	Chuck Hagel (R)	unopposed		
1996 general	Chuck Hagel (R)	379,933	(56%)	($3,564,316)
	Ben Nelson (D)	281,904	(42%)	($2,159,653)
	Other	14,952	(2%)	

Chuck Hagel, elected in 1996, is Nebraska's senior senator. Hagel grew up in the Sand Hills and small towns of Nebraska; his father died when he was 16; he became a radio DJ, then with his younger brother Tom volunteered for service in Vietnam. Promoted to sergeant because so many were dying, Chuck and Tom served together; in March 1968, when their armored personnel carrier hit a mine, Chuck, his body on fire, dragged Tom from the APC to safety. Chuck Hagel returned home, worked his way through the University of Nebraska, then got a job in Omaha

Congressman John McCollister's office. He rose to administrative assistant; after McCollister lost a Senate race in 1976, Hagel became a lobbyist for Firestone. He got the number two position in the Reagan Veterans' Affairs Administration, but resigned after only one year. He was one of two main speakers at the 1982 groundbreaking of the Vietnam Veterans' Memorial. Then he made his great break, using all of his savings—$5,000—and starting Vanguard Cellular Systems, which became the second largest independent cell phone company in the nation; Hagel traveled on business to 60 countries and installed cell phone systems in Costa Rica, Saudi Arabia and Britain. Then he went back into government, as head of World USO and then deputy director of the 1990 G-7 Summit. In 1992 he returned to Omaha, to work in investment banking; the McCarthy Group, of which he was a partner, owned a share of Election Systems & Software, which manufactures nearly half of American voting machines; he was criticized later for naming in his disclosure forms on the McCarthy Group and not the firms in which it has an interest.

In 1995 he started running for the Senate, very much the underdog. His platform was solidly conservative, sometimes riskily so: He backed school choice, opposed racial quotas and preferences, backed the Freedom to Farm Act ("less government and more open markets"), opposed the estate tax. In the primary he called state Attorney General Don Stenberg a "career politician"; Stenberg hit him for living 20 years in Virginia and for contributing to Bob Kerrey's 1992 presidential campaign. Hagel won the May primary 62%–37%. In the general he faced Governor Ben Nelson, who had won re-election in 1994 by a 73%–26% margin and had a record of tax-cutting and supported the balanced budget amendment and other conservative causes. Nelson led consistently in polls, though by lower margins in the fall. Nelson raised far more PAC money—$909,000, nearly half of his campaign funds—but Hagel spent $1 million of his own money and $3.5 million altogether. Hagel resisted advice from Republican campaign committee head Alfonse D'Amato to go negative; Nelson in the last weeks charged that Hagel had engaged in fraudulent franchising practices with Vanguard. Newspapers hit Nelson, and Hagel responded, "This is a guy who lies. This is a guy who cheats. This is a guy who will do anything." Hagel won 56%–42%, carrying all but five counties.

In the Senate, Hagel sought a seat on Foreign Relations and got it—because no one else wanted it. He quickly became, in columnist David Broder's words, "the freshman who probably has made the deepest impression on his colleagues of both parties." From a historically isolationist state, but one now heavily dependent on exports, Hagel has become a leading internationalist. His impulse is toward a bipartisan foreign policy, when possible. Hagel called on his military experience in 1997 to support the treaty against land mines, opposed by the Clinton administration; he spoke for the chemical weapons treaty ratified by the Senate in 1997 over the objections of Foreign Relations Chairman Jesse Helms; he voted against the Comprehensive Test Ban Treaty in October 1999 but joined Democrats and the administration in trying to prevent the vote. In 1999 he questioned whether the U.S. should defend Taiwan against a Chinese attack. He supported the bombing of Serbia in spring 1999, but decried the Clinton policy of ruling out the use of ground troops. In May 2000, when most Senate Republicans wanted to set a deadline for withdrawal of U.S. troops from Kosovo, Hagel was the first senator to consult George W. Bush, even though he had been campaigning for John McCain two months before, and ask his opinion; Bush, like the Clinton administration, opposed the deadline, and the measure never passed.

In Bush's first full month as president, Hagel joined Christopher Dodd in sponsoring a resolution to open Cuba to all U.S. exports and to end all restrictions on travel and credit. "Our 40-year policy toward Cuba is senseless." He was one of two senators to vote against extending trade sanctions on Iran and Libya. After September 11, he has been one of the Republicans most cautious against taking action against states that sponsor terrorism. His experience traveling abroad on business and coordinating a G-7 summit may have led him to place a high value on reaching consensus with European nations. In February 2002 he was accusing the administration of a "cavalier approach" to the rest of the world and said that the axis of evil part of George W. Bush's first State of the Union speech was "name calling." In May 2002 he said, "Our potential to lead the world at such a critical time in history calls for creativity, boldness and vision rather than nostalgia and dividing the world into simplistic categories." Before Bush's September 12, 2002, speech to the United Nations, Hagel said he had "a completely open mind" on military action in Iraq. He backed Joseph Biden and Richard Lugar in their efforts to draft a resolution endorsing military action only after diplomatic efforts were exhausted in the United Nations; that was put aside after Bush got agreement on his draft from congressional Republican leaders and House Minority Leader Richard Gephardt. He voted for the Iraq war resolution, but insisted, "Actions in Iraq must come in the context of an American-led, multilateral approach to disarmament, not as the first case for a new American doctrine involving the preemptive use of force." In December 2002 Hagel and Biden traveled to the Middle East and visited Kurdish-held areas in northern Iraq. In January 2003 Condoleezza Rice encouraged them to sound out Iranian officials in New York. Though Hagel has given Bush formal support on policy toward Iraq, it is a fair conclusion that if he had been president he would have follow a course quite different from that of Bush and his friend John McCain.

In his first two years in the Senate, Hagel was a favorite of the Republican leadership. But in 1999 and 2000, on foreign policy and other issues, he grew caustically critical of the leadership, in public. When in July 1999 Lott and others put holds on the nomination of Richard Holbrooke to be UN Ambassador he said that was "an irresponsible way to govern." He called the leadership budget devices "silly" and "a charade" in fall 1999. In June 2000, he said, "If we lose the Senate, I don't think it's too difficult to imagine that we're going to change leadership."

He spent much of his time campaigning for John McCain for president. The two had often met with other senators who were Vietnam veterans and had developed a strong bond. When McCain entered the race, Hagel endorsed him in March 1999. He was one of only four senators who did so (the others were Fred Thompson, Mike DeWine and Arizona's Jon Kyl). Hagel traveled frequently on McCain's Straight Talk Express and made appearances for him in Iowa, New Hampshire, South Carolina and other states; in the first half of 2000 he appeared on Sunday interview programs more often than any other member of Congress but McCain. He sharply criticized George W. Bush's campaign tactics in South Carolina, but he also was one of the few who would talk back to McCain. After McCain lost, Hagel was on George W. Bush's short list of vice presidential prospects. Though he did not get that nomination, the McCain campaign, plus Hagel's own work on foreign policy, made him a national figure.

Hagel did not agree with McCain on campaign finance. He favored reducing soft money contributions but not limiting them; his amendment to do that was rejected 60–40 in March 2001. He supported oil drilling in the Arctic National Wildlife Refuge and opposes limits on drilling, logging and grazing in national forests. He and John Ensign introduced a prescription drug plan very similar to George W. Bush's; it got a 51–48 margin in the Senate in July 2002, but 60 votes were needed for approval. The Senate passed his and Edward Kennedy's amendment to extend the deadline for immigrants to apply for permanent residency status in September 2001, as Mexico President Vicente Fox addressed Congress. The day before September 11 he introduced a bill requiring an economic impact analysis when the federal government impacts property rights. He opposed the farm bill passed in 2002 and criticized its conservation sections for interfering with water rights under state law; he, Charles Grassley and Byron Dorgan did get the Senate to limit payments to $275,000. To combat the effects of the drought in summer 2002 he called for the Agriculture Department to allow early haying and purchase more beef and pork as ranchers culled their herds. In late 2002 he led an uprising in the Republican Conference against riders added to the homeland security bill by House Majority Leader Dick Armey (he called that "dishonest, deceitful back room dealing") and got Trent Lott, then thought to be the next Senate Majority Leader, to make a commitment that those items would be revisited in the next Congress.

With a high job rating, Hagel seemed a cinch for reelection in 2002, and he was. His Democratic opponent couldn't afford the $1,500 filing fee and filed as a pauper. Hagel raised $3.5 million, but spent only $2 million. He won 83%–15%—that's not a misprint—by a considerable margin the biggest percentage margin ever in a Nebraska Senate race. He won 78% or more in 91 of 93 Nebraska counties, and as much as 94% in one; the other two, in the northeast corner of the state, he carried with 68% and 74%. Hagel has been mentioned as a future presidential candidate, perhaps in 2008; in 2002 and 2003 he attended political events in New Hampshire and South Carolina. He may not be averse to running. Once, when Nebraska schoolchildren asked him if he would like to be president, he said, "Maybe." But his foreign policy views may be out of sync with Republican primary voters.

Junior Senator

Ben Nelson (D)

Elected 2000, seat up 2006, 1st term; b. May 17, 1941, McCook; home, Omaha; U. of NE, B.A. 1963, M.A. 1965, LL.B. 1970; Methodist; married (Diane).

Elected Office: NE Gov., 1990–98.

Professional Career: Gen. Cnsl., Central Natl. Group Insurance, 1972–74, Pres. & CEO, 1977–81; NE Insurance Dir., 1975–76; Exec. V.P., Natl. Assn. of Insurance Commissioners, 1982–85; Practicing atty., 1985–90.

DC Office: 720 HSOB, 20510, 202-224-6551; Fax: 202-228-0012; Web site: www.senate.gov/~bennelson.

State Offices: Chadron, 308-260-2278; Lincoln, 402-437-5246; McCook, 308-340-1264; Omaha, 402-391-3411; Scottsbluff, 308-631-7614.

Committees: *Agriculture, Nutrition & Forestry*: Forestry, Conservation & Rural Revitalization; Marketing, Inspection & Product Promotion. *Armed Services*: Personnel (RMM); Readiness & Management Support; Strategic Forces. *Veterans' Affairs*.

Group Ratings

	ADA	ACLU	AFS	LCV	CON	ITIC	NTU	COC	ACU	NTLC	CHC
2002	50	60	63	24	36	75	35	63	55	9	—
2001	70	—	50	38	—	—	43	71	56	—	60

National Journal Ratings

	2001 LIB	—	2001 CONS		2002 LIB	—	2002 CONS
Economic	47%	—	49%		44%	—	55%
Social	51%	—	48%		49%	—	50%
Foreign	36%	—	54%		48%	—	49%

Key Votes of the 107th Congress

1. Approve Bush Tax Cuts	Y	5. Confirm Ashcroft as AG	Y	9. Bar Coop. with Intl. Court	Y
2. Expand Patients' Rights	Y	6. Bar Gays in the Boy Scouts	N	10. Trade Promotion Authority	Y
3. Campaign Finance Reform	N	7. $ for Hate Crime Prosecution	Y	11. Authorize Force in Iraq	Y
4. Permit ANWR Development	N	8. Overseas Military Abortions	N	12. Homeland Sec. Dept. Union	Y

Election Results

2000 general	Ben Nelson (D)	353,093	(51%)	($2,794,887)
	Don Stenberg (R)	337,977	(49%)	($1,795,402)
2000 primary	Ben Nelson (D)	105,661	(92%)	
	Al Hamburg (D)	8,482	(7%)	
1994 general	Bob Kerrey (D)	317,297	(55%)	($5,009,792)
	Jan Stoney (R)	260,668	(45%)	($1,821,778)

Ben Nelson, two-term Democratic governor of Nebraska, was elected to the Senate in 2000 in his second try. Nelson grew up in McCook, the home town of Senator George Norris and novelist Willa Cather; his high school principal, Ralph Brooks, a Democrat, was elected governor in 1958, by a 50.2%–49.8% margin. Nelson went to the University of Nebraska, practiced law, served as state insurance director and headed a major insurance company. He has collected several hundred clocks and is an avid hunter of turkeys and bears. In 1990 he ran for governor, taking on former Bob Kerrey staff aide Bill Hoppner in the primary, and won by all of 42 votes. In the general he beat Governor Kay Orr 50%–49%, because she raised taxes and her political consultants failed to place many of her paid-for TV spots in October. He cut spending increases by two-thirds and used his line-item veto to cut appropriations. In 1992 he got the Senate to pass and voters to approve a lottery, with proceeds to go to creative education and environmental projects. He built more prisons, trimmed workmen's comp and reorganized the human services department. He cut property taxes and reduced the income and sales taxes. His record won him high job ratings and re-election by a 73%–26% margin in the Republican year of 1994. When he ran for the Senate in 1996, he led in polls most of the way, but then fell behind in October and lost to Republican Chuck Hagel by a 56%–42% margin.

In 2000 Nebraska's other Senate seat came up. Everyone expected easy re-election for Senator Bob Kerrey, one of the Democratic Party's national stars—recipient of the Congressional Medal of Honor for service in Vietnam, popular governor of Nebraska in the 1980s, elected to the Senate in 1988, presidential candidate in 1992. But in January 2000 he shocked Democrats and just about everyone else when he said that he would not run for reelection that fall. Nelson, a lawyer in Omaha with an interest in a public affairs firm in Washington, was obviously the strongest possible Democratic nominee and entered the race a month later. Six Republicans ran in the May primary. The winner was Attorney General Don Stenberg, with 50% of the vote.

Nelson and Stenberg agreed on some issues; both opposed abortion and backed tax cuts. But there were significant differences in style and a considerable history of partisan differences between the two in the 1990s. Nelson never mentioned his Democratic Party affiliation, unless asked directly about it. Instead he noted, "Nebraska has always supported a bipartisan approach to things and the independent-minded approach, or we wouldn't continue to have a nonpartisan legislature." Stenberg ran as part of the "Bush-Hagel-Stenberg Team," sometimes bringing in Governor Mike Johanns as well. To which Nelson responded, "My opponent hasn't given us a single reason to vote for him apart from his party registration and the fact that he's associated with two people who are more popular than he is." Then there was style: Nelson is gregarious, has a good sense of humor, seems to enjoy campaigning; Stenberg was described as serious and studious—not a natural meeter-and-greeter. There were some serious differences on issues. Stenberg was for individual investment accounts as part of Social Security; Nelson was against. The two sparred over who was responsible for Nebraska's parlous position in a lawsuit brought by the four other states in a five-state compact to build a radioactive waste disposal site in Boyd County which Nebraska regulators blocked. Nelson led always in the polls and raised and spent more money; the big difference here was PAC contributions, of which the Democrat received three times as much as the Republican. Nelson was helped also by active campaigning by Bob Kerrey; George W. Bush, in a close national race, couldn't afford to spend time in locked-up (for him) Nebraska. Nelson's poll leads narrowed in October, to 12% in the *Omaha World-Herald*, and memories went back to 1996, when Nelson's poll leads vanished altogether. This time that didn't happen, quite. Nelson won 51%–49%. Nelson carried the Omaha area 54%–46% and the Lincoln area 60%–39%; he lost the remaining half of the state 54%–46%. Nelson ran 16% ahead of Al Gore in the Omaha area, 18% in the Lincoln area and 19% ahead in the rest of the state—just enough to win.

In February 2001 Nelson accompanied George W. Bush to Nebraska in February—the state's second presidential visit in two months—and got a Bush nickname, "Nellie"; he wrote back, "How about something more macho, like 'Tiger' or 'Killer?' I need to preserve my image." Nellie or no, Nelson turned out to be, after Zell Miller, the Senate Democrat most likely to support Bush and differ from most Democrats. He was one of three Democrats to vote against the McCain-Feingold campaign finance bill and in May was one of five Democrats to vote for the Republican budget resolution (although in April he had voted against an earlier version). He was one of 24 Democrats to vote for trade promotion authority in May 2002. Many of his legislative initiatives were aimed squarely at Nebraska problems. He and Hagel tried to amend the energy bill in March 2002 to increase consumer options for evaluating energy consumption levels—one option being the "smart metering" technology produced at the American Meter Company in Nebraska City. He got a white wheat initiative into the farm bill in April 2002; hard white wheat isn't produced in the U.S., but there's a big market for it in Asia. He voted for the farm bill in May 2002, saying that it provided $1.1 billion for Nebraska.

The Great Plains were hit by a drought in summer 2002, and Nelson argued that affected areas should get disaster relief, in the same way that places hit by hurricanes and floods do; the compensation would be for crops or livestock lost, rather than property destroyed. Twice in 2002 he got the Senate to pass disaster relief, first in the farm bill and then in the Interior Department appropriations; both times it was rejected in the House. He reintroduced the same measure in November 2002 and tried to get it included in the homeland security bill, again in vain. In January 2003, he started applying a name to the drought, as names are applied to hurricanes, and filed his bill again for relief from "Drought David." He chose the name at random, he said, and evidently was fearless of the reaction of Nebraska voters named David.

Nelson argues that, in a closely divided Senate, centrist members like him can fashion compromises that can resolve difficult issues, and he attempted to do this on the homeland security bill. Democrats claimed their version of the bill retained the collective bargaining rights of the 42,000 employees of the new department currently represented by unions; George W. Bush argued that it actually strengthened them, and made it more difficult to manage the department. Nelson came up with a compromise in September 2002 which, he said, would give federal employees whose collective bargaining rights were abolished by the president the right to an expedited non-judicial review by a federal labor relations board, with the burden of proof on the employees and their union. This was still unacceptable to Bush, and the bill was not passed before the November election. A week after the election, Bush and Trent Lott, Nelson, John Breaux and Lincoln Chafee produced another compromise that would allow the president to cancel collective bargaining rights but allow that decision to be overturned by a future president and that allowed workers to appeal to a federal mediation board new rules or salary scales; they would be imposed after one month, but the unions could bring a case in court. Outgoing Majority Leader Tom Daschle, aware now that his previous stance was politically disastrous, accepted the terms. But Nelson was infuriated when House Majority Leader Dick Armey inserted three amendments to the bill, one of which designated Texas A&M as the site for a new bioterrorism laboratory; Nelson wanted the University of Nebraska's Medical Center at Omaha to be eligible to compete for the lab, and was pleased when Lott promised the issue would be revisited in the next Congress.

Republicans have hoped that Nelson would switch parties. In September 2002 Lott said, "I think Ben is somebody who would be more comfortable on the Republican side—I really do. He is from a state that is pretty conservative and pretty Republican." But Nelson said, "As long as I am comfortable, I don't entertain the idea seriously about leaving." Nelson's seat comes up in 2006. One possible candidate is Republican Governor Mike Johanns, who will be ineligible to run for a third term then.

FIRST DISTRICT

Rep. Doug Bereuter (R)

Elected 1978, 13th term; b. Oct. 6, 1939, York; home, Cedar Bluffs; U. of NE, B.A. 1961, Harvard U., M.C.P. 1966, M.P.A. 1973; Lutheran; married (Louise).

Military Career: Army, 1963–65.

Elected Office: NE Legislature, 1974–78.

Professional Career: Urban planner, U.S. Dept. of HUD, 1965–66; Div. Dir., NE Econ. Devel. Dept., 1967–68; Dir., NE Office of Planning, 1968–70.

DC Office: 2184 RHOB 20515, 202-225-4806; Fax: 202-225-5686; Web site: www.house.gov/bereuter.

District Offices: Fremont, 402-727-0888; Lincoln, 402-438-1598.

Committees: *Financial Services* (3d of 37 R): Financial Institutions & Consumer Credit; Housing & Community Opportunity. *International Relations* (3d of 26 R): Asia & the Pacific; Europe (Chmn.). *Permanent Select Committee on Intelligence* (Vice Chmn. of 11 R): Intelligence Policy & National Security (Chmn.); Terrorism and Homeland Security (Vice Chmn.). *Transportation & Infrastructure* (20th of 41 R): Highways, Transit & Pipelines.

Group Ratings

	ADA	ACLU	AFS	LCV	CON	ITIC	NTU	COC	ACU	NTLC	CHC
2002	10	13	11	25	54	100	46	90	72	60	75
2001	10	—	10	14	—	—	50	91	72	—	—

National Journal Ratings

	2001 LIB	—	2001 CONS		2002 LIB	—	2002 CONS
Economic	43%	—	56%		50%	—	50%
Social	35%	—	63%		48%	—	52%
Foreign	43%	—	53%		24%	—	72%

Key Votes of the 107th Congress

1. Approve Bush Tax Cuts	Y	5. Faith-Based Charities	Y	9. Trade Promotion Authority	Y
2. Limit Patients' Bill of Rights	Y	6. Bar Gays in the Boy Scouts	Y	10. Bar Funds for Intl. Court	Y
3. Campaign Finance Reform	Y	7. Ban Partial-Birth Abortion	Y	11. Authorize Force in Iraq	Y
4. Ban ANWR Development	N	8. Arm Commercial Pilots	N	12. Deny Home. Sec. Dept. Union	Y

Election Results

2002 general	Doug Bereuter (R)	133,013	(85%)	($191,344)
	Robert Eckerson (Lib)	22,831	(15%)	
2002 primary	Doug Bereuter (R)	unopposed		
2000 general	Doug Bereuter (R)	155,485	(66%)	($380,036)
	Alan Jacobsen (D)	72,859	(31%)	($107,256)
	Other	6,354	(3%)	

Prior Winning Percentages: 1998 (73%); 1996 (70%); 1994 (63%); 1992 (60%); 1990 (65%); 1988 (67%); 1986 (64%); 1984 (74%); 1982 (75%); 1980 (79%); 1978 (58%)

The People		Race/Ethnic Origin	Ancestry	
Area size:	12,034 sq. mi.	90.5% White	German: 30.8%	Irish: 8.7%
Urban population:	65.1%	1.4% Black	English: 6.8%	
Rural population:	34.9%	1.5% Asian	**2000 Presidential Vote**	
Pop. 2000:	570,325	1.2% Native Am.	Bush (R)	138,799 (59%)
Median income:	$40,021	0.0% Hawaiian	Gore (D)	85,634 (36%)
Poverty status:	9.2%	1.1% Two + races	Other	12,242 (5%)
Military veterans:	12.9%	0.1% Other	**Cook Partisan Voting Index:** R + 12	
		4.2% Hispanic Origin		

Occupation	Blue collar: 26.2%	White collar: 57.7%	Gray collar: 16.1%

The eastern half of Nebraska, between the Missouri River and the 98th parallel, was laid out in relentless Midwestern mile-square grids and became some of America's prime farmland in the single decade of the 1880s. The land here has contours just regular enough and weather just favorable enough to make farming economically viable. The plains here have completed most of their gentle decline from the Rockies to sea level; above the river bottoms the land is open to the winds. This land was settled by Yankee-descended Midwestern farmers and immigrants from Germany and other countries. The immigrant heritage is not often remembered now, but traces of it can still be found. Many immigrants from Luxembourg, for example, settled along the Platte River in Butler County, where St. Mary's Presentation Parish still has a statue of Our Lady of Luxembourg. Not far away are villages with names that recall other immigrants' heritage—Prague (Czechs), Malmo (Swedes), Aloys (Germans). Now a new wave of immigrants is coming to eastern Nebraska, Latinos from Mexico and the southwest United States, to work in the meatpacking factories in the area. Wakefield (Dixon County) had the highest percentage increase in Hispanic population in the country in the 1990s, 8,700%—though that's a little less impressive when you realize that the Hispanic population went from 4 to 348. But there are larger numbers in other towns, and Nebraska's face is changing.

The 1st Congressional District is made up of 22 counties and parts of two others in the eastern part of the state. Omaha and most of its suburbs are separate, in the 2d District; the 1st District's large city is Lincoln, the state capital and home of the University of Nebraska Cornhuskers. Lincoln, with the state government, the university and telemarketing, has been growing rapidly; it is affluent, with above-national-average incomes and unemployment that is among the lowest in the United States. In smaller towns there are significant farm equipment and meat-packing factories; population growth here was robust in the 1990s. Politically, Lincoln is fond of moderate Democrats but is still on balance Republican in national contests; the district voted 59% for George W. Bush in 2000.

The congressman from the 1st District is Douglas Bereuter (pronounced *BEEwriter*), a Republican first elected in 1978. He grew up in Utica, in Seward County, graduated from the University of Nebraska, served in the Army, then got degrees in planning and public policy from Harvard. He was an aide to Governor Norbert Tiemann in the late 1960s and worked as a planning consultant and part-time professor in Lincoln in the 1970s. He was elected to the Nebraska Senate in 1974, and when Congressman Charles Thone was elected governor in 1978, Bereuter ran for the House, winning the primary 52%–48% and the general 58%–42% in what was then an expensive campaign ($167,000). He is cautious, well-prepared, with a stately manner more typical of House members when he arrived than today.

Bereuter has been a hard-working member of the International Relations Committee. He was one of the leaders in the annual fight to maintain most favored nation status for China, and for renaming the designation to the more accurate normal trade relations. In 1997 he proposed granting PNTR to China as soon as it is admitted to the World Trade Organization: That proposal became permanent normal trade relations, and Bereuter played a key role in getting it through the House in May 2000. Weeks before, PNTR was far short of the votes needed for passage; it was opposed by labor unions, by critics of China's human rights record, by advocates of a harder line policy against China's menacing military buildup. Bereuter, then chairman of the Asia and Pacific Subcommittee of International Relations, had traveled widely in China and East Asia and had been in top-level discussions with its leaders; in April 1999 Chinese Premier Zhu Rongji, evidently convinced that he could play a key role on PNTR, requested a private meeting with Bereuter in Washington. In fall 1999 Bereuter began working on amendments to address PNTR opponents' concerns while still passing the measure. Also working in that direction was Sander Levin, the ranking Democrat on the Ways and Means Trade Subcommittee; he and Bereuter had met on a congressional trip to Eastern Europe in 1984, and in early 2000 they began working together. They wrote an amendment that would create a congressional-executive commission to evaluate human rights in China, impose tough protections against import surges, create task forces on prison labor exports and rule of law and provide for the entry of Taiwan into the WTO after China entered. Bereuter and Rules Committee Chairman David Dreier convinced the Republican leadership to support the Bereuter-Levin amendment and it was combined with the PNTR bill, which passed 294–136 in May 2000. Without it, PNTR would probably not have passed, as it did a few days later. Bereuter has long wanted to exclude agricultural products from economic sanctions, and he supported the June 2000 measure to allow sale of food and medicine to Cuba.

Bereuter has been one of the most assiduous of American legislators in paying attention to NATO. He has served on the NATO Parliamentary Assembly, made up of legislators from member countries, since 1986. He was its vice president from 1993 to 1994 and in November 2002 was chosen president for a two-year term. In 2001 he sponsored a NATO expansion bill which provided for military financing for new members and named as likely candidates seven former Soviet Bloc countries, Estonia, Latvia, Lithuania, Slovakia, Slovenia, Romania and Bulgaria. The bill passed the House 372–46 in November 2001 and was signed in June 2002. Bereuter spoke at the November 2002 NATO meeting in Prague where the seven countries were offered membership in NATO. It was an historic occasion, and not only that: Nearly all publicly stated their support in 2003 for the United States in its efforts to disarm Saddam Hussein. But for all his work with NATO allies, he has little patience for the European Union's ban on genetically modified organisms, which excludes increasing percentages of U.S. farm products from Europe and, thanks to the EU's pressure on African countries, from Africa where people may actually starve in the absence of GMO produce. Bereuter points out that there is no scientific evidence of harm. In January 2003 he called the EU stand ridiculous and urged Special Trade Representative Robert Zoellick to bring a case against the EU in the WTO.

On foreign military issues, Bereuter was a strong critic of stationing ground forces in the former Yugoslavia, expressed deep skepticism on the 1998 air strikes against Iraq and was opposed to the bombing campaign against Serbia. He voted for the Iraq war resolution, but did not take a lead role in the debate. In December 2002 the Irish singer Bono made Lincoln the first stop on his Heart of America Tour to persuade Americans to support debt relief for poor countries and aid to AIDS sufferers in Africa. He clearly wanted to aim his message at Bereuter, who said in 2002 that debt relief was going nowhere because it was opposed by the Bush administration and that AIDS/Africa relief was stymied by differences between the House and the Senate; George W. Bush's proposal the next month for $10 billion in AIDS/Africa relief seemed likely to change the posture of the issue.

Though not on the Agriculture Committee, Bereuter has come up with proposals to aid farmers. In October 2001 he got some provisions added to the farm bill—making land eligible for the Conservation Reserve Program only if it has been farmed for four years, putting a litigation division in the unit inspecting grain elevators, meatpackers and stockyards, amending his Flexible Fallow plan to allow use of up to 30% of crop acreage. He is one of the few Republicans to vote with Democrats to retain the estate tax on estates over $2 million, but when that failed voted for estate tax repeal. To avoid the problems with MTBE in gasoline, he sponsored a bill to limit gasoline within four years to four standard blends, conventional gasoline, oxygenated reformulated gasoline and California reformulated gasoline. He has been the chief promoter of National Historic Trails, including the 6,357-mile American Discovery Trail from Cape Henlopen, Delaware, to Point Reyes, California. He got such designation for the California and Pony Express Trails in the 1990s. In June 2001 he called for an update of the Oregon, California, Mormon and Pony Express Trails and their offshoots; all these trails pass through Nebraska. In 2002 he got $400,000 for an expansion of the Homestead National Monument of America outside Beatrice, to be built above a 100-year floodplain.

Bereuter has been re-elected easily. In 2002 his only opponent was a Libertarian who raised no money because "I don't want to waste anybody's money." He was reelected with 85% of the vote. Bereuter is the longest-serving Nebraska House member in history, and it may seem something of a mystery why he has never sought statewide office. But he has decided four times not to run for the Senate, most recently in January 2000, when Bob Kerrey announced his retirement. One reason was that he hoped then to become chairman of the International Relations Committee; Ben Gilman, chairman since 1995, had to step down in 2001 because of House Republicans' six-year term-limit on chairmen. When he was pondering running for Kerrey's seat in 2000, Speaker Dennis Hastert gave him "every assurance that he possibly could that he wanted me to be the next chairman." Then it seemed he would have competition from Jim Leach, term-limited as Banking chairman; Leach and Bereuter, unlike competitors for other chairmanships refused to start leadership PACs to raise money to give to Republican colleagues or campaign committees. But Bereuter was foiled in his ambition. In December 2000 Henry Hyde, chairman of Judiciary and senior to Bereuter on International Relations, made a heartfelt plea for an exemption; he had lost two years of legislating, he said, for the distasteful responsibility of handling impeachment. Many strong conservatives backed Hyde, but Hastert turned him down. At the Steering Committee's closed meeting there was feeling that Hyde would prevail in a full Conference vote, and the Steering Committee gave the International Relations chairmanship to Hyde. Bereuter, deeply disappointed, announced that he would take a subcommittee chairmanship on Financial Services, even though he had probably been the hardest working International Relations subcommittee chairman. In late January 2001 Hastert found a consolation prize. Bereuter was appointed to the Intelligence Committee, on which he had served before. The rule allowing only one tour of duty on that committee was waived, and Bereuter was named vice chairman. Chairman Porter Goss had already announced he would retire from Congress in 2002; it was assumed that Bereuter was promised he would become chairman in January 2003. But after September 11, Goss, a former CIA agent, announced he would run again in 2002, and kept the chairmanship. So Bereuter has been frustrated twice. In 2002 he said that he didn't expect to serve more than six years more in the House; that would give him a chance of becoming chairman of Intelligence after the 2004 election or of International Relations after the 2006 elections—provided that Republicans maintain their majority in the House.

SECOND DISTRICT

Rep. Lee Terry (R)

Elected 1998, 3d term; b. Jan. 29, 1962, Omaha; home, Omaha; U. of NE at Lincoln, B.A. 1984; Creighton U., J.D. 1987; Methodist; married (Robyn).

Elected Office: Omaha City Cncl., 1991–98, Pres., 1995–96.

Professional Career: Practicing atty., 1988–98.

DC Office: 1524 LHOB 20515, 202-225-4155; Fax: 202-226-5452; Web site: www.house.gov/terry.

District Office: Omaha, 402-397-9944.

Committees: *Energy & Commerce* (26th of 31 R): Commerce, Trade & Consumer Protection; Environment & Hazardous Materials; Telecommunications & The Internet.

Group Ratings

	ADA	ACLU	AFS	LCV	CON	ITIC	NTU	COC	ACU	NTLC	CHC
2002	5	7	0	0	59	88	63	85	88	86	100
2001	0	—	0	0	—	—	66	91	96	—	—

National Journal Ratings

	2001 LIB —	2001 CONS		2002 LIB —	2002 CONS
Economic	7%	— 89%		40%	— 59%
Social	35%	— 63%		32%	— 63%
Foreign	4%	— 87%		44%	— 55%

Key Votes of the 107th Congress

1. Approve Bush Tax Cuts	Y	5. Faith-Based Charities	Y	9. Trade Promotion Authority	Y
2. Limit Patients' Bill of Rights	Y	6. Bar Gays in the Boy Scouts	Y	10. Bar Funds for Intl. Court	Y
3. Campaign Finance Reform	N	7. Ban Partial-Birth Abortion	Y	11. Authorize Force in Iraq	Y
4. Ban ANWR Development	N	8. Arm Commercial Pilots	Y	12. Deny Home. Sec. Dept. Union	Y

Election Results

2002 general	Lee Terry (R)	89,917	(63%)	($974,788)
	Jim Simon (D)	46,843	(33%)	($705,675)
	Other	5,254	(4%)	
2002 primary	Lee Terry (R)	unopposed		
2000 general	Lee Terry (R)	148,911	(66%)	($844,465)
	Shelley Kiel (D)	70,268	(31%)	($345,347)
	Other	7,101	(3%)	

Prior Winning Percentages: 1998 (66%)

The People		Race/Ethnic Origin	Ancestry	
Area size:	421 sq. mi.	79.6% White	German: 22.1%	Irish: 11.6%
Urban population:	97.8%	10.2% Black	English: 6.6%	
Rural population:	2.2%	1.8% Asian	**2000 Presidential Vote**	
Pop. 2000:	570,421	0.5% Native Am.	Bush (R)	125,973 (57%)
Median income:	$45,235	0.1% Hawaiian	Gore (D)	85,853 (39%)
Poverty status:	8.8%	1.5% Two+ races	Other	10,183 (5%)
Military veterans:	14.4%	0.1% Other	**Cook Partisan Voting Index:** R +10	
		6.3% Hispanic Origin		

Occupation	Blue collar: 19.5%	White collar: 66.8%	Gray collar: 13.7%

Omaha, the commercial metropolis of Nebraska, the largest city on the Great Plains north of Kansas City and west of Minneapolis, got its start from government: Abraham Lincoln picked it as the eastern terminus of the Union Pacific railroad, from which emerged the stockyards and livestock exchange that made it a top livestock town. Over the years, Omaha filled up with cattle hands from the West and European immigrants, especially Germans and Czechs; it developed fine civic institutions from the Joslyn Art Museum to the Boys Town, founded by Father Flanagan in 1917, the subject of a 1938 movie, and today gender-neutral as Boys and Girls Town but still innovative and thriving in its promotion of traditional values. Though a major city by the 1880s, Omaha has remained small enough (and famous on Wall Street as the place where Warren Buffett lives and works) to be readily comprehensible; you don't feel distant, physically or psychologically, from the other side of town, and you usually know people from a broader range of backgrounds than you would in a large homogeneous neighborhood within a big metropolitan area. The older, less affluent part of Omaha is near the river and Iowa; to the west, the city has been quietly booming, with affluent neighborhoods and new shopping malls; downtown and the riverfront are in a construction boom, the Tower at First National Center became the tallest structure between Minneapolis and Denver. Omaha's economy has been changing. It still has many processors of food products, like the hard-charging ConAgra company, and the giant Peter Kiewit construction firm; but it also has become the nation's telecommunications center, handling 20 million '800' and '900' calls a day and employing more than 20,000 people in over two dozen telemarketing centers. Its civic institutions are thriving as well: An opera company, museums, a children's theater, a zoo with the country's largest indoor jungle west of Chicago. *Parenting* magazine ranked Omaha among the top 10 cities in which to raise a family. It is also ethnically diverse: 31% of students in the Omaha public schools are black and 17% Hispanic.

The 2d Congressional District includes most of metropolitan Omaha: Douglas County with Omaha and its western suburbs; the eastern side of fast-growing Sarpy County with Bellevue and the old Strategic Air Command headquarters at Offutt Air Force Base. Politically, Omaha has long had competitive politics, with Democrats strong on the south side around the stockyards and the northeast and Republicans strong to the west. But as Omaha and Nebraska have boomed, they have become more Republican, and increasingly it is the Republican primary that decides elections here.

The congressman from the 2d District is Lee Terry, a Republican elected in 1998. Terry grew up in Omaha, and became interested in politics at 14 when his father, TV anchor Lee Terry Sr., ran for the House in 1976; a conservative, he lost 55%–45% to 31-year-old Democrat John Cavanaugh. Terry Sr. remained a prominent local commentator on politics; Terry Jr. went off to college and law school, practiced law, and was elected to the Omaha Council from an affluent west side district in 1991, at 29. There he worked to stop teenage cruising on Dodge Street and collaborated with private enterprise to build the Moylan-Tranquility IcePlex skating rink. In September 1997, Congressman Jon Christensen announced he was running for governor; he finished third in the primary. Terry announced for the House seat; he decried frivolous lawsuits, the Department of Education and "corporate welfare," and said he would apply the lessons he learned in city government and devolve power to local government.

His chief opponents were Brad Kuiper, owner of a pest control business in west Douglas County, and Steve Kupka, former chief of staff to Mayor Hal Daub and an official in Ronald Reagan's OMB. The contrast between the three was less on issues—all were for lower taxes and against abortion—than on style and approach. Kuiper, with less money than the other two, targeted religious conservatives and emphasized cultural issues. Kupka assembled Washington endorsements and, spending the most money, went on the attack. He criticized Terry for not opposing a 1991 garbage fee and said Terry had increased the city budget. Terry won 40% to 30% for Kupka and 26% for Kuiper. The general election was anticlimactic. Despite the fact that Democrats had won open seats here in 1976 and 1988, Terry won 66%–34% against Democrat Michael Scott. In April 1999, he reneged on his pledge to serve only three terms.

In Washington, Terry has had a mostly conservative voting record. He attracted attention in 1999 when he purposely bundled Clinton tax increases and user fees into one $19 billion bill and brought it to the floor; it lost 419–5. He became co-chairman of the Impact Aid Coalition to protect the interests of the Offutt base, and he reversed his previous opposition to mandatory trigger locks for guns "after a year of reflection." In the 2000 general, he had surprisingly vigorous opposition from well-financed Democratic state Senator Shelley Kiel. But Terry got a favorable response with a 66%–31% victory. In 2001 he got a seat on the Energy and Commerce Committee, where he became an advocate of what he called pro-business legislation. But in one of his early crusades, he butted heads with John Dingell and the auto industry by advocating an increase in fuel efficiency standards; his effort led the panel to compromise on smaller increases. Terry also bucked his party by opposing medical malpractice reform. Separate from his committee work, he won unanimous House passage of a bill declaring that Veterans' Day should remain separate from other federal holidays; his proposal was in response to proposals to combine the holiday with the presidential election every four years, but local opponents later called his measure "symbolism."

In 2002, Democrats initially talked up their challenger Jim Simon, an Internet millionaire and former Republican. Simon spent $230,000 of his own money, but failed to gain traction. Terry created a minor stir late in the campaign when he appeared in an TV ad for Pfizer, which offered lower costs for prescriptions. Simon suggested that it was a "disguised political ad," and Common Cause threatened to file an ethics complaint, but Terry supporters said that they were grasping at straws. Terry's 63%–33% win appears to have entrenched him in the 2d District, and he could conceivably be a strong statewide candidate.

THIRD DISTRICT

Rep. Tom Osborne (R)

Elected 2000, 2d term; b. Feb. 23, 1937, Hastings; home, Lemoyne; Hastings Col., B.A. 1959, U. of NE, M.A. 1963, Ph.D. 1965; Methodist; married (Nancy).

Military Career: Army Natl. Guard, 1960–66.

Professional Career: Pro Football Player, Natl. Football League, 1959–62; Football Coach, U. of NE, 1962–97, Head Coach 1973–97.

DC Office: 507 CHOB 20515, 202-225-6435; Fax: 202-226-1385; Web site: www.house.gov/osborne.

District Offices: Grand Island, 308-381-5555; Scottsbluff, 308-632-3333.

Committees: *Agriculture* (14th of 27 R): Conservation, Credit, Rural Development & Research (Vice Chmn.); Livestock & Horticulture. *Education & the Workforce* (18th of 27 R): 21st Century Competitiveness; Education Reform (Vice Chmn.). *Resources* (20th of 28 R): Water & Power.

Group Ratings

	ADA	ACLU	AFS	LCV	CON	ITIC	NTU	COC	ACU	NTLC	CHC
2002	10	20	0	0	8	100	55	90	80	81	75
2001	5	—	10	0	—	—	59	100	84	—	—

National Journal Ratings

	2001 LIB	—	2001 CONS		2002 LIB	—	2002 CONS
Economic	28%	—	69%		21%	—	73%
Social	20%	—	69%		32%	—	63%
Foreign	43%	—	53%		41%	—	56%

Key Votes of the 107th Congress

1. Approve Bush Tax Cuts	Y	5. Faith-Based Charities	Y	9. Trade Promotion Authority	Y
2. Limit Patients' Bill of Rights	Y	6. Bar Gays in the Boy Scouts	Y	10. Bar Funds for Intl. Court	Y
3. Campaign Finance Reform	Y	7. Ban Partial-Birth Abortion	Y	11. Authorize Force in Iraq	Y
4. Ban ANWR Development	N	8. Arm Commercial Pilots	Y	12. Deny Home. Sec. Dept. Union	Y

Election Results

2002 general	Tom Osborne (R)	163,939	(93%)	($81,357)
	Jerry Hickman (Lib)	12,017	(7%)	
2002 primary	Tom Osborne (R)	unopposed		
2000 general	Tom Osborne (R)	182,117	(82%)	($484,797)
	Roland E. Reynolds (D)	34,944	(16%)	($12,857)
	Other	5,032	(2%)	

The People		Race/Ethnic Origin	Ancestry	
Area size:	64,899 sq. mi.	91.9% White	German: 30.3%	Irish: 8.5%
Urban population:	46.1%	0.3% Black	English: 7.2%	
Rural population:	53.9%	0.5% Asian	**2000 Presidential Vote**	
Pop. 2000:	570,517	0.7% Native Am.	Bush (R)..............169,090	(71%)
Median income:	$33,866	0.0% Hawaiian	Gore (D)................60,293	(25%)
Poverty status:	11.1%	0.6% Two+ races	Other 8,952	(4%)
Military veterans:	13.9%	0.0% Other	**Cook Partisan Voting Index:** R +24	
		6.0% Hispanic Origin		

Occupation	Blue collar: 27.6%	White collar: 53.5%	Gray collar: 18.8%

West of Grand Island, Nebraska is wheat and livestock country. For miles on end you can see nothing but rolling brown fields, sectioned off here and there by barbed wire fences, and in the distance a grain elevator towering over a tiny town and its miniature railroad depot. The winds, rain and tornadoes that come suddenly out of the sky remind you that the original settlers likened this part of the country to an ocean and thought themselves in their wooden wagons almost as helpless as passengers at sea in a rowboat. Settlers passed through here on the Oregon Trail in the 1840s, then set down roots in the 1880s, but the rain they hoped for fell too unreliably, and wheatlands gave way to pasture and open range. It is a beautiful but hard land, exacting much from its people, as the novels of western Nebraska's Willa Cather make poignantly clear. Dozens of small counties today have fewer people than they did in 1940 or 1900. And the frontier may even be moving back. In November 2000 140 head of pure-bred Texas longhorn cattle were driven from the Fort Niobrara National Wildlife Refuge to Fort Robinson State Park—the last Texas longhorn drive in Nebraska, to provide more room for elk, bison and bighorn sheep. The drought in the summer of 2002 also seemed a kind of endpoint, as ranchers sold off their herds that were thinning and sickening as the grasslands turned dry and brown.

The 3d Congressional District has one-third of the state's people spread out over nearly 85% of its acreage. Except along the interstate and around Scottsbluff, the 3d has been losing population for decades and several of the western ranching counties are among the poorest in the nation; one such is Loup County, in the center of the state, which has the nation's lowest per capita income and lost its only grocery store. The district includes 69 of Nebraska's 93 counties, and has moved so far east that it's on the outskirts of Lincoln. Geographically and politically, the 3d District is where the Midwest becomes the West. For years people here welcomed farm subsidies even as they angrily opposed federal interference. Politically, it is heavily Republican and sometimes ornery: In 1992 Ross Perot got more votes than Bill Clinton. In 2000 it voted 71% for George W. Bush.

The congressman from the 3d District is Tom Osborne, a Republican elected in 2000, a man who had never run for office before but who was better known than most congressmen are after serving 20 years. He grew up in Hastings and excelled at basketball, football and track in high school and at Hastings College. He graduated in 1959 and played professional football for three years in Washington and San Francisco. Then he went to the University of Nebraska to work as a graduate assistant in the football program. He stayed for 36 years, working first under coach Bob Devaney, then becoming NU coach himself in 1973; he also got a master's degree and doctorate in educational psychology. He was head football coach for 25 years, at first compared unfavorably to Devaney, but over the whole period exceedingly successful. He won three national championships before retiring in 1998; he had perfect seasons in 1994, 1995 and 1997. His team was 87–11–1 in the 1990s and 60–3 over his last five years. After retiring he was inducted into the College Football Hall of Fame in 1999; the three-year waiting period was waived, for only the second time.

In March 1999, 3d District Congressman Bill Barrett announced that he was retiring. In January 2000, Osborne announced he was running. He had been urged to run for the Senate seat being vacated by Bob Kerrey, but declined; he said he did not want to commit to serve the six-year term. From the beginning, it was apparent that Osborne would win. Nevertheless, he campaigned hard. He traveled 60,000 miles and made more than 650 scheduled stops during the campaign; he often drove alone hundreds of miles to events to save the cost of paying a staffer to drive. At first he was uncomfortable shaking hands and asking for votes, but enjoyed talking to people in small groups; Nebraskans were delighted to meet him. He won the primary with 71% of the vote against two candidates with solid political backgrounds, former Nebraska Republican Chairman and now secretary of State John Gale and state Board of Education member Kathy Wilmot. His Democratic opponent, Rollie Reynolds, was a distant relative who called Osborne "my hero" and "everybody's hero." This was a positive campaign all around, with Osborne refusing to take PAC money; he won 82%–16%.

In the House, his voting record was in the middle of Republicans, though a bit dovish on defense issues. He got seats on the Agriculture, Education and Workforce, and Resources Committees. Although he voted for it, he was less than enthusiastic about the new farm bill, which he called too complicated but the best that could be done; he obtained additional ag research dollars for Nebraska. Osborne claimed credit for adding a new national mentoring program to George W. Bush's education bill and he increased baseline funding for rural schools. Bush also signed his bill to address the water needs of the Santee Sioux tribe. Osborne filed a bill to require the attorney general to list steroids and other performance-enhancing drugs as controlled substances, which would make over-the-counter sales illegal. But he confessed frustration with the slow pace of activity, the partisanship, and lack of discipline in the House, complaining that some things never seem to get done: he would have really hated the Senate.

Osborne had no Democratic opponent in 2002 and was reelected with 93% of the vote. He won at least 88%, and up to 98%, in every county. After the election, he voiced interest in running for governor in 2006, at age 69, when incumbent Mike Johanns will be ineligible to run. Osborne's retirement from football was good for Republicans, but has turned out worse for the Huskers: In 2002 the team lost seven games, their worst record in 41 years, and the school's athletic director quit.

★ NEVADA ★

A pyramid rising from the desert, New York skyscrapers across the street from the sphinx-like lion, a not-too-miniature Eiffel Tower and the gondolas of Venice, a flaming pirate ship next door to Roman ruins: this is what you see as the plane approaches the runway at Las Vegas. All these surrealistic monuments, and miles of spreading subdivisions, are set in one of North America's most forbidding landscapes, a bowl-shaped desert valley rimmed by barren peaks. Nature provided nothing here to encourage human settlement—Las Vegas is far from the lodes of gold and silver that attracted the first settlers of Nevada. Today's Nevada is wholly the creation of post-industrial, post-modern man. Its existence as a state is happenstance: The discovery of the Comstock Lode silver mine in 1859—$500 million worth was taken out in 20 years—brought settlers, and Abraham Lincoln's Republicans made it a state in 1864, even though Nevada did not meet the population requirement for statehood, because Republicans thought they needed an extra three electoral votes. But Nevada was not really a viable state; its population dropped by the early 20th century, and in the early 1930s there were only 91,000 Nevadans and the state government was about to go bankrupt. So Nevada decided to roll the dice. The state reduced its residency requirement for divorce to six weeks and legalized gambling. Catering to what most Americans considered sin—casinos, pawnshops, divorce mills, quick wedding chapels, even legal brothels—turned out to be good business. This has been America's fastest-growing state since 1960; in the 1990s it grew 66%, from 1.2 million to 2 million. Growth continued at only a slightly lower pace in 2001 and 2002, when the Census Bureau had 2.2 million people; at that rate, Nevada should have 3.3 million by 2010.

Las Vegas, a mere spot on the map when gambling was legalized, now is the center of a metro area of more than 1.5 million; Henderson, on the road southeast toward Hoover Dam, was the fastest-growing American city in the 1990s. Reno, known as "the biggest little city in the world," now has, together with Lake Tahoe and the capital of Carson City, another 470,000. Gaming—

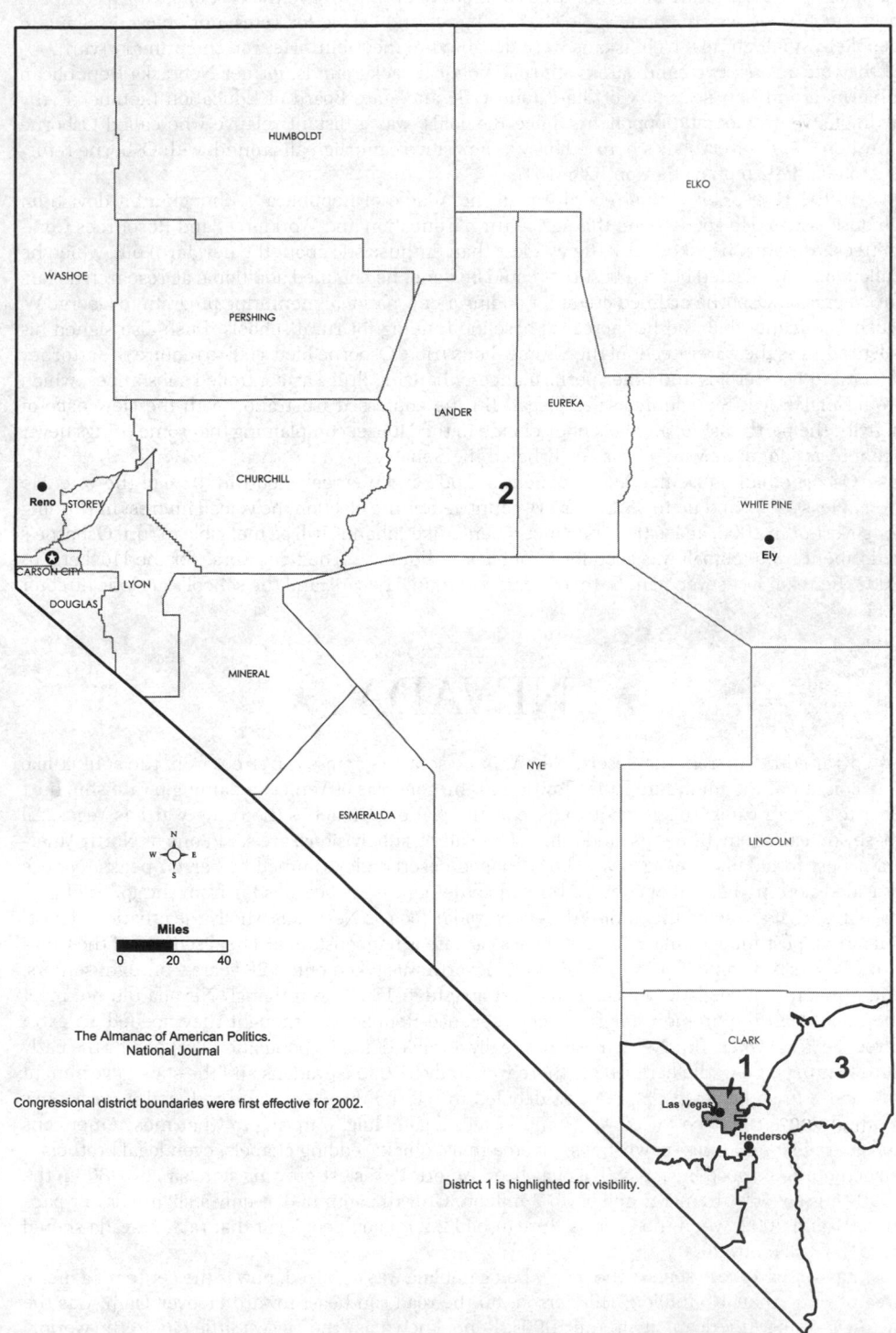

HUMBOLDT

ELKO

WASHOE

PERSHING

LANDER

EUREKA

CHURCHILL

WHITE PINE

Reno   STOREY

2

Ely

CARSON CITY

LYON

DOUGLAS

MINERAL

NYE

ESMERALDA

LINCOLN

N
W   E
S

Miles
0   20   40

The Almanac of American Politics.
National Journal

Congressional district boundaries were first effective for 2002.

CLARK

1

3

Las Vegas

Henderson

District 1 is highlighted for visibility.

the Nevada word for gambling—generates most of this growth: Las Vegas's 124,000 hotel rooms (as of early 2001) house more than 35 million visitors who spend more than $35 billion a year, Reno's nearly 5 million tourists spend almost $4 billion, and not just in casinos and hotels but in increasingly upscale restaurants and malls. They come from all over the United States and from foreign countries, especially Japan. Though at least one form of gambling is now available in 47 states, Las Vegas has made itself a destination; it has twice as much convention exhibit space as the number two city, Chicago. This is a service economy: of the more than 1 million people employed, nearly 90% produce services rather than goods. The 6.25% gambling receipts tax has generated enough revenue so that Nevada has no income, corporate or inheritance tax; even in fiscal crisis in early 2003 no one proposed one. The cost of living is low, housing is relatively inexpensive and a newcomer doesn't stand out in the crowd. As UNLV professor Hal Rothman wrote, "Las Vegas is a function of market forces, pure and simple. People move to a desert with 110 degree temperatures because there are opportunities here they can't find elsewhere."

From mining to gaming, Nevada has been a second chance state, a place for outcasts to succeed and misfits to rebound. With Alaska, it is one of the few states with more men than women. Nine out of every 1,000 Nevadans get divorced each year, the highest rate in the nation. Only 21% of Nevadans were born in the state, the lowest of any state; in Stateline, on Lake Tahoe, just 5% were born in Nevada. Nevada has been an avenue of success for ethnic groups who faced roadblocks elsewhere. The four owners of the Comstock Lode—MacKay, Fair, Flood, O'Brien—were Irishmen; the first big hotel on the Las Vegas strip, the Flamingo, was built in 1946 by Jewish gangster Bugsy Siegel, later gunned down in his Beverly Hills home; most of the big casinos were owned by mobsters until Howard Hughes—a different kind of outcast—bought them up in the late 1960s. In the 1990s Latinos moved here in large numbers, attracted by the plentiful jobs; Nevada was 20% Hispanic in 2000. Some 4% of Nevadans told the 2000 census takers they were of multiple races, the fourth highest of any state. Nevadans tend to be unchurched and not highly educated: only 34% belonged to a church in 2000, lower than in any state but Oregon and Washington; only 17% of adults in Las Vegas and Clark County had college degrees, one of the lowest numbers for any big metropolitan area. For years, the casinos catered to older tastes in entertainment, from Frank Sinatra to girlie shows, and depended on gamblers for all their trade. But in the early 1990s, as riverboat and Indian casinos opened in many states, Las Vegas became a family-friendly destination resort. Its huge and flashy hotels have glittering attractions: the 3,000-room Mirage with its tropical rainforest lobby has Siegfried and Roy's tiger-taming extravaganza, Caesars Palace has an upscale shopping center with Roman-style storefronts, the pyramid-shaped Luxor that looms over this desert has an amusement park and huge obelisk inside, New York New York imitates Gotham, and the Bellagio has a museum-class art gallery and an eleven-acre lake with 1,000 fountains. Slot machines no longer line every hallway, because that would mean keeping children out. Las Vegas has become decorous enough to attract the American Booksellers and Southern Baptist conventions. Will either political party ever dare to hold its national convention here?

There are other things in Nevada besides gambling and other places besides Las Vegas (though 69% of Nevadans live in Clark County). The state's low taxes have made it a regional distribution and credit card operations center and it has attracted warehouses and factories from California. There is still some mining—mostly gold mining—which was booming in 2003, after Clinton administration mining regulations were scrapped and the price of gold rose 25% between 2002 and 2003. Nevada also mines the less glamorous diatomaceous earth, used for swimming pool filters and kitty litter. A Wild West atmosphere remains in the "Cow Counties" beyond Las Vegas and Reno. Near Elko, a Canadian company's subsidiary in 1995 paid the federal government $9,765 for title to 1,949 acres of public lands with 30 million ounces of gold—all legal under the Mining Act of 1872. The Forest Service ranger in charge of the Humboldt-Toiyabe National Forest quit in 1999 because employees were refused service in local restaurants and local officials endorsed illegal use of federal lands.

For the past two decades, Nevada politics have been volatile. Historically, it was Democratic, sending politically shrewd Democrats to Washington and keeping them there to protect the interests of a state always heavily dependent on the federal government. The most powerful were

Key Pittman, chairman of the Senate Foreign Relations Committee, who backed FDR's foreign policy only after Roosevelt agreed to buy absurdly large amounts of Nevada's silver, and Pat McCarran, author of the repressive McCarran Act, who shamelessly pushed aid for Reno and Las Vegas (the airport there is named for him) and became suddenly solicitous of civil liberties when mobsters and casino owners were called to testify before the Kefauver committee investigating racketeering. In the 1980s, Nevada trended sharply Republican, primarily because of newcomers. This came not out of devotion to family values, for Nevada had the nation's largest percentage of non-family households, but from individualists who think they are sharper than others, have a special angle, are a step ahead of the market, and can and will beat the odds.

In the 1990s, the dice have rolled both ways. Bill Clinton, to the surprise of managers on both sides, carried Nevada in 1992, by 37%–35%, and again in 1996, by 44%–43%. The key here was his promise to veto any bill that moves toward building the national nuclear waste repository that has been approved for Yucca Mountain, some 90 miles north of Las Vegas. But that was not enough for Al Gore, who carried Clark County, but lost by wide margins in Reno and the Cow Counties; George W. Bush, without promising a veto on nuclear waste, carried the state 50%–46%. From 1988 to 2000 Nevada had two Democratic senators, but Harry Reid, an able and experienced politician, beat Republican John Ensign by only 428 votes in 1998, and when Richard Bryan retired in 2000, Ensign won his seat by a solid 55%–40%. Republicans captured the governorship in 1998 and now control all six statewide offices, the state Senate and two of the three U.S. House seats.

Nevada voters on balance seem to lean Republican, with a libertarian but sometimes culturally conservative streak. In 2000, 65% voted to approve medical marijuana, but in 2002, 61% voted against legalizing the possession of 3 ounces of marijuana and marijuana use in private and 67% voted to prohibit same-sex marriage. Nevadans in a 2002 poll opposed a ban on brothels, which are not legal anyway in Las Vegas, Reno or Carson City, by a margin of 52%–31%. This is not the cultural liberalism of college-educated baby boomers. One reason that Gore lost the state is that he didn't win the margins here that he did in other states among unmarried people without children, people who never attend church and people with graduate degrees. This is the libertarianism not of Bob Dylan but of Wayne Newton (who has an unprecedented 10-year contract on the Strip). Another unique feature of Nevada politics: since 1975 voters can vote for "none of these candidates." "None" finished second in the 1998 Democratic primary for lieutenant governor and has occasionally finished first in races for minor offices, but the law is toothless: even when there is a plurality for "none of the above," the top-running candidate wins.

Special issues are more important in Nevada than political parties. When Republican Kenny Guinn was elected in 1998 to succeed Democrat Bob Miller as governor, there was no major shift in policy: Both were supported strongly by the gaming industry. And the unions which have successfully organized Las Vegas casinos and hotels have no more been challenged by Guinn than they were by Miller.

The other raging Nevada issue is the proposed Yucca Mountain nuclear waste repository. The federal government took responsibility for nuclear waste in 1982 and the Yucca Mountain site was singled out by chosen by Congress in 1987, when the Nevada delegation was unusually weak: Harry Reid was in his first year in the Senate and Republican Chic Hecht seemed to be facing sure defeat. The plan is to bury the waste deep within the mountain, 1,300 feet above the water table, in reinforced steel containers in a 1,400-acre maze with 100 miles of storage tunnels. Many in Nevada argue that rainwater will flush the radioactive material out of the depository and into the water table; a December 1998 Energy Department study found no evidence that would happen. More recently, Yucca Mountain opponents have charged that the site is geologically flawed and within an earthquake zone, and that transportation of nuclear waste across the country would be hazardous, especially after September 11. But 39 states have nuclear plants with waste piling up alongside, and in the 1990s moves to establish a temporary site in Nevada were pressed by Larry Craig of Idaho, which agreed to take nuclear waste temporarily. Clinton promised to veto a temporary site—one reason he carried Nevada twice by narrow margins. Veto-proof majorities in the House voted for a temporary site in Nevada. Senators Bryan and Reid lobbied furiously to get enough votes to prevent a veto override in the Senate and succeeded in 1995, 1997 and 2000; a bill in the House was pulled off the calendar in 1998 by Speaker Newt Gingrich to help the candidacy of Ensign, then a Republican congressman, for the Senate. In 2000, Bush pledged not to place a temporary storage site in Nevada. But he refrained from promising to veto a permanent repository, saying that his decision would be based on "sound science and not politics." In February 2002 Bush, on the recommendation of Energy Secretary Spencer Abraham, designated Yucca Mountain as the permanent site. The law provided for a veto by the governor, which could be overridden by majorities in both houses of Congress. In April 2002, with great ceremony, Governor Kenny Guinn issued his veto. In May 2002 the House cast a large majority for Yucca Mountain. In the Senate, Reid and Ensign lobbied furiously for votes, but in July 2002 the designation of Yucca Mountain was affirmed 60–39. The permanent site, under existing law, is not supposed to open until 2010, but it may not then. The Energy Department has to apply for a permit to the Nuclear Regulatory Commission, and proceedings there could take years. Lawsuits have been filed against the project by Nevada, Clark County and Las Vegas. Guinn and the Nevada delegation have vowed not to work for concessions on the building of the repository but to fight it every step of the way.

The People		Race/Ethnic Origin			Military veterans: 238,128 (16.0%)	
Pop. 2000:	1,998,257	1,303,001	65.2%	White	WWII: 16.0%	Korea: 13.9%
Pop. 1990:	1,201,833	131,509	6.6%	Black	Vietnam: 34.8%	Gulf War: 10.4%
Change 1990–2000:	Up 66.3%	88,593	4.4%	Asian	**Most populous cities:**	
Change 1980–1990:	Up 50.1%	21,397	1.1%	Native Am.	1. Las Vegas	478,434
% of U.S. total:	0.7%	7,769	0.4%	Hawaiian	2. Reno	180,480
Pop. rank:	35th of 50	49,231	2.5%	Two+ races	3. Henderson	175,381
Area size:	110,561 sq. mi.	2,787	0.1%	Other	4. North Las Vegas	115,488
State Native:	21.3%	393,970	19.7%	Hisp. Origin	5. Sparks	66,346
Non-citizen:	10.0%	**Ancestry**			Urban population: 91.6%	
Language		German: 10.9%		Irish: 8.5%	Rural population: 8.4%	
English: 76.0%	Spanish: 14.6%	English: 7.8%		Italian: 5.1%		
Asian: 4.3%		USA: 3.7%				

Education		Work Sector		Legislature	
H.S. Grad:	80.7%	Private: 82.4%	Govt: 12.5%	Senate	13 R 8 D
College Grad:	18.2%	Self: 4.9%	Family: 0.3%	Assembly	23 D 19 R
Industry		Unemployment: 6.2%		Legislative Term Limits: Yes	
Agri: 1.6%	Con: 9.2%	**Household Income**		**Registered Voters**	
Fin: 6.5%	Info: 2.2%	<15k: 12.4%	15-35k: 25.4%	D: 361,465	(40.7%)
Mfg: 10.1%	Prof: 21.7%	35-50k: 18.1%	50-100k: 32.8%	R: 368,673	(41.5%)
Public: 4.5%	Trade: 14.0%	100-150k: 7.4%	>150k: 3.9%	I: 158,147	(17.8%)
Other: 30.3%		Median: $44,581			
Occupation		Poverty status: 10.5%			
Blue collar: 21.8%	White collar: 53.3%	**Home Value**			
Gray collar: 24.9%		<50k: 7.7% 50-100k: 19.4% 100-200k: 55.0% 200-300k: 11.3%			
		300-500k: 4.5% >500k: 2.1% Median: $132,500			

Presidential politics In the 1940s, Nevada was a Democratic state; in the 1960s, it was divided much as the nation was, voting narrowly for John Kennedy in 1960 and Richard Nixon in 1968. In the 1980s, it was heavily Republican, twice giving more than 60% to Ronald Reagan and 59%–38% for George Bush in 1988. In the 1990s, it voted twice for Bill Clinton; critical to his margin was his pledge to veto bills moving nuclear waste to Yucca Mountain or temporary storage sites. But the basic Republican proclivity of the state produced a 50%–46% margin for George W. Bush, who promised only to block a temporary storage site. Nevada, like other Rocky

2000 Presidential Vote

Bush (R)	301,575	(50%)
Gore (D)	279,978	(46%)
Nader (Green)	15,008	(2%)
Other	12,409	(2%)

1996 Presidential Vote

Clinton (D)	203,974	(44%)
Dole (R)	199,244	(43%)
Perot (I)	43,986	(9%)
Other	17,130	(4%)

Mountain states, received a big influx of white middle-aged Californians in the 1990s, an exodus that made California more Democratic and the Rocky Mountain states more Republican.

Nevada's late March presidential primary has attracted little attention; efforts to join a proposed Western states primary set for Friday, March 10, 2000, were defeated by Democrats in the Nevada House in June 1999.

Congressional districting   Nevada gained a second congressional district in the 1980 Census and a third congressional district in the 2000 Census. If growth continues at the present percentage rate, it will likely gain a fourth and may gain a fifth in the 2010 Census. Redistricting was easy in the 1980s and 1990s: the 1st District was the inner part of Clark County (the "hole in the bagel," says Congresswoman Shelley Berkley), politically marginal and won by both parties in the 1990s; the 2d District was the rest of the state, heavily Republican.

| 108th Congress Lineup |
| 2 R   1 D |
| 107th Congress Lineup |
| 1 D   1 R |

It was a little more difficult in 2001, with a third district and control of redistricting split between a Republican governor and state Senate and a Democratic Assembly. Clark County, with 69% of the Census population, was entitled to two of the seats and a small part of the third. For a time Republicans argued that two or all three of the districts should combine part of Clark County with part of the rest of the state. But that idea was dropped in the June 2001 special session. Eventually agreement was reached on a plan with an inner city Las Vegas 1st District, a 2d District including all the rest of the counties plus much of outer Clark County and a Y-shaped 3d District including much of the Las Vegas suburbs. The 1st District was safe for Democrat Berkley, the 2d safe for Republican Jim Gibbons and the 3d was drawn so that it was exactly even in party registration.

Governor

Kenny Guinn (R)

Elected 1998, term expires Jan. 2007, 2d term; b. Aug. 24, 1936, Garland, AR; home, Las Vegas; Fresno St. U, B.A. 1957, M.A. 1958; Utah St. U., Ph.D. 1970; Non-denominational; married (Dema).

Professional Career: Planning Specialist, Clark Cnty. Schl. Dist., 1964–69; Superintendent, Clark Cnty. Schl. Dist., 1969–78; Nevada Savings & Loan, 1978–80; Pres. & COO, PriMerit Bank, 1980–85; CEO, 1985–87; Pres. & COO Southwest Gas Corp., 1987–93; Chairman & CEO 1988–93; Interim Pres., U.N.L.V., 1994–95.

Office: Capitol Bldg., Carson City, 89701, 775-684-5670; Fax: 775-684-5683; Web site: www.gov.state.nv.us.

Election Results

2002 general	Kenny Guinn (R)	344,001	(68%)
	Joe Neal (D)	110,935	(22%)
	None of these	23,674	(5%)
	Other	25,469	(5%)
2002 primary	Kenny Guinn (R)	97,367	(83%)
	Shirley Cook (R)	7,717	(7%)
1998 general	Kenny Guinn (R)	223,892	(52%)
	Jan Laverty Jones (D)	182,281	(42%)
	Other	27,457	(6%)

Kenny Guinn was elected governor of Nevada in 1998 and reelected in 2002 in his only races for elective office. He grew up in the Central Valley of California, due west of Las Vegas but separated by Death Valley and Mount Whitney; he majored in physical education at Fresno State and got an education doctorate at Utah State. In 1964 he moved to Las Vegas to work for the Clark County

School District; he became school superintendent in 1969. Later he went to work for the S&L that became PriMerit Bank and became chairman in 1987, then went to Southwest Gas Corporation and became chairman in 1993. In 1994 he spent a year as interim president of the University of Nevada at Las Vegas, then recovering from a basketball scandal, and donated his salary to the school's scholarship fund. In the process he won much civic renown. In February 1996 he started running to replace term-limited Governor Bob Miller; immediately he picked up much of the support from the gaming industry Miller had, though he is a Republican and Miller a Democrat. He was christened "The Anointed One" by local political analyst Jon Ralston.

But if the Anointed One had widespread support, he also had opposition. In the September 1998 primary he faced Aaron Russo, a former Hollywood producer who moved to Las Vegas in 1996. Russo refused casino money, leaving a $1,000 check from Donald Trump on his desk ostentatiously uncashed, and called for increasing the 6.25% tax on casinos' gross. Guinn retaliated by playing in his ads a video Russo had made in 1994 when he formed a Ross Perot-like Constitution Party; it showed Russo in long hair and a dangling earring ranting in protest at politicians. Russo got within 7% in an August poll, but Guinn won handily, 58%–26%.

The Democratic nominee was Las Vegas Mayor Jan Laverty Jones. In 1994 she had run against Governor Bob Miller in the primary, and lost 63%–28%. Jones announced on filing day, only a few months after breast cancer surgery, and while still undergoing chemotherapy and radiation; she was open about this and showed great vigor. Guinn charged Jones with raising property taxes; Jones charged Guinn with raising gas rates. Russo endorsed Jones. Guinn won 52%–42%, carrying the Las Vegas and Reno areas by almost identical majorities and winning by 59%–34% in the Cow Counties.

Nevada's 63 citizen-legislators meet only four months every two years; they get $60 for postage and have no staff except secretaries. Nonetheless, the 1999 legislature proved productive. It passed Guinn's proposal for Millennium Scholarships, to allow B students in core subjects to go to college almost for free. Guinn succeeded in privatizing the state workmen's comp insurer and strengthening the ethics code. In 2001 the legislature passed a program to help pay for prescription drugs for seniors. He and the legislature backed electricity deregulation in 1999, but in 2001, facing high prices because of California's botched deregulation, he said deregulation should be abandoned for the rest of his term and called for price caps on electricity.

Guinn, like almost all Nevada politicians, has strongly opposed the proposed repository for nuclear waste at Yucca Mountain, 90 miles northwest of Las Vegas. He argues that the site is a fractured volcanic rock ridge situated among earthquake faults and that it would be a hazard to people in Las Vegas. In September 2000 he called for banning the import of water into the state to build Yucca Mountain, with fines of $1 million a gallon. Bill Clinton had opposed Yucca Mountain; George W. Bush, on the recommendation of Energy Secretary Spencer Abraham, officially approved it in February 2002. This was not the end of the process. A 1982 law gave the governor of Nevada the right to veto the proposal, subject to override by Congress. In April 2002, with great ceremony Guinn vetoed the proposal. "Yucca Mountain is not inevitable and Yucca Mountain is no bargaining chip and, so long as I am governor, it will never become one." The law gave Congress three months to override. In May 2002 the House did so, by a lopsided margin of 306–117; most House members' districts are near where nuclear waste is deposited. The Senate is where the real fight took place. Nevada Senators Harry Reid and John Ensign worked hard to round up votes, and Nevada hired former Senate Parliamentarian Robert Dove to aid its cause. But in July 2002 the Nevadans lost 60–39; Reid rounded up 36 Democrats (including Jeffords) but Ensign, opposed by the Bush administration, could only get two other Republicans. The fight will go on. Observers said the Energy Department would probably not apply to the Nuclear Regulatory Commission for a license to build the facility until December 2004, and the NRC regulatory process could take years; the state, Las Vegas and Clark County all filed lawsuits.

The other big issue in Nevada in 2002 was medical malpractice. After the biggest insurer withdrew from the business in 2002, doctors started leaving the state rather than pay vastly higher premiums; by summer 2002, 29 doctors had closed their practices, another 14 were closing them and 86 had applied for licenses or jobs in other states. Guinn called a special session of the legislature to revise Nevada's malpractice law. The legislature passed a law capping pain and suffering damages at $350,000, but provided exceptions for "gross malpractice" when proved by "clear and convincing evidence" or "exceptional circumstances." Trial lawyers predicted that without the exception, the courts would strike down the law. Doctors' organizations were not satisfied. They collected enough signature to present their own version, without the exceptions, to the legislature in February 2003; the legislature had 40 days to enact it or it would go on the November 2004 ballot. Guinn said he expected the legislature would not act. "I did what I thought was needed, but if it goes to the vote of the people, fine."

Guinn did not have strong competition in the 2002 election. In May it became apparent that the Democratic nominee would be Joe Neal, state Senator for 30 years, and an advocate of raising the gross gambling tax. He often said that Yucca Mountain was inevitable. "We don't have a Democratic party in this state," he said. "We have a gaming party." He charged that the drive to legalize marijuana in Nevada was financed by an investor with ties to the South American drug cartel, a charge based on a Lyndon LaRouche publication. Guinn suspended his fundraising in May and contributed his money to other Republicans and local charities; he did little campaigning. He had the support of Las Vegas and teachers' unions and the result was what you might expect: Guinn won 68%–22%. Republicans swept all six statewide constitutional offices for the first time since 1890, held the state Senate and reduced Democrats' margin in the state House.

During the campaign Guinn boasted that he had not raised taxes. "We're running a state with 300,000 more people now than when I came in. And we have 1,000 fewer people on the state payroll." But even before the election, the Governor's Task Force on Tax Policy called for a $336 million tax increase. In December Guinn said he would seek $800 million in tax increases over two years, even though the Economic Forum, the official estimator, said that revenue would rise 5% in each of the next two years; the Nevada economy, hit fairly hard by September 11, had rebounded in 2002 and the state still led the nation in job growth and personal income increase. The Task Force called for a .25% gross business receipts tax, a 6.5% amusements tax, a property tax increase, a near-doubling of the liquor tax and an increase in incorporation fees. The gaming industry favored the gross receipts tax, which was opposed by the Chamber of Commerce, which preferred a sales tax on services; Guinn said he was against that.

Senior Senator

Harry Reid (D)

Elected 1986, seat up 2004, 3d term; b. Dec. 2, 1939, Searchlight; home, Searchlight; S. UT St. Col., A.S. 1959, UT St. U., B.S. 1961, George Washington U., J.D. 1964, U. of NV, 1969–70; Mormon; married (Landra).

Elected Office: NV Assembly, 1968–70; NV Lt. Gov., 1970–74; U.S. House of Reps., 1982–86.

Professional Career: Practicing atty., 1969–82; Henderson City Atty., 1964–66; Chmn., NV Gaming Comm., 1977–81.

DC Office: 528 HSOB, 20510, 202-224-3542; Fax: 202-224-7327; Web site: reid.senate.gov.

State Offices: Carson City, 775-882-7343; Las Vegas, 702-388-5020; Reno, 775-686-5750.

Committees: *Minority Whip. Aging (Special). Appropriations*: Defense; Energy & Water Development (RMM); Interior; Labor, HHS & Education; Transportation, Treasury & General Government; VA, HUD & Independent Agencies. *Environment & Public Works*: Clean Air, Climate Change & Nuclear Safety; Transportation & Infrastructure (RMM). *Ethics (Select)* (Vice Chmn.). *Indian Affairs*.

Group Ratings

	ADA	ACLU	AFS	LCV	CON	ITIC	NTU	COC	ACU	NTLC	CHC
2002	85	40	100	94	36	62	11	45	10	6	—
2001	100	—	100	88	—	—	6	43	20	—	0

National Journal Ratings

	2001 LIB —	2001 CONS		2002 LIB —	2002 CONS
Economic	74% —	23%		90% —	5%
Social	70% —	20%		62% —	37%
Foreign	61% —	27%		70% —	27%

Key Votes of the 107th Congress

1. Approve Bush Tax Cuts	N	5. Confirm Ashcroft as AG	N	9. Bar Coop. with Intl. Court	Y
2. Expand Patients' Rights	Y	6. Bar Gays in the Boy Scouts	N	10. Trade Promotion Authority	N
3. Campaign Finance Reform	Y	7. $ for Hate Crime Prosecution	Y	11. Authorize Force in Iraq	Y
4. Permit ANWR Development	N	8. Overseas Military Abortions	N	12. Homeland Sec. Dept. Union	Y

Election Results

1998 general	Harry Reid (D)	208,650	(48%)	($4,939,010)
	John Ensign (R)	208,222	(48%)	($3,490,256)
	Other	18,918	(4%)	
1998 primary	Harry Reid (D)	unopposed		
1992 general	Harry Reid (D)	253,150	(51%)	($3,259,802)
	Demar Dahl (R)	199,413	(40%)	($471,371)
	Other	43,333	(9%)	

Prior Winning Percentages: 1986 (50%); 1984 House (56%); 1982 House (58%)

Harry Reid, a Democrat first elected in 1986, has held high office in Nevada for most of the last 30 years. He grew up in Searchlight, Nevada, in the scorching desert south of Las Vegas, where his father was a hardrock miner. He hitchhiked 40 miles to high school in Henderson, where his civics teacher and boxing coach Mike O'Callaghan became his political mentor. Henderson businessmen helped him pay for college, and he graduated from Utah State and George Washington Law School. He was an amateur boxer and at nights during law school he worked as a Capitol Police officer. He returned to Henderson and practiced law. Reid was elected to the Assembly in 1968, at age 28; in 1970 Callaghan was elected governor and Reid, running separately, was elected lieutenant governor. In 1974 he came within 624 votes of beating Paul Laxalt in the race for senator, lost for mayor of Las Vegas in 1976, and then became head of the Gaming Commission from 1977–81—as sensitive a post as any in Nevada. In 1982, when Nevada got two House seats for the first time and Congressman-at-Large Jim Santini ran for the Senate, Reid ran in the Las Vegas-based 1st District and won. Laxalt retired in 1986 and Reid ran for the Senate again; his opponent turned out to be Santini, who had switched parties at the last minute and was running as a Republican. Reid's ads depicted him as David to Santini's Goliath, and he won 50%–45%.

Reid is now the Democratic whip in the Senate, the number two man in the party's leadership, a constant presence on the floor and one of the reasons why Democrats became the majority in the Senate from June 2001 to January 2003. He is soft-spoken and frank, a dogged and unrelenting partisan. He has a conservative record on some issues. He is against abortion, was one of the few Democrats to vote for the Gulf War resolution in 1991 and voted for the Iraq war resolution in 2002, and has opposed environmental groups consistently on mining issues. But after winning reelection by 428 votes in 1998, he took on the job of whip and has spent most of his time on the floor, advancing the cause of his party, evidently without regard to what that might do to his popularity at home. In June 2002 he angrily called for George W. Bush to denounce conservatives who were trying to persuade trade associations to hire Republicans in their top positions. In May 2001 he contributed $500 to Torricelli's legal defense fund. Then in July 2002 Torricelli's case came before the Ethics Committee, which Reid chaired. Common Cause called on Reid to recuse himself; at first he refused, but a week later he did so. He has worked closely and cooperatively with Democratic Leader Tom Daschle, and in November 2002, when Daschle was considering running for president, he all but endorsed Reid to succeed him. "I honestly don't think he would be challenged if I weren't to run." But the point became moot when Daschle decided not to run.

Reid played a key role in persuading Jim Jeffords to leave the Republican party in May 2001. For a month Daschle, Christopher Dodd and Reid talked with Jeffords and coaxed him to switch.

Reid offered to decline the chairmanship of the Envrionment and Public Works Committee, to which he was entitled by seniority, and let Jeffords be chairman. That may have been the vital selling point, though Jeffords, Daschle and Reid deny that there was a quid pro quo.

The key federal issue for Nevada is the proposed nuclear waste repository in Yucca Mountain. The federal government assumed responsibility for nuclear waste in 1982 and a bill passed in 1987, Reid's first year in the Senate, named Yucca Mountain and one other contender as the only two sites; the other one was later ruled out. Reid has stubbornly and persistently opposed the repository with every parliamentary and political tool at his command. Both other senators with nuclear waste piling up in their states (and 39 states have it) and especially Larry Craig of Idaho, where the government established a temporary nuclear waste site, have pressed hard for designation of Yucca Mountain. Bill Clinton carried Nevada by narrow margins in 1992 and 1996 largely because he promised to veto even a temporary site in Yucca Mountain, and so Reid's task was to assemble enough votes to prevent an override of his veto. He did so in 1997, then prevented a vote in 1998 and 1999, then kept 34 votes in line in April 2000—just barely enough. George W. Bush in 2000 pledged not to support a temporary site, but he also refrained from promising to veto a permanent site, saying that his decision would be based on "sound science and not politics." In February 2002 Bush, on the recommendation of Energy Secretary Spencer Abraham, designated Yucca Mountain as the permanent site. The law provided for a veto by the governor, which could be overridden by majorities in both houses of Congress. In April 2002, with great ceremony, Governor Kenny Guinn issued his veto. In May 2002 the House cast a large majority for Yucca Mountain. Reid lobbied furiously for Democratic votes, while John Ensign, his 1998 opponent and now his Republican colleague, lobbied desperately for Republican votes.

Reid argued that the site was geologically flawed and that transporting nuclear waste to it would be hazardous, especially after September 11. Some $2 million was spent on ads in states over which trucks and trains carrying the waste would pass. Reid spoke passionately when the issue was debated in July, enough so to convert Debbie Stabenow, who had voted for the Yucca Mountain site in the House. Altogether he got 35 Democrats and Jeffords to vote his way. Ensign, opposed by the Bush administration, could get only two other Republicans, Lincoln Chafee and Ben Nighthorse Campbell. So the site was approved 60–39. But for Reid the fight was not over. Lawsuits had been filed against the plan, and the Energy Department must get approval from the Nuclear Regulatory Commission, which could take many years. Reid chaired the Appropriations subcommittee with juridiction over the Energy Department; in 2002 it cut $189 million from the Yucca Mountain budget. When retiring Utah Republican Jim Hansen, who voted for the Yucca Mountain site, got a provision in an appropriation barring transport of nuclear waste to a site in Utah, Reid got it removed in conference. He has worked for greater security around nuclear plants.

Despite his strong partisanship and the bitterness and the closeness of the 1998 campaign, Reid and Ensign have become friendly colleagues who work together on many Nevada projects. Needless to say, they both strongly support the gaming industry. They have worked to block the bill, backed by John McCain and others, to prohibit betting on college and amateur sports, which is legal only in Nevada. They worked with Congressman Jim Gibbons on a Clark County Lands Act to declare some wilderness study areas as wilderness and open others to development; it became law with scarcely a dissenting vote. In 2000 Reid supported giving permanent resident status to immigrants who have been in the United States illegally since 1986, with a five-year rolling registry; Nevada's population in 2000 was 20% Hispanic. He pushed through a "source tax" amendment barring states from taxing the state pensions of retirees who move to another state—as many have to Nevada. He has steered counterterrorism money to Nevada and has worked to get the old Nevada nuclear test site, with its hundreds of underground tunnels, made into a $250 million center for training first responders how to cope with acts of terrorists.

Despite all this, Reid has never won a Senate election with more than 51% of the vote. He was elected in 1986 by 50%–45%. In the 1992 primary he won 53%–39% over Charles Woods, a businessman badly wounded and scarred in World War II; in the general, he beat rancher Demar Dahl 51%–40%. In the 1998 race his opponent was 1st District Congressman John Ensign, who had run and won high-spending races in the Las Vegas area in 1994 and 1996. Reid in his feisty way attacked Ensign harshly as an "extremist" who called environmentalists "socialists," and would gut Social Security. This was Nevada's most expensive Senate campaign ever: Reid spent $4.9 million and Ensign $3.5 million. Unlike many small state Democrats, Reid has raised most of his money in his home state; big contributors in Las Vegas have known and supported him for many years. Reid carried Clark County, which casts two-thirds of the vote and is normally more Democratic than the rest of the state, by only 53%–44%; he may have won because he ran ahead of party lines in the usually Republican Reno area, where his work on local projects was appreciated. The election night tally showed Reid ahead by 459 votes; Ensign called for a recount, and a hand count in Reno's Washoe County took weeks. Ensign finally conceded December 9, with Reid ahead by 428 votes.

Reid's problem is that there are so many newcomers to Nevada, most of them Republicans unfamiliar with his work in almost 40 years of public life. About 4,000 people have been moving to the Las Vegas area every month—which means nearly 300,000 Nevadans in 2004 will not have been in the state the last time Reid ran. Not all of them are voters, but they will bulk large in a state where 613,000 votes were cast in 2000. In 2002 Reid contributed to three Democrats running for statewide office; all three lost, as Republicans won all six statewide constitutional offices for the first time since 1890. The only positive news for Reid is that his son Rory Reid was elected to the Clark County Commission.

In December 2002 White House political strategist Karl Rove met with 2d District Congressman Jim Gibbons and urged him to run; both Rove and Gibbons graduated, in different years, from Sparks High School near Reno. Gibbons represents everything in Nevada outside Clark County plus part of Clark County itself, and has won reelection by overwhelming margins. But the close cooperation within the Nevada delegation on many issues, especially Yucca Mountain, may prevent make it hard for Gibbons to wage an aggressive race against Reid. And George W. Bush's selection of the Yucca Mountain site may mean that Bush appearances will do less good for a Republican than they did in other states in 2002. Others mentioned as possible candidates include Secretary of State Dean Heller, Treasurer Brian Krolicki, Controller Kathy Augustine and Attorney General Brian Sandoval; the first three are term-limited and cannot run for their offices again in 2006.

Junior Senator

John Ensign (R)

Elected 2000, seat up 2006, 1st term; b. Mar. 25, 1958, Roseville, CA; home, Las Vegas; OR St. U., B.S. 1981, CO St. U., D.V.M. 1985; Christian; married (Darlene).

Elected Office: U.S. House of Reps. 1994–98.

Professional Career: Veterinarian, 1987–93; Gen. Mgr., Gold Strike Hotel, 1991–93.

DC Office: 364 RSOB, 20510, 202-224-6244; Fax: 202-228-2193; Web site: ensign.senate.gov.

State Offices: Carson City, 775-885-9111; Las Vegas, 702-388-6605; Reno, 775-686-5770.

Committees: *Armed Services:* Emerging Threats & Capabilities; Readiness & Management Support (Chmn.); Strategic Forces. *Budget. Commerce, Science & Transportation:* Aviation; Communications; Competition, Foreign Commerce & Infrastructure; Science, Technology & Space. *Health, Education, Labor & Pensions:* Aging; Children & Families; Substance Abuse & Mental Health Services. *Small Business & Entrepreneurship. Veterans' Affairs.*

Group Ratings

	ADA	ACLU	AFS	LCV	CON	ITIC	NTU	COC	ACU	NTLC	CHC
2002	15	20	0	41	84	75	70	95	85	94	—
2001	20	—	0	25	—	—	84	93	84	—	100

National Journal Ratings

	2001 LIB	—	2001 CONS		2002 LIB	—	2002 CONS
Economic	35%	—	62%		30%	—	69%
Social	31%	—	68%		0%	—	62%
Foreign	7%	—	72%		24%	—	67%

Key Votes of the 107th Congress

1. Approve Bush Tax Cuts	Y	5. Confirm Ashcroft as AG	Y	9. Bar Coop. with Intl. Court	Y
2. Expand Patients' Rights	N	6. Bar Gays in the Boy Scouts	Y	10. Trade Promotion Authority	N
3. Campaign Finance Reform	N	7. $ for Hate Crime Prosecution	N	11. Authorize Force in Iraq	Y
4. Permit ANWR Development	Y	8. Overseas Military Abortions	N	12. Homeland Sec. Dept. Union	N

Election Results

2000 general	John Ensign (R)	330,687	(55%)	($4,872,176)
	Ed Bernstein (D)	238,260	(40%)	($2,449,093)
	Other	31,303	(5%)	
2000 primary	John Ensign (R)	95,904	(88%)	
	Richard Hamzik (R)	6,202	(6%)	
	Other	6,833	(6%)	

Prior Winning Percentages: 1996 House (50%); 1994 House (48%)

John Ensign was elected to the Senate in 2000, in his second try for the office. Ensign grew up in northern Nevada and moved to Las Vegas at 16. For a time his mother was a change girl at a Reno casino, supporting three children with no help from her ex-husband. Then she married Mike Ensign, who became a top executive at Circus Circus and is now head of the Mandalay Resort Group. John Ensign graduated from Oregon State in 1981 and in 1985 graduated from veterinary school at Colorado State, where he became a born-again Christian. He built a successful veterinary practice in Las Vegas, with the first 24-hour clinic, and managed a family hotel, became involved in civic affairs and at his wife's suggestion became active in the Promise Keepers. Disturbed at trends in national life, they decided he would run for the House in 1994, against 1st District incumbent James Bilbray. This was the more Democratic of Nevada's then two seats, and Bilbray was an eight-year incumbent. But 1994 was also a Republican year, and with the help of Ensign's stepfather's connections in the gaming industry he was able to raise substantial funds. On election night, Bilbray claimed victory, but when the votes came in Ensign had won by 1,436 votes. In the House, Ensign compiled a generally conservative voting record and got a seat on the Ways and Means Committee. In the summer of 1996 he and colleague David Camp persuaded Newt Gingrich to separate the welfare and Medicaid issues and present Bill Clinton with a welfare bill, which he signed 11 weeks before the election; Ensign can reasonably claim to be one of the fathers of the 1996 Welfare Act. He was re-elected in 1996 by 50%–44%.

Ensign decided to run against Senator Harry Reid in 1998. This was a hard-fought, high-spending race, targeted by both national parties and fought with intensity by the candidates; Reid spent $4.9 million and Ensign $3.5 million. Reid attacked Ensign harshly as an "extremist" who called environmentalists "socialists," and would gut Social Security. "You send Ensign to the Senate, you send nuclear waste to Nevada," he proclaimed. Ensign responded, "Does Reid think that Dick Bryan is going to give up the fight? Bryan's a Democrat who works with Republicans, and I'm a Republican who works with Democrats." Reid ran behind only 48%–46% in Reno's usually Republican Washoe County; Ensign ran well ahead in the Cow Counties, 59%–36%. In Las Vegas' Clark County, both candidates' home base, Reid won 53%–44%. The election night tally showed Reid ahead by 459 votes; Ensign called for a recount, and it turned out that the Washoe County ballots had been misprinted, preventing some from being read by machines. The hand count there took weeks, and Ensign finally conceded December 9, with Reid ahead by 428 votes.

Then just two months later, in February 1999, Bryan announced that he would not run for re-election in 2000. Ensign, who had said he would not run against Bryan, announced his candidacy the next day. Democrats tried to enlist their strongest candidate, Bob Miller, who had just completed eight years as governor, but he preferred to remain in the private sector in Las Vegas.

Then Attorney General Frankie Sue Del Papa launched her candidacy; an April poll showed Ensign with a narrow 45%–40% lead, but he was much farther ahead in money: $1.1 million to $250,000 by the end of June. In September Del Papa abruptly withdrew from the race, as she had withdrawn from the 1998 race for governor, citing difficulties in fundraising; her bad relations with Las Vegas unions did not help. Democratic efforts to recruit Brian Greenspun, owner of the *Las Vegas Sun*, failed. What appears to have happened is that the gaming industry, developers and other leading funders in Las Vegas, who had supported Miller and then Republican Kenny Guinn to succeed him, decided that Ensign was on the road to victory and that it might suit their interests to have one Democratic and one Republican senator.

That left the Democratic banner in the hands of Ed Bernstein, a personal injury lawyer who had run ads on Las Vegas TV for years. Bernstein put in $1.1 million of his own money; his main issues were prescription drugs for seniors and abortion. The candidates engaged in six debates; one highlight came when Ensign quizzed Bernstein about a water project in northern Nevada of which Bernstein obviously had never heard. Naturally both candidates promised to fight nuclear waste storage in Nevada; Ensign was careful to return a contribution from a Yucca Mountain contractor. Bernstein managed to tighten the race for a while, but Ensign ended up winning by a large 55%–40%. Ensign carried Las Vegas and Clark County 51%–45%, Reno and Washoe County 58%–35% and the Cow Counties 68%–27%.

Ensign and Reid, bitter rivals in 1998, quickly became cooperative colleagues. In December 2000 they announced that their first priority was blocking the move by John McCain and Sam Brownback to prohibit betting on college and amateur sports—they argue that sports books are well regulated by Nevada state authorities—and Ensign tried to gut the bill in the Commerce Committee in May 2001 but his amendment to do so failed 10–10. They co-sponsored a bill to make permanent the Social HMOs permitted in Nevada under Medicare.

As a freshman senator, Ensign did much of his work by sponsoring amendments. To the election procedures bill, he added an amendment requiring paper documentation of votes so that they could be hand-counted if necessary, as in Washoe County in 1998. He and Paul Sarbanes sponsored a successful amendment to make permanent the 3% of sale price downpayment requirement in FHA-insured mortgages. To the corporate accountability bill he added an amendment to discourage regulators from treating very small non-public accounting firms the same way as large CPAs. To the HMO regulation bill he sponsored amendments to prohibit genetic discrimination, to make sure its protections were available to union members and to protect doctors doing pro bono work in poor areas from lawsuits. The bill he sponsored with Joseph Lieberman for incentives for hospitals to retain nurses passed the Senate in December 2001. With Maria Cantwell and his fellow veterinarian Wayne Allard, he sponsored a bill to ban interstate transportation of cockfighting paraphernalia and increase to two years the sentence for interstate transportation of cockfighting roosters. At the end of the session in November 2002, he blocked passage of $99 million for bus security; he said the bus industry should pay for it.

The key federal issue for Nevada is the proposed nuclear waste repository in Yucca Mountain, 90 miles northwest of Las Vegas. The federal government assumed responsibility for nuclear waste in 1982 and a bill passed in 1987, named Yucca Mountain and one other contender as the only two sites; the other one was later ruled out. Ensign strongly opposed Yucca Mountain when he was in the House, but there the odds were very heavily against him. Creation of a temporary storage site in Yucca Mountain was prevented during the Clinton years by Clinton's promise to veto it—probably the reason he carried Republican-leaning Nevada twice by narrow margins— and by Harry Reid's success in getting at least 34 senators to oppose it, enough to prevent an override of Clinton's veto. George W. Bush in 2000 also pledged not to support a temporary site, but at the same time he refrained from promising to veto a permanent site, saying that his decision would be based on "sound science and not politics." In February 2002 Bush, on the recommendation of Energy Secretary Spencer Abraham, designated Yucca Mountain as the permanent site. The law provided for a veto by the governor, which could be overridden by majorities in both houses of Congress. In April 2002, Governor Kenny Guinn issued his veto. In May 2002, the House cast a large majority for Yucca Mountain. In the Senate Reid lobbied furiously for votes among Democrats, most of whom had stood with him before on the issue, while Ensign lobbied desperately for Republican votes. This was much more difficult because of the opposition of the Bush administration. Reid got 35 Democrats and Jim Jeffords to vote his way. Ensign could get only two other Republicans, Lincoln Chafee and Ben Nighthorse Campbell. So the site was approved 60–39. But the fight was not over. Lawsuits had been filed against the plan, and the Energy Department must get approval from the Nuclear Regulatory Commission, which could take many years.

Ensign had argued in 2000 that Nevadans needed a Republican senator to argue against Yucca Mountain on his side of the aisle; now some Democrats argued that he had not swung many votes Nevada's way. He switched in January 2003 from the Banking to the Armed Services Committee, where he could look after Nellis Air Force Base and Fallon Naval Air Station. Ensign, like Reid, raises most of his money in Nevada, and there is no doubt he can raise large amounts from his gaming industry connections. His seat comes up in 2006.

FIRST DISTRICT

Rep. Shelley Berkley (D)

Elected 1998, 3d term; b. Jan. 20, 1951, South Fallsburg, NY; home, Las Vegas; U.N.L.V., B.A. 1972; U. of San Diego Law Schl., J.D. 1976; Jewish; married (Larry Lehrner).

Elected Office: NV Assembly, 1982–84; Regent, U. Commun. Col. System of NV, 1990–98.

Professional Career: Cnsl., SW Gas Corp., 1977–82; VP, Sands Hotel, 1989–98; Chair, NV Hotel & Motel Assn., 1994.

DC Office: 439 CHOB 20515, 202-225-5965; Fax: 202-225-3119; Web site: www.house.gov/berkley.

District Office: Las Vegas, 702-220-9823.

Committees: *International Relations* (17th of 23 D): International Terrorism, Nonproliferation and Human Rights; Middle East & Central Asia. *Transportation & Infrastructure* (22d of 34 D): Aviation; Highways, Transit & Pipelines. *Veterans' Affairs* (11th of 14 D): Health.

Group Ratings

	ADA	ACLU	AFS	LCV	CON	ITIC	NTU	COC	ACU	NTLC	CHC
2002	85	73	88	100	50	38	25	50	16	14	17
2001	90	—	90	79	—	—	22	43	12	—	—

National Journal Ratings

	2001 LIB	—	2001 CONS		2002 LIB	—	2002 CONS
Economic	62%	—	39%		61%	—	39%
Social	74%	—	23%		74%	—	19%
Foreign	66%	—	34%		64%	—	35%

Key Votes of the 107th Congress

1. Approve Bush Tax Cuts	Y	5. Faith-Based Charities	N	9. Trade Promotion Authority	N
2. Limit Patients' Bill of Rights	N	6. Bar Gays in the Boy Scouts	N	10. Bar Funds for Intl. Court	N
3. Campaign Finance Reform	Y	7. Ban Partial-Birth Abortion	N	11. Authorize Force in Iraq	Y
4. Ban ANWR Development	Y	8. Arm Commercial Pilots	Y	12. Deny Home. Sec. Dept. Union	N

Election Results

2002 general	Shelley Berkley (D)	64,312	(54%)	($1,717,220)
	Lynette Boggs McDonald (R)	51,148	(43%)	($983,110)
	Other	4,254	(4%)	
2002 primary	Shelley Berkley (D)	unopposed		
2000 general	Shelley Berkley (D)	118,469	(52%)	($2,062,803)
	Jon Porter (R)	101,276	(44%)	($1,386,081)
	Other	9,490	(4%)	

Prior Winning Percentages: 1998 (49%)

The People		Race/Ethnic Origin	Ancestry	
Area size:	177 sq. mi.	51.5% White	German: 8.8%	Irish: 7.1%
Urban population:	99.9%	11.9% Black	English: 5.9%	
Rural population:	0.1%	4.6% Asian	**2000 Presidential Vote**	
Pop. 2000:	666,088	0.6% Native Am.	Gore (D) 87,345	(56%)
Median income:	$39,480	0.4% Hawaiian	Bush (R) 63,163	(41%)
Poverty status:	13.9%	2.6% Two+ races	Other 4,801	(3%)
Military veterans:	14.4%	0.1% Other	**Cook Partisan Voting Index: D + 8**	
		28.2% Hispanic Origin		

Occupation   Blue collar: 23.0%   White collar: 47.8%   Gray collar: 29.2%

Las Vegas, a city whose garishness and sheer improbability are literally awesome, had a fittingly colorful beginning. It began as a Paiute Indian settlement that in the late 1700s served as a watering stop for Spanish priests making the 1,200-mile trek between New Mexico and California. By the 1800s, the Old Spanish Trail, as it came to be known, was used by horse and mule smugglers, by white explorers such as John Fremont and by Mormon emigrants heading west. Las Vegas was still a small crossroads when Nevada, its mining industry a shambles, legalized gambling in the 1930s. The *WPA Guide* to Nevada, published in 1940, when the city had 10,000 people, describes a prim Las Vegas: "Relatively little emphasis is placed on the gambling clubs and divorce facilities—though they are attractions to many visitors—and much effort is being made to build up cultural attractions. No cheap and easily parodied slogans have been adopted to publicize the city, no attempt has been made to introduce pseudo-romantic architectural themes, or to give an artificial glamour or gaiety." All that changed after World War II, when gangster Bugsy Siegel built the Flamingo hotel on what became The Strip south of the city limits. Pseudo-romantic architectural themes became the order of the day (you find flamingoes in the waters of Florida, not in the deserts of Nevada) and one casino followed another. Organized crime provided much of the money and muscle for Las Vegas, and investment capital came from Teamsters pension funds. That changed in the late 1960s, when the eccentric millionaire Howard Hughes bought most of the casinos and hired Mormons to run them. Then Hughes abruptly left town, and other operators built casinos like Caesars Palace and Circus Circus, the Mirage and Excalibur, Paris and New York, New York. In the 1970s, the casinos were the haven of flashy high rollers, of Frank Sinatra and girl shows. By the 1990s Las Vegas was producing more family-oriented entertainment and even high art, with Steve Wynn's museum-quality art collection on view, and Las Vegas built the biggest convention center in the country. September 11 hurt Las Vegas, and 15,000 casino workers were laid off. But Vegas recovered smartly in 2002 and remains one of the great leisure destinations in the world.

The 1st Congressional District consists of the inner core of Las Vegas that visitors are most likely to see. They cross into it as soon as they drive their rental cars out of the lot at McCarran International Airport and remain in the 1st as they cruise down Las Vegas Boulevard—the Strip. On the three-mile Strip—an architectural model since Robert Venturi and Denise Scott Brown's *Learning from Las Vegas*—you can find 11 of the world's 13 largest hotels, each with thousands of rooms. North of Sahara Avenue, Las Vegas Boulevard enters the city of Las Vegas, the older and less glamorous part of town, although the city has embarked on a plan to renovate downtown. The 1st continues north for another dozen miles through the housing developments and scrubland that follow the diagonal U.S. 95 and Interstate 15, to include the sizable Hispanic and black communities of North Las Vegas. The 1st is home to the University of Nevada-Las Vegas and includes the Clark County Government Center, a circular sandstone complex built in the 1990s whose beautiful Indian-inspired architecture is a testament to the power of the gambling dollar.

The population of the 1st District is 12% black and 28% Hispanic; this is also one of the parts of the west with a high percentage of union members. Overall, this is a solidly Democratic district—Al Gore won 56% here in 2000.

The congresswoman from the 1st District is Shelley Berkley, a Democrat elected in 1998. Berkley moved to Las Vegas at 11; her father worked at the Sands and rose to maitre d'; she waited tables and was a keno runner as she made her way through the UNLV, where she was student body president, and the University of San Diego law school. "My roots in this community run very, very deep," she says, and she has worked for many of its major institutions. She chaired the Nevada Hotel and Motel Associations, was government and legal affairs vice president at the Sands and in-house counsel at Southwest Gas. She was elected to one term in the state House. In 1990, she was appointed to the University of Nevada Board of Regents and then elected to serve two more terms.

After the 1996 election, she decided to run for the House. Republican John Ensign had been reelected by only 50%–44% after spending $1.9 million. Ensign decided to run against Senator Harry Reid, and Berkley—brassy, direct, effusive—seemed headed for victory. Republicans lacked a serious candidate until filing day in May 1998; 15 minutes before the deadline, Judge Donald Chairez resigned his post and filed for the seat. Then in June came a bombshell. The *Las Vegas Review-Journal* reported on tapes of Berkley's May 1997 telephone conversations to a friend and texts of a memo Berkley sent the Sands's owner Sheldon Adelson when he was seeking approvals for his Venetian megahotel. They showed her advising him to make campaign contributions to local judges to curry favor and to grant concessions to Clark County commissioners to get their votes for approval. "Those suggestions were at best unethical and at worst illegal," said the Sands's President Bill Weidner, and Adelson fired Berkley. She quickly apologized; the Clark County district attorney saw no cause for prosecution. But Chairez made his slogan, "Fairness, not favors!" Berkley argued for affordable college tuition, adequate classrooms and computers. Both candidates supported the gaming industry and opposed the temporary nuclear storage site at Yucca Mountain. With strong support from the gaming industry, Berkley outspent Chairez by $1.2 million to $554,000. She won narrowly, by 49%–46%.

In the House, Berkley's voting record has been moderate. She keeps a close watch on the interests of the gaming industry. She led opposition to a proposal by the National Collegiate Athletic Association to bar Nevada casinos from accepting bets on college sports. With the state's bipartisan delegation, she unsuccessfully fought the plan to store nuclear waste at Yucca Mountain. In 2001, she voted for Republican proposals to repeal the marriage penalty and estate taxes. She co-sponsored with Representative Pat Toomey a proposal to reduce the regulatory burden on Medicare providers. She fought to return to a local woman seven paintings that she had done for Nazi doctor Josef Mengele in the Auschwitz concentration camp and that later were taken by a Polish museum. Berkley forcefully backed George W. Bush on the use of force in Iraq.

Berkley has had tough re-election campaigns. In 2000, state senator Jon Porter revived the 1998 controversy by attacking her for failing to apologize for her conversations and notes to Adelson. After Berkley said that the state's prescription drug plan "crashed and burned," Governor Kenny Guinn said that he would do everything he could to defeat her. She refused Porter's demand to apologize to Guinn. Both candidates spent heavily on ads, with Porter helped by additional spending by pharmaceutical firms. Berkley won 52%–44%. In 2002, Republicans nominated Las Vegas Councilwoman Lynette Boggs McDonald, a former Miss Oregon and former Democrat, who hoped to become the first Republican black woman elected to the House. Boggs McDonald was well-funded, including strong support from anti-abortion groups, and she attacked Berkley for voting for spending bills that included money for the Yucca Mountain repository. But redistricting had reduced the size of the district, removing many suburban precincts, and Berkley won 54%–43%.

SECOND DISTRICT

Rep. Jim Gibbons (R)

Elected 1996, 4th term; b. Dec. 16, 1944, Sparks; home, Reno; U. of NV, B.S. 1967, M.S. 1973; Southwestern U., J.D. 1979; Mormon; married (Dawn).

Military Career: Air Force, 1967–71 (Vietnam), NV Air Natl. Guard, 1975–96 (Persian Gulf).

Elected Office: NV Assembly, 1988–94.

Professional Career: Pilot, Western Airlines, 1979–87, Delta Airlines, 1987–96.

DC Office: 100 CHOB 20515, 202-225-6155; Fax: 202-225-5679; Web site: www.house.gov/gibbons.

District Offices: Elko, 775-777-7920; Las Vegas, 702-255-1651; Reno, 775-686-5760.

Committees: *Armed Services* (13th of 33 R): Tactical Air & Land Forces; Terrorism, Unconventional Threats & Capabilities. *Permanent Select Committee on Intelligence* (4th of 11 R): Human Intelligence, Analysis & Counterintelligence (Chmn.); Technical & Tactical Intelligence; Terrorism and Homeland Security. *Resources* (Vice Chmn. of 28 R): Energy & Mineral Resources; National Parks, Recreation & Public Lands. *Select Committee on Homeland Security* (24th of 27 R): Cybersecurity, Science and Research & Development; Emergency Preparedness & Response; Intelligence & Counterterrorism (Chmn.).

Group Ratings

	ADA	ACLU	AFS	LCV	CON	ITIC	NTU	COC	ACU	NTLC	CHC
2002	5	7	0	25	58	100	59	90	92	89	92
2001	5	—	10	0	—	—	67	96	96	—	—

National Journal Ratings

	2001 LIB	—	2001 CONS		2002 LIB	—	2002 CONS
Economic	32%	—	68%		9%	—	87%
Social	20%	—	69%		39%	—	57%
Foreign	4%	—	87%		15%	—	78%

Key Votes of the 107th Congress

1. Approve Bush Tax Cuts	Y	5. Faith-Based Charities	Y	9. Trade Promotion Authority	Y
2. Limit Patients' Bill of Rights	Y	6. Bar Gays in the Boy Scouts	Y	10. Bar Funds for Intl. Court	Y
3. Campaign Finance Reform	N	7. Ban Partial-Birth Abortion	Y	11. Authorize Force in Iraq	Y
4. Ban ANWR Development	N	8. Arm Commercial Pilots	N	12. Deny Home. Sec. Dept. Union	Y

Election Results

2002 general	Jim Gibbons (R)	149,574	(74%)	($624,322)
	Travis Souza (D)	40,189	(20%)	($13,376)
	Janine Hansen (IAP)	7,240	(4%)	
	Other	4,197	(2%)	
2002 primary	Jim Gibbons (R)	unopposed		
2000 general	Jim Gibbons (R)	229,608	(65%)	($320,019)
	Tierney Cahill (D)	106,379	(30%)	
	Other	19,982	(6%)	

Prior Winning Percentages: 1998 (81%); 1996 (59%)

The People		Race/Ethnic Origin	Ancestry	
Area size:	105,635 sq. mi.	74.8% White	German: 12.8%	Irish: 9.7%
Urban population:	78.5%	2.4% Black	English: 9.6%	
Rural population:	21.5%	2.8% Asian	**2000 Presidential Vote**	
Pop. 2000:	666,087	2.1% Native Am.	Bush (R)..............134,540 (57%)	
Median income:	$43,879	0.3% Hawaiian	Gore (D)...............87,705 (37%)	
Poverty status:	10.1%	2.1% Two+ races	Other....................12,493 (5%)	
Military veterans:	17.1%	0.1% Other	**Cook Partisan Voting Index:** R +11	
		15.3% Hispanic Origin		

Occupation	Blue collar: 24.3%	White collar: 54.9%	Gray collar: 20.9%

Outside of metro Las Vegas, Nevada has only one sizable population cluster, located much further north near the border with California—the casino cities of Reno and Sparks; the small capital of Carson City; the restored Comstock Lode boomtown of Virginia City and the resort areas that surround (and endanger) the deep, impossibly blue waters of Lake Tahoe. Reno is so remote from Las Vegas that the only practical way to get there is by air; it takes more than nine hours to drive, eight of which are on two-lane highways that pass through just a handful of towns, none bigger than 7,000 people. Ghost towns that once bustled with miners dot the parched, sandswept deserts of Nevada; in some places, these lands remain distinctly rutted from the wagon trains that crossed them more than 100 years ago. Today these towns survive on mining, ranching and in some cases, servicing the human sins of greed and lust (Nevada's small counties have legal brothels, though the famous Mustang Ranch near Reno was shuttered over tax charges in 1999). Only a few roads span this huge, empty, mountainous state; the lifelines that enable this empty territory to hang on. Immigrant Basque shepherds once tended their flocks in remote portions of northern Nevada and made carvings on Aspen trees to pass the time; today, Basque festivals, social clubs and restaurants can be found in such towns as Winnemucca, Ely and Elko, while Reno is home to the national sheepherder's monument and the nation's only Basque Studies Department, at the University of Nevada-Reno.

The military has vast holdings in the Nevada interior: the Fallon Naval Air Station, home to the Navy Fighter Weapons ("Top Gun") School; the 3.1 million-acre Nellis Air Force Gunnery Range; and the Energy Department's Nevada Test Site, where more than 800 underground tests of nuclear weapons were held, plus 100 above-ground tests, all before July 1962. These explosions have left the Rhode Island-sized facility pockmarked with unstable "subsidence craters" as far as they eye can see. Many places in Nevada are dependent on other federal government programs: the Newlands Irrigation Project near Fallon was among the first projects of its kind, and Nevada's gold mining operations, booming since 2000, do not have to pay royalties to the federal government thanks to the Mining Act of 1872. Some 87% of the land in Nevada is owned by the federal government—a constant source of tension with local officials, ranchers, loggers and miners, whose pursuits, frequently solitary and often ornery, shaped Nevada's culture from its earliest days. On the desolate frontier, speculation runs wild: Until recently, Art Bell broadcast his popular radio show about the paranormal, aliens and other unexplained phenomena from tiny Pahrump, while the government's top-secret aviation experiments at places like Area 51 on the Nellis Gunnery Range, conjectured about in the 1996 box office hit *Independence Day,* have stoked UFO lore to the point that adjoining Route 375 was rededicated as the Extraterrestrial Highway in 1996. Anti-establishment views also flourish here in more mainstream ways. Nevada residents have long opposed a nuclear waste repository 1,000 feet beneath Yucca Mountain, 90 miles northwest of Las Vegas. Congress finally approved the project in 2002, with a scheduled opening of 2010, but opponents vowed to continue their battle.

The 2d Congressional District takes in all of this and the vast majority of Nevada's land territory. Excluding single member at-large states, this is the largest congressional district in the nation. When the 2000 Census results came in, the 2d District, within its then-boundaries, was the fastest-growing district in the nation, primarily because of enormous growth in Las Vegas's Clark County. But Nevada's population gains meant that reapportionment granted it a third congressional district. Two districts were created entirely within Clark County, which has 69% of the state's population; the 2d consisted of all the other counties, plus areas in Clark County that had only 44,000 people in 2000. About one-half of the 2d's population is in Washoe County, which contains Reno and Sparks. Half a century ago, Reno was Nevada's largest city ("the Biggest Little City in the World"); it has grown vastly, but vastly less than Las Vegas, and is now overshadowed by it. Its growth has been matched and more by the growth around Lake Tahoe just to the west. People here are not from Nevada, but from all over: the Tahoe communities of Stateline, Zephyr Cove and Incline Village, were three of the top eight American cities with the smallest percentage of residents born in the state.

Historically, Reno has always been Republican and Las Vegas Democratic. In the 1990s, when the federal government was widely viewed as unfriendly to mining, grazing and timber interests, the Cow Counties, as the counties outside Reno and Las Vegas are called, became even more Republican. All that has made the 2d District very heavily Republican.

The congressman from the 2d District is Jim Gibbons, a Republican first elected in 1996. Gibbons grew up in Sparks, next door to Reno, went to the University of Nevada and served in the Air Force in Vietnam. He went to law school and has practiced law, but he also was a mining geologist, a hydrologist, a pilot for Delta and Western Airlines and became vice commander of the Nevada Air National Guard. In 1988 he was elected to the Assembly; in 1990 he was called up to active duty in the Gulf War. While he was flying unarmed air reconnaissance missions of enemy targets in Kuwait, his wife took his place in the legislature. After his celebrated return, he proposed a ballot initiative to require a two-thirds supermajority to raise any state tax; it passed with more than 70% of the votes in 1994 and became law, with serious consequences in 2003 as Republican Governor Kenny Guinn sought a big tax increase. In 1994, Gibbons ran for governor. He beat Secretary of State Cheryl Lau 52%–32% in the primary, but lost the general to Democratic incumbent Bob Miller, 53%–41%.

In 1996, after Congresswoman Barbara Vucanovich retired, Gibbons ran in the 2d District. He had serious competition in the primary from Lau and Patty Cafferata, a former state treasurer (and Vucanovich's daughter). Gibbons carried the Reno area and Las Vegas suburbs to win with 42%, to 24% each for Lau and Cafferata. In the Democratic primary, former state senator Spike Wilson beat former Mustang Ranch brothel worker Jessi Winchester 62%–21%. Gibbons won the general, 59%–35%.

Gibbons opposes federal intrusion on local rights. In November 2002, George W. Bush signed his bill to create the Sloan Canyon National Conservation Area south of Henderson and broaden local input in federal land policies. His independence often has left him voting against Republican dogma and placed him toward the center of the House on cultural issues. He strongly opposed the nuclear repository at Yucca Mountain and the proposed temporary storage site at the Nevada Test Site. Despite their frequent conflicts, he joined Shelley Berkley in urging the Bush administration to move from the Justice Department to the Labor Department control of the program to compensate workers who were exposed to radiation at nuclear weapons plants. He bucked his party leadership by opposing PNTR with China but he voted for trade promotion authority.

Gibbons has been reelected easily. After the 2002 election, he unsuccessfully sought a seat on the Appropriations Committee. In December 2002 White House political strategist Karl Rove, like Gibbons a graduate of Sparks High School, tried to talk him into running against Senator Harry Reid in 2004; Gibbons said he would not make a decision until summer 2003.

THIRD DISTRICT

Rep. Jon Porter (R)

Elected 2002, 1st term; b. May 16, 1955, Ft. Dodge, IA; home, Henderson; Attended Briar Cliff College, 1974–78.; Catholic; married (Laurie).

Elected Office: Boulder City Cncl., 1983–93; Boulder City Mayor, 1987–91; NV Senate, 1994–02.

Professional Career: Indep. contractor, Farmers Insurance Group Corp., 1982–00.

DC Office: 218 CHOB 20515, 202-225-3252; Fax: 202-225-2185; Web site: www.house.gov/porter.

District Office: Henderson, 702-387-4941.

Committees: *Education & the Workforce* (21st of 27 R): 21st Century Competitiveness; Select Education (Vice Chmn.). *Transportation & Infrastructure* (41st of 41 R): Aviation; Railroads (Vice Chmn.).

Group Ratings and Key Votes: Newly Elected

Election Results

2002 general	Jon Porter (R)	100,378	(56%)	($1,916,277)
	Dario Herrera (D)	66,659	(37%)	($1,809,383)
	Pete O'Neil (I)	6,842	(4%)	($11,560)
	Other	5,115	(3%)	
2002 primary	Jon Porter (R)	25,446	(69%)	
	Barry Bilbray (R)	6,179	(17%)	
	Susan Kiger (R)	3,407	(9%)	
	Bob Daily (R)	2,052	(6%)	

The People		**Race/Ethnic Origin**	**Ancestry**	
Area size:	4,749 sq. mi.	69.3% White	German: 11.1%	Irish: 8.7%
Urban population:	96.3%	5.5% Black	English: 7.7%	
Rural population:	3.7%	5.9% Asian	**2000 Presidential Vote**	
Pop. 2000:	666,082	0.5% Native Am.	Gore (D) 104,772	(49%)
Median income:	$50,749	0.4% Hawaiian	Bush (R) 103,720	(48%)
Poverty status:	7.5%	2.7% Two + races	Other 6,119	(3%)
Military veterans:	16.4%	0.1% Other	**Cook Partisan Voting Index:** X + 00	
		15.6% Hispanic Origin		

Occupation	Blue collar: 18.4%	White collar: 56.8%	Gray collar: 24.8%

Las Vegas means The Meadows, and was the name of a place on the Old Spanish Trail from Santa Fe to California. In the early 20th century it was one of the terminuses of the Las Vegas & Tonopah Railroad, a link to Nevada's silver mines. Even at the end of the 1930s, when gambling was legalized in Nevada, Las Vegas was still a town of less than 10,000. Then came decades of amazing growth, as Las Vegas became America's greatest center of gambling and one of its greatest centers of entertainment; it grew to a metropolitan area of 1.6 million people by 2000. For the last 15 years, Las Vegas has been the fastest-growing metropolitan area in America—up 85% in the 1990s. It is still frontier country, one of the few places in the nation with more men than women. Las Vegas has spread from the few blocks around Fremont Street that it occupied in the 1930s all across the bleak desert, in every direction. It is an exuberant, undisciplined and chaotic American city, within its pattern of grid-street mile roads all manner of curved-street subdivisions and gated communities, an America uncontrolled by traditional elites.

The 3d Congressional District is a Y-shaped segment of Nevada's Clark County made up of most of the suburbs of Las Vegas. It includes the south end of the Las Vegas Strip, off South Las Vegas Boulevard, and McCarran International Airport, and spreads west, northeast and south. It includes active retiree communities, blue-collar communities such as Blue Diamond that still have a rural flavor and a variety of planned (and often gated) communities like Summerlin that cater to young families drawn by the job opportunities. Southeast of Las Vegas, the district takes in two additional population hubs: Henderson, the fastest-growing city in the United States in the 1990s, and Boulder City, originally built for federal workers at Hoover Dam (Boulder City, under an old agreement with the federal government, is the only place in Nevada where gambling is prohibited). The 3d includes the Nevada halves of Lake Mead and Lake Mohave, on the border of Arizona, and state's southernmost tip including Searchlight (hometown of Senator Harry Reid) and Laughlin, right across the Colorado River from Bullhead City, Arizona.

The 3d District is a creature of redistricting, drawn after Nevada won a third congressional district from the 2000 Census. The lines were drawn so that the new district would have almost a precisely equal number of registered Democrats and registered Republicans. Clark County historically was the most Democratic part of Nevada, but the newcomers attracted to the state in the 1990s have been tilted toward Republicans; the result is this closely divided district.

The congressman from the new 3d District is Jon Porter, a Republican elected in 2002. He grew up in Humboldt, Iowa, and attended Briar Cliff College in Sioux City. After moving to Nevada, he managed an office with more than 40 agents for the Farmers Insurance Group. He was elected mayor of Boulder City in 1987 and in 1994 won election to the state Senate, where he earned a reputation as a consensus-building moderate. An abortion opponent, he sponsored bills addressing growth management, education reform and victims rights. His legislation to streamline the state child adoption process increased the number of public adoptions in the state by 50%. He secured funding for 18-year-olds leaving foster care to assist them in living on their own.

In 2000 he ran against Democratic Congresswoman Shelley Berkley in the 1st District, attacking her for her controversial communications to a hotel owner who was seeking approvals for another hotel; he lost 52%–44%. When the new district lines were adopted in June 2001, Porter, as expected by many insiders, proceeded to run in the new 3d District. But Democrats were enthusiastic about their political *wunderkind* candidate, 28-year-old Clark County Commissioner Dario Herrera, who seemed to have the political skills and savvy that could make him in time a major statewide politician. This was one of three new, highly-competitive Mountain West districts—the other two were the Arizona 1st and the Colorado 7th— created after reapportionment; these seats seemed equally divided between the two parties, which gave Democrats the hope of pickups in states where they had been on the defensive.

But Herrera turned out to have serious problems. He spent the election season defending himself against a spate of charges over alleged ethics violations—such as his winning a no-bid consulting deal and taking a questionable loan. Herrera's ethics problems led the Nevada Conference of Police and Sheriffs to rescind its earlier endorsement of him. In turn, he sought to discredit Porter on the grounds that as an insurance agent he was furthering his own interests in restricting recoveries for medical malpractice, a raging issue in Nevada. Though both candidates strongly opposed shipping the nation's nuclear waste to the nearby Yucca Mountain site, Herrera attacked Porter for accepting contributions from House Republicans who supported the Nevada nuclear waste repository. Herrera also criticized Porter for supporting "privatization" of Social Security. Porter, who supported individual investment accounts in 2000, retreated from that position but said that he would "always look at alternatives."

It turned out to be no contest. Porter won by a 56%–37% margin, running far ahead of party lines—or perhaps it was Herrera running far behind party lines. Herrera seemed little interested in running again, but Democrats continued to hold out hope to recruit a serious challenger for 2004.

★ NEW HAMPSHIRE ★

N ew Hampshire, in an odd corner of the country, with four-tenths of 1% of the nation's population, with unusual public policies, becomes every four years the epicenter of the political universe, the site where the contest for the presidency of the most powerful nation in the history of the world is temporarily centered, where every vote is avidly sought and where members of the political press vie for access to candidates and for tables at the latest cycle's most fashionable bars and restaurants. New Hampshire has done much to change the political world— not just the United States, but the entire world: It gave a huge boost to Dwight Eisenhower's candidacy in 1952, it prompted the retirement of Lyndon Johnson in 1968, it sent on his way to power first Jimmy Carter in 1976, then Ronald Reagan in 1980 and George H. W. Bush in 1988. The lever by which this small state moves the world is New Hampshire's first-in-the-nation presidential primary, first seriously contested in 1952, then sanctioned as the first-in-the-nation primary by Democratic rules writers in the 1970s, and exploited by Republicans in the 1980s. And New Hampshire did all this when its public policies were atypical of the nation and its political terrain unusual if not eccentric. This is one of the few states that over the last half century has had more registered Republicans than Democrats, and of all the states this has been arguably the one with the most antipathy to taxes. Yet in the last dozen years, New Hampshire has changed. The last two presidents have both lost the New Hampshire primary, though Bill Clinton avoided the sting of defeat by proclaiming himself "the comeback kid" on primary night and George W. Bush recovered quickly enough to win decisively in South Carolina. By giving Patrick Buchanan 37% of the vote in the 1992 primary and 27% in the1996 primary, it gave the impression that Buchanan was a serious candidate, but he never ran as well elsewhere and has disappeared from Republican politics. New Hampshire, once a trendsetter, is in danger of being regarded as eccentric.

New Hampshire's distinctiveness started early. In a country that prides itself on its feistiness and freedom from outside direction, it has always been even feistier and less fettered by authority. Before the Revolutionary War, New Hampshire was almost an outlaw colony, its great fortunes made by poachers in the king's forests and smugglers avoiding taxes. It was the first colony with an independent government and was fighting the British before the Minutemen stood at Lexington and Concord. In this environment, 19th century entrepreneurs built textile mills along fast-flowing rivers; the Amoskeag Mills in Manchester, lining the Merrimack River for a mile, were once the largest cotton mills on the globe, employing 17,000 people and producing enough cloth every two months to put a band around the world. Around the mills grew a city of red brick dormitories and three-family frame houses filled with immigrants from Quebec, Ireland, Poland and Greece, set down amid dirt-roaded villages of flinty Yankee farmers and mechanics. New Hampshire held to its traditions of local government and little external control, and for years its refusal to join most other states and enact an income or sales tax, or to provide statewide guidance of schools and social services, seemed to doom it to continued backwardness.

Instead low taxes proved to be New Hampshire's fortune. Starting in the 1960s, New Hampshire has had the fastest growth in the Northeast, attracting businesses from Massachusetts and other high-tax states. It became a location of choice for entrepreneurs and high-tech innovators, attracting an increasing number of people skeptical of government programs. From 1965–2000, Massachusetts grew from 5.5 million to 6.3 million, up 15%; New Hampshire grew from 676,000 to 1,236,000, up 83%. The bedraggled New Hampshire of 50 years ago, of poor Yankee farmers and French Canadian mill hands, has largely disappeared, and in its place one of the nation's most prosperous economic communities has arisen. The low taxes that spurred New Hampshire's growth would probably have been raised in the late 1960s or early 1970s, as they were in so many states at the time, but for the far from gentle advocacy of the Manchester *Union Leader* and its owner William Loeb. The *Union Leader* insisted that governors and legislators "take the pledge" to vote for no sales or income tax and, from 1970 to 1998, almost all did, and the two who didn't were defeated. That meant keeping education and welfare as local responsibilities and holding down spending. At the same time, New Hampshire boasted the highest SAT scores in the country

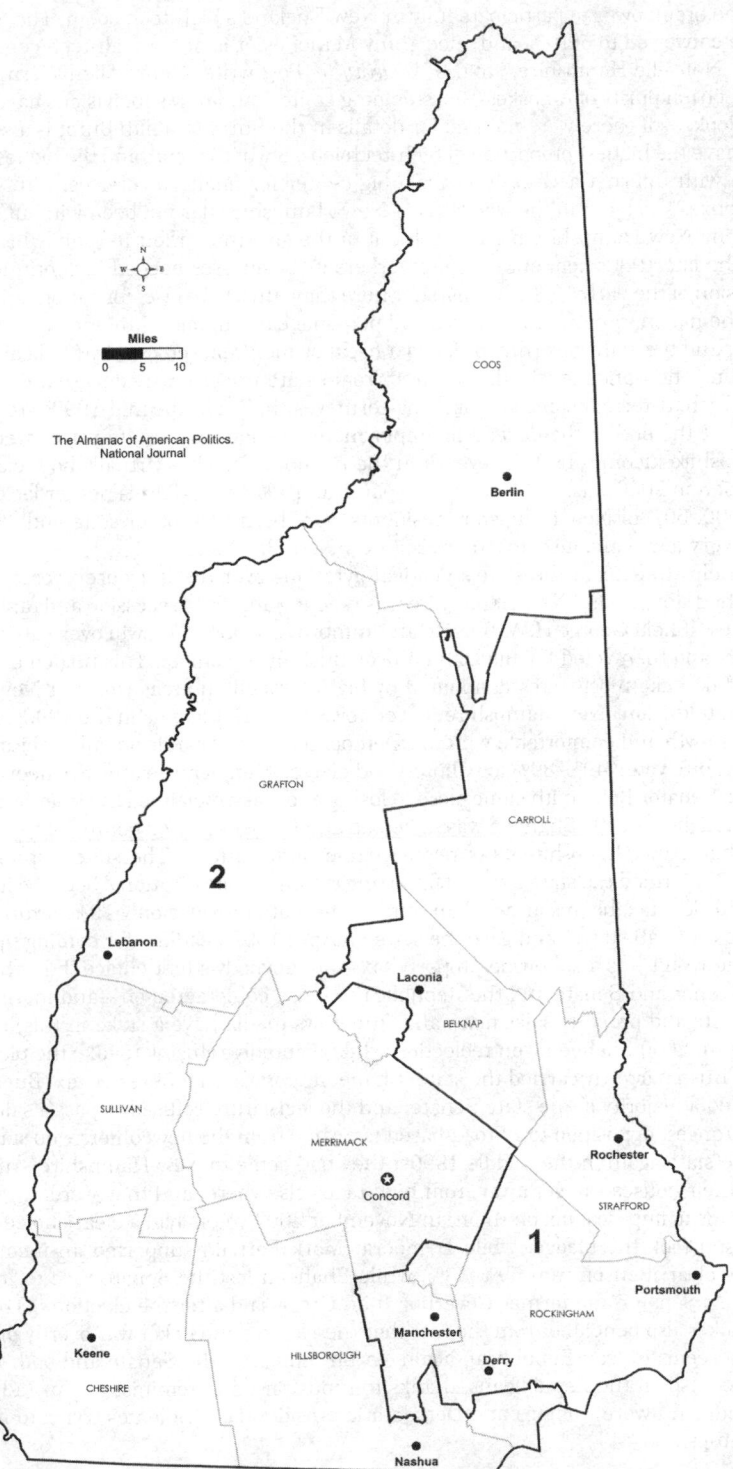

COOS

● Berlin

GRAFTON

CARROLL

2

● Lebanon

Laconia ●

BELKNAP

SULLIVAN

MERRIMACK

Rochester ●

✪
Concord

STRAFFORD

1

Portsmouth ●

ROCKINGHAM

Manchester ●

● Keene

HILLSBOROUGH

Derry ●

CHESHIRE

Nashua ●

Miles
0   5   10

N
W + E
S

The Almanac of American Politics.
National Journal

Congressional district boundaries were first effective for 2002.

and had the brainpower to participate fully in New England's high-tech boom. The old Amoskeag Mills were converted to offices, and once grimy Manchester is now a high-tech center.

This "Nouvelle Hampshire," to use *Washington Post* writer Henry Allen's term, has none of the architectural purity of Amoskeag. Its shopping centers and new subdivisions have a slap-dash, half-built look, as if there were no time for details in the hurry to build. But it is also a state that claims to have the highest proportion of high-tech jobs, 8% of the total, and the highest percentage of citizens with Internet access. It also is a big center for financial services, with giant mutual fund campuses stuck out in the woods. This New Hampshire has not been without its problems. The booming New Hampshire priced itself out of the growth market: Its giddily high real estate prices in the late 1980s kept out the new workers its businesses needed to continue expanding. The recession of the early 1990s was harsher here than anywhere else: for a moment New Hampshire led the nation in new welfare cases and personal bankruptcies; property taxes doubled over four years, and the state government faced a fiscal crunch relieved only by Medicaid accounting legerdemain. Thousands of jobs disappeared; real estate prices crashed so that ordinary people lost not only short-term income but also long-term wealth. But by the mid-1990s growth returned again, and at the end of the decade unemployment was low, real estate prices were rising and New Hampshire incomes ranked seventh in the nation. It also has virtually no racial minorities; its population in 2000 was 1% black, 2% Hispanic and 1% Asian. This is not for lack of in-migration: in 2000, 50% of New Hampshire residents were born in another state and 4% in another country. Every few years, it seems, there is a new New Hampshire.

This helps to explain the state's political gyrations over the last dozen years. By 1992 in-migration had stopped and New Hampshire was reacting angrily to recession and rapidly declining house prices. It held George H.W. Bush to an unimpressive 53%–37% win over Patrick Buchanan in February and then voted for Bill Clinton over Bush in November. This turned out not to be a one-time fluke; like most states dominated by big metropolitan areas (most of New Hampshire gets Boston television) New Hampshire moved toward the Democrats in the 1990s, reassured by economic growth and comfortable with the Democrats' liberal stands on cultural issues. In 1996 New Hampshire voted 49%–39% for Clinton and elected Democrat Jeanne Shaheen as governor; Republican Senator Bob Smith came close to losing and was proclaimed the loser by the networks on election night. In 1998 Shaheen was reelected and Democrats won control of the state Senate.

But then New Hampshire's tax regime came under attack. The state Supreme Court in December 1997 ruled the state's school financing system unconstitutional because it leaves some districts with less taxable resources than others (the state provides only 10% of funding, far less than in the other 49 states) and gave the state an April 1999 deadline for coming up with a new system. The result was a statewide property tax—not anybody's first choice, but what the Democratic governor and Senate and the Republican House could agree on—and increases in business, cigarette and property sales taxes and (the news media have a stake in this) a new tax on rental cars. In 2000 Shaheen won reelection while pointedly refusing to take the pledge, even as George W. Bush narrowly carried the state. Shaheen proposed a 2.5% sales tax. But Republicans had regained a majority in the state Senate, and the legislature refused to pass a sales or income tax. The strongest opposition to a broad-based tax came from the newcomers who started streaming into the state again in the middle 1990s; they had come to New Hampshire—and paid high prices for their houses—to get away from high taxes elsewhere, and they weren't going to allow the politicians to impose a tax on them. In November 2002 voters had a clear choice: Republican Craig Benson took the pledge, while Democrat Mark Fernald supported an income tax. The verdict was clear: Benson won 59%–38%, while Shaheen lost the Senate race to John Sununu 51%–46%. As Senator and former Governor Judd Gregg said after the election, "The entire Republican ticket also benefited from the fact that the Democratic ticket was overtly pro-tax." New Hampshire seems to lean Republican again—even though in the Senate and both House races Democrats outspent the Republicans, thanks to funds raised by feminist groups (all three Democratic candidates were women) and Democratic presidential candidates trying to make friends in New Hampshire.

The People		Race/Ethnic Origin			Military veterans: 139,038 (15.0%)	
Pop. 2000:	1,235,786	1,175,252	95.1%	White	WWII: 18.4%	Korea: 13.6%
Pop. 1990:	1,109,252	8,354	0.7%	Black	Vietnam: 33.6%	Gulf War: 8.2%
Change 1990–2000:	Up 11.4%	15,803	1.3%	Asian	**Most populous cities:**	
Change 1980–1990:	Up 20.5%	2,698	0.2%	Native Am.	1. Manchester	107,006
% of U.S. total:	0.4%	330	0.0%	Hawaiian	2. Nashua	86,605
Pop. rank:	41st of 50	11,606	0.9%	Two+ races	3. Concord	40,687
Area size:	9,350 sq. mi.	1,254	0.1%	Other	4. Rochester	28,461
State Native:	43.3%	20,489	1.7%	Hisp. Origin	5. Dover	26,884
Non-citizen:	2.3%	**Ancestry**			Urban population: 59.2%	
Language		Irish: 13.8%		English: 12.8%	Rural population: 40.8%	
English: 87.4%	Other Eur.: 9.0%	French: 10.4%		Fr. Canadian: 7.3%		
Spanish: 2.3%		German: 6.1%				

Education		Work Sector		General Court	
H.S. Grad:	87.4%	Private: 79.4%	Govt: 12.8%	Senate	18 R 6 D
College Grad:	28.7%	Self: 7.6%	Family: 0.2%	House	281 R 119 D
Industry		Unemployment: 3.8%		Legislative Term Limits: No	
Agri: 0.9%	Con: 6.8%	**Household Income**		**Registered Voters**	
Fin: 6.3%	Info: 2.7%	<15k: 10.8%	15-35k: 22.4%	D: 176,634 (25.6%)	
Mfg: 22.2%	Prof: 28.8%	35-50k: 17.2%	50-100k: 35.7%	R: 253,504 (36.7%)	
Public: 3.8%	Trade: 17.3%	100-150k: 9.1%	>150k: 4.7%	I: 260,021 (37.7%)	
Other: 11.2%		Median: $49,467			
Occupation		Poverty status: 6.5%			
Blue collar: 24.1%	White collar: 62.4%	**Home Value**			
Gray collar: 13.4%		<50k: 7.7% 50-100k: 24.8% 100-200k: 49.3% 200-300k: 12.2%			
		300-500k: 4.5% >500k: 1.4% Median: $127,500			

Presidential politics   Since 1920, New Hampshire has held the first-in-the-nation primary, and since 1952, when candidates' names were first put on the ballot, it has had extraordinary influence on the presidential selection process—a fact that will surely strike future political scientists as bizarre. To be sure, there are arguments for having early contests in small states that provide a venue for "retail politics," in which candidates meet voters in person, listen and talk to them, exchange ideas and allow them to gauge their character. In-person contact was one of the things that saved Bill Clinton in 1992, after the Gennifer Flowers charges, and John McCain's jam-packed town meetings showed a moving rapport between candidate and voter. New Hampshire is small enough physically (unlike Iowa) that candidates can efficiently meet voters; everything except the lightly populated North Country is within an hour's drive of Manchester, and for all the state's abstract dislike of government, New Hampshire does an excellent job of keeping its roads clear of snow. New Hampshire's retail politics offers little-known candidates the ability to propel themselves into the national spotlight, though over the last 20 years none of those candidates—

2000 Presidential Vote
Bush (R) 273,559   (48%)
Gore (D) 266,348   (47%)
Nader (Green) 22,188   (4%)
Other 5,700   (1%)

2000 Republican Presidential Primary
McCain (R) 115,606   (49%)
Bush (R) 72,330   (30%)
Forbes (R) 30,166   (13%)
Keyes (R) 15,179   (6%)
Other 4,925   (2%)

2000 Democratic Presidential Primary
Gore (D) 76,897   (50%)
Bradley (D) 70,502   (46%)
Other 7,240   (5%)

1996 Presidential Vote
Clinton (D) 246,166   (49%)
Dole (R) 196,486   (39%)
Perot (I) 48,387   (10%)
Other 8,014   (2%)

Gary Hart in 1984, Paul Tsongas and Patrick Buchanan in 1992, McCain in 2000—has gone on to win their party's nominations. The last to do so were George McGovern and Jimmy Carter in the 1970s.

In any case, New Hampshire retains its first-in-the-nation status not on its merits but because of threats. Democrats tried in the 1970s to confine primaries to a "window" period in which New Hampshire would have competition. But New Hampshire, with its outlaw tradition, insisted it would hold its primary before the window if necessary, confident that candidates and reporters would pay it heed even if its tiny delegation were threatened with not being seated at the national convention. Republicans made no such rules, but in 1996 let Iowa Governor Terry Branstad and New Hampshire Governor Steve Merrill, both Republicans, threaten voter retaliation against candidates who took part in caucuses or primaries held before their states' or even during the week afterwards. Democratic Governor Jeanne Shaheen continued the tradition in December 1998, demanding candidates take a pledge not to participate in such contests. In 2000 the Democrats imposed a *five-week* window of no contests after New Hampshire, which made Al Gore's 50%–46% victory here decisive; Bill Bradley's candidacy effectively died through inattention before he could reach Super Tuesday. Fortunately for George W. Bush, the *laissez faire* Republicans did not restrict other states as much as the rule-bound Democrats, and he could recover 19 days later in South Carolina. John McCain's smashing 49%–30% victory here knocked the wind out of the Bush campaign for about a week, but it turned out to be a template not for contests in other states, but for other contests in New England. Only there did registered and self-identified Republicans, as in New Hampshire, prefer McCain to Bush, and in Arizona (his home state) and Michigan (where 20% of voters were self-identified Democrats and 35% self-identified independents) was McCain able to duplicate his New Hampshire victory beyond the bounds of New England. In 2003, the Michigan Democratic Party, led by Senator Carl Levin, attempted to challenge New Hampshire's first-in-the nation status by moving the 2004 Michigan Democratic caucuses to the same January date as New Hampshire's; after a noisy debate, the Michigan Democratic State Central Committee backed down and voted to hold their caucuses in February.

A word should be said about New Hampshire media. The Manchester *Union Leader* has one of the nation's sharpest conservative tongues. Its editorials, even now after the deaths of William Loeb and his widow Nackey, scold Republicans who stray from its gospel. Its insistence that politicians take the anti-tax pledge for years set the course for New Hampshire state politics and government. But the *Union Leader* cannot automatically deliver votes on primary day—its great favorite, Patrick Buchanan, won just 27% of the vote in 1996—and its news coverage is more objective than that of many left-leaning national media outlets. New Hampshire's other great medium has been Manchester's WMUR-TV, Channel 9, which also provides tons of information to a winter-bound audience. Channel 9's rule is to cover every candidate every day he or she is in New Hampshire, allowing each to present views and make arguments without the overlay of opinionated commentary that national network reporters use; in 2000 the new WNDS, Channel 50, also based in New Hampshire, provided similar coverage.

New Hampshire is still one of the few states with more registered Republicans than Democrats—a fact of some significance for 2004, when Democrats anticipate a seriously contested primary and Republicans, for the first time in 20 years, no contest at all. Many New Hampshire voters don't bother to register in a party, and only 26% of all voters are registered Democrats. It is possible to register as a Democrat on primary day, but still this is a relatively small electorate, and one probably tilted well to the left of the political spectrum. The Democratic bastions of the state are not its two largest cities, Manchester and Nashua, which usually vote Republican, but the state capital of Concord and clusters of towns around universities—the area around Durham (the University of New Hampshire) and Dover in southeast New Hampshire, the area around Keene (Keene State College) in the southwest and the area around Hanover (Dartmouth University). Once upon a time the typical Democratic primary voters here was a textile mill worker; now she is more likely to be an assistant professor.

Where New Hampshire proved crucial in 2000 was, surprisingly, in the general election. In 2000 New Hampshire and Maine were the two Northeastern states which the Bush and Gore campaigns targeted and where the candidates made forays from Middle America to campaign in. The result was exceedingly close, but outside of recount range: Bush won 48%–47%, with a popular vote margin of 7,211 votes, just a bit larger than the 6,395 votes by which Al Gore beat Bill Bradley. How Gore won that close primary and how Bush won that close general election—something few national reporters covered closely—turned out to be more crucial than how John

McCain, thronged by congenial reporters on his Straight Talk Express, established the rapport which gave him his impressive primary victory.

Congressional districting With only slight changes, New Hampshire's two congressional districts basically have had the same boundaries since 1881, neatly separating the Merrimack River mill towns of Manchester and Nashua, the state's largest cities. That was done originally to split the Catholic Democratic vote, but now both cities are high-tech Republican towns. If the split now gives Republicans an edge in both districts, it also gives Democrats a chance for upset victories in both. For 2002 the towns of Epsom and Pittsfield were moved from the 1st District to the 2d, an uncontroversial change which does not appreciably change the political balance in either district.

108th Congress Lineup
2 R
107th Congress Lineup
2 R

Governor

Craig Benson (R)

Elected 2002, term expires Jan. 2005, 1st term; b. Oct. 8, 1954, New York, NY; home, Rye; Babson Col., B.S. 1977; Syracuse U., M.B.A. 1979; Catholic; married (Denise).

Professional Career: President and CEO, Cabletron Systems, 1983–99.

Office: State House Rm. 208, 107 N. Main St., Concord, 03301, 603-271-2121; Fax: 603-271-2130; Web site: www.state.nh.us/governor.

Election Results

2002 general	Craig Benson (R)	259,663	(59%)
	Mark Fernald (D)	169,277	(38%)
	Other	14,036	(3%)
2002 primary	Craig Benson (R)	56,099	(37%)
	Bruce Keough (R)	51,461	(34%)
	Gordon Humphrey (R)	42,698	(28%)
	Other	2,214	(1%)
2000 general	Jeanne Shaheen (D)	275,038	(49%)
	Gordon Humphrey (R)	246,952	(44%)
	Mary Brown (I)	35,904	(6%)

Craig Benson, a Republican, was elected governor of New Hampshire in 2002 in his first run for political office. Benson grew up in Chatham, New Jersey, and graduated from Babson College in 1977 and Syracuse University business school in 1979. At that time Massachusetts was perhaps the biggest high-tech center in the country, and Benson went to work for Teradyne in Boston. In 1981 he switched to Inetlan in Chelmsford, near Lowell. In 1983 he and Robert Levine started Cabletron in Levine's garage in Ashland, west of Boston. Most of Massachusetts's high-tech energy was going into producing mainframes and minicomputers, systems sold to just one customer. Benson and Levine noted the suddenly surging sales of personal computers, and saw a need for custom cables to link personal computers. In 1985 Cabletron moved to an old mill building in Rochester, New Hampshire; one attraction was the fact that New Hampshire had no income or sales tax. With an aggressive sales force and a commitment to customer service, Cabletron grew rapidly. The company went public in 1989 and had huge growth in the early 1990s. In 1990 Benson challenged New Hampshire's Business Profits Tax in court and put $12 million in escrow, at a time when Cabletron accounted for 7% of total revenues.

Cabletron's culture has been described by the *Concord Monitor*: "Cabletron was the cowboy from New Hampshire, the up-from-nothing, reflexively contrarian street fighter—outwardly confident, secretly paranoid, dazzlingly inventive, surpassingly energetic, often crass, sometimes cruel, rewarding those who thrived, expelling those who didn't—for better and for worse." In 1994 a federal court jury ruled that Benson had discriminated against a woman employee; he denied the charge, and pointed out that 40% of Cabletron's managers were women. The high-tech business is volatile, and Cabletron's successes did not go on forever. In the middle 1990s Cabletron's biggest competitor was California-based Cisco. Cabletron had the edge in switches, but Cisco had an advantage in routers. But Cisco began buying up switching companies, leaving Cabletron at a competitive disadvantage; Cisco soon captured 90% of the computer networking market; the approach championed by Cabletron's chief technology guru, a non-college graduate whose products had worked brilliantly in the past, did not prevail in the marketplace. Cabletron's stock price plummeted in 1997 and 1998, Benson left the company in 1999 and in 2000 Cabletron was split into four separate companies. But Benson had sold enough of his Cabletron stock to accumulate a fortune estimated at $600 million when he decided to run for governor in 2002.

New Hampshire has never elected a governor to four two-year terms and Democratic incumbent Jeanne Shaheen, first elected in 1996, filed an exploratory committee for a Senate race in August 2001. The great issue of Shaheen's governorship was how state government would pay for the vastly increased state aid to local schools required by the state Supreme Court in December 1997 and whether the state would end its longtime tradition and enact a sales or income tax. Shaheen had taken the pledge not to support a sales or income tax in 1996 and 1998. Her veto threat blocked an income tax in April 1999 and in June 1999 the legislature adopted a statewide property tax instead. In 2000 Shaheen refused to take the pledge, and in 2001 she supported a 2.5% sales tax. But the legislature rejected that in April, and the statewide property tax remained and business taxes were increased.

This was the backdrop to what became New Hampshire's most expensive gubernatorial race ever. There were three Republican candidates who largely self-financed their campaigns; all took the pledge. There were two serious Democratic candidates who both backed an income tax. The fiercest contest was in the Republican primary. Benson set out a platform based on his high-tech experience: upgrade state government from Version 1.0, put in real world management practices, gives incentives for saving, encourage public-private partnerships. He said he would cap state education spending at about $900 million for five years; he argued that many towns used the state education money to free up other funds for other programs. He called for a constitutional amendment capping state government spending and requiring a two-thirds vote in the legislature for tax increases and a constitutional amendment to overturn the state Supreme Court's 1997 decision.

Another Republican, Gordon Humphrey, attacked Benson vigorously. Back in 1978 and 1984 Humphrey had been elected to the U.S. Senate, and in 1990 kept his term-limit promise and did not run again. Instead, he got elected to the state Senate where he opposed a sales or income tax. In 2000 he ran against Shaheen and lost by only a 49%–44% margin. He pledged to cut property taxes by 10% and attacked Benson relentlessly—for the 1994 lawsuit, for SEC investigations into the Cabletron spinoffs, for his campaign contributions to Democrats, including Shaheen. Also running was former state Senator Bruce Keough, former chairman of the board of trustees of the state university system. He called for targeting current state education aid at the neediest schools. He did not join in the vitriolic criticism of Benson. This was a race in which money talked. Benson spent $9.2 million on the primary campaign, $8.7 million of it his own. Humphrey spent $3.9 million, $3.7 million of it his own. Keough spent $1.9 million, virtually all of it his own. Just by himself Benson spent more than was spent by all candidates in both primary and general elections in the gubernatorial race in 2000. But the primary results were not proportionate to spending. Benson won, with just 37% of the vote. Keough, moving up late in the polls, was second with 34%. Humphrey, perhaps because of his negative campaigning—always risky in a multi-candidate race—was third with 28%. Turnout was huge: 152,000, far more than in any previous state primary.

Benson, the high-tech entrepreneur, is one type of New Hampshire character; Mark Fernald, the Democratic nominee, is another. Fernald grew up in a Yankee Republican family and took a job at his father's law firm doing estate planning and business law in 1988. As a private citizen he watched New Hampshire's fiscal struggle and decided he had found the solution: an income tax. In 1998, he ran for the state Senate as (to his father's surprise) a Democrat; he won and Democrats for the first time in years won a Senate majority. The state legislature seemed on the verge of passing an income tax, but was stopped by Governor Shaheen's veto threat; Fernald walked into Shaheen's office in December 1999 and announced he would run in the primary against her if she did not reconsider; when she didn't budge, he decided to run. He lost, but by only 61%–38%, a narrow margin in a primary against an incumbent governor, he carried the western part of the state and towns hit hard by the statewide property tax. In 2002 he ran for governor again. In the Democratic primary he faced state Senator Beverly Hollingworth, also an income tax backer. This was not a big money race like the Republican primary: Fernald spent $307,000, Hollingworth $287,000. Fernald won 56%–44%.

In the two-month general election campaign Fernald stuck doggedly to his advocacy of the income tax. He charged that Benson was responsible for the Business Enterprise Tax, enacted after his lawsuit against the Business Profits Tax, and argued that an income tax would permit property taxes to be cut in half. Benson cited his own experience for his opposition to an income tax: "When Cabletron moved here, we had 17 employees. If New Hampshire had an income tax, we would never have grown to 7,000. The reason we beat 300 competitors from other states, the reason we beat IBM, HP and Digital, was because we had an advantage, the New Hampshire advantage. Other companies had to account for the income tax in their employee compensation; they had higher labor costs. It made them less competitive." Media polls never showed the race close, and much more attention went to the close Senate race between Shaheen and John Sununu. Benson, who obviously could have spent much more, spent only $880,000 between the primary and the general; Fernald spent only $168,000. New Hampshire, after flirting with the Democratic party in the 1990s, seemed to return to its old Republican roots. Benson won 59%–38%. Fernald carried only the clusters of towns around the college towns of Durham, Keene and Hanover, plus the state capital of Concord, trendy Portsmouth and his home area around Peterborough.

Benson promised to sign many of the bills Shaheen vetoed and to keep state education spending at $904 million. He called for public school choice and accountability in education. "I want to make sure every student and every teacher is measured for progress. I don't see how you can figure out whether we're doing well or poorly if you don't measure it."

Senior Senator

Judd Gregg (R)

Elected 1992, seat up 2004, 2d term; b. Feb. 14, 1947, Nashua; home, Rye; Columbia U., A.B. 1969, Boston U., J.D. 1972, LL.M. 1975; Protestant; married (Kathleen).

Elected Office: NH Exec. Cncl., 1978–80; U.S. House of Reps., 1980–88; NH Gov., 1988–92.

Professional Career: Practicing atty., 1976–80.

DC Office: 393 RSOB, 20510, 202-224-3324; Fax: 202-224-4952; Web site: gregg.senate.gov.

State Offices: Berlin, 603-752-2604; Concord, 603-225-7115; Manchester, 603-622-7979; Portsmouth, 603-431-2171.

Committees: *Appropriations*: Commerce, Justice, State & Judiciary (Chmn.); Defense; Foreign Operations; Homeland Security; Interior; Labor, HHS & Education. *Budget. Health, Education, Labor & Pensions* (Chmn.).

Group Ratings

	ADA	ACLU	AFS	LCV	CON	ITIC	NTU	COC	ACU	NTLC	CHC
2002	10	20	0	53	97	75	59	100	85	97	—
2001	0	—	8	25	—	—	85	100	88	—	100

National Journal Ratings

	2001 LIB	—	2001 CONS		2002 LIB	—	2002 CONS
Economic	35%	—	62%		39%	—	60%
Social	0%	—	79%		0%	—	62%
Foreign	30%	—	65%		24%	—	67%

Key Votes of the 107th Congress

1. Approve Bush Tax Cuts	Y	5. Confirm Ashcroft as AG	Y	9. Bar Coop. with Intl. Court	Y
2. Expand Patients' Rights	N	6. Bar Gays in the Boy Scouts	Y	10. Trade Promotion Authority	N
3. Campaign Finance Reform	N	7. $ for Hate Crime Prosecution	N	11. Authorize Force in Iraq	Y
4. Permit ANWR Development	Y	8. Overseas Military Abortions	N	12. Homeland Sec. Dept. Union	N

Election Results

1998 general	Judd Gregg (R)	213,477	(68%)	($904,448)
	George Condodemetraky (D)	88,883	(28%)	($28,547)
	Other	12,596	(4%)	
1998 primary	Judd Gregg (R)	63,729	(86%)	
	Phil Weber (R)	10,784	(14%)	
1992 general	Judd Gregg (R)	249,591	(48%)	($875,675)
	John Rauh (D)	234,982	(45%)	($1,109,467)
	Katherine Alexander (Lib)	18,214	(4%)	
	Other	15,629	(3%)	

Prior Winning Percentages: 1986 House (74%); 1984 House (76%); 1982 House (71%); 1980 House (64%)

Judd Gregg, a Republican, was first elected governor in 1988 and senator in 1992. He grew up in Nashua and was involved in politics early: in 1952, when he was 5, his father Hugh Gregg was elected governor. Hugh Gregg remained a power in presidential primary politics for many years and in 1988 provided crucial backing to George H.W. Bush. Judd Gregg was a student at Columbia during the student riots of 1968, but stayed true to New Hampshire Republicanism; he graduated from Boston University Law School and returned to Nashua and practiced law. In 1978, at 31, he was elected to the Executive Council, which dates to the colonial era and approves state appointments and expenditures. In 1980 he was elected to the House, where he was an eager participant in the Reagan revolution. In 1988, he ran for governor and won handily; he was easily reelected in 1990.

In 1992, Gregg ran for the Senate when Warren Rudman retired, and in his taciturn way seemed sure he would win. But the New Hampshire economy had turned sour, and the race turned close. In the September primary he beat a construction company owner by only 50%–38%. In the general, he faced retired businessman John Rauh, who backed the line-item veto and balanced budget amendment and attacked Gregg for opposing abortion rights. Gregg was also attacked for having received a draft deferment in 1969 for bad knees, sleepwalking and severe acne. He won by an unimpressive 48%–45% margin.

Gregg is now chairman of the Health, Education, Labor and Pensions Committee; he became ranking minority member after Jim Jeffords left the Republican party in May 2001. In 2001 he was the lead Senate supporter of the Bush education bill. He worked with Edward Kennedy on the details; his amendment to allow private school choice in 10 cities was rejected in June 2002 by a 58–41 vote. In November 2001 he and Kennedy and House members John Boehner and George Miller reached a final compromise; it left in place the Bush proposal for annual testing in math and reading from grades three to eight and flexibility for states and school districts; it included allowing disadvantaged students to use federal funds for private tutoring and summer school. Gregg has opposed mandatory funding of special education, but has worked to increase discretionary funding up toward the 40% federal commitment. He points out that federal special education funding increased from $2.4 billion in 1996 to $10.5 billion in 2002. In January 2003 he moved to add $1.5 billion to the $2 billion in increases supported by the Bush administration in 2001 and 2002. In January 2003 he also pushed through an amendment increasing education spending by $5 billion and reducing other discretionary non-military spending by a corresponding amount.

On health issues Gregg has worked to reduce the number of uninsured. To do that, he says, "We should ensure a broader choice in health insurance plans, instead of current policies that force employees to buy expensive plans only." He has worked to change FDA procedures. To combat bioterrorism, he has advocated voluntary smallpox vaccination and has called for reduction of what he calls trial lawyer and regulator barriers to the development of safe vaccines. In July 2002 he tried to amend the prescription drug bill to limit medical malpractice awards. He was one of many members calling for extension of unemployment benefits in January 2003. Gregg has been a leader in proposing changes to Social Security. He served on the 1994 Entitlements Commission and in 1995 headed the Senate Republicans' working group on entitlement reform; he drafted a Medicare reform to give seniors more choices, including the current system. In 1998 he served on the CSIS National Commission on Retirement Policy and co-sponsored its Social Security reform, which would put 2% of payroll taxes into mandatory investment accounts, lift minimum benefits levels, raise the retirement age and means-test affluent workers.

Gregg has taken on some other causes. After a young woman from Nashua was murdered by a high school classmate who had traced her down through an Internet website, he sponsored with Dianne Feinstein a bill, opposed by banks and many businesses, to ban the sale or display of Social Security numbers. It was not acted on in 2002, and they reintroduced it in 2003. His amendment to end the federal sugar program was beaten 71–29 in December 2001. He has taken a hand in foreign policy in his role as chairman of the Appropriations subcommittee with jurisdiction over the State Department. On environmental issues Gregg has backed reform of the 1872 Mining Act and higher grazing fees. He opposed the 1999 Clinton order closing off 30% of the White Mountain National Forest, and has argued that local communities should have more of a say in forest use. He has procured federal money to buy land to preserve Lake Tarleton, expand the Hubbard Brook Experimental Forest, and to purchase a conservation easement in the Ossipee Mountains. He was one of six Republicans to vote in January 2003 against the Bush administration's New Source Review rules. He has also used his seat on Appropriations to fund other New Hampshire projects and claims to have gotten $275 million for New Hampshire colleges and universities. He used an appropriations rider to seek patent protection on a drug owned by his alma mater, Columbia, and in a hand-written amendment got $1.4 million for the Advisory Commission on Electronic Commerce. He got $355,000 to repair the National Weather Radio transmitter on Pack Monadnock Mountain in Peterborough.

Gregg has maintained a network of supporters in New Hampshire, but the Gregg organization that was so effective for George H.W. Bush in 1988 was unable to deliver a victory for George W. Bush in the 2000 primary. Gregg played Al Gore in candidate Bush's debate preparation; whether he anticipated Gore's loud sighs in the first debate is not clear. Gregg's standing in New Hampshire seems strong. In 1998 he was opposed by a low-spending Democrat who called him a "draft dodger" and a "wimp" and who said at one rally that he would like to get Gregg between a dog and a fire hydrant. Gregg won 68%–28%. In December 2002 he announced he would run again in 2004. One possible opponent is state Senator Burt Cohen, who voted for a state income tax and who announced an exploratory committee in early 2003. Gregg seems likely to be the first New Hampshire senator elected to a third term since Norris Cotton in 1968.

Junior Senator

John Sununu (R)

Elected 2002, seat up 2008, 1st; b. Sept. 10, 1964, Boston, MA; home, Bedford; M.I.T., B.S. 1986, M.S. 1987, Harvard U., M.B.A. 1991; Catholic; married (Kitty).

Elected Office: U.S. House of Reps., 1996–02.

Professional Career: Design Engineer, Remec Inc., 1987–89; Mgr. & Operations Specialist, Pittiglio, Rabin, Todd & McGrath, 1990–92; C.F.O. & Dir. of Operations, Teletrol Systems Inc., 1993–95; Consultant, JHS Associates, 1995–96.

DC Office: 111 RSOB, 20510, 202-224-2841; Fax: 202-228-4131; Web site: sununu.senate.gov.

State Offices: Manchester, 603-647-7500; Portsmouth, 603-430-9560.

Committees: *Banking, Housing & Urban Affairs*: Housing & Transportation; Int'l. Trade & Finance; Securities & Investment. *Commerce, Science & Transportation*: Aviation; Communications; Competition, Foreign Commerce & Infrastructure; Oceans, Fisheries & Coast Guard; Science, Technology & Space. *Foreign Relations*: African Affairs; European Affairs; Int'l. Operations & Terrorism (Chmn.); Western Hemisphere, Peace Corps, Narcotics Affairs. *Governmental Affairs*: Financial Management, Budget & Int'l. Security; Government Management, Federal Workforce & the District of Columbia; Investigations (Permanent). *Joint Economic Committee* (4th of 10 Sens.).

Group Ratings (as Member of U.S. House of Representatives)

	ADA	ACLU	AFS	LCV	CON	ITIC	NTU	COC	ACU	NTLC	CHC
2002	0	13	0	38	89	100	61	90	92	85	100
2001	0	—	0	36	—	—	69	100	92	—	—

National Journal Ratings (as Member of U.S. House of Representatives)

	2001 LIB	—	2001 CONS		2002 LIB	—	2002 CONS
Economic	33%	—	68%		35%	—	64%
Social	20%	—	69%		29%	—	71%
Foreign	21%	—	74%		29%	—	67%

Key Votes of the 107th Congress (as Member of U.S. House of Representatives)

1. Approve Bush Tax Cuts	Y	5. Faith-Based Charities	Y	9. Trade Promotion Authority	Y
2. Limit Patients' Bill of Rights	Y	6. Bar Gays in the Boy Scouts	Y	10. Bar Funds for Intl. Court	Y
3. Campaign Finance Reform	N	7. Ban Partial-Birth Abortion	Y	11. Authorize Force in Iraq	Y
4. Ban ANWR Development	N	8. Arm Commercial Pilots	Y	12. Deny Home. Sec. Dept. Union	Y

Election Results

2002 general	John Sununu (R)	227,229	(51%)	($3,545,925)
	Jeanne Shaheen (D)	207,478	(47%)	($5,821,219)
	Other	12,428	(3%)	
2002 primary	John Sununu (R)	81,920	(53%)	
	Bob Smith (R)	68,608	(45%)	
	Other	2,694	(2%)	

Prior Winning Percentages: 2000 House (53%); 1998 House (67%); 1996 House (50%)

John E. Sununu, a Republican elected in 2002 when he defeated the state's senior senator and its governor, is the youngest member of the Senate. He grew up in Salem, on the Massachusetts border, one of eight children of John H. Sununu, who was elected to the first of three terms as governor in 1982 and served as White House Chief of Staff from 1989 to 1991. The younger Sununu graduated from M.I.T. and, like George W. Bush, got an M.B.A. at Harvard. He worked as an engineer for a microwave manufacturer, a high-tech consulting firm, the building automation manager Teletrol and as a consultant for JHS Associates. In April 1996, when Congressman Bill Zeliff announced for governor, Sununu and seven other Republicans got into the House race; Sununu won with 28%. In the general, Sununu faced Joe Keefe, former state Democratic chairman, who had run twice before in the district and who, with help from PACs, raised more money than Sununu. This was also a close race: Sununu won 50%–47%.

In the House, Sununu compiled a conservative voting record and climbed to important positions on the Appropriations and Budget Committees. He was reelected 67%–33% in 1998 but in 2000 he had spirited competition from Portsmouth state Representative Martha Fuller Clark, who spent nearly twice as much as he did and held Sununu to a 53%–45% victory. In 2002, Republican incumbent Bob Smith was obviously vulnerable in the primary and seemed likely to lose the general election. How a New Hampshire Republican got himself into this predicament is an interesting tale. Smith, a fervent opponent of abortion, ran for the Senate in 1990 and won the general election 65%–32%. In 1996 Smith had well-financed competition from former Democratic Congressman Dick Swett. Smith won by only 49%–46%; he had a near-political-death experience on election night when the VNS exit poll declared him the loser (New Hampshire exit polls have leaned Democratic since 1988).

Astonishingly, Smith proceeded to run for president. What prompted him to think he would make a plausible candidate is not clear: he had had no executive experience in government and no major legislative achievement. His standing with New Hampshire voters was shaky and support from his colleagues was nonexistent. He spent much time on the road in 1997 and 1998 and became the first candidate to formally announce for the presidency in February 1999. Much of the buzz in New Hampshire was hostile, and many feared his presence would drive out other presidential contenders, and thus reduce the importance of New Hampshire's first-in-the-nation primary. In July 1999 Smith rose on the Senate floor and made a 50-minute speech announcing that he was leaving the Republican Party and would run for president as an independent or third party candidate. He said that the Republican commitment to the rights of gun owners and the unborn "is a fraud and everyone knows it. . . . Maybe it's a party in the sense of wearing hats and blowing whistles, but it's not a party that means anything." Senate Republican leaders allowed him to keep his committee seats and seniority. Then in October 1999 Senator John Chafee died; he was chairman of the Environment and Public Works Committee and Smith held the next-ranking Republican seat. Four days later Smith abandoned his presidential candidacy, saying he could not raise enough money, and on November 1 he announced he was a Republican again. A day later he became chairman of the Environment Committee. Previously, his record on the committee had been solidly conservative, while his efforts as a subcommittee chairman to change the troubled Superfund program had gone nowhere. Now he took liberal stands on environmental issues, including opposing oil drilling in the Arctic National Wildlife Refuge.

By early 2001 New Hampshire polls showed Smith trailing Governor Jeanne Shaheen in the general election and Sununu in the primary; they also showed Sununu ahead of Shaheen. The Bush White House was officially on Smith's side: Dick Cheney assured him that the White House backed all incumbent Republican senators in March 2001. But Republican consultants believed that only a Sununu win in the primary could save the seat, and the White House appears to have made no attempt to persuade Sununu not to run. In October 2001 Sununu announced he was running for the Senate. Smith argued that with his seniority it would be a "serious matter" for Republicans to reject him. Sununu's argument was that he was the only one who could win. Smith's response: "The First District House seat is now in jeopardy. He's risking the president's agenda by running in this race. He's risking the Senate race because we have to spend money against each other and Shaheen is piling the money in the bank. So we could lose the House seat and the Senate seat. It wasn't me who did that." These arguments were undoubtedly dispositive for most primary voters, since the candidates disagreed on only a few issues—PNTR with China and oil drilling in the Arctic National Wildlife Refuge, both of which Smith opposed and Sununu favored.

It is highly unusual for leaders of both parties to refuse to support, much less oppose, one of their incumbents in a primary. But there were signs that even leaders officially on Smith's side were lukewarm in their support. Rove attended a Smith fundraiser, but White House Chief of Staff Andrew Card, who knew the Sununus for 30 years, endorsed Sununu. Majority Leader Trent Lott attended two Smith fundraisers, but in April 2002 attended a Sununu fundraiser. Senate Republican campaign committee chairman Bill Frist said he supported Smith, but in October 2001 Smith upbraided him in the cloakroom for not supporting him strongly enough. Richard Shelby and Christopher Bond endorsed Sununu early on. Chuck Hagel sent $2,500 to both candidates. Judd Gregg, Smith's New Hampshire colleague for 10 years, said he was neutral. The House Republican leadership held a fundraiser for Sununu. The Manchester *Union Leader* endorsed Sununu. Despite all his support from leading Republicans, Sununu raised far less money than Smith, who raised much by direct mail; altogether Smith raised $3.8 million and Sununu $1.5 million.

A few differences on issues surfaced during the long campaign up to the September primary. One was policy in the Middle East. Sununu is of Lebanese descent, and was one of the few Republicans to vote against recognizing Jerusalem as the capital of Israel. In October 2001 he returned a contribution from someone who turned out to be a supporter of Hamas. In December 2001 he attended a fundraiser put on by George Salem, a lawyer who once represented the Holy Land Foundation in Texas, a few days after the Bush administration froze Holy Land's bank accounts. Smith aides criticized Sununu for this; he was defended by Rudman and Anti-Defamation League director Abraham Foxman. A Sununu aide noted that Sununu had voted for and Smith against $3 billion in aid for Israel. The weekend before the primary, Smith ran an ad saying that Sununu voted to let terrorist suspects stay in the United States; Sununu replied that someone granted permanent residency status has rights under the Constitution.

New Hampshire polls often produce conflicting results, as close observers of New Hampshire presidential primaries know. In the weeks before the September 10 primary, one New Hampshire poll showed the race even and one showed Sununu with a 22% lead. Both turned out to be wrong. Turnout was a record high and Sununu won 53%–45%. Sununu carried every county and even carried Smith's hometown. Smith made a gracious concession statement and endorsed Sununu.

Now, having beaten New Hampshire's senior senator, Sununu faced New Hampshire's governor, Jeanne Shaheen. The Senate Republican campaign committee had been running ads against Shaheen since the spring, focusing especially on education funding. This had been the central issue of her governorship. She was proud of extending kindergarten, regulating HMOs and joining the tri-state pool (with Maine and Vermont) to purchase prescription drugs at discount. But the real problem was how to respond to the state Supreme Court decision outlawing New Hampshire's local-based school financing. In 1999, when the legislature, with a Democratic state Senate for the first time in years, seemed on the verge of passing an income tax, she announced that she would veto it. Instead, the legislature passed a temporary statewide property tax, plus business tax increases. But this did not solve the problem permanently. In 2000 Shaheen declined to take the pledge and was whipsawed on both sides. She won the Democratic primary by only 61%–38%, an unusually low primary showing for an incumbent governor, and in November beat state Senator (and former U.S. Senator) Gordon Humphrey by only 49%–44%..

Shaheen ran for the Senate as a moderate on key issues. She said she supported the 2001 Bush tax cut and in October 2002 came out staunchly for the Iraq war resolution. She emphasized her support of abortion rights and with help from EMILY's List and other feminist groups and from likely presidential candidates she raised far more money than Sununu. She attacked Sununu for supporting "privatization" of Social Security. He responded with an articulate advocacy of voluntary individual investment accounts as part of Social Security—"modernization", as he put it.

In late September supporters of Bob Smith launched a write-in campaign for him; eventually three different groups announced Smith write-in campaigns. Republican strategists wanted Smith to renounce them, but after the primary Smith kept busy with Senate business in Washington and did not return to New Hampshire. Three times White House political strategist Karl Rove called Smith and urged him to accompany George W. Bush to New Hampshire. But Smith wasn't interested in a last ride on Air Force One. Rove said that Smith "needed to make a decision and it could affect his future"—a not very concealed hint that the administration might find a job for him after the election. But Smith reportedly insisted on being offered a specific job—something that did not occur. In the end Smith got only 2,396 write-in votes and is now in the private sector.

The polls tightened in late October and national Democrats started to count this seat as a pickup. But the New Hampshire tax issue may have hurt Shaheen. She was on record in support of a sales tax and she was, necessarily, supporting gubernatorial nominee Mark Fernald, an outspoken advocate of an income tax. Fernald was defeated 59%–38% and Sununu defeated Shaheen

51%–47%. His margin was nearly 20,000 votes—eight times as great as the number of Smith write-ins. Elected at 38, from a mostly Republican state, Sununu may have a long Senate career ahead of him.

FIRST DISTRICT

Rep. Jeb Bradley (R)

Elected 2002, 1st term; b. Oct. 20, 1952, Rumford, ME; home, Wolfeboro; Tufts U., B.A. 1974; Protestant; married (Barbara).

Elected Office: NH House of Reps., 1990–2002.

Professional Career: Owner, Evergrain Health Food store, 1981–97; Magician.

DC Office: 1218 LHOB 20515, 202-225-5456; Fax: 202-225-5822; Web site: www.house.gov/bradley.

District Offices: Dover, 603-743-4813; Manchester, 603-641-9536.

Committees: *Armed Services* (26th of 33 R): Projection Forces; Tactical Air & Land Forces. *Small Business* (15th of 18 R): Regulatory Reform & Oversight; Workforce, Empowerment & Government Programs. *Veterans' Affairs* (13th of 17 R): Benefits; Health.

Group Ratings and Key Votes: Newly Elected

Election Results

2002 general	Jeb Bradley (R)	128,993	(58%)	($1,029,408)
	Martha Clark (D)	85,426	(39%)	($3,511,108)
	Other	7,568	(3%)	
2002 primary	Jeb Bradley (R)	23,012	(31%)	
	John Stephen (R)	16,956	(23%)	
	Sean Mahoney (R)	13,861	(19%)	
	Vivian Clark (R)	6,889	(9%)	
	Wayne Barrow (R)	6,008	(8%)	
	Fran Wendelboe (R)	4,947	(7%)	
	Other	1,648	(3%)	
2000 general	John Sununu (R)	150,609	(53%)	($578,633)
	Martha Clark (D)	128,387	(45%)	($1,055,513)
	Other	5,713	(2%)	

The People		Race/Ethnic Origin	Ancestry	
Area size:	2,688 sq. mi.	95.1% White	Irish: 14.6%	English: 12.7%
Urban population:	66.6%	0.7% Black	French: 10.5%	
Rural population:	33.4%	1.2% Asian	**2000 Presidential Vote**	
Pop. 2000:	617,575	0.2% Native Am.	Bush (R)............136,474	(49%)
Median income:	$50,135	0.0% Hawaiian	Gore (D)............128,278	(46%)
Poverty status:	6.7%	0.9% Two+ races	Other...............11,545	(4%)
Military veterans:	15.0%	0.1% Other	**Cook Partisan Voting Index:** R + 2	
		1.6% Hispanic Origin		

Occupation	Blue collar: 23.6%	White collar: 62.7%	Gray collar: 13.7%

The greatest growth in New Hampshire over the past two decades has been in the southeast and south central parts of the state—the Seacoast and the Manchester area. Manchester was once famous for the Amoskeag Mills, the world's largest textile mill complex and in the first half of the 20th century was the quintessential mill town, with a few mansions for mill owners and managers and close packed neighborhoods of frame houses for mill workers, many of them immigrants— from Quebec, Ireland and Greece (Manchester has America's largest percentage of Greek Americans). By the beginning of the 21st century it was something quite different, a high-tech city, with big shopping malls at freeway interchanges, a spiffy new airport, spruced up neighborhoods and growth extending to the wooded suburbs all around. The Seacoast, within easy commuting distance of Massachusetts, is a collection of towns of ancient pedigree and high-tech growth. The biggest city on the coast is Portsmouth, the colonial capital of New Hampshire, an old seaport with well-preserved houses and a booming economy. The successful redevelopment of Pease Air Force Base after its 1991 closing into the Pease International Tradeport, with what developers termed high-end office buildings in an international trade environment (plus a convenient airport runway), has driven the Seacoast (sometimes called e-coast) economy with more than 160 businesses and several thousand jobs. Nearby is Exeter, home of Phillips Exeter Academy, on a campus most colleges would envy; it is also the home of Tyco, the conglomerate whose flamboyant CEO Dennis Kozlowski famously cooked the books.

The 1st Congressional District includes the Manchester area and the Seacoast from Manchester and next-door Bedford, its most affluent suburb, east to Portsmouth. It also extends north to Laconia and Lake Winnipesaukee, studded with summer resorts and Ossipee in Carroll County, which promotes rock and ice climbing. Politically, this is the more Republican of New Hampshire's two congressional districts: people came here from Massachusetts not to replicate its high-tax environment but to get away from it. Manchester, the largest city in the state, still has more registered Democrats than Republicans—a relic of its mill town days—but almost always votes Republican in general elections. Portsmouth, with its trendy coffee shops, is Democratic, and so is Durham, home of the University of New Hampshire, and nearby Dover, once a mill town. But most of the smaller towns in the Seacoast and to the north are solidly Republican.

The congressman from the 1st District is Jeb Bradley, a Republican elected in 2002. He grew up in Wolfeboro on the shores of Lake Winnipesaukee and worked summers at his family's hardware store. He graduated from Tufts and met his wife—a native of Switzerland—in Nepal on a mountaineering adventure. He had a varied professional career, from running a health-food store to serving as a professional magician—arguably a useful background for his current job. In the often provincial world of New Hampshire politics, he was suspect because he switched parties in 1989, becoming a Republican one year before he ran for the state legislature, where he served for 12 years. As chairman of the Science, Technology and Energy Committee, he passed an electricity deregulation bill for the state with the nation's highest electricity costs. The Public Service Company of New Hampshire objected to the plan and sued in federal court; the state reached a settlement, which the Legislature approved at Bradley's urging.

In October 2001, 1st District Congressman John Sununu announced that he was running for the Senate. Bradley was one of eight candidates in the Republican primary. There was no obvious frontrunner, and the candidates were of different ideologies and from different parts of the district. Bradley characterized himself as a moderate in favor of abortion rights and a fiscal conservative who voted against both sales and income taxes. He also supported gay adoption and environmental restriction measures—positions too liberal for many Republicans. Meanwhile, businessman Sean Mahoney and assistant state Safety Commissioner John Stephen fought over who was the "true conservative" in the field; Stephen won the backing of some national conservative groups and the endorsement of the Manchester *Union Leader.* Bradley won the primary with 31%, as Stephen won 23% and Mahoney 19%. This race was ideological, but also regional. Stephen carried Manchester and most of the nearby towns, but Bradley edged him in Merrimack, Londonderry and Derry. Mahoney carried Portsmouth and most of the nearby towns, but Bradley led in Durham and Dover. Bradley carried all but one of the towns north of Durham; many cast only a few votes, but Bradley won a large share of them, and they added up.

In the general election, Bradley faced Martha Fuller Clark, who had held Sununu to a 53%–45% margin in 2000. Clark, from Portsmouth, served from 1990 to 2000 in the state House; she spent $1 million in 2000 and never stopped campaigning after the election. She was one of the national Democratic party's favorite candidates and benefited from contributions and campaign appearances from potential presidential candidates. For 2002 she raised the phenomenal sum of $3.5 million (including $1.6 million of her own money), while Bradley, who faced a seriously contested primary as well as the general, spent $1 million. Bradley said that funding for special education was a high priority and called for modernization of weapons systems and pay raises for military personnel. Bradley attacked Clark for her support of a state income tax—anathema to many New Hampshire voters. Clark responded by mining Bradley's legislative record and pointing to votes for business, inheritance and consumption taxes. Clark charged that Bradley favored "privatization" of Social Security. In a radio interview he said that individual investment accounts should be a matter for discussion, but afterward said that his opposition to "privatization" was "crystal clear." But this was still another district where the Social Security issue did not produce the magic Democrats expected. Instead, the income tax proved to be a millstone for Clark. Clark was also damaged by Republican attacks on her participation in a January 2002 conference hosted by Northeast Action—a coalition of labor, environmental and other liberal interest groups, which curiously included the Communist Party USA.

Bradley won by a surprisingly large 58%–39%. He carried Manchester 56%–40% and Bedford 73%–26%. Clark carried Portsmouth 56%–40% and Durham 62%–35%, plus next-door Lee and Newmarket, and lost every other city and town.

SECOND DISTRICT

Rep. Charles Bass (R)

Elected 1994, 5th term; b. Jan. 8, 1952, Boston, MA; home, Peterborough; Dartmouth Col., A.B. 1974; Episcopalian; married (Lisa).

Elected Office: NH House of Reps., 1982–88; NH Senate, 1988–92.

Professional Career: Field worker, U.S. Rep. William Cohen, 1974; Legis. Asst., U.S. Rep. David Emery, 1975–76, Chief of Staff, 1976–79; Vice Pres., High Standard Inc., 1980–93; Chmn., Columbia Architectural Products, 1980–93.

DC Office: 2421 RHOB 20515, 202-225-5206; Fax: 202-225-2946; Web site: www.house.gov/bass.

District Offices: Concord, 603-226-0249; Keene, 603-358-4094; Littleton, 603-444-1271; Nashua, 603-889-8772.

Committees: *Energy & Commerce* (22d of 31 R): Commerce, Trade & Consumer Protection; Environment & Hazardous Materials; Oversight & Investigations; Telecommunications & The Internet.

Group Ratings

	ADA	ACLU	AFS	LCV	CON	ITIC	NTU	COC	ACU	NTLC	CHC
2002	15	33	0	25	90	100	60	90	80	81	42
2001	25	—	10	57	—	—	61	91	60	—	—

National Journal Ratings

	2001 LIB	—	2001 CONS		2002 LIB	—	2002 CONS
Economic	43%	—	56%		45%	—	54%
Social	58%	—	42%		55%	—	44%
Foreign	21%	—	74%		24%	—	72%

Key Votes of the 107th Congress

1. Approve Bush Tax Cuts	Y	5. Faith-Based Charities	Y	9. Trade Promotion Authority	Y
2. Limit Patients' Bill of Rights	Y	6. Bar Gays in the Boy Scouts	Y	10. Bar Funds for Intl. Court	Y
3. Campaign Finance Reform	Y	7. Ban Partial-Birth Abortion	Y	11. Authorize Force in Iraq	Y
4. Ban ANWR Development	Y	8. Arm Commercial Pilots	Y	12. Deny Home. Sec. Dept. Union	Y

Election Results

2002 general	Charles Bass (R)	125,804	(57%)	($886,765)
	Katrina Swett (D)	90,479	(41%)	($1,457,913)
	Other	7,568	(2%)	
2002 primary	Charles Bass (R)	61,473	(87%)	
	Gene Douglass (R)	9,486	(13%)	
2000 general	Charles Bass (R)	152,581	(56%)	($812,727)
	Barney Brannen (D)	110,367	(41%)	($872,115)
	Other	8,392	(3%)	

Prior Winning Percentages: 1998 (53%); 1996 (51%); 1994 (51%)

The People		Race/Ethnic Origin	Ancestry	
Area size:	6,662 sq. mi.	95.1% White	Irish: 13.0%	English: 12.9%
Urban population:	51.7%	0.6% Black	French: 10.3%	
Rural population:	48.3%	1.3% Asian	**2000 Presidential Vote**	
Pop. 2000:	618,211	0.2% Native Am.	Gore (D)...............134,343 (48%)	
Median income:	$48,762	0.0% Hawaiian	Bush (R)...............132,336 (47%)	
Poverty status:	6.4%	0.9% Two+ races	Other...................12,801 (5%)	
Military veterans:	15.0%	0.1% Other	**Cook Partisan Voting Index:** D + 0	
		1.7% Hispanic Origin		

Occupation   Blue collar: 24.7%   White collar: 62.1%   Gray collar: 13.2%

Political reporters covering New Hampshire's first-in-the-nation political primary usually stay in Manchester, the state's largest city and within an hour or so of driving time from the rest of the state except for the North Country. Yet there are other noteworthy cities and towns in New Hampshire. Concord, north of Manchester, is the state capital; on one side of Main Street is the handsome, small, granite state Capitol and on the other you can usually find the headquarters of the two political parties and many statewide candidates. Nashua, south of Manchester and on the Massachusetts line, is the state's second largest city, a high-tech and financial services center that has been booming for two decades. To the east is Salem, the largest of the border suburbs on the Massachusetts line, prosperous and growing. To the west of Nashua, past the pleasant country around Mount Monadnock, is Keene, the hub of southwest New Hampshire and home of Keene State College. To the north are the towns along the Connecticut River, some mill towns and others once vacation home territory; New Hampshire prosperity has spread to most of these, just across the river from Vermont. Hanover, home of Dartmouth College, is an unbearably picturesque tiny town amid the mountains. And every political reporter's itinerary has to include a trip, usually by plane, to the little lumber mill city of Berlin in the midst of the North Country and perhaps also to Dixville Notch, where the town's 29 voters cast their votes a minute past midnight and provide the first reported returns in every presidential election. (Hint for election analysts: if Dixville Notch doesn't go heavily Republican, the Republicans are in trouble.)

The 2d Congressional District includes Concord, Nashua, Salem, Keene, the Connecticut River counties, Hanover, Berlin and Dixville Notch. It also includes Mount Washington, with its spectacularly violent weather, with winds measured up to 231 miles per hour, and the Bretton Woods resort where the world monetary system was established at a conference in 1944. Politically this is mixed country. Nashua is more Democratic than Manchester, Salem more Republican. The area between Mount Monadnock and Keene and roundabout is one of the most liberal parts of New Hampshire, almost as if people here would rather be in Vermont. Hanover and Berlin are Democratic strongholds in the heavily Republican North Country. Overall, this is the less Republican of New Hampshire's two districts; it was carried narrowly by Al Gore in 2000.

The congressman from the 2d District is Charles Bass, a Republican first elected in 1994. He has a long political pedigree: His grandfather Robert Bass was elected governor in 1910 and his father Perkins Bass served in the House from 1955 to 1963. Charles Bass, after graduating from Dartmouth, worked for Maine Congressmen William Cohen and David Emery, then returned to New Hampshire to run for Congress in 1980, at age 28; he finished third in the primary, with 22%, to 34% for now-Senator Judd Gregg and 25% for liberal Susan McLane. With his two brothers he ran a factory making architectural products and served in the state legislature for a decade, where he wrote the state's voluntary campaign spending law, which called on U.S. House candidates to observe a $500,000 total limit for both primary and general elections.

In 1994 Bass won the Republican nomination to oppose two-term Democratic Congressman Dick Swett. Campaigning as pro-choice on abortion and as a fiscal conservative, a supporter of welfare cuts and tougher sentencing, Bass attacked Swett for voting with Bill Clinton 90% of the time and for raising most of his money out of state, much of it generated by his father-in-law, California Congressman Tom Lantos. Swett spent over $1 million, while Bass adhered to the voluntary spending limits and spent $448,000; Bass won 51%–46%.

In the House, Bass emphasized that he is an "independent voice" as he trended toward the center on economic and cultural issues, while he maintained a more conservative record on foreign policy. He has focused on environmental issues. He opposed the Bush administration, by coming out early against oil drilling in the Arctic National Wildlife Refuge and criticizing Bush for abandoning his one-sentence campaign promise to vastly reduce the level of carbon dioxide in the air. He was one of only three Republicans to vote against the budget resolution in May 2001 and was an early supporter of the Shays-Meehan campaign finance bill. Responding to high local property taxes, he has made funding for special education a high priority. On the Energy and Commerce Committee since 2001, Bass has worked on high-tech issues and lower prescription-drug costs. In February 2003, he won House passage of his American Spirit Fraud Prevention Act, to increase Federal Trade Commission penalties for schemes in which scam artists exploit natural disasters or national emergencies on behalf of alleged charities. He has pushed persistently, but with little impact, to move toward biennial budgeting, which he said would add more stability to government programs.

Most incumbent congressmen cruise to reelection without much more than a murmur of opposition; Bass has regularly faced spirited opposition. Barney Brannen ran a lively campaign in 2000, with ads distinguishing him from Barney Rubble and the purple Barney and attacking Bass on prescription drugs for seniors. Bass attacked him for his support from trial lawyers and labor unions, and ran ads with an endorsement from John McCain. Bass ran 9% ahead of George W. Bush, and won 56%–41%.

In 2002, Bass faced his most lavishly funded challenger and won by his largest margin. Katrina Swett, wife of the incumbent whom Bass initially defeated and the daughter of California Congressman Tom Lantos, received extensive national party attention. Dick Gephardt joined to open her campaign office. Other potential presidential candidates were generous with contributions and campaign appearances. "I'll be here a lot," Lantos told New Hampshire reporters on a campaign visit. He helped her to raise an impressive $149,000 from congressional leadership PACs, plus money from California contributors such as Steven Spielberg and San Francisco financiers; altogether, she raised and spent $1.4 million. As in 1994, Bass ran ads contending that Swett's out-of-state and labor union contributions showed that she was out of touch with local voters. She attacked his contributions from big business and called Bass "the wealthy, privileged inheritor of an incredibly easy path." The NRCC kept a close eye on Bass until the closing days of the campaign. He spent $876,000, well over his former limit, but well below Swett's spending, and won by a solid 57%–41% margin. Swett carried clusters of towns around Keene, Hanover and Berlin and one small town in the south; she lost every other city and town. After the election Swett said that she might run again in 2004.

★ NEW JERSEY ★

"A valley of humility between two mountains of conceit": That is what Benjamin Franklin called New Jersey, which even in colonial days was overshadowed by the metropolises of New York and Philadelphia. New Jersey was named by King James II, then Duke of York, for the Channel Island on which he was sheltered during the English Civil War. New Jersey was plagued in its early years by rival claims from its neighbors and, still defensive, went to the Supreme Court in the 1980s to argue that it and not New York owns the Statue of Liberty and Ellis Island; New Jersey eventually got most of the islands' acreage, but New York got the immigrant museum and Great Hall which are built on fill land. But New Jersey has much to say for itself. It is "a sort of laboratory in which the best blood is prepared for other communities to thrive on," Woodrow Wilson said when he was governor, just a tad defensively.

Today, New Jersey is the nation's ninth most populous state: It boomed in the 1980s, suffered sharply in the early 1990s recession, came back strongly, and is now weathering the high-tech storms with mixed success. New Jersey was the home of Thomas Edison and of the old Bell Labs; its successors Lucent and AT&T were among its biggest employers in the 1990s, and later laid off

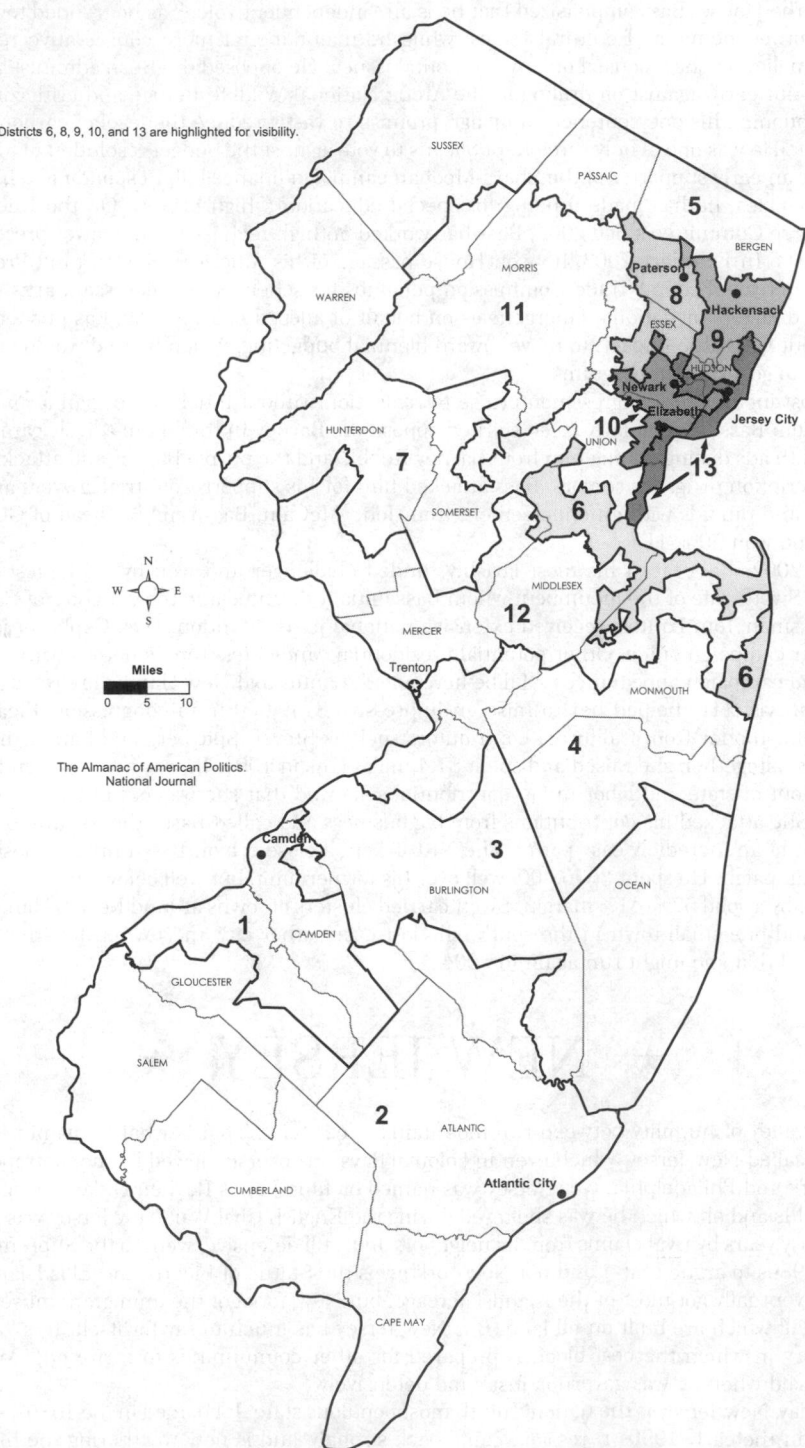

Districts 6, 8, 9, 10, and 13 are highlighted for visibility.

The Almanac of American Politics.
National Journal

Congressional district boundaries were first effective for 2002.

many workers. Other big employers include several of the nation's biggest pharmaceutical firms—Merck, Johnson & Johnson, Bristol-Myers Squibb, Novartis, Schering-Plough. These industries give the state a high-income, high-education work force, and in 2000 New Jersey passed Connecticut and had the nation's highest median household incomes. But it still trailed in per capita income and wealth and has a lower percentage of college graduates than Connecticut, Massachusetts, Maryland, Colorado and the District of Columbia; this is the home not only of high-income Ph.D.'s, but also of *The Sopranos*. This is prosperous middle income country, with more two-car than one-car families but fewer limousines than Manhattan, with an estimated 13,500 $1 million houses but not the multi-million dollar co-ops of Manhattan or mansions of Greenwich, Connecticut.

Within New Jersey's close boundaries is great diversity, geographically from beaches to mountains, demographically from old Quaker stock to new Hispanics, economically from inner city slums to hunt country mansions. Though New York writers are inclined to look on New Jersey as a land of 1940s diners and 1970s shopping malls, this state much more closely resembles the rest of America than does Manhattan, even if some of its traffic signals are arrayed horizontally rather than vertically and its accents can sometimes be incomprehensible to outsiders. The Jersey City row houses seen on emerging from the Holland Tunnel, many renovated by Wall Street commuters and Latin immigrants, give way within a few miles to the skyscrapers of Newark and its new Performing Arts Center. Farther out are comfortably packed middle-income suburbs and the horse country around Far Hills, the university town of Princeton, old industrial cities like Paterson and Trenton, and dozens of suburban towns and small factory cities where people work and raise families over generations. Among them are commuter towns like Middletown, whose commuter trails lead to Lower Manhattan, and which lost dozens of men and women on September 11. A year later, only 37% of New Jersey citizens said their lives had returned to normal and 29% said they would never be the same; 43% said they thought about the attacks every day.

Whoever has legal title to Ellis Island, New Jersey has long been a magnet for immigrants, and it is again today. In 2000, 29% of its residents were born in another country or had a parent who was. Hudson County, the land along the ridge opposite Manhattan, was the home to hundreds of thousands of Irish, Italian, Polish and Jewish immigrants in the early 20th century; in 2000 it was 40% Hispanic, with Cubans, Puerto Ricans, Dominicans and Mexicans. Immigrants are plentiful in the little middle-American towns of Bergen County, Filipinos in Bergenfield, Guatemalans in Fairview, Koreans in Leonia, Indians in Lodi, Chinese in Palisades Park. The old central cities of Elizabeth and Paterson were half-Hispanic in 2000 and Camden, opposite Philadelphia, was 39% Hispanic. There is still a black majority in Newark, but it includes many of the Brazilians in the Ironbound district. New Jersey has all the ethnic variety that America offers.

In the last two decades, a new New Jersey has sprouted. The oil tank farms and swamplands of the Jersey Meadows have become sports palaces and office complexes; the intersection of I-78 and I-287 has become a major shopping and office edge city; U.S. 1 north from Princeton to North Brunswick has become one of the nation's high-tech centers. Even some of New Jersey's long-ailing central cities are perking up. Jersey City's waterfront is sprouting office buildings, shopping malls, apartment complexes, and the *New York Daily News* printing plant; Newark is graced with a sparkling Performing Arts Center and new subdivisions; Trenton, after many years of being the only state capital without a major hotel, finally has a Marriott. New Jersey increasingly has an identity of its own. It is the home of big league football, basketball and hockey franchises and of the world's longest expanse of boardwalks on the Jersey Shore from Cape May to Sandy Hook. And New Jersey is one of America's great gambling centers: Atlantic City, an hour from Philadelphia and two hours from Manhattan, had gambling revenues in 2002 ($4.4 billion) that nearly matched the Las Vegas strip ($4.5 billion).

State government played an important role in building New Jersey identity and pride. Governor Brendan Byrne in the 1970s started the Meadowlands sports complex and got casino gambling legalized in Atlantic City. Governor Tom Kean in the 1980s started education reforms and promoted the state shamelessly. The revolt against Governor Jim Florio's tax increase in 1990 was led by the first all-New Jersey talk radio station and took on national significance with the 1993 election of Christine Todd Whitman, now EPA Administrator. In the late 1990s crime and welfare rolls dropped, but auto insurance and property taxes remained the highest in the nation. New Jersey, contained within two of the nation's biggest metropolitan areas, was also a harbinger of the national trend in the big metro areas toward Bill Clinton's Democrats. Not so long ago, suburban New Jersey was one of the most Republican of big states: It voted 56%–42% for the first George Bush in 1988. But in 1996 New Jersey voters, turned off by the congressional Republicans' Southern leaders and by the national party's opposition to abortion and gun control, voted 54%–36% for Clinton and 53%–43% for Democrat Bob Torricelli for the Senate. In 1997 Whitman, despite cutting taxes, was reelected by only 47%–46% over little-known Democrat Jim McGreevey. In 2000 New Jersey was not seriously contested; Al Gore carried the state 56%–40%. In 2001 McGreevey defeated Republican Bret Schundler for governor by 56%–42% and in 2002, after an unorthodox campaign, Democrat Frank Lautenberg defeated Republican Douglas Forrester for senator by 54%–44%—eerily similar margins. (Even more eerily, Schundler and Forrester both got 928,000 votes.) Republicans still have some suburban strength here, but in 2002 Democrats won back the position of Essex County Executive and elected their first Bergen County Executive ever.

New Jersey's politicians compete in a market that is the second most expensive in the nation, because you have to buy New York and Philadelphia television. And they have a special handicap, because those stations don't give state politics and government the in-depth coverage that voters in most states can expect. This gives an advantage to well-known candidates, like former Senator Bill Bradley, and to incumbents with a distinctive style and notable achievements, like Governors Brendan Byrne, Thomas Kean and Christine Todd Whitman. But it also means that in high-income, highly-educated New Jersey politics is often the business of county and city political machines, of varying degrees of competence, cronyism and corruption. It is, astonishingly, a great advantage in both parties to have the designation of the local county party on the primary ballot. Donald DiFrancesco, who as state Senate president became Acting Governor—not quite Governor—after Whitman's resignation, was one such politician, from the Union County Republican machine. Jim McGreevey, elected by a wide margin in 2001 after his near-defeat of Whitman in 1997, was a product of the Middlesex County Democratic machine and served as both mayor of Woodbridge and state senator—in New Jersey as in France politicians can be town mayors and state legislators at the same time. New Jersey is also notable for giving its governors more real power than any other state. They are the only statewide elected officials, they have great clout in the budget process and they appoint all judges and all 21 county prosecutors and judges.

The People		**Race/Ethnic Origin**			**Military veterans:** 672,217 (10.6%)	
Pop. 2000:	8,414,350	5,557,209	66.0%	White	WWII: 26.3%	Korea: 15.8%
Pop. 1990:	7,730,188	1,096,171	13.0%	Black	Vietnam: 28.1%	Gulf War: 6.2%
Change 1990–2000:	Up 8.6%	477,012	5.7%	Asian	**Most populous cities:**	
Change 1980–1990:	Up 5.0%	11,338	0.1%	Native Am.	1. Newark	273,546
% of U.S. total:	3.0%	2,175	0.0%	Hawaiian	2. Jersey City	240,055
Pop. rank:	9th of 50	133,689	1.6%	Two+ races	3. Paterson	149,222
Area size:	8,721 sq. mi.	19,565	0.2%	Other	4. Elizabeth	120,568
State Native:	53.4%	1,117,191	13.3%	Hisp. Origin	5. Trenton	85,403
Non-citizen:	9.4%	**Ancestry**			Urban population: 94.3%	
Language		Italian: 13.8%		Irish: 12.2%	Rural population: 5.7%	
English: 73.0%	Spanish: 11.7%	German: 9.7%		Polish: 5.3%		
Other Eur.: 10.4%		English: 4.8%				

Education		Work Sector		Legislature	
H.S. Grad:	82.1%	Private: 80.8%	Govt: 13.9%	Senate	20 D 20 R
College Grad:	29.8%	Self: 5.0%	Family: 0.2%	G. Assembly	43 D 36 R 1 I
Industry		Unemployment: 5.8%		Legislative Term Limits: No	
Agri: 0.3%	Con: 5.6%	**Household Income**		**Registered Voters**	
Fin: 8.9%	Info: 4.4%	<15k: 11.7%	15-35k: 19.4%	D: 1,170,475 (25.1%)	
Mfg: 17.9%	Prof: 31.3%	35-50k: 14.3%	50-100k: 33.3%	R: 900,969 (19.4%)	
Public: 4.5%	Trade: 15.7%	100-150k: 12.8%	>150k: 8.6%	I: 2,584,408 (55.5%)	
Other: 11.3%		Median: $55,146			
Occupation		Poverty status: 8.5%			
Blue collar: 19.7%	White collar: 66.5%	**Home Value**			
Gray collar: 13.8%		<50k: 3.0% 50-100k: 14.4% 100-200k: 46.1% 200-300k: 20.4%			
		300-500k: 11.7% >500k: 4.4% Median: $167,900			

Presidential politics For most of the 20th century New Jersey was a close state in close presidential elections, giving small margins to winners in 1960 and 1968 and losers in 1948 and 1976, but no more. In the 1980s the vast suburban expanses of New Jersey leaned toward the Republicans; since 1995 they have leaned to the Democrats. This is a state with relatively few strong-belief Christians and with a high number of seculars and Jews; sophisticated and cynical, it reacted strongly against the Southern-accented Republicans of Newt Gingrich's revolution. The 1996 results and polls in 1999 and 2000 showed New Jersey so heavily Democratic that neither party made it a target state—to the relief of fundraisers, who no longer had to raise money to buy New York TV. As it turned out, George W. Bush carried white Protestants and white Catholics by narrow margins, but was far behind among blacks, Jews and, by lesser margins, Hispanics; Al Gore won as easily as expected. For 2004, George W. Bush's managers may take a look to see if his New Jersey numbers are appreciably better after September 11, but they're not likely to spend on New York TV unless they think they have a chance to win or to tie the Democrats in New York itself.

2000 Presidential Vote

Gore (D)	1,788,850	(56%)
Bush (R)	1,284,173	(40%)
Nader (Green)	94,554	(3%)
Other	19,649	(1%)

2000 Republican Presidential Primary

Bush (R)	201,209	(84%)
Keyes (R)	39,601	(16%)

2000 Democratic Presidential Primary

Gore (D)	358,951	(95%)
LaRouche (D)	19,321	(5%)

1996 Presidential Vote

Clinton (D)	1,651,019	(54%)
Dole (R)	1,102,577	(36%)
Perot (I)	261,932	(9%)
Other	59,424	(2%)

For years, New Jersey's June presidential primary was overshadowed by California's on the same day. In 1996 California voted in March, and New Jersey did not get to the polls until two months after the nominations were sewn up. In 1998 the state Senate refused to move the primary to March 7, and so it stayed in June—far, far too late to affect the outcome. In early 2003 some legislators were trying again to move the primary back to March. But even that might be too late.

Congressional districting New Jersey's population rose 9% between the 1990 and 2000 Censuses, the most of any Northeastern state and New Hampshire, and it did not lose a House seat in 2002 as it did in 1992. New Jersey has a 10-member congressional redistricting commission, equally divided between the parties, which is supposed to agree on new lines, with a previously selected arbiter choosing a tie-breaker. In the likely event that the commission disagrees, the tie-breaker can produce a compromise plan and see if it gets a majority of the commission; if not, the tie-breaker picks one of the two parties' plans. In 1991 the tie-breaker picked the Republican plan, with grotesquely-shaped districts. But given New Jersey's post-1994 Democratic trend, by 2000 it yielded the Republicans only 6 of the state's 13 seats.

108th Congress Lineup
7 D   6 R

107th Congress Lineup
7 D   6 R

The redistricting commission first met in July 2001, two days after the 13 incumbents had agreed on a bipartisan congressional delegation plan. The biggest changes were in the 12th District, which Democrat Rush Holt had won three times by narrow margins, and by just 651 votes in 2000, and the 7th District, which freshman Republican Mike Ferguson had won by just 52%–46% in 2000. Furious attempts were made to change the plan by Republican Finn Caspersen Jr., who wanted to challenge Holt, and Democrat Susan Bass Levin, who had run unsuccessfully in the 3d in 2000 and wanted to have Cherry Hill, of which she is mayor, placed in the heavily Democratic 1st where she could run if incumbent Rob Andrews should retire. But Camden County Democratic Chairman George Norcross had other candidates in mind, and Ferguson was bound to resist the major changes needed to put Caspersen's hometown of Bedminster into the 12th. Anyway, tie-breaker Alan Rosenthal, a prominent Rutgers political scientist, liked the idea of an incumbent-protection plan.

So in October 2001 the commission adopted the delegation plan with slight changes. Holt complained loudly, even though the Bush 2000 percentage in the 12th was reduced from 45% to 40%, one of the biggest such changes in the nation. Ferguson, whose district's Bush 2000 percentage was increased from 43% to 49%, was pleased. The result is a plan with very erose district lines and oddly shaped districts, drawn explicitly to protect incumbents and blessed by a political scientist.

Governor

James McGreevey (D)

Elected 2001, term expires Jan. 2006, 1st term; b. Aug. 6, 1957, Jersey City; home, Princeton; Columbia U., B.A. 1978; Georgetown U., J.D. 1981; Harvard U., M.A. 1982; Catholic; married (Dina).

Elected Office: NJ Assembly, 1990–91; Woodbridge Mayor, 1991–01; NJ Senate, 1994–97.

Professional Career: Asst. Prosecutor, Middlesex Cnty., 1982–83; Exec. Dir., NJ Parole Bd., 1985–87; Lobbyist, Merck & Co., 1987–89.

Office: P.O. Box 001, Trenton, 08625, 609-292-6000; Fax: 609-292-3454; Web site: www.state.nj.us.

Election Results

2001 general	James McGreevey (D)	1,256,853	(56%)
	Bret Schundler (R)	928,174	(42%)
2001 primary	James McGreevey (D)	250,404	(96%)
	Elliot Greenspan (D)	11,682	(4%)
1997 general	Christine Todd Whitman (R)	1,133,394	(47%)
	James McGreevey (D)	1,107,968	(46%)
	Murray Sabrin (L)	114,172	(5%)
	Other	65,099	(2%)

Jim McGreevey, elected governor of New Jersey in 2001, likes to note that he is the grandson of a beat cop in Jersey City. He grew up in Woodbridge, a mixed working and middle class township of 97,000 which contains the wondrous interchange of the Jersey Turnpike and the Garden State Parkway, where his father was a Marine Corps drill instructor and his mother a nurse. He graduated from Columbia and Georgetown Law School and got an education degree at Harvard. He returned to Woodbridge and served as a Middlesex County assistant prosecutor, then was appointed executive director of the State Parole Board by Governor Thomas Kean in 1985; two years later he became a lobbyist for the Merck pharmaceutical company. In 1989 he was elected to the Assembly, where he voted for Governor Jim Florio's $2.8 billion tax increase in 1990; he lost his Assembly seat in a 1991 primary challenge from Woodbridge Mayor Joseph DeMarino. But McGreevey then challenged DeMarino's mayoral reelection bid that same year; he won and then easily won reelection in 1995 and 1999. In 1993 McGreevey was elected state senator; in New Jersey, as in France, politicians can and often do serve as mayors and legislators at the same time.

As mayor, he was elected to his last term in 1999 with 80% of the vote. In the state Senate he sponsored a budget cap, changes in ethical standards, a pollution prevention law and a requirement that health insurance cover mammograms.

In 1997 he ran for governor. He started off less well known than the favorite in the primary, Congressman Rob Andrews. Andrews had a strong base in South Jersey plus machine support in Hudson County and a record as a moderate. McGreevey had his own strengths. He is a natural and untiring campaigner, a hard-working candidate who stays relentlessly on message. And he won the support of several critical North Jersey county Democratic organizations and labor unions. In the June primary, with big margins in Essex, Union and Middlesex Counties, he beat Andrews 39%–37%. In the general election Whitman was a strong favorite; she had kept her promise to cut taxes and seemed to have great appeal to moderates. But McGreevey attacked her again and again for soaring property taxes and auto insurance rates. In November he came up just short, losing 47%–46%.

It was a fine showing, and one that made him the natural nominee four years later. He never stopped running. In July 2000 Senator Bob Torricelli said he was considering running for governor; McGreevey got Newark Mayor Sharpe James and other leading politicians to say they would support him, and Torricelli withdrew after twelve days. Meanwhile, the Republicans were running into trouble. Whitman resigned in January 2001 to become EPA Administrator, leaving behind problems with a firm selected to perform auto emissions tests and the EZ-Pass system. Senate President Donald DiFrancesco, a product of the Union County Republican machine, became Acting Governor and, under New Jersey law, remained Senate president, and naturally he started running to be governor in his own right. He cleared the field of opponents who had support from Republican county organizations, but he still had primary opposition from Bret Schundler, a conservative who had become mayor of heavily Democratic Jersey City. It was widely assumed that DiFrancesco would be nominated easily, and McGreevey campaigned vigorously against the in-crowd in Trenton. But DiFrancesco turned out to have ethical problems. They began with a series of disclosures of favorable financial deals that he received from friends and close family members whom he helped win state jobs and contracts, plus possible conflicts of interests in his concurrent job as the town lawyer for Scotch Plains. Then he was forced to abandon Isabel Miranda, his choice for state treasurer, who had used her expense account for personal travel when she worked for Citibank and was still on leave from a bank that was a potential trustee for state funds. After blistering news stories, DiFrancesco quit the race on April 25, weeks before the June primary.

That would seem to leave Schundler with the nomination, but this is New Jersey. The legislature, just two days earlier, had passed a bill that postponed the primary until late June and allowed the party organization to place another candidate on the ballot. The state Supreme Court, always ready to help the insiders of any party, approved this maneuver, and former Congressman Bob Franks, who lost the 2000 Senate race to Jon Corzine by only 50%–47%, became the organization candidate, endorsed by Republican organizations in 19 of 21 counties. But evidently it was a little much for Republican primary voters. Schundler won 57%–43%. Franks carried his home base, Union County, and five South Jersey counties; Schundler won big margins in his home base, Hudson County, and some big suburban counties.

Schundler's victory caused McGreevey to shift from running against the Trenton establishment to running against a supposed extremist. He made much of Schundler's opposition to abortion and support of a carry-concealed weapon law, although Schundler said he would make no attempt to change New Jersey's abortion or gun control laws. Franks endorsed Schundler, but DiFrancesco pointedly refused to do so, and many organization Republicans made it clear they preferred McGreevey as a man they could do business with. Schundler campaigned for school choice (which Republican legislators, supported by teachers' unions, had blocked for Jersey City), and promised to remove tolls on the Garden State Parkway. He also opposed any tax increases, and may have gotten some traction on the issue; in an October debate McGreevey, who had been ambiguous on the issue, said, "We're not going to raise taxes. I'm committed to not raising taxes." McGreevey won 56%–42%, a result almost identical to Al Gore's 56%–40% win in 2000. Democrats captured a majority in the Assembly; while the Senate was divided 20–20. In January 2002, New Jersey had four governors in eight days. DiFrancesco's term in the Senate and hence his status as Acting Governor ended January 8. With the new Senate evenly split, both parties selected acting governors for three-and-one-half days: Attorney General John Farmer and co-state Senate President John Bennett (his wife did considerable entertaining at Drumthwacket, the governor's mansion). Then, on January 15, McGreevey was sworn in.

"Santa isn't coming to the state legislature with Christmas tree lists this year. We need to cut back. We need to be fiscally responsible. We need to live within our means," said McGreevey in November. To avoid raising the sales or income taxes, he dipped into surplus and worker benefit funds. He did increase the cigarette tax by 70 cents and increased the corporate business tax. He held the line on state aid to education and local governments. He agreed to finance a Newark arena for the Nets and Devils after Newark Mayor Sharpe James withheld local legislators' votes on the corporate business tax; he also owed James for his support in July 2000 when Torricelli made a feint at running for governor. He moved against sprawl by issuing orders halting development in several counties and scrapped Whitman's emissions trading program. He got the legislature to pass the nation's first law requiring handguns to contain a device allowing only designated owners to fire them, but it cannot be enforced until the technology is developed. Auto emissions inspections were given back to service stations rather than a statewide contractor.

In October 2002 he played a key role in easing Torricelli off the ballot and substituting former Senator Frank Lautenberg on the ballot. He was embarrassed when two of his appointees, state police superintendent Joseph Santiago and homeland security adviser Golan Cipel, were forced to resign. He was embarrassed also when Amiri Baraka, whom he named as state poet laureate, published a poem in which he claimed that Jews were behind the World Trade Center bombing; McGreevey urged Baraka to resign, but he refused. He was criticized for spending $629,000 to renovate a parking garage in Drumthwacket. In July 2002 he made a trip to Ireland; in December he agreed to have the state Democratic party repay the state for $75,000 in expenses, including a $720 hotel suite and a chauffeured car; he himself repaid the state $3,100 for expenses for a family reunion. He also had the state repaid for $18,000 for private trips on state helicopters.

By April 2003 McGreevey's job rating had fallen to 38%–44% and he continued to face serious fiscal problems. Meanwhile he prepared to raise funds for state legislative elections in November 2003. A possible problem: In January 2003 an appellate court ordered redrawing of the state legislative districts; the commission had produced a Democratic plan.

Senior Senator

Jon Corzine (D)

Elected 2000, seat up 2006, 1st term; b. Jan. 1, 1947, Taylorville, IL; home, Summit; U. of IL (Urbana-Champaign), B.A. 1969; U. of Chicago, M.B.A. 1973; Christian; divorced.

Military Career: Marine Corps Reserves, 1969–75.

Professional Career: Officer, Continental IL Natl. Bank, 1970–73; Asst. V.P., BancOhio, 1973–75; Goldman Sachs, Bond Trader 1975–80, Partner 1980–99, Chmn. & CEO 1994–99.

DC Office: 502 HSOB, 20510, 202-224-4744; Fax: 202-228-2197; Web site: corzine.senate.gov.

State Offices: Barrington, 856-757-5353; Newark, 973-645-3030.

Committees: *DSCC Chairman. Banking, Housing & Urban Affairs:* Housing & Transportation; International Trade & Finance; Securities & Investment. *Budget. Foreign Relations:* East Asian & Pacific Affairs; International Economic Policy, Export & Trade Promotion; Near Eastern & South Asian Affairs.

Group Ratings

	ADA	ACLU	AFS	LCV	CON	ITIC	NTU	COC	ACU	NTLC	CHC
2002	100	60	100	94	81	—	20	50	5	0	—
2001	100	—	100	100	—	—	9	36	0	—	0

National Journal Ratings

	2001 LIB	—	2001 CONS		2002 LIB	—	2002 CONS
Economic	93%	—	0%		73%	—	20%
Social	95%	—	0%		82%	—	0%
Foreign	87%	—	3%		93%	—	6%

Key Votes of the 107th Congress

1. Approve Bush Tax Cuts	N	5. Confirm Ashcroft as AG	N	9. Bar Coop. with Intl. Court	Y
2. Expand Patients' Rights	Y	6. Bar Gays in the Boy Scouts	N	10. Trade Promotion Authority	N
3. Campaign Finance Reform	Y	7. $ for Hate Crime Prosecution	Y	11. Authorize Force in Iraq	N
4. Permit ANWR Development	N	8. Overseas Military Abortions	Y	12. Homeland Sec. Dept. Union	*

Election Results

2000 general	Jon Corzine (D)	1,511,237	(50%)	($63,209,506)
	Bob Franks (R)	1,420,267	(47%)	($6,389,936)
	Other	84,158	(3%)	
2000 primary	Jon Corzine (D)	251,216	(58%)	
	Jim Florio (D)	182,212	(42%)	
1994 general	Frank Lautenberg (D)	1,033,487	(50%)	($8,217,716)
	Garabed (Chuck) Haytaian (R)	966,244	(47%)	($5,110,378)
	Other	55,156	(3%)	

Jon Corzine, former chairman of Goldman Sachs, was elected senator from New Jersey in 2000 after waging the most expensive Senate campaign in American history. Corzine (pronounced *cor-ZYNE*) grew up on a family farm in Downstate Illinois, far from New Jersey; he went to college at the University of Illinois, business school at the University of Chicago and served six years in the Marine Corps Reserve. In 1975 he joined Goldman Sachs in New York; his entry-level position included fetching coffee for his superiors. Corzine was a successful bond trader and a protégé of Robert Rubin, who became Treasury Secretary in the Clinton administration. In 1980 Corzine was made a general partner and in 1994 he became co-chairman and CEO. In May 1999 Goldman Sachs went public, and the $3.66 billion initial offering netted Corzine more than $300 million; he retired in 1999 after a management shakeup. Aside from contributing to Democratic (and some Republican) candidates, he was not involved in politics, indeed did not vote in primary elections from 1988 to 1998 or in the 1991, 1995 and 1998 general elections; in 1997 he co-chaired a presidential commission on increasing investment in technology, infrastructure and schools.

In early 1999, a Senate race was probably the farthest thing from Corzine's mind. Then, in February 1999, Senator Frank Lautenberg announced he would not run again in 2000 (Lautenberg, of course, returned to win election to Senator Bob Torricelli's seat in 2002, and is now Corzine's junior colleague). Plunging immediately into the race was former Governor Jim Florio, still unpopular for the $2.8 billion tax increase he secured in 1990. In April Governor Christine Todd Whitman, presumably the strongest possible Republican candidate, announced she was running. Many Democratic insiders, including Torricelli, feared that Whitman would win the seat, and scurried around to find other contenders.

Then Torricelli and North Jersey Democratic insiders found Corzine, with $300 million and without a job. He started running, going around the state to meet leaders of the county Democratic organizations, who are considered vital in the primary, and, it was revealed much later, contributing generously to them and to community organizations. He quickly cornered organization support outside Florio's home area in South Jersey and, like most local Democratic insiders, endorsed Al Gore over New Jersey's Bill Bradley. Meanwhile, Corzine's great wealth and his willingness to spend it cleared the field; Whitman withdrew in September. Corzine's money talked even while most New Jersey voters had never heard of him.

Still Florio, backed by Camden County Democratic leader George Norcross and some labor unions, campaigned aggressively. He attacked Corzine's inexperience and spotty voting record. He said Corzine represented "Wall Street values" and was attempting a "hostile takeover of the Democratic party." He charged that under Corzine, Goldman Sachs floated a bond issue for a company that invests in Sudan, with its terrible human rights record. Even so, New Jersey Democratic leaders dreaded that Florio would lose to even the little-known candidates running for the Republican nomination. In March, three months before the primary, Corzine went up with TV ads in the New York and Philadelphia markets. He set forth his liberal stands on issues—for a universal health care system, for government payment of tuition to college or vocational or technical school for students with at least a B average, for gun control, for abortion rights. Corzine's investment—he spent $35 million up to the June primary—paid off. Florio won in South Jersey by a 67%–33% margin, but South Jersey cast only 23% of the votes. In North Jersey Corzine led 65%–35%, for an overall 58%–42% victory.

After the primary, Corzine cut back on spending—for a while. The Republican primary, with a pathetically low turnout, was won by 7th District Congressman Bob Franks—amazingly, a member of the same church as Corzine. With North Jersey support, Franks narrowly (36%–34%) edged state Senator William Gormley, who had a big financial advantage thanks to support from Atlantic City casino interests. Corzine's ads talked about his big-government positions in appealing terms, but he almost made a political neophyte's mistakes that got him bad publicity. In early September he told the Sierra Club he had voted for an open space referendum in 1998; but in 1998 he had not voted at all. Still stuck below 50% in the polls, he started running negative ads against Franks two weeks later. He had been refusing to make his income tax returns public, on the ground they violated a confidentiality agreement with Goldman Sachs. Then in mid-September he released records showing that in 1996–99 he made $145 million, paid $43 million in taxes and gave $25 million to charity. But when reporters started investigating which charities, they found that he had stepped up giving to New Jersey groups in 1999, and that he gave hundreds of thousands to groups whose leaders and sponsors later endorsed him. He gave $30,000 to a dinner honoring Lautenberg, who later endorsed him; he gave $50,000 to Operation Rainbow/PUSH, and Jesse Jackson endorsed him the night before the primary; he gave $25,000 to St. Matthew's A.M.E. Church in Orange and was endorsed by the Black Ministers Alliance of New Jersey. When he was asked whether he had contributed to any of the churches, he said no; it turned out his family foundation made the contribution.

Franks, like Florio, argued that Corzine was trying to buy a Senate seat and attacked him for failing to disclose the tax returns and for backing "universal" government programs that were unrealistic and too costly. When Corzine's numbers stalled because of his mistakes, Franks held onto his money and spent $2.5 million in the last two and a half weeks, when he also benefited from endorsements by the *New York Times* and the *Philadelphia Inquirer*. Corzine spent $7.4 million on turnout efforts including, embarrassingly, busing in residents of Philadelphia homeless shelters and halfway houses to work on his campaign. In the end Corzine spent more than $63 million, the all-time record. He won 50%–47%, with big margins in central cities—the turnout effort delivered. But that trailed the generic vote in increasingly Democratic New Jersey.

In the Senate Corzine has had a very liberal voting record; he declined to join the Democratic Leadership Council and has consistently argued that Democrats, having earned credibility on macroeconomic issues in the 1990s, should take forthright liberal stands. He continued to support universal health care, called for a national moratorium on the death penalty and a national ban of racial profiling; he voted against the Iraq war resolution in October 2002. Only on the 2002 farm bill did he strike another note: He was one of two Democrats voting against because, he said, it was too expensive. He voted against the 2001 Bush tax cuts and in August 2002 said Congress should "rescind or freeze" them; in January 2003 he led Democrats in opposing that year's Bush tax cut, arguing that by siphoning off dividends it might reduce investment and called for a $300 rebate instead. On Social Security he was one of the Democrats' leading critics of individual investment accounts.

But he got the most attention on the issue of corporate accountability raised by the collapse of Enron in December 2001. Majority Leader Tom Daschle made a point of having Corzine at his side when speaking on the issue, and it is obviously a subject on which he has special expertise. Some criticized him because Enron had been a big Goldman Sachs client and for pushing and defending monthly income preferred shares, a device promoted by Goldman Sachs by which companies sold 50-year preferred stock through an entity created on a Caribbean island, which was considered debt for tax purposes and equity for corporate purposes; but as Corzine pointed out the device was announced publicly and found to be legal by authorities. Corzine, who put his money in a blind trust and has said he would not vote on legislation affecting his portfolio, said in January 2002 that SEC Chairman Harvey Pitt should recuse himself from the SEC's review of auditing standards because he used to work for the Big Five accounting firms. He was not, however, one of the senators who called on Pitt to resign. "Contrary to popular opinion," Corzine said in February 2002. "I think he's been pretty forceful." Corzine argued that Enron and other scandals indicated the need for more regulation. In early 2002 he called for regulating hedge funds, stronger enforcement powers for the SEC and tougher limits on special purpose entities. With Barbara Boxer, he sponsored a law allowing no more than 20% of a worker's 401(k) to be invested in a single stock. On the Banking Committee, he worked with Chairman Paul Sarbanes on his corporate accountability bill, and bemoaned that it seemed stalled in June 2002. But then the WorldCom scandal came along, and the bill, slightly amended, became the Sarbanes-Oxley Act. He has argued that financial services regulation should be concentrated in the Federal Reserve and the SEC, not the Comptroller of the Currency or the Commodities Futures Trading Commission, and said that the current system provides no consolidated view of regulation of derivatives markets.

September 11 hit New Jersey especially hard—Corzine noted that 10 people from Summit, where he owns a home, died at the World Trade Center—and Corzine's major initiative in response was a chemical security bill that would require businesses that house chemicals to conduct vulnerability assessments and consider safer security technology. He sought to attach it to the homeland security bill in fall 2002, but others argued that it would put undue burdens on stores selling fertilizer and pesticide, and his provision failed. He was also a cosponsor of the Terrorism Risk Insurance Act, which became law in November 2002.

Corzine is a stronger partisan than many senators who have spent all their adult lives in politics, and from 1999 has thrown himself, and his money, into building the Democratic party in New Jersey and in the nation as a whole. He and his family gave more than $1 million to various Democratic entities in 2000, and he gave $1.6 million to New Jersey Democrats in the 2001 state elections—money that helped them gain a majority in the Assembly and a 20–20 split in the state Senate. He gave $837,000 to the First Jersey PAC run by George Norcross, his adversary in the 2000 primary. In the 2002 cycle he gave more than $1 million to Democrats across the country and $250,000 to the DSCC, including $100,000 on November 5, the last day on which such soft money contributions were legal.

Throughout the 2002 cycle he let it be known that he would like to become DSCC chairman after the election. He showed his skills at handling difficult political situations in the imbroglio over whether Bob Torricelli should drop out of the 2002 Senate race. He had backed Torricelli all along, but helped to negotiate Torricelli's departure and the selection of Frank Lautenberg to replace him; he was in the room with Jim McGreevey and other leading New Jersey Democrats when the negotiations were going on and was the one person there most concerned with the effect on the national Democratic party. In December 2002 Tom Daschle chose Corzine to head the DSCC. Corzine, as a candidate recruited just four years before, knows that candidate recruitment is important; he is expected to seek at least some self-financing millionaires like himself to run in races that might otherwise be difficult or hopeless. But he has said that the campaign finance law provision setting higher contribution limits for opponents of self-financers might reduce their advantage. His net worth of $300 million will presumably be reduced by his 2002 divorce, but the personal incomes he reported for 2000 and 2001—$71 million and $46 million— suggest that he will have enough to continue his present rate of giving for many cycles to come.

Junior Senator

Frank Lautenberg (D)

Elected 2002, seat up 2008, 1st term; b. Jan. 23, 1924, Paterson; home, Cliffside Park; Columbia U., B.S. 1949; Jewish; divorced.

Military Career: Army Signal Corps, 1942–46 (WWII).

Elected Office: U.S. Senate, 1982–00.

Professional Career: Co–founder, Automatic Data Processing, 1952–82; NY & NJ Port Authority Comm., 1978–82.

DC Office: 324 HSOB, 20510, 202-224-3224; Fax: 202-228-4054; Web site: lautenberg.senate.gov.

State Office: Newark, 973-639-8704.

Committees: *Commerce, Science & Transportation*: Aviation; Competition, Foreign Commerce & Infrastructure; Science, Technology & Space; Surface Transportation & Merchant Marine. *Governmental Affairs*: Financial Management, Budget & International Security; Government Management, Federal Workforce & the District of Columbia; Investigations (Permanent).

Group Ratings and Key Votes: Newly Elected

Election Results

2002 general	Frank Lautenberg (D)	1,138,193	(54%)	($2,929,206)
	Douglas Forrester (R)	928,439	(44%)	($10,606,843)
	Other	45,972	(2%)	
1996 general	Robert G. Torricelli (D)	1,519,154	(53%)	($9,134,854)
	Dick Zimmer (R)	1,227,351	(43%)	($8,238,181)
	Other	136,961	(5%)	

Prior Winning Percentages: 1994 (50%); 1988 (54%); 1982 (51%)

Frank Lautenberg is, once again, New Jersey's junior Senator. He was elected in 1982, 1988 and 1994 and retired in 2000, then returned to run again in October 2002 after Bob Torricelli withdrew from the race. With his personal wealth and name recognition, Lautenberg was an obvious choice to succeed Torricelli; New Jersey Democrats persuaded the state Supreme Court to let them put Lautenberg's name on the ballot. Lautenberg grew up in Paterson, the son of an immigrant silk worker. He served in the Army Signal Corps in World War II and says he never would have gone to college without the G.I. Bill of Rights. He graduated from Columbia and in 1952 started a company called Automatic Data Processing, which by the mid-1990s had almost 30,000 employees and processed the payroll for nearly 10% of private sector jobs in the United States—a brilliant success story. When ADP went public in 1961, Lautenberg's stock was worth $50,000; now his net worth is in the vicinity of $40 million. Lautenberg was a contributor to Democratic campaigns and got on Richard Nixon's enemies list when he contributed $90,000 to George McGovern in 1972.

But no one thought of him as a candidate until, not for the last time, scandal provided an opening: Democratic Senator Harrison Williams resigned in March 1982 as the Senate was considering his expulsion after his conviction in the Abscam case, and his appointed successor, Republican Nicholas Brady, made it clear he was not running for a full term (he became the first George Bush's Treasury Secretary). Lautenberg ran and spent $5 million of his own money and boasted of his high-tech experience. He beat several professional politicians in the primary and upset Republican Congresswoman Millicent Fenwick in the general 51%–48%. During the campaign he referred to the 72-year-old Fenwick, who was satirized in *Doonesbury*, as "eccentric" and a "national monument" and questioned her "fitness" and "ability to do the job."

Lautenberg believes government helped him and others work their way up, and in his first three terms had a solidly liberal voting record. He bucked the party only occasionally: In 1993, as Governor Jim Florio was being attacked for his 1990 tax increase, Lautenberg voted against the Clinton tax increase. As chairman and ranking Democrat on the Transportation Appropriations

Subcommittee, he got Congress to ban smoking first on two-hour flights, then on all domestic flights. After the tobacco settlement was announced in 1997 he pushed for an immediate $1.50 tax. He is a strong backer of gun control and author of the 1996 law barring those convicted of domestic abuse from possessing firearms.

On the Environment Committee, Lautenberg resisted Republican efforts to rewrite the Superfund law and pushed instead for separate measures to allow development of brownfields, numerous in New Jersey. He has some bipartisan achievements, including his work on the 1996 Safe Water Drinking Act and his support on the Budget Committee of the 1997 balanced budget agreement. He worked hard to maintain Amtrak funding.

New Jersey is the second most expensive state to campaign in, because candidates must buy New York and Philadelphia TV, and Lautenberg's willingness to spend large amounts of his own money helped him win reelection over retired General Pete Dawkins in 1988 by 54%–46% and Assembly Speaker Chuck Haytaian in 1994 by 50%–47%. He can be an aggressive campaigner. *Slate's* Chris Suellentrop noted, too harshly perhaps, that Lautenberg is "scrappy, sometimes mean, unpopular, occasionally nasty and insecure. In short, he's New Jersey." In 1998 he seemed primed to run again, and no well-known Republican seemed eager to challenge him. But in February 1999 he announced that he would retire in 2000. "A powerful factor in my decision was the searing reality that I would have to spend half of every day between now and the next election fundraising." So instead he enjoyed his last two years in the Senate and then returned to a comfortable private life serving on corporate and charitable boards.

One thing he surely did not miss was dealing with his colleague Bob Torricelli. Relationships between senators of the same state and party are often frayed and acrimonious; but the relationship between Lautenberg and Torricelli was probably more hostile than any since 1859, when California Senator David Broderick was killed in a duel with his colleague William Gwin's best friend. In March 1999, as Torricelli, the chairman of the Senate Democrats' campaign committee, was briefing colleagues, Lautenberg accused him of being too friendly with Republican Governor Christine Todd Whitman; Torricelli was enraged and in full view after the meeting approached Lautenberg and, as the *New York Times* daintily put it, "made a vulgar threat on his manhood." So Lautenberg was one New Jersey Democrat who was not unhappy when Torricelli fell into disfavor with voters in his 2002 reelection campaign.

In most respects, Torricelli seemed a clear favorite to win: A Democratic senator in a Democratic state, willing on occasion to take stands against his party which were popular in New Jersey. Whitman became EPA administrator and was out of the race, and the strongest possible Republican, former Governor Thomas Kean, announced in November 2001 that he would not run. Torricelli was a brilliant fundraiser and it seemed unlikely that the Senate Republicans' campaign committee would want to fund a New Jersey candidate, which would cost about as much as funding candidates in the seriously contested races in South Dakota, Missouri, South Carolina, North Carolina and Colorado put together. The best known of the Republicans to announce, Essex County Executive James Treffinger, who had finished third in the 2000 Senate primary, left the race after prosecutors began investigating him in April 2002 for campaign finance violations. The three candidates in the June primary were mostly unknown—businessman Doug Forrester, South Jersey state Senators Susan Allen and John Matheussen. Money made the difference: Forrester, who started BeneCard, a manager of prescription drug benefits, was worth some $50 million and spent $3 million in the primary and beat Allen by a 45%–37% margin.

But scandal loomed over Torricelli. For three years the U.S. Attorney's office in Manhattan had been investigating charges that businessman David Chang had given lavish gifts and cash to Torricelli and that Torricelli had worked to advance Chang's business interests in Korea. Torricelli did give such assistance, but denied receiving gifts. In January 2002 U.S. Attorney Mary Jo White announced that Torricelli would not be prosecuted. But Chang was prosecuted for $53,700 in illegal contributions to Torricelli's 1996 campaign and sentenced in May 2002 to 18 months in prison. White had sent information about the charges to the Senate Ethics Committee; in July the committee held closed-door hearings and Torricelli testified for seven hours. Torricelli admitted receiving expensive merchandise—a $9,200 Rolex watch, 10 hand-tailored Italian suits—but said that he had reimbursed Chang. On July 30 the committee "severely admonished" Torricelli for violating the Senate rule against receiving gifts over $50 but did not release the evidence to the public.

Forrester made much of Torricelli's problems. On the stump he would introduce himself by saying, "I'm the guy running against Bob Torricelli." In late July, the *New York Times* and WNBC-TV reported that a giant television and a $3,800 grandfather clock paid for by Chang had been delivered to Torricelli's house. In September, a federal judge in a lawsuit brought by news media ordered the unsealing of the memorandum on the case written by prosecutors in the U.S. Attorney's office. They found "credible" Chang's allegations that Torricelli had accepted "tens of thousands" of dollars in gifts and cash. As details poured out, Torricelli plummeted in the polls. On Saturday, September 28, a *Star-Ledger* poll showed Forrester ahead 47%–34%—a devastating result. On Sunday Governor Jim McGreevey, Senator Jon Corzine and other New Jersey Democratic leaders met in Trenton and patched in Majority Leader Tom Daschle over the phone: Obviously they were trying to get Torricelli to withdraw from the race. On Monday Torricelli's office announced he would hold a press conference at 11 a.m.; he finally appeared around 5 p.m. and, in a lugubrious speech, withdrew. "I will not be responsible for the loss of the Democratic majority in the United States Senate," he said. "I will not allow it to happen."

New Jersey Democrats were now in need of a well-known candidate to replace Torricelli. Congressman Bob Menendez, seeking a leadership position in the House, wasn't interested. Congressman Rob Andrews was presumably vetoed by McGreevey, who had narrowly beaten him in the 1997 gubernatorial primary. Congressman Frank Pallone, after giving it some thought, decided not to run. The risk of giving up a safe House seat to seek a nomination that might be rejected by a court may have seemed too great. Former Senator Bill Bradley let it be known he had no interest whatever. But Lautenberg, now evidently missing life in the Senate, said he would "seriously consider serving again if asked." It seems unlikely that Torricelli would have withdrawn if he had known that Lautenberg would get the nomination. But there was nothing he could do to stop him. Lautenberg was well known and capable of self-financing. McGreevey and the other Democrats quickly agreed on him.

New Jersey law does not contain a provision for substituting a new candidate so late in the campaign unless a candidate has died; ballots had already been printed with Torricelli's name. But the New Jersey Supreme Court is made up of judicial activists of both parties with a propensity to accommodate the insiders of both major parties. In October 2002 it quickly approved state Democrats' request to substitute Lautenberg for Torricelli and ordered the state Democratic party to pay the $800,000 needed to print new ballots. The Lautenberg campaign moved into the Torricelli headquarters and Lautenberg was again a candidate for the Senate, without having to spend months fundraising. The easiest source of funds proved unavailable: Torricelli would not send over a dime from his $5 million campaign treasury. Lautenberg spent $1.5 million of his own money, and those funds, plus $1.2 million from national and New Jersey Democrats, turned out to be enough in this Democratic state.

Now Forrester could no longer introduce himself as "the guy running against Bob Torricelli." He did run a cute ad on cable TV, showing a kid slamming his desk and saying, "I can't do this. I quit! If I fail this test, can I have Frank Lautenberg take it for me?" Forrester attacked Lautenberg as soft on defense and terrorism, citing his 1991 vote against the Gulf War resolution and he questioned whether Lautenberg at 78—six years older than Millicent Fenwick was when Lautenberg questioned her ability to do the job—was too old. Lautenberg attacked Forrester on Social Security, prescription drugs, abortion and gun control: Forrester was against state-paid abortions and had written a 1992 column in the *West Windsor-Plainsboro Chronicle* on owning semiautomatic guns. "Liberty is all about the government allowing citizens to do weird things unless there is a compelling documented public purpose which should preclude them." On October 30 they appeared together for 30 minutes on News 12 New Jersey, a cable channel available to 55% of state households; Lautenberg seemed a little ragged, but was plainly still up to the job. Forrester spent $10 million altogether, $7.5 million of it his own money; the Senate Republican campaign committee did not make New Jersey a top priority.

Unsurprisingly, Lautenberg won 54%–44%, a better showing than in 1994; but then New Jersey has become more Democratic than it was in 1994. He won big majorities in the central cities where turnout, as compared to 1994, declined; he lost the Jersey Shore and northwest New Jersey, where turnout was up. He seemed satisfied to be where he was, a satisfaction perhaps augmented by the plight of Torricelli. But he was disappointed when Senate Democrats did not give him credit for all his seniority; his previous service only entitled him to seniority over other freshmen. "What I am trying to do is to picture myself as a tenured professor who took a sabbatical after 18 years and now wants to go into my 19th year. I think some of the leadership thinks I ought to wear a freshman beanie, but that is not my style. I have too big a head."

FIRST DISTRICT

Rep. Robert Andrews (D)

Elected 1990, 7th term; b. Aug. 4, 1957, Camden; home, Haddon Heights; Bucknell U., B.A. 1979, Cornell U., J.D. 1982; Episcopalian; married (Camille).

Elected Office: Camden Cnty. Bd. of Chosen Freeholders, 1987–90.

Professional Career: Practicing atty., 1982–90; Adjunct Prof., Rutgers Law Schl., 1985–86, 1989–90.

DC Office: 2439 RHOB 20515, 202-225-6501; Fax: 202-225-6583; Web site: www.house.gov/andrews.

District Offices: Haddon Heights, 856-546-5100; Woodbury, 856-848-3900.

Committees: *Education & the Workforce* (5th of 22 D): 21st Century Competitiveness; Employer-Employee Relations (RMM). *Select Committee on Homeland Security* (12th of 23 D): Cybersecurity, Science and Research & Development; Intelligence & Counterterrorism.

Group Ratings

	ADA	ACLU	AFS	LCV	CON	ITIC	NTU	COC	ACU	NTLC	CHC
2002	90	73	89	88	92	50	23	32	8	22	8
2001	90	—	100	100	—	—	19	41	20	—	—

National Journal Ratings

	2001 LIB —	2001 CONS		2002 LIB —	2002 CONS
Economic	60% —	40%		64% —	35%
Social	74% —	23%		74% —	26%
Foreign	56% —	41%		62% —	36%

Key Votes of the 107th Congress

1. Approve Bush Tax Cuts	N	5. Faith-Based Charities	N	9. Trade Promotion Authority	N
2. Limit Patients' Bill of Rights	N	6. Bar Gays in the Boy Scouts	N	10. Bar Funds for Intl. Court	N
3. Campaign Finance Reform	Y	7. Ban Partial-Birth Abortion	N	11. Authorize Force in Iraq	Y
4. Ban ANWR Development	Y	8. Arm Commercial Pilots	*	12. Deny Home. Sec. Dept. Union	N

Election Results

2002 general	Robert Andrews (D)	121,846	(93%)	($643,964)
	Timothy Haas (I)	9,543	(7%)	
2002 primary	Robert Andrews (D)	unopposed		
2000 general	Robert Andrews (D)	167,327	(76%)	($405,723)
	Charlene Cathcart (R)	46,455	(21%)	($7,162)
	Other	5,830	(3%)	

Prior Winning Percentages: 1998 (73%); 1996 (76%); 1994 (72%); 1992 (67%); 1990 (54%); 1990 (55%)

The People		Race/Ethnic Origin	Ancestry	
Area size:	352 sq. mi.	71.2% White	Irish: 16.8%	Italian: 14.8%
Urban population:	98.6%	16.3% Black	German: 13.0%	
Rural population:	1.4%	2.6% Asian	**2000 Presidential Vote**	
Pop. 2000:	647,258	0.2% Native Am.	Gore (D)...............144,226 (63%)	
Median income:	$47,473	0.0% Hawaiian	Bush (R)................77,367 (34%)	
Poverty status:	9.9%	1.3% Two+ races	Other....................7,261 (3%)	
Military veterans:	12.4%	0.1% Other	**Cook Partisan Voting Index:** D +15	
		8.2% Hispanic Origin		

Occupation	Blue collar: 22.8%	White collar: 62.4%	Gray collar: 14.8%

The closely built streets of the little city of Camden, New Jersey, across the Delaware River from Philadelphia's skyline, have seen a fair amount of history. This was where the poet Walt Whitman lived when he wrote some of the versions of his *Leaves of Grass*. It was an immigrant-jammed industrial city then, with tinkerers and inventors. In 1894, a Camden machinist named Eldridge Johnson produced the Victor Talking Machine—the birth of the company that became RCA Victor in 1929 and the beginning of the recorded music industry. In 1897, Camden was the site of the invention of condensed soup, and the Campbell Soup Company was founded soon afterwards. Camden remained for years afterward a major industrial locus on the Jersey side of the Delaware River, not the broadest and certainly not the most picturesque of our Atlantic estuaries, but probably the East Coast's premier industrial waterway, with a concentration of steel factories, chemical plants and oil tank farms equal to any in the country. The flat lands of South Jersey all around, mostly ignored in the 19th century, had easy access to cheap water transport and plenty of skilled labor from the Philadelphia area. For a quarter-century starting in the 1940s, they became one of the country's fastest-growing industrial areas.

Now, Camden has tended to empty out, many of its factories closed, its neighborhoods beset by crime, its mostly minority residents heavily dependent on public assistance, its local government so incompetent that its mayor was convicted for doing favors for Philadelphia's organized crime leaders. The state has been paying for two-thirds of the nearly-bankrupt city's budget. But the city, the second-poorest in America, offers a few attractions: A newly-developed riverfront park, the New Jersey Aquarium and the Sony Music/Pace amphitheater; an aerospace complex and a Campbell Soup office tower have gone up; a light-rail transit system is scheduled to connect Camden and Trenton in the summer of 2003, though critics call it pork.

The 1st Congressional District is, more or less, greater Camden, the Delaware riverfront from Riverton south to a point across from the Delaware state line, and suburbs running southeast to the flat vegetable fields of South Jersey. It is traversed by Black Horse Pike and White Horse Pike, two of the most heavily traveled roads in this densely populated part of South Jersey. Both routes dates back two centuries; today, they connect Philadelphia and its middle class South Jersey suburbs. Many of these boroughs and townships developed over the past half-century as a result of flight from Camden; a few, like Gloucester City, emerged on their own rather than as an outgrowth of the city. The PATCO High-Speed Line to Philadelphia is just a quick trip over the Delaware River from here, making for an easy commute from places such as prosperous Haddonfield. The district includes a growing number of Hispanics, primarily Puerto Ricans in Camden, though Mexicans from Puebla, in central Mexico, have been arriving in the region for the past decade. Politically, this is an area with a Democratic heritage.

The 1st District is represented by Rob Andrews, first elected in 1990. Andrews grew up in Bellmawr, the son of a shipyard worker, made a splendid record in college and law school, returned home and with then-Congressman Jim Florio's support was elected to the Camden County Board of Chosen Freeholders before he was 30. When Florio left Congress to become governor in January 1990, he postponed the special election to replace him until November; he supported Andrews, though Andrews was silent on Florio's controversial state tax increase. Andrews had other help. He spent $541,000 on his campaign, and he had a Republican opponent who switched positions on abortion and claimed to have attended a college he hadn't. Even so, in the anti-Florio climate, Andrews won by only 54%–43%.

He has a rather conservative record on economics and foreign policy but is more liberal on cultural issues. He voted against tax increases, including the Clinton budget package of 1993 and announced early opposition to the Clinton health care program. To some of Andrews's Democratic critics, he is a grandstander who would cut needed government programs. But he argues that he supports government that is vigorous and serves real needs—but insists on pruning government that isn't working and on not forcing voters to pay more in taxes for the same low level of services they've been getting.

In the Republican House, Andrews has had less opportunity for such initiatives but he has remained active, often by working with Republicans. As the ranking Democrat on the Employer-Employee Relations Subcommittee, he worked with committee chairman John Boehner to expand its focus on pension and retirement issues. Unlike most Democrats, he advocates the national missile defense system. As an ardent supporter of the use of force in Iraq, Andrews joined other House Democratic supporters in several meetings with George W. Bush. On the Armed Services Committee since 1999, he has worked to protect the nation's public and private-sector computers from terrorist attacks. Andrews has been a leader among regular Democrats on several key party initiatives, including expanded health insurance, HMO reform, and education funding. Back home, he joined the three South Jersey Republicans in seeking to split the state into two federal judicial districts. He opposed the Army Corps of Engineers plan to dredge the Delaware River to permit ships to carry more freight to Philadelphia and Camden.

After the 1996 election, he announced he was running for governor; he managed to get the endorsements of Florio and Hudson County Executive Bob Janiszewski, who were both mentioned as candidates themselves. Andrews was initially favored to win the primary in June 1997, but he ran into stiff competition from then-state Senator James McGreevey, who had the backing of more Democratic county organizations in North Jersey plus key elements of organized labor. Andrews swept South Jersey and took Hudson County, but McGreevey's big margins in Middlesex, Essex and Union Counties gave him a tight 39%–37% win.

Andrews has been re-elected to the House by overwhelming margins—without Republican opposition in 2002—and he has continued to live in Haddon Heights, commuting by train to the Capitol and occasionally sleeping overnight in his office. Despite his split with the Camden County Democratic organization, his House seat seems safe as long as he wants it. His close loss in the gubernatorial primary and his $1.2 million campaign surplus suggest he may be thinking of another statewide race. But he did not challenge McGreevey in the 2001 primary, and while he made clear his interest in replacing Bob Torricelli in September 2000, McGreevey, now governor, certainly did not back him. The next statewide opportunities will be in 2008, when Senator Frank Lautenberg will probably not seek another term at 84, and 2009, when McGreevey will be barred from running by term limits if he is reelected in 2005 and will not likely be a viable candidate if he isn't. That's a long time, but Andrews will be only in his early 50s.

SECOND DISTRICT

Rep. Frank LoBiondo (R)

Elected 1994, 5th term; b. May 12, 1946, Bridgeton; home, Vineland; St. Joseph's U., B.A. 1968; Catholic; married (Jan).

Elected Office: Cumberland Cnty. Bd. of Chosen Freeholders, 1985–88; NJ Assembly, 1987–94.

Professional Career: Operations Mgr., LoBiondo Bros. Motor Express Inc., 1968–94.

DC Office: 225 CHOB 20515, 202-225-6572; Fax: 202-225-3318; Web site: www.house.gov/lobiondo.

District Office: Mays Landing, 609-625-5008.

Committees: *Armed Services* (24th of 33 R): Tactical Air & Land Forces; Terrorism, Unconventional Threats & Capabilities. *Transportation & Infrastructure* (16th of 41 R): Aviation; Coast Guard & Maritime Transportation (Chmn.); Highways, Transit & Pipelines.

Group Ratings

	ADA	ACLU	AFS	LCV	CON	ITIC	NTU	COC	ACU	NTLC	CHC
2002	15	13	22	63	75	62	52	75	80	72	75
2001	30	—	30	86	—	—	56	70	60	—	—

National Journal Ratings

	2001 LIB	—	2001 CONS		2002 LIB	—	2002 CONS
Economic	49%	—	51%		48%	—	51%
Social	38%	—	61%		44%	—	54%
Foreign	49%	—	47%		41%	—	56%

Key Votes of the 107th Congress

1. Approve Bush Tax Cuts	Y	5. Faith-Based Charities	Y	9. Trade Promotion Authority	N
2. Limit Patients' Bill of Rights	Y	6. Bar Gays in the Boy Scouts	Y	10. Bar Funds for Intl. Court	Y
3. Campaign Finance Reform	Y	7. Ban Partial-Birth Abortion	Y	11. Authorize Force in Iraq	Y
4. Ban ANWR Development	Y	8. Arm Commercial Pilots	Y	12. Deny Home. Sec. Dept. Union	Y

Election Results

2002 general	Frank LoBiondo (R)	116,834	(69%)	($646,171)
	Steven Farkas (D)	47,735	(28%)	
	Other	4,230	(3%)	
2002 primary	Frank LoBiondo (R)	unopposed		
2000 general	Frank LoBiondo (R)	155,187	(66%)	($779,831)
	Edward G. Janosik (D)	74,632	(32%)	($75,622)
	Other	4,040	(2%)	

Prior Winning Percentages: 1998 (66%); 1996 (60%); 1994 (65%)

The People		**Race/Ethnic Origin**	**Ancestry**	
Area size:	2,683 sq. mi.	71.7% White	Irish: 13.9%	Italian: 13.0%
Urban population:	79.0%	13.8% Black	German: 12.5%	
Rural population:	21.0%	2.4% Asian	**2000 Presidential Vote**	
Pop. 2000:	647,258	0.3% Native Am.	Gore (D)	134,345 (54%)
Median income:	$44,173	0.0% Hawaiian	Bush (R)	105,630 (43%)
Poverty status:	10.3%	1.4% Two+ races	Other	7,906 (3%)
Military veterans:	13.0%	0.1% Other	**Cook Partisan Voting Index:** D + 6	
		10.3% Hispanic Origin		

Occupation	Blue collar: 23.0%	White collar: 53.6%	Gray collar: 23.4%

The builders of the Camden & Atlantic Railroad in 1852 may not have known it, but when they extended their line to the little inlet town of Absecon, they were starting America's biggest beach resort, Atlantic City. Like all resorts, it was a product of developments elsewhere: Of industrialization and spreading affluence, of railroad technology and the conquest of diseases which used to make summer a time of terror for parents and doctors. In the years after the Civil War, first Atlantic City and then the whole Jersey Shore from Brigantine to Cape May became America's first seaside resort, and Atlantic City developed its characteristic features: The Boardwalk in 1870, the amusement pier in 1882, the rolling chair in 1884, salt water taffy in the 1890s, Miss America in 1921. By 1940, when 16 million Americans visited every summer, Atlantic City was a common man's resort of old traditions; it declined in the years after World War II as people could afford nicer vacations. By the early 1970s, Atlantic City was grim, with a bedraggled convention hall (site of the 1964 Democratic National Convention), empty hotels and bleak streets of rowhouses built in the ugliest Philadelphia style.

Then in 1977, New Jersey voters legalized casino gambling in Atlantic City and gleaming new hotels sprang up, big name entertainers came in and Atlantic City became more glamorous than it had been in 90 years. But not for all of its residents: Casino and hotel jobs tend to be low-wage, and the slums begin just feet from the massive parking lots of the casinos. Atlantic City's gambling business has been thriving—casinos came out ahead $4.4 billion in 2002—and huge new casinos were built on both Boardwalk and bayside. Atlantic City now has one of the nation's largest tourism economies and may be growing into what Las Vegas has become, not just a collection of gaudy casinos but also a gaggle of theme parks, with entertainment for the family as well as adults.

The Jersey Shore south of Atlantic City is a string of different resorts. There is the old Methodist town of Ocean City, where Gay Talese grew up the son of Italian immigrants, as he told movingly in *Unto the Sons*. There is Wildwood, with its gritty boardwalk, and Cape May, with its beautifully preserved Victorian houses. Together, wrote the late columnist Michael Kelly, these beaches provide a paradise of "uplifting egalitarianism" for eager eaters. "The Jersey diet takes the most fattening foods that each ethnicity offers, puts them all on the same menu and double sizes them." Behind the Shore are swamp and flatland, the Pine Barrens and vegetable fields that gave New Jersey the name "Garden State." Growth has been slow in these small towns and gas station intersections, communities in whose eerie calmness in the summer you can hear mosquitoes whining. In the flatness, you can also find towns clustered around low-wage apparel factories or petrochemical plants on the Delaware estuary; the Northeast high-tech and service economy has not reached this far south in Jersey yet.

The 2d Congressional District covers this part of South Jersey. Politically, it has strong Democratic presences in the chemical industry towns along the Delaware River and in Vineland and a strong Republican presence in Cape May; Atlantic City often votes Democratic but has an antique Republican machine that goes back generations. Democrats carried the area in all 1990s statewide elections and won easily in the 1996 and 2000 presidential races. This is prime marginal territory, off the beaten track of Northeast politics.

The congressman from the 2d District is Frank LoBiondo, a Republican elected in 1994. He grew up in Vineland, went to college in Philadelphia and worked for the family trucking firm, LoBiondo Brothers Motor Express, which originally carried produce from Jersey farms. In 1987 he was elected to the Assembly, where he stoutly opposed new taxes. LoBiondo also opposes gun control, and was backed by the National Rifle Association. In 1992 LoBiondo ran unsuccessfully against veteran Congressman William Hughes, and lost 56%–41%. After Hughes decided to retire in 1994, LoBiondo ran again and in the primary faced Atlantic County state Senator William Gormley; LoBiondo attacked him as a taxer and NRA ads called him "a liberal in Republican clothing." LoBiondo won 54%–35%, an impressive margin inasmuch as Gormley went on to carry the area in the primaries for governor in 1993 and senator in 2000. LoBiondo then easily won the 1994 general, 65%–35%. Since then, he has never fallen short of 60%.

In the House, LoBiondo has compiled a moderate voting record, especially on economic issues. He was one of six Republicans to vote against Newt Gingrich's Medicare plan in October 1995 (four were from New Jersey); he voted against a veterans' appropriation as having insufficient medical care and against exempting small businesses from the minimum wage. He is a founder and co-chair of the Congressional Gaming Caucus. He won House passage of the Honesty in Sweepstakes Act, to make clear that no purchase of merchandise is necessary to enter contests. He and Peter Visclosky won nearly unanimous passage of a bill to provide $25 million in funding for bulletproof vests for police officers. And he won enactment of his Coastal Heritage Trail Route. With his background in small business, he has become a senior member of the Small Business Committee, where he advocates for the needs of entrepreneurs such as Jersey farmers, including elimination of the estate tax. But he voted against corporate interests, including some locally, who urged support of trade promotion authority. He remains a friend of the NRA—one of two House members from New Jersey to vote for John Dingell's amendment that ended the push for gun control in 1999. He chairs the Coast Guard and Maritime Transportation Subcommittee, a useful assignment for New Jersey. In that post, he backed more spending and helped to enact steps to increase port security.

LoBiondo thought about running for the Senate in both 2000 and 2002, but he did not get close to the starting box. With the weak bench of New Jersey Republicans, he could be a candidate against Governor Jim McGreevey in 2005, especially if he honors his term-limit pledge not to run for reelection in 2006.

THIRD DISTRICT

Rep. Jim Saxton (R)

Elected 1984, 10th term; b. Jan. 22, 1943, Nicholson, PA; home, Mt. Holly; E. Stroudsburg St. Col., B.A. 1965, Temple U., 1967–68; United Methodist; divorced.

Elected Office: NJ Assembly, 1975–82; NJ Senate, 1982–84.

Professional Career: Jr. High schl. teacher, 1965–68; Real estate broker, 1968–84.

DC Office: 339 CHOB 20515, 202-225-4765; Fax: 202-225-0778; Web site: www.house.gov/saxton.

District Offices: Cherry Hill, 856-428-0520; Mt. Holly, 609-261-5800; Ocean County, 732-914-2020.

Committees: *Armed Services* (4th of 33 R): Projection Forces; Terrorism, Unconventional Threats & Capabilities (Chmn.); Total Force. *Resources* (4th of 28 R): Fisheries Conservation, Wildlife & Oceans. *Joint Economic Committee* (Vice Chmn. of 10 Reps.).

Group Ratings

	ADA	ACLU	AFS	LCV	CON	ITIC	NTU	COC	ACU	NTLC	CHC
2002	0	7	0	38	60	88	56	90	92	75	92
2001	15	—	20	71	—	—	56	82	64	—	—

National Journal Ratings

	2001 LIB — 2001 CONS		2002 LIB — 2002 CONS	
Economic	49%	51%	42%	58%
Social	20%	69%	32%	63%
Foreign	33%	60%	0%	85%

Key Votes of the 107th Congress

1. Approve Bush Tax Cuts	Y	5. Faith-Based Charities		9. Trade Promotion Authority	Y
2. Limit Patients' Bill of Rights	Y	6. Bar Gays in the Boy Scouts	Y	10. Bar Funds for Intl. Court	Y
3. Campaign Finance Reform	N	7. Ban Partial-Birth Abortion	Y	11. Authorize Force in Iraq	Y
4. Ban ANWR Development	Y	8. Arm Commercial Pilots	Y	12. Deny Home. Sec. Dept. Union	Y

Election Results

2002 general	Jim Saxton (R)	123,375	(65%)	($683,812)
	Richard Strada (D)	64,364	(34%)	
	Other	2,000	(1%)	
2002 primary	Jim Saxton (R)	unopposed		
2000 general	Jim Saxton (R)	157,053	(57%)	($2,143,518)
	Susan Bass Levin (D)	112,848	(41%)	($1,760,625)
	Other	4,182	(2%)	

Prior Winning Percentages: 1998 (62%); 1996 (64%); 1994 (66%); 1992 (59%); 1990 (58%); 1988 (69%); 1986 (65%); 1984 (61%); 1984 (62%)

The People		Race/Ethnic Origin	Ancestry	
Area size:	1,180 sq. mi.	83.4% White	Irish: 15.8%	Italian: 15.0%
Urban population:	96.2%	8.5% Black	German: 13.5%	
Rural population:	3.8%	2.7% Asian	**2000 Presidential Vote**	
Pop. 2000:	647,257	0.1% Native Am.	Gore (D)	141,964 (54%)
Median income:	$55,282	0.0% Hawaiian	Bush (R)	114,621 (43%)
Poverty status:	5.1%	1.3% Two+ races	Other	8,208 (3%)
Military veterans:	15.6%	0.1% Other	**Cook Partisan Voting Index:** D + 5	
		3.8% Hispanic Origin		

Occupation	Blue collar: 18.6%	White collar: 67.6%	Gray collar: 13.7%

The Pine Barrens of New Jersey are one of the last vacant spots on the eastern seaboard; not quite *terra incognita*, but still not thickly populated. Encroached by the Philadelphia suburbs of

South Jersey on the west and burgeoning retirement developments of the Jersey Shore on the east, they are crossed even today mostly by narrow two-lane roads; there are only a few small towns here, plus Fort Dix and McGuire Air Force Base in the center of the district. For years, the Barrens were seen as a barrier to civilization; only recently have environment-minded Jerseyites come to see them as a natural treasure.

The 3d Congressional District spans the Pine Barrens. Most of its residents live in the South Jersey suburbs of Philadelphia, in the spread-out suburb of Cherry Hill with its 1960s and 1970s shopping centers, or in the older towns along the Delaware River and newer ones inland toward McGuire. This is comfortable, but not hugely affluent, suburban country. East of the Pine Barrens is Ocean County, including the barrier islands from Normandy Beach south to Little Egg Harbor, with older beachfront communities and larger clusters of new subdivisions and condominium complexes inland. Ocean County grew rapidly in the 1980s and 1990s, a kind of frost belt Florida, with many retirees from New York and North Jersey eager to leave the urban areas' high crime and high taxes. The two big military bases have remained active, with Fort Dix especially busy after September 11 training troops for new assignments and sending war materiels to their destination. Both the west and east ends of this district once were traditionally Republican, though the district was carried by Al Gore in 2000.

The congressman from the 3d District is James Saxton. He grew up in South Jersey, worked as a teacher for three years, then became a real estate broker. In 1975 he was elected to the New Jersey Assembly, when Republicans were struggling to stop Governor Brendan Byrne's income tax. In 1984 he ran to fill a vacancy in the House, won the Republican primary 45%–41%, easily won the special election and had no serious challenge until 2000.

In the House, Saxton has compiled a moderate to conservative voting record. When Republicans won the House, he became chairman of the Fisheries Conservation, Wildlife and Oceans Subcommittee. He backed legislation to clean up 28 "nationally significant" local estuaries and has won millions of dollars to study high childhood cancer in Toms River. In April 2001, he joined with many Democrats vowing to fight the Bush administration's proposed regulations on clean air and arsenic levels in drinking water. His environment-friendly record became an obstacle when he sought to become chairman of the Resources Committee after the 2002 election. Although he was the most senior member seeking the position, most Western Republicans on the panel united against him. Saxton floated the idea of splitting the Resources panel so that he could chair a panel dealing with Merchant Marine issues, but the Republican leadership had eliminated the Merchant Marine and Fisheries Committee in 1995 and weren't about to bring it back. Shortly before the leadership met and gave the chairmanship to Richard Pombo, Saxton withdrew from consideration with an unspoken understanding that he would get a prime subcommittee at Armed Services.

Saxton is a supporter of strong anti-terrorism efforts and of aid to Israel. From 2000 to 2002 he chaired a task force to study the threat of terrorism, concluding that the nation needed prompt action to combat the risk of biological weapons. On the Joint Economic Committee, he pressured officials of the International Monetary Fund to open their operations to greater public view; after months of delay, the House in 1998 approved the Clinton administration's full $18 billion request for the IMF, but with some procedural reforms. As chairman, he cited the "steeply progressive impact of the federal income tax" and defended the Bush administration plan to return most of the tax cut to higher-income taxpayers. With his seniority on the Armed Services Committee, Saxton became chairman in 2001 of the Military Installation and Facilities Subcommittee—a useful assignment for local interests, given that both Dix and McGuire have been prime targets of base-closing review panels.

In 2003 Saxton became the first chairman of the newly-created Subcommittee on Terrorism, Unconventional Threats and Capabilities. From that position, he led anti-French sentiment in Congress during the conflict with Iraq; in March 2003 he introduced a bill that would prevent French companies from receiving any U.S. funds spent rebuilding post-war Iraq.

Democrats targeted Saxton early in the 2000 campaign with strong support for 12-year Cherry Hill Mayor Susan Bass Levin. Levin was well-funded; she depicted Saxton as too conservative and out of the mainstream locally. But he was helped by his endorsement from the local Sierra Club and New Jersey Environmental Federation and by staff resignations and other disarray in Levin's campaign. Levin carried her home area narrowly, but lost the rest of the district by solid margins; Saxton won 57%–41%. Despite some worries, redistricting left his district little changed. Levin tried to get Cherry Hill put into the 1st District, where she might try to succeed Rob Andrews if he runs for statewide office. Levin has evidently given up on the 3d, and Democrats did not seriously challenge Saxton in 2002.

FOURTH DISTRICT

Rep. Chris Smith (R)

Elected 1980, 12th term; b. Mar. 4, 1953, Rahway; home, Hamilton; Trenton St. Col., B.S. 1975; Catholic; married (Marie).

Professional Career: Sales exec., family–owned sporting goods business, 1975–80; Exec. Dir., NJ Right to Life, 1976–78.

DC Office: 2373 RHOB 20515, 202-225-3765; Fax: 202-225-7768; Web site: www.house.gov/chrissmith.

District Offices: Hamilton, 609-585-7878; Whiting, 732-350-2300.

Committees: *International Relations* (Vice Chmn. of 26 R): Asia & the Pacific; International Terrorism, Non-proliferation and Human Rights. *Veterans' Affairs* (Chmn. of 17 R).

Group Ratings

	ADA	ACLU	AFS	LCV	CON	ITIC	NTU	COC	ACU	NTLC	CHC
2002	10	13	11	50	50	62	49	80	80	86	83
2001	30	—	40	86	—	—	59	61	56	—	—

National Journal Ratings

	2001 LIB	—	2001 CONS		2002 LIB	—	2002 CONS
Economic	52%	—	49%		42%	—	57%
Social	35%	—	63%		25%	—	71%
Foreign	49%	—	47%		49%	—	50%

Key Votes of the 107th Congress

1. Approve Bush Tax Cuts	Y	5. Faith-Based Charities	Y	9. Trade Promotion Authority	N
2. Limit Patients' Bill of Rights	N	6. Bar Gays in the Boy Scouts	Y	10. Bar Funds for Intl. Court	Y
3. Campaign Finance Reform	N	7. Ban Partial-Birth Abortion	Y	11. Authorize Force in Iraq	Y
4. Ban ANWR Development	Y	8. Arm Commercial Pilots	Y	12. Deny Home. Sec. Dept. Union	Y

Election Results

2002 general	Chris Smith (R)	115,293	(66%)	($510,790)
	Mary Brennan (D)	55,967	(32%)	($73,386)
	Other	3,041	(2%)	
2002 primary	Chris Smith (R)	unopposed		
2000 general	Chris Smith (R)	158,515	(63%)	($611,785)
	Reed Gusciora (D)	87,956	(35%)	($115,392)
	Other	4,339	(2%)	

Prior Winning Percentages: 1998 (62%); 1996 (64%); 1994 (68%); 1992 (62%); 1990 (63%); 1988 (66%); 1986 (61%); 1984 (61%); 1982 (53%); 1980 (57%)

The People		Race/Ethnic Origin	Ancestry	
Area size:	762 sq. mi.	81.3% White	Italian: 15.9%	Irish: 15.2%
Urban population:	93.2%	7.5% Black	German: 11.8%	
Rural population:	6.8%	2.3% Asian	**2000 Presidential Vote**	
Pop. 2000:	647,258	0.1% Native Am.	Gore (D) 123,764	(50%)
Median income:	$54,073	0.0% Hawaiian	Bush (R) 114,309	(46%)
Poverty status:	6.6%	1.1% Two+ races	Other 8,301	(3%)
Military veterans:	13.3%	0.1% Other	**Cook Partisan Voting Index:** D + 2	
		7.6% Hispanic Origin		

Occupation   Blue collar: 20.1%   White collar: 65.3%   Gray collar: 14.5%

An invisible and not very well defined line lies across central New Jersey dividing North Jersey and South Jersey. North of the line people watch New York TV stations, eat hero sandwiches and root for the Yankees; south of the line they watch Philadelphia TV, eat hoagies and root for the Phillies. The state capital of Trenton lies south of the line, which passes east somewhere around Six Flags Great Adventure and Wild Safari in the Pine Barrens and heads southeast past Lakewood and Bricktown to the little village of Mantoloking on the Jersey Shore. But on either side of the line there has also developed over the last two decades a stronger New Jersey identity. The big cities are, after all, far away, particularly when traffic is heavy, and the economy of central New Jersey has its own special character, with big pharmaceutical companies and Fort Dix and McGuire Air Force Base. New Jersey politics is also centered here: Trenton is the state capital and also the home of the first New Jersey-oriented talk radio station, started in 1989. Some parts of this area are old: Trenton has been a manufacturing center since the 19th century, with the Lenox and Boehm china factories, the old Roebling ironworks which produced parts for many of our great bridges (the reason for the sign you see across the Delaware River, "Trenton Makes, the World Takes"). But much of this area is also spanking new, with growing subdivisions just west of the Shore and office buildings stretching north from Princeton. Even Trenton has had some growth; preservationists are eyeing its antique buildings and, long the only state capital without a hotel, it now has the Marriott Lafayette Yard Conference Hotel near the War Memorial.

The 4th Congressional District covers much of the central part of the state and the invisible line separating North Jersey and South Jersey. It stretches from the eastern part of Trenton to Mantoloking, Point Pleasant, Sea Girt and Spring Lake on the Shore. It includes the old colonial town of Burlington on the Delaware River and the new spacious subdivisions of Colts Neck just west of the Shore. It includes the Lakehurst air terminal where the zeppelin Hindenburg exploded in 1937. This is one part of America where population movement has been eastward, from the old neighborhoods of Trenton and its close-in suburbs to the new subdivisions of Ocean County and Wall Township. Politically, it is a mixed area. The Trenton area has long been solidly Democratic, but the Pine Barrens and Shore have leaned Republican. Overall the district is pretty closely divided between the parties.

The congressman from the 4th District is Christopher Smith, a youthful-looking Republican with great seniority who has applied strong moral principles to practical politics with impressive results. Smith grew up in the Trenton area, worked in his family's sporting goods business, and after graduating from college became executive director of the New Jersey Right to Life Committee in 1976. In 1980 he ran for the House in a more Trenton-centered 4th District and beat 26-year incumbent Frank Thompson, a convicted Abscam defendant. A fluke, it seemed, but Smith proceeded to beat several additional serious Democrats, winning more than 60% each time. His motivation comes from religion: "Christ said it in Matthew 25: 'Whatsoever you do to the least of my brethren, you do likewise to me.' That was my motivating scripture through all of my years in Right to Life, and it continues to be," he has said.

On abortion, Smith has worked to stop abortions in military hospitals. He has also worked to reinstate the Reagan-era restrictions that would deny federal funds to family planning organizations that promote abortions abroad. The ensuing struggle lasted more than two years, with Smith leveraging his opposition to the family planning money to prevent passage of the Clinton administration's high-priority efforts to reorganize the State Department, pay U.S. dues to the United

Nations and provide $18 billion for the International Monetary Fund. Smith finally was forced to yield in 1998 and 1999 omnibus spending bills, but he won in return White House agreement to restrict support for international abortion advocacy—which angered some Clinton loyalists. George W. Bush restored the family-planning restrictions in an executive order in his first full day in office. Smith also was a prime mover of legislation to ban partial-birth abortions; the House voted to override Clinton's vetoes, but Smith's side fell a few votes short of the two-thirds needed in the Senate.

Smith has fought not only Clinton Democrats but the House Republican leadership on the abortion issue. In July 2002 the bankruptcy bill, strongly backed by the leadership, came out of conference committee; the House had passed it 306–108 in March 2001. But it contained a provision, negotiated by Senator Charles Schumer and longtime abortion opponent Henry Hyde, providing that court judgments or fines could not be wiped out in bankruptcy: Schumer inserted this as a favor to abortion rights groups, after some abortion protesters declared bankruptcy to avoid paying fines. Smith and Joe Pitts led a group of abortion opponents and said they would vote against the bill unless the provision was removed. The leadership pulled the bill from the floor in July and kept it off in September. In November the leadership brought forward the rule to vote on the bill and Speaker Dennis Hastert took the unusual step of voting for it himself (the speaker usually does not vote). Smith and Pitts stood their ground despite furious efforts by Whip Tom DeLay, and the rule went down 243–172, with 87 Republicans voting against. It was only the second rule defeated during Hastert's first four years as speaker, and Hastert called Smith into his office to scold him in January 2003. But Smith seems likely to persist, and it will be interesting to see whether the big credit card companies, the bill's chief advocates, will try to get senators to vote against Schumer's provision in the 108th Congress.

His belief in a right to life has also led Smith to oppose embryonic stem cell research. In 2001 he held a press conference with families of children born from frozen embryos, the kind some scientists want to destroy in research. In 2002 he held a press conference with the head of a company that takes stem cells from umbilical cord blood and researches their use in replacing damaged brain cells, and he sponsored a bill providing $30 million for research into non-embryonic stem cells. Smith's principles have also led him to oppose capital punishment.

At a time when few lawmakers were focusing on events overseas, Smith worked on problems that bring him little reward at home. As chairman of the International Operations and Human Rights Subcommittee, Smith strongly criticized China for its forced sterilizations and abortions and its persecution of Christians and other religious minorities, and opposed PNTR. He decries the fact that businessmen are willing to bring lawsuits to stop piracy of copyrighted music and videotapes in China but have nothing to say about China's violations of human rights. In 2001 he handed George W. Bush a letter from the nine-year-old daughter of Li Shaomin, a scholar imprisoned in China, and asked for his help; Li was released in July when China was pushing its bid to have the 2008 Olympics held in Beijing. Smith's reaction to that: "This is like Berlin 1936 all over again. The equivalence between the Chinese government and the Nazis is compelling. American citizens are being held hostage in China. There is no other way to say this." He has condemned Russia for barring entry of foreign Catholic priests and Saudis for treating foreign servants as slaves. As co-chairman of the U.S. Helsinki Commission, he introduced a resolution condemning growing antisemitism in Europe and elsewhere; he noted that no delegates dissented, but the French delegate complained that he was speaking too loudly. In 2000 he had the signal success of pushing to passage a bill combating sex trafficking around the world, including a provision opposed by the Clinton administration requiring yearly reports on each nation's record; Clinton signed it anyway. Smith has also taken action on the subject: When he heard about Ukrainian girls being held against their will in brothels in Montenegro, he called the Montenegran prime minister, who ordered a raid on the operation.

On domestic issues, his expansive view of federal spending is a contrast to many anti-abortion Republicans. As chairman of the Veterans Committee in 2001 and 2002, he worked with ranking Democrat Lane Evans to get a $2.8 billion increase in veterans programs in the budget resolution and laws providing service dogs for veterans, increasing education and housing benefits by $3.1 billion, providing $1 billion for homeless veterans, instituting a cost of living increase for disabled veterans' compensation. Monthly education benefits were raised from $800 to $900 in October 2002 and to $985 in 2003. He said he and Evans would work in 2003 and 2004 to shift funding for veterans' health care from the discretionary to the mandatory budget—a move sure to be opposed by appropriators—and to expand programs to let the Pentagon and VA health care systems share resources and cut costs.

On September 11, 57 4th District residents were killed, and later in September, the anthrax letters sent to New York and Washington passed through the post office sorting facility in Hamilton, just outside Trenton. The facility was closed and some 800,000 pieces of mail delayed. Smith introduced a bill to waive financial penalties for people whose mail was delayed; the banking industry agreed to do that voluntarily. He also pressed for more antibiotics for those possibly exposed to anthrax and for more testing facilities.

After the 2000 election, Smith was fifth in seniority on the full International Affairs Committee and sought the chairmanship, vacant since Benjamin Gilman had served the six years House Republicans' term limits allow. But the job went instead to Henry Hyde, who was more senior and who was unhappy that he was losing the Judiciary chairmanship because of term limits. Smith got the Veterans Affairs chairmanship instead, for which he was in any case next in line.

Smith's devotion to principle and his reputation for tending to constituent problems have made him very popular in the 4th District. Redistricting closely followed the bipartisan congressional incumbents' plan; the 4th District lost the west side of Trenton and the Bush 2000 percentage was raised from 44% to 46%—pretty high for New Jersey. Smith's opponents have complained that he avoids debates, but they surely wouldn't matter much. In 2002, Smith, at 49 and after 22 years in the House, was reelected 66%–32%.

FIFTH DISTRICT

Rep. Scott Garrett (R)

Elected 2002, 1st term; b. July 9, 1959, Englewood; home, Wantage; Montclair St. U., B.A. 1981, Rutgers U., J.D. 1984; Protestant; married (Mary Ellen).

Elected Office: NJ Assembly, 1990–2002.

Professional Career: Practicing atty., 1984-present.

DC Office: 1641 LHOB 20515, 202-225-4465; Fax: 202-225-9048; Web site: www.house.gov/garrett.

District Offices: Newton, 973-300-2000; Paramus, 201-712-0330.

Committees: *Budget* (19th of 24 R). *Financial Services* (32d of 37 R): Financial Institutions & Consumer Credit; Oversight & Investigations.

Group Ratings and Key Votes: Newly Elected

Election Results

2002 general	Scott Garrett (R)	118,881	(59%)	($1,342,264)
	Anne Sumers (D)	76,504	(38%)	($1,605,385)
	Other	4,466	(2%)	
2002 primary	Scott Garrett (R)	16,234	(45%)	
	David Russo (R)	9,299	(26%)	
	Gerald Cardinale (R)	9,109	(25%)	
	Other	1,438	(4%)	
2000 general	Marge Roukema (R)	175,546	(65%)	($1,005,148)
	Linda A. Mercurio (D)	81,715	(30%)	($65,607)
	Other	11,263	(5%)	

The People		Race/Ethnic Origin	Ancestry	
Area size:	1,130 sq. mi.	86.3% White	Italian: 16.2%	Irish: 15.3%
Urban population:	82.7%	1.5% Black	German: 13.2%	
Rural population:	17.3%	6.6% Asian	**2000 Presidential Vote**	
Pop. 2000:	647,258	0.1% Native Am.	Bush (R)...............140,132	(52%)
Median income:	$72,781	0.0% Hawaiian	Gore (D)...............120,142	(45%)
Poverty status:	3.6%	1.0% Two+ races	Other...................9,431	(3%)
Military veterans:	11.6%	0.1% Other	**Cook Partisan Voting Index:** R + 4	
		4.5% Hispanic Origin		

Occupation	Blue collar: 16.3%	White collar: 72.9%	Gray collar: 10.8%

The northern edge of New Jersey was first settled three centuries ago by the Dutch, for whom this plateau of land behind the Hudson River Palisades seemed a natural part of Nieuw Amsterdam. The Dutch influence is seen in old steep-roofed farmhouses and in many of the place names—Bergen County, Cresskill, Closter. But overall, northernmost New Jersey has the well-settled look of so many northeastern suburbs, with touches both of affluence and small town hominess, criss-crossed at its edges with limited access highways lined with shopping centers—with five million square feet in Paramus, the headquarters of Toys "R" Us. Not far away are Saddle River and Franklin Lakes, with million-dollar houses on multi-acre lots, and Park Ridge, with office buildings and condominiums. This area may look like WASP suburbia on the surface, but in fact it is home to successful people of all ethnic groups, many descended from those who first saw the Statue of Liberty from the steerage deck and passed through the inspection queues at Ellis Island.

The 5th Congressional District consists of most of northern Bergen County, plus a swath of North Jersey stretching west to the hill-enclosed upper reaches of the Delaware, crossing one ridge of mountains after another, then running south to I-78. Nearly two-thirds of its population is in Bergen County; to the west, little subdivisions set amid the lakes of western Passaic County are filling up with young families; farther west are once rural, now more or less suburban Sussex and Warren counties. Politically, this area has long been solidly Republican, although like all of New Jersey it moved toward Democrats in the 1990s. It was one of the state's two districts carried by George W. Bush in 2000. Redistricting added some territory in Bergen County, but did not change the balance of the district.

The congressman from the 5th District is Scott Garrett, a Republican elected in 2002. Garrett graduated from Montclair State College and Rutgers Law School and became a trial lawyer in Sussex County. In 1989, he was elected to the state House, where he quickly became one of the most conservative members. He claimed never to have voted for a tax increase. His advocacy of limited government reached the point that he opposed measures to require radon testing at child-care centers and minimum hospital stays for mastectomies because he was not convinced these issues warranted government mandates. In 1998 and 2000, he challenged veteran Congresswoman Marge Roukema in the Republican primary. He attacked her for supporting abortion rights and gun control; she pointed to her conservative votes on economic issues and was supported by the Republican leadership. Each time, Garrett carried the western part of the district but Roukema ran strongly in her Bergen County base; she won by only 53%–47% in 1998 and 52%–48% in 2000. In November 2001, unhappy that she had been passed over for the chairmanship of the Financial Services Committee and frustrated by her party's move to the right, Roukema announced that she would not seek another term.

Garrett ran again in 2002. His challenge in the primary was to sell his views in Bergen County, where Sussex County is viewed as a distant province somewhere near Idaho. Garrett ran again as a supporter of tax cuts who wanted to streamline government and reduce bureaucracy and was opposed to abortion and gun control; the American Conservative Union and the Club for Growth endorsed him. Garrett was helped when Bergen County executive Pat Schuber declined to run, but two other well-known Republicans from Bergen entered the race, state Senator Gerald Cardinale and Assemblyman David Russo. The relatively moderate Russo unexpectedly won the Bergen County Republican Party's nominating convention against the favored Cardinale, a conservative who was endorsed by both Schuber and Roukema; Russo and Cardinale warned that the nomination of Garrett would put the seat at risk in the general election. In the June 2002 primary, Garrett won with 45% to 26% for Russo and 25% for Cardinale. Garrett won a stunning 81% of the vote in Sussex, the district's second-largest county, and 68% in Warren, which showed great regional strength. But in Bergen County, which cast 56% of the primary vote, Garrett won just 25%, raising Republican fears and Democratic hopes. The Democratic nominee was Anne Sumers, an ophthalmologist from Upper Saddle River in Bergen County, a former Republican who switched parties in early 2002 and stressed her agreement with Roukema on most issues; she promised to self-finance much of her campaign.

With help from the national party, Sumers quickly attacked Garrett as an "extremist," pointing to his opposition to abortion and support for only limited federal aid to education; she claimed to be Roukema's ideological heir. Roukema, recovering from surgery and chemotherapy, remained notably silent. Garrett pounced on Sumers's failure to vote in local school board elections and her musings on a liberal web site where she characterized American patriotism as "jingoistic." He said she was a vote for Dick Gephardt for Speaker. At the urging of the NRCC, he soft-pedaled some of his more conservative views, including his support for school vouchers, and he voiced a more generic Republican appeal. Sumers may have inflicted additional damage on her campaign with an ad in October that appeared to link Garrett's opposition to gun control with the Washington area sniper. Sumers outspent Garrett during the campaign, $1.6 million to $1.3 million, of which Garrett spent nearly $500,000 in the primary. But national Republicans spent heavily on issue ads on Garrett's behalf. This turned out to be less of a contest than many people thought; Garrett won 59%–38%. In Bergen County, which cast 64% of the total, he led 55%–43%. He won 74% and 63% of the vote in Sussex and Warren Counties.

Barring major upheaval, Garrett seems to hold a safe seat, though he may be vulnerable to united Bergen County opposition in the Republican primary.

SIXTH DISTRICT

Rep. Frank Pallone (D)

Elected 1988, 8th term; b. Oct. 30, 1951, Long Branch; home, Long Branch; Middlebury Col., B.A. 1973, Fletcher Schl. of Law & Diplomacy, M.A. 1974, Rutgers U., J.D. 1978; Catholic; married (Sarah).

Elected Office: Long Branch City Cncl., 1982–88; NJ Senate, 1983–88.

Professional Career: Asst. prof., Rutgers U., 1979–80; Practicing atty., 1981–83; Instructor, Monmouth Col., 1984–86.

DC Office: 420 CHOB 20515, 202-225-4671; Fax: 202-225-9665; Web site: www.house.gov/pallone.

District Offices: Hazlet, 732-264-9104; Long Branch, 732-571-1140; New Brunswick, 732-249-8892.

Committees: *Energy & Commerce* (7th of 26 D): Energy & Air Quality; Environment & Hazardous Materials; Health. *Resources* (6th of 24 D): Fisheries Conservation, Wildlife & Oceans (RMM).

Group Ratings

	ADA	ACLU	AFS	LCV	CON	ITIC	NTU	COC	ACU	NTLC	CHC
2002	100	73	89	100	92	38	29	35	4	11	0
2001	95	—	100	100	—	—	13	30	16	—	—

National Journal Ratings

	2001 LIB —	2001 CONS		2002 LIB —	2002 CONS
Economic	79%	—	21%	67%	—	33%
Social	74%	—	23%	84%	—	8%
Foreign	61%	—	36%	71%	—	29%

Key Votes of the 107th Congress

1. Approve Bush Tax Cuts	N	5. Faith-Based Charities	N	9. Trade Promotion Authority	N
2. Limit Patients' Bill of Rights	N	6. Bar Gays in the Boy Scouts	N	10. Bar Funds for Intl. Court	N
3. Campaign Finance Reform	Y	7. Ban Partial-Birth Abortion	N	11. Authorize Force in Iraq	N
4. Ban ANWR Development	Y	8. Arm Commercial Pilots	N	12. Deny Home. Sec. Dept. Union	N

Election Results

2002 general	Frank Pallone (D)	91,379	(66%)	($853,882)
	Ric Medrow (R)	42,479	(31%)	($28,970)
	Other	3,637	(3%)	
2002 primary	Frank Pallone (D)	unopposed		
2000 general	Frank Pallone (D)	141,698	(68%)	($836,362)
	Brian T. Kennedy (R)	62,454	(30%)	($32,021)
	Other	5,700	(2%)	

Prior Winning Percentages: 1998 (57%); 1996 (61%); 1994 (60%); 1992 (52%); 1990 (49%); 1988 (52%); 1988 (52%)

The People		Race/Ethnic Origin	Ancestry	
Area size:	388 sq. mi.	61.7% White	Italian: 12.7%	Irish: 12.6%
Urban population:	99.7%	16.1% Black	German: 8.1%	
Rural population:	0.3%	8.3% Asian	**2000 Presidential Vote**	
Pop. 2000:	647,257	0.1% Native Am.	Gore (D) 132,583	(61%)
Median income:	$55,681	0.0% Hawaiian	Bush (R) 74,828	(35%)
Poverty status:	9.1%	1.7% Two+ races	Other 8,638	(4%)
Military veterans:	10.2%	0.3% Other	**Cook Partisan Voting Index:** D +14	
		11.7% Hispanic Origin		

Occupation	Blue collar: 20.1%	White collar: 66.1%	Gray collar: 13.8%

For generations great transportation arteries have brought people out of the huge central cities of New York and Philadelphia and into the long-empty flatlands and hills of New Jersey—to vacation, to raise families and to work toward affluence and build communities. The railroads of the late 19th century created the towns of the Jersey Shore, from 1874, when the first train from New York City reached Long Branch, which quickly became the summer home of presidents from Grant to Wilson (Garfield, convalescing after he was shot, died there in 1881) and of New York racehorse owners and socialites. The great freight rail lines in the New York-Philadelphia corridor sparked big electrical and chemical industries here—building on the inventions of Thomas Edison, many produced in his Menlo Park laboratory just off the rail lines. The same corridor was the site of America's first cloverleaf intersection, at the junction of U.S. 1 and U.S. 9, and the intersection of two of America's great post-World War II highways, the New Jersey Turnpike and the Garden State Parkway. The Turnpike, now 12 lanes wide, roars past oil tank farms and petrochemical plants, major rail lines, Newark Airport and the oily waters of Raritan Bay; the Parkway links leafy affluent suburbs a dozen miles west of the Hudson with the Jersey Shore.

The 6th Congressional District inelegantly ties together these great transportation nodes and the upward mobility and economic progress that have taken place around them. The district is shaped something like an overturned capital F, with a long string of towns running from Piscataway to Sandy Hook, and two appendages running south: One along the Middlesex-Monmouth county line, the other along the Atlantic Ocean (Middlesex and Monmouth counties account for 90% of the district population). It includes the central core of Middlesex County: New Brunswick, Highland Park, Metuchen, Sayreville, parts of Edison Township and surrounding communities—a heavy industry area that also, since the time of Thomas Edison, has housed some of America's great research and development facilities, plus Rutgers, the state university of New Jersey. In recent years, Edison has seen an influx of immigrants from India, many of them engineers and doctors. Before that, immigrant factory workers in modest frame houses raised their families in nearby small towns that seem as far removed from Manhattan as any place in the Midwest. Other places are all too close, though: Middletown is still recovering from the staggering loss of 36 residents on September 11. The 6th also includes Monmouth County territory overlooking Lower

New York Bay, with spacious estates on highlands above little port towns from Sandy Hook, home to the nation's oldest lighthouse (1764), south to the mile-long boardwalk of Belmar. Between them are Asbury Park, immortalized by a Bruce Springsteen album, and Ocean Grove, founded in 1869 as a Methodist resort "free from the dissipation and follies of fashionable watering places," still dry for teetotalers who throng to its 10,000-seat 1894 Great Hall. The Shore has remained a summer vacation area that attracts millions, but also hosts year-round communities, with their own upward-striving families. Redistricters followed a bipartisan congressional delegation plan, which added heavily Democratic Plainfield and removed Republican Point Pleasant.

The congressman from the 6th District is Frank Pallone, a centrist Democrat elected in 1988. Pallone is the son of a disabled Long Branch policeman; he has been an environmentalist since 1969, when as a college freshman in Vermont he worked for that state's first-in-the-nation bottle deposit law. He was elected to the Long Branch city council in 1982, at 31, and to the New Jersey Senate in 1983, where he did not always follow party lines and concentrated on environmental issues. When Congressman Jim Howard, chairman of the Transportation and Infrastructure Committee, died in March 1988, Pallone ran for the House. The district (which then was more coastal in character) leaned Republican, but residents were angry about untreated sludge, plastic containers and medical waste washing up on the beach. Pallone's bumper sticker, without mentioning his party affiliation, said, "Stop Ocean Dumping." That, combined with his conservative stands on taxes and crime, helped him to 52% wins in the special and general elections.

Pallone started off with a reputation as a political maverick but became more partisan after Democrats lost control of the House. He has focused lately on the need for a prescription drug benefit under Medicare, accusing Republicans and pharmaceutical firms of playing a "cruel hoax" on Americans. With the district's many Indian-Americans (the most in the country, he says), he formed the Congressional Caucus for India and Indian-Americans; he is also a co-founder of the Congressional Armenian Caucus. Although he supported sanctions against India after its nuclear tests, he hailed Bill Clinton's trip to India and his chilly visit to Pakistan. After the September 11 attacks, he said that U.S. defense relations with India had improved and he called for increased democracy in Pakistan and controls on its nuclear weapons technology. At home, Pallone's environmental focus turned to the ever-lively border war with New York, opposing offshore dumping near Sandy Hook of highly contaminated material dredged from New York harbor; the Army Corps of Engineers, he complained, failed to respond to New Jersey objections. He criticized the Bush administration for cutting spending on Superfund clean-up sites, including one in Edison, where the herbicide Agent Orange had been manufactured during the Vietnam War.

When he was first elected to the House, Pallone's district was more marginal and New Jersey less Democratic. After the 1990 Census, New Jersey lost a House seat, and the new 6th District combined much of Pallone's Shore district in Monmouth County with large parts of the former Middlesex County seat; Pallone won the 1992 primary with only 55% against a Middlesex opponent. In the general, he depended on a huge money advantage and Clinton's edge in the district to win 52%–45%. Since then Pallone has been reelected with at least 60% of the vote except in 1998. That year he had a tough challenge from 28-year-old Republican Michael Ferguson, an education reformer close to former Governor Thomas Kean. An insurance group unhappy with Pallone's support for Clinton's HMO regulation plan spent nearly $2 million in an independent expenditure campaign, but in a pro-incumbent year, Pallone won 57%–40%. Two years later, Ferguson ran in the next-door 7th District and was elected; redistricting helped both of them in 2002.

Pallone's ambition for statewide office has not yet been satisfied. Rutgers political scientist Ross Baker told the *Asbury Park Press*, "His personal style is not one that commands respect. . . . It's hard for people to see him as a senator or governor. They see him as a representative." When Senator Frank Lautenberg announced his retirement in February 1999, Pallone formed an exploratory committee but did not run. When Senator Bob Torricelli quit the 2002 Senate race on September 30, and Governor Jim McGreevey offered the nomination to Pallone, he reportedly agreed to run. But Pallone quickly withdrew, reportedly because his wife opposed the move. If so, she was shrewd: He would have been giving up a safe House seat for a candidacy that could have been abruptly ended by either the New Jersey Supreme Court or the U.S. Supreme Court (in the end, Lautenberg returned to public life to replace Torricelli on the ballot). Most likely his next opportunity to move to the Senate will come when Lautenberg's seat is up in 2008.

SEVENTH DISTRICT

Rep. Michael Ferguson (R)

Elected 2000, 2d term; b. July 22, 1970, Ridgewood; home, Warren; U. of Notre Dame, B.S. 1992, Georgetown U., M.P.P. 1994; Catholic; married (Maureen Malloy).

Professional Career: H.S. teacher, Mount St. Michael Acad., 1992–93; Exec. Dir., Better Schools Fndt., 1994; Dir., Save Our Schoolchildren, 1994; Exec. Dir., Catholic Campaign for America, 1995–97; Adjunct Prof., Brookdale Com. Col., 1997–2000; Founder & Pres., Strategic Educ. Initiatives, 1997-present.

DC Office: 214 CHOB 20515, 202-225-5361; Fax: 202-225-9460; Web site: www.house.gov/ferguson.

District Office: Martinsville, 908-757-7835.

Committees: *Energy & Commerce* (28th of 31 R): Commerce, Trade & Consumer Protection; Health; Oversight & Investigations.

Group Ratings

	ADA	ACLU	AFS	LCV	CON	ITIC	NTU	COC	ACU	NTLC	CHC
2002	5	13	0	38	75	100	55	85	84	74	67
2001	20	—	20	71	—	—	58	87	58	—	—

National Journal Ratings

	2001 LIB — 2001 CONS		2002 LIB — 2002 CONS	
Economic	50% —	50%	42% —	58%
Social	46% —	54%	46% —	53%
Foreign	33% —	60%	29% —	67%

Key Votes of the 107th Congress

1. Approve Bush Tax Cuts	Y	5. Faith-Based Charities	Y	9. Trade Promotion Authority	Y
2. Limit Patients' Bill of Rights	Y	6. Bar Gays in the Boy Scouts	Y	10. Bar Funds for Intl. Court	Y
3. Campaign Finance Reform	Y	7. Ban Partial-Birth Abortion	Y	11. Authorize Force in Iraq	Y
4. Ban ANWR Development	Y	8. Arm Commercial Pilots	N	12. Deny Home. Sec. Dept. Union	Y

Election Results

2002 general	Michael Ferguson (R)	106,055	(58%)	($2,089,022)
	Tim Carden (D)	74,879	(41%)	($948,467)
	Other	2,068	(1%)	
2002 primary	Michael Ferguson (R)	unopposed		
2000 general	Michael Ferguson (R)	128,434	(52%)	($2,294,820)
	Maryanne Connelly (D)	113,479	(46%)	($1,837,766)
	Other	7,086	(3%)	

The People		Race/Ethnic Origin	Ancestry	
Area size:	603 sq. mi.	79.0% White	Italian: 15.3%	Irish: 13.0%
Urban population:	90.4%	4.4% Black	German: 11.7%	
Rural population:	9.6%	8.2% Asian	**2000 Presidential Vote**	
Pop. 2000:	647,257	0.1% Native Am.	Bush (R):	127,702 (49%)
Median income:	$74,823	0.0% Hawaiian	Gore (D):	124,699 (48%)
Poverty status:	3.4%	1.2% Two+ races	Other:	9,099 (3%)
Military veterans:	10.6%	0.2% Other	**Cook Partisan Voting Index:** R + 1	
		6.9% Hispanic Origin		

Occupation	Blue collar: 15.7%	White collar: 74.5%	Gray collar: 9.8%

The transportation arteries beneath the curve of the First Watchung Mountain are one of New Jersey's historic lines of development. The rail lines of the late 19th century opened up commuter suburbs; in the 1940s the four lanes of U.S. 22 created an automobile civilization; and finally I-78, completed in the mid-1980s, put Newark only an hour's distance from the Pennsylvania line. Interstate 78 stimulated the development of an Edge City called Bridgewater Commons, where a huge shopping mall and office developments that included the new headquarters of AT&T rose up amid horse country around Far Hills and Bernardsville, where the likes of Malcolm Forbes and Charles Engelhard owned huge estates.

The 7th Congressional District, with its contorted boundaries, covers these several generations of suburban development. It ranges across the breadth of the state, from the outskirts of Allentown, Pennsylvania, in the west almost to Staten Island in the east. It is an agglomeration of places, some of affluence, not a district with a distinct character—the 7th includes parts of 4 counties, and parts of places such as Edison, Woodbridge, Bridgewater, Linden and Union. Its easternmost points are in Union County, just shy of Newark International Airport. It includes Summit, Scotch Plains and North and South Plainfield, but not heavily Democratic Plainfield. It follows I-78 and the Watchung Mountains far into the countryside; it includes western Somerset County—prime horse farm country—and most of fast-growing Hunterdon County to the west. There is a political imperative for the weird shape of the district: The 7th was designed as part of the bipartisan congressional incumbents' plan to put heavily Democratic areas in the adjacent 12th, 6th and 10th districts while moving heavily Republican areas formerly in those districts, to this one. As a result, the Bush 2000 percentage in the 7th rose from 43% to 49%—the biggest partisan change in any New Jersey district.

The congressman from the 7th District is Michael Ferguson, a Republican elected by a narrow margin in 2000 and reelected easily in 2002. He grew up in Ridgewood; after graduating from Notre Dame, he taught history as an unpaid volunteer and coached basketball at Mount St. Michael Academy in the Bronx. He served as executive director of the Catholic Campaign for America and the Better Schools Foundations in Washington; during that time, he focused on education issues while earning a master's degree in public policy from Georgetown. He returned to New Jersey to found Strategic Education Initiatives, an education consulting firm, and became an ally of Jersey City's Republican mayor Bret Schundler and a backer of school choice. In 1998, Ferguson challenged Frank Pallone in the 6th District, spending $1 million but losing 57%–40%.

When Bob Franks decided to give up the neighboring 7th District seat to run for the Senate in 2000, Ferguson moved to the district and entered the contest. He faced serious opposition in a four-way primary. Ferguson raised the most money and focused on fiscal issues, but Tom Kean Jr., son of the popular former governor, had the highest name recognition and the most early endorsements; State Assemblyman Joel Weingarten, the only candidate previously elected to office, suffered from votes to raise taxes. A fourth candidate had little impact. Ferguson focused on cutting taxes—a unifying issue for Republicans. He won with 41% of the vote, to 28% for Kean and 23% for Weingarten. In the general, Ferguson faced Fanwood Mayor Maryanne Connelly, a retired AT&T human resources executive who in 1998 lost to Franks by 53%–44%, his closest race ever. Ferguson barely mentioned his conservative views—for school prayer and a constitutional amendment banning abortion—but emphasized his centrist positions on the environment and health care. He publicized his support for a waiting period for gun purchases and mandatory trigger locks. But his centerpiece issue was education: He strongly backed school vouchers and urged increased accountability for public schools. Against the 55-year-old Connelly, a widow without children, Ferguson highlighted his youthfulness and two children. Ferguson won by 52%–46%, running about even in the older suburbs and carrying the newer suburbs by wide margins.

In the House, Ferguson has been near the center on economic and cultural issues but more conservative on defense. He was one of 13 Republicans voting to uphold the Clinton administration's ergonomics regulation, he joined Patrick Kennedy at a press conference urging increased funding for special education and he voted against oil drilling in the Arctic National Wildlife Refuge. Health advocacy groups cheered when he removed his name as cosponsor of a tobacco-control bill backed by that industry. But he voted for the Bush tax cuts and trade promotion authority.

Ferguson's voting record plus the changes made by redistricting made him much stronger in 2002 than in 2000. House Democrats removed him from their top tier of targets. His Democratic opponent, financier Tim Carden, was a serious candidate who raised nearly $1 million; Ferguson raised more than twice that. Ferguson won 58–41%. He lost Middlesex County 54%–45%, but won with 56% in Union County, 62% in Somerset County and 68% in Hunterdon County. House Republican leaders evidently have no problems with Ferguson's liberal votes on some issues; in January 2003 they gave him a much-sought seat on the Energy and Commerce Committee. Shortly afterwards, he announced he would not run for governor in 2005.

EIGHTH DISTRICT

Rep. Bill Pascrell (D)

Elected 1996, 4th term; b. Jan. 25, 1937, Paterson; home, Paterson; Fordham U., B.A. 1959, M.A. 1961; Catholic; married (Elsie).

Military Career: Army, 1961; Army Reserves, 1962–67.

Elected Office: Pres., Paterson Bd. of Ed., 1979–82; NJ Assembly, 1987–97, Minority Ldr. Pro-Tem; Paterson Mayor, 1990–97.

Professional Career: High Schl. teacher, 1960–74; Dir., Paterson Dept. of Public Works, 1974–77; Dir., Paterson Dept. of Policy, 1977–87.

DC Office: 1722 LHOB 20515, 202-225-5751; Fax: 202-225-5782; Web site: www.house.gov/pascrell.

District Offices: Bloomfield, 973-680-1361; Passaic, 973-472-4510; Paterson, 973-523-5152.

Committees: *Select Committee on Homeland Security* (17th of 23 D): Emergency Preparedness & Response; Infrastructure & Border Security. *Transportation & Infrastructure* (17th of 34 D): Aviation; Highways, Transit & Pipelines; Water Resources & Environment.

Group Ratings

	ADA	ACLU	AFS	LCV	CON	ITIC	NTU	COC	ACU	NTLC	CHC
2002	90	60	89	88	63	38	15	50	12	8	17
2001	95	—	100	93	—	—	12	39	20	—	—

National Journal Ratings

	2001 LIB	—	2001 CONS	2002 LIB	—	2002 CONS
Economic	79%	—	21%	81%	—	18%
Social	64%	—	36%	63%	—	37%
Foreign	56%	—	41%	62%	—	36%

Key Votes of the 107th Congress

1. Approve Bush Tax Cuts	N	5. Faith-Based Charities	N	9. Trade Promotion Authority	N
2. Limit Patients' Bill of Rights	N	6. Bar Gays in the Boy Scouts	Y	10. Bar Funds for Intl. Court	Y
3. Campaign Finance Reform	Y	7. Ban Partial-Birth Abortion	Y	11. Authorize Force in Iraq	Y
4. Ban ANWR Development	Y	8. Arm Commercial Pilots	N	12. Deny Home. Sec. Dept. Union	N

Election Results

2002 general	Bill Pascrell (D)	88,101	(67%)	($864,856)
	Jared Silverman (R)	40,318	(31%)	
	Other	3,400	(3%)	
2002 primary	Bill Pascrell (D)	unopposed		
2000 general	Bill Pascrell (D)	134,074	(67%)	($1,081,808)
	Anthony Fusco Jr. (R)	60,606	(30%)	($279,545)
	Other	5,452	(3%)	

Prior Winning Percentages: 1998 (62%); 1996 (51%)

The People		Race/Ethnic Origin	Ancestry	
Area size:	110 sq. mi.	53.7% White	Italian: 15.3%	Irish: 8.0%
Urban population:	100.0%	12.7% Black	German: 6.0%	
Rural population:	0.0%	5.3% Asian	**2000 Presidential Vote**	
Pop. 2000:	647,258	0.1% Native Am.	Gore (D)..............129,906	(60%)
Median income:	$51,954	0.0% Hawaiian	Bush (R)...............78,446	(36%)
Poverty status:	10.7%	2.1% Two+ races	Other....................6,784	(3%)
Military veterans:	8.3%	0.3% Other	**Cook Partisan Voting Index:** D +12	
		25.8% Hispanic Origin		

Occupation	Blue collar: 22.4%	White collar: 64.1%	Gray collar: 13.5%

Paterson, New Jersey, is one of few American cities that have turned out pretty much as planned. The planner was Alexander Hamilton, who in the 1790s journeyed 20 miles from Manhattan into the interior of New Jersey to the Great Falls of the Passaic River. Watching the water surge down 72 feet—the highest falls along the East Coast—he predicted an industrial city would rise on this site. He formed the Society for Establishing Useful Manufactures, which opened a calico factory in 1794, and got Pierre L'Enfant, the designer of Washington, D.C., to design Paterson (named after then-Governor William Paterson). In 1836, Samuel Colt began manufacturing revolvers here; the first locomotive, the Sandusky, was built here in 1837; a walkout of Paterson cotton workers in 1828 was America's first factory strike. Paterson ultimately became America's "Silk City," employing 25,000 silk mill workers before the great strike of 1913 led by the radical Industrial Workers of the World. Paterson kept producing locomotives and, after the silk mills started closing down following another unsuccessful strike in 1924, became a cloth-dying center. Throughout, it attracted immigrants from England, Ireland and, after 1890, Italy and Poland. And it continues to attract them today, even if its economy produces more service and fewer manufacturing jobs. In 2000 Paterson's population was 50% Hispanic (up 30% since 1990); downtown's "Little Palestine" reflects the city's sizable Arab community.

The 8th Congressional District includes Paterson as its largest city, plus much suburban and industrial territory west and south of Paterson and north of Newark. Two-thirds of the population lives in Passaic County; the rest are in Essex County. It includes the mixed factory and middle-class towns south of Paterson on the Passaic River—Clifton, majority Hispanic and fast-growing Passaic, Nutley, Belleville. On higher ground are Bloomfield and affluent West Orange (most of which is in the 8th). The political heritage of the 8th District is Democratic, partly from its radical past, but more from the allegiances of its immigrant groups. In the 1980s, the central cities were outvoted by the increasingly Republican suburbs, and the district was closely divided; since then, it swung heavily Democratic, voting 60% for Al Gore in 2000. Redistricting made little change in the district in 2002.

The congressman from the 8th District is Bill Pascrell, a Democrat elected in 1996. He grew up in Paterson, the grandson of Italian immigrants, graduated from Fordham, served in the Army, then taught high school for 14 years. From there he went into politics, as director of Paterson's department of public works, school board president, then in 1987 to the New Jersey Assembly. In 1990 he was elected mayor of Paterson, but continued to serve in the Assembly—a common practice in New Jersey.

Meanwhile, he watched as the 8th District seat changed hands. After Public Works Committee chairman Robert Roe retired in 1992, liberal Democrat Herb Klein won, only to be replaced by Bill Martini in the Republican sweep in 1994. Pascrell ran against him in 1996 and attacked him as a tool of an "extremist" Republican leadership—one ad even showed Martini's face on a puppet operated by Speaker Newt Gingrich. Despite Martini's support from the Sierra Club and some labor unions, Pascrell rode the coattails of the Clinton-Gore campaign. In a district that went 58% for Clinton, Pascrell won 51%–48%.

In the House, Pascrell has compiled a liberal record on economics, more moderate on cultural and foreign issues. He called it "my proudest day" in Congress when he won approval for authorizing $400 million in federal aid to local fire departments, a provision that was included in the defense appropriation. He has voted for the partial-birth abortion ban and for parental-notification requirements for abortions across state lines. He got authorization of an Interior Department study of whether to designate Great Falls in the national park system. Pascrell gave new meaning to the "all politics is local" view by leading a move to give Italy a permanent seat on the United Nations Security Council. When he voted to condemn Palestinians for inciting Middle East violence, local Muslims rallied to protest his vote. He voted in October 2002 to authorize the use of force in Iraq.

Like others in the House delegation, Pascrell has had ambitions for statewide office. In 1999 he voiced interest in running for governor in 2001. But his support for Jim Florio in the 2000 Senate primary against Jon Corzine left him on the losing side of the North Jersey party establishment, and in early 2001 Woodbridge Mayor Jim McGreevey had the governor nomination sewed up. With the distinct Democratic trend in New Jersey politics, Pascrell remains strong in the 8th District; he won 67%–31% in 2002. His son Bill Pascrell III has gained influence as Passaic County counsel, prompting Republican criticism of a local dynasty. Following his 2002 reelection, the congressman's fortunes changed: He made an unsuccessful bid for a seat on the Ways and Means Committee. At the same time, the mayor of Passaic evicted him from City Hall, where Pascrell kept a regional office for six years, contending that Pascrell "has done nothing for the city."

NINTH DISTRICT

Rep. Steven Rothman (D)

Elected 1996, 4th term; b. Oct. 14, 1952, Englewood; home, Fair Lawn; Syracuse U., B.A. 1974, Washington U., J.D. 1977; Jewish; divorced.

Elected Office: Englewood Mayor, 1983–89; Bergen Cnty. Surrogate Court Judge, 1993–96.

Professional Career: Practicing atty., 1977–93.

DC Office: 1607 LHOB 20515, 202-225-5061; Fax: 202-225-5851; Web site: www.house.gov/rothman.

District Offices: Hackensack, 201-646-0808; Jersey City, 201-798-1366.

Committees: *Appropriations* (27th of 29 D): Foreign Operations & Export Financing; Transportation, Treasury, & Independent Agencies.

Group Ratings

	ADA	ACLU	AFS	LCV	CON	ITIC	NTU	COC	ACU	NTLC	CHC
2002	95	73	89	100	91	38	18	42	12	3	0
2001	85	—	100	100	—	—	10	26	13	—	—

National Journal Ratings

	2001 LIB —	2001 CONS	2002 LIB —	2002 CONS
Economic	92%	8%	70%	29%
Social	74%	23%	74%	19%
Foreign	61%	36%	56%	43%

Key Votes of the 107th Congress

1. Approve Bush Tax Cuts	N	5. Faith-Based Charities	N	9. Trade Promotion Authority	N
2. Limit Patients' Bill of Rights	N	6. Bar Gays in the Boy Scouts	N	10. Bar Funds for Intl. Court	Y
3. Campaign Finance Reform	Y	7. Ban Partial-Birth Abortion	N	11. Authorize Force in Iraq	Y
4. Ban ANWR Development	Y	8. Arm Commercial Pilots	Y	12. Deny Home. Sec. Dept. Union	N

Election Results

2002 general	Steven Rothman (D)	97,108	(70%)	($604,690)
	Joseph Glass (R)	42,088	(30%)	($5,476)
2002 primary	Steven Rothman (D)	unopposed		
2000 general	Steven Rothman (D)	140,462	(68%)	($880,283)
	Joseph Tedeschi (R)	61,984	(30%)	($30,099)
	Other	4,325	(2%)	

Prior Winning Percentages: 1998 (65%); 1996 (56%)

The People		**Race/Ethnic Origin**	**Ancestry**	
Area size:	100 sq. mi.	61.3% White	Italian: 16.2%	Irish: 9.0%
Urban population:	100.0%	6.6% Black	German: 6.6%	
Rural population:	0.0%	10.7% Asian	**2000 Presidential Vote**	
Pop. 2000:	647,257	0.1% Native Am.	Gore (D) 135,406	(63%)
Median income:	$52,437	0.0% Hawaiian	Bush (R) 72,695	(34%)
Poverty status:	7.6%	2.1% Two+ races	Other 6,110	(3%)
Military veterans:	8.6%	0.3% Other	**Cook Partisan Voting Index:** D +15	
		18.8% Hispanic Origin		

Occupation	Blue collar: 20.3%	White collar: 66.8%	Gray collar: 12.9%

The George Washington Bridge, one of several wondrous suspension bridges completed in America in the 1930s, strides the Hudson, its west tower almost up against the green cliff of New Jersey's Palisades. It is one of the glories of modern engineering, enabling people and goods to be transported through the irregular terrain of metropolitan New York—tidal rivers and cliffs and broad expanses of swamp. For a century the dramatic beauty of the Palisades contrasted with the ugly sprawl of the Hackensack River Valley and the Jersey Meadowlands. This giant swamp was the image of New Jersey for many—a landscape of gas station signs, oil tank farms, truck terminals and 12 lanes of New Jersey Turnpike—a smelly, ugly place that meant you were still not where you wanted to go, full of garbage and pig farms, briefly famous when Secaucus tavern owner Henry Krajewski ran for president in 1956. But the Meadowlands—which survive as 8,400 acres of wetlands and home to thousands of species of animals and plants—were the largest hunk of empty real estate near such a huge city center, and eventually they were developed. In the 1970s, the state built in East Rutherford the Meadowlands Sports Complex—Giants Stadium (where the Giants and Jets play now), the Meadowlands Racetrack, the Brendan Byrne Arena (later Continental Airlines Arena, home of the Nets and Devils). Private development followed—hotels, warehouses, light industry—in what became a small city.

The 9th Congressional District includes much of the Palisades and the Meadowlands. The scenery here is familiar to fans of the cable television series, *The Sopranos*: Jersey City, Kearny, North Arlington, Lodi (home to the fictitious Bada Bing; the actual strip club uses a different name). The 9th runs from the high-rise towers of Fort Lee, Cliffside Park and fast-growing Edgewater, where apartment houses brag about their views of New York City, west and north to the leafy suburbs of Englewood and Teaneck, and southwest to the high land overlooking the Meadowlands and the Passaic River in old small towns like Rutherford, with Polish-, German- and Italian-Americans. Blue-collar Palisades Park has become a center for Korean-Americans. Teaneck and Englewood are home to middle class blacks and young, Orthodox Jewish families. Fairview, Bergenfield and Hackensack, an old industrial town and the Bergen County seat, are home to growing numbers of Hispanics. Bergen County, which anchors the 9th, has experienced enough Hispanic growth over the past decade to warrant bilingual ballots in all 554 election districts. This area grew in the 1950s and 1960s, as New Yorkers moved out of the City; it lost population in the 1970s and 1980s, as young people moved farther out and left empty nesters behind. Now the population in some towns is rising due to new immigrants. This was Republican country in the New Deal years, an area of white-collar enclaves. But the conservative families who grew up in Bergen County are now being replaced by heavily Democratic immigrants and "tower dwellers." In 2002, these voters elected a Democratic county executive for the first time in county history.

The congressman from the 9th District is Steve Rothman, a Democrat elected in 1996. Rothman grew up in Englewood and Tenafly, went off to school at Syracuse University and Washington University law school in St. Louis, then practiced law. From 1983–89 he was mayor of Englewood; in 1993 he became a judge in the Bergen County Surrogate's Court. When 14-year Congressman Bob Torricelli ran for the Senate in 1996, Rothman resigned his judgeship and ran for the House. With the party endorsement, Rothman faced Republican Kathleen Donovan— Bergen County clerk, former assemblywoman, and chairman of the New York-New Jersey Port Authority, who was endorsed by the New Jersey Education Association and Cuban-American leader Jorge Mas Canosa. But this part of New Jersey was swinging sharply to the Democrats in the wake of the Republican takeover of the House and the 1995–96 budget struggle. The 9th District voted overwhelmingly for Bill Clinton and 56%–42% for Rothman.

In the House, Rothman has been more liberal on economic issues than on defense. During the Judiciary Committee impeachment hearings, the first-termer Rothman initially expressed unhappiness with Clinton's behavior and studied the charges intently. But as public opinion turned against impeachment, so did Rothman. He actively supported Clinton on television talk shows and complained that Republicans were ignoring the few moderate Democrats like himself; the divisive process left him more partisan. In October 2002 he voted to authorize the use of force in Iraq.

On local issues, his most innovative work has been his call to limit further development and seek federal protection for the Meadowlands. After the Fish and Wildlife Service called a local wildlife refuge too expensive and a low priority, Rothman won approval in 2001 of $1.2 million for land acquisition as a small down payment for a plan to protect the open space. During a later boat tour of the swamp, he told a reporter for *The Bergen Record*, "I think the hard part's over: changing the mindset that this was never possible." In addition, Rothman won another seemingly impossible challenge: An Internal Revenue Service apology when an internal report found that 8,500 New Jersey taxpayers were the victims of an overzealous IRS office.

Rothman has won easy re-election, with majorities comparable to Torricelli's best showings. His seat on Appropriations suggests he will have a long House career.

TENTH DISTRICT

Rep. Donald Payne (D)

Elected 1988, 8th term; b. July 16, 1934, Newark; home, Newark; Seton Hall, B.A. 1957; Baptist; widowed.

Elected Office: Essex Cnty. Bd. of Chosen Freeholders, 1972–78, Dir. 1977–78; Newark Municipal Cncl., 1982–89.

Professional Career: Elem. & High Schl. teacher, 1957–64; Exec., Prudential Insurance Co., 1964–72; Pres., YMCAs of the U.S., 1970; Vice Pres., Urban Data Systems Inc., 1975–88.

DC Office: 2209 RHOB 20515, 202-225-3436; Fax: 202-225-4160; Web site: www.house.gov/payne.

District Offices: Elizabeth, 908-629-0222; Newark, 973-645-3213.

Committees: *Education & the Workforce* (4th of 22 D): 21st Century Competitiveness; Employer-Employee Relations; Workforce Protections. *International Relations* (5th of 23 D): Africa (RMM); Western Hemisphere.

Group Ratings

	ADA	ACLU	AFS	LCV	CON	ITIC	NTU	COC	ACU	NTLC	CHC
2002	90	93	100	88	96	25	30	30	0	0	0
2001	100	—	100	100	—	—	12	22	0	—	—

National Journal Ratings

	2001 LIB —	2001 CONS		2002 LIB —	2002 CONS
Economic	95% —	0%		91% —	8%
Social	90% —	0%		94% —	3%
Foreign	96% —	0%		94% —	0%

Key Votes of the 107th Congress

1. Approve Bush Tax Cuts	N	5. Faith-Based Charities	N	9. Trade Promotion Authority	N
2. Limit Patients' Bill of Rights	N	6. Bar Gays in the Boy Scouts	N	10. Bar Funds for Intl. Court	N
3. Campaign Finance Reform	Y	7. Ban Partial-Birth Abortion	N	11. Authorize Force in Iraq	N
4. Ban ANWR Development	Y	8. Arm Commercial Pilots	N	12. Deny Home. Sec. Dept. Union	N

Election Results

2002 general	Donald Payne (D)	86,433	(84%)	($355,909)
	Andrew Wirtz (R)	15,913	(16%)	
2002 primary	Donald Payne (D)	33,851	(84%)	
	Edward Allen (D)	3,583	(9%)	
	Edmund Proctor (D)	2,818	(7%)	
2000 general	Donald Payne (D)	133,073	(88%)	($347,319)
	Dirk B. Weber (R)	18,436	(12%)	

Prior Winning Percentages: 1998 (84%); 1996 (84%); 1994 (76%); 1992 (78%); 1990 (81%); 1988 (77%)

The People		Race/Ethnic Origin	Ancestry	
Area size:	69 sq. mi.	21.4% White	West Indian: 6.4% Italian: 4.2%	
Urban population:	100.0%	56.6% Black	Irish: 3.6%	
Rural population:	0.0%	3.6% Asian	**2000 Presidential Vote**	
Pop. 2000:	647,258	0.2% Native Am.	Gore (D)................147,112	(83%)
Median income:	$38,177	0.0% Hawaiian	Bush (R)................27,718	(16%)
Poverty status:	17.5%	2.8% Two+ races	Other....................3,004	(2%)
Military veterans:	8.1%	0.5% Other	**Cook Partisan Voting Index:** D +34	
		15.0% Hispanic Origin		

Occupation	Blue collar: 23.6%	White collar: 58.0%	Gray collar: 18.4%

Newark has been the hollow core of New Jersey, the city to which main transportation arteries once led and whose corporate headquarters buildings were the tallest in the state. In 1930, 442,000 people lived here, one of every nine in New Jersey; in 2000, there were 273,000, one of 30. Recently Newark's core has been perking up; new office buildings have joined the Prudential and Public Service Electric & Gas headquarters, and the New Jersey Performing Arts Center has been a big hit. In 2002 Governor Jim McGreevey, prompted by Mayor Sharpe James, supported a new basketball and hockey arena, even in a time of budget stringency. There has been industrial development around Newark Airport, and immigrant neighborhoods like the Ironbound district are showing new vitality. At the nearby Port Newark-Elizabeth Marine Terminal, whose annual cargo makes it the largest container port on the East Coast and trails only Los Angeles and Long Beach, old warehouses are being cleared in anticipation of additional growth. What hurt Newark for so many years was the plague of horrendous schools and high crime; large parts of the city were dominated by criminals and deserted by most law-abiding residents who could get out. Now crime rates have been going down, the state has taken over the schools and life is coming back to deserted streets. The restored terminal at Newark Airport is part of a new glass and aluminum operations center that tripled its size.

The 10th Congressional District is made up of most of Newark—the Central, South and West Wards—plus Irvington, most of the Oranges and part of Montclair to the west, and much of Elizabeth, Rahway, and Linden to the south. Its boundary lines wiggle around to include blacks in Jersey City, Montclair and Elizabeth, and leave Hispanics in the next-door 13th District. Overall the district is 57% black; it cast 83% of its votes for Al Gore in 2000.

The congressman from the 10th District is Donald Payne, a Democrat elected in 1988. He grew up in Newark, was a teacher, worked for Prudential, served on the Essex Board of Chosen Freeholders in the 1970s and was vice president of Urban Data Systems for 13 years. In 1980 and 1986, he ran against Congressman Peter Rodino, chairman of the House Judiciary Committee when it voted to impeach President Richard Nixon; Payne lost, even as an African-American in a district with a black majority. But when Rodino retired in 1988, Payne got 73% in the Democratic primary and easily won the general.

Payne has an impeccably liberal voting record. He served as chairman of the Congressional Black Caucus in 1995 and 1996, just as Republicans were defunding the caucuses (the Black Caucus has raised enough money on its own to remain a vigorous force) and as senior Democrats relinquished their chairmanships.

Payne rescued the Africa Subcommittee from abolition when Republicans won the majority, and attacked cuts in aid to African countries. But he did not lionize all of Africa's leaders. He sponsored a resolution to cut off new investment in Sudan because of its practice of slavery— though he criticized as "unconscionable" the pullout from Sudan of international private-aid agencies. He traveled on Clinton's spring 1998 trip to Africa, which Payne praised as a "sea change" for viewing African issues and leaders as equals to those of other continents. In 1999, he became the ranking Democrat on the Africa Subcommittee. In recent years, roughly half the bills he has filed deal with Africa. He criticized foreign-aid spending levels for failing to meet the needs of United Nations peacekeeping operations, and has pointed out that the more than 700 million people of Africa receives far less aid from the United States than do the 6 million of Israel. In 2001, he rallied support by Black Caucus members for passage of the Zimbabwe Democracy and Economic Recovery Act, which imposed sanctions against the regime of President Robert Mugabe; his goal, Payne said, was to ensure a secure, democratic and prosperous Zimbabwe.

Nationally, Payne was a leader in passage of legislation to protect churches and other places of worship from burnings. He worked to drum up money for a revolutionary war memorial for African-Americans on Washington's Mall. As a leading Democrat on education policy, he unsuccessfully fought a Republican initiative to lower the threshold for local eligibility for special education funding of schools in poor areas. He won approval for forgiving student loans to students who choose careers as public defenders. He continues to win reelection overwhelmingly against token opposition.

ELEVENTH DISTRICT

Rep. Rodney Frelinghuysen (R)

Elected 1994, 5th term; b. Apr. 29, 1946, New York City; home, Harding; Hobart Col., B.A. 1969; Episcopalian; married (Virginia).

Military Career: Army, 1969–71 (Vietnam).

Elected Office: Morris Cnty. Bd. of Freeholders, 1974–83; NJ Assembly, 1983–94.

Professional Career: Aide, Morris Cnty. Bd. of Freeholders, 1972–74.

DC Office: 2442 RHOB 20515, 202-225-5034; Fax: 202-225-3186; Web site: www.house.gov/frelinghuysen.

District Office: Morristown, 973-984-0711.

Committees: *Appropriations* (14th of 36 R): Defense; District of Columbia (Chmn.); Energy & Water Development.

Group Ratings

	ADA	ACLU	AFS	LCV	CON	ITIC	NTU	COC	ACU	NTLC	CHC
2002	15	20	0	38	89	100	56	95	80	77	58
2001	20	—	0	64	—	—	61	91	60	—	—

National Journal Ratings

	2001 LIB	—	2001 CONS		2002 LIB	—	2002 CONS
Economic	45%	—	56%		47%	—	53%
Social	54%	—	45%		53%	—	47%
Foreign	4%	—	87%		29%	—	67%

Key Votes of the 107th Congress

1. Approve Bush Tax Cuts	Y	5. Faith-Based Charities	Y	9. Trade Promotion Authority	Y
2. Limit Patients' Bill of Rights	Y	6. Bar Gays in the Boy Scouts	Y	10. Bar Funds for Intl. Court	Y
3. Campaign Finance Reform	Y	7. Ban Partial-Birth Abortion	Y	11. Authorize Force in Iraq	Y
4. Ban ANWR Development	Y	8. Arm Commercial Pilots	Y	12. Deny Home. Sec. Dept. Union	Y

Election Results

2002 general	Rodney Frelinghuysen (R)	132,938	(72%)	($783,357)
	Vij Pawar (D)	48,477	(26%)	($15,793)
	Other	2,263	(1%)	
2002 primary	Rodney Frelinghuysen (R)	unopposed		
2000 general	Rodney Frelinghuysen (R)	186,140	(68%)	($557,937)
	John P. Scollo (D)	80,958	(30%)	($9,161)
	Other	6,740	(3%)	

Prior Winning Percentages: 1998 (68%); 1996 (66%); 1994 (71%)

The People		Race/Ethnic Origin	Ancestry	
Area size:	628 sq. mi.	82.9% White	Italian: 16.8%	Irish: 14.4%
Urban population:	93.5%	2.6% Black	German: 11.8%	
Rural population:	6.5%	6.3% Asian	**2000 Presidential Vote**	
Pop. 2000:	647,258	0.1% Native Am.	Bush (R) 151,617	(54%)
Median income:	$79,009	0.0% Hawaiian	Gore (D) 121,036	(43%)
Poverty status:	3.5%	1.0% Two+ races	Other 9,763	(3%)
Military veterans:	10.4%	0.1% Other	**Cook Partisan Voting Index:** R + 6	
		6.8% Hispanic Origin		

Occupation	Blue collar: 14.0%	White collar: 76.2%	Gray collar: 9.8%

New Jersey's Morris County, west of the Watchung Mountain ridges, was one of the first settled parts of the interior United States west of the seaboard. It has long been a place of comparative affluence, the home of skilled craftsmen during the Revolutionary War, with plenty of water mills and iron forges by the 19th century. But only in the late 20th century has it come into its own, as one of the wealthiest areas in the United States. And it is not just a collection of country estates with huddled small towns for the servants to live in, but a well-rounded community with all the appurtenances of urbanity except high crime and poverty rates. The very rich have lived here for some time, connected to Manhattan by commuter rail lines. But starting in the 1970s, new residents rushed out the newly completed I-80 and I-280 or the ring road I-287. Prompted by court-required zoning changes, old farms and woods have been cleared to make way for new subdivisions, such as the North Caldwell gated community home of television's Tony Soprano. And this is not just a bedroom community. New office complexes and corporate headquarters have been rising; much of New Jersey's economic energy, entrepreneurial creativity and research expertise are out here.

The 11th Congressional District includes all of Morris County plus small slices of Sussex, Passaic, Essex and Somerset Counties. It is one of the most affluent districts in the country: It ranks second in the nation in median household income. It is family territory, with relatively few singles; not a strongly cultural conservative area, but not aggressively liberal either. It has relatively few blacks and Hispanics, and one of its biggest immigrant populations is of Indians, whose household incomes are double the national average. Politically, it is the most Republican district in New Jersey, and one of the most Republican in the Northeast. It was one of only two New Jersey districts to vote for George W. Bush in 2000.

The congressman from the 11th District is Rodney Frelinghuysen (pronounced *FREE- ling-high-zen*), a Republican and scion of one of New Jersey's most durable political families, which moved from Germany near the Dutch border in 1720 and settled in what is now the 11th District. Four Frelinghuysens served as senator from New Jersey, starting in 1793 and as recently as 1923; Theodore Frelinghuysen was the candidate for vice president in 1844 (leading to the memorable chant, "Hurrah! Hurrah! The country's risin'/ For Henry Clay and Frelinghuysen"); Frederick Frelinghuysen was Chester Arthur's secretary of state; Peter Frelinghuysen, Rodney's father, was elected to the House in 1952 and served until his retirement in 1974. History tends to repeat itself, and Frelinghuysens have been involved in every presidential impeachment: Rodney Frelinghuysen's great-great-grandfather Frederick voted to convict Andrew Johnson in 1868; his father Peter, after the revelations of July 1974, would have voted to impeach Richard Nixon if the president had not resigned; and this generation's Frelinghuysen voted to impeach Bill Clinton in December 1998. As a child, Rodney Frelinghuysen lived in the large brick house on Georgetown's N Street now owned by former *Washington Post* editor Ben Bradlee and his wife Sally Quinn; he attended St. Albans prep school with Al Gore. After college, the congressman's son was drafted and served in the Army in Vietnam, where he built roads in the Mekong Delta. In 1972 he was appointed an aide by then-Morris County Freeholder (and later 11th District congressman) Dean Gallo; he served as a freeholder himself from 1974–83 and was elected to the Assembly in 1983.

Frelinghuysen ran for Congress in 1990 in what is now the 12th District, when its boundaries were different; he lost the primary to Dick Zimmer. In August 1994, after the primary, Gallo retired because of illness; he died two days before the election. Frelinghuysen was chosen to be the Republican nominee at a September party convention and was elected with 71% of the vote.

He showed his insider skills by winning a seat as a freshman on the Appropriations Committee, where he worked to cut spending on many programs, while maintaining a moderate voting record and concentrating on New Jersey projects for members of both parties. In 2001, after Senator Frank Lautenberg (temporarily) retired, New Jersey had no senator on Appropriations, and Frelinghuysen more than ever became the go-to guy for the entire delegation. He concentrated on big projects—$150 million for construction of the Hudson-Bergen light rail, $125 million to dredge channels in the Port of New York and New Jersey, $20 million to slow erosion on the faraway Jersey Shore. He insisted that "I look after Republican and Democratic members alike. This is totally bipartisan." But he was miffed when Senators Bob Torricelli and Jon Corzine also took credit in December 2001 for New Jersey getting $350 million for security and transportation and $655 million for military installations in the defense appropriation, plus $100 million for expanded ferry service across the Hudson.

Frelinghuysen has taken moderate or even liberal stands on some issues. He was one of five Appropriations Republicans to join Democrats in preserving the National Endowment for the Arts. He has twice won House passage of his "Know Your Caller" bill, which bars telemarketers from interfering with caller-ID systems of customers seeking to avoid such solicitations. He has said that he has more Superfund sites in his district than any other congressman and "we need to continue the cleanup and the remediation . . . I believe the polluters ought to pay." One of his favorite causes is Amber Alert, using emergency communications to track down child abductors, which is now active in 20 states and credited with recovery of 31 children. Frelinghuysen has sponsored a bill to establish a national coordinator in the Justice Department and provide $20 million for grants to enhance highway communications systems and $5 million for grants to states to develop programs supporting the alert system.

Frelinghuysen has not been seriously challenged for re-election. In June 2001, Paul Castronovo, an aide to Jersey City Mayor and 2001 gubernatorial nominee Bret Schundler, said he would run in the 2002 primary because Frelinghuysen was insufficiently conservative. But in January 2002 he bowed out of the race for lack of financial backing. Frelinghuysen showed no interest in running for governor in 2001 or for senator in 2000 or 2002; this patrician evidently believes that his gritty work in the House is more important than taking a chance on gaining the glamour of serving in the Senate. After the 2002 election, he became one of the 13 "cardinals," as chairman of the Appropriations Subcommittee on the District of Columbia.

TWELFTH DISTRICT

Rep. Rush Holt (D)

Elected 1998, 3d term; b. Oct. 15, 1948, Weston, WV; home, Hopewell Township; Carleton Col., B.S. 1970, N.Y.U., PhD. 1981; Protestant; married (Margaret Lancefield).

Professional Career: Prof., Swarthmore Col., 1981–89; Asst. Dir., Princeton Plasma Physics Lab., 1989–98.

DC Office: 1019 LHOB 20515, 202-225-5801; Fax: 202-225-6025; Web site: www.house.gov/rholt.

District Office: West Windsor, 609-750-9365.

Committees: *Education & the Workforce* (13th of 22 D): 21st Century Competitiveness; Employer-Employee Relations. *Permanent Select Committee on Intelligence* (8th of 9 D): Intelligence Policy & National Security; Technical & Tactical Intelligence.

Group Ratings

	ADA	ACLU	AFS	LCV	CON	ITIC	NTU	COC	ACU	NTLC	CHC
2002	90	87	89	100	92	50	29	40	8	8	17
2001	90	—	100	100	—	—	15	43	0	—	—

National Journal Ratings

	2001 LIB	—	2001 CONS		2002 LIB	—	2002 CONS
Economic	70%	—	29%		64%	—	35%
Social	72%	—	27%		67%	—	29%
Foreign	84%	—	16%		90%	—	8%

Key Votes of the 107th Congress

1. Approve Bush Tax Cuts	N	5. Faith-Based Charities	N
2. Limit Patients' Bill of Rights	N	6. Bar Gays in the Boy Scouts	N
3. Campaign Finance Reform	Y	7. Ban Partial-Birth Abortion	N
4. Ban ANWR Development	Y	8. Arm Commercial Pilots	Y

9. Trade Promotion Authority	N
10. Bar Funds for Intl. Court	N
11. Authorize Force in Iraq	N
12. Deny Home. Sec. Dept. Union	N

Election Results

2002 general	Rush Holt (D)	104,806	(61%)	($1,787,764)
	DeForest Soaries (R)	62,938	(37%)	($624,112)
	Other	3,969	(2%)	
2002 primary	Rush Holt (D)	unopposed		
2000 general	Rush Holt (D)	146,612	(49%)	($2,566,080)
	Dick Zimmer (R)	145,511	(49%)	($2,196,588)
	Other	8,269	(3%)	

Prior Winning Percentages: 1998 (50%)

The People		Race/Ethnic Origin	Ancestry	
Area size:	642 sq. mi.	72.4% White	Italian: 13.7%	Irish: 12.1%
Urban population:	93.2%	11.4% Black	German: 9.3%	
Rural population:	6.8%	9.1% Asian	**2000 Presidential Vote**	
Pop. 2000:	647,258	0.1% Native Am.	Gore (D) 141,568	(56%)
Median income:	$69,668	0.0% Hawaiian	Bush (R) 101,145	(40%)
Poverty status:	5.2%	1.4% Two+ races	Other 9,188	(4%)
Military veterans:	10.6%	0.2% Other	**Cook Partisan Voting Index:** D + 8	
		5.5% Hispanic Origin		

Occupation	Blue collar: 13.8%	White collar: 75.7%	Gray collar: 10.4%

It was once the main East Coast arterial highway, carrying the nation's highest volume of truck traffic. Today it is crowded with cars taking high-salaried workers and clerical help to one of the East Coast's thickest concentrations of office buildings in one of the bigger edge cities spawned in the 1980s. This is U.S. 1, which once just connected the industrial cities of Trenton and New Brunswick on its way from Philadelphia to New York; now it is better thought of around here as connecting the university towns around Princeton and Rutgers, and is a locus of telecommunications and pharmaceutical research. This had been empty bucolic country, looked out on by F. Scott Fitzgerald's undergraduates from their Gothic Princeton towers; now it is filled with postmodern office campuses and hotels and restaurants clamoring for attention.

The 12th Congressional District meanders across the breadth of New Jersey, from the Delaware River in the west to the Atlantic Ocean. It extends several dozen miles on either side of U.S. 1 as it slices through Mercer and Middlesex Counties; it is home to both an Englishtown and a Frenchtown. To the west, it takes some of the rolling country of Hunterdon County. On the other side of U.S. 1, the 12th takes in Princeton and then some various modest-income suburbs—Franklin in Somerset County, East Brunswick in Middlesex County and some fast-growing Monmouth County areas such as Rumson, part of Middletown, Holmdel, Marlboro. The 12th is one of the two New Jersey districts—the other is the adjoining 7th—most altered by redistricting. In the process, the 12th lost most of Hunterdon County and much of Somerset, gained the west side of Trenton, added some suburban territory in Middlesex County and lost some of Monmouth County. The overall result was to make the 12th, represented for most of the 1990s by a Republican, less Republican and more Democratic: The Bush 2000 percentage was reduced from 46%—a level that would allow most competitive New Jersey Republicans to carry it—to 40%.

The congressman from the 12th District is Rush Holt, a Democrat first elected in 1998. He has a political pedigree that is, however, of no importance to this district. His father Rush D. Holt, a favorite of United Mine Workers leader John Lewis, was elected as the "boy senator" from West Virginia in 1934 when he was 29; he could not take his seat until June 1935 when he turned 30. But he clashed early and often with Franklin Roosevelt and lost the Democratic primary to Harley Kilgore in 1940. Former Senator Holt died when the young Rush Holt was 6, and he grew up in Washington, D.C., where his mother Helen, who had been West Virginia Secretary of State, was an official in the Federal Housing Agency. He went off to Carleton College in Minnesota and to New York University, where he earned advanced degrees in physics, eventually becoming assistant director of the Princeton Plasma Physics Laboratory, which studies fusion. Holt—the only five-time *Jeopardy* champion to serve in Congress—also was an arms-control expert for the State Department.

Holt entered politics in 1996, when Republican Congressman Dick Zimmer ran for the Senate against Bob Torricelli and lost. He finished third in the Democratic primary behind Lawrenceville Mayor David Del Vecchio and Princeton Town Committeeman Carl Mayer; cultural conservative Mike Pappas won the Republican primary, then the general election but by only 50%–47%. Pappas immediately became a top Democratic target in 1998. Holt decided early in the year that Bill Clinton's State of the Union message gave him an agenda to appeal to suburban voters. Mayer, a wealthy investment lawyer and former Ralph Nader aide, ran again, but national and local Democrats favored Holt, who won the endorsements of all five county Democratic organizations plus all of Mayer's former colleagues on the Princeton Town Committee; he won the primary 64%–36%. Then, in July, Pappas took to the House floor to recite a poem: "Twinkle, Twinkle Kenneth Starr, now we see how brave you are. We could not see which way to go, if you did not lead us so." New Jersey was pro-Clinton, anti-impeachment territory, and Pappas's absurd ditty—replayed on network newscasts and incorporated into a Holt TV spot—proved a great liability. Holt emphasized gun control, abortion rights, the environment and preserving Social Security; he won in a 50%–47% upset.

Holt immediately became a Republican target, but he was undeterred. He compiled a generally liberal voting record, more liberal on defense than on other issues. As the second research physicist in the House, he worked with the other, Republican Vern Ehlers, to promote science education, trying to give science equal standing with reading and math in Title I. He sponsored an assortment of gun control measures, including one to require licensing and registration of all handguns (it attracted no co-sponsors).

In 2000, the Republican primary was fiercely contested. After flirting with another Senate bid, Zimmer declared for his old House seat; Pappas did too. Zimmer had support from Governor

Christine Todd Whitman, former Governor Tom Kean, Speaker Dennis Hastert, Senator John McCain and NRCC Chairman Tom Davis; Pappas was supported by former presidential candidate Steve Forbes, Majority Leader Dick Armey and Majority Whip Tom DeLay. Zimmer won convincingly, 62%–38%, carrying all parts of the district. He immediately became the target of some $2 million of DCCC negative ads. Zimmer acknowledged that the political terrain had changed. "There's a cultural divide between the Northeast and what's become the Republican base," he said during the primary. "The world looks different from suburban New Jersey than it does from Texas." Still, this turned out to be one of the closest races in the nation. At one point on election night, Zimmer was declared the winner. After all the votes were counted, Holt was the actual winner by 653 votes; his lead widened during a recount and Zimmer conceded on November 29.

As a junior member of the minority party, Holt has not played a major role in the House so far. He invoked his authority as a physicist to argue for the importance of embryonic stem cell research. When the Rules Committee blocked his proposal to reestablish the Office of Technology Assessment, which Republicans closed down in 1995, Holt snapped that they had "given up any claim to want to have informed decisions on technical issues here in this Congress." His most important work perhaps was on redistricting. He endorsed the bipartisan congressional delegation redistricting plan, which strengthened all incumbents; in particular, it traded off cities and towns to strengthen him and Republican Mike Ferguson in the adjoining 7th District. He resisted efforts by a potential challenger, Finn Caspersen Jr., son of a prominent Republican contributor, to draw quite different lines that would have kept Caspersen's hometown of Bedminster in the 12th District (it helped that Ferguson very much wanted it put in the 7th). The state redistricting commission made minor changes in the plan, which Holt alone among incumbent attacked fiercely. But the new boundaries suited him fine. The 12th sloughed off most of heavily Republican Hunterdon and Somerset Counties and added the western half of heavily Democratic Trenton. Republican towns in Monmouth County near the Shore were removed; Democratic towns in Middlesex County were added.

Holt's Republican opponent was former New Jersey Secretary of State DeForest "Buster" Soaries, a black minister with a 6,000-member Baptist church; unfortunately for him, many of the members of the congregation lived in New Brunswick, which was located in the 6th District. Soaries argued that he could assemble a coalition of blacks, conservatives, and mainstream Republicans and brought in House Republican Conference Chairman J.C. Watts to campaign for him; Holt brought in Charles Rangel, the Harlem-based ranking Democrat on the Ways and Means Committee. Soaries attracted little financial support from national Republicans; he was out-spent by more than 3–1. Holt won easily, 61%–37%. He won between 52% and 54% in the two ends of the district—Hunterdon and Somerset in the west, Monmouth in the east—but won 63% in Middlesex County and 68% in Mercer County, which includes Princeton and Trenton. This is taking shape as a safe seat for Holt, unless New Jersey moves as sharply toward Republicans in the mid-2000s as it moved toward Democrats in the mid-1990s.

THIRTEENTH DISTRICT

Rep. Robert Menendez (D)

Elected 1992, 6th term; b. Jan. 1, 1954, New York, NY; home, Union City; St. Peter's Col., B.A. 1976, Rutgers Law Schl., J.D. 1979; Catholic; married (Jane Jacobsen-Menendez).

Elected Office: Union City Board of Ed., 1974–82; Union City Mayor, 1986–92; NJ Assembly, 1987–91; NJ Senate, 1991–92.

Professional Career: Practicing atty., 1980–92.

DC Office: 2238 RHOB 20515, 202-225-7919; Fax: 202-226-0792; Web site: menendez.house.gov.

District Offices: Bayonne, 201-823-2900; Jersey City, 201-222-2828; Perth Amboy, 908-324-6212; Union City, 201-558-0800.

Committees: *Democratic Caucus Chairman. International Relations* (6th of 23 D): International Terrorism, Nonproliferation and Human Rights; Western Hemisphere (RMM). *Transportation & Infrastructure* (8th of 34 D): Aviation; Water Resources & Environment.

Group Ratings

	ADA	ACLU	AFS	LCV	CON	ITIC	NTU	COC	ACU	NTLC	CHC
2002	95	67	89	88	63	50	19	42	8	3	0
2001	95	—	100	100	—	—	12	35	16	—	—

National Journal Ratings

	2001 LIB	—	2001 CONS		2002 LIB	—	2002 CONS
Economic	72%	—	27%		69%	—	30%
Social	65%	—	34%		84%	—	8%
Foreign	49%	—	47%		61%	—	38%

Key Votes of the 107th Congress

1. Approve Bush Tax Cuts	N	5. Faith-Based Charities	N	9. Trade Promotion Authority	N
2. Limit Patients' Bill of Rights	N	6. Bar Gays in the Boy Scouts	Y	10. Bar Funds for Intl. Court	Y
3. Campaign Finance Reform	Y	7. Ban Partial-Birth Abortion	N	11. Authorize Force in Iraq	N
4. Ban ANWR Development	Y	8. Arm Commercial Pilots	N	12. Deny Home. Sec. Dept. Union	N

Election Results

2002 general	Robert Menendez (D)	72,605	(78%)	($2,197,203)
	James Geron (R)	16,852	(18%)	
	Other	3,274	(4%)	
2002 primary	Robert Menendez (D)	unopposed		
2000 general	Robert Menendez (D)	117,856	(79%)	($1.713,018)
	Theresa de Leon (R)	27,849	(19%)	($19,822)
	Other	3,893	(3%)	

Prior Winning Percentages: 1998 (80%); 1996 (79%); 1994 (71%); 1992 (64%)

The People		Race/Ethnic Origin	Ancestry	
Area size:	74 sq. mi.	32.3% White	Italian: 7.3%	Irish: 5.3%
Urban population:	100.0%	11.3% Black	Polish: 3.8%	
Rural population:	0.0%	5.5% Asian	**2000 Presidential Vote**	
Pop. 2000:	647,258	0.1% Native Am.	Gore (D)	114,586 (72%)
Median income:	$37,129	0.0% Hawaiian	Bush (R)	39,554 (25%)
Poverty status:	18.0%	2.4% Two+ races	Other	4,338 (3%)
Military veterans:	5.4%	0.6% Other	**Cook Partisan Voting Index:** D +24	
		47.6% Hispanic Origin		

Occupation	Blue collar: 28.4%	White collar: 55.7%	Gray collar: 15.9%

The Statue of Liberty, standing in New York Harbor since 1886, has been the great symbol of America welcoming immigrants to its shores. Actually, the statue is on the New Jersey side of the harbor, and so (as the Supreme Court ruled in 1998) is most of Ellis Island, where they were processed. The towns sitting on the granite and gneiss ridge of Hudson County, overlooking the harbor, have in particular been immigrant territory. When immigration was shut off in 1924, many children and grandchildren of the Irish and Italian immigrants stayed in Hudson County, living in the same neighborhoods, working on the same docks or factories and voting the dictates of the same political machine. Hudson County was the setting of one of America's classic political machines, undisciplined by any metropolitan elite. From 1917–49, the boss of Hudson County was Frank ("I am the law") Hague; his machine chose governors and U.S. Senators, prosecutors and judges, and had influence in the White House of Franklin D. Roosevelt. Hague collected high taxes from industries clustered here—who then passed them on to consumers everywhere—and in return gave them an orderly city, free of most crime and vice, and a work force insulated against racketeers and militant unions. Hague's successor, John V. Kenny, was boss from 1949–71—continuous power for 54 years.

But Hudson County began changing again, in ways little noticed by either the local machine or Manhattan sophisticates. New immigrants were coming in—refugees from Castro's Cuba, other Latinos and Asians after the 1965 immigration act. Union City became predominantly Cuban, Jersey

City neighborhoods became heavily Latino. Upscale young singles looking for lower rents moved into Hoboken's five-story Victorian apartments that sparkle with light off the Hudson, and were a quick commute through the PATH tubes to Wall Street or Greenwich Village. Starting in the 1980s, huge new condominium and office developments went up in Jersey City—Port Liberte, Newport, Liberty Place, Port Imperial South, a 45-story Goldman Sachs tower, back-office buildings for Chase Bank, Merrill Lynch, Paine Webber, U.S. Trust. In Hoboken, shopping and apartment complexes are going up on waterfront sites where Maxwell House Coffee and Lipton Tea had great factories (and where the movie classic, *On the Waterfront*, was filmed on location). Aiding this private sector growth was reform of the public sector, notably by Jersey City's Republican former mayor, Bret Schundler, a former Wall Streeter elected in 1992 after the incumbent went to jail, who was elected to full terms in 1993 and 1997; he ran unsuccessfully for governor in 2001. Meanwhile, new immigrants continue to arrive. Union City is less Cuban today, as middle class Cubans move to Bergen County suburbs, and more Colombian, Ecuadoran, Peruvian and Dominican. Old rail lines long embedded in pavement are being dug up and used for the new Hudson-Bergen light rail lines, and new ferry terminals are being built on the Hudson. Hudson County, which seemed to be dying a generation ago, is now thriving with new life.

The 13th Congressional District includes most of Hudson County plus most of the immigrant entry ports along the water, from West New York and Weehawken, where Alexander Hamilton was killed in a duel with Vice President Aaron Burr in 1804, south past Jersey City and Bayonne (where you can still find bocce courts), past the Port of New York and New Jersey to the waterfront areas of Elizabeth, Linden, Carteret (with its Sikh community), Woodbridge and Perth Amboy. It also includes the Ironbound district of Newark, with Portuguese and Brazilian immigrants, crowded stores and $300,000 houses, Harrison and part of industrial Kearny. The district's population is 48% Hispanic; black neighborhoods in Jersey City were put into the majority-black, neighboring 10th District. The 13th is heavily Democratic.

The congressman from the 13th District is Robert Menendez, a Democrat first elected in 1992. He is of Cuban descent and grew up in Union City, America's most densely populated city (in 2000 it had 60,000 people in 1.3 square miles), and got into politics early. He was elected to the school board in 1974, at 20. He worked for Union City Mayor William Musto in the 1970s, but quit and testified against Musto in a corruption trial, and ran against him and lost in 1982. Menendez was elected mayor in 1986, to the Assembly in 1987 and Senate in 1991, serving both as mayor and legislator (a common practice in New Jersey) until his 1992 election to Congress. He was the first New Jersey Latino in the legislature and Congress. When new district lines were created and incumbent Frank Guarini retired, Menendez won the 1992 primary 68%–32% and the general election 64%–31%.

In the House, Menendez serves on the International Relations Committee where he became ranking minority member on the Western Hemisphere Subcommittee in 2001. He has been a strong supporter of anti-Castro legislation—the 1992 Cuban Democracy Act, the 1996 Helms-Burton Act. He criticized the Clinton administration for not enforcing Helms-Burton and taking steps to relax the trade embargo. When Elian Gonzalez was collected by federal agents, he said grimly, "I think that the use of armed agents with automatic weapons, in the pre-dawn hours on the morning of the holiest weekend of the year, is, in my mind, something we would see in Fidel Castro's Cuba, not in the democracy of the United States." But his concerns are not limited to Cuba. He supported the Caribbean Basin Initiative and the proposal to allow Central American and Haitian refugees long in this country to remain. In May 2001 he got the committee to support for continuing negotiations "with the objective of completing the rules and guidelines for the Kyoto protocol." He spoke out in support of Israel's military actions in May 2002 even though he said his district "has far more Arabs than Jews."

Noting the increasing importance of the financial services industry in Hudson County, he broke with many Democrats to support the bankruptcy bill and financial services deregulation; one Blue Dog Democrat called him "the pro-business member of the leadership." He has pressed for more set-asides for minority contractors and Senate confirmation of Hispanic judges—though he opposed Bush nominee Miguel Estrada.

On local issues, he got $12 million for a ferry terminal near the Port Imperial South projects, whose owner is a key financial backer. "If he ends up, along with everybody else, being a beneficiary of what I'm advocating, what can I say?" He has continued to press for more ferries—whose value was shown when people fled Lower Manhattan across the Hudson on September 11.

Menendez has shown fine political skills. He aggressively supported Loretta Sanchez against the election challenge brought by Robert Dornan, whom she ousted in November 1996. In November 1998, his party colleagues elected him vice chairman of the Democratic Caucus. When Senator Frank Lautenberg announced his retirement in February 1999, Menendez was widely expected to run for the Senate. But support was not forthcoming from New Jersey Senator Bob Torricelli, the DSCC Chairman, who wanted a deep-pockets candidate and found him in Jon Corzine, whom Menendez endorsed in November 1999. In July 2000, after Torricelli said he would run for governor, Menendez choreographed an endorsement by many Hudson County Democrats of Jim McGreevey, which helped persuade Torricelli to withdraw ignominiously from the race. He is a major player in Hudson County and state politics. He helped to defeat mayors of Union City and Hoboken and install friendly replacements. McGreevey, whom he helped in July 2000, made him statewide coordinator of his 2001 campaign. Menendez claims that McGreevey's share of the Hispanic vote rose from 48% in 1997 to 72% in 2001.

One reason Menendez decided not to run for the Senate in 2000 is that Minority Leader Dick Gephardt urged him to stay in the House, arguing that as a leader of a Democratic majority he could be more important than a junior senator. Democratic caucus chairmen and vice-chairmen are limited to two two-year terms, so Menendez in 2001 began running for caucus chairman. He raised more than $1 million for House Democrats in the 2000 cycle and $3 million in the 2002 cycle and traveled around the country campaigning. His Hispanic background was an asset, and not just within the 20-member Hispanic Caucus. "There are 50 to 60 members who are not Hispanic but have significant Hispanic communities in their districts," he points out. "The Census was a real eye-opener. I have members asking me to travel with them to places I never thought I'd be invited." He issues a Latino Leadership Link every week in English and Spanish. Menendez announced his candidacy in October 2001, just after the Caucus picked Nancy Pelosi over Steny Hoyer to replace David Bonior as minority whip. Also running was Rosa DeLauro, who had been Assistant to Minority Leader Richard Gephardt.

Leadership elections are decided by secret ballot, and are sometimes bitter; the total number of commitments announced by candidates usually exceeds the number of members of the caucus. Occasionally sour notes are sounded in public. In February 2002 Menendez charged that DeLauro backers were saying, wrongly, that he did not support abortion rights; he argued that the caucus, having chosen Pelosi for the number one post, would be better off with an Hispanic than another woman in the number two post. In an unusual turn, Pelosi openly endorsed DeLauro and Hoyer openly endorsed Menendez.

Then, on September 30, came another opportunity to run for the Senate: Bob Torricelli dropped out of the race and McGreevey and other Democratic leaders sought another candidate. Menendez, with more than $2 million in his campaign treasury, probably could have had the nomination for the asking. He pondered the situation for a day, and then decided not to run; he said he was too committed to getting a Democratic majority in the House and becoming caucus chairman.

On November 5 he failed to achieve the first goal and on November 14, the day of the caucus election, he very nearly failed to achieve the second. The day before the caucus meeting, the 21 Blue Dogs met and pledged to vote as a bloc for their favorite candidate, which by a 16–5 vote was Menendez; it's not clear that all of them did. Menendez walked into the caucus with a list of 107 members who had agreed to openly support him. He won 104–103. Two members were absent. The decisive vote was cast by Mike Feeley of Colorado, who was in a still undecided race that he ended up losing by 121 votes. In similar circumstances, Democrats had let a member in an undecided race vote in 1996, and both sides agreed to follow the precedent.

Menendez has been reelected to the House easily, and spent almost all the $2 million plus he raised in the 2002 cycle helping other Democrats. In December 2002, he was asked about his future prospects. "Being speaker's a possibility. I also don't discount the possibility of running for the Senate. You know, 49 is young. By the barometer of Strom Thurmond, there's still half a century to go."

★ NEW MEXICO ★

A merica's oldest settlements and its newest technologies can be found, in surrealistic proximity, in New Mexico. For the oldest permanently inhabited city in the United States is not Plymouth, Massachusetts, or Jamestown, Virginia, or even St. Augustine, Florida, it is probably Acoma, New Mexico. Probably, because Acoma, inhabited by the Anasazi, "an agricultural, settled and architecturally sophisticated people," wrote historian Roger Kennedy in *Rediscovering America*, had perhaps 1,000 years of unrecorded history before Spanish conquistadors came upon them in 1540. Some 460 years later, much of what makes New Mexico distinctive derives from the people found here by the first European explorers—something true of no other state but Hawaii. While the Pilgrims built flimsy wood houses, the Indians in New Mexico were living in extensive dwellings hundreds of years old, made with the adobe that is still the characteristic building material here.

Other state cultures are generally based on what early white settlers brought to the land; natives have mostly disappeared or been killed off by diseases contracted from the first white settlers. Not in New Mexico. The English-speaking culture here is superimposed, at times rather lightly, on a society whose written history dates back to the Spanish settlement of Santa Fe in 1609, and to centuries long past when the Pueblo Indians set up stable agricultural societies on the sandy, rocky lands of northern New Mexico, using small pebbles as mulch to retain scarce moisture. Today, a very substantial minority of New Mexicans are descendants of these Indians or the Spanish, or both. New Mexico's population was 42% Hispanic in 2000, the highest percentage in any state, and 9% American Indian. About one-third of the people in this state speak Spanish in everyday life, but relatively few are recent migrants from Mexico: only 8% of New Mexicans are foreign-born, less than the national average.

New Mexico is the northernmost salient of the great Indian-Spanish civilizations of the Cordillera, which extend along the mountain chain through Mexico and Central and South America, to the southern Chile. Yet New Mexico also is a civilization built on modern technology. It was to a remote mesa called Los Alamos that General Leslie Groves brought his Manhattan Project scientists during World War II to build a secret town and develop a secret weapon that would in two explosions end World War II and change the course of history. Los Alamos, which remains a government high-tech laboratory, made news in early 1999 when it was revealed that Chinese spies had obtained hundreds of computer files from there. New Mexico has other high-tech sites as well—the White Sands Missile Range near Alamogordo, where the first atomic bomb was detonated, and the Sandia Laboratories near Albuquerque, run by Lockheed-Martin for the government, a non-nuclear high-tech weapons research facility, with one of the fastest computers in the world, used to simulate nuclear explosions. Near Carlsbad is the federal Waste Isolation Pilot Plant (WIPP), where the Energy Department deposits transuranic radioactive waste; after many delays, the first waste from the Idaho National Engineering and Environmental Laboratory arrived here in March 1999.

But the past intrudes on this new high-tech New Mexico. Golf courses and other resort facilities are springing up around the Indian casinos operated by 11 of New Mexico's 22 tribes; these employ many Indians, and are an opportunity for many to segue into the mainstream economy and culture; but some wonder whether they are killing off ancient traditions and religious practices.

New and old New Mexico intermingle in varying proportions in this land of majestically vast vistas. The Hispanic-Indian culture predominates north and west of Albuquerque, with picturesque old towns and still-functioning pueblos, backward Indian reservations and lavish casino resorts. "Little Texas," in the south and east, has small cities, plenty of oil wells, vast cattle ranches and desolate military bases, and resembles, economically and culturally, the adjacent west Texas High Plains. Here, as everywhere in New Mexico, government is a prime employer (accounting for 23% of jobs, one of the highest figures in the country) and often the moving force in the local economy. In the middle is Albuquerque, which, with the arrival of air conditioning, grew from a small desert town of 35,000 in 1940 into a Sun Belt metropolis of 449,000 today; it has a large

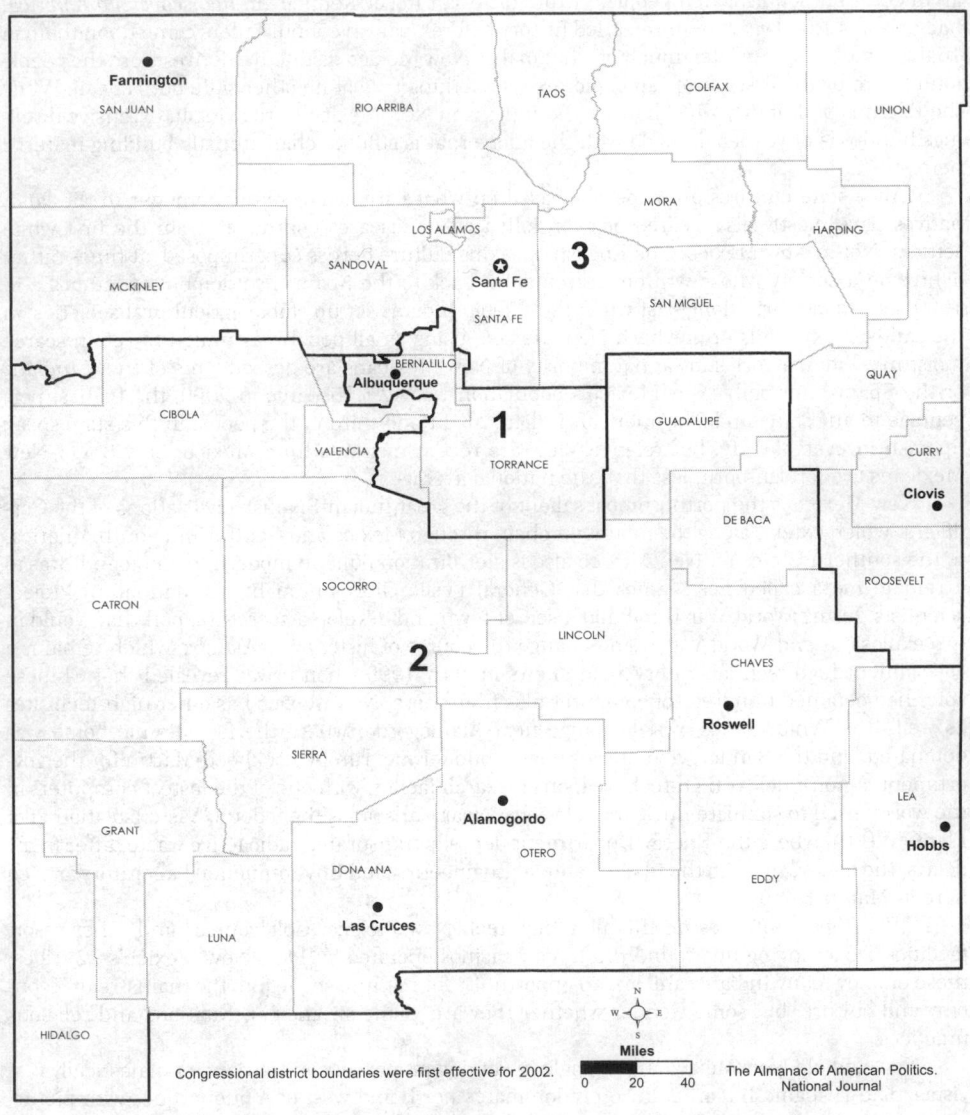

Congressional district boundaries were first effective for 2002.

Miles
0   20   40

The Almanac of American Politics.
National Journal

Hispanic minority. Its economy is based heavily on high tech, especially nuclear power, but it has relatively low income and education levels: New Mexico ranks first among states in the percentage living in poverty (18% in 2001) and 45th in median household income—the downscale Sun Belt. It also has high rates of highway fatalities, teenage pregnancies and violent crime.

For many years, New Mexico politics was a somnolent business. Local bosses—first Republican, later Democratic—controlled the large Hispanic vote. Elections in many counties featured irregularities that would have made a Chicago ward committeeman blush. New Mexico also had for years another feature of boss-controlled politics: the balanced ticket, one Spanish and one Anglo senator, with the offices of governor and lieutenant governor split as well. But for all its distinctiveness, in national politics New Mexico was a bellwether, voting for every winning presidential candidate from 1912, when it became a state, until 1976, when it backed Gerald Ford. In the 1988 and 1996 elections it was just 1% off the national mark; in 2000, after some ragged vote counting, it reported a 366-vote margin for Al Gore. Currently, Democrats have a strong base in the north, from Hispanics and from liberal newcomers in Santa Fe and Taos. Albuquerque has been politically marginal; its migrants have been conservative culturally but liberal on economics. Southeast New Mexico is as conservative and Republican as west Texas. Southwest New Mexico, around Las Cruces and Silver City, is more Hispanic and marginally Democratic.

New Mexico politics also has its peculiarities. In the 1990s a Green Party formed, in protest against the practical-minded and sometimes corrupt politics of many Democratic wheelhorses; the Green candidate for governor won 10% of the vote in 1994, and Republican Gary Johnson might well have not been elected otherwise. Johnson was also a new political force—the first strongly conservative Republican to win major office in many years, and one of the few Republicans to come out for drug legalization. But Johnson was term-limited in 2002 and was succeeded by Bill Richardson, former Congressman, Ambassador to the United Nations and Energy Secretary, occasional negotiator with North Korea and possibly the first Hispanic vice presidential nominee. The Green party was ruled off the ballot in 2001 after Ralph Nader failed to win 5%; but its gubernatorial candidate got 5% in 2002 and so it is back on—which means that there probably will be a Green presidential candidate on the ballot in very closely divided New Mexico in 2004.

From almost any point in New Mexico the physical environment is awe-inspiring: amid the vast empty plains of the east or above the peaks and mesas of the north or from the desert of the south, the sky seems enormously large and empty and the air so clear you can see for what seems like 100 miles. But it is an austere and sometimes dangerous environment. The drought of 2001 and 2002 left New Mexico's reservoirs low and the Rio Grande below Albuquerque for a time almost dry. In the summer of 2002 water conservation measures were imposed in Albuquerque and Santa Fe and lawns converted to xeriscaping. Albuquerque's future water supply is imperiled because EPA recognized the three-inch silvery minnow that used to be common in the Rio Grande as an endangered species; underground water supplies are insufficient for present needs, much less for future growth. The legislature has been grappling with water rights issues and Governor Bill Richardson in his 2002 campaign promised a statewide water plan. There are other risks: forest fires, like the Los Alamos blaze of summer 2000, which swept through 50,000 acres and was lit by Park Service employees acting under the controlled burn policies of the Clinton administration. None of New Mexico's traditional politicians, neither the machine Democrats of northern New Mexico who dominate the legislature nor the ranchers of Little Texas nor the representatives of Albuquerque, have been swept up by the environmental restriction movement and so New Mexico developed in the 1990s an active Green party. In the 1997 special election to succeed Bill Richardson in the heavily Democratic 3d Congressional District, a Green candidate won 17% of the vote and enabled Republican Bill Redmond to win the seat 43%–40%.

The People
Pop. 2000:	1,819,046	
Pop. 1990:	1,515,069	
Change 1990–2000:	Up 20.1%	
Change 1980–1990:	Up 16.3%	
% of U.S. total:	0.7%	
Pop. rank:	36th of 50	
Area size:	121,589 sq. mi.	
State Native:	51.5%	
Non-citizen:	5.4%	

Language
English: 58.2%	Spanish: 33.3%
Other Eur.: 2.1%	

Race/Ethnic Origin
813,495	44.7%	White
30,654	1.7%	Black
18,257	1.0%	Asian
161,460	8.9%	Native Am.
992	0.1%	Hawaiian
25,793	1.4%	Two+ races
3,009	0.2%	Other
765,386	42.1%	Hisp. Origin

Ancestry
German: 8.2%	English: 6.3%
Irish: 6.1%	USA: 4.2%
Italian: 2.0%	

Military veterans: 190,718 (14.5%)
WWII: 18.0%	Korea: 13.2%
Vietnam: 34.7%	Gulf War: 10.7%

Most populous cities:
1. Albuquerque	448,607
2. Las Cruces	74,267
3. Santa Fe	62,203
4. Rio Rancho	51,765
5. Roswell	45,293

Urban population: 75.0%
Rural population: 25.0%

Education
H.S. Grad:	78.9%
College Grad:	23.5%

Industry
Agri: 4.0%	Con: 7.9%
Fin: 5.5%	Info: 2.4%
Mfg: 11.2%	Prof: 31.1%
Public: 8.0%	Trade: 14.9%
Other: 14.9%	

Occupation
Blue collar: 22.2%	White collar: 59.9%
Gray collar: 17.9%	

Work Sector
Private: 68.5%	Govt: 22.7%
Self: 8.4%	Family: 0.4%

Unemployment: 7.2%

Household Income
<15k: 20.8%	15-35k: 30.2%
35-50k: 17.0%	50-100k: 24.3%
100-150k: 5.0%	>150k: 2.6%

Median: $34,133
Poverty status: 18.4%

Home Value
<50k: 22.7%	50-100k: 31.1%	100-200k: 33.4%	200-300k: 7.7%
300-500k: 3.6%	>500k: 1.6%	Median: $94,600	

Legislature
Senate	24 D 18 R
House	43 D 27 R

Legislative Term Limits: No

Registered Voters
D:	495,221	(52.1%)
R:	310,337	(32.6%)
I:	145,185	(15.3%)

Presidential politics New Mexico's near-bellwether status seems more accidental than anything else; it's hard to think of a state more atypical of the nation, yet it keeps on voting at or near the national average. It voted Republican for president in the 1980s, Democratic in the 1990s and gave Al Gore a 366-vote margin in 2000. Unlike most Rocky Mountain states, New Mexico's demographic trends favor Democrats: conservative Little Texas gained little population in the 1990s, while the Hispanic percentage rose and Indian voting increased; George W. Bush's popularity among Latinos in Texas didn't transfer at all to New Mexico's very different Hispanic voters. Whites here voted 58%–37% for Bush, Hispanics 66%–32% for Gore. The vote counting here in 2000 was as ragged as in Florida, or more so. In Bernalillo County, where one-third of the state's votes were cast, the optical scanning machine used for counting the 66,000 absentee and early ballots was misprogrammed; also, an envelope with 257 ballots was lost in the warehouse. When these glitches were finally fixed, George W. Bush ended up leading the state count by exactly 4 votes. Then someone discovered that a "620" had been misread as "120" in Dona Ana County, gaining Al Gore 500 votes. Republicans declined to ask for a recount.

2000 Presidential Vote
Gore (D)	286,783	(48%)
Bush (R)	286,418	(48%)
Nader (Green)	21,251	(4%)
Other	4,154	(1%)

2000 Republican Presidential Primary
Bush (R)	62,161	(83%)
McCain (R)	7,619	(10%)
Keyes (R)	4,850	(6%)

2000 Democratic Presidential Primary
Gore (D)	98,715	(75%)
Bradley (D)	27,204	(21%)
Other	6,361	(5%)

1996 Presidential Vote
Clinton (D)	273,495	(49%)
Dole (R)	232,751	(42%)
Perot (I)	32,271	(6%)
Other	17,566	(3%)

New Mexico traditionally held its presidential primary in June, long after every major party nomination since 1984 has been settled. But in 2003 Governor Bill Richardson signed a bill allowing parties to hold caucuses in lieu of the presidential primary; the 2004 caucuses are slated for February 3.

Congressional districting The boundaries of New Mexico's three congressional districts have been substantially the same since 1982, and seem likely to continue that way. Control of the redistricting process in 2001 was split between the Democratic legislature and Republican Governor Gary Johnson. In June 2001 the legislature passed a plan that would make the 1st District, held by Republican Heather Wilson, more Democratic. Johnson vetoed it. In September 2001 the legislature passed a plan that would make the 2d District, held by Republican Joe Skeen, more Democratic. Johnson vetoed it. Republicans had already taken the issue to court. A federal court decided to let the state court handle the issue. In January 2002, state District Judge Frank Allen, a Democrat, imposed his own plan. He said he was reluctant to make major changes and his plan shifted only 22,000 people into different districts. Democrats were disappointed; Republicans were pleased.

108th Congress Lineup
2 R   1 D
107th Congress Lineup
2 R   1 D

In February 2003 state Senate President Richard Romero, who lost to Wilson in 2002, was pressing the legislature to redistrict the House seats once again; Democratic Governor Bill Richardson would surely sign a plan. But national Democrats urged caution. House Majority Whip Tom DeLay had been pressing for another redistricting in Texas, where Republicans now controlled the legislature and held the governorship; Governor Rick Perry and the legislative leaders were at the time reluctant to take on the issue. New Mexico has only three seats, and the best New Mexico Democrats could do would be to change the delegation from 2–1 Republican to 2–1 Democratic. But Texas has 32 seats, and under the current districting plan Democrats won a 17–15 edge in 2002. A partisan Republican redistricting could easily produce a 20–12 Republican edge. In the end, the New Mexico session concluded in March with no new congressional districting plan.

Governor

Bill Richardson (D)

Elected 2002, term expires Jan. 2007, 1st term; b. Nov. 15, 1947, Pasadena, CA; home, Santa Fe; Tufts U., B.A. 1970, Fletcher Schl. of Law and Diplomacy, M.A. 1971; Catholic; married (Barbara).

Elected Office: U.S. House of Reps., 1982–97.

Professional Career: Congressional rel., U.S. Dept. of State, 1973–75; Staff, Senate Foreign Relations Subcmte., 1975–78; Exec. Dir., NM Dem. Party, 1978; Pres., Richardson Trade Group, 1978–82; U.S. Ambassador to U.N., 1997–98; Secy., U.S. Dept. of Energy, 1998–00.

Office: State Capitol, 4th Floor, Santa Fe, 87300, 505-476-2200; Fax: 505-576-2226; Web site: www.governor.state.nm.us.

Election Results

2002 general	Bill Richardson (D)	268,674	(55%)
	John Sanchez (R)	189,090	(39%)
	David Bacon (Green)	26,465	(5%)
2002 primary	Bill Richardson (D)	unopposed	
1998 general	Gary E. Johnson (R)	271,948	(55%)
	Martin Chavez (D)	226,755	(45%)

Bill Richardson, a Democrat, was elected governor of New Mexico in 2002, 20 years after he was first elected to Congress. Richardson is a unique politician—an Hispanic with an Anglo name, a newcomer when he was first elected in New Mexico where many families go back 300 years, an adept politician who has also been an international negotiator. He was born in California and grew up in Mexico City. His father was a banker from Boston and his mother Mexican; she now lives in Cuernavaca and voted for PRI candidate Francisco Labastida in the July 2000 Mexican election. He graduated from prep school in New England, where he met his wife. He was a good pitcher and in 1967 was drafted by the Kansas City Athletics. But "I was a curveball pitcher, and my elbow fell apart." He graduated from Tufts's Fletcher School of Law and Diplomacy and got a master's there. That led to a job as a "sort of go-fer" at the State Department when Henry Kissinger was secretary of state and a job on Senator Hubert Humphrey's staff. Then in 1978 he moved to New Mexico to become executive director of the state Democratic party. He was fired after a month by Governor Bruce King and proceeded to run against 1st District Congressman Manuel Lujan. This was a Republican year and Lujan had deep roots in Albuquerque and had been in office since 1968. But Richardson held him to a 51%–49% victory. New Mexico got a third congressional district from the 1980 Census, and the legislature drew a new, heavily Hispanic 3d District in northern New Mexico. Richardson, based in Santa Fe, had already carried much of this territory in the 1980 race, and he ran in 1982. He beat former Lieutenant Governor Roberto Mondragon 36%–31% in the primary and then won the general election with 64% of the vote. At age 35, after four years in New Mexico, he had a safe seat in the House.

In the House he rose in the Democratic leadership to be a Chief Deputy Whip. He had a somewhat moderate voting record and was not afraid to buck organized labor by lobbying hard for NAFTA in 1992 and 1993. From his unique background he saw the upside potential of a Mexico more closely aligned with the United States and the downside potential of a Mexico spurned and rejected. He was the lone member of the New Mexico delegation to oppose the Waste Isolation Pilot Project for several years, but supported it when tougher environmental standards were imposed. In December 1992 he came close to being named Secretary of the Interior, but that job went to Bruce Babbitt. After that he spent much time on foreign affairs. In February 1994 he traveled to Myanmar and met with imprisoned human rights advocate Aung San Suu Kyi after meeting with a head of the military junta—an important statement of American support for human rights. In July 1994 he traveled to Haiti and met with General Raoul Cedras and in a five-hour conversation tried to get him to cede power, unsuccessfully. In December 1994 he was traveling to North Korea when two U.S. helicopter pilots were gunned down for allegedly trespassing into North Korean airspace. He negotiated for the release of the surviving pilot but ended up returning with the remains of the one who died; the other pilot was soon released.

In January 1997 Richardson was nominated as ambassador to the United Nations. Here was an opportunity to be a major player in foreign policy, although Richardson was cabined in by the close supervision of his predecessor, Secretary of State Madeleine Albright. But he did negotiate agreements between the Taliban regime in Afghanistan and opposition forces and secured the release of Red Cross workers held hostage in Sudan, and the foreign policy experience he was gaining seemed likely to make him a plausible vice presidential candidate in 2000 or later. The only embarrassing thing about his service was the fact, later disclosed that, at the request of a White House staffer and without asking why, he offered a job to Monica Lewinsky; she rejected it as insufficiently grand. Then in June 1998 Energy Secretary Federico Pena resigned and Bill Clinton, eager to have at least one Hispanic in an official cabinet position, shifted Richardson to the post. This was not really a promotion: Energy is a department that is made up of several unrelated agencies, some of them with deep troubles. One of those was the Los Alamos National Laboratory, from which, it seemed, secret documents about the assembly of nuclear weapons made their way to China. The suspect was physicist Wen Ho Lee, and Richardson fired him in March 1999. Lee was indicted on 59 counts of transferring nuclear weapons data to unsecure computers, but the case against him was thoroughly botched; most charges were dropped and in September 2000 he pleaded guilty to one count of downloading sensitive material. Richardson was much criticized in Congress for his work on improving security in the national laboratories, and his connection to the case was a political liability. He was mentioned as a possible vice presidential candidate in 2000—the Democrats would have loved to run a Hispanic—but his name soon fell off the list. As he put it later, "At the time they were making the final decision for the Gore ticket in 2000, the Los Alamos hard drive issues came up and that nixed me. If I was asked by Gore, I would have accepted. But the security stuff cancelled me out."

After Al Gore's defeat, Richardson returned to Santa Fe; he did some work for Kissinger McClarty associates and served on corporate boards, but it was obvious he was running for governor. He had considered running before, especially in 1994, but decided not to. The governor elected that year, Republican Gary Johnson, had been reelected in 1998 and was ineligible to run again. There were no obvious successors: most Republican politicians were little known statewide, and well-known Democrats had malodorous reputations.

Richardson announced his candidacy in January 2002 and pledged to shake 600 hands a day; on September 16 he broke Theodore Roosevelt's record of 8,513, set on New Year's Day 1908, by shaking 13,392 hands at the New Mexico State Fair and a tailgate party at the University of New Mexico (his campaign flew in a representative of the *Guinness Book of World Records* to document the feat). He said that he would use his diplomatic skills to attract new business and abridge partisan differences. He called for lower taxes and incentives for new jobs and praised the efforts of the Greater Albuquerque Chamber of Commerce to improve the city's schools—not refrains usually heard from New Mexico Democrats. He had opposition from two Democrats, former state Representative Gary King, whose father Bruce King had served three non-consecutive terms as governor and state Land Commissioner Ray Powell. But at the state Democratic convention in March, he won 1,288 of 1,705 votes. King and Powell failed to get enough to qualify for the ballot. With his energy and his national contacts, Richardson raised and spent large sums, eventually $6.8 million, more than twice as much as both parties' candidates spent in 1998, and began running ads showing his vision for the state.

Meanwhile, there was a spirited race for the Republican nomination. The lead candidate was state Representative John Sanchez, a roofing contractor from Albuquerque's North Valley, who had won his seat in 2000 by defeating, by 206 votes, the 30-year Speaker of the New Mexico House Raymond Sanchez. He called for lower taxes, higher teacher pay and more accountability in schools; he opposed collective bargaining for state employees and pledged to continue Johnson's limits on spending. His chief competition came from Lieutenant Governor Walter Bradley, who took similar positions. Sanchez ran a series of negative ads against Bradley, charging that he was close to legislative Democrats. In April Sanchez stirred controversy when he said, "Let's empower the people of our state to . . . put an end to the banana republic that has controlled our state for the last 75 years." In June Sanchez beat Bradley 59%–35%. But Bradley and Gary Johnson were still unhappy with Sanchez's ads. Johnson did not endorse Sanchez until mid-July; Bradley withheld his endorsement even longer.

In the general election Sanchez called for vouchers, merit pay for teachers and better testing; he ran a series of ads recounting his rise from poverty under the theme of "Dream Big." But Richardson had much more money and took many more specific stands on issues. He called for cutting the state income tax—New Mexico's 8.2% top rate is much higher than those of surrounding states—and eliminating the gross receipts tax. Amid news of drought and water conservation measures, he called for a statewide water policy and sketched one out in considerable detail. He opposed vouchers, but supported charter schools and tax credits for parochial schools. Like Sanchez he favored the death penalty and a concealed weapons law.

Richardson pledged to conduct a positive campaign unless attacked. He was: Sanchez ran ads criticizing Richardson for serving on the board of Peregrine Systems, which misstated its earnings and whose CEO, Richardson's wife's brother-in-law, resigned. Richardson said he was only an outside director and had resigned that position in June 2002. Richardson ran ads criticizing Sanchez for absenteeism in the legislature and for doctoring his resume; Sanchez said he started his roofing business in 1980, but in the mid-1980s was also working as a flight attendant. "While Bill Richardson was cutting taxes for New Mexico, John Sanchez was serving orange juice at 30,000 feet." There was little suspense about the result. "The margin is important," said Richardson before the election. "I want a really good margin to be able to govern, to do the out-of-the-box solutions that are needed. I want a good victory." He got it. Richardson won 55%–39%. He ran not far behind in Little Texas, carried the Albuquerque area comfortably and won as much as 75% of the vote in Hispanic and Indian counties. He was the only one of four Clinton cabinet members running in 2002 who won. Inevitably, he was asked whether he had ambitions for national office. "I've always wanted to run for governor. I love this state, and I think the governor can make an enormous difference in people's lives—more so than any job I have held. I see this as a sort of culmination of my career. I am not interested in going back to Washington"—not even as vice president. Where did he expect to be in 10 years? "Smoking cigars in Santa Fe and riding my horses." Barbara Richardson, asked if he would run for president in 2008, said, "I'll tell you what I tell him. 'That's another life and another wife.' Honest to God. Not my bag."

Richardson appointed two Republicans and several Hispanics and Indians to his cabinet and immediately started lobbying legislators of both parties for his tax cut. Unusually in New Mexico, they brought the issue up before the budget and on Valentine's Day 2003 Richardson signed a bill cutting the top income tax rate from 8.2% in steps to 4.9% and cutting the capital gains tax in half over five years. Richardson said he planned a special session for the fall for more fundamental changes in tax laws. Richardson also made national news in January 2003 when a North Korean delegation on the way to the United Nations stopped off, with Secretary of State Colin Powell's permission, in Santa Fe and had several sessions with Richardson at the Governor's Mansion; Richardson briefed Powell and various senators on the talks and called for direct negotiations between the U.S. and North Korea.

Senior Senator

Pete Domenici (R)

Elected 1972, seat up 2008, 6th term; b. May 7, 1932, Albuquerque; home, Albuquerque; U. of NM, B.S. 1954, Denver U., LL.B. 1958; Catholic; married (Nancy).

Elected Office: Albuquerque City Comm., 1966–70, Mayor Ex–Officio, 1967–70.

Professional Career: Practicing atty., 1958–72.

DC Office: 328 HSOB, 20510, 202-224-6621; Fax: 202-228-0900; Web site: domenici.senate.gov.

State Offices: Albuquerque, 505-346-6791; Las Cruces, 505-526-5475; Roswell, 505-623-6170; Santa Fe, 505-988-6511.

Committees: *Appropriations*: Commerce, Justice, State & Judiciary; Defense; Energy & Water Development (Chmn.); Homeland Security; Interior; VA, HUD & Independent Agencies. *Budget. Energy & Natural Resources* (Chmn.). *Indian Affairs*.

Group Ratings

	ADA	ACLU	AFS	LCV	CON	ITIC	NTU	COC	ACU	NTLC	CHC
2002	15	0	14	6	65	88	56	100	88	76	—
2001	10	—	0	13	—	—	78	100	90	—	80

National Journal Ratings

	2001 LIB —	2001 CONS		2002 LIB —	2002 CONS
Economic	41%	59%		29%	70%
Social	42%	58%		0%	62%
Foreign	7%	72%		0%	76%

Key Votes of the 107th Congress

1. Approve Bush Tax Cuts	Y	5. Confirm Ashcroft as AG	Y	9. Bar Coop. with Intl. Court	Y
2. Expand Patients' Rights	*	6. Bar Gays in the Boy Scouts	Y	10. Trade Promotion Authority	Y
3. Campaign Finance Reform	Y	7. $ for Hate Crime Prosecution	N	11. Authorize Force in Iraq	Y
4. Permit ANWR Development	Y	8. Overseas Military Abortions	N	12. Homeland Sec. Dept. Union	N

Election Results

2002 general	Pete Domenici (R)	314,193	(65%)	($4,144,286)
	Gloria Tristani (D)	168,863	(35%)	($836,604)
2002 primary	Pete Domenici (R)	unopposed		
1996 general	Pete Domenici (R)	357,171	(65%)	($3,435,164)
	Art Trujillo (D)	164,356	(30%)	($155,213)
	Abraham J. Gutmann (Green)	24,230	(4%)	($12,025)

Prior Winning Percentages: 1990 (73%); 1984 (72%); 1978 (53%); 1972 (54%)

Pete Domenici, New Mexico's senior Senator, was elected to his sixth term in 2002. He grew up in Albuquerque, the son of Italian immigrants who ran a grocery wholesale business. He played baseball for the Albuquerque Dukes, practiced law, was elected to the city commission in 1966; he ran for governor in 1970, and lost 51%–46% to Bruce King. In 1972, when a Senate seat opened up in a Republican year, he ran and won 54%–46%, beating a Democrat named Jack Daniels. Ever since he has been reelected by wide margins.

Domenici is now chairman of the Senate Energy and Natural Resources Committee, but for 22 years he was chairman or ranking minority member of the Budget Committee. He has also been a member of the Appropriations Committee and brought an appropriator's mindset to his work on the budget. He got a seat on the Budget Committee in 1973, his first year in the Senate, and after Republicans gained a majority in 1980 he became chairman in January 1981; he became ranking minority member in January 1987, chairman again in January 1995 and ranking minority member in June 2001. In 1990 he turned down the ranking minority position on Energy and Natural Resources, an important committee for New Mexico, to stay on the Budget. After supporting the 1981 Reagan tax cuts, Domenici was appalled at budget deficits and pushed for entitlement cuts and tax increases, but Democrats fought the first and Republicans the second. In May 1985, Domenici and Bob Dole got Republican senators to pass a freeze on Social Security cost-of-living adjustments; then Ronald Reagan dropped the COLA freeze in a compromise with House Speaker Tip O'Neill, and Senate Republicans, left exposed, lost their majority in 1986. After Republicans became the majority party Domenici's ideas—a consumption tax, more in spending than tax cuts—were initially overruled by Speaker Newt Gingrich, but the tax increase he opposed in 1993 and the spending standstill in the budget eventually passed in early 1996 put the deficit on a downward trajectory. Domenici was the impresario in the negotiations that produced the May 1997 balanced budget agreement. He helped to shape the budget resolutions in 1999 and 2000, but as an appropriator helped work out the arrangements that resulted in exceeding the budget caps. In February 2001 he worked to pass the $1.6 trillion Bush tax cut and charged that Democrats had "anti-tax cut fever." Shy one vote in the Senate, Republicans did not end up reaching Bush's goals on the budget resolution. But they came close, and would have ended up much further away if Domenici had been lukewarm about the Bush plan. In June 2001 Domenici lost the chairmanship, but the budget resolution had already passed and in 2002 the Democrats were not able to pass one. In November 2001 he proposed a one-month $38 billion holiday from the payroll tax. In November 2002 he decided, after finding new spots for some longtime staffers, to move to the chairmanship of the Energy Committee; under Senate Republican rules he was eligible for only two more years as Budget Chairman. In early 2003 he seemed less upset with deficits than he had in the 1980s. "Obviously, deficits over long periods of time, especially when you have a good economy and are not at war, bother me very much. But I have carefully researched the projected deficits for the next few years and I am not worried about them having a negative effect on the economy. The accumulation of debt does not bother me yet. It will bother me if we keep running those kinds of deficits for seven, eight or nine more years."

Domenici took over the Energy chairmanship from his Democratic New Mexico colleague, Jeff Bingaman, who became ranking minority member; this was the first time in history senators from the same state held the top two positions on a committee. Among the reasons he did so were his continuing interest in New Mexico's Los Alamos and Sandia National Laboratories and in promoting the expansion of nuclear power. After the controversy over security lapses at Los Alamos, he sponsored the creation of a new Undersecretary of Energy for Nuclear Stewardship; this was approved 96–1. In 2001 he got the appropriation for the labs up to $5.8 billion, the highest ever and $500 million above the administration request. His knowledge of the labs' work made him interested in other programs. Since 1996 he has been a major supporter of the Nunn-Lugar program for helping Russia secure and eliminate its nuclear stockpile, and he has steadily pushed for increased funding. The labs also made him aware of homeland security problems before September 11; the Sandia Lab has one of the world's most comprehensive anthrax databases. In 1997 at Harvard he called for a national dialogue on nuclear power, which he points out produces zero pollution; in January 2002 he pointed with pride to the relicensing of six plants and the pending relicensing applications for 14 more and predicted that power companies would apply to build new nuclear plants. In 2001 he called for bringing back the Price-Anderson Act, which protected the nuclear power industry from liability for catastrophic accidents. Domenici supported the Bush energy proposals, including oil drilling in the Arctic National Wildlife Refuge; in March 2002 he criticized Tom Daschle for, with Bingaman's apparent cooperation, yanking the bill from the committee because the votes were there for ANWR drilling. But in February 2003 he admitted that he didn't have the votes on the floor for ANWR drilling. He promised to try to advance Bush's energy bill, but said that electricity deregulation would be the most contentious issue. He said that he might be open to increasing CAFE auto mileage standards and opposed putting the nuclear waste depository at Yucca Mountain in Nevada off-budget.

Domenici has been one of the leaders in the Senate to extend health insurance coverage for mental illness. He became interested in the issue after his daughter Clare, the fourth of his eight children, was diagnosed with atypical schizophrenia. Working with Paul Wellstone, and with the encouragement of Tipper Gore, he got a provision in the 1996 health care bill providing for equal dollar limits for physical and mental health coverage but allowing insurers to shift costs by raising co-payments or deductibles; it does not mandate coverage for mental illness, and some call it "mental illness coverage lite." Domenici and Wellstone pressed for broader coverage and got the Senate to agree in October 2001; the House reauthorized the 1996 version, and but it was dropped in the conference committee. Domenici was distraught when Wellstone died in a plane crash in October 2002, and cancelled many campaign events and the one debate he agreed to, which was scheduled later that day.

Domenici uses his Appropriations seat to help New Mexico projects. He opposed the Clinton administration arsenic standard in drinking water which, he said, would require New Mexico communities to spend $424 million to meet a standard "lacking a foundation of sound science" and when the Bush administration accepted it, he sought $5 billion to help communities across the nation reduce arsenic levels; he made sure fast-growing places like Rio Rancho north of Albuquerque were eligible. He has negotiated with the Sandia Pueblo on its land claim in the Sandia Mountains, got $75 million to clean up bosque in the Albuquerque corridor of the Rio Grande and proposed spending $2.5 million to improve the border crossing at Columbus, which Pancho Villa's band of soldiers attacked in 1916. He pushed through $1.5 billion in the Pentagon budget for the IOSTAR space tug, with a nuclear propulsion system developed by the Sandia Laboratory.

Domenici has not been successful in seeking Senate leadership positions. He lost the majority leadership to Bob Dole in 1984 and the post of Republican Policy Committee chairman to Don Nickles by 23–20 in November 1990. In December 2000 he made a last-minute race against Policy Committee Chairman Larry Craig; this was taken as a criticism of Majority Leader Trent Lott, although Domenici said it wasn't; in any case he lost 26–24.

Domenici has remained highly popular in New Mexico and has won reelection easily. His Pete's Political Action Committee contributed more than $80,000 to Hispanic congressional and state candidates in New Mexico, Texas and California in 2000. In 2002 he was opposed by Gloria Tristani, granddaughter of longtime (1935–62) Senator Dennis Chavez and former state Corporation Commissioner and member of the Federal Communications Commission. He campaigned heavily across the state and was endorsed by 74 mayors, including dozens of Democrats. Some raised questions about his health; he has been stricken with acute pain in two fingers in his right hand since a touch football accident in 1999, but has reportedly reduced the pain by physical therapy and medication. On Election Day Domenici won 65%–35%; he lost only three counties, and those narrowly. He reached out immediately to Governor-elect Bill Richardson, of whom he had been critical in the past, and in early 2003 the two seemed to be working together actively.

Junior Senator

Jeff Bingaman (D)

Elected 1982, seat up 2006, 4th term; b. Oct. 3, 1943, El Paso, TX; home, Santa Fe; Harvard U., B.A. 1965, Stanford U., LL.B. 1968; United Methodist; married (Anne).

Military Career: Army Reserves, 1968–74.

Elected Office: NM Atty. Gen., 1978–82.

Professional Career: NM Asst. Atty. Gen., 1969; Practicing atty., 1970–78.

DC Office: 703 HSOB, 20510, 202-224-5521; Fax: 202-224-2852; Web site: bingaman.senate.gov.

State Offices: Albuquerque, 505-346-6601; Las Cruces, 505-523-6561; Las Vegas, 505-454-8824; Roswell, 505-622-7113; Santa Fe, 505-988-6647.

Committees: *Energy & Natural Resources* (RMM). *Finance*: Health Care; Social Security & Family Policy; Taxation & IRS Oversight. *Health, Education, Labor & Pensions*: Children & Families; Substance Abuse & Mental Health Services. *Joint Economic Committee* (10th of 10 Sens.).

Group Ratings

	ADA	ACLU	AFS	LCV	CON	ITIC	NTU	COC	ACU	NTLC	CHC
2002	90	60	88	59	40	62	25	60	17	6	—
2001	90	—	100	75	—	—	7	54	29	—	0

National Journal Ratings

	2001 LIB	—	2001 CONS		2002 LIB	—	2002 CONS
Economic	68%	—	31%		64%	—	34%
Social	65%	—	32%		82%	—	0%
Foreign	74%	—	14%		74%	—	24%

Key Votes of the 107th Congress

1. Approve Bush Tax Cuts	N	5. Confirm Ashcroft as AG	N	9. Bar Coop. with Intl. Court	N
2. Expand Patients' Rights	Y	6. Bar Gays in the Boy Scouts	N	10. Trade Promotion Authority	Y
3. Campaign Finance Reform	Y	7. $ for Hate Crime Prosecution	Y	11. Authorize Force in Iraq	N
4. Permit ANWR Development	N	8. Overseas Military Abortions	Y	12. Homeland Sec. Dept. Union	Y

Election Results

2000 general	Jeff Bingaman (D)	363,744	(62%)	($2,568,649)
	Bill Redmond (R)	225,517	(38%)	($639,424)
2000 primary	Jeff Bingaman (D)	unopposed		
1994 general	Jeff Bingaman (D)	249,989	(54%)	($3,652,899)
	Colin R. McMillan (R)	213,025	(46%)	($1,537,563)

Prior Winning Percentages: 1988 (63%); 1982 (54%)

Jeff Bingaman, a Democrat first elected in 1982, is New Mexico's junior senator. He has a good political lineage: His father was a professor at Western New Mexico University in Silver City, and his uncle was campaign manager for longtime (1949–73) Senator Clinton Anderson. He graduated from Harvard and Stanford Law School, then returned to New Mexico. A year out of law school, Bingaman was counsel to the state constitutional convention; later he went into law practice in Santa Fe with former Governor Jack Campbell. Bingaman's wife, Anne, started a highly successful law practice of her own that helped finance his first campaigns; she was assistant attorney general for antitrust in the first Clinton term. In a small state, bright young people like Jeff Bingaman can rise fast. He ran for attorney general in 1978 and won; in 1982, he ran against Senator Harrison Schmitt, the former astronaut, also from Silver City, and won with 54%, partly because it was a recession year, but also because of Schmitt's misleading and negative ads.

Bingaman has followed a course in the Senate much like that of Clinton Anderson, who used his influence behind the scenes to great effect but shunned national publicity—so much so that one New Mexico magazine called him "the invisible senator." He is not well known in most of Washington, but has a close relationship with Democratic Leader Tom Daschle and stays on good terms with many senators of both parties. He got seats on two committees of great importance to the state, Armed Services and Energy. On Armed Services he became a protege of Sam Nunn, who created a subcommittee tailored to his interests; in 1997, Bingaman traded his ranking position there for one on the Strategic Forces Subcommittee. From these seats Bingaman has had some say over New Mexico's Los Alamos and Sandia labs.

On the Energy Committee, he became the top-ranking Democrat in 1999. He sparred with Chairman Frank Murkowski over electricity regulation in 1999 and 2000. Then, after Jim Jeffords switched parties, Bingaman became chairman of the Energy Committee in June 2001, with the responsibility of coming up with an energy bill in response to the Bush energy proposals. The House passed an energy bill in August, but Bingaman did not present his own version until September. It ignored the controversial proposal for oil drilling in the Arctic National Wildlife Refuge and left the issue of raising CAFE auto mileage standards to the Commerce Committee. He wanted to encourage more nuclear energy and reauthorize the Price-Anderson Act, which shields plant operators from liability, to require reporting of emissions from so-called greenhouse gases and to give FERC authority over electricity transmission systems; he said the administration and House version had too much in the way of production incentives and too little on renewable energy and energy efficiency. But the administration approach, including ANWR drilling, seemed to have majority support on the committee and in October he withdrew his bill. Republicans, including New Mexico's Pete Domenici, were furious at this and at Bingaman's and Tom Daschle's decision to bring the issue to the floor without committee consideration—a highly unusual tactic for such complex legislation.

Floor debate began in February 2001 and went on for six weeks. Bingaman was beaten by a 62–38 margin on his proposal to increase CAFE mileage standards in cars and SUVs to 35 miles per gallon but kept his proposal to require that 10% of electricity be produced by renewable energy sources by 2020. Bingaman accepted amendments on pipeline safety and maintained his provisions, opposed by environmental restriction groups, to increase the use of nuclear power and promote research in clean coal technology in New Mexico labs. He got in his provisions to encourage more oil and gas development on Indian reservations. The conference committee was delayed in June, as Bingaman claimed he should be conference chairman because the House side had chaired the conference on the Alaska Power Administration Sale Act in 1995; the House's Billy Tauzin argued that the last relevant conference was in 1992, when the Senate side got the chair, and that he should be chairman, and prevailed. The conferees met periodically, but never reached agreement; the bill died after the November election. Democrats lost their majority, and the new chairman would be Domenici, with Bingaman the ranking minority member—the first time in history senators from the same state held the top two spots on a committee.

In 2001 Bingaman supported the Bush education program except for vouchers, and got several of his amendments added to it—promoting anti-dropout programs, requiring poor schools to inform parents about teachers' qualifications. He opposed the Bush proposal to extend CHIP to unborn children, and put a hold on FDA nominee Mark McClellan and demanded to know his position on the issue. He is a physical fitness buff, and with fellow runner Bill Frist sponsored a bill to combat obesity by providing grants for schools and communities to raise awareness of the importance of exercise and healthy diets. He also co-sponsored a bill, opposed by soft drink and snack food manufacturers, to limit the availability of soft drinks and sweet snacks in schools. Many of his bills have a New Mexico angle. He sponsored a bill to pay up to $125,000 of doctors' loans, to attract specialists to states like New Mexico. He and Kay Bailey Hutchison proposed a Southwest Regional Border Authority to give grants to local communities in the four states on the Mexican border. Bingaman and Harry Reid sponsored provisions in the farm bill to fund acquisition of water rights to protect fish and wildlife and to compensate farmers who make improvements in irrigation efficiency and convert to less water-intensive crops. Bingaman helped to secure $25 million for conservation of the Ogallala Aquifer, which lies under several states including eastern New Mexico. Bingaman and Tom Udall have sought to make Santa Fe, Taos and Rio Arriba counties a National Heritage Area, to provide funding for preservation of cultural sites. Bingaman has pressed for a rider endorsing the settlement of the Sandia Pueblo's land claim on Sandia Mountain; he was opposed on some details by Pete Domenici and Heather Wilson. Bingaman and Domenici worked together to try to overrule a federal court decision ordering the release of water from the Heron Reservoir to protect the silvery minnow.

Bingaman faced his most serious challenge in the Republican year of 1994, when Republican Colin McMillan, a rancher and former assistant Defense secretary, spent over $1 million of his own money and attacked Bingaman's vote for Clinton's 1993 tax increase and for what McMillan said was a vote to increase grazing fees. Bingaman ads boasted of his work on defense conversion, national education standards and education technology. Bingaman won 54%–46%—decisive but not overwhelming. In 2000 he faced former Congressman Bill Redmond, who won the heavily Democratic 3d District in a 1997 special election and then lost to Tom Udall in 1998. Redmond, a former minister with working class roots, called for tax cuts and charged that Bingaman should have worked for forest-thinning earlier. Bingaman talked about bringing high-wage jobs to the state, improving education and expanding access to health care. People heard more of what Bingaman was saying: he spent $2.56 million, Redmond only $639,000. Bingaman won 62%–38%; he lost only six counties and ran 14% ahead of Al Gore.

FIRST DISTRICT

Rep. Heather Wilson (R)

Elected June 1998, 3d term; b. Dec. 30, 1960, Keene, NH; home, Albuquerque; U.S. Air Force Acad., B.S. 1982, Rhodes Scholar, Oxford U., M.A. 1984, Ph.D. 1985; Methodist; married (Jay Hone).

Military Career: Air Force, 1978–89.

Professional Career: Dir., European Defense Policy & Arms Control, White House NSC, 1989–91; Pres. Keystone Intl. Inc., 1991–95; NM Secy. of Children, Youth & Families, 1995–98.

DC Office: 318 CHOB 20515, 202-225-6316; Fax: 202-225-4975; Web site: www.house.gov/wilson.

District Office: Albuquerque, 505-346-6781.

Committees: *Armed Services* (15th of 33 R): Readiness; Strategic Forces. *Energy & Commerce* (15th of 31 R): Energy & Air Quality; Environment & Hazardous Materials; Health; Telecommunications & The Internet.

Group Ratings

	ADA	ACLU	AFS	LCV	CON	ITIC	NTU	COC	ACU	NTLC	CHC
2002	5	13	0	13	8	100	53	100	84	86	92
2001	5	—	10	7	—	—	60	91	84	—	—

National Journal Ratings

	2001 LIB — 2001 CONS	2002 LIB — 2002 CONS
Economic	28% — 69%	21% — 73%
Social	20% — 69%	39% — 57%
Foreign	21% — 74%	44% — 55%

Key Votes of the 107th Congress

1. Approve Bush Tax Cuts	Y	5. Faith-Based Charities	Y	9. Trade Promotion Authority	Y
2. Limit Patients' Bill of Rights	Y	6. Bar Gays in the Boy Scouts	Y	10. Bar Funds for Intl. Court	Y
3. Campaign Finance Reform	N	7. Ban Partial-Birth Abortion	Y	11. Authorize Force in Iraq	Y
4. Ban ANWR Development	N	8. Arm Commercial Pilots	Y	12. Deny Home. Sec. Dept. Union	Y

Election Results

2002 general	Heather Wilson (R)	95,711	(55%)	($2,728,165)
	Richard Romero (D)	77,234	(45%)	($1,206,962)
2002 primary	Heather Wilson (R)	unopposed		
2000 general	Heather Wilson (R)	107,296	(50%)	($2,203,322)
	John J. Kelly (D)	92,187	(43%)	($1,445,633)
	Daniel Kerlinsky (Green)	13,656	(6%)	

Prior Winning Percentages: 1998 (48%); 1998 (45%)

The People		Race/Ethnic Origin	Ancestry	
Area size:	4,720 sq. mi.	48.5% White	German: 9.6%	English: 7.0%
Urban population:	91.3%	2.3% Black	Irish: 6.9%	
Rural population:	8.7%	1.7% Asian	**2000 Presidential Vote**	
Pop. 2000:	606,400	2.9% Native Am.	Gore (D)..............106,572 (48%)	
Median income:	$38,413	0.1% Hawaiian	Bush (R)..............103,770 (47%)	
Poverty status:	14.0%	1.6% Two+ races	Other...................10,385 (5%)	
Military veterans:	15.2%	0.2% Other	**Cook Partisan Voting Index:** D + 0	
		42.6% Hispanic Origin		

Occupation	Blue collar: 18.9%	White collar: 65.2%	Gray collar: 16.0%

The future and the past of New Mexico come together in its single metropolis, Albuquerque. Its Spanish and Indian past is memorialized in its name (for a 17th century Spanish grandee) and age (founded in 1706) and its quaint Old Town, but Albuquerque's future is decidedly high-tech. For decades, the Sandia National Laboratories, Kirtland Air Force Base and the University of New Mexico have attracted scientists and engineers to Albuquerque and promoted private sector technology growth. Here in 1975, Bill Gates founded a little company called Micro-Soft; although the software maker moved its 16 employees to Seattle in 1979, Intel Corp. now employs 5,500 people here in an advanced chip-making facility.

When rocket scientist Robert Goddard moved here in 1930 and nuclear scientist J. Robert Oppenheimer reconnoitered the site in 1940, Albuquerque was still a town of 35,000 sitting at the junction of the Rio Grande and the old U.S. 66 that paralleled the Santa Fe Railroad—"a dirty red sod-hut tortilla desert highway city," Tom Wolfe wrote. Now, metro Albuquerque, spreading out from Bernalillo County into Sandoval and Valencia Counties, has more people (712,000 in 2000) than all New Mexico did when the scientists first arrived. Albuquerque's prosperous neighborhoods have climbed the gently rising heights to the east; poorer residents have spread north and south along the Rio Grande. Hemmed in by the Sandia mountains and by federal installations, growth is now moving west, across the Rio Grande, and to the north, especially to the new town of Rio Rancho, home of the Intel plant and facilities for Sprint PCS, Tricon and Victoria's Secret. The Petroglyph National Monument, a 7,200-acre preserve of ancient volcanic flows, faces Albuquerque's westward development head-on: Here, hikers in search of 500-year-old Indian carvings can witness the steady encroachment of tract housing right up to the park's borders, an evolution that has prompted a long battle over whether a road should be built through the monument to aid commuters. Albuquerque is counted as part of the Sun Belt, but its climate is sometimes very cold in the winter, and windy most of the time. Its economy also differs from those of other Sun Belt cities and despite the tech base has lower income levels than Phoenix or Denver. While Albuquerque has seen some growth in tourism—it is home of the International Balloon Fiesta every October—it is still heavily dependent on government jobs.

The 1st Congressional District includes the city of Albuquerque and some of its suburbs. It takes in most of Bernalillo County and stretches out into the desert to include sparsely populated Torrance County. But the 1st does not include most of New Mexico's big-growth suburbs, Corrales and Rio Rancho to the north in Sandoval County and Isleta and Las Lunas to the south in Valencia County. The 1st is almost 43% Hispanic. Metro Albuquerque is politically competitive: It voted for Ronald Reagan and George Bush in the 1980s and for Bill Clinton in the 1990s. In 2000 the 1st District gave a very narrow margin to Al Gore.

The congresswoman from the 1st District is Heather Wilson, a Republican first elected in a June 1998 special election. She grew up in New Hampshire, graduated from the Air Force Academy, then became a Rhodes Scholar at Oxford. She served in the Air Force until 1989, then worked two years on the National Security Council in charge of NATO and European affairs. In 1991 she moved to New Mexico, to marry her former Air Force Academy law instructor; she started a consulting firm, and then Governor Gary Johnson appointed her secretary of the Children, Youth and Families Department.

In January 1998 1st District Republican Congressman Steven Schiff announced he would not run again; he died two months later. Senator Pete Domenici, usually loath to intervene in local politics, backed Wilson strongly; after the county Republican chairman filled vacancies by appointing Wilson backers, she beat a conservative state senator for the state central committee endorsement by winning 55 votes, the minimum required. The Democratic nomination was captured by Phil Maloof, a young state senator from a wealthy family that made its fortune through beer distribution, casinos, banking interests, hotels and professional sports franchises; a statue of his late father stands in Albuquerque's Civic Plaza. Also running was Green Party candidate Bob Anderson. Wilson's first ad showed her two-year-old daughter running into her arms; she concluded speeches by talking about reading to her four-year-old son on the roof of their house. She called for a dollars-to-classroom program, with less money for bureaucracy, and for a pilot program of school vouchers. Maloof favored raising the minimum wage, opposed school vouchers and ran soft-focus ads playing on his family's 100-year history in New Mexico (next to Wilson's seven). Maloof spent $3.1 million, almost all of it his own. Wilson won 45% to 40% for Maloof and 15% for Anderson, though he spent less than $10,000. Local analysts said that the Green vote included not just left-wing environmentalists but also voters disgruntled with the negative campaign. All three candidates ran again in November. Maloof tried to appeal to environmentalists, and Anderson's former campaign manager endorsed him. But the margin was similar: Wilson 48%, Maloof 42%, Anderson 10%.

Wilson thus became the first woman veteran to serve in Congress. Her voting record has been relatively moderate. She has seats on two major committees, Armed Services and Energy and Commerce. On occasion she showed independence, as when she voted against the amendment to prevent adoptions by gays in the District of Columbia. She also worked on the bill to increase safety at public health labs. When she complained that Republicans planned to bring a bill to the House floor that would have moved the nuclear weapons program from the Energy Department to the Pentagon, party leaders made changes. Republican leaders tapped her as a leading advocate for George W. Bush's energy plan, and she filed the House-passed amendment to limit oil drilling in the Arctic National Wildlife Refuge to 2,000 acres. After September 11, House members sought her advice about war in Afghanistan and Iraq. In May 2002 the House passed her bill rescinding the policy requiring servicewomen in Saudi Arabia to wear abayas; she called it "offensive to American servicewomen and offensive to American values."

Wilson has faced well-financed challengers. John Kelly, the former U.S. Attorney for New Mexico and a friend of Bill Clinton since both were undergraduates at Georgetown, ran in 2000. The campaign was filled with controversial advertising by outside groups. Wilson won 50%–43%. In 2002, the challenger was Richard Romero, a state senator who was elected Senate President in 2001 in a coalition that ousted the Democratic incumbent. Romero at first was rated a top tier challenger by national Democrats, but he suffered from local Democratic divisions; one Democratic state senator called him Benedict Arnold. Although Democrats for the first time convinced the Greens not to run a candidate, Wilson won with her largest majority, 55%–45%. This district could be seriously contested again in 2004.

SECOND DISTRICT

Rep. Steve Pearce (R)

Elected 2002, 1st term; b. Aug. 24, 1947, Lamesa, TX; home, Hobbs; NM St. U., B.B.A. 1970, E. NM U. M.B.A. 1991; Baptist; married (Cynthia).

Military Career: Air Force, 1970–76 (Vietnam).

Elected Office: NM House of Reps., 1996–2000.

Professional Career: Owner, Lea Fishing Tools.

DC Office: 1408 LHOB 20515, 202-225-2365; Fax: 202-225-9599; Web site: www.house.gov/pearce.

District Offices: Hobbs, 505-392-8325; Las Cruces, 505-522-2219; Roswell, 505-622-0055; Socorro, 505-838-7516.

Committees: *Resources* (25th of 28 R): Energy & Mineral Resources; Forests & Forest Health; Water & Power. *Transportation & Infrastructure* (38th of 41 R): Aviation; Water Resources & Environment (Vice Chmn.).

Group Ratings and Key Votes: Newly Elected

Election Results

2002 general	Steve Pearce (R)	79,631	(56%)	($1,573,911)
	John Smith (D)	61,916	(44%)	($826,735)
2002 primary	Steve Pearce (R)	12,346	(35%)	
	Edward Tinsley (R)	9,587	(27%)	
	Phelps Anderson (R)	8,432	(24%)	
	C. Earl Greer (R)	2,428	(7%)	
	Leo Martinez (R)	2,389	(7%)	
2000 general	Joe Skeen (R)	100,742	(58%)	($699,299)
	Michael A. Montoya (D)	72,614	(42%)	($292,955)

The People		Race/Ethnic Origin	Ancestry	
Area size:	69,598 sq. mi.	44.3% White	German: 7.4%	English: 5.9%
Urban population:	71.0%	1.6% Black	Irish: 5.7%	
Rural population:	29.0%	0.5% Asian	**2000 Presidential Vote**	
Pop. 2000:	606,406	4.8% Native Am.	Bush (R) 96,161	(54%)
Median income:	$29,269	0.0% Hawaiian	Gore (D) 76,868	(43%)
Poverty status:	22.4%	1.2% Two + races	Other 5,667	(3%)
Military veterans:	14.9%	0.2% Other	**Cook Partisan Voting Index:** R + 6	
		47.3% Hispanic Origin		

Occupation	Blue collar: 26.7%	White collar: 52.9%	Gray collar: 20.4%

Southern and eastern New Mexico is a disparate landscape: endless sagebrush-strewn acreage and then, suddenly, 9,000-foot mountain peaks rising along the Continental Divide. The eastern part of this region—places like Clovis and Portales, Lovington and Hobbs—speaks with a Texas twang rather than a northern New Mexico lilt. In Little Texas, oil has long been the economic mainstay; cattle ranching is common, and cotton is grown on irrigated land. One of the larger towns is Roswell, site of a supposed flying saucer landing in 1947 and now home of the International UFO Museum and Research Center. Further west is White Sands National Monument, with its immaculate gypsum dunes and animals with specially evolved white coloration that allows them to survive predators in the harsh environment; close by is Alamogordo, where the first atomic bomb was exploded at 5:29:45 a.m. Mountain War Time on July 16, 1945. Like many places on America's high plains, population here is thinning and old economic pillars are crumbling; Carlsbad, once reliant on potash mining, aggressively sought the Waste Isolation Pilot Plant, a nuclear waste repository. In central and western New Mexico, the scrub land shades into desert, and people are crammed into small cities, protected from summer's burning heat and winter's deathly cold. The Hatch Valley, in the desert adjoining Interstate 25, is home to perhaps the world's finest chile peppers—the traditional cornerstone of the Southwest's spicy cuisine. Places like Silver City and Bayard were built on mining, and occasional discord; the story of a strike by Mexican-American workers at a zinc mine here in 1950 and 1951 was told in *Salt of the Earth*, a movie with such a volatile message that it was famously blacklisted at the height of McCarthyism.

This is also an international frontier—the tiny town of Columbus was the site of a raid by Pancho Villa and his irregular band of soldiers in 1916. Las Cruces, now New Mexico's second largest city, has grown at rates well above the statewide average, thanks to migrants from Mexico coming up the Rio Grande. For decades, Anglo and Mexican ranchers across the border spoke "the common language of cattle"; communities frequently shared public services with their cross-border neighbors and left the gates open at night for stragglers stuck too late on the wrong side of the border. But the 1990s brought enormous strains: rapid development due to NAFTA, a surge in illegal immigration and drug trafficking. Still, the New Mexico portion of U.S.-Mexico border remains far sleepier than elsewhere: Whereas El Paso sees more than one million crossings a month, the three border posts that dot New Mexico's largely empty 150-mile frontier with Mexico see less than 100,000.

The 2d Congressional District includes this southern part of the state, going as far north as the suburb of Las Lunas and the Isleta Pueblo south of Albuquerque and the Acoma Pueblo to the west. Demographically and politically, it is diverse. It includes most, but not all, of New Mexico's Little Texas—majority Anglo and solidly conservative, though with a Democratic heritage. It includes Las Cruces and the mining counties in the southwest corner of the state; Las Cruces is politically marginal and the mining counties Democratic. It includes the small towns of Socorro and Truth or Consequences on the Rio Grande, politically marginal. And it includes the Indian country around the pueblos, which is strongly Democratic.

The congressman from the 2d District is Steve Pearce, a Republican elected in 2002. He grew up in Hobbs, near the Texas line, and graduated from New Mexico State in Las Cruces; he served in the Air Force and flew missions during the Vietnam War. He returned to Hobbs and started an oil field service company. In 1996 he was elected to the state House. In 2000 he ran for the Senate, but lost the Republican primary 60%–22% to former Congressman Bill Redmond. In January 2002, 2d District Republican Congressman Joe Skeen, first elected in 1980 and stricken with Parkinson's disease, announced he would not run again; he served longer in the House than anyone else from New Mexico. Skeen's retirement had long been predicted, and Pearce plunged into the race. He had two major competitors in the Republican primary, former state representative Phelps Anderson of Roswell, the son of former Arco chairman Robert Anderson, and Ed Tinsley, the owner of the K-BOBS USA steakhouse chain who until 2000 had lived in Albuquerque but now claimed residence in the mountain town of Capitan. Anderson's Roswell is in the county next to Pearce's Hobbs, and he threatened to cut into Pearce's Little Texas base; Tinsley had enough money to run a districtwide race, and in April he got Skeen's endorsement. But Pearce ran a deft primary campaign. Using junior high and high school volunteers, he maximized his vote in Little Texas; he won 78% of the vote in Hobbs's Lea County. He built on his ties to Las Cruces, where he had gone to college, and carried its Dona Ana County with 38% of the vote. Of the district's 18 counties Pearce carried only six, but he did well enough in the rest to win 35% of the vote. Tinsley carried ten counties, but with no geographic base won only 27% of the vote. Anderson, without much support outside his home county, won 24%.

There was also a serious race in the Democratic primary; due to the historic Democratic allegiance of Little Texas, there were more registered Democrats than Republicans in the district. The competitors were Ruben Smith, mayor of Las Cruces since 1991, and John Arthur Smith, state senator from Deming since 1988. National Democrats hoped that Ruben Smith would win, on the theory that he would maximize Hispanic turnout. But he won only 58% in his home county and trailed in Little Texas; John Arthur Smith won by big majorities in his state Senate district and won the June primary 53%–47%. On issues there did not seem to be much difference between the nominees—Smith was an opponent of abortion rights, a believer in Second Amendment rights, a conservative who had not always voted with liberal Democrats in the legislature. But he proved not to be as adroit a campaigner as Pearce. Smith boasted that he had never raised any money for his state Senate campaigns; this time he did raise some money, and was the beneficiary of national Democrats and independent spenders; but Pearce, with the help of two visits from George W. Bush, raised much more. Pearce piloted his own plane around the district; Smith drove his own car (this matters in a district that covers 69,598 square miles). Pearce set up an office in Las Cruces, the district's biggest population center. Pearce said that the election was about who would be Speaker. "A lot of people are concerned with Dick Gephardt. They feel he may end up hurting the state on things like water issues and agriculture issues." Smith said that he was not committed to vote for Gephardt for speaker, and might vote for Nancy Pelosi, who of course is considerably more liberal. Pearce issued a press release saying, "Pearce takes strong stand on Iraq, Smith weak on issue." Smith said that it was important for the United States to get international support, although he ended up supporting the Iraq war resolution, the only New Mexico House or Senate Democratic candidate to do so. This was thought to be a very close race, targeted by both national parties, with polls showing little difference between the candidates. But Pearce won by a solid 56%–44%. He won large majorities, from 58% to 77%, in Little Texas and lost by only 51%–49% in Dona Ana County. Smith's margins in his home county and in the mining and Indian counties were not enough to overcome this.

THIRD DISTRICT

Rep. Tom Udall (D)

Elected 1998, 3d term; b. May 18, 1948, Tucson, AZ; home, Santa Fe; Prescott Col., B.A. 1970; Cambridge U., B.L. 1975; U. of NM, J.D. 1977; Mormon; married (Jill Cooper).

Elected Office: NM Atty. Gen., 1990–98.

Professional Career: Law clerk, 10th Circuit Court of Appeals, 1977; Asst. U.S. Atty. 1978–81; Practicing atty., 1981–83, 1985–90; Chief Cnsl., NM Health & Environment Dept., 1983–84.

DC Office: 1414 LHOB 20515, 202-225-6190; Fax: 202-226-1331; Web site: www.house.gov/tomudall.

District Offices: Clovis, 505-763-7616; Farmington, 505-324-1005; Gallup, 505-863-0582; Las Vegas, 505-454-4080; Rio Rancho, 505-994-0499; Santa Fe, 505-984-8950.

Committees: *Resources* (12th of 24 D): Energy & Mineral Resources; Forests & Forest Health; National Parks, Recreation & Public Lands. *Small Business* (3d of 17 D): Workforce, Empowerment & Government Programs. *Veterans' Affairs* (12th of 14 D).

Group Ratings

	ADA	ACLU	AFS	LCV	CON	ITIC	NTU	COC	ACU	NTLC	CHC
2002	100	93	100	100	18	38	21	35	0	6	0
2001	100	—	100	100	—	—	14	30	4	—	—

National Journal Ratings

	2001 LIB —	2001 CONS		2002 LIB —	2002 CONS
Economic	80%	— 19%		93%	— 5%
Social	79%	— 21%		82%	— 18%
Foreign	81%	— 18%		82%	— 18%

Key Votes of the 107th Congress

1. Approve Bush Tax Cuts	N	5. Faith-Based Charities	N	9. Trade Promotion Authority	N
2. Limit Patients' Bill of Rights	N	6. Bar Gays in the Boy Scouts	N	10. Bar Funds for Intl. Court	N
3. Campaign Finance Reform	Y	7. Ban Partial-Birth Abortion	N	11. Authorize Force in Iraq	N
4. Ban ANWR Development	Y	8. Arm Commercial Pilots	Y	12. Deny Home. Sec. Dept. Union	N

Election Results

2002 general	Tom Udall (D)	unopposed		($290,534)
2002 primary	Tom Udall (D)	unopposed		
2000 general	Tom Udall (D)	135,040	(67%)	($340,174)
	Lisa L. Lutz (R)	65,979	(33%)	($39,120)

Prior Winning Percentages: 1998 (53%)

The People		Race/Ethnic Origin	Ancestry	
Area size:	47,271 sq. mi.	41.4% White	German: 7.4%	English: 6.0%
Urban population:	62.8%	1.1% Black	Irish: 5.6%	
Rural population:	37.2%	0.7% Asian	**2000 Presidential Vote**	
Pop. 2000:	606,240	18.9% Native Am.	Gore (D) 102,809	(52%)
Median income:	$35,058	0.1% Hawaiian	Bush (R) 86,004	(43%)
Poverty status:	19.0%	1.4% Two+ races	Other 9,676	(5%)
Military veterans:	13.4%	0.1% Other	**Cook Partisan Voting Index:** D + 4	
		36.3% Hispanic Origin		

Occupation	Blue collar: 21.7%	White collar: 60.3%	Gray collar: 18.0%

"The dancing ground of the sun," the Pueblo Indians called the land of northern New Mexico, where the long vistas, dotted with low-lying scrub, are painted in pastel hues in the cold light and clear air. For 100 years, artists have been coming here, attracted by the scenery and by a unique civilization that is part Indian, part Anglo, part Spanish, and only a little Mexican (northern New

Mexico was under Mexican control only from 1821–46). The region's long-surviving traditions, however, hide the instabilities of this blended civilization. The adobe pueblos, including some of the world's earliest apartment buildings, were built in spurts; the Spanish conquistadors and priests brought the Catholic religion, the baroque architectural accents and the Spanish language in a rush; and successive waves of American settlement have changed New Mexico in multiple ways. The Indian crafts that thrive today nearly died out in the 1880s, while the Palace of the Governors, built in Santa Fe in 1610, had its Victorian balustrade torn off in 1913 to restore its original appearance. Yet up the back roads in Rio Arriba or Taos counties, one can find a religion that mixes Catholicism with adaptations of Indian festivals, buildings not that much different from the old pueblos and a standard of living reminiscent of the Indian past, sometimes punctuated by high rates of drug abuse—quite a contrast to the chi-chi ski lodges in the Taos Valley, the high-security research facilities of Los Alamos, or the affluent, bohemian activity in modern-day Santa Fe, with its 200-plus restaurants, its local book publishers and the third-largest art market in the country.

The 3d Congressional District contains most of the state's historic Spanish-speaking and Indian parts. The district's largest and dominant city is Santa Fe, but the 3d also runs from the High Plains along the Texas border, past the haunting Sangre de Cristo Mountains, through the vast ridges and isolated buttes in the center, to the windy and dusty desert-like plains. Its Hispanic population is 36%, the lowest of the state's three districts, but in the central part of the district it ranges from almost half in Santa Fe County to more than 80% in Mora County. Another 19% of the district population is Indian, mostly in and around the Navajo Reservation in the west, which is hard hit by poverty and poor health. (The main local highway, the curiously named U.S. 666, has unusually high rates of alcohol-related car accidents.) The politics of northern New Mexico is unique. For years, debate was conducted and votes bartered in Spanish, not by separatists, but by Republican and Democratic politicos, often cynically, sometimes corruptly; loyalties ran to families and communities more than to principles or parties. In the back country, you can still find more than just vestiges of the old communities and the old politics—though no one is going to let you in on them, even if you speak good Spanish. Although the Little Texas counties, the Albuquerque suburb of Rio Rancho, the mining and ranching country around Farmington, and the nuclear scientists of Los Alamos tend to vote Republican, this is on the whole a Democratic district; both Hispanics and Indians are very Democratic, and in Santa Fe and Taos, the affluent and hippie migrants have produced such a strong leftist tilt that in February 2003, Santa Fe's city council approved a minimum wage $3.35 over the federal level. George W. Bush managed to win only 43% of the vote here in 2000—one of his weakest performances in Rocky Mountain states.

The congressman from the 3d District is Tom Udall, a Democrat elected in 1998, the son of Arizona Congressman (1955–61) and Interior Secretary (1961–69) Stewart Udall, nephew of Arizona Congressman (1961–91) Morris Udall, first cousin of Colorado Congressman Mark Udall, and distant cousin of Oregon Senator Gordon Smith, the only Republican in the bunch. Tom Udall grew up in Tucson and McLean, Virginia, went to college in Arizona, got a degree at Cambridge University in England, and went to law school in New Mexico. He worked as a law clerk to a federal judge, then as a lawyer in New Mexico state government and went into private law practice. Politics was obviously on his mind: he ran for Congress in 1982 when the 3d District was newly created, and finished last among four candidates, with 13% of the vote. In 1988 he ran in the open Albuquerque-based 1st District, won the Democratic nomination but lost the general to Steven Schiff 51%–47%. In 1990 he was elected state Attorney General, where he later took on energy companies. In 1997, when Bill Richardson resigned and opened the 3d District seat, Udall did not run—a prudent decision, as it turned out.

That election was won in a stunning upset by Republican Bill Redmond, a self-styled "blue-collar person," an independent Christian minister from Los Alamos, who got just 31% against Richardson in 1996. The Democratic nomination, which was widely considered tantamount to election, was decided by 89 members of the Democratic central committee; in January the Democratic chairmen in the district's 11 counties selected Eric Serna, Rio Arriba County politico and member of the state Corporation Commission since 1981. This was an unfortunate choice. Charges were well known that Serna had raised money from firms with interests before his commission. Redmond attacked his "seamy past" and said it was "no secret that Eric Serna is a corrupt politician." Carol Miller, the Green Party nominee, built on a base of support in Santa Fe and Taos counties' feminist communities. Redmond courted Navajos and ran organizing drives in the high-tech areas. The result was a shocker: Redmond beat Serna 43%–40%, with 17% for Miller.

In 1998, Udall ran for the seat. He worked to consolidate the Democratic vote; drawing on lawyers, the arts community and friends of the Udall family, he raised daunting sums. The Sierra Club and the League of Conservation Voters criticized Redmond and ran waves of ads against him. As for the third party threat, Udall said, "I intend to make peace with the Greens." He was utterly successful. Udall won 53% of the vote, Redmond, for all his efforts to attract various constituencies, won the same 43% he had won 18 months before, while Carol Miller saw her 17% evaporate to 4%. Udall carried the leftish Santa Fe and Taos Counties 69%–26. Redmond carried the high-tech counties 56%–40%. And the Indian counties were 64%–34% for Udall.

In the House, Udall has a mostly liberal voting record. He has a seat on the Resources Committee, on which his father served and which his uncle once chaired. In 2000, he helped to enact the bill to buy the 95,000-acre Baca Ranch in the Jemez Mountains for $101 million. He worked to get broadband into rural areas. As chairman of the Democrats' campaign finance task force, he was a vocal advocate of the Shays-Meehan campaign finance bill; he called for opening presidential debates to third-party candidates—an odd stance for a Democrat in a seat Republicans won because of a Green candidacy. He voted against the Patriot Act and creation of the Homeland Security Department because he was concerned about civil-liberties threats, and he voted against the use of force in Iraq.

Udall was unopposed for reelection in 2002.

★ NEW YORK ★

It was a beautiful fall morning, the sunshine lighting a blue sky above the skyscrapers of Manhattan, commuters hurrying through the streets and subways to work, at 8:45 a.m. on September 11, 2001. Then, one minute later, the first plane hit the North Tower of the World Trade Center, and everything changed. When the second plane hit the South Tower 16 minutes later, it was clear that we were under attack, at war, even as office workers fled the burning buildings and New York fire fighters streamed in. The terrorists had chosen to attack Washington—the Pentagon and the building United flight 93 was heading toward when heroes brought it down—and New York, the greatest city in the nation and the world, to inflict the greatest possible damage on our country. Yet the people of New York, like those at the Pentagon and on United 93, responded with the courage and determination, the devotion to duty and the willingness to take the initiative that made this city and this country great. Fire fighters and police officers and rescue workers risked death to help others. Strangers helped strangers. People who had no experience with disaster figured out how to cope and help others. Millions volunteered to give blood, send in money, or provide food and supplies. The *Wall Street Journal*, headquartered across the street from the World Trade Center, scrambled to put out a newspaper that was distributed at the regular time across the nation the next day. In less than a week the New York Stock Exchange was reopened. Mayor Rudolph Giuliani worked tirelessly to share with the nation the tragic news of deaths and to assert the determination to recover.

The bravery, the determination, the generosity that the world saw on that terrible day and the days after were some of the same qualities that had, over the centuries, made New York what it is—America's largest city, its financial capital, its center of arts and letters and media, and its largest immigrant destination. New York's achievements were not inevitable. They happened because New Yorkers—and not least those people from elsewhere who opted to become New Yorkers—worked to make them happen. They did it in a city that has a certain enduring character that goes back to its birth as the 17th century Dutch colony of Nieuw Amsterdam. Simon Schama's *The Embarrassment of Riches* paints a picture of the old world Amsterdam: the richest city in the

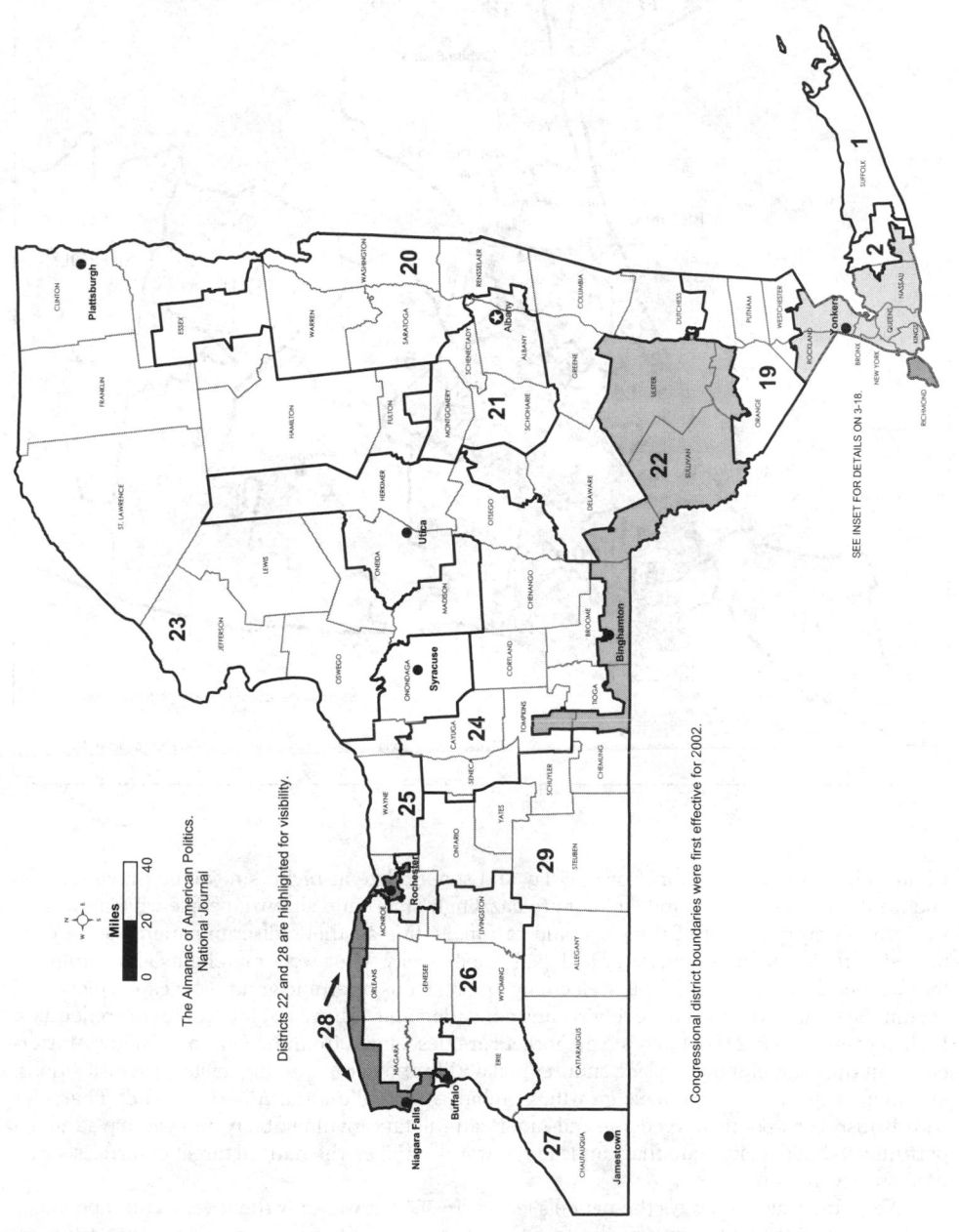

The Almanac of American Politics.
National Journal

Districts 22 and 28 are highlighted for visibility.

Congressional district boundaries were first effective for 2002.

SEE INSET FOR DETAILS ON 3-18.

Miles

0   20   40

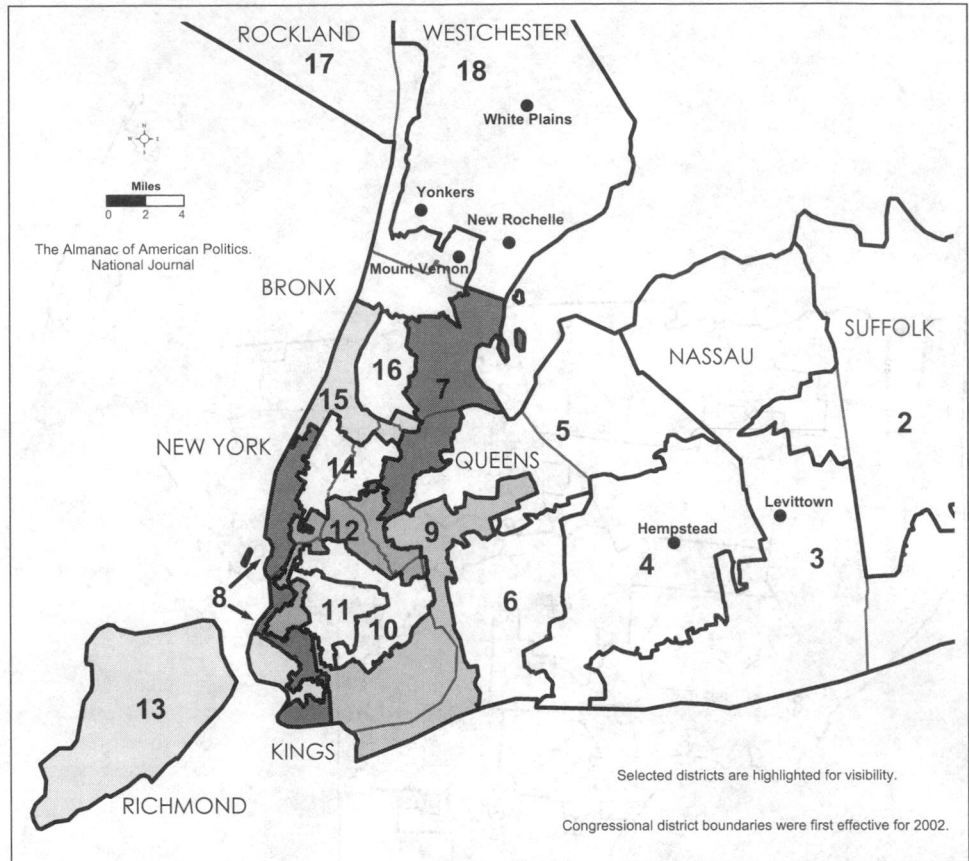

The Almanac of American Politics.
National Journal

Selected districts are highlighted for visibility.

Congressional district boundaries were first effective for 2002.

world; full of people who work hard all day and stay up late at night, smoke too much tobacco and drink too much coffee and gin, but are dazzlingly smart and shrewd; people who know their way around every corner of the globe and can make fine aesthetic discriminations, but are attached to their uncomfortable, crowded, bad-smelling city. They were merchants and manipulators with no aristocratic pedigree, welcoming any religious or ethnic group who can achieve and accumulate and show good taste, cherishing education and culture but indifferent to credentials. Probably fewer than 2% of today's New Yorkers are descended from the Dutch of Nieuw Amsterdam, but the character of the place endures in daily life and in the workings of its great institutions, and helps explain its miraculous growth. Combine Amsterdam and America: Dutch character with British-born political freedoms and American military invulnerability and you have the opportunity to build a city-state that can lead the world—and be the natural target of terrorists who hate our civilization.

New York was not always the nation's leader. In 1776 it was only the seventh most populous colony. Only in the 19th century did the descendants of Dutch patroons, Huguenot refugees, British West Indies traders and Yankee farmers become the nation's most successful merchants and capitalists, forging the first routes to the great American interior through the valleys of the Hudson and the Mohawk, and building grand brownstone mansions on broad midtown Manhattan avenues. That early diversity provides one clue to New York's success: if New York has been cynical, ready to cooperate with Loyalists and Revolutionaries, depending on who was ahead, it has also been tolerant, ready to accept anyone smart or rich enough to be counted a success. It has been propelled upward at each stage—forging ahead of London as a financial and manufacturing center by the first World War, and staying ahead of surging Chicago—by incorporating every wave of immigrants and consistently rewarding intelligence and hard work, with no concern about preserving hierarchies.

New York's success has been a product not only of market economics, but of government—and politics. The Iroquois, the most deeply-rooted and militarily strong Native Americans, kept in place for 100 years by an alliance with British troops, were driven out of Upstate New York by the Revolution. The Erie Canal, which connected western New York State with the Hudson River, was the project of Governor DeWitt Clinton's state government. And New York led the nation in political innovation: Martin Van Buren's Albany Regency was the first state political machine, an ally of New York City's Tammany Hall; Van Buren invented or institutionalized the Democratic party, the national convention and the inaugural parade. His adversaries, Thurlow Weed and William Seward, formed the Whig party and ultimately became Republicans; noting that Van Buren's Democrats were winning large margins from Irish Catholics and other immigrants, they too made bids for the newcomers' votes. Both parties served the function of mediating between the divergent interests of the New York City masses and Upstate New York's farmers and burghers, a conflict still evident in New York between city and country, immigrant and native, Catholic and Protestant, the Big Apple and the apple-knockers.

Both parties also worked to protect New Yorkers against the untrammeled workings of free economic and political markets. Old-line Democrats embarked on an unprecedented, labor-intensive building of infrastructure, of bridges and tunnels that made Greater New York possible, from the time of Mayor Abram Hewitt, elected in 1886 over the single-taxer Henry George and the young Theodore Roosevelt, up through the time of Governor Al Smith in the 1920s and his protg Robert Moses, who built bridges, tunnels, highways, beaches and two World's Fairs up through the 1960s. Progressive Republicans, from Theodore Roosevelt through Elihu Root and Henry Stimson, worked to create civil service laws and bureaucratized purchasing and spending to protect taxpayers from corrupt party machines. The Democratic Tammany machine led by Charles F. Murphy and the talented young men he advanced, Al Smith and Robert Wagner, responded to the shocking 1911 Triangle Shirtwaist fire (when hundreds of women jumped 11 floors to their death because fire escapes were blocked) by passing labor and safety measures. The results included minimum wages, maximum work hours, working-conditions regulations, encouragement of unions and state-owned electric utilities—the prototype 20 years later of the New Deal and the first American welfare state. In years after, New York pioneered public housing and fair housing laws, industry-wide unions (in the garment trades), increased minimum wages, rent control and dairy price controls to help both New York City tenants and Upstate farmers.

Statewide elections were exceedingly close, with Democrats carrying the New York City Catholic vote and Republicans winning Protestants Upstate. Swing votes were cast by the 2 million Jewish immigrants and their children, who supported a generous welfare state but mistrusted the Tammany machine and valued civil rights. The politician who combined these appeals most cannily was Fiorello LaGuardia: a nominal Republican but almost a socialist, an Episcopalian who was half-Jewish and as well as Italian, and who, as mayor of New York City from 1933–45, built much of the public housing and many of the civic monuments that still stand. But both parties produced politicians whose positions appealed to these swing voters, politicians who became nationally prominent and often presidential candidates at a time when the national media was much more concentrated in Manhattan than today: Democrats Al Smith, Robert Wagner, Franklin Roosevelt and Averell Harriman; Republicans Thomas Dewey, Wendell Willkie, Dwight Eisenhower (a New Yorker as president of Columbia University when he was elected president in 1952) and Nelson Rockefeller.

The polity that these men built was productive, generous, tolerant and closely regulated. In an America where people were becoming used to working in big units—employed by big corporations, represented by big unions, regulated by big government—this kind of New York was a natural leader. The financial dominance of Wall Street and the big banks was protected by federal regulation. The high-tech thrust of America in the mid-20th century was directed by big companies headquartered in New York's suburbs or Upstate: General Electric and IBM, Eastman

Kodak and Xerox. This New York took for granted the productivity of its thousands of entrepreneurs and the high skills of its largely immigrant-born, public and Catholic school-educated work force. It was blas about its own miraculous infrastructure—the bridges and subways, electronic cables and electric wires connecting it better than any place else with every corner of the world.

But in the last quarter of the 20th century New York's public strengths became weaknesses. The state that was clearly the national leader of a big-unit America lost the leadership of a country where growth now occurs in small economic units, where flexibility and adaptability are more important than centralized planning. The institutions, practices and infrastructure which helped produce its successes became ossified and brittle and in decline. Welfare-state benefits became too expensive, measures meant to protect against corruption stifled innovation, and both failed to achieve their objectives—ghettos throbbed with the pains of disorganization, and payoffs and rackets remained part of the everyday cost of doing business in New York as in no other place in the country. The noble aim of creating a public sector which would guarantee cheap rents, top-notch public schools and colleges, and public hospitals, instead guaranteed that none of these will be readily available: Rent control kept housing scarce, school bureaucracies stifled good teaching, public hospitals rationed care down toward nothing. The attempt to create a fail-safe government produced a government that was sure to fail. The government that intended to aid growth seemed to be cutting it off—not completely, but enough to explain why New York state, which grew 32% in population from 1940–65, grew only 2% from 1965–97, while California was growing about 74% and Texas about 87%, making both larger now than New York.

People and businesses started voting with their feet, especially during the terms of Mayor John Lindsay, a liberal Republican hailed when he was elected in 1965 by the powerful New York-based liberal media of the day as the next John Kennedy, though about all he shared with Kennedy was good looks. Lindsay denounced Democrats for being too cozy with municipal unions, but gave up more to them than any mayor before or since. He institutionalized the practice of borrowing against next year's revenues to pay this year's bills, bringing city government to the brink of bankruptcy, which came two years after he left office. He convinced New York's minorities that he cared about them, while allowing the institutions that had taught previous generations' immigrants to embrace middle-class values, to scorn those values. Antagonized middle-class New Yorkers fled not just to the suburbs, but by the hundreds of thousands to (then) low-tax New Jersey, Connecticut and Florida. In the 1970s, the population of New York, city and state, dropped by 1 million—an unprecedented hemorrhage of talent and productivity.

Retrenchment followed the mid-1970s bankruptcy crisis. Private financiers and the state government took control of city government, cut spending and negotiated cutbacks in jobs and salaries with public employees' unions. Wall Street boomed in the 1980s and Manhattan once again brimmed over with confidence. Two highly competent Democrats headed the city and state government, Edward Koch for 12 years after he was first elected mayor in 1977, Mario Cuomo for 12 years after he was first elected governor in 1982. Some taxes were cut, bureaucracy was for a time reined in, rational management was installed. But institutional problems remained. New York's legislature—"the worst governmental institution in the western world," writes former city official William Stern—remained unusually tightly controlled by the two chambers' leaders, with the Assembly dominated by New York City Democrats and the state Senate by suburban and Upstate Republicans engaged in classic political logrolling, lavishing taxpayers' dollars on each other's pet projects, with no incentives to hold spending down or deliver services. Public employee unions reestablished their stranglehold. The mild recession of the early 1990s struck New York with great force: A private sector that had grown little if at all outside Wall Street could no longer finance the countercyclically growing demands of its oversized welfare state, while big companies Upstate—Xerox, Kodak, IBM—suffered serious reverses.

By the end of the 1990s New York seemed to have adapted and changed. Leading the way to reform were two Republican executives, elected on similar government-cutting platforms, though not always political allies, Mayor Rudolph Giuliani, who beat David Dinkins in 1993, and Governor George Pataki, who beat Cuomo in 1994. Both are unsentimental men of little eloquence, without illusions, ambitious politicians who have unhesitatingly elbowed others aside, navigating with a clear eye on a lodestar of principle but willing to maneuver course to avoid political shoals and rapids. Giuliani was elected by just 51%–48%, a reversal of his 50%–48% defeat in 1989 against Dinkins. Pataki won 49%–45% after falling behind in the polls, watching Giuliani endorse Cuomo, being snubbed by the patronage-rich Nassau County Republicans and being dismissed by most of the media, led by *The New York Times*, which cheered for "our governor." The New York version of the welfare state, for all the attractiveness of its champions, was repudiated.

By 2001 it was clear that public policies—and life on the ground—in New York have greatly improved. In New York City, Giuliani and his police commissioners employed the "broken windows" police tactics urged by James Q. Wilson and George Kelling: aggressively enforcing and prosecuting perpetrators of small crimes—the graffiti vandals, turnstile jumpers, squeegee men, aggressive panhandlers. Giuliani used computers to keep track of crimes every day and to send in police to stop them, and he used accountability, demoting police precinct commanders whose numbers went up. The result was a department where patrolmen believe the mayor will know if there is a crime increase on their beats, a department that focused not on making arrests or avoiding complaints but on stopping crime. Violent crime was reduced by more than 50% in New York City, the streets everywhere were visibly safer and churning with new life. The media and protesters like Al Sharpton focused on a few widely publicized abuses, or alleged abuses, by police to delegitimize Giuliani's achievements. In fact under Giuliani the use of violence by police had sharply decreased. It is true that black voters remained hostile to Giuliani, and voted against him even as he was re-elected 58%–40% in 1997. But they were also living in safer, more economically vibrant neighborhoods as a result of his policies. And he hacked away at bureaucracy and taxes, with little regard to the log-rolling Democratic city council majority or the constantly demonstrating public employee unions.

Giuliani's reforms had national ramifications. His drive against crime set an example followed in dozens of other cities and destroyed the myth that crime is something city-dwellers just have to endure. He improved the quality of everyday life for Americans in the 1990s more than any other politician in the nation. He was barred by term limits from running again in 2001, and before September 11 he seemed to be leaving office on a sour note. In early 2000 he set out to run for the Senate against Hillary Rodham Clinton, then withdrew in May 2000 while undergoing treatment for prostate cancer. Later that year his marriage came apart publicly. Then on September 11 he became America's Mayor. The struggle to succeed him was messy. The primary had been scheduled for September 11, and was called off by Governor George Pataki. Giuliani proposed that state law be changed to let him serve two or three months more after January 1, but Assembly Democrats blocked the move. Media billionaire Michael Bloomberg, a liberal Democrat who changed his party registration to win, won the Republican nomination. Democrats had a fractious and racially-charged runoff between Public Advocate (the office used to be City Council President, and has few clear duties) Mark Green and Bronx Borough President Fernando Ferrer, both liberals and advocates of big government; Green won 51%–49%. Bloomberg won the general election 45.1% to 44.5%, a margin of just 9,000 votes out of more than 1.5 million cast, and after spending nearly $70 million of his personal fortune on his campaign. Interestingly, he carried Hispanic voters, who had come close to giving Giuliani a majority in 1997.

September 11 inflicted terrible damage on New York's economy. Officials estimated that it could cost the city's economy $100 billion and 100,000 jobs. Lower Manhattan real estate plunged in value, and Midtown real estate was affected as well. Financial services companies scrambled to decentralize their operations outside of Manhattan. Financial services had been the propelling force of New York's economic growth in the 1990s; now it seemed to be faltering. George W. Bush promised New York's Senators Charles Schumer and Hillary Rodham Clinton $20 billion to help the city and state rebuild; by late 2002 not all that had been paid, and some of it obviously would not be needed until plans were set for the World Trade Center site and its transportation facilities. State and city revenues came in much lower than expected. In the meantime, state and city politicians seemed to be abandoning the successful public policies of the 1990s. Pataki signed an expensive contract with the hospital workers' union, which helped him win Latino votes in November 2002 but saddled the state with high costs even as revenues plunged below estimates. In December 2002 Bloomberg, despite his promises not to raise taxes during the 2001 campaign, pushed through an 18% increase in the property tax and increases in other taxes. He declined to follow Giuliani's example in cutting public sector jobs and increasing efficiency, and he argued that higher taxes would not drive businesses away: the opposite of the lessons on the 1970s, 1980s and Dinkins years. As historian Fred Siegel points out, the outer boroughs are increasingly dependent on public sector jobs, with one-third of jobs in Brooklyn and half in the Bronx directly dependent on the city or state governments. Higher taxes will tend to squeeze out private sector jobs there even as the financial services industry is failing to provide the growth it did in the 1990s. The good news for New York is that it is increasing its human capital. New York City had more than 8 million people in the 2000 Census—8,008,000, more than the previous high, in 1950, of 7,984,000. Some 36% of its residents in 2000 were born in other countries—almost as high as the 1910 peak of 41%. Immigrants have been streaming into outer borough neighborhoods, creating new businesses, churches and neighborhood institutions—Caribbean blacks in Flatbush, Chinese in Flushing and Borough Park, Colombians in Corona, Pakistanis in Jackson Heights, Greeks in Astoria, Russians in Brighton Beach. The question is whether the outer boroughs will develop the private sector jobs and housing as New York did in the early 20th century surge of immigration and whether immigrants will be helped to assimilate into American society as they were then or shunted off into ghettos—not exactly appropriate in a city where 5% of the people told Census takers that they were of more than one race.

Upstate New York has its problems as well. Burdened with a state tax system constructed to support New York City's welfare state, it has been at a substantial disadvantage with nearby Northeastern states, not to mention the Sun Belt, in attracting jobs. Up through the 1980s paternalistic big corporations like IBM, Kodak and Xerox were the bedrock of the Upstate economy. But in an increasingly competitive America, these corporations faltered and cut payrolls, while big steel plants in the Niagara Frontier area around Buffalo were closed. Upstate voters have gotten into the habit of turning on governors as the area's economy stagnates. In 1994 they turned on Mario Cuomo and gave George Pataki a 59%–32% margin and in 1998, after Pataki cut taxes sharply, they voted 62%–18% to reelect him, with most of the rest of the vote going to Rochester multi-millionaire Thomas Golisano, who was running on a third party ticket. In 2002 Golisano ran again and won 18% outside of New York City, almost as much as Democrat Carl McCall's 25%; Pataki was held to 54%, and statewide he won only 49% of the vote. Hillary Rodham Clinton's listening tour of Upstate was an attempt to convince voters there that she understood and cared about their problems, and it paid off in November 2000: she lost usually Republican Upstate to Rick Lazio by only a 50%–47% margin.

But whatever New York's problems, New Yorkers now know that all of America is rooting for them. George W. Bush paid the state little heed before September 11; in his 2000 general election campaigns he came to Manhattan only to appear at the Al Smith dinner and on the David Letterman program. But in January 2003 he decided to hold the 2004 Republican National Convention in New York—the first time the Republicans have met there.

The People		Race/Ethnic Origin			Military veterans: 1,361,164 (9.5%)	
Pop. 2000:	18,976,457	11,760,981	62.0%	White	WWII: 25.4%	Korea: 15.5%
Pop. 1990:	17,990,455	2,812,623	14.8%	Black	Vietnam: 27.7%	Gulf War: 7.1%
Change 1990–2000:	Up 5.5%	1,035,926	5.5%	Asian	**Most populous cities:**	
Change 1980–1990:	Up 2.5%	52,499	0.3%	Native Am.	1. New York	8,008,278
% of U.S. total:	6.7%	5,230	0.0%	Hawaiian	2. Buffalo	292,648
Pop. rank:	3d of 50	366,116	1.9%	Two + races	3. Rochester	219,773
Area size:	54,556 sq. mi.	75,499	0.4%	Other	4. Yonkers	196,086
State Native:	65.3%	2,867,583	15.1%	Hisp. Origin	5. Syracuse	147,306
Non-citizen:	11.0%	**Ancestry**			Urban population: 87.5%	
Language		Italian: 11.4%		Irish: 10.2%	Rural population: 12.5%	
English: 70.4%	Spanish: 13.3%	German: 8.9%		English: 4.8%		
Other Eur.: 11.4%		Polish: 4.1%				

Education		Work Sector		Legislature	
H.S. Grad:	79.1%	Private: 76.8%	Govt: 17.0%	Senate	37 R 25 D
College Grad:	27.4%	Self: 6.0%	Family: 0.2%	Assembly	103 D 47 R
Industry		Unemployment: 7.1%		Legislative Term Limits: No	
Agri: 0.6%	Con: 5.2%	**Household Income**		**Registered Voters**	
Fin: 8.8%	Info: 4.1%	<15k: 17.9%	15-35k: 23.1%	D: 5,255,521 (46.7%)	
Mfg: 15.5%	Prof: 34.5%	35-50k: 14.8%	50-100k: 29.0%	R: 3,132,161 (27.9%)	
Public: 5.2%	Trade: 13.8%	100-150k: 9.1%	>150k: 6.2%	I: 2,858,680 (25.4%)	
Other: 12.3%		Median: $43,393			
Occupation		Poverty status: 14.6%			
Blue collar: 19.3%	White collar: 63.8%	**Home Value**			
Gray collar: 16.9%		<50k: 9.1%	50-100k: 25.3%	100-200k: 32.0%	200-300k: 18.5%
		300-500k: 10.0%	>500k: 5.1%	Median: $147,600	

Presidential politics In the first half of the 20th century, New York was the most pivotal—indeed, sometimes it seemed the dominant—state in presidential politics. It had the most electoral votes—45 from 1912–28, 47 from 1932–48, 45 from 1952–60—and of all the large states it was usually the most evenly divided between the two parties. But New York had just 33 electoral votes in 2000 and will have just 31 in 2004, and is among the largest states the most heavily Democratic. How has this come to pass? One reason is that Jewish voters, who did not identify strongly with either major party in the first half of the 20th century, became strong Democrats—arguably the core of the Democratic Party—in the second. Increases in the percentage of black and Puerto Rican voters raised the Democratic percentage. White Catholic voters took conservative positions on cultural issues like crime and foreign policy in the 1970s and 1980s, which was one reason Senator James Buckley was elected on the Conservative party line in 1970, Ronald Reagan won New York's electoral votes narrowly in 1980 and 1984 and George H. W. Bush was beaten by only a 52%–48% margin in 1988. But these voters now, or their

2000 Presidential Vote		
Gore (D)	4,107,697	(60%)
Bush (R)	2,403,374	(35%)
Nader (Green)	244,030	(4%)
Other	66,898	(1%)

2000 Republican Presidential Primary		
Bush (R)	1,102,850	(51%)
McCain (R)	937,655	(43%)
Keyes (R)	71,196	(3%)
Forbes (R)	49,817	(2%)

2000 Democratic Presidential Primary		
Gore (D)	639,417	(66%)
Bradley (D)	326,038	(33%)

1996 Presidential Vote		
Clinton (D)	3,756,565	(61%)
Dole (R)	1,932,900	(31%)
Perot (I)	503,356	(8%)

descendants are more likely to take liberal stands on today's salient cultural issues, gun control and abortion. So Bill Clinton carried New York by 50%–34% in 1992 and 61%–31% in 1996 and Al Gore by 60%–35% in 2000. Gore carried New York City 78%–18%—a bigger margin than Lyndon Johnson's over Barry Goldwater in 1964—the suburbs 56%–40% and historically Republican Upstate New York 49%–45%.

The tantalizing question for 2004 is whether this pattern is etched in stone, or whether it is part of what was changed on September 11. In early 2002, George W. Bush's political strategists were saying that he might have a chance of carrying New York in 2004. His performance after September 11, his appeal to the Hispanic voters among whom Michael Bloomberg and George Pataki ran so much better in 2001 and 2002 than Bush had in 2000, his appeal to Jewish and other voters who admire his strong support for Israel—all these things, Bush strategists think, could put New York within Bush's reach as it was in Ronald Reagan's. It seems likely that between March and August 2004 Bush will have a great deal of money and the putative Democrat almost none at all to advertise, send out direct mail and otherwise electioneer in New York, and probe whether New York (and New Jersey, most of which gets New York City TV) could be competitive in the fall. The Bush campaign might want to spend heavily in the New York market, if only to force the Democrats to spend money here on defense that they then will not be able to spend on offense elsewhere. If the war on terrorism goes badly or if Bush's job ratings decline significantly for other reasons, New York obviously will not be in play. But the Bush team's decision to put the Republican National Convention in New York suggests that they think there is a significant chance it will.

For years New York had boss politics, and it never had a presidential primary until 1968. Turnout is low. Democratic turnout was 1.1 million in 2000, well below the peak of 1.5 million in 1988, when Mayor Ed Koch's shrill support of Al Gore won him few votes as Michael Dukakis beat Jesse Jackson; on March 7, 2000, Gore beat Bill Bradley by a 2–1 margin. As for the Republican primary, the rules for qualifying for the ballot are so convoluted that no one but party insiders can master them; there were no contests here in the 1980s and Steve Forbes qualified in 1996 only after spending $1 million. In 2000 Republican state Chairman William Powers maneuvered to keep John McCain off the ballot, to give an uncontested victory to Bush, Governor George Pataki's candidate. But McCain went to court and got on the ballot. Then the Pataki forces ran harsh ads against McCain, including one attacking him for not supporting breast cancer funding—which drew protests from Mayor Rudolph Giuliani, even though he too was supporting Bush. But voting was limited to registered Republicans, and McCain did not have the appeal here he showed in New England; he carried affluent parts of Manhattan and the suburbs, but Bush won just about everywhere else. Voters voted for delegates, not presidential candidates; Bush delegates got 50% of the vote, McCain delegates 44%.

New York's minor parties no longer much matter. The Liberal Party and its predecessor, the American Labor Party, were founded to give Jewish garment workers a line on which to vote for Franklin Roosevelt and against local Tammany Hall candidates; the Liberal line was a help to Giuliani in the 1993 and 1997 mayoral elections. But in 2002 the Liberals endorsed Andrew Cuomo for governor, and he bowed out of the race a week before the Democratic primary. He got only 16,000 votes in November—far fewer than the 50,000 the Liberals needed to keep their position on the ballot. The Conservative Party was founded to withhold votes from liberal Republicans like Nelson Rockefeller and John Lindsay and encourage the Republican Party to nominate more conservative candidates. Lack of the Conservative line was a problem for Giuliani when he was running for senator, but the party did support the not-very-conservative Rick Lazio. It is quite comfortable with George Pataki, the first Conservative-backed governor, who got 177,000 votes on the Conservative line in 2002.

Congressional districting When John Kennedy was elected president in 1960, New York elected 43 congressmen and California 30. In 2002, New York elected 29 congressmen and California 53. Reapportionment is carnage time for New York: the state lost five districts in the 1980 Census, another three in 1990 and two more in 2000. In 2002, as in 1992, New York produced the latest and most convoluted redistricting plan. New York has more than 200 state legislators, but legislative decisions are made by three men, Governor George Pataki, Republican state Senate President Joseph Bruno and Democratic Assembly Speaker Sheldon Silver: party discipline is so strong that Bruno and Silver can always deliver majorities in their chambers, and Pataki has a veto. New York lost two seats in the 2000 Census, and before the Census numbers came in, it was assumed that the final plan would cut one Democratic district in the City and one Republican district Upstate. But the Census figures showed that, for the first time in more than 50 years, most of the state's growth had come in New York City; its population was up 9%, the suburbs up 6% and Upstate up only 1%. So congressmen hired well-wired lobbyists and negotiations began.

108th Congress Lineup	
19 D	10 R
107th Congress Lineup	
19 D	12 R

Negotiators usually don't reach agreement until they have to; in this case, the deadline was in June 2002, when candidates have to start circulating their petitions. In January Republicans talked of targeting Republican Benjamin Gilman and Rochester Democrat Louise Slaughter, the oldest members of the delegation; Silver would have none of it. In April 2002 the three-judge court appointed Frederick Lacey, a former federal judge, as a special master with orders to draft a plan that could be adopted if the legislature failed to act. To that court Pataki in May submitted a plan that targeted Maurice Hinchey and Manhattan Democrat Carolyn Maloney: an obvious negotiating ploy, since Silver would never accept it. Senate Republicans prepared a plan putting two pairs of Democrats in the same districts; Assembly Democrats prepared a plan putting two pairs of Republicans in the same districts: more negotiating ploys. On May 13 Lacey presented a plan placing two pairs of Upstate members—Republican Sherwood Boehlert and Democrat Maurice Hinchey, Republican Jack Quinn and Democrat John LaFalce—in the same districts. On May 23, the court adopted the plan, but gave the legislature more time to act and said it would gladly accept its plan if it did so.

The pressure was on. Silver wanted to protect Hinchey and other Democrats discommoded by the plan. Bruno got a call from Dick Cheney urging him to deal, since the plan put some Republican seats at risk. Nita Lowey, chairman of the House Democrats' campaign committee, and Tom Reynolds, on the inside track to become chairman of the House Republicans' campaign committee, let it be known they wanted safer districts so they could concentrate on helping their parties across the country. The three decision-makers decided to target Slaughter and Gilman, though Slaughter said she would run in the primary against LaFalce and Gilman threatened to switch parties and run against Republican Sue Kelly. The last hitch was on Long Island. State Senate Republicans there didn't like the incumbent-protection plan agreed on by the Island's two Democratic and two Republican incumbents; they wanted a better shot at Democrat Carolyn McCarthy's district. But they were brought in line. The new plan was passed and signed June 5. Slaughter went into court and asked it to adopt the Lacey plan. On June 25 the court accepted the legislature's plan and the Justice Department gave it clearance under the Voting Rights Act. On June 26 LaFalce announced that he would not run against Slaughter. On July 2, Gilman, who was 79 and had served almost 30 years in the House, announced that he would retire. All incumbents were easily reelected, except for 1st District Republican Felix Grucci, who lost for reasons having nothing to do with redistricting.

Governor

George Pataki (R)

Elected 1994, term expires Jan. 2007, 3d term; b. June 24, 1945, Peekskill; home, Garrison; Yale U., B.A. 1967, Columbia U. Law Schl., J.D. 1970; Catholic; married (Libby).

Elected Office: Peekskill Mayor, 1982–84; NY Assembly, 1984–92; NY Senate, 1992–94.

Professional Career: Practicing atty., 1970–89.

Office: State Capitol, Albany, 12224, 518-474-8390; Web site: www.state. ny.us.

Election Results

2002 general	George Pataki (R-C)	2,262,255	(49%)
	Carl McCall (D-WF)	1,534,064	(34%)
	Thomas Golisano (Ind)	654,016	(14%)
	Other	128,743	(3%)
2002 primary	George Pataki (R)	unopposed	
1998 general	George Pataki (R-C)	2,571,991	(54%)
	Peter F. Vallone (D-WF)	1,570,317	(33%)
	Thomas Golisano (Ind)	364,056	(8%)
	Other	228,872	(5%)

Prior Winning Percentages: 1994 (49%)

George Pataki, the governor of New York who helped the state recover from the attacks of September 11, was first elected in 1994. He grew up in Peekskill, a small industrial city on the Hudson in northern Westchester County, at the cusp of metropolitan New York City and Upstate New

York. His father was the son of Hungarian immigrants, his mother is of Italian and Irish ancestry; his parents had a farm in Peekskill and built it into a business; those years are the primary subject of his autobiography *Pataki*. Pataki graduated from Yale and Columbia Law School, where he was an unabashed conservative in the late 1960s; he practiced law with a big Wall Street firm, then moved to a Westchester firm in 1974. In 1982 he was elected Mayor of Peekskill, where he converted tax-exempt property to taxpaying housing, held taxes down, opened an industrial plant and approved 1,000 new housing units. In 1984 he ran against an incumbent Democratic assemblyman and won. In 1992, after eight years as a member of a powerless minority, he challenged an incumbent Republican state senator and beat her by 558 votes. In the state Senate he chafed at the leadership of Nassau County's Ralph Marino and voted against the budget—an almost unheard of rebellion in lockstep-party-voting Albany. In all this he showed ambition, ruthlessness and a penchant for cutting government, but few were paying attention.

In 1993, the almost unknown Pataki began running for governor, taking on one of America's best-known politicians, Mario Cuomo. For all his national fame, and his feints at running for president in 1987 and 1991, Cuomo was in trouble in New York: he cut the top tax rates but also created other taxes and increased spending robustly; he claimed credit for a workfare program but tended to support the public employee unions. Pataki provided a clear contrast on the issues, and he also showed political skill. He got the support of Senator Alfonse D'Amato, fresh from re-election in 1992 and in control of the state Republican party apparatus. Pataki easily won the May 1994 convention and prevented a primary challenge and a Conservative Party candidacy. In the general election, Cuomo attacked Pataki for having raised taxes in Peekskill; Democrats charged that he was a puppet of D'Amato. Thomas Golisano, a Rochester businessman, was spending millions as an independent, advised by pro-Perot pollster Gordon Black; Perot endorsed him and polls showed him with 8%. But Golisano's share of the vote fell to 4%, and Cuomo got 45%, about where he was running in polls. Pataki won 49% of the vote, losing New York City 70%–28% but carrying the suburbs 54%–43% and Upstate 59%–32%.

As governor, Pataki showed determination and even ruthlessness in seeking his goals. After the election, he declined to take a congratulatory phone call from Giuliani for three weeks and engineered a coup ousting Marino as Senate leader that was executed while the governor-elect was on vacation in Florida. Most legislation in New York is hammered out by three people: the governor, the Assembly speaker and the state Senate president. Other state legislators don't much matter. Party discipline is routinely followed; committees don't hold public hearings or markup sessions, and their chairmen can be fired by the leaders any time; most members can't offer amendments or get bills discharged from committees; legislation is typically written by the three leaders' staffers and then "jammed" through both houses without anyone reading it—and all this is enforced by the party leaders' control over expense and campaign funds. So Pataki moved suddenly from being a backbench legislator to being in the room for all the important negotiations with Democratic Assembly Speaker Sheldon Silver and Senate President Joseph Bruno. Pataki proposed cuts in taxes and a standstill in spending and, after bruising negotiations with Silver, got much of what he wanted. Pataki signed the death penalty into law in March. In 1996 he got changes in workmen's comp. With D'Amato and almost all leading New York Republicans except Giuliani, he endorsed Bob Dole for the Republican nomination; but when the Dole campaign went nowhere in New York he said coolly in November, "I wasn't involved in the campaign."

Instead he spent much effort on a $1.75 billion environmental bond issue, citing his longtime admiration for Theodore Roosevelt and gathering support from business, labor and environmental groups. In early 1997 Pataki unveiled his welfare plan, cutting benefits to recipients who do not find work by 45% over four years; he called for a three-year phase out of the estate and gift taxes, which sent many affluent New Yorkers to Florida; he pushed his STAR school tax relief plan to rebate taxes and give more aid to schools. Pataki's budgets in 1997 and 1998 had above-economic-growth spending increases; he established who was in control, however, by line-item-vetoing $1.6 billion from the legislature's budget in April 1998. All this left Pataki in strong shape for reelection in 1998. He got the support of Giuliani and former Mayor Edward Koch; potentially strong opponents like then-Congressman Charles Schumer and Comptroller Carl McCall declined to run. The Democratic nomination was won by New York City Council Speaker Peter Vallone, a competent and constructive veteran widely admired in knowledgeable circles. But he was scarcely known outside New York City, and never had a chance against the well-financed Pataki. Pataki won 54%–33%, losing New York City by 60%–33%—a slight improvement over 1994—but carrying the suburbs 62%–29% and Upstate by 64%–18%; 13% of the vote there went to Golisano, running a third-party candidacy.

Over many years now as governor, Pataki has tacked this way and that, emphasizing new issues and taking different stands that put him at different places on the political spectrum. His description of his political philosophy leaves him plenty of room: "I believe in limited government, low taxes, a tough approach to crime. But I also believe in activist government. I'm not one of those laissez faire types." During his second term he moved mostly to the left. Starting in 1999 he proposed changing the Rockefeller drug laws, with their mandatory minimum sentences. In 2001 he pushed through an expansion of children's health insurance, which covered 543,000 children. He pushed through innovative gun-control laws in 2000, including requiring ballistic fingerprinting of every gun sold. He signed a hate-crimes law and set up a DNA review commission in 2000, plus laws for tougher sentences for sex offenders. To court Latino voters, he took Spanish lessons and traveled to Puerto Rico in April 2001 for a state dinner at La Fortaleza with Governor Sila Calderon, a fundraiser and a trip to Vieques where he called for the closing of the bombing range there. He opposed a Bush administration proposal for oil drilling in the Finger Lakes National Forest.

Most of all, he courted the public employee unions. He met one of the major demands by signing in July 2000 a cost of living adjustment for public employee retiree pensions. In January 2002 he met with Dennis Rivera, head of 1199, the state's largest union, and negotiated an agreement to increase the pay of hospital employees. He signed a law allowing unionization of employees of new Indian casinos. He supported higher pensions for police and fire fighters who work 30 years, which were much appreciated by the Policemen's Benevolent Association, the United Firefighters Association and the Corrections Officers Benevolent Association. His support of teachers' pay increases was appreciated by the NEA New York and his pressure on Mayor Michael Bloomberg for a $1 billion teacher pay settlement impressed the United Federation of Teachers.

But Pataki's greatest asset in 2002 was his performance on and in the days after September 11. He worked around the clock, often making public appearances with Mayor Rudolph Giuliani; they had had edgy relations in the past, but obviously bonded in the emergency. His job rating, already in the high 50s, soared much higher in fall 2001 and early 2002, and he established a closer connection with New York City, where he had won only 28% of the vote in 1994 and 33% in 1998. His call for a total of $54 billion of aid to the state—which included some Upstate projects—was off-putting to many in Washington, but was well-received by New York voters. Democratic strategist Howard Wolfson said Pataki's greatest asset in 2002 was the "Ground Zero" effect.

Nonetheless, two well-known Democrats ran for governor. One was Andrew Cuomo, son of the former governor and the HUD Secretary in the Clinton administration. The other was state Comptroller Carl McCall, a longtime insider in New York politics, who would be the first black major party nominee for governor. McCall stressed classic Democratic themes and highlighted his own rise from modest (though not impoverished, as he suggested) beginnings to high public office. McCall played an insider's game, Cuomo an outsider's game. McCall was endorsed by hundreds of Democratic politicians, including all four Democratic borough presidents, as well as NEA New York—though other big unions, courted by Pataki, stayed out of the Democratic primary. Cuomo campaigned with his wife, a daughter of Robert Kennedy, and had more celebrity; he led in polls in the spring. Cuomo avoided the Democratic state convention and instead got on the ballot by collecting petition signatures. But both candidates made serious mistakes in off-the-cuff comments. On a bus with reporters traveling from Buffalo to Utica, Cuomo in April 2002 denigrated Pataki's role on September 11. "He stood behind the leader. He held the leader's coat. He was a great assistant to the leader. But he was not a leader." McCall, speaking at a homeless youth shelter in New York in June, was asked about education aid to ex-convicts. "Just because you're an ex-offender, you should not be denied education aid. In fact, if you're an ex-offender, I think you ought to get preference." He tried to explain he had not meant what he said, but voters got the sense he was one of New York's far left Democrats.

In July Senator Charles Schumer endorsed McCall. This put the spotlight on his junior colleague Hillary Rodham Clinton. The Clintons had always courted black voters and wanted their support in their future political endeavors, and so were uncomfortable not endorsing McCall; yet Cuomo had been an effective and politically very loyal member of the Clinton administration, who had done nothing to forfeit his claim for their support. The problem was solved when, after long negotiations in which Bill Clinton took a key part, Cuomo withdrew from the race on September 3, a week before the primary. McCall had passed him in the polls over the summer and, Cuomo said, the only way he could win was to wage a negative campaign that he didn't want to do.

That left McCall with little money for the general election and Pataki quite a lot more—but Thomas Golisano had even more. He is the founder and CEO of Paychex, a payroll processing company; his fortune is estimated at $800 million. He had run in 1994 and 1998, winning 4% and 8% of the vote, much of it in and around his hometown of Rochester. Under New York's unique system, candidates can run for the nomination of more than one party, and Pataki ran for the Conservative and Independence party nominations as well as the Republican. Golisano was running for the Conservative nomination, which he was unlikely to win; he needed the Independence nomination to get on the ballot in November. Pataki operatives evidently encouraged people to re-register in the Independence party, to knock Golisano off the ballot on September 10. They nearly succeeded, but Golisano beat Pataki by a margin of only 9,572 to 9,026. Golisano, who had already spent $30 million, proceeded to spend $43 million more, most of it on ads savaging Pataki, calling him corrupt and saying that he had neglected the economy of Upstate New York. He succeeded in depressing Pataki's vote Upstate but Pataki ran better than he ever had in New York City, losing it to McCall by only a 53%–38% margin. Pataki also nearly carried Queens, arguably the most multiethnic county in the country, losing by only a 46%–45% margin. Overall, Pataki won by a 49%–34% margin, with 14% for Golisano—not as sweeping a victory as in 1998.

Once reelected Pataki took a different tack on issues. He did press through the legislature in December a law banning discrimination against gays. But, with revenues slumping, he called for preserving previous tax cuts and said he opposed tax increases. In January 2003 he proposed a budget with cuts in spending on health care and education. Many in New York say that Pataki has ambitions for national office—perhaps a seat in the Cabinet, perhaps the vice presidency, maybe the presidency itself. During the 2002 campaign he was asked whether he would promise to serve the full four-year term; he said, "Let's take things step by step." Sheldon Silver said in December 2002 that Pataki told him that he wouldn't run again for office; Silver said he told him that four years was a long time and he might change his mind. One obvious candidate for governor in 2006 is Attorney General Eliot Spitzer, a Democrat who got great publicity from using investigative powers under a vaguely phrased state law to restructure the investment banking business; he was reelected by a 66%–30% margin.

Senior Senator

Charles Schumer (D)

Elected 1998, seat up 2004, 1st term; b. Nov. 23, 1950, Brooklyn; home, Brooklyn; Harvard U., B.A. 1971, J.D. 1974; Jewish; married (Iris).

Elected Office: NY Assembly, 1974–80; U.S. House of Reps., 1980–1998.

DC Office: 313 HSOB, 20510, 202-224-6542; Fax: 202-228-3027; Web site: schumer.senate.gov.

State Offices: Albany, 518-431-4070; Binghamton, 607-772-6792; Buffalo, 716-846-4111; Manhattan, 212-486-4430; Melville, 631-753-0978; Red Hook, 914-285-9741; Rochester, 585-263-5866; Syracuse, 315-423-5471.

Committees: *Banking, Housing & Urban Affairs*: Economic Policy (RMM); Housing & Transportation; Securities & Investment. *Energy & Natural Resources*: Energy; National Parks; Water & Power. *Judiciary*: Administrative Oversight & the Courts (RMM); Constitution, Civil Rights & Property Rights; Immigration, Border Security & Citizenship. *Rules & Administration*.

Group Ratings

	ADA	ACLU	AFS	LCV	CON	ITIC	NTU	COC	ACU	NTLC	CHC
2002	85	60	100	94	36	62	15	50	10	6	—
2001	95	—	92	88	—	—	9	43	16	—	0

National Journal Ratings

	2001 LIB —	2001 CONS		2002 LIB —	2002 CONS
Economic	79%	— 19%		90%	— 5%
Social	70%	— 20%		77%	— 18%
Foreign	74%	— 14%		81%	— 15%

Key Votes of the 107th Congress

1. Approve Bush Tax Cuts	N	5. Confirm Ashcroft as AG	N	9. Bar Coop. with Intl. Court	Y
2. Expand Patients' Rights	Y	6. Bar Gays in the Boy Scouts	N	10. Trade Promotion Authority	N
3. Campaign Finance Reform	Y	7. $ for Hate Crime Prosecution	Y	11. Authorize Force in Iraq	Y
4. Permit ANWR Development	N	8. Overseas Military Abortions	Y	12. Homeland Sec. Dept. Union	Y

Election Results

1998 general	Charles Schumer (D-Ind-L)	2,551,065	(55%)	($16,671,877)
	Al D'Amato (R-C-RTL)	2,058,988	(44%)	($24,195,287)
	Other	60,752	(1%)	
1998 primary	Charles Schumer (D)	388,701	(51%)	
	Geraldine A. Ferraro (D)	201,265	(26%)	
	Mark Green (D)	145,819	(19%)	
	Other	28,493	(4%)	

Prior Winning Percentages: 1996 House (75%); 1994 House (73%); 1992 House (89%); 1990 House (80%); 1988 House (78%); 1986 House (93%); 1984 House (72%); 1982 House (79%); 1980 House (77%)

Charles Schumer is New York's senior senator, a Democrat who is an important policymaker on many issues. Schumer grew up in Flatbush, Brooklyn, and graduated first in his class at James Madison High School, alma mater also of Justice Ruth Bader Ginsburg and Minnesota Senator Norm Coleman. He graduated from Harvard College and law school and, with the latter diploma fresh in his hand in June 1974, immediately began running for an open Assembly seat. He won, at 23. In 1980 he was elected to the House from an open Brooklyn seat, just before he turned 30. Through energy, imagination, hard work, good humor and a certain amount of chutzpah, he became a skilled legislator, and one noted—and sometimes resented—for his knack for getting publicity: Bob Dole was one of the first to say that the most dangerous place in Washington was in between Schumer and a television camera.

From the unlikely venue of the Banking Committee, a panel that most talented members lobby to get off of, Schumer spotted the perverse incentives set up by the combination of deposit insurance and letting S&Ls make risky investments. On Judiciary and, eventually, as chairman of its Crime Subcommittee, he ranged far afield, contributing key provisions to immigration acts in 1986 and 1990, leading with free marketeer Dick Armey attacks on farm subsidies, and, with Florida Republican Dan Miller, a nearly successful assault on sugar programs. Schumer sponsored the 1994 crime bill and got the House to pass the Brady bill, with its waiting period for handgun purchases, over strong opposition from the National Rifle Association.

The idea of running for statewide office was surely never far from his mind. Iin April 1997 Governor George Pataki's strong job rating, and especially his overwhelming strength Upstate, convinced Schumer to use his $5 million treasury to run for Alfonse D'Amato's Senate seat instead. It was by no means obvious that he would win. D'Amato was known for his assiduous constituent service and for his ability to win the tabloid wars that dominate campaigning in metropolitan New York. D'Amato was chairman of the Banking Committee and excelled at raising money; his early support did much to make Pataki governor. Schumer started off largely unknown outside his district and faced serious primary opposition from 1984 vice presidential nominee

Geraldine Ferraro and Mark Green, New York City Public Advocate and D'Amato's opponent in 1986. By summer, Schumer was leading in polls and was much better financed, and in September he won the primary with 51% of the vote, to 26% for Ferraro and 19% for Green.

Schumer immediately launched an attack on D'Amato, saying he had told "too many lies for too long"; it echoed D'Amato's attacks on earlier opponents as "too liberal for too long." Schumer claimed he was tougher on crime, citing his support for longer sentences, limiting death row appeals, expanding capital punishment and broadening wiretap authority; he emphasized his support of abortion rights and gun control. D'Amato concentrated heavily on Schumer's missed votes while running for Senate, but the implication that Schumer was lazy was implausible. Still, by mid-October, Schumer's poll leads were mostly less than the statistical margin of error. But in a closed meeting before a Jewish group D'Amato called Schumer a "putzhead"; when that became public, he denied it, then backtracked unconvincingly after his own supporter, former Democratic Mayor Edward Koch, confirmed it. D'Amato lost confidence and momentum, and by early November was sagging in polls. Schumer, who announced in October that he would vote against impeachment though he believed Bill Clinton lied under oath, was the beneficiary of two visits from Clinton and no less than four from Hillary Rodham Clinton (the rousing reception she got may have been what convinced her to run for the Senate in New York two years later). Though outspent, Schumer won 55%–44%, winning 74%–25% in a big turnout in New York City and losing the suburbs by only 51%–49%. He lost Upstate by only 53%–45%. Jewish voters, about 40% of whom voted for D'Amato in 1986 and 1992, now went 76%–23% for Schumer; voters with graduate degrees, the most heavily Democratic educational group in New York, went 69%–31% for Schumer.

In the Senate, Schumer has a solidly liberal voting record. He has been on the national news—he appeared 14 times on Sunday interview programs, sixth most of all senators, in his first year—but he has also taken care to keep in touch with New Yorkers. He has made a practice of visiting all 62 counties each year, and regularly spends Mondays on Upstate swings that get him on Buffalo, Rochester, Syracuse and Albany television. He is one of three Americans in history who have cast two votes on the impeachment of a president (the other two are Mike Crapo of Idaho and Jim Bunning of Kentucky); Schumer voted against impeaching Clinton in the House in December 1998 and against conviction in the Senate in February 1999.

An ally of the securities industry on both the House and Senate Banking committees, he has called for making electronic communications networks subject to the same regulations as stock exchanges and for making the New York Stock Exchange a profit-making corporation. He played a key role in the scuttling of the bankruptcy bill in 2001 and 2002. He persuaded the Senate to pass an amendment that made fines and penalties for blocking access to or attacking abortion clinics not dischargeable in bankruptcy in May 2002; some abortion opponents had taken to declaring bankruptcy to avoid paying fines. But abortion opponents in the House, led by Chris Smith and Joe Pitts, refused to vote for the bill as long as it had Schumer's amendment. Leaders in both houses got Schumer and Henry Hyde, with whom he had long worked on the House Judiciary Committee, to negotiate a compromise amendment. But that too was unacceptable to the Smith-Pitts group, and when the House leadership introduced a rule to consider the bill in November 2002 it was defeated 243–172 and the bankruptcy bill died. Advocates of the bill, primarily the credit card companies, will presumably try to block the Schumer amendment in 2003. Schumer has also taken on the pharmaceutical companies by sponsoring with John McCain an amendment that would deny them extension of their patents beyond their original time when they challenge a generic drugmaker for patent infringement. In July 2002 the amendment passed the Senate 78–21. But the underlying prescription drug bill never passed. Another Schumer cause is making the first $5,000 or so of college tuition tax deductible. But he was unable to get such a provision into the tax cut bill in May 2001.

Schumer serves on Judiciary, where he was one of the most vocal opponents of the confirmation of Attorney General John Ashcroft. He was chairman of the Subcommittee on Courts, and has argued that senators should reject Bush appointees on "purely ideological grounds"; in early 2003 he was one of the leading opponents of the confirmation of Miguel Estrada. Attention to New York interests can be detected in many of his stands. He played a leading role in shaping the election procedure bill after the Florida controversy. But he opposed Christopher Bond's amendment requiring that first-time voters be required to show photo identification—many Gothamites don't have driver's licenses. Even when the amendment was broadened to allow use of Social Security numbers, utility bills, government check stubs or other means of identification, he and Hillary Rodham Clinton voted against the final version of the bill in October 2002, the only two senators to do so. He has called a number of times for release of oil from the Strategic Petroleum Reserve—which would lower home heating costs in Upstate New York—and sponsored a bill to reclassify SUVs as cars, not trucks, and subject them to higher fuel efficiency requirements. Schumer and Orrin Hatch sponsored a bill in 2002 to allow playwrights' associations to negotiate standard royalty agreements.

On September 11 Schumer was in Washington; his daughter was in school a few blocks from the World Trade Center. Amid the terrible news, Schumer and others in the New York delegation conferred and agreed to seek $20 billion in aid for New York. In the Oval Office on September 13 Schumer and Clinton met with George W. Bush. Bush asked how much New York needed. Schumer paused and said $20 billion. Schumer later described the scene to Frank Bruni of the *New York Times*. "You could almost see in his mind he was saying, 'This is a lot of money.' But this is why I have a little faith in him, and maybe this is imagining and wishful thinking, but I don't think so. I could see he was calculating in his head, 'I have to bring America together. I know New York was not for me, the blue state and all that, but I'm going to do this." Bush's reaction: "You got it." The usually voluble Schumer's reaction? "My mouth dropped open." Of course there was more to it than that. The New Yorkers understood that some of the money would not be forthcoming immediately, since no one had decided how to reconstruct the World Trade Center site and its transportation facilities. Schumer worked to prevent OMB and House Republicans from putting off as much of the spending as they wanted and dealt with the backlash against Pataki's calling for $54 billion. The Bush administration turned to Schumer to get support for what became the USA Patriot Act, and Schumer and Clinton backed the proposal to let the FBI share information on terrorism with state and local police. In June 2002 Schumer and Jon Kyl sponsored a bill to change the Foreign Intelligence Surveillance Act to allow surveillance of terrorists not connected to a foreign government. In December 2002 he called for government tracking using new electronic devices of trucks carrying hazardous materials.

Schumer also began speaking out more on foreign policy. In general he has said he is more aligned with the "proactive and multilateral" Colin Powell than with administration "hawks." He voted for the Iraq war resolution in October 2002 and openly questioned whether the Saudis have cooperated fully with the war on terrorism.

When Hillary Rodham Clinton was elected in November 2000, many thought there would be friction between the aggressive Schumer and the more famous Clinton. There mostly hasn't been, not in public anyway. Clinton was probably irritated after Schumer said of Bill Clinton's January 2001 pardon of Marc Rich: "The pardoning of fugitives stands our criminal justice system on its head." And they must have had some disagreements as they struggled to help New York after September 11: the more earthy Schumer seemed to get along better with Bush, the more disciplined Clinton seemed to get along better with some Republican senators. But Clinton was irritated when in July 2002 Schumer endorsed Carl McCall for governor. Neither had endorsed a candidate in the fractious 2001 mayoral race, and Schumer's endorsement of McCall, who is black, over Andrew Cuomo, whom he has never cared for, put Clinton in a spot. Cuomo was, after all, a faithful member of the Clinton administration as HUD Secretary. She surely did not want to endorse either one and thus oppose the other. A solution was found when, with the active mediation of Bill Clinton, Cuomo withdrew from the race one week before the primary.

After Democrats lost their Senate majority in November 2002, Schumer said the party should follow Bill Clinton's advice. "The American people are centrist. I reject the Democrats who say 'we've got to move further to the left; that's why we lost.'" He called for the party to concentrate on homeland security, energy dependence, taxes (a one-year payroll tax cut), education and health care. He predicted that Congress would reject the Democratic prescription drug benefit as "better but too expensive" and called for support of the Republican alternative as a free-standing measure, without major changes in Medicare.

Life as a senator is not as glamorous as some may think. While Hillary Rodham Clinton holds fundraisers in her $2.8 million house in Washington, Schumer shares a Capitol Hill townhouse with Senator Dick Durbin and Congressmen Bill Delahunt and George Miller; Al Franken has been trying to fashion a television series on this, "Little House on the Hill," with an aggressive Upper West Side Congressman named Chip Weinberg. Even so, Schumer clearly wants to continue being a senator. In December 2002 he had $13.6 million cash on hand for his reelection campaign in 2004. The omens for his campaign are good. He has had a high job rating, well above 50%, and he seems far better known and liked in Upstate New York than when he started running in 1997. Precedent is in his favor: no Democratic incumbent senator has been defeated in New York since direct election of senators began (although seven incumbent Republicans have lost). His most formidable opponent would be Rudolph Giuliani; a March 2003 poll showed him leading Schumer by 45%–40%. But few think Giuliani is interested; he has embarked on a business career, he needs a high income to maintain his lifestyle and he is a national celebrity already. Long Island Congressman Peter King, Buffalo Congressman Jack Quinn and Upstate Assemblyman John Faso, who lost the 2002 comptroller race by only 50%–46%, took themselves out of the Senate race. Also mentioned as possible candidates were Erie County Executive Joel Giambra, a Democrat until 1998; Secretary of State Randy Daniels, a former newsman; and Ted Forstmann, the investment banker.

Junior Senator

Hillary Rodham Clinton (D)

Elected 2000, seat up 2006, 1st term; b. Oct. 26, 1947, Chicago, IL; home, Chappaqua; Wellesley Col., B.A. 1969; Yale U., J.D. 1973; Methodist; married (Bill).

Professional Career: Atty., Children's Defense Fund, 1973–74; Council, U.S. House of Reps. Judiciary Committee, 1974; Asst. professor, U. of AR School of Law, 1974–77, 1979–80; Practicing atty., 1977–92; Chair, Pres. Task Force on Health Care Reform, 1993.

DC Office: 476 RSOB, 20510, 202-224-4451; Fax: 202-228-0282; Web site: clinton.senate.gov.

State Offices: Albany, 518-431-0120; Buffalo, 716-854-9725; Hartsdale, 914-725-9294; Lowville, 315-376-6118; Melville, 631-249-2825; New York City, 212-688-6262; Rochester, 585-263-6250; Syracuse, 315-448-0470.

Committees: *Democratic Steering Committee Chairman. Armed Services:* Airland; Emerging Threats & Capabilities; Readiness & Management Support. *Environment & Public Works:* Clean Air, Climate Change & Nuclear Safety; Fisheries, Wildlife & Water. *Health, Education, Labor & Pensions:* Aging; Children & Families.

Group Ratings

	ADA	ACLU	AFS	LCV	CON	ITIC	NTU	COC	ACU	NTLC	CHC
2002	95	60	100	88	58	50	17	45	10	0	—
2001	95	—	100	88	—	—	3	43	12	—	0

National Journal Ratings

	2001 LIB —	2001 CONS		2002 LIB —	2002 CONS
Economic	87%	— 13%		95%	— 0%
Social	70%	— 20%		82%	— 0%
Foreign	61%	— 27%		70%	— 27%

Key Votes of the 107th Congress

1. Approve Bush Tax Cuts	N	5. Confirm Ashcroft as AG	N	9. Bar Coop. with Intl. Court	Y
2. Expand Patients' Rights	Y	6. Bar Gays in the Boy Scouts	N	10. Trade Promotion Authority	N
3. Campaign Finance Reform	Y	7. $ for Hate Crime Prosecution	Y	11. Authorize Force in Iraq	Y
4. Permit ANWR Development	N	8. Overseas Military Abortions	Y	12. Homeland Sec. Dept. Union	Y

Election Results

2000 general	Hillary Rodham Clinton (D-L-WF)	3,747,310	(55%)	($41,469,898)
	Rick Lazio (R-C)	2,915,730	(43%)	($40,576,273)
	Other	116,799	(2%)	
2000 primary	Hillary Rodham Clinton (D)	565,353	(82%)	
	Mark S. McMahon (D)	124,315	(18%)	
1994 general	Daniel Patrick Moynihan (D-L)	2,646,541	(55%)	($6,705,482)
	Bernadette Castro (R-C)	1,988,308	(42%)	($1,581,901)
	Other	155,487	(3%)	

Hillary Rodham Clinton, First Lady of the United States from 1993 to 2001, was elected junior Senator from New York in November 2000. Clinton grew up in Park Ridge, Illinois; her father owned and ran a drape and curtain factory. She excelled at her studies and was elected to student government at Maine South High School. Park Ridge is a solidly Republican Chicago suburb, near O'Hare Airport, and the young Hillary Rodham was a Goldwater girl in 1964. She went to Wellesley College, where she became a Democrat in the turbulent election year of 1968: she wrote her senior thesis (kept under lock and key by the college since 1993) on applying the theories of radical Chicago organizer Saul Alinsky and argued that antipoverty programs did not give enough power to the poor. She was elected student government president, and pushed successfully for admission of more black students and admission of men to women's dorms. At the 1969 commencement she gave a speech that won notice in *Life* magazine. She went on to Yale Law School, where she worked with the attorney for Black Panthers accused of murder and clerked for a summer with Communist attorney Robert Treuhaft in Berkeley. At Yale she met Bill Clinton, and they became partners for life.

Bill Clinton was anything but reticent about his political ambitions in his native Arkansas. He showed her around the state and together they went to Austin in 1972 to run the McGovern campaign in Texas. After graduation in 1973, Bill Clinton moved to Fayetteville to teach law at the University of Arkansas. In 1974 Hillary Rodham moved to Washington to work for the House Judiciary Committee's special counsel John Doar on the impeachment of Richard Nixon; After Nixon resigned, she returned to Arkansas to teach law, and in October 1975 she and Clinton were married. In 1976 he was elected attorney general of Arkansas; she worked for Jimmy Carter's campaign. After that she worked for the Rose Law Firm in Little Rock and in 1977 was appointed to part-time chairman of the Legal Services Corporation. Under her leadership, the Legal Services budget increased dramatically, including contributions to local political campaigns and conducting campaigns against ballot propositions. In 1978 Bill Clinton ran for governor, and after he won the Democratic nomination, tantamount to victory that year, Hillary Rodham invested $1,000 in commodities future and with the help of a friend who was general counsel of Tyson Foods, one of the state's biggest businesses, saw that turned into $100,000.

In 1980 Bill Clinton was defeated for re-election. He promptly took up a more moderate line and his wife began to call herself Hillary Clinton; in 1982 he beat the incumbent and became governor again. Hillary Clinton continued her law practice and service on the board of the Children's Defense Fund and other organizations. She served on the boards of Wal-Mart, TCBY and in 1988 and 1991 was named by the *National Law Journal* as one of the 100 most influential lawyers in the country. It was in these years also that she and her husband invested in the Whitewater real estate project and that she performed legal work for the Morgan Guaranty Savings and Loan, which invested in the project and whose failure cost the federal government $73 million. Whitewater later became the subject of congressional hearings and an independent counsel investigation, both of which were impeded when Rose Law Firm billing records were subpoenaed in July 1994 but were not found until they turned up in the residential quarters of the White House in January 1996. Independent Counsel Robert Ray in September 2000 ended the investigation, saying he could not prove that the Clintons had been involved in criminal activity or that they concealed information from investigators or obstructed justice. In his final report in March 2002 Ray noted that Rose Law Firm records were found in the family quarters of the White House in January 1996 and that three witnesses told investigators they saw her "carrying records that had the appearance of the billing records in July 1995"; but he said that that evidence was insufficient to obtain and sustain a conviction beyond a reasonable doubt.

In 1991 Bill Clinton ran for president. It was widely rumored that he had had many extramarital affairs; at a Washington press breakfast the Clintons admitted that their marriage had not been without problems. After the election, Clinton announced that the leader of his task force on health care reform would be the first lady, Hillary Rodham Clinton—the first time her maiden name was featured. The task force under her direction and that of Ira Magaziner met secretly and without input from members of Congress; a complicated plan was finally produced after a couple of deadlines were not met. Clinton eventually did testify before Congress; there and in other public forums she was crisp, articulate, knowledgeable. But she was unable to persuade Congress to adopt her plan. It never came to the floor in either house, and was abandoned in September 1994. In the meantime, the first lady had problems with scandals. In May 1993 the members of the White House Travel Office were fired, and director Billy Ray Dale was later prosecuted—and acquitted by a jury within minutes. Clinton denied that she had any role in the firings, or in apparent plans to replace the charter service with one owned by Clinton friends and Hollywood producers Harry Thomason and Linda Bloodworth-Thomason. In June 2000 Independent Counsel Robert Ray concluded that Clinton had given "factually false" testimony in a sworn deposition, but declined to prosecute her.

Clinton persevered through the humiliations of the health care fiasco and the scandals with an aplomb that showed great discipline and determination. She wrote *It Takes a Village* and donated the proceeds to children's hospitals. In January 1998, when Bill Clinton denied the charge that he had had an affair with then-White House intern Monica Lewinsky, Hillary Rodham Clinton flew to New York to appear on the *Today* show and charge that the allegations were the product of "a vast right-wing conspiracy." She continued to support him, though with obvious frostiness, when he was forced to admit in August 1998 that the charges were true.

Meanwhile, she campaigned gamely for Democratic candidates in the 1998 elections, and was particularly moved by the warm applause she received in her four appearances in New York for Senate candidate Charles Schumer. Three days after the 1998 election, Senator Daniel Patrick Moynihan announced that he would not run for re-election in New York in 2000. Moynihan, the nation's best thinker among politicians since Lincoln and its best politician among thinkers since Jefferson, a man whose public career extended back into the 1950s and included many prescient warnings and original insights, who had served four terms in the Senate after serving in the cabinet or sub-cabinets of four successive presidents, obviously was not going to be replaced by a politician of similar magnitude; there aren't any. But there also weren't any obvious Democratic successors in New York. Moynihan, who passed away in March 2003, himself suggested state comptroller Carl McCall; Congresswoman Nita Lowey of Westchester County was interested in the race, though it was not clear that either had the stature to beat the likely Republican nominee, New York City Mayor Rudolph Giuliani. In early 1999 Bob Torricelli, the aggressive head of the Senate Democrats' campaign committee, called for Clinton to run. She said she was giving "careful thought" to it. She started making more trips to New York, and Lowey said she would be glad to step aside if Clinton ran. In July 1999 she appeared at Moynihans' Upstate farm and then began a "listening tour" across Upstate New York. Giuliani responded with an appearance in Arkansas.

Clinton's early campaign was not without troubles. There was widespread ridicule of the idea of someone with no previous connection with the state running for senator from New York. In August 1999 Bill Clinton granted clemency to four Puerto Rican terrorists who never expressed remorse for their violent crimes—an obvious pitch for the Puerto Rican vote. Embarrassed, she came out against the move, without giving a heads-up to Puerto Rican leaders. That same month the Clintons left their favorite vacation spot, fashionable Martha's Vineyard, for a sojourn in Skaneateles, a pleasant town in the Finger Lakes they would never have visited otherwise. In October the Clintons bought a house in woodsy Chappaqua in Westchester County and were then embarrassed because they borrowed most of the purchase price from Democratic fundraiser Terry McAuliffe; later they got more conventional financing. In November 1999 on a trip to Israel, Clinton embraced and kissed the wife of Yasir Arafat after a speech in which she lambasted the

Israelis; Clinton explained later that she was acting in a diplomatic capacity, but her act brought back memories of her endorsement of an independent Palestinian state when that was not yet U.S. policy. In February 2000 she formally announced her candidacy, with her husband standing silently by, from a venue in Westchester. By that point her poll ratings had slipped, and she was running no better than even with Giuliani.

Carpetbagging is not necessarily a political crime in New York. Voters there in 1964 elected Robert Kennedy, though he lived in Virginia and had a technical residence in Massachusetts. Robert Kennedy won in 1964 not just because of Lyndon Johnson's coattails, but because he ran virtually even in usually Republican Upstate New York; national celebrities may be commonplace in New York City, but when they show up in Upstate towns and cities it is noted and appreciated. Hillary Rodham Clinton's strategy was similar. With her usual hard work, perseverance and intensity, she criss-crossed Upstate New York, listened to its voters' many complaints, learned about local issues and adopted appealing positions on them: the same slogging persistence she had shown in the dreary days in Arkansas and the tumultuous days after the failed health care initiative and scandal charges in Washington. And she waited for the opposition to make mistakes, which it did. In March 2000 Giuliani was under attack when police officers shot an unarmed man in Manhattan; the liberal New York press seized on this opportunity, and the mayor helped them by releasing the victim's juvenile crime record. In April Giuliani announced that he had prostate cancer; in May he announced that he was seeking a separation from his wife. Days later, in a dramatic press conference, he announced he was leaving the Senate race.

Within 24 hours the Republicans had another candidate, Long Island Congressman Rick Lazio. He had talked of running in summer 1999, until Governor George Pataki announced suddenly in August that he was backing his longtime rival Giuliani. Lazio had a moderate voting record in the House; like Giuliani he backed abortion rights. He raised plenty of money: Hillary haters from all over the country sent in contributions large and small, and he ended up spending $40 million. But his campaign was less than perfect. Lazio was vulnerable to attacks, made often by Clinton, that he had supported Newt Gingrich, a *bete noire* to most New York voters. And there were unforced errors. In the first debate on September 13, Lazio walked over to Clinton and presented her a paper with a pledge to eschew soft money ads. In a time when voters were eager for consensus, Lazio was providing them with confrontation, and this in-your-face behavior was especially repugnant to women. Nine days later they both agreed to not run ads financed by soft money, that is, contributions to parties; but this was unenforceable, since parties and others can spend what they want to, and the assumption that campaign finance was a vote-moving issue proved ill-founded. In the second debate, Lazio declined to say that he would vote for any Supreme Court nominee who opposed the key abortion rights decision of *Roe v. Wade*, a defensible position intellectually, but one difficult to sustain politically in New York; Clinton pounded him on it.

For a race that was close almost all the way in the polls, this Senate election—surpassing the 1998 New York Senate race as the most expensive in history not involving a self-financing candidate—was decided by a surprisingly wide margin. Clinton won 55%–43%, almost the same as Schumer's 55%–44% two years earlier. "Sixty-two counties, 16 months, three debates, two opponents and six black pantsuits later—here we are!" exulted Clinton on election night. She was helped, of course, by the fact that Al Gore was carrying New York 60%–35%. But she ran well on her own. She carried New York City by 74%–25%, the same margin as Schumer's in 1998. She trailed in the suburbs by only 53%–45%, despite Lazio's suburban provenance; he carried his Long Island base, but she carried her now native Westchester. And Lazio won Upstate by only 50%–47%; Clinton carried most of the large counties there, and her percentages in county after county, not usually 50% but seldom under 40%, are impressive evidence of her hard work in campaigning and mastering Upstate issues. Clinton carried the Jewish vote, according to the VNS exit poll, by only 53%–45%, which would usually mean disaster for a Democrat in New York, and she did far less well than Schumer and other Democrats among those with graduate degrees, a large percentage of whom are Jewish. But she carried Upstate women by 55%–43%, an excellent showing for a Democrat: the work paid off.

A few days after the election, Clinton took a victory lap around Upstate New York and had a harmonious meeting in Albany with Pataki. But her standing fell in the months after the election.

In December 2000 she signed a book contract with Simon & Schuster for $8 million—$4.5 million more than the book contract for which Newt Gingrich was so roundly attacked in 1995. In departing the White House, the Clintons took $190,000 in gifts—far above the Senate's $50 limit—and many had to be returned when it was revealed that they included items donated to the White House, not the Clintons. Among the gifts were $7,375 worth of coffee tables and chairs donated by Denise Rich, former wife and advocate of Marc Rich, the fugitive financier pardoned by Bill Clinton on his last day in office, despite the opposition of New York U.S. Attorney Mary Jo White. Hillary Rodham Clinton said she had no opinion on the pardon. Nor, she said, did she have any role in the pardon of four Hasidic Jews from the Rockland County community of New Square who were convicted of fleecing the federal government of millions of dollars—a pardon White also opposed. But Clinton had visited New Square in August 2000, had won the community's vote by a margin of 1,400 to 12 and had been present at a White House Map Room meeting between their leaders and Bill Clinton on December 21, 2000, where they asked for the pardons. She said she had no knowledge as well that her brother Hugh Rodham had, while living at the White House, pushed for and obtained the pardon of two other felons for which he had been paid $400,000.

Many expected that Clinton would be greeted grudgingly and suspiciously by other senators because of her obvious presidential ambitions. On at least one occasion she slipped; at the National Press Club in July 2001, when asked if she would run for president, she said, "No, I have said that I am not running and I'm having a great time being presi—being a first-term senator." In fact she has worked hard at the often tedious business of being a senator. She continued to travel around New York, especially Upstate: by June 2002 she had made 130 (!) trips to Upstate New York. She worked on federal loans for the Mohawk Valley, a theater restoration in Gloversville, the arcana of dairy price supports. She turned down many opportunities for national appearances; only after September 11 did she appear again on *Meet the Press*, in December 2001. She worked hard in the Senate, attending just about every committee and subcommittee hearing, spending time on the floor, approaching Republican colleagues to ask if she could co-sponsor their bills. At Democratic caucus meetings, she would get coffee for other senators. Republicans found themselves sheepishly admitting they like her. At the same time, by all accounts she has taken a hard partisan line behind closed doors. She advised Tom Daschle that Senate Democrats should have a war room, as the Clinton campaign and White House did. She supported George W. Bush in the war on terrorism and voted for the Iraq war resolution, and told him in their meeting on September 13, 2001, that she was one of the few who understood the loneliness of the White House, but she advised down-the-line opposition to his domestic policies. Occasionally in public she sounded a partisan note. In May 2001 she cast the single vote against the confirmation of Michael Chertoff, who had worked on the Whitewater independent counsel investigation. In November 2002, when asked by Chris Matthews about Iraq, she said, "It is clear that a lot of people in the administration have some old scores to settle." HILLPAC, her leadership PAC, raised $3.2 million in the 2002 cycle and contributed more than $1 million to Democrats across the country, including $21,000 in Iowa and $15,000 in New Hampshire; she put on fundraisers for fellow Democrats in her Washington house.

Clinton has put forward initiatives on some issues not likely to get great publicity. In 2001 she advanced an eight-point plan for dealing with health problems caused by environmental defects and tried to reduce the additional patent protection given pharmaceutical companies who test the effects of drugs on children. She supported an increase in the work requirements for welfare recipients and giving states less leeway to excuse recipients from them. She and Schumer met with Bush on September 13, 2001, and when Schumer asked for $20 billion in aid to New York, Bush said, "You got it." In the weeks and months afterward she and Schumer worked on the necessarily difficult details. She worked to get payments to same-sex partners of those killed on September 11 and to prevent deportation of illegal immigrants whose spouses died then. She tried to get a separate official in the Department of Homeland Security in charge of security on the Canadian border and called for stationing the National Guard around New York airports. In October 2001 at a rock concert in honor of rescue workers, police and fire fighters booed her. She responded graciously. "Oh, you know, I was just happy to be there. I have gotten used to being in situations in political life, either vicariously or on my own, where that just happens sometimes. . . . They can blow off steam any way they want to. They've earned it."

Clinton's propensity for bipartisanship and her partisanship were on display at the opening of the 108th Congress in January 2003. In December she had gotten agreement with Don Nickles on a compromise proposal to extend unemployment benefits. It was the first item of business in the new Congress. But unexpectedly Clinton rose and offered an amendment to extend coverage to 1 million people whose benefits had expired. This triggered several hours of debate on parliamentary motions—a tough initiation for the new Majority Leader Bill Frist. Eventually Clinton's amendment was rejected and the compromise was passed. In the new Congress, Clinton was elected head of the Democrats' Steering and Coordination Committee, a job that has never generated much publicity for its incumbent; but this gives her an institutional base for her behind-the-scenes partisan strategizing.

Will Hillary Rodham Clinton run for president? In 2004? In 2008? She has repeated many times that she has committed herself to serving out her term in the Senate and in June 2003 she told the *Associated Press* she would not consider running for president in 2004 despite being encouraged to by some Democrats. 2008 is a different matter. Unless a Democrat is elected president in 2004, Clinton seems very likely to run in 2008. Although she had a large core of detractors among the national electorate, she has an even larger core of voters who have strong positive feelings toward her. Her chances of winning reelection in 2006 are excellent, and her responses then to the inevitable question of whether she will run for president may be telling. Her poll numbers in New York are strong. New York voters have never defeated an incumbent Democratic senator, and they have never shown much resentment when their officeholders run for president.

FIRST DISTRICT

Rep. Tim Bishop (D)

Elected 2002, 1st term; b. June 1, 1950, Southampton; home, Southampton; Holy Cross Col., A.B. 1972; Long Island U., M.P.A. 1981; Catholic; married (Kathy).

Professional Career: Admin., Southampton College, 1973–02.

DC Office: 1133 LHOB 20515, 202-225-3826; Fax: 202-225-3143; Web site: www.house.gov/timbishop.

District Office: Coram, 631-696-6500.

Committees: *Education & the Workforce* (22d of 22 D): Workforce Protections. *Transportation & Infrastructure* (32d of 34 D): Highways, Transit & Pipelines; Water Resources & Environment.

Group Ratings and Key Votes: Newly Elected

Election Results

2002 general	Tim Bishop (D-WF)	84,276	(50%)	($972,095)
	Felix Grucci (R-C-Ind-RTL)	81,524	(49%)	($1,399,768)
	Other	1,991	(1%)	
2002 primary	Tim Bishop (D)	unopposed		
2000 general	Felix Grucci (R-Ind-C-RTL)	133,020	(56%)	($1,565,346)
	Regina Seltzer (D)	97,299	(41%)	($338,158)
	Other	9,285	(4%)	

The People		Race/Ethnic Origin	Ancestry	
Area size:	1,944 sq. mi.	84.5% White	Italian: 21.1%	Irish: 17.5%
Urban population:	94.0%	4.0% Black	German: 13.7%	
Rural population:	6.0%	2.4% Asian	**2000 Presidential Vote**	
Pop. 2000:	654,360	0.3% Native Am.	Gore (D).............139,490 (52%)	
Median income:	$61,884	0.0% Hawaiian	Bush (R).............116,308 (44%)	
Poverty status:	6.0%	1.2% Two + races	Other..................10,705 (4%)	
Military veterans:	12.1%	0.1% Other	**Cook Partisan Voting Index:** D + 4	
		7.5% Hispanic Origin		

Occupation	Blue collar: 20.3%	White collar: 64.4%	Gray collar: 15.3%

Long Island—"the Island" to most New Yorkers—is America's largest, most populous and in some ways most troubled island. Long Island stretches 103 miles, from the two-century-old Montauk Point lighthouse at its eastern extremity to Fort Hamilton at the foot of the Verrazano Narrows Bridge. Fluctuating between 12 and 20 miles wide, Long Island is ringed by gentle hills and cliffs above Long Island Sound and sandspit beaches that front the Atlantic Ocean. Including Brooklyn and Queens, some 7.4 million people live on Long Island, more than in all but ten states. Brooklyn, at the western end of the island, is urban and thickly settled, while the Hamptons in the east are carefully manicured countryside, preserved as a playground by a style-conscious New York elite. Demographically, the Hamptons are only a small (though growing) part of Long Island. More important are the (slower growing) suburbs created in the post-World War II rush out of the city. Developers looking for cheaper land for aircraft factories, shopping centers, subdivisions or office parks found them first in Nassau County, just east of Queens, and then further out in Suffolk County. Suffolk attracted young families, of Irish and Italian descent more often than Jewish or black, looking for more space and less crime than the city could offer. More recently Suffolk County has been attracting Latinos, Salvadorans as well as Puerto Ricans, in many of its lower income areas. In the late 1980s and 1990s, life in Long Island turned sour, as defense plants were decimated by the end of the Cold War and cost overruns on nuclear plants led to electricity-rate increases.

Such upheavals, combined with partisan rivalries, have fed political turbulence. The 1st Congressional District, consisting of the eastern end of Long Island, ousted its incumbent congressmen in both 2000 and 2002. The 1st covers eastern Suffolk County, now more populous (1.42 million people) and faster-growing (7.4% growth in the 1990s) than Nassau County, its neighbor to the west. The district runs as far east as Smithtown (on the North Shore) and Patchogue (on the South Shore). It also includes Shelter Island, located between the north and south fork of Long Island's "fishtail," and Plum Island, home to the U.S. Department of Agriculture's only animal-infection research site. The 1st includes two areas frequented in the summer by urban sophisticates: all of the Hamptons, and most of Fire Island National Seashore, the only federal wilderness area in New York state, and a magnet for gay vacationers for decades. Politically, however, the more important areas are the Brookhaven National Laboratory and the defense plants in the center of the Island. Suffolk County was long one of the most conservative parts of New York, though not very conservative by today's national standards. Republican voter registration remains high, and Suffolk voted strongly for Governor George Pataki's reelection in 2002 and for Suffolk County native Rick Lazio in the 2000 Senate race. But like many areas in the Northeast, Suffolk voted solidly for Bill Clinton and Al Gore.

The congressman from the 1st District is Tim Bishop, a Democrat elected in 2002. He grew up in Southampton and graduated from Holy Cross College and from Long Island University. He spent his entire professional career at Southampton College, where he began in 1973 as an admissions counselor and in 1986 became provost. He chaired the town of Southampton's board of ethics and was on the board of the Eastern Long Island Coastal Conservation Alliance. Few paid much attention when Bishop announced in March 2002 he would oppose Felix Grucci, the first-term Republican congressman. Grucci had won the seat in one of the more bizarre contests of 2000: Mike Forbes, a Republican elected in 1994 as part of the Gingrich revolution, switched parties in July 1999, then lost the low-turnout Democratic primary by 35 votes to Regina Seltzer, a 71-year-old retired librarian; Grucci easily won the general, 56%–41%. In the House, Grucci was a reliable back-bencher on most issues except for campaign-finance reform, with moderate-to-conservative voting typical for a New York Republican.

Bishop can thank Grucci for his House seat. In late September, Grucci ran an ad accusing Bishop of falsifying rape statistics at Southampton College and "turning his back on rape victims." This turned out to be untrue. The basis for the allegations had been several articles in the college newspaper; the articles turned out to be so riddled with inaccuracies that the editors of the student newspaper voluntarily retrieved every copy of the newspaper they could find. College officials sued to bar the ads from airing. The judge refused to ban the ad but ruled that the ad could no longer name the school. Grucci's campaign refused to repudiate the ad, on the ground that no correction had ever appeared in print. House Democrats' campaign committee quickly saw an opportunity to pick up a seat, and started funneling money to the Bishop campaign, which also benefited from fundraising by millionaire entertainment mogul Robert F.X. Sillerman, a longtime Bishop friend. Soon the airwaves became saturated with ads attacking Grucci both for the rape commercial and for his environmental voting record. In one spot, which began airing before the rape ad, the Grucci family's famed fireworks enterprise was linked to the chemical contamination of local drinking water. NRCC operatives publicly attacked Democrats for putting $550,000 of soft-money into the race, but privately fumed that Grucci had failed to tell them about the college rape ad and that he had blundered in standing by his charges and failing to offer a positive message.

In this swing district, Bishop took mostly conventional liberal views: he opposed the death penalty and the Iraqi war resolution and supported a rollback of the Bush tax cuts and abortion rights. This was one of the closest House races in the nation. The official result was delayed a week by a recount and Grucci did not concede until ten days after the election; Bishop won 50%–49%. Republicans quickly identified Bishop as one of their top targets for 2004. Possible challengers include Brookhaven Town Supervisor John Jay LaValle, Suffolk County clerk Ed Romaine, and Assembly members Patricia Acampora and Fred Thiele.

SECOND DISTRICT

Rep. Steve Israel (D)

Elected 2000, 2d term; b. May 30, 1958, Brooklyn; home, Dix Hills; George Wash. U., B.A. 1983; Jewish; married (Marlene Budd).

Elected Office: Huntington Town Bd., 1993–00, Maj. Ldr., 1997–00.

Professional Career: Legis. Asst., U.S. Rep. Richard Ottinger, 1980–83; Fundraising Dir., Touro Law Ctr., 1985–88; Pres., Steve Israel Assoc., Inc., 1992–98; Pres. & CEO, Inst. on Holocaust and Law, 1998–00.

DC Office: 429 CHOB 20515, 202-225-3335; Fax: 202-225-4669; Web site: www.house.gov/israel.

District Office: Hauppauge, 631-951-2210.

Committees: *Armed Services* (21st of 29 D): Projection Forces; Tactical Air & Land Forces. *Financial Services* (23d of 32 D): Capital Markets, Insurance & Government Sponsored Enterprises; Financial Institutions & Consumer Credit.

Group Ratings

	ADA	ACLU	AFS	LCV	CON	ITIC	NTU	COC	ACU	NTLC	CHC
2002	75	80	78	88	58	50	25	58	32	23	25
2001	90	—	80	71	—	—	16	43	8	—	—

National Journal Ratings

	2001 LIB	—	2001 CONS	2002 LIB	—	2002 CONS
Economic	59%	—	41%	55%	—	45%
Social	72%	—	27%	67%	—	29%
Foreign	65%	—	36%	57%	—	42%

Key Votes of the 107th Congress

1. Approve Bush Tax Cuts	Y	5. Faith-Based Charities	N	9. Trade Promotion Authority	N
2. Limit Patients' Bill of Rights	N	6. Bar Gays in the Boy Scouts	N	10. Bar Funds for Intl. Court	N
3. Campaign Finance Reform	Y	7. Ban Partial-Birth Abortion	N	11. Authorize Force in Iraq	Y
4. Ban ANWR Development	Y	8. Arm Commercial Pilots	Y	12. Deny Home. Sec. Dept. Union	N

Election Results

2002 general	Steve Israel (D-Ind-WF)	85,451	(58%)	($1,416,138)
	Joseph Finley (R-C-RTL)	59,117	(40%)	
	Other	1,558	(1%)	
2002 primary	Steve Israel (D)	unopposed		
2000 general	Steve Israel (D)	90,438	(48%)	($1,055,977)
	Joan B. Johnson (R)	65,880	(35%)	($1,015,225)
	Robert T. Walsh (RTL)	11,224	(6%)	($47,609)
	Richard N. Thompson (C)	10,824	(6%)	($38,967)
	David A. Bishop (Ind-Green-WF)	10,266	(5%)	($350,653)

The People		Race/Ethnic Origin	Ancestry	
Area size:	330 sq. mi.	71.5% White	Italian: 18.8%	Irish: 14.1%
Urban population:	99.7%	9.8% Black	German: 10.3%	
Rural population:	0.3%	3.0% Asian	**2000 Presidential Vote**	
Pop. 2000:	654,360	0.2% Native Am.	Gore (D)	146,723 (57%)
Median income:	$71,147	0.0% Hawaiian	Bush (R)	100,708 (39%)
Poverty status:	5.9%	1.4% Two + races	Other	8,165 (3%)
Military veterans:	10.6%	0.2% Other	**Cook Partisan Voting Index:** D + 9	
		13.9% Hispanic Origin		

Occupation	Blue collar: 20.1%	White collar: 66.3%	Gray collar: 13.6%

Shortly after World War II, hundreds of thousands of New York City residents, many of them young veterans and their families, moved to detached suburban homes built on the former potato fields of central Long Island. Those in the first wave of postwar migration settled in Nassau County, and they included a cross-section of all but the poorest New Yorkers: roughly half Catholic, a quarter Protestant and a quarter Jewish. As Long Island developed its own employment base, another wave moved further east into Suffolk County. This group was more Catholic, less Jewish and more blue-collar than the first. Ancestrally Democratic, these voters were culturally conservative, and in the 1970s and 1980s, they tended to vote Republican. But in the 1990s, voters in Suffolk County joined the rest of the New York metro area in shunning a Republican party that was being run increasingly by politicians with southern accents.

The 2d Congressional District includes most of western Suffolk County, part of the town of Islip and a small portion of Nassau County—Plainview, Woodbury and part of Jericho. For the most part, the 2d is the humbler part of Long Island: further east than most of the fashionable commuter suburbs, well south of the picturesque North Shore, not as far east as the ritzy Hamptons, and, aside from a handful of ferry-only resort towns on Fire Island, located inland from the southern shore. With some of the lowest-priced housing on the Island, this part of Long Island has been attracting young families and minorities. Brentwood—settled in 1851 as part of a free-love social experiment that lasted 13 years—is now more than half Hispanic; once a destination for Puerto Ricans, Brentwood is increasingly populated by Salvadorans, Guatemalans and Mexicans. For decades, it has been the state's largest Latino community after New York City and Yonkers. The 2d is historically Republican, and it backed its Republican congressman, Rick Lazio, in the 2000 Senate race, but in 2000 it voted solidly for Al Gore.

The congressman from the 2d District is Steve Israel, a Democrat first elected in 2000. He grew up in Wantagh and graduated from George Washington University in 1983. While in college, he worked full-time on Capitol Hill, first as a constituent correspondent for Robert Matsui of California, then as a legislative assistant for Richard Ottinger of New York. After college, Israel returned to Long Island, where he was Suffolk director for the American Jewish Congress, fund-raising director for Touro Law School and assistant for intergovernmental relations to Suffolk County Executive Patrick Halpin for three years; then he started his own public relations and marketing firm. He also was president and CEO of the Institute on the Holocaust and the Law. In 1993 Israel was the only Democrat elected to the Huntington Town Council, where he forged a reputation as a bipartisan leader who helped revive the town's finances; he eventually became majority leader.

Israel had not been planning to run until May 2000 when Rudolph Giuliani suddenly dropped out of the Senate race against Hillary Rodham Clinton and 2d District incumbent Rick Lazio announced he was running for the Senate. In the September primary, Israel faced Suffolk County Legislator David Bishop, who was better-known and a slight favorite. Bishop accused him of giving raises to Huntington employees who had volunteered for his campaign and questioned Israel's credentials and environmental record. Israel said the raises were deserved and had bipartisan support, and added that he worked to pass a $15 million bond to preserve open space in the township. Israel said that he had given Bishop his first job in politics—a claim Bishop denied. Each candidate raised more than $350,000 but Israel squeaked out a 45%–41% victory. In the general, Republican Joan Johnson had an appealing story. A 66-year old black woman who grew up in segregated Florida and moved to New York to become a schoolteacher, she would have been the first black Republican woman elected to Congress. As the elected town clerk of Islip since 1991, she had the Suffolk County party's supposed organizational muscle behind her. But, despite help from Lazio, Johnson was a disappointing candidate. She was forced to pull a TV ad attacking Israel for voting to raise taxes after Israel protested that he had opposed tax increases. Even some Republicans criticized her limited campaign skills. Israel won by a surprisingly easy 48%–35%.

In the House, Israel's voting record is moderate but a tad more liberal on cultural issues. He showed an early sign of his connections and knowledge of House politics when he was elected as the freshman on the Democratic Steering Committee and was appointed to the Financial Services Committee. But Israel has been anything but a typical New York Democrat in his legislative actions. He joined the Blue Dogs and was one of 28 House Democrats who voted for the House-Senate agreement on George W. Bush's tax cuts and supported the use of force in Iraq, but he opposed trade promotion authority. He irritated Democratic leaders by voting for the Republicans' prescription drug bill after he worked with Nancy Johnson to add a provision that increased annual Medicare payments to HMOs on Long Island that had canceled their coverage. That display of bipartisanship caused a private scolding by Minority Leader Dick Gephardt. Israel also burned some bridges when he favored Steny Hoyer over Nancy Pelosi in their contest for Minority Whip.

Israel strengthened the 2d District's Democratic base by working with legislators in Albany to exchange some of his Republican towns for Democratic towns in the adjacent 3d District. House Republican leaders urged Lazio to seek his old seat and promised that he could regain his former committee seats. When Lazio said no in March 2002, they grumbled about his delay in deciding, and quietly threw in the towel. Israel's opponent was Joe Finley, a New York City firefighter who was off duty on September 11 but worked many days in the recovery search and suffered lung damage and severe asthma symptoms. But his personal story did not compensate for his lack of political experience and Israel's 10-to-1 fundraising advantage. The Green Party nominee was John Keenan, who was a lieutenant in the New York Fire Department and was at ground zero on September 11. Israel got 58% of the vote, to 40% to Finley and 1% for Keenan. Following the election, Israel said that national Democrats should study the success of centrist Democrats on Long Island. They prevailed locally, he said, by protecting national security, balanced budgets, and civil and human rights. The party icon, Israel added, should be former Senator Scoop Jackson of Washington, not Walter Mondale—a message not likely to be embraced by many of his House Democratic colleagues.

THIRD DISTRICT

Rep. Peter King (R)

Elected 1992, 6th term; b. Apr. 5, 1944, Manhattan; home, Seaford; St. Francis Col., B.A. 1965, U. of Notre Dame, J.D. 1968; Catholic; married (Rosemary).

Military Career: Army Natl. Guard, 1968–73.

Elected Office: Hempstead Town Cncl., 1977–81; Nassau Cnty. Comptroller, 1981–92.

Professional Career: Practicing atty., 1968–72, 1978–81; Dep. Atty., Nassau Cnty., 1972–74; Exec. Asst., Nassau Cnty. Exec., 1974–76, Gen. Cnsl., 1977.

DC Office: 436 CHOB 20515, 202-225-7896; Fax: 202-226-2279; Web site: www.house.gov/king.

District Office: Massapequa Park, 516-541-4225.

Committees: *Financial Services* (7th of 37 R): Capital Markets, Insurance & Government Sponsored Enterprises; Domestic and International Monetary Policy, Trade & Technology (Chmn.); Housing & Community Opportunity. *International Relations* (11th of 26 R): Europe; International Terrorism, Nonproliferation and Human Rights. *Select Committee on Homeland Security* (19th of 27 R): Cybersecurity, Science and Research & Development; Emergency Preparedness & Response; Intelligence & Counterterrorism.

Group Ratings

	ADA	ACLU	AFS	LCV	CON	ITIC	NTU	COC	ACU	NTLC	CHC
2002	10	14	0	13	2	75	53	85	83	89	100
2001	10	—	11	29	—	—	59	83	84	—	—

National Journal Ratings

	2001 LIB —	2001 CONS		2002 LIB —	2002 CONS
Economic	41% —	60%		46% —	54%
Social	43% —	55%		0% —	75%
Foreign	21% —	74%		15% —	78%

Key Votes of the 107th Congress

1. Approve Bush Tax Cuts	*	5. Faith-Based Charities		9. Trade Promotion Authority	Y
2. Limit Patients' Bill of Rights	Y	6. Bar Gays in the Boy Scouts	Y	10. Bar Funds for Intl. Court	Y
3. Campaign Finance Reform	N	7. Ban Partial-Birth Abortion	Y	11. Authorize Force in Iraq	Y
4. Ban ANWR Development	N	8. Arm Commercial Pilots	Y	12. Deny Home. Sec. Dept. Union	Y

Election Results

2002 general	Peter King (R-C-Ind-RTL)	121,537	(72%)	($468,474)
	Stuart Finz (D)	46,022	(27%)	($137,472)
	Other	1,513	(1%)	
2002 primary	Peter King (R)	11,932	(78%)	
	Robert Previdi (R)	3,357	(22%)	
2000 general	Peter King (R-Ind-C-RTL)	143,126	(60%)	($455,110)
	Dal LaMagna (D-Green-WF)	95,787	(40%)	($285,966)
	Other	1,515	(1%)	

Prior Winning Percentages: 1998 (64%); 1996 (55%); 1994 (59%); 1992 (50%)

The People		Race/Ethnic Origin	Ancestry	
Area size:	393 sq. mi.	86.9% White	Italian: 23.1%	Irish: 17.7%
Urban population:	99.6%	2.1% Black	German: 12.0%	
Rural population:	0.4%	3.0% Asian	**2000 Presidential Vote**	
Pop. 2000:	654,361	0.1% Native Am.	Gore (D) 150,165	(52%)
Median income:	$70,561	0.0% Hawaiian	Bush (R) 127,869	(44%)
Poverty status:	4.3%	1.0% Two+ races	Other 10,251	(4%)
Military veterans:	11.8%	0.1% Other	**Cook Partisan Voting Index:** D + 4	
		6.9% Hispanic Origin		

Occupation	Blue collar: 17.0%	White collar: 69.3%	Gray collar: 13.6%

September 1947 was a pivotal moment in American history—the month when 300 families moved into 750-square-foot houses that sold for $6,990, with no money down for veterans. This was Levittown—America's first mass-produced suburb, where delivery trucks dropped off piles of pre-fabricated materials 60 feet apart, so that roving teams of specialized workers could assemble them with power tools. By the time the final house was sold for $9,500 in November 1951, "Levittown," a onetime potato field, had become synonymous with instant suburbanization. Southern State Parkway, the road that drew New York City's working- and middle-class families out to Long Island, was originally constructed in the 1920s by the legendary city-builder Robert Moses as a way of linking New Yorkers (at least those affluent enough to own a car) with the newly constructed Jones Beach State Park on Long Island. Three decades later, Moses widened the parkway to accommodate the growing ranks of long-distance commuters who populated Long Island's bedroom communities and worked in New York City. Now, a half-century later, few of the original four-room bungalows can be found, but homes here are still affordable. School enrollment has dropped, retiree workshops have proliferated, and empty nesters are common. Nassau County's population, 450,000 in 1940, zoomed to 1.3 million in 1960 and 1.4 million in 1970; but by 1990 and 2000, as the youngsters moved out, it has stabilized at 1.3 million.

Nassau County created what may have been the nation's premier county Republican machine, established before the postwar population boom. The result was one of the highest-salaried, highest-spending local governments in America—one that thrived until the late 1990s, when fiscal laxity dropped the county's credit rating to near junk-bond status, despite tax rates that were among the highest in the country. Voters rebelled in November 1999, giving Democrats their first-ever majority in the county legislature, and the following year, the state legislature approved a $105 million bailout for Nassau County, one of the most affluent parts of the state. That rebellion paralleled movement toward the national Democrats in the 1990s, as suburbanites recoiled against the Gingrich Republicans and gave majorities to Bill Clinton and Al Gore in 1996 and 2000.

The 3d Congressional District includes roughly half of Nassau County. It covers much of the southern shoreline of Long Island, taking in the old railroad resort of Long Beach, plus Baldwin, Merrick and Massapequa in Nassau County and Amityville, Lindenhurst, most of Babylon, Bay Shore and Islip in Suffolk County. From there, the 3d runs north all the way to Long Island Sound. Most of the people in the district live in towns strung along either side of Sunrise Highway or just off the Southern or Northern State Parkways: Levittown, Hicksville, Syosset and Bethpage, home to a major Northrop Grumman facility. The northern half of the district includes Oyster Bay, Old Westbury and Glen Cove, where old estates—including Sagamore Hill, the home Theodore Roosevelt built on Cold Spring Harbor in 1885, and which is now his final resting place—alternate with more modest homes built for servants and newer subdivision mansions. While few of greater New York's wealthiest live in the 3d, the overall level of affluence is high. The 3d District is the most Republican district on Long Island; it voted for Long Islander Rick Lazio in the 2000 Senate race, but it gave a plurality of its votes to Al Gore.

The congressman from the 3d District is Peter King, a Republican first elected in 1992. King grew up in Sunnyside, Queens; his parents were Irish immigrants and Democrats, his father an NYPD detective. He went to St. Francis College and law school at Notre Dame, and clerked one summer at Richard Nixon's law firm with a Long Islander named Rudolph Giuliani. After school he followed the trek to the suburbs and became part of the Nassau County Republican machine. He started working as a lawyer and staffer in county government in 1972, at 28; in 1981 he became county comptroller. When 22-year Republican Congressman Norman Lent retired in 1992, King won the Republican primary 2–1. In the general, King ran as a political insider, fiscal conservative and abortion opponent; he won by just 50%–46%. He has not faced a close reelection since then.

King has a middle-of-the-House voting record, more conservative on cultural issues, but with distinctive interests and accents. He is against abortion, racial quotas and preferences, bilingual education, gun control and the National Endowment for the Arts. He is for English-only laws and against aid to illegal immigrants. He is unapologetic about being a machine politician—he wrote a college paper on ousted New York Mayor Jimmy Walker—and seethes against campaign finance regulation proposals.

He came to the House as one of the nation's strongest supporters of the Irish Republican Army; within days of his election in 1992 he flew to Belfast to meet with leaders of Sinn Fein, the IRA's political arm. He urged the Clinton administration to drop travel and fundraising restrictions on Sinn Fein leader Gerry Adams. In the 1998 negotiations finale, King carried messages between the IRA and the Irish government. In August 1998 Clinton took him on Air Force One to Russia and Ireland and had a long late-night conversation with him. On impeachment, King was torn by party loyalty and his closeness to Clinton and support of his Northern Ireland policy. He played a visible but not pivotal role—voting for an impeachment inquiry in October, but in December worked for a censure with a financial penalty. He contended that "reform politics," which included the independent counsel law, had produced a situation that made little sense and threatened to make Republicans a minority again. He said publicly that as many as 20 Republicans were prepared to vote against impeachment; in the end only four, including King, voted against all four counts. Later, he was a rare Republican backing Clinton's military campaign in Kosovo.

King often seems more comfortable with Democrats and labor leaders—the kind of people he dealt with in Nassau County, than with southern or western Republicans. He did not support the July 1997 coup against Gingrich, on the ground that it made no sense to change leaders in mid-term.

King's efforts to secure a post in George W. Bush's cabinet went nowhere: not surprising, given King's support of John McCain in the primary, when he called Bush "politically tone-deaf" in his dealings with McCain. King supported McCain despite his previous criticism of McCain's "self-righteousness" in pushing campaign finance regulation. In early 2001, King warned Bush not to pick fights with labor unions after he threatened to intervene in an airline strike threat. After the September 11 attacks, in which 160 of his constituents died, King became more of a party regular. He pleaded for higher payments from the federal fund to the survivors of some victims. He hailed Bush's $20 billion spending pledge for New York City and state, and attacked Democrats' criticism of how that was handled. He stuck with Bush in his opposition to labor protections at the new Homeland Security Department.

Over the years, King has been a provocative presence on broadcast chat shows. "France is no longer a world power, Belgium never was and Germany started two world wars," he said in a 2003 BBC interview. Of France, he told the *New York Times*, "It seems part of their fiber to be anti-American. This ongoing struggle with terrorism could go on for 5, 10, 15 years. We're going to have to contend with France at every stage. Can we afford to have that or do we need to restructure the alliance?" He also gained attention with two novels about politics and diplomacy in Northern Ireland; Bill Clinton wrote a flattering blurb for the latest, *Deliver Us from Evil*, in which a thinly-disguised Long Island congressman is the protagonist. King sought, but with little success, to push his candidacy for the Senate seat in 2000. In redistricting, the four Long Island incumbents—there were four Republicans in 1995–96, but King is the only Republican left—agreed on new district lines that benefited all four. After the 2002 election, King talked about challenging Senator Charles Schumer in 2004. The online newsletter *Politicsny.com* offered this uncharitable assessment of his chances: "There isn't a political observer in the Empire State who doesn't want King, the most obnoxious member of the congressional delegation, to vacate his House seat and run for U.S. Senate against Chuck Schumer next year. No one (except King) thinks [he] could beat Schumer." Later, in April 2003, King announced he would not run for Senate.

FOURTH DISTRICT

Rep. Carolyn McCarthy (D)

Elected 1996, 4th term; b. Jan. 5, 1944, Brooklyn; home, Mineola; Glen Cove Nursing Schl., L.P.N. 1964; Catholic; widowed.

Professional Career: Nurse, 1964–93; Gun control activist, 1993–96.

DC Office: 106 CHOB 20515, 202-225-5516; Fax: 202-225-5758; Web site: www.house.gov/carolynmccarthy.

District Office: Garden City, 516-739-3008.

Committees: *Education & the Workforce* (8th of 22 D): 21st Century Competitiveness; Employer-Employee Relations. *Financial Services* (25th of 32 D): Capital Markets, Insurance & Government Sponsored Enterprises; Financial Institutions & Consumer Credit.

Group Ratings

	ADA	ACLU	AFS	LCV	CON	ITIC	NTU	COC	ACU	NTLC	CHC
2002	80	73	88	75	25	50	27	60	32	26	25
2001	85	—	90	93	—	—	21	48	17	—	—

National Journal Ratings

	2001 LIB	—	2001 CONS	2002 LIB	—	2002 CONS
Economic	60%	—	40%	55%	—	44%
Social	70%	—	30%	67%	—	29%
Foreign	66%	—	34%	55%	—	45%

Key Votes of the 107th Congress

1. Approve Bush Tax Cuts	Y	5. Faith-Based Charities	N	9. Trade Promotion Authority	N
2. Limit Patients' Bill of Rights	N	6. Bar Gays in the Boy Scouts	N	10. Bar Funds for Intl. Court	Y
3. Campaign Finance Reform	Y	7. Ban Partial-Birth Abortion	N	11. Authorize Force in Iraq	Y
4. Ban ANWR Development	Y	8. Arm Commercial Pilots	Y	12. Deny Home. Sec. Dept. Union	N

Election Results

2002 general	Carolyn McCarthy (D-L-Ind-WF)	94,806	(56%)	($1,794,931)
	Marilyn O'Grady (R-C-RTL)	72,882	(43%)	($318,694)
	Other	852	(1%)	
2002 primary	Carolyn McCarthy (D)	unopposed		
2000 general	Carolyn McCarthy (D-Ind-WF)	136,703	(61%)	($1,923,299)
	Gregory R. Becker (R-C-RTL)	87,830	(39%)	($269,062)
	Other	1,222	(1%)	

Prior Winning Percentages: 1998 (53%); 1996 (57%)

The People		Race/Ethnic Origin	Ancestry	
Area size:	103 sq. mi.	62.3% White	Italian: 17.5%	Irish: 12.4%
Urban population:	100.0%	17.6% Black	German: 8.0%	
Rural population:	0.0%	4.5% Asian	**2000 Presidential Vote**	
Pop. 2000:	654,360	0.1% Native Am.	Gore (D)..............156,276	(59%)
Median income:	$66,799	0.0% Hawaiian	Bush (R)...............99,263	(38%)
Poverty status:	6.4%	1.6% Two + races	Other...................8,612	(3%)
Military veterans:	9.9%	0.3% Other	**Cook Partisan Voting Index:** D +11	
		13.6% Hispanic Origin		

Occupation	Blue collar: 16.6%	White collar: 67.9%	Gray collar: 15.5%

In the mid-20th century, Nassau County changed from almost entirely rural to almost entirely suburban. One of its first suburbs was Garden City, with its wide avenues and single-family homes, laid out more than a century ago by New York retailer A.T. Stewart at a time when reformers were urging that new communities retain the commercial vitality and social interaction of the city within a setting that preserved the healthful openness of the countryside. After World War II, freeways replaced strip highways and shopping centers sprang up at intersections, but many of the middle- and upper-income residents here continue to depend on the Long Island Railroad to get them to jobs in New York City. Garden City has maintained its high real estate prices and is now surrounded by some of Nassau County's key institutions: the county seat of Mineola; Hofstra University in Hempstead; Roosevelt Field, where Charles Lindbergh took off for Paris, now a suburban shopping center; and the Nassau Coliseum, home to hockey's New York Islanders.

The 4th Congressional District includes Garden City and the towns all around. It has several suburbs just north of the Jericho Turnpike—New Hyde Park, Mineola, Westbury—as well as a large swath of southern Nassau County east of the Queens County line, and west of the Meadow-brook and Wantagh State Parkways. This territory includes communities like Uniondale, Hempstead, Rockville Center and Valley Stream, as well as the "Five Towns"—the railway suburbs of Lawrence, Inwood, Cedarhurst, Hewlett and Woodmere. Nassau County has traditionally been Republican, and both Garden City and heavily Catholic East Meadow remain that way. But the Five Towns are heavily Democratic, and about one-third of the residents here are either black or Hispanic, in places like Elmont, a community near the Queens line with a significant Caribbean and Latin American population. The 4th District has voted mostly Republican in local and state races—Rick Lazio easily won here in his race for Senate—but the 4th gave Al Gore 59% 2000; the county legislature is now led by a narrow Democratic majority. In congressional races, the 4th District elected four different congressmen in 1990s.

The congresswoman from the 4th District is Carolyn McCarthy, elected as a Democrat in 1996. She was born in Brooklyn, trained as a nurse, married and raised a family on Long Island; originally, she was a Republican. In 1993 her husband was killed and her son seriously injured in the "Long Island Railroad Massacre," when a black gunman opened fire on passengers as the train crossed the Nassau County line (he said he did not want to kill anyone in New York City lest he embarrass Mayor David Dinkins). McCarthy spoke movingly at the killer's trial and her strength in tragedy won many admirers. "You took away my husband," she said directly to him. "You took away my best friend." She began campaigning for gun control, and in 1995 lobbied her Congressman Daniel Frisa to vote against repeal of the assault weapons ban, unsuccessfully. McCarthy inquired about running against Frisa in the primary, but Nassau County Republicans discouraged this. But Democrats had been eyeing the seat for some time and recruited her. McCarthy initially knew little about politics. When told that Minority Leader Dick Gephardt wanted to meet her, she reportedly asked, "Who's Dick Gephardt?" But she learned quickly. As the Democratic nominee, she called for gun control and attacked Frisa as too close to Newt Gingrich. The political tide was going her way: House Republicans were unpopular on Long Island. Frisa disappeared in the campaign's final week, did not show up at his election night party and never made a concession statement. McCarthy won 57%–41%.

In the House, McCarthy has compiled a moderately liberal voting record and sponsored gun control measures. She called for childproof locks on handguns, fines for parents if a child gets a handgun and shows it in public, and jail terms if a crime is committed with it. She beat John Murtha's amendment to allow import of World War II-era firearms and sought to ban the sale of guns to temporary visitors to the United States. When a TV movie of McCarthy's story was broadcast, the National Rifle Association said it was inaccurate; Nassau County Republican Chairman Joseph Mondello said, "That's one hell of a campaign advertisement." But she declined a contract to write a book in time for the movie.

As she gained experience, McCarthy broadened her portfolio, using her experience as a mother and nurse to take an interest in education and health-care issues. She worked on HMO regulation with John Dingell, who had opposed her on some gun issues. She helped to reverse Medicare cutbacks for New York hospitals. She stood at the side of George W. Bush in August 2002 when he signed her bill to give incentives to hospitals in hiring more nurses and remedy the acute shortages. She worked hard and surprised people on some votes, opposing the partial-birth abortion ban and backing the use of force in Iraq. As the years passed, McCarthy also gained the expertise and patience to score modest gains in controlling guns. With support from the NRA, the House approved her bill to assist states to gain more access to the federal background check system for gun buyers. The sniper spree in the Washington D.C. area gave her the opportunity to gain voice-vote approval in the House of her bill—the Our Lady of Peace Act—to strengthen laws prohibiting the mentally ill from buying guns, again with NRA backing.

At home, Republicans have thrashed around to line up opposition. In 1998, Frisa ran early ads but withdrew from the race in July. Against 16-year Assemblyman Gregory Becker, McCarthy won 53%–47%, making her the first incumbent re-elected to this seat since 1990. In 2000 she beat him again 61%–39%. But she had a tougher time in 2002, after she failed to gain heavily Democratic Long Beach or to remove the Republican bastion of Garden City during redistricting. She was challenged by ophthalmologist Marilyn O'Grady, a first-time candidate who defeated Frisa in the primary; she took a hard line on terrorism and immigration, opposed abortions, and ran ads that attacked McCarthy for taking a 1998 contribution from Barbra Streisand. Although O'Grady received little national attention or party support, McCarthy's margin shrunk to 56%–43%. That result suggested that this district may be competitive if McCarthy retires, or perhaps sooner.

FIFTH DISTRICT

Rep. Gary Ackerman (D)

Elected Mar. 1983, 10th term; b. Nov. 19, 1942, Brooklyn; home, Jamaica Estates; Queens Col., B.A. 1965; Jewish; married (Rita).

Elected Office: NY Senate, 1978–83.

Professional Career: Jr. High schl. teacher, 1966–70; Editor & publisher, *Queens Tribune*, 1970–78; Pres., advertising agcy., 1972–78.

DC Office: 2243 RHOB 20515, 202-225-2601; Fax: 202-225-1589; Web site: www.house.gov/ackerman.

District Office: Bayside, 718-423-2154.

Committees: *Financial Services* (8th of 32 D): Capital Markets, Insurance & Government Sponsored Enterprises; Financial Institutions & Consumer Credit. *International Relations* (3d of 23 D): Asia & the Pacific; Middle East & Central Asia (RMM).

Group Ratings

	ADA	ACLU	AFS	LCV	CON	ITIC	NTU	COC	ACU	NTLC	CHC
2002	95	80	100	100	78	50	21	37	4	3	0
2001	80	—	100	100	—	—	9	35	4	—	—

National Journal Ratings

	2001 LIB	—	2001 CONS		2002 LIB	—	2002 CONS
Economic	93%	—	8%		86%	—	12%
Social	90%	—	0%		83%	—	16%
Foreign	70%	—	28%		64%	—	35%

Key Votes of the 107th Congress

1. Approve Bush Tax Cuts	*	5. Faith-Based Charities	N	9. Trade Promotion Authority	N
2. Limit Patients' Bill of Rights	N	6. Bar Gays in the Boy Scouts	N	10. Bar Funds for Intl. Court	N
3. Campaign Finance Reform	Y	7. Ban Partial-Birth Abortion	N	11. Authorize Force in Iraq	Y
4. Ban ANWR Development	Y	8. Arm Commercial Pilots	Y	12. Deny Home. Sec. Dept. Union	N

Election Results

2002 general	Gary Ackerman (D-L-Ind-WF) 68,773	(92%)	($630,086)
	Perry Reich (C) 5,718	(8%)	
2002 primary	Gary Ackerman (D) .... unopposed		
2000 general	Gary Ackerman (D-Ind-L-WF) 137,684	(68%)	($686,913)
	Edward Elkowitz (R-C) 61,084	(30%)	
	Other 3,846	(2%)	

Prior Winning Percentages: 1998 (65%); 1996 (64%); 1994 (55%); 1992 (52%); 1990 (100%); 1988 (100%); 1986 (77%); 1984 (69%); 1983 (49%)

The People		**Race/Ethnic Origin**	**Ancestry**	
Area size:	85 sq. mi.	44.2% White	Italian: 9.7%	Irish: 5.8%
Urban population:	100.0%	5.1% Black	German: 3.7%	
Rural population:	0.0%	24.5% Asian	**2000 Presidential Vote**	
Pop. 2000:	654,361	0.1% Native Am.	Gore (D)............127,288	(67%)
Median income:	$51,156	0.0% Hawaiian	Bush (R)..............56,027	(30%)
Poverty status:	12.1%	2.1% Two+ races	Other...................6,256	(3%)
Military veterans:	6.7%	0.4% Other	**Cook Partisan Voting Index:** D +19	
		23.5% Hispanic Origin		

Occupation	Blue collar: 18.2%	White collar: 65.2%	Gray collar: 16.6%

Queens is to most Americans the mystery borough, little known though it contains both LaGuardia and Kennedy airports. Some of it is almost suburban in aspect: Bayside, Douglaston and Little Neck are upper-middle income neighborhoods far beyond the subway lines, with detached houses with driveways and views across the water. Other Queens neighborhoods are more modest, with crowded houses on side streets and apartment buildings on avenues. In the past two decades, Queens has also become the number one immigrant destination in New York City and quite possibly the most diverse place in the world. Corona, the fictional home of TV's Archie Bunker, was once predominantly Italian and black (Louis Armstrong, Duke Ellington and Malcolm X lived here); today, there is a large Latin American community, with large numbers of Dominicans. Flushing, for many years a modest-income Jewish and white ethnic neighborhood is now the biggest Asian neighborhood in New York. West of 138th Street it is dominated by Taiwanese and ethnic Chinese from Malaysia, Vietnam and Thailand; shops there have a more urban, "Chinatown" feel. East of 138th Street is predominantly Korean, with development following a more suburban pattern. As Chinese businesses moved into Flushing's Main Street commercial strip, Korean storeowners moved east to Union Street, a major north-south artery, and Northern Boulevard. When Green Farm, Main Street's last remaining Korean grocery, was sold to Chinese owners in 2002, a Chinese-American weekly headlined the story, "The Last Korean Stronghold Demolished" and "Flushing Now Under Chinese Control." The area's proximity to Kennedy and LaGuardia airports has fed a boom in hotels catering to Asian businesspeople. Just east of Flushing is Flushing Meadow, the huge drainage basin and former dumping ground that hosted two World's Fairs (1939 and 1964) and which now is home to the U.S. Open tennis tournament, and countless informal soccer games played among Queens' many immigrant groups.

Just a few miles but a world away is the North Shore of Long Island. For a century it has had an upper-crust ambiance—peninsulas jutting out into Long Island Sound, the vast green lawns, and the great capitalist mansions that inspired East Egg and West Egg in *The Great Gatsby*. In the 19th century, millionaires used steam yachts to commute from Manhattan to their estates here. During Prohibition, the richest people in business and entertainment spent their leisure time playing croquet while their servants unloaded bootleggers' shipments at private docks. Inland, behind the expansive lawns, Long Island was still farm country, with little villages clustered at railroad stations, occasional colonial era houses, and acres of billboard-strewn wasteland along the highways to New York City. But by the middle of the 20th century, the city grew out, and the Great Neck and Sands Point peninsulas became affluent, predominantly Jewish suburbs with thick hedges enveloping stately Tudor homes.

The 5th Congressional District takes in this territory in Queens and suburban Nassau County.

It includes most of Queens east of Flushing Meadow and north of Union Turnpike—Flushing, Bayside, Douglaston, Little Neck (but not the airports). And it includes the northwest corner of Nassau County—Great Neck, Sands Point, and Lake Success, Port Washington, and Kings Point, home of the U.S. Merchant Marine Academy. Before the 2002 redistricting, Flushing was split between three congressional districts; now most of it is in the 5th District, whose population is 25% Asian and 24% Hispanic. Both the Queens and Nassau County portions of the district have long voted heavily Democratic, but the future voting preferences of Asian and Hispanic voters are somewhat unclear.

The congressman from the 5th District is Gary Ackerman, a Democrat first elected in a 1983 special election. Ackerman grew up in Flushing, taught junior high school, ran an advertising agency, started the weekly *Queens Tribune* in 1970 and sold it to publisher Jerry Finkelstein in 1978 (and then was part of an investment group that repurchased it in 2002). That same year he was elected to the New York Senate, where Democrats remain the permanent minority. He won his seat in the House in a special election from a district that was then centered in the heavily Jewish apartment complexes in central Queens. Ackerman is a colorful character, who always wears a white carnation and lives on a houseboat in Washington (the *Unsinkable II*, successor to the *Unsinkable I*, which sunk); he hosts an annual "Taste of New York" fundraiser, featuring pastrami sandwiches and stuffed cabbage, with waiters imported from New York. Acerbic but humorous, he is a pungent speaker, with a humor that makes even opponents smile. During the impeachment inquiry debate, frustrated by time limits, he rose and said, "I move that when the House adjourn, we do so to Salem, a quaint village in the Commonwealth of Massachusetts whose history beckons us thence."

Ackerman has a penchant for taking on worthy but neglected causes, though his once solidly liberal voting record has moderated on foreign policy issues. When Democrats held the majority and he chaired the Asia and the Pacific Subcommittee, Ackerman was one of the first Americans to meet with North Korean dictator Kim Il Sung. As chairman of the congressional India Caucus, he encouraged interest and support for that nation. On domestic issues, he helped to pass the "Baby AIDS" bill requiring HIV testing of newborns and disclosure of the results to the mother; the bill also bars insurers from terminating coverage because of AIDS test results. Manhattan liberals had opposed this measure, although many HIV-positive newborns can be saved if identified in time; it took some backbone for Ackerman to brave the wrath of New York's left wing. He worked with Republicans to stop the Center for Disease Control from opposing this and secured funding to assist states in AIDS testing. Still, he occasionally stands out as a lonely liberal, as when he was one of only three members to vote against a House resolution criticizing a federal appeals court that ruled unconstitutional the phrase "under God" in the Pledge of Allegiance.

Ackerman has also looked after North Shore and Queens issues. He opposed the inane postal regulation that requires Queens zip codes to be labeled only Jamaica, Long Island City, Flushing or Far Rockaway rather than the dozens of other community names or simply Queens. After the September 11 attacks, he criticized the Bush Administration as too slow to deliver money to New York City. But he was more supportive in 2002 of Bush's handling of the Israeli-Palestinian conflict and the conflict with Iraq, and he worked with Tom DeLay and Roy Blunt to impose sanctions against Yasir Arafat.

Ackerman survived redistricting in 1992 when it moved him farther out on Long Island and into a district where two other incumbents also lived; both of them retired. Ackerman did better in the 2002 redistricting, even though he has few friends in Albany and everyone expected that his district could easily have been sliced up among its neighbors; population increase in the immigrant neighborhoods made the slicing up more difficult. The only threat to his incumbency is the possibility of a candidacy late in the decade from immigrant communities.

SIXTH DISTRICT

Rep. Gregory Meeks (D)

Elected Feb. 1998, 3d term; b. Sept. 25, 1953, Harlem; home, Far Rockaway; Adelphi U., B.A., 1975, Howard U., J.D., 1978; Baptist; married (Simone-Marie).

Elected Office: NY Assembly, 1992–98.

Professional Career: Asst. Dist. Atty., Queens Co., NY, 1978–84; NY St. Comm. of Investigations, 1984–85; Judge, NY St. Workers Compensation Bd., 1985–92.

DC Office: 1710 LHOB 20515, 202-225-3461; Fax: 202-226-4169; Web site: www.house.gov/meeks.

District Offices: Far Rockaway, 718-327-9791; Richmond Hill, 718-738-4200; St. Albans, 718-949-5600.

Committees: *Financial Services* (12th of 32 D): Capital Markets, Insurance & Government Sponsored Enterprises; Financial Institutions & Consumer Credit. *International Relations* (12th of 23 D): Africa; Asia & the Pacific.

Group Ratings

	ADA	ACLU	AFS	LCV	CON	ITIC	NTU	COC	ACU	NTLC	CHC
2002	85	83	100	88	43	38	24	45	4	8	0
2001	85	—	100	86	—	—	13	36	5	—	—

National Journal Ratings

	2001 LIB —	2001 CONS	2002 LIB —	2002 CONS
Economic	76%	24%	63%	36%
Social	90%	0%	81%	18%
Foreign	85%	15%	93%	6%

Key Votes of the 107th Congress

1. Approve Bush Tax Cuts	N	5. Faith-Based Charities	N	9. Trade Promotion Authority	N
2. Limit Patients' Bill of Rights	N	6. Bar Gays in the Boy Scouts	*	10. Bar Funds for Intl. Court	N
3. Campaign Finance Reform	Y	7. Ban Partial-Birth Abortion	N	11. Authorize Force in Iraq	N
4. Ban ANWR Development	Y	8. Arm Commercial Pilots	Y	12. Deny Home. Sec. Dept. Union	N

Election Results

2002 general	Gregory Meeks (D-L-WF)	72,799	(97%)	($502,178)
	Other	2,632	(3%)	
2002 primary	Gregory Meeks (D)	unopposed		
2000 general	Gregory Meeks (D-WF)	unopposed		($313,591)

Prior Winning Percentages: 1998 (100%); 1998 (57%)

The People		Race/Ethnic Origin	Ancestry	
Area size:	46 sq. mi.	12.8% White	West Indian: 15.9%	Italian: 3.4%
Urban population:	100.0%	52.1% Black	USA: 3.0%	
Rural population:	0.0%	8.9% Asian	**2000 Presidential Vote**	
Pop. 2000:	654,361	0.5% Native Am.	Gore (D)	145,684 (87%)
Median income:	$43,546	0.1% Hawaiian	Bush (R)	17,632 (10%)
Poverty status:	14.5%	6.1% Two + races	Other	4,874 (3%)
Military veterans:	6.2%	2.6% Other	**Cook Partisan Voting Index:** D +39	
		16.9% Hispanic Origin		
Occupation	Blue collar: 20.5%	White collar: 57.4%	Gray collar: 22.1%	

The eastern edge of Queens has been an important transportation hub for New York for almost 250 years. In the 1750s, the British laid out what is now Jamaica Avenue to help them defend Long Island. In the 1830s—nearly a century before most present-day commuters would have guessed—the Long Island Rail Road was built here. Today, this corner of Queens is sliced through by the Belt Parkway and the Van Wyck Expressway—two integral parts of Robert Moses' mid-century highway network—and is home to the bustling John F. Kennedy International Airport, one of the leading ports of entry for overseas air travelers entering the United States. Jamaica is so well situated with transportation links that officials have worked mightily to improve its commercial vitality, after a decline hastened by the construction of regional shopping centers in Queens and Long Island. Beginning in the 1970s, the old elevated subway line on Jamaica Avenue was removed and buried underground, so that shoppers could have a less claustrophobic experience.

This part of Queens—rather than Harlem or Brooklyn—is home to New York City's largest collection of middle-class black homeowners. The neighborhoods of Springfield Gardens and Laurelton, St. Albans and Rosedale, Cambria Heights and Queens Village consist of block upon block of low-rise, frame and brick houses built mostly from the 1920s to the 1950s. There was a small black community in South Jamaica half a century ago, and since then many black families have bought houses and raised their families in neighborhoods that fan out east from Jamaica. They fought to maintain the relatively spacious streets, relishing the light in their windows, the safe schools and the good neighborhood stores; these areas never experienced the kind of riots that damaged Harlem and parts of Brooklyn.

The 6th Congressional District contains all of these southeast Queens neighborhoods, plus others less affluent and orderly, in southern Queens. It is bounded on the north, more or less, by the Jackie Robinson Parkway, on the east by the Nassau County line and on the west by Cross Bay Boulevard; to the south it includes part of the Rockaway Peninsula across Jamaica Bay from the rest of Queens. Richmond Hill and Ozone Park, previously white ethnic neighborhoods, now have sizable numbers of Latinos and South Asians. South Ozone Park is home to many immigrants from Guyana, Jamaica, Haiti, the Dominican Republic and Trinidad and Tobago. The Rockaway portions of the district, despite being just a few blocks from the beach, are a relatively undeveloped backwater, leveled by urban renewal in the late 1960s but never rebuilt, and now home to half of Queens' nursing homes; a quarter of its residents on public assistance. As a whole, the 6th is 52% black, 17% Hispanic and 9% Asian; if there is a common denominator, it is the amount of time 6th District residents spend traveling to work. The district is ranked as the nation's worst for commuters—at 48 minutes of mean travel time to work. Politically, the district is again among the nation's leaders. George W. Bush won just 10 percent here in 2000; only four districts gave him a lower percentage of the vote. Democrats here regularly win by a 9–1 margin.

The congressman from the 6th District is Gregory Meeks, a Democrat elected in 1998 to replace 11-year incumbent Floyd Flake, who resigned to devote more time to his church. Meeks grew up in Harlem, in public housing projects. After graduating from college and law school, he moved to Far Rockaway and pursued a public sector career. He became an assistant district attorney in 1978, a staffer for the Committee on Investigations in 1984, a workmen's comp judge in 1985; after losing a race for City Council in 1991, he was elected assemblyman in 1992. He became an ally of Flake, an extraordinary minister whose Allen A.M.E. Church congregation grew from 1,400 members in 1976 to 12,000 in 2000, built community schools, hundreds of housing units and encouraged private sector investment in the community.

Flake supported Meeks to succeed him, though the party's initial favorite was state Senator Alton Waldon, who lost to Flake in the 1986 Democratic primary. At the January 1998 endorsement meetings Meeks won a bare majority of committeemen and this became the Democratic nominee. Waldon ran on the Conservative and Independence lines, and spent $100,000; Assemblywoman Barbara Clark ran an independent candidacy and Republicans had a candidate as well. But Meeks had support from Flake, City Controller (now state Comptroller) Alan Hevesi, Congressman Charles Rangel, Al Sharpton and Jesse Jackson. He won with 57%, to 21% for Waldon, 13% for Clark, and 9% for Republican Celestine Miller.

Meeks got Flake's seat on the Financial Services Committee and developed a liberal voting record, though a bit more moderate on economic issues. In 2000, Meeks emerged as a player. As one of the final undecideds on PNTR with China, both sides lobbied him furiously. Various factors finally convinced him to support the deal: vigorous lobbying by Rangel and Bill Clinton; support by United Parcel Service, a major employer at Kennedy airport; a White House-sponsored trip to China where he met with senior officials and saw first-hand the economic growth; plus a last-minute agreement by the White House and Speaker Dennis Hastert to extend tax breaks and public investment to distressed urban and rural areas. But he opposed trade promotion authority, and he opposed the Iraq war resolution.

When it became clear that several party leadership positions would come up after the 2002 election, he campaigned to be vice-chairman of the Democratic Caucus. His initial approach was to claim a base among minority members, but he was forced to abandon that strategy when James Clyburn of South Carolina, the former chairman of the Congressional Black Caucus, entered the contest. Meeks then emphasized his youth and openness to a variety of viewpoints within the Caucus. But on the first ballot, Clyburn won 95 votes to 56 for Meeks and 53 for Zoe Lofgren of California. Meeks could have forced a second ballot but he decided to bow to the inevitable and avoid further divisiveness.

At home, Meeks helped to secure public and private support for a new aeronautics trade school in Far Rockaway to prepare workers for jobs at Kennedy Airport. He also worked with local officials to encourage investment in downtown Jamaica. Meeks has been reelected three times without major-party opposition, and redistricting appears to have left him in strong shape in this district. Some expect him to run for mayor some day.

SEVENTH DISTRICT

Rep. Joseph Crowley (D)

Elected 1998, 3d term; b. Mar. 16, 1962, Elmhurst, NY; home, Elmhurst; C.U.N.Y. Queens College, B.A. 1985; Catholic; married (Kasey).

Elected Office: NY Assembly, 1986–98.

DC Office: 312 CHOB 20515, 202-225-3965; Fax: 202-225-1909; Web site: www.house.gov/crowley.

District Offices: Bronx, 718-931-1400; Co-op City, 718-320-2390; Jackson Heights, 718-779-1400.

Committees: *Chief Deputy Minority Whip. Financial Services* (21st of 32 D): Capital Markets, Insurance & Government Sponsored Enterprises; Financial Institutions & Consumer Credit; Oversight & Investigations. *International Relations* (14th of 23 D): International Terrorism, Nonproliferation and Human Rights; Middle East & Central Asia.

Group Ratings

	ADA	ACLU	AFS	LCV	CON	ITIC	NTU	COC	ACU	NTLC	CHC
2002	95	60	100	100	84	38	18	50	8	6	8
2001	80	—	100	86	—	—	11	43	20	—	—

National Journal Ratings

	2001 LIB —	2001 CONS	2002 LIB —	2002 CONS
Economic	68%	32%	64%	35%
Social	65%	34%	72%	27%
Foreign	69%	31%	71%	28%

Key Votes of the 107th Congress

1. Approve Bush Tax Cuts	N	5. Faith-Based Charities	N	9. Trade Promotion Authority	N
2. Limit Patients' Bill of Rights	N	6. Bar Gays in the Boy Scouts	N	10. Bar Funds for Intl. Court	N
3. Campaign Finance Reform	Y	7. Ban Partial-Birth Abortion	Y	11. Authorize Force in Iraq	Y
4. Ban ANWR Development	Y	8. Arm Commercial Pilots	N	12. Deny Home. Sec. Dept. Union	N

Election Results

2002 general	Joseph Crowley (D-WF)	50,967	(73%)	($837,900)
	Kevin Brawley (R-C)	18,572	(27%)	
2002 primary	Joseph Crowley (D)	unopposed		
2000 general	Joseph Crowley (D)	78,207	(72%)	($657,359)
	Rose Robles Birtley (R)	24,592	(23%)	($20,776)
	Other	6,302	(6%)	

Prior Winning Percentages: 1998 (69%)

The People		Race/Ethnic Origin	Ancestry	
Area size:	42 sq. mi.	27.6% White	Italian: 9.6%	Irish: 5.0%
Urban population:	100.0%	16.5% Black	West Indian: 3.6%	
Rural population:	0.0%	12.8% Asian	**2000 Presidential Vote**	
Pop. 2000:	654,360	0.2% Native Am.	Gore (D)...............114,365	(75%)
Median income:	$36,990	0.0% Hawaiian	Bush (R)................31,682	(21%)
Poverty status:	17.7%	2.7% Two+ races	Other....................6,236	(4%)
Military veterans:	6.4%	0.6% Other	**Cook Partisan Voting Index:** D +28	
		39.5% Hispanic Origin		

Occupation	Blue collar: 21.1%	White collar: 57.4%	Gray collar: 21.6%

Over the last two decades, hundreds of thousands of immigrants have been moving into many of New York City's modest neighborhoods—neighborhoods that had been emptying out as the children of the immigrants who came to New York between 1890 and 1924 died or moved to the suburbs or Florida. These are places which affluent New Yorkers and traveling journalists seldom see as they whiz by on freeways to destinations in Manhattan—rather, these are the neighborhoods pop star Jennifer Lopez sings about. Most of the housing here was built in the decades after 1910, when the subways first started connecting these neighborhoods with job sites in Manhattan. You can find many of these neighborhoods in the East Bronx, off the Bruckner Expressway and near the cluster of highways north of the Bronx-Whitestone Bridge—places like Bruckner, Morris Park, Schuylerville, and Throgs Neck. The district includes the Hunts Point meat and produce markets, where some of the nation's toniest restaurants handpick their daily provisions. Increasingly these neighborhoods are full of Latinos, many from Puerto Rico, but many also from the Dominican Republic and other Caribbean and Latin countries. Lopez hails from Castle Hill; her *On the 6* debut album is a reference to the Number 6 train that whisked her to Manhattan auditions. Here are two massive apartment projects: Parkchester, built just after World War II by Metropolitan Life Insurance in the center of the Bronx, and Co-op City, built in the late 1960s by a consortium of labor unions on marshy land near Eastchester Bay. Out past the bay is City Island, a Cape Cod-like resort area with boatmakers and plenty of fish restaurants; it is hard to believe here that you are in New York City.

The Queens section of the 7th includes some of the most polyglot neighborhoods in New York—Jackson Heights, home to Little India and a sizable Latino community; Elmhurst, a place so diverse that one local high school counts students from 100 different countries who speak 57 different languages; and Woodside, a long-settled Irish enclave that now has residents from 49 nations who speak 34 languages. These are the places serviced by Number 7 elevated line, famously dissed by former Atlanta Braves pitcher John Rocker—you can find Pakistanis and Peruvians, Koreans and Dominicans, Indians and Filipinos, Mexicans and Bangladeshis. The district is polyglot indeed: its population is 17% black, 40% Hispanic and 13% Asian. Politically, the 7th District votes heavily Democratic in presidential and congressional elections. But more important for its political future may be those who didn't vote at all in 2000 and 2002. In 2002 only 69,000 people voted in this district of 654,000, not much more than half the 127,000 who voted in the next-door mostly Manhattan 14th District.

The congressman from the 7th District is Joseph Crowley, a Democrat elected in 1998 and effectively chosen by one man, his predecessor Tom Manton, the boss of the Queens County Democratic Party. Crowley grew up in Woodside, where his family was involved in politics; his uncle Walter Crowley was elected to succeed Manton on the City Council in 1984. When Walter

Crowley died in 1985, Crowley wanted to succeed him, though he was only 23; Manton chose his chief of staff, Walter McCaffrey, instead. In 1986 Assemblyman Ralph Goldstein from Elmhurst died; Crowley ran and, with support from Manton, won at 24, fresh from Queens College. He chaired the Racing and Waging Committee, working to revive harness racing and to get the city's Off-track Betting Corporation to make a profit (only the New York public sector could produce a bookie that loses money). Crowley was interested in Irish affairs and sponsored the law that requires public school students to be taught about the Irish potato famine. He supported legalized casino gambling and higher police pay; he opposed abortion. He played guitar and sang tenor with the Budget Blues Boys, a group of assemblymen who performed on cold Albany nights.

Crowley's elevation to Congress came suddenly. In 1998, Manton filed for re-election by the July 16 filing deadline. Then at 11 a.m. on July 21, he convened a meeting of Queens Democratic committeemen, announced he was retiring and got them to vote in Crowley as the Democratic nominee. Other potential candidates were not notified ahead of time and were naturally miffed, but quickly accepted the reality. Manton was unapologetic: "After 29 years of service, I have the right to decide when I'm going to leave." He argued that Crowley, at 36, was in a good position to accumulate seniority and power in Washington. Crowley was plainly delighted: "What you're hearing is not so much about the process, but sour grapes. What happened here is simply that I was offered an ice cream cone, and I took it." His Republican opponent had no money and no chance. Crowley won in November 69%–26%.

Once elected, Crowley voted with moderate Democrats and he demonstrated his legislative experience. He served six months as the freshman Democrats' class president, which gave him entry into party leadership circles. Despite his opposition to abortion, he worked to restore $25 million in family planning funds for the United Nations. Recounting his crowded local schools, he was a leader in Democrats' efforts to increase funding for school construction. He sought to ban gun sales on the Internet. The funds he brought home included $30 million to reduce aircraft noise in neighborhoods surrounding LaGuardia and Kennedy airports, plus $10 million for New York City's Housing Opportunities for People with AIDS. But he caused grumbling within the local delegation when he rushed to take credit for House approval of $10 million for Long Island Rail Road's East Side Access project. The September 11 attacks struck a grievous blow to Crowley's community, with the loss of many local firefighters, including his first cousin, who was a battalion chief.

Still bitter about how Crowley won the 1998 election, several Queens Democrats threatened to challenge him in the 2000 primary. But City Councilman Walter McCaffrey, the only one to actually file, withdrew in July at the prompting of party leaders after disclosures that he had spent campaign money for personal expenses. Crowley again defeated a token Republican opponent. Before the 2000 Census figures came in, many thought that Crowley's district would be divided among its neighbors; its convoluted shape made this easy, Crowley had little seniority and Manton had unsuccessfully sought to oust Assembly Speaker Sheldon Silver, who with Pataki and state Senate President Joseph Bruno would, if they could agree, draw the lines. But the Census figures showed big population growth in immigrant neighborhoods and the 7th District, with the same population as all the others in 1990, in 2000 was had the highest population of any district in the state. Redistricters abandoned the idea of eliminating a City district. Silver did not give Crowley an ideal district, however. In the old district, Queens cast 74% of the votes and the Bronx only 26%. In the new district in 2002, the Bronx cast 62% and Queens 38%. But Crowley had no primary opponent in 2002 and was reelected easily.

After the election, Minority Whip Steny Hoyer named Crowley one of eight chief deputy whips, which was partly a reward for his extensive campaigning for Democratic candidates across the nation; Crowley had supported Hoyer for Minority Whip against Nancy Pelosi in October 2001.

EIGHTH DISTRICT

Rep. Jerrold Nadler (D)

Elected 1992, 6th term; b. June 13, 1947, Brooklyn; home, Manhattan; Columbia U., B.A. 1970, Fordham U., J.D. 1978; Jewish; married (Joyce Miller).

Elected Office: NY Assembly, 1976–92.

Professional Career: Legis. Asst., NY Assembly, 1972; Law Clerk, 1976.

DC Office: 2334 RHOB 20515, 202-225-5635; Fax: 202-225-6923; Web site: www.house.gov/nadler.

District Offices: Brooklyn, 718-373-3198; Manhattan, 212-367-7350.

Committees: *Judiciary* (4th of 16 D): Commercial & Administrative Law; The Constitution (RMM). *Transportation & Infrastructure* (7th of 34 D): Highways, Transit & Pipelines; Railroads; Water Resources & Environment.

Group Ratings

	ADA	ACLU	AFS	LCV	CON	ITIC	NTU	COC	ACU	NTLC	CHC
2002	95	93	100	63	73	25	21	26	0	3	0
2001	95	—	100	100	—	—	13	26	0	—	—

National Journal Ratings

	2001 LIB	—	2001 CONS		2002 LIB	—	2002 CONS
Economic	95%	—	0%		92%	—	7%
Social	90%	—	0%		83%	—	17%
Foreign	96%	—	0%		90%	—	8%

Key Votes of the 107th Congress

1. Approve Bush Tax Cuts	N	5. Faith-Based Charities	N	9. Trade Promotion Authority	N
2. Limit Patients' Bill of Rights	N	6. Bar Gays in the Boy Scouts	N	10. Bar Funds for Intl. Court	N
3. Campaign Finance Reform	Y	7. Ban Partial-Birth Abortion	N	11. Authorize Force in Iraq	N
4. Ban ANWR Development	Y	8. Arm Commercial Pilots	Y	12. Deny Home. Sec. Dept. Union	N

Election Results

2002 general	Jerrold Nadler (D-L-WF)	81,002	(76%)	($684,568)
	Jim Farrin (R-Ind)	19,674	(18%)	($64,595)
	Other	5,805	(5%)	
2002 primary	Jerrold Nadler (D)	unopposed		
2000 general	Jerrold Nadler (D-L-WF)	150,273	(81%)	($484,835)
	Marian S. Henry (R)	27,057	(15%)	
	Other	7,639	(4%)	

Prior Winning Percentages: 1998 (86%); 1996 (82%); 1994 (82%); 1992 (81%); 1992 (100%)

The People		Race/Ethnic Origin	Ancestry	
Area size:	28 sq. mi.	68.7% White	Italian: 8.7%	Russian: 7.2%
Urban population:	100.0%	5.4% Black	Irish: 5.7%	
Rural population:	0.0%	11.0% Asian	**2000 Presidential Vote**	
Pop. 2000:	654,360	0.1% Native Am.	Gore (D) 162,240	(74%)
Median income:	$47,061	0.0% Hawaiian	Bush (R) 39,280	(18%)
Poverty status:	18.7%	2.5% Two+ races	Other 18,448	(8%)
Military veterans:	5.1%	0.5% Other	**Cook Partisan Voting Index:** D +30	
		11.7% Hispanic Origin		

Occupation	Blue collar: 10.1%	White collar: 79.2%	Gray collar: 10.7%

Over the course of the 20th century, New York City spread so far beyond its origins in lower Manhattan that, for a while, it became easy to forget how pivotal the southern end of the island had been in making the city what it is today. That all changed in an instant, on the morning of

September 11, 2001, when Al Qaeda terrorists flew two hijacked jets into the twin towers of the World Trade Center, killing approximately 2,800 people, and laying waste to at least 13 blocks. The target was chosen deliberately: The terrorists struck the tallest buildings in America's biggest city, toppling a complex whose name embodied the reach of American capitalism. Lower Manhattan has long been home to Wall Street and the Financial District, but over the years it has embodied America's striving spirit in other ways as well. The Brooklyn Bridge, begun in 1867 just a few blocks east of the Twin Towers site and completed in 1883, was half again as long as any bridge then standing, and seven times higher than any buildings in the adjoining boroughs. The Holland Tunnel, built in 1927, was the first underwater vehicular tunnel built anywhere in the world. Just offshore stands Ellis Island, where members of the great immigration wave first set foot on American soil, and the Statue of Liberty, the symbol of freedom they saw as they sailed in.

The 8th Congressional District includes all of these places. From the Battery, at the very southern tip of Manhattan Island, the 8th spreads out in two directions, north and south. As the 8th District moves up the west side of Manhattan, it takes in the Financial District; Battery Park City, the attractive modern apartments built on infill west of the now-torn down West Side Highway; the artist lofts of TriBeCa and SoHo, in former warehouses and factories; Greenwich Village and Chelsea, New York's leading gay areas and strong voting blocs; Clinton, the new, economically diverse incarnation of the old slum Hell's Kitchen; the Theater District and the recently cleaned-up Times Square; and long stretches of the Upper West Side, including Lincoln Center and the American Museum of Natural History, as far north as West 89th Street. South from the Battery, the 8th crosses into Brooklyn, running along the Brooklyn waterfront before taking in the inland neighborhood of Borough Park and the waterside enclaves of Sea Gate, Brighton Beach and Coney Island, once known as the world's largest playground.

In both halves of the 8th District, there is a strong Jewish heritage. The city's Dutch founders came from the European country then most tolerant of Jews. German Jews came to New York in large numbers in the 19th century, with many considering themselves more German than Jewish; a few founded merchant banking, retail and clothing empires. Around 1890, Ashkenazi Jews from Eastern Europe began arriving from Poland, Lithuania, Belarus, Ukraine, Hungary and Romania. In the years after World War I, as many as 400,000 Jews a year debarked at Ellis Island, until a 1924 law virtually shut down immigration. Had a malapportioned, rural-dominated, nativist Congress not done that, perhaps two million of the six million who perished in the Holocaust would instead have become Americans. Ashkenazi Jews initially lived on the Lower East Side but moved out to Brooklyn and the Bronx almost as soon as the subways were built. Their children moved up faster than any new group in memory, despite widespread prejudice in the professions and in educational institutions. They invented new businesses, from the rag trade to show biz: second-caste people from third-rate countries almost immediately becoming elite in the world's foremost country. Their descendants live all over the country, but New York remains America's most heavily Jewish city and has the largest Jewish population of any city in the world.

One big voting area of the 8th is the Upper West Side: the venerable apartments along Central Park West, West End Avenue and Riverside Drive, and the brownstones on the cross streets which house some of America's most idealistic and dedicated liberals (and radicals). These professional people—lovingly satirized on *Seinfeld,* the long-running sitcom that resonated far beyond Manhattan—include a mix of the wealthy and less-affluent intellectuals. In the 1950s, West Siders took up the reform banner and eviscerated the old Tammany Hall Democratic machine; in the 1960s, they fought the Vietnam War and helped oust a Democratic administration. Another big voting area is Greenwich Village, which in the 1910s was America's original Bohemia, now with a mix of expensive apartments and cheaper dwellings. Politically, the Village has long had a taste for what it regards as radical (as did the Lower East Side when it was heavily Jewish), though some of its ideas are now mainstream, such as the historic-preservation and urbanist policies developed in the Village's successful fight against a proposed lower Manhattan expressway, led by *The Death and Life of Great American Cities* author Jane Jacobs.

The Brooklyn part of the district is probably more Jewish than the Manhattan part. Brighton Beach and Coney Island house the largest concentration of recent Russian Jewish immigrants in

New York. Here you can see Cyrillic as well as Roman letters on store signs; Borough Park has one of the nation's largest Orthodox communities, with many living close to poverty. The 8-block shopping district along Brighton Beach Avenue hosts a handful of furriers catering to the decided preference among Russian women for fur coats. The political attitudes in these neighborhoods are quite different from those of most American Jews, who are liberal on both cultural and economic issues. The Russians favor free enterprise and are anti-socialist. The Hasidic Jews of Borough Park are conservative, hostile to racial preferences and favor tough police treatment of crime. Still, voters in these two areas tend to register as Democrats and to vote Democratic in most, though not all, elections.

The congressman from the 8th District is Jerrold Nadler, a West Side liberal Democrat elected in 1992. He was born in Brooklyn and moved around; his father was a chicken farmer in New Jersey, ran a gas station on Long Island and owned a traveling auto parts store. At Columbia he campaigned for Eugene McCarthy and was there during the 1968 campus riots. He worked as a legislative staffer and ran for the Assembly in 1976, at 29; in the primary he beat Ruth Messinger (the Democratic nominee for mayor in 1997) by 73 votes. In the Assembly, he became an expert on mass transit and advocate of rail freight into New York City. In 1992 he was suddenly presented with the opportunity to run for Congress. Two incumbents were based in the new 8th District. Stephen Solarz of Brooklyn, a lead backer of the Gulf War resolution, shied away from running in leftish Manhattan, and ran and lost in the Hispanic-majority 12th District. That left the 8th to Manhattan's Ted Weiss, long an Upper West Side icon. But he died the day before the September primary, which he won anyway. The nomination was decided by a convention of almost 1,000 county Democratic committee members, many of them involved in acerbic ideological and personal squabbles for decades. The key vote was procedural, for a system of weighted voting under which Nadler won 62% of the votes and Councilwoman Ronnie Eldridge 21%; opponents decried this system (after they lost), perhaps with reason. Nadler became the Democratic nominee and thus congressman. He has not been seriously challenged since.

Nadler's voting record has been among the most liberal in the House. Over the opposition of John Dingell, he pushed to passage the "Nadler rule" which restricted ranking members on full committees from taking any ranking subcommittee posts on their panels as well. He opposed the bankruptcy bill, saying its tighter restrictions were "a wish list of every big money special interest group." Although his district includes Wall Street, he strongly opposes individual investment accounts in Social Security. As ranking Democrat on the Constitution Subcommittee, he opposed Republican advocacy of constitutional amendments to overturn court rulings. He also has been a leading foe of abortion restrictions, including legislation designed to give legal standing to the fetus.

On local issues, he successfully fought developer Donald Trump's attempts to alter the West Side Highway to accommodate his luxury housing project on old rail yards between 59th and 72d Streets. (In a book, Trump termed Nadler "one of the most egregious hacks in contemporary politics.") He fought to get more rail competition east of the Hudson, and worked to save Amtrak. His greatest project is a rail-freight tunnel under the Hudson, from the 65th Street rail yard in Bay Ridge to little-used rail yards in either Bayonne, New Jersey or Staten Island. Lack of a rail-freight line means that New York gets only about 3% of its freight by rail, compared to 30% in the average large city; cheaper freight could lower consumer prices, help rebuild small manufacturing in New York and could revive the Brooklyn docks, which Governor Nelson Rockefeller abandoned in the 1960s when vessels began the switch to container cargo. The cost would be huge—more than $2 billion—but it could provide a way upward for the city's economy and its hundreds of thousands of new immigrants. Nadler's proposal was ridiculed for years, but he persisted. In 2001 and 2002, he got $12 million for a two-year design and environmental study of the tunnel. Mayor Rudolph Giuliani endorsed it, and others have come to appreciate it as well. Nadler made funding of the tunnel his top priority for the huge transportation bill in the 108th Congress; if it is built, it would be an impressive monument for a career.

As the representative of Ground Zero, Nadler found that his work life became both sad and frenetic. When the second airplane struck the tower, he rushed to catch a 10 a.m. train from Washington to Manhattan; after delays en route, he finally arrived at 6 p.m. to view a scene of emptiness that he later called "surrealistic." He worked with city, state and federal officials and local business leaders to identify immediate needs and then to secure $20 billion for the clean-up and eventual rebuilding. He immediately sponsored a law to expedite federal payments to families of public safety officers killed in the attack. On September 14 he formed the Ground Zero Elected Official Task Force to identify and assist residents in the "frozen zone" of Lower Manhattan. With Nydia Velazquez, he got $550 million in Community Development Block Grants earmarked for small businesses in the area that were unable to repay loans. With conservative Republican Don Manzullo, he co-sponsored the Father Mychal Judge Act to allow beneficiaries outside of a safety officer's immediate family to get federal death benefits. Always persistent, he did not lose his New Yorker sense of outrage, as when he learned that local employees of the Environmental Protection Agency approved more professional cleaning of their offices in Lower Manhattan than they recommended for residents trying to cope with the aftermath of the disaster. But, as a member of the Judiciary Committee, he vigorously opposed major legislation that the White House sought after the attack, including the USA Patriot Act (because he felt it threatened civil liberties). He opposed the Iraq war resolution in October 2002.

Nadler has been reelected without difficulty. Proving that he still has good connections in Albany, he managed to survive redistricting with the Manhattan-Brooklyn district largely intact. Following the 2002 election, Nadler disclosed that in August he had stomach-reduction surgery to force a severe reduction in his appetite; in three months he lost 60 pounds.

NINTH DISTRICT

Rep. Anthony Weiner (D)

Elected 1998, 3d term; b. Sept. 4, 1964, Brooklyn; home, Brooklyn; S.U.N.Y. Plattsburgh, B.A. 1985; Jewish; single.

Elected Office: NY City Cncl., 1991–98.

Professional Career: Aide, U.S. Rep. Charles Schumer, 1985–91.

DC Office: 1122 LHOB 20515, 202-225-6616; Fax: 202-226-7253; Web site: www.house.gov/weiner.

District Offices: Brooklyn, 718-520-9001; Kew Gardens, 718-520-9001; Rockaway, 718-318-9255.

Committees: *Judiciary* (14th of 16 D): Commercial & Administrative Law; Courts, the Internet & Intellectual Property. *Science* (19th of 22 D): Space & Aeronautics. *Transportation & Infrastructure* (28th of 34 D): Aviation; Highways, Transit & Pipelines.

Group Ratings

	ADA	ACLU	AFS	LCV	CON	ITIC	NTU	COC	ACU	NTLC	CHC
2002	100	87	100	100	79	50	21	32	8	6	0
2001	95	—	100	100	—	—	11	35	0	—	—

National Journal Ratings

	2001 LIB — 2001 CONS		2002 LIB — 2002 CONS	
Economic	88%	— 11%	85%	— 14%
Social	83%	— 11%	74%	— 19%
Foreign	86%	— 12%	74%	— 26%

Key Votes of the 107th Congress

1. Approve Bush Tax Cuts	N	5. Faith-Based Charities	N	9. Trade Promotion Authority	N
2. Limit Patients' Bill of Rights	N	6. Bar Gays in the Boy Scouts	N	10. Bar Funds for Intl. Court	N
3. Campaign Finance Reform	Y	7. Ban Partial-Birth Abortion	N	11. Authorize Force in Iraq	Y
4. Ban ANWR Development	Y	8. Arm Commercial Pilots	N	12. Deny Home. Sec. Dept. Union	N

Election Results

2002 general	Anthony Weiner (D-L-WF)	60,737	(66%)	($263,994)
	Alfred Donohue (R-C)	31,698	(34%)	
2002 primary	Anthony Weiner (D)	unopposed		
2000 general	Anthony Weiner (D-L)	98,983	(68%)	($510,247)
	Noach Dear (R-C)	45,649	(32%)	($1,521,320)

Prior Winning Percentages: 1998 (66%)

The People		Race/Ethnic Origin	Ancestry	
Area size:	103 sq. mi.	64.0% White	Italian: 12.3%	Irish: 7.5%
Urban population:	100.0%	4.0% Black	Russian: 7.2%	
Rural population:	0.0%	14.5% Asian	**2000 Presidential Vote**	
Pop. 2000:	654,360	0.1% Native Am.	Gore (D)...............123,763	(67%)
Median income:	$45,426	0.0% Hawaiian	Bush (R)...............54,699	(30%)
Poverty status:	12.2%	3.0% Two+ races	Other....................6,649	(4%)
Military veterans:	7.1%	0.7% Other	**Cook Partisan Voting Index:** D +19	
		13.6% Hispanic Origin		

Occupation	Blue collar: 17.6%	White collar: 68.4%	Gray collar: 14.0%

Forty years ago, most of the neighborhoods in New York's outer boroughs were almost all-white. A few were WASPy and high-income—Forest Hills in Queens, with its famous tennis stadium and large Tudor houses on winding lanes within view of massive high-rises, is a notable example, but most of them were filled by descendants of the great mass of immigrants who came over from eastern and southern Europe between 1890 and 1924 and from northern Europe earlier—Irish and Italians, Jews and Hungarians, Poles and Czechs and Greeks. The great pitched battles of city politics in the 1960s were between John Lindsay, a liberal Manhattan Republican, and his mostly outer borough opponents. Lindsay won big margins in Manhattan from Harlem blacks, Upper East Side Republicans, Upper West Side and Greenwich Village liberal Democrats, but he lost the other four boroughs collectively both times he ran, in 1965 and 1969, and was elected each time with only a plurality of the votes. Lindsay's attitudes and policies—soft on law enforcement, high on taxes, contempt for middle class taxpayers who wanted low taxes and safe neighborhoods—helped to lead to an exodus of middle class New Yorkers, and the city lost 1 million people in the 1970s. Some of this neighborhood change would have happened anyway: neighborhoods settled by immigrants in the 1920s were full of old people, and the increasing number of blacks were bound to move out of the old ghettoes anyway; unnoticed, increasing numbers of immigrants started coming to the United States after the 1965 changes in immigration law, and eventually large numbers came to New York.

But there are still white upper-middle and lower-middle class neighborhoods in the outer boroughs, though they are ethnically more diverse than those of 40 years ago. Many of these neighborhoods are gathered in the convoluted boundaries of the 9th Congressional District, which includes parts of Queens and Brooklyn. Its population is only 4% black and 14% Hispanic, and some of its neighborhoods, like Howard Beach on Jamaica Bay, have remained remarkably insular and seemingly unaffected by the changes swirling elsewhere. The 9th begins in Queens near Fresh Meadows, just inside Nassau County; it then runs west through Pomonok and the old rail suburbs of Kew Gardens and Forest Hills, built to resemble English cottage neighborhoods. The district continues west to Rego Park, with its 1950s high-rise apartments, Middle Village, the old German (and now more Eastern European) neighborhood of Glendale, and part of Maspeth. From there, the 9th heads south, taking in Woodhaven, Lindenwood and Howard Beach. It then crosses over open parkland to include the shoreline areas of Bergen Beach, Mill Basin, Mill Island, Marine Park and Sheepshead Bay. Manhattan Beach is commemorated in John Philip Sousa's *Manhattan Beach* March; its 20 tree-lined streets are arranged in alphabetical order, from west to east, and named after places in England. It also takes in Broad Channel, the only inhabited island in Jamaica Bay's Gateway National Recreation Area, where many descendants of the original fishing families still live. On the Rockaway Peninsula, the 9th includes the neighborhoods of Seaside; Rockaway Park, and Belle Harbor, a neighborhood of cops and firefighters where American Airlines Flight

587 crashed soon after takeoff on November 12, 2001; Roxbury; and the tight-knit, well-secured enclave of Breezy Point, once referred to as the "Irish Riviera." Like nearby Gerritsen Beach, Breezy Point is a clannish, white ethnic middle class enclave where the bungalows and brick homes often change hands by word of mouth alone. The 9th has a large and diverse Jewish population, with politically conservative Orthodox neighborhoods and liberal voters.

The congressman from the 9th District is Anthony Weiner, a Democrat elected in 1998. Weiner grew up in Brooklyn, went upstate to SUNY-Plattsburgh, then returned to work in the House for the energetic Charles Schumer. In 1991 Weiner was elected to the City Council, at 27, the youngest member ever. In 1997, as Schumer prepared to run for the Senate, Weiner began running for the House. Assemblywoman Melinda Katz, based in Forest Hills, ran with the support of the Queens Democratic organization and the Robert F. Kennedy Democratic Club. Assemblyman Daniel Feldman, based in Sheepshead Bay, had the endorsement of the Brooklyn Democratic organization and Congressman Jerrold Nadler. Councilman Noach Dear, based in Borough Park, ran with the endorsement of Orthodox leaders and was sharply more conservative. Otherwise the differences were in emphasis: Weiner talked about public safety, Katz about health care, Feldman his sponsorship of Megan's Law. This was mainly a battle of organizations and endorsements. In the last weeks, as he was sailing far ahead in the Senate primary, Schumer endorsed Weiner. The September 15 primary was so close that the results weren't certified for two weeks. In a turnout of 45,000, Weiner won with 28.1%, to 27.5% for Katz, and 22% each for Dear and Feldman. Weiner won the general election easily.

In the House, Weiner usually votes with the liberals but styled himself a moderate on issues dealing with business and crime. Conceding the political risk, he was among the handful of House Democrats to back PNTR with China. On the Judiciary Committee, he worked to expand federal DNA testing of crime scene evidence, and he sought better treatment for victims of sexual assault. Except for his eagerness to appear on cable talk shows—as befits a Schumer protégé—Weiner had few moments in the legislative spotlight and he deliberately worked as a backbencher on local issues. He claimed that retail chain stores charged exorbitant interest rates on their credit cards, and he introduced a bill to require disclosure to customers. After the crash of AA flight 587 in Belle Harbor, after it had just taken off from Kennedy Airport, he got the FAA to change its procedures at Kennedy to reduce substantially how much departing flights fly over the Rockaways.

In 2000, Dear challenged Weiner in the Democratic primary. Some thought the race would be close, but Weiner carried almost every assembly district and won 74%–26%. Dear was on the Republican and Conservative lines in November; this time Weiner beat him 68%–32%. Redistricting moved the 9th more into Queens—in 2000 50% of the votes were cast in Queens and in 2002 69%—and left Weiner with 30% new territory, but the basic character of the district remained the same and he was easily reelected. Weiner's options for political advancement seem limited for the next several years, but he has not discouraged the notion that he is a hot political commodity—perhaps, even a candidate for Mayor some day.

Weiner learned that the media spotlight also can bite the hand that feeds it. An article in *Vanity Fair* described Weiner's night out with some Democratic colleagues at the Capital Grille on Pennsylvania Avenue, when they invited three young women to join their table. One of them claimed that Weiner the next day identified himself in an email after having told her at the restaurant that he was an auto parts salesman. Other than some good-time photographs taken at the restaurant, the story identified no apparent evidence of misconduct.

TENTH DISTRICT

Rep. Edolphus Towns (D)

Elected 1982, 11th term; b. July 21, 1934, Chadbourn, NC; home, Brooklyn; NC A&T, B.S. 1956, Adelphi U., M.S.W. 1973; Baptist; married (Gwendolyn).

Military Career: Army, 1956–58.

Professional Career: Baptist Minister; Social Worker; Prof., Medgar Evers Col.; NY public schl. teacher; Dpty. Hospital Admin., 1965–71; Brooklyn Dpty. Borough Pres., 1976–82.

DC Office: 2232 RHOB 20515, 202-225-5936; Fax: 202-225-1018; Web site: www.house.gov/towns.

District Offices: Brooklyn, 718-855-8018; Brooklyn, 718-272-1175; Brooklyn, 718-774-5682.

Committees: *Energy & Commerce* (6th of 26 D): Commerce, Trade & Consumer Protection; Health; Telecommunications & The Internet. *Government Reform* (4th of 19 D): Government Efficiency & Financial Management (RMM).

Group Ratings

	ADA	ACLU	AFS	LCV	CON	ITIC	NTU	COC	ACU	NTLC	CHC
2002	80	79	100	75	15	38	22	40	4	9	8
2001	65	—	100	79	—	—	18	50	14	—	—

National Journal Ratings

	2001 LIB —	2001 CONS	2002 LIB —	2002 CONS
Economic	60%	41%	68%	31%
Social	81%	20%	97%	3%
Foreign	90%	10%	93%	6%

Key Votes of the 107th Congress

1. Approve Bush Tax Cuts	*	5. Faith-Based Charities	9. Trade Promotion Authority	N
2. Limit Patients' Bill of Rights	N	6. Bar Gays in the Boy Scouts	10. Bar Funds for Intl. Court	*
3. Campaign Finance Reform	Y	7. Ban Partial-Birth Abortion	11. Authorize Force in Iraq	N
4. Ban ANWR Development	N	8. Arm Commercial Pilots	12. Deny Home. Sec. Dept. Union	N

Key Votes middle column N's: 5. N, 6. N, 7. N, 8. N

Election Results

2002 general	Edolphus Towns (D-L)	73,859	(98%)	($741,570)
	Other	1,639	(2%)	
2002 primary	Edolphus Towns (D)	unopposed		
2000 general	Edolphus Towns (D-L)	120,700	(90%)	($1,187,226)
	Ernestine M. Brown (R)	6,852	(5%)	
	Barry Ford (WF)	5,530	(4%)	($281,004)
	Other	802	(1%)	

Prior Winning Percentages: 1998 (92%); 1996 (91%); 1994 (89%); 1992 (96%); 1990 (93%); 1988 (89%); 1986 (89%); 1984 (85%); 1982 (84%)

The People		Race/Ethnic Origin	Ancestry	
Area size:	18 sq. mi.	16.2% White	West Indian: 14.8%	USA: 3.9%
Urban population:	100.0%	60.2% Black	Subsaharan: 2.5%	
Rural population:	0.0%	2.7% Asian	**2000 Presidential Vote**	
Pop. 2000:	654,361	0.2% Native Am.	Gore (D) 149,018	(88%)
Median income:	$30,212	0.0% Hawaiian	Bush (R) 13,058	(8%)
Poverty status:	29.0%	2.6% Two+ races	Other 8,029	(5%)
Military veterans:	5.3%	0.9% Other	**Cook Partisan Voting Index:** D +42	
		17.2% Hispanic Origin		

Occupation	Blue collar: 17.5%	White collar: 60.4%	Gray collar: 22.1%

Bedford, a century ago one of Brooklyn's fashionable neighborhoods, has given its name to half of what is Brooklyn's best known—and not most downtrodden—black neighborhood. African-

Americans began settling here in the 1930s, with the opening of the new subway line that was celebrated in Duke Ellington and Billy Strayhorn's "Take the A Train." After World War II, the pace accelerated, as crime and crowding in Harlem—as well as a large migration of blacks from the South—drove black New Yorkers to the aging but solid brownstones of "Bed-Stuy." When job growth slowed, Bed-Stuy, like New York's other black neighborhoods, faced more than its share of poverty and crime. But after a 1966 visit by Robert F. Kennedy and Jacob Javits, New York's two senators, Bed-Stuy won a Model Cities designation, which brought federal development funds and the establishment of the Bedford-Stuyvesant Restoration Corporation, the first such community development organization in the United States. Even as the black community expanded far and wide across Brooklyn, Bed-Stuy grew to become almost as powerful a symbol of black New York as Harlem. As an NYU film student in 1983, Brooklyn native Spike Lee made *Joe's Bed-Stuy Barbershop: We Cut Heads*, about a tonsorial parlor that fronts for the numbers racket; five years later, he shot *Do the Right Thing* on Stuyvesant Avenue between Lexington Avenue and Quincy Street, a film that succinctly captures the racial tensions then brewing in the old neighborhood.

By the end of the 1990s, Bed-Stuy was in better shape than many other areas of Brooklyn. The neighborhood's stately, Hopperesque architecture largely avoided the wrecking ball, and community vigilance has kept the streets maintained. The area has developed a Caribbean flavor which, combined with the modest prices for handsome brownstones, has led to a modest wave of gentrification.

The 10th Congressional District takes the shape of a sideways "V" as it zigzags across Brooklyn. It takes in several neighborhoods near, but not on, the East River, including part of affluent Brooklyn Heights; downtown Brooklyn, with Borough Hall and the $500 million courthouse complex; the rising arts area of Fort Greene; and part of Williamsburg (shared with the 12th), inhabited by Hasidic families with large numbers of children. From there, it runs southeasterly through Bed-Stuy, Clinton Hill and East New York, until it hits the Queens border and turns to the southwest to take in three communities along Jamaica Bay: Spring Creek, Starrett City, and Canarsie, the site of Jonathan Reider's classic sociological study of Jewish and Italian flight from increasingly black neighborhoods. In the 1990s, Canarsie again experienced significant demographic change—the most dramatic of any neighborhood in New York City—as the neighborhood's black population grew from 10 to 60 percent, mainly due to an influx of Caribbean immigrants who prize the backyards and single-family homes. The 10th also includes Remsen Village, Flatlands and part of East Flatbush. The 1990s boom and sharp drop in crime rates helped improve even the borough's most hopeless areas, such as East New York, as gutted blocks were torn down and in many cases rebuilt. The district is 60% black—the highest of any New York district—and 17% Hispanic. Politically, it is overwhelmingly Democratic, one of the most Democratic districts in the nation.

The congressman from the 10th District is Ed Towns, first elected in 1982. He is a Democrat from East New York who is as experienced in government as in politics. He was born in North Carolina, the son of a tobacco sharecropper, graduated from North Carolina A&T, served two years in the Army and soon moved to Brooklyn, where he taught in the public schools and at Medgar Evers College. He became a social worker and hospital administrator, and was active in community affairs. In 1976, he was elected Brooklyn's deputy borough president, a position he held for six years.

In the House, Towns's voting record has lost some of its liberal edge in recent years. Starting out he worked on the Student Athlete Right-to-Know Act, which requires colleges to report the graduation rates of student athletes, and on strengthening the National Health Service Corps and the Minority Health Initiative. He worked with other Democrats on legislation to bridge the "digital divide" by earmarking telephone excise taxes to telecommunications projects. Responding to a local tragedy, he sought to ban the sale of toy guns that resemble real guns and convinced local stores to end sales of certain models. He worked on some local projects, notably a $500 million federal courthouse complex for Brooklyn.

Towns often took a community, rather than national, perspective. In 2001, as the senior Democrat on the Commerce, Trade and Consumer Protection Subcommittee, he attacked a report by the Federal Trade Commission that criticized marketing of what the agency called violent entertainment by the recording industry that targeted children. "It is simply wrong for the government to suggest that this music and its message are not suitable for America's teens because it contains, in some cases, explicit content," he said, referring to the mostly rap and hip-hop music. On the Tauzin-Dingell bill giving broadband access to the former Bell companies, Towns worked with Republican Steve Buyer to get an amendment to ensure access by competitors to the networks of the telecom giants.

For years Towns was re-elected without difficulty. In 1997 he endorsed Rudolph Giuliani for mayor; this took some courage, or showed bad judgment, since Giuliani got only 15% of the vote in two Bedford-Stuyvesant assembly districts, his worst showing in the city. In 1998 Kings County Democratic Chairman Clarence Norman recruited primary opposition for Towns. He was turned down by agitator Al Sharpton, but found an opponent in Barry Ford, a Harvard-educated Wall Street lawyer. Leftish labor unions and Democratic clubs, Public Advocate Mark Green and former Mayor David Dinkins endorsed Ford. Towns' critics concentrated on the tobacco issue. He opposed anti-tobacco legislation on the ground it would hurt farmers: "Tobacco is bad. So is starvation. Both will kill you." The Campaign for Tobacco-Free Kids put up billboards reading, "Representative Towns: Big Tobacco or Kids?" Others called him "the Marlboro man" and attacked him for accepting $54,000 from tobacco interests over 10 years. Towns beat Ford, but by only 52%–36%.

Emboldened by that result, Ford barely stopped campaigning for the next two years. This time, Ford was better known and he appeared to have a real prospect of ousting Towns. But the incumbent campaigned much harder. Towns defended his support for Giuliani by pointing to the Mayor's support for commercial development. He decided not to take campaign contributions from tobacco companies. The *New York Times* endorsed Ford as an "energetic" activist and criticized Towns for his "minimal" record and support for tobacco and other special interests. Towns won this time, 57%–43. In 2002 Towns faced token opposition. But Towns has become more involved in Brooklyn politics, leading to local speculation that he would like to pass the district to his son, Assemblyman Darryl Towns, when he retires. Towns turns 70 in 2004.

ELEVENTH DISTRICT

Rep. Major Owens (D)

Elected 1982, 11th term; b. June 28, 1936, Memphis, TN; home, Brooklyn; Morehouse Col., B.A. 1956, Atlanta U., M.L.S. 1957; Baptist; married (Maria).

Elected Office: NY Senate, 1974–82.

Professional Career: Librarian; Brooklyn Public Library, 1958–65, Community Coord., 1964–65; V.P., Metro. Cncl. of Housing, 1964; Chmn., Brooklyn Congress on Racial Equality; Exec. Dir., Brownsville Community Cncl., 1966–68; NYC Community Devel. Agency, Comm., 1968–73, Dpty. Admin., 1972–74; Dir., Community Media Library Program, Columbia U., 1973–74.

DC Office: 2309 RHOB 20515, 202-225-6231; Fax: 202-226-0112; Web site: www.house.gov/owens.

District Office: Brooklyn, 718-773-3100.

Committees: *Education & the Workforce* (3d of 22 D): 21st Century Competitiveness; Workforce Protections (RMM). *Government Reform* (3d of 19 D): Civil Service & Agency Organization; Government Efficiency & Financial Management.

Group Ratings

	ADA	ACLU	AFS	LCV	CON	ITIC	NTU	COC	ACU	NTLC	CHC
2002	90	92	100	100	63	38	27	25	4	0	0
2001	95	—	100	93	—	—	15	19	4	—	—

National Journal Ratings

	2001 LIB	—	2001 CONS		2002 LIB	—	2002 CONS
Economic	83%	—	15%		95%	—	0%
Social	90%	—	0%		74%	—	19%
Foreign	93%	—	7%		94%	—	0%

Key Votes of the 107th Congress

1. Approve Bush Tax Cuts	N	5. Faith-Based Charities	N	9. Trade Promotion Authority	N
2. Limit Patients' Bill of Rights	N	6. Bar Gays in the Boy Scouts	*	10. Bar Funds for Intl. Court	N
3. Campaign Finance Reform	Y	7. Ban Partial-Birth Abortion	N	11. Authorize Force in Iraq	N
4. Ban ANWR Development	Y	8. Arm Commercial Pilots	Y	12. Deny Home. Sec. Dept. Union	N

Election Results

2002 general	Major Owens (D-WF)	76,917	(87%)	($317,477)
	Susan Cleary (R-Ind)	11,149	(13%)	($10,580)
	Other	798	(1%)	
2002 primary	Major Owens (D)	unopposed		
2000 general	Major Owens (D-WF)	112,050	(87%)	($548,071)
	Susan Cleary (R-SCH)	8,406	(7%)	($22,790)
	Una S. T. Clarke (L)	7,366	(6%)	($265,208)
	Other	962	(1%)	

Prior Winning Percentages: 1998 (90%); 1996 (92%); 1994 (89%); 1992 (94%); 1990 (95%); 1988 (93%); 1986 (91%); 1984 (91%); 1982 (91%)

The People		Race/Ethnic Origin	Ancestry	
Area size:	12 sq. mi.	21.4% White	West Indian: 23.2%	USA: 4.1%
Urban population:	100.0%	58.5% Black	Italian: 2.8%	
Rural population:	0.0%	4.1% Asian	**2000 Presidential Vote**	
Pop. 2000:	654,361	0.2% Native Am.	Gore (D)	149,740 (83%)
Median income:	$34,082	0.0% Hawaiian	Bush (R)	15,652 (9%)
Poverty status:	23.2%	3.0% Two+ races	Other	15,828 (9%)
Military veterans:	4.1%	0.6% Other	**Cook Partisan Voting Index:** D +40	
		12.1% Hispanic Origin		

Occupation	Blue collar: 15.7%	White collar: 61.2%	Gray collar: 23.1%

Brooklyn. The single word used to arouse laughter in a comedian's monologue, applause when someone said that's where they were from. It evoked an accent that twisted the English language almost to non-recognition, a raucous and brusque confrontational style, a sense of humor with an edge, the chip-on-the-shoulder assertiveness of those sure they will always be in second place. Brooklyn would never be more important than Manhattan; the Dodgers would always lose the World Series to the Yankees or the pennant to the Giants, and when they finally did win, in 1955, they moved to Los Angeles two years later. Brooklyn, as its Dutch name testifies, was a separate community from the 17th century on, one of the largest cities in the country in the 19th century, with its own celebrities (Henry Ward Beecher, Walt Whitman, John Roebling). By 1898, when the five boroughs were welded into Greater New York, one million people lived in Brooklyn, but the Brooklyn of the comedians really came into being as the subways were built in the early 20th century. In 1913, a transit agreement was struck to interlink the city's then-independent lines and triple the track to 619 miles; this agreement helped Brooklyn expand well beyond its established neighborhoods near the Brooklyn Bridge and into then-rural southwestern Brooklyn.

Suddenly, Manhattan factory workers no longer had to live in the Lower East Side tenements that social reformer Jacob Riis had exposed in the 1890s; they moved in droves into neighborhoods of three- to five-story apartments and four-family houses. Brooklyn grew from 1.1 million in 1900 to 1.6 million in 1910 to 2 million in 1920 and 2.6 million in 1930. The old Brooklynites were mostly Protestant—Dutch, Yankee, German—plus some Catholic Irish. The new Brooklynites were heavily Italian and Jewish, and peopled the sports and entertainment businesses for a long generation, making their hometown nationally famous. In 1940, as the nation was about to go to war, Brooklyn had 2.7 million people: one of every 49 Americans lived in Brooklyn. In 2000, Brooklyn had 2.46 million people—one of every 114 Americans—and it is no longer a staple of national comedy. Some of Brooklyn's old neighborhoods have been ravaged by crime, but there is also great vitality, among upwardly mobile Hispanic, Asian, Caribbean and Russian immigrants, among the hard-working black middle class, and among a new generation of Italians and Jews.

The heart of the old Brooklyn was Ebbets Field, where the Dodgers played. Around the time

Jackie Robinson suited up for the Brooklyn Dodgers in 1947 as the first black player in Major League Baseball, Brooklyn was experiencing an influx of blacks into Brownsville and Crown Heights near Ebbets Field. Just as rapid was the flight of ethnic whites, driven away by "block-busting," in which hard-nosed real estate brokers stoked white fears, then bought their homes cheaply and re-sold high. After "Dem Bums" left for Los Angeles in 1958 and Ebbets Field was knocked down to be replaced by an apartment complex, Brooklyn's black neighborhoods continued to grow. Many of New York's black families came from the American South, but large numbers, particularly in Flatbush and Crown Heights, come from "the Islands"—Jamaica, Haiti, the Dominican Republic, Barbados, Trinidad and Tobago. Speaking deeply accented English, French, Spanish or various forms of Creole, they bring aromatic cooking (jerk chicken, spiced bread, peanut punch and Matouk's Special Hot Calypso Sauce) and reggae and calypso music—as well as strong families and an entrepreneurial spirit. The annual Labor Day West Indian Carnival reflects this strong local Caribbean presence.

The 11th Congressional District begins at the edge of downtown Brooklyn and includes some of the borough's jewels—the Grand Army Plaza, the Parisian-style Eastern Parkway (the world's first six-lane parkway), and Prospect Park, home to the Brooklyn Library, the Brooklyn Museum and the Brooklyn Botanic Garden, with its Japanese landscaping and placid duck ponds, Erasmus Hall High School, the nation's second-oldest, founded by Alexander Hamilton, John Jay and Aaron Burr. Park Slope, on Prospect Park's west side, has become increasingly affluent, filling up with professionals who appreciate the easy commute to downtown Manhattan. On the east side of Prospect Park is Crown Heights, with its mix of modest apartment buildings and nicely restored row houses; it was the scene of violent clashes between blacks and Hasidic Jews in 1991 (The Lubavitch Hasids, the largest Hasidic sect in the world, has its world headquarters at 770 Eastern Parkway in Crown Heights). Prospect Park South, also adjoining the park, is another affluent neighborhood whose suburban feel, once enforced by restrictive covenants, contrasts sharply with the vibrant Caribbean street life just around the corner on Flatbush's Church Avenue and with struggling, depopulated Brownsville to the east. Most of these neighborhoods are places of great ethnic diversity: One minute you are in "La Saline," nicknamed for the slum district of Port-au-Prince, a center of the Haitian community in the East Flatbush-Crown Heights area; the next, you are in "Little Pakistan" in Midwood, which, at least until September 11, was home to the largest concentration of Pakistanis living in America. From the 1920s to the 1960s the area defined by the 11th District had the largest concentration of Jews in America but today the population is 59% black and 12% Hispanic. Politically, the district is overwhelmingly Democratic.

The congressman from the 11th District is Major Owens, a Democrat first elected in 1982, who claims to be the first librarian elected to Congress. Owens grew up in Memphis, went to Morehouse College and Atlanta University and became a librarian. He worked in the Brownsville Community Council and with the Congress of Racial Equality, and served in Mayor John Lindsay's administration from 1968–73 as commissioner of the city's Community Development Agency; critic Charles Morris called Owens "the most capable and canny" of New York's anti-poverty program directors. In 1974, he was elected to the New York Senate. When Congresswoman Shirley Chisholm, an immigrant from Barbados and presidential candidate in 1972, announced her retirement in 1982, Owens entered the primary to succeed her and beat Chisholm's choice. Until 2000, Owens had no serious electoral competition.

Owens has one of the most liberal voting records in the House. When Democrats last controlled the House, he chaired the Subcommittee on Select Education and Civil Rights; in 2001, he became ranking member on the Workforce Protections Subcommittee. He often makes long, vigorous floor speeches after the House has finished work for the day—speaking passionately of the need to support libraries, vital institutions in immigrant communities of New York's outer boroughs. On occasion, he engages in "rap" during these late-night talks, such as this *Message to the Republican Mob*: "Before you merely mauled welfare mothers, But now you're messing with the Great American Middle Class; We'll kick your rear! Grandfathers are full of fear, New anger after every tear, Our pensions down the drain, No shelter from age old rain . . . " Owens has been outspokenly critical of the Republican majority in the House, which he said has left black lawmakers "simply shellshocked." He opposed their school vouchers plan as deceptive and dishonest, and said that the solution is to restore faith in public schools. He opposed increasing the number of H-1B visas for high-skill workers, saying that might take jobs from Americans. He called for enhanced U.S. trade with Caribbean Basin nations. As a member of the House-Senate conference committee that wrote the final version of George W. Bush's education bill in 2001, Owens pushed for more money for educational technology, including training students in high-tech programs. On the bill creating the Homeland Security Department, he tried unsuccessfully to permit legal immigrants to serve as airport screeners.

Owens had opposition in the 2000 Democratic primary from City Councilwoman Una Clarke, his Jamaican-born former protg. Although they had long been close friends and he had helped her win the council seat, their relationship became rancorous, and she accused Owens of being ineffective and anti-immigrant. "I am not a black American," she said. "I identify as a black person." He accused Clarke, whose Council seat was term-limited, of betraying their friendship. Most local party officials endorsed Owens because of his seniority. Despite Clarke's strong showing in the Caribbean precincts, Owens won 54%–46%. Redistricting made little change in the district, and Owens had no primary opposition in 2002.

TWELFTH DISTRICT

Rep. Nydia Velazquez (D)

Elected 1992, 6th term; b. Mar. 28, 1953, Yabucoa, PR; home, Brooklyn; U. of PR, B.A. 1974, N.Y.U., M.A. 1976; Catholic; married (Paul Bader).

Elected Office: NY City Cncl., 1984–86.

Professional Career: Instructor, U. of PR, 1976–81; Adjunct prof., Hunter Col., 1981–83; Special Asst., U.S. Rep. Edolphus Towns, 1983; Migration Dir., PR Dept. of Labor & Human Resources, 1986–89; Secy., PR Dept. of Community Affairs in the U.S., 1989–92.

DC Office: 2241 RHOB 20515, 202-225-2361; Fax: 202-226-0327; Web site: www.house.gov/velazquez.

District Offices: Brooklyn, 718-599-3658; Brooklyn, 718-222-5819; Manhattan, 212-673-3997.

Committees: *Financial Services* (6th of 32 D): Domestic and International Monetary Policy, Trade & Technology; Financial Institutions & Consumer Credit; Housing & Community Opportunity. *Small Business* (RMM of 17 D).

Group Ratings

	ADA	ACLU	AFS	LCV	CON	ITIC	NTU	COC	ACU	NTLC	CHC
2002	95	93	100	100	63	38	22	35	0	6	0
2001	90	—	100	100	—	—	14	35	0	—	—

National Journal Ratings

	2001 LIB	—	2001 CONS		2002 LIB	—	2002 CONS
Economic	88%	—	11%		77%	—	20%
Social	90%	—	0%		94%	—	6%
Foreign	91%	—	8%		93%	—	6%

Key Votes of the 107th Congress

1. Approve Bush Tax Cuts	N	5. Faith-Based Charities	N	9. Trade Promotion Authority	N
2. Limit Patients' Bill of Rights	N	6. Bar Gays in the Boy Scouts	*	10. Bar Funds for Intl. Court	N
3. Campaign Finance Reform	Y	7. Ban Partial-Birth Abortion	N	11. Authorize Force in Iraq	N
4. Ban ANWR Development	Y	8. Arm Commercial Pilots	N	12. Deny Home. Sec. Dept. Union	N

Election Results

2002 general	Nydia Velazquez (D-WF)	48,408	(96%)	($563,174)
	Cesar Estevez (C)	2,119	(4%)	
2002 primary	Nydia Velazquez (D)	unopposed		
2000 general	Nydia Velazquez (D-WF)	86,288	(87%)	($437,579)
	Rosemary Markgraf (R)	10,052	(10%)	($11,078)
	Other	2,740	(3%)	

Prior Winning Percentages: 1998 (84%); 1996 (85%); 1994 (92%); 1992 (77%)

The People		Race/Ethnic Origin	Ancestry	
Area size:	20 sq. mi.	23.3% White	Italian: 4.7%	Polish: 4.4%
Urban population:	100.0%	8.8% Black	Irish: 3.4%	
Rural population:	0.0%	15.9% Asian	**2000 Presidential Vote**	
Pop. 2000:	654,360	0.2% Native Am.	Gore (D)..............102,465	(77%)
Median income:	$29,195	0.0% Hawaiian	Bush (R)...............19,604	(15%)
Poverty status:	28.3%	2.5% Two+ races	Other...................11,268	(8%)
Military veterans:	4.0%	0.7% Other	**Cook Partisan Voting Index:** D +34	
		48.5% Hispanic Origin		

Occupation	Blue collar: 27.5%	White collar: 50.9%	Gray collar: 21.5%

In 1957, amid a vast wave of migration that seemed destined to make Puerto Ricans the majority in New York, Leonard Bernstein wrote his musical, *West Side Story*, with Romeo as an Italian-American and Juliet as a Manhattan Puerto Rican. But New York never became majority Puerto Rican. Before World War II, there were 60,000 Puerto Ricans in New York City; three decades later, there were 800,000. But they were among the first immigrants to arrive in a city whose industrial base was stagnant. With cheap airfares and no need to go through passport control, the inflow and outflow of Puerto Ricans balanced out by the early 1960s, and in the late 1990s the number of Puerto Ricans in New York was declining, as young New Yorkers of Puerto Rican descent increasingly moved to Puerto Rico. But by then, New York City was experiencing a vast influx of Latinos from places not under the U.S. flag, and today most New York Hispanics come not from Puerto Rico but from the Dominican Republic, Colombia, Mexico, Panama and Peru.

The 12th Congressional District was designed to stitch many of these diverse people together. The district was first created in 1992 with boundaries so convoluted it was called the "Bullwinkle" district; the boundaries were smoothed out by a court for the 1998 election, and redistricting in 2002 produced a somewhat smoother version. More than two-thirds of the people here live in Brooklyn, and most of the rest in Queens, with the rest in Manhattan. In Brooklyn the district hugs the waterfront and dips inward to include areas with large Hispanic populations—but this is New York, so it gets many others as well. Overall the district is 49% Hispanic, 16% Asian and 9% black. The 12th includes the upscale Brooklyn Heights waterfront, with its stunning but, after September 11, haunting views of Lower Manhattan, and nearby Carroll Gardens with young professionals intermingled with Italian immigrants. To the south is Sunset Park, once the home of Irish, Polish and Norwegian immigrants, now filled with Chinese, Puerto Ricans, Colombians and Ecuadorans. North of Brooklyn Heights is DUMBO (Down Under the Manhattan Bridge Overpass), with artists in old industrial lofts. North of the Brooklyn Navy Yard, a major base for the Navy until it was shuttered in 1966, and now an industrial park, is Williamsburg, with Orthodox Jews and recent Latino arrivals. Inland is Bushwick, with low-income Latinos. Just a few streets away, across the Brooklyn-Queens border, is Ridgewood, once mostly Irish, then Polish, now filled with new arrivals from Poland, Romania, Albania, Serbia and Bosnia. Nearby is industrial Maspeth. In Manhattan, the 12th District includes parts of the Lower East Side, Chinatown and Little Italy. In 1910, 373,000 people lived there, mostly Jewish and Italian immigrants. Today there are only a few Jews (Ratner's Delicatessen closed in September 2002 after 97 years in business) and virtually no Italians (only Italian restaurants remain); its population of 91,000 is mostly Chinese, with some Latinos and some young professionals renting newly converted apartments. Politically, the 12th District is heavily Democratic.

The congresswoman from the 12th District is Nydia Velazquez, chosen by a narrow margin in the 1992 Democratic primary and re-elected ever since. She was born in Puerto Rico, taught at the University of Puerto Rico in the 1970s and at Hunter College in the 1980s, worked for Congressman Ed Towns in 1983 and served on the New York City Council in 1984. Then she worked for Puerto Rico's government offices in New York. She was one of three major contenders when the district was created in 1992. The others were liberal Elisabeth Colon and incumbent Stephen Solarz; he decided to run here rather than in the Manhattan-dominated 8th or in the 9th District in which Charles Schumer had a heavy advantage. Velazquez got the endorsements of then-Mayor David Dinkins and of Jesse Jackson, and in a light turnout beat Solarz 34%–28%, with 26% for Colon. After the primary, confidential hospital records were leaked to a New York tabloid showing that in September 1991, Velazquez had attempted suicide, was hospitalized and later underwent counseling. Evidently, that was of little concern to voters: she won in November with 77%.

In the House she has a solidly liberal voting record. She was a sponsor of the Clinton administration proposals to stop money laundering in 1999, and with Republican James Talent she helped pass a bill creating 40 new renewal zones eligible for tax breaks in 2000. Since 1998, Velazquez has been ranking Democrat on the Small Business Committee. Velazquez sponsored studies that showed that small businesses' share of federal contracts fell from $6.4 billion in 1997 to $4.9 billion in 1999. In response she sponsored a bill that passed the House easily to closely monitor contract bundling—federal agencies' practice of putting small contracts together in one large package, which usually results in the contract going to a large business. Citing the 2 million minority-owned and 9 million woman-owned businesses, she spoke out for repeal of the estate tax in June 2000 and voted for it. But when Bill Clinton vetoed the bill, she voted to uphold his veto after a phone call from him. In 2001 she called for repeal of the 1996 welfare law, and wants no time limits on welfare and benefits for legal immigrants. She has sponsored legislation to clean up and allow use of brownfields, plentiful in her district. After September 11, she and Jerrold Nadler got $550 million in Community Development Block Grant aid for businesses impacted by the attacks. She called for tests of the effects of the dreadfully polluted air that blew over Brooklyn after the attacks. She asked for an investigation of Airbus planes after the crash of American Airlines flight 587 in the Rockaways in November 2001 and challenged the state permit granted for Con Edison's Hudson Avenue generating plant. She hailed the $5 million Army Corps of Engineers study of how to clean up the Gowanus Canal (at one time, it was a Mafia dumping ground) and said she envisaged a time when it was filled with gondolas and lined with restaurants.

Velazquez has been a major voice on issues relating to Puerto Rico. She used to favor independence, a cause favored by less than 5% of voters in Puerto Rico; by 1997 she favored continuation of the current commonwealth status (more accurately described in the Spanish term, *estado liberado asociado*, free associated state). She attacked the March 1998 bill setting the terms for a referendum on status—always the number one issue in Puerto Rico—as "a one-sided bill that is biased in favor of Puerto Rican statehood" that shows "a lack of respect for the people of Puerto Rico." She said its definition of commonwealth was biased, because it did not guarantee U.S. citizenship to future generations of Puerto Ricans (citizenship is now based not on the Fourteenth Amendment, but on a law passed by Congress in 1917, which could be repealed). She has strongly opposed the Navy's bombing range on the island of Vieques and in May 2000 she was one of more than 200 protesters evicted from Vieques. Velazquez strongly advocated clemency for members of the FALN terrorist group—which was responsible for the deaths of six people—who had been imprisoned for 19 years after being convicted on seditious conspiracy and weapons charges and who had not expressed regret. When Clinton granted clemency in August 1999 conditioned on a renunciation of violence, she said that the clemency should have been unconditional. When the grant was opposed by Hillary Rodham Clinton, then contemplating a run for the Senate, Velazquez said she should have come to the community and listened to the people; she was dismayed when the House condemned the clemency by a 311–41 vote.

Velazquez has been one of many combatants in New York City's political wars. She lamented the court ruling overturning the 1992 district lines, but has won easily within the more regular 1997 and 2002 lines. In September 2001, when salsa star Willie Colon, running for public advocate, took out an ad saying Velazquez supported him, her staff said she didn't and never would; Colon said she had made "supportive comments" on Dominican Independence Day in July. Newspapers took note when incoming City Controller William Thompson in early 2002 hired Velazquez's husband, Paul Bader, to a job "researching all World Trade Center-related claims" for $90,000 a year.

THIRTEENTH DISTRICT

Rep. Vito Fossella (R)

Elected Nov. 1997, 3d term; b. Mar. 9, 1965, Staten Island; home, Staten Island; U. of PA., B.S. 1993, Fordham U., J.D. 1994; Catholic; married (Mary Pat).

Elected Office: NY City Cncl., 1994–97.

Professional Career: Practicing atty., 1994.

DC Office: 1239 LHOB 20515, 202-225-3371; Fax: 202-226-1272; Web site: www.house.gov/fossella.

District Offices: Brooklyn, 718-630-5277; Staten Island, 718-356-8400.

Committees: *Energy & Commerce* (18th of 31 R): Energy & Air Quality; Environment & Hazardous Materials (Vice Chmn.); Telecommunications & The Internet. *Financial Services* (24th of 37 R): Capital Markets, Insurance & Government Sponsored Enterprises; Financial Institutions & Consumer Credit; Oversight & Investigations.

Group Ratings

	ADA	ACLU	AFS	LCV	CON	ITIC	NTU	COC	ACU	NTLC	CHC
2002	0	7	0	25	87	88	59	95	92	86	100
2001	0	—	0	29	—	—	63	100	88	—	—

National Journal Ratings

	2001 LIB	—	2001 CONS		2002 LIB	—	2002 CONS
Economic	33%	—	66%		34%	—	65%
Social	38%	—	63%		37%	—	62%
Foreign	33%	—	60%		15%	—	78%

Key Votes of the 107th Congress

1. Approve Bush Tax Cuts	Y	5. Faith-Based Charities	Y	9. Trade Promotion Authority	Y
2. Limit Patients' Bill of Rights	Y	6. Bar Gays in the Boy Scouts	Y	10. Bar Funds for Intl. Court	Y
3. Campaign Finance Reform	N	7. Ban Partial-Birth Abortion	Y	11. Authorize Force in Iraq	Y
4. Ban ANWR Development	N	8. Arm Commercial Pilots	Y	12. Deny Home. Sec. Dept. Union	Y

Election Results

2002 general	Vito Fossella (R-C-RTL)	72,204	(70%)	($893,650)
	Arne Mattsson (D-L-WF)	29,366	(28%)	($6,757)
	Other	2,123	(2%)	
2002 primary	Vito Fossella (R)	unopposed		
2000 general	Vito Fossella (R-C-RTL)	109,806	(65%)	($767,582)
	Katina M. Johnstone (D-WF)	57,603	(34%)	($39,475)
	Other	2,653	(2%)	

Prior Winning Percentages: 1998 (65%); 1997 (61%)

The People		Race/Ethnic Origin	Ancestry	
Area size:	113 sq. mi.	70.9% White	Italian: 29.5%	Irish: 11.5%
Urban population:	100.0%	6.3% Black	German: 4.3%	
Rural population:	0.0%	9.1% Asian	**2000 Presidential Vote**	
Pop. 2000:	654,361	0.1% Native Am.	Gore (D) 101,079	(52%)
Median income:	$50,092	0.0% Hawaiian	Bush (R) 85,119	(44%)
Poverty status:	11.9%	2.3% Two+ races	Other 6,538	(3%)
Military veterans:	9.0%	0.2% Other	**Cook Partisan Voting Index:** D + 4	
		11.0% Hispanic Origin		
Occupation	Blue collar: 18.3%	White collar: 65.0%	Gray collar: 16.7%	

Staten Island is part of New York City, yet a land apart, closer geographically to New Jersey than to Brooklyn. Its inclusion in Greater New York as part of the great 1898 consolidation was something of an afterthought, and for two-thirds of a century it was connected to the rest of the City only by ferry or through Bayonne, New Jersey, until the Verrazano Narrows Bridge—one of Robert Moses' last and most impressive infrastructural achievements—opened to traffic in 1965. Hilly Staten Island (or Richmond County) is the state's southernmost county, one-tenth as densely populated as Manhattan—and that's after a growth spurt of 17% during the 1990s, a faster rate than any county in New York state. Ethnically, Staten Island is the most heavily Italian part of the United States; the 13th District has the highest percentage of residents of Italian ancestry in the nation.; the signs on coffee shops here read *Caffe* and on delicatessens *Salumeria*. The Staten Island Ferry docks at St. George, the government hub and home of the Staten Island Yankees' new ballpark. The north and south shores that spread out from there are notable for their pleasant Victorian homes, while the island's west shore is industrial marshland, with new development on the now-closed Fresh Kills dump. Staten Island's interior consists of blocks of suburbia alternating with scrubland that's rapidly being turned into suburbia itself; this growth, plus a relative shortage of mass transit, has brought significant traffic congestion to this otherwise spacious island.

Culturally, Staten Islanders are deeply conservative—more so than in most of New York's suburbs, and quite a contrast from Manhattanites who live a 20-minute ferry ride away. Taking a cue from Fresh Kills, their motto is apt: "Don't dump on us." Not many people here read the *New York Times*; the local paper is the *Staten Island Advance* (emphasis on the first syllable, please), the foundation of the Newhouse publishing empire. Fed up with New York City's high income taxes and social programs, Staten Island residents voted in November 1993 for secession, but the legislature never acted. That same year, Staten Islanders provided the margin of victory for Mayor Rudolph Giuliani, whose agenda of cutting crime and welfare rolls soothed the secessionist fervor. If Staten Island were counted on its own, it would have the lowest crime rate of any city in America with more than 100,000 population: one reason is that a larger percentage of its residents are police officers. The Giuliani years also produced an economic boom, with a new ferry terminal, additional shops and hundreds of new homes near cleaned-up beaches. The biggest victory was the closing of Fresh Kills in March 2001, though it was opened again temporarily to help in the cleanup of the World Trade Center site. The September 11 terrorist attacks killed nearly 250 Staten Islanders—more than 10% of the dead, including nearly one-quarter of all the fire fighters who died.

The 13th Congressional District is made up of Staten Island plus a few adjacent neighborhoods with similar demographics over the Verrazano Narrows Bridge in Brooklyn. These include heavily Catholic and Italian Bay Ridge and Bensonhurst—middle-class enclaves with large single-family houses and small apartment buildings. The entertainment industry has found in these two neighborhoods some of its most memorable characters: The Three Stooges (Moe, Curly and Shemp) actually grew up in Bensonhurst; it was also home to the fictional Ralph Kramden of *The Honeymooners*. And it was on the streets of Bensonhurst and Bay Ridge that John Travolta danced to fame in *Saturday Night Fever*. The district also includes Fort Hamilton, the only active-duty military base in New York City and one of the oldest military outposts still in operation in the United States. The 13th is seeing a rising number of immigrants—a few white ethnic neighborhoods near St. George have experienced an influx of newcomers from West Africa, Mexico, South America and Southeast Asia—but Staten Island remains New York's whitest borough; the 13th is only 6% black and 11% Hispanic. Voters here solidly backed Republicans George Pataki for governor and Rick Lazio for senator, and Staten Island claims to have provided Republican mayoral candidate Michael Bloomberg with his winning margin in 2001. But in 1996 and 2000, the 13th (in nearly identical form to the current district) voted for Bill Clinton and Al Gore.

The congressman from the 13th District is Vito Fossella, a Republican who won a November 1997 special election. Fossella comes from a political, and Democratic, Staten Island family: his great-grandfather, James O'Leary, was a New Deal congressman from 1935–44, elected from Staten Island and the Wall Street tip of Manhattan; his father, Vito Fossella Sr., chaired the city's Board of Standards under Mayor Edward Koch; his uncle, Frank Fossella, was elected to the City Council in 1981 and was beaten in 1985 by Republican Susan Molinari, Vito Fossella Jr.'s predecessor in Congress. Despite the party difference, the families became close. Vito Fossella graduated from Penn and Fordham Law School and became a Republican in 1990, at 25, because of his conservative philosophy; he switched from pro-choice to pro-life in 1995, after the birth of his son. He worked on the campaigns of Susan Molinari, who succeeded her father, Guy Molinari, in the House. In 1994, Fossella, less than a year after finishing law school, was elected to the City Council to fill a vacancy, with the help of the Molinaris. On the council, he worked for increased school and transportation funding for Staten Island and, most important, passed a bill mandating the closing of the Fresh Kills dump by 2001.

Fossella was elected to Congress after Susan Molinari's surprise resignation. She didn't lose her political touch, however: she timed her resignation for August, which meant that the Republican nomination would go to the party committeemen, dominated by her father, then Staten Island Borough President—they rejected the pleas of two other contenders and chose Fossella. This turned out to be a high visibility contest. Democrats picked Eric Vitaliano, a 15-year assemblyman from the conservative mid-Island district, an abortion opponent and sponsor of New York's death penalty. Vitaliano criticized Fossella as inexperienced and constantly tried to link Fossella with Gingrich. Fossella hit Vitaliano for supporting higher taxes and needle exchanges, and for not taking Americans for Tax Reform's anti-tax-raise pledge. Two other factors helped Fossella. One was $750,000 in independent expenditures by the national Republican Party, attacking Vitaliano for supporting tax increases, and a group called Victory 97, which paid for posters depicting Vitaliano's allegedly silly spending programs: snow-making equipment in Ulster County, a state Museum of Cheese. The other was the re-election campaign of Giuliani, in a district where few local Democratic officeholders would admit they supported their liberal nominee Ruth Messinger. On Election Day, Giuliani carried the district 3–1 and Fossella won 61%–39%.

In the House, Fossella has a more conservative voting record than Molinari, one of the most conservative in the New York delegation. He serves on the Energy and Commerce, and Financial Services committees, both locally useful slots. He worked on interstate waste issues, pushed for rerouting Newark Airport flights away from Staten Island, and got $20 million to dredge the Arthur Kill as part of a revitalization project. He amended the Shays-Meehan campaign finance bill to ban contributions from foreigners, even if they reside in the U.S. He voted for PNTR with China. Republican leaders looked to him to reach out to Catholic voters: He sponsored the Congressional Gold Medal for New York's Cardinal John O'Connor shortly before his death. When Bill Clinton granted clemency to members of the Puerto Rican FALN terrorist group which was responsible for fatal local bombings, Fossella led the opposition, demanding that Clinton provide more details of his deliberations and sponsoring a resolution to rebuke him; it passed the House 311–41. In the 2000 presidential primary, he broke with Guy Molinari to support George W. Bush. In January 2002, Bush signed the bill that he helped to write to reduce transaction and registration fees paid to the SEC. He sponsored the law that designates September 11 as Patriot Day, a day of reflection, and he helped to organize the ceremonial session of Congress in Lower Manhattan to observe the first anniversary of the attacks.

Fossella was reelected 70%–28% in 2002.

FOURTEENTH DISTRICT

Rep. Carolyn Maloney (D)

Elected 1992, 6th term; b. Feb. 19, 1948, Greensboro, NC; home, Manhattan; Greensboro Col, A.B. 1968; Presbyterian; married (Clifton).

Elected Office: NY City Cncl., 1982–92.

Professional Career: NYC Bd. of Ed., 1970–77; Legis. aide, NY Assembly & NY Senate, 1977–82.

DC Office: 2331 RHOB 20515, 202-225-7944; Fax: 202-225-4709; Web site: www.house.gov/maloney.

District Offices: Manhattan, 212-860-0606; Queens, 718-932-1804.

Committees: *Financial Services* (4th of 32 D): Domestic and International Monetary Policy, Trade & Technology (RMM); Financial Institutions & Consumer Credit; Oversight & Investigations. *Government Reform* (6th of 19 D): Government Efficiency & Financial Management; National Security, Emerging Threats & Intl. Relations. *Joint Economic Committee* (8th of 10 Reps.).

Group Ratings

	ADA	ACLU	AFS	LCV	CON	ITIC	NTU	COC	ACU	NTLC	CHC
2002	100	87	100	100	63	50	19	53	4	6	0
2001	95	—	100	93	—	—	10	35	0	—	—

National Journal Ratings

	2001 LIB	—	2001 CONS		2002 LIB	—	2002 CONS
Economic	91%	—	9%		73%	—	27%
Social	83%	—	11%		73%	—	27%
Foreign	90%	—	10%		72%	—	26%

Key Votes of the 107th Congress

1. Approve Bush Tax Cuts	N	5. Faith-Based Charities	N	9. Trade Promotion Authority	N
2. Limit Patients' Bill of Rights	N	6. Bar Gays in the Boy Scouts	N	10. Bar Funds for Intl. Court	N
3. Campaign Finance Reform	Y	7. Ban Partial-Birth Abortion	N	11. Authorize Force in Iraq	Y
4. Ban ANWR Development	Y	8. Arm Commercial Pilots	Y	12. Deny Home. Sec. Dept. Union	N

Election Results

2002 general	Carolyn Maloney (D-L-Ind-WF)	95,931	(75%)	($916,773)
	Anton Srdanovic (R-C)	31,548	(25%)	($44,255)
2002 primary	Carolyn Maloney (D)	unopposed		
2000 general	Carolyn Maloney (D-L)	148,080	(74%)	($802,053)
	C. Adrienne Rhodes (R)	45,453	(23%)	($28,382)
	Other	6,815	(3%)	

Prior Winning Percentages: 1998 (77%); 1996 (72%); 1994 (64%); 1992 (50%)

The People		Race/Ethnic Origin	Ancestry	
Area size:	15 sq. mi.	65.9% White	Irish: 8.1%	Italian: 7.7%
Urban population:	100.0%	4.8% Black	German: 6.1%	
Rural population:	0.0%	11.4% Asian	**2000 Presidential Vote**	
Pop. 2000:	654,361	0.1% Native Am.	Gore (D) 168,842	(70%)
Median income:	$57,152	0.0% Hawaiian	Bush (R) 56,055	(23%)
Poverty status:	12.4%	3.1% Two+ races	Other 16,908	(7%)
Military veterans:	6.0%	0.6% Other	**Cook Partisan Voting Index:** D +25	
		14.0% Hispanic Origin		

Occupation	Blue collar: 7.8%	White collar: 82.1%	Gray collar: 10.2%

The Upper East Side of Manhattan, the home today of people with more accumulated wealth than anywhere else in the world, began as much of New York City did—as farmland. Its eastern border was established at Fifth Avenue when work began on Central Park in 1857, but most of the area was still farmland when the park was completed in 1873. During the 1880s, the avenues—Fifth, Madison, Park, Lexington, Third, Second, First—were paved and rich New Yorkers and many who had made their money elsewhere—Pittsburgh steel baron Andrew Carnegie, Montana mining magnate William Clark—built mansions on Fifth Avenue. Third Avenue, with its elevated train line, was lined with walkups for working class commuters, while the side streets off Fifth Avenue were lined with massive brownstone houses shielded from the industrial haze along the East River. The Upper East Side began taking on its present character in 1913, when Grand Central Terminal was opened and the New York Central rail line was buried under Park Avenue: what had been a filthy railroad cut became a broad boulevard lined with grand apartment buildings. The federal income tax, passed the same year, had the unintended consequence of encouraging New York's rich to dispense with grand mansions and live, quietly and out of sight, in apartment buildings where doormen protected their privacy.

The emergence of the modern Upper East Side represented yet another iteration of the pattern noticed by the mid-19th century New York diarists Philip Hone and George Templeton

Strong: On such a compact island, it took only a generation or so before buildings were torn down and rebuilt. Even today, New York is being transformed by gleaming postmodern skyscrapers and high-priced storefronts, though its most enduring landmarks were products of the first half of the century: the Flatiron Building in 1901; the Woolworth Building and Grand Central in 1913; the Chrysler Building, Empire State Building and Rockefeller Center in the 1920s and 1930s; and the United Nations headquarters, the world's first glass-fronted skyscraper, after World War II. Most of these landmarks are in the 14th District, which also holds the more humble distinction of being the site of the first public housing project in America—the First Houses, built in lower Manhattan in 1935 by Mayor Fiorello LaGuardia.

The 14th Congressional District includes within its irregular borders the Upper East Side and nearly all of these buildings. The district begins at East 96th Street, the historic dividing line between Manhattan's wealthiest and poorest neighborhoods, near where the railroad emerges from its tunnel and comes out in the middle of Park Avenue, and runs all the way down to East 9th Street in the East Village. It includes all of Central Park; much of the midtown corporate district; Murray Hill and Gramercy Park, and also parts of the East Village and the Lower East Side. The 14th also takes in Roosevelt Island, a 147-acre expanse in the East River that was transformed in the early 1970s from a hospital-and-prison complex to an ethnically diverse residential neighborhood (and stripped of its old name, Welfare Island). The 14th also includes part of Queens across the East River: Long Island City, Steinway, part of historically Irish Sunnyside and all of the vibrantly Greek Astoria, now with a growing number of Asians, Latinos and Arabs. Along Astoria's Steinway Street, between 28th and Astoria Blvd., there are Arabic shisha cafes, stores that offer Halal products and bakeries that make kanafa. The institutions of the 14th are famous and powerful—from the U.N. to the New York Public Library to St. Patrick's Cathedral— and its stores of culture are among the world's finest—the Metropolitan Museum of Art, the Guggenheim, the Whitney and the Frick, but also a rising arts cluster in Long Island City, including the temporarily relocated Museum of Modern Art, the contemporary art gallery P.S. 1 and the American Museum of the Moving Image adjoining the old Astoria movie studios, where most movies were made before the industry moved to sunnier Hollywood.

The 14th District is the latest version of the Upper East Side-based Silk Stocking district, originally created in 1918. The Silk Stocking district has always been dominated by its affluent and highly educated voters, leaders in securities, publishing, advertising, entertainment, broadcasting and communications. Historically, the Silk Stocking creed was confidence in its duty to lead the nation and mistrust of the city's (usually Democratic) immigrant masses—the politics of Theodore Roosevelt, the old *New York Herald Tribune* and Henry Luce's *Time* magazine. While it did not trust union leaders and Democratic Party politicians, it accepted much of the New Deal. This district believed the nation should be led by the well-educated Protestant gentlemen one saw strolling down Madison Avenue to their clubs, who held high government posts from Theodore Roosevelt's day and past Franklin's. But the attitude of the Manhattan elite was transformed from liberal Republican to leftish Democratic in a way personified by the Silk Stocking district's most famous congressman, John Lindsay. He was elected in 1958 as a liberal Republican, an advocate of civil liberties full of mistrust of machine Democrats and unions, and in 1965 he was elected Mayor of New York. While mayor, he ran up huge debts that led the city to the brink of bankruptcy in 1975, while neighborhoods deteriorated and the city lost 1 million people in the 1970s. He was succeeded as congressman and ultimately as mayor by Edward Koch, whose political travels were the reverse: Koch started as a liberal reform Democrat and became more conservative, and in the process lost the support of elite Manhattan by backing capital punishment, opposing racial quotas and questioning poverty programs. Attitudes have now changed: the troubled mayoralty of David Dinkins led Manhattanites to back Rudolph Giuliani, and they applauded his successes in cutting crime and welfare and taxes. But Giuliani and his successor Michael Bloomberg, who lives in his town house on East 79th Street, are firm cultural liberals on abortion, gay rights and gun control. To the national Republican party of Newt Gingrich in the 1990s and George W. Bush in the 2000s the Upper East Side is unremittingly hostile: these are people that seem to come from another country. The Upper East Side reacted with similar disdain to Barry Goldwater in 1964, and voted for Lyndon Johnson by a wide margin, as did the entire country; but in 2000, when the rest of the country was evenly split between George W. Bush and Al Gore, the Upper East Side voted for Gore by a wider margin than it had voted for Johnson. In American politics today, cultural issues trump economics: the affluent Upper East Side votes heavily Democratic (the 10021 zip code is the leading New York zip code for Democratic campaign contributions) while low-income Mississippi and Montana vote heavily Republican. In youth-thronged clubs and Park Avenue dinner parties, in chic restaurants and in high-fashion stores, nary a good word is to be said for the national leaders of the party that once was led by Manhattan's upper crust.

The congresswoman from the 14th District is Carolyn Maloney, a Democrat first elected in 1992. Born and educated in North Carolina, she visited New York in 1970 at the age of 22, loved it and "just stayed." She worked on welfare education programs during the 1970s, and from 1977–82 she was a legislative staffer in Albany. She was elected to the New York City Council in 1982; one observer of her time there described her as "a little spacey" until she found a cause, but then she became "a pit bull." For 1992, redistricting created a Silk Stocking district even more Democratic than its predecessor and Maloney ran against incumbent Bill Green, a thoughtful liberal Republican who shared Manhattan's cultural liberalism but could not compete with the enthusiasm of a Democratic Party dominated by the feminist left for a woman candidate. And he was poorly positioned to appeal to voters in the outer borough neighborhoods that were for the first time added to the district, who liked Republicans conservative on cultural issues but were liberal on economics. Maloney lost the Manhattan part of the district 50%–44%, but carried Queens heavily and won 50%–48% overall.

Maloney started off in the House with a certain naivete but stayed to make serious contributions on important issues and developed a relatively liberal voting record. On the Financial Services Committee, she worked to keep banks from controlling other businesses, has proposed regulation of hedge funds with assets over $1 billion, sought more oversight of the Federal Reserve, added some privacy provisions to the Gramm-Leach-Bliley financial modernization law, and in 2002 added language to the corporate accountability bill that requires a company to disclose publicly whenever its board votes to violate its own ethics code. With an eye to Astoria, she helped found the Congressional Caucus on Hellenic Issues; with an eye to the corporate suites, she voted for PNTR with China. She got $5 million to plan the long-proposed but never-built Second Avenue subway line. But the conservative Manhattan Institute contended in a report that she regularly votes against the economic well-being of the City. A leader of the Women's Caucus, she opposed separating men and women in basic training; she co-authored with John Dingell a report that documented the widening salary gap between men and women managers.

As ranking Democrat on the Census Subcommittee for four years, Maloney was a fervent backer of Census sampling; the 1990 undercount in New York City, she said, was 244,000, and the city was being deprived of needed federal funds. But in 2001, she switched off Census to become ranking Democrat on the Domestic and International Monetary Policy, Trade and Technology Subcommittee.

With part of her district in Lower Manhattan and close to Ground Zero, the aftermath of the September 11 attacks kept her busy. She was among the most outspoken House Democrats urging George W. Bush to quickly send New York the $20 billion that Congress approved for cleanup and recovery and she urged him to appoint a coordinator to work with the city on its needs. With Peter King, she passed a bill awarding the Congressional Gold Medal posthumously to emergency workers and other government employees who died while responding to the attacks. Her proposal to give a $1,000 tax credit to visitors to the city went nowhere.

Any doubts that Maloney had a firm lock on the district were dispelled in the Republican year of 1994. Manhattan Councilman Charles Millard spent almost $1 million against her; but the 14th District was voting 78% for Mario Cuomo and Maloney won 64%–35%. The 2000 Census showed, even without sampling, that New York City gained 9% in population in the 1990s, and that convinced redistricters not to eliminate a City district. Manhattan's population entitled it to only 2.3, and it was understood that Harlem's Charles Rangel must be given a district fully in Manhattan; nevertheless redistricters were able to produce two other districts, the 8th and the 14th, in which most of the votes were cast in Manhattan. This was done by adding 80,000 people in Queens, mostly in Astoria, to the 14th. Maloney was reelected easily.

FIFTEENTH DISTRICT

Rep. Charles Rangel (D)

Elected 1970, 17th term; b. June 11, 1930, New York City; home, Harlem; N.Y.U., B.S. 1957, St. John's U., LL.B. 1960; Catholic; married (Alma).

Military Career: Army, 1948–52 (Korea).

Elected Office: NY Assembly, 1966–70.

Professional Career: Asst. U.S. Atty., S. Dist. of NY, 1959–64; Legal Cnsl., NYC Housing & Redevel. Bd., Neighborhood Conservation Bureau, 1963–68; Gen. Cnsl., Natl. Advisory Comm. on Selective Svc., 1966.

DC Office: 2354 RHOB 20515, 202-225-4365; Fax: 202-225-0816; Web site: www.house.gov/rangel.

District Office: Manhattan, 212-663-3900.

Committees: *Ways & Means* (RMM of 17 D): Human Resources; Trade. *Joint Committee on Taxation* (4th of 5 Reps.).

Group Ratings

	ADA	ACLU	AFS	LCV	CON	ITIC	NTU	COC	ACU	NTLC	CHC
2002	95	80	100	88	63	50	19	32	0	3	8
2001	90	—	100	100	—	—	6	25	4	—	—

National Journal Ratings

	2001 LIB	—	2001 CONS		2002 LIB	—	2002 CONS
Economic	93%	—	7%		86%	—	12%
Social	79%	—	21%		94%	—	3%
Foreign	94%	—	5%		94%	—	0%

Key Votes of the 107th Congress

1. Approve Bush Tax Cuts	N	5. Faith-Based Charities	N	9. Trade Promotion Authority	N
2. Limit Patients' Bill of Rights	N	6. Bar Gays in the Boy Scouts	N	10. Bar Funds for Intl. Court	N
3. Campaign Finance Reform	Y	7. Ban Partial-Birth Abortion	N	11. Authorize Force in Iraq	N
4. Ban ANWR Development	Y	8. Arm Commercial Pilots	N	12. Deny Home. Sec. Dept. Union	N

Election Results

2002 general	Charles Rangel (D-WF)	84,367	(88%)	($1,749,972)
	Jessie Fields (R-Ind)	11,008	(12%)	($34,001)
2002 primary	Charles Rangel (D)	unopposed		
2000 general	Charles Rangel (D-L-WF)	130,161	(92%)	($2,032,835)
	Jose Agustin Suero (R-Ref)	7,346	(5%)	($410)
	Other	4,157	(3%)	

Prior Winning Percentages: 1998 (93%); 1996 (91%); 1994 (97%); 1992 (95%); 1990 (97%); 1988 (97%); 1986 (96%); 1984 (97%); 1982 (97%); 1980 (96%); 1978 (96%); 1976 (97%); 1974 (97%); 1972 (96%); 1970 (87%)

The People		Race/Ethnic Origin	Ancestry	
Area size:	16 sq. mi.	16.4% White	West Indian: 2.8%	German: 2.0%
Urban population:	100.0%	30.5% Black	Irish: 2.0%	
Rural population:	0.0%	2.8% Asian	**2000 Presidential Vote**	
Pop. 2000:	654,361	0.2% Native Am.	Gore (D) 165,002	(87%)
Median income:	$27,934	0.0% Hawaiian	Bush (R) 12,430	(7%)
Poverty status:	30.5%	1.8% Two+ races	Other 13,292	(7%)
Military veterans:	4.6%	0.4% Other	**Cook Partisan Voting Index:** D +43	
		47.9% Hispanic Origin		

Occupation   Blue collar: 14.8%   White collar: 63.8%   Gray collar: 21.4%

Harlem, for many years America's most famous black ghetto, is now rebounding from decades of grim times. Harlem's development came relatively late in New York City's history. When Alexander Hamilton and Roger Morris built mansions in northern Manhattan, they were far out in the countryside. Early critics of Central Park questioned the necessity of setting aside open land when picnickers could always go to Harlem. By the late 19th century, Harlem had become a commuter neighborhood for Germans and then Jews and Italians. After the turn of the century, real-estate speculators began constructing blocks of impressive brownstones, hoping to capitalize on the impending arrival of the subway. But overbuilding led to high vacancy rates, and some landlords, in desperation, agreed to rent to African-Americans as long as they were willing to pay a premium. After generations of being shunted from one neighborhood to the next as the city developed, enough black residents were willing to do so that the neighborhood soon turned into the locus of New York City's African-American community. Harlem expanded from its nucleus around Lenox Avenue and 125th Street, while the Italian neighborhood to the east later known as Spanish Harlem grew outward from 116th Street and Pleasant Avenue. In northwest Harlem's Sugar Hill lived many of the greatest black Americans—W.E.B. DuBois, Thurgood Marshall, Ralph Ellison, Joe Louis.

For a long moment Harlem was a wondrous place, a center of writers and professionals and entertainers; the rosters of the Apollo Theater on 125th Street in the 1920s and 1930s were filled with the names of great artists still remembered today. Back then, the *WPA Guide* described Harlem as "the spiritual capital of Black America." But starting with the summer 1964 riot, Harlem faced decades of deterioration. Hundreds of brownstones were abandoned or pulled down. As successful black families moved outward—to Springfield Gardens in Queens or Williamsbridge in the Bronx or to the Westchester or New Jersey suburbs—Harlem was increasingly left with welfare mothers and criminal gangs, and its population dropped by one-third between 1970 and 1990. Manufacturing jobs all but disappeared; the area's public schools declined; the Hotel Theresa closed; and antipoverty money was channeled to a tight group of successful politicians with few widespread results.

But in the 1990s, things turned up. The federal government gave $300 million in investment capital, and the huge drop in crime under Mayor Rudolph Giuliani made Harlem real estate valuable again. Brownstones were renovated, vacant city buildings sold off; neighborhood schools upgraded; commercial frontage repaired; arts spaces opened. Younger African-Americans are returning, while visitors from overseas, especially Japan and Europe, flock to the area for historical tours, prompting a boomlet in niche hotels and guest houses. Community development corporations, often linked to churches, encouraged home ownership. Supermarkets have opened, there is a big shopping center on 125th Street, with the same stores found in suburban malls, chain drug stores have opened numerous branches. And in July 2001, Bill Clinton opened his post-presidential office at 55 West 125th Street.

Politically, Harlem has been heavily Democratic ever since the 1930s, when black voters switched from the Republican party of Abraham Lincoln to the Democratic party of Franklin Roosevelt. Oddly, Harlem did not get its own congressional district until 1944; the lines, previously drawn in 1918, were based on the 1910 Census, when Harlem had far fewer people. The new congressman was Adam Clayton Powell Jr., minister at the Abyssinian Baptist Church and a brilliant orator who became the most famous (and infamous) black politician of his time: chairman of the Education and Labor Committee when it passed the Great Society programs in 1965, then excluded from Congress in 1967 (illegally, the Supreme Court ruled) for refusing to honor a New York decree in a libel case brought by a plaintiff he called a "bag woman."

Today, the 15th Congressional District includes not just Harlem but all of northern Manhattan, down to 91st Street on the west side and 96th Street on the east side. On the west side, the district's southern reaches include portions of the white-liberal Upper West Side as well as the Morningside Heights precincts around Columbia University. On the east side, 96th Street is where the railroad comes out of the tunnel that runs under Park Avenue to Grand Central Station and where real estate agents have long drawn an invisible line. Spanish Harlem, just to the north, was once Italian (it was Fiorello LaGuardia's political base and Al Pacino was born there), and later heavily Puerto Rican; today, "El Barrio" has fewer Puerto Ricans and more Latinos with roots in other Latin countries. Still further north, the district includes Washington Heights, once mainly Jewish, and Inwood, once heavily Italian. Now both are heavily Latino, the center of Dominican life in New York as Dominicans replace Puerto Ricans as New York's most numerous Latino group.

Washington Heights was hit especially hard by the crack epidemic in the late 1980s and early 1990s, but now it too is recovering thanks to reduced crime and immigrant vitality. Governor George Pataki in 2002 made a point of coming to shop on Dyckman Street, the boundary between Washington Heights and Inwood, and speaking to passers-by in his recently acquired Spanish. The district also includes imposing parts of New York's infrastructure—the huge Con Edison plant on the East River, Wards Island, home to the Triborough Bridge, and the city prison on Rikers Island: but there are no voters here. Overall, the district is 31% black and 48% Hispanic—figures that testify to decades of black flight from Harlem and the continuing inrush of immigrants from the Western Hemisphere. National Republicans seldom win as much as 10% of the vote here, but in 2002 Pataki ran much stronger in Latino neighborhoods.

The congressman from the 15th District is Charles Rangel, first elected in 1970. Rangel is now the senior member of the New York delegation and ranking Democrat on Ways and Means. He grew up in Harlem and served in the Army in Korea, where he rescued 40 men from behind the lines in Kunu-ri and was awarded the Bronze Star; he returned to Korea in June 2000 for the 50th anniversary of the outbreak of the war. He graduated from New York University and St. John's University law school, served as legal counsel in several government agencies and was elected to the Assembly in 1966; he was part of a group of young black politicians, with state Senator Basil Paterson and Carl McCall and Assemblyman Percy Sutton, who for many years have dominated Harlem and greatly influenced New York politics. In 1970 Rangel challenged Powell in the Democratic primary and narrowly won. Like most Harlem politicians, he has long argued that government aid and racial preferences are needed to solve Harlem's problems. Yet much in his own career suggests otherwise. Rangel's main emphasis for a decade was denunciation of the drug trade. From 1983 until it was abolished in 1993 with the other House select committees, Rangel chaired the Select Committee on Narcotics Abuse and Control, and seldom missed a chance to relate other problems to drugs; after all, he has seen how they can destroy a community.

On Ways and Means Rangel worked, with success, to protect state and local income tax deductibility in the 1986 tax reform and is an author of the Federal Empowerment Zone demonstration, the Low Income Housing tax credit and the Targeted Jobs tax credit. All those are aimed at turning around places like Harlem.

Rangel combines political shrewdness with a winning personality, but when Republicans took control of the House he indulged in some extravagant rhetoric. When a bipartisan majority voted to end racial preferences in broadcasting in 1995, Rangel lashed out in a letter to Ways and Means Chairman Bill Archer: "Mr. Chairman, in America we cannot afford to be colorblind. Just like under Hitler, people say they don't mean to blame any particular individuals and groups, but in the U.S. those groups always turn out to be minorities and immigrants." Archer refused to speak to Rangel except in public committee meetings and refused to meet with him in private until June 1999, when Archer and Rangel were working on Social Security. Rangel defended Bill Clinton against impeachment with great vigor, but he did not always get along with Clinton. He resented it when the administration negotiated directly with Republicans, leaving congressional Democrats out of the loop. For years he has tried to get more blacks and other minorities into the Foreign Service, sponsoring orientations for students at City College and the Charles Rangel International Affairs Program at Howard University. "As I got to Congress, I had a chance to visit foreign countries, and they would look at me as though I wasn't an American, and it was because they never had an opportunity to see diversity in this country."

Since January 1997 Rangel has been ranking Democrat on Ways and Means; if Democrats win back a majority in 2004, he would be its first New York City chairman since Fernando Wood in 1877–81. Rangel remembered how he had been beaten for House whip in 1986 by Tony Coelho, a champion Democratic fundraiser, and decided for the first time to become a major fundraiser himself: of course it helped that with only a few more Democratic seats he would chair Ways and Means. In the 1997–98 cycle he raised more than $1.3 million for Democratic candidates, drawing on successful black entrepreneurs like Robert Johnson of Black Entertainment Television. In 1999–2000 he even more actively solicited contributions from and shared his views on issues with leading corporate and financial executives. In 1999 he raised $2.3 million for the campaign committee, more than anyone else except Minority Leader Dick Gephardt and committee Chairman Patrick Kennedy; he raised another $4 million in 2000 but only $1.7 million in 2002.

Amid all this politicking, Rangel still found time for legislating. He worked hard for a bill to cut tariffs on apparel and other imports from sub-Saharan Africa, and also from the Caribbean and Central America. His chief partners in this were Republicans Ed Royce and Tom DeLay; it was opposed by unions and textile interests, and also by Jesse Jackson Jr. and other members of the Congressional Black Caucus. Jackson said it would help only multinational corporations and "African elites," but it passed the House 309–110 in May 2000. On PNTR with China, Rangel kept silent for many months, torn between union opponents and Clinton administration proponents. In May 2000 he finally came out in favor—the key vote to many observers. At that point, Tom DeLay said, "Okay, Mr. Future Chairman of Ways and Means, get the votes for passage." Rangel did: 73 Democrats joined 164 Republicans to pass it through what had been a very uncertain House. But he strongly opposed trade promotion authority in 2001 and 2002, and said that House Republican leaders' arm-twisting to get it passed was an "indictable offense." Rangel favors eliminating all sanctions on trade with Cuba; he favors allowing Haitian and Dominican immigrants into the United States on the same basis as refugees from Cuba. In early 2002 he traveled to Cuba and called Fidel Castro "a proud, brilliant man who has been able to use the U.S. trade embargo as an excuse for the failures of his socialist system. . . . Cuba continues to have one of the best and most sophisticated health care and medical research systems in the world." On the last day of 2002 he called for a revival of the military draft, contending that "a disproportionate number of the poor and members of minority groups make up the enlisted ranks of the military, while the most privileged Americans are underrepresented or absent."

Ways and Means Chairman Bill Archer was crisp and to the point; Bill Thomas, who succeeded him in 2001, is acerbic and uncollegial, and has made few moves to bipartisanship. Rangel's frustration came out when he was asked in October 2002 about a Thomas tax proposal. "It's almost accepted now that all Thomas has to do is to talk to DeLay and Armey, and then his bills come to the floor. I am embarrassed that I would hear about [the tax proposal] from you, [but] it is not unusual." But Rangel has not been an easy man to be bipartisan with. Of the fall 2001 stimulus package he said, "This isn't an economic stimulus bill. This is a corporate welfare bill." In July 2002 he opposed Thomas's proposal to compensate corporations for the tax breaks they lost when the WTO ruled that Foreign Sales Corporations were illegal; at one point he crossed the aisle and joined with Philip Crane, who was passed over for the chairmanship, to propose a 1% cut in the corporate income tax instead. On Social Security, he said in May 2002: "We're going to wrap it around [the Republican party's] neck until they come to the floor and say they didn't mean what they said. Every time they say Social Security, we'll say privatization." He did have bipartisan success when in December 2001 the House passed a bill to stop the trade in "conflict diamonds," rough diamonds sold by terrorist governments in Liberia and Sierra Leone to finance their depredations. In October 2001 Rangel proposed that Congress hold a one-day session in New York. It was done in September 2002, only the second session of Congress held outside Washington since the federal government moved out of Philadelphia in 1800.

Rangel is a major player in New York city and state politics. He strongly backed his old friend Carl McCall for governor, and in December 2001 said he would vote for George Pataki if the nomination went to McCall's rival, Andrew Cuomo. Cuomo's wife Kerry Kennedy Cuomo was furious, and chewed out Rangel ally David Dinkins in public; asked about her comments, Rangel said, "No one knows who she is." When Clinton and others tried to get Cuomo out of the race before the September primary, Cuomo's father Mario Cuomo called Rangel, who tried but failed to get McCall to appear at Cuomo's announcement. In October 2002 Rangel attacked the DNC for not backing McCall strongly enough; the DNC had put $240,000 and the RNC $1.5 million into New York.

Rangel himself has been easily reelected. In 1994 he faced primary opposition from the son of his predecessor, the Puerto Rican-raised Adam Clayton Powell IV (Adam Clayton Powell III, another son, is a respected media expert). Rangel spent $1.4 million and won 61%–33%. Redistricting did not affect Rangel in any serious way: everyone involved understood that the demands of the Voting Rights Act and the importance of Rangel's position in the House made it mandatory to give him a district very much like his previous one. In July 2002, Conrad Muhammad, the dismissed head of the Nation of Islam's Mosque No. 7, started collecting signatures to run against Rangel in the September primary. But his energies were evidently directed elsewhere. Later that month, he walked into the Abyssinian Baptist Church and declared himself a Christian, and his name did not appear on the ballot.

SIXTEENTH DISTRICT

Rep. Jose Serrano (D)

Elected Mar. 1990, 7th term; b. Oct. 24, 1943, Mayaguez, PR; home, Bronx; Lehman Col.; Catholic; married (Mary).

Military Career: Army Medical Corps, 1964–66.

Elected Office: Dist. 7 Schl. Bd., 1969–74; NY Assembly, 1974–90.

Professional Career: Banker, 1961–69.

DC Office: 2227 RHOB 20515, 202-225-4361; Fax: 202-225-6001; Web site: www.house.gov/serrano.

District Office: Bronx, 718-538-5400.

Committees: *Appropriations* (10th of 29 D): Commerce, Justice, State & Judiciary (RMM); Homeland Security.

Group Ratings

	ADA	ACLU	AFS	LCV	CON	ITIC	NTU	COC	ACU	NTLC	CHC
2002	90	93	100	100	43	50	24	37	0	3	0
2001	85	—	100	71	—	—	10	35	0	—	—

National Journal Ratings

	2001 LIB —	2001 CONS		2002 LIB —	2002 CONS
Economic	78% —	22%		92% —	7%
Social	90% —	0%		84% —	8%
Foreign	81% —	18%		92% —	7%

Key Votes of the 107th Congress

1. Approve Bush Tax Cuts	N	5. Faith-Based Charities	N	9. Trade Promotion Authority	N
2. Limit Patients' Bill of Rights	N	6. Bar Gays in the Boy Scouts	*	10. Bar Funds for Intl. Court	N
3. Campaign Finance Reform	Y	7. Ban Partial-Birth Abortion	N	11. Authorize Force in Iraq	N
4. Ban ANWR Development	Y	8. Arm Commercial Pilots	N	12. Deny Home. Sec. Dept. Union	N

Election Results

2002 general	Jose Serrano (D-WF)	50,716	(92%)	($214,152)
	Frank Dellavalle (R-C)	4,366	(8%)	
2002 primary	Jose Serrano (D)	unopposed		
2000 general	Jose Serrano (D-L)	103,041	(96%)	($210,037)
	Aaron Justice (R)	3,934	(4%)	
	Other	571	(1%)	

Prior Winning Percentages: 1998 (95%); 1996 (96%); 1994 (96%); 1992 (91%); 1990 (93%); 1990 (92%)

The People		Race/Ethnic Origin	Ancestry	
Area size:	13 sq. mi.	2.9% White	West Indian: 3.9% Subsaharan: 3.1%	
Urban population:	100.0%	30.3% Black	USA: 2.3%	
Rural population:	0.0%	1.6% Asian	**2000 Presidential Vote**	
Pop. 2000:	654,360	0.3% Native Am.	Gore (D)	112,786 (92%)
Median income:	$19,311	0.0% Hawaiian	Bush (R)	6,634 (5%)
Poverty status:	42.2%	1.6% Two+ races	Other	2,630 (2%)
Military veterans:	3.9%	0.5% Other	**Cook Partisan Voting Index:** D +44	
		62.8% Hispanic Origin		

Occupation	Blue collar: 23.6%	White collar: 46.4%	Gray collar: 30.0%

It may not quite be "the beautiful Bronx," as borough historian Lloyd Utlan calls it, but The Bronx seems to have rebounded from rock bottom. The beautiful days were in the 1930s and 1940s, when Presidents Roosevelt and Truman rode down 138th Street, when Babe Ruth, Lou Gehrig and Joe DiMaggio knocked home runs out of Yankee Stadium, when Art Deco apartment buildings were built along the Grand Concourse, when shoppers thronged Tremont Avenue stores, and when Bronx County Democratic Chairman Ed Flynn was Chairman of the Democratic National Committee. As early as the 1880s, the Bronx (then known as the Northside and only recently annexed from Westchester County) was linked to the level eastern half of Manhattan by elevated steam locomotives. But the borough really took off in 1906 with the arrival of the first subway, which allowed the children of immigrants to move from grim Lower East Side tenements to spacious walkup apartments flooded with light. The Bronx's population grew from 200,000 in 1900 to 430,000 in 1910—enough, had the borough been independent, to rank as America's sixth largest city—and 1.2 million in 1930. The Bronx's population peaked at nearly 1.5 million in 1950. But after a quarter-century of deterioration, the population shrunk to 1.2 million by 1990. Now it's up again, to 1.3 million in 2000, as new immigrants revive neighborhoods that had been given up for dead.

The downfall began in the mid-1960s. Rent control, insisted upon by tenants, guaranteed that owners of low-rent property wouldn't maintain it; once empty, many buildings were torched for the insurance money, sometimes as many as four blocks a week. At the same time, a drop in low-income, low-skill jobs in Manhattan and the Bronx—abetted by high, union-enforced wages and organized crime—led to a rise in welfare dependency and crime, with empty building shells becoming the perfect venue for drug dealing. And the 13-year, $250 million effort to build the Cross-Bronx Expressway—a brainchild of Robert Moses that crossed 113 streets and avenues, hundreds of utility mains and ten mass-transit lines—made things worse. As workers plowed through acres of tough bedrock, the project shredded entire neighborhoods, forcing 40,000 people to move from their homes and forever changing the landscape. In the upheaval, longtime residents fled in droves—whites to the suburbs or the Sun Belt, Puerto Ricans to their homeland, African Americans to the South or other cities—and the rapid turnover strained PTAs and other civic institutions. A vicious cycle emerged: Crime drove away jobs, which drove away fathers, which produced more crime. When Tom Wolfe imagined the "wrong turn" that sunk a high-flying Wall Street career in *Bonfire of the Vanities*, he set it in the South Bronx; the movie version filmed the scene under the Bruckner Expressway.

Presidents and presidential candidates came in—Jimmy Carter in 1977, Ronald Reagan in 1980—promising help. Ironically, the South Bronx was never the worst slum in New York; it just looked the worst. The borough's saviors were churches and creative community groups which, without much centralized planning, built single-family pastel bungalows and small-scale apartment projects for the elderly, single-parent families and former homeless. With their help, the South Bronx has turned a corner. The building spree of the 1990s created the Bronx's first new wave of housing starts since the 1950s, and the first new cluster of private residences since the 1930s. While Bronx County still has the third-highest percentage of single mothers in America, and while rates of childhood asthma are among the nation's highest, low-income families in the Bronx are now finding it possible to work their way up. Local institutions such as Bronx-Lebanon Hospital have helped, employing area residents and providing neighborhood stability. As immigrants from Ecuador, Ghana and Bangladesh settled in, the population once again rose; a few corners of the South Bronx have even seen yuppies and artists colonizing old industrial space. Charlotte Street, which Jimmy Carter and Ronald Reagan once visited as the worst of the slums, is now Charlotte Gardens, with owner-occupied houses worth $180,000. As with other parts of New York City, the main obstacle now for the South Bronx is its weak commercial sector—a legacy of redlining and the reality of the area's low disposable incomes. Here, bank branches are still far outnumbered by check-cashing outlets, and theaters and restaurants virtually nonexistent.

The 16th Congressional District includes most of the South Bronx. It is bounded by the Harlem River on the west, the East River on the south, the Bronx River and Bronx Park (home of the Bronx Zoo) on the east, and goes just past Fordham Road on the north. It includes the Parisian-style Grand Concourse, where single-family homes for the wealthy were replaced in the

1930s by stylish Art Deco apartment buildings; this was one of America's biggest Jewish neighborhoods up through the 1960s. It also includes Belmont, a Bronx "Little Italy" and site of an old-fashioned food market on Arthur Avenue; Belmont now has a growing number of Albanians. The 16th also includes the low-rent commercial strips of Westchester Avenue, Boston Road and the Hub, and the industrial flatlands of Bruckner Boulevard, Mott Haven and Hunts Point (though not the meat and produce markets). The 16th is 30% black, 63% Hispanic—the highest percentage in any New York district. This has long been New York's largest concentration of Puerto Ricans, but an increasing proportion of Hispanics here now are from other parts of Latin America. Politically, this was the most Democratic district in the country in 2000—92% for Al Gore and just 5% for George W. Bush.

The congressman from the 16th District is Jose Serrano (pronounced *sa-RAH-no*), chosen in a March 1990 special election. A native of Mayaguez, Puerto Rico, who grew up in the Millbrook project in the South Bronx, Serrano moved up while other Bronx politicians fell by the wayside because of corruption. He was elected to the New York Assembly in 1974 and chaired its Education Committee beginning in 1983; in 1985, he ran for Bronx borough president, bucking the Democratic organization, and nearly won. Then in January 1990, South Bronx Congressman Robert Garcia was convicted for accepting money from the minority contractor Wedtech; his conviction was later reversed, but his resignation led to Serrano's election to the House.

Serrano has one of the most liberal voting records in the House. As ranking Democrat on the Appropriations Subcommittee on Commerce, Justice, State and the Judiciary, he has used that position to redress past injustices by the FBI. In 1997, when Bill Richardson resigned from the House to become ambassador to the United Nations, Minority Leader Dick Gephardt passed over Serrano for the less senior Robert Menendez of New Jersey—a better fundraiser, with his Cuban-American connections—to be chief deputy whip. In 1998 Serrano ran for Democratic Caucus vice-chairman as "the candidate who refuses to raise money to buy your vote for leadership." But he withdrew in favor of Menendez, and supported him when he later became caucus chairman. By contrast, Serrano is known as Fidel Castro's greatest champion in the House. He says he admires Castro and has sought repeal of economic sanctions and the Helms-Burton Act. With eventual help from farm states, he led efforts to overturn the four-decade embargo of Cuba.

The pro-statehood Serrano has devoted much time to the cause of Puerto Rico, which he calls an American "colony." But the move toward statehood stalled. Serrano strongly defended Bill Clinton's 1999 clemency for Puerto Ricans members of the FALN terrorist group as an example of reconciliation. In May 2000, he was arrested for blocking passage at the White House to protest the Navy's bombing range at Vieques, Puerto Rico. When Jim Hansen condemned the protestors as ingrates who "sit down there on welfare," Serrano took offense and said that Hansen did not understand the U.S. relationship with Puerto Rico. Later, some New York City Democrats criticized him for lobbying for light rail in Puerto Rico instead of seeking transit money for New York.

In New York politics, Serrano takes strongly liberal positions. He backed Al Sharpton for mayor in 1997 and Bronx Borough President Fernando Ferrer in 2001; Sharpton lost in the Democratic primary and Ferrer in the runoff. In November 1997 he told colleagues he would run for mayor in 2001, but later said he was not interested. Meanwhile, Serrano was alert to affronts from other quarters. When Yankee owner George Steinbrenner threatened to move the team out of the South Bronx's Yankee Stadium, Serrano called on Clinton to declare it a national landmark; but as Steinbrenner's spokesman pointed out, landmark status would prevent the changes needed to make the stadium profitable and structurally sound. Serrano persuaded the House to award a Congressional Gold Medal to Frank Sinatra, whose work he has admired.

As minority leader, Nancy Pelosi named Serrano as one of three vice-chairmen of the Democratic Steering Committee, which makes committee assignments. With little change to the 16th from redistricting, Serrano appears secure for another decade.

SEVENTEENTH DISTRICT

Rep. Eliot Engel (D)

Elected 1988, 8th term; b. Feb. 18, 1947, Bronx; home, Bronx; Hunter-Lehman Col., B.A. 1969, C.U.N.Y., Lehman Col., M.A. 1973, NY Law Schl., J.D. 1987; Jewish; married (Patricia).

Elected Office: NY Assembly, 1977–88.

Professional Career: Teacher, guidance counselor, NYC public schl., 1969–77.

DC Office: 2264 RHOB 20515, 202-225-2464; Fax: 202-225-5513; Web site: www.house.gov/engel.

District Offices: Bronx, 718-796-9700; Mt. Vernon, 914-699-4100; West Nyack, 845-358-7800.

Committees: *Energy & Commerce* (14th of 26 D): Health; Telecommunications & The Internet. *International Relations* (10th of 23 D): Europe; Middle East & Central Asia.

Group Ratings

	ADA	ACLU	AFS	LCV	CON	ITIC	NTU	COC	ACU	NTLC	CHC
2002	90	79	100	88	63	38	18	50	12	3	8
2001	85	—	100	100	—	—	8	32	4	—	—

National Journal Ratings

	2001 LIB — 2001 CONS		2002 LIB — 2002 CONS	
Economic	80%	— 19%	74%	— 25%
Social	81%	— 20%	74%	— 19%
Foreign	66%	— 34%	67%	— 32%

Key Votes of the 107th Congress

1. Approve Bush Tax Cuts	N	5. Faith-Based Charities	*	9. Trade Promotion Authority	N
2. Limit Patients' Bill of Rights	N	6. Bar Gays in the Boy Scouts	N	10. Bar Funds for Intl. Court	N
3. Campaign Finance Reform	Y	7. Ban Partial-Birth Abortion	N	11. Authorize Force in Iraq	Y
4. Ban ANWR Development	Y	8. Arm Commercial Pilots	Y	12. Deny Home. Sec. Dept. Union	N

Election Results

2002 general	Eliot Engel (D-L-WF)	77,535	(63%)	($1,009,681)
	C. Scott Vanderhoef (R-C-Ind)	42,634	(34%)	($196,664)
	Other	3,674	(3%)	
2002 primary	Eliot Engel (D)	unopposed		
2000 general	Eliot Engel (D-L)	115,093	(90%)	($1,028,928)
	Patrick McManus (R-C)	13,201	(10%)	

Prior Winning Percentages: 1998 (88%); 1996 (85%); 1994 (78%); 1992 (80%); 1990 (61%); 1988 (56%)

The People		Race/Ethnic Origin	Ancestry	
Area size:	146 sq. mi.	41.3% White	West Indian: 10.1%	Irish: 8.7%
Urban population:	99.9%	30.4% Black	Italian: 8.4%	
Rural population:	0.1%	4.5% Asian	**2000 Presidential Vote**	
Pop. 2000:	654,360	0.2% Native Am.	Gore (D) 141,525	(69%)
Median income:	$44,868	0.0% Hawaiian	Bush (R) 54,362	(27%)
Poverty status:	16.0%	2.6% Two+ races	Other 8,438	(4%)
Military veterans:	7.7%	0.5% Other	**Cook Partisan Voting Index:** D +22	
		20.4% Hispanic Origin		

Occupation	Blue collar: 16.0%	White collar: 64.9%	Gray collar: 19.1%

The Bronx, settled mostly in the early 20th century, was originally a collection of middle-class neighborhoods clustered around subway stops, places where the children of immigrants left behind Manhattan's gloomy tenements and walkups and basked in the sunlight, wide avenues and hilly vistas of the Bronx. Different ethnic groups collected here and there: Irish in Kingsbridge, in the valley between Riverdale and the Grand Concourse; well-to-do WASPs and Jews in Riverdale, on the palisades above the Hudson River; middle-class blacks in Williamsbridge in the north central part of the borough. When neighboring areas in the South Bronx began to deteriorate, many of these residents fled, most often to Westchester County or the Sun Belt. Some moved to the southern cities of Westchester County on the Bronx border, some of which have taken on a central city character: Yonkers has been plagued by financial troubles and a landmark housing discrimination case; Mount Vernon now has a black majority. Others drove over the Tappan Zee Bridge to the pleasant suburbs of Rockland County, just north of Bergen County, New Jersey.

The 17th Congressional District includes the bulk of these Bronx neighborhoods, plus Baychester, Eastchester and Spuyten Duyvil, named for a now-vanished waterway separating Manhattan and the Bronx that translates as the Devil's Spate, and the century-old Van Cortlandt Park—at 1,146 acres, New York City's third-largest. It also includes leafy Woodlawn, still a magnet for Irish immigrants and more like neighboring Westchester County than the Bronx. But the district skips around Marble Hill, an African-American and Latino enclave on the Bronx mainland that, eccentrically, was kept as part of Manhattan after engineers diverted the Harlem River around it in 1895, hoping to improve shipping flow. In addition to the Bronx, the 17th reaches deep into the suburbs. It takes in Mount Vernon and Yonkers and a narrow strip of land running north from Yonkers along the Hudson River. Across the Tappan Zee, the district includes the southern half of Rockland County, including Nyack, Orangetown, Suffern, Ramapo and part of Clarkstown. This was one of the New York districts most changed by the 2002 redistricting. Much of the northeast Bronx was removed, including the huge 1960s Co-op City apartment complex; territory was added in Westchester, and for the first time, the district includes part of Rockland County. In the 2002 election, Rockland cast 40% of the vote, the Bronx cast 36% and Westchester 24%. The changes reduced the district's black percentage considerably—from 44% to 30% and its Hispanic percentage from 36% to 20%. The changes also made the district less heavily Democratic: the Bush 2000 percentage rose from 11% to 27%.

The congressman from the 17th District is Eliot Engel, a son of the Bronx who now lives in Riverdale, a political junkie who memorized the names of all 100 senators when he was a boy. He was a New York City teacher and guidance counselor who won office after an incumbent was struck by scandal. He was elected to the New York Assembly in a 1977 special election, at 30, to replace a convicted incumbent, and to the House in 1988 to replace Democrat Mario Biaggi after he was convicted in two tawdry bribery cases. Engel beat Biaggi in the primary 48%–26% and again in the general, in which Biaggi was the Republican nominee, by 56%–27%.

Engel's once strongly liberal voting record has become more moderate. On the International Relations Committee, he made his name as the backer of one ethnic cause after another; members of just about any ethnic group can be found in the Bronx. He has been a prime sponsor of the resolution to recognize Jerusalem as the capital of Israel and criticized proposals to dismantle West Bank settlements. He heads the Congressional Albanian Issues Caucus and keeps an eye on Albanian rights in the Former Yugoslav Republic of Macedonia. He met with Sinn Fein leader Gerry Adams, proposed legislation to oppose the British in Northern Ireland, and supported Bill Clinton's efforts to seek peace there. He called for investigation of the internment of Italian nationals and other harsh restrictions during World War II and filed a bill to create a clearinghouse at the Federal Communications Commission to empower Italian-Americans to monitor bias in entertainment. Engel is not a 1970s-style dove: He supported the Gulf War resolution, the bombing of Serbia to get a settlement in Bosnia, and the use of force in Iraq.

On the Energy and Commerce Committee, he worked with Henry Waxman, plus Republicans Vito Fossella and Doug Ose on a New York-California alliance to permit refiners to produce reformulated gasoline rather than more expensive ethanol. An Engel tradition: Since 1989 he has staked out an aisle seat hours before each State of the Union speech, so that he can shake the president's hand.

At home, Engel is a relentless constituency service congressman. In 1996 *The Wall Street Journal* profiled him as "Revenge of a Nerd," telling how he is known as "the mayor" in the north Bronx because of his persistent attention to local problems from broken traffic lights to congested subway trains.

When his district was mostly in the Bronx and almost 80% black and Hispanic, he faced constant primary challenges. In 1994 he was opposed by salsa singer Willie Colon, who was supported by Al Sharpton and Assemblyman Larry Seabrook. Engel won 61%–39%, not an entirely reassuring margin. In 1998 Seabrook, who is black and had become a state senator, made no secret he was running. But Democratic County Chairman Roberto Ramirez spoke to Seabrook, making vague promises about working on voter registration, and Seabrook bowed out. Finally in the September 2000 primary, there was the showdown. Seabrook argued that the district needed "real leadership" and attacked Engel for living in suburban Maryland. Ramirez and the Bronx Democratic organization backed Seabrook; he had a meeting with Congressional Black Caucus members, which brought angry comments from other Jewish members who argued that all Democrats should support their incumbent colleagues. When Seabrook produced a campaign button that said, "Vote First African-American Congressman," Engel objected to the use of race in the campaign. The contest turned uglier when a front page story in the New York *Daily News* said that Seabrook secretly divorced his wife in 1993 but continued to sign joint tax returns in violation of the law. Seabrook accused Engel of leaking sealed court documents, which Engel denied, but refused to provide his tax returns. Engel won 50%–41%. In 2001, he backed Mark Green over Fernando Ferrer for mayor.

Redistricting changed the political picture. Before the Census figures came in, many thought that Engel's district would be eliminated. But the Census showed that New York City's population had risen 9% in the 1990s, and so redistricters who needed to eliminate two districts shifted their focus to the suburbs and Upstate. They decided in June 2002 to eliminate the seat of Republican Benjamin Gilman, at 79 the oldest member of the delegation; Republicans did not strive to save the district, since they doubted they could hold it when Gilman retired. Now that only one-third of the votes are cast in the Bronx district and its black and Hispanic percentages are far lower, Engel is unlikely to be threatened by a black or Hispanic primary challenger, and neither Westchester nor Rockland provides a large enough base to support a primary challenge. Instead, in 2002 he had vigorous competition in the general election from Rockland County Executive Scott Vanderhoef, who criticized Engel's record of voting against tax cuts and defense spending. Vanderhoef carried Rockland County by 53%–45%. But his local fame did not travel well across the Hudson. Engel won 66%–31% in Westchester and 83%–13% in the Bronx, for an overall victory margin of 63%–34%—far from marginal. Naturally he has opened a district office in Rockland; this incumbent who looked like an endangered species for much of the last decade now looks stronger than ever.

EIGHTEENTH DISTRICT

Rep. Nita Lowey (D)

Elected 1988, 8th term; b. July 5, 1937, Bronx; home, Harrison; Mt. Holyoke Col., B.A. 1959; Jewish; married (Stephen).

Professional Career: Asst. for Econ. Devel. & Neighborhood Preservation, NY Secy. of State; Dep. Dir., Division of Econ. Opportunity, 1975–85; NY Asst. Secy. of St., 1985–87.

DC Office: 2329 RHOB 20515, 202-225-6506; Fax: 202-225-0546; Web site: www.house.gov/lowey.

District Offices: New City, 845-639-3485; White Plains, 914-428-1707; Yonkers, 914-779-9766.

Committees: *Appropriations* (9th of 29 D): Foreign Operations & Export Financing (RMM); Labor, HHS & Education. *Select Committee on Homeland Security* (11th of 23 D): Emergency Preparedness & Response; Intelligence & Counterterrorism.

Group Ratings

	ADA	ACLU	AFS	LCV	CON	ITIC	NTU	COC	ACU	NTLC	CHC
2002	90	87	100	88	63	50	19	40	4	6	0
2001	95	—	100	100	—	—	7	38	0	—	—

National Journal Ratings

	2001 LIB —	2001 CONS	2002 LIB —	2002 CONS
Economic	93%	7%	86%	12%
Social	83%	11%	67%	29%
Foreign	80%	20%	67%	33%

Key Votes of the 107th Congress

1. Approve Bush Tax Cuts	N	5. Faith-Based Charities		9. Trade Promotion Authority	N
2. Limit Patients' Bill of Rights	N	6. Bar Gays in the Boy Scouts	N	10. Bar Funds for Intl. Court	N
3. Campaign Finance Reform	Y	7. Ban Partial-Birth Abortion	N	11. Authorize Force in Iraq	Y
4. Ban ANWR Development	Y	8. Arm Commercial Pilots	Y	12. Deny Home. Sec. Dept. Union	N

Election Results

2002 general	Nita Lowey (D-WF)	98,957	(92%)	($1,646,414)
	Michael Reynolds (RTL)	8,558	(8%)	
2002 primary	Nita Lowey (D)	unopposed		
2000 general	Nita Lowey (D)	126,878	(67%)	($1,055,962)
	John G. Vonglis (R-C)	58,022	(31%)	
	Other	3,747	(2%)	

Prior Winning Percentages: 1998 (83%); 1996 (64%); 1994 (57%); 1992 (56%); 1990 (63%); 1988 (50%)

The People		Race/Ethnic Origin	Ancestry	
Area size:	270 sq. mi.	67.1% White	Italian: 17.2%	Irish: 11.0%
Urban population:	99.3%	9.5% Black	German: 6.2%	
Rural population:	0.7%	5.2% Asian	**2000 Presidential Vote**	
Pop. 2000:	654,360	0.1% Native Am.	Gore (D)	155,700 (58%)
Median income:	$68,887	0.0% Hawaiian	Bush (R)	103,248 (38%)
Poverty status:	7.8%	1.6% Two+ races	Other	9,268 (3%)
Military veterans:	9.2%	0.3% Other	**Cook Partisan Voting Index:** D +10	
		16.2% Hispanic Origin		

Occupation	Blue collar: 12.8%	White collar: 73.2%	Gray collar: 13.9%

The great granite ridges that form the spine of Manhattan and the Bronx move north into lower Westchester County, the thin peninsula of land between Long Island Sound and the Hudson River. This was active territory from early on. Washington Irving, the first fully professional writer in America, has his headless horseman chase schoolmaster Ichabod Crane through Sleepy Hollow, a fictionalized version of Tarrytown, on the east bank of the Hudson. Revolutionary War battles were fought here, and figures like John Peter Zenger, Alexander Hamilton and John Jay lived here. Blessed with some of America's loveliest scenery, and easily accessible to Manhattan by train since the mid-19th century, this became some of America's first suburban terrain, with grand estates built by great millionaires—Jay Gould's Gothic revival Lyndhurst and John D. Rockefeller's spectacular Kykuit, with villages for retainers clustered around the railroad stations. Today, Westchester still looks suburban, perhaps more than ever now that it has a nice patina of age. It has little commuter railroad stations across from faux Tudor drugstores, soda fountains and cobblestone post offices; it also has shopping malls and galleries and plenty of corporate headquarters, from IBM and Texaco to PepsiCo and Reader's Digest (as well as corporate watchdogs: Consumer Reports magazine is based in Yonkers). Intensive development slows down north of White Plains, for just to the north Westchester is crossed by the first of several mountain ridges—the closest the Appalachians come to the ocean. The county does have its share of homeless people and racial ghettos, and it has seedier neighborhoods if not slums. But in recent years, the greatest anxiety here has been caused by corporate restructuring and downsizing at once invincible companies like IBM—trends that have disproportionately affected the Fortune 500 managers that reside here.

The 18th Congressional District contains the heart of suburban Westchester County and also crosses over the Hudson River into Rockland County. It includes a host of affluent suburbs, many within easy reach of Grand Central via the Metro North rail lines—Bronxville, Tuckahoe, Eastchester, New Rochelle, Scarsdale, White Plains, Larchmont, Mamaroneck, Rye, Harrison, Armonk and Chappaqua, where Bill and Hillary Rodham Clinton bought a house in 2000. It also includes Haverstraw across the Hudson in Rockland County. It also includes most of the Hudson River towns of Hastings-on-Hudson, Dobbs Ferry, Irvington and Tarrytown to the east. Historically, Westchester was a Republican county, with a successful Republican political machine and an electorate made up of affluent professionals who naturally preferred the party opposed to big city political bosses and labor union leaders. But Westchester today is mostly Democratic. One reason is that Jewish voters, long Democratic, became even more so in the 1990s thanks to the visibility of Christian conservatives in the Republican party. Another reason is that on the cultural issues of greatest import recently, gun control and abortion, affluent suburbanites in America's biggest metropolitan area have been strongly on the liberal side. Still another reason is that Westchester is by no means all-white: the 18th District is 10% black, 16% Hispanic and 5% Asian. George Pataki, who began his political career as mayor of Peekskill in northern Westchester, carried the county by handsome margins in 1998 and 2002. But the county gave strong support to Bill Clinton and Al Gore in 1996 and 2000 and, unlike the Long Island suburbs, voted for Hillary Rodham Clinton in 2000.

The congresswoman from the 18th District is Nita Lowey, a Democrat first elected in 1988. She was born in the Bronx, raised her family in Queens, and now lives in upper-crust Harrison in Westchester. She went to work for Mario Cuomo in 1975, after he was appointed secretary of state, and later became assistant secretary of state. In the 1988 primary, she faced Hamilton Fish III, son and grandson of Republican Hudson River congressmen, but as a former publisher of *The Nation* considerably to the left of Lowey; she won 44%–36%. Her opponent in the general was Joseph DioGuardi, a two-term incumbent who trumpeted his experience as a CPA but was dogged by charges of illicit contributions; she won 50%–47%. Each spent over $1 million, with Lowey spending $657,000 of her own money.

In the House, Lowey has a fairly solid liberal record. She was a Clinton loyalist when it was tough to be so, voting for the 1993 budget and tax package in this high-income district, splitting with most New York Democrats and organized labor to support both NAFTA and PNTR with China. When Clinton proposed to change the health care finance system, she organized 72 members, mostly Democrats, who demanded that it cover abortions. Much of Lowey's legislative work has been done on Appropriations, and much has been connected with feminist issues. She was a leading backer of funds for international family planning, and led the unsuccessful opposition to George W. Bush's reversal of the policy when he took office. She achieved a rare feminist victory in Congress by getting into the 1998 omnibus bill a provision requiring federal employee health plans that cover prescriptions to include contraceptives; the Appropriations Committee in 2001 turned back an attempt by the Bush administration to repeal the coverage. As the senior Democrat on the Foreign Operations Subcommittee of Appropriations, she has been a strong advocate of aid to Israel. She also worked with chairman Jim Kolbe to increase funding for Afghanistan after the Taliban were routed. On other international issues, she voted for the Iraq war resolution and against trade promotion authority.

Lowey has actively supported the National Endowment for the Arts. When Republicans threatened to eliminate funding for the Public Broadcasting System, she scored points with an appearance by muppets Bert and Ernie to make their case at a congressional hearing. On local matters, she was a stalwart in 2001 in insisting that the White House deliver the full $20 billion that Congress appropriated for New York City.

Since Lowey first won, the boundaries of her district have been twice sharply changed by redistricting. She first won in an all-Westchester district similar to the current 18th. The 1992 redistricting removed much of Westchester and sent the district south through a narrow salient in the Bronx to include a large part of central Queens. This made the district more Democratic, but raised the specter of Queens-based primary opposition. In 2002 the Queens and Bronx portions were removed. Through all this Lowey has proved to be a prodigious fundraiser, never spending less than $878,000 on a campaign, and she has been reelected by wide margins. In November 1998, when Senator Daniel Patrick Moynihan announced he would retire in 2000, Lowey was mentioned as one of several Democrats interested in the seat; several others dropped out and Lowey stayed in. When talk started that Hillary Rodham Clinton might run, Lowey said she would step aside and support her enthusiastically if she did; she kept her word.

Her party loyalty and avid fundraising led Minority Leader Dick Gephardt to appoint her chairman of the Democratic Congressional Campaign Committee in January 2001. With Patty Murray of Washington chairing its Senate Democratic counterpart, they were the first two women to head party campaign committees. This was the third time Gephardt had tried to convince her to take the job, and he agreed not to control DCCC operations as he had in the past. House Democrats were dispirited after failing to win control in 2000, and Lowey faced a difficult task. She advised candidates to cooperate closely with Democratic interest groups—environmental, abortion rights, civil rights—in addition to organized labor. In early 2002 she sounded optimistic and said that Democrats' recruiting efforts, their fundraising, their apparent success in preventing Republican gains in redistricting, and their attacks on Republicans for "privatizing" Social Security would enable the party to recapture the House.

By the fall prospects were not so rosy. In key states—including New York and California— the parties had agreed on bipartisan incumbent-protection redistricting plans, and that left a small number of competitive seats. Ultimately, Democrats defeated only three Republican incumbents, while losing five of their own. The DCCC raised $95 million, but House Republicans raised nearly twice as much, and in the weeks before the election Lowey had to twist the arms of Democratic members to get much needed funds. House Republicans' six-seat gain was an acute disappointment to Lowey, who quietly bowed out of the chairmanship: she, like Patrick Kennedy and Martin Frost before her, had failed to deliver a majority that seemed in close reach.

NINETEENTH DISTRICT

Rep. Sue Kelly (R)

Elected 1994, 5th term; b. Sept. 26, 1936, Lima, OH; home, Katonah; Denison U., B.A. 1958, Sarah Lawrence Col., M.A. 1985; Presbyterian; married (Edward).

Professional Career: Owner/Mgr., Kelly & Assoc. bldg. rehab.; Researcher, Harvard U., 1958–60; Owner/Mgr., Kelly Florist, 1980–83; Prof., Sarah Lawrence Col., 1988–91.

DC Office: 1127 LHOB 20515, 202-225-5441; Fax: 202-225-3289; Web site: www.house.gov/suekelly.

District Offices: Fishkill, 845-897-5200; Goshen, 845-291-4100; Yorktown Heights, 914-962-0761.

Committees: *Financial Services* (Vice Chmn. of 37 R): Capital Markets, Insurance & Government Sponsored Enterprises; Financial Institutions & Consumer Credit; Oversight & Investigations (Chmn.). *Small Business* (3d of 18 R): Regulatory Reform & Oversight; Rural Enterprises, Agriculture and Technology. *Transportation & Infrastructure* (13th of 41 R): Aviation; Highways, Transit & Pipelines; Water Resources & Environment.

Group Ratings

	ADA	ACLU	AFS	LCV	CON	ITIC	NTU	COC	ACU	NTLC	CHC
2002	20	33	0	63	75	100	53	85	88	75	67
2001	25	—	10	86	—	—	57	91	40	—	—

National Journal Ratings

	2001 LIB	—	2001 CONS		2002 LIB	—	2002 CONS
Economic	51%	—	50%		36%	—	61%
Social	54%	—	45%		52%	—	48%
Foreign	43%	—	53%		15%	—	78%

Key Votes of the 107th Congress

1. Approve Bush Tax Cuts	Y	5. Faith-Based Charities	Y	9. Trade Promotion Authority	Y
2. Limit Patients' Bill of Rights	Y	6. Bar Gays in the Boy Scouts	Y	10. Bar Funds for Intl. Court	Y
3. Campaign Finance Reform	N	7. Ban Partial-Birth Abortion	Y	11. Authorize Force in Iraq	Y
4. Ban ANWR Development	Y	8. Arm Commercial Pilots	Y	12. Deny Home. Sec. Dept. Union	Y

Election Results

2002 general	Sue Kelly (R-Ind-C)	121,129	(70%)	($968,982)
	Janine Selendy (D)	44,967	(26%)	($13,153)
	Other	7,016	(4%)	
2002 primary	Sue Kelly (R)	unopposed		
2000 general	Sue Kelly (R-C)	145,532	(61%)	($980,892)
	Larry Otis Graham (D-L-WF)	85,871	(36%)	($314,199)
	Other	7,748	(3%)	

Prior Winning Percentages: 1998 (62%); 1996 (46%); 1994 (52%)

The People		Race/Ethnic Origin	Ancestry	
Area size:	1,470 sq. mi.	83.5% White	Italian: 17.6%	Irish: 16.5%
Urban population:	78.7%	5.0% Black	German: 10.6%	
Rural population:	21.3%	2.2% Asian	**2000 Presidential Vote**	
Pop. 2000:	654,361	0.2% Native Am.	Bush (R)	133,157　(49%)
Median income:	$64,337	0.0% Hawaiian	Gore (D)	126,785　(47%)
Poverty status:	6.4%	1.2% Two+ races	Other	11,698　(4%)
Military veterans:	11.8%	0.2% Other	**Cook Partisan Voting Index:** R + 2	
		7.7% Hispanic Origin		

Occupation	Blue collar: 18.5%	White collar: 67.2%	Gray collar: 14.3%

The great interior of America can be said to begin where the Hudson River squeezes through the series of Appalachian ridges at the Hudson Highlands. This choke point was the barrier to British military power during the Revolutionary War, when American forces built a chain across the river to keep the British from sailing north. It was over control of this part of the Hudson that Benedict Arnold betrayed his country, and it was here that the new nation built its Military Academy high on the cliffs at West Point. The Hudson was the impetus for the builders of the Erie Canal and the water-level New York Central Railroad, the great projects that made New York City the port of the American interior, as well as for the builders of the Croton Aqueduct not far away, which provided the water without which New York could not grow—and which provided a way for the first cockroaches to reach the city. Some distant day the great aqueduct may crumble, but the cockroaches will remain.

The 19th Congressional District covers much of the lower Hudson Valley, sprawling across parts of five counties. West of the Hudson, the district takes in much of Orange County, New York's third-fastest-growing county since 1990, where old villages adjoin mountains, farms and new, middle-income subdivisions on the nation's biggest deposit of muck soil outside the Everglades. The district includes Kiryas Joel, a politically controversial Satmar Hasidic settlement that became embroiled in a long-running battle over whether it could establish a government-funded but religiously run school district for disabled children. But it excludes two of Orange County's biggest population centers, Middletown and Newburgh, while taking in some adjoining portions of northern Rockland County, including Stony Point, the home of James A. Farley, Franklin Roosevelt's campaign manager in 1932 and 1936. The district crosses the Hudson where the rebels' chain did, near West Point. East of the river, the district begins in northern Westchester County, including Peekskill, where George Pataki was mayor before becoming governor; Croton-on-Hudson; Yorktown; and Mt. Kisco. Further north, the 19th takes in all of Putnam County and part of Dutchess County, including the suburbs (but not the center city) of Poughkeepsie, and Wappingers Falls. These areas are crossed by scenic highways as well as by the Appalachian Trail; the region has proved attractive to middle- and higher-income public and corporate employees seeking reasonably priced housing in safe areas, a trend that has led to modest growth at a time when other areas of New York state are losing population. Politically, this area trended Republican in the 1980s, but moved back toward Democrats in the 1990s. It has backed Pataki strongly, but the 2000 presidential election in this district was close —49% for George W. Bush, 47% for Al Gore.

The congresswoman from the 19th District is Sue Kelly, a Republican first elected in 1994. Kelly is not a Hudson Valley aristocrat but the daughter of an Ohio doctor. She met her husband while she was a botany researcher at Harvard; they raised their family in Katonah, where she volunteered in many organizations, worked as a patient advocate, rape crisis counselor and educator, and sang in a church choir. She had a business renovating buildings and owned a florist shop. She also had political experience as campaign manager for Assemblyman Jon Fossel in the 1970s. In March 1994, Congressman Hamilton Fish, a Hudson County aristocrat, decided to retire, and Kelly decided to use the $150,000 she had saved to buy a new business to help finance a campaign for Congress instead. It was a crowded field, in which Kelly emerged as the only candidate who supported lower taxes, "huge" budget cuts and abortion rights. Her chief opponent in the primary was Joseph DioGuardi, twice elected in the Westchester district to the south and twice defeated there by Nita Lowey. Kelly won the primary with 23% to DioGuardi's 20%, with two other candidates at 19% and 18%. The Democratic nominee was Hamilton Fish Jr., son of the retiring congressman but as publisher of the leftish and anti-Israel *The Nation*, with quite different politics. This was expected to be a close race. But with good margins in the northern counties Kelly beat Fish 52%–37%, and 10% for DioGuardi on the Conservative and Right-to-Life lines.

Kelly, with her middle-of-the-House voting record, has been whipsawed by criticism from right and left. She supported the Contract with America, which earned her howls from the left. In 2001, when Con Edison made mistakes in moving too quickly to reopen the Indian Point nuclear reactor in her district, Kelly criticized the utility's "keep-the-plant-running-at-all-costs mentality;" when September 11 increased security fears, she endorsed George Pataki's study of security at the plant. On abortion, Kelly irritated many conservatives by being one of the few Republicans to vote against the partial-birth abortion ban in 1996. But in 1997, when the executive director of the National Coalition of Abortion Providers admitted he lied about the frequency of partial-birth abortions, she changed her mind and came out for the ban. And in 1998 she joined other Republican women to ask why feminist Democrats were not outraged about the charges brought against Bill Clinton; she voted for two of the four impeachment counts. So when in 1999 she was chosen as the Republican co-chair of the Congressional Caucus for Women's Issues, feminists complained loudly. Kelly stood her ground—in February 2000 calling Hillary Rodham Clinton, her new constituent (though, post-redistricting, Chappaqua is now in the 18th), "a carpetbagger" who did not know New York or have the background to represent the state. The First Lady's spokesman responded by calling Kelly's comments "not very neighborly."

Kelly's difficulty in balancing conflicting pressures became apparent when she sought to circumvent seniority and seek the House Small Business Committee chairmanship in January 2001. She offered her bipartisan approach, her appeal as a woman and her positive dealings with small-business groups. But Speaker Dennis Hastert stuck with fellow Illinoisan Don Manzullo, who was next in line for the post; Kelly may have been hurt by her moderate voting record. In February 2002, she showed some partisan spirit, as chairman of the Oversight and Investigation Subcommittee of Financial Services, when she criticized Senate Democrats for failing to move more quickly on the terrorism insurance bill, which businesses and real estate developers insisted was essential after September 11. Despite huge pressure from the other side, she voted with Republican leaders against campaign finance regulation, which she called unconstitutional.

In elections, she has been challenged on all sides. Not even a plea from Speaker Newt Gingrich's office could keep DioGuardi from challenging Kelly again in the 1996 Republican primary. Kelly won the primary, but by a narrow 53%–42%. In the general, Kelly beat the Democrat by only 46%–39%, with 12% for DioGuardi. Her subsequent victories were by more convincing margins. Her 2000 opponent was Larry Otis Graham, author of best-selling *Our Kind of People: Inside America's Black Upper Class*. Graham, who boasted of campaign advice from his Chappaqua neighbor Bill Clinton, criticized Kelly as out of touch with her constituents; he lost, 61%–36%. Redistricting posed some threat to her. The plan adopted in June 2002 combined 70% of her district with many Republican towns from the district that had been held by 30-year veteran Ben

Gilman. In effect Gilman's district was carved up among his neighbors; Republican leaders considered it expendable since Gilman was 79 and they thought it likely that a Democrat would win the district when he retired. Gilman angrily threatened to switch parties and run against Kelly as a Democrat, but in July 2002 he announced he would retire. Kelly was subsequently reelected 70%–26%.

TWENTIETH DISTRICT

Rep. John Sweeney (R)

Elected 1998, 3d term; b. Aug. 9, 1955, Troy; home, Clifton Park; Russell Sage Col., B.A. 1981, W. New England Law Schl., J.D. 1990; Catholic; separated.

Professional Career: Practicing atty., 1990–92; Exec. Dir. & Chief Cnsl., NY State Repub. Cmte., 1992–95; NY Comm. of Labor, 1995–97; Dpty. Secy., Gov. George Pataki, 1997–98.

DC Office: 416 CHOB 20515, 202-225-5614; Fax: 202-225-6234; Web site: www.house.gov/sweeney.

District Offices: Clifton Park, 518-371-8839; Glens Falls, 518-792-3031; Hudson, 518-828-0181.

Committees: *Appropriations* (29th of 36 R): Commerce, Justice, State & Judiciary; Homeland Security; Transportation, Treasury, & Independent Agencies. *Select Committee on Homeland Security* (27th of 27 R): Infrastructure & Border Security; Intelligence & Counterterrorism (Vice Chmn.).

Group Ratings

	ADA	ACLU	AFS	LCV	CON	ITIC	NTU	COC	ACU	NTLC	CHC
2002	5	27	0	25	14	88	54	95	88	75	75
2001	15	—	10	43	—	—	59	96	68	—	—

National Journal Ratings

	2001 LIB —	2001 CONS	2002 LIB —	2002 CONS
Economic	43%	56%	36%	61%
Social	47%	53%	48%	52%
Foreign	14%	85%	0%	85%

Key Votes of the 107th Congress

1. Approve Bush Tax Cuts	Y	5. Faith-Based Charities	Y	9. Trade Promotion Authority	Y
2. Limit Patients' Bill of Rights	Y	6. Bar Gays in the Boy Scouts	Y	10. Bar Funds for Intl. Court	Y
3. Campaign Finance Reform	N	7. Ban Partial-Birth Abortion	Y	11. Authorize Force in Iraq	Y
4. Ban ANWR Development	Y	8. Arm Commercial Pilots	Y	12. Deny Home. Sec. Dept. Union	Y

Election Results

2002 general	John Sweeney (R-C)	140,238	(73%)	($808,955)
	Frank Stoppenbach (D)	45,878	(24%)	($18,451)
	Other	5,162	(3%)	
2002 primary	John Sweeney (R)	unopposed		
2000 general (NY 22)	John Sweeney (R-C)	167,368	(68%)	($807,676)
	Kenneth F. McCallion (D-Green-WF)	79,111	(32%)	($72,122)

Prior Winning Percentages: 1998 (55%)

The People		Race/Ethnic Origin	Ancestry	
Area size:	7,200 sq. mi.	93.4% White	Irish: 15.1%	German: 11.8%
Urban population:	44.9%	2.4% Black	Italian: 9.8%	
Rural population:	55.1%	0.8% Asian	**2000 Presidential Vote**	
Pop. 2000:	654,360	0.2% Native Am.	Bush (R)..............146,792	(51%)
Median income:	$44,239	0.0% Hawaiian	Gore (D)..............127,419	(44%)
Poverty status:	7.9%	0.9% Two+ races	Other...................15,232	(5%)
Military veterans:	14.3%	0.1% Other	**Cook Partisan Voting Index:** R + 4	
		2.2% Hispanic Origin		

Occupation   Blue collar: 22.7%   White collar: 61.1%   Gray collar: 16.2%

The Hudson River, an avenue of commerce in colonial days, an inspiration to artists in the federal republic, is still one of America's great sights, though it is no longer central, as it was not so long ago, to the nation's consciousness and politics. The classic mansions overlooking the river, like Clermont, whose builder Robert Livingston financed Robert Fulton's first steamboat, and Montgomery Place, built by Janet Livingston Montgomery, widow of the general who captured Quebec in 1775, are reminders of the cool serenity of the 18th century mind and the daring nature of its spirit. Robert Livingston (whose descendants include Eleanor Roosevelt, former Governor Thomas Kean of New Jersey and former Congressman Bob Livingston of Louisiana) administered the first oath of office to George Washington in 1789 and helped negotiate the Louisiana Purchase in 1803. It was on a visit to his lands in the 1790s that James Madison and Aaron Burr welded the Virginia-New York alliance that set the course of American political history. The Hudson was also a center of America during the Romantic Era: From Frederick Church's Moorish mansion, Olana, you can see the still unspoiled river landscape that inspired his art and that of others of the Hudson River school of painters. Later, the master photographer Alfred Stieglitz and his wife, the celebrated painter Georgia O'Keeffe, drew inspiration from the mountains and placid waters in Lake George, where they had a summer home.

The Hudson gave birth to America's passionate party politics. Nearby is Kinderhook, home of Martin Van Buren, the innkeeper's son who in alliance with Andrew Jackson invented the torchlight parade, the national party convention and, some argue, the Democratic party itself. Later in the 19th century, the Hudson was lined with the palaces of the nation's first great millionaires and the comfortable country homes of New York's gentry. One of the latter, Springwood in Hyde Park, was the birthplace and home of Franklin Roosevelt; this politician, who expanded government at home and was the victorious commander-in-chief of American military forces throughout the world, was most comfortable looking out over his sloping lawn down to the river on which he remembered iceboating during the winters of the 1880s.

The sprawling 20th Congressional District clamps around the Albany metro area and includes much of the Hudson Valley—the grand river south of Albany and the smaller river, freshly fed by the Adirondacks, to the north. It includes four full counties (Warren, Washington, Columbia and Greene), most of Saratoga County, and parts of five others (Dutchess, Essex, Rensselaer, Delaware and Otsego). The northern extreme of the 20th extends right up to Lake Placid in the Adirondacks, site of the 1980 Winter Olympics, while the southern extreme in Dutchess County is close enough for refugees from New York to travel back and forth regularly. The district extends west just short of Cooperstown, home of the National Baseball Hall of Fame, and includes Oneonta, home of the less well-known National Soccer Hall of Fame; it includes Saratoga Springs with its grand race track and the nearby battlefield where the British were decisively stopped in 1777. Despite Van Buren and Roosevelt, this has been a Republican area since the birth of the Republican Party; indeed, Roosevelt never carried his home territory except when he ran for state Senate in 1910. The 20th was one of only six New York districts to vote for George W. Bush in 2000.

The congressman from the 20th District is John Sweeney, a Republican elected in 1998. Sweeney grew up in Troy, the son of a shirt factory worker active in the Amalgamated Shirt Cutters Union; he lived for a time in a housing project. He worked his way through college, then worked for the Rensselaer County government, heading a DWI project. He went to law school part time, graduated and practiced law. He caught the eye of Republican State Chairman William Powers, an ally of then-Senator Alfonse D'Amato, who made Sweeney executive director of the party in 1992. After George Pataki was elected governor in 1994, he appointed Sweeney as Labor commissioner, then in 1997 as deputy secretary to the state Executive Chamber, one of his top aides.

In April 1998, Gerald Solomon, the local congressman for 20 years, announced he was retiring. In this heavily Republican district there was naturally a contest for the party's nomination. But it was effectively settled in a few days in May. Assemblyman John Faso, probably the best-known possibility, declined to run because he had been elected minority leader in March. Solomon backed Roy McDonald, a township supervisor in Saratoga County, the district's largest; of the nine candidates running, he said that only Sweeney was unacceptable. Facing pressure from Powers, Saratoga County Republican Chairman Jasper Nolan announced he was not supporting McDonald, who, suddenly with no chance in the endorsement convention, withdrew from the race. Powers's message, though not public, was obvious: Pataki wanted Sweeney. Sweeney had yet to officially announce, but as Solomon said, "John Sweeney is going to be the candidate." Sweeney refused to join debates but won the September primary with 52%. In the general, Sweeney vastly outspent the Democratic nominee, Jean Bordewich, a one-term council member in Red Hook in Dutchess County. Like Solomon, Sweeney opposed requiring General Electric to clean up PCBs in the Hudson—a hot local issue. He said he opposed banning abortion but backed the partial-birth abortion ban. He opposed NAFTA and GATT and said he felt strongly about the Second Amendment. Pataki also appeared in Sweeney ads, and the Civil Service Employees Union endorsed the Republican. Sweeney won 55%–42%.

In the House, Sweeney has been conservative on foreign issues and more centrist on others. He impressed Republican leaders with his fundraising and got an Appropriation Committee seat in 2001. He used that post to press the White House to deliver more rapidly on its commitment of $20 billion to New York for post-September 11 recovery. Even after that agreement, he bucked other New York House Republicans and continued to work with Nita Lowey at the Appropriations Committee to secure more money for the state. He won House approval of a bill to issue Freedom Bonds for the first time since World War II, but the Treasury Department was cool to the idea because it feared the new investment would discourage spending and slow down the economy. In 2003 he was assigned to the new Homeland Security Subcommittee.

Sweeney lobbied for Southwest Airlines service to Albany, where the airport has grown rapidly. He objected to the plan announced by EPA in the closing days of the Clinton administration requiring General Electric to spend $490 million to clean up the PCBs in the Hudson, mostly by dredging the sediment along 40 miles of the river. Although Pataki supported it, Sweeney sought to delay action until the National Academy of Sciences released a report; when the Bush White House sustained the earlier decision, he applauded the added performance standards that EPA set in its final order.

Sweeney's star is clearly on the rise: In just his 2d term, *PoliticsNY.com* called him "arguably the most effective member of the New York delegation." *The New York Times* describes his style as "alternating between street fighter and smooth political operator to get his way." This is a man who is connected both in Albany and Washington. He is known as the member of the delegation closest to Pataki and is on friendly terms with the Bush White House: his former chief of staff Brad Card is the brother of Bush's chief of staff Andrew Card. And Bush insiders will not forget that Sweeney was present in the Miami-Dade County board of canvassers meeting when the canvassers proposed to count the ballots out of view of observers in violation of Florida's sunshine law. "Thugs in that building are trying to hijack this election," Sweeney said. Sweeney continues to draw mention as a possible statewide candidate, perhaps against Senator Charles Schumer in 2004 or for governor in 2006. He has been reelected easily to the House.

TWENTY-FIRST DISTRICT

Rep. Michael McNulty (D)

Elected 1988, 8th term; b. Sept. 16, 1947, Troy; home, Green Island; Holy Cross Col., B.A. 1969; Catholic; married (Nancy Ann).

Elected Office: Green Island Town Supervisor, 1969–77; Green Island Mayor, 1977–82; NY Assembly, 1982–88.

DC Office: 2210 RHOB 20515, 202-225-5076; Fax: 202-225-5077; Web site: www.house.gov/mcnulty.

District Offices: Albany, 518-465-0700; Amsterdam, 518-843-3400; Johnstown, 518-762-3568; Schenectady, 518-374-4547; Troy, 518-271-0822.

Committees: *Ways & Means* (10th of 17 D): Oversight; Select Revenue Measures (RMM).

Group Ratings

	ADA	ACLU	AFS	LCV	CON	ITIC	NTU	COC	ACU	NTLC	CHC
2002	85	60	100	100	63	50	17	30	12	3	25
2001	80	—	100	100	—	—	9	32	24	—	—

National Journal Ratings

	2001 LIB —	2001 CONS	2002 LIB —	2002 CONS
Economic	95%	0%	93%	5%
Social	58%	42%	58%	41%
Foreign	73%	26%	77%	19%

Key Votes of the 107th Congress

1. Approve Bush Tax Cuts	N	5. Faith-Based Charities	N	9. Trade Promotion Authority	N
2. Limit Patients' Bill of Rights	N	6. Bar Gays in the Boy Scouts	Y	10. Bar Funds for Intl. Court	N
3. Campaign Finance Reform	Y	7. Ban Partial-Birth Abortion	Y	11. Authorize Force in Iraq	Y
4. Ban ANWR Development	Y	8. Arm Commercial Pilots	Y	12. Deny Home. Sec. Dept. Union	N

Election Results

2002 general	Michael McNulty (D-C-Ind-WF)	161,329	(75%)	($421,837)
	Charles Rosenstein (R)	53,525	(25%)	($20,786)
2002 primary	Michael McNulty (D)	unopposed		
2000 general	Michael McNulty (D-C-Ind)	175,339	(74%)	($334,030)
	Thomas G. Pillsworth (R)	60,333	(26%)	($12,402)

Prior Winning Percentages: 1998 (74%); 1996 (66%); 1994 (67%); 1992 (63%); 1990 (64%); 1988 (62%)

The People		Race/Ethnic Origin	Ancestry	
Area size:	1,962 sq. mi.	85.5% White	Irish: 15.0%	Italian: 12.4%
Urban population:	84.3%	7.5% Black	German: 11.8%	
Rural population:	15.7%	2.1% Asian	**2000 Presidential Vote**	
Pop. 2000:	654,361	0.2% Native Am.	Gore (D)	165,003 (56%)
Median income:	$40,254	0.0% Hawaiian	Bush (R)	114,979 (39%)
Poverty status:	11.2%	1.3% Two+ races	Other	15,101 (5%)
Military veterans:	13.1%	0.2% Other	**Cook Partisan Voting Index:** D + 9	
		3.2% Hispanic Origin		

Occupation	Blue collar: 18.9%	White collar: 66.0%	Gray collar: 15.0%

Albany, as readers of its novelist laureate William Kennedy know, is within living memory an antique city. Its solid rowhouses show its 19th century prosperity; its once teeming lumberyards and railroad car shops, old restaurants and hotels, have the patina of age and the accumulated grime of decades of coal smoke burned during six-month-long winters. Its history goes back to 1624, when the Dutch built Fort Orange on the banks of the Hudson so seagoing ships could dock at the edge of the great gloomy forests near the confluence of the Hudson and the Mohawk—

the natural crossroads of Upstate New York even before the building of the Erie Canal and the New York Central Railroad. This was one of America's early industrial centers. Troy, a few miles upriver, was a steel town rivaling Pittsburgh in the 1840s, and later the leading producer of detachable collars; Cohoes, at the junction of the Hudson and the Mohawk, became a leading textile producer; Schenectady, a few miles up the Mohawk, was the site of Charles Steinmetz's fabled General Electric laboratories and has been a big GE town ever since Albany was one of America's biggest lumber towns as well as the state capital.

Albany, with a state capitol completed in 1899 after 32 years, for the then-staggering sum of $25 million, has one of the nation's most famed Democratic political machines, dating back to 1921, when Daniel O'Connell and his brothers and local aristocrat Edwin Corning took control of City Hall. They never really relinquished it: O'Connell died in 1977 at age 91, still boss after 56 years, and his early partner's son, Erastus Corning II, was mayor from 1942 until his death in 1983. The machine was sustained by legions of city and county employees, by a certain creativity when it came to counting votes, and by the raffish atmosphere that was found in the speakeasies of so many cities during Prohibition and lingered in Albany for decades after: read Kennedy and you are there. Curiously, the machine made possible the transformation of antique Albany into the shinier metropolis it is today. Mayor Corning and Nelson Rockefeller collaborated on a smorgasbord of civic-improvement projects: the monumental South Mall, the distinctive, ovoid performing arts center known as the Egg, expressways, and a renovated Union Station. Yuppies began buying and renovating old townhouses. These days, the Albany machine can't always control the suburbs as it once could Albany; but it clings to power in the H.H. Richardson City Hall.

The 21st Congressional District includes most of the Albany metro area: all of Albany County, Schenectady County (including Schenectady), Montgomery County (including Amsterdam, a carpet-making town until the mills moved south in 1955), and rural Schoharie County; parts of Rensselaer (including Troy), Fulton and Saratoga counties. Times are not great here: The city of Albany lost 5% of its population during the 1990s, Schenectady 6% and Troy 9%. While the outer counties lean modestly Republican, the Democratic machine vote in Albany makes this a comfortably Democratic district. Even Democrat Carl McCall, who lost every other county in the state outside New York City, beat incumbent Governor George Pataki in Albany County in 2002.

The congressman from the 21st District is Michael McNulty, a Democrat first elected in 1988. McNulty's roots in Albany politics go back to his grandfather, who served as Albany County sheriff; his father was mayor of the industrial suburb of Green Island for 30 years (not consecutively) until he retired in 2002, when he was succeeded by Michael's sister, Ellen McNulty-Ryan. Michael McNulty was first elected to office in 1969, at 22, and served 13 years as town supervisor and mayor in Green Island; he was elected to the Assembly in 1982, at 35. The opening to Congress came without much warning. In 1988, four days after the July filing deadline and on the last day for withdrawal, 30-year incumbent Democrat Samuel Stratton announced he was retiring for health reasons, giving the Democratic machine a chance to name a replacement, who turned out to be McNulty. He won the general by 62%–38% against a venture capital specialist who attacked him for having been chosen by party bosses rather than primary voters. Since then, he has had no trouble in general elections.

McNulty is hard-working, serious, abstemious, pleasant and a conscientious campaigner. His voting record is like that of an old-style ethnic Democrat: liberal on economics, less so on foreign affairs, moderate on cultural issues. He is one of a handful of New York Democrats endorsed by the Conservative Party. He opposes abortion and voted for the amendment allowing penalties for flag desecration. But he supported campaign finance regulation, even though some abortion rights groups opposed it. He strongly opposed the welfare law and wants to increase payments to unemployed adults, legal immigrants and families with high shelter costs. On Ways and Means, he usually has operated independently of both parties; he was one of three Democrats to vote against a bipartisan Medicare bill in 1997.

On local issues, McNulty criticized the Army when it cut the number of jobs at the Watervliet Arsenal, and wondered whether further cuts would require closure and dependence on foreign producers; the facility was revived by a Navy contract for 450 cannons, and the Army in February 2002 turned over management to a civilian firm to attract private businesses. Its base mission will sustain the arsenal, McNulty said. "But the Army presence there has continued to decrease because of the nation's own decreased need for a large Army cannon."

McNulty in 1998 brought Hillary Rodham Clinton to Troy to commemorate Kate Mullaney, who organized the all-female Collar Laundry Union in 1864. In October 2002, the Resources Committee approved his proposal to make a national museum of her home, which had deteriorated. In April 2002, McNulty condemned Palestinian terrorist attacks on Israel and said that George W. Bush's demands for Israeli withdrawal from occupied territory were "jibberish." With Hillary Rodham Clinton, he proposed giving homeland security block grants to local communities for emergency response and public safety. Three days before he voted for the use of force in Iraq, seven anti-war protestors were arrested while staging a sit-in at his Albany office.

In 1996 he had primary opposition on the left from Lee Wasserman, head of Environmental Advocates, and won by only 57%–43%. Since then, McNulty seems to have solidified his base. Redistricting expanded him into Republican-leaning areas, but he remains secure.

TWENTY-SECOND DISTRICT

Rep. Maurice Hinchey (D)

Elected 1992, 6th term; b. Oct. 27, 1938, New York, NY; home, Saugerties; S.U.N.Y. New Paltz, B.S. 1968, M.A. 1969; Catholic; married (Ilene).

Military Career: Navy, 1956–59.

Elected Office: NY Assembly, 1974–92.

Professional Career: Cement plant worker, 1959–64; NY St. Thruway toll collector, 1959–68; Analyst, NY St. Dept. of Educ., 1971–74.

DC Office: 2431 RHOB 20515, 202-225-6335; Fax: 202-226-0774; Web site: www.house.gov/hinchey.

District Offices: Binghamton, 607-773-2768; Ithaca, 607-273-1388; Kingston, 845-331-4466.

Committees: *Appropriations* (20th of 29 D): Agriculture, Rural Development, & FDA; Interior.

Group Ratings

	ADA	ACLU	AFS	LCV	CON	ITIC	NTU	COC	ACU	NTLC	CHC
2002	100	87	100	100	55	25	21	30	4	3	0
2001	100	—	100	93	—	—	11	26	0	—	—

National Journal Ratings

	2001 LIB	—	2001 CONS		2002 LIB	—	2002 CONS
Economic	95%	—	0%		93%	—	5%
Social	90%	—	0%		82%	—	18%
Foreign	96%	—	0%		94%	—	0%

Key Votes of the 107th Congress

1. Approve Bush Tax Cuts	N	5. Faith-Based Charities	N	9. Trade Promotion Authority N
2. Limit Patients' Bill of Rights	N	6. Bar Gays in the Boy Scouts	N	10. Bar Funds for Intl. Court N
3. Campaign Finance Reform	Y	7. Ban Partial-Birth Abortion	N	11. Authorize Force in Iraq N
4. Ban ANWR Development	Y	8. Arm Commercial Pilots	Y	12. Deny Home. Sec. Dept. Union N

Election Results

2002 general	Maurice Hinchey (D-L-Ind-WF)	113,280	(64%)	($652,929)
	Eric Hall (R-C)	58,008	(33%)	($39,499)
	Other	5,196	(3%)	
2002 primary	Maurice Hinchey (D)	unopposed		
2000 general (NY 26)	Maurice Hinchey (D-Ind-L-WF)	140,395	(62%)	($795,829)
	Bob Moppert (R-C)	83,856	(37%)	($176,395)
	Other	2,328	(1%)	

Prior Winning Percentages: 1998 (62%); 1996 (55%); 1994 (49%); 1992 (50%)

The People		Race/Ethnic Origin	Ancestry	
Area size:	3,334 sq. mi.	79.9% White	Irish: 13.2%	German: 11.8%
Urban population:	67.8%	7.7% Black	Italian: 11.1%	
Rural population:	32.2%	2.5% Asian	**2000 Presidential Vote**	
Pop. 2000:	654,361	0.2% Native Am.	Gore (D)..............131,421 (51%)	
Median income:	$38,586	0.0% Hawaiian	Bush (R)..............108,460 (42%)	
Poverty status:	14.3%	1.7% Two+ races	Other...................17,578 (7%)	
Military veterans:	12.3%	0.2% Other	**Cook Partisan Voting Index:** D + 5	
		7.8% Hispanic Origin		

Occupation	Blue collar: 21.4%	White collar: 60.8%	Gray collar: 17.8%

In colonial days, the Catskills looming over the mid-Hudson River Valley were a great barrier—a mysterious place where Rip Van Winkle was said to have fallen asleep for 20 years after drinking liquor with nine pipe-playing dwarfs, and where Indians lurked in the days of James Fenimore Cooper. Eventually, the area became part of a great pathway west, along the Erie Lackawanna and Delaware & Hudson Railroad lines, with engines steaming over giant viaducts and along narrow river valleys through the hills and mountains. Later in the 19th century, huge kosher hotels were built in Sullivan County in the Catskills—the Jewish resort area popularly known as the Borscht Belt. These thrived when Jews were excluded from other resorts, but fell on hard times in the late 20th century, as discrimination ended; some still exist to cater to Russian Jewish immigrants and a kosher clientele. Today, the Catskills are no longer on great transportation lines; there is little passenger train service and the area is bypassed by major airlines. Traffic on Route 17, the gateway to the Catskills from New York City (known locally as the "Quickway"), is becoming clogged on weekends, however, and figures to get worse with the opening of three new Indian casinos (two in Sullivan and one in Ulster County) approved by Governor George Pataki in 2001.

The sprawling 22d Congressional District includes all of Sullivan and Ulster Counties and most of the Catskills area; it also covers part of the Hudson Valley and part of the Southern Tier counties along the New York-Pennsylvania border. Its two biggest population centers are on its east and west ends. On the east are Newburgh, Poughkeepsie and Kingston, old towns in the Hudson Valley, where pollution caused by General Electric's discharge of PCBs is now scheduled to be cleaned up in a $500 million, multi-year undertaking; Poughkeepsie is the home of Vassar College and Kingston, in Ulster County, was the political base of long-time Governor and two-term Vice President George Clinton. In the west, connected to the rest of the district by a narrow corridor of Southern Tier townships, are the factory town of Binghamton and the university town of Ithaca, where Cornell University sits high above the Cayuga's waters. In between are the Catskills, including Bethel, site of the misnamed 1969 Woodstock music festival. Most of this territory voted Republican for many years. But Sullivan County, with the only large rural Jewish population in the U.S., has long been Democratic. Starting in the 1960s, the university towns of Ithaca and Poughkeepsie became Democratic bastions. In the 1980s and 1990s, the sagging local economy and the specter of a southern-dominated conservative Republicanism moved other areas in a Democratic direction. The result is an Upstate district that produced a solid victory for Al Gore in 2000.

The congressman from the 22d is Maurice Hinchey, a Democrat elected in 1992. Hinchey grew up in a humble background, enlisted in the Navy at 18, labored in a cement factory for five years, then worked his way through college as a New York State Thruway toll collector. He was an analyst for the state education department; then in the Democratic year of 1974, at 36, he was elected from Ulster County to the Assembly. He served for nine terms; he was proud of the more than 600 bills he passed—on, among other things, acid rain, toxic waste, illegal dumping (and organized crime's influence over it), groundwater and wetlands protection. When he ran for Congress, Hinchey called for national health insurance, a repeal of Reagan-Bush tax cuts for the rich and corporations, and "reindustrializing America." His Republican opponent Bob Moppert, a Binghamton moving company owner, called for less government spending and bureaucracy. In a contest that was not only partisan but geographic, Hinchey beat Moppert 50%–47%.

Hinchey has one of the most liberal voting records in the House. One issue that caused

Hinchey discomfort was gun control. He backed the Brady Bill on handguns. But in 1994, as he faced a tough reelection campaign in a non-metropolitan district, he agonized over the assault weapons ban, deciding at the last minute to vote against it, despite a call from Bill Clinton. As part of the House minority, he has mostly taken on lost causes. He has called for creation of Empowerment Zones in rural areas, a patient's safety bill and a halt to shifts of veterans funds to the Sun Belt. With the election of George W. Bush as President, Hinchey sought partisan opportunities. He sparked a House debate with his proposal to prohibit the private donation of food and beverages for official events at the Vice President's residence; his amendment was defeated, with 54 Democrats opposed. After the September 11 attacks, he criticized the White House for spending disaster relief money on national security. At a March 2002 hearing, Hinchey objected to Smithsonian Secretary Lawrence Small's policy of rewarding donors by putting their names on buildings and rooms. "What we are experiencing is crass commercialization," he said. "We are selling ourselves very, very cheaply." He sought unsuccessfully to add $15 million to EPA funding for civil enforcement.

Hinchey has remained a Republican target but has built impressive strength in the district. Moppert tried again in 1994, embracing the Contract with America while trying to tie Hinchey to Clinton. Hinchey, like many Democrats, sought to localize the election, as he boasted of his efforts at local economic development. He vastly outspent the challenger but the result was one of the nation's closest races; he won 49%–48%, with the outcome uncertain until almost two weeks after the election. In 1998, the favored Republican candidate, radio station owner William (Bud) Walker, was overshadowed by Randall Terry, the Binghamton talk radio host who founded Operation Rescue in 1987 and staged anti-abortion rallies. Terry spent $1.2 million, most of it from abortion opponents across the country. Walker won the Republican primary by an unimpressive 53%–35%, and Terry kept campaigning as the Right-to-Life nominee. Hinchey won 62% to 31%, with 7% for Terry. In 2000, Moppert ran again but received little national support; Hinchey won, 62%–37%.

One of only three remaining upstate Democrats in the House, Hinchey survived redistricting with flying colors. In May 2002 Pataki presented a plan that would have sliced up Hinchey's district among its neighbors. Assembly Speaker Sheldon Silver would have none of it; Silver was a friend of Hinchey's from their time in the Assembly, and in early 2002 Hinchey hired as his redistricting lobbyist Patricia Lynch, Silver's chief of staff until 2001. On May 13, the special master appointed by a three-judge federal court, presented a plan which put Hinchey and incumbent Republican Sherwood Boehlert in the same district. On May 23 the court adopted the plan, but said that it would set it aside if the legislature and governor could reach agree on a plan before the June deadline for gathering petition signatures. Silver wanted to protect Hinchey; national Republicans feared the plan could cause them to lose two seats, and Dick Cheney called state Senate Joseph Bruno to urge him to deal. Deal they did. On June 5 the legislature adopted and Pataki signed a plan targeting the two oldest members of the delegation, Republican Ben Gilman and Democrat Louise Slaughter. The new 22d District, undoubtedly thanks to Silver, was tailor-made for Hinchey. In November he won 64%–33%, his biggest margin ever. Hinchey has shown impressive staying power for a member whose first victory seemed something of a fluke. After the election, he criticized Dick Gephardt as too timid in opposing the Bush administration as Minority Leader; he backed Nancy Pelosi's more aggressive approach to taking back the majority.

TWENTY-THIRD DISTRICT

Rep. John McHugh (R)

Elected 1992, 6th term; b. Sept. 29, 1948, Watertown; home, Pierrepont Manor; Utica Col., B.A. 1970, S.U.N.Y. Albany, M.P.A. 1977; Catholic; divorced.

Elected Office: NY Senate, 1984–92.

Professional Career: Confidential Asst., Watertown City Mgr., 1971–76; Research & Liaison Chief, NY Sen. Douglas Barclay, 1976–84.

DC Office: 2333 RHOB 20515, 202-225-4611; Fax: 202-226-0621; Web site: www.house.gov/mchugh.

District Offices: Canastota, 315-697-2063; Mayfield, 518-661-6486; Plattsburgh, 518-563-1406; Watertown, 315-782-3150.

Committees: *Armed Services* (5th of 33 R): Readiness; Total Force (Chmn.). *Government Reform* (5th of 24 R): Criminal Justice, Drug Policy & Human Resources; Energy Policy, Natural Resources and Regulatory Affairs. *International Relations* (14th of 26 R): Middle East & Central Asia.

Group Ratings

	ADA	ACLU	AFS	LCV	CON	ITIC	NTU	COC	ACU	NTLC	CHC
2002	15	13	13	25	8	75	49	85	79	73	83
2001	15	—	30	43	—	—	55	91	68	—	—

National Journal Ratings

	2001 LIB	—	2001 CONS		2002 LIB	—	2002 CONS
Economic	45%	—	55%		39%	—	61%
Social	43%	—	58%		0%	—	75%
Foreign	43%	—	53%		29%	—	67%

Key Votes of the 107th Congress

1. Approve Bush Tax Cuts	Y	5. Faith-Based Charities	Y	9. Trade Promotion Authority	N
2. Limit Patients' Bill of Rights	Y	6. Bar Gays in the Boy Scouts	Y	10. Bar Funds for Intl. Court	Y
3. Campaign Finance Reform	Y	7. Ban Partial-Birth Abortion	Y	11. Authorize Force in Iraq	Y
4. Ban ANWR Development	N	8. Arm Commercial Pilots	Y	12. Deny Home. Sec. Dept. Union	Y

Election Results

2002 general	John McHugh (R-C)	unopposed		($289,089)
2002 primary	John McHugh (R)	unopposed		
2000 general (NY 24)	John McHugh (R-C)	138,322	(74%)	($300,643)
	Neil P. Tallon (D-WF)	42,698	(23%)	
	Other	5,167	(3%)	

Prior Winning Percentages: 1998 (79%); 1996 (71%); 1994 (79%); 1992 (61%)

The People		Race/Ethnic Origin	Ancestry	
Area size:	14,739 sq. mi.	92.9% White	Irish: 12.0%	German: 9.9%
Urban population:	34.7%	2.6% Black	French: 9.9%	
Rural population:	65.3%	0.6% Asian	**2000 Presidential Vote**	
Pop. 2000:	654,361	0.9% Native Am.	Bush (R)...............119,472	(49%)
Median income:	$35,434	0.0% Hawaiian	Gore (D)...............115,611	(47%)
Poverty status:	13.5%	0.8% Two+ races	Other...................10,520	(4%)
Military veterans:	14.3%	0.1% Other	**Cook Partisan Voting Index:** R + 1	
		2.1% Hispanic Origin		

Occupation	Blue collar: 27.4%	White collar: 52.4%	Gray collar: 20.2%

Some early 19th century visionaries believed that the North Country of Upstate New York—a battleground in both the Revolutionary War and the War of 1812—was the land of the future. Financier Gouverneur Morris, French slave trader James Leray, and Dutch silver speculator David Parish bought up thousands of acres between the Adirondacks and the St. Lawrence River and tried to unload them on farmers unaware of the shortness of the growing season and the unnavigability of the river. These developers left behind grand mansions, but their hopes for huge profits were frustrated when the Erie Canal turned the stream of settlement westward, and Canadians built their new capital of Ottawa far north of the river (Queen Victoria picked the site, and wanted it as far from the U.S. border as possible). But northern New York was not without its business successes: It was in Watertown in 1878 that 26-year-old Frank Woolworth put a sign over a table of odds and ends that read "Any Article 5 Cents," starting America's first retail chain and inventing the concept of discount stores.

More recently, the North Country has looked to government for help. The St. Lawrence Seaway proved too small for most oceangoing freighters and remains frozen three months of the year; the locks are slow and icebreakers would wreck the shoreline. The state government has built prisons in Ogdensburg and Cape Vincent and Malone, and private developers have built big malls in Watertown and Massena (attracting Canadians, as even New York has lower taxes than Ontario). In the 1990s, North Country and Vermont members of Congress tried to get Lake Champlain declared one of the Great Lakes, to qualify for funding for various programs; the gambit failed as Michigan members bellowed in protest. The biggest initiative has been the enlargement of Fort Drum, near Watertown and adjacent to Lake Bonaparte, where despite the Army's preference for warm weather training sites, a 10,000-person light infantry division, the 10th Mountain Division, has been stationed since 1985; the 10th Mountain performed valiantly in Afghanistan and Iraq.

The 23d Congressional District covers most of the North Country, starting at Lake Champlain, running westward along the St. Lawrence Seaway and over the Adirondacks Forest Preserve to Lake Ontario. The district has only a few population centers, including Plattsburgh on Lake Champlain and Watertown and Oswego on Lake Ontario. Geographically it is the largest district in New York state, and one of the largest in the East. Politically, it is mostly ancestral Republican country; it gave George W. Bush a small plurality in 2000.

The congressman from the 23d District is John McHugh, a Republican first elected in 1992. McHugh has long been in government. He worked for the Watertown city manager in 1971; for eight years, he was a staffer for state Senator Douglas Barclay; in 1984, he was elected to succeed Barclay in Albany. McHugh specialized in dairy issues (New York has long price-fixed dairy products to help farmers) and military bases—both part of the North Country's economic lifeblood. When incumbent David Martin announced his retirement in June 1992, just when the district lines were redrawn, McHugh ran, with plenty of financing plus Martin's endorsement. He won the Republican primary with 70%, then won the general 61%–24%.

McHugh combines a relatively moderate voting record with a concern about local economic needs, not surprising given his district's dependence on federal spending. In 1993 he got a seat on Armed Services and hired none other than Martin to monitor the Defense Base Closure and Realignment Commission. In that year's base closure round, McHugh found himself pitted in a fierce lobbying battle against his colleague to the south, Republican Sherwood Boehlert. Griffiss Air Force Base, a major employer in Boehlert's district, and Plattsburgh Air Force Base, in McHugh's, were competing for a similar mission. In the end, the commission voted to close both bases. When the Army Corps of Engineers suggested further dredging of the St. Lawrence Seaway plus steps to keep it open year-round, McHugh objected because of the environmental consequences. Instead, he urged them to pursue a broader economic study of the Great Lakes region.

After Republicans won control of the House, McHugh chaired the Government Reform subcommittee with jurisdiction over the Postal Service, a somewhat dubious honor since it gave him responsibility for one of Congress's perennial headaches. He worked on what would have been the biggest reform of Postal Service law since the 1970s. His version passed his subcommittee in 1998 but moved no further. McHugh would have given the Postal Service more flexibility in setting prices and giving volume discounts; this pleased big advertising mailers but displeased newspapers, who feared they would lose ads. It would have reduced the limits on first-class mail that others, like FedEx and UPS, could carry. This was a heavily lobbied measure, in which most members had little interest; it may be a while before anything passes. McHugh was more successful in enacting his Semipostal Authorization Act, which allows the Postal Service to issue added-value stamps to advance causes—such as health or safety—that it considers in the public interest, with a maximum 25% surcharge made available for the cause.

McHugh now concentrates his legislative work at the Armed Services Committee, where he has been moving up in seniority. Starting in 2001, he chaired the Military Personnel Subcommittee. He asked Defense Secretary Donald Rumsfeld to investigate charges of misconduct by National Guard commanders who reportedly had inflated reports of their troop strength, and he questioned whether their forces were sufficiently prepared for their challenges in the war on terrorism. He raised concerns about the adverse reaction of some Fort Bragg soldiers to an anti-malaria drug linked to aggression and suicides. In 2003 he became chairman of the Total Force Subcommittee, a new panel that will oversee the Reserves, military health care and education, as well as personnel policy. Preserving Fort Drum in the next base-closing round will be a high priority. McHugh takes a parochial view on trade issues. He was one of the final members to announce support for PNTR with China, deciding that benefits for dairy farmers outweighed possible job losses for General Motors. He opposed trade promotion authority.

McHugh has been reelected against token opposition since 1992. Redistricting posed no problem; this geographically remote district was not on anyone's list for elimination. In 2002, McHugh had no opposition.

TWENTY-FOURTH DISTRICT

Rep. Sherwood Boehlert (R)

Elected 1982, 11th term; b. Sept. 28, 1936, Utica; home, New Hartford; Utica Col., B.A. 1961; Catholic; married (Marianne).

Military Career: Army, 1956–58.

Elected Office: Oneida Cnty. Exec., 1978–82.

Professional Career: P.R. Mgr., Wyandotte Chemicals Corp., 1961–64; A.A., U.S. Rep. Alexander Pirnie, 1964–72; A.A., U.S. Rep. Donald Mitchell, 1973–79.

DC Office: 2246 RHOB 20515, 202-225-3665; Fax: 202-225-1891; Web site: www.house.gov/boehlert.

District Offices: Auburn, 315-255-0649; Cortland, 607-758-3918; Utica, 315-793-8146.

Committees: *Permanent Select Committee on Intelligence* (3d of 11 R): Human Intelligence, Analysis & Counterintelligence (Vice Chmn.); Technical & Tactical Intelligence (Vice Chmn.). *Science* (Chmn. of 25 R). *Select Committee on Homeland Security* (10th of 27 R): Cybersecurity, Science and Research & Development. *Transportation & Infrastructure* (3d of 41 R): Highways, Transit & Pipelines; Railroads; Water Resources & Environment.

Group Ratings

	ADA	ACLU	AFS	LCV	CON	ITIC	NTU	COC	ACU	NTLC	CHC
2002	25	53	0	38	8	100	45	90	64	61	33
2001	35	—	20	86	—	—	51	83	32	—	—

National Journal Ratings

	2001 LIB	—	2001 CONS		2002 LIB	—	2002 CONS
Economic	50%	—	50%		50%	—	49%
Social	60%	—	40%		61%	—	39%
Foreign	43%	—	53%		29%	—	67%

Key Votes of the 107th Congress

1. Approve Bush Tax Cuts	Y	5. Faith-Based Charities	Y	9. Trade Promotion Authority	Y
2. Limit Patients' Bill of Rights	Y	6. Bar Gays in the Boy Scouts	Y	10. Bar Funds for Intl. Court	Y
3. Campaign Finance Reform	Y	7. Ban Partial-Birth Abortion	N	11. Authorize Force in Iraq	Y
4. Ban ANWR Development	Y	8. Arm Commercial Pilots	Y	12. Deny Home. Sec. Dept. Union	Y

Election Results

2002 general	Sherwood Boehlert (R)	108,017	(71%)	($1,063,823)
	David Walrath (C)	32,991	(22%)	($104,975)
	Mark Dunau (Green)	6,660	(4%)	
	Other	5,109	(3%)	
2002 primary	Sherwood Boehlert (R)	21,504	(53%)	
	David Walrath (R)	18,773	(47%)	
2000 general (NY 23)	Sherwood Boehlert (R-Ind)	124,132	(61%)	($808,371)
	David B. Vickers (C-RTL)	42,854	(21%)	($29,583)
	Richard W. Englebrecht (D)	38,049	(19%)	($14,129)

Prior Winning Percentages: 1998 (81%); 1996 (64%); 1994 (71%); 1992 (64%); 1990 (84%); 1988 (100%); 1986 (69%); 1984 (73%); 1982 (56%)

The People		Race/Ethnic Origin	Ancestry	
Area size:	6,356 sq. mi.	92.2% White	Irish: 12.3%	German: 11.9%
Urban population:	50.5%	3.3% Black	Italian: 10.9%	
Rural population:	49.5%	0.9% Asian	**2000 Presidential Vote**	
Pop. 2000:	654,361	0.2% Native Am.	Bush (R)	129,050 (48%)
Median income:	$36,082	0.0% Hawaiian	Gore (D)	126,021 (47%)
Poverty status:	12.6%	1.1% Two+ races	Other	12,639 (5%)
Military veterans:	14.2%	0.1% Other	**Cook Partisan Voting Index:** R + 1	
		2.3% Hispanic Origin		

Occupation	Blue collar: 24.4%	White collar: 57.3%	Gray collar: 18.3%

One of the first American frontiers was the Mohawk River Valley of Upstate New York—a frontier that remained static for 150 years. From the establishment of Fort Orange in 1624 in what now is Albany until the Revolutionary War, white settlers did not dare move west along the Mohawk. The British used their Iroquois allies as a buffer against the French and in return kept New England Yankees from moving westward. Only after the French were driven from the colonies in 1759 did the pressures for westward settlement prevail; the British tried to keep their word to the Indians, but once the Revolutionary War started, the Iroquois dominion ended.

This is the background of *Drums Along the Mohawk* and of James Fenimore Cooper's *Leatherstocking Tales*. But there is little in these rolling hills today to evoke the bloody violence whose conclusion made possible the digging of the Erie Canal and the building of the New York Central Railroad. Though the canal was soon eclipsed by the locomotive, it remains a staggering engineering feat. In 1811, it cost more to ship goods 30 miles inland from New York City than it cost to send them to England. But after eight years of work by 9,000 men, the canal opened in 1825, ahead of schedule and on budget, effectively tying together the nation and cementing the importance of New York City to America's future. As migration trade increased, the Mohawk Valley became one of the nation's early industrial centers. The little Oneida County hamlets of Utica and Rome, where the canal builders had to dig through the route's highest ground, became sizable factory towns. Even the utopian Oneida Community, with its believers in plural marriage and communal ownership, operated a stainless steel factory. First settled by New England Yankees, these towns attracted a new wave of immigration from the Atlantic coast in the early 20th century, including many Italian- and Polish-Americans.

The 24th Congressional District sprawls through parts of 11 counties in central New York, few of them heavily populated. The biggest centers are Utica and Rome in Oneida County and Auburn in Cayuga County, which sits amidst the narrow Finger Lakes and was the home of Governor, Senator and Secretary of State William Seward. Nearby Seneca Falls was the birthplace of the women's movement in 1848, when Boston transplant Elizabeth Cady Stanton and Lucretia Mott produced a Declaration of Sentiments that initiated the push for women's suffrage. Abolition and temperance were also popular here. Today, this is a part of Upstate New York that feels itself bypassed by more recent economic growth and in need of government assistance; Utica's population fell 12% in the 1990s, even as New York City's rose 9%. A proposal to build 27 high-tech windmills, each 400 feet tall, on a hill near Cherry Valley has caused soul-searching among local environmentalists, who like the idea of generating wind power but worry about the impact the complex would have on the "viewshed," especially on Otsego Lake, the model for Glimmerglass in Cooper's novels. At the south end of the lake is Cooperstown, where baseball was supposedly invented in 1839 and which is the home of the Baseball Hall of Fame. Like much of New York, the 24th District is historically Republican, but trended to Democrats in the 1990s. George W. Bush carried it by only a narrow margin in 2000.

The congressman from the 24th is Sherwood Boehlert, a Republican elected in 1982, now chairman of the Science Committee. Boehlert grew up and went to college in Utica, served in the Army, worked briefly for Wyandotte Chemical. Working as a waiter when he was a student at Utica College, he became friendly with Congressman Alexander Pirnie. In 1964, at 28, he got a job on Pirnie's staff; soon he was Pirnie's chief of staff and, after Pirnie retired in 1972, was chief of staff for his successor, Donald Mitchell, until 1978. Then he went back to Utica and was elected Oneida County Executive. When Mitchell retired in 1982, Boehlert won the seat. Boehlert has one of the most liberal voting records of any Republican House member—number three in both 1999 and 2000 *National Journal* ratings, though tenth in 2000 and 2002—and has taken a lead role in defeating what he considers extreme party positions, while maintaining party loyalty on many other matters and trying to forge bipartisan consensus on some issues. Boehlert has voted for an increased minimum wage. He sided with labor in March 2001 as one of 13 Republicans to oppose the repeal of the ergonomics rule, has voted against the partial-birth abortion ban and has supported the National Endowment for the Arts. In July 2001 he voted against the leadership on the rule to consider campaign finance regulation. He has said that Speaker Dennis Hastert's willingness to listen to moderates and respect their views means "you'll never have a Jeffords incident in the House."

Boehlert has played a particularly critical role on environmental issues. His convictions here are strong. After Republicans took control in 1995 he took the lead in opposing environmental policy riders on EPA and other appropriations. In 1995 Speaker Newt Gingrich—to whom he gave crucial support when Gingrich won the whip's post by 2 votes in 1989—named him co-head, with conservative Richard Pombo, of a task force on environmental issues. This produced some results: Republicans agreed on the bipartisan Safe Drinking Water Act of 1996 and the environmental provisions of the 1996 farm bill. But in mid-1997 the intra-party truce broke down; after Boehlert rallied votes to water down an attempt by Western Republicans to exempt flood control projects from the Endangered Species Act, they complained bitterly. In 2000 he opposed the bill to allow property rights disputes involving state and local zoning to be appealed quickly to federal court. In January 2001, he urged caution about overturning last-minute Clinton administration environmental regulations and orders, but he supported the Bush administration on reconsidering 2006 levels of arsenic in drinking water. On the Water Resources and Environment Subcommittee he chaired from 1995 until 2001, Boehlert tried to reach bipartisan agreement on Superfund reform, but without success. Republican attempts to limit presidents' power to create national monuments were frustrated by an amendment Boehlert got James Hansen to agree to; it would require Congress to vote within two months of presidential action. But Rules Chairman Gerald Solomon opposed that in 1997 and similar qualms blocked action in 2002.

As Science Committee chairman since 2001, Boehlert has been involved in some important issues. The September 11 attacks prompted action on cyberterrorism; in February 2002 the House passed Boehlert's bill for $880 million in grants to the National Science Foundation for research on cyberterrorism. In July 2002 the House passed a bill to promote investigations of building collapse, with subpoena power for investigators. On counterterrorism equipment, Boehlert insisted that local communities should pay part of the cost. In June 2002 Boehlert and subcommittee chairman Nick Smith got a 15% increase in funding for the National Science Foundation, the first step in their project to double funding over five years, as was done for the National Institutes of Health. In 2001 Boehlert supported the space program and opposed administration proposals to cut back the space station to allow just three astronauts to work there. "It's going to be more than just a vehicle up in the heavens with three people on it, two and a half of which are working minute by minute to keep the thing operating. That's not why we have the international partnerships we have." After the loss of the space shuttle Columbia, he and Senate Commerce Committee Chairman John McCain held joint hearings on the entire space program.

Some of Boehlert's votes have a local angle: he supports dairy subsidies and helped get the Northeast Dairy Compact into the House farm bill (the 24th is part of New York City's milkshed); he sponsored Pledge of Allegiance Day (the Pledge was written by Francis Bellamy in Rome in 1892). As a baseball buff, Boehlert was relieved when redistricters kept Cooperstown in his district. The foyer of his Rayburn Building office is lined with pictures of local baseball heroes—William Hulbert of Burlington Flats, the founder of the National League, Bud Fowler of Fort Plain, the first black to play professional baseball, Ben Egan of Augusta, the first catcher for Babe Ruth. Boehlert was a minority owner of Utica Blue Sox until February 2002, when the team was sold to Cal Ripken Jr. and moved to Aberdeen, Maryland. He remains chairman of the Minor League Baseball Caucus and, as an aide said, "He considers anyone ever inducted into the Hall of Fame to be his constituent."

The 24th District is a solidly Republican constituency, one of only four New York districts that voted for George W. Bush and Rick Lazio in 2000, and Boehlert has won general elections easily. But he has had serious competition in the Republican primary. In 2000 David Vickers, a high school Spanish teacher, held him to a 57%–43% margin, although the challenger spent only $27,000. Boehlert was hurt in Oneida County by his opposition to congressional ratification of old Indian treaties which would extinguish the Oneida Indians' land claims; he backed government payments in out-of-court settlements. Boehlert won the general election with 61% of the vote, but Vickers got 21% as the nominee of the Conservative and Right-to-Life parties. In June 2002 redistricting removed Madison County and added all or parts of five new counties. Vickers did not run again, but at the last minute David Walrath, a physician and Cayuga County legislator, ran. He said he was a "real Republican" and Boehlert a "big-spending liberal"; like Vickers he called for congressional action to extinguish Indian land claims, which were being asserted by the Cayuga Indians in the new parts of the district. He wrested the Conservative nomination from Boehlert and got a court to take Boehlert off the Independence party line, which meant that unless Boehlert won the Republican primary he would not be on the general election ballot. Boehlert spent $1 million over the course of the campaign and Walrath only $99,000. Outside spending also favored Boehlert. The moderate Main Street Partnership spent $10,000 on a phone bank to support Boehlert, while the conservative Club for Growth, which was spending $150,000 on a Maryland primary held the same day in which its candidate lost by a wide margin, contributed only $1,000 for Walrath. George W. Bush and Dennis Hastert endorsed Boehlert. Even so the result was very close. Boehlert won by only 53%–47%. He carried the parts of the district he had been representing since 1992 by 58%–42%. But in the new counties in the district, Walrath won 59%–41%. Steve Moore, head of the Club for Growth, said, "If I had it to do over again, I would've put the money from the Maryland race into New York." In early 2003 Walrath announced he would run again in 2004, and so would have much more time to campaign. But Boehlert will also have time to get better acquainted in the counties added in the 2002 redistricting.

TWENTY-FIFTH DISTRICT

Rep. James Walsh (R)

Elected 1988, 8th term; b. June 19, 1947, Syracuse; home, Syracuse; St. Bonaventure U., B.A. 1970; Catholic; married (Dede).

Elected Office: Syracuse Common Cncl., 1978–88, Pres. 1986–88.

Professional Career: Peace Corps, Nepal, 1970–72; Social worker, Onondaga Cnty. Social Svcs. Dept., 1972–74; Marketing exec., NYNEX, 1974–88.

DC Office: 2369 RHOB 20515, 202-225-3701; Fax: 202-225-4042; Web site: www.house.gov/walsh.

District Offices: Palmyra, 315-597-6138; Syracuse, 315-423-5657.

Committees: *Appropriations* (7th of 36 R): Agriculture, Rural Development, & FDA; Military Construction; VA, HUD & Independent Agencies (Chmn.).

Group Ratings

	ADA	ACLU	AFS	LCV	CON	ITIC	NTU	COC	ACU	NTLC	CHC
2002	15	7	11	38	17	75	49	84	75	75	83
2001	10	—	11	57	—	—	58	91	76	—	—

National Journal Ratings

	2001 LIB	—	2001 CONS		2002 LIB	—	2002 CONS
Economic	38%	—	63%		48%	—	51%
Social	38%	—	61%		43%	—	56%
Foreign	33%	—	60%		29%	—	67%

Key Votes of the 107th Congress

1. Approve Bush Tax Cuts	*	5. Faith-Based Charities	Y	9. Trade Promotion Authority	N
2. Limit Patients' Bill of Rights	Y	6. Bar Gays in the Boy Scouts	Y	10. Bar Funds for Intl. Court	Y
3. Campaign Finance Reform	Y	7. Ban Partial-Birth Abortion	Y	11. Authorize Force in Iraq	Y
4. Ban ANWR Development	Y	8. Arm Commercial Pilots	Y	12. Deny Home. Sec. Dept. Union	Y

Election Results

2002 general	James Walsh (R-Ind-C)	144,610	(72%)	($939,783)
	Stephanie Aldersley (D)	53,290	(27%)	($39,999)
	Other	2,131	(1%)	
2002 primary	James Walsh (R)	unopposed		
2000 general	James Walsh (R-Ind-C)	151,880	(69%)	($580,767)
	Francis J. Gavin (D)	64,533	(29%)	
	Other	3,830	(2%)	

Prior Winning Percentages: 1998 (69%); 1996 (55%); 1994 (58%); 1992 (56%); 1990 (63%); 1988 (57%)

The People		Race/Ethnic Origin	Ancestry	
Area size:	2,561 sq. mi.	86.6% White	German: 13.9%	Irish: 13.9%
Urban population:	79.0%	7.1% Black	Italian: 12.4%	
Rural population:	21.0%	1.8% Asian	**2000 Presidential Vote**	
Pop. 2000:	654,361	0.6% Native Am.	Gore (D)	148,623 (51%)
Median income:	$43,188	0.0% Hawaiian	Bush (R)	132,126 (45%)
Poverty status:	10.4%	1.5% Two+ races	Other	12,619 (4%)
Military veterans:	12.7%	0.1% Other	**Cook Partisan Voting Index:** D + 3	
		2.3% Hispanic Origin		
Occupation	Blue collar: 20.8%	White collar: 65.0%	Gray collar: 14.2%	

Syracuse is a middle American city in the middle of Upstate New York, halfway between Albany and Buffalo on the Erie Canal and the old New York Central Railroad, which were for years the nation's major east-west transportation routes. Built on a swamp that was a salt spring, Syracuse is the home of many practical-minded inventions—the dental chair, Stickley mission furniture, the drive-in bank teller, the foot measuring devices used in shoe stores—and was an early manufacturer of typewriters. It is the site of the New York State Fair, which attracts 1 million visitors annually, and of Syracuse University, which plays basketball inside the Carrier Dome, the only domed stadium in the northeastern U.S. The agricultural hinterland is rich with specialty crops like wine grapes, and its industrial jobs are mostly high-skill. But Onondaga County lost 2% of its population in the 1990s—the biggest percentage loss of any big New York county—and Syracuse lost 11%. To compensate, the region has sought, and received, generous federal funding: a cleanup of heavily polluted Onondaga Lake, improvements at an Air National Guard base, and other earmarks totaling $74 per constituent for fiscal year 2002, an amount 40% above the national average.

The 25th Congressional District includes all of Syracuse and Onondaga County. West of Syracuse it includes territory just south of Lake Ontario, northern Cayuga County and Wayne County, where in the village of Palmyra Joseph Smith had his vision of the angel Moroni and saw the golden tablets that led him to found the Mormon Church. The district's western end is in the suburbs of Rochester in Monroe County, which in the June 2002 redistricting plan was split up between four districts. Historically, Syracuse and Rochester have been heavily Republican, partly out of antipathy to New York City. But in the 1990s, economically ailing Upstate New York trended sharply toward national Democrats (to bring in federal dollars) even as it voted for Republican Governor George Pataki (to hold down taxes). This is a district carried by Al Gore in 2000 with 51%.

The congressman from the 25th District is James Walsh, a Republican elected in 1988. He grew up in Syracuse, the son of Syracuse mayor and Congressman (1973–79) William Walsh. He came to the House as almost a professional civic activist: He was a volunteer in the Peace Corps in Nepal, a social worker, then worked for New York Telephone and NYNEX, which detailed him to a local university. He was elected five times to the Syracuse Common Council, then ran for Congress in 1988 when a Republican incumbent nearly beaten two years earlier decided to retire. He won by a solid 57%–42%. Like other Republicans from economically sluggish Upstate areas, he is open to government intervention in the economy.

Walsh has a seat on the Appropriations Committee, and has now been chairman of three subcommittees—part of the "college of cardinals." In 1995 and 1996 he chaired the District of Columbia Subcommittee, just as Marion Barry was returned to the mayor's office after serving time in prison. In 1997 and 1998 Walsh chaired the Legislative Branch Subcommittee, which sets Congress's own budget. He suffered the embarrassment in spring 1997 of seeing his appropriation defeated because of defections by 11 Republicans, who were determined to uphold promises to cut Congress's budget.

Since 1999 Walsh has been chairman of the VA-HUD-Independent Agencies Subcommittee. In that capacity, he got into some fights with HUD Secretary Andrew Cuomo. He attacked Cuomo for using anti-drug money to fund a gun buy-back program, and said at one point that HUD employees could be arrested. He worked to create the Erie Canalway National Heritage Corridor, running 524 miles from Albany to Buffalo—and through downtown Syracuse—though it was held up because Governor George Pataki wanted to name its governing commission, to keep Clinton Democrats from control; it was approved finally in December 2000 when it was clear that George W. Bush was the next president. Walsh has not been shy about supporting what some call pork barrel projects, many for the Syracuse area. "Our economy's in tough shape right now, so we're not bashful at all in helping our own state."

The appropriations process went rather smoothly in most of 2001, but after September 11 it was more rocky. In November, Walsh and Democrat Nita Lowey pushed for $11 billion in aid to New York in the defense supplemental. This was opposed by the Bush administration, and Dick Cheney brought Walsh to the White House to ask him to defer the money until later. Walsh refused. Although Walsh and Upstater John Sweeney crossed party lines, their amendment, reduced to $9.7 billion, was defeated by two votes in committee. Walsh continued fighting and threatened to vote against the rule unless it allowed a vote on his amendment. But in a meeting with OMB Director Mitch Daniels and Deputy Whip Roy Blunt, he gave way, and agreed to accept $1.75 billion. Sweeney and New York Democrats were furious, but Walsh said, "I was concerned that we could lose everything if we just went right at the president and drew a veto." In March 2002 Walsh hailed the administration for calling for a total of $21.3 billion in aid to New York. The 2002 appropriations process was difficult because the Senate never passed a budget resolution. Walsh resisted an amendment by Sweeney that would make New York schools eligible for aid for fear of the precedent it would create. Walsh complained to Dennis Hastert in August about the level of spending allowed, but worked doggedly and in October 2002 the subcommittee approved a $90.9 billion appropriation, under both the Senate level and the president's request, though funding for some programs, like AmeriCorps, were eliminated, which Walsh said would probably be added in conference. In November 2002 House Republicans changed their rules to make Appropriations subcommittee chairmen, previously chosen by the full committee chairmen, subject to veto by the Steering Committee—clipping the cardinals' wings.

In 1998 he sponsored the "Walsh Visas" to allow 4,0000 unemployed young people a year from Northern Ireland and adjacent counties in the Irish Republic to live and work in Pittsburgh, Boston, Washington, Colorado Springs and, yes, Syracuse. Walsh is an aggressive enough political operator to oppose George Pataki's choice for U.S. attorney in Syracuse; Walsh's pick, Glenn Suddaby, prevailed.

Walsh has mostly won re-election without difficulty. After he sponsored school vouchers in Washington, D.C., the AFL-CIO targeted Walsh's district, ran an estimated $500,000 in TV ads against Walsh and a vigorous organizing campaign in 1996. With a late-spending and organizational surge, Walsh won 55%–45%. Since then, he has been reelected by overwhelming margins. One can be sure that, once the new district lines were adopted in June 2002, he began to look for worthy projects to fund in the Rochester area.

TWENTY-SIXTH DISTRICT

Rep. Tom Reynolds (R)

Elected 1998, 3d term; b. Sept. 3, 1950, Belfonte, PA; home, East Amherst; Springville-Griffith Inst., Kent St. U.; Presbyterian; married (Donna).

Military Career: NY Air Natl. Guard, 1970–76.

Elected Office: Concord Town Bd., 1974–82; Erie Cnty. Legislature, 1982–88; NY Assembly, 1988–98, Min. Ldr., 1995–98.

Professional Career: Real estate & insurance broker; Erie Cty. Repub. Chmn., 1990–96.

DC Office: 332 CHOB 20515, 202-225-5265; Fax: 202-225-5910; Web site: www.house.gov/reynolds.

District Offices: Rochester, 585-663-5570; Williamsville, 716-634-2324.

Committees: *NRCC Chairman. House Administration* (6th of 6 R). *Rules* (9th of 9 R): Technology & the House.

Group Ratings

	ADA	ACLU	AFS	LCV	CON	ITIC	NTU	COC	ACU	NTLC	CHC
2002	0	7	0	13	25	100	56	100	92	86	92
2001	5	—	10	21	—	—	62	96	88	—	—

National Journal Ratings

	2001 LIB —	2001 CONS		2002 LIB —	2002 CONS
Economic	33%	66%		16%	81%
Social	20%	69%		32%	63%
Foreign	4%	87%		15%	78%

Key Votes of the 107th Congress

1. Approve Bush Tax Cuts	Y	5. Faith-Based Charities	Y	9. Trade Promotion Authority	Y
2. Limit Patients' Bill of Rights	Y	6. Bar Gays in the Boy Scouts	Y	10. Bar Funds for Intl. Court	Y
3. Campaign Finance Reform	N	7. Ban Partial-Birth Abortion	Y	11. Authorize Force in Iraq	Y
4. Ban ANWR Development	N	8. Arm Commercial Pilots	Y	12. Deny Home. Sec. Dept. Union	Y

Election Results

2002 general	Tom Reynolds (R-Ind-C)	135,089	(74%)	($642,641)
	Ayesha Nariman (D)	41,140	(22%)	($8,377)
	Other	7,230	(4%)	
2002 primary	Tom Reynolds (R)	unopposed		
2000 general (NY 27)	Tom Reynolds (R-C)	157,694	(69%)	($832,254)
	Thomas W. Pecoraro (D)	69,870	(31%)	($27,587)

Prior Winning Percentages: 1998 (57%)

The People		Race/Ethnic Origin	Ancestry	
Area size:	2,749 sq. mi.	92.3% White	German: 20.6%	Irish: 12.3%
Urban population:	71.2%	3.0% Black	Italian: 11.9%	
Rural population:	28.8%	1.5% Asian	**2000 Presidential Vote**	
Pop. 2000:	654,361	0.3% Native Am.	Bush (R)..............144,516	(51%)
Median income:	$46,653	0.0% Hawaiian	Gore (D)..............126,693	(44%)
Poverty status:	6.9%	0.8% Two+ races	Other..................14,188	(5%)
Military veterans:	12.9%	0.1% Other	**Cook Partisan Voting Index:** R + 4	
		1.9% Hispanic Origin		

Occupation	Blue collar: 23.4%	White collar: 61.7%	Gray collar: 14.8%

The destination of the Erie Canal, the great state engineering project that made New York the Empire State—is Lake Erie, and for its last hundred miles the canal passed through the rolling countryside of western New York. This was land scarcely settled, except by Indians, when the canal was begun in 1817, and in many ways it is part of the Midwest: water here flows not into the Atlantic but into the Great Lakes; people speak not in the pungent accents of New York City but in a flat Midwestern tone; the economy, based originally on farming fertile land, by the late 19th century became dominated by heavy industry. This land was settled mostly by New England Yankees, with cultural folkways quite different from those of New York City; later they were joined by Irish, Italian and Polish immigrants who came to work in the factories of Buffalo and Rochester. For most of its history, western New York has had an economy more prosperous than that of the rest of the country, as you can still see in the solid houses and schools, stores and factories built to weather the Upstate winter. But in the 1980s and 1990s economic growth has lagged behind the rest of the nation. Many of Buffalo's factories have closed and Rochester's premier industries, Kodak and Xerox, fell on hard times: in 2002, the two employed less than two-thirds of the workforce they had a decade earlier.

The 26th Congressional District covers much of western New York. About half its people are in the suburbs of Buffalo in Erie and Niagara Counties, though none in the city of Buffalo itself. It extends from the city limits of Buffalo to the city limits of Rochester and includes that city's northwestern suburbs. In between is rural and small town territory, with many towns bearing the classical names sprinkled by state commissioners across Upstate New York. One such is Attica, scene of the terrible prison riot in 1970. Politically, this is ancestrally Republican territory. For a long time this was due to Upstaters' distrust of Democratic New York City. But as economic growth has lagged, Upstate New York has moved toward the Democratic party. Not enough to make the 26th District Democratic, however: it is one of six New York districts which voted for George W. Bush in 2000.

The congressman from the 26th District is Thomas Reynolds, a Republican elected in 1998. Reynolds grew up in Springville, in southern Erie County, and became an insurance and real estate broker there. He got into politics early: in 1973 he was aide to an assemblyman and that same year, at 23, he was elected to the Concord town council. In 1982 he was named to a vacant seat in the Erie County Legislature. In 1988 he was elected to the Assembly and also helped run the congressional campaign of Bill Paxon, who was elected to succeed Jack Kemp in Congress from the Buffalo suburbs. From 1990–96 he was Erie County Republican chairman, from 1995–98 the Assembly Minority Leader. In early 1998 it seemed sure that he would stay in Albany. Then, suddenly, what is now the 26th District seat fell open in February 1998 when Paxon announced he would not run for reelection. At his side when he made his announcement in Erie County was his long-time friend and ally Reynolds, who announced he was running for the House the next morning. No serious Republican opposition appeared; Democrats nominated a professor at SUNY-Geneseo. It was not a suspenseful or eventful campaign. Reynolds won 57%–43%.

In the House, Reynolds, with some help from Paxon, quickly won the favor of the Republican leadership and became only the second Republican freshman in a century to win a seat on the Rules Committee. That assignment gave him quick entry into the House's leadership circles and the Capitol's back rooms. Like Paxon, Reynolds proved a skillful fundraiser, gaining appointment to chair the NRCC's Battleground 2000 program, which raised $21 million from House members.

In January 2001 Speaker Dennis Hastert gave Reynolds a slot on the leadership-friendly House Administration Committee, which has responsibility for campaign finance legislation. As a further unusual sign of the leadership's gratitude to Reynolds for his campaign service and a mark of his growing influence, Hastert also got him a seat on the Ways and Means Committee; technically he is on leave on the committee, presumably pending the retirement at Ways and Means of Upstate neighbor Amo Houghton, and still serves on Rules. Reynolds became increasingly active as a legislative strategist. When the House took up the campaign finance regulation, he said that the Shays-Meehan bill had a loophole allowing Democrats to use their $40 million soft money building fund for hard money purposes; the language was fixed. After September 11, some Democrats criticized him as more interested in the priorities of the White House than the needs of New York, but Reynolds responded that he played an essential role as honest broker in getting money to his home state. Stylistically, his personal empathy—more than the specific words of his substantive appeal—can convince listeners to accept his case.

Despite his national activities and ambitions, local redistricting posed a challenge. Sluggish population growth meant that Upstate New York would lose a seat, and Reynolds's elongated district was in perfect geographical position to be carved up among its neighbors. On May 23, 2002, a three-judge federal court considering the case ordered adoption of a special master's plan which would have placed Democrat John LaFalce and Republican Jack Quinn in the same Buffalo-Niagara Falls district and which would have left Reynolds in a district with not much of a Republican edge. But the court gave the legislature more time to act and said it would happily adopt its plan if it met the June deadline for circulating nominating petitions. The legislature in this case meant Democratic Assembly Speaker Sheldon Silver, Republican state Senate President Joseph Bruno and Governor George Pataki; everyone knew that anything they agreed on would be automatically passed. Reynolds worked with Democrat Nita Lowey, then head of her party's House campaign committee, to convince Silver, Bruno and Pataki that they should agree on a plan that would give the two of them safe districts so that they could campaign for their parties across the country. Dick Cheney phoned Bruno to put on the pressure. On June 5 the legislature passed its plan, which left Reynolds with a 26th District in which he would be safe. In November he won by a 74%–22% margin.

A week after the election, House Republicans chose their new team of leaders. Both Reynolds and Jerry Weller ran vigorous campaigns to chair the NRCC. The two occasionally sniped at each other behind the scenes and among Republican lobbyists, who were pressured to contribute to the campaign fund of each. Weller's district is adjacent to that of officially neutral House Speaker Dennis Hastert, although other leadership members, especially Tom DeLay, backed Reynolds. He won 123–91.

TWENTY-SEVENTH DISTRICT

Rep. Jack Quinn (R)

Elected 1992, 6th term; b. Apr. 13, 1951, Buffalo; home, Hamburg; Siena Col., B.A. 1973, S.U.N.Y. Buffalo, M.A. 1978; Catholic; married (Mary Beth).

Elected Office: Hamburg Town Supervisor, 1983–92.

Professional Career: Teacher & coach, Orchard Park Central Schl., 1973–83.

DC Office: 2448 RHOB 20515, 202-225-3306; Fax: 202-226-0347; Web site: www.house.gov/quinn.

District Office: Buffalo, 716-845-5257.

Committees: *Transportation & Infrastructure* (9th of 41 R): Aviation; Highways, Transit & Pipelines; Railroads (Chmn.). *Veterans' Affairs* (5th of 17 R): Benefits (Vice Chmn.).

Group Ratings

	ADA	ACLU	AFS	LCV	CON	ITIC	NTU	COC	ACU	NTLC	CHC
2002	15	13	11	38	17	50	42	84	64	70	75
2001	20	—	38	43	—	—	58	82	70	—	—

National Journal Ratings

	2001 LIB — 2001 CONS		2002 LIB — 2002 CONS	
Economic	50% —	51%	46% —	53%
Social	48% —	53%	47% —	53%
Foreign	27% —	72%	29% —	67%

Key Votes of the 107th Congress

1. Approve Bush Tax Cuts	*	5. Faith-Based Charities	Y	9. Trade Promotion Authority	*
2. Limit Patients' Bill of Rights	Y	6. Bar Gays in the Boy Scouts	Y	10. Bar Funds for Intl. Court	Y
3. Campaign Finance Reform	Y	7. Ban Partial-Birth Abortion	Y	11. Authorize Force in Iraq	Y
4. Ban ANWR Development	N	8. Arm Commercial Pilots	Y	12. Deny Home. Sec. Dept. Union	Y

Election Results

2002 general	Jack Quinn (R-C)	120,117	(69%)	($772,921)
	Peter Crotty (D-WF)	47,811	(27%)	($38,359)
	Other	5,991	(4%)	
2002 primary	Jack Quinn (R)	unopposed		
2000 general (NY 30)	Jack Quinn (R-C-Ind)	138,452	(67%)	($615,608)
	John Fee (D-L-Green-WF)	67,819	(33%)	($162,267)

Prior Winning Percentages: 1998 (68%); 1996 (55%); 1994 (67%); 1992 (52%)

The People		Race/Ethnic Origin	Ancestry	
Area size:	2,444 sq. mi.	88.8% White	German: 19.2%	Polish: 14.7%
Urban population:	81.5%	4.0% Black	Irish: 12.5%	
Rural population:	18.5%	0.7% Asian	**2000 Presidential Vote**	
Pop. 2000:	654,361	0.8% Native Am.	Gore (D) 149,840	(53%)
Median income:	$36,884	0.0% Hawaiian	Bush (R) 114,859	(41%)
Poverty status:	12.0%	1.0% Two+ races	Other 16,090	(6%)
Military veterans:	14.0%	0.1% Other	**Cook Partisan Voting Index:** D + 6	
		4.6% Hispanic Origin		

Occupation Blue collar: 25.3% White collar: 57.9% Gray collar: 16.8%

Buffalo, New York's second city, with its massive 1920s skyscraper City Hall overlooking the Niagara River and Lake Erie, has been going through rough times. The butt of many jokes about the snow that piles up at the eastern end of Lake Erie and that supposedly keeps it immobilized half the year, Buffalo also should be credited with building a heavy industrial base in the late 19th and early 20th centuries, as America's number one grain milling center and as a major steel producer. Today, the Lackawanna steel mills are cold, and grain milling waned after the St. Lawrence Seaway opened in the 1950s. Buffalo is eclipsed economically by the bigger Great Lakes industrial cities of Cleveland, Detroit and Chicago, and its architecturally bold downtown skyscrapers are far overshadowed by the high-rise horizon of Toronto, not many miles away. Buffalo was one of the nation's 20 largest cities in 1950 when it had a population of 580,000; half a century later, it was not one of the top 50, with a population down to 292,000, less than it had in 1900. Surrounding Erie County, once well over 1 million, was down to 950,000. Buffalo still has considerable assets: a high-skill labor force and inexpensive real estate, including a gentrified and handsome waterfront on a now-cleaner Lake Erie and some impressive cultural institutions. Right across Buffalo's Peace Bridge is the richest part of Canada, the golden horseshoe from Niagara Falls through Hamilton to Toronto. But Buffalo's hopes of becoming Toronto's back office have faded, as the Canadian dollar has weakened; New York's taxes have declined, but so have Ontario's, and New York taxes are still high enough to leave Buffalo at a serious disadvantage. Despite incessant cheerleading on national television by the Buffalo-bred political journalist Tim Russert, the biggest news story to come out of metropolitan Buffalo in recent years was the September 2002 arrest of a half-dozen Yemeni-Americans in Lackawanna under suspicion of undergoing weapons training at an Al Qaeda terrorist training camp in Afghanistan. Media accounts inevitably dwelled on the city's decline, which began in the 1980s when the Bethlehem Steel plants were shuttered.

The 27th Congressional District consists of the eastern and southern two-thirds of Buffalo, plus most of the Erie County suburbs east and south of the city—from working-class Cheektowaga and Lackawanna to higher-income Hamburg and Orchard Park. The 27th now also includes Chautauqua County, the famed birthplace of a movement to promote high-minded discourse; it was there that a training camp for Methodist Sunday school teachers was founded in 1874, attracting some 25,000 people to educational talks and inspirational lectures from the likes of Ralph Waldo Emerson and William Jennings Bryan, and rounds of lectures continue every summer. Although some of the Buffalo suburbs are Republican, this district overall is solidly Democratic. But in the early 1990s, as Buffalo struggled, it became politically volatile. In 1992 Buffalo gave Ross Perot 28%, his best showing in a central city anywhere, and in 1994 Mario Cuomo, who had always run well in Buffalo, lost Erie County to George Pataki, who carried Erie County again in 1998 and 2002. But in contests for president and senator, Buffalo and Erie County have remained solidly Democratic.

The congressman from the 27th District is Jack Quinn, a Republican elected in 1992. He is an authentic product of Buffalo, the son of a union railroad engineer, a union member himself as a steelworker and teacher, a graduate of Siena College who became a teacher and coach at Orchard Park Central High School, and the Town of Hamburg supervisor (a full-time job) from 1983–92. When incumbent Democrat Henry Nowak retired in 1992, Quinn saw his chance to run as a reformer; he created his own Change Congress Party so his name would appear under this as well as on the Republican Party line; he ran on an 11-point program of congressional reform, including term limits (which he later said was merely a commitment to vote for term limits) and a reduction in House staff. In a stunning upset, Quinn beat Erie County Executive Dennis Gorski by 52%–46%; in effect, Quinn got the Perot vote while Gorski ran even with Bill Clinton's 46% plurality.

Quinn, sometimes compared with Ronald Reagan, is known on Capitol Hill as well as in Buffalo for his affable personality and, like Reagan, has shown that he is politically shrewd. His voting record has been moderate, though he leans conservative on foreign issues. Tagged almost immediately by Democrats as their number one target in 1994, Quinn worked to reach out to organized labor, voting against NAFTA. He was one of the few Republicans to support the defeated striker replacement bill and supported family and medical leave. Meanwhile, local Democrats were split among several contenders, and Quinn rolled over his opponent, 67%–33%.

In the Republican Congress, Quinn demonstrated further independence of his party's leadership. He was the lead Republican pushing in 1996 for an increase in the minimum wage, and in 1999 he was one of only two Republicans to vote against the Republican budget and one of four to vote against the Republican tax cut plan that year. He opposed trade promotion authority and PNTR with China, and sought quotas and other aid for the import-battered steel industry. He was a big booster of the bipartisan civility meetings, and in 1998 he led 22 other Republicans to a meeting with AFL-CIO president John Sweeney. In early 2001, he jousted with George W. Bush over his decision to ban project labor agreements. Despite his concerns that their proposal was too partisan, he succumbed to heavy pressure from Republican leaders to support its opposition to federalization of airport security workers and he was a crucial vote allowing them to prevail in the House; Quinn said that the Republican bill set tough standards for security. As the economy weakened in late 2001, he urged passage of a stimulus bill with extended unemployment compensation benefits; Republican leaders eventually agreed, and in March 2002 enacted his bill for an additional 13 weeks.

On local issues, Quinn worked on the Transportation and Infrastructure Committee to build a new Amtrak station in Memorial Auditorium. He called for lifting restrictions on imports of Canadian softwood lumber to help local homebuilders and lumber dealers. As chairman of the Railroad Subcommittee in the 107th Congress, he failed to secure a broad program of grants to bail out Amtrak; but he worked with others to keep enough money flowing to avert a threatened shutdown. When security-conscious officials after September 11 proposed new controls that might have required armed guards to inspect all passenger vehicles at the border, Quinn objected and predicted "chaos;" the idea was buried.

This record has helped Quinn hold this basically Democratic seat. In 1996 the AFL-CIO endorsed Democratic Assemblyman Frank Pordum and Bill Clinton carried what was then the 30th District 59%–29%. But Quinn won 55%–45%—an impressive example of ticket-splitting.

Impeachment was a problem for Quinn. His good relations with Clinton—he watched the 1997 Super Bowl at the White House—and the Democratic leanings of his district led everyone to assume he would oppose it. About a week before the House vote, Clinton called Quinn from *Air Force One* and Quinn gave no sign of wavering. But as he listened to the arguments of the Judiciary Committee Republicans, he did. Four days before the vote, he announced he would vote for impeachment, and eight other Republicans followed that day, deciding the issue. Much local reaction, particularly from labor, was furious. Clinton refused to shake Quinn's hand after the State of the Union in January, and journeyed to Buffalo for a rally the day after. Hillary Rodham Clinton, not yet contemplating a New York Senate race herself, promised to campaign for Quinn's 2000 opponent. Quinn said he was puzzled why labor leaders were so angry, since Clinton had deserted them on important issues like NAFTA and fast track and he had held fast. Quinn had it figured right. Dropping their earlier threats, state and local AFL-CIO unions again endorsed him. In 2000, the Democrats did not have a strong candidate, and Quinn won 67%–33%.

Redistricting was also problematic for Quinn. Upstate New York, it was recognized, would lose a district, and while it was unlikely that he would get a more Democratic district, it was quite possible that he would be thrown in with another incumbent. Against a Republican, he would be at a disadvantage in the primary; against a Democrat, he would not only have to get Democrats to cross party lines, but to get many of them to cross party lines and vote against someone they had backed for many years; at one point Quinn threatened to change parties. Quinn's fate seemed dire when on May 23, 2002, a three-judge federal court adopted a special master's plan which placed him in the same district with Buffalo area Democrat John LaFalce. But the court left time for the legislature to adopt its own plan. Leaders of both parties, up to and including Dick Cheney, put pressure on legislators to act, and on June 5 they adopted a plan which merged LaFalce's district with Democrat Louise Slaughter's Rochester area district and left Quinn with the current 27th District, made more Republican by the addition of Chautauqua County. In November Quinn won 69%–27%, his biggest victory ever.

TWENTY-EIGHTH DISTRICT

Rep. Louise Slaughter (D)

Elected 1986, 9th term; b. Aug. 14, 1929, Harlan Cnty., KY; home, Fairport; U. of KY, B.S. 1951, M.S. 1953; Episcopalian; married (Robert).

Elected Office: Monroe Cnty. Legislature, 1976–79; NY Assembly, 1982–86.

Professional Career: Regional Coord., Lt. Gov. Mario Cuomo, 1976–79.

DC Office: 2347 RHOB 20515, 202-225-3615; Fax: 202-225-7822; Web site: www.house.gov/slaughter.

District Offices: Buffalo, 716-853-5813; Niagara Falls, 716-282-1274; Rochester, 585-232-4850.

Committees: *Rules* (2d of 4 D): The Legislative & Budget Process (RMM). *Select Committee on Homeland Security* (9th of 23 D): Infrastructure & Border Security; Rules (RMM).

Group Ratings

	ADA	ACLU	AFS	LCV	CON	ITIC	NTU	COC	ACU	NTLC	CHC
2002	100	87	100	100	72	50	20	22	0	3	0
2001	95	—	100	86	—	—	9	35	0	—	—

National Journal Ratings

	2001 LIB	—	2001 CONS		2002 LIB	—	2002 CONS
Economic	95%	—	0%		92%	—	7%
Social	83%	—	11%		92%	—	6%
Foreign	90%	—	10%		81%	—	18%

Key Votes of the 107th Congress

1. Approve Bush Tax Cuts	N	5. Faith-Based Charities	N	9. Trade Promotion Authority	N
2. Limit Patients' Bill of Rights	N	6. Bar Gays in the Boy Scouts	N	10. Bar Funds for Intl. Court	N
3. Campaign Finance Reform	Y	7. Ban Partial-Birth Abortion	N	11. Authorize Force in Iraq	N
4. Ban ANWR Development	Y	8. Arm Commercial Pilots	N	12. Deny Home. Sec. Dept. Union	N

Election Results

2002 general	Louise Slaughter (D-WF)	99,057	(62%)	($982,355)
	Henry Wojtaszek (R-Ind-C)	59,547	(38%)	($215,720)
2002 primary	Louise Slaughter (D)	unopposed		
2000 general	Louise Slaughter (D)	151,688	(66%)	($167,851)
	Mark C. Johns (R-C)	75,348	(33%)	
	Other	3,820	(2%)	

Prior Winning Percentages: 1998 (65%); 1996 (57%); 1994 (57%); 1992 (55%); 1990 (59%); 1988 (57%); 1986 (51%)

The People		Race/Ethnic Origin	Ancestry	
Area size:	2,282 sq. mi.	62.0% White	German: 13.4%	Italian: 11.0%
Urban population:	93.5%	28.7% Black	Irish: 9.7%	
Rural population:	6.5%	1.4% Asian	**2000 Presidential Vote**	
Pop. 2000:	654,360	0.5% Native Am.	Gore (D) 151,402	(60%)
Median income:	$31,751	0.0% Hawaiian	Bush (R) 88,461	(35%)
Poverty status:	18.7%	1.7% Two+ races	Other 14,160	(6%)
Military veterans:	12.2%	0.1% Other	**Cook Partisan Voting Index:** D +13	
		5.5% Hispanic Origin		

Occupation	Blue collar: 23.2%	White collar: 58.3%	Gray collar: 18.5%

Rochester, with a metro area of just over one million, is one of the major cities of Upstate New York. Located where the Erie Canal, the backbone of Upstate, crosses the Genesee River, Rochester became a major industrial city—the "Flour City" in the 1830s, as it milled the wheat produced by western New York farmers, then a high-tech city, after a bank clerk named George Eastman began making photographic dry plates and marketed the first still camera and film for Thomas Edison's motion picture camera. Later, Bausch & Lomb developed its lens business here. Rochester, the home of Susan B. Anthony and Frederick Douglass, has lived on high-tech versions of the eye. Its great industries—Bausch & Lomb, Eastman Kodak, and Xerox (which started here as Haloid)—have thrived on technical innovation, precision workmanship, high reliability and customer service, lending Rochester an affluent and well-educated population as well as fine civic institutions, including the George Eastman House, one of the world's leading repositories of photographic and motion-picture history. This was the city that in 1918 invented the Community Chest and at one time had the nation's highest United Way contributions; it is also the home of Wegman's, quite possibly the nation's best supermarket chain. Unhappily, Rochester's big employers have fallen on hard times: Xerox moved away many jobs beginning in the 1970s, and in recent years Kodak has had difficulties maintaining its dominance in its fast-changing technological realm. The Rochester area still has moderate growth, but is losing many of its young people.

Not far west of Rochester is a very different part of Upstate New York, the Niagara Frontier—the local name for the Buffalo-Niagara Falls area. The Niagara Frontier was once a genuine frontier, between the United States and British-held Upper Canada, where American troops crossed the raging Niagara River during in the War of 1812 to fight the Battle of Lundys Lane. Later in the 19th century Niagara Falls became a prime vacation spot—a must-see sight for European tourists and American honeymooners. Few tourists today notice the huge water intakes farther up the river or the hydroelectric power lines strung out on giant pylons fanning out in every direction, providing cheap public power for the chemical and steel factories that made the Niagara Frontier one of the heavy industry capitals of America. But the city of Niagara Falls itself has fallen on hard times. Tourists tend to stay on the Canadian side, which has better views of the Falls. Niagara Falls has lost 70% of its manufacturing since the 1960s and had the nation's third-lowest rate of job growth in the late 1990s; its unemployment rate was over 10% in 2002 and population has been declining. The downtown, leveled by urban renewal, remains troubled but there is hope: the Seneca Nation of Indians recently opened a casino in the city's faded convention center, one of three Indian casinos scheduled to open in the Niagara Frontier.

The 28th Congressional District, in its present form, was created by redistricting in June 2002. It includes Rochester, Niagara Falls and part of Buffalo, all connected by a thin strip of land along Lake Ontario and the Niagara River. It includes the city of Rochester, but most of its suburbs are in three other districts; from Niagara Falls it goes south to include Grand Island, Tonawanda and the northeast quadrant of Buffalo, where it includes much of the city's downtown and its fine cultural institutions. This is mainly a central city district, and 29% of its residents are black, by far the highest percentage in any Upstate district. Politically, this is a solidly Democratic district.

The congresswoman from the 28th District is Louise Slaughter, a Democrat first elected in 1986. A coal miner's daughter and a descendant of Daniel Boone (which makes her a cousin of Missouri Democrat Ike Skelton), she grew up in Kentucky and still speaks with the accent and pungent phraseology of the mountains. Slaughter worked as a local staffer for Mario Cuomo when he was lieutenant governor in the 1970s and she won a seat on the Monroe County Legislature in 1976; she was elected to the New York Assembly in 1982. Four years later, she beat a one-term conservative Republican congressman 51%–49%, by charging that he did nothing to free reporter Terry Anderson, a Rochester native and hostage in Lebanon. She held what was then a marginal seat by tending carefully to local problems, by winning the support of area businessmen and the local *Democrat & Chronicle* newspaper—ironically, the flagship of Gannett, a chain founded by a diehard Upstate Republican. As Upstate New York trended Democratic in the 1990s, she became even safer.

When Democrats were in the majority, Slaughter became a member of the Rules Committee, a proponent of her party's House reforms (and a disparager of the Republicans'). Her opposition to a proposed downtown Rochester transit center placed her at the center of a local controversy. She voted against NAFTA and trade promotion authority. A major grievance has been airline deregulation, which has hurt slow-growing areas like Upstate New York; Rochester's airfares have been among the nation's highest. Slaughter's efforts at reregulation—requiring hub airlines to service smaller airports, banning temporary price cuts to drive out competition—have not prevailed. She celebrated when startup JetBlue began service from Rochester; but travelers were bedeviled by horrifying delays and Upstate flights were cancelled. Later other small carriers moved into the Rochester market. Slaughter is a prime supporter of the National Endowment for the Arts and has sponsored bills for free broadcast time for candidates. A microbiologist by training, and consistent with the Rochester-area research mindset, Slaughter opposed proposals to ban human cloning. She sometimes sounds sterner notes: The House approved her proposal for federal life-without-parole sentences for serial rapists.

Slaughter backs feminist causes and is active on health issues. In 1991 she was one of the seven women House members who marched on the Senate to protest its treatment of Anita Hill. The Lewinsky scandal and impeachment left Slaughter uncomfortable. In March 1998 she said defensively, "I have not changed a bit from my days with Anita Hill. Sexual harassment in the workplace is a terrible thing and should not be tolerated." She said she was ready to call for Bill Clinton's resignation in August, but backed away when she saw the videotape of his testimony in which she thought his rights were abridged; like many other feminists, she voted Clinton's way when the time came. In February 2002, she spearheaded opposition by House Democratic women to the nomination of Judge Charles Pickering of Mississippi.

Slaughter has been frustrated in seeking higher positions. In December 1994 she lost the race for vice chairman of the Democratic Caucus and she lost the December 1996 race for ranking Democrat on the Budget Committee. As number two Democrat on the Rules Committee, she was positioned to take the top slot if Martin Frost had been elected minority leader. But Slaughter, like most women in the Democratic caucus, supported Nancy Pelosi, and her victory meant that Frost remain ranking minority member.

Redistricting was a perils-of-Pauline nightmare for Slaughter. Rochester and Monroe County had more than enough population for one district, so she hoped her seat would be safe. But sluggish population growth meant that Upstate New York had to lose one congressional district, and there was much political manuevering to determine which it would be. On May 23, 2002, a three-judge federal court adopted a plan by a special master which would have left Slaughter with a safe seat. But the court gave the legislature time to adopt a plan of its own and indicated it would probably approve its plan. In New York the legislature is effectively controlled by three people—Democratic Assembly Speaker Sheldon Silver, Republican state Senate President Joseph Bruno and Governor George Pataki—and all are sensitive to political considerations. There was heavy political pressure—at one point Dick Cheney telephoned Bruno—to adopt a different plan. On June 5 they reached agreement on a plan that connected Rochester and Democratic parts of Monroe County in this earmuff-shaped district with Niagara Falls and part of Buffalo. It placed Slaughter in the same district as Democrat John LaFalce, the party's ranking member on the Banking Committee, whose campaign would undoubtedly be well financed. Slaughter had represented only 43% of the new district; LaFalce had represented 39% and was much better known in the remaining 18%, which had been represented by Buffalo Republican Jack Quinn. Democratic registration was higher in the Niagara Frontier than in Rochester, and so Slaughter would be at a serious disadvantage. Slaughter called the decision to carve up Monroe County between four districts "appalling" and said that the needs of Rochester and Buffalo were different and sometimes competing. She swallowed her anger and announced her candidacy on June 7. But, after sending clear signals that he would run against Slaughter, LaFalce three weeks later announced his retirement. Slaughter still faced the possibility of primary opposition from a Buffalo area Democrat, notably state Senator Byron Brown. To her amazement, none stepped forward. In the general election Slaughter had to campaign in much new territory, but most of it was Democratic. She lost in the thin strip of land connecting Rochester and Niagara Falls, but she won 73% of the vote in Monroe County and 60% in Erie County, for a 62%–38% victory.

TWENTY-NINTH DISTRICT

Rep. Amo Houghton (R)

Elected 1986, 9th term; b. Aug. 7, 1926, Corning; home, Corning; Harvard U., B.A. 1950, M.B.A. 1952; Episcopalian; married (Priscilla).

Military Career: Marine Corps, 1945–46 (WWII).

Professional Career: Exec., Corning Glass Works, 1951–86, Chmn. & CEO, 1964–86.

DC Office: 1111 LHOB 20515, 202-225-3161; Fax: 202-225-5574; Web site: www.house.gov/houghton.

District Offices: Canandaigua, 585-394-0220; Corning, 607-937-3333; Olean, 800-562-7431.

Committees: *International Relations* (13th of 26 R): Africa. *Ways & Means* (5th of 24 R): Oversight (Chmn.); Trade.

Group Ratings

	ADA	ACLU	AFS	LCV	CON	ITIC	NTU	COC	ACU	NTLC	CHC
2002	20	43	13	38	18	100	47	82	62	69	25
2001	30	—	11	36	—	—	50	82	30	—	—

National Journal Ratings

	2001 LIB	—	2001 CONS		2002 LIB	—	2002 CONS
Economic	49%	—	52%		50%	—	50%
Social	61%	—	39%		58%	—	42%
Foreign	56%	—	45%		51%	—	49%

Key Votes of the 107th Congress

1. Approve Bush Tax Cuts	*	5. Faith-Based Charities	Y	9. Trade Promotion Authority	Y
2. Limit Patients' Bill of Rights	Y	6. Bar Gays in the Boy Scouts	N	10. Bar Funds for Intl. Court	N
3. Campaign Finance Reform	Y	7. Ban Partial-Birth Abortion	Y	11. Authorize Force in Iraq	N
4. Ban ANWR Development	Y	8. Arm Commercial Pilots	Y	12. Deny Home. Sec. Dept. Union	Y

Election Results

2002 general	Amo Houghton (R-C)	127,657	(73%)	($970,302)
	Kisun Peters (D)	37,128	(21%)	
	Other	9,846	(6%)	
2002 primary	Amo Houghton (R)	unopposed		
2000 general (NY 31)	Amo Houghton (R-C)	154,238	(77%)	($801,505)
	Kisun Peters (D)	45,193	(23%)	($330)

Prior Winning Percentages: 1998 (68%); 1996 (72%); 1994 (85%); 1992 (71%); 1990 (70%); 1988 (96%); 1986 (60%)

The People		Race/Ethnic Origin	Ancestry	
Area size:	5,761 sq. mi.	92.5% White	German: 16.3%	Irish: 12.2%
Urban population:	58.4%	2.7% Black	English: 11.1%	
Rural population:	41.6%	1.8% Asian	**2000 Presidential Vote**	
Pop. 2000:	654,361	0.5% Native Am.	Bush (R)	152,004 (53%)
Median income:	$41,875	0.0% Hawaiian	Gore (D)	121,596 (43%)
Poverty status:	9.9%	1.0% Two+ races	Other	11,318 (4%)
Military veterans:	14.2%	0.1% Other	**Cook Partisan Voting Index:** R + 6	
		1.4% Hispanic Origin		

Occupation Blue collar: 23.0%   White collar: 61.3%   Gray collar: 15.7%

The Southern Tier of New York is one of the nation's forgotten stretches of territory, yet it has an interesting and distinctive history. Elmira was the hometown of Mark Twain's beloved wife, Olivia, and is where Twain is buried. Corning is the headquarters of Corning Glass Works, a company successful over the years not only in manufacturing but in its artistic distinction, which is showcased at a well-visited glass museum. This area has an Indian presence—some small reservations as well as the Seneca-Iroquois National Museum—plus miles and miles of dairy farms and much of New York's wine country. Sheltered by hills, the lands at the edge of Upstate's deep lakes are the nation's largest grape-growing area outside California, and the leader in Concord grapes, with headquarters of prime New York State wineries and a major Welch's grape juice plant. But this country is isolated, and ill-served by air travel or Interstate highways. Cattaraugus County, slightly inland from Lake Erie, is actually 110 miles closer to Washington, D.C., than it is to New York City, though getting to either destination requires considerable patience. The cruelest cut, however, was the Internet bust. Corning's prospects grew dramatically when fiber optics and other high-tech components were being installed at a feverish pace, but the reduction in orders following the bust forced the company to lay off more than 1,000 of its 8,000 local workers, in a town of only 11,000 people. In the process, a solid manufacturing giant with a strong commitment to the town it helped rebuild after Hurricane Agnes in 1972 found itself swimming with Internet sharks, and getting bitten.

The 29th Congressional District includes much of the state's Southern Tier, from Elmira to Cattaraugus County and northward, across the westernmost of the Finger Lakes to the southern suburbs of Rochester. Politically, this has been Republican country since the party's founding. The towns and countryside are no longer homogeneously Protestant, but they remain solidly Republican in most elections. Despite the 1990s trend in Upstate New York toward national

Democrats, the 29th remains solidly Republican. With 53 percent of the vote, this was George W. Bush's strongest district in the state.

The congressman from the 29th District is Amo Houghton, who carries his familiar name with considerable grace: He is a scion of the very rich family that owns the Corning Glass Works, founded in 1851. He was a top executive at Corning for 25 years and had considered retiring to be a missionary in Africa, but instead ran for Congress. The Houghtons are not just rich folks in a small town, they are charter members of the American establishment: Houghton's father was ambassador to France; his grandfather, a congressman in the 1920s, and later Ambassador to Germany and Great Britain, built one of the biggest mansions on Washington's Embassy Row; his family endowed the rare books library at Harvard; and this latest Houghton sat on boards of companies like IBM, Citicorp, and Procter and Gamble. Cheerful, articulate, used to being in comfortable command, Amo Houghton ran a chipper and well-financed campaign in 1986; he chatted with voters, competed with a serious Democratic opponent and won 60% of the vote. Houghton is not easily pigeonholed. He joined the Marine Corps in 1945, at 18, and in his campaigns has done "work days" as a disc jockey at an Elmira radio station, as a cook at the Texas Hots restaurant in Wellsville, and as a man-on-the-street reporter for the *Olean Times-Herald*. He has been reelected by wide margins.

Houghton is the only former CEO of a Fortune 500 company serving in the House, and he brings that perspective to government—he sometimes finds it wasteful and foolish, but also wants to preserve some programs with little public support. He dislikes adversariness (CEOs tend to hear little but praise) but is ready to listen to complaints (the up-to-date CEO had better know if the organization is not working). If he was not a typical freshman congressman in the 1980s, he was more what the Founding Fathers had in mind than the politically adept youngsters who win in so many districts. By one estimate, he is the richest member of Congress, though an earlier estimate of more than $700 million shrunk with the collapse of Corning's stock price when its fiber optics equipment manufacturing was crushed by the collapse of the tech industry; in October 2002, *Forbes* pegged his net worth at $475 million. Anyway, he seems to have the unassuming nature of one to whom much is given, who has been living up to his responsibilities and has mostly enjoyed himself in the process: "a wealthy Brahmin with a social conscience, a moderate congressman of grace with a spiritual bent," according to the *New York Times*.

Houghton's voting record places him among the dozen most liberal Republicans, especially on cultural issues. He was an early supporter of the Shays-Meehan campaign finance bill; he delivered a passionate speech against the school prayer amendment in 1998. He organized the Main Street Coalition, which he sees as a counterpart to the Democratic Leadership Council, a think tank for Republican moderates though it has yet to produce work of the volume or rigor as the DLC. A contributor to the arts for many years, he is a staunch advocate of the National Endowment for the Arts. He was one of four Republicans to vote against all four articles of impeachment against Bill Clinton, preferring that Congress approve a strongly-worded censure. When Dick Armey retired as Majority Leader, he sought someone to run against Tom DeLay, whose supporters were "jamming this thing down our throats;" he was unsuccessful in slowing down the conservative leader, whose combative style rubs against Houghton. Citing the need to work with the United Nations, he was one of an eclectic group of six Republicans who voted against authorizing the use of force in Iraq. As the only member of Congress who belongs to the Augusta National Golf Club, Houghton, a club member for three decades, said he was "neutral" on whether Augusta should change its policy to admit women.

On Ways and Means, he chairs the Oversight Subcommittee. He used that position to enact a modest campaign-finance reform: a requirement that "Section 527" tax-exempt political advocacy groups, an increasingly popular funding loophole for "stealth PACs," disclose their contributors and spending. Although he is not a total free trader, he supported PNTR with China and trade promotion authority. He passed in the House a bill to discourage trade in "conflict diamonds," which are used to finance illegal causes, such as the Al Qaeda terror network. The House passed his post-September 11 proposals to authorize $15 billion in tax-exempt private bonds to rebuild commercial and residential properties; it was enacted in an omnibus package.

Redistricting posed a major threat to Houghton's tenure. He was so fearful that legislators in Albany would eliminate the Southern Tier district that he rejected plans to retire in 2000, and he vigorously lobbied and made campaign contributions to state legislators to preserve the seat, rather than have its territory put into districts dominated by Buffalo and Rochester. Defying expectations, he not only preserved the district, but decided, at 76, not to retire in 2002. He has not said whether he will run for reelection in 2004. Republican state Senator John "Randy" Kuhl has been viewed as Houghton's heir apparent from the Southern Tier; the addition of the Finger Lakes and southern Rochester suburbs in redistricting could produce other candidates.

★ NORTH CAROLINA ★

N orth Carolina, in its third century as a state, has become one of the leading-edge parts of the nation, a state whose growing economy, booming demography and vibrant culture are in many ways typical of the way the nation is going—or would like to go. This was mostly unanticipated. Few people 20 years ago picked North Carolina as a state that would chart a path to the future. It had no great central city, no Atlanta primed to become another Chicago or Los Angeles, but rather a series of small metropolitan areas spaced out over thickly settled countryside. It did not have what seemed to be cutting-edge industries: the biggest employer was textiles, typically an underdeveloped nation's first industry, and the other two were stolid furniture and soon-to-be-disfavored tobacco. Geographically, it seemed to be off the nation's main lines of commerce—too steamy to be businesslike in the summer, too cold to be a resort in the winter. It did not seem socially advanced, with a population made up almost entirely of native-born Anglo-Saxons and African-Americans and with an attachment to traditional and sometimes fundamentalist religion.

Yet North Carolina has emerged as one of America's leading growth states. Its population grew by 37% from 1980 to 2000, from 5.9 million to 8 million; it ranks just behind also-fast-growing Georgia as the 11th largest state. Its economy has diversified and grown steadily. The number of textile and tobacco jobs is down, but Research Triangle Park, between Raleigh, Durham and Chapel Hill, has become one of the world's leading pharmaceutical and high-tech research centers. Charlotte has become one of the nation's leading banking centers, the headquarters of Bank of America (formerly NationsBank and NCNB) and First Union; when Florida's SunTrust sought to buy Winston-Salem-based Wachovia, the legislature passed a law to shore up the North Carolina management. Charlotte and Raleigh-Durham accounted for half the state's population growth in the 1990s, and they are now not just regional centers but major metro areas, with national sports franchises and huge hub airports. Nearly half the state's population—and more than half its affluent population— are in the Charlotte, Raleigh-Durham and Greensboro-Winston-Salem metro areas which have spread out into formerly rural counties. North Carolina is not Mayberry any more.

Not all of North Carolina is upscale. The state is the nation's number two hog producer, and the waste from big hog lots has polluted the state's rivers, most spectacularly when Hurricane Floyd drove the rivers upstream in November 1999; big national trial lawyers started targeting the hog industry. Some people are worried about the state's decline in manufacturing jobs, as low-wage factories close and work moves to lower-wage factories in less affluent states or abroad. North Carolina, number one in the percentage of workers in manufacturing jobs in 1993, was number six in 2000. But manufacturing job losses have been overwhelmed by the rise in service jobs, and the unemployment rate is low enough that thousands of Latinos moved into North Carolina seeking jobs in construction and meat and chicken factories. The state's Hispanic population rose from 77,000 to 379,000 in a decade, the biggest percentage rise in any state. Yet for all its metropolitan growth, life in North Carolina has not lost its rural tone. This has always been thickly settled rural land, and if one is never out of sight of others there is also plenty of green space and reminders of rural roots, from barbecue stands to country Baptist churches to stock car tracks. North Carolina was once known for its large number of trailers, but mobile homes have now gone upscale; in 1990, two-thirds of the trailers sold were singlewides, but in 2000 three-quarters of those sold were doublewides, and most were sold not as personal property but as real estate: Manufactured homes. Tarheels can live surrounded

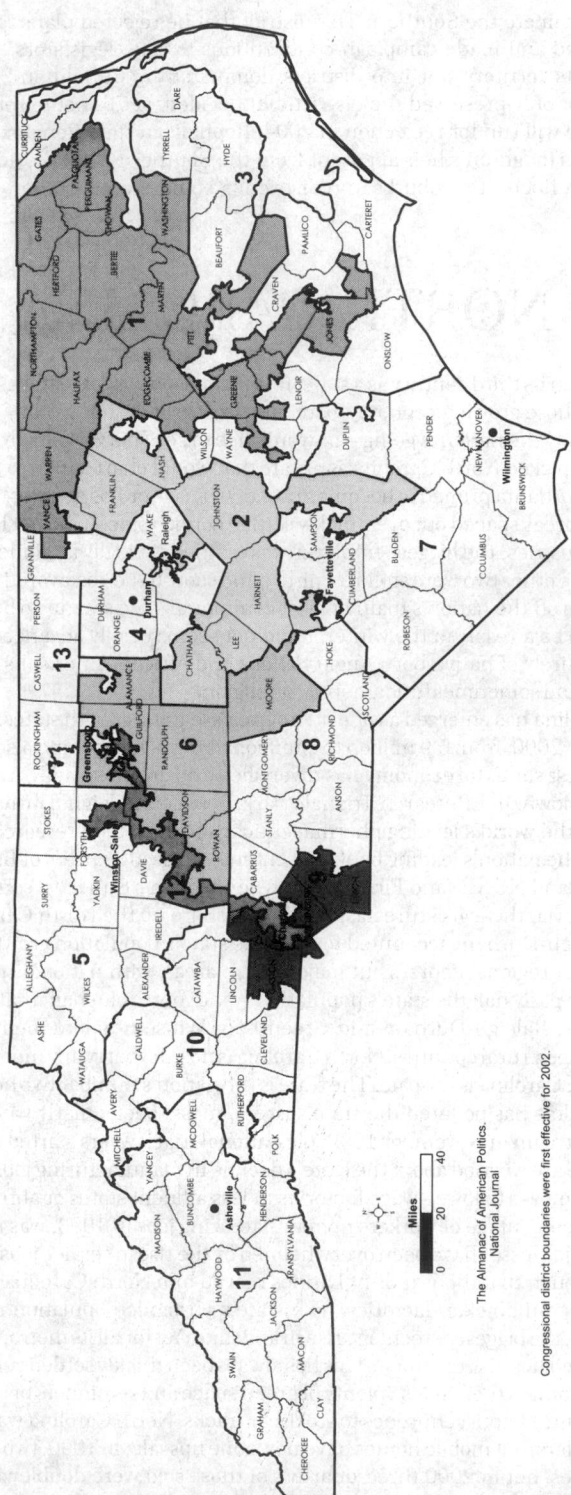

The Almanac of American Politics.
National Journal

Congressional district boundaries were first effective for 2002.

Districts 1, 2, 6, 9 and 12 are highlighted for visibility.

by forests or farms and yet be within an hour's drive of huge shopping centers and thousands of work-places.

Change has not been directed from any single establishment; the forces that have produced it are diverse and sometimes hostile. North Carolina does have a small and articulate elite, which looks for guidance from the University of North Carolina at Chapel Hill and the historically liberal editors of the state's newspapers, most prominently the Raleigh *News & Observer* and the *Charlotte Observer*. Quite different attitudes are nurtured by tradition-minded churches in a state where churchgoing is deeply ingrained, endorsed for years through Sunday blue laws and strengthened periodically by religious revivals. North Carolina's Billy Graham remains a strong voice for revealed religion; he all but endorsed George W. Bush in 2000, and his son Franklin Graham delivered the invocation at Bush's inauguration. When North Carolina was an economically backward state, infant mortality was common, indoor plumbing was not, and religion was a fountain of hope and a source of discipline; it is still, perhaps even more, in this now bustling air-conditioned, cable- and computer-wired commonwealth.

North Carolina has grown with the aid of both its progressive and tradition-minded citizens, and in spite of—sometimes because of—the polarized politics that has developed between the two sides. North Carolina's professionals tend to share progressive values; its businessmen and conservative Protestants tend to share tradition-minded values. Both groups have contributed to the state's economic dynamism and cultural energy. Liberal progressivism has provided an impetus toward building good schools and universities and highways and amenities like the nation's first state-funded symphony and state high schools for science and mathematics and the arts. North Carolina's education reforms, including stringent testing and bonuses for teachers in high-performing schools, made it one of the two states (the other was Texas) with the biggest gains in reading and math test scores in first half of the 1990s. The stringent testing has increased the number of dropouts, but it also means that a North Carolina high school diploma means something. The slowing economy led to increases in state university tuitions, but they are still a bargain by national standards.

From these two strands of North Carolina tradition developed a polarized, increasingly party-line politics that is pretty evenly balanced, waged partly on economic issues but even more on cultural attitudes. It is a politics in which Democrats and Republicans have been distinctive, sometimes bitter in their rivalries, for years not overlapping in their ideas but by the mid-1990s converging on at least some issues. This politics was built on historic partisan patterns: Coastal North Carolina settlers tended to be British Anglicans who became Methodists, slaveholders who supported the Confederacy and voted Democratic; Piedmont settlers tended to be Scots-Irish Presbyterians with a scattering of Germans sects, Union men in 1861 and Republicans ever after. The most effective paladins of both traditions for the last quarter century, Republican Senator Jesse Helms and Democratic Governor Jim Hunt, were each elected to statewide office five times over 25 years, and in 1984 waged what was then the most expensive Senate race in U.S. history; once bitter rivals, they later reconciled, and worked together on some issues. Now they have both retired from office, Hunt from the governorship after four non-consecutive terms in 2000, Helms from the Senate seat after five terms in 2002.

Most elections here have been decided by relatively narrow margins. Bill Clinton lost North Carolina twice, by less than 1% in 1992 and by 5% in 1996; in 2000, this was not a seriously contested state, and George W. Bush beat Al Gore by 56%–43%. Hunt won his last term as governor in 1996 with 56% and was succeeded in 2000 by Democrat Mike Easley, who beat Republican Richard Vinroot 52%–46%. In 1998 Democrat John Edwards upset Senator Lauch Faircloth 51%–47%, and in 2002 Republican Elizabeth Dole, living in her 100-year-old mother's house in Salisbury, beat Democrat Erskine Bowles, once Clinton's chief of staff, by 54%–45%. In 1994 Republicans took control of the North Carolina House; in 1998 Democrats took it back; in 2002 Republicans won back the state House, though a post-election party switch left the House evenly divided. This is not a state of political landslides.

North Carolina's electorate breaks along cultural, not economic lines. In the 2000 exit poll blacks, who are 21% of the population, were overwhelmingly Democratic (90% for Al Gore), while white Protestants were heavily Republican (72% for George W. Bush). Those with non-Christian or no religion voted 64%–31% for Gore, but made up only a small proportion of the electorate. Geographically, this means the centers of the Piedmont urban areas, filling up with professionals and with significant black populations, have trended Democratic; the counties farther out, filling up with middle-income families working in decentralized businesses, have switched from historic Democratic preferences to solid Republican ones. Coastal east Carolina, once overwhelmingly Democratic, is now mixed; smaller counties in and near the western mountains are heavily Republican. The result is a close balance between two cultural and political blocs which have contributed to North Carolina's unanticipated growth—though neither is inclined to give the other much credit.

The People		Race/Ethnic Origin			Military veterans: 792,646 (13.0%)	
Pop. 2000:	8,049,313	5,647,155	70.2%	White	WWII: 17.3%	Korea: 12.5%
Pop. 1990:	6,628,637	1,723,301	21.4%	Black	Vietnam: 32.3%	Gulf War: 13.3%
Change 1990–2000:	Up 21.4%	112,416	1.4%	Asian	**Most populous cities:**	
Change 1980–1990:	Up 12.7%	95,333	1.2%	Native Am.	1. Charlotte	540,828
% of U.S. total:	2.9%	3,165	0.0%	Hawaiian	2. Raleigh	276,093
Pop. rank:	11th of 50	79,965	1.0%	Two + races	3. Greensboro	223,891
Area size:	53,819 sq. mi.	9,015	0.1%	Other	4. Durham	187,035
State Native:	63.0%	378,963	4.7%	Hisp. Origin	5. Winston-Salem	185,776
Non-citizen:	3.9%	**Ancestry**			Urban population: 60.2%	
Language		USA: 11.7%		English: 8.1%	Rural population: 39.8%	
English: 90.7%	Spanish: 5.4%	German: 8.0%		Irish: 6.3%		
Other Eur.: 2.4%		Scotch-Irish: 2.7%				

Education		Work Sector			General Assembly	
H.S. Grad:	78.1%	Private: 78.8%		Govt: 14.5%	Senate	28 D 22 R
College Grad:	22.5%	Self: 6.4%		Family: 0.3%	House	60 D 60 R
Industry		Unemployment: 5.2%			Legislative Term Limits: No	
Agri: 1.6%	Con: 8.2%	**Household Income**			**Registered Voters**	
Fin: 6.0%	Info: 2.3%	<15k: 16.9%		15-35k: 27.7%	D: 2,388,679 (48.0%)	
Mfg: 24.4%	Prof: 26.9%	35-50k: 17.7%		50-100k: 28.3%	R: 1,712,992 (34.4%)	
Public: 4.1%	Trade: 14.9%	100-150k: 6.0%		>150k: 3.4%	I: 872,335 (17.5%)	
Other: 11.6%		Median: $39,184				
Occupation		Poverty status: 12.3%				
Blue collar: 29.7%	White collar: 56.0%	**Home Value**				
Gray collar: 14.3%		<50k: 18.0%	50-100k: 35.1%	100-200k: 33.7%	200-300k: 8.2%	
		300-500k: 3.6%	>500k: 1.5%	Median: $95,800		

Presidential politics North Carolina was the scene of one of the most crucial moments in the 2000 presidential campaign, when the second debate was held at Wake Forest University in Winston-Salem in October. Otherwise the state saw little of the candidates. Bill Clinton's and Al Gore's crusade against tobacco helped to put North Carolina out of reach for the Democrats, and neither campaign targeted this now fairly expensive state. Gore ran no better than even in the Raleigh-Durham metro area, and lost the Charlotte and Greensboro-Winston Salem areas by nearly 3–2 margins. In January 2001, the Democratic legislature, presumably giving up on the hope of a national Democratic candidate carrying the state, was considering whether to award 13 of the state's 15 electoral votes to the winner in each congressional district; that would guarantee the Democrats at least three more electoral votes—which would have elected Al Gore in 2000 and made the Florida count irrelevant. The bill failed to pass; it was postponed indefinitely in October 2002.

2000 Presidential Vote
Bush (R) 1,631,163 (56%)
Gore (D) 1,257,692 (43%)
Other 26,135 (1%)

2000 Republican Presidential Primary
Bush (R) 253,485 (79%)
McCain (R) 35,018 (11%)
Keyes (R) 25,320 (8%)
Other 8,694 (3%)

2000 Democratic Presidential Primary
Gore (D) 383,696 (70%)
Bradley (D) 99,796 (18%)
No Preference 49,905 (9%)
Other 11,525 (2%)

1996 Presidential Vote
Dole (R) 1,213,819 (49%)
Clinton (D) 1,098,297 (44%)
Perot (I) 167,465 (7%)

North Carolina's presidential primary has been crucial only once, in 1976, when after five straight losses, Ronald Reagan started denouncing the Panama Canal Treaty and won his first victory over Gerald Ford. It has been part of the Super Tuesday primary since 1988, but has been overshadowed by the even larger states that vote that day.

Congressional districting   North Carolina won a 12th House seat in the 1990 Census and, quite unexpectedly, a 13th seat in the 2000 Census. It beat out Utah for the latter by just 856 people, and because its apportionment population includes some 18,000 U.S. troops and diplomats who claim North Carolina as their home, Utah filed a lawsuit arguing that its apportionment population should be credited with Mormon missionaries overseas who claim Utah as their home. But in April 2001 a three-judge federal panel ruled unanimously against Utah and in November 2001 the Supreme Court affirmed that decision without opinion.

108th Congress Lineup
7 R   6 D
107th Congress Lineup
7 R   5 D

In the 1990s, North Carolina was the epicenter of race-based redistricting litigation, home to a legal controversy that has gone up to the U.S. Supreme Court four times. In 1992 the Justice Department, under the prevailing interpretation of the Voting Rights Act, required the state to create two black-majority districts—difficult because North Carolina has no concentrations of blacks as large as those in Georgia or Texas. So the Democratic legislature drew a plan with a jagged-boundaried 1st District in east Carolina and a 12th District that extended (sometimes just along the median strip of I-85) from Gastonia through Charlotte, Winston-Salem and Greensboro to Durham. In June 1993 the Supreme Court in *Shaw v. Reno*, focusing on the 12th, ordered the plan re-examined. On remand a three-judge federal panel upheld the plan in August 1994. But in June 1996 the Supreme Court declared the 12th unconstitutional and sent it back to the three-judge panel, which ruled it had to be redrawn by April 1997. In March 1997 the legislature agreed to a new plan that smoothed out the lines but, in a spirit of bipartisan compromise, left the districts much as they were. The 1st and 12th Districts, both formerly 57% black, were now 50% and 47% black, respectively (measuring by the 1990 Census). A different three-judge panel threw out that plan in April 1998. In May 1998 the legislature passed a third plan which further reduced the size of the 12th District: In the first plan it stretched from Gastonia to Durham, in the second from Charlotte to Greensboro, in the third from Charlotte to Winston-Salem. The state appealed to the Supreme Court and argued for adoption of the 1997 plan. In May 1999 the Supreme Court remanded the case for trial, and in March 2000 the district court ruled that the 1997 districts were unconstitutional. That order was stayed by the Supreme Court, and the 2000 elections were held under the 1998 plan. Three weeks after the election, the Supreme Court heard argument on the case again, and in April 2001 ruled 5–4 that the 1997 districts could stand. The issue was arguably academic in North Carolina, since new lines were drawn for the 2002 election, based on the 2000 Census, which gave the state 13 rather than 12 districts.

Democratic legislators created their plans for 2002 with the foregoing in mind. The state House and Senate passed the same plan in November 2001; in North Carolina the governor does not have a veto on redistricting bills. The plan created a new 13th District seat in the northern Piedmont which leaned Democratic in state elections, though it was even in the 2000 presidential race; the district ended up electing Democrat Brad Miller, not coincidentally the chairman of the Senate redistricting committee. The plan significantly weakened 8th District Republican Congressman Robin Hayes. It marginally improved the Republican-leaning 2d and 7th Districts seats held by Democrats Bob Etheridge and Mike McIntyre. It created six heavily Republican districts and three solidly Democratic districts, with the other four districts tailored to the needs of local Democrats. Republicans filed suit even before the plans were passed. But while their arguments about the Democratic plans for redistricting state legislative seats prevailed in the state Supreme Court, their case against the congressional district lines was dropped after the Justice Department approved the maps and the U.S. Supreme Court refused to intervene. But the case against the legislative districts did cause a delay of the primary from May to September and the legislature's cancellation of the runoff required if no candidate got 40% of the vote.

Governor

Michael Easley (D)

Elected 2000, term expires Jan. 2005, 1st term; b. Mar. 23, 1950, Rock Mount; home, Raleigh; U. of N.C. (Chapel Hill), B.A. 1972; N.C. Central U., J.D. 1976; Catholic; married (Mary).

Elected Office: NC Atty. Gen., 1992–00.

Professional Career: Asst. D.A., N.C. 13th Dist., 1976–78, 1979–82; N.C. Dist. Atty., 1982–90; private practice, 1978–79, 1990–92.

Office: State Capitol, Raleigh, 27603, 919-733-4240; Fax: 919-733-5166; Web site: www.state.nc.us.

Election Results

2000 general	Michael Easley (D)	1,530,324	(52%)
	Richard Vinroot (R)	1,360,960	(46%)
	Other	50,778	(2%)
2000 primary	Michael Easley (D)	330,764	(59%)
	Dennis Wicker (D)	203,723	(36%)
	Other	27,453	(5%)
1996 general	James B. Hunt Jr. (D)	1,436,638	(56%)
	Robin Hayes (R)	1,097,053	(43%)

Mike Easley, a Democrat, was elected governor of North Carolina in 2000, the first time either party won a third consecutive term since 1968. Easley grew up in Rocky Mount, 50 miles east of Raleigh, and graduated from the University of North Carolina and North Carolina Central University Law School. He has spent his whole adult life in government. He served as an assistant district attorney and in 1982, at 31, became district attorney in three southeast counties. There he attracted attention for programs against rape and sexual abuse, counseling child abuse victims and prosecuting drug traffickers. In 1992 he took a big step upward by winning election statewide as attorney general. In that office he won publicity by fighting a cap on prison populations imposed by a federal court. He took part in the national tobacco settlement and got some compensation for North Carolina tobacco farmers. He appeared in $1 million worth of public service ads, many warning about predatory lending to old people; his constant appearances irritated Republicans, who pushed through a law banning such appearances in election years.

Reelected in 1996, Easley started running for governor in 1999, obviously a strong candidate but by no means the favorite. His main Democratic primary opponent, Lieutenant Governor Dennis Wicker, was endorsed by teachers' unions, feminist groups and black leaders. But Easley won the May primary by 59%–36%. Meanwhile, the Republican nomination went to former Charlotte Mayor Richard Vinroot—supported by former Governor Jim Martin and former UNC basketball coach Dean Smith—who beat legislator Leo Daughtry, who was supported by the Christian Coalition and the National Rifle Association, 45%–37% (North Carolina requires a runoff only when no candidate gets 40% of the vote). Easley called for prescription drugs for seniors and HMO regulation, improvements in public schools and a lottery to fund education. He avoided the national Democratic Party and didn't attend the convention in Los Angeles. Vinroot opposed the lottery but said he would allow a referendum; he pledged not to raise taxes and called for school vouchers for low-income children in failing schools. The 6'7" Vinroot, a basketball player at UNC, got lots of notice when he referred to the 5'10" Easley as the "little fellow."

For most of the campaign, Easley ran about 10% ahead in polls. Then, when the presidential candidates debated at Wake Forest University in Winston-Salem on October 11, Vinroot tied Easley to Al Gore. One ad called Easley an "Al Gore liberal." Easley attacked Vinroot for his support of vouchers and opposition to a lottery. Easley had more money, and in the last week ran an ad with an endorsement from North Carolina's Andy Griffith. That helped portray him as a downhome, rural Carolinian, running against a city slicker. Even as George W. Bush was carrying North

Carolina, Easley won 52%–46%. He carried east Carolina and the rural areas as a whole; he carried the Raleigh-Durham area by nearly 3–2 and ran even in the Greensboro-Winston-Salem area, running behind only in Vinroot's home turf in metro Charlotte.

Easley came to the governorship at a time when voters were used to an expanding economy and used to the leadership talents of Jim Hunt, elected in 1976 and 1980 and again in 1992 and 1996. In Hunt's years state government could afford new initiatives, and Hunt had skills as an advocate to the public and as an insider dealmaker that bear comparison with Bill Clinton's. But Easley came to office when North Carolina's booming economy was slowing down, and as the first North Carolina governor never to have been a legislator in nearly 50 years he lacked the horse-trading skills that are useful in dealing with a legislature. In his first year nonetheless Easley had some success. In September 2001 he persuaded the legislature to pass his budget with money for his More at Four preschool program and smaller class sizes for early grades. He passed programs for HMO regulation and prescription drugs for seniors, character enhancement and school accountability report cards.

But as time went on he faced severe fiscal problems. In February 2002 he used executive power to take money from trust funds and withhold money from local governments to staunch a $1.2 billion shortfall. In May 2002 he presented a budget which cut overall spending and depended on receipts from an as yet unapproved lottery, but provided money for More at Four and more teachers in early grades and cut aid to local governments; they could increase their sales taxes by a half-percent if they liked. In June 2002 the state Senate rejected his education spending increases; in July 2002 the House, with Republicans solidly against, blocked his plan to cut local aid. In response Easley cut 2,600 state jobs. In September the House rejected the putting the lottery on the ballot 69–50. But a budget agreement was reached that month protecting Easley's More at Four and class size proposals and gave state agency heads greater flexibility in making cuts. In November 2002 Republicans gained seven seats in the state Senate and emerged with a 61–59 majority in the House (though a January 2003 party switch left the House evenly divided). The next day Easley astonished legislators by vetoing his first bill. The Founding Fathers of North Carolina, suspicious of executive tyranny, had written a state constitution in which the governor had no veto; only in 1996 did the voters grant the governor a limited veto. Hunt had never had occasion to use it; Easley did, on an unimportant bill designating appointments to boards and commissions. The legislature, summoned to the required special session to consider override, let it stand: The first veto by a governor of North Carolina since Josiah Martin vetoed a bill in 1774.

At the same time, Easley had to consider how to handle a shortfall estimated at $2 billion for the next fiscal year. Easley comes up for reelection in 2004. Vinroot and state Senate Minority Leader Patrick Ballantine announced their candidacies in May 2003; Southern Pines businessman George Little and Davie County Commissioner Dan Barrett were also running.

Senior Senator

John Edwards (D)

Elected 1998, seat up 2004, 1st term; b. June 10, 1953, Seneca, SC; home, Raleigh; NC St. U., B.S. 1974, U. of NC at Chapel Hill, J.D. 1977; Methodist; married (Elizabeth).

Professional Career: Practicing atty., 1977–98.

DC Office: 225 DSOB, 20510, 202-224-3154; Fax: 202-228-1374; Web site: www.edwards.senate.gov.

State Offices: Asheville, 828-285-0760; Charlotte, 704-344-6154; Greensboro, 336-333-5311; Greenville, 252-931-1111; Raleigh, 919-856-4245.

Committees: *Health, Education, Labor & Pensions*: Aging; Children & Families. *Intelligence (Select). Judiciary*: Antitrust, Competition Policy & Consumer Rights; Crime, Corrections & Victims' Rights; Immigration, Border Security & Citizenship; Terrorism, Technology & Homeland Security. *Small Business & Entrepreneurship*.

Group Ratings

	ADA	ACLU	AFS	LCV	CON	ITIC	NTU	COC	ACU	NTLC	CHC
2002	70	60	100	59	69	75	18	55	30	6	—
2001	95	—	100	88	—	—	13	50	16	—	0

National Journal Ratings

	2001 LIB —	2001 CONS	2002 LIB —	2002 CONS
Economic	74%	23%	66%	32%
Social	60%	36%	56%	38%
Foreign	61%	27%	62%	36%

Key Votes of the 107th Congress

1. Approve Bush Tax Cuts	N	5. Confirm Ashcroft as AG	N
2. Expand Patients' Rights	Y	6. Bar Gays in the Boy Scouts	N
3. Campaign Finance Reform	Y	7. $ for Hate Crime Prosecution	Y
4. Permit ANWR Development	N	8. Overseas Military Abortions	Y

9. Bar Coop. with Intl. Court	Y
10. Trade Promotion Authority	Y
11. Authorize Force in Iraq	Y
12. Homeland Sec. Dept. Union	Y

Election Results

1998 general	John Edwards (D)	1,029,237	(51%)	($8,331,382)
	Lauch Faircloth (R)	945,943	(47%)	($9,375,771)
	Other	36,963	(2%)	
1998 primary	John Edwards (D)	277,468	(51%)	
	D. G. Martin (D)	149,049	(28%)	
	Ella Scarborough (D)	55,486	(10%)	
	Robert Ayers Jr. (D)	22,477	(4%)	
	Other	35,551	(7%)	
1992 general	Lauch Faircloth (R)	1,297,892	(50%)	($2,952,102)
	Terry Sanford (D)	1,194,015	(46%)	($2,486,380)
	Other	85,984	(3%)	

John Edwards, now the senior senator from North Carolina and a presidential candidate, is a Democrat first elected in 1998. He was born in South Carolina and grew up there and in Robbins, in Moore County, North Carolina, where his father was a supervisor in a textile mill and his mother ran a furniture refinishing business. He was the first in his family to go to college, at North Carolina State, and then went to the University of North Carolina Law School. He started off defending recording companies accused of pirating Elvis Presley records, then moved to Raleigh in 1981 and became a plaintiff's personal injury lawyer, working hard to prepare cases (he was one of the first trial lawyers here to use focus groups) and fluently and persuasively presenting them in down-home style to juries. He was good at it, winning verdicts of $152 million; with 30% or more going to the lawyer, this enabled him to amass a fortune variously estimated at $20 million to $50 million. In January 1997 he won $25 million in compensatory damages for a nine-year-old girl from Cary horribly injured by a faulty swimming pool drain—the largest personal-injury verdict in North Carolina history.

At about this time, Edwards began thinking about running for the Senate. He had not run for office before, had not even voted in every election, and said he could not remember whether he had first registered as a Democrat or Republican. But he did have strong views on some issues, and proved to have acute judgment in spotting the political weakness of incumbent Republican Senator Lauch Faircloth. In the years since his surprise victory in 1992, Faircloth, a wealthy hog farmer and long-time political insider, had a voting record as conservative as Jesse Helms's and had been a strong critic of the Clintons in various investigations. Some better-known Democrats dropped out of the race, and Edwards' main rival in the May 1998 Democratic primary was D.G. Martin, former lobbyist for the University of North Carolina and a nearly successful House candidate in 1984 and 1986. He refused to take money from PACs or Washington lobbyists. His ads were criticized for suggesting that he was born in North Carolina and that he worked his way through college loading UPS trucks (he worked there for six months). But Edwards outspent Martin 4–1 and, needing 40% to avoid a runoff, won 51%–28%.

The contrast between Edwards and Faircloth was vivid. Edwards was articulate, charming, young (45 and a three-time marathon finisher); Faircloth was wrinkled with his 70 years, the embodiment of an older, rural, conservative North Carolina that many natives and newcomers wanted to leave behind. Faircloth, recognizing the threat, ran ads against Edwards in the primary, contending that he was a trial lawyer who earned millions suing doctors and driving up health care costs. He continued the negative approach, despite the voters' contented, pro-incumbent mood, throughout the campaign. Edwards proposed they pool their money and, instead of running ads, buy time for televised debates; Faircloth, less than eager for debates with a highly competent trial lawyer, would not even allow photographs one of the few times their paths crossed on the campaign trail. Edwards ran positive ads, and called for hiring teachers, building schools, regulating HMOs, and fixing Social Security. Occasionally, his inexperience showed. He said credit unions should be taxed like banks, then backed off; he refused to say how he'd vote on tobacco bill, then later said he would have voted to kill it. This was a big-spending race: Edwards spent $8.3 million, nearly three-quarters of it his own money; Faircloth spent nearly $9.4 million, including $1.7 million of his own. Faircloth started to slip in the polls and even changed pollsters in October; Edwards edged to a lead, and won 51%–47%. In this race, the Democrat carried younger voters, the Republican carried the elderly; Edwards won 55%–44% in the Raleigh-Durham area and ran well in traditionally Democratic east Carolina counties.

In the Senate, his voting record is in the moderate to conservative range of Senate Democrats. After Hurricane Floyd in September 1999, he pushed hard for disaster aid, threatening to hold up Senate proceedings in November; in time the state got more than $250 million. He did not announce his position on PNTR with China until the last minute in September 2000; he was evidently worried about the effect on the textile industry, but argued that North Carolina could gain export jobs in pork, poultry, furniture, telecommunications and software and ultimately voted for it. He brought in longtime University of North Carolina basketball coach Dean Smith to testify for his bill to outlaw betting on college and other amateur sports. Edwards made an immediate favorable impression in the impeachment debate: He was one of three Democrats to preside over the depositions of Monica Lewinsky, Vernon Jordan and Sidney Blumenthal, and his floor speeches were rated by many as the most effective during the debate.

There was little in Edwards's brief Senate record to make him a national figure, yet he was Al Gore's runner-up choice for the vice presidential nomination. The reason is his appealing manner. Though he is now rich—he sold his law practice for $5 million and in 2002 he bought an elegant $3.8 million house in Georgetown—he still has a common touch. He has an appealing family, touched by tragedy: His 16-year-old son was killed in a car crash in 1996 (a consolation call came from Jesse Helms, who had been impressed by the young man in an awards ceremony in Washington). For all Edwards' charm he is also persuasive and capable of making complex arguments understandable and undercutting an opponent's; as one Republican senator says, "Never yield the floor to John Edwards." Political consultants Bob Shrum and Tad Devine pressed Gore to pick Edwards for VP; after he was passed over he spoke to the national convention delegations from Massachusetts, New York and California—filled with big contributors—and Iowa as well. He declined to chair the DSCC and declined to be chief spokesman for the Gore campaign in Florida. And he was abashed when in November 2000 he was named as the sexiest politician in *People's* "Sexiest Man Alive" issue.

In 2001 Edwards began preparing to run for president and for the first time took a lead role on major legislation. In February 2001 he was in Iowa addressing the Drake University Law School's annual dinner in Des Moines. That same month he co-sponsored with John McCain and Edward Kennedy an HMO regulation bill similar to the Dingell-Norwood bill which had passed the House in October 1999. The Senate passed the bill in June 2001 59–36, despite a veto threat by George W. Bush; the House in August 2001 passed 226–203 a different version, based on concessions Republican Charlie Norwood made in meetings at the White House. The Senate bill provided for most lawsuits to be heard in state courts, which have tended to be more favorable to plaintiffs than federal courts, and imposed no limit on damages for pain and suffering. The House bill tried to channel cases to federal courts and limited pain and suffering damages to $1.5 million. For months no conference committee met, and Edwards, McCain and Kennedy tried to negotiate with administration officials. But negotiations fell apart in August 2002, when the administration agreed to accept a $4 million limit and Edwards and his co-sponsors refused. Trial lawyers, from whose ranks Edwards sprang, oppose such limits.

Edwards had other legislative causes. He sponsored a bill to speed up approval of generic drugs, blocked by lawsuits from pharmaceutical companies. He sponsored a privacy law, to prevent firms providing GPS equipment to sell information on customers' movements. He criticized the Bush administration for regulations he said weakened the Clean Air Act. On the Judiciary Committee he opposed the nomination of Terrence Boyle, a former aide to Helms, to a federal appeals court. He grilled appeals court nominee Judge Charles Pickering about his ex parte communication with the Justice Department in a cross-burning case; Pickering had been concerned that the ringleaders had been treated more leniently than arguably less culpable participants. Edwards's sharp questions, cutting off Pickering's responses and demanding flat yes and no answers elicited admiration from the judge's critics and cries of unfairness from his supporters. The latter included Richard Scruggs, the Mississippi trial lawyer who organized the tobacco litigation and supported Pickering. Edwards failed to return Scruggs's phone call, and Scruggs said, "He can forget my support and that of anybody I have influence with." That is possibly a potent threat: Edwards depends for much of his contributions on trial lawyers, who have made literally billions from tobacco and asbestos litigation. He supported the Iraq war resolution in October 2002.

Edwards's emergence as a presidential candidate is based more on his persona than his achievements. The *New York Times* called him "the next Bill Clinton"; *Vanity Fair* raised the question of whether he was "a perfect politician." Many in Washington would say of him what Walter Lippmann said about Franklin Roosevelt in 1932: "a pleasant man who, without any important qualifications for the office, would very much like to be president." But Lippmann was wrong about Roosevelt, and these critics may be wrong about Edwards. Certainly he was the candidate feared most by the Bush political strategists in 2002 and early 2003; they thought his Southern background, his moderate voting record on many issues and his attractive persona might put into play some Southern and Northern states which would be safe for Bush against other possible nominees. In 2001 there was little doubt Edwards was moving toward running. He traveled to Israel and Iowa, to Democratic fundraising events for candidates around the country, to Park Avenue and Beverly Hills living rooms to meet big contributors.

In 2002 the travels continued, to all of the above venues, plus Number 10 Downing Street, for a talk with Tony Blair, and Comedy Central, for jokes with Jon Stewart. Edwards's performance on *Meet the Press* in May 2002 was criticized as lightweight; he did better with George Stephanopoulos on *This Week* in January 2003. He talked frequently with Bill Clinton, as good a political strategist as there is in America today. In late 2002 he delivered a series of speeches setting out detailed positions on issues, much as Clinton had in late 1999. On foreign policy in October, despite his support of Bush on Iraq, he accused him of "arrogance without purpose" and "gratuitous unilateralism." On the economy in November he called for a $500 family tax credit, repeal of tax cuts for households with incomes over $200,000 and retention of the estate tax on estates over $7 million. On education in November he called for a tuition-free year in college for students who are in work study or community service and for incentives for better teachers. He opposed vouchers, favored public charter schools and called for tenure reform to make it easier to fire bad teachers—a proposal likely to rankle the teachers' unions. On homeland security in December he called for security clearances for police officers, new minimum standards for nuclear and chemical plants, more immigration inspectors and $1.5 billion of federal money for local police forces and firefighters. He formed a New American Optimists PAC which took in soft money contributions, mostly from lawyers, through November 2002, and on January 2, 2003, set up an exploratory committee.

"The fact that I see issues through the eyes of regular people is an enormous strength," he said in December, and in January he used the phrase "regular people" over and over. Voters usually seek in the next president qualities they miss in the incumbent; Edwards seemed to be describing himself with that in mind in January 2003: "The President has a different kind of administration that is run to a large extent by insiders and for insiders." Edwards's obvious strategy is to win over enough voters with his persona and with intensive campaigning to make a good showing in Iowa and New Hampshire against candidates who come from adjoining states—to exceed expectations. This may be more difficult because of his support of the Iraq war resolution, which will make him anathema to many of the left-wing Democrats so numerous in those states. Then comes the primary in South Carolina, where he was born, and where he must hope to win over both black and white voters; in previous contests a majority or near-majority of South Carolina Democratic primary voters have been black, but more whites may choose to vote in the contest in 2004 since there will be no contest for the Republican nomination.

Will Edwards also run for reelection in North Carolina in 2004? In late 2002 and early 2003 he would not say. North Carolina law allows him to run for both offices (and thus also for vice president and senator); the filing deadline is February 27 which under the caucus and primary schedule would allow him to make a decision knowing how well he has done in Iowa and New Hampshire. But as he has been making moves to run for president, his ratings in North Carolina polls have not been very good; a plurality of voters there say he should not run for president, and reports that he has said privately he will not seek both offices ring true. A March 2003 poll found that 43% of voters approve of his presidential bid while 49% disapprove. The Bush White House has been encouraging Congressman Richard Burr to run; in November 2002 he said he would decide by summer, and with White House backing he could raise ample funds. North Carolina Democratic leaders were encouraging Erskine Bowles, Clinton White House chief of staff and 2002 Senate nominee, to run if Edwards doesn't. Other Democrats said to be considering a race were former Speaker Dan Blue, who finished second to Bowles in the 2002 primary, and 2d District Congressman Bob Etheridge. There is a precedent that is encouraging to Republicans: Since 1968, no one has been reelected to this seat, and it has passed back and forth from party to party in each election.

Junior Senator

Elizabeth Dole (R)

Elected 2002, seat up 2008, 1st term; b. July 29, 1936, Salisbury; home, Salisbury; Duke U., B.A. 1958, Harvard U., M.A. 1960, J.D. 1965; Methodist; married (Robert).

Professional Career: Deputy Asst., U.S. Consumer Affairs, 1969–73; Fed. Trade Commission, 1973–79; Public liason, U.S. Pres. Ronald Reagan, 1981–83; Secy., U.S. Dept. of Trans., 1983–87; Secy., Dept. of Labor, 1989–90; Pres., Amer. Red Cross, 1991–95, 1997–99.

DC Office: 120 RSOB, 20510, 202-224-6342; Fax: 202-224-1100; Web site: dole.senate.gov.

State Offices: Raleigh, 919-856-4630; Salisbury, 704-633-5011.

Committees: *Aging (Special). Agriculture, Nutrition & Forestry:* Production & Price Competitiveness (Chmn.); Research, Nutrition & General Legislation. *Armed Services:* Airland; Emerging Threats & Capabilities; Personnel. *Banking, Housing & Urban Affairs:* Economic Policy; Financial Institutions; International Trade & Finance.

Group Ratings and Key Votes: Newly Elected

Election Results

2002 general	Elizabeth Dole (R)	1,248,664	(54%)	($13,735,220)
	Erskine Bowles (D)	1,047,983	(45%)	($13,306,317)
	Other	34,534	(1%)	
2002 primary	Elizabeth Dole (R)	342,631	(80%)	
	Jim Snyder (R)	60,477	(14%)	
	Other	22,998	(5%)	
1996 general	Jesse Helms (R)	1,345,833	(53%)	($14,589,266)
	Harvey B. Gantt (D)	1,173,875	(46%)	($7,992,980)

Elizabeth Dole, former Secretary of Transportation and Secretary of Labor, former President of the American Red Cross and candidate for president, was elected senator from North Carolina in 2002. She grew up in Salisbury, in the Piedmont textile country between Charlotte and Greensboro; her father was a wholesale florist and her mother had the pleasure of attending, at 101, her daughter's election night celebration. Elizabeth Hanford, as she then was graduated from Duke, got a master's in education at Harvard and taught school in Boston. She spent the summer of 1960 working in the office of North Carolina Senator B. Everett Jordan; in the fall, she worked on Lyndon Johnson's campaign train through the South. In 1962 she went to Harvard Law School, one of 29 women in a class of 550; her classmates included future Congresswomen Patricia Schroeder and Elizabeth Holtzman. In summers she worked at the Peace Corps headquarters, the United Nations and Oxford University. After graduation she practiced law briefly in Washington. With help from Democratic Governor Terry Sanford she got a job at HEW, then at the White House Office of Consumer Affairs. She stayed on after the change in administrations in 1969 and changed her registration from Democratic to Independent; she worked on projects like freshness dating on food products. In 1973 she was nominated to a six-year term on the Federal Trade Commission. In 1975 she married Senator Bob Dole and campaigned with him when he was nominated for vice president in 1976.

In all these jobs she was a hard-working perfectionist with no sharp ideological edge. She always maintained her gracious Southern manners and showed an enthusiasm and friendliness that was off-putting to some but which served her well in a series of positions that few or no women had held. When asked during the 2002 campaign if she was a feminist, she said, "I think it depends on how you define the word 'feminist.' If you are talking about equal rights and equal opportunities—absolutely. My whole career has been spent trying to help women reach their full potential—women and minorities. If you are talking about something like a prepackaged plan handed down by the political correctness club—no." In 1981 she headed Ronald Reagan's Public Liaison office and in 1983 she was appointed Secretary of Transportation; in that capacity, she likes to point out, she was the first woman to head a branch of the armed services, the Coast Guard. In 1989 George H. W. Bush appointed her Secretary of Labor. In 1991 she became head of the American Red Cross, which had grave organizational problems and whose blood bank program was in trouble. She restructured the organization and put in place new blood bank procedures. She took a leave of absence to work on her husband's presidential campaign from November 1995 to January 1997; many will remember her speech about her husband at the San Diego convention, in which she walked about and spoke fluently and fervently. In 1999 she resigned from the Red Cross to run for president. She placed third in the August 1999 Iowa straw poll, but dropped out of the race in October. She did not endorse George W. Bush at that point and did not take a job in the Bush administration.

In early 2001 it was not clear whether North Carolina Senator Jesse Helms would run for reelection. He was in poor health and would turn 80 in 2002; although his strong conservatism and outspokenness made him very popular with many voters in North Carolina, he was also highly unpopular with nearly as many others. In early 2001 White House political strategists were already looking at Dole as a possible candidate, and in August 2001 she said she would give the race "serious consideration" if Helms did not run. Later that month, he announced his retirement. Dole moved back to her mother's house in Salisbury and registered to vote. She planned a big announcement event in Salisbury for September 11 that of course was cancelled. She started out with very high ratings from the public. An October 2001 Republican poll showed her leading former Charlotte Mayor Richard Vinroot in the Republican primary, by 76%–14%, and in the general beating the strongest Democratic candidate, former White House Chief of Staff Erskine Bowles by 65%–27%. But some Republican insiders worried that Dole would be a brittle candidate. Her perfectionism and insistence on tight control of every public event would keep her distant to the voters, they feared, and a campaign based on her Washington resume would seem out of touch with North Carolina voters.

Dole did not make these mistakes. Instead she made two very shrewd decisions. One was to conduct a tour of all of North Carolina's 100 counties. Everywhere she drew crowds, not just in the big metro areas but also in small towns—175 in Hendersonville, 120 in Mars Hill, 200 in

Asheville. People mobbed her, asked for autographs, and clicked photos of her. Sometimes they also noticed Bob Dole, traveling with her over back roads. "I'll be glad to be a dollar-a-year consultant. Or I'll stay home. Whatever she wants," he said. When Elizabeth Dole was asked if she was reconnecting with North Carolina after living out of the state for 42 years, she said, "There has not been any reconnection, because I've been here so much. My roots are deep in North Carolina. I've never really left. This is home to me. Washington is where I work." She said that she had a religious renewal in the early 1980s and that her religious faith was the center of her life and that she hoped that September 11 would cause a "spiritual renewal." She called on her listeners to be "prayer warriors" for her campaign. In November 2001 Vinroot dropped out of the race; her other competitors were little-known and attracted little attention or support. When they questioned her conservatism, she said, "Just to set the record straight, in case there is any misunderstanding, I am pro-life and I am a strong supporter of the Second Amendment of the Constitution, protecting the constitutional rights of law-abiding citizens." In February 2002 Helms endorsed her. Their connections went back a long way: Helms had been a friend of her mother since his first campaign in 1972; Bob Dole had asked for Helms to vouch for him with her when he was wooing her daughter.

Dole's other wise decision was to develop a set of specific stands on issues and distribute them as the "Dole Plan." She set out a detailed plan for individual investment accounts in Social Security. On taxes she called for higher depreciation, more flexibility for Medical Savings Accounts and permanent repeal of the estate tax. On corporate accountability, she called for companies to purchase insurance policies and for the insurers to conduct independent audits. On gun control she switched her positions from her 1999 campaign, this time opposing background checks on individuals' sales of guns at gun shows and a ban on assault weapons. Tobacco and textiles have long been political issues in North Carolina: Dole presented a plan for buying out tobacco quotas and called for electronic labeling of U.S.-manufactured cloth to enable duties to be laid on imports of cloth falsely labeled Made in U.S.A.

But she favored trade promotion authority, which was opposed by all the other three Republicans and six Democrats running for the seat. It was widely believed that North Carolina had lost many textile jobs since NAFTA went into effect in 1995. Yet North Carolina Democrats like Governor Jim Hunt and Bowles, then Bill Clinton's head of the Small Business Administration, had supported NAFTA when it was voted on in 1993. The state's economy had mostly boomed in the years after NAFTA came in. But Hunt was not running, and Secretary of State Elaine Marshall, the first candidate in the race, strongly criticized NAFTA and opposed trade promotion authority. So did state Representative Dan Blue, who had been the first black Speaker of North Carolina's House. And so did Bowles. Though he had supported NAFTA and had lobbied Congress to give Clinton trade promotion authority, he opposed it now. "I made a mistake. I won't vote for fast track or slow track. We've got to make trade fair."

Bowles was an investment banker from a prominent family. His father, Hargrove "Skipper" Bowles was the Democratic nominee for governor in 1972 who lost in a Republican year but was still remembered fondly. His wife, Crandall Close, was CEO of Springs Industries, a large textile firm started by her family. Bowles, as Clinton's chief of staff, negotiated the 1997 budget package that led to a balanced budget; he had been trusted by Republican leaders when they seethed with mistrust of Clinton. But it didn't help Bowles that Blue and Marshall continued to hammer him on trade and that, because of a lawsuit against the Democratic legislature's state legislative redistricting plans, the primary was delayed from May to September 10.

Dole won the Republican primary with 80% of the vote; Bowles won the Democratic primary with 43% of the vote, to 29% for Blue and 15% for Marshall. Blue had hard feelings and did not endorse Bowles until mid-October. This was a heavy-spending race. Dole raised and spent more than $11 million, Bowles spent nearly as much; he put in $2.9 million of his money before October 15 and then another $3.6 million. Some of the ads got personal. A Dole ad criticized his wife for laying off workers in North Carolina and creating new jobs in Mexico and China; Bowles responded in an angry face-on ad and ran an ad showing racecar driver Junior Johnson saying he wouldn't let the Republicans "run Erskine Bowles into the wall." George W. Bush came in three times for Dole and Dick Cheney twice; Bill Clinton, who promised Blue he would stay neutral in the primary, helped Bowles raise money but stayed out of a state he never carried. One debate was videotaped behind locked doors in accordance with the candidates' demands. Bowles attacked Dole on trade and Social Security. She stood her ground on both issues, arguing for free trade and promoting her Dole plan for Social Security: she would hold up papers with her plan written out and then say she would show Bowles's plan—and hold up a blank sheet of paper. Bowles attacked Dole for opposing Clinton's family leave law when she was Secretary of Labor and for opposing a 1990 civil rights law; she replied that she thought the family leave measure had worked out all right and the civil rights bill was a quota bill. Dole ads often mentioned Bill and Hillary Rodham Clinton; Bowles's ads avoided mentions of the Clintons. The late surge of Bowles's spending enabled him to close the gap in the polls, but this seems mostly to have been a matter of the coalescence of the usual party constituencies.

On Election Day the VNS exit poll, widely leaked, showed Bowles ahead; Bob Dole was glum and kept the news from his wife. But VNS, realizing its data were faulty, did not publicly release the numbers, and as the returns came in it quickly became apparent that Dole had won. She led 54%–45% statewide, just shy of Bush's 56%–43% lead in 2000. She carried two of the three big metro areas by wide margins—Charlotte (57%–42%) and Greensboro-Winston Salem—and finished just behind Bowles in Raleigh-Durham (49%–50%), where the Democratic margins in Durham and Chapel Hill are balanced by the Republican margins in much faster-growing areas in Wake County like Cary. In the other half of the state, Dole led 54%–46%. West of Raleigh-Durham, Dole carried all but a few mountain and sand hill counties. She carried the central part of eastern North Carolina but lost in heavily black counties to the north and south.

FIRST DISTRICT

Rep. Frank Ballance (D)

Elected 2002, 1st term; b. Feb. 15, 1942, Windsor; home, Warrenton; NC Central U., B.A. 1963, J.D. 1965; Baptist; married (Bernadine).

Military Career: NC Natl. Guard, 1968–71.

Elected Office: NC House of Reps., 1982–86; NC Senate, 1988–02.

Professional Career: Practicing atty., 1966-present.

DC Office: 413 CHOB 20515, 202-225-3101; Fax: 202-225-3354; Web site: www.ballance.house.gov.

District Offices: Norlina, 252-456-3091; Williamston, 252-789-4939.

Committees: *Agriculture* (14th of 24 D): Conservation, Credit, Rural Development & Research; Department Operations, Oversight, Nutrition & Forestry. *Small Business* (4th of 17 D): Rural Enterprises, Agriculture and Technology (RMM); Tax, Finance & Exports.

Group Ratings and Key Votes: Newly Elected

Election Results

2002 general	Frank Ballance (D)	93,157	(64%)	($706,687)
	Greg Dority (R)	50,907	(35%)	($12,355)
	Other	2,093	(1%)	
2002 primary	Frank Ballance (D)	37,833	(47%)	
	Sam Davis (D)	20,758	(26%)	
	Janice McKenzie Cole (D)	14,410	(18%)	
	Christine Fitch (D)	7,526	(9%)	
2000 general	Eva M. Clayton (D)	142,171	(66%)	($450,199)
	Duane E. Krazter Jr. (R)	62,198	(33%)	
	Other	2,799	(1%)	

The People		Race/Ethnic Origin	Ancestry	
Area size:	7,664 sq. mi.	44.4% White	USA: 10.7%	English: 6.1%
Urban population:	47.7%	50.5% Black	Irish: 3.6%	
Rural population:	52.3%	0.5% Asian	**2000 Presidential Vote**	
Pop. 2000:	619,178	0.7% Native Am.	Gore (D)...............111,558 (57%)	
Median income:	$28,410	0.0% Hawaiian	Bush (R)................82,204 (42%)	
Poverty status:	21.1%	0.8% Two+ races	**Cook Partisan Voting Index:** D + 7	
Military veterans:	12.3%	0.1% Other		
		3.1% Hispanic Origin		

Occupation	Blue collar: 34.8%	White collar: 45.5%	Gray collar: 19.7%

Eastern North Carolina in colonial days was a smaller version of the Chesapeake Bay colonies of Virginia and Maryland—a fertile land laced by dozens of rivers and inlets, with tobacco plantations and farms with docks on the water accessible to the ocean and so to London. North Carolina was settled later than the Chesapeake colonies, and was poorer, with smaller landholdings. But vestiges of its 18th century past can still be seen in New Bern with its Tryon Palace, the governor's house when this was the capital, and the tiny, well-preserved town of Edenton on Albemarle Sound, where 51 Edenton women in 1774 protested the taxing of tea and cloth—an act considered the first women's political protest on these shores.

Today, east Carolina is still tobacco country, and is still largely inhabited by the descendants of the original white settlers and black slaves of 250 years ago. They live in small towns and cities and in some of the most thickly settled rural land in the United States. Tobacco is a labor-intensive crop that can produce yields of $4,000 an acre a family lucky enough to have a tobacco allotment can make a living off 40 acres. But anti-smoking campaigns have cut cigarette sales, and many old east Carolina tobacco fields are now planted with cucumbers, sweet potatoes, blueberries, and especially cotton. Many parts of this region are socioeconomically troubled, a fate only worsened by the flooding from Hurricane Floyd in 1999. Bertie County, lying 20-plus miles east of Interstate 95, has the lowest median income of any county in North Carolina and also the state's highest HIV infection rate; Edgecombe County, a little further west, shrunk during the 1990s even as the state's population was rising, then experienced another blow when the collapse of Enron ended construction of a major electrical generating facility there. Halifax County, which straddles I-95 near the Virginia border, even considered welcoming a big out-of-state trash disposal site before scuttling the idea in the wake of grassroots opposition. Even fast-food giant Hardee's, founded here in Rocky Mount, decamped to St. Louis on its 40th anniversary in 2001.

The 1st Congressional District covers much of the tobacco country of east Carolina. It touches Albemarle and Pamlico Sounds in the east and juts inland to reach black neighborhoods in Greenville and Goldsboro. Together, the 1st and the 3d blanket the eastern quarter of the state, with intricately drawn boundaries whose fingers reach deep into each other's territory, like hands in a tight embrace. Their demographics are intentionally distinctive. The 1st is 51% percent black, the highest percentage of any district in the state; Al Gore won here in 2000 with 57%. The 3d, by contrast, is 17% black and backed George W. Bush in 2000 by almost a 2–1 margin. Redistricting added a few small counties to counter population shrinkage, but the additions made little difference; the 1st remains strongly Democratic. It is also notable for its unique and curious sex ratio: There are 57,000 more female voters here than male voters—a far greater disparity than in any other congressional district in the state.

The congressman from the 1st District is Frank Ballance, a Democrat elected in 2002 to replace his longtime friend and ally Eva Clayton. Ballance grew up on a farm in Bertie County. He graduated from North Carolina Central University and its law school. He set up a law firm with Eva Clayton's husband Theaoseus in Warrenton. He was elected to the state House in 1982 and to the state Senate in 1988. Among the achievements he claimed were sponsorship of the state's four-year education plan that raised teacher standards and salaries from 48th in the nation to near the middle; sponsorship of voter-approved bonds for the community college system; and a mental health trust fund. In 2001, he spearheaded a legislative effort to ban the execution of mentally retarded criminals. He also held leadership positions in the North Carolina Democratic Party and the NAACP.

In November 2001 Clayton announced her retirement after five terms and encouraged Ballance to run. He considered running for the 1st District in 1992 but deferred to Clayton and instead managed her House campaigns. When he announced his candidacy in December, Clayton endorsed him and enlisted her sizable political organization on Ballance's behalf; she helped him get support from unions and PACs like the American Medical Association and the Association of Trial Lawyers of America. Other Democratic candidates were Janice McKenzie Cole, who had been a Clayton protg who served seven years as U.S. Attorney, and gained national financial support from EMILY's List; Wilson County school board chairman Christine Fitch; and Pasquotank County commissioner Sam Davis, a hardware store owner who financed most of his campaign and was the only white candidate in the field. What set him apart, Ballance argued, was his 18 years of legislative experience, "long enough to know that you can't give everybody everything they need." The primary was moved from May to September because of a pending lawsuit over state legislative redistricting, and the requirement of a runoff if no candidate gets 40% of the vote was suspended. Ballance won with 47% to 26% for Davis, and 18% for Cole. He won 17 of the 23 counties, running strongly in the population centers of Bertie, Edgecombe, Halifax and Warren Counties; Cole won four small counties in the district's northeast corner.

Ballance won the general election 64%–35%. In the House, he was elected president of the Democrats' freshman class, as Clayton had been a decade earlier. He also followed Clayton to the Agriculture Committee, a logical assignment for this rural district. He pledged to focus on economic development and the continuing recovery from the decimating effects of Hurricane Floyd in 1999.

SECOND DISTRICT

Rep. Bob Etheridge (D)

Elected 1996, 4th term; b. Aug. 7, 1941, Sampson Cnty.; home, Lillington; Campbell U., B.S. 1965; Presbyterian; married (Faye).

Military Career: Army, 1965–67.

Elected Office: Harnett Cnty. Comm., 1973–76, Chmn., 1975–76; NC House of Reps., 1978–88; NC Superintendent of Public Instruction, 1988–96.

Professional Career: Farmer, 1965–present; V.P. Sales, Sorensen Industries, 1968–87; Owner, Layton Hardware, 1973–90; Co–owner, WLLN Radio, 1979–91.

DC Office: 1533 LHOB 20515, 202-225-4531; Fax: 202-225-5662; Web site: www.house.gov/etheridge.

District Offices: Lillington, 910-814-0335; Raleigh, 919-829-9122.

Committees: *Agriculture* (7th of 24 D): Conservation, Credit, Rural Development & Research; General Farm Commodities & Risk Management; Specialty Crops & Foreign Agriculture Programs. *Select Committee on Homeland Security* (19th of 23 D): Cybersecurity, Science and Research & Development; Emergency Preparedness & Response.

Group Ratings

	ADA	ACLU	AFS	LCV	CON	ITIC	NTU	COC	ACU	NTLC	CHC
2002	80	67	89	38	43	75	24	60	24	8	25
2001	85	—	90	79	—	—	21	57	36	—	—

National Journal Ratings

	2001 LIB	—	2001 CONS		2002 LIB	—	2002 CONS
Economic	60%	—	40%		61%	—	39%
Social	65%	—	34%		63%	—	35%
Foreign	49%	—	47%		59%	—	40%

Key Votes of the 107th Congress

1. Approve Bush Tax Cuts	N	5. Faith-Based Charities	N	9. Trade Promotion Authority		Y
2. Limit Patients' Bill of Rights	N	6. Bar Gays in the Boy Scouts	N	10. Bar Funds for Intl. Court		Y
3. Campaign Finance Reform	Y	7. Ban Partial-Birth Abortion	Y	11. Authorize Force in Iraq		Y
4. Ban ANWR Development	Y	8. Arm Commercial Pilots	N	12. Deny Home. Sec. Dept. Union		N

Election Results

2002 general	Bob Etheridge (D)	100,121	(65%)	($652,178)
	Joseph Ellen (R)	50,965	(33%)	($7,423)
	Other	2,098	(1%)	
2002 primary	Bob Etheridge (D)	unopposed		
2000 general	Bob Etheridge (D)	146,733	(58%)	($911,578)
	Doug Haynes (R)	103,011	(41%)	($266,976)
	Other	2,094	(1%)	

Prior Winning Percentages: 1998 (57%); 1996 (53%)

The People		Race/Ethnic Origin	Ancestry	
Area size:	3,979 sq. mi.	59.1% White	USA: 12.3%	English: 6.7%
Urban population:	49.5%	30.1% Black	German: 5.7%	
Rural population:	50.5%	0.9% Asian	**2000 Presidential Vote**	
Pop. 2000:	619,178	0.6% Native Am.	Bush (R)	98,607 (53%)
Median income:	$36,510	0.1% Hawaiian	Gore (D)	85,552 (46%)
Poverty status:	14.3%	1.2% Two + races	Other	1,378 (1%)
Military veterans:	13.1%	0.1% Other	**Cook Partisan Voting Index:** R + 4	
		7.9% Hispanic Origin		

Occupation	Blue collar: 32.6%	White collar: 52.1%	Gray collar: 15.3%

The coastal plain of North Carolina was long bypassed by history. It was settled after Virginia and South Carolina, and only filled in with English settlers as Scots-Irish families were streaming down the valley of Virginia to the western Piedmont. This has always been tobacco country, a high-yield crop that can support a family on 40 acres (if it has a tobacco allotment). Tobacco, an important colonial crop, became even more so after James B. Duke created Bull Durham tobacco and Lucky Strike cigarettes. But this was long a backward area. Its small farms and little cities were homes mainly to tenant farmers and mill hands, people raising families in thin-walled frame houses, often with no electricity or running water.

In some ways, life here remains that way; Harnett County, a half-hour's drive south of the state capitol, is considered the state's moonshine capital, with brews (safer than in decades past) churned out for good old boys and migrant laborers alike, broken up only sporadically by law enforcement. In other ways, however, life here has improved, in large part because this region adjoins one of the nation's fastest-growing metropolitan areas, Raleigh-Durham. The population of Wake County, which includes Raleigh, grew 47% in the 1990s, the fastest growth of any North Carolina county. Its dynamic economy has generated tens of thousands of jobs, with subdivisions sprouting up all around. While some counties in this part of the state have seen denim mills close and tobacco plots replaced with less lucrative crops, other parts of the region have boomed. Raleigh combines glitzy new cultural institutions with country-cured hams and collard greens at such culinary destinations as Big Ed's City Market Restaurant. And then there is the Ava Gardner museum in Smithfield, where the actress grew up.

The 2d Congressional District consists of an irregular loop around Raleigh, taking in parts of nine counties, plus a slice of Wake County and Raleigh, which is now split between three congressional districts. Redistricting added territory in hog-producing Sampson County and in Cumberland County near Fayetteville, including parts of the Army's Fort Bragg and Pope Air Force Base, as well as the strip joints and fast-food places that service them.

The 2d has an 8% Hispanic population, the highest of any North Carolina district. Many Hispanics have been coming to work in meat and chicken processing factories; the town of Siler City in Chatham County is 39% Hispanic. This is by and large the blue collar, country music part of the booming Raleigh-Durham metro area, a place where most voters have a Democratic heritage but many have gotten into the habit of voting Republican for major offices. In 2000 it voted for George W. Bush and for Democratic Governor Mike Easley. In 2002 it voted for Republican Senator Elizabeth Dole.

The congressman from the 2d District is Bob Etheridge, a Democrat elected in 1996. His biography seems tailored to the district: He was born in the hamlet of Turkey in Sampson County, grew up in Johnston County, went to Campbell University in Harnett County, where he was a basketball star, and he owned a hardware store in Lillington, the county seat. He is a tobacco farmer, the only one currently in Congress; he served four years on the Harnett County Commission in the 1970s, was elected to the North Carolina House in 1978 and served 10 years, eventually chairing the Appropriations Committee. In 1988 and 1992 he was elected state superintendent of public instruction. In the mid-1990s, Governor Jim Hunt called for abolishing the superintendent post and transferred 300 employees to the state Board of Education. Etheridge, spying an opportunity, decided to run for the House in 1996 against freshman David Funderburk, a longtime ally of Jesse Helms. Funderburk tried to tie Etheridge to Bill Clinton's approval of FDA Commissioner David Kessler's announcement that tobacco could be regulated as a drug. Etheridge responded by citing his own tobacco credentials: "I own tobacco allotments and have for years. I'd like to know how many days Mr. Funderburk spent priming tobacco, setting tobacco, and how many days he spent under the hot sun in the tobacco fields." Etheridge won 53%–46%.

In the House, Etheridge has compiled a moderate voting record, just a bit to the left of center. Etheridge bellowed his opposition to all attempts to regulate tobacco: He voted against the 1997 budget because it included a cigarette tax increase; he opposed eliminating crop insurance for tobacco farmers; he led the fight for a $125 million bailout for tobacco farmers whose surplus did not sell on the open market, including a few thousand dollars for his own farm. After China agreed to drop its ban on tobacco products, he voted for PNTR. He defended another area crop when the Transportation Department proposed peanut-free rows on airlines to protect those with allergies to peanuts, saying, "This nutty rule is clearly an overreaction to a serious, but limited, problem faced by a fraction of the population." He pushed through a provision of the Higher Education Reorganization Act to teach values in public schools, supported the flag burning amendment and partial-birth abortion ban, and voted to override Clinton's veto of estate tax repeal. He split with his party again in December 2001 when he was among 21 House Democrats—and the only one from North Carolina—voting for trade promotion authority; North Carolina high-tech and farm interests supported the measure. The state has suffered some setbacks from expanded trade, he said, but "we've been a net winner." Etheridge also split with most House Democrats to support the use of force in Iraq. Although he called for a $17 billion buyout of tobacco farmers, he voted for the farm bill in 2002 that largely preserved the status quo. He won enactment in 2002 of his bill to assist weather forecasters to improve hurricane warnings for inland areas, which was a major problem in his area with the devastating Hurricane Floyd in 1999. With Mike McIntyre of the 7th District, he proposed a Southeast Crescent Authority for the area, on the model of the Appalachian Regional Commission.

Republicans have targeted this seat and would probably have a good chance to win it in an open seat contest. But they fell short in 1998 and 2000, when Etheridge won with 57% and 58% of the vote. The Democratic legislature's redistricting plan, by adding a part of Raleigh, made the district more Democratic; Etheridge won in 2002, 65%–33%. Etheridge considered running for the Senate in 2002, but decided not to join the large Democratic field seeking the nomination to face Elizabeth Dole; he is considered a possible Senate candidate in 2004 if John Edwards chooses not to run for reelection.

THIRD DISTRICT

Rep. Walter Jones (R)

Elected 1994, 5th term; b. Feb. 10, 1943, Farmville; home, Farmville; NC St. U., 1962–65, Atlantic Christian Col., B.A. 1967; Catholic; married (Joe Anne).

Military Career: NC Natl. Guard, 1967–71.

Elected Office: NC House of Reps., 1982–92.

Professional Career: Mgr., Walter B. Jones Office Supply Co., 1967–73; Salesman, Dunn Assoc., 1973–82; Pres., Benefit Reserves Inc., 1989–94; Pres., Judson Co., 1990–94.

DC Office: 422 CHOB 20515, 202-225-3415; Fax: 202-225-3286; Web site: www.house.gov/jones.

District Office: Greenville, 252-931-1003.

Committees: *Armed Services* (11th of 33 R): Readiness; Tactical Air & Land Forces. *Financial Services* (17th of 37 R): Financial Institutions & Consumer Credit; Housing & Community Opportunity. *Resources* (12th of 28 R): Fisheries Conservation, Wildlife & Oceans; Forests & Forest Health; National Parks, Recreation & Public Lands.

Group Ratings

	ADA	ACLU	AFS	LCV	CON	ITIC	NTU	COC	ACU	NTLC	CHC
2002	10	7	22	25	68	50	62	63	96	89	100
2001	10	—	11	21	—	—	75	80	92	—	—

National Journal Ratings

	2001 LIB —	2001 CONS	2002 LIB —	2002 CONS
Economic	27%	73%	43%	56%
Social	0%	81%	0%	75%
Foreign	41%	58%	47%	51%

Key Votes of the 107th Congress

1. Approve Bush Tax Cuts	*	5. Faith-Based Charities	
2. Limit Patients' Bill of Rights	Y	6. Bar Gays in the Boy Scouts	Y
3. Campaign Finance Reform	N	7. Ban Partial-Birth Abortion	Y
4. Ban ANWR Development	N	8. Arm Commercial Pilots	Y

9. Trade Promotion Authority	N
10. Bar Funds for Intl. Court	Y
11. Authorize Force in Iraq	Y
12. Deny Home. Sec. Dept. Union	Y

Election Results

2002 general	Walter Jones (R)	131,448	(91%)	($462,499)
	Gary Goodson (Lib)	13,486	(9%)	
2002 primary	Walter Jones (R)	unopposed		
2000 general	Walter Jones (R)	121,940	(61%)	($1,266,779)
	Leigh Harvey McNairy (D)	74,058	(37%)	($1,176,161)
	Other	2,457	(1%)	

Prior Winning Percentages: 1998 (62%); 1996 (63%); 1994 (53%)

The People		Race/Ethnic Origin	Ancestry	
Area size:	10,048 sq. mi.	76.3% White	USA: 12.9%	English: 9.9%
Urban population:	53.2%	16.6% Black	German: 7.6%	
Rural population:	46.8%	0.9% Asian	**2000 Presidential Vote**	
Pop. 2000:	619,178	0.4% Native Am.	Bush (R)	134,471 (64%)
Median income:	$37,510	0.1% Hawaiian	Gore (D)	73,035 (35%)
Poverty status:	12.4%	1.2% Two+ races	Other	1,589 (1%)
Military veterans:	15.7%	0.1% Other	**Cook Partisan Voting Index:** R +15	
		4.4% Hispanic Origin		

Occupation	Blue collar: 27.3%	White collar: 55.9%	Gray collar: 16.8%

Nearly 500 years ago, Giovanni da Verrazano sailed past the Gulf Stream and landed on a sand spit island he thought was the outer edge of China. He was wrong: It was the Outer Banks of North Carolina. These are probably America's most unstable barrier islands, constantly changing shape and cut by new inlets as they are battered by the ocean currents and storm winds. They were settled early by Europeans: Sir Walter Raleigh's Roanoke colony was founded here in 1587, then vanished shortly thereafter; Edward Teach—Blackbeard—and other pirates lurked in Pamlico and Albemarle sounds behind the islets. History is still very much alive on the Outer Banks. An antique form of English is spoken on Ocracoke Island, reachable only by ferry; the 208-foot lighthouse on Cape Hatteras, America's tallest, looks out on some of the most treacherous currents in the Atlantic; the sands along Kitty Hawk, with their constant winds, are where the Wright Brothers made mankind's first heavier-than-air flight in December 1903. Today, the Outer Banks have become vacation and retirement country, with affluent beachfront communities around Kitty Hawk, Nags Head and Duck and, much farther south, around Beaufort (BOWfort, not BEWfort as in South Carolina) and Morehead City. Inland, amid swamps, is the Marine Corps' Camp Lejeune, home base of one-fifth of the Marine Corps. The flat lands of east Carolina have long been tobacco- and peanut-growing country, and are now also hog-raising land.

The 3d Congressional District covers the Outer Banks and much of the coastal plain of North Carolina, though the northeastern tier—from the desolate Great Dismal Swamp to the affluent oceanside resort communities—move more in the orbit of Virginia's Hampton Roads than North Carolina's Research Triangle. The 3d exists in balance with the 1st, with which it shares most of eastern North Carolina. Fingers of the 3d go deep inland to include mostly white portions of Greenville and Goldsboro. These help make the 3d predominantly white and Republican, compared to the 1st, which is half-black and heavily Democratic. Party registration here is misleading: Registered Democrats outnumber Republicans by 2–1, but this district proved a Jesse Helms stronghold—in 1996, he won 62% within the lines as they exist today. A few boundary changes were instituted after the 2000 Census, with the 3d picking up part of Duplin County and a portion of Nash County adjoining Rocky Mount. These changes decreased the district's black percentage slightly and produced a district that voted 64% for George W. Bush in 2000.

The congressman from the 3d District is Walter Jones, a Republican elected in 1994. He grew up in eastern North Carolina, attended North Carolina State and Atlantic Christian College, and served in the National Guard. His father, Walter Jones Sr., was a Democratic congressman from the 1st District, which included most of northeast North Carolina, from 1966 until his death in 1992. The younger Jones was elected in 1982 to the state House, where he voted to oust the Democratic speaker and often broke with Democratic leaders. In 1992 he ran in the new black-majority 1st District after his father decided to retire, winning 38% in the Democratic primary, just 2% shy of the 40% needed to avoid a runoff, then losing the runoff to Eva Clayton 55%–45%.

In April 1993, Jones switched to the Republican Party, and later announced he was running for Congress in the 3d District: "My old party has changed and so has the world. Sadly, in my opinion, both are not for the best in far too many circumstances." This pitted Jones against four-term Congressman Martin Lancaster, a Democrat who had worked hard on local projects. But Lancaster had voted for the Clinton budget and tax package in 1993 and the crime bill in 1994, and hadn't been able to persuade the Clintons to drop the cigarette tax from their health care package. Jones ran an ad showing Lancaster jogging with Bill Clinton: "How'd Martin Lancaster get so out of touch? Well, look who he's running around with in Washington." Jones won 53%–47%.

In the House, Jones got seats on Armed Services and on Resources, which absorbed his father's old Merchant Marine and Fisheries panel. His voting record began as consistently conservative but has moderated some on non-cultural issues. In his first term one of his bills became law, the War Crimes Act of 1996, which authorizes future American prisoners of war to bring lawsuits against those who commit war crimes; this provides an enforcement mechanism for the Geneva Convention. Jones favors more defense spending, and he sponsored a bill for a $500 tax credit for military personnel on food stamps. He opposed PNTR because of the inability to trust China, which he said, "steals technology and sells it our enemies, steals our nuclear secrets and tries to influence our election process." Following crashes of the revolutionary Osprey helicopter, including one near Camp Lejeune, Jones—who has taken a demonstration flight in the aircraft—defended it as "the fighting machine that the Marines say they need." Jones, who posted the Ten Commandments in his Capitol Hill office, pursued his support for politically activist churches with his proposal to permit them to endorse candidates without losing their tax-exempt status. The bill generated lots of traffic on the Internet, but the House defeated it 178–239 in October 2002.

Jones has pursued environmental issues of local import. He passed a law protecting a herd of wild horses on Shackelford Banks. He opposes oil drilling on the North Carolina coast and won victory of a sort when Conoco gave up its federal leases for drilling off the Outer Banks, where the Gulf Stream and Labrador Current meet. He opposed a Bush administration proposal to shift to local governments a greater share of the cost for beach restoration projects. He defends beach driving along the shore, criticizing a proposed National Parks ban of off-road driving as "short-sighted" and harmful to tourism.

Jones has easily won re-election and did not have a Democratic opponent in 2002; he has been mentioned as a candidate for the Senate.

FOURTH DISTRICT

Rep. David Price (D)

Elected 1996, 4th term; b. Aug. 17, 1940, Irwin, TN; home, Chapel Hill; U. of NC, B.A. 1961, Yale U., B.D. 1964, Ph.D. 1969; Baptist; married (Lisa).

Elected Office: U.S. House of Reps., 1986–94.

Professional Career: Legis. Aide, U.S. Sen. Bartlett, 1963–67; Prof., Yale U., 1969–73, Duke U., 1973–present; Exec. Dir., NC Dem. Party, 1979–80, Chmn., 1983–84; Staff Dir., DNC Comm. on Pres. Nominations, 1981–82.

DC Office: 2162 RHOB 20515, 202-225-1784; Fax: 202-225-2014; Web site: www.house.gov/price.

District Offices: Chapel Hill, 919-967-7924; Durham, 919-688-3004; Raleigh, 919-859-5999.

Committees: *Appropriations* (15th of 29 D): Homeland Security; The Legislative Branch; VA, HUD & Independent Agencies.

Group Ratings

	ADA	ACLU	AFS	LCV	CON	ITIC	NTU	COC	ACU	NTLC	CHC
2002	95	87	100	63	43	50	14	55	0	0	0
2001	95	—	100	93	—	—	10	43	4	—	—

National Journal Ratings

	2001 LIB —	2001 CONS		2002 LIB —	2002 CONS
Economic	70%	—	29%	63%	— 36%
Social	83%	—	11%	74%	— 19%
Foreign	67%	—	32%	77%	— 19%

Key Votes of the 107th Congress

1. Approve Bush Tax Cuts	N	5. Faith-Based Charities	N	9. Trade Promotion Authority	N
2. Limit Patients' Bill of Rights	N	6. Bar Gays in the Boy Scouts	N	10. Bar Funds for Intl. Court	N
3. Campaign Finance Reform	Y	7. Ban Partial-Birth Abortion	N	11. Authorize Force in Iraq	N
4. Ban ANWR Development	Y	8. Arm Commercial Pilots	N	12. Deny Home. Sec. Dept. Union	N

Election Results

2002 general	David Price (D)	132,185	(61%)	($702,372)
	Tuan Nguyen (R)	78,095	(36%)	($7,869)
	Other	5,766	(3%)	
2002 primary	David Price (D)	unopposed		
2000 general	David Price (D)	200,885	(62%)	($686,476)
	Jess Ward (R)	119,412	(37%)	($41,009)
	Other	5,573	(2%)	

Prior Winning Percentages: 1998 (57%); 1996 (54%); 1992 (65%); 1990 (58%); 1988 (58%); 1986 (56%)

The People		Race/Ethnic Origin	Ancestry	
Area size:	1,298 sq. mi.	68.8% White	English: 10.2%	German: 9.8%
Urban population:	83.2%	20.6% Black	Irish: 7.7%	
Rural population:	16.8%	3.9% Asian	**2000 Presidential Vote**	
Pop. 2000:	619,178	0.3% Native Am.	Gore (D) 131,532 (53%)	
Median income:	$53,847	0.0% Hawaiian	Bush (R) 112,885 (46%)	
Poverty status:	9.2%	1.3% Two + races	Other 3,180 (1%)	
Military veterans:	10.3%	0.2% Other	**Cook Partisan Voting Index:** D + 4	
		5.0% Hispanic Origin		

Occupation	Blue collar: 14.3%	White collar: 74.8%	Gray collar: 10.9%

Back in the 1950s, few people would have predicted that the countryside around Raleigh and Durham, North Carolina, would become one of America's high-tech boom areas. But Governor Luther Hodges did, when he started the 6,900-acre Research Triangle Park as an R&D industrial park between the musty state capital of Raleigh, the Lucky Strike-manufacturing city of Durham and the small university town of Chapel Hill. With the drawing power of three universities—North Carolina State in Raleigh, Duke in Durham and the University of North Carolina in Chapel Hill—Research Triangle Park slowly began attracting top-tier R&D organizations, which in turn spawned a dynamic entrepreneurial sector. Today, GlaxoSmithKline, IBM, Nortel Networks and Cisco Systems are the park's largest tenants; the facility's 42,000 full-time employees earn an average salary of $56,000. In the 1990s the Raleigh-Durham metropolitan area—the Triangle to locals—became one of America's fastest growing metropolitan areas; the Raleigh-Durham airport, which had four gates in the 1970s, now has 49.

Three decades of vibrant economic growth have made the Triangle affluent, but it still prides itself on its homier touches, from slow-cooked pit barbecue to a minor-league baseball stadium in Durham that features a smoke-snorting replica of a bull, made famous by the movie, *Bull Durham*. This combination of upscale and down-home has proved to be a popular draw. In the 1990s the Raleigh-Durham metro area grew by 39%, to more than 1.2 million: The fastest metropolitan growth north and east of Atlanta. Hispanics and Asians flocked into Durham, upscale liberals who like university towns flocked into Chapel Hill and Raleigh's Wake County boomed with new suburbs, and local civic leaders worked to spruce up the Triangle's old city cores as the city fathers did in Charlotte.

The 4th Congressional District includes much of the fast-growing Research Triangle area. It includes Durham County, plus Orange County and Chapel Hill, part of Chatham County to the south and a little under half of Wake County. Politics here revolves around cultural issues. The Democratic base here made up of two parts, the black community, with 21% of the district's population, and whites with post-graduate degrees. This part of the Triangle has one of the highest concentrations of Ph.D.s in the nation, and their livelihoods—in academia, in the sciences, in the social services—tend to depend on government. Durham and Orange Counties are heavily Democratic, the strongest areas in North Carolina against Senator Elizabeth Dole and for Democrat Erskine Bowles in the 2002 Senate election except for a few rural counties with large black percentages. But the burgeoning suburbs of Wake County are pretty heavily Republican, like so many fast-growing areas at the edge of metropolitan development across the nation, and provide some counterbalance. On balance, though, this is a district that votes for Democrats, not only local moderates but also for Al Gore in 2000.

The congressman from the 4th District is David Price, a Democrat first elected in 1986; he lost his seat in 1994 and regained it in 1996. Price grew up in east Tennessee, the son of a school principal and an English teacher. He is an interesting blend of political scientist, practical politician, and a lay Baptist preacher. He came to North Carolina to go to college at Chapel Hill, earned a degree in divinity and a Ph.D. in political science at Yale and taught there for four years, then became a political science professor at Duke in 1973. He was executive director of the North Carolina Democratic Party in the 1980 election cycle and chairman from 1983–84—both, in effect, appointments of Governor Jim Hunt; he helped develop North Carolina's robust straight-ticket politics. In 1986 he ran for the House and beat a Republican who won in the 1984 sweep, the current Republican state chairman Bill Cobey. In 1994 Price lost 50.4%–49.6% to Fred Heineman, a former New York City cop and Raleigh police chief in the 1970s. In 1996 Heineman made some unforced errors and was outspent by Price, who regained the seat 54%–44%. Price has written several books, including one, *The Congressional Experience*, about his observations on Congress, which he updated in 2000.

During his first tour in the House, Price helped pass laws increasing the percentage of a home's value the FHA can insure and aiding technical education at community colleges. When he returned after 1996, Price rejoined the Appropriations Committee on which, had he not lost in 1994, he would have had enough seniority to be ranking minority member of a subcommittee. His Education Affordability Act, "my personal centerpiece," on which he had been working for a dozen years, was folded into the 1997 Balanced Budget Act; it made interest on student loans tax deductible and allowed penalty-free withdrawals from IRAs for education expenses. His next priority on education became building more classrooms. With Bob Etheridge, who also represents part of Wake County, he has pushed a federal initiative to hire 100,000 teachers to reduce class size nationwide.

In the appropriations process, Price has nurtured local projects such as $272 million for a new EPA complex in Research Triangle Park, $40 million for the Triangle Transit Authority to develop a regional rail line, nearly $1 million for North Carolina Central University to study the environmental effects of landfills on minority communities, and $4 million for hog waste research by North Carolina State University. Responding to Research Triangle urging, he was one of four North Carolina House members to vote for PNTR with China. But he pointed to labor and environmental concerns and opposed trade promotion authority in 2001 and 2002. With Republican Steve Horn, a fellow political scientist in the House, Price sponsored the "stand by your ad" requirement for candidates to appear in the full frame of TV ads reading their disclaimers on the air, so they would more likely be held responsible for negative ads. It was incorporated into the House-passed campaign-reform bill in 2002; a similar proposal has taken effect in North Carolina. On the 2002 election procedures bill he worked to improve the nation's voting equipment and voter participation.

Price won reelection in 1998 by 57%–42% and has won with more than 60% since.

FIFTH DISTRICT

Rep. Richard Burr (R)

Elected 1994, 5th term; b. Nov. 30, 1955, Charlottesville, VA; home, Winston-Salem; Wake Forest U., B.A. 1978; Methodist; married (Brooke).

Professional Career: Natl. Sales Mgr., Carswell Distributing, 1978–94; NC Taxpayers United, Co-Chmn., 1993–present.

DC Office: 1526 LHOB 20515, 202-225-2071; Fax: 202-225-2995; Web site: www.house.gov/burr.

District Office: Winston-Salem, 336-631-5125.

Committees: *Energy & Commerce* (Vice Chmn. of 31 R): Energy & Air Quality; Health; Oversight & Investigations. *Permanent Select Committee on Intelligence* (8th of 11 R): Human Intelligence, Analysis & Counterintelligence; Intelligence Policy & National Security; Terrorism and Homeland Security.

Group Ratings

	ADA	ACLU	AFS	LCV	CON	ITIC	NTU	COC	ACU	NTLC	CHC
2002	0	13	0	13	25	88	57	100	96	86	92
2001	10	—	10	0	—	—	60	96	88	—	—

National Journal Ratings

	2001 LIB	—	2001 CONS		2002 LIB	—	2002 CONS
Economic	28%	—	69%		21%	—	73%
Social	20%	—	69%		25%	—	71%
Foreign	14%	—	85%		0%	—	85%

Key Votes of the 107th Congress

1. Approve Bush Tax Cuts	Y	5. Faith-Based Charities	Y	9. Trade Promotion Authority	Y
2. Limit Patients' Bill of Rights	Y	6. Bar Gays in the Boy Scouts	Y	10. Bar Funds for Intl. Court	Y
3. Campaign Finance Reform	N	7. Ban Partial-Birth Abortion	Y	11. Authorize Force in Iraq	Y
4. Ban ANWR Development	N	8. Arm Commercial Pilots	N	12. Deny Home. Sec. Dept. Union	Y

Election Results

2002 general	Richard Burr (R)	137,879	(70%)	($420,600)
	David Crawford (D)	58,558	(30%)	($12,311)
2002 primary	Richard Burr (R)	unopposed		
2000 general	Richard Burr (R)	172,489	(93%)	($421,060)
	Steven Francis LeBoeuf (Lib)	13,366	(7%)	

Prior Winning Percentages: 1998 (68%); 1996 (62%); 1994 (57%)

The People		Race/Ethnic Origin	Ancestry	
Area size:	4,424 sq. mi.	87.9% White	USA: 15.7%	English: 9.9%
Urban population:	42.9%	6.7% Black	German: 9.5%	
Rural population:	57.1%	0.8% Asian	**2000 Presidential Vote**	
Pop. 2000:	619,178	0.2% Native Am.	Bush (R)............163,705	(66%)
Median income:	$39,710	0.0% Hawaiian	Gore (D)............81,704	(33%)
Poverty status:	9.5%	0.7% Two + races	Other...............2,147	(1%)
Military veterans:	12.3%	0.1% Other	**Cook Partisan Voting Index:** R +17	
		3.6% Hispanic Origin		

Occupation	Blue collar: 33.2%	White collar: 54.1%	Gray collar: 12.7%

From the Atlantic Ocean, the terrain of North Carolina rises slowly through the Piedmont—a transitional land of modest hills that lies between the coastal plain and the Blue Ridge mountains. The Blue Ridge, named for the mysterious blue haze that blankets it, provides the headwaters of the New River, which cuts majestic crevasses—alternately lush and mined-out—as it flows north to West Virginia. The lower Piedmont lands of North Carolina were first settled by independent-minded Scots-Irish farmers and by followers of British and German sects like the Moravians. This was hardscrabble farm country at the time of the Civil War, with few slaves. By the late 19th century, it was becoming industrialized, with textile mills alongside streams, furniture factories not far from hardwood forests and R. J. Reynolds's cigarette factories in Winston-Salem. The Piedmont economy was hailed as the basis of a progressive New South, although textile mills paid low wages and tobacco employed fewer workers.

Indeed, North Carolina's present-day affluence owes more to pharmaceuticals, banking and high-skill Piedmont factories, such as the country's most advanced tire recycling plant in Winston-Salem and a custom furniture-making operation in Kernersville. Lowe's, the $22 billion home improvement giant, is based in little Wilkesboro, population 3,000. The 2001 merger of banking giants Wachovia and First Union proved bittersweet for Winston-Salem, Wachovia's home base since 1879: First Union, the larger of the two entities, let the new company keep Wachovia's name but shifted most of the local employment presence south to First Union's headquarters in Charlotte. Yet for all the economic progress here, large swaths of the region remain rural, from chicken-raising Wilkes County to Appalachian State University in Boone, a key center for resurgent pride in the culture of Appalachia, a region toward which the rest of America has so often displayed condescension.

All these lie within the boundaries of the 5th Congressional District. The 5th begins in the heart of the Piedmont: The suburbs of Winston-Salem (though not the city, which is in the 12th). From there, it drops south just short of the outer fringes of metropolitan Charlotte; then heads west and north to the Tennessee line, taking in mountain communities like Boone. When legislators drew a new 13th District along the state's northern tier, they pushed today's 5th much further west than it had reached during the 1990s. Still, the core of its population base remains much the same: The Winston-Salem suburbs in Forsyth County, plus small industrial cities in Stokes and Surry counties, including Mount Airy, the model for Mayberry in the *Andy Griffith Show*. The district, one of only four in North Carolina where registered Republicans outnumber Democrats, is solidly Republican.

The congressman from the 5th District is Richard Burr, a Republican elected in 1994. Burr grew up in Winston-Salem, was a star football player at Reynolds High and Wake Forest, then worked for a wholesaling firm. In 1992 Burr ran against Congressman Steve Neal, a Democrat first elected in 1974, who usually won by close margins; Burr was outspent 3–1 and lost 53%–46%. Neal retired in 1994 and Burr ran again. His Democratic opponent was state Senator Sandy Sands, a rural trial lawyer who attacked Burr for using Jerry Falwell's Liberty University studios to produce his 1992 ads. Burr supported the Contract with America, promised to make defense of tobacco his number one issue, and worked hard to tie Sands to the Clinton administration. Burr won a solid 57%, carrying all but two counties and taking the Winston-Salem area by nearly 2–1. He has not had a serious challenge since then.

In the House, Burr has a mostly conservative voting record, though far from the most conservative in the North Carolina delegation. On the Commerce Committee, his early cause became streamlining the FDA drug and medical device approval process, which he claimed has kept valuable and life-saving products from patients. By the mid-1990s the FDA was moving so slowly that it took more than 10 years and $350 million to move a prescription drug from idea to market, and 773 days to approve a medical device. At first, Burr took a radical approach that aroused much opposition, but then for over two years worked with the agency, doctors, patients, consumer groups and the pharmaceutical industry to come up with a consensus. With broad bipartisan support in 1997, his FDA Modernization Act became law; it requires the FDA to establish protocol guidelines before extensive research is begun, to review applications in a more timely manner, to use due process to determine scientific disputes and to create a scientific advisory panel. As a bonus, the FDA approved the Sensor Pad, a device to help breast self-examination, which had been a Burr crusade. He strongly opposed tobacco legislation and when Bill Clinton called for the Justice Department to sue the tobacco companies, Burr said, "This is an administration whose policy is to drive the industry out." With others from North Carolina, he later called for an optional buyout of tobacco quotas. He sought a crackdown on illegal textile imports, routed by China through other countries to evade quotas, and he opposed Clinton on PNTR for China. But he backed George W. Bush's call for trade promotion authority after securing what he said were promises that the local textile industry would have a seat at the table; that was not an easy vote, he said, but it gave textiles an opportunity to regain international competitiveness. To assist furniture manufacturers against rival imports, he called for tax code changes to accelerate depreciation of their equipment.

Burr advocated electricity deregulation and sponsored a bill to give states the ability to design deregulation if they want; it barred mandatory power purchases but continued current contracts and allowed rural cooperatives to compete wherever investor-owned utilities can. He unexpectedly became a celebrity when, while testifying in opposition to the law requiring that toilets made in the U.S use no more than 1.6 gallons of water per flush, he read from a roll of toilet paper. Critics have said that he and his staff have taken excessive corporate-sponsored overseas travel, but he defended the itineraries as "fact finding." Burr became a key player in crafting the Republicans' prescription drug plan. He proposed a cap—perhaps $2,500—on how much any senior pays during a year, plus the creation of a non-profit group to negotiate lower drug prices for seniors, as the Veterans Department does for vets. His plan would give seniors more control of their coverage.

Burr has worked his district aggressively, holding women's health and electricity summits in Winston-Salem, and employing a 30-cup rule: He buys a cup of coffee everywhere he stops to talk to constituents and says he has bought as many as 30 in a day. But his ambitions have turned statewide. After Raleigh Mayor Tom Fetzer, a longtime friend, dropped out of the gubernatorial race in 1999, Burr considered running but decided he didn't have "the fire in my belly." He has made no secret of his interest in running for the Senate. He was interested in running for Jesse Helms's seat in 2002, but deferred to Elizabeth Dole when it became apparent that the Bush White House was pushing her and that her standing with voters was very high. In early 2003, he moved toward running for John Edwards's Senate seat in 2004; White House political strategist Karl Rove gave encouragement and he had promised in 1994 not to serve more than five terms in the House. He said that he would decide by summer 2003 whether to run; if he did, he would begin with the advantage of a nearly $2 million campaign treasury. Whether or not Burr runs for the Senate, the 5th District appears to be solidly Republican.

SIXTH DISTRICT

Rep. Howard Coble (R)

Elected 1984, 10th term; b. Mar. 18, 1931, Greensboro; home, Greensboro; Appalachian St. U., 1949–50, Guilford Col., B.A. 1958, U. of NC, J.D. 1962; Presbyterian; single.

Military Career: Coast Guard, 1952–56, 1977–78, Coast Guard Reserves, 1960–81.

Elected Office: NC House of Reps., 1968–70, 1978–84.

Professional Career: Asst. U.S. Atty., NC Middle Dist., 1969–73; Secy., NC Dept. of Revenue, 1973–77; Practicing atty., 1979–83.

DC Office: 2468 RHOB 20515, 202-225-3065; Fax: 202-225-8611; Web site: www.house.gov/coble.

District Offices: Asheboro, 336-626-3060; Greensboro, 336-333-5005; High Point, 336-886-5106.

Committees: *Judiciary* (3d of 21 R): Commercial & Administrative Law; Crime, Terrorism & Homeland Security (Chmn.). *Transportation & Infrastructure* (4th of 41 R): Coast Guard & Maritime Transportation; Highways, Transit & Pipelines; Railroads.

Group Ratings

	ADA	ACLU	AFS	LCV	CON	ITIC	NTU	COC	ACU	NTLC	CHC
2002	10	7	22	13	50	62	58	75	92	92	100
2001	10	—	10	7	—	—	63	87	92	—	—

National Journal Ratings

	2001 LIB	—	2001 CONS		2002 LIB	—	2002 CONS
Economic	15%	—	82%		36%	—	61%
Social	20%	—	69%		25%	—	71%
Foreign	16%	—	82%		24%	—	72%

Key Votes of the 107th Congress

1. Approve Bush Tax Cuts	Y	5. Faith-Based Charities	Y	9. Trade Promotion Authority	N
2. Limit Patients' Bill of Rights	Y	6. Bar Gays in the Boy Scouts	Y	10. Bar Funds for Intl. Court	Y
3. Campaign Finance Reform	N	7. Ban Partial-Birth Abortion	Y	11. Authorize Force in Iraq	Y
4. Ban ANWR Development	N	8. Arm Commercial Pilots	Y	12. Deny Home. Sec. Dept. Union	Y

Election Results

2002 general	Howard Coble (R)	151,430	(90%)	($316,561)
	Tara Grubb (Lib)	16,067	(10%)	
2002 primary	Howard Coble (R)	unopposed		
2000 general	Howard Coble (R)	195,727	(91%)	($301,790)
	Jeffrey Dean Bentley (Lib)	18,726	(9%)	($4,885)

Prior Winning Percentages: 1998 (89%); 1996 (73%); 1994 (100%); 1992 (71%); 1990 (67%); 1988 (62%); 1986 (50%); 1984 (51%)

The People		Race/Ethnic Origin	Ancestry	
Area size:	2,989 sq. mi.	85.3% White	USA: 15.3%	German: 10.1%
Urban population:	51.6%	8.6% Black	English: 8.9%	
Rural population:	48.4%	1.0% Asian	**2000 Presidential Vote**	
Pop. 2000:	619,178	0.4% Native Am.	Bush (R)..............160,141	(67%)
Median income:	$43,503	0.0% Hawaiian	Gore (D)................76,315	(32%)
Poverty status:	8.2%	0.7% Two+ races	Other....................1,727	(1%)
Military veterans:	13.8%	0.1% Other	**Cook Partisan Voting Index:** R +18	
		3.9% Hispanic Origin		

Occupation	Blue collar: 32.3%	White collar: 55.8%	Gray collar: 11.9%

For more than half a century, furniture store managers and owners from all over the country twice a year have converged on the huge Furniture Mart in High Point, the center of the U.S. furniture business, for the giant trade show put on by manufacturers. High Point sits amidst rolling farmland originally settled by Quakers; it was the site of the Battle of Guilford Courthouse in the Revolutionary War, then slaveholding country. The furniture business grew here early in the 20th century because of the hardwoods in the mountains not far west and the abundance of low-wage labor in the flatlands not far east. In recent years, the furniture business has proven more resilient than textiles and tobacco, but the Triad area—Greensboro, High Point, and Winston-Salem—has been forced to scramble for new engines of economic growth in the shadow of better-known success stories in Raleigh-Durham and Charlotte. Today, the region's Hispanic population is growing. The town of Robbins in Moore County—the childhood home of Sen. John Edwards—is now 48% Hispanic, as Latinos moved in to seek jobs in chicken processing and furniture making. In 2007, a new Federal Express hub is set to open at Piedmont Triad International Airport, located between Winston-Salem and Greensboro; local leaders expect it will have a $1.4 billion impact over its first 10 years.

The 6th Congressional District is centered on greater Greensboro and High Point, which collectively cast about one-third of the vote. The Furniture Mart itself is not physically located within the 6th, but the district takes in other parts of High Point, Quaker-settled Randolph County, golf-course-sprinkled Moore County to the south, plus parts of furniture-manufacturing Davidson County, most of Alamance County, part of populous Guilford County (though not downtown Greensboro) and the eastern half of Rowan County. Some of these areas are historically Republican: Davidson, Moore, Randolph and Rowan Counties have more Republicans than Democrats; Randolph County has a nearly 2–1 Republican edge.

The congressman from the 6th District is Howard Coble, a Republican first elected in 1984. He grew up in Guilford County, went to Guilford College, then after wrecking his father's car joined the Coast Guard, in which he started off collecting garbage and served for five years. He was an insurance claims representative, went to law school and became an assistant U.S. attorney, state revenue commissioner and served in the state House from 1968–70 and 1978–84. In 1984 Coble was elected to Congress in what was then a swing district; it was the third time the 6th had changed parties in three elections. Coble won reelection in 1986 by just 79 votes—in a contest that Democrats complained was decided by the Guilford County election board's refusal to hold a recount. But his personal popularity and subsequent redistricting made this a safe seat.

Coble is a friendly man who asks visitors if they mind if he smokes his cheap cigars; he likes bluegrass music and eats pork brains and eggs for breakfast. He is solidly conservative, with interesting twists. He is tightfisted, and since his first term he has tried to pass legislation to abolish congressional pensions; he boycotts that program himself, but hasn't found many cosponsors. Like many of his constituents, he is leery of free trade. He opposed fast track for NAFTA, but finally voted for it in 1993 (without visiting the White House or selling his vote, he said); but he opposed GATT and PNTR with China. He was one of three House Republicans from North Carolina to oppose trade promotion authority in 2001 and 2002.

"I see my role more as one of keeping bad legislation off the books," Coble once said. But as a subcommittee chairman he became legislatively productive. In 1995 he became chairman of the panel with jurisdiction over the Coast Guard, and steered to House passage bills replacing the maritime cartel with free markets and closing down Coast Guard stations; they went nowhere in the Senate. In 1997 he became chairman of the Courts and Intellectual Property Subcommittee of Judiciary. Suddenly this cigar-chomping and suspender-wearing Tar Heel found himself sought out by Hollywood and Nashville stars: He dined with Billy Joel and had office visits from Johnny and June Carter Cash, Michael J. Fox and Paul Reiser. Arguing that copyright industries produce more GDP than manufacturing and that patent protection is essential to technological progress, Coble supported greater protection for intellectual property—to the dismay of some. He passed a bill to extend the term of copyright by 20 years. (Otherwise, Mickey Mouse would have gone out of copyright by 2004.) He introduced measures to make it illegal to circumvent encryption technology used to protect copyrighted material and to remove digital author codes from copyrighted material, to protect creative work transmitted over the Internet. This 1998 statute conformed U.S. law to World Intellectual Property Organization treaties. When the Bush administration sought to make some budget savings by diverting funds from the Patent and Trademark Office, Coble told the appropriators to "keep their grubby paws out of the PTO's coffers." In 2002, he shepherded the enactment of additional changes in the patent law, including the development of an electronic system for the filing and processing of patent and trademark applications.

Despite his own limitations in operating a computer, Coble says that has not been an obstacle to dealing with the digital revolution and that he has come to appreciate the developers of the Internet. His bill to impose criminal penalties for unauthorized use of materials in electronic data bases generated fierce opposition; critics complained that it would permit the stock exchanges to prevent publication of stock prices. In the 106th Congress, Coble became the center of added controversy after he slipped a four-line amendment to the copyright law into an unrelated bill on home satellites; his "work for hire" provision, which recording companies requested, extended their control of recorded music to 35 years after its release; Coble thought that he was merely formalizing what already was common practice. Following strong objections from prominent musicians such as rock star Don Henley (who wrote a song complaining about the unfairness) and bluegrass banjoer Earl Scruggs—and, not incidentally, from fellow subcommittee member Mary Bono, widow of Sonny Bono—Coble agreed with ranking Democrat Howard Berman to repeal the earlier measure. Still, he enacted more than a dozen bills after taking over the copyright subcommittee and remained popular with colleagues. Based on his previous work with the Coast Guard and Justice Department, Coble voiced interest in chairing the new Homeland Security Committee in 2003; but that position went to Christopher Cox. In 2003, after the defeat of George Gekas, Coble moved up to the number-three Republican spot on the Judiciary Committee, and he took over the Crime, Terrorism and Homeland Security Subcommittee.

Since 1994, Coble has had a Democratic opponent in only one election. In 2002, his Libertarian opponent Tara Grubb criticized Coble for his excessive protection of the rights of entertainment companies and other copyright holders against users who illegally download copyrighted music. Coble defeated her 90%–10%. In February 2003, Coble stirred controversy after a radio interview in which he said that Japanese internment camps of World War II were "appropriate at the time." "I was just stating historical fact," he later explained. "If those comments were offensive to anyone, I apologize for that. I did not intend to be insensitive or uncaring."

SEVENTH DISTRICT

Rep. Mike McIntyre (D)

Elected 1996, 4th term; b. Aug. 6, 1956, Lumberton; home, Lumberton; U. of NC, B.A. 1978, J.D. 1981; Presbyterian; married (Dee).

Professional Career: Practicing atty., 1981–96.

DC Office: 228 CHOB 20515, 202-225-2731; Fax: 202-225-5773; Web site: www.house.gov/mcintyre.

District Offices: Fayetteville, 910-323-0260; Lumberton, 910-671-6223; Wilmington, 910-815-4959.

Committees: *Agriculture* (6th of 24 D): Conservation, Credit, Rural Development & Research; Specialty Crops & Foreign Agriculture Programs (RMM). *Armed Services* (13th of 29 D): Tactical Air & Land Forces; Terrorism, Unconventional Threats & Capabilities.

Group Ratings

	ADA	ACLU	AFS	LCV	CON	ITIC	NTU	COC	ACU	NTLC	CHC
2002	55	27	89	38	4	50	31	53	48	26	75
2001	60	—	67	79	—	—	29	57	64	—	—

National Journal Ratings

	2001 LIB —	2001 CONS	2002 LIB —	2002 CONS
Economic	56%	45%	54%	46%
Social	41%	59%	51%	49%
Foreign	49%	47%	52%	48%

Key Votes of the 107th Congress

1. Approve Bush Tax Cuts	*	5. Faith-Based Charities	Y	9. Trade Promotion Authority	N
2. Limit Patients' Bill of Rights	N	6. Bar Gays in the Boy Scouts	Y	10. Bar Funds for Intl. Court	Y
3. Campaign Finance Reform	Y	7. Ban Partial-Birth Abortion	Y	11. Authorize Force in Iraq	Y
4. Ban ANWR Development	Y	8. Arm Commercial Pilots	Y	12. Deny Home. Sec. Dept. Union	N

Election Results

2002 general	Mike McIntyre (D)	118,543	(71%)	($555,393)
	James Adams (R)	45,537	(27%)	
	Other	2,574	(2%)	
2002 primary	Mike McIntyre (D)	unopposed		
2000 general	Mike McIntyre (D)	160,185	(70%)	($428,263)
	James Adams (R)	66,463	(29%)	
	Other	3,018	(1%)	

Prior Winning Percentages: 1998 (91%); 1996 (53%)

The People		Race/Ethnic Origin	Ancestry	
Area size:	6,510 sq. mi.	63.0% White	USA: 11.1%	English: 7.7%
Urban population:	45.1%	23.1% Black	German: 6.1%	
Rural population:	54.9%	0.5% Asian	**2000 Presidential Vote**	
Pop. 2000:	619,178	8.5% Native Am.	Bush (R)..............108,091	(52%)
Median income:	$33,998	0.0% Hawaiian	Gore (D)..............100,025	(48%)
Poverty status:	16.7%	0.9% Two + races	Other.....................1,420	(1%)
Military veterans:	14.1%	0.1% Other	**Cook Partisan Voting Index:** R + 2	
		3.9% Hispanic Origin		

Occupation	Blue collar: 32.4%	White collar: 50.5%	Gray collar: 17.2%

Southernmost North Carolina, where the state boundary dips down along the Atlantic coast, has been historically dependent on tobacco. Tobacco, grown here for two centuries, can be cultivated profitably in only a few places in the world; it is labor-intensive, requiring close tending and serial picking (one leaf on a stalk matures before the one above it); and it produces more voters per federally assisted acre than any other crop. Southernmost North Carolina is also military country. The port city of Wilmington is home of the World War II battleship U.S.S. North Carolina, while a little further south the Army runs the 16,000-acre Military Ocean Terminal at Sunny Point—the largest ammunition port in the U.S., and the Army's main deep-water port on the east coast, built securely amidst enormous sand berms.

While these pursuits remain important to the region, the 1990s brought new ones—one clean, one dirty. Wilmington and the nearby beach towns—the second-fastest growing region in North Carolina during the decade—have become perhaps the busiest American movie- and television-production facilities outside of Los Angeles and New York, most popularly as the backdrop of the teen-oriented WB series *Dawson's Creek*. The film industry accounted for 11% of the Wilmington area's economy, with tourism accounting for another big slice. Further inland, economic growth comes from pigs—vertically integrated factory farming, loved by industry for its robotic efficiency and laser-guided precision, derided by environmentalists for its enormous output of hog waste, which is directed into high-tech waste-treatment pools known, rather euphemistically, as lagoons. One Smithfield Foods facility—located in tiny Tar Heel, along the Cape Fear River in Bladen County—recently saw its slaughter limit increased by 1 million hogs a year, to 8.48 million animals beginning in 2004. It is believed to be the largest slaughterhouse in the world.

The 7th Congressional District covers much of this territory. The district, barely altered by redistricting, consists of three main areas: the Wilmington region, with affluent condo-dwellers along the beach and retiree subdivisions reclaimed from timbered-out pinelands further inland; the outskirts of Fayetteville, heavily dependent on Fort Bragg (the training facilities on the eastern side of the installation are in the 7th District) and Pope Air Force Base; and Robeson County, which is strongly Democratic and inhabited by the Lumbee Indians, whose origins have been lost to antiquity but who were treated by state segregation laws as a race distinct from whites and blacks. For many years, this was a solidly Democratic district. In Robeson County—with 20% of the district's population, and where whites, blacks and Lumbees each comprise about a third of the population—Democrat Erskine Bowles trounced Republican Elizabeth Dole in the 2002 Senate race, 63%–36%. By contrast, Wilmington's New Hanover County, which accounts for about 30% of the district, voted Dole by 56%–43%. District-wide, the 7th supported Bill Clinton in 1996 and George W. Bush in 2000, each by modest margins; by significantly bigger margins, it backed North Carolina Democrats John Edwards for senator in 1998 and (local resident) Mike Easley for governor in 2000.

The congressman from the 7th District is Mike McIntyre, a Democrat elected in 1996. McIntyre grew up in Lumberton, in Robeson County, graduated from college and law school at Chapel Hill and practiced law in Lumberton, where his family has been prominent for 200 years. In 1974 when he was an intern in the office of Congressman Charlie Rose, then in his first term, he whispered to his father that he would like one day to run for Rose's seat. McIntyre was active in civic affairs and in his church and was often asked to run for office. In 1995, four months before Rose announced his retirement, McIntyre decided to run. When Rose chose not to run, seven Democrats and four Republicans filed. McIntyre's chief opposition in the primary was Rose Marie Lowry-Townsend, a Lumbee and a liberal, who had support from the National Education Association, labor PACs and national women's groups. Lowry-Townsend led McIntyre 30%–23% in the primary. In the runoff McIntyre called for smaller government and cited his close ties to the district and involvement in community activities and won 52%–48%. Against Republican nominee Bill Caster, a retired Coast Guard officer and New Hanover County commissioner, McIntyre's platform was almost as conservative as Caster's—on some things, more so. He was moved by state labor leaders to withdraw his support for a national right-to-work law, but continued to favor right-to-work in North Carolina. Caster ridiculed McIntyre's emphasis on his community ties: "While it's all well and good to coach Little League, that doesn't mean you're ready to go to Congress." Caster carried the coastal counties; McIntyre carried the Fayetteville area and had a huge majority in Robeson County. Overall, he won 53%–46%, even as Bill Clinton lost the district 48%–44%.

McIntyre joined the conservative Blue Dog Democrats and got seats on Armed Services and

Agriculture. His voting record—conservative among Democrats, especially on cultural issues—stands at the middle of the House. He voted for the anti-flag burning amendment, the partial-birth abortion ban, and sunset of the tax code, and he placed the Ten Commandments in his office. But he supported racial quotas and preferences and opposed school vouchers. When George W. Bush took office, he was one of 16 Democrats who voted to repeal the Clinton administration's new ergonomics rules.

McIntyre fought the proposal to end crop insurance for tobacco farmers and prevailed. Later, he proposed buyout legislation for farmers, which would end the tobacco program but continue FDA regulation of cigarettes. He got money for hurricane relief, beach nourishment for his coastal communities, and promoted deepening of the Wilmington port for an improved shipping channel along the Cape Fear River. He sought federal recognition of the Lumbees as an Indian tribe to give them "the dignity they deserve." He co-chaired the Rural Health Care Coalition, where he secured Medicaid funding relief, and he co-chaired caucuses on fatherhood and Special Operations Forces. He opposed PNTR with China and trade promotion authority, and he sought to impose a higher tariff on new imports of Caribbean Basin footwear; Converse's plant west of Lumberton was once the largest shoe factory in the United States. He proposed additional subsistence payments and job-training assistance for workers who have lost their jobs because of NAFTA; he estimated the loss of nearly 10,000 jobs in Robeson and Columbus Counties. McIntyre said that the 2002 defense bill was a huge boost for military bases in southeast North Carolina; as many of those troops headed to the Persian Gulf, he voted to authorize the use of force in Iraq. With bipartisan support from Republican Richard Burr, he proposed creation of a seven-state Southeast Crescent Authority to bring a federal focus to the region's economic development.

McIntyre has won endorsements from the U.S. Chamber of Commerce, Gary Bauer's Campaign for Working Families and the VFW; Republicans have not seriously challenged him. "I wish Mike McIntyre would make it official and switch over to the Republican Party," said a North Carolina Republican spokesman. "He's voted with the Republicans quite a bit and is one of [Democrats'] most conservative members in Congress." But McIntyre says that he has not been interested in switching, having been active in the Democratic Party since high school. He has been reelected without serious opposition. Perhaps to discourage thoughts of a party switch, Democratic legislators made the district more Democratic in redistricting.

EIGHTH DISTRICT

Rep. Robin Hayes (R)

Elected 1998, 3d term; b. Aug. 14, 1945, Concord; home, Concord; Duke U., B.A. 1967; Presbyterian; married (Barbara).

Elected Office: Concord Bd. of Aldermen, 1978–81; NC House of Reps., 1992–96, Maj. Whip, 1995–96.

Professional Career: Businessman, 1967-present; Owner, Mt. Pleasant Hosiery Mill, 1988-present.

DC Office: 130 CHOB 20515, 202-225-3715; Fax: 202-225-4036; Web site: www.house.gov/hayes.

District Offices: Concord, 704-786-1612; Rockingham, 910-997-2070.

Committees: *Agriculture* (11th of 27 R): Livestock & Horticulture (Chmn.); Specialty Crops & Foreign Agriculture Programs. *Armed Services* (14th of 33 R): Readiness; Terrorism, Unconventional Threats & Capabilities; Total Force. *Transportation & Infrastructure* (22d of 41 R): Aviation; Highways, Transit & Pipelines; Water Resources & Environment.

Group Ratings

	ADA	ACLU	AFS	LCV	CON	ITIC	NTU	COC	ACU	NTLC	CHC
2002	5	7	11	13	25	75	52	75	96	83	100
2001	5	—	0	0	—	—	61	87	96	—	—

National Journal Ratings

	2001 LIB	—	2001 CONS		2002 LIB	—	2002 CONS
Economic	15%	—	82%		21%	—	73%
Social	0%	—	81%		0%	—	75%
Foreign	4%	—	87%		24%	—	72%

Key Votes of the 107th Congress

1. Approve Bush Tax Cuts	Y	5. Faith-Based Charities	Y	9. Trade Promotion Authority	Y
2. Limit Patients' Bill of Rights	Y	6. Bar Gays in the Boy Scouts	Y	10. Bar Funds for Intl. Court	Y
3. Campaign Finance Reform	N	7. Ban Partial-Birth Abortion	Y	11. Authorize Force in Iraq	Y
4. Ban ANWR Development	N	8. Arm Commercial Pilots	Y	12. Deny Home. Sec. Dept. Union	Y

Election Results

2002 general	Robin Hayes (R)	80,298	(54%)	($2,287,339)
	Chris Kouri (D)	66,819	(45%)	($673,171)
	Other	2,619	(2%)	
2002 primary	Robin Hayes (R)	unopposed		
2000 general	Robin Hayes (R)	119,950	(55%)	($1,942,592)
	Mike Taylor (D)	89,505	(44%)	($773,202)
	Other	2,009	(1%)	

Prior Winning Percentages: 1998 (51%)

The People		Race/Ethnic Origin	Ancestry	
Area size:	3,318 sq. mi.	61.8% White	USA: 10.8%	German: 7.6%
Urban population:	69.4%	26.6% Black	English: 5.9%	
Rural population:	30.6%	1.7% Asian	**2000 Presidential Vote**	
Pop. 2000:	619,178	1.7% Native Am.	Bush (R).............105,484	(54%)
Median income:	$38,390	0.1% Hawaiian	Gore (D)...............89,672	(46%)
Poverty status:	12.4%	1.4% Two+ races	Other....................1,568	(1%)
Military veterans:	14.0%	0.2% Other	**Cook Partisan Voting Index:** R + 4	
		6.6% Hispanic Origin		

Occupation   Blue collar: 31.8%   White collar: 53.3%   Gray collar: 14.9%

In the Carolina Piedmont, ranging from Atlanta to Durham along Interstate 85, lies the thickest concentration of America's once-mighty textile industry. Within North Carolina, I-85 brushes past Concord and Kannapolis, the latter named for its founding company, Cannon Mills. While eastern Carolina was settled by Englishmen from the coast, this Piedmont land was settled mainly by Scots and diverse groups like Quakers and Moravian sects, coming down the Blue Ridge from Pennsylvania through Virginia. These migratory patterns were reflected in Civil War divisions and continue in current voting habits. The coastal counties all the way up through the Sand Hills were Confederate and are now Democratic. The textile mill towns along I-85 were anti-secession and are now Republican.

Parts of both these areas are in the 8th Congressional District. The most populous county in the district is Cabarrus County, which includes the southern end of the textile corridor around Kannapolis and Concord. In recent years, Cabarrus, fed by migration from Charlotte, has moved beyond its textile and small town roots and become an exurban county, growing by 32% in the 1990s and in 2002 it cast 25% of the district's votes. The 8th extends eastward to Fayetteville's Cumberland County, which casts 17% of the vote, but stops short of including the heavily military neighborhoods just outside the gates of Fort Bragg. The irregular boundaries of the district have a political explanation. Democratic redistricters included as much of the Democratic Sand Hills as they could, but removed most of Union County, a fast-growing and heavy Republican area just east of Charlotte. And they added central city precincts in Charlotte and Mecklenburg County with some blacks and some affluent white liberals. So this is a split personality district, with very different political leanings in the textile country, the Sand Hills and Charlotte. It has usually been carried by Republican presidential candidates and by North Carolina Democrats in close statewide contests. It has long been targeted by both Democrats and Republicans as a marginal district and has often been seriously contested, though over the past three decades it has only changed political hands twice, in 1974 and 1998.

The congressman from the 8th District is Robin Hayes, a Republican elected in 1998. He grew up in Concord, the grandson of Cannon Mills founder Charles Cannon, a legendary figure in textile country, the dominant economic and political force in this part of North Carolina. Hayes graduated from Duke and returned to Concord, where he ran several businesses—selling Mack trucks, building highways, running the Mount Pleasant Hosiery Mills. He coached football at a local college and worked in the Prison Fellowship movement. He was elected a Concord alderman, and in 1991 he switched to the Republican Party. In 1992 Hayes was elected to the North Carolina House, and became majority whip. In 1996 he ran for governor, won the Republican primary, but lost the general to Jim Hunt 56%–43%.

In November 1997 Hayes announced he was running against 8th District Congressman Bill Hefner, the winner of many close races during his 11 terms. In January 1998 Hefner surprised just about everyone by announcing that he would retire. After several better-known Democrats decided not to run, Mike Taylor, a Stanly County lawyer with an attractive biography but little name recognition, emerged as the nominee. Hayes campaigned on a standard conservative plat-form, stressing the issues he had pushed in the legislature and calling for "top-to-bottom com-prehensive tax reform." Taylor's military record helped him win the endorsement of the VFW, but Hayes outspent Taylor by 3–1, and Taylor was a non-presence in the Charlotte media market. Hayes carried the textile counties 61%–38%, but after the 1998 redistricting they cast only 36% of the votes in the district. He carried Union County even more soundly, 65%–34%. But Taylor carried the counties to the east 64%–35%, and they cast 43% of the district's votes; overall, Hayes won 51%–48%.

In the House, Hayes has compiled a conservative voting record, devoting much of his energy to getting federal money for the state and district. In December 2001, he became the focal point in the dramatic House vote on trade promotion authority. The Republican leadership took the issue to the floor without having a majority of votes in hand and held the vote open until they could squeeze them out. Hayes delayed casting his electronic vote past the usual 15-minute deadline and, with the outcome still in doubt, he found himself surrounded by Republican leaders pleading for his vote. After his "aye" vote produced a 215–214 victory for Bush, Hayes broke down in tears in the House chamber after what he called "a very intense experience." Later, he said that he got no projects for his district in exchange for the vote, but that George W. Bush had assured him that he would treat the textile industry fairly in future trade agreements, and that textiles imported from the Caribbean would have to be finished and dyed in the United States. Hayes stressed that his continued support for trade deals depended on Bush keeping his promise. When the final House-Senate agreement came for a vote in July 2002, Hayes voted against it because it permitted additional textile and apparel imports; others provided the majority this time. Republicans embraced him as a hero for putting his career on the line, and Democrats vowed that Hayes would pay the price in the next election. In a tension-filled moment of a different type, Hayes was at the Pentagon early in the morning of September 11, 2001, for a meeting with Defense Secretary Donald Rumsfeld. Toward the end of the meeting, Hayes recounted, he asked Rumsfeld what it would take to get Americans' attention focused on strengthening national de-fense. Rumsfeld responded, "Robin, I'm afraid that it's going to take an event of great signifi-cance." Less than an hour later, with Hayes back in his office, that event happened when Amer-ican Airlines Flight 77 slammed into the Pentagon's west wall.

Hayes knew in advance that he would be seriously challenged for reelection, in both 2000 and 2002. Taylor, his 1998 opponent, never stopped running, and national Democrats raised more money. But Hayes fought back. Hayes traveled the campaign trail with a four-foot-wide reusable blank check signed "Uncle Sam." At each stop he took a felt-tip pen and wrote in the federal money he had brought in: $650,000 to extend water lines to a school in Stanly County, $258,000 for a pilot housing program in Troy, $4 million for two airports. Occasionally there were snafus: He got $50,000 for the town of Hamlet to demolish the Imperial Foods chicken plant where 25 workers died in a 1991 fire, but the town council refused to spend the money because of concerns about liability. After criticism from the local media, the county accepted the grant and the Imperial plant was demolished. Hayes, who once sold heavy machinery, jumped on the backhoe and took the first hit at the building. The vote again broke down on historic lines, with Hayes winning 2-to-1 in the textile country and Taylor taking the Sand Hills counties, 3-to-2; Hayes ran about as well as George W. Bush. Overall Hayes won 55%–44%.

Democrats targeted Hayes again in 2002. Local Democratic leaders at first rallied behind wealthy former state Representative Bill Richardson, who also was backed by organized labor. But voters instead nominated 32-year-old attorney Chris Kouri, a political newcomer who was best known for having won all-Ivy League football honors as a running back at Yale before getting drafted by the Miami Dolphins. He failed to make the team and eventually became a lawyer in Charlotte. He framed his contest against Richardson in populist terms and won the primary 47%–32%; party strategists later criticized Richardson for his lackluster campaign. Although Democrats rhetorically rallied around Kouri, their financial and political commitment faded. Kouri, while attacking Hayes for his trade vote, lacked sufficient funds to convey his message. Hayes spent heavily, and renamed his opponent "a liberal trial lawyer from Charlotte." Hayes cited a thank-you letter from AFL-CIO president John Sweeney for his "principled" vote on the final version of trade promotion authority; Sweeney objected, but Hayes had made his point. Hayes won 54%–45%. Kouri won 60% in Charlotte and Mecklenburg County, which cast 15% of the vote, but Hayes won 66% in the textile counties, Cabarrus and Stanly County, which cast 37% of the total. Kouri won the Sand Hills counties, but Hayes won 54% of the vote in Cumberland County. Hayes has now twice won by decisive margins, but Democrats may target this district again.

NINTH DISTRICT

Rep. Sue Myrick (R)

Elected 1994, 5th term; b. Aug. 1, 1941, Tiffin, OH; home, Charlotte; Heidelberg Col., 1959–60; Methodist; married (Ed).

Elected Office: Charlotte City Cncl., 1983–85; Charlotte Mayor, 1987–91.

Professional Career: Pres. & CEO, Myrick Advertising, 1985–94; Pres. & CEO, Myrick Enterprises, 1992–94.

DC Office: 230 CHOB 20515, 202-225-1976; Fax: 202-225-3389; Web site: www.house.gov/myrick.

District Offices: Charlotte, 704-362-1060; Gastonia, 704-861-1976.

Committees: *Rules* (7th of 9 R): Technology & the House (Vice Chmn.).

Group Ratings

	ADA	ACLU	AFS	LCV	CON	ITIC	NTU	COC	ACU	NTLC	CHC
2002	0	7	0	25	81	100	61	100	96	100	100
2001	0	—	0	7	—	—	71	95	96	—	—

National Journal Ratings

	2001 LIB	—	2001 CONS		2002 LIB	—	2002 CONS
Economic	19%	—	82%		21%	—	73%
Social	0%	—	81%		0%	—	75%
Foreign	0%	—	97%		0%	—	85%

Key Votes of the 107th Congress

1. Approve Bush Tax Cuts	Y	5. Faith-Based Charities	Y	9. Trade Promotion Authority	Y
2. Limit Patients' Bill of Rights	Y	6. Bar Gays in the Boy Scouts	Y	10. Bar Funds for Intl. Court	Y
3. Campaign Finance Reform	N	7. Ban Partial-Birth Abortion	Y	11. Authorize Force in Iraq	Y
4. Ban ANWR Development	N	8. Arm Commercial Pilots	Y	12. Deny Home. Sec. Dept. Union	Y

Almanac 2004 Order Card

☑ YES! Send me *The Almanac of American Politics 2004.*

_____	Copies of the softcover *Almanac 2004* for $59.95	$	_____
_____	Copies of the hardcover *Almanac 2004* for $79.95	$	_____
	Add 10% shipping and handling	$	_____
	Add sales tax: DC (5.75%), CA (8.25%) or VA (4.5%)	$	_____
	TOTAL	$	_____

☐ **Check Enclosed**   ☐ **Charge:** ☐ Visa ☐ MC ☐ AMEX

_____

Account #   *Exp. Date*

_____

Name on card   *Signature*

_____

Credit card billing address

Name: _____ Title: _____

Organization: _____

Shipping Address: _____

City/State/Zip: _____

Phone: _____ Fax: _____

E-mail: _____

For even faster service, or special discounts on 10 or more
Call toll free 1-800-356-4838

National Journal Subscription Reply Card

☑ YES! I want six free issues of National Journal

The leading weekly on politics, policy and government

Please complete all of the following information:

Name: _____ Title: _____

Organization: _____

Address: _____

City/State/Zip: _____

Phone: _____ Fax: _____

E-mail: _____

Mail this postage-paid card today, or for faster service
Call toll free 1-800-424-2921

BUSINESS REPLY MAIL

FIRST-CLASS MAIL   PERMIT NO. 1338   WASHINGTON DC

POSTAGE WILL BE PAID BY ADDRESSEE

NATIONAL JOURNAL GROUP INC
PO BOX 96157
WASHINGTON DC 20077-7509

BUSINESS REPLY MAIL

FIRST-CLASS MAIL   PERMIT NO. 1338   WASHINGTON DC

POSTAGE WILL BE PAID BY ADDRESSEE

NATIONAL JOURNAL GROUP INC
PO BOX 96157
WASHINGTON DC 20077-7509

Election Results

2002 general	Sue Myrick (R)	140,095	(72%)	($916,659)
	Ed McGuire (D)	49,974	(26%)	
	Other	3,374	(2%)	
2002 primary	Sue Myrick (R)	unopposed		
2000 general	Sue Myrick (R)	181,161	(69%)	($959,304)
	Ed McGuire (D)	79,382	(30%)	($71,375)
	Other	3,677	(1%)	

Prior Winning Percentages: 1998 (69%); 1996 (63%); 1994 (65%)

The People		Race/Ethnic Origin	Ancestry	
Area size:	1,018 sq. mi.	82.9% White	German: 11.2%	USA: 9.5%
Urban population:	84.2%	10.3% Black	English: 9.0%	
Rural population:	15.8%	2.0% Asian	**2000 Presidential Vote**	
Pop. 2000:	619,178	0.3% Native Am.	Bush (R) 157,734	(63%)
Median income:	$55,059	0.0% Hawaiian	Gore (D) 91,353	(36%)
Poverty status:	6.2%	0.8% Two+ races	Other 2,066	(1%)
Military veterans:	12.4%	0.1% Other	**Cook Partisan Voting Index:** R +14	
		3.5% Hispanic Origin		

Occupation	Blue collar: 20.4%	White collar: 69.5%	Gray collar: 10.2%

"An agreeable village but in a damn rebellious country," recorded General Cornwallis when, before the unpleasantness at Yorktown, he visited Charlotte, North Carolina. "A veritable nest of hornets." This town, settled by Scots-Irish and German colonists who came down the Blue Ridge from Pennsylvania, is now a metropolitan area of 1.4 million people. Before the California gold rush, Charlotte was the gold mining capital of the country; in 1837, the U.S. Mint established a branch here. Now, Charlotte is headquarters to two of the nation's biggest banks: Bank of America, formed from the 1998 merger of Charlotte-based NationsBank and San Francisco's Bank of America; and Wachovia, created by the 2001 merger of Charlotte's First Union and Winston-Salem's Wachovia. All told, almost $1 trillion in banking resources are headquartered in Charlotte—more than in any American city except New York. Charlotte is also home to eight members of the Fortune 500, including Duke Energy, Sonic Automotive, B.F. Goodrich and Nucor; it is the center of the nation's biggest textile manufacturing region, and serves as an airline hub for USAirways.

The past two decades have brought Charlotte cultural growth worthy of its growing business stature. It now boasts a $50 million performing arts center across from 60-story Bank of America tower, and is home to the expansion NFL Panthers and a new NBA franchise owned by Black Entertainment Television founder Robert Johnson. (A feuding owner spirited away the city's first NBA expansion team, the Hornets, to New Orleans.) The rebelliousness Cornwallis noted can still be seen in this region's passion for the booming stock-car circuit: One of the nation's biggest auto-racing tracks is here, and just up the road is Mooresville, home of the sport's giant, the late Dale Earnhardt. Charlotte has also built a boosterish pride in its capacity for accommodation. It is proud that it responded amicably to a busing order approved in a landmark Supreme Court case in 1971; that it twice elected Harvey Gantt, who is black, then replaced him with Sue Myrick, a Republican woman whose grievance wasn't race but traffic.

The 9th Congressional District includes about half of Mecklenburg County; it extends west to include most of Gaston County, long a textile center, and south to take in upscale bedroom communities in fast-growing Union County. Democratic redistricters happily made this district more Republican, in order to keep Republican precincts out of the 8th and 12th Districts. Mecklenburg County as a whole is politically marginal, with a large black minority and some neighborhoods of affluent white liberals, but the 9th District is overwhelmingly Republican.

The congresswoman from the 9th District is Sue Myrick, a Republican first elected in 1994. Myrick grew up and went to college in Ohio, raised her family in Charlotte, owned an advertising agency and Amway distributorship. In 1981 she ran for the Charlotte city council and lost. She ran again and won in 1983, ran for mayor and lost in 1985, then beat Harvey Gantt in 1987. Despite nasty personal charges, she was reelected in 1989; she is proud of making infrastructure improvements, bringing the NFL Carolina Panthers to Charlotte, and preventing property tax increases for four years. Myrick ran for the Senate in 1992, but was beaten by Lauch Faircloth in the primary 48%–30%. In 1994 Charlotte Congressman Alex McMillan, passed over for the ranking position on Budget, retired. In the first round of the primary, against State House Minority Leader David Balmer, Myrick led by just 34%–28%. But before the runoff three weeks later, it was revealed that Balmer had falsely claimed on his resume to have graduated in the top 20% of his law school class and to have played varsity soccer. Myrick won 68%–32%, then easily won the general.

Myrick was a proud leader of the 1994 Republican freshman class. She served on Newt Gingrich's transition team and was her class liaison to the leadership. On the Budget Committee, she co-chaired a task force on privatizing HUD functions, supported a flat-rate income tax and sponsored a bill for civil monetary penalties for making false statements in political ads. In January 1997, she was named to the Rules Committee. But she communicated with leaders of the unsuccessful coup against Gingrich in July 1997, and later that month lost the post of Conference secretary by 110–65 to Deborah Pryce, whom Gingrich backed.

Myrick, a firm conservative, has taken a lead role on many Republican initiatives. She initiated the bill to outlaw taking a child out of state to get an abortion to avoid a state parental notification law. Representing a prosperous and growing district, she turned down the Transportation Committee's offer of $15 million for Charlotte's outerbelt because she felt the transportation bill would bust the budget: "I said when I ran for this job, 'If you want somebody to bring home the bacon, don't send me.' We get a balanced budget agreement for the first time in 30 years, and now they do this?" But she is willing to help others: She set up a database so that Charlotte residents could help those in east Carolina recover from Hurricane Floyd. Following apparent congressional leaks of post-September 11 intelligence data, Myrick proposed that members of Congress undergo the same background checks as non-elected security officials. Not surprisingly, the bill was not passed; an expert at congressional procedure said that criminal penalties already exist for any such leak, but that the law is difficult to enforce because a prosecutor must prove intent. With relatively few textile workers in her district, she voted for trade promotion authority, contending that critics in that industry were "standing outside, throwing stones."

After the 1998 election Myrick ran for another leadership position, vice chairman of the Republican Conference, but lost. She was more successful in 2000, when she was named one of two vice chairmen of the Republican platform committee; under her experienced gavel, the proceedings on the foreign policy planks proceeded briskly. Following the 2002 election, Myrick filed a change in the rules of the House Republican Conference to require that each of 13 Appropriations subcommittee chairmen secure leadership approval; Speaker Dennis Hastert modified the proposal to give the review power to the leadership's Steering Committee, and it was approved. In 2003, she became chairman of the Republican Study Committee, activist conservatives who have urged spending restraint.

Myrick had surgery for breast cancer in December 1999 and underwent three months of chemotherapy and another six weeks of radiation treatment. Following that, she sponsored the law to provide Medicaid coverage for low-income women for mammograms and Pap smears, and was critical when Bill Clinton signed it in private in October 2000 to deny a photo opportunity to co-sponsor Rick Lazio, who was running for the Senate against his wife. Myrick became co-chairman of the Cancer Caucus, and co-sponsored with Nita Lowey a bill to require the National Institutes of Health to explore the connection between the environment and cancer. Myrick was declared cancer-free and has continued to win reelection easily. She considered, but quickly decided against, Senate bids in 2002 and 2004.

TENTH DISTRICT

Rep. Cass Ballenger (R)

Elected 1986, 9th term; b. Dec. 6, 1926, Hickory; home, Hickory; U. of NC, Amherst Col., B.A. 1948; Episcopalian; married (Donna).

Military Career: Naval Air Corps, 1944–45.

Elected Office: Catawba Cnty. Bd. of Commissioners, 1966–74, Chmn. 1970–74; NC House of Reps., 1974–76; NC Senate, 1976–86.

Professional Career: Businessman; Pres., Hickory Paper Box Co., 1948–70; Founder & Pres., Plastic Packaging Inc., 1957–present.

DC Office: 2182 RHOB 20515, 202-225-2576; Fax: 202-225-0316; Web site: www.house.gov/ballenger.

District Office: Hickory, 828-327-6100.

Committees: *Education & the Workforce* (3d of 27 R): Employer-Employee Relations; Workforce Protections. *International Relations* (8th of 26 R): International Terrorism, Nonproliferation and Human Rights; Western Hemisphere (Chmn.).

Group Ratings

	ADA	ACLU	AFS	LCV	CON	ITIC	NTU	COC	ACU	NTLC	CHC
2002	0	7	0	0	60	100	55	90	96	80	100
2001	0	—	0	0	—	—	60	95	88	—	—

National Journal Ratings

	2001 LIB	—	2001 CONS		2002 LIB	—	2002 CONS
Economic	20%	—	80%		13%	—	85%
Social	41%	—	60%		32%	—	63%
Foreign	4%	—	87%		0%	—	85%

Key Votes of the 107th Congress

1. Approve Bush Tax Cuts	Y	5. Faith-Based Charities	Y	9. Trade Promotion Authority	Y
2. Limit Patients' Bill of Rights	Y	6. Bar Gays in the Boy Scouts	Y	10. Bar Funds for Intl. Court	Y
3. Campaign Finance Reform	N	7. Ban Partial-Birth Abortion	Y	11. Authorize Force in Iraq	Y
4. Ban ANWR Development	N	8. Arm Commercial Pilots	Y	12. Deny Home. Sec. Dept. Union	Y

Election Results

2002 general	Cass Ballenger (R)	102,768	(59%)	($640,420)
	Ron Daugherty (D)	65,587	(38%)	($295,383)
	Other	4,937	(3%)	
2002 primary	Cass Ballenger (R)	unopposed		
2000 general	Cass Ballenger (R)	164,182	(68%)	($266,557)
	Delmas Parker (D)	70,877	(29%)	
	Other	5,599	(2%)	

Prior Winning Percentages: 1998 (86%); 1996 (70%); 1994 (72%); 1992 (63%); 1990 (62%); 1988 (61%); 1986 (57%); 1986 (58%)

The People		Race/Ethnic Origin	Ancestry	
Area size:	3,362 sq. mi.	84.9% White	USA: 16.5%	German: 10.4%
Urban population:	49.9%	9.2% Black	English: 6.9%	
Rural population:	50.1%	1.5% Asian	**2000 Presidential Vote**	
Pop. 2000:	619,178	0.2% Native Am.	Bush (R) 143,124 (65%)	
Median income:	$37,649	0.0% Hawaiian	Gore (D) 75,592 (34%)	
Poverty status:	10.6%	0.7% Two+ races	Other 1,693 (1%)	
Military veterans:	12.8%	0.1% Other	**Cook Partisan Voting Index:** R +16	
		3.5% Hispanic Origin		

Occupation	Blue collar: 41.9%	White collar: 45.4%	Gray collar: 12.6%

Steeped in the hues that gave them the name "Blue Ridge," the heavily wooded mountains of North Carolina seem placid and ancient. Geologically, they are some of the oldest ranges in the world; economically, the region is blue collar and oriented towards manufacturing, though there is some cotton farming, too. During the 1990s, residents here benefited from investment in fiber-optic factories, which, along with the general economic boom, helped reduce the local unemployment rate to near-record lows. But the Internet bust deflated hurt the fiber optic business and textiles and furniture were also troubled, and the local unemployment rate rose. At the same time, this corner of North Carolina is adapting—as are so many other rural areas in the U.S.—to growing diversity. County seats like Morganton in Burke County are now home not just to Hispanics but to newcomers from Laos; the influx of recent arrivals have occasionally prompted anti-immigrant backlash in this previously insular region, including the occasional rejection of school bond proposals on the grounds that they could help immigrants disproportionately. Ironically, this part of North Carolina desperately needs more education: The region around Hickory, in Catawba County, ranked dead last among the state's 11 metropolitan areas in education rates. According to the most recent Census, almost a third of adults in this district lacked a high-school degree.

The 10th Congressional District stretches from Tennessee, where the mountains are tall enough to support a modest ski industry, all the way south to the South Carolina border. It is a district comprised mostly of small towns; it is still predominantly white, ranges throughout 10 counties, and is bisected by the meandering Interstate 40, which runs the length of North Carolina from Wilmington in the east to Asheville in the west. The largest population center in the 10th is Hickory, which along with the rest of Catawba County accounts for just over 20% of the district's population. This remains a very Republican area—home to a rough-hewn, hill variety of Republicanism that is unsympathetic to government regulators, from factory inspectors to revenuers on the lookout for illegal stills. In 2000 George W. Bush won 65% of the vote here.

The congressman from the 10th District is Cass Ballenger, a Republican elected in 1986. Ballenger grew up in Hickory, enlisted in the Navy at 18, went to Amherst College and headed a paper box company. In 1957 he founded Plastic Packaging Inc. to make plastic wrappings for J.C. Penney underwear, and it grew to a payroll of 250 employees. He served on the Catawba County Board of Commissioners for eight years and in the state legislature for 12. In 1986, after Congressman James Broyhill was appointed to the Senate (he lost in November), Ballenger ran for the House. Promising to be a "Broyhill Republican," he beat a primary opponent backed by Jesse Helms. Ballenger has consistently won reelection by large margins.

Ballenger combines a moderate-to-conservative voting record with a sense of civic responsibility. He and his wife have organized humanitarian trips to Central and South America, delivering donated medical supplies and second-hand fire engines; Plastic Packaging sent a half-million plastic bags to Haiti to be used to grow eucalyptus seedlings to reforest the barren hills. When Democrats were in control of Congress, he opposed the Clinton health care plan, family and medical leave and striker replacement; he amended an OSHA law by exempting employers when violations are caused by employees breaking company work rules. When Republicans gained control, Ballenger became chairman of the Workforce Protections Subcommittee.

On this subcommittee Ballenger saw his job as updating labor laws that were out of line with flexible management and family-conscious employees. One response was the comp-time (or flex-time) bill, which would allow employees who work overtime to choose whether to receive overtime pay or compensatory time within the next year; federal employees have had this option since 1985. Comp-time passed the House in 1996 and again in 1997, but was fiercely opposed by the AFL-CIO, which argued that employers will coerce employees to take leave time, and it died in the Senate. Another major initiative was OSHA reform. Two of his proposals were enacted in 1998, the first free-standing changes in OSHA since it was established in 1970. One codified OSHA's own consultation program operated by the states; businesses could get advice without inviting adversarial proceedings. The second barred enforcement quotas and using enforcement activities as performance measures. In 2000 Ballenger led the battle against OSHA's proposed ergonomic standards, arguably the most burdensome regulations on business ever. The draft regulations, he argued, did not identify the hazards being regulated nor what employers needed to do to control or eliminate the hazards; he urged that the regulations be delayed until publication of a National Academy of Sciences study. The Clinton administration went ahead anyway, putting the standards into effect four days before Clinton left office. But in March 2001 the House voted to repeal them.

Term limits barred Ballenger from that chairmanship in 2001, and he became chairman of the Western Hemisphere Subcommittee on International Relations. Forging an unusual partnership with liberal Democrat Bill Delahunt, he had several cordial discussions with Venezuela president Hugo Chavez, who had manipulated the nation's constitution through plebiscites and faced serious domestic unrest. Ballenger contended that Chavez had significant accomplishments and that "his rhetoric is worse than his actions," though others were skeptical; Chavez reinforced the friendship by visiting his home in Hickory, where they ate barbecue. Ballenger wants to extend NAFTA to Central and South America and supported PNTR for China in 2000. But he was a very reluctant supporter of trade promotion authority, and in December 2001 he paced the House floor for a long time after the usual 15 minutes before finally voting aye. Ballenger said that he worried that his vote would generate unhappiness in his district.

Perhaps it did. In 2002 Ballenger was held below 60% of the vote for the first time since 1986. Facing self-financing textile mill owner Ron Daugherty, a former Republican and political newcomer opposed to free trade, Ballenger seemed offended by the challenge. "I don't understand why [Daugherty] wants to beat up an old man," he told a local reporter two weeks before the election. He refused to debate his challenger, though they had some joint appearances. Spending more than $200,000 of his own money, Daugherty ran ads depicting Ballenger as disconnected from his constituents and more interested in foreign junkets. But he received little attention from national Democrats or the news media. Ballenger won 59%–38%.

In December 2002, Ballenger suffered an embarrassing incident when he told a reporter for *The Charlotte Observer*, "I must admit I had segregationist feelings" after dealing with acerbic Representative Cynthia McKinney, who lost reelection that year. "I mean, she was such a bitch," he added. Ballenger, whose comments came in the midst of the controversy over remarks by Senator Trent Lott and were accompanied by his statement that Lott should resign as the Republican leader, apologized a day later. He said his comments were "pretty stupid on my part." Whatever Ballenger's future, it would take a major partisan shift for the 10th District to elect a Democrat.

ELEVENTH DISTRICT

Rep. Charles Taylor (R)

Elected 1990, 7th term; b. Jan. 23, 1941, Brevard; home, Brevard; Wake Forest U., B.A. 1963, J.D. 1966; Baptist; married (Elizabeth).

Elected Office: NC House of Reps., 1966–72, Min. Ldr., 1968–72; NC Senate, 1972–74, Min. Ldr., 1972–74.

Professional Career: Tree farmer.

DC Office: 231 CHOB 20515, 202-225-6401; Fax: 202-226-6422; Web site: www.house.gov/charlestaylor.

District Offices: Asheville, 828-251-1988; Hendersonville, 828-697-8539; Murphy, 828-837-3249; Rutherfordton, 828-286-8750; Waynesville, 828-456-7559.

Committees: *Appropriations* (8th of 36 R): Commerce, Justice, State & Judiciary; Interior (Chmn.).

Group Ratings

	ADA	ACLU	AFS	LCV	CON	ITIC	NTU	COC	ACU	NTLC	CHC
2002	5	7	11	13	50	50	56	90	96	89	100
2001	10	—	10	7	—	—	65	82	92	—	—

National Journal Ratings

	2001 LIB	—	2001 CONS		2002 LIB	—	2002 CONS
Economic	13%	—	86%		28%	—	69%
Social	0%	—	81%		0%	—	75%
Foreign	16%	—	82%		35%	—	60%

Key Votes of the 107th Congress

1. Approve Bush Tax Cuts	Y	5. Faith-Based Charities	Y	9. Trade Promotion Authority	N
2. Limit Patients' Bill of Rights	Y	6. Bar Gays in the Boy Scouts	Y	10. Bar Funds for Intl. Court	Y
3. Campaign Finance Reform	N	7. Ban Partial-Birth Abortion	Y	11. Authorize Force in Iraq	Y
4. Ban ANWR Development	N	8. Arm Commercial Pilots	Y	12. Deny Home. Sec. Dept. Union	Y

Election Results

2002 general	Charles Taylor (R)	112,335	(56%)	($1,416,941)
	Sam Neill (D)	86,664	(43%)	($586,033)
	Other	3,261	(2%)	
2002 primary	Charles Taylor (R)	unopposed		
2000 general	Charles Taylor (R)	146,677	(55%)	($1,555,039)
	Sam Neill (D)	112,234	(42%)	($851,434)
	Other	7,466	(3%)	

Prior Winning Percentages: 1998 (57%); 1996 (58%); 1994 (60%); 1992 (55%); 1990 (51%)

The People		Race/Ethnic Origin	Ancestry	
Area size:	6,088 sq. mi.	89.8% White	USA: 13.2%	English: 9.8%
Urban population:	43.9%	4.6% Black	German: 8.7%	
Rural population:	56.1%	0.5% Asian	**2000 Presidential Vote**	
Pop. 2000:	619,177	1.5% Native Am.	Bush (R).............150,004	(58%)
Median income:	$34,720	0.0% Hawaiian	Gore (D).............102,321	(40%)
Poverty status:	12.0%	0.9% Two+ races	Other...................4,514	(2%)
Military veterans:	15.6%	0.1% Other	**Cook Partisan Voting Index:** R +10	
		2.6% Hispanic Origin		

Occupation	Blue collar: 31.5%	White collar: 51.9%	Gray collar: 16.6%

Western North Carolina, the protrusion of the Tarheel state deep into the eastern United States' highest and oldest mountains, is a land of long and ornery traditions. First settled by whites not long after the Revolutionary War, it still has tiny Indian communities and hollows where people are descended from the first white settlers. Its biggest city, Asheville, was memorialized in Thomas Wolfe's novels; in the early 20th century, it served as a retreat for lung patients and for Zelda Fitzgerald during her long battle with mental illness. Asheville was also the home of the brilliant eccentric George Vanderbilt, who built the chateau-like Biltmore mansion amidst vast forests on which he pioneered scientific forestry. A dozen miles east was Black Mountain College, frequented by such innovators as Buckminster Fuller and minimalist composer John Cage. Asheville's historic structures, from Gothic Revival to Art Deco, remain well preserved and are a magnet for tourists, who in turn support some of the few coffeehouses, microbreweries and artsy cinemas within hours of here. Over a ridge is the Great Smoky Mountains National Park, the nation's most heavily visited, 20 degrees cooler in the summer than the lowland towns an hour or so away. The climate and the forested, green, fog-wisped mountains have attracted millions of tourists to this area—so many that, every summer, the park's one transverse road becomes hopelessly clogged with traffic.

The 11th District of North Carolina includes the western end of the state, including Asheville's Buncombe County, which accounts for one-third of the vote. Only 5% of the voters in the district are black, the lowest percentage in any district in North Carolina; 1.5% are Indians. The orneriness of the mountain country has been manifest in its politics. This part of the state was reluctant to secede in the Civil War. There were few slaves and many small farmers loyal to the Union, and those who took up the Confederate cause did so out of loyalty to Governor Zebulon Vance, an Asheville native and reluctant secessionist. For a long time, the partisan balance here was close, and for a dozen years the 11th was one of the nation's most closely contested districts, throwing out incumbents in five of six elections between 1980 and 1990. But in the last decade, coinciding with an influx of retirees in the mountains south of Asheville, it has tilted Republican. The current round of redistricting barely changed the borders, and it is now a solidly Republican district.

The congressman from the 11th District is Charles Taylor, a Republican elected in 1990. He grew up in Brevard, where he has been a tree farmer and one of the biggest private landholders in the area; his net worth is estimated at somewhere between $12 million and $57 million. He served in the legislature from 1966–74, and ran for Congress in 1988 and narrowly lost. In 1990 he ran again and won. Taylor has a very conservative voting record and has spent much energy on district projects. He worked to delay drawdowns of area lakes each year by the Tennessee Valley Authority until August 1, and later until October 1, to keep waters high for tourist season. He has worked for years on what he calls the Magnet Triangle economic development plan, to build three federal facilities which he says will double tourism in the area: The Blue Ridge Parkway head-quarters, the Cradle of Forestry interpretive center near Brevard, and the Oconaluftee museum and visitors' center. He ran a western North Carolina workforce consortium, to encourage training in skills needed in high-tech jobs. In January 2002 he got $4.3 million for a rural fiber optic network. He is working for funding for the Western Carolinas Biotechnology Consortium. In June 2002 he called on the Bush administration to declare the 25-county Blue Ridge region a national historic site.

Early in his House career Taylor was one of the members of 1991's Gang of Seven, Republican freshmen who pushed for full disclosure of overdrafts on the House bank and other congressional reforms. In 1996, the House passed his property-rights protection amendments to the National Biological Survey and the Montana Wilderness Act. Also passed was his amendment to stop EEOC guidelines he believed would promote religious harassment in workplaces. Taylor got a seat on Appropriations in 1993, and in 1997 became chairman of the District of Columbia Subcommittee.

In 2000 Taylor received an unexpectedly strong challenge and responded with unexpected strength. In May and August, two counties threatened to garnish Taylor's congressional pay for unpaid property taxes. Taylor paid $18,466 to one county and $29,658 to the other, and his lawyer said the dispute arose because Taylor claimed a forestry tax break the counties denied. "I have always paid the property taxes I owe. But I don't believe in paying property taxes I don't owe," Taylor said in an ad. North Carolina newspapers reported that a federal grand jury was investi-gating $1 million in loans from a bank controlled by Taylor to a supporter that were never repaid and that Taylor had extended high-interest loans to a former KGB officer for construction of apartments and commercial buildings in Russia. Taylor had articulate opposition from lawyer Sam Neill, former head of the University of North Carolina governing board. A Neill ad showed Taylor's large house and said, "Congressman Charles Taylor. He cheats on his local taxes, then blames everyone else." Taylor ran his own negative ads. After the Sierra Club ran ads against him, Taylor accused them of favoring using taxpayer money to take private property, banning hunting, raising gasoline taxes and using "your tax dollars for involuntary forced abortions in China." But Taylor also made a case for himself. In July 2000 he called for a GAO study of pollution in the Great Smokies National Park and introduced a bill to force the TVA to reduce sulfur dioxide and nitrogen oxide emissions 75% from 1997 levels by 2005; environmental groups called this a "complete charade" and Neill asked why Taylor had not aiming at pollution before. In September Taylor obtained $4 million funding to help the Foothills Conservancy protect land around Lake James. In October he got $2.5 million for the Asheville Regional Airport and funding to extend the "road to nowhere" north of Lake James to provide access to a cemetery blocked since the TVA flooded the area when it built Fontana Dam in 1943. In October 2000 Bill Cosby laid the groundwork for a Deliver the Dream retreat for families of seriously ill children, on 200 acres donated by Taylor and his family.

Taylor won 55%–42%, carrying all but one county. He ran behind George W. Bush's winning margin but only slightly down from his 57%–42% in 1998 and 58%–40% in 1996. In 2002 Neill ran again, but the campaign was quite different. Taylor's legal problems were mostly clarified. The president of the Taylor bank pleaded guilty to fraud and a bank lawyer was indicted, but federal prosecutors never questioned Taylor, and there seemed to be no evidence he was involved. Taylor appealed his tax cases to state boards and lost; he paid the taxes. North Carolina's primary was put off until September because of court redistricting suits, and Neill didn't spend much money or do much campaigning this time; most of his campaign funds came from his own money. Perhaps he ran on the chance that Taylor's legal problems would explode; when they didn't he just laid low and saved his money. The result was much the same as in 2000: Taylor won 56%–43%. In January 2003 Taylor switched to become chairman of the Interior Appropriations Subcommittee, a useful position for a man who represents America's most visited national park.

TWELFTH DISTRICT

Rep. Melvin Watt (D)

Elected 1992, 6th term; b. Aug. 26, 1945, Mecklenburg; home, Charlotte; U. of NC at Chapel Hill, B.S. 1967, Yale U., J.D. 1970; Presbyterian; married (Eulada).

Elected Office: NC Senate, 1984–86.

Professional Career: Practicing atty., 1971–92; Co–owner, East Town Manor nursing home, 1989–present; Campaign Mgr., Harvey Gantt Senate Campaign, 1990.

DC Office: 2236 RHOB 20515, 202-225-1510; Fax: 202-225-1512; Web site: www.house.gov/watt.

District Offices: Charlotte, 704-344-9950; Greensboro, 336-275-9950.

Committees: *Financial Services* (7th of 32 D): Domestic and International Monetary Policy, Trade & Technology; Financial Institutions & Consumer Credit; Housing & Community Opportunity. *Judiciary* (6th of 16 D): Commercial & Administrative Law (RMM); The Constitution. *Joint Economic Committee* (9th of 10 Reps.).

Group Ratings

	ADA	ACLU	AFS	LCV	CON	ITIC	NTU	COC	ACU	NTLC	CHC
2002	90	93	89	75	67	38	25	40	4	3	0
2001	95	—	100	79	—	—	10	30	0	—	—

National Journal Ratings

	2001 LIB —	2001 CONS	2002 LIB —	2002 CONS
Economic	95% —	0%	76% —	23%
Social	90% —	0%	100% —	0%
Foreign	90% —	10%	87% —	10%

Key Votes of the 107th Congress

1. Approve Bush Tax Cuts	N	5. Faith-Based Charities	N	9. Trade Promotion Authority	N
2. Limit Patients' Bill of Rights	N	6. Bar Gays in the Boy Scouts	N	10. Bar Funds for Intl. Court	N
3. Campaign Finance Reform	Y	7. Ban Partial-Birth Abortion	N	11. Authorize Force in Iraq	N
4. Ban ANWR Development	Y	8. Arm Commercial Pilots	N	12. Deny Home. Sec. Dept. Union	N

Election Results

2002 general	Melvin Watt (D)	98,821	(65%)	($358,869)
	Jeff Kish (R)	49,588	(33%)	($3,604)
	Other	2,830	(2%)	
2002 primary	Melvin Watt (D)	33,853	(85%)	
	Kimberly Holley (D)	6,107	(15%)	
2000 general	Melvin Watt (D)	135,570	(65%)	($361,869)
	Chad Mitchell (R)	69,596	(33%)	($25,254)
	Other	3,978	(2%)	

Prior Winning Percentages: 1998 (56%); 1996 (71%); 1994 (66%); 1992 (70%)

The People		Race/Ethnic Origin	Ancestry	
Area size:	827 sq. mi.	44.6% White	USA: 8.0%	German: 6.5%
Urban population:	88.5%	44.6% Black	English: 4.6%	
Rural population:	11.5%	2.1% Asian	**2000 Presidential Vote**	
Pop. 2000:	619,178	0.4% Native Am.	Gore (D)..............115,445 (57%)	
Median income:	$35,775	0.0% Hawaiian	Bush (R)..............85,950 (42%)	
Poverty status:	15.9%	1.1% Two + races	Other...................1,495 (1%)	
Military veterans:	11.3%	0.1% Other	**Cook Partisan Voting Index:** D + 7	
		7.1% Hispanic Origin		

Occupation	Blue collar: 32.1%	White collar: 51.9%	Gray collar: 16.0%

"This is perhaps the Negro's temporary farewell to Congress," said George White, a Tarboro, North Carolina lawyer and Republican, in his last days in the House of Representatives in 1901. Segregation was being imposed by law, and blacks informally but effectively were being stricken from the voting rolls in the rural South. It was 28 years until another black candidate was elected to Congress, and 70 years until another African American won in the South. In North Carolina, blacks have played a role politically ever since the Voting Rights Act of 1965, yet White's prophecy was not overturned until 1992, when two African Americans were elected. One, Eva Clayton, hailed from the mostly rural and small-town 1st District—the kind of country where most blacks lived in White's day. The other, Melvin Watt, represents the new 12th District, whose original boundaries connected blacks in such far-flung cities as Charlotte, Winston-Salem and Greensboro.

The 12th Congressional District, was the most litigated and infamous district in the country during the 1990s, and was considered no less than four times by the Supreme Court. Its original shape—a series of scattered black precincts connected in some places by nothing wider than the lanes of Interstate 85—stretched 160 miles from Gastonia, west of Charlotte, through Winston-Salem and Greensboro all the way to Durham. In the current version, the 12th remains a 100-mile-long, snake-like agglomeration that roughly parallels I-85 and includes black voters in and near Charlotte, Winston-Salem, Greensboro, Lexington, Salisbury and High Point. A near-majority, 45%, of its residents are black. The Charlotte-area precincts account for one-third of the district population, while the Winston-Salem portion accounts for a little under 20% and Greensboro has about 10%. The district gave only 42% of the vote to George W. Bush in 2000.

The congressman from the 12th District since it was created in 1992 has been Mel Watt, a Democrat. Watt grew up in a place called Dixie outside Charlotte, now overgrown with woods, in a tin-roofed house with no electricity or running water. His dream was to attend the University of North Carolina, and he was one of the first black students there; he made a fine academic record, went on to Yale Law School, and then to a civil rights law practice in Charlotte. Today he owns an elderly care facility and is part owner of McDonald's Cafeteria and Hotel in Charlotte—and has been starting pitcher on the House Democrats' baseball team. He served one term in the state Senate, then decided not to seek office again until his sons completed high school. He managed Harvey Gantt's campaigns for city council and mayor in the 1980s and for the U.S. Senate in 1990.

In 1992 Watt decided to run in the 12th District. The contest turned out to be the kind of friends-and-neighbors Democratic primary common in the old segregated South. Watt took 47% of all votes in a four-way race, well over the 40% necessary for victory without a runoff in North Carolina; his base in Charlotte was bigger than those of his rivals, and he made inroads in other counties as well. He won the general election easily, and on election night said he was "saddened that it took 92 years" to elect another black member from the state, "and I'm disappointed, because I know that thousands and thousands of people, but for the color of their skin, would have been just as qualified to fill this office."

In the House, Watt has compiled a liberal voting record. He has voted against crime bills because of their death penalty provisions, against gun bans in urban housing projects, against increased prison sentences for crimes against children because he said that would interfere with the U.S. Sentencing Commission's autonomy. He vehemently opposed the 1996 Welfare Reform

Act; and he cast the only vote in the House against Megan's Law requiring registration of convicted sex offenders because, he said, individuals ought to be able to get on with their lives once they have paid their debt to society. On the partial-birth abortion ban, he wanted to put the burden on the state of proving a woman's life in danger. As a member of the Judiciary Committee, Watt was a vehement opponent of the impeachment of Bill Clinton. When the same committee in June 2001 debated George W. Bush's plan to assist faith-based social services, Watt said that he was made nauseous by a proposed resolution to honor George Washington for his letter to a Rhode Island synagogue in support of religious tolerance. "For us to be applauding the statements discussing bigotry that were written by a person who owned slaves is a little bit more than I can, without a churning stomach, be able to tolerate," Watt told the committee. He abstained from voting on the resolution that was offered by congressman Patrick Kennedy. When the bill reached the House floor three weeks later, Watt tried unsuccessfully to remove provisions that permit religious groups to receive federal funds to hire people only of their own faith. After September 11, he urged colleagues to protect privacy while they increased law-enforcement powers to nab terrorists.

Although it has been difficult to keep up with the many twists and turns in the composition of the 12th District since he was first elected, like many incumbents before him, Watt has shown the ability to entrench himself with voters regardless of their race. His toughest reelection contest came in the 1998 general, when the 12th District extended only from Charlotte to Winston-Salem and the black share of the population had shrunk to 36%. Republican nominee Scott Keadle, a Rowan County dentist and property developer, called for major tax cuts, attacked Watt as an "extreme liberal," and concentrated on his vote against Megan's Law. In their final debate, Watt defended his vote by saying, "Would the next step be to register everyone who commits a murder?" But later he conceded that his vote had been wrong and said that he twice voted for funding for state compliance with the law. Watt won 56%–42%, with support from the district's many white liberals, more numerous in this mostly urban district than in the mostly rural 1st District. "There are still whites who under no circumstances will vote for a black person," Watt has said. He also said, "I'd like to think it's an indication that race is becoming less of a factor as we go along." In the separate but still non-contiguous lines used in the 2000 and 2002 election, Watt ran against two political novices with little financial support and in each case raised his victory margin back to a secure 65%–33%. Some Democrats grumbled that Watt should have agreed to shift more of his black voters to either the 6th or 8th District in the interest of eventually defeating a Republican incumbent. But they were unwilling to challenge him publicly when Watt said of his constituents, "They like being in my district, and I like representing them."

THIRTEENTH DISTRICT

Rep. Brad Miller (D)

Elected 2002, 1st term; b. May 19, 1953, Fayetteville; home, Raleigh; U. of NC, B.A. 1975, London Schl. of Economics, M.S.C. 1978, Columbia U., J.D. 1979; Episcopalian; married (Esther Hall).

Elected Office: NC House of Reps., 1992–94; NC Senate, 1996–02.

Professional Career: Clerk, Judge J. Dickson Phillips Jr., U.S. Fourth Circuit Ct. of Appeals, Durham, 1979–80; Practicing atty., 1980–02.

DC Office: 1505 LHOB 20515, 202-225-3032; Fax: 202-225-0181; Web site: www.house.gov/bradmiller.

District Offices: Greensboro, 336-574-2909; Raleigh, 919-781-9101.

Committees: *Financial Services* (29th of 32 D): Capital Markets, Insurance & Government Sponsored Enterprises; Housing & Community Opportunity. *Science* (12th of 22 D): Energy; Environment, Technology and Standards. *Small Business* (16th of 17 D).

Group Ratings and Key Votes: Newly Elected

Election Results

2002 general	Brad Miller (D)	100,287	(55%)	($989,529)
	Carolyn Grant (R)	77,688	(42%)	($416,344)
	Other	5,295	(3%)	
2002 primary	Brad Miller (D)	22,130	(40%)	
	Robin Britt (D)	13,490	(24%)	
	Bill Martin (D)	8,021	(15%)	
	Lawrence Davis (D)	6,911	(13%)	
	Gene Gay (D)	2,459	(4%)	
	Ronnie Ansley (D)	2,168	(4%)	

The People		Race/Ethnic Origin	Ancestry	
Area size:	2,294 sq. mi.	63.3% White	USA: 10.0%	English: 8.7%
Urban population:	73.7%	26.9% Black	German: 6.8%	
Rural population:	26.3%	2.0% Asian	**2000 Presidential Vote**	
Pop. 2000:	619,178	0.3% Native Am.	Bush (R) 113,600 (50%)	
Median income:	$41,060	0.0% Hawaiian	Gore (D) 112,953 (49%)	
Poverty status:	11.6%	1.2% Two+ races	Other 2,429 (1%)	
Military veterans:	11.3%	0.2% Other	**Cook Partisan Voting Index:** R + 0	
		6.0% Hispanic Origin		

Occupation	Blue collar: 25.7%	White collar: 60.5%	Gray collar: 13.8%

In the last two decades, metropolitan growth has come to some of the long humble countryside of North Carolina. A generation ago, Raleigh, Durham, Burlington and Greensboro were a string of small cities connected by I-85 across the central Piedmont, moderately prosperous, with textile, tobacco and furniture factories, but not very big: just a few miles from the center of town and farm fields started, dotted by country towns with barbecue restaurants and churches. The counties to the north were almost purely rural, with a few factory towns. Today the booming metropolitan areas of North Carolina have spread far beyond the old city limits and county lines into the adjacent counties. The fastest-growing county in North Carolina in the 1990s was Wake County, which includes Raleigh, but there was also substantial growth in the counties west along I-85 and even in the counties in the north. Rural roads are now clogged in the morning with commuters headed for jobs in the new office parks and income levels have risen far above what they once were.

Much of this territory now makes up the 13th Congressional District, a district created after North Carolina, to the surprise of just about everybody, gained a new House seat from the 2000 Census. Almost half, 47%, of its residents live in Wake County. It includes the center of Raleigh, a tangent going off to North Carolina State University and much of the northern part of the county, but includes relatively few of the affluent new subdivisions that are mostly in the 4th District. Another 18% of its residents live in Guilford County, where it includes black neighborhoods and the University of North Carolina's Greensboro campus. The rest of the district includes all or almost all of four counties to the north, up to the Virginia border—Granville, Person, Caswell, Rockingham—historically rural and Democratic, with fairly large black percentages. The district lines were drawn by the Democratic legislature to produce a new Democratic district, one of the few created in the South in recent decades which does not have a majority or near-majority of blacks; only 27% of its residents are black. But the rural counties have an historical heritage, and university neighborhoods are heavily Democratic.

The congressman from the 13th District is Brad Miller, a Democrat elected in 2002. Born and raised in Fayetteville by his widowed mother, a school bookkeeper, Miller graduated from the University of North Carolina and got a master's degree at the London School of Economics and a law degree from Columbia. After clerking for a federal appeals court judge, he began practicing law in Raleigh in 1980. In 1992, he was elected to the state House, where he authored a safe gun storage law. But he was swept away after one term in the 1994 Republican landslide. He was elected in 1996 to the state Senate, where he focused on education issues, including steps to reduce class size, increase teacher pay, and improve computer and Internet access in rural communities. Like many members of the House, he had a hand in drawing his own district as chairman of the Senate's redistricting committee.

Miller drew a district very much in his political interest, but he couldn't be sure that he could run in the seat he had drawn for himself. That was because Utah brought a lawsuit against the Census Bureau, arguing that because the census counted servicemen with legal residence in a state but serving overseas as part of the state's apportionment population, it should also count Mormon missionaries domiciled in a state but serving overseas. North Carolina has a lot of servicemen, but Utah has many more Mormon missionaries, and such a count would have increased Utah's population enough that it, rather than North Carolina, would have gotten the 435th district under the formula dictated by a 1928 law. Utah lost in federal court and appealed; in June 2002 the U.S. Supreme Court unanimously affirmed and North Carolina kept its 13th District. Until then, candidates had found it difficult to raise campaign money or routinely campaign. With the Court's ruling, four experienced Democrats launched an 11-week sprint to the September 10 primary, which was likely to etermine the winner in November. Besides Miller, they were state Senator Billy Martin, who is black; former state legislator and party chairman Lawrence Davis, who ran as a conservative; and former Representative Robin Britt, who was elected in 1982 and then lost two close contests to Howard Coble in the old 6th District before becoming executive director of the United Child Development Services. Miller raised the most money and got early endorsements from labor unions, teachers' unions and the League of Conservation Voters; he also had a geographic advantage because he is from Wake County, which includes nearly half of the district's population. He got a boost when he was he was endorsed by the Raleigh-Wake Citizens Association, a group of black activists. In the primary, Miller led with 40% to 24% for Britt, 15% for Martin and 13% for Davis. Britt won the four western counties, where his name was familiar. But Wake County cast 49% of the vote, and Miller won 58% of the vote there to only 10% for Britt.

In the general, Miller faced Caroline Grant, a commercial real-estate broker and former head of the Raleigh Chamber of Commerce. Grant, who ran unsuccessfully for Raleigh Mayor as a Democrat in 1999 and then switched parties, called Miller a tax-and-spend Democrat, referring to his support for $1 billion in new taxes in the recent legislative session, but also criticizing him for voting to cut prescription drug assistance for the elderly. Miller said that North Carolina had the second-best record of any state in cutting taxes during the prior six years and that he supported elimination of the sales tax on food. When he pointed out that Grant had contributed to his campaign in 1998, she responded that she did not know "how liberal" he was. Miller ran an ad on court complaints against Grant for taking money from her son's college trust fund to buy a car and pay for her campaign expenses. She responded that she had replenished the fund. Grant, who called herself pro-choice on abortion, won support from National Right to Life because the group agreed with her position on other issues. But she got little help from national Republicans and Miller won 55%–42%. He took all seven counties, including 52% in Wake.

★ NORTH DAKOTA ★

For more than a century after statehood, North Dakota remained as close to its roots as any other state. Yet in its second century there are signs of change ahead. North Dakota was settled and its farm economy developed in a short generation. There are North Dakotans alive today who knew the men and women that settled this land and saw the state enter the Union in 1889. As children, they walked in the ruts left by the early settlers' wagon trains; they saw the Indians, recently defeated, herded onto reservations; they saw still shining new the rails that brought the world's commerce to these desolate prairies. This was the frontier to which Teddy Roosevelt came in 1884, determined to shoot one of the fast-disappearing buffalo, a place where settlers were only then breaking the sod and plowing under the natural prairies that are still preserved in a few places. This was some of the best wheat land in the world, empty by then of Indians and buffalo, connected to markets by rail, ready to become a cog in the industrial world being created by entrepreneurs and to raise its living standards to unparalleled heights.

And so, in a sudden rush of settlement during the 20 years before World War I, North Dakota filled up to pretty much its present population. There were 632,000 people here in 1920 and in

Fargo

RICHLAND

Grand Forks

PEMBINA

WALSH

TRAIL

CASS

GRAND FORKS

RANSOM

SARGENT

STEELE

NELSON

GRIGGS

BARNES

CAVALIER

RAMSEY

LAMOURE

DICKEY

EDDY

FOSTER

STUTSMAN

TOWNER

BENSON

LOGAN

MCINTOSH

ROLETTE

WELLS

PIERCE

KIDDER

SHERIDAN

BURLEIGH

EMMONS

BOTTINEAU

MCHENRY

Bismarck

Minot

MCLEAN

OLIVER

MORTON

SIOUX

WARD

RENVILLE

MERCER

GRANT

MOUNTRAIL

DUNN

STARK

HETTINGER

ADAMS

BURKE

Williston

WILLIAMS

MCKENZIE

BILLINGS

SLOPE

BOWMAN

DIVIDE

GOLDEN VALLEY

Miles

0 10 20

N
W E
S

The Almanac of American Politics.
National Journal

U.S. Representative elected at-large.

counts since, the number has fluctuated between 617,000 and 680,000. In the 2000 Census it was 642,000, and cumulatively it is the state with the lowest growth rate since 1950. Wheat is not the only crop here, there are also pinto beans and soybeans and sunflowers, and as the plains become more arid in the west, ranching and livestock grazing—along with strip mining and oil and natural gas production—are important; hardy root crops like potatoes and sugar beets grow as well. But wheat is still number one. Typically the state produces about one-tenth of the U.S. crop, and a fair percentage of the world's; its durum wheat is the main ingredient of American pasta. North Dakota has few big businesses—its leading high-tech firm Great Plains Software was bought by Microsoft in 2001—and it attracts few tourists; it is the state least visited by other Americans. It worries about losing its young people; the number of 20-to-34-year-olds declined 16% in the 1990s. But North Dakotans—who debated proposals to change the state's name to Dakota in 1947, 1983, 1989 and 2001—also has things to be proud of. North Dakota coal mine companies have gotten awards for reclamation and admiration for the respect they've shown Indian gravesites; North Dakota Air National Guard F-16s patrolled the skies of Washington after September 11; the voters of Hettinger County (population 2,715) in 2002 elected North Dakota's first black sheriff.

Its dependence on agriculture shaped North Dakota's politics. Farmers, as much as they like to extol their way of life, are seldom content with the workings of the market. When prices are high, it is often because of low production; when they are low, farmers seek protection. The boosterish optimism of the first settlers was soon followed by cries reverberating with varying intensity for government protection against market forces. Since commodity prices tend to fall during periods of economic growth, there has been a countercyclical element in North Dakota politics, a tendency to vote against the national trends, and a radical strain going back to the 1910s and still lively in recent years. That radical strain also owes much to the immigrant origins of so many of North Dakota's early settlers: Norwegians in the eastern part of the state, Canadians along the northern border, colonies of Poles and Czechs and Icelanders, and native Germans throughout the state.

These immigrants produced orderly small towns and grain and other cooperatives; they also provided support for the Non-Partisan League, which flourished from its founding in 1915 to its alliance with the Democratic Party around 1960. It appealed to marginal farmers, cut off in many cases from the wider American culture by language barriers and seemingly at the mercy of the grain millers in Minneapolis, the railroads of St. Paul, the banks of New York and the commodity traders of Chicago. The NPL's program was socialist—government ownership of railroads and grain elevators—and, like most North Dakota ethnics, it opposed going to war with Germany. The NPL often determined the outcome of the usually decisive Republican primary and sometimes swung its support to the otherwise heavily outnumbered Democrats, instituting reforms and creating a state-owned bank. By 1960, the NPL had more or less merged into the Democratic Party, a merger symbolized by the election of the late Democratic Senator Quentin Burdick, whose father, Usher Burdick, served 20 years in the House as an NPL-endorsed Republican. North Dakota's leading Democrats of recent decades, Senators Kent Conrad and Byron Dorgan, have championed a politics clearly of NPL lineage: For government farm programs, wary if not hostile to American military involvement abroad, and cheerfully championing the little guy from North Dakota against out-of-state corporations.

This is a place where everyone knows everyone else; for years there has been no voter registration because people obviously spot anyone not eligible. This communal closeness has produced an innate conservatism in North Dakota. Divorce is as uncommon here as anywhere in the United States, the two-parent family is still very much the norm and abortions are available in only one clinic in the whole state. North Dakota is proud that its students achieve some of the nation's highest math scores, even though its teacher pay is among the lowest in the country; it has one of the highest rates of students going on to college and one of the lowest rates of student loan defaults. Politics is personal, too, in a state where every politician is known to many voters. North Dakota is one of only three states with an all-Democratic congressional delegation (Massachusetts and Hawaii are the others). The two senators and congressman are all allies who have worked together for years, since the 1974 campaign when Byron Dorgan, now junior Senator, ran for the House, and lost. His campaign manager was Kent Conrad, now senior Senator, and their driver was Earl Pomeroy, now Congressman-at-large. Dorgan pioneered and Conrad followed attempts to attribute out-of-state corporations' earnings to North Dakota operations and then tax them—very small potatoes to most big companies, but very helpful for thrift-minded, suspicious-of-big-corporations traditional North Dakota voters.

Yet there are signs of change even in this settled commonwealth. And not just from natural disasters, though they have left scars. The 1997 flooding of Grand Forks left 70,000 people—11% of the state's population—out of their homes as the Red River rose 26 feet above flood stage; despite volunteer help and rallies, many homes and buildings were not replaced two years later. A devastating rainstorm hit Fargo in 2000. North Dakota's missile silos, a taken-for-granted sight in its farm fields, are now being destroyed. Meanwhile, gargantuan animal statues are raised over near-deserted highways—New Salem Sue, the world's largest Holstein cow; the Jamestown Buffalo, the world's largest catfish, a turtle crafted out of 2,000 old tires, a monster grasshopper and a giant sandhill crane, an iron pipe silhouette of Teddy Roosevelt. But most important, the land seems to be emptying out. Increasing agricultural productivity has meant fewer farmers living directly off the land, and more people living in towns and off other industries. "There's a real concern that we're probably seeing the last generation on the land," says University of North Dakota sociologist Curtis Stofferahn. In hundreds of small towns, local city halls are padlocked, banks are open just three hours a week, and bars have closed. The Freedom to Farm Act of 1996 has been replaced by the more generous 2002 farm bill, but the number of farmers continues to decline. At the same time, North Dakota's small cities have grown. Back in 1955 North Dakota-born sociologist Carl Kraenzel predicted in *The Great Plains in Transition* that sutland communities (places on transportation lines) would grow and yonland communities (places away from transportation lines); and so it has happened. North Dakota's four biggest counties, containing Fargo, Grand Forks, Bismarck and Minot, grew from 134,000 in 1930 to 317,000 in 2000, while the state's other 49 counties dropped from 546,000 to 325,000; in 2000, these four counties cast half the state's votes. The good news is that unemployment is low and the economy stable; in late 2002 North Dakota was one of 10 states with a "stable or optimistic" state budget outlook. Family farmers, as their numbers decline, no longer seem to have the critical mass to drive politics; there is less talk of helping farmers and more demands for better airline connections. In effect, North Dakota is developing the demographics of the Rocky Mountain states, with population concentrated in a few cities and towns.

On balance, these developments tend to undermine the state's radical tradition. If the typical elderly North Dakotan is a hard-working retired farmer, with fond memories of NPL agitation and a belief in government programs, the typical young North Dakotan is a family person with a college education more trusting of markets and the private sector. North Dakotans have noticed that nearby South Dakota has attracted white-collar jobs with low tax rates and that North Dakota, with its higher taxes and pro-government traditions, is the Great Plains state with the lowest population growth in the 1990s—up 3,400 people, or 0.5%. This is a state that Bill Clinton did not come close to carrying, and George W. Bush won here in 2000 by a 61%–33% margin. At the same time, Republican John Hoeven was elected governor over the strong candidacy of Democrat Heidi Heitkamp by a 55%–45% margin. To be sure, Democrats Conrad and Pomeroy have been re-elected, but Pomeroy's margin was down to 52%–48% in 2002—his closest race ever. It's too soon to say that North Dakota has moved away from its radical political roots, but a conservative strain in its heritage is asserting itself.

The People

Pop. 2000:	642,200
Pop. 1990:	638,800
Change 1990–2000:	Up 0.5%
Change 1980–1990:	Down 2.1%
% of U.S. total:	0.2%
Pop. rank:	47th of 50
Area size:	70,700 sq. mi.
State Native:	72.5%
Non-citizen:	1.1%

Language

English: 90.1%	Other Eur.: 6.5%
Spanish: 2.1%	

Race/Ethnic Origin

589,149	91.7%	White
3,761	0.6%	Black
3,566	0.6%	Asian
30,772	4.8%	Native Am.
218	0.0%	Hawaiian
6,666	1.0%	Two+ races
282	0.0%	Other
7,786	1.2%	Hisp. Origin

Ancestry

German: 30.6% Norwegian: 20.9%
Irish: 5.4% Swedish: 3.5%
English: 3.4%

Military veterans: 61,365 (12.7%)
WWII: 19.8% Korea: 14.1%
Vietnam: 32.7% Gulf War: 11.3%

Most populous cities:

1. Fargo	90,599
2. Bismarck	55,532
3. Grand Forks	49,321
4. Minot	36,567
5. Mandan	16,718

Urban population: 55.8%
Rural population: 44.2%

Education

H.S. Grad:	83.9%
College Grad:	22.0%

Industry

Agri: 8.2%	Con: 6.2%
Fin: 5.9%	Info: 2.3%
Mfg: 12.8%	Prof: 30.2%
Public: 4.8%	Trade: 16.4%
Other: 13.1%	

Occupation

Blue collar: 22.2%	White collar: 59.4%
Gray collar: 18.4%	

Work Sector

Private: 72.2%	Govt: 16.5%
Self: 10.7%	Family: 0.6%

Unemployment: 4.5%

Household Income

<15k: 19.0%	15-35k: 31.5%
35-50k: 18.6%	50-100k: 25.2%
100-150k: 3.8%	>150k: 1.9%

Median: $34,604
Poverty status: 11.9%

Home Value

<50k: 34.5%	50-100k: 41.2%	100-200k: 20.8%	200-300k: 2.4%
300-500k: 0.8%	>500k: 0.3%	Median: $68,300	

Legislative Assembly

Senate	31 R 16 D
House	66 R 28 D

Legislative Term Limits: No

Registered Voters

No state voter registration

Presidential politics

Massachusetts and Hawaii, the other states with all-Democratic congressional delegations, are heavily Democratic in presidential elections; North Dakota is heavily Republican. In olden days, North Dakota veered toward Democrats when farm prices fell; in 2000, though prices were low, it voted heavily Republican.

With a tiny number of delegates, an out-of-the-way location and frigid weather in the early primary season, North Dakota does not loom large in choosing presidential nominees. In 2000, the February 29 Republican caucuses attracted 9,100 North Dakotans; George W. Bush got 14 of the 19 delegates. A week later the 2,188 Democrats caucused, and Al Gore won 14 of 22 delegates.

2000 Presidential Vote

Bush (R)	174,852	(61%)
Gore (D)	95,284	(33%)
Nader (Green)	9,486	(3%)
Other	8,634	(3%)

1996 Presidential Vote

Dole (R)	125,050	(47%)
Clinton (D)	106,905	(40%)
Perot (I)	32,515	(12%)

Governor

John Hoeven (R)

Elected 2000, term expires Jan. 2005, 1st term; b. March 13, 1957, Bismarck; home, Bismarck; Dartmouth, B.A. 1979; Northwestern U., Kellogg Grad. Schl., M.B.A. 1981; Catholic; married (Mikey).

Professional Career: Exec. V.P., First Western Bank, 1986–93; Pres. & CEO, Bank of ND, 1993–00.

Office: State Capitol, 600 E. Boulevard, Bismarck, 58505, 701-328-2200; Fax: 701-328-2205; Web site: www.governor.state.nd.us.

Election Results

2000 general	John Hoeven (R)	159,255	(55%)
	Heidi Heitkamp (D)	130,144	(45%)
2000 primary	John Hoeven (R)	unopposed	
1996 general	Edward T. Schafer (R)	174,937	(66%)
	Lee Kaldor (D)	89,349	(34%)

John Hoeven, the governor of North Dakota, is a Republican elected in 2000. He was born in Bismarck and grew up in Minot; he graduated from Dartmouth College and received an MBA from Northwestern. In 1981, he entered the family business, First Western Bank in Minot and became executive vice president. He was active in many civic endeavors. In 1993 he was chosen to be head of the state-owned Bank of North Dakota—a Non-Partisan League creation—by a board that included his predecessor as governor, Republican Ed Schafer, and his 2000 Democratic opponent, Attorney General Heidi Heitkamp. Under Hoeven's stewardship, the bank's worth rose from $990 million to $1.6 billion and its loan portfolio increased from $200 million to $1 billion; it returns $50 million into the state's biannual budget. Hoeven was not always a Republican; in 1996, as a Democrat, he thought out loud about running against Schafer. He gave serious consideration to running in 2000 only when Schafer announced in October 1999 he would not run again.

Schafer, whose family started one of North Dakota's few big businesses, Gold Seal Wax, was widely popular and had been re-elected overwhelmingly in 1996. Republicans worried that they had no good candidate to run against the popular Heitkamp. In November Hoeven, who had never won elective office, announced his candidacy, promising to take up where Schafer left off.

This was a generally civil campaign, between two candidates who knew each other well. Bismarck is a small town, where officeholders can scarcely avoid each other, and North Dakotans are a civil people. Hoeven cited his work in attracting jobs by founding Minot's Magic Fund, a city sales tax used for business development, and by organizing to keep Minot Air Force Base off the base-closure list, as well as his work at the Bank of North Dakota. He called for economic development with high-paying jobs in technology and said that education was crucial in preparing future workers; he pledged more money for teacher training and salaries. Heitkamp, who grew up in the town of Mantador (population 77), was elected tax commissioner in 1984 and 1988 and attorney general in 1992 and 1996. She was known for her "big red hair" and her work in the tobacco lawsuit and settlement. She said she would try to keep young people in the state through a recruitment and mentoring program, by reinstating a living wage for employees of companies receiving financial assistance and by giving tax incentives to companies guaranteeing high-wage jobs. She said she would "demand a domestic farm policy that works for family farms" and "fight back against unfair foreign competition."

These were two attractive candidates running on similar, though not identical, platforms. They both raised over $1 million, Hoeven getting more from business interests, Heitkamp from labor unions and tobacco case lawyers. They were running about even in polls when, in September 2000, Heitkamp announced that she had breast cancer. She underwent a mastectomy September 25, and Hoeven suspended his ads for two days. Quickly she returned to the campaign trail. For several weeks, Heitkamp had a small lead in the polls. But then the momentum went back to Hoeven, and he won 55%–45%. He carried the state's largest counties 57%–43%; she carried only 12 rural counties. Voters over the age of 60 backed the Democrat, voters under 60 the Republican: A familiar North Dakota pattern. At the same time, Republicans won seven of nine of the statewide offices and increased their majorities in the legislature. North Dakota's skyscraper Capitol, towering over neatly-kept Bismarck and the rolling plains beyond, now contained more Republicans in high office than at any time since the NPL allied with the Democrats around 1960.

As governor, Hoeven began Phase 2 of the North Dakota Telecommunications Network and combined several state agencies—tourism, economic development, finance, job training—into a Department of Commerce. He promoted value added projects and agricultural research. In June 2002 voters, against Hoeven's advice, voted 73%–27% to require banks and credit unions to get customers' permission before selling data about them. In July 2002 Hoeven traveled to Cuba—

the second governor to do so, after Illinois's George Ryan—and signed agreements to sell $2 million of North Dakota products. But Cuba is a market not much larger than the Dominican Republic and a few months later the deals had not gone through. Democrats put on the November 2002 ballot a measure to provide an income tax credit of up to $10,000 to North Dakotans in their 20s who stayed in the state—an attempt to staunch the outflow of the young. Voters rejected it 67%–33%. At the same time Republicans lost a few seats in the legislature. In December 2002, Hoeven presented a budget that drew $50 million from two trust funds and borrowed $20 million to complete the Telecommunications Network and which provided for teacher salary increases and $10 million for a Devils Lake outlet. Some legislators were skittish about spending one-time revenue for ongoing projects; but revenues exceeded expectations in the second half of 2002 and North Dakota's fiscal problems were far less dire than those of many other states.

Senior Senator

Kent Conrad (D)

Elected 1986, seat up 2006, 3d term; b. Mar. 12, 1948, Bismarck; home, Bismarck; Stanford U., B.A. 1971, George Washington U., M.B.A. 1975; Unitarian; married (Lucy Calautti).

Elected Office: ND Tax Commissioner, 1981–86.

Professional Career: Asst., ND Tax Commissioner, 1974–80; Dir., Mgmt. Planning & Personnel, ND Tax Dept., 1980.

DC Office: 530 HSOB, 20510, 202-224-2043; Fax: 202-224-7776; Web site: conrad.senate.gov.

State Offices: Bismarck, 701-258-4648; Fargo, 701-232-8030; Grand Forks, 701-775-9601; Minot, 701-852-0703.

Committees: *Agriculture, Nutrition & Forestry*: Marketing, Inspection & Product Promotion; Production & Price Competitiveness (RMM). *Budget* (RMM). *Finance*: International Trade; Long-Term Growth & Debt Reduction; Taxation & IRS Oversight (RMM). *Indian Affairs*.

Group Ratings

	ADA	ACLU	AFS	LCV	CON	ITIC	NTU	COC	ACU	NTLC	CHC
2002	95	40	88	53	88	25	15	45	10	6	—
2001	85	—	92	63	—	—	5	50	36	—	40

National Journal Ratings

	2001 LIB	—	2001 CONS		2002 LIB	—	2002 CONS
Economic	68%	—	31%		59%	—	36%
Social	48%	—	51%		77%	—	18%
Foreign	61%	—	27%		85%	—	12%

Key Votes of the 107th Congress

1. Approve Bush Tax Cuts	N	5. Confirm Ashcroft as AG	Y	9. Bar Coop. with Intl. Court	Y
2. Expand Patients' Rights	Y	6. Bar Gays in the Boy Scouts	Y	10. Trade Promotion Authority	N
3. Campaign Finance Reform	Y	7. $ for Hate Crime Prosecution	Y	11. Authorize Force in Iraq	N
4. Permit ANWR Development	N	8. Overseas Military Abortions	Y	12. Homeland Sec. Dept. Union	Y

Election Results

2000 general	Kent Conrad (D)	176,470	(62%)	($2,312,543)
	Duane Sand (R)	110,420	(38%)	($399,584)
2000 primary	Kent Conrad (D)	unopposed		
1994 general	Kent Conrad (D)	137,157	(58%)	($1,927,866)
	Ben Clayburgh (R)	99,390	(42%)	($941,192)

Prior Winning Percentages: 1992 (63%); 1986 (50%)

Kent Conrad, North Dakota's senior senator, was first elected in 1986. He grew up in North Dakota; his parents were killed in an auto accident when he was five, and he was raised by his grandparents. One grandfather owned a bi-weekly newspaper in Bismarck and had been North Dakota chairman for Progressive Robert LaFollette in 1924; another was the physician for long-time Governor and Senator William Langer: it was a family full of connections in the small world of North Dakota politics. Conrad's first political effort was to lead, in 1968, a campaign to grant voting rights to 19-year-olds. He graduated from Stanford, and then returned in 1974 to work on Byron Dorgan's unsuccessful House campaign. When Dorgan ran for Congress again in 1980, Conrad ran for tax commissioner and won; when Dorgan declined the opportunity again, in 1986 Conrad ran against Senator Mark Andrews, and won 50%–49%. In 1986 Conrad earnestly promised not to run again unless "the federal deficit, the trade deficit and real interest rates will be brought under control." By 1992 the latter two arguably were, and he could argue that he had worked to cut the budget deficit. Early 1992 polls showed Conrad well ahead, but in April 1992, after ruminating on the issue and after his wife had been mugged and dragged down the street near their Capitol Hill home, Conrad announced he was retiring because he had not kept his pledge, and Dorgan ran for his seat.

Then, in September 1992, the elderly Senator Quentin Burdick, no ally of Dorgan and Conrad, died. State law said a special election had to be held after November but before January, so Conrad ran for this seat while serving his last month in the other. This was awkward, but Conrad's earnestness, on display in more than 1,000 town meetings over six years, helped. He was nominated unanimously at the Democratic state convention. His Republican opponent called for an absurdly expensive $5 per bushel wheat program, and an anti-abortion independent lambasted Conrad; Conrad had far more money and won easily, 63%–34%. For a few hours in December 1992, Conrad held both Senate seats: he was sworn in December 14 to fill Burdick's term, and a few hours later Dorgan was sworn in to fill his. In 1994 this seat came up again. Republican Ben Clayburgh, 70-year-old former head of the state medical association, accused Conrad of voting most of the time with Bill Clinton; Conrad responded with an ad saying he voted with Bob Dole more than 50% of the time. Dole endorsed Clayburgh, but Conrad won by a reduced margin of 58%–42%.

Conrad became ranking minority member on the Budget Committee in January 2001 and chairman in June 2001. Throughout his career he has always called for balanced budgets and decried budget deficits, and he had the pain of watching as chairman while the surplus turned to deficit. From the 1930s to the 1970s, Republicans were the great critics of deficits; since the 1980s Democrats have increasingly taken that stand, Conrad foremost among them. One reason may be that surpluses leave more room for spending, while deficits create pressure against it; as conservative Paul Gigot wrote of Conrad in *The Wall Street Journal*, "Nobody is better at using the rhetoric of fiscal conservatism to disguise demands for larger government." The tension between Conrad's desire for balanced budgets and support for government programs came out in the mid-1990s debate on a constitutional amendment to require a balanced budget. Conrad voted for such an amendment in 1994. But when his colleague Dorgan pushed an amendment taking Social Security out of the calculations, which would tend to increase deficits, Conrad hesitated, negotiating first in the Republican and then the Democratic cloakroom and emerging to cast the deciding vote against the amendment in March 1995; never since has it come as close to passing. In spring 2001 Conrad worked to get in the budget resolution $73 billion for farm programs over the next 10 years: This left room for the farm bill passed in 2002. But he also called for a continued surplus. Once chairman, he started lambasting the Bush administration and, using his trademark charts (he is known as "the chart man" on Capitol Hill), argued that the tax cut passed in May 2001 and lower than expected revenue would lead to deficits. "This new administration, only six months after assuming responsibility for the fiscal affairs of this country, after grabbing the steering wheel, has driven us right into the fiscal ditch," he said in July 2001. But he did not seek to undo the tax cut. He did threaten to hold back the reserve fund that the May 2001 budget resolution allowed the two Budget Committee chairmen to dole out. In March 2002 Conrad presented a $2.1 trillion dollar budget with a $90 billion deficit; it would pay off more of the national debt than the Bush budget. His plan passed in committee but in the 51–49 Senate there were not enough senators willing to constrain appropriators and Conrad's resolution never came to a vote. For the first time since the Budget Committees were set up in 1974, no budget resolution passed

Congress. The Republicans won back a Senate majority in November 2002 and in January 2003 Conrad became ranking minority member again; he is the only Budget chairman never to have passed a budget resolution.

On the Finance Committee, Conrad voted against the Bush tax cut and repeal of the estate tax. He seems likely to oppose changes in Medicare along the lines proposed by John Breaux, and to oppose individual investment accounts as part of Social Security. There is some political risk in these positions: Only one other Democratic senator (Nebraska's Ben Nelson) represents a state that voted by a wider margin for George W. Bush in 2000.

For years North Dakota senators tended closely to the details of farm bills, especially wheat subsidies, and then often voted against the every-four-year farm bills as insufficiently generous. In 2001 and 2002 Conrad worked on putting together a farm bill which abandoned the 1996 Freedom to Farm Act's promise of getting rid of subsidies, a promise undermined by Congress when, starting in 1997, it passed disaster relief for farmers every year. With $73 billion to spend over 10 years, the Senate Agriculture Committee was able to sharply increase the wheat subsidy at the price of increasing cotton and rice subsidies as well. Conrad defended the committee bill. "I know there are people who have cogent arguments that this farm policy encourages overproduction, but that misses the larger reality. We are engaged in a trade war, and it's not pretty. There are going to be unfortunate side effects." He was one of four Senate conferees and helped insure that the bill required country of origin labeling for meat and better treatment of pulses—peas, lentils and other crops planted in rotation on wheat fields. He followed up on implementation of the bill, charging that the "hostile" Agriculture Department wasn't reducing the sugar loan rate as the bill ordered. He didn't give up on further disaster relief, but was pessimistic in December 2002: "It's hard to envision that the drive to reduce domestic spending by billions of dollars in the current fiscal year will allow for the disaster relief that many in agriculture have been hoping for and that some of us in Congress have been pursuing." He and Dorgan welcomed the news that Special Trade Representative Robert Zoellick filed a complaint with the WTO against the Canadian Wheat Board for selling wheat under cost.

North Dakota sits astride North America's longest river, the Missouri, and Conrad has spent much time on water issues. He has worked to maintain high summer levels in Lake Sakakawea and has fought with Missouri senators who want drawdowns to keep barges afloat in their state. He and Dorgan have worked for diversion of Missouri River water to the Red River Valley in eastern North Dakota, which is opposed by Canada, Minnesota and many environmentalists.

Conrad entered the 2000 election with a good job rating. His Republican opponent was Duane Sand, Annapolis graduate and 15-year Navy veteran, who returned to North Dakota and set out running—or rather walking across the state, campaigning door-to-door in every city and town with a post office, about 300 in all. But Conrad spent far more money, $2.3 million, and national Republicans didn't target this race. Conrad ran 29% ahead of Al Gore and won 62%–38%, carrying every demographic group and all but three small counties. His seat comes up in 2006.

Junior Senator

Byron Dorgan (D)

Elected 1992, seat up 2004, 2d term; b. May 14, 1942, Dickinson; home, Bismarck; U. of ND, B.S. 1965, U. of Denver, M.B.A. 1966; Lutheran; married (Kimberly).

Elected Office: ND Tax Commissioner, 1969–80; U.S. House of Reps., 1980–92.

Professional Career: Martin–Marietta Exec. Develop. Prog., 1966–68; ND Dpty. Tax Commissioner, 1968–69.

DC Office: 713 HSOB, 20510, 202-224-2551; Fax: 202-224-1193; Web site: dorgan.senate.gov.

State Offices: Bismarck, 701-250-4618; Fargo, 701-239-5389; Grand Forks, 701-746-8972; Minot, 701-852-0703.

Committees: *Democratic Policy Committee Chairman. Appropriations*: Agriculture & Rural Development; Defense; Energy & Water Development; Interior (RMM); Transportation, Treasury & General Government. *Commerce, Science & Transportation*: Aviation; Communications; Competition, Foreign Commerce & Infrastructure (RMM); Consumer Affairs & Product Safety; Science, Technology & Space. *Energy & Natural Resources*: National Parks; Public Lands & Forests; Water & Power (RMM). *Indian Affairs*.

Group Ratings

	ADA	ACLU	AFS	LCV	CON	ITIC	NTU	COC	ACU	NTLC	CHC
2002	90	40	100	47	36	38	14	50	20	6	—
2001	85	—	92	75	—	—	6	50	36	—	40

National Journal Ratings

	2001 LIB	—	2001 CONS		2002 LIB	—	2002 CONS
Economic	67%	—	33%		56%	—	42%
Social	48%	—	51%		56%	—	38%
Foreign	61%	—	27%		74%	—	24%

Key Votes of the 107th Congress

1. Approve Bush Tax Cuts	N	5. Confirm Ashcroft as AG	Y	9. Bar Coop. with Intl. Court	Y
2. Expand Patients' Rights	Y	6. Bar Gays in the Boy Scouts	Y	10. Trade Promotion Authority	N
3. Campaign Finance Reform	Y	7. $ for Hate Crime Prosecution	Y	11. Authorize Force in Iraq	Y
4. Permit ANWR Development	N	8. Overseas Military Abortions	Y	12. Homeland Sec. Dept. Union	Y

Election Results

1998 general	Byron Dorgan (D)	134,747	(63%)	($1,681,842)
	Donna Nalewaja (R)	75,013	(35%)	($152,183)
	Other	3,598	(2%)	
1998 primary	Byron Dorgan (D)	unopposed		
1992 general	Byron Dorgan (D)	179,347	(59%)	($1,124,512)
	Steve Sydness (R)	118,162	(39%)	($498,107)
	Other	6,448	(2%)	

Prior Winning Percentages: 1990 House (65%); 1988 House (71%); 1986 House (76%); 1984 House (79%); 1982 House (72%); 1980 House (57%)

Byron Dorgan, who first held statewide office in 1969 and has often had the highest popularity ratings in North Dakota, was elected to the Senate in 1992. Dorgan grew up in Regent, North Dakota (population 268), where his family had a farm equipment and petroleum business and raised cattle and horses; he was one of nine students in his high school graduating class. After college and business school he worked for a Denver aerospace firm, then in 1969, at 26, was appointed state tax commissioner. His politics are very much out of the Non-Partisan League tradition: He has a strong mistrust of economic markets, a deep belief that government should intervene to protect the family farmer and small businessman, and a capacity to frame issues in a popular and unthreatening way. His first big issue, as tax commissioner, was taxing out-of-state corporations, which struck a chord in a state always hostile to big out-of-state money. To his work Dorgan brought the zest and cornball good humor that New Deal enthusiasts liked to summon up when liberals thought they represented the ordinary, inarticulate little guy, in contrast to the conservatives seen as old stuffed shirts.

Dorgan ran for the House in 1974, and lost to Republican Mark Andrews. In 1980, when Andrews ran for the Senate, Dorgan was elected to the House. His lowest percentage in a House race was 65%, in 1990 against Ed Schafer, who was elected governor in 1992 and 1996. On the House Ways and Means Committee, he called for more tax audits, opposed intangibles write-offs for corporate takeovers, and opposed the use of high-yield bonds for corporate takeovers. Dorgan declined to challenge Andrews for the Senate in 1986, a race his successor as tax commissioner, Kent Conrad won, and he declined to take on 80-year-old fellow-Democrat Quentin Burdick in 1988. Only with Conrad's surprise decision not to run for re-election in 1992 did Dorgan finally run for the Senate. He and his Republican opponent both backed Most Favored Nation trade status for China (a major buyer of North Dakota wheat), but remained wary of free trade otherwise and opposed the regulations that have classified hundreds of seasonal puddles in North Dakota as protected wetlands. Dorgan won by a solid 59%–39% margin.

In the Senate, Dorgan's voting record has been almost exactly the same as Conrad's; this is one case where senators of the same party from the same state have worked harmoniously together. They call themselves and Congressman Earl Pomeroy "Team North Dakota." Dorgan strongly backed fellow Dakotan Tom Daschle for Senate Democratic leader in 1994, and became an assistant floor leader; he considered running for whip against Harry Reid four years later, but withdrew. In December 1998 he became co-chairman of the Democratic Policy Committee.

Dorgan continues to be a champion of family farms, even as their numbers decline. He backed the big crop insurance and disaster relief packages starting in 1997. He has sought a ban on Canadian wheat imports, then a requirement that they all come in through one border crossing; he rejoiced when the special trade representative started investigating Canadian practices in October 2000 and brought a complaint to the WTO in December 2002. When George W. Bush signed the $5.5 billion farm relief bill in August 2001 he said, "This is just round one." Round two was the farm bill, when Dorgan and Charles Grassley led the move to limit farm subsidies. He argued that too much would go to a few rich farmers and feared that such payments would build opposition to the farm bill as a whole; anyway, not many North Dakota or Iowa farmers qualify for huge payments. It failed in committee, opposed by senators from states with big cotton and rice farms, but in February 2002, the Senate passed by voice vote a limit of $275,000 per farmer.

As an advocate of the family farm, Dorgan opposes high interest rates and mergers, but does not see taxes as such a threat. During the 1990s he often criticized Alan Greenspan for backing high interest rates and he was one of four senators to vote against his reconfirmation as Federal Reserve chairman in February 2000. He opposed financial services deregulation in 1999—"that which is true in the 1930s is true in 2010"—and wants the SEC to regulate derivatives. He wants a more vigorous antitrust policy; he called for an 18-month moratorium on agribusiness mergers in 1999 and a two-year moratorium on airline mergers in 2001. He opposes individual investment accounts for Social Security and opposed full repeal of the estate tax. His 2002 bills to allow prescription drugs to be reimported from Canada passed the Senate, but in 2000 HHS Secretary Donna Shalala said she could not certify that this would pose "no additional risk to the public's health and safety," as the law required and so it had no effect; in 2001 it was clear that her successor Tommy Thompson would do the same thing, and the bill did not pass in the House. Dorgan tried unsuccessfully in 1998 and 2001 to add to the moratorium on Internet taxes provisions authorizing the states to establish a compact to set standardized sales taxes. As chairman of a Commerce subcommittee he held widely-publicized hearings in winter 2002 on malfeasance at Enron; executives were suitably denounced. "This is disgusting to me, corporate behavior without a moral base," Dorgan said at one point. But he did not get the records of Enron's partnerships. He heads the subcommittee with jurisdiction over the White House and has sponsored a bill to require presidential libraries to raise endowments capable of paying 40%, not the current 20%, of operational expenses.

On foreign policy, Dorgan has been a prime mover in scaling back the embargo on Cuba. In 2000 he got the Senate to lift the embargo on food and medicine and to prevail against a House version that he said would limit financing of sales to Cuba. He was a strong but not successful supporter of the Comprehensive Test Ban Treaty that Bill Clinton submitted to the Senate in September 1997.

On North Dakota issues, Dorgan has sometimes disappointed environmental groups. In September 2000 he threatened to block EPA nominations unless North Dakota farmers were allowed to import a pesticide from Canada. Dorgan works closely with Conrad on water issues. They worked to limit the drawdown on Lake Sakakawea in the Missouri River and fought Missouri's senators who wanted more water let out to keep the barges floating on the river in their state. They succeeded in December 2000 in getting the $631 million Dakota Water Resources Act included in an appropriation; this would authorize diversion of Missouri River water to the Red River Valley in eastern North Dakota, and is opposed by Canada, Minnesota and many environmentalists. He voted against higher CAFE gas mileage standards for pickup trucks.

Dorgan was easily re-elected in 1998. His first opponent was Fargo nudist rights advocate Crystal Dueker who said she would "be the sacrificial virgin." She added, "I fight to win. I know how to kick a man where it hurts." But she bowed out in March after Fargo police had her hospitalized for psychiatric evaluation. In November Dorgan beat state Senator Donna Nalewaja 63%–35%, carrying every county but one; the vote in Sheridan County was 423–423. His vote was highest among elderly North Dakotans, but he carried every demographic group by wide margins. After the 2002 elections, national Republicans started talking about taking on Dorgan in 2004. George W. Bush, who carried the state 61%–33%, would be on the ballot again, and they had a potentially strong candidate in Ed Schafer, who left the governorship in 2001 with high ratings. But Schafer, who lost a House race to Dorgan in 1990, seemed reluctant. "There's no question it would be tough. Byron is smart, and he knows how to run a campaign. He's had a lot of practice." Others mentioned as possible Republican candidates were Governor John Hoeven and motivational speaker and former LSU basketball coach Dale Brown.

Representative-At-Large

Earl Pomeroy (D)

Elected 1992, 6th term; b. Sept. 2, 1952, Valley City; home, Valley City; U. of ND, B.A. 1974, J.D., 1979; Presbyterian; married (Laurie Kirby).

Elected Office: ND House of Reps., 1980–84; ND Insurance Commissioner, 1984–92.

Professional Career: Practicing atty., 1979–84; Natl. Assn. of Insurance Commissioners., Vice Pres. 1989, Pres. 1990.

DC Office: 1110 LHOB, 20515, 202-225-2611; Fax: 202-226-0893; Web site: www.house.gov/pomeroy.

District Offices: Bismarck, 701-224-0355; Fargo, 701-235-9760.

Committees: *Agriculture* (18th of 24 D): General Farm Commodities & Risk Management. *Ways & Means* (15th of 17 D): Oversight (RMM); Social Security.

Group Ratings

	ADA	ACLU	AFS	LCV	CON	ITIC	NTU	COC	ACU	NTLC	CHC
2002	70	53	89	63	43	50	18	60	32	6	25
2001	85	—	100	71	—	—	12	39	28	—	—

National Journal Ratings

	2001 LIB	—	2001 CONS		2002 LIB	—	2002 CONS
Economic	67%	—	33%		54%	—	46%
Social	60%	—	40%		54%	—	45%
Foreign	66%	—	34%		57%	—	42%

Key Votes of the 107th Congress

1. Approve Bush Tax Cuts	N	5. Faith-Based Charities	N	9. Trade Promotion Authority	N
2. Limit Patients' Bill of Rights	N	6. Bar Gays in the Boy Scouts	Y	10. Bar Funds for Intl. Court	Y
3. Campaign Finance Reform	Y	7. Ban Partial-Birth Abortion	Y	11. Authorize Force in Iraq	Y
4. Ban ANWR Development	Y	8. Arm Commercial Pilots	Y	12. Deny Home. Sec. Dept. Union	N

Election Results

2002 general	Earl Pomeroy (D)	121,073	(52%)	($1,761,813)
	Rick Clayburgh (R)	109,957	(48%)	($1,089,336)
2002 primary	Earl Pomeroy (D)	unopposed		
2000 general	Earl Pomeroy (D)	151,173	(53%)	($1,052,831)
	John Dorso (R)	127,251	(45%)	($448,823)
	Other	7,234	(3%)	

Prior Winning Percentages: 1998 (56%); 1996 (55%); 1994 (52%); 1992 (57%)

Earl Pomeroy, North Dakota's single House member, is a Democrat first elected in 1992. Pomeroy grew up in Valley City, and after college served as Byron Dorgan's driver during the 1974 campaign, then went to law school and practiced law in Valley City. In 1980, when Dorgan and Kent Conrad won statewide elections, Pomeroy at 28 won a seat in the legislature; in 1984 and 1988 he was elected insurance commissioner (his brother Glenn Pomeroy followed him in the office and he still gets more money from insurance PACs than any other industry). In 1992, he was planning to retire from politics and serve in the Peace Corps in Russia; then Dorgan ran for Conrad's seat in the Senate and Pomeroy ran for Dorgan's seat in the House. Articulate, cheerful and sincere, a critic of insurance companies yet unabrasive, he was the obvious choice for the House seat and was nominated unanimously by the Democratic convention. He won the general 57%–39%, almost exactly Dorgan's margin in the Senate race.

Pomeroy has compiled a moderate to liberal voting record, defending North Dakota interests and working with Republicans as well as Democrats on some issues. He served on the Budget Committee in his first term, and voted for both the Clinton budget and the Penny-Kasich spending cuts in 1993 and opposed the Clinton health care plan. In the Republican Congress, he strongly supported the adoption tax credit and brought his two-year-old daughter, adopted from Korea, onto the floor for the vote.

In 2001 he finally got a seat on Ways and Means; the Democratic leadership had been promising members seats on the assumption that they would win back a majority, but since they stayed in the minority they had few open seats to hand out (one Democratic aide said that "many people have been promised the seat, but Pomeroy has been promised it the most"). Social Security did not come up in 2001 or 2002, but the estate tax did. Pomeroy voted against repeal of the estate tax. When Republican leaders brought up a bill to make it permanent in June 2002, Pomeroy offered an amendment to raise the $1 million exemption to $3 million; it was rejected 231–197. He is the chief co-sponsor with Phil English to cut the beer tax back to its pre-1991 level.

Pomeroy is a former co-chairman of the House Rural Caucus. Though not averse to all change in farm programs, he opposed the 1996 Freedom to Farm Act, though he helped write its wetlands reform provisions. He has supported the crop insurance and disaster relief bills that have provided the rough equivalent of the old subsidies that the Freedom to Farm Act tried to phase out. Like other North Dakotans, he has decried Canadian wheat dumping and has sought government action against it, finally taken by Special Trade Representative Robert Zoellick in December 2002; he wants to allow North Dakota farmers to buy chemicals from Canada that are presently banned in the U.S. In the 2002 farm bill he pressed for mandatory country of origin labeling of meat, which was opposed by the Bush administration. After the bill passed with that provision, he attacked Agriculture Secretary Ann Veneman for inquiring whether labeling meat "North American" would be permissible under the law. He was a vigorous supporter of PNTR for China in 2000.

During the devastating Grand Forks flooding in April 1997, he helped man the dikes and slept in a nearby Air Force shelter in order to help residents deal with the disaster; later he worked and got nearly $500 million in flood relief, and has worked for a $300 million system of levees and walls to prevent future floods. He has worked to get a study of an emergency outlet for Devils Lake, whose water level continues to rise and has inundated 120,000 acres so far. But he has had some difficulty in the Republican House. In 2000 House Majority Whip Tom DeLay flew over Devils Lake with Pomeroy's Republican opponent. In an unusually acerbic criticism of a colleague, DeLay told reporters, "We will help Devils Lake. We will get this done in spite of Earl Pomeroy. But you ought to have a representative who knows how to work the system." He added, "He played partisan politics last year. Why should we lift a finger this year for him?"

Pomeroy has had serious challenges every two years. In 1994 businessman Gary Porter used his own money to match the incumbent's spending; Pomeroy won 52%–45%. In 1996 and 1998, state Economic Development and Finance Director Kevin Cramer opposed him. In 1996, Pomeroy outspent him by more than 2–1 and increased his margin to 55%–43%. In 1998 Cramer peppered Pomeroy with negative ads and attacked him for seeking to invest Social Security funds in the stock market. In a pro-incumbent year, Pomeroy increased his percentage to 56%–41%. In

2000, state House Majority Leader John Dorso said Pomeroy had been "ineffective" on special education and Devils Lake. Pomeroy won 53%–45%.

In 2002 Pomeroy faced Rick Clayburgh, elected in 1996 and 2000 as state tax commissioner—the job once held by Senators Dorgan and Conrad. He was Pomeroy's best-known Republican challenger yet; when approached by the American Council of Life Insurers in early 2002 and asked if he was interested in their top job, which pays more than $1 million, he said he was not interested. Instead he raised lots of money and made a $150,000 media buy in June. Clayburgh argued that North Dakota would do better with a Republican congressman. "North Dakota needs a voice," one slogan said. "We've been going into battle with one arm tied behind our back." He repeatedly attacked Pomeroy for leaving the Agriculture Committee just before it was going to consider the farm bill in order to take the seat on Ways and Means. Clayburgh brought big names into the district—Hastert, Vice President Dick Cheney. Pomeroy brought in big money—more than 70% of his campaign money came from PACs, and he spent $1.8 million against Clayburgh's $1.1 million in what was North Dakota's most expensive House race. Republicans hit Pomeroy for voting against estate tax repeal and trade Promotion Authority. And they attacked him as well for backing "privatization" of Social Security, by which they meant the Clinton plan of having the government invest payroll taxes in the stock market. Clayburgh said he would vote against that and against individual investment accounts as part of Social Security. In October Pomeroy ran an ad showing him near George W. Bush at the signing of a bill of which he was one of 39 co-sponsors continuing a tax exemption for clergy housing expenses. "President Bush signed Pomeroy's bill to stop a $2 billion tax on our rural churches," the announcer intoned. Clayburgh ran an ad assailing the "Earl Pomeroy hustle," voting for liberal measures in Washington while sounding conservative in North Dakota. Both supported the Iraq war resolution; both criticized the policies of Agriculture Secretary Ann Veneman; both said they supported a prescription drug benefit under Medicare.

This was one of the most clearly visible House races in 2002: North Dakota had no elections for senator or governor, and officeholders are well known throughout the state. The result was close. Pomeroy won 52%–48%, and by 51%–49% in the four large counties. Pomeroy carried Fargo, Minot and Grand Forks, Clayburgh's hometown; Clayburgh carried Bismarck. Pomeroy will likely get another serious challenge in 2004, unless Republicans decide to pass on this race and target Senator Byron Dorgan.

★ OHIO ★

O hio was the first entirely American state, and one which ever since has seemed an epitome of American normalcy. The original 13 states started as British colonies, and the next three, Vermont, Kentucky and Tennessee, were spun off from them. But Ohio sprung Athena-like from the head of Congress, as the first state formed from the Northwest Territory. The Northwest Ordinance of 1787 established 6 by 6 mile square townships, which imposed geometric order on diverse American landscapes west to the Pacific; it set aside one square mile per township for public schools, and the landscape was soon peppered with schoolhouses and small colleges, the foundation stones of a literate republic. The Ordinance prohibited slavery, opening the way for free labor to clear fields, raise crops, build mills and factories, and in less than half a century, make this wilderness one of the most productive parts of western civilization. Ohio, in the years after the Civil War, became one of the great industrial states, the original headquarters of John D. Rockefeller's Standard Oil, the site of major steel mills along the narrow and languidly flowing Cuyahoga and Mahoning Rivers, and home of the biggest soap companies, machine tool makers, tire manufacturers and producers of safety glass. Dayton was the home of the Wright brothers, of James Ritty and James Patterson, the inventor and manufacturer of the cash register, of Charles Kettering, who invented the automobile starter and many other things. Akron was the home of Harvey Firestone, B. F. Goodrich and F. A. Seiberling, founder of Goodyear—the great tire manufacturers. They invented their devices and built their factories in a state that was culturally split,

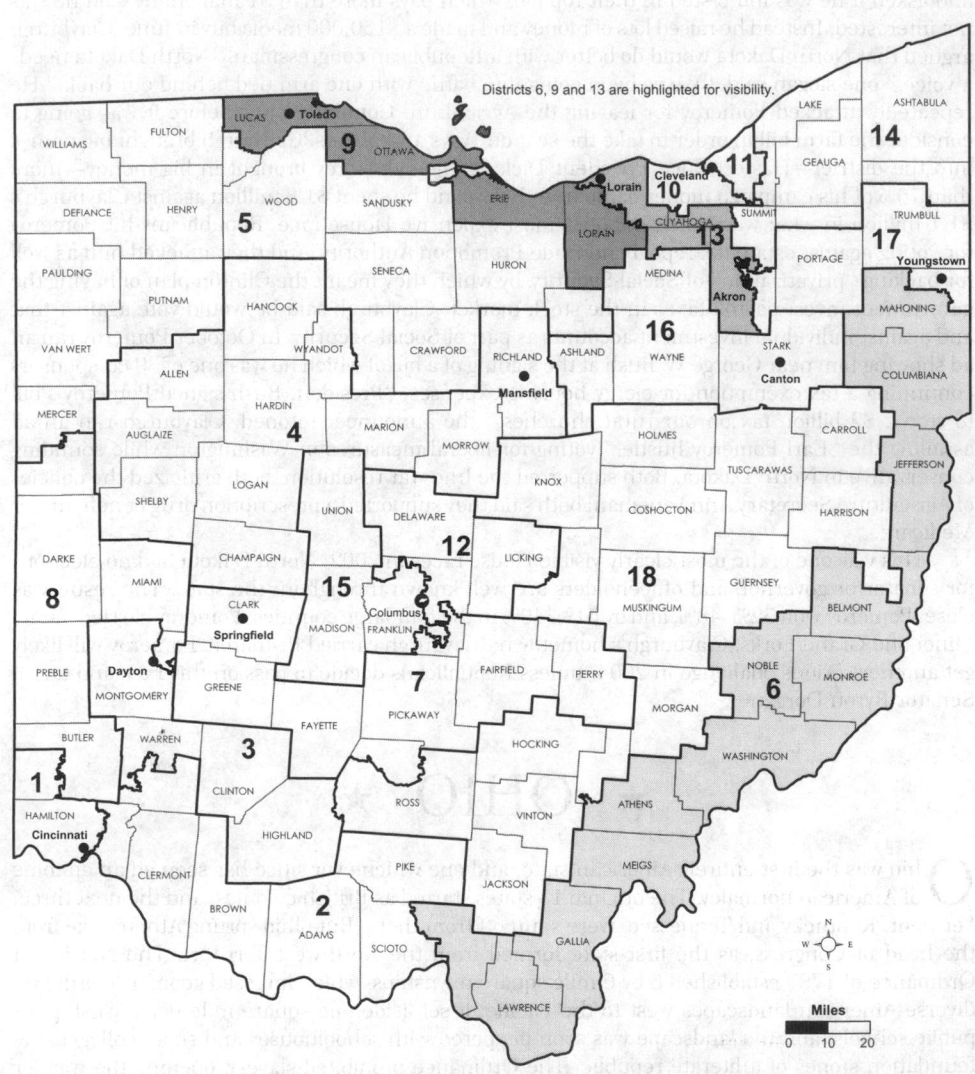

Districts 6, 9 and 13 are highlighted for visibility.

Congressional district boundaries were first effective for 2002.

The Almanac of American Politics.
National Journal

settled by New Englanders in the northeast in the Western Reserve and by Virginians in the south, split between the Southern-accented counties south of the National Road and U.S. 40 and the Northern-accented cities and towns to the north; between Butternut and Copperhead territory that didn't want to fight the Civil War and Yankee territory that fiercely prosecuted the War and Reconstruction afterwards.

This split heritage made Ohio politically a closely divided state—and a nationally pivotal one. A century ago Ohio produced the candidate and campaign manager—Governor and former Ways and Means Chairman William McKinley and iron and coal industrialist Mark Hanna; McKinley won the presidency in 1896 and 1900 and inaugurated a 34-year period of Republican national majorities. McKinley's Republicans were for high tariffs and hard money, had a friendly regard for workers and even some unions, but no patience with large union combinations and nascent socialism. They preached a nationalist Americanism tempered by a wariness about making major commitments abroad. Republicans were the majority in this increasingly industrial Ohio, losing rural Butternut counties but carrying the big industrial cities of the north.

Then came the Depression of the 1930s, and Ohio became the scene of something like class warfare, with sit-down strikes and victories for the CIO industrial unions in autos, steel and tires. CIO cities—Cleveland, Akron, Youngstown, Toledo—moved sharply toward the Democrats, while places with few CIO members—Cincinnati, Columbus, the dozens of small factory towns dotting the flat limestone plains of northern Ohio—stayed Republican. The political fighting was fierce and the stakes seemed high. CIO leaders hoped to organize the entire work force and build a Scandinavian-style welfare state; Republican leaders like Ohio's Senator Robert Taft feared union control of business would imperil freedoms and throttle the economy. In the 1930s and 1940s the unions made great gains. But Taft held them off, reducing union power with the Taft-Hartley Act of 1947, his own reelection to the Senate in 1950, and the election of his rival Dwight Eisenhower as president in 1952.

In the years since, Ohio has oscillated and been courted by national campaigns. In the 1970s it seemed to swing toward the Democrats. Jimmy Carter won crucial electoral votes by carrying Ohio by 11,000 votes and Democrats controlled the state House throughout the 1970s and 1980s. In the 1990s Ohio swung to the Republicans. Bill Clinton did carry the state twice, but by the narrowest of his margins in any large state—40%–38% in 1992, 47%–41% in 1996—and Al Gore lost here 50%–46% in 2000. Ohio Republicans won smashing victories in 1994 and 1998 and held their own in 1996 and 2000. The leading figure was George Voinovich, elected governor in 1990 by 56%–44%, reelected in 1994 by 72%–25%—by far the biggest margin since 1826, when neither Republican nor Democratic parties existed—and elected senator by 56%–44% in 1998. But this has not just been a personal victory. From 1976 to 1994 Ohio was represented by two Democrats in the Senate, but when they retired they were replaced by Republicans: Mike DeWine and Voinovich, both of whom had run unsuccessfully for the Senate before. And in 1998 Republican Bob Taft, bearer of a great Ohio name, was elected governor over Democrat Lee Fisher by 50%–45%. He was reelected against an underfinanced opponent 58%–38% in 2002. Until Taft's 1998 victory, Ohio's governorship had been passed back and forth between the two parties, with neither holding it for more than eight years, since George K. Nash won in 1899. By 2006 Republicans will have held it for a longer period than any party since 1856–74. Republicans also hold every downballot statewide office, most of which were held by Democrats between 1970 to 1994, and they have large and seemingly impervious margins in both houses of the legislature. Republicans have an 12–6 edge in the U.S. House delegation, a 22–11 margin in the state Senate and 62–37 in the state House. Twenty years ago Democrats had no difficulty finding candidates; they held most of the statewide offices and had legislators who represented swing districts and compiled records attractive to most voters. Recently they have had more difficulty. They hold no statewide offices and most of their legislators represent central city districts and have leftish records; mayors of shrinking central cities may become well known, but they too tend to tilt to the left.

The Republican trend has occurred in a state that is still more industrial than post-industrial, a state changed by the immigration of the early 20th century but little touched by the immigration of the late 20th century, a state where cultural liberalism has a far smaller constituency than it does on the East or West Coasts or even in nearby Illinois and Michigan. It used to be said that

Ohio was a typical state, a great test market, for in income levels, urban-rural balance, and ethnic mix, as well as presidential percentages, it is not very far from the national average. But economically and culturally, it is different, a template perhaps for Indiana and Missouri but not for Oregon and Arizona. Ohio trails only California, three times as large, in manufacturing jobs, yet it has 400,000 fewer of them than it did in the peak year, 1969, and its population and income have been increasing at less than the national average. Education levels are lower than the national average; the old tradition of heading straight from high school to a high-wage factory job has not entirely died out, even though low-skill factory jobs are not as plenteous as they once were and do not pay particularly well.

The reaction to these developments has been different, economically and politically, in two parts of the state. One is the part where the CIO unions organized the big factories, north-and-east Ohio, the heavy industry area along Lake Erie and reaching south to the coal-mining counties across the Ohio River from West Virginia. In north-and-east Ohio giant steel mills closed in Cleveland and the Mahoning Valley around Youngstown in the 1980s, and population declined as young people moved out. The Cleveland area developed a more white-collar economy and built a gleaming downtown, with an entertainment district on the banks of the now clean Cuyahoga River; Akron developed polymer technologies that replaced tire manufacture. Politically, the Democratic voting habits instilled by the CIO unions are still evident, though there was no movement toward Democrats on cultural issues in the 1990s here, as there was in larger metro areas. George W. Bush lost the area 55%–41% in 2000; Bob Taft carried it by only 49%–48% in 2002. The rest of Ohio is a more diversified industrial area, never so dependent on big industries like steel, tires and autos. It did not lose so many jobs or suffer such population loss in the early 1980s as north-and-east Ohio. Instead it began building a new, more supple and adaptable manufacturing economy, with smaller factories, less rigid management and fewer union members, fewer low-skill jobs with high wages and more medium-skill, high-flexibility jobs with chances for advancement. Nor did the cultural atmosphere in small towns and even its big cities become culturally much more liberal; Cincinnati and Columbus are still known as strait-laced places. Columbus, the fastest-growing metro area, developed something of a post-industrial, information-based economy. Politically, this area was and is heavily Republican; the old Butternut Democratic tradition in southern Ohio has largely disappeared. George W. Bush carried this part of the state 56%–40% in 2000 and Bob Taft carried it 65%–31% in 2002. Moreover, this part of the state is becoming more important politically. Between 1980 and 2000 turnout in north-and-east Ohio rose only 3%, while it rose 16% in the rest of Ohio.

The 2000 and 2002 elections posed a test of where Ohio stands in history. Is it New Deal Ohio, with ethnic factory workers ranged against small town businessmen, ethnic Catholics versus rural Protestants, all engaged in a contest to see how far and in what ways government should be enlarged? Or is it McKinley's Ohio, with mechanical tinkerers and can-do manufacturers, adaptive businessmen and employees, striving to work hard, raise families and serve communities that feel little class conflict or economic envy? The answer, it seems, is that it is McKinley's Ohio, but it is not clear whether this consensus and political dominance can be sustained for a long generation as it was by McKinley and Hanna and their political heirs.

The People		Race/Ethnic Origin			Military veterans: 1,144,007 (13.5%)	
Pop. 2000:	11,353,140	9,538,111	84.0%	White	WWII: 21.7%	Korea: 13.7%
Pop. 1990:	10,847,115	1,290,662	11.4%	Black	Vietnam: 30.7%	Gulf War: 8.8%
Change 1990–2000:	Up 4.7%	131,670	1.2%	Asian	**Most populous cities:**	
Change 1980–1990:	Up 0.5%	21,985	0.2%	Native Am.	1. Columbus	711,470
% of U.S. total:	4.0%	2,336	0.0%	Hawaiian	2. Cleveland	478,403
Pop. rank:	7th of 50	137,770	1.2%	Two+ races	3. Cincinnati	331,285
Area size:	44,825 sq. mi.	13,483	0.1%	Other	4. Toledo	313,619
State Native:	74.7%	217,123	1.9%	Hisp. Origin	5. Akron	217,074
Non-citizen:	1.5%	**Ancestry**			Urban population: 77.3%	
Language		German: 18.8%		Irish: 9.5%	Rural population: 22.7%	
English: 91.4%	Other Eur.: 4.1%	English: 6.9%		USA: 6.5%		
Spanish: 3.0%		Italian: 4.4%				

Education		Work Sector		General Assembly	
H.S. Grad:	83.0%	Private: 82.0%	Govt: 12.2%	Senate	22 R 11 D
College Grad:	21.1%	Self: 5.5%	Family: 0.3%	House	62 R 37 D
Industry		Unemployment: 5.0%		Legislative Term Limits: Yes	
Agri: 1.1%	Con: 6.0%	**Household Income**		**Registered Voters**	
Fin: 6.3%	Info: 2.4%	<15k: 15.6%	15-35k: 26.9%	D: 1,010,662 (14.3%)	
Mfg: 25.0%	Prof: 27.8%	35-50k: 17.3%	50-100k: 30.4%	R: 1,364,270 (19.3%)	
Public: 4.1%	Trade: 15.5%	100-150k: 6.5%	>150k: 3.3%	I: 4,683,120 (66.4%)	
Other: 12.0%		Median: $40,956			
Occupation		Poverty status: 10.6%			
Blue collar: 27.8%	White collar: 57.3%	**Home Value**			
Gray collar: 14.9%		<50k: 12.2%	50-100k: 37.5%	100-200k: 38.6%	200-300k: 7.8%
		300-500k: 2.9%	>500k: 1.0%	Median: $100,500	

Presidential politics With 20 electoral votes and a tradition of close partisan competition, Ohio is a crucial state in presidential politics. It matched the national average in 1984 and 1988, came close to doing so in 1996 and was only 2% points off in 2000. No Republican has ever been elected president without carrying Ohio; no Democrat, in today's electoral vote arithmetic, can be sure of winning without it. In 2000 George W. Bush, despite holding narrow leads in polls, made Ohio a priority state from start to finish, while the Gore campaign, looking to opportunities elsewhere, pulled out much of its advertising in mid-October, only to put more money in at the end of the month. Ohio went for Bush by only a 50%–46% margin, and he made sure to visit the state half a dozen times in 2001 and 2002 even though it had no seriously contested statewide or House races. Of the large industrial states—Pennsylvania, Ohio, Michigan, Illinois—Ohio has been consistently the most Republican for 50 years, with the single exception of 1976, when Jimmy Carter ran well in the Southern-accented counties below U.S. 40 and carried the state by 11,000 votes. In recent years this has been because Ohio's

2000 Presidential Vote
Bush (R) 2,350,363 (50%)
Gore (D) 2,183,628 (46%)
Nader (Green) 117,799 (3%)
Other 50,208 (1%)

2000 Republican Presidential Primary
Bush (R) 810,369 (58%)
McCain (R) 516,790 (37%)
Keyes (R) 55,266 (4%)

2000 Democratic Presidential Primary
Gore (D) 720,311 (74%)
Bradley (D) 241,688 (25%)
Other 16,513 (2%)

1996 Presidential Vote
Clinton (D) 2,148,309 (47%)
Dole (R) 1,860,768 (41%)
Perot (I) 483,277 (11%)

metropolitan areas have not generated as large a percentage of culturally liberal high-education voters. In 2000 Bush carried college graduates and those with post-graduate degrees; the latter went heavily for Gore in states like New York and California. There were still traces of New Deal economic voting behavior—those with incomes over $100,000 were 65%–32% for Bush while union members were 67%–30% for Gore. But there are more high-income people and fewer union members than a generation or two ago. Working women were 56%–40% for Gore, but women not working outside the household were 54%–42% for Bush: the feminist left is weaker here than in other big states.

In 1996 Ohio switched its presidential primary from May to March 19, and voted on the same day as Illinois, Michigan and Wisconsin. But even then, just four weeks after New Hampshire, the race was already over. In May 1999 the state legislature voted to move the date to March 7, and Ohio was again seriously contested. Bush and Gore, with serious organizational support, won overwhelming victories as they clinched their parties' nominations. In 2004 it is scheduled to vote on March 2, one of 13 states with 216 electoral votes voting that day; with 10 other states. California, Texas and New York may get more attention then, but Ohio may get more in the fall.

Congressional districting Ohio lost one House seat in the 2000 Census and now has a House delegation of 18 members, the smallest since the 1820s.

108th Congress Lineup	
12 R	6 D
107th Congress Lineup	
11 R	8 D

Republicans had majorities in the legislature and held the governorship, and so had control of the process for the first time since 1960. It was clear that the Republicans could eliminate the seat of 13th District Democrat Sherrod Brown and imperil the chances of 6th District Democrat Ted Strickland. Strickland threatened to run against 18th District Republican Bob Ney. Brown made it clear that if his seat was eliminated he would run for governor. Governor Bob Taft, even though he had ousted Brown as secretary of state in 1990, did not want to face a well-financed and politically adept challenger, and asked Republican legislators not to target him. The legislature did not act in 2001.

Then, in January 2002, the Republicans effectively lost control. Ohio's filing deadline for the May primary was February 21, and under the Ohio Constitution a law passed in 2002 could take immediate effect only if it had a two-thirds vote in both houses. This meant the Republicans had to get the votes of at least one Democrat in the Senate and seven in the House. In the circumstances, the Republicans constructed a pretty ingenious plan, which they unveiled January 16. All 11 Republican incumbents got districts very similar to their current ones. So did the two Cleveland Democrats. Every other Democrat got a significantly different district. The incumbent put into the most parlous position was the 17th District's Jim Traficant. But he was facing trial on bribery charges (he was convicted in April and expelled from the House in July), and had been voting with Republicans on many issues; if one Democrat had to go, Democrats obviously preferred to sacrifice him. The 3d District was made significantly more Republican, but incumbent Tony Hall had long run far ahead of party lines; at least for the time being the seat seemed safe. The 14th District's Tom Sawyer had been given much of Traficant's old territory, but he had cast some free trade votes and organized labor didn't care if he was discomfited. Ted Strickland, given a seat stretching 325 miles along the Ohio River and up to Youngstown, was happy, even though he might have to face Traficant in a primary; the seat was much more Democratic than his previous district. Brown, given a safe Democratic seat, was pleased too. So on January 17 Democrats made a deal: they would provide the votes to give the plan immediate effect and avoid having to reschedule the congressional primary for August or September at a cost to taxpayers of $7 million. The plan passed on January 22.

Then on January 26 Tony Hall said he might give up his seat for a humanitarian job; Hall had long been interested in alleviating hunger, and George W. Bush offered him the ambassadorship to the Food and Agriculture Organization in Rome, which would allow him to work on that problem around the world. Republican Dayton Mayor Mike Turner had already announced he would run for the seat; Hall did not file for reelection and resigned when he was confirmed by the Senate, and Turner easily won the seat. The upshot was that the legislature's plan, and Hall's well-timed appointment, increased the Republican edge in the delegation from 11–8 to 12–6.

Governor

Bob Taft (R)

Elected 1998, term expires Jan. 2007, 2d term; b. Jan. 8, 1942, Boston, MA; home, Cincinnati; Yale U., B.A. 1963, Princeton U., M.A. 1967, U. of Cincinnati, J.D. 1976; Protestant; married (Hope).

Elected Office: OH House of Reps., 1976–81; Hamilton Cnty. Commissioner, 1981–90; OH Secy. of State, 1991–98.

Professional Career: Peace Corps, East Africa, 1963–65; State Dept., Vietnam, 1967–69; Budget Officer & Asst. Dir., IL Budget Bureau, 1969–73.

Office: Office of the Governor, 77 S. High St., 30th Fl., 43215, 614-466-3555; Fax: 614-644-0951; Web site: www.state.oh.us/gov.

Election Results

2002 general	Bob Taft (R)	1,865,007	(58%)
	Timothy Hagan (D)	1,236,924	(38%)
	John Eastman (I)	126,686	(4%)
2002 primary	Bob Taft (R)	unopposed	
1998 general	Bob Taft (R)	1,678,721	(50%)
	Lee Fisher (D)	1,498,956	(45%)
	Other	176,536	(5%)

Bob Taft, elected governor in 1998, is from a famed Ohio family. His great-grandfather William Howard Taft was elected president in 1908 and appointed chief justice in 1921. His grandfather, Robert A. Taft, was elected senator in 1938, 1944 and 1950; a strong and principled conservative known as "Mr. Republican," he ran for president and lost the Republican nomination in 1940 and 1952, and was Senate Majority Leader when he died in 1953. His father, Robert Taft Jr., was elected to the House in 1962, 1966 and 1968 and to the Senate in 1970, then lost to Howard Metzenbaum in 1976. The increasing informality of American politics can be gauged by the style of the Tafts' names: President Taft used three full names, the first Senator Taft an initial, the second Senator Taft a Jr. and this latest Taft calls himself simply Bob—and didn't make reference to his illustrious family in his campaign ads. He grew up in Cincinnati, graduated from Yale, served two years in the Peace Corps in East Africa, got a masters degree at Princeton and worked four years as a budget officer in Illinois state government. Then he returned to Cincinnati, graduated from the·University of Cincinnati law school, and was elected to the state House in 1976. In 1981 he was elected Hamilton County commissioner. In 1990 he started to run for governor, then was persuaded by Republican National Chairman Lee Atwater in one of his last political acts to step aside for George Voinovich and run for secretary of state instead; he beat incumbent Democrat Sherrod Brown for that office, critical for redistricting the state legislature, in November.

The common expectation was that Taft would run for governor in 1998, when Voinovich would be ineligible for a third term. At first he seemed to have primary opposition from Treasurer Kenneth Blackwell, but Blackwell agreed in January 1998 to run for secretary of state instead (he won, too, and has indicated he will run for governor in 2006). But Taft had strong Democratic opposition: Lee Fisher, elected attorney general in 1990, defeated by a narrow margin in heavily Republican 1994, who from his base in the Cleveland suburbs raised nearly as much money as the Republican. On primary day, voters rejected Issue 2, a one-cent sales tax for schools and property tax relief, written in response to a court decision requiring more school funding. Both Taft and Fisher supported it, and had to scramble to come up with new ways to address the number one issue, education, without a tax increase. Fisher promised to cut property taxes by 15% over two years; Taft proposed much smaller tax cuts, a homestead exemption and a $2,500 college tuition deduction for families with incomes under $50,000. Much of the ruckus of the campaign came over attacks for backing previous tax increases. Taft won 50%–45%.

In his first year in office Taft fulfilled many of his campaign promises. Working with the Republican legislature, he required students to take reading tests in the fourth grade to be academically promoted, and created the college tuition deduction, a homestead tax cut, tougher penalties for juvenile criminals and cheats who exploit the elderly. He reduced the inheritance tax and made other state tax cuts, and got voter approval of a $400 million environmental bond issue. Even organized labor was not unhappy; he had kept his pledge not to seek anti-union legislation.

But in early 2001 Taft faced more difficulties. Because of term limits, the legislature included many new members and some new leaders. Tax revenues, which had increased at a spritely pace in 2000, increased very little in 2001. The state Supreme Court had set a June 15 deadline for a new school finance program, and Medicaid costs were skyrocketing. The legislature responded by cutting higher education spending, and Taft issued 49 line-item vetoes in June. Taft successfully opposed conservative initiatives on abortion, a concealed-weapons law and video lottery slots at race tracks. The cigarette tax was raised and the rainy day fund drained. A Golden Buckeye discount card for prescription drugs was passed. In February 2002 Taft announced his $1.6 billion, 10-year Third Frontier Project, to use tobacco settlement money and bonds (to go before voters in 2003) to fund biomedical research, scientific research centers and support industries and high-tech products with growth potential—high-tech as a substitute for manufacturing.

Taft went into the 2002 election cycle a strong favorite and raised huge sums, eventually $12 million. This deterred some opponents, and the Democratic nomination went to former Cuyahoga County Commissioner Tim Hagan, a spirited liberal who in the cynical cauldron of Cleveland politics had paid some price for adherence to liberal principle. Hagan did not trim his liberal principles in this campaign, but opposed Taft on abortion, taxes and spending, prescription drugs, capital punishment, the video lottery and medical malpractice. Hagan had trouble raising money, eventually netting $1 million and tapping friends of his wife, actress Kate Mulgrew; he aired a few witty ads, modeled on the Aflac duck, against "Taftquack." Taft angered some conservatives when he named as his lieutenant governor candidate Columbus Councilwoman Jennette Bradley, a supporter of abortion rights. He dodged questions about the budget during the campaign and his ads attacked "Taxin' Tim Hagan." Taft won 58%–38%. Hagan won big in Cuyahoga County, but carried only five other counties; Taft carried counties including Toledo and Dayton as well as Cincinnati and Columbus. He carried north-and-east Ohio 49%–48% and the rest of the state 64%–31%.

A month after the election the state Supreme Court issued its third decision ruling the state school finance system unconstitutional and ordered the legislature to change it. But it didn't retain jurisdiction, set no deadline and appointed no lower court monitor. Lieutenant Governor Maureen O'Connor in November had been elected to replace a justice who favored the decision and seemed likely to produce a 4–3 majority against it, and so Taft and the legislature appeared to ignore the decision. They had fiscal problems aplenty without it. Projections showed a $720 million shortfall in the current budget and a $4 billion deficit in 2003–05. In January 2003 Taft recommended cigarette and alcohol tax increases and sales taxes on services and also substantial reductions in Medicaid. The Republican legislature balked at the tax increases and on Taft's fallback, a temporary 1% sales tax increase. Conservative legislators argued that spending had increased too much—more than doubling in the 1990s—and that Taft had refused to challenge public employee unions. In February Taft proposed a budget with a 10% increase, $3.1 billion in new taxes and a wage freeze.

Taft is not eligible for a third term. Several Republican statewide officeholders may run, including Secretary of State Kenneth Blackwell (who could become America's first black Republican governor), Attorney General Jim Petro and Auditor Betty Montgomery. Democrats mentioned include state Senator and former Congressman Eric Fingerhut, Congressmen Sherrod Brown and Ted Strickland and Dayton Mayor Rhine McLin.

Senior Senator

Mike DeWine (R)

Elected 1994, seat up 2006, 2d term; b. Jan. 5. 1947, Springfield; home, Cedarville; Miami U. of OH, B.S. 1969, OH Northern U., J.D. 1972; Catholic; married (Fran).

Elected Office: Greene Cnty. Prosecuting atty., 1977–81; OH Senate, 1980–82; U.S. House of Reps., 1982–90; OH Lt. Gov., 1990–94.

Professional Career: Practicing atty; Greene Cnty. Asst. Prosecuting atty., 1973–75.

DC Office: 140 RSOB, 20510, 202-224-2315; Fax: 202-224-6519; Web site: dewine.senate.gov.

State Offices: Cincinnati, 513-763-8260; Cleveland, 216-522-7272; Columbus, 614-469-5186; Marietta, 740-373-2317; Toledo, 419-259-7536; Xenia, 937-376-3080.

Committees: *Appropriations*: District of Columbia (Chmn.); Foreign Operations; Labor, HHS & Education; Military Construction; Transportation, Treasury & General Government; VA, HUD & Independent Agencies. *Health, Education, Labor & Pensions*: Aging; Children & Families; Substance Abuse & Mental Health Services

(Chmn.). *Intelligence (Select). Judiciary*: Antitrust, Competition Policy & Consumer Rights (Chmn.); Immigration, Border Security & Citizenship; Terrorism, Technology & Homeland Security.

Group Ratings

	ADA	ACLU	AFS	LCV	CON	ITIC	NTU	COC	ACU	NTLC	CHC
2002	15	40	0	12	69	75	62	95	95	74	—
2001	25	—	25	13	—	—	75	79	72	—	80

National Journal Ratings

	2001 LIB —	2001 CONS	2002 LIB —	2002 CONS
Economic	42%	58%	36%	63%
Social	43%	55%	38%	61%
Foreign	30%	65%	24%	67%

Key Votes of the 107th Congress

1. Approve Bush Tax Cuts	Y	5. Confirm Ashcroft as AG	Y
2. Expand Patients' Rights	Y	6. Bar Gays in the Boy Scouts	N
3. Campaign Finance Reform	N	7. $ for Hate Crime Prosecution	N
4. Permit ANWR Development	N	8. Overseas Military Abortions	N

9. Bar Coop. with Intl. Court	Y
10. Trade Promotion Authority	Y
11. Authorize Force in Iraq	Y
12. Homeland Sec. Dept. Union	N

Election Results

2000 general	Mike DeWine (R)	2,665,512	(60%)	($5,699,889)
	Ted Celeste (D)	1,595,066	(36%)	($477,176)
	Other	188,223	(4%)	
2000 primary	Mike DeWine (R)	1,029,860	(80%)	
	Ronald Dickson (R)	161,185	(12%)	
	Frank Cremeans (R)	104,219	(8%)	
1994 general	Mike DeWine (R)	1,836,556	(53%)	($6,084,663)
	Joel Hyatt (D)	1,348,213	(39%)	($4,921,223)
	Joseph J. Slovenec (I)	252,031	(7%)	($192,867)

Prior Winning Percentages: 1988 House (74%); 1986 House (100%); 1984 House (74%); 1982 House (56%)

Michael DeWine, Ohio's senior senator, is a Republican first elected to the House in 1982 and to the Senate in 1994. DeWine grew up in Yellow Springs, the home of liberal Antioch College, where his family owned a successful seed business. He graduated from Miami of Ohio and Northern Ohio University Law School and settled in Cedarville, in a part of the state with rolling hills, winding creeks and covered bridges, where they now host an annual ice cream social. There DeWine was elected Greene County prosecutor in 1976, at 29, where he resisted plea bargaining; in order to nail a drug dealer, once put up the collateral to get $50,000 cash to stage a buy. In 1980, at 33, he was elected to the Ohio Senate. In 1982, when incumbent Clarence Brown ran for governor, he won a six-candidate Republican primary with 69% and was elected to a U.S. House seat. Elected lieutenant governor in 1990, two years later DeWine ran against Senator John Glenn. It was a hard-hitting campaign: He attacked Glenn for his part in the Keating Five case. In September 1992 Glenn was below 50% in the polls. But Democrats brought up DeWine's 31 overdrafts on the House bank and the time he fell asleep at the Iran-Contra hearings. Glenn won 51%–42%, his closest general election margin ever.

In 1994 DeWine decided to run for the Senate again. This time the incumbent, Howard Metzenbaum, was retiring, and hoped to be succeeded by his son-in-law, Joel Hyatt, founder of the storefront Hyatt Legal Services chain. But in the May primary, Hyatt defeated Cuyahoga County Commissioner Mary Boyle by only 47%–43%, while DeWine won by 53%–32% over Bernadine Healy, former director of the National Institutes of Health. From then on, DeWine had solid leads in most polls. He spent much time in the Cleveland area, cutting into the Democrats' base. DeWine's anti-crime planks, his backing of term limits and the line-item veto helped him. The 23% of voters in union households split evenly, while the 29% who were gun owners voted 58%–31% for the almost always plaid-shirt-clad DeWine. DeWine won statewide 53%–39%.

The common motif that runs through DeWine's career is a concern for children and the championing of legislation often prompted by tragedy striking a particular child, including his own: his daughter Becky died in an auto accident in 1993, at 22, and he and his wife decided to donate her organs; DeWine spends much effort on organ donor programs and awareness. With Jay Rockefeller, he sponsored a law to change the family preservation emphasis in social work, and helped pass a law requiring the best interest of the child as paramount in custody cases involving abusive or drug-problem parents. In the recesses of the Senate's impeachment trial, he made calls to try to get medical benefits for a Middletown five-year-old with xeroderma pigmentosum, a disease so rare it is not on the Social Security Administration's list of covered treatments. He took over the chairmanship of the District of Columbia Appropriations Subcommittee—generally regarded as a thankless task—with a determination to reform the District's child welfare system, which he described as "wrought with dysfunction, chaos and tragedy." He recalled that 150 complaints of sexual abuse had not been investigated for more than a year and said that he became physically ill after reading about the January 2000 death of Brianna Blackmond, a girl placed in the custody of a violent and negligent mother through the inattention and indifference of foster care workers. DeWine has split from Republicans on several high visibility issues; he voted for the hate crimes bill in 2000 and 2001, he was the one Republican co-sponsor of a bill establishing a ballistic fingerprinting database in 2002 and opposed oil drilling in the Arctic National Wildlife Refuge in 2002 and 2003.

Even before Democrats got a majority in the Senate in 2001, DeWine often worked on a bipartisan basis. As chairman of the Employment and Training Subcommittee, he assembled bipartisan support for a sweeping rewriting of job training laws, with more flexibility for cities and counties; it passed in 1998. He co-sponsored a bill authorizing FDA regulation of tobacco with Edward Kennedy, a bill providing for health screening of newborns with Christopher Dodd and a bill requiring pharmaceutical companies to test drugs on children with Hillary Rodham Clinton. He and Patrick Leahy sponsored an asbestos bill which would allow loss carrybacks without time limit of asbestos claims and providing for non-taxation of asbestos settlement funds; this would increase the pot of money available for asbestos claimants and trial lawyers but not provide an administrative apparatus to settle and preserve claims. He and Democrat Herb Kohl have run the Antitrust Subcommittee on a bipartisan basis in both the Clinton and Bush years. In 1997 a joint letter to FCC Chairman Reed Hundt prompted him to kill the proposed AT&T-SBC merger; subcommittee hearings in 1998 helped prevent the proposed American Airlines-British Airways merger. In 2001 they helped prevent the USAirways-United Airlines merger.

Although he does not serve on Foreign Relations, DeWine has taken an interest in Latin American issues. He has made many trips there—12 to Haiti and four to Colombia and others to Mexico, Panama, Chile and Peru. In the 1980s he supported the Nicaragua contras against the Sandinista government. He has pushed for tougher interdiction of drugs, supports Plan Colombia and praises Colombia's President Alvaro Uribe. He first met with Mexico's President Vicente Fox in 1997, when he was Governor of Guanajuato. He has worked for more money for AIDS treatment in Haiti. DeWine serves on the Intelligence Committee and has called for more central control of intelligence. "You couldn't ever say George Tenet didn't get it. He understood the danger to this country as much as any human being could. And yet he didn't have the troops to go get the job done, and the reason he didn't have the troops was that he didn't really command all the troops, he only commanded part of the troops." He has sponsored a bill to let the FBI obtain search warrants or wiretaps of suspected foreign terrorists if there is "reasonable suspicion" that the person is a threat.

DeWine has worked on an assortment of Ohio issues; Ohio's two senators are the only state's who have a joint office handling constituency services. He has used his seat on the Military Construction Appropriations Subcommittee to look after the interests of Wright-Patterson Air Force Base near Dayton. He has supported more money for Amtrak and said that it was shameful that the state capital of Columbus doesn't have rail passenger service. He sought to get southern Ohio designated as a High Intensity Drug Trafficking Area.

DeWine came up for reelection in 2000. Democrats thought he might be vulnerable, especially after he was put charge of screening senators' questions for Chief Justice William Rehnquist and was asked to monitor the testimony of Monica Lewinsky. But House members Sherrod Brown, Ted Strickland and Marcy Kaptur, 1998 gubernatorial candidate Lee Fisher, and former Congressman Dennis Eckhart declined to run. DeWine spent much of late 1999 and early 2000 campaigning for John McCain in Ohio and elsewhere; he was one of only four senators who endorsed McCain (the others were Jon Kyl, Chuck Hagel and Fred Thompson). DeWine's Democratic opponent turned out to be Ted Celeste, former Ohio State Board of Trustees chairman, and brother of former Governor Richard Celeste. DeWine spent $5.7 million, much of it on television. Celeste spent $477,000, and put up one ad on the Internet which focused on prescription drug prices. DeWine won 60%–36%, the first Ohio Republican senator to be reelected since John Bricker in 1952, and with the largest margin for a Republican senator here since Theodore Burton in 1928. He won 23% of the votes of blacks and 24% of Democrats and lost union members by only 55%–44%, and non-high school graduates by 52%–43% and carried all other demographic groups. He won 83 of 88 counties, losing only the two Mahoning County steel counties, two eastern Ohio coal counties and usually Republican Madison County, where there was local opposition to his proposal to create a Little Darby Creek National Wildlife Refuge.

In November 2002 DeWine announced that he would run for reelection in 2006; some had thought he might run for governor. Interestingly, Senators Don Nickles, Bill Frist and Mitch McConnell, usually not involved in local politics beyond their states, sent contributions in 2004 to his son, Cincinnati Councilman Pat DeWine.

Junior Senator

George Voinovich (R)

Elected 1998, seat up 2004, 1st term; b. July 15, 1936, Cleveland; home, Cleveland; Ohio U., B.A. 1958, Ohio St. U., J.D. 1961; Catholic; married (Janet).

Elected Office: OH House of Reps., 1966–71; Cuyahoga Cnty. Auditor, 1971–76; Cuyahoga Cnty. Commissioner, 1977–78; OH Lt. Gov., 1979; Cleveland Mayor, 1979–89; OH Gov., 1990–98.

Professional Career: OH Asst. Atty. Gen., 1963–64.

DC Office: 317 HSOB, 20510, 202-224-3353; Fax: 202-228-0501; Web site: voinovich.senate.gov.

State Offices: Cincinnati, 513-684-3265; Cleveland, 216-522-7095; Columbus, 614-469-6697; Toledo, 419-259-3895.

Committees: *Environment & Public Works*: Clean Air, Climate Change & Nuclear Safety (Chmn.); Transportation & Infrastructure. *Ethics (Select)* (Chmn.). *Foreign Relations*: East Asian & Pacific Affairs; European Affairs; International Operations & Terrorism; Near Eastern & South Asian Affairs. *Governmental Affairs*: Financial Management, Budget & International Security; Government Management, Federal Workforce & the District of Columbia (Chmn.); Investigations (Permanent).

Group Ratings

	ADA	ACLU	AFS	LCV	CON	ITIC	NTU	COC	ACU	NTLC	CHC
2002	5	40	14	0	69	62	69	95	90	88	—
2001	15	—	0	0	—	—	87	93	83	—	80

National Journal Ratings

	2001 LIB —	2001 CONS	2002 LIB —	2002 CONS
Economic	30%	66%	38%	61%
Social	43%	55%	40%	58%
Foreign	48%	51%	35%	61%

Key Votes of the 107th Congress

1. Approve Bush Tax Cuts	Y	5. Confirm Ashcroft as AG	Y
2. Expand Patients' Rights	N	6. Bar Gays in the Boy Scouts	N
3. Campaign Finance Reform	N	7. $ for Hate Crime Prosecution	N
4. Permit ANWR Development	Y	8. Overseas Military Abortions	N

9. Bar Coop. with Intl. Court	N
10. Trade Promotion Authority	Y
11. Authorize Force in Iraq	Y
12. Homeland Sec. Dept. Union	N

Election Results

1998 general	George Voinovich (R)	1,922,087	(56%)	($6,756,712)
	Mary O. Boyle (D)	1,482,054	(44%)	($2,236,137)
1998 primary	George Voinovich (R)	539,424	(72%)	
	David McCollough (R)	207,135	(28%)	
1992 general	John H. Glenn, Jr. (D)	2,444,419	(51%)	($4,974,109)
	Mike DeWine (R)	2,028,300	(42%)	($3,053,156)
	Martha Kathryn Grevatt (I)	321,670	(7%)	

George Voinovich, a Republican, was elected to the Senate in 1998 after a long career in public life. He is of Serbian and Slovenian descent and grew up in heavily ethnic Cleveland. He graduated from Ohio State and its law school, then practiced law in Cleveland. He was elected to the state House in 1966, at 30. He was elected Cuyahoga County auditor in 1971 and county commissioner in 1977. In 1978 he was selected by 69-year-old Governor James Rhodes to be lieutenant governor. In 1979, after Mayor Dennis Kucinich bankrupted Cleveland, Voinovich ran for mayor. It was a strenuous campaign, running as a Republican in a heavily Democratic city, and one touched by tragedy: his daughter was killed in an auto accident at the time. In 10 years in office, he fixed the budget and sparked the city's renaissance. His one defeat came in 1988, when he lost 57%–43% to Senator Howard Metzenbaum.

In 1990 Voinovich ran for governor and beat Attorney General Anthony Celebrezze Jr., 56%–44%; in 1994 he was re-elected by the spectacular margin of 72%–25%. Voinovich got the state government's fiscal house in order, with the help of a tax increase in 1992. He is opposed to abortion but recognizes *Roe v. Wade* as the law and says, "Let's deal in the real world." He was the first governor to endorse Bob Dole for president; he was mentioned for the vice presidential nomination but took himself out of the running.

In February 1997 Senator John Glenn announced he would retire in 1998, and Voinovich, not eligible to run for reelection as governor, was the obvious favorite; he led in polls for nearly two years. His Democratic opponent was another Clevelander (as a boy Voinovich delivered newspapers to her family's house), Cuyahoga County Commissioner Mary Boyle, who lost the 1994 Senate primary but this time had no competition for the nomination. Boyle campaigned on education, blaming Voinovich for allowing Ohio schools to decline; she called for HMO regulation and a minimum wage increase. She also attacked him for supporting the tax increase that voters rejected in the May primary. Voinovich mostly ignored her attacks and outspent her by almost 3–1, running ads that highlighted his record as governor. The results showed Voinovich a bit weaker than he had seemed when Glenn announced his retirement. An unknown won 28% against him in the May primary, and in November his margin over Boyle was a decisive but not overwhelming 56%–44%.

Voinovich came to the Senate, after 32 years in public office, as a big government Republican, willing to back tax increases as he did in 1992 but dubious about cutting them, as he was in 1999 and 2000. In his previous positions he had been required to balance budgets, and he seemed viscerally repelled by deficits. In 1999 he voted against the Republicans' $792 billion tax cut, against the smaller Democratic tax cut, and against the bipartisan moderates' compromise tax cut. To arguments that government should return money to taxpayers because there was a surplus, he said, "There's an old saying that most of us learned as children that goes, 'If it sounds too good to be true, then it is.'" He was the only Republican to vote in November 1999 against the Republican minimum wage bill, with its tax cuts for small businessmen. In April 2000 he was one of two Republicans to vote against the Republican budget. In July 2000 he was one of four Republicans to vote against estate tax repeal and the only Republican to vote against marriage penalty relief. He did support the Bush tax cuts in May 2001, when it looked as if the surplus would be permanent. In October 2001 he worked to scale back the tax cuts in House Republicans' stimulus package. In December 2002 he and Russ Feingold sponsored a bill to require CBO to calculate future deficits assuming tax cuts would be made permanent and that spending would keep rising by 8% and he warned that the annual deficit could rise to $866 billion in 10 years. He complained, "Around here nobody wants to make the hard choices. Nobody wants to prioritize. No one wants to say no to anyone." In February 2003 he came out against the $700 billion Bush tax cut and in April he and Olympia Snowe insisted they would back no cut higher than $350 billion. That led Finance Chairman Charles Grassley and Majority Leader Bill Frist to say they would insist on that figure from conference, to the rage of the House Republican leadership. When George W. Bush came to Ohio in April 2003, Voinovich was cordial but refused to budge.

Voinovich is interested not only in maintaining government's revenue flow, but in how government works. As chairman of the Government Reform subcommittee on Government Management, Restructuring and the District of Columbia, he found that agencies could not say how much they spend on training. He was concerned about the brain drain at agencies as many employees neared retirement age and at the rigidity of government hiring practices. In October 2001 he introduced a bill that he hoped would lead to the first major change in civil service laws since 1978. It provided for chief human capital officers at each agency; hiring from a wider pool of applicants rated either basically qualified, highly qualified or superior (current practice is to choose among those rated, often arbitrarily, the top three); greater leeway for demonstration projects; allowing agencies to buy out workers for $25,000 to reshape their work forces. In June 2002 Voinovich made some changes, pursuant to comments by government employee unions and others, and got the support of subcommittee Chairman Daniel Akaka. In July 2002 Voinovich and Akaka got a version of this bill inserted as the personnel section in the homeland security bill. There it became law in December 2002. This was a major achievement: the new department has 173,000 employees and, together with Defense, which has been seeking its own civil service changes, accounts for most federal government employees. Voinovich, now subcommittee chairman again, submitted another version of his bill to cover the rest in January 2003.

As an Environment and Public Works subcommittee chairman, he steered to passage in September 2000 a giant energy and water authorization, which included the $1.1 billion Everglades restoration project estimated to eventually cost $7.8 billion. But a month later he voted against a water and power appropriation, which included many Ohio projects, arguing that it spent too much money: authorizing committee members like to keep appropriators on a short leash. In November 2001 Voinovich offered up his own energy package, and in May 2002 he offered many amendments in committee to the Clean Water Act reauthorization. In January 2003 Energy Committee Chairman Jim Inhofe asked him to manage George W. Bush's Clear Skies Iniative, and he said he would have to amend it to do more to reduce greenhouse gas emissions. He also put on the omnibus appropriation an extension on the ban on oil and gas drilling in the Great Lakes.

Voinovich is the only Serbian-American in the Senate, and as a college freshman wrote a paper on how the United States sold out Yugoslavia at the February 1945 Yalta conference; in 1991 his Serbian relatives were forced out of their homes in the newly independent Croatia. In March and April 1999 he strongly opposed the bombing of Serbia, but he has called Slobodan Milosevic a "war criminal" and tried to convince the State Department to support forces to depose him.

Voinovich comes up for reelection in 2004. In early 2003 he had $2.5 million in his campaign treasury and was getting high job ratings. In January 2003 state Senator Bob Hagan of Youngstown, brother of 2002 governor candidate Tim Hagan, said that he was thinking about running. In March 2003 state Senator Eric Fingerhut, who was elected to one term in the House in 1992 and defeated in 1994, announced he was running. But the Democrat getting the most attention was Jerry Springer, the successful host of a talk show aimed at unsuccessful people. Springer's show is based in Chicago, but he is registered to vote in Ohio. He had a successful political career in the 1970s and 1980s as councilman and mayor in Cincinnati; at one point he resigned after it was revealed he had paid for a prostitute with a credit card, but he was later returned to office. In January 2003 he said he was thinking about running and figured it would take $20 million, with $5 million in the primary. When asked about his chances, he said, "There are pluses and minuses. The plus is that I'm known by everybody. The minus is that I'm known by everybody." A poll showed Springer with 71% unfavorable ratings, and he said, "I can't imagine anyone voting for me at this point." But he is articulate and knowledgeable about public policy and might be able to convince voters he is a serious candidate. Voinovich's comment: "Jerry Springer is the Democratic party's problem."

FIRST DISTRICT

Rep. Steve Chabot (R)

Elected 1994, 5th term; b. Jan. 22, 1953, Cincinnati; home, Cincinnati; William & Mary Col., B.A. 1975, N. KY U., J.D. 1978; Catholic; married (Donna).

Elected Office: Cincinnati City Cncl., 1985–90; Hamilton Cnty. Comm., 1990–94.

Professional Career: Elem. Schl. teacher, 1975–76; Practicing atty., 1978–94.

DC Office: 129 CHOB 20515, 202-225-2216; Fax: 202-225-3012; Web site: www.house.gov/chabot.

District Office: Cincinnati, 513-684-2723.

Committees: *International Relations* (12th of 26 R): Asia & the Pacific; Middle East & Central Asia. *Judiciary* (7th of 21 R): Commercial & Administrative Law; Crime, Terrorism & Homeland Security; The Constitution (Chmn.). *Small Business* (4th of 18 R): Tax, Finance & Exports.

Group Ratings

	ADA	ACLU	AFS	LCV	CON	ITIC	NTU	COC	ACU	NTLC	CHC
2002	0	7	11	25	97	100	68	90	96	100	100
2001	5	—	0	14	—	—	75	87	96	—	—

National Journal Ratings

	2001 LIB	—	2001 CONS		2002 LIB	—	2002 CONS
Economic	22%	—	74%		16%	—	81%
Social	0%	—	81%		0%	—	75%
Foreign	33%	—	60%		15%	—	78%

Key Votes of the 107th Congress

1. Approve Bush Tax Cuts	Y	5. Faith-Based Charities	Y	9. Trade Promotion Authority	Y
2. Limit Patients' Bill of Rights	Y	6. Bar Gays in the Boy Scouts	Y	10. Bar Funds for Intl. Court	Y
3. Campaign Finance Reform	N	7. Ban Partial-Birth Abortion	Y	11. Authorize Force in Iraq	Y
4. Ban ANWR Development	N	8. Arm Commercial Pilots	Y	12. Deny Home. Sec. Dept. Union	Y

Election Results

2002 general	Steve Chabot (R)	110,760	(65%)	($490,317)
	Greg Harris (D)	60,168	(35%)	($23,388)
2002 primary	Steve Chabot (R)	unopposed		
2000 general	Steve Chabot (R)	116,768	(53%)	($1,099,555)
	John Cranley (D)	98,328	(45%)	($465,561)
	Other	5,332	(2%)	

Prior Winning Percentages: 1998 (53%); 1996 (54%); 1994 (56%)

The People		Race/Ethnic Origin	Ancestry	
Area size:	420 sq. mi.	68.6% White	German: 23.6%	Irish: 9.8%
Urban population:	94.8%	27.4% Black	English: 5.4%	
Rural population:	5.2%	1.3% Asian	**2000 Presidential Vote**	
Pop. 2000:	630,730	0.2% Native Am.	Bush (R)..............136,372	(51%)
Median income:	$37,414	0.0% Hawaiian	Gore (D)..............120,927	(46%)
Poverty status:	13.9%	1.2% Two + races	Other...................8,463	(3%)
Military veterans:	12.5%	0.2% Other	**Cook Partisan Voting Index:** R + 3	
		1.1% Hispanic Origin		
Occupation	Blue collar: 23.1%	White collar: 60.5%	Gray collar: 16.5%	

From its seven hills, Cincinnati, dubbed the Queen City of the West in the 19th century, looks down on the curves of the Ohio River. Ohio's first major metropolis and a heavily German beehive of riverboats and sausage factories, known in the 1850s as Porkopolis, this was the nation's fourth-largest city and a chief destination for slaves on the Underground Railroad at the outbreak of the

Civil War. Cincinnati has long given off an air of the recent past; Mark Twain said he'd like to be there for the apocalypse because everything in Cincinnati is 20 years behind. Growing slowly over many decades, Cincinnati has long-settled good looks and urbanity somehow consistent with its natural terrain: the bottomlands along the river, the hills and rolling terrain above. In the middle of Cincinnati is Mill Creek, lined with factories; on the hills to the west, above the restored Union Terminal with the children's, historic, and natural history museums, are the modest streetcar suburbs of the 19th century and the early years of the 20th. On Mount Adams and toward the northeast are set a string of affluent neighborhoods, with stately mansions like the William Howard Taft house, and the comfortable Tudors and colonials of the 20th century bourgeoisie—Reform Jewish as well as WASP and German. In the low-income Over-the-Rhine community, riots broke out after a white police officer shot an unarmed young black man in April 2001.

Cincinnati was the site of great innovations: the first iron suspension bridge, in 1867, connecting Cincinnati to northern Kentucky and designed by John Roebling, who later built the Brooklyn Bridge; the first baseball team, the Red Stockings, in 1869; the country's leading Reform Jewish seminary, Hebrew Union College, in 1875. Cincinnati has not had the growth spurts of cities like Cleveland or Houston; it has spawned not flashy but solid industries, like the Procter & Gamble soap business, now headquartered in a striking two-towered office complex at the edge of downtown, and it has America's biggest concentration of machine tool makers. Downtown Cincinnati's spruced-up Fountain Square shows off the well-maintained skyscrapers of the past plus a revival of museums and arts institutions, and its first-class restaurants still attract a dressy clientele. Old ethnic neighborhoods, crowded with brick row houses on steep hills, keep their thick local accents and special local foods, from German sauerbrauten to Cincinnati chili.

The 1st Congressional District includes almost all of Cincinnati, except for parts of its affluent eastern edge, plus most of the middle-class suburbs that cling to the woody hills west of I-71 and south of I-275. It covers the western part of Hamilton County all the way to the Indiana border, including North Bend, the home of President William Henry Harrison. The 2002 redistricting added the southwest quarter of Butler County. Ancestrally Republican, Cincinnati was a German anti-slavery island in a Southern-stock pro-Confederate sea. City elections here were for years competitive between old-line Republicans and a combination of Democrats and Charterites (the latter started by Charles Taft, liberal brother of Senator Robert Taft Sr. and great-uncle of Governor Bob Taft). Traditionally, Cincinnati was a Republican stronghold, and culturally conservative, though the suburbs now are much more Republican than the city. In the 1990s Cincinnati's population declined by a startling 9%, with many whites leaving for suburban counties, which grew rapidly; left behind were poor blacks. Cincinnati once cast most of the votes in Hamilton County; now it casts well under half. The 1st District lost population in the 1990s, and the 2002 redistricting added 88,000 people and in the process reduced the black percentage from 34% to 27% black and increased the Bush 2000 percentage from 47% to 51%.

The congressman from the 1st District is Steve Chabot (pronounced *SHAB-butt*), a Republican first elected in 1994. Like so many of the local congressmen here over the decades, he grew up in Cincinnati and served on the city council. He graduated from William and Mary, taught elementary school for a year, then graduated from Northern Kentucky Law School and started a family law practice. In 1985, at 32, he was elected to the council in 1985, and in 1990 he was elected to the Hamilton County Commission. Chabot ran for the House in 1994 in odd circumstances. In 1992, first term Democrat Charles Luken (son of longtime incumbent Tom Luken) retired suddenly after the June primary; he later became mayor of Cincinnati. In the special primary to replace him, moderate Democratic Councilman David Mann defeated liberal state Senator William Bowen, by 416 votes, and won the general 51%–43%. In the House, Mann voted against the Clinton tax package and for NAFTA, which infuriated local unions; Bowen ran in the primary again in 1994 and this time Mann won by 667 votes. In the fall, Chabot backed the balanced budget amendment, strongly opposed abortion, and attacked Mann's support of Bill Clinton. Chabot won comfortably, 56%–44%.

Chabot has had a conservative voting record in the House, though a bit less so on foreign and defense issues. He has shown himself willing to take political risks for principle. He voted against the Appalachian Regional Commission, a $2 million study of light rail in the Cincinnati area and a bill containing $6 million for the National Underground Railroad Freedom Center in Cincinnati; he argued that the city should solve problems with local resources and not depend on Washington. He opposed farm subsidies, including the ag bill in 2002, and his tight-fistedness created unusual alliances with environmentalists fighting what they considered, for different reasons, wasteful spending.

Most of his committee work has been on the Judiciary Committee. In January 2001, he became chairman of the Constitution Subcommittee, perennially a forum for bitter ideological debate but little legislative action. After the September 11 attacks, he held a hearing on the proposed constitutional amendment by Brian Baird to permit governors to fill House vacancies in the event of a national disaster; Chabot was skeptical, and the subcommittee took no further action. He has been a House leader for a constitutional amendment to protect the rights of crime victims. In 2002, he got enactment of the Born-Alive Infants Protection Act requiring hospitals and medical personnel to protect infants who survive an abortion; abortion rights groups decided not to fight. In 2003 he worked to pass the partial-birth abortion ban by specifying its policy findings and narrowing its terms so that it would comply with Supreme Court decisions. He also has pushed measures to impose restrictions on minors who cross state lines to get an abortion and to make violence against an unborn child a crime.

Initially, Chabot was a prime Democratic campaign target. In 1996 the AFL-CIO spent over $1 million, running nearly 2,000 television ads against him. A light moment came in October when Democratic challenger Mark Longabaugh, a top aide in Dick Gephardt's 1988 presidential campaign, ran an ad showing Chabot's yellow pages listing and noting that he took clients in DUI cases; Chabot responded with an ad showing the white pages and asking, "Where's Mark Longabaugh been listed for 15 years? Not here!" Chabot won 54%–43%. In 1998 Chabot was opposed by Cincinnati Mayor Roxanne Qualls. This was one of the hardest fought races in the country, and one of the most expensive: Chabot spent $1.5 million, Qualls $1.2 million. Qualls argued that Chabot's views were too conservative for the district. Chabot called for broad-based tax cuts, and cuts in pork barrel projects and corporate welfare. They disagreed on the partial-birth abortion ban and school vouchers. Chabot won 53%–47%, just a bit closer than his earlier elections. In 2000, Chabot defeated lawyer John Cranley 53%–45%. Redistricting made the district safer. Chabot won 72% of the vote in the new Butler County territory and won overall 65%–35%.

SECOND DISTRICT

Rep. Rob Portman (R)

Elected May 1993, 5th term; b. Dec. 19, 1955, Cincinnati; home, Terrace Park; Dartmouth Col., B.A. 1979, U. of MI, J.D. 1984; Methodist; married (Jane).

Professional Career: Practicing atty., 1984–88; Assoc. Cnsl., White House, 1989; Dpty. Asst. & White House Legis. Affairs Dir., 1989–91; Alternate U.S. Rep. to UN Human Rights Comm., 1992.

DC Office: 238 CHOB 20515, 202-225-3164; Web site: www.house.gov/portman.

District Offices: Batavia, 513-732-2948; Cincinnati, 513-791-0381.

Committees: *Republican Leadership Chairman. Budget* (8th of 24 R). *Ways & Means* (14th of 24 R): Oversight.

Group Ratings

	ADA	ACLU	AFS	LCV	CON	ITIC	NTU	COC	ACU	NTLC	CHC
2002	0	7	0	25	75	100	59	95	92	92	100
2001	0	—	0	14	—	—	68	100	88	—	—

National Journal Ratings

	2001 LIB —	2001 CONS	2002 LIB —	2002 CONS
Economic	15% —	82%	16% —	81%
Social	20% —	69%	25% —	71%
Foreign	4% —	87%	15% —	78%

Key Votes of the 107th Congress

1. Approve Bush Tax Cuts	Y	5. Faith-Based Charities	Y	9. Trade Promotion Authority	Y
2. Limit Patients' Bill of Rights	Y	6. Bar Gays in the Boy Scouts	Y	10. Bar Funds for Intl. Court	Y
3. Campaign Finance Reform	N	7. Ban Partial-Birth Abortion	Y	11. Authorize Force in Iraq	Y
4. Ban ANWR Development	N	8. Arm Commercial Pilots	Y	12. Deny Home. Sec. Dept. Union	Y

Election Results

2002 general	Rob Portman (R)	139,218	(74%)	($759,363)
	Charles Sanders (D)	48,785	(26%)	($17,189)
2002 primary	Rob Portman (R)	unopposed		
2000 general	Rob Portman (R)	204,184	(74%)	($406,952)
	Charles Sanders (D)	64,091	(23%)	($12,599)
	Other	9,266	(3%)	

Prior Winning Percentages: 1998 (76%); 1996 (72%); 1994 (77%); 1993 (70%)

The People		**Race/Ethnic Origin**	**Ancestry**	
Area size:	2,630 sq. mi.	91.7% White	German: 21.3%	Irish: 11.1%
Urban population:	73.0%	4.7% Black	USA: 8.6%	
Rural population:	27.0%	1.3% Asian	**2000 Presidential Vote**	
Pop. 2000:	630,730	0.2% Native Am.	Bush (R)	175,382 (63%)
Median income:	$46,813	0.0% Hawaiian	Gore (D)	96,027 (34%)
Poverty status:	8.4%	0.9% Two+ races	Other	8,187 (3%)
Military veterans:	13.0%	0.1% Other	**Cook Partisan Voting Index:** R +15	
		1.0% Hispanic Origin		

Occupation	Blue collar: 23.2%	White collar: 63.7%	Gray collar: 13.1%

The most Republican major metro area in the nation over the longest time span has been Cincinnati. Back in the 1850s, when Harriet Beecher Stowe wrote *Uncle Tom's Cabin* here, Cincinnati was an island of German, pro-Union, Republican sentiment in a Southern, Democratic, pro-slavery sea. Later Cincinnati attracted fewer southern and eastern European immigrants than Great Lakes industrial cities like Cleveland, Detroit and Chicago; its ethnic character (like its physical appearance) and its political preference have remained pretty well fixed. Even many of the Appalachians here are Republicans, from Civil War Republican counties in the hills. Democratic constituencies here never got very large: economically, it was never a strong CIO town; culturally, it is home to a strong anti-pornography movement that, among other things, was the site of obscenity charges filed against *Hustler* publisher Larry Flynt. The local Republican record remains intact: It was the only million-plus metro area that George Bush and Bob Dole carried by more than 50% in 1992 and 1996, and George W. Bush won it handily in 2000.

For 140 years after 1852, Cincinnati and surrounding Hamilton County were divided by a north-south line into two congressional districts. But by 1990 Hamilton County no longer had enough people for two full districts, and today both the Cincinnati-based districts include territory in other counties. Ohio's 2d Congressional District includes much of eastern Hamilton County, up to the edge of downtown Cincinnati and Mount Adams and the eastern edge of the city of Cincinnati. It includes the mostly affluent suburbs of eastern Hamilton County and the fast-growing suburbs of Clermont County and southern Warren County. It also includes counties farther east on the Ohio River, all the way to the old industrial city of Portsmouth and the hills of rural Pike County. These are very different areas. The metropolitan parts of the district, with 77% of its people, are mostly affluent and politically very Republican. The counties farther east are less well off, though there has been some growth here in the 1990s. Portsmouth, however, has a depressed economy and an Appalachian frame of mind. They are close to marginal in most elections, and Pike County has an historical Democratic tradition. Overall, however, this is a very Republican district, 63% for George W. Bush in 2000, his best district in Ohio.

The congressman from the 2d District is Rob Portman, a Republican first elected in May 1993, who quickly became one of the most important legislators in the House. Portman has good connections both at home and in Washington. He grew up in Cincinnati, where his father owned a forklift company; his mother's family owned the Golden Lamb in Lebanon, Ohio's oldest inn, and his ancestors were Quaker abolitionists active in the Underground Railroad. He graduated from Dartmouth, then worked for the 1980 Bush presidential campaign as an advance man; he had already worked in the campaigns of his predecessor, Bill Gradison. He graduated from the University of Michigan Law School and worked for a big firm in Washington. In 1989 he worked in the Bush White House, first in the counsel's office and then in legislative affairs; in 1992 he was U.S. representative to the United Nations Human Rights Council. He had moved back to Cincinnati when, in January 1993, Gradison unexpectedly resigned. Portman ran for the seat with Gradison's endorsement and impressive financial backing from the Cincinnati establishment and his Bush connections. In the primary he faced former Congressman Bob McEwen, who had represented the 6th District to the east for 12 years and then lost it after a contentious primary in 1992, and businessman Jay Buchert, president of the National Association of Home Builders, who ran a vitriolic campaign against both Portman and McEwen. With help from a radio ad by Barbara Bush, Portman won with 36% of the vote, to 30% for McEwen, who carried counties he had once represented, and 25% for Buchert. Portman won the general with 70%. He has had no reelection problems since then.

In the House, Portman made himself a rising star and got a seat on Ways and Means. As part of the Contract with America, he helped floor-manage in early 1995 the unfunded mandates bill—a large responsibility for one who hadn't even been a member two years. He authored or co-authored nine bills that were signed by Clinton. He shepherded, as co-chairman with Senator Bob Kerrey of the National Commission on Restructuring the Internal Revenue Service, a bipartisan package to define taxpayer rights and make the 100,000-plus employee agency more user friendly. With Bob Matsui, he won broad support to repeal the 3% excise tax on telephone service, which critics derided as the "Spanish-American War tax" because it was instituted as a temporary measure to finance that war, which ended in 1898.

Starting in 1997, Portman worked with Democrat Ben Cardin on a bill to increase the amounts workers could set aside in 401(k)s, IRAs and other tax-free accounts and to make it easier for small businesses to offer pension plans. This was an effort not supported by the Clinton or Bush administrations and with little institutional support from the Treasury or the private sector. They worked together to forge consensus on Ways and Means; Portman resisted Republican attempts to raise the limits above $5,000 for IRAs and $15,000 for 401(k)s. Ways and Means Democrat Earl Pomeroy likened their partnership to Ginger Rogers and Fred Astaire. The House passed their bill 401–25 in 2000, but the Senate did not take it up. In April 2001 the House leadership moved it before the Bush tax cut and it was passed 308–70 in June 2001, then attached it to the Bush tax cut. It remained in the tax cut and became law in June 2001—a major bipartisan achievement for two not very senior members. In January 2002 Portman and Cardin put aside broader pension reform and concentrated on issues raised by the Enron bankruptcy. Their bill did not ban companies from putting their own stock in employees' 401(k)s but did allow workers to sell matching stock after three years, require 21 day advance notice of blackout periods and bar companies from requiring employees to invest in their own stock. Some of its provisions became law.

Portman has also addressed tax and pension issues on his own. In April 2002 he sponsored a bill to repeal the Alternative Minimum Tax for individuals and corporations and allowing those with less than $500 in dividend and interest income not to itemize. Here he was addressing an issue most serious policymakers know they will have to address some day: the AMT, passed in 1969 to affect only a handful of taxpayers, will by 2010 ensnare within its complex provisions 36 million taxpayers—30% to 40% of all voters. In early 2003 Portman told Bush administration officials that he would not support the provisions for untaxed savings accounts with much higher contributions limits, a project of outgoing Treasury Secretary Paul O'Neill. The proposal was brushed aside by Ways and Means Chairman Bill Thomas.

Among House members, Portman probably has the closest ties with the Bush White House—with George W. Bush himself, whom he briefed often during the 2000 campaign and for whom he took part in debate preparation, and with many high level members of the White House staff, with whom he is in constant touch. He is also close to Thomas and to Speaker Dennis Hastert, who arranged for him to chair Republican leadership meetings in January 2001 and in February 2003 named him officially as chairman of the leadership and liaison to the administration. He has been mentioned as a candidate for a leadership position, but has been a de facto part of the leadership for some time. He has been active as a Republican fundraiser, chairing the $25 million House and Senate Dinner in 2000 and starting his own leadership PAC in 2002 though he has declined to take PAC money himself. He has often been mentioned as a nominee for an administration position, open or not, but seems more interested in continuing in the House. But not forever; as he noted in 2002, "I am interested in the possibility of running statewide some day. And I don't know when the time might come, if ever. There are two Republican senators; I support both of them strongly."

At home, Portman has worked to keep jobs in the USEC uranium enrichment facility in Pike County and to get funds for the Portsmouth Gaseous Diffusion Plant; they are in the part of the 2d District added in redistricting, and the only part where the vote was about even in 2002.

THIRD DISTRICT

Rep. Mike Turner (R)

Elected 2002, 1st term; b. Jan. 11, 1960, Dayton; home, Dayton; OH N. U., B.A. 1982, Case Western Reserve U., J.D. 1985, U. of Dayton, M.B.A. 1992; Protestant; married (Lori).

Elected Office: Dayton Mayor, 1994–2001.

Professional Career: Practicing atty.

DC Office: 1740 LHOB 20515, 202-225-6465; Fax: 202-225-6754; Web site: www.house.gov/miketurner.

District Offices: Dayton, 937-225-2843; Wilmington, 937-383-8931.

Committees: *Armed Services* (28th of 33 R): Strategic Forces; Tactical Air & Land Forces. *Government Reform* (21st of 24 R): Government Efficiency & Financial Management; National Security, Emerging Threats & Intl. Relations (Vice Chmn.); Technology, Information Policy, Intergovernmental Relations & Census.

Group Ratings and Key Votes: Newly Elected

Election Results

2002 general	Mike Turner (R)	111,630	(59%)	($1,045,016)
	Richard Carne (D)	78,307	(41%)	($567,746)
2002 primary	Mike Turner (R)	46,952	(80%)	
	Roy Brown (R)	8,346	(14%)	
	Gregory Hunter (R)	3,702	(6%)	
2000 general	Tony P. Hall (D)	177,731	(83%)	($192,835)
	Regina Birch (NL)	36,516	(17%)	

The People		Race/Ethnic Origin	Ancestry	
Area size:	1,610 sq. mi.	79.5% White	German: 17.9%	Irish: 9.1%
Urban population:	84.7%	16.9% Black	USA: 8.5%	
Rural population:	15.3%	1.1% Asian	**2000 Presidential Vote**	
Pop. 2000:	630,730	0.2% Native Am.	Bush (R)..............130,446	(52%)
Median income:	$41,591	0.0% Hawaiian	Gore (D)..............112,102	(45%)
Poverty status:	10.2%	1.2% Two+ races	Other....................6,874	(3%)
Military veterans:	14.3%	0.1% Other	**Cook Partisan Voting Index:** R + 4	
		1.1% Hispanic Origin		

Occupation   Blue collar: 26.0%   White collar: 59.7%   Gray collar: 14.3%

Dayton, once a medium-sized city known as the home of the typical American voter, became the name of the international peace agreement reached in November 1995 that stopped the slaughter in the former Yugoslavia. The 21 days of negotiating took place at nearby Wright-Patterson Air Force Base, and the people of Dayton played a role. "From the time we landed at the airport," wrote U.S. negotiator Richard Holbrooke, "until the time we left, we felt that we were in a community that was literally praying for us. People were lighting candles in their windows, there were signs all over the airport and on the byways. That would never have happened in New York or in Washington. And it made a tremendous impression on people."

Dayton has made a difference in people's lives in America and around the world for many years. Here, just south of the old National Road that spans the Midwest, was the home of James Ritty, who in 1879 invented the cash register—that indispensable instrument of mass retail trade—and of John Henry Patterson, who bought it from Ritty for $6,500 in 1884 and established the National Cash Register company (NCR). It was home of a former Patterson employee, Tom Watson Sr., who feuded with him and went off to found IBM. It was in Dayton in the 1890s that Wilbur and Orville Wright, tinkering in their bicycle shop and observing the horseless carriages driven through Dayton's streets, experimented with kites and gliders and constructed the first wind tunnel in the world and the first heavier-than-air flying machine, which they took to ever-windy Kitty Hawk, North Carolina, to fly in December 1903. A few years later, Dayton's Charles Kettering invented the automatic starter for cars. In the 1970s and 1980s, Dayton's economy seemed to be sputtering. General Motors, the area's largest employer, was in trouble; NCR was taken over in a merger. But by the mid-1990s, the local economy had turned around. There are more scientists, engineers, computer specialists and technicians here than GM workers. The area's small manufacturers and suppliers have shown that Dayton's spirit of tinkering and innovation, practical organization and mechanical dreaming continue to thrive, as much as its neighborliness and compassion. Politically, the area has been known as a bellwether since Richard Scammon and Ben Wattenberg's *The Real Majority* of 1970 profiled the Dayton housewife. Since then, the area has mostly voted for statewide and national winners, leaning a bit more Democratic than Ohio as a whole; Al Gore beat George W. Bush in Dayton's Montgomery County 50%–48%.

The 3d Congressional District includes most of Dayton and all but the northeast corner of Montgomery County. In the 2002 redistricting, for the first time since the 1960s, it includes territory outside of Montgomery County—the northern half of fast-growing suburban Warren County just to the southeast and mostly rural and small town Clinton and Highland Counties further east. Redistricting, by removing part of Dayton and Montgomery County and adding heavily Republican Warren and Clinton Counties made the district distinctly more Republican, and raised the Bush 2000 percentage from 47% to 52%.

The congressman from the 3d District is Mike Turner, a Republican elected in 2002. Turner grew up in Dayton and graduated from Ohio Northern University, Case Western Law School and the University of Dayton business school and became a corporate lawyer. In 1993, at age 33, he narrowly defeated an ethically challenged Democratic incumbent to win the first of two terms as mayor of Dayton. Although he narrowly lost for reelection in 2001, Ohio and national Republican leaders, including Congressmen John Boehner, David Hobson and Rob Portman, considered him a prime challenger in a district which had been marginal in national contests but had been routinely electing and reelecting Democratic Congressman Tony Hall since 1978. On January 24,

2002, Turner announced he was running for Congress, the same day the Ohio legislature passed the redistricting plan which made the district more Republican. On January 31, Hall was officially nominated to succeed George McGovern as ambassador to the Food and Agriculture Organization in Rome. Hall had a long and fervent interest in anti-hunger programs at home and abroad, and it seems obvious that the Bush administration had been sounding him out for the job before January 26: here was a chance to appoint a liberal Democrat to a position where his strongly held views were congruent with administration policy and at the same time a chance to pick up a House seat that had long been safe Democratic.

In the Republican primary Turner had fierce and well-financed opposition from newspaper publisher Roy Brown, grandson and son of Congressmen Clarence Brown and Clarence Brown Jr., who represented the neighboring 7th District from 1938 to 1982. Brown spent $1.3 million of his own money in the primary, largely on ads attacking Turner's record on taxes and crime and lambasting him as not a true conservative. Also, Brown owned more than 50 newspapers, 10 in the 3d District, and Turner contended that Brown's campaign guided his newspapers' coverage of the race. He filed a complaint with the Federal Election Commission alleging that the coverage amount to an illegal corporate contribution. According to a count by Turner's campaign, 66 of 70 articles between January and April were either "pro-Brown" or "anti-Turner." He wasn't the only one upset by Brown's sharp-elbowed style. The Montgomery County Republican party censured Brown as "unfit to hold public office" for allegedly misleading voters. A few days before the election, the Ohio Election Commission ruled by a 5–2 vote that Brown violated state law with false statements in a televised ad. Voters evidently took the same view. Turner beat Brown 80%–14%; Brown spent more than $160 for each vote that he received. In Montgomery County Turner's margin was 87%–8%. NRCC chairman Tom Davis, who supported Turner in the primary, said that Brown should have sued his consultants for malpractice.

The general election was comparatively sedate. The Democratic nominee was Rick Carne, chief of staff in Hall's D.C. congressional office. Carne had little support from the national party. He called for a $500,000 spending limit but raised nearly $600,000, with help from a local appearance by Dayton native Martin Sheen, President Bartlet on *West Wing*. Turner spent about the same amount. Turner won 59%–41%; he led 55%–45% in Montgomery County and won 74%, 69% and 63% in Warren, Clinton and Highland Counties.

Turner got seats on Government Reform and Armed Services, and he pledged to work to keep Wright-Pat off the base closing list.

FOURTH DISTRICT

Rep. Michael Oxley (R)

Elected June 1981, 11th term; b. Feb. 11, 1944, Findlay; home, Findlay; Miami U. (OH), B.A. 1966, OH St. U., J.D. 1969; Lutheran; married (Patricia).

Elected Office: OH House of Reps., 1972–81.

Professional Career: FBI Spec. Agent, 1969–71; Practicing atty., 1972–1981.

DC Office: 2308 RHOB 20515, 202-225-2676; Web site: www.house.gov/oxley.

District Offices: Findlay, 419-423-3210; Lima, 419-999-6455; Mansfield, 419-522-5757.

Committees: *Financial Services* (Chmn. of 37 R).

Group Ratings

	ADA	ACLU	AFS	LCV	CON	ITIC	NTU	COC	ACU	NTLC	CHC
2002	0	7	0	25	66	100	60	100	96	85	100
2001	0	—	0	0	—	—	60	100	92	—	—

National Journal Ratings

	2001 LIB	—	2001 CONS		2002 LIB	—	2002 CONS
Economic	21%	—	80%		19%	—	80%
Social	20%	—	69%		0%	—	75%
Foreign	4%	—	87%		15%	—	78%

Key Votes of the 107th Congress

1. Approve Bush Tax Cuts	Y	5. Faith-Based Charities	Y	9. Trade Promotion Authority	Y
2. Limit Patients' Bill of Rights	Y	6. Bar Gays in the Boy Scouts	Y	10. Bar Funds for Intl. Court	Y
3. Campaign Finance Reform	N	7. Ban Partial-Birth Abortion	Y	11. Authorize Force in Iraq	Y
4. Ban ANWR Development	N	8. Arm Commercial Pilots	Y	12. Deny Home. Sec. Dept. Union	Y

Election Results

2002 general	Michael Oxley (R)	120,001	(68%)	($1,140,989)
	Jim Clark (D)	57,726	(32%)	($6,916)
2002 primary	Michael Oxley (R)	36,889	(73%)	
	James Stahl (R)	13,479	(27%)	
2000 general	Michael Oxley (R)	156,510	(67%)	($790,624)
	Daniel Dickman (D)	67,330	(29%)	($29,528)
	Ralph Mullinger (Lib)	8,278	(4%)	

Prior Winning Percentages: 1998 (64%); 1996 (65%); 1994 (100%); 1992 (61%); 1990 (62%); 1988 (100%); 1986 (75%); 1984 (78%); 1982 (65%); 1981 (50%)

The People		Race/Ethnic Origin	Ancestry	
Area size:	4,642 sq. mi.	91.7% White	German: 23.4%	USA: 9.7%
Urban population:	58.6%	5.2% Black	Irish: 8.1%	
Rural population:	41.4%	0.6% Asian	**2000 Presidential Vote**	
Pop. 2000:	630,730	0.2% Native Am.	Bush (R) 158,862	(62%)
Median income:	$40,100	0.0% Hawaiian	Gore (D) 88,760	(35%)
Poverty status:	9.4%	1.0% Two + races	Other 8,244	(3%)
Military veterans:	14.0%	0.1% Other	**Cook Partisan Voting Index:** R +15	
		1.2% Hispanic Origin		

Occupation	Blue collar: 37.5%	White collar: 47.1%	Gray collar: 15.5%

Central Ohio looks mostly like farmland to the traveler. Yet this is manufacturing country, indeed one of America's premier manufacturing areas, where the economy is based on factories in small towns and on rural highways. These places seem far from anywhere important, yet are on one of the great east-west routes—the old rail lines and newer highways—that cross the country. They seem old-fashioned and rooted in an older technological time, yet here is Wapakoneta, a typically Ohioan-Indian name, the hometown of Neil Armstrong, first man on the moon and home of the Neil Armstrong Air and Space Museum. A county away is Bellefontaine, site of the first concrete street in America. Politically, this crossroads on the flat limestone plains of northern Ohio is one of the Republican heartlands of the United States. On the B&O tracks from Dayton to Toledo that intersect the east-west rail lines used by Richard Nixon in 1968, Ronald Reagan in 1984, George Bush in 1992 and Bill Clinton in 1996 to make whistle-stop campaign tours, one can summon up memories of past campaign styles and loyalties.

Much of central Ohio makes up the 4th Congressional District. It includes Wapakoneta; Lima, whose name was pulled from a hat; Findlay, where a museum holds the captain's bathtub from the U.S.S. *Maine*, sunk in the Havana harbor in 1898; Marion, where young Socialist-to-be Norman Thomas delivered newspapers edited by President-to-be Warren Harding; and Mansfield, home of John Sherman, one of Ohio's great 19th century Republican statesmen, and his brother General William Tecumseh Sherman, who marched his troops through Georgia for the Union and refused to be considered for president. This has been a Republican stronghold since the Civil War, industrial since the late 19th century, quietly prosperous most of the years since World War II, though shaken by the collapse of the auto-steel-coal industries after the oil shock of 1979.

The congressman from the 4th District is Michael Oxley, a Republican first elected in June 1981, now chairman of the Financial Services Committee. Oxley grew up in Findlay. He graduated from Miami of Ohio and Ohio State law school, then worked three years for the FBI and returned home to practice law. He worked for his Republican congressman and in 1972, at 28, was elected to the state House. In 1981, after the incumbent died, Oxley ran for the House and won the special election during the heyday of Reagan popularity by the surprisingly narrow margin of 378 votes.

In 1983 Oxley got a seat on the Energy and Commerce Committee, which under Chairman John Dingell had a broad and expanding jurisdiction over complex regulatory issues. Although in the minority for 14 years, Oxley played a significant role in major legislation, able to unite his own Republicans and work with Democrats across the aisle. He was a major player on the 1990 Clean Air Act, working with Ohioans of both parties to protect that state's high-sulfur power plants and big factories from being saddled with high costs. On the Commerce Telecommunications Subcommittee, over opposition from Democrats, he required new frequencies of the radio spectrum to be allocated not by lottery but by auction; the resulting auctions for personal communications systems, cell phones, and pagers have been the largest in history and have supplied the Treasury with billions in revenue. He played a major role in the 1996 Telecommunications Act.

In late 1996 Oxley fought with Louisiana's Billy Tauzin for the chairmanship of the Telecommunications and Finance Subcommittee. Speaker Newt Gingrich had promised the spot to Tauzin when he switched parties in August 1995 and Tauzin, who was first elected in May 1980, has 13 months' more seniority. The solution was to split the subcommittee, whose jurisdiction was perhaps greater than that of any other in Congress. Tauzin got first choice and took Telecommunications, Trade and Consumer Protection; Oxley got Finance and Hazardous Materials. He played an important role in the landmark financial services deregulation passed in November 1999, which broke down the walls between banks, securities firms and insurance companies. Although regarded as pro-business, and although he has raised vast sums from regulated industries, Oxley has often taken stands they have vigorously opposed. He and Democrat Edward Markey pushed successfully for stock exchanges to list prices in dollars and cents rather than eighths of a dollar; their bill prompted the exchanges to do this over broker opposition. With John Dingell, Oxley moved to require mutual funds to give investors quarterly information about fees. Oxley has taken quick action to reverse regulators when convinced they are wrong. When the FCC ruled in December 1999 that a religious broadcaster with a noncommercial license must present instructional broadcasting 50% of the time, and that proselytizing did not qualify, Oxley sponsored a bill to reverse the ruling and got 50 co-sponsors; in January 2000 the FCC reversed itself 4–1. His bill to reform boxing—a longtime interest—passed the House by voice vote in May 2000; it would limit promoters' contracts to one year and bar them from having a financial interest in a boxer.

For much of 1999 and 2000 Oxley was involved in a complex behind-the-scenes fight with Tauzin over the chairmanship of the Commerce Committee. Republicans' six-year term limit on chairmen was clicking in on Thomas Bliley, who was retiring; Gingrich's decision to count Tauzin's years as a Democrat gave him the edge in seniority but Oxley proclaimed that he had spent "14 long years in the minority." As early as 1999 some members were thinking about a fallback position: Tauzin would get Commerce and Oxley Banking, with enlarged jurisdiction. The passage of financial services deregulation that fall gave power to a process argument, that it no longer made sense to have one committee with jurisdiction over securities and insurance and another with jurisdiction over banking. Oxley nonetheless pressed hard for Commerce, but lost in the Republican Steering Committee. Speaker Dennis Hastert persuaded Republicans to expand Banking's jurisdiction and rename it Financial Services. The leadership did not mind passing over senior Banking Republican Marge Roukema, and the other Republican seeking that chairmanship, Richard Baker, supported Oxley and the jurisdiction switch.

So in January 2001 Oxley became chairman of Financial Services, with all of Banking's jurisdiction plus securities and insurance. In June 2001 Oxley and subcommittee Chairman Richard Baker held hearings on whether investment bankers were unduly influencing securities analysts in securities firm; he told the industry it should develop a new rule or he would investigate. In 2002 he criticized New York Attorney General Eliot Spitzer for negotiating settlements on this issue with Merrill Lynch, Citigroup and other firms. After September 11, he and ranking Democrat John LaFalce sponsored a money-laundering bill, to attempt to cut off money from terrorists;

it was passed in October. But his Internet gambling bill was dropped from the Patriot Act. In October and November he and Baker pressed for terrorism insurance, but wanted it in the form of loans, not grants, and not on the first dollar lost—not exactly what the industry wanted. They produced a bipartisan bill out of committee, but the leadership added a provision limiting insurers' liability to lawsuits and it passed pretty much along party lines.

After the bankruptcy of Enron in December 2001, Oxley took up the issue of corporate accounting. His bill prevailed over a Democratic alternative in committee 49–12 and on the floor 334–90. It barred accounting firms hired as external auditors from doing certain consulting and inside auditing, created an accounting board within the SEC and required disclosure of off-balance-sheet deals like those at Enron. The House bill passed in April, and the Senate did not act until June, after the WorldCom collapse made the issue hot again. Senate Banking Chairman Paul Sarbanes and Republican Mike Enzi, the only accountant in the Senate, produced a bill with restrictions more stringent than Oxley's, and it passed unanimously in June. Many House Republicans, notably Tauzin, wanted the House to simply pass the Senate bill, to get on record against corporate misdeeds before the August recess. But in July Oxley persuaded Speaker Dennis Hastert to let him take the issue to conference. In the circumstances Sarbanes had the upper hand. The Senate acceded to some changes: CEOs and CFOs but not board chairmen would have to sign the certification on company reports under criminal penalties, and they could be held liable only for knowing and willful but not reckless conduct. Oxley suggested the law be called the Sarbanes Act; Sarbanes said it should be the Sarbanes-Oxley Act. George W. Bush signed it before the end of July. Oxley remained active on the issue. Oxley later announced an investigation into how investment banks manage IPOs; he said he would prefer that the SEC, the exchanges and the NASD take action, but might propose legislation, as in decimal pricing, if they didn't.

Oxley, like other House Republican committee chairmen, has raised prodigious sums for other Republicans and has stayed close to the lobbying community, an essential (though not sole) source of information on complex regulatory issues. In February 2003 some Democrats charged that two Oxley staffers had threatened to hold up hearings unless the Investment Company Institute got rid of its leading lobbyist, a Democrat, and threatened to bring charges before the ethics committee. That would have broken a six-year truce between the two parties, and some Republicans said that if that happened they would bring ethics charges against some House Democrats, including Minority Leader Nancy Pelosi, who, it was alleged, apparently broke the law by setting up two leadership PACs (she quickly shut one of them down). Democrats decided not to bring charges.

Oxley has been reelected by wide margins since 1982.

FIFTH DISTRICT

Rep. Paul Gillmor (R)

Elected 1988, 8th term; b. Feb. 1, 1939, Old Fort; home, Old Fort; Ohio Wesleyan U., B.A. 1961, U. of MI, J.D. 1964; Methodist; married (Karen).

Military Career: Air Force, 1965–66.

Elected Office: OH Senate, 1966–88.

Professional Career: Practicing atty., 1965–88.

DC Office: 1203 LHOB 20515, 202-225-6405; Web site: www.house.gov/gillmor.

District Offices: Defiance, 419-782-1996; Norwalk, 419-668-0206; Tiffin, 419-448-9016.

Committees: *Energy & Commerce* (6th of 31 R): Environment & Hazardous Materials (Chmn.); Telecommunications & The Internet. *Financial Services* (13th of 37 R): Capital Markets, Insurance & Government Sponsored Enterprises; Financial Institutions & Consumer Credit.

Group Ratings

	ADA	ACLU	AFS	LCV	CON	ITIC	NTU	COC	ACU	NTLC	CHC
2002	5	20	0	13	17	88	49	100	88	74	83
2001	15	—	11	14	—	—	55	96	79	—	—

National Journal Ratings

	2001 LIB	—	2001 CONS		2002 LIB	—	2002 CONS
Economic	41%	—	60%		36%	—	64%
Social	38%	—	63%		29%	—	70%
Foreign	21%	—	74%		15%	—	78%

Key Votes of the 107th Congress

1. Approve Bush Tax Cuts	*	5. Faith-Based Charities	Y	9. Trade Promotion Authority	Y
2. Limit Patients' Bill of Rights	Y	6. Bar Gays in the Boy Scouts	Y	10. Bar Funds for Intl. Court	Y
3. Campaign Finance Reform	N	7. Ban Partial-Birth Abortion	Y	11. Authorize Force in Iraq	Y
4. Ban ANWR Development	N	8. Arm Commercial Pilots	Y	12. Deny Home. Sec. Dept. Union	Y

Election Results

2002 general	Paul Gillmor (R)	126,286	(67%)	($666,804)
	Roger Anderson (D)	51,872	(28%)	($21,544)
	John Green (Lib)	10,096	(5%)	
2002 primary	Paul Gillmor (R)	41,711	(69%)	
	Rex Damschroder (R)	18,498	(31%)	
2000 general	Paul Gillmor (R)	169,857	(70%)	($245,036)
	Dannie Edmon (D)	62,138	(26%)	
	Other	11,345	(5%)	

Prior Winning Percentages: 1998 (67%); 1996 (61%); 1994 (73%); 1992 (100%); 1990 (68%); 1988 (61%)

The People		Race/Ethnic Origin	Ancestry	
Area size:	6,158 sq. mi.	93.7% White	German: 29.9%	Irish: 7.5%
Urban population:	48.9%	1.1% Black	USA: 7.3%	
Rural population:	51.1%	0.4% Asian	**2000 Presidential Vote**	
Pop. 2000:	630,730	0.2% Native Am.	Bush (R) 158,037	(59%)
Median income:	$41,701	0.0% Hawaiian	Gore (D) 99,818	(37%)
Poverty status:	7.6%	0.7% Two+ races	Other 9,383	(4%)
Military veterans:	12.8%	0.1% Other	**Cook Partisan Voting Index:** R +12	
		3.8% Hispanic Origin		

Occupation	Blue collar: 39.8%	White collar: 46.0%	Gray collar: 14.2%

Undergirded by limestone, as flat and fertile as any place in America, northwest Ohio sits astride the land routes in parts of the country that were economically the most productive in the years they were settled. Here were the "Firelands," reserved for Connecticut Yankees whose farms were burned in the Revolution, and the neat and substantial small towns built by German Protestants in the mid-19th century. Northwest Ohio is the beginning of the great corn and hog belt that stretches through Indiana and Illinois into Iowa, and has long been a Republican heartland. Fremont, settled by abstemious Yankees, was the home of President Rutherford B. Hayes, whose wife Lucy served only lemonade in the White House; nearby Sandusky, settled by Germans who built big wineries and breweries, has its own Merry-Go-Round Museum.

This is also prime industrial country: its limestone, rail connections and location near the Great Lakes have spurred the growth of a factory economy that financially is far more important than agriculture. After the first settlement, northwest Ohio grew steadily for many decades, surging ahead in the 1950s and 1960s as its small factories supplied the big auto plants in Detroit and Ohio cities. Growth lagged noticeably in the 1980s, when the domestic auto industry collapsed, but returned in the 1990s as small firms sold not only to the Big Three but to foreign customers. Today, this area has the highest percentage of blue-collar workers in the state.

The 5th Congressional District sweeps across northwest Ohio, from northern Ashland County, almost within the ambit of metro Cleveland, across the limestone plains through Sandusky County and Fremont, past the university town of Bowling Green and the Toledo suburb of Perrysburg, to the towns of Defiance and Napoleon and on to the northwest corner where Ohio borders Michigan and Indiana. Its factories include the Heinz ketchup plant in Fremont—the world's largest—and the largest Whirlpool washing machine plant in Clyde, both in Sandusky County. In Seneca County is the Arm and Hammer Baking Soda plant—which is, of course, the world's largest. It does not include Toledo and Lake Erie shoreline directly east. Historically, this was a solidly Republican district from the Civil War through the New Deal and up through today, and in 2000 it voted 59% for George W. Bush.

The congressman from the 5th District is Paul Gillmor, a Republican first elected in 1988. He grew up in northern Ohio, graduated from Ohio Wesleyan and Michigan Law School, practiced law and was elected, at 27, to the state Senate in 1966, where he later became Senate President. For years Gillmor eyed this House seat and waited for incumbent Delbert Latta to retire; he even passed a state law blocking the party from designating Latta's son as nominee if Latta resigned. In the 1988 primary Gillmor beat the junior Latta by exactly 27 votes out of 63,000 cast. He has not been seriously challenged since then.

Gillmor has had a relatively moderate voting record. He focused on internal reform in his first years in the House, working to freeze committee funding. He is comfortable with Republican moderates on cultural and foreign issues and has been a member of both the Tuesday Group and the Leadership's Whip Team. In 2001, he became chairman of the Subcommittee on Environment and Hazardous Materials. He sought to resolve long-deadlocked Superfund legislation, in part by giving more authority to the states. He made some progress, with enactment of a bill to limit the liability of small business owners and firms that did not account for much waste at a site.

In 2002, he had a rare primary contest with term-limited state Representative Rex Damschroder, who finished third in the 1988 primary. He criticized Gillmor for living in the Columbus area and not spending enough time in the district. Gillmor defended his record with a blast of advertising, including an endorsement from Dick Cheney, and won the primary 69%–31%. Damschroder won his home base of Sandusky County 54%–46%, but he did not come close in any other county. Gillmor won easily in November, as usual.

SIXTH DISTRICT

Rep. Ted Strickland (D)

Elected 1996, 4th term; b. Aug. 4, 1941, Lucasville; home, Lisbon; Asbury Col., B.A. 1963, M.A., 1967, U. of KY, Ph.D. 1980; Methodist; married (Frances).

Elected Office: U.S. House of Reps., 1992–94.

Professional Career: Assoc. Minister, Trinity Methodist Church, 1967–68; Dir. of Soc. Svcs., KY Methodist Home, 1968–70; Consulting psychologist, Southern OH Correctional Facility, 1985–92, 1995–96; Prof., Shawnee St. U., 1988–92, 1995–96.

DC Office: 336 CHOB 20515, 202-225-5705; Fax: 202-225-5907; Web site: www.house.gov/strickland.

District Offices: Boardman, 330-965-4220; Marrieta, 740-376-0868; Martins Ferry, 740-633-2275; Wheelersburg, 740-574-2676.

Committees: *Energy & Commerce* (18th of 26 D): Commerce, Trade & Consumer Protection; Energy & Air Quality; Health. *Veterans' Affairs* (10th of 14 D): Health.

Group Ratings

	ADA	ACLU	AFS	LCV	CON	ITIC	NTU	COC	ACU	NTLC	CHC
2002	90	67	100	88	18	38	16	40	12	3	17
2001	90	—	100	86	—	—	12	35	16	—	—

National Journal Ratings

	2001 LIB	—	2001 CONS		2002 LIB	—	2002 CONS
Economic	68%	—	32%		70%	—	29%
Social	64%	—	36%		59%	—	40%
Foreign	73%	—	26%		68%	—	31%

Key Votes of the 107th Congress

1. Approve Bush Tax Cuts	N	5. Faith-Based Charities	N	9. Trade Promotion Authority	N
2. Limit Patients' Bill of Rights	N	6. Bar Gays in the Boy Scouts	Y	10. Bar Funds for Intl. Court	Y
3. Campaign Finance Reform	Y	7. Ban Partial-Birth Abortion	Y	11. Authorize Force in Iraq	N
4. Ban ANWR Development	Y	8. Arm Commercial Pilots	Y	12. Deny Home. Sec. Dept. Union	N

Election Results

2002 general	Ted Strickland (D)	113,972	(59%)	($862,112)
	Mike Halleck (R)	77,643	(41%)	($180,074)
2002 primary	Ted Strickland (D)	41,351	(67%)	
	Lou D'Apolito (D)	13,391	(22%)	
	Charles Brown (D)	6,552	(11%)	
2000 general	Ted Strickland (D)	138,849	(58%)	($544,415)
	Michael Azinger (R)	96,966	(40%)	($202,525)
	Other	4,759	(2%)	

Prior Winning Percentages: 1998 (57%); 1996 (51%); 1992 (51%)

The People		Race/Ethnic Origin	Ancestry	
Area size:	5,236 sq. mi.	95.2% White	German: 15.2%	Irish: 9.9%
Urban population:	50.0%	2.4% Black	USA: 8.4%	
Rural population:	50.0%	0.5% Asian	**2000 Presidential Vote**	
Pop. 2000:	630,730	0.2% Native Am.	Bush (R).............129,689	(49%)
Median income:	$32,888	0.0% Hawaiian	Gore (D).............125,292	(47%)
Poverty status:	14.0%	0.8% Two+ races	Other...................11,969	(4%)
Military veterans:	14.5%	0.1% Other	**Cook Partisan Voting Index:** R + 1	
		0.8% Hispanic Origin		

Occupation	Blue collar: 31.3%	White collar: 51.7%	Gray collar: 17.0%

In the years after the American Revolution, the Ohio River was one of the great highways west. From Pittsburgh, where the Allegheny and Monongahela meet and form the Ohio, the river led south and west toward the Mississippi and the great port of New Orleans. Shipping goods down-river by raft was cheaper than sending them over the Appalachian chains, and so the Ohio became a great highway of commerce. For hundreds of miles, the Ohio twisted this way and that through rounded-off mountains and rolling hills, land that marked the boundary between post-Revolutionary Virginia and the Northwest Territory, between slaveholding territory and soil that the Confederation Congress decided in 1787 should be free. Across this boundary settlers made their way in those years—Yankees in 1788 to Marietta, Ohio's first town, and, in larger numbers, Virginians from those parts of Virginia that became Kentucky in 1792 and West Virginia in 1863. By the late 19th century the Ohio was an industrial river; coal was nearby, barge transportation was available and railroads were built in the narrow valleys between the hills, steel mills went up on the riverfront. This produced prosperity for a while, but it also produced pollution—Steubenvillle on the Ohio River once had the nation's dirtiest air—and since the old-line steel industry fell on hard times, the Ohio River was lined with some of the least prosperous parts of America.

The 6th Congressional District is made up of a string of counties running 325 miles along the Ohio River plus part of the Mahoning Valley, named after a narrow tributary of the Ohio. In the north it includes the Youngstown suburbs of Boardman, Canfield and part of Poland in Mahoning County and East Liverpool and Steubenville on the Ohio. It includes the lightly populated stretch of the river south from Marietta, the old industrial town of Ironton and it extends to the city limits of Portsmouth, where the Scioto River empties into the Ohio. Historically, the northern part of the district was Republican and the southern part Democratic, but that was a long time ago. The steel and coal areas in the north became Democratic during the 1930s and the southern counties started trending toward Republicans in the 1960s. The 2002 redistricting made substantial changes in the 6th District, which used to be centered on Portsmouth and extended far north of the Ohio and as far west as the Warren County Cincinnati suburbs; only 41% of its residents lived in the old 6th District. Redistricting also changed its political complexion. The old 6th District voted 56% for George W. Bush in 2000; the new district voted 49% for him.

The congressman from the 6th District is Ted Strickland, a Democrat first elected to the House in 1992. He grew up in Lucasville, just north of Portsmouth, site of a state prison; he was the son of a steelworker and eighth of nine children. He graduated from Asbury College and got a Ph.D. from the University of Kentucky. He was a Methodist minister, was director of a children's home, and then a prison psychologist and psychology professor at Shawnee State College. He and his wife have both made their way up as counseling professionals. He once described his goal as "building communities where children are nurtured and educated and protected and cared for." He ran for the House unsuccessfully in 1976, 1978 and 1980, and then ran again in 1992 when redistricting placed two Republican incumbents in the district. One lost in the primary 50.2%–49.8% and the other lost in the general 51%–49%. In his first term Strickland voted for the Clinton budget and tax package, but against the 1994 crime bill because of its gun control provisions and against NAFTA. As the 1994 election neared, Strickland suggested there might be a need for tax increases to pay for health care programs; Republican challenger Frank Cremeans seized on this and won 51%–49%. In 1996 Strickland attacked Cremeans for Medicare "cuts" and scaling down the Earned Income Tax Credit, which he called a tax increase on the poor. Strickland won 51%–49%, to win back the seat.

Back on Capitol Hill, Strickland got a seat on the Energy and Commerce Committee, where he sought a moratorium on implementation of Clean Air Act regulations that affect industries in his region. He complained in 2001 when the Nuclear Regulatory Commission failed to challenge the closing of the USEC uranium enrichment plant in Piketon, which would eliminate more than 1,700 local jobs and leave the nation only one other such facility, in Paducah, Kentucky. In the energy bill that the House passed in 2001, he won a provision—opposed by the Bush administration—to authorize the Energy Department to spend $170 million to keep the plant on standby. The Clean Air Trust subsequently named Strickland its "villain of the month." He has urged treatment, not imprisonment, for the mentally ill. His voting record has been moderate to liberal.

In 1998, Strickland faced Lieutenant Governor Nancy Hollister, but she was hurt by opposition from local conservatives unhappy with her support of abortion rights and resentful that party bosses pushed her candidacy, while Strickland benefited from labor unions' on-the-ground campaign. Strickland won by what was then the huge (for this district) margin of 57%–43%—the first time a 6th District incumbent was reelected since 1990. In 2000 he won 58%–40%. In 2001 Ohio Republicans had control of redistricting, and Strickland threatened to run against Republican Bob Ney in the neighboring 18th District if his own district was eliminated. Republicans failed to act before January 2002, when they needed Democratic votes to give their plan immediate effect. The result was this district, at one end of which was Strickland's home in Lucasville and at the other the home in Poland of incumbent Democrat Jim Traficant, then under indictment for bribery. But Traficant chose to run as an Independent in the new 17th District, which contained more of his old district, and Strickland won the primary and general election easily, even though 59% of the voters were new to him. He carried every county, though the margin was close in November in the northern end of the district.

SEVENTH DISTRICT

Rep. David Hobson (R)

Elected 1990, 7th term; b. Oct. 17, 1936, Cincinnati; home, Springfield; OH Wesleyan U., B.A. 1958, OH St. U., J.D. 1963; Methodist; married (Carolyn).

Military Career: OH Air Natl. Guard, 1958–63.

Elected Office: OH Senate, 1982–90, Majority Whip, 1986–88, Pres. Pro-Tem, 1988–90.

Professional Career: Real estate agent, 1969–90; Restaurant owner, 1977–93.

DC Office: 2346 RHOB 20515, 202-225-4324; Fax: 202-225-1984; Web site: www.house.gov/hobson.

District Offices: Lancaster, 740-654-5149; Springfield, 937-325-0474.

Committees: *Appropriations* (9th of 36 R): Defense; Energy & Water Development (Chmn.); VA, HUD & Independent Agencies.

Group Ratings

	ADA	ACLU	AFS	LCV	CON	ITIC	NTU	COC	ACU	NTLC	CHC
2002	0	13	0	25	34	88	59	100	88	81	83
2001	15	—	10	0	—	—	59	96	80	—	—

National Journal Ratings

	2001 LIB —	2001 CONS		2002 LIB —	2002 CONS
Economic	28%	69%		16%	81%
Social	43%	55%		39%	57%
Foreign	4%	87%		22%	78%

Key Votes of the 107th Congress

1. Approve Bush Tax Cuts	Y	5. Faith-Based Charities	Y
2. Limit Patients' Bill of Rights	Y	6. Bar Gays in the Boy Scouts	Y
3. Campaign Finance Reform	N	7. Ban Partial-Birth Abortion	Y
4. Ban ANWR Development	N	8. Arm Commercial Pilots	Y

9. Trade Promotion Authority	Y
10. Bar Funds for Intl. Court	Y
11. Authorize Force in Iraq	Y
12. Deny Home. Sec. Dept. Union	Y

Election Results

2002 general	David Hobson (R)	113,252	(68%)	($730,531)
	Kara Anastasio (D)	45,568	(27%)	($14,707)
	Frank Doden (I)	8,812	(5%)	($4,475)
2002 primary	David Hobson (R)	30,367	(73%)	
	Steven Schaefer (R)	6,110	(15%)	
	John Mitchel (R)	3,344	(8%)	
	Ralph Applegate (R)	1,941	(5%)	
2000 general	David Hobson (R)	163,646	(68%)	($706,884)
	Donald Minor (D)	60,755	(25%)	
	John Mitchel (I)	13,983	(6%)	($15,695)
	Other	3,802	(2%)	

Prior Winning Percentages: 1998 (67%); 1996 (68%); 1994 (100%); 1992 (71%); 1990 (62%)

The People		Race/Ethnic Origin	Ancestry	
Area size:	2,866 sq. mi.	88.7% White	German: 17.6%	USA: 10.1%
Urban population:	71.3%	7.5% Black	Irish: 9.3%	
Rural population:	28.7%	1.0% Asian	**2000 Presidential Vote**	
Pop. 2000:	630,730	0.3% Native Am.	Bush (R)	137,548 (55%)
Median income:	$43,248	0.0% Hawaiian	Gore (D)	102,846 (41%)
Poverty status:	8.8%	1.3% Two+ races	Other	7,644 (3%)
Military veterans:	15.3%	0.1% Other	**Cook Partisan Voting Index:** R + 8	
		1.1% Hispanic Origin		

Occupation Blue collar: 28.1% White collar: 57.1% Gray collar: 14.8%

The hills and plains of central Ohio are dotted with towns and small cities that have been manufacturing centers almost since they were settled in the early 19th century, when the dominant technologies were the waterwheel and the open forge. In the decades since, they have been replaced by one new technology after another—the automobile and the airplane—and the local manufacturing economy, sometimes with uncomfortable fits and starts, has adjusted and advanced. There were painful job losses here in the early 1980s, but small business has grown since then. As old factories shut down, new ones open that are more productive; the results are higher incomes and, though not often remembered, far less of the backbreaking hard work and drudgery that were almost everyone's lot in supposedly better times.

The 7th Congressional District is made up of a portion of south central part of Ohio southwest, south and southeast of Columbus. The largest city is Springfield, where the truck plant of Navistar, formerly International Harvester, has long been the biggest employer. Just to the south are the Greene County suburbs of Dayton around Wright-Patterson Air Force Base, whose name recalls the fathers of the airplane and the cash register, both from Dayton. The other population centers are in Fairfield County, southeast of Columbus, and a southeastern part of Columbus's Franklin County, added in the 2002 redistricting, including part of the east side of Columbus, Whitehall, Blacklick Estates, Canal Winchester and Lockbourne. The district has always been Republican territory. It backed the policies of Ohio Republican President William McKinley—tariff protection, railroad regulation, antitrust suits against monopolies, discouragement of labor unions—and of Governor James Rhodes—low taxes, promotion of new businesses and jobs. It is culturally conservative and economically mostly satisfied with free markets. It has given good margins to recent Republican presidential contenders.

The congressman from the 7th District is Dave Hobson, a Republican first elected in 1990. He grew up in Springfield, graduated from Ohio Wesleyan and Ohio State law school and worked in commercial real estate in Springfield. In 1982 he was elected to the state Senate and in 1990, when Congressman Mike DeWine ran for lieutenant governor, he was elected to the House. He is a practical-minded politician who in his second term got a seat on the Appropriations and has a moderate to conservative voting record. Hobson's steady demeanor and backroom skills continue to make him a resource for House Republican leaders; he worked on health issues with Dennis Hastert long before he became Speaker. But Hobson does not seek the spotlight on Capitol Hill: When leadership meetings break up and many head for the ever-present microphones and television cameras, Hobson typically passes them by. "That isn't my style," he says. "I'm not doing this to build Dave Hobson into a national name."

In 1999 Hobson became chairman of the Military Construction Appropriations Subcommittee, a body that usually does its legislating on a bipartisan basis and with due regard to members' local concerns. He said that his top priority is to ensure that military families have the quality housing and secure work facilities they deserve. He has traveled indefatigably to inspect military facilities, not just to Germany and Italy, but Korea (where troops described certain buildings as "crack houses") and to Bosnia and Kosovo over Thanksgiving. In early March 2002 he was in Uzbekistan and Kyrgyzstan; two weeks later he was inspecting Camp X-Ray at Guantanamo Bay, Cuba. Responding to reports of inadequate military health care, he won passage of a requirement that all military doctors hold unrestricted state medical licenses and complete education requirements. He has looked after the interests of Wright-Pat. When its 445th Airlift Wing's C-141s were about to be phased out, he met with Air Force Chief of Staff John Jumper in May 2002 and got assurances that they would be assigned C-5As (although he would have preferred the newer C-17) and that if they didn't work out another mission would be found. The 2002 redistricting added Defense Supply Center Columbus and Rickenbacker Air National Guard Base in Franklin County to the district, but Hobson, who served there after college, was aleady working for a $10 million Reserve unit facility and a $6 million fire station for Rickenbacker; he invested in a nearby office building after getting the ethics committee's approval.

Hobson was irritated by the 2002 redistricting, which stretched the district west to include Perry County, home of Ohio House Speaker Larry Householder; Hobson reportedly thought that would make his harder for state Senator Steve Austria of Greene County to succeed him. But in the 2002 Republican primary Greene and Springfield's Clark County cast 49% of the Republican primary vote and Householder's Perry County only 5%. In the general election, Hobson won only 53% in the new parts of the district, Perry and Franklin Counties. But he won 70% in the rest, for a 68%–27% victory.

EIGHTH DISTRICT

Rep. John Boehner (R)

Elected 1990, 7th term; b. Nov. 17, 1949, Cincinnati; home, West Chester; Xavier U., B.S. 1977; Catholic; married (Debbie).

Military Career: Navy, 1969.

Elected Office: Union Township Bd. of Trustees, 1981–85, Pres., 1984; OH House of Reps., 1984–90.

Professional Career: Pres., Nucite Sales Inc., 1976–90.

DC Office: 1011 LHOB 20515, 202-225-6205; Fax: 202-225-0704; Web site: www.house.gov/boehner.

District Offices: Hamilton, 513-870-0300; Troy, 937-339-1524.

Committees: *Agriculture* (Vice Chmn. of 27 R): General Farm Commodities & Risk Management. *Education & the Workforce* (Chmn. of 27 R).

Group Ratings

	ADA	ACLU	AFS	LCV	CON	ITIC	NTU	COC	ACU	NTLC	CHC
2002	0	7	0	0	38	100	62	100	88	97	100
2001	0	—	0	0	—	—	65	100	96	—	—

National Journal Ratings

	2001 LIB	—	2001 CONS		2002 LIB	—	2002 CONS
Economic	7%	—	89%		21%	—	73%
Social	20%	—	69%		32%	—	63%
Foreign	4%	—	87%		23%	—	77%

Key Votes of the 107th Congress

1. Approve Bush Tax Cuts	Y	5. Faith-Based Charities	Y	9. Trade Promotion Authority	Y
2. Limit Patients' Bill of Rights	Y	6. Bar Gays in the Boy Scouts	Y	10. Bar Funds for Intl. Court	Y
3. Campaign Finance Reform	N	7. Ban Partial-Birth Abortion	Y	11. Authorize Force in Iraq	Y
4. Ban ANWR Development	N	8. Arm Commercial Pilots	Y	12. Deny Home. Sec. Dept. Union	Y

Election Results

2002 general	John Boehner (R)	119,947	(71%)	($1,226,866)
	Jeff Hardenbrook (D)	49,444	(29%)	($18,186)
2002 primary	John Boehner (R)	27,770	(85%)	
	Roger Thomas (R)	4,839	(15%)	
2000 general	John Boehner (R)	179,756	(71%)	($1,042,008)
	John Parks (D)	66,293	(26%)	($31,098)
	Other	7,254	(3%)	

Prior Winning Percentages: 1998 (71%); 1996 (70%); 1994 (100%); 1992 (74%); 1990 (61%)

The People		Race/Ethnic Origin	Ancestry	
Area size:	2,031 sq. mi.	91.8% White	German: 22.0%	USA: 9.8%
Urban population:	78.1%	4.4% Black	Irish: 8.9%	
Rural population:	21.9%	1.2% Asian	**2000 Presidential Vote**	
Pop. 2000:	630,730	0.2% Native Am.	Bush (R)..............155,132	(61%)
Median income:	$43,753	0.0% Hawaiian	Gore (D)...............91,744	(36%)
Poverty status:	8.8%	1.1% Two+ races	Other....................7,371	(3%)
Military veterans:	13.8%	0.1% Other	**Cook Partisan Voting Index:** R +13	
		1.3% Hispanic Origin		

Occupation	Blue collar: 29.9%	White collar: 56.0%	Gray collar: 14.0%

The far west end of Ohio—where U.S. 40, the old National Road, heads straight as an arrow in its last miles across Ohio to Indiana, and the rail lines crisscross the land from Cincinnati to Dayton—has since the early 20th century housed some of the nation's prime industrial country. Here the Great and Little Miami rivers drain south into the Ohio; U.S. 40 jogs southward twice to go over the Miami and Stillwater River dams, built after the great flood of 1913 that killed 361 people in Dayton and caused $1 billion in damage. Around Dayton and Cincinnati, in large factory towns like Middletown and Hamilton and smaller factory towns like Troy and Piqua, Ohioans, after the recession of the early 1980s, adapted to new conditions and began to produce exports to Europe, Latin America and Asia as well as for the American market. At the same time people leaving the central cities of Dayton and Cincinnati moved into new subdivisions amid new shopping malls and office parks in Butler County, between those two cities; Hamilton, the Butler County seat founded in 1791 and named after the Treasury Secretary then, may have lost jobs when International Paper shut down a plant, but many more were being created all around it. Hamilton has tried to rally; in the 1950s it refused to let I-75 through town, but recently it got the state to build the Michael Fox Highway (named after a local legislator, not the Canadian-born actor) to link it with I-75 and the growth it has brought.

The 8th Congressional District covers much of this territory. It includes all of Butler County, except four lightly populated townships, and two counties north on the Indiana line and part of a third. It also includes Miami County north of Dayton and, added in redistricting in 2002, the northeastern corner of Montgomery County, including part of Dayton, all of Huber Heights and part of Wright-Patterson Air Force Base. Politically, this is very Republican territory; the district voted 61% for George W. Bush in 2000, his third-highest percentage in Ohio.

The congressman from the 8th District is John Boehner (pronounced *BAY-ner*), a Republican first elected in 1990 and now chairman of the Committee on Education and the Workforce. Boehner grew up in Cincinnati, one of 12 children, and graduated from Xavier University, the only college graduate in his family. He moved to Butler County and started a plastics packaging company, served on the Union Township Board of Trustees, and in 1984, at 34, was elected to the Ohio House. He won the congressional seat in the 1990 primary, by beating not one but two of his predecessors—incumbent Buz Lukens, who inexplicably ran after he was convicted of having sex with a 16-year-old girl, and Tom Kindness, who gave up the seat to run against Senator John Glenn in 1986 and then, as Boehner put it, deserted the district to become a Washington lobbyist. Boehner won 49%, to 32% for Kindness and 17% for Lukens. Boehner has since been reelected without difficulty.

In the House, Boehner joined the Gang of Seven, young freshman Republicans who insisted on revealing the names of all 355 members who had overdrafts at the House bank, and then went on to assail Democratic leaders and Republican go-alongers on the pay raise and the House Post Office scandal. They also argued that members of Congress should be subject to the laws they impose on other citizens; in 1992 Boehner invited OSHA inspectors to his office, where they found what would have been 15 violations if Congress were subject to its regulations. That same month Boehner took the lead in the formal adoption of the 27th Amendment to the Constitution, proposed by James Madison with the original Bill of Rights in 1789, to prohibit Congress from varying its pay during its current term. Boehner's Gang of Seven infuriated House veterans, but they struck a chord around the nation. In the process Boehner became a top lieutenant of Minority Whip Newt Gingrich, raising money for Republican candidates, and managing Gingrich's campaign for Republican leader. He was a major player in drafting and championing the 10-point Contract With America. After the 1994 election, he ran for chairman of the Republican Conference and, with Gingrich's backing, beat California's Duncan Hunter 122–102.

That made Boehner number four in the Republican leadership, and he worked hard to prepare the party message and to enforce discipline on issues from repealing the assault weapons ban to fielding ethics charges against Gingrich. Boehner also pushed for the Freedom to Farm bill in 1996, which purported to phase out most subsidies. But starting in 1998 Congress started voting disaster relief for farmers, and Boehner led the fight against the House's 2002 farm bill, which restored subsidies.

The Gingrich years were a turbulent time for Boehner. The ethics investigation on Gingrich placed Boehner in the middle of a legal altercation after a Florida couple taped Boehner's cell phone conversation with Republican leaders while he was driving through the state. The couple, Democratic activists, presented the tape to their congresswoman, Karen Thurman, who suggested they turn it over to Jim McDermott of Washington, senior Democrat on the House ethics committee, who then made the contents available to *The New York Times*. In 1998 Boehner sued McDermott in federal court for invasion of privacy; the trial judge ruled that the suit would infringe First Amendment rights, but the D.C. Circuit Court of Appeals reversed the decision. McDermott appealed to the Supreme Court, which decided another case instead and sent this one back to the D.C. Circuit, which sent it to District Court. The judge ruled in December 2002 that McDermott's conversations with a committee lawyer were not privileged. McDermott approached Boehner in 2002 (they had not spoken in the 12 years they served together) and sought to settle the case. He agreed to one of Boehner's demands, that he apologize to the House, but would not agree to the other two, that he admit he was wrong and that he make a contribution to charity. Why has Boehner continued this litigation? "The reason I did what I did then, and the reason I continue to pursue this case, is that people in politics must understand that there is a limit to what you can do to pursue your political opponents, and violating the law is at a minimum way over the line."

After Republicans lost five seats in the 1998 election, Boehner was challenged for the conference chairmanship by J.C. Watts. Some Republicans believed that Boehner had been part of the July 1997 coup against Newt Gingrich, and Boehner's fate was probably sealed when Dick Armey held the majority leadership even though he had misled members about his role in the coup. Someone had to go, and it was Boehner, who lost 121–93. After such a loss many members withdraw from legislative work. But Boehner plunged into action as chairman of the Employer-Employee Relations Subcommittee. By June 1999 the subcommittee passed eight bills restructuring managed care and health insurance; Speaker Dennis Hastert, pleased by Boehner's initiative and dismayed that other committees had not acted, adopted these as the Republican health care agenda. In 2002, after the Enron bankruptcy, pressure for pension changes increased, and Boehner, together with Rob Portman on Ways and Means, put together a bill allowing employees to sell company stock in 401(k) plans within three years, encouraging employers to give workers access to outside investment advice and giving employees advanced notice of blackout periods. It passed the House in April 2002 but nothing was passed by the Senate.

After the 2000 election Boehner sought the chairmanship of the Education and the Workforce Committee. Incumbent William Goodling was retiring; also seeking the job were second ranking Republican Tom Petri and the less senior Peter Hoekstra, who had been running the stalled investigation into illegal Teamster Union contributions. Boehner got Armey's support and Hastert told him, "If I were you, I'd go ahead." He helped Ralph Regula oust Bud Shuster from his post on the Steering Committee, which in turn chose him. Boehner, like many others, had long considered the committee a "partisan pit." Since 1960 Democrats had assigned only union loyalists to the committee and most Republican members took stands on employment issues opposed by industrial unions and stands on education opposed by teachers' unions. The basic education bill was up for reauthorization in 1999, but the committee was unable to produce a bill. Boehner knew that that would be the committee's first order of business and that George W. Bush's education proposals were one of his top priorities. So he tried to encourage a sense of bipartisanship. "We had several meetings where I said that I wanted the committee to be more productive and have a new tone." When Bush aides failed to invite the committee's ranking Democrat, George Miller, to a December 21 meeting in Austin on education, Boehner got him on the guest list and Senator Judd Gregg switched place cards at the lunch tables so that Miller sat next to Bush. In the past committee Democrats had concentrated on pumping more money into schools and opposing anything the unions disliked. But Miller had been teaching school dropouts and believed that current programs weren't teaching disadvantaged children what they should, and he became convinced that Bush and Boehner shared his concern.

So Boehner and Miller worked together on the House bill. Boehner knew he could not pass it with Republicans alone, because some were opposed to nationally required tests, a central feature of Bush's program. Committee Republicans wanted to push their Straight A's concept, replacing categorical programs with block grants. Miller said this would be anathema to committee Democrats, and Boehner agreed to drop it. Instead he backed a provision by Democrat Tim Roemer to give school districts more flexibility. Republican Bob Schaffer pressed for school vouchers, but they lacked a majority on the committee and were not pressed. Jim DeMint offered Straight A's as an amendment, but Bush talked him out of it; he had gotten Edward Kennedy to agree to greater flexibility in funding in the Senate version and didn't want to drive away Democrats in the House. The bill did include Bush's principles of annual testing and accountability. It passed committee with six Republicans and one Democrat opposed and passed on the floor 384–45 in May 2001. The Democratic takeover of the Senate in June actually helped the bill's chance. Jim Jeffords as committee chairman was fixated on getting huge funding increases for special education and had to be worked around, while Kennedy, the new chairman, was committed to compromise and accepted amendments that gave school districts flexibility and provided, in place of vouchers, private tutoring for disadvantaged students in failing schools.

Negotiations continued during summer and fall between Boehner, Miller, Kennedy and Gregg. Annual testing for grades 3–6 stayed in, but tests other than the NAEP were allowed. Some flexibility stayed in: except for Title I funds, districts could reallocate 50% of funding to suit their needs, and seven states and 150 school districts would get demonstration projects with more flexibility. The number of education programs was reduced only from 55 to 45: a victory for the constituencies of separate programs. The final agreements came in November, and in December the House passed the bill 381–41, with most of the nays from Republicans, and the Senate 87–10. Bush came to Hamilton High School to sign the bill in January.

The addition of part of Montgomery County to the district required some political adjustment; Boehner carried the area with only 56% of the vote in 2002 while winning districtwide with 71%. The Dayton area has grown accustomed to local congressmen who lavish money on local projects, but Boehner told the Miami Valley Economic Development Coalition in May 2002 that he wouldn't support anything above the president's budget request. "I told my constituents when I first ran for office if they thought my job was to rob the federal treasury on their behalf, they were voting for the wrong guy." Some have speculated that Boehner may seek another leadership position some day, but for the moment he seems content with his major committee positions.

NINTH DISTRICT

Rep. Marcy Kaptur (D)

Elected 1982, 11th term; b. June 17, 1946, Toledo; home, Toledo; U. of WI, B.A. 1968, U. of MI, M.A. 1974, M.I.T., 1981–82; Catholic; single.

Professional Career: Urban planner, Lucas Cnty. Planning Comm., 1969–75; Urban planning consultant, 1975–77; White House Asst. Dir. for Urban Affairs, 1977–80; Dpty. Secy., Natl. Consumer Coop. Bank, 1980–81; Author.

DC Office: 2366 RHOB 20515, 202-225-4146; Fax: 202-225-7711; Web site: www.house.gov/kaptur.

District Office: Toledo, 419-259-7500.

Committees: *Appropriations* (7th of 29 D): Agriculture, Rural Development, & FDA (RMM); Foreign Operations & Export Financing; VA, HUD & Independent Agencies.

Group Ratings

	ADA	ACLU	AFS	LCV	CON	ITIC	NTU	COC	ACU	NTLC	CHC
2002	95	67	100	100	1	38	20	30	18	10	8
2001	85	—	100	64	—	—	15	32	30	—	—

National Journal Ratings

	2001 LIB	—	2001 CONS		2002 LIB	—	2002 CONS
Economic	69%	—	31%		95%	—	0%
Social	68%	—	33%		65%	—	35%
Foreign	76%	—	24%		69%	—	31%

Key Votes of the 107th Congress

1. Approve Bush Tax Cuts	*	5. Faith-Based Charities	N	9. Trade Promotion Authority	N
2. Limit Patients' Bill of Rights	N	6. Bar Gays in the Boy Scouts	N	10. Bar Funds for Intl. Court	Y
3. Campaign Finance Reform	Y	7. Ban Partial-Birth Abortion	Y	11. Authorize Force in Iraq	N
4. Ban ANWR Development	Y	8. Arm Commercial Pilots	N	12. Deny Home. Sec. Dept. Union	N

Election Results

2002 general	Marcy Kaptur (D)	132,236	(74%)	($344,261)
	Ed Emery (R)	46,481	(26%)	
2002 primary	Marcy Kaptur (D)	unopposed		
2000 general	Marcy Kaptur (D)	168,547	(75%)	($285,239)
	Dwight Bryan (R)	49,446	(22%)	($86,815)
	Other	7,335	(3%)	

Prior Winning Percentages: 1998 (81%); 1996 (77%); 1994 (75%); 1992 (74%); 1990 (78%); 1988 (81%); 1986 (78%); 1984 (55%); 1982 (58%)

The People		Race/Ethnic Origin	Ancestry	
Area size:	1,244 sq. mi.	79.6% White	German: 21.3%	Irish: 8.9%
Urban population:	86.0%	13.6% Black	Polish: 6.4%	
Rural population:	14.0%	1.0% Asian	**2000 Presidential Vote**	
Pop. 2000:	630,730	0.2% Native Am.	Gore (D)	134,907 (55%)
Median income:	$40,265	0.0% Hawaiian	Bush (R)	100,704 (41%)
Poverty status:	12.0%	1.5% Two + races	Other	7,894 (3%)
Military veterans:	13.6%	0.1% Other	**Cook Partisan Voting Index:** D + 7	
		4.0% Hispanic Origin		

Occupation	Blue collar: 29.2%	White collar: 54.9%	Gray collar: 15.8%

Toledo was one of America's boomtowns in the 1920s, "a decade of fabulous figures," as historian Harlan Hatcher wrote. The Willys-Overland plant employed 25,000 workers and turned out an automobile every 30 seconds; the city built $20 million coal and iron ore docks; the Libbey-Owens-Ford merger made Toledo, with local supplies of natural gas and sand, the nation's largest glass manufacturer; the city built a new museum and transcontinental airport. Toledo had long been well-situated, where the Maumee River empties into Lake Erie, where two dozen rail lines connected it with the East Coast, Chicago, and the coal fields of Kentucky and West Virginia. It was also well positioned to be a center of the brash auto industry, a national leader when it first produced the Jeep in the 1940s. But by the early 1980s auto company management had allowed the unions to bid wages and benefits too high while watching quality decline. Subsidy, beyond the temporary Chrysler loan and a few small trade barriers, was not forthcoming, so Toledo and other auto-dependent cities went through tough times. But revival was on the way. Toledo's small manufacturers in search of markets here and abroad showed energy and ingenuity in the 1990s. They produced one of America's hottest vehicles, the Jeep Cherokee; the old plant was set to close, but the city offered Chrysler $300 million in incentives to stay, and a new plant was built along I-75. Daimler's purchase of Chrysler was a mixed blessing; in 2001, after announcing that the new Jeep Liberty would be produced at the new assembly plant, the firm scheduled cutbacks.

The 9th Congressional District is centered on Toledo, spreading east through the flatlands of Ottawa and Erie Counties on the Lake Erie shore and inland to southern Lorain County southwest of Cleveland, including Oberlin, home of Oberlin College, founded in 1833 and the first American college to admit both men and women and blacks and whites. Port Clinton, on Lake Erie, bills itself as the "Walleye Capital of the World" and drops a walleye on New Year's Eve to rival Times Square. Sandusky is home of the giant Cedar Point amusement park. Not far away is Milan, birthplace of the great inventor and capitalist Thomas Edison. Politically, Toledo has been heavily Democratic since CIO unions organized the plants in the late 1930s; the collapse of the auto industry so unnerved the district that in 1980 it voted for Ronald Reagan and elected a Republican congressman, but it switched back to the Democrats in 1982 and has stayed with them in almost all elections ever since. The other counties have also been Democratic lately, though less so.

The congresswoman from the 9th District is Marcy Kaptur, a Democrat first elected in 1982. She is now the senior female House Democrat and has worked for more portraits and statues of women in the Capitol. Kaptur is fervent and dedicated to sometimes old-fashioned principles, always a loyal daughter of Toledo. She grew up there in a blue collar neighborhood, her parents worked at local auto plants and the family operated a small grocery store. She has spent almost her entire career in public service. "The unfailingly polite, plain-spoken hometown girl," wrote the *Cleveland Plain Dealer*; she and her brother Steve live in the house where they grew up. She graduated from the University of Wisconsin, the first in her family to attend college, got a masters degree from the University of Michigan and then spent eight years as an urban planner in Toledo. She worked in the Carter White House and was shrewd enough to return home in 1980. That year Republican Ed Weber defeated 26-year incumbent Thomas Ashley. In 1982, when no other Democrat would run against Weber, she did and won 58%–39% despite being outspent 3–1. She saw Toledo's economy nosedive and felt intensely the pain of ordinary people who played by the rules but ended up losing because of larger economic forces.

Kaptur's great cause is trade. She has long been convinced that Toledo and places like it have lost jobs and industry because of unfair trade practices and low wage competition in countries like China and Mexico. She pressured the Japanese to buy more American auto parts, but has been leery of Japanese investment in the United States. She has proposed to prohibit top government officials from representing foreign corporations for five years and foreign governments forever after they leave office. Kaptur was probably Congress's most vocal and dedicated opponent of NAFTA. Bringing an emotional commitment that was genuinely moving, she visited the Mexican border and returned home with soil and water samples to demonstrate the pollution. She argued that 100,000 jobs had been transferred from Ohio to Mexico, and criticized Bill Clinton for doing nothing for sagging U.S. industries and for ignoring Democrats opposed to NAFTA. Even as the two nations' economic ties boomed, Kaptur complained that trade was one-sided toward Mexico. She was a vocal opponent of PNTR with China and trade promotion authority. Despite her liberal persona, her iconoclasm sometimes veers her voting record toward the middle. Kaptur opposes funding for abortion and favors the partial-birth abortion ban. On the Appropriations Agriculture Subcommittee, where she is the ranking Democrat, she sought to limit farm payments, which led Republicans in 2002 to threaten her favorite projects; she backed off, saying, "I may be blockheaded sometimes, but I'm not stupid." She strongly opposed the war in Iraq. Following visits to Iowa and New Hampshire in 2001, she said that she was encouraged to run for president.

Kaptur is exceedingly popular in Toledo and has run far ahead of party lines in the 9th District. She has also become something of a national figure who goes her own way from her party. In August 1995 she appeared before Ross Perot's United We Stand and made a rousing speech, mostly on trade, that had delegates cheering. Perot praised her and offered his vice presidential nomination a year later; she turned it down. She has declined opportunities to run for statewide office. She published a book on women in Congress, has hosted a weekly radio show on nearly 100 stations, and shows no sign of discouragement in representing the workers of Toledo.

After the 2002 election, she ran a one day campaign for minority leader, pledging to reform the excesses of money in politics and return to grass-roots bake sales and the like. It turned out that her chief goal was to get time to urge the Democratic Caucus to conduct a reassessment following its recent setback; on the day that super-fundraiser Nancy Pelosi took over as party leader, Kaptur got little support for her wistful plea. In March, just before military action against Iraq, she told the *Toledo Blade* that Osama bin Laden had a "religious purpose . . . very similar to those kind of atypical revolutionaries that helped to cast off the British crown" more than two centuries earlier. Local and national Republicans complained, and two weeks later she apologized at a VFW post "if my remarks have hurt anyone." Since 1984, she has been reelected with at least 74% of the vote.

TENTH DISTRICT

Rep. Dennis Kucinich (D)

Elected 1996, 4th term; b. Oct. 6, 1946, Cleveland; home, Cleveland; Cleveland St. U., 1967–70, Case Western Reserve U., B.A., M.A., 1973; Catholic; single.

Elected Office: Cleveland City Cncl., 1970–75, 1983–85; Cleveland Mayor, 1977–79; OH Senate, 1994–96.

Professional Career: Clerk, Municipal Courts, 1976–77; Radio Talk Show Host, 1979, 1989; Lecturer, 1980–83; Consultant, 1986–94; TV Reporter, Channel 8, 1989–92.

DC Office: 1730 LHOB 20515, 202-225-5871; Fax: 202-225-5745; Web site: www.house.gov/kucinich.

District Offices: Lakewood, 216-228-8850; Parma, 440-845-2707.

Committees: *Education & the Workforce* (11th of 22 D): Education Reform; Workforce Protections. *Government Reform* (8th of 19 D): Energy Policy, Natural Resources and Regulatory Affairs; National Security, Emerging Threats & Intl. Relations (RMM).

Group Ratings

	ADA	ACLU	AFS	LCV	CON	ITIC	NTU	COC	ACU	NTLC	CHC
2002	80	64	100	100	81	25	32	20	0	8	33
2001	85	—	100	93	—	—	12	17	20	—	—

National Journal Ratings

	2001 LIB —	2001 CONS		2002 LIB —	2002 CONS
Economic	88%	— 11%		95%	— 0%
Social	59%	— 41%		65%	— 35%
Foreign	96%	— 0%		90%	— 8%

Key Votes of the 107th Congress

1. Approve Bush Tax Cuts	N	5. Faith-Based Charities	N	9. Trade Promotion Authority	N
2. Limit Patients' Bill of Rights	N	6. Bar Gays in the Boy Scouts	N	10. Bar Funds for Intl. Court	N
3. Campaign Finance Reform	Y	7. Ban Partial-Birth Abortion	*	11. Authorize Force in Iraq	N
4. Ban ANWR Development	Y	8. Arm Commercial Pilots	N	12. Deny Home. Sec. Dept. Union	N

Election Results

2002 general	Dennis Kucinich (D)	129,997	(74%)	($518,620)
	Jon Heben (R)	41,778	(24%)	
	Other	3,761	(2%)	
2002 primary	Dennis Kucinich (D)	unopposed		
2000 general	Dennis Kucinich (D)	167,063	(75%)	($550,063)
	Bill Smith (R)	48,930	(22%)	($5,564)
	Other	6,762	(3%)	

Prior Winning Percentages: 1998 (67%); 1996 (49%)

The People		Race/Ethnic Origin	Ancestry	
Area size:	196 sq. mi.	87.2% White	German: 16.6%	Irish: 12.8%
Urban population:	99.4%	4.2% Black	Polish: 8.6%	
Rural population:	0.6%	1.7% Asian	**2000 Presidential Vote**	
Pop. 2000:	630,730	0.2% Native Am.	Gore (D)	122,219 (53%)
Median income:	$41,841	0.0% Hawaiian	Bush (R)	96,623 (42%)
Poverty status:	9.1%	1.5% Two+ races	Other	11,540 (5%)
Military veterans:	13.2%	0.1% Other	**Cook Partisan Voting Index:** D + 6	
		5.0% Hispanic Origin		

Occupation	Blue collar: 23.3%	White collar: 62.5%	Gray collar: 14.1%

Cleveland, one of America's great cities at the beginning of the 20th century, faced some hardships in the latter half of the century, but was on its way back in the new century. It grew as a center of heavy industry: This was the original base of John D. Rockefeller's Standard Oil; the city's twisting and deep Cuyahoga River was the site of several of the nation's largest steel mills; great industrial fortunes here built civic institutions like the museums in Wade Park, Case Western University and the Cleveland Symphony, and financed the campaigns of northeast Ohio Republican Presidents James Garfield and William McKinley. On the old Public Square, designed like a New England town green by the Yankees who settled this Western Reserve (the northeast corner of Ohio) in the early 19th century, the two eccentric Van Sweringen brothers, trolley magnates of the early 20th century, built the Terminal Tower, for many years the highest skyscraper in interior America. This yeasty, ethnic city, with more than 40 nationalities—Hungarians, Czechs, Serbs, Croatians, Poles, Italians, Germans (the Hapsburg Empire and more)—and many distinct ethnic neighborhoods, produced a robust two-party politics. In the 1930s, after CIO unions organized steel factories and auto assembly plants, Cleveland became solidly Democratic, though with some affluent Republican suburbs.

But Cleveland never led the nation as it hoped: America's fourth largest city in 1910, it was overtaken in size first by Detroit, eventually by the likes of Houston and Dallas; today, it's the center of the nation's 16th largest metropolitan area. The central city declined from 914,000 in 1950 to 478,000 in 2000, as the children who grew up in the tightly packed neighborhoods made more money and moved to the close-in suburbs and then outer suburban counties. The 1970s were a bad decade for Cleveland, which became an object of ridicule by national sophisticates. Its heavy industries were fast declining, Lake Erie and the Cuyahoga River were badly polluted (the river caught fire in June 1969). City politics became racially polarized with the election of black Mayor Carl Stokes in 1967, and in 1978 the city defaulted on bank loans under Mayor Dennis Kucinich. The city government was rescued by George Voinovich, elected mayor in 1979 and later governor and senator. Downtown Cleveland revived, with the second largest theater district center in the nation at Playhouse Square, the Jacobs Field baseball stadium, a basketball arena, and the Rock and Roll Hall of Fame. Following the departure of the city's beloved Browns to Baltimore, a new football stadium was constructed and the city gained an expansion team in 1999, retaining the Browns name and colors. People swim in now clean Lake Erie; restaurants and pleasure boat docks line the Cuyahoga where diners can sip Burning River pale ale. Although many corporate headquarters have departed and LTV shut down its steel plant with 3,200 jobs in 2001, Cleveland remains home to several of the nation's largest law firms, and some businesses, like iron ore giant Cleveland-Cliffs, have sharply revived; the city's number one employer is now health services, and the Cleveland Clinic may be its best-known firm. Although the "Comeback City" has not yet earned the title, its population declined only 5% in the 1990s, apparently bottoming out, while the metropolitan area grew.

The 10th Congressional District includes most of the west side of Cleveland and the western and southern suburbs in Cuyahoga County. Excluded is one salient of mostly black Cleveland precincts attached to the 11th District across the river. Suburbs in the 10th include Lakewood, well-established by the 1920s and still comfortable middle-class territory, plus Rocky River and Bay Village, growing more affluent westward along the lake. Inland is Parma, a creation of the 1950s, when second- and third-generation ethnics moved out to subdivision houses set amid what was once America's densest concentration of bowling alleys. The district extends east of Cleveland on the southern edge of the county in Cuyahoga Valley suburbs. The political tradition in the 10th is primarily Democratic, though Voinovich has carried the area; George W. Bush won only 42% of the vote in 2000.

The congressman from the 10th District is Dennis Kucinich, elected in 1996, still unrepentant about the day he plunged the city into default. Kucinich grew up as the oldest of seven children whose father was a truck driver; the family moved 21 times to various parts of Cleveland. Kucinich was a political prodigy who was elected to the city council in 1969, at 23; he saw himself as the champion of the working man, eager for confrontations with Cleveland's business establishment. He was elected mayor in 1977 when the city government was in terrible financial straits. Kucinich was unwilling or unable to balance the budget and meet obligations; when bankers demanded he sell city-owned properties, he refused and they called in their loans. The public verdict was negative: after surviving a recall petition by 236 votes of 120,000 cast, Kucinich was defeated in 1979. He argues that his primary goal was to preserve the city-owned Muni Light electric system, and that he saved residents millions of dollars on their electric bills. He taught at Cleveland State and Case Western Reserve, hosted a radio talk show and was a TV reporter. In 1994 Kucinich staged a political comeback and was elected to the state Senate. In 1996 he ran for the House. The Republican incumbent Martin Hoke was elected twice against Democrats with ethical problems. Kucinich campaigned against NAFTA and GATT and defended his ties with labor. Democrats, many of them former Kucinich critics, rallied around him: The Cleveland City Council named a public power plant for him on the same day Bill Clinton campaigned for him in Parma. Kucinich won, but by only 49%–46%.

Kucinich has been a vocal foe of international trade agreements. He bars his staff from parking foreign cars in congressional lots and was a leader in the fight against PNTR with China. A vegan since before he was elected to Congress, Kucinich attacked companies that produce genetically modified foods. He continues to emphasize his local roots, with a website dedicated to polka, bowling and Kielbasa. He co-chairs the Progressive Caucus with Barbara Lee, Democrats who believe their party should move to the left.

In February 2003, Kucinich decided he should run for president. His apparent motivating force was his opposition to American military action in Iraq and elsewhere. In 1999 he opposed Bill Clinton's bombing of Kosovo and was described as the "leading Democratic dove." He was one of 30 Democrats to file a lawsuit to stop George W. Bush's abrogation of the 1972 ABM Treaty. He voted to authorize the use of force after the September 11 attacks, but after the defeat of the Taliban in Afghanistan he focused on nonviolent responses and called for the creation of a Department of Peace. In February 2003 he joined five other House Democrats who filed a lawsuit to prevent Bush from invading Iraq without an explicit declaration of war. That month he also started an exploratory committee to seek the 2004 Democratic presidential nomination. He called himself an "FDR Democrat" who wanted to "return the Democratic Party to its roots," including strong ties to organized labor, and he promised "a dramatic choice for Democrats," especially those who are antiwar.

On one issue on which he had been out of line with most leftish Democrats, he switched: Long an opponent of abortion, he voted present on two anti-abortion bills in 2002. In May 2003, he flipped his position completely: "I want to state clearly that no one will be appointed to the U.S. Supreme Court if they don't commit to supporting *Roe v. Wade* and a woman's right to choose." On *Meet the Press* in February 2003, he defended his view that the war in Iraq was a battle for oil and that the oil industry would benefit: "I believe most sincerely that one of the motivating factors involved in this effort to strike against Iraq is the desire on the part of some to be able to control the oil interests in Iraq." Bush Pentagon adviser Richard Perle, appearing with him, said that was a "lie"; Kucinich replied that no one had given a better explanation of "what is this about." Undaunted, he spoke to enthusiastic audiences of peace activists on both coasts. In the first quarter of 2003 he raised $180,000, much less than most other candidates except Carol Moseley Braun.

No serious observers of American politics in early 2003 believed that Kucinich would be nominated for president. What the impact of his campaign will be in the 10th District was not clear. Cuyahoga County Elections Board Chairman and former Brook Park Mayor Tom Coyne said he was considering running against him in the 2004 House primary and said, "I don't think his views are consistent with the people of the district any more." But Kucinich has confounded the experts before, and he did win 74% of the vote in November 2002.

ELEVENTH DISTRICT

Rep. Stephanie Tubbs Jones (D)

Elected 1998, 3d term; b. Sept. 10, 1949, Cleveland; home, Cleveland; Case Western Reserve U., B.A. 1971, J.D. 1974.; Baptist; married (Mervyn Jones).

Elected Office: Cleveland Municipal Court Judge, 1981–83; Cuyahoga Cnty. Court of Common Pleas Judge, 1983–91.

Professional Career: Asst. Gen. Cnsl. & EEO Admin., NE OH Regional Sewer Dist., 1974–76; Asst. Cuyahoga Cnty. Prosecutor, 1976–79; Equal Employment Opportunity Comm., 1979–81; Cuyahoga Cnty. Prosecutor, 1991–98.

DC Office: 1516 LHOB 20515, 202-225-7032; Fax: 202-225-1339; Web site: www.house.gov/tubbsjones.

District Office: Shaker Heights, 216-522-4900.

Committees: *Standards of Official Conduct* (2d of 5 D). *Ways & Means* (17th of 17 D): Select Revenue Measures; Social Security.

Group Ratings

	ADA	ACLU	AFS	LCV	CON	ITIC	NTU	COC	ACU	NTLC	CHC
2002	85	92	100	63	56	38	26	39	0	0	0
2001	100	—	100	93	—	—	13	35	4	—	—

National Journal Ratings

	2001 LIB —	2001 CONS		2002 LIB —	2002 CONS
Economic	83%	— 15%		83%	— 16%
Social	78%	— 23%		97%	— 2%
Foreign	94%	— 5%		94%	— 0%

Key Votes of the 107th Congress

1. Approve Bush Tax Cuts	N	5. Faith-Based Charities	N	9. Trade Promotion Authority	N
2. Limit Patients' Bill of Rights	N	6. Bar Gays in the Boy Scouts	N	10. Bar Funds for Intl. Court	N
3. Campaign Finance Reform	Y	7. Ban Partial-Birth Abortion	N	11. Authorize Force in Iraq	N
4. Ban ANWR Development	Y	8. Arm Commercial Pilots	N	12. Deny Home. Sec. Dept. Union	N

Election Results

2002 general	Stephanie Tubbs Jones (D)	116,590	(76%)	($422,417)
	Patrick Pappano (R)	36,146	(24%)	($61,671)
2002 primary	Stephanie Tubbs Jones (D)	unopposed		
2000 general	Stephanie Tubbs Jones (D)	164,134	(85%)	($240,018)
	James Sykora (R)	21,630	(11%)	
	Other	7,755	(4%)	

Prior Winning Percentages: 1998 (80%)

The People		Race/Ethnic Origin	Ancestry	
Area size:	135 sq. mi.	38.8% White	German: 6.5%	Irish: 5.2%
Urban population:	100.0%	55.5% Black	Italian: 4.9%	
Rural population:	0.0%	1.6% Asian	**2000 Presidential Vote**	
Pop. 2000:	630,730	0.1% Native Am.	Gore (D)	172,146 (79%)
Median income:	$31,998	0.0% Hawaiian	Bush (R)	38,382 (18%)
Poverty status:	19.5%	1.4% Two+ races	Other	6,706 (3%)
Military veterans:	11.9%	0.2% Other	**Cook Partisan Voting Index:** D +32	
		2.3% Hispanic Origin		

Occupation	Blue collar: 21.3%	White collar: 61.4%	Gray collar: 17.3%

Like most great American cities, Cleveland grew in great bursts of migration, when capitalists' investments suddenly were paying off beyond their wildest dreams and low-wage workers were attracted from ready corners of the country and the world. Cleveland's greatest surge of growth started in the 1890s and lasted through the 1920s, as tens of thousands of immigrants from central and southern Europe arrived here, looking for jobs in steel, auto and other factories. Bohemians came to the tightly packed neighborhoods along Broadway, Hungarians a bit to the northeast, Jews north of University Circle along East 105th Street, and Italians to Little Italy along Mayfield Road. As the nation's heavy industries geared up for World War II and enjoyed years of prosperous growth afterward, a second surge of immigrants came, this time blacks from the American South. From Cleveland's old ghetto, south of Carnegie Avenue downtown to East 105th, the rapidly increasing number of blacks covered most of the east side by the middle 1960s, with only a few Bohemian and Italian enclaves remaining east of the Cuyahoga. Migration stopped around 1965, but blacks continued to move beyond the city limits to the east side suburbs. These bursts of migration led to political changes. A string of ethnic mayors—Frank Lausche, Anthony Celebrezze, Ralph Locher—was followed by the election in 1967 of Carl Stokes, the nation's first black big-city mayor, and Cleveland had racially polarized politics for much of the 1970s. Even so, the west side stayed mostly white and Cleveland did not have a black majority until the 2000 Census, according to which its population was 51% black.

The 11th Congressional District includes most of the east side of Cleveland, plus the suburbs just to the east, which together have about as many people as the city now. Some of these—East Cleveland, Warrensville Heights—are mostly black; some, notably Shaker Heights, have stable black percentages in carefully maintained neighborhoods where racial integration has succeeded. Others are the destination of blacks seeking low-crime neighborhoods and middle-class schools not often found among Cleveland's impressive museums and medical centers. Still others—Mayfield Heights and South Euclid—have been the destination of Cleveland's relatively few new immigrants, most of them from eastern Europe. Overall, 56% of the people in the 11th District are black. Politically, this is by far the most Democratic district in Ohio.

The congresswoman from the 11th District is Stephanie Tubbs Jones, for all practical purposes chosen in the May 1998 primary. She grew up in Cleveland, the daughter of a Hopkins Airport skycap, graduated from college and law school at Case Western and served her entire legal career as a federal or local government lawyer. She served eight years as judge on the Court of Common Pleas of Cuyahoga County and in 1990 narrowly lost as the Democratic nominee for Ohio Supreme Court. In 1991 she was appointed by the county's Democratic Party as the first woman and first black prosecutor in Cuyahoga County; she easily won election with 79%. When Louis Stokes announced his retirement, Tubbs Jones decided to run for the House. Her chief opponents in the primary were state Senator Jeffrey Johnson and Reverend Marvin McMickle, minister of the Antioch Baptist Church, one of the city's largest black congregations. Tubbs Jones, the early favorite, campaigned in both black and white neighborhoods, unlike her opponents. Stokes was officially neutral, but helped Tubbs Jones raise money in Washington. She won 51%, with 20% each to Johnson and McMickle. The general election was a formality in this district.

In the House, Tubbs Jones had a solidly liberal voting record. She showed her political skills by winning appointment as the freshman on the Democratic steering committee, which makes committee assignments. Later, she became president of the Democratic sophomore class. She wisely sought ways to cooperate with influential Republicans in the Ohio delegation. Bill Clinton signed the bill that she co-sponsored with Deborah Pryce that increases funding of child abuse programs. She worked with Steve LaTourette to require Medicare HMO insurers to maintain service and benefits for at least three years. She offended the sizable bloc of Jewish voters in her district when she voted present in May 2002 on a resolution to support Israel in the fight against terrorism. After some colleagues said that she had been too aggressive in questioning Fed chairman Alan Greenspan and Housing Secretary Mel Martinez at committee hearings, she said that she wouldn't change her style.

Tubbs Jones has been easily reelected. She decided not to run for mayor when Michael White retired in 2001. She generated controversy by supporting former Clinton Administration official Raymond Pierce, a black with little local experience, who was running against County Commissioner Jane Campbell, a white with whom Tubbs Jones had worked closely. When Campbell won, Tubbs Jones said they remained friends. At the urging of Democratic leaders, she considered but rejected a bid for governor in 2002. After the election, she became the first African-American woman selected to the Ways and Means Committee. In March 2003 she was one of 11 House

Democrats who voted against the resolution supporting the troops and President Bush at the start of the Iraq war.

TWELFTH DISTRICT

Rep. Pat Tiberi (R)

Elected 2000, 2d term; b. Oct. 21, 1962, Columbus; home, Columbus; OH St. U., B.A. 1985; Catholic; married (Denice).

Elected Office: OH House of Reps., 1992–2000, Maj. Ldr., 1999–2000.

Professional Career: Staff asst., U.S. Rep. John Kasich, 1984–92; Realtor, ReMax Achievers, 1995–2000.

DC Office: 113 CHOB 20515, 202-225-5355; Fax: 202-226-4523; Web site: www.house.gov/tiberi.

District Office: Columbus, 614-523-2555.

Committees: *Education & the Workforce* (16th of 27 R): 21st Century Competitiveness; Employer-Employee Relations. *Financial Services* (28th of 37 R): Capital Markets, Insurance & Government Sponsored Enterprises; Financial Institutions & Consumer Credit; Housing & Community Opportunity.

Group Ratings

	ADA	ACLU	AFS	LCV	CON	ITIC	NTU	COC	ACU	NTLC	CHC
2002	0	13	0	25	87	100	62	100	96	89	100
2001	0	—	0	0	—	—	68	100	92	—	—

National Journal Ratings

	2001 LIB — 2001 CONS		2002 LIB — 2002 CONS	
Economic	0% —	94%	0% —	91%
Social	0% —	81%	0% —	75%
Foreign	41% —	58%	46% —	53%

Key Votes of the 107th Congress

1. Approve Bush Tax Cuts	Y	5. Faith-Based Charities	Y	9. Trade Promotion Authority	Y
2. Limit Patients' Bill of Rights	Y	6. Bar Gays in the Boy Scouts	Y	10. Bar Funds for Intl. Court	Y
3. Campaign Finance Reform	N	7. Ban Partial-Birth Abortion	Y	11. Authorize Force in Iraq	Y
4. Ban ANWR Development	N	8. Arm Commercial Pilots	Y	12. Deny Home. Sec. Dept. Union	Y

Election Results

2002 general	Pat Tiberi (R)	116,982	(64%)	($777,343)
	Edward Brown (D)	64,707	(36%)	($41,214)
2002 primary	Pat Tiberi (R)	unopposed		
2000 general	Pat Tiberi (R)	139,242	(53%)	($2,349,872)
	Maryellen O'Shaughnessy (D)	115,432	(44%)	($1,340,688)
	Other	8,712	(3%)	

The People		Race/Ethnic Origin	Ancestry	
Area size:	1,031 sq. mi.	72.1% White	German: 16.8%	Irish: 9.3%
Urban population:	88.1%	21.7% Black	English: 7.5%	
Rural population:	11.9%	2.1% Asian	**2000 Presidential Vote**	
Pop. 2000:	630,730	0.2% Native Am.	Bush (R) 129,840	(51%)
Median income:	$47,289	0.0% Hawaiian	Gore (D) 115,083	(46%)
Poverty status:	10.0%	1.9% Two+ races	Other 7,340	(3%)
Military veterans:	12.5%	0.2% Other	**Cook Partisan Voting Index:** R + 3	
		1.7% Hispanic Origin		

Occupation	Blue collar: 18.0%	White collar: 68.4%	Gray collar: 13.6%

Columbus is on the verge of becoming a major metropolis. With city limits stretching toward farmland at each point of the compass, the central city of Columbus had 711,000 people in 2000, far more than Cleveland (478,000) or Cincinnati (331,000). The metropolitan area, though less populous than Cleveland and a bit smaller than Cincinnati, is growing much more rapidly; Columbus's Franklin County passed the 1 million mark in the 1990s. Columbus is centrally located, not only in the center of Ohio, but a one-day truck drive from more than one-half of the nation's population. With its growing jobs base, Columbus was the only one of the 15 largest cities in Ohio to gain population in the 1990s. It has the advantages of being a state capital, the home of Ohio State University, and a major white-collar employment town: It is the home of The Limited's Leslie Wexner, of Nationwide Insurance and AEP. Columbus likes to brag that its airfreight operations at Port Columbus, the airport, make it the largest in the country dedicated to cargo. This economic base and civic infrastructure have attracted the kind of upscale, enterprising people who have produced much of America's growth in recent years. The politics of Columbus have traditionally been Republican. It had few of the eastern European immigrants and CIO unions that made Cleveland so Democratic. But in 1999 Columbus elected a Democratic mayor, Michael Coleman, and in 2000 Franklin County was carried, though just barely, by Al Gore. The counties that ring Franklin County, however, are heavily Republican.

The 12th Congressional District is one of two districts dominated by Columbus. It includes most of the east side of the city, the affluent suburb of Bexley, home of the Governor's Mansion, and the northeastern suburbs in Franklin County. It also includes Delaware County directly north of Columbus, Ohio's fastest-growing county in the 1990s, and most of Licking County east of Columbus, including the small industrial town of Newark and the lovely college town of Granville.

The congressman from the 12th District is Pat Tiberi, a Republican elected in 2000. The son of Italian immigrants, he grew up in Columbus and graduated from Ohio State. He worked as a real estate agent and was for eight years an assistant to Congressman John Kasich, who helped Tiberi win in 1992, at age 30, a seat in the state House. He became majority leader and supported business-friendly legislation and changes in tort law. In 1999 Kasich announced his retirement, after a brief run for the presidency and six years as chairman of the Budget Committee.

Tiberi won support to replace his mentor from most of the Republican establishment plus the U.S. Chamber of Commerce. He faced a noisy but not very effective primary challenge from state Senator Gene Watts, who sought to rally the conservative base. Tiberi won 73%–21%. The resounding victory gave him a big boost heading into the general election against Maryellen O'Shaughnessy, a Columbus city council member. She told her personal story as the single mother of a 10-year-old son and set out differences with Tiberi on prescription drug benefits, campaign finance, taxes and Social Security. Tiberi played up his Columbus roots and his membership in the Ohio State marching band and attacked O'Shaughnessy for the negative Democratic party ads that labeled him as the defender of insurance companies on prescription drugs. He called for drug coverage as part of a broader overhaul of Medicare, a theme long voiced by Kasich. This was one of the most-watched House races in the nation; with campaign help from Kasich, who retained his local popularity, Tiberi won 53%–44%, running 2% ahead of George W. Bush. O'Shaughnessy won Franklin County 51%–46%. But Tiberi won 66%–31% in outlying Delaware and Licking Counties.

In the House, Tiberi's record has been solidly conservative on economic and cultural issues but more centrist on foreign and defense policy. He won House approval of an amendment to increase flexibility for local school districts in exchange for better student performance. He joined activist Republicans pushing to increase George W. Bush's tax cut above his original $1.6 trillion. He later called for scrapping the income tax code and creating a national commission to craft a new tax system by 2006. He called for lifting the embargo of Cuba. Like Kasich, he criticized the way the Appropriations Committee does business, and sought unsuccessfully to change House Republican rules to make it easier for the speaker to remove appropriators who signed a discharge petition.

In 2002 O'Shaughnessy decided to run for county commissioner, and Tiberi won reelection 64%–36%.

THIRTEENTH DISTRICT

Rep. Sherrod Brown (D)

Elected 1992, 6th term; b. Nov. 9, 1952, Mansfield; home, Lorain; Yale U., B.A. 1974, OH St. U., M.A. 1979, M.A. 1981; Lutheran; divorced.

Elected Office: OH House of Reps. 1974–82; OH Secy. of State, 1982–90.

Professional Career: Prof., OH St. U. at Mansfield, 1979–81.

DC Office: 2332 RHOB 20515, 202-225-3401; Fax: 202-225-2266; Web site: www.house.gov/sherrodbrown.

District Offices: Akron, 330-865-8450; Lorain, 440-245-5350.

Committees: *Energy & Commerce* (8th of 26 D): Commerce, Trade & Consumer Protection; Energy & Air Quality; Health (RMM). *International Relations* (7th of 23 D): Asia & the Pacific.

Group Ratings

	ADA	ACLU	AFS	LCV	CON	ITIC	NTU	COC	ACU	NTLC	CHC
2002	95	87	100	88	83	38	28	25	4	3	0
2001	95	—	100	100	—	—	15	22	4	—	—

National Journal Ratings

	2001 LIB	—	2001 CONS		2002 LIB	—	2002 CONS
Economic	95%	—	0%		88%	—	10%
Social	83%	—	11%		74%	—	19%
Foreign	91%	—	8%		87%	—	10%

Key Votes of the 107th Congress

1. Approve Bush Tax Cuts	N	5. Faith-Based Charities	N	9. Trade Promotion Authority	N
2. Limit Patients' Bill of Rights	N	6. Bar Gays in the Boy Scouts	N	10. Bar Funds for Intl. Court	N
3. Campaign Finance Reform	Y	7. Ban Partial-Birth Abortion	N	11. Authorize Force in Iraq	N
4. Ban ANWR Development	Y	8. Arm Commercial Pilots	Y	12. Deny Home. Sec. Dept. Union	N

Election Results

2002 general	Sherrod Brown (D)	123,025	(69%)	($606,396)
	Ed Oliveros (R)	55,357	(31%)	
2002 primary	Sherrod Brown (D)	unopposed		
2000 general	Sherrod Brown (D)	170,058	(65%)	($789,866)
	Rick Jeric (R)	84,295	(32%)	($28,276)
	Other	8,945	(3%)	

Prior Winning Percentages: 1998 (62%); 1996 (60%); 1994 (49%); 1992 (53%)

The People		Race/Ethnic Origin	Ancestry	
Area size:	537 sq. mi.	81.5% White	German: 17.3%	Irish: 10.1%
Urban population:	92.7%	12.1% Black	English: 6.7%	
Rural population:	7.3%	1.2% Asian	**2000 Presidential Vote**	
Pop. 2000:	630,730	0.2% Native Am.	Gore (D) 133,458	(53%)
Median income:	$44,524	0.0% Hawaiian	Bush (R) 110,812	(44%)
Poverty status:	9.4%	1.3% Two+ races	Other 9,559	(4%)
Military veterans:	14.0%	0.1% Other	**Cook Partisan Voting Index:** D + 4	
		3.5% Hispanic Origin		

Occupation	Blue collar: 26.3%	White collar: 59.2%	Gray collar: 14.4%

Fifty years ago most of the people of metro Cleveland were clustered in the city itself, in tightly packed blocks of houses on the limestone plains above the Cuyahoga River valley with its giant steel mills. Around the city there were some comfortable suburbs, then as you drove past them you found yourself amid miles of farm fields before you got to the nearby industrial cities—Akron, with its Firestone, B.F. Goodrich and Goodyear tire factories, or Lorain, a sort of mini-Cleveland, on Lake Erie with steel mills lining the narrow Black River. In the half-century since, the population of Cleveland has fallen by half and the metro area has spread out over the northern Ohio countryside. The suburbs have spread from Cleveland to Akron without interval; the shoreline from Cleveland to Lorain has been filled in; Medina County, between Lorain and Akron, has been transformed from farmland to suburbia; only the Cuyahoga River valley between Cleveland and Akron has been off limits to development, protected by the creation of the Cuyahoga Valley National Park. The economy has changed as well. In 1950 Cleveland's economy depended on heavy manufacturing, especially steel, and Akron's on tires. Today most of the steel mills have grown cold or been torn down and the old tire factories have mostly been converted to other use. Akron has developed itself as the "Polymer Center of America," with 80% of the nation's polymer research and a first class polymer engineering program at the University of Akron.

The 13th Congressional District is made up of much of this area in metro Cleveland, but none of the city itself. It includes the west side of Akron and its western suburbs; the lines separating it from the 14th and 17th Districts in Akron's Summit County are absurdly convoluted. It includes the northern part of Lorain County, including Lorain and Elyria just to the south. It includes the southern tier of suburban townships in Cleveland's Cuyahoga County—Strongsville, North Royalton, Broadview Heights—and the northern tier of suburban townships in Medina County, including Brunswick. Fifty years ago this would have been a Republican area, with Democratic precincts in Akron and Lorain. Today, as Clevelanders have spread out far and wide in the metro area, the area is Democratic, though not overwhelmingly so: George W. Bush won 44% of the vote here in 2000.

The congressman from the 13th District is Sherrod Brown, once the boy wonder of Ohio politics and now one of Ohio Democrats' few successful career politicians. He grew up in Mansfield as the son of a doctor, graduated from Yale in 1974 and won a seat in the state House later that year (a state employee, mistaking him for an intern, gave him a dollar to get her a cup of coffee). Since then, he has never stopped running. In 1982 he was elected secretary of state at 30 and worked hard to increase voter registration and turnout. In 1990 he lost that office to Bob Taft, who is now governor. In 1992 Brown ran for the open 13th District House seat. With solid labor support, he campaigned loud and hard against NAFTA and championed universal health care. He won 53%–35%, with 61% in Lorain County.

In the House, Brown has a consistently liberal voting record and has been a politically adept member of the Energy and Commerce Committee. On trade he has been one of the most voluble liberal-labor members from the Great Lakes area attacking NAFTA, GATT, PNTR with China and trade promotion authority; he opposed opening the border to Mexican trucks. But he supported the balanced budget amendment and line-item veto. His position as ranking Democrat on the Health Subcommittee has given him little influence because Republicans have written their health care proposals mostly in party task forces. He has been a critic of pharmaceutical and insurance companies, introducing with Republican Jo Ann Emerson a bill to speed approval of low cost generic drugs. He has urged adoption of a ban on the use of antibiotics on farm animals—including penicillin and tetracycline—which he claims will prevent the transmission of antibiotic resistant bacteria in food. He sponsored a successful bill to support the participation of Taiwan in international organizations. He called for enforcement of laws against importing goods made with slave labor in China. He authored *Congress from the Inside*, a book that claims that House Democrats lost their majority in 1994 because "we were blamed for everything the voters did not like."

Brown had a serious Republican challenge in 1994 from Lorain County Prosecutor Gregory White, but he survived by 49%–46%. Since then he has won easily. After the 2000 election Brown seemed threatened by redistricting. Ohio lost one House seat in the 2000 Census, and Republicans had majorities in the legislature and held the governorship. The 13th District was then shaped like a dumbbell, with Lorain and Medina Counties connected by a narrow corridor to parts of Portage, Geauga and Trumbull Counties to the east. Brown let it be known that he would run for governor if his district was eliminated. Governor Bob Taft, though he had beaten Brown for secretary of state in 1990 and had good ratings in the polls, asked legislators not to eliminate Brown. By the time the legislators were ready to act, in January 2002, they needed Democratic votes to give it immediate effect in time for the filing deadline. The result was the current 13th

District. The bad news for Brown was that he had not represented 56% of his constituents before. The good news for him was that they were much more Democratic than the constituents he lost: the Bush 2000 percentage was lowered from 50% to 44%. He has been mentioned as a candidate for governor in 2006.

FOURTEENTH DISTRICT

Rep. Steven LaTourette (R)

Elected 1994, 5th term; b. July 22, 1954, Cleveland; home, Madison; U. of MI, B.A. 1976, Cleveland St. U., J.D. 1979; Methodist; married (Susan).

Elected Office: Lake Cnty. Prosecuting atty., 1988–94.

Professional Career: Lake Cnty. Asst. Public Defender, 1980–83; Practicing atty., 1983–88.

DC Office: 2453 RHOB 20515, 202-225-5731; Fax: 202-225-3307; Web site: www.house.gov/latourette.

District Office: Painesville, 440-352-3939.

Committees: *Financial Services* (15th of 37 R): Financial Institutions & Consumer Credit (Vice Chmn.); Oversight & Investigations. *Government Reform* (8th of 24 R): Government Efficiency & Financial Management; National Security, Emerging Threats & Intl. Relations. *Standards of Official Conduct* (5th of 5 R). *Transportation & Infrastructure* (12th of 41 R): Economic Development, Public Buildings & Emergency Management (Chmn.); Highways, Transit & Pipelines; Water Resources & Environment.

Group Ratings

	ADA	ACLU	AFS	LCV	CON	ITIC	NTU	COC	ACU	NTLC	CHC
2002	15	8	11	13	13	62	51	85	76	72	67
2001	20	—	30	29	—	—	57	77	72	—	—

National Journal Ratings

	2001 LIB —	2001 CONS	2002 LIB —	2002 CONS
Economic	43%	56%	40%	59%
Social	38%	61%	44%	56%
Foreign	20%	81%	47%	51%

Key Votes of the 107th Congress

1. Approve Bush Tax Cuts	Y	5. Faith-Based Charities	Y	9. Trade Promotion Authority	N
2. Limit Patients' Bill of Rights	Y	6. Bar Gays in the Boy Scouts	Y	10. Bar Funds for Intl. Court	Y
3. Campaign Finance Reform	Y	7. Ban Partial-Birth Abortion	Y	11. Authorize Force in Iraq	Y
4. Ban ANWR Development	N	8. Arm Commercial Pilots	Y	12. Deny Home. Sec. Dept. Union	Y

Election Results

2002 general	Steven LaTourette (R)	134,413	(72%)	($532,692)
	Dale Blanchard (D)	51,846	(28%)	
2002 primary	Steven LaTourette (R)	unopposed		
2000 general (OH 19)	Steven LaTourette (R)	174,262	(69%)	($332,893)
	Dale Blanchard (D)	70,429	(28%)	
	Other	6,957	(3%)	

Prior Winning Percentages: 1998 (66%); 1996 (55%); 1994 (48%)

The People		Race/Ethnic Origin	Ancestry	
Area size:	1,820 sq. mi.	94.0% White	German: 16.9%	Irish: 11.2%
Urban population:	74.1%	2.5% Black	Italian: 9.0%	
Rural population:	25.9%	1.1% Asian	**2000 Presidential Vote**	
Pop. 2000:	630,730	0.1% Native Am.	Bush (R)..............147,148	(52%)
Median income:	$51,304	0.0% Hawaiian	Gore (D)..............124,582	(44%)
Poverty status:	5.7%	0.8% Two+ races	Other....................11,360	(4%)
Military veterans:	13.6%	0.1% Other	**Cook Partisan Voting Index:** R + 5	
		1.3% Hispanic Origin		

Occupation	Blue collar: 25.1%	White collar: 62.0%	Gray collar: 12.9%

The imprint of the westward track of New England Yankee migration is still apparent today on the shores of Lake Erie in northern Ohio. The Yankees, cooped up in New England for 200 years, shot across the country through upstate New York, west across Ohio and Michigan to Chicago, and on to Kansas and southern California in just two or three generations, providing inspiration, manpower and technical might for the Union victory in the Civil War, and leaving their imprint along the way. One place they stopped was the Western Reserve, the northeast corner of Ohio, created for the excess population of Connecticut; its towns, colleges and cultural institutions were established by Yankees. This area produced some of the strongest opposition to slavery and support of the Union armies and Republican party in the nation. Its thrifty, hard-working, well-educated citizens built communities with fine schools and, with their accumulated savings, invested in what became some of the nation's leading industries. That brought great masses of immigrants to Cleveland and the other cities of northeast Ohio. Following the Great Depression and the bloody CIO organizing drives of the late 1930s, the Western Reserve was Democratic during Ohio's class-warfare politics. Now the Western Reserve, like Connecticut and Massachusetts, may be moving toward a post-industrial economy. Factory employment has dropped, but total jobs are rising again; small, adaptive business units with highly skilled workers are the growth sectors.

The 14th Congressional District takes in parts or all of seven counties of northeast Ohio and the old Western Reserve. Its includes Lake County, northeast of Cleveland, with mixed middling-to-affluent suburbs, and Geauga County, directly east of Cleveland, with affluent suburbs amid Western Reserve villages. It includes on the east end of the state Ashtabula County and the northern part of Trumbull County, industrial country. It includes the affluent suburbs at the eastern edge of Cleveland's Cuyahoga County, comfortable suburbs in northern Summit County and the northern tier of townships in Portage County to the east. In the 19th century the Western Reserve was heavily Republican; the congressman from this area from 1863 to 1880 was James Garfield, also a general in the Civil War, who was elected with some of the highest Republican percentages in the nation; in 1880 he was elected president and in 1881 was assassinated. In the 1930s this became politically competitive, as Cleveland became heavily Democratic, and it has been in most years since. The 2002 redistricting made it more Republican: the Bush 2000 percentage rose from 46% to 52%.

The congressman from the 14th District is Steve LaTourette, a Republican first elected in 1994. LaTourette grew up in the Cleveland area and went to law school at Cleveland State University; in the 1980s he worked as a public defender and in private practice in Lake County, and became Lake County district attorney in 1988, at 34. Well-known and well-liked, he won a three-candidate 1994 Republican congressional primary with 54%. In the general he faced Eric Fingerhut, a 35-year-old political prodigy who in 1992 was elected to replace not one but two retiring Democratic incumbents. LaTourette attacked Fingerhut for backing the Clinton budget and tax increase, for being soft on crime and for hypocritically using his franking privileges. LaTourette won 48%–43%; Fingerhut now represents a solidly Democratic district in the Ohio Senate and has announced that he will run for the Senate in 2004.

In the House, LaTourette has the most moderate voting record of Ohio's Republican members and he shows more irreverence than one might expect from a former prosecutor. He invited humorist Dave Barry to spend several days on his press staff, with predictably funny results. He backs up his independence with his votes. During early debates on the bill, he was among a handful of Republicans who bucked his party on HMO regulation, which won LaTourette praise from the AFL-CIO. When the House passed a bill in 2000 to increase savings incentives, he made a seemingly minor change to calculate construction workers' pension benefits based on a worker's three highest years of earnings, instead of the three highest consecutive years; that makes a big difference for workers in carpentry and plumbing, where annual income can vary widely. He broke with House Republicans to oppose PNTR with China. He is chairman of the Transportation and Infrastructure Committee's Economic Development, Public Buildings, and Emergency Management Subcommittee—a mouthful of an assignment that gave LaTourette control of several slabs of pork that many House members find vital plus a seat at the table for the big highway bill in 2003. His high-priority projects include improvements of Ohio Routes 82 and 8. In 2000 LaTourette worked with Democrat James Traficant of the next-door 17th District to increase his comfort level with House Republicans and Traficant voted for Dennis Hastert for speaker in January 2001. LaTourette protested when several Traficant associates were subpoenaed by federal prosecutors before the March 2000 primary and defended him. "Jimmy Traficant is not being done right." In April 2002, after defending himself at the trial, Traficant was convicted on 10 counts of bribery and racketeering. That conviction triggered hearings by the ethics committee, to which LaTourette had been named to fill a vacancy in October 2001. The ethics committee in July 2002 voted unanimously to expel Traficant from the House. LaTourette unsuccessfully sought a delay of floor vote and then voted for Traficant's expulsion.

Democrats basically gave up on defeating LaTourette during the 1996 campaign, when he won 55%–41%. Since then, he has not faced a competitive challenger. In 1998 Republican governor candidate Bob Taft offered LaTourette the lieutenant governor nomination; perhaps not eager for the enforced idleness of the office, he declined. He has abandoned his 1994 term limit pledge to serve only 8 years, but has said he will not serve in the House the rest of his life.

FIFTEENTH DISTRICT

Rep. Deborah Pryce (R)

Elected 1992, 6th term; b. July 29, 1951, Warren; home, Columbus; OH St. U., B.A. 1973, Capital U. Law Schl., J.D. 1976; Presbyterian; divorced.

Elected Office: Franklin Cnty. Municipal Court Judge, 1985–92.

Professional Career: Admin. Law Judge, OH Dept. of Insurance, 1976; Columbus City Asst. Prosecutor & Asst. City Atty., 1978–85; Practicing atty., 1992.

DC Office: 221 CHOB 20515, 202-225-2015; Web site: www.house.gov/pryce.

District Office: Columbus, 614-469-5614.

Committees: *Republican Conference Chairman. Rules* (4th of 9 R): The Legislative & Budget Process (Chmn.).

Group Ratings

	ADA	ACLU	AFS	LCV	CON	ITIC	NTU	COC	ACU	NTLC	CHC
2002	5	23	0	13	58	100	58	100	88	82	58
2001	15	—	10	21	—	—	59	100	68	—	—

National Journal Ratings

	2001 LIB	—	2001 CONS		2002 LIB	—	2002 CONS
Economic	28%	—	69%		21%	—	79%
Social	54%	—	45%		44%	—	56%
Foreign	4%	—	87%		34%	—	65%

Key Votes of the 107th Congress

1. Approve Bush Tax Cuts	Y	5. Faith-Based Charities	Y	9. Trade Promotion Authority	Y
2. Limit Patients' Bill of Rights	Y	6. Bar Gays in the Boy Scouts	Y	10. Bar Funds for Intl. Court	Y
3. Campaign Finance Reform	N	7. Ban Partial-Birth Abortion	Y	11. Authorize Force in Iraq	Y
4. Ban ANWR Development	N	8. Arm Commercial Pilots	Y	12. Deny Home. Sec. Dept. Union	Y

Election Results

2002 general	Deborah Pryce (R)	108,193	(67%)	($872,928)
	Mark Brown (D)	54,286	(33%)	
2002 primary	Deborah Pryce (R)	22,048	(78%)	
	Charlie Morrison (R)	6,216	(22%)	
2000 general	Deborah Pryce (R)	156,792	(68%)	($589,675)
	Bill Buckel (D)	64,805	(28%)	($4,455)
	Scott Smith (Lib)	10,700	(5%)	

Prior Winning Percentages: 1998 (66%); 1996 (71%); 1994 (71%); 1992 (44%)

The People		**Race/Ethnic Origin**	**Ancestry**	
Area size:	1,182 sq. mi.	85.2% White	German: 18.5%	Irish: 10.4%
Urban population:	91.3%	7.2% Black	English: 8.0%	
Rural population:	8.8%	3.3% Asian	**2000 Presidential Vote**	
Pop. 2000:	630,730	0.2% Native Am.	Bush (R)	117,175 (52%)
Median income:	$43,885	0.0% Hawaiian	Gore (D)	98,204 (44%)
Poverty status:	10.8%	1.7% Two+ races	Other	8,931 (4%)
Military veterans:	11.6%	0.2% Other	**Cook Partisan Voting Index:** R + 5	
		2.3% Hispanic Origin		

Occupation Blue collar: 19.8% White collar: 66.3% Gray collar: 13.9%

Columbus, smack in the center of Ohio, was founded in 1812 to be the state capital. Its flat-domed Capitol at Broad and High, with the statue of William McKinley out front, is surrounded by high-rises, public and private, while the city has been growing in all directions into the country-side, and now is on the verge of becoming a large metropolis. It is the headquarters of state government and Ohio State, one of the nation's largest universities; it is the home as well of Nationwide Insurance and The Limited and Wendy's. It is the headquarters of the Batelle Memorial Institute, the think tank that helped invent compact discs, office copy machines and the universal product code; a major industry here is data retrieval. Columbus, which has kept annexing suburbs, is now Ohio's largest central city by far, with 711,000 people in 2000; Franklin County topped 1 million in 2000 and the metro area extends into formerly rural counties. Columbus is rapidly building civic landmarks—the Center of Science and Industry on the riverfront, the Jerome Schottenstein Center for sports and concerts at OSU, a hockey stadium for the Columbus Blue Jackets and the nation's first stadium built for a professional soccer team, the Columbus Crew. With the nation's highest proportion of residents age 25 to 34, Columbus has been attracting young professionals and immigrants more than any other Ohio city and continues to be a prime test market for products of all kinds.

The 15th Congressional District includes all of Columbus except the east side, plus southern and western Franklin County and once-rural Madison and Union Counties directly to the west; the latter is the site of the Honda plant in Marysville and grew 28% in the 1990s. The 15th includes white working class areas on the south side of the city and in nearby Grove City, and the Ohio State University campus. Politically, these Democratic areas are more than balanced by the heavily Republican suburb of Upper Arlington, across the Olentangy River from Ohio State, and by Republican subdivisions sprouting up in rural land between the old villages.

The congresswoman from the 15th District is Deborah Pryce, a Republican first elected in 1992. Pryce grew up in Warren, graduated from Ohio State and Capital University Law School, worked in state government and as a city prosecutor, and was elected municipal court judge in 1985. In 1992, when incumbent Chalmers Wylie retired after 26 years, Pryce ran for the House. She was unopposed in the primary but had tough competition in the general from Democrat Richard Cordray and from anti-abortion independent Linda Reidelbach. Pryce talked much about congressional reform—term limits, rotating chairmanships, line-item veto—and called for limiting annual spending increases to 3%. She won with 44% of the vote to Cordray's 38% and Reidelbach's 18%.

In the House, Pryce has a voting record that is mostly conservative on economic and foreign issues, more moderate on cultural issues. In her first term she was elected interim president of her Republican class and helped to write the Contract with America. Pryce has been a leadership loyalist on the Rules Committee since 1995 and headed the House Republican task force on tobacco in 1998.

Pryce has been particularly interested in issues relating to children, adoption and cancer. Her adoptive daughter developed cancer in September 1998 and died at age nine in September 1999; she adopted a newborn in 2002. Pryce started Hope Street Kids, an organization to raise funds for cancer research, using funds donated in memory of her daughter. She is co-chairwoman of the House Cancer Working Group and sponsored a bill in 2001 to require private insurers to provide coverage of routine patient costs of cancer patients who qualify to participate in a clinical trial. She sponsored the law creating the adoption stamp, which was unveiled by Wendy's founder and adoption advocate Dave Thomas. She sponsored a law signed in March 2000 giving child protective services and child welfare workers access to more court records and doubling funding for federal child abuse and domestic assistance programs to $20 million.

Pryce is now chairman of the Republican Conference, the number four position in the Republican leadership, tasked with disseminating House Republicans' message. She was elected conference secretary in July 1997, with 110 votes on the second ballot to 65 for Sue Myrick and 42 for Duke Cunningham. In November 2000 she was elected conference vice chair without opposition. In November 2002, after Conference Chairman J.C. Watts retired, she was elected to his post, with 133 votes to 61 for J.D. Hayworth and 28 for Jim Ryun. Although in charge of the party's message, Pryce has not often been seen on national television or quoted in national print media. "Controversy is part of politics, but not the part I like to participate in. Do I like being behind the scenes better than out in front? Yes. I work better. I'm more effective that way. I'm way more comfortable." She plays more of an inside role, keeping Republicans, especially moderates, together; Pryce argues for maintaining party unity and accepting bills with conservative provisions, to keep the process moving, knowing that the Senate or the administration may modify things. With Tom DeLay and Bill Paxon, she was one of the key members who got Republicans committed to Dennis Hastert for speaker after Bob Livingston stepped down on December 19, 1998. Like others in the Republican leadership, she contributes money to other Republicans, $630,000 in the 2002 cycle.

As a member of the leadership and of the Rules Committee, Pryce does not have much occasion to shepherd legislation to passage. She was a sponsor of the privacy amendment voted in the 1999 financial services deregulation bill; it gave consumers the right to block banks and financial institutions from selling personal data to outside firms, but would let them share it with affiliated companies. In 2000 she inserted into an appropriation $235 million for graduate medical programs at children's hospitals; Children's Hospital of Columbus stood to get $5 million. She got the Appropriations Committee to grant $430,000 for Columbus Mayor Michael Coleman's $20 million revolving loan fund for central-city housing initiatives. She sponsored a bill to limit coal companies' responsibility for retired mine workers' health care costs; Columbus's AEP has major coal interests.

Pryce has won reelection easily. Redistricting did not make major changes in the 15th District.

SIXTEENTH DISTRICT

Rep. Ralph Regula (R)

Elected 1972, 16th term; b. Dec. 3, 1924, Beach City; home, Navarre; Mt. Union Col., B.A. 1948, William McKinley Law Schl., LL.B. 1952; Episcopalian; married (Mary).

Military Career: Navy, 1944–46 (WWII).

Elected Office: OH House of Reps., 1964–66; OH Senate, 1966–72.

Professional Career: Teacher & schl. principal, 1948–52; Practicing atty., 1952–73; OH Bd. of Educ., 1960–64.

DC Office: 2306 RHOB 20515, 202-225-3876; Fax: 202-225-3059; Web site: www.house.gov/regula.

District Offices: Canton, 330-489-4414; Medina, 330-722-3793.

Committees: *Appropriations* (2d of 36 R): Commerce, Justice, State & Judiciary; Interior; Labor, HHS & Education (Chmn.).

Group Ratings

	ADA	ACLU	AFS	LCV	CON	ITIC	NTU	COC	ACU	NTLC	CHC
2002	5	13	11	25	8	62	53	95	88	81	83
2001	20	—	20	14	—	—	58	91	76	—	—

National Journal Ratings

	2001 LIB —	2001 CONS	2002 LIB —	2002 CONS
Economic	33% —	66%	39% —	61%
Social	38% —	61%	0% —	75%
Foreign	21% —	74%	29% —	67%

Key Votes of the 107th Congress

1. Approve Bush Tax Cuts	Y	5. Faith-Based Charities	Y	9. Trade Promotion Authority	N
2. Limit Patients' Bill of Rights	Y	6. Bar Gays in the Boy Scouts	Y	10. Bar Funds for Intl. Court	Y
3. Campaign Finance Reform	N	7. Ban Partial-Birth Abortion	Y	11. Authorize Force in Iraq	Y
4. Ban ANWR Development	N	8. Arm Commercial Pilots	Y	12. Deny Home. Sec. Dept. Union	Y

Election Results

2002 general	Ralph Regula (R)	129,734	(69%)	($252,109)
	Jim Rice (D)	58,644	(31%)	
2002 primary	Ralph Regula (R)	unopposed		
2000 general	Ralph Regula (R)	162,294	(69%)	($166,663)
	William Smith (D)	62,709	(27%)	
	Other	9,397	(4%)	

Prior Winning Percentages: 1998 (64%); 1996 (69%); 1994 (75%); 1992 (64%); 1990 (59%); 1988 (79%); 1986 (76%); 1984 (72%); 1982 (66%); 1980 (79%); 1978 (78%); 1976 (67%); 1974 (66%); 1972 (57%)

The People		Race/Ethnic Origin	Ancestry	
Area size:	1,741 sq. mi.	92.4% White	German: 21.9%	Irish: 9.5%
Urban population:	73.6%	4.8% Black	English: 7.3%	
Rural population:	26.4%	0.6% Asian	**2000 Presidential Vote**	
Pop. 2000:	630,730	0.2% Native Am.	Bush (R)..............141,311	(53%)
Median income:	$41,801	0.0% Hawaiian	Gore (D)..............112,270	(42%)
Poverty status:	8.3%	1.1% Two + races	Other...................10,908	(4%)
Military veterans:	13.6%	0.1% Other	**Cook Partisan Voting Index:** R + 6	
		0.9% Hispanic Origin		

Occupation	Blue collar: 30.5%	White collar: 54.7%	Gray collar: 14.8%

A little more than a century ago, Canton, Ohio, was at the center of American politics. Canton was already an industrial city then, though not with the huge steel factories built in Youngstown or Cleveland. Its high-skill workers were fashioning new kinds of plows and reapers, making watches and, beginning in 1899, roller bearings. Canton did not attract masses of immigrants. Its factories did not run on harsh stopwatch discipline; there were not the class warfare politics here that would be seen later in other northern Ohio industrial cities. Instead Canton was united in admiring its first citizen, William McKinley, who rose to the rank of major at 22 in the Civil War, was elected congressman and governor, and chaired the House Ways and Means Committee. As Republican nominee for president in 1896, McKinley campaigned from his front porch in Canton, meeting with delegations brought in by train from all over the country. This spectacle, with its display of technological virtuosity and personal modesty, sounds an appealing and reverberating note in American politics, as does the McKinley platform—the "full dinner pail," the gold standard, the enforcement of law and order in labor relations—which has long been viewed as antiquated but still provides useful instruction. A century later Canton is still a community still based on manufacturing—mostly high-skill, with companies like Timken, Diebold, Republic Engineered Steels, and Hoover.

The 16th Congressional District includes all of Canton and Stark County, plus Wayne County to the west and most of Ashland and Medina Counties. Wayne County is the site of the College of Wooster and the headquarters of Rubbermaid and Smuckers. In the southern part of the county (and in Holmes and Tuscarawas Counties to the south) is the largest Amish settlement in the world, where people drive horse-drawn tractors, eschew automobiles and electricity and quit school after the eighth grade. Ashland is a smaller, non-metropolitan county; Johnny Appleseed once lived on what is now the campus of Ashland University, known for its Ashbrook Center on politics. Medina County, north of Wayne, is part of the Cleveland metropolitan area, as young families buy houses in new subdivisions off I-71; its most heavily suburbanized northern townships, however, are in the 13th District. Politically, this area is generally Republican, though not always by wide margins; George W. Bush won 53% of the vote here in 2000.

The congressman from the 16th District is Ralph Regula, a Republican first elected in 1972 and the dean of the Ohio delegation. He grew up in outer Stark County, the son of a farmer and coal mine operator; he served in the Navy in World War II, worked his way through the William McKinley School of Law while teaching elementary school, and was elected to the Ohio legislature in 1964, just before turning 40. He still has a cattle farm near Canton. When the incumbent retired in 1972, Regula ran for the House and was easily elected. He is the second most senior Republican on the Appropriations Committee; from 1995 to 2001 he chaired the Interior Subcommittee, and in 2001, thanks to Republicans' six-year term limits on chairmen, began chairing the Labor-HHS Subcommittee, which oversees more domestic spending than any other.

On the Interior Subcommittee, Regula was a counterweight to the Resources Committee and its chairman, Don Young of Alaska, who added riders to Regula's appropriations strongly opposed by environmental groups and the Clinton administration. Regula resisted these, and often gave them up in end-of-session conference committees when Clinton threatened a veto. Young and Regula also got into a fight over Mount McKinley. Young introduced a bill to rename the mountain Denali, an Alaska Native name; Regula, McKinley's successor in the House, replied heatedly that that controversy had already been settled in 1980, when the McKinley name stayed on the mountain but the park was renamed Denali National Park. In his last year as Interior chairman, Regula increased the appropriation by 26%, added a ban on the Interior Department moving callers into voice mail between 7:30 a.m. and 4:30 p.m. and designated the Cuyahoga Valley National Recreation Area a national park, but not subject to national park air standards.

In January 2001 Regula took over the Labor-HHS-Education Subcommittee, whose appropriation is second only to Defense. There he worked harmoniously with ranking Democrat David Obey and produced a $123 billion appropriation approved in October 2001. Regula blocked an amendment by Melissa Hart which would have cut off aid to schools that offered the morning after pill; Speaker Dennis Hastert had promised Hart a chance to offer the amendment, but Regula said he had not been informed and that he would vote against the rule for the appropriation if it allowed Hart's amendment. Only one amendment was passed, to require pharmaceutical companies that benefit from NIH research to charge "reasonable" prices for their drugs. In summer 2002 Hastert was under pressure from conservative Republican Study Committee members to bring forward the Labor-HHS bill before any other appropriations; they wanted to hold it to the president's $129.9 billion level, while the Senate had voted $136.4 billion and Regula struggled to reconcile the demands of education and health constituencies. He took umbrage when OMB Director Mitch Daniels said the Labor-HHS appropriation was "rife with underperforming growth." Regula argued that an appropriation under the Bush limit couldn't win a majority on the floor, and as a result all appropriations except Defense and Military Construction were postponed until after the election. In February 2003, when the appropriations were finally passed, Regula's bill provided increases for Title I and special education $500 million under the Bush figure.

Regula is one of two cardinals (the term for Appropriations subcommittee chairmen) from Ohio; the other is Dave Hobson, and they both look after the interests of the state. "I see northeastern Ohio as my constituency. Cleveland, Ashland, Medina, Canton are part of an economic base. They are interconnected." His 2001 appropriation contained $1 million for Cleveland State University's K-16 urban schools program, $2 million for the Cleveland Clinic to treat sarcoidosis (which disproportionately afflicts blacks) and $500,000 for the lakefront Museum of Transportation. In the 2001 defense bill he got a provision requiring the Defense Department to buy American-made gloves; the Ansell Perry plant in Massillon, the only surgical glove manufacturer in the United States, had shut down, but there were potential buyers and this would guarantee business. He also got $1.8 million for research on a computerized device to identify biological agents at the Cleveland Clinic. In February 2003 he got $3 million to extend Cuyahoga Scenic Railroad service to Canton, $5 million for the Stark County Sheriff's office, $750,000 for renovation of Dunlap Memorial Hospital in Orrville and $990,000 for a downtown Canton bus transit center. Regula also shepherds Ohio Republicans into useful committees. He told Steve LaTourette in 1994 that he should go on Transportation, not Judiciary, and now LaTourette is a subcommittee chairman as the highway bill comes up for reauthorization. Regula has been chairman of the Congressional Steel Caucus and has often weighed in on trade issues.

In November 2002 the Republican Conference chose to give the Steering Committee a veto over the selection of Appropriations subcommittee chairmen; this is likely to make cardinals more amenable to the demands of the Republican leadership and more assiduous in raising funds for other Republicans. But Ralphus (as George W. Bush calls him) is unlikely to be bumped from his position. He is in line to chair Appropriations in 2005.

SEVENTEENTH DISTRICT

Rep. Tim Ryan (D)

Elected 2002, 1st term; b. July 16, 1973, Niles; home, Niles; Bowling Green St. U., B.A. 1995, Franklin Pierce Law Ctr., J.D. 2000; Catholic; single.

Elected Office: OH Senate, 2000–02.

Professional Career: Aide, U.S. Rep Jim Traficant, 1995–97.

DC Office: 222 CHOB 20515, 202-225-5261; Fax: 202-225-3719; Web site: www.house.gov/timryan.

District Offices: Warren, 330-373-0074; Youngstown, 330-740-0193.

Committees: *Armed Services* (29th of 29 D): Strategic Forces. *Education & the Workforce* (21st of 22 D): 21st Century Competitiveness; Select Education. *Veterans' Affairs* (14th of 14 D): Health.

Group Ratings and Key Votes: Newly Elected

Election Results

2002 general	Tim Ryan (D)	94,441	(51%)	($596,646)
	Ann Womer Benjamin (R)	62,188	(34%)	($293,316)
	James Traficant (I)	28,045	(15%)	($150,129)
2002 primary	Tim Ryan (D)	28,922	(41%)	
	Tom Sawyer (D)	19,247	(27%)	
	Anthony Latell Jr. (D)	13,858	(20%)	
	Maridee Costanzo (D)	5,148	(7%)	
	Other	2,831	(4%)	
2000 general	James Traficant (D)	120,333	(50%)	($285,165)
	Paul Alberty (R)	54,751	(23%)	($165,860)
	Randy Walter (I)	51,793	(22%)	($476,871)
	Lou D'Apolito (I)	9,568	(4%)	($39,788)
	Other	4,432	(2%)	

The People		Race/Ethnic Origin	Ancestry	
Area size:	1,033 sq. mi.	84.5% White	German: 15.5%	Irish: 10.3%
Urban population:	84.3%	11.6% Black	Italian: 9.2%	
Rural population:	15.7%	0.7% Asian	**2000 Presidential Vote**	
Pop. 2000:	630,730	0.2% Native Am.	Gore (D) 150,748	(60%)
Median income:	$36,705	0.0% Hawaiian	Bush (R) 88,184	(35%)
Poverty status:	12.3%	1.2% Two+ races	Other 10,767	(4%)
Military veterans:	14.6%	0.1% Other	**Cook Partisan Voting Index:** D +13	
		1.6% Hispanic Origin		

Occupation   Blue collar: 31.8%   White collar: 51.6%   Gray collar: 16.6%

For nearly a century, the Mahoning Valley, between the Lake Erie docks that unload iron ore from Great Lakes freighters and the coalfields of western Pennsylvania and West Virginia, was one of the steel capitals of the United States. The first coal mine here opened in 1826, canals followed, and in 1892 the first steel mill was built in Youngstown. The valley soon filled up with mills, converters, and furnaces. Now the steel mills stand empty, smokeless and silent—except those that have been dynamited or torn down. Big steel management allowed foreign producers to gain a technological edge in the 1950s and 1960s; worldwide overcapacity in steel grew as almost every developing country decided it needed its own steel mill, while cooperation between the United Steelworkers and management after the 119-day strike in 1959 boosted wages and fringe benefits to price domestic steel out of the market. Import restrictions kept the furnaces hot for a while, but the oil shock of 1979 produced sharply higher energy prices and a collapse in the U.S. auto and steel markets. Every plant in Youngstown and the Mahoning Valley closed, and in the early 1980s metro Youngstown had one of the nation's highest unemployment rates. Steel has since revived, but not here: in decentralized mini-mills or in huge new rolling plants in northern Indiana. The high-wage living standard of Youngstown in the 1970s has vanished; young people looking for opportunities routinely leave. Youngstown's population declined 14% in the 1990s to 82,000, about half of its size in the 1930s. Organized crime, it seems, has deeply infiltrated local government; a federal investigation has led to more than 70 convictions, including a prosecutor, a sheriff and a congressman.

The 17th Congressional District includes most of the Mahoning Valley industrial area—Youngstown but not its southern Mahoning County suburbs and Warren and almost all of Trumbull County to the north. But Mahoning and Trumbull Counties no longer have enough people for a congressional district, and the 17th District also includes nearly all of Portage County to the west and part of eastern Summit County and Akron. It contains two loci of 1970s protest—Kent State University, where four war-protesting students were killed by National Guardsmen in 1970, and Lordstown, site of the General Motors plant where workers purposely built shoddy cars to protest the tedium of the assembly line. The division of Akron and Summit County among three districts in the 2002 redistricting was a matter of some local controversy, but Ohio had lost a House seat in the 2000 Census and the legislature, controlled by Republicans who needed a few Democratic votes to give the bill immediate effect, considered it the least unpalatable alternative.

Politically, this area ranges from very Democratic (the Mahoning Valley) to fairly Democratic (Portage County and Akron). The new 17th District gave 60% to Al Gore in 2000.

The congressman from the 17th District is Tim Ryan, a Democrat elected in 2002 when he beat two incumbents, one in the Democratic primary and one in the general election. Ryan grew up in Niles and graduated from Bowling Green State University. His first job was with 17th District Congressman James Traficant. In 2000, after graduating from Franklin Pierce Law Center, Ryan was elected to the state Senate. His opening to run for Congress came from Traficant's downfall. For years Traficant was a colorful figure in the House, whose ranting orations and retro haircut ("I do my hair with a weed whacker," he said; it turned out to be a wig) entertained C-SPAN viewers. He was avidly protectionist and isolationist, loud and abrasive on the floor and delivered tirades against foreign aid, free trade, the Federal Reserve and the oppression visited on citizens by the Internal Revenue Service. In May 2001 Traficant was indicted on bribery charges. The Democratic leadership scorned him and Traficant voted for Dennis Hastert for speaker; Democrats stripped him of his committee assignments. In the redistricting process Traficant had no champions: Democrats figured they had to lose a seat anyway and they figured that it might as well be Traficant's. His home south of Youngstown was placed in the 6th District, which extended south along the Ohio River 325 miles to Portsmouth, where it seemed obvious he would lose a Democratic primary to incumbent Ted Strickland. But Traficant did not file to run in the Democratic primary in either district. Most insiders thought the 17th District would be won by Akron-based incumbent Tom Sawyer, first elected in 1986. But Ryan noted that 25% of the district's population and, most likely, a higher percentage of its Democratic primary voters were in Mahoning County. With a four-year state Senate term, Ryan had nothing to lose by running and a lifetime safe seat in the House to gain.

In April 2002, just before the May primary, Traficant, who defended himself in court, was convicted on 10 counts of bribery. There were altogether six candidates in the primary but inevitably much of the focus was on Traficant. Ryan's opponents seized on his two years on Traficant's staff and accused him of everything short of wearing his denim suits. After one exchange Ryan exclaimed, "Would you guys let it go about Jim Traficant?" By standard measures Sawyer should have won easily. He outspent Ryan by nearly 6–1 and had the backing, as incumbents usually do, of the DCCC. But his record on issues gave Ryan an opening. After much public agonizing he had voted for NAFTA in 1993, and he was one of the few Rust Belt Democrats to vote for PNTR for China in 1999 after Bill Clinton visited Akron a few days before the vote. Ryan hammered on these free trade votes in the Mahoning Valley, where it is gospel writ that free trade exported its high-paying jobs abroad. He also got the endorsement of the National Rifle Association in a district with more blue collar hunters than upscale suburban women who abhor guns. He did a good job of turning out the vote in Mahoning and Trumbull Counties, which cast 79% of the Democratic primary votes. Sawyer ran about as well as a longtime incumbent usually does in Summit and Portage Counties, where he led Ryan 62%–16%. But that produced a margin of only 6,846 votes. In Mahoning and Trumbull Counties, where Sawyer had never run before and which are in a different media market from Akron, Ryan led Sawyer 48%–18%. That produced a popular vote margin of 16,521. Overall Ryan beat Sawyer 41%–27%, a rare loss for an incumbent. Sawyer was stunned by his defeat and said that his polls had shown him ahead.

Republicans had some hopes of winning the district, particularly after Traficant announced he was running as an Independent. The Republican nominee was state Representative Ann Womer Benjamin. Ryan slammed Womer Benjamin and the Ohio Republican legislative majority for votes that led to higher tuitions at state universities. Republicans fired back with ads highlighting several disorderly conduct charges lodged against Ryan while he attended college. It remained an open question how strong Traficant's appeal remained in the Mahoning Valley. But in July he was expelled from the House by a 420–1 vote (the dissenter was lame duck Gary Condit) and in August he was sentenced and taken off to federal prison in Pennsylvania. The question was raised whether he was still an Ohio resident and thus able to run in the state. In the end the district's Democratic leanings and Ryan's labor support proved decisive. He won 51% of the vote to 34% for Womer Benjamin and 15% for Traficant. In Summit and Portage Counties, which cast 37% of the vote, the race was fairly close: Ryan led Womer Benjamin 49%–42%, with 6% for Traficant.

But in Mahoning and Trumbull Counties, Ryan led Womer Benjamin 52%–29%, with 18% for Traficant.

Ryan entered the House as the youngest Democrat; the youngest member remained sophomore Adam Putnam of Florida. He made a point of quietly getting to work and not looking for attention. Ryan will be under local pressure to keep the Youngstown Air Reserve Station, with its 1,500 employees, off the base-closing list.

EIGHTEENTH DISTRICT

Rep. Bob Ney (R)

Elected 1994, 5th term; b. July 5, 1954, Wheeling, WV; home, St. Clairsville; OH St. U., B.S. 1976; Catholic; married (Elizabeth).

Elected Office: OH House of Reps., 1980–82; OH Senate, 1984–94.

Professional Career: Teacher, Iran, 1978; Program Mgr., OH Office of Appalachia, 1979; Bellaire Safety Dir., 1980.

DC Office: 2438 RHOB 20515, 202-225-6265; Fax: 202-225-3394; Web site: www.house.gov/ney.

District Offices: Chillicothe, 740-779-1634; New Philadelphia, 330-364-6380; St. Clairsville, 740-699-2704; Zanesville, 740-452-7023.

Committees: *Financial Services* (10th of 37 R): Capital Markets, Insurance & Government Sponsored Enterprises; Housing & Community Opportunity (Chmn.). *House Administration* (Chmn. of 6 R). *Transportation & Infrastructure* (15th of 41 R): Highways, Transit & Pipelines; Water Resources & Environment.

Group Ratings

	ADA	ACLU	AFS	LCV	CON	ITIC	NTU	COC	ACU	NTLC	CHC
2002	0	27	0	13	8	88	56	100	92	89	92
2001	10	—	10	29	—	—	58	96	88	—	—

National Journal Ratings

	2001 LIB —	2001 CONS	2002 LIB —	2002 CONS
Economic	39%	61%	16%	81%
Social	20%	69%	0%	75%
Foreign	41%	58%	29%	67%

Key Votes of the 107th Congress

1. Approve Bush Tax Cuts	Y	5. Faith-Based Charities	Y	9. Trade Promotion Authority	Y
2. Limit Patients' Bill of Rights	Y	6. Bar Gays in the Boy Scouts	Y	10. Bar Funds for Intl. Court	Y
3. Campaign Finance Reform	N	7. Ban Partial-Birth Abortion	Y	11. Authorize Force in Iraq	Y
4. Ban ANWR Development	N	8. Arm Commercial Pilots	Y	12. Deny Home. Sec. Dept. Union	Y

Election Results

2002 general	Bob Ney (R)	unopposed		($713,837)
2002 primary	Bob Ney (R)	unopposed		
2000 general	Bob Ney (R)	152,325	(64%)	($725,334)
	Marc Guthrie (D)	79,232	(34%)	($223,429)
	Other	4,948	(2%)	

Prior Winning Percentages: 1998 (60%); 1996 (50%); 1994 (54%)

The People		Race/Ethnic Origin	Ancestry	
Area size:	6,876 sq. mi.	95.9% White	German: 16.7%	USA: 10.2%
Urban population:	43.3%	1.9% Black	Irish: 8.7%	
Rural population:	56.7%	0.3% Asian	**2000 Presidential Vote**	
Pop. 2000:	630,730	0.2% Native Am.	Bush (R)..............132,709	(55%)
Median income:	$34,462	0.0% Hawaiian	Gore (D)..............98,328	(41%)
Poverty status:	12.6%	1.0% Two + races	Other...................9,810	(4%)
Military veterans:	14.3%	0.1% Other	**Cook Partisan Voting Index:** R + 8	
		0.6% Hispanic Origin		

Occupation   Blue collar: 37.5%   White collar: 45.8%   Gray collar: 16.7%

The hills of eastern Ohio are one of those obscure parts of America, seen by most Americans, if they are at all, from speeding cars on the Interstates or U.S. highways on their way to some place else. They were settled early on in our history, in the 1790s, mostly by Virginians (there was no West Virginia until 1863), and for the most part sparsely: this was hard land to clear and hard land to farm, better suited for dairy cattle than the plains that lay beyond. In some places near the Ohio River there was industrial development early on. The local clay was used to make pottery, the coal that lies near the surface was dug up, a green vitriol works was built, and a nail factory went into operation, all before 1814, and in time the area became dotted with small factory towns. Farther south there was little industrial development and the landscape has a timeless feel today. This is a part of America little affected by the flow of immigrants from Europe in 1880–1924, southern blacks in 1940–65 or Latino and Asian immigrants since 1970. The most distinctive people here are the Amish, driving their horses and buggies over covered bridges in Holmes, Tuscarawas and Wayne Counties, the largest concentration of Amish in the world.

The 18th Congressional District covers much of this hill country, from Holmes and Tuscarawas Counties in the north to Ross and Jackson Counties in the south. It includes such cities as New Rumley, the birthplace of General George Custer; Zanesville, the birthplace of writer Zane Grey and architect Cass Gilbert and home of a famous Y-shaped bridge; and Chillicothe, the first capital of Ohio, on the Scioto River, beneath Mount Logan, which is stamped on the Great Seal of the state of Ohio. Politically, much of this area was ancestrally Democratic, but in the last two decades it has become more Republican. George W. Bush won 55% of the vote here in 2000.

The congressman from the 18th District is Bob Ney, a Republican first elected in 1994. Ney grew up in Bellaire, in Belmont County just across the Ohio from Wheeling, West Virginia, and worked as a teacher and as safety director for the city of Bellaire. He worked as a teacher in Iran in 1978 and is the only House member who speaks fluent Farsi; today he calls for dialogue with the self-styled reformers in the Iranian government. In 1979 Governor James Rhodes appointed him head of his Office of Appalachia. In 1980 he was elected to the state House, at 26, in quite an upset, beating Wayne Hays, the longtime congressman and chairman of the House Administration Committee who quit this seat in 1976 amid scandal and won a state House seat two years later. Ney lost that seat in the Democratic year of 1982 and spent some time teaching English in Saudi Arabia. In 1984 he was appointed to the state Senate and was elected later that year. When Democrat Douglas Applegate announced his retirement from the U.S. House in 1994, Ney gave up his Finance Committee chair in Columbus to run. Democrats nominated state Representative Greg DiDonato. Most unions backed DiDonato, except for teachers' unions, who backed ex-teacher Ney. His Belmont County home base turned out to be the key; while it gave only 35% to Republican Senate candidate Mike DeWine, it voted 67% for Ney, enough to clinch a 54%–46% victory.

In his first years in the House, Ney opposed the Republican leadership on several issues. He removed language eliminating provisions of the Coal Industry Retiree Health Benefits Act that make former employers pay for retirees' health care. He helped organized labor by protecting the bargaining rights of unionized bus drivers, and he opposed Republican leaders' anti-union bills. Yet he was a leader among House Republicans opposed to PNTR with China. With other Steel Belt members, he backed quotas on foreign steel and he said the Clinton administration was "dead wrong" to put international interests ahead of "working families who have been brutalized by a flood" of steel imports.

In the 107th Congress, Speaker Dennis Hastert named Ney chairman of the House Administration Committee, the very panel where Wayne Hays created his power base as "Mayor of Capitol Hill." Ney was the only 1994 freshman who asked to be on the committee, and wanted even then to be chairman; Newt Gingrich had promised him the post in 1997, but was not able to deliver in 1998. Hastert passed over the more senior Vern Ehlers, who had voted against the leadership on rules votes, to pick Ney, who dissented on substantive issues important to his district but supported the leadership on rules. Six years before, as a freshman on the committee, Ney had moved to cut each member's mail allowance by one-third. In 2001 he started off by moving to give Democrats one-third of committee staff funding—something they had been asking for in vain since Republicans took over. House Administration had been a partisan battleground since Democrats resolved the Indiana 8th District election contest in their own favor in 1985 though Indiana state officials said the Republican won. Now Ney and ranking minority member Steny Hoyer cooperated to the point of consulting each other's staffs. After September 11, that cooperation was tested under fire. From the time they helped members flee from the building, they had to make decisions about security and to balance demands for public access. They provided every member with a Blackberry and, when the congressional office buildings had to be closed because of the anthrax attacks, Ney found alternative space in the GAO building and provided every member with a laptop. He insisted on irradiating all incoming mail and resisted attempts by appropriators to make the Capitol Police chief independent of House Admin and the Senate Rules Committee.

House Administration has jurisdiction over election law, and that put Ney in the center of two fights in 2001 and 2002. The first was over campaign finance regulation. He opposed the Shays-Meehan bill and produced his own alternative, co-sponsored by Albert Wynn, a member of the Congressional Black Caucus. Hastert hoped that Ney-Wynn could prevail over Shays-Meehan, but after the rule to consider them was voted down in July 2001, both bills were pulled from the floor. In January 2002 Shays-Meehan backers got 218 signatures on a petition to discharge their bill from the Rules Committee; Ney-Wynn had become irrelevant and Shays-Meehan was passed in March. The other issue was how to change election laws after the Florida fiasco. On this Ney reached bipartisan agreement with Hoyer in November 2001. Their bill set minimum national standards but not mandates for state laws; provided $400 million to buy out punch card voting machines and upgrade others and $2.25 billion for new machines and voter education; had procedures for absentee ballots and handicapped voters; and set up an Election Assistance Commission with a Standards Board. In December it prevailed over a Democratic alternative 226–197 and was passed 326–63. The Senate took longer to act, and the conference committee took time handling difficult points, but a law similar to Ney-Hoyer was enacted in April 2002.

On other issues, Ney has continued to back trade restrictions and sponsored a bill to preempt state predatory lending laws and impose federal limits. He has worked to fund local projects like the Ohio 93 bypass around Zanesville and for changes in the Medicare reimbursement formula. He showed the power of the House Admin chairman after the White House allowed him to bring only one guest into a 2002 Christmas party (his daughter went and his wife returned to her hotel room, rather than the houseboat he lives on in Washington); soon after, Cabinet officials lost 40 of their 44 House parking spaces.

Ney was elected in a district represented by Democrats for 46 years and had serious challenges in 1996 and 1998 from former state Senator Robert Burch, a favorite of organized labor and the 1994 Democratic nominee for governor. In 1996 he won 50%–46% while Bob Dole was running far behind in the district; in 1998 he carried all but one county and won 60%–40%. In 2000 against a Democrat who invited TV show host (and former Cincinnati Mayor) Jerry Springer to appear in his behalf, Ney won 64%–34%. In 2002 the legislature removed the Ohio River counties from his district and added five new counties in the south and two in the north. That raised the Bush 2000 percentage in the district from 51% to 55%. Ney was unopposed in the primary and general election.

★ OKLAHOMA ★

Proud of its history of rising from humble beginnings, Oklahoma enjoyed the surging prosperity of the 1990s but remains uneasy about whether it is keeping pace in education and high-skill employment. It is in the middle of America geographically and perhaps spiritually as well. Oklahoma was in the national spotlight when the Oklahoma City federal building was bombed in April 1995, and all Americans marveled at the grace and determination with which Oklahomans went about rescuing the wounded and honoring the dead. But this is not the only catastrophe from which Oklahoma has rebounded. It has had exhilarating highs and sickening lows several times in its improbable history. Oklahoma was settled in a rush, first by the Five Civilized Tribes driven west by Andrew Jackson's troops over the Cherokees' Trail of Tears in the 1830s. Then came white settlers one morning in April 1889 when, in the great land rush memorialized in an Edna Ferber novel, the Rodgers and Hammerstein musical, and half a dozen Hollywood movies, thousands of would-be homesteaders drove their wagons across the territorial line at the sound of a gunshot, the most adventurous or unscrupulous of them literally jumping the gun—the Sooners.

The heritage of these rushes remains. Oklahoma has the second-largest Indian population in the country, after California—273,000 in the 2000 Census—though there is just one reservation and the status of many other tribal entities is often disputed. Some Indian tribes here have unsuccessfully sought a return of native lands and face high unemployment rates. But there has been much intermarriage over the years, and many Oklahomans proudly claim some Indian blood. Assimilation into everyday life, plus commemoration of historic traditions and efforts to keep the Cherokee, Choctaw, Chickasaw and Seminole languages from dying out—you can see street signs in the Cherokee alphabet in Tahlequah—seem to have provided a better life for most Native Americans here than other approaches have elsewhere. The counties with a large Indian heritage in the eastern part of the state have been growing smartly, even as the Great Plains farm and oil counties west of Oklahoma City and Tulsa have lost population.

Statehood came to Oklahoma late, in 1907, at which point it filled up with farmers, rising from 1.5 million people in 1907 to 2.4 million in 1930. Oil helped: The first well was drilled here in 1897 and by 1920, Tulsa was an oil boom town. Then came a decade of bust—or dust—as soil loosened by erosion was whipped into giant swirling clouds: The Dust Bowl. "On a single day, I heard, 50 million tons of soil were blown away," John Gunther reported later. "People sat in Oklahoma City, with the sky invisible for three days in a row, holding dust masks over their faces and wet towels to protect their mouths at night, while the farms blew by." Okies headed in droves west on U.S. 66 to the green land of California, and Oklahoma's population sank to 2.3 million in 1940 and 2.2 million in 1950, not to reach its 1930 level again until 1970.

Then oil brought another boom: As the oil shocks of 1973 and 1979 sent oil prices up, Oklahoma's population rose from 2.5 million in 1970 to 3 million in 1980 and 3.3 million in 1983. Then, with the collapse of oil prices and of Oklahoma's farm economy as well, it was bust again. A giddy rise was followed by a giddier fall: The rig count fell from 882 in January 1982 to 232 in February 1983, and was just 141 in February 2001. In 1999, Oklahoma's oil production fell to its lowest point in 80 years. The rising prices of 2000 stimulated little new production; 2001 production figures reflected the continued decline. Just as the dust cloud symbolized Oklahoma's 1930s bust, so the auction of oil drilling equipment was a symbol of the 1980s calamity. The 1990 Census reported just 3.1 million Oklahomans, after more than a decade of population increases. But in the 1990s, Oklahoma has been building a more diversified economy, with high-tech employers as well as oil and gas firms. Population rose 10% in the decade, to 3.45 million in 2000. Tax breaks for any business located on current or "former" Indian reservation land—nearly the entire state—have brought in new jobs. But incomes have not risen much, and thousands of Indians in Oklahoma have filed a massive class-action suit against the government charging that officials have grossly mismanaged Indian trust funds. Oklahoma continues to have above-average rates of divorce, teenage pregnancy and crime, and a low rate of college graduates. Oklahoma knows it has risen far, but still has some distance to go.

In federal elections, Oklahoma is a safely Republican state, but in state politics there is vigorous

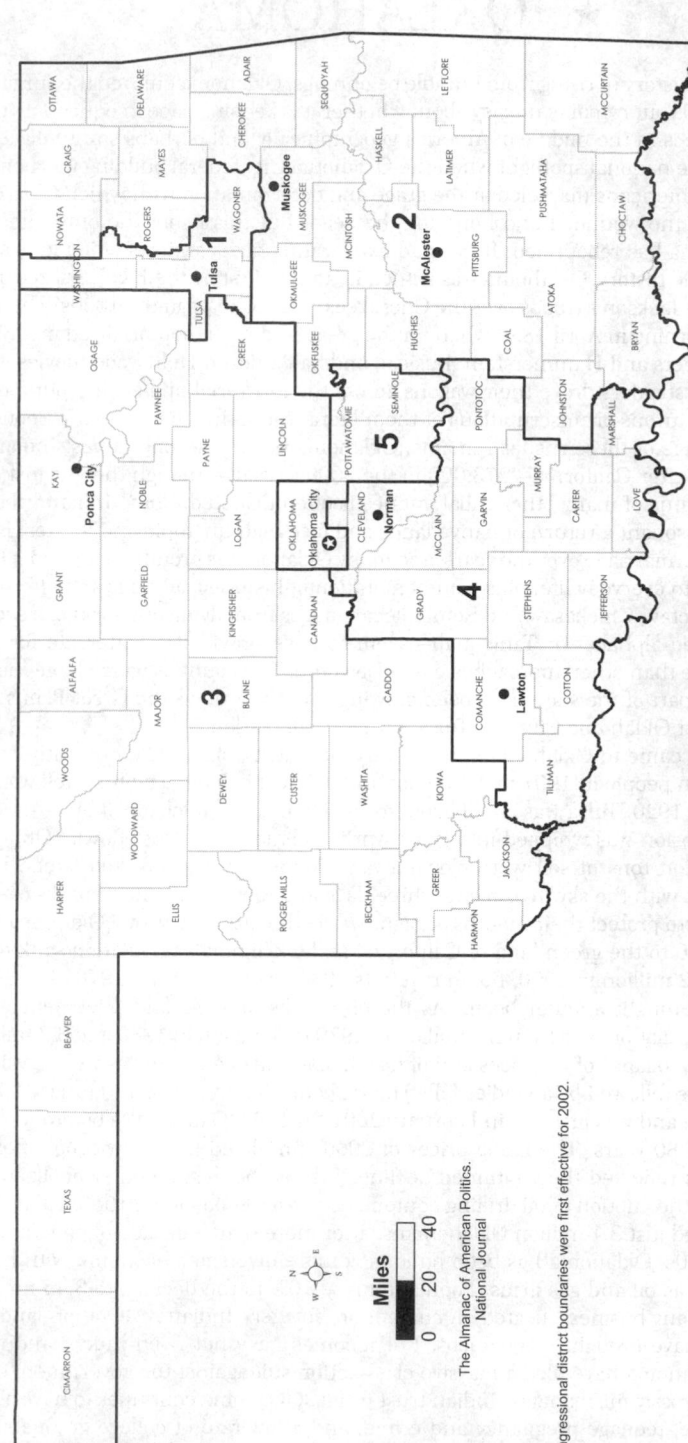

The Almanac of American Politics.
National Journal

Congressional district boundaries were first effective for 2002.

two-party competition and Democrats still have an edge in party registration. The state's House delegation was transformed from 4–2 Democratic to 6–0 Republican from 1991 to 1994, and since Senator David Boren retired in 1994, both Senate seats have been held by Republicans; Democrats picked up one House seat when an incumbent retired in 2000. Bill Clinton lost the state twice, and George W. Bush carried it by a 60%–38% margin. The VNS exit poll showed that Bush carried voters under 60 by a whopping 64%-34% margin; only among those over 60 was it close, with Bush still leading 53%–46%. From 1994 to 2002, much of Oklahoma politics was a struggle between Republican Governor Frank Keating and an aggressively partisan Democratic legislature. Keating is from Tulsa, one of Oklahoma's two big cities, and his was a brand of urban conservatism that did not go over well in some parts of rural Oklahoma. But he persuaded the voters to pass a right-to-work law, banning mandatory union membership, by a 54%–46% vote in September 2001.

On the issue that may have determined the outcome of the 2002 governor race, Keating came out on the winning side but on one that hurt his party. The issue was cockfighting: Oklahoma was one of three states that allowed it (the others are Louisiana and New Mexico); in 2000, animal rights activists tried to put the issue on the November ballot but failed to get enough valid signatures. In 2002, they succeeded. The issue split voters not on party, but on urban/rural lines. In metro Oklahoma City, 64% voted for the ban, in metro Tulsa 67%, and it passed statewide 56%–44%. But rural areas voted against, 55%–45%, and in Little Dixie (southeast and east central Oklahoma), where cockfighting is part of local culture, voters turned out in large numbers to oppose it: Counties there voted between 61% and 73% against the ban. These are, as it happens, counties with an historic Democratic tradition, the home of U.S. House Speaker (1971–76) Carl Albert, and they have been voting Democratic more in recent years; a quite liberal Democrat carried most of them against Keating in an otherwise not close 1998 reelection race. In 2002, Increased Democratic turnout in anti-cockfighting counties was probably responsible for the 6,866-vote defeat of the Republican candidate for governor, former Tulsa Congressman Steve Largent, by Democrat Brad Henry. Largent was hurt also by attacks by independent candidate Gary Richardson and by low turnout in the population-losing counties on the western plains. There were other partisan cross-currents. Republican Lieutenant Governor Mary Fallin was reelected and Republicans picked up seats in the state Senate, but they lost a seat in the much more closely divided state House and lost other downballot offices as well.

The People		Race/Ethnic Origin			Military veterans: 376,062 (14.7%)	
Pop. 2000:	3,450,654	2,556,368	74.1%	White	WWII: 18.6%	Korea: 13.2%
Pop. 1990:	3,145,585	257,981	7.5%	Black	Vietnam: 34.6%	Gulf War: 11.5%
Change 1990–2000:	Up 9.7%	46,172	1.3%	Asian	**Most populous cities:**	
Change 1980–1990:	Up 4.0%	266,158	7.7%	Native Am.	1. Oklahoma City	506,132
% of U.S. total:	1.2%	2,100	0.1%	Hawaiian	2. Tulsa	393,049
Pop. rank:	27th of 50	140,249	4.1%	Two+ races	3. Norman	95,694
Area size:	69,898 sq. mi.	2,322	0.1%	Other	4. Lawton	92,757
State Native:	62.6%	179,304	5.2%	Hisp. Origin	5. Broken Arrow	74,859
Non-citizen:	2.5%	**Ancestry**			Urban population: 65.3%	
Language		German: 10.1%		USA: 9.1%	Rural population: 34.7%	
English: 90.8%	Spanish: 5.0%	Irish: 8.2%		English: 6.7%		
Other Eur.: 1.8%		French: 1.8%				

Education		Work Sector		Legislature		
H.S. Grad:	80.6%	Private: 74.6%	Govt: 16.8%	Senate	28 D 20 R	
College Grad:	20.3%	Self: 8.2%	Family: 0.5%	House	53 D 48 R	
Industry		Unemployment: 5.2%		Legislative Term Limits: Yes		
Agri: 4.1%	Con: 6.9%	**Household Income**		**Registered Voters**		
Fin: 6.0%	Info: 2.7%	<15k: 20.7%	15-35k: 31.3%	D: 1,099,458	(53.0%)	
Mfg: 18.1%	Prof: 27.8%	35-50k: 17.1%	50-100k: 24.3%	R: 758,275	(36.6%)	
Public: 5.9%	Trade: 15.4%	100-150k: 4.3%	>150k: 2.3%	I: 215,202	(10.4%)	
Other: 13.0%		Median: $33,400				
Occupation		Poverty status: 14.7%				
Blue collar: 26.7%	White collar: 56.9%	**Home Value**				
Gray collar: 16.4%		<50k: 33.9%	50-100k: 40.6%	100-200k: 20.3%	200-300k: 3.3%	
		300-500k: 1.3%	>500k: 0.6%	Median: $67,700		

Presidential politics Oklahoma has been a solidly Republican state in presidential elections since the 1950s. There are no large blocs of voters here who back national Democrats and almost everyone finds national Republicans acceptable. Oklahoma is thus not on anyone's list of target states in October, nor is it the subject of much attention as one of the southern Super Tuesday primaries. It has voted for party nominees in the last three presidential primaries; the last time it did not was in 1988, when it voted for Al Gore (a distant relation of onetime Oklahoma Senator Thomas Gore, grandfather of writer Gore Vidal). In 2001, a Democratic state senator tried to abolish the primary and to require five of the state's electoral votes to be cast for the candidate who carries each of the five congressional districts. This would not have changed anything in 2000, when Al Gore failed to carry any of the districts but, if such a bill were passed, it could mean that the outcome of the presidency would hinge on one Oklahoma congressional district. Democrats, who control the governorship and the legislature, have no hope of winning electoral votes in Oklahoma otherwise; maybe they will pass such a law (Maine and Nebraska have them too) in time for the 2004 election.

2000 Presidential Vote		
Bush (R)	744,337	(60%)
Gore (D)	474,276	(38%)
Other	15,616	(1%)

2000 Republican Presidential Primary		
Bush (R)	98,781	(79%)
McCain (R)	12,973	(10%)
Keyes (R)	11,595	(9%)
Other	1,460	(1%)

2000 Democratic Presidential Primary		
Gore (D)	92,654	(69%)
Bradley (D)	34,311	(25%)
LaRouche (D)	7,885	(6%)

1996 Presidential Vote		
Dole (R)	582,315	(48%)
Clinton (D)	488,105	(40%)
Perot (I)	130,788	(11%)

Congressional districting Oklahoma lost one of its six House seats in the 2000 Census, and for months there was a deadlock over redistricting between Republican Governor Frank Keating and the Democratic legislature. Keating wanted to keep a Tulsa-centered district, especially before the September 2001 special election in which his wife Cathy Keating ran for the Tulsa-centered 1st District seat vacated by Steve Largent. But she lost the Republican nomination. In 2002, the solution appeared after 3d District Congressman Wes Watkins announced he was retiring. Watkins was a Republican (although he used to be a Democrat) and the 3d District was centered in Little Dixie; the seat was safe for Watkins, but Democrats carry the area in state elections and would have a good chance to win an open seat contest. The issue went to court, and in May 2002, a county judge ordered the adoption of a plan that eliminated Watkins's district and gave the other incumbents safe seats; it also had the virtue of creating an Oklahoma City-centered district rather than splitting the city between several districts as it had been since 1981. Democrats, happy that Democratic incumbent Brad Carson got a safe seat, let the matter drop.

108th Congress Lineup	
4 R	1 D

107th Congress Lineup	
5 R	1 D

Governor

Brad Henry (D)

Elected 2002, term expires Jan. 2007, 1st term; b. July 7, 1963, Shawnee; home, Shawnee; U. of OK, B.S. 1985, J.D. 1988; Baptist; married (Kim).

Elected Office: OK Senate, 1992–02.

Professional Career: Practicing atty., 1989–02; Atty., City of Shawnee, 1990–02.

Office: 212 State Capitol Bldg., Oklahoma City, 73105, 405-521-2342; Fax: 405-521-3353; Web site: www.governor.state.ok.us.

Election Results

2002 general	Brad Henry (D)	448,143	(43%)
	Steve Largent (R)	441,277	(43%)
	Gary Richardson (I)	146,200	(14%)
2002 runoff	Brad Henry (D)	135,336	(52%)
	Vince Orza (D)	122,855	(48%)
2002 primary	Vince Orza (D)	154,263	(44%)
	Brad Henry (D)	99,883	(29%)
	Kelly Haney (D)	59,044	(17%)
	Jim Dunegan (D)	28,130	(8%)
1998 general	Frank Keating (R)	505,498	(58%)
	Laura Boyd (D)	357,552	(41%)
	Other	10,535	(1%)

Brad Henry, a Democrat, was elected governor of Oklahoma in an upset in 2002. Henry grew up in Shawnee, one county east of Oklahoma City, and graduated from the University of Oklahoma and its law school. He returned home to practice law and in 1992, at 29, he was elected to the state Senate. There he achieved little statewide notice. He opposed right-to-work, but voted to put the issue on the ballot; when his committee bottled up Governor Frank Keating's covenant marriage bill, Keating called him "anti-family." At the beginning of 2002, Henry was not on anyone's political radar screen: The candidate considered most likely to win was Republican Congressman Steve Largent, a football star at the University of Tulsa and with the Seattle Seahawks, who resigned from the House in February 2002 to make the race; the favorite for the Democratic nomination was Oklahoma City area restaurateur Vince Orza, a former Republican who lost the 1990 Republican runoff for governor by a 51%–49% margin. Henry was not sure whether to run; he did not announce until the breathtakingly late date of June 24.

But he had a good campaign plan. He had one big issue (a lottery to fund education), one big vehicle (an RV in which he traveled around the state) and one big endorser (former University of Oklahoma and Dallas Cowboys football coach Barry Switzer). Voters may not be much interested in meeting politicians, but Oklahoma voters are very interested in meeting football coaches. "We like to roll into Wal-Mart parking lots and just cause a commotion," Henry said. "I've been amazed at how people are starved for personal contact." Henry's folksy, aw-shucks manner appealed to rural voters when the other major figures in gubernatorial politics—Keating, Largent, Orza—were from Oklahoma's two major cities. In the Democratic primary August 27, two months and three days after Henry announced, Orza led with 44% of the vote, short of the 50% needed to avoid a runoff, and Henry finished second with 29%; he carried only five counties. Orza called for ending reliance on the state income tax, which presumably meant a higher sales tax; Henry backed the lottery, plus an income tax exemption on seniors' retirement income. Henry had the support of third-place finisher state Senator Kelly Haney, a full-blooded Seminole-Creek; he took care to meet with tribal chiefs, who were conducting a big voter registration drive. Henry won the September 17 runoff by 52%–48%; he lost Oklahoma and Tulsa Counties, but carried their metropolitan areas and won 53%–47% in the rest of Oklahoma as well. This time he carried 49 of the state's 77 counties, sweeping virtually every one in the eastern and central parts of the state.

Against Largent in the general, there were clear contrasts. Largent opposed the lottery, called for moving from the income tax to consumption taxes over the next 10 years, and eliminating the sales tax on food. Henry was for across-the-board teacher salary increases and against merit pay—the teachers' union positions—while Largent took the other side on both. Largent, as Keating did, called for cutting administrative costs in schools; some rural Oklahomans feared that meant consolidating small school districts. Henry thought the University of Oklahoma and Oklahoma State University should be able to increase tuition more than 7% a year; Largent did not. And there was another issue that didn't qualify for the ballot until August 20: Whether to ban cockfighting. In urban Oklahoma this was a popular stand; Keating endorsed it and so did Largent. But it was highly unpopular in Little Dixie in southeastern Oklahoma, where cockfighting is part of local culture. As one enthusiast told a reporter: "It's a hobby my kids won't get to do. It hurts me that Jacky Lee can't be a cockfighter." Henry came out against the cockfighting ban.

Another factor was the independent candidacy of businessman Gary Richardson, who spent $2 million of his own money on his campaign. Richardson advocated the elimination of tolls on Oklahoma's turnpikes; both Henry and Largent were against. Richardson also called for eliminating a whole raft of taxes—the personal and corporate income taxes, the sales tax on groceries, the capital gains tax, the business franchise tax, the estate tax—and for replacing them with a tax on the gross revenues of all business operations. Polls showed Richardson with double-digit support, but his issue positions were less important than his ads attacking Largent. On September 11, 2001, though Congress was planning on going into session, Largent was bowhunting in Idaho and out of touch with his staff; he didn't hear about the attacks until two days later. In the meantime, his staff issued a statement from him, for which he had to apologize. Richardson's ads showed one of the World Trade Center towers collapsing and then asked about Largent's whereabouts, then showed Largent answering a reporter's aggressive question about the issue with an expletive. While all these things were working against Largent, Henry ran ads showing his young family and showcasing his folksy style. October polls showed the race closing. In November, Henry won by less than 7,000 votes of more than 1 million cast, 43.3%–42.6%, with 14% for Richardson. Largent led 46%–40% in the Oklahoma City area and 45%–39% in the Tulsa area—far less than the usual Republican leads there—while Henry carried the rest of Oklahoma, which cast 44% of the vote, 48%–39%. This, in many ways, was a victory for rural Oklahoma over urban Oklahoma, and stopped the Republican advance of the 1990s. On election night, Largent conceded good-naturedly, "I'll put it in a context every Oklahoman can understand: 16–13, OSU. We were the heavy favorite and the underdog won."

Henry is the third youngest governor in Oklahoma's history; the two youngest were J. Howard Edmondson, elected in 1958, and David Boren, elected in 1974. In early 2003, the lottery was the prime issue and the legislature must decide whether to put it on the ballot. Lotteries for education have been popular in southern states, helping to elect Governors Zell Miller in Georgia in 1990 and Jim Hodges in South Carolina and Don Siegelman in Alabama in 1998. But they have had mixed political results. The Georgia program is popular, but Miller was nearly defeated in 1994; Alabama voters rejected the lottery and replaced Siegelman in 2002, when Hodges lost as well.

Senior Senator

Don Nickles (R)

Elected 1980, seat up 2004, 4th term; b. Dec. 6, 1948, Ponca City; home, Ponca City; OK St. U., B.A. 1971; Catholic; married (Linda).

Military Career: OK Natl. Guard, 1970–76.

Elected Office: OK Senate, 1978–80.

Professional Career: V. P. & Gen. Mgr., Nickles Machine Co., 1976–80.

DC Office: 133 HSOB, 20510, 202-224-5754; Fax: 202-224-6008; Web site: www.senate.gov/~nickles.

State Offices: Lawton, 580-357-9878; Oklahoma City, 405-231-4941; Ponca City, 580-767-1270; Tulsa, 918-581-7651.

Committees: *Budget* (Chmn.). *Energy & Natural Resources*: Energy (Vice Chmn.); National Parks (Vice Chmn.). *Finance*: Health Care; Social Security & Family Policy; Taxation & IRS Oversight (Chmn.). *Rules & Administration. Joint Committee on Taxation* (3d of 5 Sens.).

Group Ratings

	ADA	ACLU	AFS	LCV	CON	ITIC	NTU	COC	ACU	NTLC	CHC
2002	0	20	0	0	92	75	77	95	100	100	—
2001	10	—	0	0	—	—	87	100	92	—	100

National Journal Ratings

	2001 LIB —	2001 CONS	2002 LIB —	2002 CONS
Economic	17% —	77%	0% —	94%
Social	0% —	79%	0% —	62%
Foreign	7% —	72%	0% —	76%

Key Votes of the 107th Congress

1. Approve Bush Tax Cuts	Y	5. Confirm Ashcroft as AG	Y	9. Bar Coop. with Intl. Court	Y
2. Expand Patients' Rights	N	6. Bar Gays in the Boy Scouts	Y	10. Trade Promotion Authority	Y
3. Campaign Finance Reform	N	7. $ for Hate Crime Prosecution	N	11. Authorize Force in Iraq	Y
4. Permit ANWR Development	Y	8. Overseas Military Abortions	N	12. Homeland Sec. Dept. Union	N

Election Results

1998 general	Don Nickles (R)	570,682	(66%)	($2,415,565)
	Don E. Carroll (D)	268,898	(31%)	($8,618)
	Other	20,133	(2%)	
1998 primary	Don Nickles (R)	unopposed		
1992 general	Don Nickles (R)	757,876	(59%)	($3,492,603)
	Steve Lewis (D)	494,350	(38%)	($1,455,848)
	Other	42,197	(3%)	

Prior Winning Percentages: 1986 (55%); 1980 (53%)

Don Nickles was first elected in 1980. He grew up in Ponca City, and, after his father died when he was 13, worked his way through Oklahoma State as a janitor making minimum wage; he then returned to Ponca City and helped run the family machine business. In 1978, at 29, he was elected to the Oklahoma Senate; two years later, he ran for the U.S. Senate seat being vacated by Republican Henry Bellmon. With support from Christian conservatives, he won 35% in a multi-candidate primary and 65% in the runoff; in the general, he won 53%–44%, and at 31 became the youngest Republican ever elected to the Senate. It was a signal that conservative Republicanism was the prevailing current of opinion in Oklahoma, just as Nickles's rise to a Senate leadership post is a signal of conservative Republican strength there.

In the Senate, Nickles has been a stalwart for conservative principles—"the keeper of the conservative flame," as *CongressDaily* put it. He ascribes his views to his experience running a small business. "I'm a strong proponent and believer in the free enterprise system. . . . I built up a business that was almost bankrupt. If I see government causing problems or doing things that interfere with personal freedom or economic freedom or religious freedom, I feel very strongly that we should get involved and try to change it." In his early years in the Senate, Nickles backed the successful fights to deregulate oil and natural gas prices, to repeal the windfall profits tax, and to repeal the 55-mile-per-hour speed limit. He takes sometimes lonely stands—against the confirmation of Ambassador to the UN Richard Holbrooke in 1999, against $15 billion in aid to farmers and against outlawing Section 527 campaign organizations in 2000, against the education bill in June 2001. He opposed the Conservation and Reinvestment Act as a federal power grab and called AmeriCorps a "boondoggle." He is willing to risk angering Oklahoman voters as well. He argued against the 2002 farm bill, saying that its subsidies were too generous, especially to large farmers, and would encourage overproduction. He opposed legislation to give federal loan guarantees to some oil and gas explorations companies. In May 2002, he said it was "next to impossible" to save the Army's Crusader program, expected to be located at Oklahoma's Fort Sill, against a Bush veto threat. In June 2002, he said he would seek a one-week delay of a law making Oklahoma City bombing victims eligible for federal compensation when he learned of the involvement of a St. Louis law firm. "I don't want these families victimized twice—once by the bombing and again by any attorneys or lobbyists charging unreasonable fees of 25 or 30% of the payments we intend to go solely to the victims or their families."

After 14 years in leadership positions, Nickles became chairman of the Senate Budget Committee in January 2003. He was expected to take a different approach from Pete Domenici, lead Republican on this panel since the 1981. Often troubled by deficits, Domenici was hesitant to endorse tax cuts. Nickles believes that the best way to end deficits is to "grow the economy. You'll never balance the budget if revenues aren't growing from a growing economy." In January 2003, Nickles and House Budget Committee Chairman Jim Nussle chose Douglas Holtz-Eakin, an economic adviser to George W. Bush, to head the Congressional Budget Office. In the past, Nickles has criticized CBO for not adopting dynamic scoring (taking into account the effect of tax cuts in making economic projections); Holtz-Eakin supports dynamic scoring. In December 2002, Nickles said that the recent 7% growth in domestic discretionary spending "just isn't sustainable" and said that he wanted to find savings in every program, including Social Security and Medicare.

On several issues, Nickles has put together positions that have unified Senate Republicans. In 1998, Nickles came up with his own HMO bill with 49 co-sponsors, and Democrats did not bring up their bill after a version of it passed the House. When Democrats got 51 votes for the House bill in 2000, Nickles continued to resist action, and it did not come to the floor. Nickles has resisted increases in the minimum wage, even when leavened by tax relief for small business. "By raising the minimum wage, politicians would yank the ladder up too high for some people to get on in the first place." But in the debate following the 1997 tobacco settlement, Lott would not accept the tax increases proposed by Democrats and some Republicans, and opposed Arizona Senator John McCain's bill as "one of the worst pieces of legislation I've ever seen." In summer 1998, he coordinated a three-week filibuster that killed the bill. On occasion, Nickles has taken bipartisan initiatives. With Nevada's Harry Reid, he won Senate passage of a bipartisan regulatory reform bill in March 1995—a more realistic and effective version of the moratorium on new regulations in the House's Contract With America. He and Louisiana Senator Mary Landrieu sponsored a 2000 law for automatic citizenship for foreign-born children adopted by Americans. Nickles was also the chief sponsor of the Republican $500-per-child tax credit included in the 1995 budget reconciliation bill, which was vetoed by President Clinton, but passed in 1998.

Nickles has worked to protect what he considers the interests of small business and what opponents say are K Street special interests. He played a key role in overturning the Clinton administration ergonomics regulations in March 2001 and has long worked for changes in product liability and tort law. He has long sought to bar union leaders from spending union members' dues money on politics without their permission, and when other Republicans tried to amend McCain's campaign finance bill in March 2001 to prohibit both that and executives spending corporate money on politics without shareholders' approval, he admitted that prohibiting the latter wasn't workable. With Democratic Senator John Breaux, he sponsored a bill deregulating the regional Bell companies to encourage them to provide broadband service and achieve "regulatory parity."

Nickles also can be a tenacious fighter. He has long sought to bar the Cheyenne-Arapaho tribe from claiming ancestral land at Fort Reno that has been an USDA research station (this was the tribe that lobbied Bill Clinton in the White House after making a $100,000 contribution to the Democratic National Committee). In September 2000, Nickles passed an amendment blocking the land transfer, against the strong opposition of Hawaii Senator Daniel Inouye. Nickles has also worked hard to, in effect, repeal Oregon's 1994 assisted suicide law, by sponsoring what he calls the Pain Relief Promotion Act which would bar physicians from prescribing controlled substances for purposes of suicide. This passed the House in 1999, and Nickles worked to find a vehicle to bring it to the floor of the Senate. In the process, he tangled with Oregon Democrat Ron Wyden, as he attempted to stop a vote and Nickles put holds on other Oregon legislation.

For 14 years, starting in December 1988 when he chaired the Senate Republicans' campaign committee, Nickles was part of the Republican leadership. As an opponent of the 1990 budget summit tax increase, he beat the more senior Pete Domenici for conference chairman in November 1990 by 23–20. After Bob Dole resigned from the Senate in June 1996, Nickles considered running for majority leader, but decided not to challenge Trent Lott; instead he ran for Whip, the position Lott had held, and won. During the six and one-half years they held these positions, there seemed to be tension between them. Lott, though very conservative on substance, is temperamentally a dealmaker; Nickles, though personable and pleasant, is inclined to stand solid on his convictions; neither tends to be very open about his strategy. In November 1998 he was urged to run against Lott, but declined to do so. Nickles's term as Whip expired after the 2002 elections under Republican term limit rules, and in fall 2002 he considered running against Lott again; in April 2002 he had said he wouldn't make a "Shermanesque statement" about not running, and he raised large amounts for other Republicans—$615,000 for Bill Frist's Team Ball, $1.5 million for the June President's Dinner. But in October 2002 he told Lott he wouldn't run against him, and Republican senators reelected Lott in November. Then, on December 5, Lott made his unfortunate comments at Strom Thurmond's 100th birthday party. The mainstream press didn't notice, but Lott got harsh criticism on both liberal and conservative weblogs. On December 15, on ABC's *This Week*, Nickles became the first Republican senator to say he should step aside.

"Trent has been weakened to the point that may jeopardize his ability to enact our agenda and speak to all Americans," he said. "There are several outstanding senators who are more capable of effective leadership and I hope we can have an opportunity to choose." He had notified White House strategist Karl Rove the night before and Lott on that morning that he would do this. It quickly became clear that Nickles could get the five signatures he needed to summon a Republican Conference meeting January 8 to reconsider Lott's status, and on December 20 Lott resigned the position. Nickles seems to have made no move to run for the post himself; presumably he recognized that many senators who backed Lott would resent him for undermining him. In any case, Republican senators quickly reached a consensus on supporting Bill Frist the same day Lott stepped down.

Nickles has been very popular in Oklahoma. His one tough re-election came in 1986, when he faced Tulsa Congressman Jim Jones. But Jones's ad campaign misfired and Nickles showed greater strength than many in Washington expected, winning 55%–45% in a year several other Southern Republicans elected in 1980 lost. In 1992 Nickles won easily, 59%–38%. In 1998 he had no big-name opponents and carried all but one county and won 66%–31%. Nickles has not made it clear whether he will run again in 2004. In May 2002 he said "I may not" run again. In March 2003 he told *Roll Call* he will like decide around April 2004, saying, "I have decided not to decide for a while." No one doubts he can win if he runs. If he doesn't, Republicans will be favored to keep the seat in this nationally Republican state. One possible candidate is former Congressman J. C. Watts, who did not run for reelection to the House in 2002; another is Congressman Ernest Istook. A Democrat who could make a serious race of it is 2d District Congressman Brad Carson.

Junior Senator

James Inhofe (R)

Elected 1994, seat up 2008, 2d term; b. Nov. 17, 1934, Des Moines, IA; home, Tulsa; U. of Tulsa, B.A. 1973; Presbyterian; married (Kay).

Military Career: Army, 1957–58.

Elected Office: OK House of Reps., 1966–69; OK Senate, 1969–77, Repub. Ldr., 1975–77; Repub. gubernatorial nominee, 1974; Tulsa Mayor, 1978–84; U.S. House of Reps., 1986–94.

Professional Career: Businessman, land developer, 1962–86.

DC Office: 453 RSOB, 20510, 202-224-4721; Fax: 202-228-0380; Web site: inhofe.senate.gov.

State Offices: Enid, 580-234-5105; McAlester, 918-426-0933; Oklahoma City, 405-608-4381; Tulsa, 918-748-5111.

Committees: *Armed Services*: Airland; Readiness & Management Support; Strategic Forces. *Environment & Public Works* (Chmn.). *Indian Affairs*.

Group Ratings

	ADA	ACLU	AFS	LCV	CON	ITIC	NTU	COC	ACU	NTLC	CHC
2002	10	20	0	0	43	50	64	100	100	91	—
2001	10	—	0	0	—	—	82	93	96	—	100

National Journal Ratings

	2001 LIB	—	2001 CONS		2002 LIB	—	2002 CONS
Economic	17%	—	77%		18%	—	80%
Social	0%	—	79%		0%	—	62%
Foreign	36%	—	54%		0%	—	76%

Key Votes of the 107th Congress

1. Approve Bush Tax Cuts	Y	5. Confirm Ashcroft as AG	Y	9. Bar Coop. with Intl. Court	Y
2. Expand Patients' Rights	N	6. Bar Gays in the Boy Scouts	Y	10. Trade Promotion Authority	Y
3. Campaign Finance Reform	N	7. $ for Hate Crime Prosecution	N	11. Authorize Force in Iraq	Y
4. Permit ANWR Development	Y	8. Overseas Military Abortions	N	12. Homeland Sec. Dept. Union	N

Election Results

2002 general	James Inhofe (R)	583,579	(57%)	($3,040,220)
	David Walters (D)	369,789	(36%)	($2,072,137)
	James Germalic (I)	65,056	(6%)	
2002 primary	James Inhofe (R)	unopposed		
1996 general	James Inhofe (R)	670,610	(57%)	($2,510,946)
	James Boren (D)	474,162	(40%)	($301,621)
	Other	38,378	(3%)	

Prior Winning Percentages: 1994 (55%); 1992 House (53%); 1990 House (56%); 1988 House (53%); 1986 House (55%)

James Inhofe (pronounced *IN-hoff*), Oklahoma's junior senator, is a Republican first elected in 1994. He grew up in Tulsa, served in the Army, and worked in real estate, insurance and aviation. He has for years regularly flown planes and is one of Congress's few certified commercial pilots; he flew around the world following Wiley Post's route and on short notice flew into Texas military bases to check on readiness. He was elected to the Oklahoma House in 1966, at 31, and to the Oklahoma Senate in 1969; he ran for governor in 1974 and lost to David Boren, 64%–36%. In 1976, Inhofe ran for the U.S. House against Jim Jones and lost; from 1979–84, he was mayor of Tulsa. He won the heavily Republican 1st District House seat in 1986, but held it with uninspiring margins. He was hurt by negative publicity about a family business lawsuit (he eventually was awarded $3.6 million) and charges of campaign finance irregularities, leveled often by the liberal-leaning *Tulsa World*. Inhofe's great achievement in the House was reforming the arcane discharge petition rule. For years, House rules kept secret the names of signers of petitions to discharge bills stuck in committees; members could say they had worked to bring legislation to the floor when they had done just the opposite. That was changed September 28, 1993, and one of the first bills to benefit from the new rules was the aviation liability reform bill, co-sponsored by Inhofe, which limited the liability of small airplane manufacturers in lawsuits resulting from crashes. The discharge petition was also the vehicle for House passage of campaign finance regulation in 2002, a bill Inhofe opposed.

Inhofe jumped into the 1994 Senate race when his onetime opponent David Boren, a conservative Democrat who carried not only every county but every precinct in 1990, announced he was retiring to become president of the University of Oklahoma. The Democratic nominee was Dave McCurdy, congressman since 1980 from southwest Oklahoma, chairman of the moderate Democratic Leadership Council. But in Oklahoma in 1994, the Clinton burden was too heavy for even McCurdy to carry. McCurdy had voted for the 1993 Clinton budget and tax package with its original Btu tax and for the 1994 crime bill with its assault weapons ban. Inhofe won by a solid 55%–40%. In the Senate, Inhofe was president of the conservative 11-member freshman class. He was elected to a full six-year term in 1996 over James Boren, David Boren's cousin, by 57%–40%.

Inhofe has a very conservative voting record and is not given to backslapping and banter. "I'm more of a maverick. I'm second only to John McCain," he told a reporter in October 2002. "They don't know where I'm going to be coming from. Philosophically, I'm very, very rigid in the things I believe in." He is capable of acerbic comments: He compared Clinton EPA administrator Carol Browner to Tokyo Rose and said her agency used "Gestapo tactics." He can also use sharp tactics. For two years, he stalled the nomination of openly gay James Hormel to be Ambassador to Luxembourg and has said that he will not hire gay staffers. In September 2001, two weeks after the September 11 attacks, he offered the Republican energy bill as an amendment to the defense authorization and threatened to bring it up as an amendment to every bill. For this, Democrats and editorial writers across the country denounced him. Inhofe was trying to get Majority Leader Tom Daschle to schedule floor time for the energy bill; he says he was unphased by the criticism. Inhofe also blocked the confirmation of Robert Bonner as head of Customs Service until he agreed to test contraband detection technology as a substitute for X-ray machines. "I had to play hardball. Everybody screamed and said, 'How can you do this after the tragedy? We need to have him on board.'"

In January 2003, Inhofe became chairman of the Environment and Public Works Committee; his colleague Don Nickles became chairman of Budget, and so Oklahoma has two Senate committee chairmen for the first time since 1935–36. Inhofe is committed to very different policies from those of his predecessors, Independent Jim Jeffords and Republican Bob Smith. He strongly favors oil drilling in the Arctic National Wildlife Refuge and more oil and gas drilling exploration in the United States generally. He strongly opposed the policies of the Clinton administration EPA, arguing that its air-quality standards were based on a dishonest rationale, and called for their delay. He has also argued that the Endangered Species Act has gone too far. "America has adopted an attitude that places more value on the life of a critter than on a human being. We want to protect the Arkansas River shiner, a bait fish in Oklahoma, yet we will allow unborn babies to have their brains sucked out in a partial-birth abortion." On the brownfields bill in April 2001 he got $50 million extra to clean up abandoned gas stations and petroleum sites that are not covered by the Superfund. He hailed the Bush administration policy for reducing emissions. Looking forward to the chairmanship, he struck a conciliatory note in November 2002. "I want to work in a bipartisan fashion to create fiscally responsible policies that are based on sound science and cost-benefit analyses." He called for new concrete goals to reduce emissions, increased research and development, including on renewable energy sources like wind and solar power and on fuel-cell vehicles. But he still wanted to avoid imposing what he sees as undue costs on the economy.

Inhofe has also taken an active role on the Armed Services Committee. He has been a strong supporter of missile defense. He was one of the leaders of the successful fight in October 1999 to deny ratification to the Comprehensive Test Ban Treaty. Inhofe attacked the Clinton Administration's handling of base closings as dishonest, especially the "privatization" of depot bases in electoral-vote-rich California and Texas, rather than transfer of work to bases in Oklahoma, Utah and Georgia. He has worked to maintain at least 50% of Air Force repair work in Air Force bases and has opposed further base closings.

When Puerto Ricans called for an end to live-fire amphibious exercises on the island of Vieques, Inhofe called for their continuation and said that if they were stopped the Navy should close its $3 billion Roosevelt Roads base in Puerto Rico. He harshly criticized the Bush administration for agreeing, before September 11, to close the training ranges at Vieques. Inhofe also disagreed with, and was disagreeably surprised by, Defense Secretary Donald Rumsfeld's decision in May 2002 to cancel the Army's Crusader cannon, which was to be manufactured in Elgin, Oklahoma, near Lawton, and deployed at nearby Fort Sill. In September 2002, he inserted into the defense authorization $368 million to build a different cannon and a requirement that it be deployed in 2008. "I just flat beat the White House on this thing," he boasted. "If successful, we can end up with an indirect fire cannon system that will meet the Army's needs by 2008 and still be assembled with the same Lawton, Oklahoma-based team and the same technology as Crusader." He also put in $16 million to fund two projects at Vance Air Force Base near Enid, and said that the base was safe as long as Republicans had a majority in the Senate.

Inhofe often casts lonely votes. He was one of the few votes against Richard Holbrooke for UN Ambassador, against the May 1997 budget deal and the October 1998 omnibus budget, against the bipartisan Everglades bill. Inhofe has worked with others in the Oklahoma delegation to simplify the land laws applying to the Five Tribes, so that land can be developed and mineral rights exploited more easily. Another pet measure was his provision allowing pilots to appeal a license suspension by the FAA to the National Transportation Safety Board.

In 2002, Inhofe came up for reelection. His Democratic opponent was former Governor David Walters, who in October 1993 pleaded guilty to a misdemeanor count of violating campaign finance laws in his 1990 campaign; the prosecution dropped eight felony counts. Walters had competition in the primary from businessman Tom Boetcher, who said he would be a drag on the Democratic ticket. The former governor led in the August primary, 49–34%, but was forced into a runoff which he won by the less than overwhelming margin of 57%–43%. Walters argued that he could protect Oklahoma interests better because he would be a less predictable vote; he attacked Inhofe for the cancellation of the Crusader and said he should donate $24,000 he had received from WorldCom contributors to the state teachers' retirement fund. Inhofe said that he had produced a weapon to replace the Crusader and ran ads showing Walters and a Clinton lookalike. Oklahoma voters seem to have a fixed view of Inhofe: the result was almost identical to those in 1994 and 1996. He won statewide 57%–36%, winning big margins in metro Oklahoma City (62%–31%) and metro Tulsa (60%–34%) and winning more narrowly (52%–41%) in the rest of the state.

FIRST DISTRICT

Rep. John Sullivan (R)

Elected Jan. 2002, 1st term; b. Jan. 1, 1965, Tulsa; home, Tulsa; Northeastern St. U., B.B.A., 1992; Catholic; married (Judy).

Elected Office: OK House of Reps., 1995–01.

Professional Career: Trucking salesman, 1988–92; Gas and Fleet sales rep., 1991–98; Realtor, 1997–02.

DC Office: 114 CHOB 20515, 202-225-2211; Fax: 202-225-9187; Web site: www.house.gov/sullivan.

District Office: Tulsa, 918-749-0014.

Committees: *Government Reform* (17th of 24 R): Energy Policy, Natural Resources and Regulatory Affairs; Government Efficiency & Financial Management. *Science* (18th of 25 R): Research; Space & Aeronautics. *Transportation & Infrastructure* (33d of 41 R): Aviation; Water Resources & Environment.

Group Ratings (Only Served Partial Term)

	ADA	ACLU	AFS	LCV	CON	ITIC	NTU	COC	ACU	NTLC	CHC
2002	0	0	0	0	—	100	61	89	—	100	100
2001	—	—	—	—	—	—	—	—	—	—	—

National Journal Ratings (Only Served Partial Term)

	2001 LIB — 2001 CONS	2002 LIB — 2002 CONS
Economic	* — *	32% — 68%
Social	* — *	0% — 75%
Foreign	* — *	0% — 85%

Key Votes of the 107th Congress (Only Served Partial Term)

1. Approve Bush Tax Cuts	*	5. Faith-Based Charities	*	9. Trade Promotion Authority	*
2. Limit Patients' Bill of Rights	*	6. Bar Gays in the Boy Scouts	*	10. Bar Funds for Intl. Court	Y
3. Campaign Finance Reform	*	7. Ban Partial-Birth Abortion	Y	11. Authorize Force in Iraq	Y
4. Ban ANWR Development	*	8. Arm Commercial Pilots	Y	12. Deny Home. Sec. Dept. Union	Y

Election Results

2002 general	John Sullivan (R)	119,566	(56%)	($1,470,177)
	Doug Dodd (D)	90,649	(42%)	($546,083)
	Other	4,740	(2%)	
2002 primary	John Sullivan (R)	39,992	(85%)	
	Evelyn Rogers (R)	7,280	(15%)	
2002 special	John Sullivan (R)	61,694	(54%)	
	Doug Dodd (D)	50,850	(44%)	

The People		Race/Ethnic Origin	Ancestry	
Area size:	1,790 sq. mi.	73.8% White	German: 11.1%	Irish: 8.7%
Urban population:	89.6%	9.4% Black	English: 7.9%	
Rural population:	10.4%	1.4% Asian	**2000 Presidential Vote**	
Pop. 2000:	690,131	5.8% Native Am.	Bush (R)..............165,759	(62%)
Median income:	$38,610	0.0% Hawaiian	Gore (D)................99,283	(37%)
Poverty status:	11.3%	4.2% Two + races	Other.....................3,566	(1%)
Military veterans:	14.1%	0.1% Other	**Cook Partisan Voting Index:** R +13	
		5.3% Hispanic Origin		

Occupation   Blue collar: 23.2%   White collar: 62.9%   Gray collar: 14.0%

Tulsa was one of America's oil boom towns in the early 20th Century, settled not just by people from the immediate hinterland but by Midwesterners and New Englanders of Yankee stock. In the 1920s, as its skyscrapers rose in downtown on heights above the Arkansas River, it was a raw town, intent on culture. It was optimistic and ready to seek economic change, yet culturally and politically conservative, with a Yankee elite and an Indian heritage recalled today in the Gilcrease Museum—left by one-eighth Creek Indian oil millionaire Thomas Gilcrease—and an ethnic variety suggested by the Gershon & Rebecca Fenster Museum of Jewish Art. In the decades since, Tulsa has boomed and occasionally busted. It has remained cosmopolitan and conservative; it is one of America's leading petroleum centers, and also the headquarters of Oral Roberts and his Oral Roberts University and 60-story City of Faith hospital.

The 1st Congressional District includes all of Tulsa County plus parts of several adjacent counties: Almost all of the Tulsa metropolitan area. The political tradition here is heavily Republican, strengthened in recent decades by national Democrats' cultural liberalism. Even during the collapse of oil prices in the 1980s, Tulsa remained full of a contagious enthusiasm for new business enterprises and innovations. Ordinary people here do not resent the oil companies or the new rich; they identify with them. They see not class conflict, but a coincidence of economic interests. They see government as interfering with efforts to produce desired goods and services—although Tulsans are pleased that the federal government built the McClellan-Kerr Waterway that made nearby Catoosa suburb a seaport. Redistricting added all of Wagoner County, southeast of Tulsa, and Washington County, including Bartlesville (headquarters of Phillips Petroleum prior to its recent merger with Conoco) to the north, but did not change the partisan balance much.

The congressman from the 1st District is John Sullivan, a Republican first elected in a January 2002 special election to replace Steve Largent, who resigned to run (unsuccessfully) for governor. Sullivan grew up in Tulsa and graduated from Northeastern Oklahoma State University. In Tulsa he worked in the transportation, oil and gas, and real estate industries. In 1994, at 39, he was elected to the state House, where he served as Republican whip. As a state legislator, he was involved in the creation of the Tulsa campus of Oklahoma State University, sponsorship of a large tax cut, and passage of a parental-notification bill for minors seeking abortion.

He was not the frontrunner in the special primary election in December 2001. The best-known candidate was Cathy Keating, wife of Governor Frank Keating, who enthusiastically backed her campaign. She had a big fundraising advantage, but stumbled in the brief five-week campaign. Sullivan accused her of being too moderate for a conservative district; she had no legislative record to dispute his claims. She was criticized for a TV ad that pointed out that Oklahoma had not elected a woman to Congress in 80 years (when Republican Alice Robertson won 48.8%–48.4% in the 2d District in 1920; she lost 58%–42% in 1922). Sullivan, meanwhile, built a strong grass-roots network among conservative activists. He led the first round of balloting, 46%–30%; state Senator Scott Pruitt trailed with 23%. Under state law, Sullivan's failure to win 50% entitled Keating to a runoff. But his unexpectedly large lead, plus the unlikelihood that four weeks of campaigning during the Christmas and New Year seasons would capture voter attention, convinced her to drop her candidacy. So on January 8, Sullivan faced the Democratic nominee, Doug Dodd, a Tulsa attorney and former school board member. Dodd ran a spirited campaign and raised some money from labor PACs, but this is a district George W. Bush carried 62%–37% and even the tendency of voters to vote for candidates of the nonpresidential party in special elections did not produce an upset here. Sullivan only won 54%–44%; national Democrats may have regretted they did not target this race.

In the House, Sullivan won seats on Government Reform, Science, and Transportation Committees, and pledged to fight for Tulsa's fair share of highway and transit funds. He got the Environmental Protection Agency to expedite its review of the threat to a local watershed. Sullivan received some unwanted publicity when the *Tulsa World* reported that he had a police record because of several alcohol-related offenses, mostly when he was a teenager. "I was a wild kid," he told a group of Tulsa high school students. "I would go out and have fun. I drank a lot."

In November 2002, Sullivan again faced Dodd, in a larger district because of redistricting. Sullivan cited his modest accomplishments during his months of incumbency, and was helped by an October campaign visit by Dick Cheney. Dodd criticized Sullivan for missing a vote on increased subsidies for farmers, and noted that he misrepresented his arrest record on an application to coach youth soccer. Still, Sullivan won by a slightly larger margin this time, 56%–42%.

In the 108th Congress, Sullivan sought but failed to get Largent's seat on the Energy and Commerce Committee, where oil and gas issues often are front and center. Darrell Issa of California received it instead.

SECOND DISTRICT

Rep. Brad Carson (D)

Elected 2000, 2d term; b. Mar. 11, 1967, Winslow, AZ; home, Claremore; Baylor U., B.A. 1989, Oxford U., Rhodes Scholar, M.A. 1991, U. of OK, J.D. 1994; Baptist; married (Julie).

Professional Career: Atty., 1994–96; White House Fellow, U.S. Dept. of Defense, 1997–98.

DC Office: 317 CHOB 20515, 202-225-2701; Fax: 202-225-3038; Web site: www.house.gov/bradcarson.

District Offices: Claremore, 918-341-9336; Muskogee, 918-687-2533.

Committees: *Resources* (15th of 24 D): Energy & Mineral Resources; Forests & Forest Health. *Transportation & Infrastructure* (23d of 34 D): Aviation; Economic Development, Public Buildings & Emergency Management; Highways, Transit & Pipelines.

Group Ratings

	ADA	ACLU	AFS	LCV	CON	ITIC	NTU	COC	ACU	NTLC	CHC
2002	65	67	75	38	8	75	26	75	40	6	33
2001	65	—	70	29	—	—	20	70	48	—	—

National Journal Ratings

	2001 LIB —	2001 CONS		2002 LIB —	2002 CONS
Economic	56%	45%		56%	43%
Social	58%	42%		56%	42%
Foreign	49%	47%		51%	48%

Key Votes of the 107th Congress

1. Approve Bush Tax Cuts	Y	5. Faith-Based Charities	N	9. Trade Promotion Authority	Y
2. Limit Patients' Bill of Rights	N	6. Bar Gays in the Boy Scouts	Y	10. Bar Funds for Intl. Court	Y
3. Campaign Finance Reform	Y	7. Ban Partial-Birth Abortion	Y	11. Authorize Force in Iraq	Y
4. Ban ANWR Development	N	8. Arm Commercial Pilots	Y	12. Deny Home. Sec. Dept. Union	N

Election Results

2002 general	Brad Carson (D)	146,748	(74%)	($1,021,705)
	Kent Pharaoh (R)	51,234	(26%)	($304,887)
2002 primary	Brad Carson (D)	72,612	(64%)	
	Mike Mass (D)	34,450	(30%)	
	Dorothy Vandiver (D)	6,040	(5%)	
2000 general	Brad Carson (D)	107,273	(55%)	($1,209,242)
	Andy Ewing (R)	81,672	(42%)	($988,161)
	Other	6,467	(3%)	

The People		Race/Ethnic Origin	Ancestry	
Area size:	21,225 sq. mi.	70.2% White	USA: 10.2%	Irish: 7.8%
Urban population:	35.6%	4.0% Black	German: 7.2%	
Rural population:	64.4%	0.3% Asian	**2000 Presidential Vote**	
Pop. 2000:	690,130	16.8% Native Am.	Bush (R)	123,952 (52%)
Median income:	$27,885	0.0% Hawaiian	Gore (D)	110,791 (47%)
Poverty status:	18.5%	6.2% Two+ races	Other	3,438 (1%)
Military veterans:	15.4%	0.0% Other	**Cook Partisan Voting Index:** R + 3	
		2.4% Hispanic Origin		

Occupation	Blue collar: 33.2%	White collar: 48.3%	Gray collar: 18.5%

The land that is now northeast Oklahoma a century ago was the Indian Territory, the place where in the 1830s the Five Civilized Tribes were driven from Georgia and Alabama over the Trail of Tears. Almost one in four people here report their race as American Indian, and in some counties one-third or more claim they are at least partly of Native American descent. The Indian percentage is highest in the hilly counties just west of the Ozarks of Arkansas, where county names—Cherokee, Osage, Sequoyah—recall the Civilized Tribes; the street signs in Tahlequah, once the Cherokee capital, are written in the Cherokee script as well as English. This pleasant land of gentle hills and man-made lakes grew at a healthy pace in the 1990s, from overspill from Tulsa and also from retirees and young families moving into the land that became the home of the Civilized Tribes more than 150 years ago.

South of this Indian country is Oklahoma's Little Dixie, settled between 1889 and 1907 by white Southerners, most of them poor. Some of the county names—LeFlore, Pontotoc—are straight from Mississippi. Today, Interstate highways and turnpikes connect people to jobs in more vibrant metropolitan areas, while dam-made lakes have spurred the creation of resort and retirement communities. Still, traditional cultural attitudes and cultural folkways remain strong. Oklahoma voted in November 2002 on a proposition to outlaw cockfighting, which won by 2–1 margins in metro Oklahoma City and Tulsa. But cockfighting is part of local culture in many towns in Little Dixie, and voters there turned out in large numbers and voted to keep cockfighting by similar margins—as much as 73% in some counties. The cockfighting ban won statewide. But the increased turnout in heavily Democratic Little Dixie and quite Democratic northeast Oklahoma helped elect Democrat Brad Henry as governor by a 6,866-vote margin. After the election, local judges issued injunctions against enforcement of the law; cockfighting activists hoped the Oklahoma Supreme Court would declare it unconstitutional.

The 2d Congressional District includes most of the eastern third of Oklahoma, except for metropolitan Tulsa. It includes Muskogee, subject of Merle Haggard's song, "Okie from Muskogee," Will Rogers's hometown of Claremore in Rogers County and the late Speaker of the House Carl Albert's home in McAlester in Pittsburg County in Little Dixie. McAlester is also the site of a massive army ammunition plant that manufactures non-nuclear bombs ranging in size from 500 to 5,000 pounds (during the 2003 war in Iraq it was forced to add a night shift). This area was ancestrally Democratic, but in the 1980s and early 1990s it trended Republican on cultural issues. In the late 1990s it moved back toward the Democrats, or at least Oklahoma Democrats; Al Gore's percentage here was higher than in Oklahoma's other districts, but he still lost the 2d to George W. Bush. In the 2002 race for governor, Democrat Brad Henry carried every county in the district. Redistricting created this district in its present form in 2002, combining most of the old 2d District in northeast Oklahoma with most of the Little Dixie counties of the old 3d District.

The congressman from the 2d District is Brad Carson, a Democrat elected in 2000. Carson is a sixth-generation Oklahoman, an Eagle Scout, and a member of the Cherokee Nation (the 2d is home to 60,000 Cherokees, the highest concentration in the nation). He graduated from Baylor University and won a Rhodes scholarship to Oxford, then graduated from the University of Oklahoma Law School. Carson practiced law in Oklahoma and then worked a year at the Pentagon as an aide to Defense Secretary William Cohen. In December 1998, he moved back to Oklahoma to work for a Tulsa law firm. Undoubtedly he had an eye on running in the 2d District. The incumbent congressman, Tom Coburn, was highly popular—an obstetrician who continued delivering babies even as he bucked the Republican leadership on issues ranging from abortion and the V-chip (he opposed each) to congressional perks and physician-assisted suicide (he opposed those, too). But in 1994 he promised to serve only three terms, and in 2000 he kept his word and retired.

Ten candidates ran for the seat—three Democrats and seven Republicans. Carson, running at 33, had major opposition from Bill Settle, 62, chairman of the state House Appropriations Committee. Settle emphasized health care, focusing on his legislation to allow patients to sue HMOs, and contrasted his experience with Carson's youth. Carson sought to turn his inexperience into a plus, focusing on campaign finance reform and criticized Settle for accepting large donations from nursing homes. For all his inexperience, he was a fluent and charming candidate, with flawless political instincts. In the September runoff, Carson won 57%–43%, as Settle won his Muskogee base but nothing else. The Republican primary was won easily by Andy Ewing, a political novice who shared Coburn's views on issues and on the importance of having citizen-representatives. Like Coburn, Ewing promised to serve only three terms in office, a pledge that Carson dismissed as harmful for the district. Both candidates opposed gun control, but they disagreed on abortion, with Carson supporting abortion rights. Ewing tried to portray Carson, who moved to the district two years earlier, as an outsider and a political opportunist. But Carson has roots in the district—his mother's family migrated to Oklahoma on the Trail of Tears—and he sought to portray himself as a moderate, fresh face. Health care emerged as a key issue: Carson criticized Ewing's proposal to help seniors with drug costs by stimulating competition among pharmaceutical companies and instead called for adding a prescription drug benefit for all Medicare beneficiaries. In the inexpensive Tulsa media market, both national parties spent heavily on this contest. Carson won 17 of 18 counties, and was elected by a 55%–42% margin.

In the House, Carson got seats on Resources and Transportation Committees and joined the Blue Dogs. His voting record was more conservative than those of most Democrats. The late Mike Synar held this seat for 16 years despite a liberal record far out of line with local opinion on some issues; Carson seems to avoid such positions. He voted for trade promotion authority and the use of force in Iraq. And he isn't shy about taking on his party's conventional thinking. In *The Weekly Standard* in September 2002, he wrote a thoughtful review of *The Emerging Democratic Majority*, a liberal manifesto by John Judis and Ruy Teixeira. Carson dismissed Al Gore's "people versus the powerful" theme as unpersuasive and lamented that the authors missed an opportunity to explain "the gap between the image and the reality of the Democratic party"; he concluded that they failed to make their case that a Democratic resurgence lies ahead. He added, "We [Democrats] must look for the roots of our emerging political crisis not primarily in race and class, but in culture," and predicted that a Republican majority is more likely to emerge than a Democratic one.

Carson has the look and the heft of a politician who is heading toward statewide office—and perhaps beyond. Probably not too soon, though: Oklahomans to almost everyone's surprise elected a young Democratic governor in 2002, and neither of Oklahoma's two Republican senators looks vulnerable at the moment. In 2002, Carson made it clear he has a strong political base: He was reelected with 74% of the vote, carrying every county by a wide margin.

THIRD DISTRICT

Rep. Frank Lucas (R)

Elected May 1994, 5th term; b. Jan. 6, 1960, Cheyenne; home, Cheyenne; OK St. U., B.S. 1982; Baptist; married (Lynda).

Elected Office: OK House of Reps., 1988–94.

Professional Career: Farmer & rancher.

DC Office: 2342 RHOB 20515, 202-225-5565; Fax: 202-225-8698; Web site: www.house.gov/lucas.

District Offices: Stillwater, 405-624-6407; Woodward, 580-256-5752; Yukon, 405-373-1958.

Committees: *Agriculture* (6th of 27 R): Conservation, Credit, Rural Development & Research (Chmn.); General Farm Commodities & Risk Management. *Financial Services* (9th of 37 R): Capital Markets, Insurance & Government Sponsored Enterprises; Financial Institutions & Consumer Credit. *Science* (12th of 25 R): Research; Space & Aeronautics.

Group Ratings

	ADA	ACLU	AFS	LCV	CON	ITIC	NTU	COC	ACU	NTLC	CHC
2002	0	7	0	0	8	100	55	100	96	86	92
2001	5	—	10	0	—	—	65	96	96	—	—

National Journal Ratings

	2001 LIB —	2001 CONS		2002 LIB —	2002 CONS
Economic	22% —	74%		0% —	91%
Social	20% —	69%		0% —	75%
Foreign	16% —	82%		0% —	85%

Key Votes of the 107th Congress

1. Approve Bush Tax Cuts	Y	5. Faith-Based Charities	Y	9. Trade Promotion Authority	Y
2. Limit Patients' Bill of Rights	Y	6. Bar Gays in the Boy Scouts	Y	10. Bar Funds for Intl. Court	Y
3. Campaign Finance Reform	N	7. Ban Partial-Birth Abortion	Y	11. Authorize Force in Iraq	Y
4. Ban ANWR Development	N	8. Arm Commercial Pilots	Y	12. Deny Home. Sec. Dept. Union	Y

Election Results

2002 general	Frank Lucas (R)	148,206	(76%)	($458,929)
	Robert Murphy (I)	47,884	(24%)	
2002 primary	Frank Lucas (R)	43,887	(89%)	
	Richard Hovis (R)	5,330	(11%)	
2000 general (OK 6)	Frank Lucas (R)	95,635	(59%)	($700,850)
	Randy Beutler (D)	63,106	(39%)	($414,786)
	Other	2,435	(2%)	

Prior Winning Percentages: 1998 (65%); 1996 (64%); 1994 (70%); 1994 (54%)

The People		Race/Ethnic Origin	Ancestry	
Area size:	34,384 sq. mi.	81.0% White	German: 12.4%	USA: 10.0%
Urban population:	50.7%	3.8% Black	Irish: 8.2%	
Rural population:	49.3%	0.8% Asian	**2000 Presidential Vote**	
Pop. 2000:	690,131	6.0% Native Am.	Bush (R) 163,302	(65%)
Median income:	$32,098	0.1% Hawaiian	Gore (D) 84,691	(34%)
Poverty status:	15.0%	3.0% Two+ races	Other 2,805	(1%)
Military veterans:	14.0%	0.1% Other	**Cook Partisan Voting Index:** R +16	
		5.2% Hispanic Origin		

Occupation	Blue collar: 28.2%	White collar: 54.1%	Gray collar: 17.7%

First settled just a century ago, western Oklahoma is a fertile land forever at the mercy of the elements. The western plains are scorching hot under the summer sun and snow-blown in winter;

this is one of the windiest parts of America. Visitors to the Tallgrass Prairie Preserve, maintained by the Nature Conservancy near Pawhuska, can experience what settlers of untilled land found when they arrived here: a swaying ocean of 10-foot-high grasses filled with insects emitting a dull, incessant roar. Many rural counties here are not much more populous than they were during the virgin sod era. Far fewer people live here than did before the Dust Bowl hit in the 1930s, and fewer than during the Anadarko Basin oil and natural gas boom of the 1970s. But you can still see what the old towns look like. In 1910, three years after statehood, Oklahoma moved its capital south 25 miles from Guthrie to Oklahoma City, leaving behind what has become one of the nation's largest historic preservation districts, including the Oklahoma Frontier Pharmacy Museum with racks of glass patent medicine bottles and a working soda fountain.

The 3d Congressional District includes Oklahoma's western plains, from the panhandle—an outlaw no man's land that did not officially join the Indian Territory until 1890—to the northern fringes of Oklahoma City. The third also includes north central Oklahoma, added in the 2002 redistricting, including Ponca City, the university town of Stillwater and Osage County, site of the state's one Indian reservation just west of Tulsa. A few of the southern counties, settled by farmers crossing the Red River from Texas, are ancestrally Democratic. But farmers coming south from Kansas settled most of these plains, and these have always been heavily Republican. Those divisions have been as permanent as if Oklahoma had been split down the middle during the Civil War, even though there were no whites in the area at the time. There are few blacks in this part of Oklahoma, but an increasing number of Hispanics moving here, as in other parts of the Great Plains, to work in hog farms and meatpacking plants.

The congressman from the 3d District is Frank Lucas, a Republican chosen in a 1994 special election. Lucas's roots are in western Oklahoma; he owns a farm and cattle ranch in Roger Mills County and was elected to the Oklahoma House in 1988, at 28. He got his chance to run for Congress in 1994 when Glenn English, a 19-year conservative Democrat, resigned to head the National Rural Electric Cooperative Association. Lucas had serious competition in both the primary and general elections. In the primary, he trailed state Senator Brooks Douglass 36%–34%, who campaigned from his Oklahoma City base with a Western accent. In the runoff, Lucas ridiculed "some Johnny-come-lately dressed up like a drugstore cowboy" and carried all the rural areas to win 56%–44%. In the general, he faced Dan Webber, 27-year-old press secretary to outgoing Senator David Boren. Lucas ran an ad showing the U.S. Capitol ("this is where Dan Webber has worked his entire adult life") and Oklahoma farmland ("this is where Frank Lucas has worked his entire adult life") and benefited from Oklahoma Taxpayers Union ads and Christian Coalition voting guides, winning 54%–46%.

Lucas at times has had one of the most conservative voting records in the House, but he has a practical bent. As the representative (before redistricting) of the site of the Oklahoma City bombing, he introduced the resolution condemning it, the bill for relief spending and the bill to authorize the bombing monument and make it part of the national parks system. He supported the 1995 antiterrorism bill and, after the Oklahoma City trial was moved to Denver, sponsored the amendments to allow closed-circuit broadcasting of out-of-town trials and to allow bombing victims, survivors and relatives to watch the trial and still testify in the sentencing hearing. On more traditional constituent service, he hailed the base-closing commission's decision to close two other maintenance depots and keep open Oklahoma City's Tinker Air Force Base. He delivered assistance to contemporary Indians, making it easier for seven tribes in Oklahoma to lease mineral rights to their land. He led a successful House effort to rehabilitate the nation's small watershed dams, which tend to deteriorate after 50 years—not a hot news topic on Capitol Hill, but important to the many Americans who depend on them. Of the nation's more than 10,000 dams to control flash flooding, most are on private property and almost 20% are in Oklahoma. On the 2002 farm bill, as a subcommittee chairman, he helped to unravel the 1996 Freedom to Farm Act that he had once embraced. He helped write the conservation incentives to control erosion, and protect air and water quality, and he said that the package would be good for agriculture-dependent Oklahoma.

Lucas has been re-elected by wide margins. Redistricting posed a threat, because Oklahoma lost a district in the 2000 Census, and the Democratic legislature wanted to put two Republican incumbents together in the same district. But one incumbent, Republican Wes Watkins, decided to retire, and a state court drew a plan that protected the other five. Lucas's main obstacle is the physical size of the district: From his home in Cheyenne, it extends 80 miles south, 240 miles west to the Panhandle, and 270 miles east to Tulsa's outskirts. His 2002 election proved effortless. His sole opponent was an independent with libertarian views, and Lucas was reelected with 76% of the vote. Indeed, the only trouble Lucas encounters seems to be on his ranch: he broke his nose seven years ago when a cow slammed a gate on him and lost a tooth in March 2003 while trying to attach an identification tag to a 250-pound heifer.

FOURTH DISTRICT

Rep. Tom Cole (R)

Elected 2002, 1st term; b. April 28, 1949, Shreveport, LA; home, Moore; Grinnell Col., B.A. 1971, Yale U., M.A. 1974, U. of OK, Ph.D. 1984; Methodist; married (Ellen).

Elected Office: OK Senate, 1988–91.

Professional Career: OK Repub. Party chmn, 1985–89; Exec. Dir. NRCC, 1991–95, OK Secy. of State, 1995–99; Pol. consultant, 2000-present.

DC Office: 501 CHOB 20515, 202-225-6165; Fax: 202-225-3512; Web site: www.house.gov/cole.

District Offices: Ada, 580-436-5375; Lawton, 580-357-2131; Norman, 405-329-6500.

Committees: *Armed Services* (25th of 33 R): Readiness; Total Force. *Education & the Workforce* (20th of 27 R): 21st Century Competitiveness; Employer-Employee Relations. *Resources* (24th of 28 R): Energy & Mineral Resources.

Group Ratings and Key Votes: Newly Elected

Election Results

2002 general	Tom Cole (R)	106,452	(54%)	($1,261,547)
	Darryl Roberts (D)	91,322	(46%)	($563,729)
2002 primary	Tom Cole (R)	21,789	(60%)	
	Marc Nuttle (R)	11,944	(33%)	
	Other	2,793	(8%)	
2000 general	J.C. Watts (R)	114,000	(65%)	($1,546,659)
	Larry Weatherford (D)	54,808	(31%)	($57,455)
	Other	6,876	(4%)	

The People		Race/Ethnic Origin	Ancestry	
Area size:	10,409 sq. mi.	77.6% White	USA: 10.0%	German: 9.9%
Urban population:	63.3%	6.6% Black	Irish: 8.6%	
Rural population:	36.7%	1.7% Asian	**2000 Presidential Vote**	
Pop. 2000:	690,131	5.5% Native Am.	Bush (R) 144,568	(61%)
Median income:	$35,510	0.1% Hawaiian	Gore (D) 91,078	(38%)
Poverty status:	13.1%	3.6% Two+ races	Other 2,497	(1%)
Military veterans:	15.8%	0.1% Other	**Cook Partisan Voting Index:** R +12	
		4.8% Hispanic Origin		

Occupation	Blue collar: 26.4%	White collar: 57.2%	Gray collar: 16.5%

In the years just after 1900, the brown hills west of Oklahoma City and north of the Red River suddenly filled up with farmers riding north from Texas, past the well-watered green lands of the east toward the bare pasture lands of the west. These were young people with large families, and in the years since, this land has emptied out, as children have grown up and moved elsewhere and fewer hands are needed for farming. The first settlers here arrived just as the buffalo were dying out: from an estimated 60 million animals to no more than 1,000. So in 1901, President

William McKinley established the nation's first wildlife preserve in the Wichita Mountains, 25 miles northwest of Lawton. Fifteen bison were donated by the New York Zoological Society and arrived at the preserve via rail in 1907—a major factor in the survival of the species. Government has played a role in the survival of people, too, in this part of Oklahoma. Population in southwest Oklahoma clusters around major government institutions: The state capital in Oklahoma City; the University of Oklahoma in Norman, the Army Field Artillery Center at Fort Sill, near Lawton; the giant depot at Tinker Air Force Base.

These are major landmarks in the 4th Congressional District, which begins a few miles from the oil-derrick-surrounded state Capitol in Oklahoma City, smack dab in the middle of the state, and proceeds south and west to cover half of Oklahoma's Red River Valley. Demographically, this district is becoming more suburban, but the cultural tone remains country. That is true even in the Oklahoma City suburbs, which stretch out over the mile-grid roads, where in new subdivisions dust may still get tracked indoors and people still prefer chicken-fried steak to stir-fried chicken (though they eat both). At the same time there is technical sophistication here, at OU and at Fort Sill, where the Army will try out the cannon that will replace the Crusader, which Defense Secretary Donald Rumsfeld cancelled in 2002. Ancestrally, this is Democratic country, but Norman, Lawton and the Oklahoma City fringe now have voted pretty solidly Republican over the last decade.

The congressman from the 4th District is Tom Cole, a Republican elected in 2002 to fill the seat of J.C. Watts. A former college and professional football player, conservative Christian, African-American, and chairman of the House Republican Conference, Watts decided to leave politics—at least, for a while. Cole grew up in Moore, just south of Oklahoma City and north of Norman. He is a fifth-generation Oklahoman, and his mother was a state Representative and Senator; his father served in the Air Force and later worked at Tinker. Cole graduated from Grinnell College, took a masters degree at Yale, and got a Ph.D. in British history at the University of Oklahoma, studying for a year at the University of London. From 1985 to 1989, he was the state Republican Chairman in Oklahoma. In 1988, he was elected to the state Senate. He moved to Washington in 1991 as executive director of the National Republican Congressional Committee, then returned to Oklahoma and was appointed Secretary of State—the first Republican to hold that office. He went back to Washington to serve as chief of staff at the Republican National Committee in the 2000 campaign. During much of this period he was one of the partners in a polling and political consulting firm in Oklahoma City, whose clients have included three Republican presidents, Governor Frank Keating and J.C. Watts.

When Watts announced in July 2002 that he would not seek reelection, Cole moved quickly to run. Despite his party connections, he still faced formidable opposition. Watts endorsed Cole, but that failed to dissuade attorney Marc Nuttle running. The two had much in common—their positions on most issues, their party connections. Nuttle had been Cole's predecessor at the NRCC, and then worked on Pat Robertson's 1988 campaign; Nuttle and Cole worked together to pass a right-to-work law in a September 2001 referendum. In the showdown between the strategists, Nuttle called himself a "grass-roots" activist and Cole a "party" activist who raised half his campaign funds from outside the state, much of it from other consultants. But Cole proved to be the stronger candidate. He won 60% of the vote in the August primary, in which two-thirds of the votes were cast in metro Oklahoma City (which includes Norman).

Cole also had tough competition in the general election, from former state senate Majority Leader Darryl Roberts, who defeated Watts's 1998 opponent 48%–34% in the Democratic primary. Amid talk of war in Iraq, Roberts argued that his service of more than 30 years in the Marine Corps, including a stint in Vietnam, taught him about duty and honor; he was appealing to the "yellow dog" Democratic tradition that is particularly strong in the Red River counties. Cole countered by citing the Democratic presidential nominees Roberts had supported, and described him as "pro-tax," "pro-abortion," and "pro-lawsuit." Roberts had only limited national party support; Cole had much more and won 54%–46%. Roberts carried eight of the 16 counties, all in the southern part of the district. But Cole built up larger majorities in the urban areas: In Norman-based Cleveland County, which cast nearly one-third of the total vote, he won 58%.

His strongest support was in the metro Oklahoma City counties where he won by more than 17,000 votes.

During the campaign, Speaker Dennis Hastert promised Cole a seat on the Armed Services Committee, of obvious importance to the district. With his party background, Cole seems likely to be an instant insider within the Republican Conference.

FIFTH DISTRICT

Rep. Ernest Istook (R)

Elected 1992, 6th term; b. Feb. 11, 1950, Ft. Worth, TX; home, Warr Acres; Baylor U., B.A. 1971, OK City U. Law Schl., J.D. 1976; Mormon; married (Judy).

Elected Office: OK House of Reps., 1986–92.

Professional Career: Political reporter, Oklahoma City KOMA Radio, 1972–73, WKY Radio, 1973–76; Dir., OK Alcohol Beverage Control Bd., 1977; Practicing atty., 1977–92.

DC Office: 2404 RHOB 20515, 202-225-2132; Fax: 202-226-1463; Web site: www.house.gov/istook.

District Offices: Oklahoma City, 405-234-9900; Seminole, 405-303-2868; Shawnee, 405-237-6202.

Committees: *Appropriations* (10th of 36 R): District of Columbia; Labor, HHS & Education; Transportation, Treasury, & Independent Agencies (Chmn.). *Select Committee on Homeland Security* (18th of 27 R): Infrastructure & Border Security.

Group Ratings

	ADA	ACLU	AFS	LCV	CON	ITIC	NTU	COC	ACU	NTLC	CHC
2002	5	7	11	13	56	100	61	90	92	97	100
2001	0	—	0	0	—	—	68	91	100	—	—

National Journal Ratings

	2001 LIB	—	2001 CONS		2002 LIB	—	2002 CONS
Economic	0%	—	94%		36%	—	61%
Social	0%	—	81%		0%	—	75%
Foreign	14%	—	85%		0%	—	85%

Key Votes of the 107th Congress

1. Approve Bush Tax Cuts	Y	5. Faith-Based Charities	Y	9. Trade Promotion Authority	Y
2. Limit Patients' Bill of Rights	Y	6. Bar Gays in the Boy Scouts	Y	10. Bar Funds for Intl. Court	Y
3. Campaign Finance Reform	N	7. Ban Partial-Birth Abortion	Y	11. Authorize Force in Iraq	Y
4. Ban ANWR Development	N	8. Arm Commercial Pilots	Y	12. Deny Home. Sec. Dept. Union	Y

Election Results

2002 general	Ernest Istook (R)	121,374	(62%)	($794,780)
	Lou Barlow (D)	63,208	(32%)	($232,697)
	Donna Davis (I)	10,469	(5%)	
2002 primary	Ernest Istook (R)	unopposed		
2000 general	Ernest Istook (R)	134,159	(68%)	($520,608)
	Garland McWatters (D)	53,275	(27%)	($22,401)
	Other	8,588	(4%)	

Prior Winning Percentages: 1998 (68%); 1996 (70%); 1994 (78%); 1992 (53%)

The People		Race/Ethnic Origin	Ancestry	
Area size:	2,089 sq. mi.	67.7% White	German: 9.7%	Irish: 7.7%
Urban population:	87.5%	13.6% Black	USA: 7.6%	
Rural population:	12.5%	2.5% Asian	**2000 Presidential Vote**	
Pop. 2000:	690,131	4.4% Native Am.	Bush (R) 135,761 (62%)	
Median income:	$33,893	0.1% Hawaiian	Gore (D) 82,584 (38%)	
Poverty status:	15.8%	3.3% Two + races	Other .1,338 (1%)	
Military veterans:	14.2%	0.1% Other	**Cook Partisan Voting Index:** R +13	
		8.3% Hispanic Origin		

Occupation   Blue collar: 23.6%   White collar: 60.6%   Gray collar: 15.8%

Oklahoma City, like many state capitals, was not the spontaneous creation of commerce but the deliberate creation of government, sited in the geographic center of the state, on what turned out to be oil lands. Oil rigs were pumping crude on the grounds of the then-domeless Capitol until 1989; a derrick still stands sentinel outside the governor's window. The land here is browner and more eroded by creeks than the greener, rolling Oklahoma farmland farther east. From its center Oklahoma City has grown far out into the countryside, followed, as in so many southwestern cities, by expanding city limits so that it extends into five counties and three congressional districts and covers 624 square miles. Oklahoma City became the center of the nation's attention in April 1995, when a bomb destroyed the Alfred P. Murrah Federal Building, killing 168 and injuring more than 500. The profound grief has persisted here, but was channeled effectively into the construction of a memorial on the site of the blast, dedicated movingly exactly five years later in April 2000.

The 5th Congressional District includes most of Oklahoma County and Oklahoma City, including the heavily black neighborhoods that before the 2002 redistricting were in the old 6th District; it does not include a small section of the county including Midwest City and Tinker Air Force Base. (Oklahoma, which lost a House seat in the 2000 Census, doesn't have a 6th District any more.) Added in redistricting were Pottawatomie and Seminole Counties to the east. These two counties partake of the ancestral Democratic leanings of most of Oklahoma. But Oklahoma City is solidly Republican in state as well as national politics.

The congressman from the 5th District is Ernest Istook, first elected in 1992, in his views and attitudes a forerunner of the Republican freshmen of 1994. With heavy turnover, he became in just two terms the most senior of the state's House delegation. Istook is the grandson of Hungarian immigrants; after graduating from Baylor, he was a radio reporter in Oklahoma City and went to law school at night. He attracted attention as head of Governor David Boren's alcohol control board when he refused to stop an investigation of liquor distributors. He practiced law and was elected to the Oklahoma House in 1986. In 1992, he ran for the House, taking on 16-year incumbent Republican Mickey Edwards, who had 386 overdrafts on the House bank. Edwards finished third in the primary, with 26% to 32% for Istook and 37% for 1990 gubernatorial nominee Bill Price, who harshly criticized Edwards. Istook ran on conservative issues and won the runoff 56%–44%. He won the general election by only 53%–47% over oil and gas lawyer Laurie Williams, who attacked Istook for his anti-abortion stance. He has been easily re-elected since.

Istook has a very conservative voting record and has used his seat on Appropriations to press for various controversial amendments. One was his 1995 effort to ban organizations that receive federal funds from using more than 5% of their money for lobbying. This was fought vociferously by nonprofits; both houses passed different forms of the Istook amendment, but no limit was passed.

Istook was the chief sponsor of the Religious Freedom amendment, which came to a vote in a revised form in June 1998; it stated, "The people's right to pray and to recognize their religious belief, heritage or tradition on public property, including schools, shall not be infringed. The government shall not require any person to join in prayer, initiate or designate school prayers, discriminate against religion, or deny equal access to a benefit on account of religion." It got 224 votes, well short of the required two-thirds, and short of the 240 a school prayer amendment received the last time it reached the floor, in 1971. But Istook has had some successes. A proposal to require schools and libraries to use software to screen Internet pornography was voted into a 2001 appropriation bill; in November 2002, the Supreme Court agreed to hear an appeal of a lower court ruling that it violated the First Amendment.

Istook is the only Oklahoman on an appropriations committee, but has declined to use his seat to bring home pork. He refused to back J.C. Watts' attempts to get federal funds for building a dome for the Oklahoma Capitol (the state ran out of money in 1915 and finished the project only in 2002) and he doesn't think much of Amtrak's Heartland Flyer that runs from Oklahoma City to Fort Worth (though it is a great favorite of Senator Don Nickles). But in September 2002, he did seek $3 million for the design of a Maintenance Repair Overhaul Technology Center near Tinker Air Force Base; that funding was later scaled back to $729,000. In 2002, he opposed the Democrats' prescription drug plan as "the straw that breaks the camel's back" of Medicare and the Republicans' prescription drug plan as political pandering in an election year. He voted for an Internet tax moratorium in October 2001, but now favors a moratorium only on special taxes, like an Internet access tax. He and North Dakota Senator Byron Dorgan in 2002 sponsored a bill to enable states to tax Internet transactions, by encouraging them to enter an interstate compact to write uniform definitions of taxable goods and services; he said that failure to pass it would destroy the sales tax base of states and localities.

In 1999, Istook became chairman of the D.C. Appropriations Subcommittee, and thus a member of the "College of Cardinals." In 2001, he became chairman of the Treasury-Postal Appropriations subcommittee, which supervises the White House budget. His first major project was to investigate whether taxpayers should subsidize a New York City penthouse office for President Clinton. In March 2002, he criticized the Bush administration for not providing enough information on homeland security and threatened to withhold the $329 million appropriation for the Executive Office of the President unless Homeland Security chief Tom Ridge testified before Congress.

Redistricting was Istook's major political problem in 2002. Oklahoma lost a seat in the 2000 Census, and the Democratic legislature wanted to eliminate one of the state's Republican-held districts. For two decades, the 5th District had an ungainly shape, combining Republican parts of Oklahoma City with rural and small city Republican counties to the north; Democrats wanted to siphon off Republican votes from adjacent districts. In early 2002, the state House wanted to combine part of Oklahoma City with heavily Democratic Little Dixie counties to the south and southeast; the state Senate wanted to combine part of Oklahoma City with rural northwest Oklahoma and put Istook in the same district with Republican colleague Frank Lucas. Republican Governor Frank Keating said he would veto either plan. But after 3d District Republican Wes Watkins announced his retirement, a state court judge in May 2002 approved a plan that would protect the five remaining incumbents. The 5th District now is much more compact—most of Oklahoma County with two small counties to the east—and heavily Republican, though less Republican than before redistricting. As Istook said, "We've got Oklahoma City pulled back together after decades of gerrymandering." He was reelected easily in November 2002 and seems able to win easily for the next decade.

★ OREGON ★

O regon is an experimental commonwealth and laboratory of reform on the Pacific Rim, a maker of national trends. It is far removed from where most Americans live, but closer in touch with the rest of America than sometimes appears: Within minutes after a tree branch brushed a power line in Oregon in August 1996, the entire western power grid shut down all the way from the Canadian border to San Diego, where the Republican National Convention was opening two days later. Oregon has led the nation with bike trails and Nike sneakers, light rail trams and Pendleton shirts, with assisted suicide and mail-in ballots. Oregon is an affluent high-tech civilization where one can still see much the same land and water—and rain—that Lewis and Clark saw in 1805 when they came down the Columbia River gorge, past what is now Portland, to the vast Pacific Ocean.

This Oregon was settled by Americans when John Jacob Astor set up his fur trading post at Astoria in 1811 and when New England Yankees in the 1840s rode the Oregon Trail and floated down the Columbia to the well-watered Willamette Valley. In this remote land, nearly 2,000 miles from the Mississippi River frontier and 700 miles from the small settlements of California, they built an orderly, productive society—a kind of western New England. It grew steadily over the

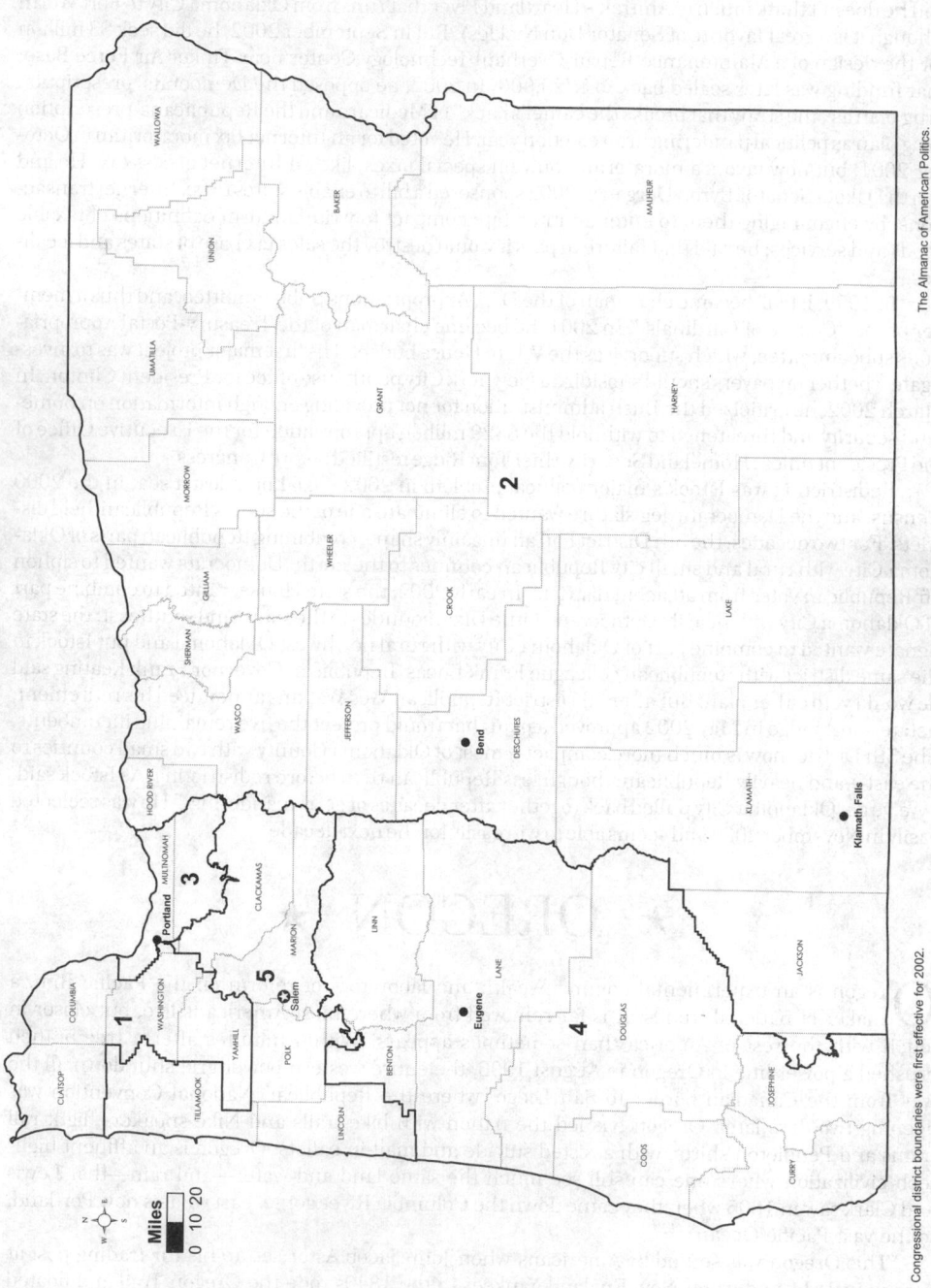

The Almanac of American Politics.
National Journal

Congressional district boundaries were first effective for 2002.

years, with a few booms—when timber, always its first industry, surged in 1900–10, during the war and after in the 1940s, and in the 1970s when home building skyrocketed and Oregon's natural environment began to be widely appreciated.

Today's Oregon seems confident it can live comfortably with growth and cope with slowdowns. In the 1990s it was the nation's 10th fastest-growing state; its population rose 20%. Its newcomers are highly educated, sparkplugs of the economic growth that leaves employers begging for workers. The newcomers fill Portland's postmodern skyscrapers and high-tech offices in Silicon Forest to the west, and they prosper and invent in the smaller cities and towns of the green Willamette Valley and the sere lands of eastern Oregon as well. The high-tech slowdown gave Oregon the highest unemployment rate in the nation, peaking at 8.1% in February 2002 but far below the levels of the early 1980s: An inconvenience, not a disaster.

Newcomers find a state that has a distinctive culture. Founded by New England Yankees accustomed to town meeting government, Oregonians nearly a century ago pioneered in bringing the people closer to government: This was the first state to pass initiative and referendum, recall of elected officials, and election of U.S. senators by popular vote. It was also the first state to institute Labor Day, workmen's compensation and the eight-hour workday for women. In recent decades Oregon, founded by New England churchmen, has become America's most unchurched state, with the lowest rate of church membership, with large numbers of believers in astrology, New Age spiritualism and the like. To the innovations of this cultural left, the public voices of Oregon's big institutions, like those of New England, have been friendly. Oregon over the last two generations produced the first bottle-deposit law, decriminalized medical marijuana, legalized most abortions before *Roe v. Wade*, and backed limits on development and use of property. It is one of two states that ban self-service gas (the other is New Jersey). A gun control law passed banning semi-automatic weapons, and weekly betting on professional sports games was legalized. The Portland area has limited development and set aside green space, to the point that metropolitan area housing prices have risen to among the highest in the nation. When Enron-owned Portland General Electric was put up for sale in 2002, the city of Portland made a bid: Publicization in an era of privatization.

Innovative health care policy has been an Oregon specialty. It legalized assisted suicide, in referenda in 1994 and 1997, to the point that doctors can prescribe but not administer lethal drugs; since 1997, 129 people have killed themselves, and Attorney General John Ashcroft angered many Oregonians by announcing in November 2001 that the federal government would prosecute doctors prescribing lethal drugs; a federal judge quickly blocked that, and the government's appeal went to court in May 2003.

Another Oregon innovation was Governor John Kitzhaber's Oregon Health Plan that went into effect in 1994. State Medicaid officials drew up a list of 696 (now 745) medical treatments and ranked them by effectiveness and importance to basic health. Then based on cost estimates, the state decides how many treatments it can afford, and draws a line—originally it was at 606, currently it is at 581. Above the line, the state will pay; below, it won't. This can raise poignant issues: Should an 18-year-old with cystic fibrosis receive a $250,000 liver and lung transplant? These questions are often avoided because the rules aren't always applied by private managed care plans that have Medicaid contracts with the state; it is said that doctors often game the system. In the meantime, costs rose from $435 million in 1993–94 to an estimated $933 million in 2003–04—nearly $130 million over the state's budget for the health plan.

In 1996 Oregonians voted by mail only for a special U.S. Senate election; in 1998 they voted by referendum to hold all elections that way. So in November 2000 and 2002 there were no polls open in Oregon on Election Day; voters had until that night to get their ballots to the election clerk. Unfortunately, Oregon has no statewide registry, so people could cast votes in multiple counties; also, some voters handed ballots to people standing outside clerks' offices who said they would file them—"snatching" ballots, some said. Proponents of mail-in ballots argue that they increase the percentage of eligibles who vote, which has always been high in Oregon anyway, and they give voters time to read over and think about the numerous ballot initiatives.

Oregon does indeed have as many ballot initiatives as any state—sometimes more. In 1998 voters approved medical marijuana, mail-in ballots and the unsealing of adoption records, and the state granted health care and other benefits to employees' domestic partners. But they rejected a ban on clear-cut logging and required notice to property owners of proposed zoning changes. In November 2000 there were 26 initiatives on the ballot, more than in any state since North Dakota in 1932; the voters' guide ran 376 pages. In 2002, there were only 12 initiatives. Voters rejected 79%–21% universal health care, to be financed by an 11.5% tax on business payrolls and an income tax rise from 9% to 17%—perhaps a gauge of national opinion on this issue. They voted to allow denturists to install partial dentures, to raise the minimum wage to $6.90 and to ban payment based on number of petition signatures obtained (will this hobble future petition drives?); they voted 70%–30% against labeling genetically-engineered foods and against allowing voters under 21 to serve as state legislators. A mixed bag, in other words: Oregonians vote conservative on some ballot initiatives, liberal on others. One common thread seems to be a regard for personal autonomy and a readiness to discard traditional rules and ways of doing things. Another seems to be a desire for putting some limits on the ability of officeholders to spend public money. Voting on most of these measures has followed similar patterns, with Portland and the university towns of Eugene and Corvallis taking liberal positions and counties east of the Cascades and outside the metro area taking more conservative stands—the same pattern seen in seriously contested partisan elections.

These cultural differences have been reflected increasingly in Oregon's partisan politics. Back in the 1960s, this state showed only the mildest of regional variations in partisan preference and was disposed to support articulate moderate Republicans, like its two long-term senators, Mark Hatfield (1967–97) and Bob Packwood (1969–95). But in the 1980s and 1990s, cultural splits have sometimes favored first Portland-oriented Democrats and sometimes conservative Republicans. The balance has shifted back and forth. Oregon voted for Michael Dukakis in 1988 and for Bill Clinton twice, but Clinton's margin was smaller in 1996 than 1992, and in 2000 Al Gore won here by only 47.0%–46.5%. Starting in 1986, Oregon has elected only Democratic governors, though only once by a wide margin; starting in 1994, it has elected Republican legislatures, except in 2002 when it produced an evenly split state Senate. Oregon's U.S. Senate elections have produced a kind of balance as well. In 1996 Oregon had two open-seat Senate contests, one in January to replace Packwood after his 1995 resignation, the other in November to replace Hatfield, who retired after 30 years. Both were decided by narrow margins. In the January election, the nation's first election conducted by mail-in ballots, Democrat Ron Wyden, from Portland, beat Republican Gordon Smith, from eastern Oregon, 48%–47%. In November Smith ran again, and beat Democrat Tom Bruggere 50%–46%.

Environmental issues have played a role in the polarization of Oregon voters, and in both directions. Limiting growth and protecting the environment are issues that have worked for Democrats in Portland and its suburbs since the 1970s, reducing or eliminating Republican margins in affluent suburbs and hugely increasing Democratic margins in the city of Portland. But in the rest of Oregon, specific environmental issues have cut the other way. Logging in the Pacific Northwest was largely wiped out because of restrictions imposed to protect the threatened spotted owl (parks officials have been known to fake evidence of owl habitation). The logging counties of southwest Oregon turned against Democrats, to the point that George W. Bush carried the 4th Congressional District which also includes the university town of Eugene in 2000. The Clinton administration entertained a proposal to breach dams on the Snake River in Idaho, which would have reduced water supplies for farmers in eastern Oregon; George W. Bush opposed breaching while Al Gore refused to take a stand on the issue, which is one reason why Bush came within a few votes of carrying this state which his father lost by a wide margin in 1988. In 2001 the Interior Department cut off water to 1,000 farmers in the Klamath Basin, to protect the endangered and in any case unhappily named sucker fish. This became a major issue in local media and helps explain why parched eastern Oregon, which once elected the Democratic Chairman of the Ways and Means Committee, has become as heavily Republican as Portland is Democratic.

The People		Race/Ethnic Origin			Military veterans: 388,990 (15.1%)	
Pop. 2000:	3,421,399	2,857,616	83.5%	White	WWII: 20.6%	Korea: 13.0%
Pop. 1990:	2,842,321	53,325	1.6%	Black	Vietnam: 33.9%	Gulf War: 8.5%
Change 1990–2000:	Up 20.4%	100,333	2.9%	Asian	**Most populous cities:**	
Change 1980–1990:	Up 7.9%	40,130	1.2%	Native Am.	1. Portland	529,121
% of U.S. total:	1.2%	7,398	0.2%	Hawaiian	2. Eugene	137,893
Pop. rank:	28th of 50	82,733	2.4%	Two + races	3. Salem	136,924
Area size:	98,381 sq. mi.	4,550	0.1%	Other	4. Gresham	90,205
State Native:	45.3%	275,314	8.0%	Hisp. Origin	5. Beaverton	76,129
Non-citizen:	5.6%	**Ancestry**			Urban population: 78.7%	
Language		German: 14.8%		English: 9.5%	Rural population: 21.3%	
English: 86.7%	Spanish: 6.7%	Irish: 8.6%		USA: 4.6%		
Other Eur.: 3.5%		Norwegian: 3.1%				

Education		Work Sector		Legislature	
H.S. Grad:	85.1%	Private: 76.3%	Govt: 14.4%	Senate	15 D 15 R
College Grad:	25.1%	Self: 8.9%	Family: 0.4%	House	35 R 25 D
Industry		Unemployment: 6.5%		Legislative Term Limits: No	
Agri: 3.2%	Con: 6.9%	**Household Income**		**Registered Voters**	
Fin: 6.1%	Info: 2.4%	<15k: 15.1%	15-35k: 27.3%	D: 726,655	(38.8%)
Mfg: 19.1%	Prof: 28.1%	35-50k: 17.7%	50-100k: 29.9%	R: 682,367	(36.5%)
Public: 4.4%	Trade: 16.5%	100-150k: 6.5%	>150k: 3.5%	I: 463,063	(24.7%)
Other: 13.2%		Median: $40,916			
Occupation		Poverty status: 11.6%			
Blue collar: 23.9%	White collar: 59.1%	**Home Value**			
Gray collar: 17.0%		<50k: 7.8% 50-100k: 16.5% 100-200k: 49.9% 200-300k: 16.2%			
		300-500k: 7.2% >500k: 2.4% Median: $145,800			

Presidential politics Oregon was once the most Republican state in the West, voting for Thomas Dewey over Harry Truman in 1948; in the 1980s and early 1990s it was one of the most Democratic. Now it seems more evenly balanced, much less Democratic than California, more Republican than the Rocky Mountain states. As compared to 1988, the 2000 Democratic percentage was flat and the Republican percentage up. One reason was the showing of Ralph Nader, who won 4% here in 1996, his best showing that year, and 5% in 2000. Oregon seems likely to be a target state in 2004.

Oregon once had an important presidential primary, scheduled in May. In 1948 Oregon ended Harold Stassen's serious presidential prospects, when he lost 52%–48% to Dewey; in 1968 Oregon gave Robert Kennedy his only defeat when it voted 44%–38% for Eugene McCarthy. Oregon in those days was part of a West Coast campaign swing, just before the California primary; at a time when campaigners were not used to flying all over the country they, like National Football League teams in the 1950s, scheduled West Coast contests together to minimize travel time. For 1992 and 1996, Oregon scheduled its primary for Super Tuesday in March, but it was overshadowed by bigger contests in the South. In 2000 the primary was held again in May. Few candidates remained. George W. Bush beat Alan Keyes and Al Gore beat Lyndon LaRouche.

2000 Presidential Vote
Gore (D)	720,342	(47%)
Bush (R)	713,577	(47%)
Nader (Green)	77,357	(5%)
Other	22,692	(1%)

2000 Republican Presidential Primary
Bush (R)	292,522	(84%)
Keyes (R)	46,764	(13%)
Other	10,545	(3%)

2000 Democratic Presidential Primary
Gore (D)	300,922	(85%)
LaRouche (D)	38,521	(11%)
Other	15,151	(4%)

1996 Presidential Vote
Clinton (D)	649,631	(47%)
Dole (R)	538,155	(39%)
Perot (I)	121,218	(9%)
Other	68,746	(5%)

Congressional districting

Oregon's new congressional map looks a lot like the one it replaced. This was not what the Republican-controlled legislature originally set out to do. Republican redistricters intended to alter the boundaries of the marginal 1st District by shifting solidly Democratic western Multnomah County (1st District Congressman David Wu's political base) from the 1st to the 3d District—an attempt to pack Democratic voters into the 3d while making the 1st more competitive for a Republican challenger. But in June 2001, Democratic Governor John Kitzhaber vetoed the Republican plan; the case was heard by a Multnomah County judge who chose the Democratic alternative in October, saying it was less disruptive and that it better preserved communities of interest. The decision, for the most part, left the old map in place with the exception of a few Multnomah County neighborhoods that were added to the 5th District.

Governor

Ted Kulongoski (D)

Elected 2002, term expires Jan. 2007, 1st term; b. Nov. 5, 1940, Missouri; home, Portland; U. of MO, B.A. 1967, J.D. 1970; Catholic; married (Mary).

Military Career: Marine Corps, 1959–63.

Elected Office: OR House of Reps., 1974–78; OR Senate, 1978–82; OR Atty. Gen., 1992–96; OR Sup. Ct., 1996–01.

Professional Career: Practicing atty., 1971–87; OR Insurance Commissioner, 1982–92.

Office: 160 State Capitol, 900 Court St., Salem, 97301, 503-378-3111; Fax: 503-378-6827; Web site: www.governor.state.or.us.

Election Results

2002 general	Ted Kulongoski (D)	618,004	(49%)
	Kevin Mannix (R)	581,785	(46%)
	Tom Cox (Lib)	57,760	(5%)
2002 primary	Ted Kulongoski (D)	170,799	(49%)
	Jim Hill (D)	92,294	(26%)
	Bev Stein (D)	76,517	(22%)
1998 general	John Kitzhaber (D)	717,061	(64%)
	Bill Sizemore (R)	334,001	(30%)
	Other	62,036	(6%)

Ted Kulongoski (pronounced *koo-lun-GAW-ski*), elected governor of Oregon in 2002, comes from as humble a background as any governor. He was born in rural Missouri; after his father died he was raised by nuns in a boys' home from age 4 to 14. He joined the Marine Corps after high school and later saved enough money working in a steel mill and as a truck driver to attend the University of Missouri; he graduated from college and law school there at 26 and 29. He moved to Eugene and practiced labor law, representing mostly labor unions; as a legislative staffer he helped write a law giving public employee unions collective bargaining rights. He was elected to the Oregon House in 1974 and the Oregon Senate in 1978; he was regarded as a champion of labor unions. In 1980 he ran against Senator Bob Packwood and held him to a 52%–44% victory in a Republican year. In 1982 he ran against Governor Victor Atiyeh and lost by the humiliating margin of 61%–36%—the last time a Republican was elected governor here. He returned to law practice and in 1987 was appointed Insurance Commissioner by Governor Neil Goldschmidt and helped reform workmen's compensation. In 1992 he was elected Attorney General (Oregon elects its downballot officials in presidential years); in 1996 he was elected to the Oregon Supreme Court. In 2001 he resigned to run for governor.

The overriding issue facing state government at the time was the budget shortfall. The great achievement of Governor John Kitzhaber, a physician elected in 1994 and 1998, was the Oregon Health Plan, which expanded Medicaid by rationing treatments. But as revenue flows weakened, the number of treatments it provided had to be reduced, and by November 2001 the budget shortfall was estimated at $720 million in a $16 billion budget. Oregon's revenue stream is especially volatile, because the state has no sales tax and relies heavily on the income tax; in addition, since 1990's Measure 5 limits property tax increases, the state provides 80% of school funding. In June 2002 Kitzhaber proposed raising the top income tax from 9% to 9.8%, but the Republican legislature refused. Budget problems kept making the news during the 2002 campaign cycle; altogether there were five special sessions of the legislature and constant news about shortfalls and cuts.

Of the six major candidates, three Democrats and three Republicans, Kulongoski was the best known: He had appeared on the statewide ballot four times in the last 22 years and had served in the legislative, executive and judicial branches of state government. He argued that he had the experience to solve the state's major problems—unemployment, the budget, school financing, the state employees' pension fund. Kitzhaber and the preceding two Democratic governors, Barbara Roberts and Goldschmidt, quickly endorsed him. With his longtime ties to unions, the AFL-CIO, the State Police Officers Association, the United Food and Commercial Workers and the Teamsters also endorsed him. So did the Confederated Tribes of Grande Ronde, operators of the state's largest casino. Against former state Treasurer Jim Hill and former Multnomah County Commission Chairman Bev Stein, Kulongoski depicted himself as the more moderate candidate and pitched his message to older voters and moderates. With late contributions from public employees unions, he outspent the others and won the May 2002 primary with 49% of the vote, to 26% for Hill and 22% for Stein.

The Republicans had a closer contest. The candidate of the party establishment was former Labor and Industries Commissioner Jack Roberts, who cast himself as a moderate. Former Portland school board member Ron Saxton also ran as a moderate and stressed that he was not a career politician. The most intriguing candidate was Kevin Mannix, a Democratic state representative from 1988 to 1996 and Democratic candidate for attorney general in 1996 (he was a young McGovern delegate at the 1972 Democratic National Convention). He switched parties in 1997 and was elected to the state Senate as a Republican in 1998 and came close to winning as the Republican candidate for attorney general in 2000. Mannix was a prolific drafter of legislation— 135 of his bills became law in 10 years—and a sponsor of ballot initiatives—his parental consent for abortion lost in 1992 but three tough on crime measures won in 1996. In 1995 he attracted attention with a bill to ban artificial insemination of unmarried women. Mannix was known in Salem for sitting at the front of the legislature, commenting on any and all legislation and quickly drafting amendments and new bills. He ran as a "populist Republican," pledged to oppose new taxes and solidly opposed to abortion. Mannix was endorsed by Oregon Right to Life and his campaign kept alive by $81,000 in loans from individuals during the last two weeks. He squeaked out a win with 35% of the vote, to 29% for Roberts and 28% for Saxton.

After the primaries, Kulongoski called Mannix "divisive" and criticized him for using the abortion issue in the primary. Mannix replied that he wouldn't focus on cultural issues as governor and would defend Oregon's assisted suicide law and not take the initiative on abortion or gay rights. The campaign focused more on fiscal issues. In September the legislature made more cuts in planned spending and authorized a January 2003 special referendum, on a three-year increase in the top income tax from 9% to 9.8%. Kulongoski supported the proposal, reluctantly he said; Mannix opposed it, and said he could make enough cuts to make it unnecessary. The measure failed 54%–46%. Kulongoski called for doubling car registration fees to $30 (which would still be the lowest in the nation) to pay for repairing bridges, and he said that localities should pay a greater share for education and that he would try to develop a consensus for a permanent, stable funding base for them, with everything on the table including a sales tax—long verboten in Oregon. He called for all children to be covered by the Oregon Health Plan and added that that would mean removing some adults now covered. He opposed the Bush forest plan and said he would continue Vermont-style civil unions. He criticized Mannix for voting for a cigarette tax increase as part of a budget package. Mannix campaigned with gusto and good humor and seemed more articulate in debate; the tax issue was one that could unite Republicans and brought large contributions in the last weeks.

By all measures—party label, experience and familiarity, the positions on abortion—Kulongoski seemed to be an easy winner. But on election night Mannix was ahead in the count. In Oregon voters cast their votes by mail or at election clerks' offices, and have up to Election Day to get them to the clerks. It takes time to process and count the votes cast on Election Day, and the clerks' offices in big counties took time to count them. The big counties, especially Multnomah (Portland) and Lane (Eugene), took several days, and it was not until Wednesday evening that it was clear that Kulongoski was well ahead and Mannix conceded. When all the votes were in, Kulongoski won 49%–46%; Mannix lost by a smaller margin than the number of votes cast for the Libertarian, as had happened in the 2000 attorney general race. Kulongoski carried Multnomah County 66%–29% and the Portland metro area by 54%–41%. Kulongoski carried only eight of 36 counties—Multnomah, the counties containing the state's two big universities, three on the Pacific coast and two on the Columbia River on either side of Portland. Mannix carried eastern Oregon 58%–37% and southwest Oregon 54%–41%.

Kulongoski was left to ponder the state's fiscal problems and to campaign for Measure 28 in December and January. He also had to deal with the Warm Springs Tribe's demand, opposed by the Grande Ronde Confederation, to build a casino at Cascade Locks, just 40 miles up the Columbia River from Portland. Observers speculated whether he would seek concessions from the public employee unions that have supported him strongly throughout his political career.

Senior Senator

Ron Wyden (D)

Elected Jan. 1996, seat up 2004, 1st term; b. May 3, 1949, Wichita, KS; home, Portland; Stanford U., B.A. 1971, U. of OR, J.D. 1974; Jewish; divorced.

Elected Office: U.S. House of Reps., 1980–96.

Professional Career: Co–Dir. & Co–Founder, OR Gray Panthers, 1974–80; Dir., OR Legal Svcs. for the Elderly, 1977–79; Prof. of Gerontology, U. of OR, 1976, Portland St. U., 1979, U. of Portland, 1980.

DC Office: 516 HSOB, 20510, 202-224-5244; Fax: 202-228-2717; Web site: wyden.senate.gov.

State Offices: Bend, 541-330-9142; Eugene, 541-431-0229; LaGrande, 541-962-7691; Medford, 541-858-5122; Portland, 503-326-7525; Salem, 503-589-4555.

Committees: *Aging (Special). Budget. Commerce, Science & Transportation*: Aviation; Communications; Consumer Affairs & Product Safety (RMM); Science, Technology & Space; Surface Transportation & Merchant Marine. *Energy & Natural Resources*: Public Lands & Forests (RMM); Water & Power. *Environment & Public Works*: Fisheries, Wildlife & Water; Superfund & Waste Management. *Intelligence (Select)*.

Group Ratings

	ADA	ACLU	AFS	LCV	CON	ITIC	NTU	COC	ACU	NTLC	CHC
2002	85	60	75	76	36	88	25	60	15	21	—
2001	95	—	92	88	—	—	17	43	8	—	0

National Journal Ratings

	2001 LIB	—	2001 CONS		2002 LIB	—	2002 CONS
Economic	74%	—	23%		73%	—	20%
Social	70%	—	20%		77%	—	18%
Foreign	87%	—	3%		76%	—	22%

Key Votes of the 107th Congress

1. Approve Bush Tax Cuts	N	5. Confirm Ashcroft as AG	N	9. Bar Coop. with Intl. Court	Y
2. Expand Patients' Rights	Y	6. Bar Gays in the Boy Scouts	N	10. Trade Promotion Authority	Y
3. Campaign Finance Reform	Y	7. $ for Hate Crime Prosecution	Y	11. Authorize Force in Iraq	N
4. Permit ANWR Development	N	8. Overseas Military Abortions	Y	12. Homeland Sec. Dept. Union	Y

Election Results

1998 general	Ron Wyden (D)	682,425	(61%)	($2,866,368)
	John Lim (R)	377,739	(34%)	($413,187)
	Other	57,583	(5%)	
1998 primary	Ron Wyden (D)	283,654	(92%)	
	John Sweeney (D)	25,456	(8%)	
	Other	853	(0%)	
1996 special	Ron Wyden (D)	571,739	(48%)	($4,237,134)
	Gordon Smith (R)	553,519	(47%)	($5,542,482)
	Other	56,392	(5%)	

Prior Winning Percentages: 1994 House (73%); 1992 House (77%); 1990 House (81%); 1988 House (99%); 1986 House (86%); 1984 House (72%); 1982 House (78%); 1980 House (72%)

Ron Wyden grew up in California, graduated from Stanford, and came to Oregon to attend the University of Oregon Law School. After graduating in 1974 he founded the Gray Panthers, an advocacy group for the elderly; his first foray into electoral politics was sponsoring a successful referendum reducing the price of dentures. In 1980, at 31, he challenged an incumbent in the heavily Democratic 3d District, which covers most of Portland, and won the primary 60%–40%. Wyden has a genius for coming up with sensible-sounding ideas no one else has thought of and a knack for making the counter-intuitive political alliances that are so helpful in passing unfamiliar measures through the House. He also worked hard to get a waiver for John Kitzhaber's Oregon Health Plan and salmon recovery plan, and to bring the abortifacient RU-486 to the United States.

When the Senate Ethics Committee recommended the expulsion of Bob Packwood in September 1995, Wyden, who had long been eyeing the seat, decided to run in the January 1996 special election to replace him—the first election Oregon conducted by mail-in ballot. With his home base in Portland, whose TV stations cover most of the state, he had greater name identification than any competitor. But he had spirited opposition in the primary from Eugene-based Congressman Peter DeFazio, who carried his own district overwhelmingly, holding Wyden to a 50%–44% win. The Republican nomination was won by state Senate President Gordon Smith, a frozen vegetable tycoon from eastern Oregon who ultimately spent $2 million of his own money. Most polls had the race in a dead heat and there were many negative ads; toward the end, Wyden said he would pull his negative spots. Wyden picked up strength the week before the January 30 deadline and won 48%–47%.

In the Senate, Wyden continued some of his crusades from the House. In April 1997 he and Republican Charles Grassley called for disclosure of the names of senators who place "holds" on legislation—a cause Wyden started working on in 1992 when a bill he backed was killed by anonymous holds. Wyden and Grassley persevered, and in March 1999 Trent Lott and Tom Daschle unveiled a new procedure: A senator putting a hold on a bill must inform the sponsor, the committee chairman and the two party leaders.

Another Wyden cause was the Internet. In summer 1996 he worked with California Congressman Christopher Cox to push their amendment prohibiting government censorship of the Internet and urging online providers to offer technologies to help parents control their children's access to Internet materials. He and Cox also sponsored the three-year ban on Internet taxation that passed in October 1998. In 2001 they sought to extend it permanently, but to set up a procedure to allow states to tax Internet sales if their adopt uniform sales tax rules, with one sales tax rate per state, and provide a means to file and remit sales taxes electronically. Wyden has also worked on Internet privacy issues and, with Conrad Burns, on anti-spam ("Can-Spam") legislation. In 2001 and 2002 he was chairman of the Science, Technology and Space Subcommittee. He sponsored a bill to encourage research in nanotechnology—the science of making changes at the molecular and atomic level—which may benefit everything from information technology to health care. He warned new NASA administrator Sean O'Keefe that there was going to be no massive infusion of new funds. He has sought to require federal agencies to systematically develop checklists to fight cyberterrorism and encouraged the development of a volunteer force of programmers and engineers to reconstruct networks damaged by emergencies like September 11. In November 2002 he became co-chairman with Bill Frist of the Congressional Forum on Technology and Innovation, which conducts frequent briefing sessions for members and staffers.

On health care, Wyden and Olympia Snowe have introduced a bill to give seniors five Medigap options, with each providing coverage of prescription drugs over $3,000 a year. Wyden voted against Oregon's assisted suicide law, but has defended it, threatening to filibuster against Don Nickles's attempts in 1999 and 2000 to repeal it and attacking Attorney General John Ashcroft's decision in 2001 to prosecute doctors who prescribe lethal drugs for terminally ill patients. He has also sought to encourage a more fundamental look at the health care system by sponsoring, with Gordon Smith and, in October 2002, Orrin Hatch a "strange bedfellows" bill devised by Families USA, the Health Insurance Association of America and the American Hospital Association and supported by the AFL-CIO, AARP and the U.S. Chamber of Commerce. It would create a process to come up with fundamental change in health care financing, with nationwide public hearings and a working group to write recommendations; Congress would have six months to write legislation embodying the recommendations and if committees did not act any member could take the issue to the floor.

Ten months after Wyden was elected, his opponent Gordon Smith won the state's other Senate seat: The first time two senators were elected who had run against each other in the same year. With the departure of Packwood and Mark Hatfield, Oregon had lost 56 years of Senate seniority and had gained two senators who everyone expected would be bitter enemies. But instead they became friends. They have held dozens of town meetings together across Oregon and meet for lunch every Thursday with their chiefs of staff. After losing a bet with Smith, Wyden answered phones for him: "Senator Smith's office; this is Ron Wyden." They began collaborating on Oregon issues, some with national application. After shooting deaths in a Springfield, Oregon, school, they sponsored a bill to require pupils who bring guns to school to be held for 72 hours and undergo psychological evaluation. Smith supported the law sponsored by Wyden and Idaho Republican Larry Craig to reimburse counties with national forests at a steady rate—fees based on logging had plummeted because of Clinton administration policies—and Wyden worked to make sure the state would send money to the counties. Wyden also worked with Oregon Republican Congressman Greg Walden to reach an agreement on protecting the environment around Steens Mountain in eastern Oregon while respecting the interests of local cattlemen; the result was the Steens Mountain Cooperative Management and Protection Area created in October 2000. In March 2001 Wyden and Smith sponsored an unsuccessful amendment to prevent California's debt-laden Southern California Edison and PG&E from declaring bankruptcy. In October 2001 they threatened a filibuster to get a limitation on a 1998 law requiring federal prosecutors to follow state ethics rules; an Oregon rule prohibits "deceit" and Wyden argued that it prevented sting operations that could be useful against terrorists. Wyden and Smith also brought the election procedures law to a halt in February 2002 with their amendment barring the requirement that first-time voters present photo identification, which passed 51–46; Smith was the one Republican in favor. Other Republicans felt strongly that photo ID was necessary to prevent fraud; Wyden and Smith argued that it would undermine Oregon's mail voting system. To save the bill, Democrats backed down, but Wyden and Smith got a provision covering Oregon and Washington (where many votes are cast by mail) to require the submission of a driver's license number or part of a Social Security number.

Wyden has also set his own course on some local issues. He has opposed the sale of the Bonneville Power Administration, opposed a restart of the experimental reactor on the Hanford Reservation and cast the lone vote against a July 1999 energy bill because he feared it would permit the reopening of a nuclear reactor in Oregon. He lobbied the Chinese ambassador and got China to accept Pacific Northwest wheat for the first time in 20 years. He got national forest land transferred to the town of Sisters for a waste treatment plan and got permanent resident status for a Russian woman whose son was being treated for cerebral palsy in Portland. As chairman of the Forestry and Public Lands Subcommittee in 2001 and 2002, he was thrust into controversies national and local. With ranking minority member Larry Craig, he developed a bill to permanently protect timber stands older than 120 years, allowing the lumber industry more access to timber west of the Cascades and setting up a system to speed up tree thinning east of the Cascades. After the huge forest fires in the summer of 2002, he worked with Dianne Feinstein on a compromise national forest thinning plan which would prevent judges from blocking projects for more than 60 days and set up procedures to speed up thinning on 7 million acres of federal land. On both the Oregon and national proposals he was opposed both by timber industries and by environmental restriction organizations like the Sierra Club. He supported permanent repeal of the estate tax, pointing out the problems it caused for family businesses that own large stands of timber.

This bipartisan tone helped Wyden win election to a full term in November 1998. He won 61%–34%, carrying all but one county. "I was bipartisan before it was p.c.," Wyden says, though not quite on everything. He voted against Bush cabinet appointees Ashcroft and Gale Norton and, after Gordon Smith started a PAC to aid Republican candidates for the Oregon legislature in the 1998 cycle, Wyden started a PAC to help Democrats in 2000. In 2002, when Gordon Smith was up for reelection, Wyden did some campaigning for Democrat Bill Bradbury, but let it be known early on that he would have nothing to do with attacks on Smith. Wyden's seat is up in 2004. In November 2002 he raised $750,000 at a fundraiser in Portland's Rose Garden and seemed well positioned for reelection. Kevin Mannix, the nearly successful Republican candidate for governor in 2002, said he would not run.

Junior Senator

Gordon Smith (R)

Elected 1996, seat up 2008, 2d term; b. May 25, 1952, Pendleton; home, Pendleton; Brigham Young U., B.A. 1976, Southwestern U., J.D. 1979; Mormon; married (Sharon).

Elected Office: OR Senate, 1992–96, Pres., 1994–96.

Professional Career: Law Clerk, NM Supreme Court, 1979–80; Practicing atty., 1980–81; Pres., Smith Frozen Foods, 1980–96.

DC Office: 404 RSOB, 20510, 202-224-3753; Fax: 202-228-3997; Web site: gsmith.senate.gov.

State Offices: Bend, 541-318-1298; Eugene, 541-465-6750; Medford, 541-608-9102; Pendleton, 541-278-1129; Portland, 503-326-3386.

Committees: *Aging (Special). Commerce, Science & Transportation:* Aviation; Communications; Competition, Foreign Commerce & Infrastructure (Chmn.); Consumer Affairs & Product Safety; Oceans, Fisheries & Coast Guard; Surface Transportation & Merchant Marine. *Energy & Natural Resources:* National Parks; Public Lands & Forests; Water & Power. *Finance:* Health Care; International Trade; Long-Term Growth & Debt Reduction (Chmn.); Taxation & IRS Oversight. *Indian Affairs. Rules & Administration.*

Group Ratings

	ADA	ACLU	AFS	LCV	CON	ITIC	NTU	COC	ACU	NTLC	CHC
2002	35	40	50	35	15	100	42	85	75	91	—
2001	25	—	25	0	—	—	76	79	80	—	80

National Journal Ratings

	2001 LIB	—	2001 CONS		2002 LIB	—	2002 CONS
Economic	39%	—	61%		43%	—	56%
Social	43%	—	55%		48%	—	51%
Foreign	47%	—	53%		44%	—	54%

Key Votes of the 107th Congress

1. Approve Bush Tax Cuts	Y	5. Confirm Ashcroft as AG	Y	9. Bar Coop. with Intl. Court	Y
2. Expand Patients' Rights	Y	6. Bar Gays in the Boy Scouts	Y	10. Trade Promotion Authority	Y
3. Campaign Finance Reform	N	7. $ for Hate Crime Prosecution	Y	11. Authorize Force in Iraq	Y
4. Permit ANWR Development	N	8. Overseas Military Abortions	N	12. Homeland Sec. Dept. Union	N

Election Results

2002 general	Gordon Smith (R)	712,287	(56%)	($5,651,098)
	Bill Bradbury (D)	501,898	(40%)	($2,104,194)
2002 primary	Gordon Smith (R)	unopposed		
1996 general	Gordon Smith (R)	677,336	(50%)	($3,527,252)
	Tom Bruggere (D)	624,370	(46%)	($3,301,736)
	Other	58,524	(4%)	

Republican Gordon Smith was born in Pendleton and grew up, after his father sold his food processing business to serve as an aide to Eisenhower Agriculture Secretary Ezra Taft Benson, in the Washington suburbs. He is a cousin of former Congressmen Morris and Stewart Udall and therefore of their sons, Congressmen Mark Udall and Tom Udall. Smith served two years as a Mormon missionary in New Zealand, then graduated from Brigham Young and from law school in Los Angeles, was a law clerk in New Mexico and practiced law in Arizona. Then he bought the family frozen vegetable processing company in Pendleton, and guided it out of debt to profitability; Smith Frozen Foods is now one of largest private label packers of frozen vegetables in the country. In 1992 he was elected to the state Senate and in 1995 became Senate president, a fast rise. In 1995 and 1996 he ran for the Senate seat from which Bob Packwood resigned. He lost, after a battle of negative ads, to Ron Wyden 48%–47% in January 1996. The month before, Mark Hatfield had announced his retirement after 30 years in the Senate. At first Smith was reluctant to run again—indeed, he is the only American in history to run in two Senate races in the same year—but Republicans urged him to do so. Attacked during the Wyden race for being endorsed by the conservative Oregon Citizens' Alliance, Smith positioned himself closer to the center and turned down the OCA endorsement this time; when OCA head Lon Mabon ran against him in the primary, Smith beat him 78%–8%. Smith's opponent in the general was Tom Bruggere, another self-made millionaire, who started Mentor Graphics near Portland and, like Smith, owned a Ferrari. In an ad shot in soft focus, Smith said he continued to oppose abortion, but promised not to back a constitutional amendment banning it and at the end of the campaign said he would vote for Medicaid to cover abortions in cases of rape, incest or threat to life of the mother; he promised to work for a balance of environmental protection, economic development and job creation. Smith won 50%–46%, carrying every county but Portland, two university towns and two northwest counties; he lost metro Portland by 53%–43%.

Against some expectations, Smith has compiled one of the more moderate voting records of Senate Republicans. He voted for mandatory background checks and for child safety locks on guns—both reversals of previous stands. He continued to oppose abortion, but in 2000 backed the use of embryonic stem cells in medical research; the cells are used in research to combat Parkinson's disease that has stricken several of his relatives. But he opposed human cloning, fearful of "embryo farms where women are induced to take superovulatory drugs to harvest lots of eggs with the deliberate intention of destroying them." He did not change his position on assisted suicide, however. While his Oregon colleague Wyden repeatedly threatened to filibuster Don Nickles's bill which would have overturned the assisted suicide law Oregon voters approved in 1994 and 1997 referenda, Smith voted for it. "For me, it's an issue of principle on which I'm prepared to stake my political career," he said later. He called on the Bush administration not to prosecute physicians for prescribing lethal drugs, but in November 2001 Attorney General John Ashcroft signaled he would do so; he was blocked from acting by a federal judge and appealed the decision. In the meantime Smith opposed congressional action.

Smith strongly supported the 2000 prescription drug bill sponsored by Wyden and Olympia Snowe in 2000 and in summer 2002 wrote his own bill with Bob Graham that at one point seemed the compromise most likely to pass the Senate. He co-sponsored Wyden's "strange bedfellows" health bill which would set up a process for a panel of experts to agree on principles and write legislation which Congress would be required to consider. With Hillary Rodham Clinton he sponsored a bill to create magnet programs for nurses. He was Edward Kennedy's chief co-sponsor of the hate crimes bill that included gays. He voted against the McCain-Feingold campaign finance regulation bill when it passed with 59 votes in April 2001, but when it came back from conference committee in February 2002 he indicated he would provide a 60th vote against a filibuster, and thus assured its passage. Smith serves on Foreign Relations and again he has steered something of a middle course. He was one of the few Republicans to vote for the Comprehensive Test Ban Treaty in October 1999. He supported the Iraq war resolution in October 2002.

The election of Wyden in January 1996 and Smith in November 1996 was the first time two senators were elected who had run against each other in the same year. Surprisingly, considering the negative character of their campaign, they became friends. They have held dozens of joint town meetings across Oregon and have issued dozens of joint press releases; they lunch together every Thursday. They have worked together when bills have special impact on Oregon. In October 2001 they threatened to filibuster the USA Patriot Act in order to get an exception from a 1998 law that requires federal prosecutor to follow state legal ethics rules; Oregon prohibits "deceit" and they said that made it impossible for federal authorities to conduct sting operations and undercover investigations. In February 2002 Smith, working with Wyden, brought consideration of the election law bill to a halt by voting to delete a provision, supported by all other Republicans, requiring first-time voters to show photo identification. Smith and Wyden argued that this would undermine Oregon's mail-in voting; they did not get the provision they first sought, but did get a provision allowing Oregon and Washington, where most votes are cast by mail, to require only submission of a driver's license number of part of a Social Security number to prove identity.

Smith has tended to oppose measures sought by environmental restriction groups as undue limits on economic activity. He has very strongly opposed breaching dams on the Snake River. He has worked on compromises on specific issues—with Wyden on expanding the Little Sandy watershed protection area, from which Portland gets drinking water; with Congressman Greg Walden to produce the Steens Mountain Cooperative Management and Protection Area; with Wyden, to question the methods by which the National Marine Fisheries Service determined that the groundfish population was declining (which resulted in limits on fishing). He championed the cause of the Klamath Basin farmers who were denied irrigation water because it was said to be needed to protect the endangered sucker fish—a heavily publicized case in Oregon; some water was restored in summer 2002. When California's electricity crisis hit in winter 2001, he and Wyden sought unsuccessfully to bar heavily indebted utilities from declaring bankruptcy. He parted with most of his fellow Republicans to vote against oil drilling in the ANWR and to vote for higher CAFE auto gas mileage standards. He worked with Tom Harkin to provide more generous conservation incentives in the 2002 farm bill and to have them apply to all farmers, not just those who produce subsidized crops.

There are signs that Smith is interested in having a long Senate career: In July 2002 he proposed repealing the Senate Republicans' term limits on chairmen; this was rejected by the Republican Conference 28–18. Heading into the 2002 cycle, it was not apparent whether this Republican senator from a state where Democrats have been winning most recent statewide elections—and which was evenly split in the 2000 presidential election—would have serious competition. His stands on abortion, assisted suicide and environmental issues were not as out of line with as many voters as some Democrats thought, but they were sure to be portrayed in the press, liberal-leaning in Oregon, as extreme right-wing positions. The toughest competitor seemed to be Governor John Kitzhaber, concluding his second term with still high ratings. But Kitzhaber, with a young family and fond of fly fishing, took his time deciding whether to run; in September 2001, on a fishing trip after the September 11 attacks, he issued a one-sentence press release saying he would not.

Two other Democrats were mentioned as possibly competitive candidates, and both had trailed but held Smith under 50% in the February poll—4th District Congressman Peter DeFazio and Secretary of State Bill Bradbury. DeFazio would have to give up his House seat to run, a seat House Democrats feared they would lose with another candidate, and in October 2001 he asked the DSCC for assurances of its "strongest possible support"—i.e., a commitment to the maximum legal financing. DSCC Chairman Patty Murray wouldn't give such a commitment and top staffer Jim Jordan said he "just might want to sit back and watch the process for a while." Translation: No serious money until you raise a lot yourself and rise in the polls. On the last day of October, DeFazio announced he would not run.

Meanwhile, Bradbury decided to run without the assurances DeFazio sought. Bradbury and Smith go back a ways. In 1993 Bradbury was Senate President and Smith a Senate freshman; at the end of the longest session in state history, Smith told Bradbury he had the votes to delay adjournment indefinitely unless Bradbury appointed more Republicans to the Emergency Board, a group of legislators with spending power when the legislature is out of session; Bradbury backed down. Smith also beat Bradbury by accepting a deal that included a cigarette tax increase but also delayed for four years imposing an employer mandate in the Oregon Health Plan—a delay that became permanent after Republicans won majorities in the legislature in 1994. In October 2001, Bradbury announced for Senate; he had no serious primary opposition. Bradbury attacked Smith's votes on environmental issues, abortion, tax cuts, education spending and assisted suicide. He had revealed to voters some time before that he has multiple sclerosis, which makes it difficult for him to walk long distances; he carried a director's chair so he wouldn't have to stand for long periods.

Smith had two strong assets. One was his work with Wyden. Wyden endorsed Bradbury and conducted fundraisers for him, but he also pledged not to attack Smith in any way and they continued to send out joint press releases. The other asset was money. By April 2002 Smith had raised $4 million—twice as much as Bradbury would during the whole campaign. And, although Smith had spent none of his own money on his November 1996 campaign, Democrats knew that he could always get out his checkbook and match whatever they raised for Bradbury. In the spring, the DSCC ran some ads attacking Smith. But for most of the spring and summer and into October Smith had a monopoly on airtime. He ran ads on his accomplishments, stressing in the Portland media market his support of expanded health care benefits for women and children and his opposition to oil drilling in ANWR. In the Medford media market, he stressed his opposition to the cutoff of irrigation water to Klamath Basin farmers. On radio ads in rural areas, he called Bradbury an "environmental extremist." In September, he ran in the Portland market an ad featuring Judy Shepard, mother of murdered student Matthew Shepard, praising him for his support of including gays in the hate crimes bill—the first pro-gay rights TV ad run by any candidate, the Human Rights Campaign said. "I'm the first candidate of either party to ever run an ad to mention the gay community in a positive way," he said. "The next time the issue comes to the floor, I'm going to have a veto-proof majority"—a way of saying he was independent of George W. Bush. Lon Mabon, running as a third party candidate, said, "If you vote for Gordon Smith, you're voting for homosexuality."

By September Smith was leading in a media poll 53%–30%. Bradbury went up with TV ads in October, attacking Smith for opposing assisted suicide and accusing Smith of preferring his own views to those of voters. But he couldn't come close to matching Smith, who ultimately spent $5.6 million to his $2.1 million. Smith won 56%–40%, carrying every county in the state but one, Multnomah (Portland). With big margins in the suburbs he carried metro Portland 51%–45% and the Willamette Valley 56%–40%; he carried southwest Oregon 63%–34% and east Oregon 70%–26%.

Smith was Oregon chairman for George W. Bush in 2000 and seems to be taking a hand in party affairs and to see that Bush carries the state this time. In November 2002 he moved to oust Christian broadcaster Perry Atkinson from the chairmanship of the Oregon Republican party and backed former legislator Lynn Snodgrass; in December 2002 both backed out, and defeated governor candidate Kevin Mannix, a former Democrat, got the post.

FIRST DISTRICT

Rep. David Wu (D)

Elected 1998, 3d term; b. Apr. 8, 1955, Taiwan; home, Portland; Stanford U., B.S. 1977; Harvard Med. Schl., 1978; Yale Law Schl., J.D. 1982; Presbyterian; married (Michelle).

Professional Career: Law clerk, 9th Circuit Court of Appeals, 1982–83; Campaign staff, Gary Hart for President, 1984; Practicing atty., 1984–98.

DC Office: 1023 LHOB 20515, 202-225-0855; Fax: 202-225-9497; Web site: www.house.gov/wu.

District Office: Portland, 503-326-2901.

Committees: *Education & the Workforce* (12th of 22 D): 21st Century Competitiveness; Employer-Employee Relations. *Science* (9th of 22 D): Energy; Space & Aeronautics.

Group Ratings

	ADA	ACLU	AFS	LCV	CON	ITIC	NTU	COC	ACU	NTLC	CHC
2002	95	80	89	100	63	38	17	45	16	14	17
2001	100	—	100	100	—	—	17	30	8	—	—

National Journal Ratings

	2001 LIB —	2001 CONS		2002 LIB —	2002 CONS
Economic	70%	— 29%		64%	— 35%
Social	67%	— 33%		65%	— 34%
Foreign	73%	— 26%		77%	— 19%

Key Votes of the 107th Congress

1. Approve Bush Tax Cuts	N	5. Faith-Based Charities	N	9. Trade Promotion Authority	N
2. Limit Patients' Bill of Rights	N	6. Bar Gays in the Boy Scouts	N	10. Bar Funds for Intl. Court	N
3. Campaign Finance Reform	Y	7. Ban Partial-Birth Abortion	N	11. Authorize Force in Iraq	N
4. Ban ANWR Development	Y	8. Arm Commercial Pilots	Y	12. Deny Home. Sec. Dept. Union	N

Election Results

2002 general	David Wu (D)	149,215	(63%)	($1,050,961)
	Jim Greenfield (R)	80,917	(34%)	
	Other	7,904	(3%)	
2002 primary	David Wu (D)	unopposed		
2000 general	David Wu (D)	176,902	(58%)	($1,437,974)
	Charles Starr (R)	115,303	(38%)	($278,345)
	Other	11,316	(4%)	

Prior Winning Percentages: 1998 (50%)

The People		Race/Ethnic Origin	Ancestry	
Area size:	3,236 sq. mi.	81.1% White	German: 15.0%	English: 9.5%
Urban population:	86.7%	1.1% Black	Irish: 8.4%	
Rural population:	13.3%	5.0% Asian	**2000 Presidential Vote**	
Pop. 2000:	684,280	0.7% Native Am.	Gore (D) 150,768	(50%)
Median income:	$48,464	0.2% Hawaiian	Bush (R).............131,808	(44%)
Poverty status:	8.7%	2.3% Two+ races	Other 17,057	(6%)
Military veterans:	13.4%	0.1% Other	**Cook Partisan Voting Index:** D + 3	
		9.4% Hispanic Origin		

Occupation	Blue collar: 20.6%	White collar: 65.3%	Gray collar: 14.1%

Postmodern skyscrapers rising above the riverfront and below a range of hills: This is downtown Portland. The city—which would have been named Boston if a coin toss had gone the other way—started here, along the Willamette River just before it flows into the Columbia, and downtown was built on the narrow margin of land west of the river and below the hills, not on the flat expanse that stretches east towards the snow-capped peak of Mount Hood. Downtown Portland was once a dowdy place, proper in a New Englandish way, with a few formal buildings above the warehouses and factories. But in the last 20 years there has been an explosion of creativity here, symbolized by handsome high-rises—the pyramid-crested brick KOIN Tower, the wedge-shaped Justice Center—restored Victorian storefronts, a downtown transit trolley and a light rail line known as MAX (Metropolitan Area Express), and just across the river the new Oregon Museum of Science and Industry. The affluent neighborhoods in the hills overlooking downtown are full of old lumber barons' mansions with splendid views.

Just over the hills are the valleys and interstices between green mountains of suburban Washington County. Not so long ago, this was farm country, with 39,000 people in 1940; now it has 445,000 and is an integral part of metro Portland. This is an affluent area, which grew by 43% in the 1990s, with clusters of towns and protected forest areas that feature a high-tech, healthy-lifestyle aura; major employers here are Tektronix, Intel, and Sequent Computer Systems. Beaverton is home to the world headquarters of Nike, housed in 16 buildings over a 175-acre spread. Like Silicon Valley, the Silicon Forest has an environment—at the foot of mountains, woodsy and even rustic, but outfitted with all the comforts and services of modern civilization— that appeals to a highly skilled work force. As they say locally, wood chips have been replaced by computer chips. Economic growth in the 1990s was so strong that at one point Washington County told Intel's officers that the company could add another 1,000 to its 4,000 employees (more than are based at its Santa Clara headquarters), but only if the company agreed to a "growth impact fee"—a $1,000 assessment for each worker over the agreed limit. With the 2000–02 high-tech slowdown and cutbacks and layoffs by Intel, TriQuint Semiconductor and Mitsubishi Silicon America, many people here might pay more to get the jobs back.

The 1st Congressional District includes downtown Portland and its western hills, and all of suburban Washington County. The 1st also proceeds nearly 100 miles northwest from Portland along the Columbia River to the rain-swept port of Astoria on the Pacific Coast, and southwest to Yamhill County, a prime site for turkey farms during the 1960s but where metro growth has been spreading. This was the fastest-growing district in Oregon in the 1990s, and redistricting removed a small slice of southwest Portland. Like Oregon, the 1st District is historically New England Republican, electing only Republican congressmen from 1892 to 1972; like New England, it then trended sharply left on cultural issues, even as its high-tech economy brought new affluence, and since 1974 it has elected liberal Democrats. But the political balance has been close here: The Portland precincts are strongly Democratic and Washington County has become increasingly Republican; no House candidate won more than 52% of the vote in the District in the 1990s.

The congressman from the 1st District is David Wu, a Democrat elected in 1998, the third Chinese-American to have served in Congress. He was born in Taiwan in 1955 and came to the U.S. with the rest of his family to join his father, studying at Rensselaer Polytechnic Institute in 1961, after restrictions on non-European immigration were softened. He grew up mostly in Orange County, California, went to college at Stanford, started medical school at Harvard (where he shared an apartment with Bill Frist), then switched to law school at Yale. He clerked for a federal judge in Portland and settled there; he worked on Jimmy Carter's campaign in 1980 and Gary Hart's in 1984. He started his own law firm in 1988 and served on the Portland Planning Commission.

In 1997, Congresswoman Elizabeth Furse, a liberal Democrat and supporter of term limits, announced she would not run again, and Wu ran. The Democratic frontrunner was Linda Peters, who was well known as Washington County Board chairwoman and had the backing of EMILY's List. Wu left his law practice and spent $100,000 of his own money. He attacked Peters in ads for taking a personal loan from a developer and for misspending tax dollars while traveling on county business. Wu's tactic drew protests from Furse, the League of Women Voters and state party leaders, but he won the primary 52%–43%. Republicans nominated 29-year-old Molly Bordonaro, the daughter of a prominent real estate man in Portland. Coming out of the primary, she had more money than Wu, a more united party behind her and was running even in the polls. Yet Wu won. One reason was that, with help from national Democrats and labor unions, he caught up in fundraising. Another was that Wu established himself early as a moderate. He talked of a balanced approach to the environment, smaller government, less business regulation. He used his own life story to extol America's system of education and to call for more spending on Head Start (his wife was a Head Start teacher) and aid to college students. Wu won 50%–47%. All of his margin and much more came from the Multnomah County part of the district, which he carried 67%–30%; Bordonaro carried Washington County 51%–47%, but that was not enough.

In the House, Wu joined the centrist New Democrat Coalition and fostered a reputation as a maverick, though he is usually a party regular: he was an early ally of Nancy Pelosi and had a voting pattern close to that of the Portland area's two other House Democrats. On education, health care, abortion and gun control, he was a reliable Democratic voice. Displeasing local business, he voted against PNTR with China because of "our commitment to American values and the sacrifices of countless families like mine," and he opposed trade promotion authority. Within the delegation, he caused a stir in 2001 by seeking a seat on Appropriations, which the more senior Darlene Hooley also wanted; neither succeeded. He sought $18 million for a new commuter rail line between Wilsonville and Beaverton. In May 2001, guards at the Energy Department for 15 minutes stopped him from entering after asking if he was a United States citizen; he was there to speak to Asian-Americans about racial profiling, and he received an apology from Energy Secretary Spencer Abraham.

Wu has been doing well at home. Against an outspoken conservative in 2000 he won 58%–38%. In 2002, against a radio talk show host who suspended his campaign in mid-October, he won 63%–34%.

SECOND DISTRICT

Rep. Greg Walden (R)

Elected 1998, 3d term; b. Jan. 10, 1957, The Dalles; home, Hood River; U. of OR, B.S. 1981; Episcopalian; married (Mylene).

Elected Office: OR House of Reps., 1988–94, Majority Ldr., 1991–93; OR Senate, 1994–96.

Professional Career: Press secy., U.S. Rep. Denny Smith, 1981–84, Chief of staff, 1984–86; Owner, Columbia Gorge Broadcasters Inc., 1986–present.

DC Office: 1404 LHOB 20515, 202-225-6730; Fax: 202-225-5774; Web site: www.house.gov/walden.

District Offices: Bend, 541-389-4408; Medford, 541-776-4646.

Committees: *Energy & Commerce* (25th of 31 R): Energy & Air Quality; Oversight & Investigations (Vice Chmn.); Telecommunications & The Internet. *Resources* (17th of 28 R): Water & Power.

Group Ratings

	ADA	ACLU	AFS	LCV	CON	ITIC	NTU	COC	ACU	NTLC	CHC
2002	5	13	0	0	25	100	56	100	96	78	83
2001	10	—	10	7	—	—	60	100	84	—	—

National Journal Ratings

	2001 LIB —	2001 CONS	2002 LIB —	2002 CONS
Economic	28%	69%	16%	81%
Social	43%	55%	44%	54%
Foreign	14%	85%	0%	85%

Key Votes of the 107th Congress

1. Approve Bush Tax Cuts	Y	5. Faith-Based Charities	Y	9. Trade Promotion Authority	Y
2. Limit Patients' Bill of Rights	Y	6. Bar Gays in the Boy Scouts	Y	10. Bar Funds for Intl. Court	Y
3. Campaign Finance Reform	N	7. Ban Partial-Birth Abortion	Y	11. Authorize Force in Iraq	Y
4. Ban ANWR Development	N	8. Arm Commercial Pilots	Y	12. Deny Home. Sec. Dept. Union	Y

Election Results

2002 general	Greg Walden (R)	181,295	(72%)	($842,862)
	Peter Buckley (D)	64,991	(26%)	($68,530)
	Other	5,998	(2%)	
2002 primary	Greg Walden (R)	unopposed		
2000 general	Greg Walden (R)	220,086	(74%)	($523,820)
	Walter Ponsford (D)	78,101	(26%)	

Prior Winning Percentages: 1998 (61%)

The People		Race/Ethnic Origin	Ancestry	
Area size:	70,227 sq. mi.	86.1% White	German: 13.6%	English: 9.9%
Urban population:	64.2%	0.4% Black	Irish: 8.7%	
Rural population:	35.8%	0.8% Asian	**2000 Presidential Vote**	
Pop. 2000:	684,280	1.9% Native Am.	Bush (R)...............182,924	(60%)
Median income:	$35,600	0.1% Hawaiian	Gore (D)...............105,971	(35%)
Poverty status:	13.0%	1.8% Two+ races	Other...................18,078	(6%)
Military veterans:	17.3%	0.1% Other	**Cook Partisan Voting Index:** R +14	
		8.8% Hispanic Origin		

Occupation	Blue collar: 26.3%	White collar: 54.0%	Gray collar: 19.7%

The Cascade Mountains that wall eastern Oregon off from the rest of the state are a magnificent chain of once (and quite possibly still) active volcanic mountains that drain almost every drop of moisture out of the air coming in from the Pacific. Thus they separate green, wet western Oregon from brown, parched east. Eastern Oregon has 70% of the state's land, but less than 400,000 of its 3.4 million people, most of whom still make their living off the land: Beef and dairy cattle, timber and lumber, fish from the Columbia River and wheat from the irrigated plains. The effect of the Cascades can be felt in the one place they are breached—by the Columbia River Gorge. There, surrounded by brown hills on both sides, funneled winds pound in steadily from the west, making the confluence of the Columbia and Hood rivers the best windsurfing site in the United States. In April 2002 the world's largest wind farm opened here; it features 400 windmills capable of generating electricity for 60,000 homes.

The 2d Congressional District covers all of the state east of the Cascades and the southern-most valley between the Cascades and the Coast Range. Much of this land is empty: Harney County, with a land area larger than that of nine states, has a population of 7,600. Population concentrations here are far apart: Pendleton, a genuine rodeo town amid the northeastern wheat fields; La Grande in the rich Grande Ronde Valley; The Dalles, where the Columbia River Gorge begins; Bend in the center of the state, near Crook County, which until it voted for George Bush in 1992 was the only county in the country to have voted for the winning presidential candidate in every election in the 20th century. In the southwestern corner, near the once huge volcano whose blown-off cone is now the 1,932-foot deep Crater Lake (the deepest in the nation), is the lumber and pear orchard country around Medford, Ashland, Klamath Falls and Grants Pass. As with the other districts in Oregon, the 2d had a scant shift in redistricting.

Politically, the 2d District has grown very suspicious of the federal government and very Republican. The cultural liberalism of Portland isn't welcome here: This is part of the leave-us-alone Rocky Mountain basin, not the culturally hip West Coast. A few government pursuits here are considered acceptable; the Army's Umatilla Chemical Depot, near Hermiston, with 3,700 tons of chemical weapons, generated no controversy for 50 years until the Army announced it would destroy the weapons by incineration. But Washington is more often viewed here as the owner of three-quarters of the district's land and the protector of the threatened spotted owl, which has forced timber companies increasingly onto Oregon's limited expanses of state and private land. In 2001, the *cause celebre* was the cutoff of water in the Klamath Basin to 1,400 farmers in order to protect the endangered sucker fish. This became a big political issue and in July 2001 some of the water started flowing again.

The congressman from the 2d District is Greg Walden, a Republican elected in 1998. He grew up on a cherry orchard near The Dalles in the Columbia gorge; his father served in the state

House. Walden served as press secretary and chief of staff to Congressman Denny Smith from 1981–87, then returned to Hood River as a radio station owner. In 1988 he was elected to the state House, and in his second term became Majority Leader. Walden was known for cobbling together consensus on issues that divided the state, working to expand the lottery and writing rules for the Oregon Health Plan. He is conservative on economic issues but more moderate on social issues; he is pro-choice but opposes federal funding of abortions.

Walden succeeded Bob Smith, who had returned to the House to serve one term as chairman of the Agriculture Committee after embarrassed Republicans decided they needed to replace Representative Wes Cooley. Walden was faced with substantial primary opposition. There was lots of grumbling about outside interference, which appeared in the form of $130,000 in ads by Americans for Limited Terms and $50,000 in ads by Gary Bauer's Family Research Council. Walden's wide support and the $500,000 he raised enabled him to win fairly easily, with 55% of the vote to 33% for religious broadcaster Perry Atkinson, later Republican state chairman, and 9% for the unembarrassable Cooley. The general election was anticlimactic. Against a Democrat who ran as a conservative, Walden won 61%–35%.

In his first term, Walden's legislative highlight was enactment of the Steens Mountain Cooperative Management and Protection Act, which was a response to Interior Secretary Bruce Babbitt's threat to create 175,000 acres of wilderness in southeast Oregon. Walden's alternative created incentives for public-private management of the land. He joined other northwest Republicans supporting a nonbinding resolution against breaching several Snake River dams to increase salmon runs. On an issue that generated huge controversy in Oregon and beyond, Walden expressed reservations about Oregon's assisted suicide law approved in referenda in 1994 and 1997, but argued that the voters' choice should be respected and not overruled by Congress. In March 2001 on the Energy and Commerce Committee, he opposed electricity price caps sought by Californians. On the Resources Committee he sought review of water management and changes in the Endangered Species Act in response to the controversy about the sucker fish in the Klamath Basin; Walden called for federal relief for the farmers deprived of irrigated water. A committee hearing in Klamath Falls drew 4,000 spectators and protestors. After a dispute between Walden and Senator Ron Wyden over who deserved credit, Congress agreed to include $50 million in the farm bill.

Walden has twice won re-election with more than 70% of the vote. He declined to run for governor in 2002. "I want to stay here [in Washington] for a while," said Walden. There is no reason to believe that he won't get his wish. After the 2002 election, Roy Blunt named him a deputy whip.

THIRD DISTRICT

Rep. Earl Blumenauer (D)

Elected May 1996, 4th term; b. Aug. 16, 1948, Portland; home, Portland; Lewis & Clark Col., B.A. 1970, J.D. 1976; no religious affiliation; divorced.

Elected Office: OR House of Reps., 1972–78; Multnomah Cnty. Comm., 1978–86; Portland City Cncl., 1986–96.

Professional Career: Asst. to Pres., Portland St. U., 1970–77.

DC Office: 2446 RHOB 20515, 202-225-4811; Fax: 202-225-8941; Web site: www.house.gov/blumenauer.

District Office: Portland, 503-231-2300.

Committees: *International Relations* (16th of 23 D): Asia & the Pacific; Europe. *Transportation & Infrastructure* (15th of 34 D): Highways, Transit & Pipelines; Railroads; Water Resources & Environment.

Group Ratings

	ADA	ACLU	AFS	LCV	CON	ITIC	NTU	COC	ACU	NTLC	CHC
2002	100	93	100	100	78	38	28	35	4	6	0
2001	90	—	100	86	—	—	19	30	0	—	—

National Journal Ratings

	2001 LIB	—	2001 CONS		2002 LIB	—	2002 CONS
Economic	86%	—	15%		74%	—	25%
Social	90%	—	0%		94%	—	6%
Foreign	96%	—	0%		86%	—	13%

Key Votes of the 107th Congress

1. Approve Bush Tax Cuts	*	5. Faith-Based Charities	N	9. Trade Promotion Authority	N
2. Limit Patients' Bill of Rights	N	6. Bar Gays in the Boy Scouts	N	10. Bar Funds for Intl. Court	N
3. Campaign Finance Reform	Y	7. Ban Partial-Birth Abortion	N	11. Authorize Force in Iraq	N
4. Ban ANWR Development	Y	8. Arm Commercial Pilots	N	12. Deny Home. Sec. Dept. Union	N

Election Results

2002 general	Earl Blumenauer (D)	156,851	(67%)	($353,543)
	Sarah Seale (R)	62,821	(27%)	
	Other	15,305	(7%)	
2002 primary	Earl Blumenauer (D)	68,893	(87%)	
	John Sweeney (D)	9,992	(13%)	
2000 general	Earl Blumenauer (D)	181,049	(67%)	($404,807)
	Jeffery L. Pollock (R)	64,128	(24%)	($92,005)
	Tre Arrow (Green)	15,763	(6%)	
	Other	10,221	(4%)	

Prior Winning Percentages: 1998 (84%); 1996 (67%); 1996 (68%)

The People		Race/Ethnic Origin	Ancestry	
Area size:	1,054 sq. mi.	77.2% White	German: 14.5%	Irish: 8.7%
Urban population:	93.1%	5.2% Black	English: 8.4%	
Rural population:	6.9%	5.4% Asian	**2000 Presidential Vote**	
Pop. 2000:	684,279	0.9% Native Am.	Gore (D) 176,831	(61%)
Median income:	$42,063	0.3% Hawaiian	Bush (R) 93,213	(32%)
Poverty status:	11.7%	3.3% Two+ races	Other 20,264	(7%)
Military veterans:	13.1%	0.2% Other	**Cook Partisan Voting Index:** D +15	
		7.6% Hispanic Origin		

Occupation	Blue collar: 24.6%	White collar: 59.4%	Gray collar: 16.0%

Portland, the Rose City set between Mount Hood to the east and the Tualatin Mountains to the west, spanning the Willamette River with its airport and industrial back to the Columbia, is still one of America's least known major cities—and one of its most distinctive. This was not always so. For most of its history Portland was a prosaic city in a magic setting; it was in many ways a muscular, blue-collar town, which piled Oregon lumber and Oregon pears into freight cars or unloaded machines from back East or autos from Japan on its docks. But in the past three decades Portland has been transformed. Out on the Pacific Rim, it increasingly makes its living on foreign trade, seeing East Asians as customers more than competitors. It has become a home of high-tech industries, particularly in the Washington County suburbs to the west—Silicon Forest. Government has also produced change. Oregon's land-use act, passed in 1973, required local governments to set geographic limits on growth; Metro, the regional government established in 1979 just as growth was accelerating, has created something of a counterweight against the endless spread outward of population into former farmland. Portland opened its first light-rail line in 1986 and has encouraged the development of high-density commercial space and housing around transit stops; bicycle paths wind throughout the metropolitan area, and downtown, west of the Willamette River, boasts proud postmodern structures amid classic masonry buildings. By 57%–43%, voters defeated in 2002 a referendum sought by developers to weaken controls on sprawl.

In the process, the central city of Portland, like San Francisco and Seattle, has come to attract political and cultural liberals. And, like those two cities, Portland has its share of traffic congestion and high home prices. But this "livable community" was rated the best city to live in by *Money* magazine in 2000 and its long-term approach to transportation, creating mixed-use neighborhoods and increasing development density, may ultimately pay off. The city dropped from the fourth-least affordable in the nation to purchase a new home in the early 1990s to 25th by the end of the decade.

The 3d Congressional District takes in the east side of Portland and Multnomah County east of the Willamette River and part of suburban Clackamas County to the south. It extends over suburban plains and hills to the splendid scenery of the Bonneville Dam in the Columbia River Gorge and Mount Hood high in the Cascades. Politically, it is dominated by a cultural liberalism, which sets Portland apart even from its suburbs and the rest of Oregon. In 2000 Portland's Multnomah County voted 64%–28% for Al Gore, and gave Ralph Nader 7% of the vote.

The congressman from the 3d District is Earl Blumenauer, elected in 1996 to replace Ron Wyden after he was elected to the Senate. Blumenauer grew up in Portland, graduated from Lewis and Clark College and its Northwestern Law School. He was inspired by the civil rights and anti-Vietnam war movements while in his teens; in 1969, in college, he headed a statewide campaign to lower Oregon's voting age. He has held public office almost all his adult life. In 1972, at 23, he was elected to the Oregon House; in 1978 he was elected to the Multnomah County Board of Commissioners; in 1986 he was elected to the Portland City Council. In these offices he has championed many of the policies that have made Portland distinctive—regional light rail transit, curbside recycling, land use planning. He initiated a law taking away the cars of repeat drunk driving offenders. He encouraged bike riding and Regional Rail Summits, which try to bring neighborhood residents into the process of planning for higher densities at transit nodes. Blumenauer has had his name on the ballot 26 times and has had some setbacks, notably when he lost the 1992 mayoral race to Vera Katz. But when Wyden was elected to the Senate, Blumenauer was the obvious successor. He won the special election 68%–25%. His campaign slogan: "Vote Earl, Vote Often."

In the House, Blumenauer has a liberal voting record and a distinctive agenda. He rides his bicycle everywhere from his Capitol Hill apartment, and formed a Bicycle Caucus with more than 100 members; he fought for showers for bike commuters and boasts that he has never driven a car in Washington. But he does get around the city in other ways: He ran the Marine Corps Marathon in slightly over four hours. He was astonished to find that the House subsidized parking for employees, but not mass transit; now, employees can get subsidized transit fares. He is interested in what seem like quixotic projects now, but may not be in a few years: An interstate highway system for bicycle paths, development of "livable communities" on the sites of Denver's closed Stapleton Airport and closed military bases. He demands that the Army Corps of Engineers show greater concern for the environment. Blumenauer has actively promoted trade across the Pacific—a key element of Portland's economy. He supported PNTR with China but he joined the 90% of House Democrats who opposed trade promotion authority in 2001 and 2002. When Portland's police chief said that he would not comply with a Justice Department request that local law enforcers interview foreign visitors about possible terrorist activities following September 11, Blumenauer defended the response as "entirely appropriate."

He proudly terms Portland a model for the future of the city, with its ample bicycle lanes, public transit and limits on sprawl. And he has taken his gospel of livability and civic values elsewhere in local visits, through his Livable Cities Task Force (more than 50 members) and his own political action committee ($200,000-plus raised). At his best, according to a profile in *The Washington Post,* Blumenauer is "directing attention to a topic most folks simply take for granted and, with a combination of realism and idealism, offering a fresh perspective." How popular his sometimes eclectic ideas become nationally, and how well their unintended consequences can be ironed out, remains to be seen. Either way, his seat seems safe. He has won reelection handily.

FOURTH DISTRICT

Rep. Peter DeFazio (D)

Elected 1986, 9th term; b. May 27, 1947, Needham, MA; home, Springfield; Tufts U., B.A. 1969, U. of OR, M.S. 1977; Catholic; married (Myrnie).

Military Career: Air Force, 1967–71.

Elected Office: Lane Cnty. Bd. of Commissioners, 1982–86.

Professional Career: Dist. Dir., U.S. Rep. James Weaver, 1977–82.

DC Office: 2134 RHOB 20515, 202-225-6416; Fax: 202-225-0032; Web site: www.house.gov/defazio.

District Offices: Coos Bay, 541-269-2609; Eugene, 541-465-6732; Roseburg, 541-440-3523.

Committees: *Select Committee on Homeland Security* (10th of 23 D): Emergency Preparedness & Response; Infrastructure & Border Security. *Transportation & Infrastructure* (4th of 34 D): Aviation (RMM); Coast Guard & Maritime Transportation; Railroads.

Group Ratings

	ADA	ACLU	AFS	LCV	CON	ITIC	NTU	COC	ACU	NTLC	CHC
2002	95	93	100	100	79	38	31	30	12	0	0
2001	100	—	100	93	—	—	13	25	16	—	—

National Journal Ratings

	2001 LIB —	2001 CONS		2002 LIB —	2002 CONS
Economic	95%	0%		77%	20%
Social	78%	22%		67%	29%
Foreign	80%	21%		81%	19%

Key Votes of the 107th Congress

1. Approve Bush Tax Cuts	N	5. Faith-Based Charities	N
2. Limit Patients' Bill of Rights	N	6. Bar Gays in the Boy Scouts	N
3. Campaign Finance Reform	Y	7. Ban Partial-Birth Abortion	N
4. Ban ANWR Development	Y	8. Arm Commercial Pilots	Y

9. Trade Promotion Authority	N
10. Bar Funds for Intl. Court	Y
11. Authorize Force in Iraq	N
12. Deny Home. Sec. Dept. Union	N

Election Results

2002 general	Peter DeFazio (D)	168,150	(64%)	($286,417)
	Liz VanLeeuwen (R)	90,523	(34%)	($150,482)
	Other	4,808	(2%)	
2002 primary	Peter DeFazio (D)	unopposed		
2000 general	Peter DeFazio (D)	197,998	(68%)	($332,650)
	John Lindsey (R)	88,950	(31%)	($34,788)
	Other	4,117	(1%)	

Prior Winning Percentages: 1998 (70%); 1996 (66%); 1994 (67%); 1992 (71%); 1990 (86%); 1988 (72%); 1986 (54%)

The People		Race/Ethnic Origin	Ancestry	
Area size:	18,034 sq. mi.	89.7% White	German: 14.7%	English: 10.1%
Urban population:	69.2%	0.5% Black	Irish: 8.8%	
Rural population:	30.8%	1.5% Asian	**2000 Presidential Vote**	
Pop. 2000:	684,280	1.2% Native Am.	Bush (R)..............156,362	(49%)
Median income:	$35,796	0.1% Hawaiian	Gore (D)..............142,123	(44%)
Poverty status:	13.7%	2.5% Two+ races	Other..................22,601	(7%)
Military veterans:	16.9%	0.1% Other	**Cook Partisan Voting Index:** R + 3	
		4.2% Hispanic Origin		

Occupation	Blue collar: 26.3%	White collar: 55.2%	Gray collar: 18.5%

Eugene is nestled in the southernmost bit of lowland at the end of Oregon's Willamette Valley, surrounded by mountains on three sides. It is a farming center, a lumber metropolis and, most notably, a leafy university town. Settlers first arrived here in 1846, farming in the valley and cutting timber in the hills. In 1876, the University of Oregon was established, a symbol of Oregon's strong Yankee cultural ethic and sparse settlement; its first graduating class had just five students. Thousands of miles from most Americans, Eugene and next-door Springfield, once a lumber town and now with computer chip factories, have grown steadily into the comfortable middle-sized towns in which many Americans would like to live. Eugene has bicycle paths along the river banks and on main streets and likes to bill itself as the Running Capital of the Universe; it is where Phil Knight and his former University of Oregon track coach, Bill Bowerman, started Nike—the first soles formed on a waffle iron. The second-largest city in Oregon and one of the most livable in the nation, it offers the ambience of a small town without the isolation.

Beyond Eugene and Springfield, southwestern Oregon is surrounded by green-clad mountains and for years cut more timber than any other place in the country. But demand for wood is volatile, dependent on the vagaries of interest rates; East Asia increasingly wants unprocessed logs rather than milled lumber, which means fewer jobs for Oregon. The early 1980s, when recession reduced the demand for housing, were tough on southern Oregon; the late 1980s, when cutting of old-growth forests was banned to protect the allegedly endangered spotted owl, were even worse. Fears grew that federal restrictions on logging would destroy the area's economy. But in the mid- and late- 1990s an otherwise robust local economy and active job retraining have resulted in local job gains and far less unemployment than forecast

The 4th Congressional District includes Eugene and Springfield and surrounding Lane County; it goes south on Interstate 5 to include Roseburg in Douglas County, once perhaps the premier logging county in the United States. It extends north to Albany and includes most of Corvallis, but not Oregon State University. It includes the entire southern half of Oregon's stunning Pacific coastline, whose craggy seastacks and surging whitecaps were stained by oil as the cargo ship New Carissa was wrecked in Coos Bay in 1999 and later washed up 60 miles north. Eugene is now heavily Democratic. Roseburg and Albany tend to be Republican, leaving a clash of left and right in the district. The travails of the logging industry have moved the area to the right: the 4th District (with only slightly different boundaries) voted 54%–44% against George H. W. Bush in 1988, but in 2000 the district voted 49%–44% for George W. Bush.

The congressman from the 4th District is Peter DeFazio (pronounced *da-FAH-zee-oh*), a Democrat first elected in 1986. He grew up in Massachusetts, came to Oregon for graduate school, and in 1977 went to work for 4th District Congressman Jim Weaver. In 1982 he moved to Springfield and won a seat on the county commission. When Weaver retired in 1986, DeFazio won the House seat in a three-way race. DeFazio beat Bill Bradbury (the 2002 Democratic candidate for governor) by a 34%–33% margin and won the general election 54%–46%. DeFazio has compiled a record that seems to satisfy both Eugene and the rest of the district—liberal on most issues, moderate or even conservative on some. An original founder of the loose-knit Progressive Caucus, he made the case that millions of Americans were suffering during the Clinton administration's booming prosperity. He has opposed NAFTA, GATT and trade promotion authority and strongly criticized the Mexican financial bailout. During the World Trade Organization protests in Seattle, he spent the week marching with coalitions from organized labor and environmental activists. When the protesters moved a few months later to the IMF meeting in Washington, he blamed international financiers for economic and social ills in developing nations. A leader of the fight against PNTR with China, he said that supporters were "a lot of well-intentioned people . . . who think it means their salvation, and actually what it means is their destruction." With the return of a Republican President, DeFazio's populist criticism grew even more outspoken—including, sometimes, of his own party.

DeFazio often takes idiosyncratic views. He authored a bill, with support from both sides of the spectrum, to allow patients greater access to alternative medical treatments, and sought to create special labels for genetically engineered food. He has been a harsh critic of airlines and their broken promises to consumers; a pet cause has been his advocacy of poor treatment of dogs and cats during flights. He also attacked the lack of regulations for cruise ships. Unlike most Democrats, he offered a specific proposal in 2002 to fix Social Security financing: Remove the payroll deduction limitation that benefits the top wage earners. On gun control, he continued to part company with many Democrats. He took the lead in the House in July 2002 with his amendment to permit airline pilots to carry guns in the cockpit. Transportation Secretary Norman Mineta and the Bush administration opposed this, and the Senate had avoided the issue. But DeFazio won by an astonishing 250–175; the Senate a few weeks later followed suit and the Bush administration went along. After the catastrophic wildfires in summer 2002, DeFazio teamed with Republican colleague Greg Walden to seek a middle ground to speed the thinning of brush in the forests. DeFazio's environmental allies denounced him as a turncoat. The bipartisan effort collapsed at the Resources Committee just before the election, but members pledged to try again.

DeFazio has won re-election by impressive margins in a district, which before him was often marginal. After Senator Bob Packwood resigned in 1995, DeFazio ran to succeed him. He had far less money than Portland Congressman Ron Wyden, whom he attacked for receiving money from Packwood contributors; in an ad, DeFazio made the best of this: "[DeFazio's] '63 Dodge tells the lobbyists and special interests he's not for sale." His opposition to gun control, NAFTA and GATT provided clear contrasts with Wyden. He ran strongly in the 4th District and the two nearby counties, leading Wyden 72%–22% there. But Wyden ran ahead 61%–32% in the rest of the state, for a 50%–44% victory in the primary, and went on to win the seat. Since then, DeFazio has called for public financing of campaigns. After Governor John Kitzhaber announced in September 2001 that he would not challenge Senator Gordon Smith, DeFazio considered running for the Senate again. This time he would have had to give up his House seat to do so, and he said he would run only with the "strongest possible support" from Democratic leaders. DSCC Chairman Patty Murray said he was the party's top choice, but executive director Jim Jordan said he "just might want to sit back and watch the process for a while." Translation: No big money till DeFazio raised lots himself and rose in the polls. So in October 2001 he announced he would not run for the Senate. In November 2002, against a 77-year-old former legislator who said every Oregon household should be required own a gun, DeFazio won 64%–34%. Should he not run in some future election, this might well be a seriously contested seat.

FIFTH DISTRICT

Rep. Darlene Hooley (D)

Elected 1996, 4th term; b. Apr. 4, 1939, Williston, ND; home, West Linn; OR St. U., B.S. 1961; Lutheran; divorced.

Elected Office: West Linn City Cncl., 1977–80; OR House of Reps., 1980–86; Clackamas Cnty. Comm., 1987–96.

Professional Career: Teacher, 1961–75.

DC Office: 2430 RHOB 20515, 202-225-5711; Fax: 202-225-5699; Web site: www.house.gov/hooley.

District Offices: Salem, 503-588-9100; West Linn, 503-557-1324.

Committees: *Budget* (3d of 19 D). *Financial Services* (9th of 32 D): Capital Markets, Insurance & Government Sponsored Enterprises; Domestic and International Monetary Policy, Trade & Technology; Financial Institutions & Consumer Credit. *Veterans' Affairs* (8th of 14 D): Health; Oversight & Investigations (RMM).

Group Ratings

	ADA	ACLU	AFS	LCV	CON	ITIC	NTU	COC	ACU	NTLC	CHC
2002	90	86	88	75	13	50	21	50	12	8	17
2001	90	—	90	93	—	—	14	43	4	—	—

National Journal Ratings

	2001 LIB	—	2001 CONS		2002 LIB	—	2002 CONS
Economic	62%	—	38%		61%	—	39%
Social	81%	—	19%		67%	—	29%
Foreign	79%	—	21%		77%	—	19%

Key Votes of the 107th Congress

1. Approve Bush Tax Cuts	Y	5. Faith-Based Charities	N	9. Trade Promotion Authority	N
2. Limit Patients' Bill of Rights	N	6. Bar Gays in the Boy Scouts	N	10. Bar Funds for Intl. Court	N
3. Campaign Finance Reform	Y	7. Ban Partial-Birth Abortion	N	11. Authorize Force in Iraq	N
4. Ban ANWR Development	Y	8. Arm Commercial Pilots	Y	12. Deny Home. Sec. Dept. Union	N

Election Results

2002 general	Darlene Hooley (D)	137,713	(55%)	($622,126)
	Brian Boquist (R)	113,441	(45%)	($158,065)
2002 primary	Darlene Hooley (D)	unopposed		
2000 general	Darlene Hooley (D)	156,315	(57%)	($762,764)
	Brian Boquist (R)	118,631	(43%)	($197,061)

Prior Winning Percentages: 1998 (55%); 1996 (51%)

The People		**Race/Ethnic Origin**	**Ancestry**	
Area size:	5,829 sq. mi.	83.6% White	German: 16.0%	English: 9.7%
Urban population:	80.4%	0.6% Black	Irish: 8.1%	
Rural population:	19.6%	1.9% Asian	**2000 Presidential Vote**	
Pop. 2000:	684,280	1.1% Native Am.	Bush (R) 149,276	(48%)
Median income:	$44,409	0.2% Hawaiian	Gore (D) 144,657	(47%)
Poverty status:	10.9%	2.2% Two+ races	Other 17,047	(5%)
Military veterans:	14.8%	0.1% Other	**Cook Partisan Voting Index:** R + 1	
		10.3% Hispanic Origin		

Occupation   Blue collar: 22.1%   White collar: 60.6%   Gray collar: 17.4%

The Willamette Valley was the great Promised Land at the end of the Oregon Trail, shielded by the Coast Range from the cold storms of the Pacific but squeezing most of the moisture out of the clouds in the form of rain, fog and persistent mist. Here, New England Yankees planted small towns they called Salem and Oregon City, founded schools and colleges, built high-spired churches and eventually Salem's cylindrical-domed Art Deco state Capitol. This was one of the few valleys in the West that settlers found readily suitable for agriculture. The Willamette Valley's soil is fertile, the plain created by the waters of the Willamette sweeping down from the mountains is broad, and the rains everyone hears about in Oregon are dependable. Into this land metro Portland has spread south, with young people leapfrogging over the lands protected from development and into counties to the south.

The 5th Congressional District includes much of the northern Willamette Valley. Near Portland it has the old pioneer town of Oregon City, and spreads south to the rapidly growing state capital of Salem (where the two bridges crossing the Willamette have become jammed at rush hour) and Corvallis (home of Oregon State University and quite liberal). Then the district hops over the Coast Range to take in Lincoln and Tillamook counties, fishing and logging and cheese-making communities; it also includes all of Polk County. Historically, the Willamette Valley was Republican, like the New England whence most of its settlers came, but, also like New England, it has been trending Democratic, and now is prime marginal territory.

The congresswoman from the 5th District is Darlene Hooley, a Democrat elected in 1996. Born in North Dakota, Hooley moved with her family to Salem at age 8. She worked as a reading and physical education teacher in rural Woodburn Gervais and raised her family in West Linn, on the Willamette north of Oregon City. Angry when council members wouldn't replace the rugged asphalt after her son fell off a playground swing and cut his head, she served on the park district board and then was elected to the city council in 1976, at 37. In 1980 she was elected to the Oregon House; in 1987 she was appointed to the Clackamas County Board of Supervisors.

In 1996, Hooley decided to run for Congress. Incumbent Republican Jim Bunn, elected 50%–47% in 1994, combined religious conservatism with a moderate record on issues and support of the Oregon Health Plan and Portland light rail. Hooley had two Democratic primary opponents, but with help from EMILY's List had far more money. She won the primary with 51% and launched attacks on Bunn for supporting Newt Gingrich and Medicare "cuts." Ultimately, she spent $1.1 million, twice as much as the incumbent. Working most strongly against Bunn was his divorce and subsequent marriage to his 31-year-old chief of staff, whom he was paying $97,500—more than any other staffer in Oregon's House delegation. Hooley won 51%–46%, carrying all but one county, though most by narrow margins.

In the House, Hooley has a mostly liberal record. She has failed repeatedly to get a seat on Appropriations and served on the Financial Services Committee instead. Hooley supported the Shays-Meehan campaign finance bill, sought to expand health insurance coverage for children, while also crossing party lines in 2002 to make permanent the elimination of the estate tax and the marriage penalty for taxpayers. She led the fight to preserve Oregon's assisted suicide law, and argued for it on states' rights ground. She joined the moderate New Democrats, contending that she wanted to work with business in a district dependent on trade; in contrast to David Wu in the adjacent suburban district, she voted for PNTR with China. But she joined the other House Democrats from Oregon in opposing trade promotion authority in 2001 and 2002. She called for a "multilateral, not unilateral" approach and voted against the authority to use military force in Iraq.

In this marginal seat, which was represented by two Republicans and two Democrats during the 1990s, Hooley faced a rematch in 2002 against Brian Boquist, an air transport executive who emphasized his knowledge of defense and intelligence and voiced doubts about attacking Iraq. Some Republicans considered Hooley vulnerable, but this was not really a serious contested race. Boquist's fundraising was modest; Hooley felt free to refuse to debate. The Oregon Farm Bureau, which endorsed her in the past, was neutral this time. Boquist criticized Hooley for taking $1,000 from Enron's PAC, which she later returned. In November Hooley won by 55%–45%, a smaller margin than in 2000. Hooley has had health problems, and close observers of these things will keep an eye on this district. Boquist said he wouldn't run again.

★ PENNSYLVANIA ★

P ennsylvania started off as the center of America: Philadelphia was the 13 colonies' largest city when it hosted the Continental Congress in 1776 and the Constitutional Convention in 1787. This was one of the newer colonies, founded 50 years after Massachusetts and 70 years after Virginia. Under the benevolent rule of the early Penns and with its Quaker traditions, Pennsylvania soon became the major settlement in the Middle Colonies: Its tolerance attracted Englishmen of all religious sects and thousands of Germans as well. Bordermen from Scotland, Yorkshire and Northern Ireland crossed the corduroy-like ridges of the Appalachians and settled the mountainous interior where General Braddock had been beaten by the French and Indians not long before, and where a decade later George Washington would again lead troops when the Whiskey Rebellion flared up. On the banks of the wide Delaware estuary, with its thriving commerce and rich hinterland, Philadelphia was, after London and Dublin, the largest Georgian city in the late 18th century. It seemed destined to be the London of America, the metropolis of government and commerce and culture.

But Philadelphia—and Pennsylvania—failed to hold the central position the Founders had expected. The nation's capital was put on the Potomac rather than the Delaware as part of a political deal, and the Erie Canal and the water-level railroad from the Hudson to Lake Erie channeled trade away from Philadelphia to New York. Philadelphia lost its chance to be the nation's financial capital when Andrew Jackson in righteous rage vetoed the rechartering of the Second Bank of the United States. Philadelphia's Quaker tradition, tolerant of diversity and indifferent to others' behavior, was overshadowed in intellectual life by New England's Puritan tradition, angrily intolerant and ready to use the state to impose cultural values from abolition to prohibition.

Instead, Pennsylvania became America's energy and heavy industry capital. The key was coal. Northeast Pennsylvania was the nation's primary source of anthracite, the hard coal used for home heating, and western Pennsylvania was laced with bituminous coal, the soft coal used in steel production. Connected with Philadelphia by the Pennsylvania Railroad, Pittsburgh, where

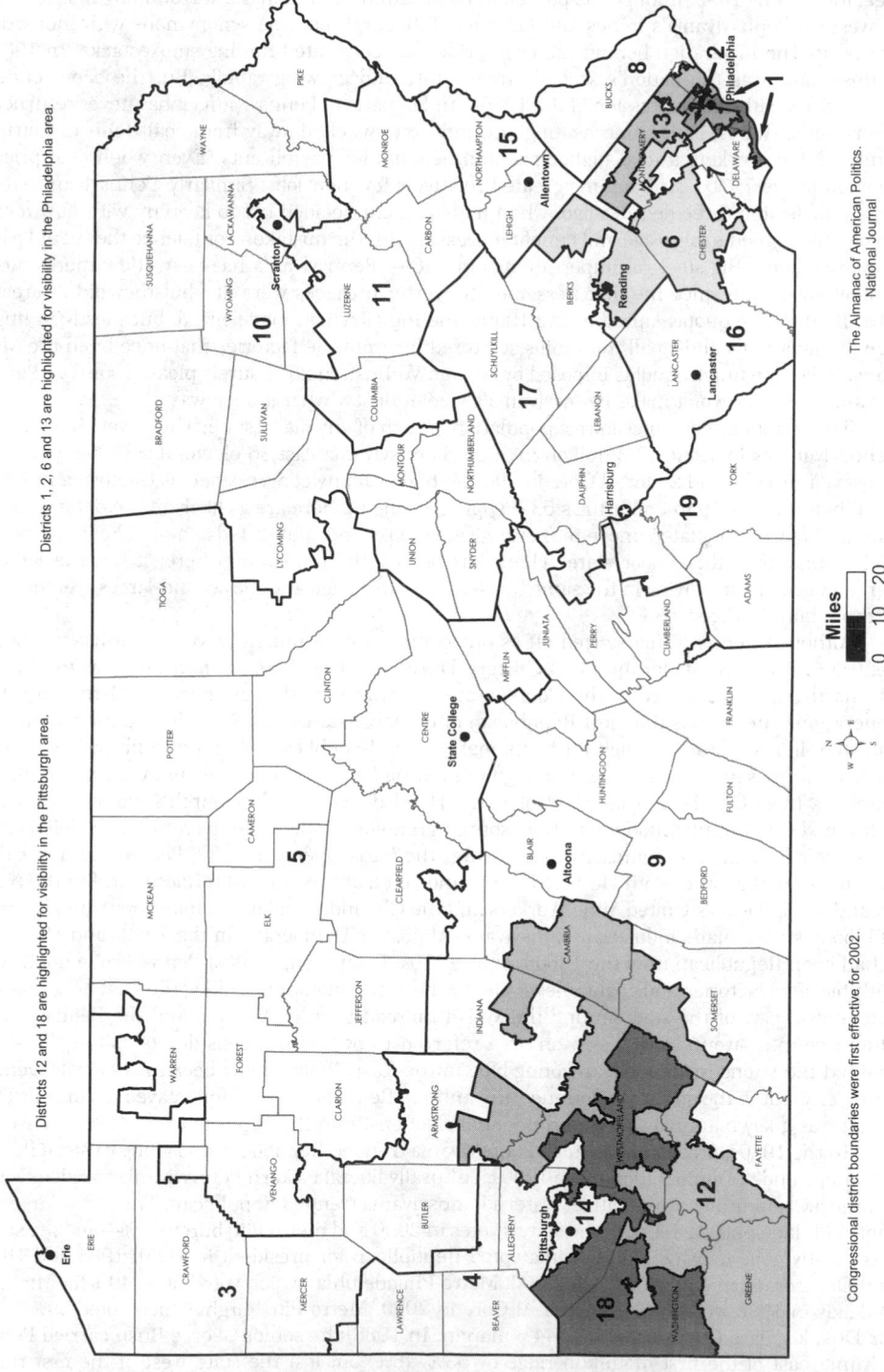

Districts 1, 2, 6 and 13 are highlighted for visibility in the Philadelphia area.

Districts 12 and 18 are highlighted for visibility in the Pittsburgh area.

Congressional district boundaries were first effective for 2002.

The Almanac of American Politics.
National Journal

the Allegheny and Monongahela Rivers join to become the Ohio, was the center of the nation's steel industry by 1890. Immigrants poured in from Europe and from the surrounding hills to work in western Pennsylvania's mines and factories. Pittsburgh became synonymous with industrial prosperity, the inspiration behind the civic pride that celebrated huffing smokestacks. In 1900, Pennsylvania was the nation's second largest state and growing rapidly. But the boom ended conclusively with the Depression of the 1930s, and in parts of Pennsylvania it has never returned. After World War II, both home heating and industry switched away from coal. John L. Lewis's United Mine Workers traded higher pay and benefits for payroll cuts. Even when coal prices boomed in the 1970s, strip mining created relatively few new jobs. Similarly, Pennsylvania steel began its decline three decades ago, when management decided not to keep up with new technology and agreed to big wage and benefit increases with the mistaken confidence they could pass the costs along. Big steel got import quotas in 1969—Pennsylvania has been the nation's most protectionist state since the first Bessemer converter furnaces were lit—but they didn't create jobs. By the time quotas lapsed in the 1990s, the industry had modernized, but mostly in huge new Indiana mills and small mini-mills scattered far from the factories that once lined the Monongahela. The import quotas imposed by George W. Bush in 2001 surely pleased some in Pennsylvania, but they won't make Pennsylvania's steel industry what it once was.

The result has been the slowest population growth of any major state: There were 9.5 million Pennsylvanians in 1930, 12.3 million in 2000. Pennsylvania cast 36 electoral votes for Franklin Roosevelt in 1940 and 23 for Al Gore in 2000; it had as many congressmen as California in 1960 (30), but now has 19 to California's 53. People growing up here are as likely to leave the state as stay, and few out-of-staters move in. Pennsylvania looks and sounds today more like it did in the 1940s than any other major state. There has been little immigration here; it has the largest percentage of people living in the same houses as 30 years ago and the second-largest percentage of those born in the state.

Although Pennsylvania started off as our center of government, government has not been central to Pennsylvania for most of its history. During the Civil War, Pennsylvania was the site of the northernmost advance of the Confederate Army, at Carlisle, just north of Gettysburg; for generations after, it was the most Republican of the large states—for Lincoln and the Union, for the steel industry and the high tariff. Its malodorous Republican machines built parties which were not representative of one ethnic segment but had a place for just about everyone: in Philadelphia's huge City Hall, a knockoff of Paris' Hotel de Ville; in Pittsburgh's massive, Roman-columned City-County Building; in Harrisburg's grandiose Capitol with its rotunda modeled after St. Peter's in Rome and staircase modeled after the Paris Opera. In 1932, Pennsylvania was the only big state that stuck with Herbert Hoover and voted against Franklin Roosevelt. But the New Deal, John L. Lewis's United Mine Workers and the CIO industrial union movement, and a series of bloody strikes made industrial Pennsylvania almost as Democratic in the 1930s and 1940s as it had been Republican from the 1860s to the 1920s. Even then, parts of Pennsylvania not heavy with big steel factories and coal mines—the northern tier of counties along the New York border, the central part of the state around the Welsh railroad town of Altoona, and the Pennsylvania Dutch country around Lancaster, an area referred to by political consultants as the "T"—remained the strongest Republican voting bloc in the East. Philadelphia became a heavily Democratic city, but in the suburban counties, the antique Republican machines stayed in control. The result was a key marginal state in presidential elections from the 1950s to the 1990s.

In the 1980s, prosperous eastern Pennsylvania trended Republican and ailing western Pennsylvania trended Democratic. In the 1990s, culturally liberal eastern Pennsylvania trended Democratic and culturally conservative western Pennsylvania trended Republican. The east is larger—metro Philadelphia cast 32% of the state's votes in 2000 and metro Pittsburgh 21%—and the state has mostly gone its way: Pennsylvania voted Republican for president in 1980, 1984 and 1988 and Democratic in 1992, 1996 and 2000. Metro Philadelphia, which voted 50%–49% for Michael Dukakis in 1988, voted 61%–36% for Al Gore in 2000. Metro Pittsburgh, which voted 59%–40% for Dukakis, gave Gore only a 53%–44% margin. In 1988, the senior George Bush carried Pennsylvania east of the first mountain ridge by 53%–46%, but lost the state west of the first ridge 48%–51%. In 2000, the regions were the other way around. George W. Bush lost Pennsylvania east of the first mountain ridge 45%–54% but carried west of the first ridge 48%–47%. These countervailing trends can best be explained by attitudes on cultural issues. Metro Philadelphia and eastern Pennsylvania are like the rest of the Northeast, liberal on issues like gun control and abortion; content with the economy, voters here moved toward Clinton-Gore Democrats in the 1990s. Pennsylvania west of the first mountain ridge, however, is full of strong-belief Catholics and Protestants and hunters who do not want their guns taken away. Relieved of economic stress, voters here moved toward Republicans in the 1990s.

In Pennsylvania, there is an unusually fine balance on cultural positions. Abortion is not political death here: The late Governor Bob Casey, a strong opponent of abortion, was re-elected by a wide margin in 1990, though he was not allowed to speak at the Democratic National Convention in 1992. And when Governor Tom Ridge first ran for the office in 1994, an anti-abortion independent got 13% of the vote, and Ridge won with only 45%. To be sure, Gore was able to carry the state in 2000 and Democrat and former Philadelphia Mayor Ed Rendell was elected governor in 2002. But Gore's margin was just 51%–46% and Rendell's not much larger, 53%–44%. Republicans have done very well otherwise. They hold both of the state's U.S. Senate seats and, thanks in part to a partisan districting plan, have a 12–7 edge in the House delegation. In 2002, they held the offices of attorney general and treasurer, held their margin in the state Senate and increased it in the state House: Rendell had no coattails. His victory was regional. He carried the historically Republican Philadelphia suburbs by wide margins and swept the Philadelphia media market, where his record as mayor from 1991 to 1999 made him the best known political figure. But he carried usually heavily Democratic metro Pittsburgh and the anthracite counties relatively narrowly and lost by a wide margin in the Pennsylvania Dutch country and the T.

The People		Race/Ethnic Origin			Military veterans: 1,280,788 (13.7%)	
Pop. 2000:	12,281,054	10,322,455	84.1%	White	WWII: 25.7%	Korea: 15.2%
Pop. 1990:	11,881,643	1,202,437	9.8%	Black	Vietnam: 28.7%	Gulf War: 6.8%
Change 1990–2000:	Up 3.4%	218,296	1.8%	Asian	**Most populous cities:**	
Change 1980–1990:	Up 0.1%	14,904	0.1%	Native Am.	1. Philadelphia	1,517,550
% of U.S. total:	4.4%	2,691	0.0%	Hawaiian	2. Pittsburgh	334,563
Pop. rank:	6th of 50	113,097	0.9%	Two+ races	3. Allentown	106,632
Area size:	46,055 sq. mi.	13,086	0.1%	Other	4. Erie	103,717
State Native:	77.7%	394,088	3.2%	Hisp. Origin	5. Reading	81,207
Non-citizen:	2.0%	**Ancestry**			Urban population: 77.0%	
Language		German: 18.6%		Irish: 11.8%	Rural population: 23.0%	
English: 89.2%	Other Eur.: 5.4%	Italian: 8.5%		English: 5.8%		
Spanish: 3.7%		Polish: 4.9%				

Education		Work Sector		General Assembly	
H.S. Grad:	81.9%	Private: 82.4%	Govt: 11.3%	Senate	29 R 21 D
College Grad:	22.4%	Self: 6.0%	Family: 0.3%	House	109 R 94 D
Industry		Unemployment: 5.7%		Legislative Term Limits: No	
Agri: 1.3%	Con: 6.0%	**Household Income**		**Registered Voters**	
Fin: 6.6%	Info: 2.6%	<15k: 16.7%	15-35k: 27.0%	D: 3,759,201 (48.2%)	
Mfg: 21.4%	Prof: 30.4%	35-50k: 16.9%	50-100k: 29.0%	R: 3,219,730 (41.3%)	
Public: 4.2%	Trade: 15.7%	100-150k: 6.6%	>150k: 3.7%	I: 818,461 (10.5%)	
Other: 11.9%		Median: $40,106			
Occupation		Poverty status: 11.0%			
Blue collar: 25.2%	White collar: 59.5%	**Home Value**			
Gray collar: 15.3%		<50k: 17.9% 50-100k: 36.0%	100-200k: 34.4% 200-300k: 7.4%		
		300-500k: 3.1% >500k: 1.2%	Median: $94,800		

Presidential politics   For the last 70 years Pennsylvania has been a swing state in every close presidential election and even in some that were not close. Yet it is not typical of the country. With its older, deeply-rooted population, it tends to be culturally more conservative than the rest of the country; with its long-dying blue-collar communities, it tends to be economically more liberal—though both tendencies are being muted with time. But it does present a problem for political strategists of both parties: Combinations of issue positions which work for Democrats on the East and West Coasts or for Republicans in the South and the Heartland do not work well here. Elderly voters—the New Deal generation— are Pennsylvania's strongest Democratic bloc; they voted 60%–38% for Al Gore in 2000. Voters 30 to 44—the Reagan generation—were the only age group to favor George W. Bush, 50%–47%. There are echoes in the VNS exit poll of the economic politics of the past, with under $15,000-income voters 61%–35% and union members 67%–29% for Gore and over $100,000 voters 60%–36% for Bush. White Protestants continue to be heavily Republican, 60%–39% for Bush; but white Catholics, overwhelmingly for John Kennedy 40 years before, gave Gore only a 50%–46% margin.

2000 Presidential Vote		
Gore (D)	2,485,967	(51%)
Bush (R)	2,281,127	(46%)
Nader (Green)	103,392	(2%)
Other	41,699	(1%)

2000 Republican Presidential Primary		
Bush (R)	472,398	(74%)
McCain (R)	145,719	(23%)
Other	24,968	(4%)

2000 Democratic Presidential Primary		
Gore (D)	525,306	(75%)
Bradley (D)	146,797	(21%)
LaRouche (D)	32,047	(5%)

1996 Presidential Vote		
Clinton (D)	2,215,819	(49%)
Dole (R)	1,801,169	(40%)
Perot (I)	430,984	(10%)

This was a state that both Gore and Bush targeted in 2000; Bush strategists were surprised and disappointed when it went for Gore. But they haven't given up. By spring 2003, Bush had made his 19th trip to Pennsylvania as president, more than in any other state. Pennsylvania is likely to see more of Bush and the Democratic nominee in the 2004 cycle.

Pennsylvania's April presidential primary has not been crucial since 1976, when Jimmy Carter clinched the Democratic nomination here by beating Henry Jackson and Morris Udall. In 1999 the legislature moved the primary date from April 25 to April 4, but it made little difference; both parties' nominations had already been cinched by then.

Congressional districting   Pennsylvania has 19 House members, the fewest since the 12th Congress assembled in 1811, when it had 18. It lost two seats in the reapportionment following the 2000 Census, just as it had after the seven preceding Censuses.

108th Congress Lineup
12 R   7 D
107th Congress Lineup
11 R   10 D

Republicans, with the governorship, a 29–21 majority in the state Senate and a 104–99 majority in the state House, were in firm control of redistricting and were determined to redraw the lines so as to transform its 11–10 margin in the House delegation to 13–6. Demographics suggested eliminating one district each from Philadelphia and the Pittsburgh area. An especial target of Republicans was 18th District Democrat Mike Doyle, who was a top aide to state Senator Frank Pecora when he switched to the Democratic party in 1992 and gave Democrats control of the chamber; he could easily be put in the same district with Pittsburgh's William Coyne. But in August 2001 Coyne announced he would retire, and Doyle ended up surviving.

In December 2001, state Senate Republicans unveiled their plan. Involved in drawing it were Senator Rick Santorum and Congresswoman Melissa Hart. Both had won Pittsburgh area House seats previously held by Democrats—Santorum in 1990 and Hart in 2000—and both wanted to eliminate one Democratic and create one Republican district in the Pittsburgh area. Hart insisted she wanted to keep heavily Democratic Beaver County in her 4th District. The Senate plan put three pairs of Democratic incumbents into the same districts: Tim Holden and Paul Kanjorski, John Murtha and Frank Mascara, and Joe Hoeffel and Robert Borski. It created new Republican-leaning districts with no incumbents in metro Philadelphia and Pittsburgh. It seemed likely to raise the Republican edge to 13–6. The Senate passed it December 11, 27–22, basically along party lines.

But House Majority Leader John Perzel of Philadelphia had a different idea. Perzel is from Northeast Philadelphia, and had been reelected by only 92 votes in 2000, after Democrats put together a registration and voter turnout drive; he was eager to get even. He also cultivated a good relationship with Bob Brady, 1st District congressman and Philadelphia Democratic chairman. Perzel and Brady wanted to preserve three Philadelphia seats, which meant putting more Philadelphia than suburban Democrats in the new district pairing Philadelphian Bob Borski and suburbanite Joe Hoeffel. Perzel's House plan protected Murtha, the second-ranking Democrat on the House Appropriations Committee, and did not create a new Republican-leaning suburban Pittsburgh district.

In the days that followed, Perzel got phone calls from NRCC Chairman Tom Davis and White House political strategist Karl Rove. Georgia Democrats had just passed a redistricting plan that seemed likely to cost Republicans seats they had counted on, and they asked Perzel to accept the Senate plan. He said there weren't enough votes to pass it in the House. But by December 20, House and Senate Republicans were close to agreement; in the days that followed, they reached agreement. Their new plan made adjustments in western Pennsylvania to please Murtha; Mascara's house was placed across the street in the new Republican-leaning district in suburban Pittsburgh. Instead of pairing Democrats Holden and Kanjorski, it put Holden and Republican George Gekas in the same district. Overall it eliminated four Democratic seats and created two Republican-leaning seats.

Lawsuits were filed in both federal and state courts. Democrats argued that the plan was unconstitutional as an obvious partisan gerrymander. But the U.S. Supreme Court in racial redistricting cases in the 1990s had said that, while it was unconstitutional to draw contorted boundaries for racial reasons, it was permissible to do so for partisan reasons. The state Supreme Court rejected the Democrats' arguments. But on April 8, the three-judge federal court ruled that the plan was unconstitutional because there was a difference of 19 between the districts' population, and that the difference should have been 1; this was based on a 1980s U.S. Supreme Court case overturning a much larger population discrepancy. The court invited the legislature to amend its plan and said the election could be put off from May 21 to July 16. The legislature passed a new plan April 15 with a population discrepancy of only 1 and with minor changes, which transferred 0.6% of the state's population into different districts. But the primary season was already on; the filing deadline was March 12. Republicans asked the court to allow 2002 elections to take place under the first plan and some Democrats, afraid that their gubernatorial candidates Ed Rendell and Bob Casey Jr. would exhaust their funds in their primary fight while Republican Mike Fisher was unopposed, joined them. The court acceded.

The plan achieved some but not all of its partisan aims. Republicans took the new suburban districts, but won only narrowly in the new 6th District. Mascara decided to run against Murtha in the primary; Murtha won handily. Borski decided to retire from the House. Democrat Holden beat Republican Gekas in the new 17th District. The result was a 12–7 Republican delegation. But the results indicate that Republicans' hold on several districts is shaky and suggest they may change partisan hands some time between 2004 and 2010. In January 2003 a three-judge federal court approved the legislature's April 15 plan; unless that is overturned by the U.S. Supreme Court, those districts will remain in place through 2010, with essentially the same partisan balance as the districts used in 2002.

Governor

Ed Rendell (D)

Elected 2002, term expires Jan. 2007, 1st term; b. Jan. 5, 1944, New York, NY; home, Harrisburg; U. of PA, B.A. 1965, Villanova U., J.D. 1968; Jewish; married (Marjorie).

Military Career: Army Reserve, 1968–74.

Elected Office: District Atty., City of Philadelphia, 1977–85; Philadelphia Mayor, 1991–99.

Office: 225 Capitol Bldg., Harrisburg, 17120, 717-787-2500; Fax: 717-772-8284; Web site: www.governor.state.pa.us.

Election Results

2002 general	Ed Rendell (D)	1,913,235	(53%)
	Mike Fisher (R)	1,589,408	(44%)
	Other	79,917	(2%)
2002 primary	Ed Rendell (D)	702,442	(57%)
	Bob Casey Jr. (D)	539,794	(43%)
1998 general	Tom Ridge (R)	1,736,844	(57%)
	Ivan Itkin (D)	938,745	(31%)
	Peg Luksik (Const)	315,761	(10%)
	Other	33,802	(1%)

Ed Rendell, a Democrat, was elected governor of Pennsylvania in 2002, the first Philadelphian elected to that position since 1914. He grew up in Manhattan, in an apartment overlooking the Hudson on Riverside Drive; his father was a middleman in the women's clothing business and an ardent New Dealer and his mother's family owned a big women's clothing manufacturer that clashed often with unions. That Rendell became a Democrat who, as mayor, clashed with unions is not perhaps a coincidence. After his father died when he was 14, he acted up and was thrown out of Riverdale Country School for a year. He graduated from the University of Pennsylvania and from the Villanova University law school, and never left Philadelphia. He got a job in Philadelphia District Attorney Arlen Specter's office prosecuting homicides. In 1977, at 33, he was elected district attorney himself, and reelected in 1981. The district attorney is a prominent figure not just in Philadelphia but also in the entire Philadelphia media market, where some 40% of Pennsylvania voters live; prominent enough that former Philadelphia district attorneys are now Pennsylvania's governor and senior U.S. senator. Brash, energetic, cheerful, rumpled (he claims to own only two pairs of shoes), Rendell became a popular public figure in Philadelphia. In 1985 he did not run for reelection but started running for governor; Pennsylvania law requires mayors and district attorneys to resign if they run for statewide office. Since 1955 the two major parties have alternated in the governor's office every eight years; Republican Governor Richard Thornburgh was ineligible to run in 1986, and it seemed the Democrats' turn. In the Democratic primary he faced former Auditor General Bob Casey, who had lost in gubernatorial primaries in 1966, 1970 and 1978. This time Casey won, 51%–40%. Rendell carried the Philadelphia market, but in the rest of the state he seemed perhaps too young, too brash, too Philadelphian. Casey, a father of eight, strong opponent of abortion, with a 76-page blueprint for developing Pennsylvania's economy, proved to be more appealing to economically liberal, culturally conservative Democrats beyond the first Appalachian ridge.

In 1987 Rendell ran unsuccessfully in the Democratic primary against Philadelphia's first black mayor, Wilson Goode. At 43, Rendell seemed to be through politically. But in 1991 he ran for mayor again. With Goode ineligible to run again and the city's finances in dreadful shape, Rendell, campaigning with his usual energy and ebullience, won the Democratic primary 49%–27%. In the general election he faced former Mayor Frank Rizzo, but Rizzo died of a heart attack in July 1991 and Rendell won easily in November, 64%–30%. As mayor, Rendell cut the city payroll, renegotiated absurdly generous union contracts, weathered a 16-hour strike by city employees and even got down on his knees and scrubbed the bathrooms of City Hall. The city employee unions shrieked, but Rendell was obdurate. It was a bravura performance, memorialized in Buzz Bissinger's *A Prayer for the City*. The city's finances were repaired, developers built glittering buildings in Center City and in his second term he managed to cut taxes. In 1999 he campaigned hard for City Council President John Street to succeed him; Street narrowly beat Republican Sam Katz, and had Rendell to thank for his victory. In January 2000 Rendell hung his shingle at the Ballard Spahr law firm and was named Democratic National Chairman. He campaigned for Al Gore, who had called him "America's mayor," but during the Florida controversy Rendell was readier to concede than Gore and his top advisers.

Immediately after the 2000 election Rendell set out to run for governor in 2002. Tom Ridge, the Republican governor elected in 1994 and 1998, was ineligible to run and became George W. Bush's homeland security adviser in October 2001; he was succeeded by Lieutenant Governor Mark Schweiker, who had previously announced he wanted to spend more time with his family and would not run for governor. In the 2002 Democratic primary, Rendell faced Auditor General Bob Casey Jr., whose father had defeated him 16 years earlier. Until May, all the focus was on the Democratic primary. A Republican contest was avoided when Treasurer Barbara Hafer, the party's hapless nominee in 1990 against the senior Casey (who died in 2000), dropped out of the race in January 2002, leaving the field open for conservative Attorney General Mike Fisher.

Early polls showed a close race in the Democratic primary, and many thought that this year, as in 1986, Rendell would be too Philadelphian for the rest of the state. There was a clear contrast between the candidates on issues. Casey, like his father, opposed abortion and said he would sign a ban on abortion if *Roe v. Wade* were reversed. He opposed gun control. Rendell favored abortion rights and gun control. There was a clear difference on economic issues as well. Rendell had an economic development initiative for parts of the state that missed the 1990s boom. Casey concentrated on extending government benefits; he advocated low-cost health insurance for unemployed workers and a $1 rise in the minimum wage. Rendell called for the state to pay for 50% of education costs to lower property taxes; he said he would pay for it by increasing the cigarette tax to 62 cents, putting slot machines in race tracks (which was bringing in a lot of revenue in Delaware) and cutting spending in Harrisburg. He was one-upped when Schweiker persuaded the Republican legislature to increase the cigarette tax to $1. There was also a contrast in demeanor. Rendell embarked on a bus caravan traveling all over the state and campaigned with his usual brio; Casey was tightly scripted, polite and earnest.

Pennsylvania allows unlimited contributions to state campaigns, and this was a big money race: the two candidates spent more than $25 million on the primary. Rendell, a tremendous fundraiser, raised huge amounts from his Philadelphia and national contacts. Casey raised over $5 million from unions, including public employee unions still bitterly opposed to Rendell. Neither campaign ran ads on Philadelphia TV stations: Rendell was so well-known and well-liked there that it would have been a waste of money. Rendell started running ads on Pittsburgh TV in January, saying that his performance in Philadelphia—20,000 new jobs, $300 million in tax cuts—showed he had "the right experience for Pennsylvania." Casey ran largely negative ads, calling Rendell's Philadelphia story a half-truth and blaming him for the conditions of the city's public schools, which had just been taken over by the state. Some of the Casey ads were scorching; a Philadelphia police officer was shown saying about Rendell, "He lies. Cops deal with liars all the time, and we have no respect for anybody who lies." The Democratic state committee endorsed Casey, and he counted on local endorsements, from influential state Senator Vince Fumo and union leaders, to dent Rendell's margin in Philadelphia.

Rendell spent $740,000 on Election Day activities, including $450,000 cash to be handed out in the city's 66 wards. But his popularity in the suburbs was even more decisive. Rendell won 79% of the vote in Philadelphia and even more in the suburbs. Altogether he carried the eight counties in the Philadelphia media market 79%–21%. Usually in Pennsylvania primaries the Pittsburgh area has higher turnout than the Philadelphia area—one reason Rendell lost in 1986. This time it was the other way around. The Philadelphia media market cast 46% of the primary votes. In the Pittsburgh media market, where the candidates had spent $7 million on ads, Rendell made some converts, and Casey won by only 58%–42%. In the rest of the state Casey won, as expected, 66%–34%. Overall Rendell won 57%–43%, though he carried only two of the 59 counties outside the Philadelphia market (Lancaster and the county containing Penn State). Analysts agreed that Casey had run too negative a campaign and had not given voters enough reason to vote for him. In contrast, Rendell ran a mostly positive campaign and presented detailed policies.

After the primary Rendell led Fisher in the polls, but not by much. Pennsylvania's pattern of alternating parties in the governorship every eight years goes back to the 1954 election, but it is not a law of nature. Ridge and Schweiker had high job ratings. Pennsylvania elects judges in off-years, the auditor and treasurer in presidential years, and so there is a statewide partisan race every year, and Republicans have been winning almost all of them since 1990. Republicans held majorities in both houses of the legislature, and in 2002 passed some liberal legislation, tripling the cigarette tax, providing $75 million promised to the Philadelphia schools, adding gays and transgendereds to the hate crime law. Fisher had more experience in state government: he had been elected to the state House in 1974 and the state Senate in 1980 and as attorney general in 1996 and 2000; he had been the unsuccessful nominee for lieutenant governor in 1986 and an unsuccessful candidate in the 1994 primary for governor. His opposition to abortion was by no means a political liability in Pennsylvania. Nor was his platform—cutting the corporate income tax from 9.9% to 7%, expanding the state's prescription drug program with slots money, increased research and development tax credits, requiring school districts to give voters a choice between the property tax and an earned income tax. After the primary, Rendell was almost out of money; he had $1 million to Fisher's $5 million.

Rendell started off on a positive note, saying that Fisher had been a good attorney general and a good state senator. Fisher started more negatively, calling Rendell a "tax-and-spend liberal" and said his success as mayor was greatly exaggerated. Fisher got some bad publicity over the proposed sale of Hershey Foods by the trust that owns the company, when it was revealed that a Fisher aide had told trustees the sale, unpopular in central Pennsylvania, was a good idea. But Fisher fought the sale in court and got a judge to halt it, turning a minus into a plus. George W. Bush raised nearly $2 million for Fisher, who eventually raised $13.8 million. But Rendell vastly outraised him, with $42 million for the entire campaign, more than any other candidate in 2002 except California Governor Gray Davis, Texas Governor Rick Perry and New York Governor George Pataki. In the end, what elected Rendell was his popularity in the Philadelphia media market. In Pennsylvania, outside the two big media markets, Fisher led 58%–39%. But in the Philadelphia media market Rendell won a smashing 68%–30% victory. He won 84% of the vote in Philadelphia, but he also won huge margins in the suburbs where Republicans have a huge registration advantage and which they usually carry in statewide races—67% in Montgomery County, 65% in Delaware County, 63% in Bucks County, 57% in Chester County. Turnout was again higher in the Philadelphia media market, which cast 41% of the state's votes. Interestingly, Rendell did not have much in the way of coattails. In only one suburban Philadelphia state House district did a Democrat oust a Republican, and overall Republicans gained four seats in the state House.

Even before he took office, Rendell started working on state problems. He held nine economic summits around the state in December and January, and put forward a plan to deal with the state's medical malpractice crisis. Physicians were threatening a walkout in northeast Pennsylvania and a suburban Philadelphia hospital shut its trauma unit as malpractice premiums spiked. Rendell proposed a one-time $220 million assessment on the surplus funds of insurance companies to cut physicians' premiums by one-quarter in 2002 and called for requiring certificates of merit from an expert panel before malpractice suits could go forward. He also set about paring the state budget, with help from the unlikely quarter of AFSCME, when sent in a proposal to save $259 million by reducing the state work force and restricting overtime; Rendell said he wouldn't rule out layoffs and benefit cuts.

Senior Senator

Arlen Specter (R)

Elected 1980, seat up 2004, 4th term; b. Feb. 12, 1930, Wichita, KS; home, Philadelphia; U. of PA, B.A. 1951, Yale U., LL.B. 1956; Jewish; married (Joan).

Military Career: Air Force, 1951–53.

Elected Office: Philadelphia Dist. Atty., 1965–73.

Professional Career: Practicing atty., 1955–56, 1974–80; Asst. Cnsl., Warren Comm., 1964; PA Asst. Atty. Gen., 1964–65.

DC Office: 711 HSOB, 20510, 202-224-4254; Fax: 202-228-1229; Web site: specter.senate.gov.

State Offices: Allentown, 610-434-1444; Erie, 814-453-3010; Harrisburg, 717-782-3951; Philadelphia, 215-597-7200; Pittsburgh, 412-644-3400; Scranton, 570-346-2006; Wilkes-Barre, 570-826-6265.

Committees: *Appropriations*: Agriculture & Rural Development; Defense; Foreign Operations; Homeland Security; Labor, HHS & Education (Chmn.); Transportation, Treasury & General Government. *Governmental Affairs*: Financial Management, Budget & International Security; Investigations (Permanent). *Judiciary*: Administrative Oversight & the Courts; Antitrust, Competition Policy & Consumer Rights; Terrorism, Technology & Homeland Security. *Veterans' Affairs* (Chmn.).

Group Ratings

	ADA	ACLU	AFS	LCV	CON	ITIC	NTU	COC	ACU	NTLC	CHC
2002	35	60	38	53	8	75	42	85	50	56	—
2001	40	—	42	50	—	—	59	79	56	—	40

National Journal Ratings

	2001 LIB — 2001 CONS	2002 LIB — 2002 CONS
Economic	52% — 48%	49% — 49%
Social	57% — 43%	43% — 56%
Foreign	58% — 41%	51% — 47%

Key Votes of the 107th Congress

1. Approve Bush Tax Cuts	Y	5. Confirm Ashcroft as AG	Y
2. Expand Patients' Rights	Y	6. Bar Gays in the Boy Scouts	N
3. Campaign Finance Reform	Y	7. $ for Hate Crime Prosecution	N
4. Permit ANWR Development	Y	8. Overseas Military Abortions	Y

9. Bar Coop. with Intl. Court	N
10. Trade Promotion Authority	Y
11. Authorize Force in Iraq	Y
12. Homeland Sec. Dept. Union	Y

Election Results

1998 general	Arlen Specter (R)	1,814,180	(61%)	($4,535,887)
	Bill Lloyd (D)	1,028,839	(35%)	($187,157)
	Other	114,753	(4%)	
1998 primary	Arlen Specter (R)	376,322	(67%)	
	Larry Murphy (R)	101,120	(18%)	
	Tom Lingenfelter (R)	82,168	(15%)	
1992 general	Arlen Specter (R)	2,358,125	(49%)	($10,454,793)
	Lynn Yeakel (D)	2,224,966	(46%)	($5,028,669)
	John F. Perry (Lib)	219,319	(5%)	($53,690)

Prior Winning Percentages: 1986 (56%); 1980 (50%)

Arlen Specter, one of the nation's most durable career politicians, has held public office and has been an important national figure off and on for nearly four decades. Specter grew up in Russell, Kansas, also the hometown of Bob Dole; his father was an immigrant who worked as a tailor, owned a junkyard and sent four children through college. Specter came to Philadelphia at 17 to attend the University of Pennsylvania. After college he served in the Air Force, went to Yale Law School and practiced law in Philadelphia. In 1964 he was a top staffer for the Warren Commission investigating the Kennedy assassination, where he helped develop the single-bullet theory; at one point, he held Oswald's weapon and aimed it out the Texas Schoolbook Depository window toward Dealey Plaza. After the Warren Commission, he returned to his law practice, switched to the

Republican Party, and was elected district attorney in Democratic Philadelphia in 1965 and again in 1969. He lost the race for D.A. in 1973, and was beaten in Republican primaries for senator in 1976 and governor in 1978. In 1980 he ran for the Senate again. He narrowly (36%–33%) edged a former state Republican chairman in the primary and beat a low-spending Democrat 50%–48% in the general. In 1986, he won re-election by a 56%–43% margin; in 1992 he was re-elected 49%–46% after he became a target of feminists for his questioning of Anita Hill during the confirmation hearings of Clarence Thomas. He ran for president in 1995, but withdrew before the first caucus or primary.

Throughout this career of narrow victories and numerous defeats, Specter's assets have been brains and hard work. He is respected by colleagues and constituents, though not always well-liked. He sides with conservatives on some divisive issues, with liberals on others, building up no permanent credit with either. He is aggressive and prosecutorial, well-prepared and persuasive once he takes a stand. These traits are both his strengths and weaknesses; they explain why he was vulnerable in 1992, and why he won; why he ran for president, and why his campaign went nowhere. His voting record is almost precisely at the midpoint of the Senate, and he has played key roles on a variety of issues. Though he switched and voted to override Bill Clinton's partial-birth abortion veto, he is generally pro-choice on abortion—an issue he featured in his presidential campaign, infuriating many Republican activists. He pushes tough penalties for crime and supports capital punishment. On a closely divided and rancorous Judiciary Committee, he played a key role on several Supreme Court nominations. More than anyone else, he defeated Robert Bork in 1987 and, more than anyone but John Danforth, he secured the confirmation of Clarence Thomas in 1991.

On impeachment, Specter took his own course. "I propose abandoning impeachment and, after the president leaves office, holding him accountable in the same way any other person would be: through indictment and prosecution for any federal crimes established by the evidence," he said in November 1998. In February 1999, in a decision he called "a lot ambiguous, maybe even a little amorphous," Specter said he would vote for the Scotch verdict of "not proven." "I think it is important to make a distinction that I do not believe that the president is not guilty," he said. "It's a trial on which you can't really come to a verdict because of the absence of witnesses and the absence of relevant evidence." In February 2001 he held hearings on Clinton's last-minute pardons of Marc Rich and others, and on one television news show said tantalizingly, "I'm not suggesting it should be done, but President Clinton technically could still be impeached." But he declined to call on Clinton to testify.

On many issues, Specter has been one of the few Republicans voting with Senate Democrats—on the Republican tax cut in August 1999, the Comprehensive Test Ban Treaty in October 1999, the minimum wage in November 1999, on the federal tobacco lawsuit in July 2000, HMO regulation in July 2000. He quickly supported the nomination of John Ashcroft, but in May 2001 he said the administration should let the American Bar Association play a role in vetting nominees before they were announced. With Lincoln Chafee and Jim Jeffords, he played a critical role in May 2001 in reducing the Bush tax cut from $1.6 trillion to $1.3 trillion. He voted for the farm bill in May 2002 because of its dairy provisions. He was one of four Republicans to vote for the Graham-Smith prescription drug bill in July 2002. He opposed George W. Bush's $250,000 limit on pain and suffering damages in medical malpractice cases, arguing that there should be no limit for egregious cases of severe bodily impairment, disfigurement or death; his son Shanin Specter is a Philadelphia malpractice lawyer who won a $49 million settlement in 2000.

To foreign policy he often brings a legalistic approach. In March 1998 he said that Saddam Hussein should be tried as a war criminal. His May 1999 amendment to the defense authorization bill, invoking the War Powers Act to prevent the deployment of ground troops in the former Yugoslavia, failed 52–48. He has taken the lead in making contacts with supposed moderates in the Iranian government, sending a letter to Tehran seeking talks in spring 2000, meeting with a delegation of Iranian legislators in August 2000 and hosting a dinner for the Iranian ambassador to the United Nations in October 2001. In November 2001 he questioned the administration's proposal for military tribunals. In July 2002 he called for a congressional vote on military action in Iraq. "We have a responsibility institutionally under the Constitution to declare war, and we have a responsibility to acquaint the American people as to what is involved." In debate on the resolution in October, he expressed doubts about whether Congress can delegate authority to president, but he voted for the resolution. In January 2003 he said it was not necessary for the United States to go back to the UN Security Council before taking action, but "realistically we should."

Specter has played a major role in encouraging medical research. He has supported changes in federal organ transplant policy in 1998 (Pittsburgh has a big organ transplant hospital) and called in 1999 for research on stem cells from human embryos. He and Tom Harkin, working from the Appropriations subcommittee they chaired, successfully completed their project of doubling the research budget of the National Institutes of Health in five years. In 2002 he sponsored one of the two major competing bills on stem cell research. Specter's bill would allow embryonic stem cell research but ban cloning for reproductive purposes; his chief co-sponsors were Harkin and Orrin Hatch. For most of the year he skirmished with Sam Brownback, sponsor of a bill that would ban embryonic stem cell research. In September 2002 Specter claimed he had 60 votes for his bill, but it was not brought to the floor. Specter is quick to act in response to breaking news. In 1999, when Pennsylvania was financing new stadiums in Philadelphia and Pittsburgh, he called for a 50% limit on public contributions to stadiums and for teams to set aside 10% of television revenues to pay for them; when a baseball strike loomed in 2002, he called for hearings on baseball's 80-year-old exemption from the antitrust laws. When the Clinton administration issued a report on medical errors, he held two quick hearings in two months, one on a day when the government was closed by a blizzard, and was the first senator with legislation on the subject.

Specter is not shy about using his place on the committee to funnel money into Pennsylvania, from the Philadelphia Navy Yard to Lake Erie. He has promised to work to keep the Tobyhanna Army Depot off the base-closing list in 2005.

After Jim Jeffords left the Republican party in May 2001, Specter was given a position in the leadership as a representative of Republican moderates. After the Jeffords switch, he proposed that members could serve only six years combined as chairman or ranking member. In August 2002 the Republican Conference voted for a somewhat different approach: the five months members served as chairmen from January to June 2001 would not be counted as a term as chairman, and members could serve up to six years as ranking minority member after serving six years as chairman, but once they had been chairman for six years they could no longer serve as ranking minority member. Specter was one moderate who stood by Trent Lott after his comments at Strom Thurmond's 100th birthday party December 5, 2002. On December 11 he said, "I know Trent Lott very well from working with him in the Senate for the last 14 years and can vouch for the fact that he is no supporter of Senator Thurmond's 1948 platform. His comment was an inadvertent slip and his apology should end the discussion." Specter is known as one of Capitol Hill's sternest taskmasters; a *PoliticsPA.com* poll of opinion leaders rated him the hardest politician to work for and a *Washingtonian* poll of Capitol Hill staffers rated him the third "meanest" senator. *The Washington Post* reported Specter is notorious for his demands on overseas trips, which include daily squash matches at 5:00 p.m., English-speaking drivers, "customs expeditors," and planned excursions for his wife.

Specter comes up for reelection in 2004. In February 2003, Congressman Pat Toomey announced he will challenge Specter in the Republican primary. Toomey, who when first elected in 1998 promised to serve only three terms, is an advocate of tax cuts and an opponent of abortion; both religious conservatives and the Club for Growth had urged him to run. White House political strategist Karl Rove made it clear to Toomey that George W. Bush would support Specter; White House Chief of Staff Andrew Card in February 2003 attended a fundraiser for Specter in Toomey's district. But the Republican primary electorate is more conservative than Pennsylvania as a whole. Specter has had primary opposition every time he has run for reelection. In 1986 he was renominated 76%–24% over a social studies teacher who said he had entered the race at God's urging; in 1992 he won 65%–35% over a state representative who opposed abortion; in 1998 he won with 67% against two candidates who won 18% and 15%. All that suggests that Toomey could probably count on one-third of the primary vote. But he is not well-known and would have to raise considerable sums to get his case to the voters. Should he surprise Washington insiders and upset

Specter, he might be vulnerable to the charge that he is an extreme conservative. But it's not clear whether the Democrats will have a strong nominee, and Specter's colleague, Rick Santorum, who has a record on issues similar to Toomey's, has won two Senate elections in Pennsylvania in the last 10 years.

Specter will not lose for lack of money or hard work. By May 2003 he had $7 million in his campaign treasury, and he can easily raise much more. At that point, no prominent Democrats appeared to be interested in making the race. Auditor General Bob Casey Jr., who lost the 2002 gubernatorial nomination to Ed Rendell, is term-limited, but was expected to run for another state post instead. Talk show host Chris Matthews, a Philadelphia native and former top aide to Speaker Tip O'Neill, was mentioned, but not after he signed a seven-year contract with NBC in 2002. Governor Ed Rendell appeared in a TV ad for Specter in 1998, and may not be eager to oust Pennsylvania's high-ranking member of the Senate Appropriations Committee. So it is possible that Specter, even if he encounters trouble in the primary, will face a general election campaign like that in 1998, when his opponent spent only $187,000 and Specter was endorsed by the AFL-CIO and the United Steelworkers and won 61%–35%, winning 58% in both big metro areas. If he is reelected, Specter will be the first Pennsylvania senator to be popularly elected to five terms, and 10 months into the term he will break the record tenure for a Pennsylvania senator, held by Boies Penrose (1897–1921).

Junior Senator

Rick Santorum (R)

Elected 1994, seat up 2006, 2d term; b. May 10, 1958, Winchester, VA; home, Penn Hills; PA St. U., B.A. 1980, U. of Pittsburgh, M.B.A. 1981, Dickinson Law Schl., J.D. 1986; Catholic; married (Karen).

Elected Office: U.S. House of Reps., 1990–94.

Professional Career: A.A., PA Sen. J. Doyle 1981–86; Exec. Dir., PA Senate Local Govt. Cmte., 1981–84; Exec. Dir., PA Senate Transportation Cmte., 1984–86; Practicing atty., 1986–90.

DC Office: 511 DSOB, 20510, 202-224-6324; Fax: 202-228-0604; Web site: santorum.senate.gov.

State Offices: Allentown, 610-770-0142; Altoona, 814-946-7023; Erie, 814-454-7114; Harrisburg, 717-231-7540; Philadelphia, 215-864-6900; Pittsburgh, 412-562-0533; Scranton, 570-344-8799.

Committees: *Republican Conference Chairman. Aging (Special). Banking, Housing & Urban Affairs:* Financial Institutions; Housing & Transportation; Securities & Investment. *Finance:* Health Care; Social Security & Family Policy (Chmn.); Taxation & IRS Oversight. *Rules & Administration.*

Group Ratings

	ADA	ACLU	AFS	LCV	CON	ITIC	NTU	COC	ACU	NTLC	CHC
2002	5	25	0	6	84	75	77	95	95	97	—
2001	10	—	0	0	—	—	82	86	100	—	100

National Journal Ratings

	2001 LIB — 2001 CONS		2002 LIB — 2002 CONS	
Economic	7%	—	86%	6%	—	90%
Social	0%	—	79%	39%	—	60%
Foreign	36%	—	54%	0%	—	76%

Key Votes of the 107th Congress

1. Approve Bush Tax Cuts	Y	5. Confirm Ashcroft as AG	Y	9. Bar Coop. with Intl. Court	Y
2. Expand Patients' Rights	N	6. Bar Gays in the Boy Scouts	Y	10. Trade Promotion Authority	Y
3. Campaign Finance Reform	N	7. $ for Hate Crime Prosecution	N	11. Authorize Force in Iraq	Y
4. Permit ANWR Development	Y	8. Overseas Military Abortions	*	12. Homeland Sec. Dept. Union	N

Election Results

2000 general	Rick Santorum (R)	2,481,962	(52%)	($10,616,262)
	Ron Klink (D)	2,154,908	(46%)	($3,641,167)
	Other	98,246	(2%)	
2000 primary	Rick Santorum (R)	unopposed		
1994 general	Rick Santorum (R)	1,735,691	(49%)	($6,732,849)
	Harris Wofford (D)	1,648,481	(47%)	($6,300,560)
	Other	129,189	(4%)	

Prior Winning Percentages: 1992 House (61%); 1990 House (51%)

Rick Santorum, a Republican elected in 1994, is the fifth-youngest senator, elected from one of the oldest states, a strong conservative elected in a state that still has many New Deal voters. Santorum is the son of an Italian immigrant who was a clinical psychologist for the Veterans' Administration; he was born in Virginia and moved to Butler, Pennsylvania, at age 7. He started in politics working for John Heinz's first Senate campaign in 1976; he went to Penn State and the University of Pittsburgh business school and worked his way through Dickinson law school as a staffer for state Senate Republicans in Harrisburg; he worked for a blue chip law firm in Pittsburgh for four years. In 1990, at 32, he challenged seven-term incumbent Congressman Doug Walgren, who outspent him $717,000 to $251,000. But Santorum knocked on 25,000 doors, amassed an army of volunteers including many right-to-lifers, attacked Walgren for voting for a pay raise seven times and for living in the Washington suburbs. Santorum opposed the congressional pay raise, backed the line-item veto and came out for limits on PAC contributions. He won 51%–49%.

In the House he had a solid conservative voting record and was one of the "Gang of Seven" freshman Republicans who helped expose the House bank scandal. Redistricting gave him a seat shorn of many Republican suburbs and centered on the industrial Monongahela Valley, historically very Democratic. Santorum beat a state senator 61%–38%—an astonishing victory. Brash and confident, Santorum immediately started running for the Senate. His opponent was Harris Wofford, appointed in May 1991 to replace John Heinz (who died in a plane crash), and subsequently elected in a November 1991 special election upset win over former Governor Dick Thornburgh 55%–45%. Wofford won the special election by emphasizing health care; he was politically hurt when the Clinton health care bill failed to pass. This was a race of sharp contrasts in issues and style: Santorum, brashly eager to chop government, backing medical savings accounts and opposing gun control; Wofford, a former civil rights activist, earnestly working for government health care financing, backing the 1994 crime bill and gun control. Wofford appealed to a long liberal tradition; Santorum scoffed at him for championing 1960s ideas in the 1990s. Santorum ran behind only 50%–47% in metro Pittsburgh, where Wofford had won 61% in 1991. Santorum did not go over so well in metro Philadelphia, which Wofford carried 54%–42%. But in the rest of the state—where half the votes are cast and where gun control hurt Wofford—Santorum won 55%–41%, for a statewide victory of 49%–47%. Since then, they have become allies of sorts. Bill Clinton appointed Wofford to head AmeriCorps, a Clinton initiative Santorum had called a "government boondoggle" that paid "hippie kids to stand around a campfire holding hands and singing 'Kumbaya.'" But Wofford transformed it into a program that provided government support for private nonprofits, and Santorum has supported it and gave Wofford credit.

Santorum was not cowed by the traditions of the Senate. In his first full month there he argued about the balanced budget amendment with Robert Byrd, who was first elected to the Senate the year Santorum was born. Then, when senior Republican Mark Hatfield cast a decisive vote against the amendment, Santorum called on Hatfield to be removed as Appropriations chairman. Senior senators and Washington insiders tut-tutted. Hatfield wasn't removed, but Senate Republicans changed the rules, limiting chairmen to six years and calling for secret ballot elections of chairmen starting in 1997. Later in 1995 Santorum took to the floor a dozen times with a "Where's Bill?" sign, asking where the President's balanced budget was; Democrats were furious.

Santorum's voting record remains one of the most conservative in the Senate, but he is not quite so brash anymore. As his colleague Arlen Specter said in November 2002, "Rick might not like my saying this, but I think he's moderated a good bit over the years." After the 2000 election he was elected chairman of the Republican Conference, the number three position in the leadership, in charge of communicating Senate Republicans' message, by a 30–20 margin over Christopher Bond. He has taken the lead on important legislation, and on occasion at some political risk. Santorum floor-managed the welfare bill to passage three times in 1995 and 1996; the first two times it was vetoed by Bill Clinton, but in August 1996, 13 weeks before the election, Clinton signed it. Santorum has also taken the lead on the partial birth abortion ban. It was vetoed twice by Clinton; in March 2003, Santorum introduced the measure one again and it passed the Senate 64–33; it awaited House action. This was not just a theoretical issue for him: In 1996 he and his wife had to decide what to do when their unborn child had a fatal defect; the baby was born in October 1996 and died two hours later.

The 1996 welfare bill contained a provision allowing more leeway for faith-based organizations to get government money to provide social services. Some use of this was made by the Clinton administration, and George W. Bush mentioned faith-based services frequently in his 2000 campaign. As president, Bush issued an executive order allowing more grants to faith-based organizations and called for Congress to pass legislation providing tax deductions and credits to strengthen such groups. This proved to be a rocky process, in which Santorum and Joe Lieberman took the lead role in the Senate. The House passed a bill in July 2001 with expanded block grants, tax breaks and a provision exempting faith-based organizations from state anti-discrimination laws, similar to that in the 1996 welfare act; some organizations want to hire members of their own faith and some refuse to hire homosexuals. In February 2002 Santorum and Lieberman introduced their bill, expanded block grants to states for child care and family welfare, providing a charitable deduction of $800 to couples who take the standard deduction, tax breaks for corporations who give money to charities, and tax deductions to banks which match individual development accounts set by low-income people for their education or starting a business. The Finance Committee passed a pared-down version in June 2002, without the corporate tax breaks. In September, Santorum tried to get the bill to the floor under a procedure allowing one amendment for each party, with Phil Gramm moving to delete the individual development accounts. But Jack Reed of Rhode Island wanted to introduce several amendments, and Tom Daschle never put the measure on the calendar. In January 2003 Santorum reintroduced the bill.

As Republican Conference Chairman, Santorum has worked aggressively to develop a unified voice for the party and to get Republican senators in touch with constituencies they have previously not had much to do with. One project has been to increase the number of Republicans hired to run business lobbies. Since the days of the New Deal, most Washington lobbyists have been Democrats, a natural development given that the Democrats held the White House from 1932 to 1952 and for most of the years from 1960 to 1980 and had majorities in the House and, except for six years, in the Senate from 1954 to 1994. Santorum and his allies argue that Democratic lobbyists tilt business interests toward Democrats, both in public policy and in campaign contributions. Santorum has held monthly breakfasts with Republican lobbyists, sometimes including White House political strategist Karl Rove. "We've been deficient in using our friends in the lobbying community who are sympathetic to our message, to let them know what we're doing and why and getting that out through their clients." With Congressman J. C. Watts and Americans for Tax Reform's Grover Norquist, Santorum objected loudly in early September 2001 when Boeing hired a Democrat to head its Washington office. Leaders of left-leaning organizations objected, and in 2002 complaints were made to the Senate Ethics Committee. In August 2002 the committee sent out a letter to all senators saying they can't deny access to lobbyists based on their political party or campaign contributions.

On internal party matters, Santorum in June 2002 asked for reconsideration or clarification of the party's six-year term limit on committee chairmen. The Republican Conference met and agreed that service as chairman from January to June 2001 did not count against the term limit, that members could serve six years as ranking minority member in addition to six years as chairman, provided that after six years as chairman they could no longer be ranking minority member; the issue was mooted, for the time being, by Republicans' recovery of the Senate majority in the 2002 election. In December 2002 Santorum was one of the staunchest defenders, in public and in private, of Majority Leader Trent Lott after his comments at Strom Thurmond's 100th birthday party December 5. On December 15 he said, "Senator Lott's affirmation that all people are equal—not only under our Constitution but also in the eyes of God—reflects the Trent Lott that I have known and worked with for so many years." On December 17 he said, "I'm confident Senator Lott will be our leader." But support for Lott was crumbling and it was clear that the required five senators would call for a meeting of the Republican Conference when Congress convened on January 6. On December 20, Lott bowed out. Santorum began calling senators seeking support for the position himself and got a public endorsement from Arlen Specter. But by the end of the afternoon it was clear that Bill Frist had the votes. Santorum convened a Conference meeting by phone call on December 23, and Frist was chosen without opposition. Before the Lott affair, Santorum was in line to become chairman of the Rules Committee and was making plans for the job. But in January he stepped aside to allow Lott to become chairman.

Santorum has taken some stands with a view to local interests and out of personal beliefs. He backed minimum wage increases in the House and Senate, and supported the steel import quota bill that died in June 1999. He backed George W. Bush's steel import quotas in March 2002 and worked to try to link oil drilling in the Arctic National Wildlife Refuge with the proposal for the government legacy payments—payments of health insurance costs for steelworkers whose companies have gone bankrupt. After the May 2002 cancellation of the Army's Crusader cannon, he sought continued work for contractor United Defense. In January 2003 he and Arlen Specter sought to allow financially troubled USAirways, whose big hub is in Pittsburgh, more time to make payments from their pension plan. He supported the compromise organ transplant bill which would have sent organs to the sickest patients instead of those who live closest to the donors (Pittsburgh has one of the country's biggest organ transplant programs). He opposed George W. Bush's proposal for a $250,000 cap on pain and suffering damages in medical malpractice cases; in 1999 his wife sued a chiropractor for $500,000 for back injuries and was awarded $175,000. He has proposed a Puppy Protection Act, to require the closing of puppy mills that have violated the Animal Welfare Act three times.

Santorum is the first Republican generally classified as conservative to have been elected senator in Pennsylvania since 1952, and some thought he would be in trouble in 2000. But he ended up winning convincingly. Three major Democrats ran in the primary: state Senator Allyson Schwartz, from Philadelphia; former state Labor Secretary Tom Foley, from Hershey, who ran unsuccessfully for lieutenant governor in 1994 and auditor general in 1996; and Congressman Ron Klink, from suburban Pittsburgh and a former anchor on KDKA-TV. This was primarily a regional contest. Klink, who opposes gun control and abortion, had great strength in his home media market; he borrowed $300,000 on his home and put most of his money into Pittsburgh TV. Klink's strategy paid off. Metro Pittsburgh, which cast 35% of the vote, voted 73% for Klink. Statewide, Klink won 41% of the vote, to 27% for Schwartz and 25% for Foley.

On paper Klink looked like a strong candidate, with vote-getting appeal in Santorum's home base and conservative issue stands appealing in the "T" between metro Philadelphia and metro Pittsburgh. Klink launched an attack at Santorum's proposal for individual investment accounts in Social Security; Santorum continued to argue for the proposal. Social Security is supposed to be a Democratic issue, especially in states with large elderly populations like Pennsylvania. But there is no evidence that the issue hurt Santorum in 2000. Santorum was way ahead in one key respect: money. Santorum had $3.7 million cash on hand after the April primary; Klink had $119,000, with debts of $446,000. And Klink had great difficulty raising more. For Democratic donors in the Philadelphia area, and for that matter in the nation generally, no issues evoke stronger emotions than abortion and gun control, and on these issues Klink's stands were totally out of line with the Democratic contributor base. In the meantime, Santorum was running positive ads about his record, campaigning as a "compassionate conservative," emphasizing his ability to work with Democrats like Joseph Lieberman and Rendell. The first Klink ads did not go up until September; he went negative against Santorum, and voters never really heard a positive case for Klink. Santorum won 52%–46%. He ran behind in metro Philadelphia 53%–45%, but this 8% margin was far less than Al Gore's 25% margin over George W. Bush there. Santorum ran slightly behind his 1994 showing in metro Pittsburgh, which Klink carried 52%–46%. But in the rest of the state, which cast 46% of the votes, Santorum won a whopping 60%–37% margin, a big improvement over 1994.

After 2000 Santorum began taking a role in other elections. He was one of the few Republican senators who backed Congressman John Sununu in the New Hampshire primary against incumbent Senator Bob Smith. Santorum also played a key role in Pennsylvania redistricting. Santorum also worked hard for the unsuccessful candidacy of Lou Barletta against 11th District Democrat Paul Kanjorski, to the point that Kanjorski charged Santorum had instigated an FBI probe of his relationship to a firm controlled by members of his family which had received $7.5 million in federal grants in three years. Kanjorski won, but the redistricting plan proved successful: Republicans went into the election with an 11–10 edge in the delegation and emerged ahead 12–7.

In April 2003 Santorum sparked controversy with his remarks regarding a landmark gay rights case before the Supreme Court. "If the Supreme Court says that you have the right to consensual [gay] sex within your home, then you have the right to polygamy, you have the right to incest, you have the right to adultery. You have the right to anything," he told the *Associated Press*. Democrats and gay rights groups harshly criticized Santorum for his comments; several Senate Republicans also criticized him. Santorum refused to apologize, explaining that he was speaking to the position taken by the high court in a previous gay rights case and did not want to elevate gay sex into a constitutional right.

FIRST DISTRICT

Rep. Robert Brady (D)

Elected May 1998, 3d term; b. April 7, 1945, Philadelphia; home, Philadelphia; Catholic; married (Debra).

Elected Office: 34th Ward Dem. Exec. Cmte. Mbr., 1967–present, Ward Ldr., 1980.

Professional Career: Carpenter; Real estate salesman; Philadelphia Dpty. Mayor for Labor, 1984–87; Chmn., Philadelphia Dem. Party, 1986; Legis. Rep., Metro. Regional Cncl. of Carpenters & Joiners, 1987–98; Lecturer, U. of PA, 1997-present.

DC Office: 206 CHOB 20515, 202-225-4731; Fax: 202-225-0088; Web site: www.house.gov/robertbrady.

District Offices: Chester, 610-874-7094; Philadelphia, 215-389-4627.

Committees: *Armed Services* (16th of 29 D): Readiness; Tactical Air & Land Forces. *House Administration* (3d of 3 D).

Group Ratings

	ADA	ACLU	AFS	LCV	CON	ITIC	NTU	COC	ACU	NTLC	CHC
2002	95	87	89	88	52	38	20	45	4	6	0
2001	95	—	100	64	—	—	13	43	16	—	—

National Journal Ratings

	2001 LIB —	2001 CONS		2002 LIB —	2002 CONS
Economic	72%	— 29%		88%	— 10%
Social	83%	— 11%		84%	— 8%
Foreign	61%	— 36%		72%	— 26%

Key Votes of the 107th Congress

1. Approve Bush Tax Cuts	N	5. Faith-Based Charities	N	9. Trade Promotion Authority	N
2. Limit Patients' Bill of Rights	N	6. Bar Gays in the Boy Scouts	N	10. Bar Funds for Intl. Court	Y
3. Campaign Finance Reform	Y	7. Ban Partial-Birth Abortion	N	11. Authorize Force in Iraq	N
4. Ban ANWR Development	N	8. Arm Commercial Pilots	N	12. Deny Home. Sec. Dept. Union	N

Election Results

2002 general	Robert Brady (D)	121,076	(86%)	($355,578)
	Marie Delaney (R)	17,444	(12%)	
	Other	1,570	(1%)	
2002 primary	Robert Brady (D)	unopposed		
2000 general	Robert Brady (D)	149,621	(88%)	($411,375)
	Steven N. Kush (R)	19,920	(12%)	($1,733)

Prior Winning Percentages: 1998 (81%); 1998 (74%)

The People		Race/Ethnic Origin	Ancestry	
Area size:	68 sq. mi.	33.1% White	Irish: 8.9%	Italian: 7.8%
Urban population:	100.0%	44.9% Black	German: 5.1%	
Rural population:	0.0%	4.8% Asian	**2000 Presidential Vote**	
Pop. 2000:	646,331	0.2% Native Am.	Gore (D)	181,274 (84%)
Median income:	$28,295	0.0% Hawaiian	Bush (R)	31,722 (15%)
Poverty status:	26.9%	1.8% Two+ races	Other	2,679 (1%)
Military veterans:	10.2%	0.2% Other	**Cook Partisan Voting Index:** D +35	
		15.0% Hispanic Origin		

Occupation	Blue collar: 21.4%	White collar: 56.8%	Gray collar: 21.8%

In Center City Philadelphia, the 1680s look out on the 1780s, 1880s and 1980s. The statue of William Penn, who founded the city in 1682, stands 37 feet high atop the 548-foot tower of the 1880s Second Empire-style City Hall at Market and Broad. To the east is Independence Hall, where Americans in the 1780s drew up the nation's Constitution; to the west is the tower of One Liberty Place, with its "romantic modernist" spire, the 1980s building that broke tradition to rise above City Hall. Philadelphia is built on a certain order. Other American colonies were settled by practical men, out to make money or replicate a farm settlement back home. But Penn was a Quaker, a member of one of those rationalizing sects of the 17th century, who intended to impose order on his new environment, and did: no cowpath street patterns here, like those in Boston or Charleston, but a grid of numbered and named streets, with precisely spaced open squares. Penn's city of brotherly love has turned out to be a commercial and industrial metropolis that grew steadily over the years, spreading out over the countryside. Yet there are still places in which you can see the distant past: in the restored townhouses of Society Hill and the tree-shaded public buildings around Independence Hall and, on the way to the ornate City Hall, the Federal and Greek Revival buildings and the temples of commerce, built when Philadelphia was the nation's largest city. Interspersed are I.M. Pei's modernist Society Hill Towers (though the rich in Philadelphia, unlike New York or Chicago, don't much like apartments) and the 1920s masonry-faced skyscrapers and 1990s glass-and-steel towers built around City Hall and in Center City farther west.

For all the grandeur of City Hall, Philadelphia has seldom had a city government of which to be proud. Corruption and incompetence have reigned here off and on for more than a century. While the city's private economy grew robustly in the 1980s, the city government lurched unknowingly toward bankruptcy under Mayor Wilson Goode. Then in 1991 Democrat Ed Rendell was elected mayor—and did well enough to become in 2002 the first former Philadelphia mayor to be elected governor since 1906. Ebullient and energetic, he literally scrubbed City Hall's grimy floors, cut spending sharply, privatized government functions and faced down unions in a strike threat; his valiant struggle to stave off the forces of urban decline was chronicled in the compelling book, *A Prayer for the City*. Unfortunately, Rendell's push for reform stalled in the mid-1990s. Philadelphia still has an inordinately expensive city government and neighborhoods ravaged by crime that have emptied out over the years; every day, 73 residents move out of the city. But there are signs of hope. Philadelphia has some of the nation's most vibrant and charitably active churches; its economy is vibrant enough to attract some Latino and Asian immigrants, though many fewer than New York or Chicago; and its Center City is still attractive, as it was when it was on display at the 2000 Republican National Convention. The Philadelphia metropolitan area is still the sixth largest in the country, but most people there live outside the city.

The 1st Congressional District contains much of Philadelphia east of Broad Street; City Hall is on the district line. The 1st includes all of 18th century Philadelphia—Independence Hall, the U.S. Mint, and Elfreth's Alley (the oldest continually occupied residential block in the country)—as well as Chinatown, Society Hill, Overbrook, Northern Liberties and Penn's Landing. It includes Philadelphia's four-square-block, 1.3 million-square-foot convention center, opened in 1993 and still one of the nation's largest. North of Center City, the 1st takes in much of heavily black North Philadelphia, a couple of wards of Northeast Philadelphia (connected to the rest by irregular boundaries), Kensington and its closely packed 19th century homes, where descendants of Irish and Italian immigrants lived for years in tiny frame houses; now the neighborhood (as well as nearby Fairhill) is increasingly Hispanic. South of Center City, the 1st includes heavily Italian South Philadelphia, where Italian families and their grocery stores and restaurants have been pressed tightly into narrow streets under a tangle of overhead wires; this is the neighborhood where the various *Rockys* were filmed and the original Philadelphia cheesesteaks are sold. Near there, the district takes in the city's stadium and arena complex, including the First Union Center, where the 2000 Republican convention was held, as well as the adjoining Navy Yard, established in 1762 and closed in 1996. From there, the 1st includes the Delaware River shore southwest into Delaware County to impoverished Chester. The district also includes three wards in heavily black West Philadelphia and a few small adjacent suburbs. The population of the district is 45% black, less than the 61% black 2d District, and 15% Hispanic (mainly Puerto Rican), the highest of any Pennsylvania district. This is a very heavily Democratic district.

The congressman from the 1st District is Bob Brady, a Democrat elected in May 1998, who is the personification of Philadelphia's old-fashioned urban politics. He grew up in Overbrook Park in West Philadelphia, with an Irish father and Italian mother; he depicts himself as a roll-up-your-sleeves guy who represents working class voters. After high school he went to work as a carpenter and quickly rose up the ranks of the carpenters' union leadership. He entered politics in 1967, at 22, when the local ward leader wouldn't replace a burnt-out streetlight. Brady was elected to the 34th Ward Democratic Executive Committee, and in 1980 he was elected ward leader. In 1975 he became assistant Sergeant-at-Arms of the city council; he was a consultant to the state Senate and member of the Pennsylvania Turnpike Commission and on the board of the city's Redevelopment Authority. In 1986 he became chairman of the Philadelphia Democratic Party, where he has been a close ally of local powerbrokers like the late state Senator Buddy Cianfrani and state Senator Vincent Fumo. Make no mistake, Bob Brady is proud to be the boss of what he calls the nation's largest big city machine—or, as he defines it, an "organization" that mostly operates below the public's radar screen, and dispenses "street money" to workers on Election Day to make sure that its candidates win. Brady is known for making "arrangements" with others—"they're always arrangements, never deals," he insists—from Rendell to Street to House Majority Leader John Perzel of Northeast Philadelphia, and that has enabled him to remain chairman for the better part of two decades.

In November 1997, Thomas Foglietta, 1st District congressman since 1980 and a veteran of South Philly politics, resigned after being confirmed as ambassador to Italy, and Brady ran for the seat. In other cities, this might have led to a primary fight with black politicians; in Philadelphia, ward leaders in the district determined the Democratic nomination for the special election. That gave Brady a great advantage; former 2d District Congressman Lucien Blackwell, probably his strongest opponent, dropped out of the race even before Brady officially declared. With the endorsement of many black leaders and a strong Election Day organization, he won the special election with 74% of the vote. He is among the last of a dying breed—the white ethnic politician who represents an urban, primarily minority district.

Even after he was elected to the House, Brady's attention focused back home. In July 1998, local officials credited him with mediating an end to the 41-day strike that had shut down parts of the SEPTA transit system. He mediated the teachers' strike in 2000, and he sought common ground between the mayor and City Council on a deal for two new stadiums. His ties to City Hall and to local unions gave him credibility with both sides. As Mayor John Street prepared for re-election in 2003, Brady worked to resolve local intra-party conflicts. According to the *Philadelphia Daily News,* he chewed out feuding city council Democrats at one memorable private meeting. "You are a [friggin'] embarrassment. You're embarrassing me, embarrassing yourselves. You're like a bunch of 10-year-old children. If you're not careful, you're not going to be here next year," he said, banging the table. "I've got 30 ward leaders who don't want to support you and 30 more who want to run against you."

In the House, where he has a liberal voting record, his positions on national issues are not always set in stone; he decided that he was in favor of abortion rights after asking his mother. But his initiatives reflect his local orientation. He claimed credit for a casting pit modernization project at the shipyard. His loyalty to unions led him to buck environmentalists and most Democrats, and vote to allow oil drilling in the Arctic National Wildlife Refuge. But these national issues and the aura of the Capitol are not what motivate Brady; his most important job remains running the party's city committee. "Ninety-five percent of my day is not Congress, " he told the *Philadelphia Inquirer* in November 2002. He did get three bills passed in 2002: each named a local post office.

Republicans controlled redistricting in 2002, and they put Northeast Philadelphia Democrat Bob Borski in the same district with suburban Democrat Joe Hoeffel. The key player was state House Majority Leader John Perzel, who had been reelected by only 92 votes in Northeast Philadelphia in 2000. Perzel led the effort to retain Brady's safe district, almost identical in form to his old one, minus some black wards in North Philadelphia and Germantown. Brady, in turn, failed to run a strong Democrat against Perzel. "I have a relationship" with Perzel, explained Brady.

Brady believes in loyalty to the organization. When he first came to the House, he delivered a signed but undated letter to Minority Leader Dick Gephardt stating, , "I, Robert A. Brady, hereby resign effective _____." He told Gephardt, "Anytime I don't do the right thing, you could turn it in." "No one's ever done that before," said Gephardt. "Or since." It is not known whether Gephardt passed the letter along to his successor Nancy Pelosi.

SECOND DISTRICT

Rep. Chaka Fattah (D)

Elected 1994, 5th term; b. Nov. 21, 1956, Philadelphia; home, Philadelphia; Community Col. of Philadelphia, U. of PA, M.A. 1986, Harvard U. Kennedy Schl. of Gov., 1984; Baptist; married (Renee Chenault).

Elected Office: PA House of Reps., 1982–88; PA Senate, 1988–94.

Professional Career: Asst. Dir., House of Umoja, 1977–79; City of Philadelphia, Spec. Asst. to Dir. of Housing & Community Dev., 1980, Spec. Asst. to Managing Director, 1981.

DC Office: 2301 RHOB 20515, 202-225-4001; Fax: 202-225-5392; Web site: www.house.gov/fattah.

District Offices: Philadelphia, 215-848-9386; Philadelphia, 215-387-6404.

Committees: *Appropriations* (26th of 29 D): District of Columbia (RMM); VA, HUD & Independent Agencies.

Group Ratings

	ADA	ACLU	AFS	LCV	CON	ITIC	NTU	COC	ACU	NTLC	CHC
2002	95	87	89	75	80	38	20	37	0	3	0
2001	100	—	100	93	—	—	11	27	0	—	—

National Journal Ratings

	2001 LIB	—	2001 CONS	2002 LIB	—	2002 CONS
Economic	83%	—	15%	86%	—	12%
Social	81%	—	19%	84%	—	8%
Foreign	86%	—	12%	94%	—	0%

Key Votes of the 107th Congress

1. Approve Bush Tax Cuts	N	5. Faith-Based Charities	N	9. Trade Promotion Authority	N
2. Limit Patients' Bill of Rights	N	6. Bar Gays in the Boy Scouts	N	10. Bar Funds for Intl. Court	N
3. Campaign Finance Reform	Y	7. Ban Partial-Birth Abortion	N	11. Authorize Force in Iraq	N
4. Ban ANWR Development	Y	8. Arm Commercial Pilots	N	12. Deny Home. Sec. Dept. Union	N

Election Results

2002 general	Chaka Fattah (D)	150,623	(88%)	($287,182)
	Thomas Dougherty (R)	20,988	(12%)	
2002 primary	Chaka Fattah (D)	unopposed		
2000 general	Chaka Fattah (D)	180,021	(98%)	($296,851)
	Other	3,673	(2%)	

Prior Winning Percentages: 1998 (87%); 1996 (88%); 1994 (86%)

The People		Race/Ethnic Origin	Ancestry	
Area size:	60 sq. mi.	29.8% White	Irish: 6.8%	Italian: 5.4%
Urban population:	100.0%	60.8% Black	German: 4.7%	
Rural population:	0.0%	4.3% Asian	**2000 Presidential Vote**	
Pop. 2000:	646,361	0.2% Native Am.	Gore (D) 221,517	(87%)
Median income:	$30,626	0.0% Hawaiian	Bush (R) 29,458	(12%)
Poverty status:	23.8%	1.7% Two+ races	Other 3,529	(1%)
Military veterans:	10.6%	0.2% Other	**Cook Partisan Voting Index:** D +38	
		3.0% Hispanic Origin		

Occupation	Blue collar: 14.6%	White collar: 65.8%	Gray collar: 19.6%

Looking out over the Schuylkill River north of Center City Philadelphia, you can still see the landscape painted 100 years ago by Philadelphia artist Thomas Eakins—the tightly-packed but formidable rowhouses, the old fieldstone houses of Germantown, the gray-blue water flowing past boat houses below the small Greek temples of the Water Works and the larger temple of the Philadelphia Museum of Art. On both sides of this romantic scene are some of Philadelphia's long-established black neighborhoods: West Philadelphia, across the Schuylkill on either side of Market Street; North Philadelphia, on either side of Broad Street; Germantown to the northwest, off the narrow diagonal of Germantown Avenue that ran through open fields in Benjamin Franklin's time. Many of these neighborhoods continue to suffer from poverty and blight, and the city has 550,000 fewer people today than in 1950.

The 2d Congressional District takes in much of the city of Philadelphia west of Broad Street, plus Cheltenham Township in suburban Montgomery County. It doesn't include the key colonial landmarks—they're in the neighboring 1st—but it does include most of the skyscrapers of Center City and well-heeled Rittenhouse Square, the Philadelphia Zoo (America's first), the University of Pennsylvania, Drexel University, and lush Fairmount Park, the largest landscaped urban park in the world, which climaxes at the grand Philadelphia Museum of Art, where a *Rocky*-like run up the steps is now *de rigueur* for tourists. The 2d includes West Oak Lane, Strawberry Mansion and, further west, the distinguished old neighborhoods of Mount Airy, Chestnut Hill and East Falls, mostly pleasant these days but dotted with some grittier precincts. The 2d also covers Roxborough and the old mill area of Manayunk, which is recently renovated. This is Pennsylvania's one black-majority district: 61% of its population in 2000 was black. Since Pennsylvania never had slavery—thanks to William Penn and his Quaker legacy—Philadelphia has been home to a large black community since before the Civil War. That heritage is reflected in places like the John Coltrane House on North 33d Street, which has been designated a national historic landmark in celebration of the jazz innovator's early years here. Suburban Cheltenham Township includes old, comfortable communities like Cheltenham, Melrose Park, Elkins Park and Glenside. Outside of five New York City-based districts, the 2d was George W. Bush's worst performing district in the nation—he won just 12 percent here in 2000.

The congressman from the 2d District is Chaka Fattah (pronounced *SHOCK-ah Fa-TAH*), first elected in 1994. Fattah grew up in Philadelphia, and in 1982, at 25, was elected to the state House—the youngest member ever. In 1988 he was elected to the state Senate, where he worked to fend off bankruptcy for Philadelphia. In 1991, much to everyone's surprise, 2d District Congressman William Gray resigned to become head of the United Negro College Fund. In the election to succeed him, local Democratic ward leaders nominated Councilman Lucien Blackwell, a former longshoreman, boxer and labor union stalwart. Fattah ran under the Consumer Party label while state Welfare Secretary John White ran as an independent. Blackwell won the November 1991 special election with 39% to 28% for Fattah and 27% for White. In 1992 Blackwell held on to the seat, but only barely, defeating C. Delores Tucker in the primary 54%–46%. Blackwell's weakness was obvious, and in 1994 Fattah ran again, as a Democrat. Blackwell relied mostly on ward politicians; Fattah was endorsed by the Black Clergy of Philadelphia and Vicinity and by state Senator Hardy Williams. This time Fattah won, 58%–42%.

Fattah's voting record has been among the most liberal in the House and he voted against Contract with America measures more often than all but one other member. Much of his focus has been on education issues. He was the prime sponsor of a law to support an educational program that encourages partnerships between colleges and public schools with at least 50% low-income students to put middle-school students on the track to college by promising federally funded scholarships. In 2000, he got 183 votes for his bill, which he now calls a Student Bill of Rights, to require each state to equalize funding for education within its borders; later, he lightened the bill's penalty provision to attract more supporters. He strongly defended Bill Clinton against impeachment charges, pointing to the benefits that he brought the black community. Unlike locally-oriented Bob Brady, the city's other congressman, Fattah's focus is more as a national Democrat. "My number one political priority is to elect a Democratic majority in Congress," he says.

In 2001, with the help of senior Pennsylvania Democrat John Murtha, he won a seat on the Appropriations Committee, a useful slot for a member who seems intent on a long House career; he said that he would use the position to push for more money for education. As senior Democrat on its District of Columbia Subcommittee, he prepared for House debate in 2001 an amendment to strike the bill's 34 restrictions on local self-rule; but he did not offer it, and instead achieved many of his priorities in the House-Senate conference committee. In 2003, he suffered an unexpected setback. He hoped to become the ranking minority member on the House Administration Committee. But Minority Leader Nancy Pelosi decided to enforce the rule barring a second committee assignment for members on Appropriations, and Fattah got bumped off House Administration altogether.

Since entering the House, Fattah has had no serious primary or general election challenge. Redistricting was no problem either. Republican redistricters were happy to leave largely intact the state's only black-majority district.

THIRD DISTRICT

Rep. Phil English (R)

Elected 1994, 5th term; b. June 20, 1956, Erie; home, Erie; U. of PA., B.A. 1978; Catholic; married (Christiane).

Elected Office: Erie City Controller, 1985–89.

Professional Career: Staff aide, PA Senate; 1980–84; Chief of Staff, PA Sen. Melissa Hart 1990–92; Exec. Dir., PA Senate Finance Cmte., 1990–94.

DC Office: 1410 LHOB 20515, 202-225-5406; Fax: 202-225-3103; Web site: www.house.gov/english.

District Offices: Butler, 724-285-7005; Erie, 814-456-2038; Hermitage, 724-342-6132; Meadville, 814-724-8414.

Committees: *Ways & Means* (15th of 24 R): Health; Human Resources; Trade. *Joint Economic Committee* (4th of 10 Reps.).

Group Ratings

	ADA	ACLU	AFS	LCV	CON	ITIC	NTU	COC	ACU	NTLC	CHC
2002	0	20	0	25	67	100	53	95	92	78	83
2001	10	—	10	36	—	—	58	95	68	—	—

National Journal Ratings

	2001 LIB —	2001 CONS		2002 LIB —	2002 CONS
Economic	46% —	54%		20% —	80%
Social	43% —	55%		32% —	63%
Foreign	49% —	47%		29% —	67%

Key Votes of the 107th Congress

1. Approve Bush Tax Cuts	Y	5. Faith-Based Charities	Y
2. Limit Patients' Bill of Rights	Y	6. Bar Gays in the Boy Scouts	Y
3. Campaign Finance Reform	N	7. Ban Partial-Birth Abortion	Y
4. Ban ANWR Development	N	8. Arm Commercial Pilots	Y

9. Trade Promotion Authority	Y
10. Bar Funds for Intl. Court	Y
11. Authorize Force in Iraq	Y
12. Deny Home. Sec. Dept. Union	Y

Election Results

2002 general	Phil English (R)	116,763	(78%)	($778,773)
	AnnDrea Benson (Green)	33,554	(22%)	($19,353)
2002 primary	Phil English (R)	unopposed		
2000 general (PA 21)	Phil English (R)	135,164	(61%)	($1,219,501)
	Marc A. Flitter (D)	87,018	(39%)	($306,378)

Prior Winning Percentages: 1998 (63%); 1996 (51%); 1994 (49%)

The People		**Race/Ethnic Origin**	**Ancestry**	
Area size:	4,762 sq. mi.	93.7% White	German: 20.8%	Irish: 10.5%
Urban population:	58.5%	3.5% Black	Italian: 7.1%	
Rural population:	41.5%	0.5% Asian	**2000 Presidential Vote**	
Pop. 2000:	646,364	0.1% Native Am.	Bush (R)..............127,598	(51%)
Median income:	$35,876	0.0% Hawaiian	Gore (D)..............116,118	(46%)
Poverty status:	11.6%	0.8% Two+ races	Other...................6,233	(2%)
Military veterans:	14.6%	0.1% Other	**Cook Partisan Voting Index:** R + 3	
		1.3% Hispanic Origin		

Occupation	Blue collar: 30.7%	White collar: 52.3%	Gray collar: 17.0%

The best natural harbor on Lake Erie is in a state with the second-shortest Great Lakes shoreline. It is Erie, Pennsylvania, protected by the Presque Isle ("almost an island") peninsula—a cowlick-shaped, seven-mile-long sand spit blanketed by mature forest. Erie is in Pennsylvania's far north-west corner, only about 100 miles from Cleveland but 428 miles from Center City Philadelphia. There is farmland here, and even some woods, but this land between the Great Lakes and the basin of the Ohio River has been prime territory for heavy industry for more than a century. But in the 1990s, under then-Governor (now Secretary of Homeland Security) Tom Ridge, the state invested $100 million in Erie's waterfront—a cruise ship terminal, a convention center, a ballpark for the single-A Erie SeaWolves baseball team, and restorations to the Warner Theatre—in an attempt to boost tourism. The effort spruced up a dying downtown, but it didn't buffer Erie from the recent economic downturn, as companies like GE, the area's largest employer, International Paper and Gunite/EMI laid off employees and closed plants. Attempts to attract other industries have been hurt by high airline fares.

The 3d Congressional District occupies this corner of the state—all of Erie County, most of Mercer, Crawford and Butler Counties and now, after the 2002 redistricting, about half of Warren, Venango, and Armstrong Counties. Erie County has 43% of the district's population; it and Mercer County, which includes most of the steel-producing area of Sharon, posted modest population gains during the 1990s, while population declined in some of the more rural counties. The rapid growth in Butler County, the northern edge of the Pittsburgh metropolitan area, did not reach the part of the county in the 3d District. Politically, the mix of industrial and rural voters makes for closely balanced territory. Erie and Mercer Counties vote Democratic in most national elections, but they have also voted for Republicans with working class appeal, like Ridge—from a

Catholic working class family in Erie—Senator Rick Santorum and 2002 governor candidate Mike Fisher, whose running mate was Erie state Senator Jane Earll. The other counties are culturally conservative and almost solidly Republican. This is a district that voted 51% for George W. Bush in 2000, 5% better than in the state as a whole.

The congressman from the 3d District is Phil English, a Republican first elected in 1994. English grew up in Erie and has worked at little else but politics and government. At 20, he was an alternate to the 1976 Republican National Convention, and he worked during the early 1980s as a Republican staffer in Harrisburg. In 1985 he became Erie Controller; in 1988, he was the unsuccessful Republican nominee for state treasurer. In 1990 he helped produce Rick Santorum's upset win in the suburban Pittsburgh 18th District, the first step on Santorum's path to the Senate; he went on to become chief of staff to state Senator Melissa Hart, who was elected to the House in the adjacent 4th District in 2000. In 1994, when Ridge ran for governor, English ran for the House and won 66% in the Republican primary. In the general, English promised to reform welfare, cut wasteful spending and create jobs for northwestern Pennsylvania with an 18-point plan for revitalizing small business and manufacturing. Key to the outcome was Erie, English's home—and probably more important, Ridge's—which supported the Republican ticket, giving English a 49%–47% victory.

In the House, the obviously vulnerable English became one of the first freshman Republicans since George H. W. Bush in 1967 to win a seat on Ways and Means, an excellent spot from which to both legislate and raise money. Early on, English made a record on local issues, getting the Army Corps of Engineers to dredge and replenish the beach at Presque Isle, working to stop Korea's dumping of steel pipe and tubing (the Shenango Valley in Mercer County is the leading U.S. producer), preserving spending on low income home heating and protecting Erie Forge & Steel from the IRS. While he supports the Republican leadership on most votes, he has a moderate record on economic and foreign issues and has dissented prominently on occasion. He has been one of the House Republicans most willing to support a minimum wage increase and was an early proponent of limiting the tax deduction for pay to corporate chief executives.

English supports fundamental tax reform to replace individual and corporate income taxes with a consumption tax to promote savings and level the playing field for U.S. businesses and workers. He enacted his innovative proposal to grant a tax break to donors to groups such as the Make-A-Wish Foundation. He was out front on behalf of the steel industry's efforts for steel import quotas imports and he won House approval of $3 million for more "trade cops" to enforce U.S. laws on unfair trade practices. He voted for trade promotion authority in 2001 and 2002 and PNTR with China.

As chairman of the Steel Caucus, English welcomed Bush's March 2002 decision to impose quotas on steel imports. He sponsored a resolution that passed opposing any changes to U.S. anti-dumping laws in the Doha trade negotiations and a bill to cover health insurance costs of retired steelworkers whose companies went bankrupt. English has conceded that his international interest has not spread much beyond economic issues. "Foreign policy is not really my thing," he told *The Washington Post*. "My constituents don't get too fired up about it either. They focus more on things like health care, and so do I."

English had a tough reelection challenge in 1996 from Democrat Ron DiNicola, who returned home from law practice in Los Angeles to run in Erie. "California office. California driver's license. And a great tan," English's campaign proclaimed. English won 51%–49%, taking just 48% in Erie County and 47% in Mercer, but carrying Butler and Crawford Counties solidly. He has had no serious challenge since, and in 2002 ran without major-party opposition. English is now one of three House Republicans from traditionally Democratic western Pennsylvania, a tribute to skillful redistricting, a cautious centrism, and hard work by local Republicans, including Santorum, Hart, Ridge and English. Democrats wondering why they are in the House minority ought to look here.

FOURTH DISTRICT

Rep. Melissa Hart (R)

Elected 2000, 2d term; b. Apr. 4, 1962, Pittsburgh; home, Bradford Woods; Washington & Jefferson Col., B.A. 1984, U. of Pittsburgh, J.D. 1987; Catholic; single.

Elected Office: PA Senate, 1991–2000.

Professional Career: Praticing atty., 1987–2001.

DC Office: 1508 LHOB 20515, 202-225-2565; Fax: 202-226-2274; Web site: www.house.gov/hart.

District Offices: Allison Park, 412-492-0161; Ellwood City, 724-752-0490.

Committees: *Financial Services* (26th of 37 R): Capital Markets, Insurance & Government Sponsored Enterprises; Financial Institutions & Consumer Credit; Housing & Community Opportunity. *Judiciary* (14th of 21 R): Courts, the Internet & Intellectual Property; Immigration, Border Security & Claims; The Constitution. *Science* (17th of 25 R): Energy; Research.

Group Ratings

	ADA	ACLU	AFS	LCV	CON	ITIC	NTU	COC	ACU	NTLC	CHC
2002	0	7	0	13	25	88	57	95	96	86	100
2001	5	—	0	14	—	—	59	96	88	—	—

National Journal Ratings

	2001 LIB	—	2001 CONS		2002 LIB	—	2002 CONS
Economic	36%	—	63%		0%	—	91%
Social	0%	—	81%		29%	—	70%
Foreign	21%	—	74%		15%	—	78%

Key Votes of the 107th Congress

1. Approve Bush Tax Cuts	Y	5. Faith-Based Charities	Y	9. Trade Promotion Authority	Y
2. Limit Patients' Bill of Rights	Y	6. Bar Gays in the Boy Scouts	Y	10. Bar Funds for Intl. Court	Y
3. Campaign Finance Reform	N	7. Ban Partial-Birth Abortion	Y	11. Authorize Force in Iraq	Y
4. Ban ANWR Development	N	8. Arm Commercial Pilots	*	12. Deny Home. Sec. Dept. Union	Y

Election Results

2002 general	Melissa Hart (R)	130,534	(65%)	($1,167,856)
	Stevan Drobac (D)	71,674	(35%)	($76,980)
2002 primary	Melissa Hart (R)	unopposed		
2000 general	Melissa Hart (R)	145,390	(59%)	($1,724,048)
	Terry Van Horne (D)	100,995	(41%)	($673,346)

The People		Race/Ethnic Origin	Ancestry	
Area size:	1,340 sq. mi.	94.3% White	German: 20.7%	Irish: 12.4%
Urban population:	78.2%	3.4% Black	Italian: 11.7%	
Rural population:	21.8%	0.9% Asian	**2000 Presidential Vote**	
Pop. 2000:	646,476	0.1% Native Am.	Bush (R) 152,313 (52%)	
Median income:	$43,628	0.0% Hawaiian	Gore (D) 134,688 (46%)	
Poverty status:	7.5%	0.7% Two+ races	Other 6,167 (2%)	
Military veterans:	14.7%	0.1% Other	**Cook Partisan Voting Index:** R + 3	
		0.6% Hispanic Origin		

Occupation	Blue collar: 22.4%	White collar: 63.7%	Gray collar: 13.9%

For a century, one of America's great industrial zones was near the intersection of the Beaver and Ohio Rivers in western Pennsylvania. This was steel country, with mills rising black and brooding from the bottomlands and filling the narrow river valleys with smoke. Immigrant families lived in small frame houses on hillsides, looking down on riverscapes lined with piles of iron ore, limestone and coal, and littered with cranes, stocks and furnaces. This was not an environmentalist's idea of perfection, but it was a land of opportunity for thousands whose lives were far worse before moving to steel country. One grandchild of a Hungarian immigrant steelworker in Beaver Falls grew up to be Joe Namath—just one of the great quarterbacks to hail from southwestern Pennsylvania (Jim Kelly, Joe Montana and Dan Marino are a few of the others). For a few heady years, high union wages and early retirement plans seemed to make working in the mills the way to affluence. But the industry crashed after the oil shock of 1979, when mills were closed and jobs vanished. Today, thousands of workers who long ago exhausted their unemployment benefits have given up and left the Beaver and Ohio valleys.

The 4th Congressional District includes much of this steel country, plus a large swath of suburban Pittsburgh, especially since the last round of redistricting, when western Pennsylvania lost one House seat and the remaining districts were given more expansive borders. The 4th begins around Farrell in Mercer County, located as close to Erie as to Pittsburgh, then travels south along Route 60 through steel-mill (and former steel-mill) country in Lawrence and Beaver Counties. It then turns to the east, taking in a fast-growing tier of suburban southern Butler County and the longer-established Pittsburgh suburbs of Allegheny County: old-money Sewickley and Fox Chapel; affluent McCandless and middle-class Ross in the North Hills. It also takes in a tiny portion of Westmoreland County. The steel mill areas tend to be Democratic, with unions still capable of flexing some muscle. In 2000, Al Gore won Beaver County easily and Lawrence County more narrowly; Democratic Senate candidate Ron Klink won both counties in 2000, as did Democratic gubernatorial candidate Ed Rendell in 2002. The suburbs of Butler County are tax-averse and strongly Republican, while the older suburbs in Allegheny County are marginal—more Democratic than Butler, but much more Republican than the city of Pittsburgh. Overall the district's heritage is Democratic but it has been trending modestly toward the Republicans.

The congresswoman from the 4th District is Melissa Hart, a Republican first elected in 2000. She grew up in the Pittsburgh area, graduated from Washington and Jefferson College and the University of Pittsburgh law school. After law school, she worked as a real estate lawyer for a Pittsburgh firm. She was elected to the state Senate in 1990 by defeating an incumbent Democrat and was reelected in 1994 and 1998. As chairman of the Finance Committee, Hart sponsored Pennsylvania's first major tax law change in more than a century; it permits school districts to reduce property taxes by implementing an earned income tax. When Democrat Ron Klink, who had held the seat for eight years, decided to challenge Senator Rick Santorum in 2000, Hart ran unopposed for the Republican nomination in this seat, which had not elected a Republican in 18 years.

In the Democratic primary, state Representative Terry Van Horne unexpectedly led the eight-candidate field, with 24% of the vote; Matthew Mangino—a pro-gun, anti-abortion prosecutor who had been supported by the DCCC—finished second with 15%. A key event in the campaign came the morning after the primary when the NRCC eagerly drew attention to a racial slur Van Horne had used in reference to a black state Representative in 1994. Van Horne, who had apologized on the floor of the state House after making the comment, said it had been taken out of context, and the target of the slur accepted Van Horne's apology long ago. But Jesse Jackson Jr. and several members of the Congressional Black Caucus expressed their concern when they learned of the comment. Van Horne and Hart clashed over prescription drug plans for seniors and campaign finance. She touted her labor roots and hoped that her anti-tax, anti-abortion, pro-gun views would play well. With a big fundraising advantage, she won by a surprisingly large 59%–41%, carrying every county.

In the House, she has had a mostly conservative voting record. Republican leaders quickly spotlighted this hard-charging newcomer, tapping her to give the party response to Bill Clinton on the Saturday after her election. She was soon mentioned as a prospective candidate for a party leadership post or for statewide office. "The sky's the limit for her," said a House Republican leader. Speaker Dennis Hastert designated her to serve as a liaison for members' concerns. On the Judiciary Committee, she passed her "safe havens" bill to permit women to leave unwanted newborns in designated institutions. After objections from the Appropriations Committee, she reluctantly agreed not to offer her amendment to bar funds for school-based health clinics that distribute "morning after" pills. She supported antiterrorism measures and said she wanted to focus more on intellectual property and other high-tech issues on Judiciary. On the Financial Services Committee, she worked on details of the money laundering bill after September 11. Despite pressure from the steel industry, she voted for trade promotion authority.

Hart played a key role in Pennsylvania's congressional redistricting. Republicans controlled the process and initially expected her to work to make the district much more Republican. But in 2001 she announced that she wanted to keep Beaver County—the most heavily Democratic part of the district—and that the only change she wanted was to add the North Hills in Allegheny County which had been in her old state Senate district; she got that and the closer-in Pittsburgh suburbs as well. That enabled state Senate Republicans to come up with a plan that created a second Republican-leaning district in the Pittsburgh suburbs, the new 18th District south of the city. Thus Hart shares credit for one of the six seats House Republicans gained in the 2002 election.

After the election, Hart ran for vice-chairman of the Republican Conference against Jack Kingston of Georgia. But Kingston had served longer and won 159–56; still, she is well-positioned to win a leadership post in the future.

FIFTH DISTRICT

Rep. John Peterson (R)

Elected 1996, 4th term; b. Dec. 25, 1938, Titusville; home, Pleasantville; PA St. U., 1974–76; Methodist; married (Sandy).

Military Career: Army, 1958–64.

Elected Office: Pleasantville Borough Cncl., 1969–77; PA House of Reps., 1977–84; PA Senate, 1984–96.

Professional Career: Owner, Peterson's Golden Dawn Food Market, 1958–84.

DC Office: 123 CHOB 20515, 202-225-5121; Fax: 202-225-5796; Web site: www.house.gov/johnpeterson.

District Offices: State College, 814-238-1776; Titusville, 814-827-3985.

Committees: *Appropriations* (25th of 36 R): Energy & Water Development; Interior (Vice Chmn.); Labor, HHS & Education. *Resources* (14th of 28 R): Forests & Forest Health; National Parks, Recreation & Public Lands.

Group Ratings

	ADA	ACLU	AFS	LCV	CON	ITIC	NTU	COC	ACU	NTLC	CHC
2002	0	13	0	13	31	100	56	100	100	88	100
2001	0	—	0	0	—	—	61	100	88	—	—

National Journal Ratings

	2001 LIB — 2001 CONS	2002 LIB — 2002 CONS
Economic	22% — 74%	32% — 67%
Social	0% — 81%	0% — 75%
Foreign	33% — 60%	35% — 60%

Key Votes of the 107th Congress

1. Approve Bush Tax Cuts	Y	5. Faith-Based Charities	Y	9. Trade Promotion Authority	Y
2. Limit Patients' Bill of Rights	Y	6. Bar Gays in the Boy Scouts	Y	10. Bar Funds for Intl. Court	Y
3. Campaign Finance Reform	N	7. Ban Partial-Birth Abortion	Y	11. Authorize Force in Iraq	Y
4. Ban ANWR Development	N	8. Arm Commercial Pilots	Y	12. Deny Home. Sec. Dept. Union	Y

Election Results

2002 general	John Peterson (R)	124,942	(87%)	($456,607)
	Thomas Martin (Lib)	18,078	(13%)	
2002 primary	John Peterson (R)	unopposed		
2000 general	John Peterson (R)	147,570	(83%)	($413,790)
	Thomas Martin (Lib)	17,020	(10%)	
	William M. Belitskus (Green)	13,857	(8%)	

Prior Winning Percentages: 1998 (85%); 1996 (60%)

The People		Race/Ethnic Origin	Ancestry	
Area size:	11,058 sq. mi.	96.1% White	German: 21.2%	Irish: 9.1%
Urban population:	46.3%	1.3% Black	English: 6.7%	
Rural population:	53.7%	1.1% Asian	**2000 Presidential Vote**	
Pop. 2000:	646,371	0.1% Native Am.	Bush (R)..............137,837	(59%)
Median income:	$33,320	0.0% Hawaiian	Gore (D)...............89,180	(38%)
Poverty status:	13.5%	0.6% Two+ races	Other...................6,197	(3%)
Military veterans:	14.4%	0.1% Other	**Cook Partisan Voting Index:** R +11	
		0.8% Hispanic Origin		

Occupation	Blue collar: 32.4%	White collar: 51.2%	Gray collar: 16.5%

North central Pennsylvania—isolated from the rest of the country by chains of mountains, and off the main east-west rail and highway lines until the 1970s—is one of those empty spaces that make even the northeastern states seem lightly populated compared to the densely packed terrain of Western Europe or East Asia. Forest and Cameron counties here are Pennsylvania's two smallest, with fewer than 6,000 people each. Pressed tightly by narrow valleys and fast-flowing rivers, roads here are often forced to switch back as they wind their way precariously over the mountains; Tioga County is home to Pine Creek Gorge, known as "Pennsylvania's Grand Canyon." This part of the state is a prime area for hunting (in 2002, 179 black bears were shot in Clinton County), fishing, all-terrain vehicles and snowmobiles, in wide-open spaces like the Allegheny National Forest which sprawls across four counties. To the west are Titusville, where Colonel Edwin Drake sank the first successful oil well in 1859, and Oil City, headquarters of Quaker State Oil from 1931 until it left for Texas in 1995. DuBois in Clearfield County is home to glass production and a powdered metal industry; timbering also remains important here. Punxsutawney in Jefferson County is home of the legendary groundhog Phil, who predicts the arrival of spring every year based on whether he sees his shadow on Gobbler's Knob on Feb. 2; the 1993 movie *Groundhog Day* sparked a tourism boomlet in the charming town of 6,000, even though the movie was filmed in Woodstock, Illinois. To the southeast is the Nittany Valley, home of State College and Pennsylvania State University. Penn State has long been known for its powerful football teams coached by Joe Paterno ("JoePa," locally); the university's cutting-edge facilities, combined with the city's gridded downtown, have spawned a high-skills job market. Tiny Coudersport in Potter County is the home of the cable giant Adelphia Communications, the company that self-destructed in 2002 amid allegations of massive embezzlement by the founding Rigas family. Yet there is something solid and grounded in this part of America. The sturdily built courthouses and banks in the center of each county seat testify to the long history of hard work and thrift in this part of the country. Interstate 80 runs through this part of Pennsylvania, making it accessible to big markets, and most of the counties here grew modestly in the 1990s.

The 5th Congressional District is the state's largest in area, taking in an enormous swath of north central Pennsylvania. Politically, this area became Republican in the 1850s when the party was founded, and it has remained heavily Republican ever since. It is the state's most rural district; in 2000, George W. Bush won 59% of the vote here.

The congressman from the 5th District is John Peterson, a Republican elected in 1996. Peterson grew up in Titusville, the son of a steelworker; he went to Penn State, served in the Army as a cook, then opened a grocery store that eventually became Peterson's Golden Dawn Supermarket chain. He served on the Pleasantville Borough Council for eight years, then in 1977, at 39, was elected to the state House in a special election. In 1984 he was elected to the state Senate, where he chaired the Public Health and Welfare Committee. In 1996 Bill Clinger announced his retirement after 18 years in the House. Peterson was an obvious candidate; his state Senate district included eight of the then-5th's 17 counties. Three other Republicans ran. The one who attracted the most attention was Bob Shuster, the brother of current 9th District Congressman Bill Shuster and son of Bud Shuster, who then was the influential chairman of the Transportation and Infrastructure Committee. "What a one-two punch we could be for central Pennsylvania," Bud Shuster said on his son's announcement day. But Shuster grew up outside the district and Peterson's chief competition was Daniel Gordeuk, a Centre County surgeon with strong local roots. Peterson won with 38%, to 28% for Gordeuk, and 18% for Shuster. In the general, Peterson attacked the Democratic nominee as "an old-fashioned liberal" and won 60%–40%.

In the House, Peterson has been a Republican loyalist. He emerged as a critic of environmental restriction advocates, complaining about their "push for world government" in the Kyoto treaty and their lawsuits to prevent logging in national forests. Curiously for an easterner, he has been a leader of the Western Caucus; he shares many of their concerns on topics such as private property rights and access to public lands, he says. "We need a strong rural, western voice." In the 171 counties where the federal government is landlord to at least half of the local land (none are in Pennsylvania), he advocated a "no net gain" rule when the government purchases land for national parks and wilderness areas. In 2002 he set off a furor among public school officials when he advocated random drug testing for junior and senior high school students in extracurricular activities. He wants to spend $1 billion a year to rehabilitate and build new technical education classrooms; that's a bit more than $2 million in every congressional district. He passed a House resolution in October 2000, urging the Clinton administration to link aid to Russia to the release of Edmond Pope, a Penn State-funded naval researcher imprisoned on spy charges, who was suffering from a rare kind of cancer. Peterson made three trips to Russia to spotlight this "sham," and when Pope was released two months later, he called Peterson "one of the two heroes" (the other was his wife) in winning his freedom. On local issues, he finally enacted in November 2002 his bill to establish the Oil Region National Heritage Area to promote the history of Titusville and Oil Creek Valley. With a seat on the Appropriations Committee, he increased spending for a program that finances vocational education. In January 2003, along with Democrat Allen Boyd of Florida, Peterson became co-chairman of the Rural Caucus, to promote the interests of rural areas in national debates.

Peterson has not had a Democratic opponent since he was first elected. Redistricting did not appreciably change the district.

SIXTH DISTRICT

Rep. Jim Gerlach (R)

Elected 2002, 1st term; b. Feb. 25, 1955, Ellwood City; home, Upper Uwchlan Township; Dickinson Col., B.A. 1977, J.D. 1980; Presbyterian; divorced.

Elected Office: PA House of Reps., 1990–94; PA Senate, 1994–02.

Professional Career: Practicing atty., 1980–02.

DC Office: 1541 LHOB 20515, 202-225-4315; Fax: 202-225-8440; Web site: www.house.gov/gerlach.

District Offices: Glenmoore, 610-458-8010; Trappe, 610-409-2780; Wyomissing, 610-376-7630.

Committees: *Small Business* (14th of 18 R): Tax, Finance & Exports. *Transportation & Infrastructure* (39th of 41 R): Aviation; Economic Development, Public Buildings & Emergency Management; Water Resources & Environment.

Group Ratings and Key Votes: Newly Elected

Election Results

2002 general	Jim Gerlach (R)	103,648	(51%)	($1,261,590)
	Dan Wofford (D)	98,128	(49%)	($1,386,721)
2002 primary	Jim Gerlach (R)	unopposed		

The People		Race/Ethnic Origin	Ancestry	
Area size:	845 sq. mi.	86.6% White	German: 19.1%	Irish: 12.5%
Urban population:	84.8%	6.7% Black	Italian: 9.8%	
Rural population:	15.2%	2.0% Asian	**2000 Presidential Vote**	
Pop. 2000:	646,483	0.1% Native Am.	Gore (D) 130,472	(49%)
Median income:	$55,615	0.0% Hawaiian	Bush (R) 129,318	(49%)
Poverty status:	5.9%	1.0% Two+ races	Other 5,589	(2%)
Military veterans:	12.7%	0.1% Other	**Cook Partisan Voting Index:** R + 0	
		3.5% Hispanic Origin		

Occupation	Blue collar: 20.3%	White collar: 67.8%	Gray collar: 11.9%

The gentle hills of southeastern Pennsylvania, settled in the 18th century by Quaker townsmen, Welsh farmers, German peasants, and members of pietistic sects who became known as the Pennsylvania Dutch, were America's first polyglot interior. Before and after independence, a diverse lot looking for tolerance in the area above Philadelphia and the Delaware River and below the first chains of the Appalachians found a land that yielded riches, first in crops, then in iron-working and other industry. Here are places like Valley Forge, where General George Washington and his men spent the terrible winter and spring of 1777–78, while the British luxuriated in Philadelphia 20 miles away. In Revolutionary times, this area was countryside, a good long day's drive from the markets and docks of Philadelphia. In the years after, the great rail lines were built from Philadelphia—the Main Line of the Pennsylvania Railroad headed west to industrial Pittsburgh and the Midwest and the Reading Railroad headed northwest to Reading and the anthracite coalfields beyond. Factories were built in some of the towns here, and many farms continued to thrive, but by the late 19th century some of this land had become commuter territory. The most lavish Philadelphia suburbs were built on the Main Line, where in mansions shaded by huge trees Philadelphia's captains of commerce could get respite from the rowhouses and narrow streets of the city. By the late 20th century highways spread over the area and giant shopping centers sprung up: this was affluent suburbia for the masses, or a large part of them. Prosperity even came to some of the factory towns. Reading, the decaying industrial town describe in John Updike's *Rabbit* novels, in the 1970s was the site of the first factory outlet store, when a company called Vanity Fair began selling seconds and overruns of stockings and lingerie at wholesale prices in what had been the Berkshire Knitting Mills; today there are more than 300 outlets there selling deeply-discounted goods on the polished wood floors of converted brick mills, bringing in more than half a billion dollars a year, generating thousands of jobs and spawning 2,200 motel and hotel rooms.

The 6th Congressional District includes parts of this countryside in Chester, Berks and Montgomery Counties; it is the new suburban Philadelphia district created by Republican redistricters in 2002. Chester County has the highest median income levels in Pennsylvania, and Lower Merion Township in Montgomery County is the home of some of Philadelphia's wealthiest people, like philanthropist Leonore Annenberg. The boundaries of the 6th District are irregular. Geographically, the main body of the district is northern Chester County (it includes Coatesville, Downingtown and Phoenixville) and southern Berks County. The district also includes a salient that runs northward in eastern Berks County. There is another salient, much more heavily populated, reaching south into Montgomery County from Pottstown to Lower Merion Township. The district includes Valley Forge and most of the Main Line suburbs—Ardmore, Bryn Mawr, part of Paoli—and it includes a part but not all of Reading. If this district had been created in 1992, one could have written with confidence that it was heavily Republican. But in the 1990s the suburbs of Philadelphia, like those in the nation's other very large metropolitan areas, trended to the Democrats. Al Gore won 49% here, and in 2002 the district voted about 2–1 for Democratic gubernatorial candidate Ed Rendell, though more out of enthusiasm for his work as mayor of Philadelphia from 1991 to 1999 than for his party label.

The congressman from the 6th District is Jim Gerlach, a Republican elected by a narrow margin in 2002. He grew up in Ellwood City, Pennsylvania, midway between Pittsburgh and Youngstown, Ohio. He graduated from Dickinson College and its law school, just west of Harrisburg. He continued moving east, settled in Chester County and practiced law. He was elected to the state House in 1990 and to the state Senate in 1994 and 1998. As chairman of the Senate Local Government Committee, he was influential in changing the welfare law (which reduced the state's welfare rolls by 120,000), property tax law (to give taxpayers more say on local taxes) and land use and growth management regulation (to provide "smart growth" planning). When Republicans wanted to create a new Republican district in suburban Philadelphia, Gerlach was the obvious intended beneficiary of their plan. The 6th included some territory previously represented by Republicans Joe Pitts and Curt Weldon and Democrats Joe Hoeffel and Tim Holden. But Pitts and Weldon were provided with new safe districts, and Hoeffel had represented relatively little of the new 6th and ran instead in the new 13th, which was far more Democratic. None of Holden's home base of Schuylkill County was included in the new 6th, and he wisely chose to run against incumbent Republican George Gekas in the new 17th, and won.

Gerlach had spirited competition in the general election from Democrat Dan Wofford, executive director of the Philadelphia Education Fund's College Access Program and a former adviser to Governor Bob Casey. Wofford had not previously run for office, but his name was well known. He is the son of former Senator Harris Wofford, winner of a 1991 special election; his theme that "working Americans should have the right to a doctor" made health care a national issue even before Bill Clinton started running for president. Gerlach centered his campaign on his twelve years of legislative experience, citing his legislative accomplishments on welfare, property taxes and growth management. He said that he had twice voted to expand Pennsylvania's prescription drug program for low-income seniors. Wofford attacked Gerlach as a career politician who believed that his 12 years in Harrisburg should be an "automatic ticket to Washington," while Gerlach countered that he "didn't hear a lot of policy substance" from Wofford. They disagreed on abortion and Medicare. Both said they were against "privatization" of Social Security and supported authorizing military action in Iraq. Polls showed the race close and national Republicans spent more than $1.5 million on ads for Gerlach; George W. Bush appeared for him in late October in Chester County. The outcome was not clear until the early morning hours; Gerlach won 51%–49%. He won 58% in his Chester County base, 52% in Berks County and only 41% in Montgomery County.

In the House, Gerlach sought and won a seat on the Transportation Committee. Democrats may well target this seat in 2004, but Gerlach likes to remind them that he won his first race to the state House by just 23 votes yet was reelected without opposition.

SEVENTH DISTRICT

Rep. Curt Weldon (R)

Elected 1986, 9th term; b. July 22, 1947, Marcus Hook; home, Aston; West Chester St. Col., B.A. 1969; Protestant; married (Mary).

Elected Office: Marcus Hook Mayor, 1977–82; Delaware Cnty. Cncl., 1982–86, Chmn. 1985–86.

Professional Career: Elem. schl. teacher & Vice Principal, 1969–76; Dir., Training & Manpower Devel., CIGNA Corp., 1976–81.

DC Office: 2466 RHOB 20515, 202-225-2011; Fax: 202-225-8137; Web site: www.house.gov/curtweldon.

District Offices: Bridgeport, 610-270-1486; Upper Darby, 610-259-0700.

Committees: *Armed Services* (Vice Chmn. of 33 R): Strategic Forces; Tactical Air & Land Forces (Chmn.). *Science* (3d of 25 R): Energy; Space & Aeronautics. *Select Committee on Homeland Security* (12th of 27 R): Cybersecurity, Science and Research & Development; Emergency Preparedness & Response (Vice Chmn.); Rules.

Group Ratings

	ADA	ACLU	AFS	LCV	CON	ITIC	NTU	COC	ACU	NTLC	CHC
2002	15	7	22	50	58	75	50	79	79	67	75
2001	15	—	30	50	—	—	55	82	70	—	—

National Journal Ratings

	2001 LIB	—	2001 CONS		2002 LIB	—	2002 CONS
Economic	51%	—	49%		49%	—	50%
Social	41%	—	60%		47%	—	52%
Foreign	55%	—	45%		46%	—	53%

Key Votes of the 107th Congress

1. Approve Bush Tax Cuts	Y	5. Faith-Based Charities	Y	9. Trade Promotion Authority	N
2. Limit Patients' Bill of Rights	Y	6. Bar Gays in the Boy Scouts	*	10. Bar Funds for Intl. Court	Y
3. Campaign Finance Reform	Y	7. Ban Partial-Birth Abortion	*	11. Authorize Force in Iraq	Y
4. Ban ANWR Development	N	8. Arm Commercial Pilots	Y	12. Deny Home. Sec. Dept. Union	Y

Election Results

2002 general	Curt Weldon (R)	146,296	(66%)	($619,156)
	Peter Lennon (D)	75,055	(34%)	
2002 primary	Curt Weldon (R)	unopposed		
2000 general	Curt Weldon (R)	172,569	(65%)	($618,319)
	Peter Lennon (D)	93,687	(35%)	($22,578)

Prior Winning Percentages: 1998 (72%); 1996 (67%); 1994 (70%); 1992 (66%); 1990 (65%); 1988 (68%); 1986 (61%)

The People		Race/Ethnic Origin	Ancestry	
Area size:	293 sq. mi.	88.4% White	Irish: 21.8%	Italian: 14.3%
Urban population:	98.6%	5.4% Black	German: 13.3%	
Rural population:	1.4%	3.7% Asian	**2000 Presidential Vote**	
Pop. 2000:	646,530	0.1% Native Am.	Gore (D) 150,805	(51%)
Median income:	$56,154	0.0% Hawaiian	Bush (R) 140,862	(47%)
Poverty status:	5.4%	0.9% Two+ races	Other 6,945	(2%)
Military veterans:	12.9%	0.1% Other	**Cook Partisan Voting Index:** D + 1	
		1.3% Hispanic Origin		

Occupation	Blue collar: 16.1%	White collar: 72.6%	Gray collar: 11.3%

The close-in suburbs of the great eastern cities were home to some of the most curious and long-lasting political machines in America. They were Republican; they conducted business in the accents of ordinary people, ethnic as well as WASP; they had a tolerance for patronage, and for what city reform liberals would call corruption, that was sharply at odds with their embodiment of middle-class morality; they were old, going back to the days when political machines were as much a part of the urban landscape as trolley lines or overhead electrical wires. One such machine was the War Board of Pennsylvania's Delaware County, a ruthlessly effective Republican organization that continues to influence local politics even in its current and greatly diminished form. But while party registration in Delaware County runs 2–1 Republican, in national races voters here recently have voted for Democrats. Delaware County voted for Bill Clinton and Al Gore, by increasing margins, and voted 2–1 for Democrat Ed Rendell for governor in 2002. The reasons are partly demographic—in recent decades many Democrats have moved out to the suburbs from Philadelphia—and partly ideological. Republicans of the Newt Gingrich stripe are unfamiliar here, and unpopular; on cultural issues like abortions and guns, voters here have taken increasingly liberal stands.

The 7th Congressional District includes almost all of Delaware County, except for a few towns (notably heavily black Chester) that are appended to Philadelphia's 1st District. The 7th extends north to include a few Montgomery County suburbs, such as modest Conshohocken, an old Schuylkill River factory town, affluent Upper Merion Township and King of Prussia, an edge city where the Schuylkill Expressway intersects the Pennsylvania Turnpike. The 7th takes in southeastern Chester County, including the commercial hub of West Chester and a few further-out suburbs such as Malvern and part of Paoli. The 7th includes the elite small colleges of Haverford and Swarthmore, and the refined farm country of Chadds Ford, home to generations of Wyeths who used wheat-brown tones to limn the region's seasonal moods on canvas. Its housing is aging but well-maintained; its population is above average in income but distinct from the inhabitants of more affluent commuter towns. People here have deep roots in greater Philadelphia, but also deep fears about crime in nearby city neighborhoods.

The congressman from the 7th District is Curt Weldon, a Republican originally backed by the War Board and with anything but an aristocratic pedigree. He grew up in Delaware County, graduated from West Chester State College and worked as a teacher and personnel trainer. He first came to public attention in 1977 as mayor of gritty Marcus Hook, Pennsylvania's southern-most town on the Delaware River, the home of oil tank farms and a rusty-looking steel mill. In 1982 he was elected to the Delaware County Council. In 1984 he ran against liberal Democratic Congressman Bob Edgar (who got to Congress when the War Board split 10 years earlier), lost by 412 votes, then ran successfully in 1986 when Edgar ran unsuccessfully for the Senate.

Weldon started off as a local congressman but has become a major force on international issues of the greatest import. Weldon is usually a partisan Republican but not always a free-market enthusiast; like Pennsylvania Republicans of yore, he supports trade restrictions and voted against NAFTA and trade promotion authority. Although he has supported unions on some issues, including family-leave legislation, he favors repeal of the Davis-Bacon Act and voted for the flextime plan to permit workers to take compensatory time off rather than overtime pay. He strongly backs the partial-birth abortion ban. Urged by Newt Gingrich to be tested, he discovered in 1996 that he has diabetes, and has become a spokesman for testing and treatment.

Weldon is now the second ranking Republican on the Armed Services Committee and chairman of the Tactical Air and Land Forces Subcommittee. After he spotlighted the discovery of the Soviet radar at Krasnoyarsk in the 1980s, a violation of the ABM treaty, he has been for more than a decade a strong advocate of missile defense. His warnings were vindicated by the July 1998 Rumsfeld report revealing that missile threats could come from rogue states without notice. With the election of George W. Bush, a strong missile defense supporter, a less adversarial approach was required. In December 2002 Weldon predicted that Congress would approve the administration's plans to deploy ballistic missile defense systems in Alaska and California and on Aegis ships by the end of 2005, and he called for more support for the Airborne Laser program.

From 1995 to 2001 Weldon chaired the Research and Development Subcommittee; after the death of Floyd Spence in August 2001 he became chairman of Military Procurement. He has long charged that the Clinton administration undermined national security and has supported higher defense spending than the Bush administration. He has said that his priorities are more ship-building and getting the Navy to decide which two of three fighters to produce—the Joint Strike Fighter, the F-22 Raptor or the F/A-18E/F Super Hornet. Working with ranking member Gene Taylor, he got unanimous approval of a $73.4 billion authorization in April 2002, which provided $1 billion more than the administration requested for shipbuilding and provided $810 million for an additional DDG-51 to be built (in Taylor's district) if the Navy wins that much in a Court of Claims case against A-12 contractors.

Weldon is the House's strongest advocate of the Marine Corps's V-22 Osprey, one of whose prime contractors, the Boeing helicopter division, is located in Ridley Park in Delaware County. The tilted-rotor aircraft takes off and lands like a helicopter and flies like a plane. The Marine Corps says it flies faster and further than helicopters and can carry more passengers; in October 2001 Weldon said it would have been perfect in Afghanistan. But the Osprey has had serious troubles. It was cancelled by Defense Secretary Dick Cheney in 1989, but reinstated by Congress soon after. Since then, Weldon has assembled an Osprey coalition that has kept it alive despite crashes in 1991, 1992 and 2000. "We had a coalition broad and deep. We had the ex-Marines in Congress. We brought in the retired Marine reserve officers' association. I brought in the United Auto Workers and the civil aviation people." Two Ospreys crashed in late 2000 and the plane was grounded in December 2000. A panel headed by Norman Augustine in April 2001 called for major design and engineering changes. In October 2001 Weldon said the problems were nearly fixed and the Osprey could be ready to fly in two months; Augustine said it would take longer. In 2002 the House voted for 12 Ospreys, the Senate for nine. In the meantime, Weldon bristled in December 2001 when Boeing announced layoffs of 1,500 employees at Ridley Park. "If Boeing wants to eventually phase out [at the Ridley Park plant], then I have to know. Then I can do what I have to do in Washington," he said, in effect threatening retaliation against the firm's other contracts.

Weldon has made no secret of his ambition to become Armed Services Chairman. In 2000 Floyd Spence was about to leave the chairmanship because of House Republicans' term limits, and next in seniority was the elderly and quiet Bob Stump. Weldon, then seventh-ranking Republican in seniority, ran for chairman, with a detailed program for action and proposals to involve junior members more in decision-making and to encourage members to reach out to labor unions and other constituencies favoring defense spending. Duncan Hunter, the next in seniority after Stump, supported Stump but said he would be a candidate for the chairmanship if the Republican Steering Committee rejected him. Weldon lost by 1 vote and charged that Republican leaders had reneged on promises not to support Stump. But the chairmanship of the Military Procurement Subcommittee somewhat assuaged him. In April 2002 Stump announced that he would not run for reelection. Hunter promptly said he would seek the chairmanship; Weldon kept mum. In May Weldon announced he would support Hunter, with whom he had worked closely on many issues.

Weldon's accomplishments have not been limited to committee work. He has taken a special interest in Russia. He was a Russian studies major in college and is fluent in Russian; as of May 2002 he had made 28 trips to Russia. In the late 1980s he initiated a U.S. Congress-Duma Study Group and met regularly with senior Russian officials, both in Moscow and Washington. He worried that crime, corruption and internal disintegration are so rampant in Russia that nuclear-weapons theft "seems entirely plausible." He notes that 80 Russian portable nuclear weapons were unaccounted for in 2002 and worries that Russian nuclear, chemical and biological weapons could have made their way to America's enemies in the Middle East. He harshly criticized the Clinton administration approval of export licenses for sensitive equipment to Russia and China. He presented the Bush administration with a 41-page outline of how to foster partnerships between the U.S. and Russia in preparation for George W. Bush's 2001 meeting with Vladimir Putin in Crawford, Texas. He was outraged when the State Department concealed the whereabouts of a diplomat who had injured a Russian in a car crash in Vladivostok and encouraged support of oil development on Sakhalin and in the Timan-Pechora region of Siberia. In 2002, Weldon took an approach to North Korea that was similar to his approach to Russia in the 1980s. His plans for a trip there in spring 2002 were sidetracked by George W. Bush's inclusion of North Korea in the "axis of evil" in his January 2002 State of the Union. In December 2002, after the North Koreans announced that they had violated the 1994 Agreed Framework, he called for talks again. "The North Koreans just don't understand our intentions. I don't want to see Kim Jong Il do something stupid which could lead to significant loss of life. We need to convince him America does not want to have a war with the North." In 2003 he led a congressional delegation on a three-day visit to Pyongyang.

For Weldon September 11 was a case of the "government failing the American people." Back in 1998 he called for a National Operations Analysis Hub to coordinate agencies dealing with threats of terrorism, and after September 11 he criticized intelligence agencies for not sharing information. Weldon has drawn on his experience as a former volunteer firefighter and as founder of the Congressional Fire Services Caucus. He put into the 2002 defense authorization a provision for the transfer of military technology to firefighters and other first responders, our "domestic defenders" as he calls them. He was skeptical of Tom Ridge's ability to adequately coordinate homeland security without budget authority and supported creation of the Department of Homeland Security. In September 2002, before the homeland security bill passed, he said the House should see that it reported to only one authorizing committee and one appropriations subcommittee, instead of to the 88 committees and subcommittees currently with jurisdiction over its activities. He proposed a resolution to that effect at the Republican Conference meeting after the November election, and no one rose in opposition. Committees and subcommittees do not give up jurisdiction readily, but in 2003 the House adopted his proposals. Speaker Dennis Hastert created a new Select Committee on Homeland Security; Appropriations Committee chairman Bill Young reorganized his committee and created a Homeland Security Subcommittee.

Weldon has been reelected every two years by robust margins. Republicans controlled redistricting in 2002 and accommodated Weldon by adding Republican territory in Montgomery County. He was reelected with 66% of the vote.

EIGHTH DISTRICT

Rep. Jim Greenwood (R)

Elected 1992, 6th term; b. May 4, 1951, Philadelphia; home, Erwinna; Dickinson Col., B.A. 1973; Protestant; married (Christina).

Elected Office: PA House of Reps., 1980–86; PA Senate, 1986–93.

Professional Career: Legis. Asst., PA Rep. John Renninger, 1972–76; Social worker, Woods Schools, 1974–76; Caseworker, Bucks Cnty. Children & Youth Social Svc. Agency, 1977–80.

DC Office: 2436 RHOB 20515, 202-225-4276; Fax: 202-225-9511; Web site: www.house.gov/greenwood.

District Offices: Doylestown, 215-348-7511; Langhorne, 215-752-7711.

Committees: *Education & the Workforce* (8th of 27 R): Education Reform; Select Education. *Energy & Commerce* (7th of 31 R): Environment & Hazardous Materials; Health; Oversight & Investigations (Chmn.).

Group Ratings

	ADA	ACLU	AFS	LCV	CON	ITIC	NTU	COC	ACU	NTLC	CHC
2002	20	47	0	50	31	100	55	95	78	80	42
2001	25	—	0	64	—	—	57	91	48	—	—

National Journal Ratings

	2001 LIB	—	2001 CONS		2002 LIB	—	2002 CONS
Economic	41%	—	58%		44%	—	55%
Social	59%	—	41%		62%	—	37%
Foreign	33%	—	60%		28%	—	71%

Key Votes of the 107th Congress

1. Approve Bush Tax Cuts	Y	5. Faith-Based Charities	Y	9. Trade Promotion Authority	Y
2. Limit Patients' Bill of Rights	Y	6. Bar Gays in the Boy Scouts	Y	10. Bar Funds for Intl. Court	Y
3. Campaign Finance Reform	Y	7. Ban Partial-Birth Abortion	N	11. Authorize Force in Iraq	Y
4. Ban ANWR Development	Y	8. Arm Commercial Pilots	Y	12. Deny Home. Sec. Dept. Union	Y

Election Results

2002 general	Jim Greenwood (R)	127,475	(63%)	($889,736)
	Timothy Reece (D)	76,178	(37%)	
2002 primary	Jim Greenwood (R)	31,327	(69%)	
	Tom Lingenfelter (R)	13,981	(31%)	
2000 general	Jim Greenwood (R)	154,090	(59%)	($889,821)
	Ronald L. Strouse (D)	100,617	(39%)	($146,563)
	Other	5,394	(2%)	

Prior Winning Percentages: 1998 (63%); 1996 (59%); 1994 (66%); 1992 (52%)

The People		Race/Ethnic Origin	Ancestry	
Area size:	634 sq. mi.	90.8% White	German: 18.5%	Irish: 18.1%
Urban population:	90.9%	3.4% Black	Italian: 10.6%	
Rural population:	9.1%	2.4% Asian	**2000 Presidential Vote**	
Pop. 2000:	646,340	0.1% Native Am.	Gore (D)..............144,878	(51%)
Median income:	$59,184	0.0% Hawaiian	Bush (R)..............130,500	(46%)
Poverty status:	4.5%	0.9% Two+ races	Other....................9,050	(3%)
Military veterans:	12.9%	0.1% Other	**Cook Partisan Voting Index:** D + 2	
		2.3% Hispanic Origin		

Occupation   Blue collar: 20.9%   White collar: 68.0%   Gray collar: 11.1%

Bucks County was one of William Penn's three original settlements and the launching point for George Washington's crossing of the frigid Delaware River to surprise English and Hessian forces on Christmas Day 1776. But it had a split personality from the start. Upper Bucks County was at once a paradise of bucolic hills and creeks running into the Delaware River and, after Penn's secretary James Logan built the Durham Furnace iron works in 1727, one of the nation's major industrial sites. In the 1920s, Bucks County's well-settled farmland, old fieldstone houses and covered bridges in its northern parts captured the imagination of writers and artists, attracting the New York theatrical crowd—Oscar Hammerstein, Moss Hart, Dorothy Parker, S. J. Perelman. After World War II, its location between Philadelphia and Trenton, New Jersey, brought industrial Lower Bucks County to the forefront. The ocean-navigable Delaware River and several rail lines resulted in huge new developments: U.S. Steel's Fairless Works, one of the few big postwar steel plants, down by the river, and the Levitt organization's second Levittown, in what had been farmland and swamp between U.S. 13 and U.S. 1. But now the steel mill is closed, and Bucks County's economy depends more on modern technologies.

Bucks County's political tradition was heavily Republican and protectionist; more recently it has been marginally Republican and environmentalist. This was the home of Senator Joseph Grundy, longtime head of the Pennsylvania Manufacturers Association, who opposed the 1930 Smoot-Hawley tariff as insufficiently protectionist. Development in Bucks came after the New Deal, unlike other suburban Philadelphia counties where most blue collar immigration occurred years earlier, when county political organizations were ready to enroll new residents in their party. So Lower Bucks around the Fairless Works and Levittown, with its tightly-packed homes filled with blue collar workers, became Democratic. And Upper Bucks, faster-growing and still attracting trendy New Yorkers, is Republican but environment-conscious.

The 8th Congressional District includes all of Bucks County, a tiny finger of Montgomery County around Willow Grove and parts of two Far Northeast wards in Philadelphia. Bucks has the third highest income of any county in the state and the district as a whole has the highest percentage of married persons; the county's population grew by 10% in the 1990s. Bucks County's population has been just slightly less than that of a full congressional district for several decades, and so the 8th District has been one of the few districts in the country in states with multiple districts that has been left virtually unchanged during the last three redistricting cycles. The 8th was marginal in congressional elections between 1976 and 1992; since then, it has moved like other Philadelphia suburbs toward national Democrats and voted for Bill Clinton in 1992 and 1996 and Al Gore in 2000. It also joined the rest of southeastern Pennsylvania in voting decisively for Democrat Ed Rendell for governor in 2002. But Rendell had no coattails; three Republican state legislative candidates fended off concerted Democratic opposition; one of the failed Democrats was Peter Kostmayer, who had been congressman from the 8th from 1976 to 1980 and 1982 to 1992.

The congressman from the 8th District is Jim Greenwood, a Republican elected in 1992. Greenwood grew up in Newtown, on the margin between Lower Bucks and Upper Bucks. After college he worked for a state legislator, then was a social worker in Langhorne. He was elected to the state House in 1980 and the state Senate in 1986. In 1992 he ran against Kostmayer, an environment-minded, defense-cutting liberal. But Kostmayer had 50 overdrafts on the House bank and other financial problems, and Greenwood won 52%–46%.

In the House, Greenwood's voting record has been moderate-to-conservative on economic and foreign issues and moderate-to-liberal on cultural issues. He has worked closely with Republican leaders and was the moderate Tuesday Group's representative at Republican leadership meetings; in 1997 Speaker Newt Gingrich appointed him to head the House Republican long-term planning team after Bill Paxon resigned after the failed coup against Gingrich. On impeachment, he was undecided nearly until the vote, and displayed his balancing act by voting for two of the four House charges but urging the Senate to quickly end the trial with a bipartisan rebuke of Clinton. One of Greenwood's big causes has been to maintain funding of international family planning, insisting the issue wasn't abortion. "The whole planet is too fragile to support a runaway population," he says. Domestically, he wants to ensure that all private health insurance covers contraceptives. He has been among the handful of House Republicans opposing the ban on partial-birth abortions.

Greenwood has been busy on consumer issues at Energy and Commerce. He won committee approval of changes in the Superfund program to relieve liability from small businesses, recyclers and municipalities, and to allocate more money to clean up abandoned brownfield sites. On another Commerce issue, he helped to write legislation restricting Internet pornography's availability to kids, but it was overturned by the Supreme Court. As chairman of the Oversight and Investigations Subcommittee since 2001, he has targeted rising prices by insurance and pharmaceutical companies, demanded proof that government agencies protect against computer hackers and held lengthy hearings on the collapse of Enron that produced extensive documentation of the corporate abuses. He ran a separate investigation into the alleged stock manipulation by Martha Stewart; he called the scope of his influence as chairman "very liberating." In 2001, he tried to help organize a bipartisan coalition in the House, but it didn't get far. Likewise, he has sought centrist alternatives on health care in vain. As the House was about to vote a sweeping ban on human cloning, Greenwood offered an amendment to permit limited "therapeutic cloning" for medical research; it lost 249–178. Pat Toomey of the neighboring 15th District was a leader on the other side of the issue; Greenwood criticized the "hysteria" surrounding the debate. In April 2002, he introduced a bipartisan bill to limit to $250,000 claims for medical malpractice, which have become particularly troublesome in Pennsylvania; he cited low malpractice premiums in California, which sets that limit. In July George W. Bush endorsed the bill and it passed the House in September, but went nowhere in the Senate. The House again passed the bill in March 2003; the Senate has yet to act.

Greenwood's political formula still seems to suit the 8th District well. He has been reelected comfortably against poorly funded Democrats. Not surprisingly, given his continuing warnings that Republicans should not bow to the right wing on social issues, his problem has been in the Republican primary. In the past four cycles, he had primary challenges from conservatives and won each time with at least 60% of the vote. Greenwood has said he might be interested in running for the Senate if Arlen Specter retires in 2004. In June 2003, he announced he would break the 12-year term limit pledge he made in 1992. "What I didn't know then . . . is that it takes a long time in the U.S. Congress to develop the expertise for incredibly complex issues," Greenwood said at a press conference. "It takes a very long time to develop clout and influence in Washington." The new Bucks County Democratic chairman promised a more aggressive challenge against Greenwood for neglecting everyday problems while playing on the national stage.

NINTH DISTRICT

Rep. Bill Shuster (R)

Elected May 2001, 1st term; b. Jan. 10, 1961, McKeesport; home, Hollidaysburg; Dickinson Col., B.A. 1983; American U., M.B.A. 1987; Lutheran; married (Rebecca).

Professional Career: Mgr., Goodyear Tire & Rubber Co., 1983–87; District Mgr., Bandag Inc., 1987–90; Gen. Mgr., Shuster Chrysler, 1990–01.

DC Office: 1108 LHOB 20515, 202-225-2431; Web site: www.house.gov/shuster.

District Offices: Chambersburg, 717-264-8308; Hollidaysburg, 814-696-6318; Indiana, 724-463-0516.

Committees: *Small Business* (11th of 18 R): Rural Enterprises, Agriculture and Technology. *Transportation & Infrastructure* (31st of 41 R): Aviation; Highways, Transit & Pipelines; Water Resources & Environment.

Group Ratings (Only Served Partial Term)

	ADA	ACLU	AFS	LCV	CON	ITIC	NTU	COC	ACU	NTLC	CHC
2002	0	15	0	13	37	100	56	95	96	93	86
2001	5	—	14	8	—	—	—	94	94	—	—

National Journal Ratings (Only Served Partial Term)

	2001 LIB —	2001 CONS		2002 LIB —	2002 CONS
Economic	* —	*		21% —	73%
Social	34% —	67%		0% —	75%
Foreign	21% —	80%		0% —	85%

Key Votes of the 107th Congress (Only Served Partial Term)

1. Approve Bush Tax Cuts	Y	5. Faith-Based Charities	Y	9. Trade Promotion Authority	Y
2. Limit Patients' Bill of Rights	Y	6. Bar Gays in the Boy Scouts	Y	10. Bar Funds for Intl. Court	Y
3. Campaign Finance Reform	N	7. Ban Partial-Birth Abortion	Y	11. Authorize Force in Iraq	Y
4. Ban ANWR Development	N	8. Arm Commercial Pilots	Y	12. Deny Home. Sec. Dept. Union	Y

Election Results

2002 general	Bill Shuster (R)	124,184	(71%)	($1,099,169)
	John Henry (D)	50,559	(29%)	($8,723)
2002 primary	Bill Shuster (R)	33,538	(74%)	
	David Keller (R)	6,319	(14%)	
	David Bahr (R)	5,457	(12%)	
2001 special	Bill Shuster (R)	55,670	(52%)	($490,469)
	Scott Conklin (D)	47,220	(44%)	($237,971)
	Alanna Hartzok (Green)	4,437	(4%)	
2000 general	Bud Shuster (R)	unopposed		($1,150,318)

The People		Race/Ethnic Origin	Ancestry	
Area size:	7,284 sq. mi.	96.4% White	German: 24.4%	Irish: 9.0%
Urban population:	39.9%	1.6% Black	USA: 7.6%	
Rural population:	60.1%	0.4% Asian	**2000 Presidential Vote**	
Pop. 2000:	645,612	0.1% Native Am.	Bush (R)	149,393 (64%)
Median income:	$34,850	0.0% Hawaiian	Gore (D)	80,008 (34%)
Poverty status:	11.1%	0.5% Two+ races	Other	4,079 (2%)
Military veterans:	14.6%	0.0% Other	**Cook Partisan Voting Index:** R +15	
		0.9% Hispanic Origin		
Occupation	Blue collar: 34.4%	White collar: 48.7%	Gray collar: 16.9%	

Today, the old towns of south central Pennsylvania look much as they did 60 years ago: farmhouses and red barns set amidst rolling hills in the shadow of mountain ridges, seemingly isolated from the pulsing rhythms of 21st Century America. But this tranquility was shattered on September 11, 2001, when United Airlines Flight 93, crashed into an empty former coalfield near Shanksville in Somerset County, killing all 40 passengers and crew on board. To Americans, the crash site became a symbol of both sadness and pride at the passengers' effort to wrest back control of the plane, initiated by the now-famous cry of "Let's roll!" The plane was headed to Washington; the bravery of the passengers prevented its reaching the hijackers' target, probably the Capitol or perhaps the White House. Just as Shanksville's 245 residents were grappling with the aftermath of Flight 93—the influx of visitors, the fears of commercialization—Somerset County was struck by another bolt of lightning, less than a year later and only 13 miles away. Nine miners at the Quecreek coal mine were trapped by rising waters 240 feet underground, and as a breathless nation looked on, rescuers strained to dig rescue shafts. After 77 hours in confinement, the miners were lifted one by one to safety—a joyous counterpoint to the heartbreak just 10 months earlier.

The area's usual placidity owes much to the Appalachian mountains, which run like a series of vertebrae up and down central Pennsylvania, long posing a formidable barrier. Up close, the mountains look tantalizingly low: you imagine that you could hike over them in an hour or so. But they are much more daunting than they seem. The colonials and British regulars led by General Braddock to defeat near Pittsburgh in 1754 found it hard going, despite guidance from George Washington; 19th century pioneers in Conestoga wagons found it not much easier, for there are few gaps in the ridges. During the 18th century, the mountains provided Quaker Pennsylvania with a rampart against Indian attacks and allowed the commonwealth to become the richest and most populous of the colonies. But in the 19th century, when businessmen were ready to trade throughout the vast interior, the mountains proved to be a barrier, and people flocked to the easier routes through New York: the Erie Canal and the New York Central Railroad. It took the aggressive capitalists who built the Pennsylvania Railroad to get trains over these ridges. Conquering the mountains near Altoona required the work of several hundred Irish laborers, equipped with hand tools, gunpowder and pack animals, to build Horseshoe Curve between 1851 and 1854—one of the finest examples of railroad engineering anywhere, and today a National Historic Landmark that is celebrated by "railfans" who come from all over the world to visit it and a nearby railroaders museum.

Though Pennsylvania's rail links remained important—the Nazis considered them key sabotage targets during World War II—the war-bound nation in 1940 opened the road of the future here: the Pennsylvania Turnpike, the first highway in America that was able to move vehicles dependably at high speeds over long distances. "The Pennsylvania Turnpike is a triumph of engineering," writes Tom Lewis in *Divided Highways*, a recent study of the Interstate highway system. "The road tunnels under the Allegheny Mountains and cuts about five hours off the journey between the cities. It is like no other road in America: a maximum rise at any point of just three feet in every 100; a minimum sight distance of 600 feet; bridges and underpasses that do away with cross traffic; and wide, banked curves that eliminate the need to slow down." Federal officials set a seemingly impossible 20-month deadline for construction, but despite technical obstacles, racial animosities in the workforce and two dozen worker deaths, the road was completed only three months late, after 30,000 workers—five times the number that built the Hoover Dam—converged on western Pennsylvania during the project's final months. Driving it was a breathtakingly unfamiliar experience to most Americans: "I never thought I could drive at 75 miles an hour around mountain curves in heavy rain and live to write about it," began one contemporary news report cited by Lewis.

Pennsylvania's 9th Congressional District takes in a wide swath of south and central Pennsylvania, including six full counties and parts of eight others. Most of the 9th is not coal country and was thus spared the boom-bust cycles of northeastern Pennsylvania and West Virginia. But this is a slow-growth, low-income area today. The largest city is Altoona, which withered from 82,000 people in 1930 to 49,000 in 2000 as the once-prosperous Pennsylvania Railroad succumbed to competition from truck traffic and became the bankrupt Penn Central and now privatized Conrail. Since the 1940s, Hollidaysburg near Altoona has been home to the small and scrupulously independent company that manufactures the Slinky, the inexpensive wire-coil toy invented accidentally by Navy engineer Richard James. Redistricting in 2002 pushed the 9th significantly west, to take in Frank Lloyd Wright's Fallingwater in Fayette County and far enough east to take in part of Carlisle, the home of Dickinson College. Politically, this part of Pennsylvania has been solidly Republican since 1860, when Mercersburg native James Buchanan left the White House, and has not come close to electing a Democrat to Congress for decades. George W. Bush won 64% of the vote here in 2000.

The congressman from the 9th District is Bill Shuster, a Republican first elected in a May 2001 special election. His father Bud Shuster, for six years the powerful chairman of the Transportation and Infrastructure Committee, announced his resignation in January 2001, after he failed to get an exemption from the Republicans' six-year term limit on chairmanships. As Transportation chairman, Bud Shuster was both a generous local benefactor and a serious national policymaker; his work can be seen not only in the Bud Shuster Highway (as Interstate 99 in Bedford and Blair Counties is known) but also in transportation projects sprinkled across the country by the giant 1998 TEA-21 bill. Bill Shuster grew up in the Pittsburgh area, where his father started a successful business. After graduating from Dickinson College and American University business school, he moved to Blair County, where he owned the family's car dealership, Shuster Chrysler in East Freedom, near Altoona. Although he was a newcomer to politics, he had plenty of experience observing his father.

The contest for the House seat was for all practical purposes decided at a district-wide Republican convention, when Bill Shuster won 69 of 133 votes, two more than the required majority. Facing nine other contenders, Shuster—with back-room help from his father—ran an insider campaign that took advantage of the family's years of service. Although there was some local grumbling about a Shuster dynasty, opponents failed to coalesce behind a single candidate. In a key move, Shuster's allies obtained a state court injunction forcing a vote on a new slate of delegates for Blair County after claiming that the original slate supporting his opponent had been seated in violation of the rules. In the general election in a heavily Republican district that had not elected a Democrat since the New Deal, Shuster ran ads touting his "hard work, real world experience" and "conservative values." National Democrats ignored the race, which seemed to them hopeless; Governor Tom Ridge and Speaker Dennis Hastert came in for Shuster and George W. Bush cut a radio spot. But Democrat H. Scott Conklin campaigned vigorously as an opponent of abortion and gun control, Shuster won by a closer than expected 52%–44%. National Republicans attributed the narrow margin to residual intra-party ill will over his nomination; national Democrats dismissed second-guessing and said the district was just too Republican for a Democrat to win.

In the House, Bill Shuster has had a voting record a bit more conservative than his father's. He won his father's former seat on the Transportation Committee, although this time it was at the bottom rank of seniority. His chief legislative focus was renewal of the dam safety program, with technical assistance to improve post-9/11 security. He claimed credit for new local water and sewer projects that his father had earlier written into law; local officials call them "Shuster grants." Working with local officials, he struggled to find ways to keep open the Letterkenny Army Depot in Franklin County.

Shuster was easily reelected in 2002.

TENTH DISTRICT

Rep. Don Sherwood (R)

Elected 1998, 3d term; b. Mar. 5, 1941, Nicholson; home, Tunkhannock; Dartmouth Col., B.A. 1963; Methodist; married (Carol).

Military Career: Army, 1964–66.

Elected Office: Tunkhannock Area Schl. Bd., 1975–98, Pres., 1992–98.

Professional Career: Businessman; Auto dealer, 1967–present.

DC Office: 1223 LHOB 20515, 202-225-3731; Fax: 202-225-9594; Web site: www.house.gov/sherwood.

District Offices: Clarks Summit, 570-585-8190; Williamsport, 570-327-8161.

Committees: *Appropriations* (31st of 36 R): Homeland Security; Interior; Labor, HHS & Education.

Group Ratings

	ADA	ACLU	AFS	LCV	CON	ITIC	NTU	COC	ACU	NTLC	CHC
2002	5	20	0	13	8	100	56	100	96	89	100
2001	0	—	0	14	—	—	62	100	88	—	—

National Journal Ratings

	2001 LIB	—	2001 CONS		2002 LIB	—	2002 CONS
Economic	22%	—	74%		21%	—	73%
Social	32%	—	67%		0%	—	75%
Foreign	33%	—	60%		0%	—	85%

Key Votes of the 107th Congress

1. Approve Bush Tax Cuts	Y	5. Faith-Based Charities	Y	9. Trade Promotion Authority	Y
2. Limit Patients' Bill of Rights	Y	6. Bar Gays in the Boy Scouts	Y	10. Bar Funds for Intl. Court	Y
3. Campaign Finance Reform	N	7. Ban Partial-Birth Abortion	Y	11. Authorize Force in Iraq	Y
4. Ban ANWR Development	N	8. Arm Commercial Pilots	Y	12. Deny Home. Sec. Dept. Union	Y

Election Results

2002 general	Don Sherwood (R) 152,017	(93%)	($1,001,321)
	Kurt Shotko (Green) 11,613	(7%)	
2002 primary	Don Sherwood (R) .... unopposed		
2000 general	Don Sherwood (R) 124,830	(53%)	($2,107,286)
	Pat Casey (D) 112,580	(47%)	($1,619,801)

Prior Winning Percentages: 1998 (49%)

The People		Race/Ethnic Origin	Ancestry	
Area size:	6,689 sq. mi.	95.5% White	German: 18.5%	Irish: 11.0%
Urban population:	44.6%	1.9% Black	Italian: 7.4%	
Rural population:	55.4%	0.5% Asian	**2000 Presidential Vote**	
Pop. 2000:	646,537	0.1% Native Am.	Bush (R)...............140,387	(56%)
Median income:	$35,984	0.0% Hawaiian	Gore (D)...............100,754	(40%)
Poverty status:	10.3%	0.6% Two + races	Other....................7,887	(3%)
Military veterans:	15.3%	0.1% Other	**Cook Partisan Voting Index:** R + 9	
		1.4% Hispanic Origin		

Occupation	Blue collar: 31.1%	White collar: 52.6%	Gray collar: 16.4%

The northeast corner of Pennsylvania is a land of crevassed valleys and rugged mountains, criss-crossed by giant viaducts built for the railroads linking the East Coast with the Great Lakes and mines to the big cities that heated their houses with the region's anthracite coal. Except for a row of anthracite coal cities from Scranton to Wilkes-Barre, this part of Pennsylvania still has a wild look to it: the superstructure of railroads and Interstate 80 pass through an area that seems otherwise little touched by late 20th century prosperity. This is a land of numerous long-established small towns, with solidly built courthouses and banks and elderly citizens—a part of the Northeast that seems worlds away from the region's huge central cities and growing suburbs. The biggest towns here are Lewisburg, home of Bucknell University and a major federal penitentiary, and Williamsport, home of the Little League World Series. Only at the eastern edge is there significant growth; rural Pike County on the Delaware River grew 65% in the 1990s, largely because of an influx of New Yorkers and Latinos.

The 10th Congressional District includes all of northeast Pennsylvania except for Scranton, Wilkes-Barre and fast-growing Monroe County, which are in the 11th District. Redistricting changed the configuration of districts in this part of the state. Since 1888, there had been separate districts centered on Scranton and Wilkes-Barre. Since the New Deal years both cities have been far more Democratic than the rest of northeast Pennsylvania, which has been Republican since 1850; a Democratic congressman this area in the 1840s, David Wilmot, introduced the Wilmot Provisio barring slavery from the New Mexico and California Territories acquired in the Mexican War. This became one of the great causes of the Republican party in the 1850s; Wilmot was one of the founders of the Republican party and was elected as a Republican to the Senate. Most people in this part of Pennsylvania have been Republicans ever since. In 2002 Republican redistricters put Scranton and Wilkes-Barre together in the 11th District, leaving the 10th a solidly Republican constituency.

The congressman from the 10th District is Don Sherwood, a Republican elected in 1998. He has deep roots in Tunkhannock in Wyoming County, 40 winding miles northwest of Scranton. After graduating from Dartmouth and serving in the Army, Sherwood became a Chevrolet dealer in 1967—at age 26, the youngest Chevy dealer in the East. He served 24 years on the Tunkhannock school board. He raises and grooms Belgian horses, which he shows throughout the state. When Joseph McDade, a Scranton Republican who had showered projects on Scranton from his seat on the Appropriations Committee, announced that he would not run again in 1998, Sherwood ran for the seat, assembling a grass-roots organization of 1,800 volunteers and announcing an agenda that combined small business goals to cut taxes and "eliminate the IRS as we know it" with calls for a minimum wage increase and HMO regulation. With a personable style and an open wallet—he ultimately spent $795,000 of his own money on the campaign—he won 43% in the eight-candidate Republican primary, well ahead of the 23% for Scranton Mayor James Connors. In the general election he faced Pat Casey, son of former Governor Robert Casey, a Scranton native and strong opponent of abortion. Casey argued that by entering Congress at a young age he would put money in the district for years to come, and said that Sherwood's ideas on Social Security and education are "walking in lockstep with Dick Armey and Newt Gingrich." Sherwood argued that he was "a proven job creator" and that his support of a higher minimum wage showed he was alert to the district's needs. Sherwood got a big boost in the closing days when Speaker Newt Gingrich came in and pledged to assign him to fill McDade's seat on the Appropriations; when Gingrich resigned after the election, the offer was not honored and the seat was given to John Peterson. This was one of the closest races in the nation: Sherwood won by just 515 votes, 49%–48%.

In the House, Sherwood has compiled a mostly conservative voting record. He supported a bipartisan plan for a $1 increase in the minimum wage. But he opposed organized labor with his votes for PNTR with China and trade promotion authority. He sponsored an amendment of the Death on the High Seas Act to allow damage claims for airline crashes at sea; the victims of the TWA 800 crash off Long Island in 1996 included 21 students and chaperones from the local Montoursville High School, most of whose families had been unable to file claims because of maritime law.

Democrats again nominated Casey to oppose Sherwood in 2000, and both again spent heavily. In vivid contrast to 1992, when then-Governor Casey was barred from speaking to the Democratic convention because of his anti-abortion views, Pat Casey paid tribute to his father, who died in May 2000, from the convention podium in Los Angeles. The AFL-CIO ran an ad that said Sherwood sided with the pharmaceutical industry on drug coverage for seniors. Sherwood said that he was working to strengthen Medicare and that Casey would say anything to get elected. Sherwood won by a larger margin this time, 53%–47%, losing Lackawanna County 62%–38% but piling up sizable majorities elsewhere. After the election, Republican leaders gave him the Appropriations seat that he was denied two years earlier.

Redistricting transformed what had been one of the most closely divided districts in the nation in 1998 to an utterly safe Republican seat. The Republican redistricters, by putting Scranton and nearby towns in the 11th District, removed practically every precinct that voted against Sherwood in 1998 or 2000. No Democrat filed to run against Sherwood; he was reelected with 93% of the vote.

ELEVENTH DISTRICT

Rep. Paul Kanjorski (D)

Elected 1984, 10th term; b. Apr. 2, 1937, Nanticoke; home, Nanticoke; Temple U., 1957–61, Dickinson Law Schl., 1962–65; Catholic; married (Nancy).

Military Career: Army Reserves, 1960–61.

Professional Career: Practicing atty., 1966–85; Nanticoke City Solicitor, 1969–81; Admin. Law Judge, 1971–80.

DC Office: 2353 RHOB 20515, 202-225-6511; Fax: 202-225-0764; Web site: www.house.gov/kanjorski.

District Office: Wilkes-Barre, 570-825-2200.

Committees: *Financial Services* (2d of 32 D): Capital Markets, Insurance & Government Sponsored Enterprises (RMM); Domestic and International Monetary Policy, Trade & Technology; Financial Institutions & Consumer Credit. *Government Reform* (5th of 19 D): Energy Policy, Natural Resources and Regulatory Affairs; Government Efficiency & Financial Management.

Group Ratings

	ADA	ACLU	AFS	LCV	CON	ITIC	NTU	COC	ACU	NTLC	CHC
2002	75	53	89	88	43	50	22	50	24	14	33
2001	65	—	100	64	—	—	20	43	36	—	—

National Journal Ratings

	2001 LIB	—	2001 CONS		2002 LIB	—	2002 CONS
Economic	74%	—	25%		82%	—	17%
Social	50%	—	50%		54%	—	46%
Foreign	61%	—	36%		60%	—	39%

Key Votes of the 107th Congress

1. Approve Bush Tax Cuts	N	5. Faith-Based Charities	N	9. Trade Promotion Authority	N
2. Limit Patients' Bill of Rights	N	6. Bar Gays in the Boy Scouts	Y	10. Bar Funds for Intl. Court	Y
3. Campaign Finance Reform	Y	7. Ban Partial-Birth Abortion	Y	11. Authorize Force in Iraq	Y
4. Ban ANWR Development	N	8. Arm Commercial Pilots	Y	12. Deny Home. Sec. Dept. Union	N

Election Results

2002 general	Paul Kanjorski (D)	93,758	(56%)	($1,179,632)
	Louis Barletta (R)	71,543	(42%)	($566,407)
	Other	3,304	(2%)	
2002 primary	Paul Kanjorski (D)	unopposed		
2000 general	Paul Kanjorski (D)	131,948	(66%)	($271,258)
	Stephen A. Urban (R)	66,699	(34%)	($18,760)

Prior Winning Percentages: 1998 (67%); 1996 (68%); 1994 (67%); 1992 (67%); 1990 (100%); 1988 (100%); 1986 (71%); 1984 (59%)

The People		Race/Ethnic Origin	Ancestry	
Area size:	2,249 sq. mi.	93.3% White	German: 14.5%	Irish: 13.2%
Urban population:	72.6%	2.5% Black	Italian: 12.0%	
Rural population:	27.4%	0.7% Asian	**2000 Presidential Vote**	
Pop. 2000:	646,209	0.1% Native Am.	Gore (D) 127,140	(54%)
Median income:	$34,979	0.0% Hawaiian	Bush (R) 101,629	(43%)
Poverty status:	11.3%	0.7% Two+ races	Other 6,983	(3%)
Military veterans:	15.3%	0.1% Other	**Cook Partisan Voting Index:** D + 5	
		2.5% Hispanic Origin		

Occupation	Blue collar: 29.8%	White collar: 54.0%	Gray collar: 16.1%

"Coal is the theme song of this city in the hills," the *WPA Guide* said of Scranton in 1940, but even as those words were written, the anthracite kingdom around Scranton and Wilkes-Barre was crumbling. In the 19th century anthracite had become America's main home heating fuel and the valley along the East Branch of the Susquehanna River and the creek that extends north was America's number one source of anthracite. Thousands of immigrants flocked to this valley, settling in a chain of little cities north and south of Wilkes-Barre (named for two backers of the American revolution) and Scranton (named for the leading founding family). There, they took honest jobs with long hours, modest pay, poor working conditions and high death rates—facts of life that made the violently pro-union Molly Maguires popular here, and which spawned periodic clashes between them and the Pinkerton security forces hired by the industrial moguls. While the supply of coal was endless—the area produced 40% of the world's hard coal—demand proved fleeting. Anthracite production peaked in 1917, with long strikes in 1922 and 1925 quickening the conversion to oil and gas. Demand for anthracite began to fall in the 1920s and plummeted in the 1940s; the counties containing Wilkes-Barre and Scranton, Luzerne and Lackawanna, had 755,000 people in 1930 and 528,000 in 2000. As the area's 50 collieries shut down, the once-ubiquitous coal dust vanished; the local ethnic mix—Irish and Polish, Ukrainian and Welsh—grew less distinctive; and former boomtowns full of young families became time-worn communities of senior citizens. Visitors can see how suddenly growth stopped here: at the edge of town streets with houses obviously built in the 1910s and 1920s suddenly end, with only open space beyond. In the 1960s and 1970s, textile and apparel mills brought low-wage, non-union jobs to a formerly high-wage, unionized area. But the anthracite kingdom, created by unbridled (and often exploitative) free enterprise, increasingly looked to the government for sustenance. Two longtime congressmen, Democrat Daniel Flood of Luzerne (1945–47, 1949–53, 1955–80) and Republican Joseph McDade of Lackawanna (1963–99) specialized in funneling money and projects into the area, of which the most visible today is Scranton's $66 million Steamtown train historic site.

The 11th Congressional District is the anthracite district. It includes almost all of Luzerne County and Scranton and surrounding towns in Lackawanna County. It also includes Columbia County west of Luzerne, Carbon County south of Luzerne and Monroe County to the east. Monroe is a different sort of place: it contains most of the Pocono resort area and the Interstate 80 bridge to New Jersey; in the 1990s, New Yorkers and New Jerseyites looking for lower taxes and pleasant scenery moved here in large numbers and the county's population rose 45%. More typical of the district are small towns like Centralia, site of a massive underground fire that has burned unchecked since 1962, forcing out all but a dozen stubborn residents, and Jim Thorpe, created in 1953 from the unification of neighboring (and rival) Mauch Chunk and East Mauch Chunk. The cities changed their name after offering to provide a gravesite for the great football, baseball and Olympic track star when Thorpe's widow was shopping his remains to whichever town agreed to build him a suitable memorial. Downtown, however, is lively today, with hilly streets, high-ceilinged craft shops and homey restaurants that the Molly Maguires would have recoiled from—and they are here largely because of tourists drawn by the Oklahoma Indian who never came to Carbon County until his death. Since the 1930s, the miners have always been a large Democratic voting bloc, and this is a solidly Democratic district. But these Democrats tend to be cultural conservatives, pro-gun and anti-abortion.

The congressman from the 11th District is Paul Kanjorski, first elected in 1984. Kanjorski grew up in Nanticoke, near Wilkes-Barre. As a 16-year-old page in the House of Representative in 1954, he was on the floor when Puerto Rican terrorists started shooting from the gallery; five congressmen were wounded and Kanjorski was sprayed by dust from the gunfire. He attended, but did not graduate from, college and law school, then passed the bar exam and returned home to practice law; he was a workmen's compensation administrative law judge for nine years and Nanticoke city solicitor for 12. In 1984 he ran for Congress and won the May Democratic primary by pointing out the incumbent was in Central America while flood-soaked Wilkes-Barre area residents had to boil tap water because of contamination.

In the House, Kanjorski's voting record has been liberal on economics and moderate on cultural issues. He opposes abortion rights but has voted for international family planning aid. He is a tough partisan. While chairing a subcommittee with jurisdiction over White House operations, he sharply attacked the first Bush White House for lavish spending; Bush once apologized at a breakfast meeting for the skimpy meal, blaming Kanjorski's investigations. But with Bill Clinton in the White House, Kanjorski vociferously attacked fellow Pennsylvanian Bill Clinger's investigation of the White House travel office firings and delayed issuance of the report. When Dan Burton chaired the Government Reform Committee's hearings on campaign finance abuses, Kanjorski said the panel "should be holding its meeting in a chamber with padded walls." In October 1998, he was one of five House Democrats who voted against all impeachment inquiry resolutions. Legislatively, Kanjorski helped to enact a bill allowing expanded membership in credit unions. That measure, which he termed "a victory of David over Goliath," was a setback for banks since it overturned a Supreme Court ruling that limited credit union membership to one occupational group. In 2000, he won compensation for workers who were harmed by exposure to beryllium at nuclear weapons plants, including the former facility in Hazle Township in Luzerne County. In November 2001, he sponsored a bill for tax credit bonds to finance reclamation of abandoned coalmines. On the Financial Services Committee he helped to write in 2002 the post-Enron bill designed to crack down on corporate fraud. He voted to authorize the use of force in Iraq. In 2003, he became the second-ranking Democrat on the committee.

Most important to Kanjorski is helping his economically ailing district. The *New York Times* called him "a master of earmarking" for getting millions of dollars for the Earth Conservancy Applied Research Center, a public-private project for developing new technologies to reclaim mine-ravaged northeastern Pennsylvania. When Clinton called for 10 more National Historic

Rivers, Kanjorski's intervention led Clinton to expand the list to 14—including the Susquehanna. But his eagerness to deliver money to the district got him into trouble in 2002. A federal probe prompted by local union and civic leaders divulged that Kanjorski had obtained $7.5 million in federal grants for Cornerstone Technologies, a high-tech research and development company partly-owned by his nephew and other family members. Kanjorski insisted there was no wrong-doing and that he had not violated House rules or profited personally. No charges have been filed against Kanjorski; local newspapers reported that the FBI was investigating possible wrongdoing at the companies. Kanjorski accused Senator Rick Santorum of instigating the FBI investigation in an attempt to oust him in the 2002 election. House Republican leaders planned to refer the case to the Ethics Committee for its review, but they reportedly backed off when Democrats threatened to retaliate with an ethics challenge against a Republican.

Republicans targeted Kanjorski in 2002. Their first redistricting plan, passed by the state Senate in December 2001, put him in the same district with fellow Democrat Tim Holden, whose base, Schuylkill County, is an anthracite county south of Luzerne. But that plan could not get support from state House Majority Leader John Perzel, and the final plan paired Holden and Republican George Gekas and left Kanjorski with a Democratic district. Nevertheless Republicans found a serious challenger in Hazleton Mayor Lou Barletta, who hammered Kanjorski on the newspaper allegations. The NRCC ran ads asking, "And who does Paul Kanjorski create jobs for? Not average Pennsylvania families. But his own family. Like his nephews." Kanjorski conceded that he had been investigated, but said that his partisan opponents manufactured the allegations to damage him politically. Reports of grand jury investigations continued throughout his reelection campaign. This was Kanjorski's closest contest since he was first elected, but he won decisively, 56%–42%. About one-third of his victory margin came from Lackawanna County, which had been added to the district but cast only 15% of the total vote. Barletta said that might run again in 2004.

TWELFTH DISTRICT

Rep. John Murtha (D)

Elected Feb. 1974, 15th term; b. June 17, 1932, New Martinsville, WV; home, Johnstown; U. of Pittsburgh, B.A. 1962, Indiana U. of PA, 1963–64; Catholic; married (Joyce).

Military Career: Marine Corps, 1952–55, 1966–67 (Vietnam); Marine Corps Reserves, 1955–66, 1967–90.

Elected Office: PA House of Reps., 1969–74.

Professional Career: Owner, Johnstown Minute Car Wash.

DC Office: 2423 RHOB 20515, 202-225-2065; Fax: 202-225-5709; Web site: www.house.gov/murtha.

District Office: Johnstown, 814-535-2642.

Committees: *Appropriations* (2d of 29 D): Defense (RMM); Interior.

Group Ratings

	ADA	ACLU	AFS	LCV	CON	ITIC	NTU	COC	ACU	NTLC	CHC
2002	55	50	88	50	68	62	21	61	32	24	33
2001	65	—	100	36	—	—	24	52	48	—	—

National Journal Ratings

	2001 LIB — 2001 CONS	2002 LIB — 2002 CONS
Economic	72% — 27%	66% — 34%
Social	52% — 47%	52% — 47%
Foreign	61% — 36%	56% — 44%

Key Votes of the 107th Congress

1. Approve Bush Tax Cuts	N	5. Faith-Based Charities	N	9. Trade Promotion Authority	N
2. Limit Patients' Bill of Rights	N	6. Bar Gays in the Boy Scouts	Y	10. Bar Funds for Intl. Court	Y
3. Campaign Finance Reform	N	7. Ban Partial-Birth Abortion	Y	11. Authorize Force in Iraq	Y
4. Ban ANWR Development	N	8. Arm Commercial Pilots	Y	12. Deny Home. Sec. Dept. Union	N

Election Results

2002 general	John Murtha (D)	124,201	(73%)	($2,386,861)
	Bill Choby (R)	44,818	(27%)	($17,584)
2002 primary	John Murtha (D)	60,687	(64%)	
	Frank Mascara (D)	33,837	(36%)	
2000 general	John Murtha (D)	145,538	(71%)	($968,531)
	Bill Choby (R)	56,575	(28%)	($8,310)
	Other	3,324	(2%)	

Prior Winning Percentages: 1998 (68%); 1996 (70%); 1994 (69%); 1992 (100%); 1990 (62%); 1988 (100%); 1986 (67%); 1984 (69%); 1982 (61%); 1980 (59%); 1978 (69%); 1976 (68%); 1974 (58%); 1974 (50%)

The People		Race/Ethnic Origin	Ancestry	
Area size:	2,783 sq. mi.	94.9% White	German: 17.2%	Irish: 9.9%
Urban population:	62.5%	3.3% Black	Italian: 9.2%	
Rural population:	37.5%	0.3% Asian	**2000 Presidential Vote**	
Pop. 2000:	646,079	0.1% Native Am.	Gore (D)	131,960 (55%)
Median income:	$30,614	0.0% Hawaiian	Bush (R)	105,451 (44%)
Poverty status:	13.6%	0.7% Two + races	Other	3,595 (1%)
Military veterans:	15.3%	0.1% Other	**Cook Partisan Voting Index:** D + 5	
		0.6% Hispanic Origin		

Occupation Blue collar: 30.5% White collar: 51.3% Gray collar: 18.1%

The mountains and valleys within a 100-mile radius of Pittsburgh comprise one of America's most beautiful—and economically troubled—regions. This has been tough, hard-working country ever since Scots-Irish farmers settled here in the 1790s. Their first big product was whiskey—this was the site of the Whiskey Rebellion of 1794—but historically the most important product was bituminous coal. Discovered in the 19th century, it was the basic energy source for the production of iron and steel. The offspring of the original settlers were joined by immigrants from Italy, Poland and Czechoslovakia, living in little frame houses packed into the towns on interstices between hills and rivers, within walking distance of steel factories, foundries and coal mine shafts. It is an industrial landscape and yet there are spots of natural beauty, like the swirling waters of the Youghiogheny River, now much enjoyed by rafters. But the water coming down from the mountains can be dangerous. Its best known community is Johnstown, where on May 31, 1889 floodwater from the ruptured South Fork Dam, gaining speed during an 18-mile trip down steepwalled valleys, poured into the little industrial city with a force equal to Niagara Falls. During 10 awful minutes buildings crumpled like paper, the tumbling hearths and gaslights ignited the wreckage, a flaming pile of debris converged on a 30-acre expanse, and 2,209 people died. This was the worst single-day civilian loss of life in American history until September 11, 2001, when airliners crashed into the World Trade Center and the Pentagon and came down in a field just 50 miles southwest of Johnstown. The 1889 flood and its class overtones (the dam, built at a rural retreat owned by western Pennsylvania's richest families, had been negligently maintained) are documented thoughtfully by the Johnstown Flood Museum in the old Carnegie Library. The museum provides an offset to the economic woes of Johnstown, whose population fell from 67,000 in 1920 to 23,000 in 2000—a decline similar to that of many communities in this region. Life was never easy here; after some prosperous years in the 1960s and 1970s, the coal country was hit hard by the recession that followed the 1979 oil shock. Young people have been leaving the area for years, and it now has the highest percentage of elderly residents of any of the state's 19 congressional districts.

The 12th Congressional District, with highly irregular boundaries, contains much of this coal and steel country. It includes all of Greene County and parts of Fayette, Somerset, Cambria,

Indiana, Armstrong, Washington and Westmoreland Counties. The boundaries were drawn by Republican legislators who wanted to create a new Republican-leaning 18th District in the southern suburbs of Pittsburgh while also accommodating Democratic Congressman John Murtha, second ranking minority member on the Appropriations Committee, where he has worked assiduously to help Pennsylvania. The district includes Murtha's home base of Johnstown and Democratic territory in northern Westmoreland County, plus parts of Armstrong and Indiana Counties to the north. It includes part of rural Somerset County and much of the industrial country in Fayette, Greene and Washington Counties south of Pittsburgh. Its boundaries were carefully drawn so as to exclude Republican-leaning suburbs and to leave out the hometown of former 20th District Congressman Frank Mascara.

Politically, this was one of the most Republican parts of America from the Civil War up to the 1930s. Republican policies, including high tariffs and hostility to labor unions, were seen as protecting jobs and increasing growth in the steel economy centered on Pittsburgh. With the coming of the New Deal, and success of the United Mine Workers and the United Steelworkers, the area began voting mostly Democratic. Since 1945, on the Monday before primary and general elections, Democratic pols from across southwestern Pennsylvania have attended the "rally in the valley" held at the Slovak Home in the mill town of Monessen. But it has not followed the national Democratic Party on all issues. Voters here have strongly favored trade restrictions on steel imports, even when most other Democrats were free traders in the 1960s and 1970s; more recently most House Democrats have been opposing free trade measures. Voters here also tend to take conservative stands on cultural issues and foreign policy. Metro Pittsburgh in 2000 gave Al Gore a much smaller percentage than metro Philadelphia. But this carefully carved out district was solidly Democratic and cast 55% of its votes for Al Gore in 2000.

The congressman from the 12th District is John Murtha, a Democrat first elected in a February 1974 special election that signaled the political weakness of Richard Nixon. Murtha grew up in this area, served in the Marine Corps, then graduated from the University of Pittsburgh and re-enlisted in the Marines in 1966, at 34; he was the first Vietnam veteran to serve in Congress. For his service there he was awarded the Bronze Star, two Purple Hearts and the Vietnamese Cross for Gallantry. Murtha is a member of the Appropriations Committee and the ranking Democrat on the Defense Subcommittee, his party's key man on the defense budget. His voting record—hawkish and patriotic on foreign policy, interventionist on economics and usually tradition-minded on cultural issues—seems perfectly suited to the steel and coal country. Murtha is also one of those old-time politicians who operate best in secret, holding court in the back corner of the House chamber where he trades gossip and votes to colleagues who crowd around him as if they were kissing his ring (Gene Taylor has twice cast votes for him as Speaker). He speaks for attribution to few national or local reporters, hardly ever appears on television, and rarely speaks in the House chamber except for the annual defense spending bill. He wields power not only on his committee work but also on many back-room issues dear to his colleagues, including pay raises, committee assignments and, after the trial and acquittal of Pennsylvania Republican Joseph McDade, a provision requiring the Justice Department to reimburse members of Congress who are indicted but acquitted. With John Dingell, he is one Democrat who has opposed some gun control proposals.

On foreign issues, Murtha voted for the Gulf War resolution in 1991 and the use of force in Iraq in 2002, but opposed intervention in Bosnia and deployment in Somalia, arguing that UN officials lacked the know-how to command U.S. troops. He supported the Nunn-Lugar program to decommission former Soviet nuclear weapons and favored technology that provides "force multipliers" for U.S. weapons. With Defense subcommittee chairman Jerry Lewis, he raised questions about production of the F-22 fighter plane, but worked on changes and testing to avoid its elimination. He is caught sometimes between Democratic demands for lower defense spending to make more money available for domestic programs and Republican desires to spend even more on defense, but he seeks to come up with appropriations that a broad cross-section of the House will sustain. When a bipartisan group of 14 members met in Austin with George W. Bush in January 2001, Murtha urged him to reduce his proposed tax cut to assure adequate money for the Pentagon. He opposed PNTR with China because of its threat to use force against Taiwan; as a stalwart of organized labor, he opposed trade promotion authority. After the September 11 attacks, he won enactment of a bill creating a national memorial at the Somerset County crash site to commemorate the passengers and crew of United Flight 93. Inside the Democratic Caucus, he gained additional respect and influence as the campaign manager for Nancy Pelosi in her contest against Steny Hoyer for Democratic Whip, adding his old-style influence to her new-age style. But he retained his independence, voting against campaign finance reform despite Pelosi's plea that his vote would be "an embarrassment to her."

After a close 1990 primary, Murtha spent more time traveling around the district and developed a more secure electoral base. His tending to local concerns paid off handsomely in 2002, when redistricting added much of the territory represented by four-term Democrat Frank Mascara. Republicans had consulted Murtha during the redistricting process and made adjustments to the boundaries to suit him; one was to put Mascara's house in the new Republican-leaning 18th District. Mascara took a month to decide which district to run in, then finally decided that his chances in the general election in the 18th were poor and that he would run against Murtha. Each had represented about half of the new 12th District. Mascara's campaign was poorly financed and organized. Murtha campaigned actively around the new district, emphasizing his "record of getting things done." Mascara attacked Murtha for ducking debates, and for being "the David Copperfield of politics . . . handing out checks and then disappearing from his district." Murtha won 64%–36%. He had huge leads in his base of Cambria and Indiana Counties, while Mascara led only narrowly in Washington and Greene Counties. In Westmoreland County, parts of which both had represented, Murtha won 67%–33%. The general election was no contest; Murtha won with 73% of the vote.

Murtha returned to business as usual at the Capitol: protecting the Pentagon and the troops, cutting deals wherever he could, and receiving visitors from his throne in the Pennsylvania corner of the House. Meanwhile, the Republican redistricting plan reduced the number of Pennsylvania Democrats from 10 to seven.

THIRTEENTH DISTRICT

Rep. Joe Hoeffel (D)

Elected 1998, 3d term; b. Sept. 3, 1950, Philadelphia; home, Abington; Boston U., B.A. 1972, Temple U. Law Schl., J.D. 1986; Protestant; married (Francesca).

Military Career: Army Reserves, 1970–76.

Elected Office: PA House of Reps., 1976–84; Montgomery Cnty. Comm., 1991–98.

Professional Career: Practicing atty., 1986–91.

DC Office: 426 CHOB 20515, 202-225-6111; Fax: 202-226-0611; Web site: www.house.gov/hoeffel.

District Offices: Ambler, 215-540-8444; Philadelphia, 215-335-3355.

Committees: *International Relations* (15th of 23 D): Europe; Middle East & Central Asia. *Transportation & Infrastructure* (30th of 34 D): Highways, Transit & Pipelines; Water Resources & Environment.

Group Ratings

	ADA	ACLU	AFS	LCV	CON	ITIC	NTU	COC	ACU	NTLC	CHC
2002	95	87	89	88	35	38	16	50	4	8	0
2001	100	—	100	93	—	—	12	35	0	—	—

National Journal Ratings

	2001 LIB	—	2001 CONS		2002 LIB	—	2002 CONS
Economic	70%	—	31%		77%	—	20%
Social	83%	—	11%		74%	—	19%
Foreign	77%	—	22%		72%	—	26%

Key Votes of the 107th Congress

1. Approve Bush Tax Cuts	*	5. Faith-Based Charities	N	9. Trade Promotion Authority	N
2. Limit Patients' Bill of Rights	N	6. Bar Gays in the Boy Scouts	N	10. Bar Funds for Intl. Court	N
3. Campaign Finance Reform	Y	7. Ban Partial-Birth Abortion	N	11. Authorize Force in Iraq	Y
4. Ban ANWR Development	Y	8. Arm Commercial Pilots	N	12. Deny Home. Sec. Dept. Union	N

Election Results

2002 general	Joe Hoeffel (D)	107,948	(51%)	($1,554,821)
	Melissa Brown (R)	100,295	(47%)	($1,827,440)
	Other	3,627	(2%)	
2002 primary	Joe Hoeffel (D)	unopposed		
2000 general	Joe Hoeffel (D)	146,026	(53%)	($1,772,923)
	Stewart J. Greenleaf (R)	126,501	(46%)	($1,481,942)
	Other	4,224	(2%)	

Prior Winning Percentages: 1998 (52%)

The People		Race/Ethnic Origin	Ancestry	
Area size:	251 sq. mi.	85.6% White	Irish: 19.5%	German: 15.5%
Urban population:	98.7%	5.9% Black	Italian: 10.4%	
Rural population:	1.3%	4.1% Asian	**2000 Presidential Vote**	
Pop. 2000:	646,167	0.1% Native Am.	Gore (D) 155,903	(56%)
Median income:	$49,311	0.0% Hawaiian	Bush (R) 117,773	(42%)
Poverty status:	7.1%	1.0% Two + races	Other 5,972	(2%)
Military veterans:	12.7%	0.1% Other	**Cook Partisan Voting Index:** D + 7	
		3.1% Hispanic Origin		

Occupation   Blue collar: 19.2%   White collar: 68.3%   Gray collar: 12.5%

Montgomery County, Pennsylvania, is the proximate hinterland of Philadelphia: rolling hills cut on one side by the Schuylkill River and at intervals by the Pennsylvania and Reading Railroad lines radiating outward from Center City. Older suburbs, both rich and modest, grew up around rail stations, with comfortable houses within walking distance for commuters. Further out are 18th and 19th century villages, once surrounded by farm fields, now encroached by subdivisions where people depend on cars, not rail lines, to get to work. Montgomery County has its shopping malls and office parks, but there are not many freeways here; most of the traffic here is along roads on the area's diagonal grid or along the old pikes laid out when Pennsylvania was a colony. Statistically, Montgomery County is the most populous and second most affluent county in metropolitan Philadelphia.

Quite a different place, though adjacent to southern Montgomery County, is Northeast Philadelphia. This is relatively new urban territory, with more than half its houses built after 1950. When the alley-wide streets of North and South Philadelphia and the river wards were already teeming and the Main Line suburbs were already well-settled, the workers of Philadelphia's docks, factories and Center City offices were just starting to fill up vacant land here. They settled in neighborhoods like Bustleton, Somerton and Torresdale. Many of Philadelphia's Hispanics live in the industrial river wards along the Delaware River, but the other wards of Northeast Philadelphia are still mostly white and ethnic, the kind of places where city cops and firefighters live and the kind that gave big margins to Mayor Frank Rizzo in the 1970s and 1980s.

The 13th Congressional District includes much of southeastern and central Montgomery County and most of Northeast Philadelphia. Historically Montgomery was quintessentially Republican, with a style of politics set for years by Ivy-educated Republican men, and with Republicans of more modest and sometimes ethnic backgrounds manning the local precincts and staffing local offices. But Montgomery County, like other affluent suburbs in the Boston-Washington corridor, swung toward the Democratic Party in national politics in the 1990s, with abortion and other cultural issues usually trumping economic interests. The same county that voted by large margins for Ronald Reagan and George H.W. Bush in the 1980s voted for Bill Clinton in the 1990s and Al Gore in 2000. In 2002 Montgomery County backed Democrat and former Philadelphia Mayor Ed Rendell for governor by a 2–1 margin. Northeast Philadelphia has a different political heritage. Operating in a city where Democrats hold most local offices, Northeast Philadelphia's feisty Republican organization has won some elections and shown facility in making deals to get their share of patronage. There are enough Republican voters here for Republicans to occasionally carry the area, most recently Senator Arlen Specter in 1998. The current boundaries of the district are a departure from tradition. Historically, Philadelphia has had separate districts; only occasionally has one included a small bit of Montgomery, and for many years Montgomery County was a single district by itself. But the 2000 Census results left Philadelphia with enough people for only two-and-one-half districts. Republicans in charge of redistricting decided to divide Montgomery among six districts and to create a Montgomery-Northeast Philadelphia district containing the homes of two incumbent Democrats and with enough Republicans to make it competitive in the general election. In 2002, 58% of the district's votes were cast in Montgomery County, 42% in Northeast Philadelphia.

The congressman from the 13th District is Joseph Hoeffel, a Democrat elected in 1998. Hoeffel grew up in the Philadelphia area and has spent most of his adult life in politics and public office. He was elected to the state House in 1976, at 26, and re-elected three times. In 1984 he challenged Republican Congressman Lawrence Coughlin and was beaten 56%–44%—a respectable showing in the Reagan landslide. In 1986 he ran again and lost 59%–41%. After five years in law practice, he was elected a Montgomery County commissioner in 1991. Coughlin retired in 1992, and the 13th District became fiercely contested by the two parties. In 1992 Democrat Marjorie Margolies-Mezvinsky beat Republican Jon Fox 50%–47%. In 1994 Fox beat Margolies-Mezvinsky after she cast the decisive vote to pass the Clinton tax increase by 49%–45%. In 1996 Hoeffel ran and Fox beat him by 84 votes. In 1998 Hoeffel ran again. Fox was peppered by Republican opponents from both left and right, and won only 49% of the primary votes—an obvious sign of trouble. Hoeffel linked Fox to Newt Gingrich and said he did not fit the district's "moderate, progressive community." Although Hoeffel said he initially feared that the Lewinsky scandal would harm Democrats, he later argued Republicans overplayed their hand and impeachment produced a voter backlash by October. Hoeffel won 52%–47%.

In the House, Hoeffel's record has been to the liberal side of House Democrats. He was torn on PNTR with China between his claims to be a pro-trade New Democrat and the opposition from labor unions who have been crucial campaign supporters; he decided to vote no, he said, to maintain "leverage" on the Chinese. In January 2002, he said that Congress should repeal the Bush tax cut rather than return to deficit spending. He voted for the use of force in Iraq, while urging George W. Bush to pledge reconstruction of that nation once the conflict was over.

Hoeffel has won two close, but quite different, reelection contests. In 2000, he started as a top target of Republicans. His opponent was Stewart Greenleaf, a state senator for 22 years. Hoeffel emphasized their differences on prescription-drug legislation and criticized Greenleaf for supporting HMOs. Greenleaf emphasized his support for tax cuts and individual investment accounts in Social Security. But Greenleaf's reputation for leisurely campaigning persuaded Republicans to take the district off their top priority list; Hoeffel won 53%–46%. Then the January 2002 redistricting put Hoeffel in the same district with Northeast Philadelphia Democrat Bob Borski. But Borski decided to retire, and Hoeffel had no opposition in the primary. The Republican nominee was Montgomery County ophthalmologist Melissa Brown, a supporter of abortion rights who was more aggressive than Greenleaf. Brown had an issue that resonated in Northeast Philadelphia: the Section 8 federal housing program that subsidizes low-income residents to help them pay rent. Brown mailed a flyer to predominantly white neighborhoods in the Northeast with a picture of Hoeffel and Mayor John Street, and implied that Hoeffel wanted to expand the controversial program. Opponents of the program argue that it is widely abused and contributes to the degradation of area neighborhoods because tenants pay little in rent and invest little in their properties. Hoeffel's camp quickly countered that he had already been working on ways to systematically change the Section 8 program. Democrats charged she was making a racial appeal by linking Hoeffel and his support of Section 8 to Philadelphia Mayor John Street. Brown also criticized Hoeffel's opposition to limiting damages in medical malpractice cases. Hoeffel linked his opponent to a failed health-insurance firm, in which she invested with her husband. In late October national Republicans, sniffing an upset, put large amounts of money into the race. Hoeffel won by only 51%–47%, and by that same margin in Montgomery County, and Northeast Philadelphia. Brown ran 5% ahead of George W. Bush's 2000 showing in the district, and against an incumbent; this is a seat that could be seriously contested again, for the seventh election in a row, in 2004.

In January 2003 Hoeffel tried to get a seat on Ways and Means Committee and failed; as the minority party, Democrats have few seats to give out. He promised to spend more time getting to know his voters in Northeast Philadelphia, but he has also been mentioned as a possible Senate candidate in either 2004 or 2006.

FOURTEENTH DISTRICT

Rep. Mike Doyle (D)

Elected 1994, 5th term; b. Aug. 5, 1953, Pittsburgh; home, Swissvale; PA St. U., B.S. 1975; Catholic; married (Susan).

Elected Office: Swissvale Borough Cncl., 1977–81.

Professional Career: Insurance agent, 1975–77; Exec. Dir., Turtle Creek Valley Citizens Union, 1977–79; Chief of Staff, PA Sen. Frank Pecora, 1978–94; Co–Founder/Owner, Eastgate Insurance Agency, 1983–present.

DC Office: 401 CHOB 20515, 202-225-2135; Fax: 202-225-3084; Web site: www.house.gov/doyle.

District Offices: McKeesport, 412-664-4049; Penn Hills, 412-241-6055; Pittsburgh, 412-261-5091.

Committees: *Energy & Commerce* (21st of 26 D): Energy & Air Quality; Environment & Hazardous Materials; Telecommunications & The Internet. *Standards of Official Conduct* (5th of 5 D).

Group Ratings

	ADA	ACLU	AFS	LCV	CON	ITIC	NTU	COC	ACU	NTLC	CHC
2002	80	53	100	88	83	25	22	45	8	3	42
2001	85	—	100	57	—	—	13	43	32	—	—

National Journal Ratings

	2001 LIB	—	2001 CONS		2002 LIB	—	2002 CONS
Economic	79%	—	21%		77%	—	20%
Social	54%	—	45%		55%	—	44%
Foreign	61%	—	36%		72%	—	26%

Key Votes of the 107th Congress

1. Approve Bush Tax Cuts	N	5. Faith-Based Charities	N	9. Trade Promotion Authority	N
2. Limit Patients' Bill of Rights	N	6. Bar Gays in the Boy Scouts	Y	10. Bar Funds for Intl. Court	N
3. Campaign Finance Reform	Y	7. Ban Partial-Birth Abortion	Y	11. Authorize Force in Iraq	N
4. Ban ANWR Development	Y	8. Arm Commercial Pilots	N	12. Deny Home. Sec. Dept. Union	N

Election Results

2002 general	Mike Doyle (D)	....	unopposed		($648,209)
2002 primary	Mike Doyle (D)	....	unopposed		
2000 general (PA 18)	Mike Doyle (D)	....	156,131	(69%)	($421,732)
	Craig C. Stephens (R)	....	68,798	(31%)	($7,729)

Prior Winning Percentages: 1998 (68%); 1996 (56%); 1994 (55%)

The People		Race/Ethnic Origin	Ancestry	
Area size:	169 sq. mi.	72.9% White	German: 15.5%	Irish: 12.1%
Urban population:	99.8%	22.5% Black	Italian: 9.8%	
Rural population:	0.2%	1.7% Asian	**2000 Presidential Vote**	
Pop. 2000:	646,196	0.2% Native Am.	Gore (D) 183,640	(70%)
Median income:	$30,140	0.0% Hawaiian	Bush (R) 74,085	(28%)
Poverty status:	17.1%	1.4% Two+ races	Other 6,007	(2%)
Military veterans:	14.1%	0.3% Other	**Cook Partisan Voting Index:** D +21	
		1.1% Hispanic Origin		

Occupation	Blue collar: 18.6%	White collar: 61.7%	Gray collar: 19.7%

The Golden Triangle is the inevitable focus of Pittsburgh, the tip of land where the Allegheny and Monongahela Rivers come together to form the Ohio. It has been a strategic site for more than 200 years. It was there, to Fort Duquesne during the French and Indian War, that Braddock's army was heading (with George Washington helping lead the way) when it was ambushed and defeated in 1754. A few years later, the first American city west of the Appalachian chain was carved out of the wilderness here and named after the English statesman William Pitt. Pittsburgh grew rapidly in the days when most of the nation's commerce moved over water. When railroads became ascendant, Pittsburgh still did nicely, since rail lines tend to run along the riverside rather than scaling the mountains. Then came Andrew Carnegie, a Scottish immigrant working as a telegrapher for the Pennsylvania Railroad who foresaw that steel would replace iron for railroad bridges; he built a steel factory in Pittsburgh, then not much more than a rail junction but blessed with ready deposits of coal and access to iron ore from the Great Lakes. With associates like Henry Clay Frick and Henry Phipps, Carnegie built his capacity to the point that when he sold out in 1901, the resulting U.S. Steel Corporation held a near-monopoly.

The Pittsburgh that Carnegie and his steel men built is one of giant mills in the bottomlands along the rivers and massive buildings downtown, such as H.H. Richardson's classic stone City-County Building. There were once 12 cable cars going up the Duquesne Incline and other routes, connecting mills with the neighborhoods above. Back then, the smog—a word used here before it was in Los Angeles—was so bad that street lights had to stay on all day downtown; a 1947 photograph shows a midnight-like darkness at nine in the morning. But then an alliance of local elected officials and corporate titans (including the leaders of such local Fortune 500 companies as USX, Heinz, Alcoa, and PPG) pushed through a series of forceful and visionary projects designed to improve the city's quality of life. Early on, this model produced tremendous successes: In the 1950s, Mayor David Lawrence and financier Richard King Mellon led efforts to cut air pollution, control river flooding, and construct an advanced network of highways and tunnels. They also turned a derelict industrial zone at the three-rivers confluence into Point State Park—a triangular gem that remains popular with office workers from the adjoining downtown.

But Pittsburgh is not just a downtown; it is a city of neighborhoods, built on or beneath vertiginous hills; neighborhoods that look right next to each other on the map are in fact quite separate and distinct. There is the uptown neighborhood around Carnegie-Mellon University and the University of Pittsburgh with its neo-Gothic "cathedral of learning"; they have helped to spur a robust high-tech sector that has replaced many of the manufacturing jobs lost in previous decades. Among and atop the hills are neighborhoods as different as the predominantly black Hill District, where baseball Hall of Famers Josh Gibson, Satchel Paige and "Cool Papa" Bell once played for the Negro Leagues' Pittsburgh Crawfords, and Shady Side and Squirrel Hill, with fine mansions and fashionable shops. Along the Monongahela River in Pittsburgh and southeast are small industrial neighborhoods and towns, like Clairton (where the classic movie *The Deer Hunter* was set and filmed) with less than half as many residents as a half-century ago.

The 14th Congressional District includes all of Pittsburgh and mostly working class suburbs to the east, south and west. There is some verdant suburbia here, but much of the district is in the Monongahela (or Mon) Valley, where the old steel mills stand or once stood, and the hills above. More affluent suburbs to the north and south are in the Republican held 4th and 18th Districts. This is a heavily Democratic district.

The congressman from the 14th is Mike Doyle, a Democrat first elected in 1994. Of Irish and Italian descent, Doyle grew up in the Mon Valley town of Swissvale, worked in steel mills during summers off from Penn State, worked as an insurance agent, for a nonprofit agency and was elected to the Swissvale Borough Council in 1977, at 24. In 1978 he became chief of staff to state Senator Frank Pecora, who was then a Republican. Pecora switched parties in 1992 and briefly gave Democrats control of the state Senate—the Jim Jeffords of the Mon Valley. In 1994 Doyle ran as a Democrat for the 18th District seat held then by Rick Santorum, who was running for the Senate; Doyle was one of seven Democrats and four Republicans to seek the open seat. The Democrats were close to evenly matched. Doyle, who had just switched to the Democratic Party himself, was assisted by endorsements from unions and community leaders and won with 20% of the vote; the next finisher had 18%. In the general, he faced John McCarty, an aide to the late Senator John Heinz; interestingly, McCarty was pro-choice and Doyle anti-abortion. Doyle campaigned for sweeping health care reform, against the new General Agreement on Tariffs and Trade, and for rebuilding the Mon Valley's industrial base. In a Republican year, he won 55%–45%.

In the House, Doyle has a mixed voting record, toward the right on cultural issues, toward the left on economics. He supported the Blue Dogs in opposing tax cuts, and called for higher Medicare co-payments for high-income recipients. Clinton signed his bill to develop methane hydrates as a clean energy source. He opposed EPA's new air quality standards for fear of further local job losses. As a Steel Caucus member, while working to reduce foreign imports, he pushed a bill to create a national historic site at the former U.S. Steel facilities along the Mon River as part of the local Rivers of Steel program. He lives on Capitol Hill with his "family" of bipartisan House colleagues and is one of the dwindling number of members who drive back home after each week's final vote.

Republicans controlled redistricting after the 2000 Census, and state Senate Republicans had not forgotten Doyle's role in Pecora's party switch. Their obvious strategy was to merge his 18th District with the Pittsburgh-based 14th District. But in August 2001, before any redistricting bill was passed, 14th District Democrat Bill Coyne, a low-profile liberal who held the seat for 22 years, announced he would retire. Republicans concentrated on creating a new Republican-leaning 18th District in Pittsburgh's southern suburbs; they attached Doyle's Mon Valley base to the 14th District. Doyle had reason to worry that a Pittsburgh-based Democrat might run for the seat. But in January 2002, his most likely opponent, Allegheny County Controller Dan Onorato, said he would not run. Doyle was renominated and reelected without opposition. In the House, he settled in to build seniority at Energy and Commerce.

FIFTEENTH DISTRICT

Rep. Pat Toomey (R)

Elected 1998, 3d term; b. Nov. 17, 1961, Providence, RI; home, Allentown; Harvard U., B.S. 1984; Catholic; married (Kris).

Elected Office: Allentown Govt. Study Comm., 1994.

Professional Career: Investment Banker, 1984–89; Financial Consultant, 1990; Restaurateur, 1990-present.

DC Office: 224 CHOB 20515, 202-225-6411; Fax: 202-226-0778; Web site: www.house.gov/toomey.

District Offices: Allentown, 610-439-8861; Pennsburg, 215-541-1423; Wilson Borough, 610-515-1906.

Committees: *Budget* (6th of 24 R). *Financial Services* (21st of 37 R): Capital Markets, Insurance & Government Sponsored Enterprises; Financial Institutions & Consumer Credit; Housing & Community Opportunity. *Small Business* (5th of 18 R): Rural Enterprises, Agriculture and Technology; Tax, Finance & Exports (Chmn.).

Group Ratings

	ADA	ACLU	AFS	LCV	CON	ITIC	NTU	COC	ACU	NTLC	CHC
2002	0	13	0	25	94	100	66	100	100	100	100
2001	0	—	0	7	—	—	76	95	100	—	—

National Journal Ratings

	2001 LIB	—	2001 CONS		2002 LIB	—	2002 CONS
Economic	0%	—	94%		28%	—	69%
Social	20%	—	69%		0%	—	75%
Foreign	49%	—	47%		41%	—	56%

Key Votes of the 107th Congress

1. Approve Bush Tax Cuts	Y	5. Faith-Based Charities	Y
2. Limit Patients' Bill of Rights	Y	6. Bar Gays in the Boy Scouts	Y
3. Campaign Finance Reform	N	7. Ban Partial-Birth Abortion	Y
4. Ban ANWR Development	N	8. Arm Commercial Pilots	Y

9. Trade Promotion Authority	Y
10. Bar Funds for Intl. Court	Y
11. Authorize Force in Iraq	Y
12. Deny Home. Sec. Dept. Union	Y

Election Results

2002 general	Pat Toomey (R)	98,493	(57%)	($1,029,593)
	Ed O'Brien (D)	73,179	(43%)	($824,636)
2002 primary	Pat Toomey (R)	unopposed		
2000 general	Pat Toomey (R)	118,307	(53%)	($975,795)
	Ed O'Brien (D)	103,864	(47%)	($772,988)

Prior Winning Percentages: 1998 (55%)

The People		Race/Ethnic Origin	Ancestry	
Area size:	817 sq. mi.	86.4% White	German: 21.9%	Irish: 9.0%
Urban population:	87.4%	2.8% Black	Italian: 8.1%	
Rural population:	12.6%	1.7% Asian	**2000 Presidential Vote**	
Pop. 2000:	646,495	0.1% Native Am.	Gore (D) 119,393	(49%)
Median income:	$45,419	0.0% Hawaiian	Bush (R)..............116,817	(48%)
Poverty status:	8.2%	1.0% Two+ races	Other 8,865	(4%)
Military veterans:	13.5%	0.1% Other	**Cook Partisan Voting Index:** D + 0	
		7.9% Hispanic Origin		

Occupation   Blue collar: 26.4%   White collar: 59.5%   Gray collar: 14.1%

Allentown, Pennsylvania, has long been derided by show-biz songwriters, from "42nd Street" back in 1933, in which it was scorned as nowhere, the polar opposite of Broadway, to Billy Joel's "Allentown" in 1982, with its grim picture of closed factories and unemployment. Though both contain nuggets of truth, neither is an entirely fair portrait of Pennsylvania's Lehigh Valley today: Allentown and next-door Bethlehem did suffer when big employers—Mack Truck in Allentown and Bethlehem Steel in Bethlehem—closed down big plants in the 1980s. But the Lehigh Valley around Allentown and Bethlehem had solid growth and low unemployment rates in the late 1990s, thanks to a mix of regional health care networks, telephone call-centers for insurance companies (Aetna) and banks (Wachovia), long-surviving industries (such as Air Products and Chemicals, energy utility PPL and the remnants of Mack Truck's local operations), and small startups that don't earn the visibility of the big closedowns but which together have created more new jobs than have been lost. In the Lehigh Valley, 43% of employees now work for companies with 100 or fewer workers, and 10% for companies with 10 or fewer. Some 8% of the population here is Hispanic, higher than in any other Pennsylvania metropolitan area—a sure sign that the area is generating new jobs. The redevelopment of Bethlehem includes a convention center, hotel complex and National Museum of Industrial History housed in part of the old steel plant. If the Lehigh Valley is off the main lines of traffic, it does at least have several features that make it attractive to people from the big city. It is connected by I-78 to New York and by the Turnpike Extension to Philadelphia; it has lower taxes and living costs; it has a cluster of colleges (Lehigh, Muhlenberg, Moravian) and a strong regional newspaper (the Allentown *Morning Call*); and it has both Dorney Park, one of the nation's oldest amusement parks, and the Crayola Crayon factory in Easton. Easton's old industrial buildings, just across the Delaware River from New Jersey, have become something of a magnet for artists seeking inexpensive loft and warehouse space.

The 15th Congressional District consists of the Lehigh Valley plus a small adjoining slice of northern Montgomery County. Politically, this has long been a classic swing area, located at the intersection of heavily Democratic industrial precincts and the Republican farmlands of the Pennsylvania Dutch Country. The valley backed Ronald Reagan twice, the elder George Bush in 1988 and Bill Clinton twice; in the past five governors' races, it voted twice for Democrat Robert Casey, twice for Republican Tom Ridge and, in 2002, for Democrat Ed Rendell. The only losing candidate to receive the valley's support in recent years was Al Gore.

The congressman from the 15th District is Pat Toomey, a Republican elected in 1998. Toomey grew up in a blue collar Rhode Island family, got enough scholarship aid to attend Harvard, then turned to a career in investment banking. After getting wealthy by creating an international financial services consulting firm, he moved to Allentown in 1990, where he and his brothers started Rookies' Restaurants. In 1994 he was elected to the Allentown Government Study Commission, where he authored tax limitation plans, including requiring a supermajority on the city council to raise taxes.

In November 1997, Democratic Congressman Paul McHale announced he was retiring; a year later, he became the first House Democrat to call for Bill Clinton's resignation and was one of five Democrats to vote for impeachment. Toomey was one of six candidates in the Republican primary. He called for individual investment accounts in Social Security reform and a 17% flat tax; he pledged to serve no more than six years and promised never to vote to raise taxes. He spent heavily and narrowly won the Republican primary. In the general election Toomey put the Democratic nominee, state Senator Roy Afflerbach, on the defensive early with an ad highlighting his votes for tax increases, calling him "the tax man" and attacking him for voting against repeal of a tax on toothpaste and dental floss. Afflerbach criticized Toomey's tax plan as a threat to Social Security and the budget surplus, and tried to appeal to conservative, blue-collar voters by calling Toomey an outsider. But Toomey won by the surprisingly large margin of 55%–45%. Toomey's win demonstrated the growing strength of suburbs over the declining Democratic strongholds of Allentown and Bethlehem, where Afflerbach won by only single-digit margins.

In the House, Toomey quickly went to work on national economic issues and ruffled many influential feathers. He took on the task for conservative Republicans of challenging excessive spending by the Appropriations Committee and won the leadership's support for setting aside an additional $4 billion for debt reduction. "We've got three parties in Congress—Republicans, Democrats and Appropriators," Toomey complained. He led opposition among Republicans to waiving the six-year term limits for committee chairmen. After the 2000 election, he urged a larger tax cut than George W. Bush's plan, with additional savings incentives and lower capital gains taxes. When the fiscal spigots were opened after the September 11 attacks, Toomey sought to impose some restraint and worried that terrorism would become "an opportunity for some to spend more money across the board." In 2002, his opposition helped to force Republicans to keep appropriations bills from the House floor before the election; Appropriations chairman Bill Young accused Toomey of trying to "destroy the appropriations process." He won enactment in 2001 of parts of his bill to reduce 130,000 pages of Medicare regulatory requirements on doctors and other providers. Keeping his district's political concerns in mind, Toomey inserted a provision in a House-passed bill that restricted Export-Import Bank subsidies from hurting domestic industries; this followed reports of a loan guarantee to a Chinese steel company that was undercutting domestic steel firms. In May 2002, he criticized the farm bill as a step "in the direction of Soviet-style agricultural policy." He voiced early support for removing Saddam Hussein in Iraq.

In both the 2000 and 2002 elections, Toomey was challenged by Ed O'Brien, a former blast-furnace worker at Bethlehem Steel and the number two United Steelworkers official in Pennsylvania. With strongly divergent views, the contests had elements of class warfare. Toomey backed limits on how much a patient can sue an HMO, and individual investment accounts for Social Security. O'Brien opposed each, and called for strengthening Social Security. Their initial contest was closer than expected. Toomey won 53%–47%, drawing 54% in Lehigh County but only 51% in Northampton. In 2002, after Republican redistricters made slight adjustments to the lines in

Montgomery County, O'Brien tried to link Toomey to corporate scandals, calling him "Mr. Wall Street." Toomey ran an effective campaign ad with a steelworker complaining that O'Brien did a poor job for the union. This time, Toomey won 57%–43%, with 58% in Lehigh and 55% in Northampton.

After the 2002 election, Toomey kept his term limit pledge not to run for reelection in 2004. Instead, he announced in February 2003 that he would challenge Senator Arlen Specter in the 2004 primary. He took on a daunting task: Specter is a hard worker, an assiduous fundraiser, an aggressive opponent who has run six statewide campaigns and was first elected to the Senate in 1980. White House political strategist Karl Rove told Toomey that George W. Bush would support Specter in the primary; in February 2003 White House Chief of Staff Andrew Card attended a Specter fundraiser in the Lehigh Valley. But Toomey has taken on daunting odds before and prevailed; he is well liked by national conservative groups such as the anti-tax Club for Growth.

In the 15th District, Toomey's announcement opened up a competitive contest. Mentioned as likely candidates in mid-2003 were two state senators, Republican Charlie Dent and Democrat Lisa Boscola.

SIXTEENTH DISTRICT

Rep. Joe Pitts (R)

Elected 1996, 4th term; b. Oct. 10, 1939, Lexington, KY; home, Kennett Square; Asbury Col., B.A. 1961, West Chester U., M.Ed. 1972; Protestant; married (Virginia).

Military Career: Air Force, 1963–69 (Vietnam).

Professional Career: High schl. teacher, 1969–72; PA House of Reps., 1972–96; Owner, Landscape & Nursery Co., 1974–90.

DC Office: 204 CHOB 20515, 202-225-2411; Fax: 202-225-2013; Web site: www.house.gov/pitts.

District Offices: Kennett Square, 610-429-1540; Lancaster, 717-393-0667; Reading, 610-374-3637.

Committees: *Energy & Commerce* (23d of 31 R): Commerce, Trade & Consumer Protection; Environment & Hazardous Materials; Health. *International Relations* (18th of 26 R): International Terrorism, Nonproliferation and Human Rights; Middle East & Central Asia.

Group Ratings

	ADA	ACLU	AFS	LCV	CON	ITIC	NTU	COC	ACU	NTLC	CHC
2002	0	7	11	25	81	88	64	94	100	100	100
2001	0	—	0	0	—	—	76	91	100	—	—

National Journal Ratings

	2001 LIB	—	2001 CONS		2002 LIB	—	2002 CONS
Economic	0%	—	94%		0%	—	91%
Social	0%	—	81%		0%	—	75%
Foreign	21%	—	74%		29%	—	67%

Key Votes of the 107th Congress

1. Approve Bush Tax Cuts	Y	5. Faith-Based Charities	Y	9. Trade Promotion Authority	Y
2. Limit Patients' Bill of Rights	Y	6. Bar Gays in the Boy Scouts	Y	10. Bar Funds for Intl. Court	Y
3. Campaign Finance Reform	N	7. Ban Partial-Birth Abortion	Y	11. Authorize Force in Iraq	Y
4. Ban ANWR Development	N	8. Arm Commercial Pilots	Y	12. Deny Home. Sec. Dept. Union	Y

Election Results

2002 general	Joe Pitts (R)	119,046	(88%)	($432,695)
	Will Todd (Green)	8,720	(6%)	
	Kenneth Brenneman (CNP)	6,766	(5%)	
2002 primary	Joe Pitts (R)	unopposed		
2000 general	Joe Pitts (R)	162,403	(67%)	($366,418)
	Bob Yorczyk (D)	80,177	(33%)	($9,809)

Prior Winning Percentages: 1998 (71%); 1996 (59%)

The People		Race/Ethnic Origin	Ancestry	
Area size:	1,330 sq. mi.	84.3% White	German: 25.2%	Irish: 8.8%
Urban population:	76.0%	4.0% Black	English: 6.1%	
Rural population:	24.0%	1.4% Asian	**2000 Presidential Vote**	
Pop. 2000:	646,156	0.1% Native Am.	Bush (R) 144,862	(62%)
Median income:	$45,941	0.0% Hawaiian	Gore (D) 82,729	(35%)
Poverty status:	9.5%	0.9% Two+ races	Other 5,713	(2%)
Military veterans:	11.5%	0.1% Other	**Cook Partisan Voting Index:** R +14	
		9.2% Hispanic Origin		

Occupation   Blue collar: 29.6%   White collar: 54.7%   Gray collar: 15.8%

The Pennsylvania Dutch Country, settled by Germans in the 18th century when it was Pennsylvania's frontier, remains a distinctive part of America. These Germans were Amish and Mennonite, pietistic sects seeking religious liberty and determined to farm rich lands in the same intensive way they had in Germany. Today, many of their descendants—the Eisenhower family is the most famous example—have blended into mainstream America, but in the Dutch area around Lancaster, many "Plain People" still live in the old way. Though larger communities exist in Ohio and Indiana, tourists can still see families of Plain People clad in black, clattering over the back roads in horse-drawn carriages, with scrupulously tended farms set amid rolling hills and barns decorated with hex signs (the scene was captured memorably in the 1983 film *Witness*). Beneath the surface, Amish communities are facing the strains of modernity: In recent years, Amish teens have attracted public attention for using drugs and alcohol while participating in the "rumschpringes"—a period when adolescents are freed from their community's rigid rules and mores, before being given the choice of returning to the fold as an adult. Still, the community remains robust, and tourism, much of it linked to interest in the Amish, brings in more than five million people annually. Agriculture is the other pillar of the local economy: Farmers here produce some of the highest per-acre yields on earth, and Lancaster is home to the largest stockyards east of Chicago. Given the easy drive from Philadelphia, Baltimore and Washington, this area has also become home to many outlet malls. Lancaster County and Chester County each grew by double-digit rates in the 1990s—partly from religious families, partly from growth out from the city—making this the heart of one of Pennsylvania's fastest-growing regions.

The 16th Congressional District includes all of Lancaster County, plus parts of southwestern Chester County that adjoin the Maryland and Delaware borders, as well as a small slice of Berks County that reaches as far as Reading (the city is now split among three districts; a little over half is in the 16th). Outside the regional hub of Lancaster, the 16th is mostly small-town territory, with numerous quaint and quirkily named, if somewhat touristy, villages, such as Bird-in-Hand, Blue Ball and Intercourse (the first two named for the posted logos of old pubs, the third for reasons that are obscure, but almost certainly non-sexual). Closer to Philadelphia, the district takes in the metropolis' spreading suburbs, including West Chester, Kennett Square, fragrant with the manure that makes it America's leading mushroom-growing center as well as the glorious perfumes of the flowers at Longwood Gardens, and the fringe of the Wyeth country west of Chadds Ford. During the 1990s, Reading and Berks County attracted a large number of Hispanics, who found jobs in a growing if not terribly affluent economy. But their inclusion in this district—now the second-most Hispanic in the state, at 9%—has not altered the political equation greatly. This is one of the most Republican districts in Pennsylvania and, for that matter, in the whole Northeast. It has favored the party of Lincoln ever since it abandoned the party of Pennsylvania's only president, Lancaster resident James Buchanan, on the eve of the Civil War. The 16th gave George W. Bush 62% of the vote in 2000, and Lancaster County was the only county within an hour's drive of Philadelphia to back Republican Mike Fisher over Democrat Ed Rendell in the 2002 gubernatorial race, and by more than a 2–1 margin.

The congressman from the 16th District is Joe Pitts, a Republican elected in 1996. Pitts was born in Kentucky, spent time in the Philippines with his parents where they served as religious missionaries, joined the Air Force after college, served three tours of duty and flew 116 B-52 combat missions in Vietnam. He returned to become a math and science teacher in Malvern, in Chester County, and later owned a nursery near Kennett Square. He and his daughter have exhibited their artwork, everything from painting to sculpture, at local galleries. In 1972, at 33, he was elected to the Pennsylvania House. In 1989 he became chairman of the Appropriations Committee; he oversaw the restoration of the glorious Pennsylvania Capitol. In December 1995, when Congressman Bob Walker, one of the conservative reformers close to Newt Gingrich who helped revolutionize the House, cited the "Pennsylvania Dutch tradition" of not serving over 20 years and said he was retiring, Pitts plunged into the primary. He spoke favorably of home-schooling and unfavorably of gambling, and ran as a "true conservative." He raised the most money and won with 45% to 26% for the runner-up, a moderate. In the general, Pitts easily defeated newspaper publisher James Blaine, a descendant of James G. Blaine, the "Plumed Knight" and Republican presidential nominee in 1884.

In the House, Pitts has had a firmly conservative record. He was an early advocate of repeal of the estate and gift tax, which became a core component of the Bush tax cut in 2001. He won House passage of an "Amish bill" to permit Amish youth an exemption from child labor laws to work with adult supervision at sites with heavy machinery. He co-chairs the Renewal Alliance, seeking ways to encourage local and faith-based groups in low-income neighborhoods to work on the needs of the poor. He led the Pro-Life Caucus and headed the Republicans' "values action team" that worked with the Christian Coalition and other family groups to promote a pro-family agenda. He founded two diverse groups: the religious prisoners' congressional task force, to plead for human rights around the world, and the Electronic Warfare Working Group. After the liberation of Afghanistan from the Taliban, he visited refugee camps and national leaders there. He also traveled to Pakistan, on what he called a humanitarian mission to review the impact of American aid. On local issues, in March 2002, after a federal judge ordered removal of the Ten Commandments from the Chester County courthouse, an angry Pitts criticized the court's reasoning. "Chester County is not Congress, posting a plaque is not making a law and the Ten Commandments are not a church."

Pitts played a key role in killing the bankruptcy bill in 2002. He joined Chris Smith of New Jersey in objecting to a provision, added by Senator Charles Schumer, which would make fines and criminal penalties for abortion protesters non-dischargeable under bankruptcy. Pitts and Smith rallied anti-abortion Republicans and said they would vote against the bill if the provision was not removed. The leadership pulled the bill from the floor in July. In November, the leadership brought forward the rule to vote on the bill and Speaker Dennis Hastert took the unusual step of voting for it himself (the Speaker usually does not vote). Despite a determined effort by Tom DeLay, Pitts and Smith held their ground. The rule failed 243–172, with 87 Republicans voting against it. The Pitts initiative scuttled the bankruptcy bill, disappointing Republican leaders and many business groups.

Pitts has been re-elected easily; in 2002, without major party opposition. In November 2002, several days before the election, he announced he was reneging on his 1996 term limits pledge to serve only 10 years. "It was a political type of decision," he told the Lancaster *Intelligencer Journal*, explaining his initial support for term limits. "I felt like, as the only politician who had been in the legislature at that point, that that was what I should have done."

SEVENTEENTH DISTRICT

Rep. Tim Holden (D)

Elected 1992, 6th term; b. Mar. 5, 1957, Pottsville; home, St. Clair; U. of Richmond, 1976–78, Bloomsburg St. U., B.A. 1980; Catholic; married (Gwen).

Elected Office: Schuylkill Cnty. Sheriff, 1985–92.

Professional Career: Real estate agent; Insurance broker, Holden Insurance Agency, 1980–85; Probation Officer, 1980–85.

DC Office: 2417 RHOB 20515, 202-225-5546; Fax: 202-226-0996; Web site: www.house.gov/holden.

District Offices: Harrisburg, 717-234-5904; Lebanon, 717-270-1395; Pottsville, 570-622-4212; Reading, 610-371-9931.

Committees: *Agriculture* (4th of 24 D): Conservation, Credit, Rural Development & Research (RMM); Department Operations, Oversight, Nutrition & Forestry. *Transportation & Infrastructure* (19th of 34 D): Aviation; Highways, Transit & Pipelines.

Group Ratings

	ADA	ACLU	AFS	LCV	CON	ITIC	NTU	COC	ACU	NTLC	CHC
2002	65	40	89	75	43	38	18	60	40	11	50
2001	80	—	100	57	—	—	17	41	48	—	—

National Journal Ratings

	2001 LIB	—	2001 CONS		2002 LIB	—	2002 CONS
Economic	63%	—	37%		58%	—	41%
Social	43%	—	55%		44%	—	54%
Foreign	49%	—	47%		53%	—	46%

Key Votes of the 107th Congress

1. Approve Bush Tax Cuts	N	5. Faith-Based Charities	N	9. Trade Promotion Authority	N
2. Limit Patients' Bill of Rights	N	6. Bar Gays in the Boy Scouts	Y	10. Bar Funds for Intl. Court	Y
3. Campaign Finance Reform	Y	7. Ban Partial-Birth Abortion	Y	11. Authorize Force in Iraq	Y
4. Ban ANWR Development	Y	8. Arm Commercial Pilots	Y	12. Deny Home. Sec. Dept. Union	N

Election Results

2002 general	Tim Holden (D)	103,483	(51%)	($1,714,892)
	George Gekas (R)	97,802	(49%)	($1,427,486)
2002 primary	Tim Holden (D)	unopposed		
2000 general (PA 6)	Tim Holden (D)	140,084	(66%)	($417,147)
	Thomas G. Kopel (R)	71,227	(34%)	($30,913)

Prior Winning Percentages: 1998 (61%); 1996 (59%); 1994 (57%); 1992 (52%)

The People		Race/Ethnic Origin	Ancestry	
Area size:	2,334 sq. mi.	87.3% White	German: 26.0%	Irish: 8.7%
Urban population:	69.6%	7.3% Black	Italian: 5.2%	
Rural population:	30.4%	1.1% Asian	**2000 Presidential Vote**	
Pop. 2000:	646,465	0.1% Native Am.	Bush (R)	139,932 (56%)
Median income:	$40,334	0.0% Hawaiian	Gore (D)	103,603 (41%)
Poverty status:	8.4%	0.9% Two+ races	Other	6,994 (3%)
Military veterans:	14.9%	0.1% Other	**Cook Partisan Voting Index:** R + 8	
		3.2% Hispanic Origin		

Occupation Blue collar: 30.1% White collar: 55.1% Gray collar: 14.8%

Through the center of Pennsylvania flows the Susquehanna, the longest river in the East if you include the Chesapeake Bay, which is actually the flooded lower Susquehanna Valley. Starting in Cooperstown, New York, emptying into the Chesapeake next to the antique town of Havre de Grace, Maryland, the Susquehanna is the one river strong enough to break through the Appalachian chains of central Pennsylvania. But few songs are written to celebrate the Susquehanna—

it has not given a name to a fever (Potomac), a school of painting (Hudson) or economics (Charles), or to a state (Delaware, Connecticut, Ohio, Mississippi, Alabama, Illinois, Missouri, Colorado)—and today its dams are silting up and threatening to wreak environmental havoc on the tenuously recovering Chesapeake, unless the unwieldy grouping of states through which the Susquehanna runs can find a solution.

The 17th Congressional District includes two distinct areas: the agricultural lands adjoining the Susquehanna River and the industrial areas of Schuylkill and Berks Counties. The first is centered on the state capital of Harrisburg; it includes Dauphin County, part of Perry County just across the river and Lebanon County to the east. Harrisburg features a string of mansions-turned-lobbying headquarters gracefully lining the banks of the Susquehanna and boasts Pennsylvania's marvelously restored Capitol building—its dome is modeled after St. Peter's in Rome, its stairway on the Paris Opera. Nearby is Hershey, the town erected by chocolate magnate Milton S. Hershey as a carefully planned, almost utopian village for his factory workers and their families. Hershey left his fortune to a school for orphans and disadvantaged children; when its board proposed to sell the firm in summer 2002, it sparked political controversy, and Attorney General Mike Fisher, the Republican candidate for governor, persuaded a judge to block the sale. The surrounding area, fed by a steady flow of tourists to Hersheypark, has attracted top-flight hospitals and cultivated a prosperous air; the U.S. House of Representatives held a number of "civility retreats" here during the 1990s. Directly south of Hershey is Middletown, whose leafy, gridded streets and handsome homes give no hint that it is the location of the Three Mile Island nuclear plant, site of the worst nuclear accident in American history in 1979.

The eastern half of the district has a grittier heritage. In Berks and Schuylkill Counties the farmers were rough-hewn and more violence-prone, and the towns existed solely to mine rich veins of anthracite coal, the primary energy source of late 19th and early 20th century America. These mountain towns were less orderly, filled with tough-talking miners and factory workers who stayed menacingly in the background unless a character stumbled into the wrong roadhouse at night or the wrong diner at dawn—the Pennsylvania that John O'Hara grew up in and wrote about in the 1930s and 1940s. Pottsville, nestled amid mountains and the home of Yuengling lager (known locally as "Vitamin Y"), produced the Maroons, the team that may have won the 1925 National Football League championship (the league disputed the claim, to Pottsville's eternal chagrin) and whose ties to coal country are emblematic of the game's hardscrabble roots. Pottsville and its neighbors have never rebounded from the switch from anthracite coal to oil and natural gas for home heating: With a disproportionately aging population, Schuylkill County had 228,000 people in 1940 and 150,000 in 2000.

Politically, the 17th leans Republican. Harrisburg, unlike Democratic-machine dominated Albany, has been a Republican town from the days when the party seemed to conquer all in Pennsylvania; Republicans held the governorship for all but eight years from 1860 to 1934 and filled the ornate halls of the Capitol with Republican patronage hacks. Lebanon County is even more solidly Republican. Schuylkill County, in contrast, has a Democratic heritage from its mining days, though its Democrats tend to take conservative stands on cultural issues like abortion and guns. Berks County is somewhat more Republican. Overall, the district voted 56% for George W. Bush in 2000.

The congressman from the 17th District is Tim Holden, a Democrat first elected from the old 6th District in 1992 and the winner of a 2002 battle between incumbents. Holden comes from a political family from the coal mining hamlet of St. Clair; his great-grandfather was a coal miner who founded the forerunner to the United Mine Workers, and his father served four terms as Schuylkill County commissioner. Holden gained fame as a local football player, although tuberculosis cut short his college career. In 1985, at age 28, after selling insurance and real estate in the family business for five years, he was elected Schuylkill County sheriff. Holden's opponent in the 1992 race for an open seat was the better-financed John Jones III, a lawyer who called Holden "clueless" and backed term limits and congressional salary cuts; Holden said he represented "the hardworking men and women" of the district. This appeal sold in culturally conservative but economically polarized Schuylkill County, and Holden won 52%–48%.

Holden has a moderate voting record, though a bit more conservative on cultural issues: He is one of the centrist Blue Dog Democrats and has consistently been near the middle of the House. "The problems our country is facing need to be solved in a bipartisan manner," he says. "There's about 70 liberals and 70 ultraconservatives still in the House. They need to be left behind." He opposed PNTR with China, NAFTA and the Clinton health care plan, but backed welfare reform and health insurance portability. After voting in 2000 to override Bill Clinton's veto of the marriage penalty tax repeal and for cutting back the estate tax, he voted against the Bush tax cut a year later. He is anti-abortion and opposed the FDA's approval of the RU-486 drug. On the Agriculture Committee, Holden looks after dairy programs; he wants the government to buy more cheese, increase the flow of dairy products in international food aid and resume a dairy export subsidy program. With the departure of two colleagues, in 2003 he became the senior Democrat from Pennsylvania on the Transportation and Infrastructure Committee. Most of all, he had worked hard at home, talking issues and solving constituents' problems. As the Pottsville *Republican & Evening Herald* wrote, "It would be hard to imagine a legislator more precisely in tune with his county on virtually any and every issue that has come before Congress." Holden won reelection four times easily even as the district went Republican for other offices.

That experience proved vital to Holden after redistricting in 2002. Republicans controlled redistricting; the initial plan passed by the state Senate split Holden's district and put him in the same district with 11th District Democrat Paul Kanjorski. But the state House would not accept that plan, and instead the two houses agreed on a plan which created a new 6th District based in the Philadelphia suburbs—a district in which Holden's record would be a liability—and a new 17th District which combined Holden's Schuylkill County base with the Harrisburg base of 17th District Republican incumbent George Gekas. A 20-year veteran and senior member of the Judiciary Committee, where he was an impeachment manager, Gekas had not been seriously tested since he was first elected in 1982. At age 72, he was slow to learn modern campaign techniques and was showing his age. The Republican edge in the district favored Gekas, but Holden raised more money—though each was well-funded by additional expenditures by their party and interest groups. The candidates agreed on abortion and gun control; both voted to authorize the use of force in Iraq. But they had plenty of differences. Gekas usually supported business and favored more trade overseas; Holden is pro-union and has opposed new trade agreements. They also disagreed on tax cuts and oil drilling in the Arctic National Wildlife Refuge. As the campaign began, each showed strength in his base but was not well known in the other part of the new district. In what proved to be a key factor in the contest, Holden spent endless time knocking on doors in Dauphin and Lebanon County emphasizing his independence, while Gekas was slower to introduce himself to voters in Schuylkill County. Supporters of Gekas, who trailed in late campaign polls, hoped that a late appearance by George W. Bush would turn the tide.

It didn't. Holden won 51%–49%. The county breakdown showed that he won by his own hard work. In Dauphin County, which had the largest turnout, Gekas won 56%–44%, about the same as losing gubernatorial candidate Mike Fisher's 56%–42% in the county; in Lebanon, the other strong part of his base, Gekas won 61%–39%. But Holden was far stronger in his base, winning Schuylkill 72%–28%, with support from local Republican officials. By contrast, Democratic gubernatorial candidate Ed Rendell carried Schuylkill County by only 51%–46%. There were four contests in 2002 between Democratic and Republican incumbents; this is the only one in which the Republican lost. After this setback, Republicans said Holden was a prime target for 2004. But he will have two more years to get acquainted with voters in the Harrisburg area. He rejected overtures to switch parties. In January 2003 two well-known Republicans, state Representative David Argall and state Senator Jeffrey Piccola, said they would not run. Other possible Republican candidates include former professional football player Ron Hostetler and accounting consultant Frank Ryan.

EIGHTEENTH DISTRICT

Rep. Tim Murphy (R)

Elected 2002, 1st term; b. Sept. 11, 1952, Cleveland, OH; home, Upper St. Clair; Wheeling Jesuit U., B.S. 1974, Cleveland St. U., M.S. 1976, U. of Pittsburgh, Ph.D. 1979; Catholic; married (Nan Missig).

Elected Office: PA Senate, 1996–2002.

Professional Career: Practicing psychologist, 1976–02; author.

DC Office: 226 CHOB 20515, 202-225-2301; Fax: 202-225-1844; Web site: www.house.gov/murphy.

District Office: Pittsburgh, 412-344-5583.

Committees: *Financial Services* (33d of 37 R): Domestic and International Monetary Policy, Trade & Technology; Financial Institutions & Consumer Credit; Oversight & Investigations. *Government Reform* (20th of 24 R): Civil Service & Agency Organization (Vice Chmn.); National Security, Emerging Threats & Intl. Relations; Technology, Information Policy, Intergovernmental Relations & Census. *Veterans' Affairs* (17th of 17 R): Health.

Group Ratings and Key Votes: Newly Elected

Election Results

2002 general	Tim Murphy (R)	119,885	(60%)	($893,568)
	Jack Machek (D)	79,451	(40%)	($126,488)
2002 primary	Tim Murphy (R)	unopposed		
2000 general (PA 20)	Frank R. Mascara (D)	145,131	(64%)	($509,444)
	Ronald J. Davis (R)	80,312	(36%)	

The People		Race/Ethnic Origin	Ancestry	
Area size:	1,433 sq. mi.	95.4% White	German: 19.4%	Irish: 12.3%
Urban population:	84.2%	2.0% Black	Italian: 11.8%	
Rural population:	15.8%	1.3% Asian	**2000 Presidential Vote**	
Pop. 2000:	646,817	0.1% Native Am.	Bush (R)............154,252	(52%)
Median income:	$44,864	0.0% Hawaiian	Gore (D)............139,346	(47%)
Poverty status:	6.3%	0.6% Two+ races	Other..................5,240	(2%)
Military veterans:	14.9%	0.1% Other	**Cook Partisan Voting Index:** R + 3	
		0.6% Hispanic Origin		

Occupation	Blue collar: 20.0%	White collar: 66.3%	Gray collar: 13.7%

Pittsburgh was built on the unlikeliest terrain of any of our major cities. Just about the only level places in the city and its suburbs are the bottomlands along the rivers. Everything else is hills that approach the magnitude of mountains. Only a propitious location, where the Allegheny and Monongahela rivers join to form the Ohio, and the confluence of economically valuable natural resources, coal from the mountains and iron ore from the Great Lakes, can explain the fact that a vast metropolitan area has been built on such land. The great cities of California were built around and over mountains, but for the most part not on top of them; they are vast expanses of contiguous communities most of them little distinguishable from the next. The cities and towns of greater Pittsburgh, in contrast, are discontinuous, separated from each other not just by miles but by altitude. So the region's high-income suburbs and its gritty factory towns are not concentrated in one quarter, but are scattered all around. This is long-settled country, with many more old towns than sparkling new suburbs.

The 18th Congressional District, entirely redrawn by redistricters in 2002, covers an irregularly shaped swath of the southern part of the Pittsburgh metropolitan area. It includes most of southern Allegheny County, most of Westmoreland County to the east and most of Washington County to the west; it stretches from the Pittsburgh city limit to the West Virginia border. It contains the Pittsburgh airport in Moon Township, Monroeville to the east and towns like Ligonier, green with prosperity and dotted with the vast estates of Mellons and other scions of Pittsburgh's industrial elite, and Canonsburg, which recently unveiled a "singing sculpture" of its most famous son, the crooner Perry Como. But the district's backbone are middle- to upper-middle-class bedroom suburbs, like Mount Lebanon and Upper St. Clair in Allegheny County and Penn Township and Greensburg in Westmoreland County. These areas lean Republican, but not overwhelmingly so. Democrats grumble that the Republican trend in Westmoreland reflects the local influence of the *Tribune-Review*, the Greensburg-based newspaper owned by conservative Richard Mellon Scaife, named by Clintonite conspiracy theorists as the mastermind of the vast right wing conspiracy. Republicans controlled redistricting in 2002, and they worked carefully to make this a Republican district; within its boundaries George W. Bush won 52% of the vote in 2000.

The congressman from the 18th District is Tim Murphy, a Republican first elected in 2002. He grew up in Cleveland in a family of 11 children. He graduated from Wheeling Jesuit University, got a Ph.D. from the University of Pittsburgh and became a child psychologist. He worked in several Pittsburgh area hospitals and was an adjunct faculty member in public health and pediatrics at the University of Pittsburgh. He became a public figure while offering medical advice as "Dr. Tim" in television appearances and on radio talk shows; he co-authored *The Angry Child: Regaining Control When Your Child is Out of Control*. In 1996 Murphy was elected to the state Senate. As chairman of the Aging and Youth Committee and vice chairman of the Public Health and Welfare Committee, he helped to enact HMO regulation, licensing requirements for pediatric care centers for medically fragile children and price controls for prescriptions in the state's program for the elderly. In the process, he won notice for his ability to work both sides of the aisle.

The redistricters drew the 18th with Murphy in mind. But they also included in the district the house of 20th District Democrat Frank Mascara, so that he would not be in the same district with 12th District Democrat John Murtha, whom even Republicans valued as a dispenser of aid to Pennsylvania from his high-ranking seat on the Appropriations Committee. Mascara took a month to decide which district to run in, then ran against Murtha anyway and lost by a wide margin. Mascara's decision showed a recognition of Murphy's strength: Murphy had already shown an ability to run ahead of party lines. He announced his candidacy soon after redistricting plan was passed in January 2002. A day later his campaign released a poll showing him leading Mascara 45%–30%.

Murphy was unopposed in the Republican primary. Jack Machek, an administrator in the Norwin School District tax office, won the Democratic nomination over the early favorite Washington County Sheriff Larry Maggi. Murphy presented himself as an experienced and accomplished legislator who opposed abortion and supported gun rights. When Dick Armey came in to campaign for him, he said that the combative Armey's approach to politics was "not my style." Murphy had extensive support from Pennsylvania and national Republicans and spent $894,000 to Machek's $126,000. Murphy's support of the Republican plan for prescription drugs for seniors was evidently not a handicap in a district that has a high percentage of elderly residents. Murphy won 60%–40%—an impressive showing in an open seat race in a district with 74,000 more registered Democrats than Republicans.

NINETEENTH DISTRICT

Rep. Todd Platts (R)

Elected 2000, 2d term; b. Mar. 5, 1962, York; home, York; Shippensburg U., B.S. 1984, Pepperdine U., J.D. 1991; Episcopalian; married (Leslie).

Elected Office: PA House of Reps., 1993–2000.

Professional Career: Practicing atty.

DC Office: 1032 LHOB 20515, 202-225-5836; Fax: 202-226-1000; Web site: www.house.gov/platts.

District Offices: Carlisle, 717-249-0190; Gettysburg, 717-338-1919; York, 717-600-1919.

Committees: *Education & the Workforce* (15th of 27 R): Education Reform; Employer-Employee Relations. *Government Reform* (12th of 24 R): Government Efficiency & Financial Management (Chmn.); National Security, Emerging Threats & Intl. Relations. *Transportation & Infrastructure* (28th of 41 R): Highways, Transit & Pipelines; Railroads.

Group Ratings

	ADA	ACLU	AFS	LCV	CON	ITIC	NTU	COC	ACU	NTLC	CHC
2002	5	13	11	38	25	100	58	85	88	75	75
2001	5	—	10	21	—	—	60	83	80	—	—

National Journal Ratings

	2001 LIB — 2001 CONS	2002 LIB — 2002 CONS
Economic	47% — 53%	49% — 51%
Social	20% — 69%	44% — 54%
Foreign	41% — 60%	24% — 72%

Key Votes of the 107th Congress

1. Approve Bush Tax Cuts	Y	5. Faith-Based Charities	Y	9. Trade Promotion Authority	Y
2. Limit Patients' Bill of Rights	Y	6. Bar Gays in the Boy Scouts	Y	10. Bar Funds for Intl. Court	Y
3. Campaign Finance Reform	Y	7. Ban Partial-Birth Abortion	Y	11. Authorize Force in Iraq	Y
4. Ban ANWR Development	N	8. Arm Commercial Pilots	Y	12. Deny Home. Sec. Dept. Union	Y

Election Results

2002 general	Todd Platts (R)	143,097	(91%)	($224,480)
	Ben Price (Green)	7,900	(5%)	
	Michael Paoletta (Lib)	6,008	(4%)	
2002 primary	Todd Platts (R)	34,026	(77%)	
	Tom Glennon (R)	7,150	(16%)	
	Lester Searer (R)	1,921	(4%)	
	Other	1,332	(3%)	
2000 general	Todd Platts (R)	168,722	(73%)	($308,158)
	Jeff Sanders (D)	61,538	(26%)	($33,709)
	Other	2,234	(1%)	

The People

Area size:	1,657 sq. mi.
Urban population:	71.3%
Rural population:	28.7%
Pop. 2000:	647,065
Median income:	$45,363
Poverty status:	6.8%
Military veterans:	14.3%

Race/Ethnic Origin

92.2% White
2.9% Black
1.1% Asian
0.1% Native Am.
0.0% Hawaiian
0.9% Two+ races
0.1% Other
2.7% Hispanic Origin

Ancestry

German: 28.1% Irish: 9.0%
USA: 6.7%

2000 Presidential Vote

Bush (R)	153,892	(61%)
Gore (D)	90,125	(36%)
Other	6,766	(3%)

Cook Partisan Voting Index: R +13

Occupation Blue collar: 29.3% White collar: 57.1% Gray collar: 13.7%

The Mason-Dixon Line, the historic boundary between Maryland and Pennsylvania, runs through some of the country's most pleasant rolling farmlands, west of the Susquehanna River up through the first of the Appalachian chains. This area was home to the westernmost capital of the United States during the Revolutionary War: the small city of York, capital from September 1777 to June 1778. York is where the Continental Congress passed the Articles of Confederation, received word from Benjamin Franklin in Paris that the French would help the colonies with money and ships and issued the first proclamation calling for a national day of thanksgiving. A little more than four score years later, Robert E. Lee's Confederate troops crossed over this invisible line and were repulsed in the Battle of Gettysburg in July 1863. Not much today suggests that this region was either a frontier or the object of bloody struggle: The green farmland seems peaceful, prosperous and mostly undisturbed by the current era's commercial trappings and stylistic excesses; this is where Dwight D. Eisenhower, a man of Pennsylvania Dutch stock, chose to quietly spend his retirement years.

For more than 50 miles, the Mason-Dixon Line forms the southern boundary of the 19th

Congressional District, which includes all of Adams and York Counties and part of Cumberland County to the north—areas that grew by 10% or more during the 1990s. The 19th takes in the fruit belt of Adams County, the Harrisburg suburbs across the Susquehanna and part of the old town of Carlisle, with Dickinson College, the Carlisle Barracks, and the U.S. Army War College. Hanover, in York County, is one of the world's snack headquarters—home to Snyder's of Hanover, which makes one of every four pretzels sold in the U.S., as well as potato-chip giant Utz Quality Foods. The district's biggest city is York, the site of Harley-Davidson's largest manufacturing plant and the USA Weightlifting Hall of Fame at the York Barbell Company. York is a place where many residents commute an hour (or less) to work in Baltimore and where the Orioles, not the more distant Phillies, are the baseball team of choice. The city also hosts a rapidly growing Hispanic population, mainly Puerto Rican, but with increasing numbers of Mexicans. Politically, the 19th is heavily Republican. George W. Bush won 61% of the vote here in 2000, and most other Republicans do as well or better.

The congressman from the 19th District is Todd Platts, a Republican elected in 2000. Platts grew up in York, graduated from Shippensburg University and Pepperdine University School of Law. In 1992, at age 30, after practicing law in Lancaster, he was elected to the state House of Representatives, where he served four terms. He was active in community affairs in York, including service on transportation and urban planning boards.

In 2000, Platts was the first to announce his candidacy after longtime Congressman Bill Goodling, chairman of the Education and the Workforce Committee, announced his retirement in early 1999. Platts's chief primary opponents were state Representative Al Masland, attorney and Goodling-endorsed Dick Stewart and Charlie Gerow, head of the state Citizens Against Government Waste. The campaign motto for Platts, who refused contributions from political action committees and was outspent by his chief Republican rivals, was "Putting People First" (his conservative supporters apparently weren't bothered by the fact that the phrase had been the title of a book by Bill Clinton). He emphasized his views on campaign finance, education, shoring up Social Security and health care issues. Platts won with 33% to 29% for Masland and 19% for Stewart, rolling up huge margins in his home base of York County; Masland had a big edge in his base of Cumberland County, but it had less than half as many votes. The general election was no contest. Platts won 73%–26%, after spending about one-third the amount of the average House freshman that year.

In the House, Platts has a comparatively moderate voting record. He was elected freshman class representative on the Republican Policy Committee. Showcasing his independence, he caused unhappiness among Republican leaders when he signed the discharge petition to bring the campaign reform bill to the House floor and when he voted against a school choice amendment. Platts claimed credit for a requirement that airport screeners must meet a citizenship requirement.

Redistricting, controlled by Republicans, made few changes in the district lines, and Platts had no Democratic opponent in 2002.

★ RHODE ISLAND ★

The tiny little city-state with a mouthful of an official name, Rhode Island and Providence Plantations, has as turbulent a political history as any state in the Union. A successful trading community since the 1600s, a leader in manufacturing since Samuel Slater replicated from memory an English water-powered cotton textile mill in Pawtucket in 1791, Rhode Island also had its beginning as an upstart community, a refuge for religious dissenters, "the sewer of New England," as the orthodox Cotton Mather put it. Rhode Island profited from slavery (two-thirds of America's slaves arrived on ships owned by Rhode Islanders) and war (the state boomed during the Civil War), and carried its tradition of tolerating just about anything into its politics. Rhode Island refused to pay its share for the Revolutionary War, declined to send delegates to the 1787 Constitutional Convention, and delayed joining the Union until the other 12 states had, prompting George Washington to say, "Rhode Island still perseveres in that impolitic, unjust—and one might add without much impropriety—scandalous conduct, which seems to have marked all her public counsels of late." The new nation's first bank failure occurred here in 1809, when a bank capitalized at $45 issued $800,000 in bank notes. In the 1840s, conflict between hard money merchants and soft money farmers resulted in two state governments and a conflict known as Dorr's War, with the outcome determined when merchant Dorr's two ancient cannons failed to fire.

Then, in the 1930s, Rhode Island had something resembling a political revolution. Thousands of immigrants from French Canada, Ireland and Italy came to Rhode Island to work in the textile mills and this colony of dissident Protestants became the most heavily Catholic state in the nation. Yankee Republicans tried to appeal to Catholics by running French Canadians for office. But national events—Al Smith's candidacy in 1928, when he carried Rhode Island, and Franklin Roosevelt's New Deal—moved the Catholics toward the Democrats. Then came the revolution: in 1935, the Democrats under Governor Theodore Green, although they had won only 20 of the 42 state Senate seats, refused to seat two Republicans. With the lieutenant governor's tie-breaker, they voted Democrats into the seats, and proceeded in 14 minutes to declare the state Supreme Court seats vacant, abolish state boards that controlled Democratic cities, strengthen the power of the governor and reorganize state government to purge Republicans. This ended the direct political control of Rhode Island's "Five Families"—the Browns, Metcalfs, Goddards, Lippitts and Chafees—who owned or ran many of the textile mills, the Rhode Island Hospital Trust (long the largest bank), the Providence *Journal-Bulletin*, Brown University, the Rhode Island School of Design and the state Republican Party. The Democrats have won most elections with the lion's share of votes from Rhode Island's 64% Catholic majority, starting with Green's election in 1936, at age 69, to the first of his four terms as U.S. senator. From 1940 to 1980, Democrats won every election for U.S. House seats; its Democratic percentages in presidential elections from 1968 to 1996 are rivalled only by Massachusetts. Republicans have won when they've been able to capitalize on scandal or Democratic disarray, as Governors Lincoln Almond and Donald Carcieri did in 1994 and 2002. But the only really durable Republican politician has been John Chafee, elected governor in 1962, 1964 and 1966, senator in 1976, 1982, 1988 and 1994, who died in 1999; and even he lost twice, in 1968 and 1972.

Rhode Island has gone through a long and painful economic transformation, from blue collar to white collar, from textiles to high-tech. It suffered economic problems in the early 1990s, but has smartly recovered and entered the new century more productive and confident than it has been in decades. The Census Bureau estimated that Rhode Island's population fell below the 1 million mark in 1996, but the 2000 Census showed it up to 1,048,000, a 5% increase for the decade. The submarine factory and Navy base at Quonset Point lost thousands of jobs; employment in costume jewelry, Rhode Island's major manufacturer, fell from 32,500 in 1977 to 6,300 in 2000; overfishing has cut the lobster and winter flounder stocks sharply. But Republican Governor Lincoln Almond, elected in 1994 and 1998, persuaded the overwhelmingly Democratic legislature (44–6 in the Senate, 85–15 in the House) to gradually cut income taxes and eliminate the car tax, and Providence Mayor Buddy Cianci promoted brilliantly successful redevelopment in the state's capital and largest city. Tourism became Rhode Island's second largest industry, and

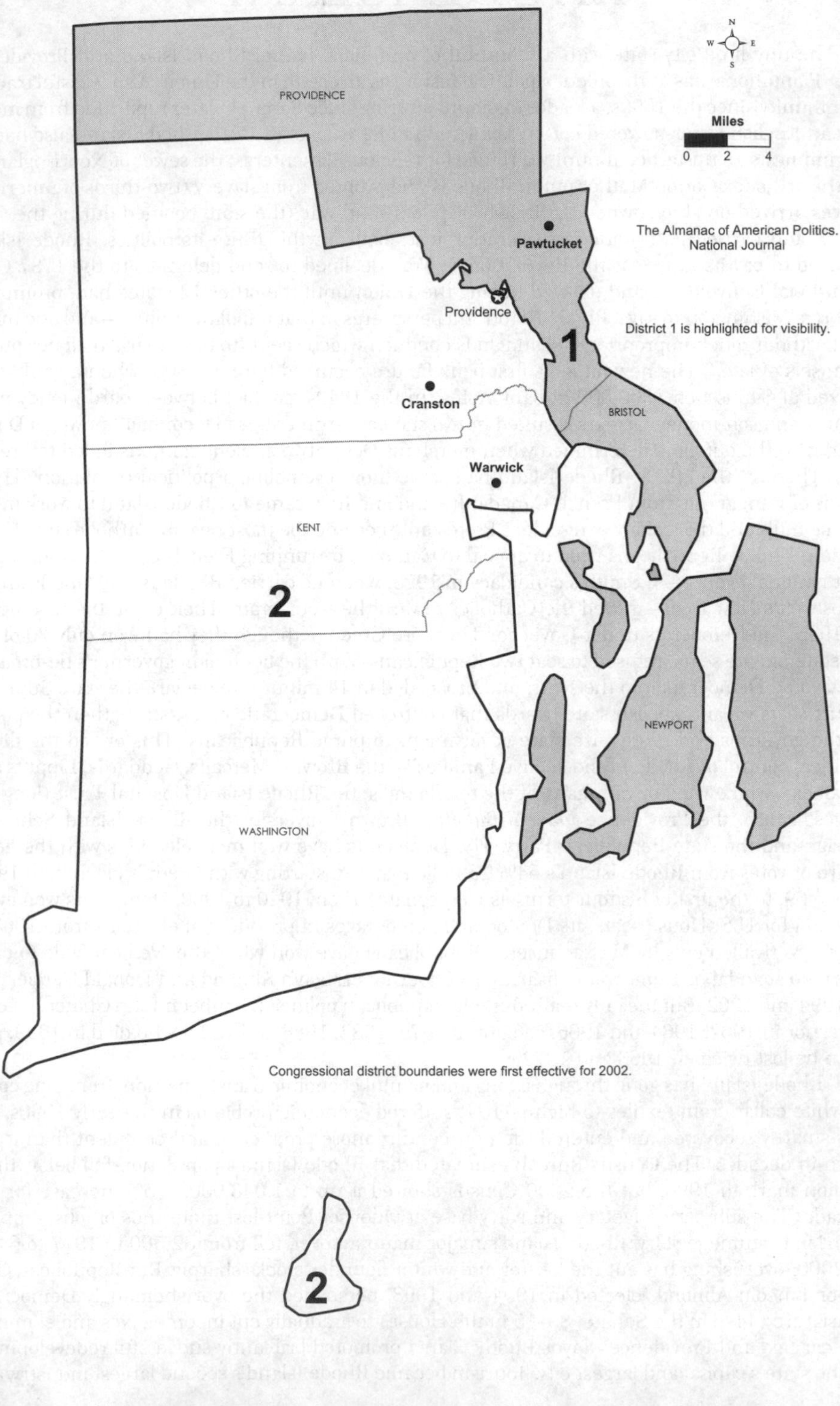

PROVIDENCE

Miles
0 2 4

Pawtucket

Providence

The Almanac of American Politics.
National Journal

District 1 is highlighted for visibility.

1

Cranston

BRISTOL

Warwick

KENT

2

NEWPORT

WASHINGTON

Congressional district boundaries were first effective for 2002.

2

computer data processing a major part of the economy; Rhode Island's university hospitals drew a far-above-average number of federal research dollars; Rhode Island's research and development tax credit, claimed to be the largest in the nation, encouraged high-tech startups; Providence's T.F. Green Airport boomed, as a low-cost alternative to Boston's Logan. Providence, after losing population for decades, grew 8% in the 1990s, the biggest gain since 1900–10, and Latino immigrants—from the Dominican Republic and Guatemala, Peru and Ecuador—brought vitality to neighborhoods long given up for dead.

There seemed to be a new sense of optimism—and fun. Tourists came to see Nibbles Woodaway, the 58-foot-long termite built by the New England Pest Control Company and the state marketed Mr. Potato Head, created in Pawtucket, as the symbol of "Rhode Island—the birthplace of fun." The television show *Providence* painted the city's booming East Side in soft and golden hues. Yet there were also problems. Cianci, mayor from 1975 to 1984, when he was convicted of assaulting and burning a man he accused of having an affair with his wife, and mayor again from 1991, was indicted in April 2001 and convicted in June 2002 of racketeering and conspiracy—just two days before the filing deadline for mayor. He left office in September and went to prison. His successor, David Cicilline, son of a prominent mob lawyer, is part Italian, part Jewish and openly gay: a new combination for a successful politician.

The People		**Race/Ethnic Origin**			**Military veterans:** 102,494 (12.8%)	
Pop. 2000:	1,048,319	858,433	81.9%	White	WWII: 25.4%	Korea: 14.9%
Pop. 1990:	1,003,464	41,922	4.0%	Black	Vietnam: 29.6%	Gulf War: 7.0%
Change 1990–2000:	Up 4.5%	23,416	2.2%	Asian	**Most populous cities:**	
Change 1980–1990:	Up 5.9%	4,181	0.4%	Native Am.	1. Providence	173,618
% of U.S. total:	0.4%	320	0.0%	Hawaiian	2. Warwick	85,808
Pop. rank:	43d of 50	20,816	2.0%	Two+ races	3. Cranston	79,269
Area size:	1,545 sq. mi.	8,411	0.8%	Other	4. Pawtucket	72,958
State Native:	61.4%	90,820	8.7%	Hisp. Origin	5. East Providence	48,688
Non-citizen:	6.0%	**Ancestry**			Urban population: 90.9%	
Language		Italian: 14.1%		Irish: 13.7%	Rural population: 9.1%	
English: 77.2%	Other Eur.: 12.8%	English: 8.9%		French: 8.1%		
Spanish: 7.5%		Portuguese: 6.5%				

Education		**Work Sector**		**General Assembly**	
H.S. Grad:	78.0%	Private: 80.6%	Govt: 13.8%	Senate	32 D 6 R
College Grad:	25.6%	Self: 5.4%	Family: 0.2%	House	63 D 11 R 1 I
Industry		Unemployment: 5.6%		Legislative Term Limits: No	
Agri: 0.5%	Con: 5.4%	**Household Income**		**Registered Voters**	
Fin: 6.9%	Info: 2.3%	<15k: 17.7%	15-35k: 24.2%	No party registration	
Mfg: 20.3%	Prof: 31.3%	35-50k: 15.7%	50-100k: 30.8%		
Public: 4.5%	Trade: 15.5%	100-150k: 7.6%	>150k: 3.9%		
Other: 13.3%		Median: $42,090			
Occupation		Poverty status: 11.9%			
Blue collar: 22.9%	White collar: 61.1%	**Home Value**			
Gray collar: 16.0%		<50k: 2.0% 50-100k: 21.0% 100-200k: 59.6% 200-300k: 11.1%			
		300-500k: 4.5% >500k: 1.8% Median: $130,500			

Presidential politics Rhode Island is almost always one of the most Democratic states in presidential elections—over the last generation, the most Democratic. It voted 61%–32% for Al Gore in 2000. Bush carried the towns of East Greenwich and (by 6 votes) Scituate; Gore carried every other city and town. White Protestants, once the Republican base here, voted 51%–41% for Gore; white Catholics voted 59%–35% for Gore. Rhode Island's Catholic majority is heavily Democratic and, interestingly, pro-choice on abortion: In states where Catholics are beleaguered minorities they may stand together and strongly oppose abortion; here, where they're the strong majority and where the mostly Mediterranean Catholics traditionally didn't pay strict attention to the mostly Irish priests, they come out against the church position.

Rhode Island holds a presidential primary the same day as Massachusetts, usually with the lowest turnout rate in the nation. It has not won much attention. In 1992 only 66,000 of 1 million Rhode Islanders voted in both parties' primaries; in 2000, when the primary was held on March 7 and the outcomes not entirely clear, 82,000 voted. Al Gore beat Bill Bradley 57%–41%—one of Bradley's better performances—and John McCain beat George W. Bush 60%–36%.

2000 Presidential Vote		
Gore (D)	249,508	(61%)
Bush (R)	130,555	(32%)
Nader (Green)	25,052	(6%)
Other	3,668	(1%)

2000 Republican Presidential Primary		
McCain (R)	21,754	(60%)
Bush (R)	13,170	(36%)
Other	1,196	(3%)

2000 Democratic Presidential Primary		
Gore (D)	26,801	(57%)
Bradley (D)	19,000	(41%)
Other	1,043	(2%)

1996 Presidential Vote		
Clinton (D)	233,050	(60%)
Dole (R)	104,683	(27%)
Perot (I)	43,723	(11%)
Other	8,674	(2%)

Congressional districting The Rhode Island legislators had a heck of a time redrawing the boundaries of their own districts in 2001 and 2002; voters in 1994 adopted a constitutional amendment reducing the size of the state House after the 2000 Census from 100 to 75 seats and the state Senate from 50 to 38. But redistricting the two congressional districts was much easier. Rhode Island's two congressional districts have remained pretty much the same since 1842, except for the period from 1912 to 1932 when the state had three districts. Providence is split and both districts are overwhelmingly Democratic. For 2002, 14,000 people needed to be moved from the 2d District to the 1st. Incumbents Patrick Kennedy and James Langevin agreed on a change in Providence that gave Kennedy his old state representative district near Providence College.

108th Congress Lineup
2 D
107th Congress Lineup
2 D

Governor

Donald Carcieri (R)

Elected 2002, term expires Jan. 2007, 1st term; b. Dec. 16, 1942, East Greenwich; home, East Greenwich; Brown U., B.A. 1965; Catholic; married (Suzanne).

Professional Career: High schl. teacher, 1965–71; Banker, Old Stone Bank, 1971–81; Director, Catholic Relief Services, Jamaica, 1981–83; CEO, Cookson America, 1983–97.

Office: The State House, Room 115, Providence, 02903, 401-222-2080; Fax: 401-861-5894; Web site: www.governor.state.ri.us.

Election Results

2002 general	Donald Carcieri (R)	181,687	(55%)
	Myrth York (D)	150,147	(45%)
2002 primary	Donald Carcieri (R)	17,227	(67%)
	James Bennett (R)	8,518	(33%)
1998 general	Lincoln Almond (R)	156,180	(51%)
	Myrth York (D)	129,105	(42%)
	Robert J. Healey (Cool Moose)	19,250	(6%)
	Other	1,910	(1%)

Donald Carcieri, elected governor of Rhode Island in 2002, grew up in East Greenwich, on Narragansett Bay, where his father was a teacher and coach at the town high school and a quahogger in the summer. East Greenwich today is one of Rhode Island's most affluent suburbs; in the 1950s, Carcieri says, it was a modest town of fishermen and farmers. Carcieri was class president and a top athlete in high school and attended Brown on scholarship and played varsity football and baseball. He taught high school math in Newport and then in Concord, Massachusetts. Then he went to work for Old Stone Bank and in 10 years became executive vice president. In 1981 he moved to Kingston, Jamaica, to be head of the Catholic Relief Service's West Indies operation. In 1983 he returned to Rhode Island and went to work for Cookson America, the U.S. branch of a London conglomerate that owns dozens of manufacturing, electronic and precious metals companies around the world. He rose to become CEO of Cookson America and a joint managing director of Cookson Group Worldwide. He moved Cookson America's headquarters to the former Providence train station, overlooking Burnside Park and the State House. He retired in 1997 and in 2002 started running for governor.

The incumbent, Republican Lincoln Almond, was ineligible to run for a third term. For many years—from 1969 to 1978 and from 1981 to 1993, he was United States Attorney in Rhode Island, a stern enforcer of the law in an often politically corrupt state. He was elected in 1994 by 47%–44% over state Senator Myrth York and beat her again in 1998 by 51%–42%. Almond was not a gregarious politician, and the heavily Democratic legislature took over the budget and increased spending 46% between 1996 and 2001; when Almond vetoed the budget in 2002, his veto was overridden.

Three Democrats and two Republicans ran to succeed Almond; Carcieri was the only one with no experience in public office, though he did serve as the Bush chairman in Rhode Island in 2000. His primary opponent was James Bennett, former chairman of the Convention Center Authority and owner of Mitkem, an environmental testing laboratory. Carcieri and Bennett mostly agreed on priorities—rein in the legislature, cut spending increases, promote economic development. Both avoided Rhode Island's matching fund public financing and spent their own money on their campaigns—$600,000 for Carcieri and $275,000 for Bennett. Bennett spent much of his money on fierce negative ads against Carcieri, charging that under his leadership Cookson's debt rose, layoffs increased, trade secrets disclosed and Carcieri was given a $2.6 million golden handshake. Carcieri retaliated with a mailer (there aren't many Rhode Island Republican primary voters, 26,000 in 2002, and it makes sense to reach them through direct mail) showing a hand digging through sopping wet mud. "Why is Jim Bennett throwing mud? Maybe Jim Bennett has to cover up his own failed record. Jim Bennett got caught not paying his company's sales taxes for seven years." Mitkem withheld $235,000 in sales taxes from 1994 to 1999 while it sought a tax exemption; in 2002 it was forced to pay nearly $500,000 in back taxes, interest and penalties. Carcieri won the September primary 67%–33%.

The Democratic contest got more attention. Running again was Myrth York, with a liberal message. She had a new team of consultants and ran ads showing her family. Her father started a chemical equipment company, and she manages her family's money; she spent $2 million of her own money before the primary. Also running was her Federal Hill neighbor in Providence, Attorney General Sheldon Whitehouse, who spent some of his own money as well. He was supported by the AFL-CIO and was probably the candidate closest to Democratic legislative leaders. The third candidate was state Representative Antonio Pires, who had been ousted from the chairmanship of the Finance Committee by Speaker John Harwood in 2001; he depended on $25 contributions raised by the Portuguese American Committee of Northern Rhode Island for his matching funds. The real race was between the two self-financing candidates. The result was not clear until the absentee ballots were counted election night. York beat Whitehouse 39%–38%, with 22% for Pires.

The *Providence Journal* post-primary poll showed York ahead 49%–35%, but she had led in early polls in 1994 and 1998 as well. Their differing stances were apparent in a September debate. York said, "I have a knowledge of government and a knowledge of how to get things done in government. Government is there to provide opportunity for folks." Carcieri said, "I believe if real change is going to happen in the state, it's going to have to come from somebody who owes nothing to the system, somebody from outside." Carcieri pledged not to raise taxes in his first year; York said she didn't want to but wouldn't make a pledge. Republicans recalled that she had voted for a 20% income tax increase in the early 1990s. York called for new prescription drug and education programs; Carcieri said economic development was his goal. The *Providence Journal's* M. Charles Bakst said that York sounded scripted and Carcieri likeable. When he asked them about spending their own money, York said "I believe I can really make a difference for Rhode Islanders and I'm willing to invest in that opportunity to make a difference," while Carcieri told him that when a voter asked him how it felt to drop a million, he said, "Sometimes you feel kind of stupid!" and talked about his commitment to change.

In mid-October York started running a series of negative ads about Cookson. One said the company brokered a "tin mining deal" that ravaged an Amazon rain forest, another that it owned a plant in Philadelphia that released hazardous lead into the neighborhood, a third with neighbors of the plant denouncing Carcieri. A radio ad talked about an accident in which 15 Amazon miners were killed. Carcieri's pollster said that his polls showed Carcieri behind after the primary, drawing even in mid-October and gaining rapidly as York's negative spots were airing. The *Journal's* polls and the election result suggest this was accurate. Carcieri won 55%–45%. York won big in Providence but in the rest of the state carried only East Providence and the tiny textile mill town of Central Falls. Altogether York spent $3.8 million of her own money, Carcieri $1.5 million of his.

In early 2003 the shortfall for the rest of the fiscal year was estimated at $200 million and the projected deficit for the next was $520 million, in a $2.6 billion budget. It did not appear that the legislature would increase taxes over Carcieri's veto, so it began cutting spending. Almond had lost control of spending because of the Democrats' huge majorities in the legislature and because, like Massachusetts's Republican governors from 1990 to 2002, he had done nothing to build a Republican party. Carcieri promised during the campaign to do more. Carcieri put off the budget for a week after the nightclub fire in West Warwick killed 100 people in February 2003.

Senior Senator

Jack Reed (D)

Elected 1996, seat up 2008, 2d term; b. Nov. 12, 1949, Providence; home, Cranston; U.S. Military Acad., West Point, B.S. 1971, Harvard U., M.P.P. 1973, J.D. 1982; Catholic; single.

Military Career: Army, 1967–79; Army Reserves, 1979–91.

Elected Office: RI Senate, 1984–90; U.S. House of Reps., 1990–96.

Professional Career: Assoc. Prof., U.S. Military Acad. at West Point, 1978–79; Practicing atty., 1982–90.

DC Office: 728 HSOB, 20510, 202-224-4642; Fax: 202-224-4680; Web site: reed.senate.gov.

State Offices: Cranston, 401-943-3100; Providence, 401-528-5200.

Committees: *Armed Services*: Emerging Threats & Capabilities (RMM); Seapower; Strategic Forces. *Banking, Housing & Urban Affairs*: Financial Institutions; Housing & Transportation (RMM); Securities & Investment. *Health, Education, Labor & Pensions*: Children & Families; Substance Abuse & Mental Health Services. *Joint Economic Committee* (7th of 10 Sens.).

Group Ratings

	ADA	ACLU	AFS	LCV	CON	ITIC	NTU	COC	ACU	NTLC	CHC
2002	100	60	100	100	81	38	16	40	0	0	—
2001	100	—	100	100	—	—	8	36	4	—	0

National Journal Ratings

	2001 LIB — 2001 CONS		2002 LIB — 2002 CONS	
Economic	93%	0%	95%	0%
Social	81%	8%	82%	0%
Foreign	87%	3%	85%	12%

Key Votes of the 107th Congress

1. Approve Bush Tax Cuts	N	5. Confirm Ashcroft as AG	N	9. Bar Coop. with Intl. Court	N
2. Expand Patients' Rights	Y	6. Bar Gays in the Boy Scouts	N	10. Trade Promotion Authority	N
3. Campaign Finance Reform	Y	7. $ for Hate Crime Prosecution	Y	11. Authorize Force in Iraq	N
4. Permit ANWR Development	N	8. Overseas Military Abortions	Y	12. Homeland Sec. Dept. Union	Y

Election Results

2002 general	Jack Reed (D)	253,773	(78%)	($1,767,967)
	Robert Tingle (R)	69,808	(22%)	
2002 primary	Jack Reed (D)	unopposed		
1996 general	Jack Reed (D)	230,676	(63%)	($2,732,011)
	Nancy J. Mayer (R)	127,368	(35%)	($773,789)

Prior Winning Percentages: 1994 House (68%); 1992 House (71%); 1990 House (59%)

Jack Reed, Rhode Island's senior senator, was elected to the House in 1990 and the Senate in 1996. He grew up in working-class Cranston, the son of a school custodian; he graduated from West Point, served in the 82d Airborne, got a degree at Harvard's Kennedy School, then taught at West Point. In 1979 he retired from the Army and went to Harvard Law School. He practiced law briefly in Washington and then in Providence. In 1984, at 35, he beat an incumbent in the primary for state Senate, where he served for six years, was close to the party leadership and built a good reputation. When Republican Claudine Schneider left the House to run against Senator Claiborne Pell in 1990, Reed ran for the House seat, overcoming several better-known candidates in the primary, and winning with 59% over Save the Bay Executive Director Trudy Coxe in the general.

Reed compiled a substantially, though not quite totally, liberal record in the House. On the Education and the Workforce Committee he worked for the Goals 2000 Act and on reauthorization of the Elementary and Secondary Education Act. He tried to amend the 1996 welfare act to have block grants increase when national unemployment is more than 6%. On local issues, Reed worked for the freight rail connection at the Quonset Point port and introduced legislation to require indelible country-of-origin markings on foreign-made jewelry and jewelry boxes; Rhode Island's jewelry industry produces about a third of the costume jewelry in the United States.

In 1995, when Senator Claiborne Pell announced his retirement after 36 years in the Senate, Reed almost immediately started running. Reed was easily nominated and faced state Treasurer Nancy Mayer in the general. National Republicans spent nearly $1 million on ads attacking Reed as a liberal for opposing workfare and for supporting labor unions; in liberal, heavily unionized Rhode Island these did not hurt him and may have helped. Mayer's support for campaign finance regulation and opposition to soft money were parried when Reed in debate asked her why she didn't call off the Republican soft money campaign against him. Mayer's campaign was overshadowed by Reed's: She spent $773,000 and he spent $2.7 million. His biography was his message: Reed launched his campaign in a school conference room named after his late father; he stressed how he came up from humble beginnings by hard work and called for education spending to help others rise as he had. That message, and his own pleasant, unassuming demeanor evidently touched a chord. He won 63%–35%, an impressive first Senate victory.

In the Senate, Reed has a liberal voting record. He serves on the HELP Committee and has sought to amend major bills. The 1998 Higher Education law included his TEACH program, grants to teacher colleges for partnerships with K-12 schools. He has been a strong supporter of requiring continual teacher training. He believes that school libraries have been underfunded and in 2001 with Thad Cochran sponsored a bill to provide them $500 million. He has sought to increase Medicare spending for home health care and to promote purchasing pools for health insurance. In October 2000 he put a hold on a bill granting citizenship to foreign children adopted by American parents, in an effort to get permanent refugee status for 10,000 Liberians who came to the United States, many of them to Rhode Island. When the Bush administration called for cuts in Low-Income Home Energy Assistance in 2002, he called for increases. He has worked on the national project to eliminate lead poisoning in children by 2010, and criticized the administration for not spending more. With Barbara Mikulski and Christopher Bond, he sponsored a $75 million demonstration project to fight lead poisoning in cities with the highest rates of lead poisoning.

Reed is one of the few senators of his generation with military experience. He was appointed to the governing board of West Point in 1998 and got a seat on the Armed Services Committee in January 1999. He wants to consolidate the Naval War College and the Naval Undersea Warfare Center, two of the remaining Rhode Island military facilities; defense jobs in the state declined from 44,000 in 1970 to 8,000 in 1999. In October 2002 he voted against the Iraq war resolution. The 2002 defense appropriation included $1.5 billion for a Virginia class submarine and $645 million for retooling two Trident submarines, with much of the work to be done at Electric Boat in Groton, Connecticut, where many Rhode Islanders work. In December 2002 he led the successful fight in committee to cut $15 million off research into a bunker buster nuclear weapon and $812 million off the missile defense budget. In 2003 he became ranking Democrat on the Emerging Threats and Capabilities Subcommittee.

In July 2001, after Democrats got their majority in the Senate, Reed got a seat on Appropriations. He promised to be a team player: "Senator Daschle and Chairman [Robert] Byrd have difficult, demanding jobs. If you respect that and try to help out, I think that ultimately is appreciated." He has worked for $2 million for the Save the Bay Education Center in Providence, $3.25 million for Narragansett Bay Commission new sewers, $9.3 million for an undersea combat vehicle at the Naval Undersea Warfare Center in Middletown, $100,000 for Charlestown Breachway navigation safety and $120,000 for a federal breakwater at the Port of Galilee Harbor of Refuge at Narragansett. When Democrats lost their majority, Reed lost his Appropriations seat.

In Rhode Island politics, Reed has always been his own man, unentangled with the various machine politicians who come and go. In 2002, against a pit manager at Foxwoods Resort Casino, he was reelected 78%–22%. This is a Senate seat whose members have had long tenures. Theodore Green, elected at 69, served 24 years; Claiborne Pell, elected at 41, served 36 years. Reed, elected just before turning 47, has the prospect of long service before him.

Junior Senator

Lincoln Chafee (R)

Appointed Nov. 1999, seat up 2006, 1st term; b. Mar. 26, 1953, Warwick; home, Warwick; Brown U., B.A., 1975; Episcopalian; married (Stephanie).

Elected Office: Warwick city council, 1986–92; Warwick mayor, 1992–99.

Professional Career: Farrier, 1976–83; Cranston Print Works, 1984–85; Rhode Island Forging Steel, 1985–86; Planner, General Dynamics, 1986–90; Exec. dir., Northeast Corridor Initiative, 1990–92.

DC Office: 141-A RSOB, 20510, 202-224-2921; Fax: 202-228-2853; Web site: chafee.senate.gov.

State Offices: Newport, 401-845-0700; Providence, 401-453-5294.

Committees: *Banking, Housing & Urban Affairs*: Financial Institutions; Housing & Transportation; International Trade & Finance. *Environment & Public Works*: Superfund & Waste Management (Chmn.); Transportation

& Infrastructure. *Foreign Relations*: European Affairs; International Economic Policy, Export & Trade Promotion; Near Eastern & South Asian Affairs (Chmn.); Western Hemisphere, Peace Corps, Narcotics Affairs.

Group Ratings

	ADA	ACLU	AFS	LCV	CON	ITIC	NTU	COC	ACU	NTLC	CHC
2002	45	60	50	76	100	50	52	63	53	36	—
2001	65	—	42	50	—	—	49	64	44	—	20

National Journal Ratings

	2001 LIB	—	2001 CONS		2002 LIB	—	2002 CONS
Economic	53%	—	47%		53%	—	46%
Social	55%	—	44%		46%	—	52%
Foreign	48%	—	51%		48%	—	49%

Key Votes of the 107th Congress

1. Approve Bush Tax Cuts	Y	5. Confirm Ashcroft as AG	Y	9. Bar Coop. with Intl. Court	N
2. Expand Patients' Rights	Y	6. Bar Gays in the Boy Scouts	N	10. Trade Promotion Authority	Y
3. Campaign Finance Reform	Y	7. $ for Hate Crime Prosecution	Y	11. Authorize Force in Iraq	N
4. Permit ANWR Development	N	8. Overseas Military Abortions	Y	12. Homeland Sec. Dept. Union	Y

Election Results

2000 general	Lincoln Chafee (R)	222,588	(57%)	($2,265,221)
	Robert A. Weygand (D)	161,023	(41%)	($2,297,885)
	Other	7,742	(2%)	
2000 primary	Lincoln Chafee (R)	unopposed		
1994 general	John H. Chafee (R)	222,856	(65%)	($2,086,236)
	Linda J. Kushner (D)	122,532	(35%)	($805,867)

Lincoln Chafee, the junior senator from Rhode Island, was appointed to the office in November 1999, a week after the death of his father, Senator John Chafee. He was only the second son appointed to the Senate to succeed his father; the other was Harry Byrd, Jr., in 1965. Lincoln Chafee grew up in Warwick, Rhode Island, on a 20-acre estate; there he developed his love of horses. "The outside of a horse is good for the inside of a man," he likes to say. His father was elected governor when he was eight, and he remembers going to the 1964 Republican National Convention, at 11, and the hostility of the Goldwater supporters there for Rockefeller Republicans. In 1969 John Chafee became Secretary of the Navy; Lincoln Chafee was at Andover, where one of his schoolmates was Jeb Bush. In 1976 John Chafee was elected to the Senate; the year before, Lincoln Chafee graduated from Brown, where he was captain of the wrestling team, and went off to horseshoeing school at Montana State University. For seven years he worked as a farrier at racetracks in the United States and Canada. In 1984 he returned to Rhode Island. In 1985 he was elected to the Rhode Island Constitutional Convention and in 1986 was elected to the city council in Warwick, the state's second largest city. In 1992 he was elected mayor of Warwick, by 335 votes, the first Republican in 32 years. He was reelected three times, and as mayor privatized the solicitor's office, produced an economic development plan for the T.F. Green Airport area and left the city with a $6.6 million surplus. In March 1999, John Chafee announced that he would not seek re-election in 2000; the next day Lincoln Chafee announced he would run for the seat. The older Chafee was a productive legislator who was greatly beloved in Rhode Island, respected as a member of one of Rhode Island's "Five Families," who had volunteered for the Marine Corps and served in combat in World War II and Korea.

John Chafee died in October 1999. After a week of mourning, Governor Lincoln Almond appointed Lincoln Chafee to the Senate. He had not been running strong in the polls against possible Democratic opponents, and some thought he was hurt when in August 1999 he admitted he had used cocaine. In the Senate he promised to continue in his father's tradition and pursued many of his interests. On one of his first votes he was one of four Republicans to vote against the party's minimum wage bill. In 2000 he voted with Democrats on the estate tax and HMO regulation. But he said he would not switch parties—"I'm named after Abraham Lincoln"—and said that Senate Republican leaders "have been very understanding of my votes." Obviously they understood that only a Republican who often voted with Democrats, and probably only a Chafee, could hold this seat in the nation's most Democratic state.

Certainly he could expect Democratic competition. Senate seats don't come up often in Rhode Island: John Chafee held his for 23 years, Claiborne Pell for 36, John Pastore for 26, Theodore Green for 24—they, plus Jack Reed, were the state's only senators from 1950 to 1999. The first Democrat to announce was 2d District Congressman Robert Weygand, who was not on good terms with machine Democrats. Democrat Patrick Kennedy of the 1st District, busy traversing the country as chairman of the Democratic Congressional Campaign Committee, was expected to back state House Speaker John Harwood, but when he didn't run backed former Lieutenant Governor Richard Licht. For five months the two Democrats battered each other with charges and countercharges. Weygand backers pointed out that Licht's wife and children lived in Massachusetts, where she was a state judge; Licht said they lived together on weekends in the Rhode Island resort town of Little Compton. Weygand won the September 12 primary by a 57%–43% margin, but wounds still stung: Not until September 30 did Patrick Kennedy and Senator Jack Reed endorse Weygand.

In the meantime, the Republican Senate campaign committee was running ads praising Chafee for his independence and citing his votes against Republican positions on HMO regulation and prescription drugs. One Chafee ad accused Weygand of "embroidering the truth" in an ad about his Labrador retriever taking the arthritis drug Lodine. Weygand ran negative spots attacking Chafee's record as mayor, linking him with right-wing Republicans, depicting him as a pawn of the pharmaceutical industry. Democrats made much of a $6,000 fund Chafee used as mayor to buy presents for children of city employees and contribute to charity. Chafee actually spent less than Weygand. Chafee won 57%–41%, running 25% ahead of George W. Bush in Rhode Island.

After the election Chafee said he liked the tone of the Bush campaign, but he did not like many of the early Bush policies—the ban on aid to international organizations that provide abortion counseling, support of oil drilling in the Arctic National Wildlife Refuge, renunciation of the Kyoto treaty, moves toward abrogation of the ABM treaty, reversal of Bush's little noticed one-sentence commitment to reduce levels of carbon dioxide. Chafee was the first Senate Republican to oppose the Bush tax cut in 2003. He voted with Democrats and John McCain on campaign finance in March 2001. In the spring Democratic Whip Harry Reid approached Chafee and asked if he wanted to switch parties. Chafee said no; as he explained later, "Back in the spring of 2001, it was just this avalanche—we had the tax cuts and were getting out of the missile defense treaty. And I thought, I have to do something. What can I do? But the next step that had to be taken, as you say, I was just constitutionally incapable." But he didn't discourage Jim Jeffords from switching in May. Again and again he broke ranks with Republicans—on the budget and tax cut in May 2001, on HMO regulation in June, on a letter urging Tom Daschle to bring up the defense appropriation first in March 2002, on the Department of Homeland Security in September. With John Breaux and Ben Nelson, he developed a compromise on homeland security in September; Bush refused to accept it. He said in June 2001 he would consider switching parties if Republicans won back a majority in the Senate. But when they gained two seats in and a 51–49 majority in November 2002, he said, "No. I've always said that's an extreme step." Of course a switch in those circumstances would not give the Democrats a majority. He was one of the Republican senators who said Trent Lott had to go in December 2002. "I believe it's time to make a change. I think the process is happening." And he was dismayed by the Bush tax cut and other proposals in January 2003.

On the Environment Committee his father once chaired, he is now chairman of the Superfund Subcommittee. With ranking member Barbara Boxer he has backed the reimposition of the Superfund tax on oil and chemical companies that lapsed in 1995. After MTBE seeped into the water supply in Pascoag in September 2001 he wrote a bill for stronger regulation of underground storage tanks. He is also chairman of the Near Eastern and South Asian Affairs Subcommittee of Foreign Relations. He has generally opposed Bush administration policy in the region. In September 2001 he struggled before voting to authorize military action against the Taliban and expressed fears that it would have grave unintended consequences in the region; in October he said his fears had not been borne out. He fervently opposed military action in Iraq up through March

2003. Some conservatives wanted to keep him out of the chairmanship, but he was third in seniority (because more senior members were denied waivers to stay or get back on the committee) and that entitled him to his choice of subcommittee chairs. But he noted that subcommittees are not very powerful.

Chafee comes up for reelection in 2006. In early 2003 there was speculation about which of Rhode Island's many fractious Democrats would run against him. It focused on newly elected Secretary of State Matt Brown and Attorney General Patrick Lynch and term-limited Lieutenant Governor Charles Fogarty.

FIRST DISTRICT

Rep. Patrick Kennedy (D)

Elected 1994, 5th term; b. July 14, 1967, Brighton, MA; home, Portsmouth; Providence Col., B.A. 1991; Catholic; single.

Elected Office: RI House of Reps., 1988–94.

DC Office: 407 CHOB 20515, 202-225-4911; Fax: 202-225-3290; Web site: www.house.gov/patrickkennedy.

District Office: Pawtucket, 401-729-5600.

Committees: *Appropriations* (18th of 29 D): Commerce, Justice, State & Judiciary; Labor, HHS & Education.

Group Ratings

	ADA	ACLU	AFS	LCV	CON	ITIC	NTU	COC	ACU	NTLC	CHC
2002	90	71	100	100	70	38	16	40	8	0	0
2001	95	—	100	93	—	—	8	32	4	—	—

National Journal Ratings

	2001 LIB	—	2001 CONS		2002 LIB	—	2002 CONS
Economic	70%	—	31%		88%	—	10%
Social	83%	—	11%		66%	—	34%
Foreign	70%	—	28%		59%	—	40%

Key Votes of the 107th Congress

1. Approve Bush Tax Cuts	N	5. Faith-Based Charities	N	9. Trade Promotion Authority	N
2. Limit Patients' Bill of Rights	N	6. Bar Gays in the Boy Scouts	N	10. Bar Funds for Intl. Court	N
3. Campaign Finance Reform	Y	7. Ban Partial-Birth Abortion	Y	11. Authorize Force in Iraq	Y
4. Ban ANWR Development	Y	8. Arm Commercial Pilots	Y	12. Deny Home. Sec. Dept. Union	N

Election Results

2002 general	Patrick Kennedy (D)	95,233	(60%)	($2,935,810)
	David Rogers (R)	59,316	(37%)	($1,972,236)
	Other	4,314	(3%)	
2002 primary	Patrick Kennedy (D)	unopposed		
2000 general	Patrick Kennedy (D)	123,442	(67%)	($1,263,102)
	Stephen Cabral (R)	61,522	(33%)	($8,902)

Prior Winning Percentages: 1998 (67%); 1996 (69%); 1994 (54%)

The People		Race/Ethnic Origin	Ancestry	
Area size:	565 sq. mi.	82.6% White	Irish: 12.9%	Italian: 11.4%
Urban population:	95.5%	4.1% Black	Portuguese: 9.3%	
Rural population:	4.5%	1.9% Asian	**2000 Presidential Vote**	
Pop. 2000:	524,157	0.3% Native Am.	Gore (D)................125,174	(63%)
Median income:	$40,616	0.0% Hawaiian	Bush (R)................61,396	(31%)
Poverty status:	11.9%	2.3% Two+ races	Other..................12,705	(6%)
Military veterans:	12.5%	1.3% Other	**Cook Partisan Voting Index:** D +17	
		7.5% Hispanic Origin		

Occupation	Blue collar: 23.2%	White collar: 61.3%	Gray collar: 15.5%

The 1st Congressional District is the eastern half of Rhode Island, east of Narragansett Bay, a line that cuts through Providence and then proceeds west and north to the Massachusetts-Connecticut-Rhode Island border. It includes much of Providence (including elite East Side and College Hill around Brown University) and all of next-door Pawtucket whose Slater Mill is known as the birthplace of the American Industrial Revolution. The onetime textile mill towns of the Blackstone Valley, Woonsocket and Central Falls are also in the 1st, along with high-income Barrington and Bristol and, south on the ocean, the old city of Newport, with its restored 18th century houses and the summer "cottages" that are really palaces. Newport was once home to the America's Cup races and now hosts a famous jazz festival; it is also the site of the oldest synagogue in North America, to whose congregation George Washington declared that the United States gives "to bigotry no sanction, to persecution no assistance." Ethnically, this district is the more French-Canadian and the less Italian of the two Rhode Island districts; politically, it is strongly Democratic.

The congressman from the 1st District is Patrick Kennedy, a Democrat elected in 1994. Patrick Kennedy was born in 1967, his father Edward Kennedy's fifth year in the Senate; a week after his second birthday came the terrible accident at Chappaquiddick. He grew up in McLean, Virginia, and had a somewhat troubled youth, spending time in a drug rehabilitation clinic in 1986 before enrolling at Providence College, at 20, in 1987. Almost immediately, in 1988, he ran for a seat in the state House and beat the longtime incumbent John Skeffington as the tiny (population 9,800) district was inundated with visits by Kennedy family members and funds raised by the Kennedy national fundraising network. He became chairman of the Rules Committee in 1992, a year after spending the now-infamous Easter weekend in Palm Beach with his father and cousin William Kennedy Smith. In 1994, when the 1st District's Congressman Ron Machtley ran for governor, Kennedy decided to run for Congress. Kennedy had an attractive and energetic Republican opponent, Kevin Vigilante, a doctor who worked with handicapped orphans in Romania and with female prison inmates infected with HIV. Vigilante was a moderate on issues and raised enough to spend $803,000. But Kennedy had the advantages of money and his family name, and won 54%–46% in a Republican year.

In the House Kennedy has had a liberal voting record and has proven an excitable if not always eloquent debater. He started off by avoiding national media and working on local issues, from the Naval Undersea Warfare Center in Newport to visas for Portuguese immigrants. He voted for the partial-birth abortion ban and unsuccessfully backed casino gambling rights for the Narragansett Indians. He has been strongly opposed to Fidel Castro, whom he blames for the death of his uncle John F. Kennedy; he voted for the Helms-Burton Act and backed the 2000 bill that would have made Elian Gonzalez a U.S. citizen. He has strongly supported gun control—another issue with family reverberations—and embarrassed himself in June 1999 when he told reporters House Democrats had "written off the rural areas" because of gun control. In February 2001 he sought permanent residence status for Liberian refugees, many of whom live in Rhode Island.

After winning re-election by 69%–28% in 1996, he took on a more combative role and seemed to be eyeing a race for the Senate seat held by John Chafee. He criticized Chafee sharply for several votes but Chafee fought back gamely, returning often to the state, working hard on local projects, and his standing in the polls, never weak, slowly rose. Meanwhile, the harshness of Kennedy's attacks evidently grated; his job approval fell from 62% to 44% during the year. In 1998

Kennedy's career took another turn. In April he said he wanted a seat on Appropriations—not a likely goal if he intended to seek only one more term in the House. He struck up a friendship with Minority Leader Dick Gephardt; Kennedy let it be known that he would support Gephardt for president against Al Gore. When Gephardt decided not to run for president, but to concentrate on helping Democrats win a House majority, he enlisted Kennedy as a key ally. In November 1998, after Kennedy easily won reelection, Gephardt named him chairman of the DCCC. A few days later Kennedy announced what was already pretty plain, that he would not run for the Senate.

As DCCC chairman, Kennedy excelled not as a strategist but as a fundraiser. He traveled indefatigably around the country to fundraisers, and made yeoman efforts to raise soft money, even while calling for campaign finance legislation that would outlaw it. As a result, the DCCC in 1999 and 2000 raised nearly $50 million in soft money, reaching parity with its Republican counterpart, the NRCC; the NRCC raised more hard money, but Kennedy vastly reduced the disadvantage his party labored under in the 1996 and 1998 cycles. He was less successful in other respects. In May 2000 he brought a RICO racketeering suit against Republican Whip Tom DeLay, arguing that he was extorting contributions from various groups. But some Democrats as well as many Republicans said that this was a misuse of the RICO statute, and after DeLay threatened to take depositions of every House Democrat, the suit was dropped. Nor were Democrats successful in their efforts to regain a majority in the House. They needed only a net gain of six seats, and they benefited from Gephardt's success in persuading senior Democrats and incumbents who held their districts more through personal popularity than party strength to run for one more term. But voters in 2000, as in 1998 and 1996, were in a pro-incumbent mood, and it proved hard to persuade them to oust Republican incumbents. Despite Gephardt's and Kennedy's efforts to recruit locally strong candidates, Democrats won only nine of the 35 open seats. A week after the election, Kennedy announced he would not serve another term as DCCC chairman. Gephardt tried to change his mind, but did not succeed.

Instead he seemed to be moving from national politics to concentration on Rhode Island, where he had spent only 40 days in 1999 and 2000, and where his standing was decline because of a series of imbroglios. In March 2000, he shoved an airport security guard in Los Angeles, sending her backward and jostling the metal detector archway. A police complaint was filed, but the Los Angeles city attorney decided against prosecution. In an informal hearing in May 2000, Kennedy apologized to the woman. But she sued him in March 2001, and Kennedy said his insurance company would handle the suit. The insurance company, it appeared, had already been busy settling claims against Kennedy by owners of sailboats he had chartered. In August 1999 a rented boat required assistance from the Coast Guard after becoming entangled in fishing nets, and suffered several thousand dollars damage; Kennedy docked the boat and drove off, leaving his security deposit to pay for it. In July 2000, the Coast Guard was summoned to a boat Kennedy had rented; it was revealed in November 2000 that Kennedy had ruined the engine and damaged the rigging. In November 2000 his insurance company settled a claim that he had damaged a 42-foot sloop rented in Mystic, Connecticut, and abandoned it off Martha's Vineyard in August 2000. None of this hurt him in the 2000 election. Against a Republican who spent $9,000, he won 67%–33%. But his job approval in the district fell from 63% in February 2000 to 42% in September 2001. Republicans were talking about making a serious challenge in 2002.

In January 2001 Kennedy took back the seat on Appropriations to which he had been named in 1998, but from which he had taken a leave of absence to chair the DCCC. He worked on some other legislation, co-sponsoring the mental health parity bill which passed in the Senate but did not come to a vote in the House, but he mostly concentrated on getting federal money, especially defense dollars, for Rhode Island. In the 2002 campaign Kennedy claimed he had brought $90 million to the district, more per capita, he boasted, than his father's colleague and erstwhile rival Robert Byrd. His involvement in military issues may help to explain his differences with his father on the B-1 bomber and the Iraq war resolution, both of which Patrick Kennedy supported. He spoke often about Iraq with his father, who asked him sharp questions about his stand but didn't seem perturbed by it.

Three Republicans ran for the seat. The early favorites were former state Human Services Director Christine Ferguson and Michael Battles, a former Army Ranger. But the winner of the primary, with 38% of the vote, was the most conservative candidate, David Rogers, a Portsmouth technical analyst and former Navy Seal. He raised money through direct mail—you can raise a lot that way running against a Kennedy—and ultimately spent $2 million. Rogers attacked Kennedy for holding a fundraiser in April in Harrah's in Las Vegas and for paying his chief of staff an extra $40,000 for campaign work; the man resigned the congressional staff job in September. That month Rogers reported that someone had loosened all the lugnuts on his tire and that his campaign manager's windshield was smashed and laptop stolen. Kennedy called a talk show in October and told Rogers that he had concocted the story. Kennedy ran ads portraying Rogers as a friend of the National Rifle Association and questioning his stand on prescription drugs. Rogers ran ads asking, "How does Patrick Kennedy feel about airport security?" and showing a tape of the LAX incident and another saying his behavior with the rented boats was "arrogant, unstable and embarrassing." Kennedy's standing seems to have improved as the year went on, as he spent time in the state (Rhode Island is small enough that people expect to see their officeholders) and argued that he was bringing in money. In November he won 60%–37%.

Patrick Kennedy's political career has taken several courses. At first it seemed he was headed to a lifetime Senate seat, like his father; but he turned aside from running for the Chafee seat. Then he seemed to be a transforming figure in national politics, when he was chairman of the DCCC; but when his standing with voters declined, he backed away from that. Now he seems to be that stock figure, the long-serving congressman who quietly and behind the scenes funnels federal money into his district for many years. He did take some part in national politics in January 2003, when he endorsed Dick Gephardt for president. But instead of flying with him around the country, he asked him to come up to Rhode Island and invited all the local Democratic politicians.

SECOND DISTRICT

Rep. Jim Langevin (D)

Elected 2000, 2d term; b. Apr. 22, 1964, Warwick; home, Warwick; RI Col., B.A. 1990, Harvard U., M.P.A. 1994; Catholic; single.

Elected Office: RI House of Reps., 1988–94; RI Sec. of State, 1994–00.

DC Office: 109 CHOB 20515, 202-225-2735; Fax: 202-225-5976; Web site: www.house.gov/langevin.

District Office: Warwick, 401-732-9400.

Committees: *Armed Services* (20th of 29 D): Projection Forces; Terrorism, Unconventional Threats & Capabilities. *Select Committee on Homeland Security* (22d of 23 D): Cybersecurity, Science and Research & Development; Intelligence & Counterterrorism (RMM).

Group Ratings

	ADA	ACLU	AFS	LCV	CON	ITIC	NTU	COC	ACU	NTLC	CHC
2002	85	53	100	100	89	38	20	45	8	3	42
2001	85	—	100	93	—	—	10	35	28	—	—

National Journal Ratings

	2001 LIB	—	2001 CONS		2002 LIB	—	2002 CONS
Economic	77%	—	23%		82%	—	17%
Social	58%	—	42%		53%	—	46%
Foreign	61%	—	36%		69%	—	30%

Key Votes of the 107th Congress

1. Approve Bush Tax Cuts	N	5. Faith-Based Charities	N	9. Trade Promotion Authority	N
2. Limit Patients' Bill of Rights	N	6. Bar Gays in the Boy Scouts	N	10. Bar Funds for Intl. Court	Y
3. Campaign Finance Reform	Y	7. Ban Partial-Birth Abortion	Y	11. Authorize Force in Iraq	N
4. Ban ANWR Development	Y	8. Arm Commercial Pilots	Y	12. Deny Home. Sec. Dept. Union	N

Election Results

2002 general	Jim Langevin (D)	129,312	(76%)	($774,848)
	John Matson (R)	37,740	(22%)	($5,964)
	Other	2,323	(1%)	
2002 primary	Jim Langevin (D)	unopposed		
2000 general	Jim Langevin (D)	123,805	(62%)	($1,041,752)
	Rodney R. Driver (CFC)	42,625	(21%)	($274,183)
	Robert G. Tingle (R)	27,932	(14%)	
	Other	4,536	(2%)	

The People		Race/Ethnic Origin	Ancestry	
Area size:	980 sq. mi.	81.2% White	Italian: 16.7%	Irish: 14.4%
Urban population:	86.3%	3.9% Black	English: 9.8%	
Rural population:	13.7%	2.6% Asian	**2000 Presidential Vote**	
Pop. 2000:	524,162	0.5% Native Am.	Gore (D)...............124,314	(60%)
Median income:	$44,129	0.0% Hawaiian	Bush (R)...............69,076	(33%)
Poverty status:	11.9%	1.6% Two+ races	Other 14,366	(7%)
Military veterans:	13.1%	0.3% Other	**Cook Partisan Voting Index:** D +14	
		9.8% Hispanic Origin		

Occupation	Blue collar: 22.6%	White collar: 60.8%	Gray collar: 16.6%

The 2d Congressional District is the western half of Rhode Island. While the 1st includes many mill towns, the 2d has most of its population in working- and middle-class towns like Cranston and Warwick which, despite their British names, are inhabited mostly by people with Irish, Italian, French and Portuguese surnames. The 2d also includes the fastest-growing part of the state: South County, which is not an official place but the common name for Rhode Island south of East Greenwich, including the affluent suburbs to the south along Narragansett Bay, the Kingston home of the University of Rhode Island, and the area around Westerly, where many residents work at the Electric Boat shipyards in Groton, Connecticut. It includes Rhode Island's rolling farm land, though there is not that much acreage, and the communities along the Bay and the Ocean, where many people still make their living building boats and catching fish. Redistricting exchanged only small parts of Providence between the 1st District and the 2d, and politically both are heavily Democratic districts.

The congressman from the 2d District is Jim Langevin, a Democrat first elected in 2000. Langevin grew up in Warwick, and as a boy hoped to become an FBI agent. But in 1980, at age 16, when he was a police cadet in the Boy Scout Explorer program, he was shot by a police officer when a gun accidentally discharged. The bullet went through his upper back and throat and damaged the upper part of his spinal column; ever since, he has been a quadriplegic, getting around in a wheelchair, the first to serve in Congress. He received $2.2 million in a settlement with the city of Warwick and currently hires a home health care aide; it takes him two and a half hours to get dressed each morning. This tragic accident focused attention on him, at first unwanted, but he says it made him determined to make something of his life. He worked as an intern in the State House and for Senator Claiborne Pell. In 1988, while he was a student at Rhode Island College, he was elected to the state House of Representatives, where he styled himself as a reformer; his 1st District colleague Patrick Kennedy was also elected that year to the state House as a college student. While in the state House Langevin graduated from college and received a master's degree from the Kennedy School at Harvard. In 1994 Langevin was elected Rhode Island's secretary of state. In 1998 he issued a report called "Access Denied," exposing secret meetings held by legislators in violation of Rhode Island's open meetings laws.

When Congressman Bob Weygand ran for the Senate in 2000, Langevin decided to run for his House seat. It was a four-way race in the Democratic primary, and Langevin's most strenuous opposition came from Kate Coyne-McCoy, executive director of the Rhode Island Association of Social Workers. Langevin had support from many Democratic Party leaders and some unions, and won the party endorsement at the April convention, from which Coyne-McCoy angrily withdrew. But she waged an aggressive campaign, financed by unions, health care workers and EM-

ILY's List. "There's no such thing as being too liberal," Coyne-McCoy said. Langevin called her positions "unrealistic and extreme." He backed non-government universal health care coverage, prescription drug coverage in Medicare and HMO regulation—the standard Democratic program that year. He favored less stringent forms of gun control and said, "No one has to tell me how dangerous weapons can be." Coyne-McCoy attacked Langevin for opposing abortion rights. He said, "because of what happened to me, I became aware of how precious life is . . . I'm pro-life." He spoke often of the accident that paralyzed him: "Certainly, being disabled is part of who I am, but it doesn't define me." In the September primary, he led Coyne-McCoy 47%–29%. In the general, his chief opposition came from Rodney Driver, nominee of the Conscience for Congress Party, a retired mathematics professor who spent $300,000 of his retirement savings. Langevin won with 62%, to 21% for Driver.

In the House, Langevin has been liberal on economic issues and more centrist on cultural and foreign issues. The House chamber was made wheelchair-accessible for Langevin, with two of the fixed seats removed to give him space to maneuver and talk to colleagues. He used his experience as Secretary of State in the House debate on election procedures; he favored setting minimum federal standards but giving ultimate responsibility to state officials. He served as a liaison with disability groups on that bill and worked closely with Steny Hoyer of the House Administration Committee. Because he has only limited use of his hands, Langevin was unable to cast a secret ballot until Rhode Island purchased special voting machines. Despite the opposition of anti-abortion groups, he urged George W. Bush to support stem-cell research, arguing that it might alleviate suffering from certain diseases and injuries and assist infertile couples to have children. He filed several gun control bills. After the September 11 attacks, he urged steps to permit Congress to conduct its business electronically in the event of a disaster. He won reelection easily.

★ SOUTH CAROLINA ★

S outh Carolina, at times beleaguered and under attack, stands proud but not untroubled, a state that has made much progress but still feels it has some distance to go. Within living memory, this state looked like an underdeveloped country: Beneath a thin veneer of rich people, it was among the poorest of states, with income levels less than half the national average and with high levels of illiteracy and disease. South Carolina was founded by planters from Barbados and even today there are reminders of the West Indies—the semitropical climate, the lush foliage and trademark palmettos, and the billions of damage from hurricanes. But economically and culturally, South Carolina is now clearly part of the booming South Atlantic region from Maryland to Florida, filling up with new retirement condominiums, factories and office buildings, giant shopping centers, growing robustly in the 1990s.

South Carolina started off with a plantation economy built on the swampy Low Country below the Fall Line, where the great 18th and 19th century planters built rice paddies and cultivated exotic crops like indigo in the days before cotton was king. The great wealth of these Low Country planters was destroyed by the Civil War which they, more than any other Southerners, provoked. But their pride and way of life continued as did that of former slaves. As late as 1940, 43% of South Carolinians were black, most living in conditions inconceivable today. South Carolina's economic growth started only in the 1920s, with that lowest-wage of industries, textiles. Mills were built in the Up Country above Columbia, hiring poor whites (never blacks) from the hardscrabble farms in the area. Politics remained a rough business, with harsh appeals to racial fear and economic envy, and with limited participation: in 1940, just 99,000 South Carolinians voted for president, 96% of them Democratic—the highest Democratic percentage in the nation. In the 1946 Democratic primary, the year Strom Thurmond was elected governor, only 271,000 people voted in a state of more than 2 million.

Now this once underdeveloped country has joined the First World: The 2000 Census counted 4 million South Carolinians, 30% of them black, 2% Hispanic. Personal incomes rose 40% in the

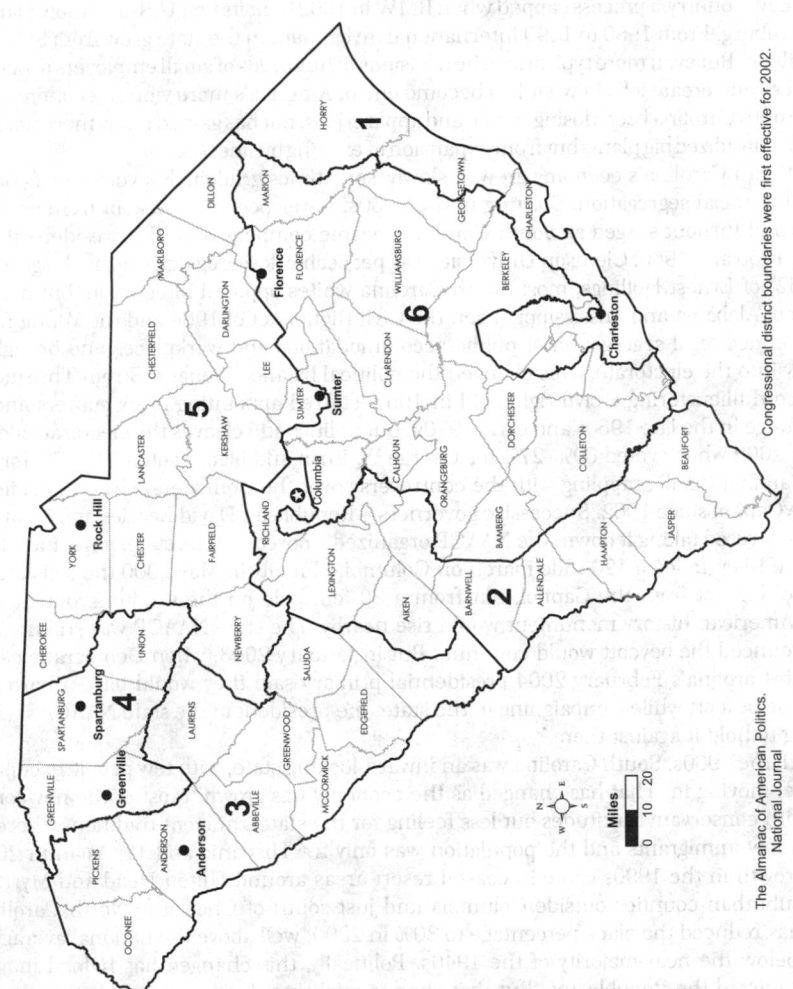

1990s, up toward national levels, and poverty fell sharply; health standards are as good as those in the rest of the nation; educational achievement still lags, though not nearly so much as before, with 80% of white and 65% of black adults high school graduates; homeownership is above the national average. South Carolina was helped for some years by the military bases clustered around Charleston, by the big textile mills around Greenville and Spartanburg, and by the outmigration of Low Country blacks to big cities of the Northeast. Then, starting in the 1970s, South Carolina became the most aggressive state in the South in attracting new industry. It advertised its business climate (the nation's lowest rates of unionization), its taxes (low) and its willingness to meet local employers' needs (very high). It enticed French and German firms to set up major operations in the Piedmont and the Low Country, a process capped when BMW in 1992 built its first U.S. assembly plant off I-85 in Spartanburg. From 1960 to 1990 international investment in the state grew from $80 million to $16.4 trillion. But even more typical are the decisions of hundreds of small employers to open plants, rent offices and create jobs in what has become one of America's more vibrant economic environments. South Carolina keeps losing textile and apparel jobs, but has gained many more not from government-subsidized big plants but from expansion of existing businesses.

As South Carolina's economy grew, it slowly, sometimes grudgingly, overcame its heritage of slavery and racial segregation. Starting in the 1950s, fewer people were kept from voting by the poll tax, and turnout surged as South Carolina became competitive in the presidential elections of 1952, 1956 and 1960. Clemson University was peaceably desegregated during the governorship (1959–62) of Ernest Hollings; most South Carolina whites opposed integration, but not with the violence of Alabama and Mississippi. Then the Civil Rights Act of 1964 and the Voting Rights Act of 1965 ended legal segregation of public accommodations and workplaces and brought blacks suddenly into the electorate. This changed the political balance. Senator Strom Thurmond, who set a record filibustering a civil rights bill in 1957, started appointing black staffers and a black federal judge in the late 1960s and early 1970s. But politics still cleaves the electorate along racial lines: In 2000 whites voted 69%–27% for George W. Bush and blacks voted 91%–7% for Al Gore. South Carolina is still grappling with the controversy over the Confederate battle flag, flown over the state Capitol since 1962. Successive governors—Republican David Beasley and Democrat Jim Hodges—favored taking it down; the NAACP organized a boycott of the state; longtime Charleston Mayor Joe Riley Jr. led a 120-mile march on Columbia. Finally in May 2000 the legislature voted to fly the flag not from the Capitol, but from a 30-foot pole on the Capitol grounds, while an African-American history monument would rise nearby. The state NAACP was still not satisfied, and announced the boycott would continue. But in January 2003, when Democratic candidates for South Carolina's February 2004 presidential primary said they would have a hard time observing the boycott while campaigning in the state, the president of the state NAACP said, "We're not going to hold it against them."

Until the 1960s, South Carolina was an inward-looking state, with few people except military personnel moving in. That has changed as the economy has grown. Most of the newcomers are white, with conservative attitudes but less feeling for the state's ancient traditions; there have as yet been few immigrants and the population was only 2% Hispanic and 1% Asian in 2000. The fastest growth in the 1990s came in coastal resort areas around Hilton Head and Myrtle Beach and in suburban counties outside Columbia and just south of Charlotte, North Carolina. This growth has reduced the black percentage to 30% in 2000, well above the national average of 12% but far below the near-majority of the 1940s. Politically, this changed has helped move South Carolina toward the Republicans. But that change might not have occurred without the efforts of two individuals. One was Strom Thurmond, who had voted for Franklin Roosevelt at the 1932 Democratic National Convention, but who switched to the Republican party in September 1964 and provided critical votes to nominate Richard Nixon at the 1968 Republican National Convention. South Carolina voted for Barry Goldwater in 1964 and Nixon in 1968 and has only voted once—and narrowly—for a Democrat since then (Jimmy Carter in 1976). The other individual was Carroll Campbell, elected governor in 1986 and 1990, who with the aid of Lee Atwater built a Republican party capable of electing statewide officials and majorities in the legislature. In 1988 Campbell and Atwater, by then George H. W. Bush's campaign manager, set up the early Republican primary, on the Saturday before Super Tuesday, which enabled George H. W. Bush to clinch the Republican nomination that year; it did the same for Bob Dole in 1996 and, against John McCain's strong challenge, for George W. Bush in 2000. In 1989 Campbell and Atwater seemed to be Thurmond's heirs. But Atwater died of a brain tumor at 39 in 1991. In 1994 Campbell helped his protege David Beasley win the governorship and supported Thurmond's campaign for an unprecedented eighth Senate term. It was widely assumed that Campbell, making good money as a Washington lobbyist, would be appointed to fill Thurmond's seat if it should become vacant. But Beasley was defeated for reelection in 1998 and in 2001 Campbell announced that, at 61, he was battling Alzheimer's disease. Thurmond served out his eighth term as he had the other seven and as a United States senator celebrated his 100th birthday in December 2002.

South Carolina politics now belongs to a new generation, with the vivid exception of Senator Ernest Hollings, who after 36 years as a junior senator—the longest in history—became senior senator when Thurmond's term expired in January 2003. The state continues to be heavily Republican, though Democrats have been competitive and cannot be counted out. In 1998 Hollings was reelected to a sixth full term by a 53%–46% margin over Congressman Bob Inglis, and Democrat Jim Hodges upset Beasley 53%–45%. Beasley was hurt by his switch on the Confederate battle flag and by his opposition to video poker. But in 2000, voters went Republican up and down the line: George W. Bush carried the state 57%–41% and Republicans, after a party switch, took control of the state Senate 24–22; they already had a majority in the state House. Bush carried the Greenville metro area 65%–33%, the Columbia-Aiken metro area 57%–41%, the Charleston metro area and the coastal counties 56%–42% and the rest of the state, with its rural black-majority counties and lingering Democratic tradition, 52%–46%. In 2002 the Republican trend continued. Republicans had a fierce primary and runoff for governor, and the surprise winner, former Congressman Mark Sanford, who moved to the state as an adult, beat Hodges 53%–47%. In the race to succeed Thurmond Democrats put up an attractive and articulate candidate, College of Charleston President Alex Sanders. But Congressman Lindsey Graham, famous after his lead role in the impeachment of Bill Clinton, won 54%–44%. Interestingly, both Sanford and Graham had actively backed John McCain in the 2000 presidential primary, when most party leaders backed George W. Bush. Republicans won six of the eight downballot races and won majorities of 25–21 in the state Senate and 73–51 in the state House.

The People		Race/Ethnic Origin			Military veterans: 420,971 (14.0%)	
Pop. 2000:	4,012,012	2,652,291	66.1%	White	WWII: 16.1%	Korea: 12.0%
Pop. 1990:	3,486,703	1,178,486	29.4%	Black	Vietnam: 34.1%	Gulf War: 13.1%
Change 1990–2000:	Up 15.1%	35,568	0.9%	Asian	**Most populous cities:**	
Change 1980–1990:	Up 11.7%	12,765	0.3%	Native Am.	1. Columbia	116,278
% of U.S. total:	1.4%	1,270	0.0%	Hawaiian	2. Charleston	96,650
Pop. rank:	26th of 50	33,290	0.8%	Two+ races	3. North Charleston	79,641
Area size:	32,020 sq. mi.	3,266	0.1%	Other	4. Greenville	56,002
State Native:	64.0%	95,076	2.4%	Hisp. Origin	5. Rock Hill	49,765
Non-citizen:	1.8%	**Ancestry**			Urban population: 60.5%	
Language		USA: 11.9%		German: 7.2%	Rural population: 39.5%	
English: 92.6%	Spanish: 4.0%	English: 7.0%		Irish: 6.8%		
Other Eur.: 2.5%		Scotch-Irish: 2.5%				

Education		Work Sector		General Assembly	
H.S. Grad:	76.3%	Private: 78.1%	Govt: 15.9%	Senate	25 R 21 D
College Grad:	20.4%	Self: 5.7%	Family: 0.3%	House	73 R 51 D
Industry		Unemployment: 5.7%		Legislative Term Limits: No	
Agri: 1.1%	Con: 8.3%	**Household Income**		**Registered Voters**	
Fin: 5.6%	Info: 2.1%	<15k: 18.8%	15-35k: 28.3%	No party registration	
Mfg: 24.4%	Prof: 25.5%	35-50k: 17.6%	50-100k: 27.3%		
Public: 4.7%	Trade: 15.2%	100-150k: 5.3%	>150k: 2.8%		
Other: 13.0%		Median: $37,082			
Occupation		Poverty status: 14.1%			
Blue collar: 30.4%	White collar: 54.2%	**Home Value**			
Gray collar: 15.3%		<50k: 24.3%	50-100k: 38.3%	100-200k: 26.9%	200-300k: 6.1%
		300-500k: 3.0%	>500k: 1.5%	Median: $83,100	

Presidential politics In presidential general elections South Carolina is reliably Republican. It was the only Deep South state to vote for Richard Nixon over George Wallace in 1968 and since then has voted Democratic only once, for Jimmy Carter in 1976. It was one of the top three Republican states in 1988 and 1992; it was solidly Republican in 1996 and 2000.

South Carolina does not set one day for presidential primaries or caucuses; each of its two major party selects a date and decides whether it will be a primary or caucus. In 1987 Lee Atwater purposefully scheduled the Republican primary here for the Saturday before Super Tuesday, and in 1988 George Bush won a 49%–21%–19% victory over Bob Dole and Pat Robertson, forecasting the Southern sweep that clinched his nomination four days later. Democrats chose their delegates by caucus; a Democratic primary would have had an electorate about 50% black and would surely have produced a victory for South Carolina

2000 Presidential Vote		
Bush (R)	786,892	(57%)
Gore (D)	566,039	(41%)
Nader (Green)	20,279	(1%)
Other	10,832	(1%)

2000 Republican Presidential Primary		
Bush (R)	305,998	(53%)
McCain (R)	239,964	(42%)
Keyes (R)	25,966	(5%)

1996 Presidential Vote		
Dole (R)	573,458	(50%)
Clinton (D)	506,283	(44%)
Perot (I)	64,386	(6%)

native Jesse Jackson, which would not have been helpful to the party in state elections. In 1992 Bush beat Pat Buchanan 67%–26%, squashing Buchanan's claims to Southern support. Democrats held a primary the same day, which Bill Clinton won with 63% of the vote; 148,000 voted in the Republican primary and 116,000 in the Democratic. In 1996 former Governor Carroll Campbell and Governor David Beasley led a grass-roots campaign that gave Bob Dole, after his disappointing showings elsewhere, an impressive 45%–29% victory over Buchanan; turnout was 276,000. And in 2000 Campbell and Beasley, both now ex-governors, supported George W. Bush, as he beat John McCain 53%–42%. Turnout was 573,000 of which 10% were self-identified Democrats and 30% were self-identified Independents; McCain carried both those groups, but lost by a wide margin among self-identified Republicans. Democrats chose their delegates by caucus in 1996 and 2000.

In 2004 Democrats will hold a primary February 3, one week after New Hampshire; Republicans will choose their delegates by caucus. South Carolina was the first of several primaries scheduled for that date, and one that was paid heavy attention by the candidates and the press; as early as May 2, 2003, all nine announced candidates and the press trouped down to Columbia for the earliest presidential candidates' debate in history. The big mystery about the South Carolina primary is the turnout. It will certainly be the first contest with a significant number of black voters; Iowa's population is 2% black and New Hampshire's 1%. Blacks could turn out to be a majority of primary voters; the November 2000 exit poll showed that 53% of South Carolina Gore voters were black. But because there is no simultaneous Republican contest, self-identified Independents and Republicans can vote in the Democratic primary, and may—to an unknown extent. In early 2003 Democratic candidates were paying plenty of attention to 6th district Congressman Jim Clyburn, who said he will not make an endorsement until late in the campaign, and to other black politicians and prominent black ministers. But it is possible that some—particularly John Edwards and Joe Lieberman—might strike themes designed to appeal to white South Carolinians who usually or often vote Republican.

Congressional districting Control of the South Carolina redistricting process was split between Democratic Governor Jim Hodges and the Republican-controlled legislature. The legislature, after toying with proposals for major changes, passed in September 2001 a plan with no major changes. It expanded the black-majority 6th District, which extends from Columbia to Charleston and includes much of the Low Country and Pee Dee area, and increased its black percentage from 61% to 63%. Hodges vetoed the plan and Republicans failed to override. A three-judge

108th Congress Lineup	
4 R	2 D
107th Congress Lineup	
4 R	2 D

federal court took over, and in March 2002 decided on a plan that smoothed out the lines considerably and reduced the black percentage in the 6th District to 57%. The delegation seems likely to remain 4–2 Republican for some time.

Governor

Mark Sanford (R)

Elected 2002, term expires Jan. 2007, 1st term; b. May 28, 1960, Ft. Lauderdale, FL; home, Charleston; Furman U., B.A. 1983; U. of VA, M.B.A. 1988; Episcopalian; married (Jenny).

Elected Office: U.S. House of Reps., 1994–00.

Professional Career: Real estate investor, 1988–92; Owner, Norton & Sanford real estate investment firm, 1992–02.

Office: P.O. Box 12267, Columbia, 29211, 803-734-2100; Fax: 803-734-5167; Web site: www.state.sc.us/governor.

Election Results

2002 general	Mark Sanford (R)	585,422	(53%)
	Jim Hodges (D)	521,140	(47%)
2002 runoff	Mark Sanford (R)	183,820	(60%)
	Bob Peeler (R)	121,881	(40%)
2002 primary	Mark Sanford (R)	122,143	(39%)
	Bob Peeler (R)	119,026	(38%)
	Charlie Condon (R)	49,469	(16%)
	Ken Wingate (R)	12,366	(4%)
1998 general	Jim Hodges (D)	574,035	(53%)
	David Beasley (R)	486,342	(45%)
	Other	16,758	(2%)

Mark Sanford, a Republican and something of a maverick, was elected governor of South Carolina in 2002. He grew up in Fort Lauderdale, the son of a heart surgeon; the family spent summers and vacations on 3,000-acre farm in Beaufort County, once known as Coosaw Plantation, and moved there permanently when Mark was 18. He graduated from high school in South Carolina and from Furman University in Greenville and the University of Virginia business school. He worked in real estate investment in New York where he met his wife, a Midwesterner; in 1992 he started a real estate investment firm in Charleston. He lives in the suburb of Sullivans Island and is perpetually tanned from windsurfing in the ocean. In 1994, 1st District incumbent Arthur Ravenel ran for governor, and Sanford, with no political experience, ran for the House. It was a family campaign, managed by his wife and financed by $100,000 of his own money. Sanford campaigned as an outsider: he called for term limits and cutting the deficit; he said citizen-legislators needed to replace career politicians; he pledged to serve only three terms, to take no PAC money, to vote for no tax increases and to refuse any salary increase until the budget was balanced. Emphasizing his outsider status, he finished second in the primary and then won the runoff 52%–48%. He carried the general election with 66%.

In the House Sanford voted more often than almost any other member against spending increases. But he took moderate positions on some issues and often bucked the Republican leadership. He strongly advocated term limits and made a point of sleeping on a futon in his office and returning home as often as possible. He was one of the few members voting against measures passed by nearly unanimous votes: a bill to preserve sites significant to the Underground Railroad, a defense appropriation that included funds for Charleston harbor. He opposed what he considered pork barrel spending, including demonstration projects for Charleston's Cooper River

South Carolina / *Governor*

bridges; he opposed building I-73 to Charleston. He spent much of late 1999 and early 2000 campaigning for John McCain across the state, as did Lindsey Graham, even though most state Republican insiders backed George W. Bush.

Back in South Carolina full-time in 2001 Sanford started running for governor. Well known and well liked in Charleston and the coast, he was unknown in the rest of the state, and he set about getting better acquainted. In April 2001 he launched a "working tour," taking his turn at doing various jobs. He moved his family to Greenville for the month of June 2001, where he attended community functions and delivered the commencement address at Furman. He was not the only Republican running. Lieutenant Governor Bob Peeler, originally from Cherokee County east of Greenville-Spartanburg, was traveling around the state in his trademark red pickup truck; he had backed George W. Bush in 2000 and was supported by most of the state Republican establishment, although former Governor Carroll Campbell endorsed Sanford. Attorney General Charlie Condon, who had won much publicity from his conservative stands on hot-button issues, had been running for the Senate, but switched abruptly to the governor race.

Their ultimate target was Governor Jim Hodges, the Democrat who had upset Republican incumbent David Beasley in 1998. Hodges was an obscure legislator whose main accomplishment was an all-day kindergarten bill. His chief plank was a lottery to pay for college scholarships, similar to Zell Miller's HOPE scholarships in Georgia, and for school construction and all-day kindergarten. Beasley was hurt when he switched and called for removal of the Confederate battle flag from the Capitol; Hodges, who backed a statewide referendum on video poker, was helped by video poker operators' heavy spending against Beasley, and won 53%–45%. In July 1999 the legislature passed a bill banning video poker unless voters decided in a referendum to keep it. But one small video poker filed a lawsuit to overturn the law, and in October 1999 the state Supreme Court upheld the ban but overturned the referendum: on July 1, 2000, video poker was gone, and with it much of Hodges's financial base. Hodges played a major role in getting the legislature to vote in May 2000 to take the Confederate flag off the dome and put it up on the Capitol grounds; he also got the legislature to pass a Martin Luther King Holiday, plus a Confederate Memorial Day in May. Hodges's biggest success came when voters approved the lottery in November 2000 and it was passed by the legislature in June 2001. In his first three years Hodges raised teacher pay and increased school construction, while tests scores improved. But he also sparked controversy when in June 2001 he vetoed a plan to reduce the sales tax on food by 1% to curb state college tuition increases. Despite his achievements, Hodges's job ratings were not particularly high, and Republicans were confident they could beat "the accidental governor," as some called him, in this basically Republican state.

The three Republicans called for major changes in taxes and spending. Sanford liked to say, "People pay a wealth premium to live in South Carolina" and pointed out that the 7% top income tax rate kicked in at $12,000. He proposed phasing out the income tax over 18 years and making up for fluctuations in revenues with a transition fund established by a sales tax on gas. He also called for school vouchers. Peeler called for eliminating state property taxes and car taxes in two years and called for tax credits for the textile and high-tech industries and called for changing Hodges's early school programs to focus on reading-accountability. Condon called for cutting state spending 15%. Sanford, capitalizing on his ties in the business world and from the McCain campaign, raised more money and ran more ads than the other two. Peeler led in polls in the run up to the June 11 primary, and many expected that Condon would cut into Sanford's Low Country base. Instead, Sanford finished first with 39% of the vote, just ahead of Peeler's 38%; Condon, who carried only one small county, was far behind with 16%. Sanford had huge strength in metro Charleston and the coast, where he beat Peeler 59%–16%, with 19% for Condon; Sanford also beat Peeler 42%–35% in metro Columbia-Aiken. In metro Greenville in the Up Country, Sanford's early campaigning helped him hold Peeler to a 51%–26% lead, while in the rest of the state Peeler led by 48%–29%.

Still, Sanford carried only 11 of 46 counties, and standard analysis would suggest that more of the culturally conservative Condon's votes would go to Peeler in the June 25 runoff. But the race was not defined ideologically. Peeler's strategists felt this "looks like more of a Bush-McCain thing" and that he would win if he could argue that Sanford was not a real conservative. Peeler criticized Sanford for votes on the breast cancer stamp, military housing and supporting military action; Sanford said these issues were taken out of context and were "negative." Congressman Lindsey Graham, nominated unopposed for senator on June 11, cut a spot endorsing Sanford; Sanford won 60%–40%. He carried metro Charleston and the coast 84%–16% and metro Columbia-Aiken 63%–37%. And he cut deep into Peeler's base, holding him to just over 50% in metro Greenville and the rest of the state.

Hodges approached the general election campaign much as Peeler had the runoff. The day after the runoff negative ads started running, spotlighting Sanford's votes in the House. Hodges played up his modest background and recalled working in a textile mill for $2.10 an hour, and called Sanford a wealthy Charleston plantation owner from south Florida. But Hodges had embarrassments of his own. One of his ads attacked Sanford for having voted "against programs for disabled kids." But then it was revealed that Hodges had transferred $300,000 from the Continuum of Care for Emotionally Disturbed Children fund to the operating account for the governor's office. Hodges had also been embarrassed by his failure to keep an oft-repeated promise to block the shipment of spent plutonium to the Savannah River Site for reprocessing. Energy Secretary Spencer Abraham promised that the reprocessed fuel would be shipped out of state, but Hodges wanted a commitment in writing and in April 2002 brought a suit in federal court. This backfired: in June 2002, a week before the runoff, a federal judge ordered Hodges not to block the shipment; Hodges backed down on his promise to stand in the road in front of the convoy. "It is a sad day for South Carolina when the governor . . . who has taken an oath to uphold the Constitution must be ordered by a court to obey it," the judge said.

Hodges had more money, but Sanford seemed to attract more attention. Dressed usually in khakis and a plaid shirt, he talked about his plans for change and getting away from politics as usual. He criticized the state Republican party, run by Peeler backers, when it hired as executive director a man who had been fired from a similar job in Virginia after listening in clandestinely to a Democratic strategists' conference call. In November Sanford won 53%–47%. Metro Charleston and the coast, which had voted for Hodges in 1998, this time went 55%–45% for Sanford. So did metro Columbia-Aiken. The Greenville area gave Sanford a 60%–40% margin. Hodges carried the rest of the state by only 55%–45%.

As governor, Sanford continued to defy convention. He invited a black minister who was one of the leaders of the NAACP boycott to deliver a prayer at his inauguration; some Republican legislators complained. He instituted an "open door at four" policy: citizens could line up to get five-minute audiences with the governor (they sometimes went longer). He wondered out loud whether he should quit the Air Force Reserve, lest he be called to active duty; he decided to stay in and arranged that Lieutenant Governor Andre Bauer, 33, another McCain supporter, should become acting governor. He was not called up but did spend two weeks in the spring in training. From the legislature he asked some pretty major changes: abolishing the elective offices of secretary of state, treasurer, comptroller, adjutant general, superintendent of education and agriculture commissioner, and putting their functions under the governor; putting the state universities, accustomed to lobbying for themselves, under a single board of regents; enacting school vouchers ("education passports") for children in failing schools. He seemed more likely to have success on expanding incentives to business and requiring full disclosure of contributions to state political parties. And he faced serious fiscal problems.

Senior Senator

Ernest Hollings (D)

Elected 1966, seat up 2004, 6th term; b. Jan. 1, 1922, Charleston; home, Charleston; The Citadel, B.A. 1942, U. of SC, LL.B. 1947; Lutheran; married (Peatsy).

Military Career: Army, 1942–45 (WWII).

Elected Office: SC House of Reps., 1948–54, Speaker Pro-Tem, 1951–54; SC Lt. Gov., 1954–58; SC Gov., 1958–62.

Professional Career: Practicing atty., 1947–55, 1963–66.

DC Office: 125 RSOB, 20510, 202-224-6121; Fax: 202-224-4293; Web site: hollings.senate.gov.

State Offices: Charleston, 843-727-4525; Columbia, 803-765-5731; Greenville, 864-233-5366.

Committees: *Appropriations*: Commerce, Justice, State & Judiciary (RMM); Defense; Energy & Water Development; Homeland Security; Interior; Labor, HHS & Education. *Budget. Commerce, Science & Transportation* (RMM): Aviation; Communications (RMM); Oceans, Fisheries & Coast Guard.

Group Ratings

	ADA	ACLU	AFS	LCV	CON	ITIC	NTU	COC	ACU	NTLC	CHC
2002	85	60	100	65	58	38	19	55	15	9	—
2001	90	—	83	88	—	—	7	50	29	—	40

National Journal Ratings

	2001 LIB —	2001 CONS		2002 LIB —	2002 CONS
Economic	66%	34%		66%	32%
Social	65%	32%		52%	46%
Foreign	51%	43%		64%	33%

Key Votes of the 107th Congress

1. Approve Bush Tax Cuts	N	5. Confirm Ashcroft as AG	N	9. Bar Coop. with Intl. Court	Y
2. Expand Patients' Rights	Y	6. Bar Gays in the Boy Scouts	Y	10. Trade Promotion Authority	N
3. Campaign Finance Reform	Y	7. $ for Hate Crime Prosecution	Y	11. Authorize Force in Iraq	Y
4. Permit ANWR Development	N	8. Overseas Military Abortions	Y	12. Homeland Sec. Dept. Union	Y

Election Results

1998 general	Ernest Hollings (D)	563,296	(53%)	($4,968,456)
	Bob Inglis (R)	488,217	(46%)	($2,143,278)
	Other	17,444	(2%)	
1998 primary	Ernest Hollings (D)	unopposed		
1992 general	Ernest Hollings (D)	591,030	(50%)	($4,188,829)
	Tommy Hartnett (R)	554,175	(47%)	($886,816)
	Other	35,233	(3%)	

Prior Winning Percentages: 1986 (63%); 1980 (70%); 1974 (70%); 1968 (62%); 1966 (51%)

Ernest Hollings, after 36 years as South Carolina's junior senator, the longest-serving junior senator in history, became senior senator in January 2003, at 80, on the retirement of 100-year-old Strom Thurmond. Hollings grew up in Charleston, in moderate but not aristocratic circumstances, graduated from The Citadel and served in the Army in combat in World War II. Returning home, he worked as a trial lawyer and was elected to the legislature in 1948, at 26, and was a member of the leadership two years later; he was elected governor in 1958, at 36, serving as South Carolina first faced school desegregation, which thanks to his efforts proceeded in an orderly fashion—a considerable achievement at the time. Hollings also set up the state's technical colleges, which he credits for some of South Carolina's manufacturing growth. He then spent four years out of office until he beat another former governor in the 1966 special election Senate race. In 1968 he went on hunger tours in the Low Country and in 1970 wrote *The Case Against Hunger,* and later co-authored the WIC program. Hollings has one of the quickest and sharpest tongues in the Senate and an instinct for zeroing in on others' weaknesses—though he sometimes gets himself in trouble.

Hollings has served on the Senate Budget Committee longer than anyone else. In the early 1980s he argued for a budget freeze. In 1983 and 1984 he ran for president; his candidacy did not get far, but when spending was frozen a dozen years later the budget was balanced not long after. In 1985 he co-sponsored the Gramm-Rudman-Hollings deficit-cutting bill, which did in fact lead to lower deficits. When the May 1997 budget agreement was reached, Hollings insisted that it would not produce a surplus, since the total of government and intragovernmental debt (including Social Security's Treasury IOUs) would still be rising; he offered to jump off the Capitol dome if the Treasury ever reported a surplus.

Hollings spent much of the 1990s working on telecommunications issues, as Chairman or ranking minority member on the Commerce Committee and its Communications Subcommittee. Telecom issues were probably the most intellectually demanding and certainly the most heavily lobbied issues in Congress during many of those years, and Hollings managed to keep an even keel—and to get legislation passed. Hollings's instinct is to regulate at the federal level, which puts him at odds with many trends of the times. He was the major opponent of deregulating broadcasting and a major proponent of the 1992 Cable Reregulation Act, the one law on which Congress overrode George H. W. Bush's veto. But he has also been the most persistent backer of what became the telecommunications act of 1996, for more competition between long distance companies and the regional Bells. He first raised the issue in the early 1990s, then worked hard as a bill passed the House in 1994; but it died in the Senate because Hollings insisted that regional Bell companies get actual competition in local service before they were permitted to enter the long distance or cable markets. In 1995 and 1996, Hollings worked with new Chairman Larry Pressler to produce a bipartisan bill, which was signed into law in February 1996.

Hollings has worked since then to superintend the deregulatory process, working to block the regional Bells from the long distance market and Internet business. He continued to insist on FCC rather than state regulation of the rates regional Bells could charge long distance companies for interconnecting their wires, but at the same time criticized the FCC for its enforcement, or non-enforcement, of the act. In 2001 and 2002 he vigorously opposed the Dingell-Tauzin bill, passed in the House, to allow the Bells to provide broadband service; after he became Chairman of the committee in June 2001 it was apparent it was going nowhere in the Senate. He has decried the 1995 FCC rule change that lifted the limit on the number of radio stations a media company can buy and opposes FCC Chariman Michael Powell's moves to lift other limits. He has taken the side of the media content providers over high-tech companies on the issue of copying, and sponsored a bill to require anti-piracy chips to be installed in personal computers, handheld organizers and other electronic equipment. Another Hollings bill would require the high-tech and media industries to agreeing on devices to prevent unauthorized copying of copyrighted material or have one imposed on them by the FCC; but that has been blocked by the Judiciary Committee.

In 2002 Democrats lost their majority, and the chairmanship went back to John McCain, with whom Hollings has had stormy relations. In May 1998 Hollings vigorously opposed the tobacco bill that McCain passed through the committee 19–1 after it was changed to phase out tobacco price supports; there are many tobacco farmers in the corner of South Carolina around Marlboro and Chesterfield counties. In early 1999 he seemed to mistrust McCain for his presidential candidacy, though he did join with him in sponsoring a bill to require software to block inappropriate material from the Internet wired up to schools under a Gore-backed FCC measure. After September 11, Hollings was skeptical when the airlines sought a bailout; on September 15 he said, "I would be willing to consider compensation if they give up monopolistic control of the nation's hub airports." But he held hearings September 20 and worked for a bill imposing tough conditions; he added provisions guaranteeing service for small communities and capping executives' pay raises for airlines that got federal money. In October 2001 Hollings and McCain agreed that airline security should be turned over to federal employees; that view prevailed unanimously in the Senate and in conference committee, despite opposition from the House and the Bush administration. Hollings was a staunch opponent of allowing pilots to carry guns, but in July 2002, when it was clear that large majorities in both houses were in favor, he said he would not block a vote. "I am not the mother superior. Let them vote." He sponsored a port security bill which passed. On the committee he has been a great supporter of Amtrak, backing in 2002 and 2003 a $4.6 billion package with $1.3 billion for security, $1.3 billion for development of high-speed corridors in the Northeast and $1.5 billion for them in the rest of the country, plus $580 million for long distance trains; he has plans for a passenger rail network linking Greenville, Columbia, Florence, Charleston and Myrtle Beach with Atlanta, Charlotte and Raleigh.

Hollings has been one of the Senate's strongest opponents of free trade and one of its strongest backers of trial lawyers. On trade, he has worked to protect textile jobs in South Carolina, even though they are in long-term decline and the state has been growing anyway. He opposed NAFTA and caused GATT to be postponed until after the 1994 elections over the objections of then-Majority Leader George Mitchell, and then voted against. He filibustered the Africa and Caribbean trade bill in November 1999 until cloture was voted 74–23. He delivered a long speech against PNTR with China in September 2000 and sought to retain annual review and to drop the words "permanent" and "normal." He remembers his own days as a trial lawyer and regards plaintiff's attorneys as fighters for the rights of the little guy. He opposed the 1999 Y2K relief bill as an infringement on the right to sue. He was one of three Democrats to oppose the McCain-Feingold campaign finance bill. Twice he has sponsored amendments to the First Amendment to allow Congress to set "reasonable limits" on campaign contributions and spending; they were defeated 61–38 in March 1997 and 67–33 in March 2000. A longtime supporter of Israel, in 2002 he referred to Ariel Sharon as "the Bull Connor of Israel" and added, "You can't be bulldozing houses and wonder why little kids are throwing rocks."

In increasingly Republican South Carolina, Hollings won his fifth and sixth terms by relatively narrow margins—50%–47% over former Congressman Tommy Harnett in 1992 (his January 1991 vote against the Gulf war resolution may have hurt) and 53%–46% over Congressman Bob Inglis in 1998. Inglis eschewed pork barrel spending and promised to serve only 12 years and asked Hollings to join him in a "courteous" campaign. This is not Hollings's style; in mid-October Hollings described Inglis to the *Rock Hill Herald* in mid-October thusly: "He finesses all around. He is Jack be nimble, Jack be quick. He's all around the damn clock, so oozing and goozing and such a nice little choirboy and so pleasant, and everybody's rude, and he wants to be courteous. He is a goddamn skunk." He apologized the next day, and said he was angered by "the gross distortions of my record and the callous accusations that have been leveled against me"—obviously staff-written language, without the authentic Hollings touch. Hollings's not-so-secret weapon was money; he outspent Inglis, who promised not to take PAC money, by $4.9 million to $2.1 million. Hollings organized a turnout drive that had a major effect on election day; he also benefited from the lively campaign of Governor Jim Hodges, financed heavily by video poker money.

Will Hollings run again in 2004, when he turns 82? In August 2000 he told a cheering South Carolina Democratic convention that he would, but in late 2002 and early 2003 he was more circumspect, while his staffers said they were assuming he would. Certainly age should not be a barrier in a state that reelected Strom Thurmond just one month before he turned 82, 88 and 94. But if he does run he seems likely to have strong competition again and, if George W. Bush is as strong in November 2004 as he was in early 2003, this will be the first time he will have run in a year when a Republican presidential candidate is sweeping the state. Announced candidates in early 2003 were 4th District Congressman Jim DeMint, Myrtle Beach Mayor Mark McBride and former Attorney General Charlie Condon, who started to run for the Senate in 2001 and in 2002 switched to the governor race and finished third in the Republican primary. It was widely understood that DeMint had the backing of the Bush White House. If Hollings does not run, the Democratic field is thin. "If not Fritz, then who?" asked local political columnist Lee Bandy. "There just aren't any Democrats, which tells you something about the condition of the party. It's in bad shape."

Junior Senator

Lindsey Graham (R)

Elected 2002, seat up 2008, 1st term; b. July 9, 1955, Central; home, Seneca; U. of SC, B.A. 1977, J.D. 1981; Baptist; single.

Military Career: Air Force, 1982–88; SC Air Natl. Guard, 1989–94 (Operation Desert Storm); Air Force Reserves, 1995–present.

Elected Office: SC House of Reps., 1992–94; U.S. House of Reps., 1994–02.

Professional Career: U.S. Air Forces Europe Circuit Trial Counsel, 1984–88; Asst. Oconee Cnty. Atty., 1988–92; Practicing atty., 1988–94; Judge Advocate, McEntire Air Natl. Guard Base, 1989–94; Central SC City Atty., 1990–94.

DC Office: 290 RSOB, 20510, 202-224-5972; Fax: 202-224-1189; Web site: lgraham.senate.gov.

State Offices: Columbia, 803-933-0112; Florence, 843-669-1505; Greenville, 864-250-1417; Mount Pleasant, 843-849-3887; Washington, 202-224-5972.

Committees: *Armed Services*: Emerging Threats & Capabilities; Seapower; Strategic Forces. *Health, Education, Labor & Pensions*: Children & Families. *Judiciary*: Antitrust, Competition Policy & Consumer Rights; Constitution, Civil Rights & Property Rights; Crime, Corrections & Victims' Rights (Chmn.). *Veterans' Affairs*.

Group Ratings (as Member of U.S. House of Representatives)

	ADA	ACLU	AFS	LCV	CON	ITIC	NTU	COC	ACU	NTLC	CHC
2002	15	0	11	25	72	62	54	70	83	89	83
2001	15	—	10	14	—	—	64	78	88	—	—

National Journal Ratings (as Member of U.S. House of Representatives)

	2001 LIB —	2001 CONS	2002 LIB —	2002 CONS
Economic	22%	74%	47%	53%
Social	0%	81%	39%	57%
Foreign	21%	74%	24%	72%

Key Votes of the 107th Congress (as Member of U.S. House of Representatives)

1. Approve Bush Tax Cuts	Y	5. Faith-Based Charities	Y	9. Trade Promotion Authority	N
2. Limit Patients' Bill of Rights	Y	6. Bar Gays in the Boy Scouts	Y	10. Bar Funds for Intl. Court	Y
3. Campaign Finance Reform	Y	7. Ban Partial-Birth Abortion	Y	11. Authorize Force in Iraq	Y
4. Ban ANWR Development	N	8. Arm Commercial Pilots	Y	12. Deny Home. Sec. Dept. Union	Y

Election Results

2002 general	Lindsey Graham (R)	600,010	(54%)	($6,213,563)
	Alex Sanders (D)	487,359	(44%)	($4,211,812)
2002 primary	Lindsey Graham (R)	unopposed		

Prior Winning Percentages: 2000 House (68%); 1998 House (100%); 1996 House (60%); 1994 House (60%)

South Carolina's junior senator is Lindsey Graham, a Republican elected in 2002. Graham grew up in Pickens County, where his parents owned a beer joint. His parents died after he went to college at the University of South Carolina; he became his younger sister's legal guardian. He was the first in his family to graduate from college, then received a master's and a law degree from the University of South Carolina, and then served in the Air Force as a prosecutor in Germany, Crete and other distant locales. In 1988 he returned home and practiced law in Seneca, the same town where North Carolina Senator John Edwards grew up; he also served as a judge advocate at McEntire Air National Guard Base. He was called up to active duty and served stateside during the Gulf war. In 1992 he was elected to the state House. In 1994, with the retirement of 20-year Congressman Butler Derrick, Graham ran for the House. Both parties had contested primaries, but the Republican contest attracted more votes—41,000 versus 35,000—and Graham won without a runoff with 52% of the vote. In the general he faced state Senator Jim Bryan. Graham called for term limits, supported more defense spending and opposed gays in the military. His attitude toward the Clinton administration and the Democratic leadership was unequivocal: "I'm one less vote for an agenda that makes you want to throw up." Bryan also campaigned as a conservative—pro-life, anti-gays in the military, against employer mandates in health care, against defense cuts—and boasted of his legislative experience. Graham modeled his campaign after Bob Inglis's successful 1992 race in the next-door 4th District and won 60%–40%—a smashing victory in a district represented only by Democrats since Reconstruction.

In the House Graham had a solidly conservative voting record but did not always support the Republican leadership. In July 1997 he helped organize the fight to overthrow Speaker Newt Gingrich. This coup soon foundered, and in a Republican Conference meeting, when Dick Armey said no member of the leadership was involved, Graham lunged to the microphone to contradict him.

As a member of the Judiciary Committee, Graham played a major role in the impeachment of Bill Clinton. When Clinton defenders quibbled about the meaning of words and insisted that Clinton's deposition testimony was "legally accurate," Graham exploded in opposition. He was especially upset at the way Clinton used the official powers of the White House to discredit Monica Lewinsky. Yet he voted against impeaching Clinton for lying in the Paula Jones deposition, on the ground that it was later ruled immaterial by the judge. In the Senate trial Graham's folksy manner and clear description of Clinton's offenses—"Where I come from, a man who calls someone up at 2:30 in the morning is up to no good"—made him one of the most effective managers. On other issues, he passed in the House in 1999 and 2001 the Unborn Victims of Violence Act which makes it a separate crime to injure an unborn child when assaulting a pregnant woman. He defied most South Carolina Republican leaders and supported John McCain in 2000 and was a tireless and highly visible supporter all over South Carolina.

Senator Strom Thurmond, reelected to his eighth term in 1996 one month before he turned 94, promised not to run again in 2002. Thurmond's political career spanned most of the 20th century: As a delegate to the Democratic National Convention he voted for Franklin Roosevelt in 1932, he was on the beach on D-Day (he had to get an exemption because he was over age) in 1944, was elected Governor of South Carolina in 1946 and was the presidential candidate of the State's Rights Democratic party in 1948. In 1954 he was elected to the Senate as a write-in candidate and in 1964 he switched to the Republican party; at the 1968 Republican National Convention he provided critical support for Richard Nixon. A segregationist for years, he switched after the Voting Rights Act was passed and was the first Southern senator to hire black staffers and nominate a black federal judge. He worked assiduously on South Carolina projects, sent out thousands of letter to South Carolinians and was reelected without difficulty to more Senate terms than anyone else in American history. He celebrated his 100th birthday as a U.S. senator at a party in the Capitol that made news.

It is not often that a Senate seat comes open in South Carolina; the last time one did was in 1941 (Thurmond and Ernest Hollings both won their seats by beating incumbent senators appointed to fill vacancies). Yet in this now heavily Republican state Graham had no opposition in the Republican primary: his work on impeachment and in the McCain campaign made him well known and well liked statewide. He was endorsed by three former governors and Bob Dole; Strom Thurmond added his endorsement in November 2001. Democrats portrayed him as lacking in substance, and state Democratic Chairman Dick Harpootlian said on the day Graham announced in February 2001 that he was "light in the loafers"; Graham accused him of slander since the phrase is sometimes used as a pejorative reference to homosexuality. Harpootlian, perhaps disingenuously, denied any such imputation. But for all their bravado, state and national Democrats had a hard time coming up with a candidate; eight prominent Democrats turned them down. Finally they found a candidate, and an attractive one at that, Alex Sanders, president of the College of Charleston, with a colorful resume. Sanders ran off as a teenager and joined the circus, and was briefly a juggler and fire eater; in 1966 he was elected to the state House, in 1974 he lost a race for lieutenant governor, in 1976 he was elected to the state Senate, in 1985 he was appointed to the state Court of Appeals and in 1992 he was named college president. Sanders was also a folksy raconteur, gifted at telling hundreds of old stories, charming and well connected around the state. He resigned as college president and announced for the Senate September 5, 2001.

Sanders was an active and energetic candidate. He dialed assiduously for dollars, even as he complained about being handed a script, and raised eventually $4.2 million, below Graham's $5.8 million, but a considerable achievement for a candidate who was always behind in the polls. He charmed reporters and was profiled by Joe Klein in the *New Yorker* and on *60 Minutes*. He said that he "hadn't been a very good Democrat" and that he was a member of the National Rifle Association and the Sons of Confederate Veterans as well as the NAACP. He supported the Bush tax cuts (though he said he was for more tax cuts only to create jobs) and military action in Iraq. But he opposed the death penalty, on religious grounds. And he opposed a constitutional amendment to allow criminalization of flag burning. Graham hammered him on the death penalty and the flag amendment but most of all on his party. "Let me tell you, the big difference between my opponent and myself is who's in control of the U.S. Senate." He said Sanders would advance the liberal agenda of Tom Daschle, Hillary Rodham Clinton and Edward Kennedy, and pointed to his contributions from Democratic celebrities. "Barbra Streisand, great singer, very liberal. My opponent is a nice guy, but he's getting Democratic support out the ying-yang." Democratic ads hit Graham for supporting individual investment accounts in Social Security. Graham stood his ground and argued that the system would be broke by 2040, when many of today's voters would be about to retire. Sanders attacked Graham for supporting gubernatorial nominee Mark Sanford's gas tax increase. In one of their four debates Sanders, perhaps weary of being attacked for associating with glamorous liberals, said of Graham's endorsement by Rudolph Giuliani, "He's an ultraliberal. His wife kicked him out and he moved in with two gay men and a Shih Tzu. Is that South Carolina values? I don't think so." But Sanders was put on the defensive by his own comment that South Carolinians could prove they were not racists by voting for him. Trying to explain, he said, "When I said I would show America that we are not ignorant, racist, redneck Dixiecrats, I was referring to the false stereotype many people in the North have of us in South Carolina. None of these terms are applicable to Senator Thurmond, and I most certainly was not referring to him."

Graham won 54%–44%, about the margin one might have projected from the polls. Graham ran just a little bit better than Mark Sanford in all parts of the state and came close to carrying the part of the state outside the big metro areas. So Graham took the place of a senator first elected in the year before he was born. He said that his goals were legislation to state that South Carolina is not the permanent depository for plutonium, a teacher loan forgiveness bill and supporting George W. Bush, although he differed from him on trade, military retiree pay, drought relief and trial lawyer issues.

FIRST DISTRICT

Rep. Henry Brown (R)

Elected 2000, 2d term; b. Dec. 20, 1935, Bishopville; home, Hanahan; The Citadel; Baptist Col.; Baptist; married (Billye).

Military Career: SC Natl. Guard, 1953–62.

Elected Office: Hanahan City Council, 1981–85; SC House of Reps., 1985–00.

Professional Career: V.P., Piggly Wiggly Carolina Co., 1958–85.

DC Office: 1124 LHOB 20515, 202-225-3176; Fax: 202-225-3407; Web site: www.house.gov/henrybrown.

District Offices: Myrtle Beach, 843-445-6459; N. Charleston, 843-747-4175.

Committees: *Budget* (10th of 24 R). *Transportation & Infrastructure* (25th of 41 R): Highways, Transit & Pipelines; Water Resources & Environment. *Veterans' Affairs* (10th of 17 R): Benefits (Chmn.).

Group Ratings

	ADA	ACLU	AFS	LCV	CON	ITIC	NTU	COC	ACU	NTLC	CHC
2002	0	13	0	0	50	100	53	95	96	86	100
2001	0	—	0	7	—	—	61	96	92	—	—

National Journal Ratings

	2001 LIB	—	2001 CONS		2002 LIB	—	2002 CONS
Economic	22%	—	74%		21%	—	73%
Social	0%	—	81%		0%	—	75%
Foreign	33%	—	60%		24%	—	72%

Key Votes of the 107th Congress

1. Approve Bush Tax Cuts	Y	5. Faith-Based Charities	Y	9. Trade Promotion Authority	Y
2. Limit Patients' Bill of Rights	Y	6. Bar Gays in the Boy Scouts	Y	10. Bar Funds for Intl. Court	Y
3. Campaign Finance Reform	N	7. Ban Partial-Birth Abortion	Y	11. Authorize Force in Iraq	Y
4. Ban ANWR Development	N	8. Arm Commercial Pilots	Y	12. Deny Home. Sec. Dept. Union	Y

Election Results

2002 general	Henry Brown (R)	127,562	(89%)	($189,806)
	James Dunn (UCIT)	9,841	(7%)	
	Other	5,022	(4%)	
2002 primary	Henry Brown (R)	47,084	(79%)	
	Bob Batchelder (R)	12,680	(21%)	
2000 general	Henry Brown (R)	139,597	(60%)	($606,776)
	Andy Brack (D)	82,622	(36%)	($485,733)
	Other	9,227	(4%)	

The People		Race/Ethnic Origin	Ancestry	
Area size:	3,419 sq. mi.	73.7% White	German: 9.6%	USA: 9.3%
Urban population:	78.4%	20.9% Black	English: 8.9%	
Rural population:	21.6%	1.2% Asian	**2000 Presidential Vote**	
Pop. 2000:	668,668	0.4% Native Am.	Bush (R)	139,758 (59%)
Median income:	$40,713	0.1% Hawaiian	Gore (D)	91,510 (38%)
Poverty status:	11.5%	1.1% Two+ races	Other	6,849 (3%)
Military veterans:	17.2%	0.1% Other	**Cook Partisan Voting Index:** R +11	
		2.5% Hispanic Origin		

Occupation   Blue collar: 23.0%   White collar: 59.7%   Gray collar: 17.3%

Looking out across the harbor to Fort Sumter are the glorious mansions of the Battery, gazing on the same view that the hot-blooded young swells of Charleston saw in April 1861 when they fired the shots that began the Civil War. Today there are few more beautiful urban scenes in America than the pastel "single houses" of Charleston, built flush with the sidewalk, turning their shoulders to the streets, with open piazzas inside their iron gateways facing south to catch the breeze. Charleston, founded in 1670, was blessed with one of the finest harbors on the Atlantic, at the point where, Charlestonians say, the Ashley and Cooper Rivers meet to form the Atlantic Ocean. It was one of the South's two leading cities through the Civil War; across its docks went cargoes of rice, indigo, cotton and slaves, enriching the white planters and merchants who dominated the state's economic and political life. After the Civil War, Charleston became an economic backwater, enabling the old buildings to survive; more recently, prosperity and insurance payouts after Hurricane Hugo in 1989 have funded loving restorations, making the center city look better than ever—and able to attract an annual $3 billion in tourism revenue.

This old society, descended from Barbados planters and French Huguenots, Sephardic Jews and the second sons of English gentry, was once a leading force in American political life. The hotheads in the gallery disrupted the 1860 Democratic National Convention here so boisterously that it was adjourned and reconvened in Baltimore, while Southern Democrats split off and nominated their own candidate, enabling Abraham Lincoln to win with 38% of the popular vote. The local accent, which seems to outsiders to have a touch of New Jersey and which can be incomprehensible when rapidly spoken, is best appreciated in the speech of Charlestonian Senator Ernest Hollings on C-SPAN2 (you may want to click the closed caption button). The history of black South Carolinians, memorialized in George Gershwin's *Porgy and Bess*, is long and note-worthy, but the tale of slavery, once hidden under a blanket of politeness, is only now emerging, as many, though not all, plantations near Charleston add programs on the history of slavery to tours once dominated by romantic tales of the old South.

Some 25 years ago, Navy and Air Force bases accounted for 20% of payrolls in metropolitan Charleston. Many of these bases are now closed, but a vibrant private economy with lots of small companies has emerged, most notably at the 1,600-acre Charleston Naval Base, which, thanks to concerted efforts by regional officials, has created thousands of new jobs since its 1996 closure. One hundred miles north, Myrtle Beach has also bounced back impressively from the loss of an air force base. Despite being the only major South Carolina population center not located near an Interstate, Myrtle Beach's Horry County has doubled in population since 1980 and now attracts more than 13 million tourists annually. The number of golf rounds played there soared from 2.1 million in 1988 to almost 4.3 million a decade later, while the number of miniature-golf courses rose 60%. Myrtle Beach has recently taken steps to rein in its visual clutter, hoping to join the rest of the Low Country as one of the most gracefully growing regions of the United States.

The 1st Congressional District stretches along the coast roughly between Charleston and Myrtle Beach, including Murrells Inlet, Pawleys Island and Litchfield Beach. It includes the heavily white Battery and the area west of the Ashley River but not the heavily black areas to the north and in North Charleston; the 1st District's population is still 21% black. It also includes the heavily white burgeoning suburbs in Berkeley and Dorchester Counties. The 1st voted 59% for George W. Bush in 2000, and was solidly Republican in the 2002 elections. But the conservatism of the Low Country district is more economic and less cultural than the conservatism of Up Country South Carolina; many voters here favor environmental restrictions and efforts to curb sprawl. This area was strong for John McCain in the 2000 presidential primary and for nearly unanimous for Mark Sanford, the former 1st District congressman, in the 2002 primary and runoff for governor.

The congressman from the 1st District is Henry Brown, a Republican first elected in 2000. Brown grew up on a small farm in Cordesville in Berkeley County, worked at the Charleston Naval Shipyard as his father had, and then spent almost 30 years working for the Piggly Wiggly grocery chain, where he eventually became a vice president. In 1981, at age 45, Brown was elected to the City Council in Hanahan, north of North Charleston. In 1985 he was elected to the state House in a special election; after the 1994 election he became chairman of the Ways and Means Committee, where he claimed credit for enacting in 1995 the largest tax cut in the state's history.

Sanford, first elected to the House in 1994, had promised to serve only three terms, and Brown and other Republicans started running for the seat immediately after the 1998 election. Brown stressed issues of concern to the district's many senior citizens, property tax relief and shoring up Social Security. To boost his name recognition, he distributed 20,000 "Oh! Henry" chocolate bars. His chief opponent, Buck Limehouse, was best known as head of the state's Transportation Commission. Brown won endorsements from many legislators and from Christian conservatives. Limehouse, a Charleston developer, spent $790,000 to Brown's $315,000 and had the support of most party leaders, including Senator Strom Thurmond and former Governor Carroll Campbell. In the six-candidate primary Brown led 44%–34%. In the runoff two weeks later, Limehouse won the Grand Strand along the beaches. But Brown won Charleston County 53%–47% and his home base, Berkeley County, by 70%–30%; overall Brown won overall 55%–45%. The general election was anticlimactic. Brown won 60%–36%.

In the House, Brown has had a conservative voting record with occasional dashes of mod-eration on economic and foreign issues. He promoted the interests of the Charleston port in expanding the cruise ship business with a bill to waive the 1886 law that restricts foreign-flag vessels from using the port. Responding to recent court decisions, he filed a constitutional amend-ment to ban child pornography, and he won unanimous House passage of his resolution expressing support for public schools that display "God Bless America." He had no Democratic opponent in 2002. He tried to get a seat on Ways and Means in 2003 but it went to Eric Cantor of Virginia.

SECOND DISTRICT

Rep. Joe Wilson (R)

Elected Dec. 2001, 1st term; b. July 31, 1947, Charleston; home, Springdale; Washington & Lee U., B.A., 1969, U. of S.C., J.D., 1972; Presbyterian; married (Roxanne).

Military Career: Army Reserves, 1972–75; SC Natl. Guard, 1975–01.

Elected Office: SC Senate, 1985–01.

Professional Career: Practicing atty., 1972–01.

DC Office: 212 CHOB 20515, 202-225-2452; Fax: 202-225-2455; Web site: www.house.gov/joewilson.

District Offices: Beaufort, 843-521-2530; West Columbia, 803-939-0041.

Committees: *Armed Services* (23d of 33 R): Tactical Air & Land Forces; Terrorism, Unconventional Threats & Capabilities. *Education & the Workforce* (19th of 27 R): Education Reform; Employer-Employee Relations.

Group Ratings (Only Served Partial Term)

	ADA	ACLU	AFS	LCV	CON	ITIC	NTU	COC	ACU	NTLC	CHC
2002	10	17	11	25	—	75	57	80	92	100	75
2001	—	—	0	—	—	—	—	100	—	—	—

National Journal Ratings (Only Served Partial Term)

	2001 LIB	—	2001 CONS		2002 LIB	—	2002 CONS
Economic	0%	—	94%		21%	—	73%
Social	*	—	*		0%	—	75%
Foreign	*	—	*		24%	—	72%

Key Votes of the 107th Congress (Only Served Partial Term)

1. Approve Bush Tax Cuts	*	5. Faith-Based Charities	*	9. Trade Promotion Authority	*
2. Limit Patients' Bill of Rights	*	6. Bar Gays in the Boy Scouts	*	10. Bar Funds for Intl. Court	Y
3. Campaign Finance Reform	N	7. Ban Partial-Birth Abortion	Y	11. Authorize Force in Iraq	Y
4. Ban ANWR Development	*	8. Arm Commercial Pilots	Y	12. Deny Home. Sec. Dept. Union	Y

Election Results

2002 general	Joe Wilson (R)	144,149	(84%)	($1,305,481)
	Mark Whittington (UCIT)	17,189	(10%)	($8,178)
	James Legg (Lib)	9,650	(6%)	
2002 primary	Joe Wilson (R)	unopposed		
2001 special	Joe Wilson (R)	40,355	(73%)	($886,123)
	Brent Weaver (D)	14,034	(25%)	($86,732)

The People		Race/Ethnic Origin	Ancestry	
Area size:	5,237 sq. mi.	68.0% White	German: 10.0%	USA: 9.9%
Urban population:	66.0%	26.2% Black	English: 7.9%	
Rural population:	34.0%	1.1% Asian	**2000 Presidential Vote**	
Pop. 2000:	668,668	0.3% Native Am.	Bush (R) 145,953	(58%)
Median income:	$42,915	0.0% Hawaiian	Gore (D) 97,985	(39%)
Poverty status:	11.0%	0.9% Two + races	Other 6,374	(3%)
Military veterans:	15.1%	0.1% Other	**Cook Partisan Voting Index:** R + 10	
		3.3% Hispanic Origin		
Occupation	Blue collar: 22.6%	White collar: 63.1%	Gray collar: 14.3%	

Soon after the Revolutionary War, in 1786, the South Carolina legislature decided to move the state's capital away from the Charleston aristocracy and into the Up Country interior, away from a city named after a king to a new city named after a discoverer of America: so began Columbia. The State House was built on high ground above the Congaree River in a town of one-and-a-half story houses with first floor porticoes, dormers and raised brick basements—"Columbia cottages." In 1865, General William Tecumseh Sherman's army burned almost everything here but the

State House. Columbia recovered, but grew slowly, with state government and the university, the Army's Fort Jackson and local insurance companies providing steady employment. Manufacturing boomed in the 1970s, pushing up the metro area population to 536,000 and making Columbia a confident city, not just a village-capital. For a time, Columbia was personified by Jimmy Byrnes, the Democrat who returned from top posts in Washington to serve as governor and lament the *Brown v. Board of Education* decision in 1954. Since then, upwardly mobile South Carolinians, transplanted from underdeveloped rural areas to comfortable two-car-garage subdivisions, turned Republican, first in national and then in state and local elections. The Columbia area has been mostly Republican: the increasing black percentage in Columbia's Richland County has helped Democrats carry it, but faster-growing Lexington County across the river has remained heavily Republican.

The 2d Congressional District includes most of metro Columbia, except for black neighborhoods in northern and western Columbia and the eastern part of Richland County which are in the black-majority 6th District. It contains the city's affluent white neighborhoods and the spread-out towns of Richland and Lexington Counties, with their shopping centers, churches and the Army's huge training center, Fort Jackson. The district extends south, taking in Barnwell, which includes half the Savannah River Site, one of the nation's major storage sites for radioactive waste; it includes horse farm country around Aiken and takes in several lightly populated, black-majority rural counties, including Allendale and Hampton, two of the state's poorest. The 2d also includes fast-growing Beaufort County on the coast, with the old county seat of Beaufort, the carefully manicured developments of Hilton Head Island and the Marine Corps's Parris Island training base. This part of the district distinctively blends old and new: Beaufort's wonderful mansions and evocative Spanish moss provided the backdrop for the prose of Pat Conroy and the 1983 movie *The Big Chill*, while the posh condominium developments and golfing resorts around Hilton Head helped drive up Beaufort County's population by 40% during the 1990s—the state's highest growth rate. A notable feature is the Gullah culture centered on St. Helena Island. Slave owners, hating the heat and mosquitoes, ran largely absentee operations, thus allowing Gullah culture— a fusion of English and African elements—to thrive. Recent tourist interest has helped provide a market that sustains some once-threatened cultural practices, from storytelling to hair-braiding and boatbuilding. The current lines of the 2d make the district 26% black—enough to whittle down but not eliminate its Republican margins. George W. Bush won 58% of the vote here in 2000.

The congressman from the 2d District is Joe Wilson, a Republican who won a December 2001 special election after the death of Floyd Spence, who was first elected in 1970 and was chairman of the House Armed Services Committee from 1995 to 2001. Wilson grew up in Charleston and graduated from Washington and Lee and the University of South Carolina Law School. He worked as aide to Spence and Senator Strom Thurmond and was deputy general counsel at the Energy Department in the Reagan administration. He practiced law in West Columbia for 25 years and worked on and managed many campaigns, including Spence's, and in 1984 was elected to the state Senate, where he chaired the Transportation Committee. He has remained a member of the Army National Guard and he has sons in the Army National Guard, the Navy and Army ROTC. When Spence died in August 2001 after extended illnesses, Wilson became the immediate frontrunner to replace his longtime ally and pledged to continue his focus on national defense. He won the special Republican primary in October 2001 with 76% of the vote and in the December 2001 special he won 73%–25%.

In the House, Wilson got seats on Armed Services, and Education and the Workforce and has had a conservative voting record. Citing the need for a stronger military relationship with India in the war on terrorism, he became co-chairman of the Caucus on India and Indian Americans. He joined most other Carolina Republicans in opposing trade promotion authority in 2002, but was an early supporter of Bush's proposal to eliminate double taxation of dividends. During a shared C-SPAN appearance in September 2002, he called California's Bob Filner, an opponent of military action in Iraq, "viscerally anti-American" and said he harbored a "hatred of America" after Filner suggested the U.S. supplied biological and chemical weapons technology to Saddam

Hussein. Filner told a South Carolina reporter that he was "incredulous"; Wilson responded that he did not intend to question his patriotism or insult him.

Wilson had no Democratic opponent in 2002. He briefly considered running for the Senate in 2004 but in December 2002 ruled it out.

THIRD DISTRICT

Rep. Gresham Barrett (R)

Elected 2002, 1st term; b. Feb. 14, 1961, Westminster; home, Westminster; The Citadel, B.S. 1983; Baptist; married (Natalie).

Military Career: Army, 1983–87.

Elected Office: SC House of Reps., 1996–02.

Professional Career: Furniture store owner, 1987–96.

DC Office: 1523 LHOB 20515, 202-225-5301; Fax: 202-225-3216; Web site: www.house.gov/barrett.

District Offices: Aiken, 803-649-5571; Anderson, 864-224-7401; Greenwood, 864-223-8251.

Committees: *Budget* (20th of 24 R). *Financial Services* (35th of 37 R): Domestic and International Monetary Policy, Trade & Technology; Financial Institutions & Consumer Credit; Oversight & Investigations.

Group Ratings and Key Votes: Newly Elected

Election Results

2002 general	Gresham Barrett (R)	119,644	(67%)	($960,402)
	George Brightharp (D)	55,743	(31%)	($64,187)
	Other	2,808	(2%)	
2002 runoff	Gresham Barrett (R)	38,366	(65%)	
	Jim Klauber (R)	20,505	(35%)	
2002 primary	Gresham Barrett (R)	27,499	(43%)	
	Jim Klauber (R)	13,865	(22%)	
	George Ducworth (R)	13,836	(22%)	
	Bob Waldrep (R)	3,983	(6%)	
	Stan Jackson (R)	2,702	(4%)	
	Other	1,360	(2%)	
2000 general	Lindsey Graham (R)	150,176	(68%)	($725,118)
	George L. Brightharp (D)	64,920	(29%)	($41,713)
	Other	6,525	(3%)	

The People		Race/Ethnic Origin	Ancestry	
Area size:	5,568 sq. mi.	76.0% White	USA: 15.0%	Irish: 8.0%
Urban population:	50.3%	20.5% Black	English: 7.3%	
Rural population:	49.7%	0.6% Asian	**2000 Presidential Vote**	
Pop. 2000:	668,669	0.2% Native Am.	Bush (R) 142,414 (63%)	
Median income:	$36,092	0.0% Hawaiian	Gore (D) 77,694 (34%)	
Poverty status:	13.3%	0.7% Two+ races	Other 5,185 (2%)	
Military veterans:	13.5%	0.1% Other	**Cook Partisan Voting Index:** R +15	
		1.9% Hispanic Origin		

Occupation	Blue collar: 36.8%	White collar: 48.7%	Gray collar: 14.5%

The South Carolina Up Country, many days' travel by wagon from the Low Country plantations, was first settled by Scots-Irish farmers, including the family of John C. Calhoun around the time of the Revolutionary War. The pioneers wanted to make big plantations of these forests, but the land was too hilly for the labor-intensive rice crops grown in the Low Country and sometimes too cold for cotton. So relatively few slaves were brought here, and the land became mostly small farms owned by whites. Today, the racial and cultural tone of Up Country South Carolina shows traces of these roots. This is a mostly white part of the South, with a hell-of-a-fella tone to daily life and a tradition-minded slice of Middle America. Yet even this area has been touched by change. Aiken, with its horsey trappings, has long attracted affluent transplants, and the nearby Savannah River Site—a 310-square-mile federal weapons plant that for four decades produced tritium and plutonium that fueled America's nuclear arsenal—has employed generations of highly trained engineers (though its nuclear legacy has aroused environmental concern in some parts of the state). Today, Interstate 85—once the main street of America's textile belt—sits amidst a booming southeastern corridor that runs from Raleigh-Durham to Atlanta. In some retirement communities, newcomers cheer for Ohio State and Michigan, though Clemson, the university founded here by Calhoun's son-in-law, retains intense loyalty most everywhere else.

The 3d Congressional District follows the Georgia border north from the Savannah River Site through the tree-harvesting country around McCormick County north to mountains along the North Carolina border. The southern part of the 3d has a few heavily black communities, such as Edgefield, where Strom Thurmond grew up and first won public office in the 1930s, and where he now lives in retirement; Edgefield County grew significantly in the 1990s as it became part of the metropolitan area around Aiken and Augusta, Georgia. This part of South Carolina, ancestrally Democratic, began trending Republican in the 1950s, first in Yankified Aiken, well before Thurmond's party switch in 1964, as cultural issues took center stage in this fervently religious area. The 3d voted Republican even as Democrats swept the state in 1998, and George W. Bush won 63% of the vote here in 2000.

The congressman from the 3d District is Gresham Barrett, a Republican elected in 2002. Barrett grew up in Westminster in Oconee County and graduated from The Citadel in Charleston. After serving as an artillery captain in the First Cavalry Division at Fort Hood, he returned home to run his family's furniture store. In 1996 he was elected to the state House. In his three terms, he sponsored tort reform legislation and a state constitutional amendment guaranteeing the right to hunt and fish, sought more accountability and local control of education and advocated the mandatory posting of "In God We Trust" signs in school lunchrooms and auditoriums.

In February 2001 3d District incumbent Lindsey Graham, the first Republican to hold this seat since Reconstruction, announced he was running for the Senate, and Barrett became the early frontrunner for the seat. He issued a four-point plan to fight terrorism, including barring immigrants from nations like Iraq and Iran except in cases of asylum and military patrols on the nation's borders.

A social conservative, Barrett opposes abortion rights and defends gun-owner rights. He intends to "work to welcome God back to our public-squares, public schools, and our public life." He said he would vote to eliminate the capital gains tax and to make the income tax code fairer, flatter and shorter. In the six-candidate June primary, Barrett got 43% of the vote. In second place was state Representative and financial consultant Jim Klauber, just 29 votes ahead of former 10th Circuit Solicitor and 1970s Strom Thurmond staffer George Ducworth. Barrett won 82% of the vote in Oconee County and 53% in Pickens County, just to the west; he won nearly 50% in Aiken and Edgefield Counties, not the home area of any of the three leading candidates. He eliminated Ducworth by holding his lead in his home in Anderson County to 40%–35%; Klauber ran stronger in his home in Greenwood County, 68%–19%, but it cast many fewer votes. In the two-week runoff campaign Klauber argued that Barrett wasn't tough enough in cracking down on illegal immigrants; Barrett continued to insist that military issues were paramount. He raised more money, won more endorsements and won the runoff 65%–35%. Klauber won four counties in the central part of the district, but Barrett won 90% in Oconee County, 77% in Pickens County and 69% in Anderson and Aiken Counties. Barrett won the general election 67%–31%.

In the House, Barrett hoped for a seat on Armed Services but instead got Budget and Financial Services. Roy Blunt named him an assistant whip.

FOURTH DISTRICT

Rep. Jim DeMint (R)

Elected 1998, 3d term; b. Sept. 2, 1951, Greenville; home, Greenville; U. of TN, B.S. 1973, Clemson U., M.B.A. 1981; Presbyterian; married (Debbie).

Professional Career: Sales Rep., Scott Paper, 1973–75; Acct. Rep., Henderson Advertising, 1975–81; V.P., Leslie Advertising, 1981–84; Pres., DeMint Marketing, 1983–98.

DC Office: 432 CHOB 20515, 202-225-6030; Fax: 202-226-1177; Web site: www.house.gov/demint.

District Offices: Greenville, 864-232-1141; Spartanburg, 864-582-6422; Union, 864-427-2205.

Committees: *Education & the Workforce* (12th of 27 R): Education Reform; Employer-Employee Relations (Vice Chmn.). *Small Business* (6th of 18 R): Tax, Finance & Exports; Workforce, Empowerment & Government Programs. *Transportation & Infrastructure* (19th of 41 R): Coast Guard & Maritime Transportation; Highways, Transit & Pipelines; Railroads.

Group Ratings

	ADA	ACLU	AFS	LCV	CON	ITIC	NTU	COC	ACU	NTLC	CHC
2002	0	7	0	25	87	88	62	90	100	100	100
2001	0	—	0	0	—	—	73	96	100	—	—

National Journal Ratings

	2001 LIB —	2001 CONS	2002 LIB —	2002 CONS
Economic	0% —	94%	0% —	91%
Social	0% —	81%	0% —	75%
Foreign	0% —	97%	24% —	72%

Key Votes of the 107th Congress

1. Approve Bush Tax Cuts	Y	5. Faith-Based Charities	Y	9. Trade Promotion Authority	Y
2. Limit Patients' Bill of Rights	Y	6. Bar Gays in the Boy Scouts	Y	10. Bar Funds for Intl. Court	Y
3. Campaign Finance Reform	N	7. Ban Partial-Birth Abortion	Y	11. Authorize Force in Iraq	Y
4. Ban ANWR Development	N	8. Arm Commercial Pilots	Y	12. Deny Home. Sec. Dept. Union	Y

Election Results

2002 general	Jim DeMint (R)	122,422	(69%)	($458,695)
	Peter Ashy (D)	51,462	(29%)	
	Other	3,533	(2%)	
2002 primary	Jim DeMint (R)	39,142	(62%)	
	Phil Bradley (R)	24,423	(38%)	
2000 general	Jim DeMint (R)	150,436	(80%)	($303,967)
	Ted Adams (CNP)	16,532	(9%)	($15,968)
	April Bishop (Lib)	12,757	(7%)	($69,869)
	Other	9,326	(5%)	

Prior Winning Percentages: 1998 (58%)

The People		Race/Ethnic Origin	Ancestry	
Area size:	2,165 sq. mi.	74.6% White	USA: 13.7%	English: 8.0%
Urban population:	73.5%	19.7% Black	Irish: 7.5%	
Rural population:	26.5%	1.3% Asian	**2000 Presidential Vote**	
Pop. 2000:	668,669	0.2% Native Am.	Bush (R)	151,975 (64%)
Median income:	$39,417	0.0% Hawaiian	Gore (D)	78,449 (33%)
Poverty status:	11.4%	0.8% Two+ races	Other	5,843 (2%)
Military veterans:	12.8%	0.1% Other	**Cook Partisan Voting Index:** R +16	
		3.2% Hispanic Origin		

Occupation	Blue collar: 30.8%	White collar: 56.0%	Gray collar: 13.2%

A century ago, Northern investors seeking sites for textile mills looked at the Up Country of South Carolina and "were attracted by the mild climate, abundant water power, proximity to the cotton fields and plenty of native [white] labor already accustomed to a low standard of living." As mills fled New England, textile factories settled along the Southern Railway and Seaboard Coast Line tracks between Charlotte and Atlanta, especially in the Piedmont of South Carolina. The textile country might look bucolic, but Greenville, Spartanburg and the dozens of mill towns thick in the surrounding countryside were as industrial as Lancashire or the Ruhr, with mills rising up on what were once twisting woodland paths. In the days before child labor laws, factory work sometimes began at age six, condemning workers to a life of illiteracy; escapes to a brighter future, such as the brilliant but brief baseball career of West Greenville's Shoeless Joe Jackson, were rare.

Today, this same stretch of land along Interstate 85, which parallels the Southern Railway, remains the number one textile-producing area in the United States. But it is now much more than that. Textile and apparel work has steadily declined, but so many other jobs were created in the 1990s that the South Carolina Manufacturers Alliance dropped "textiles" from its name. Financial sweeteners, low taxes, nonexistent unions and solid infrastructure—airports, interstate highways, and the busy port of Charleston—have attracted an enormous BMW plant, the American headquarters of Michelin and a big Fuji film factory, among many others. Greenville's revitalized downtown now boasts fancy hotels and restaurants, including Korean, Thai and Vietnamese cuisine—each catering to the new corporate manager class.

The 4th Congressional District includes all of Greenville and Spartanburg Counties, plus much smaller Union County and a sliver of Laurens County. Culturally, the 4th ranges from conservative to very conservative, with strong influence by Greenville's many evangelical and fundamentalist churches. Bob Jones University is here; it has dropped its longtime ban on interracial dating and has an impressive collection of religious paintings. Newcomers to the area have brought religious diversity. Greenville has growing populations not only of Catholics and Jews, but also Muslims, Buddhists, Hindus, Baha'is, and the only gay-oriented church within a 60-mile radius. Still, this is a heavily Republican district, with the smallest black percentage in the state and the highest vote share by George W. Bush in 2000 (64%). Here the real political divide is between religious and economic conservatives.

The congressman from the 4th District is Jim DeMint, a Republican elected in 1998. DeMint grew up in Greenville, graduated from the University of Tennessee and Clemson Business School, and returned to Greenville to work as a paper salesman and in the advertising business. In 1983 he founded DeMint Marketing, a research firm with businesses, schools, colleges and hospitals as clients. In 1992 he went to work for 33-year-old lawyer Bob Inglis's House campaign. As he explains, "I became increasingly concerned that the freedoms we take for granted in America are under attack in such a subtle way that no one is noticing it. I developed the feeling that I had a burden to try to change things." Inglis pledged to serve only three terms, to take no PAC money, to oppose pork barrel projects even in South Carolina; DeMint honed the Inglis message using focus groups and advertising expertise. Inglis upset an incumbent Democrat by 50%–48%, and kept his promises.

In 1998 Inglis kept his term-limit promise and ran for the Senate. DeMint ran, with Inglis' support, in the 4th District. Like Inglis, he pledged to serve only three terms and take no PAC money. He called for a national sales tax or flat tax, for individual retirement accounts in Social Security, for the right-to-life amendment, for the English rule (loser pays winner's attorney fees) in tort cases. In the primary, the favorite was state Senator Mike Fair, a former University of South Carolina quarterback. In the primary Fair led with 32%; DeMint came in second with 23%, 699 votes ahead of hospital executive Howell Clyborne. In the runoff two weeks later, Fair bragged about his experience, but DeMint called him a "career politician." The result was a 53%–47% upset win for DeMint. He trailed in Greenville County 51%–49%, but carried Spartanburg County by 60%–40%. DeMint won the general election 58%–40%.

In the House DeMint was elected president of the freshman class and quickly became a strong conservative voice. He used his background in marketing research to work on developing and communicating the Republican message. He joined other junior Republicans seeking to rein in spending by the appropriators. He resisted local pressures and was the only South Carolina

House member to vote for PNTR with China, arguing that the best way to remedy human-rights abuses was "to export our products and principles." The libertarian Cato Institute ranked DeMint in the top 1% of "free traders" in the House. But DeMint refused to support trade promotion authority and accused Ways and Means Chairman Bill Thomas of undermining a written pledge from Republican leaders to protect the domestic textile industry by requiring that Caribbean textile imports be dyed and finished in the United States. A few weeks later, DeMint won the showdown with Thomas when House leaders restored the textile provision; he ultimately voted for trade promotion authority.

When Bush in 2001 proposed his $1.6 trillion tax-cut package, DeMint was among a small group who immediately pushed for more; he was a leading advocate of the expanded adoption tax credits in the final package. He sponsored an amendment to Bush's education bill to create a state-based block-grant program; to preserve his bipartisan coalition, Education and the Work-force Chairman John Boehner tried to discourage DeMint. Bush, in a meeting in the Oval Office, got DeMint to back down. He worked to advance individual investment accounts in Social Security by getting 117 House members to sign a letter of support for the Social Security Commission.

DeMint's votes on trade aroused some loud opposition in the district, and in May 2001 Public Service Commissioner and former state Representative Phil Bradley announced he would challenge him in the Republican primary. Bradley had the support of textile titan Roger Milliken, long a financer of conservative and protectionist candidates. DeMint defended his support for free trade as beneficial for international investment in the district, and said that he also sought to protect domestic workers. This turned out to be a more serious challenge than most incumbents get. DeMint led by only 52%–48% in Spartanburg County, which cast 36% of the votes. He did better, 68%–32%, in more diversified Greenville County, which cast 61% of the votes. Overall DeMint won 62%–38%. After the election, DeMint said that he would keep his promise to serve only three terms in the House and that he would run for Ernest Hollings's Senate seat in 2004; he soon gained the backing of White House political strategist Karl Rove. Continuing their partnership, Bob Inglis said that he would run again in the 4th District, but refused to make another term limits pledge, which he said would be "unilateral disarmament" for local interests.

FIFTH DISTRICT

Rep. John Spratt (D)

Elected 1982, 11th term; b. Nov. 1, 1942, Charlotte, NC; home, York; David-son Col., A.B. 1964, Oxford U., M.A. 1966, Yale U., LL.B. 1969; Presbyterian; married (Jane Stacy).

Military Career: Army Operations, U.S. Dept. of Defense, 1969–71.

Professional Career: Practicing atty., 1971–82; Pres., Bank of Ft. Mill, 1973–82; Pres., Spratt Insurance Agcy., 1973–82.

DC Office: 1401 LHOB 20515, 202-225-5501; Fax: 202-225-0464; Web site: www.house.gov/spratt.

District Offices: Darlington, 843-393-3998; Rock Hill, 803-327-1114; Sumter, 803-773-3362.

Committees: *Armed Services* (2d of 29 D): Strategic Forces; Tactical Air & Land Forces. *Budget* (RMM of 19 D).

Group Ratings

	ADA	ACLU	AFS	LCV	CON	ITIC	NTU	COC	ACU	NTLC	CHC
2002	80	50	100	63	43	50	16	55	16	0	17
2001	85	—	90	71	—	—	11	45	36	—	—

National Journal Ratings

	2001 LIB —	2001 CONS		2002 LIB —	2002 CONS
Economic	65% —	36%		77% —	20%
Social	54% —	45%		63% —	35%
Foreign	56% —	41%		58% —	42%

Key Votes of the 107th Congress

1. Approve Bush Tax Cuts	N	5. Faith-Based Charities	N	9. Trade Promotion Authority	N
2. Limit Patients' Bill of Rights	N	6. Bar Gays in the Boy Scouts	Y	10. Bar Funds for Intl. Court	Y
3. Campaign Finance Reform	Y	7. Ban Partial-Birth Abortion	Y	11. Authorize Force in Iraq	Y
4. Ban ANWR Development	*	8. Arm Commercial Pilots	N	12. Deny Home. Sec. Dept. Union	N

Election Results

2002 general	John Spratt (D)	121,912	(86%)	($406,711)
	Doug Kendall (Lib)	11,013	(8%)	
	Steve Lefemine (CNP)	8,930	(6%)	
2002 primary	John Spratt (D)	unopposed		
2000 general	John Spratt (D)	126,877	(59%)	($1,070,965)
	Carl L. Gullick (R)	85,247	(39%)	($342,397)
	Other	3,714	(2%)	

Prior Winning Percentages: 1998 (58%); 1996 (54%); 1994 (52%); 1992 (61%); 1990 (100%); 1988 (70%); 1986 (100%); 1984 (92%); 1982 (68%)

The People		Race/Ethnic Origin	Ancestry	
Area size:	7,141 sq. mi.	64.1% White	USA: 14.8%	Irish: 5.6%
Urban population:	46.7%	32.2% Black	English: 5.6%	
Rural population:	53.3%	0.5% Asian	**2000 Presidential Vote**	
Pop. 2000:	668,668	0.6% Native Am.	Bush (R)	119,052 (55%)
Median income:	$35,416	0.0% Hawaiian	Gore (D)	93,637 (43%)
Poverty status:	15.2%	0.7% Two+ races	Other	3,979 (2%)
Military veterans:	13.0%	0.1% Other	**Cook Partisan Voting Index:** R + 6	
		1.8% Hispanic Origin		

Occupation	Blue collar: 37.5%	White collar: 48.5%	Gray collar: 14.1%

Some of the fiercest battles of the Revolutionary War were fought in South Carolina's Up Country, on hilly lands just being settled by Scots-Irish farmers moving up from the Low Country or down the Virginia Piedmont valley. This was a country of violent passions and unclear lines; Carolinians have long argued over which side of the North and South Carolina boundary Andrew Jackson was born in 1767. Ever since, the fighting spirit and Calvinist faith of Up Country Carolinians have never wavered. This "Olde English District" remains intensely religious and pro-military. But it is no longer impoverished. For many years, the dominant industry here was textiles, traditionally the first factory enterprise of industrializing countries, with low pay and poor working conditions. But in the 1980s and 1990s the number of textile jobs declined, and small business prosperity more recently has been barreling out the interstates from Greenville-Spartanburg and Columbia and Charlotte, to transform counties once dependent on tobacco fields and textile mills.

The 5th Congressional District consists of all or part of 14 counties, mostly in the Up Country. It includes just one small county in the Greenville metro area and fast-growing (up 25% in the 1990s) York County, part of the Charlotte, North Carolina, metro area; growth accelerated here after settlement of the Catawba Indians' land claims in 1993. To the east, the 5th includes Dillon County, site of the pink, orange and turquoise South of the Border tourist attraction heralded on 250 billboards on I-95, and Darlington, site of the Southern 500 stock car race every Labor Day. It also includes lowland tobacco country, including Marlboro and Chesterfield Counties. In the west, it includes Fort Mill and Rock Hill in York County, just south of Charlotte, the site of rapid development after a 1993 land settlement with the Catawba Indians. Politically, this homeland of Andrew Jackson is ancestrally Democratic. But Republicans are now competitive if not dominant here: the tobacco counties are heavily Democratic but York County is trending Republican. George

W. Bush won 55% of the vote here in 2000; in 2002 the 5th was carried by Democratic Governor Jim Hodges, who lives in the district, and by Republican Senate candidate Lindsey Graham.

The congressman from the 5th District is John Spratt, ranking minority member on the House Budget Committee and assistant to the minority leader, a Democrat first elected in 1982. He comes from a prominent York County family and graduated from Davidson College, Yale Law School and Oxford University. He served two years in the Army, in the Operations Analysis Group in the office of the Pentagon comptroller. He first got involved in politics in Charles Ravenel's unsuccessful 1974 campaign for governor. In 1982 the 5th District incumbent announced his retirement a week before the filing deadline; Spratt put a campaign together fast and won 38% in the primary, 55% in the runoff against a high-spending candidate, and 68% in the general. And so a campaign quickly put together has given Spratt a seat in the House for more than 20 years and a key role in shaping national legislation.

Spratt is the second-ranking Democrat on the Armed Services Committee. In the 1980s, he worked with Chairman Les Aspin and, in his thick Carolina accent and with impressive knowledge of details, stitched together compromises on the MX missile, binary nerve gas weapons, the Strategic Defense Initiative, and the Savannah River Site and other nuclear plants—keeping military projects flowing through the House, many of whose members were constantly looking to cut military spending. Starting in the mid-1990s Spratt has been the House Democrats' lead man on missile defense. He conceded that the ABM Treaty will have to be abandoned some day, but was cautious about rapid development and deployment of missile defense. His amendment on the subject prevailed in February 1995 by 218–212, the first significant defeat of a Contract with America promise in the Republican House. In August 1998, a month after the Rumsfeld Commission report on missile defense, he joined Curt Weldon and other Republicans in support of a one-sentence bill declaring "the policy of the United States is to deploy a national missile defense." This passed the House, but Senate Democrats (except for South Carolina's Ernest Hollings and three others) filibustered against any missile defense measure in September 1998. In late May 1999 the House passed a bill that would make the construction of a national missile defense a top priority. In May 2000 Spratt argued that near-term deployment of missile defense would be a mistake, but said that missile defense tests were promising; he said that much work needed to be done diplomatically with Russia and our European allies before withdrawing from the ABM Treaty, and that he preferred modification of the agreement over withdrawal. George W. Bush did not take his advice, but abrogated the Treaty and increased the pace of development, which Spratt continues to monitor.

On the Iraq war resolution Spratt played a key role for House Democrats. He had voted for the Gulf War resolution in January 1991 and had strong defense credentials from his work on Armed Services. In September 2002, after George W. Bush's speech at the United Nations, Minority Leader Dick Gephardt turned to Spratt and Ike Skelton, ranking Democrat on Armed Services, for help in drafting an alternative to the broad White House resolution authorizing the use of force. Spratt sought another round of weapons inspections and wanted Bush to ask for U.N. approval and suggested removing a phrase authorizing any action to ensure peace and security in the region; the administration agreed to delete it. He sought advice from Anthony Zinni, Joseph Hoar and other retired generals with experience in the region, and found that they were wary of military action against Iraq. When Gephardt went to the White House and agreed on a resolution, Spratt continued to prepare a Democratic alternative, working with Minority Whip Nancy Pelosi. He saw "no need to invoke preemptive intervention or to draw a tenuous connection between Iraq and al Qaeda." His resolution authorized military action if the U.N. approved and left room for the administration to seek another resolution from Congress if the U.N. did not approve. "Iraq's defiance of Security Council resolutions is enough to warrant force, particularly if it does not comply with a new, tougher round of arms inspections," Spratt said, but he also argued that it was worth getting approval from others. He offered his resolution as an amendment and it was defeated 270–155; Democrats favored it 147–60 but Republicans opposed it 210–8. Spratt joined the majority and voted for the resolution sponsored by the administration and Gephardt, which passed 296–133. Spratt worked closely with Pelosi in seeking support for his alternative. After the election, Gephardt stepped down and Pelosi was elected minority leader;

one of her first acts was to appoint Spratt assistant to the leader and name him her designee on budget issues—a sign, it appeared, that she would be paying attention to moderates in the Democratic Caucus.

In 1991 Spratt got a seat on the Budget Committee. His moderate voting record made him a natural point of contact between the parties, but Democrats did not see him as their leader: In their November 1992 caucus, he was beaten for Budget chairman by the more liberal Martin Sabo by 149–112. He rotated off the committee in 1992, then ran for the ranking Democrat position on Budget again in December 1996. Democrats, now in the minority, were more ready for his leadership; he beat the more liberal Louise Slaughter by 106–83. He played a major role in putting together the May 1997 agreement to reach a balanced budget, holding together Democrats who disliked the concessions to high-income taxpayers and staying in touch with Republicans who wanted more spending cuts. In the process, he got support from Bill Archer and Al Gore against a proposed Medicaid funding cut that would have hurt South Carolina, and came up with an alternative Republican Governor David Beasley praised. Spratt continued to work with the White House, House Republicans and House Democrats in establishing the specific details of the balanced budget package, which finally were agreed on in August 1997.

The bipartisanship of that period has not continued, and Spratt has been given the role of offering Democratic alternatives which are beaten on party lines. His March 2000 budget resolution would have provided for more non-defense spending and less defense spending (though an increase) than Chairman John Kasich's. In early 2001 he urged George W. Bush to approach the budget as Bill Clinton did in 1997, with negotiations between leaders of both parties. But the new Budget chairman, Jim Nussle, instead offered a budget resolution based on Bush's program, with a $1.6 trillion tax cut over 10 years and a 4% increase in non-defense spending. Spratt's alternative offered a smaller tax cut, with one-third of the surplus going to tax cuts, one-third to increased spending and one-third to a "strategic reserve fund." He decried the size of the Republican tax cuts. In August 2001 he was warning that administration economic projections were too optimistic. "You can only fudge these numbers so far before the real numbers come in and start undoing your numbers, if they're too optimistic." But he cooperated with Nussle on creating a Commission on Federal Budget Concepts. After September 11, he issued a report predicting that the budget surplus would disappear in 2002 and, pessimistically, it would disappear for several years. In 2002 he called for negotiations like those that produced the 1997 budget agreement or the 1990 budget summit in which George W. Bush's father agreed to break his promise and raise taxes. "He can take a page from his father's experience and hope it doesn't cost him what it cost his dad. But his dad did the right thing." In 2002 Republicans once again passed a budget resolution along party lines; surveying the deficits ahead, Spratt blamed them on the 2001 Bush tax cuts, but said that he would not urge their repeal. "We think they have the first move." In February 2003, as House Republicans moved toward another monopartisan budget resolution, Spratt and his Senate counterpart Kent Conrad wrote, "We warned two years ago that the president was betting his budget on a blue sky forecast and making his tax cuts so large that no margin was left for error. Now we are watching 15 years of fiscal effort unravel." On other issues, Spratt has a moderate record, a bit to the left of the middle of the House. He has been co-chair of the Textile Caucus and criticized the Clinton FDA's attempts to regulate tobacco as unjustified by law.

Spratt had two tough races, in 1994 and 1996, when he won by margins of 52%–48% and 54%–45%. Since then he has been reelected easily; he had no Republican opponent in 2002.

SIXTH DISTRICT

Rep. James Clyburn (D)

Elected 1992, 6th term; b. July 21, 1940, Sumter; home, Columbia; SC St. U., B.A. 1962; African Methodist Episcopal; married (Emily).

Professional Career: Teacher, 1962–66; Dir., Charleston Neighborhood Youth Corps, 1966–68; Exec. Dir., SC Comm. for Farm Workers, 1968–71; Asst., SC Gov. West, 1971–74; SC Human Affairs Comm., 1974–92.

DC Office: 2135 RHOB 20515, 202-225-3315; Fax: 202-225-2313; Web site: www.house.gov/clyburn.

District Offices: Charleston, 843-965-5578; Columbia, 803-799-1100; Florence, 843-622-1212.

Committees: *Democratic Caucus Vice Chairman. Appropriations* (19th of 29 D): Energy & Water Development; The Legislative Branch; Transportation, Treasury, & Independent Agencies.

Group Ratings

	ADA	ACLU	AFS	LCV	CON	ITIC	NTU	COC	ACU	NTLC	CHC
2002	95	71	100	75	48	50	20	50	0	6	17
2001	70	—	90	64	—	—	14	61	20	—	—

National Journal Ratings

	2001 LIB	—	2001 CONS		2002 LIB	—	2002 CONS
Economic	65%	—	36%		93%	—	5%
Social	68%	—	32%		92%	—	6%
Foreign	86%	—	12%		87%	—	10%

Key Votes of the 107th Congress

1. Approve Bush Tax Cuts	N	5. Faith-Based Charities	N	9. Trade Promotion Authority	N
2. Limit Patients' Bill of Rights	N	6. Bar Gays in the Boy Scouts	N	10. Bar Funds for Intl. Court	N
3. Campaign Finance Reform	Y	7. Ban Partial-Birth Abortion	N	11. Authorize Force in Iraq	N
4. Ban ANWR Development	N	8. Arm Commercial Pilots	N	12. Deny Home. Sec. Dept. Union	N

Election Results

2002 general	James Clyburn (D)	116,586	(67%)	($398,652)
	Gary McLeod (R)	55,760	(32%)	($10,616)
2002 primary	James Clyburn (D)	34,106	(89%)	
	Ben Frasier (D)	4,304	(11%)	
2000 general	James Clyburn (D)	138,053	(72%)	($449,439)
	Vince Ellison (R)	50,005	(26%)	($39,945)
	Other	4,322	(2%)	

Prior Winning Percentages: 1998 (73%); 1996 (69%); 1994 (64%); 1992 (65%)

The People		Race/Ethnic Origin	Ancestry	
Area size:	8,490 sq. mi.	40.3% White	USA: 9.0%	English: 4.1%
Urban population:	48.0%	56.7% Black	German: 3.7%	
Rural population:	52.0%	0.5% Asian	**2000 Presidential Vote**	
Pop. 2000:	668,670	0.3% Native Am.	Gore (D) 126,287	(58%)
Median income:	$28,967	0.0% Hawaiian	Bush (R) 87,252	(40%)
Poverty status:	22.4%	0.7% Two+ races	Other 2,991	(1%)
Military veterans:	12.4%	0.1% Other	**Cook Partisan Voting Index:** D + 9	
		1.5% Hispanic Origin		

Occupation	Blue collar: 33.0%	White collar: 48.1%	Gray collar: 18.9%

South Carolina was first settled by planters from Barbados, bringing with them a tropical plantation economy, which they transferred to the not-quite-tropical climate of the Carolina coastal lowlands. Here the flat Low Country and many islands are laced with sluggish-flowing rivers and swamps, and here the planters brought thousands of slaves directly from Africa. Colonial South

Carolina was one of the richest parts of North America, with dazzling Georgian architecture in Charleston and classic plantation gardens; the planters built great irrigation systems and grew rice and cotton and the dye-plant indigo, all heavily in demand in Britain and elsewhere. All this wealth, of course, was built on the slave labor of countless African Americans. In colonial times, a majority of South Carolinians were slaves, as were a majority of lowlands residents when Fort Sumter was fired upon (although there were also many free blacks in Charleston, a few of whom owned slaves themselves).

South Carolina's black heritage has left a lasting imprint on American culture, and the African-influenced Gullah language still can be heard here. The poverty that was the almost universal lot of lowland blacks after the Civil War has eased only in the last generation, as development came to the coast and long cultural isolation dissipated. But such rural, landlocked counties as Bamberg and Williamsburg still rank among the state's poorest, and over the years, many blacks decided not to wait, abandoning South Carolina for opportunities in the North. Today, rural, heavily black counties are suffering steeper losses in manufacturing jobs than urban areas are.

The 6th Congressional District, created in 1992 as a black-majority district, with its boundaries modified in 1994 and 2002, includes only a bit of the South Carolina coast, which is increasingly lined with affluent retirement and recreational communities. The district's boundaries, less jagged since the 2002 redistricting, take in the black, central-city neighborhoods of Charleston, North Charleston and Columbia but leave their affluent white areas, both urban and suburban, in the adjacent 1st and 2d Districts. The 6th includes Orangeburg, home of the historically black South Carolina State University, and Florence, at the center of the Pee Dee tobacco-growing country in eastern South Carolina. The 6th, with a 57% black population, gave George W. Bush only 40% of the vote in 2000—the only South Carolina district he failed to carry.

The congressman from the 6th District is James Clyburn, a Democrat first elected in 1992. Clyburn grew up in Sumter, the son of a minister. In 1960 he was one of seven young people who organized the state's first sit-ins, at a five-and-dime store in the Orangeburg town square; in February 2001, Governor Jim Hodges apologized for the massacre that took place there in 1968, when highway patrolmen killed three protestors and wounded 27 others. Clyburn worked as a teacher, in government antipoverty programs and on the staff of Governor John West. In 1974 he became state Human Affairs commissioner, serving 18 years under Republican and Democratic governors; when criticized for working for Republican Carroll Campbell, Clyburn got him to back the state's first fair housing act. Twice he ran for secretary of state, losing narrowly. In 1992 Clyburn effectively won the 6th District seat in the Democratic primary, with 56% of the vote against four black opponents, all with serious claims for the nomination; the white Democratic incumbent in the old 6th District, Robin Tallon, at the last minute decided not to run. Clyburn, well known statewide, ran first or second in every part of the district and piled up 88% of the vote in his home county of Sumter.

Clyburn, the first black to represent South Carolina in Congress since 1897, has a moderate-to-liberal voting record. He has good working relationships with leading businessmen and Republicans and—like many South Carolinians before him—has focused on local priorities first. He supported the balanced budget amendment and joined the moderate New Democrat Coalition at its inception in 1997, the only black to do so. Against campaign finance critics in his own party, he has defended PACs as the voice of the little guy. When cigarette tax increases were proposed, he urged safeguards for tobacco farmers.

In 1999, he got a seat on the Appropriations Committee, where he continued his focus on local projects, including $30 million for the Cooper River bridge replacement in Charleston. Also that year he became chairman of the Congressional Black Caucus, where he showed his reputation for being conciliatory and non-confrontational. He urged the Democratic National Committee to become more responsive to blacks, and sought to create a Policy and Leadership Institute for the Black Caucus to develop new liberal positions and protect black lawmakers in redistricting. But he ran into opposition when he supported the King efforts to have the Library of Congress purchase Dr. Martin Luther King's papers for perhaps $20 million. Following the 2002 election, he won a three-candidate contest to become vice-chairman of the Democratic Caucus with 95 votes to 56 for Gregory Meeks and 53 for Zoe Lofgren, placing him among the top half-dozen

House Democratic leaders; it was vital, he said, that the leadership reflect the party's diversity and not "just white men." He pledged to sharpen the party's message.

Back home, Clyburn relished his role as a major player and potential kingmaker in the 2004 Democratic presidential primary and found himself wooed by candidates for support in the potentially crucial South Carolina primary. Blacks may well cast a majority of the votes in the primary and if not will cast a large minority, and Clyburn is the most prominent black politician in the state. "You try to play the hand you've been dealt to the best of your ability," he told *National Journal*. He has been close to Dick Gephardt, but in early 2003 he said he would not endorse anyone until late in the year—perhaps as a Christmas present.

★ SOUTH DAKOTA ★

When the Census Bureau proclaimed the closing of the American frontier in 1890, one of the last places where it had closed was the southern part of the Dakota Territory, just admitted to the Union in 1889 as the state of South Dakota. For years this land had been the home of the Oglala Sioux, one of the largest Native American tribes, who had built a buffalo hunting civilization by becoming masters of the horses the Spaniards had imported to North America 350 years earlier. It was the Sioux warrior chief Sitting Bull, now buried on a bluff above the Missouri River, who destroyed Custer at Little Big Horn in 1876; it was Oglala Sioux who were the victims at the massacre of Wounded Knee in 1890. After half a century of horrifying disease and a decade of defeat, the Sioux were a traumatized people, and still are today, living on reservations with proud traditions but in terrible poverty. They are isolated far from the mainstream economic marketplace, beset by high rates of crime, alcoholism and suicide, with life expectancy and disease rates like those of sub-Saharan Africa. But infant mortality has been reduced and the American Indian population has been growing—by 23% in the 1990s. Indians are in the process of getting a great monument, the late Korczak Ziolkowski's Crazy Horse sculpture, which—when and if finished—will dwarf Mount Rushmore (which was left unfinished itself at the start of World War II).

Less tragic and more successful, though not without its moments of violence, was the whites' settlement of South Dakota. It was a rapid process: the first gold strikes in the Black Hills came in 1876, and soon the mountains swarmed with settlers. Deadwood became a city of 20,000 where Calamity Jane ruled the saloons and Wild Bill Hickok was shot in the back while holding two pair—aces and eights. Ranchers, knowing that the buffalo could not be contained by barbed wire fences, massacred them so thoroughly that when Teddy Roosevelt got to the Dakota Territory in 1884, he had a hard time finding one to shoot. It was not long before the railroad came through, and then settlers, many of them German and Scandinavian immigrants recruited by the railroads, had built sodhouses, broken the land and set down enough roots to justify making both the two Dakota states.

Geographically, South Dakota has never entirely filled up. In the 25 years between statehood and World War I, the eastern third of the state, sectioned off Midwestern style into 640-acre square miles, was settled by farmers. But moving westward, before a traveler reaches the Missouri River in the middle of the state, green turns to brown, cultivation grows sparse and then stops; the plains are open grazing land, scarcely touched by the white men who were so eager to establish dominion over them a century ago. The land is punctuated, not by roads meeting every mile at precise angles, but by buttes, gullies and grasslands sweeping to the horizon with no sign of human habitation except the occasional missile silos that once pointed toward the Soviet Union.

South Dakota's political patterns were fairly well set by the early 1900s. Its early settlers were mostly Midwesterners who brought their Republicanism with them. Voters here never had much use for the Non-Partisan League, which caught on in the more Scandinavian soil of North Dakota, and there was never anything here comparable to the Farmer-Labor Party of Minnesota. But the nature of the farm economy—its dependence on the great railroads and milling companies, and on the vagaries of international markets—meant that South Dakota was subject to periodic farm

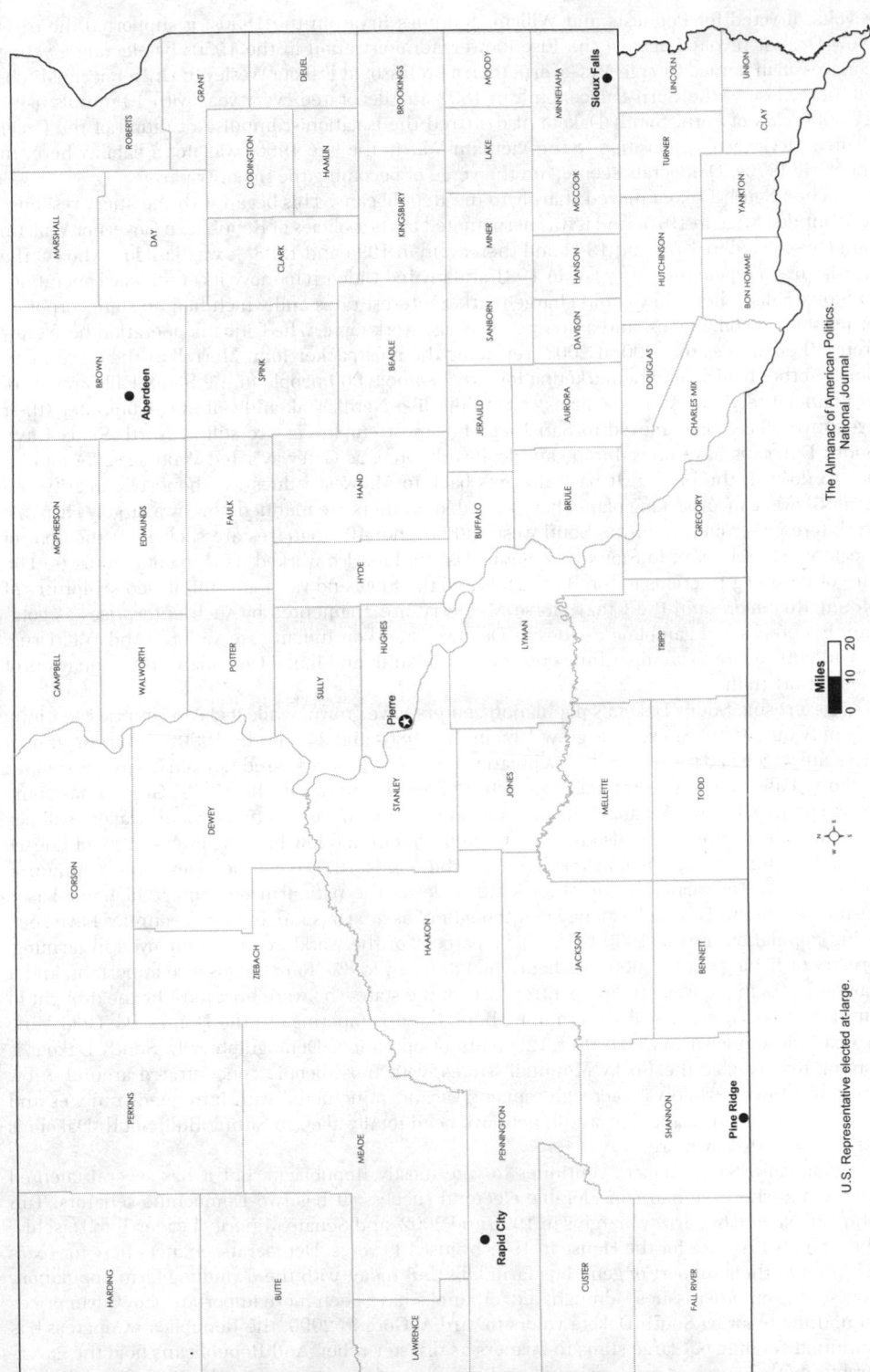

The Almanac of American Politics.
National Journal

U.S. Representative elected at-large.

revolts. It voted for Populists and William Jennings Bryan in the 1890s; it supported the early New Deal; it revolted against the Eisenhower Administration in the 1950s by electing a young congressman named George McGovern, then a professor at Dakota Wesleyan University in Mitchell, home also of the Corn Palace, built in 1892 and decorated every year with 13 murals using 275,000 ears of corn. South Dakota also shared the isolationist impulse of much of the Great Plains; McGovern's opposition to the Vietnam War in the late 1960s was not a liability here. In the early 1970s, Democrats seemed on the verge of becoming the majority party.

Then South Dakota moved sharply to the Republicans. This began with the angry response to Wounded Knee in 1975. And it was perpetuated by the policies of Republican Governor William Janklow, elected in 1978 and 1982 and then again in 1994 and 1998. It was Janklow who got the legislature to repeal the usury law in 1981 and invited Citicorp to move its credit card operations to Sioux Falls, where they could charge market interest rates and which had no state corporate or personal income taxes, and a literate low-wage work force. The Citibank operation here grew from 50 employees to 3,200 in 2003, replacing the meatpacker John Morrell as the biggest employer; other banks and telemarketing followed; some 9,000 people in the Sioux Falls area work in financial services. And new firms started up, like NordicTrak and Gateway Computer (their executive offices have moved to San Diego but most employees are still in North Sioux City). South Dakotans have proved to be an ideal work force; as Gateway's Ted Waitt says, "A lot of it has to do with the people. It basically gets back to Midwest values . . . honesty, integrity and loyalty." Some meatpacking plants have closed, but others are manned now by a largely Hispanic work force, recruited from the Southwest and beyond; 40 languages are spoken on the floor of the John Morrell plant in Sioux City. South Dakota has also worked hard to court tourists. The lure of natural attractions in the Black Hills and the huge and varyingly unfinished sculptures of Mount Rushmore and the Crazy Horse Memorial are augmented by such enterprises as gold-panning creeks and gambling casinos in Deadwood and on Indian reservations. And Wall Drug, the 46,000-square foot emporium between the Badlands and Rapid City, snares three-quarters of the freeway traffic.

As a result, South Dakota's population centers have grown, while its farm counties continue to empty out. Metro Sioux Falls grew 13% in the 1980s and 24% in the 1990s—amazing growth in a state which had sometimes lost population between censuses—and Lincoln County, just south of Sioux Falls, was one of the nation's fastest growing counties in the 1990s. Growth has come along counties in the I-29 and I-90 corridors and on Indian reservations. South Dakota still has a low-wage economy, but it also has low unemployment and low housing prices (10% of houses in rural counties are vacant); its residents and those in North Dakota spend less time commuting to work than Americans in any other state. It leads the nation in percentage of home-based businesses. South Dakota has long been thought of as a farm state, but farm counties have been losing population; in the 1990 Census, 11 percent of the workforce was employed in farming, forestry or fishing but by 2000 that figure had dropped to 8%. Ranching is also important, and it was ranchers in the western and central parts of the state who were hurt most by the drought in summer 2002. There is still some mining here, but it is tapering off; the Homestake Gold Mine in Lead closed down in 2001 after 127 years of operation. Demographically, South Dakota is coming to resemble the Rocky Mountain states, with most people concentrated around a few cities and towns, while vast acreage remains vacant, punctuated with infrequent ranches and resort areas—a landscape that would not have been totally alien to Sitting Bull. South Dakota is not a farm state any more.

Politically, South Dakota continues to vote mostly Republican, but it has several talented Democrats who have had considerable electoral success. It has two Democratic senators, Tim Johnson, elected by narrow margins in 1996 and 2002, and Senate Minority Leader Tom Daschle, who won his first race for the House in 1978 by just 139 votes. Democrats' chances here for years were tied to their support of generous farm bills, but today, with the dwindling farm population, their stands on other issues—drought aid, ethanol—have been more important. Low farm prices did nothing to swing South Dakota voters toward Al Gore in 2000; the Republican Congress has continued sending out large sums to farmers as disaster relief. And Republicans hold the governorship, both houses of the legislature and the state's lone House seat. In 2002 South Dakota was the scene of two of the nation's most strenuously contested congressional elections. Tim Johnson held his Senate seat over Congressman John Thune by just 524 votes. Bill Janklow, governor for 16 of the last 24 years, was able to win the House seat by only 53%–46% over 31-year-old Democrat Stephanie Herseth. Personal campaigning is still important here. This is a state where voters expect to meet and talk with the candidates, and with some frequency. In 2004, there may be another hotly contested race here: in early 2003, Thune seemed to be preparing to run for Daschle's Senate seat. Daschle's years of meeting with South Dakota voters will undoubtedly help his candidacy, but South Dakota voters have been willing to reject incumbent senators—Democrat George McGovern in 1980 and Republicans Jim Abdnor in 1986 and Larry Pressler in 1996.

The People		Race/Ethnic Origin			Military veterans: 79,370 (14.4%)	
Pop. 2000:	754,844	664,585	88.0%	White	WWII: 19.3%	Korea: 16.1%
Pop. 1990:	696,004	4,563	0.6%	Black	Vietnam: 31.3%	Gulf War: 11.0%
Change 1990–2000:	Up 8.5%	4,316	0.6%	Asian	**Most populous cities:**	
Change 1980–1990:	Up 0.8%	60,988	8.1%	Native Am.	1. Sioux Falls	123,975
% of U.S. total:	0.3%	219	0.0%	Hawaiian	2. Rapid City	59,607
Pop. rank:	46th of 50	8,960	1.2%	Two+ races	3. Aberdeen	24,658
Area size:	77,116 sq. mi.	310	0.0%	Other	4. Watertown	20,237
State Native:	68.1%	10,903	1.4%	Hisp. Origin	5. Brookings	18,504
Non-citizen:	1.1%	**Ancestry**			Urban population: 51.9%	
Language		German: 29.1%	Norwegian: 10.9%		Rural population: 48.1%	
English: 91.0%	Other Eur.: 3.8%	Irish: 7.4%	English: 5.0%			
Spanish: 2.2%		Dutch: 3.4%				

Education		Work Sector		Legislature	
H.S. Grad:	84.6%	Private: 72.9%	Govt: 15.3%	Senate	26 R 9 D
College Grad:	21.5%	Self: 11.0%	Family: 0.8%	House	49 R 21 D
Industry		Unemployment: 4.4%		Legislative Term Limits: Yes	
Agri: 8.1%	Con: 6.3%	**Household Income**		**Registered Voters**	
Fin: 7.4%	Info: 2.1%	<15k: 18.4%	15-35k: 31.2%	D: 183,343	(38.5%)
Mfg: 15.7%	Prof: 27.0%	35-50k: 19.0%	50-100k: 25.5%	R: 228,200	(47.9%)
Public: 4.8%	Trade: 15.3%	100-150k: 3.8%	>150k: 2.1%	I: 64,441	(13.5%)
Other: 13.3%		Median: $35,282			
Occupation		Poverty status: 13.2%			
Blue collar: 23.3%	White collar: 59.1%	**Home Value**			
Gray collar: 17.6%		<50k: 31.1%	50-100k: 39.4%	100-200k: 23.6%	200-300k: 3.7%
		300-500k: 1.4%	>500k: 0.7%	Median: $74,300	

Presidential politics   South Dakota has voted Democratic for president just four times since statehood, in 1896, 1932, 1936 and 1964. But it was fairly close in five of the seven elections between 1972, when South Dakota's George McGovern was the Democratic nominee, and 1996, when Bill Clinton came within 3% of winning. In 2000 the cultural liberalism and environmental policies of Al Gore were far from popular here, and George W. Bush carried the state 60%–38%. Gore carried only Indians, a rising but small percentage of the electorate, and ran even among the elderly, but the percentage of voters who remember Franklin Roosevelt is on the wane. South Dakota's three electoral votes seem unlikely to be seriously contested in 2004. In 2002 Republicans passed a law barring candidates from running for president and other office at the same time. This was obviously aimed at preventing Tom Daschle from running for president and

2000 Presidential Vote		
Bush (R)	190,700	(60%)
Gore (D)	118,804	(38%)
Other	6,765	(2%)

2000 Republican Presidential Primary		
Bush (R)	35,418	(78%)
McCain (R)	6,228	(14%)
Keyes (R)	3,478	(8%)

1996 Presidential Vote		
Dole (R)	150,543	(46%)
Clinton (D)	139,333	(43%)
Perot (I)	31,250	(10%)

for senator in 2004, but it was mooted when Daschle announced in January 2003 that he wouldn't run for president.

South Dakota's presidential primary for years was held in June, on the same day as California's, and eclipsed by it. Since 1988 it has been held in February, just one week after New Hampshire. So far it has been not a trendsetter, but a booster of Great Plains candidates who do not fare well elsewhere: Bob Dole in 1988 and 1996, Dick Gephardt in 1988, Bob Kerrey and Tom Harkin in 1992. In 2000 the primary was moved back to June and attracted little notice.

Governor

Mike Rounds (R)

Elected 2002, term expires Jan. 2007, 1st term; b. Oct. 24, 1954, Pierre; home, Pierre; SD St. U., B.S. 1977; Catholic; married (Jean).

Elected Office: SD Senate, 1990–00; Maj. Ldr. 1996–00.

Professional Career: Practicing atty., 1979-present.

Office: 505 E. Capitol Ave., Pierre, 57501, 605-773-3212; Fax: 605-773-5844; Web site: www.state.sd.us/governor.

Election Results

2002 general	Mike Rounds (R)	189,920	(57%)
	Jim Abbott (D)	140,263	(42%)
	Other	4,376	(1%)
2002 primary	Mike Rounds (R)	49,331	(44%)
	Mark Barnett (R)	32,868	(30%)
	Steve Kirby (R)	29,065	(26%)
1998 general	Bill Janklow (R)	166,621	(64%)
	Bernie Hunhoff (D)	85,473	(33%)
	Other	8,093	(3%)

Mike Rounds, a Republican, was elected governor of South Dakota in 2002. He grew up in a family of 11 children in Pierre, the state's tiny state capital; his father was director of the Office of Highway Safety and worked as a lobbyist for the petroleum industry. Rounds graduated from South Dakota State University, the first governor to do so. He worked as a partner in an insurance and real estate agency in Pierre and participated, as you would expect, in many civic activities. In 1990 he was elected to the state Senate and in 1996 he became Senate majority leader. In that job he worked on overhauling the education aid formula, reducing property taxes, changing workmen's comp, wiring schools to the Internet and funding leases of long-term hunting rights. He opposed a state income tax and opposed abortion. He was prevented by term limits from running for reelection in 2000. In December 2001 he announced he was running for governor.

Rounds sought to replace the governor who had dominated state government for the past quarter-century, Bill Janklow. Janklow was elected attorney general in 1974; in 1978 and 1982 he was elected governor. Term-limited, he ran for the Senate and lost in 1986; his successor, George Mickelson, died in an April 1993 plane crash; Mickelson was succeeded by 67-year-old Walter Dale Miller. Janklow challenged Miller in the 1994 Republican primary and won by a 54%–46% margin, and won the general election 55%–41%. He was reelected 64%–33% in 1998. In his second two terms, Janklow cut the state payroll and cut property taxes by 30%; the inheritance tax, which brought in $25 million, was abolished. As voters considered outlawing video lotteries, which have been legal since 1989 and bring $95 million annually to the state, he said the video games were a "lousy" way to raise money but warned that outlawing them would require the biggest tax increase in state history; voters came out for the games 54%–46%. For most of the

1990s, sales tax revenues increased 5% to 7% a year, but in 2001–02 they increased by only 1%, and by November 2001 it was apparent that the state faced a budget shortfall.

In the Republican primary Rounds faced two much more well-financed opponents, former Lieutenant Governor Steve Kirby and Attorney General Mark Barnett. Rounds ran on property tax relief and opposition to an income tax and abortion. "No gimmicks, no grandstanding, just good government," read his fliers. He was willing to tell people what they didn't want to hear. He told a truckers' group that he was responsible for applying the sales tax to transportation services and said he might favor a higher gas tax if it would bring in much more federal money. He was the only candidate in either party to oppose mandated use of ethanol fuel, despite the state's many ethanol plants and corn growers. He told the South Dakota Education Association that there were "very limited funds" for education spending increases. He refused to pledge to oppose all tax increases. "Very seldom should a candidate totally eliminate all possible need for some revenue action," he said.

His opponents made more news. Kirby, an investor who had built several businesses, called for a multimillion dollar economic development fund to create 50,000 jobs over four years. He proposed increasing the state's take of video lottery money to 65% and using the proceeds for prescription drugs for seniors. He pledged to oppose any tax increase. Barnett also pledged not to increase taxes, although at one candidate forum said he might support a gas tax increase. Rounds's approach to economic development was more *laissez faire*. "Our job, when we talk economic development, is to give people the opportunity to succeed. This starts at the local level up, not at the state down. When people get the idea, government should do whatever it can to help." At candidate forums and then in their ads and direct mail, Kirby and Barnett bitterly attacked each other, on economic development and on other substantive and character issues. They had plenty of money to launch these attacks: Kirby spent over $2.5 million and Barnett $1.75 million. Rounds spent just $147,000. But he had a strategy. In April 2002 he spelled it out, "For the time being, I haven't minded being considered by the other two candidates as this fly buzzing away over in the corner. I've heard several people say just stay out of the negative, there's enough of that. I'd like to run my spots right between Kirby and Barnett. Hopefully, people will see some differences."

Evidently they did. South Dakota is a small state in which voters expect to see candidates in person; candidate forums held in small towns can make some difference here. While Kirby and Barnett attacked each other, Rounds always seemed to be smiling. He certainly was on primary night. In the June primary Rounds won 44% of the vote, to 30% for Barnett and 26% for Kirby. Rounds carried 52 of South Dakota's 66 counties. It was a classic illustration of the rule that it is not wise to launch a negative campaign in a multicandidate race.

The Democratic nominee was Jim Abbott, a businessman who served in the legislature, lost races for lieutenant governor in 1994 and the House in 1996 and was on leave as president of the University of South Dakota. This was a gentlemanly race between old friends; after the primary Abbott said, "Mike Rounds is just a good guy. I really think the people of South Dakota like the idea of a positive message for the future, and this contest offers interesting options." Abbott called for state-sponsored research for economic development and for higher education to work with the private sector to create jobs. He revealed something of his attitude when he said, after shots were fired at a car occupied by girls from the Crow Creek Indian Reservation, "I don't know if that was about race or not, but of course it wouldn't be surprising in this state. When we're really being honest, we know darned well that you can't be at least a white male in this state and not have almost from birth some prejudice." While negative ads were hitting the air in the Senate race, the dialogue in the governor race was positive. Rounds led in polls from the primary on and in November won 57%–42%. Abbott carried Indian reservations and the area around the University of South Dakota in Vermillion.

After the election Rounds went to work on the state budget problems. In December Janklow presented figures showing spending requests $54 million higher than projected revenue, with $90 million in the state reserve. In 2003 Rounds proposed tax increases on cigarettes and alcoholic beverages and making more interstate phone calls subject to the sales tax. Though the legislature failed to pass his proposed tax on alcohol, it ended up passing 19 of the 22 bills requested by

Rounds. Even without revenues from the tax measures he requested, he successfully cut the cost of prescription drugs for senior citizens and managed to increase state aid to school districts by $15.1 million.

Senior Senator

Tom Daschle (D)

Elected 1986, seat up 2004, 3d term; b. Dec. 9, 1947, Aberdeen; home, Aberdeen; SD St. U., B.A. 1969; Catholic; married (Linda).

Military Career: Air Force, 1969–72, Air Force Reserves, 1975–78.

Elected Office: U.S. House of Reps., 1978–86.

Professional Career: Legis. Asst., U.S. Sen. James Abourezk, 1973–77.

DC Office: 509 HSOB, 20510, 202-224-2321; Fax: 202-224-7895; Web site: daschle.senate.gov.

State Offices: Aberdeen, 605-225-8823; Rapid City, 605-348-7551; Sioux Falls, 605-334-9596.

Committees: *Minority Leader. Agriculture, Nutrition & Forestry*: Forestry, Conservation & Rural Revitalization; Production & Price Competitiveness. *Finance*: Health Care; International Trade; Social Security & Family Policy. *Rules & Administration.*

Group Ratings

	ADA	ACLU	AFS	LCV	CON	ITIC	NTU	COC	ACU	NTLC	CHC
2002	85	60	75	59	36	75	18	58	22	0	—
2001	100	—	100	88	—	—	6	43	8	—	0

National Journal Ratings

	2001 LIB	—	2001 CONS		2002 LIB	—	2002 CONS
Economic	82%	—	15%		73%	—	20%
Social	81%	—	8%		68%	—	28%
Foreign	74%	—	14%		59%	—	38%

Key Votes of the 107th Congress

1. Approve Bush Tax Cuts	N	5. Confirm Ashcroft as AG	N	9. Bar Coop. with Intl. Court	N
2. Expand Patients' Rights	Y	6. Bar Gays in the Boy Scouts	N	10. Trade Promotion Authority	Y
3. Campaign Finance Reform	Y	7. $ for Hate Crime Prosecution	N	11. Authorize Force in Iraq	Y
4. Permit ANWR Development	N	8. Overseas Military Abortions	Y	12. Homeland Sec. Dept. Union	Y

Election Results

1998 general	Tom Daschle (D)	162,884	(62%)	($4,861,541)
	Ron Schmidt (R)	95,431	(36%)	($492,854)
	Other	3,796	(1%)	
1998 primary	Tom Daschle (D)	unopposed		
1992 general	Tom Daschle (D)	217,095	(65%)	($3,981,548)
	Charlene Haar (R)	108,733	(33%)	($478,421)
	Other	8,667	(3%)	

Prior Winning Percentages: 1986 (52%); 1984 House (57%); 1982 House (52%); 1980 House (66%); 1978 House (50%)

Tom Daschle, first elected to the Senate in 1986, was Senate majority leader from June 2001 to January 2003 (and for 17 days in January 2001) and is now, as he was from January 1995 to June 2001, minority leader. He grew up in Aberdeen, where his father was a bookkeeper at an auto parts store, and graduated from South Dakota State, the first in his family to graduate from college. His entire career has been in government. He served as an intelligence officer in the Air Force in the years George McGovern was running for president. In 1973 he became a Washington staffer for Senator James Abourezk. In 1978, as Abourezk was about to retire, Daschle returned to South Dakota, ran for the eastern House district that Larry Pressler was vacating to run for the Senate, and won by exactly 139 votes over Vietnam P.O.W. Leo Thorsness, who had come close to beating McGovern for the Senate in 1974. Daschle was a generally faithful follower of the Democratic leadership in the House, trapped far behind others in seniority. In 1982, when South Dakota lost one of its two House seats, he ran against incumbent Republican Cliff Roberts and won 52%–48%.

It was natural for Daschle, already representing the entire state, to run in 1986 for the Senate seat held by Republican Jim Abdnor. Daschle had the additional good luck that Governor Bill Janklow was opposing Abdnor in the primary, putting Abdnor on the defensive and forcing him to use much of his money. Daschle again won 52%–48%, in one of the key victories that returned control of the Senate to the Democrats for eight years. Two years later, in January 1989, new Senate Majority Leader George Mitchell named Daschle co-chairman of the Senate Democratic Policy Committee—in effect, though not in title, the number two man in the Senate leadership. When Mitchell announced his retirement in March 1994, Daschle immediately started running for majority leader—too soon to suit some traditionalists. His opponent Jim Sasser seemed to have enough votes to win, but Sasser lost to Republican Bill Frist in Tennessee in November. That was the good news for Daschle; the bad news was that Democrats had lost enough seats that the race was for minority rather than majority leader. Connecticut's Christopher Dodd immediately entered the race, with encouragement from some older committee chairmen; but Daschle relinquished his seat on the Finance Committee to Carol Moseley-Braun of Illinois, whose vote gave him a 24–23 victory.

Daschle's capacity for dogged hard work, his seemingly mild manner and ability to stay unruffled, and his efforts at building consensus made the Democratic Caucus more united than in many years—maybe ever—and more effective legislatively than almost anyone expected. His first big test was on the balanced budget amendment. Daschle segued smoothly from his former support of the amendment to opposition, with the argument that any such amendment should exclude Social Security. That provided cover for him and five other Democrats who had previously supported balanced budget amendments to switch and defeat the amendment by one vote in March 1995.

Through all this, Daschle's soft-spoken style, about which many Democrats had qualms, proved effective on television. He maintained his generally liberal voting record. Once rather skeptical of American foreign involvements, and an opponent of the Gulf War resolution, he steadily supported the Clinton administration on Bosnia and Kosovo and on PNTR with China. After Republicans gained two seats in the 1996 election, Daschle advanced his own priorities. One was change in campaign finance regulation: he backs a constitutional amendment to limit spending by candidates, parties and independent groups. On impeachment, Daschle steadily defended Bill Clinton and advanced partisan positions in his pleasant but steely manner. But as Clinton's lawyers kept trying to insist that he had not lied under oath in August 1998 about lying under oath in January 1998, Daschle called on Clinton to stop "hairsplitting" in September. During the impeachment trial, as on other issues, he stayed in close and constant touch with Majority Leader Trent Lott, which led to the 100-senator caucus in the Old Senate Chamber and a much more harmonious proceeding than had been expected.

Daschle's success in holding Senate Democrats together during their years in the minority in the 1990s and again today has been accomplished not by intimidation—there was not much he can threaten them with—but by dialogue. He understands that colleagues will sometimes disagree with the party position, but he asks them not to go off the reservation without talking to him first—and then often gets them to agree to delay going public. As a result, Democrats who might be publicly committed to opposing the party often end up supporting it instead: inertia works for party unity. From 1995 to 2000 Daschle used the Senate rules allowing non-germane amendments to advantage, advancing to the floor Democratic proposals which test well in the polls—the minimum wage, prescription drugs for seniors, HMO regulation—even while using procedure to obstruct popular Republican measures to move forward.

The emergence of a 50–50 Senate and the election of George W. Bush—neither of them apparent until December 2000—made Daschle one of the pivotal figures in American politics. He was majority leader for 17 days, from January 3 to January 20, 2001, when the new Senate took office and the tie-breaking vote was still cast by Vice President Al Gore. But Daschle sensibly made no move to capitalize unduly on that temporary majority. Instead, by threatening to tie up Senate business for months, he forced Trent Lott to agree on January 5 to equal membership on all committees for both parties, with the proviso that on tied committee votes nominations and bills could be brought to the floor: both parties' ability to obstruct was reduced. From January to May 2001 he complained that Bush's pleas for bipartisan action were not matched by any willingness to negotiate with the Democratic leadership. He reacted sharply when Democrat Zell Miller, appointed in July 2000 to replace Republican Paul Coverdell, endorsed Bush's tax cut and backed Attorney General nominee John Ashcroft; Miller had broken Daschle's unwritten rule of not consulting with him first, and giving Daschle an opportunity to persuade him to delay any break with the party. He was angered when ranking Finance Committee Democrat Max Baucus worked out a bipartisan tax cut with Chairman Charles Grassley.

It was the tax cut, nevertheless, that led to Daschle regaining his post as majority leader. Vermont Republican James Jeffords had helped force Republicans to compromise on the tax cut, and Daschle and Democratic Whip Harry Reid reached out to Jeffords just as his relations with Republican leaders began to deteriorate. In May 2001 Jeffords announced he was becoming an Independent and would vote with Democrats to organize the Senate. Daschle now became majority leader and negotiated a new organizing resolution with Republicans. Democrats would have one-vote majorities on all committees and Daschle would be able to use the majority leader position to bring—or refuse to bring—legislation to the floor. Like Bush, he sounded a bipartisan note. But, also like Bush, he pursued partisan goals. He insisted on a floor vote on HMO regulation before the July 4 recess.

Then came September 11. Congressional leaders of both parties literally found themselves in the same bunker, feeling the same outrage at the attacks and the same determination to respond. When George W. Bush came to speak to Congress he hugged Daschle. Daschle, Lott, Speaker Dennis Hastert and Minority Leader Dick Gephardt met with Bush in weekly breakfasts and worked on legislation together. On October 15 a letter addressed to Daschle that contained anthrax was opened in his Hart Senate Office Building; he and his staff were tested and the building was closed for months. But the bipartisan mood didn't last. Daschle opposed the administration's stimulus package, and the Senate Finance Committee voted out a Democratic version November 9; Republicans used procedural votes to kill it November 14. Daschle said he was "disappointed" (his trademark word of disapproval) that the issue had become so "partisan." There was an impasse on the issue in December; Daschle said he would support a bill only if it had support from two-thirds of the Democratic Caucus. A $51 billion stimulus bill was eventually signed into law March 9; Daschle voted for it. Back in South Dakota, in December, a conservative group ran a TV ad showing next to each other pictures of Daschle and Saddam Hussein. In Washington, Daschle put more money for homeland security in the defense supplemental.

Partisan conflict became more visible. In December 2001 Dick Cheney said Daschle "unfortunately has decided . . . to be more of an obstructionist." In January 2002 Daschle delivered a speech arguing that the Bush tax cut "probably made the recession worse" and set the stage for "the most dramatic fiscal deterioration in our nation's history." In February 2002 he said of the situation in Afghanistan, "I don't think the success has been overstated, but the continued success, I think, is still somewhat in doubt. Clearly we've got to find Mohammed Omar. We've got to find Osama bin Laden . . . or we will have failed." Increasingly Republicans attacked Daschle for obstructionism and Democrats rallied to his defense. Ads ran in South Dakota attacking and backing him. In the meantime, Daschle in March 2002 pushed to passage the McCain-Feingold campaign finance regulation bill. Daschle also stepped in and took over bills from Democratic committee chairmen. After Max Baucus cooperated, while in the minority, on the Bush tax cut, Daschle reportedly threatened to take away his chairmanship if he made his own deal on prescription drug legislation. In October 2001 he snatched the energy bill from the Energy Committee when it appeared likely to approve oil drilling in the Arctic National Wildlife Refuge. In December 2001 he arranged for another version to come to the floor, into which he inserted a provision tripling by 2012 the amount of ethanol refiners were required to produce; California and New York Democrats protested. In May 2002 he shaped the farm bill behind the scenes, increasing limits on subsidies and providing for higher loan rates. But on his own list of successes there were more instances of blocking Republican initiatives than advancing Democratic bills. The Senate never passed a budget resolution, for the first time since the budget process began in 1974. That meant that any prescription drug bill required 60 votes to pass; after long debate in July 2002, none was able to do so. In September 2002, in a widely publicized speech, he attacked the Bush economic policies as "tragic, deplorable, abysmal," but did not offer alternatives.

In June 2002 Bush called for a new Department of Homeland Security, something previously championed mostly by Democrats. But Bush said that the labor relations provisions of the Senate Democrats' bill were unacceptable. Sponsor Joe Lieberman and Daschle said they found it hard to believe that Bush would veto the bill over the issue, but Bush seemed implacable. "The Senate is more interested in special interests in Washington and not interested in the security of the American people," said Bush at a September 23 campaign appearance in New Jersey. Two days later Daschle rose in the Senate and spoke with evident anger, saying that Bush was "politicizing" the debate. This came two weeks after Bush's speech to the United Nations and his announcement that he would ask for congressional authorization of military action in Iraq. At first, in September, Daschle suggested that the Senate would not vote until after the election; this was interpreted by some as an attempt to shield Democrats up in 2002 from pressure to vote in favor. Shortly afterwards, Daschle said the Senate should debate only a few days and move on to other issues; this was interpreted by some as an attempt to shift attention to domestic issues on which Democrats were thought to have an advantage. Daschle encouraged Foreign Relations leaders Joseph Biden and Richard Lugar to write a resolution that would limit authorization to Iraq and removal of weapons of mass destruction. But on October 2 House Minority Leader Dick Gephardt, House and Senate Republicans and the White House agreed on a broader resolution, and Daschle's position was effectively undercut; Daschle cancelled his usual press conference that day. The Senate voted on the resolution October 11 and Daschle and his South Dakota colleague Tim Johnson, running about even in the polls with Republican challenger John Thune, were two of 29 Democrats to vote in favor. But the homeland security bill was the subject of continued debate, and no version passed the Senate before the election.

In June 2002 Daschle told *National Journal*, "I have one focus, and that focus is exclusively on maintaining a majority of the Senate—hopefully winning a couple of additional seats—and I will do whatever it takes, within the confines of what is prudent and appropriate, to accomplish that goal." But Daschle's insistence on solidarity with federal employees' unions on homeland security and his changes of course on an Iraq war resolution helped to undermine Democrats' credibility on national security. On Election Day Democrats picked up one seat in Arkansas but lost three in Georgia, Minnesota and Missouri; Tim Johnson held on by 524 votes. The next day Daschle's face was etched with disappointment. But, perhaps heeding some Democrats who argued that their party had not opposed Bush vociferously enough, he seemed determined to carry on, from the minority, much as before. In January 2003 he led Democrats in refusing to agree on divisions in committees and on staffs similar to those that obtained before 2001; he insisted on something more like the June 2001 organizing resolution. Senate Democrats embarked on a filibuster of a lower court nomination—the first in history. It was not clear whether, as Minority Leader, Daschle could or would rein in committee ranking Democrats as he had, as majority leader, committee chairmen. On March 17, 2003, as Bush was to address the nation that evening announcing a final 48-hour ultimatum to Saddam Hussein, Daschle said, "I'm saddened, saddened that this president failed so miserably at diplomacy that we're now forced to war. Saddened that we have to give up one life because this president couldn't create the kind of diplomatic effort that was so critical for our country." Republicans chastised him for criticizing the president at an inappropriate time.

Throughout his years as leader, Daschle has kept his eye on South Dakota issues. He was not able to stop the drastic revision of farm laws in 1996, but in 1998, as farm prices sagged, he helped put together a $6 billion package of emergency aid—the first of several annual disaster relief packages that delivered more money to farmers of favored crops than the old subsidy system. And he intervened to increase payments in the 2002 farm act. Into the defense appropriation in December 2001 he put a provision giving the federal government responsibility for environmental damage at the Homestake mine near Lead, which will help his project to build a national laboratory for subatomic particle research there. Into the defense supplemental in July 2002 he inserted a provision exempting South Dakota from environmental regulations and lawsuits against logging operations to thin forest after disastrous forest fires; Republicans from Rocky Mountain states complained that they wanted similar provisions for their states too, which Daschle, at the behest of environmental restriction groups, did not back.

Daschle has made a practice of traveling each year, usually in August, to all 66 South Dakota counties; he sometimes just drives by himself, dressed casually, and over coffee or at gas stations asks voters about their concerns. He was reelected by wide margins in 1992 and 1998 against lightly funded opponents. In 1998 he was helped by solid support from Republican Governor Bill Janklow, who was cruising to reelection himself.

But he may have more trouble winning reelection in 2004. In 2001 and 2002 he was one of several national Democrats considering running for president; he promised a decision after the 2002 election. In February 2002 the Republican legislature passed and Janklow signed a bill prohibiting anyone for running for president and another office; Daschle said, "Under no circumstances would I ever run for both offices, the presidency and the Senate." In December 2002 his aides started interviewing staffers for a presidential campaign and set up media interviews. But on January 7 he announced he would not run for president. "To be honest, I came very close to deciding in favor of running," he said, but late on the night before he decided not to. Standing in the Capitol he said, "I'm not going to run for president because my passion is right here."

He did say that he would run for reelection to the Senate. But some are not sure; in November 2002, after Democrats lost their Senate majority, South Dakota's premier political reporter, Dave Kranz of the Sioux Falls *Argus-Leader*, wrote that "betting people who are close to him think he won't seek reelection to a fourth term." The example of his predecessor as Democratic leader, George Mitchell, may be tantalizing: Mitchell retired in 1994, when he could easily have won reelection, and has since taken an important part in public affairs while making an excellent living as a Washington lawyer-lobbyist. And it is not clear that Daschle could win easily. True, his colleague and friend Tim Johnson did win in 2002, but by only 524 votes. Republican candidate John Thune was urged by other Republicans to contest the election, but he refused to do so. Thune's favorable ratings continue to be very high, and Republican polls in November 2002 and March 2003 showed Thune 1% to 2% ahead of Daschle—the same kind of dead heat in almost every poll taken during the Johnson-Thune race. If Thune runs he will have the advantage of all-out support from the Bush White House and fundraising prowess as great as Daschle's, assets that none of Daschle's previous opponents have had. And George W. Bush, who carried South Dakota 60%–38% in 2000, will be at the top of the ballot. All of this is not to say that Daschle cannot win. He is hard-working and disciplined, he has built up good will with South Dakota voters over many years and he will have strong financial backing. But this man whose congressional career began when he won by 139 votes and whose career as Democratic leader began when he won by one vote may be facing the race of his life.

Junior Senator

Tim Johnson (D)

Elected 1996, seat up 2008, 2d term; b. Dec. 28, 1946, Canton; home, Vermillion; U. of SD, B.A. 1969, M.A. 1970, J.D. 1975, MI St. U., 1970–71; Lutheran; married (Barbara).

Military Career: Army, 1969.

Elected Office: SD House of Reps., 1978–82; SD Senate, 1982–86; U.S. House of Reps., 1986–96.

Professional Career: Budget Analyst, MI Senate, 1971–72; Practicing atty., 1975–85; Clay Cnty. Dpty. Atty., 1985.

DC Office: 136 HSOB, 20510, 202-224-5842; Fax: 202-228-5765; Web site: johnson.senate.gov.

State Offices: Aberdeen, 605-226-3440; Rapid City, 605-341-3990; Sioux Falls, 605-332-8896.

Committees: *Appropriations*: Agriculture & Rural Development; Foreign Operations; Legislative Branch; Military Construction; VA, HUD & Independent Agencies. *Banking, Housing & Urban Affairs*: Financial Institutions (RMM); International Trade & Finance; Securities & Investment. *Budget. Energy & Natural Resources*: Energy; Public Lands & Forests; Water & Power. *Indian Affairs*.

Group Ratings

	ADA	ACLU	AFS	LCV	CON	ITIC	NTU	COC	ACU	NTLC	CHC
2002	90	40	100	47	8	50	14	53	15	9	—
2001	85	—	92	63	—	—	16	64	32	—	40

National Journal Ratings

	2001 LIB —	2001 CONS	2002 LIB —	2002 CONS
Economic	57%	43%	56%	42%
Social	53%	46%	77%	18%
Foreign	61%	27%	64%	33%

Key Votes of the 107th Congress

1. Approve Bush Tax Cuts	Y	5. Confirm Ashcroft as AG	N	9. Bar Coop. with Intl. Court	Y
2. Expand Patients' Rights	Y	6. Bar Gays in the Boy Scouts	Y	10. Trade Promotion Authority	N
3. Campaign Finance Reform	Y	7. $ for Hate Crime Prosecution	Y	11. Authorize Force in Iraq	Y
4. Permit ANWR Development	N	8. Overseas Military Abortions	Y	12. Homeland Sec. Dept. Union	Y

Election Results

2002 general	Tim Johnson (D)	167,481	(50%)	($6,152,991)
	John Thune (R)	166,957	(50%)	($5,989,043)
2002 primary	Tim Johnson (D)	65,438	(95%)	
	Herman Eilers (D)	3,558	(5%)	
1996 general	Tim Johnson (D)	166,533	(51%)	($2,990,554)
	Larry Pressler (R)	157,954	(49%)	($5,138,298)

Prior Winning Percentages: 1994 House (60%); 1992 House (69%); 1990 House (68%); 1988 House (72%); 1986 House (59%)

Tim Johnson, a Democrat, was elected to the Senate in 1996. He grew up in Canton, Flandreau and Vermillion in southeast South Dakota, graduated from the University of South Dakota and served briefly in the Army (he was discharged because of a hearing problem). He graduated from Michigan State University business school and worked for the state Senate. Then he graduated from the University of South Dakota Law School and started a law practice in Vermillion. He was elected to the state House in 1978, at 31, and reelected in 1980; in 1982 and 1984 he was elected to the state Senate. When Congressman Tom Daschle ran for the Senate in 1986, Johnson ran for the House. He beat state Senator Jim Burg in the primary 48%–45%. He won the general by 59%–41%, and was reelected with larger percentages every two years thereafter.

In the House, Johnson compiled a generally liberal voting record, though he voted for the balanced budget amendment and was the only Democrat to switch his vote to support lifting the Bosnia arms embargo. He successfully managed reauthorization of crop insurance as a subcommittee chairman in 1994 and helped relax the "swampbuster" provisions penalizing farmers who violated wetlands regulations in the 1996 Freedom to Farm Act; he warned that the phasing out of farm supports would hurt in drought years.

In 1996 Johnson ran against Republican Senator Larry Pressler, then chairman of the Commerce Committee. This was a high-spending, high-stakes race: Pressler spent $5.1 million, with over $1.7 million from PACs; Johnson spent almost $3 million, with $850,000 from PACs. TV ads began in August 1995, when the race was about even, and it stayed that way for 15 months. Since South Dakota TV is cheap, that meant one barrage of ads after another—plus seven debates. Pressler attacked Johnson as too liberal, going back to a 1981 vote in the legislature against workfare. Johnson attacked Pressler as a Newt-oid Medicare cutter and charged that he switched from opposition to support of maritime subsidies after receiving $29,000 from maritime PACs. Pressler spent much time in 1995 and 1996 on the telecommunications bill, the most-lobbied and arguably most complex bill before the 104th Congress. He succeeded in passing the bill, the first major rewrite of communications law in 63 years, but back home Johnson was charging that phone and cable rates were going up. The final result was a 51%–49% Johnson victory, narrower than the final month's polls suggested.

In the Senate, Johnson's voting record has been generally liberal, except on some cultural issues; he supported the partial-birth abortion ban. He co-sponsored a bill prohibiting meatpackers from owning, feeding or keeping livestock. He opposed a measure that would label as "Made in the U.S.A." beef from cattle that had fed in the United States for only 100 days. The ban on meatpacker ownership of livestock and country-of-origin labeling of meat went into the 2002 farm bill. He helped pass a six-state pilot project to allow farmers to enroll plots of five acres and less of wetlands into the Conservation Reserve Program: good for South Dakota pheasant habitat. He worked quietly on a bill to overhaul the FDIC, co-sponsored by Chuck Hagel, Mike Enzi and Jack Reed. Johnson seldom got much publicity. "There are enough showhorses in Washington to go around," he says.

By early 2001 it was apparent that Johnson would face a tough challenge in 2002. He had been elected with 51% of the vote in a state that voted 60%–38% for George W. Bush. Early 2001 polls showed him trailing Republican Congressman John Thune, who had succeeded him in the House and won reelection by wide margins. In late 2000 Thune seemed poised to run for governor. But Bush, on a trip to South Dakota in March 2001 and at a White House dinner with spouses in April, talked him into running for Senate. But if the race was important to Bush, it was even more important to Tom Daschle, who often said it was "the most important political effort for me" in 2002. Daschle helped Johnson by getting him a seat on the Appropriations Committee, from which he could funnel money into South Dakota. And Johnson was careful to cast some moderate votes on important issues. He voted for the Republican Social Security lockbox in March 2001 and for the $1.3 trillion tax cut in May 2001.

Thune announced in October 2001. He argued that the state would have been better off with a bipartisan Senate delegation. Of course, there was a caveat: a Thune victory could give the Republicans a Senate majority and make Daschle Minority Leader again. Johnson argued that he and Daschle made a uniquely powerful team. "This is the first time in a very, very long time that our state has had a seat [on Appropriations]. South Dakota's priorities are now the nation's priorities. We have the Senate majority leader from South Dakota and a senator on this committee. We've only had this power for only a year. I think we need to keep the team that's been incredibly powerful for this state."

This was a campaign waged, as all South Dakota campaigns are, by personal campaigning but also, to a greater extent than any in South Dakota history, over television. The candidates, both incumbent members of Congress, had to spend much of their time in Washington. The two candidates spent record amounts for South Dakota—Johnson $6.1 million, Thune $6.0 million— and the national parties and independent expenditure groups on both sides spent much more. A week of TV ads costs only about $80,000 in South Dakota, as compared to about $1.5 million in

Los Angeles. The ads started running in late 2001 and by November 2002 the average voter had seen more than 1,000 of them.

Thune was the more outgoing of the two, a candidate who loved shaking hands and seldom forgot a face. Johnson, more reserved, was nevertheless tenacious and moderate in demeanor. At one point Johnson said of Thune, "He's a nice guy. He'd make a great next-door neighbor. You just wouldn't want him representing you in the United States Senate." Thune replied, "He'd be a good neighbor too, because he'd be quiet. He wouldn't make a lot of noise." Of all the seriously contested Democratic senators in 2002, Johnson ran the most conservative-sounding campaign. "Tim Johnson has strongly supported President Bush, the war against terrorism, his tax cut and his education reform," one ad said. Thune nonetheless attacked him for voting against making the tax cut permanent. Johnson replied that he supported eliminating the estate tax for family farmers and ranchers and family-owned businesses and to increase the exemption to $4 million for individuals. On some issues both candidates seemed to take stands in opposition to their own parties. Thune attacked Johnson for favoring "privatization" of Social Security and called for no changes in the program; he was referring to Johnson's positive statements in the 1990s about a proposal advanced by Bill Clinton for the federal government to invest part of Social Security revenues in the stock market. Johnson replied that he now backed nothing of the sort. Thune also said that Johnson "voted seven times to raise $300 billion from Social Security;" this was a reference to votes on the entire budget, and used national Democrats' device of claiming that such spending robs Social Security.

Both local and international issues got some airing during the campaign. The biggest local issue was the drought that hit western South Dakota for most of 2002. Ranchers were selling off their herds for low prices; business losses were estimated at $1.8 billion. Daschle and Johnson responded by sponsoring $5 billion in disaster aid for farmers and ranchers, arguing that if floods and tornadoes triggered disaster relief, then droughts should too. But this was opposed by the Bush administration, which wanted any aid to come out of the $190 billion approved for farm spending. On August 15 George W. Bush came to South Dakota amid speculation that he would offer more. But, to the disappointment of the Thune campaign, he didn't. By this time, there seemed to be some improvement in Johnson's showing in the polls, though almost no polls throughout the campaign showed a margin for either candidate outside the statistical margin of error. But in mid-September Agriculture Secretary Ann Veneman announced $750 million in aid for 30 states. Democrats grumbled that $750 million was a pittance, but Daschle's $5 billion, now raised to $6 billion, was stalled in the Senate.

Defense was another issue often stressed. Thune attacked Johnson for voting against the Gulf War resolution in January 1991 and for joining the group of Democratic members of Congress who sued George H.W. Bush challenging his conduct of the war. Johnson pointed out that his son, Brooks Johnson, served in the 101st Airborne Division in Afghanistan from December 2001 to June 2002 and could be sent to Iraq (which he later was) if the United States went in. "Our understanding as father and son is, 'You do what is best for the country, and I'll do my job.'" While Daschle was still publicly undecided, Johnson announced that he would vote for the Iraq war resolution. On the floor of the Senate he said, "There is a strong possibility that I may be voting to send my own son into combat, and that gives me special empathy for the families of other American servicemen and women whose own sons and daughters may also be sent to Iraq. Nevertheless, I am willing to cast this vote—one of the most important in my career both as a senator and certainly as a father—because I recognize the threat that Saddam Hussein represents to world peace." Republicans continued to attack Johnson on defense issues and his support of the Democratic position on homeland security.

There was one more issue blazing in October: fraudulent Indian voter registrations. The state Democratic party set up offices on each of the state's Indian reservations and paid bonuses to contractors who brought in signed voter registration cards. One such contractor was fired in October and charged with submitting scores of illegally filled out registration cards, including one purportedly signed by a woman who had died two weeks before, and many more with mismatched birth dates and nonexistent addresses. On October 22, a consultant for the Sioux Tribes Voter Education and Registration Committee was indicted on five counts of forgery of voter registration cards. Attorney General Mark Barnett and the U.S. attorney launched investigations. All this made headlines in a state with a tradition of squeaky-clean voting and a memory of the violent Indian movement of the 1970s. Johnson said that the voter registration operation was run by the state Democratic party and that his campaign had nothing to do with it. At one debate Johnson challenged Thune to stop his negative ads. Thune said he would do so as soon as Johnson held a news conference to explain what he knew about this vote fraud.

This election turned out to be the closest in the nation. During most of election night and into the morning Thune led in the counting. Then the last two precincts came in, from Shannon County, which includes most of the Pine Ridge Indian Reservation. Those two precincts put Johnson over the top, by a margin of 524 votes—in percentage terms, 50.1%–49.9%. In Shannon County, 3,118 votes were cast, as compared to 1,953 in the 2000 presidential election. The county voted 92%–8% for Johnson. In the six main reservation counties, turnout was 11,275, up from 7,500 in 2000 and 7,000 in 1994. These six counties voted 78%–21% for Johnson. In 43 of the other 60 counties, including the 10 largest, Johnson's percentage declined from 1996, when he won 51% statewide. It was an Indian registration drive that was either very successful or partly fraudulent, or both, that reelected Tim Johnson. Investigations were continuing after the election, but no further specific evidence of fraud surfaced. Many Republicans urged Thune to contest the election. But on November 13, he announced he would not. "The people of South Dakota have been subjected to one of the longest and most expensive campaigns in South Dakota history. I choose not to subject them to more." Johnson has now won two full terms in the Senate by the smallest combined popular vote margin, 9,103, of any senator since George Malone of Nevada, elected by a combined margin of 7,970 in 1946 and 1952.

Representative-At-Large

Bill Janklow (R)

Elected 2002, 1st term; b. Sept. 13, 1939, Chicago, IL; home, Brandon; U. of SD, B.S. 1964, LL.B 1966; Lutheran; married (Mary Dean).

Military Career: Marine Corps, 1956–59.

Elected Office: SD Atty. Gen., 1974–78; SD Gov., 1978–86; 1994–2002.

Professional Career: Director, Legal aid program for Rosebud Indian Reservation, 1966–73; SD Special Prosecutor, 1973–75; Practicing atty., 1987–94.

DC Office: 1504 LHOB, 20515, 202-225-2801; Fax: 202-225-5832; Web site: www.house.gov/janklow.

District Offices: Aberdeen, 605-626-3440; Rapid City, 605-394-5280; Sioux Falls, 605-367-8371.

Committees: *Agriculture* (19th of 27 R): Department Operations, Oversight, Nutrition & Forestry; Livestock & Horticulture. *Government Reform* (23d of 24 R): Energy Policy, Natural Resources and Regulatory Affairs (Vice Chmn.); National Security, Emerging Threats & Intl. Relations. *International Relations* (25th of 26 R): Europe; Middle East & Central Asia.

Group Ratings and Key Votes: Newly Elected

Election Results

2002 general	Bill Janklow (R)	180,023	(53%)	($1,314,087)
	Stephanie Herseth (D)	153,656	(46%)	($1,511,189)
	Other	3,128	(1%)	
2002 primary	Bill Janklow (R)	60,575	(55%)	
	Larry Pressler (R)	29,992	(27%)	
	Tim Amdahl (R)	10,593	(10%)	
	Roger Hunt (R)	7,799	(7%)	
2000 general	John Thune (R)	231,083	(73%)	($953,757)
	Curt Hohn (D)	78,321	(25%)	($115,038)
	Other	5,357	(2%)	

South Dakota's single member of the House is Bill Janklow, a Republican elected in 2002 after serving 16 years as governor and four as attorney general. Janklow grew up first in Chicago; then after the death of his father, a prosecutor at the Nuremberg war crimes trial, the family moved to his mother's hometown, Flandreau, South Dakota. Janklow dropped out of high school and joined the Marines; he returned in 1960, married, and without a high school diploma talked his way into the University of South Dakota, where he worked his way through college and law school. After law school he worked in the legal aid program at the Rosebud Indian Reservation. He was elected state attorney general in 1974, with 67% of the vote; this was just a year after the American Indian Movement seized the town of Wounded Knee on the Pine Ridge Indian Reservation. Janklow vigorously prosecuted AIM members and other Indians for violent crimes and compiled a high conviction record. In 1978 he was elected governor with 56% of the vote; in 1982 re-elected with 71%. During this time, he attracted Citicorp to the state, reduced agricultural and residential property taxes, cut state payrolls, stimulated new business, and converted a state college into a prison. Term-limited in 1986, Janklow ran against incumbent Republican Senator Jim Abdnor and lost 55%–45% in the primary; it is a tantalizing question whether Janklow would have beaten Tom Daschle in the fall. Janklow proceeded to practice law for eight years in Sioux Falls. In 1994 he ran for governor again, against Walter Miller, who succeeded to the office in 1993 after incumbent George Mickelson died in a plane crash. Janklow won the Republican primary by a 54%–46% margin. He won the general election 55%–41%.

Janklow is a blunt, plain-spoken, often tactless politician given to hands-on management of crises. In 1994 he promised to cut homeowners' property taxes by 30%, and delivered by 2000. He cut the state payroll, and even cut total spending in 1996. He welcomed more new businesses including the headquarters of IBP meatpackers to South Dakota. After the town of Spencer was destroyed by a May 1998 tornado he camped out there and superintended evacuation and recovery plans. In September 1998, in protest of what he considered unfair Canadian trade practices, he ordered state troopers to stop and inspect trucks carrying Canadian livestock and grain; they were to be searched and not allowed in the state if the livestock was not proved free of drugs legal in Canada but not in the U.S., and if the grain was not certified as free of disease and wild oats. The searches continued for three weeks, until Agriculture Secretary Dan Glickman promised to raise the issues with Canadian officials.

In 1998 he ran for a fourth term. During the campaign he lavished praise on Tom Daschle, who was also running for reelection. Their friendship went back to 1994, when Daschle was accused of exerting undue influence with the FAA; Janklow wrote a letter to *The New York Times* affirming his integrity, and Daschle responded with a handwritten letter. Janklow was re-elected 64%–33%, and Daschle was re-elected 62%–36%. According to the VNS exit poll, 62% of Daschle voters voted for Janklow, and 60% of Janklow voters voted for Daschle.

It was long obvious that South Dakota's House seat was going to be open in 2002; incumbent John Thune had promised to serve just three terms and in 2001 was deciding whether to run for governor or senator. At first Janklow seemed uninterested, and most South Dakotans thought that a governor used to dominating state government would not be happy as one of 435 members of the House. But after September 11, he started thinking about it, and thought about it harder when former Senator and Congressman Larry Pressler entered the race in November 2001. In March 2002, just three months before the primary, Janklow announced he would run for the House, pledged to be a "sledgehammer" and "the toughest junkyard dog that's ever gone to Congress to fight for South Dakota." Polls showed him far ahead; he beat Pressler 55%–27%.

In the general election he faced Democrat Stephanie Herseth, who beat the 1996 Democratic House nominee, Rick Weiland, by a 58%–32% margin. Herseth, who started running when she was only 30, had a fine political pedigree. Her grandfather Ralph Herseth was governor from 1958 to 1960. Her grandmother Lorna Herseth was secretary of state from 1972 to 1978. Her father Lars Herseth served in the legislature from 1974 to 1986 and 1988 to 1996; in 1986 he ran for governor and lost by only 52%–48%. Herseth graduated from Georgetown University and its law school, interned with Senator Tim Johnson (a college classmate of her father), clerked for a federal judge in South Dakota, taught at Georgetown Law School and worked for big law firm in Washington. She was in her own right a dynamic candidate, articulate and eager to meet people.

She also proved to be a great fundraiser; with help from EMILY's List she raised $1.5 million, more than Janklow's $1.3 million.

Herseth argued that South Dakota had "a tradition of sending young passionate leaders to Congress," and cited Democrats Tom Daschle and Tim Johnson and Republicans Larry Pressler and John Thune, all first elected in their 30s. She called for more spending on renewable energy sources, for fair trade in farm products, for changes in loan rates in farm payments, for barring the USA label for meat when the animals were only briefly in the United States. She avoided phrases that might be construed as "liberal," saying, "that's not a term that's respected here." When asked about abortion, she would typically say she wanted to make it "as rare as possible." When asked about gun control she noted that she grew up on a farm in pheasant hunting country and said she saw no need for new restrictions on guns. For her part, Herseth was respectful of Janklow. "When I made the decision to seek office, I never thought I would be running against Bill Janklow. He is larger than life, especially for people of my generation." She noted that, while she was still in high school, then-Governor Janklow took time from his schedule to answer questions from her for a report she was writing.

The two candidates agreed on many local issues. They both wanted to take control of Missouri River levels away from the Army Corps of Engineers. They both backed ethanol and renewable energy. They differed in their approaches to Iraq. In September 2002 Janklow said, "I'd love to have the support of our allies, but it's the American World Trade Center they flew the planes into. I'd love to have the support of our allies, but if we can't get the support of these people, then in this war they're not our allies, and we may have to go it alone." Herseth said, "We are looking at putting our men and women in urban warfare, hand-to-hand combat on the streets of Baghdad. I view it as a sliding scale. To the extent that we have little support from allies, the need goes way up for congressional approval. With more allied support, the bar goes down a little for congressional approval."

By September the polls suggested that this was an even race. Herseth was an attractive and energetic candidate, while some South Dakotans thought that Janklow had just run to block Pressler and was not really interested in the job. Janklow stepped up his campaign pace and the NRCC bought up a block of TV time for the six weeks before the election. But in contrast to the Senate race, the ads in this contest were all positive. When the NRCC ran a spot attacking Herseth as a carpetbagger, Janklow insisted it be pulled. Janklow evidently pulled ahead in October, as the nation contemplated military action in Iraq, and on Election Day he won 53%–46%; it is interesting to note that each time he has run for a legislative position he has gotten less than 55%, his lowest percentage for governor. In his last month as governor, he submitted revenue and spending estimates, but no budget, and he pardoned AIM leader Russell Means.

In November 2002 Janklow indicated he would run for the Senate in 2004 if Tom Daschle ran for president rather than for reelection. But in January 2003 Daschle announced he would not run for president, and White House political strategist Karl Rove made it clear that the White House would support John Thune, the narrow loser in 2002, for Daschle's seat, even though George W. Bush and Janklow had become friends at governors' conferences. Later in the month, when Bush came to the House chamber for his State of the Union speech, he embraced Janklow and had a brief conversation with him. One possible opponent in 2004 is Tony Dean, host of the popular television program *Tony Dean Outdoors*, who cut a key TV spot for Tim Johnson in 2002; in early 2003 Dean said he was considering switching his party registration to Democratic to run against Janklow.

★ TENNESSEE ★

T ennessee is a battleground state, with a fighting temperament since it was settled 200 years ago by the likes of Andrew Jackson and went on to produce so many soldiers it came to be known as the Volunteer State. This was a frontier battleground in the 1790s, from which Jackson launched his wars on the Indians and the British. It was a military battleground in the 1860s, when Yankee troops swept down the Tennessee and Cumberland Rivers on their way to Mississippi and through Chattanooga's Lookout Mountain on their way to Atlanta and the sea. It has been a cultural battleground for much of this century. On one side were the Fugitives, writers like John Crowe Ransom and Allen Tate, who contributed to "I'll Take My Stand," a manifesto calling for retaining the South's rural economy and heritage. On the other side have been business leaders and politicians who have made Tennessee the fastest-growing state of the interior South: Tennessee has given birth to the first supermarket (a Piggly Wiggly), the Holiday Inn, Federal Express and Goo-Goo Clusters.

This state has also been a marshaling ground for the music traditions that have a large place in Americans' lives. East Tennessee is one of the homes of bluegrass music and mountain fiddling, with string bands and vocal harmony; Knoxville's *Tennessee Barn Dance* has been broadcast since 1942. Gospel music has long been centered in Nashville, which is also the nation's leading center of religious publishing. Country music got its commercial start in Nashville, with broadcasts of the Grand Ole Opry from Ryman Auditorium starting in 1925 and then the Opryland U.S.A. theme park; Nashville remains indisputably the capital of country music. The Mississippi lowlands around Memphis, economically and culturally the metropolis of the Mississippi Delta, gave birth to the blues in the years from the 1890s to 1920; and the blues were in turn the inspiration for the jazz musicians of Beale Street in the 1920s and Elvis Presley, whose Graceland mansion is now a major tourist destination, in the 1950s and 1960s.

Tennessee is and has long been a political battleground. Its political divisions have their roots in the Civil War, and many counties today still vote their 1860s loyalties: The Union counties, mainly in the east but with a scattering to the west, vote solidly Republican, while the Confederate counties in middle and west Tennessee have long been heavily Democratic. Within the limits of these enduring party loyalties, political entrepreneurs have set the tone for the state. From the 1920s to 1948, Edward Crump, longtime mayor of Memphis, used his total control of Democratic primary votes there to elect governors and senators. The Tennessee Valley Authority and the cheap electric power it generated provided an institutional base for reform liberal Democrats Estes Kefauver and Albert Gore Sr., elected to the Senate in 1948 and 1952. They were soon national figures, with reliable enough backing from Tennessee's yellow-dog Democratic majority to vote for civil rights bills and to refuse to sign the segregationist Southern Manifesto, and still thrive electorally. Kefauver died in 1963 and Gore was defeated in 1970, but lived on to see his son twice elected vice president, before dying in December 1998. Tennessee has never had a large black population—16% in 2000, half of whom live in and around Memphis—and the state was not riven by the racial animosity that seared so much of the South in the 1950s and 1960s, thanks in large part to the actions of its leading politicians, but also to the continuing hold of ancestral partisan preferences.

Today the political balance has changed, and Tennessee has become a mostly Republican state—witness the fact that Al Gore lost his home state, and thus the presidency, by 51%–47% in 2000. Democrats' cultural liberalism has moved rural voters in west and middle Tennessee away from their ancestral loyalties, and the surging growth in the ring of counties around Nashville in the 1990s has created a new voting bloc that is conservative on both economic and cultural issues. The first movement toward the Republicans occurred in the 1960s and 1970s, symbolized by the elections of Republican Senators Howard Baker and Bill Brock in 1966 and 1970, and Republican Governor Lamar Alexander in 1978. Then, as Jimmy Carter changed the image of the Democratic Party, Democrats rallied; Democrats Jim Sasser and Al Gore were elected to the Senate in 1976 and 1984, and Democrat Ned Ray McWherter was elected governor in 1986.

This movement was still strong enough for the Clinton-Gore ticket to carry Tennessee

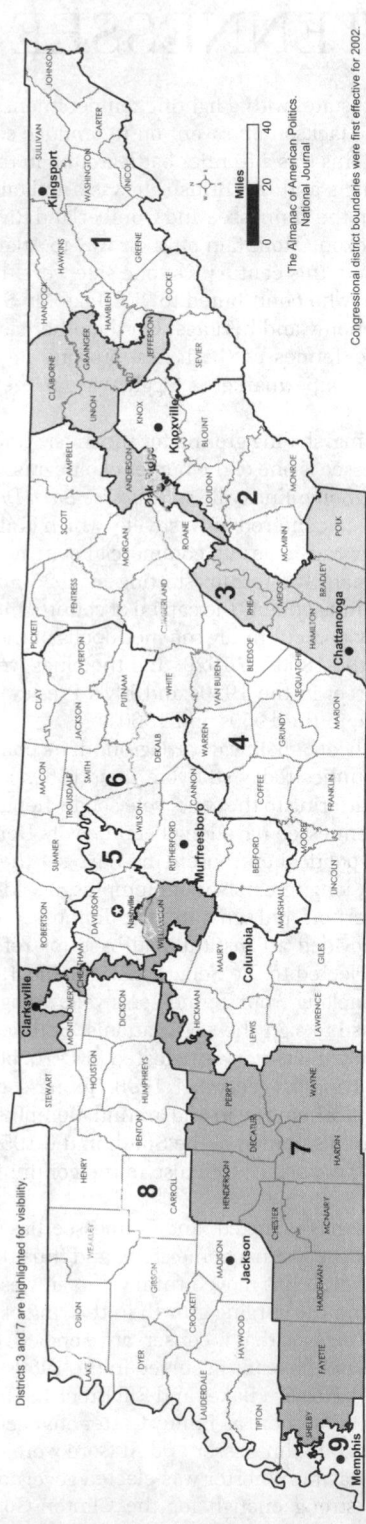

Districts 3 and 7 are highlighted for visibility.

The Almanac of American Politics.
National Journal

Congressional district boundaries were first effective for 2002.

Miles
0   20   40

47%–42% in 1992. But the narrowness of the margin was a warning of what was ahead. In 1994 Tennessee turned against the Clinton administration and produced a kind of political revolution. Republican Fred Thompson, famous as a Watergate investigator and movie actor, won the remainder of Gore's Senate term by a landslide, surgeon Bill Frist beat Sasser, and Republican Don Sundquist was elected governor. Republicans won a majority of the vote for the U.S. House, gaining two seats and coming close in a third. The Republican trend was strong enough in 1996 that only after extraordinary efforts—Gore made 16 appearances here and the campaign pumped in money for late ads—was the Clinton-Gore ticket able to win by a narrow 48%–46% margin.

In 2000 the tide was even stronger. George W. Bush targeted the state early and worked it energetically; the Gore campaign, though headquartered in Nashville, seemed to assume it would come around in the end, and only campaigned hard here in the last few days. Bush carried the state and Gore became only the fourth major party nominee to lose his home state in 85 years (the others were South Dakota's George McGovern in 1972, Kansas' Alf Landon in 1936 and New Jersey's Woodrow Wilson in 1916). In his gracious concession speech, Gore noted that he had some fence-mending to do in Tennessee, but the problem was not that he was personally unpopular; the problem was that the issue positions and cultural tone of the Clinton-Gore administration, so appealing to voters in the great suburban expanses of the largest non-Southern metropolitan areas, was alien and grating in rural Tennessee and in the suburban subdivisions expanding from Nashville and other cities out into the countryside. The 2002 election saw some move back to Tennessee Democrats. Former Nashville Mayor Phil Bredesen won the governorship by a 51%–48%; Tennessee has now alternated the parties in the governor's office at eight-year intervals for a quarter-century. Democrats, aided by partisan redistricting, also picked up one congressional district and maintained control of the legislature. But Republican Lamar Alexander, 20 years after he won his second election as governor, was elected to the U.S. Senate by a 54%–44% margin and Republicans won the total popular vote for the House.

This is a Tennessee that is expanding economically but is not abandoning its cultural roots. If its economy lagged behind the nation's through much of the 20th century, its respect for hard work and its open climate for entrepreneurism have enabled it to grow mightily in its last decades and in the first years of the 21st. The expansion started in the early 1980s, when Alexander helped bring big auto plants to middle Tennessee. The lack of strong unions and of bitter racial divisions—Tennessee was mostly untouched by the racial strife of the 1930s and the civil rights strife of the 1960s—attracted the many Japanese companies here, which in turn attracted General Motors. The country music business boomed, and so did tourism. Nashville is also a health care center; the headquarters of Columbia/ HCA was rescued after some problems by Thomas Frist Jr., (the brother of Senator Bill Frist). The Nashville establishment traditionally supported Democrats in Tennessee politics, but now Nashville money has become heavily Republican: Lamar Alexander's presidential campaigns raised so much money locally that 37205 and 37215 became two of the Republicans' top five fundraising zip codes in 1996, and have continued to be big contributors since.

Despite all that growth, Tennessee state politics has become, well, a battleground. Tennessee grew more rapidly than most of its neighboring states in the 1990s in part because of its low taxes. It has no income tax (the state Supreme Court ruled in 1931 that the state Constitution didn't list the income tax as one the legislature could impose, and so it couldn't) and it has been ranked 50th in state and local taxes as a percentage of per capita income. But state government spending has sharply increased. Expenditures for TennCare, established with Medicaid waivers by Democratic Governor Ned Ray McWherter in 1994, have risen much more sharply than predicted and more than twice as fast as most other state Medicaid programs. And Sundquist, first elected in 1994, came to share the view of many business leaders and teachers' union leaders that Tennessee needed to spend more on education in order to continue to attract new business. Sundquist ran in 1994 as an opponent of an income tax, but in October 1999 he called for a 3.5% income tax. Most Democrats were in favor, and most Republicans opposed. At the special session of the legislators, motorists prompted by radio talk show hosts honked their horns outside the State House; the income tax failed. In 2000 Sundquist vetoed the state budget because it did not include an income tax; it was passed over his veto (only a majority of votes is needed to override a veto in

Tennessee). After the 2000 election Sundquist said he would not try for an income tax again, but in 2001 he did; again horns honked and protesters chanted anti-tax slogans in front of the State House, and the budget was passed over Sundquist's veto. In July 2002 the legislature compromised and raised the sales tax from 6% to 7%. Sundquist was prevented from seeking reelection by term limits; Democrat Phil Bredesen, elected in 2002, promised not to seek an income tax.

The People

Pop. 2000:	5,689,283			
Pop. 1990:	4,877,185			
Change 1990–2000:	Up 16.7%			
Change 1980–1990:	Up 6.2%			
% of U.S. total:	2.0%			
Pop. rank:	16th of 50			
Area size:	42,143 sq. mi.			
State Native:	64.7%			
Non-citizen:	1.9%			

Language

English: 93.5%	Spanish: 3.3%
Other Eur.: 2.0%	

Race/Ethnic Origin

4,505,930	79.2%	White
928,204	16.3%	Black
56,077	1.0%	Asian
13,820	0.2%	Native Am.
1,810	0.0%	Hawaiian
54,824	1.0%	Two+ races
4,780	0.1%	Other
123,838	2.2%	Hisp. Origin

Ancestry

USA: 14.7%	Irish: 7.8%
English: 7.6%	German: 7.0%
Scotch-Irish: 2.2%	

Military veterans: 560,141 (13.1%)

WWII: 17.3%	Korea: 12.8%
Vietnam: 33.9%	Gulf War: 11.0%

Most populous cities:

1. Memphis	650,100
2. Nashville	569,891
3. Knoxville	173,890
4. Chattanooga	155,554
5. Clarksville	103,455

Urban population: 63.6%
Rural population: 36.4%

Education

H.S. Grad:	75.9%
College Grad:	19.6%

Industry

Agri: 1.4%		Con: 7.3%
Fin: 5.8%		Info: 2.4%
Mfg: 25.2%		Prof: 26.0%
Public: 4.0%		Trade: 15.6%
Other: 12.3%		

Occupation

Blue collar: 30.2%	White collar: 55.6%
Gray collar: 14.2%	

Work Sector

Private: 78.4%	Govt: 13.9%
Self: 7.3%	Family: 0.3%

Unemployment: 5.4%

Household Income

<15k: 19.2%	15-35k: 28.9%
35-50k: 17.4%	50-100k: 26.2%
100-150k: 5.2%	>150k: 3.1%

Median: $36,360
Poverty status: 13.5%

Home Value

<50k: 19.0%	50-100k: 40.1%	100-200k: 29.9%	200-300k: 6.8%
300-500k: 2.9%	>500k: 1.3%	Median: $88,300	

General Assembly

Senate	18 D 15 R
House	54 D 45 R

Legislative Term Limits: No

Registered Voters

No party registration

Presidential politics Tennessee has been about evenly divided in presidential politics at several different points in the last half-century, even as its basic political leanings have switched from Democratic to Republican. It was close in the Eisenhower-Stevenson races in the 1950s, in the Carter-Reagan race of 1980 and again in 1992, 1996 and 2000. But the fact that native son Al Gore was unable to win here as the representative of the incumbent party in a time of peace and prosperity suggests that Tennessee is likely to be out of reach for presidential Democrats in the near future.

Tennessee's presidential primary has been held on Super Tuesday (though Tennessee holds its state primaries on Thursdays, the only state to do so). But it is far from the biggest state to vote that day, and so receives relatively little attention from presidential candidates.

2000 Presidential Vote

Bush (R)	1,061,949	(51%)
Gore (D)	981,720	(47%)
Nader (Green)	19,781	(1%)
Other	12,731	(1%)

2000 Republican Presidential Primary

Bush (R)	193,166	(77%)
McCain (R)	36,436	(15%)
Keyes (R)	16,916	(7%)
Other	4,273	(2%)

2000 Democratic Presidential Primary

Gore (D)	198,264	(92%)
Bradley (D)	11,323	(5%)
Other	5,616	(3%)

1996 Presidential Vote

Clinton (D)	909,146	(48%)
Dole (R)	863,530	(46%)
Perot (I)	105,918	(6%)

Congressional districting Tennessee's Democratic legislature controlled redistricting after the 2000 Census; Republican Governor Don Sundquist's veto could be overridden by majority votes in both houses. But in January 2002 the Democrats, with help from 6th District Democrat Bart Gordon, drew lines which were agreed to by most Republicans. The congressional district plan cut across party lines far more often than ever before in Tennessee. It took six Democratic-leaning counties out of Republican Zach Wamp's 3d District and placed them in the 4th District, whose incumbent Republican Van Hilleary was running for governor. That enabled Democratic state Senator Lincoln Davis to win the 4th: He led by only 2,000 votes in the counties formerly in the district, but by nearly 8,000 in the counties added, and would surely have trailed in the Republican East Tennessee counties that were subtracted. Heavily Republican Williamson County south of Nashville was taken out of Gordon's 6th and split between the 4th and the heavily Republican 7th District. The last time an incumbent Tennessee congressman was defeated was in 1974, when a Republican lost in an increasingly black central Memphis district.

108th Congress Lineup
5 D   4 R
107th Congress Lineup
5 R   4 D

Governor

Phil Bredesen (D)

Elected 2002, term expires Jan. 2007, 1st term; b. Nov. 21, 1943, Oceanport, NJ; home, Nashville; Harvard U., B.S. 1967; Catholic; married (Andrea Conte).

Elected Office: Lexington, MA, City Cncl., 1972–73; Nashville Mayor, 1991–99.

Professional Career: Founder, HealthAmerica Corp., 1975–86.

Office: State Capitol, Nashville, 37243, 615-741-2001; Fax: 615-532-9711; Web site: www.state.tn.us/governor.

Election Results

2002 general	Phil Bredesen (D)	837,284	(51%)
	Van Hilleary (R)	786,803	(48%)
2002 primary	Phil Bredesen (D)	426,418	(79%)
	Randy Nichols (D)	38,322	(7%)
	Charles Smith (D)	34,547	(6%)
1998 general	Don Sundquist (R)	669,973	(69%)
	John Jay Hooker (D)	287,750	(29%)
	Other	18,513	(2%)

Phil Bredesen, elected governor of Tennessee in 2002, won the office on his second try. He is an outdoorsman who likes risky sports: Rock climbing, sky diving, scuba diving, piloting a glider. Bredesen grew up far from Nashville, in Shortsville, New York, 30 miles southeast of Rochester; his parents were divorced and his mother worked as a bank teller. He got a scholarship at Harvard and graduated with a degree in physics, and in 1967 he moved to Lexington, Massachusetts, and went to work for Itek; it was classified work and he got a draft deferment for it. He caught the political bug early. In 1968 he volunteered for Eugene McCarthy in New Hampshire and then for Robert Kennedy and for John Lindsay for mayor in New York in 1969. In 1970 he ran for the Massachusetts state Senate and lost to a longtime incumbent. In 1972 he won a seat on the Lexington Town Meeting. He went to work for Searle, a pharmaceutical firm, and went to London, where he met his wife. She was recruited by Hospital Corporation of America; he quit his job to follow her to Nashville in 1975. There he got a job with Hospital Affiliates International, negotiating management contracts with hospitals. He wanted to start his own business and in 1980, with $50,000 cash and $250,000 in backing from local venture capitalists, he started Health-

America, which began acquiring and operating HMOs across the country. When it went public in 1983, it ran 20 HMOs with 400,000 members. His backers decided to sell the firm in 1986, and got $400 million from MaxiCare; Bredesen pocketed $47 million, while MaxiCare, under other management, later went bankrupt.

The political bug bit again. This time his goal was not the Lexington Town Meeting, but the mayoralty of Nashville, a particularly powerful position since the city includes all of Davidson County and the mayor has broad powers. Bredesen spent $2 million on his 1987 mayoral campaign but lost in the runoff to Congressman Bill Boner. Bredesen ran again in the January 1988 special election to succeed Boner, but lost 40%–36% to former gubernatorial candidate Bob Clement (who lost to Lamar Alexander in the 2002 Senate race). Boner proved to be a dud of a mayor; in 1990 he outraged the city by divorcing his third wife and appearing with wife number four on the Phil Donahue Show to discuss his sexual prowess. In 1991 Bredesen ran for mayor again and won with 71%. As mayor, Bredesen had some spectacular successes. He lined up financing for a hockey arena and, later, a football stadium and brought the NHL Predators and NFL Tennessee Titans to Nashville. He got voters to approve $100 million to build schools. He engineered a merger that saved Meharry-Hubbard Hospital. He got approval of a new garbage site. He enticed Dell to locate a facility in Nashville. Nashville boomed in the 1990s and he took credit for 106,000 new jobs. Once a regional center, Nashville now seemed to be a major national metro area.

Nashville is Tennessee's largest media market, covering almost all of Middle Tennessee, and a successful Nashville mayor is a natural candidate for statewide office. In 1994 Bredesen spent $6 million on running for governor and won the Democratic nomination with 53% of the vote in a 10-candidate field. But he did not campaign heavily in East and West Tennessee and lost to Republican Don Sundquist by a 54%–45% margin. But in the years that followed, Bredesen had a more successful record than Sundquist. The state government's problem is that it had an increasingly expensive health care program, TennCare, and one of the nation's lowest revenue bases, with no state income tax. TennCare was Democratic Governor Ned Ray McWherter's idea; with federal waivers, it covered not only those eligible for Medicaid but others with relatively low incomes; enrollment zoomed and costs increased higher than average. In his second term, Sundquist went back on a campaign promise and sought an income tax. Most Republicans opposed him, arguing that Tennessee's low taxes helped account for the fact that the state had had much more economic growth than most neighboring states. The legislature, barraged at critical points by honking motorists and slogan-chanting anti-tax crusaders mobilized by radio talk show hosts, refused to pass one.

Against this background Bredesen, who had not run for reelection as mayor in 1999, decided to run for governor again. He said that he opposed an income tax and argued that his experience managing health care systems would enable him to straighten out TennCare. He won the Democratic primary easily, but Republicans had more of a fight. The favorite was Congressman Van Hilleary, whose district had been made more Democratic by redistricting. Hilleary based his campaign on opposition to an income tax, and in May 2002 Sundquist said he would make "a horrible governor," while he called Bredesen a "me too candidate." He had questions for both of them. "How are you going to educate my children and grandchildren? How are you going to pay for health care? How are you going to pay for these raises you are promising teachers? How can you be an 'education governor' with no money? You can't." Former Republican Governor Winfield Dunn endorsed Hilleary's primary opponent, former state Representative Jim Henry. Hilleary won the Republican primary 64%–30%, but the intraparty strife was not helpful. Bredesen had similar problems. House Speaker Jimmy Naifeh, a strong income tax backer, refused to take his calls. "I've been too engaged in trying to keep the state afloat, unlike some people who don't know enough about state government but sure seem to have a lot to say. No, I have nothing to say to him."

Much of Hilleary's campaign was based on the premise that Bredesen didn't really oppose an income tax. In an August debate Bredesen said, "I'm not for the income tax. I'm certainly not for it in the first term, and if I were to change my mind, and I don't think that's going to happen, I would certainly say to you that I would run for reelection with that, or anything else that I wanted to do with the tax system, as a matter to be decided in that process." In September Hilleary ran an ad saying that "Phil BredeSundquist" had raised property taxes three times in Nashville (as indeed Bredesen had). Bredesen responded the next day with an on-camera ad: "Well, Mr. Hilleary, I'll say it again as clearly as I know how. I do not support an income tax." In debate Hilleary said, "Read my lips. Not on the first term, not on the second term, will I ever support an income tax. An income tax will not happen on my watch." Perhaps this issue did not work as well for Hilleary as he hoped because neither candidate could assure voters he would prevent an income tax: Tennessee allows the governor's veto to be overridden by a mere majority of both houses, and so the legislature could impose an income tax over a contrary-minded governor.

Bredesen focused more on fixing TennCare. "Everybody in the state of Tennessee knows somebody on TennCare they don't think should be on TennCare. It needs to be the bronze package, not the platinum package," he said. "TennCare is a good program, it's just been horribly mismanaged." Hilleary, who said TennCare was "not my passion," said he would cut $300 to $400 million from TennCare. Already during the campaign changes were being made. In July 2002 the program was closed to new enrollees not eligible for Medicaid, and in October 2002 the existing 450,000 non-Medicaid enrollees (there were 900,000 Medicaid-eligible enrollees) were required to meet strict new eligibility requirements. On other issues, there was agreement: Both candidates opposed gun control, supported scheduled teacher pay raises, called for children to learn to read by the third grade, wanted more spending on higher education, more spending to promote tourism and expansion of the Tennessee Industrial Infrastructure Program.

Bredesen spent $3 million of his own money on his campaign, to counter, he said, money raised for Hilleary by George W. Bush. This turned out to be the closest Tennessee governor's race since 1896; Bredesen won 51%–48%. This time he had campaigned across the state, raising money in small fundraisers, holding chili suppers is rural counties. He broke into the Republican base in East Tennessee, carrying Knoxville's Knox County—and holding Hilleary to a narrow lead in his region. Bredesen carried Nashville solidly and carried or held Hilleary to narrow margins in all but one of the Republican-trending counties around Nashville. Bredesen had a big lead in Memphis and carried rural West Tennessee, often a swing area in Tennessee elections. After the election Bredesen, facing a predicted $800 million budget shortfall, predicted that there would be no new initiatives except for a lottery, teacher pay equalization and TennCare reforms and said he wanted "the dullest budget session on record."

Senior Senator

Bill Frist (R)

Elected 1994, seat up 2006, 2d term; b. Feb. 22, 1952, Nashville; home, Nashville; Princeton U., A.B. 1974, Harvard Med. Schl., M.D. 1978; Presbyterian; married (Karyn).

Professional Career: Practicing surgeon, 1978–94; Dir., Vanderbilt Medical Ctr. Heart–Lung Transplant Program, 1986–93.

DC Office: 461 DSOB, 20510, 202-224-3344; Fax: 202-228-1264; Web site: frist.senate.gov.

State Offices: Chattanooga, 423-756-2757; Jackson, 731-424-9655; Kingsport, 423-323-1252; Knoxville, 865-602-7977; Memphis, 901-683-1910; Nashville, 615-352-9411.

Committees: *Majority Leader. Finance*: Health Care; International Trade; Social Security & Family Policy. *Health, Education, Labor & Pensions. Rules & Administration.*

Group Ratings

	ADA	ACLU	AFS	LCV	CON	ITIC	NTU	COC	ACU	NTLC	CHC
2002	10	20	0	0	62	88	67	100	100	100	—
2001	10	—	0	0	—	—	84	100	100	—	100

National Journal Ratings

	2001 LIB	—	2001 CONS		2002 LIB	—	2002 CONS
Economic	15%	—	84%		6%	—	90%
Social	0%	—	79%		0%	—	62%
Foreign	7%	—	72%		0%	—	76%

Key Votes of the 107th Congress

1. Approve Bush Tax Cuts	Y	5. Confirm Ashcroft as AG	Y	9. Bar Coop. with Intl. Court	Y
2. Expand Patients' Rights	N	6. Bar Gays in the Boy Scouts	Y	10. Trade Promotion Authority	Y
3. Campaign Finance Reform	N	7. $ for Hate Crime Prosecution	N	11. Authorize Force in Iraq	Y
4. Permit ANWR Development	Y	8. Overseas Military Abortions	N	12. Homeland Sec. Dept. Union	N

Election Results

2000 general	Bill Frist (R)	1,255,444	(65%)	($4,664,737)
	Jeff Clark (D)	621,152	(32%)	($173,406)
	Other	52,017	(3%)	
2000 primary	Bill Frist (R)	unopposed		
1994 general	Bill Frist (R)	834,226	(56%)	($7,017,424)
	Jim Sasser (D)	623,164	(42%)	($5,020,515)
	Other	23,001	(2%)	

Bill Frist, first elected to the Senate in 1994, is now the 20th Senate majority leader (the title goes back only to 1925). Frist grew up in Nashville, in a well-known Tennessee family: His father practiced medicine for 55 years and was the physician for six Tennessee governors. Both his brothers are doctors, too. Frist graduated from Princeton and Harvard Medical School, studied at Massachusetts General Hospital, in England and at Stanford, and became a heart and lung transplant surgeon, setting up the transplant program at Vanderbilt. He performed 250 transplants and in 1989 wrote a book, *Transplant*, on the social and ethical issues of these surgeries; he has written more than 100 peer-reviewed articles. In 1968 his father and brother, Thomas Frist Jr., set up HCA (which through a 1994 merger became Columbia/ HCA), the world's largest hospital company; the Frists lost control of the firm in the late 1980s. After it was hit with charges of Medicare violations in 1997, Thomas Frist Jr. came back from semi-retirement to run it. He piloted his first plane at 16, and flew small planes to pick up donated organs; he runs marathons (two within 13 days in 1999). He still practices some medicine, at clinics in Washington, and on five trips to Africa, where he has tended patients in war zones in Sudan and in Uganda. He resuscitated a constituent in the Dirksen Building in September 1995, treated the wounded in the Capitol shooting in July 1998, tended Strom Thurmond when he collapsed on the Senate floor in October 2001, and treated accident victims on Florida's Alligator Alley on New Year's Day 2003.

Frist is a man of intensity and focus, and for years that focus was medicine, not politics; he never voted until he was 36, after he moved back to Nashville. He decided to switch careers and run in 1994 as a Republican against Democrat Jim Sasser. Frist seemed unlikely to win: Sasser was chairman of the Budget Committee and running for majority leader, and he had won his last race in 1988 with 65% of the vote. And Frist had tough primary opposition from east Tennessee businessman Bob Corker, who attacked him for not voting and for obtaining cats from animal shelters for experiments as a medical student (which he mentioned in *Transplant*). But Frist, spending liberally, carried the Nashville and Memphis media markets and beat Corker 44%–32%. In the general, Frist backed welfare reform, federal spending cuts, school prayer and term limits; he followed Howard Baker in calling for citizen-politicians and pledged to serve just two terms. Sasser emphasized school prayer, the balanced budget amendment and cracking down on illegal immigrants; he ridiculed Frist as a bored, rich surgeon. Frist outspent Sasser, spending $3.7 million of his own money. Sasser led in polls up through October, but in November Frist won 56%–42%, carrying all the large metro areas and losing only scattered traditionally Democratic rural counties.

Frist is the first practicing physician to serve in the Senate since Royal Copeland of New York died in June 1938. Naturally he got involved in health issues—the Senate ethics committee ruled that he is not prohibited from voting on any "legislation of general applicability to the health care industry." He played a key role on the 1996 health care bill on portability and pre-existing conditions, working to include Medical Savings Accounts. He worked to reauthorize the Ryan White CARE Act for the treatment and support of AIDS patients. He put on the income tax form a box to check off for information on organ donor cards. He worked to make sure Tennessee was not penalized for extending TennCare to uninsured children.

On some health issues, Frist has worked with Democrats. With Jay Rockefeller, he sponsored a law to allow physicians and hospitals to establish service provider organizations to contract directly with Medicare; they also founded a Forum on Technology and Innovation that holds frequent cram sessions for members and staffers. He backed the 1997 Clinton bill to ban discrimination by insurers by genetic traits and to assure privacy of genetic information. In 2000 he worked with Ted Kennedy to forge a compromise on organ transplants, to try to reduce regional disparities; the House, which backed the United Network of Organ Sharing, with its 62 separate geographic regions, refused to compromise. In 2000, Frist and Kennedy steered through a $919 million authorization for public health laws, including $540 million for research on bioterrorism and $180 million to refurbish Centers for Disease Control labs. He passed a law with incentives for primary care physicians in rural and inner city areas, and worked to reauthorize the bone marrow registry, with recruitment of minorities. Frist supported the partial-birth abortion ban, "because it is needlessly risky to the woman, because it is an unnecessary procedure, because it is inhumane to the fetus, and because it is medically unacceptable and offends the very basic civil sensibilities of people all across this country."

On HMO regulation and prescription drugs, Frist has taken the lead in forging Republican positions. He served on the Medicare Commission that presented its premium support plan in March 1999. In June 2000 he sponsored a Medicare reform bill with commission chairman John Breaux. Their plan would have private insurers competing to provide coverage to Medicare beneficiaries, overseen by a new government agency that would approve the content of plans; the idea is to evade the cumbersome HCFA bureaucracy in HHS. They seek to include prescription drug coverage as part of a larger reform of Medicare, with subsidies for all seniors and a progressive sliding scale of subsidies depending on income. The Breaux-Frist proposal went nowhere in 1999 because of opposition from the Clinton administration. But George W. Bush campaigned on the issue in 2000 and in early 2003 made it one of his priorities. Republicans had campaigned on the issue of prescription drugs for seniors in 2002 and House Republicans passed their version of a freestanding bill. But Frist has argued all along that it makes better sense to make a prescription drug benefit part of a larger Medicare revision, and in 2003 he gained his chance to bring it forward. Frist has also been a leader on stem-cell research. In July 2001 he set out ten "essential components" of policy, including funding adult stem-cell research, banning human cloning and using excess embryos from in vitro fertilization procedures which otherwise would be discarded. He co-sponsored with Congressman Tom Davis a bill, supported by Philip Morris, which would provide some FDA regulation of tobacco products.

Frist became a member of the Africa Subcommittee in 1997, which led to his medical trips to Africa. He criticized the Clinton administration for not supervising humanitarian relief that was being manipulated by the Sudan government and worked for a change in policy. After treating AIDS patients, he showed Jesse Helms pictures of them and got him to co-sponsor $500 million for a global AIDS fund. He backed down to the Bush administration and agreed to seek only $200 million, and was much criticized by Democrats, but he got Bush in 2003 to commit to spending $15 billion over several years.

After letters with anthrax were sent to Majority Leader Tom Daschle's office, Frist stepped forward and used his expertise to provide information and reassurance. He emphasized anthrax's sensitivity to antibiotics and encouraged anyone who might be exposed to take drugs; mistakenly, as he admitted, he underestimated the danger from anthrax in envelopes. Colleagues and citizens went to Frist for information; his website received 40,000 hits a day. In November 2001 he and Kennedy sponsored a bioterrorism preparedness bill, with $3 billion to expand the nation's supply of vaccines, expand the Centers for Disease Control and Prevention, beef up state public health laboratories and provide training for response to a bioterrorism attack. It became law in June 2002. In March 2002, his book, *When Every Moment Counts: What You Need to Know About*

Bioterrorism from the Senate's Only Doctor, was published in English and Spanish, with royalties going to the Tennessee Public Health Association. In August 2002 he argued that all Americans should have the option to get vaccinated against smallpox and to require vaccination of health care workers and military personnel likely to be exposed in a smallpox attack. In 2002 he wrote a bill restricting lawsuits against pharmaceutical companies that used the mercury-based preservative thimerosal as a preservative; his approach was that parents claiming that thimerosal caused autism in their children should go through the vaccination compensation process established by Congress in the 1980s. This provision was put into the homeland security bill by House Majority Leader Dick Armey in November 2002, and was attacked as a special interest provision to help Eli Lilly, which had contributed to Republicans. Frist continued to argue it was good public policy, but after he was elected majority leader agreed to honor Trent Lott's commitment to several Republican senators to allow the issue to be revisited in 2003, and said he would argue for the bill on its merits.

Frist got his start as a national Republican leader when he was chosen to deliver the response to Bill Clinton's State of the Union address in January 2000. In July 2000, after Paul Coverdell died, he was named to replace him as the liaison between George W. Bush's campaign and Republican senators. He chaired the Platform Committee at the Republican National Convention and spoke Thursday night just before Bush and was on an early list of possible vice presidential candidates. In December 2000, this surgeon who had no experience in politics a few years before was elected chairman of the NRSC, with the assignment of regaining a Senate majority in 2002 when 20 Republican and 14 Democratic Senate seats were up. He did it. He excelled in fundraising—the NRSC outspent its Democratic counterpart by $66 million—and in political strategy. He kept in close touch with White House political strategist Karl Rove but also made decisions on his own, as when he ran ads showing George W. Bush in March 2002 in five states where Democratic incumbents seemed vulnerable; Republicans picked up seats in two of the states. He worked with Rove and Bush to recruit candidates and clear the field for the challenger they thought had the best chance.

Overall, Republicans gained two seats. Never since popular election of senators came in had a president's party regained a Senate majority in an off-year election. Frist was suddenly a party hero and, interested in concentrating on health care issues, declined a second term at the NRSC three days after the election. Then Majority Leader Trent Lott made his now famous but then little-noticed statement at Thurmond's 100th birthday party December 5. As the furor began, Frist told a reporter December 10, "The statement was unfortunate, and it was off the cuff and casual. I know Trent Lott and he's not a racist. It's important people understand the Republican party leads on issues of equity and fairness and nondiscrimination. Any implication otherwise would be a disappointment to me." On December 15 Don Nickles called for a Republican Conference meeting January 6 to reconsider Lott's leadership. Frist, who had voted for Lott for Whip in December 1994, when Lott won by one vote, started making calls by December 19 seeking support should Lott step down. On the morning of December 20 Lott bowed out. By the end of the day it was clear that Frist would be the new majority leader. He was officially chosen in a conference call December 23.

Frist was elevated after only eight years in the Senate (Lyndon Johnson had only six years in the Senate when he was elected majority leader in 1954) and to a position that confers less power than many people assume. The majority leader can keep legislation off the schedule, but Senate rules require supermajorities and unanimous consent for many procedures; the majority leader is less often the tamer of lions than the herder of cats. He can be expected to take a particularly active part on Medicare and other health care issues, like medical malpractice awards; with a new seat on the Finance Committee he is particularly well positioned on Medicare. He can act without much concern about opinion in Tennessee. He was reelected in 2000 against weak opposition by a 65%–32% margin, with the highest number of votes cast for a senator in Tennessee history; he carried all but 5 of 95 counties. But he said in 1994 that he would only seek two terms, and in December 2002 said, "I've always said and I still say that I'm interested in serving a total of 12 years in the Senate. That means, in 2006, it will be very likely that I won't run for reelection." Already two young congressmen—Republican Zach Wamp of Chattanooga and Democrat Harold Ford of Memphis—have been making moves toward running then. But there is another office Frist could run for. Even before the 2002 elections, many Republicans and others mentioned him as a possible presidential candidate. "Bill Frist could become president," Phil Gramm said then. "Quote me on that." (He is not likely to be picked for the vice presidency should Dick Cheney not run again; Tennessee Governor Phil Bredesen is a Democrat, and George W. Bush will want Frist in the Senate through 2006.) In December 2002 Frist said, "That's not my purpose in life, to be president. There are a lot of people who would like to be president, but that's not my goal."

Junior Senator

Lamar Alexander (R)

Elected 2002, seat up 2008, 1st term; b. July 3, 1940, Maryville; home, Nashville; Vanderbilt U., B.A. 1962, N.Y.U., J.D. 1965; Presbyterian; married (Honey).

Elected Office: TN Governor, 1978–86.

Professional Career: Pres., Univ. of TN, 1988–91; U.S. Edu. Sect., 1991–93; Co-director, Empower America, 1994–95; Prof., Harvard U. JFK Schl. of Govt., 2001–02.

DC Office: 302 HSOB, 20510, 202-224-4944; Fax: 202-228-3398; Web site: alexander.senate.gov.

State Offices: Chattanooga, 423-752-5337; Jackson, 731-423-9344; Knoxville, 865-545-4253; Memphis, 901-544-4224; Nashville, 615-736-5129; Tri-Cities, 423-325-6240.

Committees: *Energy & Natural Resources*: Energy (Chmn.); National Parks; Public Lands & Forests. *Foreign Relations*: African Affairs (Chmn.); East Asian & Pacific Affairs; International Economic Policy, Export & Trade Promotion. *Health, Education, Labor & Pensions*: Aging; Children & Families (Chmn.); Employment, Safety & Training. *Joint Economic Committee* (5th of 10 Sens.).

Group Ratings and Key Votes: Newly Elected

Election Results

2002 general	Lamar Alexander (R)	891,420	(54%)	($3,761,804)
	Bob Clement (D)	728,295	(44%)	($2,832,990)
2002 primary	Lamar Alexander (R)	295,052	(54%)	
	Ed Bryant (R)	233,678	(43%)	
	Other	19,752	(3%)	
1996 general	Fred D. Thompson (R)	1,091,554	(61%)	($3,469,369)
	Houston Gordon (D)	654,937	(37%)	($795,969)
	Other	32,173	(2%)	

Lamar Alexander, former governor of Tennessee and Secretary of Education, was elected Tennessee's junior senator in 2002. Alexander grew up Maryville, in East Tennessee between Knoxville and the Smoky Mountains, the son of a principal and a teacher; he started piano lessons at 4 and still plays. Like Bill Clinton, he was elected governor of Boys State. He graduated from Vanderbilt, where he wrote editorials in the *Hustler* urging integration, and New York University Law School; he clerked for Judge John Minor Wisdom of the Fifth Circuit federal appeals court. Alexander was always a Republican, and in 1966 he wrote Howard Baker, then the Republican candidate for Senate, and volunteered for his Senate campaign against Frank Clement; Baker gave him a job—the critical connection in Alexander's career. In 1967 he served on Baker's staff in Washington; briefly he lived in a group house with a Democratic congressional staffer named Trent Lott. In 1969, on Baker's recommendation, Alexander got a job working for Bryce Harlow in Richard Nixon's White House. On a trip back to Tennessee to scout the possibilities of running against Senator Albert Gore Sr. in 1970, he met Memphis dentist Winfield Dunn, who was running for governor; Alexander agreed to manage his campaign and Dunn became the first Republican elected governor in 50 years. He decided that next time he would be the candidate, so in 1974, at 34, he ran for governor. He ran a conventional campaign and in that Watergate year lost 55%–44% to Democratic Congressman Ray Blanton.

He ran again in 1978, but differently this time: Wearing a red plaid shirt, he walked 1,000 miles across Tennessee. This time he won 56%–44%. After the election Blanton started issuing many pardons of criminals: It turned out that he was taking bribes. To stop him, the U.S. Attorney, a Democrat, urged that Alexander be sworn in three days early; Democratic legislative leaders and the state's Chief Justice agreed. In a hurried ceremony, Alexander took the oath and announced that he was naming Fred Thompson, famous from his work as Baker's chief counsel in the Senate Watergate hearings, as a special prosecutor. As governor, Alexander got Nissan to build its first American plant in Rutherford County, and General Motors to build its Saturn plant in Williamson County; they became the sparkplugs of rapid growth in the counties around Nashville. He passed a Master Teacher program, with merit pay. He was reelected 60%–40% in 1982. In 1987, out of office and with young children, Alexander and his family moved to Australia for six months; he later wrote a book about the experience. In 1988 he became president of the University of Tennessee and in 1991 he became the first George Bush's Education Secretary. In these years he also reaped big profits from small investments: An option to buy the *Knoxville Journal* was sold to Gannett and yielded $620,000; an option given for his consultant work at Whittle Communications became $330,000. Alexander started a company called Corporate Child Care and is still part-owner. Critics said he benefited from good connections; he said, "I plead guilty to being a capitalist."

In 1993 he went to work at the Nashville office of Baker's law firm. The next year turned out to be a good Republican year in Tennessee: Fred Thompson and Bill Frist were elected to the Senate and Don Sundquist was elected governor. Alexander probably could have won either office. But he was after bigger things: He was running for president. His 1996 campaign was keyed to the mood of 1994: He campaigned as an outsider, wore his red plaid shirt and called, as Baker often had, for citizen-politicians. Of members of Congress, he said, "Cut their pay and bring them home!" His bumper stickers said, "Lamar!" But he also had a sophisticated message, based on the idea that the nation needed more decentralized government; he had a superb fundraising organization that made Nashville one of the leading Republican money sources in the nation; and he hired top notch political consultants and brilliant organizers in Iowa and New Hampshire. Alexander finished third in the Iowa caucuses, behind Bob Dole and Pat Buchanan and ahead of Steve Forbes. New Hampshire was his best chance for a breakthrough. He flew from Des Moines to Manchester the night of the caucuses and began rallying the impressive organization he had built. Dole, the favorite, had been concentrating his fire on Buchanan. But five days before the primary Dole began running ads attacking Alexander. This was shrewd strategy: Buchanan was likely to do well into New Hampshire but obviously could never be nominated; the candidate who finished second in New Hampshire would likely be his chief rival and would easily win the nomination. So it turned out. But the second-place finisher in New Hampshire nearly wasn't Dole. Buchanan did win, with 27% of the vote, to 26% for Dole and 23% for Alexander. Alexander finished just 7,590 votes behind Dole; if those negative ads hadn't run, he might have finished second, Dole might have dropped out and Alexander might have been the Republican nominee in 1996. If he had run well—and he was the candidate Clinton strategists feared most—he might have had a head start in the 2000 presidential race, and a lot of recent history might have been different.

In 1999 Alexander started running for president again. But the plaid shirt and the 1994-style themes failed to resonate. George W. Bush, with his celebrity and his fundraising, dominated the race and Steve Forbes's extensive, expensive campaigning in Iowa left little room for Alexander. His fundraising faltered and after his disappointing sixth-place finish in the August 1999 Ames, Iowa, straw poll, he dropped out within days and endorsed Bush. He didn't go to the 2000 Republican National Convention; he said he had run his last race for public office. He concentrated on his business interests and taught courses at Harvard in the 2002 spring semester.

Then, on Friday, March 8, just 27 days before the filing deadline, Senator Fred Thompson announced that he would not run for reelection. In 2001 Thompson openly pondered not running, then finally was persuaded to do so by Republicans who were confident he could win easily. Then his daughter died; he decided not to seek reelection. He gave Alexander a head-up on his decision, and on Monday, March 11 Alexander announced.

Alexander's candidacy was welcome to the Bush White House and to Bill Frist, chairman of the Republicans' Senate campaign committee; a 2001 poll by Alexander's pollster Whit Ayres showed that 93% of voters could identify him, though he had not campaigned in Tennessee in 20 years, and that 66% of voters had favorable feelings toward him and only 16% unfavorable. But other politicians wanted to run. Nashville's Democratic Congressman Bob Clement, son of three-term Governor Frank Clement, made it clear he was interested. Gore said he wasn't interested, but for a few days Tipper Gore considered running; on March 17, after a meeting with Clement, she said she would not. Clement announced the next day. When suburban Memphis Congressman Ed Bryant said he might run, some Republicans tried to talk him out of it; it was clear he would start out behind in a four-month race. But on April 1 he announced.

Bryant's campaign theme was that he was the real conservative in the race. "I'm emphasizing consistency," he said. "Depending on where he is in the country, he tends to get more moderate. It's a little like Al Gore." But Alexander campaigned as a conservative, backing individual investment accounts in Social Security, permanent tax cuts, school vouchers (a "G.I. Bill for kids") and a two-year federal budget cycle. On talk radio shows, whose listeners are very likely to be Republican primary voters, he ran a series of "plain talk" ads taking conservative stands on taxes, campaign finance, the Pledge of Allegiance, Judge Charles Pickering, charter schools and oil drilling in the Arctic National Wildlife Refuge. Bryant's ads called him "the one without the plaid shirt" and urged, "Don't be plaid. Be solid for Bryant." Alexander was endorsed on March 12 by Governor Don Sundquist, unpopular with many of his fellow Republicans for his advocacy of a state income tax. Bryant charged that Alexander had favored an income tax when he was governor. Alexander replied that he had considered an income tax as one of several alternatives and "rejected it." Bryant noted that he did increase the sales and gasoline taxes. The results of the August 1 primary suggest that voters were divided not on ideological but on regional grounds. Alexander won overall 54%–43%; Bryant had made some gains from initial polls. But Alexander carried the smaller counties of East and Middle Tennessee by 2–1 margins and carried the Knoxville and Chattanooga metro areas by wide margins; he led narrowly in metro Nashville.

Alexander began running ads immediately after the primary and did not stop until November; Clement didn't put ads up until mid-September. But Clement started with good name identification: He had been elected congressman from Nashville, the center of the state's largest media market, starting in January 1988. He like Alexander was a university president (Cumberland University). Clement had a relatively moderate voting record: He voted for the Bush tax cuts and in October 2002 for the Iraq war resolution. They differed on Social Security, prescription drugs, and campaign finance regulation. But much of the campaign dialogue concerned their business investments. Clement said Alexander was a political insider who became wealthy through political connections. Alexander charged that Clement, while Public Service Commissioner in the 1970s, served on the board of one of the banks of Jake Butcher—Alexander's opponent in 1978, and whose banks imploded in scandal in the 1980s. Clement at first denied that he'd served on the board, then said it was just an advisory board, and that he had served a decade before the scandal. Alexander said that Clement had voted 143 times to raise taxes and attacked him for backing Senate Democrats' stand on homeland security; he said Clement would be part of "that crowd" voting against George W. Bush.

Alexander led in polls all along, though the lead narrowed as partisan lines strengthened: He won 54%–44%. He won 63% in his native (and ancestrally Republican) East Tennessee, which cast nearly 40% of the votes. Clement carried Nashville's Davidson County and rural counties in Middle Tennessee, but Alexander carried the fast-growing ring of suburban counties around Nashville and held Clement to 53% in his home area. In West Tennessee, Alexander made some inroads among Memphis blacks and carried the rural counties, for 50% in this (ancestrally Democratic) region. Memphis Mayor Willie Herenton introduced him at his victory party.

And so a politician who ran for governor at 34 became a senator at 62. As a former governor and cabinet secretary, he got a little seniority over other freshmen, and he joined his Tennessee colleague, Majority Leader Bill Frist, on the Health Education Labor and Pensions Committee.

FIRST DISTRICT

Rep. Bill Jenkins (R)

Elected 1996, 4th term; b. Nov. 29, 1936, Detroit, MI; home, Rogersville; TN Tech., B.B.A. 1957, U. of TN, J.D. 1961; Baptist; married (Kathryn).

Military Career: Army, 1960–62.

Elected Office: TN Assembly, 1962–71, Speaker, 1969–71; TN Circuit Court Judge, 1990–96.

Professional Career: Farmer, 1961–present; Practicing atty., 1961–90; Commissioner, TN Dept. of Conservation, 1971–72; Dir., TN Valley Authority, 1971–78.

DC Office: 1207 CHOB 20515, 202-225-6356; Fax: 202-225-5714; Web site: www.house.gov/jenkins.

District Office: Kingsport, 423-247-8161.

Committees: *Agriculture* (8th of 27 R): General Farm Commodities & Risk Management; Specialty Crops & Foreign Agriculture Programs (Chmn.). *Judiciary* (8th of 21 R): Courts, the Internet & Intellectual Property; The Constitution.

Group Ratings

	ADA	ACLU	AFS	LCV	CON	ITIC	NTU	COC	ACU	NTLC	CHC
2002	0	7	0	0	31	88	56	95	100	89	100
2001	5	—	0	0	—	—	60	87	96	—	—

National Journal Ratings

	2001 LIB —	2001 CONS	2002 LIB —	2002 CONS
Economic	22%	74%	21%	73%
Social	0%	81%	0%	75%
Foreign	16%	82%	0%	85%

Key Votes of the 107th Congress

1. Approve Bush Tax Cuts	Y	5. Faith-Based Charities	Y	9. Trade Promotion Authority	Y
2. Limit Patients' Bill of Rights	Y	6. Bar Gays in the Boy Scouts	Y	10. Bar Funds for Intl. Court	Y
3. Campaign Finance Reform	N	7. Ban Partial-Birth Abortion	Y	11. Authorize Force in Iraq	Y
4. Ban ANWR Development	N	8. Arm Commercial Pilots	Y	12. Deny Home. Sec. Dept. Union	Y

Election Results

2002 general	Bill Jenkins (R)	unopposed		($107,482)
2002 primary	Bill Jenkins (R)	65,421	(88%)	
	Larry Edgell (R)	8,740	(12%)	
2000 general	Bill Jenkins (R)	unopposed		($92,463)

Prior Winning Percentages: 1998 (69%); 1996 (65%)

The People		Race/Ethnic Origin	Ancestry	
Area size:	4,174 sq. mi.	95.0% White	USA: 18.9%	English: 8.2%
Urban population:	55.4%	2.1% Black	Irish: 7.8%	
Rural population:	44.6%	0.4% Asian	**2000 Presidential Vote**	
Pop. 2000:	632,143	0.2% Native Am.	Bush (R)............132,304	(61%)
Median income:	$31,228	0.0% Hawaiian	Gore (D)..............81,335	(37%)
Poverty status:	14.8%	0.7% Two+ races	Other..................3,441	(2%)
Military veterans:	14.2%	0.1% Other	**Cook Partisan Voting Index:** R +12	
		1.5% Hispanic Origin		
Occupation	Blue collar: 34.4%	White collar: 50.0%	Gray collar: 15.6%	

Between the corduroy-like ridges of the Appalachian chains, as they bend west and then south, the valley of Virginia extends far into northeastern Tennessee. The communities of this region— a hilly patchwork of industrial centers, small farms and federal land—were largely shaped by the building of railroads in the 1850s. The land rush immediately after the Revolutionary War populated the area; here in tiny Jonesborough the early settlers established the free state of Franklin in 1784, and many pioneer cabins, federal mansions and Greek Revival churches are lovingly preserved. It was the railroads, however, that determined the winners and losers. Other Appalachian areas were cut off from the rest of America, with tracks running only to the coal mines, but the small industrial cities that had grown up here—Johnson City, Kingsport, Bristol—were on the main lines of national commerce even before the Civil War. The War had a different political effect here than in most of the South: Northeast Tennessee, the home of wartime Governor and then Vice President Andrew Johnson, had few slaves and with its connection to northern industry was Union territory. It remains heavily Republican to this day.

The political continuity may be surprising because this area has had continuous economic growth and has developed the sort of industrial economy that produced unions and Democrats in the North. Its growth has been helped by modest wage levels, a skilled and hard-working labor force, low electric power rates because of the Tennessee Valley Authority and good transportation routes (rail lines and now Interstate 81). Its small cities boast major paper and printing plants, and have the look of comfortable, clean, 1920s factory towns. Growth has been rapid only in Sevier County near Knoxville, where Gatlinburg and Pigeon Forge (home of Dolly Parton's Dollywood theme park) with more than 14,000 hotel rooms are the entry point to the Great Smoky Mountains National Park, the nation's most-visited national park.

The 1st Congressional District takes in the far northeastern end of Tennessee, a district so heavily Republican that it has not elected a Democrat to the House for more than 100 years. Nonetheless, it has had turbulent politics on occasion. For almost 40 years (1921–61, with one four-year and one two-year hiatus), the seat was held by B. Carroll Reece, a fierce mountain politician who was Republican national chairman from 1946–48. After Reece died in 1961, and his widow was elected to fill out his term, there was a hotly contested primary in 1962. The winner, Jimmy Quillen, a bread-and-butter politician and former owner of the *Johnson City Times*, represented the 1st for the next 34 years.

The congressman from the 1st District is Bill Jenkins, elected in 1996. Jenkins is a lawyer from Rogersville in Hawkins County, and a farmer who raises beef cattle and grows burley tobacco. He was elected to the state House in 1962, at 25. In 1969 the state House was evenly split between Democrats and Republicans; Jenkins was elected Speaker, the only Republican to hold that position in the 20th century. In 1971 he was named to the TVA Board of Directors; in 1990 he was elected Circuit Court judge. When Quillen announced his retirement, Jenkins resigned his judgeship to run for Congress. He was one of 11 Republicans—the Quillen 11—who filed to run in the primary. Tennessee has no runoff, and this was what political scientist V.O. Key called a "friends and neighbors" primary: There were few perceptible differences on issues, and candidates struggled to get enough votes out in their home areas to win. Jenkins won with just 18% of the votes, including 74% in Hawkins County. In second, just 331 votes behind, was state Senator Jim Holcomb, who had conservative Christian activist support. Jenkins won in November 65%–32%.

In the House, Jenkins has a conservative voting record and avoids the spotlight. He wants to restore the deductibility of state sales taxes, a move that would help Tennesseans, who have no state income tax. He defended TVA against advocates of competition, contending that other utilities would not necessarily have lower fuel or labor costs.

In 1998 Jim Holcomb, the second place finisher two years before, attacked Jenkins's vote for PNTR with China and announced his candidacy. But House Majority Leader Dick Armey attended a Jenkins fundraiser in April and Jimmy Quillen appeared at Jenkins' re-election announcement. Holcomb, unable to raise much money, dropped out of the race in May. Jenkins has had only token opposition since. Asked during the 2002 campaign about his most significant accomplishment, Jenkins responded that it was balancing the federal budget; he may need a different answer in 2004. In 2003, Jenkins moved up from the back benches to become chairman of the Agriculture Specialty Crops and Foreign Agriculture Programs Subcommittee.

SECOND DISTRICT

Rep. John Duncan (R)

Elected 1988, 8th term; b. July 21, 1947, Lebanon; home, Knoxville; U. of TN, B.S. 1969, George Washington U., J.D. 1973; Presbyterian; married (Lynn).

Military Career: Army Natl. Guard & Army Reserves, 1970–87.

Professional Career: Practicing atty., 1973–81; Knox Cnty. judge, 1981–88.

DC Office: 2267 RHOB 20515, 202-225-5435; Fax: 202-225-6440; Web site: www.house.gov/duncan.

District Offices: Athens, 423-745-4671; Knoxville, 865-523-3772; Maryville, 865-984-5464.

Committees: *Government Reform* (16th of 24 R): National Security, Emerging Threats & Intl. Relations. *Resources* (6th of 28 R): Forests & Forest Health; National Parks, Recreation & Public Lands. *Transportation & Infrastructure* (5th of 41 R): Aviation; Highways, Transit & Pipelines; Water Resources & Environment (Chmn.).

Group Ratings

	ADA	ACLU	AFS	LCV	CON	ITIC	NTU	COC	ACU	NTLC	CHC
2002	5	7	11	25	97	50	71	75	92	97	100
2001	10	—	10	14	—	—	71	70	92	—	—

National Journal Ratings

	2001 LIB —	2001 CONS	2002 LIB —	2002 CONS
Economic	46%	— 54%	16%	— 81%
Social	0%	— 81%	0%	— 75%
Foreign	43%	— 53%	52%	— 48%

Key Votes of the 107th Congress

1. Approve Bush Tax Cuts	Y	5. Faith-Based Charities		9. Trade Promotion Authority	N
2. Limit Patients' Bill of Rights	Y	6. Bar Gays in the Boy Scouts	Y	10. Bar Funds for Intl. Court	Y
3. Campaign Finance Reform	N	7. Ban Partial-Birth Abortion	Y	11. Authorize Force in Iraq	N
4. Ban ANWR Development	N	8. Arm Commercial Pilots	Y	12. Deny Home. Sec. Dept. Union	Y

Election Results

2002 general	John Duncan (R)	146,887	(79%)	($362,876)
	John Greene (D)	37,035	(20%)	
	Other	2,059	(1%)	
2002 primary	John Duncan (R)	67,582	(92%)	
	Jim Pendergrass (R)	6,095	(8%)	
2000 general	John Duncan (R)	187,154	(89%)	($342,829)
	Kevin J. Rowland (Lib)	22,304	(11%)	

Prior Winning Percentages: 1998 (89%); 1996 (71%); 1994 (90%); 1992 (72%); 1990 (81%); 1988 (57%); 1988 (56%)

The People		Race/Ethnic Origin	Ancestry	
Area size:	2,492 sq. mi.	90.1% White	USA: 14.0%	English: 8.9%
Urban population:	71.4%	6.2% Black	German: 8.9%	
Rural population:	28.6%	1.0% Asian	**2000 Presidential Vote**	
Pop. 2000:	632,144	0.3% Native Am.	Bush (R) 144,412	(59%)
Median income:	$36,796	0.0% Hawaiian	Gore (D) 95,100	(39%)
Poverty status:	12.2%	1.0% Two+ races	Other 4,246	(2%)
Military veterans:	13.5%	0.1% Other	**Cook Partisan Voting Index:** R +11	
		1.3% Hispanic Origin		

Occupation	Blue collar: 25.9%	White collar: 59.6%	Gray collar: 14.5%

Knoxville, the largest city in East Tennessee, is nestled between mountain ridges where the Holston and French Broad Rivers join to form the Tennessee River. It was established not long after the first wave of pioneers came through the gaps and down between the mountains of the Appalachian chain. During the Civil War it was Union territory, and it has remained Republican in allegiance ever since: The ancestral tug of Tennessee politics. But its Republican heritage is tempered by another tradition, that of the Tennessee Valley Authority. A venturesome program when created in the 1930s, it is now part of the fabric of life in East Tennessee, sometimes criticized as its cheap hydroelectric power capacity was filled and more of its production came from expensive and sometimes poorly functioning nuclear plants.

Both TVA and the region have undergone turbulent changes in recent years. TVA has cut its payroll sharply and held down rates; in a newly competitive electricity market, its director proposed abandoning federal subsidies and spinning off navigation and flood control functions to state or federal agencies; but TVA is laboring under billions of dollars in debt mostly incurred in building its nuclear plants. Knoxville is one of those cities which has overcome setbacks and grown robustly without much notice in the national press. Education entrepreneur Christopher Whittle's campus in downtown Knoxville is now a federal courthouse complex; the 1982 World's Fair site is now the home of the Women's Basketball Hall of Fame. And the University of Tennessee's football stadium on fall Saturdays contains one of the nation's largest crowds—it qualifies as the state's 5th largest city during games—cheering the Vols. Knoxville is also the home base of InstaPundit.com, the weblog of University of Tennessee law professor Glenn Reynolds, "the Grand Central Station" of weblogs. It was one of the first weblogs to skewer Trent Lott for his comments at Strom Thurmond's 100th birthday party, comments that the national press had ignored: One man at his desktop in Knoxville can be a player in national politics.

The 2d Congressional District includes Knoxville and Knox County, plus four mountainous counties and part of one other to the south. It is heavily Republican and has not elected a Democratic congressman since the Civil War. Knox County surprised many by giving a narrow plurality to Democratic Governor Phil Bredesen in 2002, but Republican Van Hilleary carried the rest of the district by a wider margin.

The congressman from the 2d District is John Duncan, a Republican elected in 1988; his father, who was senior Republican on the House Ways and Means Committee, represented the 2d from 1964 until his death in May 1988. Duncan studied in Knoxville and Washington, practiced law and was a trial judge in the 1980s. When his father died, he won the seat despite a spirited challenge from Democrat Dudley Taylor, a scion of another prominent East Tennessee political family. Taylor attacked Duncan for signing up with the National Guard in 1970 and for his ties to scandal-tarred banker and Democratic politician Jake Butcher, but Duncan won with 56% in the special election and 57% in November.

Duncan has been an occasional maverick on economic and foreign policy issues. For six years, the House Republicans' term limit, he chaired the Aviation Subcommittee on Transportation and Infrastructure, dealing with airline ticket taxes, aviation safety and treatment of unruly airplane passengers. In 2001 he switched and became chairman of the Water Resources Subcommittee. Duncan opposed PNTR with China, trade promotion authority and he was one of 10 Republicans to vote against the new Homeland Security Department. In October 2002 he was one of six Republicans—and the only Tennessean—who voted against the use of force in Iraq. Duncan said that this was his most difficult vote in 14 years in the House; he argued that there was not sufficient proof that Saddam Hussein had weapons of mass destruction. He also showed independence from party lines when he voted against term limits and initially favored the Shays-Meehan campaign finance bill, though he voted against the final version in February 2002. He was a team player in helping to negotiate the final deal on the airline security bill after the September 11 attacks. Duncan's independence had its price. He was a candidate for the chairmanship of the Resources Committee in 2003. But Speaker Dennis Hastert's Steering Committee passed over Duncan and five other senior members and gave the post to Richard Pombo.

Duncan sometimes takes his thrifty approach to unusual extremes. He voted in 1997 to end subsidies for sugar, peanuts and tobacco. He questioned excessive bonuses and pensions for TVA executives and won enactment of his bill to have TVA's inspector general appointed by the President rather than the TVA board. Duncan hasn't been shy about seeking funding for other local projects, from resurfacing the Foothills Parkway in the Great Smoky Mountains National Park to a rail and trolley system for downtown Knoxville. Duncan is chief sponsor of a National Parks check-off on the income tax form, which would provide more funding for U.S. parks, including Great Smoky Mountains. In Knoxville, his annual barbecue dinner draws as many as 10,000 people.

In 2002, against his first Democratic challenger since 1996, Duncan won 79%–20%.

THIRD DISTRICT

Rep. Zach Wamp (R)

Elected 1994, 5th term; b. Oct. 28, 1957, Fort Benning, GA; home, Chattanooga; U. of NC, 1976–77, 1979–80, U. of TN, 1978–79; Baptist; married (Kim).

Professional Career: Regional Sales Super., 1981–82, Partner, Wamp Alliance Architectural Devel. Co., 1983–89; Real Estate broker, 1989–94.

DC Office: 2447 RHOB 20515, 202-225-3271; Fax: 202-225-3494; Web site: www.house.gov/wamp.

District Offices: Chattanooga, 423-756-2342; Oak Ridge, 865-576-1976.

Committees: *Appropriations* (19th of 36 R): Energy & Water Development (Vice Chmn.); Homeland Security; Interior.

Group Ratings

	ADA	ACLU	AFS	LCV	CON	ITIC	NTU	COC	ACU	NTLC	CHC
2002	5	7	0	13	97	88	59	80	96	81	75
2001	15	—	10	7	—	—	62	87	88	—	—

National Journal Ratings

	2001 LIB —	2001 CONS		2002 LIB —	2002 CONS
Economic	41%	— 58%		40%	— 59%
Social	0%	— 81%		32%	— 63%
Foreign	29%	— 69%		0%	— 85%

Key Votes of the 107th Congress

1. Approve Bush Tax Cuts	Y	5. Faith-Based Charities	Y	9. Trade Promotion Authority	Y
2. Limit Patients' Bill of Rights	Y	6. Bar Gays in the Boy Scouts	Y	10. Bar Funds for Intl. Court	Y
3. Campaign Finance Reform	Y	7. Ban Partial-Birth Abortion	Y	11. Authorize Force in Iraq	Y
4. Ban ANWR Development	N	8. Arm Commercial Pilots	Y	12. Deny Home. Sec. Dept. Union	Y

Election Results

2002 general	Zach Wamp (R)	112,254	(65%)	($644,166)
	John Wolfe (D)	58,824	(34%)	($35,550)
	Other	2,843	(2%)	
2002 primary	Zach Wamp (R)	unopposed		
2000 general	Zach Wamp (R)	139,840	(64%)	($737,216)
	William L. Callaway (D)	75,785	(35%)	($232,095)
	Other	3,315	(2%)	

Prior Winning Percentages: 1998 (66%); 1996 (56%); 1994 (52%)

The People		Race/Ethnic Origin	Ancestry	
Area size:	3,597 sq. mi.	85.2% White	USA: 16.4%	Irish: 8.0%
Urban population:	64.2%	11.1% Black	English: 7.9%	
Rural population:	35.8%	0.9% Asian	**2000 Presidential Vote**	
Pop. 2000:	632,143	0.3% Native Am.	Bush (R)..............132,792	(57%)
Median income:	$35,434	0.0% Hawaiian	Gore (D)................96,441	(41%)
Poverty status:	13.4%	1.0% Two+ races	Other.....................3,843	(2%)
Military veterans:	13.6%	0.1% Other	**Cook Partisan Voting Index:** R + 8	
		1.6% Hispanic Origin		

Occupation	Blue collar: 31.7%	White collar: 54.3%	Gray collar: 14.0%

Through some of the most vivid scenery of the Appalachian chain, etching its way through the serrated ridges of East Tennessee, is the river that gave Tennessee its name. From Knoxville, the river cuts through a ridge and then plunges down a long valley to the city of Chattanooga at the Georgia line. There it switches course again, winding around the table-top Lookout Mountain and then moving into northern Alabama. Chattanooga, the city at the base of Lookout Mountain, was just a village when it was a Civil War battlefield; after the war, it became the industrial "Dynamo of Dixie." Three decades ago it was labeled America's most polluted city. But regional political leaders, prodded by the influential and civic-minded remnants of its Industrial Age aristocracy, used creative measures, such as a locally built electric shuttle bus, to reduce pollution and spruce up the city's scenic river banks. Chattanooga is now the proud home of the 12-story-high Tennessee Aquarium, the world's largest fresh water aquarium, with an exhibit in which you can follow the course of a drop of rain from the headwaters of the Tennessee until it flows out the Mississippi River into the Gulf. In recent years, the region has pinned its hopes for growth more on the private sector and less on the public sector institutions that had heretofore shaped it. The Tennessee Valley Authority, buffeted by a changing energy market and pro-competition moves in Congress, has slashed its workforce from its 1980 peak of more than 50,000 to less than 13,000 in 2002.

The 3d Congressional District includes Chattanooga and runs northeasterly from the Tennessee-Georgia border in the south to the Virginia border. Most of the population is in Chattanooga and the counties around it. But it reaches north through a thin strip of land that includes Dayton, where John Scopes was tried for teaching evolution in 1925 and was defended by Clarence Darrow and prosecuted by William Jennings Bryan, and Oak Ridge, which was secretly constructed in virgin Appalachian forest during World War II in order to house the key nuclear facility that is now the Oak Ridge National Laboratory; Oak Ridge today is a highly educated enclave which tends to vote Republican. North and east of Oak Ridge, the Democratic redistricters attached five heavily Republican mountain counties previously in the 1st and 2d districts, making this one of three Tennessee districts that span the state from north to south. Six Democratic counties west of the last mountain ridge were removed from the 3d District to make the 4th more Democratic.

The congressman from the 3d District is Zach Wamp, a Republican elected in 1994. Wamp left college before graduating to become a real estate developer in Chattanooga, selling $22 million in real estate in five years. In 1992 he ran a high-voltage race for Congress against 20-year Democratic incumbent Marilyn Lloyd. Lloyd won by just 49%–47%, the closest margin of her career; she decided to retire in 1994. Wamp ran again as a strong conservative; one proposal was to pay members of Congress the same as a lieutenant colonel and billet them in officer housing. Democrat Randy Button won a close primary and attacked Wamp's character. Wamp accused Button of flip-flopping on issues and, like many Republicans, ran an ad showing his opponent's face morphing into Bill Clinton's. Wamp won 52%–46%.

In the House, Wamp got a seat on the Appropriations Committee. He has a conservative record laced with locally appealing stands. He called himself "a heat-seeking missile on behalf of Tennessee and my district." He supported study of a Chattanooga-to-Atlanta high-speed rail route, secured funding to repair the deteriorating Chickamauga Lock in Chattanooga, and has sought to attract new industries to parts of the Oak Ridge reservation and Chattanooga's former Army ammunition plant. He won Bill Clinton's approval of additional benefits for employees with work-related illnesses at Oak Ridge, a city with a tongue-in-cheek reputation for people who "glow in the dark." In 2002, the House and Senate passed separate versions of his proposal to create a 780-acre national archeological district at Chattanooga's Moccasin Bend, but they failed to resolve their differences.

Despite his generally conservative record, Wamp has taken some maverick stances. His support for TVA, including opposition to Rodney Frelinghuysen's attempt to sell off its non-hydro power plants, annoyed many conservatives. He is co-chairman of the House Renewable Energy and Efficiency Caucus, which he uses to cite Chattanooga's successes in this area. He has never accepted PAC money and he vocally supported the McCain-Feingold campaign finance bill, a stance that irritated the Republican leadership and prompted the National Right to Life Committee to run radio ads against him, even though he is opposed to abortion; the committee feared that the new law would prevent it from running issue-advocacy ads at campaign time. When the bill was enacted in 2002, he offered a vital amendment for Republicans to double the maximum individual contribution to $2,000 per candidate. He called for reforming managed health care to ensure that patients "get the treatment they need," showed little zeal to abolish racial preferences and placed preservation of Social Security above tax cuts. He tacked to the conservatives in sponsoring a bill to permit local governments to post the Ten Commandments in public buildings, and he sought to restrict Internet access to pornography for children. He unsuccessfully tried after the 2000 election to repeal the House Republicans' three-term limit on chairmanships. He rented a home on Capitol Hill with three other House Republicans and three Democrats. "My attitude toward the Congress has changed," Wamp told *The New York Times Magazine*. "We must realize public service is a great way of life. I came in with the attitude there were a bunch of thieves here. That's not true."

In 1996 he faced a spirited challenge from the second-place finisher in the 1994 Democratic primary. With Marilyn Lloyd's endorsement, Wamp won 56%–43%, nearly 10% ahead of Bob Dole. In 2002, he won 65%–34%. In 1994 Wamp said he would serve only 12 years in the House and Bill Frist, running for the Senate, said he would only serve two terms there. Wamp has made no secret that he is interested in running for the Senate in 2006 if Frist doesn't.

FOURTH DISTRICT

Rep. Lincoln Davis (D)

Elected 2002, 1st term; b. Sept. 13, 1943, Pall Mall; home, Pall Mall; TN Tech. U., B.S. 1966; Baptist; married (Lynda).

Elected Office: Byrdstown Mayor, 1978–82; TN House of Reps, 1980–84; TN Senate, 1996–02.

Professional Career: Owner, Diversified Construction Co.

DC Office: 504 CHOB 20515, 202-225-6831; Fax: 202-225-5172; Web site: www.house.gov/lincolndavis.

District Offices: Columbia, 931-490-8699; Jamestown, 931-879-2361; Rockwood, 865-354-3323.

Committees: *Agriculture* (24th of 24 D): Department Operations, Oversight, Nutrition & Forestry; General Farm Commodities & Risk Management. *Science* (13th of 22 D): Energy; Environment, Technology and Standards. *Transportation & Infrastructure* (34th of 34 D): Economic Development, Public Buildings & Emergency Management; Water Resources & Environment.

Group Ratings and Key Votes: Newly Elected

Election Results

2002 general	Lincoln Davis (D)	95,989	(52%)	($1,280,211)
	Janice Bowling (R)	85,680	(46%)	($556,643)
	Other	2,631	(1%)	
2002 primary	Lincoln Davis (D)	48,843	(57%)	
	Fran Marcum (D)	36,779	(43%)	
2000 general	Van Hilleary (R)	133,622	(66%)	($1,320,424)
	David H. Dunaway (D)	67,165	(33%)	($417,105)
	Other	2,423	(1%)	

The People		Race/Ethnic Origin	Ancestry	
Area size:	10,155 sq. mi.	92.6% White	USA: 20.0%	Irish: 8.1%
Urban population:	32.1%	4.4% Black	English: 7.2%	
Rural population:	67.9%	0.3% Asian	**2000 Presidential Vote**	
Pop. 2000:	632,143	0.3% Native Am.	Bush (R) 111,639	(50%)
Median income:	$31,645	0.0% Hawaiian	Gore (D) 109,559	(49%)
Poverty status:	15.2%	0.8% Two+ races	Other 3,507	(2%)
Military veterans:	13.2%	0.0% Other	**Cook Partisan Voting Index: R + 1**	
		1.6% Hispanic Origin		

Occupation   Blue collar: 40.4%   White collar: 45.1%   Gray collar: 14.4%

The invisible line between Civil War Republican and Civil War Democratic territory runs along the Cumberland Plateau, the westernmost upswelling of the Appalachians, west of the valley where the Tennessee River runs south from Knoxville to Chattanooga. It separates the Tennessee Valley, which had few slaves and whose economic ties were with the North, from the rolling farmlands of middle Tennessee, first settled by Andrew Jackson in the 1790s and resolutely Democratic from the time he became the first president to call himself a Democrat in the 1830s. Here are places like Sewanee, the pleasant home of the University of the South; Bledsoe County, the pumpkin capital of the world; Columbia, home of President James K. Polk and the site of Maury County's Mule Day celebration every April; and Lynchburg, where Jack Daniels whiskey has been made for generations and which is every bit the idealized small town that the distillery's folksy, black-and-white advertisements make it out to be.

The 4th Congressional District runs across this line and crosses Tennessee northeast to southwest for some 200 miles. It reaches almost to Virginia in the northeast and almost to Mississippi in the southwest. It is comparatively svelte and compact, though, compared to the 4th District before the 2002 redistricting, which stretched 300 miles and actually bordered on both Virginia and Mississippi. There was a political motive behind the 2002 redistricting: Democratic redistricters hoped to make a safe district for a moderate Democrat after Van Hilleary left the seat to run for governor in 2002. Democratic redistricters removed five heavily Republican counties from the northeast end of the district and two Republican-leaning counties from the southwest and added six Democratic counties northwest of Chattanooga from the 3d District and three Democratic-leaning counties, including Maury, in the west. In the process they reduced the district's Bush 2000 percentage from 53% to 50%, enough, they hoped, to enable a Tennessee Democrat to win. And so it turned out.

The congressman from the 4th District is Lincoln Davis, a Democrat elected in 2002. Davis grew up in Fentress County on his family farm, which was purchased from World War I hero Sergeant Alvin York, who was a great celebrity in the 1920s and 1930s and who was played by Gary Cooper in an Academy Award performance in the 1941 movie *Sergeant York*. Davis started his own construction company, which builds homes and businesses, and develops land. He also has been a soil scientist and farms cattle and tobacco. He began his political career in 1978 as mayor of Byrdstown near the Kentucky border and was elected to the state House in 1980. In 1984, when Al Gore left the House to run for the Senate, Davis was a candidate to replace him in the old 6th District, but he lost the Democratic primary to Bart Gordon 28%–22%. He lost another House primary 31%–27% in 1994, for the seat won by Republican Van Hilleary. Davis returned to office in 1996 as a state senator.

Davis was the early favorite in 2002 to take this more Democratic-friendly seat; he gained a cross-section of support in the Democratic primary from national and local party leaders, organized labor, anti-abortion groups, and the National Rifle Association. But he had a more difficult time than expected in winning the nomination against political newcomer Fran Marcum from Tullahoma in the southern part of the district. A wealthy businesswoman with EMILY's List backing, she spent $1.6 million of her own money on her campaign. Her ads depicted Davis as a political retread, tied him to the legislature's politically unpopular handling of state budget problems and emphasized her support for abortion rights. Davis won, 57%–43%, carrying 20 of the 24 counties. Republicans also had a competitive primary: Janice Bowling, a Tullahoma alderwoman and district director for Hilleary, won the six-candidate Republican primary by 37%–24% over former state Safety Commissioner Mike Greene.

In the general, self-described "pistol-packing Mama" Bowling attempted to seize on Gore's endorsement of Davis in the primary by asking voters to vote against Gore one more time. As part of her folksy message, she campaigned in a white chenille dress, red boots and an American flag scarf, and was a strong backer of George W. Bush's defense policy. She was significantly outspent by her opponent, and complained that Republican financial backing came too late. Davis promised not to let any opponent "out-gun me, out-pray me, or out-family me," and held true to that. In the words of *The Tennessean*, Davis combined a "folksy, slap-on-the-back attitude with the oratorical punch of a revival preacher." When the Democrats' House campaign committee advised him to tone down his focus on values, he said, "I just giggled at them." He won 52%–46%. Redistricting made the difference. Davis carried the counties added to the district by nearly 8,000 votes—almost all of his 10,000-vote margin. Bowling would probably have carried the Republican counties removed by redistricting by more than Davis's 2,000-vote margin in the counties in both the old and new 4th Districts.

Aware that his conservative views may be ill-suited for the House Democratic Caucus, Davis pledged to stay in close touch with the grass roots and said that he probably will differ from most national Democrats on cultural issues. Republicans might try to regain this district by riding on Bush's coattails in 2004.

FIFTH DISTRICT

Rep. Jim Cooper (D)

Elected 2002, 1st term; b. June 19, 1954, Nashville; home, Nashville; U. of NC, B.A. 1975, Oxford U., B.A./M.A. 1977, Harvard U., J.D. 1980; Episcopalian; married (Martha).

Elected Office: U.S. House of Reps., 1982–94.

Professional Career: Practicing atty., 1980–82; Investment banker, 1995–99; Founder and partner, investment bank, 1999–02.

DC Office: 1536 LHOB 20515, 202-225-4311; Fax: 202-226-1035; Web site: cooper.house.gov.

District Office: Nashville, 615-736-5295.

Committees: *Armed Services* (23d of 29 D): Tactical Air & Land Forces; Terrorism, Unconventional Threats & Capabilities; Total Force. *Budget* (15th of 19 D). *Government Reform* (18th of 19 D): Civil Service & Agency Organization; Energy Policy, Natural Resources and Regulatory Affairs.

Group Ratings and Key Votes: Newly Elected

Election Results

2002 general	Jim Cooper (D)	108,903	(64%)	($1,888,568)
	Robert Duvall (R)	56,825	(33%)	($17,615)
	Other	5,158	(3%)	
2002 primary	Jim Cooper (D)	32,651	(47%)	
	John Arriola (D)	16,878	(24%)	
	Gayle Ray (D)	16,087	(23%)	

Prior Winning Percentages: 1992 (66%); 1990 (69%); 1988 (100%); 1986 (100%); 1984 (75%); 1982 (66%)

The People		Race/Ethnic Origin	Ancestry	
Area size:	932 sq. mi.	68.2% White	USA: 10.8%	Irish: 7.6%
Urban population:	88.7%	23.4% Black	English: 7.6%	
Rural population:	11.3%	2.0% Asian	**2000 Presidential Vote**	
Pop. 2000:	632,143	0.3% Native Am.	Gore (D) 130,111	(57%)
Median income:	$40,419	0.1% Hawaiian	Bush (R) 95,309	(42%)
Poverty status:	12.2%	1.6% Two + races	Other 4,015	(2%)
Military veterans:	11.7%	0.2% Other	**Cook Partisan Voting Index:** D + 7	
		4.2% Hispanic Origin		
Occupation	Blue collar: 21.9%	White collar: 64.2%	Gray collar: 13.8%	

Nashville is the home of country music, the buckle of the Bible Belt, and in almost every way the heart of Tennessee. This was one of the first American cities established west of the Appalachians; Andrew Jackson built his Hermitage nearby above the banks of the Cumberland River, and his political home base has remained Democratic ever since. It was the capital of Tennessee early on, just as it was, and still is, the center of the state's political life and discourse: Home to *The Tennessean,* a classically partisan Democratic paper, and the state's biggest television market. Nashville is proud of its universities and of its columned Capitol and its Parthenon; this is perhaps the greatest center of Greek Revival architecture in America. Nashville is also firmly established as the religious publishing center of the country, producing more bibles than any other city in the world. Country music, an art form that emerged from the hardscrabble, mountainous counties of East Tennessee, now is a $2 billion-a-year business and is one of the nation's dominant radio formats. The industry, run from a series of deceptively modest homes-turned-offices on what's called Music Row, congregated in Nashville because local radio station WSM had a clear channel from which to beam its weekly "barn dances" throughout the South in the 1920s; these later became known as the Grand Ole Opry, the longest continuously running radio show in history. An expanded Country Music Hall of Fame and Museum opened in the downtown revitalization project.

For years, both the city's Parthenon-building elite and its religious leadership resented the growing local influence of country music; the former looked down on the music's uneducated practitioners, while the latter cringed at the musicians' unwholesome travails and occasional indecorous deaths. But all three groups made their peace in the 1970s, and since then Nashville has become one of the South's boom cities—the fastest growing metropolitan area between Atlanta and Dallas-Fort Worth. New-generation industry moved in, with Nissan building a big plant in nearby Smyrna and General Motors setting up its Saturn plant in nearby Spring Hill. There were commercial and apartment real estate booms as well, though naturally followed by some busts. An agreeable quality of life, plenty of medium-wage, high-skill labor, a central location, and absence of urban strife and militant unions have all helped Nashville boom, with the metropolitan area surpassing the Memphis region as the largest in the state. The rapid growth has caused local concern, with Mayor Bill Purcell lamenting that he doesn't want his city "to become like Atlanta." The dominant cultural tone remains conservative, and fast-growing surrounding counties have become increasingly Republican, but Nashville and Davidson County remain Democratic bulwarks of Republican-trending Tennessee.

The 5th Congressional District includes most of Nashville-Davidson County, plus the bulk of suburban Wilson County to the east and Cheatham to the west. The 5th is reliably Democratic in statewide elections; to Congress it has long elected rather liberal Democrats—this is, after all, the home of the first Democratic president. It was the home of Al Gore when he was a divinity student at Vanderbilt and reporter for *The Tennessean*, and was the site of his headquarters for his 2000 presidential campaign; in June 2002, he and Tipper bought a house in the elegant Belle Meade neighborhood. The 5th was one of only three Tennessee districts he carried in 2000.

The congressman from the 5th District is Jim Cooper, a Democrat elected in 2002; he was elected from 1982 to 1992 in the very different 4th District and ran unsuccessfully for the Senate in 1994. His father, Prentice Cooper, was elected governor in 1938, 1940 and 1942. In the 1982 election, Jim Cooper beat the bearer of another famous name, Cissy Baker, the daughter of then-Senate Majority Leader Howard Baker. When he first took office, he was the youngest member of the House. Notable for his frankness, he spoke out against tobacco use and opposed the National Rifle Association. He participated actively in the "group of nine" Democrats on the Energy and Commerce that helped to produce a compromise between John Dingell and Henry Waxman on the Clean Air Act of 1990. In 1994, he ran against Fred Thompson for the Senate seat Gore vacated when he was elected vice president. Ads captured a personal contrast between the two candidates: Thompson appeared in workshirts, speaking confidently to the camera while walking up porch stairs; the much shorter and youthful-looking Cooper appeared before a church in starched white shirt and tie. Cooper got squeezed out of the middle ground he had long worked to occupy, and Thompson won 60%–39%.

In March 2002, less than a month before the filing deadline, Thompson announced he would not run for reelection, and 5th District Congressman Bob Clement jumped into the Senate race. Cooper, who had been working as an investment banker in Nashville, quickly joined a flurry of candidates for the Democratic nomination. His toughest opponent was Davidson County Sheriff Gayle Ray, who had support from EMILY's List. The first female sheriff in Tennessee, Ray attacked Cooper's voting record on health care, particularly on women's health issues. Cooper, an abortion-rights supporter, recalled his actions as a key player on health care initiatives and said that Ray's charges were inaccurate. He ran an ad showing his children describing what he does well (banjo playing, helping with homework, getting health care for senior citizens) and what he doesn't do well (cooking, playing basketball). The AFL-CIO and *The Tennessean* endorsed Ray; Cooper had support from the Sierra Club and several smaller newspapers. Cooper raised twice as much money as Ray, including more than $700,000 of his own. Cooper won with 47%, Ray faded at the end and got 23%, while state representative John Arriola had 24% in the seven-candidate field. In the general, Cooper easily defeated Nashville businessman Robert Duvall 64%–33%.

Cooper returned to the House with more seniority than other freshmen because of his previous House service. But he was not able to get back his old seat on the Commerce Committee, because his 6th District colleague Bart Gordon is now a member.

SIXTH DISTRICT

Rep. Bart Gordon (D)

Elected 1984, 10th term; b. Jan. 24, 1949, Murfreesboro; home, Murfreesboro; Middle TN St. U., B.S. 1971, U. of TN, J.D. 1973; United Methodist; married (Leslie).

Military Career: Army Reserves, 1971–72.

Professional Career: Practicing atty., 1974–84; Chmn., TN Dem. Party, 1981–83.

DC Office: 2304 RHOB 20515, 202-225-4231; Fax: 202-225-6887; Web site: gordon.house.gov.

District Offices: Cookeville, 931-528-5907; Murfreesboro, 615-896-1986; Springfield, 615-382-9712.

Committees: *Energy & Commerce* (9th of 26 D): Health; Telecommunications & The Internet. *Science* (2d of 22 D): Space & Aeronautics (RMM).

Group Ratings

	ADA	ACLU	AFS	LCV	CON	ITIC	NTU	COC	ACU	NTLC	CHC
2002	70	53	88	63	3	50	33	68	40	29	58
2001	65	—	70	71	—	—	33	65	42	—	—

National Journal Ratings

	2001 LIB —	2001 CONS		2002 LIB —	2002 CONS
Economic	54% —	47%		54% —	45%
Social	54% —	45%		56% —	42%
Foreign	56% —	41%		55% —	45%

Key Votes of the 107th Congress

1. Approve Bush Tax Cuts	Y	5. Faith-Based Charities	Y	9. Trade Promotion Authority	N
2. Limit Patients' Bill of Rights	N	6. Bar Gays in the Boy Scouts	Y	10. Bar Funds for Intl. Court	Y
3. Campaign Finance Reform	Y	7. Ban Partial-Birth Abortion	Y	11. Authorize Force in Iraq	Y
4. Ban ANWR Development	Y	8. Arm Commercial Pilots	Y	12. Deny Home. Sec. Dept. Union	N

Election Results

2002 general	Bart Gordon (D)	117,034	(66%)	($595,537)
	Robert Garrison (R)	57,401	(32%)	
	Other	3,112	(2%)	
2002 primary	Bart Gordon (D)	69,121	(92%)	
	Harvey Howard (D)	6,255	(8%)	
2000 general	Bart Gordon (D)	168,861	(62%)	($1,135,811)
	David Charles (R)	97,169	(36%)	($174,937)
	Other	5,869	(2%)	

Prior Winning Percentages: 1998 (55%); 1996 (54%); 1994 (51%); 1992 (57%); 1990 (67%); 1988 (76%); 1986 (77%); 1984 (63%)

The People		Race/Ethnic Origin	Ancestry	
Area size:	5,576 sq. mi.	89.0% White	USA: 19.0%	English: 8.1%
Urban population:	53.2%	6.3% Black	Irish: 8.1%	
Rural population:	46.8%	0.9% Asian	**2000 Presidential Vote**	
Pop. 2000:	632,143	0.3% Native Am.	Bush (R)..............112,096 (49%)	
Median income:	$39,721	0.0% Hawaiian	Gore (D)..............111,872 (49%)	
Poverty status:	11.1%	0.8% Two + races	Other....................3,729 (2%)	
Military veterans:	12.3%	0.1% Other	**Cook Partisan Voting Index:** R + 0	
		2.6% Hispanic Origin		

Occupation	Blue collar: 33.9%	White collar: 52.9%	Gray collar: 13.1%

The rolling countryside of Middle Tennessee, west of the Cumberland Plateau and the last chain of Appalachians, has been called "the dimple of the universe." This is hilly and fertile land, cut by deep rivers ambling along in S-curves. The terrain here was never much suited for plantation crops; this has long been a land of small farmers and small county seat towns, nestled amid what people here regard as some of the loveliest scenery on earth. Middle Tennessee has also been one of the heartlands of the Democratic Party. It was the political home base of Andrew Jackson and supported him nearly unanimously; during the Civil War, though it had very few slaves, it resisted the invading Union armies. For 140 years after Jackson, it voted solidly Democratic and elected as its congressmen some of the luminaries of the national Democratic Party: James K. Polk (1825–39), speaker of the House and later president; Cordell Hull (1907–21, 1923–31), later senator and secretary of State; Albert Gore Sr., (1939–53), later senator; and Albert Gore Jr., (1977–85), later senator and vice president.

The 6th Congressional District includes 14 Middle Tennessee counties east and south of Nashville, plus the eastern half of Wilson County just east of Nashville. The heritage here is old and rural, but economic growth has fanned out into the farmland from Nashville, evident in thousands of jobs created by Japanese companies and American startups, firms fleeing the North and entrepreneurs fleeing taxes. This was the fastest growing district in Tennessee during the

1990s. Many new voters here are Republican: The 6th District, in its 1990s boundaries, voted for the Clinton-Gore ticket by 47%–40% in 1992, for Bob Dole by 47%–45% in 1996 and in 2000 it voted 54%–45% for the Bush-Cheney ticket against its former representative, Al Gore. But Democrats who controlled redistricting in 2002 were determined to stop the Republican advance; they lopped off half of Wilson County and all of fast-growing and heavily Republican Williamson County, just south of Nashville. They added the more Democratic Robertson County north of Nashville, whose small towns have only started to become bedroom communities. The changes reduced the Bush 2000 percentage in the 6th from 54% to 49%.

The congressman from the 6th District is Bart Gordon, a Democrat first elected in 1984 when Gore gave up his House seat to run for the Senate. Gordon grew up in Murfreesboro in Rutherford County and went to Middle Tennessee State University. He practiced law and became Tennessee Democratic chairman in 1981: Politics has been most of his life. In 1984, he ran a computerized fund-raising operation and voter contact system—then a novelty in this district where a personal handshake from a candidate was the norm. He won a multi-candidate primary with 28% of the vote (the 4th District's freshman Congressman Lincoln Davis was second with 22%) and won the general election 63%–37%.

In the House, Gordon has built a firmly moderate record and he used his insider skills to build a close relationship with the Democratic leadership. Gordon, who lost his seat on the Rules Committee and moved to Commerce when the Republicans took control of the House in 1995, has worked to limit children's access to adult material by phone, on television, and on the Internet. On the 2001–02 energy bill he worked to protect the Tennessee Valley Authority from proponents of electricity deregulation. He has voted with House Republicans to make permanent the repeal of the marriage penalty and the estate tax. He voted to authorize the use of force in Iraq, but opposed trade promotion authority. From his perch on the Space Subcommittee, he voiced concern that, in the wake of the 2003 Columbia space shuttle crash, NASA was "rapidly losing credibility;" he called for a presidentially-appointed panel to take over the investigation.

Gordon's voting record and his ties to the Democratic leadership in this Republican-trending district caused him trouble in the 1990s. In 1994 he faced Steve Gill, a lawyer from Williamson County. In a good Republican year, Gill voiced anti-Clinton themes. Gordon spent $1.4 million with $608,000 of it from PACs—more than Gill spent altogether. Gordon carried the smaller rural counties 58%–42%, for a slim overall margin of 51%–49%. Two years later, when Clinton was in better esteem, Gordon beat Gill 54%–42%, with 51% in the counties outside Nashville and 64% in the rural counties. By 2000, against less well-financed opposition, Gordon won 62%–36%, winning every county but Williamson and a precinct in Nashville. Gordon was Tennessee House Democrats' point man in redistricting, and the changes in the district lines seem to have made him invulnerable; in 2002 he won 66%–32%. A notable accomplishment in the increasingly fit House: Gordon has won for several years the 5K race as the fastest member of Congress.

SEVENTH DISTRICT

Rep. Marsha Blackburn (R)

Elected 2002, 1st term; b. June 6, 1952, Laurel, MS; home, Brentwood; MS St. U., B.S. 1973; Presbyterian; married (Chuck).

Elected Office: TN Senate, 1998–2002.

Professional Career: Retail marketing consultant, 1973–98.

DC Office: 509 CHOB 20515, 202-225-2811; Fax: 202-225-3004; Web site: www.house.gov/blackburn.

District Offices: Clarksville, 931-503-0391; Franklin, 615-591-5161; Memphis, 901-382-5811.

Committees: *Education & the Workforce* (25th of 27 R): Employer-Employee Relations; Workforce Protections. *Government Reform* (24th of 24 R): Civil Service & Agency Organization; Criminal Justice, Drug Policy & Human Resources; Government Efficiency & Financial Management (Vice Chmn.). *Judiciary* (21st of 21 R): Commercial & Administrative Law; Immigration, Border Security & Claims.

Group Ratings and Key Votes: Newly Elected

Election Results

2002 general	Marsha Blackburn (R)	138,314	(71%)	($552,213)
	Tim Barron (D)	51,790	(26%)	($18,969)
	Other	5,454	(3%)	
2002 primary	Marsha Blackburn (R)	36,633	(40%)	
	David Kustoff (R)	18,392	(20%)	
	Brent Taylor (R)	14,139	(16%)	
	Mark Norris (R)	13,104	(14%)	
	Forrest Shoaf (R)	7,319	(8%)	
2000 general	Ed Bryant (R)	171,056	(70%)	($727,131)
	Richard P. Sims (D)	71,587	(29%)	($10,493)
	Other	3,006	(1%)	

The People		Race/Ethnic Origin	Ancestry	
Area size:	6,349 sq. mi.	83.5% White	USA: 12.3%	English: 9.1%
Urban population:	61.0%	11.4% Black	Irish: 9.1%	
Rural population:	39.0%	1.5% Asian	**2000 Presidential Vote**	
Pop. 2000:	632,139	0.2% Native Am.	Bush (R)..............146,213	(59%)
Median income:	$50,090	0.1% Hawaiian	Gore (D)...............99,423	(40%)
Poverty status:	8.0%	1.1% Two+ races	Other...................3,098	(1%)
Military veterans:	14.2%	0.1% Other	**Cook Partisan Voting Index:** R + 10	
		2.2% Hispanic Origin		

Occupation	Blue collar: 24.0%	White collar: 64.0%	Gray collar: 12.0%

Rural Tennessee north of Mississippi is one of the most sparsely settled areas in the state. Along each side of the Tennessee River, as it flows north and widens out into Kentucky Lake amid heavy forests, are small rural communities; many go back to pre-Civil War days and some have not grown much since. One of those towns is Waynesboro, where Davy Crockett delivered campaign speeches from the base of a huge natural stone double bridge overlooking the Buffalo River. Farther west is McNairy County, where Sheriff Buford Pusser of *Walking Tall* fame carried his big stick until his untimely death in 1974; here, the land is flatter and more open, a northward extension economically and demographically of the northern Mississippi farmlands. This mostly empty land is bounded on two sides by large metropolitan areas, Nashville to the east and Memphis to the west, with Nashville now the largest in Tennessee. South of Nashville is booming Williamson County, with its bedroom communities of Franklin and Brentwood; this is the most affluent, highly educated and fastest-growing county in Tennessee. To the north, along the Cumberland River, is fast-growing Clarksville, with many well-restored 19th century homes plus the sprawling Fort Campbell army base, which has more than 20,000 military personnel just across the Kentucky border.

The 7th Congressional District spans this territory, packing Republican voters from Montgomery County's seat of Clarksville, south to the western fringe of Cheatham County and most of Williamson County plus a bite of Nashville-Davidson, then rambling west across the Tennessee River and south to the Mississippi border and finally to the white neighborhoods on the east side of Memphis and Shelby County. Almost 40% of its votes are cast in metro Memphis and 30% in metro Nashville, mostly in Williamson County; another 11% are in Montgomery County and only 21% in the smaller rural counties. On the map, this looks like a rural district. In reality, it's mostly suburban. Redistricting, which added suburban and Republican Williamson County, increased the Bush 2000 percentage from 53% to 59%, making it nearly as solidly Republican as the 1st District in faraway East Tennessee.

The congresswoman from the 7th District is Marsha Blackburn, a Republican first elected in 2002. She grew up in a Farm Bureau family in Laurel, Mississippi, where her father sold oil-field production equipment. Her interest in gardening and canning won her a 4-H college scholarship, which she used at Mississippi State University, where she majored in merchandising and clothing. After that, she sold books and became a sales manager with Southwestern Company, which sells educational materials, and moved to Williamson County. (Her hilltop home is known as "Up Yonder," named by its former owner, Grand Ole Opry star Minnie Pearl). Blackburn then became director of retail fashion for a Nashville department store, and was appointed by Governor Don Sundquist as executive director of the Tennessee Film, Entertainment and Music Commission. In 1992, she was the Republican nominee against Bart Gordon in the 6th District, which then included Williamson County, and attacked his spending record and the congressional pay raise; she carried Williamson County but lost 57%–41%. She was elected in 1998 to the Tennessee Senate, where she became an outspoken opponent of Sundquist's proposed income tax. She was well known there for her appearances on conservative radio talk shows and for organizing rallies opposed to the income tax. When Blackburn e-mailed an aide, "We need troops at 5," more than 1,200 responded and the angry crowd of protesters moved into the Capitol; three windows were broken. She said she had no regrets about "letting people know." There's nothing subtle about Blackburn: She once burned her travel receipts and presented the ashes to an inquisitive boss, just "to make a point."

In March 2002, less than a month before the filing deadline, Senator Fred Thompson announced that he wouldn't run for reelection. Within days, 7th District Congressman Ed Bryant decided to run for the Senate, and Blackburn decided to run in the 7th District. Seven candidates ran in the Republican primary; three were well known in the Memphis area—Tennessee Bush-Cheney Chairman David Kustoff, Memphis City Councilor Brent Taylor and state Senator Mark Norris. Blackburn was the only well-known candidate from the Nashville area. Norris called her "an uncomplicated obstructionist," and a *Tennessean* columnist said her career was "marked by unblemished negativism." Blackburn benefited from $100,000 in advertising and another $90,000 in contributions by the anti-tax Club for Growth, and from attacks by the Shelby County candidates on one another. She ran as pro-life, pro-gun and pro-military. The Memphis area cast 50% of the votes in the primary and the Nashville area only 25%. But Blackburn won with 40% of the vote while Kustoff finished second with 20%. She won 78% of the vote in the Nashville area, and she ran competitive in the Memphis area, where she got 24% and her Memphis-based opponents got between 19% and 28%. Blackburn called the victory a celebration of the defeat of the state income tax.

The general election was not seriously contested, and Blackburn won, 71%–26%.

EIGHTH DISTRICT

Rep. John Tanner (D)

Elected 1988, 8th term; b. Sept. 22, 1944, Halls; home, Union City; U. of TN, B.S. 1966, J.D. 1968; Disciples of Christ; married (Betty Ann).

Military Career: Navy, 1968–72; TN Natl. Guard, 1974–2000.

Elected Office: TN House of Reps., 1976–88.

Professional Career: Practicing atty., 1973–88.

DC Office: 1226 LHOB 20515, 202-225-4714; Fax: 202-225-1765; Web site: www.house.gov/tanner.

District Offices: Jackson, 731-423-4848; Millington, 901-873-5690; Union City, 731-885-7070.

Committees: *Ways & Means* (12th of 17 D): Oversight; Trade.

Group Ratings

	ADA	ACLU	AFS	LCV	CON	ITIC	NTU	COC	ACU	NTLC	CHC
2002	70	38	75	13	73	88	26	80	39	21	42
2001	60	—	78	43	—	—	25	70	50	—	—

National Journal Ratings

	2001 LIB —	2001 CONS	2002 LIB —	2002 CONS
Economic	55% —	45%	57% —	42%
Social	54% —	47%	51% —	48%
Foreign	49% —	47%	53% —	46%

Key Votes of the 107th Congress

1. Approve Bush Tax Cuts	N	5. Faith-Based Charities	N
2. Limit Patients' Bill of Rights	N	6. Bar Gays in the Boy Scouts	Y
3. Campaign Finance Reform	Y	7. Ban Partial-Birth Abortion	Y
4. Ban ANWR Development	N	8. Arm Commercial Pilots	Y

9. Trade Promotion Authority	Y
10. Bar Funds for Intl. Court	Y
11. Authorize Force in Iraq	Y
12. Deny Home. Sec. Dept. Union	N

Election Results

2002 general	John Tanner (D)	117,811	(70%)	($553,863)
	Mat McClain (R)	45,853	(27%)	
	Other	4,306	(3%)	
2002 primary	John Tanner (D)	66,015	(87%)	
	Richard Ward (D)	10,069	(13%)	
2000 general	John Tanner (D)	143,127	(72%)	($621,357)
	Billy Yancy (R)	54,929	(28%)	($3,658)

Prior Winning Percentages: 1998 (100%); 1996 (67%); 1994 (64%); 1992 (84%); 1990 (100%); 1988 (62%)

The People		Race/Ethnic Origin	Ancestry	
Area size:	8,528 sq. mi.	74.4% White	USA: 15.8%	Irish: 7.6%
Urban population:	47.0%	22.3% Black	English: 6.3%	
Rural population:	53.0%	0.4% Asian	**2000 Presidential Vote**	
Pop. 2000:	632,142	0.3% Native Am.	Gore (D) 109,221	(51%)
Median income:	$33,001	0.0% Hawaiian	Bush (R) 102,998	(48%)
Poverty status:	15.0%	0.8% Two+ races	Other 2,633	(1%)
Military veterans:	13.5%	0.1% Other	**Cook Partisan Voting Index:** D + 1	
		1.6% Hispanic Origin		

Occupation	Blue collar: 37.0%	White collar: 47.7%	Gray collar: 15.3%

West of Nashville and the lakes along the Tennessee River and north of Memphis, the rivers roll lazily through flat or gently rolling land that almost could be the northern end of Mississippi. Cotton and soybeans are the main crops; more blacks remain in rural areas here than in any other part of Tennessee, a reminder of its old plantation economy. The towns here are small, edged in by farm fields; the river bottoms, often flooded, are heavily forested. Here is Henning, the hometown of Alex Haley, where he used to sit on his porch and listen to his aunts tell him stories about slave ships and the Civil War that became *Roots*.

The 8th Congressional District includes much of this West Tennessee farmland, from the lakes west to the Mississippi. Its largest city is Jackson, which has a Toyota plant; it also includes the northern fringes of Memphis. Historically, this is Democratic country; Republicans haven't represented most of the counties that make up the 8th since the end of Reconstruction. The region trended Republican in national races in the 1960s and 1970s, then turned back toward the Democrats with the help of some smart local politicians. One of them was Ned Ray Mc-Wherter, first elected to the legislature from Weakley County in 1968, speaker from 1973–86, then governor until 1994. In the 1990s, movement was back toward the Republican party; this has been a key marginal area in Tennessee politics. Rural Carroll County is something of a bell-wether, voting 50%–49% for George W. Bush over Al Gore in 2000. But Democratic strength still remains in the 8th District—it was one of the three Tennessee congressional districts carried, in this case narrowly, by Gore. Redistricting did not much change the political balance.

The congressman from the 8th District is John Tanner, a Democrat elected in 1988. Tanner, who is a cousin of McWherter, grew up in Obion County, went to college and law school at the University of Tennessee, served four years in the Navy, then practiced law in Union City. In 1976, at 32, he successfully ran for the Tennessee House, where he served 12 years. In 1988, when the incumbent retired, Tanner ran for Congress and won with a whopping 66% in a four-candidate primary and 62% in the general.

Tanner's voting record put him solidly in the middle of the Democratic House, slightly to the left of midpoint after Republicans took control. In 1997, he got a seat on Ways and Means; his 8th District predecessor Jere Cooper served there from 1932 to 1957, the last three years as chairman. He went to work on tax issues, including elimination of estate taxes on family-owned farms and small businesses and opposition to the IRS's current-year taxation of farmers' income from deferred payment contracts. In 1999 he joined Republican Jennifer Dunn in sponsoring legislation to eliminate the estate tax. The bill passed but was vetoed by Bill Clinton. George Bush made it a centerpiece in the tax cuts that were part of his first legislative initiative; but Tanner voted against that bill because of its overall size. Tanner has long supported the balanced budget amendment and line-item veto, though he has opposed some Republican versions. He supported trade promotion authority when sought by both Clinton and Bush, and PNTR with China in 2000. His advocacy of those measures at Ways and Means angered many Democrats and their interest-group allies.

In 1992 Tanner could have been a senator for the asking. McWherter was ready to appoint him to succeed Al Gore, but Tanner refused the post and chose instead to stay in the House. If he had accepted he might have become a more nationally prominent figure, but he would also have had to defend the seat against Fred Thompson in what turned out to be the very Republican year of 1994. Instead, Tanner became a major force in the House. He was a founder of a group of moderate-to-conservative Democrats called the Blue Dogs who advanced their own proposals for fiscal responsibility. Tanner co-sponsored the Blue Dogs' welfare reform proposal, which, he claims with some legitimacy, was "the genesis for the broad welfare reform plan that Clinton signed" in 1996. When Republicans brought the bill to the House, Tanner passed amendments allowing states to provide non-cash assistance such as baby formula and diapers and providing that no one loses Medicaid because of federally imposed time limits. These provisions helped win the support of half the House's Democrats at the time; that bipartisanship, as well as Tanner's support, collapsed when House Republicans sought to extend the law in 2002. Also that year, he filed a resolution to amend House rules to require a three-fifths vote to pass any bill that would increase the federal deficit.

In the 8th District, Tanner has held more than 1,000 town hall meetings and has been re-elected by wide margins. In 2000, the United Steelworkers backed his Democratic primary opponent because of Tanner's free trade votes; Tanner won the primary 87%–13%. In 2002, his primary challenger attacked Tanner as a part of "Republican-Democrat one-partyism;" again, he won 87%–13%. He won more than 70% of the vote in the 2000 and 2002 general elections. When columnist Robert Novak wrote that Tanner might switch parties, he was furious and responded, "it's just grotesquely irresponsible to write something like that." Novak apologized for relying on a Republican source and not checking with Tanner.

NINTH DISTRICT

Rep. Harold Ford (D)

Elected 1996, 4th term; b. May 11, 1970, Memphis; home, Memphis; U. of PA, B.A. 1992, U. of MI, J.D. 1996; Baptist; single.

Professional Career: Staff Aide, U.S. Senate Budget Cmte., 1992; Spec. Asst., Clinton/Gore Transition Team, 1992; Spec. Asst., DNC Chairs Ron Brown & Alexis Herman, 1993; Spec. Asst., U.S. Dept. of Commerce, 1993.

DC Office: 325 CHOB 20515, 202-225-3265; Fax: 202-225-5663; Web site: www.house.gov/ford.

District Office: Memphis, 901-544-4131.

Committees: *Budget* (11th of 19 D). *Financial Services* (18th of 32 D): Capital Markets, Insurance & Government Sponsored Enterprises; Financial Institutions & Consumer Credit.

Group Ratings

	ADA	ACLU	AFS	LCV	CON	ITIC	NTU	COC	ACU	NTLC	CHC
2002	70	60	78	50	43	75	24	63	24	12	33
2001	85	—	100	86	—	—	18	55	8	—	—

National Journal Ratings

	2001 LIB —	2001 CONS		2002 LIB —	2002 CONS
Economic	58%	43%		61%	38%
Social	70%	30%		65%	35%
Foreign	70%	28%		64%	35%

Key Votes of the 107th Congress

1. Approve Bush Tax Cuts	N	5. Faith-Based Charities	N	9. Trade Promotion Authority	N
2. Limit Patients' Bill of Rights	N	6. Bar Gays in the Boy Scouts	N	10. Bar Funds for Intl. Court	N
3. Campaign Finance Reform	Y	7. Ban Partial-Birth Abortion	Y	11. Authorize Force in Iraq	Y
4. Ban ANWR Development	Y	8. Arm Commercial Pilots	Y	12. Deny Home. Sec. Dept. Union	N

Election Results

2002 general	Harold Ford (D)	120,904	(84%)	($863,754)
	Tony Rush (I)	23,208	(16%)	
2002 primary	Harold Ford (D)	unopposed		
2000 general	Harold Ford (D)	unopposed		($475,376)

Prior Winning Percentages: 1998 (79%); 1996 (61%)

The People		Race/Ethnic Origin	Ancestry	
Area size:	340 sq. mi.	34.9% White	English: 4.9%	Irish: 4.7%
Urban population:	99.6%	59.5% Black	USA: 4.5%	
Rural population:	0.4%	1.5% Asian	**2000 Presidential Vote**	
Pop. 2000:	632,143	0.2% Native Am.	Gore (D) 147,898	(63%)
Median income:	$33,806	0.0% Hawaiian	Bush (R) 83,531	(36%)
Poverty status:	19.4%	0.9% Two+ races	Other 2,758	(1%)
Military veterans:	11.2%	0.1% Other	**Cook Partisan Voting Index:** D +14	
		3.0% Hispanic Origin		

Occupation	Blue collar: 24.0%	White collar: 60.4%	Gray collar: 15.6%

Memphis, the largest city in Tennessee, is in the state's far southwestern corner, 500 miles from the Appalachian border with Virginia but only 20 miles from Mississippi's cotton fields and riverboat casinos. Metropolitan Memphis has one of the highest percentages of blacks in the country—evidence of the city's economic heritage as a capital of the Cotton Kingdom. Big Mississippi planters used to come north to sell their crop in the courtyard of the Peabody Hotel where the ducks march each day, then make financial arrangements for the next growing season.

Such facts have shaped the city's most celebrated tradition, the blues—a musical form worlds apart from Nashville's country music, which emerged from mountainous, mainly white Middle and East Tennessee. The Memphis sound originated from the self-taught musical stylings of poor, rural blacks in the Mississippi Delta. Throughout the first half of the 20th century, the most talented black musicians migrated north to Memphis and congregated downtown on Beale Street. The blues sound was later adapted by Elvis Presley, a poor white from rural Mississippi, in pivotal sessions in July 1954 at Sam Phillips' Sun Studio in Memphis—the birth of rock 'n' roll, and the beginnings of an Elvis cult that long outlived the man. In the early 1960s Memphis once again became the crucible of a new sound, soul music, which emerged as a counterpoint to rock, its increasingly white-dominated cousin. For some years Memphis tried to live down this musical heritage; much of Beale Street was razed and set on a misguided path toward urban renewal. But more recently, the city has come to recognize its history as an asset. Graceland, Presley's garishly decorated mansion, attracts hordes of musical pilgrims from all over the world, and a Museum of American Soul Music opened in 2003 on the site of the Stax studio, demolished in 1989, where Otis Redding, Isaac Hayes, the Staple Singers and Sam & Dave once made their records.

Music is not the city's only asset. Geographically central in the U.S., and with some of its workers crossing over from Arkansas as well as Mississippi, Memphis is the home of the first supermarket chain (the Piggly Wiggly, founded in 1916; its symbol, Mr. Pig, has slimmed down) and the first Holiday Inn. Home of the world's busiest cargo airport, Memphis calls itself "America's distribution center": by far its biggest employer is FedEx, which ships its domestic packages in and out of Memphis Airport every night. Despite such enterprises, racial discord has scarred the political life of Memphis. It is the city where Martin Luther King Jr. was assassinated in 1968; the site of the murder, the Lorraine Motel, was converted into a civil rights museum. Even today, the resurgent Beale Street is one of the few racially integrated spaces in the city, a division that holds equally true in voting. Blacks vote almost unanimously Democratic; whites vote Republican by percentages almost as high. For the first time, blacks now outnumber whites in Shelby County; many have moved into the middle class, although Memphis continues to have the highest poverty rate in Tennessee.

The 9th Congressional District consists of most of the city of Memphis, some of its suburban fringe and about 30 precincts in east Shelby County. Redistricting dropped the black percentage in the district from 66% to 60%, and the Bush 2000 percentage increased from 32% to 36%, though it was still by far his poorest performance in Tennessee.

The congressman from the 9th District is Harold Ford Jr., a Democrat elected in 1996 at age 26; his father, Harold Ford Sr., had been elected in 1974 at 29 and represented the 9th for 22 years. Harold Ford Jr. grew up in Memphis until 1979, when the family moved to Washington. He graduated from the elite St. Albans School, a classmate of Jesse Jackson's son Yusef, and then graduated from the University of Pennsylvania in 1992. He worked on the Clinton transition team and as a special assistant in the Economic Development Administration (and thus technically worked for Commerce Secretary Ron Brown, whom he has praised as a "profound influence"). In 1993 he went off to the University of Michigan law school.

The Fords are a large family—Harold Ford Sr. has 11 siblings and Harold Ford Jr. has 75 first cousins—from a humble background. Ford Sr. grew up in a house with no plumbing, but the family built a successful funeral home business. Harold Ford Sr. was elected to the state legislature in 1970, and there has been a Ford on the Memphis Council since 1971; other Fords have served on the county commission and in the state Senate. In 1996, Ford Sr. became a lobbyist after retiring from Congress in favor of his son, who had cut an ad for him at age 4, calling for "lower cookie prices." Ford won the primary 60%–34%. In the general, "Jr."—as his campaign buttons read—won 61%–37%, slightly better than the 58% his father had won during his last three general elections.

In the House, Harold Ford Jr. has been notably more moderate on issues than his father and most members of the Black Caucus, although he has the most liberal voting record in the Tennessee delegation. He says that he talks regularly with his father, but that they often disagree on issues. A member of the New Democrat Coalition, he voted against needle exchanges, for prayer in school and anti-flag burning constitutional amendments, for the balanced budget amendment, the capital gains tax cut, repeal of the estate tax, PNTR with China, aid to tobacco farmers, and the use of force in Iraq. He has sided with conservatives on national education testing and trade promotion authority, but he has taken liberal stands on affirmative action and against cutting tax rates.

At home in Memphis, Ford's appeal has crossed racial lines. He was reelected with 79% in 1998 and has been unopposed by a major party candidate since then. In the summer of 1999 he crisscrossed Tennessee testing the ground for a run against Republican Senator Bill Frist. In sharp partisan terms he criticized Frist for voting on health care issues while owning large amounts of Columbia/ HCA stock and for opposing the Democrats' HMO regulation bill. He promised he would decide whether to run by Labor Day, but the deadline passed and, while campaigning less, he did not announce he was not running until February 2000; some Democrats groused that he had left the party without a serious candidate. But in his announcement he left little doubt about his future intentions: "I absolutely look forward to serving the entire state of Tennessee some day." In March 2002, when Senator Fred Thompson announced just weeks before the filing deadline that he would not run for reelection, Ford resumed his exploratory tour. In Knoxville he told National Rifle Association members that the debate over guns had become too polarized and that he would join their organization. Asked whether his race would cost him votes, he said, "I have confidence that the better angels will prevail. I don't believe race will play as pernicious a role as some suggest. If it does, obviously I won't have a chance." When it became clear that most of the party establishment was backing Congressman Bob Clement, Ford said he would not run. The key year for Ford may be 2006, since Bill Frist has long said he would only serve 12 years. Though Tennessee has been trending Republican, Ford's moderate record and his appeal across racial boundaries could make him a strong candidate.

After the 2002 election, Ford shook up the Democratic Caucus for a few days when he challenged Nancy Pelosi for minority leader. Pledging a "clean break" in the party's strategy, he made a flood of media appearances in the six days before the Caucus vote. He said Pelosi was too far to the left. On November 14, Pelosi won 177–29. Afterwards Ford said he planned to meet often with Washington think tanks, and to take overseas trips to learn about national security and foreign policy.

His temporary setbacks have not quelled Ford's ambitions, or clouded his prospects for future higher office. In 2001, *People* magazine listed him among the "50 most beautiful people in the world." It is possible to imagine this still very young-looking man as some day the first black president of the United States. That thought certainly has occurred to him. In the meantime, he obviously can win reelection to the House.

★ TEXAS ★

Texas is a nation-sized state, one of four to have been an independent republic (the others are California, Vermont and Hawaii) and the one that stuck to it the longest. It is a state with an international image and international impact. The nation has voted for president 11 times since 1960: four times it has voted for Californians, four times for Texans. These two largest states have put their stamp on national politics in our times, just as New York did up through 1960, when it was the residence of five of the winners elected in the 15 contests starting in 1900. Texas has been the second-largest state in area since Alaska was admitted to the Union in 1959; it became the second largest in population in 1994, when it passed New York. The key to Texas's history is that this is a society with no aristocratic past, a state not formed by plantation owners or plutocrats but by dirt farmers. Texas was founded by Southerners, mainly Tennesseans, who wanted to establish their own republic in what were empty spaces within the borders of Mexico, a republic with Anglo-Saxon freedoms and black slavery. They defended their dream to the death at the Alamo and to a bloody victory at San Jacinto; they entered the Union willingly in 1845 and left it enthusiastically in 1861. The Texas that emerged from the Civil War was still young and poor; it was only in 1901 that oil was discovered at Spindletop, and the Texas wildcatters made their first fortunes.

Without the underpinnings and burdens of tradition, 20th century Texas has produced fabulous wealth, generously rewarding success while being unforgiving of failure. It has respect for learning and style—think of its great universities, or Neiman Marcus—and it revels in rough manners and western wear. Texans are prone to wild swings in fortune—think of Sam Houston, or the great wildcatters, or Lyndon Johnson. And as the 20th century ended, Texans, for all their history of slavery and segregation, have proved open to immigrants and friendly with their neighbors in Mexico. NAFTA, the opening up of the border and the coming together of these two countries which are at such different economic levels and have such different cultures, is a project mainly of Texans of both political parties, of President George H. W. Bush and Treasury Secretary Lloyd Bentsen, Governors Ann Richards and George W. Bush. At the same time, Texas has become a high-tech powerhouse, a country with some of the nation's most creative businesses. But its success is not just economic. There are large elements of heroism—some mythical, some genuine—in the Texas history that every high school student here learns.

Texas started off as a marchland on the border of the Third World, with an economy based

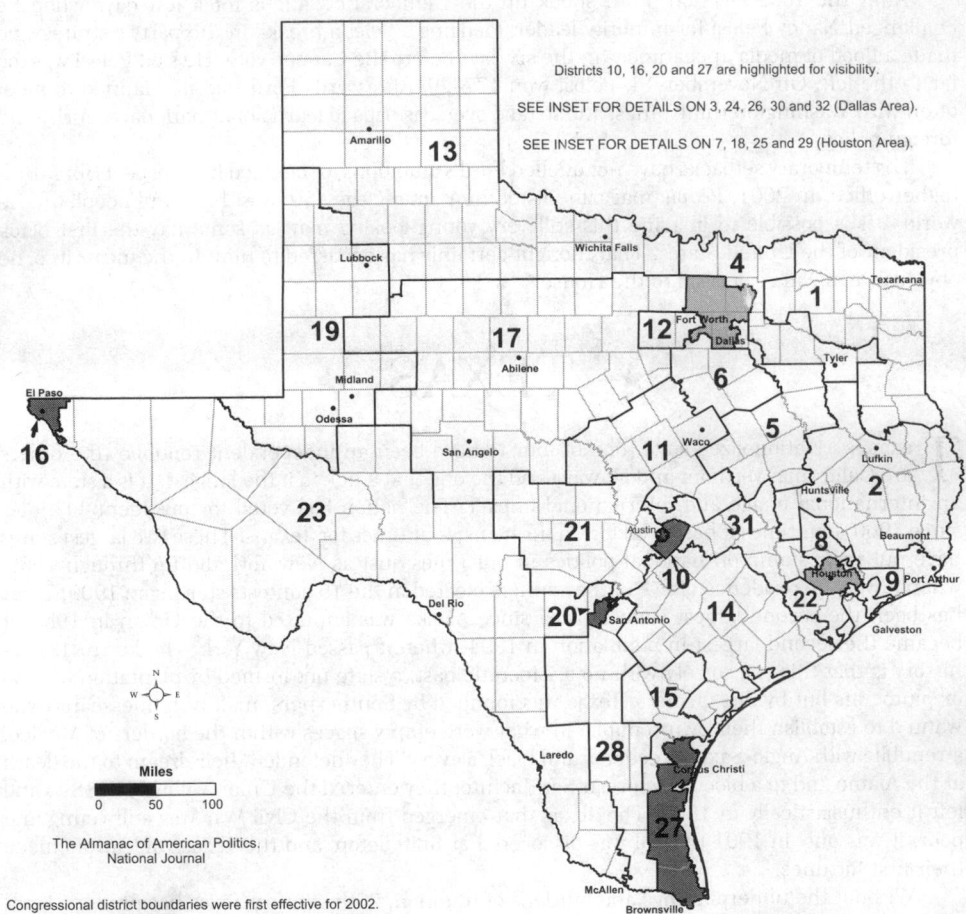

Districts 10, 16, 20 and 27 are highlighted for visibility.

SEE INSET FOR DETAILS ON 3, 24, 26, 30 and 32 (Dallas Area).

SEE INSET FOR DETAILS ON 7, 18, 25 and 29 (Houston Area).

The Almanac of American Politics.
National Journal

Congressional district boundaries were first effective for 2002.

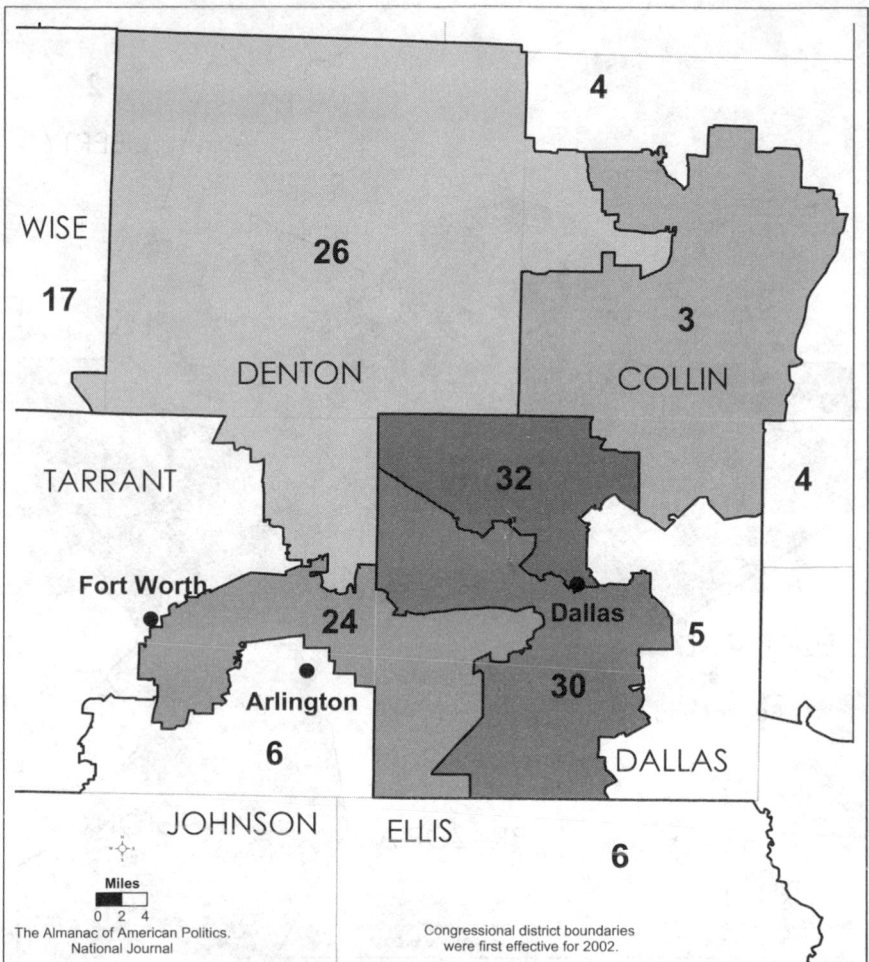

WISE

17

TARRANT

Fort Worth ●

DENTON

26

4

COLLIN

3

4

32

Dallas ●

24

30

5

Arlington ●

6

DALLAS

JOHNSON

6

ELLIS

6

Miles

0 2 4

The Almanac of American Politics.
National Journal

Congressional district boundaries
were first effective for 2002.

on commodities, mainly cotton, whose prices were in long-term decline. Its farmers felt like part of a colonial economy controlled by bankers and Wall Street financiers. After Spindletop, Texas became the nation's—and for a time the world's—leading producer of oil. But oil prices, too, fell in free markets, and were propped up by politicians—the 1936 "hot oil" act that Sam Rayburn, as chairman of the House Commerce Committee, pushed through and the oil depletion allowance maintained for years by Rayburn when he was speaker, Senate Majority Leader Johnson, Senate Finance Committee Chairman Bentsen and others. These politicians also got subsidies for cotton growers and contracts for defense plants and space facilities in World War II and through the long years of the Cold War. Most Texas voters stayed Democratic up to 1970 because of Confederate memories, New Deal affections, and the clout and competence of Texas's Democratic politicians.

But as Texas's economy became complex and creative, Texas's politics changed from a mostly Democratic effort to prop up the price of commodities to an increasingly Republican push to open up markets. By the 1970s Texas's economy was no longer dependent on raw commodities. The "awl bidness" here is less a matter of extracting oil from Texas; instead, Texas has the greatest concentration of high-skill specialists in extracting oil and natural gas in any part of the world. Also, beginning in the 1960s Texas has become a center for high tech, with the critical mass of

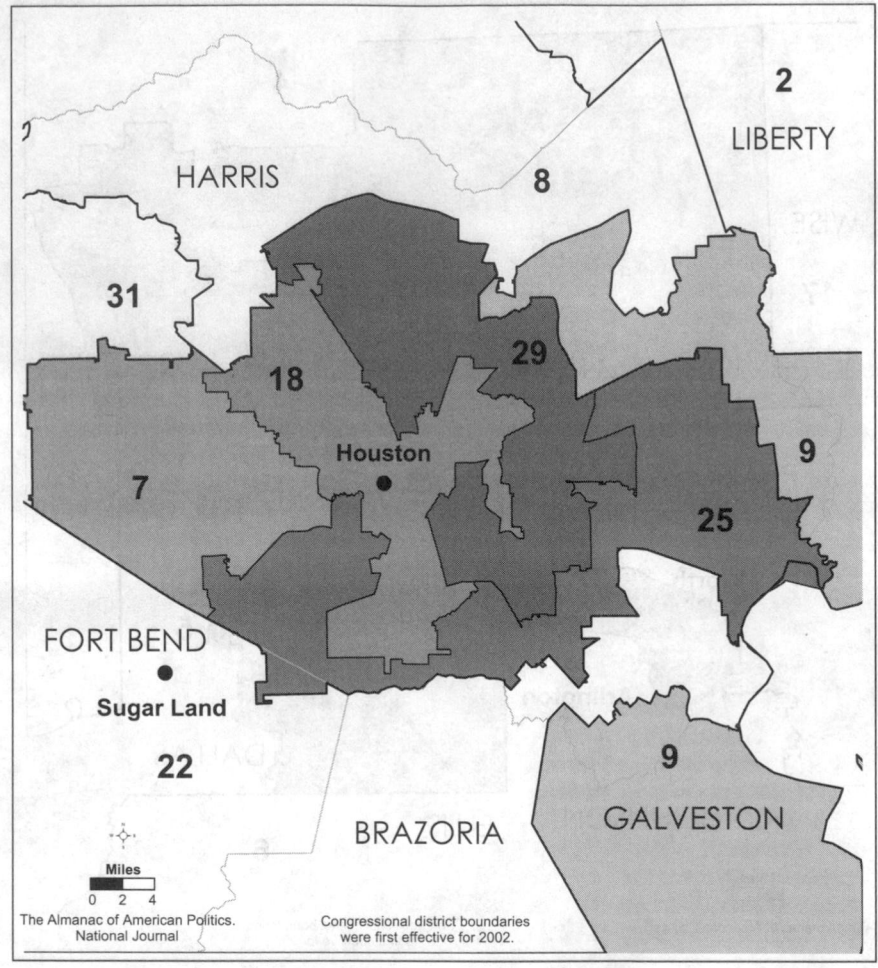

Congressional district boundaries
were first effective for 2002.

knowledge and finances needed to produce firms like Texas Instruments and Dell Computer, and a university infrastructure in the University of Texas and Texas A&M to match the highway system that ties the state together. The Dallas-Fort Worth Metroplex is rich with defense contractors and with small firms that have become large with exports to Mexico. Houston is home to firms like Compaq (which merged with Hewlett-Packard in 2002) and to once-thriving Enron, to many of the high-tech spinoffs from the space program, and to the enormous Texas Medical Center. San Antonio, with the Air Force's prime hospital, has significant medical technology and biotech industries. Austin, as UT doubled its number of engineering professors, became a high-tech center vying for second place after Silicon Valley in California. Texas's low taxes (and lack of a state income tax) helped attract corporate headquarters like American Airlines, GTE, J.C. Penney and Exxon. The result has been to put Dallas-Fort Worth and Houston solidly on the list of the top ten metro areas, ahead of old industrial centers like Cleveland, Pittsburgh and St. Louis, and on their way to overtaking Detroit, Boston and Philadelphia.

The early and middle 1980s were rough in Texas, when oil prices crashed and the commercial real estate market collapsed and banks failed in the wake of the politically-created savings and loan crisis. Defense spending cuts in the early 1990s hurt as well. But Texas has stormed ahead nevertheless. The Dallas metro area created more jobs in 2000 than any other in the nation. Once the government disposed of failed S&L assets, Texas real estate prices started booming again. Oil is just a small part of the Texas economy now; as *The Wall Street Journal* put it, "The new wildcatters are striking it big in personal computers, telecommunications, plastics, home building and airlines."

Texas has also surged ahead because it, in vivid contrast to that other onetime republic, California, has nurtured and profited from its relationship with its southern neighbor, Mexico. California, for all the proud liberalism of its articulate elite, has shown its scorn, disgust and, worst of all, indifference to Mexico; it has portrayed its southern neighbor as generating illegal aliens and criminals California taxpayers must pay for; for most of the 1990s, both its right and its left did little to assimilate Mexican-Americans and other Latinos into a united America. Texas has taken a different course. Its border with Mexico is longer, and more often crossed; southern Texas along the Rio Grande is a kind of transition zone. As Laredo Mayor Betty Flores says, "The border is not where the U.S. stops and Mexico begins. It's where the U.S. blends into Mexico." Monterrey, 140 miles from Laredo, is perhaps Mexico's most America-friendly city. Despite a history of racial segregation, Texas has shown a friendly face to Mexicans, while Mexican immigrants have shown they wanted to become Texans and Americans. Fewer Latinos have crossed the border here to take advantage of welfare programs, which are much less generous in Texas than in California. Political leadership has made a difference. California's former Governor Pete Wilson had little contact with Mexico and strongly championed Proposition 187 against services for illegal immigrants in 1994 and Proposition 209 banning racial quotas and preferences in 1996; a chilly tone was set, which has only been partially warmed by Wilson's successor Gray Davis. George W. Bush, like Governor Ann Richards before him, journeyed often to Mexico and invited Mexican leaders to Texas, emphasizing the positive in public and leaving any negative details to private negotiations. Governor Rick Perry, who has been taking Spanish lessons, has followed Richards's and Bush's lead. So, increasingly, has the Texas economy. Nearly half of U.S. merchandise exports to Mexico are from Texas, significantly more than California; 70% of U.S. exports to Mexico go through Texas. The NAFTA secretariat of labor is in Dallas, the North American Development Bank is headquartered in San Antonio, the Border Environmental Cooperation Commission is in Juarez, across the Rio Grande from El Paso, and the busiest truck crossing between the countries is the new World Trade Bridge near Laredo and Nuevo Laredo. The only thing marring the relationship is a dispute over the distribution of Rio Grande water.

Texas stands as a model for the American future, a model admired by many and disparaged by others. Quite explicitly in the 2000 campaign George W. Bush constantly cited his Texas record; Al Gore highlighted the state's shortcomings. Texas is an open society, unpretentious, delivered from its heritage of racial and ethnic discrimination. But it also has vast income disparities, between struggling and population-losing rural counties and the surging cities, and between the gleaming affluent neighborhoods spreading out into the countryside and the poor and crime-ridden neighborhoods of rickety frame houses not far from the urban cores. Texas presents a contrast with and a challenge to the traditions of other megastates—New York which pioneered the American welfare state, California which used high taxes to build highways and schools, the Great Lakes industrial states with their big labor unions. For Texas has some of the lowest taxes in the country and some of the lowest welfare levels; it has few union members and a relatively small public sector; it has resisted court-ordered moves to equalize spending among school districts; it continues to be a violent state, with a high crime rate and the highest number of executions. For years, out-of-state elites and liberals in Texas have called on the state to become more like New York or California or Michigan. But most Texans prefer their own model. Indeed, in important respects New York and California and Michigan are choosing to become more like Texas. Low taxes and high tech, few barriers to opportunity but a less elaborate safety net, moving away from reliance on agriculture and oil, bypassing the era of big factories and big unions of the Great Lakes and eschewing the liberal cultural values of the two coasts: This is Texas's way, and increasingly the way of the other 49 states and of Mexico.

Politically, Texas is now an indisputably Republican state: George W. Bush carried it in 2000 by a 59%–38% margin, significantly larger than the 56%–43% margin his father won 12 years before. It was not always so: both George Bushes and Senator Kay Bailey Hutchison and former

Senator Phil Gramm each lost an election before they started winning. One-party Democratic dominance ended in the 1960s, and for two decades Democratic victories were largely the product of Lloyd Bentsen, when he was on the ballot in 1970, 1976, 1982 and 1988 and when he exerted his influence for Ann Richards for governor in 1990. The old Democratic strength in the Texas countryside is gone—in 1998 George W. Bush carried 239 of 254 counties and in 2000 he carried 230—and the Republican hold on the big cities is solid. Bush carried the Dallas-Forth Worth Metroplex 61%–37% in 2000 and metro Houston 57%–40%; together those two areas cast 47% of Texas's votes.

In 2002, Texas Democrats made a game effort to turn the tide but the results were unambiguous. Except on the Border, Democrats did not produce the high black and Hispanic turnouts they hoped for. Attorney General John Cornyn beat former Dallas Mayor Ron Kirk 55%–43% for an open Senate seat and Governor Rick Perry defeated Laredo banker Tony Sanchez 58%–40%. Cornyn and Perry won big margins in the Metroplex and metro Houston; they carried the combined Austin and San Antonio areas; they lost by wide margins in the Border, which casts 8% of the vote; but they won 62% and 64% of the vote in the rest of Texas—call it rural Texas—once heavily Democratic, which casts 30% of the state's votes. In U.S. House races, as they have since 1994, Republicans won more votes than Democrats, but fewer seats, thanks to a 1991 Democratic redistricting plan which was closely followed by a court in 2001. But they won all the downballot races; the closest margin was in the race for lieutenant governor (an important position, because its holder runs the state Senate), in which Republican David Dewhurst beat Democrat John Sharp 51%–46%. Republicans now hold all 29 statewide elective offices, including all seats on the state Supreme Court. They turned a 72–78 deficit in the state House into an 88–62 majority and elected Tom Craddick the first Republican Speaker since 1871. Craddick is from Midland, the Permian Basin town in the west Texas desert which is also the home town of George W. Bush, Laura Bush and, Commerce Secretary Donald Evans and General Tommy Franks. Who in the late 1950s and early 1960s, when they were all in Midland public schools, imagined that this one small town (there were 25,000 people in Midland County in 1950 and 67,000 in 1960) would produce so many leaders?

Back then the only Republican parts of Texas were Midland and affluent neighborhoods in Dallas and Houston. In time the two big metro areas became more Republican. In 1976 Jimmy Carter lost both of them, but carried Texas because he carried rural Texas, which then cast 36% of the state's votes, 53%–46%. By 1988, rural Texas had crossed over: George H.W. Bush carried rural Texas, even though Texan Lloyd Bentsen was on the Democratic ticket, by 57%–42%, a showing 1% better than in the rest of the state. In 2000, rural Texas voted 67%–31% for George W. Bush. Over these years the Dallas-Fort Worth Metroplex and metro Houston remained solidly Republican, and the San Antonio-Austin area, once the home base of many feisty Texas liberals, became mildly Republican too. The cultural liberals who hang out on Austin's Sixth Street are now being joined by high-tech engineers and hard-charging entrepreneurs in the new subdivisions and office centers running north of the pink marble Capitol and the UT campus, and Anglos in the San Antonio area vote more solidly Republican than Latinos vote Democratic. To be sure, Dallas County and Houston's Harris County have become less Republican, as their black and Hispanic percentages have increased. But the rapidly growing surrounding counties, full of Christian conservatives and free marketeering entrepreneurs and engineers, have become overwhelmingly Republican. The prime example is Collin County, north of Dallas County, whose population increased 86% in the 1990s, from 264,000 to 491,000 in the 1990s. It has long been heavily Republican, voting a nearly identical 74%–25% for George Bush in 1988 and 73%–24% for George W. Bush in 2000. But the senior Bush's popular vote margin here was 44,000 votes; the younger Bush carried it by 85,000. In 2002 Collin County voted 70% for John Cornyn and 74% for Rick Perry.

The one threat to this Republican dominance is the inevitable increase in the number of Latino voters. In 2000, 32% of Texas residents were Hispanic; more than half of Texas's population increase in the 1990s was accounted for by the increase in the number of Hispanics. To be sure, very many of these people are not U.S. citizens, and many who are citizens do not vote: Hispanic turnout in 2002 was, despite the "dream team," disappointing to Democrats everywhere but in the Rio Grande Valley. White House political strategist Karl Rove has long been aware that Republicans must win a large share of the Latino vote if they are to remain dominant in the state. George W. Bush has cultivated Latino voters, starting in 1994 when he had little chance of reducing Ann Richards's margins among them; in 1998 the two exit polls showed him winning 49% and 39% of Hispanic votes. He carried the Lower Rio Grande Valley and El Paso, where more than 80% of residents are Hispanic. In 2000 against Al Gore he did not do as well: the exit poll showed Gore carrying Texas Hispanics 54%–42%. Rick Perry, despite the Spanish lessons, did not do as well in 2002, but then he was running against a Latino who spent $60 million on his campaign. The Fox News Election Day poll showed Perry carrying 35% of Hispanics—a good showing in the circumstances. Latino Democrats challenged that number and pointed out that in essentially all-Hispanic counties in the Lower Rio Grande Valley Perry's percentages were far lower—10% in Webb County (his opponent Tony Sanchez's home), 11% in Starr County, 12% in Duval County, 14% in Brooks County. But in the much more populous and 78% to 88% Hispanic border counties Perry ran better—31% in Hidalgo County, 39% in Cameron County, 35% in El Paso County. Many of the Perry votes there were cast by Anglos, but not all. And it's not clear that Hispanics in the big cities of Texas are as heavily Democratic as those on the Border were in 2002: the majority-Hispanic 29th Congressional District in Houston voted 39% for George W. Bush in 2000. West Texas rural counties where Hispanics are 30% to 50% of the population voted 2–1 for Perry, but it's not clear how many Hispanics there voted. In 2001 Perry signed a bill providing for in-state tuition at state colleges and universities for illegal immigrants—a measure that provides a chance at upward mobility for many young Latinos whose parents crossed the border without a green card. The increasing number of Latino voters may make the Democrats more competitive in Texas over the years, but Republicans are not going to allow this to happen without fighting for those votes.

The People		**Race/Ethnic Origin**			**Military veterans:** 1,754,809 (11.7%)	
Pop. 2000:	20,851,820	10,933,313	52.4%	White	WWII: 17.1%	Korea: 11.7%
Pop. 1990:	16,986,510	2,364,255	11.3%	Black	Vietnam: 34.6%	Gulf War: 13.3%
Change 1990–2000:	Up 22.8%	554,445	2.7%	Asian	**Most populous cities:**	
Change 1980–1990:	Up 19.4%	68,859	0.3%	Native Am.	1. Houston	1,953,631
% of U.S. total:	7.4%	10,757	0.1%	Hawaiian	2. Dallas	1,188,580
Pop. rank:	2d of 50	230,567	1.1%	Two+ races	3. San Antonio	1,144,646
Area size:	268,581 sq. mi.	19,958	0.1%	Other	4. Austin	656,562
State Native:	62.2%	6,669,666	32.0%	Hisp. Origin	5. El Paso	563,662
Non-citizen:	9.5%	**Ancestry**			Urban population: 82.5%	
Language		German: 8.4%		USA: 6.3%	Rural population: 17.5%	
English: 68.6%	Spanish: 25.9%	Irish: 6.1%		English: 6.0%		
Other Eur.: 2.8%		French: 1.9%				

Education		**Work Sector**		**Legislature**		
H.S. Grad:	75.7%	Private: 78.0%	Govt: 14.6%	Senate	19 R 12 D	
College Grad:	23.2%	Self: 7.1%	Family: 0.3%	House	88 R 62 D	
Industry		Unemployment: 6.0%		Legislative Term Limits: No		
Agri: 2.7%	Con: 8.1%	**Household Income**		**Registered Voters**		
Fin: 6.8%	Info: 3.1%	<15k: 17.0%	15-35k: 27.0%	No party registration		
Mfg: 17.6%	Prof: 28.8%	35-50k: 16.5%	50-100k: 27.9%			
Public: 4.5%	Trade: 15.9%	100-150k: 7.2%	>150k: 4.3%			
Other: 12.5%		Median: $39,927				
Occupation		Poverty status: 15.4%				
Blue collar: 24.1%	White collar: 60.6%	**Home Value**				
Gray collar: 15.3%		<50k: 27.6%	50-100k: 38.4%	100-200k: 24.6%	200-300k: 5.5%	
		300-500k: 2.6%	>500k: 1.3%	Median: $77,800		

Presidential politics In 2000 Texas was the counterweight to New York in presidential politics. Neither was seriously contested: it was always clear that Texas would cast 32 electoral votes for George W. Bush and New York 33 votes for Al Gore. In 2004 it will be different: Texas will cast 34, New York 31, and in early 2003 some Republican strategists were wondering whether the Bush campaign might be able credibly to try to make a serious contest of New York. No Democratic strategist imagined that their nominee would have any chance in Texas. In 2000, 73% of Texas whites, 42% of Texas Hispanics and 5% Texas blacks voted for Bush; in early 2003 it looked like all of those percentages would be higher in 2004. The best the Democratic ticket has done here in recent years was 43% in 1988, when Lloyd Bentsen was on the ticket, and 44% in 1996, as Ross Perot split the opposition to Bill Clinton and Bob Dole carried the state anyway with 49%.

Texas's presidential primary, originally in May, was moved to March for Super Tuesday in 1988. The Republican primary electorate is heavily conservative; the Democratic primary electorate is increasingly liberal. In 1988, Michael Dukakis won the Democratic primary here with 33% and Jesse Jackson got 25%, ahead of Al Gore, running as a southern moderate, with 20%. And that was with a turnout of 1.7 million. Turnout in 2000 was 787,000, with many fewer rural conservatives.

2000 Presidential Vote		
Bush (R)	3,799,639	(59%)
Gore (D)	2,433,746	(38%)
Nader (Green)	137,994	(2%)
Other	36,258	(1%)

2000 Republican Presidential Primary		
Bush (R)	986,416	(88%)
McCain (R)	80,082	(7%)
Keyes (R)	43,518	(4%)
Other	16,741	(2%)

2000 Democratic Presidential Primary		
Gore (D)	631,428	(80%)
Bradley (D)	128,564	(16%)
LaRouche (D)	26,898	(3%)

1996 Presidential Vote		
Dole (R)	2,730,085	(49%)
Clinton (D)	2,455,853	(44%)
Perot (I)	378,117	(7%)

Congressional districting Before 2001, redistricting in Texas has always been the prerogative of Democrats. For many years it was not particularly partisan; there weren't enough Republicans to matter. By the 1990s there were, and the Democrats produced their masterpiece, the 1991 redistricting plan drawn by Bob Mansker, aide to Democratic Congressman Martin Frost. Modified slightly by a 1996 court ruling, it clumped heavily Republican areas into hugely Republican districts, then carved out with incredibly convoluted lines three new districts for Democrats. Starting in 1994, Republicans outpolled Democrats in House races and Anglo Democrats found themselves increasingly imperiled. Still, Democrats held a 17–13 majority in the delegation up through the 2000 election.

108th Congress Lineup	
17 D	15 R

107th Congress Lineup	
17 D	13 R

Things looked different in 2001. Republicans held the governorship and a 16–15 edge in the state Senate; the state House was still Democratic by 78–72, but many of those Democrats were conservative or not very partisan. Texas gained two new seats after the 2000 Census, and Republicans like House Majority Whip Tom DeLay predicted that their party would pick up six to eight seats. It didn't happen. The House Redistricting Committee approved a map that would have split the two new seats between the parties, but it never came to the floor. In the Senate, which requires a two-thirds vote to approve almost anything, a competing plan died on the floor in May 2001. Democrats welcomed the logjam; their lawyers filed suit in state court in Austin's Travis County before a Democratic judge (judges are elected on partisan ballots in Texas). A three-judge federal court in Tyler, with two Democratic- and one Republican-appointed judges, agreed to hear a case in October and consider the state court ruling. On October 3 the Austin judge unexpectedly approved a plan that would have produced 16 Republican and 13 Democratic districts, with three tossups. Martin Frost and other Democrats led attacks on it. One week later, the Austin judge reversed himself and approved a plan with 17 Democrat and 15 Republican seats. On October 18 Attorney General John Cornyn asked the state Supreme Court to sweep that plan aside, which the court did, but it failed to approve their own alternative and instead returned the case to the Austin judge.

The federal court then took control and on November 14 came up with its own plan. It protected all incumbents and created two new Republican districts, one in west Houston and one in north Dallas. In its opinion the court said its decision to protect incumbents was motivated by the "unique, major" leadership positions held by members of the Texas delegation and recognized "a traditional state interest in the power of its congressional delegation distinct from party affiliation." Redistricting law, which started off as a device to protect the equal rights of voters, had become a device to protect the interests of incumbents. In effect, the partisan Democratic plan of 1991 was given new life, with the Republicans given two new seats as a consolation prize. The result was, predictably, a 17–15 Democratic delegation, although Charles Stenholm and Chet Edwards were pressed more closely in 2002 than in the recent past; the statewide popular vote for the House was 53% Republican and 44% Democratic.

But Republicans now had majorities in the legislature—88–62 in the House and 19–12 in the Senate—plus all statewide elected officials. In early 2003 Tom DeLay, now House Majority Leader, urged the legislature to pass a new plan; Senate Republicans were reluctant. DeLay continued to press new House Speaker Tom Craddick, a longtime ally. As the legislative session neared adjournment, the House Redistricting Committee approved a new map on May 6. It would have added five to seven new Republican seats and jeopardized each of the delegation's 10 Anglo Democrats, though it protected the five incumbent Latino Democrats and two African-Americans; it appeared to create two additional open seats designed for Latinos and one for a black candidate. The disciplined Republican majority ignored Democrat protestations, including their objection to reopening the redistricting process without a court order.

Recognizing that the legislature would likely pass some version of this plan, on the eve of the House's scheduled May 12 debate, 51 Democrats resorted to a final desperate measure: They fled the state and secretly settled in a Holiday Inn in Ardmore, Oklahoma, in an effort to bust the House quorum, which requires the presence of two-thirds of members to do business. The spectacle of Texas Democrats holed up in an Oklahoma motel attracted national attention; the bizarre scene attracted further national notice after it was revealed that the state police—possibly with the assistance of the new federal Homeland Security Department personnel—had been dispatched to track down the self-styled "Killer D's." Once their location was revealed, the Democrats insisted they would not return to Austin until after May 15, the final day the House could take up the bill in its regular session. The maneuver worked, at least temporarily. But Governor Rick Perry announced on June 18 that he would convene a special session of the legislature on June 30, primarily to deal with redistricting. If such a plan were passed in a special session, Democrats would almost certainly challenge it in court.

Odds favor a Republican majority in the delegation sooner or later. Ralph Hall, a conservative Democrat who turns 81 in May 2004, represents a district that voted 70% for George W. Bush in 2000; if he should retire, no one doubts the district would elect a Republican. Republicans would have a great advantage if the seats represented by Democrats Jim Turner, Max Sandlin, Chet Edwards and Charles Stenholm should become open, and may seriously contest one or more of these incumbents in 2004, regardless of redistricting action.

Governor

Rick Perry (R)

Assumed office Dec. 2000, term expires Jan. 2007, 1st term; b. Mar. 4, 1950, Paint Creek; home, Austin; Texas A&M U., B.S. 1972; United Methodist; married (Anita).

Military Career: Air Force, 1972–77.

Elected Office: TX House of Reps., 1984–90; Comm., TX Dept. of Agriculture, 1990–98; Lt. Gov., 1998–00.

Professional Career: Farmer & rancher.

Office: State Capitol, P.O. Box 12428, Austin, 78711, 512-463-2000; Fax: 512-463-1849; Web site: www.governor.state.tx.us.

Election Results

2002 general	Rick Perry (R)	2,632,541	(58%)
	Tony Sanchez (D)	1,819,843	(40%)
	Other	101,598	(2%)
2002 primary	Rick Perry (R)	unopposed	
1998 general	George W. Bush (R)	2,550,821	(68%)
	Garry Mauro (D)	1,165,592	(31%)
	Other	21,665	(1%)

Rick Perry succeeded George W. Bush as governor of Texas on December 21, 2000 and was elected to a four-year term on November 5, 2002. Perry grew up on his family's farm in Paint Creek, in Haskell County, near where his great-great grandfather settled after fighting in the Civil War, and was elected to the Texas House in the 1890s. His family owns a 10,000-acre ranch, and his father served 28 years as a county commissioner, as a Democrat. Rick Perry was an Eagle Scout and went to Texas A&M to study to be a veterinarian; that didn't pan out, though he did receive a degree in animal science. There, he became a yell leader—cheerleader on lesser campuses, and a coveted position at A&M. These were the years of great student rebellions, but apparently not at College Station; Perry says he never saw a war protest. After college he served five years in the Air Force, piloting C-130 transports. In 1977 he returned to work on the family ranch. In 1984 he was elected to the state House, as a Democrat; this part of West Texas was for a very long time strong Democratic territory. He got on the Appropriations Committee and was one of three young legislators known there as the "pit bulls." In 1989 he was passed over for a leadership position and switched to the Republican Party. In 1990 he ran for agriculture commissioner against the picaresque incumbent Jim Hightower, a populist who was perhaps the most liberal Democrat ever elected to statewide office. Perry, with the help of Karl Rove, got the support of the Farm Bureau and won an upset victory even while Democrat Ann Richards was winning the governorship. In an increasingly Republican Texas, Perry was easily reelected in 1994.

Then in 1998, when storied Democratic incumbent Bob Bullock retired, Perry ran for lieutenant governor. This is an important position in Texas, more powerful than the governorship, some say; the lieutenant governor not only presides over the state Senate but controls its proceedings and appoints its committee members and chairmen. Governors and lieutenant governors are elected separately in Texas, and Bush and Perry ran separate campaigns; Karl Rove, worked for Perry in 1990 and 1994 but not in 1998. Nevertheless there were clear signs that Bush was vitally interested in Perry's candidacy, for without a Republican lieutenant governor he would be open to criticism in a presidential campaign that he was leaving the governorship to a Democrat. Perry, interestingly, had no Republican primary opposition for a post that obviously could lead directly to the governorship. Perry and his Democratic opponent, state Comptroller John Sharp, managed to raise $15 million for the campaign; George H.W. Bush and Barbara Bush appeared at some of Perry's fundraisers. Sharp was a new Democrat who had done some interesting work on government reform, and served as student body president at A&M when Perry was yell leader.

Perry's 50%–48% victory opened the way to the governor's office for him, and to the presidency for Bush.

As lieutenant governor, Perry—contrary to the expectations of many—followed the Bush tradition of bipartisanship, working with senators of both parties, and breaking an impasse that threatened to turn the end of the 1999 session into chaos. He helped to pass record tax cuts, a teacher pay increase and more money for public schools. His relations with Democratic Speaker Pete Laney, whom he had opposed for that office in 1992, were frayed, and Laney criticized him for campaigning for Republicans running against Democratic incumbents in 2000. For five weeks after the election it was not clear whether he would become governor, but he was obviously preparing. On December 21 he was sworn in—interestingly, the first Aggie governor of Texas. In his first major policy speech in January 2001 he made little mention of some of his trademark conservative issues—school vouchers, more prison construction, opposition to hate crime bills that mention special groups. Instead he called for $300 million for college scholarships, $40 million for teacher training in math education, affordable health insurance for teachers: where Bush had emphasized reading, Perry emphasized math; where Bush had emphasized the early grades, Perry called for doing more on higher education. Perry signed a bill giving in-state tuition at state colleges and universities to illegal immigrants who graduated from high school. But he vetoed a record 82 bills, including a bill banning the execution of mentally retarded persons and a bill allowing illegal immigrants to get driver's licenses. In November 2001 voters approved his initiative to allow the state to use public and private toll road revenues for transportation projects, including paving roads in the colonias along the Border.

Democrats believed that Perry was vulnerable in 2002 and gamely tried to put together a winning ticket. The chief organizer was John Sharp, whose record as Comptroller enabled him to run within 2% of Perry in the lieutenant governor race in 1998. Sharp decided to run for lieutenant governor again, not governor, and worked to get a gubernatorial candidate who could swell Democratic turnout among Latinos. His dream candidate was Tony Sanchez, chief share-holder of International Bank of Commerce and Sanchez Oil & Gas in Laredo, who was said to have a net worth of $600 million. Sanchez was no political naif: in the early 1970s, he had worked for Lieutenant Governor Ben Barnes, one of Texas's canniest politicians and still a major lobbyist today. Sanchez returned to Laredo and with his father developed a huge pool of natural gas on the Mexican border near Laredo and started International Bank of Commerce and Tesoro Savings & Loan; the latter went under in the Texas S&L crisis in 1989, but overall this was a classic Texas business success story. In 1994, when Ann Richards opposed and George W. Bush supported the Camino Colombia toll road bypassing Laredo and connecting to the new bridge to Mexico, Sanchez supported Bush and contributed $300,000 to his campaign; Bush appointed him to the University of Texas Board of Regents—for many, the most prized appointment a governor can make. Sharp and former San Antonio Mayor Henry Cisneros persuaded Sanchez to run for governor; they helped to push aside former UT quarterback Marty Akins, who in September 2001 announced he would run for comptroller instead.

Sanchez seemed to be sweeping toward an easy victory in the March 2002 primary. Then in January 2002 former Attorney General Dan Morales filed for governor. Morales had been elected attorney general in 1990 and 1994 and had retired in 1998; he hired the private lawyers who won the state a $17.3 billion tobacco settlement and who received $3.3 billion in legal fees. After he left office, his successor John Cornyn questioned the legal fees and choice of lawyers; in March 2003 Morales was indicted for trying to fraudulently obtain a $260 million fee for one of the lawyers he chose who did little work on the case. Morales hinted that taxes might have to be raised, but otherwise campaigned as the more moderate candidate. He opposed racial quotas and preference—illegal in Texas colleges and universities since a 1996 federal court decision—and when the two candidates held one of their debates in Spanish he insisted on translating his answers into English. He accused Sanchez of running as if he were running for governor in a state in Mexico, as a *patron* who feels entitled to buy the election because he already owns ev-erything else. In response Sanchez spent $18 million on ads, most of them positive, and won the primary 61%–33%. But the primary fight was an offputting spectacle to many Anglo voters. They were willing enough to vote for Latinos—Morales was elected statewide twice as a Democrat and

Republican Tony Garza was elected to the Railroad Commission (it regulates oil) in 1998—but the spectacle of Sanchez outflanking Morales on the left on ethnic issues was not appealing, and Sanchez entered the general election campaign with about one-quarter of voters having unfavorable feelings toward him. Meanwhile, in the April 2002 runoff, Democrats nominated for senator the black and business-friendly former mayor of Dallas, Ron Kirk. Sharp had got his "dream team," which he hoped would drive Latino and black turnout up even while he maintained greater appeal to Anglo voters than either of the two at the top of the ticket.

Perry and Sanchez agreed on many issues: they favored a moment of silence in schools, for example, and both ruled out higher taxes. Water was an issue on which they had differences. Mexico is in arrears on providing water to the Rio Grande as required by a 1944 treaty, and south Texas farmers have claimed that they have lost $1 billion as a result. In other parts of the state aquifers are threatened with depletion. Perry proposed that the state build reservoirs and desalination plants to prevent water shortages; Sanchez said the state should concentrate on water conservation measures. Another hot issue was homeowners insurance. Texas insurers have been hit for huge claims for mold damage—$500 million in 2000, $1.2 billion in 2001. Insurers, claiming they could not make money at state-written rates, have taken advantage of a Texas law that allows them to shift businesses to subsidies that have unregulated rates. As a result, rates skyrocketed and in 2002 the top two insurers stopped selling policies in the state. Sanchez called for a special session of the legislature and argued that the insurance companies should be brought back into state-written rates. Perry wanted to authorize the insurance companies to charge national rates and said the matter should be taken care of in the 2003 regular session.

Much of the campaign consisted of vitriolic negative ads. Sanchez's general theme was that Perry was beholden to campaign contributors and did their bidding. Perry hit Sanchez for not voting in some elections and for his business practices. In the fall he ran a number of hard-hitting ads linking Sanchez to drug kingpins' money laundering. It was undisputed that some $25 million was laundered through Tesoro Savings & Loan in the early 1980s; Sanchez claimed that the S&L followed regulations and that he did not know of the transactions and that no one in the S&L was charged with a crime. Nevertheless Perry ads linked the money laundering to the murder in 1985 of a Drug Enforcement Administration agent in Mexico. In one Perry ad another DEA agent said, "We investigated the murder. The same drug dealers who killed Kiki laundered millions in drug money through Tony Sanchez's bank." Sanchez was outraged. He said that Perry was "by far the most disgusting human being I have ever known. This is an absolute bald-faced lie and he knows it. Going into this race, I thought he was a man of no substance. I didn't realize just how bad he really is. He is a disgusting human being."

Election night was a nightmare for the "dream team." Perry beat Sanchez 58%–40%, although Sanchez spent $67 million to Perry's $28 million, and Republicans won up and down the line. And Ron Kirk and John Sharp, who led the Democratic ticket, both lost. Perry carried the Dallas-Fort Worth Metroplex 61%–38% and metro Houston 58%–40%. In the San Antonio and Austin metro areas, once Democratic, Perry led 54%–42%. Sanchez carried the Border 66%–33%, but Perry carried the much larger rural Texas 64%–34%. The high Latino turnout that Democrats had hoped for did materialize, but only in the Rio Grande Valley. In Laredo's Webb County, turnout was up 130% from 1994, the last big turnout election, and turnout was up 18% and 13% in the big Lower Rio Grande Valley counties and 12% in El Paso County. But elsewhere in the state, turnout in Latino neighborhoods in Houston, Dallas and San Antonio was not up much; the big increases were in heavily Republican counties at the edge of metro areas. Democrats spent three times as much as before on turnout operations, but Republicans registered 420,000 new voters, many in the fast-growing suburban counties, and that proved much more productive. The Fox News Election Day poll showed Perry winning the votes of 35% of Hispanics, 15% of blacks and 72% of Anglos. Republicans won big margins in the legislature—19–12 in the state Senate and 88–62 in the state House. The new leaders of the legislature were Lieutenant Governor David Dewhurst in the Senate and Speaker Tom Craddick in the House—the first Republican speaker since 1871. Both continued the practice of appointing committee chairmen from both parties, but Craddick removed most of the chairmen appointed by his predecessor Pete Laney, who had thrown him out of the chairmanship of Ways and Means in 1999. Craddick is the senior member of the House, first elected in 1968, and in his first session was one of eight Republicans in the House; now there are 88. Dewhurst, a former Air Force officer and CIA agent, self-financed his campaigns for land commissioner and lieutenant governor, and is one of several Republicans who might run for governor if Perry retires—but that may be a long way off.

Perry called his victory a mandate for restricting tort lawsuits, providing rate relief on home-owner insurance and changes in medical malpractice law; he also sought a school vouchers pro-gram. Facing forecasts that state revenues would fall $10 billion short of the cost of maintaining current levels of spending, he ordered 7% cuts for the rest of the fiscal year in all programs except education, Medicaid and children's health in January 2003. The state Senate voted for disclosure of homeowners insurance rates to regulators in February 2003. In January 2003 the federal government and Mexico reached an agreement obliging Mexico to release 350,000 acre-feet of water into the Rio Grande, where it could be used by south Texas farmers. But this was far short of the 1.4 million acre-feet Mexico owes under a 1944 treaty and Perry called it "unacceptable."

Senior Senator

Kay Bailey Hutchison (R)

Elected June 1993, seat up 2006, 2d term; b. July 22, 1943, Galveston; home, Dallas; U. of TX, B.A. 1962, J.D. 1967; Episcopalian; married (Ray).

Elected Office: TX House of Reps., 1972–76; TX Treasurer, 1990–93.

Professional Career: Political & legal corresp., KPRC–TV, 1967–70; Vice Chmn., Natl. Transp. Safety Bd., 1976–78; V.P. & Gen. Cnsl., RepublicBank Corp., 1978–82; Owner, McCraw Candies, 1984–88.

DC Office: 284 RSOB, 20510, 202-224-5922; Fax: 202-224-0776; Web site: www.hutchison.senate.gov.

State Offices: Abilene, 325-676-2839; Austin, 512-916-5834; Dallas, 214-361-3500; Harlingen, 955-425-2253; Houston, 713-653-3456; San Antonio, 210-340-2885.

Committees: *Republican Conference Vice Chair. Appropriations:* Commerce, Justice, State & Judiciary; Defense; District of Columbia; Labor, HHS & Education; Military Construction (Chmn.); Transportation, Treasury & General Government; VA, HUD & Independent Agencies. *Commerce, Science & Transportation:* Aviation; Communications; Oceans, Fisheries & Coast Guard; Science, Technology & Space; Surface Transportation & Merchant Marine (Chmn.). *Rules & Administration. Veterans' Affairs.*

Group Ratings

	ADA	ACLU	AFS	LCV	CON	ITIC	NTU	COC	ACU	NTLC	CHC
2002	5	25	13	6	29	88	68	95	100	97	—
2001	10	—	0	0	—	—	79	85	96	—	100

National Journal Ratings

	2001 LIB —	2001 CONS	2002 LIB —	2002 CONS
Economic	26%	73%	13%	86%
Social	33%	59%	0%	62%
Foreign	0%	94%	0%	76%

Key Votes of the 107th Congress

1. Approve Bush Tax Cuts	Y	5. Confirm Ashcroft as AG	Y	9. Bar Coop. with Intl. Court	Y
2. Expand Patients' Rights	N	6. Bar Gays in the Boy Scouts	Y	10. Trade Promotion Authority	Y
3. Campaign Finance Reform	N	7. $ for Hate Crime Prosecution	N	11. Authorize Force in Iraq	Y
4. Permit ANWR Development	Y	8. Overseas Military Abortions	*	12. Homeland Sec. Dept. Union	N

Election Results

2000 general	Kay Bailey Hutchison (R)	4,082,091	(65%)	($3,518,862)
	Gene Kelly (D)	2,030,315	(32%)	($4,602)
	Other	164,246	(3%)	
2000 primary	Kay Bailey Hutchison (R)	unopposed		
1994 general	Kay Bailey Hutchison (R)	2,604,218	(61%)	($6,114,755)
	Richard Fisher (D)	1,639,615	(38%)	($3,360,850)

Prior Winning Percentages: 1993 (67%)

Kay Bailey Hutchison, senior senator from Texas, is a Republican who first won her seat in a June 1993 special election. She is of old Texas stock, the great-great-granddaughter of Charles S. Taylor, a signer of the Texas Declaration of Independence, who was a friend and business partner of Senator Thomas Jefferson Rusk, the first man to hold this seat; Hutchison is the first woman. She grew up in LaMarque, near the refinery town of Texas City, a prom queen who went to college and then law school at the University of Texas; unable to get a law job in 1967, she worked for a Houston TV station as a reporter. In 1972, she won a seat in the legislature, its first Republican woman. In 1976 she went to Washington to fill the number two position at the National Transportation Safety Board. She married her former colleague Ray Hutchison, moved to Dallas and went into banking and became a small business owner in 1978. In 1982, she lost a House race to Steve Bartlett, later mayor of Dallas. But she stayed active in Republican politics and in 1990 was elected state treasurer, a breakthrough race for state Republicans. Hutchison began her political career when it was no advantage to be a woman and has been mocked by liberals for her tight-lipped good manners and by Washington conservatives as a "Texas pompom girl." Her response: "This is what I have faced all my life—the trivialization of me—which I have not ever let bother me. I have always been able to rise above the expectations." Indeed: She is a senator from the nation's second-largest state, one of three senators in history (Dianne Feinstein and Daniel Patrick Moynihan are the others) to have been elected with 4 million votes.

Her big break came in January 1993 when Lloyd Bentsen resigned his Senate seat after 22 years to become secretary of the Treasury. To replace him, Governor Ann Richards appointed Bob Krueger, a two-term congressman in the 1970s who nearly beat Senator John Tower in 1978, then ran third in a three-way Senate primary in 1984 and was elected Railroad commissioner (actually, oil regulator) in 1990. Running against him in the May 1993 all-party primary were three Republicans, Hutchison and Congressmen Joe Barton and Jack Fields. Krueger opposed the Clinton budget and tax plan, but Democrats were so unpopular in Texas then—Bill Clinton had a 73% negative job rating—that Krueger won only 29% of the total vote, just behind Hutchison, also with 29%; Barton and Fields won 14% each. Hutchison kept the focus on Clinton and won the June runoff by an astonishing 67%–33%.

Three serious Democrats were running as she entered the race for the full term in 1994. The potentially strongest candidate, moderate Houston Congressman Mike Andrews, was eliminated in the March primary. In the April runoff, former Attorney General and bitter Richards enemy Jim Mattox lost 54%–46% to Richard Fisher, a free-spending moderate who campaigned extensively in the Border counties in Spanish. Fisher's credentials seemed a bit fishy—he claimed to have been an adviser to former British Prime Minister Margaret Thatcher, though Thatcher said their acquaintance was minor—and Hutchison cruised to a solid 61%–38% victory.

Hutchison has a mostly conservative voting record. She is opposed to outlawing abortion and favors embryonic stem cell research, but voted for the partial-birth abortion ban. In her first years she worked on the 1996 welfare act, helping to write a funding formula helpful to Texas and getting funding for colonias and other border infrastructure. She beat a Democratic filibuster and inserted in a September 1999 appropriation a ban on Clinton administration plans to increase oil and gas royalties on federal land. She supported the Bush energy bill, including oil drilling in the Arctic National Wildlife Refuge.

Hutchison has long sought to repeal the marriage penalty; in 1997 she sponsored a bill to do so that was vetoed by Clinton. She supported it as part of the 2001 Bush tax cut and advanced her own version with relief for homemakers. In January 2003 she co-sponsored with Evan Bayh a bill to repeal it immediately and permanently. She also co-sponsored with two Democrats a bill to allow IRA holders over 59 to withdraw money for charitable donations without paying tax. On the Aviation Subcommittee she sponsored a 2000 law strengthening airport security that was being put into effect on September 11. After that tragedy she worked with Chairman Jay Rockefeller and strongly supported federalization of airport security. That position prevailed unanimously in the Senate; in conference committee she worked out a compromise with the House, which had voted for private security personnel, which seems likely to effectively federalize the program. In November 2002 she called for a speedup of the registered traveler program, which would issue identity cards with biometric information. That month the Senate passed unanimously the cargo security bill she and Dianne Feinstein co-sponsored; the House did not act and in January 2003 they introduced it again. Hutchison had hoped to be chairman of the Aviation Subcommittee, but in January 2003 Trent Lott returned to the committee and with greater seniority, claimed the post; she became chairman of the Surface Transportation Subcommittee instead. She has been a longtime supporter of the Amtrak system and of Amtrak lines in Texas. But she argues that Amtrak should get tougher on its unions. Hutchison is also a strong supporter of the manned space program; she grew up near what is now the Johnson Space Center. Before the February 2003 Columbia disaster she warned of underfunding, and afterwards she expressed confidence in the program and called for more funding. "If you see how many times they've aborted takeoffs for one little malfunction or signal that came through, I do think they put safety first. But I don't think you can continue draconian cuts and continue to do the mission safely."

Hutchison has weighed in on a number of health issues. In May 2001 she introduced a bill to reverse the proposed $735 million cut in reimbursement of teaching hospitals; she was supported by other senators with little in common except that they represent states with big teaching hospitals—Charles Schumer, Hillary Rodham Clinton, Edward Kennedy, Jesse Helms. She and Barbara Mikulski co-sponsored a bill for $250 million research in blood cancers; at a hearing she introduced those struck by such cancers, including former Congresswoman Geraldine Ferraro and her brother Allan Bailey. The bill became law in May 2002, with a research program named after former Congressman Joe Moakley and an education program named after Ferraro. With Dianne Feinstein, she has co-sponsored continuation of the breast cancer stamp. Also with Feinstein, she co-sponsored the national AMBER Alert bill in 2002; it is named after Amber Hagerman, who was abducted in 1996 in Arlington, Texas. It passed the Senate in 2002 and became law in April 2003.

Hutchison is vice-chairman of the Senate Republican Conference. Six days after Trent Lott's comments at Strom Thurmond's 100th birthday party she called his words "overboard" and defended his record of support of blacks and Hispanics. She talked with him frequently and conveyed the opinions of other Republican senators; the last call was the morning of December 20, when he bowed out of the majority leader post. During the Clinton years, Hutchison was critical of administration foreign policy; she was wary of U.S. involvement in the former Yugoslavia, called for an eventual pullout from Bosnia, and decried Clinton administration policy in Kosovo. "We have seen the United States stumble into a series of regional crises—displacing local powers that share our objectives and are otherwise able to act on their own. This has led to strategic missteps—a hallmark of Clinton administration foreign policy." She has generally supported the foreign policy of the Bush administration.

On Texas issues, Hutchison has worked to protect Texas's military bases against another round of base closings. San Antonio, with four bases and two military medical centers, is a particular concern; Kelly Air Force Base there was closed in 2001, costing the area 10,900 civilian jobs. In July 2002 she sponsored an amendment to change the base closing ranking and evaluation systems, which she says have produced mistakes in previous base closing rounds. In July 2001 she used her seat on the Appropriations Committee to earmark $25 million for Houston Metro, for either a study of expanding its rail line or for improvements in the Katy Freeway; that put her in a fight with Tom DeLay, who on House Appropriations put in a provision barring federal funds for Houston Metro rail. She met with officials from the Mexican state of Chihuahua in May 2002 and disagreed when they said they did not have any water to release to the Rio Grande, as required by a 1944 treaty; Mexico is in arrears on its obligations, and south Texas farmers say they have lost $1 billion in the last decade. For a time she opposed the Bush administration and her colleague Phil Gramm on Mexican trucks, calling for more inspections before they are allowed into the United States.

Hutchison was reelected in 2000 by a 65%–32% margin over an opponent named Gene Kelly who had no visible support; she carried 237 of 254 counties. After the election she showed some interest in running for governor in 2002, but that would have meant a primary against Rick Perry; in March 2001 she announced she would not do so. In August and November 2001 Hutchison and her husband adopted two infants from an adoption agency; she and Christopher Dodd are two senators approaching 60 who became parents for the first time.

Junior Senator

John Cornyn (R)

Elected 2002, seat up 2008, 1st term; b. Feb. 2, 1952, Houston; home, San Antonio; Trinity U., B.A. 1973, St. Mary's Law Schl., J.D. 1977, U. of VA, L.L.M. 1995; Church of Christ; married (Sandy).

Elected Office: San Antonio Dist. Ct. judge, 1984–90; TX Sup. Ct., 1990–97; TX Atty. Gen., 1998–02.

Professional Career: Practicing atty., 1977–84.

DC Office: 517 HSOB, 20510, 202-224-2934; Fax: 202-228-2856; Web site: cornyn.senate.gov.

State Offices: Austin, 512-469-6034; Dallas, 972-239-1310; Harlingen, 956-423-0162; Houston, 713-572-3337; Lubbock, 806-472-7533; San Antonio, 210-224-7485; Tyler, 903-593-0902.

Committees: *Armed Services*: Emerging Threats & Capabilities; Personnel; Readiness & Management Support; Strategic Forces. *Budget. Environment & Public Works*: Clean Air, Climate Change & Nuclear Safety; Transportation & Infrastructure. *Judiciary*: Administrative Oversight & the Courts; Constitution, Civil Rights & Property Rights (Chmn.); Crime, Corrections & Victims' Rights; Immigration, Border Security & Citizenship.

Group Ratings and Key Votes: Newly Elected

Election Results

2002 general	John Cornyn (R)	2,496,243	(55%)	($9,769,780)
	Ron Kirk (D)	1,955,758	(43%)	($9,426,763)
	Other	62,011	(1%)	
2002 primary	John Cornyn (R)	478,825	(77%)	
	Bruce Lang (R)	46,907	(8%)	
	Douglas Deffenbaugh (R)	43,611	(7%)	
	Dudley Mooney (R)	32,262	(5%)	
	Other	17,757	(3%)	
1996 general	Phil Gramm (R)	3,027,680	(55%)	($14,078,131)
	Victor M. Morales (D)	2,428,776	(44%)	($978,862)

John Cornyn, a Republican, was elected to the Senate in 2002. He was born in Houston and grew up in San Antonio. He graduated from high school in Japan; his father was an oral pathologist in the Air Force stationed there and after retiring from the service settled in San Antonio and taught at the University of Texas Health Science Center. John Cornyn graduated from Trinity University and St. Mary's University Law School, both in San Antonio, in the 1970s. He practiced law for five years with a firm that defended doctors and insurance companies in medical malpractice cases. In 1984 he ran for District Court Judge on the Republican ticket in Bexar County and upset a strong favorite in the race.

In 1990 he was elected to the state Supreme Court as a Republican. This was at a time when Texas voters were regularly replacing pro-trial lawyer Democrats with Republicans who believed that their predecessors had made law unduly favorable to plaintiffs. Cornyn generally ruled for defendants in tort cases, but not always; he dissented in 1995 from a decision that stripped juries of the right to determine the credibility of expert witnesses. The same year he wrote a 5–4 decision upholding the "Robin Hood" school finance system in which property-wealthy school districts had to send money to property-poor districts. In 1997 he resigned from the court to run for attorney general. In the March 1998 Republican primary and runoff he defeated two better-known opponents. In the general election he faced a grizzled veteran of Texas politics, Jim Mattox, a populist-sounding Democrat, congressman from Dallas from 1976 to 1982, attorney general from 1982 to 1990, second place finisher to Ann Richards in the 1990 primary and runoff for governor. Cornyn won 54%–44%.

Cornyn was the first Republican attorney general since Reconstruction. He recruited top law school graduates to serve two-year stints in the office, supplementing civil service lawyers. He collected over $3 billion in overdue child support, up 63%, $4 million in penalties from nursing home operators and $5 million from insurance companies that underpaid on auto insurance claims. He launched a program called Texas Exile, to confiscate firearms from career criminals. He won a $35 million settlement from Koch Industries under the federal Clean Water Act. He ruled that federal law bars public hospitals from giving illegal immigrants anything but emergency care, immunizations and treatment of communicable diseases. He sued Farmers Insurance, the state's largest homeowners insurance company, for deceptive trade practices. He argued two cases before the U. S. Supreme Court, including the Santa Fe Independent School District's defense of reading the Lord's Prayer at football games (the Court nixed it).

Cornyn had been planning to run for reelection in 2002. But on September 4, 2001, Senator Phil Gramm announced that he would not run for reelection. Cornyn immediately set out to run for the Senate and seemed to have the support of George W. Bush. Other Republicans considered the race but quickly ran for something else—Land Commissioner David Dewhurst for lieutenant governor, Congressmen Joe Barton and Henry Bonilla for reelection. Cornyn announced September 21 and said he hoped to raise $6 million for the March primary, he had no serious opposition there and didn't raise that much until later. National Democrats found a Texas candidate they liked: Dallas Mayor Ron Kirk. Kirk had an interesting life story: he is black, the son of the first black mailman in Austin and a teacher; he graduated from the University of Texas and its law school and was an aide to Senator Lloyd Bentsen, known for hiring top-notch staffers. In 1995 he was elected mayor of Dallas and in 1999 he was reelected by a wide margin. He soothed an often fractious Council and won wide support from the business community for pushing for approval of a downtown arena and supporting the Trinity River Project. Before Gramm's announcement he had said he would run for the Senate only if Gramm retired. In 2001 he announced he was resigning as mayor and in January 2002 he announced he was running for the Senate.

Kirk was not the only Democrat who ran. Another was Congressman Ken Bentsen of metro Houston, nephew of Senator and Treasury Secretary Lloyd Bentsen. Bentsen had a moderate record and a well-known name; at the time he was threatened with an unfavorable redistricting. But neither Kirk nor Bentsen ran first in the March primary. That place went to Victor Morales, a geography teacher and track coach from the Dallas suburb of Crandall, who raised $7,000 for his campaign. Morales had won the nomination to run against Phil Gramm in 1996 with 36% of the vote against two former congressmen; his main assets were his Hispanic identity and the fact that he had the same last name as Attorney General Dan Morales. (This scenario may recur as more Hispanics enter politics. There are many fewer surnames among American Hispanics than among American Anglos.) In 2002 Morales won 33.2% of the vote in the primary, to 33.1% for Kirk and 27% for Bentsen. This contest split voters on geographic and ethnic lines. Kirk carried most counties in the Dallas-Fort Worth and Austin media markets. Bentsen carried the Houston media market and the Wichita Falls, Lubbock and Amarillo media markets. Morales carried, often with large majorities, counties with large Hispanic populations. There was a big turnout in the Rio Grande Valley inspired by Laredo-based governor candidate Tony Sanchez; this helped Morales and sank Bentsen. In the four weeks before the runoff, Kirk was endorsed by Bentsen and Houston Mayor Lee Brown. In the lower-turnout runoff, in which two-thirds of votes were cast by blacks and Hispanics, Kirk won 60%–40%. Again Morales won big majorities in most heavily Hispanic communities, but Kirk won just about everywhere else.

In the general election Cornyn ran as a supporter of George W. Bush, and of making the 2001 tax cuts permanent, extending the research and development tax credit and raising Texas's share of gas tax funds from 90.5 cents to 95 cents per dollar of gas tax revenues. He supported school vouchers, individual investment accounts as part of Social Security and colorblind standards nationally in college and university admissions. Kirk took an opposite stand on all these issues, but portrayed himself as a moderate Democrat who would often support Bush. Cornyn favored Bush-level spending on missile defense; Kirk did not. On Iraq, Kirk equivocated, taking different stands at different times.

Kirk was a favorite of Democratic contributors and spent much time—50 days, Cornyn's spokesman charged—outside Texas schmoozing with Democratic contributors in Washington, on the Upper East Side of Manhattan, in Beverly Hills and in similar venues. Republicans ran ads linking him to Hillary Rodham Clinton and liberal out-of-state moneygivers. Eventually he spent $8.9 million—almost as much as Cornyn's $9.5 million, most of it raised in Texas. Kirk was helped here by his sense of humor and a considerable charm, making fun of his bald pate and answering—mindful of Texas mores—when asked whether he owned a gun, "I have a wife and two little girls. You figure it out." But in the course of the campaign Kirk made some mistakes. He opposed the nomination to a federal judgeship of Texas Supreme Court Justice Priscilla Owen—something Republicans seized on in ads. He refused to disclose his income tax returns, except for allowing reporters one peek at his 2001 return. When Cornyn came out for a bill in the legislature requiring district attorneys to seek the death penalty for killers of law enforcement officials (the liberal Austin district attorney had not sought the death penalty for the killer of a Travis County sheriff's deputy), Kirk said Cornyn was acting like he was running for district attorney—and then had to apologize abjectly to a convention of law enforcement officials a few days later, while Cornyn met with the deputy's widow. In San Antonio on September 12 he said that Cornyn might not support military action in Iraq if our military forces were not "disproportionately ethnic [and] disproportionately minority." He said he supported military action only if it met with international approval. Four days later he apologized and then said he backed Bush's position; he endorsed the Iraq war resolution in October.

Texas Democrats called their ticket of Kirk for senator and Tony Sanchez for governor the "dream team." They hoped it would draw a large turnout of blacks and Hispanics. Phil Gramm in June said the Democrats were trying to divide Texas along racial lines; Cornyn's spokesman in April said the Democratic ticket was the product of a "racial quota system," a comment that Cornyn said was "shocking and inappropriate." Democrats at one point they said they would register 500,000 new Hispanics, though they later scaled that back and concentrated on Election Day get-out-the-vote. Meanwhile Republicans quietly registered thousands of new voters in the heavily Republican fast-growing suburban counties around Dallas-Fort Worth, Houston, San Antonio and Austin.

Polls showed the race close in the spring, with Cornyn well under 50%; one nonpartisan firm and Kirk's pollster showed Kirk ahead or leading in the summer and fall. But this race may never have been as close as it seemed to some. Neither candidate started off very well known in most of the state, and Kirk had the regional advantage—he was quite well known in his larger home media market of Dallas-Fort Worth than Cornyn was in his smaller home media market of San Antonio. Spending on this race was dwarfed by the spending in the governor's race, so that Cornyn's relatively low substantive identification may have depressed his poll numbers to the end. Democrats operated on the assumption that Kirk had to win 85% of blacks, 65% of Hispanics and 35% of whites to win. He clearly achieved the first and probably achieved the second of those goals, but failed by a solid margin to achieve the third. Cornyn won 55%–43%—almost the same numbers as in his race for attorney general in 1998, and a fair reflection of basic party identification in Texas in recent times. Kirk carried historically Republican Dallas County 50%–49%. But Cornyn carried the entire Dallas-Fort Worth Metroplex 58%–41%. Cornyn carried metro Houston 55%–43% and the combined San Antonio and Austin metro areas 51%–47%. The Border went 69%–29% for Kirk, a 148,000-vote margin. But rural Texas, much larger, went 62%–37% for Cornyn, a 346,000-vote margin. Kirk may have increased black turnout in Dallas, and Sanchez clearly increased Hispanic turnout in Laredo, but otherwise black and Hispanic turnout does not seem to have risen much above that in 1994, the last big-turnout off-year election. In contrast, turnout was up from 25% to 52% in fast-growing counties around Dallas-Fort Worth (Collin, Denton, Rockwall), Houston (Fort Bend, Montgomery), San Antonio (Comal, Kendall, Bandera) and Austin (Williamson, Hays, Bastrop, Burnet). Cornyn holds the seat once held by Sam Houston, Lyndon Johnson and John Tower and is the first Texas senator to come from San Antonio, which in the state's first decades was its largest city and which he argues is the most representative.

Cornyn won seats on Armed Services, on which he will try to protect Texas military bases from base closing; Environment, on which he will fight for a more favorable highway spending formula; Budget and Judiciary, on which he is chairman of the Constitution Committee.

FIRST DISTRICT

Rep. Max Sandlin (D)

Elected 1996, 4th term; b. Sept. 29, 1952, Texarkana; home, Marshall; Baylor U., B.A. 1975, J.D. 1978; Baptist; divorced.

Elected Office: Harrison Cnty. Judge, 1986–89; Judge, Harrison Cnty. Court at Law, 1989–96.

Professional Career: Practicing atty., 1978–96; V.P., Howell & Sandlin Inc., 1989–96; Pres., E. TX Fuels, Inc., 1992–96.

DC Office: 324 CHOB 20515, 202-225-3035; Fax: 202-225-5866; Web site: www.house.gov/sandlin.

District Offices: Marshall, 903-938-8386; New Boston, 903-628-5594; Sulphur Springs, 903-885-8682.

Committees: *Chief Deputy Minority Whip. Ways & Means* (16th of 17 D): Oversight; Select Revenue Measures.

Group Ratings

	ADA	ACLU	AFS	LCV	CON	ITIC	NTU	COC	ACU	NTLC	CHC
2002	70	67	89	50	3	38	31	60	40	22	25
2001	80	—	90	29	—	—	24	52	32	—	—

National Journal Ratings

	2001 LIB	—	2001 CONS	2002 LIB	—	2002 CONS
Economic	54%	—	46%	56%	—	43%
Social	65%	—	34%	62%	—	37%
Foreign	67%	—	32%	56%	—	44%

Key Votes of the 107th Congress

1. Approve Bush Tax Cuts	Y	5. Faith-Based Charities	N	9. Trade Promotion Authority	N
2. Limit Patients' Bill of Rights	N	6. Bar Gays in the Boy Scouts	Y	10. Bar Funds for Intl. Court	Y
3. Campaign Finance Reform	Y	7. Ban Partial-Birth Abortion	Y	11. Authorize Force in Iraq	Y
4. Ban ANWR Development	N	8. Arm Commercial Pilots	Y	12. Deny Home. Sec. Dept. Union	N

Election Results

2002 general	Max Sandlin (D)	86,384	(56%)	($1,070,933)
	John Lawrence (R)	66,654	(44%)	($81,432)
2002 primary	Max Sandlin (D)	unopposed		
2000 general	Max Sandlin (D)	118,157	(56%)	($1,147,002)
	Noble Willingham (R)	91,912	(43%)	($246,827)
	Other	1,779	(1%)	

Prior Winning Percentages: 1998 (59%); 1996 (52%)

The People		Race/Ethnic Origin	Ancestry	
Area size:	12,900 sq. mi.	74.7% White	USA: 13.0%	Irish: 7.8%
Urban population:	40.1%	16.2% Black	English: 6.7%	
Rural population:	59.9%	0.3% Asian	**2000 Presidential Vote**	
Pop. 2000:	651,619	0.5% Native Am.	Bush (R) 142,544	(64%)
Median income:	$31,894	0.0% Hawaiian	Gore (D) 79,801	(36%)
Poverty status:	16.8%	0.9% Two + races	**Cook Partisan Voting Index:** R +14	
Military veterans:	14.2%	0.1% Other		
		7.4% Hispanic Origin		

Occupation	Blue collar: 31.9%	White collar: 51.0%	Gray collar: 17.1%

Texarkana, with a population of 35,000 and a rural and small town hinterland somewhat larger, for years was noteworthy mainly because its neat grid streets cross the Texas-Arkansas state line.

The downtown post office straddles the boundary; those who work in Texarkana, Texas, and live in Texarkana, Arkansas, are exempted from the Arkansas state income tax because Texas has none. Yet this small city and its hinterland produced two presidential candidates in the 1990s: Ross Perot grew up in Texarkana, Texas, while Bill Clinton's boyhood home of Hope, Arkansas, is only 30 miles east on Interstate 30.

Texarkana was populist country then, a place where farmers producing crops felt themselves at the mercy of Dallas cotton brokers, Wall Street financiers and railroad magnates who, they felt, were grabbing all the gains of their hard work. Outside Texarkana, in landscape littered with small houses amid lazily winding rivers, there was little protection from the sun and wind, and precious little ornament. The politics here has always been Democratic: Clinton, who remembers his grandfather as an FDR fan, has never been anything else, while Perot was more at ease with moderate Democrats Lloyd Bentsen and Ann Richards than with the Republican Bushes. And in Texarkana this politics was surely affected by Wright Patman, congressman from this area from 1929 until he died in office in 1976, a populist who began his career in the House by moving to impeach Treasury Secretary Andrew Mellon, punctuated it by calling constantly for low interest rates and ended it after 12 years as Banking Committee chairman. But culture here was always traditional: this is an area of heavy churchgoing and proud patriotism. Another kind of culture is recalled at Texarkana's Perot Theater—which Ross helped to restore with an $800,000 donation; the stage once featured performers such as Will Rogers and Annie Oakley.

The 1st Congressional District includes most of the northeastern corner of Texas—from Texarkana west to within two counties of Dallas and south to include Nacogdoches. Politically, it is traditionally Democratic but has been voting Republican in most statewide races since the early 1990s. It was the scene of an epic 1985 special election, contrived by Phil Gramm as an example of how Republicans could capture southern Democratic seats, opposed by Jim Wright and Tony Coelho who wanted to hold on; the result was a narrow 51%–49% win for Democrat Jim Chapman and a delay of nine years before the Republicans won most of the seats in the South. Yellow Dog Democrats crossing party lines are now the norm here, but the district still has not elected a Republican to Congress.

The congressman from the 1st District is Max Sandlin, a Democrat first elected in 1996 to replace Chapman. Sandlin grew up in East Texas, graduated from Baylor, practiced law in Marshall and got involved in oil and gas exploration. He was Harrison County judge, an elected administrative position, when he ran for the House in 1996. Local politics here was still Democratic, and the Democratic primary attracted four times as many voters as the Republican. Sandlin led attorney Jo Ann Howard, wife of a longtime Chapman opponent, 42%–34%. In the runoff, Sandlin, spending his own money and using his oil business connections to raise more, beat Howard 56%–44%. Sandlin pointed to his local tax-cutting experience and promised to find "common sense" solutions to Medicare and education. He attacked Republican Ed Merritt, an insurance lawyer with no political experience, for backing Medicare "cuts." Merritt attacked him for appearing with Bill Clinton. Overall Sandlin spent $1.7 million, including $784,000 of his own money—a total almost four times Merritt's. Sandlin won 52%–47%, losing counties only in the periphery of the district.

In the House, Sandlin has a moderate voting record that carefully straddles Democratic wings, joining the centrist Blue Dogs but also taking on populist causes like HMO regulation. He urged national Democrats to abandon gun control and worked with Arkansas Democrats to rescue Interstate 49, now a dotted line on the map from Shreveport to Texarkana, after George W. Bush cut funding. He led the Blue Dogs' energy task force and charged that the Bush energy program did not do enough for production; he backed additional tax incentives for domestic production plus support for renewable energy sources. After meeting with Dick Cheney, he voted for the bill that passed in the House. He supported Bill Clinton on PNTR with China and he voted for the final agreement on President Bush's tax cuts, but he opposed Bush's request for trade promotion authority. Those tax and trade positions became relevant to lobbyists in January 2003, when Nancy Pelosi unexpectedly secured for him a seat on the Ways and Means Committee. Sandlin had been a vocal supporter of Pelosi's rise in leadership, and his conservative background gave her an entry into a wing of the party where she had fewer contacts. As thanks, she also named him a chief deputy whip and Sandlin became a frequent presence in her leadership office; for a time, he dated Pelosi's daughter Christine, an aide to Congressman John Tierney. Sandlin considered, but abandoned, his own bid for Caucus vice-chairman. In April 2002 he won *Chile Pepper* magazine's Zestiest Legislator contest by eating eight jalapeno peppers in five minutes. In February 2003, against four of his colleagues from the chile pepper states (Louisiana, Texas, New Mexico, Arizona, California) Sandlin ate 40 peppers (with a glass of milk nearby). Yet he was beaten by Joe Baca of California who ate 43.

Sandlin was targeted in 2000 by national Republicans, who helped fund the candidacy of Noble Willingham, a native of Wood County who gained renown as the barkeeper C.D. Parker on the long-running TV show *Walker, Texas Ranger.* Willingham criticized Sandlin's bringing Clinton to the district for a fundraiser and his support of the Democratic agenda. But Sandlin won the Chamber of Commerce endorsement and showed that yellow dog Democrats still prevail in east Texas. He won 56%–43%, even as George W. Bush was winning 64% in the district; he carried all but two counties. In 2002, against a candidate not so well-known and who spent far less money, Sandlin won by a nearly identical 56%–44%. If a new congressional map is passed for the 2004 election, Sandlin's seat could be at risk; a reconfiguration of the district boundaries could put heavily Republican Longview or Tyler in the district and change the political balance.

SECOND DISTRICT

Rep. Jim Turner (D)

Elected 1996, 4th term; b. Feb. 6, 1946, Ft. Lewis, WA; home, Crockett; U. of TX, B.B.A. 1968, M.B.A. 1971, J.D. 1971; Baptist; married (Ginny).

Military Career: Army, 1970–78.

Elected Office: TX House of Reps., 1981–84; Crockett Mayor, 1989–91; TX Senate, 1991–96.

Professional Career: Exec. Asst., Gov. Mark White, 1984–86; Practicing atty., 1986–96; Chmn., TX Comm. on Children & Youth, 1993–94.

DC Office: 330 CHOB 20515, 202-225-2401; Fax: 202-225-5955; Web site: www.house.gov/turner.

District Offices: Huntsville, 936-291-3097; Lufkin, 936-637-1770; Orange, 409-883-4990.

Committees: *Armed Services* (10th of 29 D): Tactical Air & Land Forces; Terrorism, Unconventional Threats & Capabilities. *Select Committee on Homeland Security* (RMM of 23 D).

Group Ratings

	ADA	ACLU	AFS	LCV	CON	ITIC	NTU	COC	ACU	NTLC	CHC
2002	75	53	100	25	31	62	17	55	32	14	33
2001	60	—	80	36	—	—	18	57	48	—	—

National Journal Ratings

	2001 LIB	—	2001 CONS	2002 LIB	—	2002 CONS
Economic	57%	—	43%	58%	—	41%
Social	52%	—	47%	56%	—	42%
Foreign	61%	—	36%	54%	—	46%

Key Votes of the 107th Congress

1. Approve Bush Tax Cuts	Y	5. Faith-Based Charities	N	9. Trade Promotion Authority	N
2. Limit Patients' Bill of Rights	N	6. Bar Gays in the Boy Scouts	Y	10. Bar Funds for Intl. Court	Y
3. Campaign Finance Reform	Y	7. Ban Partial-Birth Abortion	Y	11. Authorize Force in Iraq	Y
4. Ban ANWR Development	N	8. Arm Commercial Pilots	Y	12. Deny Home. Sec. Dept. Union	N

Election Results

2002 general	Jim Turner (D)	85,492	(61%)	($330,840)
	Van Brookshire (R)	53,656	(38%)	($27,861)
	Other	1,353	(1%)	
2002 primary	Jim Turner (D)	unopposed		
2000 general	Jim Turner (D)	162,891	(91%)	($138,491)
	Gary Lyndon Dye (Lib)	15,939	(9%)	

Prior Winning Percentages: 1998 (58%); 1996 (52%)

The People		Race/Ethnic Origin	Ancestry	
Area size:	14,214 sq. mi.	75.6% White	USA: 12.5%	Irish: 7.5%
Urban population:	38.1%	13.8% Black	German: 6.5%	
Rural population:	61.9%	0.4% Asian	**2000 Presidential Vote**	
Pop. 2000:	651,619	0.4% Native Am.	Bush (R) 133,641 (63%)	
Median income:	$32,986	0.0% Hawaiian	Gore (D) 78,493 (37%)	
Poverty status:	15.9%	0.9% Two+ races	**Cook Partisan Voting Index:** R +13	
Military veterans:	13.9%	0.0% Other		
		8.8% Hispanic Origin		

Occupation   Blue collar: 33.3%   White collar: 48.2%   Gray collar: 18.5%

East Texas is thick with landmarks of Lone Star history. There's still an Indian reservation in Polk County, and the swampland of the Big Thicket National Preserve reminds you of what this area once looked like. Near Beaumont is Spindletop, where the world's first gusher spewed out in 1901 and started the Texas oil boom. Not far away is the huge oil field that wildcatter H. L. Hunt found in 1931, the foundation of a billion-dollar fortune. Much of East Texas looks little different from the wildcat days of 50 years ago: the town squares with churches and courthouses (Cherokee County's courthouse square features a 546-foot footbridge, the longest in the nation); the stands of fast-growing pine; the rough farmland. It was in the fields and woodlands of Nacogdoches County and other nearby counties that the debris, including human remains, fell when Space Shuttle Columbia was lost in February 2003.

The 2d Congressional District includes all or part of 18 East Texas counties, most of them still largely rural; it runs from Huntsville in the west to the oil port of Orange just east of Beaumont then north past Lufkin to Jacksonville. The political tradition here is Democratic and populist, devoted to traditional values but with a military posture and a certain Texas rowdiness. This is the kind of district Democrats must carry to win Texas, but lately have failed to do so: George W. Bush won 63% of the vote here in 2000.

The congressman from the 2d District is Jim Turner, a Democrat first elected in 1996. He grew up in East Texas, went to college and law school at the University of Texas in Austin, served eight years in the Army, then returned to Crockett in Houston County, practiced law and was active in church and community organizations. In 1980 he was elected to the Texas House and served four years; he was mayor of Crockett for two years; in 1990 he returned to Austin in the state Senate. His opportunity to run for the House came when Congressman Charlie Wilson decided to retire after 24 years. With Wilson's support, he won a three-candidate Democratic primary in 1996 with 59%, carrying everything but his opponents' home counties. Donna Peterson, a West Point graduate who opposed Wilson three times, lost the Republican runoff by 2–1 to Christian conservative Brian Babin. Turner outspent Babin by nearly 2–1 and won 52%–46%.

In the House, Turner joined the conservative-leaning New Democrat Coalition and Blue Dogs, and has taken a centrist posture. Like other skillful Texas Democrats over the years, he took on legislative tasks in the House, like playing a leading role to promote the Shays-Meehan campaign finance bill by filing a discharge petition. After voting to sustain Clinton's vetoes of the marriage-penalty and estate and gift tax repeals, he was among the 28 House Democrats who approved final passage of tax cuts in 2001. With Republican Kevin Brady and Democrat Lloyd Doggett, he proposed that Congress apply to the federal government the sunset review process used in Texas. As the Blue Dogs policy co-chair in 2001, he urged George W. Bush to devote half of the surplus to reducing the debt, one-fourth to tax cuts, and one-fourth to spending priorities.

When the surplus disappeared, he led the Blue Dogs' efforts to control the deficit by enforcing spending caps, revising House rules to require a three-fifths vote to increase the deficit and requiring the president to submit a balanced budget each year. Working with Tom Davis and Joe Lieberman, he enacted his bill to establish a federal chief information officer within the Office of Management and Budget, and requiring Internet access to government information and services. He proposed a memorial on the National Mall to honor the victims of September 11.

In January 2003, Nancy Pelosi named him as ranking Democrat of the new Select Homeland Security Committee. Turner had been disappointed over his failure to gain a seat on the Energy and Commerce Committee, but said this was more significant. With Chairman Christopher Cox, he moved quickly to assert the committee's oversight authority within the House and to strengthen the law that created the Homeland Security Department. He has been especially interested in assuring rapid development of information technology in homeland defense.

Turner was reelected with 58% of the vote in 1998, 91% in 2000 and was reelected with 61% of the vote in 2002. If a new congressional map is passed for the 2004 election, Turner's seat could be at risk; under one proposal that circulated in May 2003, Turner and 1st District Congressman Max Sandlin were paired together in a distinctly Republican district.

THIRD DISTRICT

Rep. Sam Johnson (R)

Elected May 1991, 6th term; b. Oct. 11, 1930, San Antonio; home, Dallas; S. Methodist U., B.B.A. 1951, George Washington U., M.S. 1974; Methodist; married (Shirley).

Military Career: Air Force, 1950–79 (Korea & Vietnam).

Elected Office: TX House of Reps., 1984–91.

Professional Career: Home builder.

DC Office: 1211 LHOB 20515, 202-225-4201; Fax: 202-225-1485; Web site: www.samjohnson.house.gov.

District Office: Richardson, 972-470-0892.

Committees: *Education & the Workforce* (7th of 27 R): 21st Century Competitiveness; Employer-Employee Relations (Chmn.). *Ways & Means* (11th of 24 R): Health; Oversight; Social Security.

Group Ratings

	ADA	ACLU	AFS	LCV	CON	ITIC	NTU	COC	ACU	NTLC	CHC
2002	0	7	0	0	81	88	61	90	100	89	100
2001	0	—	0	7	—	—	73	91	100	—	—

National Journal Ratings

	2001 LIB	—	2001 CONS		2002 LIB	—	2002 CONS
Economic	0%	—	94%		0%	—	91%
Social	0%	—	81%		0%	—	75%
Foreign	0%	—	97%		0%	—	85%

Key Votes of the 107th Congress

1. Approve Bush Tax Cuts	Y	5. Faith-Based Charities	Y	9. Trade Promotion Authority	Y
2. Limit Patients' Bill of Rights	Y	6. Bar Gays in the Boy Scouts	Y	10. Bar Funds for Intl. Court	Y
3. Campaign Finance Reform	N	7. Ban Partial-Birth Abortion	Y	11. Authorize Force in Iraq	Y
4. Ban ANWR Development	N	8. Arm Commercial Pilots	Y	12. Deny Home. Sec. Dept. Union	Y

Election Results

2002 general	Sam Johnson (R)	113,974	(74%)	($921,485)
	Manny Molera (D)	37,503	(24%)	($78,120)
	Other	2,656	(2%)	
2002 primary	Sam Johnson (R)	17,153	(84%)	
	Thomas Caiazzo (R)	3,184	(16%)	
2000 general	Sam Johnson (R)	187,486	(72%)	($892,324)
	Billy Wayne Zachary (D)	67,233	(26%)	($6,702)
	Other	7,178	(3%)	

Prior Winning Percentages: 1998 (91%); 1996 (73%); 1994 (91%); 1992 (86%); 1991 (53%)

The People		Race/Ethnic Origin	Ancestry	
Area size:	489 sq. mi.	69.6% White	German: 11.3%	English: 8.3%
Urban population:	96.0%	6.6% Black	Irish: 8.2%	
Rural population:	4.0%	7.4% Asian	**2000 Presidential Vote**	
Pop. 2000:	651,620	0.4% Native Am.	Bush (R) 154,525 (72%)	
Median income:	$65,546	0.0% Hawaiian	Gore (D) 59,357 (28%)	
Poverty status:	5.7%	1.5% Two+ races	**Cook Partisan Voting Index:** R +23	
Military veterans:	10.4%	0.1% Other		
		14.4% Hispanic Origin		

Occupation	Blue collar: 14.8%	White collar: 75.9%	Gray collar: 9.3%

Dallas, a synonym in popular culture for newly-gotten riches, is actually a community with a long history, and in its early years was one of the poorest and most backward parts of the nation. Dallas was named, improbably, for the stuffy and otherwise forgotten Philadelphia lawyer who was James K. Polk's vice president. The city got its commercial start as the place where the first railroad in Texas stopped at the three forks of the Trinity River, surrounded by dirt-poor farm country. "Its wealth originally came from cotton," John Gunther wrote in 1946, "but primarily it is a banking and jobbing and distributing center, the headquarters of railroads and utilities." In the 1960s Dallas was at the cutting edge of high-tech, the home of Texas Instruments and Ross Perot's EDS and of many defense contractors. The defense business is not as robust as it was in the 1980s but the Dallas-Fort Worth Metroplex thrived in the 1990s, with growth from corporate headquarters relocated from less business-friendly precincts, from small businesses growing quickly in an entrepreneur-friendly climate with no state income tax and from companies making money trading with Mexico; Dallas has been the nation's greatest beneficiary of NAFTA. The Metroplex, one way or the other, continues to thrive.

Dallas's growth has now extended far into the countryside. The home of the city's elite may still be in the mansion-lined streets of Highland Park, only a few miles north of downtown. But the center of Dallas's entrepreneurial economy has moved north to the LBJ Freeway and edge cities beyond, and the residential center of Dallas's business and professional classes has moved ever farther north in Dallas county, to the rolling, scrub-covered hills, as they recently were, of Collin County to the north. Over the last 20 years Collin County has moved from a countrified area of 144,000 to an affluent urban area of half a million; its 86% growth in the 1990s made it the fastest-growing county in Texas. It grew another 10% between 2000 and 2001, one of the 10 fastest-growing counties in the nation. The most Republican areas in the Metroplex now are in Collin County and Plano, a corporate headquarters and edge city, site of mega-mansion subdivisions, the state's ninth-largest city, its richest and most educated county, the new face of successful Texas. In Plano, 10% of the population is Asian, a bit more than the total of Latinos; many are of Chinese ancestry.

The 3d Congressional District includes most of Collin County and is centered on Plano; it also includes the northeastern corner of Dallas County, northeast of the LBJ Freeway, including much of Garland and Richardson. This was the fastest-growing district in Texas in the 1990s and is very Republican, casting 72% of its votes for George W. Bush in 2000.

The congressman from the 3d District is Sam Johnson, a Republican first elected in 1991, a former Air Force fighter pilot with 86 combat missions during the Korean and Vietnam Wars and a prisoner of war in Vietnam, including 42 months in solitary confinement. Johnson grew up in Dallas, graduated from SMU and George Washington University. After his F-4 was shot down over North Vietnam during his 25th mission, he was imprisoned from 1966 to 1973 in the "Hanoi Hilton" and was left with a slight stoop in his walk and a disfigured hand. On his return, Johnson started a homebuilding company and was elected to the Texas House in 1984. He was elected to the House in a 1991 special election after incumbent Steve Bartlett was elected mayor of Dallas. Johnson ran second in the primary to former Peace Corps head Tom Pauken. In the runoff, he emphasized his war record and, although he was less familiar with legislative issues in debate, won 53%–47% over Pauken, later a sharp critic of Governor George W. Bush as Texas Republican chairman.

In the House, Johnson had the most conservative record for three consecutive years, opposing pork barrel projects of all kinds, voting for more IRAs and against extending unemployment benefits. He was a founder and chair of the Conservative Action Team, which pressed Republican leaders to stick with goals from budget targets to shutting down the National Endowment for the Arts. Every Congress he offers a constitutional amendment to repeal the 16th Amendment, which authorized the federal income tax. On the Ways and Means Committee, he was an early advocate and, then, sponsor of the successful repeal in 2000 of the earnings limit for Social Security recipients. He proposed the Good Samaritan Tax Act to permit corporations to take a tax deduction for charitable giving of food. He chairs the Subcommittee on Employer-Employee Relations, where he has encouraged small business owners to expand their pension benefits for employees. Johnson has been a defender of the F-22 fighter jet, partly produced at the Lockheed Martin plant in Fort Worth.

Unlike some other former POWs in Congress, Johnson strongly opposed Bill Clinton's decision to extend diplomatic and trade recognition to Vietnam. Even though he was a POW with John McCain for a year and a half, Johnson strongly backed George W. Bush in the 2000 primaries; McCain "cannot hold a candle to George Bush," he said. After the election, he and Mac Thornberry introduced legislation to make the voting process easier for military personnel.

This is a safe Republican seat—one of the safest in the country. In his first term Johnson pledged to serve only 12 years, but has changed his mind.

FOURTH DISTRICT

Rep. Ralph Hall (D)

Elected 1980, 12th term; b. May 3, 1923, Fate; home, Rockwall; U. of TX, TX Christian U., S. Methodist U., LL.B. 1951; United Methodist; married (Mary Ellen).

Military Career: Navy, 1942–45 (WWII).

Elected Office: Rockwall Cnty. Judge, 1950–62; TX Senate, 1962–72.

Professional Career: Practicing atty., 1951–80; Pres. & CEO, TX Aluminum Corp., 1967–68; Spec. Cnsl., Howmet Corp., 1970–74.

DC Office: 2405 RHOB 20515, 202-225-6673; Fax: 202-225-3332; Web site: www.house.gov/ralphhall.

District Offices: Rockwall, 972-771-9118; Sherman, 903-892-1112; Tyler, 903-597-3729.

Committees: *Energy & Commerce* (4th of 26 D): Energy & Air Quality; Health. *Science* (RMM of 22 D).

Group Ratings

	ADA	ACLU	AFS	LCV	CON	ITIC	NTU	COC	ACU	NTLC	CHC
2002	15	13	33	0	3	100	42	85	88	75	100
2001	25	—	10	7	—	—	62	83	96	—	—

National Journal Ratings

	2001 LIB —	2001 CONS	2002 LIB —	2002 CONS
Economic	39%	— 61%	49%	— 51%
Social	35%	— 63%	25%	— 71%
Foreign	33%	— 60%	35%	— 60%

Key Votes of the 107th Congress

1. Approve Bush Tax Cuts	Y	5. Faith-Based Charities	Y	9. Trade Promotion Authority	Y
2. Limit Patients' Bill of Rights	N	6. Bar Gays in the Boy Scouts	Y	10. Bar Funds for Intl. Court	Y
3. Campaign Finance Reform	N	7. Ban Partial-Birth Abortion	Y	11. Authorize Force in Iraq	Y
4. Ban ANWR Development	N	8. Arm Commercial Pilots	Y	12. Deny Home. Sec. Dept. Union	Y

Election Results

2002 general	Ralph Hall (D)	97,304	(58%)	($635,633)
	John Graves (R)	67,939	(40%)	($160,820)
	Other	3,042	(2%)	
2002 primary	Ralph Hall (D)	unopposed		
2000 general	Ralph Hall (D)	145,887	(60%)	($739,496)
	Jon Newton (R)	91,574	(38%)	($132,984)
	Other	4,417	(2%)	

Prior Winning Percentages: 1998 (58%); 1996 (64%); 1994 (59%); 1992 (58%); 1990 (100%); 1988 (66%); 1986 (72%); 1984 (58%); 1982 (74%); 1980 (52%)

The People		Race/Ethnic Origin	Ancestry	
Area size:	6,335 sq. mi.	76.6% White	USA: 12.4%	Irish: 7.9%
Urban population:	54.2%	11.7% Black	German: 7.9%	
Rural population:	45.8%	0.6% Asian	**2000 Presidential Vote**	
Pop. 2000:	651,620	0.6% Native Am.	Bush (R) 157,678	(70%)
Median income:	$38,677	0.0% Hawaiian	Gore (D) 66,995	(30%)
Poverty status:	12.5%	1.1% Two+ races	**Cook Partisan Voting Index:** R +21	
Military veterans:	14.0%	0.1% Other		
		9.4% Hispanic Origin		

Occupation   Blue collar: 28.6%   White collar: 56.4%   Gray collar: 15.1%

The Red River Valley is just one of the hearts of Texas. It is hardscrabble farm country along an unnavigable river. First settled in the 1830s, in the days of the Texas Republic, many counties here reached their population peak around 1900, when a large extended farm family worked every 160 acres. This was the part of Texas that sent Sam Rayburn to Congress in 1912; he served as speaker from 1940 until his death in 1961, except for two terms when Republicans had the majority. The Red River Valley then was one of the strongest Democratic parts of the country, with a sentimental regard for Confederate veterans and a seething hatred of Wall Street bankers. This was Rayburn's politics, and he was a skillful lawmaker: He helped write the securities laws that have for nearly 70 years provided the basis for confidence in American securities markets and other regulatory measures that have fared less well. Today Rayburn's politics has almost completely vanished from the area. The cause of the Confederacy has been left behind, populist suspicion of Wall Street has been replaced by active brokerage accounts and allegiance to the Democratic Party is a thing of the distant past.

The 4th Congressional District is the lineal descendant of the seat that Rayburn held, and still includes his home town of Bonham in Fannin County, which houses a Rayburn museum. But it is quite a different district. Only about one-quarter of its population is in the Red River Valley counties, in places like Denison and Sherman, now just beyond the Dallas-Fort Worth Metroplex. Nearly half the population is in and around the small oil (and now high-tech) cities of Tyler (famous for its annual Texas Rose Festival and the East Texas State Fair) and Longview, which are now entirely in the district. Connecting them is a thin corridor of land at the eastern edge of the Metroplex, in Collin, Kaufman and Rockwall Counties. Rockwall carries the curious distinction of being the smallest county in Texas (in land size) and the fastest growing county in the nation (in percentage population growth between 2001 and 2002). These were rural, heavily

Democratic counties in Rayburn's day; now they are home to upwardly mobile families, far more trusting of free markets than of government regulation, and more than 2–1 Republican. The Tyler and Longview area is similarly Republican. And even the Red River Valley counties have been giving Republicans good-sized majorities. In 1940, when Rayburn first became speaker, his district voted 90% for Franklin Roosevelt. In 2000, the 4th District voted 70% for George W. Bush. After Charles Stenholm's 17th District of Texas, this is the most Republican district in the nation that is held by a Democrat.

The congressman from the 4th District is Ralph Hall, a firmly conservative Democrat who votes almost always with Republicans, and the oldest member of the House. He was first elected in 1980 after a 30-year career in local politics and business; he was a county judge as long ago as 1950 and from 1962 to 1972 served in the Texas Senate. He usually has the most conservative voting record of any House Democrat and rarely backs his leadership except on purely party or procedural matters, and not always on those. During the 2002 campaign he promised to vote for Republican Speaker Dennis Hastert if his vote made the difference in which party controlled the House. In January 2003 he voted "present" rather than vote for Nancy Pelosi, because "she just don't think like we do." He supported just about everything in the Contract with America in 1995 and voted with George W. Bush on key tax, trade and foreign policy votes. He was one of five House Democrats who voted to impeach Bill Clinton; his lying under oath "was perjury and perjury is a felony and it's impeachable," Hall said. "I'm not a big fan of his." He continues as a prime sponsor of the constitutional amendment to require two-thirds House and Senate votes to raise taxes. But Hall is not a pure free marketeer: He voted against NAFTA. On the Energy and Commerce Committee he backed limits on the FCC's authority to regulate religious broadcasters but was skeptical about allowing the regional Bells into long distance and favored cable re-regulation.

Those views, plus his ancestral heritage, help to explain why Hall has not switched parties. "I think it's my duty to stay [a Democrat] and try to pull them back toward the middle," he said. Hall has been a hunting pal of John Dingell, and he was the ranking Democrat on the Energy and Power Subcommittee, a convenient slot for a booster of the oil and gas industry. In 2001 he became ranking Democrat on the Science Committee, where he has emphasized the use of space for biomedical research. In late 2002, he voiced concern about long-term operations and financing of the space station, and called for a fleet of "lifeboats" as transfer vehicles. Following the Columbia disaster, he defended NASA and its performance. In 2003 he proposed changes in Social Security to improve the rate of return on its trust funds.

In recent years there has been speculation that Hall would retire or face serious competition because of the district's growing Republican base. But Hall has continued to win handily. His affection for the Bushes was solidified in 1992 when George H.W. Bush telephoned Hall to extend best wishes while he was at the Texas bedside of his grandson, who was suffering from a brain tumor; he spoke favorably about George W. Bush in 2000. After the 2001 redistricting, local and national Republicans voiced interest in a serious challenge to Hall; Tyler Mayor Kevin Eltife made plans to run. But they backed off after Hall met with Bush at the White House and said that the President strongly opposed a challenge; Hall said then that he would vote for the "most conservative" candidate for Speaker if his vote determined which party organized the House. He was reelected by a 58%–40% margin; during the campaign, he said that unless Bush asked him to run again, "This is absolutely it." In 2000 his son Brett Hall was elected district judge back home, as a Republican. Democrats concede that a Republican will take this district when Hall retires.

FIFTH DISTRICT

Rep. Jeb Hensarling (R)

Elected 2002, 1st term; b. May 29, 1957, Stephenville; home, Dallas; TX A&M U., B.A. 1979, U. of TX, J.D. 1982; Christian; married (Melissa).

Professional Career: Practicing atty., 1982–84; TX Dir., U.S. Sen. Phil Gramm, 1985–89; Exec. Dir., NRSC, 1991–93; Communications Exec., 1993–02.

DC Office: 423 CHOB 20515, 202-225-3484; Fax: 202-226-4888; Web site: www.house.gov/hensarling.

District Offices: Athens, 903-675-8288; Dallas, 214-349-9966.

Committees: *Budget* (23d of 24 R). *Financial Services* (31st of 37 R): Domestic and International Monetary Policy, Trade & Technology; Financial Institutions & Consumer Credit; Oversight & Investigations.

Group Ratings and Key Votes: Newly Elected

Election Results

2002 general	Jeb Hensarling (R)	81,439	(58%)	($2,040,082)
	Ron Chapman (D)	56,330	(40%)	($914,592)
	Other	2,139	(2%)	
2002 primary	Jeb Hensarling (R)	10,475	(54%)	
	Dan Hagood (R)	3,628	(19%)	
	Mike Armour (R)	3,247	(17%)	
	Phil Sudan (R)	1,632	(8%)	
	Other	574	(3%)	

The People		Race/Ethnic Origin	Ancestry	
Area size:	7,455 sq. mi.	63.0% White	USA: 9.2%	German: 7.5%
Urban population:	76.7%	15.8% Black	Irish: 7.1%	
Rural population:	23.3%	1.8% Asian	**2000 Presidential Vote**	
Pop. 2000:	651,620	0.4% Native Am.	Bush (R)	118,703 (62%)
Median income:	$39,227	0.0% Hawaiian	Gore (D)	72,507 (38%)
Poverty status:	12.3%	1.2% Two + races	**Cook Partisan Voting Index:** R + 12	
Military veterans:	12.2%	0.1% Other		
		17.7% Hispanic Origin		

Occupation	Blue collar: 26.5%	White collar: 58.1%	Gray collar: 15.4%

Not all of Dallas is glitz and postmodern marble. From each side of downtown, on one of the three street grids that run skew to each other, is an older Dallas, with neighborhoods of high-ceilinged old mansions, modest bungalows and shotgun houses running out toward the old airport at Love Field or the State Fair Grounds and the Cotton Bowl in east Dallas, or south to the desolate treeless parks along the cement-lined Trinity River. Some of this older Dallas is being renovated and rebuilt, with chic cafes and trendy stores serving those who make their livings catering to the rich farther north. Other once middle-class neighborhoods are filling up with immigrants from Mexico and other parts of Latin America, once again noisy with children as they were in the 1950s when people moved here not from Mexico or Central America but from the almost all-Anglo counties of north and central Texas. The 2000 Census showed that 30% of the population in Dallas County is Hispanic.

The 5th Congressional District includes much of east and southeast Dallas County, including many such neighborhoods in Dallas and suburban Mesquite. It also includes a more upscale slice of Dallas inside the Freeway extending to White Rock Lake and Lake Highlands. But the 5th District also contains all or part of 10 counties in central Texas, connected to the Dallas County portions by a thin strip of land in suburban Kaufman County; the 2001 court that produced the redistricting plan followed almost exactly the same lines as the 1991 partisan Democratic redistricting plan. The Democrats' original aim was to avoid including much Republican suburban territory and connecting hip inner-city neighborhoods with yellow-dog Democratic rural counties. But their strategy has not worked. The 5th District is 16% black and 18% Hispanic, but it is not very Democratic. As rural areas swung away from Bill Clinton's Democrats, the affluent Dallasites within the district stuck with Republicans and George W. Bush attracted support from Latinos. In 2000, Bush won 62% districtwide.

The congressman from the 5th District is Jeb Hensarling, a Republican elected in 2002. Pete Sessions, who had represented the 5th for the previous six years, decided to run in the new and slightly more Republican 32d District on the north side of Dallas, even though the new 5th included 74% of his old district while the 32d included only 16%; Sessions said that he wanted to spend less time traveling around his district. Hensarling grew up in Morris County in east Texas and Lubbock County in west Texas. He worked on his father's poultry farm near College Station as a teenager and decided that he did not want to be a farmer. In high school, he started a Republican club and began organizing political events. He graduated from Texas A&M and the University of Texas Law School and practiced law for two years in San Antonio. Then he got a job on the staff of Senator Phil Gramm. He managed Gramm's 1990 campaign and was executive director of the NRSC when Gramm was chairman. He returned to Texas to become vice president of communications for Green Mountain Energy, a local utility, and he was co-founder of Family Support Assurance, a firm that has tried to modernize child support collections.

After Sessions announced he would not run again in the 5th District, Hensarling announced and became the frontrunner for the Republican nomination. Like his mentor, he listed cutting taxes as his top priority. Against four opponents he got 54% of the vote in the March 2002 primary and won the nomination without a runoff. His most curious opponent was attorney Phil Sudan, who ran two years earlier in the 25th District on the south and east side of Houston, and lost to Congressman Ken Bentsen 60%–39% despite largely self-financing his $3.2 million bid; running in the 2002 primary in the Dallas-based district, he got 8% of the vote.

Democrats tried to recruit state Senator David Cain, but he declined to run. Instead, they nominated Ron Chapman, a former Dallas County appellate judge who had been on the Dallas County ballot since 1978 and shared the name of a popular Dallas radio disc jockey. Actively backed by Texas Democratic delegation leader Martin Frost, Chapman described himself as a loyal Democrat who could work with Republicans. By the fall, Hensarling referred to his opponent as "Judge Softie" for twice allowing a man charged with attempted murder to go free from his courtroom. The folksy Chapman emphasized his public service, fiscal conservatism and deep local roots. He tried to paint Hensarling as too extreme for the district, but his message failed to take hold as a parade of Republican luminaries paraded into the district on his behalf, including George W. Bush, Dick Cheney, Bush adviser Karen Hughes and Phil Gramm. Perhaps the most significant endorsement came when Ron Chapman the disc jockey backed Hensarling at a press conference and sought to make clear that he was not the Democrat running for Congress. Hensarling won 58%–40%, with almost identical margins in Dallas County and the rest of the district.

SIXTH DISTRICT

Rep. Joe Barton (R)

Elected 1984, 10th term; b. Sept. 15, 1949, Waco; home, Ennis; Texas A&M U., B.S. 1972, Purdue U., M.S. 1973; United Methodist; divorced.

Professional Career: Asst. to V.P., Ennis Business Forms, 1973–81; White House Fellow, U.S. Dept. of Energy, 1981–82; Consultant, Atlantic Richfield Co., 1982–84.

DC Office: 2109 RHOB 20515, 202-225-2002; Fax: 202-225-3052; Web site: www.house.gov/barton.

District Office: Arlington, 817-543-1000.

Committees: *Energy & Commerce* (3d of 31 R): Energy & Air Quality (Chmn.); Health; Telecommunications & The Internet. *Science* (5th of 25 R): Space & Aeronautics.

Group Ratings

	ADA	ACLU	AFS	LCV	CON	ITIC	NTU	COC	ACU	NTLC	CHC
2002	0	7	0	0	15	75	60	100	96	97	100
2001	5	—	0	7	—	—	69	91	96	—	—

National Journal Ratings

	2001 LIB —	2001 CONS		2002 LIB —	2002 CONS
Economic	7% —	89%		0% —	91%
Social	0% —	81%		0% —	75%
Foreign	0% —	97%		33% —	66%

Key Votes of the 107th Congress

1. Approve Bush Tax Cuts	Y	5. Faith-Based Charities	Y	9. Trade Promotion Authority	Y
2. Limit Patients' Bill of Rights	Y	6. Bar Gays in the Boy Scouts	Y	10. Bar Funds for Intl. Court	N
3. Campaign Finance Reform	N	7. Ban Partial-Birth Abortion	Y	11. Authorize Force in Iraq	Y
4. Ban ANWR Development	N	8. Arm Commercial Pilots	Y	12. Deny Home. Sec. Dept. Union	Y

Election Results

2002 general	Joe Barton (R)	115,396	(70%)	($1,324,767)
	Felix Alvarado (D)	45,404	(28%)	($13,367)
	Other	3,237	(2%)	
2002 primary	Joe Barton (R)	unopposed		
2000 general	Joe Barton (R)	222,685	(88%)	($936,534)
	Frank Brady (Lib)	30,056	(12%)	

Prior Winning Percentages: 1998 (73%); 1996 (77%); 1994 (76%); 1992 (72%); 1990 (66%); 1988 (68%); 1986 (56%); 1984 (57%)

The People		Race/Ethnic Origin	Ancestry	
Area size:	3,961 sq. mi.	71.8% White	USA: 9.4%	German: 9.3%
Urban population:	75.6%	10.2% Black	Irish: 7.8%	
Rural population:	24.4%	2.6% Asian	**2000 Presidential Vote**	
Pop. 2000:	651,620	0.4% Native Am.	Bush (R)..............146,931	(67%)
Median income:	$49,763	0.1% Hawaiian	Gore (D)...............72,754	(33%)
Poverty status:	8.2%	1.3% Two+ races	**Cook Partisan Voting Index:** R +17	
Military veterans:	13.1%	0.1% Other		
		13.5% Hispanic Origin		

Occupation	Blue collar: 25.4%	White collar: 62.2%	Gray collar: 12.3%

The Dallas-Fort Worth Metroplex—yes, the name is part of everyday speech there—has spread outward from its historic nodes in downtown Dallas and Fort Worth. Although Dallas is the larger population center, much of the development has moved west, across the dusty plains where one crosses the barely perceptible Balcones Escarpment, the geologist's boundary between green and grassy East Texas and the brown and barren West. This was empty territory a few decades ago; now it has mostly been filled in, with subdivisions and shopping centers that leave some feeling of the shape of this land under the enormous Texas sky. The biggest city here is Arlington, once seemingly all suburban, with all-American attractions like Six Flags over Texas, Wet 'n' Wild and the Ballpark in Arlington, commissioned by the former part owner of the Texas Rangers, George W. Bush. But this is not just white bread suburbia any more. Arlington's population in 2000 was 18% Hispanic, 14% black and 6% Asian; just a couple miles south of Six Flags is a mixed Latino-Vietnamese area with Mexican restaurants and Asian delis, and the Arlington police gives extra pay to officers who can speak Spanish or Vietnamese.

The 6th Congressional District includes most of Arlington (although not Six Flags and the others) and the southern edge of Fort Worth to the west. More than one-third of its people live in Johnson and Ellis Counties, once rural and dusty, now fast-growing suburbia just south of Fort Worth and Dallas. The district also includes still unsuburbanized Hill and Navarro Counties to the south. Redistricting changed the boundaries of the 6th District considerably. In the 1980s it consisted mostly of rural counties and stretched almost all the way from Fort Worth to Houston. After the 1991 and 1996 redistrictings, it stretched odd tentacles all around Fort Worth and Tarrant County. The 2001 redistricting smoothed out the boundaries and extended the district to the south. Politically, this is a heavily Republican part of the Metroplex; George W. Bush won 67% here in 2000.

The congressman from the 6th District is Joe Barton, a Republican first elected in 1984. Barton grew up in rural Ennis, in then rural Ellis County just south of Dallas. He graduated from Texas A&M and Purdue, worked as an engineer and was a White House Fellow. When Phil Gramm ran for the Senate in 1984, Barton ran for his 6th District House seat, and won the Republican runoff by only 10 votes and the general with 57%. At first, Barton had two great causes, one defunct, the other successful—in a way. The first was the superconductor Supercollider, an enormous scientific laboratory that was to have been built in Waxahachie, in Ellis County. In retrospect this was a Texas project, alive only so long as George H.W. Bush was president; despite Barton's efforts, the House voted 282–143 to zero it out in 1993. His other cause has been sponsorship of a constitutional amendment requiring a two-thirds vote to raise taxes. When the House took up the issue in early 1995, leadership whispered there was no way the tax limitation measure could win the needed 290 votes. In fact it got 253. Newt Gingrich promised to schedule the two-thirds amendment for a vote on subsequent April 15ths until it passed, but the number of votes has never exceeded the 1995 count. Barton claimed progress across the country, where many states have approved tax-limitation plans. But the budget surpluses starting in 1998 changed the conversation, and the amendment has been mostly forgotten.

In 1995 Barton became chairman of the Energy and Commerce Oversight and Investigation Subcommittee and conducted extensive hearings on food and drug laws. These resulted in enactment, with bipartisan support, of major FDA modernization, encouraging the agency to more quickly review innovative drugs and medical devices. In 1999 Barton became chairman of the Energy and Power Subcommittee. One of his bills was to restructure federal electricity regulation to adjust to the states' moves toward deregulation. But he clashed with full committee Chairman Thomas Bliley, and Bliley declined to take the issue up. Bliley retired from the House in 2000 and amid the fight for the chairmanship between Billy Tauzin and Mike Oxley, Barton maneuvered to expand his subcommittee's jurisdiction to include energy and air quality.

In 2001 he concentrated first on a bill to relieve California's electricity crisis; it did not include the price caps sought by Democrats and passed in subcommittee on a 17–13 party line vote in May. But in June Tauzin, now chairman of the full committee, said he would not bring it up. In July Barton got into a tiff with Democrats who objected to the Navy's paying for the electricity in the Vice President's House, which is on the grounds of the Naval Observatory; Barton replied that Congress, with its old electric power plant, wasted more energy than the vice president. Barton's subcommittee had jurisdiction over part of the Bush energy plan, which Barton generally supported. He surprised some by supporting higher fuel economy standards. "A lot of people have been surprised that I would support any increase. But I think when you have a responsibility, you also have accountability." His bill, passed in subcommittee in July 2001, required a cut of 5 billion gallons in light truck gas consumption by 2010. He held hearings on the Clean Air Act in 2002 and in July 2002 sponsored a bill embodying Bush's Clear Skies proposal, which was intended to reduce power plant emissions with market incentives.

All the while he pressed for action on electricity regulation. In December 2001, despite the implosion of Enron, heretofore the nation's largest electricity trader, he was pressing for subcommittee action and seeking agreement with Democrat Rick Boucher, though their positions continued to differ. In February 2002 the subcommittee held markup hearings but Barton suspended them, at Tauzin's request, to assess the Enron collapse more fully. In July, he circulated another draft, which differed considerably from the version that passed the Senate. Barton retreated from requiring utilities to join regional transmission organizations and sought to encourage them to do so, to produce an easy basis for exchanges of traded electricity. His version repealed the 1930s Public Utility Holding Company Act (PUHCA) and repealed also the 1978 Public Utility Regulatory Policies Act except to the extent it was maintained in the Senate bill. Interestingly, this was an issue on which a Republican like Barton was trying to increase federal regulatory power while

Democrats like John Dingell and Henry Waxman were trying to maintain state primacy. In September Tauzin took the issue before the full committee and, amid an onslaught of Democratic amendments, pushed it through. Later in September a House-Senate conference committee took it up but it went no farther. Tauzin reintroduced the bill in the 108th Congress; it passed the House again in April 2003. Electricity regulation is one of those Energy and Commerce issues that has tremendous ramifications for the national economy and affects so many interests that major legislation is seldom passed more often than every generation or two; it is the sort of issue which is carried over from Congress to Congress. So Barton has plenty of work ahead of him.

The House Republicans' three-term limit on chairmanships, if enforced and if Republicans maintain their majority, means that Barton will not chair this subcommittee in the next Congress; Tauzin has one more term to go as full committee chairman. Presumably Barton will find another subcommittee to chair. But he also has his eye on the full committee chairmanship. So does Mike Oxley, who got the chairmanship of an expanded Financial Services Committee in 2001 after his fight with Tauzin for the Energy and Commerce chairmanship. Oxley has greater seniority, but Barton has argued that his seniority lapsed when he left for Financial Services. This looks like a future headache for the Republican leadership.

Barton has been a headache to the leadership before. He got along well with Majority Leader Dick Armey but not his successor Tom DeLay. He has voted against compromise budgets backed by Republican leaders, opposed PNTR with China and sought unsuccessfully to require a three-fifths vote to break budget spending caps. Barton has also had some political disappointments. He ran for the Senate in 1993 after Lloyd Bentsen resigned to be Treasury secretary but finished third with just 14% of the vote in the May all-party primary. In 1994 he was outgoing Republican state Chairman Fred Meyer's choice to succeed him but Barton lost at the state convention. In September 2001, when Phil Gramm announced his retirement from the Senate, Barton considered running for his seat. But in early October, busy with electricity and energy legislation and amid talk that the Bush White House favored Attorney General John Cornyn, he announced he would not run.

Barton has been reelected easily in the 6th District.

SEVENTH DISTRICT

Rep. John Culberson (R)

Elected 2000, 2d term; b. Aug. 24, 1956, Houston; home, Houston; Southern Methodist U., B.A. 1981, S. TX Col. of Law, J.D. 1988; Methodist; married (Belinda).

Elected Office: TX House of Reps., 1986–00, Maj. Whip, 1999–00.

Professional Career: Jim Culberson Advertising, 1981–85; Practicing atty., 1988–00.

DC Office: 1728 LHOB 20515, 202-225-2571; Fax: 202-225-4381; Web site: www.house.gov/culberson.

District Office: Houston, 713-682-8828.

Committees: *Appropriations* (34th of 36 R): District of Columbia; The Legislative Branch; Transportation, Treasury, & Independent Agencies.

Group Ratings

	ADA	ACLU	AFS	LCV	CON	ITIC	NTU	COC	ACU	NTLC	CHC
2002	0	7	0	13	87	100	63	90	100	100	100
2001	0	—	0	0	—	—	74	96	100	—	—

National Journal Ratings

	2001 LIB —	2001 CONS	2002 LIB —	2002 CONS
Economic	7% —	89%	0% —	91%
Social	0% —	81%	0% —	75%
Foreign	4% —	87%	0% —	85%

Key Votes of the 107th Congress

1. Approve Bush Tax Cuts	Y	5. Faith-Based Charities	Y	9. Trade Promotion Authority	Y
2. Limit Patients' Bill of Rights	Y	6. Bar Gays in the Boy Scouts	Y	10. Bar Funds for Intl. Court	Y
3. Campaign Finance Reform	N	7. Ban Partial-Birth Abortion	Y	11. Authorize Force in Iraq	Y
4. Ban ANWR Development	N	8. Arm Commercial Pilots	Y	12. Deny Home. Sec. Dept. Union	Y

Election Results

2002 general	John Culberson (R)	96,795	(89%)	($472,911)
	Drew Parks (Lib)	11,674	(11%)	
2002 primary	John Culberson (R)	unopposed		
2000 general	John Culberson (R)	183,712	(74%)	($1,085,071)
	Jeff Sell (D)	60,694	(24%)	($13,122)
	Other	4,187	(2%)	

The People		**Race/Ethnic Origin**	**Ancestry**	
Area size:	194 sq. mi.	49.6% White	German: 8.4%	English: 7.1%
Urban population:	99.9%	11.3% Black	Irish: 5.9%	
Rural population:	0.1%	10.9% Asian	**2000 Presidential Vote**	
Pop. 2000:	651,620	0.2% Native Am.	Bush (R)	130,053 (68%)
Median income:	$48,561	0.0% Hawaiian	Gore (D)	61,498 (32%)
Poverty status:	10.6%	2.0% Two + races	**Cook Partisan Voting Index:** R +18	
Military veterans:	8.6%	0.2% Other		
		25.9% Hispanic Origin		

Occupation	Blue collar: 15.5%	White collar: 71.8%	Gray collar: 12.7%

When the senior George Bush moved from Midland in West Texas to Houston in 1960, he bought a house in Briarwood, in what was then the western edge of the fast-growing city, beyond Memorial Park and Loop 610, before the Galleria and high-rises went up around the intersection of Post Oak and Westheimer. Bush returned to Houston in 1993 and built a new house a mile from his old one, just west of lush Memorial Park. Bush's favorite shopping mall is nearby on Sage and San Felipe and his favorite barbecue joint a mile east on Memorial; his office is atop the Park Laureate building at 10000 Memorial. Today these landmarks are no longer at the edge of the vastly bigger and economically vibrant Houston metropolitan area, but near its epicenter, certainly its retail center and not far from its commercial center, though the industrial center of gravity remains far to the east, near the Ship Channel. Near the lavish Galleria, business leaders have made this area more than a shopping center. With extensive landscaping and art, they have sought to give it a unique and inviting image, and they have made improvements on the 610 to increase mobility for commuters and shoppers.

The 7th Congressional District is the lineal descendant of the district that elected George H.W. Bush its first member of the House in 1966, and the first Republican to represent Houston. It occupied far more territory then, but its boundaries have been pared back as the population of the west side of Houston has skyrocketed. Today more than 1.5 million people live in the area where 350,000 lived when Bush was first elected. The 7th District now starts just inside Loop 610 at Memorial Park and radiates westward on either side of the busy Katy Freeway in Harris County, beyond the Addicks-Satsuma Road and adjacent state parks. It remains firmly Republican, 68% for George W. Bush in 2000.

The congressman from the 7th District is John Culberson, a Republican first elected in 2000 and only the second man to hold the seat after Bush. Culberson grew up in Houston and graduated from Southern Methodist University, then worked for his father's advertising agency. He graduated from South Texas College of Law and worked as a civil defense attorney. In 1986, at 29, Culberson won a seat in the Texas House, where he served for 14 years. In 2000 Bill Archer, Bush's successor in the House, retired after serving the maximum of six years permitted under House Republican rules as chairman of the Ways and Means Committee. Naturally there was a seriously contested Republican primary in this safe Republican seat. The frontrunners among the eight candidates were Culberson and Peter Wareing, a Houston merchant banker and son-in-law of Texas oilman Jack Blanton. Culberson led Wareing in the first round 38%–27%. Wareing had a financial advantage: he spent nearly $4 million to Culberson's $650,000. But Culberson had an extensive grassroots campaign and won the runoff four weeks later 60%–40%. "I wouldn't change one Culberson volunteer for all the $4 million," he said. The general election was no contest.

Culberson calls himself a "Jeffersonian Republican" and is passionate about transferring power from the federal to local governments; he has had a solidly conservative voting record. He opposes racial quotas and preferences, gun control, and abortion (except in cases of rape, incest, or to save the life of the mother). In the Archer tradition, he says his goal is to junk the current tax system and replace it with a national sales tax. He quickly showed his political instincts when he became the freshman representative on the Republican Steering Committee, which makes House committee assignments. On the Transportation and Infrastructure Committee, he proposed a "trusted traveler" card to assist frequent flyers to circumvent some airport screening based on previous background checks.

Though 25% of the district was new to him after redistricting, Culberson had no major party opposition in 2002. He supported John Carter and criticized his former opponent Wareing (who ran against Carter) in the 2002 Republican primary for the adjacent 31st District. He sponsored a Houston fundraising event in April 2002 for four of his more vulnerable freshman colleagues. After the election he sought a seat on the Energy and Commerce Committee. He didn't get that, but he did get his neighbor Tom DeLay's seat on Appropriations.

EIGHTH DISTRICT

Rep. Kevin Brady (R)

Elected 1996, 4th term; b. Apr. 11, 1955, Vermillion, SD; home, The Woodlands, TX; U. of SD, B.S. 1990; Catholic; married (Cathy).

Elected Office: TX House of Reps., 1990–96.

Professional Career: Exec., Woodlands Chamber of Commerce, 1978–96.

DC Office: 428 CHOB 20515, 202-225-4901; Fax: 202-225-5524; Web site: www.house.gov/brady.

District Offices: Conroe, 936-441-5700; Houston, 281-895-8892.

Committees: *Ways & Means* (22d of 24 R): Select Revenue Measures; Social Security.

Group Ratings

	ADA	ACLU	AFS	LCV	CON	ITIC	NTU	COC	ACU	NTLC	CHC
2002	0	7	0	0	58	100	61	100	100	94	100
2001	0	—	0	0	—	—	69	100	96	—	—

National Journal Ratings

	2001 LIB	—	2001 CONS		2002 LIB	—	2002 CONS
Economic	0%	—	94%		0%	—	91%
Social	0%	—	81%		0%	—	75%
Foreign	33%	—	60%		24%	—	72%

Key Votes of the 107th Congress

1. Approve Bush Tax Cuts	Y	5. Faith-Based Charities	Y	9. Trade Promotion Authority	Y
2. Limit Patients' Bill of Rights	Y	6. Bar Gays in the Boy Scouts	Y	10. Bar Funds for Intl. Court	Y
3. Campaign Finance Reform	*	7. Ban Partial-Birth Abortion	Y	11. Authorize Force in Iraq	Y
4. Ban ANWR Development	N	8. Arm Commercial Pilots	Y	12. Deny Home. Sec. Dept. Union	Y

Election Results

2002 general	Kevin Brady (R)	140,575	(93%)	($222,082)
	Gil Guillory (Lib)	10,351	(7%)	
2002 primary	Kevin Brady (R)	unopposed		
2000 general	Kevin Brady (R)	233,848	(92%)	($370,246)
	Gil Guillory (Lib)	21,368	(8%)	

Prior Winning Percentages: 1998 (93%); 1996 (59%)

The People		Race/Ethnic Origin	Ancestry	
Area size:	1,193 sq. mi.	77.2% White	German: 12.8%	Irish: 9.0%
Urban population:	83.8%	5.2% Black	English: 8.6%	
Rural population:	16.2%	3.0% Asian	**2000 Presidential Vote**	
Pop. 2000:	651,619	0.3% Native Am.	Bush (R)..............187,243	(78%)
Median income:	$60,198	0.1% Hawaiian	Gore (D)...............53,843	(22%)
Poverty status:	6.7%	1.2% Two + races	**Cook Partisan Voting Index:** R +28	
Military veterans:	12.3%	0.1% Other		
		13.0% Hispanic Origin		

Occupation	Blue collar: 18.6%	White collar: 70.0%	Gray collar: 11.4%

When Houston Intercontinental Airport opened in 1969, it was located far north of the city, in vacant ground near the small town of Humble (named for a wandering fisherman, and later home of the oil company that was the predecessor of Exxon)—25 miles away from downtown Houston or from just about any other concentration of population. Today, the airport, known now as George Bush Intercontinental, is still a jaunt from downtown Houston. But it's in the middle of a zone of rapid metropolitan expansion and growth, of commercial office space and upscale residential subdivisions rising on land that once held roadside stands and barbecues and unpainted farm-houses with water pooling on low swampy fields. Greater Houston has spread far out into the countryside, past Loop 610 in the inner city, past the Sam Houston Tollway, past the now misla-beled Farm-Market Route 1960, out past The Woodlands, Conroe and Woodbranch Village in once rural Montgomery County.

The 8th Congressional District occupies most of this territory. The district includes Humble and the developments north of Bush Intercontinental Airport. It includes the suburban areas around Tomball and Jersey City in Harris County, which includes 60% of its population. It also includes all but the eastern edge of Montgomery County just to the north. In past decades the affluent, highly educated west side of Houston that made up the 7th District was the most Republican congressional district in the nation. But after the 1990s, in which cultural issues tended to determine party preference, the not quite so affluent and not quite as highly educated 8th District, where many people are still close to their country roots, became even more Republican, and in 2000 the 8th voted 78% for George W. Bush, a higher percentage than in any other congressional district in the nation.

The congressman from the 8th District is Kevin Brady, a Republican first elected in 1996. Brady grew up and went to college in South Dakota, moved to Montgomery County in 1978 and headed The Woodlands Chamber of Commerce for 18 years. In 1990 he was elected to the Texas House. When Congressman Jack Fields announced in 1995 he was retiring, Brady decided to run. His main opponent in the decisive Republican primary was Eugene Fontenot, a physician who wanted "to restore America to its Christian heritage." Brady was the choice of party regulars; Fontenot was endorsed by conservatives. Fontenot attacked Brady for being one of two Republicans to vote against the concealed weapons law. Brady had opposed most gun control bills, but not this one; when he was 12, his father was shot and killed while trying a case in a South Dakota courtroom. Brady and Fontenot ran against each other four separate times in that one year. In the March primary, Fontenot led Brady 36%–22% in a six-candidate field. In the April runoff Brady won 53%–47%. After the U.S. Supreme Court in June ordered a redrawing of 13 districts, there was an all-party primary in November, in which Brady led Fontenot 41%–39%. Finally, in the December runoff, turnout was sharply down. This evidently helped party regular Brady, who won 59%–41%.

In the House, Brady has compiled a conservative voting record, though a bit less so on foreign issues. He gained a reputation as more of a pragmatist than other Texas Republicans. With the murder of his father always a fresh memory, Brady has been an advocate of victims' rights and the death penalty. In January 2001, he took Bill Archer's seat on Ways and Means; he is an advocate of abolishing the IRS and moving toward a consumption tax. He strongly backed the Bush tax cuts, and helped to win House passage of a scaled-back version of Bush's plan to give tax breaks for contributions to faith-based groups. In 2002, he reached a compromise with advocates of campaign finance regulation and got enacted a modification of a recent tax code change to reduce paperwork requirements for tax-exempt state and local political party committees that raised less than $100,000 a year. In March 2002, he sponsored a proposal to establish at Texas A&M a national center for homeland security research. In December this became controversial when Dick Armey inserted it in the homeland security bill; the bill passed the Senate only after Trent Lott, the majority leader-designate, promised a vote on the provision in 2003. Brady said that critics were using the issue to take "cheap shots" at Republican leaders. In early 2003, he called for a U.S. free trade agreement with Central America.

Since his four contests in 1996, Brady has had no problem winning reelection. In 2003, Roy Blunt appointed Brady one of his deputy whips.

NINTH DISTRICT

Rep. Nick Lampson (D)

Elected 1996, 4th term; b. Feb. 14, 1945, Beaumont; home, Beaumont; Lamar U., B.S. 1968, M.Ed. 1971; Catholic; married (Susan).

Elected Office: Jefferson Cnty. Assessor, 1977–95.

Professional Career: Public schl. teacher, 1968–71; Instructor, Lamar U., 1971–76; Pres., Jefferson Cnty. Home Health Care, 1993–95.

DC Office: 405 CHOB 20515, 202-225-6565; Fax: 202-225-5547; Web site: www.house.gov/lampson.

District Offices: Beaumont, 409-838-0061; Galveston, 409-762-5877; Houston, 281-333-4884.

Committees: *Science* (6th of 22 D): Energy (RMM); Space & Aeronautics. *Transportation & Infrastructure* (20th of 34 D): Coast Guard & Maritime Transportation; Highways, Transit & Pipelines; Water Resources & Environment.

Group Ratings

	ADA	ACLU	AFS	LCV	CON	ITIC	NTU	COC	ACU	NTLC	CHC
2002	75	64	88	38	20	62	21	55	21	6	8
2001	85	—	100	57	—	—	14	48	21	—	—

National Journal Ratings

	2001 LIB —	2001 CONS		2002 LIB —	2002 CONS
Economic	66%	35%		63%	37%
Social	62%	38%		61%	38%
Foreign	70%	28%		68%	31%

Key Votes of the 107th Congress

1. Approve Bush Tax Cuts	N	5. Faith-Based Charities	N	9. Trade Promotion Authority	N
2. Limit Patients' Bill of Rights	N	6. Bar Gays in the Boy Scouts	Y	10. Bar Funds for Intl. Court	Y
3. Campaign Finance Reform	Y	7. Ban Partial-Birth Abortion	Y	11. Authorize Force in Iraq	Y
4. Ban ANWR Development	Y	8. Arm Commercial Pilots	Y	12. Deny Home. Sec. Dept. Union	N

Election Results

2002 general	Nick Lampson (D)	86,710	(59%)	($1,076,495)
	Paul Williams (R)	59,635	(40%)	($29,261)
	Other	1,613	(1%)	
2002 primary	Nick Lampson (D)	unopposed		
2000 general	Nick Lampson (D)	130,143	(59%)	($1,343,927)
	Paul Williams (R)	87,165	(40%)	($104,570)
	Other	2,508	(1%)	

Prior Winning Percentages: 1998 (64%); 1996 (53%)

The People		**Race/Ethnic Origin**	**Ancestry**	
Area size:	3,023 sq. mi.	60.1% White	German: 8.4%	Irish: 6.9%
Urban population:	89.6%	21.1% Black	USA: 6.2%	
Rural population:	10.4%	2.7% Asian	**2000 Presidential Vote**	
Pop. 2000:	651,619	0.3% Native Am.	Bush (R)................124,758 (55%)	
Median income:	$41,416	0.0% Hawaiian	Gore (D)...............100,778 (45%)	
Poverty status:	13.6%	1.1% Two+ races	**Cook Partisan Voting Index:** R + 6	
Military veterans:	13.3%	0.1% Other		
		14.4% Hispanic Origin		

Occupation   Blue collar: 24.0%   White collar: 60.3%   Gray collar: 15.6%

The spongy land of the Texas Gulf Coast, where the French explorer LaSalle and the Spanish colonizer Galvez dreamed of thriving settlements, remained mostly unsettled until well into the 19th century. The elements here are not gentle, as Galveston learned when a hurricane in 1900 destroyed this city-on-a-sand spit. The summer heat is ferocious and the rains torrential; few crops grow well here. But this is a land of oil. When oil was found at the Spindletop field near Beaumont in 1901, the area all around boomed. First oil exploration, then petroleum refining, then petrochemicals: The straight-edged metal of oil rigs and the intricate curving metalwork of refineries shine through the swampy landscape of southeast Texas. The rig workers and mechanical engineers they brought here have given a kind of permanent roughneck air to the region. In the early days of Spindletop, the town was so overrun by boomers who drained the local water supply that some doctors advised people to drink whiskey instead of water. The Women's Christian Temperance Union jumped in to create a counterforce.

The 9th Congressional District occupies much of this territory. About 40% of its people live in and around Beaumont and Port Arthur, still very much oil country, an active industrial area with some of the country's largest oil refineries and chemical plants and often-dense pollution. It is among the few places in Texas where labor unions have had any strength. Beaumont is the home of several trial lawyers who have become billionaires through asbestos and tobacco cases; Beaumont juries are known for their willingness to bring in large verdicts against big corporations. Nearly half live south of Houston—in Galveston, now restoring its grand historic buildings (and the unlikely site of a Dickensian Christmas celebration every year); the refinery town of Texas City, where more than 500 died after two freighters containing ammonium nitrate fertilizer exploded in 1947; and the Lyndon B. Johnson Space Center, where America's space missions are planned, brought here originally by then-Vice President Johnson and longtime Houston Congressman Albert Thomas. The rest live in Chambers County, between Houston and Beaumont, and in an irregularly shaped part of Harris County northeast of Houston.

The congressman from the 9th District is Nick Lampson, a Democrat first elected in 1996. Lampson grew up in Beaumont; he got his first job at age 12 when his father died. After graduating from Lamar University, he taught science in Beaumont schools, leading the first local Earth Day celebration in 1970, and then a real estate management course at Lamar; he also headed a home health care company. In 1977, at 32, he was elected Jefferson County tax assessor; he claimed to cut the cost of tax collections during 18 years on the job. In 1996 Lampson ran against Congressmen Steve Stockman, who won the seat by upsetting 42-year incumbent and Judiciary Committee Chairman Jack Brooks. Stockman stirred controversy by writing a letter to Attorney General Janet Reno expressing concern about raids allegedly planned on militias and for a garbled report about a threatening fax from a militia group his office received the day of the 1995 Oklahoma City bombing. Lampson won the five-candidate primary with 69%, but then the Supreme Court ruled 3 Texas districts unconstitutional, which marginally altered the boundaries of the 9th. The court required holding a whole new all-party election on November 5; the going then got nasty. Stockman said Lampson's home health care company had been accused of defrauding Medicare, while Lampson accused Stockman of failing to repay his college loans on time. Democrats cried foul when one of their losing primary candidates, Geraldine Sam, ran in the November 5 election (which became an open contest after the Supreme Court ruling); the Democratic vote was split, and Stockman led Lampson 46%–44%. Then Sam endorsed Stockman: more screams from Democrats. Labor unions worked Beaumont hard to get Lampson votes in the December runoff. Lampson won 53%–47%, winning more than his entire margin in the Beaumont area.

In the House, Lampson has a moderate voting record typical of Anglo Texas Democrats and is known for his low-key style. He promoted the Johnson Space Center and expanded space exploration from his seat on the Science Committee. Following the abduction and murder of a local 12-year-old girl, he became a national advocate for missing and exploited children and formed a Congressional Missing and Exploited Children's Caucus. Although a member of the moderate New Democrat Coalition, he has remained faithful to his labor allies. He voted against PNTR with China and trade promotion authority. He wants to lift the trade embargo on Cuba so that local rice farmers can have a new market. He organized local meetings in Port Arthur to coordinate steps with EPA to seek air-pollution reduction. Following the 2003 Columbia shuttle disaster, he said that the Houston delegation had been a weak advocate of the NASA program and that it must do more to promote the benefits of space travel.

Lampson has been reelected with relative ease. In 2000 and 2002, he was opposed by Republican Paul Williams, an oil and gas executive who was a fill-in quarterback during the 1987 National Football League strike. Each time, Lampson won 59%–40%. If a new congressional map is passed for the 2004 election, Lampson's seat could be at risk; under one May 2003 proposal, his residence was moved to a more rural district and the new 9th District was made more attractive for an African-American primary challenger.

TENTH DISTRICT

Rep. Lloyd Doggett (D)

Elected 1994, 5th term; b. Oct. 6, 1946, Austin; home, Austin; U. of TX, B.B.A. 1967, J.D. 1970; Methodist; married (Libby).

Elected Office: TX Senate, 1973–85; TX Supreme Ct. Justice, 1989–94.

Professional Career: Practicing atty., 1970–89; Adjunct Prof., U. of TX Law Schl., 1989–94.

DC Office: 201 CHOB 20515, 202-225-4865; Fax: 202-225-3073; Web site: www.house.gov/doggett.

District Office: Austin, 512-916-5921.

Committees: *Ways & Means* (14th of 17 D): Health; Select Revenue Measures.

Group Ratings

	ADA	ACLU	AFS	LCV	CON	ITIC	NTU	COC	ACU	NTLC	CHC
2002	100	87	100	100	94	50	32	30	4	19	0
2001	85	—	100	93	—	—	21	35	4	—	—

National Journal Ratings

	2001 LIB	—	2001 CONS		2002 LIB	—	2002 CONS
Economic	76%	—	25%		88%	—	10%
Social	90%	—	0%		72%	—	27%
Foreign	91%	—	8%		94%	—	0%

Key Votes of the 107th Congress

1. Approve Bush Tax Cuts	*	5. Faith-Based Charities	N	9. Trade Promotion Authority	N
2. Limit Patients' Bill of Rights	N	6. Bar Gays in the Boy Scouts	N	10. Bar Funds for Intl. Court	N
3. Campaign Finance Reform	Y	7. Ban Partial-Birth Abortion	N	11. Authorize Force in Iraq	N
4. Ban ANWR Development	Y	8. Arm Commercial Pilots	N	12. Deny Home. Sec. Dept. Union	N

Election Results

2002 general	Lloyd Doggett (D)	114,428	(84%)	($190,484)
	Michele Messina (Lib)	21,196	(16%)	
2002 primary	Lloyd Doggett (D)	33,083	(90%)	
	Jennifer Gale (D)	3,554	(10%)	
2000 general	Lloyd Doggett (D)	203,628	(85%)	($232,268)
	Michael Davis (Lib)	37,203	(15%)	

Prior Winning Percentages: 1998 (85%); 1996 (56%); 1994 (56%)

The People		Race/Ethnic Origin	Ancestry	
Area size:	555 sq. mi.	49.7% White	German: 10.1%	Irish: 6.6%
Urban population:	95.6%	10.9% Black	English: 6.5%	
Rural population:	4.4%	4.3% Asian	**2000 Presidential Vote**	
Pop. 2000:	651,619	0.3% Native Am.	Gore (D)	101,534 (53%)
Median income:	$41,374	0.0% Hawaiian	Bush (R)	89,738 (47%)
Poverty status:	14.8%	1.6% Two+ races	**Cook Partisan Voting Index:** D + 3	
Military veterans:	9.5%	0.2% Other		
		33.0% Hispanic Origin		

Occupation	Blue collar: 19.6%	White collar: 66.2%	Gray collar: 14.2%

Austin, the capital of the second largest state in the U.S. and site of its largest Capitol building, is also the southernmost capital in the continental 48 states. It is one of many capitals with a first-rate university, but one of the few (Nashville is the other) with its own musical tradition. Not long ago, Austin seemed as laid-back and countrified. There had never been much commerce here, and for much of the year the Capitol basked in a sun that seemed to ban gainful employment. Its skies were untainted with the smoke of industry, its ground unpocked with pumping oil rigs, its downtown streets lined not with business offices but with buildings holding a few lobbyists and the antique Driskill Hotel. Its biggest industry was the University of Texas—with 50,000 students and endowed with thousands of west Texas acres that turned out to sit on top of oil. The university has long had a distinguished faculty and some of the world's great scholarly collections; it houses the LBJ Presidential Library with its 35 million documents, has spawned a community of liberal intellectuals since the 1940s and helped spark Austin's high-tech boom in the 1980s and 1990s.

Half a century ago, in Lyndon Johnson's time, Austin had a metropolitan population of 132,000. The compact Austin that was Johnson's headquarters in 1948 when the Duval County returns came in and gave him the 87-vote victory that made his national career is a very different Austin from the town that waited up in the rain, alternatively enthused and downcast, hoping to celebrate the election of George W. Bush in 2000. Today's high-tech Austin has grown out miles from the comfortable precincts of the old downtown and university, up and down the vast sloping hills to the west and north and south, bringing together subdivisions on dozens of square miles that were empty land in 1980, not to speak of 1948. Today's Austin is no longer just a creation of the public sector, of state government and the University, though they are still prominent; it is also the home of Dell Computer, of the fourth largest number of high-tech employees in the nation. In the 1990s, the Austin metro area had some of the nation's fastest population growth, up 48% to 1,250,000, and 60% job growth in the 1990s. Austin has a new airport, the converted Bergstrom Air Force Base, handsome and conveniently located—one of the few closed military bases put to this obvious use. One of America's most charming and idiosyncratic small cities has become one of America's fastest-growing and creative metropolitan areas.

Growth has also brought political change. For many years Austin was the central focus of Texas's hardy but almost always outnumbered liberals, based in the university, state government and *The Texas Observer*. Confident that the future was theirs, that Texas would follow America into the New Deal and the welfare state, they mocked the conservative business lobbyists who called the shots when the "lege" was in session and celebrated Texas zaniness with the verve of a Sixth Street band. But history—or at least Austin—has not moved in the direction Texas liberals expected. As the Austin area has grown, it has become more conservative; as its private sector has led the local economy, the techies who settled in the Silicon Hills going from Austin's Travis County to once-rural Williamson County have tended to vote Republican. The city core and the University area are still Democratic, Texas liberals still are potent in the media, and 31% of the population is Latino—with 10% black and 5% Asian. But this is a state capital, with an Hispanic mayor, in which George W. Bush could feel more at home than he would have 30 years before (when his application for admission was rejected by the UT Law School). Bush lost Austin and Travis County 59%–41% when he first ran for governor in 1994, but he carried Travis 60%–38% in 1998 for re-election and 47%–42% in 2000 for president (with 10% for Ralph Nader).

The 10th Congressional District, which once spread over the Hill Country to the west and south, is now entirely contained within Travis County. It contains the city of Austin east of a line that runs, at various points, along the Capital of Texas ring road and the MoPac Freeway. It includes downtown, the Capitol, the University area and most of the Austin that was settled before the 1980s. The district also includes eastern Travis County. The 10th District takes in all the more Democratic parts of metro Austin; the new Republican areas of western Travis County and Williamson County are in the heavily Republican 21st and 31st Districts. Even so, the 10th is not as heavily Democratic as it once was; it cast 47% of its votes for George W. Bush in 2000. This is the descendant of the district represented in the House by Lyndon Johnson from 1937 until he was elected to the Senate in 1948. Johnson was succeeded by his friend Homer Thornberry, who held the seat until he became a federal judge in December 1963; another LBJ backer, Jake Pickle, was elected that month and served until he retired in 1994—57 years of representation by three political allies, all born between 1908 and 1913.

The congressman from the 10th District is Lloyd Doggett, first elected in 1994. He is a liberal Democrat with a dream resume and an up-and-down political career. Doggett grew up in Austin, finished first in his class and was president of UT's student body in 1967. In 1972, he was elected to the state Senate at 26, and as part of a surprisingly large liberal bloc in the 1970s, he pushed laws against job discrimination and cop-killer bullets and for generic drugs; he has always been a close ally of trial lawyers, the one strong institutional force supporting liberal Democrats in Texas. In the "lege," he was one of the "killer bees" who hid out to prevent a quorum on changing the rules in the Democratic primary and filibustered—wearing sneakers—against what he called anti-consumer bills. In 1984 he ran for the U.S. Senate, narrowly edging two congressmen to win the Democratic nomination. Then, despite the campaign help of James Carville and Paul Begala, Doggett lost the general 59%–41% to party-switching Congressman Phil Gramm, who sharply attacked him for holding a fundraiser at a San Antonio gay strip bar. Doggett came back and, with strong support from trial lawyers, was elected to the Texas Supreme Court in 1988. When Pickle retired, Doggett left the bench and ran for Congress. He won the Democratic primary with token opposition and in the general won by the solid, but not quite overwhelming, margin of 56%–40%.

In the House, Doggett's voting record has placed him among the most liberal Texans. He was a vocal critic of Newt Gingrich, and a close ally of Minority Whip David Bonior and Nancy Pelosi, and backed her against Texan Martin Frost in her race for minority leader. With Judy Biggert of Illinois, he co-chairs the Information Technology Working Group, which he helped to form. In 1999, he outmaneuvered other aspirants to become the first Texas Democrat assigned to the Ways and Means Committee since Pickle retired. Along with other Ways and Means Democrats, he sought to restrict the use of offshore tax havens. He voted with Bill Clinton on most key votes, and has voted against most of George W. Bush's major proposals. Three days after September 11, his parliamentary objections stymied late-night action on a $15 billion airline aid bill and forced more thorough debate. He was a leader in opposing the resolution authorizing the use of force in Iraq; even Doggett was surprised that 126 House Democrats voted to oppose it. Still, he is not everyone's cup of tea. Rich Oppel, editor of *The Austin American-Statesman*, said that while he often agrees with Doggett, he has gained "a reputation for rhetoric with the subtlety of a stevedore's punch."

Doggett was re-elected 56%–41% in 1996 over Teresa Doggett (no relation) and has won easily since. In 2002, he had no Republican opponent. The 2002 redistricting made the district more Democratic by removing west Austin neighborhoods and western Travis County. Party leaders have privately criticized him as one of several House Democrats sitting on a huge campaign account (more than $2 million) that could have been profitably shared with other candidates; perhaps Doggett is keeping his options open to run for statewide office. But if a new congressional map is passed for the 2004 election, Doggett may need every penny to win reelection. Under a May 2003 proposal, western Harris County would be added to Doggett's district and the seat would become considerably more Republican.

ELEVENTH DISTRICT

Rep. Chet Edwards (D)

Elected 1990, 7th term; b. Nov. 24, 1951, Corpus Christi; home, Washington D.C.; TX A&M U., B.A. 1974, Harvard U., M.B.A. 1981; Methodist; married (Lea Ann).

Elected Office: TX Senate, 1982–90.

Professional Career: Legis. & Dist. Dir., U.S. Rep. Olin Teague, 1975–77; Marketing Rep., Trammell Crow Co., 1981–85; Pres., Edwards Communications, 1985–90.

DC Office: 2459 RHOB 20515, 202-225-6105; Fax: 202-225-0350; Web site: www.house.gov/edwards.

District Offices: Belton, 254-933-2904; Georgetown, 512-864-3192; Waco, 254-752-9600.

Committees: *Appropriations* (16th of 29 D): Energy & Water Development; Military Construction (RMM). *Budget* (9th of 19 D).

Group Ratings

	ADA	ACLU	AFS	LCV	CON	ITIC	NTU	COC	ACU	NTLC	CHC
2002	75	67	78	38	43	50	21	65	36	8	25
2001	80	—	100	43	—	—	15	57	40	—	—

National Journal Ratings

	2001 LIB — 2001 CONS		2002 LIB — 2002 CONS	
Economic	63%	— 37%	56%	— 43%
Social	60%	— 40%	61%	— 39%
Foreign	61%	— 36%	58%	— 41%

Key Votes of the 107th Congress

1. Approve Bush Tax Cuts	N	5. Faith-Based Charities	N	9. Trade Promotion Authority	N
2. Limit Patients' Bill of Rights	N	6. Bar Gays in the Boy Scouts	Y	10. Bar Funds for Intl. Court	Y
3. Campaign Finance Reform	Y	7. Ban Partial-Birth Abortion	N	11. Authorize Force in Iraq	Y
4. Ban ANWR Development	N	8. Arm Commercial Pilots	Y	12. Deny Home. Sec. Dept. Union	N

Election Results

2002 general	Chet Edwards (D)	74,678	(52%)	($1,566,761)
	Ramsey Farley (R)	68,236	(47%)	($614,493)
	Other	1,943	(1%)	
2002 primary	Chet Edwards (D)	unopposed		
2000 general	Chet Edwards (D)	105,782	(55%)	($1,281,637)
	Ramsey Farley (R)	85,546	(44%)	($558,727)
	Other	1,590	(1%)	

Prior Winning Percentages: 1998 (82%); 1996 (57%); 1994 (59%); 1992 (67%); 1990 (53%)

The People		Race/Ethnic Origin	Ancestry	
Area size:	9,074 sq. mi.	64.2% White	German: 11.4%	Irish: 7.1%
Urban population:	72.6%	15.4% Black	USA: 7.1%	
Rural population:	27.4%	1.5% Asian	**2000 Presidential Vote**	
Pop. 2000:	651,620	0.4% Native Am.	Bush (R)..............129,701	(67%)
Median income:	$36,378	0.2% Hawaiian	Gore (D)..............62,465	(33%)
Poverty status:	13.6%	1.7% Two+ races	**Cook Partisan Voting Index:** R +18	
Military veterans:	17.0%	0.1% Other		
		16.4% Hispanic Origin		

Occupation   Blue collar: 25.6%   White collar: 57.1%   Gray collar: 17.3%

Waco, at the intersection of lines from Dallas to Austin and Houston to Amarillo, is arguably the geographic and cultural heart of Texas. The city was named after Indians the Mexicans called Huecos; by the late 19th century it was one of the largest cotton markets in the world, a rip-roaring town with legalized prostitution and with a graceful ox-cart-wide suspension bridge across the Brazos which, when it opened in 1870, was the longest single-span suspension bridge in the United States and the second longest in the world. Waco was the home of atheist William Cowper Brann, author and publisher of *The Iconoclast* magazine, who was shot down in the streets but managed to kill his attacker. Waco is famous now as the site of the tragedy of February 1993, when agents of the Bureau of Alcohol, Tobacco and Firearms moved in on David Koresh's Branch Davidian compound, Ranch Apocalypse, near Waco, and Koresh and his followers were burned to death. But Waco should be famous for other things as well. It is the home of Baylor University, the oldest college in Texas and the largest Baptist university in the world; its Armstrong Browning Library houses the papers of Robert and Elizabeth Barrett Browning. It is the largest city near Fort Hood, the largest U.S. military base in the world, which occupies much of next-door Bell and Coryell Counties and is home to 43,000 Army soldiers. Even closer, in Waco's McLennan County, are the tiny town of Crawford, with its Rainey Creek, which traverses the George W. Bush's Prairie Chapel Ranch. Waco is only a little more than an hour away from the gallerias of the Dallas-Fort Worth Metroplex, but it is still in touch with Texas's rural roots, with the days when cotton was the basis of Texas's economy.

The 11th Congressional District is centered on Waco and the Fort Hood area. It includes all of nine counties, most of them still quite rural, all of them ancestrally Democratic, and part of one other, Williamson County north of Austin, including the county seat of Georgetown and the heavily Republican retirement community in nearby Sun City Texas. But the Democratic tradition here has slowly waned. This area voted for Democrat Hubert Humphrey in 1968, when most of the rural South went for George Wallace and Richard Nixon; it voted Democratic when Texas first elected a Republican governor in 1978 and voted for Democrat Ann Richards, a Waco native, in 1990. But in 1994 it voted for George W. Bush, and in 2000 Bush won 67% of the votes in this district. Williamson County, added in the 2002 redistricting, is even more Republican; this is a fast-growing area, prospering from Austin's booming economy with little affection for the liberal Democrats of the past.

The congressman from the 11th District is Chet Edwards, a Democrat elected in 1990, and only the third congressman from this district since 1936. Edwards is one of those highly skilled and motivated Democrats who has made politics his life—and who kept the Texas legislature and the U.S. House Democratic for so many years. He grew up in Corpus Christi, was a junior golf champion and graduated from Texas A&M, where he studied economics under Phil Gramm, then a conservative Democrat. From there, Edwards went to work as district director for 6th District Congressman Olin Teague. In 1978, Teague retired and Edwards, at 27, ran for the seat. In the Democratic primary, Edwards wound up in third place, just 115 votes behind Gramm, who went on to win the seat; if Edwards had won just 116 more votes, a lot of Texas and national political history would be different. Edwards went off to Harvard to get an M.B.A., returned and moved to Duncanville in southwest Dallas County, and at age 31 ran for the state Senate in 1982 and won.

In 1990 when 11th District Democrat Marvin Leath retired, Edwards moved his residence to Waco, and ran for the 11th District seat unopposed in the Democratic primary. With a promise of an Armed Services Committee slot from Speaker Thomas Foley and strong support from Leath, Edwards won a 53%–47% victory. In the House, Edwards worked for Fort Hood and eventually won a seat on Appropriations, where he claims credit for nearly a quarter-billion dollars in construction there; the 2001 appropriation included $99 million for a new barracks, command and control center, training range and two vehicle maintenance outfits. He is co-chairman of the Army Caucus and opposes proposals to reduce the force structure of the Army.

When Democrats were in the majority Edwards took conservative stands on some but by no means all issues. He worked successfully to stop the designation of 33 Texas counties as a critical habitat for the allegedly endangered golden-cheeked warbler and supported the Private Property Owners Bill of Rights. He voted against the Brady bill but for the assault weapons ban and the 1994 crime bill.

After Democrats lost their majority in 1994, Minority Leader Dick Gephardt asked Edwards to serve as one of four chief deputy whips. Edwards accepted, but promptly voted for the Contract with America's balanced budget amendment and line-item veto. In 1998 and 1999 he led opposition to the school-prayer constitutional amendment and opposed a resolution for a national day of prayer and fasting after the Columbine shootings in 1999. Later that year, he sponsored an amendment to ban government funds for "pervasively sectarian" groups. He has been critical of George W. Bush's proposals to fund services provided by faith-based organizations. But he supported the Fort Hood commander's granting of a request to have a Wiccan religious service on the base; he also opposed the partial-birth abortion ban.

On several measures, he has worked with the Democratic leadership, supporting a waiting period for sales at gun shows and opposing repeal of the estate tax; he opposed the leadership and backed the Clinton administration in voting for PNTR with China. He has worked on Appropriations for funding of the Nunn-Lugar program to secure nuclear weapons in Russia. He voted against the appropriations conference report on this issue in November 2001 and in 2002 was able to get $226 million more. He has not been shy about using his seat on Appropriations to fund local projects; when an allocation of $1.9 million for an area groundwater study was no longer needed, he doled the funds out elsewhere—$400,000 for a flood control study of the Colorado River, $500,000 to renovate a Lake Belton park and $1 million for Lake Georgetown in Williamson County just after it had been added to the district. Edwards has won reelection in an increasingly Republican district by narrowing margins. In 1998, the expected Republican candidate decided at the last minute not to run, and Edwards had a free ride. In 2000, against retired Texaco executive Ramsey Farley, who raised over $500,000 and attacked him on education, taxes and abortion, he won 55%–44%. In 2002 Farley ran again and easily won the Republican primary. The NRCC began running ads against him in July, saying that he had the voting record of a northeastern liberal. Edwards argued that he supported Bush on terrorism, education, welfare, energy and the Iraq war resolution. Edwards gleefully pointed out that Farley had said he "very vehemently" opposed Bush's education bill. But for all his skills, Edwards was sorely pressed. He spent $1.6 million to Farley's $614,000. Yet he won by only a 52%–47% margin—his closest ever in a general election. He won 56%–43% in Waco's McLennan County and only 51%–48% in Bell County, the second largest in the district, which contains part of Fort Hood. He lost the district's portion of Williamson County 63%–35% and also lost, more narrowly, in rural San Saba and Lampasas Counties, which he had represented for 10 years.

In 2003 House Majority Leader Tom DeLay was pressing the now Republican legislature to redistrict the state once again; it would be easy to draw a district that would put Edwards at a greater disadvantage. Even if that doesn't happen, he could easily be seriously challenged again in 2004. He points out that he has two more years in which to become known in Williamson County and to shower local projects on the area. In January 2003 he resigned his position as chief deputy whip to spend more time on district affairs. But in 2004 George W. Bush will be on the ballot, and this district is likely to give Bush a majority even greater than the 67% he won in 2000. If a new district is drawn for the 2004 election, Edwards's standing will be even more tenuous. As early as April 2003, one Republican candidate confirmed that she planned to challenge Edwards: former Waco school board president Dot Snyder.

TWELFTH DISTRICT

Rep. Kay Granger (R)

Elected 1996, 4th term; b. Jan. 18, 1943, Greenville; home, Ft. Worth; TX Wesleyan U., B.S. 1965; Methodist; divorced.

Elected Office: Ft. Worth City Cncl., 1989–91; Ft. Worth Mayor, 1991–96.

Professional Career: Teacher, 1965–78; Life Insurance Agent, 1978–85; Chmn., Ft. Worth Zoning Comm., 1981–88; Founder & Pres., Kay Granger Insurance Co., Inc., 1985–present.

DC Office: 435 CHOB 20515, 202-225-5071; Fax: 202-225-5683; Web site: www.house.gov/granger.

District Office: Ft. Worth, 817-338-0909.

Committees: *Appropriations* (24th of 36 R): Homeland Security; Labor, HHS & Education; Military Construction. *Select Committee on Homeland Security* (25th of 27 R): Cybersecurity, Science and Research & Development; Emergency Preparedness & Response; Infrastructure & Border Security (Vice Chmn.).

Group Ratings

	ADA	ACLU	AFS	LCV	CON	ITIC	NTU	COC	ACU	NTLC	CHC
2002	0	14	0	0	14	88	53	95	96	78	92
2001	0	—	0	7	—	—	63	100	80	—	—

National Journal Ratings

	2001 LIB	—	2001 CONS		2002 LIB	—	2002 CONS
Economic	7%	—	89%		9%	—	87%
Social	43%	—	55%		25%	—	71%
Foreign	4%	—	87%		0%	—	85%

Key Votes of the 107th Congress

1. Approve Bush Tax Cuts	Y	5. Faith-Based Charities	Y	9. Trade Promotion Authority	Y
2. Limit Patients' Bill of Rights	Y	6. Bar Gays in the Boy Scouts	Y	10. Bar Funds for Intl. Court	Y
3. Campaign Finance Reform	N	7. Ban Partial-Birth Abortion	Y	11. Authorize Force in Iraq	Y
4. Ban ANWR Development	N	8. Arm Commercial Pilots	Y	12. Deny Home. Sec. Dept. Union	Y

Election Results

2002 general	Kay Granger (R)	121,208	(92%)	($989,881)
	Edward Hanson (Lib)	10,723	(8%)	
2002 primary	Kay Granger (R)	20,769	(87%)	
	Philip Hillery (R)	3,067	(13%)	
2000 general	Kay Granger (R)	117,739	(63%)	($671,838)
	Mark Greene (D)	67,612	(36%)	($83,280)
	Other	2,565	(1%)	

Prior Winning Percentages: 1998 (62%); 1996 (58%)

The People		Race/Ethnic Origin	Ancestry	
Area size:	1,363 sq. mi.	71.4% White	German: 9.4%	USA: 9.0%
Urban population:	88.7%	4.5% Black	Irish: 8.1%	
Rural population:	11.3%	2.3% Asian	**2000 Presidential Vote**	
Pop. 2000:	651,619	0.5% Native Am.	Bush (R) 141,032	(67%)
Median income:	$44,624	0.1% Hawaiian	Gore (D) 70,751	(33%)
Poverty status:	9.8%	1.3% Two+ races	**Cook Partisan Voting Index:** R +17	
Military veterans:	13.4%	0.1% Other		
		19.9% Hispanic Origin		
Occupation	Blue collar: 25.5%	White collar: 61.2%	Gray collar: 13.3%	

Fort Worth, Texas, has a fair claim to being the quintessential mid-American city: halfway across the continent, just west of the Balcones Escarpment that divides the dry treeless grazing lands of West Texas from the humid green croplands of East Texas. It is Southern in heritage and Northern in its advanced post-industrial economy. It has the nation's longest row of Western wear shops and one of the nation's richest families, the Basses, whose steel-sheen skyscrapers, outlined at night by lights, dominate the skyline. This is where the West begins, Fort Worth boosters say, adding, as Will Rogers said, that Dallas is "where the East peters out."

But this is not a primitive West. Fort Worth has a high-tech economy, though one hard hit by defense cuts. The big Lockheed Martin (formerly General Dynamics) plant has produced the B-24, B-36, B-52, F-111 and F-16 bombers and fighters; since Lockheed Martin won the contract for the Joint Strike Fighter in October 2002, it is likely to stay in production well beyond 2010. Next door is Carswell Air Force Base, the home of B-52s for years, slated for closure in 1993 but turned into a Joint Reserve Base. The assembly lines at Bell Helicopter Textron's nearby plant were kept going only when the Texas delegation and others overruled the cancellation of the accident-prone V-22 Osprey. Fort Worth also has some of the nation's premier small museums, the Amon Carter Museum of Western Art designed by Philip Johnson, the Kimbell Museum designed by Louis Kahn and the new Museum of Modern Art opened in December 2002. The downtown Bass Performance Hall has been acclaimed for its superb architectural design. Other cities have their claims, but the visitor from abroad who wants to see what is quintessentially American would be well advised to fly to Dallas/Forth Worth International Airport and head west.

The 12th Congressional District includes half of Fort Worth and some of suburban Tarrant County, plus all of Parker County to the west. It includes the northern and western neighborhoods of the city and the affluent southwest quarter beyond Texas Christian University; the heavily black areas of the city are in the neighboring 24th District. It includes most of the modest northeast suburbs—Haltom City, Richland Hills and North Richland Hills, Watauga, Keller, Hurst. Parker County to the west was once rural, windwept open land around the courthouse town of Weatherford; now it is sprouting new subdivisions and growing rapidly. The historical heritage here is Democratic: Fort Worth stayed Democratic in the 1950s when Dallas went Republican, and Speaker Jim Wright grew up in Weatherford and was first elected to the House in 1954. But in the 1980s and 1990s Fort Worth and Tarrant County have trended Republican. Their heavily Democratic areas are in other districts, and the 12th, represented by the Democratic Speaker of the House as recently as 1989, is now solidly Republican—67% for George W. Bush in 2000.

The congresswoman from the 12th District is Kay Granger, a Republican elected in 1996. Granger grew up in Fort Worth, graduated from Texas Wesleyan College, worked as a teacher in North Richland Hills, raised three children and started her own insurance agency. In 1989 she was elected to the Fort Worth Council, and two years later was elected as the nonpartisan mayor. She became very popular for her "Code: Blue" anti-crime initiatives and encouragement of citizen patrols, and violent crime dropped 49%. In 1995 Congressman Pete Geren, a conservative Democrat elected to replace Wright in 1989, announced his retirement; both Republican and Democratic leaders tried to recruit Granger. She said she was a Republican and ran in the Republican primary. Attacked as a liberal, partly for her pro-choice stand on abortion, she won 69% in a three-candidate race. Granger's Democratic opponent was Hugh Parmer, a former Fort Worth mayor and the Democratic nominee against Senator Phil Gramm in 1990. That turned out to be a liability: it was revealed that he had large unpaid debts left over from that campaign. Parmer attacked Republican Medicare plans and Newt Gingrich. Granger called for a balanced budget and tax cuts for business and ran on her record as mayor. Granger won 58%–41%, a stunning victory in Jim Wright's old district.

In the House, Granger's voting record has tended to be moderate on cultural issues and more conservative on economics. She became a favorite of Republican leaders, winning enactment of tax-free savings accounts for higher education expenses and serving as the only freshman on Dennis Hastert's health care task force. She split with most Republicans in applauding the FDA's approval of the RU-486 abortion pill. One setback was the Republican leadership's support of legislation that diluted the Wright Amendment's protection of Dallas/Fort Worth International Airport from competition by Dallas's Love Field; after that, Granger worked to create a local regional airport authority to encourage cooperation between the DFW and Love. Granger had served on the DFW board, and in summer 2002 it became apparent to her that DFW and other big airports were not going to be able to meet the November 19 deadline for having federal security officers in place and the December 31 deadline for X-ray screening of all baggage. In July 2002 she sponsored a bill to give flexibility to the 40 largest airports in meeting the deadlines. A compromise version made its way into the homeland security bill in November 2002, covering all airports and requiring TSA monitoring and reports.

In 1999 Granger became the third Texas Republican on the Appropriations Committee, where her seat on the Military Construction Subcommittee allows her to keep a close eye on local Pentagon spending. She and the 24th District's Martin Frost have kept a vigilant eye open on the F-16, the F-22, the V-22 and the Joint Strike Fighter. In September 2002 she proposed a $256 million program to fight obesity—with money for the Center for Disease Control and Prevention, health care professionals' training, programs at schools and hospitals and a $1 million study of diets. But she has not supported every proposal that has come her way. When Fort Worth Mayor Kenneth Barr, eager to keep the Texas Eagle running through Fort Worth, lobbied for $1.2 billion funding of Amtrak in October 2002, she stuck with the House committee's choice of $762 million. "I would love to see passenger rail. They can't continue to exist on having those trips where the taxpayer pays the first $258 of every trip they take, which is what happens in Fort Worth, and then only 21% of the time do the trains even run on time." After September 11, Granger came up with the idea of auctioning off for eBay a flag that has flown over the Capitol with matting signed by every member of the 107th Congress to raise money for victims of the attacks. In mid-November the bids had only gone to $17,000, much less than she expected, so she went on the *Today* show, and the flag and matting sold for $80,100.

Granger was reelected in 1998 and 2000 by wide margins. Redistricting treated her kindly. Though one-third of the district was new to her, the Bush 2000 percentage in the 12th District rose from 59% to 67%. In 2002 no Democrat bothered to run in Jim Wright's old district, and Granger was reelected with 92% of the vote.

THIRTEENTH DISTRICT

Rep. Mac Thornberry (R)

Elected 1994, 5th term; b. July 15, 1958, Clarendon; home, Clarendon; TX Tech. U., B.A. 1980, U. of TX Law Schl., J.D. 1983; Presbyterian; married (Sally).

Professional Career: Legis. Cnsl., U.S. Rep. Tom Loeffler, 1983–85; Chief of Staff, U.S. Rep. Larry Combest, 1985–88; Dpty. Asst. Secy. of State for Legis. Affairs, 1988–89; Practicing atty., 1989–94; Rancher 1989–94.

DC Office: 2457 RHOB 20515, 202-225-3706; Fax: 202-225-3486; Web site: www.house.gov/thornberry.

District Offices: Amarillo, 806-371-8844; Wichita Falls, 940-692-1700.

Committees: *Armed Services* (9th of 33 R): Strategic Forces; Terrorism, Unconventional Threats & Capabilities. *Budget* (4th of 24 R). *Select Committee on Homeland Security* (23d of 27 R): Cybersecurity, Science and Research & Development (Chmn.); Emergency Preparedness & Response; Intelligence & Counterterrorism.

Group Ratings

	ADA	ACLU	AFS	LCV	CON	ITIC	NTU	COC	ACU	NTLC	CHC
2002	0	7	0	0	25	100	58	95	92	94	100
2001	0	—	0	0	—	—	63	100	96	—	—

National Journal Ratings

	2001 LIB	—	2001 CONS		2002 LIB	—	2002 CONS
Economic	7%	—	89%		0%	—	91%
Social	20%	—	69%		0%	—	75%
Foreign	4%	—	87%		44%	—	55%

Key Votes of the 107th Congress

1. Approve Bush Tax Cuts	Y	5. Faith-Based Charities	Y	9. Trade Promotion Authority	Y
2. Limit Patients' Bill of Rights	Y	6. Bar Gays in the Boy Scouts	Y	10. Bar Funds for Intl. Court	Y
3. Campaign Finance Reform	N	7. Ban Partial-Birth Abortion	Y	11. Authorize Force in Iraq	Y
4. Ban ANWR Development	N	8. Arm Commercial Pilots	Y	12. Deny Home. Sec. Dept. Union	Y

Election Results

2002 general	Mac Thornberry (R)	119,401	(79%)	($441,738)
	Zane Reese (D)	31,218	(21%)	
2002 primary	Mac Thornberry (R)	unopposed		
2000 general	Mac Thornberry (R)	117,995	(68%)	($741,039)
	Curtis Clinesmith (D)	54,343	(31%)	($208,541)
	Other	2,137	(1%)	

Prior Winning Percentages: 1998 (68%); 1996 (67%); 1994 (55%)

The People		Race/Ethnic Origin	Ancestry	
Area size:	39,621 sq. mi.	70.0% White	USA: 10.2%	German: 9.0%
Urban population:	73.2%	5.6% Black	Irish: 7.3%	
Rural population:	26.8%	1.1% Asian	**2000 Presidential Vote**	
Pop. 2000:	651,619	0.6% Native Am.	Bush (R)	156,330 (75%)
Median income:	$33,361	0.0% Hawaiian	Gore (D)	53,146 (25%)
Poverty status:	14.4%	1.1% Two+ races	**Cook Partisan Voting Index:** R +25	
Military veterans:	13.0%	0.1% Other		
		21.6% Hispanic Origin		

Occupation   Blue collar: 26.7%   White collar: 53.3%   Gray collar: 20.0%

Heading west in Texas, the population thins out, the land becomes browner until you can travel through whole counties containing only a few hundred people each—plus quite a few more head of cattle. And then the land rises nearly 1,000 feet in elevation, up steep hillsides from the gullies that surround the rivers that for most of the year are just tiny trickles, to the tilted tableland that is the High Plains of West Texas. The winds here sweep down from the Rockies, the land is barren except where irrigated, often with the now dangerously depleted waters of the Ogallala Aquifer; and so one passes through grazing land to cotton fields and then grazing land again. But here and there in this demanding environment—sticky-hot in the summer, swept by north winds from Canada in winter, always threatened in "Tornado Alley"—comfortable cities have been built to house the people and businesses that bring forth some of the nation's most abundant oil, natural gas, helium and other elements from the earth.

The 13th Congressional District is larger than 13 states; it spans 40,000 square miles and includes all of 41 counties and small parts of two others. Population declined here in the 1980s, in some rural counties by as much as 30%, with only small gains in and around two of the three biggest cities, Wichita Falls and Amarillo. In the 1990s, the district's population increased 5%, but that was the smallest gain in any Texas district, with population increasing in the larger cities but declining in most rural counties. Around Wichita Falls, in the eastern part of the district, is the agricultural land of the Red River Valley—dusty land with empty skylines, like Archer City, the boyhood and current home of novelist Larry McMurtry, chronicled in *The Last Picture Show* and *Texasville*. The area claims to produce more cotton than any other congressional district, produces much of the world's milo (a variety of sorghum), and is home to one of the nation's oldest and largest cattle auctions. This was long white Anglo Texas: few blacks got this far west and there were not many Latinos either. But in the 1990s Latinos started moving in in large numbers, to work in the fields or in crop processing. Today, the district is 6% black and 22% Hispanic. Much of the High Plains economy is based on natural resources. The largest city here is Amarillo, once the helium capital of North America (before Congress shut down production), now the center of the largest natural gas development in the world, and still—not Chicago—the windiest city in the United States. It has become the site of one of Bell Helicopter's V-22 Osprey plants. Just outside town is the Pantex Plant that secretly assembled the nation's thousands of nuclear warheads and was the epicenter of American defense in the Cold War; its 16,000 acres have been used to dismantle some disarmed weapons and now maintain the remainder of the arsenal.

Political traditions here differ. The Red River Valley, settled by Confederate veterans, was heavily Democratic up through the 1970s. The High Plains, settled overland from Kansas wheatlands, was for years more Republican. By 2000, both the Red River Valley and the High Plains were overwhelmingly for George W. Bush, giving him county percentages as high as he won anywhere in the United States. Overall he won 75% here in 2000.

The congressman from the 13th District is Mac Thornberry, a Republican elected in 1994. His great-great-grandfather Amos Thornberry, a Union Army veteran and staunch Republican, moved to Clay County, just east of Wichita Falls, in the 1880s; a year after Amos died in 1925, his son bought the cattle ranch that Mac Thornberry, his brothers and father now run. From the window of his ranch house, writes *The Texas Techsan,* "as far as the eye can see is the Golden Spread of Texas for which this part of the state is named. There are no buildings, no roadways, no signs of life. Gaze out long enough and you begin to think you can actually see the curvature of the earth." But Thornberry is not just a local farmer: After college and law school in Texas he worked for Congressmen Tom Loeffler and Larry Combest and at the State Department in Washington. Then he returned to practice law in West Texas. In 1994 the well-connected Thornberry took on three-term Democratic Congressman Bill Sarpalius. He attacked Sarpalius for voting for the Clinton budget and tax package. He profited from news stories about how Sarpalius did not pay a moving company that shipped his furniture to Washington, then accepted a fee for speaking at the company's convention in Las Vegas. The FBI investigated in October 1994: not helpful for Sarpalius's campaign. Thornberry won a solid 55%–45% victory.

In the House, Thornberry has compiled a conservative voting record, though hardly the most ideological in the Texas delegation. His hard work on defense and homeland security issues has earned him a reputation as one of the brainiest and most accessible lawmakers on those issues. In March 2001, he took the recommendations of a commission chaired by former Senators Gary Hart and Warren Rudman and authored the first bill to create a homeland security agency; a year later, with Joseph Lieberman, he played a key role in the bipartisan effort to create the new department. On the Armed Services Committee, he has weighed in on military policy. He has enthusiastically championed missile defense and has called for better coordination of military space programs.

Thornberry has also been active on domestic issues. He pressed hard for estate tax repeal and tax credits to encourage production in marginal wells.

Thornberry has been reelected easily every two years.

FOURTEENTH DISTRICT

Rep. Ron Paul (R)

Elected 1996, 4th term; b. Aug. 20, 1935, Pittsburgh, PA; home, Surfside; Gettysburg Col., B.A. 1957, Duke U., M.D. 1961; Protestant; married (Carol).

Military Career: Flight Surgeon, Air Force, 1963–68.

Elected Office: U.S. House of Reps., 1976, 1978–84.

Professional Career: Practicing physician, 1968–96.

DC Office: 203 CHOB 20515, 202-225-2831; Fax: 202-226-4871; Web site: www.house.gov/paul.

District Offices: Freeport, 979-230-0000; Victoria, 361-576-1231.

Committees: *Financial Services* (12th of 37 R): Domestic and International Monetary Policy, Trade & Technology; Oversight & Investigations (Vice Chmn.). *International Relations* (16th of 26 R): Asia & the Pacific; Western Hemisphere. *Joint Economic Committee* (6th of 10 Reps.).

Group Ratings

	ADA	ACLU	AFS	LCV	CON	ITIC	NTU	COC	ACU	NTLC	CHC
2002	30	67	38	50	99	38	88	50	76	89	50
2001	20	—	44	36	—	—	88	62	70	—	—

National Journal Ratings

	2001 LIB —	2001 CONS		2002 LIB —	2002 CONS
Economic	49% —	52%		47% —	52%
Social	50% —	50%		49% —	51%
Foreign	75% —	26%		58% —	42%

Key Votes of the 107th Congress

1. Approve Bush Tax Cuts	Y	5. Faith-Based Charities	N	9. Trade Promotion Authority	N
2. Limit Patients' Bill of Rights	*	6. Bar Gays in the Boy Scouts	Y	10. Bar Funds for Intl. Court	Y
3. Campaign Finance Reform	N	7. Ban Partial-Birth Abortion	Y	11. Authorize Force in Iraq	N
4. Ban ANWR Development	N	8. Arm Commercial Pilots	Y	12. Deny Home. Sec. Dept. Union	Y

Election Results

2002 general	Ron Paul (R)	102,905	(68%)	($1,309,118)
	Corby Windham (D)	48,224	(32%)	($40,410)
2002 primary	Ron Paul (R)	unopposed		
2000 general	Ron Paul (R)	137,370	(60%)	($2,353,816)
	Loy Sneary (D)	92,689	(40%)	($1,033,842)

Prior Winning Percentages: 1998 (55%); 1996 (51%); 1982 (99%); 1980 (51%); 1978 (51%); 1976 (56%)

The People		Race/Ethnic Origin	Ancestry	
Area size:	16,067 sq. mi.	58.2% White	German: 14.1%	Irish: 6.2%
Urban population:	55.1%	7.7% Black	English: 5.3%	
Rural population:	44.9%	0.8% Asian	**2000 Presidential Vote**	
Pop. 2000:	651,620	0.3% Native Am.	Bush (R)	136,460 (66%)
Median income:	$35,966	0.0% Hawaiian	Gore (D)	71,434 (34%)
Poverty status:	15.0%	0.9% Two + races	**Cook Partisan Voting Index:** R +16	
Military veterans:	13.8%	0.1% Other		
		32.0% Hispanic Origin		

Occupation	Blue collar: 30.3%	White collar: 52.1%	Gray collar: 17.6%

Retreating east from the Alamo, the ragtag army led by Sam Houston passed over what would become, after their bloody and conclusive victory at San Jacinto, some of the prime cropland in the new Republic and later the state of Texas. The hilly and river-crossed land between Houston and Austin, both named after Texas' first leaders, was settled early. The first capital of the Republic of Texas was in Brazoria County. The flat coastal plains, steamy and humid so much of the year, were settled later when the railroads came in. The Gulf of Mexico coastline, though it has plenty of inlets, never had any important ports in the stretch between Houston and Corpus Christi until the discovery of oil here made it worthwhile to build channels to ship the oil out.

This is the land of the 14th Congressional District. Made up of rural countrysides, small towns and a couple of small cities, it runs along the Gulf Coast and inland toward the old Texas German country. It is a district between the big metropolitan areas of Houston, Austin, San Antonio and Corpus Christi, including some of their suburban fringe. Victoria, which passes for the urban center of the district, is a rail hub that serves Gulf ports; it also includes large industrial plants, including DuPont, Union Carbide, Alcoa and BP Chemicals. This country is ancestrally Democratic except for a couple of counties settled by Texas Germans, who were pro-Union in the Civil War and have remained Republican ever since. But it has trended Republican since the 1980s, culminating in 66% for George W. Bush in 2000.

The congressman from the 14th District is Ron Paul, a Republican elected in 1996, but also once a Libertarian candidate for president. Paul grew up in Pennsylvania, graduated from Duke Medical School, served as a Air Force flight surgeon, then moved to Texas to practice obstetrics and gynecology in Brazoria County, just southwest of Houston. Paul was dismayed when Richard Nixon cut the connection between the dollar and gold in 1971 and became interested in politics.

After winning election to the House in 1976 and serving four terms, he ran for the Senate in 1984 and lost the primary to Phil Gramm 73%–16%. His House seat was won by a young legislator and exterminating firm owner, Tom DeLay. In 1988, as the Libertarian candidate for president, Paul ran third with 432,000 votes, 0.47% of the total (more than Patrick Buchanan's 0.43% in 2000, which was achieved with the help of $12 million in federal funding). In his first stint in the House, Paul advanced some ideas that in the mid-1990s became mainstream—term limits and abolition of the income tax. Other Paul ideas remain outside the political pale—endorsing a group that wants to end all government funding of education, cutting $150 billion from the defense budget and returning to the gold standard. Paul practices what he preaches. He will not accept payment by Medicare or Medicaid, he wouldn't let his children accept federal student loans and he refuses his congressional pension.

Following his presidential campaign, Paul reentered politics after 14th District Congressman Greg Laughlin switched parties and became a Republican in June 1995. Laughlin had a moderate voting record, by no means the most conservative of Texas Democrats. Republicans offered him a seat on Ways and Means if he switched, and he did. Paul decided to run again in 1996, raising money from his nationwide network of Libertarians, gold bugs and subscribers to the *Ron Paul Political Report*. After Laughlin led the primary with 43%, Paul won the runoff 54%–46%. This set up an excruciating situation for Republican leaders. They did not want to lose the seat to Democrat Charles "Lefty" Morris, who ran as a "conservative Democrat," but omitted from his resume the fact that he had been president of the state trial lawyers' association. Nor did they want to be associated with Paul's wackier-seeming views. Morris ("Lefty is right") hit Paul for favoring abolition of the minimum wage, repealing federal anti-drug laws and anti-prostitution laws. Researchers reported that Paul's newsletter in 1992 said that 95% of black men in Washington, D.C. are "semi-criminal or entirely criminal" and that black teenagers are "unbelievably fleet of foot." Paul ran 1% ahead of Bob Dole and won 51%–48%.

With his libertarian views, Paul's voting record is anything but rock-solid Republican; *National Journal* ratings place him near the middle of the House. Frequently, his insistence on limited government made Paul the House's lonely dissenter—against bills to require states to report on their progress in improving student achievement, to award Rosa Parks and Pope John Paul II with Congressional Gold Medals, to pass the Patriot Act for increased law-enforcement authority after September 11. He was the only Republican to vote "present" on the resolution expressing support for the military forces at the start of the war with Iraq. He filed a lawsuit challenging the McCain-Feingold campaign finance act as a violation of the First Amendment. He supports virtually no role for the U.S. government overseas—from military defense to international trade; he calls himself a "non-interventionist," not an isolationist. His iconoclasm has reached the point that he is probably the least dependable and persuadable Republican in the House—all the more frustrating for Tom DeLay in his role as majority whip and now majority leader. Interestingly, many liberals have begun to praise him.

Paul has appeared on House Democrats' target lists, but easily survived in 1998 and 2000 against Loy Sneary, a local rice farmer. Redistricting made many changes at the edges of the district, but none that caused him any problem in 2002, when he was reelected with 68% of the vote. Democrats do not really have a chance in this district; more regular Republicans may have their eyes on it, but have not yet made a serious challenge in the primary: it may not be wise to underestimate someone who, however offbeat, has managed to be elected to the House eight times, at least once in each of the past four decades.

FIFTEENTH DISTRICT

Rep. Ruben Hinojosa (D)

Elected 1996, 4th term; b. Aug. 20, 1940, Mercedes; home, Mercedes; U. of TX, B.B.A. 1962, M.B.A. 1980; Catholic; married (Marty).

Elected Office: TX Bd. of Educ., 1974–84.

Professional Career: Pres. & CEO, H&H Foods Inc., 1962–present.

DC Office: 2463 RHOB 20515, 202-225-2531; Fax: 202-225-5688; Web site: www.house.gov/hinojosa.

District Offices: Beeville, 361-358-8400; McAllen, 956-682-5545.

Committees: *Education & the Workforce* (7th of 22 D): 21st Century Competitiveness; Select Education (RMM). *Financial Services* (19th of 32 D): Capital Markets, Insurance & Government Sponsored Enterprises; Financial Institutions & Consumer Credit; Oversight & Investigations. *Resources* (21st of 24 D).

Group Ratings

	ADA	ACLU	AFS	LCV	CON	ITIC	NTU	COC	ACU	NTLC	CHC
2002	80	73	78	75	43	75	21	61	20	8	8
2001	85	—	90	64	—	—	15	52	13	—	—

National Journal Ratings

	2001 LIB	—	2001 CONS		2002 LIB	—	2002 CONS
Economic	64%	—	36%		60%	—	39%
Social	69%	—	31%		71%	—	28%
Foreign	65%	—	35%		67%	—	33%

Key Votes of the 107th Congress

1. Approve Bush Tax Cuts	N	5. Faith-Based Charities	N	9. Trade Promotion Authority	Y
2. Limit Patients' Bill of Rights	N	6. Bar Gays in the Boy Scouts	N	10. Bar Funds for Intl. Court	N
3. Campaign Finance Reform	Y	7. Ban Partial-Birth Abortion	Y	11. Authorize Force in Iraq	N
4. Ban ANWR Development	Y	8. Arm Commercial Pilots	N	12. Deny Home. Sec. Dept. Union	N

Election Results

2002 general	Ruben Hinojosa (D)	unopposed		($271,632)
2002 primary	Ruben Hinojosa (D)	46,688	(87%)	
	Mel Hawkins (D)	7,138	(13%)	
2000 general	Ruben Hinojosa (D)	106,570	(88%)	($470,513)
	Frank Jones (Lib)	13,167	(11%)	
	Other	711	(1%)	

Prior Winning Percentages: 1998 (58%); 1996 (62%)

The People		Race/Ethnic Origin	Ancestry	
Area size:	6,435 sq. mi.	19.2% White	German: 4.3%	USA: 2.7%
Urban population:	87.3%	1.3% Black	English: 2.5%	
Rural population:	12.7%	0.6% Asian	**2000 Presidential Vote**	
Pop. 2000:	651,619	0.1% Native Am.	Gore (D) 76,161	(55%)
Median income:	$27,530	0.0% Hawaiian	Bush (R) 63,495	(45%)
Poverty status:	30.5%	0.4% Two+ races	**Cook Partisan Voting Index:** D + 4	
Military veterans:	8.8%	0.0% Other		
		78.3% Hispanic Origin		

Occupation   Blue collar: 25.5%   White collar: 53.5%   Gray collar: 21.0%

The Lower Rio Grande Valley of south Texas is one of America's 20th century frontiers. A century ago, there was little here but desert wilderness. Only a handful of people lived anywhere near the shallow, sluggish Rio Grande; there was no Border Patrol because in this desert land very few people bothered to cross it. Then came pioneers like Lloyd Bentsen Sr., father of the former senator and Treasury secretary, who arrived after World War I with $5 in his pocket and became one of the biggest Valley landowners. Bentsen and others cleared the land and dug canals, hired Mexican and Mexican-American workers, and with irrigated water from the Rio Grande planted citrus groves, cornfields and palm windbreaks, ran cattle and drilled for oil and gas. Along U.S. 83 north of the Rio Grande these pioneers built a string of towns with Anglo names and storefronts. But most of the people here were Latino in culture and language. Wage levels higher than in Mexico (though low by U.S. standards) brought more Mexicans over the border. But if wages are low, so is the cost of living—which makes this a haven for low-income "winter Texan" retirees coming from the North in their RVs. The days are past when ranchers and oil men wielded absolute political power here. There is instead a robust, mostly Hispanic, politics.

The 15th Congressional District is one of three districts dividing up the Lower Rio Grande Valley. Some 73% of its residents live just north of the river in Hidalgo County, in or near the string of towns from Mercedes through McAllen to Edinburg. The county grew by 49% in the 1990s and the local infrastructure has barely kept up. The 15th then stretches through a narrow corridor of land between Corpus Christi and San Antonio to include on its northern tip Goliad, where 352 captured Texans were massacred by Santa Ana's troops in 1836, and Bee County. In the northern end of the district, around, but not including Corpus Christi, and up to Goliad County, the population is 44% Hispanic. Overall, the 15th's population is 78% Hispanic and mostly but not entirely Democratic: George W. Bush won 45% of the vote here in 2000.

The congressman from the 15th District is Ruben Hinojosa, a Democrat first elected in 1996. His background is not in politics but in business and civic affairs. He grew up in Mercedes, where his family owns H&H Foods, which produces Mexican foods and beef patties and is one of the largest employers in the Valley. Hinojosa graduated from the University of Texas, then went into the family business and was active in civic affairs, primarily in education and regional development. He served on the state Board of Education and led an effort to create three regional magnet schools, including the South Texas School for Health Professions, a high school. After former House Agriculture Committee Chairman Kika de la Garza announced he would not seek reelection in 1996, Hinojosa ran in the Democratic primary. In the primary he led Anglo lawyer Jim Selman 34%–33%. Selman promised to fight corruption; he questioned Hinojosa's Democratic credentials and said he profited from government contracts. Hinojosa emphasized his interest in improving educational opportunities in the Lower Rio Grande Valley and extending I-69 to the Valley. Not the kind of liberal who leads most national and Texas Hispanic organizations, he called for reducing the capital gains tax and giving investment tax credits to those making capital improvements. Hinojosa won the runoff 52%–48% and easily won the general.

Hinojosa has had a moderate-to-conservative voting record among House Democrats. He has sought to protect benefits for legal immigrants, to promote NAFTA, and to demand that Mexico deliver on its agreement for water to south Texas farmers. He has a proclivity for holding out on last-minute legislative deals. With Democrat Gregory Meeks, he was one of only two undecided congressmen who took up Bill Clinton's offer of a visit to China to assess whether to approve PNTR; Hinojosa got assurances of funding for the Cross-Border Institute for Regional Development before voting for it. He again was one of the final members to decide on George W. Bush's proposal for trade promotion authority. This time, he shook hands with Tom DeLay on the House floor in a deal for earmarked funding for a job training project that Hinojosa wanted. In 2001, with other Democrats, he opposed subcommittee lines proposed by new Education and the Workforce Committee chairman John Boehner because of jurisdiction over historically black and Hispanic-serving colleges; they boycotted initial meetings until Boehner worked out a compromise. He had support in 2003 from the Texas delegation for a Democratic opening on Ways and Means, but it went to Max Sandlin, and Hinojosa became ranking Democrat on the Select Education Subcommittee, which has jurisdiction over black and Hispanic colleges.

In the past two elections Hinojosa has had no Republican opposition.

SIXTEENTH DISTRICT

Rep. Silvestre Reyes (D)

Elected 1996, 4th term; b. Nov. 10, 1944, Canutillo; home, El Paso; El Paso Commun. Col., A.A. 1977; Catholic; married (Carolina).

Military Career: Army, 1966–68 (Vietnam).

Elected Office: Canutillo Schl. Board, 1968–70.

Professional Career: Border Patrol Agent, 1969–95.

DC Office: 1527 LHOB 20515, 202-225-4831; Fax: 202-225-2016; Web site: www.house.gov/reyes.

District Office: El Paso, 915-534-4400.

Committees: *Armed Services* (8th of 29 D): Readiness; Strategic Forces (RMM). *Permanent Select Committee on Intelligence* (3d of 9 D): Human Intelligence, Analysis & Counterintelligence; Terrorism and Homeland Security. *Veterans' Affairs* (9th of 14 D): Benefits.

Group Ratings

	ADA	ACLU	AFS	LCV	CON	ITIC	NTU	COC	ACU	NTLC	CHC
2002	75	64	100	50	43	38	15	39	19	0	17
2001	90	—	100	57	—	—	13	43	30	—	—

National Journal Ratings

	2001 LIB	—	2001 CONS		2002 LIB	—	2002 CONS
Economic	70%	—	31%		65%	—	34%
Social	68%	—	33%		60%	—	39%
Foreign	29%	—	72%		64%	—	36%

Key Votes of the 107th Congress

1. Approve Bush Tax Cuts	N	5. Faith-Based Charities	N	9. Trade Promotion Authority	N
2. Limit Patients' Bill of Rights	N	6. Bar Gays in the Boy Scouts	N	10. Bar Funds for Intl. Court	*
3. Campaign Finance Reform	Y	7. Ban Partial-Birth Abortion	Y	11. Authorize Force in Iraq	N
4. Ban ANWR Development	N	8. Arm Commercial Pilots	Y	12. Deny Home. Sec. Dept. Union	N

Election Results

2002 general	Silvestre Reyes (D)	unopposed		($413,161)
2002 primary	Silvestre Reyes (D)	unopposed		
2000 general	Silvestre Reyes (D)	92,649	(68%)	($406,530)
	Daniel S. Power (R)	40,921	(30%)	($30,621)
	Other	2,080	(2%)	

Prior Winning Percentages: 1998 (88%); 1996 (71%)

The People		Race/Ethnic Origin	Ancestry	
Area size:	582 sq. mi.	17.4% White	German: 3.9%	Irish: 2.6%
Urban population:	98.3%	2.9% Black	USA: 2.4%	
Rural population:	1.7%	0.9% Asian	**2000 Presidential Vote**	
Pop. 2000:	651,619	0.3% Native Am.	Gore (D) 81,860	(59%)
Median income:	$31,245	0.1% Hawaiian	Bush (R) 56,276	(41%)
Poverty status:	23.6%	0.7% Two+ races	**Cook Partisan Voting Index:** D + 9	
Military veterans:	11.6%	0.1% Other		
		77.7% Hispanic Origin		

Occupation	Blue collar: 24.7%	White collar: 58.1%	Gray collar: 17.2%

El Paso, Texas, and Juarez, Mexico, face each other across the narrow Rio Grande, their tree-shaded streets spread out below the rough brown face of Comanche Peak. The two border cities are surrounded by hundreds of miles of some of North America's most rugged and desolate landscape, 600 miles from Dallas-Fort Worth. There is much history here: Texas claims the first Thanksgiving took place in San Elizario near El Paso in 1598, and there were Spanish conquistadors coming through the pass of the north, El Paso del Norte, years before that. In the 1950s, El Paso and Juarez each had a population of 140,000; in 2000 U.S. Census counted 679,000 in El Paso County (78% of them counted as Hispanic) and the Mexican census counted 1.2 million in metro Juarez. This is a bilingual, bicultural pair of cities, where most people have a Mexican heritage; the thrust of growth comes from the fertile union of a Spanish-speaking people and an English-speaking economy. El Paso is one of the lowest-wage and lowest-education cities in the U.S.; Juarez is one of the highest-wage in Mexico. *Maquiladora* plants pioneered a cross-border economy and the NAFTA strengthened it, and it is not all low-skill either; south of the border, there is a big General Motors technical center.

The 16th Congressional District is made up of much of El Paso County—the city itself, the suburban fringe and giant Fort Bliss to the north and the colonias spread out to the east and south. El Paso feels distant from the rest of Texas—it's closer to Los Angeles than to Beaumont, and El Paso is in a different time zone from the rest of the state. As governor, George W. Bush paid close attention to El Paso, and in his 1998 reelection he carried El Paso County 50%–49%— a considerable achievement given the overwhelmingly Latino electorate. In 2000 though, Bush lost the county to Al Gore.

The congressman from the 16th District is Silvestre Reyes, a Democrat first elected in 1996. He grew up on a farm in Canutillo, five miles north of El Paso, the oldest of 10 children; he went to college in El Paso and Austin. He served in the Army in Vietnam, then "took as many civil service tests as I could, and the Border Patrol called" in 1969. He worked for the Immigration and Naturalization Service in four cities in Texas and Glynco, Georgia, and returned to El Paso in 1993 as chief patrol agent. When he got there he found that "people could basically cross the border at any time, wherever they wanted to." More than 40 boatmen ran "what were essentially international ferries" with 8,000 illegals crossing the border every day. In September 1993, Reyes started Operation Hold the Line, positioning 400 officers on the border instead of trying to intercept illegals after they had already crossed into El Paso (amazingly enough, that had been firmly-rooted INS policy). Mexico complained about threats to its sovereignty, merchants worried about loss of sales, homeowners fretted about finding domestic help, border agents feared losing credit for apprehending aliens. But in El Paso auto thefts were down 30%, burglaries and robberies were down, beggars were absent from the streets, fewer Mexicans were having babies in El Paso hospitals; the move was almost universally popular north of the border and has been accepted to the south. The law finally was being enforced by an agency that had long said it was impossible; he reduced the flow by more than half.

By November 1995 Reyes's name recognition was 65%, higher than most elected officials; he resigned from the INS and ran for Congress. Reyes talked of the need for integrity and common sense. His target was Ron Coleman, a Democrat first elected in 1982, around whom scandals lurked: he had 673 overdrafts at the House bank and he was accused by Texas Attorney General Dan Morales of trying to block prosecution of a local developer. In December 1995, Coleman announced he was retiring, but he and labor unions backed Jose Luis Sanchez, his legislative assistant. Sanchez harshly attacked Reyes as a crypto-Republican and for backing a capital gains tax cut. Reyes hewed to his moderate platform, including water conservation research, more high-tech jobs, more highways and border crossings. After Reyes led the primary 42%–28%, Sanchez and the unions pressed hard in the runoff, but Reyes won 51%–49% and easily won the general.

In the House, Reyes' voting record fell among moderates in the Democratic Caucus. He said that the permanent solution for the border is economic stabilization for Mexico and spoke out against decertification of Mexico for its drug enforcement record, saying it would upset the Mexican economy. He backed retraining for workers displaced by NAFTA, which he said has been a great success overall. He backed PNTR with China, but he opposed trade promotion authority. From the Armed Services Committee, where he is ranking Democrat on the Strategic Forces Subcommittee, Reyes has worked to protect Fort Bliss from possible base closing. On the Intelligence Committee, he blamed flaws in U.S. intelligence for the September 11 attacks and said that he saw no evidence of a link between Iraq and al Qaeda terrorists; he opposed the use of force in Iraq.

In 2001, he became chairman of the Hispanic Caucus, and set as a major priority the expansion of its membership by recruiting and providing financial help to prospective candidates; he set a goal of electing an additional six to 10 Hispanics to Congress in the 2002 election. But redistricting did not result in many new Hispanic-majority seats as Anglo and black Democrats concentrated on protecting incumbents in California and Florida, and only three new Hispanics were elected, two Democrats in California and Arizona and one Republican in Florida. Reyes urged the four Hispanic Republicans—three Cuban-Americans from Miami-Dade County and Henry Bonilla from San Antonio—to return to the Hispanic Caucus, but they demanded that the Caucus support free elections in Cuba; it is not clear why Hispanic Democrats, who have called for and supported free elections elsewhere in Latin America, found this unacceptable. Reyes briefly considered running for the Senate in 2002 after Phil Gramm retired, but decided not to. He was unopposed for reelection in 2002.

SEVENTEENTH DISTRICT

Rep. Charles Stenholm (D)

Elected 1978, 13th term; b. Oct. 26, 1938, Stamford; home, Avoca; TX Tech. U., B.S. 1961, M.S. 1962; Lutheran; married (Cynthia).

Professional Career: Farmer; Vocational educ. teacher, 1962–65; Exec. V.P., Rolling Plains Cotton Growers, 1965–68; Mgr., Stamford Electric Co–op., 1968–76.

DC Office: 2409 RHOB 20515, 202-225-6605; Fax: 202-225-2234; Web site: www.house.gov/stenholm.

District Offices: Abilene, 915-673-7221; San Angelo, 915-942-8881; Stamford, 915-773-2833.

Committees: *Agriculture* (RMM of 24 D).

Group Ratings

	ADA	ACLU	AFS	LCV	CON	ITIC	NTU	COC	ACU	NTLC	CHC
2002	40	33	67	13	100	75	27	70	50	31	50
2001	50	—	80	14	—	—	28	74	64	—	—

National Journal Ratings

	2001 LIB	—	2001 CONS		2002 LIB	—	2002 CONS
Economic	53%	—	48%		53%	—	47%
Social	43%	—	55%		44%	—	54%
Foreign	33%	—	60%		47%	—	51%

Key Votes of the 107th Congress

1. Approve Bush Tax Cuts	N	5. Faith-Based Charities	N	9. Trade Promotion Authority	Y
2. Limit Patients' Bill of Rights	N	6. Bar Gays in the Boy Scouts	Y	10. Bar Funds for Intl. Court	Y
3. Campaign Finance Reform	Y	7. Ban Partial-Birth Abortion	Y	11. Authorize Force in Iraq	Y
4. Ban ANWR Development	N	8. Arm Commercial Pilots	Y	12. Deny Home. Sec. Dept. Union	Y

Election Results

2002 general	Charles Stenholm (D)	84,136	(51%)	($1,555,669)
	Rob Beckham (R)	77,622	(47%)	($472,591)
	Other	2,046	(1%)	
2002 primary	Charles Stenholm (D)	unopposed		
2000 general	Charles Stenholm (D)	120,670	(59%)	($871,201)
	Darrell Clements (R)	72,535	(35%)	($68,388)
	Debra M. Monde (Lib)	11,180	(5%)	($50,824)

Prior Winning Percentages: 1998 (54%); 1996 (52%); 1994 (54%); 1992 (66%); 1990 (100%); 1988 (100%); 1986 (100%); 1984 (100%); 1982 (97%); 1980 (100%); 1978 (68%)

The People		Race/Ethnic Origin	Ancestry	
Area size:	33,836 sq. mi.	74.7% White	USA: 11.4%	German: 8.6%
Urban population:	61.0%	3.8% Black	Irish: 7.6%	
Rural population:	39.0%	0.5% Asian	**2000 Presidential Vote**	
Pop. 2000:	651,619	0.4% Native Am.	Bush (R)...............161,877	(72%)
Median income:	$32,413	0.0% Hawaiian	Gore (D)................62,241	(28%)
Poverty status:	15.1%	1.0% Two+ races	**Cook Partisan Voting Index:** R +23	
Military veterans:	14.1%	0.1% Other		
		19.6% Hispanic Origin		

Occupation	Blue collar: 26.8%	White collar: 53.9%	Gray collar: 19.3%

West from Fort Worth, the West Texas plains stretch miles beyond the horizon, thousands and thousands of acres of rolling grazing land punctuated occasionally by oases of irrigated farmland (often in circles that show the reach of the sprinklers). This is primarily cattle country, with ranches specializing in Angora goats and sheep and exotic animals like ostriches, emus and aoudad sheep; there are cotton fields and pecan trees and mesquite, and many oil wells. Scurry County, far west of Fort Worth, is said to be the number one oil-producing county in the United States. On the interstate going west from Fort Worth, settlements start thinning out quickly. Before long, you are on open plains, with enormous skies and no people in sight: parched country in the drought of 2000. Then in the distance is a good-sized town, an oasis of activity. The largest towns here are Abilene and San Angelo; at Dyess Air Force Base near Abilene are stationed some of the nation's B-1 bombers, while Goodfellow Air Force Base near San Angelo houses electronic intelligence operations training and advanced imagery training. The communities here maintain their traditions and keep close to nature: Sweetwater in Nolan County has an annual Rattlesnake Roundup; Olney in Young County stages a One-Armed Dove Hunt. The local congressman's website describes the area: "The people of West Central Texas are independent, proud, good-natured, religious and family-oriented. In many of the smaller communities activities still center around local church and school events. From a political perspective, the region maintains a conservative outlook." The biggest problem here is water: the aquifers are at risk of being drained, and local communities have been clearing brush to improve the water flow and seeding clouds to get more rain.

The 17th Congressional District takes up much of this "God's country," starting a few miles from Fort Worth and including 35 whole counties and most of another and extending westward almost to New Mexico. Settled by Confederate veterans suspicious of Eastern bankers and Yankee businessmen, this was one of the Democratic heartlands of America up through the 1970s. Since then it has become Republican, at first at the top of the ticket, then going farther down. In 2000 it cast 72% of its votes for George W. Bush. There is a growing Hispanic population, 20% in 2000, but that has not perceptibly tipped the district toward Democrats.

The congressman from the 17th District is Charles Stenholm, one of several conservative Texas Democrats elected in 1978, and the only one still in the House; no other Democrat represents a district which cast a higher percentage of its votes for George W. Bush in 2000. Stenholm is a farmer from a small town settled by Swedes near Abilene; he graduated and received a masters degree at Texas Tech University. He returned to farm the family land and headed the Rolling Plains Cotton Growers Association and the Stamford Electric Cooperative. Stenholm became a Democrat because in the 1970 Senate race Lloyd Bentsen was interested in his issues and the senior George Bush wasn't. In 1978, when 32-year incumbent Omar Burleson retired, Stenholm ran for the seat and easily won.

In the House, Stenholm and Phil Gramm were leaders of the "Boll Weevils," backing the 1981 Reagan budget and tax cuts. He threatened momentarily to run against Speaker Tip O'Neill in January 1985, but desisted when conservatives were promised more attention. His voting record is relatively conservative, at about the center of the House. In the 1980s and early 1990s Stenholm was the lead conservative Democrat on budget issues, as head of the Conservative Democratic Forum and on the Budget Committee. But that role faded as Republican leaders started viewing Stenholm as a conservative talker but a partisan Democratic doer, and the spotlight passed to other members of the Democratic Blue Dogs. He was one of five Democrats who voted to impeach Bill Clinton. But he has stood with Democrats on tax issues. House Democratic leaders let Stenholm and other Blue Dogs take the lead in arguing against the Bush income tax cut in March 2001. Later he opposed making the tax cut permanent and called for retaining the estate tax on estates over $4 million.

In 1997 he became ranking Democrat on the Agriculture Committee, just after the Republicans had passed the Freedom to Farm Act, which purported to phase out farm subsidies. Stenholm argued that that bill was the product of Speaker Newt Gingrich, not the Agriculture Committee, and that it was based on the assumption—a faulty one, he says—that American farmers would be able to sell surplus production on the world market. He pointed out that the European Union pays $55 billion yearly in subsidies to farmers and that, after farm prices collapsed in 1998, Congress started voting roughly half that yearly in "disaster relief" to farmers, and that government payments amount to one-third to one-half of net farm income. Starting in 1999 the committee chairman was Larry Combest, from the next-door 19th District; these districts are both big producers of cotton, historically a heavily subsidized crop. In 2001 the farm bill was up for reauthorization, and the political stars were in alignment for a return to subsidies. In 1996 the House bill had been a project of the Republican leadership and the chairman and ranking members of the Senate Agriculture Committee were from Vermont and Indiana, states with no interest in subsidized crops. In June 2001, when Democrats took over the Senate, the chairman of the Agriculture Committee was Tom Harkin of Iowa, with much historically subsidized corn and wheat. Combest and Stenholm worked together to shape the House bill, just as they worked together to open up China to U.S. farm exports. Some $79 billion was set aside for 10 years of farm programs in the 2001 budget resolution, and Stenholm in August hoped for passage by December, before that number might be reduced in a new budget resolution—another reason, Stenholm said, he opposed the Bush tax cut. Markup was scheduled for the week of September 10, and had to be put off.

But by October it had passed the committee nearly unanimously and was ready for the floor. There was something for almost everyone: resurrection of the cotton, rice, corn, wheat, soybeans, honey, wool and mohair programs; increased food stamps for "the nutrition community"; $12 billion more in land conservation programs, to please environmentalists; a new peanut program to buy up peanut quotas and pay off peanut farmers. Left out, at the insistence of the Republican leadership, was the Northeast Dairy Compact, which expired September 30. Warnings from the Bush administration that the bill was too expensive were brushed aside; Stenholm said that the administration needed votes from farm bill supporters to pass trade promotion authority (he himself was persuaded to vote for that only after a phone call from George W. Bush). The bill passed by a 291–120 vote.

It took Harkin longer to get a bill through the Senate, and it had somewhat different provisions. Eventually the differences were hammered out in conference, and a generous new farm act was passed in May 2002. Few in the Bush administration liked the bill, which expanded government programs; but with two Texans in charge of the bill in the House, Bush had little choice but to sign it. It might not have happened: in November 2002, one week after the election, Combest announced he was resigning, effective May 2003, for personal reason; if he had done that two years before, the chairman would have been Bob Goodlatte of Virginia, from a district with no significant subsidized crops. Stenholm then took to defending the bill. In August 2002 he opposed the Bush plan to tap farm bill funds for drought relief. In December 2002 he started working to make sure appropriators would not impose payment limitations.

Since 1995 Stenholm has been working to change Social Security by instituting individual investment accounts. In July 2001 he and his partner on this issue, Jim Kolbe, introduced a bill with individual investment accounts and with cuts in the guaranteed benefit, especially for those with high incomes, an increase in the level of earnings subject to FICA tax, a reduction in COLAs, an accelerated schedule for raising the retirement age and reductions in benefits in line with increases in life expectancy. Opponents of individual accounts said this showed that they were too costly; Stenholm and Kolbe said they were putting their proposal forward for discussion. Minority Leader Dick Gephardt, a longtime opponent of individual accounts, immediately opposed it; so did Speaker Dennis Hastert, who opposed increasing taxes and reducing benefits. In May 2002 Stenholm conceded that the 107th Congress wouldn't act; in December 2002 he urged action in the 108th and the next month took comfort in the fact that George W. Bush took two sentences in his State of the Union speech to plug Social Security changes, one more than he had before. Stenholm pointed to the success in 2002 of candidates who had actively backed individual investment accounts—Elizabeth Dole, Lindsey Graham, John Sununu, Wayne Allard, Jim DeMint, all Republicans. In early 2003 it seemed unlikely that the issue would be acted on in the 108th Congress, and that it could be passed only with Republican and a very few Democratic votes. But Stenholm promised to persist. "We can either make some tough choices today to honestly deal with the challenges facing Social Security, or we can leave a fiscal time bomb for future generations." Far more quixotic is another Stenholm proposal, advanced in January 2003: a constitutional amendment setting House terms at four years.

Stenholm's relationship with the Democratic leadership has varied—not at all close in the early 1980s, much closer in the late 1980s and early 1990s. In December 1994 he tried to get into the leadership himself when he ran for minority whip; predictably, he lost to the far more liberal David Bonior 145–60. There have been far fewer conservative Democrats in the Caucus when the party has been in the minority than when it was the majority. At the same time, there has been no challenge in the Caucus to his ranking position on Agriculture; he produces bills that most Democrats like, and most committee Democrats are pretty conservative anyway. In 2001 he supported Steny Hoyer in his unsuccessful race against Nancy Pelosi for minority whip. Unlike his Texas colleague Ralph Hall, Stenholm in 2002 flatly refused to pledge that he would vote for the most conservative candidate for speaker if his vote made the difference in which party organized the House. But when the roll was first called in January 2003, he, like Hall and Ken Lucas, voted "present" for speaker.

When Stenholm first ran for Congress in 1978, the Democratic party label was still a political asset in the 17th District. By the middle 1990s it had become a political liability. In 1994 he won by only 54%–46%, far less than his previous majorities. In 1996, Republican Rudy Izzard, a dentist and former San Angelo councilman, carried Abilene and eight other counties and Stenholm won by only 52%–47%. In 1998 Izzard ran again. Stenholm argued that Newt Gingrich and Dick Armey wanted to defeat him because they opposed the needs of agriculture. Stenholm won 54%–45%. In 2000, running against a former judge who moved into the district from North Dallas, Stenholm won with a solid 59%–35%. The 2001 redistricting added most of San Angelo's Tom Green County; this raised the Bush 2000 percentage in the district from 70% to 72%.

In 2002 his Republican opponent was Rob Beckham, a broker and former Abilene Councilman. Stenholm emphasized his position on the Agriculture Committee and his conservative stands on many issues; he ran an ad showing a photo of him with George W. Bush. This was a race that the national Republicans, perhaps unwisely, did not target. The difference may have been made by the fact that Stenholm spent $1.5 million and Beckham $472,000. Stenholm won by only 51%–47%, a margin fractionally narrower than in 1996. Beckham carried the counties containing the district's two biggest cities, Abilene and San Angelo, which cast 33% of the district's votes; he also carried three of the new rural counties and four that Stenholm had previously represented. This is likely to be a seriously contested district in 2004; by April 2003, Beckham and Russell Gill, a Desert Storm fighter pilot, had already announced their intentions to run. Stenholm's seat will become even more precarious if the Texas legislature, now controlled by Republicans, adopts a new redistricting plan for the 2004 election. In any new territory—especially any in the fast-growing counties at the edge of the Dallas-Fort Worth Metroplex—Stenholm would be at a disadvantage.

EIGHTEENTH DISTRICT

Rep. Sheila Jackson Lee (D)

Elected 1994, 5th term; b. Jan. 12, 1950, Queens, NY; home, Houston; Yale U., B.A. 1972, U. of VA Law Schl., J.D. 1975; Seventh Day Adventist; married (Elwyn).

Elected Office: Houston City Cncl., 1990–94.

Professional Career: Practicing atty., 1975–77, 1978–87; Staff Cnsl., U.S. House Select Assassinations Cmte., 1977–78; Houston Assoc. Municipal Judge, 1987–90.

DC Office: 2435 RHOB 20515, 202-225-3816; Fax: 202-225-3317; Web site: www.house.gov/jacksonlee.

District Offices: Houston, 713-691-4882; Houston, 713-861-4070; Houston, 713-655-0050.

Committees: *Judiciary* (8th of 16 D): Crime, Terrorism & Homeland Security; Immigration, Border Security & Claims (RMM). *Science* (14th of 22 D): Research; Space & Aeronautics. *Select Committee on Homeland Security* (16th of 23 D): Cybersecurity, Science and Research & Development; Infrastructure & Border Security.

Group Ratings

	ADA	ACLU	AFS	LCV	CON	ITIC	NTU	COC	ACU	NTLC	CHC
2002	100	93	100	63	53	25	20	26	4	0	0
2001	100	—	100	71	—	—	9	35	8	—	—

National Journal Ratings

	2001 LIB	—	2001 CONS		2002 LIB	—	2002 CONS
Economic	94%	—	6%		95%	—	0%
Social	90%	—	0%		84%	—	8%
Foreign	70%	—	31%		94%	—	0%

Key Votes of the 107th Congress

1. Approve Bush Tax Cuts	N	5. Faith-Based Charities	N	9. Trade Promotion Authority	N
2. Limit Patients' Bill of Rights	N	6. Bar Gays in the Boy Scouts	N	10. Bar Funds for Intl. Court	N
3. Campaign Finance Reform	Y	7. Ban Partial-Birth Abortion	N	11. Authorize Force in Iraq	N
4. Ban ANWR Development	Y	8. Arm Commercial Pilots	N	12. Deny Home. Sec. Dept. Union	N

Election Results

2002 general	Sheila Jackson Lee (D)	99,161	(77%)	($395,662)
	Phillip Abbott (R)	27,980	(22%)	($21,455)
	Other	1,785	(1%)	
2002 primary	Sheila Jackson Lee (D)	31,563	(94%)	
	Lenwood Johnson (D)	1,871	(6%)	
2000 general	Sheila Jackson Lee (D)	131,857	(76%)	($516,613)
	Bob Levy (R)	38,191	(22%)	($18,244)
	Other	2,330	(1%)	

Prior Winning Percentages: 1998 (90%); 1996 (77%); 1994 (73%)

The People		Race/Ethnic Origin	Ancestry	
Area size:	186 sq. mi.	21.2% White	German: 4.0%	English: 2.9%
Urban population:	99.9%	42.2% Black	Irish: 2.7%	
Rural population:	0.1%	2.8% Asian	**2000 Presidential Vote**	
Pop. 2000:	651,620	0.2% Native Am.	Gore (D) 138,059	(74%)
Median income:	$31,725	0.0% Hawaiian	Bush (R) 47,335	(26%)
Poverty status:	23.7%	0.9% Two+ races	**Cook Partisan Voting Index:** D +24	
Military veterans:	8.6%	0.1% Other		
		32.6% Hispanic Origin		

Occupation	Blue collar: 27.3%	White collar: 55.2%	Gray collar: 17.4%

Houston contains, within its vast bounds, disparities of income and wealth as striking as any city in the United States. This is what one must expect in an expanding city with dynamic economic growth, vast immigration, absence of centralized planning and openness to cultural diversity. The contrast is most glaringly apparent at the edge of Houston's gleaming downtown with its keynote Pennzoil, Heritage Plaza and Bank of America buildings, plus Minute Maid Park (formerly, "Enron Field") for baseball's Astros and the new basketball and hockey arena, and newly renovated housing in what was once the city's warehouse district. Only a few blocks away are the slums where blacks and Mexican-Americans live in unpainted frame houses full of cracks wide enough to let in Houston's humid, smoggy air. But the contrasts are less obvious as one moves out from Houston's historic center. Half a century ago, when Houston pioneers like Jesse Jones, millionaire cotton broker and newspaper publisher, started building downtown skyscrapers, they were operating in a town with a Third World economy, a low-skill producer of basic commodities, where a few got rich and many lived near subsistence level. Since then, Houston has had a high-tech advanced economy offering a myriad of opportunities and wide range of economic outcomes. As Houston's blacks and Hispanics have moved outward from the city, increasingly they are living in comfortable middle-class neighborhoods. The entire area recently suffered from a series of man-made and natural disasters. The biggest headlines came with the collapse and bankruptcy of the Enron Corporation, the local energy and energy trading company whose executives cooked the books to conceal huge debt. Its collapse cost thousands of Houstonians their jobs, as did the merger of Compaq into Hewlett-Packard. There were big headlines also when there was extensive flooding in downtown and there was smaller, embarrassed notice when one publication proclaimed that Houston was the nation's most obese city.

The 18th Congressional District contains central Houston and many of these outlying neighborhoods. The district has three spokes running out from Loop 610 and beyond: northeast between the Eastex Freeway and Beaumont Highway, south along the South Freeway, and northwest between the Northwest Freeway and Hempstead. In 2000 the population here was 42% black, the highest percentage in any Texas district, and 33% Hispanic. Politically, it is overwhelmingly Democratic, far more so than any other metro Houston district; the 18th gave George W. Bush his lowest vote percentage in the state in 2000—just 26%.

The congresswoman from the 18th District is Sheila Jackson Lee, a Democrat first elected in 1994. A native of Queens, New York, she was educated at Yale and Virginia law school, worked on Capitol Hill and practiced law in Houston, served as a local judge and won two terms in an at-large seat on the Houston Council. After a local term limits law took effect in 1994, she ran for Congress. The incumbent was Craig Washington, a talented but storm-tossed legislator, an iconoclast who voted against the space station and NAFTA, both of which are big pluses for the Houston area economy. Jackson Lee supported NAFTA and raised lots of money from business interests who favored it—including Kenneth Lay, then a rising star at Enron. She won the Democratic primary unambiguously, 63%–37%, and has been re-elected easily since.

In the House, Jackson Lee has a liberal voting record and has been prolific in proposing bills and offering amendments on the floor. Several of those that passed required studies, added small amounts to spending bills, or were non-controversial, such as prohibiting the use of children as soldiers in Afghanistan. More often than not, her more substantive proposals—for example, in favor of NASA funding and abortion—have been defeated, though she has won funds for science research at minority colleges. On the bankruptcy bill, she unsuccessfully sought to give child support payments priority over everything except taxes. With the collapse of Enron, Jackson Lee turned to seeking steps to assist its former employees. In February 2003, she was one of six House Democrats who filed a lawsuit to prevent George W. Bush from invading Iraq without action by Congress; in March, she was raucously jeered and booed at a "Rally for America" held in her district by a local talk radio station.

Jackson Lee emerged into national prominence as an outspoken and contentious defender of President Clinton during impeachment. She called for censure as "right, punitive and just" and called impeachment a "preposterous" trampling of the Constitution. She has modeled herself on Barbara Jordan, the first representative elected by the 18th District and an eloquent advocate of the impeachment of Richard Nixon in the Judiciary Committee. But she has drawn some negative publicity. *The Weekly Standard* alleged that she violated House ethics rules by having an aide drive her one block to and from her Capitol Hill apartment in a daily commute in her government-leased car.

Jackson Lee is ranking Democrat on the Immigration, Border Security and Claims Subcommittee, where she faces conflicting desires among her constituents: Latinos tend to favor greater immigration and more generous treatment of immigrants, but some African-Americans and union leaders see immigrants as dangerous competition for jobs. Frequently, but not always, she takes the pro-immigrant side. After she lectured high-tech firms about their failure to reach out to Black Caucus members, she opposed the bill to expand temporary H-1B visas for foreign workers because the proposal "does nothing" to recruit, hire or train domestic workers.

Jackson Lee was easily reelected in 2002.

NINETEENTH DISTRICT

Rep. Randy Neugebauer (R)

Elected June 2003, 1st term; b. Dec. 24, 1949, Lubbock; home, Lubbock; TX Tech. U., B.B.A. 1972.; Baptist; married (Dana).

Elected Office: Lubbock City Cncl., 1992–98; Mayor Pro Tempore, Lubbock, 1994–96.

Professional Career: Mgr., Sentry Property Mngt., 1972–75; Instructor, South Plains College, 1975–78; V.P., First National Bank, 1975–82; Pres., Prestige Homes, 1983–87; Pres., Lubbock Land Co., 1987-present.

DC Office: 1026 LHOB 20515, 202-225-4005.

Committees: *Agriculture; Resources; Science*

Group Ratings and Key Votes: Newly Elected

Election Results

2003 spec. runoff	Randy Neugebauer (R)	28,546	(51%)	
	Mike Conaway (R)	27,959	(49%)	
2003 spec. prim.	Randy Neugebauer (R)	13,091	(22%)	
	Mike Conaway (R)	12,270	(21%)	
	Carl Isett (R)	11,015	(19%)	
	David Langston (R)	8,053	(14%)	
	Stace Williams (R)	2,609	(4%)	
	Other	11,331	(19%)	
2002 general	Larry Combest (R)	117,092	(92%)	($389,333)
	Larry Johnson (Lib)	10,684	(8%)	
2002 primary	Larry Combest (R)	unopposed		
2000 general	Larry Combest (R)	170,319	(92%)	($556,470)
	John Turnbow (Lib)	15,579	(8%)	

The People		Race/Ethnic Origin	Ancestry	
Area size:	17,528 sq. mi.	58.2% White	USA: 8.4%	German: 7.4%
Urban population:	81.3%	5.6% Black	English: 6.5%	
Rural population:	18.7%	0.8% Asian	**2000 Presidential Vote**	
Pop. 2000:	651,619	0.4% Native Am.	Bush (R)...............149,350 (76%)	
Median income:	$32,409	0.0% Hawaiian	Gore (D)...............48,400 (24%)	
Poverty status:	17.5%	0.8% Two+ races	**Cook Partisan Voting Index:** R +26	
Military veterans:	10.9%	0.0% Other		
		34.1% Hispanic Origin		

Occupation	Blue collar: 24.4%	White collar: 57.8%	Gray collar: 17.8%

More than 400 years ago, in the 1540s, the conquistador Francisco Coronado and his men rode their horses over the plains of the land they called the Llano Estacado, land that is now the plains of west Texas. What they saw was a vast empty land, gradually and imperceptibly rising in elevation to the west, with only scrub vegetation and small bands of Comanche Indians. What they did not see, lying far beneath the surface, were the two commodities that would make this productive land today, water and oil. And for more than 300 years the water and oil lay hidden; this was Indian country, then a land of Army forts and cattle ranches, until well into the 20th century. The water is the giant Ogallala Aquifer that lies under the area around Lubbock, and it was tapped first, and what had been grazing land suddenly became cotton fields, with green crops grown in circles where sprinklers reached, separated by parched land. Lubbock became the great regional center, the home of Texas Tech, and grew rapidly at mid-century: Lubbock County's population increased from 51,000 in 1940 to 101,000 in 1950 and 156,000 in 1960—lots of people in sparsely settled west Texas. Since then the regional economy has grown more slowly; the Aquifer seemed to be going dry; in 2000, Lubbock County's population reached 242,000, as the populations of the neighboring, much smaller, counties declined. Lubbock has had its problems—a killer tornado in 1970, an infestation of prairie dogs in 2002—but it has also made a great and outsized contribution to American popular culture. This one small city and the nearby counties have produced a slew of fine musicians: Buddy Holly, Tanya Tucker, Jimmy Dean, Waylon Jennings, Mac Davis, Joe Ely, Roy Orbison, Don Williams. The only discordant note came from the most recent, Natalie Maines of the Dixie Chicks, who told a London audience in March 2003 that she was ashamed that George W. Bush came from Texas; the Dixie Chicks quickly disappeared from the playlists of country stations. As the local congressman once noted in his website, people around here are "fiercely independent as Texans, steeped in patriotism when it comes to Flag and Country."

After water came oil, discovered in the 1940s in large amounts in the Permian Basin, 120 miles south of Lubbock. This is desert country, barren and open to the hot sun in the cloudless summer and cold north winds in the winter. When oil was found, two tiny county seats 25 miles apart suddenly became small cities—Odessa, home of the roughneck oil well workers, and Midland, the more upscale town where oil entrepreneurs lived and started their own Petroleum Club. The Permian Basin boomed in the years just after World War II: in 1940, Ector and Midland Counties had a population of 26,000, in 1950 67,000 and in 1960 158,000. Since then growth has slowed, as new discoveries have grown fewer and oil prices, after shooting upward in the 1970s, fell; in 2000, Ector and Midland Counties had 237,000 people. It was to the Permian Basin in 1948 that George and Barbara Bush moved, in search of oil wealth and to raise a growing family. They moved around a lot, to three rented houses in Odessa (two since torn down and the third pretty grim) and then, after a year in Bakersfield, California, to three larger but by no means grand houses in Midland (typical 1950s ranches, one now a museum). Those houses, the Bushes' previous houses in New Haven and Houston and the Adams farmhouse in Braintree, Massachusetts, are the only houses in the United States where one president of the United States has raised another.

Midland in the 1950s was an affluent town by west Texas standards, but hardly a luxurious town to today's tastes; air conditioning had not yet become standard in homes or schools, and there were no mansions at the edge of town, just barren desert and oil derricks. There was a lively civic culture, with lots of volunteer organizations and new churches; today Midland has its own cultural institutions such as the Museum of the Southwest and the Petroleum Museum (the largest such museum in the world). And this small city in the 1950s was producing more than its share of the leaders of America today. Passing through the Midland public schools were George W. Bush, Laura Bush, Commerce Secretary Donald Evans and General Tommy Franks.

The 19th Congressional District includes Lubbock, Odessa, Midland and most of the rural counties in the vicinity; the big three counties account for 74% of its population, and the next biggest city, Big Spring, has only 25,000 people. Politically, west Texas in the 1940s was, like every place in Texas except a few Texas German counties, almost totally Democratic. That began to change in the 1950s as Midland, together with a few affluent neighborhoods in Dallas and Houston, moved toward Republicans; newcomers like the Bushes were an important part of this trend. In 1962 a Republican was also elected to the U.S. House in a district then made up of the Permian Basin and El Paso, but that was mostly because the incumbent was ensnared in the Billie Sol Estes scandal, and he was defeated in 1964. That same year Midland elected a Republican to the state House, where he was outnumbered by Democrats by 149–1. He was replaced in 1968 by another Republican, Tom Craddick, who has remained in the legislature ever since and in January 2003 was elected speaker; by this time Republicans outnumbered Democrats 88–62. The 19th District, originally centered on Lubbock, was first created in 1934, and for 68 years was represented by only three congressmen, the first two of them Democrats. George Mahon, elected in 1934, stayed around long enough to become chairman of the Appropriations Committee. He retired in 1978, and there was a two-party battle between Democrat Kent Hance of Lubbock and 32-year-old George W. Bush of Midland. In the Republican primary, Bush carried only Midland County, but there were enough Republican voters there for him to prevail district-wide. Hance campaigned as a conservative Democrat, and Republican margins in the Permian Basin were not enough to overcome the still Democratic Lubbock, and Hance won the general election 53%–47%. By 1984 the Lubbock area had trended Republican too, and Hance was replaced by Lubbock Republican Larry Combest. In 2000 the congressional district which had refused to elect George W. Bush to the House cast 76 percent of its votes for him—more than any other congressional district in the country except the Texas 8th in northern metro Houston, which contains part of George Bush Intercontinental Airport.

The congressman from the 19th District is Randy Neugebauer (pronounced *NAW-ga-bauer*), a Republican who won a June 2003 special election to become 435th in House seniority. The contest was prompted by the unexpected resignation, announced a week after the November 2002 election, of Larry Combest. As chairman of the Agriculture Committee since 1999, he had played a critical part in shaping the 2002 farm bill. Combest regretted the 1996 farm bill, which purported to phase out subsidies, and restored them in the House bill he fashioned with ranking member Charles Stenholm from the next-door 17th District. In the all-party 17-candidate contest to succeed him, there was little doubt that a runoff would be required and no question that a Republican would win. Once again, a Lubbock native prevailed in the final showdown with a Midland contender. That was Neugebauer, who graduated from Texas Tech, and became a banker and then ran his own land-development company. From 1992 to 1998, he was a Lubbock city councilman.

In the May 3 primary, there were four leading candidates in the crowded field, all Republican. They were Mike Conaway, a Midland accountant, plus three from Lubbock: Neugebauer, state representative Carl Isett, and former Mayor David Langston. The question appeared to be which Lubbock candidate would face Conaway in the runoff. Neugebauer benefited as the biggest spender. He also was helped because Isett—the only active office-holder—was tied down by legislative business in Austin. Langston, who previously won election as a Democrat, pitched himself as a Bush-like "compassionate conservative." The candidates struggled for attention amid the public focus on the war in Iraq, which ended little more than two weeks before their contest. With the most advertising, Neugebauer emphasized homeland defense and the need for secure borders. He also focused on his business connections to oil and farming. In the closing days, he and Langston attacked Isett for his fund-raising and legislative votes at odds with local interests. Neugebauer surprisingly finished first, with 821 more votes than Conaway. In third place, Isett trailed Conaway by 1,255 votes; Langston finished farther back. The top four got 76% of the ballots in the primary. In Lubbock County, which cast nearly half of the total vote, Neugebauer won 30% to 28% for Isett and 21% for Langston. Conaway swept the Midland and Odessa areas.

The runoff featured few differences on the issues. Not surprisingly, both supported Combest's farm bill and Bush's national-security policy. Conaway played up his friendship and oil-business partnership with Bush during the 1980s and his appointment by Bush to the state board of public accountancy. Neugebauer won Isett's endorsement, and spotlighted his advocacy in Washington of local economic development. The two barely criticized each other. Predictably, each sought to maximize the vote in his geographic base and to steal some votes from his opponent's turf. Regional patterns again held firm in the June 3 vote. In the combined vote from Midland and Odessa areas, Conaway carried an eye-opening 85% of the vote. But in Lubbock County, which cast 47% of the vote, Neugebauer led 71% to 29%. Overall, Neugebauer won 51%–49%. Key to his 587-vote victory were wins in 10 of the 16 remaining counties.

TWENTIETH DISTRICT

Rep. Charles Gonzalez (D)

Elected 1998, 3d term; b. May 5, 1945, San Antonio; home, San Antonio; U. of TX, B.A. 1969; St. Mary's Law Schl., J.D. 1972.; Catholic; divorced.

Military Career: TX Air Natl. Guard, 1969–75.

Elected Office: Judge, San Antonio Municipal Court; Judge, Bexar Cnty. Court at Law, 1983–87; Judge, 57th State Judicial Dist. Court, 1988–97.

Professional Career: Elem. schl. teacher, 1969–71; Practicing atty., 1972–82.

DC Office: 327 CHOB 20515, 202-225-3236; Fax: 202-225-1915; Web site: www.house.gov/gonzalez.

District Office: San Antonio, 210-472-6195.

Committees: *Financial Services* (16th of 32 D): Capital Markets, Insurance & Government Sponsored Enterprises; Financial Institutions & Consumer Credit; Oversight & Investigations. *Select Committee on Homeland Security* (20th of 23 D): Cybersecurity, Science and Research & Development; Infrastructure & Border Security. *Small Business* (8th of 17 D).

Group Ratings

	ADA	ACLU	AFS	LCV	CON	ITIC	NTU	COC	ACU	NTLC	CHC
2002	100	86	100	75	52	50	17	45	0	3	0
2001	95	—	100	71	—	—	12	43	4	—	—

National Journal Ratings

	2001 LIB	—	2001 CONS		2002 LIB	—	2002 CONS
Economic	70%	—	31%		77%	—	20%
Social	83%	—	11%		84%	—	8%
Foreign	70%	—	28%		77%	—	19%

Key Votes of the 107th Congress

1. Approve Bush Tax Cuts	N	5. Faith-Based Charities	N	9. Trade Promotion Authority	N
2. Limit Patients' Bill of Rights	N	6. Bar Gays in the Boy Scouts	N	10. Bar Funds for Intl. Court	N
3. Campaign Finance Reform	Y	7. Ban Partial-Birth Abortion	N	11. Authorize Force in Iraq	N
4. Ban ANWR Development	Y	8. Arm Commercial Pilots	N	12. Deny Home. Sec. Dept. Union	N

Election Results

2002 general	Charles Gonzalez (D)	unopposed		($633,493)
2002 primary	Charles Gonzalez (D)	unopposed		
2000 general	Charles Gonzalez (D)	107,487	(88%)	($619,173)
	Alejandro (Alex) De Pena (Lib)	15,087	(12%)	

Prior Winning Percentages: 1998 (63%)

The People		Race/Ethnic Origin	Ancestry	
Area size:	304 sq. mi.	23.7% White	German: 6.0%	Irish: 3.6%
Urban population:	97.7%	5.3% Black	English: 3.0%	
Rural population:	2.3%	1.3% Asian	**2000 Presidential Vote**	
Pop. 2000:	651,619	0.2% Native Am.	Gore (D) 86,133	(57%)
Median income:	$31,801	0.1% Hawaiian	Bush (R) 64,659	(43%)
Poverty status:	20.3%	1.1% Two+ races	**Cook Partisan Voting Index:** D + 7	
Military veterans:	13.7%	0.1% Other		
		68.2% Hispanic Origin		

Occupation	Blue collar: 24.3%	White collar: 56.7%	Gray collar: 19.0%

San Antonio, with its antique past and theme-park future, its Hispanic heritage, its military superstructure and its high-tech hopes, is unlike any other city in the United States. Here on a plaza is the Alamo, preserved by the Daughters of the Republic of Texas, where Davy Crockett, Jim Bowie and 184 others were wiped out in 1836 (Crockett was a Tennessee congressman for three terms; if he had not lost his reelection in 1834, he presumably would not have left Tennessee for Texas). The Spanish architecture recalls San Antonio's days as the most important town in Texas, when the state was part of Mexico, and contrasts with the 31-story Tower Life Building, which contrasts with the armadillo-like Alamodome; the stark terrain contrasts with the lushness of the Paseo, the 1970s-redeveloped Riverwalk along the tiny San Antonio River. The city includes old neighborhoods redolent of the Texas Germans who were its chief Anglo citizens for many years.

For most of the 20th century, San Antonio's economy was built on the military. What the locals call "Military City, U.S.A." remains the home of three Air Force bases, Fort Sam Houston and two military hospitals. In 1995 Bill Clinton bent the rules of the base closing process to keep in San Antonio the thousands of depot jobs at Kelly Air Force Base, a move so resented that Congress blocked new rounds of base closings. Kelly was finally closed in 2001; now the largest local employer is the health industry, which includes the Texas Health Science Center. San Antonio also has many military retirees and it has become a tourist center. Toyota plans a new truck assembly plant on the city's southwest edge.

San Antonio is Texas's third largest city and the ninth largest in the country, with a 22% increase in the 1990s, though its metro area of 1.6 million is only about one-third the size of metro Houston or the Dallas-Fort Worth Metroplex. Its low education and income levels are affected by the proximity of the Mexican border. Yet it has mostly avoided polarized politics and ethnic anger as it has made progress as a low-wage, high-tech center, with some linkage to nearby Austin.

The 20th Congressional District includes most of central San Antonio and its west side. The district is wholly contained within Bexar County; affluent Anglo neighborhoods are set off and placed in the 21st District. On the west it extends beyond Lackland Air Force Base to the county line. This is one of Texas' seven Hispanic-majority districts, and the first to elect a Hispanic congressman. It is solidly Democratic.

The congressman from the 20th District is Charles Gonzalez, a Democrat first elected in 1998. He is one of eight children of Henry B. Gonzalez, who held the seat for 37 years after a 1961 special election. Charles Gonzalez grew up in San Antonio, graduated from the University of Texas and St. Mary's University School of Law, and served in the Texas Air National Guard. He was an elementary school teacher, practiced law and served as a judge from 1982 to 1997. In late 1997, at 81 and in poor health, his father announced his retirement. Charles Gonzalez was the frontrunner for the seat, but the contest was more competitive than many had expected. He campaigned as a consensus-builder, emphasizing his background in negotiation and compromise. Symbolizing the economic transformation of San Antonio, he said he would work for the entire district, not simply the low-income groups. Taking a more feisty tone was Maria Berriozabal, a former city council member, who called for more outspoken leadership. In a brash move, she used a picture of Henry Gonzalez in her campaign literature and claimed that she was more his model than was Charles. Just before the March primary, his father issued a brief statement endorsing his son. Gonzalez led Berriozabal in the primary 44% to 22%. In the April runoff, Gonzalez benefited from a fundraising advantage of more than 2–1 and mostly ignored his opponent. He won 62%–38% and easily took the general election.

In the House, Gonzalez has a generally liberal voting record and took his father's seat on the now renamed Financial Services Committee. For both the Democratic Caucus and the Hispanic Caucus—which his father had refused to join—he became a leading proponent of census sampling; Census Bureau professionals and Commerce Secretary Donald Evans ruled that there was no evidence that sampling was more accurate than the head count. Perhaps surprisingly, he opposed Latino activists who wanted to create an additional Hispanic-majority district for Texas in the 2001 redistricting; because of low voter turnout among Hispanics, he said, such a step would reduce the Democratic majorities in other seats. After the 2002 election, he made a big push for a seat on the Energy and Commerce Committee, and was endorsed by the Hispanic Caucus. But Nancy Pelosi selected Hilda Solis of California. Some thought that Gonzalez suffered because he had backed other candidates against Pelosi in her races for minority whip and minority leader.

Since his initial election, Gonzalez has had no major party opposition.

TWENTY-FIRST DISTRICT

Rep. Lamar Smith (R)

Elected 1986, 9th term; b. Nov. 19, 1947, San Antonio; home, San Antonio; Yale U., B.A. 1969, S. Methodist U., J.D. 1975; Christian Scientist; married (Beth).

Elected Office: TX House of Reps., 1981–82; Bexar Cnty. Comm., 1982–85.

Professional Career: U.S. Small Business Admin., 1969–70; Business writer, *Christian Science Monitor*, 1970–72; Practicing atty., 1975–76.

DC Office: 2231 RHOB 20515, 202-225-4236; Fax: 202-225-8628; Web site: www.house.gov/lamarsmith.

District Office: San Antonio, 210-821-5024.

Committees: *Judiciary* (4th of 21 R): Courts, the Internet & Intellectual Property (Chmn.); Immigration, Border Security & Claims. *Science* (2d of 25 R): Research; Space & Aeronautics. *Select Committee on Homeland Security* (11th of 27 R): Cybersecurity, Science and Research & Development; Infrastructure & Border Security; Intelligence & Counterterrorism.

Group Ratings

	ADA	ACLU	AFS	LCV	CON	ITIC	NTU	COC	ACU	NTLC	CHC
2002	0	7	0	0	25	100	51	100	96	85	100
2001	0	—	0	0	—	—	61	100	96	—	—

National Journal Ratings

	2001 LIB	—	2001 CONS		2002 LIB	—	2002 CONS
Economic	15%	—	86%		32%	—	68%
Social	0%	—	81%		0%	—	75%
Foreign	14%	—	85%		15%	—	78%

Key Votes of the 107th Congress

1. Approve Bush Tax Cuts	Y	5. Faith-Based Charities	Y	9. Trade Promotion Authority	Y
2. Limit Patients' Bill of Rights	Y	6. Bar Gays in the Boy Scouts	Y	10. Bar Funds for Intl. Court	Y
3. Campaign Finance Reform	N	7. Ban Partial-Birth Abortion	Y	11. Authorize Force in Iraq	Y
4. Ban ANWR Development	N	8. Arm Commercial Pilots	Y	12. Deny Home. Sec. Dept. Union	Y

Election Results

2002 general	Lamar Smith (R)	161,836	(73%)	($798,990)
	John Courage (D)	56,206	(25%)	($167,000)
	Other	4,051	(2%)	
2002 primary	Lamar Smith (R)	unopposed		
2000 general	Lamar Smith (R)	251,049	(76%)	($543,754)
	Jim Green (D)	73,326	(22%)	
	Other	6,503	(2%)	

Prior Winning Percentages: 1998 (91%); 1996 (76%); 1994 (90%); 1992 (72%); 1990 (75%); 1988 (93%); 1986 (61%)

The People		Race/Ethnic Origin	Ancestry	
Area size:	11,088 sq. mi.	77.2% White	German: 16.1%	English: 10.1%
Urban population:	69.4%	2.1% Black	Irish: 8.7%	
Rural population:	30.6%	2.0% Asian	**2000 Presidential Vote**	
Pop. 2000:	651,619	0.3% Native Am.	Bush (R)	206,157 (73%)
Median income:	$52,751	0.1% Hawaiian	Gore (D)	77,056 (27%)
Poverty status:	7.0%	1.1% Two+ races	**Cook Partisan Voting Index:** R +23	
Military veterans:	16.5%	0.1% Other		
		17.2% Hispanic Origin		

Occupation Blue collar: 15.7% White collar: 72.6% Gray collar: 11.7%

The Balcones Escarpment is the invisible line, or rather the physiographic break, that separates the flat lands of coastal Texas from the stony hills to the north and west. The Hill Country is a lyrical part of Texas, part of its story told in *The Path to Power*, the first volume of Robert Caro's biography of Lyndon Johnson; he describes a dirt poor southern backwater, saved from poverty by dams that prevented floods and generated electricity. But the Hill Country west of Austin and northwest San Antonio is also the home of some of the oldest Texas German communities, established by immigrants who fled after the failure of the democratic revolutions of 1848. The Texas German country has always been a set of orderly communities in rip-roaring Texas, economically prosperous in a state that considered itself poor until it struck oil. It was anti-slavery and politically Republican in a state whose enthusiasm for the Democratic Party had roots in Confederate loyalties and populist rebellions. You can see the contrast today if you travel from Johnson City, LBJ's boyhood home, west past his LBJ Ranch in Gillespie County to the county seat of Fredericksburg. Johnson City is a small town of wooden structures, where the Hill Country Cupboard boasts "the world's best chicken-fried steak" and the one industry produces beef jerky, better off than in Johnson's day but not by any measure affluent. Fredericksburg, 30 miles west, is a town of two-story stone structures, with many restaurants and antique stores; Zweite Weihnachten, a German Christmas celebration, is an annual tradition.

The Hill Country today has a new group of settlers. From Austin, rapidly growing and increasingly affluent in the 1990s, and San Antonio, not as affluent but also growing, have come young families with high incomes seeking homesites in spacious new subdivisions spread out over the hills. Some are in western Travis County, where Austin has spread out into land that was vacant 20 years ago; some in northern Hays County around Dripping Springs, a vivid contrast with the low-income trailer parks east of I-35 (lined with outlet malls) and the Balcones Escarpment; some in Comal County as the old German town of New Braunfels spreads into the hills; some in Kendall County, directly north of San Antonio, where the flatness of the Alamo's city gives way to the hills. To the west is the old Texas German city of Kerrville, now increasingly prosperous and, with its relatively cool summers, a magnet for retirees. Going west, the Hill Country eventually peters out, and turns into rolling grazing land.

The 21st Congressional District includes all of this Hill Country. Its eastern boundary runs, roughly, along I-35 and the Balcones Escarpment. It includes much of the north side of San Antonio, its jagged boundaries enclosing most of the affluent and heavily Anglo parts of the city, although 24% of its Bexar County residents are Hispanic. It includes the western geographic half of Austin, west of the Capital of Texas Parkway and the MoPac freeway that run on the west side of Austin; this was mostly empty land 20 years ago. It includes all of New Braunfels and fast-growing Comal County just northeast of San Antonio and the part of western fast-growing Hays County, just southwest of Austin, west of San Marcos, where Johnson went to San Marcos State Teachers College. And it includes 10 counties to the west: the Hill Country and sheep-grazing country beyond. The 21st includes much of the territory represented by Johnson when he served in the House from 1937 to 1948. Johnson's career is entwined with the story of the Texas Germans, who were Texas's one usually Republican voting bloc from Reconstruction to the 1950s. The death of Republican Congressman Harry Wurzbach who represented San Antonio gave Democrats a majority in the House in 1931 and enabled them to elect John Nance Garner of Uvalde as speaker, while Wurzbach's replacement in the House, Democrat Richard Kleberg (of the King Ranch family) gave the then 23-year-old Johnson to his first Washington job. And, though Johnson never emphasized this, his LBJ Ranch was not in Blanco County or Johnson City, where he grew up, but west in Gillespie County near Fredericksburg. Today, the Texas German country continues to be Republican, indeed just about as Republican as any part of the country, and the new affluent subdivisions outside Austin and San Antonio are very heavily Republican too. George W. Bush won 73% of the vote in 2000.

The congressman from the 21st District is Lamar Smith, a Republican first elected in 1986. Smith is from an old San Antonio and south Texas ranching family; their Jim Wells County ranch has been in the family for four generations. He graduated from Yale and SMU law school, worked as a reporter and a lawyer, was elected to the Texas House in 1980 and the Bexar County Commission in 1982. In 1986, when Congressman Tom Loeffler ran for governor, Smith ran for the

House; at that time the 21st District ranged even wider and had more acreage than Ohio. Smith won by beating two other San Antonio-based candidates in the primary and then winning the runoff 54%–46% against a religious conservative; his campaign was run by then little-known Texas political consultant Karl Rove.

Smith compiled a conservative voting record and pursued original initiatives when Democrats held the majority. One bill added 100,000 acres to Big Bend National Park along the Rio Grande; another sponsored the first Bush administration's government-wide ethics act. In the majority, Smith chaired the Immigration Subcommittee of Judiciary from 1995 to 2001. He had long believed in stronger action to stop illegal immigration and to reduce legal immigration, and in 1995 he steered his immigration bill through subcommittee. But on the House floor, a bipartisan group including liberal Democrats and freshmen Republicans successfully moved to strip almost all provisions on legal immigration—the effective end of Smith's move to reduce legal immigration. The bill passed by a wide margin, but House-Senate conferees removed almost all aid for illegals, even as the welfare bill barred states from aiding legal immigrants. The final version had stricter deportation and asylum proceedings, doubled the number of Border Patrol agents and mandated a 14-mile fence on the California-Mexico border. In the midst of his reelection campaign, Bill Clinton signed it.

Smith has supported some liberalizing immigration provisions but he opposed Bill Clinton's proposal for, and George W. Bush's suggestion of legalization of, illegal immigrants living in the United States for many years. His bill to split the INS into two agencies, one concentrating on law enforcement, the other on aid to immigrants, was passed as part of the homeland security bill in November 2002. Smith was initially skeptical about increasing the number of H-1B visas for high-skill immigrants. But in 2000 data convinced him that foreigners were needed to fill high-tech jobs, and he sponsored the House bill that removed the cap on the visas through 2002; a different version became law in October 2000. In a 1999 subcommittee hearing, Smith recalled the 1993 World Trade Center bombing and said, with eerie prescience, "The time to act is now before either [Canada or the United States] has another World Trade Center bombing." In July 2002 he pointed out that he had proposed, unsuccessfully, changes that were made after the attack. "I am not saying I told you so, but it is interesting that the Bush administration just in the last few months has increased the Border Patrol agents, which we called for in '96. They're doing a better job of tracking foreign students, which we called for in '96. They're planning an entry-exit system, which we had in 1996. So I suspect, as Mark Twain said, imitation is the sincerest form of flattery."

In 2001, having served the six years permitted by House Republican rules as chairman of the Immigration Subcommittee, Smith became chairman of what was then the Crime Subcommittee. There he focused on cybercime and high-tech issues. He strongly supported the Patriot Act, which passed in October 2001. In December 2001, he introduced a bill providing for sentences up to life for malicious computer hacking, better coordinating the FBI's National Infrastructure Protection Center, raising the stature of the Justice Department's Office of Science and Technology and providing protection from legal liability for Internet service providers which alert government officials to possible criminal activity. The House passed the bill in July 2002, 385–3, but the Senate failed to act. The second bill came in response to an April 2002 Supreme Court decision that held that previous child pornography laws did not apply to electronically produced images of children. Smith's bill expanded the definition to include computer imaging and to rule out any defense based on a claim that the pornography was an electronic creation. It passed the House in June, 413–8, but the Senate did not take it up. After the 2002 election, the chairmanship of the Courts, the Internet and Intellectual Property Subcommittee came open because of term limits, and Smith was appointed the new chairman. Before the election he had represented part of Williamson County, just north of Austin; starting in 2002, he represents western Travis County; both of these are full of people who have brought about the Austin area's high-tech boom. Some high-tech groups had opposed Smith's initial position on H-1B visas, but on other high-tech issues he has been in accord with the industry's thinking. He has worked on these and on other issues of local importance with Austin Democrat Lloyd Doggett; now the Austin area has three congressmen with the election of Republican John Carter from Williamson County in the newly created 31st District.

Smith is second in seniority among Republicans on the Science Committee. Most Texans have been strongly supportive of the manned space program. But after the loss of space shuttle Columbia in February 2003, Smith expressed some skepticism. "I think we need to revisit the question of whether manned missions are absolutely necessary. That's not to say we ought to exclusively do one or the other. Maybe we should undertake fewer manned missions." From January 1999 to January 2001, Smith chaired the ethics committee but the practice of bringing ethics complaints for partisan reasons has been discontinued, and Smith had few cases to contend with. In February 2003, he was named to the new Homeland Security Committee.

Smith has been easily reelected by wide margins, 73%–25% in 2002. In that contest 222,000 votes were cast in the 21st District, more than three times as many as in the next-door 20th District, and 53,000 more than in any other district in Texas.

TWENTY-SECOND DISTRICT

Rep. Tom DeLay (R)

Elected 1984, 10th term; b. Apr. 8, 1947, Laredo; home, Sugar Land; U. of Houston, B.S. 1970; Baptist; married (Christine).

Elected Office: TX House of Reps., 1978–84.

Professional Career: Owner, Albo Pest Control, 1973–84.

DC Office: 242 CHOB 20515, 202-225-5951; Fax: 202-225-5241; Web site: www.majorityleader.gov.

District Office: Stafford, 281-240-3700.

Committees: *Majority Leader.*

Group Ratings

	ADA	ACLU	AFS	LCV	CON	ITIC	NTU	COC	ACU	NTLC	CHC
2002	0	7	0	0	79	88	59	95	92	100	100
2001	0	—	0	0	—	—	73	100	100	—	—

National Journal Ratings

	2001 LIB — 2001 CONS	2002 LIB — 2002 CONS
Economic	0% — 94%	0% — 91%
Social	0% — 81%	0% — 75%
Foreign	0% — 97%	15% — 78%

Key Votes of the 107th Congress

1. Approve Bush Tax Cuts	Y	5. Faith-Based Charities	Y	9. Trade Promotion Authority	Y
2. Limit Patients' Bill of Rights	Y	6. Bar Gays in the Boy Scouts	Y	10. Bar Funds for Intl. Court	Y
3. Campaign Finance Reform	N	7. Ban Partial-Birth Abortion	Y	11. Authorize Force in Iraq	Y
4. Ban ANWR Development	N	8. Arm Commercial Pilots	Y	12. Deny Home. Sec. Dept. Union	Y

Election Results

2002 general	Tom DeLay (R)	100,499	(63%)	($1,274,921)
	Tim Riley (D)	55,716	(35%)	($192,709)
	Other	2,869	(2%)	
2002 primary	Tom DeLay (R)	22,179	(80%)	
	Mike Fjetland (R)	5,619	(20%)	
2000 general	Tom DeLay (R)	154,662	(60%)	($1,298,995)
	Jo Ann Matranga (D)	92,645	(36%)	($6,597)
	Other	8,960	(3%)	

Prior Winning Percentages: 1998 (65%); 1996 (68%); 1994 (74%); 1992 (69%); 1990 (71%); 1988 (67%); 1986 (72%); 1984 (65%)

The People		Race/Ethnic Origin	Ancestry	
Area size:	1,706 sq. mi.	60.1% White	German: 10.5%	English: 6.9%
Urban population:	87.5%	10.1% Black	Irish: 6.8%	
Rural population:	12.5%	8.3% Asian	**2000 Presidential Vote**	
Pop. 2000:	651,619	0.3% Native Am.	Bush (R)...............156,219 (68%)	
Median income:	$62,678	0.0% Hawaiian	Gore (D)................72,806 (32%)	
Poverty status:	6.6%	1.4% Two+ races	**Cook Partisan Voting Index:** R +19	
Military veterans:	11.2%	0.1% Other		
		19.7% Hispanic Origin		

Occupation	Blue collar: 19.7%	White collar: 69.3%	Gray collar: 11.0%

Those seeking the story of Houston's booming growth over the last dozen years would be well advised to go out the Southwest Freeway 45 minutes or so (if the traffic is not too bad) to Sugar Land. Here in once rural Fort Bend County, on the site of the old Imperial Sugar Mill, is a privately planned city of 63,000, with privatized water and other services, immaculately clean and fast-growing (there were 33,000 people here in 1990). The entrepreneurial spirit is alive and well, with thousands of new and growing businesses, and so is a communitarian spirit, with dozens of churches and civic associations buzzing with activity. People welcome the new freeways and toll roads being built, to link them with Houston's airports and other business nodes. The image of suburbia has long been one of an all-white haven, but Sugar Land and Fort Bend County are welcoming to immigrants and minorities. Some 20% of the county population is black, and 77% of its blacks own their own homes; another 21% are Hispanic and 11% are Asian, the highest of any county in Texas. A reporter from the *San Francisco Chronicle* came to Sugar Land to see "the anti-San Francisco" and seemed charmed by a community that "welcomes immigrants, shopping centers and jogging paths." Sugar Land has elected David Wong, from Macao, to the city council and Dinesh Shah, from India, to the board of the Chamber of Commerce. "Sugar Landers consider themselves thoroughly diverse. There are Chinese Republicans and Indian Republicans. Palestinian Catholics run the town's popular Brookstreet Barbeque. Muslims have a bagpipe band. Hindus are building a temple." This is America 2003.

The 22d Congressional District is made up of all of Fort Bend County except for 32,000 people, mostly black, inside the Houston city limits. It also includes three-quarters of Brazoria County, from fast-growing Pearland, just south of Houston, south to Lake Jackson, almost up to the Brazosport area on the Gulf of Mexico. About one-quarter of its residents are in Harris County, in the far southeast extension of Houston and in Deer Park and LaPorte south of the Houston Ship Channel; the Johnson Space Center is just outside its boundaries. Overall the district's population is 60% Anglo, 10% black, 20% Hispanic and 8% Asian—the last the highest percentage in any Texas district. Politically, the 22d District is heavily Republican, though not as much so as the ethnically less diverse 8th District in the northern part of metro Houston. The 8th District voted 78% for George W. Bush in 2000 and the 22d District only 68%—but that is still 20% more Republican than the national average.

The Congressman from the 22d District is Tom DeLay, of Sugar Land, a Republican first elected in 1984 and now House Majority Leader. He was born in Laredo, on the border. His father was in the oil business, and between ages 9 and 14 he lived in Venezuela; he claims to have come close to being killed in one of its revolutionary upheavals. He attended Baylor University for two years and was asked to leave, and graduated from the University of Houston. Then he settled in Sugar Land and started a pest control business—he is our only political leader who is a former exterminator. In his business he developed a hatred for the Environmental Protection Agency, which he has called "the Gestapo of government." In 1978 he was elected to the state House, the first Republican legislator from Fort Bend County in the 20th century. When 22d District Congressman Ron Paul (now congressman from the 14th District) ran for the Senate in 1984, DeLay ran for the House. He won a five-candidate primary with 53% of the vote and won the general election 65%–35%.

DeLay's voting record in the House has been very conservative; he has combined a strong ideological motivation and a knack for practical politics. The motivation comes at least partly from a profound religious experience he had in 1985—at about the same time and about the same point in his life as George W. Bush. In his second term he got a seat on the Appropriations Committee. But he opposed a $1.2 billion monorail and has opposed any extension of Houston's light rail line into Fort Bend County without approval of the voters. In the House he showed early on an interest in leadership positions and prowess as a vote-counter. In March 1989 he managed the campaign of moderate Edward Madigan to replace Dick Cheney as minority whip; but Madigan lost 87–85 to Newt Gingrich—a result that made a revolutionary change in the House. Madigan's loss didn't stop DeLay from running in December 1992 against incumbent Bill Gradison for the post of Republican Conference Secretary; DeLay won 95–71. It was clear that Robert Michel would retire as Minority Leader in 1994, and that Gingrich would run to succeed him. DeLay started running for whip, presumed to be the second highest leadership post at a time when almost no one thought Republicans would win a majority in the 1994 elections; that meant that DeLay was trying to leapfrog Dick Armey on the leadership ladder. After the Republicans won their majority in 1994, Gingrich was easily elected speaker and Armey majority leader and DeLay kept running for whip. He had serious opposition from Robert Walker, Gingrich's best friend in the House, and Bill McCollum. But he had done much more to prepare, campaigning in 25 states and contributing $2 million to Republican candidates. DeLay showed his vote-counting acumen by proclaiming that he was not interested in the second-ballot votes he would need if no one had a majority. He won with 119 votes to 80 for Walker and 28 for McCollum.

So DeLay came to the whip position as an independent operator, capable of amassing a majority of Republican members. As whip, his job was to assemble majorities on the House floor, and he proved himself a master of that. Over his eight years as whip he built a massive and loyal organization of as many as 67 deputy whips. Through them he could keep in close touch with Republican members of all stripes. He became known as "the Hammer," for his ability to hammer out majorities on the floor of the House over eight years when there were never more than 236 Republican members and at one time as few as 221—just three more than the majority of 218. But he kept Republicans together not just by hammering them, but by serving their needs. His first floor office—invaded by a gun-wielding maniac in July 1998 who killed two Capitol policemen—was always stocked with food during late night sessions; his staff was happy to make travel arrangements for members. As one Republican member said, "His whip operation is a cross between the concierge at the Plaza and the mafia. They can get you anything you want, but it will cost you." Like Democratic whips before him, he expected members to support the leadership on procedural votes, especially the rules limiting debate voted by the Rules Committee, and, with others in the leadership, made committee assignments in light of such votes. "I looked at what kind of a team member have they been. Have they participated and acted like they were a member of the team?" Moderate Republican members have often been unhappy, but he insists that he has supported them in campaigns. His vote-counting ability has enabled him to make the minimum substantive concessions to amass a majority; no need for more concessions to get votes that aren't needed. And on occasion he has brought measures to the floor without a majority in hand and has, while Speaker Dennis Hastert keeps the roll call running, squeezed out the critical votes on the floor, as he did twice on trade promotion authority, in December 2001 and July 2002.

In all these respects DeLay has followed the pattern of Democratic whips before him, except that he seems to have been better at corralling majorities than they mostly were. But he has also tried to change the culture of Washington. In his first years as whip, he tried to change the culture of regulatory commissions by riders on environmental issues, demanding cost-benefit analyses or placing a moratorium on new regulations. On these he was mostly frustrated by Clinton vetoes and by moderate Republican dissenters. He also sought to change the culture of K Street—the shorthand term for Washington's lobbying community. He worked closely with sympathetic lobbyists, bringing them in on the drafting of legislation, and has also raised money from them in very large amounts. K Street from New Deal days until 1994 had been overwhelmingly Democratic. DeLay insisted that trade associations and big corporations must hire Republicans as lobbyists. That brought him bad publicity and a private rebuke from the ethics committee when in October 1998 he attacked the Electronics Industries Alliance for hiring as its president former Democratic Congressman Dave McCurdy. But as Republicans kept winning House elections, it became clear to K Street denizens that they must hire Republicans if they wanted to be effective, and they have hired more and more, including prominently many former members of DeLay's staff. DeLay has also had great success raising money, from K Street and elsewhere. After the 1998 election, DeLay worked to replace NRCC Chairman John Linder, a Georgian and ally of Newt Gingrich, with Tom Davis of Virginia, a moderate with a detailed knowledge of the politics of every district. DeLay promoted a group called the US Family Network, a 501(c)4 group that raised $1.3 million in 1998 from five donors and to which the NRCC gave $500,000 in October 1999, and he started the Republican Majorities Issues Campaign, a Section 527 organization also not required to disclose contributors. In May 2000 Patrick Kennedy, then head of DCCC, brought a RICO suit charging that DeLay "extorted" funds from donors and laundered them through groups like US Family Network and RMIC, and the House in June 2000 passed a law requiring disclosure by Section 527 organizations. Many Democrats admitted that Kennedy's suit was an abuse of the RICO law, and DeLay threatened to take depositions of every House Democrat; the suit was eventually settled in April 2001.

DeLay's relationship with Gingrich was tense; he supported him when his reelection as speaker was uncertain in January 1997, but in July 1997 he met with leaders of the coup against Gingrich, telling them the leadership would support a floor vote to oust him. But the coup failed, and at a Republican Conference meeting a few days later, DeLay came dramatically forward and admitted his participation in the coup attempt, while Dick Armey seemed to deny his. From that point forward, it was clear DeLay had much more support in the conference than Armey. In November 1998, when Gingrich quit after the disappointing results of the election, DeLay supported Bob Livingston for speaker. But on the morning of the impeachment vote in December 1998, Livingston shocked everyone by announcing that he would resign. Members began hovering around DeLay at the back of the chamber. Armey clearly did not have the support to win the speakership; DeLay, aware that he was "too nuclear," made no move to run. Instead he turned to the man he had named Chief Deputy Whip, Dennis Hastert, little known outside the House but respected by Republican members as a hard worker, consensus builder and party loyalist. "And so I pulled Denny aside and told him that he had to run for speaker. And he turned white as a sheet." Within hours it would be clear that Hastert would be the next speaker.

Many assumed that Hastert would be DeLay's puppet, but Hastert and DeLay often disagreed on basic strategy, and Hastert usually prevailed. In October 1999 DeLay wanted to pass stripped-down appropriations, even if they would be vetoed by Bill Clinton, so that Republicans could argue that they preserved the Social Security surplus. But Hastert preferred to cut compromises with the Clinton White House. In October 2000 they agreed on not reaching an agreement with Clinton before the election, by refusing to drop language delaying the ergonomics rule. In the delayed session after the election, DeLay wanted to pass a one-year continuing resolution, daring Clinton to veto it; Hastert and Trent Lott preferred to negotiate with Clinton and avoid a government shutdown. DeLay's relations with George W. Bush's campaign were not always smooth. In October 1999 Bush attacked the leadership's—and DeLay's—proposal to save $8 billion in the next budget by sending out EITC payments every month instead of in one check in the spring. Bush said that was balancing the budget on the backs of the working poor; DeLay said, "It's obvious the governor's got a lot to learn about Congress." But DeLay was a loyal and aggressive Bush supporter during the Florida controversy.

For the most part, Hastert, Armey and DeLay delivered for the administration; Bush, unlike his father, could count on a favorable vote in the House and then could negotiate with the Senate. The danger for House Republicans is that that they would be left hanging out there with an unpopular issue stand while Bush and the Democratic (from June 2001 to January 2003) Senate would get the credit. This didn't happen often. The most notable example was on airline security, in which DeLay squeezed out a 218–214 vote in November 2001 against federalizing employees. But the Senate voted 100–0 for federal security employees, and Bush didn't fight it hard. In December 2001 Dick Armey announced that he would not run for reelection in 2002 (Texas has a March primary and an early filing deadline, forcing him to announce then), and hours later DeLay began quietly running for the post. Ray LaHood, often a critic of the leadership, said he wanted to run; some Republicans pressed John Boehner, voted out of the leadership in 1998 and fresh from his success managing the education bill, to run. But Tom Reynolds announced that DeLay had 140 votes, far more than a majority, and Boehner showed no interest. So instead of a long and divisive leadership battle, the succession passed quietly and smoothly. In November 2002 DeLay was elected majority leader without opposition and his chief deputy whip Roy Blunt was elected whip. Reynolds was elected chairman of the NRCC.

Many Democrats crowed that DeLay, with his outspoken and blunt conservatism, would be a target Democrats could run against, as they had run against Newt Gingrich. But DeLay is much less known to the public than Gingrich was, and as a member of the House leadership of the president's party he is not likely to be a prominent agenda-setter. To be sure, DeLay is a conviction politician willing to take unpopular stands in the glare of the public spotlight, as he did during the impeachment of Bill Clinton; Clinton would probably not have been impeached without him. But in 2002 and early 2003 DeLay sought the spotlight mainly to advance his views on foreign policy issues on which his stances were widely popular.

Emphasizing foreign policy was not out of character. He called the return of Elian Gonzalez to totalitarian Cuba "the lowest point of the Clinton administration's tenure, a statement I make with full knowledge of its considerable excesses and transgressions." In February 2000 he sponsored the Taiwan Security Act, despite the opposition of the Clinton administration; it passed the House 341–70. In June 2000 he sponsored a bill to bar the U.S. from cooperating with the International Criminal Court established in the 1998 Rome treaty unless and until the Senate ratified it. In May 2001 a similar amendment, barring cooperation with the Court and denying U.S. military assistance to non-NATO countries who cooperate with it passed 282–137; the Bush administration did not oppose it.

In 2002 he emerged as the House's loudest voice in support of Israel. In April, when the Bush administration was still talking about encouraging talks between Israel and Palestinians and was ambiguous on the role of Yasir Arafat, DeLay went to Westminster College in Fulton, Missouri, where Winston Churchill had named the Iron Curtain in 1946, and delivered a speech linking Yasir Arafat with terrorism. It was a prod to Bush, who had said he would not negotiate with terrorists, and a jab at State Department Arabists, who argued that Arafat was the only person to negotiate with. "The defense of freedom demands more of us than value-neutral brokerage. It is time for us to stand squarely against the terrorist organizations which systematically attack Israel." Later in the month at the American Israel Public Affairs Committee meeting he said, "We cannot act as a mere broker. Israel is resisting a campaign of death. America must stick to our policy of unending hostility to terrorism. Let me make something clear to those who urge the United States to pressure Israel. America does not run out on her friends." He received six standing ovations and impressed many lifelong Democratic supporters in the audience. In the House DeLay was co-sponsoring with Democrat Tom Lantos, Congress's only Holocaust survivor, a resolution supporting Israel and denouncing Arafat. On April 29, at the urging of Secretary of State Colin Powell, DeLay agreed to delay taking the resolution to the floor. But on May 1 Bush told Majority Leader Tom Daschle that he had no objection to Senate action on a resolution sponsored by Joe Lieberman, which supported Israel but did not condemn Arafat as much. DeLay scheduled a House vote on his and Lantos's resolution, with minor changes in wording, on May 2, and it passed 352–21, with 29 voting present; almost all of the nays and abstentions came from Democrats.

One issue on which DeLay has surprised his detractors is foster care. In September 1994 Christine DeLay became a trained Court Appointed Special Advocate and the DeLays became foster parents to several children. DeLay was infuriated in January 2000 at the violent death of two-year-old Brianna Blackmond, supposedly under the care of the District of Columbia foster care agency, after she was returned to the custody of her biological mother by a judge who heard nothing from the agency or the lawyer appointed to represent the girl. DeLay angrily confronted District officials. He sought action in the House to change the D.C. system; D.C. Delegate Eleanor Holmes Norton, usually opposed to congressional interference in District affairs, said, "His commitment is sincere, and it's deep, and he has special credibility because he and his wife have had foster children." Liberal columnist Mary McGrory, who has long crusaded for better treatment of foster children, wrote admiring columns about DeLay. Back in Texas, Christine DeLay has been raising money for a $5 million foster home, The Oaks at Rio Bend, to serve 250 abandoned and abused children, with sports facilities, a chapel, counseling—and no government money.

In the 22d District, DeLay has regularly been reelected by wide margins. The increasing black, Hispanic and Asian populations in the district have led some Democrats to think he might be vulnerable, and his percentage did go down from 65% in 1998 to 60% in 2000. In 2002 pollster John Zogby, polling in August for a nonpolitical client, found that district voters favored DeLay over his Democratic opponent by only 54%–34%. Usually polls tend to understate the percentage for unknown challengers and come pretty close to the percentages for well-known incumbents. This one was the other way around: DeLay won 63%–35%. In 2003 DeLay pressed Texas's Republican legislature to redraw the state's congressional district lines, arguing that the partisan composition of the congressional delegation failed to reflect the state's Republican dominance at the polls. A 2001 federal court decision had mostly kept in place the district configurations from the 1991 partisan Democratic districting; DeLay backed a map that would dramatically alter that—and create a solidly Republican delegation. But in May 2003 state House Democrats fled the state (to prevent a quorum) rather than vote on a new map.

TWENTY-THIRD DISTRICT

Rep. Henry Bonilla (R)

Elected 1992, 6th term; b. Jan. 2, 1954, San Antonio; home, San Antonio; U. of TX, B.A. 1976; Baptist; married (Deborah).

Professional Career: TV Reporter, 1976–80; Asst. Press Secy., PA Gov. Thornburgh, 1981; Writer/producer, WABC, New York, 1982–85; Asst. News Dir., WATF–TV, Philadelphia, 1985–86; KENS–TV, San Antonio, Exec. News Producer, 1986–89, Public Affairs, 1989–92.

DC Office: 2458 RHOB 20515, 202-225-4511; Fax: 202-225-2237; Web site: www.house.gov/bonilla.

District Offices: Alpine, 915-837-1313; Del Rio, 830-774-6547; Laredo, 956-726-4682; San Antonio, 210-697-9055.

Committees: *Appropriations* (11th of 36 R): Agriculture, Rural Development, & FDA (Chmn.); Defense; Foreign Operations & Export Financing.

Group Ratings

	ADA	ACLU	AFS	LCV	CON	ITIC	NTU	COC	ACU	NTLC	CHC
2002	0	7	0	0	8	100	53	95	92	83	100
2001	0	—	0	0	—	—	61	96	92	—	—

National Journal Ratings

	2001 LIB	—	2001 CONS		2002 LIB	—	2002 CONS
Economic	15%	—	82%		9%	—	87%
Social	20%	—	69%		0%	—	75%
Foreign	0%	—	97%		15%	—	78%

Key Votes of the 107th Congress

1. Approve Bush Tax Cuts	Y	5. Faith-Based Charities	Y	9. Trade Promotion Authority	Y
2. Limit Patients' Bill of Rights	Y	6. Bar Gays in the Boy Scouts	Y	10. Bar Funds for Intl. Court	Y
3. Campaign Finance Reform	N	7. Ban Partial-Birth Abortion	Y	11. Authorize Force in Iraq	Y
4. Ban ANWR Development	N	8. Arm Commercial Pilots	Y	12. Deny Home. Sec. Dept. Union	Y

Election Results

2002 general	Henry Bonilla (R)	77,573	(52%)	($2,413,172)
	Henry Cuellar (D)	71,067	(47%)	($1,055,342)
	Other	1,912	(1%)	
2002 primary	Henry Bonilla (R)	unopposed		
2000 general	Henry Bonilla (R)	119,679	(59%)	($1,050,250)
	Isidro Garza, Jr. (D)	78,274	(39%)	($364,440)
	Other	3,801	(2%)	

Prior Winning Percentages: 1998 (64%); 1996 (62%); 1994 (63%); 1992 (59%)

The People		Race/Ethnic Origin	Ancestry	
Area size:	55,536 sq. mi.	29.8% White	German: 6.8%	English: 4.2%
Urban population:	80.4%	1.4% Black	Irish: 3.9%	
Rural population:	19.6%	1.0% Asian	**2000 Presidential Vote**	
Pop. 2000:	651,619	0.3% Native Am.	Bush (R)..............105,789 (59%)	
Median income:	$36,158	0.0% Hawaiian	Gore (D)................74,727 (41%)	
Poverty status:	22.1%	0.7% Two+ races	**Cook Partisan Voting Index:** R + 9	
Military veterans:	10.9%	0.1% Other		
		66.8% Hispanic Origin		

Occupation   Blue collar: 21.8%   White collar: 61.0%   Gray collar: 17.1%

"On the streets of Laredo," runs an old country song, summoning up images of lonely cowboys on dusty streets outside a row of saloons in a tiny town. But this is not the Laredo of today. Laredo, on the Rio Grande 150 miles south of San Antonio, is the main border crossing for U.S.-Mexico trade: some 9,000 trucks and 1,200 rail cars cross its three bridges (one 17 miles upriver) every day, with merchandise worth upward of $100 billion a year, more than through all the other border crossings combined. Laredo was America's second fastest-growing city in the 1990s, with more warehouse space than San Antonio and Austin combined; its old downtown streets with their bargain stores are still filled with Mexicans who cross the border on foot, but those with cars head up the freeway to malls, and the Wal-Mart here is said to be the chain's top producer per square foot. Incomes and housing prices in Laredo (population 310,000 in 2000) are low by U.S. standards, but far above those of Nuevo Laredo (population 500,000 in 2000) across the Rio Grande, and there is money to be made here. Laredo's Tony Sanchez, proprietor of a family oil and gas business and owner of International Bank of Commerce, became rich enough to spend $60 million on his campaign for governor of Texas in 2002.

The border country along the Rio Grande is in some ways a zone all its own, a mixture of the U.S. and Mexico, where many people have roots on both sides of the border. As Laredo Mayor Betty Flores says, "The river for us is more like some street that we cross; it's really not a border." Webb County, almost all of whose people live in Laredo, had a population 94% Hispanic in 2000, and fast food restaurants here feature enchiladas more than hamburgers. Los Dos Laredos share a minor league baseball team. Yet the predictions that Latinos would Mexicanize the United States don't seem to be panning out. Years ago, movements like La Raza Unida—which got its beginnings here in 1969 when Hispanic youngsters wanted to elect high school cheerleaders in Crystal City— wanted the border country to become more like Mexico, with its union and party apparatchiks. More recently, Mexico, with its economic reforms and NAFTA, and with the election of President Vicente Fox in July 2000, has been trying to become more like the United States, and particularly like Texas, with open markets and privatized companies, less controlled by political or labor bosses.

The 23d Congressional District includes Laredo and nearly 800 miles of the U.S.-Mexican border. Geographically, it is roughly the size of Illinois. Most of the borderland is barren scrub, like most of the land between Laredo and San Antonio. Some of it is mountainous: the mountains around Big Bend National Park have attracted artists and other eccentrics, enchanted with the landscape, the clear air in which you can see for 180 miles and the wide variety of birds you can watch. On the north it stretches from the north side of San Antonio west almost to El Paso. Most of the population is clustered in urban areas—27% in Laredo and 20% in San Antonio. Some 5% each are in and around Del Rio and Eagle Pass. Overall, the district population is 67% Hispanic. Politically, there are wide differences within the district. Laredo and the border counties are mostly very Democratic. The district's portion of San Antonio and Bexar County is quite affluent and heavily Republican. The ranching counties with low Hispanic populations are also Republican. In 2000 the district voted 59% for George W. Bush. But in 2002, when Tony Sanchez's campaign produced a huge increase in turnout in Laredo and Webb County, the House race here was very closely contested.

The congressman from the 23d District is Henry Bonilla, a Republican first elected in 1992, when he beat a scandal-tarred incumbent. He was raised in a Latino neighborhood on the south side of San Antonio. His grandmother worked as a maid, and his father held down two jobs. Bonilla graduated from the University of Texas and then worked as a TV reporter, producer and executive in San Antonio, New York, Philadelphia and, starting in 1986, San Antonio again; his wife is an anchor for a San Antonio station. In 1991, Bexar County Republican leaders recruited Bonilla to run for Congress against incumbent Democrat Albert Bustamante, who reportedly was being investigated by the FBI for racketeering, who had 30 overdrafts on the House bank and who, after the election, was convicted of two counts of misuse of office for racketeering and bribery. Bonilla backed standard conservative planks but developed his own issues as well. Bustamante called Bonilla "a eunuch for the plantation owners" for opposing a minimum wage bill, but Bonilla won by a large 59%–38%, with most of his margin in San Antonio's Bexar County, which he won 81%–16%.

Republicans gave Bonilla a seat on Appropriations, where he has displayed a talent for placing deregulatory riders on appropriations bills—to eliminate funding for enforcing a rule on cardboard balers and to block the Labor Department from developing ergonomic standards. Bonilla voted enthusiastically for NAFTA and against gun control. He and Solomon Ortiz of the 27th District have been co-chairmen of the Border Caucus since 1997, and have worked successfully to get Mexico to abandon deposits on cars brought from the U.S. and to withdraw tax proposals which would affect U.S. companies operating maquiladoras and have sought equality in duty-free rules and reversal of a decision not to allow commuter students to attend U.S. colleges and universities. Bonilla has refused to join the Hispanic Caucus, lamenting that it lacks a bipartisan agenda, but he is cautious about banning racial quotas and preferences. He criticized a National Council of La Raza survey report. "All too often Hispanics are portrayed as victims, cowering in the neighborhoods, waiting for the federal government to rescue them. This is simply not the case," he wrote in July 2001. "There is a booming Hispanic middle class, with good prospects for future growth. Average Latino income has almost doubled in the past decade, and the amount of Latinos with a college education has risen almost 50%. . . . I don't know about the people who represent these 'professional minority' groups, but when I look in the mirror every morning I first see an American. I'm proud of my culture, but more proud and grateful to say I live in this country."

In January 2001 he became chairman of the Agriculture Appropriations Subcommittee, one of the "college of cardinals." As an appropriator, Bonilla was hostile to the Republican leadership's attempt to confine the committee to the administration's $759 billion total for discretionary spending. In May 2002 he was one of three Republican appropriators who voted "present" on a rule that would impose that limit; three others voted no, but the leadership prevailed anyway 216–209. As chairman, he received in 2002 some 2,700 requests for special projects, some of which he wrote into the appropriations, most not. His appropriation was approved early by the full committee, on July 11, but it was not filed with the leadership until July 26, to avoid amendments. When there was talk that ranking minority member Marcy Kaptur would file an amendment to limit farm subsidies, a Bonilla aide let it be known that if she did Bonilla was prepared to zero out all her projects in the 2003 appropriation. He has earmarked money for district projects—$7 million for El Paso desalinization, $3 million for I-69 and $3.5 million for El Metro in Laredo, $461,000 for Texas A&M International University's English as a second language program—and he made sure to keep in money for a rail spur from San Antonio to the site of the newly announced Toyota plant. He serves on the Defense Appropriations Subcommittee and announced in September 2002 that San Antonio's Fort Sam Houston was chosen as the new home of the U.S. Army South. In March 2003 he announced a $16 million Colonias Gateway Initiative, a nonprofit entity to coordinate aid to colonias.

Bonilla was an early and enthusiastic supporter of George W. Bush for president. Redistricting in November 2001 did not change the district much, and he seemed to be on the way to easy reelection. Instead he had tough competition from Henry Cuellar, a state representative from Laredo from 1986 to 2000, who was appointed secretary of state by Governor Rick Perry in December 2000 and resigned in January 2002.

Bonilla said that he didn't need Laredo to win; he had never won more than 49% of the vote in Webb County. That didn't go over well with outgoing Webb County Republican Chairman Gene Belmares, who in January 2002 endorsed Cuellar. "If Henry Bonilla has said publicly that he does not need Laredo to win, and if he does not want to include us as Republicans, fine. I will support Henry Cuellar." It was clear that Tony Sanchez's campaign for governor would produce a big increase in voter turnout in Webb County, and Democrats hoped that would make Cuellar competitive. In February 2002, a Bonilla aide parked outside Democratic headquarters to see who would emerge from a Cuellar fundraiser; after that Bonilla was said to have threatened to retaliate against colleagues who did, and he exchanged harsh words with Ruben Hinojosa, Charles Gonzalez and Ciro Rodriguez. Cuellar attacked Bonilla for his votes against funding the CHIP program, passage of the Family and Medical Leave Act, funding Pell grants, student loans, work study and classroom construction. And he accused him of being insufficiently Hispanic. "He said he 'doesn't wake up in the morning thinking he's Hispanic.' I don't know what he means by that."

Bonilla had the money advantage; he spent $2.4 million to Cuellar's $1 million. For most of the campaign, this race was not on either national party's radar screen. Bonilla had, after all, never won less than 59% of the vote. But despite miscues—he ended up hiring three campaign managers—Cuellar came up with an effective strategy given his comparative lack of funds. He started off by flying around to all the small communities in the district. Then he conducted an extensive blockwalking campaign in San Antonio and elsewhere; by August he claimed that he and his teams had walked every street in the district except in Laredo. He spent much of the last two months concentrating on turning out the vote in Webb County and only in the last month ran television ads. In Laredo he was helped by the great local enthusiasm for Tony Sanchez; Cuellar carried the county 84%–15%. On election night, that seemed to make the difference. Cuellar's 26,000-vote margin in Webb County gave him a 15,000 vote lead as the evening went on. But in San Antonio Bexar County officials were having trouble with their vote scanning machines. The final Bexar County totals were not reported until Wednesday night, and Bonilla's 75%–24% lead there erased Cuellar's lead and showed a 6,000-vote, 52%–47% victory for Bonilla. Cuellar acknowledged the loss, but seemed as if he were interested in a rematch. In 2003, national and Texas Democrats grumbled that Cuellar ran a flawed campaign; they were seeking a different challenger for 2004. How competitive this district will be in 2004 depends on whether Bonilla attracts a strong opponent and on whether the Webb County turnout was a onetime show of support for a local hero or the beginning of increased voter participation on the border.

TWENTY-FOURTH DISTRICT

Rep. Martin Frost (D)

Elected 1978, 13th term; b. Jan. 1, 1942, Glendale, CA; home, Arlington; U. of MO, B.A., B.J., 1964, Georgetown U., J.D. 1970; Jewish; married (Kathy).

Military Career: Army Reserves, 1966–72.

Professional Career: Staff writer, Congressional Quarterly, 1965–1967; Legal commentator, KERA–TV, Dallas, 1971–72; Practicing atty., 1972–78.

DC Office: 2256 RHOB 20515, 202-225-3605; Fax: 202-225-4951; Web site: www.house.gov/frost.

District Offices: Arlington, 817-303-1530; Dallas, 214-948-3401; Ft. Worth, 817-293-9231.

Committees: *Rules* (RMM of 4 D): The Legislative & Budget Process.

Group Ratings

	ADA	ACLU	AFS	LCV	CON	ITIC	NTU	COC	ACU	NTLC	CHC
2002	95	73	100	75	48	50	13	50	4	0	0
2001	85	—	100	64	—	—	9	50	25	—	—

National Journal Ratings

	2001 LIB	—	2001 CONS	2002 LIB	—	2002 CONS
Economic	74%	—	27%	77%	—	20%
Social	70%	—	30%	74%	—	19%
Foreign	43%	—	53%	69%	—	30%

Key Votes of the 107th Congress

1. Approve Bush Tax Cuts	N	5. Faith-Based Charities	N	9. Trade Promotion Authority	N
2. Limit Patients' Bill of Rights	N	6. Bar Gays in the Boy Scouts	N	10. Bar Funds for Intl. Court	N
3. Campaign Finance Reform	Y	7. Ban Partial-Birth Abortion	N	11. Authorize Force in Iraq	Y
4. Ban ANWR Development	Y	8. Arm Commercial Pilots	N	12. Deny Home. Sec. Dept. Union	N

Election Results

2002 general	Martin Frost (D)	73,002	(65%)	($1,566,087)
	Mike Rivera Ortega (R)	38,332	(34%)	($39,910)
	Other	1,560	(1%)	
2002 primary	Martin Frost (D)	unopposed		
2000 general	Martin Frost (D)	103,152	(62%)	($1,983,181)
	James (Bryndan) Wright (R)	61,235	(37%)	($205,245)
	Other	2,561	(2%)	

Prior Winning Percentages: 1998 (57%); 1996 (56%); 1994 (53%); 1992 (60%); 1990 (100%); 1988 (93%); 1986 (67%); 1984 (59%); 1982 (73%); 1980 (61%); 1978 (54%)

The People		Race/Ethnic Origin	Ancestry	
Area size:	261 sq. mi.	35.3% White	German: 5.3%	USA: 4.8%
Urban population:	99.5%	21.7% Black	English: 4.5%	
Rural population:	0.5%	3.1% Asian	**2000 Presidential Vote**	
Pop. 2000:	651,619	0.4% Native Am.	Gore (D) 83,806 (54%)	
Median income:	$36,962	0.1% Hawaiian	Bush (R) 70,665 (46%)	
Poverty status:	17.2%	1.3% Two+ races	**Cook Partisan Voting Index:** D + 4	
Military veterans:	9.7%	0.1% Other		
		38.0% Hispanic Origin		

Occupation	Blue collar: 30.4%	White collar: 55.0%	Gray collar: 14.6%

The geographical heart of the Dallas-Fort Worth Metroplex was open country as late as the 1950s, when the Dallas-Fort Worth Turnpike was built over empty land to link the two downtowns. Then, over the next three decades, the bottomlands of the West Fork of the Trinity River and the barren hills overlooking them filled up. Whole new Dallases and Fort Worths, with as many people as the central cities had in the 1950s—Grand Prairie and Arlington—grew up along the highway in these once impoverished lands and became central to one of America's richest and most productive metropolitan areas. Major civic landmarks have arisen here as well, such as The Ballpark in Arlington, the new old-style baseball stadium for the Texas Rangers built by managing partner George W. Bush. It also attracted some big employers with plants here or nearby—Northrop Grumman, General Motors, Hughes Training, Bell Textron Helicopter, Lockheed Martin. Now Arlington and Grand Prairie are in their second generation, taking on the patina of age, but above them you still see the big Texas sky and, in the distance, the small bluffs that mark the Balcones Escarpment, the geological divide between flat and lush east Texas and rolling and dry west Texas. In some neighborhoods, old houses are being torn down to be replaced by bigger, gaudier ones; in others, immigrants from Latin America or East Asia are moving in in large numbers.

The 24th Congressional District contains much of this area. Its eastern and western edges touch on downtown Dallas and downtown Fort Worth. It includes part of the old Oak Cliff neighborhood of Dallas, across the Trinity River south of downtown; this was a heavily black area in the 1980s, but now is heavily Hispanic. It also includes most of the modest suburbs of Duncanville and Cedar Hill to the south. The 24th includes most of Grand Prairie and the northern part of Arlington, including Six Flags Over Texas and The Ballpark. It also includes the eastern part of Fort Worth, including most of the city's predominantly black areas. About half the population is in the central cities of Fort Worth and Dallas and half in cities that are classified as suburban but have taken on an urban character of their own. Ethnically, the district is diverse: 35% Anglo, 22% black, 38% Hispanic, 3% Asian. Politically, it is a diverse area as well. The Fort Worth portion is heavily Democratic, the Dallas portion somewhat less so; Arlington and Grand Prairie tend to vote Republican. Overall the district voted 54% for Al Gore in 2000. This is the closest thing to an evenly balanced district in the Dallas-Fort Worth Metroplex.

The congressman from the 24th District is Martin Frost, a Democrat first elected in 1978. He is the only member of Congress married to a general, Major General Kathy George Frost, whom he met on a courtesy visit to the Army and Air Force Exchange Service in Oak Cliff; she is commanding officer of the Army and Air Force Exchange Service, based in Dallas. Martin Frost grew up in Fort Worth and had some political blood; his maternal grandfather was mayor of Henderson and his uncle a Rusk County judge and state senator. He graduated from the University of Missouri and Georgetown Law School. He clerked for Judge Sarah Hughes, who swore in Lyndon Johnson as president in November 1963, worked for *Congressional Quarterly* in Washington and for Jim Lehrer at public TV in Dallas and appeared as a commentator himself on the channel. But politics has been most of his professional life. The first Mid-Cities district was created in 1972, and Frost first ran for the seat in 1974, at 32, and lost the primary to incumbent Dale Milford. He ran again in 1978 and reversed the result. As a freshman he got a seat on the Rules Committee, thanks to Majority Leader Jim Wright of Fort Worth. Frost was a stalwart supporter of Wright to the end and has been close to the leadership, or in it, for years. He lost two leadership bids in the 1980s, backing off a bid to chair the Budget Committee in 1984 and losing the race for caucus vice chairman to Vic Fazio in 1989. But he came back to chair the IMPAC 2000 redistricting panel from 1991, coordinating Democratic redistricting efforts across the country, and was the chief architect of the Texas redistricting plan of 1991, which gave Democrats a 21–9 lead in the delegation in 1992. The federal court that drew new district lines in November 2001 followed that plan fairly closely.

After the debacle of 1994, Frost was appointed chairman of the DCCC. He led Democrats to gains of 9 seats in 1996 and, against off-year precedent, 5 in 1998, but they were left achingly short of a majority; he succeeded in holding down the number of Democratic retirees and, despite Republican Tom DeLay's efforts, maintained the flow of PAC money to Democratic incumbents and even to Democrats running in open seats. In November 1998 Frost defeated Rosa DeLauro 108–97 to replace Vic Fazio as Democratic Caucus chairman, a rare case of the moderate defeating the more liberal Democrat. Frost became the ranking Democrat on the Rules Committee after Joe Moakley died in May 2001.

Frost has worked on local causes, including funding the V-22 Osprey at Bell Helicopter Textron in Fort Worth; in October 2002 he helped secure $1.6 billion for 11 Ospreys in the defense appropriations bill. He is proud of having sponsored the Amber Hagerman Child Protection Act, tacked onto an appropriation bill in October 1996 and named for an Arlington 9-year-old who was kidnapped and murdered; it mandates life in prison for anyone twice convicted of a sex offense against a child. In 2002 he co-sponsored a national AMBER Alert, to complement state and local programs; the bill was enacted in April 2003.

Frost continued to work hard on nationwide redistricting as head of IMPAC 2000 after the 2000 Census. In 2001 he said that Republicans were overreaching in partisan plans in Pennsylvania and Michigan and predicted that court challenges would help Democrats. He argued that Republicans made no net gains in redistricting; Republicans claimed a net gain of between five and 10 seats. Judgment on this is subjective, and the truth may be somewhere in between. In Texas Frost stayed in touch with Speaker Pete Laney, who had a 78–72 Democratic majority, and contributed generously to Democratic candidates for the legislature in 1998 and 2000. He kept Democrats together while Republicans submitted several plans. Democrats' deftness at filing lawsuits found them in favorable state and federal courts. The federal court plan adopted in November 2001 explicitly set out to protect incumbents, which meant that many features of Frost's 1991 plan stayed in place and Democrats eked out a 17–15 majority in the delegation.

In 2001 and 2002 Frost was serving his final term as Caucus chairman under House Democrats' rules and after all his work on redistricting and in the leadership, he announced in February 2002 that he was seeking to move up. If Democrats were to win a majority, Dick Gephardt would become speaker and Frost would run for majority leader. If they stayed in the minority, it was widely assumed that Gephardt would step down as minority leader to run for president, and Frost would run for minority leader. In either case his likely opponent would be Nancy Pelosi, elected as minority whip by a 118–95 vote over Steny Hoyer in October 2001. As he had in past cycles, Frost had been raising money for other Democrats. Altogether he raised or contributed $7.5 million in 2001 and 2002, including $4.5 million to the DCCC and $1 million through his Lone Star Fund, which accepted soft money; nearly half that money came from four of the five Texas trial lawyers who collected $3.3 billion as their fee in the Texas tobacco settlement. Frost ran as "someone who is a consensus-builder and someone who can help build toward a majority." Many Democrats said that Pelosi would beat Frost as she had beaten Hoyer, with a coalition of Californians, women, liberals and some old-timers who admired her energy and political savvy. Frost hoped to beat her, as he had beaten DeLauro, with a coalition of Texans, southerners, Jews, blacks and moderates. But this would be a different Democratic Caucus. In 1976 the Caucus had 29 Californians, 22 Texans and 80 southerners. In 2002 it would have 33 Californians, 17 Texans and 57 southerners. And Pelosi won the support of three Texans—Max Sandlin, Lloyd Doggett and Frost's Dallas neighbor Eddie Bernice Johnson.

In retrospect, the vote on the Iraq war resolution forecast the outcome of the leadership contest. Frost was one of the first Democrats to openly support the use of military force in Iraq. Pelosi adamantly opposed it. During the debate on the Iraq war resolution, she busily counted votes and, some said, lobbied for Democrats to vote no. Frost, like Dick Gephardt, supported the resolution but did not lobby. To the surprise of many, House Democrats voted against the resolution by a margin of 126–81.

Two days after the election, Gephardt announced he would not run for minority leader again and Frost immediately announced he would. He posed the issue squarely. "I think that her politics are to the left, and I think that the party, to be successful, must speak to the broad center of the country." But a day after his announcement, Frost sent out a letter withdrawing from the race. "It is clear to me that Nancy Pelosi has the votes of a majority of the caucus. Nancy Pelosi is a talented and capable party leader. I intend to support her for Democratic leader in next week's election, and I will work with her to do everything I can to return Democrats to control of the House of Representatives."

In December 2002 there was speculation that Pelosi would appoint him chairman of the DCCC. His qualifications were strong: House Democrats had gained more seats during his chairmanship than in any cycle since 1982; he had good contacts among contributors, he had top-notch political staffers and an in-depth knowledge of the political situation across the country. But Pelosi decided instead to nominate fellow Californian Robert Matsui, who has had little experience in electoral politics outside his safe Democratic district.

Interestingly, Frost got a more favorable 24th District from the federal court redistricting plan of 2001 than from his own plan of 1991. But neither district is overwhelmingly Democratic. Frost's active constituency service probably helped him get through the Republican year of 1994 when he beat homebuilder Ed Harrison by only 53%–47%. His margin came from black precincts in Fort Worth. In a 1996 rematch he won 56%–39%. In 2000 and 2002 against poorly financed Republicans he won 62%–37% and 65%–34%. Redistricting remains a perilous proposition for Frost, however. If a new congressional map is passed for the 2004 election, he is almost certain to be put in jeopardy; Republicans have made clear he is a prime target.

TWENTY-FIFTH DISTRICT

Rep. Chris Bell (D)

Elected 2002, 1st term; b. Nov. 23, 1959, Abilene; home, Houston; U. of TX, B.J. 1982, South TX Col. of Law, J.D. 1992; Episcopalian; married (Alison).

Elected Office: Houston City Cncl., 1997–01.

Professional Career: Television and radio reporter, 1982–92; Practicing atty., 1992–02.

DC Office: 216 CHOB 20515, 202-225-7508; Fax: 202-225-2947; Web site: www.house.gov/bell.

District Offices: Baytown, 281-837-8225; Houston, 713-383-8600; Pasadena, 281-991-1300.

Committees: *Government Reform* (19th of 19 D): Criminal Justice, Drug Policy & Human Resources; National Security, Emerging Threats & Intl. Relations. *International Relations* (23d of 23 D): International Terrorism, Nonproliferation and Human Rights; Middle East & Central Asia. *Science* (11th of 22 D): Space & Aeronautics.

Group Ratings and Key Votes: Newly Elected

Election Results

2002 general	Chris Bell (D)	63,590	(55%)	($1,107,790)
	Tom Reiser (R)	50,041	(43%)	($4,538,270)
	Other	2,495	(2%)	
2002 runoff	Chris Bell (D)	9,572	(54%)	
	Carroll Robinson (D)	8,056	(46%)	
2002 primary	Chris Bell (D)	7,443	(36%)	
	Carroll Robinson (D)	5,597	(27%)	
	Paul Colbert (D)	4,307	(21%)	
	Stephen King (D)	3,274	(16%)	
2000 general	Ken Bentsen (D)	106,112	(60%)	($1,354,444)
	Phil Sudan (R)	68,010	(39%)	($3,247,033)
	Other	2,400	(1%)	

The People		Race/Ethnic Origin	Ancestry	
Area size:	280 sq. mi.	36.6% White	German: 5.8%	English: 4.9%
Urban population:	99.5%	22.7% Black	USA: 4.5%	
Rural population:	0.5%	4.8% Asian	**2000 Presidential Vote**	
Pop. 2000:	651,619	0.2% Native Am.	Gore (D) 86,764 (52%)	
Median income:	$38,048	0.0% Hawaiian	Bush (R) 81,359 (48%)	
Poverty status:	16.3%	1.3% Two+ races	**Cook Partisan Voting Index:** D + 1	
Military veterans:	8.6%	0.1% Other		
		34.3% Hispanic Origin		

Occupation	Blue collar: 24.2%	White collar: 60.0%	Gray collar: 15.8%

Spreading out in all directions from its historic center at Allen's Landing on Buffalo Bayou, Houston has become one of the great metropolises of North America. A half-century ago, the steaming flatlands south of Houston running down to the Gulf of Mexico did not seem a likely site for one of the world's most advanced civilizations. But they are today. It was Houston where most of the scientific work was done that put the first man on the moon—the first word spoken on the moon was "Houston." Houston is the undisputed center of expertise in the oil business, where the greatest concentration of experts in the world is within a few miles of each other. Houston has also become one of the great medical centers of the world, with the giant Texas Medical Center looming as impressively massive as any great office skyscraper complex. And Houston became one of the great surprise growth cities of the 1990s, creating thousands of small businesses, with special growth among immigrants. All this success and sophistication are testimony to human—

and Texan—creativity, and to the triumph of air conditioning. For who supposed that all these people would move here if they had to sweat through Houston's steamy five-month summer?

The 25th Congressional District includes many widely separated parts of metro Houston on the streets and freeways and waterways spreading out from the center of the city. It is astonishing that a federal court produced a district with such convoluted boundaries; the judges in this case said they were obliged to safeguard incumbents and preserve the political balance established by the partisan Democratic redistricting plan of 1991. In its eastern reaches it includes parts of industrial Baytown and Pasadena; areas with many white blue-collar workers. In the center it includes a large part of southwest Houston around Hobby Airport; this is an area where many Latinos are moving in. In the west it includes the affluent neighborhoods around the Texas Medical Center and Rice University and wealthy River Oaks. To the south of the old Astrodome it includes predominantly black neighborhoods. This is a mixed area in every way; many of its residents would be astonished to learn that they are in the same congressional district with some of the others. Politically, it is just about evenly divided, the only such district in metro Houston; in 2000 George W. Bush won 48% of the vote here.

The congressman from the 25th District is Chris Bell, a Democrat elected in 2002. He was born in Abilene and graduated from the University of Texas, where he was president of the Interfraternity Council, and from South Texas College of Law. Before law school, he worked as a television and radio reporter in Houston and in 1990 the Texas *Associated Press* named him the state's best radio reporter. He later served four years on the Houston City Council and ran a distant third in the Democratic primary for mayor in early 2001 after spending $1.1 million. In September 2001, when it looked like redistricting might put him in a heavily black district with Sheila Jackson Lee, 25th District Congressman Ken Bentsen decided to run for the Senate, and Bell quickly jumped into the race with the support of Mayor Lee Brown and the AFL-CIO. In the primary his toughest competitor was Councilman Carroll Robinson, a law professor at Texas Southern University, who had the backing of the Democratic Leadership Council: this was a contest between a white backed by liberals and a black backed by moderates. Bell led in the March 2002 primary 36%–27%. In the runoff Robinson attacked Bell for smoking marijuana in college more than 20 years earlier and for having temporarily lost his law license for failing to pay bar dues and some bills. Bell won the endorsements of the third and fourth-place finishers in the primary and refused Robinson's demand that he take a drug test. Bell won the April runoff 54%–46%.

Unopposed in the Republican primary was Tom Reiser, a wealthy Houston insurance executive specializing in high risk oil businesses; he had lost the 2000 primary to Phil Sudan, a lawyer who spent $3 million on his campaign. Both supported the use of force against Iraq and the Bush tax cuts, although Bell expressed doubts about making them permanent. Reiser attacked Bell for accepting a gift of flatware from a city contractor while serving on the Council, an act that resulted in a grand jury investigation. Bell criticized Reiser for claiming to have an economics minor from the College of William & Mary when the school actually had no such program. Reiser spent $4.5 million, included $1.7 million of his own money, which was far more than what Bell spent in the primary and general combined. With large margins in black precincts, Bell won 55%–43%.

If a new congressional map is passed for the 2004 election, Bell could be the odd man out in Houston; under one May 2003 proposal, Bell was left without a district and his home was placed in a heavily Republican district represented by John Culberson.

TWENTY-SIXTH DISTRICT

Rep. Michael Burgess (R)

Elected 2002, 1st term; b. Dec. 23, 1950, Rochester, MN; home, Highland Village; N. TX St. U., B.S. 1972, M.S. 1976, U. of TX Med. Schl., M.D. 1977, U. of TX Dallas, M.S. 2000; Episcopalian; married (Laura).

Professional Career: Practicing obstetrician, 1981–03.

DC Office: 1721 LHOB 20515, 202-225-7772; Fax: 202-225-2919; Web site: www.house.gov/burgess.

District Office: Lewisville, 972-434-9700.

Committees: *Science* (22d of 25 R): Environment, Technology and Standards; Space & Aeronautics. *Transportation & Infrastructure* (36th of 41 R): Economic Development, Public Buildings & Emergency Management; Highways, Transit & Pipelines.

Group Ratings and Key Votes: Newly Elected

Election Results

2002 general	Michael Burgess (R)	123,195	(75%)	($461,328)
	Paul William LeBon (D)	37,485	(23%)	($20,367)
	Other	3,998	(2%)	
2002 runoff	Michael Burgess (R)	10,522	(55%)	
	Scott Armey (R)	8,737	(45%)	
2002 primary	Scott Armey (R)	11,487	(45%)	
	Michael Burgess (R)	5,700	(23%)	
	Keith Self (R)	5,609	(22%)	
	Roger Sessions (R)	1,627	(6%)	
	Other	879	(3%)	
2000 general	Dick Armey (R)	214,025	(72%)	($1,325,516)
	Steve Love (D)	75,601	(26%)	($8,040)
	Other	5,646	(2%)	

The People		Race/Ethnic Origin	Ancestry	
Area size:	1,148 sq. mi.	77.8% White	German: 12.9%	Irish: 9.3%
Urban population:	91.7%	5.0% Black	English: 9.1%	
Rural population:	8.3%	4.0% Asian	**2000 Presidential Vote**	
Pop. 2000:	651,619	0.5% Native Am.	Bush (R)..............166,762	(73%)
Median income:	$61,287	0.2% Hawaiian	Gore (D)..............60,771	(27%)
Poverty status:	5.7%	1.4% Two+ races	**Cook Partisan Voting Index:** R +24	
Military veterans:	11.4%	0.1% Other		
		11.0% Hispanic Origin		

Occupation	Blue collar: 15.8%	White collar: 73.5%	Gray collar: 10.7%

Until the Texian Land and Immigration Company settled this portion of northeast Texas with a land grant from the Texas Congress in 1841, settlers were scarce and Indian raids were common. The area now known as Denton County takes its name, in fact, from John Bunyan Denton, a Methodist pioneer preacher and lawyer killed in a skirmish with Indians. Today, this area on the northern edge of the Dallas-Fort Worth Metroplex is teeming with new arrivals: Denton County is part of America's fastest-growing metropolitan area in the 1990s. It is booming and filled with young, well-educated, middle-class families. Its chief cities are Denton and Lewisville, Carrollton and Flower Mound; its largest private employers are truck-manufacturer Peterbilt Motors Company and Boeing, which are based in those two cities. And a quick look at the county map reveals that there is plenty more room for growth along the Interstate 35E and 35W corridors as they converge on the city of Denton in the heart of the county. In 1940, there were 33,000 people in

Denton County and they voted 88% Democratic for president. In 2000 there were 432,000 people in Denton County and they voted 70% Republican for president.

The 26th Congressional District is at the heart of the northern expansion of the Dallas-Fort Worth Metroplex. It includes all of Denton County, a sliver (257 people) of Wise County to the west, a fair-sized chunk (34,000) of Collin County to the east including part of the county seat of McKinney and the northeast corner of Tarrant County. This area includes the heavily Anglo cities of Grapevine, Colleyville, Euless and Bedford and most of the giant (larger than Manhattan Island) Dallas-Fort Worth International Airport. This is a very heavily Republican district—73% for George W. Bush in 2000.

The congressman from the 26th District is Michael Burgess, a Republican elected in 2002. He succeeded Dick Armey, the House Majority Leader. When Armey announced in December 2001 that he would not run again, there was no doubt that he would be succeeded by a Republican. The widespread expectation, in Texas and in Washington, was that his successor would be his son Scott Armey, a former Denton County judge. But the election did not turn out that way.

Almost no one expected that the winner would be Michael Burgess. He grew up in Denton County and graduated from the University of North Texas and the University of Texas Medical School. He trained at Parkland Hospital in Dallas and set up an obstetrical-gynecological practice in Lewisville. After 21 years of practice, in which he delivered more than 3,000 babies, he decided to run for Congress in 2002—his first run for elective office. He was so intimidated at his first campaign forum that he nearly walked out. Scott Armey, in contrast, had already won an election in Denton County, which has two-thirds of the district's population. He quickly made the rounds on Capitol Hill and among lobbyists: he was only 32 and it seemed likely he would be a congressman for many years to come. Up through the March 2002 primary Armey outspent Burgess by more than 6–1. But turnout in the primary was light, only 25,000 in a heavily Republican district with 456,000 voting age residents; there were no Republican primary contests at the top of the ticket and there didn't seem to be much suspense about the outcome of this race. Armey won 45% of the vote, not enough to avoid a runoff. Burgess won 23%, just 91 votes ahead of the third place finisher. Altogether Burgess got only 5,700 votes; one wonders how many of them were cast by parents of babies he had delivered or by the babies themselves. Interestingly, Armey got only 41% of the votes in Denton County, where voters presumably knew him best; if he had won a majority there, he would have won the nomination.

Burgess said later that his initial goal in the four-week runoff campaign was to "not get embarrassed." But he benefited from a series of hard-hitting articles in *The Dallas Morning News*, owned by the Belo Corporation, about Armey's record as county judge. The paper reported that Armey had used his position to steer county jobs and contracts to close friends, including a $1.5 transportation consulting contract. Armey responded, "[T]hose very few circumstances or situations where it was someone I knew, we went the extra step to make sure it was thoroughly ventilated and went above and beyond what we had to do." Burgess focused primarily on two issues— health care and taxes. A patients' rights advocate, he helped draft and pass the Texas Patients' Bill of Rights, and he vowed to do the same on a national level. Like Dick Armey, he is a supporter of a flat tax. Burgess's campaign was helped by the support of local physicians who urged their patients to vote for him; he was endorsed by medical societies in Denton, Tarrant and Collin counties as well as from the Texas Medical Association and the American Medical Association. Only 19,000 people turned out to vote in the April runoff and Burgess won 55%–45%. Armey carried Collin and Tarrant Counties (and got the only 2 votes cast in Wise County) but lost 60%–40% in Denton County. After the runoff, Dick Armey spoke bitterly of the Belo papers' "vicious unprofessionalism" and said they had conducted a vendetta against the Armey family; he sponsored a bill that would have forced Belo to sell one of its newspapers, but that did not get very far. *The Dallas Morning News* in an editorial called Armey's response "a troubling way" for him to end his congressional career. In the general election Burgess won 75%–23% over a Democrat whose son he had delivered.

Democrats are unlikely to offer much competition in this district, so Burgess is unlikely to face serious general election opposition. But *National Review* called him a "place-holder" for his political ally, conservative state Senator Jane Nelson, who encouraged him to run.

TWENTY-SEVENTH DISTRICT

Rep. Solomon Ortiz (D)

Elected 1982, 11th term; b. June 3, 1937, Robstown; home, Corpus Christi; Del Mar Col., Natl. Sheriffs Training Inst., 1977; Methodist; divorced.

Military Career: Army, 1960–62.

Elected Office: Nueces Cnty. Constable, 1965–68, Commissioner, 1969–76, Sheriff, 1976–82.

DC Office: 2470 RHOB 20515, 202-225-7742; Fax: 202-226-1134; Web site: www.house.gov/ortiz.

District Offices: Brownsville, 956-541-1242; Corpus Christi, 361-883-5868.

Committees: *Armed Services* (3d of 29 D): Readiness (RMM); Tactical Air & Land Forces. *Resources* (5th of 24 D): Energy & Mineral Resources; Fisheries Conservation, Wildlife & Oceans.

Group Ratings

	ADA	ACLU	AFS	LCV	CON	ITIC	NTU	COC	ACU	NTLC	CHC
2002	85	47	100	63	43	62	14	42	25	3	42
2001	70	—	90	36	—	—	17	65	60	—	—

National Journal Ratings

	2001 LIB —	2001 CONS	2002 LIB —	2002 CONS
Economic	63% —	37%	66% —	34%
Social	52% —	47%	53% —	47%
Foreign	21% —	74%	56% —	44%

Key Votes of the 107th Congress

1. Approve Bush Tax Cuts	N	5. Faith-Based Charities	N	9. Trade Promotion Authority	Y
2. Limit Patients' Bill of Rights	N	6. Bar Gays in the Boy Scouts	Y	10. Bar Funds for Intl. Court	Y
3. Campaign Finance Reform	Y	7. Ban Partial-Birth Abortion	Y	11. Authorize Force in Iraq	*
4. Ban ANWR Development	N	8. Arm Commercial Pilots	Y	12. Deny Home. Sec. Dept. Union	N

Election Results

2002 general	Solomon Ortiz (D)	68,559	(61%)	($539,401)
	Pat Ahumada (R)	41,004	(37%)	($19,648)
	Other	2,646	(2%)	
2002 primary	Solomon Ortiz (D)	unopposed		
2000 general	Solomon Ortiz (D)	102,088	(63%)	($443,821)
	Pat Ahumada (R)	54,660	(34%)	($34,318)
	Other	4,324	(3%)	

Prior Winning Percentages: 1998 (63%); 1996 (65%); 1994 (59%); 1992 (56%); 1990 (100%); 1988 (100%); 1986 (100%); 1984 (64%); 1982 (64%)

The People		Race/Ethnic Origin	Ancestry	
Area size:	5,531 sq. mi.	24.6% White	German: 4.9%	Irish: 3.4%
Urban population:	90.1%	2.1% Black	English: 3.4%	
Rural population:	9.9%	0.8% Asian	**2000 Presidential Vote**	
Pop. 2000:	651,619	0.2% Native Am.	Gore (D) 79,716	(51%)
Median income:	$30,431	0.0% Hawaiian	Bush (R) 75,600	(49%)
Poverty status:	26.5%	0.6% Two+ races	**Cook Partisan Voting Index:** D + 1	
Military veterans:	11.3%	0.1% Other		
		71.6% Hispanic Origin		
Occupation	Blue collar: 25.0%	White collar: 55.1%	Gray collar: 19.9%	

South from Corpus Christi to the Rio Grande and the Mexican border are two Texan versions of dreamland. One, fronting the Gulf of Mexico, is the sand spit of Padre Island, for most of its 80-mile length a barrier reef island and national seashore, at the southern tip of which is a high-rise resort to which college students throng for spring break and which developers have built 5,500 rental units. Remains of a 1554 Spanish shipwreck have been found offshore, and Portuguese settlers began cattle ranching here not long after. The other, inland from the Laguna Madre, is the vast grazing and oil lands of the 825,000-acre (that's 1,289 square miles, partner) King Ranch. This still seemingly vacant land between the Nueces and the Rio Grande was the territory in contention in the Mexican-American War. The United States won that war and established its sovereignty. But today most people here are of Mexican ancestry, some from families who have lived for generations this side of the border, some recent immigrants. The culture here is *Tejano*, proudly American but with Mexican flair and vitality.

The 27th Congressional District includes this land from Corpus Christi south to the Rio Grande. Its population is concentrated at the northern and southern ends of the district. Corpus Christi and surrounding Nueces County have a mixed population, 56% Hispanic; it is the southernmost natural port on Texas's Gulf Coast and the nation's fifth largest in trading volume with big petrochemical plants. At the southern end is Cameron County, which includes South Padre Island; the population here is 84% Hispanic. The biggest city is Brownsville, on the Lower Rio Grande opposite Matamoros, Mexico, one of the major border crossings in Texas; not far away is the colonia of Cameron Park, where people live in trailers or makeshift structures without water or sewage service, rated by the Census Bureau as the poorest place in the nation. NAFTA has lifted the economy here, and growth in Mexico and the United States will lift it more. Politically, the 27th District is Democratic, but not so Democratic as one might expect. In 1998 the 27th District gave a majority of its votes for Governor George W. Bush; in 2000, Bush won 49% of the votes here for president.

The congressman from the 27th District is Solomon Ortiz, a Democrat and the only representative for this district since its creation in the 1982 redistricting. He grew up inland from Corpus in the Canta Ranas (singing frogs) neighborhood of Robstown, which is known for its political activism. His father died when he was 14, leaving him the eldest of four children who scratched out a living as migrant farm workers, sometimes working as far away as Colorado and Michigan. When his father died, his employer at the local newspaper raised his wage and then urged him to join the Army. Ortiz worked as an Army investigator and translator, using his Spanish to learn French, took a correspondence course in police work and returned home to run for constable. "If it wasn't for the military, I wouldn't be here today," he said. In 1976 he was the first Hispanic elected Nueces County Sheriff. When he ran for Congress in 1982, he got only 26% in the primary, but he made a propitious alliance with Democratic leaders in the Brownsville area and won the runoff with 52% and the general with 64%.

Ortiz's voting record has been moderate, especially on cultural issues. As the third-ranking Democrat on the Armed Services Committee, he watches out for the four military installations in the Coastal Bend, as he calls the area; they emerged from the 1995 base-closing review with more jobs than before. As ranking Democrat on the Readiness Subcommittee, he remains an advocate of depot maintenance and is adamantly opposed to additional rounds of base closings; he co-chairs the Depot Caucus. Five months after the Port of Corpus Christi dedicated its new conference center in his name, the *San Antonio Express-News* reported that Ortiz received favored treatment when the Port awarded a contract to provide security to a firm that he owned even though it was not the low bidder. The newspaper claimed he was bringing home "political pork and eating it too." Ortiz defended the contract as awarded in open competition and his supporters said that the original low bidder was unqualified.

Ortiz is a sturdy internationalist: an enthusiastic supporter of NAFTA and PNTR with China, and one of 21 Democrats to vote for trade promotion authority in 2001, though he switched and voted against it in 2002. He spoke against decertification of Mexico as a partner in good standing in the drug war. As co-chairman with Henry Bonilla of the Border Caucus, Ortiz convinced Mexican authorities to drop regulations requiring refundable deposits for U.S. automobiles traveling into Mexico; he has urged Mexico to repay its long-running water debt, which comes from runoff of the Rio Grande. He also worked with a local consortium that built a spaceport in the Valley that had its first launch in early 2003.

Ortiz has generally won reelection without difficulty. In 2002, former Brownsville Mayor Pat

Ahumada ran again after losing 63%–34% two years earlier and tried to take advantage of the controversy over the Port's contract with Ortiz. But he was poorly funded and Ortiz won 61%–37%. Ortiz reportedly is grooming his son Solomon Ortiz Jr., chairman of the Nueces County Democratic Party, as his successor.

TWENTY-EIGHTH DISTRICT

Rep. Ciro Rodriguez (D)

Elected April 1997, 3d term; b. Dec. 9, 1946, Piedras Negras, Coah., Mexico; home, San Antonio; St. Mary's U., B.A. 1973, Our Lady of the Lake U., M.S.W., 1978; Catholic; married (Carolina).

Elected Office: Harlandale Schl. Bd., 1975–87; TX House of Reps., 1986–97.

Professional Career: Substance Abuse Counselor, 1971–74, 1978–80; Educ. Consultant, 1980–87; Faculty, Our Lady of the Lake U., 1987–97.

DC Office: 1507 LHOB 20515, 202-225-1640; Fax: 202-225-1641; Web site: www.house.gov/rodriguez.

District Offices: Roma, 956-847-1111; San Antonio, 210-924-7383; San Diego, 361-279-3907.

Committees: *Armed Services* (14th of 29 D): Readiness; Terrorism, Unconventional Threats & Capabilities. *Resources* (22d of 24 D). *Veterans' Affairs* (6th of 14 D): Health (RMM); Oversight & Investigations.

Group Ratings

	ADA	ACLU	AFS	LCV	CON	ITIC	NTU	COC	ACU	NTLC	CHC
2002	95	79	100	63	17	50	18	40	0	3	8
2001	85	—	100	71	—	—	12	39	12	—	—

National Journal Ratings

	2001 LIB	—	2001 CONS		2002 LIB	—	2002 CONS
Economic	72%	—	29%		84%	—	15%
Social	74%	—	23%		74%	—	19%
Foreign	75%	—	25%		77%	—	19%

Key Votes of the 107th Congress

1. Approve Bush Tax Cuts	*	5. Faith-Based Charities	N	9. Trade Promotion Authority	N
2. Limit Patients' Bill of Rights	N	6. Bar Gays in the Boy Scouts	N	10. Bar Funds for Intl. Court	N
3. Campaign Finance Reform	Y	7. Ban Partial-Birth Abortion	N	11. Authorize Force in Iraq	N
4. Ban ANWR Development	Y	8. Arm Commercial Pilots	Y	12. Deny Home. Sec. Dept. Union	N

Election Results

2002 general	Ciro Rodriguez (D)	71,393	(71%)	($409,446)
	Gabriel Perales (R)	26,973	(27%)	($39,889)
	Other	2,054	(2%)	
2002 primary	Ciro Rodriguez (D)	unopposed		
2000 general	Ciro Rodriguez (D)	123,104	(89%)	($294,228)
	William A. Stallknecht (Lib)	15,156	(11%)	

Prior Winning Percentages: 1998 (91%); 1997 (67%)

The People		Race/Ethnic Origin	Ancestry	
Area size:	11,930 sq. mi.	21.2% White	German: 5.4%	Irish: 2.8%
Urban population:	82.1%	7.5% Black	USA: 2.7%	
Rural population:	17.9%	0.7% Asian	**2000 Presidential Vote**	
Pop. 2000:	651,620	0.2% Native Am.	Gore (D) 90,202	(59%)
Median income:	$29,127	0.0% Hawaiian	Bush (R) 62,275	(41%)
Poverty status:	26.7%	0.7% Two+ races	**Cook Partisan Voting Index:** D + 9	
Military veterans:	12.3%	0.1% Other		
		69.6% Hispanic Origin		

Occupation	Blue collar: 30.3%	White collar: 48.6%	Gray collar: 21.1%

The Mexican-American tradition in the part of South Texas radiating from San Antonio is anchored in two culturally conservative but adaptive institutions, the Catholic Church and the United States military. Both are a major presence in San Antonio, just 150 miles north of the border, which for many years had the largest Mexican-American population of any American city, where Spanish has long been widely spoken and political refugees from Mexico's revolution could be sure of freedom. The church in San Antonio was led for years by liberal bishops who also ran St. Mary's University, which educated many Hispanic politicians and leaders, including two longtime House Democratic committee chairmen, Henry B. Gonzalez and Kika de la Garza—and also Senator John Cornyn, who graduated from St. Mary's law school. Just as visible a presence in San Antonio are the Army and Air Force, with huge Fort Sam Houston, Lackland Air Force Base, Randolph Air Force Base, and the Brooks City Base, all in or near the city limits. At the site of the former Brooks Air Force Base, Toyota plans a truck-manufacturing plant. Mexican-Americans have long volunteered for military service in numbers higher than most ethnic groups, and for many years Mexican-Americans in San Antonio worked in civilian jobs for the military service: Uncle Sam has long been an equal opportunity employer. San Antonio's Mexican-American community has produced many politicians who are liberal on economic issues, civil rights and civil liberties. But it has not produced many who are hostile to the military or to traditional religious and cultural values.

The 28th Congressional District stretches from the southern half of San Antonio to the Mexican border. Some 57% of its people are in Bexar County, with Hispanics heavily on the south side of San Antonio and a smaller number of blacks on the east side. The district extends south, through thinly settled ranch and oil well country, to the Lower Rio Grande. There it includes Starr County, home of many blatant and wealthy drug smugglers, and, to the north, Duval County, sometimes the most Democratic county in the United States, whose boss George Parr provided the key votes Lyndon Johnson needed for his 87-vote victory in the 1948 Democratic Senate runoff (conveniently, many people voted in alphabetical order). The district also includes part of Hidalgo County, the most populous county in the Lower Rio Grande Valley. Overall the district is 70% Hispanic and heavily Democratic, but it did cast 41% of its votes for George W. Bush in 2000.

The congressman from the 28th District is Ciro Rodriguez, a Democrat chosen in a special election in April 1997. Rodriguez grew up in San Antonio, worked as a social worker, teacher and educational consultant, and spent 12 years on the Harlandale school board. In 1986 he was elected to the Texas House, where he had a liberal record. He started running for the U.S. House soon after incumbent Frank Tejeda died of a brain tumor. Critical in the campaign was his endorsement by the San Antonio Central Labor Council; he raised $280,000 from PACs, mostly union PACs, more than half of his $505,000 total. His only serious competition for the House seat came from San Antonio Councilman Juan Solis. Like Tejeda, Solis was pro-life on abortion and against gun control, and he backed term limits and school vouchers; he called Rodriguez "more of a wild-eyed liberal, and that's not what we need in Congress." Rodriguez was backed by prominent politicians, including several members of Congress, and was promised Tejeda's seat on the Armed Services Committee by House Democratic leaders. Even more important, Rodriguez had the money to go on television and Solis didn't. In the March primary, Rodriguez led Solis 46%–27%; Rodriguez won the low-turnout runoff 67%–33%.

Rodriguez has the most liberal voting record of Texas's six Hispanic congressmen, five of whom represent districts touching the border. He got Tejeda's seat on Armed Services and strongly opposes the closing of more military bases, contending that the money would be better spent on improvements to crumbling installations. He won House passage in 2001 of his bill to designate the 2,600-mile El Camino Real de los Tejas, the Spanish "Royal Road," from Laredo to Natchitoches, Louisiana, as a National Historic Trail, which he said would symbolize the immigration and trade route's critical link between Mexico and the new American frontier. Unlike others from South Texas, he opposed PNTR with China because he feared that local farmers would be hurt by "price-busting Chinese imports;" he also opposed trade promotion authority. In 2003, he became the Hispanic Caucus chairman, and led opposition to the judicial nomination of Miguel Estrada.

Despite speculation that Bexar County Commissioner Robert Tejeda would seek to regain the seat his cousin once held, Rodriguez has not faced a significant challenge. In the 2002 campaign, he charged that San Antonio Republican Henry Bonilla was threatening San Antonio area projects at the Appropriations Committee; but Bonilla won narrowly despite the discord in the San Antonio delegation.

TWENTY-NINTH DISTRICT

Rep. Gene Green (D)

Elected 1992, 6th term; b. Oct. 17, 1947, Houston; home, Houston; U. of Houston, B.A., 1971, Bates Col. of Law at U. of Houston, 1973–77; Methodist; married (Helen).

Elected Office: TX House of Reps., 1972–84; TX Senate, 1985–92.

Professional Career: Practicing atty., 1977–92.

DC Office: 2335 RHOB 20515, 202-225-1688; Fax: 202-225-9903; Web site: www.house.gov/green.

District Offices: Houston, 713-330-0807; Houston, 281-999-5716.

Committees: *Energy & Commerce* (16th of 26 D): Commerce, Trade & Consumer Protection; Environment & Hazardous Materials; Health; Telecommunications & The Internet. *Standards of Official Conduct* (3d of 5 D).

Group Ratings

	ADA	ACLU	AFS	LCV	CON	ITIC	NTU	COC	ACU	NTLC	CHC
2002	90	73	100	75	43	38	16	35	16	3	8
2001	90	—	100	50	—	—	17	43	36	—	—

National Journal Ratings

	2001 LIB	—	2001 CONS		2002 LIB	—	2002 CONS
Economic	67%	—	33%		74%	—	26%
Social	62%	—	38%		74%	—	19%
Foreign	49%	—	47%		59%	—	40%

Key Votes of the 107th Congress

1. Approve Bush Tax Cuts	N	5. Faith-Based Charities	N	9. Trade Promotion Authority	N
2. Limit Patients' Bill of Rights	N	6. Bar Gays in the Boy Scouts	Y	10. Bar Funds for Intl. Court	Y
3. Campaign Finance Reform	Y	7. Ban Partial-Birth Abortion	N	11. Authorize Force in Iraq	Y
4. Ban ANWR Development	N	8. Arm Commercial Pilots	Y	12. Deny Home. Sec. Dept. Union	N

Election Results

2002 general	Gene Green (D)	55,760	(95%)	($549,217)
	Paul Hansen (Lib)	2,833	(5%)	
2002 primary	Gene Green (D)	unopposed		
2000 general	Gene Green (D)	84,665	(73%)	($626,951)
	Joe Vu (R)	29,606	(26%)	($50,896)
	Other	1,204	(1%)	

Prior Winning Percentages: 1998 (93%); 1996 (68%); 1994 (73%); 1992 (65%)

The People		Race/Ethnic Origin	Ancestry	
Area size:	240 sq. mi.	20.0% White	USA: 3.7%	German: 2.9%
Urban population:	99.5%	14.7% Black	Irish: 2.7%	
Rural population:	0.5%	2.1% Asian	**2000 Presidential Vote**	
Pop. 2000:	651,620	0.2% Native Am.	Gore (D) 65,863	(61%)
Median income:	$32,128	0.0% Hawaiian	Bush (R) 42,770	(39%)
Poverty status:	21.5%	0.8% Two + races	**Cook Partisan Voting Index:** D +10	
Military veterans:	7.1%	0.1% Other		
		62.2% Hispanic Origin		

Occupation	Blue collar: 40.4%	White collar: 43.1%	Gray collar: 16.5%

"What built Houston," wrote John Gunther in *Inside U.S.A.* , "was a combination of cotton, oil, and the ship canal." The cotton and oil were gifts of nature, though they required much human effort and ingenuity to produce in commercial quantities; the 54-mile Houston Ship Channel, by contrast, was almost totally man's creation. After the sand spit port of Galveston was destroyed by a hurricane and tidal wave in 1900, Houston's elders decided to dredge out Buffalo Bayou and make their inland city a seaport. And so a sluggish, 6-foot-deep creek became a 40-foot-deep channel—recently deepened to 45 feet—and Houston turned into the nation's busiest port for foreign trade, with more than 400 vessels daily generating 205,000 jobs and $7.7 billion a year for the local economy. On the west side of town, Houston—a world-class metropolis of 4.7 million people—seems entirely a white-collar, office-bound city. But on the east and north, around the turning basin in the port and through the maze of refinery towers and tubing, Houston remains vibrant and blue collar, with blacks, Mexican-Americans and large numbers of whites from the rural South and even Michigan and California, who have come here to move up in the world.

The 29th Congressional District covers much of the Ship Channel area and working-class Houston—like a reverse "C" on the east side of the city surrounding the downtown. Included is much of the area on Houston's Northside, between the Eastex and North Freeways all the way out to George Bush Intercontinental Airport and FM 1960, and blue-collar neighborhoods in northeast Houston. This is an 80% minority population district and solidly Democratic.

The congressman from the 29th District is Gene Green, a Democrat elected in 1992. Green grew up in Houston, worked as a printer's apprentice and was admitted to the bar at age 30; he was elected to the state House in 1972, at 25, and to the state Senate in a special election in 1985. He has been a faithful union and trial lawyer man in Austin and Washington, and also an opponent of gun control—a politician whose natural base is Texas' small union, blue-collar class. He is a compulsive campaigner who goes door to door, with lawn signs and a hammer in his trunk; and a good thing, for him anyway, since otherwise he never would have won in the 29th. In the 1992 primary he faced Ben Reyes, a tempestuous Houston councilman who once protested official inaction by demolishing a crack house. In the primary, Reyes led 34%–28% over Green. For the runoff, Green came out ahead by 180 votes out of 31,508 cast. Then Reyes went to court and charged that Republican voters had illegally crossed over and voted in the runoff. That got him a July re-runoff, but to no avail. This time Green won with 52%; he won the general election with 65%.

In the House, Green has had a relatively moderate voting record for a member in a heavily minority urban district. After a spirited fight with other Texas Democrats in 1997, he won a seat on the Commerce Committee. Following the 2000 election, he called for abolition of the Electoral College. He called the HMO regulation bill that House Republicans passed in 2001 a "sham compromise." He opposed trade promotion authority but voted for the use of force in Iraq.

Green's most satisfying victory may have been to wrest the bulk of Harris County's grant money from the county's longstanding Head Start contractor. Always sensitive to his Hispanic constituents, Green complained to the Health and Human Services Department that Latinos in his district were being shut out of Head Start by the contractor's dysfunctional bureaucracy. This was "awkward," Green explained to *National Journal*, because the bureaucracy in question was run by blacks and supported, at least tacitly, by virtually all of the city's black leadership. After careful negotiations, a deal was struck to open three-quarters of the contract to bidding—a constructive agreement for a city that prides itself on easing racial discord rather than letting hostility into the open.

Since 1996, no other Democrat has challenged him and he has been reelected easily. At a time when national and state Hispanic leaders are pressing for more Hispanic members, the 29th remains an inviting opportunity for an ambitious Hispanic politician. Perhaps in anticipation, Green organized a Spanish class for members of Congress. Those language skills will come in handy if a new congressional map is passed for the 2004 election—under one May 2003 proposal, the 29th District became even more inviting to an Hispanic challenger.

THIRTIETH DISTRICT

Rep. Eddie Bernice Johnson (D)

Elected 1992, 6th term; b. Dec. 3, 1935, Waco; home, Dallas; St. Mary's at Notre Dame, B.A. 1955, TX Christian U., B.S. 1967, S. Methodist U., M.B.A. 1976; Baptist; divorced.

Elected Office: TX House of Reps., 1972–1977; TX Senate, 1986–92.

Professional Career: Registered nurse; Regional Dir., U.S. Dept. of HEW, 1977–80; Mgmt. consultant, Sammons Corp., 1979–81; Owner, Eddie Bernice Johnson & Assoc., 1981–present.

DC Office: 1511 LHOB 20515, 202-225-8885; Fax: 202-226-1477; Web site: www.house.gov/ebjohnson.

District Offices: Dallas, 214-922-8885; Irving, 972-253-8885.

Committees: *Science* (4th of 22 D): Research (RMM). *Transportation & Infrastructure* (11th of 34 D): Aviation; Highways, Transit & Pipelines; Water Resources & Environment.

Group Ratings

	ADA	ACLU	AFS	LCV	CON	ITIC	NTU	COC	ACU	NTLC	CHC
2002	95	93	100	63	43	50	18	45	0	0	0
2001	95	—	100	79	—	—	10	48	4	—	—

National Journal Ratings

	2001 LIB —	2001 CONS		2002 LIB —	2002 CONS
Economic	83% —	15%		74% —	25%
Social	90% —	0%		84% —	8%
Foreign	77% —	22%		86% —	13%

Key Votes of the 107th Congress

1. Approve Bush Tax Cuts	N	5. Faith-Based Charities	N	9. Trade Promotion Authority	N
2. Limit Patients' Bill of Rights	N	6. Bar Gays in the Boy Scouts	N	10. Bar Funds for Intl. Court	N
3. Campaign Finance Reform	Y	7. Ban Partial-Birth Abortion	N	11. Authorize Force in Iraq	N
4. Ban ANWR Development	Y	8. Arm Commercial Pilots	N	12. Deny Home. Sec. Dept. Union	N

Election Results

2002 general	Eddie Bernice Johnson (D)	88,980	(74%)	($462,419)
	Ron Bush (R)	28,981	(24%)	($1,973)
	Other	1,856	(2%)	
2002 primary	Eddie Bernice Johnson (D)	unopposed		
2000 general	Eddie Bernice Johnson (D)	109,163	(92%)	($243,072)
	Kelly Rush (Lib)	9,798	(8%)	

Prior Winning Percentages: 1998 (72%); 1996 (55%); 1994 (73%); 1992 (72%)

The People		Race/Ethnic Origin	Ancestry	
Area size:	290 sq. mi.	24.7% White	German: 3.7%	USA: 3.6%
Urban population:	99.1%	40.5% Black	Irish: 3.1%	
Rural population:	0.9%	2.2% Asian	**2000 Presidential Vote**	
Pop. 2000:	651,620	0.3% Native Am.	Gore (D)	109,507 (69%)
Median income:	$35,612	0.0% Hawaiian	Bush (R)	48,916 (31%)
Poverty status:	19.1%	1.0% Two+ races	**Cook Partisan Voting Index:** D +19	
Military veterans:	9.0%	0.1% Other		
		31.1% Hispanic Origin		

Occupation	Blue collar: 29.3%	White collar: 54.4%	Gray collar: 16.2%

Dallas is, among other things, the westernmost city of the Deep South. Cotton was originally the major crop in this part of Texas, and many of Dallas's first enterprising businessmen, when the railroad reached the Trinity River here in the 1870s, were cotton brokers. Geographically, Dallas is directly west of the Black Belt of Alabama and the Mississippi Delta, both heavy cotton-producing areas in the days before the boll weevil. Many blacks and whites came west on U.S. 80—and now

Interstate 20—to this metropolis, which is now the largest metro area in the South. The south side of Dallas, not much visited by tourists, is predominately black.

The 30th Congressional District, designed to be the Dallas-Fort Worth Metroplex's black-majority district, includes most of Dallas's predominantly black neighborhoods. Its creation in 1991 was insisted on by Eddie Bernice Johnson, then chairman of the Texas Senate's redistricting committee, and the result was one of the most grotesquely shaped districts in the country: Attached to the central body in south and east Dallas, were tentacles that appeared as complex and attenuated as a series of DNA molecules. A lawsuit was filed, claiming racial gerrymandering, and the Supreme Court ruled the 30th and two Houston districts unconstitutional. In August 1996 a three-judge federal court drew new lines. In November 2001 another three-judge federal court drew new lines for all of the state's 32 districts and in the process smoothed out the lines even more. Today the 30th District includes two compact geographic units connected by downtown Dallas. One consists of most of the south side of Dallas; the other runs northwest out Stemmons Freeway and includes most of Irving. It includes the corporate headquarters for American Airlines, Southwest Airlines and Exxon Mobil. The district's population is 41% black and 31% Hispanic.

The congresswoman from the 30th District is Eddie Bernice Johnson, who created the district in 1991. She grew up in Texas and graduated from Texas Christian University as a registered nurse. She worked at St. Paul Hospital and was chief psychiatric nurse at the VA Hospital in Dallas. In 1972 she was elected to the Texas House—the first black woman elected to anything in Dallas. She became a regional HEW director in the Carter administration and was elected to the state Senate in 1986; in 1991 she was chairman of the Senate Redistricting Committee. She has never had effective opposition in the 30th District; she won the 1992 Democratic primary with 92% of the vote. After the 1996 redistricting, she won comfortably with 55% against seven opponents in the November special election. After the 2001 redistricting, she was reelected without serious contest.

In the House, Johnson has a mostly liberal voting record, but she has been attentive to business interests in Dallas. Though she once pledged to unions to oppose NAFTA, she changed her mind and voted for it; Dallas probably exports more to Mexico than any other American city, and many jobs depend on those exports. Johnson also sided with business on PNTR with China, but she later opposed trade promotion authority. On the Science Committee, where she is ranking Democrat on the Research Subcommittee, she shared credit for passing the Networking and Information Research and Development Act to double federal information research spending. She also sought to double spending for the National Science Foundation.

As a health care professional, Johnson has taken an interest in minorities' health care problems. Serving on the Transportation and Infrastructure Committee, she got a seat on the Aviation Subcommittee, of great importance here: The 30th District includes part of Dallas-Fort Worth International Airport and three others, Love Field, Dallas Executive Airport and Lancaster Airport.

Johnson was chairwoman of the Congressional Black Caucus in 2001 and 2002. The Democratic primary defeats of Black Caucus members Earl Hilliard and Cynthia McKinney to other African-Americans led Johnson to voice concern that "Jewish people are attempting to pick our leaders." She supported Nancy Pelosi for minority leader over her Metroplex neighbor Martin Frost and unsuccessfully urged Pelosi to name Bill Jefferson of Louisiana chairman of the House Democrats' campaign committee.

THIRTY-FIRST DISTRICT

Rep. John Carter (R)

Elected 2002, 1st term; b. Nov. 6, 1941, Houston; home, Round Rock; TX Tech. U., B.A. 1964, U. of TX, J.D. 1969; Christian; married (Erika).

Elected Office: Dist. Ct. judge, 1982–01.

Professional Career: Practicing atty., 1969–81.

DC Office: 408 CHOB 20515, 202-225-3864; Web site: www.house.gov/carter.

District Offices: College Station, 979-846-6068; Round Rock, 512-246-1600.

Committees: *Education & the Workforce* (23d of 27 R): 21st Century Competitiveness; Employer-Employee Relations. *Government Reform* (22d of 24 R): Criminal Justice, Drug Policy & Human Resources. *Judiciary* (19th of 21 R): Commercial & Administrative Law; Courts, the Internet & Intellectual Property.

Group Ratings and Key Votes: Newly Elected

Election Results

2002 general	John Carter (R)	111,556	(69%)	($811,681)
	David Bagley (D)	44,183	(27%)	($23,763)
	Other	5,745	(4%)	
2002 runoff	John Carter (R)	13,150	(57%)	
	Peter Wareing (R)	9,986	(43%)	
2002 primary	Peter Wareing (R)	12,987	(37%)	
	John Carter (R)	9,144	(26%)	
	Brad Barton (R)	5,751	(16%)	
	C. Patrick Meece (R)	3,653	(10%)	
	Other	3,629	(10%)	

The People		Race/Ethnic Origin	Ancestry	
Area size:	5,090 sq. mi.	69.4% White	German: 14.7%	Irish: 7.6%
Urban population:	77.0%	9.0% Black	English: 7.5%	
Rural population:	23.0%	3.1% Asian	**2000 Presidential Vote**	
Pop. 2000:	651,620	0.3% Native Am.	Bush (R)...............160,802	(72%)
Median income:	$50,252	0.0% Hawaiian	Gore (D)................63,903	(28%)
Poverty status:	11.3%	1.2% Two+ races	**Cook Partisan Voting Index:** R +22	
Military veterans:	10.9%	0.1% Other		
		16.9% Hispanic Origin		

Occupation   Blue collar: 19.9%   White collar: 67.7%   Gray collar: 12.5%

In a one-story, unfinished wood building in the village of Washington-on-the-Brazos, delegates of the people of Texas assembled and signed the Texas Declaration of Independence, wrote a new constitution and adopted an interim government. This was Texas's first Capitol building; not far away was the story-and-a-half Anson Jones house with hand-hewn timbers and a wide city hall, the White House of the Texas Republic. Ten miles away is Independence, where Sam Houston was converted to the Baptist faith and baptized, and where Baylor College was founded in 1845; it moved to Waco in 1887 and is now the world's largest Baptist university. Such were the humble beginnings of a state now of 21 million people, with a productive and creative economy larger than those of most nations, the home of a president of the United States who has sent American military forces to liberate nations halfway around the world.

Set amid a rolling region of grassy prairies, rich alluvial bottom lands and wooded slopes, Washington-on-the-Brazos and Independence today are tiny rural backwaters. Yet not too far away are some of the communities that have made Texas a nation-state. Seventy miles southeast is metro Houston, with 4.5 million people, the center of the world's oil and oil service industries.

Eighty miles north is College Station, home of Texas A&M University, whose agricultural and military tradition sets it apart from the University of Texas; it has a more conservative atmosphere and is the site of the George H.W. Bush Presidential Library. And 120 miles west of Washington-on-the-Brazos is Austin, the state capital since 1839. In the 1990s metro Austin boomed with high-tech growth and spread out far into the countryside. One of its most successful companies has been Dell Computer, headquartered in Round Rock in rapidly-growing Williamson County just north of Austin; this was the fourth fastest-growing county in the nation between 2000 and 2001, according to Census Bureau estimates.

The 31st Congressional District, newly created for the 2002 election, includes all these booming parts of Texas as well as Washington-on-the-Brazos and Independence, including six small, still rural, counties and parts of three others. About one-quarter of the district's residents are in the far western section of Houston's Harris County, not heavily built up in 2000 but likely to become so by 2010. Another one-quarter are in Brazos County, whose main cities are College Station and next-door Bryan. And 30% are in the district's portion of Williamson County, including Round Rock and the affluent suburbs along U.S. 183 running north from Austin. Politically, it is a very Republican district: Williamson, Brazos and the district's portion of Harris County are all very heavily Republican: liberals in Austin live closer to the center of town, liberal students go to UT rather than A&M and liberal Houstonians wouldn't think of moving so far out in Harris County. And all of the rural counties voted for Governor Rick Perry and Senator John Cornyn in the 2002 election.

The congressman from the 31st District is John Carter, a Republican elected in 2002. He grew up in Houston and graduated from Texas Tech and the University of Texas Law School. He practiced law in Williamson County and served as a municipal judge in Round Rock. He was appointed a district judge in 1981 by Governor Bill Clements and in 1982 stood for election; judicial elections are partisan in Texas, and he was the first Republican judge elected in Williamson County. Other Republicans started sweeping county offices as well, and Carter became known as the father of the county Republican party. In November 2001 a three-judge district court drew Texas's new congressional district lines, creating the new 31st District. Two weeks later Carter retired from the bench and started running for Congress. He is a social and fiscal conservative who opposes abortion rights, supports voluntary prayer in schools and promises to bring a faith-based family agenda to Washington.

The real contest in this district was the race for the Republican nomination. Eight candidates ran in the Republican primary. Carter's main rivals were Peter Wareing, the son-in-law of Texas oilman Jack Blanton, who was the runner-up for the Republican nomination in the 7th District in Harris County in 2000, and Brad Barton, son of 6th District Congressman Joe Barton, whose district once included Brazos County and College Station. In the March 2002 primary, Wareing led with 37% to 26% for Carter and 16% for Barton. Wareing got 67% in his home base in Harris County, which cast 18% of the votes; Carter got 58% in Williamson County, which cast 26%. In the four-week of runoff campaign Carter attacked Wareing for campaign contributions to Democrats like Congresswoman Sheila Jackson Lee and Carter argued that Wareing was a liberal in disguise. When Wareing proposed that each candidate sign a "clean campaign pledge," Carter offered what he called a "homestead pledge"—a ploy to highlight his charge that Wareing was a Houston carpetbagger who rented an apartment in the district for the sole purpose of running for office. Barton endorsed Carter as "the only true conservative in this race," even though Carter earlier called him a carpetbagger from the Dallas area. Wareing spent $1.7 million of his own money; Carter spent only $811,000 in the primary and general election combined. But Carter won 57%–43%. He got 78% of the vote in Williamson County, which cast 33% of the vote; Wareing got 65% of the vote in Harris County, which cast 16% of the vote. In Brazos County, with its two local candidates eliminated in the primary, Carter increased his percentage from 12% in March to 46% in April. He won the general election easily.

In the House, Carter became the freshman class representative on the Republican Steering Committee, which makes committee assignments. He can be expected to push for putting the main homeland security research center at Texas A&M.

THIRTY-SECOND DISTRICT

Rep. Pete Sessions (R)

Elected 1996, 4th term; b. Mar. 22, 1955, Waco; home, Dallas; SW U., B.A. 1978; Methodist; married (Juanita).

Professional Career: District Mgr., SW Bell Telephone Co., 1978–93; V.P., Public Policy, Natl. Center for Policy Analysis, 1994–95.

DC Office: 1318 LHOB 20515, 202-225-2231; Fax: 202-225-5878; Web site: www.house.gov/sessions.

District Office: Dallas, 972-392-0505.

Committees: *Rules* (8th of 9 R): Technology & the House. *Select Committee on Homeland Security* (26th of 27 R): Cybersecurity, Science and Research & Development (Vice Chmn.); Emergency Preparedness & Response; Rules.

Group Ratings

	ADA	ACLU	AFS	LCV	CON	ITIC	NTU	COC	ACU	NTLC	CHC
2002	0	7	0	0	55	88	62	100	100	97	100
2001	0	—	0	0	—	—	76	96	100	—	—

National Journal Ratings

	2001 LIB — 2001 CONS		2002 LIB — 2002 CONS	
Economic	0%	94%	0%	91%
Social	35%	63%	0%	75%
Foreign	16%	82%	0%	85%

Key Votes of the 107th Congress

1. Approve Bush Tax Cuts	Y	5. Faith-Based Charities	Y	9. Trade Promotion Authority	Y
2. Limit Patients' Bill of Rights	Y	6. Bar Gays in the Boy Scouts	Y	10. Bar Funds for Intl. Court	Y
3. Campaign Finance Reform	N	7. Ban Partial-Birth Abortion	Y	11. Authorize Force in Iraq	Y
4. Ban ANWR Development	N	8. Arm Commercial Pilots	Y	12. Deny Home. Sec. Dept. Union	Y

Election Results

2002 general	Pete Sessions (R)	100,226	(68%)	($530,671)
	Pauline Dixon (D)	44,886	(30%)	($10,578)
	Other	2,790	(2%)	
2002 primary	Pete Sessions (R)	19,973	(93%)	
	Danny Davis (R)	1,391	(7%)	
2000 general (TX 5)	Pete Sessions (R)	100,487	(54%)	($1,826,456)
	Regina Montoya Coggins (D)	82,629	(44%)	($1,636,875)
	Other	2,842	(2%)	

Prior Winning Percentages: 1998 (56%); 1996 (53%)

The People		Race/Ethnic Origin	Ancestry	
Area size:	166 sq. mi.	55.2% White	German: 8.7%	English: 8.2%
Urban population:	99.8%	9.1% Black	Irish: 6.7%	
Rural population:	0.2%	6.3% Asian	**2000 Presidential Vote**	
Pop. 2000:	651,619	0.3% Native Am.	Bush (R)...............129,527	(65%)
Median income:	$48,848	0.0% Hawaiian	Gore (D)................70,029	(35%)
Poverty status:	11.3%	1.5% Two+ races	**Cook Partisan Voting Index:** R +15	
Military veterans:	8.9%	0.1% Other		
		27.4% Hispanic Origin		

Occupation	Blue collar: 16.4%	White collar: 71.3%	Gray collar: 12.4%

North Dallas has long been the home of the city's elite—indeed, of a good portion of the nation's elite. Early in the 20th century, Dallas's richest citizens started moving away from old neighborhoods next to downtown and out past Turtle Creek to the area around the suburbs of Highland Park and University Park—the Park Cities. Dallas grew lustily from midcentury on, and beyond the Park Cities miles of affluent neighborhoods were built, especially between the Central Expressway and the Dallas North Tollway. Gallerias and office complexes followed; increasingly North Dallasites were working near where they lived. Not all of North Dallas is like that; there is an entertainment and singles apartment corridor along Greenville Avenue, working class black neighborhoods here and there, pockets of Latino neighborhoods near the freeways. But overall the tone has been set by the Dallas elite. In the 1960s and 1970s this was one of the politically most conservative parts of the country: people believed firmly in free markets, personal responsibility and the Republican party. In the 1990s North Dallas moved, like elite areas in other big metropolitan areas, toward Democrats—but here only just a little bit. Gun control is not much more popular here than in rural Texas, and the number of affluent women willing to vote Democratic on the abortion issue is very much less than in similarly affluent quadrants of New York or Los Angeles. A decade ago, both George W. Bush and Dick Cheney lived in North Dallas, in or near the Park Cities; Bush moved to Austin in January 1995 when he became governor and Cheney changed his residence to Wyoming in July 2000 so that he could be nominated vice president.

The 32d Congressional District includes all of the area commonly thought of as North Dallas. This was a new district created by a federal court in November 2001; the districts that had recently included much of North Dallas, the 3d and the 26th, were moved farther north into the suburbs. The 32d includes the Park Cities, the Turtle Creek area, and affluent North Dallas north to the Dallas County line. It also includes all or part of affluent suburbs in Dallas County: parts of Richardson and Garland northeast of the city and Farmers Branch, Coppell and parts of Irving and Carrollton to the northwest. Politically this is a solidly Republican area, but not so Republican as some of the fast-growing suburban counties in the state. It voted 65% for George W. Bush in 2000.

The congressman from the 32d District is Pete Sessions, a Republican first elected in 1996. Sessions grew up in Waco, graduated from Southwestern University, then worked at Southwestern Bell in Dallas for 16 years; his father William Sessions, a federal judge, served as FBI director from 1987 to 1993. Sessions has shown he is willing to move around to different House districts. In 1991 he ran and finished sixth in the special election in the 3d District, which then included much of North Dallas. In 1993 he resigned from the phone company to run against Democratic incumbent John Bryant in the 5th District, which included much of the east side of Dallas and several rural counties to the south. The district had been designed to reelect Bryant, a liberal and active legislator. But Sessions ran a vigorous campaign, making a two-day, 12-city tour of the district's rural portions with a livestock trailer full of horse manure and a sign saying "the Clinton health care plan stinks worse than this trailer." "A vulgar thing," Bryant sniffed. This was a heavily Republican year and, although he outspent Sessions 2–1, Bryant won by just 50%–47%. In 1996 Bryant ran unsuccessfully for the Senate; Sessions ran again and won the March primary. The district lines were changed by a federal court in the summer, and in the fall he faced Democrat John Pouland, a former regional GSA administrator, in November. Sessions charged that Pouland was a big government liberal and would abandon U.S. military bases overseas; Pouland criticized subsidizing the foreign bases while pursuing Medicare "cuts." Pouland charged that Sessions had changed to an anti-abortion stance after his 1991 race. This was a seriously contested race; Sessions won 53%–47%.

In the House, Sessions has a solidly conservative voting record. In 1999 he got a seat on the Rules Committee, a sure sign that he is regarded as a leadership loyalist. He sponsored the constitutional amendment to require a two-thirds vote to raise taxes, and was a leading advocate of the Republicans proposal to put Social Security and Medicare surpluses in a lockbox. He also joined with Democrats Charles Grassley, Ted Kennedy and Henry Waxman on a bill to permit families with disabled children to keep their Medicaid coverage even if their income rises; Sessions and his wife have a son with Down's syndrome. He was an early House organizer of the bandwagon for George W. Bush's presidential candidacy.

In the 5th District, Sessions faced serious challenges. His opponent in 1998 was Victor Morales, who lost to Phil Gramm two years earlier and again ran a shoestring campaign, criticizing

Sessions for taking contributions from special interests. Sessions won 56%–43%. In 2000, Democrats spoke well of his challenger Regina Montoya Coggins, who was a Clinton White House liaison to local elected officials and whose husband was Clinton's U.S. attorney in the Dallas area; she was well known for her on-air work at KERA-TV in Dallas. She attacked the "politics of selfishness" and said that the incumbent was "in the pocket of the big drug companies." Sessions termed her "at the outer edges of the liberal agenda" and said that she was a "liar" in describing how he would benefit from tax cuts. With her Clinton and feminist contacts, Coggins was competitive financially. In a strong Republican year in Texas, Sessions had a slightly smaller victory margin, 54%–44%.

When the federal court issued its redistricting map in November 2001, the new 5th District was considerably more Republican: the Bush 2000 percentage rose from 58% to 62%. The 32d district, which voted 65% for Bush, seemed only marginally more Republican. But Sessions surprised almost everyone by abandoning the 5th District and running instead in the 32d, which included only 16% of his old district. Sessions explained that he wanted to spend less time traveling around his district (the 32d covers just 166 square miles, making it the state's smallest seat; the 5th covers 7,455 square miles) and that the new district was compatible with his pro-business philosophy; certainly the 32d has a stronger fundraising base. Some Republicans criticized Sessions. But state Representative Ken Marchant abandoned his plan to run in the 32d and Sessions had only token primary opposition. In the general, Sessions won 68%–30%. After the election he urged the legislature to order a new round of congressional redistricting to replace the "current partisan interim map." Depending on the result, he could find himself in yet another district.

★ UTAH ★

U tah is a triumph of man over nature, the creation of a productive and orderly civilization in a remote expanse of desert and mountain, arrayed around a desolate salt sea. Today's Utah and Mormonism have their roots in a very different landscape of more than 150 years ago, when a wave of religious enthusiasm, prophecy and utopianism swept across the "burnt-over district" of Upstate New York in the 1820s and 1830s. There Joseph Smith, a 14-year-old farmer, experienced a vision in which the angel Moroni appeared and told him where to unearth several golden tablets inscribed with hieroglyphic writings. With the aid of special spectacles, Smith translated the tablets and published them as the Book of Mormon in 1831. He later declared himself a prophet and founded the Church of Jesus Christ of Latter-day Saints.

The Mormons, as they were called, attracted thousands of converts and created their own communities; persecuted for their beliefs, they moved west to Ohio, Missouri and then Illinois. In 1844, the Mormon colony at Nauvoo, Illinois, had some 15,000 members living under the theocratic rule of Smith. It was here that Smith received a revelation sanctioning the practice of polygamy, which led to his death at the hands of a mob in 1844. After the murder, the new church president, Brigham Young, decided to move the faithful, "the saints," farther west into territory that was still part of Mexico and far beyond white settlement. In 1847 Young led a well-organized march across the Great Plains and into the Rocky Mountains on a path where Mormons re-enacted the march 150 years later in 1997. In 1847, they stopped on the western slope of the Wasatch Range and, as Young gazed over the valley of the Great Salt Lake spread out below, he uttered the now famous words, "This is the place."

The place was Utah. Young was governor of the territory for many years, and it is the only state that largely continues to live by the teachings of a church. The early pioneers laid out towns foursquare to the points of the compass with huge city blocks, built sturdy houses and planted dozens of trees. Young's home still stands a block away from Temple Square, where the Temple, closed to non-Mormons, stands in gleaming marble, topped by the golden angel Moroni, across from the oval Mormon Tabernacle where its great choir sings. For 150 years this "Zion" has attracted thousands of converts from the Midwest, the north of England and Scandinavia. The object of religious fear and prejudice, Utah was not granted statehood until 1896, after the church

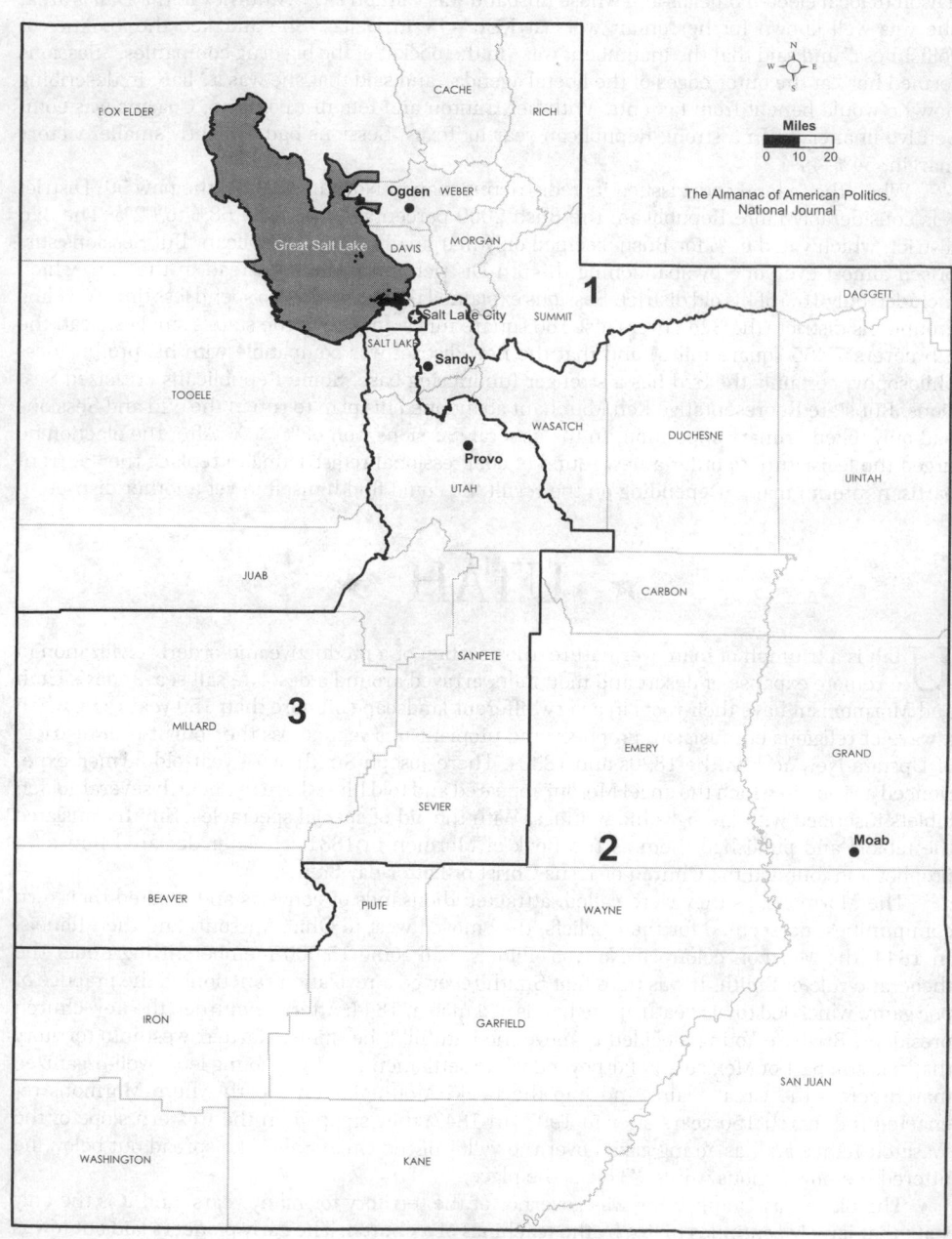

Congressional district boundaries were first effective for 2002.

renounced polygamy. Utah has grown steadily since then, and remains heavily Mormon, its basic character is stamped on the desert, mountain-shadowed, often surrealistic landscape that without the Mormons would probably have remained as unpopulated as Nevada without gambling.

The LDS church remains distinctive in many ways. It cares deeply about its past: In caves in the mountains of Utah, the Church preserves America's most complete genealogical records in its Family History Library, which is also on the Internet. It tries to spread the faith: Young Mormons, 65,000 every year, spend missionary years in the United States and abroad, and their experiences in turn give Utah the biggest inventory of people with knowledge of obscure foreign languages of any state in the union, a nice commercial advantage. The church prohibits the consumption of tobacco, alcohol and caffeine; it encourages hard work and large families. Mormons are healthier than the average American; better educated, they work longer hours and earn more money. In an individualist country, the church fosters communitarian attitudes: The LDS Church has no clergy, but members serve in positions for which they are chosen, conducting religious services but also keeping in touch with members and counseling them when they need help. The church also maintains its own social service organizations. It evidently works: While American mainline denominations are losing members, the Mormon Church is growing. There were 2.9 million Mormons in 1970 and nearly 11 million in 2000, with more than half outside the United States and just 15% in Utah; this was the fastest-growing church in the United States in the 1990s and the nation's fifth largest denomination in 2002.

The church's influence in Utah has long been great and has sometimes been resented. It owns one of the two leading Salt Lake City newspapers and a TV station; it has holdings in an insurance company, several banks, real estate; it is the state's largest employer. But church President Gordon Hinckley barred church general authorities from serving on business boards and though about 70% of Mormons vote Republican church leaders have insisted that there is no "church party" and that one can be a good Mormon and a Democrat. Power is diffuse in this rapidly growing state and the days are gone when the church president could sit down with four or five business leaders and make civic decisions. In politics the church weighs in only on what it considers moral issues—abortion (Utah has the strictest anti-abortion law in the nation), gambling (leave that to Nevada), tobacco (this was the first state to ban cigarette vending machines), alcohol (the state's restrictive liquor laws are slowly being liberalized). But on these issues the church is in line with public opinion. Polls show Utahns more conservative than Americans generally on every cultural issue except school prayer; Mormons, originally a discriminated-against minority, are wary of imposing their religion on others. They get converts enough anyway: Polynesian converts have moved to Utah and are joining in disproportionate numbers its police forces.

If the moral underpinnings of life in Utah have not changed in 50 years, Utah's view of its place in the nation has. Before World War II, Utah saw itself as a colonial victim of East Coast bankers and financiers and Mormons saw themselves as suffering religious discrimination and bigotry—all with some cause. Utah's income levels were well below the national average, its cost of living higher, the prices paid for the things it produced seemed to be controlled elsewhere. In political terms, this perspective translated into a Democratic allegiance: In 1940 Utah was represented by staunch New Dealers in Congress and cast 62% of its votes for Franklin Roosevelt. Today, Utah sees itself as a busy generator of wealth, with a raft of successful businesses and a knack for high-tech innovation. It has the youngest and most productive workforce of any state in the nation. Its population grew 30% in the 1990s, the fourth highest rate in the nation (after Nevada, Arizona and Colorado). Work weeks average 48 hours here, more than Japan and far more than anywhere else in America. It has had fast-rising incomes and in the mid-1990s America's fastest-rising house prices as thousands of people migrated from California. Utah has the largest families and the largest proportion of children of any state, by far, and low rates of divorce. It has the lowest median age of any state (27.1), Utah County has the lowest median age of any county (23.3) and Provo has the lowest median age of any city (22.9). Church doctrine discriminated against blacks until 1978, and Utah's population was only 1% black in 2000, but it was also 9% Hispanic, 2% Asian and 1% Pacific Islander. In many ways, Utah looks like the America of the 1950s, but with 21st century high-tech: in 2000 it was the number one state in households with computers.

Utah is also a place with community spirit—and with its problems. It rejoiced when it won the 2002 Winter Olympics, and started a $1.6 billion reconstruction of I-15, an airport expansion, a downtown light rail system and building a winter sports park, new stadium space and an athlete's village. Then in late 1998 it was revealed that members of the International Olympics Committee had received gifts—$400,000 for college scholarships, $28,000 in medical care, airline tickets, guns and skis—from Salt Lake Olympics organizers. Six members of the IOC resigned in January 1999, and two organizers were indicted in July 2000. Utah brought in Massachusetts entrepreneur (and now Massachusetts Governor) Mitt Romney to get the Olympics back on track, and he succeeded. The Games went off on schedule; Utah showed its mountains and its new Olympic facilities to the world—Utah Olympic Park and Utah Olympic Oval, Soldier Hollow and the Olympic Caldron and Legacy Park. But Utah also made less happy news. Polygamist Tom Green, with five wives and 29 children, was convicted of bigamy in 2001 and child rape in 2002: an unhappy reminder of the Mormon past. And in 2002 Utah's economic boom and the in-migration of people into the state seemed to end. Governor Mike Leavitt called it "the toughest year for Utah's economy since 1954," and he and the legislature had to grapple with serious budget problems. Farmers meanwhile had been grappling with a population explosion of the Mormon crickets and grasshoppers that Brigham Young's followers had found in Zion.

Politically, Utah's special characteristics have made it a heavily Republican state since the middle 1960s. The arithmetic is pretty similar: about 75% of voters are Mormon and about 70% of them usually vote Republican; that puts the Republicans over 50% without a single non-Mormon vote. This was not always so, but in the last 30 years, as traditional values thriving in Utah have come under attack elsewhere, Utahns, Mormons and gentiles alike, have made it arguably the most Republican of states—standing out in national statistics politically just as it does demographically. Interestingly, the Salt Lake City neighborhoods close to the church headquarters, with gracious old houses and a smaller street grid that attract academic and professional newcomers, have become the most heavily "gentile" and politically liberal parts of the state. As the Yankee hub of Boston filled up with Irish Catholic Democrats in the 1890s, so Salt Lake City is getting more than its share of secular liberal Democrats in the 1990s, people who cheer on the non-Church-owned *Salt Lake Tribune* when it runs stories attacking the church for converting a block of Main Street into a plaza with restrictions on speech, dress, and conduct; the church lost that case in court but has appealed. But for the most part, Democrats are competitive only if they seem consistent with Utah values and attitudes, and even then are in jeopardy: Utah's one Democratic congressman, son of a respected two-term governor, only narrowly held onto his seat in 2002.

The People		Race/Ethnic Origin			Military veterans: 161,351 (10.6%)	
Pop. 2000:	2,233,169	1,904,265	85.3%	White	WWII: 21.0%	Korea: 13.9%
Pop. 1990:	1,722,850	16,137	0.7%	Black	Vietnam: 31.7%	Gulf War: 11.5%
Change 1990–2000:	Up 29.6%	36,483	1.6%	Asian	**Most populous cities:**	
Change 1980–1990:	Up 17.9%	26,663	1.2%	Native Am.	1. Salt Lake City	181,743
% of U.S. total:	0.8%	14,806	0.7%	Hawaiian	2. West Valley City	108,896
Pop. rank:	34th of 50	31,308	1.4%	Two + races	3. Provo	105,166
Area size:	84,899 sq. mi.	1,948	0.1%	Other	4. Sandy	88,418
State Native:	62.9%	201,559	9.0%	Hisp. Origin	5. Orem	84,324
Non-citizen:	4.9%	**Ancestry**			Urban population: 88.3%	
Language		English: 21.4%		German: 8.5%	Rural population: 11.7%	
English: 83.1%	Spanish: 9.1%	USA: 5.0%		Danish: 4.8%		
Other Eur.: 4.5%		Irish: 4.3%				

Education		Work Sector		Utah	
H.S. Grad:	87.7%	Private: 78.2%	Govt: 15.7%	Senate	22 R 7 D
College Grad:	26.1%	Self: 5.8%	Family: 0.3%	House	56 R 19 D
Industry		Unemployment: 4.9%		Legislative Term Limits: No	
Agri: 1.9%	Con: 8.2%	**Household Income**		**Registered Voters**	
Fin: 6.8%	Info: 3.3%	<15k: 10.8%	15-35k: 25.1%	No party registration	
Mfg: 17.0%	Prof: 28.6%	35-50k: 19.0%	50-100k: 33.9%		
Public: 5.5%	Trade: 16.3%	100-150k: 7.5%	>150k: 3.7%		
Other: 12.4%		Median: $45,726			
Occupation		Poverty status: 9.4%			
Blue collar: 24.1%	White collar: 61.4%	**Home Value**			
Gray collar: 14.5%		<50k: 4.8% 50-100k: 15.9% 100-200k: 57.0% 200-300k: 14.3%			
		300-500k: 5.9% >500k: 2.0% Median: $142,600			

Presidential politics Utah has been the most Republican state in five of the last seven presidential elections. Arguably it was in 2000 as well. The percentage of votes for George W. Bush, 67%, was slightly behind that in Wyoming and Idaho. But the Bush margin of 40.49% over Al Gore was larger than in either of those two other states. As far back as 1960, Richard Nixon carried Utah with 55% of the vote; in 1972 he won with 68%. Ronald Reagan won 73% here in 1980 and 75% in 1984; George Bush won 66% here in 1988 and George W. Bush 67% in 2000. In 1992, this was also the least Democratic state: Ross Perot finished ahead of Bill Clinton, 27% to 25%.

Governor Mike Leavitt spent much time and effort promoting a Western regional primary for the Friday following Southern Super Tuesday, March 10, 2000. But only Colorado and Wyoming (with a caucus, not a primary) adopted the date, and candidates paid little attention to western issues as Leavitt had hoped. Bill Bradley and John McCain pulled out of their races before March 10, and only 10% of Utah's registered voters bothered to vote.

2000 Presidential Vote		
Bush (R)	515,096	(67%)
Gore (D)	203,053	(26%)
Nader (Green)	35,850	(5%)
Other	16,755	(2%)

2000 Republican Presidential Primary		
Bush (R)	57,617	(63%)
Keyes (R)	19,367	(21%)
McCain (R)	12,784	(14%)
Other	1,285	(1%)

2000 Democratic Presidential Primary		
Gore (D)	12,527	(80%)
Bradley (D)	3,160	(20%)

1996 Presidential Vote		
Dole (R)	361,911	(54%)
Clinton (D)	221,633	(33%)
Perot (I)	66,461	(10%)
Other	15,623	(2%)

Congressional districting Utahns expected that the 2000 Census would give Utah a fourth seat in the House of Representatives. But, under the formula used for reapportionment, Utah fell 857 residents short of getting a new district; instead, North Carolina got an unexpected 13th seat. Utah did what comes naturally to Americans today: it sued, twice. The first lawsuit contended that if military personnel stationed abroad should be counted in their states of residence, so also should be Mormon missionaries, who also can be accurately tracked and matched with their home states. As it happens, North Carolina had thousands of military personnel stationed abroad and only 107 attributable Mormon missionaries. Utah had fewer military personnel stationed abroad but 11,176 Mormon missionaries. In April 2001 a three-judge federal court threw out Utah's case, and one judge called its theory "wildly unfair." In late November 2001 the Supreme Court affirmed that ruling without opinion. Utah's other theory was that the Census Bureau violated the Constitution's injunction that it conduct an "actual enumeration" of the population when it employed what statisticians call "hot-deck imputation": when Census takers after repeated efforts cannot contact residents of one housing unit, they assume that it contains the same number of people in similar housing units nearby. Utah argued that this is "sampling," prohibited, the Supreme Court ruled in another case, by a 1957 statute. This argument did better in court:

108th Congress Lineup	
2 R	1 D

107th Congress Lineup	
2 R	1 D

Utah lost by a 2–1 margin in a three-judge district court in early November 2001 and by 5–4 in the Supreme Court in June 2002. But the upshot was that North Carolina, not Utah, got the 435th district in the 2000 reapportionment.

Utah's legislature drew new congressional district lines in September 2001. Aware that the state was suing for another district, it adopted both three and four district plans. The large Republican majorities in the legislature argued that all districts should contain both urban and rural areas; this policy was followed when Utah had two congressional districts, but when it gained a third district in the 1980 Census, and then again after the 1990 Census, the legislature drew plans which had one district entirely inside Salt Lake County. This 2d District had had the temerity in 2000 to elect a Democratic congressman. The Republicans' principle, honored in the breach for the preceding 20 years, forced them to draw three districts which combined urban and rural areas and which increased the Bush 2000 percentage in the 2d District from 57% to 67%. Naturally, the Democratic congressman, Jim Matheson, protested; he had the TV savvy to go to a trendy Salt Lake City neighborhood within easy reach of camera crews and put red and blue tape down the pavement of the streets which divided his new 2d District from the 1st. Neighbors, some of them Republicans, said how unfair it was that their communities were being split between two districts. At the same time, the Republican legislators drew a four-district plan, which would go into effect should Utah win one of its then two pending court cases. This plan included a new 4th District entirely within Salt Lake County—nothing urban-and-rural about it—but within the southern portion of the county, which is heavily Republican. Democrats, understandably, assailed this as hypocrisy, but it availed them nothing. Utah conducted its 2002 election with the three-district plan in place, and the Supreme Court decision narrowly rejecting the state's attack on "hot-deck imputation" came just five days before the June 2002 primary. Democrats thought of challenging the three-district plan on the ground that it reduced the Hispanic percentage in the 2d District from 9% to 6% and therefore violated the Voting Rights Act but, understandably, got nowhere with this flimsy argument.

Governor

Michael Leavitt (R)

Elected 1992, term expires Jan. 2005, 3d term; b. Feb. 11, 1951, Cedar City; home, Salt Lake City; S. UT U., B.A. 1976; Mormon; married (Jacalyn).

Military Career: Army Natl. Guard, 1969–78.

Professional Career: Pres. & CEO, Leavitt Group Insurance Co., 1984–92; Chmn., S. UT U. Bd. of Trustees, 1985–89; UT Board of Regents, 1989–92.

Office: 210 State Capitol, Salt Lake City, 84114, 801-538-1000; Fax: 801-538-1528; Web site: www.utah.gov/governor.

Election Results

2000 general	Michael Leavitt (R)	424,837	(56%)
	Bill Orton (D)	321,979	(42%)
	Other	14,990	(2%)
2000 primary	Michael Leavitt (R)	122,289	(62%)
	Glen P. Davis (R)	75,719	(38%)
1996 general	Michael Leavitt (R)	503,693	(75%)
	Jim Bradley (D)	156,616	(23%)
	Other	11,570	(2%)

Prior Winning Percentages: 1992 (42%)

Mike Leavitt, a Republican, was elected governor of Utah in 1992 and reelected in 1996 and 2000. He grew up in Cedar City, in the southwest corner of the state, graduated from Southern Utah University, worked for and in the 1980s ran the family businesses, including an insurance company that has spread all over the West and has land holdings in southern Utah and Nevada. In between, he managed the campaigns of Governor Norman Bangerter and Senator Jake Garn. In 1992, when Bangerter retired after two terms, Leavitt ran himself. He won the Republican primary 56%–44% over Richard Eyre, who backed a $1,200 school choice voucher; Leavitt had his own Strategic Plan for Education and opposed vouchers. In the general, liberal Democrat Stewart Hanson ran third, with only 23%; second was anti-tax crusader and later 2d District Congressman Merrill Cook, with 34%; Leavitt won with 42%.

As the economy surged in the mid-1990s Leavitt cut taxes and pushed activist programs with catchy labels. One was the 1994 Healthprint insurance reforms; he boasted that Utah had lower health care costs than all but one other state. Another was a $120 million, seven-year Technology 2000 initiative. In 1995 he convened a Growth Summit, which proposed a $2.6 billion highway-building program, to make I-15 in Salt Lake County a 12-lane highway in time for the 2002 Winter Olympics; for that he raised gas taxes while cutting the sales tax. In 1996 he proposed a Legacy Highway, to be built parallel to and west of I-15, to be built after the Olympics. He worked to start, with other Western states, a Western Virtual University, and is completing UtahLINK, giving Internet access to all Utah schools.

On environmental issues, he backed a quality growth initiative, with incentives to local communities to preserve valuable open space, but no mandates. After discussions with Oregon's Democratic Governor John Kitzhaber, he advanced what he called Enlibra, "a symbol of balance and stewardship," based on collaboration, local decision-making and free market incentives rather than government command and control, "not to eliminate conflict but to shorten the conflict so as to increase the velocity of environmental problem-solving." Leavitt engineered land swaps with Clinton Interior Secretary Bruce Babbitt, but he was blindsided when in fall 1996 while campaigning in Arizona Bill Clinton announced the creation of the Grand Staircase-Escalante National Monument. Leavitt, other western governors and environmental groups developed an Enlibra National Fire Plan to allow thinning and logging of forests to avoid disastrous fires, but in 2002 Utah's James Hansen, chairman of the House Resources Committee, moved to sweep it aside and substitute the Bush administration's approach. In April 2003 he signed a memo of understanding with Interior Secretary Gale Norton: the state and localities would stop suing the federal government to gain title to pre-1976 roads and trails on national park, wildlife refuge and wilderness land, and the Bureau of Land Management would cede title to such roads on its lands if Utah could prove they existed before 1976.

In 1996 Democrats had to scrounge to find a candidate to run against Leavitt; he was reelected 75%–23%. But as the 2000 election approached he was embroiled in controversy, often with members of his own party. He signed a carrying concealed weapon bill in 1995, but ordered state employees to leave their guns home in 1996 and in 1999 called for a ban on guns in churches and schools; that, and a threat to call a special session on guns, infuriated conservatives. In March 2000 he vetoed a bill substituting abstinence advocacy for sex education, but said he would work to see that schools stressed abstinence. In December 1999 Leavitt seemed to avoid primary opposition when he got House Speaker Marty Stephens to endorse him. But four little-known candidates ran anyway, and at the May 2000 state Republican convention, amid boos and catcalls, he failed to get the 60% required to win the nomination outright; on the final ballot he prevailed over the little-known Glen Davis by only 54%–46%. "I am in the mainstream of Republican thought," Leavitt insisted. "I'll take my message to the people." That message was a very conservative one in the primary; he stressed tax cuts, abstinence education, opposition to federal confiscation of private lands and opposition to trigger locks, without mentioning his abstinence veto, gun control measures and Enlibra. Leavitt spent more than $1 million, Davis only $70,000; but Leavitt won by an uninspiring 62%–38% margin.

His Democratic opponent was Bill Orton, three-term congressman from the heavily Republican 3d District until he was defeated in 1996. Orton said the well-financed Leavitt was beholden to special interests and criticized him for not taking a stand on guns; he frequently cited LDS

Church President Gordon Hinckley's admonition that there was no reason a good Mormon could not be a Democrat. Leavitt spent $1.9 million altogether, Orton just $140,000; Leavitt won again by an unimpressive margin, 56%–42%, as Orton carried Salt Lake County, Summit County (which contains Park City and voted 10% for Ralph Nader) and three small traditionally Democratic rural counties.

In his third term Leavitt faced more severe fiscal problems than in his first two. In 2002 he called no less than three special sessions of the legislature to cut spending. Then and in the budget session in early 2003 he managed to avoid cuts in education spending, which had risen more than 50% since he first took office. Instead the rainy day fund was drained, one-time fixes applied and highway spending stretched out. Leavitt tried in vain to use a water tax that subsidized urban water use diverted to general spending. In 2003 legislators of both parties came together on a plan somewhat different from Leavitt's; he responded with four vetoes.

Utah imposes no term limit on governors, but it has never elected a governor to a fourth term and polls in late 2002 showed pluralities thought Leavitt shouldn't run again in 2004. He said he would decide in summer 2003. Speaker Marty Stephens, who did not run in 2000, was expected to run in 2004 whatever Leavitt's decision. Other Republicans mentioned in early 2003 were University Regents Nolan Karras and David Jordan and Jim Hansen, who retired from the House in 2002. Democrats mentioned include 2000 candidate Bill Orton, former Attorney General Jan Graham, former Congresswoman Karen Shepherd and Congressman Jim Matheson, whose father Scott Matheson was elected governor in 1976 and 1980.

Senior Senator

Orrin Hatch (R)

Elected 1976, seat up 2006, 5th term; b. Mar. 22, 1934, Pittsburgh, PA; home, Salt Lake City; Brigham Young U., B.S. 1959; U. of Pittsburgh, J.D. 1962; Mormon; married (Elaine).

Professional Career: Practicing atty., 1962–76.

DC Office: 104 HSOB, 20510, 202-224-5251; Fax: 202-224-6331; Web site: hatch.senate.gov.

State Offices: Cedar City, 435-586-8435; Ogden, 801-625-5672; Provo, 801-375-7881; Salt Lake City, 801-524-4380; St. George, 435-634-1795.

Committees: *Aging (Special). Finance*: Health Care; International Trade; Taxation & IRS Oversight. *Indian Affairs. Intelligence (Select). Judiciary* (Chmn.): Antitrust, Competition Policy & Consumer Rights; Crime, Corrections & Victims' Rights; Terrorism, Technology & Homeland Security. *Joint Committee on Taxation* (2d of 5 Sens.).

Group Ratings

	ADA	ACLU	AFS	LCV	CON	ITIC	NTU	COC	ACU	NTLC	CHC
2002	5	20	13	6	27	100	63	100	95	94	—
2001	5	—	0	0	—	—	81	86	96	—	100

National Journal Ratings

	2001 LIB	—	2001 CONS		2002 LIB	—	2002 CONS
Economic	28%	—	71%		23%	—	76%
Social	0%	—	79%		0%	—	62%
Foreign	0%	—	94%		24%	—	67%

Key Votes of the 107th Congress

1. Approve Bush Tax Cuts	Y	5. Confirm Ashcroft as AG	Y	9. Bar Coop. with Intl. Court	Y
2. Expand Patients' Rights	N	6. Bar Gays in the Boy Scouts	Y	10. Trade Promotion Authority	Y
3. Campaign Finance Reform	N	7. $ for Hate Crime Prosecution	N	11. Authorize Force in Iraq	Y
4. Permit ANWR Development	Y	8. Overseas Military Abortions	N	12. Homeland Sec. Dept. Union	N

Election Results

2000 general	Orrin Hatch (R)	504,803	(66%)	($3,130,550)
	Scott N. Howell (D)	242,569	(31%)	($296,839)
	Other	22,332	(3%)	
2000 primary	Orrin Hatch (R)	unopposed		
1994 general	Orrin Hatch (R)	357,297	(69%)	($4,209,993)
	Pat Shea (D)	146,938	(28%)	($311,491)
	Other	15,088	(3%)	

Prior Winning Percentages: 1988 (67%); 1982 (58%); 1976 (54%)

Orrin Hatch, Utah's senior senator, is a Republican now serving his fifth term, a man who didn't plan a political career but won his seat after filing on the last possible day in 1976. Hatch grew up in Pittsburgh, where his father was a metal lather; he worked his way through Brigham Young University, then Pittsburgh Law School, practiced law there and then moved to Salt Lake City. For a time he was an amateur boxer and at one point he and his wife lived in a refurbished chicken coop. He got into the 1976 Senate race late; an endorsement from Ronald Reagan helped him win the Republican nomination, and in the general he upset three-term Democrat Frank Moss 54%–45%. His toughest re-election fight came in 1982, when he was opposed by Salt Lake City Mayor Ted Wilson; Hatch won 58%–41%.

Hatch's Senate career has been shaped by two impulses that are sometimes in tension with each other: a strong conservative philosophy and a sense of responsibility for the superintendency of legislation. He wrote a book about his thinking titled *Square Peg*. He first attracted attention in a Senate dominated by Democrats when he successfully filibustered the AFL-CIO's labor law bill, which had been expected to pass. Then, after just four years, he became chairman of the Labor Committee after Republicans won a Senate majority in 1980. He worked to convert federal programs to block grants to states, but became a fan of some programs, like the Job Corps. But he remained a strong opponent of the striker replacement law sought by unions. On the Judiciary Committee, he fought abortion and a civil rights bill that produced racial quotas and preferences, and staunchly defended Supreme Court nominees Robert Bork and Clarence Thomas. He was the author of the 1994 law limiting the FDA's authority to test and regulate food supplements; Hatch, like many Mormons, is a consumer of food supplements, and Utah has a $3 billion food supplement industry.

In 1993 Hatch switched from ranking Republican on Labor to the same post on Judiciary, when it was vacated by Strom Thurmond; in 1995 he became chairman of Judiciary and left Labor altogether. On Judiciary he worked on limiting tort liability and regulatory law and managed the balanced budget amendment to one-vote defeats in 1995 and 1997. He worked also on the flag amendment, which fell four votes short of passage in March 2000, the anti-terrorism law and the Religious Freedom Restoration Act. On judicial appointments, Hatch promised in 1995 to cooperate with the Clinton administration; by early 1997 some Democrats were charging that he was stalling approval of nominees, while some Republicans were complaining that he was allowing too many liberal, activist judges on the bench. In 1997 and 1998 Hatch passionately defended Independent Counsel Kenneth Starr against attacks by Clinton advisors.

In 1997 Hatch again surprised some on both sides of the aisle when he joined Edward Kennedy in sponsoring a $24 billion program to get states to provide health insurance for children of low-income working parents who don't qualify for Medicaid. Hatch praised the Microsoft antitrust suit in May 1998; one of Microsoft's major competitors was Utah-based Novell. Hatch has worked to allow homeowners to claim capital losses on sales of homes, to bar the federal government from using racial or gender quotas, to stop operation of Oregon's assisted suicide law and to ban stalking of celebrities by paparazzi. He tried to ban lawsuits against gun manufacturers, which he called "extortion." In 2000 he sponsored a bill to extend Schering-Plough's patent on Claritin, for which he was widely criticized. Presiding over hearings on Napster, he opined that the recording industry was going to have to sit down with Napster and owners of other copying software. In 2000 he sponsored a number of bills which were signed into law—a law giving religious groups a federal remedy when their religious rights are violated by land use policies, an increase in the number of H1-B visas, funding for agents and training aimed at methamphetamines.

As chairman and, after June 2001, ranking minority member of Judiciary, Hatch defended the Bush Justice Department and judicial nominees against Democrats' attacks; he decried their refusal to hold hearings on many appointees when they were in the majority and their filibusters of judicial appointees after January 2003. After September 11, he was one of the framers of the USA Patriot Act. In January 2003 he said he would not honor the blue slip procedure, by which one senator could stop the nomination of a judicial appointee from his state. But he also took some surprising and bipartisan positions. He and Jeff Sessions sponsored a bill to increase the amount of crack cocaine required for an automatic five-year sentence from 5 grams to 20 grams. He and Herb Kohl sponsored a Safe Explosives Act to require permits, background checks and fingerprinting to buy explosives. He and Charles Schumer sponsored a bill to allow the Dramatists Guild of America to negotiate standard contracts for playwrights. He and Joseph Biden sponsored the provision of the corporate accounting bill requiring CEOs and CFOs to sign their companies' statement of earnings with criminal penalties for inaccurate reporting. He sponsored a successful cyberterrorism amendment and co-sponsored with Joe Lieberman a bill to stimulate private sector development of medicines, vaccines and antidotes to combat bioterrorism. Despite his longstanding opposition to abortion, he supported embryonic stem-cell research and argued that life is created in the womb, "not in a petri dish." He was a co-sponsor of the tripartisan prescription drug plan that came to the floor in July 2002. In February 2003 the Senate passed his bill outlawing computer-enhanced child pornography, which the Supreme Court said was not covered by a previous law. With Charles Grassley and Kohl, he sponsored a bill to restrict class action lawsuits. He said that he would work on the issues raised by digital technology and the movie and record industries' complaints about file sharing. He and Bennett supported a permanent nuclear waste repository in Yucca Mountain, Nevada: better to have the waste transported over Utah than deposited there. The Senate passed his bills to protect the Virgin River dinosaur footprints found in St. George and to make alternate routes of the Pony Express, Oregon, California and Mormon Trails part of the National Historic Trails system.

Every senator, it sometimes seems, must run for president, and the time came for Hatch in June 1999. He admitted that it would take a "miracle" to win, but argued that he had more experience in federal office than the other candidates and could work with Democrats, and that he was not "beholden to the Republican establishment." At the August 1999 Iowa straw poll he came in last, with 2% of the votes. He managed to raise $2 million, much of it in $36 "skinny cat" contributions. But in the Iowa caucuses in January 2000 he won only 1% of the votes, fewer than John McCain, who did not campaign in the state. Two days later he withdrew from the race and endorsed George W. Bush. He had one complaint. "I did find that there was a certain amount of prejudice against Mormons. The Gallup Poll said that 17% would not vote for a Mormon for president. . . . These people think that Mormons are not Christians, when the name of the church is 'Church of Jesus Christ of Latter-Day Saints.' We're very Christian."

Hatch's seat came up for election in the fall. He attracted competition for the Republican nomination, and was greeted with jeers as well as applause at the very conservative May 2000 state party convention. But he got 61% of the votes, just above the 60% required to win the nomination without a primary. For the fall campaign he was able to raise much more than he had for his presidential candidacy, and spent $3.1 million; his opponent, for eight years the Democratic leader in the Utah Senate, spent $296,000. Hatch won 66%–31%, and became the first Utahn popularly elected five times to the Senate; the only other five-term senator in Utah history, Reed Smoot, who served from 1903 to 1933, was elected to his first term by the legislature. Hatch's talents, by the way, extend beyond the political. He has long written poetry and in 1995 began writing songs. They have been recorded by a Utah firm, first in a 13-song album of Christmas music; some have been recorded by Gladys Knight, a convert to the LDS Church, and after Christian music publishers seemed uninterested in what Hatch has called his Latter-Day Sound, he began distributing his songs on www.hatchmusic.com. He also appeared in the movie *Traffic*, but criticized the movie for its frequent obscenities.

Junior Senator

Robert Bennett (R)

Elected 1992, seat up 2004, 2d term; b. Sept. 18, 1933, Salt Lake City; home, Salt Lake City; U. of UT, B.S. 1957; Mormon; married (Joyce).

Military Career: Chaplain, Army Natl. Guard, 1957–60.

Professional Career: Staff Aide, U.S. Rep. Sherm Lloyd, 1962; Staff Aide, U.S. Sen. Wallace F. Bennett, 1963; Cong. Liaison, U.S. Dept. of Transp., 1969–70; Pres., Robert Mullen P.R., 1970–74; P.R. Dir., Summa Corp., 1974–78; Pres., Osmond Communications, 1978–79; Chmn., American Computers Corp., 1979–81; Pres., Microsonics Corp., 1981–84; CEO, Franklin Quest Co., 1984–91; Chmn., UT Educ. Strategic Plng. Comm., 1988.

DC Office: 431 DSOB, 20510, 202-224-5444; Fax: 202-228-1168; Web site: bennett.senate.gov.

State Offices: Cedar City, 435-865-1335; Ogden, 801-625-5676; Provo, 801-379-2525; Salt Lake City, 801-524-5933; St. George, 435-628-5514.

Committees: *Appropriations*: Agriculture & Rural Development (Chmn.); Energy & Water Development; Foreign Operations; Interior; Legislative Branch; Transportation, Treasury & General Government. *Banking, Housing & Urban Affairs*: Financial Institutions (Chmn.); Housing & Transportation; Securities & Investment. *Governmental Affairs*: Financial Management, Budget & International Security; Government Management, Federal Workforce & the District of Columbia; Investigations (Permanent). *Small Business & Entrepreneurship. Joint Economic Committee* (Chmn. of 10 Sens.).

Group Ratings

	ADA	ACLU	AFS	LCV	CON	ITIC	NTU	COC	ACU	NTLC	CHC
2002	5	20	13	6	51	88	61	100	100	97	—
2001	5	—	0	0	—	—	83	100	100	—	100

National Journal Ratings

	2001 LIB	—	2001 CONS	2002 LIB	—	2002 CONS
Economic	7%	—	86%	18%	—	80%
Social	0%	—	79%	0%	—	62%
Foreign	7%	—	72%	0%	—	76%

Key Votes of the 107th Congress

1. Approve Bush Tax Cuts	Y	5. Confirm Ashcroft as AG	Y	9. Bar Coop. with Intl. Court	Y
2. Expand Patients' Rights	N	6. Bar Gays in the Boy Scouts	Y	10. Trade Promotion Authority	Y
3. Campaign Finance Reform	N	7. $ for Hate Crime Prosecution	N	11. Authorize Force in Iraq	Y
4. Permit ANWR Development	Y	8. Overseas Military Abortions	N	12. Homeland Sec. Dept. Union	N

Election Results

1998 general	Robert Bennett (R)	316,652	(64%)	($1,546,219)
	Scott Leckman (D)	163,172	(33%)	($265,494)
	Other	15,085	(3%)	
1998 primary	Robert Bennett (R)	unopposed		
1992 general	Robert Bennett (R)	420,069	(55%)	($3,339,325)
	Wayne Owens (D)	301,228	(40%)	($1,904,750)
	Other	37,182	(5%)	

Bob Bennett, Utah's junior senator, is a Republican who was first elected in 1992. He grew up in Salt Lake City, and was 17 when his father Wallace Bennett was elected in 1950 to the first of four terms in the Senate. Bob Bennett worked as a congressional staffer and was the Transportation Department's chief lobbyist during the Nixon administration. He also headed the public relations firm (and CIA front) that employed Watergate burglar Howard Hunt, but was involved in no wrongdoing himself; some Watergate buffs believe that Bennett was Bob Woodward's "Deep Throat," but both Bennett and Woodward have denied it. After that, Bennett headed Microsonics Corporation, which makes audio discs for talking toys, for three years, then became head of Franklin Quest, which produces the Franklin day planners and organizers; he increased it from four to 700 employees and brought in sales of $80 million; he sold his interest in 1991 for a reported $25 million. He headed a commission that produced Utah's Strategic Plan for Education and wrote *Gaining Control*, a book on how to control your daily life.

In 1992, when Jake Garn retired from the Senate, Bennett decided to run for the seat his father once held. He was not the only millionaire in the race. The initial favorite was Republican Joseph Cannon, who had taken over the old Geneva Steel plant and made it profitable, and who spent $5 million of his own money. But Bennett spent $1.4 million of his own and effectively attacked Geneva's environmental record and won 51%–49%. The Democratic nominee, Congressman Wayne Owens, was a familiar face, with a voting record that was moderate—perhaps too liberal for Utah. Bennett won 55%–40%.

Bennett has had a moderate to conservative voting record and became Chief Deputy Whip in January 2003. He has worked for several years on bills to protect the confidentiality of medical records, with uniform rules for access by researchers and law enforcement personnel. He sponsored a bill to limit liability on debit cards as it is on credit cards, and one to establish a uniform minimalist framework for digital signatures and electronic verification over the Internet. In 1997, before most other senators were thinking about the problem, Bennett sponsored a bill to require businesses to disclose what they were doing to fix Y2K errors. In April 1998 Trent Lott made him chairman of a Select Committee on the Year 2000 Technology Problem. His first priorities were public utilities, telecommunications and transportation; later he spotlighted the unpreparedness of health care providers, and got the SEC to require disclosure of business spending on the problem. In July 2000 he moved successfully to reduce the time to review computer export controls from 180 days to 60 days; in March 2001 he moved to change the MTOPS (millions of theoretical operations per second) standards for exports, with new ones to be set by the Bush administration. In 2001 and 2002 he worked for a law that would exempt from the Freedom of Information Act information on computer intrusions that businesses share with the federal government; he argued that this was necessary to protect the Internet from hackers and cyberterrorists. He has embraced some new technology himself: He drives a gasoline-electric hybrid 2000 Honda Insight that gets 61 miles per gallon. He has come out in favor of sales taxes on Internet transactions; in his mail order business, he says, he charged customers sales tax in every state and no one protested.

In the debate on homeland security, Bennett strongly supported the personnel provisions backed by the Bush administration. He cited his experiences at the then new Department of Transportation, where only the secretary's power to transfer personnel as needed enabled him to meld the congressional liaison offices of the FAA, Urban Mass Transit Authority, Coast Guard and Federal Highway Administration into a single responsive unit. In the debate over corporate accounting in July 2002, Bennett warned against making too many changes that might have unanticipated effects; he cited a 1993 law which barred companies from expensing executive salaries over $1 million, which he said led to more companies granting stock options. In the March 2001 debate he offered an amendment to bar PACs from using soft money for fundraising and operating expenses; opposed by unions, it was defeated by advocates of the McCain-Feingold bill.

Bennett has pressed for land exchanges between Utah and the federal government, to eliminate the checkerboard pattern of land ownership which prevents Utah from producing revenue for education from mining on state lands; he notes that the idea was pushed by his father 40 years ago and by Democratic Governor Scott Matheson 20 years ago. In September 2000 he came out against the proposed nuclear waste depository on the lands of the Skull Valley Band of the Goshute Indians; in July 2002 he and Orrin Hatch supported the nuclear waste repository in Yucca Mountain, Nevada: better to have the waste transported over Utah than stored in Utah. On the Appropriations Committee, he got $34.5 million extra for security at the 2002 Winter Olympics in Salt Lake City after September 11. In September 2002 Bennett led the effort by Western state Republicans to get the same flexibility in forest management for their states that Tom Daschle, using his power as majority leader, got for South Dakota. On Appropriations he secured $15 million for the Natural History Museum at the University of Utah (75% of the collection is federally owned), $3.5 million to preserve 15,000 acres in Summit County, more payments in lieu of taxes on federal lands, $2 million for the Castle Rock Ranch, $300,000 for the Wasatch Canyons water quality initiative, $16 million for a computer support facility at Hill Air Force Base, $650,000 for Mormon cricket control (there has been a population explosion of these crop-eating insects) and $1.2 million for the Sevier County Multi-Events Center.

Bennett was re-elected 64%–33% in 1998 against a Democrat who was a surgeon with an interest in the microloan programs in Bangladesh. In 1992 he said he would run for only two terms, but in 1998 Bennett said he would not rule out running again in 2004, and just before September 11 he said, "I'm leaning strongly toward running again." In mid-2003 no candidate had appeared; state Democratic Chairman Meg Holbrook said, "Don't be surprised if it's not a regular politician." Bennett might be good for many more terms. Longevity runs in the family: his father lived to be 95, and his grandfather Heber Grant was president of the LDS Church, a job that goes to the longest serving member of the Quorum of the Twelve Disciples.

FIRST DISTRICT

Rep. Rob Bishop (R)

Elected 2002, 1st term; b. July 13, 1951, Salt Lake City; home, Kaysville; U. of UT, B.A. 1974; Mormon; married (Jeralyn Hansen).

Elected Office: UT House of Reps., 1979–94; Speaker, 1992–94.

Professional Career: H.S. teacher, 1974–02.

DC Office: 124 CHOB 20515, 202-225-0453; Fax: 202-225-5857; Web site: www.house.gov/robbishop.

District Office: Ogden, 801-625-0107.

Committees: *Armed Services* (27th of 33 R): Readiness; Strategic Forces. *Resources* (26th of 28 R): Energy & Mineral Resources; National Parks, Recreation & Public Lands. *Science* (21st of 25 R): Space & Aeronautics.

Group Ratings and Key Votes: Newly Elected

Election Results

2002 general	Rob Bishop (R)	109,265	(61%)	($670,302)
	Dave Thomas (D)	66,104	(37%)	($704,616)
	Other	4,043	(2%)	
2002 primary	Rob Bishop (R)	25,280	(60%)	
	Kevin Garn (R)	16,957	(40%)	
2000 general	Jim Hansen (R)	180,591	(69%)	($338,572)
	Kathleen Collinwood (D)	71,229	(27%)	($74,137)
	Other	2,380	(4%)	

The People		Race/Ethnic Origin	Ancestry	
Area size:	22,700 sq. mi.	83.3% White	English: 20.9%	German: 8.3%
Urban population:	88.7%	1.1% Black	USA: 5.0%	
Rural population:	11.3%	1.6% Asian	**2000 Presidential Vote**	
Pop. 2000:	744,389	0.7% Native Am.	Bush (R)..............167,716 (68%)	
Median income:	$45,058	0.6% Hawaiian	Gore (D)................66,792 (27%)	
Poverty status:	9.5%	1.4% Two+ races	Other....................13,415 (5%)	
Military veterans:	11.7%	0.1% Other	**Cook Partisan Voting Index:** R +22	
		11.1% Hispanic Origin		

Occupation	Blue collar: 26.2%	White collar: 58.7%	Gray collar: 15.1%

In May 1869, a motley crowd of Irish and Chinese laborers, teamsters, engineers, train crews, officials and guests from California and Salt Lake City gathered in Promontory Point, Utah, to watch the opening of the transcontinental railroad. The Union Pacific train was late and Leland Stanford's raised hammer totally missed the golden spike, but an alert telegrapher mimicked the sound over the wire and a photographer recorded the scene for posterity: United at last were the civilized East and the mostly untamed West. Here, beyond sight of the snow-capped mountains crossed by Mormon pioneers, the salt flats still stretch out endlessly; the rail lines now pass north of here, and Promontory Point lies on an uninhabited peninsula that dips into the Great Salt Lake. Back in the mid-1980s the lake was rising and threatened to cover the historic site; the state legislature passed a law forbidding it to rise above a certain level. For whatever reason, the lake level fell. In 1987, the Newfoundland Evaporation Basin was completed, enabling the Great Salt Lake to be drained if its rise ever again threatens populated areas.

In Salt Lake City, the center of the Mormon Church—and of Utah—is Temple Square, illuminated by 300,000 lights during Christmas week and nestled beneath the towering, snow-capped mountains that flank Salt Lake City. Here you can find the Mormon Tabernacle, home of the famous choir, and the Temple itself, crowned with the golden angel Moroni. This place has been the focal point of Utah since Brigham Young, looking down at this valley, said, "This is the place." Ironically, Salt Lake City is the least Mormon and most cosmopolitan part of Utah, with the state university and businesses bringing in outsiders who, flouting Mormon strictures, keep purveyors of alcohol and caffeine in business. Salt Lake County voted 56% for George W. Bush in 2000, as compared to 74% in the rest of the state, and even voted 7% for Ralph Nader.

The 1st Congressional District consists of the northern end of the state. It includes most of Salt Lake City's historic downtown, its distinctive Avenues District and the airport, but little of the fast-growing suburbia that stretches south of the city. More than half the people in the district live in the stretch of the Wasatch Front, between the mountains and the lake, just north of Salt Lake City, in Davis and Weber Counties. Davis County is suburban and fairly affluent; Ogden is the old working class railroad town, an industrial center that depends on nearby Hill Air Force Base. To the north in the Cache Valley is Logan, home of Utah State University. This is farming country and very heavily Mormon. Over the mountains to the east of Salt Lake City is Park City, the old mining town that is now an increasingly fashionable ski resort and home of the Sundance Film Festival. West of Salt Lake City are the desolate Bonneville Salt Flats, where land speed records have been set. This land of stark beauty, much of it federally owned, has been used roughly by man: as a repository for hazardous wastes at civilian and military dumps in Tooele County and as a place for military experimentation on the the Dugway Proving Ground, where scientists test defenses against chemical and biological agents, and the Wendover Range, where the designs of "Fat Man" and "Little Boy" were assessed before being dropped on Japan. Politically this is a heavily Republican area, with patches of Democratic strength. The district's portions of Salt Lake County are trendy and working class Democratic; they were kept out of the 2d District by Republican redistricters who wanted to beat a Democratic incumbent. Park City is on its way to becoming another Aspen, Democratic with leftist third party voters; its county voted 51% for Bush and 10% for Nader. The Cache Valley is very heavily Republican, though, and overall the district voted 68% for George W. Bush.

The congressman from the 1st District is Rob Bishop, a Republican elected in 2002. He grew up in Davis County and graduated from the University of Utah. He became a high school history and government teacher in Box Elder County. In 1978, at 27, he was elected to the state House; in 1993 and 1994 he was Speaker. He remained a teacher after leaving the legislature and also worked as a lobbyist for state Republicans and for the National Rifle Association (though he does not own a gun). In 2002 incumbent Jim Hansen, first elected in 1980, decided to retire. Bishop ran and so did former House Majority Leader Kevin Garn. As a former state party chair, Bishop was able to win 58% of the vote at the Republican nominating convention in May. The two had similar conservative views, and the difference came down to a contentious local issue in Utah, the ongoing battle between banks and credit unions. The credit union lobby endorsed Bishop who, as a lobbyist in 1999, helped defeat legislation to curtail the credit unions' tax-exempt status. Garn, as the wealthy chairman of a Layton bank, had the support of Utah bankers. Bishop portrayed Garn as a pawn of the banking industry. Garn accused Bishop of being in the "pocket" of the credit unions. The credit unions turned out to be the more valuable ally: They poured at least $100,000 in independent expenditures into an anti-Garn campaign, which helped even the financial balance since Garn outspent Bishop by 4–1. In the low turnout June 25 primary, Bishop won 60%–40%.

Democrats believed they had a chance in the general election with the slightly more favorable redistricting lines and the candidacy of Dave Thomas, a wealthy advertising executive and an anti-abortion Mormon bishop who also presented himself as a fiscal conservative and "a regular guy" not tied to special interests. Thomas, who had done volunteer work for Democrats but did not produce their advertising, narrowly won the primary over Donald Dunn, a former intern in the Clinton White House who lost 59%–37% against 3d District incumbent Chris Cannon in 2000. There was some bad blood between Bishop and Garn. But Bishop appealed to the strong Republican base in the district and emphasized his experience in government, especially on the reorganization of the state retirement system, which he said could be useful in dealing with Social Security. Thomas, a longtime member of his local Chamber of Commerce, was miffed when the national Chamber endorsed Bishop without giving Thomas a chance to make his case. Bishop won by a wider margin than expected, 61%–37%. Thomas carried Salt Lake County 59%–35% and Park City's Summit County 52%–43%, but they cast only 5% of the vote. Bishop won 67%–31% in Davis County and 56%–42% in Weber County and by even more in the Cache Valley.

SECOND DISTRICT

Rep. Jim Matheson (D)

Elected 2000, 2d term; b. Mar. 21, 1960, Salt Lake City; home, Salt Lake City; Harvard U., B.A. 1982, U.C.L.A., M.B.A. 1987; Mormon; married (Amy).

Professional Career: Staff, Environmental Policy Inst., 1982–85; Project Dev. Mgr., Bonneville Pacific, 1987–91; Sr. Assoc., Energy Strategies Inc., 1992–98; Founder & Pres., The Matheson Group, 1998–99.

DC Office: 410 CHOB 20515, 202-225-3011; Fax: 202-225-5638; Web site: www.house.gov/matheson.

District Offices: Salt Lake City, 801-486-1236; St. George, 435-627-0880.

Committees: *Financial Services* (27th of 32 D): Capital Markets, Insurance & Government Sponsored Enterprises; Oversight & Investigations. *Science* (20th of 22 D): Environment, Technology and Standards; Research. *Transportation & Infrastructure* (24th of 34 D): Aviation; Highways, Transit & Pipelines.

Group Ratings

	ADA	ACLU	AFS	LCV	CON	ITIC	NTU	COC	ACU	NTLC	CHC
2002	80	73	67	88	25	75	27	65	40	28	42
2001	70	—	80	57	—	—	25	65	32	—	—

National Journal Ratings

	2001 LIB	—	2001 CONS		2002 LIB	—	2002 CONS
Economic	55%	—	46%		55%	—	45%
Social	57%	—	43%		65%	—	34%
Foreign	49%	—	47%		64%	—	35%

Key Votes of the 107th Congress

1. Approve Bush Tax Cuts	Y	5. Faith-Based Charities	N	9. Trade Promotion Authority	Y
2. Limit Patients' Bill of Rights	N	6. Bar Gays in the Boy Scouts	Y	10. Bar Funds for Intl. Court	N
3. Campaign Finance Reform	Y	7. Ban Partial-Birth Abortion	N	11. Authorize Force in Iraq	Y
4. Ban ANWR Development	Y	8. Arm Commercial Pilots	Y	12. Deny Home. Sec. Dept. Union	N

Election Results

2002 general	Jim Matheson (D)	110,764	(49%)	($1,405,199)
	John Swallow (R)	109,123	(49%)	($1,163,612)
	Other	4,211	(2%)	
2002 primary	Jim Matheson (D)	unopposed		
2000 general	Jim Matheson (D)	145,021	(56%)	($1,305,202)
	Derek W. Smith (R)	107,114	(41%)	($1,681,135)
	Other	7,466	(3%)	

The People		Race/Ethnic Origin	Ancestry	
Area size:	46,034 sq. mi.	88.0% White	English: 21.8%	German: 9.0%
Urban population:	84.9%	0.6% Black	Irish: 5.0%	
Rural population:	15.1%	1.5% Asian	**2000 Presidential Vote**	
Pop. 2000:	744,390	2.2% Native Am.	Bush (R)...............183,387	(67%)
Median income:	$45,583	0.3% Hawaiian	Gore (D)................84,266	(31%)
Poverty status:	9.0%	1.4% Two+ races	Other....................6,573	(2%)
Military veterans:	11.3%	0.1% Other	**Cook Partisan Voting Index:** R +19	
		5.9% Hispanic Origin		

Occupation   Blue collar: 20.1%   White collar: 65.6%   Gray collar: 14.3%

Demographically, Utah is an urban state; geographically, it is not just rural but, over most of its acreage, scarcely inhabited. Three-quarters of its people live in the Wasatch Front, from Ogden south through Salt Lake City to Provo, between the Great Salt Lake and Utah Lake and the Wasatch Mountains. The scenery here has grandeur, but is surpassed by the landscape of much of southern Utah, much of it preserved in five national parks, five national monuments and a national recreation area. The terrain of southern Utah ranges from the soaring cliffs of Zion National Park to the popsicle-like outcroppings of Bryce Canyon National Park to the red-walled river cuts of Canyonlands National Park to the surreal moonscape of Arches National Park. Monument Valley, on Navajo land in far southeastern Utah, has become familiar to Americans as the site of countless car commercials. Land here is mostly owned by one agency or another of the federal government, and there have been bitter fights between locals dependent on mining and environmentalists who want to preserve scenery: you can see evidence of old uranium mines in some of the national parks. Bill Clinton's campaign-year creation of the Grand Staircase-Escalante National Monument in 1996, in a ceremony across the border in Arizona, enraged many Utahns, since it effectively removed 1.7 million acres from mineral development, much of it land owned by the state which used the proceeds for schools. Areas adjoining Dead Horse Point State Park and Arches National Park have been eyed for oil and gas projects by the Bush administration. But the towns of Moab and Springdale have found success as hubs for recreation-based tourism.

The 2d Congressional District consists of a combination of these parts of Utah and borders five different states. Most of its people, 59% of them, live in Salt Lake County. But it stretches far east and south to include the whole eastern part of the state and the southwest corner, including all the scenic territory described above. It includes almost all of Salt Lake County east of a wobbling line between I-15 and the often dry Jordan River, including most of the affluent neighborhoods in Salt Lake City and the suburbs of South Salt Lake, Murray (an old smelter city settled by southern and central Europeans), Midvale, Sandy and Draper. Before the 2001 redistricting, the 2d District was entirely within Salt Lake County, and the legislature could have drawn a similar district if it had wanted to. But in 2000 the 2d District elected a Democratic congressman; the legislature was heavily Republican and wanted to defeat him, and so it sloughed off the most Democratic parts of Salt Lake County into the otherwise overwhelmingly Republican 1st District and added the less affluent western suburbs and city neighborhoods to the even more Republican 3d District. Just to make sure, it added a heavily Republican part of Utah County just south of Salt Lake County. The changes raised the Bush 2000 percentage in the 2d District from 57% to 67% and made it the strongest Bush district held by a Democrat outside of Texas.

The congressman from the 2d District is Jim Matheson, a Democrat first elected in 2000. Matheson grew up in Salt Lake City, graduated from Harvard and interned on Capitol Hill for

Speaker Tip O'Neill. His father Scott Matheson, a prominent lawyer, was elected governor of Utah in 1976 and 1980. Jim Matheson worked for the Environmental Policy Institute, and then earned an M.B.A. from UCLA. He returned to Salt Lake City to join Bonneville Pacific, an energy development company, where he was a project development manager. He moved in 1992 to Energy Strategies, a consulting firm, where he was a senior associate. In 1998, he started the Matheson Group to help businesses adapt to electricity deregulation, but he closed it a year later to run for the House. He served four years on the Salt Lake Public Utilities Board.

Matheson was running in a district with a turbulent politics: in the five elections from 1992 to 2000 it elected two Democratic and two Republican congressmen. Much of the turbulence was caused by the volatile behavior of Congressman Merrill Cook. Cook was elected in 1996 after running as an Independent in the 1992 governor and 1994 House races; once elected to the House he became known for his temper tantrums, high staff turnover and his feud with Utah colleague Chris Cannon. He was challenged in the 2000 Republican primary by businessman Derek Smith; Cook charged him with financial misconduct and aides had to pull them apart after a 45-minute confrontation near the end of the campaign. Smith won the primary 59%–41%. In the general, Matheson played down his party affiliation and criticized Al Gore's prescription drug plan. Smith denounced Democrats, and especially Clinton's creation of the Grand Staircase-Escalante National Monument, and charged that Matheson was trying to look like a Republican. Smith sold $830,000 in stock to finance his campaign and benefited from $1 million in advertisements by national Republicans, more than four times what Democrats spent on Matheson. But Matheson won 56%–41%.

In the House, Matheson had a voting record near the center of the House, and he joined the New Democrat Coalition. He supported the Bush tax cuts, and voted for trade promotion authority and was one of eight Democrats who voted for the Republicans' prescription drug plan in 2002. He worked with Chris Cannon to win House passage of a bill, backed by the Bush administration and opposed by environmentalist groups, to swap federal and state lands in the San Rafael Swell to permit mineral development. He opposed the cost-of-living increase for members of Congress, but was unable to get a vote to stop it. After the June 2002 disappearance of Elizabeth Smart in a Salt Lake City suburb, he became a vocal supporter of the nationwide "AMBER alert" to track down missing and abducted children; that proposal was became law in April 2003, a few weeks after she was found.

Matheson was a target of national as well as Utah Republicans in 2002. John Swallow, a three-term state legislator, won the Republican primary 52%–48% over venture capitalist Tim Bridgewater. Swallow emphasized his strong support of tax cuts and gun ownership rights, and reminded voters of Matheson's Democratic Party affiliation at every opportunity; he harshly criticized his vote against a partial-birth abortion ban. Matheson reminded rural voters of his family's local connections and said that Swallow would harm public schools by giving tax money to parents who send their kids to private schools (the 2d has the lowest private school enrollment in the nation). Both national parties spent lavishly. Matheson won 49.4%–48.7%. Swallow won most of the rural counties with percentages as high as 76% and carried everything but Salt Lake County by 63%–36%. But Matheson carried the old mining area of Carbon County and Grand County, which includes the hip outdoorsmen of Moab (the county voted 15% for Ralph Nader in 2000). Salt Lake County cast 60% of the votes, and Matheson won there 59%–39%, an impressive achievement given the fact that most of the county's most Democratic precincts were no longer in the district.

Even so, Matheson seems likely to face serious challenges every two years in this seat, and he might very well choose to run for statewide office, perhaps to succeed Governor Mike Leavitt in 2004. If he does not run, Democrats will be hard pressed to hold this district.

THIRD DISTRICT

Rep. Chris Cannon (R)

Elected 1996, 4th term; b. Oct. 20, 1950, Salt Lake City; home, Mapleton; Brigham Young U., B.S. 1974, J.D. 1980; Mormon; married (Claudia).

Professional Career: Practicing atty., 1980–83; Asst. Assoc. Solicitor, Dept. of Interior, 1983–84; Assoc. Solicitor, 1984–86; Co–owner, Geneva Steel, 1987–90; Founder, Cannon Industries Inc., 1990–96.

DC Office: 118 CHOB 20515, 202-225-7751; Fax: 202-225-5629; Web site: www.house.gov/cannon.

District Offices: Provo, 801-379-2500; West Valley City, 801-955-3631.

Committees: *Government Reform* (13th of 24 R): Energy Policy, Natural Resources and Regulatory Affairs; Wellness & Human Rights (Vice Chmn.). *Judiciary* (9th of 21 R): Commercial & Administrative Law (Chmn.); Immigration, Border Security & Claims. *Resources* (13th of 28 R): Energy & Mineral Resources; National Parks, Recreation & Public Lands.

Group Ratings

	ADA	ACLU	AFS	LCV	CON	ITIC	NTU	COC	ACU	NTLC	CHC
2002	0	7	0	13	38	100	65	94	95	94	100
2001	0	—	0	7	—	—	67	100	100	—	—

National Journal Ratings

	2001 LIB —	2001 CONS		2002 LIB —	2002 CONS
Economic	7% —	89%		0% —	91%
Social	0% —	81%		30% —	68%
Foreign	16% —	82%		40% —	59%

Key Votes of the 107th Congress

1. Approve Bush Tax Cuts	Y	5. Faith-Based Charities	Y	9. Trade Promotion Authority	Y
2. Limit Patients' Bill of Rights	Y	6. Bar Gays in the Boy Scouts	Y	10. Bar Funds for Intl. Court	*
3. Campaign Finance Reform	N	7. Ban Partial-Birth Abortion	Y	11. Authorize Force in Iraq	Y
4. Ban ANWR Development	N	8. Arm Commercial Pilots	Y	12. Deny Home. Sec. Dept. Union	Y

Election Results

2002 general	Chris Cannon (R)	103,598	(67%)	($345,073)
	Nancy Woodside (D)	44,533	(29%)	($66,491)
	Kitty Burton (Lib)	5,511	(4%)	
2002 primary	Chris Cannon (R)	unopposed		
2000 general	Chris Cannon (R)	138,943	(59%)	($340,723)
	Donald Dunn (D)	88,547	(37%)	($378,565)
	Other	9,858	(4%)	

Prior Winning Percentages: 1998 (77%); 1996 (51%)

The People		Race/Ethnic Origin	Ancestry	
Area size:	16,165 sq. mi.	84.5% White	English: 21.5%	German: 8.2%
Urban population:	91.2%	0.5% Black	USA: 5.2%	
Rural population:	8.8%	1.7% Asian	**2000 Presidential Vote**	
Pop. 2000:	744,390	0.7% Native Am.	Bush (R) 163,983	(75%)
Median income:	$46,568	1.1% Hawaiian	Gore (D) 51,878	(24%)
Poverty status:	9.7%	1.4% Two+ races	Other 4,002	(2%)
Military veterans:	8.8%	0.1% Other	**Cook Partisan Voting Index:** R +26	
		10.0% Hispanic Origin		

Occupation	Blue collar: 26.2%	White collar: 59.7%	Gray collar: 14.1%

The heartland of the Mormon Church in America is in a geographically isolated valley between 11,000-foot peaks of the Wasatch Range and the shores of Utah Lake. Here is Provo, the home of Brigham Young University, an institution long known for the rigorously conservative views of its faculty, the old-fashioned moral standards it encourages, and its welcoming of technological innovation. The Mormon commonwealth, after all, started off with a terrific shortage of both labor and water and was eager to use technology to compensate and prosper in this fearsome terrain. Provo produced Philo Farnsworth, the inventor of television, and Harvey Fletcher, inventor of the hearing aid. In the 1990s this was one of America's high-tech centers, the home of Novell and hundreds of other computer-related firms, some fleeing California's high taxes and cultural liberalism. Overseas missionary work has also bequeathed the area with unusual resources in foreign languages. But this area is not immune to recession. In 2001 Geneva Steel shut its factory in Utah County, and Utah, with its relatively low wages, large families and frequent tithing, had the nation's highest rate of bankruptcy.

The 3d Congressional District includes all or part of seven counties in central and western Utah. Many of them are remote; during World War II, Japanese Americans were interned near Topaz in Millard County. But almost 90% of its people live in Utah or Salt Lake Counties. The 3d includes the west side of Salt Lake City and the west side suburbs south of the city, including West Valley City (the state's second-largest city, home to many recent Mormon converts from Polynesia), West Jordan, South Jordan and Riverton. Kennecott, the old mining conglomerate that owns 90,000 acres in Salt Lake and Tooele Counties, has been rapidly unloading its landholdings to real estate developers, who have built many subdivisions and the unique Sunrise, a "walkable" community of 30,000 in South Jordan. The district includes almost all of Utah County, including Provo and the string of counties between high-jutting mountains and Utah Lake. Politically, this is very much Republican country. Utah County is one of the most heavily Republican large counties in the United States: Bill Clinton finished a poor third here in 1992 with 22% of the vote and lost 58%–29% to Bob Dole in 1996, and George W. Bush carried the county 82%–14% in 2000. Overall the 3d District voted 75% for Bush, one of his 5 top districts in the country.

The congressman from the 3d District is Chris Cannon, a Republican first elected in 1996. Cannon is a great-grandson of Utah's first territorial delegate and counselor to Church President Brigham Young, George Q. Cannon, who had five wives and a lot of progeny. Chris Cannon grew up in Salt Lake City, graduated from Brigham Young and its law school and practiced law. From 1983 to 1986 he worked, sometimes controversially, in the Reagan Interior and Commerce Departments, on surface coal mining and other issues. In 1987, with his brother Joe, he purchased and reopened the Geneva Steel plant near Provo, restoring 2,500 jobs. In 1990 Chris Cannon was bought out and set up his own venture capital investment firm. He was active in Republican politics, as was Joe, who ran for the Senate in 1992 and lost the primary 51%–49% to Bob Bennett and who is now Republican state chairman.

In 1996, Chris Cannon ran for the 3d District seat held by Democrat Bill Orton, a conservative Democrat who won it in 1990 after a fractious Republican primary. To get the nomination, Cannon faced Tom Draschil, who called Cannon (a backer of Lamar Alexander for president) too moderate; Cannon said that Draschil was an extremist and had a lawn sign backing militia favorite Bo Gritz for president in 1992. Cannon won by only 56%–44%. In the general election, Cannon spent $1.8 million, $1.5 million of it his own money, against Orton's $709,000. He was helped when Bill Clinton in September, speaking in Arizona without consultation with Utah officials (including Orton), announced that he was establishing the 1.7 million-acre Grand Staircase-Escalante National Monument in southern Utah. This was heartily opposed in the area: much of the land was owned by a state school fund, which wanted to lease it for coal mining, and now would not get the revenue. Cannon ran an ad showing himself denim-clad, leading a horse, attacking Clinton, "I feel like I'm back in the 1850s again with the federal government encamped all around us." Orton said the designation was "a monumental blunder—pun intended." Cannon, with a big margin in Utah County, won 51%–47%.

In the House, Cannon has had a conservative voting record and continued to attack the national monument. He served on the Judiciary Committee during impeachment and was one of the House managers in the Senate trial; afterward, he set up a House Managers PAC in 1999, but it failed to generate much enthusiasm or money and he shut it down in 2000. He enacted several resource bills after George W. Bush became President, including one that approved the

Central Utah Project to shift its water from rural areas to Salt Lake County. He also sponsored a law to help state and local governments fight the spread of methamphetamines. On Judiciary Cannon has worked to set up a regulatory framework for the Internet. He filed a bill to ban willful distribution of copyrighted material on the Internet; when the committee in June 2002 approved a ban on Internet casino gambling, he argued that the bill would be difficult to enforce and would pose hardships to small Internet service providers. He co-sponsored with Democrat Rick Boucher a bill designed to increase competition for digital music on the Internet. Citing the close connections between Mormons and Jews, he has been a prominent booster of the Holocaust Museum, and he serves on the memorial council. In 2003, Cannon became chairman of the Judiciary Subcommittee on Commercial and Administrative Law, which handles bankruptcy and tort law. Also in 2003, he became chairman of the Western Caucus, a group of more than 50 House members who advocate "rational, balanced and sound resource management." Cannon has been supportive of providing amnesty to illegal immigrants; he cosponsored the Central American Security Act, which would legalize the status of more than 250,000 Central American immigrants living in the U.S.

In 2000 Cannon was opposed by a former Clinton White House intern who outspent him, but Cannon won 59%–37%. Perhaps the biggest jolt in the campaign came the day before the election when Cannon was driving alone in his pickup truck in Provo, hit a patch of ice, slid off the road and tumbled down an embankment. Cannon had some bruises and his truck was totaled. In 2002 he won 67%–29%.

★ VERMONT ★

Vermont is a mixture of the 19th and the 21st centuries—maple syrup and Ben & Jerry's Ice Cream, tiny clapboard villages and carefully zoned towns complete with unobtrusively signed outlet malls, covered bridges and civil unions—with much of the 20th, its factories and suburbs, skyscrapers and shopping malls, mostly left out. Not so long ago, Vermont seemed an entirely antique state, almost as carefully preserved as its Shelburne Museum, with a barn and jail, railroad station and blacksmith shop, covered bridge, and 37 buildings full of folk art. Yet it has been transformed by newcomers, who came here attracted to its antique look but have transformed its culture in their own image.

Vermont was first settled by flinty Yankees from Connecticut, and showed an independent streak from the beginning. After Ethan Allen's Green Mountain Boys repulsed the British in 1777, this was an independent republic for 14 years, claimed by New York and New Hampshire without avail, their argument settled when Vermont was admitted as the 14th state in 1791. The economy was almost entirely agricultural, as second sons and daughters from small New England farms struggled to scratch out livings from the rocky soil. In time, they quit struggling and raised dairy cows instead, producing milk for the masses of New York City. Vermont developed commerce as well. With its legendary thriftiness, it accumulated capital that, invested wisely, was used to build the solid stone office buildings and courthouses, the thick-timbered houses and gold-topped state Capitol that have remained long after ramshackle wooden buildings of the 19th century have crumbled into dust. But Vermont never developed labor-intensive industry, and so over the years it exported people, and it aged. Today, millions of Americans have Vermont blood—far more than the 609,000 who live here now, many of whom have no Vermont roots at all. Two presidents were born here, but both made their careers elsewhere—Chester Arthur in New York, Calvin Coolidge in Massachusetts. Vermont made no visible impression on two great writers who lived here for years—Rudyard Kipling and Aleksandr Solzhenitsyn. From 1850 to the 1960s, as a result of continuous outmigration, Vermont's population hovered between 300,000 and 400,000.

Since then—perhaps the key date was 1963, when people first outnumbered cows—Vermont has changed rapidly. Its economy has boomed, led by leisure-time industries—ski resorts, summer homes—and IBM, with several big high-tech facilities around the Burlington area on the mostly undeveloped shores of glorious Lake Champlain. Here you can find big box retailers in Williston

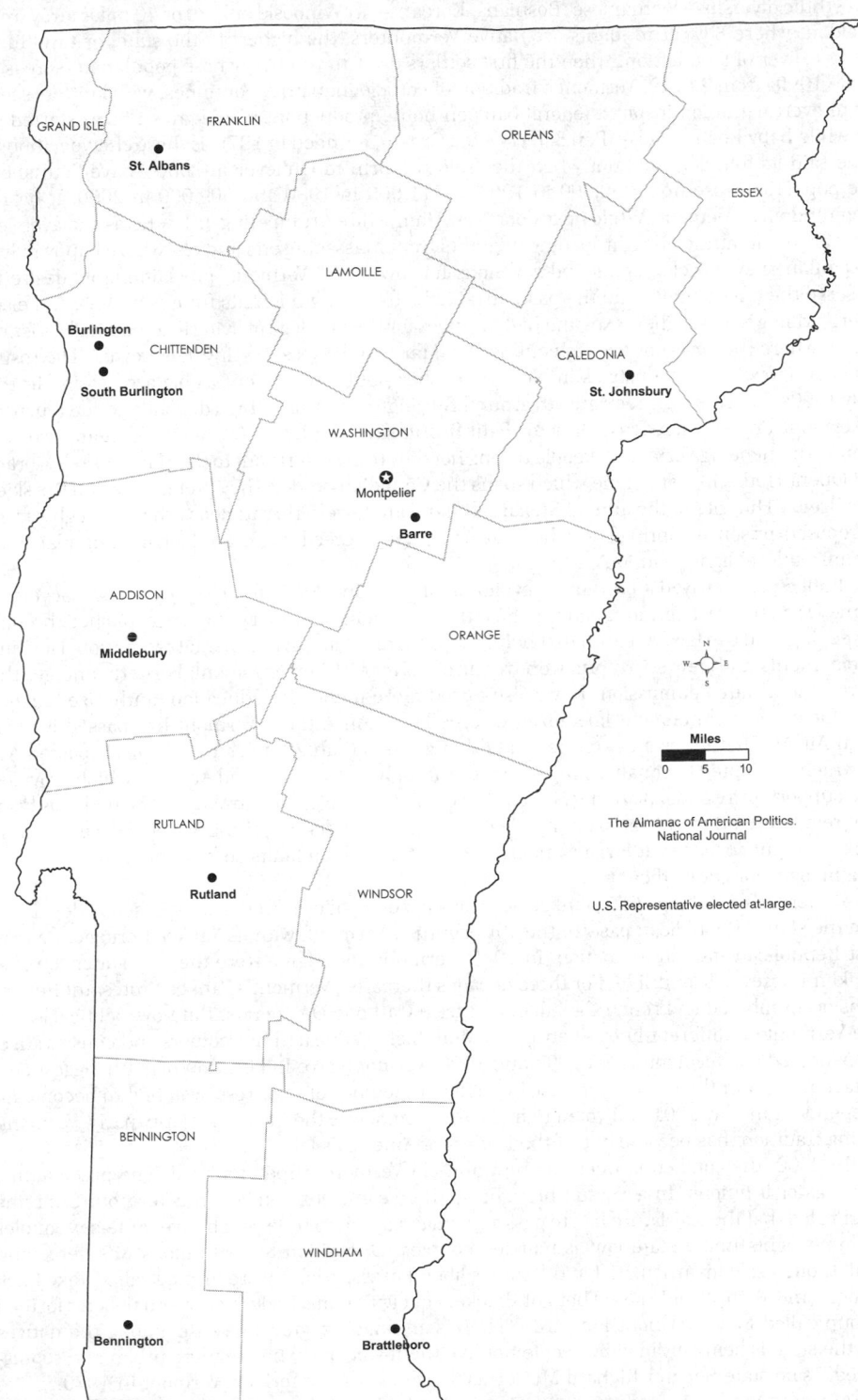

The Almanac of American Politics.
National Journal

U.S. Representative elected at-large.

and ethnic diversity—Vietnamese, Bosnians, Koreans—in Winooski only 30 or 40 miles away from Sheldon, where 83% of residents are native Vermonters, the highest in the state, or tiny Buels Gore, a sliver of land left out when the first settlers drew town lines, whose population increased in the 1990s from 2 to 12. Vermont's tradition of cottage industries continues, with knitters seeking to overturn union-inspired federal bans on home production. Home-grown firms started by erstwhile Baby Boom rebels—Ben & Jerry's Ice Cream, founded in 1978, is the archetype, though some said its founders sold out when they sold the firm to Unilever in 2000—have flourished. The population rose from 390,000 in 1960 to 511,000 in 1980 and 609,000 in 2000. It hasn't been random settlement: While next-door New Hampshire, trumpeting its low taxes and aversion to government, attracted right-leaning migrants from Massachusetts and elsewhere happy to live in spanking-new developments and ravenous for low taxes, Vermont, proclaiming its desire to preserve the environment and the past, attracted left-leaning migrants from New York and elsewhere, willing to pay higher taxes and higher prices for the privilege of living in a seemingly pristine setting where the governor tries to confine Wal-Marts to the existing tiny downtowns. The result has been growth, not as lusty as in New Hampshire, but also without as big a recession in the early 1990s. There is high-tech growth around Burlington, but also a high dependence on tourism; as Vermont Preservation Trust Director Paul Bruhn says, "At least 30% of our economy is based upon Vermont being Vermont." People throng not only to ski resorts but to the Haskell Free Library and Opera House in Derby Line which spans the Canadian border; they protested when the skies over Breezy Hill, site of the annual Stellafane star watch, were threatened with bright lights from a proposed prison in Springfield (the state eventually agreed to an outdoor lighting plan that minimized local light pollution).

Public policy played a part in the evolution of Vermont. Back in 1970, Republican Governor Deane Davis (the last Vermont native to hold the job), facing a primary challenge, pushed through a sweeping land use law (Act 250) that helped give Vermont its environmental reputation. Housing developments and new ski resorts were required to meet 10 environmental criteria and get the approval of a state commission. Davis also raised more money for education, authorized higher fines for water polluters and liberalized divorce laws. Since then, Vermont has passed its own Clean Air Act that levies a tax on new cars that get less than 20 miles per gallon. It passed Act 60, which attempted to equalize property taxes throughout the state, and Act 200, which provided state support for regional planning boards. Although it has no gun control laws, Vermont has been busy regulating other things, banning clear-cutting of forests, requiring seat belt use, banning smoking in public places. It has a campaign finance law, which limits contributions and spending in campaigns for state office.

If there is something of the Yankee busybody in such policies, they also represent a departure from the state's Republican past. In the 19th century, Vermont, with its Yankee heritage, was the most Republican state in the nation; in 1936, Vermont and Maine were the only states to resist Franklin Roosevelt's landslide. For three decades thereafter Vermont's Yankee Protestant Republicans outnumbered its French Canadian and Irish Catholic Democrats. But now, political issues slice Vermont on different lines—between liberal, highly educated newcomers and conservative, less educated old Vermonters. In 1992 and 1996, Vermont gave Bill Clinton his fifth biggest percentage margin in the country; its last Republican member of Congress switched to become an Independent in May 2001 and voted to make the Democrats the Senate majority party. Vermont, valuing tradition, has become one of the leaders of America's left.

In 2000, the conflict between the new and old Vermont came to a head. The precipitating issue was civil unions. In a lawsuit brought by three same-sex couples, the Vermont Supreme Court ruled that the legislature had to pass a gay marriage law or one which gave same-sex couples the same rights under state law as married couples. Opposition to civil unions was fierce and vocal, though seldom articulated in the state's liberal press; groups were formed called Take Back Vermont and Who Would Have Thought. Backers of civil unions and other liberal policies formed a group called Move Vermont Forward. "There's an ongoing, growing sense among the natives that the state is being invaded by people not like them—people who are more urban and sophisticated," said state Senator Richard McCormack, who left New York for Vermont in 1970.

A civil union law passed the legislature in April 2000 and was signed by Governor Howard

Dean out of sight of cameras. That law and other liberal policies were opposed vociferously by Republican gubernatorial candidate Ruth Dwyer. Several pro-civil union Republican legislators lost their seats in the September primary, but Republicans won control of the state House in November. Democrats, though, held the Senate and in statewide races, the Move Vermont Forward side unequivocally prevailed. Dean—one of the nation's last two governors who serves a two-year term—beat Dwyer by 50%–38% vote, with another 10% for Anthony Pollina, who ran on the Progressive Party of Vermont ticket. Dwyer carried only the northeast part of the state and small towns in the mountainous south; Dean won by more than 2–1 in the Burlington area and swept most of the Connecticut River valley. Al Gore carried the state comfortably, 51%–41%, and Congressman Bernie Sanders, a former New Yorker who was elected mayor of Burlington as a Socialist in the 1980s, won 69% as an independent, to 18% for a transsexual moderate Republican and 5% for a left-wing Democrat. James Jeffords was reelected for the last time as a Republican by 66%–25%. The VNS exit poll showed that 27% of voters were enthusiastic about and 25% supportive of the civil unions law, while 32% were opposed and 14% angry. As Dwyer said on election night, with candor unusual for a politician, "The people of Vermont clearly don't believe what we believe, and we've got to accept that."

Since 2000, the controversy over civil unions abated; both major party candidates for governor in 2002 opposed repeal and the 2000 Census showed that only 1% of households were same-sex unions. At the same time, some of Vermont's liberalism seemed to wane. Job losses at IBM and slow economic growth in what had been the booming Burlington area were accompanied by a questioning of the costs of Act 250 and Act 60. Dean decided not to run for governor again, and set out to run for president on a platform of fiscal conservatism and cultural liberalism. Longtime Republican officeholder Jim Douglas beat Lieutenant Governor Doug Racine by 45%–42%, while Democrats gained seats in both houses of the legislature: A mixed result and an unclear political future.

The People		Race/Ethnic Origin			Military veterans: 62,809 (13.6%)		
Pop. 2000:	608,827	585,431	96.2%	White	WWII: 19.4%		Korea: 14.3%
Pop. 1990:	562,758	2,921	0.5%	Black	Vietnam: 32.2%		Gulf War: 7.4%
Change 1990–2000:	Up 8.2%	5,160	0.8%	Asian	Most populous cities:		
Change 1980–1990:	Up 10.0%	2,325	0.4%	Native Am.	1. Burlington		38,889
% of U.S. total:	0.2%	120	0.0%	Hawaiian	2. Rutland		17,292
Pop. rank:	49th of 50	6,809	1.1%	Two+ races	3. South Burlington		15,814
Area size:	9,614 sq. mi.	557	0.1%	Other	4. Barre		9,291
State Native:	54.3%	5,504	0.9%	Hisp. Origin	5. Montpelier		8,035
Non-citizen:	1.8%	**Ancestry**			Urban population: 38.2%		
Language		English: 13.1%		Irish: 11.7%	Rural population: 61.8%		
English: 90.8%	Other Eur.: 6.8%	French: 10.3%		German: 6.5%			
Spanish: 1.6%		Fr. Canadian: 6.3%					

Education		Work Sector		General Assembly	
H.S. Grad:	86.4%	Private: 75.3%	Govt: 14.2%	Senate	19 D 11 R
College Grad:	29.4%	Self: 10.3%	Family: 0.3%	House	74 R 69 D 7 I
Industry		Unemployment: 4.2%		Legislative Term Limits: No	
Agri: 3.0%	Con: 6.7%	**Household Income**		**Registered Voters**	
Fin: 4.7%	Info: 2.7%	<15k: 14.5%	15-35k: 27.9%	No party registration	
Mfg: 18.8%	Prof: 31.2%	35-50k: 18.6%	50-100k: 30.3%		
Public: 4.6%	Trade: 15.1%	100-150k: 5.7%	>150k: 3.0%		
Other: 13.3%		Median: $40,856			
Occupation		Poverty status: 9.4%			
Blue collar: 23.3%	White collar: 60.8%	**Home Value**			
Gray collar: 15.9%		<50k: 8.6%	50-100k: 33.8%	100-200k: 43.9%	200-300k: 8.8%
		300-500k: 3.6%	>500k: 1.5%	Median: $111,200	

Presidential politics James A. Farley had a good laugh on Vermont in 1936 when he updated an adage to say "As goes Maine, so goes Vermont." Today's Vermont, liberal on cultural and foreign issues, not very conservative on economics, has become pretty solidly Democratic in presidential campaigns. Back in 1980, Ronald Reagan got his seventh lowest percentage here and John Anderson his best, 15%; in 1984 and 1988, Vermont was more Democratic than the nation; in 1992 and 1996, it gave Bill Clinton his fifth largest percentage margins. In 2000 Al Gore won 51%–41%, with 7% for Ralph Nader. The conflict between the old and new Vermonts is apparent in the VNS exit poll. Those without college degrees voted 48%–46% for Bush, but Gore carried college graduates 51%–36% and those with postgraduate degrees 62%–29%. The old divide between Protestants and Catholics has vanished; Bush carried them both by narrow margins. But Gore won those with no religion 64%–21%, with 12% for Nader.

The Vermont presidential primary, abolished for 1992, reappeared in 1996, but has achieved little notice; all the action is next door in New Hampshire.

2000 Presidential Vote		
Gore (D)	149,022	(51%)
Bush (R)	119,775	(41%)
Nader (Green)	20,374	(7%)
Other	5,137	(2%)

2000 Republican Presidential Primary		
McCain (R)	49,045	(60%)
Bush (R)	28,741	(35%)
Other	3,569	(4%)

2000 Democratic Presidential Primary		
Gore (D)	26,774	(54%)
Bradley (D)	21,629	(44%)
Other	880	(2%)

1996 Presidential Vote		
Clinton (D)	137,894	(53%)
Dole (R)	80,352	(31%)
Perot (I)	31,024	(12%)
Other	9,179	(4%)

Governor

Jim Douglas (R)

Elected 2002, term expires Jan. 2007, 1st term; b. June 21, 1951, Springfield, MA; home, Middlebury; Middlebury Col., B.A. 1972; Congregationalist; married (Dorothy).

Elected Office: VT House of Reps., 1972–79; Maj. Ldr., 1977–79; VT Secy. of St., 1980–92; VT Treasurer, 1994–02.

Office: 109 State St., Montpelier, 05609, 802-828-3333; Fax: 802-828-3339; Web site: www.gov.state.vt.us.

Election Results

2002 general	Jim Douglas (R)	103,436	(45%)
	Doug Racine (D)	97,565	(42%)
	Cornelius Hogan (I)	22,353	(10%)
	Other	6,807	(3%)
2002 primary	Jim Douglas (R)	unopposed	
2000 general	Howard Dean (D)	148,059	(50%)
	Ruth Dwyer (R)	111,359	(38%)
	Anthony Pollina (PRG)	28,116	(10%)
	Other	5,939	(2%)

The key decision that led to Jim Douglas being elected governor of Vermont in 2002 may have been his decision 34 years earlier to attend Middlebury College. Douglas grew up in Longmeadow, Massachusetts, a political junkie and a strong Republican, passing out AuH2O stickers for Barry Goldwater in 1964, at 13. In 1968, he enrolled at Middlebury and almost immediately decided to live in the town that gave name to the college; his wife is from Middlebury and they have lived there ever since. Douglas's college years were a time of campus protests against the Vietnam War, but he became an active Republican and organized a rally for President Richard Nixon in Middlebury in 1970. In 1972, the year he graduated, he ran for state representative from Middlebury and was elected; he was elected majority leader in 1977. In 1979, he lost a race for Speaker and became an aide to Republican Governor Richard Snelling. In between sessions of the legislature he worked as a radio announcer and became executive director of the local United Way. In 1980, he was elected secretary of state and served for 12 years. In 1992, he ran against Senator Patrick Leahy and lost 54%–43%—the closest race Leahy has had since 1980. In 1994, after working for the Porter Medical Center in Middlebury, he spotted an opening for state treasurer and was elected to the first of four terms. The Democratic party produces many gifted political entrepreneurs who win office even in unlikely years and districts; the Republican party has one in Douglas. He has been on the Vermont ballot every two years since 1972, and for most of that time has gotten up before 6 a.m. to commute over the Green Mountains to the tiny state capital of Montpelier.

His opening to run for governor came when Democratic Governor Howard Dean announced on September 5, 2001 that he would not run again. Dean is a physician who succeeded to the governorship when Richard Snelling (the only Republican elected governor between 1970 and 2002) died suddenly in August 1991; Dean was given the news while he was treating a patient. Returned to office every two years—Vermont and New Hampshire are the last two states with two-year gubernatorial terms—he advanced a number of innovative policies which, in the minds of many observers, entitled him to serious consideration as a candidate for president in 2004. He takes liberal positions on many cultural issues (but not gun control, verboten in peaceful Vermont) but prides himself on fiscal tightness. He did not succeed in his 1992 goal of creating a universal health insurance system, but using the Medicaid program and exemptions obtained from the Clinton administration he has provided a health insurance coverage for 94% of children and 92% of adults. Prompted by a state Supreme Court ruling, Dean in 1997 got the legislature to pass Act 60, which levied a statewide property tax to provide each school district with $5,010 per student; taxes would be limited to 2% of income for those earning under $75,000. Districts wishing to raise money beyond that are required to donate a percentage of revenues to the state sharing pool, which ladles it out to other districts. Prompted again by the state Supreme Court, he got the legislature to institute civil unions for same-sex couples. A great furor rose over the issue and Dean, who was reelected with 75% of the vote in 1992, 69% in 1994 and 71% in 1996, won by lesser margins of 56%–41% and 50%–38% in 1998 and 2000.

But by 2001, there was starting to be discontent over what had seemed to be settled Vermont consensus. Not on civil unions—seemingly widely, if in some cases grudgingly, accepted—but over the high property taxes engendered by Act 60, the long delays in development caused by the environmental reviews under 30-year-old Act 250 and, most of all, by frequent news of job loss and a rising sense that Vermont has a reputation for being unfriendly to business. Douglas and his Democratic opponent, Lieutenant Governor Douglas Racine, agreed that Act 60 and Act 250 needed some changes; so did Con Hogan, former director of state human services, who started running for the Republican nomination but decided in February to run as an Independent. But there was a clear difference in emphasis. Douglas called for tax cuts, if spending cuts could be achieved, and promised to "create a more business-friendly environment." He advocated major modification in Act 60 and ending the sharing pool. He charged that despite its high spending on education, Vermont was still getting mediocre test scores. He called for a Megan's Law requiring registration of addresses of convicted drug dealers. It was "time for a change," he said, in a state which had had Democratic governors 17 of the last 18 years. "With each new announcement of job losses, officials in Montpelier act surprised and helpless. It's time to stop making excuses and start making a difference."

Racine had a political career as long as Douglas's. He, too, was a teenage political junkie, watching the 1964 conventions on television; but he was rooting for the Democrats. At home, he worked in his father's service station and Jeep dealership in Burlington; at Princeton, he wrote a senior thesis on the rise of the Democratic party in Vermont. In 1974 he worked on the Senate campaign of the young Burlington prosecutor, Patrick Leahy. When Leahy won and became Vermont's first Democratic senator ever, he asked Racine to work on his staff in Washington and then Montpelier. Racine ran for the state Senate and lost in 1980, then won five terms; he lost the race for lieutenant governor in 1994 but won in 1996, 1998 and 2000. In the 2002 campaign, Racine said that as lieutenant governor he had helped fashion consensus on school funding, children's services and the budget. He called for conservation, environmental protection and broad access to health care. He conceded the need for simplifying Act 60 and speeding up Act 250.

There were more than three dozen debates between the candidates, and Racine led in most public polls. The turning point evidently came in the last week. Douglas ran a tough ad accusing Racine of flip-flopping on issues—switching to support the Circumferential Highway sought by IBM in the Burlington area, allowing local school districts to raise local taxes with lesser penalties in the form of the sharing pool. The implication was that Racine did not really stand for change and that Douglas did. Racine may have been hurt as well by a leaflet his campaign mailed out charging Douglas with cutting programs for women and featuring a large hatchet; at least some people objected.

The result was something of an upset. Douglas led Racine 45%–42%, with 10% for Hogan. Under Vermont law, if no candidate receives 50% of the vote, the governor is chosen by a combined vote of the two houses of the legislature. Republicans entered the campaign with a large majority of legislative seats; Racine announced that he would not take his candidacy to the legislature if he won under 50%, while Douglas said he would. Then, contrary to most expectations, Democrats made gains in the legislature and their majority in the Senate was larger than the Republicans' narrow margin in the House. But Racine kept his word and Douglas became governor.

Senior Senator

Patrick Leahy (D)

Elected 1974, seat up 2004, 5th term; b. Mar. 31, 1940, Montpelier; home, Burlington; St. Michael's Col., B.A. 1961, Georgetown U., J.D. 1964; Catholic; married (Marcelle).

Elected Office: VT St. Atty., Chittenden Cnty., 1966–74.

Professional Career: Practicing atty., 1964–74.

DC Office: 433 RSOB, 20510, 202-224-4242; Web site: leahy.senate.gov.

State Offices: Burlington, 802-863-2525; Montpelier, 802-229-0569.

Committees: *Agriculture, Nutrition & Forestry*: Forestry, Conservation & Rural Revitalization; Research, Nutrition & General Legislation (RMM). *Appropriations*: Commerce, Justice, State & Judiciary; Defense; Foreign Operations (RMM); Homeland Security; Interior; VA, HUD & Independent Agencies. *Judiciary* (RMM): Administrative Oversight & the Courts; Antitrust, Competition Policy & Consumer Rights; Immigration, Border Security & Citizenship.

Group Ratings

	ADA	ACLU	AFS	LCV	CON	ITIC	NTU	COC	ACU	NTLC	CHC
2002	95	60	100	94	16	50	14	55	0	3	—
2001	100	—	100	100	—	—	8	38	8	—	0

National Journal Ratings

	2001 LIB —	2001 CONS		2002 LIB —	2002 CONS
Economic	92% —	8%		80% —	15%
Social	70% —	20%		82% —	0%
Foreign	87% —	3%		96% —	0%

Key Votes of the 107th Congress

1. Approve Bush Tax Cuts	N	5. Confirm Ashcroft as AG	N	9. Bar Coop. with Intl. Court	N
2. Expand Patients' Rights	Y	6. Bar Gays in the Boy Scouts	N	10. Trade Promotion Authority	N
3. Campaign Finance Reform	Y	7. $ for Hate Crime Prosecution	Y	11. Authorize Force in Iraq	N
4. Permit ANWR Development	N	8. Overseas Military Abortions	Y	12. Homeland Sec. Dept. Union	Y

Election Results

1998 general	Patrick Leahy (D)	154,567	(72%)	($1,014,751)
	Fred H. Tuttle (R)	48,051	(22%)	
	Other	11,418	(5%)	
1998 primary	Patrick Leahy (D)	18,643	(97%)	
	Other	647	(3%)	
1992 general	Patrick Leahy (D)	154,762	(54%)	($1,202,445)
	Jim Douglas (R)	123,854	(43%)	($195,737)
	Other	7,123	(2%)	

Prior Winning Percentages: 1986 (63%); 1980 (50%); 1974 (50%)

Patrick Leahy, the only Democrat ever elected to the Senate in Vermont, has held public office for most of his adult life. He grew up in Burlington, went to Georgetown law school, then returned home to Burlington to practice law. He was elected Chittenden County state's attorney in 1966, at 26, and, after eight years in that post—and few public officials are scrutinized as closely as a local prosecutor—he was elected to the U.S. Senate at 34. If he is reelected in 2004, he will be set to become the longest-serving senator in Vermont history; his predecessor George Aiken served 33 years.

Leahy is the ranking Democrat on the Judiciary Committee and served as Chairman from June 2001 to January 2003. He was also formerly chairman of the Agriculture Committee. Judiciary handles many of the cultural issues which polarize the two parties and their constituencies—issues like gun control and abortion—and the committee has been sharply polarized at least since the hearings on the nomination of Judge Robert Bork to the Supreme Court in 1987. This was certainly true in the 1990s when Republicans were in the majority. Then, Leahy criticized Republicans for holding up Bill Clinton's judicial appointments and stoutly defended Clinton on impeachment. When Leahy became chairman, he began to hold up judicial nominations himself, as Republicans had done in the past. Most appointments to district court judgeships were approved, but very many nominated in May 2001 and later to the federal courts of appeals did not even get hearings until the end of the 2002 session. By April 2002, Leahy drew criticism as a "champion nomination squelcher," for confirming only 9 of 30 Bush nominees to that point. But at the conclusion of the 107th Congress, Leahy reported that 100 White House judicial nominees had been confirmed since the change in majority; he announced that this record compared favorably to the 38 judicial confirmations averaged per year during the six-and-a-half years of a Republican Senate majority. The committee, however, rejected on party-line votes two appointees to the Fifth Circuit Court of Appeals, Charles Pickering and Priscilla Owen. Leahy even demanded from one nominee the memos he had written while working in the office of the solicitor general during the Clinton administration—something never before sought, and a demand denounced by all former solicitors general in administrations of both parties and by *The Washington Post*. Republicans complained that Leahy and the other Democrats were following the lead and, in some cases, the script of lobbyists Ralph Neas and Nan Aron. With Republicans in the majority again, Leahy and his allies will have much less leverage, but they will probably try to make cases against some appointees that they hope will win a few Republican votes. They will surely scrutinize very closely and very hostilely any appointments to the United States Supreme Court.

Judiciary had jurisdiction over much of the antiterrorism legislation brought forward after September 11. Leahy approached the task with some concern lest federal powers override individual rights. He and his staff worked with the Bush administration to hammer out the planks in the USA Patriot Act; it was essentially the Senate version, not the House version, which was passed in October 2001. It authorized roving wiretaps (to cover the target's cell phones and wireless communications devices as well as his home phone), imposed tougher penalties for terrorism, provided for tighter security on the U.S.-Canada border and toughened the laws against money laundering. But Leahy also criticized some of the Bush administration's actions and proposals. He opposed the administration's first proposal for broader powers to detain and deport immigrants suspected of terrorism without presenting evidence in court. Leahy was angry when the committee was not consulted on the administration's proposal to establish military tribunals (they would be administered by the Defense Department, not Justice) and in December 2001, demanded that Ashcroft explain and defend the administration's assertion of police, detention and prosecutorial powers. In August 2002, he disclosed the May 2002 decision by the Foreign Intelligence Surveillance Act trial court that declared that FBI agents had lied to the court in applying for 75 warrants (almost all of this was during the Clinton administration). In September 2002, he said Justice should be required to disclose the number of U.S. citizens being spied on, the number of secret foreign intelligence wiretaps that had become part of criminal proceedings and the total number of persons targeted by foreign intelligence surveillance warrants; and he pointed out that the Foreign Intelligence Surveillance Act has a sunset date—an implicit threat to hold up its reauthorization.

Amid the publicity about corporate wrongdoing by Enron and others, Leahy in July 2002 fashioned criminal penalties for violations of the disclosure provisions of what became the Sarbanes-Oxley financial disclosure act. Appearing with former Death Row inmates who were exonerated, he sought to provide DNA testing for death row inmates who challenge their convictions. He has sought to legalize the presence in the U.S. of Haitian and Central American refugees living here for many years.

Leahy is a gadgeteer and fine amateur photographer, and he was one of the first senators to go online; he has worked on various bills that affect high-tech and telecommunications. He cosponsored with Orrin Hatch the Digital Millennium Copyright law, passed to comply with the WIPO treaty, and with Arizona Sen. Jon Kyl, the law making the theft of personal identification information a crime. After considerable negotiation, he worked out an e-signature bill which passed the Senate unanimously, setting a national framework for giving on-line signatures legal status; it allowed consumers to agree to electronically signed contracts and consent to receiving records, while businesses had to verify electronic addresses.

Another Leahy cause has been the elimination of land mines. Since 1989, he has been crusading against the export and use of landmines, which are easy and cheap to implant yet difficult and expensive to remove, and which injure thousands of civilians long after hostilities have ended. In 1994, he got the United Nations to approve unanimously their eventual elimination. In 1997, he and Nebraska Sen. Chuck Hagel moved to support the treaty ban worked out in Ottawa, but the Clinton administration, worried especially about U.S. forces in Korea, refused to support a total ban. Leahy continues to work to aid land mine victims and to deactivate the thousands of land mines still active in many parts of the world and to find alternatives for them. On foreign and defense issues, he tends to stand to the left of the Senate: He was one of three senators to vote against authorization of missile defense in March 1999 and has called for an end to the ban on travel to Cuba.

Leahy is the only member on the Agriculture Committee not from a state with heavily subsidized crops like wheat, corn, soybeans or cotton; from his lead position, he worked with Richard Lugar in the 1990s to phase out the old subsidy system. Their great success was the Freedom to Farm Act of 1996, but soon crop prices fell and Congress took to voting huge annual subsidies in the form of emergency relief; the 2002 farm bill largely rolled back the 1996 act. In that act, Leahy shaped the bill's conservation provisions to establish the Northeast Dairy Compact, to set milk prices in the six New England states; the Compact, however, expired in September 2001. As Congress moved back to subsidize the long-protected crops, Leahy helped to establish an Eggplant Caucus to represent the interests of Eastern farmers who produce specialty crops; he worked to get money for conservation grants, environmental initiatives and transition to organic farming for such farmers.

Leahy serves on Appropriations and has procured funding for Vermont projects—$3 million for the Lake Champlain Basin Science Center, $4 million for Waterbury dam repairs, $3.7 million for Missisquoi Bay Bridge repairs, $1.5 million for downtown Winooski revitalization (Winooski is the most densely populated city in the state). After the education act was signed into law in January 2002, Leahy and Jeffords co-sponsored a bill to undercut one of its main features by allowing states and school districts to opt out of national student testing requirements.

Leahy is a strong partisan who usually expresses himself in a quiet, thoughtful way and sometimes with a puckish sense of humor, part of the Yankee heritage of Vermont, though his Irish and Italian ethnic origin is not standard Yankee. He is a Batman buff who had a bit part in the movie *Batman and Robin*. His standing in Vermont has been strong over the years: He narrowly survived the Republican sweep in 1980 and beat popular Governor Richard Snelling 63%–35% in 1986. In anti-incumbent 1992, his opponent was Jim Douglas, then state treasurer and now governor. He attacked Leahy for voting for the congressional pay raise and for the loss of dairy jobs; Leahy won 54%–43%—a decisive margin, but no landslide. In 1998, he had an easier time. The favorite for the Republican nomination, a Massachusetts businessman who had moved to Bennington to run, was upset 55%–45% by 77-year-old dairy farmer Fred Tuttle, the star of a 1996 documentary *A Man with a Plan* in which he is shown running for Congress. In October 1998, when the film aired on PBS, Leahy had dinner at the Tuttles' home and contrasted this contest with the negative campaigns being waged elsewhere. Leahy won 72%–22%.

Leahy comes up for reelection in 2004, and in a Vermont that has been increasingly Democratic in national politics, he is considered a strong favorite to win. In summer 2002, there were reports that former Governor Thomas Salmon might challenge him in the Democratic primary. Salmon had declined to run for the seat in 1974 because he was in only his second year as governor, and evidently the thought has struck him that if he had pushed aside Leahy, then only a state's attorney, he and not Leahy would have been elected to serve 30 years in the Senate. But that musing seems unlikely to persuade many Vermont Democrats to oust one of the national leaders of their party. Nor does it seem likely that Douglas, after two years as governor, will choose to run against Leahy again.

Junior Senator

James Jeffords (I)

Elected 1988, seat up 2006, 3d term; b. May 11, 1934, Rutland; home, Shrewsbury; Yale U., B.S. 1956, Harvard U., LL.B. 1962; Congregationalist; married (Elizabeth).

Military Career: Navy, 1956–59, Naval Reserves, 1959–90.

Elected Office: VT Senate, 1966–68; VT Atty. Gen., 1968–72; U.S. House of Reps. 1974–88.

Professional Career: Law clerk, 1962–63; Practicing atty., 1963–69, 1973–75; Shrewsbury Repub. Party Chmn., 1963–74; Town Agent, Grand Juror, 1964.

DC Office: 413 DSOB, 20510, 202-224-5141; Fax: 202-228-0776; Web site: jeffords.senate.gov.

State Offices: Burlington, 802-658-6001; Montpelier, 802-223-5273; Rutland, 802-773-3875.

Committees: *Aging (Special). Environment & Public Works* (RMM). *Finance:* Health Care; International Trade; Taxation & IRS Oversight. *Health, Education, Labor & Pensions:* Children & Families; Employment, Safety & Training. *Veterans' Affairs.*

Group Ratings

	ADA	ACLU	AFS	LCV	CON	ITIC	NTU	COC	ACU	NTLC	CHC
2002	95	60	86	76	8	75	18	53	6	16	—
2001	40	—	58	75	—	—	49	64	29	—	40

National Journal Ratings

	2001 LIB —	2001 CONS	2002 LIB —	2002 CONS
Economic	47% —	49%	72% —	27%
Social	58% —	42%	82% —	0%
Foreign	51% —	43%	78% —	21%

Key Votes of the 107th Congress

1. Approve Bush Tax Cuts	Y	5. Confirm Ashcroft as AG	Y	9. Bar Coop. with Intl. Court		*
2. Expand Patients' Rights	N	6. Bar Gays in the Boy Scouts	N	10. Trade Promotion Authority		Y
3. Campaign Finance Reform	Y	7. $ for Hate Crime Prosecution	Y	11. Authorize Force in Iraq		N
4. Permit ANWR Development	N	8. Overseas Military Abortions	Y	12. Homeland Sec. Dept. Union		Y

Election Results

2000 general	James Jeffords (R)	189,133	(66%)	($1,889,243)
	Ed Flanagan (D)	73,352	(25%)	($1,054,977)
	Other	26,015	(9%)	
2000 primary	James Jeffords (R)	60,234	(78%)	
	Rick Hubbard (R)	15,991	(21%)	
	Other	1,204	(2%)	
1994 general	James Jeffords (R)	106,505	(50%)	($1,174,973)
	Jan Backus (D)	85,868	(41%)	($308,069)
	Gavin T. Mills (I)	12,465	(6%)	
	Other	6,834	(3%)	

Prior Winning Percentages: 1988 (70%); 1986 House (89%); 1984 House (65%); 1982 House (69%); 1980 House (79%); 1978 House (75%); 1976 House (67%); 1974 House (53%)

Jim Jeffords, the senator whose departure in May 2001 from the Republican Party gave the Democrats a majority in the Senate for 18 months, was first elected to the House in 1974 and to the Senate in 1988. He grew up in Rutland, the son of a Vermont chief justice, went to Yale, served in the Navy, went to Harvard Law School and then returned to Shrewsbury in the Green Mountains to practice law. He was elected state senator in 1966, at 32, and then state attorney general in 1968 and 1970. In 1974, he was elected to the House and in 1988, when Senator Robert Stafford retired, to the Senate. For 27 years he had one of the most liberal voting records of any congressional Republican; now his voting record is very similar to those of liberal Democrats.

In the 1990s, he became one of Bill Clinton's favorite Republicans. He voted for family and medical leave, motor voter, national service, the Brady bill and the 1994 crime package, despite Vermont's anti-gun control sentiment; in July 1993, he announced he was supporting the not-yet-written Clinton health care plan—the only Republican member of Congress who ever did. Jeffords was one of four Republican senators to vote for the Comprehensive Test Ban Treaty in October 1999, and one of four to vote for the Democratic version of the minimum wage in November 1999. As chairman of the Health, Education, Labor and Pensions Committee from 1997 to June 2001—a post he got with help from Majority Leader Trent Lott, he promised not to hold up legislation backed by all other Republicans, but otherwise mostly voted with ranking Democrat Edward Kennedy. He did, however, take the lead on the Republican bill to allow worker-management consultation, vehemently opposed by labor unions. His bill to allow import of prescription drugs from other countries passed 74–21 in July 2000 and was ultimately signed. He was the principal Republican co-sponsor of hate crimes legislation and of the bill to ban discrimination because of sexual orientation; he supported the Vermont civil unions law.

What prompted Jeffords to switch parties? He later said he had pondered doing so off and on for 20 years; he was obviously out of line with most other Republicans on many issues. He made his announcement on May 24, 2001, and said though he would call himself an Independent, he would caucus with the Democrats; the new organizing resolution giving Democrats the majority leadership and majorities on committees was not passed until June. Precipitating the issue was the Bush tax cut. His refusal to support the $1.6 trillion Bush tax cut left it one vote short in the Senate; the result was a $1.3 trillion cut, which Jeffords voted for even as he announced he was leaving the Republican Party. In his negotiations with the White House, he says he asked for and got a commitment to a $180 billion increase over 10 years for special education, a program for which he has great affection. Bush aides said he asked for $1.5 billion in a meeting April 3 with Bush, and got it, and then evidently decided that wasn't enough and demanded more. He may have been more disturbed by conservative columnists' reports of further White House retaliation, including possible opposition to the Northeast Dairy Compact, set to expire in September 2001, which gives New England dairy farmers far higher prices than those in the Midwest. Certainly he was attracted by the offer from Democratic Whip Harry Reid of the chairmanship of the Environment and Public Works Committee. At the time it was widely thought that Democrats might get a majority if and when 98-year-old Strom Thurmond died and was replaced by a Democrat (as it happened, Thurmond lived to celebrate his 100th birthday in December 2002 in the Senate); a chairmanship would not be on offer to a switcher who only added to a Democratic majority. Jeffords's account, at the time and in his 2001 book *My Declaration of Independence*, was that he "had to be true to what I thought was right, and leave the consequences to sort themselves out."

The consequences did not sort themselves out too favorably for him. The Northeast Dairy Compact expired in September 2001. Jeffords and colleague Patrick Leahy cobbled together a national dairy compact in December 2001, which would fix prices paid by milk processors and subsidize dairy farmers when prices fell below a certain level, but they were never able to reach agreement with critical colleagues from Wisconsin and no separate bill passed. The farm bill passed in spring 2002 did provide some retroactive payments to farmers, but they didn't arrive until October 2002, and in Vermont, since they were paid by the government rather than by milk processors, they were labeled "welfare." Meanwhile, in December 2001, Democrats in conference committee refused to hold out against House Republicans for the amount of special education spending Jeffords wanted. Jeffords was reported to be "depressed."

On the Environment Committee, Jeffords pressed for environmental causes, with varying success. In March 2001, he had sponsored a bill to scale back carbon emissions to 1990 levels—a quixotic goal. A more limited bill covering power plants—to scale back emissions of sulfur 95%, nitrogen oxides 85%, carbon dioxide 25% and mercury 90%—passed the committee by a 10–9 vote in June 2002. But Democrat Max Baucus immediately announced he'd vote against it, because it would close down many power plants in 2008, and it was clear the bill was going nowhere. In April 2002, Jeffords opposed a proposed treaty phasing out a dozen toxic chemicals because it didn't provide for eliminating other pollutants in the future. In June 2002, he considered issuing a subpoena for documents relating to EPA's consideration of rules for new-source pollution; he decided against it when the EPA agreed to provide some of the documents. In July 2002, he held hearings on a national bottle deposit law like those in Vermont and other states—another nonstarter. That same month, he switched his long-held position and voted against permanent storage of nuclear waste in Nevada's Yucca Mountain—an obvious thank you to Harry Reid, its most strenuous opponent.

One reason that Jeffords may have switched is that, in a politically polarized Vermont where Republicans were increasingly conservative, he would always be vulnerable in a Republican primary. Even in the general, he could be threatened: In 1994, he beat state Senator Jan Backus by only a 50%–41% margin, and a February 1999 poll showed him leading Congressman Bernie Sanders, the Burlington socialist who runs as an Independent but caucuses with Democrats, by only 42%–37%. But Sanders didn't run in 2000, and Jeffords won easily over state Auditor Ed Flanagan, 66%–25%— it helped that Trent Lott and Speaker Dennis Hastert agreed in November 1999 to a two-year extension of the Northeast Dairy Compact to save his seat. Jeffords's seat does not come up until 2006, but now he is positioned to run either as an Independent with no serious Democratic opposition (Democrats have been giving Sanders a bye for years) or as a Democrat (he was the star attraction at a big Senate Democrats fundraiser in February 2002), in either case against a presumably conservative Republican who would be at a disadvantage in what is now a pretty solidly Democratic state. And there is historic precedent: Since popular election of senators came in, no elected senator from Vermont has been defeated for reelection.

Representative-At-Large

Bernie Sanders (I)

Elected 1990, 7th term; b. Sept. 8, 1941, New York, NY; home, Burlington; U. of Chicago, B.A. 1964; Jewish; married (Jane).

Elected Office: Burlington Mayor, 1981–89.

Professional Career: Writer; Dir., Amer. People's History Soc.; Lecturer, Harvard U., 1989; Prof., Hamilton Col., 1989–90.

DC Office: 2233 RHOB, 20515, 202-225-4115; Fax: 202-225-6790; Web site: bernie.house.gov.

District Offices: Brattleboro, 802-254-8732; Burlington, 802-862-0697.

Committees: *Financial Services* (1st of 1 I): Domestic and International Monetary Policy, Trade & Technology; Financial Institutions & Consumer Credit (RMM); Housing & Community Opportunity. *Government Reform* (1st of 1 I): National Security, Emerging Threats & Intl. Relations; Wellness & Human Rights.

Group Ratings

	ADA	ACLU	AFS	LCV	CON	ITIC	NTU	COC	ACU	NTLC	CHC
2002	95	93	100	88	67	25	22	16	0	3	8
2001	100	—	100	100	—	—	11	22	8	—	—

National Journal Ratings

	2001 LIB	—	2001 CONS		2002 LIB	—	2002 CONS
Economic	95%	—	0%		95%	—	0%
Social	71%	—	29%		74%	—	19%
Foreign	90%	—	10%		94%	—	0%

Key Votes of the 107th Congress

1. Approve Bush Tax Cuts	N	5. Faith-Based Charities	N	9. Trade Promotion Authority	N
2. Limit Patients' Bill of Rights	N	6. Bar Gays in the Boy Scouts	N	10. Bar Funds for Intl. Court	N
3. Campaign Finance Reform	Y	7. Ban Partial-Birth Abortion	N	11. Authorize Force in Iraq	N
4. Ban ANWR Development	Y	8. Arm Commercial Pilots	Y	12. Deny Home. Sec. Dept. Union	N

Election Results

2002 general	Bernie Sanders (I)	144,880	(64%)	($622,639)
	William Meub (R)	72,813	(32%)	($184,845)
	Other	7,783	(3%)	
2002 primary	Bernie Sanders (I)	unopposed		
2000 general	Bernie Sanders (I)	196,118	(69%)	($323,561)
	Karen Ann Kerin (R)	51,977	(18%)	
	Pete Diamondstone (LU)	14,918	(5%)	
	Stewart Skrill (I)	11,816	(4%)	($21,501)
	Other	8,537	(3%)	

Prior Winning Percentages: 1998 (63%); 1996 (55%); 1994 (50%); 1992 (58%); 1990 (56%)

Vermont's single House member is Bernie Sanders, a Socialist elected as an Independent since 1990 but treated as a Democrat in the House. Sanders grew up in Flatbush, Brooklyn, the son of a paint salesman who had immigrated from Poland. "I know what it's like to live in a family without any money. Lack of money was a constant stress on my parents' relationship and in our household." He became involved in radical politics at the University of Chicago, then came to Vermont as part of the hippie invasion of 1968. His rumpled, tieless, sincere persona helped him win election as mayor of Burlington in 1981 by 10 votes, after losing four statewide races. In 1988, when Congressman Jim Jeffords ran for the Senate, Sanders ran for the House and lost to Republican Peter Smith. Two years later he ran again and reversed the result by capitalizing on Smith's support of the 1990 budget summit agreement and his vote for the ban on semiautomatic weapons. The National Rifle Association came out against Smith, and Sanders' opposition to gun control helped this urban-based Socialist carry 227 of Vermont's 251 cities and towns, plus three gores and one grant. Sanders became only the third Socialist elected to the House, after Victor Berger of Milwaukee (1911–13, 1923–29) and Meyer London of Manhattan's Lower East Side (1915–23). His views haven't changed much since his first election. In July 2002, he wrote an article in *People's Weekly World*, which proclaims itself the newspaper of the Communist Party USA, arguing that "a handful of corporations control the flow of information in the United States" and that as a result "the most important issues facing the middle class and working people are rarely discussed"—the lack of a national health care system, workers working longer hours for lower wages, the trade deficit, the impact of trade policy in driving down wages. "The U.S. has the most unfair distribution of wealth and income in the industrialized world," he wrote, "and the highest rate of childhood poverty."

At first, Democrats balked at accepting him in their caucus, but they have granted him seniority as a Democrat since 1991; he became ranking minority member on a subcommittee in 1997 over the objections of Elijah Cummings and, when a Banking subcommittee ranking position opened up in November 1997, he got that over the claims of Carolyn Maloney. Sanders adds to a heavily liberal voting record his own particular stamp. He formed a Progressive Caucus, with 52 members in the 108th Congress, with what is for the moment a quixotic agenda: progressive tax reform, a Canadian-style single-payer health care system, a 50% cut in military spending over five years, a national energy policy and—here Vermont speaks—support for family farms. He decries the tumbling of the barriers to international capital movement, and says the world economy is growing more slowly than at any time in the last 30 years; he joined conservative Republicans in voting against IMF funding.

But Sanders has also been a practical and sometimes successful legislator, gaining Republican allies in targeting what they consider corporate welfare. With Chris Smith of New Jersey, for example, he passed an amendment barring spending for defense contractor mergers ("payoffs for layoffs"). As a Banking subcommittee ranking member, he has criticized the IMF for subsidizing Russian mafias, undermining foreign economies and hurting the poor and middle class. He has been the House's leading backer of the Northeast Dairy Compact, which props up Northeast dairy prices, and after the Compact expired, his bill to establish a national dairy compact passed the House. It was killed in conference committee when Vermonters were unable to come up with a version acceptable to Midwestern dairy states.

As much as any member of Congress, he has made the cost of prescription drugs a national issue. Since the 1980s, he has called for government programs to pay for prescription drugs, and was the first member of Congress to lead bus trips to Canada to buy drugs there. He strongly backed Senator Jim Jeffords's bill to allow the import of prescription drugs and squawked loudly when he thought Jeffords and Republican leaders were watering it down. But then-HHS Secretary Donna Shalala ruled that under the terms of the law, she could not certify that reimported drugs were less expensive or safe; Sanders wants a new law that would reverse that decision. In early 2001, he sponsored a bill to provide prescription drugs for seniors under Medicare, with a 20% co-payment and full reimbursement for annual drug costs over $2,000. Seniors would pay the same prices that government agencies do, and prices would not allow companies to profit from government research. This became one of the Democrats' lead issues in the House and in the 2002 elections. Sanders denounces the pharmaceutical industry repeatedly for making profits on research done by NIH and for successfully lobbying against proposals like his. "But one organization never loses, and that organization has hundreds of victories to its credit and zero defeats in the United States Congress. And that is the pharmaceutical industry."

Another Sanders initiative actually became law. In February 2001, he proposed a $300 per person income tax rebate. Other Democrats picked up on this and it became party policy. George W. Bush, in assembling majorities for his tax cut, embraced it in diluted form—a $300 rebate for income taxpaying adults. Sanders and Democrats noted ruefully, and accurately, that Bush claimed credit for a tax cutting proposal which was initially theirs and which Republicans for a time resisted. Sanders noted that the rebate sent $90 million back to Vermonters. Over the years, he has pushed for Vermont projects characteristic of his interests—$1 million for a wind energy project in central Vermont; $850,000 for Burlington's Good News Garage, which provides cars to poor working people; $750,000 for his Israel-Arab Peace Partners Program, which brings young Jews and Arabs together in the United States.

Sanders was re-elected 58%–31% in 1992, and considered running against Jeffords in 1994. In 1994, after voting for the assault weapons ban and the crime bill with its gun control provisions, Sanders was opposed by the National Rifle Association-backed Vermont Sportsmen's Coalition. Sanders outspent state Senator John Carroll, but won by only 50%–47%. He has won by solid margins since, in 2000 against Karen Ann Kerin, a woman who was formerly a man; he has not had a Democratic opponent since 1996. Sanders again gave serious consideration to running against Jeffords, then a Republican, in 2000. One poll showed him trailing only narrowly, and Senators Tom Daschle and Bob Torricelli tried to recruit him. But House Democratic Leader Dick Gephardt promised him a seat on Appropriations if he remained in the House and Democrats won a majority. In September 2001, after Governor Howard Dean announced his retirement, he considered running for governor, but in November 2001, decided not to. In 2002, against a vigorous opponent, he was reelected by a 64%–32% margin.

★ VIRGINIA ★

T raditions endure in Virginia. Through nearly 400 years of history, Virginians have honored, and sometimes been fixated by, traditions going back to the Revolution and before. For the last half-century, Virginia has been growing lustily, in the first years about World War II thanks mainly to government, in recent years thanks more to a vibrant private sector, but the first state in the nation to elect a black governor still hews to a course close to its roots. The first Virginia was a commonwealth ruled by a landed gentry that was, in the words of historian David Hackett Fischer, "elitist and libertarian." From the tobacco-growing counties emerged in the 1770s a group of leaders—George Washington, George Mason, Patrick Henry, Thomas Jefferson, Richard Henry Lee, James Madison—who in learning, wisdom and strength of character, equal any such group from any similarly sized polity since Periclean Athens or republican Rome. They were slaveholders who insisted on liberty, armed men living on the marches of civilization who insisted on the rule of law, believers in racial inequality who set forth principles of equality that would in time form the basis of a non-racist society. The Virginia they led into the American Revolution was not only the most populous and the richest of the 13 colonies, it also was the indispensable creator of the Republic and the Constitution that has held together the world's greatest democracy.

After the Revolutionary War, gentry control continued even as Virginia was eclipsed in population and wealth by Pennsylvania and New York and, its tobacco fields, all but exhausted, became a breeding ground for slaves. But Virginia had two more great heroes, Robert E. Lee and Stonewall Jackson, both of whom reluctantly and brilliantly fought for their state rather than their country. The state's leadership class was impoverished and embittered by the Civil War, so much of which was fought on Virginia soil. Industrialization was haphazard: Railroads were constructed to ship cotton up from the South and coal east to the seaports; textile mills were built in Southside towns and tobacco factories in Richmond; the giant Newport News Shipbuilding & Drydock Company was built by railroad magnate Collis Huntington. Politically, Virginia was ruled by a local gentry who worshipped their Revolutionary past and mourned their Lost Cause. They were pessimists, looking not for economic growth but for stability, bent on maintaining Virginia's segregation and content with its second-class economy. County courthouse organizations became the political machine of Harry Byrd, who ran Virginia politics from 1925, when he was elected governor, until 1965, when he retired from the Senate. In national politics, this machine lost battles more often than Lee lost on the battlefield, and less gallantly. For years the machine succeeded in keeping most vestiges of the welfare state and racial equality out of Virginia, to the point of closing public schools in the 1950s rather than obeying federal court desegregation orders.

This "massive resistance" collapsed in the late 1950s; Virginia's demographics changed and it went through a quarter-century of political flux. The government-employee filled northern Virginia suburbs of Washington D.C. and the industrial Tidewater region around Norfolk and

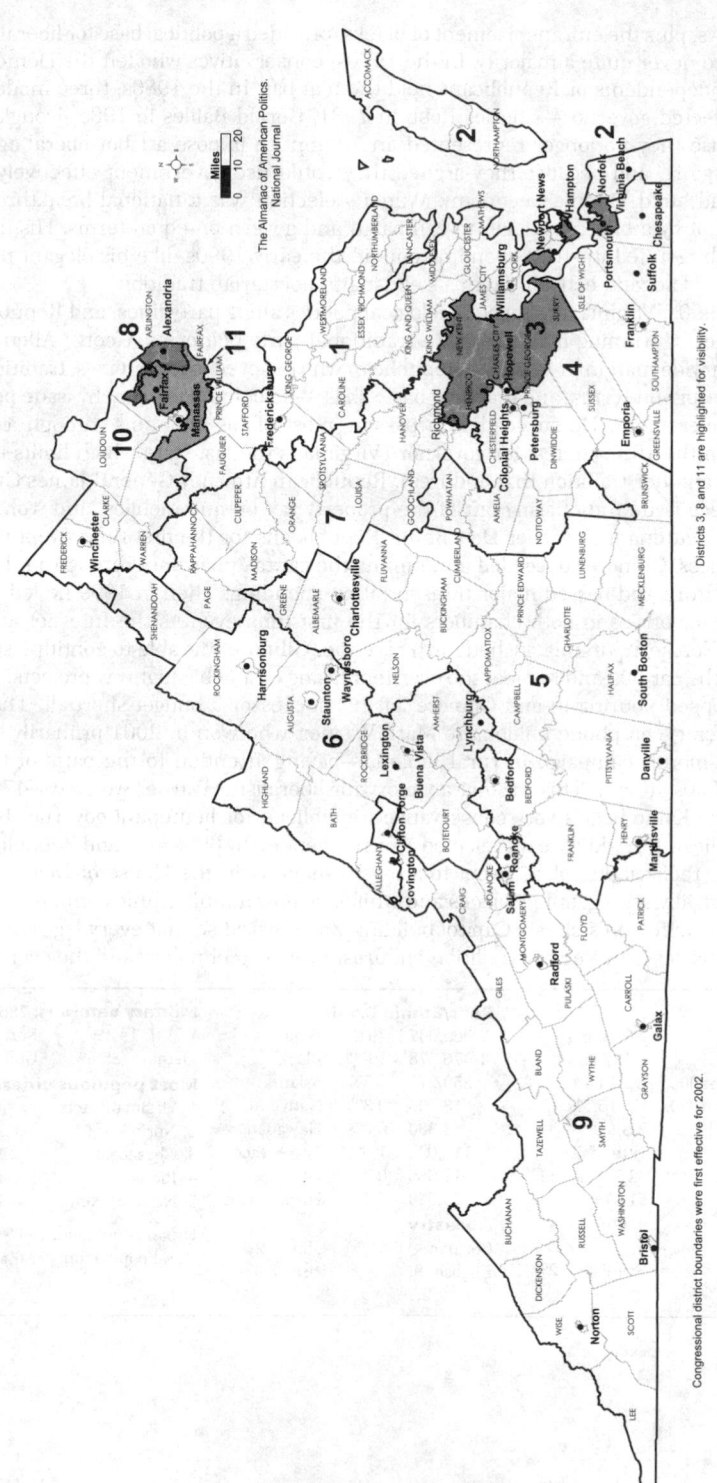

The Almanac of American Politics.
National Journal

Districts 3, 8 and 11 are highlighted for visibility.

Congressional district boundaries were first effective for 2002.

Newport News, plus the enfranchisement of blacks, provided a political base for liberal Democrats. But they were never quite a majority. In the 1970s, conservatives who left the Democratic Party and ran as independents or Republicans held them at bay. In the 1980s, three moderate Democrats were elected governor—Charles Robb in 1981, Gerald Baliles in 1985, Douglas Wilder in 1989—because they no longer represented an attempt to impose a labor-liberal agenda on an unwilling Virginia, and because they argued they could use government effectively to improve education and build Virginia's economy. Wilder's election was a national breakthrough, a successful attempt by a black politician to campaign and govern on equal terms. His fiscal conservatism, which resulted in sharp spending cuts in the early 1990s, like his elegant manners and thick Richmond accent, echoed Virginia's elitist and libertarian tradition.

In the 1990s, Virginia developed ideological politics along party lines, and Republicans made historic strides by winning majorities with traditional party platforms. George Allen was elected governor by a wide margin in 1993 as a Republican who believed in lower taxes, traditional cultural values, longer prison terms, and teaching basic skills—he combined crunchy issue positions with a sunny temperament. He succeeded in passing most of his programs through a Democratic legislature. In the 1997 contest for governor (Virginia is the last state which limits its governors to one term, another tradition that endures), Republican Attorney General James Gilmore made his centerpiece issue the phasing out of the property tax on automobiles, and won a 56%–43% victory over Lieutenant Governor Don Beyer. Republicans for the first time swept the top three statewide offices. Gilmore succeeded in ramming the car tax phase-out through a reluctant Democratic legislature and passed major transportation spending. Then in 1999 he led Republicans to legislative majorities in both chambers for the first time ever. As the Internet and high-tech economy of Northern Virginia gushed forth revenue, Gilmore was able to continue spending and phasing out the car tax, and to meet the ever-increasing cost of big highway projects. But in 2000, revenues stopped pouring in and Gilmore left his successor a budget shortfall. That successor was a Democrat, cell phone millionaire Mark Warner, who won in 2001 primarily thanks to an intensive 18-month campaign in rural Virginia—paying attention to the parts of the state not blessed by 1990s growth. This was not a victory for liberalism: Warner won 52%–47% and Democrat Timothy Kaine beat a very conservative Republican for lieutenant governor by 50%–48%, while Republican Jerry Kilgore was elected attorney general by 60%–40% and Republicans, helped by a partisan redistricting plan, swept to a 64–36 majority in the House of Delegates. Virginia, which once rigidly segregated its blacks and whites, is now a multiethnic commonwealth. And in 2000 Thomas Jefferson's classic Capitol building was rewired so that every legislator could have a laptop on his desk: In Virginia tradition endures, even as technology and the economy change.

The People		Race/Ethnic Origin			Military veterans: 786,359 (14.7%)	
Pop. 2000:	7,078,515	4,965,637	70.2%	White	WWII: 14.1%	Korea: 10.5%
Pop. 1990:	6,187,358	1,376,378	19.4%	Black	Vietnam: 35.4%	Gulf War: 16.8%
Change 1990–2000:	Up 14.4%	259,277	3.7%	Asian	**Most populous cities:**	
Change 1980–1990:	Up 15.7%	18,596	0.3%	Native Am.	1. Virginia Beach	425,257
% of U.S. total:	2.5%	3,380	0.0%	Hawaiian	2. Norfolk	234,403
Pop. rank:	12th of 50	114,022	1.6%	Two+ races	3. Chesapeake	199,184
Area size:	42,774 sq. mi.	11,685	0.2%	Other	4. Richmond	197,790
State Native:	51.9%	329,540	4.7%	Hisp. Origin	5. Newport News	180,150
Non-citizen:	4.8%	**Ancestry**			Urban population: 73.0%	
Language		German: 9.5%		USA: 9.2%	Rural population: 27.0%	
English: 87.3%	Spanish: 5.2%	English: 9.0%		Irish: 7.9%		
Other Eur.: 4.0%		Italian: 2.9%				

Education		Work Sector		General Assembly	
H.S. Grad:	81.5%	Private: 74.7%	Govt: 19.6%	Senate	23 R 17 D
College Grad:	29.5%	Self: 5.5%	Family: 0.2%	House of Del.	65 R 33 D 2 I
Industry		Unemployment: 4.1%		Legislative Term Limits: No	
Agri: 1.3%	Con: 7.3%	**Household Income**		**Registered Voters**	
Fin: 6.6%	Info: 3.8%	<15k: 13.2%	15-35k: 23.5%	No party registration	
Mfg: 16.0%	Prof: 29.9%	35-50k: 16.5%	50-100k: 31.7%		
Public: 8.3%	Trade: 14.2%	100-150k: 9.4%	>150k: 5.7%		
Other: 12.6%		Median: $46,677			
Occupation		Poverty status: 9.6%			
Blue collar: 22.1%	White collar: 63.7%	**Home Value**			
Gray collar: 14.2%		<50k: 10.6% 50-100k: 30.2%	100-200k: 37.4% 200-300k: 12.9%		
		300-500k: 6.7% >500k: 2.3%	Median: $118,800		

Presidential politics   Virginia remains one of the more Republican states in presidential races, but not as solidly Republican as in the 1980s. In 1996, Bill Clinton lost here by only 48%–46%, and in 2000, George W. Bush won by 52%–44%, running only even in Northern Virginia and the Hampton Roads area around Norfolk, but winning 55% in the Richmond area and 56% in the rest of the state. In Virginia, as elsewhere, big metro areas have trended Democratic in the 1990s. Until 2000, Virginia's national convention delegates were chosen at state conventions, but Republicans held an open primary in 2000, in which and Bush took 53% of the vote to John McCain's 44%. In early 2003, Virginia passed a law moving the state presidential primary to February 2004, in order to gain the attention of presidential candidates and the national media. But until now Virginia, within sight of the White House and the Capitol, has seen relatively little presidential politicking.

2000 Presidential Vote		
Bush (R)	1,437,490	(52%)
Gore (D)	1,217,290	(44%)
Nader (Green)	59,398	(2%)
Other	25,269	(1%)

2000 Republican Presidential Primary		
Bush (R)	350,588	(53%)
McCain (R)	291,488	(44%)
Other	22,017	(3%)

1996 Presidential Vote		
Dole (R)	1,137,171	(48%)
Clinton (D)	1,090,219	(46%)
Perot (I)	159,795	(7%)

Congressional districting   Republicans won control of both houses of the Virginia legislature in 1999 and, with Republican Jim Gilmore as governor, controlled the redistricting process in 2001 for the first time ever. Republican legislators promptly drew new lines, which made relatively minimal changes. They moved some black precincts from the 4th District to the 3d and increased its black majority while making the 4th more secure. They followed the wishes of the three Northern Virginia incumbents, two Republicans and one Democrat, who all strengthened themselves. They made the 9th District, held by Democrat Rick Boucher, a little more Republican, but it would have been difficult to do otherwise without drawing a geographical monstrosity. Oliver North, the Iran-contra figure, unsuccessful 1994 Senate candidate and radio talk show host, volunteered to run against Boucher if legislators would connect his district in southwest Virginia with North's home in the far northern end of the state; the offer was politely rejected. Bobby Scott of the black-majority 3d District raised questions about the 3d and 4th District lines, but the Justice Department approved the plan, and a lawsuit went nowhere.

108th Congress Lineup	
8 R	3 D

107th Congress Lineup		
7 R	3 D	1 I

Governor

Mark Warner (D)

Elected 2001, term expires Jan. 2006, 1st term; b. Dec. 15, 1954, Indianapolis, IN; home, Alexandria; George Washington U., B.A., 1977; Harvard U., J.D., 1980; Presbyterian; married (Lisa).

Professional Career: Mng. Dir., Columbia Capitol Corp., 1989–01.

Office: State Capitol, Richmond, 23219, 804-786-2211; Fax: 804-371-6351; Web site: www.governor.state.va.us.

Election Results

2001 general	Mark Warner (D)	984,177	(52%)
	Mark Earley (R)	887,234	(47%)
2001 primary	Mark Warner (D)	unopposed	
1997 general	Jim Gilmore (R)	969,062	(56%)
	Don Beyer (D)	738,971	(43%)
	Sue Harris DeBauche (I)	25,777	(2%)

Mark Warner was elected governor of Virginia in 2001, the first Democrat to be elected since 1989, when Warner managed Douglas Wilder's successful campaign. Warner was born in Indianapolis and moved to Hartford, Connecticut in the 8th grade. He was the first in his family to graduate from college, from George Washington University in 1977; then he graduated from Harvard Law School in 1980. After law school he worked in the fundraising office of the Democratic National Committee. There, former Congressman Tom McMillen told him about the potential of cell phone markets just as the Reagan administration was about to award almost 1,500 free licenses for metropolitan cell phone markets. Warner cobbled together investor groups and packaged their applications in exchange for a fee and a five percent ownership stake if they received the licenses. He made millions; his net worth in 2001 was estimated at $200 million.

In 1989, the same year he managed Wilder's campaign, Warner set up Columbia Capital, a venture capital fund which provided financing for more than 70 telecommunications and information technology firms, many of which went public; the best known is Nextel. From 1993 to 1995, he served as Virginia Democratic chairman. In 1996, he ran against Republican Senator John Warner (no relation) and spent $10 million of his own money on the campaign; he ran well throughout the state and held the Republican Warner to a 52%–47% margin, his closest since his first election in 1978. Over the next several years, Warner put millions into philanthropic efforts: In 1997 to a Virginia High-Tech Partnership to give internships in high-tech firms to students in Virginia's five historically black colleges and universities; in 2000 to TechRiders, which provided demonstrations in using computers in houses of worship around the state. He also set up four regional small business investment funds in Southwest Virginia, Southside Virginia, metro Richmond and Hampton Roads. By 1999, it was plain that Warner was going to run for governor in 2001. With no experience in elected office, he presented himself as an entrepreneur who could bring business methods to government.

Warner picked a good year to run. In 1993 and 1997, Republicans George Allen and Jim Gilmore had been elected governor by advancing popular proposals which their Democratic opponents opposed—Allen called for an end to parole and Gilmore for elimination of the car tax. In 2000, Allen was elected to the Senate, but Gilmore spent much of the year battling the Republican-controlled General Assembly over the budget; revenues were coming in lower than expected, and Gilmore wanted to keep phasing out the car tax. In 2000 and 2001, the two Republicans elected to downballot offices in 1997—Lieutenant Governor John Hager and Attorney General Mark Earley—were battling each other for the Republican nomination for governor. Against this background, Warner called for an end to old-style politics, regional divisions, partisan bickering and personal attacks. Earley won the June primary, but had little money and no clear campaign strategy—no bold proposal like Allen's in 1993 or Gilmore's in 1997. Warner had plenty of money: He ultimately spent $5 million of his own money on the campaign, but used his finely honed talents at fundraising to raise more in Virginia and around the nation. He ran ads starting in August and straight through November; Earley made a smaller time buy starting in mid-October.

Nor would Warner, who lives in a restored mansion in Alexandria's beautiful Old Town, be tabbed as an urban liberal. He called himself a "fiscal conservative" and pledged not to raise the income or sales taxes. Responding to complaints from traffic-choked Northern Virginia, he called for regional referendums on local sales tax increases: This pleased business interests and local legislators who feared congestion would stop growth and propitiated tax opponents who felt they would get a chance to vote no. He hired a rural strategist, David "Mudcat" Saunders of Roanoke. He opposed any new gun control laws and wooed the National Rifle Association, which remained neutral—a victory for a Democrat. He ran ads featuring old pickup trucks and blue grass music. He sponsored a NASCAR race truck. He traveled to all parts of rural Virginia, showing that this rich entrepreneur was in touch with folks and reminding them of his investment funds and his philanthropic initiatives. In October, Earley came out against the regional referendum, but this evidently hurt him with both sides: The businessmen and legislators were angry at him for opposing their project, while some tax opponents outside Northern Virginia thought it made a statewide tax increase more likely. Earley's ads were on hot-button issues like taxes and abortion, but Warner had inoculated himself on taxes and Earley's opposition to abortion put off some suburban Republicans.

The surprise is not that Warner won, but that he won by a small margin, 52%–47%, a reversal of the numbers in his 1996 Senate race. That time Warner had lost narrowly each of the major regions of the state; this time by narrow margins he carried them all. He carried Northern Virginia 54%–46% and the Hampton Roads region 53%–47%. He did well in the Richmond suburbs and carried metro Richmond 51%–48%. And in the rest of Virginia, he carried dozens of rural counties that national Democrats usually lose. Al Gore had won only 41% in this region the year before; Warner carried it 51%–48%, losing badly only in the Shenandoah Valley but carrying Southside and Southwest Virginia.

Once in office, Warner had to cope with unpleasant fiscal realities. The car tax phase-out was put on hold in November 2001, and Gilmore resigned as Republican National Chairman later that month. Warner got the legislature to approve November 2002 transportation tax referenda in Northern Virginia and in Hampton Roads, but the House of Delegates killed his education initiative in March 2002. As the budget shortfall kept growing, Warner continued to rule out a tax increase, cut $858 million in spending and laid off 1,800 state employees. Meanwhile, opinion was moving against the tax increases in Northern Virginia and Hampton Roads. They were opposed by tax opponents who argued that the politicians would just shuffle the money around and by "smart growth" advocates, environmentally-minded activists who argued that more highways just meant more growth and more traffic congestion. In November 2002, Northern Virginia voted 55%–45% against the referendum and Hampton Roads rejected it by 62%–38%. These are not two insignificant areas: Together they cast a majority of the state's votes. Warner said the results showed a "sobering" mistrust of politicians. The prospect was for a battle for scarce highway dollars between the traffic-choked suburbs and rural areas. In December 2002, Warner presented a budget balanced by one-time financial maneuvers that suggested that more fiscal troubles lay ahead.

Virginia is the last state to limit its governors to one term. In November 2002 Warner called for changing this, but in a way that would not make him eligible to run again in 2005; the House killed his measure in February 2003. From this distance the two likeliest candidates then are the two statewide downballot elected officials, Democratic Lieutenant Governor Timothy Kaine, a former mayor of Richmond, who won 50%–48% in 2001, and Republican Attorney General Jerry Kilgore, a former federal and state prosecutor, who won 60%–40% in 2001.

Senior Senator

John Warner (R)

Elected 1978, seat up 2008, 5th term; b. Feb. 18, 1927, Washington, D.C.; home, Alexandria; Washington & Lee U., B.S., 1949, U. of VA, LL.B. 1953; Episcopalian; divorced.

Military Career: Navy, 1944–46 (WWII), Marine Corps, 1950–52 (Korea).

Professional Career: Law Clerk, U.S. Court of Appeals, Chief Judge Barrett Prettyman, 1953–54; Practicing atty., 1954–56, 1960–69; Asst. U.S. Atty., 1956–60; U.S. Navy, Undersecy., 1969–72, U.S. Navy, Secy., 1972–74; Dir., Amer. Rev. Bicentennial Comm., 1974–76.

DC Office: 225 RSOB, 20510, 202-224-2023; Fax: 202-224-6295; Web site: warner.senate.gov.

State Offices: Abingdon, 276-628-8158; Norfolk, 757-441-3079; Richmond, 804-771-2579; Roanoke, 540-857-2676.

Committees: *Armed Services* (Chmn.). *Environment & Public Works*: Fisheries, Wildlife & Water; Superfund & Waste Management; Transportation & Infrastructure. *Health, Education, Labor & Pensions*: Aging; Children & Families. *Intelligence (Select)*.

Group Ratings

	ADA	ACLU	AFS	LCV	CON	ITIC	NTU	COC	ACU	NTLC	CHC
2002	15	20	38	12	12	100	51	95	79	82	—
2001	20	—	8	25	—	—	77	86	96	—	100

National Journal Ratings

	2001 LIB —	2001 CONS	2002 LIB —	2002 CONS
Economic	35%	62%	40%	59%
Social	33%	59%	0%	62%
Foreign	36%	54%	33%	65%

Key Votes of the 107th Congress

1. Approve Bush Tax Cuts	Y	5. Confirm Ashcroft as AG	Y	9. Bar Coop. with Intl. Court	Y
2. Expand Patients' Rights	Y	6. Bar Gays in the Boy Scouts	Y	10. Trade Promotion Authority	Y
3. Campaign Finance Reform	Y	7. $ for Hate Crime Prosecution	N	11. Authorize Force in Iraq	Y
4. Permit ANWR Development	Y	8. Overseas Military Abortions	N	12. Homeland Sec. Dept. Union	N

Election Results

2002 general	John Warner (R)	1,229,893	(83%)	($1,709,202)
	Nancy Spannaus (I)	145,102	(10%)	($61,984)
	Jacob Hornberger (I)	106,055	(7%)	($66,480)
2002 primary	John Warner (R)	unopposed		
1996 general	John Warner (R)	1,235,744	(52%)	($5,819,157)
	Mark Warner (D)	1,115,982	(47%)	($11,600,424)

Prior Winning Percentages: 1990 (81%); 1984 (70%); 1978 (50%)

John Warner, first elected in 1978, is the chairman of the Senate Armed Services Committee. He grew up in Washington, D.C., with Virginia roots; his grandparents lived in Amherst County, Virginia. His father was a field surgeon in World War I; a great-uncle served in the Confederate Army and lost his arm in the Battle of the Wilderness. Warner volunteered for both the Army and Navy in 1944, at 17; the Navy snapped him up first. (There are only six World War II veterans left in the Senate: Ted Stevens, Daniel Inouye, Daniel Akaka, Frank Lautenberg, Ernest Hollings, John Warner; 43 of the 100 senators were not born until after World War II.) He went to college at Washington & Lee and then interrupted his years at the University of Virginia Law School when he volunteered to serve in the Marine Corps in Korea. He worked as an assistant U.S. attorney and then practiced law in Washington and had a house in the horse country in Middleburg, Virginia. During the Nixon administration, he was Secretary of the Navy and negotiated with the Soviets the Incidents at Sea Executive Agreement, still in effect and a model often imitated. From 1974 to 1976 he headed the American Revolution Bicentennial Commission. He ran for the

Senate in 1978 with few political assets other than his then-wife, Elizabeth Taylor. Finishing second at the huge Republican state convention, he graciously supported winner Richard Obenshain; then, when Obenshain died in a plane crash, Republican leaders reluctantly named Warner to fill his place. Warner won the general over Democrat Andrew Miller by a 4,721-vote margin and was easily re-elected in 1984, 1990 and 2002. He had serious competition only in 1996 from now-Governor Mark Warner (no relation).

Warner can be grandiloquent and showy, yet he works hard on important issues and has shown steadfastness in his beliefs. His voting record is moderately conservative, sometimes liberal on cultural issues. He has voted for government funding of abortions in some cases, but favors parental consent laws and the partial-birth abortion ban. He voted for the Brady gun control bill and in May 1999 to control gun sales by non-licensed dealers at gun shows. Representing a state that still has a large number of public employees (though the proportion is dropping), he favors higher federal pay and supported repeal of the Hatch Act. In the 2001 tax cut, he sponsored successfully a $250 credit for educational supplies and a $500 deduction of professional development for teachers.

On some issues he has joined Democrats and opposed most Republicans, on gun control in May 1999 and on amendments to HMO regulation in July 1999. He led the bipartisan Virginia-Maryland delegation and in October 2000 raised the federal funding of the Woodrow Wilson Bridge across the Potomac to $1.5 billion.

Warner was the ranking Republican on the Armed Services committee from 1987–93, and was looking forward to becoming chairman when the more senior Senator Strom Thurmond bumped him. When both were re-elected in 1996, Warner expressed the hope he might be chairman some time within six years. In December 1997, on the day before his 95th birthday, Thurmond announced he would step down in January 1999 to give the younger generation a chance; he kept his word and Warner became chairman at 71. For years on the committee he had worked closely with Democratic chairman Sam Nunn; but he opposed Nunn and led the fight in 1991 for the Gulf War resolution, which passed by only 52–47. Warner made harsh criticisms of Clinton administration defense policy. He had supported previous rounds of base closings, but after Bill Clinton's politically-motivated tampering with the 1995 round of closings, he voted against another round in May 1999, saying, "Politics have destroyed the credibility of the process for closing bases." Warner voted against the Comprehensive Test Ban Treaty in October 1999, arguing that it was impossible to monitor Russian compliance. He opposed NATO expansion and was wary of U.S. troop commitments in the Balkans. But when Clinton sent in troops in May 1999 he said, "Once the president made the decision to join NATO in the Balkans, we have to support the troops." In May 2000, he and Robert Byrd sponsored an amendment to end U.S. deployment in Kosovo by July 2001; it was beaten by only 53–47. In the first major bill of the 106th Congress, he hammered through the biggest military pay and pension increases in nearly 20 years. In October 2000, he secured coverage under the military Triad medical care plan of all military retirees, a change with a price tag of $60 billion over 10 years.

Warner has shown some prescience about problems others did not discern. In early 2001, before September 11, he created a new Emerging Threats Subcommittee to focus on terrorism, chemical and biological warfare and cyberwarfare; he was concerned about what might happen if the military's high-tech computers fail or are somehow jammed by low-tech countermeasures. Noting the unwillingness of the military and its civilian leaders to accept casualties, he called for a new set of unmanned weapons, and wants one-third of military aircraft to be unmanned by 2010 and one-third of ground vehicles to be unmanned by 2015. He strongly backs missile defense. In a secret markup session in May 2000, he got approval of five new nuclear submarines of the Virginia class—a major increase in the submarine fleet.

The evening of September 11 he appeared at a press conference with Rumsfeld and the Joint Chiefs at the Pentagon. "We call upon the entire world to step up and help—because terrorism is a common enemy to all." Because of the danger of terrorism at home, he called in October 2001 for reexamination of the 1878 Posse Comitatus law that bars use of federal troops domestically. Defense authorization bills usually pass with bipartisan support, but in May 2002 he voted against the bill because Democrats led by Chairman Carl Levin shifted $812 million away from missile defense; his opposition plus a Bush veto threat got the Democrats to back down. Shipbuilding is a major Warner interest, and much of it is done at Virginia's Newport News Shipbuilding & Drydock. In 2001 Warner favored Northrop Grumman's acquisition of the company; he was opposed by Trent Lott, who worried that Northrop Grumman might transfer business from Mississippi's Ingalls shipyard, which it already owned, to Newport News. Warner put into the 2002 defense bill $229 million to keep on schedule the $10 billion CVNX aircraft carrier to be built at Newport News; this is a transformational ship, with a new nuclear plant and electromagnetic catapults to hurl planes into flight. He continued to press Rumsfeld to keep work going forward to meet the delivery date of 2013 (when Warner will be 84). Warner sponsored the Iraq war resolution in October 2002. "We cannot let the United Nations think in any way that they can veto the authority of this president or the ability of this nation to defend itself."

For a time in the 1990s, Warner seemed to be in a war with many Virginia Republicans. In 1993, he refused to endorse lieutenant governor candidate Michael Farris, the leader of the national home schooling movement, and in 1994 he announced he could not support Senate nominee Oliver North, whose conviction on Iran-Contra charges was overturned on the grounds of inadmissibility of some critical evidence. Instead Warner backed independent (and twice Republican gubernatorial candidate) Marshall Coleman, and many blamed Warner for North's narrow loss to Charles Robb. Farris and North backers hoped to deny Warner renomination in 1996 at the gigantic Virginia Republican state convention. But Warner invoked a Virginia law that entitled him to insist on a primary. There he defeated James Miller, budget director under President Ronald Reagan and North's opponent at the 1994 convention, by 66%–34%. In the general election, against former Democratic state chairman and now-Governor Mark Warner, John Warner called himself a "common sense conservative" and, citing seniority, said, "Virginia's got an investment in me." John Warner won, but only narrowly, 52%–47%. He carried by narrow 51%–49% margins the usually Republican Richmond areas and non-metropolitan Virginia: evidence that some Farris and North enthusiasts cut him. He carried the Norfolk area by only 52%–47%: He was not yet Armed Services chairman. He ran best, 55%–45%, in Northern Virginia, where his highly visible opposition to Farris and North was an asset.

In 2002, by contrast, he had no serious opposition. Republicans had mostly forgotten Farris and North. Democrats were content not to run a candidate. Mark Warner, now governor, called John Warner "a great guy and a great senator" and said, "I think Senator Warner represents Virginia well and fights very, very hard on a number of critical issues." Think shipbuilding and highways: Warner fights for Newport News on Armed Services and, after getting a waiver from the Republican Conference to serve on Environment and Public Works, will be in on the markup of the next highway bill—important in traffic-clogged Virginia. For his part, Senator Warner joined Governor Warner in campaigning for passage of the November 2002 transportation tax referenda in Northern Virginia and Hampton Roads. "I fully recognize that taxation is a highly volatile thing—especially when you're seeking reelection—but, you know, duty calls. I put politics aside when the issue requires a team effort." The referenda were defeated, but John Warner was reelected with 83% of the vote. Warner played a critical role in December 2002 in easing Trent Lott out of the Majority Leader position. After Don Nickles called for a new leader, Warner went on CNN and said, "Let's make it clear. This nation is at war. We're approaching very serious decisions with regard to future action we may take. . . . And we have the integrity of the institution which we love and serve, the U.S. Senate. To leave this very fine leader—and he's been a good leader through the years; I've worked with him carefully—just out there by himself and leaving it to the journalists and the people to pick us off individually and singularly, I think, is not in the interest of the nation." Translation from senatorial into English: Lott must go.

Virginia has elected 51 men to the United States Senate, and Warner has served longer than all but two of them. He will pass the record of Carter Glass in April 2005 and, if he is elected to another term, of Harry Byrd Sr. in September 2011.

Junior Senator

George Allen (R)

Elected 2000, seat up 2006, 1st term; b. Mar. 8, 1952, Whittier, CA; home, Earlysville; U. of VA, B.A. 1974, J.D. 1977; Presbyterian; married (Susan).

Elected Office: VA House of Delegates, 1982–91; U.S. House of Reps., 1991–92; VA Gov., 1993–97.

Professional Career: Practicing atty., 1977–91, 1998–99.

DC Office: 204 RSOB, 20510, 202-224-4024; Fax: 202-224-5432; Web site: allen.senate.gov.

State Offices: Abingdon, 276-676-2646; Herndon, 703-435-0039; Richmond, 804-771-2221; Roanoke, 540-772-4236; Virginia Beach, 757-518-1674.

Committees: *NRSC Chairman. Commerce, Science & Transportation*: Aviation; Communications; Science, Technology & Space; Surface Transportation & Merchant Marine. *Foreign Relations*: East Asian & Pacific Affairs; European Affairs (Chmn.); International Operations & Terrorism; Western Hemisphere, Peace Corps, Narcotics Affairs. *Small Business & Entrepreneurship*.

Group Ratings

	ADA	ACLU	AFS	LCV	CON	ITIC	NTU	COC	ACU	NTLC	CHC
2002	10	20	13	0	12	100	55	95	84	85	—
2001	15	—	0	0	—	—	80	100	96	—	100

National Journal Ratings

	2001 LIB	—	2001 CONS	2002 LIB	—	2002 CONS
Economic	17%	—	77%	32%	—	66%
Social	29%	—	70%	0%	—	62%
Foreign	7%	—	72%	24%	—	67%

Key Votes of the 107th Congress

1. Approve Bush Tax Cuts	Y	5. Confirm Ashcroft as AG	Y
2. Expand Patients' Rights	N	6. Bar Gays in the Boy Scouts	Y
3. Campaign Finance Reform	N	7. $ for Hate Crime Prosecution	N
4. Permit ANWR Development	Y	8. Overseas Military Abortions	N

9. Bar Coop. with Intl. Court	Y
10. Trade Promotion Authority	Y
11. Authorize Force in Iraq	Y
12. Homeland Sec. Dept. Union	N

Election Results

2000 general	George Allen (R)	1,420,460	(52%)	($9,995,980)
	Charles S. Robb (D)	1,296,093	(48%)	($6,610,252)
2000 primary	George Allen (R)	unopposed		
1994 general	Charles S. Robb (D)	938,376	(46%)	($5,501,697)
	Oliver L. (Ollie) North (R)	882,213	(43%)	($20,607,367)
	J. Marshall Coleman (I)	235,324	(11%)	($813,409)

Prior Winning Percentages: 1991 House (62%)

George Allen, a Republican elected in 2000, is one of only six Virginians to serve as governor and senator (the others were James Monroe, John Tyler, Claude Swanson, Harry Byrd Sr. and the man he beat, Charles Robb). Allen grew up in Illinois and California, graduating from high school in Palos Verdes. At that point his father had moved to Virginia to become the highly successful coach of the Washington Redskins ("Hit hard and good things will happen"), and he advised his son to go to college in the area. The younger George Allen graduated from college and law school at the University of Virginia. In 1977 he moved to a country home near Charlottesville and practiced law—wearing boots and chewing tobacco. In 1982 he was elected to the Virginia House of Delegates, where he was a conservative backbencher while Robb was governor. In a 1991 special election he won a seat in the U.S. House, which the Democratic legislature promptly redistricted out from under him.

Out of office, he started running for governor in 1993. He maneuvered to get the support of religious conservatives at the 13,000-delegate June 1993 state convention, perhaps the largest legislative body in the history of democracy (and whose real enthusiasm was reserved for its lieutenant governor nominee, home schooling advocate Michael Farris). The Democratic nominee, Attorney General Mary Sue Terry, was better known and had a moderate record on many issues, though she backed some forms of gun control and was pro-abortion rights. Democrats thought gun control and the religious right would hurt Republicans. But Allen won by a whopping 58%–41% margin.

Allen's term as governor (Virginia is the last state to limit governors to one term) was more successful than many had expected. His achievements included a more permissive concealed weapons law, abolition of parole (a big issue in the 1993 campaign), parental notification for abortions and welfare reform that required recipients to work after 90 days and cut off benefits after two years—which resulted in a big decline in welfare rolls. Allen was regarded by his foes as an intellectual lightweight, but his education reforms included Standards of Learning that were probably the toughest in the nation. But in 1995 the legislature rejected Allen's tax cut, and in elections that fall, despite a major effort by Allen, Republicans fell short of winning majorities in the legislature (they finally did so in 1999). Democrats disliked him for his partisanship and activist conservatism; he has a cheerful, sunny temperament but also a penchant for harsh conservative rhetoric. To the 1994 Republican state convention, he said, "My friends—and I say this figuratively—let's enjoy knocking their soft teeth down their whining throats." But he had 68% job approval when he left the governorship.

Out of office in 1998, Allen joined a Richmond law firm, but it was widely expected that he would run against Charles Robb in 2000. Robb was elected lieutenant governor of Virginia in 1977 and governor by a 54%–46% margin in 1981. His record in the Senate was among the more conservative of Democrats, but he found himself in political trouble in 1994 because of scandal. In the Democratic primary Robb beat Delegate Virgil Goode (later, as congressman, an Independent and then a Republican) by the unimpressive margin of 58%–34% and in the general, against Oliver North, the epicenter of the Iran-contra scandal, who spent $20 million, Robb won by only 46%–43%. Robb continued to compile a moderate voting record and worked hard on military issues and on programs with appeal in rural areas, but Allen led in early polls. The centerpiece of Allen's campaign was a $1,000 per child tax credit for educational expenses for both public and private schools. He also called for cutting the cost of public college and for smaller elementary school class sizes. Robb argued that the money would be better invested in federal spending for education. Allen, a bit on the defensive on gun control, said he would vote to renew the assault weapons ban. Robb gained, at last, a lukewarm endorsement from his longtime adversary, former Governor Douglas Wilder; Allen gained a strong endorsement, and backing for his tax credits for education, from that sometime adversary of conservative Republicans, Senator John Warner. In the last weeks of the campaign, Robb accused Allen of an "intolerable" and "appalling" record on racial issues; Democratic flyers attacked him for opposing a federal Martin Luther King Holiday, for displaying a Confederate flag in his house and for displaying a noose in his law office.

Allen won by a narrow 52%–48% margin. His votes tracked very closely with George W. Bush's. Robb, targeting the suburbs, carried Northern Virginia, but by only a 51%–49% margin. With his military credentials, he won in Tidewater Virginia, but by only 52%–48%. Allen carried the Richmond area 55%–45%, and won an even bigger margin, 57%–43%, in the one-third of the state outside these metropolitan areas. A bad sign for Democrats in the future: Robb, elected governor in 1981, carried voters 60 and older; Allen, elected governor in 1993, carried voters under 60, and by wider margins

Majority Leader Trent Lott named Allen head of a Republican high-tech task force. He was the lead sponsor of extending the ban on Internet taxes, which became law in November 2001; in January 2003 he called for making the ban permanent, a measure sure to be opposed by many governors of both parties. Soon after September 11, he called for reopening Reagan National Airport and sponsored the law which provided closed-circuit television of terrorist trials so that victims' relatives could watch. In 2002 he sponsored a bill to enable injured civilian federal workers to receive retirement benefits they were losing while convalescing. In a move opposed by advocates of autonomy for the District of Columbia, he voted to overturn the District's needle exchange program. In May 2002 he and Maryland Democrat Paul Sarbanes called for $3.5 billion more for

Navy shipbuilding. In November 2002 he called for including the scheduled 4.1% federal wage increase in the continuing resolution. In 2001 he sponsored a bill to give citizenship to a Chinese scholar arrested while on vacation in Beijing.

After the 2002 election, Allen was picked to succeed Bill Frist as head of the National Republican Senatorial Committee; he had been co-chairman of the Senate and House Republicans' President's Dinner in June 2002. Allen was troubled by Lott's comments at Strom Thurmond's 100th birthday party December 5 and on December 14 he began urging Frist to run for majority leader and started calling other senators to get their support. On December 18 Allen picked up the phone and called Lott—he was the first senator to tell him he should step down. "I got to the point, which was that we needed a new leader."

FIRST DISTRICT

Rep. Jo Ann Davis (R)

Elected 2000, 2d term; b. June 29, 1950, Rowan Cnty., NC; home, Yorktown; Hampton Roads Bus. Col.; Assembly of God; married (Chuck).

Elected Office: VA House of Del., 1997–2000.

Professional Career: Real estate broker, 1984-present; Founder, Davis Mngmt. Co., 1988; Founder, Jo Ann Davis Realty, 1990.

DC Office: 1123 LHOB 20515, 202-225-4261; Fax: 202-225-4382; Web site: www.house.gov/joanndavis.

District Offices: Fredericksburg, 540-548-1086; Tappahanock, 804-443-0668; Yorktown, 757-874-6687.

Committees: *Armed Services* (18th of 33 R): Projection Forces; Terrorism, Unconventional Threats & Capabilities. *Government Reform* (11th of 24 R): Civil Service & Agency Organization (Chmn.); Criminal Justice, Drug Policy & Human Resources. *International Relations* (20th of 26 R): Europe; Middle East & Central Asia.

Group Ratings

	ADA	ACLU	AFS	LCV	CON	ITIC	NTU	COC	ACU	NTLC	CHC
2002	5	7	11	13	87	75	56	75	96	94	100
2001	5	—	0	14	—	—	66	83	100	—	—

National Journal Ratings

	2001 LIB	—	2001 CONS		2002 LIB	—	2002 CONS
Economic	32%	—	68%		28%	—	69%
Social	0%	—	81%		0%	—	75%
Foreign	29%	—	69%		24%	—	72%

Key Votes of the 107th Congress

1. Approve Bush Tax Cuts	Y	5. Faith-Based Charities	Y	9. Trade Promotion Authority	Y
2. Limit Patients' Bill of Rights	Y	6. Bar Gays in the Boy Scouts	Y	10. Bar Funds for Intl. Court	Y
3. Campaign Finance Reform	N	7. Ban Partial-Birth Abortion	Y	11. Authorize Force in Iraq	Y
4. Ban ANWR Development	N	8. Arm Commercial Pilots	Y	12. Deny Home. Sec. Dept. Union	Y

Election Results

2002 general	Jo Ann Davis (R)	113,168	(96%)	($280,852)
	Other	4,829	(4%)	
2002 primary	Jo Ann Davis (R)	unopposed		
2000 general	Jo Ann Davis (R)	151,344	(58%)	($393,119)
	Lawrence A. Davies (D)	97,399	(37%)	($152,592)
	Sharon A. Wood (I)	9,652	(4%)	
	Other	4,619	(2%)	

The People		Race/Ethnic Origin	Ancestry	
Area size:	4,612 sq. mi.	74.7% White	English: 10.7%	German: 10.4%
Urban population:	64.0%	18.4% Black	Irish: 8.8%	
Rural population:	36.0%	1.7% Asian	**2000 Presidential Vote**	
Pop. 2000:	643,514	0.4% Native Am.	Bush (R)..............146,914	(58%)
Median income:	$50,257	0.1% Hawaiian	Gore (D)...............98,731	(39%)
Poverty status:	6.7%	1.6% Two + races	Other....................6,060	(2%)
Military veterans:	17.7%	0.2% Other	**Cook Partisan Voting Index:** R + 10	
		3.0% Hispanic Origin		

Occupation	Blue collar: 22.1%	White collar: 62.8%	Gray collar: 15.0%

When English settlers first sailed up the estuaries that flow into the Chesapeake Bay, they were searching for gold, hoping to sail back soon with fortunes. But they couldn't help noticing that the spot where the James River feeds into the bay, now Hampton Roads, was a fine natural harbor, with calm, deep water and good anchorages. There they established a civilization whose elegance is recalled in the craftsmanship of restored Williamsburg and whose coarseness and brutality is brought to life by the story of Jamestown and the other beleaguered settlements. Tidewater Virginia brought slavery to America and tobacco to the world, and slave-raised tobacco was the center of its economy in the colonial era and in the years afterward, when its most talented sons left its depleted soil for better opportunities elsewhere.

Now the economy and tone of life in Tidewater Virginia are set by the American military. Sixty years ago, as America faced world war, the Navy base at Norfolk and the shipbuilding centers in Newport News across Hampton Roads became the center of American naval might in the Atlantic. There were fewer than 370,000 people living then on both sides of Hampton Roads. Today there are nearly 1.6 million—a population collected from all over the country, making this a metropolitan area that is not so much Southern in atmosphere as it is, in the manner of military bases abroad, national.

Virginia's 1st Congressional District contains much of this territory. The district ranges as far north from the Peninsula as rural Fauquier County, outside the Washington, D.C., but the bulk of the population lives between the Potomac and James Rivers. Redistricting parceled most of the major Hampton Roads military installations into the surrounding congressional districts, but the 1st remains steeped in military culture, both past and present, and the Department of Defense continues to be a significant employer. Within the district lines, in 1781, George Washington's tattered and exhausted army at Yorktown finally pushed General Cornwallis to the sea where the French Navy waited: The final victory of the Revolutionary War. Today, historic Yorktown is adjacent to a Naval Weapons Station on the banks of the York River. To the north, in Caroline County, Fort A.P. Hill serves as a valuable training site for active and reserve-component units. The 1st includes within its boundaries all of 13 counties and parts of five others; all of the cities of Fredericksburg and colonial Williamsburg; the Marine Corps Base at Quantico; the more populous and developed part of Spotsylvania County; and the Northern Neck between the Rappahannock and Potomac Rivers, where Robert "King" Carter, one of the great landowners of colonial Virginia, reigned, and where George Washington and Robert E. Lee were born. In the Hampton Roads area, the 1st includes parts of Hampton, Newport News, Poquoson, Williamsburg and York County—primarily north of Mercury Boulevard, once known as Military Highway but renamed to honor the Mercury 7 astronauts. About 40% of the district's votes are cast in the Hampton Roads area and about 40% in the metro Washington orbit. Ancestrally, much of this area was Democratic. But with a large military population drawn from across the country (and with heavily black precincts placed in the adjoining 3d District), the 1st District is now reliably Republican in most elections.

The congresswoman from the 1st District is Jo Ann Davis, a Republican first elected in 2000. She grew up in the Hampton Roads area; her father worked at a gas station and drove city buses in Hampton. She graduated from Hampton Roads Business College and went to work as an executive secretary for a real estate firm for several years before becoming a stay-at-home mom, then started a real estate career in 1988. Davis was elected to the House of Delegates in 1997, defeating a 15-year incumbent who outspent her 3-to-1. When 1st District Congressman Herbert Bateman, suffering from cancer and after heart surgery, announced his retirement in January 2000, she jumped into the race three days later. She faced four other candidates for the Republican nomination, including real estate entrepreneur Paul Jost, who spent almost $1 million of his own money and won the endorsement of Governor James Gilmore. Davis, who spent less than one-tenth that sum, appealed to conservative activists, especially in the district's rural counties. She favored a Social Security lockbox, more flexibility to the states on education funding, elimination of the marriage penalty and estate taxes, and protection of Second Amendment rights. Her religious faith and modest background are a stark contrast to the Richmond aristocrats who once ruled the local Republican Party—and the state. She defeated Jost 35%–30%, with just 14,274 votes. Political consultant Michael Rothfeld was third with 22%. In the general, she faced Democrat Lawrence Davies, a Baptist minister and mayor of Fredericksburg for 20 years. The two biggest issues of the campaign were abortion rights—Davis against, Davies for—and the proposed King William reservoir, which many local officials said is required to meet the Peninsula's future water demand: Davis considered it too expensive and Davies defended it as necessary for growth. Davis won 58%–37%, with Davies winning Williamsburg, his home city of Fredericksburg plus two small counties.

In the House, Davis has been a strict conservative on cultural issues but toward the middle of House Republicans on economic and foreign policy. Not surprisingly, she got a seat on the Armed Services Committee—as did the two other freshman Republicans from the Tidewater area who took office in 2001. She joined with Virginia Rep. Bobby Scott to get signatures from nearly 200 lawmakers to urge Defense Secretary Rumsfeld to make sure that President Bush's fiscal 2004 budget includes money for timely construction of the CVNX nuclear-powered aircraft carrier, which is scheduled to be built at Newport News. Davis won passage in early 2001 of a bill to assure that survivors of military personnel killed on duty receive the full additional life insurance benefit up to $250,000; her bill, which closed an unintended loophole in a bill enacted, applied to 18 Virginia National Guard members who died in an airplane crash in Georgia, plus the victims of the terror attack on the USS *Cole* off the coast of Yemen. In early 2003, she reintroduced a bill to require the Navy to have no fewer than 375 vessels in active service, including 15 aircraft carrier battle groups and 15 amphibious ready groups.

Davis's "district first" approach gives her little visibility on Capitol Hill, but she had only write-in opposition at home in 2002 and is not likely to have much trouble winning reelection.

SECOND DISTRICT

Rep. Ed Schrock (R)

Elected 2000, 2d term; b. Apr. 6, 1941, Middletown, OH; home, Virginia Beach; Alderson Broaddus Col., B.S. 1964, American U., M.A. 1974; Baptist; married (Judy).

Military Career: U.S. Navy, 1964–88 (Vietnam).

Elected Office: VA Senate, 1995–2000.

Professional Career: Stockbroker, Kidder Peabody, 1988–94.

DC Office: 322 CHOB 20515, 202-225-4215; Fax: 202-225-4218.

District Office: Virginia Beach/Norfolk, 757-497-6859.

Committees: *Armed Services* (19th of 33 R): Projection Forces; Tactical Air & Land Forces; Total Force. *Budget* (9th of 24 R). *Government Reform* (15th of 24 R): Criminal Justice, Drug Policy & Human Resources; National Security, Emerging Threats & Intl. Relations. *Small Business* (8th of 18 R): Regulatory Reform & Oversight (Chmn.).

Group Ratings

	ADA	ACLU	AFS	LCV	CON	ITIC	NTU	COC	ACU	NTLC	CHC
2002	0	7	0	0	77	100	59	100	100	89	100
2001	0	—	0	0	—	—	67	100	100	—	—

National Journal Ratings

	2001 LIB — 2001 CONS		2002 LIB — 2002 CONS	
Economic	7% —	89%	16% —	81%
Social	0% —	81%	0% —	75%
Foreign	4% —	87%	0% —	85%

Key Votes of the 107th Congress

1. Approve Bush Tax Cuts	Y	5. Faith-Based Charities	Y
2. Limit Patients' Bill of Rights	Y	6. Bar Gays in the Boy Scouts	Y
3. Campaign Finance Reform	N	7. Ban Partial-Birth Abortion	Y
4. Ban ANWR Development	N	8. Arm Commercial Pilots	Y

9. Trade Promotion Authority	Y
10. Bar Funds for Intl. Court	Y
11. Authorize Force in Iraq	Y
12. Deny Home. Sec. Dept. Union	Y

Election Results

2002 general	Ed Schrock (R)	103,807	(83%)	($483,440)
	D.C. Amarasinghe (Green)	20,589	(16%)	($12,415)
2002 primary	Ed Schrock (R)	unopposed		
2000 general	Ed Schrock (R)	97,856	(52%)	($1,067,074)
	Jody M. Wagner (D)	90,328	(48%)	($1,117,345)
	Other	145	(1%)	

The People

Area size:	2,776 sq. mi.
Urban population:	91.7%
Rural population:	8.3%
Pop. 2000:	643,510
Median income:	$44,193
Poverty status:	8.7%
Military veterans:	20.3%

Race/Ethnic Origin

67.4% White
21.4% Black
4.0% Asian
0.4% Native Am.
0.1% Hawaiian
2.2% Two + races
0.2% Other
4.4% Hispanic Origin

Ancestry

German: 10.1%   Irish: 9.1%
English: 9.0%

2000 Presidential Vote

Bush (R)	115,512	(55%)
Gore (D)	90,256	(43%)
Other	4,940	(2%)

Cook Partisan Voting Index: R + 6

Occupation

Blue collar: 21.1%   White collar: 63.0%   Gray collar: 15.9%

The United States Navy Atlantic fleet berthed in its homeport of Norfolk is one of the great awe-inspiring sights in America, or anywhere. The aggregation of destructive power in the line of towering gray ships is probably greater than in any other single port in history. There are 76 ships based here—aircraft carriers, cruisers, destroyers, large amphibious ships, submarines, supply and logistics ships—and 133 aircraft. Norfolk has been a Navy port since 1801, and has long been recognized as one of the best natural harbors on the East Coast, one that never freezes, has a channel 50 feet deep and is within 750 miles of three-quarters of U.S. manufacturing capacity. The Norfolk Naval Station is now the world's largest naval station, situated on 4,300 acres on Sewells Point, and the Hampton Roads region as a whole is considered the world's largest naval base, where residents are always within minutes of one naval installation or another. The local Navy community—retirees, dependents, active duty and civilian personnel, workers at the Newport News Shipbuilding & Drydock—is estimated at more than 300,000 and military spending pours over $11 billion annually into the local economy.

Norfolk, once a small city, is now the state's second-largest; next-door Virginia Beach, once a beach resort and acres of swamp, is now the largest, with 425,000 people in 2000. Virginia Beach began attracting tourists when rail service began in 1883. But the city is now, like Norfolk, infused with military culture. It is home to four military installations—Oceana Naval Air Station is the city's largest employer—with 35,000 service and civilian employees and an annual payroll of over $1 billion. In a corner of Virginia Beach near shopping centers and Interstate 64 is the larger-than-life Williamsburg-style headquarters of Pat Robertson's Christian Broadcasting Network (the *700 Club* is produced here) and other Robertson operations.

The 2d Congressional District includes all of Virginia Beach, which accounts for 72% of its votes. It also includes parts of Norfolk and Hampton with mostly white residents, including the

Norfolk Navy base and Langley Air Force Base and, on a spit of land in the bay, Fort Monroe, where Jefferson Davis was confined after the Civil War. The 2001 redistricting added the two counties of the Delmarva Peninsula, Virginia's Eastern Shore, site of the annual roundup of wild Chincoteague ponies; these isolated rural counties with their fishing villages are two of the state's poorest. Surrounded by water on three sides, far from markets, they are connected to Virginia Beach by the Chesapeake Bay Bridge-Tunnel with its $10 toll. Back in the 1960s and 1970s, most of the people in the 2d District were in Norfolk, and the district often voted Democratic. Now the overwhelming majority live in communities that are suburban, and the district is heavily Republican. In 1968, the 2d voted for Hubert Humphrey, as Norfolk cast 65,000 votes and Virginia Beach 37,000. In 2000, the two cities voted for George W. Bush, as Norfolk cast 62,000 votes and Virginia Beach 150,000.

The congressman from the 2d District is Edward Schrock, one of three freshman Republicans who entered the House from Tidewater in 2001 and the one who made the biggest initial impact. He grew up in Ohio, joined the Navy in 1964 before graduating from college and served until 1988, retiring as a captain. He worked on public affairs throughout his Navy career, which included two tours in Vietnam and stints at the Pentagon, the White House, and on the West Coast, where his assignment was to ensure that Hollywood accurately portrayed the Navy. From 1989 until 1995, he was an investment adviser in Norfolk. In 1995, he was elected to the Virginia Senate, defeating a veteran Democrat. Late in the 2000 campaign, he revealed that he suffered non-Hodgkin's lymphoma in 1975, possibly as the result of exposure in Vietnam to the chemical defoliant Agent Orange. At the time, his doctors gave him six months to live and he spent months drifting in and out of a coma, while dropping to 98 pounds. As a cancer survivor, he has participated in victim support activities.

Schrock was exploring a House race even before seven-term Democrat Owen Pickett announced his retirement in 1999. With no primary opposition, Schrock became the early frontrunner in the Republican-trending district. He emphasized his military experience, legislative record and many campaign donors. He endorsed a national missile defense system, increased defense spending and improved health care for military retirees. Although he's an anti-abortion conservative who wants lower taxes, he sounded bipartisan notes on paying down the national debt, improving the environment and saving Social Security and Medicare. Schrock faced an unexpectedly strong challenge from Democratic nominee Jody Wagner, a securities lawyer, who made the race after better-known Democrats declined to run. Though a political novice, she was a successful fund-raiser, more than matching Schrock's $1 million-plus. Schrock won 52%–48%, winning 55% in Virginia Beach and 42% in Norfolk.

In the House, Schrock has taken conservative positions. He was elected president of his Republican freshman class, which gave him additional contact with the House leadership and George W. Bush, including two trips on Air Force One. On the Armed Services and Budget committees, he pushed for more money for ships and security at defense facilities. He said the Bush 2003 budget's proposed delay in construction of the CVNX aircraft carrier "makes absolutely no sense at all," and he worked with others in the House to add $229 million for that year's spending.

Although Virginia Beach has a Democratic mayor, Democrats could not find an opponent for Schrock in 2002. The Green Party candidate, Norfolk physician D.C. Amarasinghe, was jailed three weeks before the election for failure to make court-ordered payments to his ex-wife. Schrock won 83%–16%. In the 108th Congress, he sought a seat on Appropriations, but Virgil Goode's February 2002 switch to the Republican party meant there were already two Virginia Republicans on the committee; he did not get the seat.

THIRD DISTRICT

Rep. Bobby Scott (D)

Elected 1992, 6th term; b. Apr. 30, 1947, Washington, D.C.; home, Newport News; Harvard U., B.A. 1969, Boston Col., J.D. 1973; Episcopalian; single.

Military Career: Army Natl. Guard, 1970–73; Army Reserves, 1973–76.

Elected Office: VA House of Delegates, 1977–82; VA Senate, 1983–92.

Professional Career: Practicing atty., 1973–91.

DC Office: 2464 RHOB 20515, 202-225-8351; Fax: 202-225-8354; Web site: www.house.gov/scott.

District Offices: Newport News, 757-380-1000; Richmond, 804-644-4845.

Committees: *Budget* (10th of 19 D). *Judiciary* (5th of 16 D): Crime, Terrorism & Homeland Security (RMM); The Constitution.

Group Ratings

	ADA	ACLU	AFS	LCV	CON	ITIC	NTU	COC	ACU	NTLC	CHC
2002	95	100	100	63	43	25	17	42	4	6	8
2001	100	—	100	71	—	—	12	35	4	—	—

National Journal Ratings

	2001 LIB —	2001 CONS	2002 LIB —	2002 CONS
Economic	83%	15%	74%	26%
Social	90%	0%	100%	0%
Foreign	77%	22%	84%	14%

Key Votes of the 107th Congress

1. Approve Bush Tax Cuts	N	5. Faith-Based Charities	N
2. Limit Patients' Bill of Rights	N	6. Bar Gays in the Boy Scouts	N
3. Campaign Finance Reform	N	7. Ban Partial-Birth Abortion	N
4. Ban ANWR Development	Y	8. Arm Commercial Pilots	N

9. Trade Promotion Authority	N
10. Bar Funds for Intl. Court	N
11. Authorize Force in Iraq	N
12. Deny Home. Sec. Dept. Union	N

Election Results

2002 general	Bobby Scott (D)	87,521	(96%)	($195,537)
	Other	3,552	(4%)	
2002 primary	Bobby Scott (D)	unopposed		
2000 general	Bobby Scott (D)	unopposed		($250,417)

Prior Winning Percentages: 1998 (76%); 1996 (82%); 1994 (79%); 1992 (79%)

The People		Race/Ethnic Origin	Ancestry	
Area size:	1,306 sq. mi.	37.7% White	English: 5.6%	USA: 5.3%
Urban population:	92.2%	56.0% Black	German: 5.3%	
Rural population:	7.8%	1.4% Asian	**2000 Presidential Vote**	
Pop. 2000:	643,476	0.5% Native Am.	Gore (D) 134,020 (66%)	
Median income:	$32,238	0.1% Hawaiian	Bush (R) 65,724 (32%)	
Poverty status:	18.9%	1.6% Two+ races	Other 3,603 (2%)	
Military veterans:	15.5%	0.2% Other	**Cook Partisan Voting Index:** D +17	
		2.6% Hispanic Origin		

Occupation   Blue collar: 25.8%   White collar: 55.4%   Gray collar: 18.7%

The history of African-American slavery literally began along the tidal expanse of the James River. In 1607, the first English colonists chose one of the marshiest, least healthy spots along the broad river as the site of their settlement at Jamestown. Only a dozen years later, the first slave ship sailed up the James and offloaded its human cargo, giving birth to the biracial society of the American South. In the 21st century, the great plantation houses of the Tidewater, entire communities once adorned by the most impressive architecture of the day and attended by hundreds of slaves, still dot the banks of the James. Charles City County—the site of William Byrd II's Westover, Benjamin Harrison III's Berkeley, and John Carter's Shirley—also was the birthplace of two successive presidents, William Henry Harrison and John Tyler. The county's population continues to be heavily black: The demography of the plantation remains.

The 3d Congressional District is the descendant of a black-majority district formed in 1992, and redrawn twice in the 1990s after a federal court ruled it unconstitutional and then again after the 2000 Census. Now, as in earlier plans, the district jumps back and forth across the James River to string together black precincts and communities in Norfolk, Hampton and Newport News, then upriver on the Peninsula past Jamestown and Charles City County all the way to Richmond and eastern suburban Henrico County. It includes the Army's Fort Eustis and all of the majority-black city of Portsmouth—a Navy port and industrial town with a charming old section. Politically, the 3d is by far the most Democratic district in Virginia and the only black-majority district. The economy of much of the district depends heavily on the Newport News Shipbuilding & Drydock Company (acquired by Northrop Grumman in 2001). The shipyard lies over the flat neighborhoods lining the baysides, with ships looming larger than life, their turrets and superstructures bristling with armored might. During the Cold War era, Newport News built the two of the largest tankers ever made in the western hemisphere, in addition to its *Nimitz* class nuclear aircraft carriers and *Los Angeles* class nuclear attack submarines; the Navy plans to build its CVNX class nuclear carriers here. It is the biggest private employer in Virginia after Wal-Mart and Food Lion.

The congressman from the 3d District is Bobby Scott, a Democrat elected when the district was created in 1992. He grew up in Newport News, the son of a doctor, went to Harvard, where he was a classmate of Al Gore, and then to Boston College Law School. He served in the National Guard and Army Reserves and returned home to practice law in 1973. In 1977, he was elected to the Virginia House of Delegates and in 1983 to the state Senate, representing a multi-racial district in a community where, because of the military tradition of integration, biracial politics came more naturally than in other places. While there, he helped to raise the state's minimum wage and to give tax credits to businesses that donate to certain social services. In 1986 he ran a credible race for Congress in the 1st District and lost to Republican Herb Bateman, 56%–44%. In 1992 he ran in the new 3d. With his base in the Peninsula, and against two Richmond-based candidates, Scott won the crucial Democratic primary with 67% of the vote. He is the first black member of Congress elected from Virginia since Reconstruction.

Scott has had a solidly liberal voting record, except on occasional foreign and defense issues. He has become one of the House's most outspoken civil libertarians. He opposes the death penalty. He sought unsuccessfully to delete language mandating a life sentence for a second sex offense against a minor. When bipartisan coalitions passed legislation to permit states to display the Ten Commandments in schools or government buildings, he raised First Amendment objections, as he did to George W. Bush's plan to fund faith-based social programs. After September 11 he opposed the USA Patriot Act, arguing that it might promote racial profiling. In June 2002, he was one of three members to oppose the condemnation of a federal court decision declaring unconstitutional the words "one nation under God" in the Pledge of Allegiance. "We ought to be standing up for unpopular decisions" and not voting for a resolution that "everyone knows is stupid, but it sounds popular." Occasionally, he has stood against the liberal mainstream, as when he was one of 12 Democrats voting against the Shays-Meehan campaign reform bill, which he viewed as unconstitutional. Scott has had some success on civil liberties, as with enactment of the bipartisan Death in Custody Act requiring states to report such information. "Bobby Scott is our conscience," said Massachusetts Rep. William Delahunt.

On the Judiciary Committee, Scott spoke out often against what he considered an unfair and partisan proceeding in the Clinton impeachment. He was the only Democrat to vote against Rick Boucher's motion to censure Clinton. But he also has shown skill as a consensus-builder. At the same time that he was engaging in partisan warfare in the highly publicized impeachment hearings, Scott took an active role in the highly technical and carefully bipartisan proceedings in the special committee on China chaired by Rep. Christopher Cox. He helped build consensus for a unanimous report on an intellectually difficult and politically sensitive issue. One of his goals is affordable health care for all. Remembering how his father had been denied staff privileges in a

Newport News hospital, he vowed during the Clinton health care debate that any health care bill would prohibit racial discrimination against patients and health care providers.

Scott is eager to defend his views with voters. In 2002, he objected when Republican redistricters increased the Democratic percentage in his district; he thought, correctly, that they were trying to put the next-door 4th District out of Democrats' reach. "I think that your best shot is telling the truth. Then, if somebody comes and challenges you on it, you respond." But he has had little need to do so lately: he was unopposed in 2000 and 2002. He has considered running for governor, but yielded to party leaders who had other ideas.

FOURTH DISTRICT

Rep. Randy Forbes (R)

Elected June 2001, 1st term; b. Feb. 17, 1952, Chesapeake; home, Chesapeake; Randolph-Macon Col., B.A. 1974, U. of VA, J.D. 1977; Baptist; married (Shirley).

Elected Office: VA House of Del., 1989–97; VA Senate, 1997–01.

Professional Career: Practicing atty., 1977-present.

DC Office: 307 CHOB 20515, 202-225-6365; Fax: 202-226-1170; Web site: www.house.gov/forbes/.

District Offices: Chesapeake, 757-382-0080; Colonial Heights, 804-526-4969; Emporia, 434-634-5575.

Committees: *Armed Services* (21st of 33 R): Readiness; Tactical Air & Land Forces. *Judiciary* (17th of 21 R): Courts, the Internet & Intellectual Property; Crime, Terrorism & Homeland Security; The Constitution. *Science* (19th of 25 R): Space & Aeronautics.

Group Ratings (Only Served Partial Term)

	ADA	ACLU	AFS	LCV	CON	ITIC	NTU	COC	ACU	NTLC	CHC
2002	0	8	0	0	95	100	61	85	100	91	50
2001	0	—	0	0	—	—	—	94	100	—	—

National Journal Ratings (Only Served Partial Term)

	2001 LIB —	2001 CONS		2002 LIB —	2002 CONS
Economic	*	—	*	28%	69%
Social	0%	—	81%	0%	75%
Foreign	16%	—	85%	0%	85%

Key Votes of the 107th Congress (Only Served Partial Term)

1. Approve Bush Tax Cuts	*	5. Faith-Based Charities	Y	9. Trade Promotion Authority	Y
2. Limit Patients' Bill of Rights	Y	6. Bar Gays in the Boy Scouts	Y	10. Bar Funds for Intl. Court	Y
3. Campaign Finance Reform	N	7. Ban Partial-Birth Abortion	Y	11. Authorize Force in Iraq	Y
4. Ban ANWR Development	N	8. Arm Commercial Pilots	Y	12. Deny Home. Sec. Dept. Union	Y

Election Results

2002 general	Randy Forbes (R)	108,733	(98%)	($1,668,314)
	Other	2,308	(2%)	
2002 primary	Randy Forbes (R)	unopposed		
2001 special	Randy Forbes (R)	70,926	(52%)	($305,662)
	Louise Lucas (D)	65,189	(48%)	($375,018)
2000 general	Norman Sisisky (D)	unopposed		($56,828)

The People		Race/Ethnic Origin	Ancestry	
Area size:	4,575 sq. mi.	62.0% White	USA: 10.0%	English: 8.6%
Urban population:	70.9%	33.1% Black	German: 7.2%	
Rural population:	29.1%	1.3% Asian	**2000 Presidential Vote**	
Pop. 2000:	643,477	0.3% Native Am.	Bush (R)..............131,834 (54%)	
Median income:	$45,249	0.0% Hawaiian	Gore (D)..............107,553 (44%)	
Poverty status:	9.5%	1.1% Two+ races	Other....................3,690 (2%)	
Military veterans:	16.2%	0.1% Other	**Cook Partisan Voting Index:** R + 5	
		2.0% Hispanic Origin		

Occupation	Blue collar: 27.6%	White collar: 57.8%	Gray collar: 14.6%

The clash of arms resounds through much of the history of Tidewater Virginia. The Tidewater was the scene of the final victory of the Revolutionary War and saw bitter fighting more than 80 years later in the Civil War, as Union troops invested the battlements of the small industrial city of Petersburg, 25 miles south of Richmond. Today, the Tidewater region boasts one of the densest concentrations of military power in the world: The Hampton Roads area has the United States's largest accumulation of Navy bases, while Fort Lee, the big Army base near Petersburg, provides 6,800 local jobs and an estimated $686 million impact on the local economy.

The 4th Congressional District includes much of the Tidewater south of the James River. About half its people are in the Hampton Roads area, mostly in the fast-growing suburbs of Chesapeake and Suffolk. Suffolk's sandy loam soil is the eastern edge of Virginia's Peanut Belt, nearly all of which is in the 4th, where farmers begin planting in late April or early May and wait five months for the crop to reach maturity. The district also takes in the flat lands of Southside Virginia fanning south from the James River. These were tobacco lands when the English first settled them in the 17th century; today they also produce peanuts and Smithfield hams. The district also includes all of Petersburg and Hopewell, with its Honeywell plant facing 18th century plantations. The 2001 redistricting removed majority-black Portsmouth from the district and added heavily white parts of suburban Chesterfield County outside Richmond; this reduced the 4th's black percentage from 39% to 33% and raised its Bush 2000 percentage 50% to 54%.

The congressman from the 4th District is Randy Forbes, a Republican who won a June 2001 special election. Forbes grew up in Chesapeake, majored in government at Randolph-Macon and graduated from the University of Virginia Law School. His first job in politics was as an aide to the Democratic member of the House of Delegates from Chesapeake. When his boss retired in 1989, Forbes ran for and won the seat as a Republican. Four years later, when Republicans were still in the minority, he became the party's floor leader. In 1997 he was elected to the state Senate. Forbes was a classmate and friend of Governors George Allen and Jim Gilmore in law school, and in 1996 Allen made him Republican state chairman; he helped engineer the historic Republican 1997 sweep of all three statewide offices.

In early 2001, Forbes was a leading candidate for lieutenant governor. When 10-term Democratic Congressman Norman Sisisky died in March eight days after cancer surgery, national and state Republican leaders asked Forbes to run in what was then a competitive seat. The nominee was chosen at a convention, and Forbes won by forging unity in the delegations from Chesapeake and Portsmouth, then the district's two largest cities. He got a break when the strongest Democrat, Sisisky's son Mark, declined to run. Democrats chose state Senator Louise Lucas of Portsmouth, who is African-American and since 1992 held a majority-black seat. Lucas worked for 18 years at the Norfolk Naval Shipyard, where she became its first woman shipfitter. Both national parties and their interest-group allies spent heavily. Republicans attacked Lucas for opposing repeal of the sales tax on non-prescription drugs and for supporting a gasoline tax increase. Democrats criticized Forbes for backing "privatization" of Social Security. In what became an early battleground for similar exchanges in 2002, Forbes said that he favored George W. Bush's proposal to let younger workers invest some of their payroll taxes in individual investment accounts, but his ads emphasized that he would preserve current benefits—"every penny of it." The Lucas campaign did an effective job of turning out her base vote. In a half-dozen heavily black precincts in Portsmouth, Lucas got more than 98% of the vote; she carried the city 63%–37%. But Forbes more than overcame this by winning 61%–39% in more populous Chesapeake and won a majority in seven of the 10 rural counties, for an overall win of 52%–48%. Forbes's victory was only the fourth time since 1977 that the president's party won a special election for a House seat that the other party has held.

In the House, Forbes voted with conservatives and got seats on the Armed Services, Judiciary and Science committees. The Republicans' redistricting, by removing Portsmouth and adding part of Chesterfield County, significantly strengthened Forbes. Lucas pondered a rematch but decided not to run. And so a district held for 19 years by a Democrat went Republican by default.

FIFTH DISTRICT

Rep. Virgil Goode (R)

Elected 1996, 4th term; b. Oct. 17, 1946, Richmond; home, Rocky Mount; U. of Richmond, B.A. 1969, U. of VA, J.D. 1973; Baptist; married (Lucy).

Military Career: VA Natl. Guard, 1969–75.

Elected Office: VA Senate, 1973–96.

Professional Career: Practicing atty., 1973–96.

DC Office: 1520 LHOB 20515, 202-225-4711; Fax: 202-225-5681; Web site: www.house.gov/goode.

District Offices: Charlottesville, 804-295-6372; Danville, 804-792-1280; Farmville, 804-392-8331; Rocky Mount, 540-484-1254.

Committees: *Appropriations* (26th of 36 R): Agriculture, Rural Development, & FDA; Military Construction; VA, HUD & Independent Agencies (Vice Chmn.).

Group Ratings

	ADA	ACLU	AFS	LCV	CON	ITIC	NTU	COC	ACU	NTLC	CHC
2002	5	7	11	13	25	50	65	75	96	97	100
2001	10	—	10	7	—	—	72	83	96	—	—

National Journal Ratings

	2001 LIB — 2001 CONS		2002 LIB — 2002 CONS	
Economic	12%	88%	33%	67%
Social	0%	81%	0%	75%
Foreign	29%	69%	46%	53%

Key Votes of the 107th Congress

1. Approve Bush Tax Cuts	Y	5. Faith-Based Charities	Y	9. Trade Promotion Authority	N
2. Limit Patients' Bill of Rights	Y	6. Bar Gays in the Boy Scouts	Y	10. Bar Funds for Intl. Court	Y
3. Campaign Finance Reform	N	7. Ban Partial-Birth Abortion	Y	11. Authorize Force in Iraq	Y
4. Ban ANWR Development	N	8. Arm Commercial Pilots	Y	12. Deny Home. Sec. Dept. Union	Y

Election Results

2002 general	Virgil Goode (R)	95,360	(63%)	($707,704)
	Meredith Richards (D)	54,805	(36%)	($215,406)
2002 primary	Virgil Goode (R)	unopposed		
2000 general	Virgil Goode (I)	143,312	(67%)	($581,016)
	John W. Boyd, Jr. (D)	65,387	(31%)	($38,455)
	Other	4,006	(2%)	

Prior Winning Percentages: 1998 (100%); 1996 (61%)

The People		Race/Ethnic Origin	Ancestry	
Area size:	9,054 sq. mi.	72.4% White	USA: 14.7%	English: 9.0%
Urban population:	36.0%	23.9% Black	German: 6.6%	
Rural population:	64.0%	1.0% Asian	**2000 Presidential Vote**	
Pop. 2000:	643,497	0.2% Native Am.	Bush (R)..............137,223	(55%)
Median income:	$35,739	0.0% Hawaiian	Gore (D)..............102,814	(41%)
Poverty status:	13.2%	0.8% Two+ races	Other.....................8,907	(4%)
Military veterans:	13.1%	0.1% Other	**Cook Partisan Voting Index: R + 8**	
		1.6% Hispanic Origin		

Occupation   Blue collar: 31.7%   White collar: 53.3%   Gray collar: 15.0%

Southside Virginia is a geographic name that for years was shorthand for a state of mind. Here is Appomattox Court House, in the serene little hamlet where Robert E. Lee surrendered to his onetime subordinate Ulysses S. Grant; here is Danville, where the tobacco auction originated in 1858; here also is Prince Edward County, where Harry Byrd's massive resistance shut down public schools in 1957 rather than obey a federal court desegregation order. This land north of the dividing line Colonel William Byrd surveyed in 1728 has some variety. Its eastern counties are flat and humid—frontier in the late colonial period, plantation country by 1800, now peanut fields and pine forests. Along U.S. 58, just north of Byrd's dividing line, are the vestiges of Virginia's Tobacco Road. In South Hill, the Tobacco Farm Life Museum pays tribute to that heritage, though only one of six tobacco warehouses is still in business. To the west, into the Piedmont, the land gradually gets hillier. Here are abandoned textile mills and furniture manufacturing centers of Danville and Martinsville, places that reminisce fondly about the last period of textile industry growth that peaked in 1973. Nearby is Bedford, site of the new D-Day Memorial, which lost more men per capita, 23 of its 35 soldiers, in the Normandy invasion than any other in the nation. Westward, nearer to the mountains, are more livestock and less tobacco, and the thick syrupy tones of the Southside Virginia accent turn to mountain twangs.

The 5th District consists of much of Southside Virginia, west of metropolitan Richmond, and spreads as far north as the Blue Ridge Mountains. It includes all of liberal Charlottesville and surrounding Albemarle County (a rapidly growing swing county), but skirts around Lynchburg. Historically, politics here were Democratic, segregationist and conservative, run by chain-smoking local bankers and courthouse lawyers. Such Democrats are a rare breed these days, on the way to becoming extinct, and Southside is becoming part of the Republican heartland of Virginia.

The congressman from the 5th District is Virgil Goode (rhymes with mood), elected as a Democrat in 1996, an Independent for two years, and officially a Republican since February 2002. Goode grew up in Franklin County, where his father was a prominent enough figure that part of U.S. 220 was named after him. He graduated from the University of Richmond and the University of Virginia Law School. In 1973, the same year he graduated from law school, he was elected to the Virginia Senate, at 27. In 1994, Goode ran against scandal-beleaguered Senator Charles Robb in the Democratic primary; he lost 58%–34%, but showed local strength. In 1995, his re-election in a Republican-leaning state Senate district enabled Democrats to hold control of the Senate. In 1996, when conservative Democrat L.F. Payne retired, Goode seemed the only Democrat with a strong chance to win the district. He ran emphasizing bipartisan cooperation with the slogan on the pencils and emery boards he handed out to voters: "Work together in Congress." Republicans ran George Landrith, a former Albemarle County school board member, who lost 53%–47% to Payne in 1994. Goode won by an impressive 61%–36%.

In the House, Goode compiled an increasingly conservative voting record. He joined the Blue Dogs and supported the Shays-Meehan campaign finance bill. By 1999 he had the most conservative voting record of any House Democrat. He passionately opposed one of the Clinton White House's favorite projects, the bill to curb tobacco consumption: "I'm not going to support legislation that bankrupts the companies, destroys the family farm and relegates land to a place where hope is a stranger and mercy will never reach!"

Goode was one of 31 Democrats to vote for the Republicans' impeachment inquiry, and in December 1998 he voted for the impeachment of Clinton, evidently not a close issue for him.

"The party line says that lying under oath in a court proceeding is not an impeachable offense. I disagree with that." In 1999 he kept voting with Republicans on key issues—on gun control in June, on the tax cut in July, on the budget that passed in October. Republican leaders had kept in touch with him through Republican neighbor Bob Goodlatte, who frequently urged him to switch parties. In January 2000, Goode announced that he would no longer be a member of the Democratic Caucus and would run for re-election as an Independent. He said that he opposed Democrats' positions on spending and tobacco, and would attend meetings of the House Republican Conference and contribute to their campaign committee. Republicans promptly gave him a seat on the Appropriations Committee. In February, in Danville at the Piedmont Big Sale tobacco warehouse, he endorsed George W. Bush for president.

In his well-financed 2000 campaign, he attacked the Clinton administration for neglecting the woes of the Southside textile and apparel industries—Goode has voted against free trade agreements, including PNTR for China and trade promotion authority—and campaigned with George Allen. Opposed by a Democrat who headed a black farmers' advocacy group, he won 67%–31%, carrying every city and county except the university town of Charlottesville. In February 2002, when he completed his evolution by formalizing his affiliation as a Republican, he offered a practical explanation: On certain voting machines, independents are listed "off-center," and "we had to do significant advertising" to alert voters. He said that the switch would not change his stand on issues, including his continued opposition to trade promotion authority. Some observers thought that redistricting was the reason Goode left the Democratic party; it was clear in January 2000 that Republicans would control the process, and they could have put his Franklin County home into the 9th District represented by Democrat Rick Boucher. Instead, they made only minor adjustments to the lines in their June 2001 plan. In 2002, Goode was challenged by a Charlottesville councilwoman and psychologist who had help from Goode's top aide when he was a Democrat. Goode won handily, 63%–36%, losing only liberal Charlottesville (by a 2-to-1 margin) and heavily black Brunswick County.

SIXTH DISTRICT

Rep. Bob Goodlatte (R)

Elected 1992, 6th term; b. Sept. 22, 1952, Holyoke, MA; home, Roanoke; Bates Col., B.A. 1974, Washington & Lee Law Schl., J.D. 1977; Christian Scientist; married (Maryellen).

Professional Career: Dist. Dir., U.S. Rep. Caldwell Butler, 1977–79; Practicing atty., 1979–92.

DC Office: 2240 RHOB 20515, 202-225-5431; Fax: 202-225-9681; Web site: www.house.gov/goodlatte.

District Offices: Harrisonburg, 540-432-2391; Lynchburg, 804-845-8306; Roanoke, 540-857-2672; Staunton, 540-885-3861.

Committees: *Agriculture* (Chmn. of 27 R). *Judiciary* (6th of 21 R): Courts, the Internet & Intellectual Property; Crime, Terrorism & Homeland Security. *Select Committee on Homeland Security* (17th of 27 R): Cybersecurity, Science and Research & Development; Infrastructure & Border Security.

Group Ratings

	ADA	ACLU	AFS	LCV	CON	ITIC	NTU	COC	ACU	NTLC	CHC
2002	0	7	0	0	25	100	60	95	100	100	100
2001	0	—	0	0	—	—	72	91	96	—	—

National Journal Ratings

	2001 LIB	—	2001 CONS		2002 LIB	—	2002 CONS
Economic	0%	—	94%		21%	—	73%
Social	0%	—	81%		0%	—	75%
Foreign	4%	—	87%		0%	—	85%

Key Votes of the 107th Congress

1. Approve Bush Tax Cuts	Y	5. Faith-Based Charities	Y	9. Trade Promotion Authority	Y
2. Limit Patients' Bill of Rights	Y	6. Bar Gays in the Boy Scouts	Y	10. Bar Funds for Intl. Court	Y
3. Campaign Finance Reform	N	7. Ban Partial-Birth Abortion	Y	11. Authorize Force in Iraq	Y
4. Ban ANWR Development	N	8. Arm Commercial Pilots	Y	12. Deny Home. Sec. Dept. Union	Y

Election Results

2002 general	Bob Goodlatte (R)	105,530	(97%)	($562,236)
	Other	3,202	(3%)	
2002 primary	Bob Goodlatte (R)	unopposed		
2000 general	Bob Goodlatte (R)	unopposed		($395,342)

Prior Winning Percentages: 1998 (69%); 1996 (67%); 1994 (100%); 1992 (60%)

The People		Race/Ethnic Origin	Ancestry	
Area size:	5,664 sq. mi.	84.8% White	USA: 13.4%	German: 11.9%
Urban population:	64.7%	10.9% Black	English: 8.9%	
Rural population:	35.3%	0.9% Asian	**2000 Presidential Vote**	
Pop. 2000:	643,504	0.2% Native Am.	Bush (R)	147,961 (60%)
Median income:	$37,773	0.0% Hawaiian	Gore (D)	92,407 (37%)
Poverty status:	11.0%	1.0% Two+ races	Other	6,984 (3%)
Military veterans:	13.7%	0.1% Other	**Cook Partisan Voting Index:** R +12	
		2.0% Hispanic Origin		

Occupation   Blue collar: 28.5%   White collar: 55.9%   Gray collar: 15.6%

The sturdy men and women who settled the Valley of Virginia west of the Blue Ridge were quite different from the "second sons" of the European aristocracy who cleared the marshy forests of the Tidewater and built grand plantations there. Even before the Revolutionary War, Englishmen and Scots, German Protestants and Mennonites and Moravians—members of religious communities and fiercely independent farmers—poured down the great Wagon Road from Pennsylvania to the Valley. They were looking not for the flat, mahogany-brown land that eastern tobacco growers sought, but for fields, which could support wheat, corn and hay, crops which could be rotated, and which an individual farmer and his family could handle. That same independent spirit nurtured the growth of higher education here. In Lexington alone are Washington and Lee University, which Robert E. Lee headed, and the Virginia Military Institute, where Stonewall Jackson taught philosophy and artillery tactics, and which began admitting women in 1996 under order from the U.S. Supreme Court. A quartet of the South's most distinguished private women's colleges are only a short drive away: Mary Baldwin College at Staunton, Randolph-Macon Woman's College at Lynchburg, Sweet Briar College at Sweet Briar, and Hollins College at Roanoke, farther south in the Valley. Industry flourished here more than in most of Virginia east of the Blue Ridge. In the 19th century the Norfolk and Southern Railroad established its chief junction at Roanoke; as the years passed the city became the railroad's headquarters, and many major companies have plants here.

The 6th Congressional District covers the heart of the Valley of Virginia, from Strasburg south to Roanoke, and crosses over the Blue Ridge to take in Lynchburg, the home of Jerry Falwell's Thomas Road Baptist Church and Liberty University. Politically, this area has a Republican tradition hospitable to economic assistance for the little guy, and it fiercely opposed Harry Byrd Democrats. But in more recent years, the ancestral conservatism of Byrd Democrats and the feisty politics of the mountain rebels have melded into a single conservative Republicanism, more populist than elite in tone, as concerned with moral values as economic freedom, prickly about interference from Washington or even Richmond. Statewide, the 6th was only slightly behind the 7th District as the strongest supporter of George W. Bush in 2000.

The congressman from the 6th District is Bob Goodlatte (pronounced *GOOD-lat*), a Republican first elected in 1992. Goodlatte grew up in Massachusetts, attended college in Maine and then law school at Washington & Lee, and went to work in Congressman Caldwell Butler's office in Roanoke. Goodlatte then practiced law and stayed active in politics; in 1992, when Democratic

Congressman Jim Olin retired, Goodlatte was nominated by convention and won the general 60%–40%.

Goodlatte has compiled a mostly conservative voting record. He sponsored the House-passed bill to limit class-action lawsuits against tobacco companies, gun makers and others companies, and a separate bill to give federal courts jurisdiction over all class-action suits with claims exceeding $2 million. He favors scrapping the current tax code and replacing it with a much simpler tax. He has proposed limited campaign finance measures including requiring candidates' supporters to identify themselves on polls of more than 1,200 respondents, repealing voter registration by mail, banning fundraising in the White House and requiring disclosure of contributions and expenditures by computer.

With 9th District neighbor Rick Boucher, Goodlatte has become a leader among House members working on technology issues. He is chairman of Speaker Dennis Hastert's High-Tech Working Group and co-chairs the Congressional Internet Caucus with Boucher where they have encouraged open and non-taxed access to broadband technology. "Really, this technology is the future of my district," he told *National Journal.* The Judiciary Committee, on which each has served, has handled some of these issues. He has been chief sponsor, with Silicon Valley Democrat Zoe Lofgren, of bills to liberalize export controls on encryption technology. Although these were opposed by the NSA and FBI, which wanted law enforcement and intelligence agencies to possess keys to encryption, the Clinton White House agreed to the legislation. Goodlatte sponsored the Communications Decency Act, allowing censorship of obscene material on the Internet, which was overturned by the Supreme Court. He sponsored a law imposing tougher penalties on commercial counterfeiters, especially important in the software industry.

In 2003, Goodlatte became chairman of the Agriculture Committee. Although he had been less active on farm issues, he sponsored proposals to expand federal assistance to food banks. As a subcommittee chairman during the previous Congress, he chaired a score of hearings on the operations of the Agriculture Department. And he contends that his heavily agricultural district has given him an understanding of the issues that affect rural America and the nation.

Goodlatte has been consistently reelected without difficulty. His only modest challenge came in 1998 from David Bowers, mayor of Roanoke. Goodlatte was confident enough to leave $460,000 cash on hand after the campaign, which he won 69%–31%, carrying every city and county and winning in Roanoke 58%–42%. In the past two cycles, he got only write-in opposition. Goodlatte announced in July 2002 that he will abandon his self-imposed 12-year term limit, which would have expired in 2004.

SEVENTH DISTRICT

Rep. Eric Cantor (R)

Elected 2000, 2d term; b. June 6, 1963, Richmond; home, Richmond; George Washington U., B.A. 1985, Col. of William & Mary, J.D. 1988, Columbia U., M.S., 1989; Jewish; married (Diana).

Elected Office: VA House of Del., 1991–2000.

Professional Career: Practicing atty., 1990–00.

DC Office: 329 CHOB 20515, 202-225-2815; Fax: 202-225-0011; Web site: cantor.house.gov.

District Offices: Culpeper, 540-825-8960; Richmond, 804-747-4073.

Committees: *Chief Deputy Majority Whip. Ways & Means* (24th of 24 R): Human Resources; Oversight.

Group Ratings

	ADA	ACLU	AFS	LCV	CON	ITIC	NTU	COC	ACU	NTLC	CHC
2002	0	7	0	0	67	100	57	100	100	97	100
2001	0	—	0	0	—	—	70	100	100	—	—

National Journal Ratings

	2001 LIB —	2001 CONS	2002 LIB —	2002 CONS
Economic	0% —	94%	9% —	87%
Social	0% —	81%	0% —	75%
Foreign	33% —	60%	0% —	85%

Key Votes of the 107th Congress

1. Approve Bush Tax Cuts	Y	5. Faith-Based Charities	Y	9. Trade Promotion Authority	Y
2. Limit Patients' Bill of Rights	Y	6. Bar Gays in the Boy Scouts	Y	10. Bar Funds for Intl. Court	Y
3. Campaign Finance Reform	N	7. Ban Partial-Birth Abortion	Y	11. Authorize Force in Iraq	Y
4. Ban ANWR Development	N	8. Arm Commercial Pilots	Y	12. Deny Home. Sec. Dept. Union	Y

Election Results

2002 general	Eric Cantor (R)	113,658	(69%)	($1,402,415)
	Ben "Cooter" Jones (D)	49,854	(30%)	($166,332)
2002 primary	Eric Cantor (R)	unopposed		
2000 general	Eric Cantor (R)	192,652	(67%)	($1,336,548)
	Warren A. Stewart (D)	94,935	(33%)	($70,430)

The People		Race/Ethnic Origin	Ancestry	
Area size:	3,556 sq. mi.	78.2% White	English: 12.1% USA: 10.6%	
Urban population:	70.0%	16.1% Black	German: 10.2%	
Rural population:	30.0%	2.3% Asian	**2000 Presidential Vote**	
Pop. 2000:	643,499	0.3% Native Am.	Bush (R)................172,425	(61%)
Median income:	$50,990	0.0% Hawaiian	Gore (D)................105,504	(37%)
Poverty status:	6.1%	1.1% Two+ races	Other....................6,261	(2%)
Military veterans:	13.5%	0.1% Other	**Cook Partisan Voting Index:** R +12	
		2.0% Hispanic Origin		

Occupation	Blue collar: 19.4%	White collar: 68.4%	Gray collar: 12.2%

In the center of Virginia, on a hill in downtown Richmond above the James River, is Thomas Jefferson's Capitol, one of the first classical-style buildings in North America, chaste and simple in the Jefferson style. A mile or so west is Monument Avenue, Richmond's grand 140-foot-wide boulevard, punctuated by circles, each with a statue of a Confederate hero—Robert E. Lee (62 feet tall, dedicated Memorial Day 1890), Jeb Stuart, Jefferson Davis, Stonewall Jackson, Matthew Fountain Maury, "the Pathfinder of the Sea." Richmond is a monument to Jefferson and to the Confederacy; its metro area is only the third largest in the state, but it still sets the tone for Virginia, and is the home of many of the state's great institutions—Dominion Resources, Main Street banks, big law firms, and the *Richmond Times-Dispatch*. Richmond's metro area has long since grown out past its city borders, covering almost all of suburban Henrico and Chesterfield counties and spreading out into what was until recently countryside. For many years Richmond was riven by sharp racial differences. It was from here that Virginia's leaders called for massive resistance to desegregation in the 1950s, and when Richmond elected its first black-majority council in the 1970s, the outgoing council deeded the statue of Lee to the state for fear it would be torn down. Now Richmond has come to a better place. Blacks have been a majority in the city for two decades now, and in 1989 Virginia elected a black governor, Douglas Wilder, who grew up on Church Hill, in a segregated neighborhood overlooking the Capitol. The state's Martin Luther King Jr. holiday pays homage to Confederate heroes and to the civil rights leader, and a statue of Richmond-born African-American tennis champion Arthur Ashe has been added to Monument Avenue. Politically there remain differences. Black-majority Richmond is solidly Democratic; Henrico and Chester-field and the counties beyond are heavily Republican.

The 7th Congressional District includes most of the area surrounding Richmond, but the black precincts in the city and Henrico County are mostly in the black-majority 3d District, which extends downriver along the James to Newport News and Norfolk. The growth in the suburbs has led activists to criticize the sprawl as jeopardizing the local quality of life. The district also has an extension that runs north past James Madison's home at Montpelier to Rappahannock County and the Blue Ridge Mountains. But 76% of the 7th's population is in metro Richmond. Even after redistricting moved half of Chesterfield County to the 4th District in an effort to strengthen the party there, this remains the most heavily Republican district in Virginia.

The congressman from the 7th District is Eric Cantor, a Republican elected in 2000. He grew up in Henrico County, graduated from George Washington University and William and Mary Law School and got a master's degree in real estate from Columbia University. He then began practicing law in his family's firm in Richmond. In 1991, he was elected to the first of five terms in Virginia's House of Delegates. In the legislature, he was a leading ally of business, sponsoring a bill to limit the liability of Philip Morris in a Florida court decree and opposing restrictions on telemarketers. When 7th District Congressman Tom Bliley, after 20 years in the House, announced his retirement, Cantor entered the race. He had a big advantage: He served as Bliley's campaign chairman for six years and had the backing of Bliley's political organization. He endorsed a $1,000 per child education tax credit, elimination of the marriage tax penalty, and an increase in the maximum IRA contribution. Cantor, who is the only Jewish Republican in the House, has strongly supported Israel, and secured funding for a new building for the Virginia Holocaust Museum.

Still, Cantor faced a serious contest in the Republican primary, which was tantamount to victory here. His opponent was state Senator Stephen Martin. Martin emphasized his low-income background and he had a solid base of social and religious conservatives. Their contest turned negative: Cantor attacked Martin for supporting a back-door pay raise for legislators; Martin questioned Cantor's business dealings. Both supported gun rights and abolition of the National Endowment for the Arts, and opposed racial quotas and most abortions. Cantor supported PNTR with China; Martin was opposed. Cantor, who was well-known in his Henrico County base, had a big fundraising advantage and put on a substantial advertising campaign. Martin raised less than $200,000—a quarter of what Cantor spent in the primary. Cantor got the endorsement of Governor Jim Gilmore, but won the primary by only 263 votes. Cantor won 74% in Henrico, while Martin won 77% in his Chesterfield County base; each county cast about one-third of the total vote. In the general election, Cantor beat former Goochland County school superintendent Warren A. Stewart by 67%–33%.

In the House, Cantor has been reliably conservative in the Richmond tradition. His first term seemed uneventful. His first bill provided a tax credit of $1,000 per child for all parents with school-age children in public or private schools until they graduate from high school. He passed in the House a bill that would retain the image of Monticello on the nickel starting in 2006, after the U.S. Mint had announced a redesign to commemorate the bicentennial of the Louisiana Purchase and the Lewis and Clark expedition. With his knowledge of the Middle East and his outspoken support for Israel, Cantor also became chairman of the House Republican task force on terrorism and unconventional warfare. But his more significant activity was outside the public spotlight as a member of Tom DeLay's Whip team. His laborious and mostly behind-the-scenes efforts to assure support for Republican initiatives impressed House leaders and presaged a meteoric rise to leadership. In December 2002, incoming Majority Whip Roy Blunt unexpectedly named Cantor as his chief deputy whip, giving him a seat at the party's leadership table and handing him the often thankless task of keeping track of his colleagues' sentiments on pending legislation. The appointment also was seen as part of DeLay's efforts to reach out to Jewish voters. Cantor also sought and won a seat on the Ways and Means Committee.

Cantor's reelection probably received more public attention than it warranted. His opponent was Ben Jones, who served two terms in the House from Georgia before he lost a 1992 Democratic primary, but who remains better known for his "Cooter" character in *The Dukes of Hazzard*. Jones settled in Rappahannock County, where he opened two stores capitalizing on Cooter's popularity and was a member of a successful band. But his campaign was hardly a joy ride. Jones picked up little national Democratic support, and Cantor largely ignored Jones and won 69%–30%; Jones carried Rappahannock County, which usually votes Republican. Even before he was tapped for the Republican leadership, the *Times-Dispatch* editorialized that Cantor's victory margin showed that he had become "indispensable" in Washington. It's not likely that he will have to worry about reelection for the remainder of this decade.

EIGHTH DISTRICT

Rep. Jim Moran (D)

Elected 1990, 7th term; b. May 16, 1945, Buffalo, NY; home, Alexandria; Col. of Holy Cross, B.A. 1967, City U. of NY, 1968, U. of Pittsburgh, M.P.A. 1970; Catholic; divorced.

Elected Office: Alexandria City Cncl., 1979–82; Alexandria Vice Mayor, 1982–84, Alexandria Mayor, 1985–90.

Professional Career: Budget analyst & auditor, U.S. Dept. of H.E.W., 1968–74; Fiscal policy spec., Library of Congress, 1974–76; Staff, U.S. Senate Approp. Cmte., 1976–80; Investment broker, 1980–88.

DC Office: 2239 RHOB 20515, 202-225-4376; Fax: 202-225-0017; Web site: www.house.gov/moran.

District Office: Alexandria, 703-971-4700.

Committees: *Appropriations* (12th of 29 D): Defense; Interior; The Legislative Branch (RMM). *Budget* (2d of 19 D).

Group Ratings

	ADA	ACLU	AFS	LCV	CON	ITIC	NTU	COC	ACU	NTLC	CHC
2002	70	73	89	63	91	88	30	68	21	11	0
2001	85	—	90	86	—	—	15	57	8	—	—

National Journal Ratings

	2001 LIB —	2001 CONS	2002 LIB —	2002 CONS
Economic	64%	36%	58%	42%
Social	72%	27%	74%	19%
Foreign	75%	25%	66%	33%

Key Votes of the 107th Congress

1. Approve Bush Tax Cuts	N	5. Faith-Based Charities	N	9. Trade Promotion Authority	Y
2. Limit Patients' Bill of Rights	N	6. Bar Gays in the Boy Scouts	N	10. Bar Funds for Intl. Court	N
3. Campaign Finance Reform	Y	7. Ban Partial-Birth Abortion	Y	11. Authorize Force in Iraq	N
4. Ban ANWR Development	Y	8. Arm Commercial Pilots	N	12. Deny Home. Sec. Dept. Union	N

Election Results

2002 general	Jim Moran (D)	102,759	(60%)	($1,615,275)
	Scott Tate (R)	64,121	(37%)	($83,860)
	Other	4,919	(3%)	
2002 primary	Jim Moran (D)	unopposed		
2000 general	Jim Moran (D)	164,178	(63%)	($1,203,058)
	Demaris H. Miller (R)	88,262	(34%)	($204,046)
	Other	6,759	(3%)	

Prior Winning Percentages: 1998 (67%); 1996 (66%); 1994 (59%); 1992 (56%); 1990 (52%)

The People		Race/Ethnic Origin	Ancestry	
Area size:	125 sq. mi.	57.1% White	German: 9.6%	Irish: 9.0%
Urban population:	100.0%	13.4% Black	English: 8.4%	
Rural population:	0.0%	9.5% Asian	**2000 Presidential Vote**	
Pop. 2000:	643,503	0.2% Native Am.	Gore (D) 152,940	(57%)
Median income:	$63,430	0.1% Hawaiian	Bush (R) 101,788	(38%)
Poverty status:	7.5%	3.0% Two+ races	Other 11,692	(4%)
Military veterans:	11.3%	0.3% Other	**Cook Partisan Voting Index:** D +10	
		16.4% Hispanic Origin		
Occupation	Blue collar: 10.7%	White collar: 77.0%	Gray collar: 12.3%	

More than two hundred years ago, when George Washington trod the brick sidewalks of Alexandria, Virginia, on his way to market or court or church, this was the largest city in northern Virginia, and dwarfed Georgetown, Maryland, just up the Potomac River; what are now Capitol

Hill and downtown Washington were hills above the river's mud flats. As Washington grew, Northern Virginia seemed left behind. In 1846, the District of Columbia retroceded its land south of the Potomac—now Alexandria and Arlington—to Virginia because it seemed obvious that the federal government would never need it, and it was 97 years before the first federal building was built on the Virginia side—the Pentagon; Franklin Roosevelt wondered out loud what they would do with all that space after the war. When the Pentagon was built, Alexandria and the rural countryside of Northern Virginia were represented in Congress by Judge Howard W. Smith, a Harry Byrd Democrat, who saw as his mission the maintenance of the standards of George Washington, Thomas Jefferson and Robert E. Lee. Yet by the 1960s, even as Judge Smith kept his law offices in Old Town, Alexandria, the area was changing around him. New subdivision dwellers with white-collar jobs and lots of children wanted schools with good academic programs—not the segregated schoolhouses Judge Smith's friends were willing to finance. The new generation wanted freeways and traffic lights, parks and recreation facilities. Smith's district was moved farther out into the countryside, two-party politics came to the suburbs, and local governments got to work. The congressional seat here, though often bitterly contested, was held from 1952–74 by Republican Joel Broyhill, a real estate developer who ran a fine constituency service operation in a district more than one-third of whose residents were federal employees.

Now the onetime suburbs of Alexandria and Arlington have become central cities of a sort—"edge cities," using Joel Garreau's term—themselves. Giant office developments sprang up from rail yards in Crystal City and from used car lots in Rosslyn. Vietnamese and Salvadorans, immigrants from Asia and Latin America have moved into these neighborhoods, and one of America's biggest Vietnamese commercial districts is in Clarendon, about a mile from Arlington National Cemetery and Fort Myer. Politically, Alexandria and Arlington, once hotly contested, are now solidly Democratic.

The 8th Congressional District consists of all of Arlington County and the cities of Alexandria and Falls Church. It also takes in two separate parts of Fairfax County: A stretch of land from Tysons Corner west to Reston, and several areas south of Alexandria's Old Town—the gentle landscapes of Mount Vernon, lower-income Groveton along the old U.S. 1, suburban Springfield and the more rural areas around Fort Belvoir; it transferred to the 10th District the portion of high-income McLean inside the Capital Beltway, and north and west Springfield, Newington and Lorton went to the 11th District. Two local landmarks here were severely affected by the September 2001 attacks: The Pentagon was struck by American Airlines Flight 77 which caused a loss of 189 lives and nearly $1 billion in damage, and Ronald Reagan Washington National Airport was shut down because of security concerns for three weeks and did not return to nearly full operations until April 2002. The district now is more firmly entrenched as solidly Democratic, while the 11th has become more safely Republican and the 10th remains that way.

The congressman from the 8th District is Jim Moran, an oft-embattled Alexandria politician with traces in his accent of his Massachusetts roots. He graduated from Holy Cross and got a master's degree from the University of Pittsburgh, worked in Washington for HEW, the Library of Congress and the Senate Appropriations Committee. He was elected to the Alexandria City Council in 1979 and vice mayor in 1982; in 1984 he pleaded no contest to a conflict of interest charge and resigned from the Council. The charges were eventually dropped (the law he supposedly violated had been changed), and in 1985 Moran was elected mayor. In 1990, he ran for Congress in what had become one of the most populous districts in the country, stretching from Alexandria south almost to Fredericksburg, against Republican incumbent Stanford Parris. It was a nasty race: Parris said Moran was a supporter of Saddam Hussein; Moran said he wanted to "break [Parris's] nose," and called him "a deceitful, fatuous jerk." The major substantive issue was abortion, on which Moran ran a pro-choice ad portraying Lady Liberty behind bars. With a big margin in Alexandria, Moran won 52%–45%.

He jousted—literally—with other Republicans, shoving Californian Duke Cunningham off the floor and out the House chamber doors in 1995 after Cunningham said that Moran had "turned his back on Desert Storm." He balked at Clinton's health care reform because it threatened the federal employees' plan; he blasted Al Gore's reinventing government plan as "politically expedient" and based on "sound bites" and viewed it as a threat to the most talented federal employees. He was strongly critical of Bill Clinton's conduct in the Lewinsky scandal and in September 1998 suggested the president should resign. He was one of 31 Democrats who voted for the Republicans' impeachment inquiry, but he voted against impeachment in December.

Moran, with Cal Dooley and Tim Roemer, founded the New Democrat Coalition in 1997, made up of moderate Democrats mostly from suburban districts to support alternatives to "traditional Democratic policies." Working with other New Democrats and with Virginians, he became a strong ally of the local high-tech industry. He was an early supporter of trade promotion authority, which he struggled to pass for several years until George W. Bush became President, and of PNTR with China. He was the only Democrat to vote for a Republican program to allow local governments to consolidate federal grants into more flexible spending plans—his Alexandria experience counted. He criticized senior Democratic Rep. John Dingell for "doing the NRA's bidding" and harming Democrats in weakening gun-control legislation. On the Appropriations Committee, from his seat on the District of Columbia Subcommittee, he has put in much bipartisan labor to straighten out the District's finances—and in the process helped force the District to close Lorton prison in Virginia; he also worked to reverse the federal ban on adoptions by gay couples in the District. Also on Appropriations, he has been ranking Democrat on the Legislative Subcommittee, a strategic slot to distribute perks to colleagues. He strongly opposed the Republican initiative to rename Washington National Airport after Ronald Reagan. In 2002, the House passed his amendment to prohibit federal agencies from using quotas to privatize their jobs.

The 1992 redistricting gave Moran a solidly Democratic district, but he had serious competition in 1992 and 1994 and he won with 56% and 59% of the vote; in 1996 and 1998, he won by more than 2–1. He received negative headlines just before the 2000 election when *The Washington Post* reported that Maryland 8th District Democratic challenger—and pharmaceutical-company lobbyist—Terry Lierman gave his financially-troubled friend Moran a $25,000 loan on generous terms; but Moran quickly agreed to repay the loan and he suffered no apparent political damage. More trouble followed in 2002 with reports that he borrowed $50,000 from the founder of America Online, and that MBNA, the big credit-card company, had given him a favorable rate on a mortgage while Moran was arguing vehemently for the bankruptcy bill MBNA was strongly backing. Although NRCC chairman Tom Davis, who represents the neighboring district, said that he saw no ethical problems with Moran's actions, *The Washington Post* was highly critical and called for his defeat. Republican challenger Scott Tate, a member of the Arlington County planning commission, attacked Moran's "twenty year history of self-inflicted ethical difficulties." But Tate raised little money. Moran won 60%–37%, a drop from his 63%–34% margin in a district that was 3% more Democratic.

In February 2003 Moran said the House ethics committee told him it would not open a formal investigation into the MBNA matter, though he declined to release the letter he received from the committee. In March 2003, Moran's reelection prospects grew cloudy. At an anti-war forum, Moran said, "If it were not for the strong support of the Jewish community for this war with Iraq we would not be doing this. The leaders of the Jewish community are influential enough that they could change the direction of where this is going and I think they should." The furious reaction to his remarks led Moran to apologize; six Jewish Democratic members wrote to Minority Leader Nancy Pelosi that they "cannot and will not support" Moran's candidacy in 2004. Katherine Hanley, chairman of the Fairfax County Board of Supervisors, announced in May 2003 that she would not seek reelection and would challenge Moran in the 2004 Democratic primary; former Congresswoman Leslie Byrne, now a state senator, said she also may challenge Moran in the primary.

NINTH DISTRICT

Rep. Rick Boucher (D)

Elected 1982, 11th term; b. Aug. 1, 1946, Abingdon; home, Abingdon; Roanoke Col., B.A. 1968, U. of VA, J.D. 1971; United Methodist; single.

Elected Office: VA Senate, 1975–1983.

Professional Career: Practicing atty., 1971–83.

DC Office: 2187 RHOB 20515, 202-225-3861; Fax: 202-225-0442; Web site: www.house.gov/boucher.

District Offices: Abingdon, 540-628-1145; Big Stone Gap, 540-523-5450; Pulaski, 540-980-4310.

Committees: *Energy & Commerce* (5th of 26 D): Energy & Air Quality (RMM); Telecommunications & The Internet. *Judiciary* (3d of 16 D): Courts, the Internet & Intellectual Property.

Group Ratings

	ADA	ACLU	AFS	LCV	CON	ITIC	NTU	COC	ACU	NTLC	CHC
2002	80	100	89	75	43	38	22	70	21	17	17
2001	90	—	100	79	—	—	12	57	16	—	—

National Journal Ratings

	2001 LIB —	2001 CONS		2002 LIB —	2002 CONS
Economic	62%	39%		58%	41%
Social	71%	29%		73%	26%
Foreign	67%	32%		68%	32%

Key Votes of the 107th Congress

1. Approve Bush Tax Cuts	N	5. Faith-Based Charities	N	9. Trade Promotion Authority	N
2. Limit Patients' Bill of Rights	N	6. Bar Gays in the Boy Scouts	Y	10. Bar Funds for Intl. Court	N
3. Campaign Finance Reform	N	7. Ban Partial-Birth Abortion	N	11. Authorize Force in Iraq	Y
4. Ban ANWR Development	Y	8. Arm Commercial Pilots	Y	12. Deny Home. Sec. Dept. Union	N

Election Results

2002 general	Rick Boucher (D)	100,075	(66%)	($1,085,883)
	Jay Katzen (R)	52,076	(34%)	($231,108)
2002 primary	Rick Boucher (D)	unopposed		
2000 general	Rick Boucher (D)	137,488	(70%)	($676,127)
	Michael D. "Oz" Osborne (R)	59,335	(30%)	($33,501)

Prior Winning Percentages: 1998 (61%); 1996 (65%); 1994 (59%); 1992 (63%); 1990 (97%); 1988 (63%); 1986 (99%); 1984 (52%); 1982 (50%)

The People		Race/Ethnic Origin	Ancestry	
Area size:	8,838 sq. mi.	93.3% White	USA: 20.0%	English: 7.7%
Urban population:	34.1%	3.8% Black	German: 7.7%	
Rural population:	65.9%	0.8% Asian	**2000 Presidential Vote**	
Pop. 2000:	643,514	0.1% Native Am.	Bush (R)	129,110 (55%)
Median income:	$29,783	0.0% Hawaiian	Gore (D)	100,298 (42%)
Poverty status:	16.2%	0.7% Two+ races	Other	7,011 (3%)
Military veterans:	11.9%	0.1% Other	**Cook Partisan Voting Index:** R + 7	
		1.1% Hispanic Origin		

Occupation	Blue collar: 35.3%	White collar: 49.1%	Gray collar: 15.5%

One of the first areas to be settled from the seacoast to the great American interior was what is now southwest Virginia. As early as 1765, settlements were carved out of the great Valley of Virginia, which bends westward and south toward Tennessee and the Cumberland Gap. Most settlers were of Scots-Irish lineage, and the mountainous area where they moved developed almost apart from the rest of Virginia. The fiercely independent settlers were first farmers, later often coal miners, as in West Virginia, which wasn't a separate state until 1863. Politically, this virtually all-white area opposed slavery and was skeptical if not hostile to the Confederacy. Out of the crucible of struggle between secessionists and unionists, southwest Virginia developed a robust two-party politics after the Civil War, with both parties resembling their national counterparts more closely than in the rest of Virginia. The state's extreme southwest corner is a shorter distance to the Mississippi River than to the Potomac.

The 9th Congressional District covers all of southwest Virginia west of Roanoke. Over the years, the district became known as the "Fighting Ninth," because of its taste for raucous politics, culturally conservative and economically populist. Lately, it has become somewhat more like the rest of Virginia, as development has moved down Interstate 81 to, and even past, Blacksburg, home of Virginia Tech. It now includes Patrick County, the site of the R.J. Reynolds Homestead plus annual peach and cabbage festivals. Mountain counties farther west continue to depend on coal and to lose population. The Fighting Ninth voted for Republican Governors George Allen and James Gilmore and for 1994 Republican Senate candidate Oliver North. It voted narrowly for Bill Clinton in 1992 and 1996 and for 1996 Democratic Senate candidate Mark Warner and by a much wider margin for George W. Bush in 2000. No other Virginia district voted for that combination.

The congressman from the 9th is Rick Boucher, a Democrat first elected in 1982. Boucher grew up in the antique town of Abingdon, went to Roanoke College and then the University of Virginia law school; he practiced law in Abingdon and was elected to the Virginia Senate in 1975, at 29. Politics runs in the family: His father was the Republican commonwealth's attorney in Washington County, while his mother was county Democratic chairwoman; his grandfather and great-grandfather were Democratic members of the House of Delegates. In 1982 Boucher ran for the House against veteran Representative William Wampler and won with big margins in coal counties on the Kentucky border. Boucher tends to vote with House Democrats but he sometimes strays, especially on economic issues.

Boucher says that he has devoted 80% of his legislative time to technology issues, including his work on the Commerce Committee's Telecommunications subcommittee. Back in 1988, he co-sponsored with then-Senator Al Gore a bill to allow phone companies to offer cable TV, and he sponsored the Satellite Home Viewers Act, so viewers without over-the-air network reception could subscribe to satellite services carrying network channels: The beginning of the now booming satellite TV business. Cable TV had its start in mountainous areas where network TV signals were weak, and Boucher sees new technologies, from satellite TV to the Internet, as a means for out-of-the-way places like the 9th to compete on an equal commercial basis with urban areas. On the 1996 Telecommunications Act, he helped write provisions intended to open up competition in the local telephone and cable TV markets. He convinced Colorado-based EchoStar Communications Corp. to establish a presence in southwest Virginia. *Network Computing* magazine called him one of the 10 most important people of the 1990s.

Boucher was a co-founder of the House Internet Caucus in 1996; he became co-chair with Bob Goodlatte of the next-door 6th District. He worked on the Judiciary Subcommittee on Courts, the Internet and Intellectual Property with Goodlatte to update copyright laws for the digital age and for a consensus on a National Information Infrastructure. He sponsored the law that permitted messages with commercial content to traverse the Internet backbone. With Goodlatte, he established a loan-guarantee program for private businesses to deliver television signals to satellite TV viewers in rural areas. In 2002, he voiced concern that the recording industry's anti-piracy technology on CDs might override the consumer's ability to copy albums for personal use, as permitted by law. He later introduced a bill with California Rep. John Doolittle to permit circumventing such technology in digital content for "fair use."

On other issues, Boucher has worked for binding arbitration to settle Superfund suits, for allowing state and local governments to engage in interstate shipment of municipal waste, and for electricity deregulation, which he hopes will benefit the coal industry and stimulate investment in mine facilities. He opposed PNTR with China and trade promotion authority, voicing concern about the impact on jobs in his district. He won approval for a $182 million Army Corps of Engineers project to move part of the often-flooded town of Grundy to higher ground from the Levisa River.

Boucher came into the national spotlight in the hearings on Clinton's impeachment. Far less strident than most other Judiciary Committee Democrats, speaking with old-fashioned formality in a businesslike manner, he pressed Kenneth Starr on whether a president can be prosecuted after leaving office. He was the author of the Democratic resolution to conduct a limited impeachment inquiry in October 1998. In December he was the author of the Democrats' censure resolution. In each case, he lost in the House but his views mirrored a consensus of political sentiment.

In this usually partisan district, Boucher has become highly popular. He conducts an active constituency service operation in an area where many people have problems with Social Security, veterans' benefits and black lung payments. His Commerce Committee seat helps him to raise large sums of money and he usually wins comfortably. When the Republican legislature was preparing to redistrict, Oliver North volunteered to run against Boucher if legislators connected southwest Virginia, where he had run well in 1994, with his home county in the northern end of the state; legislators declined his offer. Redistricting added territory that did Boucher no political damage. After redistricting, former Delegate Jay Katzen moved into the district and ran for the House; he was the unsuccessful Republican nominee for lieutenant governor in 2001, but had carried the 9th District. Those votes proved non-transferable. Boucher won 66%–34% and took all 27 counties and cities. With his support from organized labor and the National Rifle Association, the high-tech oriented Boucher appears secure.

TENTH DISTRICT

Rep. Frank Wolf (R)

Elected 1980, 12th term; b. Jan. 30, 1939, Philadelphia, PA; home, Vienna; PA St. U., B.A. 1961, Georgetown U., LL.B. 1965; Presbyterian; married (Carolyn).

Military Career: Army, 1962–63, Army Reserves 1963–67.

Professional Career: Legis. Asst., U.S. Rep. Edward Biester, 1968–71; Asst., U.S. Interior Secy. Rogers Morton, 1971–74; Dep. Asst. Secy., U.S. Dept. of Interior, 1974–75; Practicing atty., 1975–80.

DC Office: 241 CHOB 20515, 202-225-5136; Fax: 202-225-0437; Web site: www.house.gov/wolf.

District Offices: Herndon, 703-709-5800; Winchester, 540-667-0990.

Committees: *Appropriations* (5th of 36 R): Commerce, Justice, State & Judiciary (Chmn.); Homeland Security; Transportation, Treasury, & Independent Agencies.

Group Ratings

	ADA	ACLU	AFS	LCV	CON	ITIC	NTU	COC	ACU	NTLC	CHC
2002	5	0	0	25	34	88	57	80	92	78	83
2001	10	—	0	7	—	—	59	91	79	—	—

National Journal Ratings

	2001 LIB — 2001 CONS		2002 LIB — 2002 CONS	
Economic	27%	73%	36%	61%
Social	0%	81%	32%	63%
Foreign	27%	72%	29%	67%

Key Votes of the 107th Congress

1. Approve Bush Tax Cuts	Y	5. Faith-Based Charities	Y	9. Trade Promotion Authority	Y
2. Limit Patients' Bill of Rights	Y	6. Bar Gays in the Boy Scouts	Y	10. Bar Funds for Intl. Court	Y
3. Campaign Finance Reform	Y	7. Ban Partial-Birth Abortion	Y	11. Authorize Force in Iraq	Y
4. Ban ANWR Development	N	8. Arm Commercial Pilots	Y	12. Deny Home. Sec. Dept. Union	Y

Election Results

2002 general	Frank Wolf (R)	115,917	(72%)	($691,008)
	John Stevens (D)	45,464	(28%)	($20,344)
2002 primary	Frank Wolf (R)	unopposed		
2000 general	Frank Wolf (R)	238,817	(84%)	($465,729)
	Brian M. Brown (I)	28,107	(10%)	($6,826)
	Marc A. Rossi (I)	16,031	(6%)	

Prior Winning Percentages: 1998 (72%); 1996 (72%); 1994 (87%); 1992 (64%); 1990 (62%); 1988 (68%); 1986 (60%); 1984 (63%); 1982 (53%); 1980 (51%)

The People		Race/Ethnic Origin	Ancestry	
Area size:	1,864 sq. mi.	77.2% White	German: 12.9%	Irish: 10.5%
Urban population:	83.3%	6.7% Black	English: 9.5%	
Rural population:	16.7%	6.6% Asian	**2000 Presidential Vote**	
Pop. 2000:	643,512	0.2% Native Am.	Bush (R) 148,211	(56%)
Median income:	$71,560	0.0% Hawaiian	Gore (D) 109,063	(41%)
Poverty status:	4.4%	1.9% Two + races	Other 8,106	(3%)
Military veterans:	13.5%	0.2% Other	**Cook Partisan Voting Index:** R + 8	
		7.1% Hispanic Origin		

Occupation	Blue collar: 15.9%	White collar: 72.5%	Gray collar: 11.6%

When George Washington decided to place the new nation's capital on the Potomac just upriver from Mount Vernon, where the falls block navigation above the port of Georgetown, the land above the fall line on the Virginia side of the river—the rolling green Piedmont of northern Virginia and the fertile mountain-bound lands of the Shenandoah Valley—was buzzing with new settlers. They came up the Potomac and the runs (a Virginia word) that flow into it and into the Valley from the great Wagon Road south from Pennsylvania, moving onto lands speculated on by George Washington and his peers. During the Civil War, this was some of the most heavily contested land on the continent; afterwards, the land was quiet: The frontier was very far to the west, and on these lands farmers quietly raised hay and grazed cattle and kept horses for fox hunting. During World War II and immediately after this was still open country: General George Marshall, driving from his office in the Pentagon to the old house he bought in the courthouse town of Leesburg 30 miles away, would pass a few gas stations and crossroads villages and hundreds of acres of farm fields. If he could make the trip today, he would see something very different. For metropolitan Washington has spread out into this bucolic land. There are still some horse farms in the Piedmont, long the first or second homes of some of the richest people in America, but they are increasingly flanked by subdivisions that sprout up in the fields overnight. Fairfax County, by many measures the highest-income county in the nation, had 98,000 people in 1950; it has ten times as many people today. Loudoun County, just past Dulles Airport, was the third-fastest growing county in the United States in the 1990s, doubling its population to 170,000 in just one decade; the growth triggered a movement called Voters to Stop Sprawl which won every seat on the county Board of Supervisors in 1999. The Washington metropolitan area, as defined by the government, now extends past Fairfax and Loudoun and over the Blue Ridge into the Shenandoah Valley.

In the 1950s and 1960s, the Northern Virginia suburbs of Washington were just that: Bedroom communities where most workers headed into the District of Columbia and where one-third of them were employed by the federal government. Today Northern Virginia is an employment center and focus of innovation on its own. The Dulles Access Road, which ran through rural-looking territory 20 years ago, is now lined with office buildings holding high-tech firms and entrepreneurial startups. Along intersecting Route 28, crossing the Fairfax-Loudoun County line, are the headquarters of tech giants such as America Online and Telos Corp. The federal government is no longer the dominant employer here. Some of Northern Virginia's private sector is the spawn of government—"Beltway Bandits" and defense contractors—but this area has also become one of the nation's major centers of high-tech and telecommunications firms.

The 10th Congressional District covers much of Northern Virginia. It starts inside the Capital Beltway and includes most of McLean, home to much of Washington's political and lawyer-lobbyist elite, and goes beyond the Beltway to include woodsy Great Falls, Herndon and the Route 28 corridor around Dulles Airport. It includes Manassas, site of the Civil War's first battle, in Prince William County; all of Loudoun County, heavily built-up in the east with some still rural areas west of Leesburg; and the northern half of Fauquier County, which has limited development and is still mostly horse farms. It includes three counties in the northern end of the Shenandoah Valley, the country around Front Royal and Winchester. About 40% of the votes are cast in Fairfax County, 30% in Loudoun County, about 10% in Prince William and Manassas, 5% in Fauquier and 15% in the Shenandoah Valley. The political leanings of parts of metro Washington reflect the government agencies that predominate there and the private economy that has grown up around them: Northern Virginia, with its defense and high-tech base, tends to be Republican, while Montgomery County, Maryland, with its health and biotech base, tends to be Democratic. The 10th District is a heavily Republican district, with a more rural flavor than Virginia's other Washington metro area districts. It voted solidly for George W. Bush in 2000, even as he was losing across the river in Montgomery by 2–1.

The congressman from the 10th District is Frank Wolf, first elected in 1980. Wolf grew up in Philadelphia, went to law school at Georgetown, worked as a staffer on Capitol Hill and as an Interior Department appointee in the Nixon and Ford administrations and practiced law. In 1978 he ran for Congress against Joseph Fisher, a liberal who had won the district in 1974, and lost 53%–47%; in 1980 he ran again and won 51%–49%. He started off, in the suburban Washington manner, maintaining a crackerjack constituency service operation and concentrating on issues affecting federal employees. He has promoted on-site child care centers at federal workplaces, flextime and flexplace arrangements, leave-sharing and telecommuting (the first center was in Winchester and he keeps pressing for more employees to be eligible). He opposed the Clinton health care reform in 1994 because it would have gutted the federal employee health plan, and he opposed the Contract with America tax cut in 1995 because it would have required higher pension payments by federal employees. He pushed the 4.1% federal pay increase in 2002 and sought extra pay for SEC employees. He has tried to use the appropriator's leverage to change the culture of the FBI.

Over the 20 years Wolf has come to specialize in three other areas—transportation, human rights and gambling. He used his seat on the Transportation Appropriations Subcommittee to work on projects in traffic-choked Northern Virginia. He got permanent Customs entry status for Front Royal and enactment of the Cedar Creek and Belle Grove National Historical Parks in the Shenandoah Valley. Other projects have not been as successful. A proposed Metro rail link to Dulles is behind schedule, and costs are rising. In October 2000, Wolf called for a study of a proposed "Techway" bridge over the Potomac linking Rockville and Dulles. But protests by home-owners in Great Falls and other areas convinced him to oppose the study in May 2001. From 1995 to 2000, Wolf was Chairman of the Transportation Appropriations subcommittee; he op-posed earmarking proposals for specific congressmen, even as the chairman of the authorizing committee, Bud Shuster made the practice an art form; Wolf thus lost most of the appropriators' leverage. He used the subcommittee chairmanship to put through a national .08% blood alcohol limit for drunk driving and to promote truck safety. In January 2001, House Republicans' six year limits on chairmanships caught up with both Wolf and Shuster: Shuster resigned from Congress, while Wolf took the chairmanship of the Commerce, Justice and State Subcommittee.

Wolf has been one of the House's leading crusaders for human rights and is co-chairman of the Congressional Human Rights Caucus. He traveled to El Salvador in 1982, Sudan in 1989, Romania in 1990, East Timor and Tibet in 1997 (only the second time a congressman has been there since the Chinese takeover in 1959), Sierra Leone in 1999 and Ethiopia in 2003, where he saw starvation as ghastly as he had in 1984. Recently he has focused on human rights abuses in Kuwait and Saudi Arabia. With California's Nancy Pelosi, he led the annual moves to withdraw PNTR for China because of human right violations; he strongly opposed PNTR in 2000, citing China's acts of jailing dissidents, killing Catholic priests, jailing evangelical pastors, persecuting Tibetan Buddhists and aiming missiles at the United States. "Did trade change Nazi Germany?" he asked. "I don't think appeasement ever works." In 2000 he sought sanctions against oil companies doing business in Sudan, called for labeling the country of origin of diamonds (to identify those from Sierra Leone).

Wolf is probably Congress's leading opponent of gambling. "It leaves in its path the wreckage of human misery. Addiction, crime, corruption, loss of revenue to local business, bankruptcy and even suicide—these are the fruits of this industry which is sweeping America." He first proposed the National Gambling Impact Study Commission, passed in 1997, but was not pleased by the appointees; he hailed its call in June 1999 for a pause in granting licenses for new casinos and for federal oversight of Indian and Internet gambling. He called on George W. Bush to reform the Bureau of Indian Affairs, citing a *Boston Globe* series on the creation of phony Indian tribes, and pointed out that just 2% of Indians earn 50% of the $10 billion in Indian gambling revenues, and two-thirds of Indians get nothing. He opposes federal recognition of Indian tribes in Virginia.

Wolf has been reelected by overwhelming margins. Redistricting was not a problem. He sat down with neighbors Republican Tom Davis of the 11th District and Democrat Jim Moran of the 8th District and agreed on boundaries for Northern Virginia, which were enacted by the Republican legislature. He was reelected in 2002 by a 72%–28% margin.

ELEVENTH DISTRICT

Rep. Tom Davis (R)

Elected 1994, 5th term; b. Jan. 5, 1949, Minot, ND; home, Annandale; Amherst Col. B.A. 1971, U. of VA, J.D. 1975; Christian Scientist; married (Peggy).

Military Career: Army, 1971–72; Army Reserves, 1972–79.

Elected Office: Fairfax Cnty. Bd. of Supervisors, 1979–94, Chmn., 1991–94.

Professional Career: Vice Pres. & Gen. Cnsl., PRC Inc., 1977–94.

DC Office: 2348 RHOB 20515, 202-225-1492; Fax: 202-225-3071; Web site: www.house.gov/tomdavis.

District Offices: Annandale, 703-916-9610; Prince William, 703-590-4599.

Committees: *Government Reform* (Chmn. of 24 R).

Group Ratings

	ADA	ACLU	AFS	LCV	CON	ITIC	NTU	COC	ACU	NTLC	CHC
2002	10	33	0	50	36	100	57	84	88	69	75
2001	15	—	10	43	—	—	60	90	60	—	—

National Journal Ratings

	2001 LIB — 2001 CONS	2002 LIB — 2002 CONS
Economic	41% — 58%	28% — 69%
Social	49% — 51%	39% — 57%
Foreign	21% — 74%	22% — 77%

Key Votes of the 107th Congress

1. Approve Bush Tax Cuts	Y	5. Faith-Based Charities	Y	9. Trade Promotion Authority	Y
2. Limit Patients' Bill of Rights	Y	6. Bar Gays in the Boy Scouts	Y	10. Bar Funds for Intl. Court	Y
3. Campaign Finance Reform	N	7. Ban Partial-Birth Abortion	Y	11. Authorize Force in Iraq	Y
4. Ban ANWR Development	Y	8. Arm Commercial Pilots	Y	12. Deny Home. Sec. Dept. Union	Y

Election Results

2002 general	Tom Davis (R)	135,379	(83%)	($1,591,381)
	Frank Creel (CNP)	26,892	(16%)	($8,797)
	Other	1,027	(1%)	
2002 primary	Tom Davis (R)	unopposed		
2000 general	Tom Davis (R)	150,395	(62%)	($1,515,583)
	M.L. (Mike) Corrigan (D)	83,455	(34%)	($72,833)
	Other	9,118	(4%)	

Prior Winning Percentages: 1998 (82%); 1996 (64%); 1994 (53%)

The People		Race/Ethnic Origin	Ancestry	
Area size:	404 sq. mi.	66.8% White	German: 11.5%	Irish: 10.0%
Urban population:	95.9%	10.1% Black	English: 9.4%	
Rural population:	4.1%	10.9% Asian	**2000 Presidential Vote**	
Pop. 2000:	643,509	0.2% Native Am.	Bush (R)..............140,961	(52%)
Median income:	$80,397	0.1% Hawaiian	Gore (D)..............123,702	(45%)
Poverty status:	3.8%	2.6% Two+ races	Other....................8,087	(3%)
Military veterans:	15.9%	0.2% Other	**Cook Partisan Voting Index:** R + 4	
		9.1% Hispanic Origin		

Occupation	Blue collar: 11.7%	White collar: 76.5%	Gray collar: 11.8%

When author and *Washington Post* reporter Joel Garreau coined the term "edge city" to describe the autonomous urban centers developing on the rims of some of the nation's oldest municipalities, his prime example was Tysons Corner, Virginia. Rising on a hill west of Washington, Tysons Corner was a back-country intersection 50 years ago and a junction of several suburban roads 25 years ago; today it is home to the largest concentration of office space to be found anywhere between Washington and Atlanta, with a modern skyline and busy multi-lane avenues that serve as arteries to the Capital Beltway. Fairfax County, which includes all of Tysons Corner, has changed just as dramatically since the end of World War II. At first only a few District of Columbia residents seeking breathing room in the suburbs trickled into Northern Virginia; initially they went to Arlington and Alexandria. But that trickle became a rush as young marrieds with large families and whites avoiding the increasingly high-crime District pushed farther out into Fairfax. Now Fairfax County is no longer Washington's country cousin. By 2000 it had 969,000 residents, nearly twice D.C.'s. 572,000; it reached 1 million by 2003. It had in 1999 the nation's highest median household income ($81,050), almost half its residents have a bachelor's degree or more and nearly 70% of its households have two or more vehicles. It also has plenty of immigrants, from Koreans and Vietnamese to Afghanis and Africans.

The 11th Congressional District consists of much of Fairfax County and most of fast-growing Prince William County to the south. The district straddles the Capital Beltway and includes Tysons Corner. Inside the Beltway are Baileys Crossroads and Annandale; beyond are Vienna, Fairfax, much of Springfield, Burke, Clifton, Centreville, part of Mount Vernon. In Prince William County it includes Woodbridge and Dale City and stretches west to Haymarket. This is a cosmopolitan district: 10% black, 9% Hispanic, 11% Asian; some 25% of residents speak a language other than English at home. The district is made up largely of two-income families, many with at least one spouse employed in one of the many divisions of high-tech companies that dot Fairfax County. The district was first created in 1991, after Virginia got a new seat in the 1990 Census. It was originally designed to be equally divided between the parties, and within its 1991 boundaries it voted 43%–42% for George Bush in 1992, 49%–47% for Bill Clinton in 1996 and 49%–47% for Al Gore in 2000. In its post-redistricting 2002 form, the district voted 52% for George W. Bush.

The congressman from the 11th District is Tom Davis, a Republican elected in 1994. Davis grew up in Northern Virginia, and was always interested in politics; by seventh grade he could name every member of the House. He got a job as a Senate page and was president of his class at the Capitol Page School; he was a friend of David Eisenhower at Amherst College, where almost everyone else was a Democrat or something further left; he served on active duty in the Army before earning a law degree. He practiced law in Northern Virginia and was general counsel to computer services firm PRC. In 1979 he was elected to the Fairfax County Board of Supervisors, a high visibility position. In 1991 he was elected board chairman, something in the nature of a mayor.

In 1994 Davis ran for the 11th District seat against Democrat Leslie Byrne, who had won 50%–45% in 1992. Byrne had voted solidly for Clinton administration positions and called for discipline against members of the Democratic Caucus who did not; she had strong support from labor and feminist groups and spent $1.1 million. But Davis was able to raise and spend even more, $1.4 million. He won 53%–45%.

As soon as he arrived on Capitol Hill, Davis was handed by Speaker Newt Gingrich one of the hottest potatoes of the new Congress: Dealing with the affairs of the troubled District of Columbia government and its just re-elected mayor, Marion Barry. As chairman of the House Government Reform and Oversight Committee's D.C. Subcommittee, Davis first rejected Barry's request for massive federal aid, working closely with Gingrich and District Delegate Eleanor Holmes Norton to cut District spending. Together they passed in April 1995 a law establishing a five-member control board to oversee the D.C. government. He tended to oppose the appropriators' detailed policy prescription as micromanagement, but went along with the 1997 law taking power over nine agencies from Barry and giving it to the control board. In February 1999 Davis and Norton sponsored a bill restoring full management powers to the District and its new mayor, Anthony Williams; it was speedily passed. Davis and Norton also passed a bill suggested by *Washington Post* publisher Donald Graham to enable District students to attend Virginia and Maryland public colleges and universities at in-state tuition rates.

Davis has a moderate voting record, near the midpoint of the House. He opposed the Contract with America tax cut in 1995 because it would have required higher pension payments by federal employees; he and suburban Washington's Frank Wolf and Connie Morella were three of only 11 Republicans who voted against the tax cut. He has worked for legislation to protect high-tech firms from the depredations of trial lawyers, including the securities litigation reform that was passed over Bill Clinton's veto in 1996. He co-sponsored a bill, supported by Philip Morris, to buy out tobacco farmers and allow the FDA to regulate tobacco products. He has kept in touch with the many immigrant groups in the 11th District, and favored amnesty to former refugees who have lived in the United States for many years. Over several years Davis worked on getting federal financing for the new Woodrow Wilson Bridge, which totaled $1.58 billion in federal aid; he has worked with Northern Virginia colleagues Jim Moran and Frank Wolf for new Potomac and Rappahannock buses and Job Access and Reverse Commute funds. He and Maryland Rep. Steny Hoyer got the House to pass a bill giving U.S. Park Police and the Secret Service Uniformed Division the same locality pay as other federal workers, and they pushed for the 4.1% federal pay increase in 2002.

Davis is a political buff with a detailed knowledge of political statistics across the country. In Virginia's 1997 elections, he criss-crossed the state and created a PAC that gave some $150,000 to state legislative candidates. In September 1997, NRCC Chairman John Linder named Davis to be his chief recruiter. He specialized in raising money from high-tech sources and argued that despite their cultural liberalism they were better protected by Republican principles of free trade, small government and laissez faire economic policies. The NRCC chairmanship became an elective post after the November 1998 election, and after Republicans lost seats in the cycle Davis ran against Linder. Tom DeLay put his whip organization to work for Davis, and Davis won 130–77.

Davis had a delicate balancing act as a moderate in a mostly conservative party; he insisted that he was just trying to maximize the number of Republicans elected. He was criticized by the Family Research Council for meeting with the Log Cabin Republicans of Northern Virginia in February 1999 and criticized by moderates for giving $750,000 to the U.S. Family Network and the National Right to Life Committee. He spent $1 million on 1999 state legislative races in Virginia, in which Republicans captured both houses and won control of redistricting; within a few months conservative incumbent Congressman Virgil Goode left the Democratic Party and announced he would caucus with Republicans and conservative Democrat Owen Pickett retired— a two-seat gain a year before an election in which Democrats needed only a five- or six-seat gain to win control.

Through most of the cycle Democrats were supremely confident they would win the House in 2000, and they matched, and at some points exceeded, Republicans' fundraising—a considerable achievement that owed much to the fame of their campaign committee chairman Patrick Kennedy. But Kennedy and those who advised him did not quite match Davis's political knowledge and instincts. He early on spotted open seats which had long voted Democratic but where conservative non-economic issues helped Republicans—Pennsylvania's 4th, West Virginia's 2d, Missouri's 6th, Michigan's 8th, Virginia's 2d—and won them all. Against party-switcher Michael Forbes in New York's 1st, he spent money on billboards thanking him for his solid support of Newt

Gingrich and the Contract With America; Forbes was upset in the September Democratic primary, and the seat went Republican in November. He spotted the weakness of 20-year incumbent Democrat Sam Gejdenson in Connecticut's 2d, which led to another gain. The Republican nomination in the open seat in Florida's 8th was not determined until the October runoff; but for two months before the NRCC spent heavily on ads attacking the Democratic nominee, who lost 51%–49%. Only four Republican incumbents lost, three in California and one in the Arkansas 4th District (the one district where a vote for impeachment hurt).

Davis was re-elected campaign committee chairman in November 2000. During the 2002 cycle Republicans far outraised the Democrats, whose campaign committee staff was headed by Hillary Rodham Clinton's 2000 campaign spokesman. Once again Davis did a fine job of targeting vulnerable seats, but his most valuable work was on redistricting. Not since the death of California Democrat Phillip Burton in 1983 has a member of Congress with such a detailed knowledge of the political demography of the entire country taken such a lead role in redistricting. Davis and White House political strategist Karl Rove persuaded the chief Democratic redistricter in California, Michael Berman, brother of Congressman Howard Berman, to settle for a plan that gave the state's one new seat to Democrats but otherwise maintained the status quo: Not a bad deal for Democrats, who had just picked up three seats there, but not as much as they might have won in 2002, admittedly with a greater risk of losing seats later in the decade. After Democrats put through an aggressively partisan redistricting plan in Georgia, Davis worked to see that Republicans in Pennsylvania put through a similarly aggressive plan. As a result, Republicans gained seats in a state that lost two seats while Democrats failed to achieve the gains they expected in a state that gained two seats. Davis urged the appointment of Ohio Democrat Tony Hall to the FAO in Rome; redistricting made Hall's seat more Republican, and a Republican won it easily. Davis predicted that Republicans would pick up as many as eight seats; they picked up five, and he savored the victory after dinner with George W. Bush and other Republican congressional leaders at the White House election night. "I'll quote the great one, Wayne Gretzky," he told a reporter soon after. "'Most people skate to where the puck is. I skate to where the puck is going to be.' In politics you have to understand not where the voters are when a poll is taken, but where they are likely to end up on Election Day."

Davis also took care of himself in redistricting in Virginia. He and Republican Frank Wolf and Democrat Jim Moran drew new district lines for Northern Virginia that helped all three. He had no Democratic opponent in November 2002 and won with 83% of the vote; in 2000, against a Democrat in a district closely divided between the parties, Davis won 62%–34%. After the 2002 election he was faced with a deadline for spending NRCC soft money on party headquarters: he gave $250,000 and $50,000 to the Fairfax and Prince William County Republican parties for that purpose. When asked if he had given disproportionate favor to parties in his district, he said. "Of course. I'm the chairman. What do you expect?" Davis has not been shy about running for statewide office, perhaps for governor in 2005, more likely for the Senate in 2008 if John Warner retires.

In the meantime, he remained active in the House. On the Government Reform Committee, Davis ranked only ninth in seniority among Republicans in early 2002, but he was nevertheless seen as a likely candidate to replace Chairman Dan Burton, who would reach the end of his six-year term limit in January 2003. Also in the running were Christopher Shays, whose use of a discharge petition to get his campaign finance regulation bill to the floor irked the leadership, and Christopher Cox, already in a leadership post himself. But the leadership decided on Davis; Cox became head of the new Homeland Security Committee, and Shays seemed to accept this, saying "I felt like I was dealt with very, very fairly by the leadership." "We're going to focus legislatively on areas of reform—civil service, federal procurement," Davis said. "We're going to move from 75–25 investigative to legislative to maybe 60–40 legislative to investigative." Davis is an expert on both subjects, on good terms with government employee unions but willing to vote against them and with Bush on personnel rules in the Homeland Security Department. Davis promptly abolished the District of Columbia Subcommittee and announced that he would superintend District legislation himself.

★ WASHINGTON ★

For a brief moment in the late 1990s, the eyes of the nation—and the world—were on Washington—Washington state, that is, not Washington, D.C. From Starbucks coffee to grunge music, from America's leading exporter, Boeing, to America's leading software maker, Microsoft, to America's most visible dot-com, amazon.com, Washington was a national trend-setter. An unusual environment and human creativity combined to produce these achievements: Seattle's cold misty air and 225 overcast days a year stimulate the appetite for strong aromatic coffee, and the shapeless blue jeans and sweatshirts worn year-round in this moist climate by professionals and teenagers alike created a trend made famous by Nirvana and Soundgarden and other grunge artists. Boeing's airframe business took off during World War II because the Pacific Northwest's abundant hydroelectric power made cheap aluminum possible, and the boom in air travel in the 1980s and 1990s kept Boeing's huge assembly lines humming. Microsoft, founded by the usually tie-less and tousle-haired Bill Gates and based in Redmond, across Lake Washington from Seattle, became one of America's great success stories as its software became embedded in the vast majority of the world's computers. With flannel shirts and umbrellas, blue-collar types working off hangovers as if in a Raymond Carver story, and professionals relaxing on woodsy acreage, Washington set a tone for the 1990s, a style plainly Middle American but with attitude, an ordinariness so hip it is no longer ordinary. As the end of the century approached, Washington was a commonwealth of nearly 6 million people, economically booming, pleased to the point of smugness with its physical environment and lifestyle. Since that high point Washington has had its woes, but it is useful to see how it got there, and what strengths it has to approach another peak ahead.

For Washington is a state which is not much more than a century old, one which in the two decades after statehood in 1889 built a new civilization, as transcontinental railroads reached the great ports of Puget Sound, the wheat-processing city of Spokane inland, orchard towns and fishing ports and lumber settlements. Shielded from the storms of the Pacific by the Olympic Mountains and the Sound, Seattle quickly became a serious American city, a lusty town full of lumbermen and railroad workers. When gold was struck in the Klondike and Alaska, Seattle became a metropolis of miners, prospectors and get-rich-quick operators, the site of the original "Skid Road" (skid row is a corruption propagated by a 1937 magazine article), where logs were rolled downhill to the port; today it's the focus of the restored Pioneer Square area. Booming young Seattle had a turbulent class-warfare politics in the years before World War I, pitting the Industrial Workers of the World (the IWW, or Wobblies) against city business and civic leaders; the businessmen, after some violence, prevailed. Adding to the area's distinctiveness was its large numbers of Scandinavian immigrants, with their favorable views of cooperative enterprises and government ownership.

Over time, Washington was transformed by a series of national decisions that set its course for decades. One was government development of hydroelectric power. The Columbia River and its tributary, the Snake, falling thousands of feet in a relatively short distance, had far greater hydroelectric potential than any other American river system, and Franklin Roosevelt was always interested in these river valley projects. In 1937 Bonneville Dam was completed on the lower Columbia; in 1940 Grand Coulee Dam, the largest man-made structure in the world at the time, was opened where the Columbia cuts through the arid, surrealistically contoured plains of eastern Washington. Washington proved hospitable to the industrial union movement of the 1930s and became one of the nation's most heavily unionized states. When war came, Washington's hydroelectric power—the cheapest electricity in the country—made it the natural site for huge aluminum production plants, which require vast amounts of electricity, and the Seattle area became the home not only of shipbuilders, but of what became the biggest aircraft manufacturer in the country, Boeing, founded in 1916 by William Boeing after he bought a shipyard on the Duwamish River and turned it into an airplane factory. After the war, the Hanford plant on the Columbia was one of the government's main nuclear weapons manufacturing sites. Cheap power, aluminum, aircraft, nuclear weapons and high unionized wages: these became Washington's economic foundations in the post-World War II years.

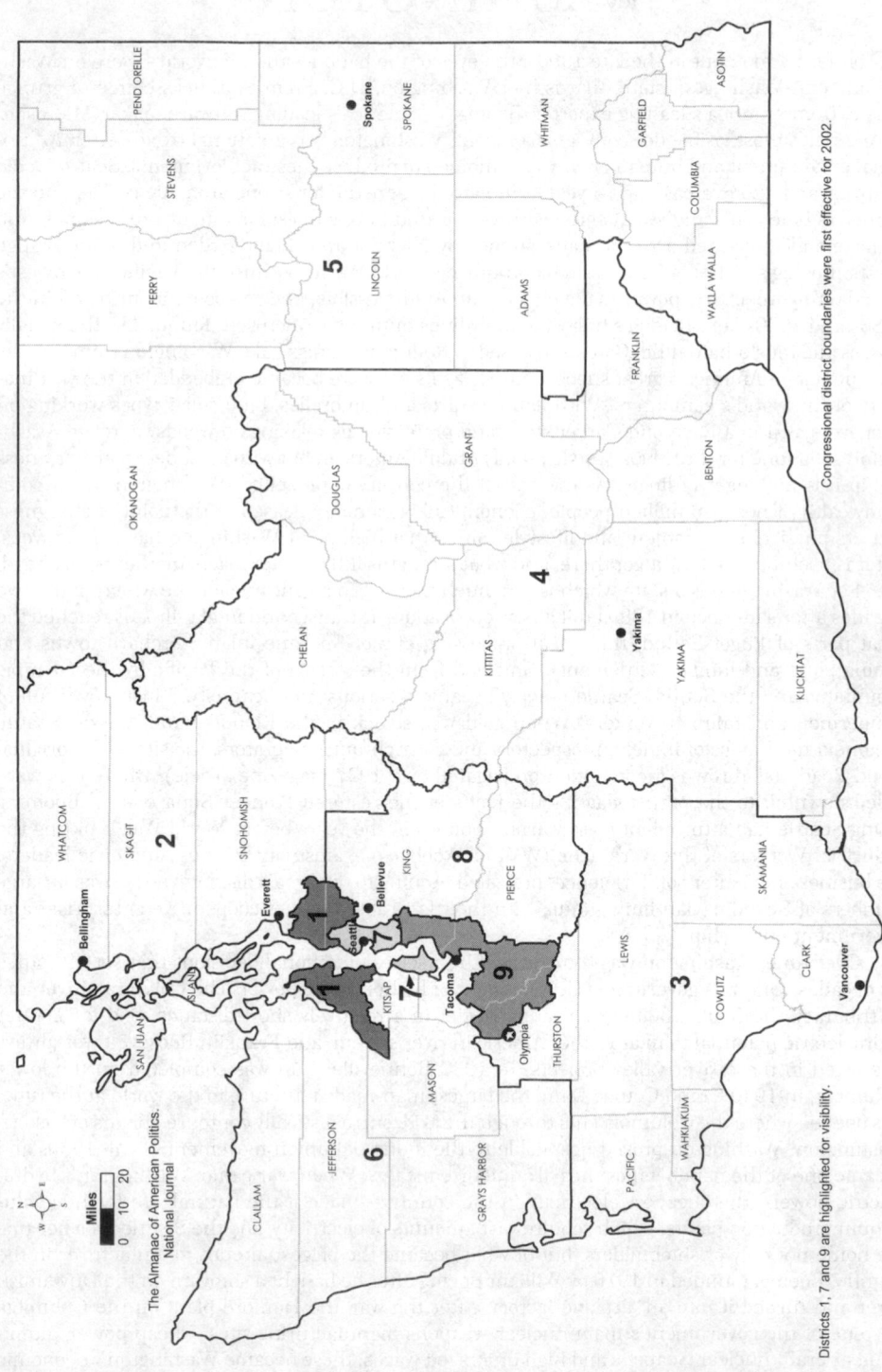

The Almanac of American Politics.
National Journal

Congressional district boundaries were first effective for 2002.

Districts 1, 7 and 9 are highlighted for visibility.

Today's Washington lives less off the brawn of hydroelectric power and rail and ship tonnage and more off the brains that made Boeing the world leader in aircraft and Microsoft the world leader in software. Yet since 1999 there has been trouble in this moist paradise. The turning point may have come in December 1999, when Seattle hosted a meeting of the World Trade Organization. This was supposed to be an occasion for the city to shine in the international spotlight. But 50,000 demonstrators took control of the streets, smashing Starbucks' windows and preventing leaders from Bill Clinton on down from attending meetings; Seattle's police chief and mayor did little to stop the violence, and even came out with statements, echoed by Clinton, expressing sympathy for the lawbreakers. Seattle became a symbol of mindless protest and lawless violence. The image was reinforced in the Mardi Gras riots in February 2001; Mayor Paul Schell carried only 22% of the vote in the September 2001 primary to become the first Seattle mayor in 45 years to lose a reelection bid. Washington was hurt also by the dot.com bust; the high-tech industry boomed as businesses retooled to avoid Y2K problems, then it suddenly became apparent that customers had all the high-tech they needed, the stock market started tanking in March 2000, takings thousands of dot.coms down. Microsoft was sued by the Justice Department's Antitrust Division in 1998; in November 1999 Judge Thomas Penfield Jackson ruled that Microsoft was a monopoly, and in June 2000 ordered the firm broken up. That decision was reversed on appeal in June 2001 and the company's leaders fought to preserve its aggressive and innovative culture. Boeing has had its problems as well. In March 2001 Boeing's chairman announced that the firm's headquarters would be moved out of Seattle, to Chicago. Politicians were aghast; Boeing executives, removed from Seattle, can cast a cold eye on its expensive and strike-prone Washington operations. Then, after September 11, the airline industry was hard hit and cut back its orders; Boeing cut back its Seattle area employment from 102,000 in 1997 to 62,000 in 2002, and more cuts seemed certain. Washington's unemployment rate was among the highest in the nation, with no net job growth from 1998 to 2002.

Amid this turbulence, the fundamentals undergirding Washington's affluent life seemed threatened. Light snowpacks threatened to reduce the supply of hydroelectric power even as demand from energy-starved California seemed likely to draw down supply. Proposals by Clinton administration officials to breach the dams on the Snake River threatened to reduce hydroelectric supply and to destroy the agriculture of eastern Washington just as the court decision to protect the endangered spotted owl largely shut down Washington's logging industry in the early 1990s. The Hanford Nuclear Reservation, which produced plutonium for the military, for years leaked radioactive waste and now must be cleaned up at the cost of billions, while new underground storage procedures have been criticized as unsafe. And in the Seattle area traffic congestion remained monumental on I-405 and I-5; the Alaskan Way viaduct along the port was damaged by the March 2001 earthquake and the pontoon bridge on Route 520 was approaching obsolescence.

All these problems may turn out to be no more than footnotes to what is mainly a story of success. Look at a map that shows elevation of mountains and density of population. On both sides of the Pacific, vast numbers of people are squeezed into small margins of level land between steeply rising volcanic mountains and the sea, or tucked into valleys. These islands of settlement are surrounded by vast wildernesses—desert and mountains, open sea and Arctic lands. Yet the inhabitants of these pockets of the Pacific Rim in the last three decades have produced more economic growth than anywhere else in the world and, if there are occasional slumps, the Pacific Rim (except for Japan) has always come surging back, as East Asia did in 1999. The question is whether Washington's laid-back tolerance can be so excessive as to undermine its impressive achievements.

Politically, Washington, with its Scandinavian and labor union heritage, was once one of the most Democratic states: Franklin Roosevelt's campaign manager James Farley used to refer to "the 47 states and the Soviet of Washington." Its mainstream Democrats—notably Warren Magnuson and Henry Jackson, who represented the state in Congress for a total of 87 years—believed in an active and compassionate federal government that built dams, aluminum plants and the Hanford Works at home, and pursued an internationalist, anti-Communist foreign policy abroad. Their political strength was built on a blue collar base, augmented by the respect big businesses had for their political clout. Today, the fulcrum of the electorate has moved from blue collar to white collar, from economic class warfare to cultural wars. The balance is fairly close. In presidential races, Washington leans Democratic: big Seattle-area margins delivered the state for Michael Dukakis in 1988, Bill Clinton in 1992 and 1996 and Al Gore in 2000. Democrats have also won most downballot races in presidential years. Three different Democrats have held the governorship since 1984, and Democrats hold both Senate seats and six of its nine U.S. House seats.

The political lines are fairly clear. The central city of Seattle is increasingly the liberal bastion, while old blue-collar lumber country strongholds have soured on many Democrats: Seattle's King County, by a wide margin the most affluent county in the state, is also its liberal stronghold. Republicans run best in the arid country east of the Cascades, with far lower income levels, this is a marchland between the culturally liberal Pacific Rim and the culturally conservative Rocky Mountains. Culture wars also are fought out in referenda. In 1997 voters rejected easing penalties for marijuana use and a ban on discrimination against (or for) gays; a gun control measure, requiring trigger locks for guns and safety tests for handgun owners, was rejected 71%–29%. In 1998, despite opposition from nearly every newspaper, all Democratic and some Republican politicians, Boeing, Starbucks, Microsoft and Eddie Bauer, voters approved by 58%–42% a ban on racial and gender quotas and preferences in state government. In 1999, against business and union opposition, voters passed 56%–44% Initiative 695, which eliminated the 2.2% car tax and replaced it with a $30 annual fee; this reduced state revenue $750 million, or 7.5% of the state budget—the state courts later ruled the initiative was unconstitutional so the legislature passed a law to do it instead. Washington likes its politicians liberal, but operating under conservative restraints.

Washington had a humdrum political year in 2002, with neither the governorship nor a Senate seat up. But in 2004 it may be a focus of national politics. George W. Bush, who lost the state 50%–45% in 2000, did not visit it in 2001 or 2002, but might target it in 2004. This is a state sharply divided on cultural issues, where the outcome of elections can depend on whether turnout is high in liberal King County or conservative eastern Washington.

The People		Race/Ethnic Origin			Military veterans: 670,628 (15.3%)
Pop. 2000:	5,894,121	4,652,490	78.9%	White	WWII: 16.3% Korea: 11.4%
Pop. 1990:	4,866,692	184,631	3.1%	Black	Vietnam: 35.9% Gulf War: 12.2%
Change 1990–2000:	Up 21.1%	319,401	5.4%	Asian	**Most populous cities:**
Change 1980–1990:	Up 17.8%	85,396	1.4%	Native Am.	1. Seattle 563,374
% of U.S. total:	2.1%	22,779	0.4%	Hawaiian	2. Spokane 195,629
Pop. rank:	15th of 50	175,926	3.0%	Two+ races	3. Tacoma 193,556
Area size:	71,300 sq. mi.	11,989	0.2%	Other	4. Vancouver 143,560
State Native:	47.2%	441,509	7.5%	Hisp. Origin	5. Bellevue 109,569
Non-citizen:	6.1%	**Ancestry**			
Language		German: 13.7% English: 8.8%			Urban population: 82.0%
English: 84.2%	Spanish: 6.1%	Irish: 8.3% Norwegian: 4.6%			Rural population: 18.0%
Asian: 4.6%		USA: 3.9%			

Education		Work Sector		Legislature	
H.S. Grad:	87.1%	Private: 76.1%	Govt: 16.5%	Senate	25 R 24 D
College Grad:	27.7%	Self: 7.2%	Family: 0.3%	House	52 D 46 R
Industry		Unemployment: 6.1%		Legislative Term Limits: No	
Agri: 2.5%	Con: 7.0%	**Household Income**		**Registered Voters**	
Fin: 6.1%	Info: 3.4%	<15k: 13.1%	15-35k: 24.2%	No party registration	
Mfg: 17.9%	Prof: 29.1%	35-50k: 17.1%	50-100k: 33.0%		
Public: 5.0%	Trade: 16.2%	100-150k: 8.3%	>150k: 4.3%		
Other: 12.8%		Median: $45,776			
Occupation		Poverty status: 10.6%			
Blue collar: 22.1%	White collar: 61.4%	**Home Value**			
Gray collar: 16.4%		<50k: 5.8% 50-100k: 15.2% 100-200k: 45.7% 200-300k: 19.3%			
		300-500k: 10.1% >500k: 3.9% Median: $158,800			

Presidential politics For three decades Washington was one of the most contrarian states in presidential politics, voting for losers Richard Nixon in 1960, Hubert Humphrey in 1968, Gerald Ford in 1976 and Michael Dukakis in 1988. In the 1990s it was in sync with the nation, voting for Bill Clinton twice, but there has been an increasing divergence between coastal and interior voting patterns. In 1996 Clinton carried the state 50%–37%, winning by solid margins in Seattle's King County (57%–32%), which includes about one-third of the voters, and the rest of the west (49%–38%), with about half. He lost eastern Washington (45%–42%), with about one-fifth of the voters. In 2000 Al Gore carried the state 50%–45%, with the same percentage as Clinton. But the vote was more polarized. Gore carried King County overwhelmingly (60%–34%) but only won narrowly in the rest of the west (49%–46%). He lost by a wide margin in eastern Washington (58%–37%). Clinton would have carried the state without King County; Gore would not. Gore carried union voters by a solid 62%–32% margin, while running marginally ahead among high income voters, who are heavily concentrated in culturally liberal King County. By the way the racial mix here is very different from back east: 5% Asian, 8% Hispanic and 3% black.

2000 Presidential Vote		
Gore (D)	1,247,652	(50%)
Bush (R)	1,108,864	(45%)
Nader (Green)	103,002	(4%)
Other	27,915	(1%)

2000 Republican Presidential Primary		
Bush (R)	402,287	(48%)
McCain (R)	399,980	(48%)
Other	31,391	(4%)

2000 Democratic Presidential Primary		
Gore (D)	310,406	(65%)
Bradley (D)	162,727	(34%)

1996 Presidential Vote		
Clinton (D)	1,123,323	(50%)
Dole (R)	840,712	(37%)
Perot (I)	201,003	(9%)
Other	90,465	(4%)

Washington switched from a caucus system to primaries in 1992, when Pat Robertson won among Republicans and Jesse Jackson finished a solid second among Democrats: not much precedent for November there. In April 1999 Washington, which has never seen much of presidential primary candidates, set its primary for leap-year day, February 29, 2000. For the Democrats, this was a "beauty contest," since under party rules delegates chosen within five weeks of New Hampshire were not entitled to seating at the convention. In 2000 Bill Bradley, without any other contests in which to pick up momentum, campaigned here for six days, to no avail; Al Gore won by about 2–1. George W. Bush beat John McCain by a razor-thin margin.

Congressional districting In 1983 Washington voters approved a constitutional amendment which provided that congressional and legislative districts be drawn by a bipartisan commission; the lines can be changed by a two-thirds vote of the legislature. If the commission is deadlocked, the issue goes to the state Supreme Court. In 1991 the commission created four districts that were pretty evenly divided between the parties: only three of the nine districts were won by the same party in the five elections during which the lines were in effect. The problem was that even minor alterations in the closely divided districts—the 1st, 2d, 3d and 9th—can make changes that will turn out to be partisanly significant at some point in the next decade. But 6th District Democrat Norm Dicks and 8th District Republican Jennifer Dunn pressed the commissioners to compromise. As one commissioner said, "It's hard not to pass a plan when you have Norm Dicks calling you every day." Just before the constitutional deadline expired on January 1, 2002, they reached agreement. Attorney General Christine Gregoire pushed the legislature to change the statutory December 15 deadline to eliminate any question of the plan's legality; the legislators were happy to do so and made no changes in the plan. This 2002 plan followed pretty closely the lines drawn in 1991. The Washington plan has been lauded by many for taking partisanship out of redistricting and for creating more districts that both parties can win. But in Washington, where the commission is not bound by the mathematical requirements that in Iowa have resulted in districts not tailored to incumbents, incumbent protection has been the result. It is possible that

108th Congress Lineup	
6 D	3 R

107th Congress Lineup	
6 D	3 R

some of Washington's districts may be seriously contested between 2004 and 2010, and it is almost certain that some will be if the incumbent does not run for reelection. But only one, the 2d District, was seriously contested in 2002.

Governor

Gary Locke (D)

Elected 1996, term expires Jan. 2005, 2d term; b. Jan. 21, 1950, Seattle; home, Olympia; Yale U., B.A. 1972, Boston U., J.D. 1975; Protestant; married (Mona).

Elected Office: WA House of Reps., 1982–93; King Cnty. Chief Exec., 1994–97.

Professional Career: Dpty. King Cnty. Prosecuting atty., 1976–80; Staff atty., WA Senate, 1981; Legal Advisor, Seattle Human Rights Dept., 1981–82; Community Relations Mgr., U.S. West, 1988–92.

Office: P.O. Box 40002, Olympia, 98504, 360-902-4111; Fax: 360-753-4110; Web site: www.governor.wa.gov.

Election Results

2000 general	Gary Locke (D)	1,441,973	(58%)
	John Eric Carlson (R)	980,060	(40%)
	Other	47,819	(2%)
2000 primary	Gary Locke (D)	701,929	(54%)
	John Eric Carlson (R)	446,142	(35%)
	Harold Hochstatter (R)	93,467	(7%)
	Other	50,764	(4%)
1996 general	Gary Locke (D)	1,296,492	(58%)
	Ellen Craswell (R)	940,538	(42%)

Gary Locke, a Democrat, was elected governor of Washington in 1996 and 2000, the first governor of Chinese descent in American history. Locke grew up in Seattle, the son of immigrants from Guandong and Hong Kong; he lived six years in a housing project and worked in his father's restaurant and grocery store; his grandfather worked as a houseboy less than a mile from the state Capitol. Locke graduated from Yale (a beneficiary of affirmative action, he says) and Boston University Law School, returned to Seattle and worked as a deputy prosecutor and community relations manager for USWest. In 1982, at 32, he was elected to the state House from a liberal district in Seattle and rose to chair the Appropriations Committee; he supported an income tax (Washington still doesn't have one) and the 1993 tax increases that helped to make Democratic Governor Mike Lowry unpopular. That same year, Locke was elected King County Executive. His father was once shot at the family's grocery store, and Locke has been a supporter of tough penalties for crime and victim's rights legislation.

In February 1996 Lowry, a liberal and former congressman who was staggering under charges of sexual harassment, announced his retirement, and Locke decided to run for governor. It was a crowded field in what was then an all-party primary. Locke's main opponent, Seattle Mayor Norm Rice, shared the same base; they also faced former Congressman Jay Inslee from east of the mountains (he has since moved to the Seattle area and is now congressman from the 1st District). Locke won with 24% of the total vote to 18% for Rice and 10% for Inslee. The Republican field was more fragmented, and the nomination was won by former state Senator Ellen Craswell, who emphasized her religious faith. Altogether Democrats won 52% of votes, Republicans 48%, indicating a close race in November. Craswell emphasized what she called "God's plan" to cut state taxes 30% (later modified to 15%) and to privatize state universities, which evidently struck many voters as bizarre. Republican ads accused Locke of supporting prostitution (King County had a county prostitute counseling service). Locke, despite his liberal record in the legislature, took a moderate tack, abjuring tax increases and calling for more spending on education, with higher standards and accountability. Although some polls showed a close race, Locke won 58%–42%, with a 62%–38% lead in the Seattle area; Craswell just barely carried the east.

Locke cultivated an image of moderation and compromise even as he vetoed more bills than any previous governor in his first months. But he and the legislature operate under the constraints of Initiative 601, passed in 1993, which limits spending increases to a formula based on population and inflation. Locke vetoed some changes in welfare reform but approved a business tax cut. He vetoed a bill banning gay marriage in February 1998; that was overridden in five hours as Democrats scampered to keep the issue off the November 1998 ballot. Left on was Referendum 49, a proposal to cut the auto tax and dedicate the revenue, plus money from a huge bond issue, into a fund devoted to transportation; that passed 57%–43%.

In 1998 Democrats won a 27–22 margin in the Senate and a 49–49 tie in the House, which left Locke to stick to the middle ground. The evenly divided House, with co-speakers and co-chairmen of committees, in time worked out compromises on major state issues—regulating HMOs and changing unemployment insurance. In November 1999 voters passed Initiative 695, eliminating the 2.2% car tab tax, which had provided 7.5% of state revenue and was replaced by a $30 annual fee; it also provided that voters would have to approve any new state or local tax increase or fee. It was opposed by business groups, unions and Locke, but a volunteer campaign led by Mukilteo wristwatch salesman Tim Eyman prevailed and voters approved it by a 56%–44% margin. Locke offered health benefits for the same-sex partners of state employees and offered senior citizens a chance to buy prescription drugs through the state employees' health plan. His Republican opponent in 2000 was radio talk show host John Carlson, a strong backer of the 1993 initiative to limit spending increases to inflation and population increase and the 1998 initiatives to end racial quotas and preferences. Carlson called for lower taxes, more lanes on the Evergreen Point Floating Bridge and a new bridge to Portland to clear up traffic and more teachers. In August Republicans ran ads criticizing Locke for vetoing a bill to bring methamphetamine crimes under the three-strikes law, and for the death of a three-year-old killed by her mother after state social workers removed her from foster home and gave the mother custody. But voters were in a consensus-minded, pro-incumbent mood, and Locke won 58%–40% margin. He carried King County 66%–32% and the rest of western Washington by 56%–42%; he even carried eastern Washington 51%–47%, thanks to a large margin in Spokane County.

Locke had convened Competitive Council that identified transportation as the state's leading problem: in the boom of the late 1990s Seattle's freeways were clogged and the bridges over Lake Washington were deteriorating. Locke responded by proposing a 9-cent increase in the gas tax to yield $8.5 billion for transportation. In July 2001 the legislature rejected this; Republicans would not support it unless it was put before the voters as a referendum. Locke tried again in January 2002, and this time the legislature, in which the Democrats had the narrowest of majorities, approved it with a November referendum. With a budget shortfall looming, Locke put in a hiring and equipment freeze and laid off some employees. With support from business and unions and from former Republican Senator Slade Gorton, Locke campaigned hard for the transportation referendum. But it lost 62%–38% in November; only in San Juan County, dependent on state ferries, did voters approve. Voters gave Republicans a 25–24 majority in the state Senate and Democrats a 52–46 majority in the state House.

In December 2002 Locke became chairman of the Democratic Governors Association and in January 2003 he delivered the Democratic response to George W. Bush's State of the Union address. Locke told his family's story and said that Americans were "still far too vulnerable" to terrorism and that Bush's tax cuts were "upside down economics." At home the state faced a $2 billion shortfall in the next budget. In constructing his budget, Locke ranked spending according to 10 Priorities of Government. That led him to call for suspending two initiatives passed in 2000, providing for a teacher pay increase and class size reduction, and for removing 60,000 of the 125,000 people on the state's Basic Health Plan, insurance for those who don't qualify for Medicaid. He flatly ruled out major tax increases. He called for modification of the state's high school graduation requirements (many students were failing tests) and for cleanup efforts in Puget Sound. Many Democrats angrily denounced Locke's education and health care proposals, but Republicans seemed to favor them and John Carlson praised them warmly. By the end of the regular session in April 2003, the legislature had not reached agreement on class size reduction, teacher pay or the Basic Health Plan; they made no changes to the graduation requirements. In May, Locke signed a $4.2 billion transportation plan funded by a 5-cent gas tax.

In early 2003 Locke said he had not decided whether to run for a third term in 2004. His job approval rating in January 2003 was only 30%, down from 67% in summer 1998. If he does run, he seems likely to have primary opposition. Former state senator and state Supreme Court Justice Phil Talmadge announced he was running and said, "Everywhere I go, people say the same thing—the Democratic party has no policies and no soul. We seem tired, distracted and aimless." One potentially strong Republican candidate drew mention: John Stanton, founder of Western Wireless and the co-owner of the Seattle Mariners and the Supersonics.

Senior Senator

Patty Murray (D)

Elected 1992, seat up 2004, 2d term; b. Oct. 11, 1950, Seattle; home, Seattle; WA St. U., B.A. 1972; Catholic; married (Rob).

Elected Office: Shoreline Schl. Bd., 1985–89, Pres., 1985–86; WA Senate, 1988–92.

DC Office: 173 RSOB, 20510, 202-224-2621; Fax: 202-224-0238; Web site: murray.senate.gov.

State Offices: Everett, 425-259-6515; Seattle, 206-553-5545; Spokane, 509-624-9515; Vancouver, 360-696-7797; Yakima, 509-453-7462.

Committees: *Appropriations*: Commerce, Justice, State & Judiciary; Energy & Water Development; Homeland Security; Labor, HHS & Education; Transportation, Treasury & General Government (RMM). *Budget. Health, Education, Labor & Pensions*: Aging; Children & Families; Employment, Safety & Training (RMM). *Veterans' Affairs*.

Group Ratings

	ADA	ACLU	AFS	LCV	CON	ITIC	NTU	COC	ACU	NTLC	CHC
2002	90	60	88	76	31	88	19	55	10	3	—
2001	85	—	100	75	—	—	9	64	4	—	0

National Journal Ratings

	2001 LIB	—	2001 CONS		2002 LIB	—	2002 CONS
Economic	70%	—	30%		80%	—	15%
Social	81%	—	8%		72%	—	25%
Foreign	98%	—	0%		67%	—	30%

Key Votes of the 107th Congress

1. Approve Bush Tax Cuts	N	5. Confirm Ashcroft as AG	N	9. Bar Coop. with Intl. Court	N
2. Expand Patients' Rights	Y	6. Bar Gays in the Boy Scouts	N	10. Trade Promotion Authority	Y
3. Campaign Finance Reform	Y	7. $ for Hate Crime Prosecution	Y	11. Authorize Force in Iraq	N
4. Permit ANWR Development	N	8. Overseas Military Abortions	Y	12. Homeland Sec. Dept. Union	Y

Election Results

1998 general	Patty Murray (D)	1,103,184	(58%)	($5,600,592)
	Linda Smith (R)	785,377	(42%)	($5,159,527)
1998 primary	Patty Murray (D)	479,009	(46%)	
	Linda Smith (R)	337,407	(32%)	
	Chris Bayley (R)	155,864	(15%)	
	Other	72,109	(7%)	
1992 general	Patty Murray (D)	1,197,973	(54%)	($1,342,038)
	Rod Chandler (R)	1,020,829	(46%)	($2,504,777)

Patty Murray is the senior senator from Washington, first elected in 1992. Murray grew up in the Seattle suburb of Bothell, the daughter of a disabled veteran. She graduated from Washington State University in 1972, married and stayed home to raise her children. In 1980, when she was in Olympia trying to save from budget cuts a parent education class she was teaching at Shoreline Community College, a state legislator told her gruffly, "You're just a mom in tennis shoes; you can't make a difference." As she had said later, "Almost every woman I've ever met in politics got into it because she was mad about something." But like many committed public employees, she won her fight; then she ran for the Shoreline School District board, lost, was appointed and then elected, and served as president. In 1988 she challenged a Republican state senator, knocked on 17,000 doors and won the seat. Her first great cause there was extending a family leave bill to include leave for a parent whose child is sick or dying; she threatened to put the proposal on the ballot, and won the issue. Then in late 1991 she decided to run against U.S. Senator Brock Adams, who was under a cloud from charges of sexual harassment and later decided not to seek reelection.

Amid a crowd of better-known conventional male politicians, Murray, with her flat accent and "mom in tennis shoes" line, attracted most of the attention and most of the votes. In the all-party primary, her main Democratic opponent was former Congressman Don Bonker, who had narrowly lost a Senate nomination in 1988. But Murray won 28% of the total vote to Bonker's 19%. Meanwhile, three well-known Republicans vied: Congressman Rod Chandler won 20% to 16% for state Senator Leo Thorsness and 11% for King County Executive Tim Hill. Murray sprinted to a big lead in polls, and in November won 54%–46%. Her margins over Chandler were similar to Bill Clinton's over George Bush, except in eastern Washington, which Clinton nearly carried but where Murray ran 10% behind.

In the Senate Murray has had a largely liberal voting record. In her first years she refused to see Washington industry lobbyists; in a scathing *Seattle Times* profile in 1996, Robert Nelson wrote of Murray, "Colleagues, lobbyists and former staff members view her as indifferent to issues that can't be explained through anecdotes about her family and neighbors." She got a seat on Appropriations and became involved in Washington issues: seeking funding for cleanup of the Hanford Nuclear Reservation, trying to preserve the undammed Hanford Reach of the Columbia as a wild and scenic river. Murray defended Microsoft against the antitrust case brought by the Clinton Justice Department; she criticized Judge Thomas Penfield Jackson's decision in November 1999. Murray was one of the Senate's strongest proponents of PNTR with China—a position strongly backed by Boeing; she also favors relaxing export restrictions on encryption technology. In January 2001 she mediated a 45-day strike by the Pacific Northwest Newspaper Guild against the *Seattle Times*.

When Democrats gained their Senate majority in June 2001, Murray became chairman of the Transportation Appropriations Subcommittee. By December 2001 her appropriation had $190 million of projects for Washington, more than twice as much as in 2000—$20 million for the Sounder Commuter Rail between Tacoma and Lakewood, $9.5 million for Puget Sound transit hubs, $12.6 million for repair of Seattle's earthquake-damaged Pier 36. John McCain, in his campaign against what he considers pork barrel spending, singled out two items for abuse: $3 million for the Odyssey Maritime Project, actually a Seattle museum (the owner gave the Senate campaign committee Murray headed $25,000) and $4.65 million for the Coast Guard to purchase a fast boat built by Guardian Marine International which it hadn't requested. Her appropriation also included money for the Air Force to lease up to 100 Boeing 767s over 10 years, to replace aging KC-135 tankers at a potential cost of $26 billion. McCain called this one of "the great rip-offs in the history of the United States of America" and "war profiteering." In July 2001 she and ranking minority member Richard Shelby sought to restrict Mexican trucks in the United States. Under the NAFTA treaty ratified in 1993, they were supposed to be able to venture beyond a 20-mile border zone in January 2002. Murray and Shelby argued that Mexican trucks were unsafe and called for requiring them to undergo inspections and weigh-in-motion scales on the border and to obtain insurance from U.S. licensed insurers. This was a big priority for the Teamsters Union, long a major presence in Washington. The House had passed an even stricter bill, but the Bush administration threatened to veto the appropriation if it stayed in. In conference committee in November, under threat of veto, Murray and Shelby compromised by relaxing their inspection and insurance provisions.

Murray and Olympia Snowe have long sought to have abortions allowed in military hospitals; they lost by narrow margins in May 1999 and June 2000, but prevailed 52–40 in June 2002. They also co-sponsored a bill to create a national sales tax holiday during the 10 days after Thanksgiving 2001; the federal government would reimburse states $6.5 billion for lost revenues. Murray clashed with the senior Republican from Washington, Representative Jennifer Dunn, on the issue of federal judges. Murray and Republican Slade Gorton had had a bipartisan panel to select judges but Dunn, when Republicans had the Senate majority, rejected that approach. She set up her own panel and either (Dunn's version) invited Murray and Maria Cantwell to participate or (Murray's version) simply named her own nominee, whom Murray and Cantwell blocked.

In December 1998 Murray was named vice-chairman of the DSCC and in December 2000, when no one else seemed to want the job, she succeeded Bob Torricelli as chairman. Torricelli had set records in fundraising and helped Democrat gain five seats and get within reach of a majority. Murray nearly doubled Torricelli in fundraising and brought in $158 million during the cycle. She also did a fine job of recruiting candidates. But she did less well at the polls. Democrats took only one seat from Republicans and lost three to them—and the Senate majority. After the election Murray said, "We need to not feel we lost, as everyone likes to portray at this point. Had we not had those two plane crashes"—one which killed Democratic nominee Mel Carnahan in October 2000 and the other which killed incumbent Paul Wellstone in October 2002—"we would still be in the majority."

In December 2002, at a meeting with an honors class at Columbia River High School in Vancouver, Murray, who voted against the Iraq war resolution in October, was asked about Osama bin Laden. She said, "We've got to ask, 'Why is this man [Osama bin Laden] so popular around the world? Why are people so supportive of him in many countries . . . that are riddled with poverty?' He's been out in these countries for decades, building schools, building roads, building infrastructure, building day care facilities, building health care facilities, and the people are extremely grateful. We haven't done that. How would they look at us today if we had been there helping them with some of that rather than just being the people who are going to bomb in Iraq and go to Afghanistan?" Republicans and conservatives in the media immediately criticized this comment in harsh tones. Murray aides, playing defense, pointed out that the State Department website said that bin Laden had in fact built roads, tunnels, hospitals and storage depots in Afghanistan, but could not point to other countries except perhaps Sudan where he had done such good works, nor could they point to any day care centers he had built. For several days Murray refused to comment and then, rather than defend the substance of her remarks, she complained that she was being criticized. "What is important is that we have to have thoughtful debates and discussions in this country and raise questions and answer them without being pulled into some right wing media frenzy. That is truly frightening to me."

All this prompted some Republicans to speculate that Murray might be vulnerable when she comes up for reelection in 2004, even though she won reelection by a solid margin in 1998. Her opponent that year was Congresswoman Linda Smith, another mom in tennis shoes—a strong opponent of abortion, backer of campaign finance regulation and opponent of free trade, a favorite of Ross Perot who was mistrusted by the Republican leadership. In the all-party primary (California's was ruled unconstitutional in 2000 by the U.S. Supreme Court) in September, Smith won the Republican nomination with 32% of all votes; Murray won 46%. The all-party primary used to be a good predictor of November results, and these numbers made it look like a close race. But the primary came when Bill Clinton's numbers were at their lowest that year, before release of the Starr report, when they jumped back up. Murray campaigned as a public official who had addressed issues of importance to Washington voters—"apples to aerospace, high-tech to Hanford, saving salmon to educating kids." She raised far more money than Smith, who spent much of her money on direct mail rather than TV ads. On Election Day and before (about one-third of Washington's votes that year were cast by absentee ballot) Murray won 58%–42%, winning 63% in the Seattle area and 55% in west Washington; Smith carried the east by only 51%–49%. After the November 2002 election, Murray said that she was "absolutely, positively" running again.

Congresswoman Jennifer Dunn, often mentioned as a possible opponent, took herself out of the race in April 2003. Also frequently mentioned as a candidate was Congressman George Nethercutt.

Junior Senator

Maria Cantwell (D)

Elected 2000, seat up 2006, 1st term; b. Oct., 13, 1958, Indianapolis, IN; home, Edmonds; Miami U. (OH), B.A. 1981; Catholic; single.

Elected Office: WA House of Reps., 1987–92; U.S. House of Reps., 1992–94.

Professional Career: RealNetworks, 1995–2000.

DC Office: 717 HSOB, 20510, 202-224-3441; Fax: 202-228-0514; Web site: cantwell.senate.gov.

State Offices: Richland, 509-946-8106; Seattle, 206-220-6400; Spokane, 509-353-2507; Vancouver, 360-696-7838.

Committees: *Commerce, Science & Transportation*: Aviation; Communications; Competition, Foreign Commerce & Infrastructure; Oceans, Fisheries & Coast Guard. *Energy & Natural Resources*: Energy; Water & Power. *Indian Affairs. Small Business & Entrepreneurship.*

Group Ratings

	ADA	ACLU	AFS	LCV	CON	ITIC	NTU	COC	ACU	NTLC	CHC
2002	80	60	88	82	84	88	20	55	25	6	—
2001	100	—	100	75	—	—	7	50	12	—	0

National Journal Ratings

	2001 LIB —	2001 CONS	2002 LIB —	2002 CONS
Economic	79%	19%	90%	5%
Social	95%	0%	72%	25%
Foreign	87%	3%	62%	36%

Key Votes of the 107th Congress

1. Approve Bush Tax Cuts	N	5. Confirm Ashcroft as AG	N	9. Bar Coop. with Intl. Court	N
2. Expand Patients' Rights	Y	6. Bar Gays in the Boy Scouts	N	10. Trade Promotion Authority	Y
3. Campaign Finance Reform	Y	7. $ for Hate Crime Prosecution	Y	11. Authorize Force in Iraq	Y
4. Permit ANWR Development	N	8. Overseas Military Abortions	Y	12. Homeland Sec. Dept. Union	Y

Election Results

2000 general	Maria Cantwell (D)	1,199,437	(49%)	($11,533,295)
	Slade Gorton (R)	1,197,208	(49%)	($6,402,488)
	Other	64,734	(3%)	
2000 primary	Slade Gorton (R)	560,787	(44%)	
	Maria Cantwell (D)	472,609	(37%)	
	Deborah Senn (D)	168,110	(13%)	
	Other	85,732	(7%)	
1994 general	Slade Gorton (R)	947,821	(56%)	($4,792,764)
	Ron Sims (D)	752,352	(44%)	($1,228,098)

Prior Winning Percentages: 1992 House (55%)

Maria Cantwell is a Democrat elected in the closest Senate race of 2000. Cantwell grew up in Indianapolis, where her father, a construction worker, served as county commissioner, city councilman and state legislator. She graduated from Miami University (Ohio) in 1980—the first in her family to graduate from college—and worked in Ohio for Jerry Springer's 1982 campaign for governor. Then she worked for Senator Alan Cranston's presidential campaign and went to Seattle to set up a regional campaign office. The Cranston campaign went nowhere, and so did Cantwell: she loved the Pacific Northwest and decided to stay. She moved to Mountlake Terrace, a suburb in Snohomish County just north of Seattle, where she organized a coalition to build a new library. In 1986, at 28, she was elected to the Washington House.

In 1992 Cantwell ran for the House, for the just redrawn 1st District seat being vacated by Republican John Miller. She won a solid 55%–42% victory. In the House she supported the family and medical leave bill and the Clinton economic plan; she did not support the Clinton health care plan and only supported NAFTA at the last minute. She was a strong supporter of abortion rights and of stands backed by environmental advocacy groups. But by fall 1994 some of those positions had become unpopular. In the September 1994 all-party primary she got just 44% of the vote, compared to 52% for three Republican candidates. In November she lost 52%–48% to Republican nominee Rick White.

Back in the Seattle area, she joined a startup firm called Progressive Networks in 1995; five years later it had become RealNetworks, a leader in Internet-based audio and visual software. In late 1999 her stock was worth about $40 million, and she decided to run against Republican Senator Slade Gorton. A brainy and hard-working veteran of Washington politics, Gorton served as attorney general from 1968 to 1980 and was elected senator in 1980, 1988 and 1994 (he lost a race in 1986). Gorton had an increasingly conservative record on environmental and economic issues; he was also Microsoft's leading advocate on Capitol Hill. Cantwell was an answer to Democrats' prayers; their well-known House members had declined to run, and Insurance Commissioner Deborah Senn, who was running, was widely considered too liberal to win. They had different role models: Cantwell called herself a New Democrat in the Clinton mode, while Senn said her role model was Senator Barbara Mikulski. But the real difference was money. Cantwell, who liquidated more than $5 million of her RealNetworks stock, spent freely, while Senn was on TV only during the last two weeks before the September all-party primary. Cantwell won 37% of the total vote, to only 13% for Senn; Gorton, with 44% of the vote, was ahead but short of a majority.

For the general Cantwell said she would spend "whatever it takes" to win. At the same time, she made her support of McCain-Feingold-type campaign finance regulation a major issue, and refused to take contributions from PACs or soft money from the Democratic Party (though it put $640,000 into the state before Cantwell won the primary). She charged that Gorton was beholden to special interest contributors, singling out his last-night amendment to open a cyanide-leach gold mine in Okanogan County. Gorton called Cantwell an old-style liberal Democrat who would have government meddling in health care, education and local environmental issues. Cantwell highlighted her experience in the high-tech private sector. She called Gorton divisive, saying he pit eastern Washington against Seattle on environmental and other issues. Overall, Cantwell spent $11.5 million, $10.3 million of which she contributed; Gorton spent $6.4 million.

Gorton led on election night, but not by much. Washington allows absentee voting, and 54% of the votes were cast absentee; two days after the election, one-quarter of the votes had yet to be counted. During the three weeks of counting, Gorton seemed to have the advantage. But the last two day's absentee ballots from King County put Cantwell over the top by 1,953. A mandated recount left the margin at 2,229 for Cantwell, out of 2.4 million cast. Cantwell carried only five counties—King, Snohomish, Thurston (which includes the state capital of Olympia) and two small counties in the west. She won King County 59%–39%; she also carried the rest of western Washington 50%–47%. Gorton carried eastern Washington 61%–36%—a lot but not quite enough to win. Cantwell's victory created a tie in the Senate, until James Jeffords became an independent in May 2001 and gave Democrats a razor-thin majority. This race was a very big loss for the Republican Party.

In the Senate Cantwell worked hard on campaign finance in the March 2001 two-week session on the issue. After September 11, she put an amendment into the Patriot Act tripling the number of border guards on the Canadian border and another to require the administration to develop a form of biometric identification, perhaps by facial recognition software. On the Judiciary Committee she advanced a bill to give consumers redress against identity theft. In May 2002 she urged FERC to cancel electricity contracts entered into during 2001; the Bonneville Power Authority had raised rates 46%. The bill she and Bob Smith sponsored to end the requirement that military women stationed in Saudi Arabia be required to wear abayas off base passed in June

2002. Her bill to provide federal funding of DNA analysis passed the Senate in September 2002. In January 2003 her amendment to require the Bush administration to release $300 million in low income heating assistance passed overwhelmingly; two days later the administration released $200 million. In February 2003 she and Texas's Kay Bailey Hutchison introduced a bill to allow taxpayers to deduct state sales taxes as well as state income taxes on their federal income tax forms; Texas like Washington has a sales tax but no income tax. In January 2003 she moved off the strife-torn Judiciary Committee to Commerce, where she promised to look after Washington interests. In December 2001 and February 2003 she traveled to Cuba and tried to spur interest in Washington peas, lentils and wine. Unlike her colleague Patty Murray, she voted for the Iraq war resolution in October 2002.

A strong supporter of campaign finance regulation, Cantwell had campaign finance problems of her own. To finance her 2000 campaign she had sold $5.6 million of her RealNetworks stock and had borrowed $3.8 million from a bank with RealNetworks stock as collateral. But Real-Network, like so many high-tech firms, saw its stock price plummet, from $80 in spring 2000 to $6 in spring 2001. Suddenly she owed far more than the collateral was worth. She negotiated another loan due December 2001, guaranteed by the DSCC, which of course could use soft money to pay it off. And she began raising money, from committed Democrats and from Washington lobbyists. She raised $3.3 million in 2001 and 2002, but in early 2003 her campaign was still in debt and her personal net worth was evidently below $1 million. But she had never shown much interest in an affluent lifestyle, and she proved the old rule that the smart thing to do with bubble money is to use it to buy something you want. Her 2006 campaign will presumably not be self-financed, and presumably will be conducted in different style; she has been traveling by car, not plane, to keep her promise to visit each of Washington's 39 counties every year.

FIRST DISTRICT

Rep. Jay Inslee (D)

Elected 1998, 3d term; b. Feb. 9, 1951, Seattle; home, Bainbridge Island; Stanford U., 1969–70, U. of WA, B.A. 1973, Willamette U., J.D. 1976.; Christian; married (Trudi).

Elected Office: WA House of Reps., 1988–92; U.S. House of Reps., 1992–94.

Professional Career: Practicing atty., 1976–92, 1995–96; Regional Dir., U.S. Dept. of H.H.S., 1997–98.

DC Office: 308 CHOB 20515, 202-225-6311; Fax: 202-226-1606; Web site: www.house.gov/inslee.

District Offices: Mountlake Terrace, 425-640-0233; Poulsbo, 360-598-2342.

Committees: *Financial Services* (14th of 32 D): Capital Markets, Insurance & Government Sponsored Enterprises; Oversight & Investigations. *Resources* (10th of 24 D): Forests & Forest Health (RMM); Water & Power.

Group Ratings

	ADA	ACLU	AFS	LCV	CON	ITIC	NTU	COC	ACU	NTLC	CHC
2002	95	87	100	88	63	50	19	45	4	0	0
2001	90	—	100	100	—	—	10	41	4	—	—

National Journal Ratings

	2001 LIB —	2001 CONS		2002 LIB —	2002 CONS
Economic	80%	— 21%		68%	— 32%
Social	83%	— 11%		84%	— 8%
Foreign	73%	— 26%		77%	— 19%

Key Votes of the 107th Congress

1. Approve Bush Tax Cuts	N	5. Faith-Based Charities	N	9. Trade Promotion Authority	N
2. Limit Patients' Bill of Rights	N	6. Bar Gays in the Boy Scouts	N	10. Bar Funds for Intl. Court	Y
3. Campaign Finance Reform	Y	7. Ban Partial-Birth Abortion	N	11. Authorize Force in Iraq	N
4. Ban ANWR Development	Y	8. Arm Commercial Pilots	N	12. Deny Home. Sec. Dept. Union	N

Election Results

2002 general	Jay Inslee (D)	114,087	(56%)	($643,505)
	Joe Marine (R)	84,696	(41%)	($205,550)
	Other	6,251	(3%)	
2002 primary	Jay Inslee (D)	65,368	(56%)	
	Joe Marine (R)	42,473	(37%)	
	Mike The Mover (D)	5,291	(5%)	
	Other	3,025	(3%)	
2000 general	Jay Inslee (D)	155,820	(55%)	($2,009,131)
	Daniel McDonald (R)	121,823	(43%)	($1,462,965)
	Other	7,993	(3%)	

Prior Winning Percentages: 1998 (50%); 1992 (51%)

The People		Race/Ethnic Origin	Ancestry	
Area size:	616 sq. mi.	81.6% White	German: 13.6%	English: 10.0%
Urban population:	95.4%	1.8% Black	Irish: 8.7%	
Rural population:	4.6%	7.9% Asian	**2000 Presidential Vote**	
Pop. 2000:	654,904	0.8% Native Am.	Gore (D)	154,583 (53%)
Median income:	$58,565	0.3% Hawaiian	Bush (R)	123,879 (42%)
Poverty status:	5.6%	3.1% Two + races	Other	13,803 (5%)
Military veterans:	14.5%	0.2% Other	**Cook Partisan Voting Index:** D + 5	
		4.3% Hispanic Origin		

Occupation   Blue collar: 18.0%   White collar: 69.4%   Gray collar: 12.6%

In the past 30 years, metropolitan Seattle spread out to the north and the east, as a growing wave of newcomers arrived seeking this area's distinctive blend of natural environmental beauty, free-wheeling culture and briskly expanding economy. In the process some of the distinctiveness of the old Seattle is left behind. The fishy odor of its docks does not permeate the new subdivisions built on what were once vegetable fields or vineyards; the Scandinavian heritage of old neighborhoods like Ballard has been mixed into a Pacific Northwest blend.

The heart of this new Seattle is east of Lake Washington, in the edge city of Redmond. Here are the turquoise, pine-shaded low-rise buildings of the Microsoft campus—a tranquil environment for a booming and boisterously aggressive company. Microsoft set the standard for computer software and made billions for its founder Bill Gates by taking advantage of others' oversights, cobbling together innovative software that is sometimes barely "good enough" to put on the marketplace, and keeping fierce watch to see if its market niches are threatened by the new developments of others—too fierce, said the Clinton Justice Department and one trial judge. The company disagreed, and won most of its case on appeal with the D.C. Circuit; with that burden lifted, the optimistic corporate culture appeared to reassert itself under the Redmond pines. With 26,000 employees in Washington—one-half of its worldwide total—the company had expanded its 300-acre campus and made plans for a new campus to the south in Issaquah, which could house 15,000 more employees. Not far away is the eastern shore of Lake Washington, home to many of the newly super-rich, where motorists on the causeway can make out from miles away the $60 million mansion that Bill and Melinda Gates took six years to complete—a 66,000-square-foot complex with a trampoline room with vaulted ceilings, video walls that can be electronically programmed with art from the world's great museums, and a garage large enough to hold 30 cars: Seattle's Xanadu.

The 1st Congressional District includes Redmond, Kirkland and other suburbs east of Seattle, plus Shoreline in the northwest corner of King County; it also includes suburban territory—Edmonds, Lynnwood, Bothell, Mukilteo—in Snohomish County to the north. Across Puget Sound it includes the northern tip of Kitsap County and Bainbridge Island, where you can commute by ferry to downtown Seattle each day and return home to what looks like the perfect American small town in the evening. Politically, this has been an area torn by forces of roughly equal strength, cultural liberalism and economic conservatism. Most Seattle area residents appreciate, and want to preserve, the region's unique natural aura: the evergreen smell of a well-watered land; the subtle regional style that is plainly American yet distinct from most of the nation. But it is impossible not to recognize the spectacular success of market economics in the 1st District.

The congressman from the 1st District is Jay Inslee, a Democrat first elected here in 1998. Inslee grew up in north Seattle, the son of a high school biology teacher and football coach, and graduated from the University of Washington and Willamette School of Law. He moved to Selah, in Yakima County east of the Cascades, to practice law and served on the State Trial Lawyers board of directors. In 1988, at 37, he was elected to the state House over a former Yakima mayor. In 1992, when 4th District Congressman Sid Morrison ran for governor, Inslee won the general 51%–49% over Doc Hastings, a conservative supported by the Christian Coalition. In the House, Inslee voted for the Clinton budget and tax increase and for the crime bill with the assault weapons ban, despite promising to vote against gun control bills. In 1994 Hastings ran again and beat Inslee, 53%–47%.

After his defeat, Inslee moved to Bainbridge Island and practiced law in Seattle. In 1996 he ran for governor, attacking the Seattle Seahawks football stadium deal. He finished fifth, with 10% of the total vote, in the all-party primary. Briefly he was a regional director of HHS. Then he ran in the 1st District against Republican Congressman Rick White. White was an economic conservative with liberal votes on some cultural issues, but he also had problems. In April 1998 he was divorced, though he had portrayed himself as a family man in his first campaign. And Bruce Craswell, whose wife Ellen Craswell lost to Governor Gary Locke in 1996, decided to run against him on the line of the conservative American Heritage Party. Inslee attacked White for voting to reduce spending on education and the environment and for supporting electricity deregulation, claiming that White was "willing to sell our reasonably priced electricity to California." White tried to paint Inslee as an opportunist. To the carpetbagger issue, Inslee replied that he had grown up in the 1st District and had lived there more years than White. In the September all-party primary, White led 50%–44%; Craswell got 7%. By November, two issues changed the balance. One was White's divorce: Although Inslee never mentioned it, his ad claimed that White intended to spend 10 years in the House and then be a lobbyist—a reference to a statement by his wife in the divorce papers. The second issue was impeachment: After White voted for the impeachment inquiry, Inslee ran an ad saying, "Rick White and Newt Gingrich shouldn't be dragging us through this. Enough is enough." In the acrimony, the primary numbers were reversed in November: Inslee won 50%–44%.

In the House, Inslee voted as a liberal-leaning Democrat and found ways to work on high-tech issues. He joined in protecting the privacy of consumer financial records—a cause that is important to Microsoft. Congress approved his amendment to require that government inspectors general report how agencies collect and use personal information on their web sites. When Congress passed the electronic signature bill, Inslee included an amendment to require that terms of consumer consent to receive electronic records be obvious and separate from other terms. On other issues, he helped to defeat a pipeline safety bill that he said failed to require stronger enforcement. He voted for PNTR with China but against trade promotion authority. He voted to override Bill Clinton's veto of the estate tax and marriage penalty repeal. After failing to win a seat on Energy and Commerce, he settled in as ranking Democrat on the Forest and Forest Health Subcommittee, where he attacked the Bush administration for cutting $500 million from a forest fire fighting program. He narrowly won House approval of his amendment to prohibit Bush officials from suspending or revising new mining regulations. The House defeated his amendment to prohibit the Navy Department from paying the utility bills at Vice President Cheney's mansion. After September 11 and the airline slowdown, he sought increased unemployment benefits for aerospace workers. His vote against the use of force in Iraq led an Internet site called Move-OnPAC.org, which was supported by some Silicon Valley executives, to direct $150,000 to his campaign.

In 2000 against former state Senate Republican leader Dan McDonald, Inslee won 55%–43%—virtually the same as Al Gore's margin in the district. In 2002 he won 56%–41% over state Representative Joe Marine, with comfortable margins in each of the three counties.

SECOND DISTRICT

Rep. Rick Larsen (D)

Elected 2000, 2d term; b. June 15, 1965, Arlington; home, Lake Stevens; Pacific Lutheran U., B.A. 1987, U. of MN, M.P.A. 1990; Methodist; married (Tiia).

Elected Office: Snohomish City Cncl., 1998–2000, Pres., 1999–2000.

Professional Career: Econ. Dev. Ofcl., Port of Everett, 1990–91; Dir., Pub. Affairs, WA St. Dental Assn., 1991–98.

DC Office: 1529 LHOB 20515, 202-225-2605; Fax: 202-225-4420; Web site: www.house.gov/larsen.

District Offices: Bellingham, 360-733-4500; Everett, 425-252-3188.

Committees: *Agriculture* (23d of 24 D): General Farm Commodities & Risk Management; Livestock & Horticulture. *Armed Services* (22d of 29 D): Readiness; Terrorism, Unconventional Threats & Capabilities. *Transportation & Infrastructure* (26th of 34 D): Aviation; Highways, Transit & Pipelines.

Group Ratings

	ADA	ACLU	AFS	LCV	CON	ITIC	NTU	COC	ACU	NTLC	CHC
2002	85	87	78	38	8	62	27	60	24	17	25
2001	85	—	90	93	—	—	16	48	12	—	—

National Journal Ratings

	2001 LIB	—	2001 CONS		2002 LIB	—	2002 CONS
Economic	58%	—	42%		59%	—	40%
Social	68%	—	32%		67%	—	29%
Foreign	73%	—	26%		68%	—	31%

Key Votes of the 107th Congress

1. Approve Bush Tax Cuts	Y	5. Faith-Based Charities	N	9. Trade Promotion Authority	N
2. Limit Patients' Bill of Rights	N	6. Bar Gays in the Boy Scouts	N	10. Bar Funds for Intl. Court	Y
3. Campaign Finance Reform	Y	7. Ban Partial-Birth Abortion	N	11. Authorize Force in Iraq	N
4. Ban ANWR Development	Y	8. Arm Commercial Pilots	Y	12. Deny Home. Sec. Dept. Union	N

Election Results

2002 general	Rick Larsen (D)	101,219	(50%)	($1,768,783)
	Norma Smith (R)	92,528	(46%)	($555,564)
	Other	8,403	(4%)	
2002 primary	Rick Larsen (D)	59,238	(48%)	
	Norma Smith (R)	26,365	(22%)	
	Herb Meyer (R)	22,168	(18%)	
	Warren Hanson (R)	8,541	(7%)	
	Other	6,087	(5%)	
2000 general	Rick Larsen (D)	146,617	(50%)	($1,529,101)
	John Koster (R)	134,660	(46%)	($1,092,585)
	Other	11,903	(4%)	

The People		Race/Ethnic Origin	Ancestry	
Area size:	7,976 sq. mi.	85.6% White	German: 13.7%	English: 9.2%
Urban population:	69.4%	1.1% Black	Irish: 8.4%	
Rural population:	30.6%	2.8% Asian	**2000 Presidential Vote**	
Pop. 2000:	654,903	1.9% Native Am.	Gore (D).............133,216 (48%)	
Median income:	$45,441	0.2% Hawaiian	Bush (R).............129,027 (46%)	
Poverty status:	10.0%	2.4% Two+ races	Other.................16,765 (6%)	
Military veterans:	16.3%	0.2% Other	**Cook Partisan Voting Index:** D + 1	
		5.8% Hispanic Origin		

Occupation	Blue collar: 27.6%	White collar: 55.1%	Gray collar: 17.3%

The 172 San Juan Islands, in the waters of Puget Sound at the far northwest corner of Washington, were the last part of the continental United States to be turned over to this country; these waters were great whaling ground, and not until 1860 did the British relinquish them. Today, ferryboats ply the waters of the Sound, connecting the islands to mainland Washington, and to British Columbia directly to the west. Whale watching is popular not only with tourists, but also among scientists on both sides of the border. This is some of the most beautiful land and water of North America, the steely blue Sound with green forested hills rising behind; it is wet country, shielded from the full force of Pacific rains by the Olympic Mountains, but still seldom dry. The little towns, on bits of level land between the water and mountains, have the look of pristine New England villages or midwestern historic towns, but are better preserved than the originals; the stores are full of fresh produce and local seafood. Here the Seattle metropolitan area has marched north along the shore of Puget Sound, beyond the old lumber port and railroad terminus of Everett, with the huge Boeing plant—the largest building in the world—where 747s, 767s and 777s are built. To the north are the small city of Bellingham and the town of Blaine on the 49th parallel, with America's most attractively landscaped border crossing and International Peace Arch, just south of British Columbia.

The 2d Congressional District includes the San Juan Islands, Whidbey Island and Puget Sound from Everett north, plus most of the margin of mainland along the Sound and the huge Cascade mountains, topped by snow-capped Mount Baker to the east. The district has several military installations, including the navy base at Everett and naval air station on Whidbey Island. This was the fastest-growing district in Washington during the 1990s. The political tradition in most of the lumbering and fishing areas here is Democratic, while the rich agricultural areas, like the flower-bulb-growing Skagit Valley, are more Republican. Everett tends to be Democratic, some of the nearby new suburban towns Republican. Overall, this is a pretty evenly balanced district that tends to vote as the state does.

The congressman from the 2d District is Rick Larsen, a Democrat first elected in 2000. He grew up in Arlington, in Snohomish County, graduated from Pacific Lutheran University and got a masters degree at the University of Minnesota. He spent a year doing research on economic development for the Port of Everett. For six years he was director of public affairs for the Washington State Dental Association. In 1998 he won a seat on the Snohomish County Council and he later became its president. In 2000, Republican Jack Metcalf kept his promise to retire after serving three terms; he had won the formerly Democratic seat three times by relatively narrow margins, and the 2d District became one of the premier open seat battles of the year. The Democratic field was cleared for Larsen when a state legislator unpopular with labor union leaders withdrew. The Republican field was cleared for conservative state Representative John Koster when a moderate legislator was unable to raise much money and dropped out. In the September all-party primary, Koster unexpectedly led 49%–46%. The contest became a major battleground for political action committees: anti-abortion groups and the National Rifle Association backed Koster, and unions and abortion rights groups fought for Larsen. Larsen turned up the heat on abortion, saying that the contest offered "a clear choice," and criticizing Koster for referring to "our American holocaust." Larsen won 50%–46%, improving his performance in each major county from the primary: winning 51%–46% in Snohomish and 50%–45% in Whatcom, and losing Skagit by only 76 votes.

In the House, Larsen joined the New Democrat Coalition and got seats on the Agriculture, Armed Services, and Transportation and Infrastructure Committees. He voted for the Bush tax cuts in 2001. He voted against trade promotion authority in December 2001 but he was one of five Democrats who switched to vote for the conference agreement in July 2002. But he voted against the Iraq war resolution in October 2002. Spurred by a fatal pipeline explosion in Bellingham in 1999, he filed legislation to require more aggressive inspection and testing plus improved training for pipeline operators. He worked with Republican Jennifer Dunn on a bipartisan approach that became the basis for passage in November 2002, although many Democrats criticized it as "sham reform."

In 2002 Larsen was opposed by Norma Smith, a former top aide to Metcalf. Smith criticized Larsen's vote on Iraq and his vote against creation of the Homeland Security Department. She ran an ad that morphed the face of liberal Seattle Congressman Jim McDermott, who traveled to Baghdad in September 2002 and said that he believed Saddam Hussein more than George W. Bush, into Larsen's. Larsen spent three times as much money as Smith, who received no money from the national party. Larsen won 50%–46%, almost exactly the same as his margin in 2000. This second narrow victory could place Larsen higher on the Republicans' target list in 2004.

THIRD DISTRICT

Rep. Brian Baird (D)

Elected 1998, 3d term; b. Mar. 7, 1956, Chama, NM; home, Olympia; U. of UT, B.A. 1977, U. of WY, M.S. 1980, Ph.D. 1984; Protestant; married (Rachel).

Elected Office: Dem. nominee for U.S. House of Reps., 1996.

Professional Career: Prof., Pacific Lutheran U., 1986–98.

DC Office: 1421 CHOB 20515, 202-225-3536; Fax: 202-225-3478; Web site: www.house.gov/baird.

District Offices: Olympia, 360-352-9768; Vancouver, 360-695-6292.

Committees: *Budget* (14th of 19 D). *Science* (17th of 22 D): Environment, Technology and Standards. *Transportation & Infrastructure* (21st of 34 D): Highways, Transit & Pipelines; Water Resources & Environment.

Group Ratings

	ADA	ACLU	AFS	LCV	CON	ITIC	NTU	COC	ACU	NTLC	CHC
2002	90	73	100	75	63	50	19	58	12	3	17
2001	85	—	100	100	—	—	14	41	12	—	—

National Journal Ratings

	2001 LIB — 2001 CONS		2002 LIB — 2002 CONS	
Economic	66%	— 35%	68%	— 32%
Social	62%	— 38%	74%	— 19%
Foreign	96%	— 0%	72%	— 26%

Key Votes of the 107th Congress

1. Approve Bush Tax Cuts	N	5. Faith-Based Charities	N	9. Trade Promotion Authority	N
2. Limit Patients' Bill of Rights	N	6. Bar Gays in the Boy Scouts	Y	10. Bar Funds for Intl. Court	N
3. Campaign Finance Reform	Y	7. Ban Partial-Birth Abortion	N	11. Authorize Force in Iraq	N
4. Ban ANWR Development	Y	8. Arm Commercial Pilots	Y	12. Deny Home. Sec. Dept. Union	N

Election Results

2002 general	Brian Baird (D)	119,264	(62%)	($781,953)
	Joseph Zarelli (R)	74,065	(38%)	($198,886)
2002 primary	Brian Baird (D)	77,540	(57%)	
	Joseph Zarelli (R)	58,939	(43%)	
2000 general	Brian Baird (D)	159,428	(56%)	($1,368,592)
	Trent Ross Matson (R)	114,861	(41%)	($487,812)
	Other	8,375	(3%)	

Prior Winning Percentages: 1998 (55%)

The People		Race/Ethnic Origin	Ancestry	
Area size:	7,961 sq. mi.	87.7% White	German: 14.3%	English: 8.9%
Urban population:	70.9%	1.2% Black	Irish: 8.3%	
Rural population:	29.1%	2.6% Asian	**2000 Presidential Vote**	
Pop. 2000:	654,898	1.0% Native Am.	Bush (R)............131,958 (48%)	
Median income:	$44,426	0.3% Hawaiian	Gore (D)............127,292 (46%)	
Poverty status:	10.5%	2.5% Two+ races	Other..................15,732 (6%)	
Military veterans:	16.2%	0.1% Other	**Cook Partisan Voting Index:** R + 1	
		4.6% Hispanic Origin		

Occupation	Blue collar: 26.8%	White collar: 57.0%	Gray collar: 16.2%

From the Pacific Ocean to the majestic row of active and inactive volcanoes from Mount Rainier to Mount St. Helens to Oregon's Mount Hood, southwest Washington was long one of America's most productive lumber areas. The moist air and almost constant rains blown in from the Pacific keep the trees on the coast growing rapidly; in the valleys just past the Coast Range there is plenty of precipitation and fast-growing forest. Then come the high mountains: The Cascades are a genuine divide, wrenching almost all precipitation out of the air so the climate eastward for a thousand miles is arid. Americans were reminded of the force of the volcanoes when Mount St. Helens, dormant for 123 years, erupted in 1980, killing 65 people, destroying its own peak and paving the land around with lava. Americans used to be taught that there were no active volcanoes in the lower 48 states; but Mount St. Helens proved that wrong, and one of her sisters may prove it again.

Lewis and Clark came here in 1805, down the Columbia River to a rainy and foggy winter by the ocean, and for many years this part of Washington was sparsely settled, with lumber-mill and fishing-boat towns interspersed between mountains and water. It was flannel shirt country, Democratic since the New Deal days. In the early 1990s its resource-based economy was threatened by the environmental movement, which restricted fishing practices and got a court decision shutting down old growth forest logging to save spotted owl habitat. This roiled local politics and gave Republicans an opening. More important recently has been the spread of the Pacific Northwest's great metropolitan areas into these valleys. Clark County across the Columbia from Portland, Oregon, has filled up with new residents, eager to avoid Oregon's income tax and still able to make big purchases in Oregon free of sales tax; its population grew by 45% in the 1990s, the largest increase in the state. The Seattle-Tacoma metro area has been moving down from the north past the small state capital of Olympia. This is one of America's great international trading areas, with big exports of logs and timber and vast imports on the docks of Portland and the Puget Sound.

The 3d Congressional District covers the land between the ocean and the Cascades, from Olympia on an inlet of Puget Sound, south to Vancouver in Clark County, site of the Hudson Bay Company headquarters in the 19th century. Economic growth and diversification and the coming of many new residents with no roots in the old industries have made the 3d a politically marginal district; George W. Bush got 48% of the vote here in 2000.

The congressman from the 3d District is Brian Baird, a Democrat first elected in 1998. Baird grew up in northern New Mexico and western Colorado. He got a Ph.D. in clinical psychology from the University of Wyoming, and worked with veterans and families dealing with cancer, with juvenile delinquents in prison and with families of murder victims. He wrote a book called *Are*

We Having Fun Yet? for couples on vacation. He moved to Washington in 1980 and was a professor at Pacific Lutheran University in Tacoma and living in Olympia when he ran for the House in 1996 against Republican incumbent Linda Smith, who was a backer of campaign finance regulation and had strong supported from Christian conservatives. On election night Baird was ahead by 2,400 votes and was pronounced the winner by an overeager media. But when the more than 40,000 absentee votes outstanding were counted, Smith won by 887 votes, 50.2%–49.8%. Taking a leave from his job, Baird never stopped running, while Smith ran unsuccessfully against Senator Patty Murray in 1998. Campaigning constantly, Baird picked up the consensus-minded inclination of voters and emphasized how confrontation-minded the Republicans were. Republicans nominated state Senator Don Benton, who called for a flat tax and respect for gun rights and property rights. He started far behind Baird in fundraising and took confrontational stands on issues. Baird spent twice as much money and won 55%–45%, exceeding 60% in the Olympia area and the coast and running barely ahead around Vancouver, Benton's home base.

In the House, Baird has had a moderate voting record that trends liberal on foreign policy. He was elected president of the Democratic freshman class. He kept a campaign promise by filing a bill to restore income tax deductibility for state sales taxes, a perennial favorite in Washington which has no state income tax. He voted to override Bill Clinton's vetoes of the estate tax and marriage penalty repeal, but opposed George W. Bush's tax cuts. He was among a handful of white Democrats who joined Black Caucus members in walking out of the Electoral College vote to protest the Florida result. When Bush canceled U.S. assistance to international family planning agencies, Baird said that he was "saddened" by the failure to deal with overpopulation: He proposed incentives for owners of gas-electric hybrid cars and owns one himself. He also voted against Bush on trade promotion authority and the use of force in Iraq.

After September 11, he gained some national attention when he focused on what would happen if many members of Congress were killed or incapacitated; he noted that United flight 93, which was brought down in Pennsylvania, was heading to Washington and its intended target might very well have been the Capitol. He proposed a constitutional amendment providing that, if one-fourth of House seats became vacant, governors must appoint a successor within seven days. This would be quite a change; as House members like to note, under the Constitution no one has ever served in the House without winning an election. And Baird's amendment could result in a change of party balance. Baird argued that if many members were killed or incapacitated, the House might not be able to act during a crisis. Speaker Dennis Hastert did not consider the issue a priority, but Baird did elicit interest from Christopher Cox, who proposed changes in rules which would help the House adjust to such a catastrophe and they were adopted in January 2003. Baird was active on a bipartisan commission on continuity of government that was expected to offer recommendations in June 2003. Some members thought that Baird's and other similar proposals were too radical, and Congress usually moves cautiously on constitutional amendments, only 17 of which have been ratified since 1790. Baird also proposed that the House change its rules on a less lofty topic: with Scott McInnis, he proposed that House members should be prohibited from romantic relationships with interns in their offices; this was evidently a reaction to Gary Condit's involvement with an intern, though she was working in the Executive Branch.

Baird has been reelected easily. In 2000, against a 29-year-old lobbyist who raised nearly $500,000, he won 56%–41%; he won 55% in Clark County even as George W. Bush was beating Al Gore there 50%–46%. His 2002 opponent, state Senator Joseph Zarelli, was damaged when he acknowledged that he drew unemployment checks while serving in the legislature. Baird won 62%–38%.

FOURTH DISTRICT

Rep. Doc Hastings (R)

Elected 1994, 5th term; b. Feb. 7, 1941, Spokane; home, Pasco; Columbia Basin Col., 1959–61, Central Washington U., 1963–64; Protestant; married (Claire).

Military Career: Army Reserves, 1964–69.

Elected Office: WA House of Reps., 1979–87.

Professional Career: Pres., Columbia Basin Paper & Supply, 1967–94.

DC Office: 1323 LHOB 20515, 202-225-5816; Fax: 202-225-3251; Web site: www.house.gov/hastings.

District Offices: Tri-Cities, 509-543-9396; Yakima, 509-452-3243.

Committees: *Budget* (7th of 24 R). *Rules* (6th of 9 R): The Legislative & Budget Process. *Standards of Official Conduct* (2d of 5 R).

Group Ratings

	ADA	ACLU	AFS	LCV	CON	ITIC	NTU	COC	ACU	NTLC	CHC
2002	0	7	0	0	8	100	56	100	92	89	100
2001	0	—	0	0	—	—	62	96	96	—	—

National Journal Ratings

	2001 LIB —	2001 CONS	2002 LIB —	2002 CONS
Economic	12%	— 88%	0%	— 91%
Social	20%	— 69%	0%	— 75%
Foreign	0%	— 97%	15%	— 78%

Key Votes of the 107th Congress

1. Approve Bush Tax Cuts	Y	5. Faith-Based Charities	Y	9. Trade Promotion Authority	Y
2. Limit Patients' Bill of Rights	Y	6. Bar Gays in the Boy Scouts	Y	10. Bar Funds for Intl. Court	Y
3. Campaign Finance Reform	N	7. Ban Partial-Birth Abortion	Y	11. Authorize Force in Iraq	Y
4. Ban ANWR Development	N	8. Arm Commercial Pilots	Y	12. Deny Home. Sec. Dept. Union	Y

Election Results

2002 general	Doc Hastings (R)	108,257	(67%)	($250,574)
	Craig Mason (D)	53,572	(33%)	($37,657)
2002 primary	Doc Hastings (R)	75,745	(70%)	
	Craig Mason (D)	18,726	(17%)	
	Thor Amundson (D)	7,342	(7%)	
	Gordon Allen Pross (R)	6,500	(6%)	
2000 general	Doc Hastings (R)	143,259	(61%)	($761,774)
	Thomas James Davis (D)	87,585	(37%)	($433,054)
	Other	4,260	(2%)	

Prior Winning Percentages: 1998 (69%); 1996 (53%); 1994 (53%)

The People		**Race/Ethnic Origin**	**Ancestry**	
Area size:	19,430 sq. mi.	67.8% White	German: 13.1%	English: 7.8%
Urban population:	70.5%	0.8% Black	Irish: 6.9%	
Rural population:	29.5%	1.2% Asian	**2000 Presidential Vote**	
Pop. 2000:	654,901	1.9% Native Am.	Bush (R)	141,891 (62%)
Median income:	$37,764	0.1% Hawaiian	Gore (D)	78,768 (34%)
Poverty status:	16.2%	1.7% Two+ races	Other	8,629 (4%)
Military veterans:	13.3%	0.1% Other	**Cook Partisan Voting Index:** R +15	
		26.4% Hispanic Origin		

Occupation	Blue collar: 23.7%	White collar: 52.8%	Gray collar: 23.5%

The rugged peaks of the Cascade Mountains divide Washington State into two starkly different climate zones and two almost as starkly different political cultures. West of the Cascades, Washington is moist, green, full of watery inlets; to the east it is barren and brown, except where irrigation ditches feed the waters of the Columbia River into thirsty valleys, or where mountaintop waters fall east, as they do to water the apple orchards in the Yakima Valley. The federal government has been a presence in the East-of-the-Cascades since the 1930s, when it began to build dams that provided cheap power and boosted economic development in this forbidding, often surreal, landscape: A giant bust of Franklin Roosevelt gazes from a bluff on the Columbia out over 550-foot-high Grand Coulee Dam, which Roosevelt initiated and which was one of his favorite projects. Other dams are strung along downriver, like beads on the necklace of the Columbia, most of the way to Bonneville Dam near Portland, where the river breaks through the Cascades.

The one exception is the Hanford Reach, the last undammed, undeveloped stretch of the upper Columbia River, near the 560-square mile Hanford Nuclear Reservation, north of the Tri-Cities of Richland, Kennewick and Pasco. Hanford was built by the Army to manufacture plutonium for the Manhattan Project and was where the Nagasaki bomb was constructed. After the war, the Hanford Works became the primary producer of materials for America's nuclear weapons and eastern Washington's largest employer. Then in 1989 Hanford's plutonium plant, which produced two-thirds of the nation's plutonium, was shut down because of hazardous leaks and contaminated waste; the spent fuel is scheduled to be shipped to Yucca Mountain in Nevada, when the nuclear waste repository there is completed. In 2001 the Department of Energy abandoned a proposal to restart the Fast Flux Test Facility reactor to produce plutonium for space batteries and medical isotopes. Construction began in September 2001 on a plant to convert million of gallons of nuclear waste to glass starting in 2007 at a cost of $4 billion.

The 4th Congressional District covers much of the western part of the state east of the Cascades, running from Grand Coulee and the Columbia River through the Hanford Works down to the Dalles Dam and the Columbia River Gorge. One tends to think of this area as ethnically unvaried, but 26% of the district's residents, and 36% in Yakima County, are Hispanic: farm workers, in many cases, who have settled here permanently. Sentiment toward the federal government has soured in other parts of the district almost as much as around the Tri-Cities. Farmers in the Yakima Valley, which produces most of the nation's apples and many other crops have been enraged at environmental groups' proposals to breach the Snake River dams upriver to save salmon. Lumber towns in the Cascades responded angrily when those who wanted to preserve the spotted owl tried to shut down logging businesses. In an area once narrowly split between the parties and that as recently as 1992 elected a Democrat to Congress, opinion has shifted sharply, making this the most Republican district in the state; the cultural liberalism of Seattle seems very far away here. Said one Democrat when he looked at a party poll in 1998, "I don't know what Democrats did to these people, but it sure must have been bad."

The congressman from the 4th District is Doc Hastings, a Republican first elected in 1994. Hastings grew up in the Tri-Cities, went to college in Ellensburg, served in the Army Reserves and for 27 years ran the Columbia Basin Paper and Supply Company in Pasco, where he was president of the Chamber of Commerce. In 1979 he was elected to the state House, served as a Republican leader, then retired in 1987. In 1992 he ran for Congress, won the Republican nomination, but was beaten 51%–49% by Democrat Jay Inslee. But Inslee voted for the Clinton budget and tax package in 1993 and the crime bill with its gun control provisions in 1994—big liabilities when Hastings ran again. Hastings led with 50% in the September 1994 all-party primary, to only 41% for Inslee. In November he won 53%–47%. Since then, Democrats no longer seriously compete and this has become a safe seat.

In the House, Hastings has had a solidly conservative voting record and, with a seat on the Rules Committee, has usually been a leadership loyalist. Much of his time has been spent on Hanford. Initially, he sponsored a bill with bipartisan support in the delegation to make the state government responsible for the cleanup, allowing privatization of cleanup work and avoiding the plethora of often impractical and duplicative federal regulations. But he abandoned that approach and has advocated maximum federal funding to meet federal deadlines. He opposed Senator Patty Murray's proposal to designate the 51-mile Hanford Reach of the Columbia a wild and scenic river; it has been kept free from development by the Hanford Reservation and as a result is the closest thing to a free-flowing part of the Columbia, producing most of its wild salmon run. He argued for a county-state-federal management panel, with a quarter-mile on each side of the river kept free from development. In June 2000 Bill Clinton unilaterally acted to create the Hanford Reach National Monument to be managed by the Fish and Wildlife Service, with the assistance of a local advisory board; Hastings opposed the action as an abuse of presidential authority. But Clinton signed Hastings's bill to promote salmon recovery in the Yakima River and Hastings got $11 million for the Yakima River Basin Water Enhancement Project. When George W. Bush proposed cuts in the Energy Department budget, Hastings warned that cuts in the cleanup program were not acceptable; within a few months, he secured sufficient funding for local projects to avoid an overall reduction.

As chairman of the Investigating Subcommittee of the Ethics Committee, Hastings had the thankless task in 2002 of reviewing the case against James Traficant, who was convicted of bribery in federal court in April 2002. The subcommittee and the full ethics committee voted unanimously to expel Traficant from the House, only the second such action since the Civil War. The House voted 420–1 for expulsion.

FIFTH DISTRICT

Rep. George Nethercutt (R)

Elected 1994, 5th term; b. Oct. 7, 1944, Spokane; home, Spokane; WA St. U., B.A. 1967, Gonzaga U. Law Schl., J.D. 1971; Presbyterian; married (Mary Beth).

Professional Career: Law Clerk, Fed. Judge Ralph Plumer, 1971–72; Chief of Staff & Cnsl., U.S. Sen. Ted Stevens, 1972–76; Practicing atty., 1976–94.

DC Office: 2443 RHOB 20515, 202-225-2006; Fax: 202-225-3392; Web site: www.house.gov/nethercutt.

District Offices: Colville, 509-684-3481; Spokane, 509-353-2374; Walla Walla, 509-529-9358.

Committees: *Appropriations* (16th of 36 R): Agriculture, Rural Development, & FDA; Defense (Vice Chmn.); Interior. *Science* (11th of 25 R): Energy; Space & Aeronautics.

Group Ratings

	ADA	ACLU	AFS	LCV	CON	ITIC	NTU	COC	ACU	NTLC	CHC
2002	0	13	0	0	8	100	55	100	92	86	100
2001	0	—	0	0	—	—	65	96	96	—	—

National Journal Ratings

	2001 LIB —	2001 CONS		2002 LIB —	2002 CONS
Economic	7%	89%		0%	91%
Social	20%	69%		0%	75%
Foreign	29%	69%		50%	50%

Key Votes of the 107th Congress

1. Approve Bush Tax Cuts	Y	5. Faith-Based Charities	Y	9. Trade Promotion Authority	Y
2. Limit Patients' Bill of Rights	Y	6. Bar Gays in the Boy Scouts	Y	10. Bar Funds for Intl. Court	*
3. Campaign Finance Reform	N	7. Ban Partial-Birth Abortion	Y	11. Authorize Force in Iraq	Y
4. Ban ANWR Development	N	8. Arm Commercial Pilots	Y	12. Deny Home. Sec. Dept. Union	Y

Election Results

2002 general	George Nethercutt (R)	....	126,757	(63%)	($857,642)
	Bart Haggin (D)	....	65,146	(32%)	($37,039)
	Rob Chase (Lib)	....	10,379	(5%)	($4,433)
2002 primary	George Nethercutt (R)	....	83,972	(64%)	
	Bart Haggin (D)	....	38,630	(30%)	
	Rob Chase (Lib)	....	10,379	(6%)	
2000 general	George Nethercutt (R)	....	144,038	(57%)	($1,749,203)
	Thomas Keefe (D)	....	97,703	(39%)	($651,225)
	Greg Holmes (Lib)	....	9,473	(4%)	($5,688)

Prior Winning Percentages: 1998 (57%); 1996 (56%); 1994 (51%)

The People		Race/Ethnic Origin	Ancestry	
Area size:	23,166 sq. mi.	87.7% White	German: 16.5%	Irish: 9.0%
Urban population:	71.9%	1.3% Black	English: 8.8%	
Rural population:	28.1%	1.7% Asian	**2000 Presidential Vote**	
Pop. 2000:	654,904	2.3% Native Am.	Bush (R)..............150,013	(56%)
Median income:	$35,720	0.1% Hawaiian	Gore (D)..............106,610	(40%)
Poverty status:	14.4%	2.3% Two+ races	Other....................13,262	(5%)
Military veterans:	16.2%	0.2% Other	**Cook Partisan Voting Index:** R + 9	
		4.5% Hispanic Origin		

Occupation	Blue collar: 21.1%	White collar: 60.0%	Gray collar: 18.9%

Eastern Washington is a land of great rivers and bare parched land, where the Columbia, Spokane and Snake Rivers wind among vast plateaus, bringing water from the Rockies to the desert. Spokane grew up at the falls of the Spokane River when the railroads first came through, and became a major wheat, mining, electrical and railroad center early in the 20th century, the center of the so-called "Inland Empire;" it celebrated with the 1974 World's Fair and Exposition on the downtown riverfront. Nearby are some of the most fascinating landscapes in the United States: surreally undulating yellow wheatfields, the rolling ridges of the Palouse where the wheat-growing topsoil is 200 feet deep, the bare-rock coulees rising above dammed-up lakes and barren desert, the vast wilderness of Okanogan County that has long been gold county and where the locals recently have battled over whether to open a new mine. This is remote and inhospitable land: the summers can be blazing hot and winters bitter cold; many rivers run wildly. But much of it has been tamed by man, and the water from the Grand Coulee and other dams irrigates some of the richest farmland in the country.

The 5th Congressional District covers the easternmost part of the state. Two-thirds of the people here live in greater Spokane, a city whose voting habits are a fairly good proxy of the nation's. Its heritage leans Republican, but it is not as Republican as most of the nearby Rocky Mountain states. It is open to Democrats: Spokane County voted for Bill Clinton in 1992 and 1996, but George W. Bush won the county 52%–43% in 2000; he won 56% in the district overall.

The congressman from the 5th District is George Nethercutt, a Republican elected in 1994 when he defeated House Speaker Thomas Foley—the first time a House speaker had been defeated in his home district since Galusha Grow lost in Pennsylvania in 1862. (Contrary to some local expectations, this did not make Nethercutt the new speaker.) Nethercutt grew up in Spokane, graduated from Washington State University in Pullman and Gonzaga Law School in Spokane, served four years on the staff of Alaska Senator Ted Stevens, then returned home and practiced law. He was involved in civic work, representing clients in adoptions, heading the local Diabetes Foundation (his daughter was diagnosed with the disease), and starting a crisis nursery for abused children. Foley had served the district for 30 years and had wide personal popularity. But in 1992 his margin was not much larger than that of Bill Clinton's, and many in the state were angry with Foley for filing a lawsuit against the congressional term limits imposed by the voters in 1992. Nethercutt announced his candidacy in April 1994. In May two former Foley opponents also announced: Duane Alton, owner of a chain of tire stores who ran in 1976 and 1978; and John Sonneland, a physician who ran in 1980, 1982 and 1992. Nethercutt ran ahead of the other Republicans in the September all-party primary with 29% of the total vote, to 20% for Alton and 15% for Sonneland. But the big news was that Foley won only 35% of the total vote. Immediately Foley began spending heavily, emphasizing the work he had done for the district and what he could do in the future. However, he had to buck not only Nethercutt's ads but also campaigns by the National Rifle Association (furious that Foley, a longtime gun control opponent, backed the 1994 crime bill) and the National Taxpayers Union. Nethercutt in an ad promised never to sue the people of Washington, a swipe at Foley's lawsuit against the term-limits initiative, and pledged to serve only three terms. Foley spent $2.1 million to Nethercutt's $1.1 million, but even he could not withstand the national Republican tide and an election-eve appearance by Ross Perot. Foley narrowly carried Spokane County and lost all but one of the smaller counties; that gave Nethercutt a 51%–49% win.

In the House Nethercutt got a seat on Appropriations and supported most of the Contract with America. His voting record has trended more conservative in recent years. He has pushed hard for increased diabetes research, and made the Congressional Diabetes Caucus the largest such group on Capitol Hill; but he broke with many medical researchers by voting for the bill to ban cloning and embryonic stem-cell research. Nethercutt has strongly opposed proposals to dismantle or breach the Columbia River dams. In 2000 the House narrowly approved his attempt to stifle the Clinton administration's management rules for the Columbia River Basin. The House passed his proposal in 2002 to block federal agencies from releasing certain firearms data; when it became part of the giant spending bill that finally was enacted in February 2003, the Supreme Court returned to a lower court a lawsuit against gun manufacturers. After Nethercutt threatened in early 2002 to oppose any legislation sought by Boeing if it closed its West Plains assembly plant west of Spokane, the company announced late in the year that it would sell the plant but would sign an eight-year sole source contract to buy parts made at the plant by the new owner.

Nethercutt has been a persistent advocate of lowering international trade barriers to benefit local products, even at the risk of offending conservative orthodoxy. In 1998 he helped put together the repeal of sanctions against Pakistan, the single largest buyer of winter wheat, in time for Washington grain sellers to qualify for a $35 million purchase. Assembling a coalition of free traders, left wingers sympathetic to Fidel Castro and farm state members eager to export local products, he became the leader of the successful House attempt in 2000 to end the food and drug embargo on Communist Cuba. The deal also expanded travel rights to Cuba by American grain and food exporters. Nethercutt called it "a fundamental shift in American foreign policy, and a new day for American agriculture." With the Bush White House firmly allied with the Cuban-American community in Florida, he was unable to expand the provision. But he welcomed the benefits secured under that law by Northwest apple and peas producers, and he criticized the approach of Cuban-American advocates: "They don't like anything to do with Fidel Castro, even if helps Americans." After the September 11 attacks, the Bush administration sought to include in its anti-terrorism package the repeal of a provision that Nethercutt had helped to enact a year earlier that made it difficult to include food or medicine in unilateral trade sanctions; when he and other farm state members objected, the proposal died.

Nethercutt generated some controversy by seeking reelection in 2000 in breach of his self-imposed term limit. He defended his decision by saying he had found the issues so complicated that six years "is probably not enough," and he talked about the possibility of becoming a member of the college of cardinals—the 13 Appropriations subcommittee chairmen. U.S. Term Limits launched a $100,000 ad campaign that started with an ad showing Richard Nixon, George Bush and Bill Clinton making promises they were not to keep, then posing the question "Will George Nethercutt be next?" Nethercutt responded: "I've changed my mind. . . . I made a mistake when I chose to set a limit on my service." *Doonesbury* lampooned him as "the Weasel King." Polls and political forecasters listed him in deep trouble for reelection. But Nethercutt had one big factor going his way: weak opposition. In the all-party primary, he easily won the Republican nomination with 45% of the total vote to 20% for Spokane talk radio host and term-limits advocate Richard Clear. Clear supported Democratic nominee Tom Keefe, who had received 21% of the total vote, in the general. But Keefe was a former congressional staffer and Washington lobbyist and a Seattle native who moved to Spokane a month before he declared his candidacy: a flawed messenger for a grass roots cause. Nethercutt won 57%–39%, including 55%–41% in Spokane. He was easily reelected in 2002. After the election, he sought leadership support for the chairmanship of the Interior Appropriations Subcommittee; they rejected his argument that regional interests should trump seniority.

Nethercutt has voiced interest in challenging Senator Patty Murray in 2004. In February 2003 he said he would not run if Jennifer Dunn did; with White House encouragement, he became the favorite for the Republican nomination in April 2003 when Dunn said she would not run. Washington has not elected a senator from east of the Cascades since 1944. But Nethercutt has a way of beating the odds. In early 2003, possible candidates in the 5th District if Nethercutt does not run there included state Senator Larry Sheahan and state House Minority Leader Cathy McMorris, both Republicans and Senate Minority Leader Lisa Brown, a Democrat.

SIXTH DISTRICT

Rep. Norm Dicks (D)

Elected 1976, 14th term; b. Dec. 16, 1940, Bremerton; home, Bremerton; U. of WA, B.A. 1963, J.D. 1968; Lutheran; married (Suzanne).

Professional Career: Legis. Asst., U.S. Sen. Warren Magnuson, 1968–73, A.A., 1973–76.

DC Office: 2467 RHOB 20515, 202-225-5916; Fax: 202-226-1176; Web site: www.house.gov/dicks.

District Offices: Bremerton, 360-479-4011; Tacoma, 253-593-6536.

Committees: *Appropriations* (3d of 29 D): Defense; Interior (RMM); Military Construction. *Select Committee on Homeland Security* (5th of 23 D): Infrastructure & Border Security; Intelligence & Counterterrorism.

Group Ratings

	ADA	ACLU	AFS	LCV	CON	ITIC	NTU	COC	ACU	NTLC	CHC
2002	80	80	89	63	43	88	19	60	13	0	0
2001	90	—	89	86	—	—	12	50	8	—	—

National Journal Ratings

	2001 LIB	—	2001 CONS		2002 LIB	—	2002 CONS
Economic	74%	—	25%		73%	—	26%
Social	68%	—	32%		74%	—	19%
Foreign	61%	—	36%		61%	—	38%

Key Votes of the 107th Congress

1. Approve Bush Tax Cuts	N	5. Faith-Based Charities	N	9. Trade Promotion Authority	Y
2. Limit Patients' Bill of Rights	N	6. Bar Gays in the Boy Scouts	N	10. Bar Funds for Intl. Court	Y
3. Campaign Finance Reform	Y	7. Ban Partial-Birth Abortion	N	11. Authorize Force in Iraq	Y
4. Ban ANWR Development	Y	8. Arm Commercial Pilots	Y	12. Deny Home. Sec. Dept. Union	N

Election Results

2002 general	Norm Dicks (D)	126,116	(64%)	($914,657)
	Bob Lawrence (R)	61,584	(31%)	($62,571)
	John Bennett (Lib)	8,744	(4%)	
2002 primary	Norm Dicks (D)	83,455	(63%)	
	Bob Lawrence (R)	35,639	(27%)	
	Douglas Milholland (D)	9,758	(7%)	
	Other	3,549	(3%)	
2000 general	Norm Dicks (D)	164,853	(65%)	($596,375)
	Bob Lawrence (R)	79,215	(31%)	($95,540)
	John A. Bennett (Lib)	10,645	(4%)	

Prior Winning Percentages: 1998 (68%); 1996 (66%); 1994 (58%); 1992 (64%); 1990 (61%); 1988 (68%); 1986 (71%); 1984 (66%); 1982 (63%); 1980 (54%); 1978 (61%); 1976 (74%)

The People		Race/Ethnic Origin	Ancestry	
Area size:	8,592 sq. mi.	77.7% White	German: 13.2%	English: 8.5%
Urban population:	78.8%	5.5% Black	Irish: 8.5%	
Rural population:	21.2%	4.4% Asian	**2000 Presidential Vote**	
Pop. 2000:	654,902	2.2% Native Am.	Gore (D)..............139,643	(52%)
Median income:	$39,205	0.7% Hawaiian	Bush (R)..............115,736	(43%)
Poverty status:	13.2%	4.1% Two+ races	Other...................15,098	(6%)
Military veterans:	19.8%	0.2% Other	**Cook Partisan Voting Index:** D + 4	
		5.1% Hispanic Origin		

Occupation   Blue collar: 25.3%   White collar: 54.8%   Gray collar: 19.8%

The rainiest part of the continental United States is at its far northwest corner, where the Olympic Mountains of Washington thrust into the Pacific Ocean. The waters of the Pacific evaporate, condense and then mist or rain down on the hills and mountains that jut up from the ocean and Puget Sound. The mountains here are always green, the trees that line the inlets towering, and during heavy rainfalls the rivers can rise six feet a day. This has long been lumbering and fishing country, where men go out to work at 6 a.m. in air cold enough to see your breath year round, and where dependence on the vagaries of nature plus harsh environmental laws—like the ban on old-growth logging to protect the habitat of the spotted owl—have strengthened a traditional surly independence and suspicion of authority. Still, respect for the beauty of Nature endures at the 3,310 square mile Olympic Coast National Marine Sanctuary, which probes a vast underwater reserve.

The inlets of Puget Sound, winding sinuously through the mountains, are among America's most picturesque waterways and strategically among its most important. Here during World War II, shipyards built and sheltered much of the U.S. Navy's Pacific fleet, and here during the Cold War much of the nuclear submarine fleet anchored at the giant Bremerton Navy base. To the south is the Tacoma Straits Bridge, the replacement of the narrow span that, in a scene preserved on newsreel (and still viewed by civil engineering students), started vibrating on the wrong harmonic in high winds and collapsed in 1940. On the other side is Tacoma, long the second-ranking city on Puget Sound, with its massive docks, former pulp mills and pleasant hilly residential neighborhoods.

The 6th Congressional District includes the Olympic Peninsula, Bremerton and much of surrounding Kitsap County amid various inlets of Puget Sound, and most of Tacoma. Politically, the Olympic Peninsula and Bremerton are working-class Democratic. Tacoma also is traditionally Democratic. But as cultural issues have become more important, and as Seattle latte liberals come to symbolize the Democratic party, these areas have become somewhat less Democratic, and far less Democratic than Seattle. In 2000 the 6th District cast 43% of its votes for George W. Bush, far more than the 21% cast for him in Seattle's 7th District.

The congressman from the 6th District is Norm Dicks, a Democrat first elected in 1976. Dicks grew up in Bremerton, graduated from the University of Washington where he was on the football team and became a top aide to Senator Warren Magnuson when his staff was one of the best on Capitol Hill. Dicks returned home to Bremerton to run for Congress in 1976, when the 6th District incumbent got a judgeship. Dicks was elected easily that year, and in every year since except 1980, when Magnuson lost. He has passed up several chances to run for the Senate, and has become a senior Democrat in the House. Dicks has brought to the House the aggressiveness and political shrewdness that were the hallmarks of the Magnuson staff in its golden days, plus a hard-nosed interest in defense and intelligence reminiscent of Magnuson's colleague for 40 years, Henry Jackson. Before November 1994 it never occurred to him that he would serve in the minority party, but he has adapted smoothly to that fate, helped by the fact that on some issues, though not all, his goals are more congenial to Republicans than Democrats.

Dicks has a moderate voting record, especially on foreign issues, and has a seat on the

Appropriations Committee and on its Defense Subcommittee—a vital post for Kitsap County, where most workers depend on Pentagon payrolls, and for Washington generally. In these posts Dicks has exerted pivotal influence on vital policies, usually operating behind the scenes. In the early 1980s Dicks took the lead in restoring Export-Import Bank loan authority—Boeing is America's biggest exporter and user of the loans—when the Reagan administration wanted to cut it, and led a campaign that switched 80 House votes overnight. During the post-Cold War downsizing of the Pentagon, he has looked out for the F-117 Stealth aircraft and especially for expanded production of the B-2 Stealth bomber. In 1996 and 1997 he won four straight votes on the B-2: "We are undefeated, untied, unscored on. That's the way I like it." Dicks complained when B-2s weren't used in 1998 air attacks on Iraq; he was vindicated when the B-2 was used in the bombing of Serbia and Kosovo in 1999, Afghanistan in 2001 and Iraq in 2003, delivering weapons with pinpoint accuracy and, in Afghanistan, flying halfway around the world to do so.

As ranking Democrat on the Interior Subcommittee, Dicks has used his Appropriations seat to help additional Washington communities, funneling money to lumber mill towns when logging in old-growth forests was banned, passing timber salvage riders to keep mills going, dealing with the cost of maintaining salmon runs in dammed rivers. Naturally he looks after the interests of the Bremerton waterfront and pushed for funding of a Tacoma waterfront development from which visitors can gaze upon Mount Rainier and see I-705, the last of the original interstate routes to be built. He sought to maintain Washington's military bases during the Pentagon's base-closing reviews. Dicks worked for five years to settle the Puyallup Indian land claims and advanced the claim that Lewis and Clark ended their journey on the Washington, not the Oregon, side of the Columbia River. He was vital in defending Bill Clinton's "lands legacy" from attacks by Western Republicans, and he was instrumental in the bipartisan approval of billions of dollars for new conservation projects. Dicks has been a strong supporter of PNTR with China; Washington accounts for one-quarter of U.S. exports to China and Boeing foresees a great market there. But when he was appointed ranking Democrat on a special committee to study technology transfers and espionage losses to China in 1998, he worked effectively and in a bipartisan manner with Chairman Christopher Cox, even amid the impeachment controversy. There were no leaks and the committee's report was unanimous, with 38 specific recommendations for improving security and regulating technology transfers.

Dicks's friendship with Al Gore began when they entered the House in January 1977; they worked together on defense issues in the 1980s and on Northwest issues when Gore was Vice President. There was talk that Gore, if elected, would have given Dicks a prime national security job. Instead Dicks found himself meeting with George W. Bush to urge building more B-2s. Dicks was one of 21 House Democrats who voted for trade promotion authority in 2001. During the slowdown in aircraft building in 2001, he successfully pushed for a $20 billion, 10-year lease of up to 100 Boeing 767s to replace aging KC-135 tankers. Opponents argued that was more expensive in the long run, but Dicks said, "We don't have the money to buy them." And he worked quietly and behind the scenes to build Democratic support for the Iraq war resolution even as his 7th District neighbor Jim McDermott went to Baghdad to try to stop military action.

Dicks was reelected easily in 2002, as he has been since 1982. In February 2003 he got a seat on the Homeland Security Committee.

SEVENTH DISTRICT

Rep. Jim McDermott (D)

Elected 1988, 8th term; b. Dec. 28, 1936, Chicago, IL; home, Seattle; Wheaton Col., B.S. 1958, U. of IL, M.D. 1963; Episcopalian; married (Therese Hansen).

Military Career: U.S. Navy Medical Corps., 1968–70.

Elected Office: WA House of Reps., 1970–72; WA Senate, 1974–87; Dem. gubernatorial nominee, 1980.

Professional Career: Asst. Prof., U. of WA, Practicing psychiatrist, 1970–83; Medical Officer, U.S. Foreign Svc., Zaire, 1987–88.

DC Office: 1035 LHOB 20515, 202-225-3106; Fax: 202-225-6197; Web site: www.house.gov/mcdermott.

District Office: Seattle, 206-553-7170.

Committees: *Ways & Means* (6th of 17 D): Health; Human Resources.

Group Ratings

	ADA	ACLU	AFS	LCV	CON	ITIC	NTU	COC	ACU	NTLC	CHC
2002	95	93	89	88	47	38	28	28	0	3	0
2001	95	—	100	100	—	—	17	29	0	—	—

National Journal Ratings

	2001 LIB —	2001 CONS	2002 LIB —	2002 CONS
Economic	82%	19%	92%	7%
Social	90%	0%	98%	0%
Foreign	96%	0%	94%	0%

Key Votes of the 107th Congress

1. Approve Bush Tax Cuts	*	5. Faith-Based Charities		9. Trade Promotion Authority	N
2. Limit Patients' Bill of Rights	N	6. Bar Gays in the Boy Scouts	N	10. Bar Funds for Intl. Court	N
3. Campaign Finance Reform	Y	7. Ban Partial-Birth Abortion	N	11. Authorize Force in Iraq	N
4. Ban ANWR Development	Y	8. Arm Commercial Pilots	N	12. Deny Home. Sec. Dept. Union	N

Election Results

2002 general	Jim McDermott (D)	156,300	(74%)	($436,384)
	Carol Cassady (R)	46,256	(22%)	($18,775)
	Stan Lippmann (Lib)	8,447	(4%)	
2002 primary	Jim McDermott (D)	84,876	(77%)	
	Carol Cassady (R)	20,688	(19%)	
	Other	4,112	(4%)	
2000 general	Jim McDermott (D)	193,470	(73%)	($322,022)
	Joseph Brian Szwaja (Green)	52,142	(20%)	($33,331)
	Joel Grus (Lib)	20,197	(8%)	

Prior Winning Percentages: 1998 (88%); 1996 (81%); 1994 (75%); 1992 (78%); 1990 (72%); 1988 (76%)

The People		Race/Ethnic Origin	Ancestry	
Area size:	246 sq. mi.	66.9% White	German: 11.1%	Irish: 8.5%
Urban population:	98.5%	8.3% Black	English: 8.2%	
Rural population:	1.5%	13.2% Asian	**2000 Presidential Vote**	
Pop. 2000:	654,902	0.9% Native Am.	Gore (D) 228,988	(72%)
Median income:	$45,864	0.6% Hawaiian	Bush (R) 66,066	(21%)
Poverty status:	11.5%	3.9% Two+ races	Other 23,952	(8%)
Military veterans:	10.6%	0.3% Other	**Cook Partisan Voting Index:** D +27	
		5.8% Hispanic Origin		

Occupation	Blue collar: 14.7%	White collar: 70.9%	Gray collar: 14.4%

Seattle rises from the Puget Sound harbor of Elliott Bay on steep hills, once covered with 300-foot-high Douglas firs. Behind the hills and buildings you can see on a clear day, from almost anywhere, the nimbus of Mount Rainier. On the waterfront, below gleaming high-rises, is the Pike Place market, where you can get fresh salmon and Dungeness crabs; nearby is Pioneer Square, where stores and warehouses from the turn of the century have been restored; and Yesler Way, America's original "Skid Road," now has upscale shops but still some homeless people. Seattle's upper class, like San Francisco's, continues to be anchored downtown, with its upscale stores and busy sidewalks. Seattle first zoomed into the national consciousness with the 1897 Klondike gold strike, has been a major American city since around 1910 and hosted its own World's Fair in 1962. Then in the 1990s its combination of economic growth and creativity plus its physical beauty and distinctive style made it a national leader. Seattle still has its old ethnic neighborhoods, like Scandinavian Ballard, and comfortable working-class frame houses on steep hillsides. But it also has a new ethnic mix, with thousands of Asian immigrants, and the Capitol Hill neighborhood with shoppers jamming busy stores and clubs. The dominant tone is set by highly educated, affluent, single professionals—the kind of people who have made the Victorian houses of Queen Anne overlooking the harbor or the 1940s houses lining the streets of Capitol Hill among the nation's highest priced residential real estate. There are still blue-collar workers on the south side of the city and in valleys; factories, warehouses and railroad yards are concentrated in a flat plain near Puget Sound and south of downtown. Boeing, long based in Seattle, is America's biggest exporter, but Seattle has exported other institutions: more than 100 Nordstrom department stores offer their famously polite service and fashionable goods; Seattle espresso bars—especially Starbucks, named after the coffee-crazed first mate in Herman Melville's *Moby Dick*—have brought caffe latte across America.

But as the new century dawned, all was not well in the nation's new industrial center. In December 1999 rioters protesting globalism made a shambles of an international trade meeting at which Bill Clinton had hoped to chart new reductions in trade barriers. The city cancelled its New Year's Eve gala at the Space Needle because of terrorist threats. Then a federal judge back in the other Washington ruled that Microsoft was a monopoly. In perhaps the most stunning blow, Boeing chairman Phil Condit announced in May 2001 that the company would relocate its corporate headquarters to Chicago. That decision followed a series of bitter labor disputes plus less than hospitable treatment by Seattle area officials. The headquarters account for relatively few jobs, but top executives will no longer feel the neighborly pressures to accommodate querulous workers and maintain economically marginal operations. Seattle's affinity for protest politics and unionism came to seem, in post-September 11 America, as an indulgence that could no longer be afforded. Even Seattle's leftish voters took notice: when the dithering mayor came up for reelection in September 2001 he finished third in the primary with only 22% of the vote.

The 7th Congressional District includes all of the city of Seattle, some industrial suburban fringe to the south and white collar suburban fringe to the north and rural looking Vashon Island in Puget Sound. This is the Seattle area's minority district: 13% Asian, 8% black and 6% Hispanic. Seattle shares more with San Francisco than hills and scenery: it is heavily populated by singles, gays, young professionals and elderly pensioners. A generation ago, the city of Seattle was roughly split between the parties; today, it is heavily Democratic and liberal. Al Gore won 72% of the vote in this district in 2000.

The congressman from the 7th District is Jim McDermott, one of the most liberal members of the House and its only (credentialed) psychiatrist. McDermott grew up in Chicago and was the first in his family to attend college; interestingly he went to conservative religious Wheaton College, also the alma mater of Speaker Dennis Hastert. After service in the Navy and stints in New York and Illinois hospitals, he came to the University of Washington Hospital in Seattle. Almost immediately, he was elected to the state House in 1970, ran for governor in 1972 and finished third in the primary, and was elected to the state Senate in 1974, where he worked on issues from clean water to health care. He ran for governor again in 1980, beat incumbent Dixy Lee Ray in the primary, then lost to Republican John Spellman; in 1984 he ran for governor a third time and lost the primary to Booth Gardner. In 1987 he retired from the legislature and went to Zaire (now Congo) as a medical officer in the Foreign Service. When Congressman Mike Lowry ran for the Senate in 1988, McDermott returned to Seattle and ran for the 7th District seat and easily won, beating Norm Rice 38%–29% in the primary and winning 76% in the general.

In the House, McDermott's great cause has been health care but he has shared the frustration that many have met on the issue. He has long backed a single-payer, Canadian-style national health insurance program. In August 1994, as the Clinton health care plan was failing and Democratic leaders were scrambling to come up with an alternative, McDermott urged Congress to abandon all health care bills for the year. He evidently expected a more favorable political environment after the elections, and, like many, was surprised by the result. After Republicans took control, he said: "A lot of people around here have never been in the minority. I have. I know what to do: attack." In 2001, he joined Republican Jim McCrery on an innovative plan to replace the employer-based health insurance system with one that relied on tax credits to provide universal coverage.

Another measure, which seemed quixotic when McDermott first pushed it, was enacted in 2000. This was the African Growth and Opportunity Act, which reduces import quotas and tariffs on African goods and includes investment funds. McDermott was a co-sponsor with free-market Republican Philip Crane and Democrat Charles Rangel; as large parts of Africa moved toward free markets and political democracy, it became an idea whose time had come. He was among the handful of Democrats who actively supported PNTR with China. But he opposed trade promotion authority.

After the September 11 attacks, McDermott had trouble sleeping and recognized that he was having symptoms of post-traumatic stress disorder. He urged other lawmakers to talk to their constituents about their reaction to terrorism. When George W. Bush ordered military strikes against Afghanistan, he was the first member to criticize him for acting too quickly. He continued to oppose the new foreign policy Bush propounded in speeches in January and June 2002, and in late September went to Baghdad with former Minority Whip David Bonior and Mike Thompson of California. There, much to the astonishment of George Stephanopoulos, he told the audience of *This Week* that Bush was willing to "mislead the American people" and that he found Saddam Hussein more credible. This sparked harsh criticism from some Republicans and dismay from those Democrats who sensed, probably accurately, that his comments helped destroy their party's chances in the November 2002 elections. McDermott retreated a bit and argued that Bush had failed to make the case for military action. McDermott voted against military action against Iraq in October and, in February 2003, joined five other Democrats in bringing a lawsuit to stop military action. He was one of 11 Democrats who voted against the resolution supporting the troops and the president at the start of the war in March 2003.

In the meantime, McDermott was still dealing with another controversy that arose when he was ranking minority member on the ethics committee during its consideration of charges brought against Speaker Newt Gingrich in 1996 and 1997. McDermott was angry that Republicans would not make public the report of special counsel James Cole before the House voted for speaker in January 1997. A few days later, the committee voted for a House reprimand and a $300,000 penalty.

In the midst of the controversy, in December 1996 a Florida couple, Democratic activists, happened to tape a conversation between Ohio's John Boehner, talking on a cell phone, and other House Republican leaders. They presented the tape to their congresswoman, Karen Thurman, who suggested they turn it over to McDermott. A few days later excerpts from the tape appeared in the *New York Times*. Evidence suggested that McDermott was the source, and in 1998 Boehner sued McDermott in federal court for invasion of privacy. The trial judge ruled that the suit would infringe First Amendment rights, but the D.C. Circuit Court of Appeals reversed the decision. McDermott appealed to the Supreme Court, which decided another case instead and sent this one back to the D.C. Circuit, which sent it to District Court. The judge ruled in December 2002 that McDermott's conversations with a committee lawyer were not privileged. McDermott approached Boehner in 2002 (they had not spoken in the 12 years they served together) and sought to settle the case. He agreed to one of Boehner's demands, that he apologize to the House, but would not agree to the other two, that he admit he was wrong and that he make a contribution to charity.

McDermott considered running against Senator Slade Gorton in 2000, but backed away soon after he underwent open-heart surgery; he said that he didn't want to raise the $8 million that would be required. He has been reelected easily in this overwhelmingly Democratic district; his words in Baghdad may have hurt many Democrats elsewhere but they did not hurt McDermott in Seattle.

EIGHTH DISTRICT

Rep. Jennifer Dunn (R)

Elected 1992, 6th term; b. July 29, 1941, Seattle; home, Bellevue; U. of WA, 1960–62, Stanford U., B.A. 1963; Episcopalian; divorced.

Professional Career: Systems Engineer, IBM, 1964–69; P.R., King Cnty. Assessors Office, 1978–80; Chmn., WA Repub. Party, 1981–92; Delegate, U.N. Comm. on Status of Women, 1984 & 1990.

DC Office: 1501 LHOB 20515, 202-225-7761; Fax: 202-225-8673; Web site: www.house.gov/dunn.

District Office: Mercer Island, 206-275-3438.

Committees: *Select Committee on Homeland Security* (2d of 27 R): Infrastructure & Border Security; Intelligence & Counterterrorism; Rules. *Ways & Means* (12th of 24 R): Health; Trade. *Joint Economic Committee* (3d of 10 Reps.).

Group Ratings

	ADA	ACLU	AFS	LCV	CON	ITIC	NTU	COC	ACU	NTLC	CHC
2002	5	14	0	13	34	100	57	100	92	92	92
2001	10	—	0	21	—	—	66	95	88	—	—

National Journal Ratings

	2001 LIB —	2001 CONS		2002 LIB —	2002 CONS
Economic	36% —	65%		34% —	65%
Social	47% —	53%		43% —	57%
Foreign	4% —	87%		15% —	78%

Key Votes of the 107th Congress

1. Approve Bush Tax Cuts	Y	5. Faith-Based Charities	Y	9. Trade Promotion Authority	Y
2. Limit Patients' Bill of Rights	Y	6. Bar Gays in the Boy Scouts	Y	10. Bar Funds for Intl. Court	Y
3. Campaign Finance Reform	N	7. Ban Partial-Birth Abortion	Y	11. Authorize Force in Iraq	Y
4. Ban ANWR Development	Y	8. Arm Commercial Pilots	Y	12. Deny Home. Sec. Dept. Union	Y

Election Results

2002 general	Jennifer Dunn (R)	121,633	(60%)	($1,031,727)
	Heidi Behrens-Benedict (D)	75,931	(37%)	($120,333)
	Other	5,771	(3%)	
2002 primary	Jennifer Dunn (R)	68,199	(64%)	
	Heidi Behrens-Benedict (D)	35,681	(34%)	
	Other	2,606	(2%)	
2000 general	Jennifer Dunn (R)	183,255	(62%)	($1,731,507)
	Heidi Behrens-Benedict (D)	104,944	(36%)	($377,825)
	Other	6,269	(2%)	

Prior Winning Percentages: 1998 (60%); 1996 (65%); 1994 (76%); 1992 (60%)

The People		Race/Ethnic Origin	Ancestry	
Area size:	2,621 sq. mi.	82.1% White	German: 14.0%	English: 9.4%
Urban population:	87.6%	2.0% Black	Irish: 8.3%	
Rural population:	12.4%	7.8% Asian	**2000 Presidential Vote**	
Pop. 2000:	654,905	0.8% Native Am.	Gore (D)..............140,387	(49%)
Median income:	$63,854	0.3% Hawaiian	Bush (R)..............136,575	(47%)
Poverty status:	5.1%	2.8% Two+ races	Other...................11,838	(4%)
Military veterans:	14.0%	0.2% Other	**Cook Partisan Voting Index:** D + 0	
		4.0% Hispanic Origin		

Occupation   Blue collar: 19.7%   White collar: 68.6%   Gray collar: 11.8%

The land east of Seattle's Lake Washington half a century ago was quiet countryside. Orchards and vineyards flourished in the rich, moist soil just below the rise of the Cascades Mountains, while farms and broad pasturelands spread toward 14,410-foot Mount Rainier like a living green quilt. But as Seattle has grown over the years, people have crossed the pontoon bridge across Mercer Island to Bellevue and have made this Eastside area one of the most vibrant parts of metropolitan Seattle. Bellevue now has 109,000 people and enough office space to make it an edge city; its population in 2000 was 17% Asian, the highest percentage in Washington's 15 largest cities. While downtown Seattle specialized in banks and law firms and trading companies, Bellevue and other communities in Overlake specialized in high-tech startups. Redmond, just to the north, is the headquarters of Microsoft, and there are dozens of other firms here that make this one of America's leading high-tech centers.

The 8th Congressional District includes most of the eastern edge of metro Seattle. It includes most of Bellevue, Mercer Island and the affluent suburbs on Lake Washington—Medina, Clyde Hill, Yarrow Point, Hunts Point, Beaux Arts—where Bill Gates has built his 66,000-square foot high-tech home (the 8th does not include Redmond, however). It also includes the suburbs to the south in King and Pierce Counties. It goes up to the crest of the Cascades Mountains and includes all of Mount Rainier. This is the most affluent district in Washington, rivaled only by the 1st; politically it is market-oriented on economics, more liberal on the environment and other cultural issues. Historically it is Republican, but cast only 47% of its votes for George W. Bush.

The congresswoman from the 8th District is Jennifer Dunn, a Republican first elected in 1992. She grew up in Bellevue, graduated from Stanford, worked as a systems engineer for IBM in the 1960s and then stayed home to raise her children (her younger son is named Reagan, after the then-California governor, whom she supported over Gerald Ford in 1976). In 1981 she became Washington Republican Party chairwoman and served for 12 years. She is a peppery partisan, vigorous and knowledgeable about issues, persevering through bad times for her party and working to make them better. In 1992, when Congressman Rod Chandler ran for the Senate, she ran for the House and won in a walkover. In the House she was a vocal deficit hawk. Her voting record has been conservative on economic and foreign policy, moderate on cultural issues.

When Republicans won their majority in 1994, Dunn was put on the transition team and Speaker Newt Gingrich's task force on committee review, and given a seat on Ways and Means. She worked on the child support provisions of the welfare reform bill and pushed for medical savings accounts in the 1996 health care bill. She worked to allow software firms to lower their taxes by setting up foreign sales corporations as other businesses can.

Dunn, as one might expect of a longtime state party chairman, took political initiatives as well. She was a loyal supporter of Gingrich through his travails. In November 1996 she was elected secretary of the Republican Conference. In May 1997, when Susan Molinari announced her resignation from the House, Dunn ran for her post of Conference vice chair. Just as the coup against Gingrich was disintegrating, Dunn had leadership support and defeated Jim Nussle of Iowa, by 129–85. Having won that position, she decided not to run against Senator Patty Murray in 1998. Dunn had already moved to challenge Majority Leader Dick Armey, who was in low regard after the collapse of the anti-Gingrich coup. But the Tuesday Group and liberal Republicans did not endorse her, her longtime supporter Gingrich had announced his retirement and Steve Largent, one of the most ardent 1994 freshmen, was running as well. Dunn stressed the importance of having a woman in the Republican leadership, but other women were running for other leadership positions. Armey led the first ballot, led with 100 votes to 58 for Largent, 45 for Dunn and 18 for Dennis Hastert, whose name was advanced by others as he stuck by a commitment to support Armey. Largent asked Dunn to withdraw, in return for a new post as assistant majority leader; Dunn declined. On the second ballot, Armey got 99 votes, Largent 73 and Dunn 49— which meant that she was eliminated; Armey won on the third ballot, 127–95. After that setback, Dunn returned to her strong support of tax cuts: in income tax rates, in the estate tax, in capital gains and through Education Savings Accounts. She has worked on addressing the gender gap for Republicans, urging candidates to relate their policies to women's lives—she talks often about how she coped as a divorced working mom, and of how two-thirds of new small businesses are being formed by women. She has been a strong backer of free trade and PNTR with China.

In December 1998 she had dinner in Austin with George W. and Laura Bush and a few aides and agreed to support him. Among other things, she was impressed with how Bush related to his wife. She was one of three co-chairs of the 2000 national convention in Philadelphia, and then became a co-chair of the "Victory 2000" drive during the fall campaign. "She understands politics and she understands issues, and it's rare that you get someone who understands both," Bush political adviser Karl Rove said. But Dunn did not get a job in the Bush Cabinet; Rove may not have wished to risk a special election in a district that had gone for Al Gore. Dunn played a lead role on estate tax repeal and in 2003 moved to make it permanent. She led an effort to get 37 Republican congressmen to sign a letter in July 2001 supporting embryonic stem-cell research. In 2002 and 2003 she and Martin Frost co-sponsored the Amber Alert bill, which became law in April 2003. She supports individual investment accounts in Social Security and argues that the current program gives unfairly low benefits to women who spend some time at home rather than at a job, because the benefit formula depends on the 35 highest years of pay and because their earnings often don't qualify them for anything more than the spousal benefit and so they get nothing for the taxes they paid. Support for environmental restriction is high in the 8th District. In June 2002 Dunn supported the Wild Sky wilderness area sought by Murray and the 2d District's Rick Larsen; she got them to allow float planes in Lake Isabel. In 2003 she worked successfully on the Ways and Means Committee to get tax-exempt status for bonds floated to enable the Evergreen Forest Trust to buy the 104,000-acre Weyerhaeuser property in the Snoqualmie Tree Farm and for the Cascade Conservation Partnership to purchase the Plum Creek timber land.

Dunn clashed with Murray and Cantwell over Washington judicial nominations. Murray and former Senator Slade Gorton had created a bipartisan panel to consider possible nominees during the Clinton years. Dunn, as the senior Republican in the delegation, refused to do that after George W. Bush became president. She convened her own panel; she said Murray and Cantwell declined to participate in it. They said they were not asked. In any case, when the first nomination was made, Murray and Cantwell placed a hold on it.

Dunn has been reelected by wide margins, though less wide as the Seattle area became more Democratic in the Clinton years. In December 2002 it was reported that she was meeting with leaders of the Air Transport Association about the $700,000 executive directorship, but she was not offered the job. At that time she was also being urged to run against Murray in 2004—George W. Bush took to calling her "Senator," and 5th District Congressman George Nethercutt said he would not run if Dunn did. The Republican campaign committee took a poll showing her trailing the incumbent by only 46%–42%. But after being conspicuously undecided for several weeks, in April 2003 she announced that she would not run for the Senate. In February 2003 she got a seat on the Homeland Security Committee.

NINTH DISTRICT

Rep. Adam Smith (D)

Elected 1996, 4th term; b. June 15, 1965, Washington, DC; home, Tacoma; Fordham U. B.A. 1987, U. of WA, J.D. 1990; Christian; married (Sara).

Elected Office: WA Senate, 1990–96.

Professional Career: Practicing atty., 1991–92; Seattle Prosecutor, 1992–95.

DC Office: 227 CHOB 20515, 202-225-8901; Fax: 202-225-5893; Web site: www.house.gov/adamsmith.

District Office: Tacoma, 253-593-6600.

Committees: *Armed Services* (11th of 29 D): Tactical Air & Land Forces; Terrorism, Unconventional Threats & Capabilities. *International Relations* (21st of 23 D): Asia & the Pacific.

Group Ratings

	ADA	ACLU	AFS	LCV	CON	ITIC	NTU	COC	ACU	NTLC	CHC
2002	85	64	88	75	94	75	28	63	23	12	17
2001	80	—	100	86	—	—	18	48	20	—	—

National Journal Ratings

	2001 LIB —	2001 CONS		2002 LIB —	2002 CONS
Economic	58%	42%		63%	37%
Social	64%	36%		67%	29%
Foreign	73%	26%		61%	39%

Key Votes of the 107th Congress

1. Approve Bush Tax Cuts	N	5. Faith-Based Charities	N	9. Trade Promotion Authority	N
2. Limit Patients' Bill of Rights	N	6. Bar Gays in the Boy Scouts	N	10. Bar Funds for Intl. Court	Y
3. Campaign Finance Reform	Y	7. Ban Partial-Birth Abortion	N	11. Authorize Force in Iraq	Y
4. Ban ANWR Development	Y	8. Arm Commercial Pilots	Y	12. Deny Home. Sec. Dept. Union	N

Election Results

2002 general	Adam Smith (D)	95,805	(59%)	($769,600)
	Sarah Casada (R)	63,146	(39%)	($61,073)
	Other	4,759	(3%)	
2002 primary	Adam Smith (D)	57,250	(60%)	
	Sarah Casada (R)	36,368	(38%)	
	Other	2,555	(3%)	
2000 general	Adam Smith (D)	135,452	(62%)	($1,046,195)
	Christopher M. Vance (R)	76,766	(35%)	($634,816)
	Other	7,405	(3%)	

Prior Winning Percentages: 1998 (65%); 1996 (50%)

The People		Race/Ethnic Origin	Ancestry	
Area size:	691 sq. mi.	73.3% White	German: 13.2%	Irish: 7.9%
Urban population:	95.0%	6.3% Black	English: 7.7%	
Rural population:	5.0%	7.1% Asian	**2000 Presidential Vote**	
Pop. 2000:	654,902	1.1% Native Am.	Gore (D)............128,076	(53%)
Median income:	$46,495	0.9% Hawaiian	Bush (R)..............104,549	(43%)
Poverty status:	9.2%	4.2% Two+ races	Other..................10,874	(4%)
Military veterans:	17.2%	0.3% Other	**Cook Partisan Voting Index:** D + 5	
		6.7% Hispanic Origin		
Occupation	Blue collar: 24.7%	White collar: 59.4%	Gray collar: 15.9%	

The misty shores of Puget Sound have seen some of America's most vibrant economic growth over the last two decades. It has spread south from Seattle, over the mixed suburban territory, south and west to the outskirts of the once industrial city of Tacoma. The subdivisions along the Sound, which have some of the loveliest views in America, tend to be high-income. But much of greater Seattle's prime industrial territory lies between the ridges that run north and south inland. Weyerhaeuser, the world's largest private owner of softwood timber, has its headquarters here in Federal Way. Boeing is a major presence in Renton, on the south end of Lake Washington; its aircraft and electronic components plants have made it America's number one exporter for many years. A host of smaller factories cluster near the rail lines that run from Minneapolis-St. Paul across the Great Plains to Puget Sound.

The 9th Congressional District covers much of this area. It includes SeaTac Airport, Burien and Renton, not far south of Seattle, and Kent, Des Moines, most of Auburn and Federal Way farther south in King County. It includes the port area of Tacoma, though most of the rest of the city is in the 6th District, and in surrounding Pierce County includes Edgewood and Puyallup, Fort Lewis and McChord Air Force Base. It also includes a part of Thurston County outside the small state capital Olympia. This district was created after the 1990 Census and politically was almost perfectly balanced in the mid-1990s: it elected a Democratic congressman in 1992, a Republican in 1994 and a Democrat in 1996. But as the Seattle area trended toward Democrats it has become more Democratic. It gave George W. Bush only 43% of its votes in 2000.

The congressman from the 9th District is Adam Smith, a Democrat first elected in 1996. He grew up in the Sea-Tac area; his father, a baggage handler for United Airlines and active in the Machinists' Union, died when Smith was 17. The family went on welfare; Smith worked his way through Fordham driving trucks for UPS, then went to the University of Washington Law School. He worked as a lawyer, then as a Seattle prosecutor, handling drunk driving and domestic abuse cases. In 1990, at 25, he was elected to the state Senate, beating an incumbent Republican by doorbelling the district twice. In July 1995, he decided to run against Congressman Randy Tate. The two were born the same year, to families of modest backgrounds, were first elected to office at young ages and were firm believers in doorbelling. Tate, a religious conservative and strong supporter of Speaker Newt Gingrich, was a prime target in 1996 of the AFL-CIO, which spent perhaps $1 million on ads against him. Smith campaigned as a moderate Democrat, a supporter of the death penalty and three-strikes legislation. Smith's campaign steadily attacked Tate for supporting Gingrich on 96% of House votes and for backing Medicare "cuts." Tate attacked Smith for opposition to channeling youthful offenders to adult courts and prisons and for voting for Governor Mike Lowry's $1.2 billion tax increase in 1993. This was one of the closest races in the country. In the September all-party primary, usually a good indicator of the final result in Washington, Smith led 49%–48%. In November, his edge was 50%–47%.

In the House, Smith won the locally useful assignment to the Armed Services Committee, joined the New Democrat Coalition, had a decidedly moderate voting record and was willing to take on established interests within his party. He voted for the balanced budget and for charter schools, but against school vouchers; he supported term limits and voted to allow concealed weapons permits to be transferred from state to state. In 1999 he was one of four House Democrats to vote for the Republicans' budget; a year later, he voted to override Bill Clinton's vetoes of the estate tax and marriage penalty repeals. Smith voted against the Bush tax cuts and opposed permanent repeal of the estate tax because of its fiscal impact; he opposed trade promotion authority in December 2001, but then voted for the version that came out of conference committee in July 2002. Also in 2002, he, Jim Davis and Ron Kind became co-chairmen of the New Democrats. He voted to authorize military action in Iraq in October 2002, and sought to improve compensation and other "quality of life" benefits for military personnel.

Smith's independence has worked well for him back home. He has won reelection easily, and Republicans have quit targeting this district. In 2002 he won 59%–39%.

★ WEST VIRGINIA ★

Almost heaven—that's what the song says about West Virginia. And indeed some things are looking up for this state, whose people have never lost their sense of hope or their affection for the hills and mountains that make this the most unhorizontal state in the nation. But West Virginia has had more than its share of tragedy and heartbreak. It was born out of the tragedy of the Civil War, when 55 mountain counties with few slaves seceded from Virginia, and it has made its living most of the years since on that cruelest of commodities, coal. Coal kept the sons of large mountaineer families here for much of the 20th century, men who would otherwise have left for big cities; coal brought immigrants in, a few from odd corners of Europe, but more from adjacent areas of the South where the local farming economies were stagnant when West Virginia's coal economy was booming. Coal and local rock salt and brines brought the large concentration of chemical plants 50 years ago to the Kanawha Valley around Charleston; it built steel mills and glass factories in the panhandle and the Monongahela River valley, not far south of Pittsburgh.

But coal did not build a self-sustaining economy. When America was beleaguered abroad, demand for coal increased and energy prices rose, and West Virginia boomed, during World War II (the state reached its all-time population peak of 2 million in 1950) and the oil shocks of the 1970s. Coal changed the state's politics too. West Virginia's heritage from the Civil War days was Republican, though some counties tilted toward the Confederacy and the Democrats. But after John L. Lewis's United Mine Workers organized most of the West Virginia mines, the coal country shifted toward the New Deal Democrats, and West Virginia for more than half a century was one of the most Democratic states, deserting the national ticket only in Republican landslide years (1956, 1972, 1984) until George W. Bush carried it in 2000; its legislature has been controlled by Democrats since 1930. But neither Democratic administrations nor the pensions and medical benefits the UMW negotiated for retired miners were able to provide the economic growth to keep thousands of West Virginians from leaving their mountains to find work elsewhere—now more often south on I-77 to the booming Carolinas than north to the Great Lakes' industrial cities. As underground miners were replaced by strip-mining machines, coal tonnage went way up but coal mine employment dropped from 22% of the state's work force in 1950 to 10% in 1980 and only 4% in the late 1990s; coal employed 126,000 West Virginians in 1948, 63,000 in 1978, 13,500 in 2002. The state's population, 2.0 million in 1950 and 1.95 million in 1980, fell to 1.8 million in 2000—the largest decrease, absolutely and in percentage terms, of any state. In the 2000 Census West Virginia ranked 50th among states in household income, 50th in median value of housing (but first in percentage of home ownership), 48th in percentage of adults with a high school diploma and second in percentage living in poverty. Still, West Virginians have a strong attachment to this unique state, where the accent sounds Southern and the early 20th century factories and houses look Northern, where the landscape is rural and the economy industrial.

In the 1990s West Virginia was on the rebound, only to be threatened at the end of the decade with economic disaster. Population increased during the decade, though at the second-lowest rate of any state, and the number of jobs rose by 8%. Unemployment was down to 4.3% in 2001, the lowest since 1975. Government has played a role. Senator Robert Byrd, as both chairman and ranking Democrat on the Appropriations Committee, achieved his career goal of channeling $1 billion of federal projects into West Virginia, and more. They include offices for the FBI, Fish and Wildlife Service, NASA and the National Institute of Occupational Safety; federal jobs in West Virginia have grown 20% since 1988. West Virginia's universities have received directed funds for a biotech center, forensic science research and positron emission tomography. Old mining towns like Nellis and Matewan have been given new firewalls and preservation funds to keep up their historic buildings; a memorial to the 130,000 men killed in underground coal mining is being planned for Nellis. State tax breaks promoted by Governor Gaston Caperton (1988–96) attracted investments from Georgia Pacific, Swearingen Aircraft, NGK Sparkplugs and Toyota; Lexus engines are produced in Buffalo, West Virginia. Forest products are replacing coal in rural counties, health care is growing as everywhere and telemarketing is growing as well. Even the number of farms is increasing. West Virginia has finally completed its interstate highway network

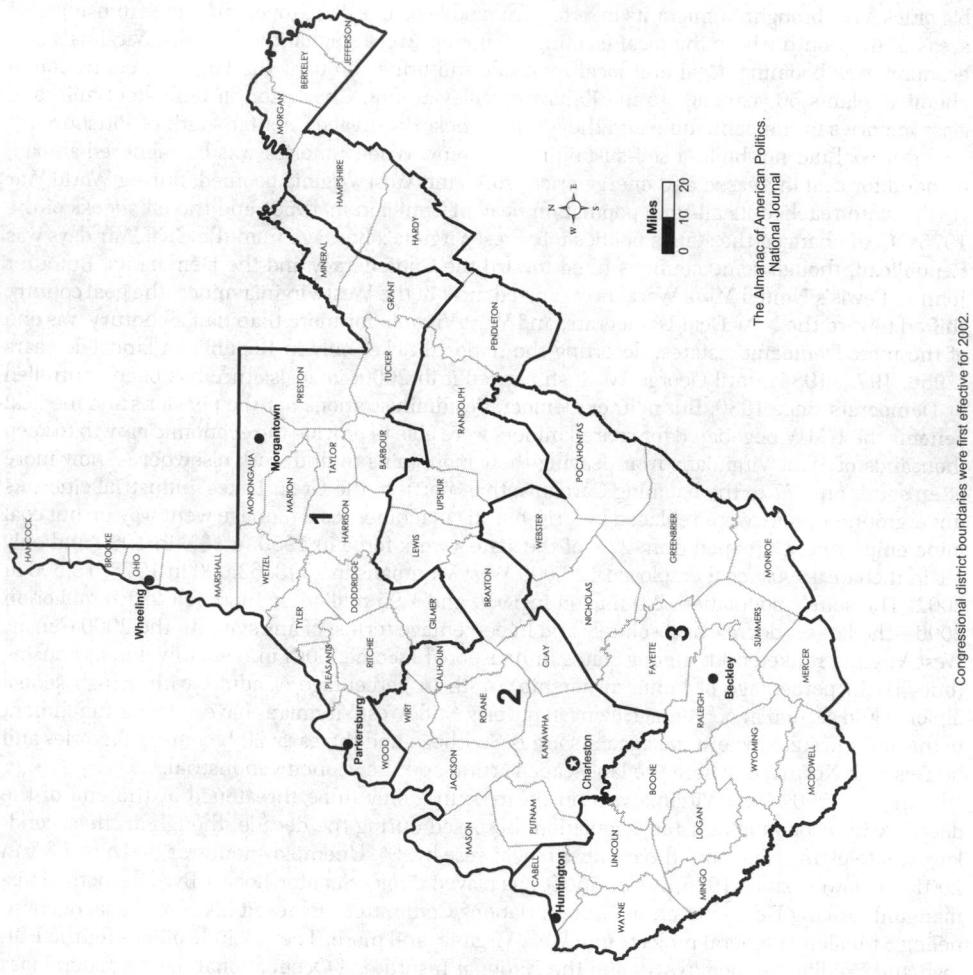

The Almanac of American Politics.
National Journal

Congressional district boundaries were first effective for 2002.

and in a computer age it is no longer isolated; with low wages, good work habits, low land costs, the state has even developed a software industry in the I-79 corridor between Morgantown and Clarksburg.

The threat to West Virginia's economy came in October 1999 when, in a case brought by environmental groups, federal judge Charles Haden ruled that mountaintop mining violates federal environmental laws. Most underground mines in West Virginia have been closed; they were uneconomic and the most unsafe workplaces in the country except for Alaskan fishing ships. Since the 1970s, mining companies have been leveling mountaintops with 20-story removal machines, exploding the loose dirt and rock and extracting low-sulfur coal from the resulting surface, and filling in local rivers and streams with piles of slag; when a mountain is mined, the companies are supposed to reclaim the land. Far fewer miners are needed for this work than in underground mining, but the pay is good and the jobs highly valued in counties which, in some cases, have half as many people as they did 50 years ago. Mining companies said that Judge Haden's decision would end coal mining in West Virginia. Senator Robert Byrd threatened to overturn the decision in an appropriations bill; Bill Clinton said he would veto any such bill, and the provision was dropped. But the issue became important—arguably crucial—in the 2000 presidential race. The Clinton administration came out in April 2000 opposing a ban on mountaintop mining, but calling for stricter regulation; Al Gore was caught in the middle between environmentalists who supported it and West Virginia's all-Democratic congressional delegation which opposed it. George W. Bush, spotting an opening quickly, came out in favor of mountaintop mining and called for increased federal support of clean coal technology; he said that the Clinton administration "fears coal" and managed to mention coal in one of the presidential debates. Bush's support of coal and his opposition to gun control enabled him to carry West Virginia 52%–46%—a stunning upset in a state that hadn't voted for a Republican in an open presidential race since 1928. Its five electoral votes were crucial: Without them, it would not have mattered who won Florida. The environmental stands which helped Gore in large East and West Coast states proved fatal to his candidacy in West Virginia. Bush ran well ahead of local Republicans: Democratic Congressman Bob Wise beat incumbent Republican Governor Cecil Underwood 50%–47%, and Republican Shelley Moore Capito, who won Wise's 2d District House seat 48%–46%—the first Republican victory in a congressional race here since 1980—ran 6% behind Bush. In April 2001, the Fourth Circuit Court of Appeals reversed Judge Haden and ruled that under the 1977 Surface Mining Control and Reclamation Act, West Virginia's mining standards superseded federal standards; *The Washington Post* wrote, "There's a growing feeling here that coal is back." West Virginia now produces only half as much coal as Wyoming, but much of it is high-quality bituminous coal and West Virginia's production is worth more.

That doesn't leave West Virginia without problems. High-paying chemical and steel jobs are being eliminated, and even during the growing 1990s the number of people aged 25 to 34 fell by 33,000. Students at the state's three medical schools are now required to spend month-long rotations at rural medicine clinics (and the number of doctors specializing in rural medicine has risen), but a rapid rise in malpractice insurance costs and the withdrawal of the state's largest insurer from the business has forced some doctors to quit obstetrics or leave the state altogether. On New Year's Day 2003, dozens of surgeons at four West Virginia hospitals went on strike in protest of rising malpractice premiums. The state Supreme Court is notoriously sympathetic to trial lawyers, and the resulting bitter fights between trial lawyers and doctors and insurance companies occupy much of the legislature's time. There are bitter fights as well over the treatment of overweight trucks. In early 2003, state government faced a revenue shortfall amid a consensus that there is little room to raise taxes. And there are other controversies as well. As the result of a poorly drafted statute on two highly sensitive issues in West Virginia—guns and God—35 counties held referenda in May 2002 and voted to ban hunting on Sundays; this is an issue that is likely to be revisited.

The People		Race/Ethnic Origin			Military veterans: 201,701 (14.3%)	
Pop. 2000:	1,808,344	1,709,966	94.6%	White	WWII: 21.4%	Korea: 14.9%
Pop. 1990:	1,793,477	56,825	3.1%	Black	Vietnam: 32.5%	Gulf War: 8.4%
Change 1990–2000:	Up 0.8%	9,356	0.5%	Asian	**Most populous cities:**	
Change 1980–1990:	Down 8.0%	3,456	0.2%	Native Am.	1. Charleston	53,421
% of U.S. total:	0.6%	335	0.0%	Hawaiian	2. Huntington	51,475
Pop. rank:	37th of 50	14,983	0.8%	Two+ races	3. Parkersburg	33,099
Area size:	24,230 sq. mi.	1,144	0.1%	Other	4. Wheeling	31,419
State Native:	74.2%	12,279	0.7%	Hisp. Origin	5. Morgantown	26,809
Non-citizen:	0.5%	**Ancestry**			Urban population: 46.1%	
Language		USA: 14.8%		German: 11.0%	Rural population: 53.9%	
English: 95.5%	Other Eur.: 2.0%	Irish: 8.6%		English: 7.7%		
Spanish: 1.8%		Italian: 3.0%				

Education		Work Sector		Legislature	
H.S. Grad:	75.2%	Private: 75.8%	Govt: 17.9%	Senate	24 D 10 R
College Grad:	14.8%	Self: 5.9%	Family: 0.4%	House	68 D 32 R
Industry		Unemployment: 7.3%		Legislative Term Limits: No	
Agri: 4.1%	Con: 7.0%	**Household Income**		**Registered Voters**	
Fin: 4.6%	Info: 2.2%	<15k: 25.4%	15-35k: 32.0%	D: 641,442	(60.5%)
Mfg: 17.9%	Prof: 29.7%	35-50k: 16.4%	50-100k: 21.2%	R: 309,280	(29.1%)
Public: 5.8%	Trade: 15.9%	100-150k: 3.3%	>150k: 1.8%	I: 110,170	(10.4%)
Other: 12.9%		Median: $29,696			
Occupation		Poverty status: 17.9%			
Blue collar: 28.7%	White collar: 54.0%	**Home Value**			
Gray collar: 17.3%		<50k: 35.4%	50-100k: 41.0%	100-200k: 19.0%	200-300k: 3.0%
		300-500k: 1.0%	>500k: 0.5%	Median: $66,000	

Presidential politics West Virginia was on few political reporters' radar screens in the 2000 presidential elections; after all, over the past 70 years the only Republican nominees it voted for were incumbents headed for landslide victories—Dwight Eisenhower in 1956, Richard Nixon in 1972, Ronald Reagan in 1984. But George W. Bush targeted the state early, and Al Gore paid it little heed until the very end of the campaign, when it was too late. Bush shrewdly took advantage of West Virginia's conservative cultural attitudes and of the threat to the coal industry. He carried two of the three congressional districts, and held Gore's margin to far below usual Democratic levels in the southern coal counties. This was the only state Bush carried which his father lost in 1988, though he came close in four others (Iowa, Minnesota, Oregon and Wisconsin); he ran ahead of his father's showing in almost every county except in the eastern panhandle, which is part of the Washington metropolitan area. Gore had only a 51%–47% margin among union members; Bush ran well ahead, 57%–37%, among voters under 30.

West Virginia's presidential primary, held in May, has not attracted much attention in years. But in 1960 it was the focus of the nation's attention when John F. Kennedy, reportedly fortified with large injections of cash from his father, took on Hubert Humphrey and beat him, proving that a Catholic could carry a virtually all-Protestant state.

2000 Presidential Vote
Bush (R)	336,475	(52%)
Gore (D)	295,497	(46%)
Nader (Green)	10,680	(2%)
Other	5,472	(1%)

2000 Republican Presidential Primary
Bush (R)	87,050	(80%)
McCain (R)	14,121	(13%)
Keyes (R)	5,210	(5%)
Other	3,023	(3%)

2000 Democratic Presidential Primary
Gore (D)	182,403	(72%)
Bradley (D)	46,710	(18%)
McDonald (D)	19,374	(8%)
LaRouche (D)	4,823	(2%)

1996 Presidential Vote
Clinton (D)	327,812	(52%)
Dole (R)	233,946	(37%)
Perot (I)	71,639	(11%)

Congressional districting West Virginia's three congressional districts, created after the state lost one House seat in the 1990 Census, were not signifi-

108th Congress Lineup
2 D   1 R
107th Congress Lineup
2 D   1 R

cantly altered in redistricting—even though the process was dominated by Democrats and the sole Republican, Shelley Moore Capito, who won an open seat narrowly in 2000, could have been harmed by a partisan redrawing of the lines. But one or both of the state's two Democratic incumbents might have been weakened, if not for the general election, then in a possible primary, by such a plan. One Democratic legislator suggested removing the eastern panhandle counties from Capito's 2d District, and her 2000 opponent, trial lawyer Jim Humphreys, called for a plan that removed three Republican counties west of Charleston and substituted three heavily Democratic coal-mining counties to the south. But most legislators, preoccupied with redrawing their own districts, were content to please all three incumbents. In a September 2001 special session, the legislature with one dissenting vote removed Gilmer County from the 2d and placed it in the 1st and removed Nicholas County from the 2d and placed it in the 3d: Both are Democratic counties that had no significant impact on the 2002 results.

Governor

Robert Wise (D)

Elected 2000, term expires Jan. 2005, 1st term; b. Jan. 6, 1948, Washington, D.C.; home, Clendenin; Duke U., B.A. 1970, Tulane U., J.D. 1975; Episcopalian; married (Sandy).

Elected Office: WV Senate, 1980–82; U.S. House of Reps. 1982–00.

Professional Career: Practicing atty., 1975–80; Dir., WV for Fair & Equitable Assessment of Taxes, 1977–80.

Office: State Capitol, Charleston, 25305, 304-558-2000; Fax: 304-558-2722; Web site: www.state.wv.us/governor.

Election Results

2000 general	Robert Wise (D)	324,822	(50%)
	Cecil H. Underwood (R)	305,926	(47%)
	Other	17,299	(3%)
2000 primary	Robert Wise (D)	174,202	(63%)
	Jim Lees (D)	101,774	(37%)
1996 general	Cecil H. Underwood (R)	324,518	(52%)
	Charlotte Pritt (D)	287,870	(46%)
	Other	16,171	(3%)

Bob Wise, a Democrat, was elected governor of West Virginia in 2000. He grew up in Charleston in an affluent family and graduated from Duke and Tulane Law School. He returned home to start a law practice geared to low- and middle-income clients, and led a movement to force coal companies to pay higher taxes. A strong advocate of West Virginia culture—he is renowned for his clog dancing and sensitive to stereotypes about his state—he urges West Virginia students to make their careers, as he did, in their home state. In 1980, he was elected to the state Senate, at 32; with the support of the teachers' union he beat the state Senate President in the Democratic primary. In 1982, he ran for the 3d District House seat (it was renumbered the 2d in 1992), occupied by a Republican who had won in the Reagan year of 1980. It was widely assumed that the Democratic nominee would win the seat and hold it for a long time, and there was serious competition. But Wise, after just two years in office, beat the state House majority leader and a former Kanawha County sheriff with 45% of the vote and then knocked off the Republican incumbent 58%–42%.

In the House, Wise had a generally liberal and often interesting voting record; he supported some conservative policies—repeal of the assault weapons ban, the flag amendment, welfare reform. His biggest legislative success was a 1990 amendment to provide benefits for workers displaced by compliance with the Clean Air Act, with a $250 million cap. He moved to delay EPA's 1998 Clean Air guidelines which would require reductions of nitrous oxide in West Virginia to 44% below 1990 levels, the biggest drop in the nation.

In May 1999, he announced that he would run for governor. Incumbent Republican Cecil Underwood had won in 1996 largely because Democratic nominee Charlotte Pritt, backed by labor unions, was seen as too unfriendly to business and too far to the left; outgoing two-term Democratic Governor Gaston Caperton made little effort to hide the fact that he preferred Underwood. Once in office, Underwood gamely set about running for re-election and in 2000 proceeded to disperse $16 million from the governor's discretionary funds to presumably worthy projects throughout the state. Wise ran with the support of the state's teachers' unions and the United Mine Workers, but sought to avoid the split between labor and business so prominent in the gubernatorial primary of 1996. He had spirited opposition from Jim Lees, who had run third in the 1996 primary and was now spending large sums of his own money on his campaign. He profited from the split among Democrats on mountaintop mining. Articulate liberals and environmentalist groups wanted to abolish the practice, and brought a lawsuit in federal court to do so; most elected officials, including Wise, were against, though in August 1998 Wise called for a moratorium on new permits for mountaintop mining pending the outcome of the court case. In October 1999, a federal judge ruled that mountaintop mining violated federal environmental laws; Wise backed Senator Robert Byrd's attempt to overturn the ruling through legislation. Lees outspent Wise 2–1 in the final two months before the May primary and was endorsed by the Charleston newspapers, the state Sierra Club and the social workers association, but Wise won 63%–37%.

In the general election, Wise said that the economy was not growing fast enough and issued a 28-page job growth plan. He charged that Underwood had failed to implement the CHIP child health care program and had taken the side of big insurance companies on HMO regulation. Education funding would come from taxing and regulating video poker machines—called 'gray machines' in West Virginia—which were then unlicensed and untaxed. In September, Underwood unleashed a series of ads stressing his support for the partial-birth abortion ban and prayer in schools; he touted his support for mountaintop mining and criticized Wise for seeking a moratorium in 1998. Wise got key endorsements from leading state Democrats. Caperton and Senator Jay Rockefeller, who had backed Pritt ardently in 1996, backed Wise in 2000. Senator Byrd, who seldom endorsed other candidates, cut a TV spot for Wise and traveled across the state urging West Virginians to vote for him. Byrd's support may have made the difference. While George W. Bush was carrying the state 52%–46%, Wise won 50%–47%; 21% of Bush voters voted for him. He did especially well in Charleston's Kanawha County, his home base, and in the northern panhandle; his support in the southern coal counties was below historic Democratic levels, and he carried only one county in the Republican-leaning eastern panhandle, though he had represented much of the area for eight years.

In 2001, Wise got the legislature to increase teachers' salaries and legalize and tax gray machines to fund Promise scholarships for college. Interestingly, such programs tend to redistribute money from the less affluent (who are more likely to play video poker) to the more affluent (who are more likely to have children who get good grades in college), but similar programs advocated by Democratic governors have been highly popular in Georgia and other states. He called a special session in October 2001 to deal with the crisis in malpractice insurance: Rates were rising, insurance companies were dropping coverage, and doctors were abandoning specialties or leaving the state. Wise got the legislature to authorize state issuance of malpractice policies and for review by a medical specialist of malpractice cases before a court could hear them. He wanted state insurance to be cheaper than private insurance; the legislature disagreed, except in the event only one company offered coverage—which appeared to be the case in late 2002.

But problems continued and in late 2002, doctors and hospital groups were seeking additional curbs on malpractice cases. He also got an increase in the coal industry tax to fund cleanup of abandoned mines.

In 2002, Wise got much of his agenda through, with some changes: The legislature voted for a bigger increase in teachers' salaries than he asked, but restored half the cuts he asked for in higher education and gave him $1.5 million, not $3 million, for a Sunny Day Fund to give him flexibility to attract businesses to the state. Wise vetoed a bill passed by large majorities to give women risk information 24 hours in advance of having an abortion. As revenues came in lower than expected, Wise made spending cuts in late 2002, and the possibility of state payroll cuts loomed in 2003. Wise remained opposed to tax increases, though some legislators called for an increase in the cigarette tax.

Wise comes up for reelection in 2004. Republicans surprised many when they beat the chairmen of the state Senate Finance and Judiciary Committees in November 2002, but Democrats still have large majorities in both the Senate and the House of Delegates. Among those mentioned as possible Republican candidates in 2004 are state Senate Minority Leader Vic Sprouse and Underwood's tax and revenue secretary Robin Capehart; Congresswoman Shelley Moore Capito seemed uninterested in seeking the office her father Arch Moore won in 1968, 1972 and 1984. Wise's political fortunes took a turn for the worse in May 2003 when he admitted to an affair with an employee of the state development office. The relationship was revealed after the woman's husband alleged in divorce papers that his wife was involved in a relationship with a man he identified as Wise. "That weasel-faced bastard," said the angry cuckold to the *Charleston Daily Mail*. "Typical Democrat."

Senior Senator

Robert Byrd (D)

Elected 1958, seat up 2006, 8th term; b. Nov. 20, 1917, North Wilkesboro, NC; home, Sophia; American U., J.D. 1963; Baptist; married (Erma).

Elected Office: WV House of Delegates, 1946–50; WV Senate, 1950–52; U.S. House of Reps., 1952–58; U.S. Senate Majority Whip, 1971–76, Majority Ldr., 1977–80, 1987–88, Minority Ldr., 1981–86.

DC Office: 311 HSOB, 20510, 202-224-3954; Fax: 202-228-0002; Web site: byrd.senate.gov.

State Office: Charleston, 304-342-5855.

Committees: *Appropriations* (RMM): Defense; Energy & Water Development; Homeland Security (RMM); Interior; Transportation, Treasury & General Government; VA, HUD & Independent Agencies. *Armed Services*: Emerging Threats & Capabilities; Readiness & Management Support; Strategic Forces. *Budget. Rules & Administration.*

Group Ratings

	ADA	ACLU	AFS	LCV	CON	ITIC	NTU	COC	ACU	NTLC	CHC
2002	75	20	88	47	47	25	15	40	15	12	—
2001	85	—	75	75	—	—	13	21	40	—	60

National Journal Ratings

	2001 LIB —	2001 CONS	2002 LIB —	2002 CONS
Economic	64%	35%	59%	36%
Social	47%	53%	50%	48%
Foreign	61%	27%	76%	22%

Key Votes of the 107th Congress

1. Approve Bush Tax Cuts	N	5. Confirm Ashcroft as AG	Y	9. Bar Coop. with Intl. Court	N
2. Expand Patients' Rights	Y	6. Bar Gays in the Boy Scouts	Y	10. Trade Promotion Authority	N
3. Campaign Finance Reform	Y	7. $ for Hate Crime Prosecution	Y	11. Authorize Force in Iraq	N
4. Permit ANWR Development	N	8. Overseas Military Abortions	Y	12. Homeland Sec. Dept. Union	N

Election Results

2000 general	Robert Byrd (D)	469,215	(78%)	($1,045,993)
	David T. Gallaher (R)	121,635	(20%)	
	Other	12,627	(2%)	
2000 primary	Robert Byrd (D)	unopposed		
1994 general	Robert Byrd (D)	290,495	(69%)	($1,550,354)
	Stan Klos (R)	130,441	(31%)	($267,165)

Prior Winning Percentages: 1988 (65%); 1982 (69%); 1976 (100%); 1970 (78%); 1964 (68%); 1958 (59%); 1956 House (57%); 1954 House (63%); 1952 House (56%)

Robert Byrd, longtime chairman and ranking minority member of the Senate Appropriations Committee, third in line for the presidency as President Pro Tempore of the Senate from June 2001 to January 2003, may come closer to the kind of senator the Founding Fathers had in mind than any other. He comes from the humblest of beginnings, and when first elected to the Senate, as part of the large and talented Democratic class of 1958, he was scarcely noticed. Now he is the last member of that class still in the Senate, and an authentic power whether in majority or minority. From a background as grindingly poor as that of any American politician, he has continually moved up with awesome persistence. "I lived in a house without electricity," he lectured Treasury Secretary O'Neill in one hearing. "No running water, no telephone, little wooden outhouse." (O'Neill told him that he had grown up dirt poor too.) Son of a coal miner, he was a welder in wartime shipyards and a meat cutter in a coal company town when he won his seat in the House of Delegates in 1946; he campaigned in every hollow in the county, playing his fiddle and even going to the length of joining the Ku Klux Klan (which he quickly quit and has ever since regretted joining). He worked hard in the legislature, and won a U.S. House seat when the incumbent retired in 1952; he made such a name for himself in West Virginia that by 1958, when he was 40, he was elected to the Senate—even though the United Mine Workers initially opposed him and the coal companies never supported him.

In the Senate, he became a supporter of Majority Leader Lyndon B. Johnson and in return got a seat on Appropriations his first year. He backed Hubert Humphrey against John Kennedy in the 1960 West Virginia presidential primary not because he shared Humphrey's liberal politics—his voting record then was as conservative as any Southerner's and he opposed the Civil Rights Act of 1964—but because Johnson wanted to stop Kennedy. Then, in the 1960s, Byrd's career took what in retrospect was a helpful detour. He became assistant majority whip, an unimportant position in 1965; in 1971, when Edward Kennedy neglected his duties as whip after Chappaquiddick, Byrd quietly lined up support and, with Richard Russell's deathbed vote, ousted Kennedy. There Byrd performed ably, managing Senate business and accommodating colleagues' needs, and when Majority Leader Mike Mansfield retired in 1976, Byrd easily won the job. All the while Byrd was working hard to keep in touch with West Virginians, to the point that he won 78% of the vote in 1970, becoming the first West Virginian in history to carry all 55 counties.

Byrd did not like being majority leader. Contrary to most people's assumptions, the post carries little power, because Senate rules requiring unanimous consent or supermajorities allow minorities and even individual senators to block action. Byrd was aware that his power came from meeting other senators' needs and did not have a national issues agenda of his own, though his voting record became notably less conservative. In 1987, with Democrats back in the majority after six years out of power, Byrd established some legislative priorities and then announced he would leave the post after the 1988 election.

In 1989, Byrd got the position he had been aiming for all along—chairman of the Appropriations Committee. "I want to be West Virginia's billion dollar industry," he announced in 1990, and in the next dozen years succeeded handsomely. An FBI office went to Clarksburg, Treasury and IRS offices to Parkersburg, the Fish and Wildlife Training Center in Harper's Ferry, a Bureau of Alcohol, Tobacco and Firearms in Martinsburg, a NASA Research center in Wheeling. "All roads, they say, lead to Rome," he said in 1994 in Logan, West Virginia. "They haven't seen anything yet. All roads lead to Logan." The December 2000 final appropriations included more than $1 billion of spending in West Virginia. Some of it represents the ordinary operations of government, but much of it is Byrd's work. Since 1990, he has attached more than $270 million to appropriations bills for the construction of one interstate highway alone. He boasts that when he was in the state House of Delegates in 1947, West Virginia had just four miles of divided, four-lane highway. Today, there are more than 1,033 miles. Byrd has worked hard to find funds for the depleted United Mine Workers health care program for retired miners and their widows. He has supported the state's coal mining industry, seeking funds for miners displaced by the Clean Air Act in 1990, co-sponsoring the 1997 resolution opposing the Kyoto Protocol so long as it excluded developing countries like China, and opposing EPA's 1999 proposed air quality standards. When a federal judge ruled in October 1999 that mountaintop mining violated federal environmental laws, Byrd tried to pass an appropriations rider reversing the decision; he was angry when the Clinton administration, at first agreeable, decided to oppose such a rider with a veto. The issue helped George W. Bush carry West Virginia in 2000; in April 2001, a federal appeals court reversed the decision and ruled that state laws governed mountaintop mining.

It should be added that Byrd's positions are not just parochial but are the product of serious study of the Constitution and of history. He always carries a copy of the Constitution in his left breast pocket. With the assistance of Senate historian Richard Baker, he wrote *The Senate 1789–1989*, a two-volume history, plus two volumes of classic speeches and statistics; based on impressive research, gracefully written, full of arresting anecdotes and sound insights, it surpasses any previous work on the subject. Byrd earned his law degree while in the Senate and had his diploma presented to him by President Kennedy at the 1963 American University commencement where Kennedy delivered his most important foreign policy speech. In 1994, he was awarded his B.A. summa cum laude by Marshall University, which he had attended for one semester 43 years before and could not afford to continue, and where he earned A's in all eight courses he took. Byrd has been educating himself as well, systematically reading the classics, and takes to quoting Shakespeare, Thucydides or Cato the Younger in debates on the balanced budget amendment and the line-item veto. He said passage of the line-item veto in 1996 was "one of the darkest moments in the history of the republic," and with five other members of Congress brought suit against it. The Supreme Court rejected their challenge in July 1997, but it was ruled unconstitutional in June 1998. "After 200 years," he wrote in his history, the Senate "is still the anchor of the Republic, the morning and evening star in the American constitutional constellation."

As might be expected, Byrd played a leading role on impeachment. In October 1998, when the White House sought to forestall a House vote by getting 34 Democratic senators to sign a letter saying they would never vote to remove Clinton, Byrd responded, "Don't tamper with this jury." The tampering stopped. After Clinton and most Democratic House members held a campaign-style rally at the White House after the House voted for impeachment, Byrd called it, "an egregious display of shameless arrogance the likes of which I don't think I have seen." Later in January, he introduced a resolution to dismiss the charges, but that was defeated 56–44. Though he evidently continued to believe that Clinton committed high crimes, he decided that a vote to remove would abet partisanship.

Byrd has upheld the Senate's prerogatives consistently and has responded fiercely when he believes the Senate has been slighted. He opposed PNTR with China in June 2000 and complained particularly about the administration's insistence that the Senate approve the House legislation: "What weak dishwater is the excuse that we cannot add anything to the House-passed bill? What a sorry spectacle is a Senate completely cowed by the possibility that we might upset the Chinese."

If Byrd is determined to uphold the prerogatives of the Senate, he is determined also to uphold the prerogatives of the Appropriations Committee. George W. Bush went out of his way to shake Byrd's hand at his first speech to a joint session of Congress; Byrd had not attended State of the Union addresses since 1994 out of distaste for Bill Clinton: "His lifestyle and mine were so different I didn't care about coming to hear him." But Byrd opposed Bush's tax cut as "sheer madness," arguing that it was based on inevitably untrustworthy economic forecasts and complaining that it would cut off funds for appropriators. At Democratic caucuses he made impassioned pleas that Democrats not support tax cuts, and in February 2001, he clashed with Senate Parliamentarian Robert Dove over his interpretation that budget resolution procedures, which allow debate to be shut off by 50 senators, could be used on the tax cut. Byrd obviously resented Bush OMB Director Mitch Daniels, whom he referred to as "little Caesar" and complained Daniels was "always meddling in the Congress always lecturing the Congress . . . I'm fed up to my ears." What infuriated him was Daniels' insistence that appropriators not exceed spending limits set by the administration. In December 2001, he fought to appropriate more money for fighting terrorism than the administration wanted and held up the defense appropriations bill; Majority Leader Tom Daschle, evidently unwilling to have Democrats be seen as withholding money for defense, cut a deal with Minority Leader Trent Lott to pass the bill. In July 2002, Byrd again had to back down on an emergency spending bill, but arranged with Appropriations ranking Republican Ted Stevens to take the cuts out of programs the administration wanted.

Byrd's insistence on maintaining what he regards as the Senate's constitutional prerogatives and his distaste for Bush administration policies led him to embark on two crusades in 2002 which may have helped lead to the Democrats' loss of their Senate majority in November. One was his opposition to the bill setting up the Department of Homeland Security. "Have we all completely taken leave of our senses?" he asked in July 2002. "If ever there was a time for the Senate to throw a bucket of cold water on an overheated legislative process that is spinning out of control, it is now. Now!" He insisted that the biggest reorganization of the federal government since the creation of the Department of Defense required more scrutiny, and he opposed giving the president authority to shift money between agencies without regard for congressional appropriators. His persistent speeches meant that the Senate, unlike the House, couldn't vote on it before the August recess or the September 11 anniversary that many senators had as a goal. In September, Byrd spoke frequently and at great length on the issue. He never used the word filibuster, but this was one in effect. It also gave government unions time to unite Democrats against the provisions for flexibility insisted on by Bush—a stand that hurt Democratic senators gravely in Georgia and Missouri on Election Day. In September, Byrd sought to require the president to get approval of the new department in three stages over the next year; that lost 70–28. After the election, Democrats realized it was in their political interest to pass the bill, and a motion to limit debate passed 65–29. Byrd still regarded the new department as a "snake" and said, "If I could, I would chop off its head and kill it, dead, dead, dead."

The other crusade was against military action in Iraq. In September, he accused Bush of political motivation, saying out loud what some other Democrats believed but were too politick to say. "All of a sudden the president was dropping in the polls, and the domestic situation was such that the administration was appearing to be much like the emperor who had no clothes. All of a sudden, bam! All of this war talk—the war fervor, the drums of war, the bugles of war, the clouds of war, this war hysteria—has blown in like a hurricane. And what has that done to the president's polls? Seventy percent." In October, he threatened to delay action on the Iraq war resolution by insisting on votes on individual clauses; he was foiled when Connecticut Sen. Joe Lieberman and Daschle made a change in wording that made his motion out of order. Most Democrats wanted to get the issue out of the way and to talk about the domestic issues they thought would help them in November. Not Byrd. "Congress might as well just close the doors, put a sign over the doors and say, 'Going fishing.' Congress is being stampeded, pressured, adjured, importuned into acting on this blank check." But the Senate passed the resolution 77–23.

Does Byrd's lack of success on homeland security and Iraq mean that his power is fading? Certainly he does not operate with a view to positioning his party in line with public opinion, but he can make an eloquent case that he has responsibilities higher than that. And, well past 80, he seems to speak with less inhibition than in previous years, and to make mistakes: On Fox News Channel he spoke in 2001 of "white niggers," a phrase for which he quickly apologized. But Byrd's power in the Senate comes largely from his position on Appropriations, and it has not been greatly lessened because Republicans now have a majority. Appropriators have worked together for years and cooperate against party lines against institutional adversaries like OMB and the authorizing and Budget committees. Byrd has served on Appropriations with his predecessor and successor as chairman, Ted Stevens, since 1973, and contributed $2,000 to his 2002 campaign.

In November 2000, Byrd was re-elected by a 78%–20% margin, his largest percentage margin ever, carrying all 55 counties for the third time. At a spirited rally at the end of the campaign he said, "West Virginia has always had four friends. God Almighty, Sears Roebuck, Carter's Liver Pills and Robert C. Byrd." He is the second senator to have been elected to eight six-year terms (the other was Strom Thurmond of South Carolina); he has served longer than any other senator but Thurmond and, if reelected in 2006, stands to beat his record in February 2007.

Junior Senator

Jay Rockefeller IV (D)

Elected 1984, seat up 2008, 4th term; b. June 18, 1937, New York, NY; home, Charleston; Harvard U., B.A. 1961, Intl. Christian U., Tokyo, Japan, 1957–60; Presbyterian; married (Sharon).

Elected Office: WV House of Delegates, 1966–68; WV Secy. of State, 1968–72; WV Gov., 1976–84.

Professional Career: Natl. Advisory Cncl., Peace Corps, 1961; Asst., Peace Corps Dir. Sargent Shriver, 1962–63; VISTA worker, 1964–66; Pres., WV Wesleyan Col., 1973–75.

DC Office: 531 HSOB, 20510, 202-224-6472; Fax: 202-224-7665; Web site: rockefeller.senate.gov.

State Offices: Beckley, 304-253-9704; Charleston, 304-347-5372; Fairmont, 304-367-0122; Martinsburg, 304-262-9285.

Committees: *Commerce, Science & Transportation*: Aviation (RMM); Communications; Science, Technology & Space; Surface Transportation & Merchant Marine. *Finance*: Health Care (RMM); International Trade; Social Security & Family Policy. *Foreign Relations*: East Asian & Pacific Affairs; International Economic Policy, Export & Trade Promotion; Near Eastern & South Asian Affairs. *Intelligence (Select)* (Vice Chmn.). *Veterans' Affairs*. *Joint Committee on Taxation* (5th of 5 Sens.).

Group Ratings

	ADA	ACLU	AFS	LCV	CON	ITIC	NTU	COC	ACU	NTLC	CHC
2002	90	60	100	71	27	38	10	45	15	6	—
2001	100	—	100	100	—	—	7	43	12	—	0

National Journal Ratings

	2001 LIB	—	2001 CONS	2002 LIB	—	2002 CONS
Economic	88%	—	9%	73%	—	20%
Social	69%	—	31%	68%	—	28%
Foreign	61%	—	27%	81%	—	15%

Key Votes of the 107th Congress

1. Approve Bush Tax Cuts	N	5. Confirm Ashcroft as AG	N	9. Bar Coop. with Intl. Court	Y
2. Expand Patients' Rights	Y	6. Bar Gays in the Boy Scouts	N	10. Trade Promotion Authority	N
3. Campaign Finance Reform	Y	7. $ for Hate Crime Prosecution	Y	11. Authorize Force in Iraq	Y
4. Permit ANWR Development	N	8. Overseas Military Abortions	Y	12. Homeland Sec. Dept. Union	Y

Election Results

2002 general	Jay Rockefeller IV (D)	275,281	(63%)	($2,299,519)
	Jay Wolfe (R)	160,902	(37%)	($136,935)
2002 primary	Jay Rockefeller IV (D)	198,327	(90%)	
	Bruce Barilla (D)	11,178	(5%)	
	William Galloway (D)	11,173	(5%)	
1996 general	Jay Rockefeller IV (D)	456,526	(77%)	($5,819,157)
	Betty A. Burks (R)	139,088	(23%)	

Prior Winning Percentages: 1990 (68%); 1984 (52%)

Jay Rockefeller's full name, John D. Rockefeller IV, has a familiar ring to those who remember his great-grandfather as the oil billionaire who was America's richest man, and his grandfather as the heir who had more than enough money to build New York's Rockefeller Center, restore Colonial Williamsburg, and found the Museum of Modern Art during the Depression of the 1930s. Jay Rockefeller's father and uncles were men of impressive achievement in different fields. His uncle, Winthrop Rockefeller, moved to an impoverished state in the southern hills—in his case Arkansas—and won two terms as governor, running an honest and reforming administration. His other uncle, Nelson Rockefeller, became governor of the nation's then-biggest state and spent money expansively on generous welfare and gigantic monuments. Jay Rockefeller became governor of what turned out to be America's number one population-losing state of the 1980s, leaving behind a network of roads and highways and a progressive tax structure. Both Rockefellers—Nelson and Jay—were mentioned early on as presidential candidates: Nelson, never very shy about running, finally did so in 1964 at 56, and again in 1968, and served as Vice President from 1974 to 1977. Jay for years avoided projecting his name forward, then almost decided to run in the summer of 1991 at 54, but in 2001 said, "No, I'm not interested. If I'd wanted to do it, I would have in 1991."

The parallels stop here, for Jay Rockefeller lacks the aloof, imperial bearing of his Uncle Nelson; he is affable, full of self-deprecating humor, tall enough so that he stoops to get through doorways and uses hearing aids because of noise damage from frequent helicopter travel. He was careful to work his way up the political ladder. He grew up in New York, graduated from Harvard, and lived and studied in Japan for three years. He first came to West Virginia as a VISTA volunteer in Emmons in 1964. "Although I went to Emmons to help that community," he reminisced in 2002, "they helped me much more. My experience in Emmons set the course for the rest of my life." He was elected to the House of Delegates in Kanawha County in 1966 and as secretary of state in 1968, and then had the chastening experience of losing a 1972 race for governor to Republican Arch Moore. He served three years as president of West Virginia Wesleyan College in Buckhannon, and became more practical, dropping his opposition to strip mining. He was not shy about spending his own millions—his net worth was estimated at $200 million in 2002—and was elected governor in 1976 and, against Moore, in 1980, after which the state was plunged into deep recession. In 1984, he ran for the U.S. Senate and beat Republican businessman John Raese by just 52%–48% after spending $12 million.

Initially in the Senate, Rockefeller deferred to Robert Byrd and compiled a conventional liberal voting record, though somewhat more inclined to free trade because of his experience in East Asia. Then he began his concentration on health care. With a seat on the Finance Committee, he got a place on the Pepper Commission on long-term health care. As chairman, he got majorities on the commission to back long-term care for all Americans regardless of age and, by 8–7, universal medical insurance coverage. But getting others to agree was harder. Rockefeller talked mostly about health care financing when he was mulling a presidential race; but he warmly endorsed Bill Clinton and applauded his emphasis on health care. He was motivated in part by anger at his mother's treatment during a long terminal illness—an experience that would be much worse for people of ordinary incomes, he thought—and he worked to increase the number of general practitioners, especially in states like West Virginia and Arkansas, at the risk of harming the major teaching hospitals. Efforts at compromise came far too late, after voters had turned against a government takeover of health care, and the health care bill crashed and burned in September 1994.

Rockefeller has worked on other health care issues since. Perhaps his biggest legislative achievement was his 1992 law, passed over furious opposition from Western coal states, which forced union and non-union coal companies and "reachback" companies that had gone out of the coal business to pay for the exploding cost of the United Mine Workers' health care trust funds; he has worked ever since to continue funding of this program for retired miners and their widows. Rockefeller was a member of the Medicare commission set up under a 1997 law. He opposed the recommendations of John Breaux of a premium-support system, under which seniors would be given a certain amount of money and could choose between offerings from different insurance companies, much as federal employees choose from among a series of approved plans today. Breaux won a 10–7 margin for his plan, but it was below the 11-vote supermajority required to make it an official recommendation; Rockefeller vigorously opposed the proposal. On the Finance Committee and, if it comes to that, on the floor he is likely to be a staunch opponent of similar proposals if advanced by George W. Bush, Frist and Breaux. Rockefeller still would like a system-wide health care reform but recognizes that it cannot pass, and so he works on incremental changes, like the amendment he got passed unanimously in July 2002 to route $6 billion to Medicaid programs in the states.

On some issues, Rockefeller has not taken stands on the left. He supported the 1996 Welfare Reform Act, working to maintain programs for abused and neglected children. For a dozen frustrating years, one of his major causes was a uniform federal product liability law, to reduce the burden of expensive lawsuit settlements on manufacturers. Bill Clinton vetoed one version in May 1996; another was sidelined by the production of the Starr report in September 1998.

In 2001, Rockefeller vehemently opposed the Bush tax cuts and argued that West Virginians, with the lowest incomes in the nation, received relatively little. "I understand that we are in a war against terrorism and money is tight," he wrote in May 2002. "But I have trouble understanding why money is tight when it comes to funding health care programs that benefit the poor and middle class but is readily available when it comes to funding a tax cut that dramatically favors the rich."

Steel has been a preoccupation of Rockefeller for a long time. He was one of those who helped Weirton Steel, now West Virginia's fourth largest employer, become employee-owned in 1984. In the late 1990s, he called for aid to steel makers in the face of what he regarded as a flood of subsidized steel imports, arguing that workers and companies that have "played by the book" should get government help to allow them to continue in their jobs and their homes. In 2002, he called for 40% tariffs for four years on steel imports. The Bush administration in March 2002 imposed a 24% tariff in the second year and 18% in the third; Rockefeller complained when the administration made exceptions. Rockefeller has worked for several years to provide health care benefits to retired steelworkers whose former employers have gone out of business or filed for bankruptcy. He scaled down his original proposal to a $179 million refundable tax credit to cover 70% of health care costs. In May 2002, the Senate voted for this 56–40; not enough for approval, which required 60 votes, but it did signal progress for Rockefeller on a long-term project which he says will make possible a consolidation of the steel industry.

Rockefeller is vice chairman on the Intelligence Committee and participated in the joint intelligence committees' investigation of intelligence before September 11. In January 2003 he was involved in a dispute with Chairman Pat Roberts over the apportionment of funding for the committee; the rift nearly prevented the organization of the Senate for the 108th Congress. According to Roberts, Rockefeller also proposed firing the entire staff of the traditionally non-partisan committee and rehiring the positions on a partisan basis. On Iraq and homeland security, Rockefeller took stands opposite to those vehemently urged by his West Virginia colleague Robert Byrd. In October 2002, Rockefeller voted for the Iraq war resolution. After the November 2002 election, he voted for the Department of Homeland Security as a "bold and necessary step." But he took care to thank Byrd for leading the opposition to it with "clarity, conviction and passion," and with Byrd, he voted against limiting debate on the measure.

Rockefeller is in strong shape politically—strong enough that he no longer spends any of his own money and wins handsomely. He won by 68%–32% in 1990, 77%–23% in 1996 (duplicating Robert Byrd's feat of winning all 55 counties) and 63%–37% in 2002.

FIRST DISTRICT

Rep. Alan Mollohan (D)

Elected 1982, 11th term; b. May 14, 1943, Fairmont; home, Fairmont; Col. of William & Mary, A.B. 1966, WV U., J.D. 1970; Baptist; married (Barbara).

Military Career: Army, 1970, Army Reserves, 1970–83.

Professional Career: Practicing atty., 1970–82.

DC Office: 2302 RHOB 20515, 202-225-4172; Fax: 202-225-7564; Web site: www.house.gov/mollohan.

District Offices: Clarksburg, 304-623-4422; Morgantown, 304-292-3019; Parkersburg, 304-428-0493; Wheeling, 304-232-5390.

Committees: *Appropriations* (6th of 29 D): Commerce, Justice, State & Judiciary; Homeland Security; VA, HUD & Independent Agencies (RMM). *Standards of Official Conduct* (RMM of 5 D).

Group Ratings

	ADA	ACLU	AFS	LCV	CON	ITIC	NTU	COC	ACU	NTLC	CHC
2002	75	47	100	63	53	38	24	40	24	14	50
2001	65	—	90	29	—	—	17	48	48	—	—

National Journal Ratings

	2001 LIB	—	2001 CONS		2002 LIB	—	2002 CONS
Economic	62%	—	38%		64%	—	35%
Social	48%	—	52%		52%	—	48%
Foreign	60%	—	40%		62%	—	36%

Key Votes of the 107th Congress

1. Approve Bush Tax Cuts	N	5. Faith-Based Charities	Y	9. Trade Promotion Authority	N
2. Limit Patients' Bill of Rights	N	6. Bar Gays in the Boy Scouts	Y	10. Bar Funds for Intl. Court	Y
3. Campaign Finance Reform	N	7. Ban Partial-Birth Abortion	Y	11. Authorize Force in Iraq	N
4. Ban ANWR Development	N	8. Arm Commercial Pilots	Y	12. Deny Home. Sec. Dept. Union	N

Election Results

2002 general	Alan Mollohan (D)	.... unopposed		($326,462)
2002 primary	Alan Mollohan (D)	.... unopposed		
2000 general	Alan Mollohan (D)	 170,974	(88%)	($335,864)
	Richard Kerr (Lib)	 23,797	(12%)	($16,469)

Prior Winning Percentages: 1998 (85%); 1996 (100%); 1994 (70%); 1992 (100%); 1990 (67%); 1988 (75%); 1986 (100%); 1984 (54%); 1982 (53%)

The People		Race/Ethnic Origin	Ancestry	
Area size:	6,344 sq. mi.	95.8% White	German: 14.1%	USA: 10.7%
Urban population:	53.7%	1.7% Black	Irish: 10.0%	
Rural population:	46.3%	0.7% Asian	**2000 Presidential Vote**	
Pop. 2000:	602,545	0.2% Native Am.	Bush (R)...............122,827	(54%)
Median income:	$30,303	0.0% Hawaiian	Gore (D)................97,432	(43%)
Poverty status:	17.0%	0.8% Two+ races	Other....................7,399	(3%)
Military veterans:	14.8%	0.1% Other	**Cook Partisan Voting Index:** R + 6	
		0.7% Hispanic Origin		

Occupation	Blue collar: 28.5%	White collar: 54.0%	Gray collar: 17.5%

The northern part of West Virginia is in many ways an extension of the Pittsburgh metropolitan area. People here are Steelers and Pirates fans, they drink Iron City and Rolling Rock beer, they watch Pittsburgh TV, they live in the crevasses between hills cut by the Monongahela and Ohio rivers, on terrain that seems forbidding to industrial and urban development. Yet this has been one of America's prime industrial areas; northern West Virginia is part of the same coal-and-steel economy that made Pittsburgh one of the nation's largest cities and filled the narrow bottomlands along the rivers with steel and glass factories, foundries and coal yards. For more than two decades, these have been declining industries, or rather industries that have become far less labor-intensive. Replacing these jobs are service jobs—West Virginia's largest employer now is Wal-Mart—and the government jobs brought in by Senator Robert Byrd (the largest employer in Harrison County is the U.S. Dept. of Justice).

The 1st Congressional District includes the northern third of the state. On the panhandle along the Ohio River are Victorian Wheeling, once one of the richest cities in the country with its steel and glass company investors and executives, and where the country music radio show "Jamboree U.S.A." has been broadcast every Saturday night for more than 50 years, and Weirton, a steel company town that is home to the nation's second-largest producer of tin-plated steel. South of Pittsburgh on the Monongahela are Morgantown, site of West Virginia University, and Clarksburg and Fairmont. To the west, the district includes three lonely Republican mountain counties—Doddridge, Ritchie and Tyler— that never heavily industrialized and have remained Republican since the Civil War. West of these, on the Ohio River, is the plastics and manufacturing hub of Parkersburg. Politically, most of this territory has been solidly Democratic. But dissatisfaction with the Clinton-Gore policies on coal and the environment gave George W. Bush a rare Republican presidential win in this district in 2000. Bush's March 2002 decision to limit steel imports, as unpopular as it was among free trade advocates, foreign steel producers and domestic steel users, was popular in northern West Virginia; executives at Weirton Steel praised Bush for putting their industry on the right path (though Weirton filed for bankruptcy protection in May 2003).

The congressman from the 1st District is Alan Mollohan, a Democrat elected in 1982. His father Robert Mollohan was elected congressman in 1952 and 1954, ran for governor and lost in 1956, and then won back the House seat a dozen years later when his Republican successor, Arch Moore, was elected governor. Mollohan, a Washington lawyer for Consolidated Coal, among other clients, returned home in 1982 when his father retired and promptly won the seat. His one major challenge came in the 1992 primary, when he was redistricted into a seat with another congressman, Harley Staggers Jr., who was also the son of a congressman, as well as an ally of the National Rifle Association. Mollohan, who had represented more of the new district than Staggers, won 62%–38%.

Mollohan has compiled a moderately liberal voting record—though more to the center on cultural issues—and has concentrated on bringing projects to the district. He is a member of the Appropriations Committee and in 1994, became briefly the chairman of the Commerce, Justice, State and Judiciary Subcommittee; he is now the ranking member on the VA-HUD and Independent Agencies Subcommittee. The culture of appropriators is bipartisan, so even in the minority Mollohan got an SBA Business Information Center in Fairmont, favorable language on the use of high-sulfur coal for the Kammer power plant in Marshall County, plus an expansion of Morgantown's federal prison and renovation of the city's historic theater. Still far from moribund, he has been memorialized with the Alan B. Mollohan Innovation Center, a computer software testing center in Fairmont; also headquartered there are a First District Federal Procurement Team and a West Virginia High-Technology Consortium, for which Mollohan takes credit. Citizens Against Government Waste designated him a "porker of the month," for securing a $6 million appropriation for a non-profit community development project in Vandalia. But Mollohan remains unapologetic: "I'm very proud of every one of my projects. If I was not very convinced of their merit, then I wouldn't fund the projects in the first place."

On national issues, Mollohan strongly opposed the Bush tax cut and in protest cast the House's sole no vote in May 2002 on making the marriage penalty provisions permanent. "I think it's just been the worst piece of legislation, the most damaging piece of legislation, since I've been here," he said of the tax cut. "The Republicans are going to grab everything while the grabbing's good." He supported Bush's steel import restrictions as a vital step against unfair competition from foreign steelmakers, but protested when the administration subsequently granted a series of waivers in response to pressure from domestic steel users complaining about price increases.

The failure of Congress to pass most of the 13 appropriations bills in 2002 left Mollohan, like other appropriators, less favorably positioned to advocate his local projects.

Mollohan has been reelected without Republican opposition since 1994. He is not one of those Democrats champing at the bit to regain a majority; as a minority member of Appropriations, he is still well positioned to strengthen his position in the district. In the 2002 redistricting, he rebuffed Democrats who wanted a radical redrawing of West Virginia's district lines to disadvantage 2d District Republican Shelley Moore Capito. That would have meant relinquishing some Democratic counties and gaining Republican-leaning counties in the eastern panhandle that might have provided a base for serious Republican opposition. Mollohan eventually agreed to a plan that transferred just one small county from Capito's district to his. He was reelected against a write-in with 99.73% of the vote.

SECOND DISTRICT

Rep. Shelley Moore Capito (R)

Elected 2000, 2d term; b. Nov. 26, 1953, Glen Dale; home, Charleston; Duke U., B.S. 1975, U. of VA, M.Ed. 1976; Presbyterian; married (Charles).

Elected Office: WV House of Del., 1996–00.

Professional Career: Career counselor, WV State Col., 1976–78; Dir., Educ. Info. Center, WV Board of Regents, 1978–81.

DC Office: 1431 LHOB 20515, 202-225-2711; Fax: 202-225-7856; Web site: www.house.gov/capito.

District Offices: Charleston, 304-925-5964; Martinsburg, 304-264-8810.

Committees: *Financial Services* (27th of 37 R): Capital Markets, Insurance & Government Sponsored Enterprises; Financial Institutions & Consumer Credit. *Small Business* (10th of 18 R): Rural Enterprises, Agriculture and Technology; Workforce, Empowerment & Government Programs. *Transportation & Infrastructure* (24th of 41 R): Economic Development, Public Buildings & Emergency Management; Highways, Transit & Pipelines; Railroads.

Group Ratings

	ADA	ACLU	AFS	LCV	CON	ITIC	NTU	COC	ACU	NTLC	CHC
2002	15	7	11	50	8	62	49	85	76	72	75
2001	20	—	20	43	—	—	56	87	76	—	—

National Journal Ratings

	2001 LIB —	2001 CONS	2002 LIB —	2002 CONS
Economic	39%	61%	45%	55%
Social	43%	55%	44%	54%
Foreign	33%	60%	41%	56%

Key Votes of the 107th Congress

1. Approve Bush Tax Cuts	Y	5. Faith-Based Charities	Y
2. Limit Patients' Bill of Rights	Y	6. Bar Gays in the Boy Scouts	Y
3. Campaign Finance Reform	Y	7. Ban Partial-Birth Abortion	Y
4. Ban ANWR Development	N	8. Arm Commercial Pilots	Y

9. Trade Promotion Authority	N
10. Bar Funds for Intl. Court	Y
11. Authorize Force in Iraq	Y
12. Deny Home. Sec. Dept. Union	Y

Election Results

2002 general	Shelley Moore Capito (R)	98,276	(60%)	($2,530,078)
	Jim Humphreys (D)	65,400	(40%)	($8,150,237)
2002 primary	Shelley Moore Capito (R)	unopposed		
2000 general	Shelley Moore Capito (R)	108,769	(48%)	($1,288,226)
	Jim Humphreys (D)	103,003	(46%)	($6,964,933)
	John Brown (Lib)	12,543	(6%)	

The People		Race/Ethnic Origin	Ancestry	
Area size:	8,512 sq. mi.	93.9% White	USA: 14.7%	German: 11.7%
Urban population:	46.2%	3.6% Black	Irish: 8.1%	
Rural population:	53.8%	0.5% Asian	**2000 Presidential Vote**	
Pop. 2000:	602,243	0.2% Native Am.	Bush (R)..............118,839	(54%)
Median income:	$33,198	0.0% Hawaiian	Gore (D)...............96,524	(44%)
Poverty status:	14.8%	0.9% Two+ races	Other...................4,787	(2%)
Military veterans:	14.8%	0.1% Other	**Cook Partisan Voting Index: R + 6**	
		0.8% Hispanic Origin		

Occupation   Blue collar: 28.9%   White collar: 55.1%   Gray collar: 16.1%

Not all of West Virginia is coal country, not all of its valleys are industrial hollows choked with workingmen's homes and small factories, and not all of its hills are scarred with strip mining wounds or piled with tailings. It's true that for miles you can see gentle hills and rugged mountains, stands of green trees and vistas stretching to far horizons. Yet over another hill you may find, amid scenery primeval and rural, sudden evidence of industrialization: A pulp mill or charcoal factory in a clearing scraped out of the forest; a small factory town, built close to a river in a cleft bordered with hills, its houses built in the same 1910s style as in the factory suburbs of Pittsburgh; the entrance to an underground coal mine or a mountaintop blasted open to allow surface mining. Large parts of this naturally beautiful state look as verdant and unchanged as they must have when George Washington was speculating in land here or taking the waters in Berkeley Springs, or when John Brown launched his assault at the federal arsenal at Harper's Ferry.

The 2d Congressional District is the central part of West Virginia, a belt of land from Berkeley Springs and Harper's Ferry in the Washington exurbs all the way west to the Ohio River town of Point Pleasant, where the Kanawha River (pronounced *kaNAW*) flows into the Ohio. It could easily take a full day to drive through this mountainous district that, if ironed out, would probably spread across the continent. The 2d District includes the few fast-growing parts of West Virginia—the eastern panhandle counties, some of which are technically within the Washington, D.C., metro area, and chemical-producing Putnam County just west of Charleston, where Toyota built an engine plant. The major urban center here is Charleston, where on the banks of the Kanawha rises West Virginia's Capitol, built in 1932 and designed by Cass Gilbert with a dome higher than the U.S. Capitol and a chandelier with 10,000 pieces of cut glass. Charleston, with its two partisan newspapers, the Democratic *Gazette* and the Republican *Daily Mail*, is the state capital and the center of the state's political culture. Charleston is a major industrial center, with coal in the hills all around and, downriver from the Capitol, huge petrochemical plants that convert coal tar into everyday products. This was a center of American high tech in the 1940s, when it produced all the nation's lucite, polyethylenes and nylon, as well as much of its artificial rubber and antifreeze. Today, the state boasts it is home to more polymer producers than any other place on the planet; the chemical industry makes products used in the manufacturing of cosmetics, detergents, shampoo, rubber, paints and coatings, fire retardants and agricultural products. Charleston is also West Virginia's white-collar and professional center, with a few downtown skyscrapers and some affluent residential districts. But like much of the state, it lost population in the 1990s. Politically, this is a Democratic district, though the eastern Panhandle has begun to vote like a Republican exurb. Still, George W. Bush carried the 2d 54%–44% in 2000—which helped him win the state's five electoral votes. It is a seat that has now twice in a row elected a Republican member of the House—the first West Virginia district to do that since the current member's father served in the House in the 1950s and 1960s.

The congresswoman from the 2d District is Shelley Moore Capito, a Republican who has confounded the political oddsmakers. She grew up in northern West Virginia and in the Washington area, when her father, Arch Moore, served in the House from 1957–69. He was elected governor in 1968 and (against Jay Rockefeller) in 1972, and then again in 1984; later he was convicted and served three years in jail for fraud and extortion. Shelley Moore Capito graduated from Duke University and the University of Virginia. She worked for two years as a career counselor at West Virginia State College, and then was director of the state's Educational Information

Center from 1978–81, when Rockefeller was governor. She served two terms in the West Virginia state House. Her opportunity to follow in her father's footsteps came when Bob Wise, a Democratic congressman since 1982, ran for governor in 2000. She benefited from a divisive Democratic primary that was won by Jim Humphreys, a trial lawyer, former state senator and ally of labor unions, who made a fortune in asbestos litigation and spent $3 million of his own money to win the Democratic nomination. In the general, Humphreys spent another $3 million from his own pocket and focused on health care issues. Capito, who supported abortion rights, started as the underdog but Humphreys proved to be a poor candidate. Capito may have been one of the few congressional candidates in 2000 who benefited from George W. Bush's coattails: She won 48%–46%, with big margins in the eastern panhandle counties.

In the House, Capito got special attention from Republican leaders because of her precarious district. She helped to make the case for her party's prescription drug plan for seniors, and against the Democratic alternative. She joined a congressional delegation to Afghanistan in July 2002, and praised the determination of that nation's new leader Hamid Karzai; en route, she met more than a dozen West Virginians serving in tents or at sea. She demonstrated her partisan loyalty by voicing support for individual investment accounts as part of Social Security. In return, Capito was one of the few House Republicans to get a free pass from party leadership to vote against trade promotion authority.

In the 2002 election, Capito was an obvious Democratic target. But Democrats gave her a big break by again nominating Humphreys. Once again, he dug deep in his pockets to win the primary against Margaret Workman, a former state Supreme Court justice, who received national support from EMILY's List. Humphreys and Workman sliced up each other with more than $3 million in ads—money that the party could have spent more profitably elsewhere; Humphreys won 51%–49%. Discouraged national Democrats gritted their teeth; a new team of national consultants could not change his approach, and his 2002 campaign was even more ineffective than in 2000. Humphreys's big spending again made it easy for Capito to say he was trying to buy the seat, and she was probably helped by George W. Bush's late campaign visit to Charleston. She won 60%–40%, winning with 59% in Kanawha County, 67% in Putnam County to the west and 64% in fast-growing Berkeley County in the eastern panhandle. Humphreys carried only one small county, and redistricting, which sloughed off one small county each to the 1st and 3d Districts, made no difference.

Capito has said she does not regard her district as safe, and it's possible that she could be seriously challenged in 2004 or later. But she looks now to be a well-positioned incumbent, with some potential as a statewide candidate.

THIRD DISTRICT

Rep. Nick Rahall (D)

Elected 1976, 14th term; b. May 20, 1949, Beckley; home, Beckley; Duke U., B.A. 1971; Presbyterian; divorced.

Professional Career: Civil Air Patrol, 1977–88; Staff Asst., U.S. Sen. Robert Byrd, 1971–74; Bd. of Dir., Rahall Communications Corp. 1974–76; Pres., Mountaineer Tour & Travel Agency, 1974–76; Pres., WV Broadcasting Corp. 1980–present.

DC Office: 2307 RHOB 20515, 202-225-3452; Fax: 202-225-9061; Web site: www.house.gov/rahall.

District Offices: Beckley, 304-252-5000; Bluefield, 304-325-6222; Huntington, 304-522-6425; Logan, 304-752-4934.

Committees: *Resources* (RMM of 24 D). *Transportation & Infrastructure* (2d of 34 D): Aviation; Highways, Transit & Pipelines; Railroads.

Group Ratings

	ADA	ACLU	AFS	LCV	CON	ITIC	NTU	COC	ACU	NTLC	CHC
2002	80	67	100	100	1	38	20	40	24	14	50
2001	80	—	100	79	—	—	21	39	36	—	—

National Journal Ratings

	2001 LIB	—	2001 CONS	2002 LIB	—	2002 CONS
Economic	66%	—	35%	77%	—	20%
Social	51%	—	49%	49%	—	51%
Foreign	73%	—	26%	74%	—	25%

Key Votes of the 107th Congress

1. Approve Bush Tax Cuts	*	5. Faith-Based Charities		9. Trade Promotion Authority	N
2. Limit Patients' Bill of Rights	N	6. Bar Gays in the Boy Scouts	Y	10. Bar Funds for Intl. Court	Y
3. Campaign Finance Reform	N	7. Ban Partial-Birth Abortion	Y	11. Authorize Force in Iraq	N
4. Ban ANWR Development	Y	8. Arm Commercial Pilots	Y	12. Deny Home. Sec. Dept. Union	N

Election Results

2002 general	Nick Rahall (D)	87,783	(70%)	($374,850)
	Paul Chapman (R)	37,229	(30%)	
2002 primary	Nick Rahall (D)	72,655	(87%)	
	Theodore Hamb (D)	11,110	(13%)	
2000 general	Nick Rahall (D)	146,807	(91%)	($354,164)
	Jeff Robinson (Lib)	13,979	(9%)	

Prior Winning Percentages: 1998 (87%); 1996 (100%); 1994 (64%); 1992 (66%); 1990 (52%); 1988 (61%); 1986 (71%); 1984 (67%); 1982 (81%); 1980 (77%)

The People		Race/Ethnic Origin	Ancestry	
Area size:	9,375 sq. mi.	93.9% White	USA: 19.7%	Irish: 7.7%
Urban population:	38.4%	4.1% Black	English: 7.1%	
Rural population:	61.6%	0.4% Asian	**2000 Presidential Vote**	
Pop. 2000:	603,556	0.2% Native Am.	Gore (D) 101,541	(51%)
Median income:	$25,630	0.0% Hawaiian	Bush (R) 94,809	(47%)
Poverty status:	21.9%	0.8% Two + races	Other 3,942	(2%)
Military veterans:	13.5%	0.0% Other	**Cook Partisan Voting Index:** D + 1	
		0.6% Hispanic Origin		

Occupation	Blue collar: 28.8%	White collar: 52.6%	Gray collar: 18.5%

Early in this century, the coalfields of southern West Virginia were one of America's boom areas. Into rural farmland and hollows, inhabited by the same families since they first arrived at these mountains 100 years before, came coal company lawyers with mineral rights' leases to sign, coal company engineers to design and sink the mineshafts, and men from other mountain counties, as well as Europe, to work the mines. Company houses were built, company stores were stocked with goods as the company dictated and company paymasters kept close tabs on the finances of every employee. These conditions bred dull discontent, ignited into the fire of industrial unionism by the tongue of John L. Lewis, president of the United Mine Workers, who organized most of the mines in the 1930s. Lewis was not only a militant unionist, but also an isolationist, and during and after World War II he called out his coal miners on strikes, to the fury of Franklin Roosevelt and Harry Truman. The entire national war effort and postwar economic recovery seemed gravely threatened by these labor stoppages involving some 300,000 workers, centered in back corners of the country like southern West Virginia.

All that is history now. Coal is no longer central to the U.S. economy and there are only a few thousand coal miners left in southern West Virginia—and many are not UMW members anymore. Most of the old underground mines have been abandoned, leaving behind mineshafts and piles of tailings—and lives that were snuffed out by cave-ins or simple carelessness in America's deadliest industry. In 1950, when coal area population peaked, there were 560,000 people in the eight counties that made up the heart of southern West Virginia's coal country; in 2000, those same counties had a population of 334,000. There are few parts of the United States, apart from some central city neighborhoods and Great Plains farm counties, which have suffered such depopulation over the last half-century. But this region has still not hit bottom: Of seven counties in the nation with more than 20,000 residents that suffered more than 10% population loss in the 1990s, four—Logan, McDowell, Mingo and Wyoming—were in southern West Virginia, which has the oldest median age in the nation.

The 3d Congressional District includes most of the mountainous coal country in the southern part of the state that are among America's most heavily Democratic jurisdictions (6 of the state's 10 top coal-producing counties are in the 3d). Democratic voter registration is around 90 percent in Logan and McDowell Counties; nearby Mingo County—"Bloody Mingo," where coal company enforcers battled Matewan miners seeking to escape economic serfdom—is equally monolithic. But the coal mining counties now make up less than half of the 3d District. About a quarter of the population is in and around the industrial city of Huntington on the Ohio River, which includes Marshall University. Another quarter is to the east, at the interstate junction at Beckley and in the farming uplands around the resorts of White Sulphur Springs where, at the Greenbrier Hotel resort, the government built a massive secret fallout shelter (code-named "Project Greek Island," the bunker was intended to house the entire U.S. Congress in the event of nuclear war) that was finally exposed in 1992. These two areas are much less Democratic than the coal counties.

The congressman from the 3d District is Nick Rahall, a Democrat first elected in 1976, at 27; he was the youngest member of the 95th Congress. He comes from the thin economic upper crust of the coal country; his family owned radio and TV stations in Beckley and in St. Petersburg, Florida. Rahall has concentrated on bringing public works projects and jobs to his district. He got seats on Transportation and Infrastructure, and Resources early on, and now has great seniority. He was the chief sponsor in the House of the law requiring union and non-union coal operators to bail out the United Mine Workers health care funds. In 1998, Rahall criticized West Virginia regulators for improperly permitting mountaintop mining operations. This is a contentious local issue: 61 of 81 active mountaintop removal mines approved by state regulators since 1978 did not receive variances for flattening the land after mining is complete, according to an investigation by *The Charleston Gazette*. Rahall helped obtain $21 million in abandoned mine reclamation funds for 1999 and later sought to assure that the abandoned mine land reclamation program was used only to clean up high-priority projects.

In January 2001, Rahall replaced California Rep. George Miller as ranking Democrat on the Resources Committee. That is undoubtedly a source of disappointment to environmental restriction groups, for Rahall is far more interested in parochial West Virginia issues than in the sort of issues—stopping oil drilling in the Arctic National Wildlife Refuge (ANWR), expanding wilderness areas in the West—which the groups use to raise money through direct mail from affluent East and West Coast urbanites. He did come out against opening more public lands—including ANWR—to energy production, and called for development in the National Petroleum Reserve in Alaska, which the Clinton administration approved in 1998. He spent more effort, and was opposed by Republicans, in getting money for a fund to cover the health costs of retired coal miners and their families. Two months before the 2002 election, Rahall traveled to Iraq on what was termed a humanitarian mission to assess that nation's health and nutrition. Rahall—whose family's roots are in Lebanon, and who often is in the small minority of members voicing support for Arab causes and voting against Israel—said, "I feel the Iraqis want to give peace a chance."

Rahall has mostly won re-election easily; since his first election in 1976, he's dropped below 61% only once. That was in 1990, after opponents revisited negative publicity over gambling debts and a drunk driving arrest. But he had little to worry about in 2002. An auto-parts storeowner ran against him in the primary, but refused to debate because he said Rahall had better information; Rahall won 87% of the vote. In the general, his Republican opponent refused to campaign outside his home county; his only campaign expense was his $1,500 filing fee. He criticized Rahall for alleged financial ties to radical Islamic groups. Rahall responded that he backed George W. Bush's fight against terrorism. In the only West Virginia district carried by Al Gore, Rahall won 70%–30%.

★ WISCONSIN ★

W isconsin, tucked off north of the main east-west routes across the country and squeezed between Lake Michigan and the Mississippi River, was at the beginning of the 20th century one of America's premier "laboratories of reform," in Justice Louis Brandeis's phrase—and was again at the end of the 20th century: a state originating new public policies, seeing how they work, serving as an example for others. Wisconsin's first fame as a laboratory came during the Progressive era that began around 1900, and its primacy was due to an extraordinary governor, Robert LaFollette Sr., and to the state's unique history and German heritage. Wisconsin is the first state of that vast stretch of the United States reaching all the way to the Pacific, settled first by New England Yankees but even more by immigrants from Germany and Scandinavia. The German language is seldom heard now, the once plainly German beer brands now seem quintessentially American and few ties remained with the old country after two world wars, though in 2000 30% of Wisconsin residents were of German descent. But in the late 19th and early 20th centuries, Germans were among America's most numerous immigrants and until the 1890s probably the most distinct. They implanted, on the rolling dairyland of Wisconsin and the orderly streets of Milwaukee, their separate religions, often retaining their language and maintaining old customs, from country weddings to drinking beer—a source of friction in temperance-minded America—to eating bratwurst.

Politically, the Germans were not monolithic. Their origins were diverse and they were spread too widely across the nation. But where they were concentrated, there was a distinctive politics, basically American, but with echoes of progressive ideas current in German-speaking countries in Europe. Nowhere was the politics of German-Americans more apparent than in Wisconsin. This is one of the two states that gave birth to the Republican Party in 1854 (the other is Michigan), and Germans, then arriving in America in vast numbers, heavily favored it. They abhorred slavery and welcomed the free lands Republicans advocated in the Homestead Act, the free education promised by setting up land grant colleges, and the transportation routes constructed by subsidizing railroad builders. Then came the Progressive movement of LaFollette, elected governor of Wisconsin in 1900. Up to that time a conventional Republican politician, LaFollette completely revamped the state government before going to the Senate in 1906. At a time when Germany was the world's leader in graduate education and the application of science to government, LaFollette had professors from the University of Wisconsin, just across town in Madison, help develop the state workmen's compensation system and income tax. The Progressive movement favored rational use of government to improve the lot of the ordinary citizen—an idea borrowed partly from German liberals and adopted by the New Dealers a generation later. All these programs were an attempt to bring bureaucratic rationality—Germanic systematization—to the seemingly disordered America of free markets and multiple cultures, gigantic fortunes and vast open spaces.

LaFollette became a national figure. He tried to run for president in 1912 as a Progressive, but was shoved aside by Theodore Roosevelt. He did run in 1924 on his Progressive ticket and won 18% of the vote, the best third-candidate showing between 1912 and 1992. He was strongest in the northern tier of states from Wisconsin west and along the West Coast—the same area of strength of later liberals George McGovern, Walter Mondale and Michael Dukakis. After LaFollette died in 1925, his sons carried on his tradition, progressive at home and isolationist abroad: Robert LaFollette Jr., for 22 years in the Senate; Philip, elected governor in 1930, 1934 and 1936. Philip created his own Progressive Party in 1934, with ominous overtones: a "Cross in Circle" symbol his critics called a circumcised swastika, huge rally-like parades reminiscent of some in Europe at the time and a call for the governor to propose all legislation. But Philip lost in 1938 and did not run again, and Robert Jr. decided to run for re-election in 1946 as a Republican but lost the primary to Joseph McCarthy. McCarthy's charges that Communists were influencing American foreign policy fed on the inarticulate convictions of many in Wisconsin and elsewhere that the U.S. should have been fighting Russia as well as Germany in World War II.

McCarthy's national prominence made Wisconsin seem like a Republican state. But he won by narrow margins and the LaFollette Progressive tradition was taken up by liberal Democrats like Sen-

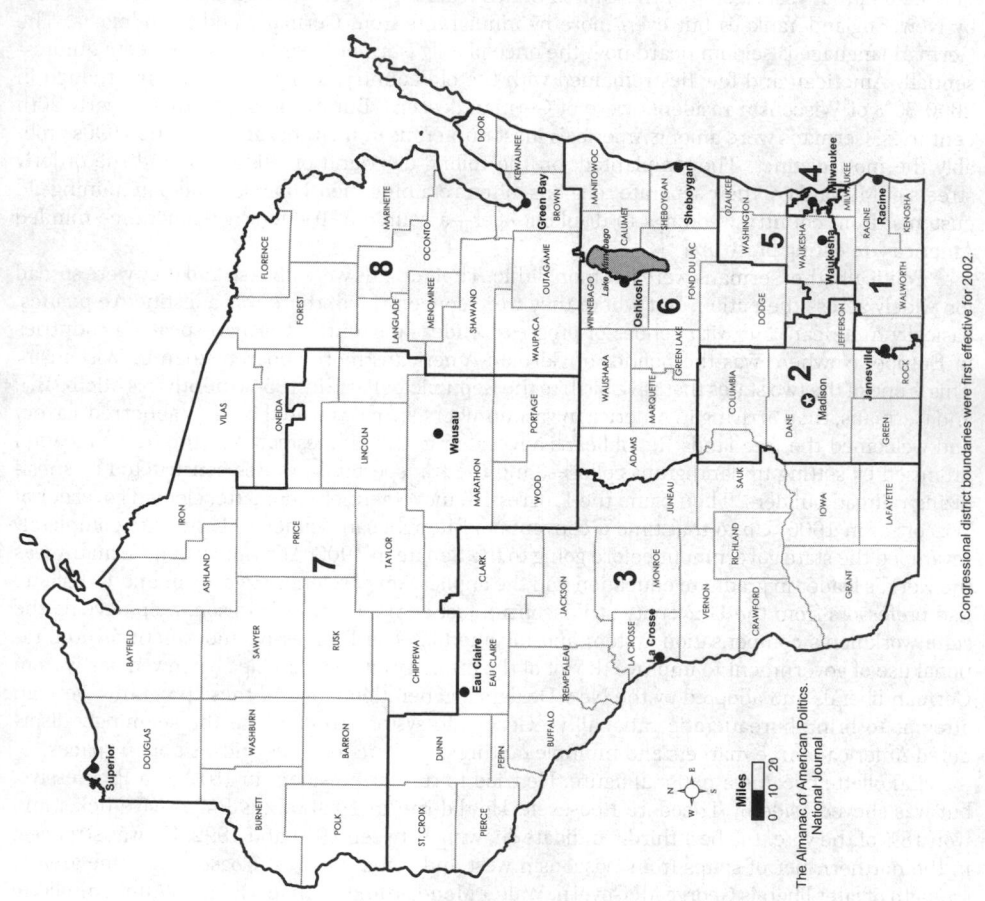

Congressional district boundaries were first effective for 2002.

The Almanac of American Politics.
National Journal

ators William Proxmire and Gaylord Nelson, and Governor Patrick Lucey. Like most liberals of their era, these progressives saw Washington rather than Madison as the main site of their laboratory of reform. Wisconsin, a mostly Republican state in the mostly Democratic years from 1944 to 1964, became a mostly Democratic state in the mostly Republican years from 1968 to 1988.

In the 1990s Wisconsin moved in another direction, and was a laboratory for different reforms, for which the state's economy provided a favorable environment. Wisconsin's high-skill, precision manufacturing economy jumped into gear in the late 1980s, and helped lead the nation's export boom of the 1990s. The labor force is highly skilled and famously productive, with fewer hours lost to health, weather or strikes than average; unemployment fell to 3.5% in 2000, entry level-wages were $2 over the legal minimum wage, and Wisconsin's major economic problem was a shortage of workers. Population has been rising robustly, particularly in the ring of counties around Milwaukee, around Madison and in the Fox River Valley from Oshkosh to Green Bay, and in the once rural counties within commuting range of greater Minneapolis-St. Paul. Yet much of the political focus remains on the dwindling number of dairy farmers. Wisconsin ranks number two in milk production, number one in cheese, but thanks to improved productivity the number of dairy farms has declined from 105,000 in 1960 to 45,000 in 1980 and 21,000 in 2000. Waukesha County outside Milwaukee, once Cow County, U.S.A., now has only 67 dairy farms. The federal milk price fixing system is biased against Wisconsin, with prices higher the farther the farming operation is from Eau Claire; Wisconsin's members of Congress have spent much time and psychic energy trying to change this.

The motivating force for reform in the 1990s was, as in the early 1900s, a Republican governor, in this case Tommy Thompson, who beat a liberal Democrat in 1986 and went on to win some of the nation's highest job approval ratings. He cut taxes, sponsored a school choice program, and passed a series of welfare reforms—the nation's most thoroughgoing—which since 1987 cut caseloads by 93%. Across the nation other governors and leaders of the Republican Congress have looked to learn from Wisconsin's experiments: it's a fair question whether the 1996 federal Welfare Reform Act would have passed without Wisconsin's example to give its backers confidence.

Thompson did not carry all before him and left some fiscal problems behind him, while Wisconsin, proud of its clean politics since the LaFollette era, was suddenly beset by political scandal. Neither party is dominant. Al Gore carried the state in 2000 by a margin of 47.8%–47.6%. Wisconsin has two Democratic U.S. senators, one elected twice by narrow margins; its U.S. House delegation is split 4–4. In 2002 it replaced Thompson's successor as governor, Scott McCallum, with Democrat Jim Doyle. But he won with less than a majority of the vote. Republicans won control of the state Senate and increased their majority in Assembly. Previous legislative leaders were swept aside by scandal, though their misdeeds might not be classified as such in many other states. The scandal broke when legislative staffers were accused of running partisan campaigns from state offices; it escalated when legislative leaders were charged with seeking contributions from lobbyists during discussions about legislation. But this is a state where in the 1970s two legislators were defeated after they used state credit cards for less than $100 of personal phone calls, a state senator was prosecuted for accepting $100 for giving a speech and in 1987 a state senator was charged with accepting food and drinks at a Packers game. Even after the reforms of the late 20th century, the spirit of the LaFollette reformers of the early 20th century lives on.

The People		Race/Ethnic Origin			Military veterans: 514,213 (12.9%)	
Pop. 2000:	5,363,675	4,681,630	87.3%	White	WWII: 21.1%	Korea: 14.5%
Pop. 1990:	4,891,769	300,245	5.6%	Black	Vietnam: 30.6%	Gulf War: 8.3%
Change 1990–2000:	Up 9.6%	87,995	1.6%	Asian	**Most populous cities:**	
Change 1980–1990:	Up 4.0%	43,980	0.8%	Native Am.	1. Milwaukee	596,974
% of U.S. total:	1.9%	1,346	0.0%	Hawaiian	2. Madison	208,054
Pop. rank:	18th of 50	51,921	1.0%	Two+ races	3. Green Bay	102,313
Area size:	65,498 sq. mi.	3,637	0.1%	Other	4. Kenosha	90,352
State Native:	73.4%	192,921	3.6%	Hisp. Origin	5. Racine	81,855
Non-citizen:	2.2%	**Ancestry**			Urban population: 68.3%	
Language		German: 29.9%	Irish: 7.6%		Rural population: 31.7%	
English: 90.5%	Spanish: 4.1%	Polish: 6.5%	Norwegian: 5.9%			
Other Eur.: 3.9%		English: 4.5%				

Education		Work Sector		Legislature	
H.S. Grad:	85.1%	Private: 81.1%	Govt: 12.5%	Senate	18 R 15 D
College Grad:	22.4%	Self: 6.1%	Family: 0.3%	Assembly	58 R 41 D
Industry		Unemployment: 4.7%		Legislative Term Limits: No	
Agri: 2.8%	Con: 5.9%	**Household Income**		**Registered Voters**	
Fin: 6.1%	Info: 2.2%	<15k: 13.0%	15-35k: 25.9%	No party registration	
Mfg: 26.7%	Prof: 26.6%	35-50k: 18.1%	50-100k: 33.6%		
Public: 3.5%	Trade: 14.8%	100-150k: 6.4%	>150k: 3.0%		
Other: 11.3%		Median: $43,791			
Occupation		Poverty status: 8.7%			
Blue collar: 28.4%	White collar: 56.6%	**Home Value**			
Gray collar: 15.0%		<50k: 10.0%	50-100k: 33.8%	100-200k: 43.6%	200-300k: 8.7%
		300-500k: 3.0%	>500k: 1.0%	Median: $109,900	

Presidential politics Wisconsin has been seriously contested in six of the last seven presidential elections, and probably will be again in 2004. It was one of 10 states which voted for Michael Dukakis over the older George Bush in 1988, and came within 5,709 votes of voting for George W. Bush over Al Gore in 2000. In the process, some historic patterns were reversed. The younger Bush carried metro Milwaukee, which casts about one-third of the state's votes, by 49%–47%, thanks to big margins in the suburban counties, where he ran well ahead of his father's showing—the opposite of the pattern in most very large metro areas across the nation. But Gore carried many historically Republican or marginal counties in western Wisconsin, just as he carried many rural counties across the Mississippi River in eastern Iowa. Indeed, this was the only rural part of the country where Gore carried large numbers of counties and ran ahead of Democratic norms. Gore's biggest percentage margins were in Madison's Dane County and in Menominee County, which is an Indian reservation. Bush carried the Fox River Valley, though not by as big a margin as his father had, and ran well ahead of Republican norms in the far north, as he did in the Upper Peninsula of Michigan and northern Minnesota. The eastern

2000 Presidential Vote		
Gore (D)	1,242,987	(48%)
Bush (R)	1,237,279	(48%)
Nader (Green)	94,070	(4%)
Other	22,375	(1%)

2000 Republican Presidential Primary		
Bush (R)	343,292	(69%)
McCain (R)	89,684	(18%)
Keyes (R)	48,919	(10%)
Other	13,874	(3%)

2000 Democratic Presidential Primary		
Gore (D)	328,682	(89%)
Bradley (D)	32,560	(9%)
Other	9,954	(3%)

1996 Presidential Vote		
Clinton (D)	1,071,970	(49%)
Dole (R)	845,028	(38%)
Perot (I)	227,310	(10%)
Other	51,881	(2%)

half of the state, with its high precision manufacturing base humming during the 1990s and welfare rolls dropping toward zero, has become fairly solidly Republican. Western Wisconsin, with ailing dairy farms and an economy not so dynamic, has become the Democratic bastion of the state, with metro Madison providing the big Democratic majorities that metro Milwaukee no longer provides in the east.

Wisconsin once had one of the nation's most influential presidential primaries. It knocked Wendell Willkie out of the race in 1944, helped John Kennedy establish his lead over Hubert Humphrey in 1960, and prompted Lyndon Johnson to withdraw as Eugene McCarthy was about to beat him here in 1968. But now Wisconsin's primary, even after it was moved from April to March, tends to get lost—so in 2003 the legislature moved the date up another month to February 2004. The national Democrats, incidentally, have allowed Wisconsin to continue its open primary (that is, there is no party registration), one of Bob LaFollette's reforms.

Congressional districting Wisconsin lost a congressional district in the 2000 Census. Ordinarily that would trigger a fierce battle between a Republican governor and Assembly and Democratic state Senate. But in May 2001 5th District Democrat Tom Barrett announced he was running for governor. His north Milwaukee district had lost population and was easy to eliminate. The result was a consensus plan, approved by the House delegation, passed by both houses of the legislature and signed by the governor in March 2002. A lawsuit brought a year earlier was dismissed a day later. This is one state that produced a plan with regularly shaped districts with obvious communities of interest; it was also a plan that enabled all eight incumbents running to win reelection easily.

108th Congress Lineup
4 D   4 R
107th Congress Lineup
5 D   4 R

Governor

James Doyle (D)

Elected 2002, term expires Jan. 2007, 1st term; b. Nov. 23, 1945, Washington, DC; home, Maple Bluff; Attended Stanford U. 1963–66, U. of WI, B.A. 1967, Harvard U., J.D. 1972; Catholic; married (Jessica).

Elected Office: Dane Cnty. D.A., 1976–82; WI Atty. Gen. 1990–02.

Professional Career: Peace Corps, Tunisia, 1967–69; Atty., Navajo Indian Reservation (Chinle, AZ), 1972–75; Practicing atty., 1982–90.

Office: 115 E. State Capitol, Madison, 53707, 608-266-1212; Fax: 608-267-8983; Web site: www.wisgov.state.wi.us.

Election Results

2002 general	James Doyle (D)	800,515	(45%)
	Scott McCallum (R)	734,779	(42%)
	Ed Thompson (Lib)	185,455	(11%)
2002 primary	James Doyle (D)	212,066	(38%)
	Tom Barrett (D)	190,605	(34%)
	Kathleen Falk (D)	150,161	(27%)
1998 general	Tommy G.Thompson (R)	1,047,716	(60%)
	Ed Garvey (D)	679,553	(39%)
	Other	28,745	(2%)

James Doyle, a Democrat, was elected Governor of Wisconsin in 2002. He grew up in Madison, in a political family. His parents were part of a group of Madison liberals in the rising Democratic party of the 1950s and the dominant Democratic party of the 1960s—Governor and Senator Gaylord Nelson, Senator William Proxmire, Governor Pat Lucey, Governor John Reynolds, *Capital Times* editor Miles McMillan. Doyle's mother was elected to the Wisconsin Assembly in 1948, only the second woman there, but the fourth generation of her family (the Bachhubers) to serve there. His father ran for governor in 1954 and lost the primary to Proxmire; in 1967 he became a federal judge, for years the only judge in the Western District of Wisconsin, and issued dozens of liberal rulings disallowing state and federal government actions. Jim Doyle was a star basketball player and top student in high school in Madison, went to Stanford for three years and then graduated from the University of Wisconsin. With his wife, a niece of Congressman and Defense Secretary Melvin Laird, he spent two years in the Peace Corps in Tunisia; back in the U.S. they marched in Washington in protest of the Vietnam War and then met Laird in his office in the Pentagon. Doyle graduated from Harvard Law School, then worked for three years as a lawyer on the Navajo Reservation in Arizona.

He returned to Madison in 1975 and in 1976 ran against Dane County District Attorney Humphrey Lynch, a Democrat, and beat him. He served for six years, then went into private practice in Madison. In 1990 he ran for attorney general. Most Democratic legislators supported another candidate, but he won the primary and defeated the incumbent Republican. His best publicized accomplishment was the state's $6 billion tobacco settlement, but he was criticized for paying the state's lawyers $847 million; Ed Garvey, a Democrat who had run for governor, sued and got the fee blocked. He pushed through a truth-in-sentencing law, for longer prison sentences; he also pushed a "truth-in-legislating" law, requiring the cost of changes in criminal penalties to be attached to any bill. He took initiatives against school violence, sexual predators, Publishers Clearinghouse and domestic violence. He defended Governor Tommy Thompson on his creative use of Wisconsin's broad veto power—Thompson used his veto pen to delete single words or phrases from bills. But in four cases he disagreed with Thompson, who hired special counsels, and prevailed in all four.

Thompson was long the dominant figure in state politics. He was first elected in 1986, and his waves of successive changes in the welfare laws served as the leading model for the nation and the foundation of one of the major public policy successes of the 1990s. But the unbeatable Thompson left Madison in January 2001 to become Secretary of Health and Human Services, and Scott McCallum, lieutenant governor for 14 years, became governor. McCallum was faced with more serious budget problems than Thompson had faced in many years, and in January 2002 he proposed that the state cut $1 billion in aid to local governments over the next three years. He argued that that would allow the state to maintain education and healthcare spending and build a Milwaukee-to-Madison light rail line. But the cut in local aid was unpopular and McCallum's job rating, hovering around 50% in fall 2001, fell to about 35% in spring 2002.

Four Democrats lined up to run against McCallum. Doyle set out a specific program; he would meet the state's budget problems by cutting the work force from 67,000 to 56,000, which is what it was when Thompson became governor in 1987, and would not increase taxes; he would tax business only on Wisconsin sales, not on Wisconsin payroll and property; he would continue current funding levels or more on education and health care. He was endorsed by former Governors Gaylord Nelson, Patrick Lucey (who had managed his father's campaign for governor in 1954) and Martin Schreiber. But he was backed by few legislators, many of whom were angry at his prosecutorial attitude toward state Senate Majority Leader Chuck Chvala, who was in trouble because his staffers had been politicking in his state office. Doyle started off much better known than his Democratic rivals, none of whom had a statewide base. Milwaukee Congressman Tom Barrett was well known in his district and, from previous service in the state Senate and Assembly, popular among Democratic legislators, most of whom endorsed him, as did 7th District Congressman David Obey. Dane County Executive Kathleen Falk ran as a candidate with executive experience and provided detailed proposals, including increase the cigarette tax from 77 cents to $1.62 to increase spending on health care. She obviously was relying on her Madison area base and EMILY's List. State Senator Gary George ran as the candidate with the most experience in state government and hoped to build on his base among teachers' unions and Milwaukee blacks. But Wisconsin's population is only 6% black (with three-quarters of them in Milwaukee) and George was thrown off the ballot in July for invalid signatures.

The Democratic candidates avoided negative campaigning; the ads were mostly positive; Doyle's showed his two grown sons, who are adopted and of African-American descent, praising him. In the September primary Doyle ran pretty evenly statewide, in no county above 54% or below 30%; the others' support was mostly in their bases. Barrett carried the Milwaukee metro area, which cast 33% of the votes, 44%–33% over Doyle. Falk won 50% in Dane County, which cast 13% of the vote, well ahead of Doyle's 32%, but she carried no other county. In the rest of the state, which cast 41% of the votes, Doyle led with 43% to 29% for Barrett and 26% for Falk. Overall, Doyle won with 38% of the vote to 34% for Barrett and 27% for Falk.

Doyle came out of primary night swinging at McCallum who, he said, had "squandered Wisconsin's greatest resources, our trust in government and our faith in the future." He added, "He's living proof that not all on-the-job training programs are successful." He continued to run on cutting $1 billion by reducing the number of state employees and attacked McCallum for spending the state's entire tobacco settlement on balancing one year's budget. McCallum, who emerged from the primary with three times as much money, ran an ad showing a messy desk and spilled coffee and attacked Doyle for missing deadlines while doing the state's legal business. McCallum said he would balance the budget through revenue growth and said Doyle had promised teachers' unions and other groups programs that would cost $2.7 billion on top of an anticipated $2.8 billion shortfall. Into the fray also stepped a third candidate, Libertarian nominee Ed Thompson, who ran the Tee-Pee Supper Club in Tomah and was elected mayor of the town. But the real reason Thompson attracted attention was because he is Tommy Thompson's brother. Ed Thompson called for cutting prison building in half and cutting spending by $2.2 billion by accountability budgeting. In public polls Doyle had the lead, but never took off, while McCallum never seemed to rise above his lackluster job rating and Thompson ran in the high single digits.

In November Doyle beat McCallum 45%–42%, with 11% for Ed Thompson; Thompson carried the county where he lived and the next-door county where he grew up. It was a narrow win for Doyle, and one accompanied by Republican gains in legislative races: Republicans won control of the state Senate 18–15 and enlarged their Assembly majority to 58–41. In many ways this was a different race in different media markets. In the Milwaukee market McCallum led 47%–44%, with Thompson at 7%; in the Fox River Valley McCallum led 47%–41%, with Thompson at 8%. This eastern part of Wisconsin, with 57% of votes, went Republican. Where Doyle won was in the Madison market, where he led 49%–30%, and Thompson got 17%, and in the Wausau and Eau Claire markets, where he led 44%–37%, and Thompson got 15%. These two areas cast 35% of the state's votes. In the farthest west counties, served by Twin Cities and Duluth TV, Thompson was not much of a factor, with just 5% of the votes; here Doyle led 50%–24%.

In February 2003 he presented his plan to cut 2,900 state jobs and raise university tuition; balancing the budget still depended on getting $237 million from Indian tribes by renegotiating casino deals and $408 million from changing the Medicaid reimbursement formula. "We have cut as no administration has cut before," Doyle said.

Senior Senator

Herb Kohl (D)

Elected 1988, seat up 2006, 3d term; b. Feb. 7, 1935, Milwaukee; home, Milwaukee; U. of WI, B.A. 1956, Harvard U., M.B.A. 1958; Jewish; single.

Military Career: Army Reserves, 1958–64.

Professional Career: Businessman; Pres., Kohl Corp., 1970–79; Chmn., WI Dem. Party, 1975–77; Pres., Herbert Kohl Investments, 1979–88; Owner, Milwaukee Bucks pro basketball team, 1985–present.

DC Office: 330 HSOB, 20510, 202-224-5653; Fax: 202-224-9787; Web site: kohl.senate.gov.

State Offices: Appleton, 920-738-1640; Eau Claire, 715-832-8424; La Crosse, 608-796-0045; Madison, 608-264-5338; Milwaukee, 414-297-4451.

Committees: *Aging (Special). Appropriations*: Agriculture & Rural Development (RMM); Commerce, Justice, State & Judiciary; Homeland Security; Labor, HHS & Education; Transportation, Treasury & General Government. *Judiciary*: Antitrust, Competition Policy & Consumer Rights (RMM); Crime, Corrections & Victims' Rights; Terrorism, Technology & Homeland Security.

Group Ratings

	ADA	ACLU	AFS	LCV	CON	ITIC	NTU	COC	ACU	NTLC	CHC
2002	85	60	88	53	23	88	18	60	15	6	—
2001	90	—	92	88	—	—	20	54	16	—	20

National Journal Ratings

	2001 LIB	—	2001 CONS		2002 LIB	—	2002 CONS
Economic	64%	—	35%		59%	—	36%
Social	81%	—	8%		63%	—	36%
Foreign	74%	—	14%		67%	—	30%

Key Votes of the 107th Congress

1. Approve Bush Tax Cuts	Y	5. Confirm Ashcroft as AG	N	9. Bar Coop. with Intl. Court	Y
2. Expand Patients' Rights	Y	6. Bar Gays in the Boy Scouts	N	10. Trade Promotion Authority	Y
3. Campaign Finance Reform	Y	7. $ for Hate Crime Prosecution	Y	11. Authorize Force in Iraq	Y
4. Permit ANWR Development	N	8. Overseas Military Abortions	Y	12. Homeland Sec. Dept. Union	Y

Election Results

2000 general	Herb Kohl (D)	1,563,238	(62%)	($4,991,364)
	John Gillespie (R)	940,744	(37%)	($582,221)
	Other	35,199	(1%)	
2000 primary	Herb Kohl (D)	184,920	(90%)	
	Jim Sigl (D)	20,858	(10%)	
1994 general	Herb Kohl (D)	912,662	(58%)	($8,249,531)
	Robert T. Welch (R)	636,989	(41%)	($1,180,382)

Prior Winning Percentages: 1988 (52%)

Herb Kohl, a Democrat first elected in 1988, is one of the richest members of Congress, and one of the least flamboyant, a mild-mannered but persistent and successful politician. His parents immigrated to Milwaukee from Russia and Poland in the 1920s and opened a food store, which became a Wisconsin supermarket and retail chain. He grew up in Milwaukee and graduated from the University of Wisconsin and Harvard Business School. He worked at Kohl's and was president in the 1970s; the firm was sold in 1979, and today is one of the fastest-expanding national retail chains. Kohl was a Democratic contributor and chairman of the Wisconsin Democratic party in the mid-1970s. In 1985 he became a local celebrity, in a city smarting from sports franchises with lousy records and eager to move elsewhere, when he bought for $18 million the Milwaukee Bucks basketball team to keep it from moving out of Milwaukee; in January 2003 he said he was willing to sell, but only to those who would keep the team in Milwaukee (Forbes estimated the team was worth $168 million). In 1976 he bought a ranch near Jackson, Wyoming, from Senator Clifford Hansen, a Republican who says Kohl has been a "good steward of the land"; like the Bucks, the property is worth far more today than when he bought it.

When Senator William Proxmire retired in 1988, Kohl decided to run for the Senate. He spent his own money liberally, running an extensive ad campaign with the theme, "Nobody's senator but yours." He won 47% in the primary to 38% for former Governor Tony Earl. In the general, against moderate Republican Susan Engeleiter, Kohl stressed his support of defense cuts—popular in dovish Wisconsin—and for requiring businesses to provide medical insurance; Engeleiter stressed her environmental stands, her legislative experience and her status as a wife and mother. This turned out to be one of the closest Senate races in the country, with Kohl winning 52%–48% after spending $7 million of his own money.

Kohl is a pleasant, shy, almost painfully earnest man, of transparent good will and seemingly little guile. He personally funds the Herb Kohl Educational Foundation, which has given more than $3.6 million in scholarships and grants to Wisconsin students, teachers and schools, and he donated $25 million to the University of Wisconsin for the Kohl Center arena which opened in 1998. His voting record has been moderate to liberal; he dislikes the clash of partisan fighting. He opposed the Supercollider, the space station, and Trident II missiles, and has tried to keep defense spending increases down to Clinton budget levels. He was one of 12 Democratic senators who voted for the Bush tax cut in 2001 but he opposed the Bush tax cut in 2003.

Kohl has supported gun control and wrote the 1990 law banning guns in schools; when that was overturned by the Supreme Court in 1995 (on the ground it had nothing to do with interstate commerce). His amendment to require child safety locks on guns was rejected 61–39 in July 1998. But after the Littleton, Colorado, murders a version requiring that safety locks be sold with, but separate from, guns passed 78–20 in May 1999. Since 2000 he has sponsored bills to provide for national use of ballistic fingerprinting. On the bankruptcy bill Kohl persuaded the Senate in March 2001 to limit state homestead exemptions to $125,000. In 2002 he used the Enron scandal to press the issue in conference committee; Texas has an unlimited homestead exemption and Enron executives forced into bankruptcy could keep their multimillion-dollar houses. The conference approved a $125,000 limit for convicted felons, or those owing debts under federal or state securities laws and those who have not lived in the state for five years. He and DeWine have run the Antitrust Subcommittee on a bipartisan basis in both the Clinton and Bush years. In 1997 a joint letter to FCC Chairman Reed Hundt prompted him to kill the proposed AT&T-SBC merger; subcommittee hearings in 1998 helped prevent the proposed American Airlines-British Airways merger. In 2001 they helped prevent the USAirways-United Airlines merger. As the only sports team owner in the Senate, he has recused himself on the issue of Major League Baseball's anti-trust exemption. With DeWine, he pushed through a law making it a felony to cross state lines to avoid paying child support in cases after one year or more than $5,000 in arrears. He and Judd Gregg sponsored a bill to make permanent the ban on Internet sales taxes; Kohl cited the plight of small Wisconsin cheese sellers. With Orrin Hatch and Charles Grassley he has sponsored a bill to allow class action suits with damages over $2 million and plaintiffs from other states to be removable to federal courts. He and Hatch sponsored a Safe Explosives Act to require permits, background checks and fingerprinting to buy explosives. He has opposed the judicial nominations of Charles Pickering, Priscilla Owen and Miguel Estrada. Noting that there is no security screening of the chartered flights he takes to get around Wisconsin, he pressed the Bush administration for screening of passengers on chartered planes large enough to do great damage if taken over by terrorists. Four days after September 11 he was wary of military action. "We would take a tragic situation and make it infinitely worse if we just lash out." But in October 2002 he voted for the Iraq war resolution saying, "I believe Saddam Hussein's acquisition of weapons of mass destruction is a great threat." But he added, "If Saddam Hussein no longer rules as a result of our actions, then I say fine. But for us to take action with the primary purpose of overthrowing the Iraqi government would be wrong."

Kohl has fought with uncharacteristic fierceness to change what he considers the unfair treatment of Wisconsin dairy farmers. Since 1937, the Agriculture Department has fixed milk prices by a formula that allows higher prices the farther a farmer is from Eau Claire, Wisconsin. This increases prices to consumers, creates an oversupply of milk and reduces dairy prices in the Upper Midwest. Further aggravating the problem is the Northeast Dairy Compact set up in the 1980s, which allows the New England states to set even higher prices; other Northeastern states have sought to join. In debate on the 1996 Freedom to Farm Act, Kohl got the Senate to vote 50–46 to end the Northeast Dairy Compact, but in conference it was extended to 1999 and the Agriculture Secretary was ordered to set new milk marketing rules by then. In October 1999 New England senators inserted into an appropriations bill a two-year extension of the Northeast Dairy Compact and a rejection of Agriculture Secretary Dan Glickman's new rules; this was in part an effort to help then-Republican Jim Jeffords of Vermont, who was up for reelection in 2000. Kohl was outraged, and threatened to filibuster the bill and obstruct all business of the Senate. "This is very much unlike me," he told a reporter. "I hate it. I don't like to be a pain. I've never been an obstructionist before. But if this is what it takes, this is what I'll do." On November 18 and 19 he held the floor and filibustered. He was forced to desist, but got verbal support on the issue from party leaders Trent Lott and Tom Daschle and Agriculture Chairman Richard Lugar who promised the issue would be revisited. In 2001 he got 41 senators to sign a letter opposing the Northeast Dairy Compact, enough to threaten a filibuster if the issue was brought up, and on September 30 the Compact expired. In February 2003 he helped get $15.9 million to battle Chronic Wasting Disease, which affected deer in woods west of Madison.

Kohl has been reelected easily. His sincere, unprepossessing demeanor has helped—so has his money. He spent $6.5 million of his own money in 1994 (far more per voter, incidentally, than the much-ridiculed Michael Huffington was spending in California) and $5 million of his own money in 2000. His ability to self-finance has deterred many well-known Republicans from running against him. In 1994, against legislator Robert Welch, he won 58%–41%. In 2000 he beat John Gillespie, founder of the Rawhide Boys Ranch for troubled teens, 62%–37%. Kohl said in May 2003 that he would run for reelection in 2006.

Junior Senator

Russell Feingold (D)

Elected 1992, seat up 2004, 2d term; b. Mar. 2, 1953, Janesville; home, Middleton; U. of WI, B.A. 1975, Rhodes Scholar, Oxford U., 1977, Harvard Law Schl., J.D. 1979; Jewish; married (Mary).

Elected Office: WI Senate, 1982–92.

Professional Career: Practicing atty., 1979–83; Prof., Beloit Col., 1985–93.

DC Office: 506 HSOB, 20510, 202-224-5323; Fax: 202-224-2725; Web site: feingold.senate.gov.

State Offices: Green Bay, 920-465-7508; La Crosse, 608-782-5585; Middleton, 608-828-1200; Milwaukee, 414-276-7282; Wausau, 715-848-5660.

Committees: *Aging (Special). Budget. Foreign Relations*: African Affairs (RMM); East Asian & Pacific Affairs; International Operations & Terrorism. *Judiciary*: Administrative Oversight & the Courts; Antitrust, Competition Policy & Consumer Rights; Constitution, Civil Rights & Property Rights (RMM).

Group Ratings

	ADA	ACLU	AFS	LCV	CON	ITIC	NTU	COC	ACU	NTLC	CHC
2002	90	80	75	88	99	0	43	20	5	14	—
2001	95	—	92	75	—	—	17	29	20	—	20

National Journal Ratings

	2001 LIB —	2001 CONS	2002 LIB —	2002 CONS
Economic	79%	19%	73%	20%
Social	65%	32%	82%	0%
Foreign	60%	40%	85%	12%

Key Votes of the 107th Congress

1. Approve Bush Tax Cuts	N	5. Confirm Ashcroft as AG	Y	9. Bar Coop. with Intl. Court	N
2. Expand Patients' Rights	Y	6. Bar Gays in the Boy Scouts	N	10. Trade Promotion Authority	N
3. Campaign Finance Reform	Y	7. $ for Hate Crime Prosecution	Y	11. Authorize Force in Iraq	N
4. Permit ANWR Development	N	8. Overseas Military Abortions	Y	12. Homeland Sec. Dept. Union	N

Election Results

1998 general	Russell Feingold (D)	890,059	(51%)	($3,846,089)
	Mark W. Neumann (R)	852,272	(48%)	($4,373,953)
1998 primary	Russell Feingold (D)	unopposed		
1992 general	Russell Feingold (D)	1,290,662	(53%)	($2,056,079)
	Robert W. Kasten Jr. (R)	1,129,599	(46%)	($5,427,163)

Russ Feingold is a Democrat first elected to the Senate in 1992. He grew up in Janesville and said he wanted to be a senator someday; his father ran for district attorney as a Progressive and once lost an election to the county board by one vote. Feingold nurtured his ambition at the University of Wisconsin, as a Rhodes Scholar, and at Harvard Law School; he moved to Middleton, a not-so-academic suburb of Madison, and beat an incumbent state senator in 1982, at 29, by 31 votes. Feingold has a flair for publicity, and for political reform issues and novel arguments. His great goal in the legislature was to ban the use of bovine growth hormones, a Luddite measure aimed at keeping in business Wisconsin's numerous and long-subsidized dairy farmers, whose chief problem is that Americans drink less milk today than in the 1950s while cows are much more productive. Feingold decided to run in 1992 for the Senate seat held by Bob Kasten, a free-market conservative who had won by narrow margins in 1980 and 1986. In the Democratic primary, while Milwaukee businessman Joseph Checota and Congressman Jim Moody battered each other with negative ads, Feingold ran clever, humorous spots: one showing Elvis, alive and endorsing Feingold; another showing Feingold at home, opening up a closet and saying, "No skeletons." He also had detailed position papers, including an 82-point plan for reducing the deficit. Near primary day, Checota apologized for his ads and asked voters to vote for Feingold if they didn't vote for him. Feingold, already ahead in polls, zoomed to an astonishing 70% win in this three-way race. Feingold also bounced way ahead of Kasten, who ran his own Elvis ads attacking Feingold on issues; Feingold attacked Kasten's negativity and avoided engaging on specifics. The race narrowed, but Feingold won 53%–46%.

In the Senate, Feingold has had a liberal record on cultural and foreign issues, somewhat more moderate on economics. He attacked many spending programs: the Pentagon's medical school, helium subsidies and the Supercollider; he moved to eliminate the Extremely Low Frequency radio system—"a Cold War relic" in his words—embedded in northern Wisconsin. Feingold did not respond in lockstep with other Democrats on the Clinton scandals. In February 1997 he called for an independent counsel on the Clinton-Gore fundraising operations. In January 1999 he was the only Democrat to vote against Robert Byrd's motion to dismiss the charges against Clinton. "I simply cannot say that the House managers cannot prevail," he said. He voted against removal in February.

Feingold has long said that the campaign finance system is "legalized bribery and influence-peddling"; democracy, he once said, "has been almost entirely corrupted in the last few years by soft money." In December 1995 he was surprised when John McCain called and asked if he would work with him against pork barrel spending—which McCain seems to regard as intended to please contributors, rather than voters. Out of this collaboration came the various versions of McCain-Feingold campaign finance bills, which were filibustered to death in July 1996 and in February 1998. The House passed one version in August 1998, but it was filibustered in the Senate in September. In October 1999 McCain-Feingold was again beaten, but McCain and Feingold did push through the bill requiring disclosure by Section 527 committees in June 2000. McCain's presidential campaign and his threats to bring up the issue at every turn forced Trent Lott to schedule two weeks of debate on campaign finance in March 2001. This time McCain and Feingold prevailed. They beat an amendment for lesser changes by Chuck Hagel by 60–40 and beat non-severability by 57–43, important because most senators considered at least some provisions constitutionally dubious. The bill passed 59–41 in April. In July it seemed about to come to the floor of the House, but the Republican leadership's rule was defeated and Speaker Dennis Hastert pulled it off the calendar. Then, after the Enron bankruptcy, pressure mounted. The bill's advocates got 218 signatures on a discharge petition and it was brought to the floor and passed. The Senate passed a final version in March. George W. Bush expressed doubts about the constitutionality of some provisions but signed it anyway, without ceremony and without inviting McCain and Feingold. Behind the scenes not all Democrats were happy; some thought it would hurt their party. At a Democratic Policy Committee lunch in July 2002, Hillary Rodham Clinton cited one provision. Feingold disputed her interpretation. She said, "Russ, live in the real world." He said, "I also live in the real world, Senator, and I function quite well in it." The argument switched to another venue in December 2002, when several plaintiffs challenged the bill before a three-judge federal court. In May 2003 the court, deeply divided, issued 1,700 pages of opinions and upheld some of the provisions but not others. The law requires the Supreme Court to review their decision; oral arguments are scheduled to take place September 8, 2003.

Feingold has pursued other ethics issues. He was one of the crusaders against lobbyists' gifts to lawmakers. He sought to prohibit members of Congress from using for personal travel frequent flier miles earned on business trips. He has tried to ban cost-of-living adjustments to congressional pay. In October 2001, even as he was seeking more debate on the Patriot Act, he once again objected. Majority Leader Tom Daschle, who had said he was "disappointed" with Feingold on the Patriot Act, said he was "very disappointed." Feingold said, "I am wondering when he will be very, very disappointed." He tried to attach repeal of the COLA to various measures and failed until he got a vote on it as an amendment to the homeland security bill in November 2002; it lost 58–36.

To the Patriot Act Feingold tried to offer amendments to limit secret searches, computer surveillance and roving wiretaps. Daschle got them all tabled, and Feingold cast the sole vote against the bill. That is not an unusual posture for him: he voted against the 1996 anti-terrorism bill and he was the only Democrat to vote against Robert Byrd's $15 billion homeland security package in 2001. He was the only Democrat on the Budget Committee to join Republicans and vote for five-year caps on spending in 2002. He has called for repeal of all federal death penalty statutes. He was one of eight Democrats who voted to confirm John Ashcroft; he argues that a president should be given great deference in Executive Branch appointments. But not in judges: he joined other Democrats in opposing Charles Pickering, Priscilla Owen and Miguel Estrada. In March 1999 he was one of three Democratic senators to vote against air strikes in Serbia and Kosovo. In October 2002 he voted against the Iraq war resolution, and argued that the administration had presented "confused" and "seemingly shifting" justifications. He objected when the Bush administration abrogated the ABM Treaty and argued that it could so only with the advice and consent of two-thirds of the Senate. He criticized the 2002 arms control treaty with Russia for having no timetable for reductions and no requirement that nuclear warheads be destroyed. As chairman of the Africa Subcommittee he traveled to Kenya, Tanzania and Mozambique in February 2002; his visa for Zimbabwe was revoked by the Mugabe government. He argues that the U.S. must do more to encourage democracy and economic development in Africa.

Prompted by a complaint by a musician, he embarked on a crusade against Clear Channel Worldwide, which runs 70% of the pop music concerts and owns 10% of radio stations in the country. He argued that such companies are squeezing out artists and charging consumers high prices, and prepared a bill which would impose a freeze on the number of radio stations companies could buy and prohibit anti-competitive behavior. He and Herb Kohl secured $15.9 million to attack Chronic Wasting Disease, which has afflicted deer in woods west of Madison. He has opposed the Northeast Dairy Compact and wants to change the milk marketing system to provide Wisconsin dairy farmers a level playing field.

Feingold has made it a practice to hold listening sessions in all 72 Wisconsin counties every year, speaking for five minutes and then taking all questions. And he has submitted voluntarily to some of the campaign restrictions he sought to place on all candidates. In 1998 he faced a strong opponent in Congressman Mark Neumann, a conservative elected in 1994 who proposed to reserve all the budget surplus for paying down the national debt and retain money for Social Security—similar though not identical to Feingold's views—and touted his independence by saying he had been thrown off an Appropriations subcommittee for voting against the leadership. After some negotiation, they agreed to limit their campaign spending, Feingold to $3.8 million, Neumann to $4.7 million (he actually spent $4.4 million), and to limit PAC money to 10% of donations and out-of-state contributions to 25% and to impose a $2,000 limit on candidate contributions (more of a handicap for Neumann, a self-made home-builder millionaire, who spent $700,000 of his own money on a losing race in 1992). To Democrats who complained that Feingold was risking his seat in a race that was close in the polls, he said, "The issue is my issue now. We're on my playing field. Is Wisconsin going to become another state where money rules?" The NRSC, then headed by Mitch McConnell, who led the fight against Feingold's campaign finance bill, spent heavily on this race, running anti-Feingold ads. But when the DSCC starting running anti-Neumann ads, Feingold responded: "Get the hell out of my state with those things"; the ads continued until the buy was finished. Neumann argued that Feingold's stand was hypocritical, since the Sierra Club, League of Conservation Voters and AFL-CIO all spent heavily on ads against Neumann. Republican attacks dominated the TV screens in August and into September; Feingold's leads of 10% or so melted away and the race became about even. Neumann ran humorous ads attacking Feingold for sending dollars to Russia to study monkeys in space and for voting for a study of cow flatulence (the ad showed smock-clad scientists out in a field trying to isolate samples of cow gas). In one of the nation's closest Senate races, Feingold won 51%–48%. This was not a big-city victory: metro Milwaukee voted for Feingold by only 50%–49%. His biggest margin came in Madison's Dane County, and he carried and ran ahead of Democratic norms in most counties in the Madison media market and along the Mississippi River—where Al Gore would run well in 2000 and Jim Doyle in 2002—as well as in the Democratic Lake Superior counties. Neumann ran only about even in his own 1st District, but ran well ahead in the prosperous Fox River Valley and the Lake Michigan counties.

In 2001 Feingold talked occasionally about running for president; in the fall he made a campus speaking tour. But he said it was unlikely and that he would decide by his 50th birthday in March 2003. He spent that evening at the Harmony Bar in Madison and, as he put it, "I turned to a couple of friends and family members and said, 'By the way, I'm not running for president in 2004.' They said, 'OK. Fine. Now listen to the band.'" All along he had said it was "extemely likely" that he would run for reelection in 2004. After the Democrats' setbacks in November 2002 he said, "To sort of act like, 'Oh, gee, a few things kind of went bad, and we just lost by a few votes here and there,' to me, that's a failure. . . . Let's admit we made some mistakes." He said Democrats should be "progressive" and at the same time "deficit hawks." Feingold's 1998 numbers and his job rating—48% positive in February 2003—made many Republicans think he might be vulnerable. But few seemed to want to run against him. Congressman Paul Ryan of the 1st District ruled it out adamantly. HHS Secretary and former Governor Tommy Thompson has never shown any interest in running for the Senate. In March 2003 Neumann said he would not run and recommended former Lieutenant Governor Margaret Farrow. But she said, "I just don't see at this point doing it." The closest thing to a declared candidate at the time was state Senator Robert Welch, who lost 58%–41% to Herb Kohl in 1994. A straw poll taken by *WisPolitics.com* at the Republican state convention in May 2003 showed Farrow winning 109 votes and Welch 55 out of 278 cast; Farrow said she might be a little more interested.

FIRST DISTRICT

Rep. Paul Ryan (R)

Elected 1998, 3d term; b. Jan. 29, 1970, Janesville; home, Janesville; Miami U. of OH, B.A., 1992; Catholic; married (Janna).

Professional Career: Aide, U.S. Sen. Bob Kasten, 1992; Advisor & speechwriter, Empower America, 1993–95; Legis. Dir., U.S. Sen. Sam Brownback, 1995–97; Mktg. consultant., Ryan Inc. Central, 1997–98.

DC Office: 1217 LHOB 20515, 202-225-3031; Fax: 202-225-3393; Web site: www.house.gov/ryan.

District Offices: Janesville, 608-752-4050; Kenosha, 262-654-1901; Racine, 262-637-0510.

Committees: *Ways & Means* (23d of 24 R): Oversight; Select Revenue Measures; Social Security. *Joint Economic Committee* (2d of 10 Reps.).

Group Ratings

	ADA	ACLU	AFS	LCV	CON	ITIC	NTU	COC	ACU	NTLC	CHC
2002	0	13	0	25	52	100	63	100	96	97	100
2001	0	—	0	29	—	—	69	96	88	—	—

National Journal Ratings

	2001 LIB — 2001 CONS		2002 LIB — 2002 CONS	
Economic	22%	— 74%	32%	— 67%
Social	0%	— 81%	25%	— 71%
Foreign	56%	— 41%	41%	— 56%

Key Votes of the 107th Congress

1. Approve Bush Tax Cuts	Y	5. Faith-Based Charities	Y	9. Trade Promotion Authority	Y
2. Limit Patients' Bill of Rights	Y	6. Bar Gays in the Boy Scouts	Y	10. Bar Funds for Intl. Court	Y
3. Campaign Finance Reform	N	7. Ban Partial-Birth Abortion	Y	11. Authorize Force in Iraq	Y
4. Ban ANWR Development	N	8. Arm Commercial Pilots	Y	12. Deny Home. Sec. Dept. Union	Y

Election Results

2002 general	Paul Ryan (R)	140,176	(67%)	($962,417)
	Jeffrey Thomas (D)	63,895	(31%)	($206,799)
	Other	4,542	(2%)	
2002 primary	Paul Ryan (R)	unopposed		
2000 general	Paul Ryan (R)	177,612	(67%)	($1,055,707)
	Jeffrey Thomas (D)	88,885	(33%)	($11,374)

Prior Winning Percentages: 1998 (57%)

The People		Race/Ethnic Origin	Ancestry		
Area size:	1,724 sq. mi.	87.4% White	German: 27.0%	Polish: 8.5%	
Urban population:	84.4%	4.6% Black	Irish: 8.3%		
Rural population:	15.6%	1.0% Asian	**2000 Presidential Vote**		
Pop. 2000:	670,458	0.3% Native Am.	Bush (R).............163,040	(51%)	
Median income:	$50,372	0.0% Hawaiian	Gore (D).............144,138	(45%)	
Poverty status:	6.3%	1.0% Two+ races	Other..................11,656	(4%)	
Military veterans:	13.2%	0.1% Other	**Cook Partisan Voting Index:** R + 3		
		5.7% Hispanic Origin			
Occupation	Blue collar: 29.4%	White collar: 57.4%	Gray collar: 13.2%		

Rolling dairy country, blanketed by snow during most of the winter, gloriously green under sunny blue skies in summer, the southern tier of Wisconsin from Lake Michigan inland to the Rock River Valley, is some of America's prime industrial country. Settled by Yankee and German farmers 170 years ago, it was once primarily dairyland. By the early 20th century, the steady habits and high skills of the local dairy farmers provided a good labor pool for factories. Today there are still major plants here: the operations center for SC Johnson Wax (and its Frank Lloyd Wright-designed tower and Wingspread Center) in Racine, a DaimlerChrysler engine plant in Kenosha and a Chevrolet plant in Janesville. In between are lake resorts, most notably Lake Geneva, a favorite of wealthy Chicagoans. Increasingly, most of this area is becoming metropolitan, part of the almost continuously suburban zone where metro Milwaukee melds into metro Chicago. To the untrained eye, this part of southern Wisconsin looks much the same as nearby northern Illinois; politically, there is a vast difference. The dotted line on the map is the boundary between corruption-prone machine politics of Illinois and mostly squeaky-clean (there were legislative scandals in 2002) progressive politics of Wisconsin.

This is the land of the 1st Congressional District, from Lake Michigan west into Rock County. It includes all of Racine and Kenosha Counties on the lake and Walworth County, with Lake Geneva, inland. It also includes, after the 2002 redistricting, the southern Milwaukee County suburbs up to Oak Creek and Greenfield and the southern tier of townships in suburban Waukesha County. It extends as far west as Janesville in the middle of Rock County. Politically, it tilts a bit to the Republican side; Waukesha County is heavily Republican, while Beloit in Rock County, which is Democratic, was removed from the district. This increased the Bush 2000 percentage in the district from 47% to 51%.

The congressman from the 1st District is Paul Ryan, a Republican first elected in 1998. He grew up in Janesville, where in 1884 his great-grandfather started a family construction firm now run by his cousins. Ryan got started in politics early, as a staffer for Senator Bob Kasten during college; then he worked as a speechwriter for Jack Kemp and William Bennett at Empower America and was legislative director to Kansas Senator Sam Brownback. Ryan returned to the 1st District in anticipation of the Senate candidacy of Congressman Mark Neumann, who lost to Russ Feingold in 1998. Ryan won the Republican primary with 81% of the vote. Democrats renominated Kenosha County official Lydia Spottswood, who had lost to Neumann in 1996. Ryan was for local control, against tax increases, in favor of gun ownership rights. He seized on her statement that she would consider removing the cap on the Social Security payroll tax, and accused her in ads, recalling her support of tax increases in Kenosha, of wanting to increase taxes by "a trillion dollars." This was a strenuously contested election, one of the Democrats' top 10 priorities in the nation. Spottswood spent $1.33 million, Ryan $1.24 million. But the final result was not that close. Ryan won 57%–43%.

In the House, Ryan became a mainstream Republican who was not afraid to occasionally challenge his party. He worked for a Social Security lockbox. But he lost on the House floor when he pressed for language to require that any funds cut from appropriations bills be set aside to reduce total spending; appropriators in both parties objected that the provision would tie their hands. In 2001, he won a seat on the Ways and Means Committee. He immediately became an ally of the Wall Street-based Club for Growth by criticizing George W. Bush's proposed tax cut as too small. On Ways and Means, Ryan called for individual investment accounts in Social Security. He has advocated business tax cuts to spur economic growth. During the debate on welfare in 2002, he shaped legislation creating a "super-achiever" credit for Wisconsin that lowered the requirement for future welfare reduction because the state had already cut the caseload by 76% since 1995. With Mark Green, he proposed changes in dairy policy to narrow price differences across the nation.

Ryan was reelected 67%–33% in 2000 and 67%–31% in 2002—big margins in a district held by Democrats from 1970 to 1994. His success has been held up by national conservatives as an example for Republicans across the nation. Ryan has also been mentioned as a candidate against Senator Russ Feingold in 2004, though he has adamantly ruled that race out. If George W. Bush is reelected and Republicans hold their majorities in Congress, Ways and Means may well be considering major changes in Social Security, and Ryan as a member of the Social Security Sub-committee would be in a position to get in on the action. He has not ruled out the possibility of a statewide race some time in the future.

SECOND DISTRICT

Rep. Tammy Baldwin (D)

Elected 1998, 3d term; b. Feb. 11, 1962, Madison; home, Madison; Smith Col., A.B. 1984; U. of WI Law Schl., J.D. 1989; No religious affiliation; companion (Lauren Azar).

Elected Office: Dane Cnty. Bd. of Supervisors, 1986–94; WI Assembly, 1992–98.

Professional Career: Practicing atty, 1989–92.

DC Office: 1022 LHOB 20515, 202-225-2906; Fax: 202-225-6942; Web site: www.house.gov/baldwin.

District Offices: Beloit, 608-362-2800; Madison, 608-258-9800.

Committees: *Budget* (4th of 19 D). *Judiciary* (13th of 16 D): Commercial & Administrative Law; Courts, the Internet & Intellectual Property.

Group Ratings

	ADA	ACLU	AFS	LCV	CON	ITIC	NTU	COC	ACU	NTLC	CHC
2002	100	93	100	100	73	38	27	25	0	3	0
2001	100	—	100	100	—	—	14	30	0	—	—

National Journal Ratings

	2001 LIB —	2001 CONS	2002 LIB —	2002 CONS
Economic	80%	21%	95%	0%
Social	90%	0%	84%	8%
Foreign	96%	0%	94%	0%

Key Votes of the 107th Congress

1. Approve Bush Tax Cuts	N	5. Faith-Based Charities	N	9. Trade Promotion Authority	N
2. Limit Patients' Bill of Rights	N	6. Bar Gays in the Boy Scouts	N	10. Bar Funds for Intl. Court	N
3. Campaign Finance Reform	Y	7. Ban Partial-Birth Abortion	N	11. Authorize Force in Iraq	N
4. Ban ANWR Development	Y	8. Arm Commercial Pilots	N	12. Deny Home. Sec. Dept. Union	N

Election Results

2002 general	Tammy Baldwin (D)	163,313	(66%)	($1,238,876)
	Ron Greer (R)	83,694	(34%)	($171,865)
2002 primary	Tammy Baldwin (D)	unopposed		
2000 general	Tammy Baldwin (D)	163,534	(51%)	($1,680,093)
	John Sharpless (R)	154,632	(49%)	($637,530)

Prior Winning Percentages: 1998 (53%)

The People		Race/Ethnic Origin	Ancestry	
Area size:	3,602 sq. mi.	89.0% White	German: 28.4%	Irish: 9.4%
Urban population:	75.6%	3.6% Black	Norwegian: 9.1%	
Rural population:	24.4%	2.4% Asian	**2000 Presidential Vote**	
Pop. 2000:	670,457	0.3% Native Am.	Gore (D).............201,738	(58%)
Median income:	$46,979	0.0% Hawaiian	Bush (R).............125,442	(36%)
Poverty status:	8.7%	1.3% Two+ races	Other..................19,398	(6%)
Military veterans:	11.1%	0.1% Other	**Cook Partisan Voting Index:** D +11	
		3.4% Hispanic Origin		

Occupation Blue collar: 22.3% White collar: 63.6% Gray collar: 14.1%

On a narrow isthmus between Lakes Mendota and Monona is the center of Madison and, in many ways, the center of Wisconsin. Here the state Capitol rises at the one end of State Street; at the other end of several commercial blocks is the main campus of the University of Wisconsin, on a beautiful, parklike, sometimes windswept setting above Lake Mendota. For most of the 20th century, Wisconsin politics was dominated by the Madison-based LaFollettes and their liberal Democratic successors. And the traffic on State Street was two-way, with university faculty devoted to Bob LaFollette's "Wisconsin idea" of an apolitical bureaucracy, his Wisconsin Tax Commission and workmen's compensation law—both firsts in the nation. Now there is more division, with the liberal campus at odds with the welfare and school choice law enacted while Tommy Thompson was governor. But there is a steady debate carried on here between the very liberal Madison *Capital Times* and its more conservative rival, the *Wisconsin State Journal,* with a larger circulation; the two newspapers practice the kind of competitive journalism still seen in only a few major cities and state capitals. Meanwhile, Madison's varied economy is thriving, with unemployment as low as 1.2% in recent years.

Madison is the center of Wisconsin's 2d Congressional District, which includes surrounding Dane County and dairy and alfalfa country to the north and south, as well as several rural dairy counties that have traditionally been Republican; they include such picturesque scenes as the birthplace of the Ringling Brothers Circus in Baraboo, and the Swiss-settled town of New Glarus. Madison spawned an activist and sometimes violent student movement (during the Vietnam War, a grad student was killed in a laboratory by a bomb set off by a protester) and a permanent postgraduate proletariat. In the 1990s, public sector employment rose 12% in Madison, while private sector jobs grew by 21%; *Money* magazine rated it among the best places to live in America. For many decades Madison and Dane County have been heavily Democratic and the surrounding rural counties heavily Republican. In the 1990s things got more fluid: Dane County was open to Republicans like Thompson and former 2d District Congressman Scott Klug, while the rural counties became more Democratic. In 2000 and 2002, both Dane County and the rural counties voted solidly Democratic.

The congresswoman from the 2d District is Tammy Baldwin, a Democrat elected in 1998. She grew up in Madison, where she was raised by her mother (a University of Wisconsin student when she was born) and her maternal grandparents, a UW biochemist and the theater department's head costume designer. She graduated first in her class at Madison West High School and went on to Smith College and UW Law School. In 1986, at 24, while still in law school, she was elected to the Dane County Board of Supervisors. In 1992 she was elected to the Wisconsin Assembly from a heavily Democratic Madison seat; in her first term she chaired the Elections Committee.

In 1998, when moderate Republican Scott Klug honored his promise to serve only four terms, this seemed a good chance for Democrats to pick up an open seat. Four Democrats and six Republicans ran. Baldwin had special advantages. As a woman with great political skills, she was supported by EMILY's List, which helped raised about one-quarter of her $1.5 million. And as a lesbian, she had support from national gay and lesbian organizations, which raised money from a large and affluent national constituency. With almost all (86%) of Democratic primary votes cast in Dane County, this was mostly a Madison contest. Baldwin won with 37% of the vote. Republicans nominated former state Insurance Commissioner Jo Musser. The primary results guaranteed that Wisconsin would elect its first woman member to Congress (the states that still have not are an odd bunch: Delaware, Iowa, Mississippi, New Hampshire and Vermont; Alaska has a woman senator, but she was appointed, not elected). Baldwin's candidacy roused the enthusiasm of Madison liberals in a way not seen in years. She called for a single-payer health insurance system and suggested that Musser was dominated by cash from insurance companies; Musser, a nurse who founded the Madison Employers Health Care Alliance, argued that single-payer would reduce choices and create long waiting periods for elective surgery. Both sides were well-financed. Dane County, which cast 73% of the district's votes, went 57%–42% for Baldwin, and she won the district 53%–47%.

Baldwin thus became the first openly homosexual non-incumbent to win a seat in the House; the two other openly gay members of the House, Barney Frank and Jim Kolbe, divulged their sexual orientation after they had served several terms. Baldwin said that she did not want to be seen primarily as a lesbian congresswoman. Befitting Madison, she has a strongly liberal voting record, though she prefers to be called a progressive. She sponsored the Health Security for All Americans Act to guarantee universal coverage. After September 11, she proposed the Service Members Health Protection Act to create a national center to study military health issues. She sought to broaden hate crimes to include people targeted because of gender, sexual orientation or disability. Baldwin joined an odd alliance with Republican Bob Barr to outlaw distribution over the Internet of recipes for methamphetamine, but a bipartisan coalition on the Judiciary Committee defeated them. After the House defeated an amendment to shift money from commodity programs to conservation, she voted against the farm bill. With Melissa Hart she successfully co-sponsored a bill in 2002 to make it illegal to tamper with consumer products to distribute offensive literature; their proposal was prompted by incidents in which pornography and other material was found in cereal boxes. Baldwin was an outspoken opponent of the Iraq war resolution; she said Iraq "poses no imminent threat."

In the 2000 campaign Baldwin faced Republican John Sharpless, whose ads in UW newspapers called him "our professor, our Congressman, our voice"; he had students in senior campaign positions. He said that Baldwin had sparse accomplishments, had ignored farmers and raised most of her campaign money out of state. Baldwin won by only 51%–49%, a smaller margin than when she was first elected, a reversal of the usual pattern. Baldwin ran far behind Al Gore: he carried Dane County 61%–33% in a high turnout, while she won there by 55%–45%. In 2002, Baldwin faced Ron Greer, a black minister and firefighter who was suspended from the force for distributing what many considered anti-gay literature when he ran in the 1998 House Republican primary, which he lost by 395 votes. In 2002 Greer vigorously opposed gay rights laws; he complained that Republican officials abandoned him because "they find me too conservative." Baldwin won 66%–34%, with a 70%–30% lead in Dane County and comfortable margins in the other counties.

THIRD DISTRICT

Rep. Ron Kind (D)

Elected 1996, 4th term; b. Mar. 16, 1963, La Crosse; home, La Crosse; Harvard U., B.A. 1985, London Schl. of Econ., 1986, U. of MN, J.D. 1990; Lutheran; married (Tawni).

Professional Career: Practicing atty., 1990–92; Asst. St. Prosecutor, La Crosse Cnty., 1992–96.

DC Office: 1406 LHOB 20515, 202-225-5506; Fax: 202-225-5739; Web site: www.house.gov/kind.

District Offices: Eau Claire, 715-831-9214; La Crosse, 608-782-2558.

Committees: *Chief Deputy Minority Whip. Budget* (19th of 19 D). *Education & the Workforce* (10th of 22 D): 21st Century Competitiveness; Education Reform. *Resources* (9th of 24 D): Energy & Mineral Resources (RMM); National Parks, Recreation & Public Lands.

Group Ratings

	ADA	ACLU	AFS	LCV	CON	ITIC	NTU	COC	ACU	NTLC	CHC
2002	90	73	100	75	92	62	24	47	8	8	8
2001	90	—	100	100	—	—	15	39	12	—	—

National Journal Ratings

	2001 LIB — 2001 CONS	2002 LIB — 2002 CONS
Economic	70% — 29%	64% — 36%
Social	65% — 36%	67% — 29%
Foreign	79% — 21%	76% — 23%

Key Votes of the 107th Congress

1. Approve Bush Tax Cuts	N	5. Faith-Based Charities	N	9. Trade Promotion Authority	N
2. Limit Patients' Bill of Rights	N	6. Bar Gays in the Boy Scouts	Y	10. Bar Funds for Intl. Court	N
3. Campaign Finance Reform	Y	7. Ban Partial-Birth Abortion	N	11. Authorize Force in Iraq	Y
4. Ban ANWR Development	Y	8. Arm Commercial Pilots	Y	12. Deny Home. Sec. Dept. Union	N

Election Results

2002 general	Ron Kind (D)	131,038	(63%)	($554,120)
	Bill Arndt (R)	69,955	(34%)	($12,325)
	Other	7,588	(3%)	
2002 primary	Ron Kind (D)	unopposed		
2000 general	Ron Kind (D)	173,505	(64%)	($564,246)
	Susan Tully (R)	97,741	(36%)	($124,818)

Prior Winning Percentages: 1998 (71%); 1996 (52%)

The People		Race/Ethnic Origin	Ancestry	
Area size:	13,849 sq. mi.	96.1% White	German: 29.7%	Norwegian: 14.1%
Urban population:	43.1%	0.5% Black	Irish: 8.5%	
Rural population:	56.9%	1.2% Asian	**2000 Presidential Vote**	
Pop. 2000:	670,462	0.5% Native Am.	Gore (D) 155,832	(49%)
Median income:	$40,006	0.0% Hawaiian	Bush (R) 144,948	(46%)
Poverty status:	9.8%	0.7% Two+ races	Other 16,626	(5%)
Military veterans:	12.9%	0.0% Other	**Cook Partisan Voting Index:** D + 2	
		0.9% Hispanic Origin		

Occupation	Blue collar: 29.2%	White collar: 53.3%	Gray collar: 17.5%

On the rolling land of western Wisconsin, in the knobby hills just east of the Mississippi River, is some of the most beautiful river landscape in the country. This is where Laura Ingalls Wilder's family built the "little house in the big woods" in the 1870s, before the first railroad came steaming up the narrow floodplain alongside the Mississippi River. Today, it is hard to imagine the big woods: The trees have long since been cut and the hillsides are covered with grass grazed by placid dairy cattle. Where pioneers tried to scratch out diversified crops, farmers soon created America's premier dairy region, producing milk, butter and especially cheese. But more than half of family dairy farmers have gone out of business since 1980. Cows are more productive, while demand for milk has decreased. And Wisconsin has trouble competing against the European Common Market's hugely subsidized cheese and butter. But other businesses have risen. Dodgeville in Iowa County (which is not on the Iowa border) is the headquarters of Lands' End, the catalog retailer. In the 1980s many communities here lost population, but in the 1990s there was steady 10% growth, especially rapid in the northern counties within commuting distance of Minneapolis-St. Paul.

The 3d Congressional District follows the Mississippi and St. Croix River counties from the southern border of the state to St. Croix County, just east of St. Paul, and extends east two or three counties. This is probably the nation's number one dairy district, with nearly as many cows as people. It was settled largely by German and Scandinavian immigrants (Laura's Yankee family moved away as Swedes were moving into the area), and it once voted for LaFollette Progressives. More recently, it has been fairly closely divided between Democrats and Republicans. In 2000 it voted 49%–46% for Al Gore; western Wisconsin and eastern Iowa were the one segment of rural America where Gore ran even with or ahead of historic Democratic percentages in 2000, which was vital to his narrow victory in each state. In 2002 the Democratic trend continued, as Democratic Governor Jim Doyle carried all but four counties in the district. He lost to Republican Scott McCallum in one northern rural county and St. Croix County, which trended Republican (as did the nearby Minnesota suburban counties in the Twin Cities), and he lost two counties to Libertarian nominee Ed Thompson, the brother of former Governor Tommy Thompson, who carried the county he lived in and the one he grew up in on his way to 10% of the statewide vote.

The congressman from the 3d District is Ron Kind, a Democrat first elected in 1996. He grew up in a large family in La Crosse, the son of a telephone repairman and a secretary. He went to Harvard on scholarship and played quarterback, and worked as a summer intern for Senator William Proxmire, doing research for his Golden Fleece awards. He attended the London School of Economics and University of Minnesota Law School, practiced law in a big firm in Milwaukee, then returned home to La Crosse to work as an assistant prosecutor on rape and sexual abuse cases. Kind started running for Congress soon after Republican Steve Gunderson announced during the 1994 campaign that he would not run again in 1996. He talked of cutting corporate welfare and aiding the poor, and won the September primary 46%–29%. Republican former state Senator Jim Harsdorf won the Republican primary after Gunderson rejected pleas to run again even though he might have become Agriculture Committee chairman. Harsdorf took hard-edged stands for the balanced budget and Governor Tommy Thompson's "Wisconsin Works" welfare program. Kind talked instead of campaign finance regulation and presented his own balanced budget proposal. On November 1 Gunderson announced he was neutral on the candidates because he didn't agree with Harsdorf's views on civil and human rights and thought him too close to the Christian Coalition. Kind won 52%–48%.

In the House, Kind has compiled a moderate record on economics and cultural issues, and was a bit more liberal on foreign and defense issues. Like other Wisconsin members, he worked to reform the Federal Milk Marketing Order System, instituted in 1937, which pays higher prices the farther the farmer is from Eau Claire, which is in the northern part of the district, which means that 3d District dairy farmers get the lowest prices in the nation. He focused attention on nitrogen fertilizer runoff from farms. In 2001, as an Agriculture Committee member, he sponsored the bipartisan amendment on the farm bill to shift $19 billion of commodity support dollars to environmental conservation of idle land. "Farmers are the best stewards of the land, but we have not given them the resources they need for conservation," he said. That was defeated 226–200. Later, he lost an attempt to impose a maximum payment limit of $275,000 per farmer.

Kind is a founder and co-chairman of the Upper Mississippi River Congressional Task Force. His own home is on the river and was flooded in 2001; the 3d District's entire western border is the Mississippi River. With members from Illinois and Iowa, he got the House to pass a bill to establish a water quality monitoring network in the Upper Mississippi River Basin. After strong lobbying by union leaders and dairy interests, he opposed trade promotion authority in 1997, but he sided with Bill Clinton and local farmers in favor of PNTR with China. In 2001 and 2002, he again opposed trade promotion authority. In 2002, he became a co-chairman of the New Democrat Coalition and said that he wanted to expand access to broadband in rural areas and to make his area "the Silicon Valley of agricultural research." Although he voted for the use of force in Iraq, in January 2003 he voiced concern about what he viewed as the rush to war after he took some heat from liberals back home (in November, more than 500 anti-war voters wrote in the name of Mark Twain to protest Kind's vote on the war).

After a heavily contested campaign in 1996, Kind has been reelected easily. Local union organizers have complained that he has not been sufficiently supportive on trade issues, but they have not put up a primary challenger. He briefly considered running for governor in 2002, but decided against it.

FOURTH DISTRICT

Rep. Jerry Kleczka (D)

Elected April 1984, 10th term; b. Nov. 26, 1943, Milwaukee; home, Milwaukee; U. of WI; Catholic; married (Bonnie).

Military Career: Air Natl. Guard, 1963–69.

Elected Office: Milwaukee Cnty. Cncl., 1965–68; WI Assembly, 1968–74; WI Senate, 1974–84, Asst. Majority Ldr., 1977–82.

Professional Career: Accountant, 1982–84.

DC Office: 2217 RHOB 20515, 202-225-4572; Fax: 202-225-8135; Web site: www.house.gov/kleczka.

District Offices: Milwaukee, 414-297-1140; Milwaukee, 414-297-1331.

Committees: *Ways & Means* (7th of 17 D): Health; Oversight.

Group Ratings

	ADA	ACLU	AFS	LCV	CON	ITIC	NTU	COC	ACU	NTLC	CHC
2002	95	73	100	100	88	50	27	35	4	3	8
2001	95	—	100	100	—	—	11	43	4	—	—

National Journal Ratings

	2001 LIB —	2001 CONS	2002 LIB —	2002 CONS
Economic	79%	21%	82%	17%
Social	79%	21%	63%	35%
Foreign	94%	7%	87%	10%

Key Votes of the 107th Congress

1. Approve Bush Tax Cuts	N	5. Faith-Based Charities	N	9. Trade Promotion Authority	N
2. Limit Patients' Bill of Rights	N	6. Bar Gays in the Boy Scouts	N	10. Bar Funds for Intl. Court	N
3. Campaign Finance Reform	Y	7. Ban Partial-Birth Abortion	Y	11. Authorize Force in Iraq	N
4. Ban ANWR Development	Y	8. Arm Commercial Pilots	N	12. Deny Home. Sec. Dept. Union	N

Election Results

2002 general	Jerry Kleczka (D)	122,031	(87%)	($478,091)
	Brian Verdin (Green)	18,324	(13%)	($1,593)
2002 primary	Jerry Kleczka (D)	54,258	(72%)	
	Nathaniel Stampley (D)	21,244	(28%)	
2000 general	Jerry Kleczka (D)	163,622	(61%)	($632,355)
	Tim Riener (R)	101,811	(38%)	($46,119)
	Other	3,705	(1%)	

Prior Winning Percentages: 1998 (57%); 1996 (58%); 1994 (54%); 1992 (66%); 1990 (69%); 1988 (100%); 1986 (100%); 1984 (67%); 1984 (65%)

The People		Race/Ethnic Origin	Ancestry	
Area size:	113 sq. mi.	50.4% White	German: 18.3%	Polish: 8.9%
Urban population:	100.0%	33.0% Black	Irish: 5.4%	
Rural population:	0.0%	2.7% Asian	**2000 Presidential Vote**	
Pop. 2000:	670,458	0.7% Native Am.	Gore (D) 183,810	(66%)
Median income:	$33,121	0.0% Hawaiian	Bush (R) 84,823	(30%)
Poverty status:	19.8%	1.8% Two+ races	Other 11,814	(4%)
Military veterans:	11.1%	0.2% Other	**Cook Partisan Voting Index:** D +18	
		11.2% Hispanic Origin		

Occupation	Blue collar: 27.8%	White collar: 54.0%	Gray collar: 18.2%

Milwaukee is America's most German city, with an ethnic heritage noticeable not just in the names of its beers and its old German restaurants but in the solidness of its houses and the orderliness of its streets. Until World War I made this German character seem un-American, German was spoken on the streets and read in newspapers, German beer was produced in dozens of breweries and German cultural traditions breathed in churches, union halls and parlors. There was a German-type politics, with a Socialist mayor and an efficient, honest city government. The world's largest four-sided clock faces outward from all sides of the tower on the Allen-Bradley factory, looking out over the manufacturing city. It is an apt symbol, a piece of precision engineering, in this high-skill manufacturing town, with its skyline of smokestacks and church steeples, the closest thing in America to the factory cities of the Germany whence so many Milwaukeeans' ancestors came. Milwaukee leads the nation in industrial control equipment, mining gear, cranes and independent foundries. The work force, with German, Polish, Mitteleuropean work habits, is highly skilled and hard-working.

Though some neighborhoods here are beset by crime and drug use, most of Milwaukee is solid and upstanding, and some of it—Brewers Hill near the old Schlitz brewery—is gentrifying. There is an Oktoberfest (as well as an Irish Fest, a huge musical Summerfest, etc.), and there are large and efficiently run factories that pay high wages to highly-skilled and well-disciplined workers.

The 4th Congressional District, which had been the south side Milwaukee district since 1892, now covers the entire city. The 2002 redistricting eliminated the old 5th District on the north side in the northern half of Milwaukee, which had suffered significant population loss and moved its black and white neighborhoods to the 4th. Removed from the 4th were almost all of its suburbs in Waukesha and Milwaukee County; the only remaining suburbs are working class—St. Francis, Cudahy and South Milwaukee on Lake Michigan and West Milwaukee and part of West Allis west of the Allen-Bradley tower. This lowered the Bush 2000 percentage in the 4th District from 50% to 30%, the biggest change in partisan percentage in any district in the nation in the 2001–02 redistricting cycle. Both parties agreed on this change. For Republicans it was an easy call: the state was losing one seat and the Democrats would lose it. For Democrats it was an easy call as well: 5th District Democrat Tom Barrett was running for governor, and so there would be no matchup between two incumbents, and expanding the 5th District to meet the population requirement would have made the 4th District more Republican. Local black leaders complained that the district included three-quarters of Wisconsin's blacks—the opposite of the usual complaint that black voters are being spread among too many districts. Overall, the district's population is 33% black and 11% Hispanic.

The congressman from the 4th District is Jerry Kleczka (pronounced *KLETCH-kuh*), a Democrat first elected in 1984. Kleczka is a product of the south side of Milwaukee, the sort of man who has remodeled his house from top to bottom and maintains the best lawn in the neighborhood. He has spent his adult lifetime in politics. He was elected to the Milwaukee County Council in 1965, at 21, and to the Wisconsin Assembly in 1968 and the state Senate in 1974. There he chaired several committees. In April 1984 he won the special election held after the death of Clement Zablocki, who had first been elected in 1948.

In the House Kleczka has a moderate-to-liberal voting record and has weighed in on many tax, health and trade issues as a member of the Ways and Means Committee. He wants to protect employee contributions to pension funds from being seized by banks and other creditors in bankruptcy proceedings. He has stood strongly against allowing private contracts between Medicare beneficiaries and doctors; that would create a two-tier system, he argues. With Pete Stark, he has proposed a crackdown on doctors who refer Medicare patients to boutique hospitals in which they have invested. In 2002, he said that the Republican prescription drug plan "benefits drug companies more than seniors" and would be a step toward privatization of Medicare. On other matters, he has sponsored bills to require school buses to be equipped with seat belts and—joined at his office by his dog Colby—to extend the ban on dog and cat fur in domestic clothing to imported clothing. He was the only Wisconsin Democrat to vote for the partial-birth abortion ban. Citing his district's sizable Serb constituency, he voted in 1999 against Bill Clinton's air war against Yugoslavia; in October 2002 he voted against the use of force in Iraq.

Kleczka was in the middle of a bitter House conflict in 2000 over the selection of a new House chaplain. He recommended Father Tim O'Brien, a Marquette University professor, who was initially favored by a bipartisan committee and would have been the first Roman Catholic chaplain. But Kleczka said that Republican leaders "rigged" the process to select a Presbyterian minister. O'Brien said that he was the victim of anti-Catholic discrimination. Later, Speaker Dennis Hastert selected Father Daniel Coughlin, a Catholic priest from Chicago. Kleczka remained angry, contending that Republicans had "gone over the line" in politicizing the position.

Before the 2002 redistricting, Kleczka had some serious challenges. In 1994 Tom Reynolds, a Christian conservative printer whose backyard print shop churned out anti-abortion as well as campaign literature, held him to a 54%–45% margin. In May 1995, after a second drunk driving arrest, Kleczka gave up drinking. He won the next two elections against Reynolds, 58%–42% in 1996 and 57%–43% in 1998. In 2000 he won 61%–38%. The 2002 redistricting removed the possibility of any serious competition from a Republican. Kleczka did have opposition in the Democratic primary from Nathaniel Stampley, a black minister who had served on the Milwaukee County Board but was convicted in Senegal on charges arising from a business deal there. Kleczka won 72%–28%. There was no Republican nominee.

FIFTH DISTRICT

Rep. Jim Sensenbrenner (R)

Elected 1978, 13th term; b. June 14, 1943, Chicago, IL; home, Menomonee Falls; Stanford U., A.B. 1965, U. of WI, J.D. 1968; Episcopalian; married (Cheryl).

Elected Office: WI Assembly, 1968–74; WI Senate, 1974–78.

Professional Career: Practicing atty., 1968–69; Staff asst., U.S. Rep. Arthur Younger, 1965.

DC Office: 2332 RHOB 20515, 202-225-5101; Fax: 202-225-3190; Web site: www.house.gov/sensenbrenner.

District Office: Brookfield, 262-784-1111.

Committees: *Judiciary* (Chmn. of 21 R). *Select Committee on Homeland Security* (5th of 27 R): Rules.

Group Ratings

	ADA	ACLU	AFS	LCV	CON	ITIC	NTU	COC	ACU	NTLC	CHC
2002	0	7	0	38	97	75	72	95	92	97	100
2001	10	—	0	29	—	—	84	74	96	—	—

National Journal Ratings

	2001 LIB — 2001 CONS		2002 LIB — 2002 CONS	
Economic	22%	74%	19%	80%
Social	0%	81%	39%	57%
Foreign	33%	60%	35%	60%

Key Votes of the 107th Congress

1. Approve Bush Tax Cuts	Y	5. Faith-Based Charities	Y	9. Trade Promotion Authority	Y
2. Limit Patients' Bill of Rights	Y	6. Bar Gays in the Boy Scouts	Y	10. Bar Funds for Intl. Court	Y
3. Campaign Finance Reform	N	7. Ban Partial-Birth Abortion	Y	11. Authorize Force in Iraq	Y
4. Ban ANWR Development	Y	8. Arm Commercial Pilots	Y	12. Deny Home. Sec. Dept. Union	Y

Election Results

2002 general	Jim Sensenbrenner (R)	191,224	(87%)	($493,305)
	Robert Raymond (I)	29,567	(13%)	
2002 primary	Jim Sensenbrenner (R)	unopposed		
2000 general (WI 9)	Jim Sensenbrenner (R)	239,498	(74%)	($464,515)
	Mike Clawson (D)	83,720	(26%)	($7,355)

Prior Winning Percentages: 1998 (91%); 1996 (74%); 1994 (100%); 1992 (70%); 1990 (100%); 1988 (75%); 1986 (78%); 1984 (73%); 1982 (100%); 1980 (78%); 1978 (61%)

The People		Race/Ethnic Origin	Ancestry	
Area size:	1,301 sq. mi.	94.0% White	German: 34.6%	Irish: 8.8%
Urban population:	84.9%	1.3% Black	Polish: 7.7%	
Rural population:	15.1%	1.5% Asian	**2000 Presidential Vote**	
Pop. 2000:	670,458	0.2% Native Am.	Bush (R) 233,005 (62%)	
Median income:	$58,594	0.0% Hawaiian	Gore (D) 132,310 (35%)	
Poverty status:	3.4%	0.7% Two+ races	Other 13,080 (3%)	
Military veterans:	12.4%	0.1% Other	**Cook Partisan Voting Index: R +14**	
		2.2% Hispanic Origin		

Occupation	Blue collar: 21.3%	White collar: 68.2%	Gray collar: 10.5%

For decades, the orderly, heavily German-American factory city of Milwaukee has been spreading slowly, mostly west and north, into Wisconsin dairy country. There are high-income enclaves here, like close-in Elm Grove and Oconomowoc spread out to the west around its lakes. There is office development in Brookfield; subdivisions spread out in Mequon and Menomonee Falls and farther, to reach small towns with roots deep in the 19th century. This is comfortable but not fancy territory, and the economy here is still based heavily on skilled manufacturing. Not far from Milwaukee are Port Washington, with Allen-Edmonds shoes; West Bend, with West Bend kitchen appliances; Pewaukee, with Quad/Graphics printing. Closer to Milwaukee are its tonier suburbs along Lake Michigan—Shorewood, Whitefish Bay, and Fox Point—where wealthy neighborhoods are just a few miles from the poorest neighborhoods in the state on the other side of I-43.

The 5th Congressional District, numbered the 9th before 2002 redistricting, includes most of the western, northwestern and northern suburbs of Milwaukee. It includes the close-in lake-front suburbs in Milwaukee County, Ozaukee County north of Milwaukee and Washington County to the west. It includes most of the Milwaukee County suburbs of Wauwatosa and West Allis and most of the northern three tiers of townships in Waukesha County just to the west. It also includes a part of Jefferson County further west. This is by far the most Republican district in the state; it voted 62% for George W. Bush in 2000.

The congressman from the 5th District is Jim Sensenbrenner, a Republican first elected in 1978. Sensenbrenner grew up in the Milwaukee area, graduated from Stanford and the University of Wisconsin Law School, and has spent most of his adult life in politics. He served briefly as a staffer in the House, then was elected to the Wisconsin Assembly in 1968 and the Wisconsin Senate in 1974. When incumbent Bob Kasten ran for governor in 1978, Sensenbrenner ran in this district and won the Republican primary by 589 votes. Of such narrow victories are long congressional careers made. His Wisconsin roots are strong; his great-grandfather was a founder of Kimberly-Clark. He reports a net worth of $11 million, and *Roll Call* ranks him the 24th richest member of Congress; but that may be misleading, since Sensenbrenner lists his investments in detail and calculates his net worth with precision, while most wealthy members value their assets within broad categories. In December 1997 he won $250,000 in the District of Columbia lottery after buying two tickets at a Capitol Hill liquor store.

During most of Sensenbrenner's long political career he was in the minority, gamely undertaking the Sisyphean task of moving amendments certain to lose. But he persevered out of a dogged sense of mostly conservative principle. Since 1994 he has been in the majority and in January 2001 he became chairman of the House Judiciary Committee. He immediately moved to rein in the number of hearings by subcommittee chairmen and he sought to reduce the committee's reputation for partisanship and to protect its jurisdiction from raids by other House committees, notably Energy and Commerce. He made the bankruptcy bill a top priority. "Every dollar that is written off in a bankruptcy is a dollar that's added to the cost of goods and services that are paid for by people who pay their bills." But in November 2002 the rule to put the conference committee report onto the floor of the House failed when abortion opponents opposed it because of a provision, agreed to by Sensenbrenner's predecessor Henry Hyde and Senator Charles Schumer, making non-dischargeable in bankruptcy fines and damages for violence or protest against abortion providers. He was proud of enacting the first congressional authorization of the Department of Justice in many years, citing the vital role that it gave his committee in improving oversight of the department. "I am a hawk on oversight," he said. "I don't back down because the president is in my party." Prompted by the Microsoft case, he proposed and won enactment in 2002 of a 12-member commission to examine the need to modernize the antitrust laws, particularly the role of intellectual property, the global economy and the role of state attorneys general; it is scheduled to report in 2005. After September 11, he pressed for a thorough congressional review of Attorney General John Ashcroft's call for additional law enforcement investigative powers. Concerned about possible violations of civil liberties, he insisted on a sunset provision under which the law would expire in four years. But a bipartisan House-Senate leadership group preempted the Judiciary Committees and rewrote many of the final details. When Ashcroft in April 2003 pushed to extend the law's scheduled sunset, Sensenbrenner objected. He passed a bill to split the Immigration and Naturalization Service into two different agencies; when they were placed in the new Homeland Security Department, Sensenbrenner expressed concern that longstanding internal problems would remain unresolved. In early 2003, he supported the partial-birth abortion ban and helped enact the nationwide AMBER Alert, a communications network to track down missing and abducted children. He has long opposed racial quotas and preferences.

Sensenbrenner has long been a stickler for ethics, and was one of the first to urge that Congress apply to itself the laws it imposes on the rest of the country. He served on the ethics committee in the early 1980s, when in the Abscam case the committee secured the first expulsion from the House since the Civil War era. In the Clinton impeachment, he was one of the 13 House managers and was chosen by Hyde to start the managers' presentation to the Senate. He was the first Republican to call for the expulsion of Jim Traficant after he was convicted of bribery in April 2002. From 1997 to 2001 Sensenbrenner was chairman of the Science Committee. He supported the space station and most manned space flight, but was persistently critical of the U.S.-Russia space agreement, particularly the condition of the Russian Mir spacecraft. He generally backed the NASA policy of "faster, better, cheaper" small missions, and called for more privatization of the space program. On local issues, Sensenbrenner has spoken out strongly for Milwaukee's school choice experiment. He has opposed the Northeast Dairy Compact, which he argues suffuses the national market with unfairly priced milk, butter and cheese. Sensenbrenner has not had a serious electoral challenge since the 1978 primary. In 2002, as in 1994 and 1998, he had no Democratic opponent.

SIXTH DISTRICT

Rep. Tom Petri (R)

Elected April 1979, 12th term; b. May 28, 1940, Marinette; home, Fond du Lac; Harvard U., B.A. 1962, J.D. 1965; Lutheran; married (Anne).

Elected Office: WI Senate, 1972–79.

Professional Career: Peace Corps, Somalia, 1966–67; Law Clerk, Fed. Judge James Doyle, 1965–66; White House aide, 1969; Practicing atty., 1970–79.

DC Office: 2462 RHOB 20515, 202-225-2476; Fax: 202-225-2356; Web site: www.house.gov/petri.

District Offices: Fond du Lac, 920-922-1180; Oshkosh, 920-231-6333.

Committees: *Education & the Workforce* (Vice Chmn. of 27 R): 21st Century Competitiveness. *Transportation & Infrastructure* (Vice Chmn. of 41 R): Aviation; Highways, Transit & Pipelines (Chmn.); Railroads.

Group Ratings

	ADA	ACLU	AFS	LCV	CON	ITIC	NTU	COC	ACU	NTLC	CHC
2002	10	13	0	50	67	88	63	85	80	86	83
2001	25	—	10	50	—	—	76	65	72	—	—

National Journal Ratings

	2001 LIB — 2001 CONS	2002 LIB — 2002 CONS
Economic	47% — 53%	48% — 51%
Social	34% — 66%	39% — 57%
Foreign	21% — 74%	44% — 55%

Key Votes of the 107th Congress

1. Approve Bush Tax Cuts Y	5. Faith-Based Charities Y	9. Trade Promotion Authority Y
2. Limit Patients' Bill of Rights Y	6. Bar Gays in the Boy Scouts Y	10. Bar Funds for Intl. Court Y
3. Campaign Finance Reform Y	7. Ban Partial-Birth Abortion Y	11. Authorize Force in Iraq Y
4. Ban ANWR Development Y	8. Arm Commercial Pilots Y	12. Deny Home. Sec. Dept. Union Y

Election Results

2002 general	Tom Petri (R)	.... unopposed		($344,870)
2002 primary	Tom Petri (R)	.... unopposed		
2000 general	Tom Petri (R)	 179,205	(65%)	($703,496)
	Dan Flaherty (D)	 96,125	(35%)	($213,059)

Prior Winning Percentages: 1998 (93%); 1996 (73%); 1994 (100%); 1992 (53%); 1990 (100%); 1988 (74%); 1986 (97%); 1984 (76%); 1982 (65%); 1980 (59%); 1979 (50%)

The People		Race/Ethnic Origin	Ancestry	
Area size:	5,816 sq. mi.	94.1% White	German: 38.8%	Irish: 6.8%
Urban population:	60.7%	1.0% Black	Polish: 5.4%	
Rural population:	39.3%	1.5% Asian	**2000 Presidential Vote**	
Pop. 2000:	670,440	0.4% Native Am.	Bush (R)..............170,134	(53%)
Median income:	$44,242	0.0% Hawaiian	Gore (D)..............134,926	(42%)
Poverty status:	6.1%	0.7% Two + races	Other...................13,499	(4%)
Military veterans:	13.7%	0.0% Other	**Cook Partisan Voting Index:** R + 6	
		2.3% Hispanic Origin		

Occupation	Blue collar: 35.4%	White collar: 49.1%	Gray collar: 15.5%

Central Wisconsin is solid country, a producer of basic commodities—milk, butter and cheese, paper products, Mirro pots and pans, Mercury outboard motors, Oshkosh overalls and Kleenex. Settled first by Yankee Protestants, it was one of the birthplaces of the Republican Party in February 1854, when a group of Whigs, Free Soilers and Democrats met in a small white schoolhouse in Ripon, Wisconsin, and proclaimed themselves Republicans; Jackson, Michigan, also claims to be the birthplace of the party. Whichever, the party grew rapidly, winning a near-majority in the House in the 1854 elections. But Republican roots here are not just Yankee. The 1850s brought the first surge of German migration into the United States, and central Wisconsin was a favorite destination. Here they built the dairy farms and factory towns that seemed steadfastly prosperous 50 years ago, and developed a manufacturing economy that boomed in the 1990s. The German influence is still felt: Sheboygan, on Lake Michigan, is the Bratwurst Capital of the World. Here also was the testing ground, in Fond du Lac County, of Governor Tommy Thompson's W-2 welfare program; the welfare rolls there, never high, fell to zero after the program began in 1997.

The 6th Congressional District is a slice of central Wisconsin from Lake Michigan to the Wisconsin River. It has the highest percentage of residents of German ancestry (39%) in the nation and includes Sheboygan and Manitowoc on Lake Michigan, Oshkosh and Fond du Lac on Lake Winnebago in the Fox River Valley, and the towns of Menasha and Kimberly, just outside Appleton. It also includes most of five rural counties to the west and south. Politically, this has been mostly Republican territory since that first meeting in Ripon and remains so today, and it has elected Republican congressmen who have come up with thoughtful and original solutions to problems. One was William Steiger, first elected in 1966, who put on his staff a University of Wisconsin graduate student named Dick Cheney; Steiger's chief monuments are the all-volunteer military and the 1978 Steiger amendment cutting capital gains tax rates—considerable accomplishments for a member of the minority party, and for one who died at age 40 in 1978.

The congressman from the 6th District is Tom Petri, a Republican first elected in the 1979 contest to succeed Steiger. Petri grew up in Fond du Lac, graduated from Harvard, was a Peace

Corps volunteer in Somalia and was elected to the state Senate in 1972, at 32. In 1974 he was the Republican nominee against Senator Gaylord Nelson; he walked across the state campaigning but in that Democratic year lost 62%–36%. When he ran for the House, Petri beat Tommy Thompson in the primary 35%–19% and then won the special with 50.4%.

Some of Petri's ideas have been adopted. He long boosted the Earned Income Tax Credit, which results in payments to low-income people who work, targeting aid to families much better than the minimum wage; the Clinton administration agreed and increased the EITC when Democrats were in control. Petri called for expanding the EITC concept with a $1,000 tax credit per child, in place of the current deduction; Congress and Bill Clinton agreed on a $500 per child credit, leaving the deduction in place. In 2000, he called for expanding the EITC to coordinate it with other programs for the poor, including housing subsidies and Medicaid. In 2003 he called for a commission to examine what he called the poverty trap—as low income people increase their earnings, they lose eligibility for the EITC and other federal benefits and are in effect taxed at rates up to 100%.

Petri hoped to become chairman of the Education and the Workforce Committee after the 2000 elections. He was the most senior Republican on the committee, but the Republican Steering Committee passed over him and installed the fourth most senior Republican, John Boehner. Petri's office put out a statement saying this was part of a "purge of moderate Republicans," and Petri's voting record has been more liberal than it was before 2000. He was one of 13 Republicans to vote against repeal of the Clinton ergonomics rule in March 2001, one of 34 Republicans to vote against oil drilling in the Arctic National Wildlife Refuge in August 2001 and one of four Republicans to vote against the resolution backing Israel in May 2002. He backed the Shays-Meehan campaign finance bill for some time and in July 2001 he was one of 19 Republicans to vote against the rule for debate on the bill; the rule failed, one of only two that did in the 107th Congress. He was urged by Shays-Meehan backers to sign the discharge petition to bring the bill to the floor, but hung back for several months. Then in January 2002, after the Enron bankruptcy raised serious questions for him, he was one of two Republicans who signed to provide the decisive 218th vote and brought the issue to the floor. Later that year he and Paul Kanjorski sponsored a bill to provide a tax credit up to $200 or a tax deduction up to $600 for campaign contributions.

As chairman of the often renamed Highways, Transit and Pipelines Subcommittee, Petri played a major role in shaping the 1998 transportation bill. He strongly supported Chairman Bud Shuster's move to require all gas tax revenues to be taken off-budget and used for transportation; he passed an amendment raising Wisconsin's return on its gas tax dollars, which meant a 54% increase for the state. After losing the Education chairmanship, Petri got a waiver from the three-term limit on subcommittee chairmanships, and remains as he has been since 1995 the chairman of the Highways Subcommittee in time for the reauthorization of TEA-21. Petri had added $4.4 billion to the Bush request in 2002. He argues that even that is not enough. "We're still in a catch-up mode when it comes to maintaining infrastructure. We've not kept up with the growth in the system. Lane miles haven't equaled miles traveled." In January 2003 he said the federal government was spending $40 billion on highways and transit and needs to spend $60 billion on highways and $12 billion on transit. Don Young, chairman of the full committee, was rounding up support for an increase in the gas tax; Petri was suggesting other possibilities—indexing the gas tax, raising the tax on ethanol 5.2 cents to the gas tax level. The Bush administration is opposed and the Republican leadership hostile, but Petri wants to go ahead. Another transportation cause is his bill to authorize individuals or states to bring action under state laws against rogue moving companies, who hold furniture hostage for higher than agreed on fees.

Petri has been reelected easily; he had no opposition in either the primary or the general election in 2002.

SEVENTH DISTRICT

Rep. David Obey (D)

Elected April 1969, 17th term; b. Oct. 3, 1938, Okmulgee, OK; home, Wausau; U. of WI, B.S. 1960, M.A., 1962; Catholic; married (Joan).

Elected Office: WI Assembly, 1962–69.

Professional Career: Asst., family-run supper club & motel, 1962–68.

DC Office: 2314 RHOB 20515, 202-225-3365; Web site: www.house.gov/obey.

District Offices: Superior, 715-398-4426; Wausau, 715-842-5606.

Committees: *Appropriations* (RMM of 29 D): Labor, HHS & Education (RMM).

Group Ratings

	ADA	ACLU	AFS	LCV	CON	ITIC	NTU	COC	ACU	NTLC	CHC
2002	90	67	100	88	70	38	25	26	8	3	17
2001	95	—	100	93	—	—	9	30	13	—	—

National Journal Ratings

	2001 LIB	—	2001 CONS		2002 LIB	—	2002 CONS
Economic	80%	—	19%		86%	—	12%
Social	65%	—	36%		63%	—	37%
Foreign	93%	—	7%		74%	—	25%

Key Votes of the 107th Congress

1. Approve Bush Tax Cuts	N	5. Faith-Based Charities	N	9. Trade Promotion Authority	N
2. Limit Patients' Bill of Rights	N	6. Bar Gays in the Boy Scouts	*	10. Bar Funds for Intl. Court	N
3. Campaign Finance Reform	Y	7. Ban Partial-Birth Abortion	Y	11. Authorize Force in Iraq	N
4. Ban ANWR Development	Y	8. Arm Commercial Pilots	N	12. Deny Home. Sec. Dept. Union	N

Election Results

2002 general	David Obey (D)	146,364	(64%)	($860,378)
	Joe Rothbauer (R)	81,518	(36%)	($19,932)
2002 primary	David Obey (D)	unopposed		
2000 general	David Obey (D)	173,007	(63%)	($1,085,618)
	Sean Cronin (R)	100,264	(37%)	($192,479)

Prior Winning Percentages: 1998 (61%); 1996 (57%); 1994 (54%); 1992 (64%); 1990 (62%); 1988 (62%); 1986 (62%); 1984 (61%); 1982 (68%); 1980 (65%); 1978 (62%); 1976 (73%); 1974 (71%); 1972 (63%); 1970 (68%); 1969 (52%)

The People		Race/Ethnic Origin	Ancestry
Area size:	19,391 sq. mi.	95.1% White	German: 30.4% Polish: 8.6%
Urban population:	42.0%	0.3% Black	Norwegian: 7.6%
Rural population:	58.0%	1.5% Asian	**2000 Presidential Vote**
Pop. 2000:	670,462	1.5% Native Am.	Gore (D).............152,177 (47%)
Median income:	$39,026	0.0% Hawaiian	Bush (R).............150,068 (47%)
Poverty status:	8.6%	0.8% Two+ races	Other...................18,294 (6%)
Military veterans:	14.5%	0.0% Other	**Cook Partisan Voting Index:** X +00
		0.9% Hispanic Origin	

Occupation	Blue collar: 31.8%	White collar: 51.5%	Gray collar: 16.7%

In the late 19th century, on the rail lines radiating northwest from Chicago and Milwaukee, came thousands of migrants whose descendants have made the northern reaches of Wisconsin the most thickly settled land this far north in the United States east of the Mississippi. What brought people up so far was not cropland—there are no industrial-sized wheat farms as in the Red River Valley of North Dakota—but trees, iron and cows. This was one of America's largest virgin timberlands, and the river towns are still dotted with paper mills. Farther north, iron brought Finns and Italians to the port of Superior, Wisconsin, right next to Duluth, Minnesota, and to smaller towns on the chilly lake. Then on the cleared forestlands came dairy farms. Dairy cattle, properly cared for, thrive in these northern uplands, and the sons of Wisconsin dairymen, many of them immigrants from Germany and Norway, moved their dairy herds even farther north. On this base small cities grew, some with big enterprises. Wausau has paper mills and Wausau Insurance, Wisconsin Rapids has Stora Enso, and Stevens Point has Sentry Insurance. While many rural areas have declined, the area around Wausau, Wisconsin Rapids and Stevens Point has generated new businesses and jobs and retained a high-skill work force. The number of dairy farmers is in sharp decline, but farmers are turning to potatoes, vegetables, cranberries and ginseng.

All these places are in Wisconsin's 7th Congressional District, which stretches from Stevens Point in the south to Lake Superior in the north. The politics of northern Wisconsin and the 7th District has a rough-hewn quality, a certain lumberjack populist flavor. Ancestrally Republican, this area favored the progressivism of the LaFollettes. Today, Superior and Stevens Point are heavily Democratic and so is Stevens Point's Portage County; Wausau and Marathon County and many of the smaller counties have been more Republican. This was a closely divided district in 2000; it cast 46.8% of its votes for George W. Bush and 47.5% for Al Gore.

The congressman from the 7th District is David Obey, a Democrat first elected in April 1969. Chairman of the Appropriations Committee from March 1994 to January 1995, and since then ranking minority member, he is one of the most capable and strongly motivated legislators on either side of the aisle. He grew up in Wausau, where his father worked in a roofing factory; he started off as a Republican, but was influenced by history teacher Arthur Henderson—who assigned papers on the politics of the 1920s and was attacked by McCarthyites—and between 1952 and 1956 Obey switched from supporting Dwight Eisenhower and Joe McCarthy to Adlai Stevenson and William Proxmire. Obey graduated from the University of Wisconsin and in 1962, when he was 24, he was elected to the Wisconsin Assembly even before he got his master's degree. When Melvin Laird resigned his House seat to become Richard Nixon's Defense secretary, Obey won an upset victory in the April 1969 special election.

In the state legislature, Obey was inspired by older New Deal Democrats who fought hard for the little guy; when he entered the House, the driving energy came from liberal Democrats opposed to the Vietnam war. Obey preserves something of the force of each group. He is not a sentimental liberal: He has a prickly personality and a vigorous temper and does not suffer gladly those he considers fools or knaves. But he can leaven that with humor: he likes to quote Archy the Cockroach, the supposed writer of Don Marquis's *Archy and Mehitabel*, and he is part of a band called The Capitol Offenses, which plays rock music and hymns. Even as he has moved to the top of the seniority ladder, Obey has retained his sense of outrage and his eagerness to fight for what he believes in—a quality that even some Democrats complain has been too intense. But he continues to display abundant energy and leadership on a host of fronts. He has had his disappointments. He lost the Budget Committee chairmanship to Oklahoma's Jim Jones in 1980 by 121–116. In 1984 he wanted to become Democratic Caucus chairman, but demurred when it became clear that Dick Gephardt had the votes. Even so, informally Obey became a key leader of liberal Democrats, in 1989 pushing Gephardt for majority leader when Jim Wright and Tony Coelho were resigning.

Obey remains a true believer in traditional liberalism, in Keynesian economics and economic redistribution. He thinks that government should provide economic security, create jobs and build infrastructure through public investment, that it should control health care costs and guarantee coverage and a choice of providers. In two stints as chairman of the Joint Economic Committee, he prepared studies arguing that Reagan-Bush policies enriched the rich and hurt the middle class. He bucked the Clinton administration, vocally opposing NAFTA and, when Bill Clinton seemed to be backing away from universal health care coverage in July 1994, said "then I will walk away from the Clinton health care plan" and supported his real preference, a single-payer system. In June 1995, when Clinton accepted the Republicans' goal of a budget balanced in seven years, Obey immediately issued a written statement reading, "I think most of us learned some time ago that if you don't like the president's position on a particular issue you simply need to wait a few weeks." Obey also opposed some administration positions from the right. He has long opposed abortion, and backs the partial-birth abortion ban; he opposes gun control, and once pointed out that one of the guns singled out in the assault weapons ban was owned by 23,000 residents of the 7th District, including two sheriffs.

Obey is above all an appropriator, and takes some justifiable pride in his skill at this work. He first got his seat on Appropriations in August 1969, when he was just 30; when he became chairman in March 1994, he was the youngest person to hold the post since James Good of Iowa in 1919. Obey has shown great skill, plus a determination to get things done on time—which is not always how appropriating works. For years much of his work was on the Foreign Operations Subcommittee, which he chaired from 1985 to 1995. This panel handles rather small sums of money but deals with some very sensitive issues, and it was often rocked in disputes about aid to the Nicaraguan Contras, the pace of negotiations in the Middle East, the treatment of the liberated nations of Eastern Europe. Obey has not always gotten his way, but in each case he worked to move appropriations bills forward in an orderly manner. He passed separate foreign operations appropriation bills nine out of 10 years, something that had only been accomplished twice in 10 years by his predecessors. Similarly, when Obey became chairman of the full committee, all 13 appropriations bills were signed into law prior to the beginning of the new fiscal year for the first time in 47 years; it hasn't happened since.

Obey's climb to the chairmanship was sudden. In January 1993 Jamie Whitten, whose health was impaired, was voted out after 14 years as chairman. William Natcher, holder of the record for consecutive roll call votes, performed ably for a year, but then his health visibly failed in January 1994. When he died in March 1994, Obey challenged the next Democrat in line, 74-year-old Neal Smith of Iowa. Smith had the support of other cardinals (Appropriatese for subcommittee chairmen), but Obey had more from non-committee liberals and less senior members, and won in the Democratic Caucus 152–106. When Republicans took control in 1995, Obey and Chairman Bob Livingston managed to work together on numerous occasions, sometimes to reach agreement, often to frame disagreement in orderly choices for other members; and he has worked amicably with Livingston's successor Bill Young. He has opposed holding up appropriations on what he considers extraneous issues.

After September 11, Obey and other Appropriations leaders backed George W. Bush's emergency appropriation of $40 billion, but put restrictions on spending—the first $10 billion could be spent after consultation with congressional leaders, the next $10 billion only after giving Congress 15 days of notice in which members could make objections, the last $20 billion only with congressional approval. Obey said, "Congress has only two powers that mean diddly, outside of the power to investigate: the power to declare war and the power of the purse. As a practical measure, it's the president who decides these days when the trigger is going to be pulled, so it is even more imperative for us to exercise the power of the purse." In October Bush asked for $20 billion more for homeland security; Obey, like Robert Byrd in the Senate, thought that more was needed. He delayed the measure for two days in November because the Republican leadership would not allow a vote on his amendment for $7 billion more; Obey argued that more was needed for, among other things, protecting nuclear sites, but the Republicans passed a rule 216–211 blocking the amendment. In June 2002, when Appropriations approved allocations to subcommittees of $748 billion in discretionary spending, Obey called that a "fiction"; he blamed not Young but the Republican leadership. In July he and Henry Waxman signed a letter criticizing the administration's homeland security bill for undermining congressional oversight and calling for changes. Obey is ranking Democrat on the Labor-HHS Subcommittee, the focus of the appropriations process in fall 2002; the conservative Republican Study Committee was pressuring the leadership to bring up Labor-HHS and hold it to the Bush budget limits, while Obey and subcommittee Chairman Ralph Regula, who have worked together harmoniously, argued that they would be forced to cut worthy programs. Obey asked Speaker Dennis Hastert to allow four alternatives on the floor, with the one getting the most votes prevailing—the Bush budget level, Regula's preferred version, his own and a Republican Study Committee alternative. "This would take the weight for congressional inaction off the shoulders of the leadership and put the responsibility back on the House. The obvious advantage is that at the end of the day the issue would be resolved one way or the other and the House could move forward to complete its business." This was the last thing Hastert would allow, and all but the defense and military construction appropriations were delayed until after the election and not passed until February 2003.

Obey is not one of those appropriators who load up their districts with earmarked projects, though he has supported some. But he has paid close attention to district interests. He and Senator Tom Daschle effectively killed the Clinton administration's ban on snowmobiles on federal lands. More important is the plight of Wisconsin dairy farmers; since 1937 the Agriculture Department has fixed milk prices by a formula that allows higher prices the farther a farm is from Eau Claire, Wisconsin. This increases prices to consumers, creates an oversupply of milk and reduces dairy prices in the Upper Midwest. Obey opposed the Northeast Dairy Compact, which allowed New England states to set higher prices, and it finally expired in September 2001. He voted against the farm bill in 2002; he said it provided a modest safety net for dairy farmers and more regional equity but left in place unfair Federal Milk Marketing orders. He has tried to limit import of dairy products, especially Milk Protein Concentrates. He worked aggressively to get funding to deal with Chronic Wasting Disease, which may be akin to mad cow disease and has affected deer herds west of Madison; in May 2002 he got $10 million in funding and in September he criticizing the administration for not releasing funds. He criticized the Agriculture Department for creating a "public panic" by not allowing testing for the disease by a private lab in Wisconsin. He and Tammy Baldwin sought $15 million for the University of Wisconsin's IceCube neutrino telescope, to be mounted in Antarctica. Obey can be roused to action by what he considers corporate excess: he attached a rider that the Smithsonian Institution reconsider its decision to name the IMAX Theater at the Air and Space Museum after Lockheed Martin after the company donated $10 million.

Obey is the third most senior member of the House and one of four who served in the 1960s. He has been reelected by wide margins, except in 1994, when he won 54%–46%. When rumors spread that he would retire in 2004, he said, "There isn't a snowball's chance in hell. Not a prayer." He said he planned to run at least through 2010, before the next round of redistricting.

EIGHTH DISTRICT

Rep. Mark Green (R)

Elected 1998, 3d term; b. June 1, 1960, Boston, MA; home, Hobart; U. of WI, B.A. 1983, J.D. 1987; Catholic; married (Sue).

Elected Office: WI Assembly, 1992–98.

Professional Career: Teacher, Kenya, 1987–88; Practicing atty., 1988–98.

DC Office: 1314 LHOB 20515, 202-225-5665; Fax: 202-225-5729; Web site: www.house.gov/markgreen.

District Offices: Appleton, 920-380-0061; Green Bay, 920-437-1954.

Committees: *Financial Services* (20th of 37 R): Capital Markets, Insurance & Government Sponsored Enterprises; Housing & Community Opportunity (Vice Chmn.); Oversight & Investigations. *International Relations* (21st of 26 R): Africa; International Terrorism, Nonproliferation and Human Rights. *Judiciary* (12th of 21 R): Courts, the Internet & Intellectual Property; Crime, Terrorism & Homeland Security.

Group Ratings

	ADA	ACLU	AFS	LCV	CON	ITIC	NTU	COC	ACU	NTLC	CHC
2002	0	7	0	25	25	100	60	95	88	94	100
2001	0	—	0	29	—	—	65	96	88	—	—

National Journal Ratings

	2001 LIB	—	2001 CONS	2002 LIB	—	2002 CONS
Economic	33%	—	66%	36%	—	61%
Social	0%	—	81%	25%	—	71%
Foreign	33%	—	60%	15%	—	78%

Key Votes of the 107th Congress

1. Approve Bush Tax Cuts	Y	5. Faith-Based Charities	Y	9. Trade Promotion Authority	Y
2. Limit Patients' Bill of Rights	Y	6. Bar Gays in the Boy Scouts	Y	10. Bar Funds for Intl. Court	Y
3. Campaign Finance Reform	N	7. Ban Partial-Birth Abortion	Y	11. Authorize Force in Iraq	Y
4. Ban ANWR Development	N	8. Arm Commercial Pilots	Y	12. Deny Home. Sec. Dept. Union	Y

Election Results

2002 general	Mark Green (R)	152,745	(73%)	($428,296)
	Andrew Becker (D)	50,284	(24%)	
	Other	7,418	(4%)	
2002 primary	Mark Green (R)	unopposed		
2000 general	Mark Green (R)	211,388	(75%)	($553,153)
	Dean Reich (D)	71,575	(25%)	($13,904)

Prior Winning Percentages: 1998 (55%)

The People		Race/Ethnic Origin	Ancestry	
Area size:	10,118 sq. mi.	92.2% White	German: 30.8% Irish: 6.9%	
Urban population:	56.0%	0.6% Black	Polish: 6.5%	
Rural population:	44.0%	1.4% Asian	**2000 Presidential Vote**	
Pop. 2000:	670,480	2.6% Native Am.	Bush (R)	165,819 (52%)
Median income:	$43,274	0.0% Hawaiian	Gore (D)	138,056 (43%)
Poverty status:	6.8%	0.9% Two+ races	Other	13,974 (4%)
Military veterans:	13.9%	0.0% Other	**Cook Partisan Voting Index:** R + 5	
		2.2% Hispanic Origin		

Occupation	Blue collar: 31.3%	White collar: 53.9%	Gray collar: 14.8%

In 1673, the French explorer and priest Father Marquette sailed from the open waters of Lake Michigan into what is now Green Bay. He had hoped to find the Northwest Passage to the Pacific. He actually found the Fox River, which leads to Lake Winnebago and, after a not-too-difficult portage, the Wisconsin River, which flows into the Mississippi. Green Bay and the Fox River Valley remained mostly wilderness and Indian country for more than 150 years. But once settled by Europeans, they became, as Father Marquette would have liked, one of the most heavily Catholic parts of the United States, though Indians still remain a presence; there was a long dispute over Chippewa Indian spearfishing rights and Green Bay's best hotel is now next to the Oneida Indian casino. This has been a thriving area economically, with traditional paper mills joined by high-skill manufacturing in Green Bay and Appleton in the Fox River Valley. Green Bay is of course known nationally as the home of the Green Bay Packers, owned by 110,000 shareholding Wisconsinites and never likely to move (under the team's charter, if the Packers are ever sold, the proceeds would go to the local Sullivan-Wallen American Legion Post 11 "for the purposes of erecting a proper soldier's memorial"). Appleton has produced a number of famous Americans—Senator Joseph McCarthy, novelist Edna Ferber and escape artist Harry Houdini.

The 8th Congressional District includes Green Bay and the Fox River Valley south to Appleton. It also includes several north woods and dairy counties inland, plus the Door County peninsula that juts out into Lake Michigan, a favorite summer vacation spot for Chicago and Milwaukee families. Politically, this has often been malleable country. Democrats, especially Catholics, can win here: John Kennedy carried the Fox River Valley in the primary and general election in 1960, and Bill Clinton carried it in 1996. But the 8th District more often votes Republican; it voted 52% for George W. Bush 2000.

The congressman from the 8th District is Mark Green, a Republican first elected in 1998, the only Republican to beat a Democratic incumbent that year. Green grew up in the Green Bay area; his father was from South Africa and his mother from Britain. In high school and college he was a champion swimmer; after graduating from the University of Wisconsin at Eau Claire and UW Law School in Madison, he and his wife spent a year in Kenya, working in a WorldTeach program. He practiced law and in 1992, at 32, was elected to the Wisconsin Assembly, where he became Republican Caucus chairman. In 1998 he challenged freshman Democratic Congressman Jay Johnson, a former TV news anchor. Green brought a conceptual framework to his campaign. He listed 55 issues on which he would vote differently from Johnson, one for each day between the primary and general election; they ranged from taxes and spending to education to abortion and defense. It was a solidly conservative platform, in opposition to Johnson's moderate-to-liberal voting record. Green called for "restoration of American values," an end to partial-birth abortions, scrapping the tax code, increasing local control of education and tougher crime laws. He carefully avoided any reference to the Clinton-Lewinsky scandal or to impeachment, saying that he had called for Clinton's resignation only to get the issue out of the way. Green spent $823,000, about the same as Johnson's $830,000, and won 55%–45%.

In the House, Green's voting record has been fairly conservative. His achievements included enactment of his "disabled housing initiative," a HUD pilot program that seeks to raise the fewer than 5% of individuals with disabilities who own homes. Four times the House has passed his two strikes law, for mandatory life sentences for second-time child sex offenders, but the Senate has not taken up the cause. He sponsored a DNA testing bill, to provide $400 million for "rape kits," to eliminate the backlog of DNA evidence collected in sexual assault cases. He has introduced resolutions to require electronic posting of lobbyist disclosure reports, but they have been referred to the Judiciary Committee and ignored. Concerned about foreigners who overstay their visas, he sponsored a law to require states to have driver's licenses expire when the applicant's visa does, or earlier. With Tammy Baldwin, he sponsored a bill to increase testing capacity and require a federal strategy to deal with Chronic Wasting Disease, which has afflicted deer near Madison. He would eliminate the capital gains tax on sales of farms to family members.

Green was reelected 75%–25% in 2000 and 73%–24% in 2002. In 1998 he said he would only serve three terms. He has been mentioned as a possible candidate for governor in 2006.

★ WYOMING ★

Wyoming is "the land of the cowboy," as the WPA Guide called it 60 years ago. "Its mountains, plains, and valleys are essentially livestock country. A cowboy astride a bucking bronco greets the visitor from enameled license plates, from newspapers, magazines and painted signs." The cowboy is still on the license plates, and Wyoming remains the most western of states in spirit—largely unsettled, the least populous state, a thin veneer of civilization stretched over a forbidding and beautiful land. Wyoming "has a 'lean-to' look," writes Gretel Ehrlich. "Instead of big, roomy barns and Victorian houses, there are dugouts, low sheds, log cabins, sheep camps and fence lines that look like driftwood blown haphazardly into place. People here still feel pride because they live in such a harsh place, part of the glamorous cowboy past." "What you see now in Wyoming is the promotion of things we used to apologize for," says the state Commerce Department director. "Wide open spaces, a huge expansive sky with no pollution, uncluttered clean rivers with maybe a lone fly fisherman, a cowboy and his dog and a herd of cattle."

But Wyoming's economy now depends not on cowboys and cattle but on mining and minerals. Wyoming boomed with oil prospectors during the energy price surge of the 1970s, but was hit hard by drops in oil prices in the early 1980s and again in the late 1990s. As the exploration for oil slumped, the production of other minerals has surged. The Clean Air Act put a premium on Wyoming's low-sulfur coal, and this is now the number one coal state, producing as much as West Virginia and Kentucky combined. Wyoming produces one-third of the nation's coal and a new $1.4 billion rail line is being built to the Mississippi River, the biggest U.S. rail construction project in a century. Wyoming is also the number seven oil and number four natural gas producer, and the nation's top producer of the mineral bentonite (used in oil drilling and cosmetics) and has the world's largest reserve of trona (used in glass and baking soda). Much of the natural gas is

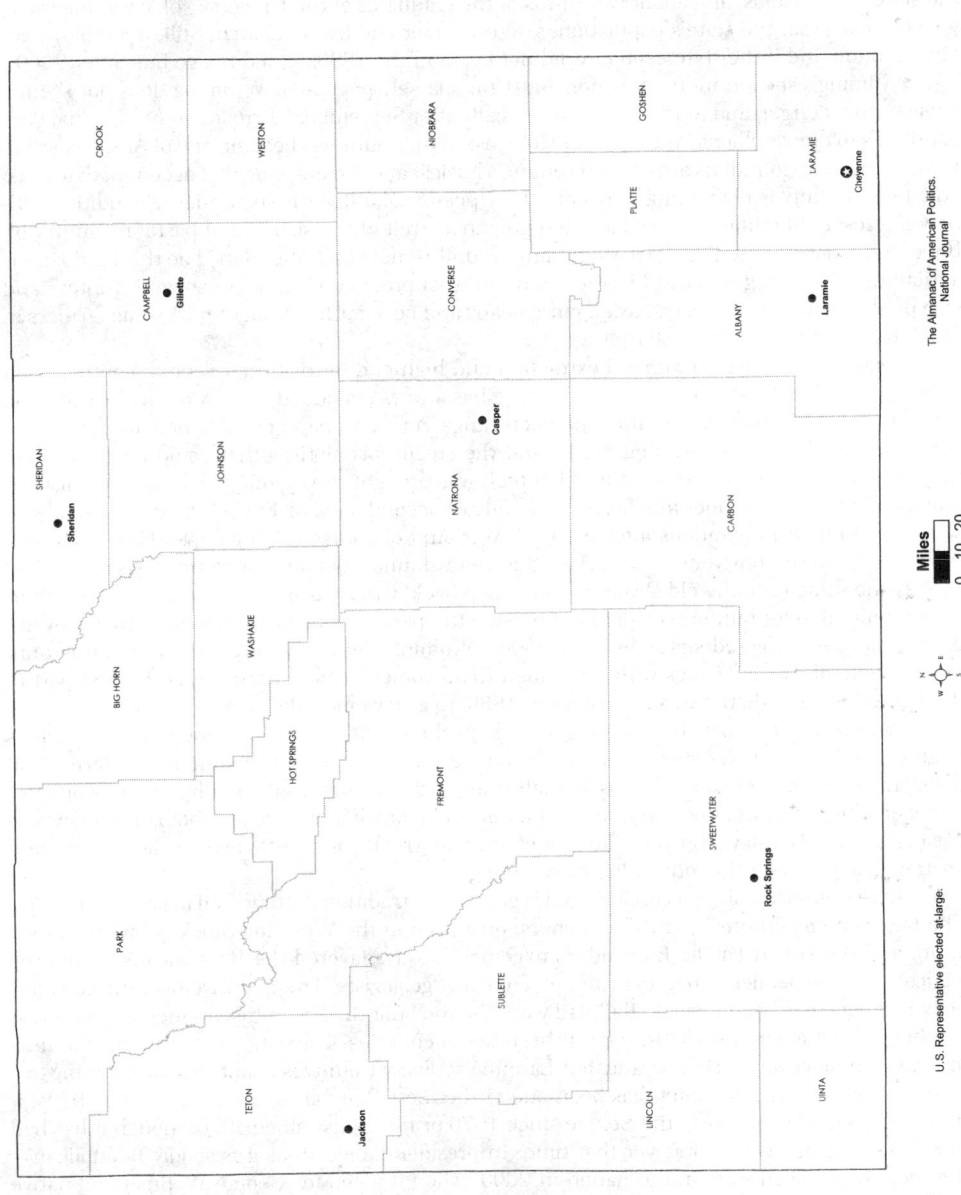

U.S. Representative elected at-large.

The Almanac of American Politics.
National Journal

Miles

0 10 20

coal-bed methane, mixed with water next to coal seams; only in 1989 did engineers figure out how to separate the natural gas from the water. Now 200-foot drilling rigs are sinking wells as deep as 25,000 feet, and production has jumped enormously since 2000. But ranchers without mineral rights complain that they are inundated with salty water. And these capital-intensive industries produce relatively few jobs for young people. About one-quarter of people 25 to 34 left the state in the 1990s, and about two-thirds of the graduates of the University of Wyoming leave, which means that the state's population is getting older and less educated. Still, unemployment has been low and if the state economy did not boom in the 1990s, it did not go bust after 2000.

Wyoming's second industry is now tourism; sparsely populated Wyoming does not seem a likely terrorist target, and tourism remained steady after September 11. Yellowstone National Park continues to draw millions, and Jackson Hole just to the south has become one of America's elite resort areas year-round; its airport is Wyoming's busiest and the only one that accommodates jets, and Teton County is now trying to restore the Upper Snake River to its pre-levee condition with new islands and braiding. There has been growth as well in the scenic and pastoral country on the eastern slope of the Big Horn Mountains around Buffalo and Sheridan. The third industry is agriculture: Wyoming is second in the nation in wool production, third in sheep inventory and also produces hay, sugar beets, barley, pinto beans and beef cattle. Drought hurt some farmers in 2002, but farm exports were sharply up.

Reliance on high-tech mineral extraction and high-end tourism may seem a contradiction of Wyoming's Old West heritage. But Wyoming has always depended on new technology to tame age-old nature. Cattle ranches after the open-range era were made possible only by the barbed wire that could fence in roaming herds, and the steam locomotives that could carry cattle to markets back east. This 19th century high tech was brought to Wyoming by large capitalist operators, some of them onetime Texas cowhands or second sons of English landed gentry, who started the first big operations after the Civil War. And of course mining depends on high-tech machinery and responsiveness to markets that reward innovation and penalize stasis.

At the same time the old Wyoming is coming back. Grizzly bears have done well enough in Yellowstone, despite hunters luring them outside the park with artificial salt licks, that they are likely to lose endangered status by early 2004. Wyoming still is a kind of frontier: It was until recently one of the few states with more men than women—one reason it was the first part of the United States, when it was a territory in 1869, to give women the vote.

There is a settled part of Wyoming as well, in the medium-sized towns that are the state's largest cities, and among sheep and cattle ranches, sugar beet and malting barley farms and denizens of tiny settlements. This is a small state, a single community really, where people remember who played what position, when and how well, for what high-school football team; where because all locals know who your father's cousins married, you mostly live on the straight and narrow. The locals set the tone of life in Wyoming.

There was once a sharp economic and regional split traditionally reflected in partisan politics. The big economic interests—cattle ranchers, organized in the Wyoming Stock Growers' Association, and the Union Pacific Railroad management always favored the Republicans, as did the wildcatters, independent producers and oil company geologists. The main Democratic constituency had been the Union Pacific Railroad workers who built the first transcontinental line across southern Wyoming in the 1860s; the southern tier of counties, from Cheyenne through Laramie to Evanston, once voted Democratic, but Laramie's Albany County is about the closest thing to a Democratic area left. Wyoming has been one of the most Republican states since the 1970s; it hasn't elected a Democrat to the Senate since 1970 or the House since 1976, though it has had mostly Democratic governors over that time. In presidential elections it is solidly Republican—the most Republican state in the nation in 2000, when it voted for George W. Bush and native son Dick Cheney, a running back on the Natrona High School football team, by a 69%–28% margin.

Wyoming's Republican tendencies in the 1990s was strengthened by the Clinton administration's environmental policies—proposing grazing fee increases, the reintroduction of gray wolves into Yellowstone, proposing threatened species status on the black-tailed prairie dog, banning snowmobiles in national parks, the moratorium on road building in the national parks. But the policies of the Bush administration—removing endangered status from the gray wolves, opening the way to proving title to land currently controlled by the Bureau of Land Management—have removed some of these grievances. This is a small state and the least populous—with not even half a million people, three-quarters the population of the average congressional district—and Wyoming voters expect to talk person-to-person with their governors, senators and congressmen every few years. Personal campaigning is important, and Democrats have won six of the last eight races for governor. But party tends to trump personality when it comes to federal office. Democrat Mike Sullivan, a popular two-term governor, was nonetheless beaten 59%–39% by Republican Craig Thomas in 1994; Democrats haven't won a Senate election here since 1970 or a House election since 1976.

The People		Race/Ethnic Origin			Military veterans: 57,860 (15.8%)	
Pop. 2000:	493,782	438,799	88.9%	White	WWII: 16.8%	Korea: 12.3%
Pop. 1990:	453,588	3,504	0.7%	Black	Vietnam: 36.2%	Gulf War: 12.8%
Change 1990–2000:	Up 8.9%	2,670	0.5%	Asian	**Most populous cities:**	
Change 1980–1990:	Down 3.4%	10,238	2.1%	Native Am.	1. Cheyenne	53,011
% of U.S. total:	0.2%	264	0.1%	Hawaiian	2. Casper	49,644
Pop. rank:	50th of 50	6,164	1.2%	Two+ races	3. Laramie	27,204
Area size:	97,814 sq. mi.	474	0.1%	Other	4. Gillette	19,646
State Native:	42.5%	31,669	6.4%	Hisp. Origin	5. Rock Springs	18,708
Non-citizen:	1.2%	**Ancestry**			Urban population: 65.2%	
Language		German: 18.4%		English: 11.3%	Rural population: 34.8%	
English: 90.7%	Spanish: 5.7%	Irish: 9.4%		USA: 4.6%		
Other Eur.: 2.3%		Norwegian: 3.0%				

Education		Work Sector		Legislature	
H.S. Grad:	87.9%	Private: 70.2%	Govt: 20.4%	Senate	20 R 10 D
College Grad:	21.9%	Self: 8.9%	Family: 0.5%	House	45 R 15 D
Industry		Unemployment: 5.2%		Legislative Term Limits: Yes	
Agri: 10.7%	Con: 8.7%	**Household Income**		**Registered Voters**	
Fin: 4.7%	Info: 2.2%	<15k: 16.7%	15-35k: 29.2%	D: 57,062	(27.7%)
Mfg: 11.4%	Prof: 27.4%	35-50k: 18.3%	50-100k: 29.1%	R: 129,606	(62.9%)
Public: 6.3%	Trade: 14.1%	100-150k: 4.5%	>150k: 2.2%	I: 19,371	(9.4%)
Other: 14.5%		Median: $37,892			
Occupation		Poverty status: 11.4%			
Blue collar: 27.5%	White collar: 54.2%	**Home Value**			
Gray collar: 18.2%		<50k: 18.4% 50-100k: 39.0% 100-200k: 31.7% 200-300k: 6.0%			
		300-500k: 2.5% >500k: 2.4% Median: $91,500			

Presidential politics Wyoming is one of the least likely states in the nation to be seriously contested in presidential general elections: it is too Republican, too remote and has only three electoral votes. Candidates have seldom visited, except when Dick Cheney has gone to his home in Jackson.

Wyoming holds presidential caucuses in early March. In 2000 they were held on March 10, the same day as the Colorado and Idaho primaries—a sort of western primary, which attracted little attention.

2000 Presidential Vote
Bush (R)	147,947	(69%)
Gore (D)	60,481	(28%)
Other	5,298	(2%)

1996 Presidential Vote
Dole (R)	105,388	(50%)
Clinton (D)	77,934	(37%)
Perot (I)	25,928	(12%)

Governor

Dave Freudenthal (D)

Elected 2002, term expires Jan. 2007, 1st term; b. Oct. 12, 1950, Thermopolis; home, Cheyenne; Amherst Col., B.A. 1973, U. of WY, J.D. 1980; Episcopalian; married (Nancy).

Professional Career: Practicing atty. 1980–94; U.S. Atty. for WY, 1994–01.

Office: State Capitol Bldg., Rm. 124, Cheyenne, 82002, 307-777-7434; Fax: 307-632-3909; Web site: www.state.wy.us.

Election Results

2002 general	Dave Freudenthal (D)	92,662	(50%)
	Eli Bebout (R)	88,873	(48%)
	Other	3,924	(2%)
2002 primary	Dave Freudenthal (D)	19,732	(54%)
	Paul Hickey (D)	13,793	(37%)
	Toby Simpson (D)	1,918	(5%)
	Kenneth Casner (D)	1,356	(4%)
1998 general	Jim Geringer (R)	97,235	(56%)
	John P. Vinich (D)	70,754	(40%)
	Other	6,899	(4%)

Dave Freudenthal, a Democrat, was elected governor of Wyoming in 2002. He grew up on a farm north of Thermopolis, the seventh of eight children. Freudenthal (pronounced *FREE-den-thal*) graduated from Amherst College and then returned to Wyoming to work for the state Department of Economic Planning and Development. Ed Herschler, a Democrat elected to the first of his three terms as governor in 1974, appointed him state planning coordinator in 1975 and administrative aide in 1978. In 1980 he graduated from the University of Wyoming Law School. From 1981 to 1993 he practiced law in Cheyenne; he also served on the Blueprint for Business Committee, the Wyoming Futures Project and the Economic Development and Stabilization Board and from 1981 to 1985 he was Wyoming Democratic chairman. In 1994 he was appointed U.S. Attorney for Wyoming and served until 2001. Then he started running for governor.

The incumbent, Republican Jim Geringer, was ineligible to run for a third term. Five Republicans and four Democrats got into the race. All agreed that economic development was a key concern. Freudenthal's chief competitor in the Democratic primary was Paul Hickey, son of Joseph Hickey, who was elected governor in 1958 and who was appointed to the Senate in January 1961 after Senator-elect Keith Thomson died in December; Hickey was defeated 58%–42% in 1962 by Milward Simpson, father of Senator Alan Simpson. In the August primary Freudenthal beat Hickey 54%–37%; the race was close in most of the historically Democratic counties in the southern part of the state, and Freudenthal ran well ahead in most others. The winner in the Republican primary was state House Speaker Eli Bebout, with 49% of the vote. Bebout and his brother owned a mining business in Riverton that repaired cave-ins in old mines; he also had other mining investments. He had been elected to the state House in 1986 as a Democrat, but switched parties in 1994.

The two nominees had similar positions on many issues—for the death penalty, against gun control, for economic diversification, against a state income tax. Freudenthal called for putting about $15 million of the interest from the Permanent Mineral Trust Fund each year into the state budget for economic development. He called for a more efficient audit of oil and gas companies; he noted that the legislature insisted on auditing schools, but not the companies whose taxes furnished one-third of the state budget. Bebout claimed there were "huge differences" between him and Freudenthal and pointed out that, as U.S. Attorney, Freudenthal was a Clinton nominee.

But his business interests caused him some problems. One of his primary opponents attacked him because a company on whose board he served had applied to build a temporary storage facility for spent nuclear rods. After the August primary the *Casper Star-Tribune* reported that SEC documents showed that he had not repaid a $468,000 loan made in 1983 by a company on whose board he served; Bebout presented the paper with a copy of the loan with "PAID" stamped on it. In June 2002 Bebout's 24-year-old son was arrested for drunk driving and the policemen said he said, "You don't want to do this. I'll have your job when my dad is elected governor." Polls showed many voters undecided, and on Election Day Freudenthal won 50%–48%. He won 59%–39% in the five counties in the southern end of the state—the traditionally Democratic Union Pacific counties. In the rest of the state he carried the counties including Casper, the state's second-largest city, his hometown of Hot Springs and Jackson Hole, and held Bebout's lead to 53%–45%.

Freudenthal entered office with state government in a good fiscal position. Increases in land values due to mining activity had produced surging increases in state revenue and the state budget was in surplus. "I would sure rather be in my position than that of most other governors," he said. Freudenthal sought more personnel to process coal-bed methane applications and more auditors for the Wyoming Natural Gas Pipeline Authority. He sought to direct money going to the advisory Wyoming Energy Commission for a study of pipeline needs instead to the Wyoming Natural Gas Pipeline Authority, which can act to increase pipeline capacity. He called for increasing the state contribution to employees' health insurance. Republicans had majorities in the legislature big enough to override vetoes; he said they convinced him to hold off on making the Tourism Division a department, but he vetoed a bill removing the sunset from the Wyoming Business Council and the effort to override failed. Freudenthal called for more Medicaid spending, expansion of community colleges and added capacity at state prisons.

Senior Senator

Craig Thomas (R)

Elected 1994, seat up 2006, 2d term; b. Feb. 17, 1933, Cody; home, Casper; U. of WY, B.S. 1954, LaSalle U.; Methodist; married (Susan).

Military Career: Marine Corps, 1955–59.

Elected Office: WY House of Reps., 1984–89; U.S. House of Reps., 1989–94.

Professional Career: V.P., WY Farm Bureau, 1959–66; Legis. staff, Amer. Farm Bureau, 1966–75; Gen. Mgr., WY Rural Electric Assn., 1975–89.

DC Office: 307 DSOB, 20515, 202-224-6441; Fax: 202-224-1724; Web site: thomas.senate.gov.

State Offices: Casper, 307-261-6413; Cheyenne, 307-772-2451; Riverton, 307-856-6642; Rock Springs, 307-362-5012; Sheridan, 307-672-6456.

Committees: *Energy & Natural Resources*: Energy; National Parks (Chmn.); Water & Power. *Environment & Public Works*: Clean Air, Climate Change & Nuclear Safety; Fisheries, Wildlife & Water. *Ethics (Select)*. *Finance*: Health Care; International Trade (Chmn.); Taxation & IRS Oversight. *Indian Affairs*.

Group Ratings

	ADA	ACLU	AFS	LCV	CON	ITIC	NTU	COC	ACU	NTLC	CHC
2002	10	50	0	0	55	75	73	90	100	100	—
2001	5	—	8	0	—	—	83	100	96	—	80

National Journal Ratings

	2001 LIB	—	2001 CONS		2002 LIB	—	2002 CONS
Economic	24%	—	75%		0%	—	94%
Social	0%	—	79%		0%	—	62%
Foreign	29%	—	71%		0%	—	76%

Key Votes of the 107th Congress

1. Approve Bush Tax Cuts	Y	5. Confirm Ashcroft as AG	Y	9. Bar Coop. with Intl. Court	Y
2. Expand Patients' Rights	N	6. Bar Gays in the Boy Scouts	Y	10. Trade Promotion Authority	Y
3. Campaign Finance Reform	N	7. $ for Hate Crime Prosecution	N	11. Authorize Force in Iraq	Y
4. Permit ANWR Development	Y	8. Overseas Military Abortions	*	12. Homeland Sec. Dept. Union	N

Election Results

2000 general	Craig Thomas (R)	157,622	(74%)	($762,833)
	Mel Logan (D)	47,087	(22%)	($4,187)
	Margaret Dawson (Lib)	8,950	(4%)	
2000 primary	Craig Thomas (R)	unopposed		
1994 general	Craig Thomas (R)	118,754	(59%)	($1,068,335)
	Mike Sullivan (D)	79,287	(39%)	($712,991)
	Other	3,669	(2%)	

Prior Winning Percentages: 1992 House (58%); 1990 House (55%); 1989 House (53%)

Craig Thomas grew up in Cody, where he knew his later Senate colleague Alan Simpson. He graduated from the University of Wyoming and served in the Marine Corps. For years he worked for the Wyoming Farm Bureau and the Wyoming Rural Electric Association, organizations with conservative political leanings that kept him in touch with hundreds of people active in their communities. In 1984 he was elected to the Wyoming House. In March 1989, when Congressman-at-Large Dick Cheney was appointed secretary of Defense, Thomas ran for his seat. He had serious competition from veteran Democrat John Vinich, who had just run a close race against Senator Malcolm Wallop. Vinich noted that national Republicans were backing Thomas and said voters shouldn't let outsiders make decisions for Wyoming. Thomas rallied and won with 53%.

In the House Thomas concentrated on Wyoming issues and was reelected with 55% in 1990 and 58% in 1992. When Wallop retired in 1994, Thomas was the obvious Republican candidate and had no primary opposition. In the general, he faced Governor Mike Sullivan, personally popular and with a conservative record, but handicapped by his association with Bill Clinton; Clinton personally asked him to run for the Senate. Thomas relentlessly attacked Sullivan as a "Friend of Bill" and ally of locally unpopular Interior Secretary Bruce Babbitt. Thomas won 59%–39%, losing only one southern tier county—by 6 votes.

Thomas is the chairman of the National Parks Subcommittee. In 1998, despite his disagreements with Babbitt, he steered to passage a national parks reauthorization bill which reformed the granting of park concessions, mandated that peer-reviewed scientific research should take primacy in park management, and set up a new process for studying potential park areas. He opposed Babbitt's higher grazing fees on federal lands and opposed the ban on snowmobiles in national parks, calling instead for stricter pollution and noise limitations. Since 1999 he has proposed changes in the Endangered Species Act, to require use of peer-reviewed scientific data open to the public; it would set minimum requirements for petitions rather than the current "postage stamp" petition, would give a more substantial role to states and local citizens and would make delisting species easier. "The critical listing decisions ought to be made with quality, peer-reviewed science and not by federal bureaucrats reacting only to the threat of environmental lawsuits." In 2000 he pushed to passage a law increasing the amount of federal land coal companies could lease. In 2002 he proposed using $4 million of Bureau of Land Management funds to purchase the Devil's Canyon Ranch in Big Horn County, an inholding that would give access to more public land. In October 2001 he got the Senate to pass a land swap, trading state-owned land in Grand Teton National Park for mineral-producing federal land of similar value elsewhere in Wyoming. But it was bottled up in the House after Thomas opposed House Resource Committee James Hansen's bill to allow the Mormon Church to buy from the government Martin's Cove, where nearly 150 Mormon pioneers died in a blizzard in 1856. Hansen eventually allowed the land swap before retiring in 2002, and it passed the House in September 2002. Thomas said he would work with Senator Orrin Hatch to get the BLM to cooperate with the Mormon Church on proper commemoration of Martin's Cove.

From his former seat on the East Asian and Pacific Affairs Subcommittee of Foreign Relations, Thomas strongly backed PNTR with China, noting that nearly half of Wyoming's products are sold abroad. Thomas played a key role in amending the electricity restructuring parts of the energy bill in March 2002. Over the opposition of Energy Chairman Jeff Bingaman, he got an amendment passed that would establish an industry-run organization, regulated by FERC, rather than run by FERC itself, to oversee power transmission access and conduct. And he got Bingaman to agree to a provision reducing FERC's authority to oversee mergers, regulate transmission construction and pass judgment on rates. Other Thomas causes include rural health: He wants higher Medicare reimbursement for rural areas, incentives to attract health care professionals and increased use of telemedicine. With Charles Grassley and two Democrats he moved to bar meatpackers from owning livestock; in December 2002 he and Conrad Burns and Pat Roberts called for $3.2 billion in drought aid. He takes an interest in special education; his wife teaches special needs children in Northern Virginia. Frustrated with air service to Wyoming, he has complained about United Airlines's near-monopoly in Denver.

Thomas had little trouble winning reelection in 2000. A backer of Lyndon LaRouche won the low-turnout Democratic primary, and Thomas, campaigning on rural health care, highway spending and expanding agricultural trade, won the general 74%–22%. In August 2001 he said he was thinking about running for governor, but in late September he said he would not do so. His seat comes up in 2006.

Junior Senator

Michael Enzi (R)

Elected 1996, seat up 2008, 2d term; b. Feb. 1, 1944, Bremerton, WA; home, Gillette; George Washington U., B.S. 1966, Denver U., M.B.A. 1968; Presbyterian; married (Diana).

Military Career: WY Natl. Guard, 1967–73.

Elected Office: Gillette Mayor, 1975–82; WY House of Reps., 1986–90; WY Senate, 1990–96.

Professional Career: Owner, NZ Shoes, 1969–95; Dir. & Chmn., First WY Bank of Gillette, 1978–88; Accounting Mgr. & Computer Programmer, Dunbar Well Service, 1985–97; Educ. Comm. of States, 1989–93; Dir., Black Hills Corp., 1992–96; Western Interstate Comm. for Higher Educ., 1995–96.

DC Office: 379-A RSOB, 20510, 202-224-3424; Fax: 202-228-0359; Web site: enzi.senate.gov.

State Offices: Casper, 307-261-6572; Cheyenne, 307-772-2477; Cody, 307-527-9444; Gillette, 307-682-6268; Jackson, 307-739-9507.

Committees: *Aging (Special). Banking, Housing & Urban Affairs*: Housing & Transportation; International Trade & Finance; Securities & Investment (Chmn.). *Budget. Foreign Relations*: International Economic Policy, Export & Trade Promotion; International Operations & Terrorism; Western Hemisphere, Peace Corps, Narcotics Affairs. *Health, Education, Labor & Pensions*: Children & Families; Employment, Safety & Training (Chmn.); Substance Abuse & Mental Health Services. *Small Business & Entrepreneurship.*

Group Ratings

	ADA	ACLU	AFS	LCV	CON	ITIC	NTU	COC	ACU	NTLC	CHC
2002	10	40	13	0	51	62	73	89	100	94	—
2001	10	—	9	0	—	—	83	100	92	—	80

National Journal Ratings

	2001 LIB	—	2001 CONS		2002 LIB	—	2002 CONS
Economic	17%	—	77%		0%	—	94%
Social	0%	—	79%		0%	—	62%
Foreign	7%	—	72%		24%	—	67%

Key Votes of the 107th Congress

1. Approve Bush Tax Cuts	Y	5. Confirm Ashcroft as AG	Y	9. Bar Coop. with Intl. Court	Y
2. Expand Patients' Rights	N	6. Bar Gays in the Boy Scouts	Y	10. Trade Promotion Authority	Y
3. Campaign Finance Reform	N	7. $ for Hate Crime Prosecution	N	11. Authorize Force in Iraq	Y
4. Permit ANWR Development	Y	8. Overseas Military Abortions	N	12. Homeland Sec. Dept. Union	N

Election Results

2002 general	Michael Enzi (R)	133,710	(73%)	($884,114)
	Joyce Corcoran (D)	49,570	(27%)	($8,467)
2002 primary	Michael Enzi (R)	78,612	(86%)	
	Crosby Allen (R)	12,931	(14%)	
1996 general	Michael Enzi (R)	114,116	(54%)	($953,572)
	Kathy Karpan (D)	89,103	(42%)	($814,258)
	Other	7,858	(4%)	

Wyoming's junior senator is Michael Enzi, elected in 1996. Enzi grew up in Thermopolis and Sheridan, the son of a shoe salesman, got degrees in accounting and marketing, moved to Gillette and became an oil company accountant and founded NZ Shoes. He served eight years as mayor of Gillette, the center of Wyoming's coal belt and its fastest-growing town. In 1986 he was elected to the state House and in 1990 to the state Senate.

After Senator Alan Simpson announced his retirement in December 1995, Enzi was one of nine Republicans and two Democrats to run for the seat. With support from a grass roots network of conservatives, Enzi finished first in a straw poll at the May 1996 Republican state convention; in second place was John Barrasso, an orthopedic surgeon from Casper who had appeared on statewide TV discussing health issues for 12 years. Their chief difference was on abortion; Barrasso supported and Enzi opposed abortion rights. Barrasso had more money, but Enzi won 32%–30%, with a big majority in his home area in northeast Wyoming and narrow margins in the Casper and Cheyenne areas.

In the Democratic primary Kathy Karpan, secretary of state from 1986 to 1994 and gubernatorial candidate in 1994, beat a man who called for construction of a 22,000-mile-high tower into space to promote world peace. A moderate, Karpan's opposition to gun control led the National Rifle Association to stay neutral; her opposition to federally funded abortions kept her off EMILY's List. But she had the liabilities of having supported the presidential candidacies of Bill Clinton in 1992 and Bruce Babbitt (unpopular in Wyoming as Clinton's Interior Secretary) in 1988. It was a game effort by Karpan, but Enzi led in polls all the way and won 54%–42%.

Enzi started off in the Senate by presiding for 100 hours in the chair by July and seeking permission to bring his laptop on the floor. The Rules Committee said no by a 6–1 vote; Enzi renewed his request in June 2002, noting that even the Senate is in a new century. In 2000 he denounced U.S. acquiescence to a United Nations agreement allowing countries to ban imports of genetically modified food. In 1999 he managed to get unanimous support in the Banking Committee for reauthorizing the lapsed Export Administration Act, adding higher fines and dropping useless restrictions. But this and other attempts failed, and in 2003 he was still working for reauthorization. He has opposed meatpacker ownership of livestock and in January 2003 he and Charles Grassley introduced a bill to ban ownership within seven days of slaughter; a similar provision was removed from the 2002 farm bill by the House. With colleague Craig Thomas, he got an amendment to help livestock producers to benefit from anti-dumping laws. Enzi has sought to get a veterans cemetery at Francis E. Warren Air Force Base in Cheyenne and to get Minuteman III missiles assigned there as its Peacekeeper missiles are dismantled; the base is Cheyenne's biggest employer and bases without missions are vulnerable in the base closing process.

In 2002, his sixth year in the Senate, Enzi was still little known in most of Washington, but he played a key role on a major piece of legislation. The issue was corporate accountability, and as the only accountant in the Senate Enzi could claim special expertise. In July 2000 he was one of 13 senators who signed a letter urging then-SEC Chairman Arthur Levitt to delay a decision on his proposal to bar accounting firms from doing auditing and consulting work for the same corporation. After the Enron bankruptcy in December 2001 raised questions about accounting, Enzi still urged caution and said he feared overregulation; he returned contributions from the

Arthur Andersen and Enron PACs and said he was confident they would be contributed to funds aiding employees. Banking Chairman Paul Sarbanes held extensive hearings on the issue and Enzi, the fifth ranking Republican, paid close attention. The bill Sarbanes introduced to the committee did not go so far as the Levitt proposal, but did go farther than the bill passed by the House in April 2002. It included an accounting board independent of the SEC with power to set rules, investigate, punish violations and conduct regular inspections of accounting firms' work. Enzi worked closely with lobbyists for the big accounting firms but kept the perspective of a Wyoming small business accountant. He decided that some bill needed to be passed and Sarbanes, not wanting to report a bill supported only by Democrats, consulted him. "I knew there would be people on his side of the aisle who would be looking to him," Sarbanes said later. On the evening of June 17, Enzi flew in from Wyoming and went to Sarbanes's office where they negotiated a compromise. Enzi got Sarbanes to agree that two of the four members of the board must be accountants, that the board could adopt rules favored by the accounting industry and that the board would not be financed by accountants. Disciplinary proceedings would be confidential. On June 18 in the office of Phil Gramm, the ranking Republican on the committee, Enzi told committee Republicans that he would vote for Sarbanes's bill. Others agreed: six of the 10 Republicans supported it. It still looked as if the bill would not come up until the fall. But on June 26 the WorldCom accounting scam was made public. The Senate wanted to act, and Sarbanes could go to the floor with bipartisan support. On July 15 the Senate approved the bill 97–0. House negotiators got minor concessions from the Senate side in the conference committee, and the bill was passed and signed before the August recess. Without Enzi the bill might never have been passed.

Enzi did not have serious opposition in 2002. He won the Republican primary 86%–14% and the general election 73%–27%.

Representative-At-Large

Barbara Cubin (R)

Elected 1994, 5th term; b. Nov. 30, 1946, Salinas, CA; home, Casper; Creighton U., B.S. 1969; Episcopalian; married (Frederick).

Elected Office: WY House of Reps., 1986–92; WY Senate, 1992–94.

Professional Career: Office Mgr., Dr. Frederick Cubin, 1975–94.

DC Office: 1114 LHOB, 20515, 202-225-2311; Fax: 202-225-3057; Web site: www.house.gov/cubin.

District Offices: Casper, 307-261-6595; Cheyenne, 307-772-2595; Rock Springs, 307-362-4095.

Committees: *Energy & Commerce* (13th of 31 R): Commerce, Trade & Consumer Protection; Health; Telecommunications & The Internet. *Resources* (10th of 28 R): Energy & Mineral Resources (Chmn.); National Parks, Recreation & Public Lands.

Group Ratings

	ADA	ACLU	AFS	LCV	CON	ITIC	NTU	COC	ACU	NTLC	CHC
2002	0	0	0	13	82	50	61	88	100	93	100
2001	5	—	0	0	—	—	77	93	100	—	—

National Journal Ratings

	2001 LIB	—	2001 CONS		2002 LIB	—	2002 CONS
Economic	0%	—	94%		13%	—	85%
Social	0%	—	81%		0%	—	75%
Foreign	0%	—	97%		0%	—	85%

Key Votes of the 107th Congress

1. Approve Bush Tax Cuts	*	5. Faith-Based Charities	Y	9. Trade Promotion Authority	Y
2. Limit Patients' Bill of Rights	Y	6. Bar Gays in the Boy Scouts	Y	10. Bar Funds for Intl. Court	Y
3. Campaign Finance Reform	*	7. Ban Partial-Birth Abortion	Y	11. Authorize Force in Iraq	Y
4. Ban ANWR Development	N	8. Arm Commercial Pilots	Y	12. Deny Home. Sec. Dept. Union	Y

Election Results

2002 general	Barbara Cubin (R)	110,229	(61%)	($635,271)
	Ron Akin (D)	65,961	(36%)	($19,154)
	Other	5,962	(3%)	
2002 primary	Barbara Cubin (R)	unopposed		
2000 general	Barbara Cubin (R)	141,848	(67%)	($640,700)
	Michael Allen Green (D)	60,638	(29%)	
	Lewis Stock (Lib)	6,411	(3%)	
	Other	3,415	(1%)	

Prior Winning Percentages: 1998 (58%); 1996 (55%); 1994 (53%)

Wyoming, the nation's least populous state, has elected one congressman-at-large since it was admitted to the Union in 1890. The current incumbent is Barbara Cubin, a Republican first elected in 1994. The great-great-granddaughter of one of Wyoming's original homesteaders, she grew up in Casper, where she worked as a teacher, social worker, chemist and realtor; for 19 years she managed her husband's medical practice. She was divorced after an early first marriage, worked as a single mother, was subjected to sexual harassment, but insists: "I am not a feminist. I am not gender sensitive." She notes that Susan B. Anthony and all the early advocates of women's rights were opposed to abortion. In 1986 she was elected to the state House and in 1992 to the state Senate; she was prime sponsor of a 1994 ballot measure authorizing life without parole sentences.

In 1994, when Congressman Craig Thomas ran for the Senate, Cubin was one of five Republicans and two Democrats to run for the House. She sharply attacked "the Clinton-Babbitt war on the West." In the Republican primary, she won with 39%. The Democratic nominee was Bob Schuster, a law partner of high-profile Wyoming trial lawyer Gerry Spence. He spent $2.4 million, most of it his own money, on what was the third-highest spending campaign in the country. Schuster's big issue was abortion; she called him a "a slick trial-lawyer Clinton Democrat." Cubin won 53%–41%.

In the House Cubin has a solidly conservative voting record and quickly became chairman of the Energy and Mineral Resources Subcommittee. She has opposed bills to fund federal purchases of private lands and wants to limit the federal government to no-net-gain. In 2000 a Cubin bill passed the House to stop the federal government from charging states for the administrative expenses on mineral leases; Wyoming's $7.5 million savings, she said, would go for education. She sponsored the successful bill to allow coal companies larger leases of federal lands. She decried the October 2000 decision to ban snowmobiling in national parks. She spearheaded the effort to obtain Medicare coverage for the breast cancer treatment Xeloda. In November 2000 she was elected Republican Conference Secretary, the number six position in the House leadership.

In April 2002 Cubin expressed interest in succeeding James Hansen, who had announced he was not running for reelection, as chairman of the Resources Committee. She was only the 12th Republican on the committee in seniority, but the most senior was James Saxton of New Jersey, who had voted against conservatives on many committee issues, and only one more senior committee Republican represented a district with large amounts of federally owned land. She suggested reviving the old Merchant Marine and Fisheries Committee, abolished by Republicans in 1995, and making Saxton its chairman. She admitted this would cause jurisdictional disputes, but asked, "Is there anything more aggravating than putting jurisdiction over good government?" She may have damaged her case in September 2002, when she sponsored a bill for $6 billion in drought relief; this was the position taken by Senate Democrats and opposed by the Bush administration and the House Republican leadership. The Republican Steering Committee interviewed

Cubin and other candidates for the chairmanship in January 2003, and awarded it to Richard Pombo of California, who had been 11th in seniority. Cubin was a good sport. "The western states have a friend in the chair in Chairman Pombo."

Cubin endured personal difficulties in 2001 and 2002. Her husband had multiple surgeries for nonmalignant tumors and autoimmune disease; he and their two sons rallied to appear with her when she announced for reelection in Cheyenne, Casper and Evanston in April 2002. She considered not running again, but her husband persuaded her to do so. Her Democratic opponent in 2002 criticized her for missing votes; she had missed the vote on Resources Chairman James Hansen's proposal to allow the Mormon Church to buy Martin's Cove in Wyoming, the site of the death of Mormon pioneers in a blizzard in 1856, a proposal opposed by the Wyoming delegation, because she had been caught in traffic returning from a doctor's appointment. She was reelected 61%–36% and said afterwards, "It's actually the first time I've felt pleasure in defeating someone. My husband's very life was hanging in the balance, and they tried to capitalize on that. It was pretty low." She did not seek reelection to the Conference Secretary position. In February 2003 she was felled by a viral infection complicated by meningitis. In April 2003 Cubin drew sharp criticism for a disputed statement during a debate over restricting lawsuits against gun manufacturers. Cubin said, "My sons are 25 and 30. They are blond-haired and blue-eyed. One amendment today said we could not sell guns to anybody under drug treatment. So does that mean if you go into a black community, you cannot sell a gun to any black person, or does that mean because my—" at which point, Mel Watt demanded that her statement be "taken down" (a motion to limit her debate privileges for the day and strike her words from the Congressional Record) because he said it promoted stereotypes about drug abuse and black neighborhoods. By a largely party-line vote, the House refused to condemn her statement. Cubin later said Watt interrupted her before she could finish her point. "I don't believe in stereotyping anyone, anytime, ever, for anything," she said. "That's what I believe, and I believe that from the bottom of my heart."

PUERTO RICO, VIRGIN ISLANDS,
★ GUAM, AMERICAN SAMOA ★

Four American insular territories—Puerto Rico, Virgin Islands, Guam, American Samoa—are represented in Congress by elected delegates who, like the District of Columbia's delegate, have floor privileges and votes on committees but not votes on the floor (though House Democrats let them vote in committee of the whole proceedings in the 103d Congress). Each territory's status—its relationship to the United States—is different, governed by a separate law, and status is often the pivot around which territorial politics turn.

PUERTO RICO

Puerto Rico has a unique history. For four centuries, from Columbus's landing here in 1493 until the Spanish-American War of 1898, Puerto Rico was a Spanish colony, and the port of San Juan was the gathering place for its annual convoy of gold and silver from the Americas to Spain. Today, with 4 million people, it is the largest American territory—about the same population as South Carolina; also, perhaps 3 million people of Puerto Rican descent live on the mainland. Fifty years ago, it was "the poorhouse of the Caribbean," heavily populated, devoted almost entirely to sugar and coffee cultivation. Now it has a recognizably First World economy, with per capita incomes about half of those of the least affluent American states and among the highest in Latin America.

Puerto Rico has elected a resident commissioner to Congress since 1900 (the only member of Congress with a four-year term) and its residents have been American citizens since 1917, but it didn't elect its own governor until 1948. In the 1940s, 1950s and early 1960s, Puerto Rico was transformed by Governor Luis Munoz Marin and his Popular Democratic Party. Munoz initiated "Operation Bootstrap" (called "Operation Hands to Work" by Puerto Ricans) to lure businesses to Puerto Rico with promises of low-wage labor and government-built factories and tax exemptions. Munoz also developed Puerto Rico's commonwealth form of government—better understood in Spanish, Estado Libre Asociado (ELA): Free Associated State—approved by plebiscite in 1952. Under ELA, Puerto Rico is part of the United States for purposes of international trade, foreign policy and war, but has its own separate laws, taxes and representative government; it is not subject to federal income taxes and is not eligible for federal benefits (though some have been approved). Some 200,000 Puerto Ricans have served in the U.S. military; 2,000 died and four were awarded the Congressional Medal of Honor. Puerto Rico has also developed its own political parties: Munoz's Popular Democrats (the Spanish acronym is PPD), the New Progressives (PNP) who favor statehood, and two Independence parties.

The commonwealth solution, by its own terms, was open to amendment; ever since Munoz's voluntary retirement in 1964, the central issue in Puerto Rico's politics has been status: Should this island continue or modify ELA, should it seek statehood, or should it seek independence? For many years there was gradual movement toward statehood. In the July 1967 referendum, conducted when the Popular Democrats were in power, Puerto Ricans voted for ELA over statehood by 60%–39%; in the November 1993 referendum, conducted with PNP Governor Pedro Rossello in office, the vote was 48% for ELA, 46% for statehood. In March 1998 the U.S. House voted 209–208 for a referendum setting terms for statehood; this was a project of Speaker Newt Gingrich, who hoped to attract Hispanic votes, and of Resources Committee Chairman Don Young, who saw in statehood backers' demands echoes of Alaska's fight for statehood. But the bill went nowhere in the Senate. Rossello ordered a referendum on his terms (which are unlikely ever to be accepted in Congress) in December 1998; 47% voted for statehood and 50% for "none of the above," the option favored by the Popular Democrats. Independence has negligible support—4% in 1993, 3% in 1998—primarily from university students; nor are there many pro-independence abstentions, for voter turnout in the enthusiastic politics of Puerto Rico is the highest under the American flag, higher than in even the most affluent, long-settled suburbs of the mainland. Now, with the election of Popular Democrat Governor Sila Calderon in 2000, the move toward statehood has been halted. For years younger and more affluent voters have tilted toward statehood, but as they have aged and the island has grown more prosperous, support for statehood has stopped growing. In 2002 Calderon established a Consensus and Unity Commission, to agree on choices that might be put before voters and Congress, but the PNP refused to participate; at the celebration of the 50th anniversary of ELA, PNP 2000 candidate Carlos Pesquera rushed into the hall and installed an American flag next to the Puerto Rican flag.

As Puerto Ricans were debating status in the 1990s, the island's economy was changing. In 1996 Congress voted to phase out over 10 years Section 936, the provision that shelters earnings of some Puerto Rico manufacturers from federal taxes and allows their products into the U.S. duty-free. Pharmaceutical companies in particular have set up highly visible plants in Puerto Rico—half of U.S. prescription drugs are manufactured in Puerto Rico—and ELA supporters claimed that the island's economy depended on the tax exemptions. Since then Puerto Rico has lost 27,000 manufacturing jobs, but its overall economy has kept pace with the mainland; unemployment has hovered around 11%, but it was 22% in the 1980s. Puerto Rico has long since lost low-wage garment jobs to lower-wage countries in the Caribbean and Latin America, and is developing new jobs in services, tourism, trading and exports. Calderon and Resident Commissioner (non-voting delegate in the U.S. House) Anibal Acevedo-Vila are pushing for an amendment of Section 956, to allowed foreign registered subsidiaries of U.S. companies to repatriate their profits to the mainland at a lower tax rate; they argued that this would produce more jobs for Puerto Rico and more profits for the mainland.

Calderon has also changed the thrust of Puerto Rico's internal policies from those of Pedro Rossello, the PNP governor from 1992 to 2000. Rossello sold the government-owned Navieras shipping line and telephone company, privatized hospitals and the Aqueduct and Sewer Authority's facilities. He reduced the corporate tax rate, eliminated taxes on distributed dividends and started massive public works projects. Puerto Rico provides health insurance to the poor via *la tarjetita* (the little card) and Rossello instituted school vouchers and five minutes of daily reflection in schools. Calderon has halted privatizations. In June 2001 she announced a plan to create 100,000 new jobs with $379 million in agricultural initiatives and job training programs. In August

2002 she announced that the government would invest $1 billion in the 700 poorest communities on the island, in infrastructure—water, electricity, roads—and education and health care programs. Calderon and Acevedo-Vila are also seeking from Congress power to enter into trade agreements with neighboring countries and exemption from federal maritime laws.

A raging issue in Puerto Rico is corruption. In 1999 federal prosecutors started investigating what appears to have been pervasive corruption in Rossello's administration. In August 2001 29 police officers were indicted for protecting cocaine shipments and in January 2002 another 23 were charged with protecting drug traffickers. The PNP House speaker was indicted in October 2001 for extortion in a hospital sale; he was jailed in August 2002 and charged with the rape of a 17-year-old high schooler. In January 2002 the former education secretary was charged with extorting $4.3 million from contractors and channeling $1.5 million to the PNP and keeping $300,000 in cash at home; a dozen others were indicted and the former education secretary pleaded guilty. In August 2002 Rossello's former executive aide was convicted of taking $125,000 in payoffs from contractors. On taking office in January 2001 Calderon appointed a Blue Riband Commission to review all transactions of the Rossello administration, particularly the privatization of the telephone company. Corruption of this sort had been unknown in previous administrations of both parties in Puerto Rico, and if Calderon does not succeed in stamping it out the island will lose what has been an asset of great value.

The other raging issue in Puerto Rico has been Vieques. The Vieques bombing range was established in 1941, and had long sparked protests from those who claimed the bombing jeopardized islanders' safety and polluted the environment; the Navy claimed that it was their most important training ground, the best place in the world for combined sea-land-air training exercises. For a year protesters streamed onto the range and prevented exercises, and many were arrested. Rossello and politicians of all parties demanded that the range be shut down. In January 2000 Rossello reached agreement with the Clinton White House. The Navy would set a date for a referendum in which voters in Vieques (population 9,300) would decide whether to end the bombing in May 2003 or allow it to continue, with $40 million of federal aid for the town; in the meantime, exercises would continue 90 days a year. In December 2000 the Navy announced the Vieques referendum would be held in November 2001. Bombing exercises using inert ordnance began again in April 2001 and were met with continued demonstrations; among those detained were mainland politicians and protest figures.

Sila Calderon campaigned for an immediate end to the bombing on Vieques and made that and corruption her two top issues. Some feared that George W. Bush would not follow Clinton's policy. But in June 2001 Bush announced that the Navy would halt all military exercises on Vieques by May 2003 and provide $40 million in local aid. Calderon engineered an advisory referendum in Vieques in July 2001; 68% voted for immediate closure, 30% for indefinite continuation of the bombing and 2% for closure in May 2003. In October 2001 a Puerto Rico judge ruled the November referendum was unauthorized by law; a lawsuit brought by Puerto Rico to stop the bombing as contrary to the Federal Noise Control Act was dismissed in December 2001. September 11 obviously made military priorities seem more important, and in the December 2001 defense bill Congress barred the Navy from moving until an "equivalent or superior" site was found. In January 2002 at a bill signing, Bush assured Calderon that he would keep his word. In June 2002 the Navy turned over the western part of the island to the Interior Department. In January and February 2003 the Navy held its last military exercises there, and on May 1 the base was closed.

The Vieques controversy raised the possibility that the ties between the United States and Puerto Rico would be frayed or ruptured. With the closure of the base that threat seems greatly diminished. The status issue seems off the table, for the time being: the PNP's corruption problems seem likely to weaken the cause of statehood, and consensus on the terms of a referendum seems unlikely at best. Independence continues to be favored by only a splinter of the electorate. Instead, new ties seem to be developing between the island and the mainland, and between the island, the mainland and Latin America. In 2002 Calderon led a voter registration drive among Puerto Ricans in the mainland, from the 12 Puerto Rico Federal Affairs Administration offices in mainland cities. Thirty years ago, almost all Puerto Ricans on the mainland were in New York City. Now there are large numbers in Boston, Hartford, northern New Jersey, Cleveland, Chicago, Houston, Orlando and Broward County, Florida, and the drive registered over 75,000 voters.

Previous Puerto Rico politicians identified with one of the two mainland parties: the PPD all with Democrats, some PNP with Republicans and some with Democrats. Calderon has said she identifies with neither party and cooperated with governors of both parties—Republicans George Pataki and Jeb Bush, Democrats Jim McGreevey and Rod Blagojevich. Calderon has also set a new course in regional affairs. Thirty years ago, as Puerto Rico had developed a First World economy, its Caribbean and Central American neighbors were still in the Third World, dependent on export of agricultural commodities, with tiny middle classes and ruling elites. Today they are moving ahead, with low-wage factory jobs that Puerto Rico, with its higher wages, can no longer compete for, and growing middle classes and electoral democracies. Calderon has cultivated close ties with regional leaders. Enactment of the Free Trade of the Americas treaty or of a Caribbean Free Trade Agreement could lead to greater trade and to a role for Puerto Rico as a helpful elder sister, with money to invest and expertise gained from of its own economic development.

And wisdom gained from its own political development. Puerto Rico's ELA status is a compromise, often an uneasy one. But Munoz Marin's achievement, creating enthusiasm for a compromise, is an astonishing political feat. Amid the noisy clash of the partisans of ELA and statehood and independence, the Puerto Rican people have developed a polity that is tolerant of divergence of opinion, determined to uphold personal liberty, intolerant of corruption and capable of fostering sustained economic growth. That is an achievement worthy of attention in Latin America and of respect on the mainland.

Presidential politics One of the complaints of Puerto Rico's New Progressives is that it cannot vote for president, and in 2000 Governor Pedro Rossello tried to remedy that. On August 29, 2000, a federal judge in Puerto Rico ruled that Puerto Rican voters have a right to vote for president emanating from their U.S. citizenship and ordered that a vote be held and that Congress count eight electoral votes for Puerto Ricans' choice (eight was the number of electoral votes Puerto Rico would have had under the 1990 Census if it were a state). This ruling went against precedent and the language of the Constitution, which gives votes only to states that have been admitted to the Union and, in an amendment, to the District of Columbia. But Rossello and the legislature were happy to pass a law putting the presidential election on the November 7 ballot. On October 13, the First Circuit Court of Appeals predictably reversed the rules and ordered the presidential contest off the ballot. So no one knows for sure which candidate Puerto Rico would have preferred, George W. Bush (who nominally favored statehood, as Republican platforms long have) or Al Gore (who favored "self-determination" for Puerto Rico), although almost everyone assumes Gore would have won.

Puerto Rico does send delegates to the two mainland parties' national conventions. The Republicans, long identified with the New Progressives, though its two leading figures in 2000 identify with Democrats, held a primary in February in which Bush beat John McCain 93%–6%. That gave him 14 convention delegates, more than were elected by Vermont or Delaware and the same as Maine, Rhode Island and Hawaii. Al Gore won the March Democratic caucus, giving him 59 delegates, more than 24 states. Since Puerto Rico's Democratic delegates in the past have voted as a bloc, while Democratic rules require other states' delegates to be split proportionately, in a divided Democratic convention (if there ever is one again) Puerto Rico actually has more leverage than all but a half dozen or so states, as it did in the bitterly split convention in 1980.

Governor Sila Maria Calderon, the first woman governor of Puerto Rico, was elected in 2000. She grew up in San Juan, graduated from Manhattanville College in New York and became a vice president of Citibank in Puerto Rico. In 1985 she became chief of staff to PPD Governor Rafael Hernandez Colon. In 1996 she was elected mayor of San Juan—a notable upset victory, since San Juan ordinarily votes PNP. As mayor she was one of the most visible public figures in Puerto Rico and, as the most prominent PPD officeholder, the party's logical candidate for governor in 2000. When incumbent Pedro Rossello announced his retirement in June 1999, Calderon led him in a public poll by a solid 47%–30% margin.

Calderon, a supporter of ELA over statehood, did not campaign much on status. Instead, she emphasized her support of *paz para Vieques* and criticism of corruption in the Rossello administration. This was enough to change the 1990s balance of opinion in Puerto Rico and give her a

49%–46% victory over former Transportation Secretary Carlos Pesquera. The PPD won majorities in the legislature and won most mayoralties on the island, though the PNP won in San Juan, Bayamon and Guaynabo, the first, second and seventh-largest *municipios*.

In May 2003, Calderon unexpectedly announced she would not seek reelection in 2004; she immediately backed lawyer Jose Alfredo Hernandez Mayoral, son of the former three-term Governor Rafael Hernandez Colon, for the PPD nomination.

Resident Commissioner

Anibal Acevedo-Vila (D)

Elected 2000, 1st term; b. Feb. 13, 1962, Hato Rey; home, Guaynabo; U. of PR, B.A. 1982, J.D. 1985; Harvard U., J.D. 1987; Catholic; married (Luisa Gandara).

Elected Office: PR House of Reps., 1991–00.

Professional Career: Clerk, PR Supreme Court, 1985–86; clerk, 1st Circuit Court of Appeals, Boston, 1987–88; Aide, Gov. Rafael Hernandez Colon, 1989–92; Pres., Popular Democratic Party, 1997–00.

DC Office: 126 CHOB, 20515, 202-225-2615; Fax: 202-225-2154; Web site: www.house.gov/acevedo-vila.

District Offices: Mayaguez, 787-831-3400; Ponce, 787-841-3209; San Juan, 787-723-6333.

Committees: *Agriculture* (11th of 24 D): Conservation, Credit, Rural Development & Research; Department Operations, Oversight, Nutrition & Forestry. *Resources* (14th of 24 D): Forests & Forest Health; National Parks, Recreation & Public Lands. *Small Business* (10th of 17 D): Regulatory Reform & Oversight; Tax, Finance & Exports.

Anibal Acevedo-Vila, former president of the PPD, was elected to a four-year term as Puerto Rico's Resident Commissioner—actually, non-voting delegate in Congress—in 2000. Acevedo-Vila was born in San Juan and lives in Guaynabo. He graduated from the University of Puerto Rico and Harvard Law School and was a law clerk in the First Circuit Court of Appeals in Boston, which has jurisdiction over Puerto Rico. He returned to Puerto Rico to work on the staff of Governor Rafael Hernandez Colon from 1989 to 1992. In 1992 he was elected to the Puerto Rico House. Like all Puerto Rican politicians, he opposed the continuation of the Navy bombing range in Vieques and said he was "not satisfied" by the January 2000 agreement between Governor Pedro Rossello and Bill Clinton. He said Vieques would be his first priority, and said that he would try to create tax breaks for American companies in Puerto Rico—although the main tax break, Section 936, is being phased out.

His opponent in the 2000 election was incumbent Carlos Romero Barcelo, who was elected mayor of San Juan in 1968 and 1972, governor in 1976 and 1980 and resident commissioner in 1992 and 1996. Romero was known for his pugnacious temperament and strong advocacy of statehood, and unlike many other New Progressives always identified with the mainland Democratic Party. But Puerto Ricans tend to vote on straight party lines, and as the Popular Democrats' Sila Maria Calderon was winning the governorship 49%–46%, Acevedo-Vila was elected by a 50%–45% margin, with 5% for the Independence Party candidate. He identifies with the Democratic party.

VIRGIN ISLANDS

The United States's other insular territory in the Caribbean is the Virgin Islands, a very different sort of place from Puerto Rico. It is much smaller, with a resident population of only 120,000, mainly on the three islands of St. Thomas, St. John and St. Croix. They were settled not by Spaniards but by Dutch and Danes, and had a polyglot colonial society with one of the oldest Jewish communities in the Western Hemisphere; their most famous son is Alexander Hamilton, who grew up in St. Croix. Puerto Rico is multiracial and not self-conscious about it, but most

Virgin Islanders are black, and resent the clear divide between the races. While Puerto Rico has attracted all kinds of light industry, the Virgin Islands lives off tourism and refineries (the Hovensa refinery on St. Croix is the largest refinery in the Western Hemisphere; it was built by Amerada Hess in the 1960s and is now half-owned by the Venezuela government oil company). These are industries that have produced high incomes for a few employees but have not provided the basis for a steady economy. One-third of the work force is on government payrolls, and the Virgin Islands government in late 2001 had a crushing debt of more than $1 billion; in July 2001 it agreed to pay $22.4 million in overdue bills to the state-owned water and power authority to avoid loss of service. The regional director of the Inspector General's office said in July 2001 that the Virgin Islands government had ignored the recommendations of 36 federal audits since 1991, failing to resolve 125 recommendations and failing to implement 81 others. One agency had a 70% delinquency rate on its loans, prompting state Senator Donald Cole to say, "It will only be a matter of time before the feds force the local government into action, unless we want a federal control board to come down and take over."

One reason for these problems is that the Virgin Islands, blessed with beauty, has been cursed by bad weather for a decade. Hurricane Hugo in September 1989 destroyed 90% of the buildings on St. Croix, and tourism has never recovered; Hurricanes Luis and Marilyn in September 1995 caused terrible damage on St. Thomas; Hurricane Georges in September 1998 was not as bad, but still slowed down recovery; Hurricane Lenny in November 1999 caused $31.5 million of damage to St. Croix. St. Thomas has one-half the islands' population and four-fifths of its hotel rooms, but some 75% of tourists arrive on cruise ships and spend only about one-quarter as much time on shore as those who arrive by plane. St. John, lightly inhabited, remains mostly a natural paradise, with a few very high-end hotels. St. Croix is trying to stimulate tourism by building gambling casinos, the first of which opened in December 2000. But the islands' interests diverge: St. Thomas is against gambling, while Cruzans (the residents of St. Croix) resent the amount the V.I. government spends on promoting tourism.

The Virgin Islands has several political parties, but Democrats have won recent elections. They are not necessarily in line with their national party. Governor Charles Turnbull and Delegate Donna Christian-Christiansen opposed Bill Clinton's designation in January 2001 of 12,708 undersea acres as the U.S. Virgin Islands Coral Reef National Monument. They said it would hurt local fishermen and that Gerald Ford had turned the acreage over to the Virgin Islands government in 1974. The government has taken some actions to spur the local economy. In July 2001 it approved Internet gambling, to provide a legal base for the enterprise. In March 2002 it agreed to require more thorough tax reporting to get off the Organization for Economic Cooperation and Development's list of tax havens. But problems still abound. In May 2002 the Virgin Islands's high schools lost U.S. accreditation; Turnbull immediately fired Education Commissioner Ruby Simmonds.

Governor Charles Turnbull was born in St. Thomas, the son of immigrants from the British Virgin Islands. He earned undergraduate and graduate degrees from Hampton University and a doctorate in education from the University of Minnesota, then returned home to teach. As Virgin Islands's Education commissioner, Turnbull upgraded the curriculum and built enough new schools to eliminate double school-day sessions. Promising a "grander vision" than offered by Independent Governor Roy Schneider—who focused on downsizing government, reducing spending and fighting drugs—Turnbull in 1998 defeated the one-term incumbent 59%–41%.

In April 1999, Turnbull said the government would be unable to pay its 10,000 workers because of $1 billion in debt from the previous administration. Turnbull tried to tackle this huge debt by cutting the government payroll through attrition and negotiated a memorandum of understanding with Interior Secretary Bruce Babbitt, promising to cut the budget, change the labor relations law and scrap five government holidays. But fiscal problems continued, and it appears that there has been no proper accounting of Virgin Islands government for many years. Nonetheless Turnbull was reelected on November 5, 2002, with 50.4% of the vote, just enough to avoid a runoff. In second place with 24% was Independent John deJongh, president of the Chamber of Commerce. "The people of the Virgin Islands have spoken," Turnbull said. "They have seen a turnaround in the economy and we are moving to reduce crime and improving education." He went on, "You know where we were. We were on the brink of bankruptcy."

Delegate

Donna Christian-Christensen (D)

Elected 1996, 4th term; b. Sept. 19, 1945, Teaneck, NJ; home, St. Croix; St. Mary's Col., B.S. 1966, George Washington U., M.D. 1970; Moravian; married (Christian).

Professional Career: Practicing physician, 1975–97; Territorial Asst., Commissioner of Health, 1988–94; Acting Commissioner of Health, 1994–95.

DC Office: 1510 LHOB, 20515, 202-225-1790; Fax: 202-225-5517; Web site: www.house.gov/christian-christensen.

District Offices: St. Croix, 340-778-5900; St. Thomas, 340-774-4408.

Committees: *Resources* (8th of 24 D): National Parks, Recreation & Public Lands (RMM). *Select Committee on Homeland Security* (18th of 23 D): Cybersecurity, Science and Research & Development; Emergency Preparedness & Response. *Small Business* (6th of 17 D): Regulatory Reform & Oversight; Rural Enterprises, Agriculture and Technology.

The delegate from the Virgin Islands is Donna Christian-Christensen, first elected in 1996, when she beat Victor Frazer, a Republican who ran as an independent and was the upset winner in 1994. Christensen (as her name is given in her press releases) is from an old St. Croix family; her father was Virgin Islands Chief District Court Judge Almeric Christian. She graduated from St. Mary's College and George Washington Medical School; she practiced medicine for more than 20 years in the Virgin Islands, in a family practice and in several public positions. She was elected a Democratic National committeewoman in 1984 and ran one losing race for delegate in 1994. In 1996 she attacked Frazer, who after some hesitation caucused with the Democrats, for foreign travel (11 trips to four continents) and for inaction in opposing the welfare bill. Christensen led Frazer 38%–34% on November 5; in the runoff two weeks later she won 52%–48%. It was a regional race: Christensen won 69% on St. Croix, Frazer 64% on St. Thomas and St. John.

In the House, Christensen has forged alliances with the Congressional Black Caucus and, when it was in office, the Clinton administration to achieve her goals; she works on health issues for the Black Caucus. She objected to government health guidelines recommending milk, since many blacks, Asians and Hispanics are lactose intolerant. She fought for the Virgin Islands to get the total rum tax of $13.50 per gallon, instead of the current $10.50; but the clout behind this proposal comes from Puerto Rico's friends in the New York delegation. She got the support of Resources Chairman Don Young, who can remember when his Alaska was a territory and subject to the whims of Congress, to a proposal to allow the Virgin Islands to write a constitution and to reduce the V.I. Senate from 15 to nine members. She opposed Bill Clinton's designation in January 2001 of 12,708 undersea acres as the U.S. Virgin Islands Coral Reef National Monument, arguing that it would hurt local fishermen. She is ranking minority member of the Parks Subcommittee and got a hearing on the issue in the Virgin Islands in July 2002. She was reelected easily in 2002.

GUAM

Some 3,500 miles west of Hawaii, 19 hours of flying time from Washington, D.C., is Guam, where America's day begins. Guam lies west of the International Date Line, and it is in the early hours of Tuesday there when the rest of us are just trying to get through Monday afternoon; the Interior Department came to Guam to see whether there were Y2K problems, as the clock struck midnight, January 1, 2000, while it was 9 a.m., December 31, in Washington. Geographically in the center of the Mariana Islands, Guam is legally separate: The Northern Marianas were administered by the U.S. as a United Nations trust territory until they became a commonwealth in 1978. Guam was ruled by Navy captains from 1898 to 1950, except for 32 months of Japanese occupation during World War II; in 1950 the Guam Organic Act made Guamanians U.S. citizens and allowed them to elect a local government, but Congress still retained final power over the territory; it started electing a non-voting delegate to Congress in 1972.

Guam is 36 miles long by four to nine miles wide, with 154,000 people; nearly half are Chamorro (descendants of the original islanders), 25% Filipino, 13% other Asian and 10% Caucasian; more than 75% of Guamanians are Catholic. (In 1990 Guam passed a law barring almost all abortions; it was overturned by a federal court in 1992, as clearly contrary to *Roe v. Wade*, and the Supreme Court dodged a direct challenge to that decision by refusing to hear the case.) There are about 4,000 U.S. military personnel here, on bases which occupy one-third of the island. Guam is tropical, but not an easy environment: in August 1993 it lived through an earthquake rated at 8.2 on the Richter scale, comparable to San Francisco in 1906; in December 1997 Typhoon Paka raged through with winds of 236 miles per hour. In December 2002 Supertyphoon Pongsona, with winds up to 184 miles per hour, cut off all electric power and caused hundreds of millions in damage.

Economically, Guam depends heavily on U.S. military bases; 60% of income comes from the federal government and it makes for a pretty good living: Guam's gross domestic product per capita is the second highest in the Pacific, after Hawaii's. In the early 1990s there was a tourism boom, and the number of hotel rooms tripled. But the slump in the Japanese economy has hit Guam too: tourism was down from 1.3 million in 2000 to 1 million in 2002. Tourism seemed like the wave of the future when the military was being drawn down; Agana Naval Air Station was closed in 1995. But September 11 changed that. Popular protests in South Korea and Japan against the U.S. military presence there, the threats of the North Korean government and the need to supply operations in South Asia have made Guam much more important militarily. In fall 2002 two Los Angeles class submarines were stationed in Guam, with another to follow in 2003. In February 2003 12 B-52s and 12 B-1s were stationed on Guam. An Air Force general speculated that F-22s, 767 tankers and C-17s may be stationed there. The Navy and Air Force are in the process of investing $500 million in Guam facilities. Guam officials were delighted. Governor Felix Camacho said, "While many communities may shun having the military in their back yards, we on Guam welcome them, embrace them." Delegate Madeleine Bordallo said, "We have learned that we may not be able to ride on tourism alone, we need something else. We are very anxiously looking forward to an increase of military activity in Guam." The 2002 defense authorization bill contained provisions to accommodate Guam—cooperation with local authorities on water and sewers, access to Jinaspen Beach for Jess Pangelinan's ecotourism business, exemption from the Migratory Bird Act for a local airfield. The local economy has been reviving somewhat: unemployment fell from 15% in 2000 to 11% in 2002. But local GovGuam (the name for Guam's government) in 2002 cut welfare payments 60% and terminated medical assistance and in 2003 laid off hundreds of government employees.

For much of the 1990s Guam sought a change in status, to give the Guam government control over immigration. Chamorros said they want to block others from coming in, establishing citizenship and making them a minority; another motive was to bring in guest workers as the surrounding Commonwealth of the Northern Mariana Islands has done, with local enforcement of labor laws. The first Bush administration rejected the bill as inconsistent with the constitutional provision giving Congress full powers over territories. For a time the Clinton administration seemed sympathetic and inclined to agree to "mutual consent." But the election of the Republican Congress abruptly changed the provision's prospects. Guamanians attempted to counter that in 1996 by showering the Democratic National Committee with $892,000 in contributions, the most per capita anywhere under the American flag. But in October 1997 a Clinton official said he saw no constitutional way to do what Guam wanted. There has been no revival of this issue since George W. Bush became president. Instead Guam Delegate Robert Underwood sought increased Compact-Impact Aid and a War Reparations Commission. The latter, a goal of Guam delegates since 1972, was finally signed in December 2002, as Underwood was leaving office (he ran for governor and lost). It sets up a five-member commission to decide whether Guamanians who were victims of torture, forced labor, internment and deprivation during the Japanese occupation should get more than the $5,000 that was paid them under the 1940s Guam Meritorious Claims Act.

Guam votes for Democrats more often than Republicans, but politics here is a family matter.

Governor Felix Camacho's father was also governor; his lieutenant governor, Kaleo Moylan, is the son of the elder Camacho's lieutenant governor. Robert Underwood ascribed his first victory as delegate to his large number of cousins; he was weakened in the 2002 governor race by primary competition from Geri Gutierrez, wife of term-limited Governor Carl Gutierrez. The 2002 Republican candidate for delegate, Joseph Ada, was elected governor in 1986 and 1990. His opponent in the latter race was Madeleine Bordallo, who beat him for delegate and whose husband Ricardo Bordallo was elected governor in 1974 and 1982. Bordallo won the 2002 Democratic nomination by beating Judith Won Pat, daughter of Antonio Borja Won Pat, Guam's first elected Delegate who served from 1972 to 1984 and after whom Guam's civilian airport is named.

Guam of course does not cast any electoral votes for president, but has a part in presidential politics. It elects delegates to party national conventions—4 for Bush and 6 for Gore in 2000. In November Guam has conducted a straw poll for president, and has voted for the winner every time since 1984; in 2000 George W. Bush won 52%–47%.

Governor Felix Camacho, a Republican, was elected governor of Guam in 2002. Camacho grew up in Guam and attended Catholic schools; his father Carlos Camacho was appointed governor in 1969 and elected to a single term in 1970. He graduated from Marquette University in Milwaukee and returned to Guam and worked for Pacific Financial Corporation and IBM. When he was 31, IBM proposed to transfer him off island, and he paused to set out his short-term and long-term goals; one of the long-term goals was "governor of Guam." Republican Joseph Ada was governor, and in March 1988 he appointed Camacho deputy chief of the Public Utility Agency, and in November 1988 he was appointed executive director of the Civil Service Commission. In 1992 he was elected to the Guam Legislature, where he was assistant majority leader.

In 2002 Carl Gutierrez was ineligible to run for a third term, and Camacho ran; he defeated Tony Unpingco, the Speaker of the Guam Legislature, 54%–46%. In the Democratic primary, between Delegate Robert Underwood and Geri Gutierrez, Carl Gutierrez's wife, both Democrats spent more than $400,000 on this race, which got somewhat angry; Underwood won 64%–36%. Afterward there was talk that some Gutierrez backers were supporting Camacho in return for promises of jobs. The candidates debated in both English and Chamorro; Underwood spoke in Chamorro the whole time, while Camacho had to break into English. They disagreed on issues like casinos, waste treatment and return of military land. Underwood was supported by the teachers' union and the AFL-CIO, Camacho by the Committee to Get Guam Working. Camacho won 55%–45%, carrying some normally Democratic areas, but Democrats won a 9–6 majority in the Legislature.

Camacho announced that he was yanking all government-issued credit cards; officials at the Airport Authority had racked up $1 million in charges. He assured Guamanians that, with his civil service experience, he would hire on merit. He said that he would work on big construction projects at Antonio Won Pat Airport, strengthen the water and waste water system and try to encourage tourism from Japan and South Korea.

Delegate

Madeleine Bordallo (D)

Elected 2002, 1st term; b. May 31, 1933, Graceville, MN; home, Tamuning; St. Mary's Col. 1952, St. Katherine's Col., A.A. 1953; Catholic; widowed.

Elected Office: GU Senate, 1981–82, 1986–94; GU LT. Gov., 1994–02.

DC Office: 427 CHOB, 20515, 202-225-1188; Fax: 202-226-0341; Web site: www.house.gov/bordallo.

District Office: Hagatna, 671-477-4272.

Committees: *Armed Services* (26th of 29 D): Readiness; Total Force. *Resources* (18th of 24 D): Fisheries Conservation, Wildlife & Oceans; National Parks, Recreation & Public Lands. *Small Business* (12th of 17 D): Rural Enterprises, Agriculture and Technology; Workforce, Empowerment & Government Programs.

Madeleine Bordallo, a Democrat, was elected delegate from Guam in 2002. She grew up in Minnesota and, from age 14, on Guam. She graduated from St. Katherine's College in St. Paul with a degree in vocal music and worked as a program director and program host on Guam radio stations. In 1953 she married Ricardo Bordallo, from a prominent Guam family, who owned an auto dealership and had many business interests and was well connected in island politics. Madeleine Bordallo became Guam's Democratic National Committeewoman in 1964 and has held that position ever since (she is the most senior member of the Democratic National Committee). Ricardo Bordallo was elected governor in 1974, defeated for reelection in 1978, then elected governor again in 1982. With her husband's encouragement, Madeleine Bordallo ran for the Guam Legislature and was elected in 1980, 1986, 1988, 1990 and 1992. In 1990 Ricardo Bordallo wrapped himself in the Guam flag, chained himself to the statue of Chief Quipuha and shot himself to avoid a prison term for bribery. Madeleine Bordallo was a candidate for governor that year, but lost 57%–43% to incumbent Joseph Ada. In 1994 she was elected lieutenant governor and was reelected in 1998.

In 2002, when Delegate Robert Underwood decided to run for governor, Bordallo ran for delegate. In the primary she faced Judith Won Pat, daughter of Guam's first delegate, Antonio Borja Won Pat, who served from 1974 to 1986. In this contest between longtime friends, Bordallo won 59%–41%. In the general she faced Joseph Ada, who beat her in 1990. This time she won by an impressive 65%–35% margin. Bordallo promised to increase Compact-Impact Aid; she said the federal government had delivered only $38 million of $164 million owed. She backed the use of military hospitals for immigrants brought in by Compact-Impact Aid and said that she would welcome the military "as much as they care to bring to Guam."

AMERICAN SAMOA

American Samoa, the only American territory south of the Equator, has been little influenced by Western settlers and remains almost as Polynesian today as it was when the United States took possession in 1900. These seven islands are 2,300 miles southwest of Hawaii, 1,600 miles northeast of New Zealand. American Samoa has 64,000 people, 90% of them on the island of Tutuila, 89% of them Polynesian, mostly Christian (50% Congregationalist, 20% Catholic); they are U.S. nationals but not U.S. citizens. An estimated 50,000 Samoans live on the U.S. mainland and 20,000 in Hawaii. Its population has doubled in the last 20 years, and fear that outsiders will change the culture has prompted some demands for stricter immigration standards. American Samoa is an unincorporated territory administered by the Interior Department since 1951; minimum wages are set for industries by the U.S. Department of Labor. American Samoa elects a governor and a two house legislature known as the Fono. It is a bilingual society and government: Government is mostly conducted in English, Fono proceedings are in Samoan, and court sessions are conducted in English with each sentence then translated into Samoan. The islands of Ofu, Tau and Tutuila are the site of the National Park of American Samoa, opened in April 1997, preserving fruit bat habitat, tropical forests and coral reefs.

The market economy has not made much progress here: American Samoa lives off the federal government, which spends some $23 million annually, plus varying amounts for construction (the Army in 2002 pitched in $1 million for a 55-year lease of six acres at Pago Pago Airport for a Reserve County), and two big tuna canneries, which employ 4,000 workers, 30% of the work force, earn $451 million and provide one-third of all U.S. canned tuna. Another 4,000 work for the American Samoan government, most at $2.60 an hour. Residents are eligible for U.S. food stamps and welfare; local agriculture is minimal and sheltered (the territorial government in 2000 wanted to quadruple tariffs on bananas and taro). The bedrock of the local economy is the territorial government, which under the late Governor Tauese Sunia, who died in March 2003, maintained payroll levels even though it stiffed creditors from the local utility to the IRS and was not been able to send out tax refunds on time.

Efforts to attract investment brought in just one garment factory, which was closed in January 2001 after it was found that the Korean owner was paying Chinese and Vietnamese workers less than minimum wage, withholding their passports and return plane tickets, feeding them weak broth with rice and cabbage and withholding meals if they complained; the owner was indicted for involuntary servitude and in April 2002 was ordered to pay $3.5 million in back wages and penalties to workers. In February 2001 Governor Tauese Sunia announced that there would be no more foreign-owned garment factories in American Samoa. Tourism has been minimal: 2000 saw the opening of the first McDonalds here, but plans for a 104-room hotel went nowhere. The territorial government controls immigration and in August 2002 Attorney General Fiti Sunia, the late governor's nephew, called for exclusion of anyone from 24 countries in the Middle East and "heightening scrutiny for entry into the territory of individuals of Middle Eastern descent and features." Michael Homsany, a Samoan resident born in Brooklyn of Middle Eastern ancestry was afraid he would not be allowed back on the island if he left, and sued. Congressman Nick Rahall, of Middle Eastern descent himself and ranking Democrat on the House Resources Committee— someone American Samoa should pay attention to—expressed concern, and the order was revised in December.

One cause celebre is the renaming of nearby Samoa, formerly British Samoa and Western Samoa. The single name suggests to many in American Samoa that they are regarded as not full Samoans, and the legislature threatened not to recognize Samoan passports—a problem, since 85% of the cannery work force is from Samoa. But Sunia, a nephew of the Samoan prime minister, promised to veto any such bill. But if American Samoans are proud Samoans, they are also proud Americans: On April 17, 2000, they celebrated the 100th anniversary of the American takeover, with a 60-foot American flag raised on Sogelau Hill, where the American flag was first raised; there was traditional singing and dancing at Veterans Stadium and a long boat race in Pago Pago Harbor, and a commemorative stamp was unveiled showing a Samoan alia (two-hull canoe) sailing in easterly winds near Suniatu Mountain in the Manu'a island group.

American Samoa does not cast electoral votes for president, but does send delegates to the parties' national conventions. In February 2000, George W. Bush won four delegates in a caucus. In March 2000, Al Gore beat Bill Bradley by 21–4—those are not percentages, but the actual number of votes; Bradley got one convention vote split between four delegates.

Governor Togiola T.A. Tulafono was sworn in as American Samoa's governor on April, 7, 2003, following the sudden death of Governor Tauese Sunia March 26. Tauese (it is Samoan tradition to refer to chieftains by their first names) was elected governor in 1996 and reelected in 2000. In office he had to struggle with American Samoa's $35.6 million debt and its difficulty in paying bills and in collecting taxes and fees. In the early 1990s, it owed $6 million to the IRS for unpaid payroll deductions, $7 million to the authority providing trash collection, electricity and drinking water, which in turn owed $2.5 million to three oil companies. None of these issues seemed to bother Tauese, who, when running for reelection in 2000, said he could balance the budget in an hour, but he preferred preserving government jobs to paying off the government debt. He wanted to restrict immigration and property-holding rights, and he fought unsuccessfully to repeal the death penalty. He sought to strike a balance between preserving local cultures and traditions and recognizing what he viewed as inevitable economic globalization. Tauese died unexpectedly while on a plane to Honolulu for medical treatment.

Togiola was elected lieutenant governor in 1996 and served under Tauese until his 2003 death. A native of American Samoa, Togiola left after high school to attend Chadron State College in Nebraska; he graduated from the Washburn University law school in Topeka, Kansas, and National Judicial College in Reno, Nevada. He returned to American Samoa, where he practiced law for 20 years and served in a variety of executive posts: administrative assistant to the Secretary of Samoan Affairs, Samoan Assistant to the Attorney General, the first chairman of the American Samoa Power Authority, and the first chairman of the Board of High Education. Togiola also served as a policeman and for 12 years in the American Samoa Senate. In April 2003, one of his first acts as governor was to appoint Treasurer Aitofele Toese Sunia—Tauese's brother—as lieutenant governor.

Delegate

Eni F.H. Faleomavaega (D)

Elected 1988, 8th term; b. Aug. 15, 1943, Vailoatai; home, Pago Pago; Brigham Young U., B.A. 1972, U. of CA, LL.M. 1973; Mormon; married (Hinanui).

Military Career: Army, 1966–69 (Vietnam).

Elected Office: AS Lt. Gov., 1984–89.

Professional Career: A.A., U.S. Del. from AS, 1973–75; Cnsl., U.S. House Interior Cmte., 1975–81; AS Dpty. Atty. Gen., 1981–84.

DC Office: 2422 RHOB, 20515, 202-225-8577; Fax: 202-225-8757; Web site: www.house.gov/faleomavaega.

District Office: Pago Pago, 684-633-1372.

Committees: *International Relations* (4th of 23 D): Asia & the Pacific (RMM); Western Hemisphere. *Resources* (3d of 24 D): Energy & Mineral Resources; Fisheries Conservation, Wildlife & Oceans. *Small Business* (5th of 17 D).

American Samoa has elected a delegate to Congress since 1980. Delegate Eni F. H. Faleomavaega is a Democrat first elected in 1988. He went to high school in Hawaii, to Brigham Young University, then to law school in Houston and Berkeley; he served in Vietnam in the Army. In the 1970s he worked on the Natural Resources Insular subcommittee staff and for Utah Democrat Gunn Mc-Kay. In 1981 he became deputy attorney general of American Samoa, and in 1985 lieutenant governor.

Faleomavaega (he uses his last name in his press releases, rather than the first name used to refer to Samoan chiefs) serves on the Resources Committee, where he has been ranking Democrat on three subcommittees—Native Americans and Insular Affairs in January 1995; National Parks and Public Lands in January 1998; Fisheries, Conservation, Wildlife and Oceans in January 1999. He is also a member of International Affairs and ranking member on its East Asian and the Pacific Subcommittee. Faleomavaega worked to improve conditions at the StarKist tuna plant and to get the British Ceramic Tile Company to make the largest investment in American Samoa since the canneries were built decades ago. He led the congressional protest against the French nuclear tests in the Pacific, and was stopped by the French for approaching the French nuclear testing site at Mururoa Atoll and imprisoned in Tahiti in 1996. In September 2000 he met in Washington with Indian Prime Minister Atal Bihari Vajpayee and discussed the political strife in Fiji between island natives and the descendants of Indian laborers; he said it was not solely a racial conflict, but was rooted in colonialism.

Faleomavaega has expressed fears that American Samoa will be threatened by an "invasion" of Asian small businessmen, comparing it to Fiji. With help from Senator Daniel Inouye and Pennsylvania Democrat John Murtha, Faleomavaega got into the October 1998 omnibus budget free transportation on military aircraft for veterans approved for VA health care in Hawaii; in July 2000 he complained that the VA was not cooperating and only one veteran had flown to Hawaii. In late 2000 he urged American Samoa veterans to enroll as a first step in establishing a VA medical clinic in American Samoa. In January 1998 he congratulated two Samoans who played in the Super Bowl, Maa Tanuvasa of the Denver Broncos and Esera Tuaolo of the Atlanta Falcons; he hailed other Samoan athletes, professional wrestler Dwayne Johnson, known as "The Rock," and heavyweight fighter David Tua, and helped arrange for the November 2000 championship fight between Tua and Lennox Lewis to be seen on free TV in American Samoa. In 2000 Faleomavaega's Fisheries Subcommittee passed bills to increase funding for coral reef preservation, to transfer a NOAA research vessel to the American Samoa government for future transport of cargo and passengers to the Manu'a islands and to prohibit the practice of shark finning in American waters. In December 2001 he expressed fears that expanding the Andean Trade Preference Act to include tuna would result in StarKist moving its cannery from American Samoa to Ecuador, where wages are much lower; a company spokesman said it had no intention of leaving. When Guam's Robert Underwood in February 2002 amended the National Sea Grant college program in the Resources Committee to earmark money for five colleges in the northern Pacific, Faleomavaega offered and then withdrew an amendment to earmark $2 million for American Samoa Community College and the University of the Virgin Islands (presumably to get Donna Christian-Christiansen's vote). When the Science Committee considered the bill a month later, Vern Ehlers's motion to delete the Underwood amendment passed by voice vote. In August 2002 Faleomavaega and three Florida congressmen asked the Justice Department to investigate the shooting by a Pasco County Sheriff's deputy of a woman with many relatives in American Samoa. That month he also appeared at a House Resources Committee hearing in Pago Pago, where members—Chairman Jim Hansen of Utah, Dan Miller of Florida, Jeff Flake of Arizona, Dennis Rehberg of Montana and Anibal Acevedo-Vila of Puerto Rico—reviewed Interior Secretary Gale Norton's comprehensive report on American Samoa's economic and development needs, prepared over the last two years.

In three of the last four elections, Faleomavaega has failed to get 50% of the vote and has been forced into runoffs, which are held two weeks later; he has argued for a longer interval, since two weeks is not enough to get ballots to and from Samoans serving in the U.S. military. On Election Day 2000 he won 46% of the vote, to 30% for Independent Gus Hannemann and 22% for Republican Aumua Amata Coleman. There was some bitterness here: Faleomavaega had endorsed Honolulu Mayor Jeremy Harris in his September 2000 primary against Hannemann's brother, Honolulu Councilman Mufi Hannemann. In the runoff two weeks later Faleomavaega won 61%–39%. In 2002 he faced Fagafaga Langkilde, Tufele Lia's running mate in the 1996 governor election and a former chairman of the territory's Democratic party, and, once again, Aumua Amata Coleman. Faleomavaega talked of his accomplishments in Washington, Fagafaga Langkilde said he would take "us to a level where the interests of American Samoa will once again be put at the top of our political agenda" and Aumua Amata Coleman said she would work on "bread and butter" issues like education, jobs, vocational training and health care. On November 5 Faleomavaega got 41% of the vote, Langkilde 32% and Coleman 27%. Faleomavaega stayed on island for the two weeks of the runoff campaign, thereby missing the November 14 Democratic Caucus where Bob Menendez defeated Rosa DeLauro for Caucus chairman by one vote (he would have voted for Menendez); given the infrequency of flights to and from American Samoa, there was no way he could have attended the caucus meeting and done any campaigning. Staying home paid off: He won the runoff 55%–45%. Fewer votes are cast in American Samoa than in any other House race—10,393 on November 5 and 9,042 in the runoff.

FILING DEADLINES

STATE	CONGRESSIONAL FILING DEADLINE	CONGRESSIONAL PRIMARY DATE	RUNOFF DATE	ELECTIONS DIVISION PHONE NUMBER
Alabama	April 2, 2004	June 1, 2004	June 29, 2004	334-242-7205
Alaska	June 1, 2004	August 24, 2004		907-465-4611
Arizona	June 9, 2004	September 7, 2004		602-542-4285
Arkansas	March 30, 2004	May 18, 2004	June 8, 2004	501-682-1010
California	December 5, 2003	March 2, 2004		916-657-2166
Colorado	June 1, 2004	August 10, 2004		303-894-2200
Connecticut	TBD	August 10, 2004		860-509-6100
Delaware	July 30, 2004	September 11, 2004		800-273-9500
Florida	May 7, 2004	August 31, 2004		850-245-6200
Georgia	April 30, 2004	July 20, 2004	August 10, 2004	404-656-2871
Hawaii	July 20, 2004	September 18, 2004		808-453-8683
Idaho	March 19, 2004	May 25, 2004		208-334-2852
Illinois	December 15, 2003	March 16, 2004		217-782-4141
Indiana	February 20, 2004	May 4, 2004		317-232-3939
Iowa	March 19, 2004	June 8, 2004		515-281-5865
Kansas	June 10, 2004	August 3, 2004		785-296-4564
Kentucky	January 27, 2004	May 18, 2004		502-573-7100
Louisiana	August 6, 2004	November 2, 2004	December 4, 2004	225-342-4970
Maine	March 15, 2004	June 8, 2004		207-624-7650
Maryland	December 22, 2003	March 2, 2004		410-269-2840
Massachusetts	June 1, 2004	September 14, 2004		617-727-2828
Michigan	May 11, 2004	August 3, 2004		517-373-2540
Minnesota	July 20, 2004	September 14, 2004		651-215-1440
Mississippi	January 9, 2004	March 9, 2004	March 30, 2004	601-576-2550
Missouri	March 30, 2004	August 3, 2004		573-751-2301
Montana	March 25, 2004	June 8, 2004		406-444-4732
Nebraska	February 15, 2004	May 11, 2004		402-471-3229
Nevada	May 17, 2004	September 7, 2004		775-684-5705
New Hampshire	June 11, 2004	September 14, 2004		603-271-3242
New Jersey	April 12, 2004	June 8, 2004		609-292-3760
New Mexico	February 10, 2004	June 1, 2004		505-827-3600
New York	TBD	TBD		518-474-6220
North Carolina	February 27, 2004	May 4, 2004	June 21, 2004	919-733-7173
North Dakota	April 12, 2004	June 8, 2004		701-328-4146
Ohio	January 2, 2004	March 2, 2004		614-466-2585
Oklahoma	June 23, 2004	July 27, 2004	August 24, 2004	405-521-2391
Oregon	March 9, 2004	May 18, 2004		503-986-1518
Pennsylvania	February 17, 2004	April 27, 2004		717-787-5280
Rhode Island	June 30, 2004	September 14, 2004		401-222-2345
South Carolina	March 30, 2004	June 8, 2004		803-734-9060
South Dakota	April 6, 2004	June 1, 2004	June 15, 2004	605-773-3537
Tennessee	April 1, 2004	August 5, 2004		615-741-7956
Texas	January 2, 2004	March 9, 2004		800-252-8683
Utah	March 17, 2004	June 22, 2004		801-538-1041
Vermont	July 19, 2004	September 14, 2004		802-828-2363
Virginia	April 9, 2004	June 8, 2004		804-786-6551
Washington	July 30, 2004	September 21, 2004		360-902-4180
West Virginia	January 31, 2004	May 11, 2004		304-558-6000
Wisconsin	July 13, 2004	September 14, 2004		608-266-8005
Wyoming	May 28, 2004	August 17, 2004		307-777-7186

TBD: To be determined
All dates and deadlines as of June 26, 2003.

CONGRESSIONAL APPORTIONMENT

SEATS IN THE U.S. HOUSE BY STATE

Seats allocated by Decennial Apportionments for Elections 1942–2002

	1942	1952	1962	1972	1982	1992	2002	Gain/Loss 1942–2002
Alabama	9	9	8	7	7	7	7	−2
Alaska	—	1*	1	1	1	1	1	0
Arizona	2	2	3	4	5	6	8	+6
Arkansas	7	6	4	4	4	4	4	−3
California	23	30	38	43	45	52	53	+30
Colorado	4	4	4	5	6	6	7	+3
Connecticut	6	6	6	6	6	6	5	−1
Delaware	1	1	1	1	1	1	1	0
Florida	6	8	12	15	19	23	25	+19
Georgia	10	10	10	10	10	11	13	+3
Hawaii	—	1*	2	2	2	2	2	+1
Idaho	2	2	2	2	2	2	2	0
Illinois	26	25	24	24	22	20	19	−7
Indiana	11	11	11	11	10	10	9	−2
Iowa	8	8	7	6	6	5	5	−3
Kansas	6	6	5	5	5	4	4	−2
Kentucky	9	8	7	7	7	6	6	−3
Louisiana	8	8	8	8	8	7	7	−1
Maine	3	3	2	2	2	2	2	−1
Maryland	6	7	8	8	8	8	8	+2
Massachusetts	14	14	12	12	11	10	10	−4
Michigan	17	18	19	19	18	16	15	−2
Minnesota	9	9	8	8	8	8	8	−1
Mississippi	7	6	5	5	5	5	4	−3
Missouri	13	11	10	10	9	9	9	−4
Montana	2	2	2	2	2	2	1	−1
Nebraska	4	4	3	3	3	3	3	−1
Nevada	1	1	1	1	2	2	3	+2
New Hampshire	2	2	2	2	2	2	2	0
New Jersey	14	14	15	15	14	13	13	−1
New Mexico	2	2	2	2	3	3	3	+1
New York	45	43	41	39	34	31	29	−16
North Carolina	12	12	11	11	11	12	13	+1
North Dakota	2	2	2	1	1	1	1	−1
Ohio	23	23	24	23	21	19	18	−5
Oklahoma	8	6	6	6	6	6	5	−3
Oregon	4	4	4	4	5	5	5	+1
Pennsylvania	33	30	27	25	23	21	19	−14
Rhode Island	2	2	2	2	2	2	2	0
South Carolina	6	6	6	6	6	6	6	0
South Dakota	2	2	2	2	1	1	1	−1
Tennessee	10	9	9	8	9	9	9	−1
Texas	21	22	23	24	27	30	32	+11
Utah	2	2	2	2	3	3	3	+1
Vermont	1	1	1	1	1	1	1	0
Virginia	9	10	10	10	10	11	11	+2
Washington	6	7	7	7	8	9	9	+3
West Virginia	6	6	5	4	4	3	3	−3
Wisconsin	10	10	10	9	9	9	8	−2
Wyoming	1	1	1	1	1	1	1	0

*The admission of Alaska and Hawaii in 1959 caused a temporary increase in the House to 437 for the 86th and 87th Congresses. Source: Polidata.

TOP RANKED CONGRESSIONAL DISTRICTS

All rankings and calculations compiled by Polidata from 2000 Census Bureau datasets

Largest*
(*in square miles*)

1. NV-2	105,635
2. OR-2	70,227
3. NM-2	69,598
4. NE-3	64,899
5. AZ-1	58,714

*excludes at-large seats

Smallest
(*in square miles*)

1. NY-11	12
2. NY-16	13
3. NY-14	15
4. NY-15	16
5. NY-10	18

Rural
(*as a % of total population*)

1. KY-5	78.7
2. AL-4	73.5
3. ME-2	71.0
4. TN-4	67.9
5. MI-1	66.6

Married
(*as a % of persons 15 + years*)

1. GA-7	67.8
2. CO-6	67.5
3. TX-22	66.0
4. TN-7	65.8
5. GA-6	65.7
TX-8	65.7

One-Person Households
(*one person as a % of households*)

1. NY-14	49.6
2. NY-8	45.8
3. DC-AL	43.8
4. CA-8	40.9
5. CO-1	39.2

Median Household Income

1. VA-11	$80,397
2. NJ-11	$79,009
3. CA-14	$77,985
4. GA-6	$75,611
5. CA-15	$74,947

Household Income Over $150,000
(*% over $150,000 in annual income*)

1. CA-14	20.8
2. CT-4	19.2
3. NY-18	19.0
4. IL-10	18.4
5. NJ-11	18.2

Graduate/Professional Degrees
(*as a % of 25 + years*)

1. MD-8	28.1
2. NY-14	25.9
3. VA-8	24.9
4. CA-14	24.5
5. CA-30	22.3

Most Government Workers
(*as a % of employed workers*)

1. MD-4	29.0
2. MD-5	28.8
3. FL-2	28.5
4. AK-AL	26.8
5. DC-AL	25.9

In Military
(*as a % of 16 + years*)

1. VA-2	11.7
2. TX-11	8.2
3. NC-3	7.6
4. CA-49	6.3
5. NC-2	6.0

Military Veterans
(*as a % of voting age persons*)

1. FL-1	21.7
2. FL-5	21.5
3. VA-2	20.3
4. CO-5	19.9
5. FL-14	19.8
WA-6	19.8

German
(*estimated % of population*)

1. WI-6	38.8
2. WI-5	34.6
3. MN-1	31.7
4. IA-1	31.5
5. NE-1	30.8
WI-8	30.8

Irish
(estimated % of population)

1. MA-10	23.9
2. MA-9	23.2
3. PA-7	21.8
4. PA-13	19.5
5. MA-6	18.6

Italian
(estimated % of population)

1. NY-13	29.5
2. NY-3	23.1
3. NY-1	21.1
4. NY-2	18.8
5. CT-3	18.7

Black, non-Hispanic
(as a % of total population)

1. IL-1	65.2
2. LA-2	63.7
3. MS-2	63.2
4. IL-2	62.0
5. AL-7	61.7

Asian, non-Hispanic
(as a % of total population)

1. HI-1	53.6
2. CA-15	29.2
3. CA-8	28.7
4. CA-12	28.5
5. CA-13	28.3

Chinese
(number of persons)

1. CA-8	113,625
2. CA-12	82,235
3. NY-12	81,529
4. CA-29	71,572
5. NY-5	69,593

Filipino
(number of persons)

1. HI-1	95,404
2. HI-2	75,231
3. CA-12	61,777
4. CA-51	61,364
5. CA-13	54,369

Hispanic
(as a % of total population)

1. TX-15	78.3
2. TX-16	77.7
3. CA-34	77.2
4. IL-4	74.5
5. TX-27	71.6

Mexican
(number of persons)

1. TX-16	424,035
2. TX-15	412,449
3. CA-38	376,162
4. CA-34	373,330
5. IL-4	363,653

Puerto Rican
(number of persons)

1. NY-16	183,125
2. NY-12	137,314
3. NY-7	103,384
4. NJ-13	89,992
5. PA-1	73,791

American Indian, non-Hispanic
(as a % of voting age population)

1. AZ-1	18.0
2. NM-3	16.3
3. OK-2	14.5
4. AK-AL	13.7
5. NC-7	7.7

Cherokee
(number of persons)

1. OK-2	59,902
2. OK-1	19,494
3. OK-3	9,004
4. NC-11	7,475
5. OK-4	4,860

Navajo
(number of persons)

1. AZ-1	107,639
2. NM-3	87,146
3. UT-2	10,014
4. NM-1	7,876
5. NM-2	7,264

CLOSEST 2002 HOUSE ELECTIONS

District	Member	2002 %	2000 Bush %	District	Member	2002 %	2000 Bush %
CA-39	Sanchez (D)	55	36	MD-8	Van Hollen (D)	52	31
CO-4	Musgrave (R)	55	57	ND-AL	Pomeroy (D)	52	61
FL-13	Harris (R)	55	54	TN-4	Davis (D)	52	50
GA-12	Burns (R)	55	45	TX-11	Edwards (D)	52	67
IL-19	Shimkus (R)	55	56	TX-23	Bonilla (R)	52	59
IA-4	Latham (R)	55	49	CA-18	Cardoza (D)	51	44
MS-2	Thompson (D)	55	41	GA-3	Marshall (D)	51	52
NM-1	Wilson (R)	55	47	IN-8	Hostettler (R)	51	56
NC-13	Miller (D)	55	50	IN-9	Hill (D)	51	56
OR-5	Hooley (D)	55	48	KY-4	Lucas (D)	51	61
TX-25	Bell (D)	55	48	OH-17	Ryan (D)	51	35
CT-2	Simmons (R)	54	40	PA-6	Gerlach (R)	51	49
CT-5	Johnson (R)	54	43	PA-13	Hoeffel (D)	51	42
MD-2	Ruppersberger (D)	54	41	PA-17	Holden (D)	51	56
NV-1	Berkley (D)	54	41	TX-17	Stenholm (D)	51	72
NC-8	Hayes (R)	54	54	AL-3	Rogers (R)	50	52
OK-4	Cole (R)	54	61	IN-2	Chocola (R)	50	53
IN-7	Carson (D)	53	43	KS-3	Moore (D)	50	53
IA-3	Boswell (D)	53	48	LA-5	Alexander (D)	50	57
MN-2	Kline (R)	53	51	NY-1	Bishop (D)	50	44
SD-AL	Janklow (R)	53	60	WA-2	Larsen (D)	50	46
GA-11	Gingrey (R)	52	51	UT-2	Matheson (D)	49	67
IA-2	Leach (R)	52	43	AZ-1	Renzi (R)	49	51
KY-3	Northup (R)	52	48	FL-5	Brown-Waite (R)	48	54
ME-2	Michaud (D)	52	46	CO-7	Beauprez (R)	47	49

PRESIDENTIAL PERFORMANCE: BEST AND WORST CONGRESSIONAL DISTRICTS

Top 10 Best-performing Bush districts 2000			Top 10 Worst-performing Bush districts 2000		
District	*Member*	*Bush %*	*District*	*Member*	*Bush %*
TX-8	Brady (R)	77.7	NY-16	Serrano (D)	5.4
TX-19	Neugebauer (R)	75.5	NY-15	Rangel (D)	6.5
TX-13	Thornberry (R)	74.6	NY-10	Towns (D)	7.7
UT-3	Cannon (R)	74.6	NY-11	Owens (D)	8.6
AL-6	Bachus (R)	73.6	NY-6	Meeks (D)	10.5
TX-26	Burgess (R)	73.3	PA-2	Fattah (D)	11.6
TX-21	Smith (R)	72.8	CA-9	Lee (D)	13.4
TX-17	Stenholm (D)	72.2	CA-33	Watson (D)	13.5
TX-3	Johnson (R)	72.2	NY-12	Velazquez (D)	14.7
TX-31	Carter (R)	71.6	PA-1	Brady (D)	14.7

SENATE SEATS

2004 ELECTION CYCLE

REPUBLICANS (15)	PREVIOUS %	DEMOCRATS (19)	PREVIOUS %
Robert Bennett (UT)	64%	Evan Bayh (IN)	64%
Christopher (Kit) Bond (MO)	53%	Barbara Boxer (CA)	53%
Sam Brownback (KS)	65%	John Breaux (LA)	64%
Jim Bunning (KY)	50%	Tom Daschle (SD)	62%
Ben Nighthorse Campbell (CO)	62%	Christopher Dodd (CT)	65%
Mike Crapo (ID)	70%	Byron Dorgan (ND)	63%
Peter Fitzgerald (IL)*	50%	John Edwards (NC)	51%
Charles Grassley (IA)	68%	Russell Feingold (WI)	51%
Judd Gregg (NH)	68%	Bob Graham (FL)	62%
John McCain (AZ)	69%	Ernest Hollings (SC)	53%
Lisa Murkowski (AK)	+	Daniel Inouye (HI)	79%
Don Nickles (OK)	66%	Patrick Leahy (VT)	72%
Richard Shelby (AL)	63%	Blanche Lincoln (AR)	55%
Arlen Specter (PA)	61%	Barbara Mikulski (MD)	71%
George Voinovich (OH)	56%	Zell Miller (GA)*	58%
		Patty Murray (WA)	58%
		Harry Reid (NV)	48%
		Charles Schumer (NY)	55%
		Ron Wyden (OR)	61%

*Will not seek reelection in 2004.
+Lisa Murkowski was appointed Dec. 20, 2002 to serve the remainder of Frank Murkowski's term.

2006 ELECTION CYCLE

REPUBLICANS (15)	PREVIOUS %	DEMOCRATS (17)	PREVIOUS %
George Allen (VA)	52%	Daniel Akaka (HI)	73%
Conrad Burns (MT)	51%	Jeff Bingaman (NM)	62%
Lincoln Chafee (RI)	57%	Robert Byrd (WV)	78%
Mike DeWine (OH)	60%	Maria Cantwell (WA)	49%
John Ensign (NV)	55%	Thomas Carper (DE)	56%
Bill Frist (TN)	65%	Hillary Rodham Clinton (NY)	55%
Orrin Hatch (UT)	66%	Kent Conrad (ND)	62%
Kay Bailey Hutchison (TX)	65%	Jon Corzine (NJ)	50%
Jon Kyl (AZ)	79%	Mark Dayton (MN)	49%
Trent Lott (MS)	66%	Dianne Feinstein (CA)	56%
Richard Lugar (IN)	67%	Edward Kennedy (MA)	73%
Rick Santorum (PA)	52%	Herb Kohl (WI)	62%
Olympia Snowe (ME)	69%	Joe Lieberman (CT)	63%
Jim Talent (MO)	51%	Bill Nelson (FL)	51%
Craig Thomas (WY)	74%	Ben Nelson (NE)	51%
		Paul Sarbanes (MD)	63%
		Debbie Stabenow (MI)	49%

INDEPENDENTS (1)	PREVIOUS %
James Jeffords (VT)	66%

GUBERNATORIAL ELECTION CYCLE

2003, 3 States

Kentucky (D)
Louisiana (R)

Mississippi (D)

2004, 11 States

Delaware (D)
Indiana (D)
Missouri (D)
Montana (R)
New Hampshire (R)
North Carolina (D)

North Dakota (R)
Utah (R)
Vermont (R)
Washington (D)
West Virginia (D)

2005, 2 States

New Jersey (D)

Virginia (D)

2006, 36 States

Alabama (R)
Alaska (R)
Arizona (D)
Arkansas (R)
California (D)
Colorado (R)
Connecticut (R)
Florida (R)
Georgia (R)
Hawaii (R)
Idaho (R)
Illinois (D)
Iowa (D)
Kansas (D)
Maine (D)
Maryland (R)
Massachusetts (R)
Michigan (D)

Minnesota (R)
Nebraska (R)
Nevada (R)
New Hampshire*
New Mexico (D)
New York (R)
Ohio (R)
Oklahoma (D)
Oregon (D)
Pennsylvania (D)
Rhode Island (R)
South Carolina (R)
South Dakota (R)
Tennessee (D)
Texas (R)
Vermont*
Wisconsin (D)
Wyoming (D)

Partisan control of governorships (as of June 26, 2003): 26 Republicans, 24 Democrats
*New Hampshire and Vermont have two-year terms. All others are four years.
Boldface indicates governors who cannot succeed themselves in the next election.

CAMPAIGN FINANCE

All data is derived from candidate and party reports as well as other official studies available from the Federal Election Commission. Individuals listed in italics were losing candidates in that election. Zip code analysis is compiled by The Center for Responsive Politics.

TOP DONOR ZIP CODES FOR 2001–2002 ELECTION CYCLE

Rank	Zip Code	Location	Total Amount	Democrat	Republican
1.	20005	Washington, DC	23,677,537	44%	56%
2.	20036	Washington, DC	22,669,351	61%	39%
3.	20001	Washington, DC	16,730,941	85%	15%
4.	20004	Washington, DC	15,345,621	34%	66%
5.	20006	Washington, DC	13,896,245	66%	34%
6.	10021	New York, NY	12,202,916	76%	24%
7.	60614	Chicago, IL	9,393,492	96%	3%
8.	90024	Los Angeles, CA	8,286,138	90%	10%
9.	10022	New York, NY	8,024,339	59%	40%
10.	90067	Los Angeles, CA	7,697,428	84%	16%
11.	90035	Los Angeles, CA	5,853,320	100%	0%
12.	94022	Los Altos, CA	5,556,917	90%	10%
13.	20007	Washington, DC	5,413,009	75%	25%
14.	22314	Alexandria, VA	5,163,936	21%	79%
15.	10017	New York, NY	5,035,603	38%	62%
16.	20003	Washington, DC	5,034,544	72%	28%
17.	10036	New York, NY	4,774,687	92%	8%
18.	10019	New York, NY	4,480,190	68%	31%
19.	20016	Washington, DC	4,272,637	52%	48%
20.	22101	McLean, VA	3,983,653	40%	60%
21.	20854	Potomac, MD	3,941,423	55%	45%
22.	77002	Houston, TX	3,753,765	47%	53%
23.	90210	Beverly Hills, CA	3,673,950	71%	29%
24.	10023	New York, NY	3,590,686	83%	17%
25.	75201	Dallas, TX	3,580,949	20%	80%

U.S. SENATE

The following charts show the 15 top 2002 Senate candidates in terms of the highest total net receipts, net expenditures, political action committee (PAC) contributions, individual contributions, cash-on-hand and debts owed during the 2001-2002 election cycle as of June 18, 2003.

2002 SENATE: TOP RAISERS

1. Elizabeth Dole (R-NC) — $13,840,946
2. *Erskine Bowles (D-NC)* — $13,335,229
3. *Paul Wellstone (D-MN)** — $12,631,608
4. *Jean Carnahan (D-MO)* — $12,316,325
5. *Douglas Forrester (R-NJ)* — $10,623,030
6. Norm Coleman (R-MN) — $10,206,511
7. John Cornyn (R-TX) — $9,798,366
8. *Ron Kirk (D-TX)* — $9,517,216
9. Jim Talent (R-MO) — $9,131,603
10. John Kerry (D-MA) — $8,609,757
11. *Max Cleland (D-GA)* — $8,170,080
12. Saxby Chambliss (R-GA) — $7,797,139
13. Mary Landrieu (D-LA) — $6,829,025
14. Tom Harkin (D-IA) — $6,754,658
15. *Bob Torricelli (D-NJ)*† — $6,386,901

2002 SENATE: TOP SPENDERS

1. Elizabeth Dole (R-NC) — $13,735,220
2. *Erskine Bowles (D-NC)* — $13,306,317
3. *Paul Wellstone (D-MN)** — $12,617,876
4. *Jean Carnahan (D-MO)* — $12,293,579
5. *Douglas Forrester (R-NJ)* — $10,606,843
6. Norm Coleman (R-MN) — $10,035,279
7. John Cornyn (R-TX) — $9,769,780
8. *Ron Kirk (D-TX)* — $9,426,763
9. *Max Cleland (D-GA)* — $9,116,775
10. John Kerry (D-MA) — $8,776,915
11. Jim Talent (R-MO) — $8,577,033
12. Saxby Chambliss (R-GA) — $7,743,004
13. Mary Landrieu (D-LA) — $7,436,458
14. Tom Harkin (D-IA) — $6,897,168
15. Lindsey Graham (R-SC) — $6,197,982

2002 SENATE: TOP PAC RECIPIENTS

1.	Mary Landrieu (D-LA)	$2,634,646
2.	Max Baucus (D-MT)	$2,627,382
3.	Wayne Allard (R-CO)	$2,107,023
4.	Tim Johnson (D-SD)	$1,999,096
5.	Norm Coleman (R-MN)	$1,938,483
6.	Jim Talent (R-MO)	$1,780,200
7.	*Max Cleland (D-GA)*	$1,772,512
8.	*Tim Hutchinson (R-AR)*	$1,701,081
9.	John Cornyn (R-TX)	$1,654,561
10.	Gordon Smith (R-OR)	$1,645,341
11.	Elizabeth Dole (R-NC)	$1,588,296
12.	Susan Collins (R-ME)	$1,575,376
13.	*Jean Carnahan (D-MO)*	$1,561,984
14.	Saxby Chambliss (R-GA)	$1,433,134
15.	Tom Harkin (D-IA)	$1,396,254

2002 SENATE: TOP INDIVIDUAL CONTRIBUTIONS

1.	*Paul Wellstone (D-MN)**	$11,699,925
2.	Elizabeth Dole (R-NC)	$11,149,786
3.	*Jean Carnahan (D-MO)*	$9,943,621
4.	John Kerry (D-MA)	$8,488,322
5.	John Cornyn (R-TX)	$7,904,777
6.	*Ron Kirk (D-TX)*	$7,672,926
7.	Jim Talent (R-MO)	$6,803,449
8.	Norm Coleman (R-MN)	$6,372,650
9.	*Max Cleland (D-GA)*	$5,995,192
10.	*Erskine Bowles (D-NC)*	$5,235,680
11.	Saxby Chambliss (R-GA)	$4,928,954
12.	Tom Harkin (D-IA)	$4,911,188
13.	*Bob Torricelli (D-NJ)†*	$4,457,464
14.	*Jeanne Shaheen (D-NH)*	$4,403,926
15.	Lamar Alexander (R-TN)	$4,204,731

2002 SENATE: TOP CASH-ON-HAND

1.	*Bob Torricelli (D-NJ)†*	$2,918,115
2.	Richard Durbin (D-IL)	$1,830,445
3.	John Warner (R-VA)	$1,338,535
4.	Jay Rockefeller IV (D-WV)	$1,168,812
5.	Jack Reed (D-RI)	$1,148,583
6.	Carl Levin (D-MI)	$985,373
7.	*Walter Mondale (D-MN)*	$893,880
8.	Jeff Sessions (R-AL)	$681,271
9.	Ted Stevens (R-AK)	$672,745
10.	Jim Talent (R-MO)	$655,317
11.	*Suzanne Haik Terrell (R-LA)*	$633,564
12.	Thad Cochran (R-MS)	$604,726
13.	Pat Roberts (R-KS)	$543,436
14.	Chuck Hagel (R-NE)	$491,534
15.	Mitch McConnell (R-KY)	$428,116

2002 SENATE: TOP DEBTS OWED

1.	*Douglas Forrester (R-NJ)*	$7,489,555
2.	*Erskine Bowles (D-NC)*	$6,801,344
3.	Gordon Smith (R-OR)	$2,293,119
4.	Frank Lautenberg (D-NJ)	$1,530,000
5.	*Alan Blinken (D-ID)*	$1,510,000
6.	Lamar Alexander (R-TN)	$1,246,565
7.	*John Cox (R-IL)*	$1,130,580
8.	*Julian McPhillips (D-AL)*	$1,024,650
9.	Elizabeth Dole (R-NC)	$558,877
10.	*Bob Irvin (R-GA)*	$496,843
11.	*James Oberweis (R-IL)*	$490,000
12.	Saxby Chambliss (R-GA)	$462,316
13.	*Greg Ganske (R-IA)*	$400,000
14.	John Cornyn (R-TX)	$385,783
15.	*Lois Weinberg (D-KY)*	$351,010

*Paul Wellstone died October 25, 2002
†Withdrew from race

U.S. HOUSE OF REPRESENTATIVES

The following charts show the 25 top 2002 House candidates in terms of the highest total net receipts, net expenditures, political action committee (PAC) contributions, individual contributions, cash-on-hand and debts owed during the 2001-2002 election cycle as of June 18, 2003.

2002 HOUSE: TOP RAISERS

1.	Jim Humphreys (D-WV)	$8,163,840
2.	Dick Gephardt (D-MO)	$5,756,676
3.	Wayne Hogan (D-FL)	$4,667,211
4.	Tom Reiser (R-TX)	$4,563,312
5.	Roger Kahn (D-GA)	$4,101,181
6.	Harry Jacobs (D-FL)	$4,023,332
7.	Martha Fuller Clark (D-NH)	$3,537,316
8.	Nancy Johnson (R-CT)	$3,405,858
9.	Katherine Harris (R-FL)	$3,320,493
10.	Bob Barr (R-GA)	$3,249,602
11.	Rahm Emanuel (D-IL)	$3,149,644
12.	John Dingell (D-MI)	$3,073,004
13.	Anne Northup (R-KY)	$3,025,943
14.	Dennis Hastert (R-IL)	$2,995,170
15.	Chris Van Hollen (D-MD)	$2,989,215
16.	Connie Morella (R-MD)	$2,855,043
17.	Chip Pickering (R-MS)	$2,781,337
18.	Mark Kennedy Shriver (D-MD)	$2,736,614
19.	Heather Wilson (R-NM)	$2,735,478
20.	Shelley Moore Capito (R-WV)	$2,581,019
21.	Patrick Kennedy (D-RI)	$2,563,800
22.	David Fink (D-MI)	$2,468,156
23.	Robert Menendez (D-NJ)	$2,461,931
24.	John Murtha (D-PA)	$2,405,385
25.	Robin Hayes (R-NC)	$2,322,512

2002 HOUSE: TOP SPENDERS

1.	Jim Humphreys (D-WV)	$8,150,237
2.	Wayne Hogan (D-FL)	$4,659,352
3.	Tom Reiser (R-TX)	$4,538,270
4.	Roger Kahn (D-GA)	$4,215,536
5.	Harry Jacobs (D-FL)	$3,989,408
6.	Nancy Johnson (R-CT)	$3,752,161
7.	Martha Fuller Clark (D-NH)	$3,511,108
8.	John Dingell (D-MI)	$3,461,009
9.	Dick Gephardt (D-MO)	$3,389,306
10.	Bob Barr (R-GA)	$3,336,214
11.	Katherine Harris (R-FL)	$3,293,690
12.	Anne Northup (R-KY)	$3,128,295
13.	Chip Pickering (R-MS)	$3,071,060
14.	Connie Morella (R-MD)	$2,996,119
15.	Chris Van Hollen (D-MD)	$2,985,329
16.	Rahm Emanuel (D-IL)	$2,971,514
17.	Dennis Hastert (R-IL)	$2,970,554
18.	Patrick Kennedy (D-RI)	$2,935,810
19.	Heather Wilson (R-NM)	$2,728,165
20.	Mark Kennedy Shriver (D-MD)	$2,626,638
21.	Shelley Moore Capito (R-WV)	$2,530,078
22.	Joe Knollenberg (R-MI)	$2,524,728
23.	Henry Bonilla (R-TX)	$2,413,172
24.	John Murtha (D-PA)	$2,386,861
25.	David Fink (D-MI)	$2,321,103

2002 HOUSE: TOP PAC RECIPIENTS

1.	John Dingell (D-MI)	$1,715,280
2.	Nancy Johnson (R-CT)	$1,657,576
3.	Dick Gephardt (D-MO)	$1,476,066
4.	Billy Tauzin (R-LA)	$1,473,095
5.	Roy Blunt (R-MO)	$1,343,167
6.	Dennis Hastert (R-IL)	$1,318,868
7.	Earl Pomeroy (D-ND)	$1,242,469
8.	Shelley Moore Capito (R-WV)	$1,228,951
9.	Karen Thurman (D-FL)	$1,168,393
10.	Chip Pickering (R-MS)	$1,161,934
11.	Connie Morella (R-MD)	$1,120,872
12.	Heather Wilson (R-NM)	$1,115,394
13.	John Shimkus (R-IL)	$1,067,795
14.	Anne Northup (R-KY)	$1,034,883
15.	Robin Hayes (R-NC)	$1,032,197
16.	Henry Bonilla (R-TX)	$1,030,054
17.	Martin Frost (D-TX)	$1,010,993
18.	Jim Maloney (D-CT)	$1,000,831
19.	Jim Nussle (R-IA)	$986,844
20.	Charles Rangel (D-NY)	$958,571
21.	Tom Latham (R-IA)	$956,210
22.	Mark Kennedy (R-MN)	$939,716
23.	Bill Thomas (R-CA)	$937,948
24.	Bill Luther (D-MN)	$937,278
25.	Don Young (R-AK)	$912,243

2002 HOUSE: TOP INDIVIDUAL CONTRIBUTIONS

1.	Dick Gephardt (D-MO)	$3,196,238
2.	Bob Barr (R-GA)	$2,986,883
3.	Katherine Harris (R-FL)	$2,857,988
4.	Mark Kennedy Shriver (D-MD)	$2,430,253
5.	Chris Van Hollen (D-MD)	$2,275,297
6.	Rahm Emanuel (D-IL)	$2,256,010
7.	David Rogers (R-RI)	$1,889,328
8.	Anne Northup (R-KY)	$1,881,953
9.	Patrick Kennedy (D-RI)	$1,841,387
10.	Jay Dickey (R-AR)	$1,801,140
11.	Robert Menendez (D-NJ)	$1,793,725
12.	John Murtha (D-PA)	$1,659,772
13.	Connie Morella (R-MD)	$1,646,611
14.	Stephen Lynch (D-MA)	$1,613,009
15.	Dennis Hastert (R-IL)	$1,588,870
16.	Denise Majette (D-GA)	$1,560,532
17.	Nancy Johnson (R-CT)	$1,546,989
18.	Lynn Rivers (D-MI)	$1,519,572
19.	Joe Knollenberg (R-MI)	$1,517,260
20.	Chip Pickering (R-MS)	$1,516,227
21.	Heather Wilson (R-NM)	$1,503,693
22.	Ron Paul (R-TX)	$1,487,825
23.	Martha Fuller Clark (D-NH)	$1,417,737
24.	Rush Holt (D-NJ)	$1,413,289
25.	Carolyn McCarthy (D-NY)	$1,388,013

2002 HOUSE: TOP CASH-ON-HAND

1.	David Dreier (R-CA)	$2,563,095
2.	Peter Deutsch (D-FL)	$2,514,397
3.	Dick Gephardt (D-MO)	$2,442,118
4.	Lloyd Doggett (D-TX)	$2,132,499
5.	Robert Menendez (D-NJ)	$1,947,579
6.	Martin Meehan (D-MA)	$1,805,202
7.	Mark Foley (R-FL)	$1,721,788
8.	Richard Burr (R-NC)	$1,694,191
9.	Sherrod Brown (D-OH)	$1,656,372
10.	Nick Rahall (D-WV)	$1,630,577
11.	Ileana Ros-Lehtinen (R-FL)	$1,505,727
12.	Scott McInnis (R-CO)	$1,462,629
13.	Loretta Sanchez (D-CA)	$1,456,092
14.	Cliff Stearns (R-FL)	$1,444,500
15.	William Delahunt (D-MA)	$1,369,494
16.	Roy Blunt (R-MO)	$1,338,181
17.	Tom Reynolds (R-NY)	$1,310,081
18.	Rob Portman (R-OH)	$1,267,201
19.	Anthony Weiner (D-NY)	$1,235,726
20.	Robert Andrews (D-NJ)	$1,209,066
21.	Don Young (R-AK)	$1,163,533
22.	Jim Turner (D-TX)	$1,128,351
23.	Nita Lowey (D-NY)	$1,126,489
24.	Jerry Lewis (R-CA)	$1,101,127
25.	Johnny Isakson (R-GA)	$1,094,830

2002 HOUSE: TOP DEBTS OWED

1.	Jim Humphreys (D-WV)	$13,953,152
2.	Roger Kahn (D-GA)	$5,732,500
3.	Phil Sudan (R-TX)	$3,830,810
4.	Harry Jacobs (D-FL)	$3,270,000
5.	Tom Reiser (R-TX)	$2,223,986
6.	Darrell Issa (R-CA)	$1,820,000
7.	Chris Cannon (R-UT)	$1,713,427
8.	Janet Robert (D-MN)	$1,592,100
9.	Martha Fuller Clark (D-NH)	$1,580,000
10.	Melissa Brown (R-PA)	$1,485,800
11.	Doug Ose (R-CA)	$1,362,069
12.	Roy Brown (R-OH)	$1,352,500
13.	Peter Wareing (R-TX)	$1,218,191
14.	David Fink (D-MI)	$1,200,000
15.	Noel Hentschel (R-CA)	$1,131,250
16.	Beth Rogers (R-CA)	$1,110,474
17.	Mike Sodrel (R-IN)	$1,005,000
18.	Mark Johnson (R-CA)	$1,000,000
19.	Mike Ferguson (R-NJ)	$814,541
20.	Kevin Garn (R-UT)	$736,172
21.	Jim Cooper (D-TN)	$727,038
22.	Sean Mahoney (R-NH)	$685,000
23.	Merrill Cook (R-UT)	$634,691
24.	Chris Chocola (R-IN)	$611,804
25.	Oz Bengur (D-MD)	$585,000

CONGRESSIONAL LEADERSHIP

U.S. SENATE

REPUBLICANS

Majority Leader	Bill Frist (TN)
Majority Whip	Mitch McConnell (KY)
President Pro Tempore	Ted Stevens (AK)
Conference Chairman	Rick Santorum (PA)
Conference Secretary	Kay Bailey Hutchison (TX)
Policy Committee Chairman	Jon Kyl (AZ)
NRSC Chairman	George Allen (VA)

DEMOCRATS

Minority Leader	Tom Daschle (SD)
Minority Whip	Harry Reid (NV)
Conference Secretary	Barbara Mikulski (MD)
Policy Committee Chairman	Byron Dorgan (ND)
Steering and Coordination Committee Chairman	Hillary Rodham Clinton (NY)
DSCC Chairman	Jon Corzine (NJ)

U.S. HOUSE OF REPRESENTATIVES

REPUBLICANS

Speaker of the House	Dennis Hastert (IL-14)
Majority Leader	Tom DeLay (TX-22)
Majority Whip	Roy Blunt (MO-7)
Chief Deputy Whip	Eric Cantor (VA-7)
Conference Chairman	Deborah Pryce (OH-15)
Conference Vice Chairman	Jack Kingston (GA-1)
Conference Secretary	John Doolittle (CA-4)
Policy Committee Chairman	Christopher Cox (CA-48)
Leadership Chairman	Rob Portman (OH-2)
Chairman, Committee on Rules	David Dreier (CA-26)
NRCC Chairman	Tom Reynolds (NY-26)

DEMOCRATS

Minority Leader	Nancy Pelosi (CA-8)
Minority Whip	Steny Hoyer (MD-5)
Caucus Chairman	Robert Menendez (NJ-13)
Caucus Vice Chairman	James Clyburn (SC-6)
Assistant to the Democratic Leader	John Spratt (SC-5)
DCCC Chairman	Robert Matsui (CA-5)
Steering Committee Co-Chair	Rosa DeLauro (CT-3)
Steering Committee Co-Chair	George Miller (CA-7)
Senior Chief Deputy Whip	John Lewis (GA-5)
Chief Deputy Whip	Joe Crowley (NY-7)
Chief Deputy Whip	Baron Hill (IN-9)
Chief Deputy Whip	Ron Kind (WI-3)
Chief Deputy Whip	Ed Pastor (AZ-4)
Chief Deputy Whip	Max Sandlin (TX-1)
Chief Deputy Whip	Jan Schakowsky (IL-9)
Chief Deputy Whip	Maxine Waters (CA-35)

COMMITTEE CHAIRMEN

SENATE COMMITTEES	CHAIRMAN	RANKING MEMBER
Aging (Special)	Larry Craig (ID)	John Breaux (LA)
Agriculture, Nutrition & Forestry	Thad Cochran (MS)	Tom Harkin (IA)
Appropriations	Ted Stevens (AK)	Robert Byrd (WV)
Armed Services	John Warner (VA)	Carl Levin (MI)
Banking, Housing & Urban Affairs	Richard Shelby (AL)	Paul Sarbanes (MD)
Budget	Don Nickles (OK)	Kent Conrad (ND)
Commerce, Science & Transportation	John McCain (AZ)	Ernest Hollings (SC)
Energy & Natural Resources	Pete Domenici (NM)	Jeff Bingaman (NM)
Environment & Public Works	James Inhofe (OK)	James Jeffords (VT)
Ethics (Select)	George Voinovich (OH)	Harry Reid (NV)
Finance	Charles Grassley (IA)	Max Baucus (MT)
Foreign Relations	Richard Lugar (IN)	Joseph Biden (DE)
Governmental Affairs	Susan Collins (ME)	Joe Lieberman (CT)
Health, Education, Labor & Pensions	Judd Gregg (NH)	Edward Kennedy (MA)
Indian Affairs	Ben Nighthorse Campbell (CO)	Daniel Inouye (HI)
Intelligence (Select)	Pat Roberts (KS)	Jay Rockefeller IV(WV)
Judiciary	Orrin Hatch (UT)	Patrick Leahy (VT)
Rules & Administration	Trent Lott (MS)	Christopher Dodd (CT)
Small Business	Olympia Snowe (ME)	John Kerry (MA)
Veterans' Affairs	Arlen Specter (PA)	Bob Graham (FL)

HOUSE COMMITTEES	CHAIRMAN	RANKING MEMBER
Agriculture	Bob Goodlatte (VA-6)	Charles Stenholm (TX-17)
Appropriations	Bill Young (FL-10)	David Obey (WI-7)
Armed Services	Duncan Hunter (CA-52)	Ike Skelton (MO-4)
Budget	Jim Nussle (IA-1)	John Spratt (SC-5)
Education & The Workforce	John Boehner (OH-8)	George Miller (CA-7)
Energy & Commerce	Billy Tauzin (LA-3)	John Dingell (MI-15)
Financial Services	Michael Oxley (OH-4)	Barney Frank (MA-4)
Government Reform	Tom Davis (VA-11)	Henry Waxman (CA-30)
Homeland Security (Select)	Christopher Cox (CA-48)	Jim Turner (TX-2)
House Administration	Bob Ney (OH-18)	John Larson (CT-1)
Intelligence (Select)	Porter Goss (FL-14)	Jane Harman (CA-36)
International Relations	Henry Hyde (IL-6)	Tom Lantos (CA-12)
Judiciary	Jim Sensenbrenner (WI-5)	John Conyers (MI-14)
Resources	Richard Pombo (CA-11)	Nick Rahall (WV-3)
Rules	David Dreier (CA-26)	Martin Frost (TX-24)
Science	Sherwood Boehlert (NY-24)	Ralph Hall (TX-4)
Small Business	Donald Manzullo (IL-16)	Nydia Velazquez (NY-12)
Standards of Official Conduct	Joel Hefley (CO-5)	Alan Mollohan (WV-1)
Transportation & Infrastructure	Don Young (AK-AL)	James Oberstar (MN-8)
Veterans' Affairs	Chris Smith (NJ-4)	Lane Evans (IL-17)
Ways & Means	Bill Thomas (CA-22)	Charles Rangel (NY-15)

SENATE COMMITTEES

Aging (Special)
aging.senate.gov
Majority (R 11): Craig (ID), Chmn.; Shelby (AL), Enzi (WY), Collins (ME), Smith (OR), Talent (MO), Fitzgerald (IL), Hatch (UT), Dole (NC), Stevens (AK), Santorum (PA)
Minority (D 9): Breaux (LA), RMM; Reid (NV), Kohl (WI), Feingold (WI), Wyden (OR), Bayh (IN), Lincoln (AR), Carper (DE), Stabenow (MI)
Independent (1): Jeffords (I-VT)

NO SUBCOMMITTEES

Agriculture, Nutrition & Forestry
agriculture.senate.gov
Majority (R 11): Cochran (MS), Chmn.; Lugar (IN), McConnell (KY), Roberts (KS), Fitzgerald (IL), Chambliss (GA), Coleman (MN), Crapo (ID), Talent (MO), Dole (NC), Grassley (IA)
Minority (D 10): Harkin (IA), RMM; Leahy (VT), Conrad (ND), Daschle (SD), Baucus (MT), Lincoln (AR), Miller (GA), Stabenow (MI), Nelson (NE), Dayton (MN)

SUBCOMMITTEES

Forestry, Conservation & Rural Revitalization
Majority (R 6): Crapo, Chmn.; Lugar, Coleman, Talent, McConnell, Roberts
Minority (D 5): Lincoln, RMM; Dayton, Leahy, Daschle, Nelson

Marketing, Inspection & Product Promotion
Majority (R 5): Talent, Chmn.; Roberts, Fitzgerald, Chambliss, Grassley
Minority (D 4): Baucus, RMM; Nelson, Conrad, Stabenow

Production & Price Competitiveness
Majority (R 6): Dole, Chmn.; McConnell, Roberts, Chambliss, Coleman, Grassley
Minority (D 5): Conrad, RMM; Daschle, Miller, Baucus, Lincoln

Research, Nutrition & General Legislation
Majority (R 5): Fitzgerald, Chmn.; Lugar, McConnell, Crapo, Dole
Minority (D 4): Leahy, RMM; Stabenow, Miller, Dayton

Appropriations
appropriations.senate.gov
Majority (R 15): Stevens (AK), Chmn.; Cochran (MS), Specter (PA), Domenici (NM), Bond (MO), McConnell (KY), Burns (MT), Shelby (AL), Gregg (NH), Bennett (UT), Campbell (CO), Craig (ID), Hutchison (TX), DeWine (OH), Brownback (KS)
Minority (D 14): Byrd (WV), RMM; Inouye (HI), Hollings (SC), Leahy (VT), Harkin (IA), Mikulski (MD), Reid (NV), Kohl (WI), Murray (WA), Dorgan (ND), Feinstein (CA), Durbin (IL), Johnson (SD), Landrieu (LA)

SUBCOMMITTEES

Agriculture & Rural Development
Majority (R 8): Bennett, Chmn.; Cochran, Specter, Bond, McConnell, Burns, Craig, Brownback
Minority (D 7): Kohl, RMM; Harkin, Dorgan, Feinstein, Durbin, Johnson, Landrieu

Commerce, Justice, State & Judiciary
Majority (R 7): Gregg, Chmn.; Stevens, Domenici, McConnell, Hutchison, Campbell, Brownback
Minority (D 6): Hollings, RMM; Inouye, Mikulski, Leahy, Kohl, Murray

Defense
Majority (R 10): Stevens, Chmn.; Cochran, Specter, Domenici, Bond, McConnell, Shelby, Gregg, Hutchison, Burns
Minority (D 9): Inouye, RMM; Hollings, Byrd, Leahy, Harkin, Dorgan, Durbin, Reid, Feinstein

District of Columbia
Majority (R 3): DeWine, Chmn.; Hutchison, Brownback
Minority (D 2): Landrieu, RMM; Durbin

Energy & Water Development
Majority (R 7): Domenici, Chmn.; Cochran, McConnell, Bennett, Burns, Craig, Bond
Minority (D 6): Reid, RMM; Byrd, Hollings, Murray, Dorgan, Feinstein

Foreign Operations
Majority (R 8): McConnell, Chmn.; Specter, Gregg, Shelby, Bennett, Campbell, Bond, DeWine
Minority (D 7): Leahy, RMM; Inouye, Harkin, Mikulski, Durbin, Johnson, Landrieu

Homeland Security
Majority (R 9): Cochran, Chmn.; Stevens, Specter, Domenici, McConnell, Shelby, Gregg, Campbell, Craig
Minority (D 8): Byrd, RMM; Inouye, Hollings, Leahy, Harkin, Mikulski, Kohl, Murray

Interior
Majority (R 8): Burns, Chmn.; Stevens, Cochran, Domenici, Bennett, Gregg, Campbell, Brownback
Minority (D 7): Dorgan, RMM; Byrd, Leahy, Hollings, Reid, Feinstein, Mikulski

Labor, HHS & Education
Majority (R 8): Specter, Chmn.; Cochran, Gregg, Hutchison, Craig, Stevens, DeWine, Shelby
Minority (D 7): Harkin, RMM; Hollings, Inouye, Reid, Kohl, Murray, Landrieu

Legislative Branch
Majority (R 3): Campbell, Chmn.; Bennett, Stevens
Minority (D 2): Durbin, RMM; Johnson

Military Construction
Majority (R 5): Hutchison, Chmn.; Burns, Craig, DeWine, Brownback
Minority (D 4): Feinstein, RMM; Inouye, Johnson, Landrieu

Transportation, Treasury & General Government
Majority (R 8): Shelby, Chmn.; Specter, Bond, Bennett, Campbell, Hutchison, DeWine, Brownback
Minority (D 7): Murray, RMM; Byrd, Mikulski, Reid, Kohl, Durbin, Dorgan

VA, HUD & Independent Agencies
Majority (R 7): Bond, Chmn.; Burns, Shelby, Craig, Domenici, DeWine, Hutchison
Minority (D 6): Mikulski, RMM; Leahy, Harkin, Byrd, Johnson, Reid

Armed Services
armed-services.senate.gov

228 Russell
202-224-3871

Majority (R 13): Warner (VA), Chmn.; McCain (AZ), Inhofe (OK), Roberts (KS), Allard (CO), Sessions (AL), Collins (ME), Ensign (NV), Talent (MO), Chambliss (GA), Graham (SC), Dole (NC), Cornyn (TX)
Minority (D 12): Levin (MI), RMM; Kennedy (MA), Byrd (WV), Lieberman (CT), Reed (RI), Akaka (HI), Nelson (FL), Nelson (NE), Dayton (MN), Bayh (IN), Clinton (NY), Pryor (AR)

SUBCOMMITTEES

Airland
Majority (R 7): Sessions, Chmn.; McCain, Inhofe, Roberts, Talent, Chambliss, Dole
Minority (D 6): Lieberman, RMM; Akaka, Dayton, Bayh, Clinton, Pryor

Emerging Threats & Capabilities
Majority (R 9): Roberts, Chmn.; Allard, Collins, Ensign, Talent, Chambliss, Graham, Dole, Cornyn
Minority (D 8): Reed, RMM; Kennedy, Byrd, Lieberman, Akaka, Nelson (FL), Bayh, Clinton

Personnel
Majority (R 4): Chambliss, Chmn.; Collins, Dole, Cornyn
Minority (D 3): Nelson (NE), RMM; Kennedy, Pryor

Readiness & Management Support
Majority (R 9): Ensign, Chmn.; McCain, Inhofe, Roberts, Allard, Sessions, Talent, Chambliss, Cornyn
Minority (D 8): Akaka, RMM; Byrd, Nelson (FL), Nelson (NE), Dayton, Bayh, Clinton, Pryor

Seapower
Majority (R 4): Talent, Chmn.; McCain, Collins, Graham
Minority (D 3): Kennedy, RMM; Lieberman, Reed

Strategic Forces
Majority (R 6): Allard, Chmn.; Inhofe, Sessions, Ensign, Graham, Cornyn
Minority (D 5): Nelson (FL), RMM; Byrd, Reed, Nelson (NE), Dayton

Banking, Housing & Urban Affairs
banking.senate.gov

534 Dirksen
202-224-7391

Majority (R 11): Shelby (AL), Chmn.; Bennett (UT), Allard (CO), Enzi (WY), Hagel (NE), Santorum (PA), Bunning (KY), Crapo (ID), Sununu (NH), Dole (NC), Chafee (RI)
Minority (D 10): Sarbanes (MD), RMM; Dodd (CT), Johnson (SD), Reed (RI), Schumer (NY), Bayh (IN), Miller (GA), Carper (DE), Stabenow (MI), Corzine (NJ)

SUBCOMMITTEES

Economic Policy
Majority (R 3): Bunning, Chmn.; Dole, Shelby
Minority (D 2): Schumer, RMM; Miller

Financial Institutions
Majority (R 8): Bennett, Chmn.; Dole, Chafee, Allard, Santorum, Hagel, Bunning, Crapo
Minority (D 7): Johnson, RMM; Miller, Carper, Dodd, Reed, Bayh, Stabenow

Housing & Transportation
Majority (R 7): Allard, Chmn.; Santorum, Bennett, Chafee, Enzi, Sununu, Shelby
Minority (D 6): Reed, RMM; Stabenow, Corzine, Dodd, Carper, Schumer

International Trade & Finance
Majority (R 6): Hagel, Chmn.; Enzi, Crapo, Sununu, Dole, Chafee
Minority (D 5): Bayh, RMM; Miller, Johnson, Carper, Corzine

Securities & Investment
Majority (R 8): Enzi, Chmn.; Crapo, Sununu, Hagel, Bunning, Bennett, Allard, Santorum
Minority (D 7): Dodd, RMM; Johnson, Reed, Schumer, Bayh, Stabenow, Corzine

Budget
624 Dirksen
202-224-0642
budget.senate.gov
Majority (R 12): Nickles (OK), Chmn.; Domenici (NM), Grassley (IA), Gregg (NH), Allard (CO), Burns (MT), Enzi (WY), Sessions (AL), Bunning (KY), Crapo (ID), Ensign (NV), Cornyn (TX)
Minority (D 11): Conrad (ND), RMM; Hollings (SC), Sarbanes (MD), Murray (WA), Wyden (OR), Feingold (WI), Johnson (SD), Byrd (WV), Nelson (FL), Stabenow (MI), Corzine (NJ)

NO SUBCOMMITTEES

Commerce, Science & Transportation
508 Dirksen
202-224-5115
commerce.senate.gov
Majority (R 12): McCain (AZ), Chmn.; Stevens (AK), Burns (MT), Lott (MS), Hutchison (TX), Snowe (ME), Brownback (KS), Smith (OR), Fitzgerald (IL), Ensign (NV), Allen (VA), Sununu (NH)
Minority (D 11): Hollings (SC), RMM; Inouye (HI), Rockefeller (WV), Kerry (MA), Breaux (LA), Dorgan (ND), Wyden (OR), Boxer (CA), Nelson (FL), Cantwell (WA), Lautenberg (NJ)

SUBCOMMITTEES

Aviation
Majority (R 11): Lott, Chmn.; Stevens, Burns, Hutchison, Snowe, Brownback, Smith, Fitzgerald, Ensign, Allen, Sununu
Minority (D 10): Rockefeller, RMM; Hollings, Inouye, Breaux, Dorgan, Wyden, Nelson, Boxer, Cantwell, Lautenberg

Communications
Majority (R 11): Burns, Chmn.; Stevens, Lott, Hutchison, Snowe, Brownback, Smith, Fitzgerald, Ensign, Allen, Sununu
Minority (D 10): Hollings, RMM; Inouye, Rockefeller, Kerry, Breaux, Dorgan, Wyden, Boxer, Nelson, Cantwell

Competition, Foreign Commerce & Infrastructure
Majority (R 6): Smith, Chmn.; Burns, Brownback, Fitzgerald, Ensign, Sununu
Minority (D 5): Dorgan, RMM; Boxer, Nelson, Cantwell, Lautenberg

Consumer Affairs & Product Safety
Majority (R 3): Fitzgerald, Chmn.; Burns, Smith
Minority (D 2): Wyden, RMM; Dorgan

Oceans, Fisheries & Coast Guard
Majority (R 6): Snowe, Chmn.; Stevens, Lott, Hutchison, Smith, Sununu
Minority (D 5): Kerry, RMM; Hollings, Inouye, Breaux, Cantwell

Science, Technology & Space
Majority (R 8): Brownback, Chmn.; Stevens, Burns, Lott, Hutchison, Ensign, Allen, Sununu
Minority (D 7): Breaux, RMM; Rockefeller, Kerry, Dorgan, Wyden, Nelson, Lautenberg

Surface Transportation & Merchant Marine
Majority (R 8): Hutchison, Chmn.; Stevens, Burns, Lott, Snowe, Brownback, Smith, Allen
Minority (D 7): Inouye, RMM; Rockefeller, Kerry, Breaux, Wyden, Boxer, Lautenberg

Energy & Natural Resources
364 Dirksen
202-224-4971
energy.senate.gov
Majority (R 12): Domenici (NM), Chmn.; Nickles (OK), Craig (ID), Campbell (CO), Thomas (WY), Alexander (TN), Murkowski (AK), Talent (MO), Burns (MT), Smith (OR), Bunning (KY), Kyl (AZ)
Minority (D 11): Bingaman (NM), RMM; Akaka (HI), Dorgan (ND), Graham (FL), Wyden (OR), Johnson (SD), Landrieu (LA), Bayh (IN), Feinstein (CA), Schumer (NY), Cantwell (WA)

SUBCOMMITTEES

Energy
Majority (R 8): Alexander, Chmn.; Nickles, Vice Chmn.; Talent, Bunning, Thomas, Murkowski, Craig, Burns
Minority (D 7): Graham, RMM; Akaka, Johnson, Landrieu, Bayh, Schumer, Cantwell

National Parks
Majority (R 7): Thomas, Chmn.; Nickles, Vice Chmn.; Campbell, Alexander, Burns, Smith, Kyl
Minority (D 6): Akaka, RMM; Dorgan, Graham, Landrieu, Bayh, Schumer

Public Lands & Forests
Majority (R 8): Craig, Chmn.; Burns, Vice Chmn.; Smith, Kyl, Campbell, Alexander, Murkowski, Talent
Minority (D 7): Wyden, RMM; Akaka, Dorgan, Johnson, Landrieu, Bayh, Feinstein

Water & Power
Majority (R 8): Murkowski, Chmn.; Campbell, Vice Chmn.; Smith, Kyl, Craig, Talent, Bunning, Thomas
Minority (D 7): Dorgan, RMM; Graham, Wyden, Johnson, Feinstein, Schumer, Cantwell

Environment & Public Works
410 Dirksen
202-224-6176
epw.senate.gov
Majority (R 10): Inhofe (OK), Chmn.; Warner (VA), Bond (MO), Voinovich (OH), Crapo (ID), Chafee (RI), Cornyn (TX), Murkowski (AK), Thomas (WY), Allard (CO)
Minority (D 8): Baucus (MT), Reid (NV), Graham (FL), Lieberman (CT), Boxer (CA), Wyden (OR), Carper (DE), Clinton (NY)
Independent (1): Jeffords (I-VT), RMM

SUBCOMMITTEES

Clean Air, Climate Change & Nuclear Safety
Majority (R 5): Voinovich, Chmn.; Crapo, Bond, Cornyn, Thomas
Minority (D 4): Carper, RMM; Lieberman, Reid, Clinton

Fisheries, Wildlife & Water
Majority (R 5): Crapo, Chmn.; Warner, Murkowski, Thomas, Allard
Minority (D 4): Graham, RMM; Baucus, Wyden, Clinton

Superfund & Waste Management
Majority (R 4): Chafee, Chmn.; Warner, Allard, Bond
Minority (D 3): Boxer, RMM; Wyden, Carper

Transportation & Infrastructure
Majority (R 6): Bond, Chmn.; Warner, Voinovich, Chafee, Cornyn, Murkowski
Minority (D 5): Reid, RMM; Baucus, Graham, Lieberman, Boxer

Ethics (Select)

220 Hart
202-224-2981

ethics.senate.gov
Majority (R 3): Voinovich (OH), Chmn.; Roberts (KS), Thomas (WY)
Minority (D 3): Reid (NV), Vice Chmn.; Akaka (HI), Lincoln (AR)

NO SUBCOMMITTEES

Finance

219 Dirksen
202-224-4515

finance.senate.gov
Majority (R 11): Grassley (IA), Chmn.; Hatch (UT), Nickles (OK), Lott (MS), Snowe (ME), Kyl (AZ), Thomas (WY), Santorum (PA), Frist (TN), Smith (OR), Bunning (KY)
Minority (D 9): Baucus (MT), RMM; Rockefeller (WV), Daschle (SD), Breaux (LA), Conrad (ND), Graham (FL), Bingaman (NM), Kerry (MA), Lincoln (AR)
Independent (1): Jeffords (I-VT)

SUBCOMMITTEES

Health Care
Majority (R 10): Kyl, Chmn.; Snowe, Frist, Bunning, Nickles, Thomas, Santorum, Smith, Hatch, Lott
Minority (D 8): Rockefeller, RMM; Daschle, Graham, Bingaman, Kerry, Lincoln, Breaux, Baucus
Independent (1): Jeffords (I)

International Trade
Majority (R 8): Thomas, Chmn.; Hatch, Grassley, Smith, Snowe, Frist, Lott, Bunning
Minority (D 6): Baucus, RMM; Rockefeller, Conrad, Graham, Daschle, Kerry
Independent (1): Jeffords (I)

Long-Term Growth & Debt Reduction
Majority (R 3): Smith, Chmn.; Lott, Kyl
Minority (D 2): Graham, RMM; Conrad

Social Security & Family Policy
Majority (R 7): Santorum, Chmn.; Grassley, Kyl, Bunning, Nickles, Snowe, Frist
Minority (D 6): Breaux, RMM; Daschle, Kerry, Rockefeller, Bingaman, Lincoln

Taxation & IRS Oversight
Majority (R 7): Nickles, Chmn.; Hatch, Lott, Snowe, Thomas, Santorum, Smith
Minority (D 5): Conrad, RMM; Bingaman, Lincoln, Breaux, Baucus
Independent (1): Jeffords (I)

Foreign Relations

450 Dirksen
202-224-4651

foreign.senate.gov
Majority (R 10): Lugar (IN), Chmn.; Hagel (NE), Chafee (RI), Allen (VA), Brownback (KS), Enzi (WY), Voinovich (OH), Alexander (TN), Coleman (MN), Sununu (NH)
Minority (D 9): Biden (DE), RMM; Sarbanes (MD), Dodd (CT), Kerry (MA), Feingold (WI), Boxer (CA), Nelson (FL), Rockefeller (WV), Corzine (NJ)

SUBCOMMITTEES

African Affairs
Majority (R 4): Alexander, Chmn.; Brownback, Coleman, Sununu
Minority (D 3): Feingold, RMM; Dodd, Nelson

East Asian & Pacific Affairs
Majority (R 5): Brownback, Chmn.; Alexander, Hagel, Allen, Voinovich
Minority (D 4): Kerry, RMM; Rockefeller, Feingold, Corzine

European Affairs
Majority (R 5): Allen, Chmn.; Voinovich, Hagel, Sununu, Chafee
Minority (D 4): Biden, RMM; Sarbanes, Dodd, Kerry

International Economic Policy, Export & Trade Promotion
Majority (R 5): Hagel, Chmn.; Chafee, Enzi, Alexander, Coleman
Minority (D 4): Sarbanes, RMM; Rockefeller, Corzine, Dodd

International Operations & Terrorism
Majority (R 5): Sununu, Chmn.; Enzi, Allen, Voinovich, Brownback
Minority (D 4): Nelson, RMM; Biden, Feingold, Boxer

Near Eastern & South Asian Affairs
Majority (R 5): Chafee, Chmn.; Hagel, Brownback, Voinovich, Coleman
Minority (D 4): Boxer, RMM; Corzine, Rockefeller, Sarbanes

Western Hemisphere, Peace Corps & Narcotics Affairs
Majority (R 5): Coleman, Chmn.; Chafee, Allen, Enzi, Sununu
Minority (D 5): Dodd, RMM; Boxer, Nelson, Biden, Kerry

Governmental Affairs
340 Dirksen
202-224-4751
govaffairs.senate.gov
Majority (R 9): Collins (ME), Chmn.; Stevens (AK), Voinovich (OH), Coleman (MN), Specter (PA), Bennett (UT), Fitzgerald (IL), Sununu (NH), Shelby (AL)
Minority (D 8): Lieberman (CT), RMM; Levin (MI), Akaka (HI), Durbin (IL), Carper (DE), Dayton (MN), Lautenberg (NJ), Pryor (AR)

SUBCOMMITTEES

Financial Management, Budget & International Security
Majority (R 7): Fitzgerald, Chmn.; Stevens, Voinovich, Specter, Bennett, Sununu, Shelby
Minority (D 6): Akaka, RMM; Levin, Carper, Dayton, Lautenberg, Pryor

Government Management, Federal Workforce & the District of Columbia
Majority (R 6): Voinovich, Chmn.; Stevens, Coleman, Bennett, Fitzgerald, Sununu
Minority (D 5): Durbin, RMM; Akaka, Carper, Lautenberg, Pryor

Investigations (Permanent)
Majority (R 8): Coleman, Chmn.; Stevens, Voinovich, Specter, Bennett, Fitzgerald, Sununu, Shelby
Minority (D 7): Levin, RMM; Akaka, Durbin, Carper, Dayton, Lautenberg, Pryor

Health, Education, Labor & Pensions
428 Dirksen
202-224-5375
labor.senate.gov
Majority (R 11): Gregg (NH), Chmn.; Frist (TN), Enzi (WY), Alexander (TN), Bond (MO), DeWine (OH), Roberts (KS), Sessions (AL), Ensign (NV), Graham (SC), Warner (VA)
Minority (D 9): Kennedy (MA), RMM; Dodd (CT), Harkin (IA), Mikulski (MD), Bingaman (NM), Murray (WA), Reed (RI), Edwards (NC), Clinton (NY)
Independent (1): Jeffords (I-VT)

SUBCOMMITTEES

Aging
Majority (R 6): Bond, Chmn.; Alexander, DeWine, Roberts, Ensign, Warner
Minority (D 5): Mikulski, RMM; Kennedy, Murray, Edwards, Clinton

Children & Families
Majority (R 9): Alexander, Chmn.; Enzi, Bond, DeWine, Roberts, Sessions, Ensign, Graham, Warner
Minority (D 7): Dodd, RMM; Harkin, Bingaman, Murray, Reed, Edwards, Clinton
Independent (1): Jeffords (I)

Employment, Safety & Training
Majority (R 5): Enzi, Chmn.; Alexander, Bond, Roberts, Sessions
Minority (D 3): Murray, RMM; Dodd, Harkin
Independent (1): Jeffords (I)

Substance Abuse & Mental Health Services
Majority (R 4): DeWine, Chmn.; Enzi, Sessions, Ensign
Minority (D 3): Kennedy, RMM; Bingaman, Reed

Indian Affairs
838 Hart
202-224-2251
indian.senate.gov
Majority (R 8): Campbell (CO), Chmn.; McCain (AZ), Domenici (NM), Thomas (WY), Hatch (UT), Inhofe (OK), Smith (OR), Murkowski (AK)
Minority (D 7): Inouye (HI), RMM; Conrad (ND), Reid (NV), Akaka (HI), Dorgan (ND), Johnson (SD), Cantwell (WA)

NO SUBCOMMITTEES

Intelligence (Select)
211 Hart
202-224-1700
intelligence.senate.gov
Majority (R 9): Roberts (KS), Chmn.; Hatch (UT), DeWine (OH), Bond (MO), Lott (MS), Snowe (ME), Hagel (NE), Chambliss (GA), Warner (VA)
Minority (D 8): Rockefeller (WV), Vice Chmn.; Levin (MI), Feinstein (CA), Wyden (OR), Durbin (IL), Bayh (IN), Edwards (NC), Mikulski (MD)

NO SUBCOMMITTEES

Judiciary
judiciary.senate.gov
Majority (R 10): Hatch (UT), Chmn.; Grassley (IA), Specter (PA), Kyl (AZ), DeWine (OH), Sessions (AL), Graham (SC), Craig (ID), Chambliss (GA), Cornyn (TX)
Minority (D 9): Leahy (VT), RMM; Kennedy (MA), Biden (DE), Kohl (WI), Feinstein (CA), Feingold (WI), Schumer (NY), Durbin (IL), Edwards (NC)

SUBCOMMITTEES

Administrative Oversight & the Courts
Majority (R 5): Sessions, Chmn.; Grassley, Specter, Craig, Cornyn
Minority (D 4): Schumer, RMM; Leahy, Feingold, Durbin

Antitrust, Competition Policy & Consumer Rights
Majority (R 5): DeWine, Chmn.; Hatch, Specter, Graham, Chambliss
Minority (D 4): Kohl, RMM; Leahy, Feingold, Edwards

Constitution, Civil Rights & Property Rights
Majority (R 5): Cornyn, Chmn.; Kyl, Graham, Craig, Chambliss
Minority (D 4): Feingold, RMM; Kennedy, Schumer, Durbin

Crime, Corrections & Victims' Rights
Majority (R 6): Graham, Chmn.; Hatch, Grassley, RMM; Sessions, Craig, Cornyn
Minority (D 5): Biden, RMM; Kohl, Feinstein, Durbin, Edwards

Immigration, Border Security & Citizenship
Majority (R 7): Chambliss, Chmn.; Grassley, Kyl, DeWine, Sessions, Craig, Cornyn
Minority (D 6): Kennedy, RMM; Leahy, Feinstein, Schumer, Durbin, Edwards

Terrorism, Technology & Homeland Security
Majority (R 6): Kyl, Chmn.; Hatch, Specter, DeWine, Sessions, Chambliss
Minority (D 5): Feinstein, RMM; Kennedy, Biden, Kohl, Edwards

Rules & Administration
rules.senate.gov
Majority (R 10): Lott (MS), Chmn.; Stevens (AK), McConnell (KY), Cochran (MS), Santorum (PA), Nickles (OK), Hutchison (TX), Frist (TN), Smith (OR), Chambliss (GA)
Minority (D 9): Dodd (CT), RMM; Byrd (WV), Inouye (HI), Feinstein (CA), Schumer (NY), Breaux (LA), Daschle (SD), Dayton (MN), Durbin (IL)

NO SUBCOMMITTEES

Small Business & Entrepreneurship
sbc.senate.gov
Majority (R 10): Snowe (ME), Chmn.; Bond (MO), Burns (MT), Bennett (UT), Enzi (WY), Fitzgerald (IL), Crapo (ID), Allen (VA), Ensign (NV), Coleman (MN)
Minority (D 9): Kerry (MA), RMM; Levin (MI), Harkin (IA), Lieberman (CT), Landrieu (LA), Edwards (NC), Cantwell (WA), Bayh (IN), Pryor (AR)

NO SUBCOMMITTEES

Veterans' Affairs
veterans.senate.gov
Majority (R 8): Specter (PA), Chmn.; Campbell (CO), Craig (ID), Hutchison (TX), Bunning (KY), Ensign (NV), Graham (SC), Murkowski (AK)
Minority (D 6): Graham (FL), RMM; Rockefeller (WV), Akaka (HI), Murray (WA), Miller (GA), Nelson (NE)
Independent (1): Jeffords (I-VT)

NO SUBCOMMITTEES

HOUSE COMMITTEES

Agriculture
agriculture.house.gov
Majority (R 27): Goodlatte (VA), Chmn.; Boehner (OH), Vice Chmn.; Pombo (CA), Smith (MI), Everett (AL), Lucas (OK), Moran (KS), Jenkins (TN), Gutknecht (MN), Ose (CA), Hayes (NC), Pickering (MS), Johnson (IL), Osborne (NE), Pence (IN), Rehberg (MT), Graves (MO), Putnam (FL), Janklow (SD), Burns (GA), Bonner (AL), Rogers (AL), King (IA), Chocola (IN), Musgrave (CO), Nunes (CA), Neugebauer (TX)
Minority (D 24): Stenholm (TX), RMM; Peterson (MN), Dooley (CA), Holden (PA), Thompson (MS), McIntyre (NC), Etheridge (NC), Hill (IN), Baca (CA), Ross (AR), Acevedo-Vila (PR), Case (HI), Alexander (LA), Ballance (NC), Cardoza (CA), Scott (GA), Marshall (GA), Pomeroy (ND), Boswell (IA), Lucas (KY), Thompson (CA), Udall (CO), Larsen (WA), Davis (TN)

SUBCOMMITTEES

Conservation, Credit, Rural Development & Research
Majority (R 10): Lucas, Chmn.; Moran, Osborne, Vice Chmn.; Graves, Putnam, Burns, Bonner, Rogers, King, 1 vacancy
Minority (D 9): Holden, RMM; Case, Ballance, Peterson, Dooley, Etheridge, Acevedo-Vila, Marshall, McIntyre

Department Operations, Oversight, Nutrition & Forestry
Majority (R 10): Gutknecht, Chmn.; Pombo, Smith, Ose, Rehberg, Vice Chmn.; Putnam, Janklow, Bonner, King, Nunes
Minority (D 9): Dooley, RMM; Baca, Acevedo-Vila, Cardoza, Holden, Hill, Ballance, Thompson, Davis

General Farm Commodities & Risk Management
Majority (R 18): Moran, Chmn.; Boehner, Smith, Vice Chmn.; Everett, Lucas, Jenkins, Pickering, Johnson, Pence, Rehberg, Graves, Burns, Chocola, Musgrave, 4 vacancies
Minority (D 17): Peterson, RMM; Thompson (MS), Alexander, Ross, Dooley, Pomeroy, Boswell, Etheridge, Hill, Case, Cardoza, Marshall, Larsen, Davis, 3 vacancies

Livestock & Horticulture
Majority (R 11): Hayes, Chmn.; Pombo, Ose, Vice Chmn.; Pickering, Osborne, Pence, Putnam, Janklow, Rogers, Chocola, Musgrave
Minority (D 10): Ross, RMM; Cardoza, Scott, Peterson, Alexander, Lucas, Boswell, Udall, Larsen, Baca

Specialty Crops & Foreign Agriculture Programs
Majority (R 8): Jenkins, Chmn.; Everett, Vice Chmn.; Gutknecht, Hayes, Rehberg, Rogers, Nunes, 1 vacancy
Minority (D 7): McIntyre, RMM; Etheridge, Hill, Scott, Marshall, Thompson (MS), Alexander

Appropriations
www.house.gov/appropriations

H-218 The Capitol
202-225-2141

Majority (R 36): Young (FL), Chmn.; Regula (OH), Lewis (CA), Rogers (KY), Wolf (VA), Kolbe (AZ), Walsh (NY), Taylor (NC), Hobson (OH), Istook (OK), Bonilla (TX), Knollenberg (MI), Kingston (GA), Frelinghuysen (NJ), Wicker (MS), Nethercutt (WA), Cunningham (CA), Tiahrt (KS), Wamp (TN), Latham (IA), Northup (KY), Aderholt (AL), Emerson (MO), Granger (TX), Peterson (PA), Goode (VA), Doolittle (CA), LaHood (IL), Sweeney (NY), Vitter (LA), Sherwood (PA), Weldon (FL), Simpson (ID), Culberson (TX), Kirk (IL), Crenshaw (FL)
Minority (D 29): Obey (WI), RMM; Murtha (PA), Dicks (WA), Sabo (MN), Hoyer (MD), Mollohan (WV), Kaptur (OH), Visclosky (IN), Lowey (NY), Serrano (NY), DeLauro (CT), Moran (VA), Olver (MA), Pastor (AZ), Price (NC), Edwards (TX), Cramer (AL), Kennedy (RI), Clyburn (SC), Hinchey (NY), Roybal-Allard (CA), Farr (CA), Jackson (IL), Kilpatrick (MI), Boyd (FL), Fattah (PA), Rothman (NJ), Bishop (GA), Berry (AR)

SUBCOMMITTEES

Agriculture, Rural Development, FDA & Related Agencies
Majority (R 8): Bonilla, Chmn.; Walsh, Kingston, Nethercutt, Latham, Vice Chmn.; Emerson, Goode, LaHood
Minority (D 5): Kaptur, RMM; DeLauro, Hinchey, Farr, Boyd

Commerce, Justice, State & Judiciary
Majority (R 8): Wolf, Chmn.; Rogers, Kolbe, Taylor, Regula, Vitter, Vice Chmn.; Sweeney, Kirk
Minority (D 5): Serrano, RMM; Mollohan, Cramer, Kennedy, Sabo

Defense
Majority (R 9): Lewis, Chmn.; Young, Hobson, Bonilla, Nethercutt, Vice Chmn.; Cunningham, Frelinghuysen, Tiahrt, Wicker
Minority (D 5): Murtha, RMM; Dicks, Sabo, Visclosky, Moran

District of Columbia
Majority (R 6): Frelinghuysen, Chmn.; Istook, Cunningham, Vice Chmn.; Doolittle, Weldon, Culberson
Minority (D 3): Fattah, RMM; Pastor, Cramer

Energy & Water Development
Majority (R 8): Hobson, Chmn.; Frelinghuysen, Latham, Wamp, Vice Chmn.; Emerson, Doolittle, Peterson, Simpson
Minority (D 5): Visclosky, RMM; Edwards, Pastor, Clyburn, Berry

Foreign Operations & Export Financing
Majority (R 8): Kolbe, Chmn.; Knollenberg, Lewis, Wicker, Vice Chmn.; Bonilla, Vitter, Kirk, Crenshaw
Minority (D 5): Lowey, RMM; Jackson, Kilpatrick, Rothman, Kaptur

Homeland Security
Majority (R 9): Rogers, Chmn.; Young, Vice Chmn.; Wolf, Wamp, Latham, Emerson, Granger, Sweeney, Sherwood
Minority (D 6): Sabo, RMM; Price, Serrano, Roybal-Allard, Berry, Mollohan

Interior
Majority (R 8): Taylor, Chmn.; Regula, Kolbe, Nethercutt, Wamp, Peterson, Vice Chmn.; Sherwood, Crenshaw
Minority (D 5): Dicks, RMM; Murtha, Moran, Hinchey, Olver

Labor, HHS & Education
Majority (R 10): Regula, Chmn.; Istook, Wicker, Northup, Vice Chmn.; Cunningham, Granger, Peterson, Sherwood, Weldon, Simpson
Minority (D 7): Obey, RMM; Hoyer, Lowey, DeLauro, Jackson, Kennedy, Roybal-Allard

Military Construction
Majority (R 8): Knollenberg, Chmn.; Walsh, Aderholt, Vice Chmn.; Granger, Goode, Vitter, Kingston, Crenshaw
Minority (D 5): Edwards, RMM; Farr, Boyd, Bishop, Dicks

The Legislative Branch
Majority (R 5): Kingston, Chmn.; LaHood, Vice Chmn.; Tiahrt, Culberson, Kirk
Minority (D 3): Moran, RMM; Price, Clyburn

Transportation, Treasury & Independent Agencies
Majority (R 9): Istook, Chmn.; Wolf, Lewis, Rogers, Tiahrt, Vice Chmn.; Northup, Aderholt, Sweeney, Culberson
Minority (D 6): Hoyer, Olver, RMM; Pastor, Kilpatrick, Clyburn, Rothman

VA, HUD & Independent Agencies
Majority (R 9): Walsh, Chmn.; Hobson, Knollenberg, Northup, Goode, Vice Chmn.; Aderholt, LaHood, Weldon, Simpson
Minority (D 6): Mollohan, RMM; Kaptur, Price, Cramer, Fattah, Bishop

Armed Services
www.house.gov/hasc
2120 Rayburn
202-225-4151
Majority (R 33): Hunter (CA), Chmn.; Weldon (PA), Vice Chmn.; Hefley (CO), Saxton (NJ), McHugh (NY), Everett (AL), Bartlett (MD), McKeon (CA), Thornberry (TX), Hostettler (IN), Jones (NC), Ryun (KS), Gibbons (NV), Hayes (NC), Wilson (NM), Calvert (CA), Simmons (CT), Davis, J. (VA), Schrock (VA), Akin (MO), Forbes (VA), Miller (FL), Wilson (SC), LoBiondo (NJ), Cole (OK), Bradley (NH), Bishop (UT), Turner (OH), Kline (MN), Miller (MI), Gingrey (GA), Rogers (AL), Franks (AZ)
Minority (D 29): Skelton (MO), RMM; Spratt (SC), Ortiz (TX), Evans (IL), Taylor (MS), Abercrombie (HI), Meehan (MA), Reyes (TX), Snyder (AR), Turner (TX), Smith (WA), Sanchez, Lo. (CA), McIntyre (NC), Rodriguez (TX), Tauscher (CA), Brady (PA), Hill (IN), Larson (CT), Davis (CA), Langevin (RI), Israel (NY), Larsen (WA), Cooper (TN), Marshall (GA), Meek (FL), Bordallo (GU), Alexander (LA), Ruppersberger (MD), Ryan (OH)

SUBCOMMITTEES
Projection Forces
Majority (R 9): Bartlett, Chmn.; Simmons, Davis (VA), Schrock, Saxton, Hostettler, Calvert, Bradley, Kline
Minority (D 7): Taylor, RMM; Abercrombie, Tauscher, Langevin, Israel, Marshall, Alexander

Readiness
Majority (R 16): Hefley, Chmn.; McKeon, Hostettler, Jones, Ryun, Hayes, Wilson (NM), Calvert, Forbes, Miller (FL), Cole, Bishop, Miller (MI), Rogers, Franks, McHugh
Minority (D 14): Ortiz, RMM; Evans, Taylor, Abercrombie, Reyes, Snyder, Rodriguez, Brady, Hill, Larson, Davis (CA), Larsen, Marshall, Bordallo

Strategic Forces
Majority (R 8): Everett, Chmn.; Thornberry, Weldon, Wilson (NM), Bishop, Turner, Rogers, Franks
Minority (D 6): Reyes, RMM; Spratt, Sanchez, Tauscher, Meek, Ryan

Tactical Air & Land Forces
Majority (R 16): Weldon, Chmn.; Gibbons, Akin, Bradley, Turner, Gingrey, Everett, McKeon, Jones, Ryun, Simmons, Schrock, Forbes, Hefley, Wilson (SC), LoBiondo
Minority (D 14): Abercrombie, RMM; Skelton, Spratt, Ortiz, Evans, Turner, Smith, McIntyre, Brady, Larson, Israel, Cooper, Meek, Alexander

Terrorism, Unconventional Threats & Capabilities
Majority (R 12): Saxton, Chmn.; Wilson (SC), LoBiondo, Kline, Miller (FL), Bartlett, Thornberry, Gibbons, Hayes, Davis (VA), Akin, Hefley
Minority (D 10): Meehan, RMM; Turner, Smith, McIntyre, Rodriguez, Hill, Davis (CA), Langevin, Larsen, Cooper

Total Force
Majority (R 8): McHugh, Chmn.; Cole, Miller (MI), Gingrey, Saxton, Ryun, Schrock, Hayes
Minority (D 6): Snyder, RMM; Meehan, Sanchez, Tauscher, Cooper, Bordallo

Budget
budget.house.gov
309 Cannon
202-226-7270
Majority (R 24): Nussle (IA), Chmn.; Shays (CT), Vice Chmn.; Gutknecht (MN), Thornberry (TX), Ryun (KS), Toomey (PA), Hastings (WA), Portman (OH), Schrock (VA), Brown (SC), Crenshaw (FL), Putnam (FL), Wicker (MS), Hulshof (MO), Tancredo (CO), Vitter (LA), Bonner (AL), Franks (AZ), Garrett (NJ), Barrett (SC), McCotter (MI), Diaz-Balart, M. (FL), Hensarling (TX), Brown-Waite (FL)
Minority (D 19): Spratt (SC), RMM; Moran (VA), Hooley (OR), Baldwin (WI), Moore (KS), Lewis (GA), Neal (MA), DeLauro (CT), Edwards (TX), Scott (VA), Ford (TN), Capps (CA), Thompson (CA), Baird (WA), Cooper (TN), Emanuel (IL), Davis (AL), Majette (GA), Kind (WI)

NO SUBCOMMITTEES

Education & the Workforce
edworkforce.house.gov
2181 Rayburn
202-225-4527
Majority (R 27): Boehner (OH), Chmn.; Petri (WI), Vice Chmn.; Ballenger (NC), Hoekstra (MI), McKeon (CA), Castle (DE), Johnson (TX), Greenwood (PA), Norwood (GA), Upton (MI), Ehlers (MI), DeMint (SC), Isakson (GA), Biggert (IL), Platts (PA), Tiberi (OH), Keller (FL), Osborne (NE), Wilson (SC), Cole (OK), Porter (NV), Kline (MN), Carter (TX), Musgrave (CO), Blackburn (TN), Gingrey (GA), Burns (GA)
Minority (D 22): Miller (CA), RMM; Kildee (MI), Owens (NY), Payne (NJ), Andrews (NJ), Woolsey (CA), Hinojosa (TX), McCarthy (NY), Tierney (MA), Kind (WI), Kucinich (OH), Wu (OR), Holt (NJ), Davis (CA), McCollum (MN), Davis (IL), Case (HI), Grijalva (AZ), Majette (GA), Van Hollen (MD), Ryan (OH), Bishop (NY)

SUBCOMMITTEES

21st Century Competitiveness
Majority (R 16): McKeon, Chmn.; Isakson, Vice Chmn.; Petri, Castle, Johnson, Upton, Ehlers, Tiberi, Keller, Osborne, Cole, Porter, Carter, Gingrey, Burns, 1 vacancy
Minority (D 13): Kildee, RMM; Tierney, Kind, Wu, Holt, McCollum, McCarthy, Van Hollen, Ryan, Owens, Payne, Andrews, Hinojosa

Education Reform
Majority (R 11): Castle, Chmn.; Osborne, Vice Chmn.; Greenwood, Upton, Ehlers, DeMint, Biggert, Platts, Keller, Wilson, Musgrave
Minority (D 9): Woolsey, RMM; Davis (CA), Davis (IL), Case, Grijalva, Kind, Kucinich, Van Hollen, Majette

Employer-Employee Relations
Majority (R 13): Johnson, Chmn.; DeMint, Vice Chmn.; Ballenger, McKeon, Platts, Tiberi, Wilson, Cole, Kline, Carter, Musgrave, Blackburn, 1 vacancy
Minority (D 10): Andrews, RMM; Payne, McCarthy, Kildee, Tierney, Wu, Holt, McCollum, Case, Grijalva

Select Education
Majority (R 6): Hoekstra, Chmn.; Porter, Vice Chmn.; Greenwood, Norwood, Gingrey, Burns
Minority (D 4): Hinojosa, RMM; Davis (CA), Davis (IL), Ryan

Workforce Protections
Majority (R 8): Norwood, Chmn.; Biggert, Vice Chmn.; Ballenger, Hoekstra, Isakson, Keller, Kline, Blackburn
Minority (D 6): Owens, RMM; Kucinich, Woolsey, Majette, Payne, Bishop

Energy & Commerce

2125 Rayburn
202-225-2927
energycommerce.house.gov
Majority (R 31): Tauzin (LA), Chmn.; Bilirakis (FL), Barton (TX), Upton (MI), Stearns (FL), Gillmor (OH), Greenwood (PA), Cox (CA), Deal (GA), Burr (NC), Vice Chmn.; Whitfield (KY), Norwood (GA), Cubin (WY), Shimkus (IL), Wilson (NM), Shadegg (AZ), Pickering (MS), Fossella (NY), Blunt (MO), Buyer (IN), Radanovich (CA), Bass (NH), Pitts (PA), Bono (CA), Walden (OR), Terry (NE), Fletcher (KY), Ferguson (NJ), Rogers (MI), Issa (CA), Otter (ID)
Minority (D 26): Dingell (MI), RMM; Waxman (CA), Markey (MA), Hall (TX), Boucher (VA), Towns (NY), Pallone (NJ), Brown (OH), Gordon (TN), Deutsch (FL), Rush (IL), Eshoo (CA), Stupak (MI), Engel (NY), Wynn (MD), Green (TX), McCarthy (MO), Strickland (OH), DeGette (CO), Capps (CA), Doyle (PA), John (LA), Allen (ME), Davis (FL), Schakowsky (IL), Solis (CA)

SUBCOMMITTEES

Commerce, Trade & Consumer Protection
Majority (R 15): Stearns, Chmn.; Upton, Whitfield, Cubin, Shimkus, Shadegg, Vice Chmn.; Radanovich, Bass, Pitts, Bono, Terry, Fletcher, Ferguson, Issa, Otter
Minority (D 12): Schakowsky, RMM; Solis, Markey, Towns, Brown, Davis, Deutsch, Stupak, Green, McCarthy, Strickland, DeGette

Energy & Air Quality
Majority (R 17): Barton, Chmn.; Cox, Burr, Whitfield, Norwood, Shimkus, Vice Chmn.; Wilson, Shadegg, Pickering, Fossella, Buyer, Radanovich, Bono, Walden, Rogers, Issa, Otter
Minority (D 14): Boucher, RMM; Wynn, Allen, Waxman, Markey, Hall, Pallone, Brown, Rush, McCarthy, Strickland, Capps, Doyle, John

Environment & Hazardous Materials
Majority (R 15): Gillmor, Chmn.; Greenwood, Shimkus, Wilson, Fossella, Vice Chmn.; Buyer, Radanovich, Bass, Pitts, Bono, Terry, Fletcher, Issa, Rogers, Otter
Minority (D 12): Solis, RMM; Allen, Pallone, Doyle, Davis, Schakowsky, Deutsch, Rush, Stupak, Wynn, Green, DeGette

Health
Majority (R 17): Bilirakis, Chmn.; Barton, Upton, Greenwood, Deal, Burr, Whitfield, Norwood, Vice Chmn.; Cubin, Wilson, Shadegg, Pickering, Buyer, Pitts, Fletcher, Ferguson, Rogers
Minority (D 14): Brown, RMM; Waxman, Hall, Towns, Pallone, Eshoo, Stupak, Engel, Green, Strickland, Capps, Gordon, DeGette, John

Oversight & Investigations
Majority (R 8): Greenwood, Chmn.; Bilirakis, Stearns, Burr, Bass, Walden, Vice Chmn.; Ferguson, Rogers
Minority (D 6): Deutsch, RMM; DeGette, Davis, Schakowsky, Waxman, Rush

Telecommunications & the Internet
Majority (R 17): Upton, Chmn.; Bilirakis, Barton, Stearns, Vice Chmn.; Gillmor, Cox, Deal, Whitfield, Cubin, Shimkus, Wilson, Pickering, Fossella, Bass, Bono, Walden, Terry
Minority (D 14): Markey, RMM; Rush, McCarthy, Doyle, Davis, Boucher, Towns, Gordon, Deutsch, Eshoo, Stupak, Engel, Wynn, Green

Financial Services
www.house.gov/financialservices　　　　　　　　　　　　**2129 Rayburn**
202-225-7502

Majority (R 37): Oxley (OH), Chmn.; Leach (IA), Bereuter (NE), Baker (LA), Bachus (AL), Castle (DE), King (NY), Royce (CA), Lucas (OK), Ney (OH), Kelly (NY), Vice Chmn.; Paul (TX), Gillmor (OH), Ryun (KS), LaTourette (OH), Manzullo (IL), Jones (NC), Ose (CA), Biggert (IL), Green (WI), Toomey (PA), Shays (CT), Shadegg (AZ), Fossella (NY), Miller (CA), Hart (PA), Capito (WV), Tiberi (OH), Kennedy (MN), Feeney (FL), Hensarling (TX), Garrett (NJ), Murphy (PA), Brown-Waite (FL), Barrett (SC), Harris (FL), Renzi (AZ)

Minority (D 32): Frank (MA), RMM; Kanjorski (PA), Waters (CA), Maloney (NY), Gutierrez (IL), Velazquez (NY), Watt (NC), Ackerman (NY), Hooley (OR), Carson (IN), Sherman (CA), Meeks (NY), Lee (CA), Inslee (WA), Moore (KS), Gonzalez (TX), Capuano (MA), Ford (TN), Hinojosa (TX), Lucas (KY), Crowley (NY), Clay (MO), Israel (NY), Ross (AR), McCarthy (NY), Baca (CA), Matheson (UT), Lynch (MA), Miller (NC), Emanuel (IL), Scott (GA), Davis (AL)

Independent (1): Sanders (I-VT)

SUBCOMMITTEES

Capital Markets, Insurance & Government Sponsored Enterprises

Majority (R 26): Baker, Chmn.; Ose, Vice Chmn.; Shays, Gillmor, Bachus, Castle, King, Lucas, Royce, Manzullo, Kelly, Ney, Shadegg, Ryun, Fossella, Biggert, Green, Miller, Toomey, Capito, Hart, Kennedy, Tiberi, Brown-Waite, Harris, Renzi

Minority (D 23): Kanjorski, RMM; Ackerman, Hooley, Sherman, Meeks, Inslee, Moore, Gonzalez, Capuano, Ford, Hinojosa, Lucas, Crowley, Israel, Ross, Clay, McCarthy, Baca, Matheson, Lynch, Miller, Emanuel, Scott

Domestic and International Monetary Policy, Trade & Technology

Majority (R 14): King, Chmn.; Biggert, Vice Chmn.; Leach, Castle, Paul, Manzullo, Ose, Shadegg, Kennedy, Feeney, Hensarling, Murphy, Barrett, Harris

Minority (D 11): Maloney (NY), RMM; Watt, Waters, Lee, Kanjorski, Sherman, Hooley, Gutierrez, Velazquez, Baca, Emanuel

Independent (1): Sanders (I)

Financial Institutions & Consumer Credit

Majority (R 25): Bachus, Chmn.; LaTourette, Vice Chmn.; Bereuter, Baker, Castle, Royce, Lucas, Kelly, Gillmor, Ryun, Jones, Biggert, Toomey, Fossella, Hart, Capito, Tiberi, Kennedy, Feeney, Hensarling, Garrett, Murphy, Brown-Waite, Barrett, Renzi

Minority (D 21): Maloney (NY), Watt, Ackerman, Sherman, Meeks, Gutierrez, Moore, Gonzalez, Kanjorski, Waters, Velazquez, Hooley, Carson, Ford, Hinojosa, Lucas, Crowley, Israel, Ross, McCarthy, Davis

Independent (1): Sanders (I), RMM

Housing & Community Opportunity

Majority (R 14): Ney, Chmn.; Green, Vice Chmn.; Bereuter, Baker, King, Jones, Ose, Toomey, Shays, Miller, Hart, Tiberi, Harris, Renzi

Minority (D 11): Waters, RMM; Velazquez, Carson, Lee, Capuano, Watt, Clay, Lynch, Miller, Scott, Davis

Independent (1): Sanders (I)

Oversight & Investigations

Majority (R 11): Kelly, Chmn.; Paul, Vice Chmn.; LaTourette, Green, Shadegg, Fossella, Hensarling, Garrett, Murphy, Brown-Waite, Barrett

Minority (D 9): Gutierrez, RMM; Inslee, Moore, Crowley, Maloney, Gonzalez, Hinojosa, Matheson, Lynch

Government Reform
www.house.gov/reform　　　　　　　　　　　　　　　**2157 Rayburn**
202-225-5074

Majority (R 24): Davis, T. (VA), Chmn.; Burton (IN), Shays (CT), Vice Chmn.; Ros-Lehtinen (FL), McHugh (NY), Mica (FL), Souder (IN), LaTourette (OH), Ose (CA), Lewis (KY), Davis, J. (VA), Platts (PA), Cannon (UT), Putnam (FL), Schrock (VA), Duncan (TN), Sullivan (OK), Deal (GA), Miller (MI), Murphy (PA), Turner (OH), Carter (TX), Janklow (SD), Blackburn (TN)

Minority (D 19): Waxman (CA), RMM; Lantos (CA), Owens (NY), Towns (NY), Kanjorski (PA), Maloney (NY), Cummings (MD), Kucinich (OH), Davis (IL), Tierney (MA), Clay (MO), Watson (CA), Lynch (MA), Van Hollen (MD), Sanchez, Li. (CA), Ruppersberger (MD), Norton (DC), Cooper (TN), Bell (TX)

Independent (1): Sanders (I-VT)

SUBCOMMITTEES

Civil Service & Agency Organization

Majority (R 7): Davis, J. Chmn.; Murphy, Vice Chmn.; Mica, Souder, Putnam, Deal, Blackburn

Minority (D 5): Davis (IL), RMM; Owens, Van Hollen, Norton, Cooper

Criminal Justice, Drug Policy & Human Resources

Majority (R 9): Souder, Chmn.; Deal, Vice Chmn.; McHugh, Mica, Ose, Davis, J., Schrock, Carter, Blackburn

Minority (D 7): Cummings, RMM; Davis (IL), Clay, Sanchez, Ruppersberger, Norton, Bell

Energy Policy, Natural Resources and Regulatory Affairs

Majority (R 8): Ose, Chmn.; Janklow, Vice Chmn.; Shays, McHugh, Cannon, Sullivan, Deal, Miller

Minority (D 6): Tierney, RMM; Lantos, Kanjorski, Kucinich, Van Hollen, Cooper

Government Efficiency & Financial Management

Majority (R 6): Platts, Chmn.; Blackburn, Vice Chmn.; LaTourette, Sullivan, Miller, Turner

Minority (D 4): Towns, RMM; Kanjorski, Owens, Maloney

National Security, Emerging Threats & International Relations
Majority (R 11): Shays, Chmn.; Turner, Vice Chmn.; Burton, LaTourette, Lewis, Platts, Putnam, Schrock, Duncan, Murphy, Janklow
Minority (D 8): Kucinich, RMM; Lantos, Lynch, Maloney, Sanchez, Ruppersberger, Bell, Tierney
Independent (1): Sanders (I)

Technology, Information Policy, Intergovernmental Relations & Census
Majority (R 5): Putnam, Chmn.; Miller, Vice Chmn.; Ose, Murphy, Turner
Minority (D 3): Clay, RMM; Watson, Lynch

Wellness & Human Rights
Majority (R 4): Burton, Chmn.; Cannon, Vice Chmn.; Shays, Ros-Lehtinen
Minority (D 2): Watson, RMM; Cummings
Independent (1): Sanders (I)

House Administration
1309 Longworth
202-225-8281
www.house.gov/cha
Majority (R 6): Ney (OH), Chmn.; Ehlers (MI), Mica (FL), Linder (GA), Doolittle (CA), Reynolds (NY)
Minority (D 3): Larson (CT), RMM; Millender-McDonald (CA), Brady (PA)

NO SUBCOMMITTEES

International Relations
2170 Rayburn
202-225-5021
www.house.gov/international_relations
Majority (R 26): Hyde (IL), Chmn.; Leach (IA), Bereuter (NE), Smith (NJ), Vice Chmn.; Burton (IN), Gallegly (CA), Ros-Lehtinen (FL), Ballenger (NC), Rohrabacher (CA), Royce (CA), King (NY), Chabot (OH), Houghton (NY), McHugh (NY), Tancredo (CO), Paul (TX), Smith (MI), Pitts (PA), Flake (AZ), Davis, J. (VA), Green (WI), Weller (IL), Pence (IN), McCotter (MI), Janklow (SD), Harris (FL)
Minority (D 23): Lantos (CA), RMM; Berman (CA), Ackerman (NY), Faleomavaega (AS), Payne (NJ), Menendez (NJ), Brown (OH), Sherman (CA), Wexler (FL), Engel (NY), Delahunt (MA), Meeks (NY), Lee (CA), Crowley (NY), Hoeffel (PA), Blumenauer (OR), Berkley (NV), Napolitano (CA), Schiff (CA), Watson (CA), Smith (WA), McCollum (MN), Bell (TX)

SUBCOMMITTEES

Africa
Majority (R 5): Royce, Chmn.; Houghton, Tancredo, Flake, Green
Minority (D 4): Payne, RMM; Meeks, Lee, McCollum

Asia & the Pacific
Majority (R 11): Leach, Chmn.; Burton, Bereuter, Smith (NJ), Rohrabacher, Royce, Chabot, Paul, Flake, Weller, Tancredo
Minority (D 9): Faleomavaega, RMM; Brown, Blumenauer, Watson, Smith, Ackerman, Sherman, Wexler, Meeks

Europe
Majority (R 7): Bereuter, Chmn.; Burton, Gallegly, King, Davis, McCotter, Janklow
Minority (D 6): Wexler, RMM; Engel, Delahunt, Lee, Hoeffel, Blumenauer

International Terrorism, Nonproliferation and Human Rights
Majority (R 10): Gallegly, Chmn.; Smith (NJ), Rohrabacher, King, Pitts, Green, Ballenger, Tancredo, Smith (MI), Pence
Minority (D 8): Sherman, RMM; Menendez, Crowley, Berkley, Napolitano, Schiff, Watson, Bell

Middle East & Central Asia
Majority (R 10): Ros-Lehtinen, Chmn.; Chabot, McHugh, Smith (MI), Davis, Pence, McCotter, Janklow, Pitts, Harris
Minority (D 8): Ackerman, RMM; Berman, Engel, Crowley, Hoeffel, Berkley, Schiff, Bell

Western Hemisphere
Majority (R 6): Ballenger, Chmn.; Paul, Weller, Harris, Leach, Ros-Lehtinen
Minority (D 5): Menendez, RMM; Delahunt, Napolitano, Faleomavaega, Payne

Judiciary
2138 Rayburn
202-225-3951
www.house.gov/judiciary
Majority (R 21): Sensenbrenner (WI), Chmn.; Hyde (IL), Coble (NC), Smith (TX), Gallegly (CA), Goodlatte (VA), Chabot (OH), Jenkins (TN), Cannon (UT), Bachus (AL), Hostettler (IN), Green (WI), Keller (FL), Hart (PA), Flake (AZ), Pence (IN), Forbes (VA), King (IA), Carter (TX), Feeney (FL), Blackburn (TN)
Minority (D 16): Conyers (MI), RMM; Berman (CA), Boucher (VA), Nadler (NY), Scott (VA), Watt (NC), Lofgren (CA), Jackson Lee (TX), Waters (CA), Meehan (MA), Delahunt (MA), Wexler (FL), Baldwin (WI), Weiner (NY), Schiff (CA), Sanchez, Li. (CA)

SUBCOMMITTEES

Commercial & Administrative Law
Majority (R 7): Cannon, Chmn.; Coble, Flake, Carter, Blackburn, Chabot, Feeney
Minority (D 5): Watt, RMM; Nadler, Baldwin, Delahunt, Weiner

Courts, the Internet & Intellectual Property
Majority (R 12): Smith, Chmn.; Hyde, Gallegly, Goodlatte, Jenkins, Bachus, Green, Keller, Hart, Pence, Forbes, Carter
Minority (D 10): Berman, RMM; Conyers, Boucher, Lofgren, Waters, Meehan, Delahunt, Wexler, Baldwin, Weiner

Crime, Terrorism & Homeland Security
Majority (R 8): Coble, Chmn.; Feeney, Goodlatte, Chabot, Green, Keller, Pence, Forbes
Minority (D 5): Scott, RMM; Schiff, Jackson Lee, Waters, Meehan

Immigration, Border Security & Claims
Majority (R 8): Hostettler, Chmn.; Flake, Blackburn, Smith, Gallegly, Cannon, King, Hart
Minority (D 5): Jackson Lee, RMM; Sanchez, Lofgren, Berman, Conyers

The Constitution
Majority (R 8): Chabot, Chmn.; King, Jenkins, Bachus, Hostettler, Hart, Feeney, Forbes
Minority (D 5): Nadler, RMM; Conyers, Scott, Watt, Schiff

Permanent Select Committee on Intelligence
intelligence.house.gov

H-405 The Capitol
202-225-4121

Majority (R 11): Goss (FL), Chmn.; Bereuter (NE), Vice Chmn.; Boehlert (NY), Gibbons (NV), LaHood (IL), Cunningham (CA), Hoekstra (MI), Burr (NC), Everett (AL), Gallegly (CA), Collins (GA)
Minority (D 9): Harman (CA), RMM; Hastings (FL), Reyes (TX), Boswell (IA), Peterson (MN), Cramer (AL), Eshoo (CA), Holt (NJ), Ruppersberger (MD)

SUBCOMMITTEES

Human Intelligence, Analysis & Counterintelligence
Majority (R 7): Gibbons, Chmn.; Boehlert, Vice Chmn.; Cunningham, Hoekstra, Burr, Everett, Collins
Minority (D 5): Boswell, RMM; Ruppersberger, Reyes, Peterson, Cramer

Intelligence Policy & National Security
Majority (R 6): Bereuter, Chmn.; LaHood, Vice Chmn.; Cunningham, Hoekstra, Burr, Gallegly
Minority (D 4): Eshoo, RMM; Hastings, Holt, Ruppersberger

Technical & Tactical Intelligence
Majority (R 7): Hoekstra, Chmn.; Boehlert, Vice Chmn.; Gibbons, Cunningham, Everett, Gallegly, Collins
Minority (D 5): Cramer, RMM; Holt, Eshoo, Peterson, Ruppersberger

Terrorism & Homeland Security
Majority (R 7): LaHood, Chmn.; Bereuter, Vice Chmn.; Gibbons, Burr, Everett, Gallegly, Collins
Minority (D 5): Hastings, RMM; Reyes, Peterson, Boswell, Cramer

Resources
www.house.gov/resources

1324 Longworth
202-225-2761

Majority (R 28): Pombo (CA), Chmn.; Young (AK), Tauzin (LA), Saxton (NJ), Gallegly (CA), Duncan (TN), Gilchrest (MD), Calvert (CA), McInnis (CO), Cubin (WY), Radanovich (CA), Jones (NC), Cannon (UT), Peterson (PA), Gibbons (NV), Vice Chmn.; Souder (IN), Walden (OR), Tancredo (CO), Hayworth (AZ), Osborne (NE), Flake (AZ), Rehberg (MT), Renzi (AZ), Cole (OK), Pearce (NM), Bishop (UT), Nunes (CA), Neugebauer (TX)
Minority (D 24): Rahall (WV), RMM; Kildee (MI), Faleomavaega (AS), Abercrombie (HI), Ortiz (TX), Pallone (NJ), Dooley (CA), Christian-Christensen (VI), Kind (WI), Inslee (WA), Napolitano (CA), Udall (NM), Udall (CO), Acevedo-Vila (PR), Carson (OK), Grijalva (AZ), Cardoza (CA), Bordallo (GU), Miller (CA), Markey (MA), Hinojosa (TX), Rodriguez (TX), Baca (CA), McCollum (MN)

SUBCOMMITTEES

Energy & Mineral Resources
Majority (R 10): Cubin, Chmn.; Tauzin, Cannon, Gibbons, Souder, Rehberg, Cole, Pearce, Bishop, Nunes
Minority (D 8): Kind, RMM; Faleomavaega, Ortiz, Napolitano, Udall (NM), Carson, Markey, 1 vacancy

Fisheries Conservation, Wildlife & Oceans
Majority (R 6): Gilchrest, Chmn.; Young, Tauzin, Saxton, Souder, Jones
Minority (D 5): Pallone, RMM; Faleomavaega, Abercrombie, Ortiz, Bordallo

Forests & Forest Health
Majority (R 10): McInnis, Chmn.; Duncan, Jones, Peterson, Tancredo, Hayworth, Flake, Rehberg, Renzi, Pearce
Minority (D 9): Inslee, RMM; Kildee, Udall (NM), Udall (CO), Acevedo-Vila, Carson, McCollum, 2 vacancies

National Parks, Recreation & Public Lands
Majority (R 11): Radanovich, Chmn.; Gallegly, Duncan, Gilchrest, Cubin, Jones, Cannon, Peterson, Gibbons, Souder, Bishop
Minority (D 9): Christian-Christensen, RMM; Kildee, Kind, Udall (NM), Udall (CO), Acevedo-Vila, Grijalva, Cardoza, Bordallo

Water & Power
Majority (R 9): Calvert, Chmn.; Radanovich, Walden, Tancredo, Hayworth, Osborne, Renzi, Pearce, Nunes
Minority (D 8): Napolitano, RMM; Dooley, Inslee, Grijalva, Cardoza, Miller, Rodriguez, Baca

Rules
www.house.gov/rules

H-312 The Capitol
202-225-9191

Majority (R 9): Dreier (CA), Chmn.; Goss (FL), Vice Chmn.; Linder (GA), Pryce (OH), Diaz-Balart, L. (FL), Hastings (WA), Myrick (NC), Sessions (TX), Reynolds (NY)
Minority (D 4): Frost (TX), RMM; Slaughter (NY), McGovern (MA), Hastings (FL)

SUBCOMMITTEES

Technology & the House
Majority (R 5): Linder, Chmn.; Myrick, Vice Chmn.; Sessions, Reynolds, Dreier
Minority (D 2): McGovern, RMM; Hastings (FL)

The Legislative & Budget Process
Majority (R 5): Pryce, Chmn.; Diaz-Balart, Vice Chmn.; Goss, Hastings (WA), Dreier
Minority (D 2): Slaughter, RMM; Frost

Science
www.house.gov/science
2320 Rayburn
202-225-6371

Majority (R 25): Boehlert (NY), Chmn.; Smith (TX), Weldon (PA), Rohrabacher (CA), Barton (TX), Calvert (CA), Smith (MI), Bartlett (MD), Ehlers (MI), Gutknecht (MN), Nethercutt (WA), Lucas (OK), Biggert (IL), Gilchrest (MD), Akin (MO), Johnson (IL), Hart (PA), Sullivan (OK), Forbes (VA), Gingrey (GA), Bishop (UT), Burgess (TX), Bonner (AL), Feeney (FL), Neugebauer (TX)

Minority (D 22): Hall (TX), RMM; Gordon (TN), Costello (IL), Johnson, E. (TX), Woolsey (CA), Lampson (TX), Larson (CT), Udall (CO), Wu (OR), Honda (CA), Bell (TX), Miller (NC), Davis (TN), Jackson Lee (TX), Lofgren (CA), Sherman (CA), Baird (WA), Moore (KS), Weiner (NY), Matheson (UT), Cardoza (CA), 1 vacancy

SUBCOMMITTEES

Energy
Majority (R 9): Biggert, Chmn.; Weldon, Bartlett, Ehlers, Nethercutt, Akin, Hart, Gingrey, Bonner
Minority (D 7): Lampson, RMM; Costello, Woolsey, Wu, Honda, Miller, Davis

Environment, Technology & Standards
Majority (R 8): Ehlers, Chmn.; Smith (MI), Gutknecht, Biggert, Gilchrest, Johnson (IL), Burgess, 1 vacancy
Minority (D 6): Udall, RMM; Miller, Davis, Baird, Matheson, Lofgren

Research
Majority (R 10): Smith (MI), Chmn.; Smith (TX), Rohrabacher, Gutknecht, Lucas, Akin, Johnson (IL), Hart, Sullivan, Gingrey
Minority (D 8): Johnson (TX), RMM; Honda, Lofgren, Cardoza, Sherman, Moore, Matheson, Jackson Lee

Space & Aeronautics
Majority (R 14): Rohrabacher, Chmn.; Smith (TX), Weldon, Barton, Calvert, Bartlett, Nethercutt, Lucas, Sullivan, Forbes, Bishop, Burgess, Bonner, Feeney
Minority (D 12): Gordon, RMM; Larson, Bell, Lampson, Udall, Wu, Johnson (TX), Jackson Lee, Sherman, Moore, Weiner, 1 vacancy

Select Committee on Homeland Security
hsc.house.gov
433 Cannon
202-226-8417

Majority (R 27): Cox (CA), Chmn.; Dunn (WA), Young (FL), Young (AK), Sensenbrenner (WI), Tauzin (LA), Dreier (CA), Hunter (CA), Rogers (KY), Boehlert (NY), Smith (TX), Weldon (PA), Shays (CT), Goss (FL), Camp (MI), Diaz-Balart, L. (FL), Goodlatte (VA), Istook (OK), King (NY), Linder (GA), Shadegg (AZ), Souder (IN), Thornberry (TX), Gibbons (NV), Granger (TX), Sessions (TX), Sweeney (NY)

Minority (D 23): Turner (TX), RMM; Thompson (MS), Sanchez, Lo. (CA), Markey (MA), Dicks (WA), Frank (MA), Harman (CA), Cardin (MD), Slaughter (NY), DeFazio (OR), Lowey (NY), Andrews (NJ), Norton (DC), Lofgren (CA), McCarthy (MO), Jackson Lee (TX), Pascrell (NJ), Christian-Christensen (VI), Etheridge (NC), Gonzalez (TX), Lucas (KY), Langevin (RI), Meek (FL)

SUBCOMMITTEES

Cybersecurity, Science and Research & Development
Majority (R 12): Thornberry, Chmn.; Sessions, Vice Chmn.; Boehlert, Smith, Weldon, Camp, Goodlatte, King, Linder, Souder, Gibbons, Granger
Minority (D 10): Lofgren, RMM; Sanchez, Andrews, Jackson Lee, Christian-Christensen, Etheridge, Gonzalez, Lucas, Langevin, Meek

Emergency Preparedness & Response
Majority (R 12): Shadegg, Chmn.; Weldon, Vice Chmn.; Tauzin, Shays, Camp, Diaz-Balart, King, Souder, Thornberry, Gibbons, Granger, Sessions
Minority (D 10): Thompson, RMM; Harman, Cardin, DeFazio, Lowey, Norton, Pascrell, Christian-Christensen, Etheridge, Lucas

Infrastructure & Border Security
Majority (R 12): Camp, Chmn.; Granger, Vice Chmn.; Dunn, Young (AK), Hunter, Smith, Diaz-Balart, Goodlatte, Istook, Shadegg, Souder, Sweeney
Minority (D 10): Sanchez, RMM; Markey, Dicks, Frank, Cardin, Slaughter, DeFazio, Jackson Lee, Pascrell, Gonzalez

Intelligence & Counterterrorism
Majority (R 12): Gibbons, Chmn.; Sweeney, Vice Chmn.; Dunn, Young (FL), Rogers, Smith, Shays, Goss, King, Linder, Shadegg, Thornberry
Minority (D 10): Langevin, RMM; Markey, Dicks, Frank, Harman, Lowey, Andrews, Norton, McCarthy, Meek

Rules
Majority (R 8): Diaz-Balart, Chmn.; Dunn, Sensenbrenner, Dreier, Weldon, Goss, Linder, Sessions
Minority (D 6): Slaughter, RMM; Thompson, Sanchez, Lofgren, McCarthy, Meek

Small Business
www.house.gov/smbiz
2361 Rayburn
202-225-5821

Majority (R 18): Manzullo (IL), Chmn.; Bartlett (MD), Kelly (NY), Chabot (OH), Toomey (PA), DeMint (SC), Graves (MO), Schrock (VA), Akin (MO), Capito (WV), Shuster (PA), Musgrave (CO), Franks (AZ), Gerlach (PA), Bradley (NH), Beauprez (CO), Chocola (IN), King (IA)

Minority (D 17): Velazquez (NY), RMM; Millender-McDonald (CA), Udall (NM), Ballance (NC), Faleomavaega (AS), Christian-Christensen (VI), Davis (IL), Gonzalez (TX), Napolitano (CA), Acevedo-Vila (PR), Case (HI), Bordallo (GU), Majette (GA), Marshall (GA), Michaud (ME), Miller (NC), Sanchez, Li. (CA)

SUBCOMMITTEES

Regulatory Reform & Oversight
Majority (R 7): Schrock, Chmn.; Bartlett, Kelly, Franks, Bradley, King, 1 vacancy
Minority (D 6): Christian-Christensen, Acevedo-Vila, Majette, 3 vacancies

Rural Enterprises, Agriculture and Technology
Majority (R 6): Graves, Chmn.; Shuster, Kelly, Capito, Musgrave, Toomey
Minority (D 5): Ballance, RMM; Michaud, Christian-Christensen, Case, Bordallo

Tax, Finance & Exports
Majority (R 8): Toomey, Chmn.; Chabot, Musgrave, Gerlach, Beauprez, Franks, DeMint, Chocola
Minority (D 7): Millender-McDonald, RMM; Marshall, Ballance, Davis, Acevedo-Vila, Majette, Michaud

Workforce, Empowerment & Government Programs
Majority (R 7): Akin, Chmn.; DeMint, Capito, Bradley, Chocola, King, 1 vacancy
Minority (D 6): Udall, Davis, Napolitano, Case, Bordallo, 1 vacancy

Standards of Official Conduct
HT-2 The Capitol
www.house.gov/ethics
202-225-7103
Majority (R 5): Hefley (CO), Chmn.; Hastings (WA), Biggert (IL), Hulshof (MO), LaTourette (OH)
Minority (D 5): Mollohan (WV), RMM; Tubbs Jones (OH), Green (TX), Roybal-Allard (CA), Doyle (PA)

NO SUBCOMMITTEES

Transportation & Infrastructure
2165 Rayburn
www.house.gov/transportation
202-225-9446
Majority (R 41): Young (AK), Chmn.; Petri (WI), Vice Chmn.; Boehlert (NY), Coble (NC), Duncan (TN), Gilchrest (MD), Mica (FL), Hoekstra (MI), Quinn (NY), Ehlers (MI), Bachus (AL), LaTourette (OH), Kelly (NY), Baker (LA), Ney (OH), LoBiondo (NJ), Moran (KS), Miller (CA), DeMint (SC), Bereuter (NE), Isakson (GA), Hayes (NC), Simmons (CT), Capito (WV), Brown (SC), Johnson (IL), Rehberg (MT), Platts (PA), Graves (MO), Kennedy (MN), Shuster (PA), Boozman (AR), Sullivan (OK), Chocola (IN), Beauprez (CO), Burgess (TX), Burns (GA), Pearce (NM), Gerlach (PA), Diaz-Balart, M. (FL), Porter (NV)
Minority (D 34): Oberstar (MN), RMM; Rahall (WV), Lipinski (IL), DeFazio (OR), Costello (IL), Norton (DC), Nadler (NY), Menendez (NJ), Brown (FL), Filner (CA), Johnson (TX), Taylor (MS), Millender-McDonald (CA), Cummings (MD), Blumenauer (OR), Tauscher (CA), Pascrell (NJ), Boswell (IA), Holden (PA), Lampson (TX), Baird (WA), Berkley (NV), Carson (OK), Matheson (UT), Honda (CA), Larsen (WA), Capuano (MA), Weiner (NY), Carson (IN), Hoeffel (PA), Thompson (CA), Bishop (NY), Michaud (ME), Davis (TN)

SUBCOMMITTEES

Aviation
Majority (R 25): Mica, Chmn.; Petri, Duncan, Quinn, Ehlers, Bachus, Kelly, Baker, LoBiondo, Moran, Isakson, Hayes, Johnson, Rehberg, Graves, Kennedy, Shuster, Boozman, Sullivan, Chocola, Vice Chmn.; Beauprez, Pearce, Gerlach, Diaz-Balart, Porter
Minority (D 21): DeFazio, RMM; Boswell, Lipinski, Costello, Norton, Menendez, Brown (FL), Johnson, Millender-McDonald, Tauscher, Pascrell, Holden, Berkley, Carson (OK), Matheson, Honda, Larsen, Capuano, Weiner, Rahall, Filner

Coast Guard & Maritime Transportation
Majority (R 7): LoBiondo, Chmn.; Coble, Gilchrest, Hoekstra, DeMint, Simmons, Diaz-Balart, Vice Chmn.;
Minority (D 6): Filner, RMM; DeFazio, Brown (FL), Millender-McDonald, Lampson, Thompson

Economic Development, Public Buildings & Emergency Management
Majority (R 5): LaTourette, Chmn.; Capito, Burgess, Burns, Gerlach
Minority (D 4): Norton, RMM; Davis, Carson (OK), Michaud

Highways, Transit & Pipelines
Majority (R 30): Petri, Chmn.; Boehlert, Coble, Duncan, Mica, Hoekstra, Quinn, LaTourette, Kelly, Baker, Ney, LoBiondo, Moran, DeMint, Bereuter, Isakson, Hayes, Simmons, Capito, Brown (SC), Johnson, Rehberg, Platts, Graves, Kennedy, Shuster, Boozman, Beauprez, Vice Chmn.; Burgess, Burns
Minority (D 25): Lipinski, RMM; Rahall, Nadler, Johnson, Taylor, Millender-McDonald, Cummings, Tauscher, Pascrell, Holden, Baird, Berkley, Carson (OK), Matheson, Honda, Larsen, Capuano, Blumenauer, Lampson, Weiner, Carson (IN), Hoeffel, Thompson, Bishop, Michaud

Railroads
Majority (R 14): Quinn, Chmn.; Petri, Boehlert, Coble, Mica, Bachus, Moran, Miller, DeMint, Simmons, Capito, Platts, Graves, Porter, Vice Chmn.;
Minority (D 12): Brown, RMM; Rahall, DeFazio, Nadler, Filner, Cummings, Blumenauer, Boswell, Carson (IN), Michaud, Lipinski, Costello

Water Resources & Environment
Majority (R 19): Duncan, Chmn.; Boehlert, Gilchrest, Ehlers, LaTourette, Kelly, Baker, Ney, Miller, Isakson, Hayes, Brown (SC), Shuster, Boozman, Sullivan, Chocola, Pearce, Vice Chmn.; Gerlach, Diaz-Balart
Minority (D 15): Costello, RMM; Menendez, Taylor, Lampson, Baird, Hoeffel, Thompson, Bishop, Davis, Norton, Nadler, Johnson, Blumenauer, Tauscher, Pascrell

Veterans' Affairs
335 Cannon
veterans.house.gov   **202-225-3527**
Majority (R 17): Smith (NJ), Chmn.; Bilirakis (FL), Vice Chmn.; Everett (AL), Buyer (IN), Quinn (NY), Stearns (FL), Moran (KS), Baker (LA), Simmons (CT), Brown (SC), Miller (FL), Boozman (AR), Bradley (NH), Beauprez (CO), Brown-Waite (FL), Renzi (AZ), Murphy (PA)
Minority (D 14): Evans (IL), RMM; Filner (CA), Gutierrez (IL), Brown (FL), Snyder (AR), Rodriguez (TX), Michaud (ME), Hooley (OR), Reyes (TX), Strickland (OH), Berkley (NV), Udall (NM), Davis (CA), Ryan (OH)

SUBCOMMITTEES

Benefits
Majority (R 5): Brown (SC), Chmn.; Quinn, Vice Chmn.; Miller, Bradley, Brown-Waite
Minority (D 4): Michaud, RMM; Davis, Reyes, Brown (FL)

Health
Majority (R 11): Simmons, Chmn.; Moran, Vice Chmn.; Baker, Miller, Boozman, Bradley, Beauprez, Brown-Waite, Renzi, Stearns, Murphy
Minority (D 9): Rodriguez, RMM; Filner, Snyder, Strickland, Berkley, Ryan, Gutierrez, Brown (FL), Hooley

Oversight & Investigations
Majority (R 5): Buyer, Chmn.; Bilirakis, Vice Chmn.; Everett, Boozman, 1 vacancy
Minority (D 4): Hooley, RMM; Evans, Filner, Rodriguez

Ways & Means
1102 Longworth
waysandmeans.house.gov   **202-225-3625**
Majority (R 24): Thomas (CA), Chmn.; Crane (IL), Shaw (FL), Johnson (CT), Houghton (NY), Herger (CA), McCrery (LA), Camp (MI), Ramstad (MN), Nussle (IA), Johnson (TX), Dunn (WA), Collins (GA), Portman (OH), English (PA), Hayworth (AZ), Weller (IL), Hulshof (MO), McInnis (CO), Lewis (KY), Foley (FL), Brady (TX), Ryan (WI), Cantor (VA)
Minority (D 17): Rangel (NY), RMM; Stark (CA), Matsui (CA), Levin (MI), Cardin (MD), McDermott (WA), Kleczka (WI), Lewis (GA), Neal (MA), McNulty (NY), Jefferson (LA), Tanner (TN), Becerra (CA), Doggett (TX), Pomeroy (ND), Sandlin (TX), Tubbs Jones (OH)

SUBCOMMITTEES

Health
Majority (R 8): Johnson (CT), Chmn.; McCrery, Crane, Johnson (TX), Camp, Ramstad, English, Dunn
Minority (D 5): Stark, RMM; Kleczka, Lewis, McDermott, Doggett

Human Resources
Majority (R 8): Herger, Chmn.; Johnson (CT), McInnis, McCrery, Camp, English, Lewis, Cantor
Minority (D 5): Cardin, RMM; Stark, Levin, McDermott, Rangel

Oversight
Majority (R 8): Houghton, Chmn.; Portman, Weller, McInnis, Foley, Johnson (TX), Ryan, Cantor
Minority (D 5): Pomeroy, RMM; Kleczka, McNulty, Tanner, Sandlin

Select Revenue Measures
Majority (R 8): McCrery, Chmn.; Hayworth, Weller, Lewis, Foley, Brady, Ryan, Collins
Minority (D 5): McNulty, RMM; Jefferson, Sandlin, Doggett, Tubbs Jones

Social Security
Majority (R 8): Shaw, Chmn.; Johnson (TX), Collins, Hayworth, Hulshof, Lewis, Brady, Ryan
Minority (D 5): Matsui, RMM; Cardin, Pomeroy, Becerra, Tubbs Jones

Trade
Majority (R 9): Crane, Chmn.; Shaw, Houghton, Camp, Ramstad, Dunn, Herger, English, Nussle
Minority (D 6): Levin, RMM; Rangel, Neal, Jefferson, Becerra, Tanner

JOINT COMMITTEES

Joint Committee on Taxation
1015 Longworth
www.house.gov/jct   **202-225-3621**
House (5): Thomas (CA), Chmn.; Crane (IL), Shaw (FL), Rangel (NY), Stark (CA)
Senate (5): Grassley (IA), Vice Chmn.; Hatch (UT), Nickles (OK), Baucus (MT), Rockefeller (WV)

Joint Economic Committee
G-01 Dirksen
www.house.gov/jec   **202-224-5171**
House (10): Saxton (NJ), Vice Chmn.; Ryan (WI), Dunn (WA), English (PA), Putnam (FL), Paul (TX), Stark (CA), RMM; Maloney (NY), Watt (NC), Hill (IN)
Senate (10): Bennett (UT), Chmn.; Brownback (KS), Sessions (AL), Sununu (NH), Alexander (TN), Collins (ME), Reed (RI), Kennedy (MA), Sarbanes (MD), Bingaman (NM)

Joint Committee on Printing

www.house.gov/jcp/

House (5): Ney (OH), Chmn.; Doolittle (CA), Linder (GA), Larson (CT), Brady (PA)
Senate (5): Chambliss (GA), Vice-Chmn.; Cochran (MS), Smith (OR), Inouye (HI), Dayton (MN)

Joint Committee on the Library

House (5): Ehlers (MI), Vice-Chmn.; Ney (OH), Kingston (GA), Larson (CT), Millender-McDonald (CA)
Senate (5): Stevens (AK), Chmn.; Lott (MS), Cochran (MS), Dodd (CT), Schumer (NY)

Secretary of the Senate

Emily Reynolds

Clerk of the House

Jeff Trandahl

INDEX

The names of all the Governors, Senators and Representatives appear in boldface type. The number of the page that includes Members' corresponding biographical information also appears in bold.

THE AUTHORS

MICHAEL BARONE, senior writer at *U.S. News and World Report*, is a regular panelist on *The McLaughlin Group* and a Fox News Channel contributor. The *Chicago Tribune* says, "Michael Barone is to politics what statistician-writer Bill James is to baseball, a mix of historian, social observer, and numbers cruncher who illuminates his subject with perspective and a touch of irreverence." He is the author of *The New Americans: How the Melting Pot Can Work Again,* published by Regnery in 2001.

RICHARD E. COHEN brings to the *Almanac* 26 years of experience covering Capitol Hill. He is the 1990 winner of the Everett McKinley Dirksen Award for distinguished reporting on Congress and *National Journal*'s congressional correspondent since 1977. Cohen is the author of several books about Congress, including a biography of former Rep. Dan Rostenkowski.

THE PUBLISHER

66 The nation's most respected nonpartisan source of information about how Washington's policymaking machinery really works. 99

That's how *Newsweek* described *National Journal*. For more than 30 years, *National Journal* has reached subscribers with an award-winning weekly magazine noted for its dedication to "facts only" reporting. *National Journal* speaks to people who make it their business to know what's going on in the world's largest business—the United States Government.

Only *National Journal* is exclusively devoted to the coverage of what the government is doing today, what it's going to do tomorrow, and how its actions affect our lives.

This 2004 edition of *The Almanac of American Politics* marks the eleventh volume to be published by National Journal Group. In addition to the *Almanac* and *National Journal*, National Journal Group publishes *Government Executive*, a monthly magazine for senior federal managers; *CongressDaily*, a twice-daily news service covering Congress; *The Hotline*, the premier daily publication on campaign politics; National Journal's *Technology Daily*, a twice-daily news service on information technology politics and policy; NationalJournal.com, the online source for political and policy professionals; *UN Wire*, a daily briefing on the United Nations; *The Capital Source*, a semi-annual Washington directory; and the *National Journal Convention Daily*, a daily newspaper published at the Democratic and Republican Conventions.

National Journal GROUP

1501 M Street, NW, Washington, DC 20005 Telephone (202) 739-8400